Architectural GRAPHIC Standards

JOHN WILEY & SONS

THE AMERICAN INSTITUTE OF ARCHITECTS

Peggy Burns
Publisher

Robert J. Fletcher IV
Production Director

Dean Gonzales
Illustration Manager

Jean Morley
Design Director

Meg Hudak
Marketing

Janet Rumbarger
Managing Editor

Anthony Lewandowski
Consulting Editor

Richard J. Vitullo, AIA
Contributing Editor

James V. Vose
Graphics Editor

STAFF CONSULTANTS
Pamela James Blumgart
Stacy Droneburg
Jenifer Tennant-Dwyer
Nora Richter Greer
Christopher Keane
Fredj Khlifi
Ruthann Mackey
Scot C. McBroom, AIA
Elyse C. Tipton
Laird Ueberroth, AIA
Pilar Wyman

COMPUTER GRAPHICS
Samir Ali
Steve Dehanas, RIBA
Tom Epps
Jeffery Madsen
Scott Peterson
Ed Rahme
David Salela
Jason Sturniolo
Jerry L. Smith
Antonio Vercillo

ARCHITECTURAL GRAPHIC STANDARDS TASK FORCE CHAIRMEN
William G. Miner, AIA
Darrel Rippeteau, AIA

TASK FORCE MEMBERS
Edward Allen, AIA
William A. Brenner, AIA
Fred Dubin, PE
James M. Duda
James Freehof, AIA
H. Ward Jandl
John Loss, FAIA
Robert Odermatt, FAIA
John Reynolds, AIA
Theodore D. Sherman, AIA
Norma Sklarek, FAIA
James L. Terry, AIA
Douglas Stenhouse, AIA

AMERICANS WITH DISABILITIES ACT TASK FORCE MEMBERS
Kim Beasley, AIA
Steve Cotler, AIA
Ruth Hall Lusher
Thomas L. McGrath
Mark Mazz, AIA
John Sorrenti, AIA
Susan B. Tusick, AIA

JOHN WILEY & SONS, INC.

New York • Chichester • Brisbane • Toronto • Singapore

RAMSEY/SLEEPER

Architectural GRAPHIC Standards

Ninth Edition

JOHN RAY HOKE, JR., FAIA
EDITOR IN CHIEF

THE AMERICAN INSTITUTE OF ARCHITECTS

SUBSCRIPTION NOTICE

Architectural Graphic Standards is updated on a periodic basis to reflect important changes in the subject matter. If you purchased this product directly from John Wiley & Sons, we have already recorded your subscription for this update service.

If, however, you purchased this product from a bookstore and wish to receive future updates or editions billed separately with a 15-day examination review, please send your name, company name (if applicable), address, and the title of this product to:

Supplement Department
John Wiley & Sons, Inc.
One Wiley Drive
Somerset, NJ 08875
1-(800)-225-5945

The drawings, tables, data, and other information in this book have been obtained from many sources, including government organizations, trade associations, suppliers of building materials, and professional architects or architecture firms. The American Institute of Architects (AIA), the Architectural Graphic Standards Task Force of the AIA, and the publisher have made every reasonable effort to make this reference work accurate and authoritative, but do not warrant, and assume no liability for, the accuracy or completeness of the text or its fitness for any particular purpose. It is the responsibility of users to apply their professional knowledge in the use of information contained in this book, to consult the original sources for additional information when appropriate, and, if they themselves are not professional architects, to consult an architect when appropriate.

Library of Congress Cataloging-in-Publication Data

Ramsey, Charles George, 1884–1963.
    [Architectural graphic standards]
    Ramsey/Sleeper architectural graphic standards. — 9
Ray Hoke, Jr., editor-in-chief.
        p.   cm.
    "The American Institute of Architects."
    Includes index.   e,
    ISBN 0-471-53369-6
    1. Building—Details—Drawings. I. Sleeper, Institute
1893–1960. II. Hoke, John Ray, 1950– . III
of Architects. IV. Title.   93-31757
TH2031.R35 1994
721'.028'4—dc20

Printed in the United States of America
10 9 8 7 6

CONTENTS

PUBLISHER'S NOTE

In the fall of 1932, the lowest point of the Great Depression, Chairman Emeritus W. Bradford Wiley joined the House of Wiley and soon learned a promising new book had been published in May. Martin Matheson, then manager of marketing, had persuaded Charles George Ramsey, AIA, author of an earlier Wiley textbook, and his younger colleague, Harold Reeve Sleeper, FAIA, to develop their ideas and prepare the plates for what became *Architectural Graphic Standards*. Subsequently, Matheson directed the design and layout of the book and personally oversaw its production and manufacture.

The immediate acceptance and success of *Architectural Graphic Standards* extended far beyond its anticipated audience of architects, builders, draftsmen, engineers, and students. Interior designers, real estate agents and brokers, homeowners, insurance underwriters, and lovers of fine books all came to be among its users and admirers.

Soon after the publication of *Architectural Graphic Standards*, suggestions and requests came from many enthusiastic readers. These called for changes and additions and inevitably the decision was made to publish a second edition, which was almost 25 percent larger. It appeared in 1936, not long after the first. Recovery from the Great Depression had begun when the second edition came out, and with rising construction activity the demand for *Architectural Graphic Standards* increased. To serve its users' growing needs, work soon began on a third edition which, when published in 1941, was almost twice as large as the original edition.

World War II lengthened the interval between editions; the fourth edition, prepared by Sleeper, appeared in 1951; the book had grown to 614 pages. The fifth edition (with 758 pages), Sleeper's last revision, was issued in 1956. The coauthors' achievements in the initial decade, followed by the efforts of Sleeper, provided untold thousands of users with an invaluable resource for almost 30 years.

Harold Sleeper's foresight led to his suggestion, heartily supported by John Wiley & Sons, that The American Institute of Architects be asked to assume the editorial responsibility for the sixth and subsequent editions. This was proposed at the June 1964 annual convention of The American Institute of Architects, and within a month a contract between John Wiley & Sons and the Institute led to the fulfillment of Harold Sleeper's wish.

Now, more than 60 years after publication of the first edition, we look back on a remarkable record. Each edition has surpassed its predecessors. The book has grown fourfold in size and immeasurably in depth. The collected editions are a chronicle of twentieth-century architectural practice and reflect as well those times when progress has meant preserving (and hence respecting) our architectural heritage. This edition presents substantial material on historic preservation, leading to the satisfying notion that buildings created with the aid of the first edition may now benefit from material presented in the ninth.

John Wiley & Sons takes pride in the part the firm has played in the enduring success of *Architectural Graphic Standards* and in the association with The American Institute of Architects. Three generations of readers have benefited from this work, and we look forward to meeting the needs of generations to come.

W. BRADFORD WILEY
Chairman Emeritus

BRADFORD WILEY II
Chairman
John Wiley & Sons, Inc.

FOREWORD

The ninth edition of *Architectural Graphic Standards* reflects the collaborative, creative relationship that has developed over the years between The American Institute of Architects and John Wiley & Sons. In fact, it is the fourth time the AIA has assumed editorial responsibility for a new edition. This collaborative relationship fits well into the AIA's mission, which calls for the Institute to "coordinate the building industry and the profession of architecture." Put simply, *Architectural Graphic Standards* is one of the most unifying and focused reference works available to a historically fragmented industry.

W. Bradford Wiley, chairman emeritus of John Wiley & Sons, set a high standard of caring, from the time he first became associated with *Architectural Graphic Standards* as a copy editor in 1932. His commitment to excellence in serving all those who work in the profession of architecture—from architects and engineers to interior designers and contractors—has earned him the deep respect and affection of a grateful industry. The new chairman, Bradford Wiley II, carries on this tradition of excellence.

The work of the building industry depends on the careful orchestration of many and varied hands. When the process works well, it can be compared to the rainbow of colors that make up a stained glass window; however, when the process does not work well, it risks being considerably less than the sum of its parts. *Architectural Graphic Standards* is a catalyst for coherence and coordination. It offers the industry a common graphic vocabulary so that each segment of it can speak clearly and persuasively to another. One could say that it visualizes the art and craft of design—the planning, landscaping, materials, and everything else that goes into creating the environment in which we live and work. *Architectural Graphic Standards* is, in short, an illustrated and well-thumbed "dictionary" that belongs on the desk of anyone who is involved in architecture.

Providing a unifying visual vocabulary for the design professions is only one goal of *Architectural Graphic Standards*. Each edition is also a kind of benchmark or snapshot of the state of the art of the professions and crafts that make up this rapidly evolving (some might say transforming) industry. Readers of the first edition learned about T squares, triangles, and pencils; the tens of thousands of users of this latest edition will discover the language of light pencils and key-boards. Indeed, much of this ninth edition was generated electronically. But more than simply reflecting the state of the art, this publication will help mold the identity of tomorrow's drafting room. The ninth edition of this invaluable resource and the design professions will go hand in hand into the next century.

No introduction to the content of this edition would be complete without some acknowledgment of the individuals who brought it to life. In this edition, there are innumerable contributions from AIA members who gave tirelessly, unselfishly, and creatively so that those in their professions, and the building industry as a whole, would benefit from their knowledge. To that list I would add the many individuals, firms, trade associations, professional societies, and manufacturers who have given this publication its authority. Their contributions are credited throughout this book on the appropriate pages.

I would also like to acknowledge and thank the founding authors, as well as three editors—Joseph N. Boaz, AIA; Robert T. Packard, AIA; and our current editor in chief, John Ray Hoke, Jr., FAIA—all of whom are AIA members. They have tilled the fields of *Architectural Graphic Standards* to ensure a rich harvest of good information time and time again. Each author and editor has taken his own special approach to define and, when necessary, redefine the technical data that are essential to a new generation of architects. Because of their collective wisdom and dedication, the basic principles of service to the industry that were set forth in the original edition have been maintained.

Earlier I made reference to the AIA's mission, which is, in part, to help coordinate the building industry. However, another important part of the AIA's mission is to "make the profession of ever-increasing service to society." This statement reminds us that the value of the design process ultimately is determined by how well the industry serves the public's health, safety, and well-being. *Architectural Graphic Standards* is an indispensable resource in carrying out this high calling. As such, it is a milestone on the road to excellence.

JAMES P. CRAMER, HON. AIA
Executive Vice President/CEO

PREFACE

This book began with the architects Charles George Ramsey, AIA, and Harold Reeve Sleeper, FAIA, who, amidst the Great Depression, were approached by publisher Frederick L. Ackerman of John Wiley & Sons to publish the graphic standards used in their studio. In March 1932, waiting in their office to receive the first copy of their new book, these two New York City architects could not have imagined that, more than three generations later, architects would still consider the book they published as the bible in the profession. Their idea of producing a simple office reference for drafters has become the indispensable standard reference that architects today trust and rely on in their work.

Although the first edition of *Architectural Graphic Standards* consisted of only 213 individual pages, a nation of architects soon discovered that a single volume of standard details and design data was just what they needed to improve their practices. This catalog of building materials, components, equipment, systems, details, charts, graphs, tables, and "odds and ends" has been used by generations of architects because it is the most trusted reference book in architecture. Ramsey and Sleeper's desire to define standards, to establish uniformity, and to clearly present complex and diverse information from thousands of industry sources was then and still is the mission of *Architectural Graphic Standards*.

The research done by John Wiley & Sons affirms that the audience for *Architectural Graphic Standards* is the largest and most loyal for any book ever published in this market. The primary market includes architects and interns; drafters; construction specifiers; civil, structural, and mechanical engineers; and students in these fields. An important secondary market includes general contractors, subcontractors, home builders, estimators, and specialty contractors; developers; planners; landscape architects; interior designers; building code officials; building owners and building engineers; construction trade associations; historians and preservationists; facility space planners; librarians; and lawyers.

Since the sixth edition, *Architectural Graphic Standards* has been organized, generally, according to the principles of *Masterformat*, published by the Construction Specifications Institute. *Masterformat* organizes construction data and information into classifications based on building trade or specialty, reflecting the assembly-line character of the modern construction industry. In this ninth edition, an effort has been made to conform even more to the *Masterformat* system. As a result, most pages have new and improved page headings and section titles. Chapters 2 through 16 conform to *Masterformat*, whereas Chapters 1, 17, 18, 19, and 20 contain sections that are compatible with, or complementary to, *Masterformat*.

The ninth edition consists of 20 chapters—one more than the previous edition. It contains 918 pages, as compared with 854 pages in the eighth edition, and more than 10,000 illustrations. For those who keep a record, we omitted 156 pages, revised 298 pages, added 233 new pages, and kept 344 pages unchanged from the eighth edition.

Since the publication of the eighth edition of *Architectural Graphic Standards* in 1988, we have published annual supplements that help keep the current edition up to date. The first supplement appeared in 1991, and over the past four years some 400 new and revised pages have been published; these pages were produced entirely on a computer.

This process of revision has helped enrich the book by making room for new material. The *Architectural Graphic Standards* Task Force and the editor in chief selected the pages that have been eliminated, most of which were out of date or of little interest to today's professional.

There are some highlights and new features in the ninth edition. We have developed, with the help of masonry industry leaders, a new chapter on masonry that helps redefine the use and application of one of the most reliable building materials used today. Special thanks go to the fine team of experts responsible for this chapter: Ted Sherman, AIA, chairman of the committee; Brian Trimble, of the Brick Institute of America; Stephen S. Szoke, PE, of the National Concrete Masonry Association; and Darrel Rippeteau, AIA, and Grace Lee of Rippeteau Architects, P.C. Chapter 20, on building types and space planning, is also new. Here an attempt has been made for the first time in *Architectural Graphic Standards* to discuss total building planning and design. We plan to expand this chapter in future supplements.

Another important new feature is the addition of 60 pages based on the 1990 Americans with Disabilities Act. Today, both existing buildings and new buildings must be in compliance with ADA requirements with regard to accessibility. A special team of experts, led by James L. Terry, AIA, helped develop these pages. The ADA Task Force members included Kim Beasley, AIA; Steve Cotler, AIA; Ruth Hall Lusher; Thomas L. McGrath; Mark Mazz, AIA; John Sorrenti, AIA; and Susan B. Tusick, AIA.

A resource section has been added at the end of each chapter, which lists published references, trade associations, government agencies, and regulatory organizations pertaining to the material in the chapter, including addresses and phone numbers.

One last, significant new feature of the ninth edition is the 18 pages on site, community, urban, and regional land planning by Gary Greenan of the University of Miami and Andres M. Duany, AIA, and Elizabeth Plater-Zyberk, AIA, of Andres Duany & Elizabeth Plater-Zyberk Architects, Inc. These important pages should become a new standard for land development.

Other highlights to the ninth edition include pages on the following topics: AIA documents introduction, asbestos abatement, building and site security planning, building systems integration, CAD layer guidelines, classical orders, construction cost estimating, door hardware, economy of concrete formwork, chutes and dumbwaiters, energy management systems, environmental impact analysis of building materials, garden structures, geometric proportions, glass fiber reinforced concrete panels, glazed metal curtain wall systems, handrails and rails, historic eaves and overhangs, workstation lighting, indoor air quality, wall paneling, life-cycle costing, metric system, Palladian windows, prefabricated fireproofed steel columns, preservation of historic landscapes, specialty modules, wood trusses, stair design, steel frame systems, structural plastics, structural welds, telecommunications cabling distribution, waterproofing of foundations, water tables, and wine storage cellars.

The publication of a new edition of *Architectural Graphic Standards* requires the time, energy, and expertise of many people. At Wiley, I would like to thank Peggy Burns, publisher, and Meg Hudak, senior marketing manager, for their commitment to this undertaking. I am grateful also to my dear friend Robert J. Fletcher IV, production director, who managed all aspects of the production of this fine book, and I thank him for his attention to detail as well as his professionalism. Two other key people at Wiley who lent their support in shaping this project are Tom Conter, vice president and general manager, and Stephen Kippur, senior vice president.

I would also like to thank W. Bradford Wiley, who retired as chairman of Wiley last year, for his many years of tender loving care of *Architectural Graphic Standards* and this editor. Brad started his career at Wiley at about the same time the first edition was published in 1932, and he has always considered *Architectural Graphic Standards* to be Wiley's flagship publication. We are truly indebted to this publishing giant. The torch has been passed to his son and successor, Bradford Wiley II, who will lead John Wiley & Sons and this book into the next century.

On the *Architectural Graphic Standards* Task Force, William G. Miner, AIA, and Darrel Rippeteau, AIA, have each served as chairman for three years of supplements. I have worked with both of these dedicated professionals on this project in various roles for 15 years and am grateful for their leadership in challenging the Task Force to find a new vision of how the book can be improved in the years to come. I also wish to thank the other members of the Task Force for their contributions: Edward Allen, AIA; William A. Brenner, AIA; Fred Dubin, PE; James M. Duda; James Freehof, AIA; H. Ward Jandl; John Loss, FAIA; Robert Odermatt, FAIA; John Reynolds, AIA; Theodore D. Sherman, AIA; Norma Sklarek, FAIA; James L. Terry, AIA; Douglas Stenhouse, AIA. Special thanks go to Ed Allen for his ideas about shaping the ninth edition.

I am delighted with the dedication of the professionals at the AIA. My special thanks go to three people who made things happen: Janet Rumbarger, managing editor; Anthony Lewandowski, consulting editor; and Richard J. Vitullo, AIA, contributing editor. I am fortunate to have them as my associates.

In addition to this core group, we were supported by a group of staff and consultants: Pamela James Blumgart; Stacy Droneburg; Jenifer Tennant-Dwyer; Nora Richter Greer; Christopher Keane; Fredj Khlifi; Ruthann Mackey; Scot C. McBroom, AIA; Wendy Talarico; Elyse C. Tipton; Laird Ueberroth, AIA; and Jim Vose. Our computer graphic artists were Samir Ali; Steve Dehanas, RIBA; Tom Epps; Jeffery Madsen; Scott Peterson; Ed Rahme; David Salela; Jason Sturniolo; Jerry L. Smith; and Antonio Vercillo. Special thanks go to Jim Vose for pioneering electronic illustrations that helped shape this new edition and to Pilar Wyman for her fine work on the index.

I would also like to take this opportunity to thank James P. Cramer, Hon. AIA, executive vice president/CEO; Fred DeLuca, chief operating officer/CFO; and Steve Etkin, group vice president, for their counsel.

In conclusion, I would like to express my appreciation to the firms, AIA members, and other contributors for their good work on this ninth edition. They are honored with credit lines on each of their pages and also are listed in the Acknowledgments, which follows this Preface. Their valuable service to The American Institute of Architects is a fine example of how the profession continues its undaunted support of *Architectural Graphic Standards* year after year.

JOHN RAY HOKE, JR., FAIA
Editor in Chief

ACKNOWLEDGMENTS

Edward Allen, AIA
Robert E. Anderson, AIA
Dennis A. Andrejko, AIA
Randall Arendt
William R. Arnquist, AIA
Randall Atlas, Ph.D., AIA, CPP
Brian J. F. Baer
B. J. Baldwin
Gordon B. Batson, P.E.
William C. Bauman, Jr.

Eric K. Beach
Christine Beall, AIA, CCS
Kim A. Beasley, AIA
Peter Binnie, BA
Charles A. Birnbaum
Eric A. Borch
Donald Bosserman, AIA
A. Larry Brown
John L. Bryan
Timothy A. Buehner

Robert P. Burns, AIA
Ted Cameron, AIA
John Carmody
Chester Chellman, P.E.
Linda Clark, AIA
D. L. Collins
L. James Cooke, Jr., P.E.
David Cooper, AIA
Timothy J. Cowan
Mattie F. Cox

Edwin B. Crittenden, FAIA
John N. Crittenden, AIA
Graham Davidson, AIA
Thomas D. Davies, Jr., AIA
J. T. Devine, AIA
David M. DiCiuccio, P.E.
Michael Dienesch
Charles Driesen
G. Lawson Drinkard, III, AIA
Andres Duany, AIA

James M. Duda
Charles Easterberg
M. David Egan, P.E.
Charles F. D. Egbert, AIA
A. A. Erdman
Robert T. Faass, CE
Leslie Farrel
Anthony L. Felder
Kenneth D. Franch, AIA, P.E.
James N. Freehof, AIA

Peter H. Frink
Richard L. Gaines
Eric Gastier
Frank Giese
T. John Gilmore, AIA
Carleton Granbery, FAIA
Terry Graves
Gary Greenan
Onkal K. Guzey
Mark R. Hafen, AIA

Roger W. Haines, P.E.
Gary A. Hall
Jane Hansen, AIA
David A. Harris, FAIA
John D. Harvey, AIA
David Hayes
Fred W. Hegel, AIA
Deborah Hershowitz
Ed Hesner
Charles R. Heuer, FAIA

John D. Hilberry, AIA
F. Holdorf
Richard F. Humenn, P.E.
Mary Hurd
Joseph Iano
Norman Jaffe, FAIA
H. Ward Jandl
Roger W. Kipp, AIA
Don Klabin, AIA
William A. Klene, AIA

Stuart L. Knoop
Kenneth Labs
Grace Lee
Randall S. Lindstrom, AIA
Tom Lokey
Alfred F. Lyons
J. David Mack, P.E.
William T. Mahan, AIA
Harold E. Marshall
Derek Martin, FAIA

Mark J. Mazz, AIA
Scot McBroom, AIA
Jess McIlvain, AIA, CCS, CSI
McCain McMurray
Attila L. Mocsary, P.E.
Harold C. Munger, FAIA
Barbara Munson
Don Neubauer, P.E.
Jesse Oak
Tom O'Connor, AIA, FASTM

W. David Owen
Charles J. Parise, FAIA, FASTM
Sharon C. Park, AIA
Nicholas A. Phillips, AIA
Elizabeth Plater-Zyberk, AIA
Gary L. Powell, Ph.D.
Kurt N. Pronske, P.E.
Robert Prouse, IALD, IES
Paul D. Purnell
J. Paul Raeder

Janet B. Rankin
Alan H. Rider, AIA
Boyd C. Ringo
Darrel Rippeteau, AIA
Carl J. Rosenberg, AIA
Laurence Saint Germain, AIA
Ferdinand R. Scheeler, AIA
Michael Schley, AIA
Iskandar Shafie
Theodore D. Sherman, AIA

Robert K. Sherrill
Walter H. Sobel, FAIA
Neil Spencer, AIA
Andrew Sumners
Stephen S. Szoke, P.E.
Charles A. Szoradi, AIA
James L. Terry, AIA
Barry R. Thalden, AIA
Brian E. Trimble
J. Trost, AIA

Laird Ueberroth, AIA
Charles W. Vanderlinden, P.E.
Jeffrey R. Vandevoort
James van Sweden
Don Velsey, AIA
Rudolph R. Verderber
Richard J. Vitullo, AIA
Glenn J. Ware, AIA
Brooks Washburn, AIA
Donald Watson, FAIA

James W. G. Watson, AIA
Kay D. Weeks
Joseph A. Wilkes, FAIA
Joseph J. Williams, AIA
Kent Wong
Dan E. Woosley, AIA
Pilar Wyman
Kamal Zaharin

CHAPTER

1

GENERAL PLANNING AND DESIGN DATA

INTRODUCTION TO ANTHROPOMETRIC DATA

The following anthropometric drawings show three values for each measurement: the top figure is for the large person or 97.5 percentile; the middle figure, the average person or 50 percentile; and the lower figure, the small person or 2.5 percentile. The chosen extreme percentiles thus include 95%. The remaining 5% include some who learn to adapt and others, not adequately represented, who are excluded to keep designs for the majority from becoming too complex and expensive. Space and access charts are designed to accept the 97.5 percentile large man and will cover all adults except a few giants. Therefore, use the 97.5 percentile to determine space envelopes, the 2.5 percentile to determine the maximum "kinetospheres" or reach areas by hand or foot, and the 50 percentile to establish control and display heights. To accommodate both men and women, it is useful at times to add a dimension of the large man to the corresponding dimension of the small woman and divide by 2 to obtain data for the average adult. This is the way height standards evolve. Youth data are for combined sex. Although girls and boys do not grow at the same rate, differences are small when compared with size variations.

Pivot point and link systems make it easy to construct articulating templates and manikins. Links are simplified bones. The spine is shown as a single link; since it can flex, pivot points may be added. All human joints are not simple pivots, though it is convenient to assume so. Some move in complicated patterns like the roving shoulder. Reaches shown are easy and comfortable; additional reach is possible by bending and rotating the trunk and by extending the shoulder. Stooping to reach low is better than stretching to reach high. The dynamic body may need 10% more space than the static posture allows. Shoes have been included in all measurements; allowance may need to be made for heavy clothing. Sight lines and angles of vision given in one place or another apply to all persons.

The metric system of measurement has been included, since it is used in scientific work everywhere and is the most practical system of measurement ever devised. Millimeters have been chosen to avoid use of decimals. Rounding to 5 mm aids mental retention while being within the tolerance of most human measurements.

Disabilities are to be reckoned as follows: 3.5% of men and 0.2% of women are color blind; 4.5% of adults are hard of hearing; over 30% wear glasses; 15 to 20% are handicapped, and 1% are illiterate. Left-handed people have increased in number to more than 10%.

SAFETY INFORMATION

Maximum safe temperature of metal handles is 50°C (122°F) and of nonmetallic handles, 62°C (144°F); maximum air temperature for warm air hand dryers is 60°C (140°F); water temperatures over 46.1°C (115°F) are destructive to human tissue. Environmental temperature range is 17.2 to 23.9°C (63 to 75°F). Weights lifted without discomfort or excessive strain are 22.7 kg (50 lb) for 90% of men and 15.9 kg (35 lb) for women; limit weight to 9.07 kg (20 lb) if carried by one hand for long distances. Push and pull forces, like moving carts, are 258 N (58 lbf) and 236 N (53 lbf) initially, but 129 N (29.1 lbf) and 142 N (32 lbf) if sustained. Noise above the following values can cause permanent deafness: 90 dB for 8 hr, 95 dB for 4 hr, 100 dB for 2 hr, 105 dB for 1 hr, and 110 dB for 0.5 hr.

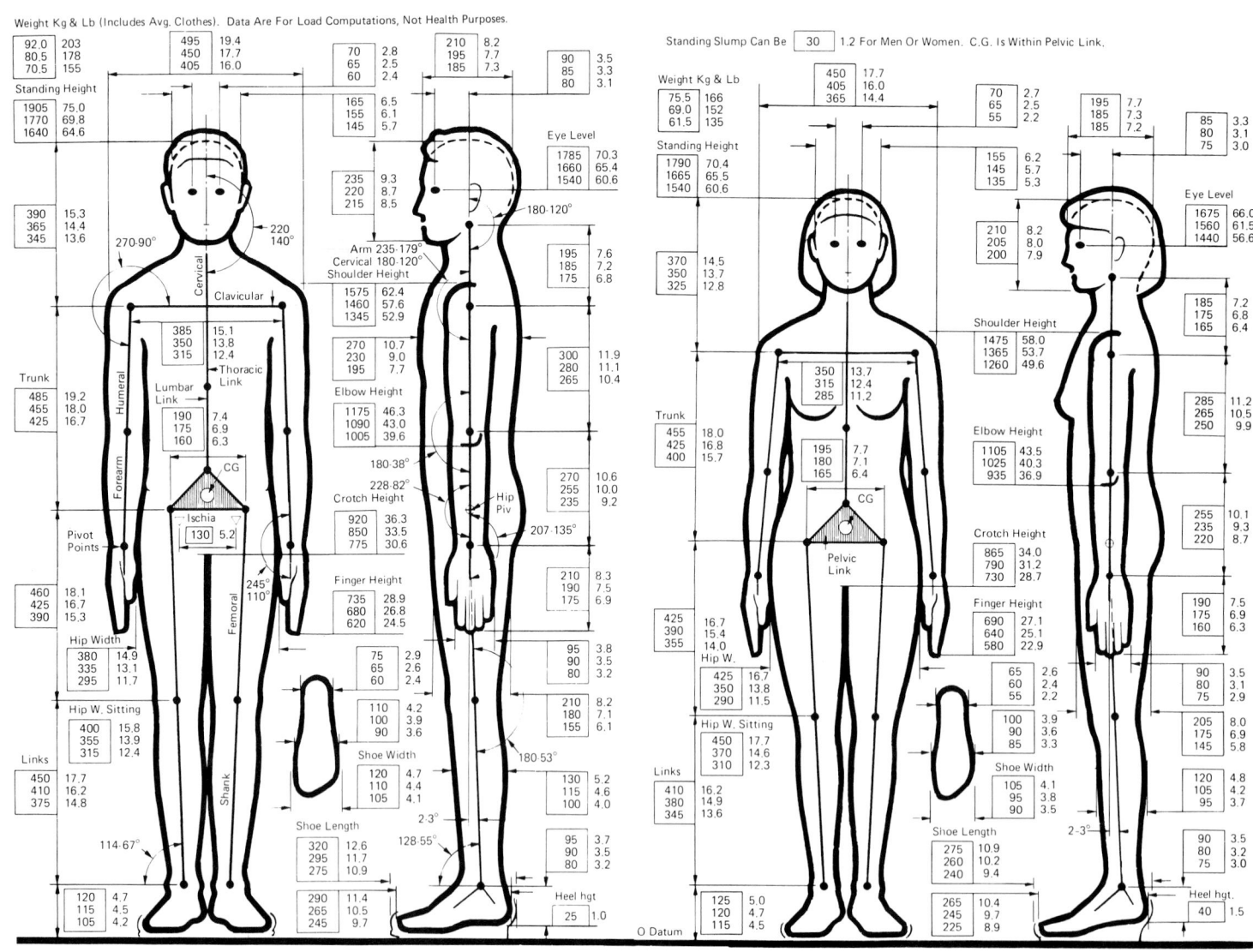

Weight Kg & Lb (Includes Avg. Clothes). Data Are For Load Computations, Not Health Purposes.

Standing Slump Can Be 30 / 1.2 For Men Or Women. C.G. Is Within Pelvic Link.

Male and female standing heights (including shoes):

1905	75.0	1790	70.4 large = 97.5 percentile	includes
1775	69.8	1665	65.5 average = 50 percentile	95% U.S.
1640	64.6	1540	60.6 small = 2.5 percentile	adults.

Dimensional notation system:

1000	39.3	Numbers appearing in boxes are measurements
100	3.9	in millimeters. Numbers outside boxes are
25.4	1.0	measurements in inches.

Niels Diffrient, Alvin R. Tilley; Henry Dreyfuss Associates; New York, New York

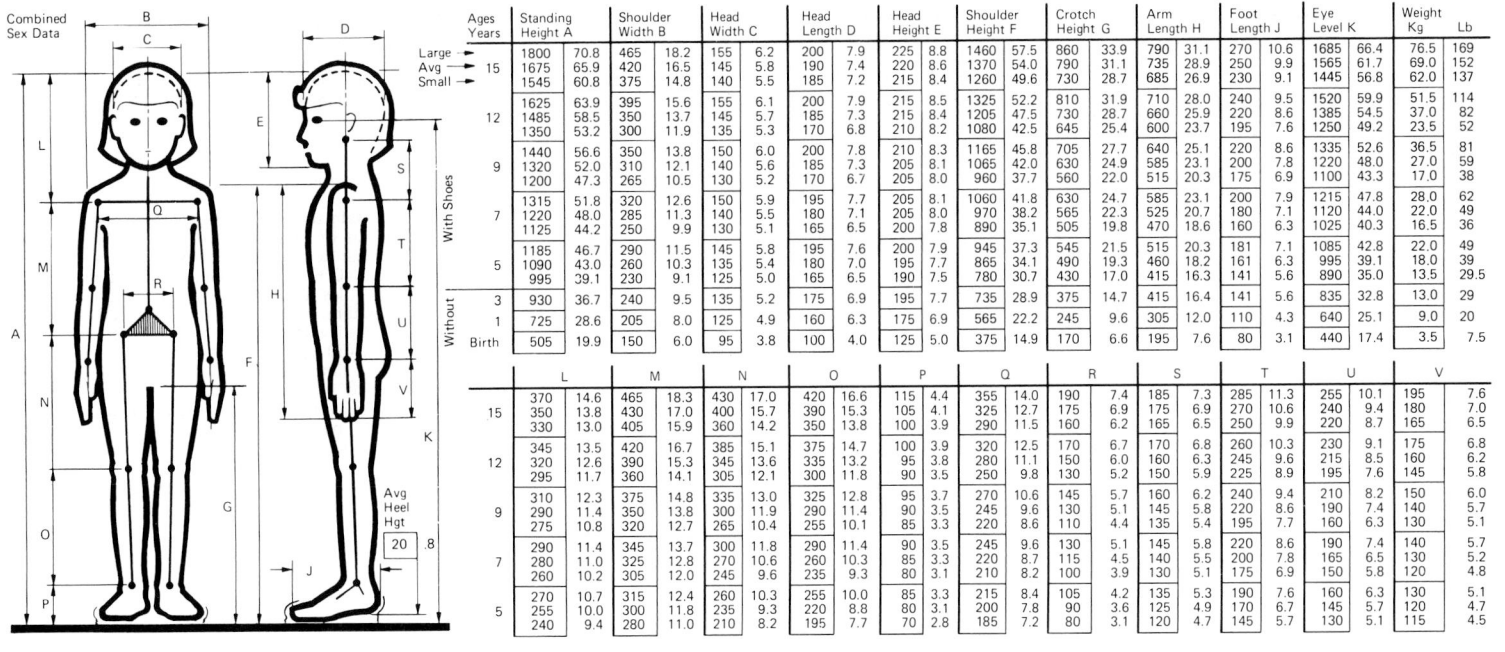

Ages Years	Standing Height A		Shoulder Width B		Head Width C		Head Length D		Head Height E		Shoulder Height F		Crotch Height G		Arm Length H		Foot Length J		Eye Level K		Weight Kg	Lb
15 (Large)	1800	70.8	465	18.2	155	6.2	200	7.9	225	8.8	1460	57.5	860	33.9	790	31.1	270	10.6	1685	66.4	76.5	169
(Avg)	1675	65.9	420	16.5	145	5.8	190	7.4	220	8.6	1370	54.0	790	31.1	735	28.9	250	9.9	1565	61.7	69.0	152
(Small)	1545	60.8	375	14.8	140	5.5	185	7.2	215	8.4	1260	49.6	730	28.7	685	26.9	230	9.1	1445	56.8	62.0	137
12	1625	63.9	395	15.6	155	6.1	200	7.9	215	8.5	1325	52.2	810	31.9	710	28.0	240	9.5	1520	59.9	51.5	114
	1485	58.5	350	13.7	145	5.7	185	7.3	215	8.4	1205	47.5	730	28.7	660	25.9	220	8.6	1385	54.5	37.0	82
	1350	53.2	300	11.9	135	5.3	170	6.8	210	8.2	1080	42.5	645	25.4	600	23.7	195	7.6	1250	49.2	23.5	52
9	1440	56.6	350	13.8	150	6.0	200	7.8	210	8.3	1165	45.8	705	27.7	640	25.1	220	8.6	1335	52.6	36.5	81
	1320	52.0	310	12.1	140	5.6	185	7.3	205	8.1	1065	41.9	630	24.9	585	23.1	200	7.8	1220	48.0	27.0	59
	1200	47.3	265	10.5	130	5.2	170	6.7	205	8.0	960	37.7	560	22.0	515	20.3	175	6.9	1100	43.3	17.0	38
7	1315	51.8	320	12.6	150	5.9	195	7.7	205	8.1	1060	41.8	630	24.7	585	23.1	200	7.9	1215	47.8	28.0	62
	1220	48.0	285	11.3	140	5.5	180	7.1	205	8.0	970	38.2	565	22.3	525	20.7	180	7.1	1120	44.0	22.0	49
	1125	44.2	250	9.9	130	5.1	165	6.5	200	7.8	890	35.1	505	19.8	470	18.6	160	6.3	1025	40.3	16.5	36
5	1185	46.7	290	11.5	145	5.8	195	7.6	200	7.9	945	37.3	545	21.5	515	20.3	181	7.1	1085	42.8	22.0	49
	1090	43.0	260	10.3	135	5.4	180	7.1	195	7.7	865	34.1	490	19.3	460	18.2	161	6.3	995	39.1	18.0	39
	995	39.1	230	9.1	125	5.0	165	6.5	190	7.5	780	30.7	430	17.0	415	16.3	141	5.6	890	35.0	13.5	29.5
3	930	36.7	240	9.5	135	5.2	175	6.9	195	7.7	735	28.9	375	14.7	415	16.4	141	5.6	835	32.8	13.0	29
1	725	28.6	205	8.0	125	4.9	160	6.3	175	6.9	565	22.2	245	9.6	305	12.0	110	4.3	640	25.1	9.0	20
Birth	505	19.9	150	6.0	95	3.8	100	4.0	125	5.0	375	14.9	170	6.6	195	7.6	80	3.1	440	17.4	3.5	7.5

Ages	L		M		N		O		P		Q		R		S		T		U		V	
15	370	14.6	465	18.3	430	17.0	420	16.6	115	4.4	355	14.0	190	7.4	185	7.3	285	11.3	255	10.1	195	7.6
	350	13.8	430	17.0	400	15.7	390	15.3	100	3.9	325	12.7	175	6.9	175	6.9	270	10.6	240	9.4	180	7.0
	330	13.0	405	15.9	360	14.2	350	13.8	100	3.9	290	11.5	160	6.2	165	6.5	250	9.9	220	8.7	165	6.5
12	345	13.5	420	16.7	385	15.1	375	14.7	100	3.9	320	12.5	170	6.7	170	6.8	260	10.3	230	9.1	175	6.8
	320	12.6	390	15.3	345	13.6	335	13.2	95	3.8	280	11.1	150	6.0	160	6.3	245	9.6	215	8.5	160	6.2
	295	11.7	360	14.1	305	12.1	300	11.8	90	3.5	250	9.8	130	5.2	150	5.9	225	8.9	195	7.6	145	5.8
9	310	12.3	375	14.8	335	13.0	325	12.8	95	3.7	270	10.6	145	5.7	160	6.2	240	9.4	210	8.2	150	6.0
	290	11.4	350	13.8	300	11.9	290	11.4	90	3.5	245	9.6	130	5.1	145	5.8	220	8.6	190	7.4	140	5.7
	275	10.8	320	12.7	265	10.4	255	10.1	85	3.3	220	8.6	110	4.4	135	5.4	195	7.7	160	6.3	130	5.1
7	290	11.4	345	13.7	300	11.8	290	11.4	90	3.5	245	9.6	130	5.1	145	5.8	220	8.6	190	7.4	140	5.7
	280	11.0	325	12.8	270	10.6	260	10.3	85	3.3	220	8.7	115	4.5	140	5.5	200	7.8	165	6.5	130	5.2
	260	10.2	305	12.0	245	9.6	235	9.3	80	3.1	210	8.2	100	3.9	130	5.1	175	6.9	150	5.8	120	4.8
5	270	10.7	315	12.4	260	10.3	255	10.0	85	3.3	215	8.4	105	4.2	135	5.3	190	7.6	160	6.3	130	5.1
	255	10.0	300	11.8	235	9.3	220	8.8	80	3.1	200	7.8	90	3.6	125	4.9	170	6.7	145	5.7	120	4.7
	240	9.4	280	11.0	210	8.2	195	7.7	70	2.8	185	7.2	80	3.1	120	4.7	145	5.7	130	5.1	115	4.5

	Ages	High Reach A		Low Reach B		Reach Distance C		High Reach D		Reach Radius E		Eye Level F	
HS	15	2085	82.0	815	32.0	735	29.0	1440	56.7	660	25.9	1215	47.8
		1915	75.3	730	28.7	685	27.0	1375	54.1	610	24.1	1160	45.6
		1765	69.4	665	26.2	635	25.1	1315	51.7	570	22.4	1100	43.3
Jr. HS	12	1860	73.2	705	27.6	665	26.2	1320	52.0	600	23.6	1100	43.3
		1705	67.1	630	24.7	620	24.3	1250	49.2	555	21.9	1040	41.0
		1545	60.9	560	22.1	565	22.3	1185	46.6	510	20.1	990	38.9
4th.	9	1645	64.8	605	23.8	600	23.6	1175	46.3	540	21.2	975	38.4
		1510	59.4	555	21.8	550	21.7	1120	44.0	495	19.5	925	36.5
		1345	53.0	510	20.0	485	19.1	1040	40.9	435	17.1	880	34.6
2nd.	7	1505	59.3	545	21.5	550	21.7	1080	42.6	500	19.6	890	35.0
		1370	53.9	510	20.1	495	19.5	1015	40.0	445	17.5	850	33.5
		1245	49.0	485	19.0	445	17.5	960	37.7	395	15.6	815	32.0
KDG	5	1330	52.3	500	19.7	480	19.0	970	38.1	430	16.9	815	32.1
		1210	47.7	465	18.3	435	17.1	915	36.1	385	15.2	770	30.4
		1085	42.7	425	16.7	390	15.3	865	34.1	345	13.6	720	28.4

Starting School Grades

Up To Ages	Hat Shelf Height G		Lavatory Height H		Work Top J		Work Depth K		Table Height L		Seat Length M	
15	1675	66.0	760	30.0	915	36.0	460	18.0	650	25.5	370	14.6
12	1485	58.5	685	27.0	795	31.3	420	16.5	590	23.3	340	13.3
9	1320	52.0	635	25.0	695	27.3	380	15.0	525	20.7	300	11.8
7	1220	48.0	585	23.0	635	25.0	355	14.0	480	18.9	275	10.8
5	1090	43.0	485	19.0	570	22.5	330	13.0	445	17.5	250	9.9

Ages	Seat Height N		Seat To Backrest O		Min Backrest Height P		Armrest Spacing Q		Seat Width R		Basic Table Width S	
15	405	15.9	150	6.0	175	6.8	445	17.5	380	15.0	760	30.0
12	370	14.6	145	5.7	160	6.2	420	16.5	370	14.5	710	28.0
9	325	12.8	135	5.4	140	5.6	355	14.0	330	13.0	610	24.0
7	290	11.4	130	5.1	130	5.1	330	13.0	305	12.0	610	24.0
5	265	10.4	120	4.8	125	5.0	305	12.0	280	11.0	535	21.0

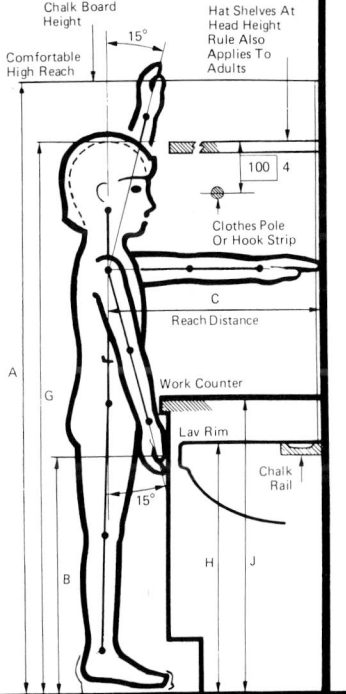

Chalk Board Height
Comfortable High Reach
15°
Hat Shelves At Head Height Rule Also Applies To Adults
100 4
Clothes Pole Or Hook Strip
C Reach Distance
Work Counter
Lav Rim
Chalk Rail
15°

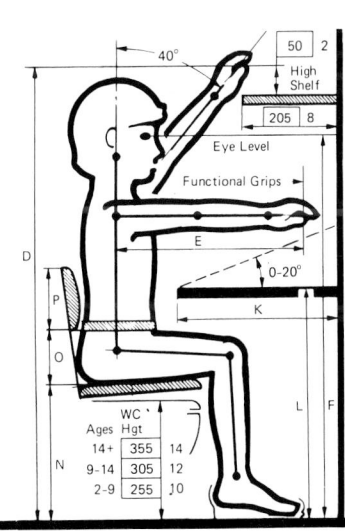

40°
50 2 High Shelf
205 8
Eye Level
Functional Grips
0-20°
E
K
D
P
O
N

Ages	WC Hgt	
14+	355	14
9-14	305	12
2-9	255	10

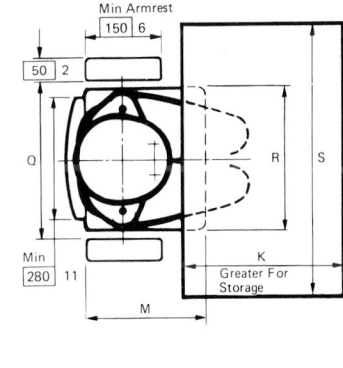

Min Armrest
150 6
50 2
Q
R S
Min 280 11
K Greater For Storage
M

Standing heights (including shoes)—typical example:
1800 70.8 large 15 year youth = 97.5 percentile
1675 65.9 average 15 year youth = 50 percentile
1545 60.8 small 15 year youth = 2.5 percentile
combined sex data U.S. youths

Dimensional notation system:
1000 39.3 Numbers appearing in boxes are measurements in millimeters. Numbers outside boxes are measurements in inches.
100 3.9
25.4 1.0

Niels Diffrient, Alvin R. Tilley; Henry Dreyfuss Associates; New York, New York

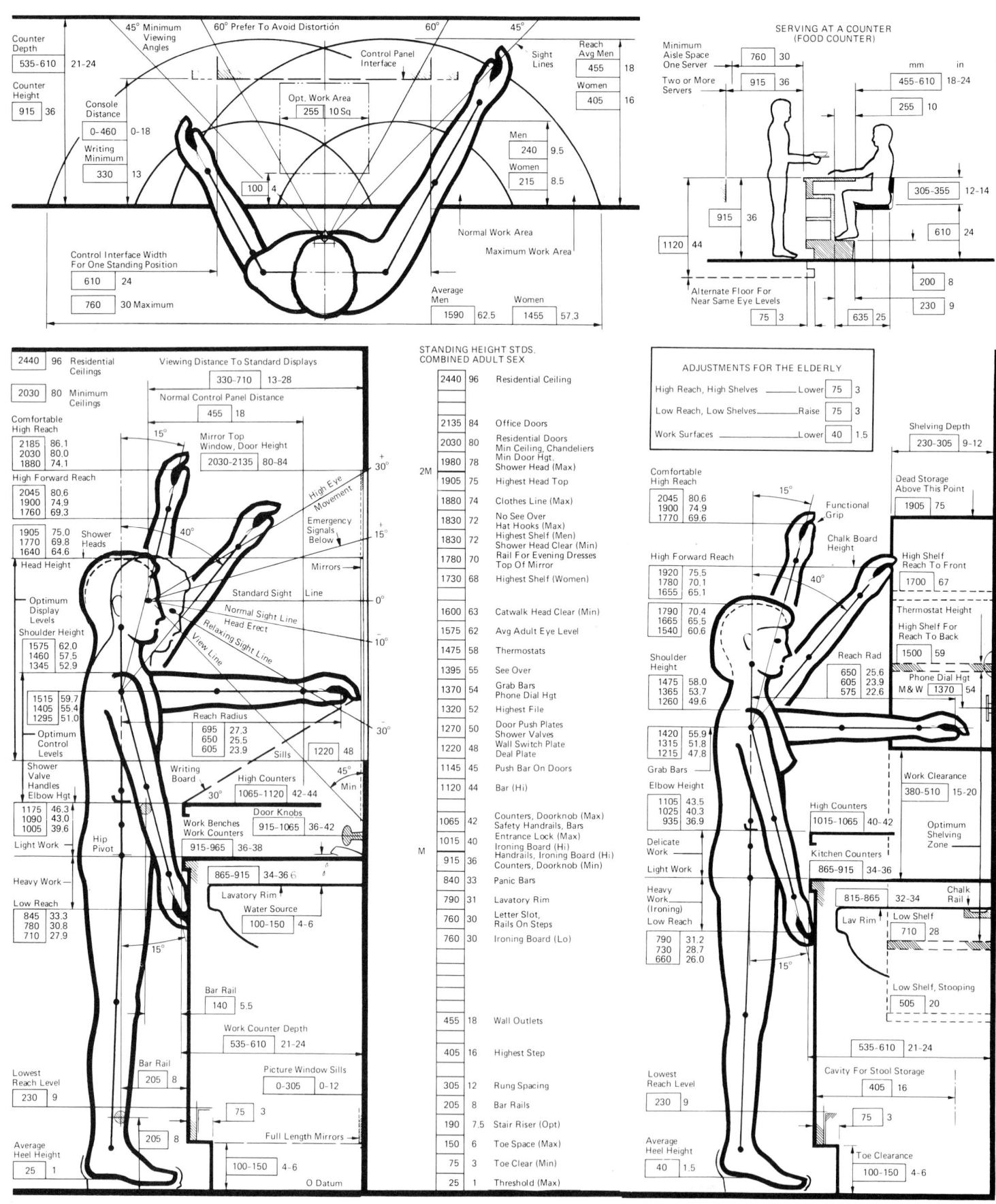

Niels Diffrient, Alvin R. Tilley; Henry Dreyfuss Associates; New York, New York

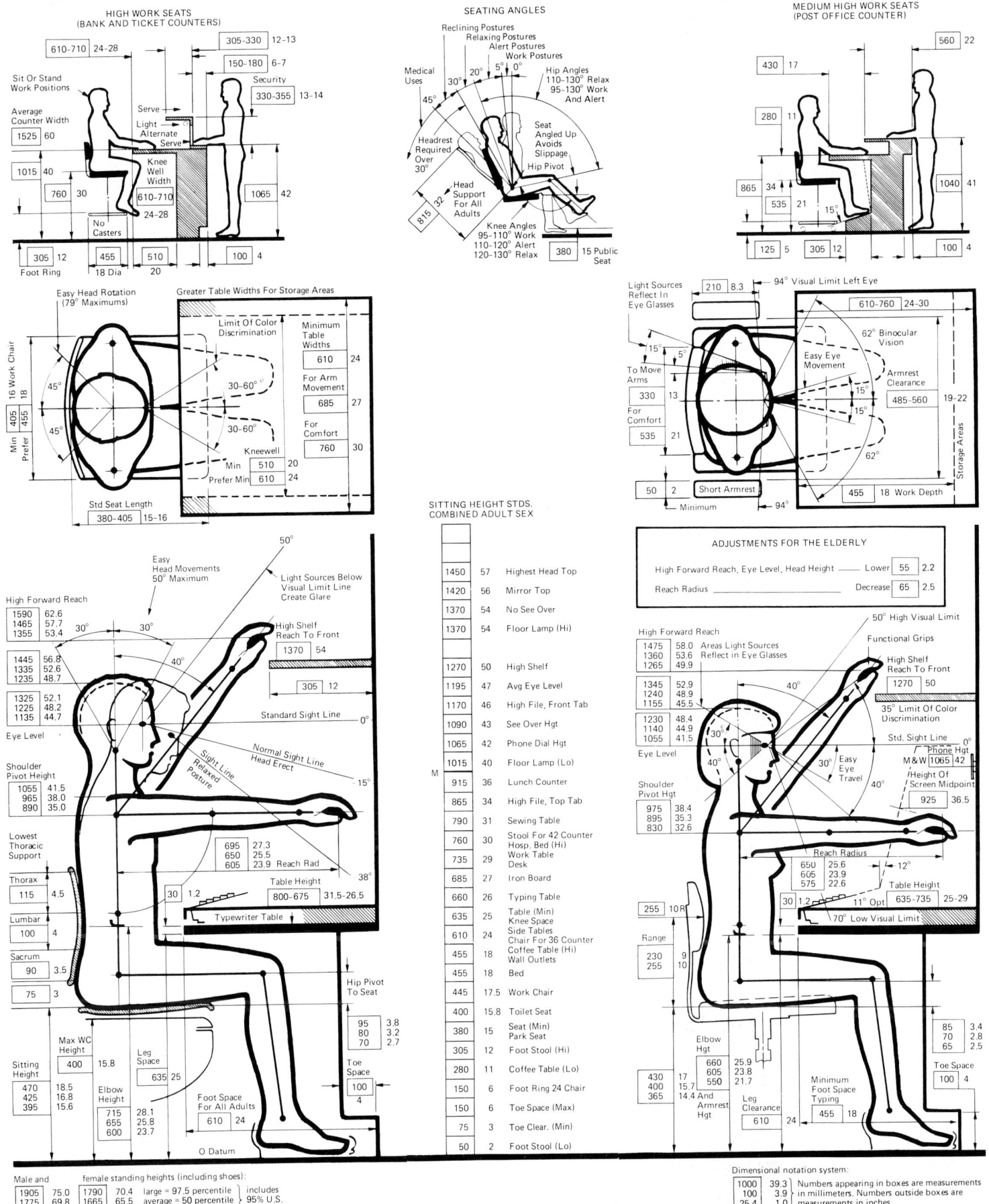

HIGH WORK SEATS
(BANK AND TICKET COUNTERS)

SEATING ANGLES

MEDIUM HIGH WORK SEATS
(POST OFFICE COUNTER)

SITTING HEIGHT STDS.
COMBINED ADULT SEX

1450	57	Highest Head Top
1420	56	Mirror Top
1370	54	No See Over
1370	54	Floor Lamp (Hi)
1270	50	High Shelf
1195	47	Avg Eye Level
1170	46	High File, Front Tab
1090	43	See Over Hgt
1065	42	Phone Dial Hgt
1015	40	Floor Lamp (Lo)
915	36	Lunch Counter
865	34	High File, Top Tab
790	31	Sewing Table
760	30	Stool For 42 Counter / Hosp. Bed (Hi)
735	29	Work Table / Desk
685	27	Iron Board
660	26	Typing Table
635	25	Table (Min) / Knee Space
610	24	Side Tables / Chair For 36 Counter
455	18	Coffee Table (Hi) / Wall Outlets
455	18	Bed
445	17.5	Work Chair
400	15.8	Toilet Seat
380	15	Seat (Min) / Park Seat
305	12	Foot Stool (Hi)
280	11	Coffee Table (Lo)
150	6	Foot Ring 24 Chair
150	6	Toe Space (Max)
75	3	Toe Clear. (Min)
50	2	Foot Stool (Lo)

ADJUSTMENTS FOR THE ELDERLY

High Forward Reach, Eye Level, Head Height — Lower 55 / 2.2

Reach Radius — Decrease 65 / 2.5

Male and female standing heights (including shoes):

1905	75.0	1790	70.4	large = 97.5 percentile	includes
1775	69.8	1665	65.5	average = 50 percentile	95% U.S.
1640	64.6	1540	60.6	small = 2.5 percentile	adults

Dimensional notation system:
1000 / 39.3 — Numbers appearing in boxes are measurements
100 / 3.9 — in millimeters. Numbers outside boxes are
25.4 / 1.0 — measurements in inches.

Niels Diffrient, Alvin R. Tilley; Henry Dreyfuss Associates; New York, New York

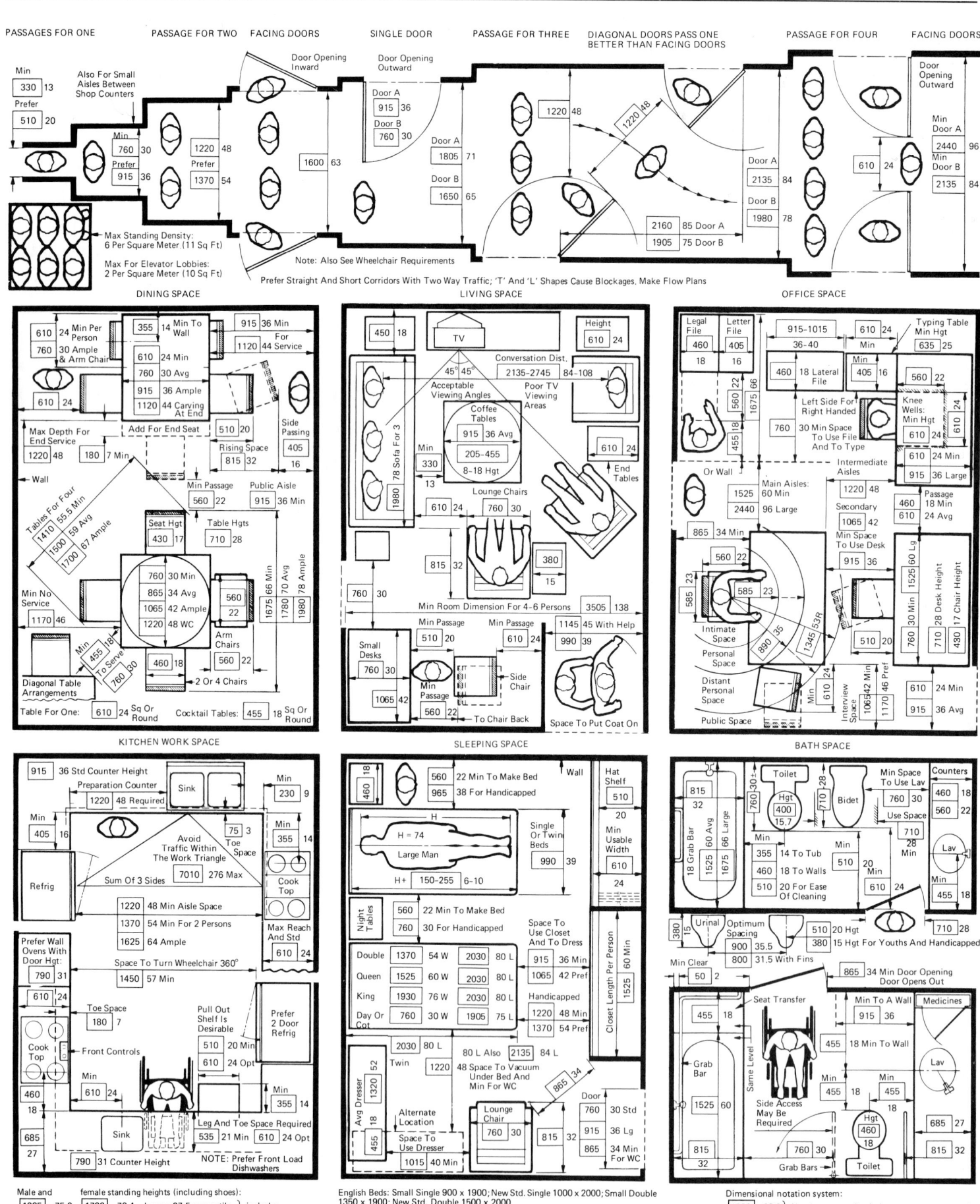

Niels Diffrient, Alvin R. Tilley; Henry Dreyfuss Associates; New York, New York

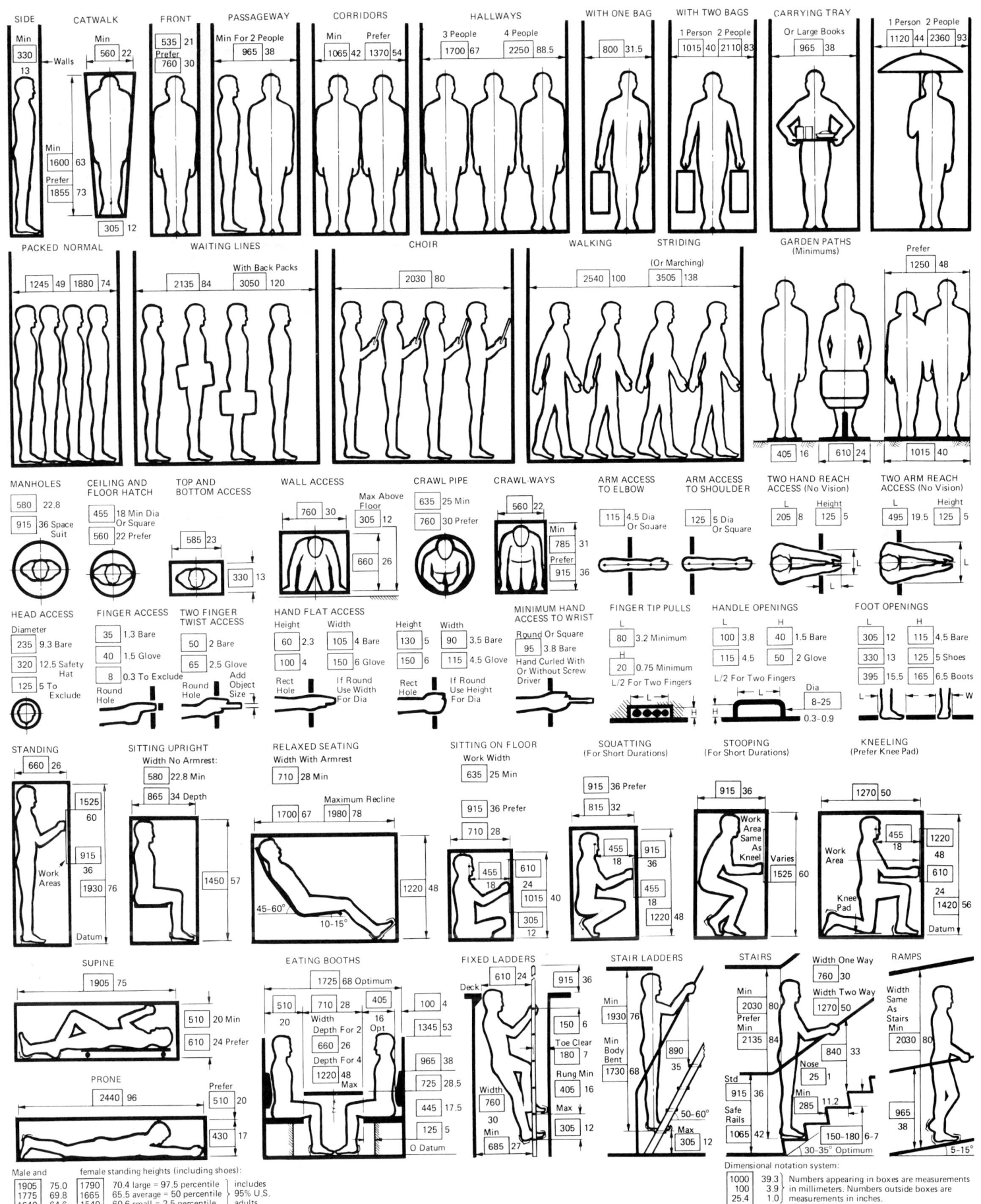

Niels Diffrient, Alvin R. Tilley; Henry Dreyfuss Associates, New York, New York

HUMAN DIMENSIONS 1

ACCESS LAWS AND REGULATIONS

Designing a barrier-free environment may be easier than understanding the laws and regulations that attempt to define what is needed to ensure accessibility for persons with disabilities. Four federal laws, two federal standards, a consensus standard, model codes, state codes, and even local codes and ordinances can all have jurisdiction, depending upon the type and location of a project.

AMERICANS WITH DISABILITIES ACT OF 1990 (ADA)

The ADA makes it a civil rights violation to fail to provide barrier-free access in state and local government projects and in commercial facilities and public accommodations by private entities. The ADA has five titles or sections that prohibit discrimination on the basis of disability in employment, public services (including transportation), state and local governments, public accommodations and commercial facilities operated by private entities, and telecommunications. Title II of the ADA applies to state and local government (public) entities, while title III applies to public accommodations and commercial facilities. The Department of Justice's regulations under titles II and III and the Department of Transportation's (DOT) regulations under title II establish standards for accessible design that must be followed in new construction and alteration projects. The title III standards for accessible design that apply to public accommodations and commercial facilities are the ADA Accessibility Guidelines for Buildings and Facilities (ADAAG). Under title II, state and local governments must use DOT's regulations, which include ADAAG with Section 10—Transportation Facilities. For other facilities, entities may choose between ADAAG (without the elevator exemption) and the Uniform Federal Accessibility Standards (UFAS) for facilities.

FAIR HOUSING AMENDMENTS ACT OF 1988 (FHAA)

Multifamily projects consisting of four or more dwelling units must be accessible in common areas and adaptable in dwelling units based on Fair Housing Accessibility Guidelines (FHAG).

THE ARCHITECTURAL BARRIERS ACT OF 1968 (ABA)

All facilities that are designed, constructed, altered, or leased by or on behalf of the government and certain other facilities that are financed with federal funds must comply with the Architectural Barriers Act of 1968. Under the ABA, four federal agencies set the standards: the Department of Housing and Urban Development sets requirements for housing; Department of Defense sets requirements for defense facilities; U.S. Postal Service sets requirements for postal facilities; and the General Services Administration (GSA) sets requirements for all other facilities that fall under the act. Since 1984 the standard used by the four agencies for design, construction, and alterations has been UFAS.

THE REHABILITATION ACT OF 1973 (SECTION 504)

Programs and activities that receive federal financial assistance may not discriminate on the basis of disability in providing benefits and services. New construction and alteration projects must be accessible and comply with standards referenced by funding agencies in their section 504 regulations. Under almost all section 504 regulations, UFAS is the operant standard. Entities that do not comply face the loss of federal funds.

ACCESSIBILITY GUIDELINES FOR BUILDINGS AND FACILITIES (ADAAG)

Standards for accessible design that apply to new construction and alteration projects (including historic properties) of public accommodations and commercial facilities under title III of the ADA. Under title II, ADAAG is the standard for design, construction, and alteration of transportation facilities of state and local government entities. State and local governments may choose to use ADAAG (without the elevator exemption) or UFAS for other buildings and facilities. ADAAG will be modified and adopted to cover all title II facilities (see Resources, below).

UNIFORM FEDERAL ACCESSIBILITY STANDARDS (UFAS)

The accessibility standard that applies to new construction and alteration of all federal buildings, most federally funded projects, and those of most programs and activities that receive federal financial assistance. UFAS may also be used by state and local governments under the ADA for facilities other than transit facilities which must follow ADAAG (see Resources, below).

John A. Raeber, AIA, FCSI; San Francisco, California
Ruth Hall Lusher; Washington, D.C.

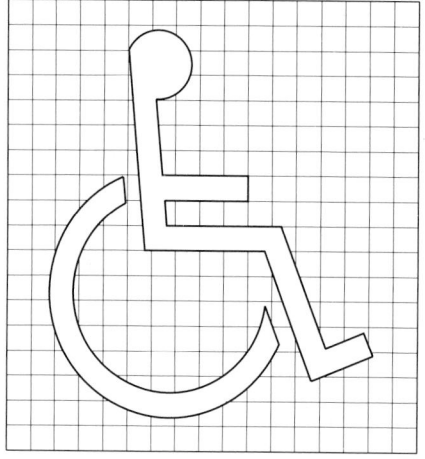

INTERNATIONAL SYMBOL OF ACCESSIBILITY

AMERICAN NATIONAL STANDARD INSTITUTE (ANSI)

ANSI A117.1 has been a national consensus standard providing guidance for barrier-free design for over thirty years. The ADAAG, FHAA guidelines, UFAS, and model codes access requirements, although they contain differences, are all based on ANSI A117 in one way or another.

MODEL CODES

(Uniform, National, and Standard)

When a state or local government adopts a model code, it becomes an applicable regulation. At this writing all three model codes reference ANSI A117.1-1986 as the basis for technical conformance but include their own scoping requirements.

STATE CODES

During the last twenty years more than a dozen states have developed their own special regulations defining what constitutes a barrier-free environment.

LOCAL CODES AND ORDINANCES

Although most local jurisdictions have adopted one of the model codes, some larger jurisdictions have either adopted special ordinances or provided written interpretations relating to barrier-free design.

DESIGNING FOR PEOPLE WITH DISABILITIES

Passage of the Americans with Disabilities Act emphasizes the importance of design professionals understanding the needs of persons with disabilities. The act's full effect on design will not be known for many years as a variety of needs are identified and standards are developed.

Understanding the specific needs of persons with mobility impairments, both ambulatory and nonambulatory, has been growing. The needs of persons with visual and hearing impairments have also been given special attention.

Under the definition of persons with disabilities, the ADA includes those who are physically and mentally impaired and those regarded or treated as physically or mentally impaired.

At present there are no standards for designing an environment for persons with mental disabilities. And, though the disabilities that develop with age often fall into one of the other categories, the specific needs of elderly persons may prove to be more comprehensive than presently suggested. New understanding will lead to new regulations. Creating a barrier-free environment will require a continuing educational process for the design professional.

Further, the ADA regulations allow for "equivalent facilitation": the use of alternative designs and technology as long as equivalent or greater accessibility is provided. With understanding of the basis for requirements in the standards, architects will be able to take advantage of this provision.

REGULATION APPLICABILITY EXAMPLES

The ADA, as well as regulations issued under the act, build on the requirements that have applied to federal facilities and federally assisted programs and activities for many years. The ADA does not replace existing federal, state, or local accessibility requirements. It does, however, bring under coverage of federal accessibility standards state and local government entities, some of which were not previously covered by Section 504, as well as privately owned public accommodations and commercial facilities. To determine whether a privately owned facility houses a place of public accommodation or is considered a commercial facility, use the following list.

PUBLIC ACCOMMODATIONS

- Places of lodging
- Establishments serving food or drink
- Places of exhibition or entertainment
- Places of public gathering
- Sales or rental establishments
- Service establishments
- Stations used for specified public transportation
- Places of public display or collection
- Places of recreation
- Places of education
- Social service center establishments
- Places of exercise or recreation

COMMERCIAL FACILITIES

- Facilities whose operations will affect commerce such as factories, warehouses, industrial facilities, and office buildings.

Where more than one set of regulations applies, the most restrictive must be used unless otherwise stipulated in one of the regulations.

1. U.S. POST OFFICE IN A SHOPPING CENTER: When a government agency leases space, the UFAS is used in conjunction with other applicable laws and regulations. In this case, any alterations would be subject to state and local regulations and ADA, as well as UFAS.
2. STATE LIBRARY: The ADA allows use of either the ADAAG without the elevator exemption or the UFAS for determining compliance. In addition, any state regulations would apply.
3. SHOPPING CENTER: In addition to applicable state and local regulations, ADA's ADAAG would apply.
4. CONDOMINIUMS: In addition to applicable state and local regulations, FHAA's FHAG applies where four or more dwelling units are built.
5. HOTEL: In addition to applicable state and local regulations, the ADAAG applies. If a portion of the hotel is used as long-term lodging such as a residential hotel, the FHAG would apply to that portion.
6. MULTI-USE FACILITY: Each part of the facility must comply with the regulations applicable to that particular part. Common use facilities have to comply with the most restrictive applicable regulations.

PROJECT CONSIDERATIONS

It is appropriate to begin each project with the assumption that everything being designed should be barrier free. Work areas must be on an accessible path, and maneuvering space and clearances must be provided at doors to work areas. Workstations, however, are not required to be usable by a person with a disability unless they are assigned to such persons. Dwelling units within complexes covered by the FHAA require common areas to be fully accessible, but the dwelling units themselves are only required to be adaptable for accessibility.

FEDERAL PROJECTS

Federal projects must comply with UFAS. UFAS scoping and occupancy classifications, together with the technical provisions, define what areas are required to be accessible.

STATE AND LOCAL GOVERNMENT PROJECTS

Under ADA new construction, additions, and alterations require barrier-free design. For transportation facilities, public entities must follow DOT's rule which includes ADAAG with Section 10—Transportation Facilities. For other facilities, design may be based on either the UFAS or ADAAG, although the elevator exception in ADAAG does not apply.

Although many provisions in ADAAG and UFAS are the same or similar, there are major differences, particularly in the alteration provisions of each. The Justice Department's ADA Technical Assistance Manual for title II provides an overview of the differences (see Resources, below).

Since many facility types such as public housing and prisons are not covered in ADAAG 1991, public entities are advised to use UFAS provisions for such facilities.

1 UNIVERSAL ACCESSIBILITY

PRIVATE ENTITY PROJECTS

The ADA has different requirements for commercial facilities and public accommodations. New construction and alteration projects for both public accommodations and commercial facilities must comply with accessibility requirements in the Justice Department's title III rule, which incorporates ADAAG. Only public accommodations must comply with the requirements for barrier removal.

1. New construction: Two exemptions allow certain smaller buildings to not provide an elevator. There is also an exception for structural impracticability based on site constraints. Neither exception is intended to have broad application, and access is required to the extent possible. Thus a two-story building without an elevator would still require accessible toilet compartments with grab bars in the second floor bathrooms.

2. Additions and alterations: Modifications to existing facilities are required to be barrier free. Where a primary functional area is modified, the path of travel, which includes toilet rooms, drinking fountains, and telephones servicing the altered area, is also required to be made barrier free. The costs for the path of travel work can be limited to 20% of the original project cost.

3. Barrier removal: The ADA requires removal of existing barriers in public accommodations, where readily achievable, even where no alterations are planned. "Readily achievable" means able to be carried out without much difficulty or expense.

Projects undertaken strictly for barrier removal are not considered alterations, and path-of-travel requirements do not apply. Such modifications must comply with the technical provisions for alterations contained in ADAAG if compliance is readily achievable.

HISTORIC PRESERVATION PROJECTS

Alteration of existing historically significant public and private facilities requires barrier-free access. However, where barrier-free design would threaten the historic significance of the facility, alternative methods of providing access are permitted and are in some cases defined in the title II and title III regulations of ADAAG and UFAS.

1. Barrier removal: Privately owned public accommodations of historic significance must comply with requirements for removal of existing barriers.

2. Public entities, state and local governments, and federal assisted programs must comply with program accessibility requirements.

RESIDENTIAL PROJECTS

New complexes with four or more dwelling units are required to have common areas fully accessible and dwelling units on the ground floor and on accessible levels adaptable for accessibility (capable of being easily modified).

1. In complexes without elevators, site impracticability due to terrain or unusual characteristics may allow the number of adaptable units to be limited to 20% of the total units provided.

2. Townhouses in buildings without elevators are exempt from the FHAA adaptability requirements; however, in buildings with elevators, the dwelling unit spaces on the level with an elevator would have to comply.

3. Residential buildings, including single-family units, that include public accommodations such as a rental office are required to comply with ADAAG in areas used as a public accommodation, including the building entrance and sanitary facilities made available to customers or clients.

4. New public housing projects must also comply with the requirement for 5% fully accessible units and other requirements contained in UFAS and in regulations issued by the Department of Housing and Urban Development under Section 504 (see Resources, below).

CONSIDERATIONS FOR VISUALLY IMPAIRED PERSONS

1. Protruding objects along circulation paths.
   a. Objects in path: keep lower than 27 in. for cane detectability
   b. Protrusions: maximum 4 in. if bottom edge is over 27 in.
2. Minimum height clearance: 80 in.
3. Emergency signals: both audible and visual
4. Raised character and Braille signs
5. Visual signage requirements
6. Audible elevator signals

CONSIDERATIONS FOR HEARING IMPAIRED PERSONS

1. Assistive listening systems in assembly areas with fixed seating
2. Visual alarms in public and common use area
3. Telephone requirements (see below)
4. Visual notification devices required in transient housing, hotels, and motels
5. Hall lanterns and other visual elevator indicators

ACCESSIBLE ROUTE

An accessible route must connect an accessible building entrance to public transportation stops, accessible parking, accessible passenger loading zones, and public streets and sidewalks. An accessible route must connect the accessible building entrance to rooms, spaces, and accessible elements in the facility.

PLATFORM (WHEELCHAIR) LIFTS

ADA limits use of lifts for access in new construction to very specific applications to achieve access goals and in alterations and additions projects where no other method of access is available.

DRINKING FOUNTAINS

Both high and low fountains are required, no fewer than 50% wheelchair accessible; others are to be located at a standard height convenient to those with difficulty stooping. Hi-low fountains are required when only one fountain is provided.

TELEPHONES

Requirements are for public pay telephones, public closed circuit telephones (such as apartment entry phones and hotel house phones), and other public telephones.

VOLUME CONTROL TELEPHONES

Provide magnetic field receivers; volume control required for accessible telephones and for at least 25% of all other telephones.

TEXT TELEPHONES

One required where four or more public pay telephones are provided in a facility or on the exterior, where at least one is provided in interior location. Also required in specific facility types and areas (e.g., hospitals, convention centers, transit facilities).

ACCESSIBLE EXITS AND AREAS OF RESCUE ASSISTANCE

1. Accessible routes shall also serve as accessible means of egress.
2. Provide areas of rescue assistance in new buildings with occupiable levels above and below grade without exit directly to grade; except where buildings have a supervised automatic sprinkler system
3. Number per floor: same as required by applicable code for exits, typical minimum 2
4. Area of rescue assistance size: provide space for at least two wheelchairs
5. Stairway width: minimum 48 in. clear between handrails

ADDITIONAL PROVISIONS UNIQUE TO ADAAG:

1. Dressing rooms: One dressing room in each cluster for each type of use must be accessible, including bench and mirror.
2. Hotels, motels, and other transient housing: Roll-in/transfer showers must be provided in some wheelchair accessible rooms, and visual alarms, visual notification devices, and accommodations for TDD use by individuals with hearing impairments must be provided.
3. Auditorium seating: In addition to accessible wheelchair seating, transfer seats with movable aisle armrests must be provided.
4. Automated teller machines: Must be accessible to persons with visual, hearing, and mobility impairments.
5. Special facility types: Detailed provisions are provided in special sections for restaurants and cafeterias, medical care facilities, libraries, accessible transient lodging, and transportation facilities.

RESOURCES

Public Access Section
Civil Rights Division
U.S. Department of Justice
P.O. Box 66738
Washington, D.C. 20035-6738

ADA Information Line operates from 1:00 p.m. to 5:00 p.m. EST, Monday - Friday, except holidays.
(202) 514 - 0301 (V)
(202) 514 - 0383 (TDD)

PUBLICATIONS

Title II ADA Regulations (28 CFR Part 35), Nondiscrimination on the Basis of Disability in State and Local Government Services

Title III ADA Regulations (28 CFR Part 36), Nondiscrimination on the Basis of Disability by Public Accommodations and in Commercial Facilities, including ADAAG as the Standards for Accessible Design

ADA Title II and ADA Title III Technical Assistance Manuals

ADA Handbook: contains title I, title II, and title III rules, including ADAAG and UFAS.

U.S. Architectural and Transportation
Barriers Compliance Board
1331 F Street, N.W.
Suite 1000
Washington, D.C. 20004-1111

ADA Information Line operates from 9:00 a.m. to 5:00 p.m. EST, Monday - Friday, except holidays.
(800) 872 - 2253 (V)
(202) 272 - 5434 (V)
(202) 272 - 5449 (TDD)

PUBLICATIONS

Uniform Federal Accessibility Standards (UFAS).

UFAS Accessibility Checklist

ADA Guidelines Accessibility Checklist for Buildings and Facilities

Accessible Design Bulletins" on a growing list of topics related to ADAAG requirements, including no. 1, "Detectable Warnings"; no. 2, "Visual Alarms"; no. 3, "Text Telephones"; no. 4, "Entrances/Exits"; no. 5, "Using ADA Regulations and the ADA Accessibility Guidelines for Buildings and Facilities."

Fair Housing Information Clearinghouse
P.O. Box 6091
Rockville, Maryland 20850
(800) 343 - 3442 (V)
(800) 877 - 8339 (TDD)

PUBLICATIONS

24 CFR, chapter 1, Final Fair Housing Accessibility Guidelines.

24 CFR, part 14, et al. Implementation of the Fair Housing Amendments Act of 1988.

Section 504 Rule (24 CFR Part 8), Nondiscrimination Based on Handicap in Federally Assisted Programs and Activities of the Department of Housing and Urban Development.

U.S. Department of Transportation
400 Seventh Street, S.W.
Room 10424
Washington, D.C. 20590
(202) 366 - 9305 (V)
(202) 755 - 7687 (TDD)

PUBLICATIONS

ADA Regulations (49 CFR Parts 27, 37, and 38), Transportation for Individuals with Disabilities; Final Rule.

CANES

1. Provide support while walking.
2. Assist balance, relieve pain in extremities.
3. Assist seeing-impaired and blind.
4. Canes are adjustable or nonadjustable, and are made with a variety of handgrips.
   a. Ortho-cane: 27 to 42 in. high.
   b. Quad cane: four legs for a wider base of support. Height adjusts from 26 1/2 to 36 1/2 in. Wide base is 9 x 13 in., narrow is 5 x 7 in.
   c. Long cane: used by the blind, 36 to 48 in.

CRUTCHES

1. Reduce stress of weight on lower extremities.
2. User must have good shoulder muscles and good balance.
3. User must be able to maintain hand functions while standing.
4. Because crutches are angled away from the body, wider doors and corridors may be necessary.
   a. Axillary crutches have an underarm support piece to transmit forces to the shoulder.
   b. Nonaxillary crutches have handgrips and a forearm or upper arm cuff and distribute weight to the forearm.

WALKERS

1. Aid balance and decrease stress on joints and muscles.
2. Require wider doors and additional maneuvering space.
3. Generally made of aluminum, and may have wheels or a seat for resting.

WHEELCHAIRS

1. Come in many models and sizes and have a variety of removable accessories, such as footrests and armrests.
2. The U.S. model is the most popular, with large, rear drive wheels, and smaller, front caster wheels.
3. Frames are usually aluminum and may be collapsible.

MOTORIZED WHEELCHAIRS

1. Driven by electric motors powered by storage batteries below the seat.
2. Controlled by a hand mechanism on the chair arm (more clearance is needed under tables, desks, etc.).
3. Similar in size to manual wheelchairs, but heavier, less maneuverable, and noncollapsible.

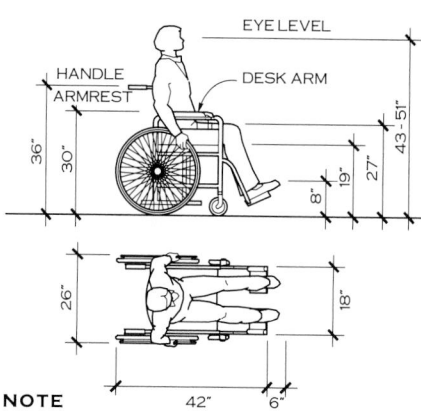

NOTE

Footrest may extend further for tall people

STANDARD WHEELCHAIR DIMENSIONS

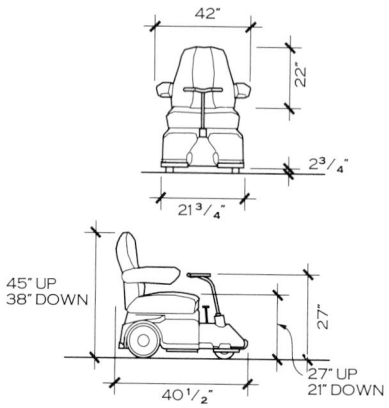

THREE-WHEELED ELECTRIC WHEELCHAIR

NOTES

1. Steers like a bicycle.
2. Maneuvering clearances similar to conventional chairs.

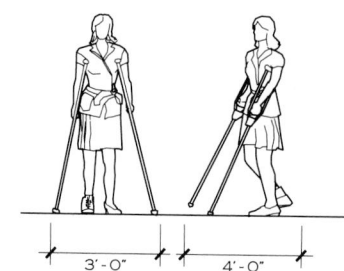

AXILLARY CRUTCH DIMENSIONS

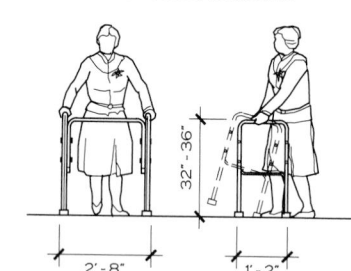

WALKER DIMENSIONS

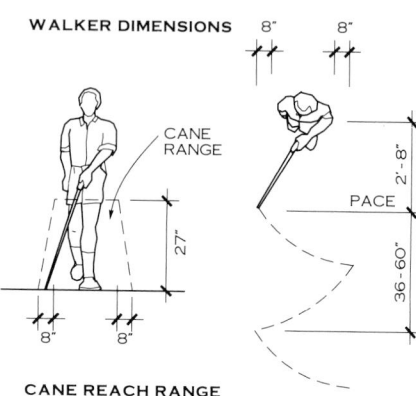

CANE REACH RANGE

MOBILITY AIDS

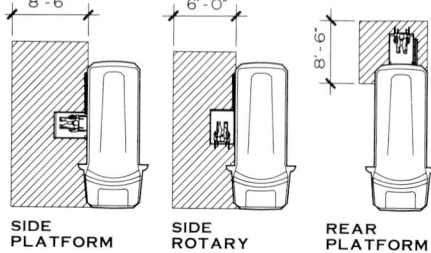

SIDE PLATFORM   SIDE ROTARY   REAR PLATFORM

NOTES

1. Three types of lifts are available to allow users to enter and exit vans:

   SIDE AND REAR PLATFORM LIFTS: Platform lifts are stowed in a vertical position. To board, the operator opens the vehicle's door and activates the platform to unfold to a horizontal position, flush with the floor of the van. The lift is then lowered to ground level. When passenger boards, lift is raised to van floor level and stored.

   SIDE ROTARY LIFTS: Rotary lifts and lowers passenger vertically, parallel to the van. This type of lift requires the smallest aisle.

2. Each lift requires different clearances at parking spaces and passenger loading zones. For each lift, the access aisle should include a clear path to the operating controls, usually located in the passenger-side rear quarter-panel.

3. Lifts can be attached to most standard vans.

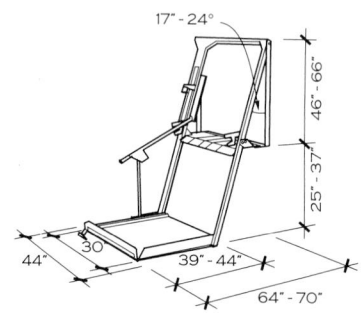

PLATFORM LIFT DIMENSIONS

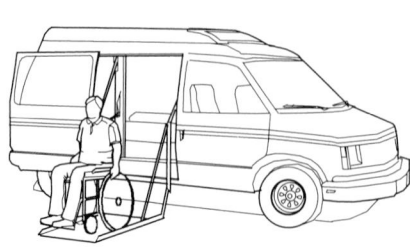

PLATFORM LIFT

VAN LIFTS

MODIFIED VAN DIMENSIONS (IN.)

Wheelbase	112 – 120
Overall length	175 – 191
Overall width	69 – 72
Overall height	66 – 70
Interior height	58 – 62
Interior width	65 – 76
Ramp length	54 – 54

NOTES

1. Entire van is modified by manufacturer to include a lowered floor, removable or adjustable seating, hand controls, and an access ramp. Vans with lowered floors have a lower overall height than other modified vans. Dimensions below are for lowered floor vans.

2. Vans may have raised tops to permit drivers and passengers in wheelchairs to move about inside. Raised tops typically increase the total height of a standard van to approximately 8 ft 10 in. Minimum required canopy clearance is 9 ft 0 in., only 2 in. greater than van height; therefore, a clearance of 9 ft 6 in. is recommended.

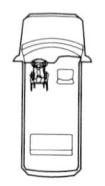 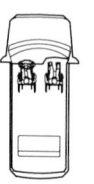 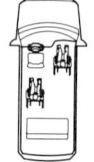

A variety of seating options is possible.

MODIFIED VANS

Janet B. Rankin, AIA; Rippeteau Architects; Washington, D.C.
Thomas D. Davies, Jr., AIA, Kim A. Beasley, AIA; Paradigm Design Group; Washington, D.C.

1 UNIVERSAL ACCESSIBILITY

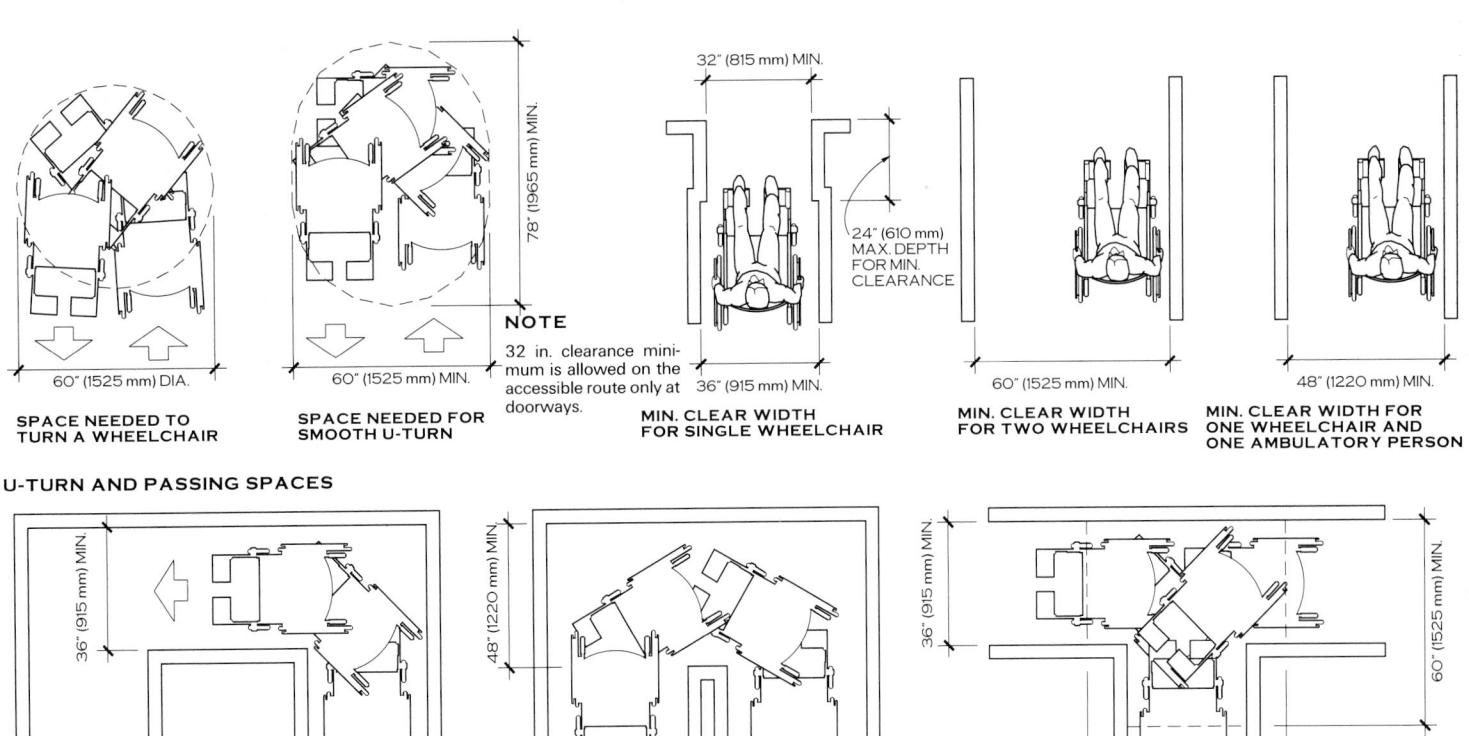

SPACE NEEDED TO TURN A WHEELCHAIR
60" (1525 mm) DIA.

SPACE NEEDED FOR SMOOTH U-TURN
60" (1525 mm) MIN.
78" (1965 mm) MIN.

NOTE
32 in. clearance minimum is allowed on the accessible route only at doorways.

MIN. CLEAR WIDTH FOR SINGLE WHEELCHAIR
32" (815 mm) MIN.
24" (610 mm) MAX. DEPTH FOR MIN. CLEARANCE
36" (915 mm) MIN.

MIN. CLEAR WIDTH FOR TWO WHEELCHAIRS
60" (1525 mm) MIN.

MIN. CLEAR WIDTH FOR ONE WHEELCHAIR AND ONE AMBULATORY PERSON
48" (1220 mm) MIN.

U-TURN AND PASSING SPACES

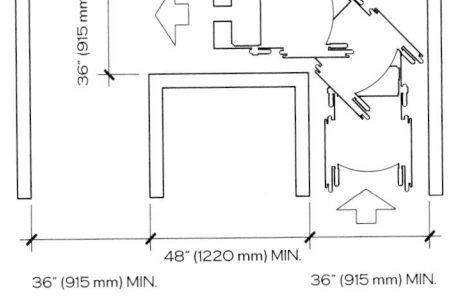

90° TURN
36" (915 mm) MIN.
48" (1220 mm) MIN.
36" (915 mm) MIN.

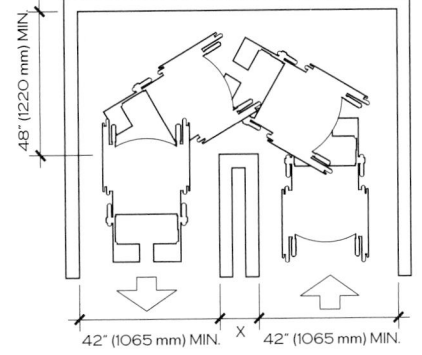

NOTE
Dimensions shown apply when x < 48 in. (1220 mm).

U-TURN AROUND AN OBSTRUCTION
48" (1220 mm) MIN.
42" (1065 mm) MIN. x 42" (1065 mm) MIN.

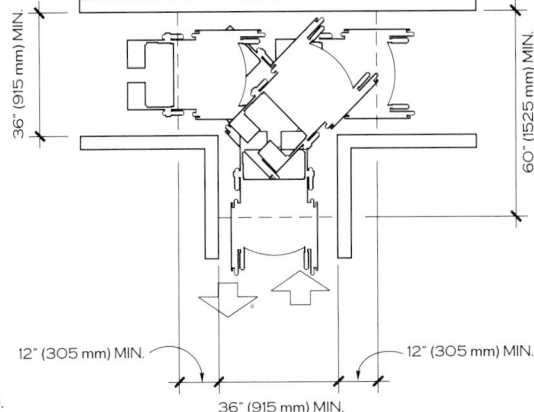

T-SHAPED SPACE FOR 180° TURN
36" (915 mm) MIN.
60" (1525 mm) MIN.
12" (305 mm) MIN.   12" (305 mm) MIN.
36" (915 mm) MIN.

TURNAROUNDS

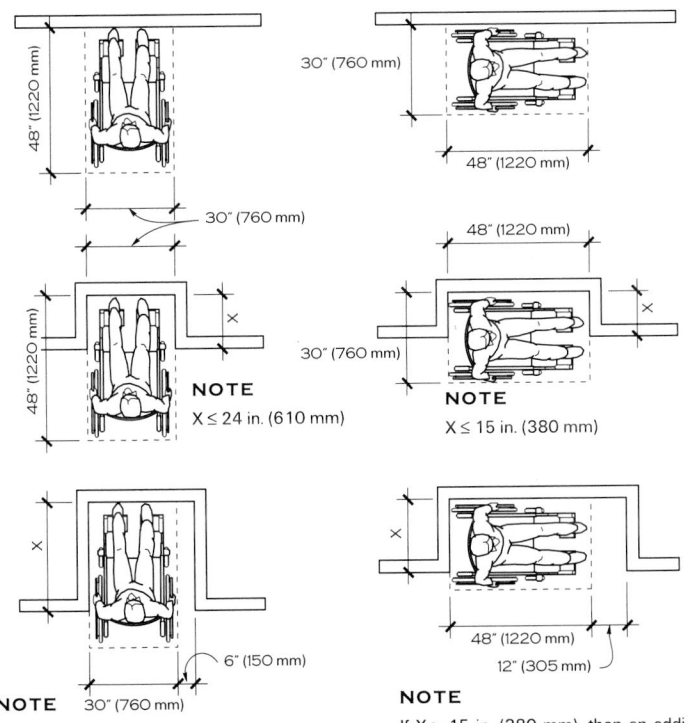

48" (1220 mm)
30" (760 mm)

30" (760 mm)
48" (1220 mm)

48" (1220 mm)

NOTE
X ≤ 24 in. (610 mm)

48" (1220 mm)
30" (760 mm)

NOTE
X ≤ 15 in. (380 mm)

48" (1220 mm)
6" (150 mm)

48" (1220 mm)
12" (305 mm)

NOTE
If X > 24 in. (610 mm), then an additional maneuvering clearance of 6 in. (150 mm) shall be provided as shown

FORWARD APPROACH
30" (760 mm)

NOTE
If X > 15 in. (380 mm), then an additional maneuvering clearance of 12 in. (305 mm) shall be provided as shown.

PARALLEL APPROACH

MINIMUM CLEAR FLOOR SPACE IN ALCOVES

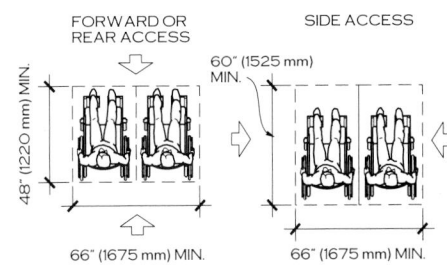

FORWARD OR REAR ACCESS
SIDE ACCESS
60" (1525 mm) MIN.
48" (1220 mm) MIN.
66" (1675 mm) MIN.   66" (1675 mm) MIN.

SEATING SPACES IN SERIES

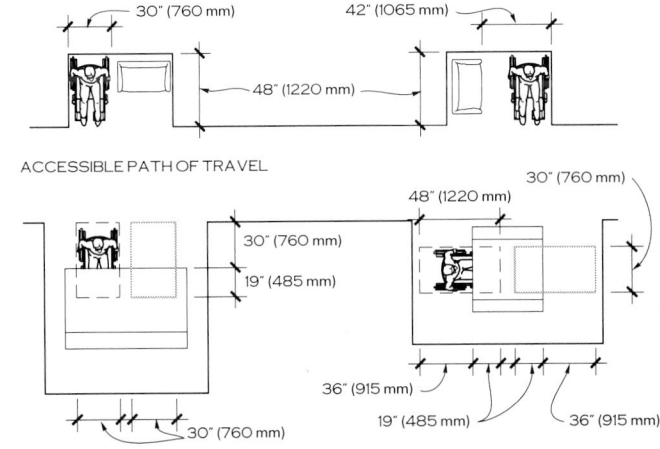

30" (760 mm)   42" (1065 mm)
48" (1220 mm)

ACCESSIBLE PATH OF TRAVEL

48" (1220 mm)   30" (760 mm)
30" (760 mm)
19" (485 mm)
36" (915 mm)   19" (485 mm)   36" (915 mm)
30" (760 mm)

MINIMUM CLEARANCES FOR SEATING AND TABLES

Scot C. McBroom, AIA; Alexandria, Virginia
Thomas D. Davies, Jr., AIA, Kim A. Beasley, AIA; Paradigm Design Group; Washington, D.C.

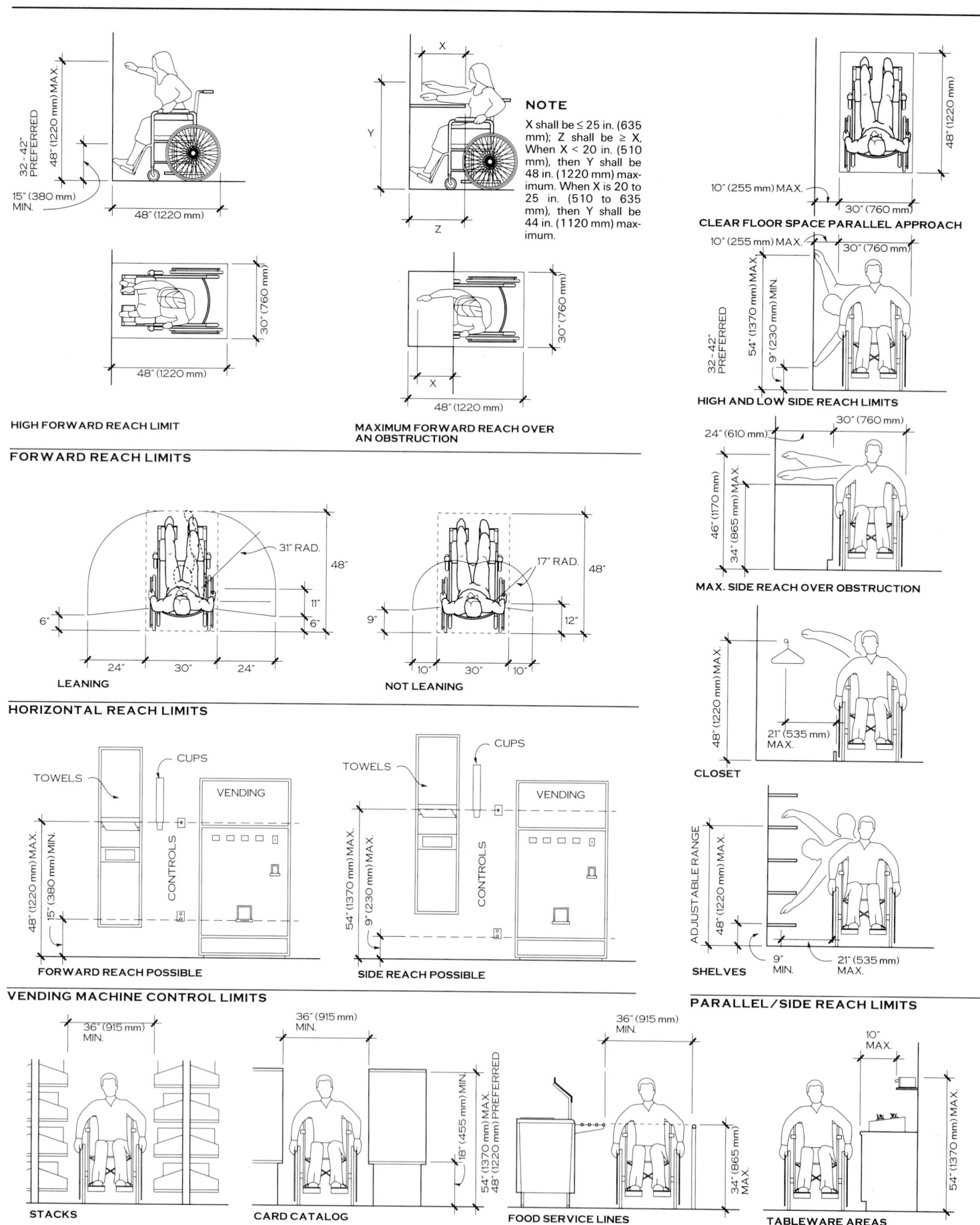

NOTE

X shall be ≤ 25 in. (635 mm); Z shall be ≥ X, When X < 20 in. (510 mm), then Y shall be 48 in. (1220 mm) maximum. When X is 20 to 25 in. (510 to 635 mm), then Y shall be 44 in. (1120 mm) maximum.

CLEAR FLOOR SPACE PARALLEL APPROACH

HIGH FORWARD REACH LIMIT

MAXIMUM FORWARD REACH OVER AN OBSTRUCTION

HIGH AND LOW SIDE REACH LIMITS

FORWARD REACH LIMITS

MAX. SIDE REACH OVER OBSTRUCTION

LEANING

NOT LEANING

CLOSET

HORIZONTAL REACH LIMITS

FORWARD REACH POSSIBLE

SIDE REACH POSSIBLE

SHELVES

VENDING MACHINE CONTROL LIMITS

PARALLEL/SIDE REACH LIMITS

STACKS

CARD CATALOG

FOOD SERVICE LINES

TABLEWARE AREAS

EXAMPLES

Scot C. McBroom, AIA; Alexandria, Virginia

1   UNIVERSAL ACCESSIBILITY

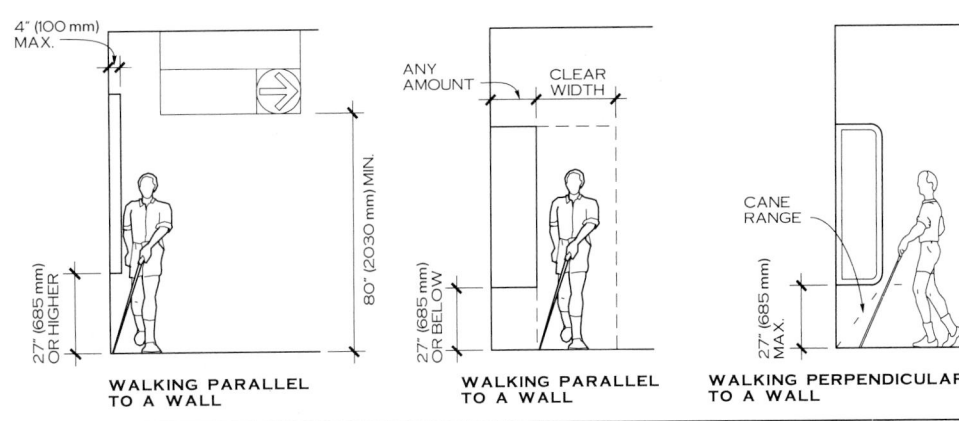

CANE CLEARANCES

WALKING PARALLEL TO A WALL

WALKING PARALLEL TO A WALL

WALKING PERPENDICULAR TO A WALL

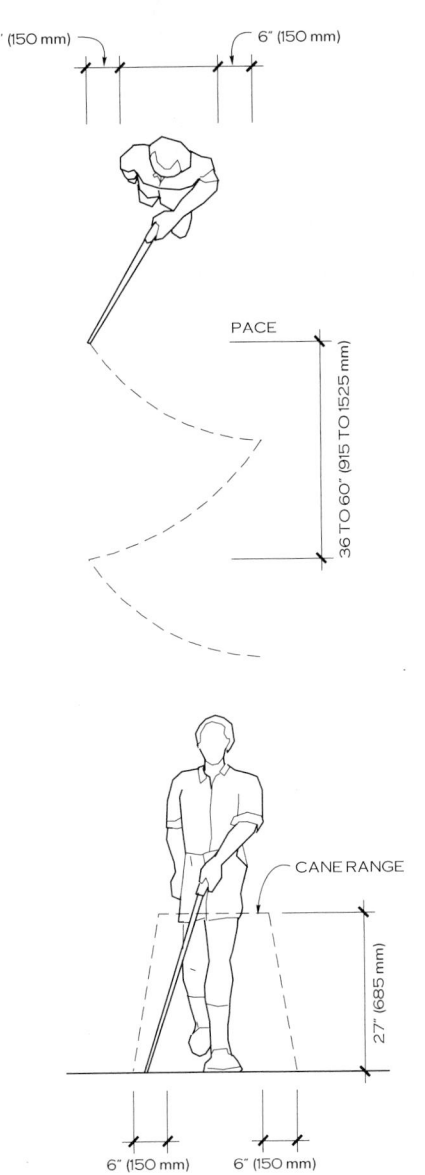

CANE TECHNIQUE

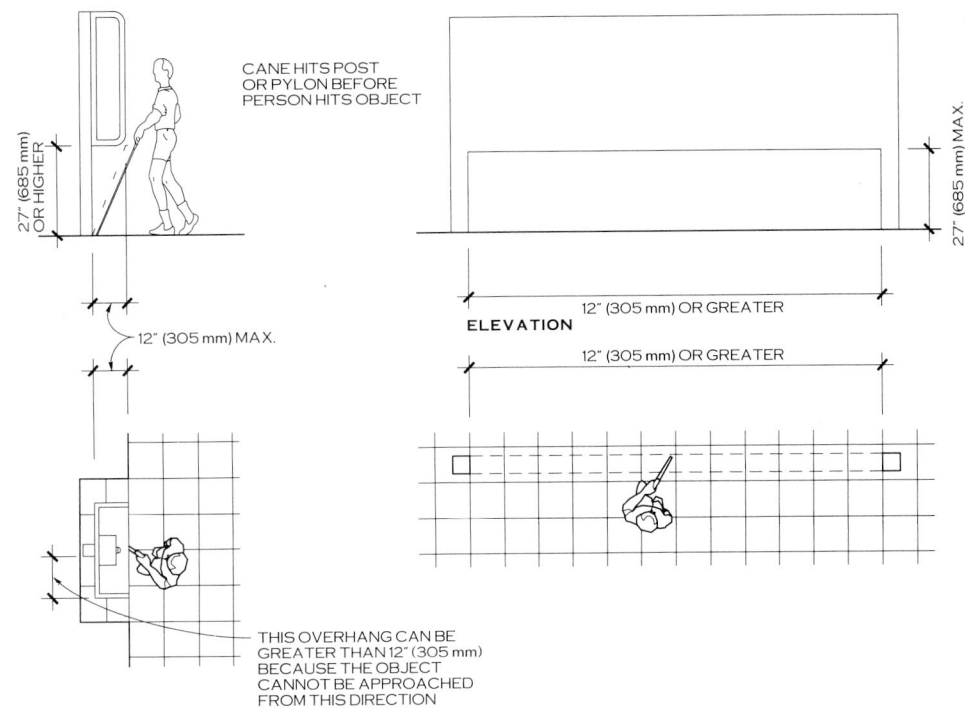

CANE HITS POST OR PYLON BEFORE PERSON HITS OBJECT

ELEVATION

12" (305 mm) OR GREATER

12" (305 mm) OR GREATER

THIS OVERHANG CAN BE GREATER THAN 12" (305 mm) BECAUSE THE OBJECT CANNOT BE APPROACHED FROM THIS DIRECTION

OBJECTS MOUNTED ON POSTS OR PYLONS

FREESTANDING OVERHANGING OBJECTS

FREESTANDING OBJECTS

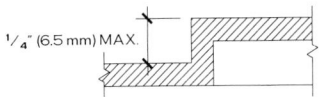

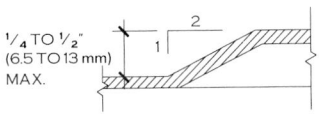

CHANGES IN LEVEL

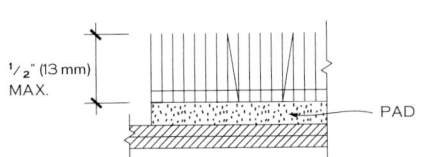

CARPET PILE THICKNESS

Scot C. McBroom, AIA; Alexandria, Virginia

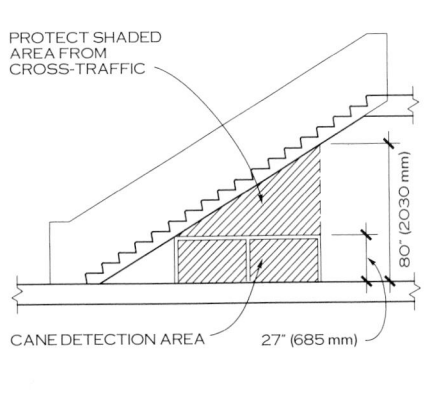

PROTECT SHADED AREA FROM CROSS-TRAFFIC

CANE DETECTION AREA   27" (685 mm)

ADDITIONAL PROTECTION NOT REQUIRED BETWEEN WING WALLS

OVERHEAD HAZARDS — EXAMPLE

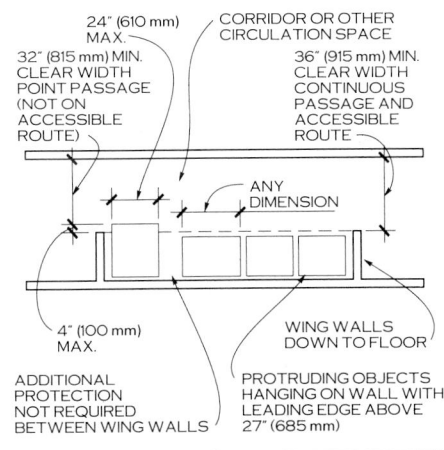

24" (610 mm) MAX.

32" (815 mm) MIN. CLEAR WIDTH POINT PASSAGE (NOT ON ACCESSIBLE ROUTE)

CORRIDOR OR OTHER CIRCULATION SPACE

36" (915 mm) MIN. CLEAR WIDTH CONTINUOUS PASSAGE AND ACCESSIBLE ROUTE

ANY DIMENSION

4" (100 mm) MAX.

WING WALLS DOWN TO FLOOR

PROTRUDING OBJECTS HANGING ON WALL WITH LEADING EDGE ABOVE 27" (685 mm)

WALL-MOUNTED OBJECTS — EXAMPLE

UNIVERSAL ACCESSIBILITY

1

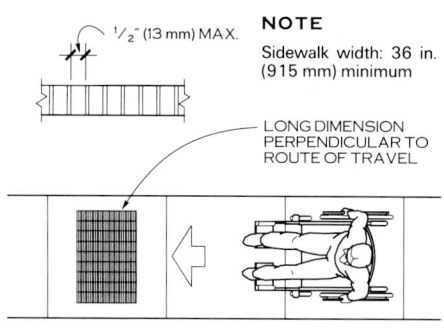

NOTE

Sidewalk width: 36 in. (915 mm) minimum

LONG DIMENSION PERPENDICULAR TO ROUTE OF TRAVEL

GRATING ORIENTATION

NOTE

ADAAG standardizes detectable warnings as raised truncated domes with a nominal 0.9 in. diameter, 0.2 in. height, and nominal 2.35 in. on center which must contrast visually with adjoining surfaces.

DETECTABLE WARNING

Detectable warnings identify potentially hazardous conditions to persons with visual impairments. Because curb ramps take away the curb, the traditional warning that one is approaching a street, detectable warnings are required where the transition between sidewalk and street is smooth. Warnings may be required at all curb ramps and hazardous vehicular area boundaries with walks.

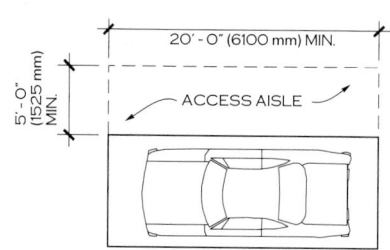

PASSENGER LOADING ZONES
NOTES

1. On accessible route
2. Vertical clearance: 114 in. (2900 mm), for vehicle route and loading area

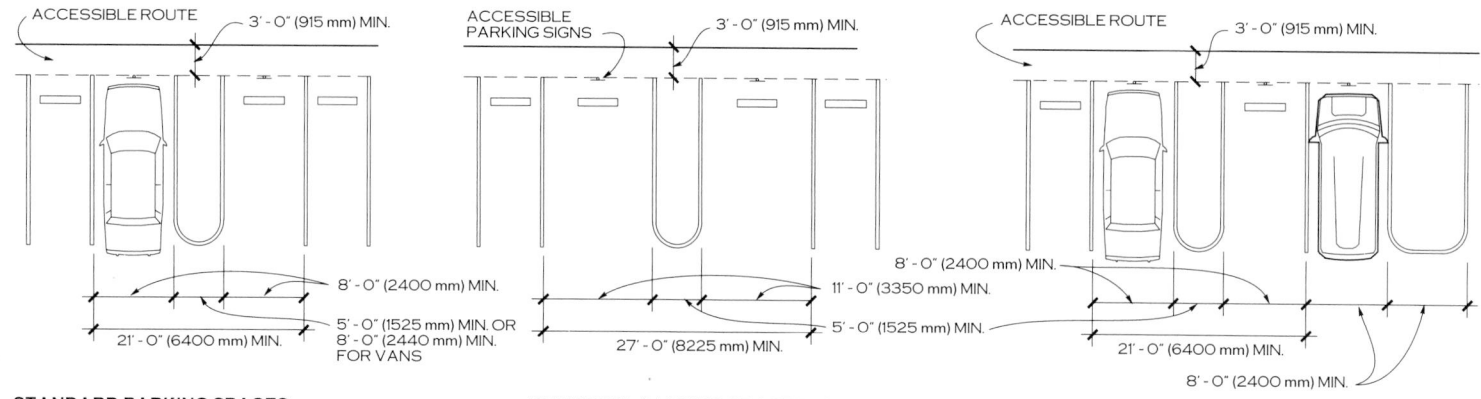

STANDARD PARKING SPACES

UNIVERSAL PARKING SPACE DESIGN (ACCOMMODATES CARS OR VANS)

VAN ACCESSIBLE SPACE AT END ROW

ACCESSIBLE PARKING SPACES

ACCESSIBLE PARKING NOTES

1. As close as possible to building entry; on an accessible route. Maximum slope of spaces and access aisle is 1:50.
2. Vertical clearance: 98 in. (2490 mm) to, at, and from accessible van parking.
3. See ADAAG 4.1.2 for the percentage of accessible spaces required based on lot size and facility type.

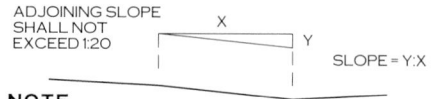

ADJOINING SLOPE SHALL NOT EXCEED 1:20

SLOPE = Y:X

NOTE

Design storm drain system to shed water away from curb ramps.

CURB RAMP SLOPES

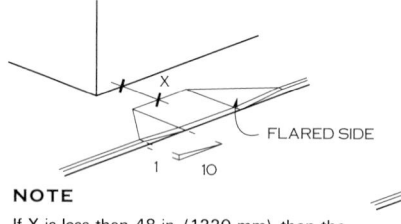

FLARED SIDE

NOTE

If X is less than 48 in. (1220 mm), then the slope of the flared side shall not exceed 1:12.

FLARED SIDES

PLANTING OR OTHER NONWALKING SURFACE

36" (915 mm) MIN.

RETURNED CURB

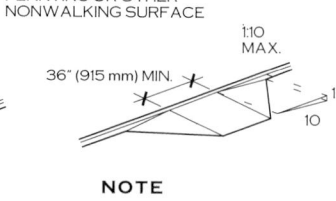

1:10 MAX.

NOTE

Ramp must not project into vehicular traffic lane.

BUILT-UP CURB RAMP

CURB RAMPS

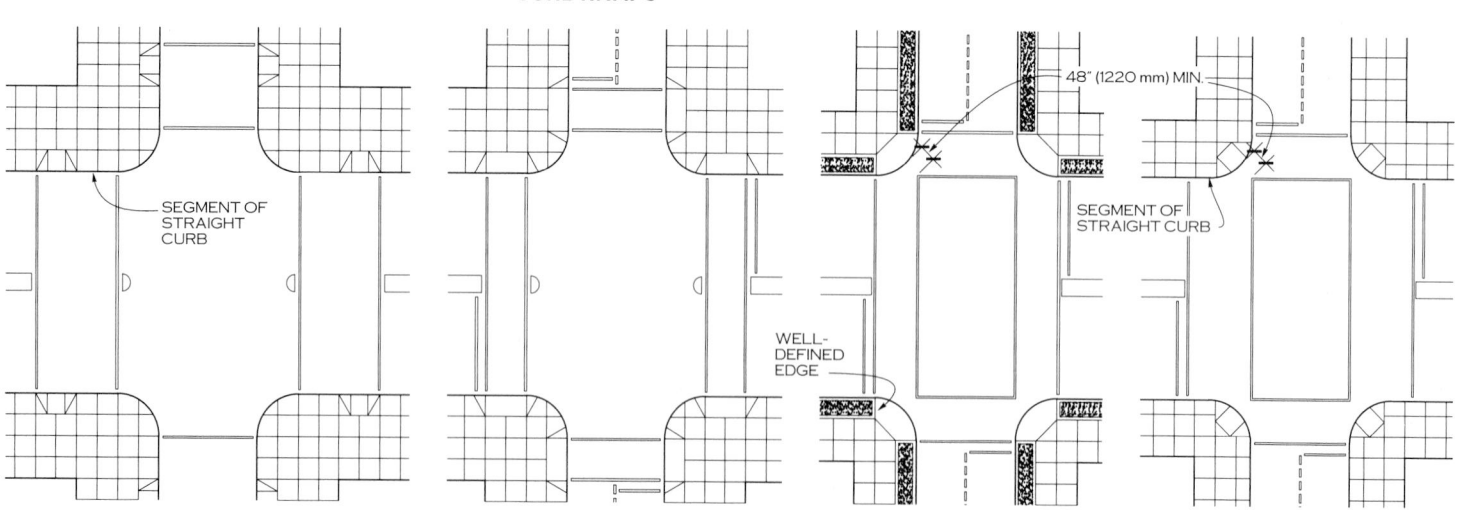

SEGMENT OF STRAIGHT CURB

48" (1220 mm) MIN.

SEGMENT OF STRAIGHT CURB

WELL-DEFINED EDGE

CURB RAMPS AT MARKED CROSSINGS (SHOWN IN ORDER OF PREFERENCE FOR ACCESSIBILITY)

Scot C. McBroom, AIA; Alexandria, Virginia

DOORS AND ENTRANCES

1. Accessible entrances to and exits from a building must be provided, according to ADAAG 4.1.3 (8) and applicable codes.
2. Maneuvering clearances at doors shall be level (1:50 maximum slope) and clear if doors are not automatic or power-assisted.
3. Gates must meet accessible requirements for doors.
4. Provide accessible doors or gates adjacent to revolving doors and turnstiles.
5. Double-leaf doors shall have at least the active leaf meet all door requirements.
6. All doors in alcoves shall comply with the clearances for front approaches.

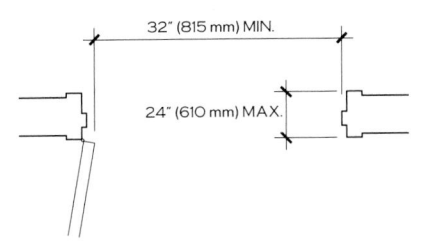

DOORWAY CLEARANCES

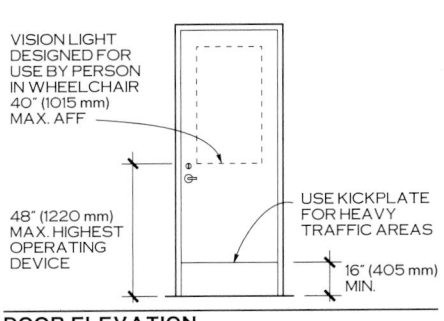

DOOR ELEVATION

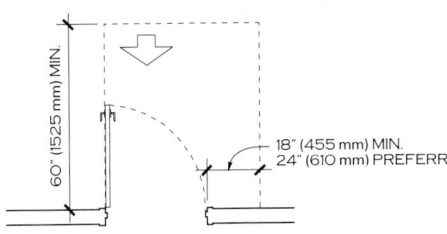

PULL SIDE

NOTE

X = 12 in. (305 mm) if door has both a closer and latch.

PUSH SIDE

FRONT APPROACHES — SWINGING DOORS

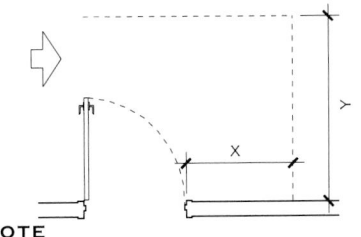

PULL SIDE

NOTE

X = 36 in. (915 mm) minimum if Y = 60 in. (1525 mm)
X = 42 in. (1065 mm) minimum if Y = 54 in. (1370 mm)

PULL SIDE

NOTE

Y = 48 in. (1220 mm) minimum if door has both a latch and closer.

PUSH SIDE

HINGE SIDE APPROACHES — SWINGING DOORS

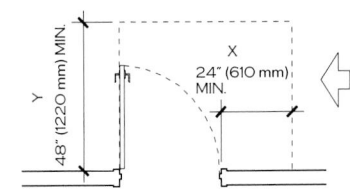

NOTE

Y = 54 in. (1370 mm) minimum if door has closer.

PULL SIDE

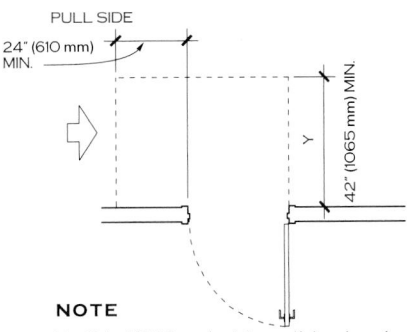

NOTE

Y = 48 in. (1220 mm) minimum if door has closer.

PUSH SIDE

LATCH SIDE APPROACHES — SWINGING DOORS

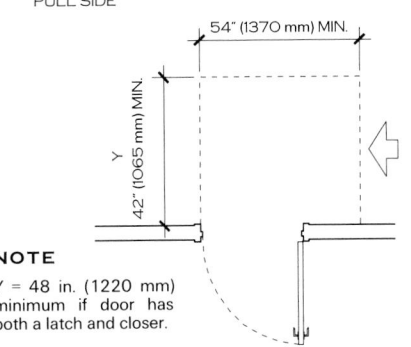

FRONT APPROACH — SLIDING AND FOLDING DOORS

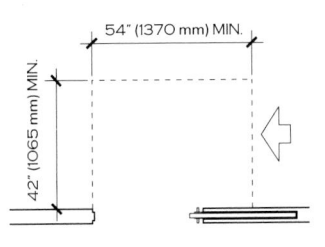

SLIDE SIDE APPROACH — SLIDING AND FOLDING DOORS

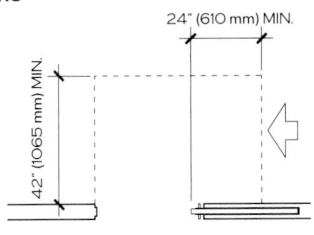

LATCH SIDE APPROACH — SLIDING AND FOLDING DOORS

MANEUVERING CLEARANCES AT DOORS

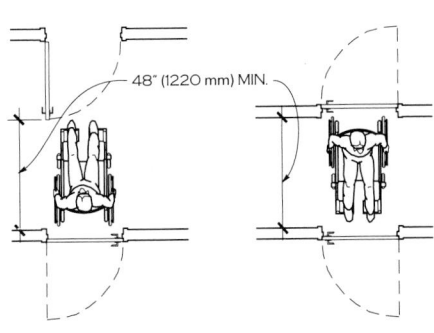

TWO HINGED DOORS IN SERIES

Scot C. McBroom, AIA; Alexandria, Virginia

THRESHOLD OR SADDLE

HARDWARE AND CONTROLS

1. Door passage hardware: shape easy to grasp with one hand; does not require tight grasping, pinching, or twisting of wrist.
2. Interior door opening force: no more than 5 lbf (22.2 N) unless greater required for fire doors.
3. Automatic and power-assisted doors are accessible; see Americans with Disabilities Act Accessibility Guidelines for further requirements.

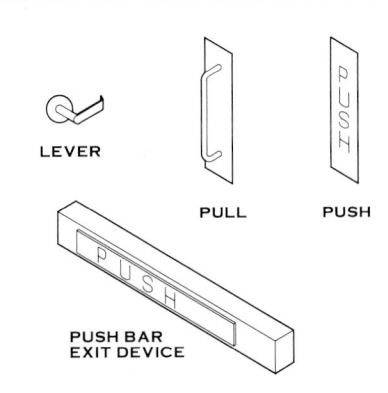

ACCEPTABLE HARDWARE

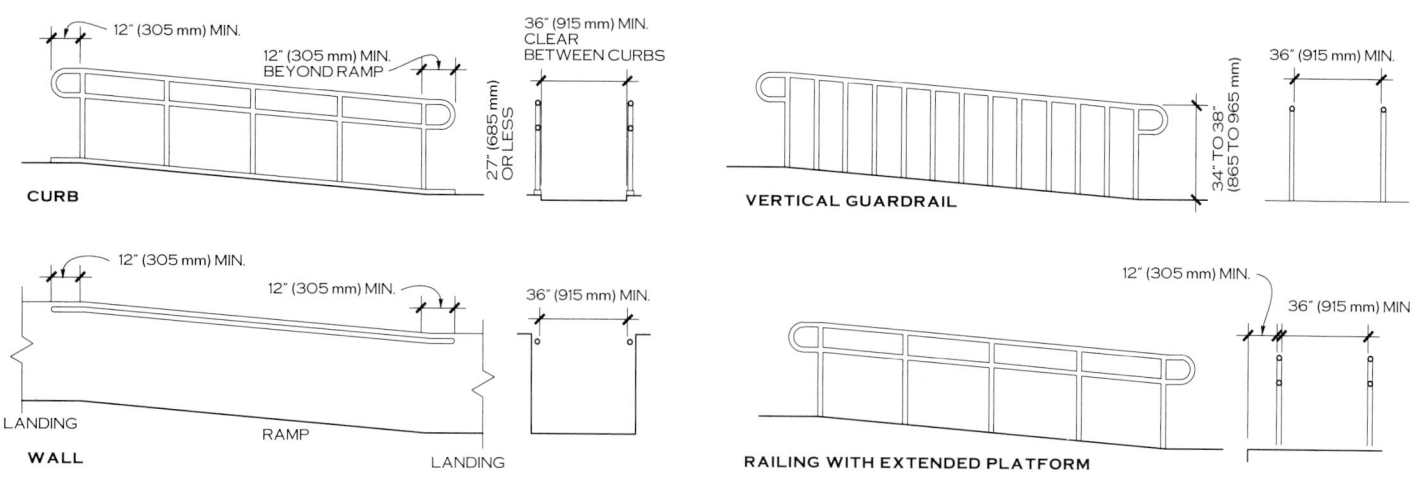

CURB

VERTICAL GUARDRAIL

WALL

RAILING WITH EXTENDED PLATFORM

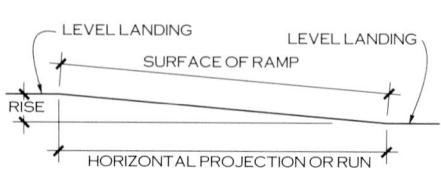

COMPONENTS OF A SINGLE RAMP

SAMPLE RAMP DIMENSIONS

SLOPE	MAXIMUM RISE		MAXIMUM RUN	
	IN.	MM	FT	M
1:12 to < 1:16	30	760	30	9
1:16 to < 1:20	30	760	40	12

NOTE

Slope < 1:20 is not a ramp so no handrails are required.

NOTE

X is the 12 in. minimum handrail extension required at each top riser. Y is the minimum handrail extension of 12 in. plus the width of one tread that is required at each bottom riser.

RAMPS

1. Provide at accessible route; slopes greater than 1:20 are considered ramps.
2. Slope maximum 1:12; provide least slope possible; maximum rise of 30 in. per run.
3. Landings should be level at top and bottom of each ramp run and at least as wide as the run leading to it. A 60 x 60 in. landing is required where ramp changes direction. If there is a door at the landing, provide level maneuvering clearances.
4. Handrails required: where rise is greater than 6 in. or run is greater than 72 in.; both sides; see handrail examples and notes.
5. Edge protection required at ramps and landings with drop-offs; see examples.
6. Design outdoor ramps and approaches so that water will not accumulate on surface; maximum cross slope of 1:50.

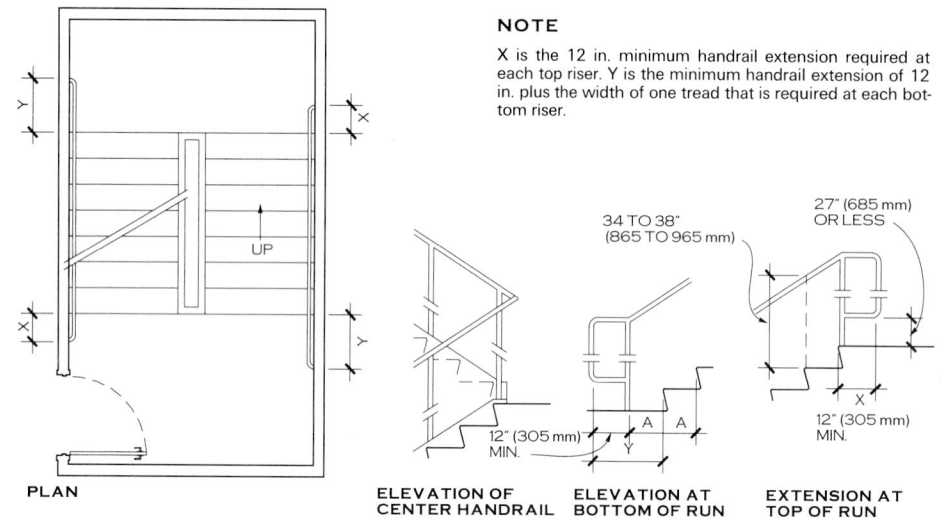

PLAN

ELEVATION OF CENTER HANDRAIL

ELEVATION AT BOTTOM OF RUN

EXTENSION AT TOP OF RUN

STAIR HANDRAILS

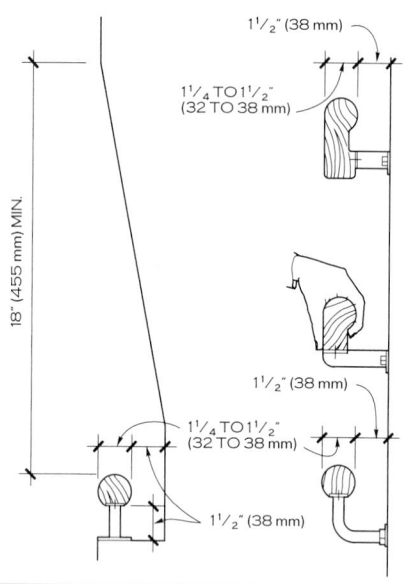

SIZE AND SPACING OF HANDRAILS

HANDRAILS

1. Provide continuous handrails at both sides of ramps and stairs; the inside handrail of switchback or dogleg ramps and stairs to be continuous.
2. If handrails are not continuous at bottom, top, or landings, provide handrail extensions as shown in the ramp and stair examples; ends of handrails to be rounded or returned smoothly to floor, wall, or post.
3. Provide handrails of size and configuration shown; gripping surfaces to be uninterrupted by newel posts or other construction elements; handrails shall not rotate within their fittings.

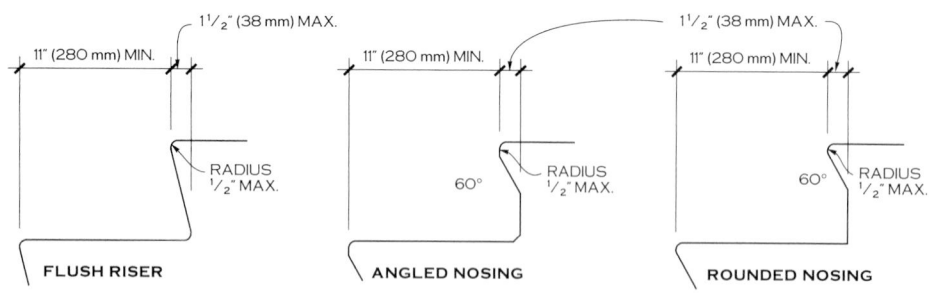

FLUSH RISER

ANGLED NOSING

ROUNDED NOSING

STAIR TREADS, RISERS, AND NOSINGS

STAIRS

Interior or exterior stairs connecting levels not connected by elevator, ramp, or lift must comply with the following:

1. Uniform risers and treads; minimum 11 in. tread; open risers not permitted.
2. Nosings as shown.
3. Handrails as shown and described.
4. Design outdoor stairs and approaches so that water does not accumulate on walking surfaces.

Scot C. McBroom, AIA; Alexandria, Virginia

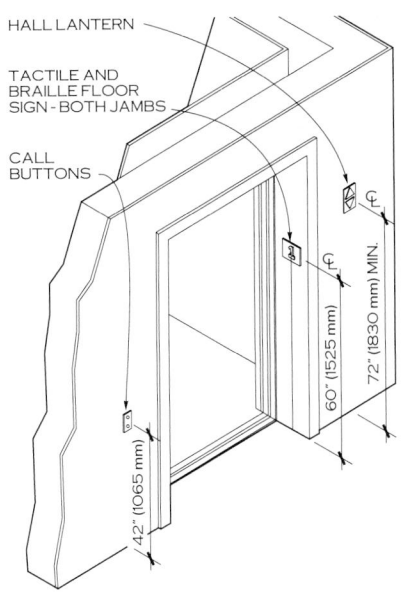

HALL LANTERN

TACTILE AND BRAILLE FLOOR SIGN - BOTH JAMBS

CALL BUTTONS

60" (1525 mm)

72" (1830 mm) MIN.

42" (1065 mm)

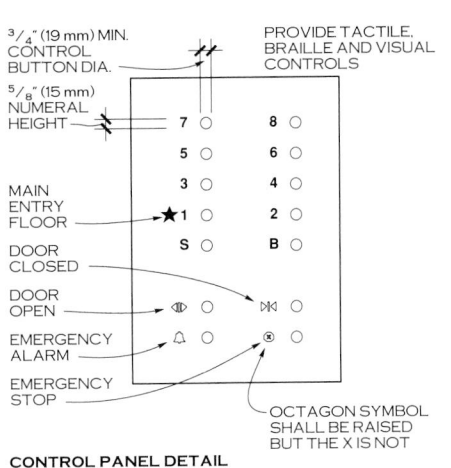

3/4" (19 mm) MIN. CONTROL BUTTON DIA.

5/8" (15 mm) NUMERAL HEIGHT

PROVIDE TACTILE, BRAILLE AND VISUAL CONTROLS

MAIN ENTRY FLOOR

DOOR CLOSED

DOOR OPEN

EMERGENCY ALARM

EMERGENCY STOP

OCTAGON SYMBOL SHALL BE RAISED BUT THE X IS NOT

CONTROL PANEL DETAIL

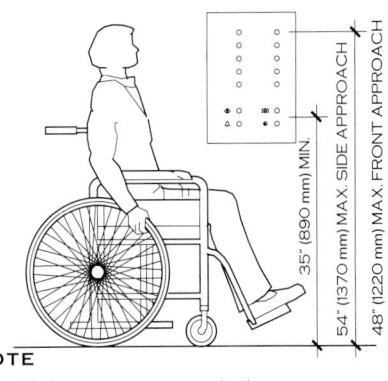

35" (890 mm) MIN.

54" (1370 mm) MAX. SIDE APPROACH

48" (1220 mm) MAX. FRONT APPROACH

NOTE

If provided, emergency communications must be accessible per ADAAG.

CONTROL PANEL HEIGHT

NOTES

1. Floor designations: 2 in. high letters, including Braille, 60 in. above floor on both sides of elevator doorjamb.
2. Hall lanterns: sound once for up direction, twice for down; mount minimum 72 in. high; minimum 2 1/2 in. smallest dimension.
3. Visual and audible car position indicator.
4. See Americans with Disabilities Act Accessibility Guidelines (ADAAG) for mechanical requirements.

PLATFORM (WHEELCHAIR) LIFTS

The Americans with Disabilities Act (ADA) limits use of lifts for access in new construction to very specific applications to achieve access goals and in alterations and additions where no other method of access is available.

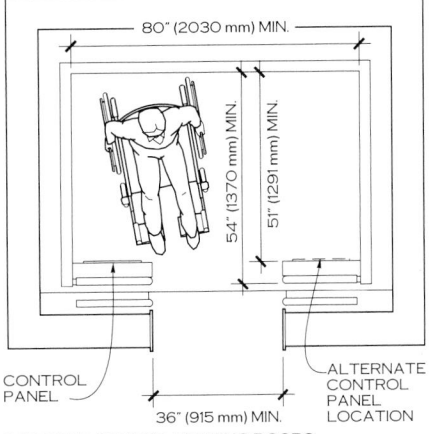

80" (2030 mm) MIN.

54" (1370 mm) MIN.

51" (1291 mm) MIN.

CONTROL PANEL

ALTERNATE CONTROL PANEL LOCATION

36" (915 mm) MIN.

CAR WITH CENTER OPENING DOORS

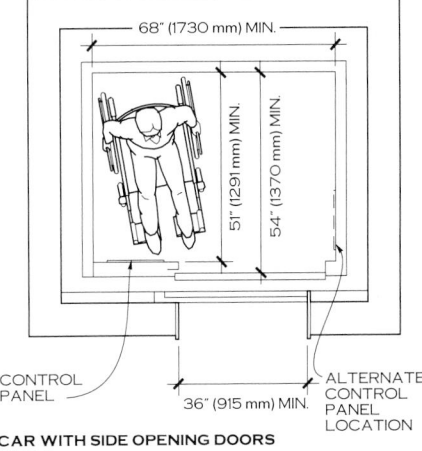

68" (1730 mm) MIN.

51" (1291 mm) MIN.

54" (1370 mm) MIN.

CONTROL PANEL

ALTERNATE CONTROL PANEL LOCATION

36" (915 mm) MIN.

CAR WITH SIDE OPENING DOORS

ELEVATORS

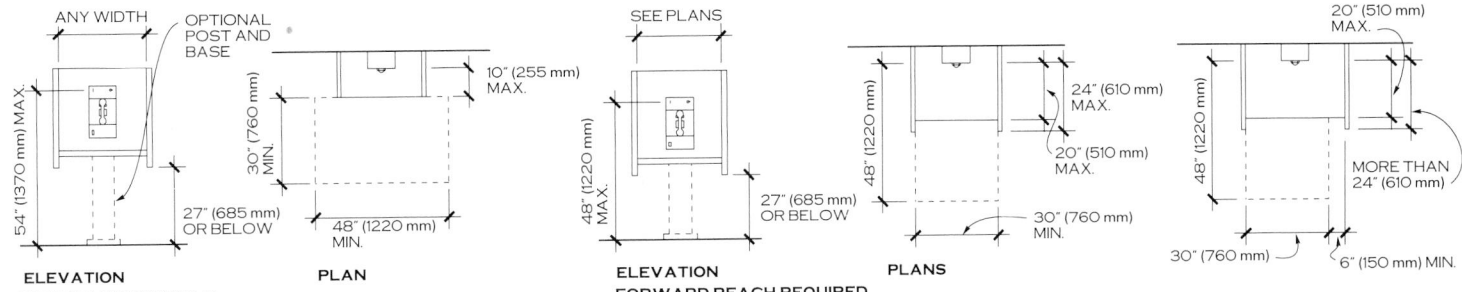

ANY WIDTH

OPTIONAL POST AND BASE

54" (1370 mm) MAX.

10" (255 mm) MAX.

30" (760 mm) MIN.

27" (685 mm) OR BELOW

48" (1220 mm) MIN.

ELEVATION
SIDE REACH POSSIBLE

PLAN

SEE PLANS

48" (1220 mm) MAX.

27" (685 mm) OR BELOW

ELEVATION
FORWARD REACH REQUIRED

48" (1220 mm)

24" (610 mm) MAX.

20" (510 mm) MAX.

30" (760 mm) MIN.

PLANS

VOICE CONTROL TELEPHONES

20" (510 mm) MAX.

48" (1220 mm)

MORE THAN 24" (610 mm)

30" (760 mm)

6" (150 mm) MIN.

TEXT TELEPHONES

NOTE

Requirements are for public telephones, including closed circuit (such as apartment entry phones and hotel house phones), pay, and other types.

Provide hearing aid compatible telephones; volume control required for accessible telephones and for at least 25% of all other telephones.

One required where four or more public pay telephones are provided in a facility and at least one is provided at an interior location. Also required in specific facility types and areas (e.g., stadiums, arenas, hospitals, convention centers, transit facilities).

TELEPHONES

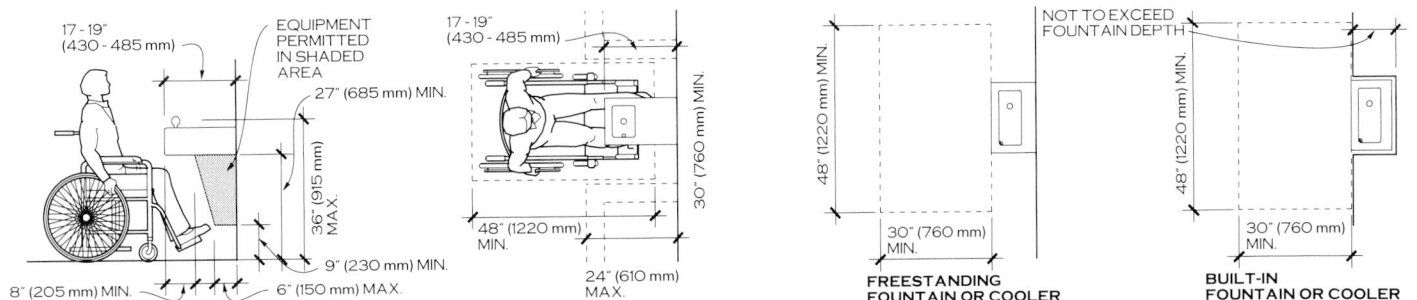

17 - 19" (430 - 485 mm)

EQUIPMENT PERMITTED IN SHADED AREA

27" (685 mm) MIN.

36" (915 mm) MAX.

9" (230 mm) MIN.

8" (205 mm) MIN.

6" (150 mm) MAX.

17 - 19" (430 - 485 mm)

30" (760 mm) MIN.

48" (1220 mm) MIN.

24" (610 mm) MAX.

48" (1220 mm) MIN.

30" (760 mm) MIN.

FREESTANDING FOUNTAIN OR COOLER

NOT TO EXCEED FOUNTAIN DEPTH

48" (1220 mm) MIN.

30" (760 mm) MIN.

BUILT-IN FOUNTAIN OR COOLER

NOTE

Both high and low fountains are required, no fewer than

50% wheelchair accessible; others are to be located at a standard height convenient to those with difficulty stooping. High-low fountains are required when only one fountain is provided.

DRINKING FOUNTAINS

Scot C. McBroom, AIA; Alexandria, Virginia

TOILET ROOMS, FIXTURES, AND ACCESSORIES

1. All public and common use toilet rooms must be accessible. Private toilet rooms off a private office must be adaptable.
2. At least one type of each fixture and accessory must be accessible; provide path to accessible fixtures.
3. Turning space: 60 in. diameter or 5 x 5 ft T-shape.
4. Where 6 or more toilet stalls are provided in addition to the standard 5 x 5 ft wheelchair stall, at least one stall must be 36 in. wide with grab bars on both sides.
5. Stall doors may not swing into clear floor space required for fixture; in standard stalls, the front partition and at least one side partition must provide a toe clearance of 9 in. above finish floor (AFF). If stall depth is greater than 60 in., toe clearance not required.

6. Flush, lavatory, and accessory controls: operable with one hand; no tight grasping, pinching, or twisting of wrist; 5 lbf max.; 44 in. AFF max.; automatic is okay. Toilet flush controls to be mounted on wide side of toilet area.
7. Hot water and drainpipes under lavatories must be insulated or otherwise configured to protect against contact. No sharp or abrasive surfaces under lavatories.
8. Toilet paper dispensers that control delivery or do not permit continuous flow may not be used.
9. For paper towel and other dispensers and disposals, see page on reach dimensions.
10. Coordinate ADAAG with state and local code requirements.
11. All dimensions on this page are for adult use facilities.

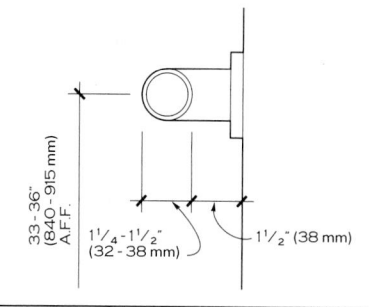

GRAB BAR

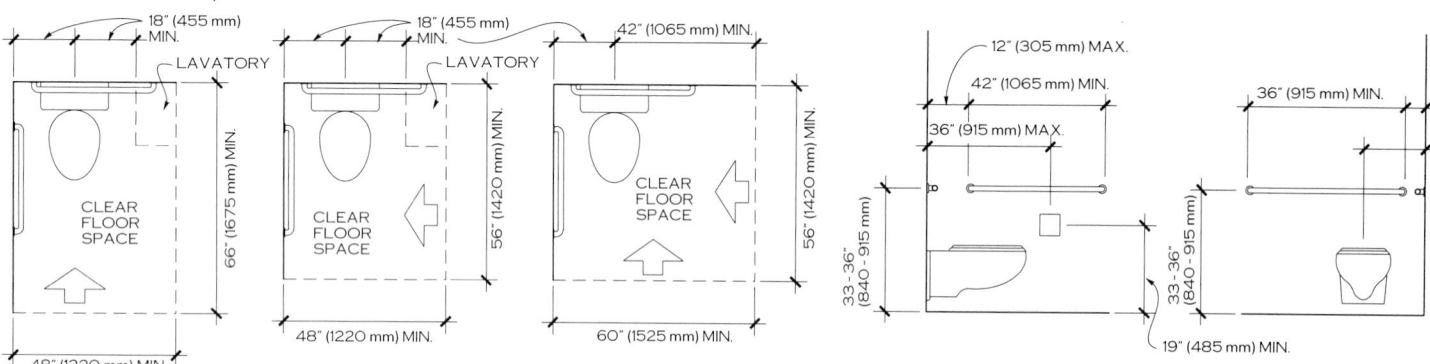

CLEAR FLOOR SPACE AT WATER CLOSETS

ELEVATIONS

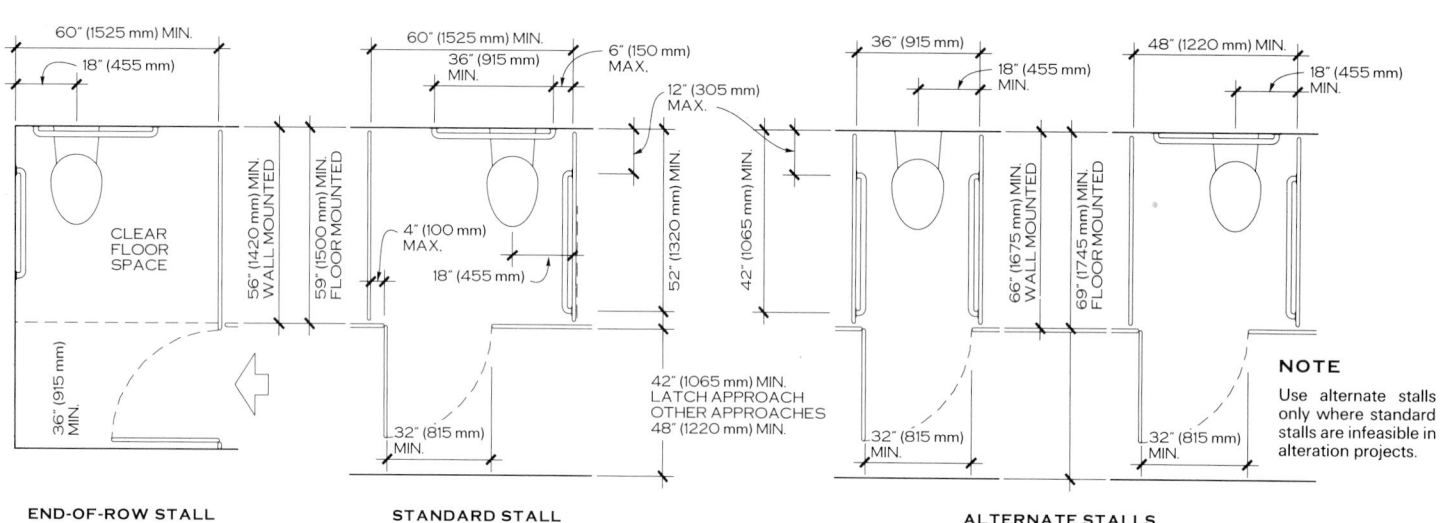

END-OF-ROW STALL   **STANDARD STALL**   **ALTERNATE STALLS**

NOTE

Use alternate stalls only where standard stalls are infeasible in alteration projects.

TOILET STALLS

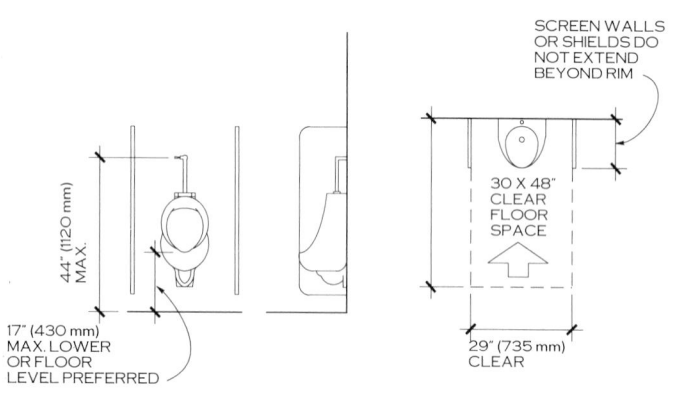

ELONGATED WALL-HUNG URINAL

LAVATORY CLEARANCES

Scot C. McBroom, AIA; Alexandria, Virginia

1   UNIVERSAL ACCESSIBILITY

NOTE

All dimensions on this page are for adult-use facilities.

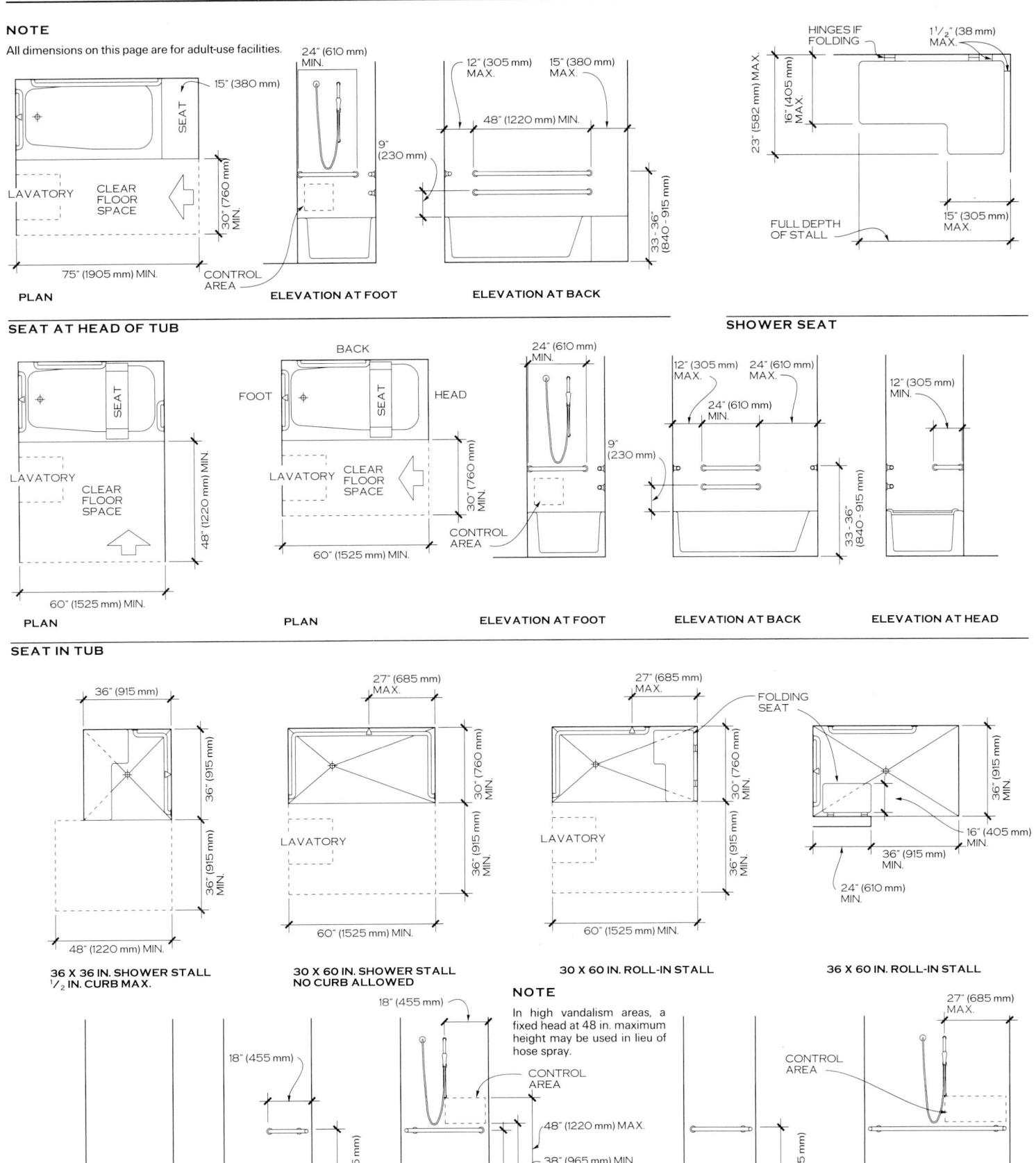

SEAT AT HEAD OF TUB

PLAN

15" (380 mm)
SEAT
CLEAR FLOOR SPACE
LAVATORY
30" (760 mm) MIN.
75" (1905 mm) MIN.
CONTROL AREA

ELEVATION AT FOOT

24" (610 mm) MIN.
9" (230 mm)
30" (760 mm) MIN.

ELEVATION AT BACK

12" (305 mm) MAX.
15" (380 mm) MAX.
48" (1220 mm) MIN.
33 - 36" (840 - 915 mm)

SHOWER SEAT

HINGES IF FOLDING
1 1/2" (38 mm) MAX.
23" (582 mm) MAX.
16" (405 mm) MAX.
FULL DEPTH OF STALL
15" (305 mm) MAX.

SEAT IN TUB

PLAN

BACK
FOOT
SEAT
HEAD
LAVATORY
CLEAR FLOOR SPACE
48" (1220 mm) MIN.
60" (1525 mm) MIN.

PLAN

LAVATORY
CLEAR FLOOR SPACE
30" (760 mm) MIN.
60" (1525 mm) MIN.

ELEVATION AT FOOT

24" (610 mm) MIN.
9" (230 mm)
30" (760 mm) MIN.
CONTROL AREA

ELEVATION AT BACK

12" (305 mm) MAX.
24" (610 mm) MAX.
24" (610 mm) MIN.
33 - 36" (840 - 915 mm)

ELEVATION AT HEAD

12" (305 mm) MIN.

36 X 36 IN. SHOWER STALL
1/2 IN. CURB MAX.

36" (915 mm)
36" (915 mm)
36" (915 mm) MIN.
48" (1220 mm) MIN.

30 X 60 IN. SHOWER STALL
NO CURB ALLOWED

27" (685 mm) MAX.
LAVATORY
30" (760 mm) MIN.
36" (915 mm) MIN.
60" (1525 mm) MIN.

30 X 60 IN. ROLL-IN STALL

27" (685 mm) MAX.
FOLDING SEAT
LAVATORY
30" (760 mm) MIN.
36" (915 mm) MIN.
60" (1525 mm) MIN.

36 X 60 IN. ROLL-IN STALL

FOLDING SEAT
36" (915 mm) MIN.
16" (405 mm) MIN.
36" (915 mm) MIN.
24" (610 mm) MIN.

36 X 36 IN. SHOWER STALL ELEVATIONS

SEAT WALL
17 - 19" (430 - 485 mm)

BACK WALL
18" (455 mm)
33 - 36" (840 - 915 mm)

CONTROL WALL
18" (455 mm)
48" (1220 mm) MAX.
38" (965 mm) MIN.
33 - 36" (840 - 915 mm)

NOTE

In high vandalism areas, a fixed head at 48 in. maximum height may be used in lieu of hose spray.

30 X 60 IN. SHOWER STALL ELEVATIONS

33 - 36" (840 - 915 mm)
27" (685 mm) MAX.
CONTROL AREA

SHOWER STALLS

Scot C. McBroom, AIA; Alexandria, Virginia

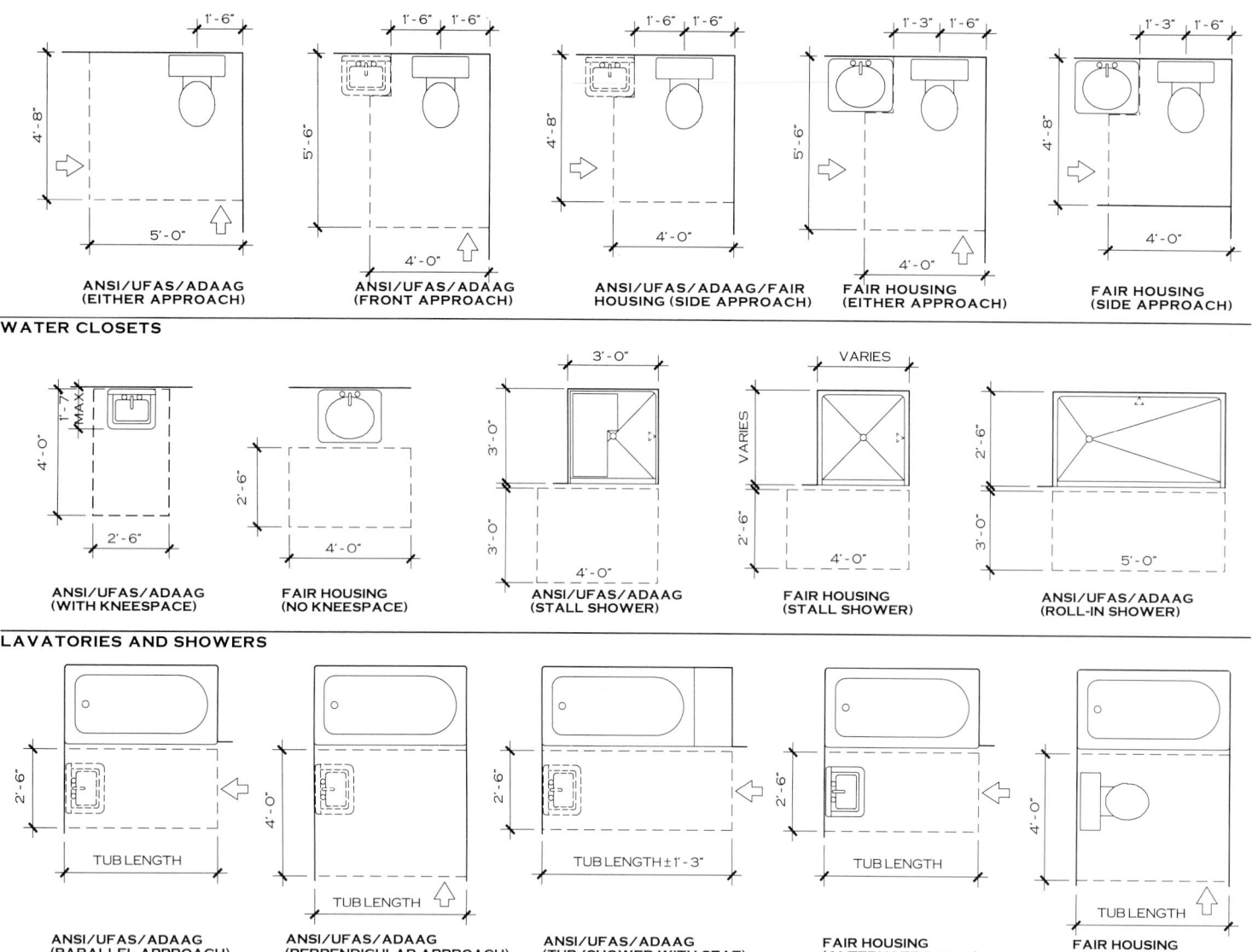

ANSI/UFAS/ADAAG
(EITHER APPROACH)

ANSI/UFAS/ADAAG
(FRONT APPROACH)

ANSI/UFAS/ADAAG/FAIR
HOUSING (SIDE APPROACH)

FAIR HOUSING
(EITHER APPROACH)

FAIR HOUSING
(SIDE APPROACH)

WATER CLOSETS

ANSI/UFAS/ADAAG
(WITH KNEESPACE)

FAIR HOUSING
(NO KNEESPACE)

ANSI/UFAS/ADAAG
(STALL SHOWER)

FAIR HOUSING
(STALL SHOWER)

ANSI/UFAS/ADAAG
(ROLL-IN SHOWER)

LAVATORIES AND SHOWERS

ANSI/UFAS/ADAAG
(PARALLEL APPROACH)

ANSI/UFAS/ADAAG
(PERPENDICULAR APPROACH)

ANSI/UFAS/ADAAG
(TUB/SHOWER WITH SEAT)

FAIR HOUSING
(ALTERNATE A OR B)

FAIR HOUSING
(ALTERNATE A)

BATHTUBS

GUIDELINES FOR ACCESSIBILITY

Residential bathrooms and toilet rooms can be divided into two general categories: private facilities such as those in single or multifamily dwellings, and institutional bathrooms such as those in nursing homes, hospitals, dormitories, hotels, or motels. Design standards for toilet room fixtures have been an important part of most accessibility codes since the first American National Standards Institute (ANSI) A117.1 standards were published in 1961. Standards specifically intended for private dwellings did not become a part of the ANSI document, however, until the 1981 edition. Four years later, the Uniform Federal Accessibility Standard (UFAS) published nearly identical standards for dwellings in federal projects. The ANSI/UFAS standards are typically applied to between 1% and 5% of the total dwellings in multifamily projects, depending on the local or federal code.

In 1988 the Fair Housing Amendments Act was enacted; guidelines for this federal law included different standards for residential bathroom designs. Though less strict than those found in ANSI and UFAS, the Fair Housing standards must be more broadly applied, typically to between 30% and 100% of the total units in a project, depending on the building configuration and whether it has a passenger elevator. Two alternative design standards are included in Fair Housing. In dwellings with more than one bathroom, the more strict of these can be used for one bath; minimal standards for an accessible route can be applied to the second bathroom.

The Americans with Disabilities Act Accessibility Guidelines (ADAAG) are not typically applied to private residen-

tial facilities because Fair Housing addresses these dwellings. However, bathrooms located in public accommodations and commercial facilities, such as hotels or hospitals, may be required to meet ADA standards.

Architects should verify bathroom requirements because accessibility codes and interpretations of standards change.

ADAPTABLE FEATURES

In residential bathroom design, "adaptability" is a technical term first described in the 1980 edition of the ANSI Standards. It is defined as "the capability of certain... elements... to be altered or added so as to accommodate the needs of persons with or without disabilities, or to accommodate the needs of persons with different types or degrees of disabilities." For accessible bathrooms, the adaptable elements might typically include "removable" base cabinets that can be eliminated, when necessary, to provide kneespace below vanities, and wall reinforcing that will permit the later installation of grab bars around certain fixtures.

PLUMBING FIXTURE REQUIREMENTS

Categories of accessibility standards for bathrooms are 1) requirements for individual plumbing fixtures, and 2) requirements for maneuvering space within bathrooms or toilet rooms. Fixture requirements vary among common accessibility standards and guidelines. There are significant differences between the fixture requirements for Fair Housing and the requirements for ANSI/UFAS. The requirements for ADAAG are essentially similar to ANSI/

UFAS except for some very subtle technical differences. The floor space requirements for these accessibility standards are illustrated in the plan drawings. There are additional requirements, such as grab bars and other accessories, that are associated with most fixtures, so architects should reference the applicable code for each project.

WATER CLOSETS

The clear floor space required adjacent to water closets is similar for Fair Housing, ANSI/UFAS, and ADAAG. The arrows illustrated on the floor plans indicate a direction of approach by a wheelchair user, though the significance of this is never explicitly stated in the standards and guidelines. The major differences between Fair Housing and the other standards are the minimum space required behind the water closet (33 in. vs. 36 in.) and the configuration of the lavatory or vanity that may be located adjacent to the toilet. To meet Fair Housing, the adjacent lavatory or vanity does not need to include kneespace, whereas this is an important requirement for ANSI/UFAS and ADAAG. Designers should also be aware of other technical requirements such as grab bars, wall reinforcement, and toilet seat heights. For all the standards except Fair Housing, the requirements for grab bars or wall reinforcement can significantly affect the location of the water closet and the overall arrangement of the bathroom. As a practical matter, water closets that meet ANSI/UFAS and ADAAG must be located adjacent to a wall. Therefore they cannot be positioned next to a bathtub.

Thomas D. Davies, Jr., AIA, Kim A. Beasley, AIA, Paradigm Design Group; Washington, D.C.

1   **UNIVERSAL ACCESSIBILITY**

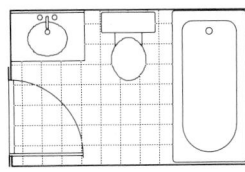

CONVENTIONAL 1 - WALL CONFIGURATION (NOT ACCESSIBLE)

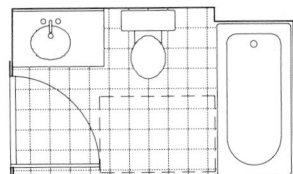

FAIR HOUSING 2 - WALL CONFIGURATION (ALTERNATE A AND B)[1]

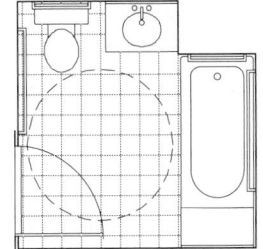

ANSI/UFAS

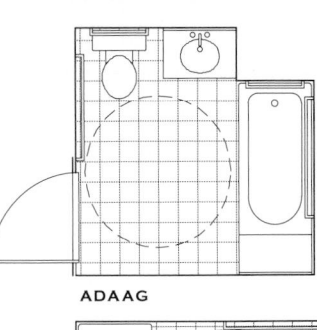

ADAAG

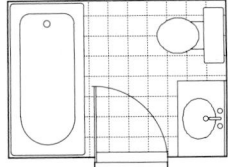

CONVENTIONAL 2 - WALL CONFIGURATION (NOT ACCESSIBLE)

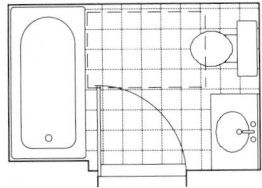

FAIR HOUSING 1 - WALL CONFIGURATION (ALTERNATE A AND B WITH TUB)

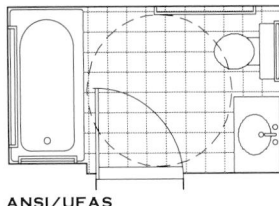

ANSI/UFAS

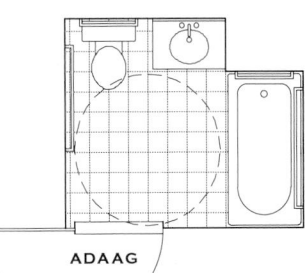

ADAAG

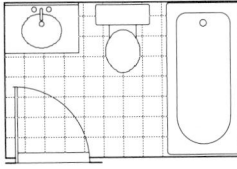

CONVENTIONAL 2 - WALL CONFIGURATION (NOT ACCESSIBLE)

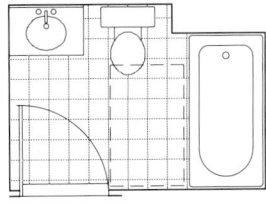

FAIR HOUSING 1 - WALL CONFIGURATION (ALTERNATE A AND B)[1]

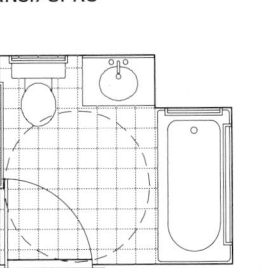

ANSI/UFAS

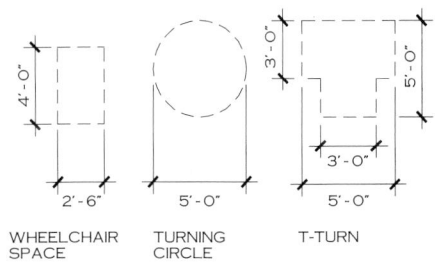

ADAAG

NOTE

1. For alternate B, reverse the plumbing at the tub.

BATHROOM ARRANGEMENTS

LAVATORIES AND VANITIES

The major differences between accessibility standards for these types of plumbing fixtures are based on the need to provide kneespace under the basin. For example, Fair Housing does not require a kneespace to be provided below the basin at the lavatory or vanity, but the other standards do require this space to accommodate a front approach. In some cases, the height of the kneespace has been increased in ADAAG as compared to both ANSI and UFAS. There are also additional requirements in all accessibility standards, except Fair Housing, for the maximum depth of the sink basin and for the design of the faucets, mirror, and medicine cabinet.

BATHTUBS AND TUB/SHOWERS

There are also subtle differences between standards for accessible bathtubs. The clear floor space requirements for these fixtures are similar to those for water closets in that a specific direction of approach is indicated (either perpendicular or parallel) in the standards. The significance of the approach direction is not clear, particularly for ANSI, UFAS, and ADAAG where a lavatory adjacent to the tub will always have kneespace. Therefore, wheelchair access to the faucets and controls is available in either case, though access for ambulatory bathers is compromised when a lavatory is installed in this location. Under the Fair Housing guidelines, either a water closet or a lavatory or vanity without kneespace can be located in this position.

Fair Housing has different requirements for clear space; the designer may choose from two different standards. Of these alternatives, the second option (Alternative B) is the more strict. This requires clear space adjacent to the foot of the tub.

For any of the accessibility standards, there are also requirements for grab bars or wall reinforcement. Except for Fair Housing, the grab bar/reinforcement requirements essentially dictate that the tub basin be enclosed on three sides. There is also an alternate tub configuration illustrated in ANSI, UFAS, and ADAAG that includes a small built-in seat at the head of the basin. The intended use of this seat, however, is not completely clear. These standards also address the design and location of the mixing valve and other operating controls as well as the shower-spray head.

STALL SHOWERS AND ROLL-IN UNITS

Accessible showers include both transfer stalls (where a bather moves from the wheelchair to a bench or portable seat) and roll-in shower units (where the bather remains seated in a special shower chair and is either pushed by an attendant or is propelled by the bather into the stall). The design requirements for stall showers vary among the different standards. Fair Housing has less strict requirements for the stall size and requires a smaller clear space in the bathroom outside the shower entrance. ANSI, UFAS, and ADAAG require a built-in seat in the stall and also address the location and design of the mixing valve, operating controls, and shower-spray head. All accessibility standards require either wall reinforcing or grab bars in the shower. ANSI, UFAS, and ADAAG include a maximum limit on the height of the dam or threshold for stall showers.

All the accessibility standards except Fair Housing include roll-in showers. These stalls are much larger and have no threshold to restrict wheelchair access. Therefore the floor structure or slab beneath the shower must typically be either lowered or depressed to provide an essentially flush transition from the bathroom floor.

MANEUVERING SPACE

An accessible bathroom must meet different arrangement requirements, depending on the standards used. Each bathroom must provide the fixture clearances required by the applicable standard. In addition, some maneuvering space must typically be provided, though the amount of space and the rules vary.

Bathrooms that comply with Fair Housing must be "usable." If the door swings into the bathroom, there must be enough clear space to position a wheelchair clear of the door swing. This requirement is described diagrammatically as rectangular space 30 by 48 in. For ANSI, UFAS, and ADAAG, the maneuvering space is described as either a 5 ft diameter circle or a 5 ft T-shaped area.

All of the standards permit the floor space for fixtures to overlap with required clear floor space. ADAAG, however, does not permit the bathroom door to swing into any fixture clearances. In almost all cases, this will effectively require the door to swing out.

DOORS

There is also a difference in the size of the doors serving bathrooms designed to different standards. For Fair Housing, a 2 ft 10 in. door can be used to provide a "nominal" 32 in. clear opening. For ANSI, UFAS, and ADAAG a 3 ft 0 in. door must typically be used to provide the full 32 in. opening.

GRAB BARS

The arrangement of grab bars can also influence the floor plan of an accessible bathroom. For Fair Housing, the standards for grab bars are less strict and this permits the design of small bathrooms. For example, the grab bar adjacent to a water closet can be shorter than that required by ANSI. In fact, Fair Housing permits swing-down grab bars so that the water closet does not need to be adjacent to a wall. The more strict grab bar requirements of ANSI, UFAS, and ADAAG will become critical factors in water closet and bathtub arrangements and therefore impact the overall design of the bathroom.

WHEELCHAIR SPACE 2'-6" × 4'-0"

TURNING CIRCLE 5'-0"

T-TURN 3'-0" / 3'-0" / 5'-0" / 5'-0"

WHEELCHAIR SPACES

Thomas D. Davies, Jr., AIA, Kim A. Beasley; AIA, Paradigm Design Group; Washington, D.C.

GUIDELINES FOR ACCESSIBILITY

The first design standards for kitchens were included in the 1980 edition of the American National Standards Institute (ANSI) A117.1. In 1984, the Uniform Federal Accessibility Standards (UFAS) incorporated identical standards, with minor exceptions. The ANSI/UFAS kitchen standards are very specialized design requirements that focus on the needs of wheelchair users. For multifamily projects, the minimum number of dwelling units to which these standards must be applied is typically between 1 and 5% of the total, depending on local or federal codes.

The 1988 Fair Housing Amendments Act guidelines include a different set of kitchen standards with less specialized design features. The standards for Fair Housing, however, must be more broadly applied to those multifamily units that are covered by this federal law. Typically the Fair Housing standards are applied to between 30 and 100% of the total units in a project, depending on the building configuration and whether it has a passenger elevator.

Architects should verify kitchen requirements because accessibility codes and interpretation of standards change.

FIXTURE AND APPLIANCE REQUIREMENTS

For most kitchens, there are two types of standards for accessible design:

1. General maneuvering space
2. Fixture and appliance requirements.

The table below outlines design standards for appliances and plumbing fixtures specified by different accessibility codes. ANSI/UFAS standards are much more restrictive than Fair Housing.

CLEAR FLOOR SPACES

Under both design standards, clear floor space at fixtures or appliances must accommodate wheelchair approach. This can be either a parallel or front approach, depending on the fixture or appliance.

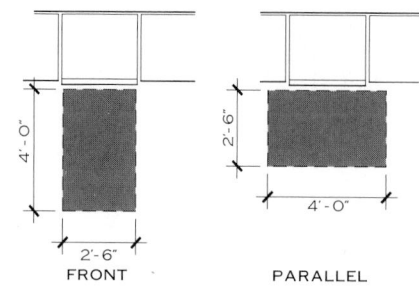

APPROACH DIAGRAM

ADAPTABLE FEATURES

In accessible kitchen design, "adaptability" is a technical term first described in the ANSI standards. It is defined as "... the capability of certain... elements... to be altered or added so as to accommodate the needs of persons with or without disabilities, or to accommodate the needs of persons with different types or degrees of disabilities." For accessible kitchens, the adaptable elements might typically include "removable" base cabinets that can be eliminated, when necessary, to provide kneespace below countertops, and adjustable sections of countertops that can be raised and lowered to suit individual tenants. These countertop sections sometimes include plumbing fixtures, such as sinks.

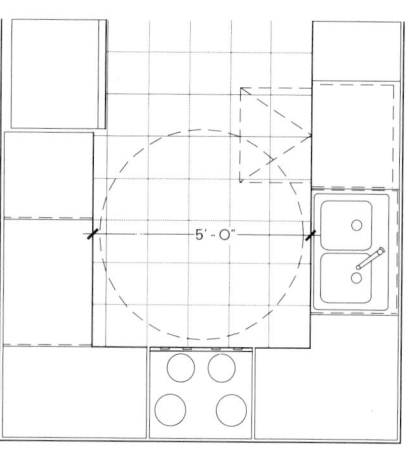

ANSI/UFAS KITCHEN PLAN

Kitchens designed to meet these standards include fixture and appliance requirements outlined in the table at left. The kitchen plan must also include a 5 ft diameter wheelchair turning space if the countertops are in a U-shaped configuration, as illustrated above.

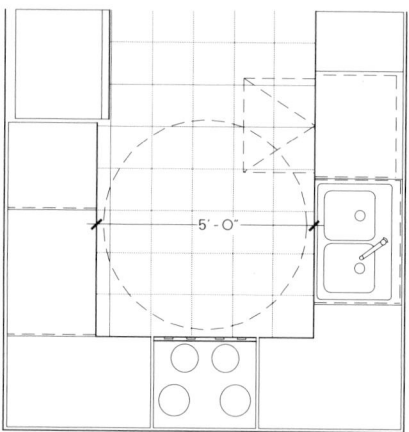

FAIR HOUSING KITCHEN PLAN

Kitchens have less stringent requirements for fixtures and appliances, as indicated in the table at left. For example, a lower work counter is not required on the base cabinets and a kneespace is not required at the kitchen sink. Fair Housing kitchens must also be sufficiently wide, however, to provide a similar 5 ft diameter turning space.

DESIGN STANDARDS FOR KITCHEN APPLIANCES AND PLUMBING FIXTURES

	FAIR HOUSING		ANSI/UFAS	
Sink		• Clear floor space (front or parallel approach)		• Clear floor space (front approach) • Kneespace • Lowered countertop • Shallow sink • Faucets and controls
Range and cooktop		• Clear floor space (parallel approach)		• Clear floor space (front or parallel approach) • Optional kneespace • Location of burner controls
Work space		(Not required)		• Clear floor space (front approach) • lowered countertop section • kneespace
Refrigerator		• Clear floor space (front or parallel approach)		• Clear floor space (front or parallel approach) • storage compartment heights • control locations
Dishwasher		• Clear floor space (front or parallel approach)		• Clear floor space (front or parallel approach)
Oven (wall or range unit)		• Clear floor space (front or parallel approach)		• Clear floor space • Ovens that are not self-cleaning require adjacent kneespace. Self-cleaning ovens need only provide floor space similar to Fair Housing.

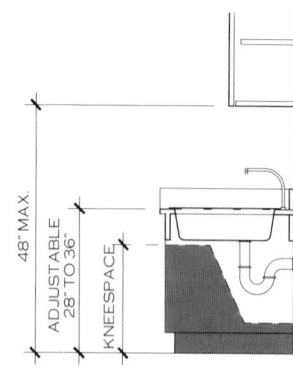

COUNTERS AND CABINETS

To comply with the ANSI or UFAS standards, wall cabinets and some counters in accessible kitchens must also meet specialized design requirements. Counters at work surfaces and sinks with kneespaces can be either fixed at a height of 34 in. or adjustable between 28 and 36 in. The configuration of the sink and garbage disposal unit must conform to a specific profile to ensure adequate kneespace. Upper cabinets must be mounted with the lowest shelf no higher than 48 in. (approximately 4 to 8 in. lower than standard kitchens).

Thomas D. Davies, Jr., AIA, Kim A. Beasley; AIA, Paradigm Design Group; Washington, D.C.

GENERAL

Information to determine occupant load is from three model building codes in use in the United States:

1. Uniform Building Code (UBC), 1985 edition, copyright 1985, with permission of the International Conference of Building Officials, publisher.
2. BOCA National Building Code (BOCA), 1986 edition, copyright 1986, with permission of the Building Officials and Code Administrators International, Inc., publisher.
3. Standard Building Code (SBC), 1985 edition, copyright 1985, with permission of the Southern Building Code Congress International, Inc., publisher, with all rights reserved.

Occupant load generally is defined as the maximum capacity of a building or room given as the total number of people present at any one time. For occupant loads, generally it is assumed that all areas of a building will be occupied at the same time, with some exceptions noted in specific codes. For example, the UBC states: "Accessory use areas, which ordinarily are used only by persons who occupy the main areas of an occupancy, shall be

provided with exits as though they are completely occupied, but their occupant load need not be included in computing the total occupant load of the building" (UBC-Sec. 3302.(a)].

Most codes require that to determine multiple use building or area occupancies, the occupant load (O.L.) be based on the use that produces the most occupants. For example, the occupant load for a school multiple use room, which also will be used for classroom activities (O.L. factor = 20), as well as for assembly space (O.L. factor = 15), is calculated using the 15 sq. ft. per occupant factor.

If buildings or areas contain two or more separate occupancies, the overall occupant load is determined by computing occupant loads for various areas and adding them together for an aggregate occupant load.

When calculating occupant load for areas with fixed seating in benches or pews, the number of occupants is based on one seat for each 18 in. of bench or pew. In dining areas with booth seating, the number of seats is based on 24 in. for each seat.

EXITS

All three major codes use occupant loads to determine the size and number of required exits. Based on occupant loads and area usages, it is possible to determine the required exits, arrangement, and sizes of exit components. All three codes (BOCA, SBC, and UBC) consider an exit to be more than merely a door. Although specific definitions vary with each code, exits usually are considered to be continuous and unobstructed means of egress to a public way and may include such building elements as doors, corridors, stairs, balconies, lobbies, exit courts, etc. Elevators are not considered exits. Requirements for arrangements, size, and operation of exits vary; consult appropriate code for specific information.

OCCUPANT LOADS

USE	MAXIMUM FLOOR AREA PER OCCUPANT (SQ. FT. PER OCCUPANT)		
	BOCA	SBC	UBC[1]
Assembly areas[2]—concentrated use (without fixed seats): auditoriums, bowling alleys[3], churches, dance floors, lodge rooms, reviewing stands, stadiums	7 net	7 net	7
Assembly areas—less concentrated use: conference rooms, dining/drinking areas, exhibit rooms, gymnasiums, lounges, stages[4]	15 net	15 net	15
Assembly areas—standing space	3 net	3 net	—
Business areas[7]	100 gross	100 gross	100
Courtrooms—(without fixed seats)	40 net	40 net	—
Daycare facilities	—	—	35
Dormitories	—	—	50
Educational			
classroom areas	20 net	20 net	20
shops and vocational rooms	50 net	50 net	50
Industrial areas[5]	100 gross	100 gross	200
Institutional[6]			
children's homes, homes for aged, nursing homes, sanitariums, hospitals	—	—	80
inpatient treatment areas	240 gross	240 gross	—
outpatient areas	100 gross	100 gross	—
sleeping areas	120 gross	120 gross	—
Kitchens (commercial)	—	—	300
Library			
reading rooms	50 net	50 net	50
stack areas	100 gross	100 gross	—
Lobbies (accessory to assembly area)	—	—	7
Locker rooms	—	—	50
Mechanical equipment areas	300 gross	300 gross	300
Mercantile[8]			
basements	30 gross	30 gross	20
ground floors	30 gross	30 gross	30
upper floors	60 gross	60 gross	50
storage, stockrooms, shipping areas	100 gross	100 gross	300[9]
Parking garages	200 gross	200 gross	200
Residential[10]	200 gross	200 gross	—
hotels and apartments	—	—	200
dwellings	—	—	300
Skating rinks[11]	—	15 net	—
rink area	—	—	50
deck	—	—	15
Storage areas	300 gross	300 gross	300
Swimming pools			
pool	—	—	50
deck	—	—	15
All other areas	—	—	100

MINIMUM EXITS BASED ON USAGE

USAGE	MINIMUM TWO EXITS REQUIRED WHERE O.L. IS AT LEAST:
Aircraft hangars	10
Auction rooms	20
Assembly areas	50
Children's homes and homes for the aged	6
Classrooms	50
Dormitories	10
Dwellings	10
Hospitals, sanitariums, and nursing homes	6
Hotels and apartments	10
Kitchens (commercial)	30
Library reading rooms	50
Locker rooms	30
Manufacturing areas	30
Mechanical equipment rooms	30
Nurseries for children (daycare)	7
Offices	30
Parking garages	30
School shops and vocational rooms	50
Skating rinks	50
Storage and stockrooms	30
Stores (retail sales rooms)	
basements	2 exits minimum
ground floors	50
upper floors	10
Swimming pools	50
Warehouses	30
All other	50

TABLE NOTES

1. Both BOCA and SBC use net and gross floor areas to determine occupant load. UBC does not differentiate between gross and net areas.
2. Occupant loads for assembly areas with fixed seats are determined by the actual number of installed seats.
3. Occupant load calculations for bowling alleys under BOCA and SBC use 5 persons per alley in addition to tabular values indicated.
4. Stages are considered assembly areas—less concentrated use (15 sq. ft. per occupant) in UBC; not separately classified in BOCA or SBC.
5. UBC classifies industrial areas as manufacturing areas.
6. BOCA and SBC classify areas within institutional occupancies, UBC classifies by occupancy description only.
7. UBC classifies business areas as office occupancy.
8. UBC classifies mercantile areas as store-retail sales rooms.
9. UBC considers storage and stockroom areas as storage occupancy (300 sq. ft. per occupant).
10. BOCA and SBC do not separate hotel/apartment and dwelling occupancies.
11. BOCA does not classify separately skating rinks from other assembly areas—less concentrated use (15 sq. ft. per occupant). SBC does not separate areas within skating rinks.

International Conference of Building Officials; Southern Building Code Congress International
Building Officials and Code Administrators International, Inc.
James O. Rose, AIA; University of Wyoming; Laramie, Wyoming

GENERAL

An Area of Rescue Assistance (ARA) is defined in the Americans with Disabilities Act Accessibility Guidelines (ADAAG) as "an area, which has direct access to an exit, where people who are unable to use stairs may remain temporarily in safety to await further instructions or assistance during emergency evacuation." ARAs are also known as "Area for Evacuation Assistance" in the Uniform Building Code and as "Area of Refuge" in NFPA 101 and CABO/ANSI A117.1 - 1992. Note the exception in ADAAG section 4.1.3(9) for facilities having a supervised automatic sprinkler system. ADAAG does not require ARAs in alterations or existing facilities.

These seven case studies provide examples of several ways to configure the ARA to meet ADAAG and UBC requirements. They provide a starting point for designing facilities and meeting the requirements of building officials. Verify design for compliance with local and state building codes.

The ADA requires that the design of ARAs satisfy the building official having jurisdiction over the project. The ARA provisions in ADAAG were modeled after similar requirements in the 1991 edition of the UBC. The order of case studies corresponds to the seven options under ADAAG section 4.3.11.1.

LEGEND

A. Wheelchair space: 30 x 48 in. Minimum of two required with one per 200 occupants served by the ARA.

B. "Area of Rescue Assistance" sign with symbol of accessibility, illuminated if required for exit signs. Directional signs also required.

C. Audible and visual two-way communication unit.

D. Instructions on use of space.

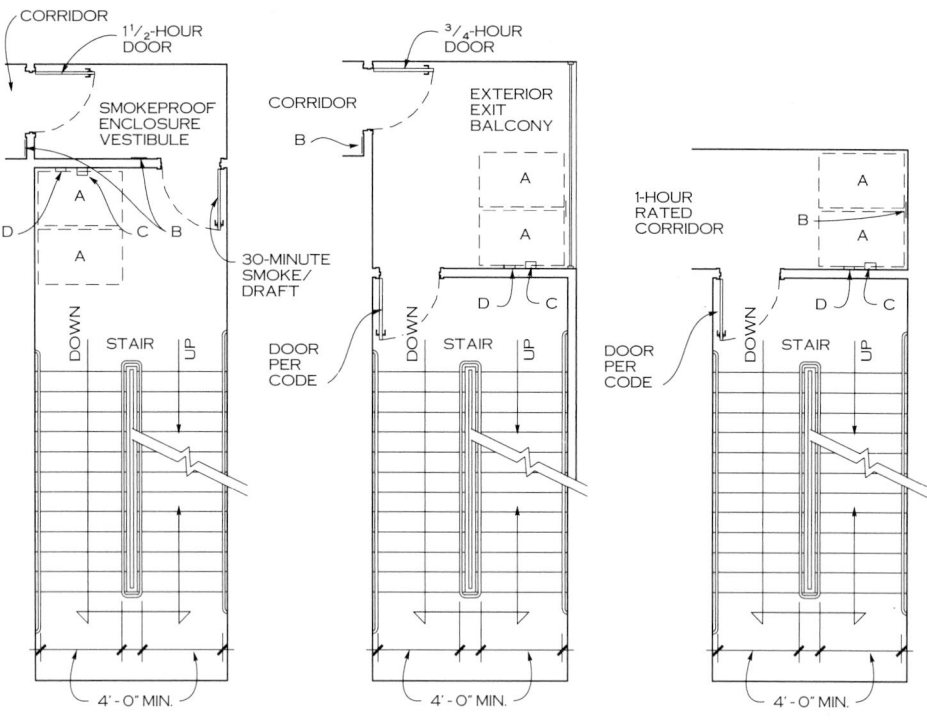

CASE STUDY I
STAIRWAY LANDING
OPTION I

CASE STUDY II
EXTERIOR EXIT
BALCONY OPTION

CASE STUDY III
PORTION OF
CORRIDOR OPTION

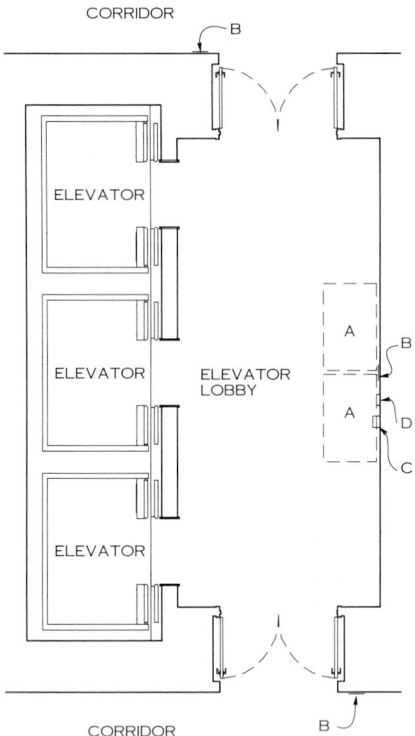

CASE STUDY VII

NOTE

Elevator lobby and shaft shall be pressurized for smokeproof enclosure as required by the local building official. The pressurization system shall be activated by smoke detectors in locations approved by the local building official. The system's equipment and ducts shall be 2-hour fire resistive construction.

ELEVATOR LOBBY OPTION

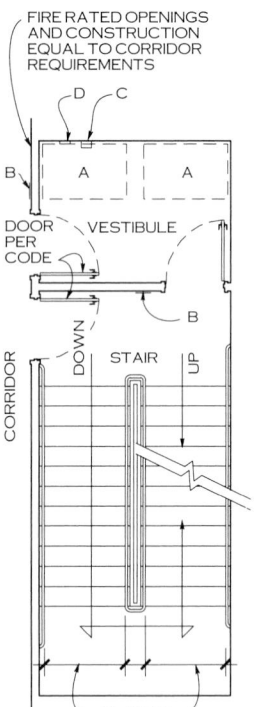

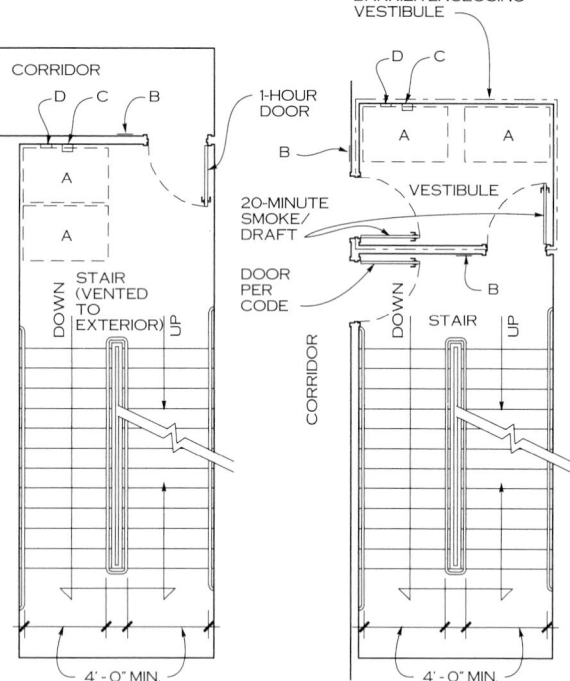

CASE STUDY IV
VESTIBULE NEXT TO
EXIT ENCLOSURE OPTION

NOTE

4 ft 0 in. dimension at stair is clear between handrails (typical).

CASE STUDY V
STAIRWAY LANDING
OPTION II

CASE STUDY VI
VESTIBULE
OPTION II

STAIRCASE OPTIONS

Bill Hecker, AIA, Dan E. Woosley, AIA, and James L. Terry, AIA; Evan Terry Associates, P.C.; Birmingham, Alabama

1 **EGRESS PLANNING**

GENERAL

Stairways are an essential component in the circulation and egress systems of most buildings. They are also the site of accidents resulting in approximately 4000 deaths and one million injuries requiring hospital treatment annually in the United States. For these reasons stairway design is strictly controlled by building regulations.

The information on this and the following page summarizes most common building code and access regulation requirements. Be sure to check local regulations as well. Follow the steps below to complete a stair design:

1. Minimum requirements: Consult the Building Code Stairway Requirements table below to determine dimensional limits for treads, risers, and stair width. Verify that local codes are not more restrictive.
2. Tread and riser sizes: Use the Stair Proportioning Graph on the following page to find the number of risers, riser height, and optimum tread depth.
3. Stair width: In addition to the minimums shown on this page, stair widths must also meet occupant load requirements based on Use Group and floor area. Consult the local building code.
4. Landings: Landings at least as wide as the stair itself are required at the top and bottom of the stair, and at intermediate points if necessary to ensure that no single flight has a rise greater than 12 ft (3658 mm).
5. Stair Layout: See the example stairway plan and section on the following page. Maintain headroom a minimum of 6 ft 8 in. (2032 mm) for nonresidential and 6 ft 6 in. (1981 mm) for residential stairs. Avoid flights with fewer than 3 risers to minimize tripping hazards. The use of door alcoves is recommended to prevent stairway doors from obstructing the egress travel path (as noted on the diagrams). For prefabricated stairs, oversize the stairwell enclosure by several inches for ease of stair installation and to avoid structural conflicts.

TREAD AND RISER PROPORTIONING

Most interior stairs are designed to the steepest limits permitted by code so as to occupy the least amount of space. However, tread and riser combinations that are less steep may be considered for exterior stairs, grand stairs, or stairs of just a few risers. The most common rule for the comfortable proportioning of stairs in these cases is: 2 x riser height + tread depth = 25 in. (635 mm). Consider testing life-size mock-ups of stairs of unusual proportions to verify their ease of use.

HANDRAILS

The accompanying diagrams summarize most handrail requirements for nonresidential stairs. For residential stairs not covered by ADA, most codes permit handrails on only one side of the stair, without top and bottom extensions. In some cases a greater range of heights is also permitted. The ADA recommends (but does not require) additional handrails at lower heights where stairs are used by children.

GUARDRAILS

Guardrails 42 in. (1067 mm) in height are typically required on the open sides of nonresidential stairs. When handrails are used in combination with a guardrail, handrail heights up to 42 in. (1067 mm) are permitted by some building codes. Intermediate rails or balusters must be spaced so that a sphere of either 4 or 6 in. (102 or 152 mm), depending on the code and Use Group, cannot pass through any part of the guard. Guardrail designs with horizontal rails that are easily climbed are not recommended and, in some cases, are restricted. For residential stairs, guardrails 36 in. (914 mm) in height are usually permitted.

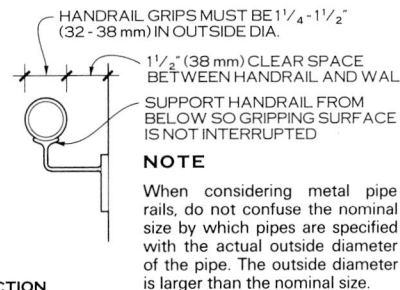

HANDRAIL GRIPS MUST BE 1¼-1½" (32-38 mm) IN OUTSIDE DIA.

1½" (38 mm) CLEAR SPACE BETWEEN HANDRAIL AND WALL

SUPPORT HANDRAIL FROM BELOW SO GRIPPING SURFACE IS NOT INTERRUPTED

NOTE
When considering metal pipe rails, do not confuse the nominal size by which pipes are specified with the actual outside diameter of the pipe. The outside diameter is larger than the nominal size.

SECTION

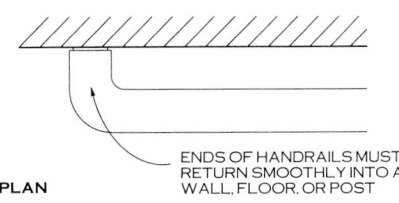

ENDS OF HANDRAILS MUST RETURN SMOOTHLY INTO A WALL, FLOOR, OR POST

PLAN

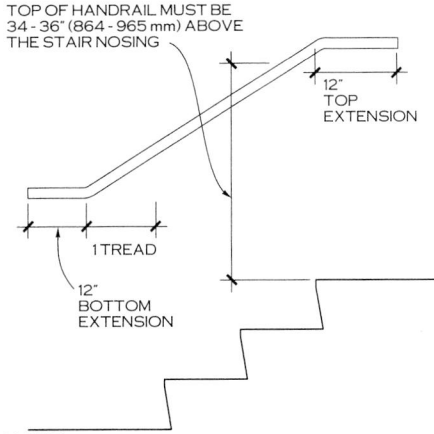

TOP OF HANDRAIL MUST BE 34-36" (864-965 mm) ABOVE THE STAIR NOSING

12" TOP EXTENSION

1 TREAD

12" BOTTOM EXTENSION

NOTE
Handrails must be continuous on both sides of a stair. Ends of handrails must extend beyond the stair as shown above.

ELEVATION

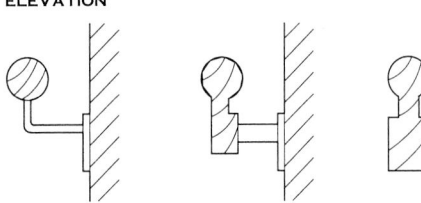

NOTE
The gripping portion of a handrail must be equivalent to a 1¼ to 1½ in. (32 to 38 mm) diameter round rail.

HANDRAIL DETAILS CONFORMING TO ADA AND MOST BUILDING CODE REQUIREMENTS

STAIR DETAILS

Treads and risers within a flight must be uniform in size within close tolerances. Treads must be slip resistant. The shape of nosings and risers must meet the requirements shown below. Carpeting or other stair coverings should be applied securely and should not create a nosing radius greater than permitted. Handrails, guardrails, and stairways themselves must meet structural load requirements.

Access regulations in some localities require floor material strips of contrasting color located at the top approach to a stair and at the lowest tread. These markings are intended to aid the visually impaired in identifying the limits of the stair. The application of such markings may be appropriate even where not required, particularly where a high proportion of elderly or visually impaired users are anticipated..

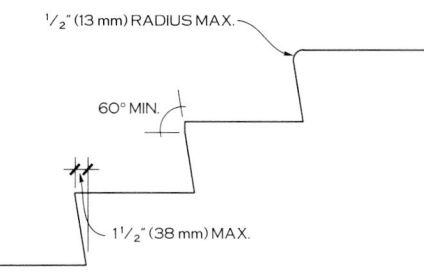

½" (13 mm) RADIUS MAX.

60° MIN.

1½" (38 mm) MAX.

ACCEPTABLE NOSINGS AND RISERS

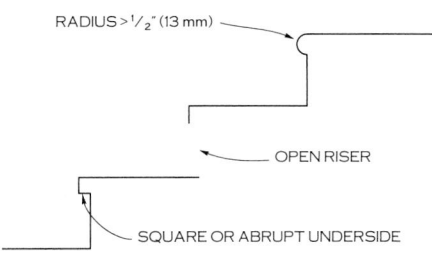

RADIUS > ½" (13 mm)

OPEN RISER

SQUARE OR ABRUPT UNDERSIDE

UNACCEPTABLE NOSINGS AND RISERS

SPECIAL STAIR CONFIGURATIONS

Winders (radiating risers) in stairs normally are permitted only in single-family residences. Minimum tread depth requirements at the inside of the winders may limit the inside radius of the stair. Spiral stairs typically are permitted in single-family residences and for access to mezzanines of limited area in other building types. With certain tread depth restrictions, circular stairways are permitted in most buildings. Alternating tread stairways are permitted for some mezzanines and for access to rooftops. The use of fixed ladders is limited to access to restricted areas, such as rooftops and elevator pits.

REFERENCES

National Association of Architectural Metal Manufacturers. *Metal Stairs Manual.* Chicago, 1992.

Templer, John. *The Staircase* (2 vols). Cambridge, Mass.: MIT Press, 1992.

See pages elsewhere in this volume for stair construction details of various materials.

BUILDING CODE STAIRWAY REQUIREMENTS

	BUILDINGS OTHER THAN SINGLE-FAMILY RESIDENCES			SINGLE-FAMILY RESIDENCES		
	MINIMUM TREAD DEPTH	RISER RESTRICTIONS	MINIMUM STAIR WIDTH	MINIMUM TREAD DEPTH	RISER RESTRICTIONS	MINIMUM STAIR WIDTH
1991 ADAAG	11" (279 mm)	No limits	48" (1219 mm) clear between handrails for stairs adjacent to an area of rescue assistance	No limits	No limits	No limits
1993 BOCA National Building Code	11" (279 mm)	7" (178 mm) maximum 4" (102 mm) minimum	44" (1118 mm) 36" (914 mm) for occupancy of 50 or fewer	9" (229 mm)	8¼" (210 mm)	36" (914 mm)
1991 Standard Building Code	9" (229 mm)	7¾" (197 mm) maximum 2R + T must equal 25" (635 mm)	44" (1118 mm) 36" (914 mm) for occupancy of 50 or fewer in some cases 66" (1676 mm) for shopping malls	9" (229 mm)	7¾" (197 mm)	36" (914 mm)
1991 Uniform Building Code	11" (279 mm)	7" (178 mm) maximum 4" (102 mm) minimum	44" (1118 mm) 36" (914 mm) for occupancy of 49 or fewer 60" (1524 mm) for educational use group with occupancy of 100 or more	9" (229 mm)	8" (203 mm)	36" (914 mm)

Joseph Iano, Architect; Boston, Massachusetts
Edward Allen, AIA; South Natick, Massachusetts

EXAMPLE 1

An exit stairway in a theater rises a total of 20 ft 3 in. This dimension is off the graph, meaning that at least one landing must be inserted in the stair. Select two flights of 10 ft 1 1/2 in. rise each. Looking for the highest possible riser, read across to the 18-riser sloping line (before crossing the 7in. maximum riser height line), then upward to read a riser height of 6.75 in. Reading downward to the bottom horizontal axis, the optimum tread dimension is 11.5 in. This can be rounded down to the legal minimum of 11 in. to make the stair as compact as possible.

EXAMPLE 2

A stairway in a single-family house rises 8 ft 10 in. and needs to be as compact as possible according to CABO requirements. Read across to the 13-riser sloping line, then upward to read a riser height of 8.15 in. Read downward to find that the tread depth must be 9 in.

NOTE

Stairways may also be designed in metric units using this graph.

NOTES

1. Stairs should be laid out in both plan and section. The dimensions shown are examples only.
2. Landings must be at least as wide as the stair.
3. No single flight may rise more than 12 ft 0 in. (3658 mm) vertically.
4. In each flight, there is one more riser than tread.
5. Handrails may project up to 3 1/2 in. (89 mm) into the required stairway width. They must be continuous, or the ends must extend beyond the top and bottom of the stair. Stairs serving areas of rescue assistance must have 4 ft clear between handrails.
6. Stairway doors must swing with the direction of egress travel and must not obstruct more than one-half of the required landing width at any point in the swing. When fully open, doors must not strike handrails (including extensions) and not project more than 7 in. (178 mm) into the travel path.

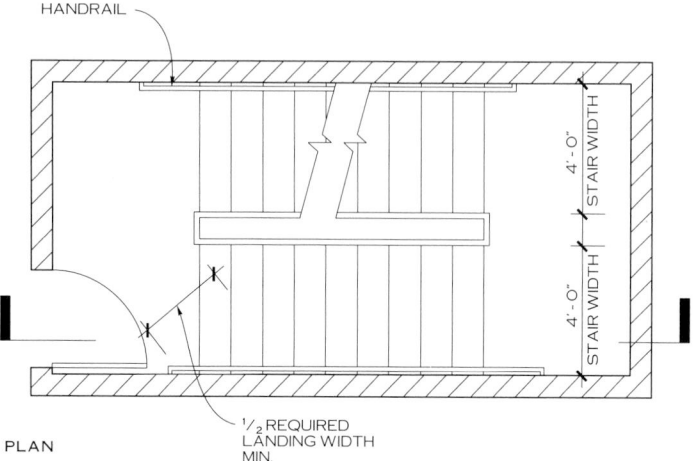

PLAN

STAIR PROPORTIONING GRAPH

Joseph Iano, Architect; Boston, Massachusetts
Edward Allen, AIA; South Natick, Massachusetts

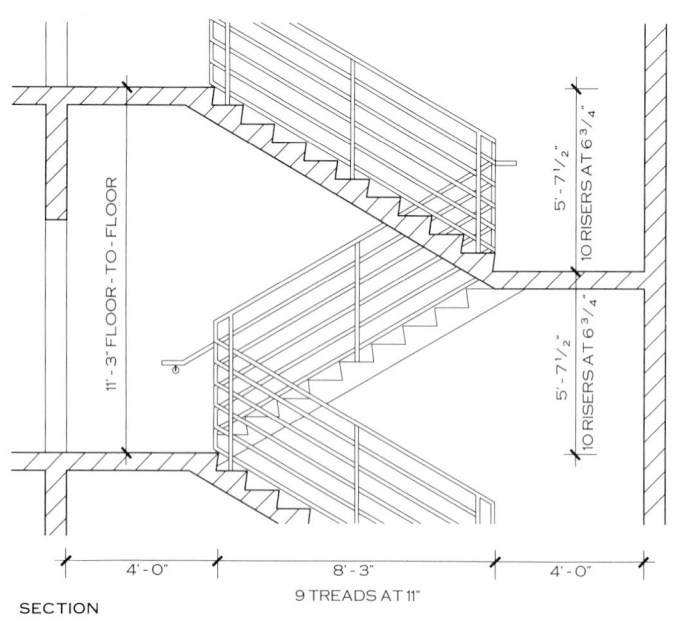

SECTION

EXAMPLE STAIRWAY PLAN AND SECTION

1 EGRESS PLANNING

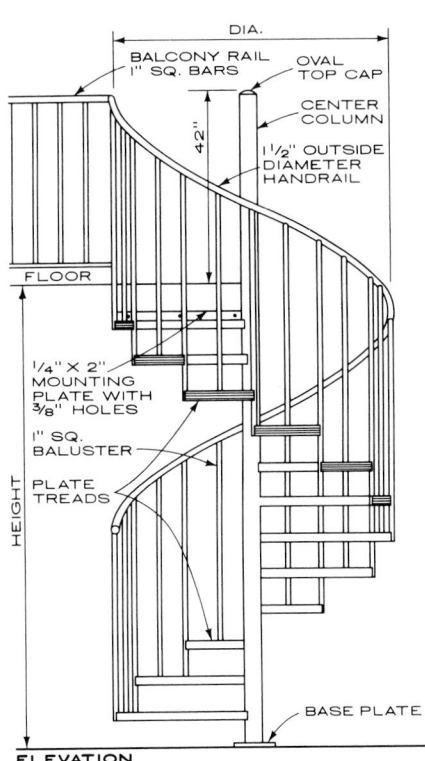

ELEVATION

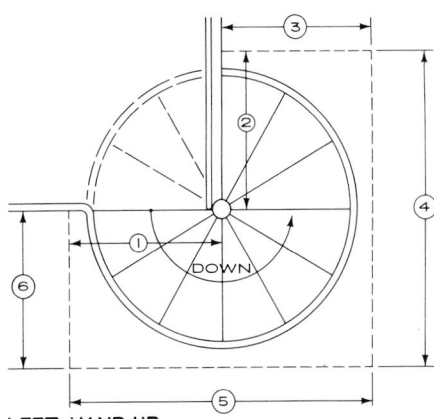

LEFT-HAND UP
12 TREADS/CIRCLE 8" TO 9½" RISERS
MAY BE RIGHT-HAND UP

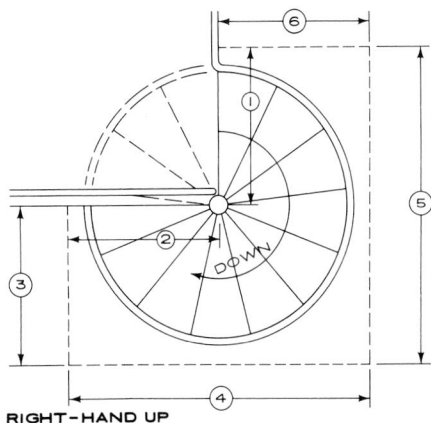

RIGHT-HAND UP
13 TREADS/CIRCLE 7½" TO 8" RISERS
MAY BE LEFT-HAND UP

Framing dimensions are used when the stair passes through the flooring. The opening is "L" shaped, not square. For maximum head room, taper joist #2 45°. For standard 27° treads and 10 in. or over joist, delete one step to increase head room.

SPIRAL STAIRS

David W. Johnson; Washington, D.C.

NOTES

1. Dimensions: Spiral stairs are manufactured in a variety of diameters. Larger diameters increase perceived comfort, ease of use, and safety.
2. Tread and platform materials: The most common materials are steel, aluminum, and wood. Steel and aluminum can be smooth plate, checker plate, pan type, and bar. A variety of hardwoods can be used, although many manufacturers use steel substructures to support the finish wood surface. Plywood usually is used under carpeting.
3. Factory finishes: Standard for exterior and wet area interiors are zinc-chromated rust inhibitor or hot-dipped galvanized. Other coatings are black acrylic enamel and black epoxy.
4. Handrails and balusters: A large variety of materials are available, including steel, aluminum, brass, bronze, wood, glass, and plastic laminate.
5. Platform dimensions usually are 2 in. larger than the stair radius. Various anchorage connections are available to suit the floor structure.
6. Refer to local and national codes for dimension and construction requirements and allowable uses.

SPECIFICATIONS (IN.)

Diameter	40	48	52	60	64	72	76	88	96
Center Column	4	4	4	4	4	4	4	6⅝	6⅝
Lb per 9 ft	205	220	235	250	265	310	325	435	485
Tread Detail A	4	4	4	4	4	4	4	6⅝	6⅝
Tread Detail B	18	22	24	28	32	34	36	42	48
27° Tread Detail C	9¼	11⅛	12⅛	13¹⁵/₁₆	14⅞	16¾	17⅝	20½	22⁵/₁₆
27° Tread Detail D	7⅝	8	8¼	8⅜	8½	8⅝	8¾	10	10½
30° Tread Detail C	10½	12⁹/₁₆	13⅝	15¾	16¾	18⅞	19⅞	23	25½
30° Tread Detail D	8½	8⅝	8¾	8⅞	9	9¼	9⅜	11⅜	11½
Landing Size	22	26	28	32	34	38	40	46	52

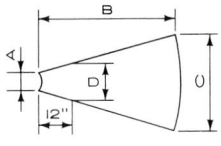

TREAD DETAIL

27° RISER TABLE

FINISH FLOOR HEIGHT (IN.)	NUMBER OF STEPS	CIRCLE DEGREE
90 to 96	11	297°
97 to 104	12	324°
105 to 112	13	351°
113 to 120	14	375°
121 to 128	15	405°
129 to 136	16	432°
137 to 144	17	459°
145 to 152	18	486°
153 to 160	19	513°
161 to 168	20	540°

30° RISER TABLE

FINISH FLOOR HEIGHT (IN.)	NUMBER OF STEPS	CIRCLE DEGREE
85 to 95	9	270°
96 to 104	10	300°
105 to 114	11	330°
115 to 123	12	360°
124 to 133	13	390°
134 to 142	14	420°
143 to 152	15	450°
153 to 161	16	480°
162 to 171	17	510°
172 to 180	18	540°

FRAMING DIMENSIONS (IN.)

STAIR DIAMETER	1	2	3	4	5	6
40	20	20	24	44	44	24
48	24	24	28	52	52	28
52	26	26	30	56	56	30
60	30	30	34	64	64	34
64	32	32	36	68	68	36
72	36	36	40	76	76	40
76	38	38	42	80	80	42
88	44	44	48	92	92	48
96	48	48	52	100	100	52

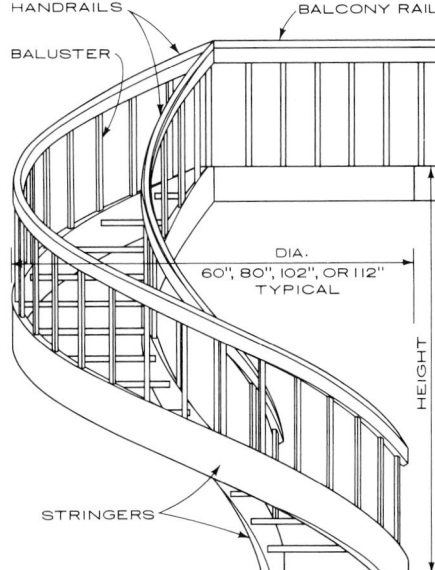

ELEVATION

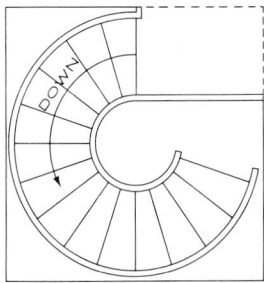

PLAN

Design considerations are similar to those for spiral stairs. Made of fabricated steel tube one-piece stringer with treads bolted or welded to the stringer. Treads also are made of laminated wood. Numerous finishes are available, with wood the most common. Risers can be open or closed, and they can be carpeted.

CIRCULAR STAIRS

EGRESS PLANNING **1**

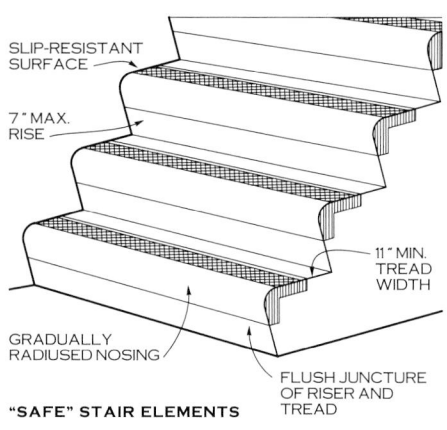

SLIP-RESISTANT SURFACE

7" MAX. RISE

11" MIN. TREAD WIDTH

GRADUALLY RADIUSED NOSING

FLUSH JUNCTURE OF RISER AND TREAD

"SAFE" STAIR ELEMENTS

TREADS AND RISER SIZES

Riser and tread dimensions must be uniform for the length of the stair. ANSI specifications recommend a minimum tread dimension of 11 in. nosing-to-nosing and a riser height of 7 in. maximum. Open risers are not permitted on stairs accessible to persons with disabilities.

TREAD COVERING

OSHA standards require finishes to be "reasonably slip resistant" by using nosings of slip-resistant finish. Treads without nosings are acceptable provided that the tread is serrated or is of a definite slip-resistant design. Uniform color and texture are recommended for clear delineation of edges.

NOSING DESIGN

ANSI specifications recommend nosings without abrupt edges that project no more than 1/2 in. beyond the edge of the riser. A safe stair uses a 1/2 in. radius abrasive nosing firmly anchored to the tread, with no overhangs and a clearly visible edge.

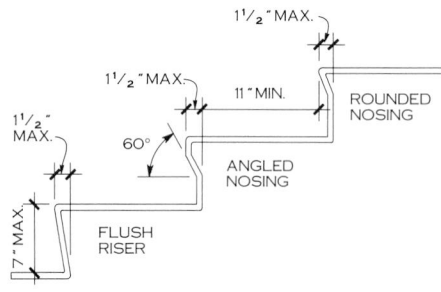

1 1/2" MAX.

1 1/2" MAX.

11" MIN.

ROUNDED NOSING

1 1/2" MAX.

60°

ANGLED NOSING

7" MAX.

FLUSH RISER

ACCEPTABLE NOSING PROFILES (ANSI 117.1-86)

DESIGN OF A "SAFE" STAIR

NOTE

Abrasive materials are used as treads, nosings, or inlay strips for new work and as surface-mounted replacement treads for existing work. A homogeneous epoxy abrasive is cured on an extruded aluminum base for a smoother surface, or it is used as a filler between aluminum ribs.

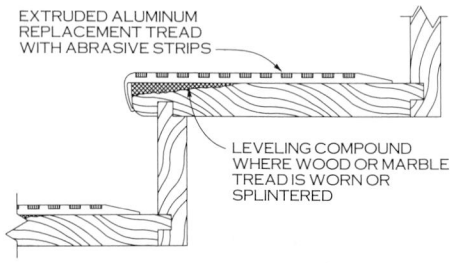

EXTRUDED ALUMINUM REPLACEMENT TREAD WITH ABRASIVE STRIPS

LEVELING COMPOUND WHERE WOOD OR MARBLE TREAD IS WORN OR SPLINTERED

REPLACEMENT OF TREAD

Eric K. Beach, Rippeteau Architects, PC; Washington, D.C.

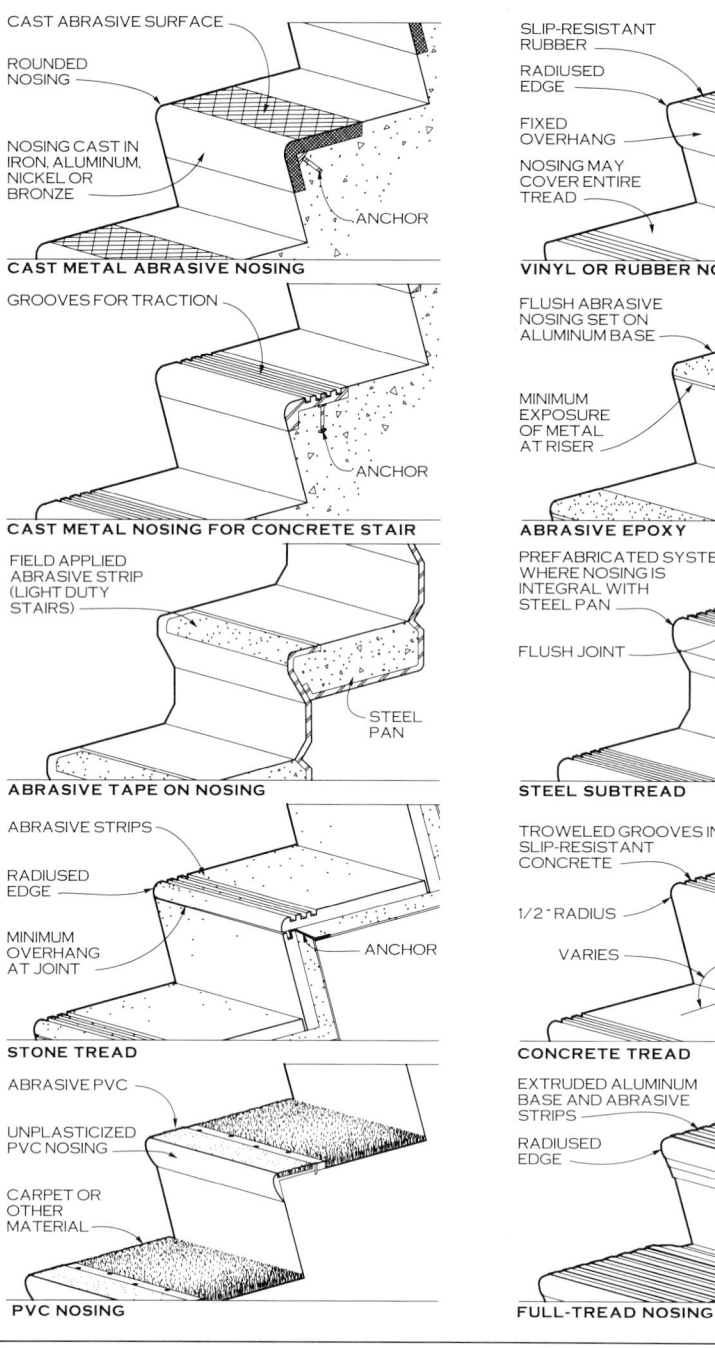

CAST ABRASIVE SURFACE

ROUNDED NOSING

NOSING CAST IN IRON, ALUMINUM, NICKEL OR BRONZE

ANCHOR

CAST METAL ABRASIVE NOSING

GROOVES FOR TRACTION

ANCHOR

CAST METAL NOSING FOR CONCRETE STAIR

FIELD APPLIED ABRASIVE STRIP (LIGHT DUTY STAIRS)

STEEL PAN

ABRASIVE TAPE ON NOSING

ABRASIVE STRIPS

RADIUSED EDGE

MINIMUM OVERHANG AT JOINT

ANCHOR

STONE TREAD

ABRASIVE PVC

UNPLASTICIZED PVC NOSING

CARPET OR OTHER MATERIAL

PVC NOSING

SLIP-RESISTANT RUBBER

RADIUSED EDGE

FIXED OVERHANG

NOSING MAY COVER ENTIRE TREAD

VINYL OR RUBBER NOSING

FLUSH ABRASIVE NOSING SET ON ALUMINUM BASE

MINIMUM EXPOSURE OF METAL AT RISER

CONCRETE ANCHORS

ABRASIVE EPOXY

PREFABRICATED SYSTEM WHERE NOSING IS INTEGRAL WITH STEEL PAN

FLUSH JOINT

STEEL SUBTREAD

TROWELED GROOVES IN SLIP-RESISTANT CONCRETE

1/2" RADIUS

VARIES

CONCRETE TREAD

EXTRUDED ALUMINUM BASE AND ABRASIVE STRIPS

RADIUSED EDGE

TAPERED END

FULL-TREAD NOSING

NOTE

Cast nosings for concrete stairs are iron, aluminum, nickel, or bronze in custom-made or stock sizes. Nosings and treads come with factory-drilled countersunk holes, with riveted strap- or wing- type anchors.

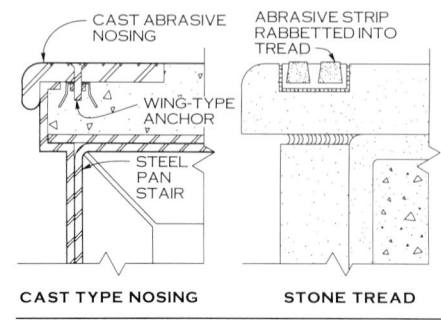

CAST ABRASIVE NOSING

WING-TYPE ANCHOR

STEEL PAN STAIR

ABRASIVE STRIP RABBETTED INTO TREAD

CAST TYPE NOSING   **STONE TREAD**

NOSING DETAILS

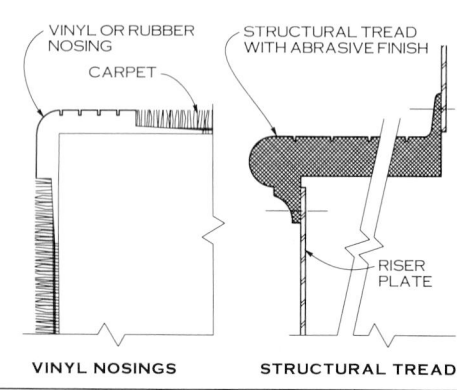

VINYL OR RUBBER NOSING

CARPET

STRUCTURAL TREAD WITH ABRASIVE FINISH

RISER PLATE

VINYL NOSINGS   **STRUCTURAL TREAD**

INTRODUCTION

Combining a wide range of common building technologies, the building systems presented on this and the following pages reflect basic approaches to design, construction, and use of materials in response to a variety of occupancy requirements. Such building systems embody key integration issues that arise when components and subsystems are merged to produce complete buildings.

Each example includes a summary of the unique system features, a description of the system's most appropriate or particularly advantageous uses, and a discussion of the main opportunities and challenges for systems integration. The drawings stress the essential interconnectedness among design decisions, illustrating the design process as a fusion of the knowledge of many disciplines, each with an understanding of the value and import of the others' contributions.

The examples encompass structural, envelope, mechanical, and interior systems. In most examples one system (usually structural) or a pair of systems tends to dominate the integration potentials and priorities, clearly circumscribing the prudent and possible uses of the other systems. The examples represent common and reasonable combinations and variations, but they are not the only possibilities within a given building vocabulary.

STRUCTURAL

Roof: Steel decking and open web steel joists (C)

Floor: Slab on grade (M)

Walls: Concrete masonry bearing wall and concrete footing (H)

Principal advantages and characteristics: Bearing wall and bar joist roof building systems employ masonry walls bearing on a turndown slab on grade or conventional spread footings. The walls support a roof structure of open web steel bar joists, through which mechanical distribution systems are threaded. Spans for J- and H-series open web joists generally may not exceed more than 20 times the joist depth, or more than 50 to 60 ft. Long-span joists are available, as are a wide variety of special shapes. By nature, open web joists spaced at even intervals are best suited to relatively light, uniform loads; joists may be doubled or tripled to accommodate heavier, concentrated loads or may be combined with other steel framing for roof openings and rooftop mechanical equipment. The roof deck may be precast concrete plank, tongue and groove wood decking, or, more commonly, steel decking. Small openings in the roof area can be framed between joists by means of specially designed headers.

In buildings with masonry bearing walls, each joist should be anchored to the masonry by means of a joist anchor embedded in the masonry. Steel joists can be designed to cantilever beyond the edges of the bearing walls. Continuous horizontal bracing of both top and bottom joist chords is possible with spot-welded connections at each joist and with the ends of the bracing members anchored to a bearing wall; this type of system is well suited to seismic risk zones.

ENVELOPE

Roof: Built-up roofing and rigid insulation (B)

Walls: Window assembly (N), exterior insulation and finish system (EIFS) (D), and canopy assembly (K)

Floor: Vapor barrier and dampproofing (L)

Principal advantages and characteristics: The concrete masonry unit (CMU) bearing walls are insulated on the exterior to take better advantage of the wall's thermal mass by placing it toward the occupied side. Long-span open web steel joist roofs can deflect substantially, and the camber of the joists alone is often not sufficient to maintain the necessary slope to roof drains.

MECHANICAL

HVAC: Rooftop unit (A) and ductwork (G)

Electrical: Surface-mounted conduit or behind furred-out walls

Plumbing: In partition walls, then through roof

Fire safety: Sprinkler system suspended from structure in ceiling plenum (E)

Principal advantages and characteristics: If ductwork is to be housed within the depth of the joist, headers or branches must be fed through the joist webs, perpendicular to the spanning direction. The webs of joists must be aligned, and bearing walls with projections must be worked around. Because beams running transverse to the joists may block the threading of piping, ductwork, and wiring, care must be taken that variations in the configuration of perimeter walls do not disrupt the regular pattern of the

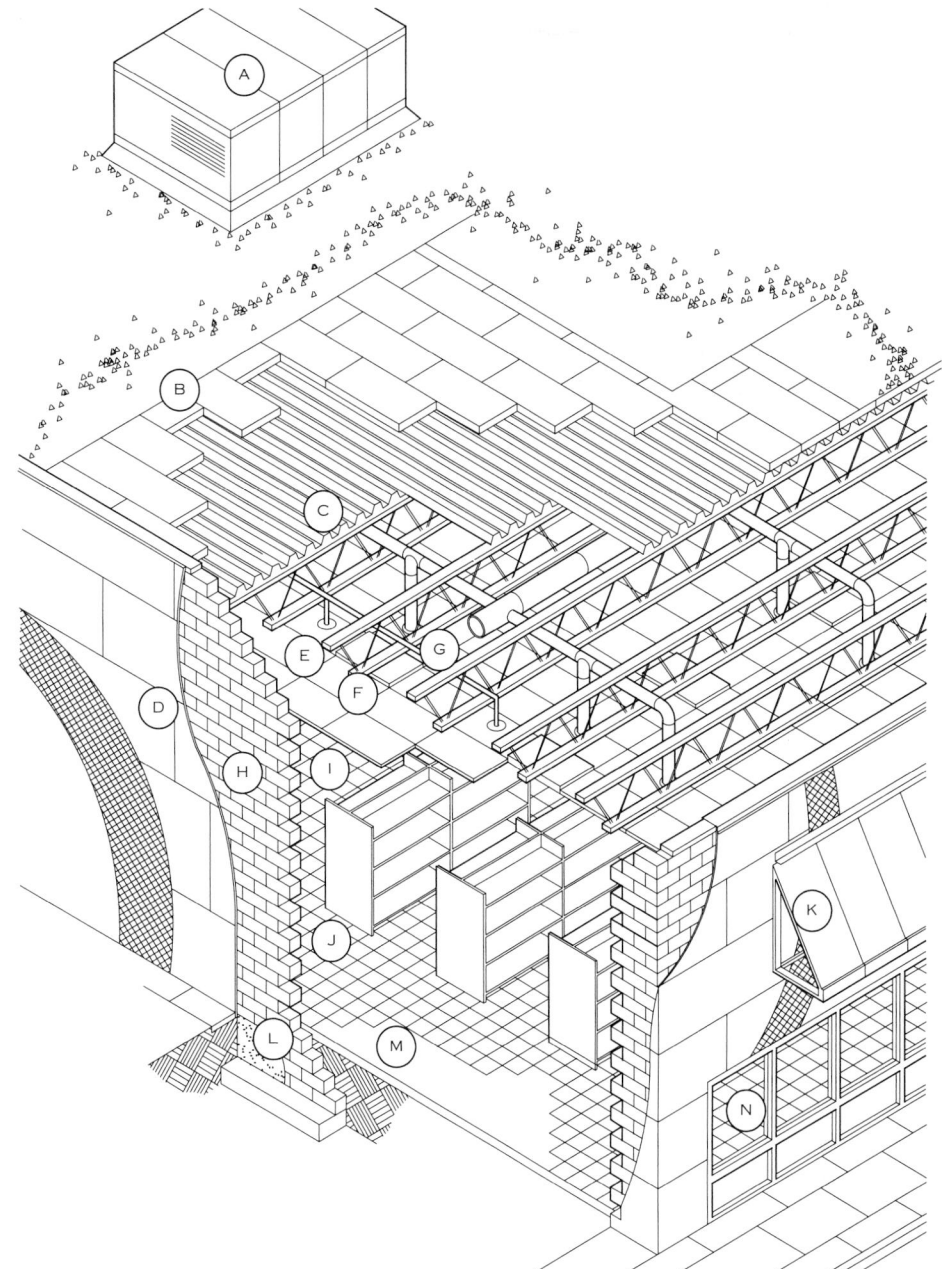

STEEL BAR JOIST WITH BEARING WALL

joist web elements, interfering with straight runs for mechanical components. If the building owners will also be tenants, relatively fixed interior lighting and mechanical systems may be planned. Otherwise, overhead and in-floor systems should be laid out for maximum flexibility. If the joist depth is insufficient to carry the ductwork, such equipment can be suspended from the bottom chord of the steel joist.

INTERIOR

Ceilings: Suspended acoustical tile (E)

Floors: Resilient tile (J)

Walls: Glazed interior face on CMU (I)

Lighting: Fluorescent light fixture in ceiling (F) and natural light (N)

Furnishings: Movable displays

Principal advantages and characteristics: Suspended interior ceilings are nearly always preferred to directly attached interior ceilings. Finished ceilings attached directly to the joist bottom chord are not only difficult to alter but must be designed to accommodate the high degree of deflection the roof assembly will experience.

SYSTEM SUMMARY

Steel open web joist and bearing wall construction yields buildings that have relatively large interior clear spans and flexible interior layouts. The open webbing of the joists provides a lightweight structure that is easily penetrated by mechanical systems. The bottom chords of the joists are used for suspension of interior finishes, lighting fixtures, and air diffusers in finished areas, although they may be left uncovered. Masonry bearing walls and metal joist roofs are among the simplest and easiest to design and build. The relatively low cost of the system makes it attractive for speculative projects, as does the fact that contractors find this construction method familiar and easy to erect. Retail commercial facilities usually require flexibility in lighting, partitioning, and mechanical systems and large expanses of column- and wall-free space; the envelope and structural systems chosen often reflect these demands.

The height to which masonry bearing walls can be built without resorting to lateral bracing is limited, so they are used most frequently in one-story structures. Roof spans up to 60 ft can generally be accommodated. The spacing and depth of joists is related to the spanning capability of the roof decking material and the requirements for loads on the roof structure.

Richard J. Vitullo, AIA; Oak Leaf Studio; Crownsville, Maryland
Based on The Building Systems Integration Handbook, by Richard D. Rush, AIA (John Wiley & Sons, 1986)

STRUCTURAL

Frame: Steel, with welded and bolted connections (F)
Roof: Steel decking welded to frame (A)
Floors, upper: Steel decking welded to primary frame members, with cast-in-place concrete topping (M)
Floors, basement: Slab on grade, with concrete foundation (O)
Core: Central service core of cast-in-place concrete

Principal advantages and characteristics: Core shear walls add rigidity to frame; composite action of structural steel framing and a steel and concrete floor diaphragm result in relatively long, uninterrupted clear spans with smaller depth of construction. Heights can range from one to more than 100 stories. System allows for off-site fabrication of frame components, easy shipping to site, and rapid assembly; corrugated steel deck becomes a working surface as soon as it is placed and provides formwork for concrete topping.

ENVELOPE

Roof: Built-up roofing or single-ply membrane on rigid insulation (B)
Walls: Curtain wall units of glass/frame assemblies (E) and insulated spandrel panels (I), attached to structural frame
Basement: Waterproofing and protective board, with foundation drain (N); vapor barrier under slab (P)

Principal advantages and characteristics: The envelope is structurally independent of the steel frame, providing flexibility in weight, size, and configuration of the envelope system. Curtain wall units preassembled at the factory must be designed with shipping, storage, installation, and general handling in mind, emphasizing protection from damage at all stages.

MECHANICAL

HVAC: Ducts, with diffusers, either suspended from structure in ceiling plenum or placed in floor plenum beneath access floor (D)
Electrical and telecommunications: Electrical wires and cables placed mainly in access floor plenum and structural/electrified floor (H); can also be located in ceiling plenum, for lighting, and in interior wall at spandrel panel
Plumbing: Most plumbing functions placed in core area for efficient vertical circulation of systems
Fire safety: Sprinkler system suspended from structure in ceiling plenum

Principal advantages and characteristics: Mechanical systems, hidden in floor or ceiling plenums or both, can be accessed through removable panels in ceiling or floor systems.

INTERIOR

Ceilings: Suspended acoustical tile (C)
Floors: Carpeted access floor system (L) and structural electrified floor (H)
Walls: Gypsum wallboard (J)
Lighting: Fluorescent light fixture in ceiling (G) and natural light (E)
Furnishings: Open office furniture (K)

Principal advantages and characteristics: Suspended ceiling provides space for distribution of internal services, but it tends to be used principally for overhead lighting and ductwork. Structural/electrified floors and access floor systems keep all wires and cables in space below finish floor, easily accessible by removable floor panels, allowing high degree of flexibility for interior environment. Buildup of static electricity and the ensuing risk of equipment damage and shocks need to be considered. Access floors are not suited to situations involving heavy point loads or shifting heavy equipment. Stringerless systems are among the most flexible and least costly varieties, but they lack the stability of fully gridded systems and depend on perimeter walls for restraint. Use of access floors as air plenum, requiring tight and uniform joints between access panels, may hinder access to wires, cables, and pipes; ductwork in floor plenums may eliminate the advantages of access floors by blocking the path for wiring, cables, and pipes.

SYSTEM SUMMARY

Steel frame and curtain wall construction allows for off-site fabrication of frame and envelope components, easy ship-

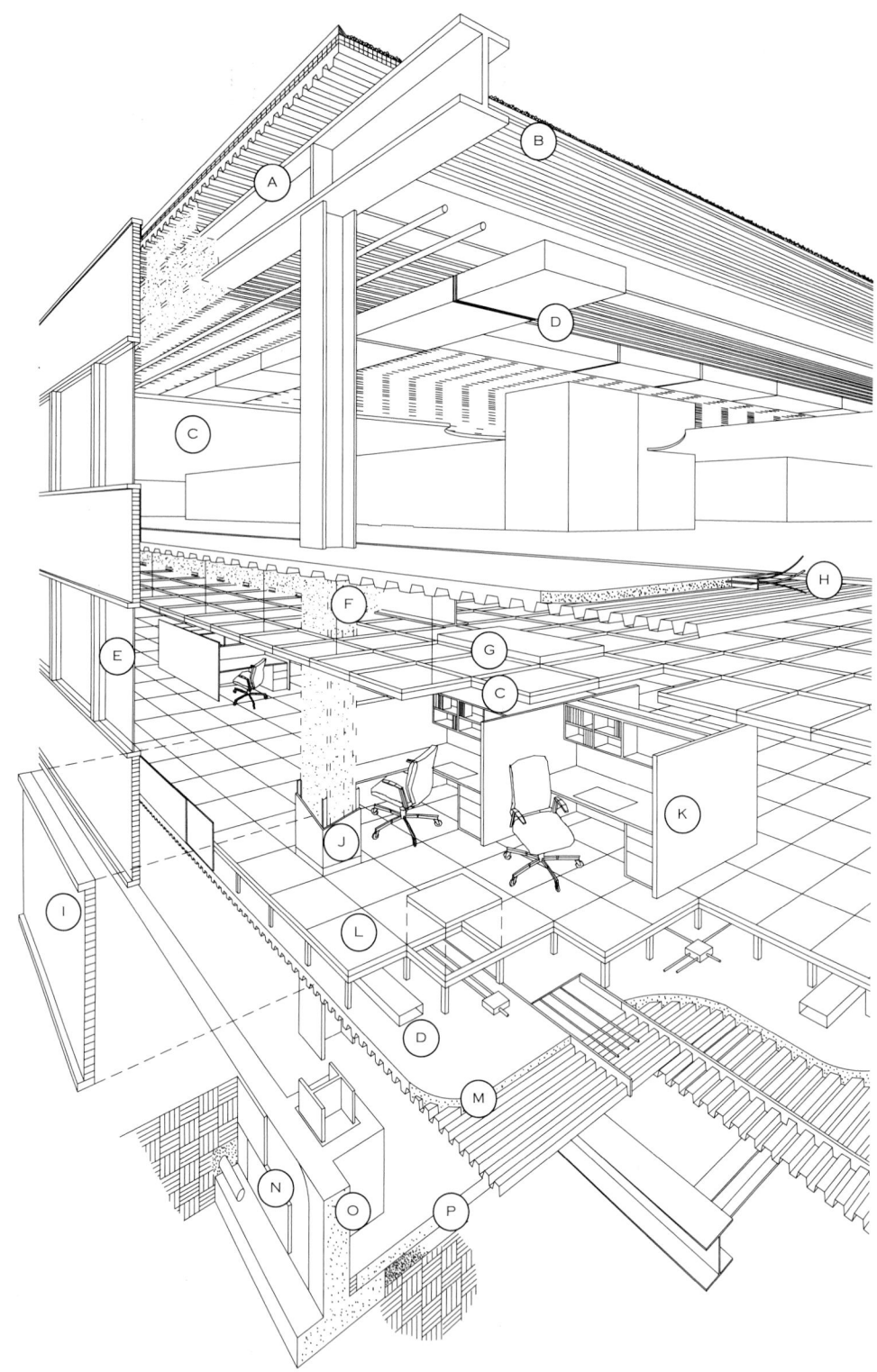

STEEL FRAME WITH ACCESS FLOOR AND CURTAIN WALL

ping to the site, and rapid assembly at the site. The steel and concrete in the floors are designed to act as a composite diaphragm, providing a thin, lightweight structural element with or without an access floor. The access floor shown is advantageous in office environments that need especially flexible interior layouts. This system keeps all wires and cables in the space below the finish floor (generally not less than 4 in. deep) and out of wall cavities. Although access floors may add to overall floor-to-floor heights, the access floor conceals the most visually obtrusive distribution elements.

Richard J. Vitullo, AIA; Oak Leaf Studio; Crownsville, Maryland
Based on The Building Systems Integration Handbook, by Richard D. Rush, AIA (John Wiley & Sons, 1986)

STRUCTURAL

Frame: Staggered story-high steel trusses (D) on steel columns (I) support floor slabs on both top and bottom chords

Roof: Precast hollow-core concrete plank deck (C)

Floors, upper: Precast hollow-core concrete plank deck (C)

Floor, lowest: Slab on grade, with concrete foundation (M)

Walls: Precast shear panels (H) and precast stiffener beams (O) stabilize structure

Principal advantages and characteristics: This system is best suited to multiunit residential or hotel buildings of 7 to 30 stories with repetitive floor plans. Floor-height Pratt trusses are placed atop every other column in a staggered pattern, strengthening the structural system while reducing overall weight; precast hollow-core concrete planks serve as the floor without a topping slab, allowing for bays of approximately 60 x 60 ft (twice the truss spacing). A fire-resistant membrane, such as drywall, is usually added to each side of a truss to provide protection; these walls also serve to divide individual units. Lower floors in this system can be finished and trimmed while upper-level structural members are still being laid; the structure becomes rigid as soon as the precast exterior wall panels and the outer concrete deck elements have been installed.

ENVELOPE

Roof: Rigid insulation, single-ply roofing and ballast (A)

Walls: Window assembly (G), precast concrete panels (L), precast stiffener beams (O), and precast shear panels (H)

Basement: Vapor barrier, and waterproofing and protective board (N)

Principal advantages and characteristics: Precast concrete wall members act as an envelope system as well as a structural system.

MECHANICAL

HVAC: Ducts, with diffusers, and sprinkler system (B); separate unit-by-unit HVAC systems can be used

Electrical: Conduit fed through vertical chases at outer walls (J)

Plumbing: Pipes fed through vertical interior chases

Fire safety: Sprinkler system supply at central corridor (B)

Principal advantages and characteristics: Because the Pratt-type trusses extend from floor to ceiling, with openings for corridors and elevator doors only, horizontal running of pipes, wiring, and ductwork can be difficult. For this reason separate unit-by-unit heating and air conditioning systems are often preferable; also, unitary HVAC systems offer economic and maintenance advantages in multifamily residential construction. Utilities are typically fed upward through chases and risers on outer walls, with service or supply units placed to either side on each floor; end wall stair enclosures are also used for this purpose. Most sprinkler systems are laid out in this fashion as well.

INTERIOR

Ceilings: Underside of concrete planks is either painted or covered with acoustical ceiling tile; corridors may have suspended ceiling tile (B)

Floors: Joints at floor planks are grouted and tops carpeted (K) or tiled (E)

Walls: Gypsum wallboard (F)

Lighting: Surface-mounted fixtures or suspended fluorescent fixtures at corridor (B)

Principal advantages and characteristics: The smooth surface of concrete deck planks can provide interior ceiling finishes, if desired.

SYSTEM SUMMARY

Staggered truss construction is most often used for double-loaded residential-type occupancies, including hotels, high-rise apartments, nursing homes, and hospitals. Such building types usually have highly repetitive floor plans and

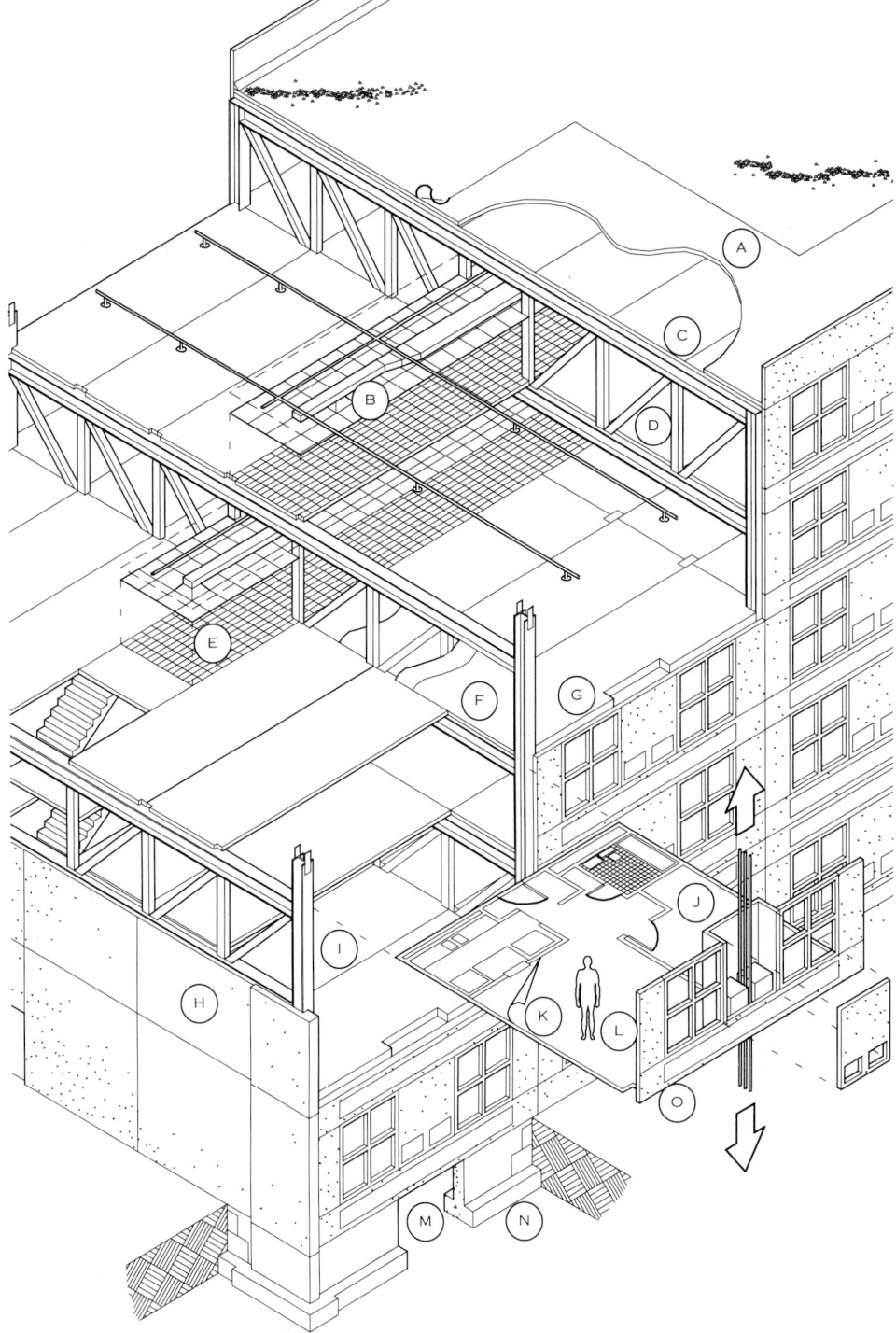

STAGGERED STEEL TRUSS

can benefit from systems that integrate objectives regarding structure, interior unit separations, fire-compartmentalization, and acoustical privacy. The system is not generally considered economical for low-rise buildings due to the manufacturing costs of the jigs for the trusses and the forms for the spandrel precasting. The system easily allows

for long structural bays, permitting a high degree of flexibility in unit interiors. The ground floor is free of trusses and interior columns and thus suitable for parking or retail commercial use. The system's light weight reduces foundation size.

Richard J. Vitullo, AIA; Oak Leaf Studio; Crownsville, Maryland
Based on The Building Systems Integration Handbook, by Richard D. Rush, AIA (John Wiley & Sons, 1986)

STRUCTURAL

Roof: Metal roof frame (C-stud brace, C-rafter, C-channel, C-joist) (C), with plywood sheathing

Floor, upper: Metal floor frame (C-joist), steel deck, and concrete topping (L)

Floor, ground: Slab on grade with concrete foundation (P)

Walls: C-stud assembly (M)

Principal advantages and characteristics: The lightweight cold-formed steel members are load bearing, and beams, columns, channels, headers, and other elements can be built up from standard steel shapes and sections. The frame's rigidity depends on cross bracing, the distance from exterior corner to exterior corner, and the type and layout of fasteners used. Sheathing both sides of the frame also provides some lateral stability. Steel studs used for masonry backup should be cross braced with steel straps. Horizontal and diagonal bracing increases the frame's rigidity. Welded connections are stronger than self-tapping screws. The method of attachment can affect costs substantially. The positioning and types of fasteners for affixing both interior and exterior sheathing should be carefully specified, because these factors significantly affect lateral stability.

Cold-rolled steel framing is detailed and fastened quite differently than wood framing, and special noncarpentry tools and equipment are required. Advantages of cold-formed steel framing include its light weight, dimensional stability, speed and ease of assembly, resistance to moisture and decay, and, in some cases, readier availability than wood framing members. Also, steel framing members are frequently made from recycled scrap and can themselves be endlessly recycled.

ENVELOPE

Roof: Shingles and roofing felt (B)

Grade: Dampproofing (O) and vapor barrier under slab

Walls: Batt insulation (K), window assembly (H), and brick veneer (G)

Principal advantages and characteristics: Deflection in lightweight steel frame construction can be several times greater than deflection in exterior masonry veneer; such differentials must be accommodated in anchoring details or overcome by adding structural rigidity to the wall frame. The masonry ties that anchor the veneer to the steel frame should permit free and independent movement of the two materials. Where the veneer depends on the steel frame for lateral stability, anchors should be flexible and should not resist shear; wire ties that allow independent movement are recommended. The framing design and method of fastening windows and doors should account for the differences in movement. In general, fenestration components should be attached to either the framing or the veneer, but not attached rigidly to both. When filled with batt insulation and fully sheathed, the lightweight steel frame wall is thermally isolated from the single wythe of masonry veneer. This results in greater differential thermal movement in the veneer than would occur with solid double-wythe masonry construction; the interior heat is not transferred as readily to the exterior masonry.

MECHANICAL

HVAC: Ducts, with diffusers (D)

Electrical: Wiring threaded through C-stud wall assembly (M)

Plumbing: In partition walls, then through roof

Principal advantages and characteristics: Prepunched holes in the studs provide easy routing of plumbing and electrical lines. Most codes require the use of electrical conduit or sheathing of the prepunched stud opening to avoid stripping the insulation as wires are drawn through. Electrolytic action between framing members and nonferrous plumbing pipes must also be considered, and pipes on exterior walls must be adequately insulated.

INTERIOR

Ceilings: Suspended acoustical tile (E)

Floors: Ceramic floor tile (J), resilient floor tile (N), and carpet (I)

Walls: Gypsum wallboard (F)

Principal advantages and characteristics: Interior gypsum wallboard, along with exterior sheathing, applied to steel studs provides additional lateral bracing and an interior finish.

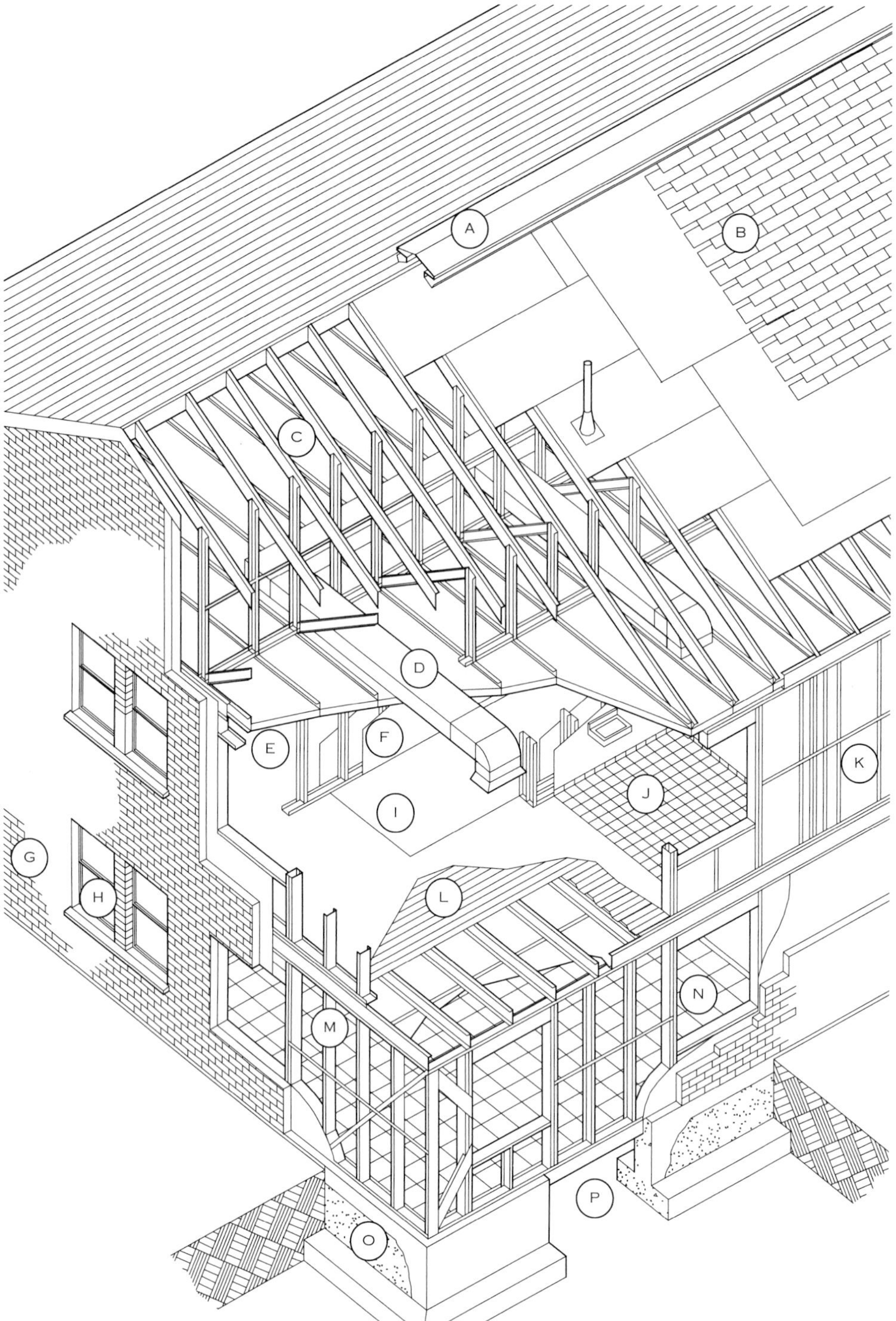

LIGHTWEIGHT STEEL FRAME AND BRICK VENEER

SYSTEM SUMMARY

Lightweight steel frame bearing wall construction is often used in low-rise commercial and residential buildings. The long-term performance of lightweight steel framing in structures over three stories is a concern. To date, its use in medium- and high-rise buildings has been mainly for exterior partitions or as nonbearing backup for exterior veneers.

Speed of construction, noncombustibility, and relative light weight are key advantages of this system. The space between studs eases insulation and accommodates piping and electrical distribution. Because the framing can be completed independent of the masonry veneer, the interior is out of the weather quickly and can be finished while the exterior brick veneer is laid. In nonresidential construction, which is likely to have fewer bracing walls and longer vertical spans and horizontal runs, added cold-formed bridging or bracing of the frame increases lateral stability. This can also be accomplished by decreasing the stud spacing or increasing the stud gauge.

Richard J. Vitullo, AIA; Oak Leaf Studio; Crownsville, Maryland
Based on The Building Systems Integration Handbook, by Richard D. Rush, AIA (John Wiley & Sons, 1986)

1   BUILDING SYSTEMS

STRUCTURAL

Roof: Wood roof truss and plywood sheathing (B)

Floor, upper: Wood floor truss and plywood subfloor (G)

Floor, ground: Slab on grade, concrete masonry foundation wall, and concrete footing (K)

Walls: Wood frame and sheathing (F)

Principal advantages and characteristics: In this example, a standard wood framing system is employed with prefabricated roof and floor trusses and exterior sheathing. The trusses are built at the factory to engineering specifications. The exterior panels act in concert with wall studs as a structural skin and weathering surface. The wood frame system unifies envelope and structure when this external skin acts as a diaphragm over the studs, joists, and rafters. Often built of 2 x 4 elements, the floor trusses also provide a nailing edge nominally 4 in. wide along the top and bottom chords for subflooring and decking, an improvement over the thinner edges presented by dimension lumber. Because trusses are made up from commonly available dimension lumber, there is little chance that supply shortages will delay projects. Assuming proper factory quality control, the variations often seen in dimension lumber from different mill lots should not be a problem. Also, the smaller wood components are more readily available from sustainable forest reserves, as opposed to large dimension lumber sections, which are available only from older growth forests.

Bridging between floor trusses may be eliminated, depending on the depth of the truss and the application and rigidity of subflooring and ceiling finishes. If needed, bridging may be accomplished by running continuous 2 x 4s perpendicular to the truss chords within the open web and nailing them to truss struts. When such bridging is used, it should not block possible transverse duct runs. Most floor truss systems allow for a continuous-edge ribbon at the truss ends in lieu of a header. Before truss units are lifted into place, it is wise to inspect them for uniformity of depth and camber and for general tightness. If substantial fieldwork is contemplated, it may be desirable to use plywood I-trusses, which can be cut to length and drilled to allow threading of pipes and wires.

ENVELOPE

Roof: Shingles, roofing felt, with metal flashing (A)

Grade: Vapor barrier under slab, with dampproofing at foundation

Walls: Batt insulation (E), window assembly (J), and lapped wood siding (I)

Principal advantages and characteristics: Wood components treated with fire retardants can now be used in many applications for which untreated wood is unsuitable. Some fire-retarding treatments may discolor wood, accelerate corrosion of metal fasteners, or alter the structural properties of the wood. For example, plywood can become delaminated, a particularly difficult problem when the plywood sheathing itself acts as the exterior finish surface.

MECHANICAL

HVAC: Ducts and diffusers (H), with below-slab perimeter ducts (M)

Electrical: Wiring threaded through holes drilled through wood studs

Plumbing: Pipes set in partition walls, then through roof

Principal advantages and characteristics: Open web trusses allow threading of wiring, piping, and ductwork without on-site drilling or cutting, thus greatly speeding and easing the installation of heating, plumbing, and electrical systems.

INTERIOR

Ceilings: Acoustical tile (C)

Floors: Carpet (L)

Walls: Gypsum wallboard (D)

Principal advantages and characteristics: The open web wood trusses permit longer clear spans than conventional timber framing, leaving greater flexibility for the location of interior partition walls that need not be load bearing.

SYSTEM SUMMARY

Prefabricated roof and floor trusses eliminate much field labor, thus speeding on-site construction; help ensure dim-

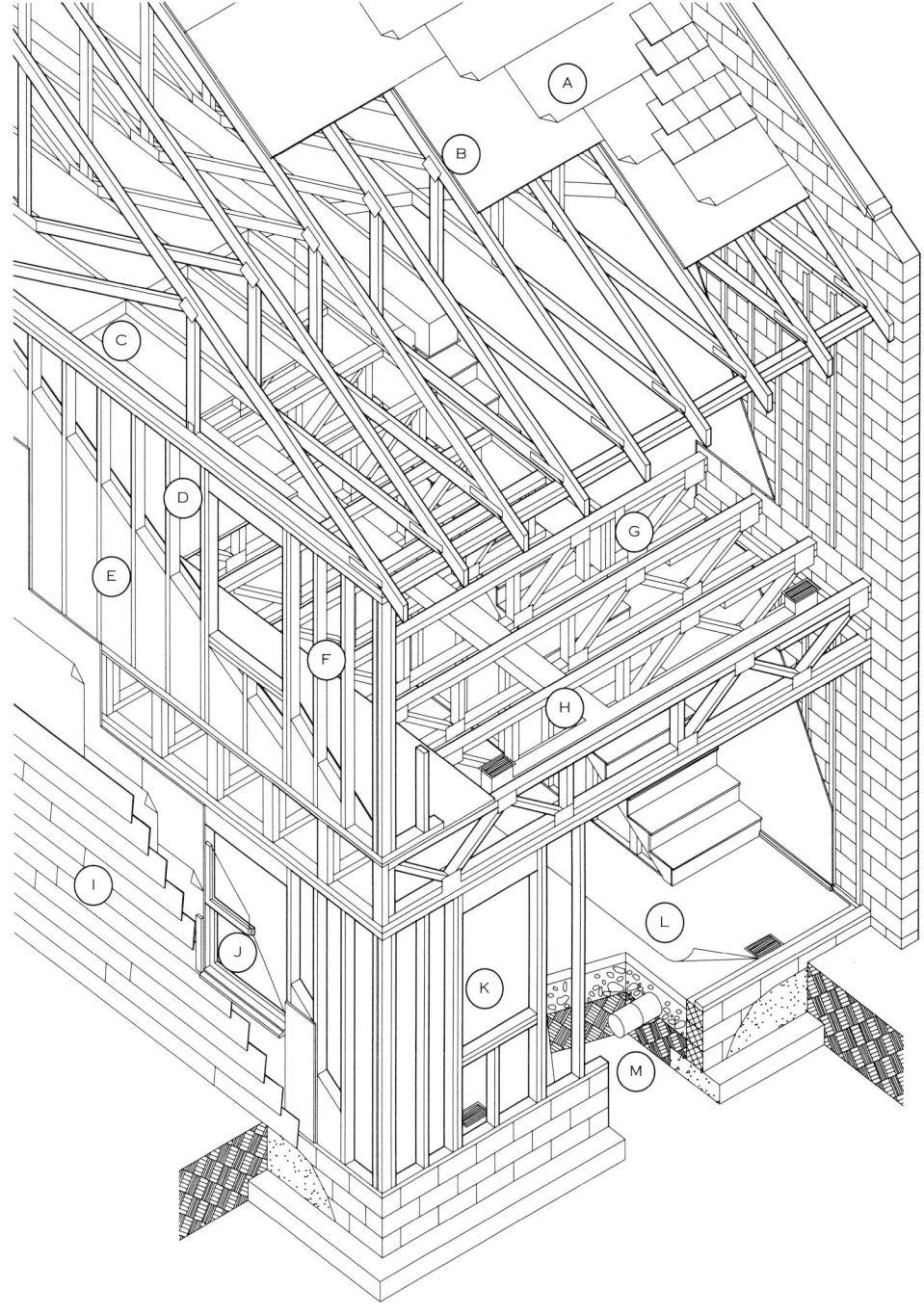

WOOD ROOF TRUSS AND WOOD FLOOR TRUSS

ensional stability; and may eliminate the need for intermediate load bearing partitions. Longer clear spans are possible with floor trusses than with generally available dimension lumber, and recent advances in manufacturing techniques make it possible to specify many special features. Open web trusses are lighter in weight than dimension lumber and can be lifted easily in gangs by a small crane or lift. Trusses are available in standard configurations between 12 and 24 in. deep and allow threading of mechanical systems without cutting the members, speeding installation. The smaller wood components used in these trusses are more readily available from sustainable forests, as opposed to the older growth trees harvested for larger standard lumber sections.

Richard J. Vitullo, AIA; Oak Leaf Studio; Crownsville, Maryland
Based on The Building Systems Integration Handbook, by Richard D. Rush, AIA (John Wiley & Sons, 1986)

STRUCTURAL

Columns:	Cast-in-place concrete (K)
Roof:	Cast-in-place concrete flat plate (E)
Floors, upper:	Cast-in-place concrete flat plate (E)
Floors, basement:	Slab on grade and concrete pile foundation (N)
Core:	Central service core of cast-in-place concrete

Principal advantages and characteristics: Combines cast-in-place concrete columns with two-way concrete slab plates of uniform thickness. Two-way flat plate concrete floors are among the simplest concrete structures for reinforcing, formwork, and detailing. Exterior precast concrete panels can be attached on lower floors, even with flat plate shoring still in place, while concrete is being poured for upper-floor columns and plates. When crane hoists are used to lift concrete buckets or large equipment, a hole is generally left in a section of each plate to allow for passage of the hoist; this hole is filled later, when large components have been moved and concrete pouring is complete. Elevator shafts are not used for this purpose, as elevators are usually installed before construction work is complete. In this system, precast concrete or composite spandrel units are welded in place to a series of angle clips fastened into the concrete flat plates at their edges.

Flat plate concrete construction permits more stories to be fitted into a given building height than any other system. This is because its floor structure has minimum thickness, especially when post-tensioned. In addition, in many building types the underside of the floor plate can serve as the finish ceiling.

ENVELOPE

Roof:	Rigid insulation and ballast (C), on protected roof membrane (B)
Walls:	Window assembly (D) and precast concrete spandrel panels (M), batt insulation (I)
Basement:	Waterproofing and protective board at foundation, with vapor barrier under slab (O)

Principal advantages and characteristics: Exterior precast concrete panels can be attached on lower floors, even with flat plate shoring still in place, while concrete is being poured for upper-floor columns and plates. Window-framing elements and glazing are installed after the spandrels have been set. Tolerances within the system grow progressively tighter: the concrete structure requires the least attention; placement of steel angles for welding to the spandrels requires greater exactitude; and positioning the spandrels to accommodate framing and glass requires greatest care.

MECHANICAL

HVAC:	Ducts, with diffusers, suspended from structure in ceiling plenum (G)
Electrical and tele-communications:	Power and communication poles (H)
Plumbing:	Most plumbing functions in core area for efficiency in vertical circulation of systems
Fire safety:	Sprinkler system suspended from structure in ceiling plenum
Conveying system:	Elevator equipment in penthouse (A)

Principal advantages and characteristics: Centralized core permits relatively uniform, short horizontal runs for power, plumbing, lighting, and other systems.

INTERIOR

Ceilings:	Suspended acoustical tile (F)
Floors:	Carpeting (L)
Walls:	Gypsum wallboard, metal stud assembly (J)
Lighting:	Fluorescent light fixture in ceiling and natural light (D)

Principal advantages and characteristics: Workstations in unpartitioned interior offices can be serviced unobtrusively by ceiling height power and communications poles, in furred-out areas around columns, and in corridor partition walls. Office workstations require daylight exposure and views. Because the central core is farthest from perimeter zones, usable floor area in the perimeter can be maximized. On constrained urban sites, the central core may be moved against an unfenestrated wall and still retain this advantage.

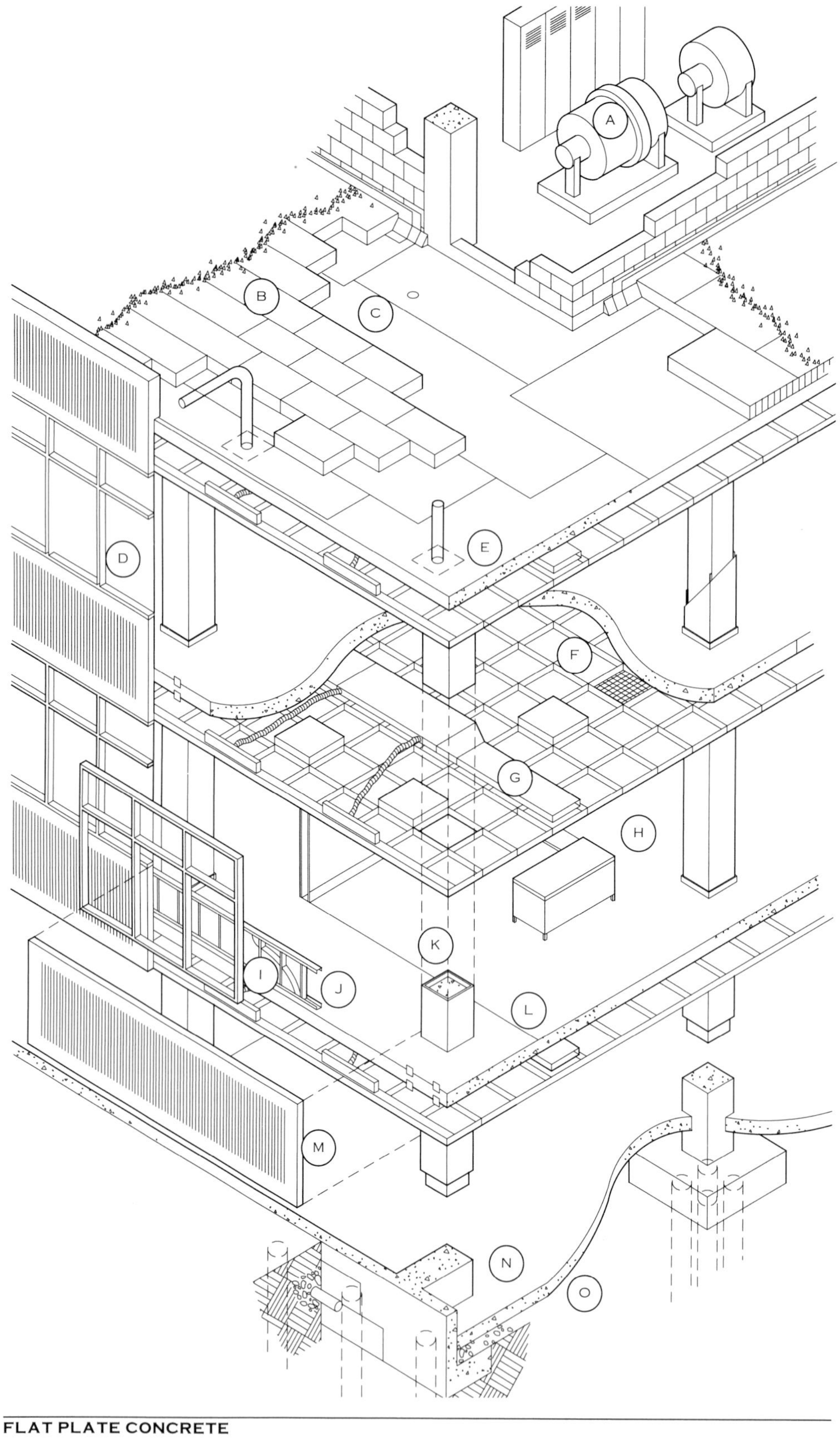

FLAT PLATE CONCRETE

SYSTEM SUMMARY

This example combines cast-in-place columns and two-way concrete flat plates of uniform thickness, with precast concrete spandrel panels. The system usually has a central core for vertical circulation and services, and it is typically employed for low- to medium-rise construction because of the costs and difficulties associated with placement of materials and labor in higher buildings. The central core also permits consolidation of vertical service risers, increasing fire protection by reducing or eliminating through-floor penetrations in office areas.

Flat plate concrete construction is especially applicable to apartments, hotels, and dormitories, in which no suspended ceiling is required. Story height can be minimized in these applications by using the undersides of the slabs as finish ceiling.

Richard J. Vitullo, AIA; Oak Leaf Studio; Crownsville, Maryland
Based on The Building Systems Integration Handbook, by Richard D. Rush, AIA (John Wiley & Sons, 1986)

BUILDING SYSTEMS

STRUCTURAL

Frame:	Rigid concrete (J)
Roof:	Rigid concrete slab
Floors, upper:	Concrete slab (B)
Floor, basement:	Slab on grade and concrete foundation (L)

Principal advantages and characteristics: Post-tensioning is a highly sensitive integration of the compressive strength of concrete with the tensile strength of steel. Plastic-sheathed, high-strength steel tendons are cast in the slab and, after curing, are placed in the tubes, anchored, and jacked into tension from one end. After stresses are applied, the tendon channels may be grouted to bond the tendons to the slab. For lengths greater than 100 ft, stresses must be applied simultaneously from two ends. Integration of mechanical services is influenced greatly by the positioning of tendons, which controls the locations of through-slab penetrations. Post-tensioning permits the use of shallower beams and slabs, reducing overall building height and permitting longer spans with thinner structural members; structure is quite rigid and less subject to movement and creep, allowing use of masonry infill envelope. Alterations and demolition can be difficult due to potential forces latent in post-tensioned tendons.

ENVELOPE

Roof:	Built-up roofing or single-ply membrane on rigid insulation (A)
Walls:	Window assembly (I), and brick and concrete masonry with rigid insulation (K)
Basement:	Waterproofing and protective board at foundation (N), vapor barrier under slab

Principal advantages and characteristics: Envelope rests on the concrete frame by means of steel shelf angles attached to spandrel beams.

MECHANICAL

HVAC:	Ducts, with diffusers, suspended from structure in ceiling plenum (C)
Electrical and tele-communications:	Wires and cables placed in wall assemblies
Plumbing:	Most plumbing functions placed in centralized locations, avoiding tendons
Fire safety:	Sprinkler system suspended from structure in ceiling plenum

Principal advantages and characteristics: Mechanical systems hidden in ceiling plenums can be accessed through removable panels. This system is optimal for additions to hospitals and other medical facilities, which often require floor-to-floor heights that match those of the existing structure. Although contemporary standards for servicing and mechanical equipment require deeper interstitial spaces than are found in older medical buildings, the shallower slabs and beams of post-tensioned concrete construction can conserve such space.

INTERIOR

Ceilings:	Suspended acoustical tile ceilings (E)
Floors:	Resilient flooring (F)
Walls:	Metal stud and drywall assembly (H)
Lighting:	Fluorescent light fixture in ceiling (D) and natural light (I)
Specialties:	Operable partitions (G)

Principal advantages and characteristics: Suspended ceiling provides space for distribution of internal services but tends to be used only for overhead lighting and ductwork.

SYSTEM SUMMARY

Post-tensioned concrete construction is virtually identical to the flat plate concrete construction described on the preceding page. The major difference lies in the thickness of the concrete slab, which is slightly reduced in this type of construction.

Post-tensioning is a method of reinforcing concrete by stretching steel reinforcing tendons after placement and curing of the concrete structure. This prestressing reduces or eliminates tensile stresses on the concrete under use loading and strengthens the slab without increasing its thickness or adding the dead loads introduced by additional steel reinforcing rods. Post-tensioning is useful when the thickness is important to economical or functional design aspects or when concentrated live loads are high and the building height must be kept to a minimum. It is also effective when project conditions require minimal floor-to-floor heights but maximum ceiling heights with generous space above the ceilings.

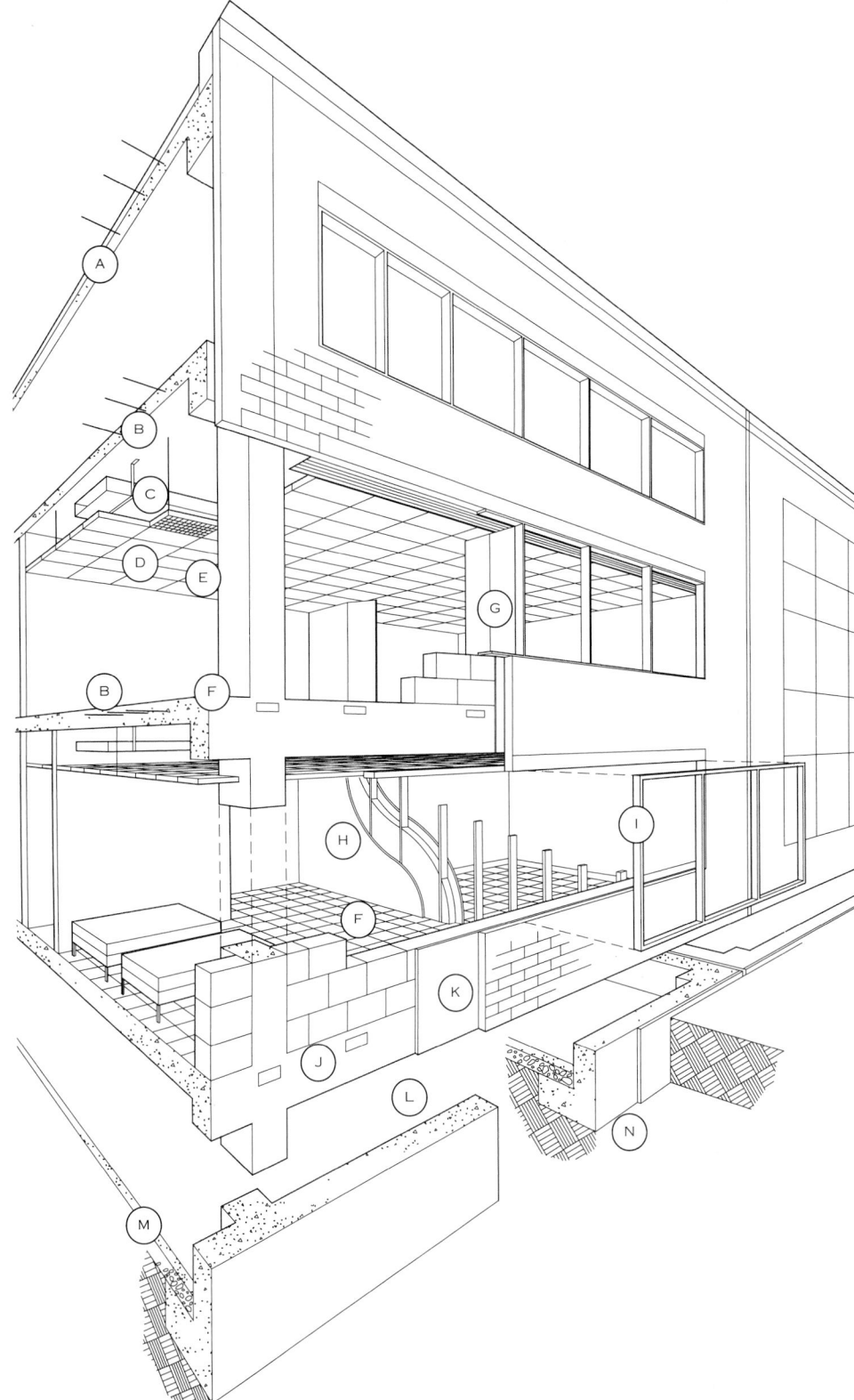

POST-TENSIONED CONCRETE

Richard J. Vitullo, AIA; Oak Leaf Studio; Crownsville, Maryland
Based on The Building Systems Integration Handbook, by Richard D. Rush, AIA (John Wiley & Sons, 1986)

STRUCTURAL

Frame:	Prestressed precast concrete columns and spandrel beams (D)
Roof:	Prestressed precast concrete double T (B)
Floors, upper:	Prestressed precast concrete double T (B)
Floors, basement:	Slab on grade, with cast-in-place concrete piles (F)
Core:	Cast-in-place concrete vertical circulation (E)

Principal advantages and characteristics: This system is most commonly used for parking garages. Double-T joists are generally 8 or 12 ft wide, at a depth of 18 to 36 in., depending on the spanning requirements; spans of 60 ft are considered maximum, due to the constraints of shipping and lifting the pieces, but longer spans and deeper sections are possible. It is advantageous to use as many similar elements as possible; that is, floors, inverted T girders, and columns should all be of the same length and design. Off-site precasting can conserve time and materials for concrete forming, and on-site erection time is considerably faster than for cast-in-place construction. Cast-in-place core provides lateral stability to frame. Adding final finishes and installation hardware to prestressed components before erection helps reduce on-site construction time. Temporary shoring and bracing may be required during construction, particularly (if the structure is composite) until the toppings have cured to service strength. Lifting loops are generally embedded in the precast pieces and then covered with the topping or cut off after installation.

ENVELOPE

Roof:	Concrete topping slab (A)
Walls:	Spandrel beams act as finish walls (D); no glazing in openings

Principal advantages and characteristics: For parking garages, the most common application of precast concrete frame, a weather-tight condition is not needed; therefore, structural components can be directly exposed to the elements. Some aesthetic treatments can be cast in or applied to surfaces but are not needed for moisture protection.

MECHANICAL

Electrical:	Conduit, exposed at underside of concrete structure
Plumbing:	Pipes from roof and floor drains, exposed to view throughout structure
Conveying system:	Elevator equipment for hydraulic elevator (G)
Fire safety:	Sprinkler heads dropped from supply lines set into channels at upper face of precast floor Ts

Principal advantages and characteristics: In parking structures the requirements for through-floor penetrations are minimal. However, holes or sleeves can be cast in the stems and flanges of the Ts, to allow for passage of conduit and piping. These holes and openings can be as great as one-third of the stem's total depth but must avoid the reinforcing tendons; openings toward the top of the stem in midspan and toward the bottom at the ends are most common. Preplanning of all openings is essential to minimize sitework and to realize the inherent economies of the system. Ts may be notched at the ends to permit passage of conduit along girders or bearing walls. Also, channels can be formed by chamfering mated edges of adjacent Ts at the upper surface, setting the conduit, then pouring a concrete topping slab.

INTERIOR

Floors:	Concrete topping acts as floor finish (A)
Walls:	Concrete structure surface acts as wall finish (D)
Lighting:	Fluorescent light fixtures attached to structure (C), and natural light between spandrel beams
Specialties:	Curbs, handrails, and signage

Principal advantages and characteristics: Most typical interior elements are not needed because of the open air nature of the building type; however, all elements provided are attached directly to the exposed structure. In parking garages, the depth of the structural Ts and concerns for minimizing floor-to-ceiling height present special challenges for the integration of lighting and signs.

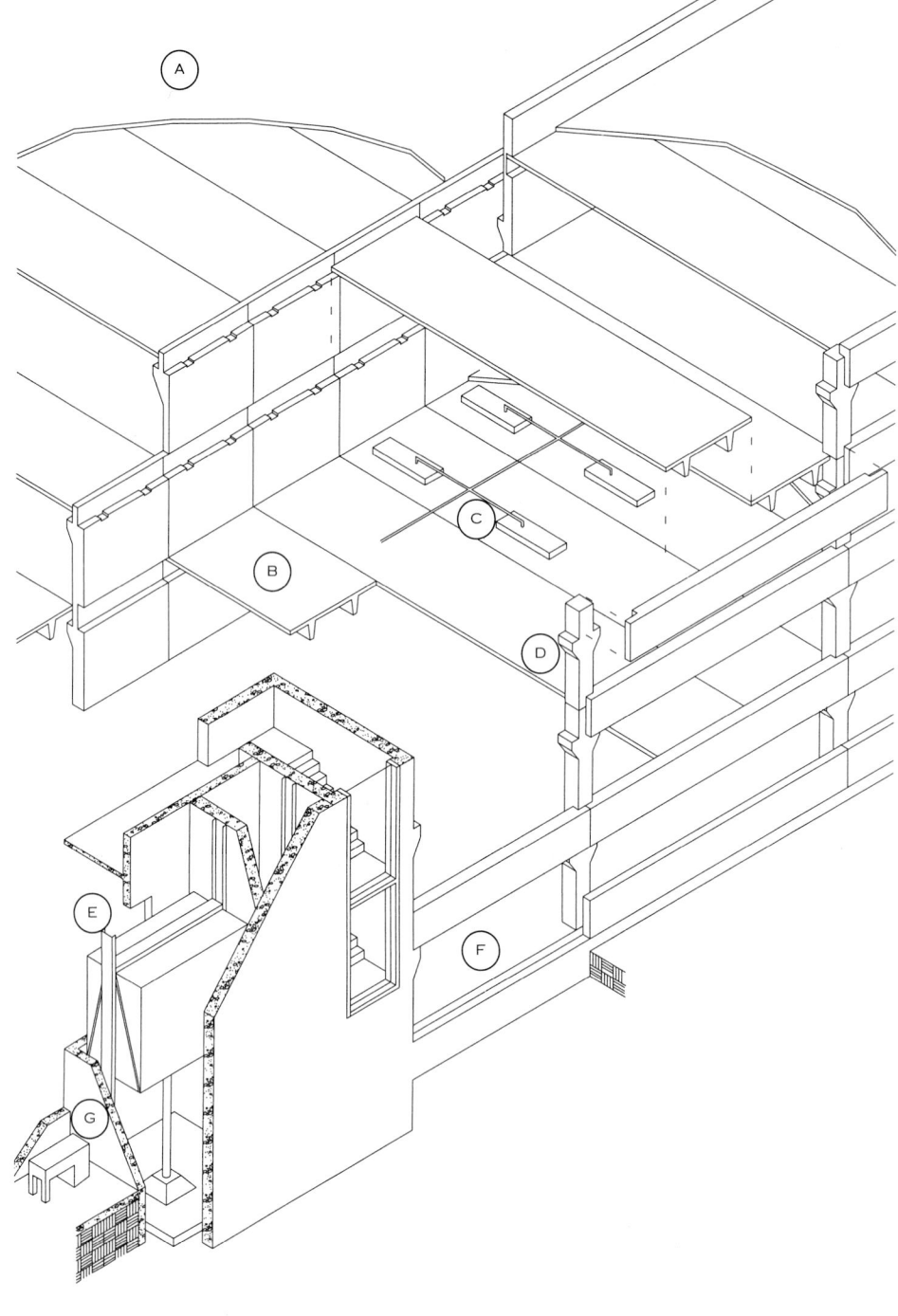

PRECAST CONCRETE FRAME

SYSTEM SUMMARY

Precast concrete components are usually pretensioned. Pretensioning is a method of prestressing concrete in which steel tendons are stretched prior to placement of concrete and maintained in tension until the concrete is cured. The external tension on the tendons is then released to compress the concrete. This example employs prestressed columns, inverted T girders, ledger girders, and double-T joists, all of the same length and design. Once the floor and roof Ts are set, the surface is covered with a thin concrete topping that provides the finished, weather-exposed surface and a horizontal structural diaphragm. The precast components are fabricated off site and lifted into place by crane. A variety of finished surfaces is possible, and the unity of materials presents an opportunity for natural visible integration of elements. Thin brick or tile can also be used as a surface material.

Richard J. Vitullo, AIA; Oak Leaf Studio; Crownsville, Maryland
Based on The Building Systems Integration Handbook, by Richard D. Rush, AIA (John Wiley & Sons, 1986)

FLOOR STRUCTURE ASSEMBLIES FOR ADDITIONAL INFORMATION CONSULT MANUFACTURERS' LITERATURE AND TRADE ASSOCIATIONS		DEPTH OF SYSTEM (IN.)	STANDARD MEMBER SIZES (IN.)	DEAD LOAD OF STRUCTURE (PSF)	SUITABLE LIVE LOAD RANGE (PSF)	SPAN RANGE (FT)	DIMENSIONAL STABILITY AFFECTED BY
WOOD JOIST	PLYWOOD SUBFLOOR / WOOD JOIST / CEILING	7–13	Nominal joist 2 x 6, 8, 10, and 12	5–8	30–40	Up to 18	Deflection
WOOD TRUSS OR PLYWOOD JOIST	PLYWOOD SUBFLOOR / PLYWOOD JOIST (OR WOOD TRUSS) / CEILING	13–21	Plywood joists 12, 14, 16, 18, and 20	6–12	30–40	12–30	Deflection
WOOD BEAM AND PLANK	WOOD PLANK / WOOD BEAM	10–22	Nominal plank 2, 3, and 4	6–16	30–40	10–22	—
LAMINATED WOOD BEAM AND PLANK	WOOD PLANK / GLUE LAMINATED WOOD BEAM	8–22	Nominal plank 2, 3, and 4	6–20	30–40	8–34	—
STEEL JOIST	PLYWOOD SUBFLOOR / WOOD NAILER / STEEL JOIST / CEILING	9–31	Steel joists 8–30	8–20	30–40	16–40	Deflection
STEEL JOIST	CONCRETE SLAB / STEEL CENTERING / STEEL JOIST / CEILING	11–75	Steel joists 8–72	30–110	30–100	16–60 (up to 130)	Deflection
LIGHT-WEIGHT STEEL FRAME	PLYWOOD SUBFLOOR / LIGHTWEIGHT STEEL FRAME / CEILING	7–12	Consult manufacturers' literature	6–20	30–60	10–22	—
STEEL FRAME	CONCRETE SLAB / STEEL CENTERING / STEEL BEAM / CEILING	9–15	—	35–60	30–100	16–35	Deflection
STEEL FRAME	CONCRETE TOPPING / PRECAST CONCRETE PLANK / STEEL BEAM / CEILING	8–16	Concrete plank 16–48 W 4–12 D	40–75	60–150	Up to 50 Generally below 35	Deflection and creep
PRECAST CONCRETE	CONCRETE TOPPING / PRECAST CONCRETE PLANK / CONCRETE BEAM	6–12	Concrete plank 16–48 W 4–12 D	40–75	60–150	Up to 60 Generally below 35	Deflection and creep
ONE-WAY CONCRETE SLAB	CONCRETE SLAB / CONCRETE BEAM	4–10	—	50–120	40–150	10–20 More with prestressing	—
TWO-WAY CONCRETE SLAB	CONCRETE SLAB / CONCRETE BEAM	4–10	—	50–120	40–250	10–30 More with prestressing	—
ONE-WAY RIBBED CONCRETE SLAB	CONCRETE SLAB / RIB (JOIST)	8–22	Standard pan forms 20 and 30 W 6–20 D	40–90	40–150	15–50 More with prestressing	Creep
TWO-WAY RIBBED CONCRETE SLAB	CONCRETE SLAB / RIB (JOIST)	8–22	Standard dome forms 19 x 19, 30 x 30 6–20 D	75–105	60–200	25–60 More with prestressing	Creep
CONCRETE FLAT SLAB	CONCRETE SLAB / DROP PANEL / CAPITAL / COLUMN	6–16	Min. slab thickness 5 without / 4 with } Drop panel	75–170	60–250	20–40 Up to 70 with prestressing	Creep
PRECAST DOUBLE TEE	CONCRETE TOPPING / PRECAST DOUBLE TEE	8–18	4', 5', 6', 8', and 10' W 6–16 D	50–80	40–150	20–50	Creep
PRECAST TEE	CONCRETE TOPPING / PRECAST SINGLE TEE	18–38	16–36 D	50–90	40–150	25–65	Creep
COMPOSITE	CONCRETE SLAB / WELDED STUD (SHEAR CONNECTOR) / STEEL BEAM	4–6	—	35–70	60–200	Up to 35	Deflection
CONCRETE FLAT PLATE	COLUMN / CONCRETE FLAT PLATE	5–14	—	60–175	60–200	18–35 More with prestressing	Creep

Roger K. Lewis, FAIA, and Mehmet T. Ergene, Architect; Roger K. Lewis, FAIA, & Associates; Washington, D.C.

BAY SIZE CHARAC-TERISTICS	REQUIRES FINISHED FLOOR SURFACE	REQUIRES FINISHED CEILING SURFACE	SERVICE PLENUM	COMPARATIVE RESISTANCE TO SOUND TRANSMISSION		FIRE RESISTIVE RATING PER CODE AND UNDERWRITERS		CONSTRUC-TION TYPE CLASSIFI-CATION	REMARKS
				IMPACT	AIRBORNE	UNPRO-TECTED HOURS	MAXIMUM PROTECTED HOURS		
—	Yes	Visual or fire protection purposes	Between joists —one way	Poor	Fair	—	2 (combustible)	4B (A) 3C (B)	Economical, light, easy to construct. Limited to lowrise construction
—	Yes	Visual or fire protection purposes	Between trusses and joists —two ways	Poor	Fair	—	2 (combustible)	4B (A) 3C (B)	Close dimensional tolerances; cutting holes through web permissible
Maximum beam spacing 8'-0"	Optional	No	Under structure —one way	Poor	Fair	—	2	3A 6" x 10" frame min. 4" planks min.	Most efficient with planks continuous over more than one span
—	Optional	No	Under structure —one way	Poor	Fair	—	2	3A 6" x 10" frame min. 4" planks min.	—
Light joists 16" to 30" o.c. Heavy joists 4'-12' o.c.	Yes	Visual or fire protection purposes	Between joists —two ways	Poor	Poor	—	1	3C (B)	—
Light joists 16" to 30" o.c. Heavy joists 4'-12' o.c.	No	Visual or fire protection purposes	Between joists —two ways	Poor	Fair	—	1-3	1, 2 and 3	Economical system, selective partition placement required. Cantilevers difficult
—	Yes	Visual or fire protection purposes	Under structure	Poor	Poor	—	1	3C (B)	—
—	No	Visual or fire protection purposes	Under structure	Poor	Fair	1-3	1-4	1, 2, and 3	—
—	Optional	Visual or fire protection purposes	Under structure	Fair	Fair	—	1-4	1, 2, and 3	—
—	Optional	No	Under structure	Fair	Fair	2-4	3-4	1 and 2	—
—	No	No	Under structure	Good	Good	1-4	3-4	1 and 2	Restricted to short spans because of excessive dead load
L ≤ 1.33 W	No	No	Under structure	Good	Good	1-4	3-4	1 and 2	Suitable for concentrated loads, easy partition placement
—	No	No	Between ribs —one way	Good	Good	1-4	3-4	1 and 2	Economy through re-use of forms, shear at supports controlling factor
L ≤ 1.33 W	No	No	Under structure	Good	Good	1-4	3-4	1 and 2	For heavy loads, columns should be equidistant. Not good for cantilevers
L ≤ 1.33 W	No	No	Under structure	Good	Good	1-4	3-4	1 and 2	Drop panels against shear required for spans above 12 ft
—	Optional	Visual purposes; differential camber	Between ribs —one way	Fair	Good	2-3	3-4	1 and 2	Most widely used pre-stressed concrete product in the medium span range
—	Optional	Visual purposes; differential camber	Between ribs —one way	Fair	Good	2-3	3-4	1 and 2	Easy construction, lack continuity, poor earthquake resistance
—	No	Visual or fire protection purposes	Under structure	Good	Good	—	1-4	1, 2, and 3	—
L ≤ 1.33 W	No	No	Under structure	Good	Good	1-4	3-4	1 and 2	Uniform slab thickness, economical to form, easy to cantilever

Roger K. Lewis, FAIA, and Mehmet T. Ergene, Architect; Roger K. Lewis, FAIA, & Associates; Washington, D.C.

1　　**BUILDING SYSTEMS**

ROOF STRUCTURE ASSEMBLIES FOR ADDITIONAL INFORMATION CONSULT MANUFACTURER'S LITERATURE AND TRADE ASSOCIATIONS		DEPTH OF SYSTEM (IN.)	STANDARD MEMBER SIZES (IN.)	DEAD LOAD OF STRUCTURE (PSF)	SUITABLE LIVE LOAD RANGE (PSF)	SPAN RANGE (FT)	BAY SIZE CHARAC-TERISTICS	DIMENSIONAL STABILITY AFFECTED BY
WOOD RAFTER	PLYWOOD SHEATHING / WOOD JOIST / CEILING	5–13	Nominal rafters 2 x 4, 6, 8, 10, and 12	4–8	10–50	Up to 22	—	Deflection
WOOD BEAM AND PLANK	WOOD PLANK / WOOD BEAM (OR LAMINATED BEAM)	8–22	Nominal planks 2, 3, and 4	5–12	10–50	8–34	Maximum beam spacing 8'-0''	—
PLYWOOD PANEL	PLYWOOD (STRESSED SKIN) PANELS	3¼ and 8¼	—	3–6	10–50	8–32	4'-0'' modules	—
WOOD TRUSS	SHEATHING / WOOD TRUSS / CEILING	Varies (1'–12')	—	5–15	10–50	30–50	2'-8' between trusses	Deflection
STEEL TRUSS	STEEL DECK / PURLIN / STEEL TRUSS	Varies	—	15–25	10–60	100–200	—	Deflection
STEEL JOIST	CONCRETE / STEEL CENTERING / STEEL JOIST / CEILING	11–75	Steel joists 8–72	10–28	10–50	Up to 96	Light joists 16''–30'' o.c. Heavy joists 4'–12' o.c.	Deflection
STEEL JOIST	PLYWOOD DECK / WOOD NAILER / STEEL JOIST / CEILING	10–32	Steel joists 8–30	8–20	10–50	Up to 96	Light joists 16''–30'' o.c. Heavy joists 4'–12' o.c.	Deflection
STEEL JOIST	INSULATION / STEEL DECK / STEEL JOIST / CEILING	11–75	Steel joists 8–72	6–24	10–50	Up to 96	—	Deflection
STEEL FRAME	PRECAST CONCRETE PLANK / STEEL BEAM / CEILING	4–12 plus beam depth	Concrete plank 16–48 W 4–12 D	40–75	30–70	20–60 Generally below 35	—	Deflection and creep
PRECAST CONCRETE	PRECAST CONCRETE PLANK / CONCRETE BEAM	4–12 plus beam depth	Concrete plank 16–48 W 4–12 D	40–75	30–70	20–60 Generally below 35	—	Deflection and creep
ONE-WAY CONCRETE SLAB	CONCRETE SLAB / CONCRETE BEAM	4–10 slab plus beam depth	—	50–120	Up to 100	10–25 More with prestressing	—	—
TWO-WAY CONCRETE SLAB	CONCRETE SLAB / CONCRETE BEAM	4–10 slab plus beam depth	—	50–120	Up to 100	10–30 More with prestressing	L ≤ 1.33 W	—
ONE-WAY RIBBED CONCRETE SLAB	CONCRETE SLAB / RIB (JOIST)	8–22	Standard pan forms 20 and 30 W 6–20 D	40–90	Up to 100	15–50 More with prestressing	—	Creep
TWO-WAY RIBBED CONCRETE SLAB	CONCRETE SLAB / RIB (JOIST)	8–24	Standard dome forms 19 x 19, 30 x 30 6–20 D	75–105	Up to 100	25–60 More with prestressing	L ≤ 1.33 W	Creep
PRECAST TEE		16–36	16–36 deep	65–85	20–80	30–100	—	Creep
PRECAST DOUBLE TEE		6–16	4', 5', 6', 8', and 10' wide 6''–16'' deep	35–55	25–60	20–75	—	Creep
CONCRETE FLAT PLATE	CONCRETE FLAT PLATE / COLUMN	4–14	—	50–160	Up to 100	Up to 35 More with prestressing	L ≤ 1.33 W	Creep
CONCRETE FLAT SLAB	CONCRETE SLAB / DROP PANEL / CAPITAL / COLUMN	5–16	Min. slab thickness 5 w/o Drop 4 w/ panel	50–200	Up to 100	Up to 40 More with prestressing	L ≤ 1.33 W Equal column spacing required	Creep
GYPSUM DECK	GYPSUM CONCRETE / FORM BOARD / SUBPURLIN / CEILING	3–6	—	5–20	Up to 50	Up to 10	Up to 8' between subpurlins	Deflection and creep

Roger K. Lewis, FAIA, and Mehmet T. Ergene, Architect; Roger K. Lewis, FAIA, & Associates; Washington, D.C.

SUITABLE FOR INCLINED ROOFS	REQUIRES FINISHED CEILING SURFACE	SERVICE PLENUM	RELATIVE THERMAL CAPACITY	COMPARATIVE RESISTANCE TO SOUND TRANSMISSION		FIRE RESISTIVE RATING PER CODE AND UNDERWRITERS		CONSTRUCTION TYPE CLASSIFICATION	REMARKS
				IMPACT	AIRBORNE	UNPROTECTED HOURS	MAXIMUM PROTECTED HOURS		
Yes	For visual or fire protection purposes	Between rafters —one way	Low	Poor	Fair	–	2 (combustible)	4B (A) 3C (B)	
Yes	For fire protection purposes	Under structure —one way	Medium	Poor	Fair	–	2	3A 6'' x 10'' frame min. 4'' plank min.	
Yes	No	Under structure only	Low	Poor	Fair	–	2	4B (A) 3C (B)	
Yes	For visual or fire protection purposes	Between trusses	Low	Poor	Fair	–	2 (combustible)	4B (A) 3C (B)	Truss depth to span ratio 1:5 to 1:10
Yes Pitched trusses usually used for short spans	For visual or fire protection purposes	Between trusses	Low	Fair	Fair	–	1–4	1, 2, and 3	Truss depth to span ratio 1:5 to 1:15
No	For visual or fire protection purposes	Between joists	Medium	Fair	Fair	–	1–4	1, 2, and 3	
Yes	For visual or fire protection purposes	Between joists	Low	Poor	Fair	–	1	1, 2, and 3	
Yes	For visual or fire protection purposes	Between joists	High	Excellent	Good	–	2	1, 2, and 3	
Yes	For visual or fire protection purposes	Under structure	High	Fair	Fair	–	1–4	1, 2, and 3	Easy to design; quick erection
Yes	No	Under structure	High	Fair	Fair	2–4	3–4	1 and 2	Provides finished flush ceiling. May be used with any framing system
No	No	Under structure	High	Good	Good	1–4	3–4	1 and 2	
No	No	Under structure	High	Good	Good	1–4	3–4	1 and 2	
No	For visual purposes	Between ribs —one way	High	Good	Good	1–4	3–4	1 and 2	
No	No	Under structure	High	Good	Good	1–4	3–4	1 and 2	Economy in forming; suitable for two-way cantilevering
Yes	For visual or fire protection purposes	Between ribs —one way	High	Fair	Good	2–3	3–4	1 and 2	Generally used for long spans
Yes	For visual or fire protection purposes	Between ribs —one way	High	Fair	Good	2–3	3–4	1 and 2	Most widely used prestressed concrete element.
No	No	Under structure	High	Good	Good	1–4	3–4	1 and 2	Uniform slab thickness; easy to form; suitable for vertical expansion of building
No	No	Under structure	High	Good	Good	1–4	3–4	1 and 2	Suitable for heavy roof loads
No	For visual or fire protection purposes	Under structure	High	Good	Good	–	2	1, 2, and 3	Provides resistance to wind and seismic loads

Roger K. Lewis, FAIA, and Mehmet T. Ergene, Architect; Roger K. Lewis, FAIA, & Associates; Washington, D.C.

EXTERIOR WALL ASSEMBLIES FOR ADDITIONAL INFORMATION CONSULT MANUFACTURERS LITERATURE AND TRADE ASSOCIATIONS		WALL THICKNESS (NOMINAL) (IN.)	WEIGHT (PSF)	VERTICAL SPAN RANGE (UNSUPPORTED HEIGHT) (FT)	WIND RESIST.	RACKING RESISTANCE	SERVICE PLENUM SPACE	HEAT TRANS-MISSION COEFFICIENT (U-FACTOR) (BTU/HR·SQ FT·°F)
C.M.U.	C.M.U. (GRAVEL AGGREGATE)	8 12	55 85	Up to 13 Up to 20	Wind resistance depends on geographical location and height of building; wind velocity; wall material thickness, strength; workmanship; axial loads; and horizontal span. Design walls for both inward and outward pressures	Good	None	0.56 0.49
C.M.U. (INSULATED)	C.M.U. / INSULATION / INT. WALL FIN.	8 + 12 +	60 90	Up to 13 Up to 20		Good	Through insulation	0.21 0.20
C.M.U. AND BRICK VENEER (INSULATED)	BRICK VENEER / C.M.U. / INSULATION / INT. WALL FIN.	4 + 4 + 4 + 8 +	75 100	Up to 13 (w/filled cavity) Up to 20 (w/filled cavity)		Good	Through insulation	0.19 0.18
CAVITY	BRICK VENEER / CAVITY (MIN. 2") / INSULATION (WATER REPELLENT) / C.M.U. / INT. WALL FIN.	4 + 2 + 4 4 + 2 + 8	75 100	Up to 9 Up to 13		Fair	None	0.12 0.11
C.M.U. AND STUCCO (INSULATED)	STUCCO / C.M.U. / INSULATION / INT. WALL FIN.	8 +	67	Up to 13		Good	Through interior insulation	0.16
WOOD STUD	EXT. WALL FIN. / SHEATHING WITH MOISTURE BARRIER / WOOD STUD / INSULATION WITH VAPOR BARRIER / INT. WALL FIN	4 6	12 16	Up to 14 Up to 20 (L/d ≤ 50)		Poor to fair	Between studs	0.06 0.04
BRICK VENEER	BRICK VENEER / SHEATHING WITH MOISTURE BARRIER / WOOD STUD / INSULATION WITH VAPOR BARRIER / INT. WALL FIN.	4 + 4	52	Up to 14		Poor to fair	Between studs	0.07
METAL STUD	EXT. WALL FIN. / METAL STUD AT 16" O.C. / INSULATION WITH VAPOR BARRIER / INT. WALL FIN.	4 5	14 18	Up to 13 Up to 17		Poor	Between studs	0.06 0.04
BRICK VENEER	BRICK VENEER / SHEATHING WITH MOISTURE BARRIER / METAL STUD AT 16" O.C. / INSULATION WITH VAPOR BARRIER / INT. WALL FIN.	4 + 4	54	Up to 15		Good	Between studs	0.07
INSULATED SANDWICH PANEL	METAL SKIN / AIRSPACE / INSULATING CORE / METAL SKIN	5	6	See manufacturers' literature		Fair to good	None	0.05 See manufacturers' literature
CONCRETE	CONCRETE	8 12	92 138	Up to 13 (w/reinf. 17) Up to 20 (w/reinf. 25)		Excellent	None	0.68 0.55
CONCRETE (INSULATED)	CONCRETE / INSULATION / INT. WALL FIN.	8 +	97	Up to 13 (w/reinf. 17)		Excellent	Through insulation	0.13
CONCRETE AND BRICK VENEER (INSULATED)	BRICK VENEER / CONCRETE / INSULATION / INT. WALL FIN.	4 + 8 +	112	Up to 13 (w/reinf. 17)		Excellent	Through insulation	0.13
PRECAST CONCRETE	CONCRETE (REINFORCED) / INSULATION / INT. WALL FINISH	2 + 4 +	23 46	Up to 6 Up to 12		Fair to good	Through insulation	0.99 0.85
PRECAST CONCRETE SANDWICH	CONCRETE / INSULATION	5	45	Up to 14		Fair to good	None	0.14

GLASS	SEE INDEX UNDER "GLASS"			SIZE RANGE — MAXIMUM ALLOWABLE GLASS AREA	WIND LOAD	SHADING COEFFICIENT S.C.	
SINGLE GLAZING	¼" GLASS	¼	3.2	Four side supported 110 SF @ 10 PSF 20 SF @ 60 PSF Two side supported 40 SF @ 10 PSF 17 SF @ 60 PSF		Clear 0.94 Tinted 0.70	Clear/tinted 1.1 Reflective 0.8–1.1
DOUBLE GLAZING	¼" GLASS / ¼" CAVITY	¾	6.4	Four side supported 55 SF @ 30 PSF 28 SF @ 60 PSF Heat strengthened 70 SF @ 80 PSF 30 SF @ 200 PSF		Reflective 0.44	Clear/tinted 0.5–0.6 Reflective 0.3–0.6
TRIPLE GLAZING	¼" GLASS / ¼" CAVITY	1¼	9.6				Clear/tinted 0.3–0.4 Reflective 0.2–0.4

Roger K. Lewis, FAIA, and Mehmet T. Ergene, Architect; Roger K. Lewis, FAIA, & Associates; Washington, D.C.

The HAZARD CLASSIFICATION (FIRE) column contains this explanatory block:

Classification provides data in regard to (1) flame spread, (2) fuel contributed, and (3) smoke developed during fire exposure of materials in comparison to asbestos-cement boards as zero and untreated red oak lumber as 100 when exposed to fire under similar conditions

	FLAME SPREAD	FUEL CON-TRIB-UTED	SMOKE DEVEL-OPED
Paint on CMU	5–25	0–5	0–10
Gypsum board surfaced on both sides with paper	15	15	0
Gypsum board surfaced on both sides with paper, vinyl faced	25–35	0–10	15–45
Untreated wood particle board	180	75	190
Treated wood particle board with untreated wood face veneer	25–180	10–160	10–250
Vermiculite acoustical plaster	10–20	10–20	0
Glass fiber batts and blankets (basic)	20	15	20
(foil kraft faced)	25	0	0
Treated lumber (Douglas fir)	15	10	0–5
(Hemlock)	10–15	5–15	0
Laminated plastic (fr)	20–30	0–15	5–30

NFPA CLASSIFICATION:

CLASS	FLAME SPREAD	SMOKE DEVELOPED
A	0–25	0–450
B	26–75	0–450
C	76–200	0–450

For lesser classifications, permitted in residential construction only, refer to regulating agency guidelines

Main assembly table:

RESISTANCE TO EXTERIOR AIRBORNE SOUND TRANSMISSION	FIRE RESISTIVE RATING PER CODE AND UNDERWRITERS (HRS)	CONSTRUCTION TYPE CLASSIFICATION	SUBCONTRACTORS REQUIRED FOR ERECTION (PLUS FINISHES)	EXTERIOR MAINTENANCE REQUIREMENTS	REMARKS
Fair to good	2–4 / 4	1, 2, and 3	Masonry	Washing, re-pointing joints, painting, sand blasting	Properties of non-engineered masonry are drastically reduced
Fair to good	2–4 / 4	1, 2, and 3	Masonry Carpentry Drywall	Washing, re-pointing joints, painting, sand blasting	
Excellent	3–4 / 4	1, 2, and 3	Masonry Carpentry Drywall	Washing, re-pointing joints, sand blasting	
Excellent	4	1, 2, and 3	Masonry Drywall (Carpentry)	Washing, re-pointing joints, sand blasting	Cavity increases heat storage capacity and resistance to rain penetration
Good	2–4	1, 2, and 3	Masonry Drywall Lath and plaster (Carpentry)	Washing, painting, and re-stuccoing	The assembly is reversed for optimum energy conservation
Poor to fair	1 (combustible)	4	Carpentry Drywall (Lath and plaster)	Washing, painting, and replacing exterior finish	Exterior wall finishes: • wood, plywood, • aluminum siding • stucco
Good to excellent	1–2 (combustible)	3B, C	Masonry Carpentry Drywall	Washing, re-pointing joints, sand blasting	
Poor to fair	1–2	1 (nonbearing) 2 and 3	Carpentry Drywall (Lath and plaster)	Washing, painting, and replacing exterior finish	Exterior wall finishes: • wood, plywood, • aluminum siding • stucco
Good to excellent	1–2	1 (nonbearing) 2 and 3	Masonry Carpentry Drywall	Washing, re-pointing joints, sand blasting	
Poor to good; see manufacturers' literature	See manufacturers' literature	See manufacturers' literature	Curtain walls —erection	Washing, steam cleaning, painting, replacing joint sealers	Temperature change critical. Minimize metal through connections
Good	4 / 4	1, 2, and 3	Concrete work	Washing, sand blasting	Concrete walls have very high heat storage capacity
Good	4 / 4	1, 2, and 3	Concrete work Drywall (Carpentry)	Washing, sand blasting	
Excellent	4	1, 2, and 3	Concrete work Masonry Drywall (Carpentry)	Washing, re-pointing joints, sand blasting	
Poor to fair	1–3	1A (nonbearing) 1B, 2, and 3	Curtain walls —erection Drywall (Carpentry)	Washing, sand blasting, replacing joint sealers	Large size economical (fewer joints) units available with various finishes
Fair	1–3	1A (nonbearing) 1B, 2, and 3	Curtain walls —erection	Washing, sand blasting, replacing joint sealers	8' x 20' max. size for concrete sandwich panels. Plant quality control is very essential
Poor	—	—	Curtain walls —erection (Glazing)	Washing, replacing joint sealers, gaskets	Anchorage to building is critical. Anchors must isolate wall to limit building movement transmitted to glass
Fair	—	—	Curtain walls —erection (Glazing)	Washing, replacing joint sealers, gaskets	Wall design must limit wall movement transmitted to glass. Mullions should accommodate movement through gaskets, sliding connections, etc.
Good	—	—	Curtain walls —erection (Glazing)	Washing, replacing joint sealers, gaskets	

Roger K. Lewis, FAIA, and Mehmet T. Ergene, Architect; Roger K. Lewis, FAIA, & Associates; Washington, D.C.

MINIMUM UNIFORMLY DISTRIBUTED LIVE LOADS

OCCUPANCY OR USE	LIVE LOAD (PSF)
Armories and drill rooms	150
Assembly halls and other places of assembly	
Fixed seats	50
Movable seats	100
Platforms (assembly)	100
Attics	
Nonstorage	10
Storage	30[5]
Bakeries	150
Balconies	
Exterior	60
Interior (fixed seats)	50
Interior (movable seats)	100
Bowling Alleys, poolrooms, and similar recreational areas	75
Broadcasting studios	100
Catwalks	25
Cold storage rooms	
Floor	150
Roof	250
Corridors	
First floor	100
Other floors, same as occupancy served except as indicated	
Dance halls and ballrooms	100
Dining rooms and restaurants	100
Dormitories	
Nonpartitioned	80
Partitioned	40
File rooms	
Card	125[1]
Letter	80[1]
High-density storage	150[5]
Fire escapes on multifamily or single family residential buildings only	100
Foundries	600[2]
Fuel rooms, framed	400[2]
Garages (passenger cars only). For trucks and buses use AASHO[3] lane load	50
Grandstands	100[6]
Greenhouses	150
Gymnasiums, main floor and balconies	100
Hospitals	
Operating rooms and laboratories	60
Private rooms	40
Wards	40
Corridors, above first floor	80
Hotels (see residential)	
Kitchens, other than domestic	150[2]
Laboratories, scientific	100
Laundries	150[2]
Libraries	
Reading rooms	60
Stack rooms (books and shelving at 65 pcf) but not less than indicated	150
Corridors, above first floor	80
Manufacturing	
Light	75
Heavy	125
Ice	300
Marquees	75
Morgues	125
Office buildings	
Office	50
Business machine equipment	100[2]
Lobbies	100
Corridors, above first floor	80
File and computer rooms require heavier loads based on anticipated occupancy	
Penal Institutions	
Cell blocks	40
Corridors	100
Printing plants	
Composing rooms	100
Linotype rooms	100
Paper storage rooms	4
Pressrooms	150[2]

OCCUPANCY OR USE	LIVE LOAD (PSF)
Public rooms	100
Residential	
Multifamily houses	
Private apartments	40
Public rooms	100
Corridors	80
Dwellings	
First floor	40
Second floor and habitable attics	30
Inhabitable attics	20
Hotels	
Guest rooms	40
Public rooms	100
Corridors serving public rooms	100
Rest rooms and toilet rooms	40
Schools	
Classrooms	40
Corridors	80
Sidewalks, vehicular driveways, and yards subject to trucking	250
Skating rinks	100
Stairs and exit-ways	100
Storage warehouses	
Light	125
Heavy	250
Hay or grain	300
Stores	
Retail	
First floor, rooms	75
Upper floors	75
Wholesale	100
Telephone exchange rooms	150[2]
Theaters	
Aisles, corridors, and lobbies	100
Orchestra floors	50
Balconies	50
Stage floors	150
Dressing rooms	40
Grid iron floor or fly gallery grating	75
Projection room	100
Transformer rooms	200[2]
Vaults, in offices	250[1]
Yards and terraces, pedestrians	100

NOTES

1. Increase when occupancy exceeds this amount.
2. Use weight of actual equipment when greater.
3. American Association of State Highway Officials.
4. Paper storage 50 lb/ft of clear story height.
5. Verify with design criteria.
6. Additional loads—120 lb/linear ft vertical, 24 lb/ft parallel lateral, and 10 lb/ft perpendicular to seat and footboards.

LIVE LOAD

Live load is the weight superimposed by the use and occupancy of the building or other structure, not including the wind, snow, earthquake, or dead load.

The live loads to be assumed in the design of buildings and other structures shall be the greatest loads that probably will be produced by the intended use or occupancy, but in no case less than the minimum uniformly distributed unit load.

THRUSTS AND HANDRAILS

Stairway and balcony railing, both exterior and interior, shall be designed to resist a vertical and a horizontal thrust of 50 lb/linear ft applied at the top of the railing. For one- and two-family dwellings, a thrust of 20 lb/linear ft may be used instead of 50.

CONCENTRATED LOADS

Floors shall be designed to support safely the uniformly distributed live load or the concentrated load in pounds given, whichever produces the greater stresses. Unless otherwise specified, the indicated concentration shall be assumed to occupy an area of $2\frac{1}{2}$ sq ft (6.26 ft²) and shall be located so as to produce the maximum stress conditions in the structural members.

PARTIAL LOADING

The full intensity of the appropriately reduced live loads applied only to a portion of the length of a structure or member shall be considered if it produces a more unfavorable effect than the same intensity applied over the full length of the structure or member.

IMPACT LOADS

The live loads shall be assumed to include adequate allowance for ordinary impact conditions. Provision shall be made in structural design for uses and loads that involve unusual vibration and impact forces.

1. ELEVATORS: All elevator loads shall be increased 100% for impact, and the structural supports shall be designed within limits of deflection prescribed by American National Standard Safety Code for elevators and escalators, A17.1 - 1981, and American National Standard Practice for the Inspection of Elevators, Escalators, and Moving Walks (Inspector's Manual) A17.2 - 1979.

2. MACHINERY: For the purpose of design, the weight of machinery and moving loads shall be increased as follows to allow for impact:

   a. Elevator machinery, 100%.
   b. Light machinery, shaft or motor driven, 20%.
   c. Reciprocating machinery or power driven units, 50%.
   d. Hangers for floors or balconies, 33%.

   All percentages to be increased if so recommended by the manufacturer.

3. CRANEWAYS: All craneways, except those using only manually powered cranes, shall have their design loads increased for impact as follows:

   a. A vertical force equal to 25% of the maximum wheel load.
   b. A lateral force equal to 20% of the weight of trolley and lifted load only, applied one - half at the top of each rail.
   c. A longitudinal force of 10% of the maximum wheel loads of the crane applied at top of rail.

4. PARKING GARAGE GUARDRAILS: Guardrails and walls acting as impact rails in parking structures shall be designed for a minimum horizontal ultimate load of 10,000 lb applied 18 in. above the floor at any point of the guardrail.

MINIMUM ROOF LOADS

1. FLAT, PITCHED, OR CURVED ROOFS: Ordinary roofs – flat, pitched, or curved – shall be designed for the live loads or the snow load, whichever produces the greater stress.

2. PONDING: For roofs, care shall be taken to provide drainage or the load shall be increased to represent all likely accumulations of water. Deflection of roof members will permit ponding of water accompanied by increased deflection and additional ponding.

3. SPECIAL PURPOSE ROOFS: When used for promenade purposes, roofs shall be designed for a maximum live load of 60 psf; 100 psf when designed for roof garden or assembly uses. Roofs used for other special purposes shall be designed for appropriate loads, as directed or approved by the building official.

LIVE LOAD REDUCTION

In general, design live loads should not be in excess of 100 psf on any member, supporting an area of 150 sq ft or more, except for places of public assembly, repair garages, parking structures, and roofs. The reduction shall not exceed the value of R from the following formulas:

$$R = .08(A-150)$$
$$R = 23(1+D/L)$$

where R = reduction (%)
D = dead load per square foot of area supported by the member
L = live load per square foot of area supported by the member
A = area supported by the member

In no case should the reduction exceed 60% for vertical members, nor 40 to 60% for horizontal members.

For live loads in excess of 100 psf, some codes allow a live load reduction of 20% for columns only.

CODES AND STANDARDS

The applicable building code should be referred to for specific uniformly distributed live loads, movable partition load, special and concentrated load requirements.

In addition to specific code requirements, the designer must consider the effects of special loading conditions, such as moving loads, construction loads, roof top planting loads, and concentrated loads from supported or hanging equipment (radiology, computer, heavy filing, or mechanical equipment).

The live loads given in this table are obtained by reference to ASCE, UBC, BOCA, and SBCCI.

Charles W. Vanderlinden, PE; Hansen Lind Meyer, Inc.; Orlando, Florida

GENERAL

When selecting a long span roof system, it is appropriate to consider life safety of equal concern to cost. Egress must be carefully evaluated by simulating the most adverse conditions rather than simply complying with building codes. Fire safety begins by limiting the fire load, as codes rarely require fire protection or sprinkler systems. Auxiliary uses having any fire risk (e.g., food handling) should be carefully fire separated from the rest of the structure.

DESIGN CONSIDERATION FACTORS

Examples of long span structures shown in the table are rated for their ability to address the following design factor conditions.

NATURAL CONDITIONS

a. Uneven or excessive snow and ice loads: Geometry, equipment, or exterior structure may contribute to snow drifting or ice buildup.
b. Ponding: Provide positive drainage to remove water from the structure when roof drains clog.
c. Wind: Evaluate potential of wind induced destructive vibration in members or connections.
d. Thermal: Diurnal and seasonal temperature cycles can cause significant changes in structural shape and member stresses and may lead to fatigue failure.
e. Freeze/thaw cycles or corrosive atmosphere: Evaluate long-term effects on structural performance, particularly for exposed concrete structures.

PRIMARY STRESSES

f. Two or more load paths for all loads should be provided wherever possible. The greater the area a single member supports, the greater should be its safety factor.
g. Compression failure: Resistance to lateral buckling of long members is crucial. Use members that assure initial and verifiable alignment.
h. Tension failure: Dynamic stability under wind or other vibration loading should be carefully verified.

SECONDARY STRESSES

i. Deflection: Changes in orientation of members at joints from loads can increase stresses destructively.
j. Member interaction: Load flows through structures in such a way as to minimize strength. Check all possible load paths of complex geometric structures.
k. Nonstructural connections: Assemblies attached to a structure will influence structural load flow and even become part of the load flow if the attachment changes the deflected shape.
l. Scale: Most systems have a span beyond which self weight becomes a severe limit.
m. Stress concentration: Check stresses at changes of cross sections, holes, and connections. High-strength materials are particularly sensitive.

TOLERANCES

n. Erection alignment: True member length and spatial position are crucial for proper alignment and load flow.
o. Creep: Length changes over time will influence both primary and secondary stresses.
p. Supports and foundations: Supports must accept movements due to deflections from primary and secondary stresses and differential foundation settlement.

QUALITY CONTROL

q. Engineering design must not be compromised by time, scheduling, design changes, or building codes. Computerized design must be carefully verified to resolve all primary and secondary stresses.
r. Construction methods should be selected carefully to safely locate the structural components accurately in space.
s. Site observation: Only when the structure is properly established in space should it be accepted. Changes in construction should be carefully checked.
t. Structural building maintenance: Conditions and alignment of various members, especially crucial nonredundant members, should be verified on a regular schedule. Consider using equipment to detect excessive deflection.
u. Nonstructural building maintenance: Condition of building components should not adversely affect the structure (e.g., keep roof drains open, prevent excessive equipment vibration, and maintain expansion joints).

LONG SPAN SYSTEMS

SYSTEM	MATERIAL (OR SHAPE)	ONE WAY	TWO WAY	FLAT SURFACE	PITCHED PLANE	CURVED PLANE	CURVED SURFACE	SPAN RANGE (FT)	SPAN/DEPTH RATIO	FACTORS STRONG AGAINST	FACTORS SENSITIVE TO
Joist	Steel	•		•	-				20 - 24	p,q,s	a,b,f,g
Truss	Steel	•		•	•	-			16 - 22		a,b,f,g,m,t
			•	•		-			16 - 20	a,b,f	m
	Wood	•		•	•	-			9 - 12		a,b,f,g
			•	•					9 - 12	b,f	
Space frame	Steel		•	•					16 - 20	f	a,b,i,j,m,n, p,q,s,u
Stressed skin	Steel	•		•					14 - 18	f	a,b,i,j,m,n, p,q,s,u
Beam	Steel	•	-	•					18 - 22	a,q	b,f,t
	Wood	•		•					16 - 20		b,f,t
	Prestressed concrete	•	-	•					22 - 26		b,f,t
Rigid frame	Steel	•	-	•	-				20 - 24	a,b	f
	Wood	•	•		-				18 - 22		f
	Prestressed concrete	•	-		-				24 - 28		f
Cabke stayed										i,p	c,e,h,q,t
Folded plate	Steel	•			•				18 - 22	b	a,f,m
	Wood	•			•				12 - 16	b	a,f,m
	Concrete	•			•				10 - 14	b	a,f,l,m
Cylindric shell	Concrete	•				•			10 - 14	b	a,l,m,o
Vault	Concrete	•	•			•			6 - 10	b	c,o
Arch	Steel	•	•			•			4 - 8	b	a,d,f,g
	Wood	•	•			•			3 - 7	b	a,d,f,g
	Concrete	•	•			•			3 - 7	b	a,d,f,g
Dome	Radial steel		•				•		4 - 8	b,c	a,d,f,g
	Geodesic dome		•				•		2 - 5	a,b,c,f,g	d,n,r
	Radial wood		•				•		3 - 6	b,c	a,d,f,g
	Lamella wood		•				•		3 - 6	a,b,c,f,g	d,n,r
	Concrete		•				•		5 - 8	b,c,f,g	a,d,l,o
Pneumatics	Steel		•				•		4 - 7	d	a,b,c,e
Cabke	Parallel	•				•			8 - 16	d	a,b,c,f
	Radial		•				•		6 - 12	d	a,b,c,f
	Hyperbolic		•				•		4 - 8	b,d,f	a,c
	Tent		•				•		3 - 6	b,f	a,c
Hyperbolic	Concrete		•				•		3 - 6	f	a,d,l,o

NOTES

1. Steel is A-36; wood is laminated, sometimes heavy timber; concrete is reinforced with steel; prestressed concrete is prestressed with steel.
2. Cable-stayed system can give auxiliary support to trusses, beams, or frames, greatly reducing span and member sizes, but providing additional tensional strength.
3. Lamella arches provide two-way arch structures and improve redundancy.
4. Domes may also be constructed of aluminum.
5. Pneumatics are fabric roofs, pressurized, and stabilized with steel cables.
6. For each system the following notation applies:
   - • is the typical configuration
   - - is occasionally used

William C. Bauman, Jr.; University of Oklahoma; Norman, Oklahoma

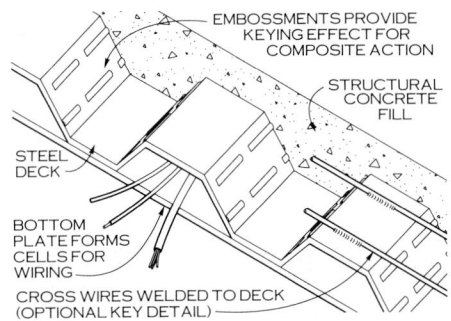

CONCRETE TOPPED STEEL DECK

Labels: EMBOSSMENTS PROVIDE KEYING EFFECT FOR COMPOSITE ACTION; STRUCTURAL CONCRETE FILL; STEEL DECK; BOTTOM PLATE FORMS CELLS FOR WIRING; CROSS WIRES WELDED TO DECK (OPTIONAL KEY DETAIL)

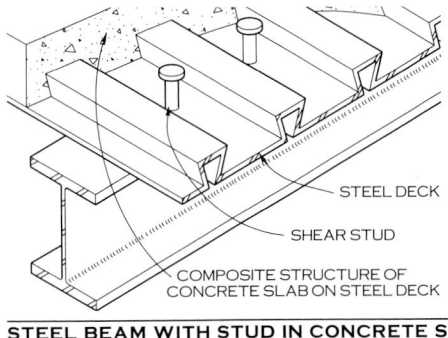

STEEL BEAM WITH STUD IN CONCRETE SLAB

Labels: STEEL DECK; SHEAR STUD; COMPOSITE STRUCTURE OF CONCRETE SLAB ON STEEL DECK

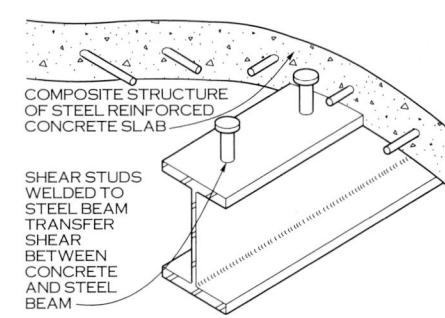

Labels: COMPOSITE STRUCTURE OF STEEL REINFORCED CONCRETE SLAB; SHEAR STUDS WELDED TO STEEL BEAM TRANSFER SHEAR BETWEEN CONCRETE AND STEEL BEAM

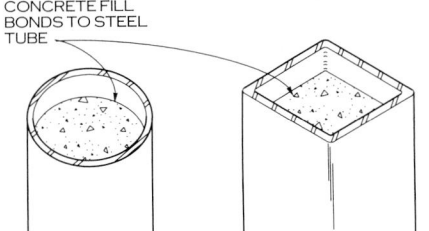

STEEL-ENCASED CONCRETE COLUMNS

Labels: CONCRETE FILL BONDS TO STEEL TUBE

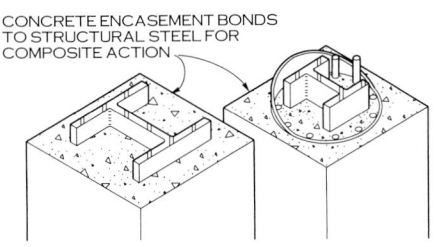

CONCRETE ENCASED STEEL COLUMNS

Labels: CONCRETE ENCASEMENT BONDS TO STRUCTURAL STEEL FOR COMPOSITE ACTION

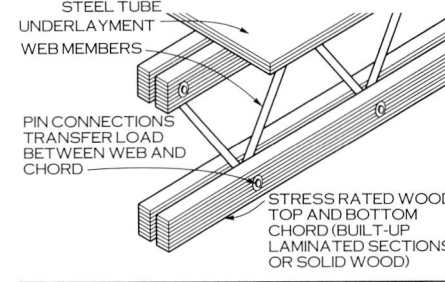

WOOD AND STEEL JOISTS

Labels: STEEL TUBE UNDERLAYMENT; WEB MEMBERS; PIN CONNECTIONS TRANSFER LOAD BETWEEN WEB AND CHORD; STRESS RATED WOOD TOP AND BOTTOM CHORD (BUILT-UP LAMINATED SECTIONS OR SOLID WOOD)

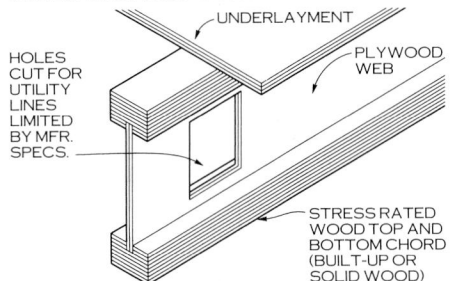

WOOD AND PLYWOOD COMPOSITE JOISTS

Labels: UNDERLAYMENT; PLYWOOD WEB; HOLES CUT FOR UTILITY LINES LIMITED BY MFR. SPECS.; STRESS RATED WOOD TOP AND BOTTOM CHORD (BUILT-UP OR SOLID WOOD)

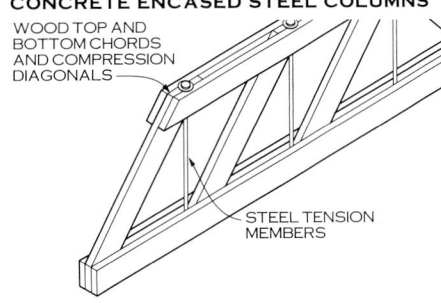

WOOD AND STEEL TRUSSES

Labels: WOOD TOP AND BOTTOM CHORDS AND COMPRESSION DIAGONALS; STEEL TENSION MEMBERS

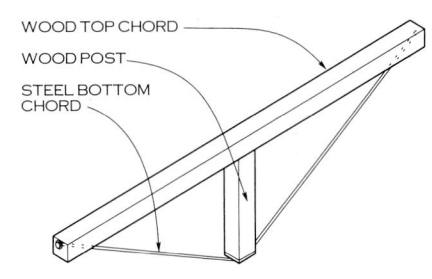

Labels: WOOD TOP CHORD; WOOD POST; STEEL BOTTOM CHORD

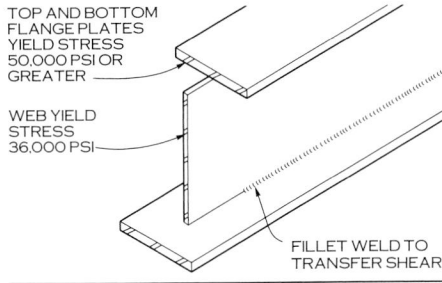

HYBRID STEEL GIRDERS USING STEELS OF DIFFERING STRENGTH

Labels: TOP AND BOTTOM FLANGE PLATES YIELD STRESS 50,000 PSI OR GREATER; WEB YIELD STRESS 36,000 PSI; FILLET WELD TO TRANSFER SHEAR

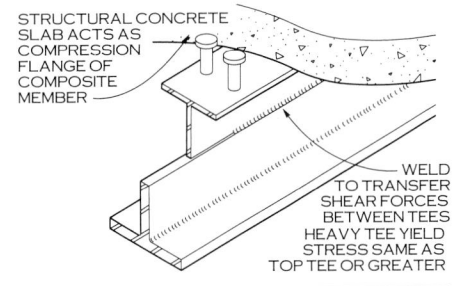

Labels: STRUCTURAL CONCRETE SLAB ACTS AS COMPRESSION FLANGE OF COMPOSITE MEMBER; WELD TO TRANSFER SHEAR FORCES BETWEEN TEES HEAVY TEE YIELD STRESS SAME AS TOP TEE OR GREATER

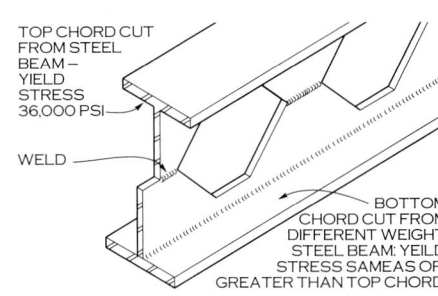

CASTELLATED BEAMS

Labels: TOP CHORD CUT FROM STEEL BEAM—YIELD STRESS 36,000 PSI; WELD; BOTTOM CHORD CUT FROM DIFFERENT WEIGHT STEEL BEAM: YEILD STRESS SAMEAS OR GREATER THAN TOP CHORD

NOTES

Individual elements of the composite unit must be securely fastened to prevent slippage, especially at points where load is transferred from one element of the composite member to another.

TYPES OF COMPOSITE ELEMENTS

1. Concrete topped composite steel decks.
2. Steel beams acting compositely with concrete slabs.
3. Steel columns encased by or filled with concrete.
4. Open web joists of wood and steel or joists with plywood webs and wood chords.
5. Trusses combining wood and steel.
6. Hybrid girders utilizing steels of different strengths.
7. Cast-in-place concrete slab on precast concrete joists or beams.

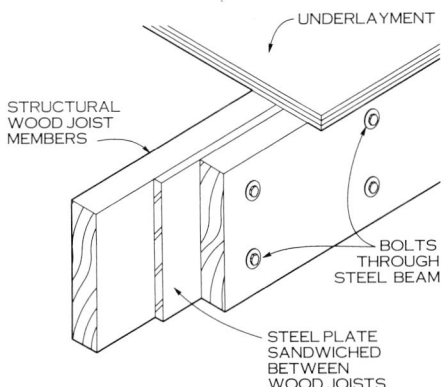

FLITCH BEAMS

Labels: UNDERLAYMENT; STRUCTURAL WOOD JOIST MEMBERS; BOLTS THROUGH STEEL BEAM; STEEL PLATE SANDWICHED BETWEEN WOOD JOISTS

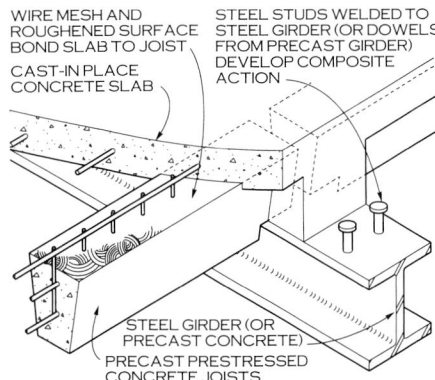

REINFORCED CONCRETE SLAB AND PRECAST JOIST

Labels: WIRE MESH AND ROUGHENED SURFACE BOND SLAB TO JOIST; CAST-IN PLACE CONCRETE SLAB; STEEL STUDS WELDED TO STEEL GIRDER (OR DOWELS FROM PRECAST GIRDER) DEVELOP COMPOSITE ACTION; STEEL GIRDER (OR PRECAST CONCRETE); PRECAST PRESTRESSED CONCRETE JOISTS

Composite construction combines different materials, or different grades of a material, to form a structural member that utilizes the most desirable properties of each. Perhaps the earliest composite structural unit was the mud brick reinforced with straw. More recently fiberglass-reinforced plastics, wire-reinforced safety glass, and glued laminated plywood and wood beams have been used.

COMPARATIVE DESIGN

A 30 ft beam with a 2.25 kip/ft uniform load carrying $2/_2$ in. concrete fill on a 2 in. metal deck slab uses a W24x55 in a noncomposite design and only a W18x40 with 38 steel studs of $3/_4$ in. diameter in a composite design.

Richard J. Vitullo, AIA; Oak Leaf Studio; Crownsville, Maryland

SEISMIC DESIGN

Earthquake forces result from random vertical and horizontal ground vibrations where a structure rests. Vertical forces are frequently neglected in seismic design because of a combination of safety factors in vertical system designs. Some nonstructural elements also require consideration for vertical forces. Earthquake forces may vary in direction, magnitude, and duration, and they are influenced strongly by geological conditions at and around a specific site.

Seismic resistance is achieved by structural elements, including braced frames, moment-resisting frames, shear walls, or a combination of each, connected by horizontal diaphragms. A building's seismic performance is greatly affected by its architectural concept. A building's fundamental period, primarily determined by the building height and proportions, is affected by the nature of the seismic forces. Irregular plan forms can cause torsion and high stress concentrations. The center of mass and the center of rigidity of horizontal resisting elements should coincide or be close to one another.

In the vertical plane, abrupt changes in strength of stiffness should be avoided because these produce dangerous stress concentration. Horizontal offsets, or "setbacks," should be analyzed with special care for the same reason. All shear walls must be continuous from roof to foundation. Major building form units either should be tied together to respond to earthquake forces as an entity or adequate structural separations must be provided to ensure that pounding-damage does not occur between them.

Most structural materials can be used effectively as elements of a seismic resisting system, although brittle material, such as concrete, requires special detailing when used in highly stressed structures. Because of its ductility, steel is a particularly suitable material. Small conventional wood-framed structures have performed well because they give when subjected to stress.

Seismic building codes emphasize life safety and aim to safeguard against structural collapse. Nonstructural elements, building equipment, and contents also can be life threatening under seismic conditions. Even if a building structure meets the code intentions, it still can suffer considerable damage and be rendered nonfunctional. This is especially true of essential facilities such as hospitals, fire and police stations, and the like. Equipment and utilities in such buildings need special design attention; some seismic codes specifically mandate it.

METHOD OF SEISMIC DESIGN
EQUIVALENT-STATIC-FORCE PROCEDURE

The essential feature of all seismic codes is to provide a standard and simple way to determine seismic forces for design use. The California Uniform Building Code is typical. It states that every structure shall be designed to resist minimum lateral forces that act nonconcurrently in the direction of the main axis. The total lateral force is calculated by applying the formula: $V = ZICW/R_w$. V represents dynamic lateral forces as an equivalent shear force applied at the structure's base and distributes to various structure levels on a basis that is described in the code. Coefficient Z defines the seismicity of the site. It is determined by maps provided in the code. The importance factor I is used to increase the margin of safety for "essential" and hazardous facilities. The site coefficient C is dependent on the soil characteristics of the site and the fundamental vibration period of the building. W is the building's total weight. R_w is the structural system coefficient. It measures the ductility and is based primarily on the performance of similar systems in past earthquakes.

Dynamic analysis is a more complex form analysis that yields more precise information about the nature of seismic forces; it is used for buildings of large size, unusual form, or special importance.

Two general methods exist. The first, and most common, is the response spectrum method. Critical modes of vibration, their period, and size are determined by this technique. The second method is more exact since it reviews the structure with respect to the earthquake time history (divided into small increments of time). This type of analysis results in estimates of building motion, building distortion, building forces, and accelerations for specific locations in the building at defined intervals of earthquake motion.

Dynamic analysis can be used to determine resonant frequencies, which, coupled with similar ground motion frequencies, may result in dangerous amplification of forces within the building. It also is valuable in establishing seismic characteristics of complex systems such as nuclear power plants where utility systems performance may be critical for continued operation and safety.

Attila L. Mocsary, PE; Hope Design Group; San Diego, California

DESIGN JUDGMENT

While analysis can establish design forces, the correct selection and detailing of the structural system remains a matter of engineering judgment in both economy and the ultimate safety of the building. In this, the extent to which the architectural concept assists the engineering design by eliminating potential torsion, stress concentrations, and geometrically induced points of weakness, is of great importance. Recent building damage studies have shown that many apparent structural failures can be traced to architectural decisions.

OCCUPANCY IMPORTANCE FACTOR, I

NATURE OF OCCUPANCY	I FACTOR
All buildings and structures except those listed below	1.0
Buildings and structures that are used or designed for gathering together of persons for purposes such as civic, social or religious functions, recreation, food or drink consumption, or awaiting transportation	1.25
Buildings and structures designated as essential facilities including, but not limited to:	1.5

1. Buildings and structures used for medical, surgical, psychiatric, nursing or custodial care on a 24-hour basis of six or more persons who are not capable of self-preservation having surgery or emergency treatment areas
2. Fire or rescue and police stations
3. Primary communication facilities and disaster operation centers
4. Power stations and other utilities required in an emergency
5. Structures having critical national defense capabilities
6. Designated shelters for hurricanes

SEISMIC ZONES FACTOR, Z

Zone	1	2A	2B	3	4
Coefficient Z	0.075	0.15	0.20	0.30	0.40

NOTE

The five seismic zones, numbered 1, 2A, 2B, 3, and 4, are defined in the Uniform Building Code, UBC-1991 edition. The zone for a particular site is determined from a seismic map (see below). The value of the coefficient can be viewed as the peak ground acceleration, in percentage of gravity, in each zone.

LABORATORY TESTING

Full-size structures or details, model structures, and equipment sometimes are tested seismically by laboratory experiment. These involve either shaking tables that realistically can represent ground motion or by various forms of static or pseudodynamic testing. Shaking-table testing is time-consuming and generally is used only for long-term research, although it has been used for critical equipment testing such as computers.

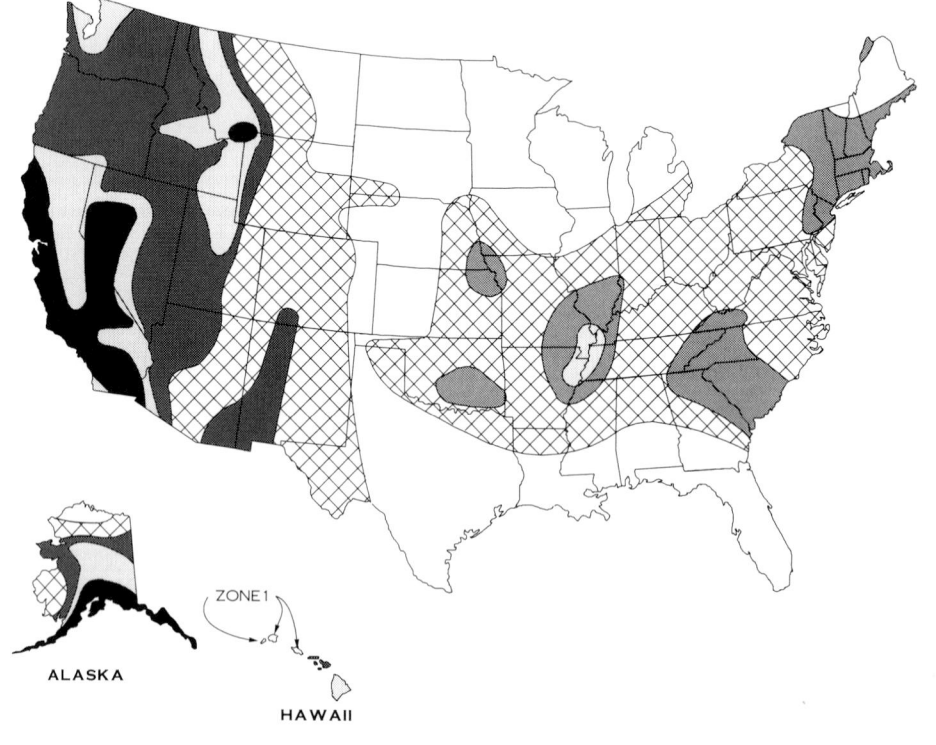

SEISMIC ZONES - UNITED STATES

THE EARTHQUAKE GENERATES GROUND MOTIONS THAT CAN BE EXPRESSED IN THREE MUTUALLY PERPENDICULAR AXES

GROUNDSHAKING, NOT GROUNDRUPTURE, GENERALLY CAUSES MOST BUILDING DAMAGE

GROUNDSHAKING

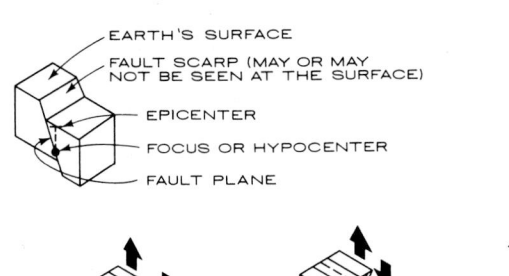

- EARTH'S SURFACE
- FAULT SCARP (MAY OR MAY NOT BE SEEN AT THE SURFACE)
- EPICENTER
- FOCUS OR HYPOCENTER
- FAULT PLANE

STRIKE SLIP – LEFT LATERAL

STRIKE SLIP – RIGHT LATERAL

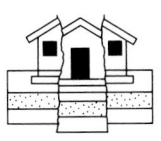

DIP SLIP NORMAL   DIP SLIP REVERSE   THRUST   CONTINUOUS FAULT CREEP

FAULT TERMINOLOGY AND TYPES

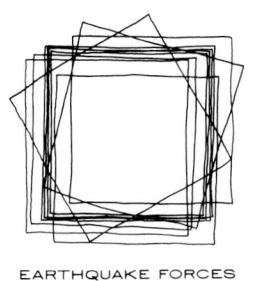

GROUNDRUPTURE   GROUNDSHAKING   DIFFERENTIAL SUBSIDENCE   LIQUEFACTION

FOUNDATION FAILURES - MAIN CAUSES

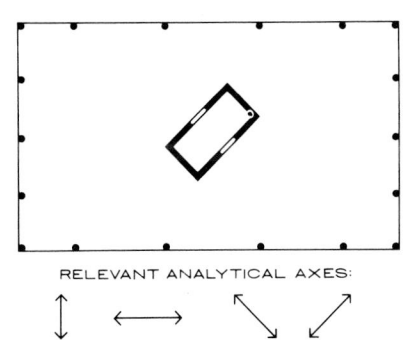

EARTHQUAKE FORCES   THE REALITY

RELEVANT ANALYTICAL AXES:

FOR COMPLICATED CONFIGURATIONS, MORE THAN TWO AXES MAY BE USED FOR ANALYSIS

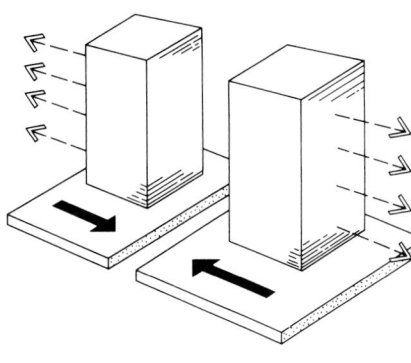
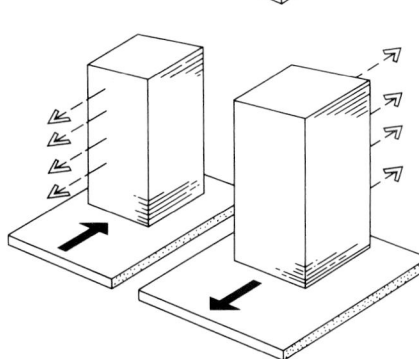

TYPICAL ANALYTICAL DIAGRAM OF EARTHQUAKE FORCES

Attila L. Mocsary, PE; Hope Architects & Engineers; San Diego, California
Gary L. McGavin; Wyle Laboratories; El Segundo, California
Alfred M. Kemper & Associates; Los Angeles, California

EARTHQUAKE RELATED EVENTS

SURFACE FAULTING

An earthquake is the result of slippage along a fault plane, sometimes miles below the surface, that creates large earth movement. The fault slippage sometimes, but not always, moves upward through the earth to create visible cracks in the earth's surface known as surface faults. A building located across the surface fault will suffer severe damage. Structures should not be sited over active geologic faults.

SOIL LIQUEFACTION

A threatening condition and common occurrence in loose sands and silts with high groundwater table (sites located adjoining rivers, lakes, and bays). Earthquake motion can transform the soil into a semi-liquefied state that resembles quicksand.

TSUNAMI (TIDAL WAVES)

These are earthquake-caused wave movements originating in the ocean. The wave front may move at 400 mph to 500 mph. Pacific Coast sites must be investigated carefully. When a tsunami reaches the coast, its energy is concentrated in a smaller and smaller wave front because the ocean depth decreases.

SEICHE

A sloshing wave movement in enclosed lakes, bays, or dams created during an earthquake. It can top dams and damage adjacent structures.

LANDSLIDE

Slope failure, rock fall, avalanche, or earth flow can be triggered by earthquake ground motion. Many landslide-prone areas have been mapped. For projects in these areas, geological evaluation must be conducted before planning.

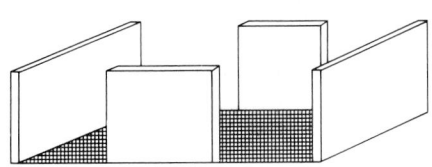

SHEAR WALLS

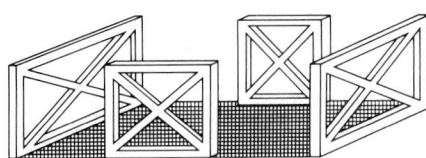

BRACED FRAMES

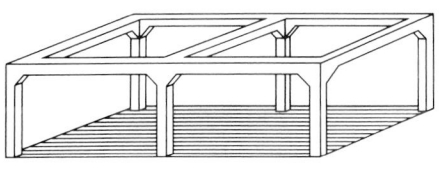

MOMENT-RESISTANT FRAMES

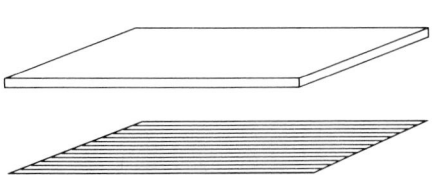

DIAPHRAGMS

COMPONENTS FOR SEISMIC RESISTANCE

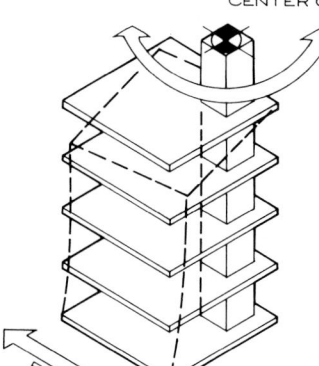

CENTER OF RESISTANCE

FORCE

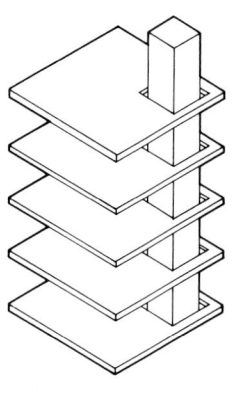

PROBLEM: TORSION FROM
STIFF ASYMMETRIC CORE

SOLUTION: DISCONNECT CORE
(AS SHOWN) OR USE FRAME WITH
NON-STRUCTURAL CORE WALLS

FALSE SYMMETRY

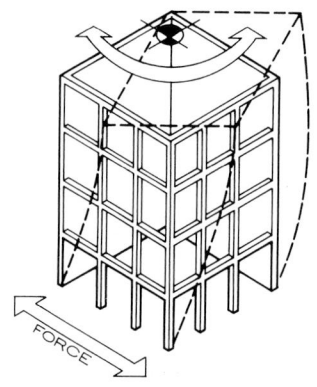

CENTER OF RESISTANCE

FORCE

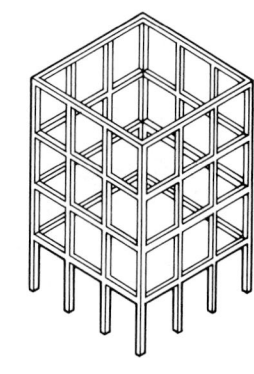

PROBLEM: TORSION CAUSED BY
EXTREME VARIATION IN STIFFNESS
AND STRENGTH

SOLUTION: USE FRAMES
AND LIGHTWEIGHT WALLS

VARIATION IN PERIMETER STRENGTH-STIFFNESS

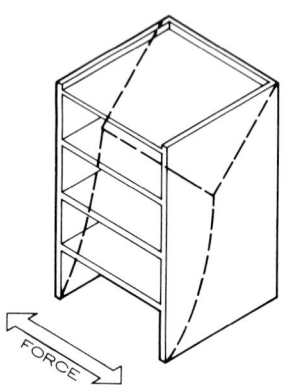

FORCE

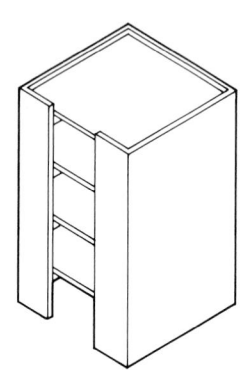

PROBLEM: TORSION FROM
EXTREME VARIATION IN
STRENGTH AND STIFFNESS

SOLUTION: ADD SHEAR WALL
OR STIFF FRAME AT OR
NEAR OPEN FRONT

VARIATION IN PERIMETER STRENGTH-STIFFNESS

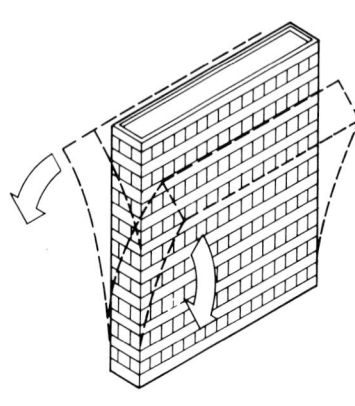

HIGH OVERTURNING FORCES
AND LARGE DRIFT

EXTREME HEIGHT-DEPTH RATIO

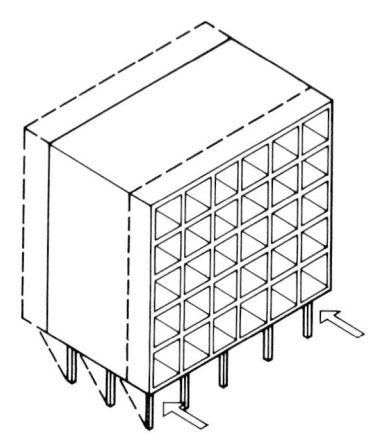

DISCONTINUITIES IN LOAD PATH
AND STRESS CONCENTRATION
AT HEAVILY LOADED COLUMNS

DISCONTINUOUS SHEAR WALL

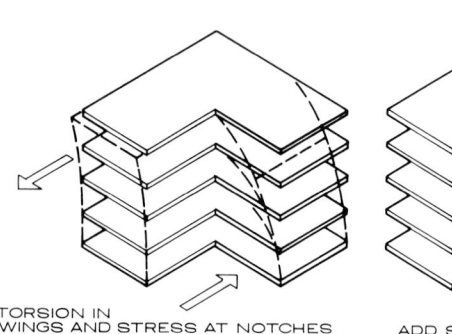

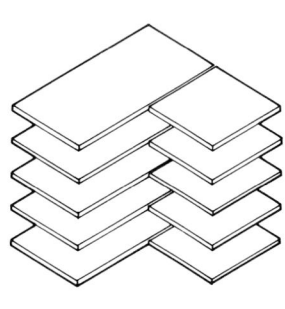

TORSION IN
WINGS AND STRESS AT NOTCHES

ADD SEISMIC JOINT

RE-ENTRANT CORNER

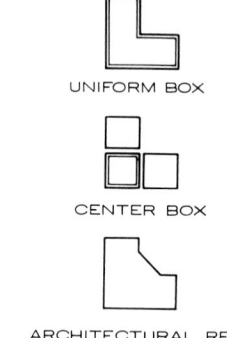

UNIFORM BOX

CENTER BOX

ARCHITECTURAL RELIEF

Building configuration has tremendous influence on the performance of structures under seismic loading conditions. Code design forces used for calculation are based on uniform buildings and conditions. If a building is irregular in plan, section, or elevation, the code forces calculated are probably unrealistic. Some examples of structural irregularity are shown here to illustrate seismic responses. Variations in perimeter strength and stiffness, reentrant corner designs, discontinuous shear walls, extreme height–depth or length–depth ratios, and extreme plan area are among the configuration problems which should be studied carefully. In high risk areas, unsuitable building configurations can result in intolerable stresses placed on some specific material or connection causing failure. Those design solutions which perform most successfully are simple, straightforward, symmetrical, continuous and repetitive.

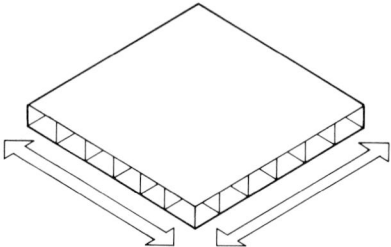

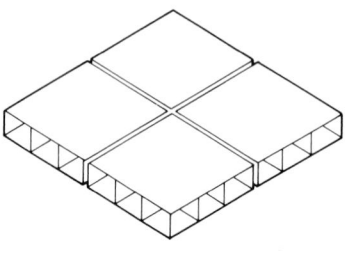

LARGE DIAPHRAGM FORCES

ADD SEISMIC JOINTS

EXTREME PLAN AREA

Christine Beall, R.A., CCS Architectural Consultant; Austin, Texas

1   SEISMIC DESIGN

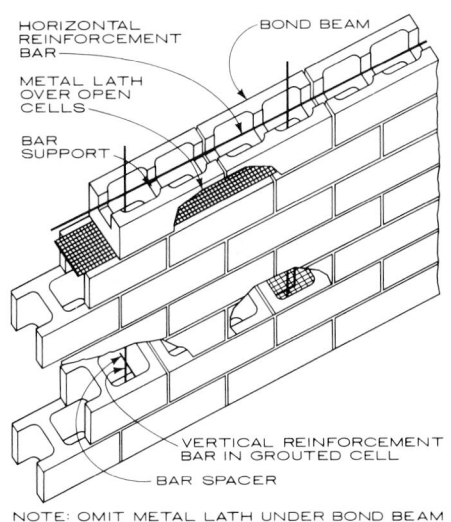

HORIZONTAL REINFORCEMENT BAR
BOND BEAM
METAL LATH OVER OPEN CELLS
BAR SUPPORT
VERTICAL REINFORCEMENT BAR IN GROUTED CELL
BAR SPACER

NOTE: OMIT METAL LATH UNDER BOND BEAM BLOCK WHERE ALL CELLS ARE SOLID GROUTED.

SECURING OF REINFORCEMENT

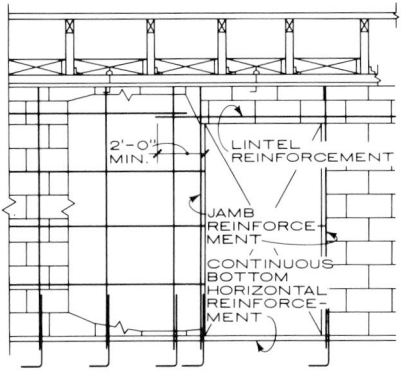

2'-0" MIN.
LINTEL REINFORCEMENT
JAMB REINFORCEMENT
CONTINUOUS BOTTOM HORIZONTAL REINFORCEMENT

NOTE: SEE APPLICABLE CODE FOR MIN. REINFORCEMENT REQUIRED.

MASONRY WALL

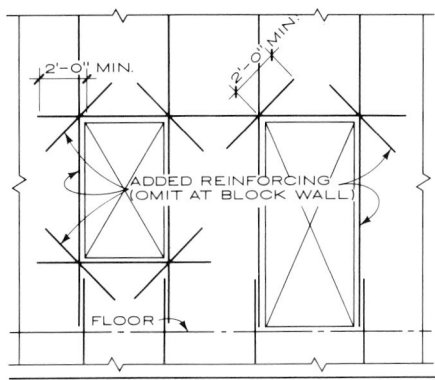

2'-0" MIN.
2'-0" MIN.
ADDED REINFORCING (OMIT AT BLOCK WALL)
FLOOR

CONCRETE WALL

OPENINGS IN MASONRY AND CONCRETE WALLS

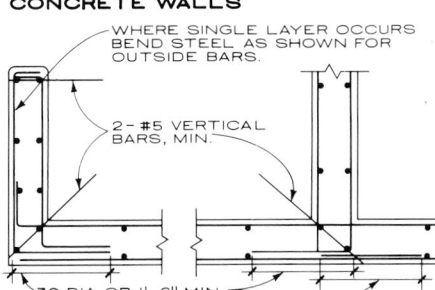

WHERE SINGLE LAYER OCCURS BEND STEEL AS SHOWN FOR OUTSIDE BARS.
2 - #5 VERTICAL BARS, MIN.
30 DIA. OR 1'-6" MIN.

INTERSECTION OF CONCRETE OR REINFORCED MASONRY WALLS

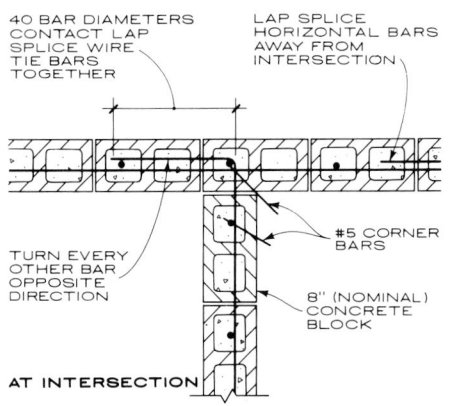

40 BAR DIAMETERS CONTACT LAP SPLICE WIRE TIE BARS TOGETHER
LAP SPLICE HORIZONTAL BARS AWAY FROM INTERSECTION
TURN EVERY OTHER BAR OPPOSITE DIRECTION
#5 CORNER BARS
8" (NOMINAL) CONCRETE BLOCK

AT INTERSECTION

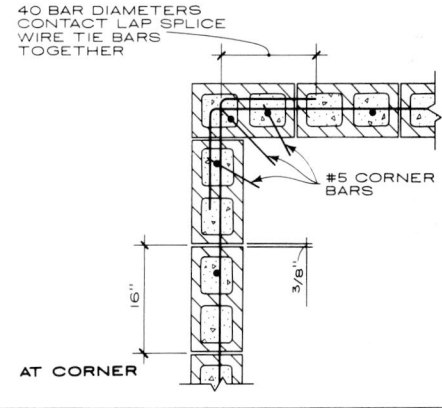

40 BAR DIAMETERS CONTACT LAP SPLICE WIRE TIE BARS TOGETHER
#5 CORNER BARS
16"
3/8"

AT CORNER

CONCRETE BLOCK MASONRY

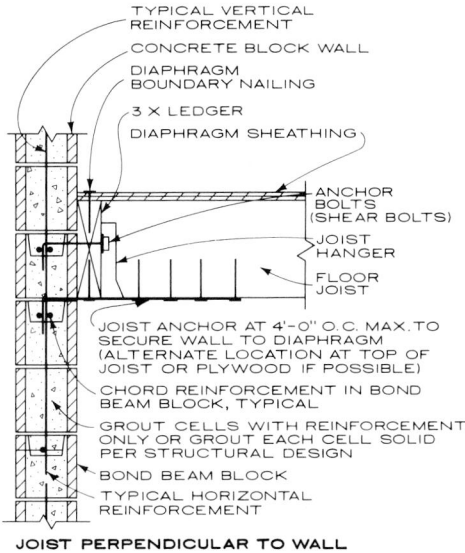

TYPICAL VERTICAL REINFORCEMENT
CONCRETE BLOCK WALL
DIAPHRAGM BOUNDARY NAILING
3 X LEDGER
DIAPHRAGM SHEATHING
ANCHOR BOLTS (SHEAR BOLTS)
JOIST HANGER
FLOOR JOIST
JOIST ANCHOR AT 4'-0" O.C. MAX. TO SECURE WALL TO DIAPHRAGM (ALTERNATE LOCATION AT TOP OF JOIST OR PLYWOOD IF POSSIBLE)
CHORD REINFORCEMENT IN BOND BEAM BLOCK, TYPICAL
GROUT CELLS WITH REINFORCEMENT ONLY OR GROUT EACH CELL SOLID PER STRUCTURAL DESIGN
BOND BEAM BLOCK
TYPICAL HORIZONTAL REINFORCEMENT

JOIST PERPENDICULAR TO WALL

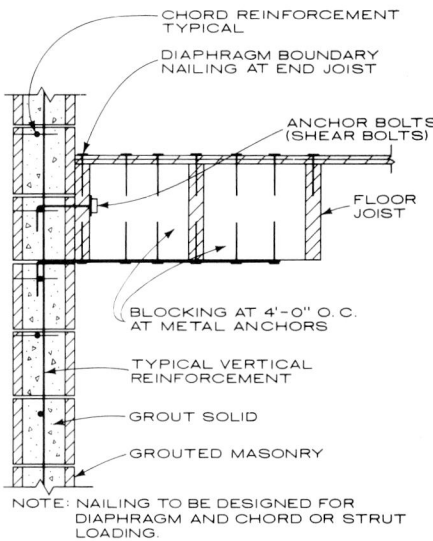

CHORD REINFORCEMENT TYPICAL
DIAPHRAGM BOUNDARY NAILING AT END JOIST
ANCHOR BOLTS (SHEAR BOLTS)
FLOOR JOIST
BLOCKING AT 4'-0" O.C. AT METAL ANCHORS
TYPICAL VERTICAL REINFORCEMENT
GROUT SOLID
GROUTED MASONRY

NOTE: NAILING TO BE DESIGNED FOR DIAPHRAGM AND CHORD OR STRUT LOADING.

JOIST PARALLEL TO WALL

WOOD DIAPHRAGM WITH MASONRY SHEAR WALL CONNECTIONS

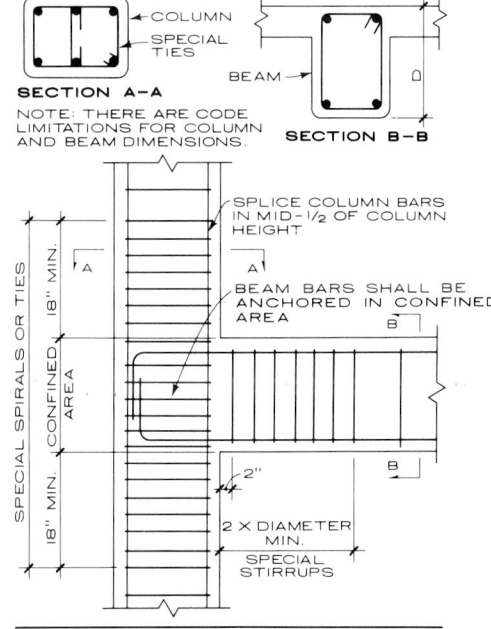

COLUMN
SPECIAL TIES

SECTION A-A

NOTE: THERE ARE CODE LIMITATIONS FOR COLUMN AND BEAM DIMENSIONS.

BEAM

SECTION B-B

SPECIAL SPIRALS OR TIES
18" MIN.
18" MIN. CONFINED AREA
CONFINED AREA
SPLICE COLUMN BARS IN MID-1/2 OF COLUMN HEIGHT
BEAM BARS SHALL BE ANCHORED IN CONFINED AREA
2"
2 X DIAMETER MIN.
SPECIAL STIRRUPS

REINFORCING DETAIL FOR DUCTILE MOMENT RESISTING SPACE FRAME CONFINED JOINT

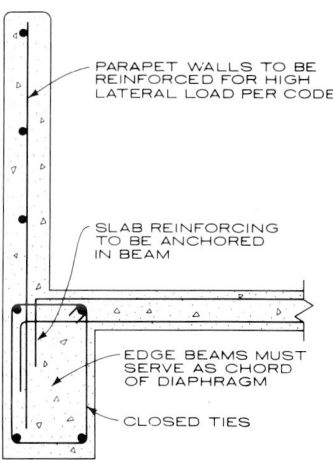

PARAPET WALLS TO BE REINFORCED FOR HIGH LATERAL LOAD PER CODE
SLAB REINFORCING TO BE ANCHORED IN BEAM
EDGE BEAMS MUST SERVE AS CHORD OF DIAPHRAGM
CLOSED TIES

CONCRETE DIAPHRAGM WITH CONCRETE SPANDREL BEAM AND PARAPET

NOTE

Details shown are representative of possible construction detailing. In addition to code-defined structural requirements, safety considerations require nonstructural building elements and furnishings to be anchored in areas subjected to seismic movement. These pages show selected details as samples of recommended bracing and anchorage.

Attila L. Mocsary, PE; Hope Architects & Engineers; San Diego, California
Gary L. McGavin; Wyle Laboratories; El Segundo, California
Alfred M. Kemper & Associates; Los Angeles, California

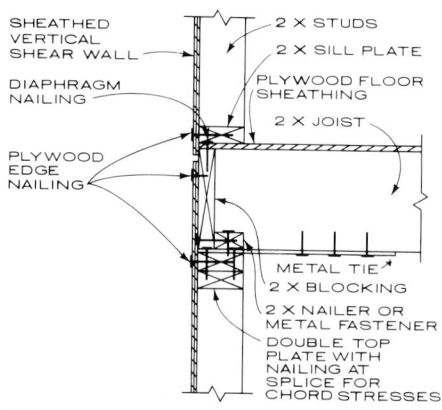

JOIST PERPENDICULAR TO WALL

SHEATHED VERTICAL SHEAR WALL
DIAPHRAGM NAILING
PLYWOOD EDGE NAILING
2 × STUDS
2 × SILL PLATE
PLYWOOD FLOOR SHEATHING
2 × JOIST
METAL TIE
2 × BLOCKING
2 × NAILER OR METAL FASTENER
DOUBLE TOP PLATE WITH NAILING AT SPLICE FOR CHORD STRESSES

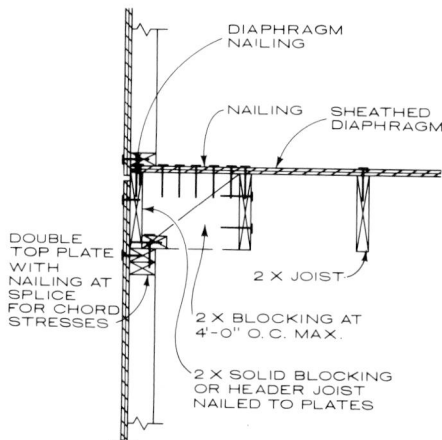

JOIST PARALLEL TO WALL

DIAPHRAGM NAILING
NAILING
SHEATHED DIAPHRAGM
DOUBLE TOP PLATE WITH NAILING AT SPLICE FOR CHORD STRESSES
2 × JOIST
2 × BLOCKING AT 4'-0" O.C. MAX.
2 × SOLID BLOCKING OR HEADER JOIST NAILED TO PLATES

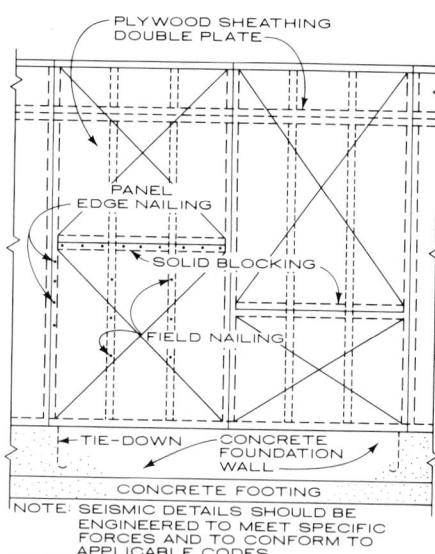

NOTE: SEISMIC DETAILS SHOULD BE ENGINEERED TO MEET SPECIFIC FORCES AND TO CONFORM TO APPLICABLE CODES.

PLYWOOD SHEATHED SHEAR WALL WITH TIE-DOWNS

PLYWOOD SHEATHING
DOUBLE PLATE
PANEL EDGE NAILING
SOLID BLOCKING
FIELD NAILING
TIE-DOWN
CONCRETE FOUNDATION WALL
CONCRETE FOOTING

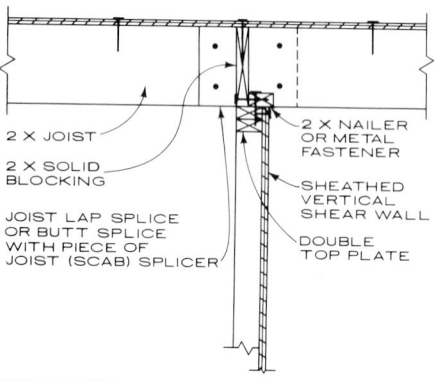

JOIST PERPENDICULAR TO WALL

2 × JOIST
2 × SOLID BLOCKING
JOIST LAP SPLICE OR BUTT SPLICE WITH PIECE OF JOIST (SCAB) SPLICER
2 × NAILER OR METAL FASTENER
SHEATHED VERTICAL SHEAR WALL
DOUBLE TOP PLATE

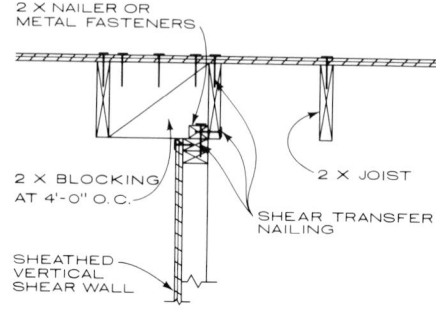

JOIST PARALLEL TO WALL

2 × NAILER OR METAL FASTENERS
2 × BLOCKING AT 4'-0" O.C.
2 × JOIST
SHEAR TRANSFER NAILING
SHEATHED VERTICAL SHEAR WALL

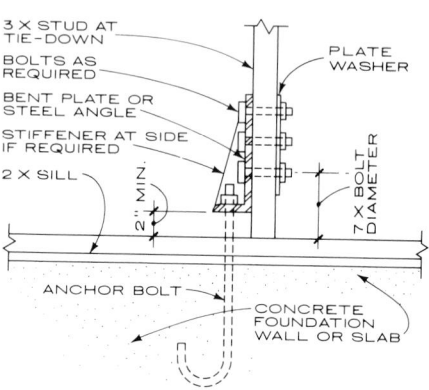

TIE DOWN

3 × STUD AT TIE-DOWN
BOLTS AS REQUIRED
BENT PLATE OR STEEL ANGLE
STIFFENER AT SIDE IF REQUIRED
2 × SILL
2" MIN.
ANCHOR BOLT
PLATE WASHER
7 × BOLT DIAMETER
CONCRETE FOUNDATION WALL OR SLAB

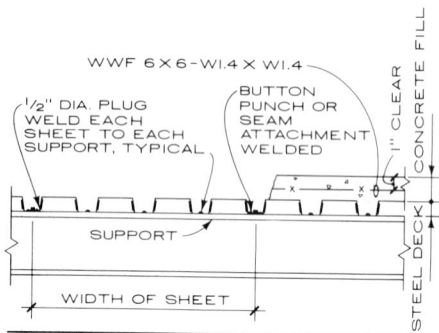

DECK FLUTES PERPENDICULAR TO SUPPORT

WWF 6 × 6 - W1.4 × W1.4
1/2" DIA. PLUG WELD EACH SHEET TO EACH SUPPORT, TYPICAL
BUTTON PUNCH OR SEAM ATTACHMENT WELDED
1" CLEAR
CONCRETE FILL
STEEL DECK
SUPPORT
WIDTH OF SHEET

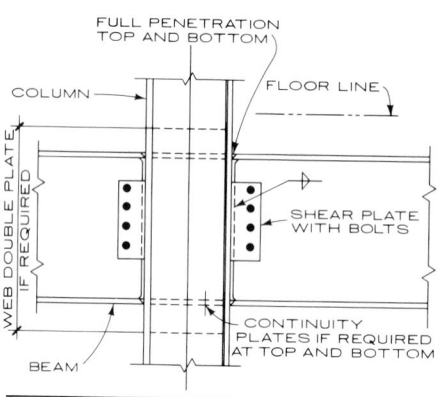

TYPICAL GIRDER AND COLUMN MOMENT CONNECTION

FULL PENETRATION TOP AND BOTTOM
COLUMN
FLOOR LINE
WEB DOUBLE PLATE IF REQUIRED
SHEAR PLATE WITH BOLTS
BEAM
CONTINUITY PLATES IF REQUIRED AT TOP AND BOTTOM

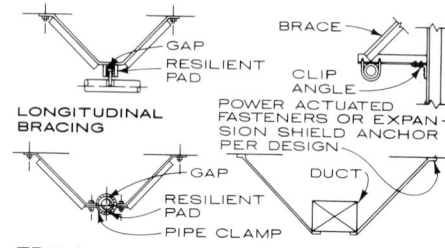

BRACING FOR PIPES AND DUCTS

GAP
RESILIENT PAD
LONGITUDINAL BRACING
BRACE
CLIP ANGLE
POWER ACTUATED FASTENERS OR EXPANSION SHIELD ANCHOR PER DESIGN
GAP
RESILIENT PAD
PIPE CLAMP
DUCT
TRANSVERSE BRACING

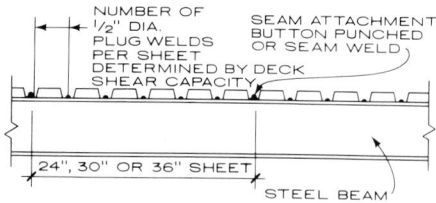

NUMBER OF 1/2" DIA. PLUG WELDS PER SHEET DETERMINED BY DECK SHEAR CAPACITY
SEAM ATTACHMENT BUTTON PUNCHED OR SEAM WELD
24", 30" OR 36" SHEET
STEEL BEAM

DECK PERPENDICULAR TO SUPPORT

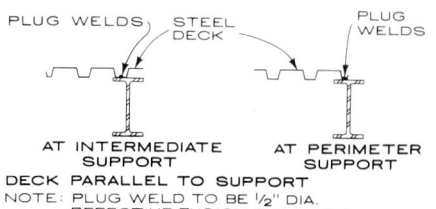

PLUG WELDS
STEEL DECK
PLUG WELDS
AT INTERMEDIATE SUPPORT
AT PERIMETER SUPPORT

DECK PARALLEL TO SUPPORT
NOTE: PLUG WELD TO BE 1/2" DIA. EFFECTIVE FUSION DIAMETER

1-1/2" STEEL DECK WELDING PATTERN

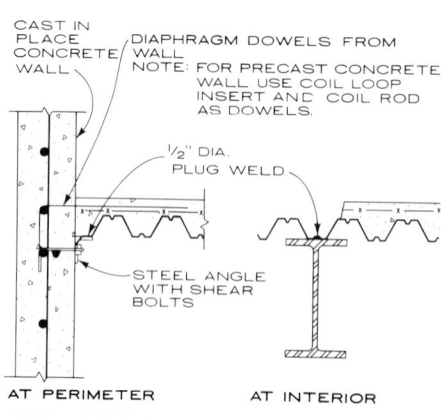

CAST IN PLACE CONCRETE WALL
DIAPHRAGM DOWELS FROM WALL
NOTE: FOR PRECAST CONCRETE WALL USE COIL LOOP INSERT AND COIL ROD AS DOWELS.
1/2" DIA. PLUG WELD
STEEL ANGLE WITH SHEAR BOLTS
AT PERIMETER
AT INTERIOR

DECK FLUTES PARALLEL TO SUPPORT

STEEL DECK WITH CONCRETE FILL

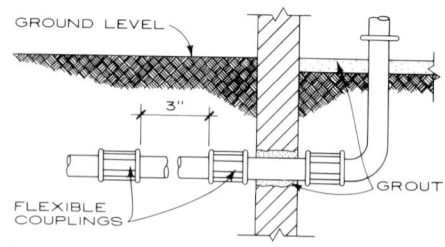

GROUND LEVEL
3"
FLEXIBLE COUPLINGS
GROUT

PIPE ENTERING BUILDING

NOTE
Details shown are representative of possible construction detailing. In addition to code defined structural requirements, safety considerations require nonstructural building elements and furnishings to be anchored in areas subjected to seismic movement. These pages show selected details as samples of recommended bracing and anchorage.

Attila L. Mocsary, PE; Hope Architects & Engineers; San Diego, California
Gary L. McGavin; Wyle Laboratories; El Segundo, California
Alfred M. Kemper & Associates; Los Angeles, California

1 **SEISMIC DESIGN**

FUNCTIONS OF LIGHTING

Light is one of many tools available to help us design space. It is wise at the beginning of any project to recall the functions of lighting and to be certain that each function has been examined.

1. PERFORMANCE OF TASKS: Lighting to perform work, whether it be reading, assembling parts, or seeing a blackboard, is referred to as task lighting. Visual work is a primary reason for providing lighting.

2. ENHANCEMENT OF SPACE AND STRUCTURE: It is only through the presence of light that spatial volume, planes, ornament, and color are revealed. For centuries, structural systems evolved partly in response to aesthetic as well as functional desires for light of a certain quality. The progress from bearing wall to curtain wall was driven by the push of newly discovered technologies (both in materials and in technique), by evolving cultural desires for certain spatial characteristics, and by a desire to admit light of a particular quality—as with the Gothic church window, the Baroque oculus, or the Bauhaus wall of glass. With the advent of electric lighting systems, this connection of structure to light was no longer entirely necessary, but most architects continue to pay homage to this historic tie.

3. FOCUSING ATTENTION: The quality of light in a space profoundly affects one's perception of that space. The timing and the direction of one's gaze—which are the vanguards of understanding of the space—are often a function of the varying quality and distribution of light throughout the space. Lighting draws attention to points of interest and helps to guide the user of a space about.

4. PROVISION OF SECURITY: Lighting can enhance visibility and thereby engender a sense of security. Lighting can also be used to illuminate hazards, such as a changing floor plane or moving objects.

ISSUES TO CONSIDER IN GOOD LIGHTING DESIGN

Good lighting design promotes (1) seeing—in the sense of performing such visual tasks as reading or operating equipment—and (2) perceiving the space and its various qualities (volume, color, texture, etc.).

To do visual work, a sufficient amount of light is required for the task. Most lighting standards discuss the quantity of light in terms of incident light or light that falls onto a surface. This light, called illuminance, is measured in footcandles or lux (S.I.). Although convenient to calculate, illuminance is not, of course, what actually enters our eyes.

When performing a visual task, the light that reaches our eyes and is therefore laden with whatever raw information our mind takes in is usually reflected light—that is, light reflected off the details of the task (typed letters), the immediate background (paper), and the surround (desk top and room). Important exceptions are electronic visual displays using CRTs and LEDs, which emit their own light. In these visual tasks, light reflected off their surfaces generally reduces their legibility, and much attention needs to be given to the lighting of the surround.

It should be recognized that exitance or luminance or even brightness is only one factor in a list of criteria for seeing, including contrast, task size, time (duration of gaze), and environmental distractions (noise, odors, etc.). While these items are by and large not part of the lighting design, contrast must be taken into account quite specifically. Tasks have their own inherent contrast, but under different lighting systems can produce differing perceived contrasts. This is primarily a matter of the position of the source of light relative to the task and the observer's eye.

Another factor in lighting design is the choice of the light source. Two issues are involved: color and size.

COLOR: Each lamp family has its own inherent color characteristics. The chart below describes in general terms the various perceived color effects.

SIZE: It is useful to think of sources and source/fixture combinations classified into point, line, or area sources. Point sources [for instance, bare incandescent lamps and recessed incandescent or high-intensity discharge (HID) fixtures with small apertures and specular reflectors] can be precisely controlled in terms of where light is and is not and can provide sparkle in a space by means of reflections off of polished room surfaces. Line sources

Robert Prouse, IALD, IES; H.M. Brandston & Partners, Inc.; New York, New York

(bare fluorescent tubes and linear fluorescent fixtures) can be controlled in their transverse axis of output, but not longitudinally. This makes them useful for lighting large open areas where repetitive rows of fixtures are suitable. The most common area source is a window, but also included in this category are arrays of line sources covered by a diffusing element. These sources usually provide medium to high levels of light with little directional control.

The human eye/brain combination is a complex and sensitive perceptual apparatus and does not simply function as a camera, projecting pictures into the mind. The many nerves and tissues necessary for translating the information carried as radiant energy by light into an image in the brain results in some anomalies that are significant to consider in lighting design.

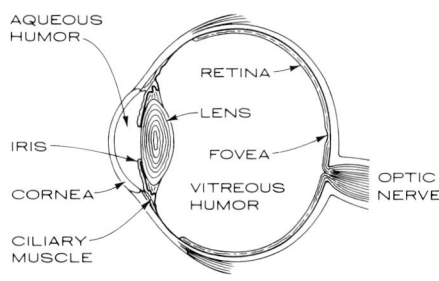

Light passes into the eye through a flexible lens, which passes the image through the vitreous humor and focuses it on the retina. The retina is actually a layer of light-sensitive receptors of two types: rods and cones. Millions of these receptors are spread over the retinal area, but they are not distributed evenly. The rods predominate in the peripheral zone, away from the center or fovea. Rods do not discriminate between colors, but are very sensitive to low light levels and movement. They are the primary transmitters of information at night when light levels are said to be in the scotopic range ("night vision"). Toward the center of the retina, and especially at the fovea, cones predominate. Cones are active at higher light levels (photopic range) and are divided into types that are sensitive to red, blue, and green light, which makes these hues the primary colors of light. The rods and cones are not equally sensitive to all wavelengths (colors) of light. Sensitivity peaks at about 550 nm for cones (a yellow-green color) and at about 500 nm for the rods, which do not "see" this wavelength as a color.

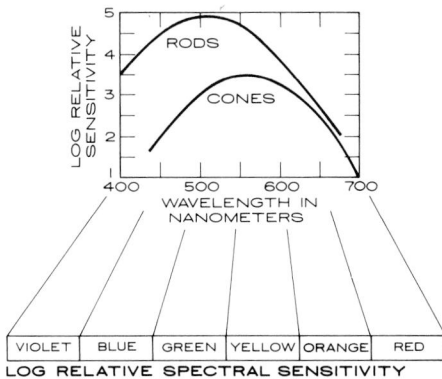

LOG RELATIVE SPECTRAL SENSITIVITY CURVES FOR CONE AND ROD VISION

Two important features of the human visual system for lighting design are adaptation to different light levels and color adaptation.

1. Adaptation to light levels: The visual system does not see a patch of a given luminance as a constant brightness across differing ambient light levels. Rather, it sees the patch as a brightness relative to another adjacent patch, or relative to the general surround. The visual system can be very discriminating in side-by-side, simultaneous comparisons of brightness. But judging the absolute brightness of a scene is near impossible, since the system adapts to the ambient light level. Also, because two different kinds of receptors (rods and cones) are used for night and daytime light levels, a transition from one extreme to the other—such as entering a movie theater at midday—requires time for the system to shift from photopic to scotopic sensitivity.

2. Adaptation of color: Analogously to brightness adaptation, the visual system does not have an absolute color sensitivity. When in an environment illuminated with light that primarily triggers the red sensitive cones, for instance, the blue and green receptors become acutely sensitive, and the red receptors become saturated or dulled to the dominant color. Because the visual system works in this way, two phenomena occur: (1) After a period of time (the adaptation), we see the red-light-dominated scene as more or less normal, since the sensing of red is attenuated and the sensing of blue and green is enhanced; (2) When we leave the red-light-dominated space and pass into one with less redness in the light, the blues and greens will, for a time (the adaptation period), be more apparent than their absolute value suggests. Color sensitivity is very much dependent on one's state of adaptation.

PERCEIVED COLOR EFFECTS FROM LAMPS

LAMP NAME	COLOR APPEARANCE	OBJECT COLORS ENHANCED	OBJECT COLORS DULLED
Incandescent, including tungsten halogen	Yellowish white	Warm colors	Cool colors
Fluorescent			
Cool white	White	Orange, yellow, blue	Red
Warm white	Yellowish white	Orange, yellow, blue	Red, blue
Cool white deluxe	White	All nearly equal	None appreciable
Warm white deluxe	Yellowish white	Red, orange, yellow	Blue
High-intensity discharge (HID)			
Clear mercury	Blue/green	Yellow, green, purple	Red, orange
Deluxe mercury	Purplish white	Orange, yellow, purple	Deep reds
Deluxe warm mercury	Yellowish white	Orange, yellow, purple	Deep reds
Metal halide	White	Orange, yellow, blue	Deep reds
High-pressure sodium	Yellow/orange	Yellow, orange	Green, blue
Low-pressure sodium	Yellow	Yellow	All except yellow

TERMS COMMONLY USED IN LIGHTING DESIGN

ENGLISH	SI	MEASURE OF
Footcandle (FC) Lumens/sq ft	Lux (LX) Lumens/sq m	Illuminance; incident light
Candlepower (CP) CP/D^2 (ft)	Candela (CD) CP/D^2 (meters)	Intensity of a "ray" of light in a given direction (used for point-by-point calculations)
Lumen (LM)	Lumen (LM)	Flux; total amount of light emitted by a source (used for lumen method calculations)
Candela/sq ft (CD/sq ft)	Candela/sq m (CD/sq m)	Luminance or luminous exitance, or simply exitance; flux leaving a surface at a point (formerly measured in footlamberts)
Reflectance (R)	Reflectance	$R(\%) = \dfrac{\text{Luminance of sample material}}{\text{Luminance of reflectance standard}}$ or $\dfrac{\text{Flux reflected}}{\text{Flux incident}}$
Transmission (T)	Transmission	$T(\%) = \dfrac{\text{Flux emerging}}{\text{Flux incident}}$

ILLUMINANCE VALUES FOR VARIOUS TYPES OF ACTIVITIES IN INTERIORS

TYPES OF ACTIVITY	FOOTCANDLES	REFERENCE WORK PLANE
Public spaces with dark surroundings	2–3–5	Hospital corridors (night)
Simple orientation for short temporary visits	5–7.5–10	CRT areas (veiling reflections need special consideration), transportation terminal concourses
Working spaces where visual tasks are only occasionally performed	10–15–20	Auditoriums, banks (general), hotel corridors and lobbies, hospital corridors (days)
Performance of visual tasks of high contrast or large size	20–30–50	Conference rooms, offices (high contrast), factory (simple assembly)
Performance of visual tasks of medium contrast or small size	50–75–100	Drafting rooms (high-contrast tasks), classrooms, offices, factory (low contrast), factory (moderately difficult assembly)
Performance of visual tasks of low contrast or small size	100–150–200	Drafting rooms (low-contrast tasks), laboratories, factory (difficult assembly)
Performance of visual tasks of low contrast and very small size over a prolonged period	200–300–500	Factory (very difficult assembly)
Performance of very prolonged and exacting visual tasks	500–750–1000	Factory (exacting assembly)
Performance of very special visual tasks of extremely low contrast and small size	1000–1500–2000	Cloth inspection areas

ENERGY MANAGEMENT

Many state governments have or are in the process of formulating laws, codes, and guidelines to control the use of energy. While the major impact is on building HVAC systems, lighting systems are also considered. The federal government is in the process of developing a model code for use by states and municipalities.

Most of these energy management guidelines are based on a procedure to limit the total connected load in units of overall watts per square foot. Most also recognize that time is a factor since power is measured in units of kilowatt hours (KWHRS).

The procedures being developed require that some assumptions be made about space use, but should not be confused with actual design of lighting systems. While the process will set an overall limit of connected load for a building, individual spaces within the building may vary widely from the watts-per-square-foot average. The procedure must often be invoked at a point in design when not enough is known about all the activities in the building; however, enough latitude is generally given to allow the law of averages to take its course.

Many special areas are typically excluded, although one must always check with the current local code. These typically include:

1. Performance spaces
2. Outdoor activities
3. Special lighting for medical or dental uses
4. Display lighting for art
5. Special lighting for research
6. Lighting for plant growth used only in off-peak hours
7. Normally off emergency lighting
8. Lighting for high-risk security areas
9. Classrooms for the visually handicapped
10. Store display windows
11. Lighting for dwelling units

To determine a building's power limit, each space type must be analyzed to determine a "base unit power density" (UPD). The UPD is stated in units of watts per square foot. The formula for UPD is:

$$\text{UPD} = \frac{(FC_t \times \text{task area \%}) + (FC_g \times \text{general area \%})}{GCU \times LSF \times LLF} \times AF$$

where:

FC_t = recommended task area illuminance (in footcandles)

Task area % = percent that the task area is of the total

FC_g = recommended illuminance for the general area around the task area (usually $\frac{1}{3} \times FC_t$)

General area % = percent that the general area is of the total (100% − task area %)

GCU = generalized coefficient of utilization for a broad space or task type (the range is 0.50–0.75)

LSF = light source factor based on lamp efficacy (lumens/watt) appropriate for the space or task (the range is 20–90)

LLF = light loss factor taking into account the accumulation of dirt on fixture and room surfaces (the range is 0.70–0.75)

AF = adjustment factor to account for special conditions (rarely used).

Robert Prouse, IALD, IES; H.M. Brandston & Partners, Inc.; New York, New York

LIGHTING THE HORIZONTAL PLANE

The most commonly used measure of a lighting system's performance is the resulting illuminance (the amount of footcandles delivered to the work surface). This is not because illuminance is an effective measure of all aspects of quality, but because the illuminance characteristics of lighting systems are well understood and easily predicted.

The work surface is usually a horizontal plane such as a desk top, a drafting board, or the floor. Hence, the most commonly used calculation technique (the lumen method described on the following page) permits the selection of fixtures and layouts to achieve approximate uniformity of illuminance (footcandles) at any desired horizontal plane in a room.

UNIFORMITY

Uniformity is of interest to the lighting designer for two reasons. One is that it is thought that excessive variations in brightness in the observer's field of view in a work environment can be unpleasant and lead to feelings of fatigue and subsequently reduced performance. The most common example is looking up from one's desk at a bright, sunlit window, which causes the visual system to begin to adapt to that high brightness, and then looking back down at one's work surface, which has a lower brightness, causing the visual system to begin to readapt. A day full of such attempted adaptation to such extreme contrasts can be a tiring one. The second interest in uniformity has to do with the relatively common need to provide a fixed lighting system for a flexible (or unknown at the time of design) furniture plan. This situation requires uniformity of illuminance so that the required amount of footcandles is present wherever a work surface might be positioned.

Therefore, in addition to achieving a particular illuminance level, understanding of the uniformity of a lighting plan is necessary. In a typical room it is possible to achieve virtually any illuminance level with only one very powerful fixture. However, that one fixture would create unacceptably high brightness gradients.

To understand the uniformity aspect of any lighting system, it is necessary to look at the distribution of light from one fixture and consider how it relates to an adjacent one. As an example, here is a diagram of the output from a downlight:

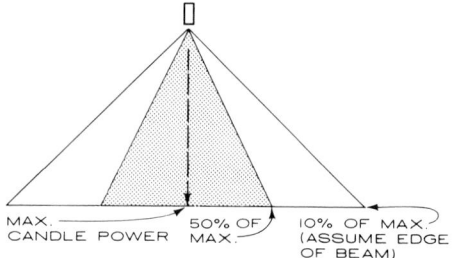

MAX. CANDLE POWER   50% OF MAX.   10% OF MAX. (ASSUME EDGE OF BEAM)

Manufacturers provide the angles off center of the points at which the intensity of light has dropped to 50% of the maximum value and 10% of the maximum value.

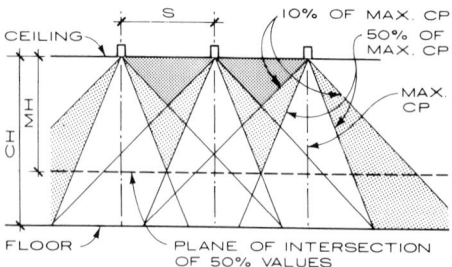

The maximum spacing (S) at a given mounting height (MH) above the work plane is chosen such that the illuminance halfway between fixtures due to two adjacent fixtures is equal to the illuminance under one fixture due to that one fixture. The MH and the ceiling height (CH) may or may not be the same, depending on the selection of the work plane height (i.e., floor vs. desk). The ratio of a suitable spacing to the mounting height (S/MH) is known as the spacing criterion (SC).

AVOIDING VEILING REFLECTIONS

The area above and directly in front of the task is called the offending zone, since it is the most likely to cause veiling reflections (reflected glare).

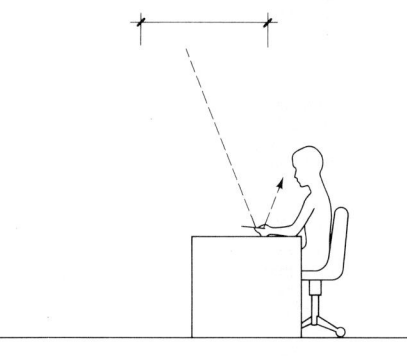

Fixtures located off to each side in an area 25°–45° off the task surface will tend not to produce veiling reflections:

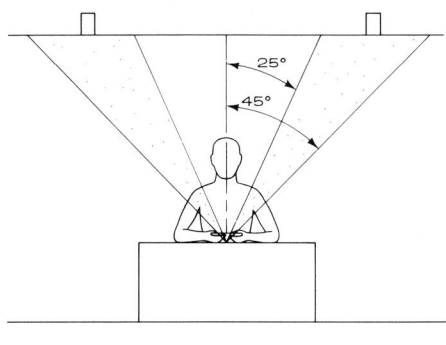

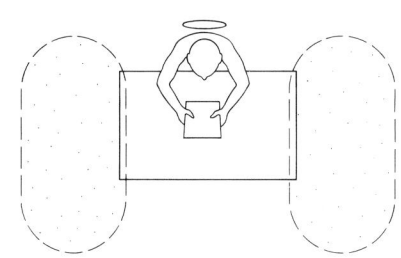

LUMEN METHOD

The lumen method, also known as the zonal cavity system, is a way to calculate either horizontal illuminance from a proposed lighting fixture section and layout or quantity of fixtures from proposed fixture selection and horizontal illuminance value.

The lumen method is based on the definition of average footcandles over an area which is lumens per square foot. The method modifies this fundamental equation (FC = lumens/sq ft) to account for room size and proportion; reflectance of walls, ceiling, and floors; fixture efficiency; and the effects of time in reducing output due to dirt accumulation, deterioration of reflecting surfaces, and reduction of lumen output.

Robert Prouse, IALD, IES; H.M. Brandston & Partners, Inc.; New York, New York

The lumen method requires the following information:

1. Room dimensions (adequate to compute wall area and floor area)
2. Height of fixtures above work plane
3. Reflectances of major surfaces (ceiling, walls, and floor)
4. An estimate of the light loss factor (LLF)
5. Initial lamp lumens
6. A target illuminance level

The coefficient of utilization (CU) is the percentage of total lamp lumens that reaches the work plane. As such, it has nothing to do with the intensity of the fixture, but rather with the efficiency of the fixtures (lumens emitted from the fixture divided by lamp lumens) and the direction of the light output. (This direction of output is graphically represented by the candlepower distribution curve.) Since for purposes of this procedure, the plane of interest is invariably a horizontal plane (typically either the floor or desk level), a fixture that throws the greatest percentage of its lumens downward will necessarily have a higher CU [room cavity ratio (RCR) and reflectance values being equal] than one that distributes light in any other direction. A higher CU is not necessarily a virtue; it only ranks fixtures according to their ability to provide horizontal illuminance.

The lumen method/zonal cavity system is limited by the following:

1. It is based on a single number, average value, from which follows:
2. It assumes a uniform array of lighting fixtures.
3. It assumes that all room surfaces are a matte (lambertian) finish.
4. It assumes that the room is devoid of obstruction, at least down to the level of the work plane.

The LLF is used in calculating illuminance at a specific point in time in the life of a lighting system under given conditions. It incorporates variations from test conditions in temperature and voltage, dirt accumulation on lighting fixtures and room surfaces, lamp lumen output depreciation, maintenance procedures (mainly frequency of cleaning), and atmospheric conditions. The LLF is also known as the maintenance factor.

In order to use a CU table, one must first make assumptions about the reflectances of the major room surfaces: ceiling, walls, and floor. Then the RCR must be determined according to one of the following formulas:

RCR = (5 x H(L + W))/(L x W), for rectangular rooms

where H is the cavity height (see diagram)

RCR = 2.5 wall area/floor area, for odd-shaped rooms

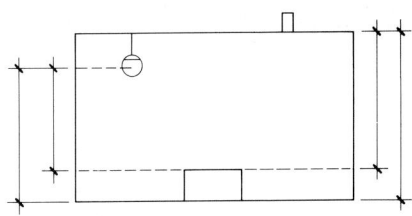

Any one of these dimensions may be the cavity height, depending on the location of the work plane of interest and the fixture mounting.

BATWING DISTRIBUTION

Fixture manufacturers have developed luminaires (mostly fluorescent) that produce a light distribution that tends to reduce direct glare and veiling reflections if used in large, uniform arrays and typical open office geometries. This distribution pattern is called batwing and has the following characteristics:

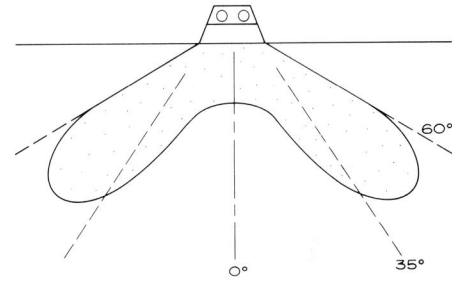

The intensity of light straight below the fixture (0°) is minimized so that even a fixture placed in the "offending zone" will not be as objectionable as it otherwise might. The intensity at angles between 35° and 60° is maximized so that at typical spacings, peak intensities overlap at the work surface:

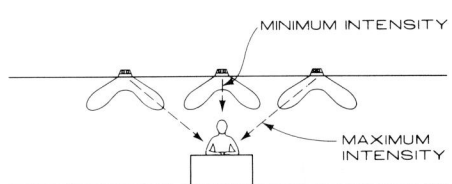

SOME USEFUL FORMULAS FOR AVERAGE LIGHTING CALCULATIONS

$$\text{NUMBER OF LUMINAIRES} = \frac{\text{footcandles desired} \times \text{room area}}{\text{CU} \times \text{LLF} \times \text{lamps/luminaire} \times \text{lumens/lamp}}$$

$$\text{AVERAGE FOOTCANDLES} = \frac{\text{lumens/lamp} \times \text{lamps/luminaire} \times \text{CU} \times \text{LLF}}{\text{area of room (sq ft)}}$$

$$\text{POWER DENSITY (W/sq ft)} = \frac{\text{footcandles desired}}{\text{source efficacy (lumens/watt)} \times \text{CU} \times \text{LLF}}$$

where CU = Coefficient of Utilization (percentage of light that actually reaches task)
LLF = Light loss factor (time-dependent depreciation factors)

NOTE

See manufacturer's photometric tables or the Lighting Handbook of the Illuminating Engineering Society for tables giving values of CU, LLF, lumens/lamp, and so on.

TYPICAL EXAMPLES

Room size 25 x 40 ft; ceiling height 9 ft; office area 70 ft-c; 2 x 4 ft recessed troffers with 4–40 W T12 lamps (3100 lm) each. From IES tables, Room Index = E and CU = 0.67 (plastic lens):

$$\text{NUMBER OF FIXTURES} = \frac{70 \times 25 \times 40}{0.67 \times 0.7 \times 4 \times 3100} = 12.03 \text{ (use 12 luminaires)}$$

$$\text{POWER DENSITY (W/sq ft)} = \frac{70 \text{ FC}}{78 \text{ lumens/W} \times 0.67 \times 0.70} = 1.9 \text{ W/sq ft}$$

LUMINAIRE SELECTION PARAMETERS

In selecting luminaires that will contribute to the making of an appropriate environment in a space, several factors are usually considered:

1. DISTRIBUTION is the shape of the light output from a luminaire. It is illustrated by the candlepower distribution curve, a polar plot of intensities at specific angles. Luminaires are classified by the percentage of their luminous output sent in various directions.

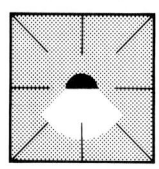

$$\frac{0-10\%}{90-100\%}$$

DIRECT

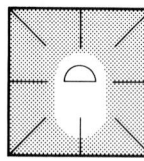

$$\frac{10-40\%}{60-90\%}$$

SEMIDIRECT

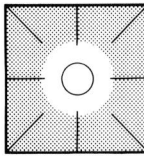

$$\frac{40-60\%}{40-60\%}$$

GENERAL DIFFUSE

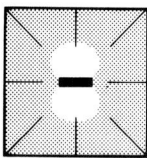

$$\frac{40-60\%}{40-60\%}$$

DIRECT-INDIRECT

$$\frac{60-90\%}{10-40\%}$$

SEMIINDIRECT

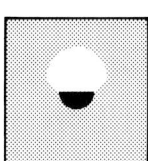

$$\frac{90-100\%}{0-10\%}$$

INDIRECT

2. WHERE IS THE FIXTURE relative to the space? Is it outside (i.e., recessed), inside on a surface (ceiling or wall), or within: portable (table or floor)?

Recessed fixtures primarily light major planes: downlights for floors and horizontal work surfaces (desks, drafting tables, lab tables, etc.) and wall washers for walls. Recessed adjustable accent lights can be used to highlight selected areas. Since their distributions are entirely "direct," the lighting quality tends to the dramatic: full of contrasts and shadows. Fixtures located in the space (surface, pendant, or portable) can illuminate the ceiling as well as the floor, work surfaces, and walls. These types of fixtures (except for those whose distribution is totally direct) tend to soften shadows and contrasts.

Robert Prouse, IALD, IES; H.M. Brandston & Partners, Inc.; New York, New York

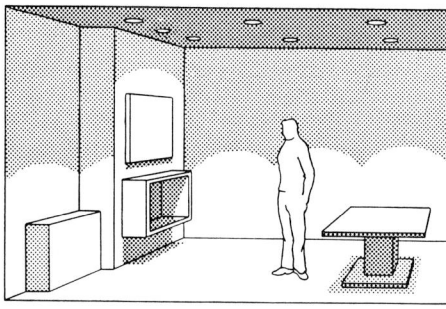

DIRECT

All recessed lighting is an example of a direct lighting system, but a pendant fixture could be direct if it emits virtually no light above the horizontal. Unless extensive wall-washing is used, the overall impression of a direct lighting system is one of low general brightness with the possibility of higher intensity accents.

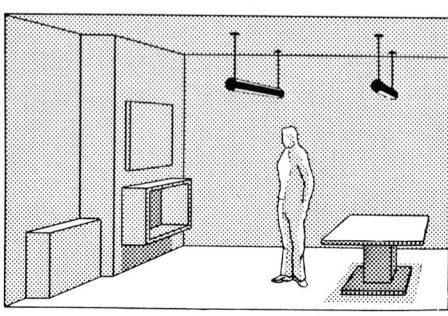

SEMIDIRECT

All systems other than direct ones necessarily imply that the lighting fixtures are in the space, whether pendant mounted, surface mounted, or portable. A semidirect system will provide good illuminance on horizontal surfaces, with moderate general brightness.

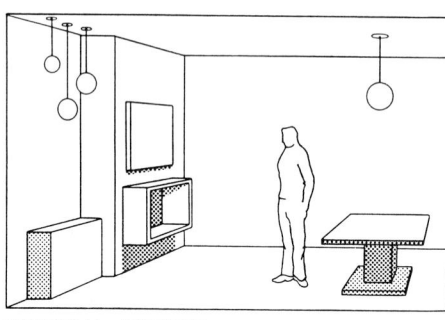

GENERAL DIFFUSE

A general diffuse system most typically consists of suspended fixtures, with predominantly translucent surfaces on all sides.

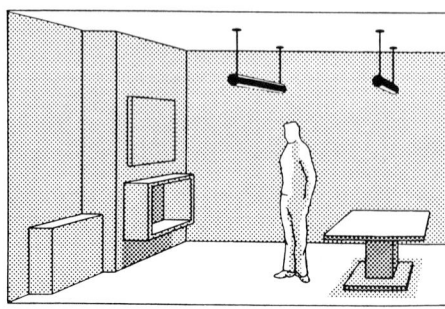

DIRECT-INDIRECT

A direct-indirect lighting system will tend to equally emphasize the upper and lower horizontal planes in a space (i.e., the ceiling and the floor).

SEMIINDIRECT

A semiindirect system will place the emphasis on the ceiling, with some downward or outward-directed light.

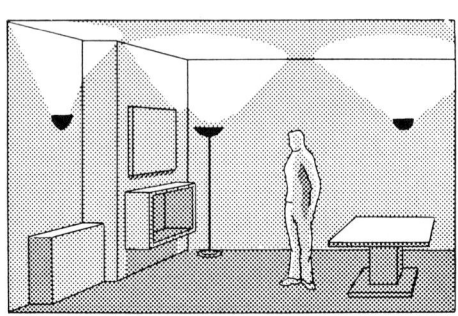

INDIRECT

A fully indirect system will bounce all the light off the ceiling, resulting in a low-contrast environment with little shadow.

3. DIRECT GLARE is produced by excessive luminance in the visual field which affects the visual systems as the individual looks around the environment. It is usually associated with the luminaire zone from 45° to 90°. To minimize direct glare, the luminous intensity should be kept out of the 45°–90° zone.

The design of a good lighting fixture is—in photometric terms—often a balance between a fixture that is efficient at delivering illuminance to a work surface (high CU) and one that is comfortable to live with (low glare). Excessive brightness at high angles (above 45°) will tend to cause fixtures to be perceived as glaring. Some manufacturers publish charts of luminous exitance values at critical angles, and some sense of this can be obtained from inspection of the candlepower distribution curve.

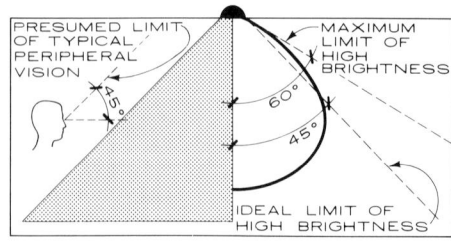

4. SOURCE TYPE AND MAGNITUDE: The lumen output of a fixture must be proportionate to the desired illuminance level and the size of the space. The color of the source must also be appropriate to the area/space and activity being lighted.

NOISE

Because they contain no magnetic coils that can loosen over time and cause a buzzing sound, electronic ballasts are less noisy.

COST

Electronic ballasts typically cost several times more than a magnetic ballast, but those costs are expected to decrease as more are manufactured. Even at today's costs, the payback on electronic ballasts is typically between one and two years. Additionally, utility companies are starting to offer incentives in the form of rebates on utility bills for the use of electronic ballasts, which can reduce this payback period dramatically.

HARMONIC DISTORTION

Harmonic distortion is a phenomenon that is produced by electrical, and especially electronic, devices that use power. Almost all electronic devices distort power that passes through them. For many years this distortion was of no concern because it was negligible. However, with the advent of the modern technology of computers, facsimile machines, copiers, and computers, the distortion is no longer insignificant. The effect of the distortion is to increase the load on a building's wiring system, causing overheating of wires and transformers, and tripping of breakers that do not appear to be overloaded. When the distortion from poorly designed electronic ballasts is added to that from other electronic devices in a typical office, the results can be serious overloading of the electrical system.

There is another issue that electronic ballasts have raised. In the days of magnetic ballasts, the only commonly used fluorescent lamps that used instant-start ballasts were the single-pin T-12 lamps called slimlines. These were not widely used for interior lighting (compared with the use of rapid-start lamps). The lampholders for rapid-start and slimline lamps were physically incompatible, and there was no possibility of inadvertently interchanging the two.

It is, however, possible to operate a lamp designed to be used on a rapid-start circuit on an instant-start ballast designed for such a purpose. While this was not customarily done with magnetic ballasts, such ballasts are available in an electronic form. There are two significant results from this: (1) an instant-start electronic ballast operating a rapid-start lamp will typically draw a little less power, thus saving energy; but (2) it will shorten the expected lamp life by about 25%, thus raising a different operating cost.

GLARE CONTROL

The control of glare has always been a primary component of a good lighting design. Recently the discussion of glare has been reinvigorated by concerns related to the use of visual display terminals (VDTs) associated with computers in the workplace.

Glare is difficult to evaluate because a fixture may be a source of glare in one environment and perfectly unobtrusive in another. The reason for this has to do with how the human visual system works. We can perceive – "see" – over an enormous range of brightnesses: from the noon day sun at one end of the spectrum to the darkness of night at the other. However, we cannot see well when there are widely varying brightnesses present in our field of view at the same time: we couldn't do our work in a setting with both the noon day sun and the darkness of night present simultaneously. We see comfortably in discrete ranges of adaptation whose maximum-to-minimum values are on the order of one 100:1. While the total from the top of the uppermost range to the bottom of the lowest is on the order of a billion-to-one, we become adapted to a sort of weighted average of the prevailing brightnesses in our field of view at the moment.

This is important to realize because glare is a point or area of luminance (the measurable version of brightness) near or beyond the maximum luminance of the current range of adaptation. Thus a fixture's surface brightness may be in the middle of one adaptation range (and therefore be quite comfortable), but be at the upper limit of another and thereby be a source of glare in that range.

Likewise a fixture may be a source of glare from one viewing position, and not from another. Some fixtures are more or less uniform in their distribution of brightnesses in all directions. Others – and these include many commonly used in office lighting today – are highly nonuniform in their dispersal of brightness. These are specifically designed this way so that as much light as possible is emitted in certain directions, and so that it is very well shielded in other directions. When these fixtures are misused, or when the work environment changes, unwanted glare may be introduced.

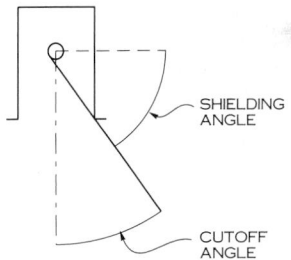

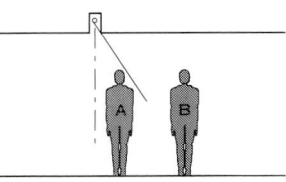

NOTE

Person standing at "A" has some direct view of the bare source and thus a potential for glare. Person standing at "B" does not.

GLARE CONTROL DIAGRAM

COMMON PRINCIPLES USED TO CONTROL GLARE IN LIGHTING FIXTURES

Several techniques are commonly used to control glare in electrically lighted interior environments. Most revolve around trying to shield the bare light bulb from direct view at most normal viewing positions. Other techniques are directed toward keeping the brightness of the materials used in shielding the view of the light bulb at an acceptable level. Some of the terms and techniques are summarized here:

The first line of defense in glare control is to hide the lamp from the typical lines of sight. It happens that most configurations are such that as shielding is increased, the overall efficiency of the fixture is decreased. A successful fixture design balances these competing needs, usually tailoring fixture geometry to the typical space proportions in which the fixture is intended to be used.

Cutoff angle: "the angle, measured up from nadir, between the vertical axis and the first line of sight at which the bare source is not visible" (IES)

Shielding angle: "the angle between a horizontal line through the light center and the line of sight at which the bare source first becomes visible" (IES)

Using the geometric principles listed above, glare control strategy tends to divide into two parts, depending on the size of the source. Small sources such as incandescent, compact fluorescent, and high-intensity discharge lamps usually have a single reflector or lens designed to control the brightness of the source. Larger sources such as fluorescent lamps tend to use a lens or a large baffle to shield the lamp.

A reflector cone for a downlight (whether incandescent or compact fluorescent) sets the cutoff and shielding angles based on the size of the lamp, the width of the aperture, and the distance from the bottom of the fixture to the bottom of the lamp. The key to a successful fixture design is a properly formed and finished reflector surface. A fully specular (mirror finish) surface would redirect a ray of light off of its surface at exactly the same angle (reflected) as that ray struck the surface.

If a fully matte surface were used, the ray of light would be scattered equally in all directions. This would send much of the light back up into the fixture, and much of it in directions above the shielding angle.

Such fixtures are normally designed with a semi-specular finish so that most of the light reflected by the surface is redirected within the cutoff angle. A small portion of the light is scattered above the angle, to smooth the visual transition when one passes from the shielded viewing zone into the cutoff angle.

Another method is to use a ridged baffle lining in a cylinder to absorb high angle emissions of light. This is an inherently less efficient approach compared to the specular reflector design, but is sometimes preferred for reasons of appearance.

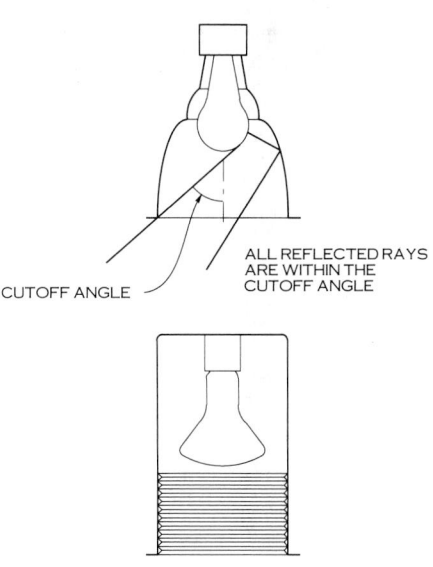

LAMP DESIGNS

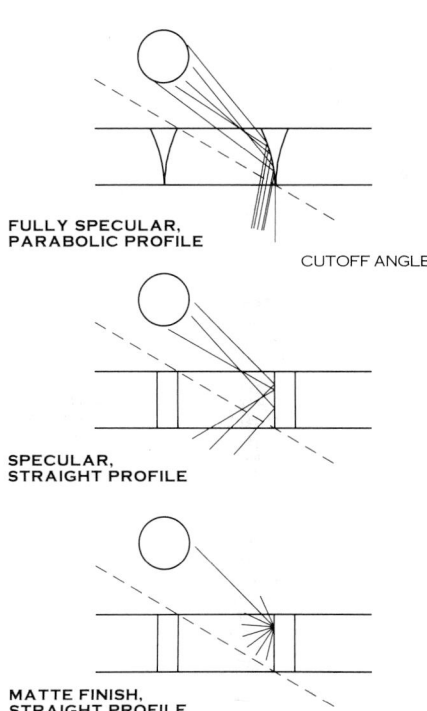

FULLY SPECULAR, PARABOLIC PROFILE

CUTOFF ANGLE

SPECULAR, STRAIGHT PROFILE

MATTE FINISH, STRAIGHT PROFILE

LOUVERS AND BAFFLES

LOUVERS AND BAFFLES

A baffle is "a single opaque or translucent element to shield a source from direct view at certain angles, or to absorb unwanted light" (IES) The term "baffle" is typically used to refer to a metal or plastic blade that is part of a louver that shields fluorescent lamps. It also refers to the ridges on the inside of a cylindrical aperture piece that shields an incandescent lamp and controls glare by absorbing light above the cutoff angle.

A louver is "a series of baffles used to shield a source from view at certain angles or to absorb unwanted light. The baffles are usually arranged in a geometric pattern" (IES)

Louvers are sized so that the height of the baffles and the spacing between them create the desired cutoff angle. Flat louvers simply block the sightline from a viewer to the lamps. Louvers with a parabolic profile not only block sightlines, but also redirect rays of light that strike them downward within the cutoff angle.

Robert Prouse, IALD, IES; H.M. Brandston & Partners, Inc.; New York, New York

INDIRECT LIGHTING

Another method of dealing with the potential for glare from electric lamps is to hide them entirely by using them in what is called indirect lighting. Opaque or translucent elements are placed fully between the lamps and any possible sightline. The fixture is designed to direct light first upward to the ceiling and then down to the work surface.

THE CHANGING WORKPLACE

Indirect lighting has been applied to office spaces where intensive work is done on visual display terminals (computer screens). Before the widespread use of VDTs in the workplace, lighting designers often thought of the visual environment as being divided into "heads down" tasks and "heads up" tasks. The more critical task in the office was thought to be the former: looking down to the desk top and reading typed, handwritten, or photocopied material. Thus the emphasis was often placed on providing a recommended level of illumination on the desk top.

RELECTED SIGHTLINES   DIRECT, PERIPHERAL SIGHTLINES

SIGHTLINES

NEW SIGHTLINES

That orientation has changed with the introduction of VDTs. Now the typical sightline is more nearly horizontal. This puts a large area of the ceiling and surrounding wall or work station into peripheral view in the form of background brightness. Both the overall level as well as the uniformity of brightness of these surfaces can have an impact on the visibility of the VDT screen and surrounding paperwork.

REFLECTED IMAGES

The VDT introduces another surrounding brightness problem. The screen of course reflects the brightnesses of the scene behind the worker. The scope of that scene is quite large due to the curvature and tilt of the typical VDT screen. And a VDT "sees" much more of the ceiling than one might at first imagine: most screens are convex and many are tilted slightly. Such a surface is like a convex security mirror used in retail establishments or parking garage entrances to provide a wide angle reflected view. So too, a VDT screen reflects a larger area of the ceiling than a flat mirror in the same location would. Between this reflected view and the change in orientation described above, great areas of the ceiling and surrounding walls or partitions now need to be considered carefully in the balancing of brightnesses.

It has been found that in spaces lighted with direct fixtures, a fixture is often inappropriately located relative to a VDT, and a reflected sightline would fall within the cutoff angle, where no direct sightline would. Depending on surrounding surface reflectance, even a fixture that is comfortable to view directly might be distracting when viewed reflected in the VDT.

Simply using an indirect lighting strategy will not necessarily result in a comfortable VDT viewing environment since the patches of light reflected from the ceiling may cause distracting contrast in the terminal displays. Thus the burden of the indirect lighting fixture is to spread the light evenly across the ceiling. It is, of course, easier to do this if the distance from the fixture to the ceiling is comfortably large, and so the higher the ceiling, the more successful the results are likely to be.

INDIRECT LIGHTING AND ENERGY USE

It might at first seem that indirect lighting is an inherently inefficient way to light interior space. The light must first travel upward (and be subjected to the vitiating effects of the inverse square law), and then bounce off a ceiling which, however white, still absorbs some light, and only then start its journey to the desk top. In spite of all this, there are several factors that tend to compensate.

POTENTIAL FOR INCREASED EFFICIENCY. Because the configuration of indirect fixtures totally shields the bare lamps from view, it is possible to design fixtures that emit a greater percentage of the bare lamp lumens than well shielded direct fixtures. Efficiency in a fixture that directs most of its output downward is usually a trade-off between good glare control and efficiency, whereas an indirect fixture can be more efficient without producing glare.

The only limit on efficiency (percentage of light escaping the fixture divided by the total lamp lumens) is the geometrical relationship between the source size and the fixture size: a very large fixture (in cross section) containing a very small source is very efficient; a very small fixture employing a relatively large source is less efficient. Since the trend in both fluorescent and HID sources has been toward smaller sizes of greater efficacy (lumens produced per watt consumed), it is possible to design indirect fixtures that emit enough "extra" light to compensate for the greater distance the light must travel.

The typical modern open-plan VDT workplace derives greater benefit from lower, uniform light levels, than higher, less uniform levels: Unlike the printed paper visual tasks that dominated the workplace of ten to twenty years ago, most VDT screens have their own internal brightness. But since typical work patterns involve much moving of the eyes back and forth from the screen to nearby documents or the surrounding surfaces, it is important to provide a luminous environment that produces roughly equal brightness on the document or surrounding surface as that of the screen. Because of the range of typical VDT display brightness, this has meant that overall recommended light levels are lower than in the all-paper visual tasks. So a lighting system that provides a somewhat lower lighting level, with a corresponding reduction in power consumed, may be a good approach to the modern office.

SPATIAL GEOMETRY CRITICAL. Good visibility of a VDT screen is primarily a matter of avoiding the reflections from the surface of the screen interfering with the clarity of the image on the screen. In most circumstances, the absolute brightness of the surfaces reflected in the screen are not as important as the uniformity of brightness. The screen brightness can be adjusted to an appropriate level for the surrounding environment, if that surround is of uniform brightness. Annoying reflections in the screen are caused by spots or areas of brightness that noticeably exceed that of the general surface brightness. These spots can be lighting fixtures that are not well shielded, or are inappropriately located; or they could be from surfaces that have a noticeable gradient of contrast. A wall with small windows or a ceiling with "hot spots" from improperly selected indirect fixtures are examples of such contrast.

PROBLEMS IN AN OPEN-OFFICE PLAN. No single lighting approach holds a monopoly on producing good results for a VDT environment. But it sometimes takes a special design strategy to eliminate the hot spots and other contrast gradient problems in an open office plan with an entirely direct system. This is because, as the partitions around the individual workstations increase in height, a great deal of shadowing occurs, and the system that produces a uniform field of brightness in the open room no longer produces such uniformity within the confines of each cubicle, which may be the primary surfaces reflected in the VDT screen.

When panels of a height greater than 42 inches are used, an indirect or partially indirect lighting scheme may yield better system performance than a direct one. This is because the amount and quality (shadowing, uniformity, etc.) of light at the desk is very much dependent on the geometrical relationship of the desk to the ceiling pattern in a direct lighting system. With an indirect or partially indirect system, the light is more evenly diffused throughout the space by the time it begins its downward path from the ceiling to the desk top, resulting in less dependence on fixture location relative to desk surface.

WORKSTATION PANEL HEIGHT

The illumination reaching a desk top in a direct lighting system is a combination of light that arrives directly from the lighting fixture and indirectly after it has been reflected off various room surfaces.

A partition not only interferes with the indirect component of light, but can drastically reduce the potential direct component. Consider the example shown in the diagram below. In diagram "A", the work station is contained within 42 in. high panels. Extending "sightlines" (as if the desk top could "see" the ceiling) from the center of the station out to the ceiling over the top of the panels, it can be seen that in a 10 by 10 ft workstation, a ceiling area of 4,225 square feet (65 by 65 ft) has the potential for contributing light to the workstation. If the lighting fixtures are on an 8' spacing, there would be an average of 66 fixtures [4,225 sq ft ÷ (8 x 8 ft)] that could contribute light directly to the desk top.

If the same 10 by 10 ft work station had partitions 60 in. tall, the projected lines would enclose a ceiling area of 676 square feet (26 by 26 ft). This area would include only ten or eleven fixtures [676 sq ft ÷ (8 x 8 ft)]. While this 80% decrease in the number of lighting fixtures that could possibly contribute light directly to the desk top will not translate into an 80% drop in light levels at the desk top, it will cause a significant decrease. The amount would be influenced by factors such as the distribution pattern of the lighting fixture and the finishes of the partitions.

Clearly, task lighting is important to consider when partitions are more than 42 in. high.

CALCULATIONS IN SPACES WITH PARTITIONs. A rough approximation of the magnitude of the effect of partition height can be calculated as follows (this technique should not be used for totally direct lighting systems unless several luminaires directly contribute light to the cubicle):

1. Use the fixture's Coefficient of Utilization (CU) table to calculate the average illuminance at the top of the partitions. Use the distance from the luminaires to the top of the partitions as the cavity height, and use actual reflectance except for the floor. Use "0" for the floor cavity reflectance.

2. Determine the transfer coefficient of a virtual ceiling cavity luminaire: Use the distance from the top of the partition to the desk top as the cavity height. Use the cubicle's partition reflectance as the wall reflectance, use the effective ceiling cavity reflectance of the actual ceiling cavity above the top of the partitions. Use the table below to find the transfer coefficient.

3. Multiply the illuminance from the first step (at the top of the partitions) by the transfer coefficient to find the approximate average illuminance at the desk top.

TRANSFER COEFFICIENTS

Ceiling	80			50		
Walls	50	30	10	50	30	10
RCR:						
0	1.19	1.19	1.19	1.11	1.11	1.11
1	1.03	0.98	0.94	0.96	0.93	0.89
2	0.89	0.81	0.75	0.83	0.78	0.73
3	0.77	0.69	0.62	0.73	0.66	0.60
4	0.68	0.59	0.52	0.64	0.57	0.51
5	0.61	0.51	0.45	0.58	0.50	0.44
6	0.55	0.45	0.39	0.52	0.44	0.38
7	0.49	0.40	0.34	0.47	0.39	0.34
8	0.45	0.36	0.30	0.43	0.35	0.30
9	0.41	0.33	0.27	0.39	0.32	0.27
10	0.38	0.30	0.25	0.36	0.29	0.24

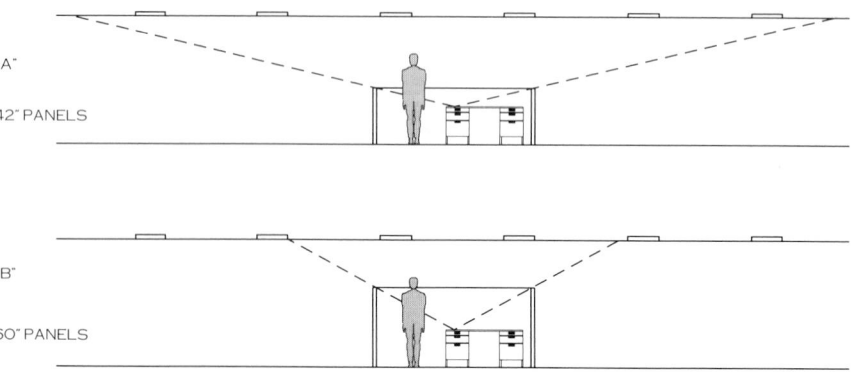

"A"

42" PANELS

"B"

60" PANELS

PANEL HEIGHT COMPARISON

Robert Prouse, IALD, IES; H.M. Brandston & Partners, Inc.; New York, New York

1 **LIGHTING DESIGN**

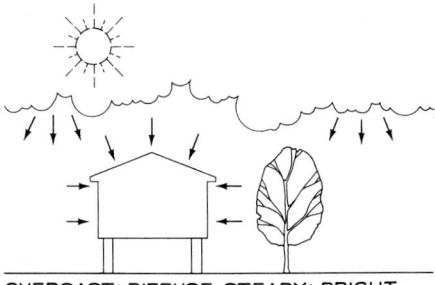

OVERCAST: DIFFUSE, STEADY; BRIGHT OR DARK

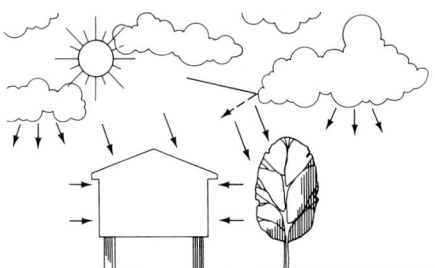

PARTLY CLOUDY: INTENSE/DIFFUSE; DIRECT BRIGHT

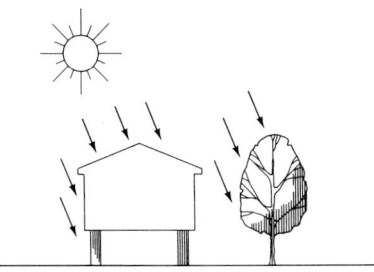

CLEAR: INTENSE, DIRECT BRIGHT, BLUE

DAYLIGHT

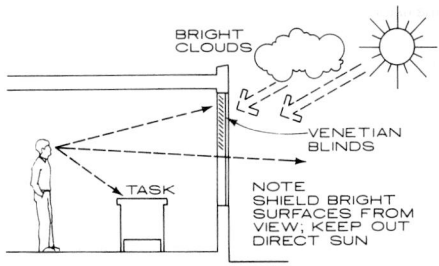

QUALITY DAYLIGHTING

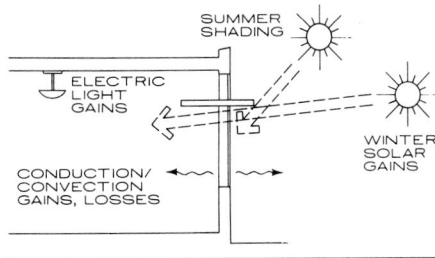

SOLAR GAIN OPTIMIZATION

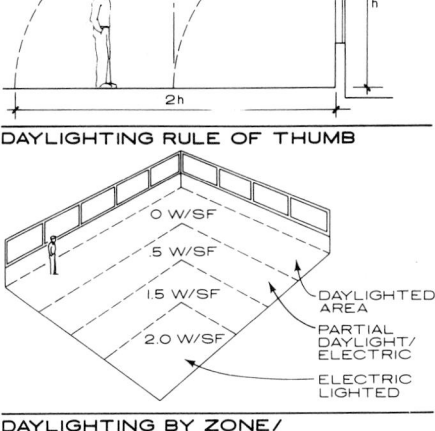

DAYLIGHTING RULE OF THUMB

DAYLIGHTING BY ZONE/ THREE-STEP SWITCHING

INTRODUCTION

Ample daylight is available throughout most of North America for lighting interior spaces during a large portion of the working day. This daylight may be used for critical visual tasks or for ambient lighting, to be supplemented with electric task lights. Daylight is thought by most to be psychologically desirable and there is much evidence that it is biologically beneficial. The variability of daylight from one moment to the next produces visual stimulus and provides a psychological contact with the outdoors which most people find extremely satisfying. Its use in place of, or in conjunction with, other lighting sources can conserve energy, but energy is conserved only if electric light sources are adequately controlled through on-off switching and/or dimming.

SOURCE

Daylight comes from the sun, bright and direct; it often comes filtered, diffused, and scattered by clouds, and it is reflected by the ground and other surfaces. The availability of daylight for a particular location can be determined from charts published by the Illuminating Engineering Society (IES), "Recommended Practice of Daylighting"; from the Solar Energy Research Institute (SERI), "Daylight Availability Data for Selected Cities in the U.S."; and from "Daylight in Architecture," by Benjamin Evans, McGraw-Hill, 1981.

It has been traditional, particularly in Europe, to consider the overcast sky as the minimum daylighting condition and to design buildings accordingly, but in North America the clear sky with sun and the partly cloudy sky are more common and generally more critical to building design for good daylighting.

Direct sun contains the maximum quantity of all wavelengths of radiation, including infrared which causes the sensation of heat. Smaller quantities of infrared as well as ultraviolet, which can cause material deterioration, come from the diffuse light of the sky and clouds.

QUALITY IN DAYLIGHTING

The principles of good lighting apply equally to daylight and electric light. Of principal concern in daylighting is the glare that may result when building occupants peripherally see bright clouds or sunlighted surfaces while trying to perform visual tasks.

Direct sun in interiors where critical visual tasks are performed is generally to be avoided. Thus, apertures that allow vision to the exterior must provide for shielding (or filtering) of exterior excessive brightnesses, or work stations must be oriented away from the apertures. Partly cloudy skies may contribute major quantities of daylight but also can be excessively bright and, therefore, should be shielded from view. Energy savings from switching or dimming of electric lights depend on daylight intensity and on the percentage of the year that daylight is available.

SOLAR-THERMAL GAINS/LOSSES

Daylight includes a significant amount of radiation that produces heat. This may be beneficial during the heating season, allowing for a reduction in other interior heating, or it may be detrimental during the cooling season, requiring additional air conditioning. Shading can be configured to reduce direct sun heating during warm weather while allowing some sun penetration in winter.

The quantity of radiant heat gain from the direct sun through glazing can be determined using the following formula:

Solar heat gain (Btu/hr) = insolation* x exposed area of glazing x transmissivity of glazing x hours of exposure

(* in Btu/hr/sq ft)

Glazing also allows for transmission of heat between outdoors and indoors via conductivity and convection. These heat losses or gains can be determined with the following formula:

Thermal gains/losses (Btu/hr) = exposed area of glazing x outdoor temperature x maintained indoor temperature x U factor of glazing x hours of exposure

ENERGY USE CONTROLS

Energy-efficient lighting design requires that electric lights remain off when daylighting levels are sufficient. The two principal types of lighting controls are selective switching (on/off) and dimming. These controls can eliminate or reduce work plane footcandles from electric lights by task, area, or zone. The simplest version of this is switching off the luminaires near the windows or at other points when and where the daylight is sufficient. Automatic dimming of luminaires can ensure that the total quantity of illumination on the work plane is maintained even as the daylight disappears or is reduced by clouds.

Switches can be controlled manually or by photosensors that switch luminaires off or on depending on the levels of daylight available; by timers that switch lights according to some preselected times (e.g., off at 8:00 am and on at 6:00 pm); by a sensor that responds to the presence of occupants.

Switching can be categorized as two, three, four, or five step. The two step is a simple on/off of all lamps on the circuit. The three-step mode requires a luminaire with two lamps or multiples of two. The three steps are all on, all off, or half on. Similar switching can be with luminaires with multiples of three or four lamps. Multilevel switching can maintain illumination levels more evenly and increase energy savings over two-step systems.

Most incandescent lamps can be dimmed, and lamps that require ballasts (e.g., fluorescent) can be dimmed if equipped with an appropriate ballast. Automatic switching and dimming controls combined with thoughtfully selected control zones allow electric lighting levels to reliably and economically respond to available daylight levels.

Energy-efficient design is a function of not only the energy used by electric lights, but also of the effect of heat given off by lights on cooling and heating systems. The approximate heat gain from an average electric lighting system can be calculated as follows:

Heat gain (Btu/hr) = footcandles/sq ft x area x .06 watt/footcandle x 3.41 Btu/hr/watt

Calculation of the electric energy used in the operation of a lighting system can be determined by the following equation:

Energy (watts/hr) = watts per luminaire* x number of luminaires x hours of operation

(* including watts for ballast)

Determining the amount of daylight that any interior space will receive during the course of the day or year is a complex process involving the determination of (1) the amount of daylight available on any aperture at appropriate times, (2) the amount of daylight that will reach interior areas, through calculations or by studies using scale models, (3) the results of step two modified by local weather data according to the percentage of cloud cover expected, and (4) the percentage of electric lighting that can be reduced or eliminated. (For scale model studies see "Daylight in Architecture," by Benjamin Evans, McGraw-Hill, 1981; see also "A Method for Predicting Energy Savings Attributed to Daylighting," by Claude L. Robbins and Kerry C. Hunter, Solar Energy Research Institute, 1982.)

Benjamin Evans, FAIA; Blacksburg, Virginia

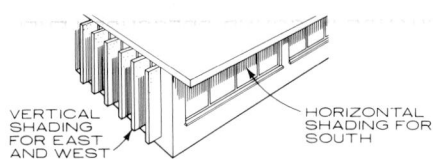

VERTICAL SHADING FOR EAST AND WEST   HORIZONTAL SHADING FOR SOUTH

SHADING DEVICES BY ORIENTATION

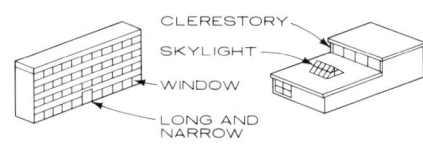

CLERESTORY
SKYLIGHT
WINDOW
LONG AND NARROW

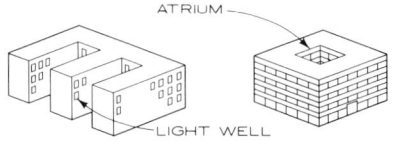

ATRIUM
LIGHT WELL

BUILDING CONFIGURATIONS

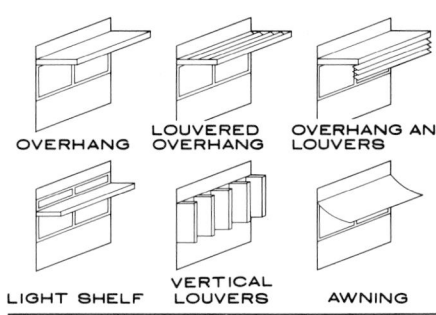

OVERHANG   LOUVERED OVERHANG   OVERHANG AND LOUVERS

LIGHT SHELF   VERTICAL LOUVERS   AWNING

SHADING DEVICES

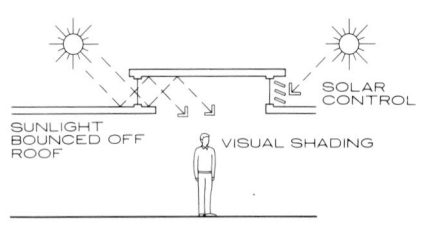

SUNLIGHT BOUNCED OFF ROOF   SOLAR CONTROL   VISUAL SHADING

CLERESTORY

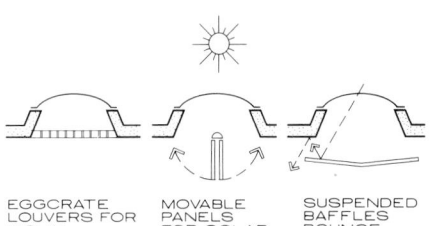

EGGCRATE LOUVERS FOR VISUAL SHIELDING   MOVABLE PANELS FOR SOLAR CONTROL AND NIGHT INSULATION   SUSPENDED BAFFLES BOUNCE LIGHT ONTO CEILING

SKYLIGHT CONTROLS

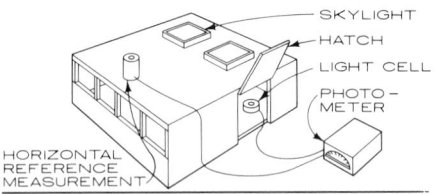

SKYLIGHT
HATCH
LIGHT CELL
PHOTO-METER
HORIZONTAL REFERENCE MEASUREMENT

DAYLIGHTING SCALE MODELS

ORIENTATION

Usable daylight is available to apertures oriented in any direction, although the amount will differ with each orientation. Of principal concern is the location of the sun relative to a building fenestration. Apertures to the north receive only sky-contributed illumination and so will require larger areas of glazing than orientations with exposure to direct sun. Advantages of north apertures include the resulting soft, diffuse north sky light and lack of need for sun controls. However, sky glare controls still need to be considered.

East and west facades require treatment to avoid the bright early and late direct sun. This is usually best accomplished with vertical louvers or a mix of vertical and horizontal (eggcrate) louvers. The location of the sun at any time relative to any aperture can be determined using the charts on the Solar Angles pages.

South facades provide the best opportunity for daylighting. Horizontal controls (e.g., overhangs, light shelves, louvers, venetian blinds) respond best to the sun in the southern sky quadrant. Apertures can be designed such that when the sun is high in the sky during the summer there is no sun penetration, but in the winter some low-altitude sun can be admitted.

CONFIGURATION

Building configuration is also important in daylighting. Multistory buildings will be most effective if they are long and narrow, allowing maximum vertical glazing per square foot of floor space. A rule of thumb is that daylighting (allowing electric lights to be turned off) can be achieved to a depth of about 2.5 times the height of the windows, or about 15–20 ft from the windows.

Buildings wrapped around courtyards, light wells, and atria can be effectively daylighted if properly designed. Open spaces must be large enough so as not to block light from the sky from reaching interior spaces. The effectiveness of such light wells can be improved by using high-reflecting, diffuse exterior finishes such as white paint, light-colored tile, or concrete. Direct sun illuminating these surfaces, however, may make them very bright when viewed from the building interior.

In single-story buildings the configuration is not so important, since roof apertures (e.g., skylights, clerestories) can be used to illuminate interior spaces, with or without peripheral windows.

ARCHITECTURAL CONTROLS

Shading/Reflecting Devices: Shading devices can be used to prevent penetration of direct sun and to shield view of the sky. Some shading devices also reflect daylight toward the interior (e.g., light shelves). Light shelves, however, are not very effective in reflecting diffuse light from the sky and are cost-effective only when necessary to shade direct sun. Venetian blinds are very effective for shading direct sun, and they can be adjusted for total blackout and raised and lowered as needed. Sun screen consisting of tiny horizontal louvers can also be effective in shading.

Glazing: Tinted glazing (glass or plastic) reduces the apparent brightness of exterior objects from the interior, but it also reduces the amount of transmitted daylight, which must be supplemented by electric light. Heat-reflecting and other variable spectrum transmission glazing is available that tends to reduce the transmission of heat more than light, but may produce only a small advantage (check manufacturer's data). Directional glass block is useful in directing incoming light toward the ceiling, providing a low brightness image from the interior. Translucent materials exposed to direct sun diffuse incoming light and can be excessively bright when viewed from the interior.

Benjamin Evans, FAIA; Blacksburg, Virginia

Finishes/Surfaces: All surfaces absorb and reflect light to varying degrees. Light-colored surfaces, particularly the ceiling, generally increase the light available on the interior. Floors are usually the least effective surface in reflecting light to the work plane. Avoid highly reflective or slick finishes on large areas.

Apertures: Windows, clerestories, and skylights can be used for effective daylighting, provided they are equipped with proper shading devices. Glazing located above the work plane (e.g., high windows) is more effective in producing work plane illumination than glazing close to the floor. Clerestories and skylights are valuable in single-story buildings. The effect of clerestories can be improved by using light-colored roof surfaces to reflect exterior daylight into the aperture, but direct sun penetration may still be a concern. Clerestories and skylights both may produce glare if the sky is not properly shielded from interior view.

Geometry: The geometry or shape of interior spaces is generally not significant in achieving good daylighting. Interior walls and partitions, of course, can prevent or reduce daylight penetration into other areas, but this can often be offset by using glass in the upper portions of interior partitions. The shape and slope of the ceiling can increase interior daylight by very small amounts, but usually not enough to be cost-effective.

Spectral Transmission: The amount of light radiation received on earth depends on the amount and content of atmosphere through which the light must pass. Therefore, the color of the daylight received in buildings varies by time of day and quantity of air pollution. Generally, daylight tends to be warm (i.e., more light from the red/orange end of the spectrum) early and late in the day and cooler (i.e., blue/violet) toward midday.

Coordination of daylighting with electric lighting requires selection of interior lamps that will produce colors compatible with that of daylight. Some fluorescent lamps, particularly the new triphosphorus lamps, and metal halides are similar to daylight in color.

Ultraviolet radiation is considered to cause damage to materials such as paintings, drapes, carpets, and furniture coverings. While regular glass eliminates much of the ultraviolet energy, additional protection can be achieved by using ultraviolet filters. This is especially useful in museums.

ANALYSIS

Physical Scale Models: Daylight in a scale model will behave exactly as in the full-scale building provided that all details are identical and the model is tested under an identical sky. Relatively simple models can be used to compare design alternatives (e.g., horizontal vs. vertical window) and to determine approximate footcandle levels. Certain details and surface finishes, however, are critical for meaningful model studies, and proper instruments must be used.

Computers: Several computer programs have been developed for analyzing building designs. Each program is designed to produce a particular sophistication of analysis using a limited variety of parameters.

For further discussion of these issues, see Benjamin Evans, "Daylight in Architecture" (McGraw-Hill, 1981) and Fuller Moore, "Concepts and Practice of Architectural Daylighting" (Van Nostrand Reinhold, 1985).

REFLECTION FACTORS OF TYPICAL SURFACES

SURFACE TYPE	PERCENT
Concrete	20–40
Red brick	10–25
Dark stone	10–30
Light stone	20–50
Grass	5–10
Dirt	10–20
Snow	70–80
White ceiling	75–80
Wood floor	20–30
Tile floor	15–20

TRANSMISSIVITY OF TYPICAL GLAZING ⅛" THICK

GLAZING MATERIAL	PERCENT
Clear glass	85–90
Tinted glass	30–60
Bronze glass	65–75
Reflective glass	8–50
Heat-absorbing glass	70–80
Glass block	60–80
Clear plastic	80–92
Translucent plastic	10–80

NOTES

Sound is produced by a vibrating object or surface. In order for sound to be transmitted or propagated, it requires an elastic medium. The most common medium for transmission is the air. Such sound is called "air-borne sound." However, sound can also be easily transmitted through common building materials and components such as steel, concrete, wood and metal framing, piping, and gypsum wallboard. This type of sound is called "structure-borne sound."

A-weighted decibel [dB(A)] is a standard single-number rating representing the overall sound energy of a given source. The A-weighting network in a sound level meter filters sound in a manner similar to the human ear by downgrading low frequencies.

DECIBEL SCALE

The decibel (dB) scale is a logarithmic scale based on 10 times the logarithm of a ratio of sound pressures. The decibel levels of two noise sources can not be added directly; instead use this simplified method:

difference between two sound levels, in dB	0–1	2–3	4–9	>10
add to the higher level	3	2	1	0

For example: 90 dB + 20 dB = 90 dB
60 dB + 60 dB = 63 dB

OCTAVE BAND

An octave band covers the range from one frequency (Hz) to twice that frequency, f to 2f.

SUBJECTIVE FACTORS: EFFECT OF CHANGE IN SOUND PRESSURE LEVEL

CHANGE IN SOUND PRESSURE LEVEL (+ OR −) (dB)	CHANGE IN APPARENT LOUDNESS
3	Barely perceptible
5	Clearly noticeable
10	Dramatic: Twice as loud (OR ½)
15	Dramatic: Three times as loud (OR ⅓)
20	Dramatic: Four times as loud (OR ¼)

FREQUENCY OF COMMON SOUNDS

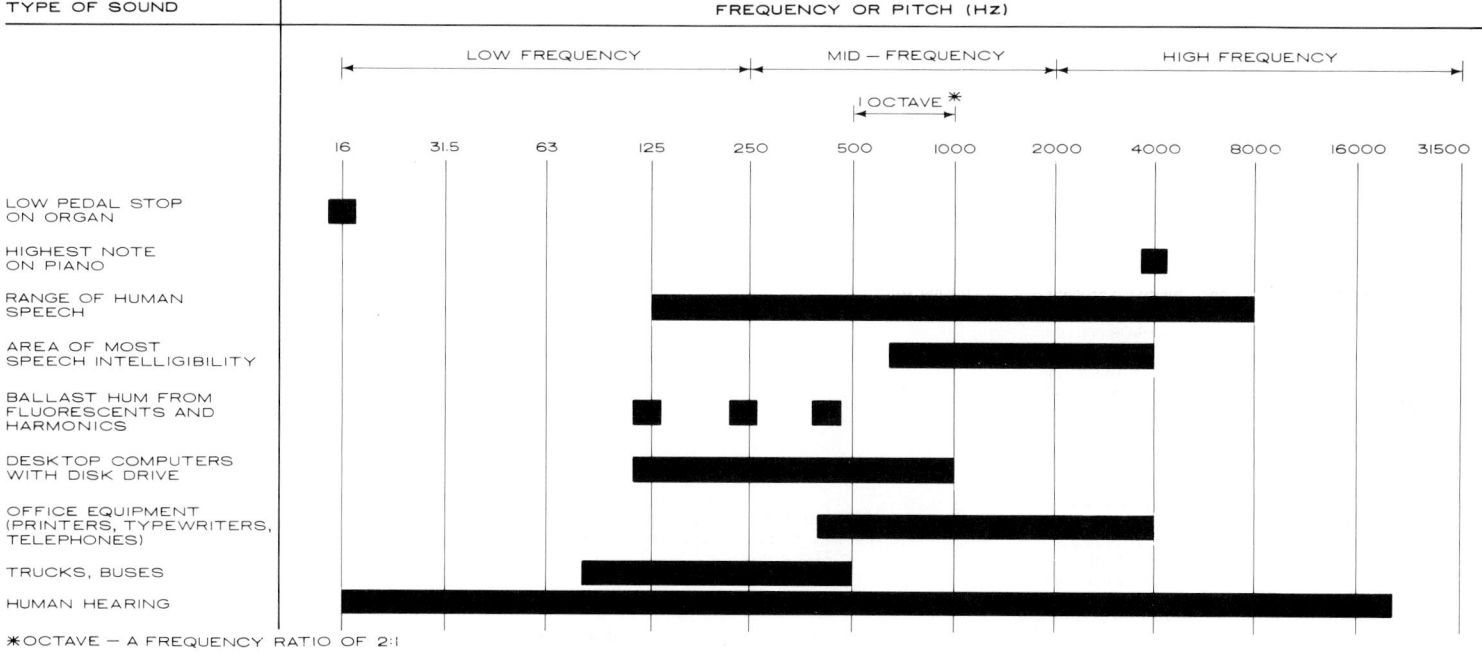

✳ OCTAVE — A FREQUENCY RATIO OF 2:1

RELATIONSHIP OF SOUND LEVEL AND SUBJECTIVE LOUDNESS

SOUND LEVEL (dBA)	SUBJECTIVE EVALUATIONS	ENVIRONMENT OUTDOOR	INDOOR	COMMENTS
140	Deafening	Near jet aircraft and artillery fire		
130	Threshold of pain			
120	Threshold of feeling	Elevated train	Hard rock band	
110		Jet flyover at 1000 ft	Inside propeller plane	
100	Very loud	Power mower, motorcycle at 25 ft, auto horn at 10 ft		Continuous exposure above here is likely to degrade the hearing of most people
90		Propeller plane flyover at 1000 ft, noisy urban street	Full symphony or band, food blender, noisy factory	
80	Moderately loud	Diesel truck at 40 mph at 50 ft	Inside auto at high speed, garbage disposal, dishwasher	
70	Loud		Face-to-face conversation, vacuum cleaner, electric typewriter	
60	Moderate	Air conditioning condenser at 15 ft, near freeway auto traffic	General office	Range of Speech
50	Quiet	Large transformer at 100 ft		
40		Birdcalls	Private office, soft radio music in apartment	
30	Very quiet	Quiet residential neighborhood	Bedroom, average residence without stereo	
20		Rustling leaves	Quiet theater, whisper	
10	Just audible			
0	Threshold of hearing			

Carl J. Rosenberg, AIA; Accentech Inc.; Cambridge, Massachusetts

NOTE

The material below outlines a design procedure, in abbreviated form, for the architect to use in analyzing a noise control problem and developing a solution or solutions. The three major elements of an acoustical circuit—source, path, and receiver—can each be quantified as shown here; hence there is no need for guesswork.

1. SELECT RECOMMENDED BACKGROUND NOISE DESIGN CRITERIA FOR TYPICAL OCCUPANCIES

TYPE OF SPACE	RECOMMENDED MAXIMUM BACKGROUND NOISE CRITERION CURVE*
Broadcast studios, concert halls	NC 15–25
Legitimate theaters, churches (no amplification)	NC 20–30
Large conference rooms, small auditoriums, orchestra rehearsal rooms, movie theaters, courtrooms, teleconferencing	NC 25–30
Bedrooms (residences, apartments, hotels, hospitals)	NC 25–35
Small conference rooms, classrooms	NC 30–35
Small private offices, libraries	NC 30–35
Hospitals, clinics	NC 30–45
Restaurants, stores, general offices	NC 35–40
Coliseums for sports only (with amplification)	NC 40
Computer rooms	NC 40–50

*Noise Criteria (NC) Curves—The noise criteria curves provide a convenient way of defining the ambient noise level in terms of octave band sound pressure levels. The NC curves consist of a family of curves relating the spectrum of a noise to the environment being specified. Higher noise levels are permitted at the lower frequencies, since the ear is less sensitive to noise in this frequency region. By using one NC number, the complete octave band frequency of an acceptable ambient noise can be specified.

2. IDENTIFY ALL NOISE SOURCES—INTERIOR AND EXTERIOR:
Note proximity of noise sensitive areas to all exterior and interior sources of intrusive background noise—whether speech (in corridors, outdoor play areas, etc.), music (auditorium, rehearsal and practice rooms, etc.), impact noise (pedestrian traffic, etc.), activity noise (recreation areas, workrooms, traffic, etc.), or mechanical equipment noise (rooftop, perimeter, basement, etc.). Measured sound pressure level data for all these sources are generally available or can be calculated.

3. CALCULATE REQUIRED NOISE REDUCTION (NR) =
SOURCE LEVEL—NC: To minimize NR requirements, locate noisy spaces next to spaces having a relatively high NC; when this is not possible, a heavier and more expensive construction assembly is required. See Figs. 1 and 2.

4. SELECT PARTITION TYPES (AND FLOOR/CEILING ASSEMBLIES) WHOSE TRANSMISSION LOSS (TL) CURVES EXCEED REQUIRED NR CURVES.

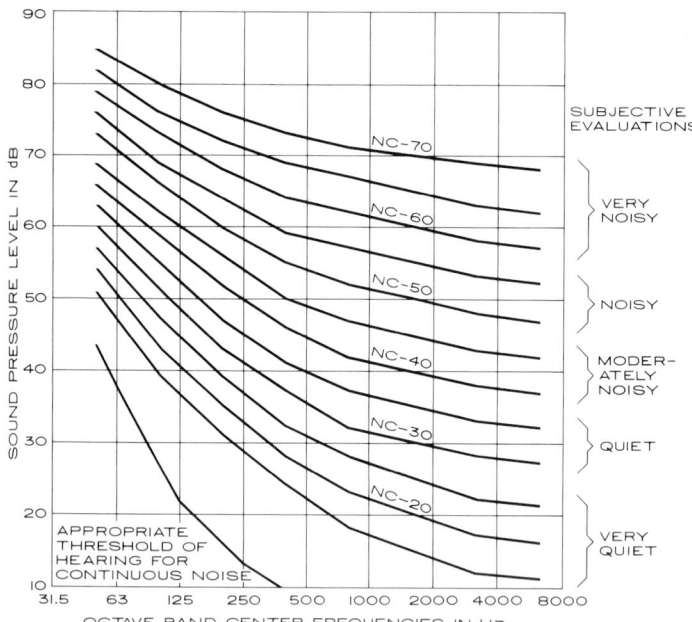

NOISE CRITERIA SOUND PRESSURE LEVEL TABLE*

NC CURVE	SOUND PRESSURE LEVEL, dB							
	63 Hz	125 Hz	250 Hz	500 Hz	1000 Hz	2000 Hz	4000 Hz	8000 Hz
NC-70	83	79	75	72	71	70	69	68
NC-65	80	75	71	68	66	64	63	62
NC-60	77	71	67	63	61	59	58	57
NC-55	74	67	62	58	56	54	53	52
NC-50	71	64	58	54	51	49	48	47
NC-45	67	60	54	49	46	44	43	42
NC-40	64	57	50	45	41	39	38	37
NC-35	60	52	45	40	36	34	33	32
NC-30	57	48	41	36	31	29	28	27
NC-25	54	44	37	31	27	24	22	21
NC-20	50	41	33	26	22	19	17	16
NC-15	47	36	29	22	17	14	12	11

*For convenience in using noise criteria data, the table lists the sound pressure levels (SPLs) in decibels for the NC curves from the above chart.

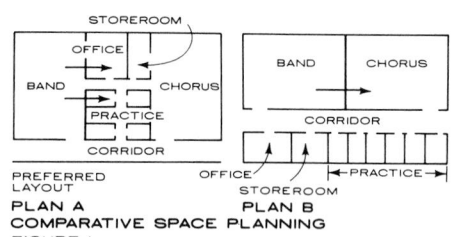

PREFERRED LAYOUT
PLAN A

PLAN B

COMPARATIVE SPACE PLANNING
FIGURE 1

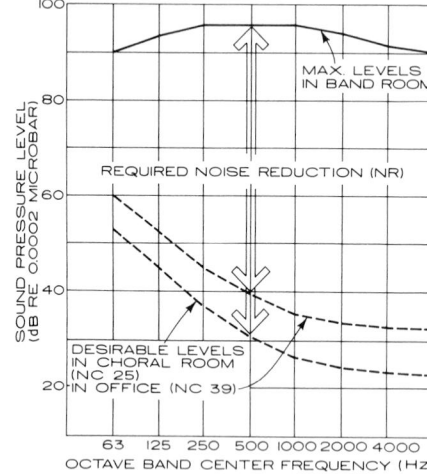

FIGURE 2

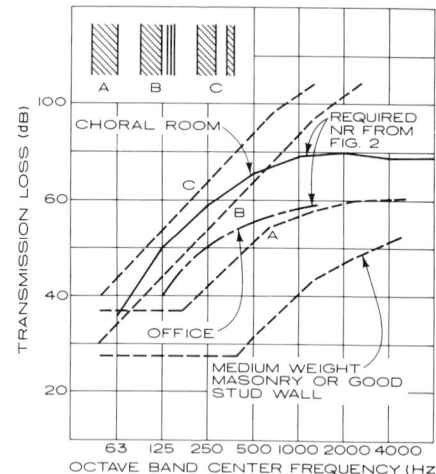

FIGURE 3

ACOUSTICAL DESIGN CHECKLIST

1. Build in good acoustical design—sound isolation and reverberation control—from the beginning. It is much cheaper to avoid noise problems in the initial design than to correct them later. Good acoustics is not cosmetics; it must be an integral part of the building design and is not a superficially applied treatment either before or after the fact.
2. Select materials with adequate mass and sound isolation design; choose the simplest construction that meets the NR criteria. Detail well and build well; min-

imize penetrations of walls, floors, and ceilings and make all holes and openings airtight to maintain acoustical integrity. Use materials wisely: Do not confuse lightweight, porous, sound-absorbing materials (for echo and reverberation control) with heavy, impervious, sound-isolating materials (for sound transmission control). Both may be needed, but both cannot be achieved with the same material.
3. Consider the mechanical and electrical equipment as an integral part of the acoustical design. Choose quiet-

rated fixtures and equipment and beware of the sound "leaks" that the ductwork, piping, and conduit provide. Use as needed vibration isolators and sound-absorbing duct lining together with flexible connections and low flow velocities in ducts and pipes.
4. Seek out qualified professional advice for all spaces with critical acoustical requirements. Do not rely solely on rules of thumb.

Carl J. Rosenberg, AIA; Accentech Inc.; Cambridge, Massachusetts

1 **ACOUSTICAL DESIGN**

INSTRUCTIONS FOR THE PROPER USE OF SOUND TRANSMISSION CLASS (STC) DATA

DESIGN CRITERIA FOR PARTITIONS

STC ratings are a measure of the effectiveness of a given partition construction in reducing airborne sound transmission, not the transmission of impact noise, low frequency noise sources (e.g., HVAC equipment and vehicular traffic), or amplified music. Because of the limited frequency range covered (125–4000 Hz), STC ratings are limited to evaluating the speech privacy potential of the various partitions and therefore are best used in the design of partitions separating adjacent offices, hospital patient rooms, classrooms (with little or no amplified speech or playback of recordings), dormitories, apartments, courtrooms, small conference rooms, etc. The single number STC ratings should not be relied on, solely, for the selection of partitions separating, say, movie theaters, large conference rooms, auditoriums, music practice rooms, computer and business machine rooms, and mechanical equipment rooms, from, say, private offices and apartments. Typically, a more extensive acoustical analysis is required for such adjacent locations; consult an acoustical consultant for additional information.

Note also that the STC ratings are based on test data measured in a laboratory installation of the given partitions, that is, under ideal construction conditions. Drywall manufacturers admit to a 5–15 point reduction in the lab ratings for the actual field performance, depending on the quality of detailing and workmanship. The importance of communication between the design team and the construction team cannot be overemphasized. The presence of flanking paths—interconnecting ductwork, nonairtight edge joints, inadequate door and window construction, untreated piping and conduit penetrations, and so on—in a completed building can result from improper design, improper construction, or both. The stated criteria assume no flanking paths.

Partitions with STC ratings within 1–2 points (1–2 dB) of the listed criteria would still be acceptable given the anticipated tolerances in test results. (Subjectively, the human ear would consider a 1–2 dB change as "just barely audible" at best, which is insignificant.)

The stated performance criteria assume acceptable background noise levels in the source and receiver rooms, that is, some masking of intrusive sounds without loss of speech intelligibility or other interference in listening conditions. The stated criteria are for buildings that fall into an average construction cost range and thus are not weighted toward any one type of construction or geographic region. The primary concern on which these criteria are based is the desire to provide adequate acoustical privacy for the building user. It is clear, however, that these acoustical criteria must be tempered by the designer's consideration of other design parameters—fire ratings, structural loads, energy conservation, and so on—which may downgrade (or even upgrade) the quality of the acoustical design.

For this reason the acoustical criteria listed here tend to be reasonably conservative, rather than lenient, given the many possible compromises.

DESIGN CRITERIA FOR FLOOR/CEILING ASSEMBLIES

1. AIRBORNE SOUND: STC ratings for floor/ceiling assemblies should be equal to or greater than those for the partitions.
2. STRUCTUREBORNE (IMPACT) SOUND: Impact Isolation Class (IIC) ratings should be equal to or greater than the STC ratings.

Both criteria must be met to ensure adequate acoustical privacy.

STC values for constructions built in the field range from 10 (practically no isolation; an open doorway) to 65 or 70 (such performance requires special constructions). Average constructions might provide noise reduction in the range of STC 30 to STC 60.

It is extremely difficult to measure the STC performance of a single wall or door in the field because of the many flanking paths and nonstandard conditions. Field performance is measured as Noise Isolation Class (NIC), which includes the contribution of all sound transfer between rooms.

Carl J. Rosenberg, AIA; Accentech Inc.; Cambridge, Massachusetts

SOUND ISOLATION CRITERIA

SOURCE ROOM OCCUPANCY	RECEIVER ROOM ADJACENT	SOUND ISOLATION REQUIREMENT (MINIMUM) FOR ALL PATHS BETWEEN SOURCE AND RECEIVER
Executive areas, doctors' suites, personnel offices, large conference rooms; confidential privacy requirements	Adjacent offices and related spaces	STC 50–55
Normal offices, regular conference rooms for group meetings; normal privacy requirements	Adjacent offices and similar activities	STC 45–50
Large general business offices, drafting areas, banking floors	Corridors, lobbies, data processing; similar activities	STC 40–45
Shop and laboratory offices in manufacturing laboratory or test areas; normal privacy	Adjacent offices; test areas, corridors	STC 40–45
Mechanical equipment rooms	Any spaces	STC 50–60+[1]
Multifamily dwellings	Neighbors (separate occupancy)	
(a) Bedrooms	Bedrooms	STC 48–55[2]
	Bathrooms	STC 52–58[2]
	Kitchens	STC 52–58[2]
	Living rooms	STC 50–57[2]
	Corridors	STC 52–58[2]
(b) Living rooms	Living rooms	STC 48–55[2]
	Bathrooms	STC 50–57[2]
	Kitchens	STC 48–50[2]
School buildings		
(a) Classrooms	Adjacent classrooms	STC 50
	Laboratories	STC 50
	Corridors	STC 45
(b) Large music or drama area	Adjacent music or drama area	STC 60[3]
(c) Music practice rooms	Music practice rooms	STC 55[3]
Interior occupied spaces	Exterior of building	STC 35–60[4]
Theaters, concert halls, lecture halls, radio and TV studios	Any and all adjacent	Use qualified acoustical consultants to assist in the design of construction details for these critical occupancies

NOTES

1. Use acoustical consultants for mechanical equipment rooms housing other than air handling equipment—e.g., chillers, pumps, compressors—and for heavy manufacturing areas employing equipment generating noise levels at or above OSHA allowable levels or generating high vibration levels.
2. Depends on nighttime, exterior background levels, and other factors that affect actual location of building. Grades I, II, and III are discussed in "Guide to Airborne, Impact and Structureborne Noise Control in Multifamily Dwellings," HUD TS-24, 1974.
3. The STC ratings shown are guidelines only. These situations require, typically, double layer construction with resilient connections between layers or, preferably, structurally independent "room-within-a-room" construction. The level of continuous background noise, such as that provided by the HVAC system or an electronic masking system, has a significant impact on the quality of construction selected and must be coordinated with the other design parameters.
4. Depends on the nature of the exterior background noise—its level, spectrum shape, and constancy—as well as the client's budget and on thermal considerations. Use qualified acoustical consultants for analysis of high noise outdoor environments such as airport areas, highways (with heavy truck traffic especially), and industrial facilities.

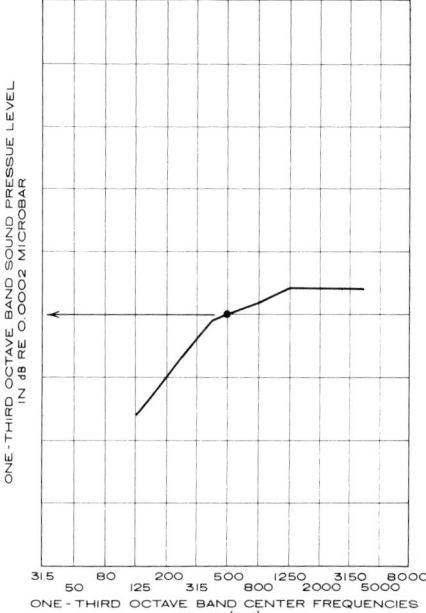

ONE-THIRD OCTAVE BAND SOUND PRESSURE LEVEL IN dB RE 0.0002 MICROBAR

31.5   80   200   315   1250   3150   8000
50   125   315   800   2000   5000

ONE-THIRD OCTAVE BAND CENTER FREQUENCIES IN Hz (cps)

STC RATING CURVE

DERIVATION AND USE OF THE STC CURVE

To determine the STC rating for a given construction, the STC curve shown in the adjacent figure is applied over the transmission loss (TL) curve for a laboratory test of that construction. Typical TL curves are shown on the next page, Fig. 2. The STC curve is then manipulated in accordance with prescribed rules to obtain the highest possible rating. The procedure states that the TL curve can not be less than the STC curve by more than 8 dB in any one-third octave band; nor can the TL curve be less than the STC curve by more than a total of 32 dB (average of 2 dB for each of 16 one-third octave band frequencies). Any values from the TL curve that are above the STC curve are of no benefit in the rating. The object is to move the STC curve up as high as possible, and to read the STC rating number from the point where the STC curve at 500 Hz crosses the TL curve.

The STC curve has three segments: the first segment, from 125 to 400 Hz, rises at the rate of 9 dB per octave (3 dB per one-third octave); the second segment, from 400 to 1250 Hz, rises at the rate of 3 dB per octave (1 dB per one-third octave); the third segment, from 1250 to 4000 Hz, is flat.

ACOUSTICAL DESIGN 1

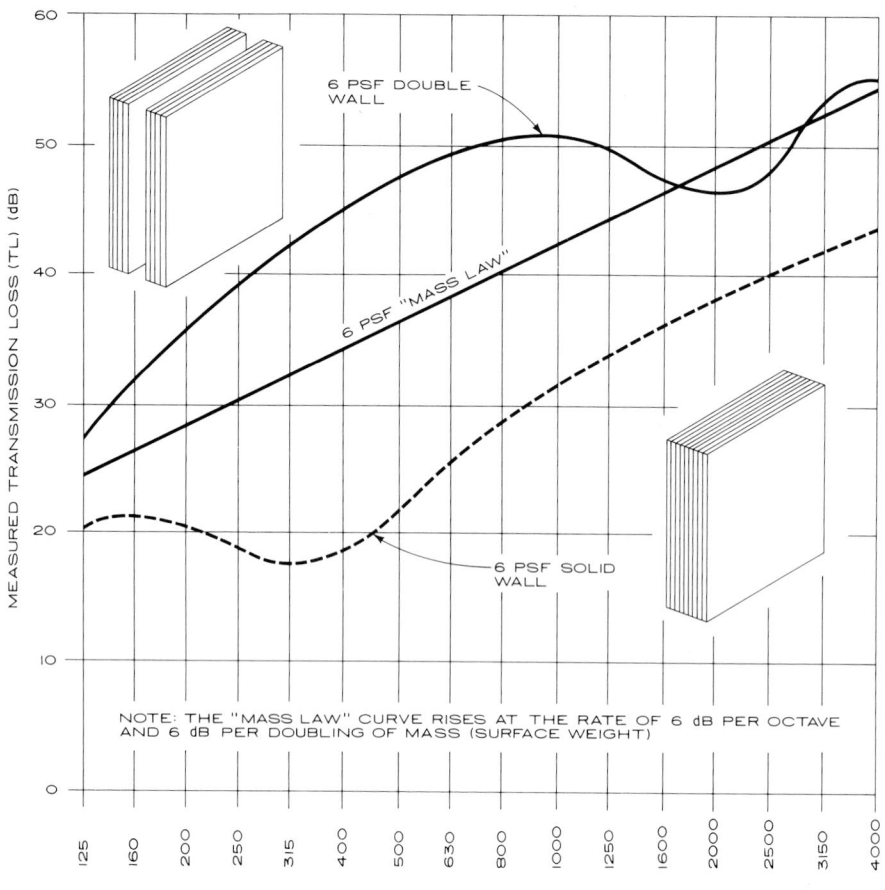

NOTE: THE "MASS LAW" CURVE RISES AT THE RATE OF 6 dB PER OCTAVE AND 6 dB PER DOUBLING OF MASS (SURFACE WEIGHT)

ONE-THIRD OCTAVE BAND CENTER FREQUENCY (Hz)

FIGURE 1

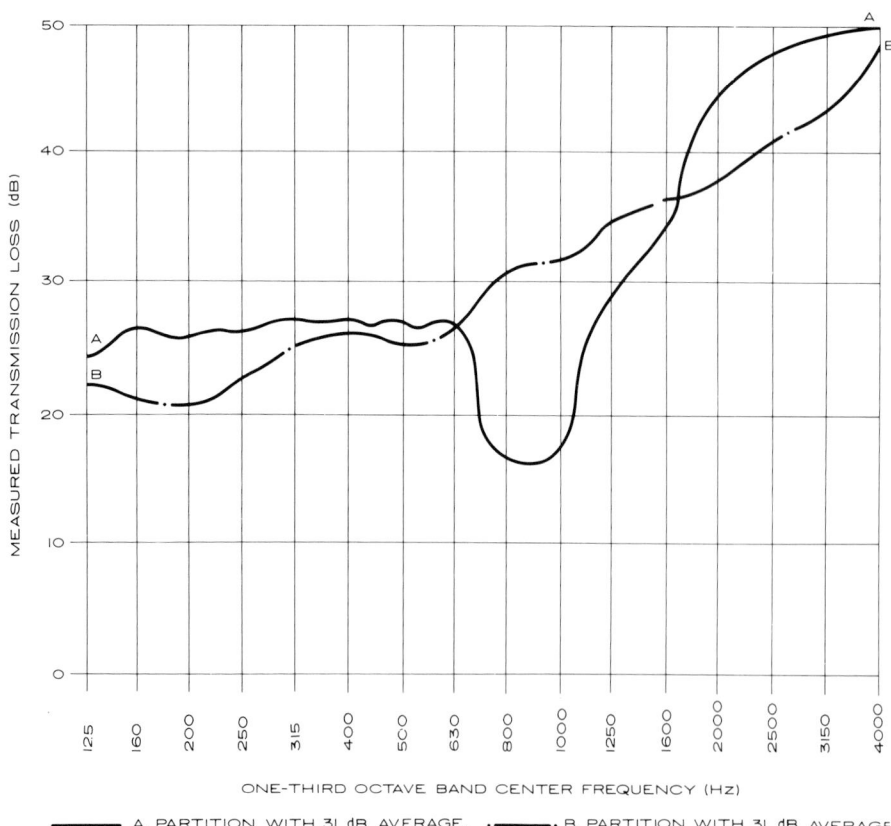

ONE-THIRD OCTAVE BAND CENTER FREQUENCY (Hz)

A. PARTITION WITH 31 dB AVERAGE, STC 22   B. PARTITION WITH 31 dB AVERAGE, STC 32

FIGURE 2

Carl J. Rosenberg, AIA; Accentech Inc.; Cambridge, Massachusetts

ACOUSTICAL DESIGN

NOTES AND DEFINITIONS

1. TRANSMISSION LOSS (TL): The measure of the properties of a material to block sound; specifically, the attenuation of air-borne sound transmitted through construction when tested in a laboratory according to ASTM E90. The measured test data, as opposed to calculations, provide the most accurate information on which to base the single-number sound transmission class descriptor. (See note 2 below.)

   Design of construction and materials for high transmission loss builds on three principles:

   a. MASS: Lightweight materials do not block sound. Sound transmission through walls, floors, and ceilings varies with the frequency of sound, the weight (or mass), the stiffness of the construction, and the cavity absorption. Theoretically, the transmission loss varies at the rate of 6 dB per doubling (or halving) of the surface weight of the construction.

   A single solid panel behaves less well than the mass law would predict, since the mass law assumes a homogeneous, infinitely resilient material/wall.

   b. SEPARATION: Improved TL performance without undue increase of mass can be achieved by separating materials. A true double wall of the same weight with separate unconnected wythes performs better than the mass law predicts. Note in Figure 1 the significant improvement in transmission loss with increased resiliency—approximately 15 dB ±, depending on the octave band. The transmission loss tends to increase about 5 dB for each doubling of the airspace between wythes (minimum effective space approximately 2 in.).

   Resilient attachment of surface skins to studs or structural surfaces provides similar benefit, as do separate wythes.

   c. ABSORPTION: Soft, resilient absorptive materials in the cavity between wythes, particularly for lightweight staggered stud construction, increase transmission loss significantly. Viscoelastic (somewhat resilient but not fully elastic) materials, such as certain insulation boards, dampen or restrict the vibration of rigid panels such as gypsum board and plywood and thus increase transmission loss appreciably. Installation details recommended by manufacturers should be followed.

2. SOUND TRANSMISSION CLASS (STC): A single-number rating system that compares the laboratory TL test curve for a particular material or assembly with a standard contour as described in ASTM E413. The contour is fitted to the test curve of the constructions, allowing for a certain maximum amount of deviation. See Figure 2 for an example that compares two constructions with identical average TL values but widely differing effectiveness (10 points) shown by the STC rating.

   The sound transmission loss at all frequencies, from 125 to 4000 Hz, is important (in varying degrees), so a single TL number or an average is meaningless. The shape of the entire TL test curve as related to the standard contour is important. Deep dips (as in curve A) are harmful, and yet the numerical average misses this dip; the sound transmission class contour properly evaluates its effect by downgrading the overall performance accordingly.

3. NOISE REDUCTION (NR): This depends on the properties of the rooms and is the actual difference in sound pressure level between two spaces being considered. It is what the ear hears and what is actually of interest to us and consists of the noise reduction of the walls, floors, and ceilings as well as the sound absorption present in the receiver room being considered.

   Noise reduction also depends on the relative size of the room in question. If the noise source is in a small room next to a large receiving room, like an office next to a gymnasium, then the noise reduction will be greater than the transmission loss performance alone of the wall, because the sound radiating from the common wall between office and gym has such a large space to be dissipated into. On the contrary, if the noise source is in a large room next to a small one, like the gym next to the office, then the noise reduction will be far less than the transmission loss, because the common wall, which is radiating sound, is such a large part of the surface of the smaller room. This adjustment, plus the contribution of the absorptive finishes in the receiving room, enter into our calculation of actual noise reduction.

IMPACT NOISE DESIGN CRITERIA

Floors are subject to impact or structure-borne sound transmission—noises such as footfalls, dropped objects, and scraping furniture. Parallel to development of laboratory Sound Transmission Class (STC) ratings for partition constructions is Impact Insulation Class (IIC), a single-number rating system to evaluate the effectiveness of floor construction to prevent impact sound transmission to spaces underneath the floor. The current IIC rating method replaces the previously used Impact Noise Rating (INR) method. To compare the ratings, note that IIC = INR + 51 ±. [The amount of deviation is relatively small (±2), but should still be noted.] For example, INR = +4 would be equivalent basically to IIC = 55.

SUMMARY OF IMPACT SOUND PRESSURE LEVELS MEASUREMENT (ASTM E492.77)

$$L_n = L_p - 10 \log (A_0/A_2)$$

where L_n = normal impact sound pressure

L_p = sound pressure level in the receiving room

A_2 = sound absorption of the receiving room

A_0 = reference absorption (108 sabins)

A standard tapping machine is used on a test floor specimen, which forms a horizontal separation between two rooms, one directly above the other. The transmitted impact sound is characterized by the one-third octave band spectrum of the average sound pressure level produced by the tapping machine in the receiving room located directly beneath the test floor specimen. This spectrum is then rated by comparing it with standardized curves to determine the matching IIC class (see accompanying figure).

Since the noise levels depend on the absorption of the receiving room, it is desirable to normalize the impact sound pressure levels to a reference absorption for purposes of comparing results obtained in receiving rooms that have different absorption.

To achieve adequate acoustical privacy in multifamily dwellings and other structures where both air-borne and structure-borne sound transmission are concerns, controlling impact sound transmission is as important as the control of air-borne sound transmission, or, expressed in its simplest terms: IIC ≥ STC for a given construction. Again, as with STC ratings, the higher the IIC number, the greater the sound control.

PRACTICAL CONSIDERATIONS

Because it is portable, the tapping machine cannot simulate the weight of a human walker. Therefore, the creak or boom of a timber floor caused by such footsteps cannot be reflected in the single-figure impact rating. The correlation between tapping machine tests in the laboratory and field performance of floors under typical conditions may vary greatly, depending on floor construction and the nature of the impact.

Often the greatest annoyance caused by footfall noise is generated by low-frequency sound energy beyond standardized test frequency range. Sometimes it is near or at the resonant frequency of the building structure.

To summarize, think resiliency. Wherever possible, use carpet with padding on floors of residential buildings. Use resilient, suspended ceilings with cavity insulation. For especially critical situations such as those involving pedestrian bridges or tunnels, use an acoustics consultant.

Other sources of impact noise are slamming of doors or drawers of cabinets. If possible, bureaus should not be placed directly against a wall. Door closers or stops can be added to cushion the impact of the energy so that it is not imparted directly into the structure. Common sense arrangements can help minimize problems in multi-family dwellings. Kitchen cabinets should not be placed on a common wall to a neighbor's bedroom, for example.

Carl J. Rosenberg, AIA; Accentech Inc.; Cambridge, Massachusetts

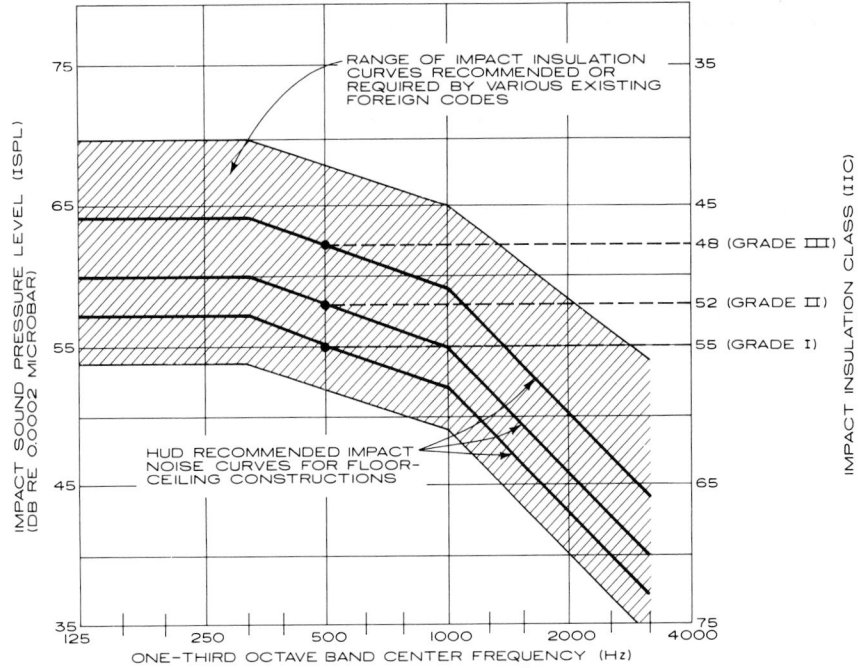

IMPACT NOISE INSULATION CRITERIA

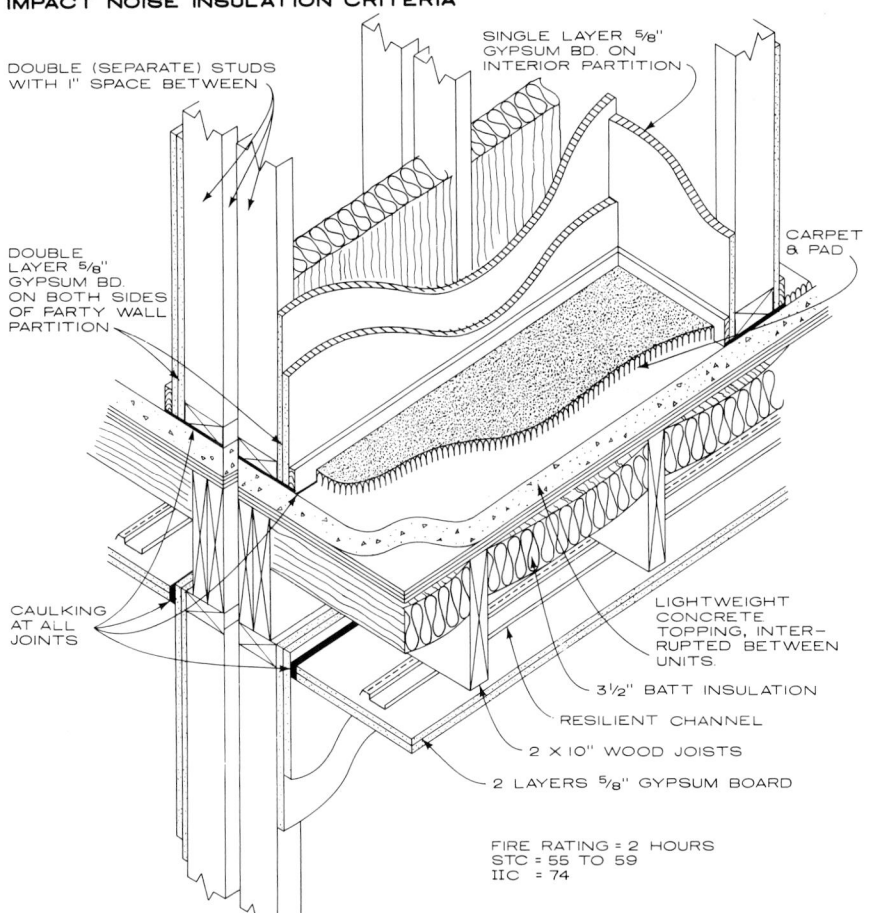

GOOD SOUND ISOLATION CONSTRUCTION

NOTE

Edge attachment and junctions of walls, partitions, floors, and ceilings can cause large differences in TL performance. The transverse waves set up in continuous, stiff, lightweight walls or floors can carry sound a long distance from the source to other parts of the structure with little attenuation. Curtain walls, thin concrete floors on bar joists, and wood framed structures are particularly subject to this weakness.

Properly designed discontinuities such as interrupted floor slab/toppings are helpful in reducing structural flanking.

A resilient (airtight) joint between exterior wall and partition or partition and floor can appreciably improve TL.

Continuous pipes, conduits, or ducts can act as transmission paths from room to room. Care must be taken to isolate such services from the structure.

USE OF ABSORPTION IN COMMON OCCUPANCIES

ROOM OCCUPANCY	CEILING TREATMENT	WALL TREATMENT	SPECIAL
Auditoriums, churches, theaters, concert halls, lecture halls, radio, recording and T.V. studios, speech and music rooms			●
Boardrooms, teleconferencing	●	●	
Classrooms	●	○	
Commercial kitchens	●		
Computer and business machine rooms	●		
Corridors and lobbies	○		
Gymnasiums, arenas, and recreational spaces	●	●	
Health care patient rooms	●		
Laboratories	●		
Libraries	●		
Mechanical equipment rooms			●
Meeting and conference rooms	●	○	
Open office plan	●	●	
Private offices	●		
Restaurants	●	○	
Schools and industrial shops, factories	●	●	
Stores and commercial shops	●		

● Strongly recommend
○ Advisable

NOTES

1. This table lists conservative rule-of-thumb recommendations for use of absorption.
2. Wall treatment is advisable in addition to ceiling treatment for the reduction of reflections, flutter, or echo. This treatment will further reduce noise and control reverberation.
3. Complex applications require an acoustical consultant.

DEFINITIONS

The percentage of sound energy absorbed by a material is the coefficient of absorption (x), which ranges from 0 to .99; the coefficient varies with frequency.

The total sound-absorbing units (sabins) provided by a given material are a function of its absorptive properties and surface area, as defined by this formula:

$$a = S\alpha$$

where a = sabins, units of sound absorption
S = surface area, in square feet or square meters
α = coefficient of absorption

The total sound absorption for a space is the sum of sabins for all surfaces in the room.

Reverberation time is directly proportional to the volume of a space and inversely proportional to the units of absorption:

$$R_t = \frac{KV}{a}$$

where R_t = reverberation time, in seconds
K = .161
V = volume, in cubic meters
a = total absorption, m²-sabins

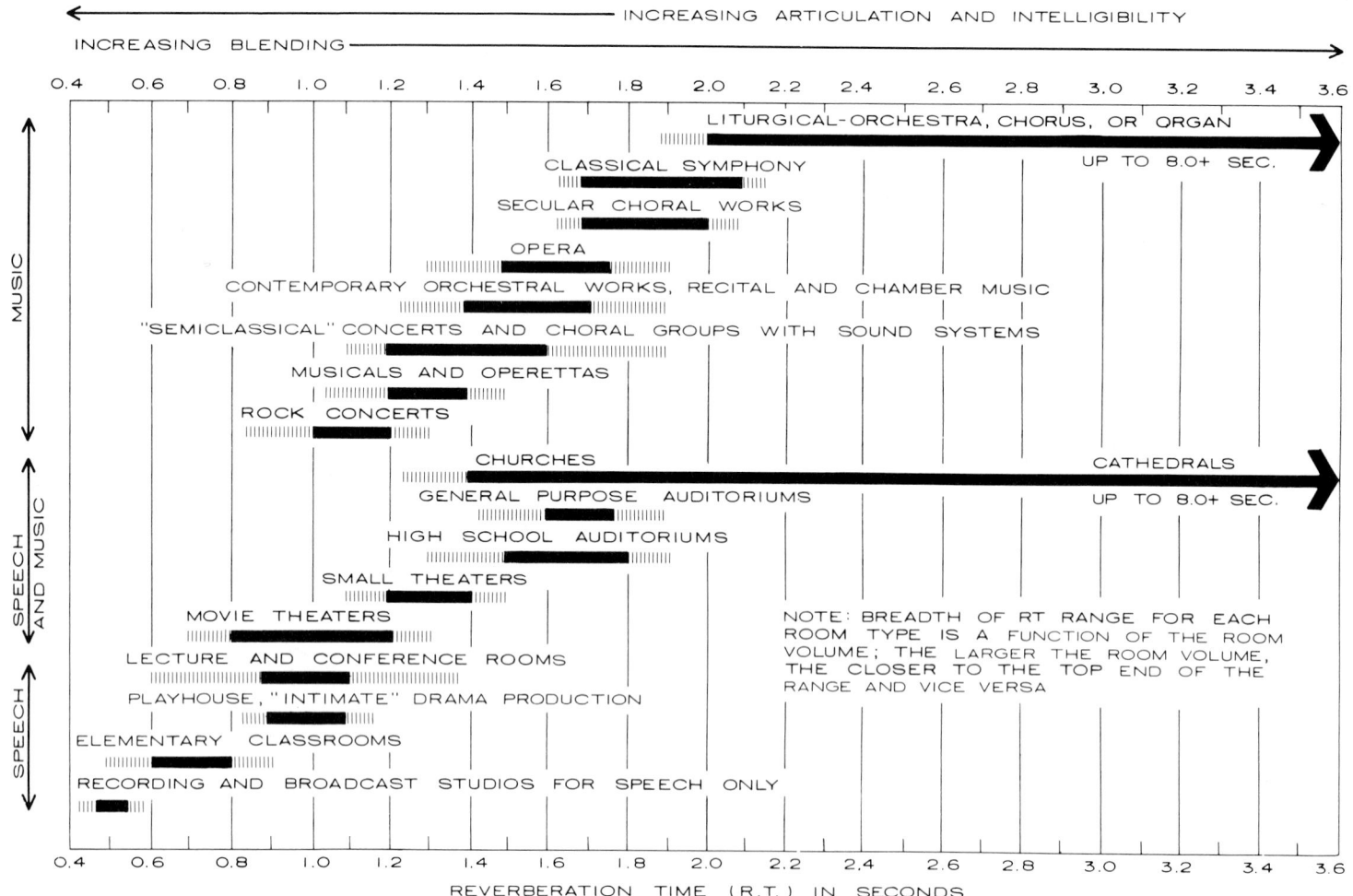

OPTIMUM REVERBERATION TIMES AT MID-FREQUENCIES (500/1000 Hz) FOR AUDITORIUMS AND SIMILAR FACILITIES

Carl J. Rosenberg, AIA; Accentech Inc.; Cambridge, Massachusetts

1   **ACOUSTICAL DESIGN**

THERMAL COMFORT

Human thermal comfort is determined by the body's ability to dissipate the heat and moisture that are produced continuously by metabolic action. The rate of heat production varies with the size, age, sex, and degree of activity of the individuals whose comfort is under consideration. For men of average size, seated and doing light work, the metabolic rate is about 450 Btu/hr; for women under similar circumstances the comparable rate is about 385 Btu/hr. For a 155 lb man seated and doing moderate to heavy work, the rate ranges from 650 to 800 Btu/hr; standing and walking about while doing moderately heavy work will raise the rate to 1000 Btu/hr while the hardest sustained work will result in a metabolic rate of 2000 to 2400 Btu/hr. For an office with the usual complement of men and women, an average metabolic rate will range from 400 to 450 Btu/hr per person.

Thermal comfort is attained when the environment surrounding the individual can remove the bodily heat and moisture at the rate at which they are being produced. The removal, accomplished by convection, evaporation, and radiation, is regulated by the dry bulb temperature, the vapor pressure, and rate of movement of the air and the mean radiant temperature (MRT) of the surrounding surfaces. MRT is defined by ASHRAE as the temperature of an imaginary black enclosure in which the individual experiences the same rate of radiant heat exchange as in the actual environment. (See 1985 ASHRAE Handbook of Fundamentals, Chapter 8, for more information on MRT and human comfort.)

Heat and moisture removal are also strongly affected by the nature and amount of clothing being worn and by its insulating value. This quality can be evaluated in terms of a thermal resistance unit designated by clo, where 1 clo = 0.88°F/(Btu/hr · sq ft). Typical masculine office attire, complete with warm jacket and light trousers, has an insulating value of 1.12 clo while a woman's office dress is rated at 0.73 clo. Values for other combinations are given in the ASHRAE reference cited above, page 8.6, Table 1-D. Uncomfortably low ambient air temperatures can be made tolerable by putting on more and heavier clothing, thus increasing the clo value; the converse, unfortunately, is not true.

The properties of atmospheric air-water vapor mixtures in the temperature range normally experienced by the human body can be shown effectively on psychrometric charts, which can take many different forms. The most familiar is that put forth by Willis H. Carrier, who is generally regarded as the originator of the air-conditioning industry in the U.S.A. On the Carrier-type chart, shown in modified form in Fig. 1, the humidity ratio of moist air, in pounds or grains (1 lb = 7000 grains) of water vapor per pound of dry air, is plotted against the dry bulb temperature of the air. Significant psychrometric data are given in the table at temperature intervals of 5°F from 50 to 90°F.

The relative humidity of moist air is the ratio, expressed as a percentage, of the amount of water vapor actually present in a given quantity of that air to the amount that the same quantity of air could contain if it were completely saturated at the same temperature and pressure. The uppermost curved line on the chart, called the saturation line, denotes 100% relative humidity. The wet bulb temperature, measured by a thermometer with a water wetted sensor over which the air-vapor mixture is flowing rapidly (800 to 900 fpm) is used in combination with the dry bulb temperature to find the % RH at conditions other than saturation. For example, at 75°F dry bulb and 60°F wet bulb the relative humidity is seen to be 40%.

The humidity ratio at this condition is 53 grains/lb of dry air while the dew point temperature, found by following the horizontal line of constant humidity ratio to its intersection with the saturation line, is 50°F.

The relatively restricted range of conditions within which most lightly clothed sedentary adults in the U.S.A. will experience thermal comfort is shown by the cross-hatched area on Fig. 1. Known as the ASHRAE comfort zone (also called "comfort envelope"), this area on the psychrometric chart represents the combinations of dry bulb temperature and relative humidity, which, when combined with an air movement of 45 fpm or less, will meet the thermal needs of most adults. For this chart, MRT = dry bulb temperature.

The effective temperature lines shown on Fig. 1 represent combinations of dry bulb temperature and relative humidity that will produce the same rate of heat and moisture dissipation by radiation, convection, and evaporation as an individual would experience in a black enclosure at the specified temperature and 50% relative humidity. As the % RH rises, the dry bulb temperature must be slightly reduced to produce the same feeling of comfort; as the % RH falls toward the 10 to 20% level experienced in desert climates, the dry bulb temperature may rise slightly without inducing discomfort.

An indoor temperature between 70°F and 80°F will be tolerable for most lightly clothed adults. Additional clothing (higher clo values) may help offset the discomfort of most building occupants at the lower end of the comfort range regardless of the % RH, but extremities will be uncomfortably cold.

Thermal comfort is directly related to the manner in which heat flows through or about building materials, whether by means of convection, radiation, or conduction.

Convection takes place when a fluid, such as gas, or a liquid is heated and moved from one place to another. When warm air in a room rises and forces the cooler air down, convection is taking place.

Radiation is the transfer of heat by electromagnetic waves from a warmer surface to a cooler one. A person sitting in the sun by a window absorbs radiant heat.

Conduction is heat transfer between adjacent molecules within a single or two separate bodies in direct contact. This occurs when a person touches a sun-warmed window or when the handle of a poker gets warm after a few minutes when the other end is placed in a fire.

The upper range of the comfort zone for summer operation of public buildings will be tolerable for most lightly clothed adults until the relative humidity rises above 60 to 65%. At that condition, discomfort will be experienced by many building occupants because of their inability to dissipate metabolic moisture. Increases in air velocity are beneficial under these conditions, but velocities above about 70 fpm will generally result in unpleasant working conditions because of drafts, blowing papers, and so on.

Figure 2 shows another version of the psychrometric chart in which wet bulb temperatures are plotted against dry bulb temperatures, with straight lines of constant % RH running upward from lower left to upper right. The effect of air velocity and clothing thermal resistance (expressed as clo units) is shown by the curved lines near the center of each diagram.

For these conditions, in which the mean radiant temperature equals the dry bulb temperature, relative humidity has only a small effect. As the activity level of the room occupants is lowered, reducing the metabolic rate, the comfortable air temperature range moves upward; as the activity level is increased, cooler air is required.

The effects of radiant energy transfer between individuals and the surfaces surrounding them can have significant influence on sensations of comfort or discomfort. An increase of 1°F in MRT is approximately equivalent to a 1.5°F increase in ambient air temperature. The use of radiant heating from moderately warm surfaces can help to offset the discomfort caused by air temperatures that are significantly below the ASHRAE comfort zone. Conversely, discomfort can be caused by large heated areas, such as sun warmed windows. An excessively high MRT can require a significant reduction in air temperature to create comfort. For an individual exposed to direct sunshine entering through an unshaded window, discomfort is almost certain to result.

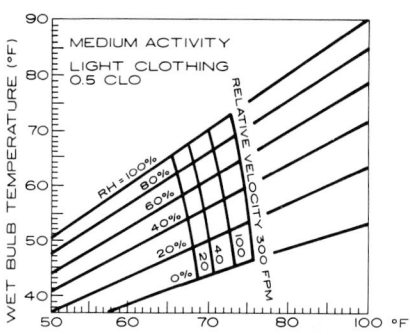

AIR TEMPERATURE = MEAN RADIANT TEMPERATURE

FIGURE 2

NOTE: Modified comfort chart for men, medium activity = 750 Btu/hr, thermal resistance of "light-clothing" = 0.5 clo.

MODIFIED COMFORT CHART

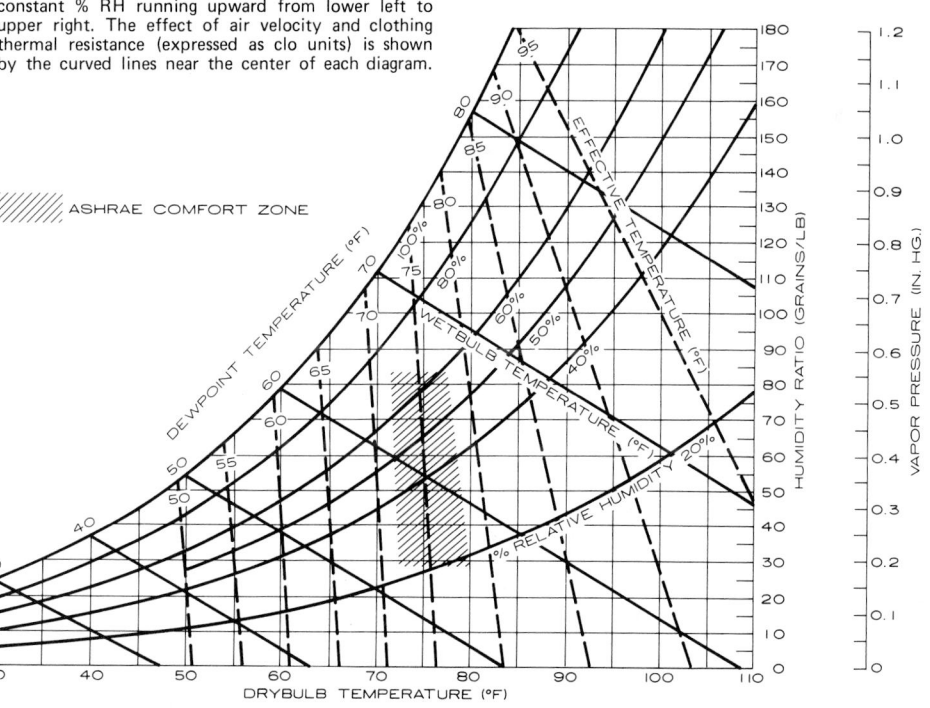

FIGURE 1

PSYCHROMETRIC CHART

John I. Yellott, P.E.; College of Architecture, Arizona State University; Tempe, Arizona

INTRODUCTION

Buildings must meet specific functional criteria, and the design evolves from these functions. Buildings must permit efficient job performance, meet the needs of the user, and protect the user from safety hazards and criminal acts.

Crimes such as vandalism, terrorism, burglary, shoplifting, employee theft, assault, and espionage endanger lives and threaten our built environment. Nonetheless, security is a design consideration that is often inadequately addressed and poorly funded. The most efficient time and least expensive way to provide security is in the design process. Thus, as crime increases, architects are being called on to address security and crime concerns in their building designs, challenging them to

1. Determine security requirements
2. Know security technology
3. Understand the architectural implications of security needs

This section on security design will demonstrate the process of designing security into the architecture of a building.

Security design is more than bars on windows, a security guard in a booth, a camera, or a wall. Security involves the systematic integration of design, technology, and operation for the protection of three critical assets: people, information, and property (PIP). Protection of these assets is a concern in all building types and should be considered throughout the design and construction process—from programming, schematic design, design development, construction documents, bidding, through construction.

Designing without security in mind can lead to expensive retrofitting with security equipment and a need for more security personnel. If not properly planned for, security equipment can distort key design elements and building function. Additional personnel costs for security are expensive. But most important, overlooking security can lead to successful claims against owners, architects, and building managers.

DEFINING THE ROLES

Role of the client
1. Define precisely the vulnerabilities and threats to people, information, and property.
2. Define the importance of each asset worth protecting.
3. Assess and describe threats to these assets
4. Develop a pragmatic description of protection requirements in light of the perceived threats and the value of the assets

Role of the security manager/consultant
1. Help the client describe the level of protection required in each area
2. Help the client identify security needs and vulnerabilities to crime
3. Help plan access control, security zoning, and surveillance systems
4. Define the basic security concepts, operational procedures, and security manpower allocation
5. Define the types, locations, and tasks of security personnel

Role of the architect
1. Incorporate the security program into effective space and circulation planning
2. Provide clear sightlines for surveillance and planned access controls at entrances and exits
3. Provide appropriate locations for sensitive or restricted areas
4. Accommodate the placement of security personnel in the design
5. Use design elements that will coordinate security technology and personnel requirements

DESIGNING FOR SECURITY IS A PROCESS

To create a security master plan that can be incorporated into the architecture a sequence of evaluations should be conducted before the security system design begins. These steps are outlined below:

ASSET DEFINITION

What are the vital assets—people, information, property? What are the secondary assets? What level of protection is needed for each asset?

THREAT DEFINITION

What are the threats to each asset—vandalism, espionage, burglary, theft, assault, sabotage, robbery? How would threats be accomplished? When? Why? By whom? Where? What kind of attack or approach might be used? Are the threats highly probable, possible, or unlikely?

VULNERABILITY ANALYSIS

Are the threats real or perceived? Compare the cost of protecting each asset with the potential loss. Compare the cost and effectiveness of different security measures.

SECURITY MEASURES

A security system usually is composed of technical systems, security personnel, and physical barriers:

1. Mechanical measures—electronic security needs, access control, surveillance devices, technical solutions.
2. Organizational features—policies and procedures of staff, such as information flow and types (armed or unarmed), numbers, and deployment of security personnel.
3. Natural features—physical barriers, circulation patterns, building materials, fenestration, and other physical elements.

THE PURPOSE OF SECURITY

A comprehensive security system should detect a threat or intrusion, delay the intrusion with barriers, and notify security personnel of the threat in sufficient time for them to respond and neutralize it.

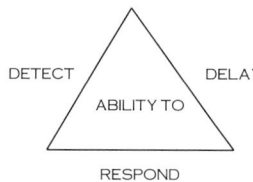

For a security design to be effective, it must allow for each of these actions: detection, delay, and response. Detection and delay are worthless is there is no one to respond to an emergency or threat. If there are no barriers, a burglar can commit a crime and leave before a response team arrives. Barriers with no detection give no advance warning of a problem to security personnel or police.

DETECTION

Before a problem can be delayed or responded to, it must be detected or perceived. Detection options include fixed guard posts, closed-circuit television (CCTV), and intrusion detection equipment.

DELAY

A series of barriers must be established to delay the intruder. These can be walls, fences, vehicle barriers, blocked access, razor ribbon, or any device or design measure that creates time and distance between a threat and the target.

RESPONSE

The ability to respond is made possible by the devices in the "detection" phase, and the time for apprehension is created in the "delay" phase. Official response is usually provided by law enforcement or private security forces. Unofficial sources of response include building occupants, doormen, neighborhood watch patrols, etc.

WHAT IS BEING PROTECTED

A threat and vulnerability analysis identifies the assets to be protected, including people, information, and property.

PEOPLE

Employees, visitors, patrons, service providers, and executive VIPs must be protected from assault, kidnapping, murder, robbery, and terrorism. Failure to protect invited and uninvited guests on a property can be grounds for premises liability litigation.

INFORMATION

Computer records, financial information, proprietary secrets, personnel records, and accounting systems are the backbone of any business. Protection of such information is a critical part of a security plan. Knowing who has the information, where it is, when it is accessible, and how it could be compromised are critical issues for design.

PROPERTY

Property includes cars on a parking lot, airplanes in a hangar, or office supplies in a closet. A threat analysis will help identify which property assets need protection.

CRIME PREVENTION THROUGH ENVIRONMENTAL DESIGN—"3D"

The crime prevention through environmental design approach (CPTED) to security design recognizes a building environment's intended use of space. This practice differs from the traditional approach to crime prevention, which focuses on denying access to a crime target with barrier techniques such as locks, alarms, fences, and gates. CPTED takes advantage of opportunities for natural access control, surveillance, and territorial reinforcement. Sometimes natural and normal uses of the environment can meet the same security goals as physical and technical protection methods.

Natural access control strategies deny access to crime targets and create a perception of risk to offenders. Surveillance strategies primarily keep intruders under observation. Territorial reinforcement strategies create or extend the building's sphere of influence. Occupants develop a sense of proprietorship that offenders perceive as protective. Mechanical, natural, and organizational means are used to achieve CPTED-style security.

Environmental security design or CPTED is based on three functions of human space—the 3Ds:

1. Designation—What is the space used for?
2. Definition—How is the space defined? How do social, cultural, legal, and psychological considerations affect this definition?
3. Design—How does the space support its intended use?

CPTED strategies are implemented by

1. Mechanical methods—technical products, target hardening techniques, locks, alarms, CCTV, gadgets
2. Natural methods—architectural design and layout, site planning, landscaping, signage, circulation control
3. Organizational methods—manpower, police, security guards, receptionists, doormen, and business block watches

The CPTED security design process is applied on three levels—site security design, building perimeter protection, and inner building space or point protection.

SITE SECURITY DESIGN

Goal: To protect people, information, and property

Threats: How will attacks be initiated?

Strategies for protection:

1. Access control strategies control entry to the site.
   a. Mechanical solutions, e.g., electronic or microwave sensors detect intrusions.
   b. Natural solutions, e.g., walls, fences, canals, thorn bushes, delay intruders by creating barriers.
   c. Organizational solutions, e.g., patrol roads, guard houses, watch towers, make it possible to respond.
2. Surveillance strategies watch for intruders.
   a. Mechanical solutions, e.g., CCTV, exterior site lighting, use technology to assist watching.
   b. Natural solutions, e.g., window placement, location of entrances, walkways, reduce blind spots and permit building users to observe pedestrian movement.
   c. Organizational solutions use assigned or remote observers, e.g., police, security guards, or building users, to detect, delay, and respond to intruders. For example, the building may be designed to focus outward to allow observation of parking lots or playgrounds.
3. Territorial reinforcement strategies use the building design and the ability of occupants to challenge intruders.
   a. Mechanical solutions define boundaries and territory with perimeter detection systems.
   b. Natural solutions create boundaries with building forms or landscaping to delineate public, semipublic, semiprivate, and private spaces.
   c. Organizational solutions provide the building occupants with ways to distinguish outsiders or criminals from legitimate users of the site. Vehicle stickers, decals, ID cards, access control badges, or personnel verification are possible means of accomplishing this.

Randall Atlas, Ph. D., AIA, CPP; Atlas Safety and Security Design, Inc.; Miami, Florida

BUILDING PERIMETER

Goal: To protect the building perimeter from intruders

Threats: What threats are there from criminals, explosions, terrorism, burglary?

Strategies for protection:

1. Access control strategies control ingress and egress into the building.
   a. Mechanical solutions, e.g., locking systems, access control systems, strengthen vulnerable points such as doors, windows, utility openings, and basements.
   b. Natural solutions clearly define the entrance, allow for careful placement of fire exits, and offer control and surveillance of those doors. Glazing and wall materials should be consistent with the threat level. Entry may be controlled with sallyports or security vestibules.
   c. Organizational solutions place a receptionist, guard station, or doorman to permit screening.
2. Surveillance strategies allow building points to be monitored by on-site or remote observers.
   a. Mechanical solutions include CCTV.
   b. Natural solutions use design to avoid blind spots and circulation conflicts.
   c. Organizational solutions allow security personnel and/or building users to observe unusual activity.
3. Territorial reinforcement strategies permit security staff or building users to challenge intruders or users who violate the building's intended use.

VOLUMETRIC SPACE PROTECTION OR POINT PROTECTION

Goal: To protect a specific interior space, item, person, or object

Threats: Are threats from within, such as espionage; or from outside, such as fire, explosion, terrorism, or burglary?

Strategies for protection:

1. Access control strategies delay entrance to areas defined as off limits. Security layering protects by allowing open, limited, or restricted movement in a facility.
2. Surveillance strategies.
3. Territorial strategies.

CHECKLIST FOR SECURITY DESIGN

The following checklist may be useful in designing security environments.

1. Site planning
   - Access
   - Service delivery
   - Circulation patterns on site
   - Exterior lighting quality and quantity
   - Perimeter fencing
2. Main lobby
   - Visitor control
   - Location of fire alarms
   - Architectural barriers—turnstiles, glass enclosures, reception areas, etc.

- Retail tenant security requirements
- Unobtrusive CCTV surveillance
- Access to adjacent emergency stairwells
- After-hours access control
- Alarm monitoring of perimeter doors
- Lighting
3. Parking garage
   - Valet or self-parking
   - Public, private, or mixed use
   - Segregation of parking uses
   - Parking security for executives
   - Surveillance, emergency signaling, and intercom systems and guard tours
   - Type, intensity, and number of lighting fixtures
4. Loading docks
   - Traffic flow expected
   - Relationship to street traffic or pedestrian walkways
   - Storage of delivered items
   - Distribution of deliveries in the building
   - CCTV surveillance and intercom systems
   - Remote door release controls and monitoring
5. Emergency stairwells
   - Restricted access for interior traffic
   - Communication provisions
   - Emergency exit alarms on doors
   - Alarm monitoring
   - Control of access
6. Miscellaneous
   - Elevator bank access control
   - Communication provisions in elevator cabs and vestibules on individual floors
   - Public washroom security
   - Scheduling and control of deliveries, including mail
   - Security in mechanical equipment areas
   - Door hardware for telephone, electrical, and storage closets
   - Security for fuel and water storage areas and emergency generator
   - Roof access
   - Access to tunnel or skyway connections to other nearby buildings
7. Building tenant security
   - Control of access to elevator cars and individual floors
   - Security measures for individual departments and operations
   - Executive floor security
   - Receptionist workstation protection
   - Access to boardroom or executive conference rooms
   - Freight elevator lobbies
   - Console room design
   - Secured storage areas, vaults, and safes within tenant spaces
   - Space for accessible storage of security-related equipment
   - HVAC and power requirements for security operations
8. Major systems to consider
   - Fire and life safety
   - Public address

- CCTV surveillance
- Access control
- Alarm monitoring
- Radio communication
- Emergency signaling
- Intercom
- Guard force
- Door control
- Uninterrupted power supply

DESIGN GUIDELINES

The following design guidelines are provided to assist in effective security system planning.

1. Isolate unsafe activities.
2. Design the exterior of a building to prevent access.
3. Minimize the number of exterior openings at or below grade level.
4. Protect all building openings against entry or attack.
5. Provide for expansion of security control systems.
6. Design walls to resist penetration by intruders.
7. Provide space in entry areas for equipment for verification, identification, and screening of building occupants and visitors.
8. Provide adequate space for maintaining security equipment.
9. Protect all utilities and security system control panels from disruption by unauthorized persons.
10. Design elevators, stairways, and automated locking mechanisms to avoid compromising security during emergency evacuations.
11. Design lighting for proper illumination, glare reduction, and increased field of view for CCTV.
12. Design site perimeter so it is well defined and supported by natural barriers such as landscaping; mechanical barriers such as walls, fences, buried sensors, motion sensors, and proximity sensors; and organizational methods such as guard patrols.

SUMMARY

Maintain records of the decision-making process; security design should be incorporated in all buildings. Design for security now, or the owner will pay for it later at much greater cost. In fact, design with security system expansion in mind by providing for extra conduit. The health, safety, and welfare of building users depends on good security planning and design.

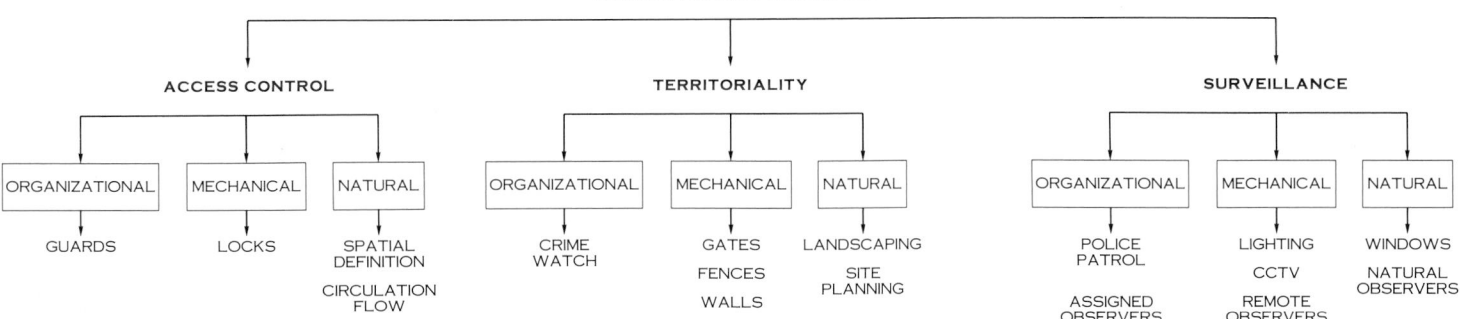

SECURITY DESIGN STRUCTURE

SECURITY DESIGN STRUCTURE

Randall Atlas, Ph. D., AIA, CPP; Atlas Safety and Security Design, Inc.; Miami, Florida

SITE SELECTION

The development of an effective protection for a building site begins with identification of five issues:

1. The potential target(s): persons, goods, information.
2. The potential adversaries: amateur or professional individuals; criminal or political organizations; unstructured groups acting together in an episode.
3. The potential means: human body; commonly available tools; specialized tools; weapons; explosives; vehicles.
4. The availability and types of response personnel.
5. The balance between the cost of deterrence or resistance and the level of acceptable risk.

RESCUE   PARKING   FIRE   HOSPITAL   POLICE

SYMBOL LEGEND

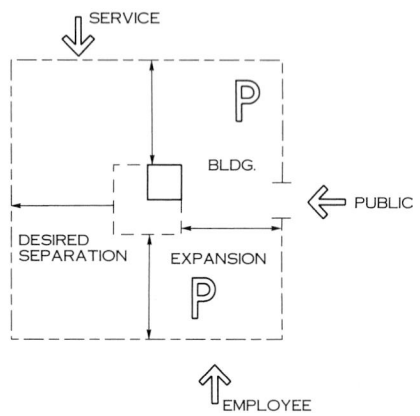

CONSIDERATIONS

1. Sufficient for desired separation between building and perimeter.
2. Sufficient to maintain separation with future expansion.
3. Sufficient for segregation of parking and access.

SITE SIZE

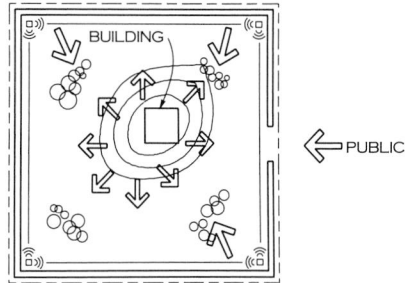

CONSIDERATIONS

1. Allows for siting building out of sight of adjacent uses.
2. Allows economical perimeter protection.
3. Allows good surveillance and intrusion detection sightlines.
4. Allows needed elevations for antennae.

SITE TOPOGRAPHY

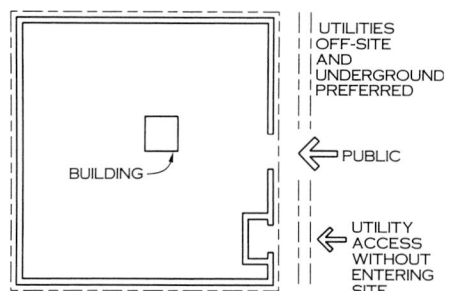

UTILITIES OFF-SITE AND UNDERGROUND PREFERRED

PUBLIC

UTILITY ACCESS WITHOUT ENTERING SITE

CONSIDERATIONS

1. No easements through site.
2. Utility suppliers' access to site can be controlled.
3. Reliable utility services.
4. Utility services not vulnerable to sabotage.

SITE UTILITIES

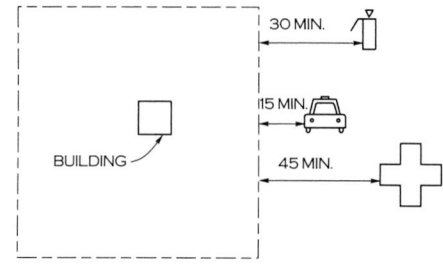

CONSIDERATIONS

1. Public fire protection.
   a. Max. 30 minute response.
   b. Well-trained and equipped.
   c. Acceptable for secure area fire control.
2. Public law enforcement.
   a. Max. 15 minute response.
   b. Well-trained and equipped.
   c. Willing to work with owner's security personnel.
3. Medical care.
   a. 30-45 minute response time.
   b. Well-trained and equipped.

SITE EMERGENCY SERVICES

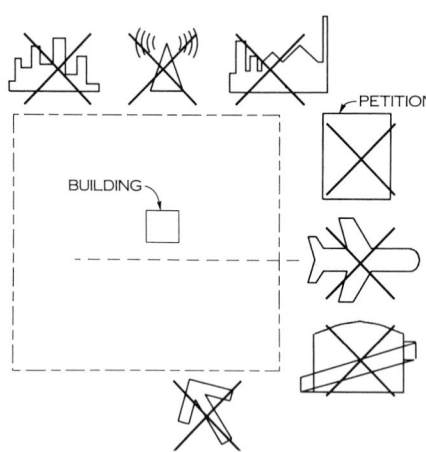

PETITION

CONSIDERATIONS

1. Compatibility of permitted uses.
2. Acceptability of adjacent structures.
   a. No intruding visual sightlines.
   b. No hostile occupancies.
   c. No radio interference.
   d. No nearby aircraft pathways.
   e. No congested adjacent arterial roads.

SITE SURROUNDING USES

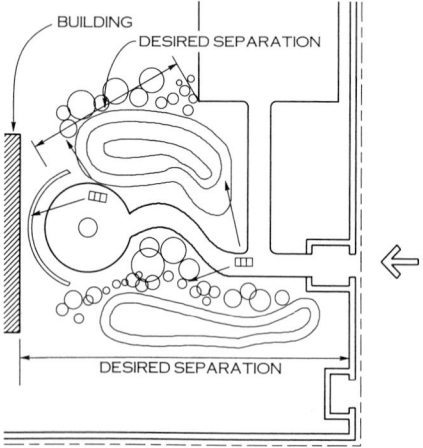

ACCESS TO SITE CONSIDERATIONS

1. Parking needs can be met in controlled areas on site at desired distance from building.
2. Parking needs can be met off site.
3. Public transportation available.
4. Alternative routes available to potential target personnel.
5. Adjacent streets not congested, and not preventing access by emergency vehicles and rapid evacuation.
6. No unimpeded high-speed approaches to site perimeter.

COMMUNITY CONSIDERATIONS

1. Not hostile toward proposed use.
2. Will accept well-designed, visible security measures (perimeter enclosures, lighting, etc.).

SITE ACCESS

The vehicular approach to sensitive buildings should be contained by landscape. Berms and plantings can shield sensitive areas from vision as well as denying direct off-roadway access to building. Indirect or curving approach toward a building minimizes speed of vehicular approach. All drop-off access to a building should be limited access, and desired separations from parking and site perimeter should be maintained.

SITE APPROACH DIAGRAM

Stuart L. Knoop, W. David Owen, Brian J. F. Baer; Oudens + Knoop Architects P.C.; Washington, D.C.

SITE PERIMETER SECURITY

The design of the defensive measures consists of three interrelated factors:

1. Detection systems sensitive to intrusion attempts or other hostile acts must alert response personnel promptly and with minimal false alarms.
2. Delay systems, barriers, or distances must impede the intruder sufficiently to allow time for action by response personnel.
3. Whether public law enforcement or on-site forces, response personnel must be able to take the required neutralizing action in the time afforded by the detection and delay systems.

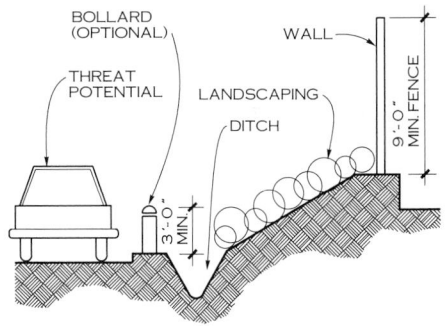

DITCH AND WALL PERIMETER SECURITY

RATES OF PENETRATION

TYPE	PENETRATION MODE TIME IN MINUTES		
	OVER	THROUGH	UNDER
8' high chain link fence	4-12	8-24	3-9
Same with barbed top concertina	5-15	-	-
Same with cable or rail	-	8-24	5-27
Same with mesh buried 2'	-	-	75
Same with concrete security sill	-	-	75
8' high reinforced 8" concrete wall	15-30	7-21	N/A

NOTE

Selected rates in minutes for penetration activities using commonly available articles or tools.

VEHICLE BARRIER EFFECTIVENESS

TYPE	ADVANTAGES	DISADVANTAGES
Earth ditch 13-20' wide and 5' deep	Penetrated but stops and damages vehicle	Can be bridged
Chain-link fence with ³/₄" cable	Penetrated but stops and damages vehicle	Personnel can follow through
Concrete vehicle barrier	Penetrated but demolishes vehicle	Second vehicle or personnel can follow through
8" high reinforced concrete antiram wall	Vehicle does not penetrate	Costly

NOTES

Comparative effectiveness of generic, nonproprietary vehicle barriers. Vehicle used is a ³/₄ ton pickup traveling at 50 mph.

Proprietary active barriers, such as ramp barricades, crash beams, pop-up bollards, tire traps, specially reinforced gates, etc., are rated by each manufacturer by specific model. These devices have been in widespread use for some years.

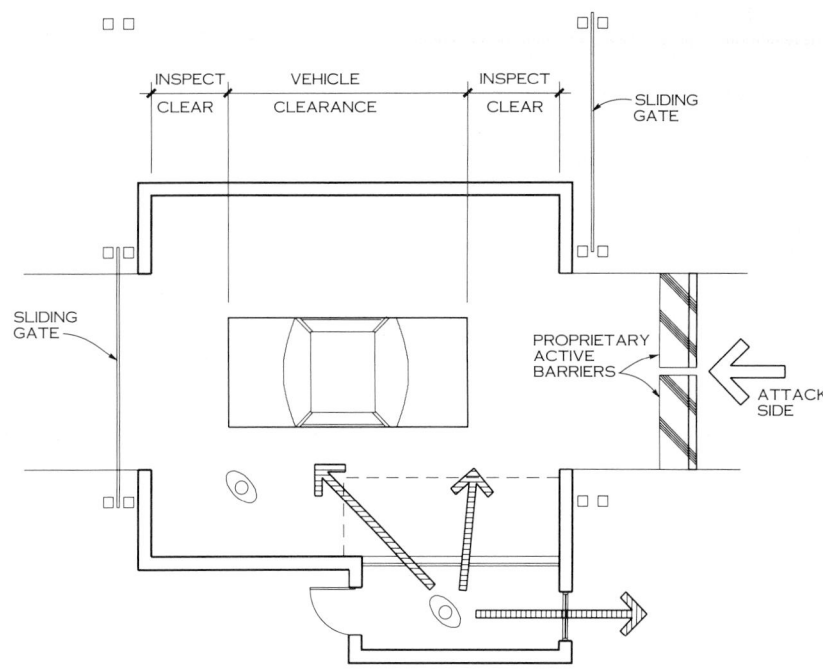

NOTE

In areas of high risk a screening facility is needed to detect guns, explosives, or other threats. A sally-port detains a vehicle for inspection and prevents access by tailgating.

A typical sally port consists of a detainment area of size sufficient for vehicle clearance and space to operate inspection equipment. The entry and exit of the sally port is operated from an adjacent guard booth. The entry to the sally port is often guarded by an active barrier. In areas of extreme sensitivity a secondary guard is needed to perform the vehicle inspection.

SITE ACCESS — SALLY PORTS

PROTECTION TECHNIQUE EVALUATION: (ON A SCALE OF 1 AS MOST TO 5 AS LEAST)

	DEPENDABILITY[1]	ACCURACY[2]	SPEED OF PROCESS	SKILLED LABOR INTENSITY[3]	TECHNOLOGICAL INTENSITY[4]	RESISTANCE TO DEFEAT	USER CONVENIENCE
IDENTIFICATION							
Visual/oral	4	4	3	1	5	4	1
Badge	4	4	3	3	2	5	2
Card	2	2	1	2	4	3	2
Card and PIN	1	1	1	2	5	1	3
Biometric	2	2	3	2	5	1	4
Card and Biometric	1	1	4	3	5	1	5
SCREENING							
Visual/oral	5	5	5	1	5	2	4
Body search	1	2	5	1	5	3	5
Walk-through detector	3	3	2	2	3	4	3
X-ray	4	4	3	2	2	2	4
Parcel inspection	2	2	5	2	5	2	5
SEGREGATION							
Oral/graphic	5	5	1	5	5	5	1
Guard/controller	3	3	2	4	2	4	3
Key	5	-	1	5	5	4	2
Card access	2	3	1	2	4	4	2
Digital combination	4	4	3	4	5	4	4
DUAL DIGITAL							
Combinations	5	5	2	4	5	2	5
Biometric	2	2	3	3	1	2	4
Two or more techniques	1	1	4	4	5	1	4

NOTES

1. Dependability refers to performance reliability with least maintenance and repair.
2. Accuracy refers to precision of task performance.
3. Skilled labor intensity refers to quality and number of experienced personnel needed.
4. Technological intensity refers to amount and sophistication of supporting equipment or software for optimal performance.

Stuart L. Knoop, W. David Owen, Brian J. F. Baer; Oudens + Knoop Architects P.C.; Washington, D.C.

GENERAL

Comprehensive, effective site security provides deterrents to hostile acts, barriers to unauthorized entry, access/egress control, detection of unauthorized entry or exit, and positions for security personnel. Design of the system includes:

1. Perimeter physical barriers preventing penetration by intruders and vehicles
2. Entry/exit control
3. Protective lighting
4. Standoff distance from blasts
5. Intrusion detection, alert, and notification
6. Guard posts and guard walls

Perimeter and site security are augmented by a comprehensive building security system.

SITE ACCESS

A screening facility at perimeter access points should be considered in high risk areas to detect explosives, firearms, and other weapons. A sally port detains vehicles for inspection and prevents other vehicles from gaining access by tailgating.

A protected guard booth should be located so that the guard can control entry/exit of pedestrians and vehicles. Guard booths in high risk areas should be constructed to appropriate ballistic and forced entry resistant standards. Where extensive vehicle inspection is required, a roving guard should augment guards in the booth.

PERIMETER PROTECTION

Perimeter security addresses issues of protection against forced entry by unauthorized personnel and vehicles, and against explosive blast.

PERSONNEL BARRIERS: FENCES AND WALLS

Walls and opaque fences to deter and resist intruders should be smooth-faced with no easy foot or handholds, and be a minimum 9 ft high. Open fencing should be constructed of vertical elements with 9 ft minimum between horizontal elements.

SITE SECURITY LIGHTING

A comprehensive system of security lighting should include illumination of the perimeter, structures within, and site passageways.

Continuous lighting using fixed luminaires to flood an area with overlapping cones of light is most common. Lighting across an area makes it difficult for intruders to see inside the area. Controlled lighting, which adjusts light to fit a particular strip inside and/or outside the perimeter, is less intrusive to adjacent properties.

Auxiliary standby lighting is turned on if suspicious activity is detected. Movable lighting supplements continuous or standby lighting.

EXPLOSIVE BLAST RESISTANCE

The most effective protective measure against explosive blast is to maximize the standoff distance from perimeter barriers to buildings or other assets. Blast walls are of limited effectiveness.

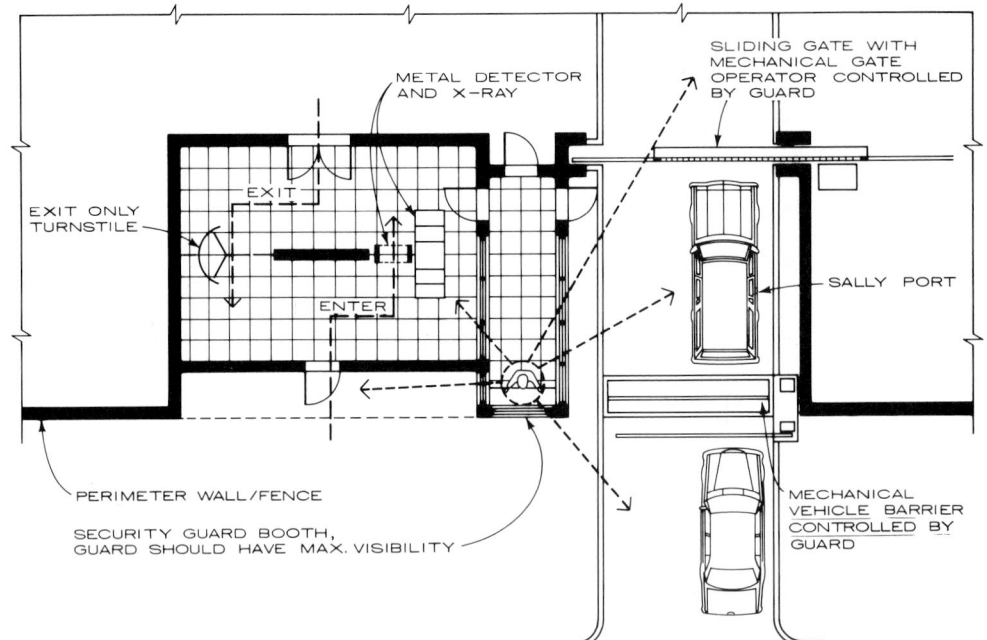

SITE ACCESS DIAGRAM

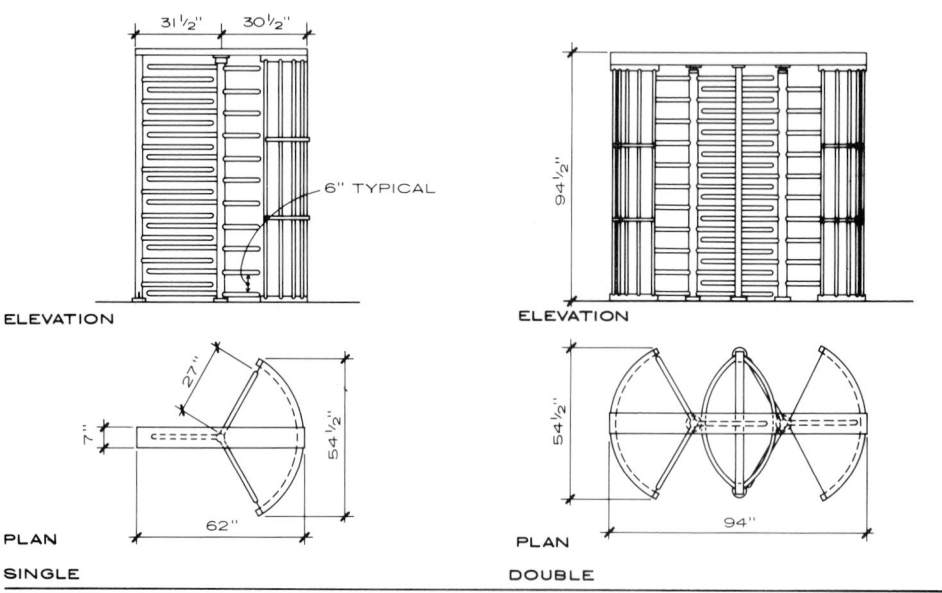

SINGLE   DOUBLE

TURNSTILES

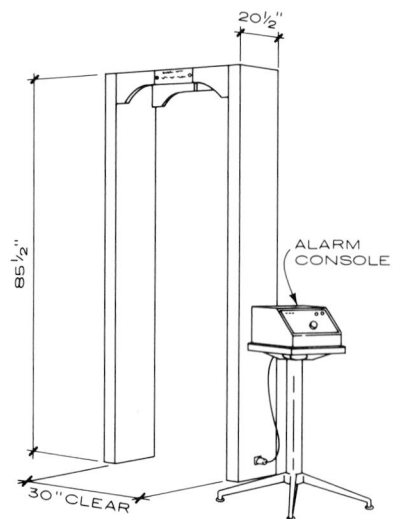

WALK THROUGH METAL DETECTOR

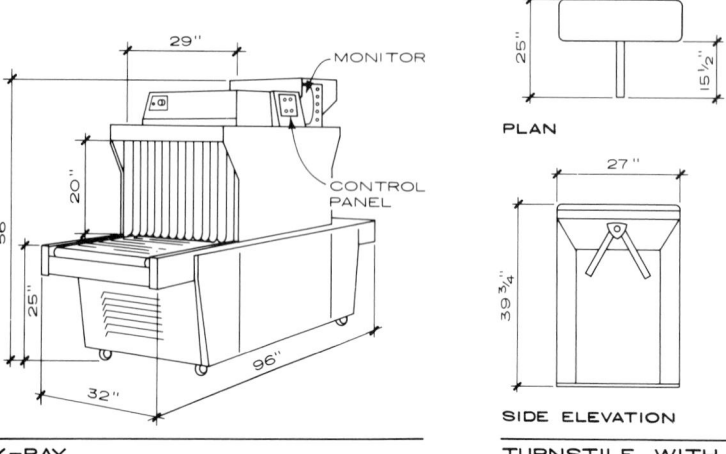

X-RAY   **TURNSTILE WITH CARD READER**

Edwin Daly, AIA; Joseph Handwerger, Architects; Washington, D.C.;
William G. Miner, AIA; Washington, D.C.

BUILDING SECURITY

ACCESS CONTROL

The illustrations on this page are intended to show a range of access control spaces and techniques that, in practice, could take any number of combined forms; for instance, within the same point of control, such as a lobby, several techniques might be applied depending on the nature and volume of the persons being screened. In Diagram A, the control is a little more than one encounters in the waiting room of a physician's office; in Diagram D, the control is such as might be used at a nuclear facility.

In any situation, the following must be defined:

1. The potential target(s): persons, goods, information.
2. The potential adversaries: amateur or professional individuals; criminal or political organizations; unstructured groups acting together in an episode.
3. The potential means: human body; commonly available tools; specialized tools; weapons; explosives; vehicles.
4. The availability and types of response personnel.
5. The balance between the cost of deterrence or resistance and the level of acceptable risk.

CARD KEY   GUARD   BADGE   BUTTON PAD

BIOMETRIC   WALK THROUGH METAL DETECTOR   BAG X-RAY   RECEPTION

TURNSTILE   SECURE WHEN ACTIVATED   ALWAYS SECURE

SYMBOL LEGEND

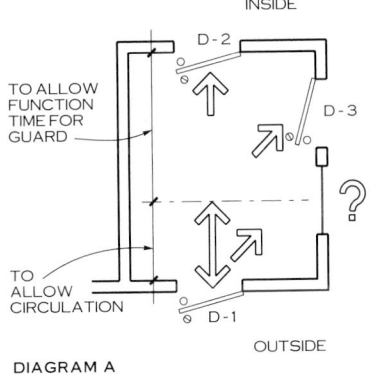

DIAGRAM A

FEATURES

1. Identification: visual, oral
2. Screening: visual
3. Segregation: oral or graphic instructions
4. Traffic handling: same for all persons; entrance and exit combined
5. Operation: all doors normally operable for entry and exit; doors secured by receptionist as needed

BASIC ACCESS CONTROLS

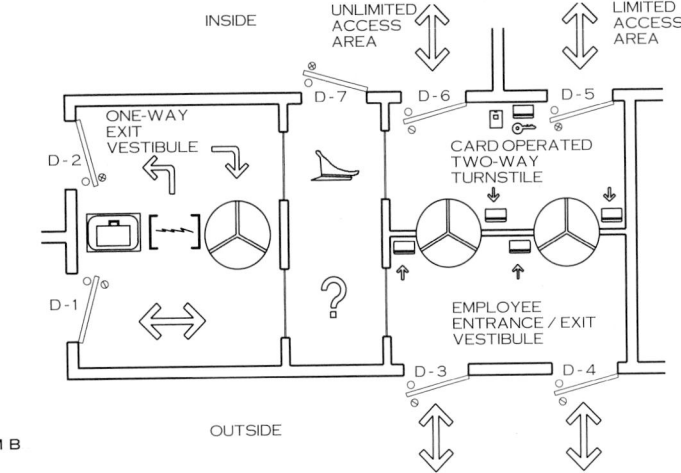

DIAGRAM B

FEATURES

1. Identification: visual/oral, except door D-5 to limited access area requires card and personal ID number (PIN).
2. Screening: visual/oral for employees; walk-through metal detector, parcel X-ray, visual/oral for pass issuance by receptionist.
3. Segregation: separated employee and visitor control. Visitors admitted by guard after identification, pass issuance, and screening. Employees segregated by card, key, PIN, code.
4. Traffic handling: visitors issued passes, screened, exit on surrender of pass. Employees enter and exit using card at turnstile.
5. Operation: exterior entrance doors D-1, D-3, and D-4 usually operable both directions; locked after hours. Door D-2 always locked; unlocked by guard after screening. Door D-6 normally locked; locked by guard in emergency. Door D-5 always locked, unlocked by card, key, PIN, guard, or combination. All doors operable in exit direction.

LOW VOLUME VISITOR ENTRY/EXIT AND HIGH VOLUME EMPLOYEE ENTRY/EXIT

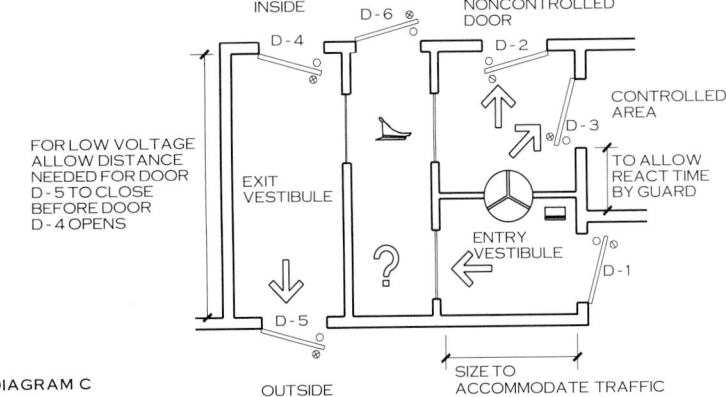

DIAGRAM C

FEATURES

1. Identification: visual, oral
2. Screening: visual
3. Segregation: oral or graphic instructions
4. Traffic handling: same for all persons; entrance and exit separated
5. Operation: Door D-1 normally operable, secure after hours; turnstile card operated by employees, released by guard or receptionist for visitors. Door D-2 normally operable to noncontrolled area, can be locked by guard in emergency. Door D-3 to controlled area always locked, unlocked by guard. Doors D-4 and D-5 always locked on outside; unlocked for exit. Distance needed to allow D-4 to close before D-5 opened. Doors can be interlocked, but not recommended for high volume.

SEPARATE EXIT AND ENTRANCE

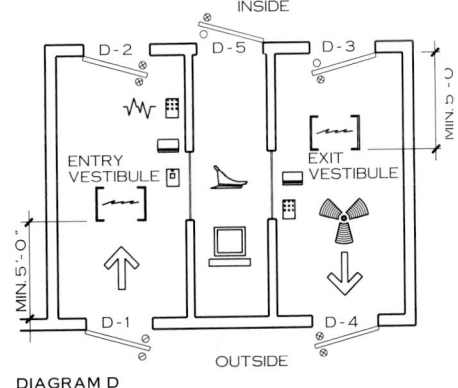

DIAGRAM D

FEATURES

1. Identification: visual, magnetic card, PIN, biometric combination.
2. Screening: walk-through metal detectors, radioactive and explosive materials "sniffers" etc. in and out.
3. Segregation: by identification.
4. Traffic handling: one person at a time.
5. Operation: all doors except D-1 locked from outside. D-1 locks when entry vestibule in use. Door D-2 unlocks only after successful screening and identification. D-1 locks for containment by guard; D-4 unlocks after successful exit screening and log-out.

HIGH SECURITY ENTRY/EXIT SALLY-PORT

Stuart L. Knoop, W. David Owen, Brian J. F. Baer, Oudens + Knoop Architects P.C.; Washington, D.C.

BUILDING SYSTEMS
THREAT ANALYSIS AND RESPONSE

The illustration on this page exemplifies a building in which information or processes might be the threatened targets. The intention is to screen the public and to segregate employees as to their access to certain parts of the building.

In any building, the threat must be determined preferably before a site is selected. Threat analysis consists of five considerations:

1. The potential targets: persons, goods, information.
2. The potential adversaries: amateur or professional individuals; criminal or political organizations; unstructured groups acting together in an episode.
3. The potential means: human body; commonly available tools; specialized tools; weapons; explosives; vehicles.
4. The availability and types of response personnel: public law enforcement; military; contract security forces; owner personnel. Use of force as a response governed by law.
5. The balance between the cost of deterrence or resistance and the level of acceptable risk.

As the threats are determined, the means of countering them must be evaluated.

1. Visibility of security measures and the inconvenience of them to the public may be an unacceptable public image or may have a desirable deterrent effect.
2. The skill and legal authority of response personnel varies widely. At best, physical security design affords time to take action such as by force, to defuse a situation by negotiation or to escape peril. No physical measures are undefeatable by determined, skilled, and well-financed adversaries.
3. Designs to counter response to security threats must be tempered by life safety and access needs for persons with disabilities. These are often in conflict, especially in cases where emergency egress must be through an access-controlled lobby or where heavy ballistic doors must be operated by elderly or wheelchair-confined persons. Usually alternative assisted access is preferable to attempting to reconcile the demands of security with those of easy accessibility.

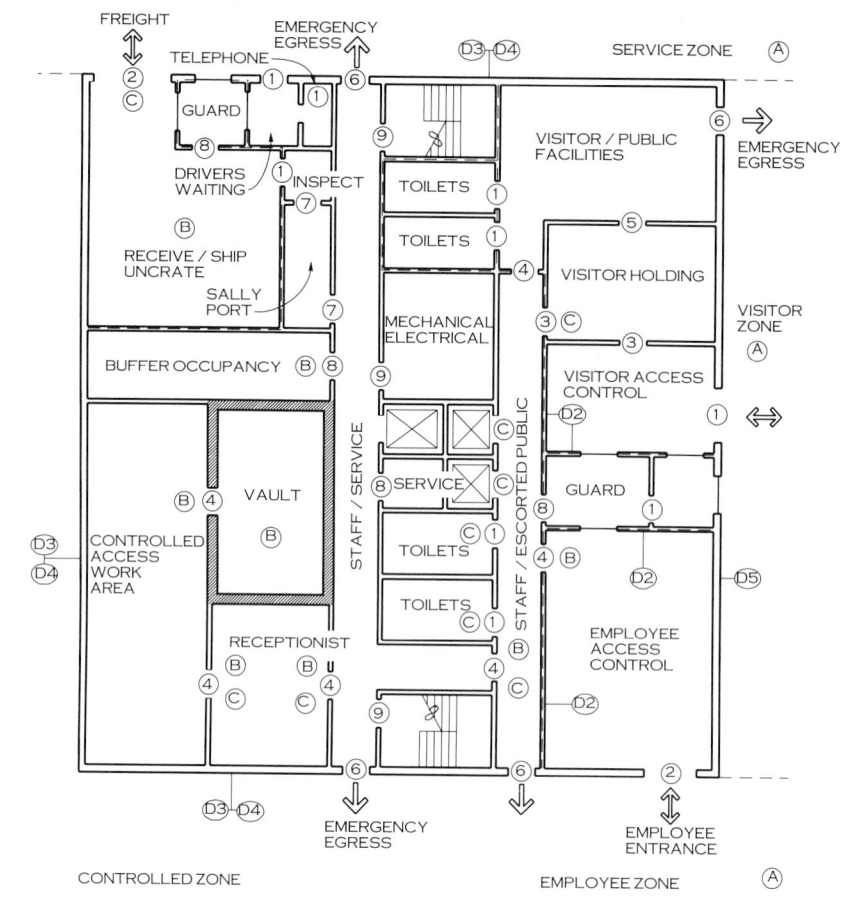

BUILDING SECURITY DIAGRAM

NOTES

1. Exterior zones separated from each other; access to each from public rights-of-way controlled.
2. Employees controlled by monitored selective access system such as access control cards. Coded for level of permitted access.
3. Visitors must have escorted access by employees in access control system.
4. Wall construction depends on threat:
   - D-1 Blast
   - D-2 Ballistic
   - D-3 Forced entry
   - D-4 Surreptitious entry
   - D-5 All of the above

DOOR FUNCTIONS FOR BUILDING SECURITY DIAGRAM

DOOR FUNCTION	1	2	3	4	5	6	7	8	9
No control function					•				
Outside normally locked			•	•		•	•	•	•
Inside normally operable			•	•	•	•	•	•	•
Outside locked by guard/controller	•	•							
Outside unlocked by guard/controller			•				•	•	
Outside unlocked by card, key, I.D., etc.				•			•	•	
Inside locked under emergency						•			
Outside unlocked under emergency									•
Outside locked after hours only			•	•					
After hours unlocked by guard/controller				•					
Doors interlocked						•			

BUILDING SYSTEMS MEAN PENETRATION TIME

4 IN. THICK, 3,000 PSI CONCRETE WITH ONE LAYER $\frac{1}{2}$ IN. - 6 X 6 MESH

Sledge, hand bolt-cutters	3.2 min.	1 person
Sledge, cutting torch	3.3 min.	2 persons

6 IN. THICK, 3,000 PSI CONCRETE WITH ONE LAYER #5 – 6 IN. X 6 IN.

Sledge, hand hydraulic bolt-cutters	4.7 min.	1 person
Sledge, cutting torch	4.0 min.	2 persons

8 IN. THICK 3000 PSI CONCRETE WITH TWO LAYERS #5 - 6 IN. X 6 IN.

Rotohammers, sledge, punch, hand-held power hydraulic bolt-cutters, generator	30 min.	2 persons

4 IN. THICK CMU, UNFILLED, NO REBAR

Sledge	0.4 min.	1 person

8 IN. THICK CMU VOL. #8 REBAR IN MORTAR-FILLED CORES

Sledge, cutting torch	2.7 min.	2 persons

8 IN. HOLLOW CMU FILLED WITH MORTAR, 1 IN. X 9 GAUGE EXPANDED STEEL MESH BONDED TO BLOCK, 4 IN. SOLID CMU

Sledge, punch, wrecking bar, rotohammer, drill, cutting torch, generator	4.9 min.	2 persons
Bolt-cutters, battering ram	10 min.	3 persons

NOTE

1. Explosives not included.

Stuart L. Knoop, W. David Owen, Brian J. F. Baer, Oudens + Knoop Architects P.C.; Washington, D.C.

1 **BUILDING SECURITY**

GENERAL NOTES

1. Technology is changing constantly, affecting size, cost, and capability of equipment.
2. Generally the same types of detectors and alarms are available for residential and commercial systems.
3. Specific examples are shown for each type of equipment. A wide variety of each type is available, varying in size, shape, and capability. Check with manufacturers for latest information.

SECURITY SYSTEM DESIGN

Determine if security consultant is required.

1. Identify need for security: prevent loss; reduce loss; internal and external loss; personnel safety; terrorism; trade secrets
2. Determine the level of risk: type of business; geographic location; response time available from police and fire department.
3. Establish budget based on risk, need, and cost including the cost to maintain and operate the system.
4. Determine basic system: local alarm, central station, or proprietary.
5. Begin security system design during initial site planning and schematic building design. Continue to review and develop the system with the building. Consideration of security during design of the building can reduce the cost of the security system and improve its capability.
6. Test all systems thoroughly after installation to avoid false alarms and to ensure complete coverage.

SYSTEM LAYOUT

1. Systems can range from basic, such as perimeter detectors at exterior doors that trigger an on site alarm, to elaborate systems with access control, fire detection, and environmental systems monitoring and control.
2. Systems are usually built up in layers. An example would be site detection as the first layer, perimeter detection of the exterior building wall openings as the second, space and motion detection third, perimeter of special areas or rooms, fourth, and, finally, specific objects as the fifth layer.

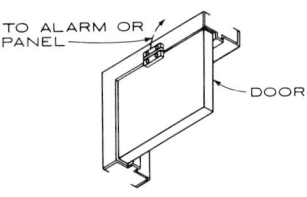

Increasing gap between magnets triggers alarm. Can be used for sliding doors.

MAGNETIC DETECTOR

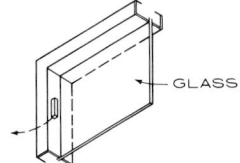

Break in tape opens electrical circuit and sets off alarm.

METAL FOIL TAPE

Detects vibration caused by breaking glass or moving window.

SHOCK DETECTOR

Attached directly to glass. One required on each pane.

GLASS BREAK DETECTOR

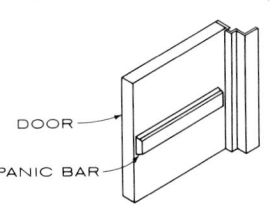

Detects cutting, breaking, or removal of screen.

SCREEN DETECTOR

Available with electronic operation to signal use and to allow unlocking from a remote location.

PANIC BAR

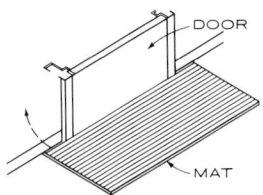

Weight of person on mat triggers alarm.

PRESSURE DETECTOR

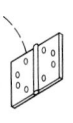

Detects opening of door. Another type conducts power to electric lock.

ELECTRIC HINGE

PERIMETER DETECTORS

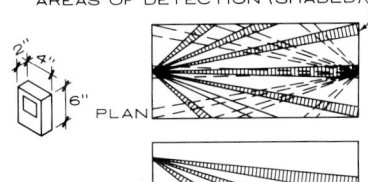

Detects object in heat range of body temperature. Detectors can overlap coverage to eliminate blind spots.

PASSIVE INFRARED

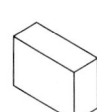

Detects change in sound wave pattern. Not recommended in areas with high acoustical absorption or with equipment emitting high pitched noises.

ULTRASONIC

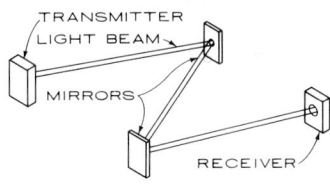

Detects interruption of light beam. Modulated beam is more difficult to bypass. Infrared and photoelectric available.

LIGHT BEAM

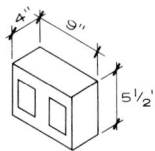

Alarm signal from both detectors is required to trigger alarm. Reduces possibility of false alarms.

PASSIVE INFRARED WITH ULTRASONIC OR MICROWAVE

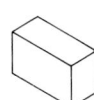

Subject to false alarms from aircraft radar and from movement outside building through windows, wood doors, and the like. Radio waves penetrate glass, wood, and gypsum board and can cover several rooms at once. Must be certified by the FCC and less than 10 milliwatts for safety.

MICROWAVE

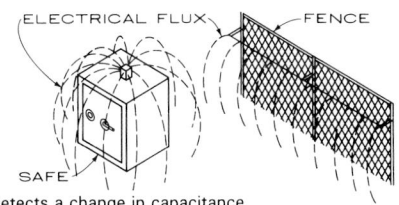

Detects a change in capacitance of the area covered, caused by intrusion. Very versatile and sensitive. Object becomes part of the detector.

PROXIMITY/CAPACITANCE

SPACE AND MOTION DETECTORS

Fred W. Hegel, AIA; Denver, Colorado

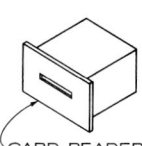
CARD READER

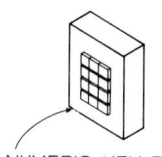
NUMERIC KEY PAD

COMBINED CARD READER AND NUMERIC KEY PAD

LOCKSET AVAILABLE IN MORTISE AND CYLINDRICAL MODELS

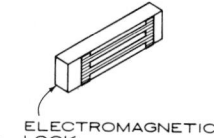
ELECTROMAGNETIC LOCK

Access control devices can operate a lockset directly with an electronic signal, or through a computer to verify and record access card, code used, time and date, or to notify security personnel to operate the lock.

Available with audio or audio video monitor and remote control to unlock security door.

APARTMENT LOCK

ELECTRIC LOCKS

ACCESS CONTROL

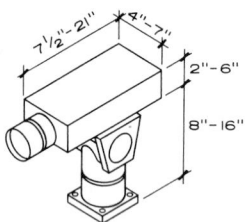

Available with remote controlled base and lens, high resolution, and low light level capability.

VIDEO CAMERA

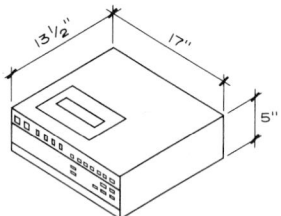

Available with variable speed time lapse or continuous record at alarm signal. Can encode tape with the time and date of event and locate event for playback.

VIDEO RECORDER

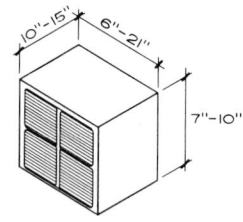

Controls can sequence automatically to view all cameras, or split screen to view four at one time. High resolution screens are available.

VIDEO MONITOR

Alarm sensitivity can be set to reduce false alarms. Can monitor remotely by radio or telephone line.

AUDIO DETECTOR/MICROPHONE

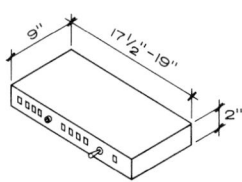

Can control one or multiple cameras and bases adjusting pan, tilt, focus, zoom, and iris from remote location.

VIDEO CAMERA CONTROL

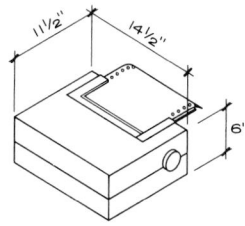

Automatically prints a record of all events with date, time, and alarm location. Can include access card use and instructions for evacuation, etc.

EVENT PRINTER

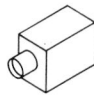

Triggered by alarm signal and preset to take time-lapse pictures at a selected rate.

FILM RECORDER

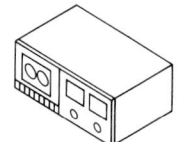

AUDIO RECORDER

SURVEILLANCE AND RECORDING

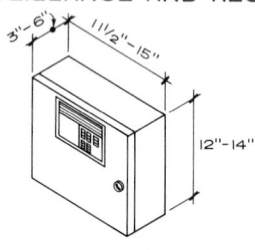

Can monitor security, fire, and environmental systems, and can notify security company of alarm.

MICROPROCESSOR

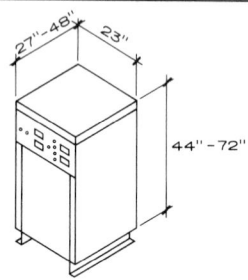

Battery pack with charger to maintain security during power failure.

UNINTERRUPTIBLE POWER

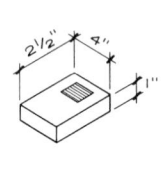

Portable or fixed location alarm button.

WIRELESS ALARM

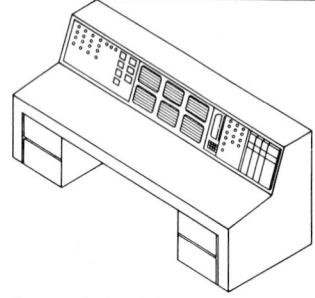

Custom designed for each installation. Can include security, fire, and environmental systems monitoring and control.

MAIN CONTROL CONSOLE

PANELS AND MISCELLANEOUS

DETECTORS

ALARM

Any detector automatically triggers alarm.

LOCAL ALARM

DETECTORS   ALARM

DEDICATED PHONE LINE

SECURITY COMPANY   BUILDING MAIN PANEL   LIGHTS

Any detector signals off-site security company that notifies public safety, owner, etc.

CENTRAL STATION ALARM

SECURITY   ACCESS CONTROL   FIRE   HVAC

MAIN CONSOLE

PUBLIC SAFETY FIRE DEPT.   LIGHTS   HVAC ELEC. EQUIP LOCKS

Owner's on-site personnel monitor alarm signals, and they notify the public safety and fire departments directly. Monitoring and access control, HVAC, etc. also can be included.

PROPRIETARY CONTROL SYSTEM

ALARM AND NOTIFICATION

Fred W. Hegel, AIA; Denver, Colorado

INTRODUCTION

The following pages provide the essential elements of town design. Included are an abstract, a set of diagrams, and criteria for town and community design.

Site planning for development projects should be a sequential process that begins with information gathering and ends with detailed design drawings. The process involves three stages: analysis, design, and implementation. The chart below indicates a planning process; however, this can vary to accommodate the specifics of a particular project. Physical site characteristics, urban or suburban location, and community criteria modify the process. The site planning process includes both architect and landscape architect and, in some cases, biologists, civil engineers, and others. An integrated approach to site development and architecture helps create a quality environment. The text on this page is presented as a checklist for structuring a project.

CLIENT CONTACT AND INPUT

The first step is contact between the client and the site planner. The client may have some development objectives based on financial capabilities and market feasibility. It is important for the site planner to obtain all client data relative to planning the site.

LITERATURE REVIEW

Site planning covers a variety of situations from rural and suburban to high-intensity urban.

There is substantial literature on planning sites and designing neighborhoods of all densities. Recent publications

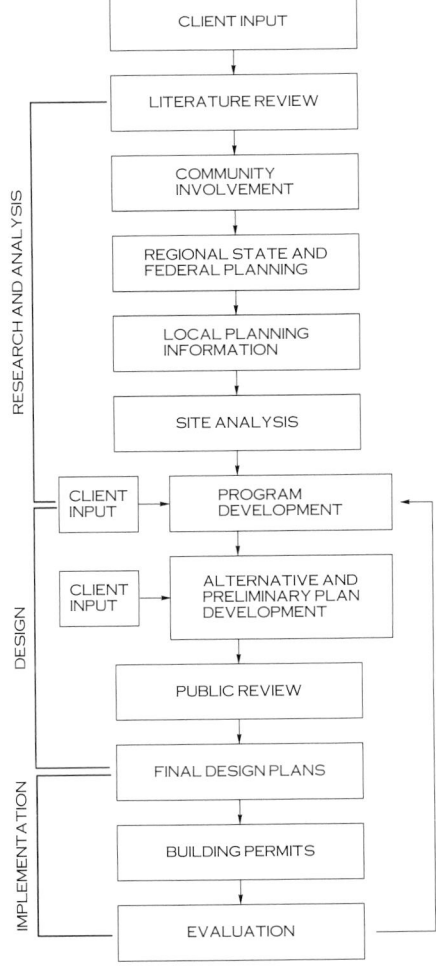

TOWN PLANNING PROCESS

demonstrate a return to the basic town planning principles that have produced orderly community design throughout history.

COMMUNITY INVOLVEMENT

Early in the planning process, contact community groups with an interest in the proposed project. Such efforts yield useful information for community design and are particularly important when a proposed project is adjacent to existing development. Compatibility issues are typically resolved with community participation.

One method of involving the community is the "charrette," a participatory planning process with a limited time frame, usually one day to a week, in which residents, municipal staff, elected leaders, and others participate in the physical design of a project. The planner receives local information useful for the design, and individuals and groups bring their interests to bear at the beginning of the design process, thereby expediting final approvals.

REGIONAL, STATE, AND FEDERAL PLANNING

Some areas of the country have established regional agencies for intercommunity issues, such as water management, transportation, population studies, and pollution control. Some communities have adopted regional planning guidelines.

State and/or federal criteria can also affect projects. State plans may address broad issues applicable to large sites or impose constraints on sites involving issues of statewide concern. Also, some states require environmental impact statements for large-scale projects. The U.S. Army Corps of Engineers is responsible for environmental review of proposed dredge and fill operations in navigable waters and wetlands. The Federal Flood Insurance Program establishes minimum elevations for potential flood areas. Other state, regional, and local authorities also may oversee the protection of air and water quality and other environmental issues.

LOCAL PLANNING INFORMATION

The planner must collect local planning information. Personal contact with planning and zoning agencies is important in order to comprehend local criteria. Following is a list of information to review.

PLANNING DOCUMENTS

Many communities have adopted comprehensive plans that indicate the particular land use and intensity of the site. In addition, information on the availability and/or phasing of public services and utilities, environmental criteria, traffic planning, and population trends can be found in most comprehensive plans. Some communities require that rezoning meet the criteria provided in their comprehensive plans.

In addition to the comprehensive plan, communities may also adopt neighborhood or area plans that refine the comprehensive plan as it relates to a particular locale. Many of these studies stipulate specific zoning categories for individual parcels of land.

URBAN DESIGN PLANS

Some communities have adopted urban design plans for creating a harmonious physical environment. These documents may range from conceptual to those that incorporate specific requirements. Some provide bonuses in land use intensities for incorporating urban amenities such as plazas and squares. There may also be criteria for retrofitting existing areas, a critical need in American cities where a substantial amount of urban area is deteriorated or developed incoherently.

ZONING

Land zoning prescribes the intensity and type of land use allowed. A zoning change is required if the planned project differs. Regulations often need to be modified to allow good community design. Common examples of regulations discouraging good urban form include excessive setbacks and restricted mixed-use development.

PUBLIC WORKS STANDARDS

Local public works criteria significantly affect the design of large sites. Roadway layout, cross sections, and drainage are typical requirements. Excessive roadway standards designed for automobile convenience, with little regard for

the pedestrian are typical of today's public works regulations. Such standards should be modified to allow coherent neighborhood design.

PUBLIC SERVICES AND UTILITIES

Other information that may require additional research includes

1. Availability of potable water, including local and state regulations on wells
2. Availability of public sewer service, access to trunk lines, and available increases in flow. If sewage lines are not immediately available, determine projected phasing of these services, as well as alternatives to sewage collection and treatment, including septic tanks.
3. Access to public roads, existing and projected carrying capacities, and levels of services of the roads. (State and local road departments can provide this information.)
4. Availability and capacities of schools and other public facilities, such as parks and libraries

SITE ANALYSIS

Site analysis is one of the planner's major responsibilities. All the on- and off-site design determinants must be evaluated before design begins. For details, see the following pages on environmental site analysis.

PROGRAM DEVELOPMENT

At the program development stage, background research, citizen input, and site analysis are combined with client input and synthesized into a set of program strategies. Basic elements for program development include market and financial criteria; federal, state, regional, and local planning information; local political climate development costs; the client's objectives; and site opportunities and constraints as developed in the synthesis of environmental site determinants. Balancing the various determinants will lead to an appropriate approach to site development. Consider dwelling unit type, density, marketing, time phasing, and similar criteria, as well as graphic studies of the site, to finalize the program. Develop clear graphic representations of design concepts to present to the client and others who may have input to the process. If the project cannot be accomplished under the existing zoning or public works requirements, requesting a regulatory change becomes a part of the program.

ALTERNATIVE PLAN PREPARATION

Once the program has been accepted by the client, develop several design solutions to meet the program objectives. When an alternative has been accepted, develop it into the preliminary plan. This plan should be relatively detailed, showing all spatial relationships, infrastructure, landscaping, and other relevant information.

PUBLIC REVIEW

A zoning change requires public review. Some communities require substantial data, such as impact statements and other narrative and graphic exhibits, while others may require only an application for the zoning change. Local requirements for changes can be complex, and it is imperative that the planner and the client's attorney are familiar with local criteria.

FINAL DESIGN PLANS

At this stage, the preliminary plans are refined into final site development plans that include fully dimensioned drawings, landscape plans, and site details. Final development plans also include drawings prepared by the engineer or surveyor, such as legal plats and utilities, street, and drainage plans. Upon approval, final design plans are recorded in the public records in the form of plats. Homeowner association agreements, deed restrictions, and similar legal documents must also be recorded, and they become binding on all owners and successive owners, unless changed legally. Bonding may be required for infrastructure and other public facilities. In some instances, the planner may develop specific design standards for the total buildout of the project.

Gary Greenan, Andres Duany, Elizabeth Plater-Zyberk, Kamal Zaharin, Iskandar Shafie; Miami, Florida

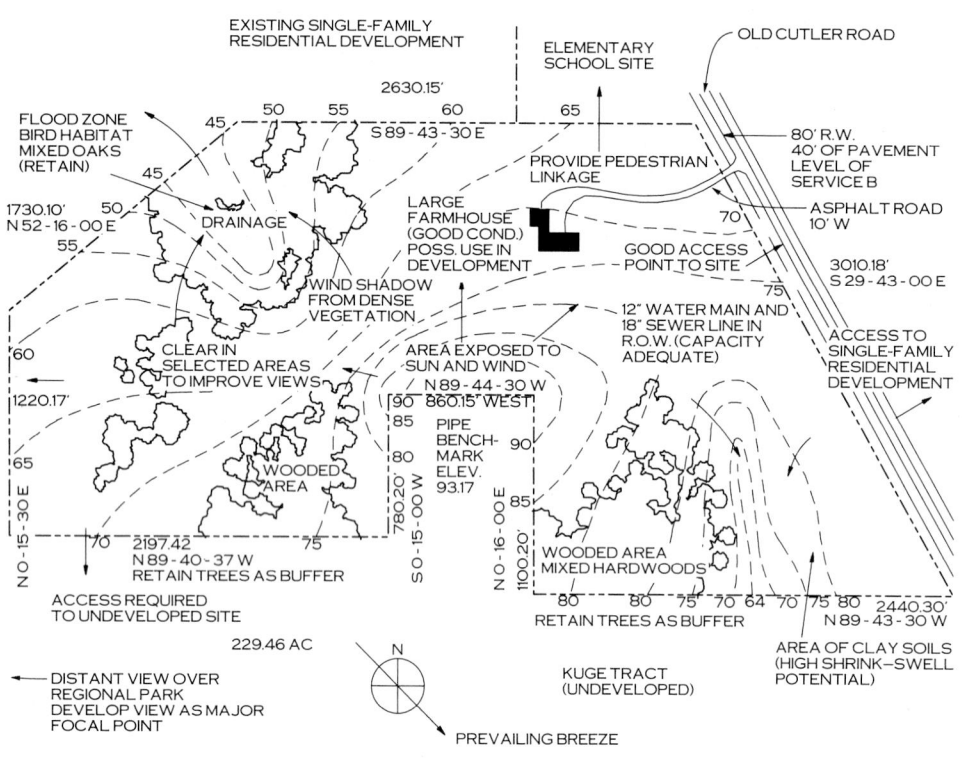

TOPOGRAPHICAL SURVEY

SURVEY DATA

The first step in any site analysis is the gathering of physical site data. An aerial photograph and an accurate survey showing the following information are basic to any site analysis process:

1. Scale, north arrow, benchmark, and date of survey
2. Tract boundary lines
3. Easements: location, width, and purpose
4. Names and locations of existing road rights-of-way on or adjacent to the tract, including bridges, curbs, gutters, and culverts
5. Position of buildings and other structures such as foundations, walls, fences, steps, and paved areas
6. Utilities on or adjacent to the tract—location of gas lines, fire hydrants, electric and telephone poles, and street lights; and direction, distance to, and size of nearest water mains and sewers and invert elevation of sewers
7. Location of swamps, springs, streams, bodies of water, drainage ditches, watershed areas, flood plains, and other physical features
8. Outline of wooded areas with names and condition of plant material
9. Contour intervals of 2 to 5 ft, depending on slope gradients, and spot elevations at breaks in grade, along drainage channels or swales, and at selected points as needed

Considerable additional information may be needed, depending on design considerations and site complexities such as soil information and studies of the geological structure of the site. Federal regulations for wetland mapping and conservation may also be relevant.

SUBURBAN SITE ANALYSIS

The site analysis is a major responsibility of the site planner. The physical analysis of the site is developed primarily from field inspections. Using the survey, the aerial photograph, and, where warranted, infrared aerial photographs, the site designer, working in the field and in the office, verifies the survey and notes site design determinants. These should include, but not be limited to, the following:

1. Areas of steep and moderate slopes
2. Macro- and microclimatic conditions, including sun an-

gles during different seasons; prevailing breezes; wind shadows; frost pockets; and sectors where high or low points give protection from sun and wind
3. Solar energy considerations. If solar energy appears feasible, a detailed climatic analysis must be undertaken considering factors such as detailed sun charts; daily averages of sunlight and cloud cover; daily rain averages; areas exposed to the sun at different seasons; solar radiation patterns; and temperature patterns
4. Potential flood zones and routes of surface water runoff
5. Possible road access to the site, including potential conflicts with existing road systems and carrying capacities of adjacent roadways (usually available from local or state road departments)
6. Natural areas that from an ecological and aesthetic standpoint should be saved; all tree masses with name and condition of tree species and understory planting
7. Significant wildlife habitats that would be affected by site modification
8. Soil conditions relative to supporting plant material, areas suitable for construction, erosion potential, and septic tanks, if relevant
9. Geological considerations relative to supporting structures
10. Exceptional views; objectionable views (use on-site photographs)
11. Adjacent existing and proposed land uses with notations on compatibility and incompatibility
12. Potential noise sources, particularly noise generated from traffic that can be mitigated by using plants, berming, and walls and by extending the distance between the source and the receiver

URBAN SITE ANALYSIS

Although much of the information presented for suburban sites may apply equally to urban sites, additional site design criteria may be necessary. The urban environment has numerous design determinants in the form of existing structures, city patterns, and microclimatic conditions.

ENVIRONMENTAL CONSIDERATIONS

1. Air movement: Prevailing breezes characteristic of a region may be greatly modified by urban high-rise structures. Predominant air movement patterns in a city may be along roadways and between buildings. The placement, shape, and height of existing buildings can create air turbulence caused by micro air movement patterns. These patterns may influence the location of building elements such as outdoor areas and balconies. Also, a building's design and placement can mitigate or increase local wind turbulence.
2. Sun and shadow patterns: The sun and shadow patterns of existing structures should be studied to determine how they would affect the proposed building. This is particularly important for outdoor terraces and balconies where sunlight may be desirable. Sun and shadow patterns also should be considered as sources of internal heat gain or loss. Building orientation, window sizes, and shading devices can modify internal heat gain or loss. Studies should include daily and seasonal patterns and the shadows the proposed building would cast on existing buildings and open spaces.
3. Reflections: Reflections from adjacent structures such as glass-clad buildings may be a problem. The new building should be designed to compensate for such glare or, if possible, oriented away from it.

URBAN CONTEXTUAL ANALYSIS

1. Building typology and hierarchy: An analysis of the particular building type (residential, commercial, public) relative to the hierarchy of the various building types in the city is useful in deciding the general design approach of a new building. For example, public buildings may be dominant in placement and design, while residential buildings are subdominant. It is important to maintain any existing hierarchy that reinforces visual order in the city. Any predominant architectural solutions and details characteristic of a building type incorporated in the new building's design can help maintain a recognizable building type.
2. Regional character: An analysis of the city's regional architectural characteristics is appropriate in developing a design solution that responds to unique regional characteristics. Regional characteristics may be revealed through unique architectural types, through vernacular building resulting from local climatic and cultural characteristics, and from historically significant architecture. Historic structures should be saved by modifying them for the proposed new use or by incorporating parts of the existing structure(s) into the proposed design.
3. City form: The delineation of city form created by road layout, location of major open spaces, and architecture-created forms should be analyzed. Elements that delineate city form should be reinforced by architectural development solutions for a particular place within the city. For example, a building proposed for a corner site should be designed to reinforce the corner through building form, entrance, and design details. A building proposed for midblock may be a visually unifying element providing connection and continuity with adjacent buildings. Sites at the ends of important vistas or adjacent to major city squares probably should be reserved for important public buildings.
4. Building scale and fenestration: It is important to analyze building scale and fenestration of nearby structures. Reflecting, although not necessarily reproducing, such detailing in the proposed building can provide visual unity and continuity in the architectural character of the city. One example is the use and placement of cornice lines to define the building's lower floors in relation to adjacent buildings. Cornice lines also can define the building's relationship to pedestrians in terms of scale and use.
5. Building transition: Sometimes it may be appropriate to use arcades and porches to provide transition between the building's private interior and the public sidewalk. Including them may be especially worthy if adjacent buildings have these elements.
6. Views: Important city views of plazas, squares, monuments, and natural features such as waterfronts and parks should be considered. It is important to design the proposed structure to enhance and preserve such views for the public and for inhabitants of nearby buildings, as well as incorporating them as views from the proposed building.

Gary Greenan, Andres Duany, Elizabeth Plater-Zyberk, Kamal Zaharin, Iskandar Shafie, Rafael Diaz; Miami, Florida

1 **SITE, COMMUNITY, AND URBAN PLANNING**

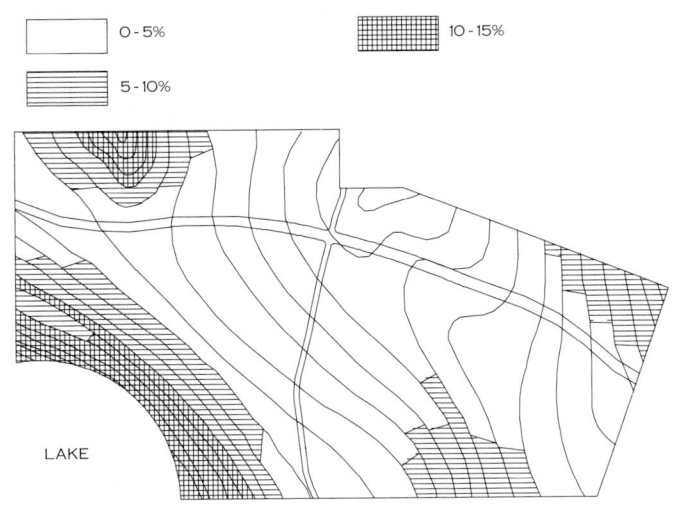

☐ 0 - 5%	⊞ 10 - 15%		
☰ 5 - 10%			

SLOPE

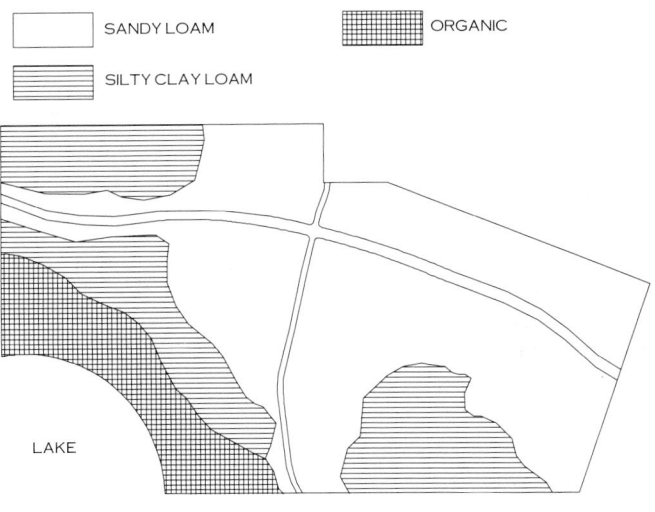

☐ SANDY LOAM	⊞ ORGANIC
☰ SILTY CLAY LOAM	

SOILS

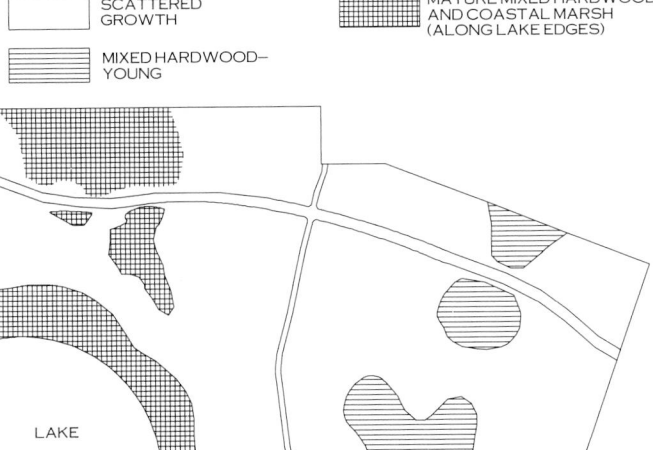

☐ SCATTERED GROWTH	⊞ MATURE MIXED HARDWOOD AND COASTAL MARSH (ALONG LAKE EDGES)
☰ MIXED HARDWOOD— YOUNG	

VEGETATION

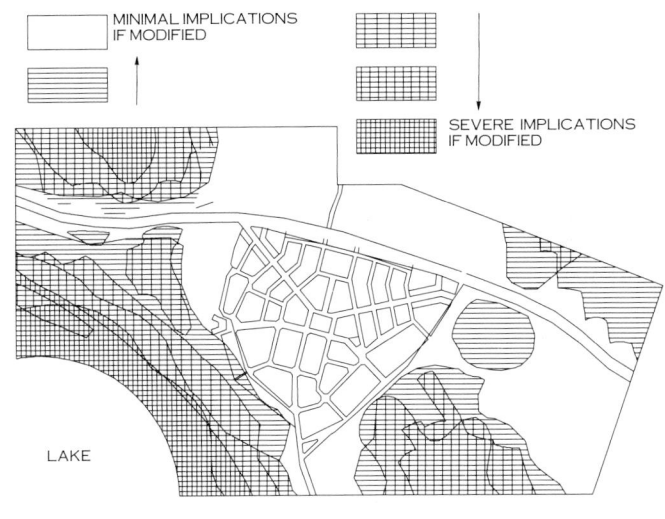

☐ MINIMAL IMPLICATIONS IF MODIFIED	⊞
☰	⊞
	⊞ SEVERE IMPLICATIONS IF MODIFIED

COMPOSITE

ENVIRONMENTAL SITE ANALYSIS PROCESS

If a site has numerous environmental design determinants, the site planner may analyze each environmental system individually in order to comprehend the environmental character of the site more clearly. This can be a complex process, and a site planner/landscape architect with expertise in environmental analysis should be retained to coordinate such an effort.

By preparing each analysis on transparencies, the site planner can use the overlay approach. Values are assigned to each sheet based on impact, ranging from areas of the site where change would have minimal effect to areas where change would result in severe disruption of the site. In essence, the separate sheets become abstractions with values assigned by the site planner and associated professionals. As each sheet is superimposed, a composite develops that, when completed, constitutes the synthesis of the environmental design determinants. Lighter tones indicate areas where modification would have minimal influence, darker tones indicate areas more sensitive to change. The sketches shown simulate the overlay process. The site planner may give greater or lesser weight to certain parameters depending on the particular situation. In assigning values that help determine the site design process, the site planner should consider such factors as the value of maintaining the functioning of the individual site systems, the uniqueness of the specific site features, and the cost of modifying the site plan.

Following is a list of the environmental design determinants that, depending on the particular site, may be considered and included in an overlay format:

1. SLOPE: The slope analysis is developed on the contour map; consideration should include the percentage of slope and orientation of slope relative to the infrastructure and land uses.
2. SOIL PATTERNS: Consideration may include the analysis of soils by erosion potential, compressibility and plasticity, capability of supporting plant growth, drainage capabilities, possible sources of pollution or toxic wastes, septic tank location (if relevant), and the proposed land uses and their infrastructure.
3. VEGETATION: Consideration of indigenous species (values of each in terms of the environmental system) includes their size and condition, the succession of growth toward climax conditions, uniqueness, the ability of certain species to tolerate construction activities, aesthetic values, and density of undergrowth.
4. WILDLIFE: Consideration of indigenous species includes their movement patterns, the degree of change each species can tolerate, and feeding and breeding areas.
5. GEOLOGY: Consideration of underlying rock masses studies the depth of different rock layers and the suitability of different geological formations in terms of potential infrastructure and building.
6. SURFACE AND SUBSURFACE WATER: Consideration of natural drainage patterns covers aquifer recharge areas, erosion potential, and flood plains.
7. CLIMATE: Consideration of microclimatic conditions includes prevailing breezes (at different times of the year), wind shadows, frost pockets, and air drainage patterns.

COMPUTER APPLICATION

The above process is labor intensive when developed by hand on individual sheets of mylar; however, this particular method of environmental analysis is easily adaptable to the CAD (computer-aided drafting) system. Commercial drafting programs suitable for the overlay approach are readily available. Simplified, the method is as follows:

1. A map, such as a soil map, is positioned on the digitizer and the information is transferred to the processor through the use of the stylus. One major advantage to the use of a computer is that the scale of the map being recorded will be transferred to the selected scale by the processor. A hatched pattern is selected, with a less dense pattern for soil types that would have minimal influence and more dense patterns for soil types more sensitive to change. Once this information is programmed into the computer, it is stored.
2. The same process is repeated for development of the next overlay; for example, vegetation. Once again any scale map may be used. This process is repeated until all overlays have been stored. At any time one or all overlays can be produced on the screen.
3. The individual overlays or any combination of overlays can be drawn on mylar with a plotter. If appropriate for the particular analysis, the plotter will draw in color. The resulting overlay sheets take considerably less time than by hand and may be more accurate. Other benefits are that the site can be studied directly on the computer screen and any part of the overlay can be enlarged for greater detail.
4. The overlay process can be recorded by videotape or by slides from the screen for use in presentations.

Gary Greenan, Andres Duany, Elizabeth Plater-Zyberk, Kamal Zaharin, Iskandar Shafie, Rafael Diaz; Miami, Florida

SITE ANALYSIS MAP

Locate natural, cultural, and scenic features first. These include many buildable areas, such as farm fields, pastures, meadows, and mature woodland; special features, such as stone walls, springhouses, cellar holes, and views into and out of the site; and unbuildable areas, such as steep slopes, wetlands, springs, streams, and ice ponds.

CONVENTIONAL LAYOUT OR "YIELD PLAN"

Sketch an unimaginative but legally correct conventional layout to demonstrate the density that could realistically be achieved on the site and, by comparison, to show local officials and abutters how different a rural village approach is. The sketch here shows how, under 1.5-acre zoning, a 520-acre site would ordinarily be checkerboarded into 300 lots, each with a required minimum area of 60,000 sq ft, leaving no open space whatsoever.

VILLAGE PLAN

Designing the development as a traditional village, with lots ranging from 5000 sq ft to 1 acre, achieves slightly greater density on less than one-quarter of the land and preserves nearly 400 acres. This layout is based closely on the site analysis map, with the village located to avoid disturbing the woodlands that provide the only natural habitat in this largely agricultural community. The most special site features are protected by designing around them. Nine "conservancy lots," varying in area from 20 to 60 acres, are limited to one principal dwelling plus two accessory units. This assures significant open space around the perimeter of this 300-lot village. Permanent conservation easements protect these lands from further subdivision and preserve the 150 acres of undivided open space and its trail system, which connects the old springhouse to the lakeshore and leads back to the schoolyard. This open space could be owned by the village government, a local land trust, or a homeowners' association (with automatic membership and authority to place liens on properties of members who fail to pay their dues). Rural views outward from three village streets have also been preserved, with open countryside terminating their vistas. Terminated vistas are also provided by three large public or semipublic buildings (churches, libraries, etc.) positioned at the ends of several streets.

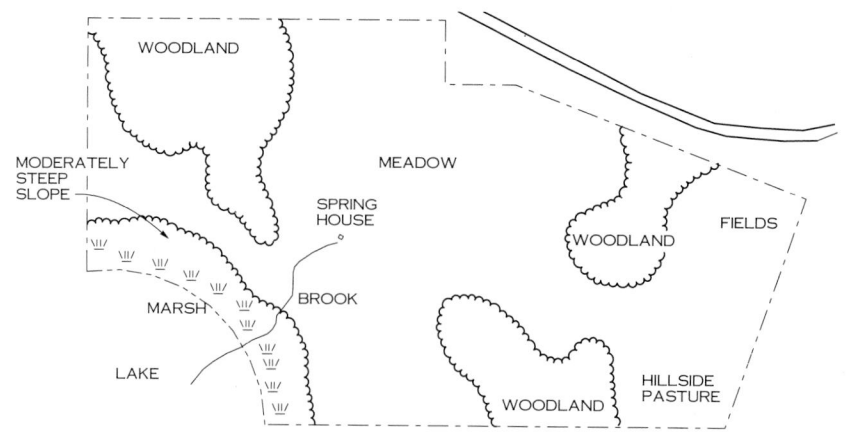

SITE ANALYSIS MAP

CONVENTIONAL LAYOUT

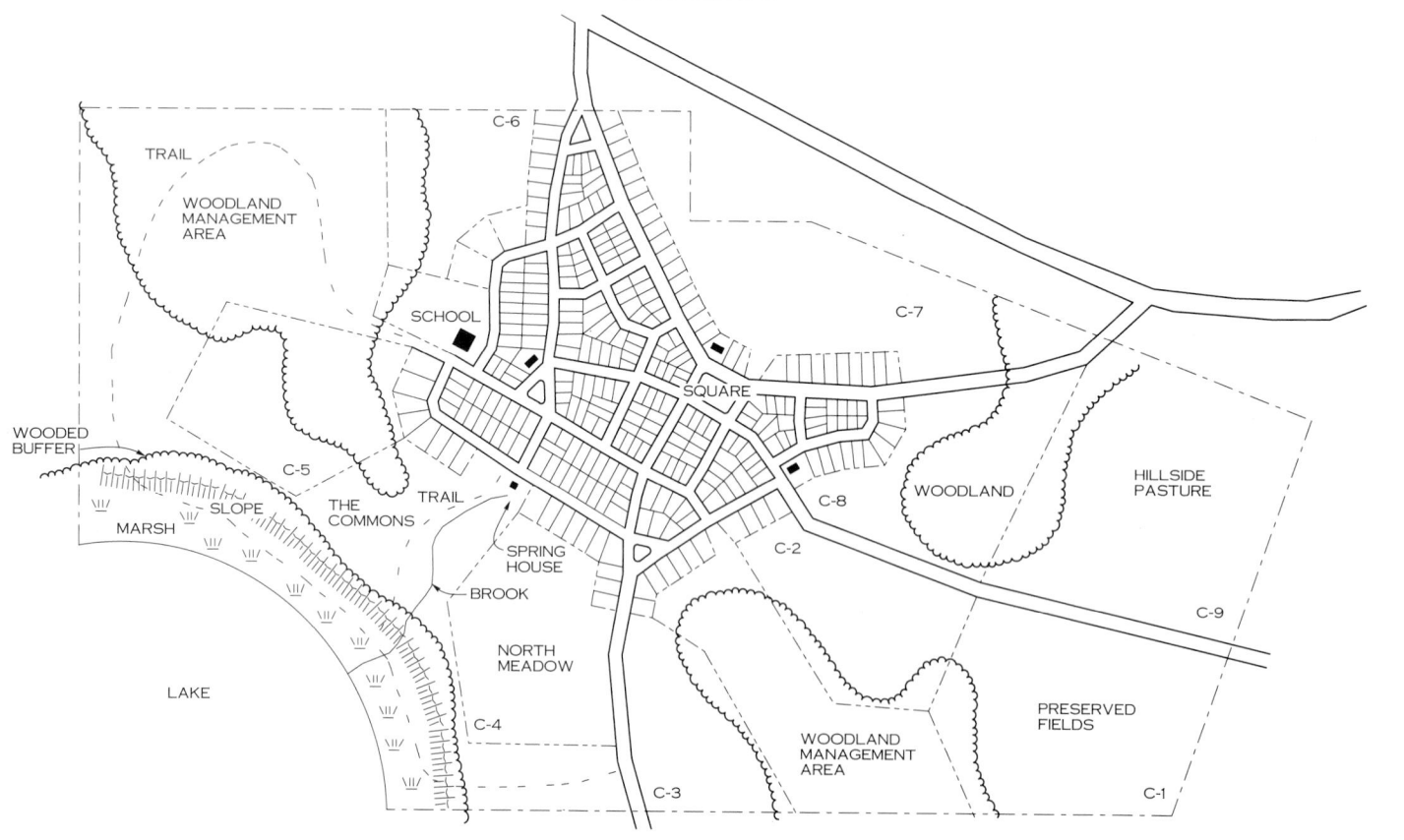

RURAL VILLAGE DESIGN

Randall Arendt, MRTPI; Natural Lands Trust; Media, Pennsylvania
Gary Greenan, Andres Duany, Elizabeth Plater-Zyberk, Kamal Zaharin, Iskandar Shafie; Miami, Florida

1   SITE, COMMUNITY, AND URBAN PLANNING

THE NEIGHBORHOOD, THE DISTRICT, AND THE CORRIDOR

The fundamental elements of urbanism are the neighborhood, the district, and the corridor. Neighborhoods are urbanized areas with a full and balanced range of human activity. Districts are urbanized areas organized around a predominant activity. Neighborhoods and districts are connected and isolated by corridors of transportation or open space.

Neighborhoods, districts, and corridors are complex urban elements. Suburbia, in contrast, is the result of simplistic zoning concepts that separate activities into residential subdivisions, shopping centers, office parks, and open space.

THE NEIGHBORHOOD

Cities and towns are made up of multiple neighborhoods. A neighborhood isolated in the landscape is a village.

The nomenclature may vary, but there is general agreement regarding the physical composition of a neighborhood. The neighborhood unit of the 1929 New York Regional Plan, the *quartier* identified by Leon Krier, traditional neighborhood design (TND), and transit-oriented development (TOD) share similar attributes. The population, configuration, and scale may vary, but all of these models propose the following:

1. The neighborhood has a center and an edge. This combination of a focus and a limit contributes to the social identity of the community. The center is a necessity, the edge less so. The center is always a public space–a square, a green, or an important street intersection–located near the center of the urbanized area, unless compelled by geography to be elsewhere. Eccentric locations are justified by a shoreline, a transportation corridor, or a promontory with a compelling view.

   The center is the locus of the neighborhood's public buildings. Shops and workplaces are usually here, especially in a village. In the aggregations of neighborhoods that create towns and cities, retail buildings and workplaces are often at the edge, where they can combine with others to draw customers.

   The edges of a neighborhood vary in character. In villages, the edge is usually defined by land designated for cultivation or conservation of its natural state. In urban areas, the edge is often defined by rail lines and boulevards, which best remain outside the neighborhood.

2. The neighborhood has a balanced mix of activities: shops, work, school, recreation, and dwellings of all types. This is particularly useful for young, old, and low-income populations who, in an automobile-based environment, depend on others for mobility.

   The neighborhood provides housing for residents with a variety of incomes. Affordable housing types include backyard apartments, apartments above shops, and apartment buildings adjacent to workplaces.

3. The optimal size of a neighborhood is 1/4 mile from center to edge, a distance equal to a five-minute walk at an easy pace. Its limited area gathers the population within walking distance of many of its daily needs.

   The location of a transit stop within walking distance of most homes increases the likelihood of its use. Transit-oriented neighborhoods create a regional network of villages, towns, and cities accessible to a population unable to rely on cars. Such a system can provide the major cultural and social institutions, variety of shopping, and broad job base that can only be supported by the larger population of an aggregation of neighborhoods.

4. The neighborhood consists of blocks on a network of small thoroughfares. Streets are laid out to create blocks of appropriate building sites and to shorten pedestrian routes. An interconnecting street pattern provides multiple routes, diffusing traffic. This pattern keeps local traffic off regional roads and through traffic off local streets.

   Neighborhood streets of varying types are detailed to provide equitably for pedestrian comfort and automobile movement. Slowing the automobile and increasing pedestrian activity encourage the casual meetings that form the bonds of community.

5. The neighborhood gives priority to public space and to appropriate location of civic buildings. Public spaces and public buildings enhance community identity and foster civic pride. The neighborhood plan creates a hierarchy of useful public spaces: a formal square, an informal park, and many playgrounds.

THE DISTRICT

The district is an urbanized area that is functionally specialized. Although districts preclude the full range of activities of a neighborhood, they are not the single-activity zones of suburbia. Rather, multiple activities support its primary identity. Typically complex examples are theater districts, capital areas, and college campuses. Other districts accommodate large-scale transportation or manufacturing uses, such as airports, container terminals, and refineries.

The structure of the district parallels that of the neighborhood. An identifiable focus encourages orientation and identity. Clear boundaries facilitate the formation of special taxing or management organizations. As in the neighborhood, the character of the public spaces creates a community of users, even if they reside elsewhere. Interconnected circulation encourages pedestrians, supports transit viability, and ensures security. Districts benefit from transit systems and should be located within the regional network.

THE CORRIDOR

The corridor is the connector and the separator of neighborhoods and districts. Corridors include natural and technical components ranging from wildlife trails to rail lines. The between is not the haphazardly residual space remaining outside subdivisions and shopping centers in suburbia. It is a civic element characterized by its visible continuity and bounded by neighborhoods and districts, to which it provides entry.

The transportation corridor's trajectory is determined by its intensity. Heavy rail corridors should remain tangent to towns and enter only the industrial districts of cities. Light rail and trolley corridors may occur as boulevards at the edges of neighborhoods. As such, they are detailed for pedestrian use and to accommodate building sites. Bus corridors may pass into neighborhood centers on conventional streets.

The corridor may also be a continuous parkway, providing long-distance walking and bicycling trails and natural habitat. Parkway corridors can be formed by the systematic accretion of recreational open spaces, such as parks, schoolyards, and golf courses. These continuous spaces can be part of a larger network, connecting urban open space with rural surroundings.

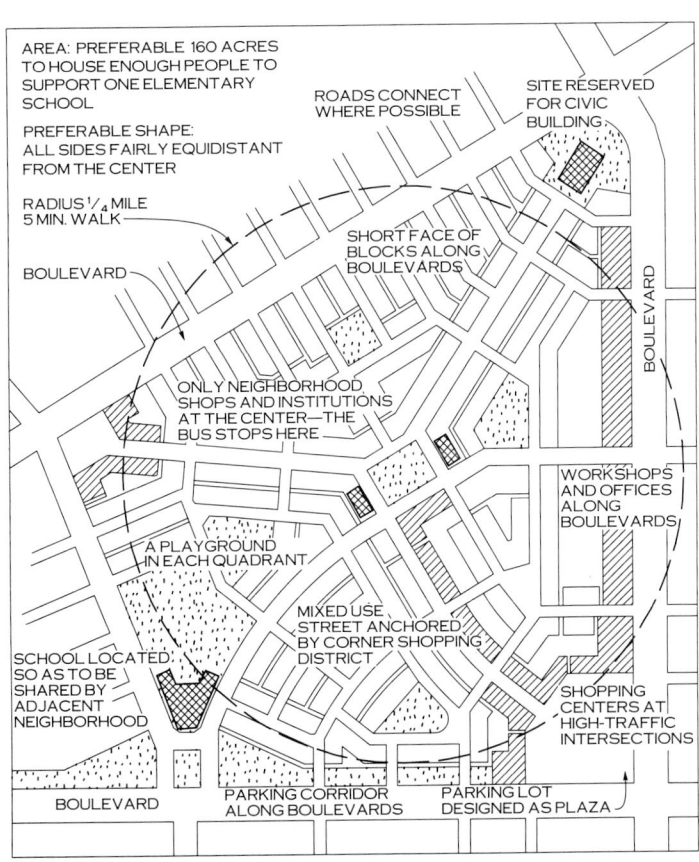

AREA: PREFERABLE 160 ACRES TO HOUSE ENOUGH PEOPLE TO SUPPORT ONE ELEMENTARY SCHOOL

PREFERABLE SHAPE: ALL SIDES FAIRLY EQUIDISTANT FROM THE CENTER

RADIUS 1/4 MILE 5 MIN. WALK

BOULEVARD

ROADS CONNECT WHERE POSSIBLE

SITE RESERVED FOR CIVIC BUILDING

SHORT FACE OF BLOCKS ALONG BOULEVARDS

BOULEVARD

ONLY NEIGHBORHOOD SHOPS AND INSTITUTIONS AT THE CENTER—THE BUS STOPS HERE

WORKSHOPS AND OFFICES ALONG BOULEVARDS

A PLAYGROUND IN EACH QUADRANT

MIXED USE STREET ANCHORED BY CORNER SHOPPING DISTRICT

SCHOOL LOCATED SO AS TO BE SHARED BY ADJACENT NEIGHBORHOOD

SHOPPING CENTERS AT HIGH-TRAFFIC INTERSECTIONS

BOULEVARD

PARKING CORRIDOR ALONG BOULEVARDS

PARKING LOT DESIGNED AS PLAZA

AN URBAN NEIGHBORHOOD (PART OF A TOWN)

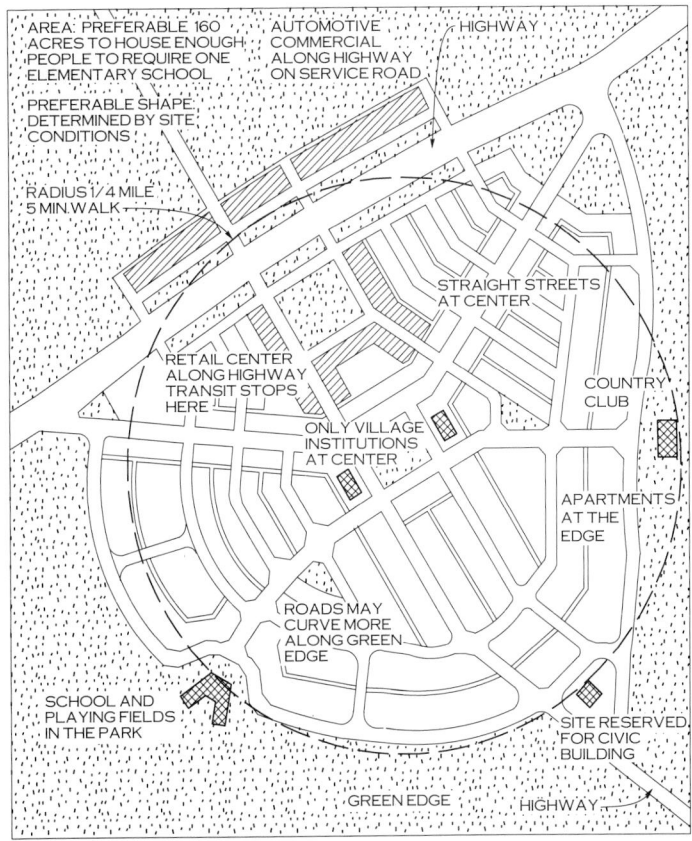

AREA: PREFERABLE 160 ACRES TO HOUSE ENOUGH PEOPLE TO REQUIRE ONE ELEMENTARY SCHOOL

AUTOMOTIVE COMMERCIAL ALONG HIGHWAY ON SERVICE ROAD

HIGHWAY

PREFERABLE SHAPE: DETERMINED BY SITE CONDITIONS

RADIUS 1/4 MILE 5 MIN. WALK

STRAIGHT STREETS AT CENTER

RETAIL CENTER ALONG HIGHWAY TRANSIT STOPS HERE

ONLY VILLAGE INSTITUTIONS AT CENTER

COUNTRY CLUB

APARTMENTS AT THE EDGE

ROADS MAY CURVE MORE ALONG GREEN EDGE

SCHOOL AND PLAYING FIELDS IN THE PARK

SITE RESERVED FOR CIVIC BUILDING

GREEN EDGE

HIGHWAY

A RURAL NEIGHBORHOOD (A VILLAGE)

Gary Greenan, Andres Duany, Elizabeth Plater-Zyberk, Kamal Zaharin, Iskandar Shafie; Miami, Florida
The Cintas Foundation

GENERAL

In its short history as a discipline, regional planning has generated a substantial number of models, usually presented as diagrams. Redrawing the main types in a standard graphic form reduces options to a few fundamental models. Most regional plans are hybrids of these few.

Most cities expand through incremental decisions, not by following clear regional plans. But even when followed closely, such plans tend to be implemented in distorted form, due to pressures from natural and man-made conditions. The diagrams of each planning model to the right are accompanied by examples of their application to actual places.

GARDEN CITY/NEIGHBORHOODS, TOWNS AND VILLAGES

This is the ancient natural pattern. A clearly defined core city, composed of neighborhoods, is surrounded by towns and villages that are separated by open landscape. Ideally, each element is relatively self-sufficient. This historical pattern has been overwhelmed as mechanical transportation has permitted the city to absorb the surrounding landscape and to erase its neighborhood structure.

A rationalization of this pattern, designating fixed greenbelts and creating independent new towns (garden cities), was proposed by Howard, and restructuring the core city into self-contained neighborhoods was proposed by Saarinen and Perry.

The garden city has been the underlying concept for suburban growth, although its current form is unrecognizably degenerated. With the late arrival of the office park into the residential/retail suburb, the functional elements of the city are now available in the suburb, and the core city has lost its importance. As conceptualized by Fishman and Garreau, this regional pattern is no longer centroidal. The automobile is able to move equally in all directions, although it tends to reinforce major intersections. These intensified points support commercial development, around which residential areas cluster.

This automobile model can be made pedestrian-oriented by traditional neighborhood development (TND), which reconfigures the activities of the shopping center, office park, and housing subdivision into the form of towns and villages. Of the three models described, this is the one most influenced by market conditions.

LINEAR CITY/CORRIDORS AND WEDGES

The linear city evolved with the advent of the streetcar. Moving along defined axes, the streetcar extended the boundaries of the centroidal city, creating corridors whose width was limited by the walking distance to the tracks. The arrival of the automobile, with its ability to go anywhere, destroyed the disciplined edges of the corridors, creating undifferentiated sprawl.

The remedial model (corridors and wedges) was conceptualized by Olmsted and MacKaye. Through legislation, the urban fabric is channeled along the transportation axes while wedges of open landscape are preserved between these corridors. The wedges are ideally continuous, formed by an irregular agglomeration of valuable natural features. This is the model most influenced by ecological concerns.

TRANSIT-ORIENTED DESIGN

This pattern emerged naturally with the advent of the railroad. Moving along a single axis like the streetcar, but unable to stop as frequently, the railroad creates nodal points of commercial development with residential settlement around them. The advent of the automobile permitted the expansion of these settlements beyond any limit, consuming the landscape.

This model was rationalized and modernized by Calthorpe and Kelbaugh as transit-oriented design (T.O.D.). The T.O.D. creates nodes at intervals most efficient for rail transportation. These mixed-use areas, limited in size by walking distance, are usually surrounded by a residential hinterland connected to the rail system by feeder bus. The commercial uses and other businesses at the nodes may not offer all the services that would make the area self-sufficient (i.e., a town). However, together, several areas linked by rail may be self-sufficient.

This is the model most influenced by the requirements of transportation.

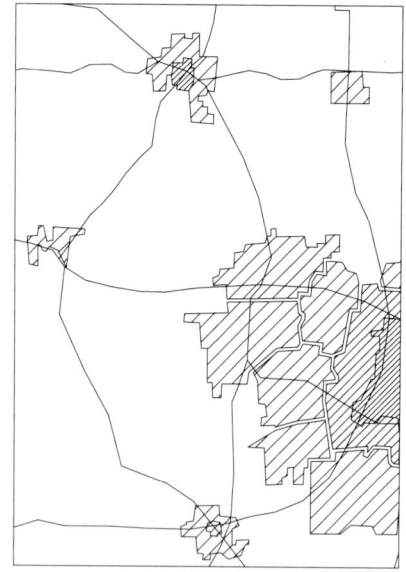

MADISON 1993

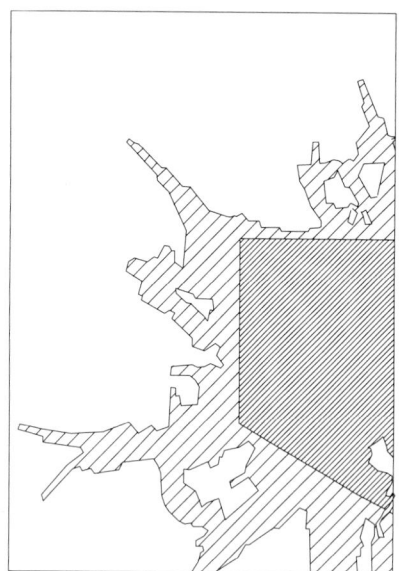

BALTIMORE 1950

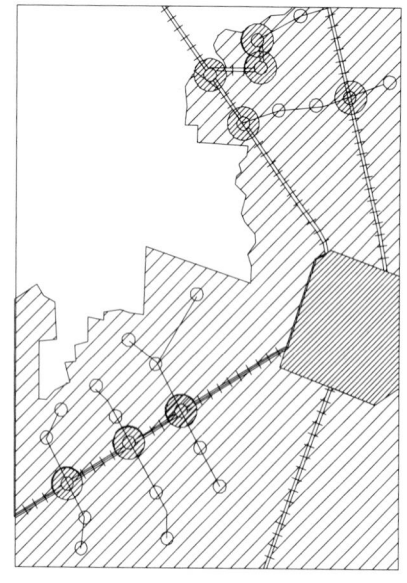

PORTLAND 2020

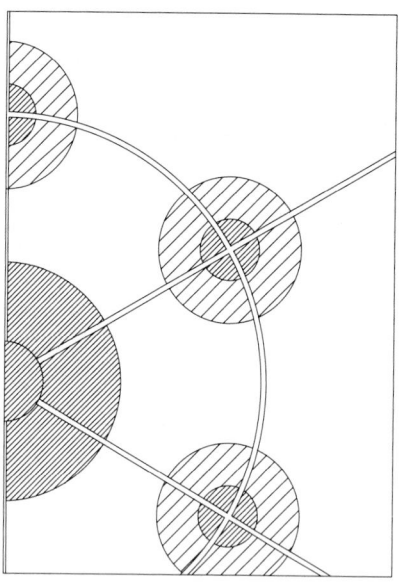

TOWNS AND VILLAGES

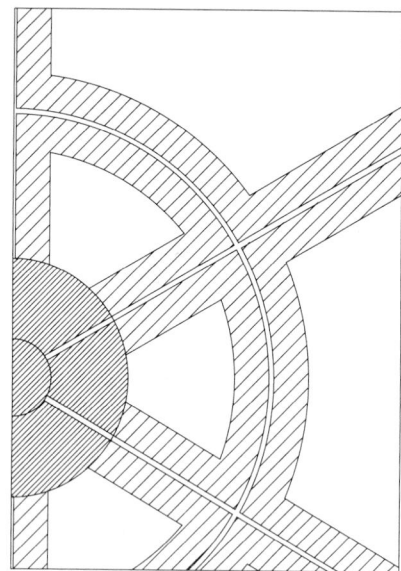

LINEAR CITY

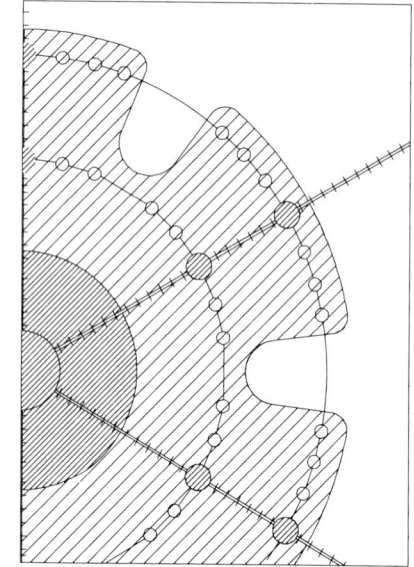

TRANSIT-ORIENTED DESIGN

Gary Greenan, Andres Duany, Elizabeth Plater-Zyberk, Kamal Zaharin, Iskandar Shafie, Rafael Diaz; Miami, Florida
The Cintas Foundation

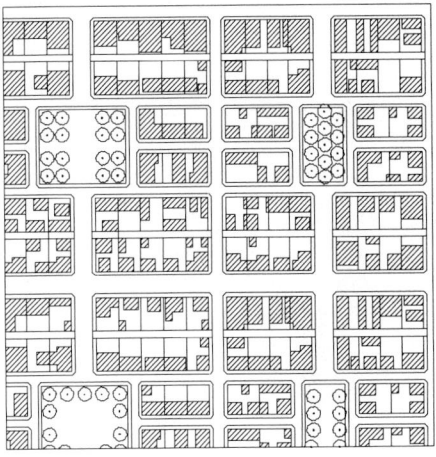

SAVANNAH

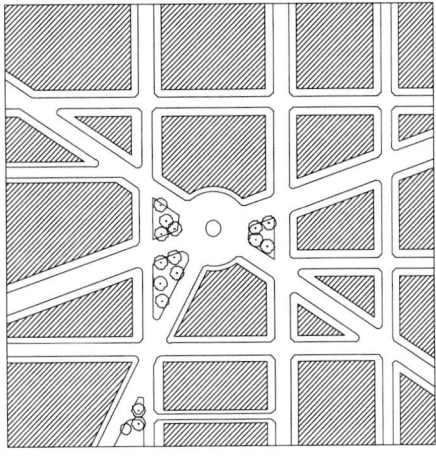

WASHINGTON, D.C.

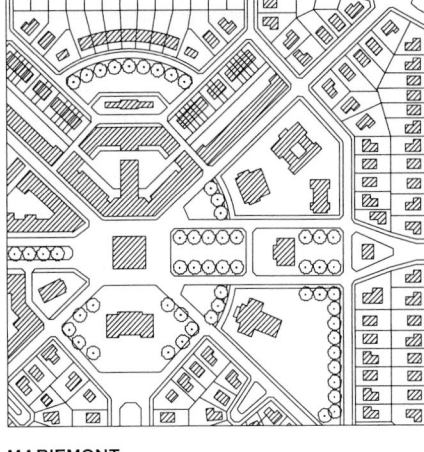

MARIEMONT

ADVANTAGES

1. Excellent directional orientation
2. Lot shape controllable
3. Street hierarchy with end blocks for through traffic
4. Even dispersal of traffic through the grid
5. Straight lines enhance rolling terrain
6. Efficient double-loading of alleys and utilities

DISADVANTAGES

1. Monotonous unless periodically interrupted
2. Does not accommodate environmental interruptions
3. Unresponsive to steep terrain

ORTHOGONAL GRID

ADVANTAGES

1. Street hierarchy with diagonals for through traffic
2. Even dispersal of traffic through the grid
3. Diagonals respond to the terrain
4. Diagonals interrupt monotony of the grid

DISADVANTAGES

1. Uncontrollable variety of blocks and lots
2. High number of awkward lot shapes
3. Diagonal intersections spatially ill defined

GRID WITH DIAGONALS

ADVANTAGES

1. Street hierarchy with diagonals for through traffic
2. Even dispersal of traffic through the network
3. Diagonals respond to terrain
4. Intrinsically interesting by geometric variety
5. Controllable shape of blocks and lots
6. Efficient double-loading of alleys for utilities
7. Diagonal intersections spatially well defined

DISADVANTAGES

1. Tends to be disorienting

DIAGONAL NETWORK

NANTUCKET

RIVERSIDE

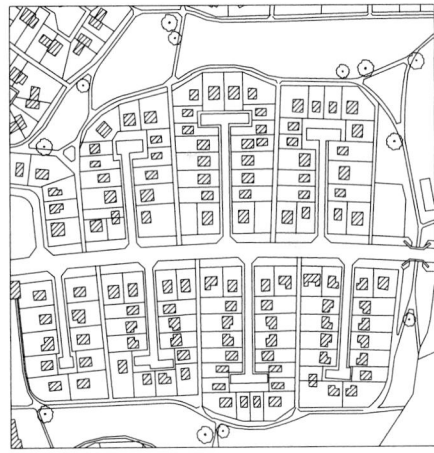

RADBURN

ADVANTAGES

1. Street hierarchy with long routes for through traffic
2. Even dispersal of traffic through network
3. Intrinsically interesting by geometric variety
4. Responsive to terrain
5. Easily accommodates environmental interruptions
6. Short streets, terminated vistas

DISADVANTAGES

1. None

ORGANIC NETWORK

ADVANTAGES

1. Intrinsically interesting by deflecting vistas
2. Easily accommodates environmental interruptions
3. Highly responsive to terrain
4. Even dispersal of traffic through the network

DISADVANTAGES

1. Little directional orientation
2. Uncontrollable variety of lots
3. No natural hierarchy of streets

CURVILINEAR NETWORK

ADVANTAGES

1. Street hierarchy with collectors for through traffic
2. Controllable variety of blocks and lots
3. Easily accommodates environmental interruptions
4. Highly responsive to p terrain

DISADVANTAGES

1. Concentration of traffic by absence of network

DISCONTINUOUS NETWORK

Gary Greenan, Andres Duany, Elizabeth Plater-Zyberk, Kamal Zaharin, Iskandar Shafie, Rafael Diaz; Miami, Florida
The Cintas Fountain

SITE, COMMUNITY, AND URBAN PLANNING 1

GENERAL

The urban plan must be assembled of blocks before building frontage and landscape types are assigned. The disposition of blocks has distinct socioeconomic implications.

THE SQUARE BLOCK

This type was an early model for planned settlements in America, particularly in Spanish colonies. It was sometimes associated with agricultural communities, providing four large lots per block, each lot with a house at its center. When the growth of the community produced additional subdivision, replatting created irregular lots (Fig. 1). While this may provide a useful variety, it is more often regarded as a nuisance by a society accustomed to standardized products. A further disadvantage is that discontin-uous rear lot lines make alleys and rear-access utilities impractical. Despite these shortcomings, the square block is useful as a specialized type. When platted only at its perimeter, with the center left open, it can accommodate the high parking requirements of certain buildings. The open center, well insulated from traffic, may also be used as a common garden or a playground (Fig. 2).

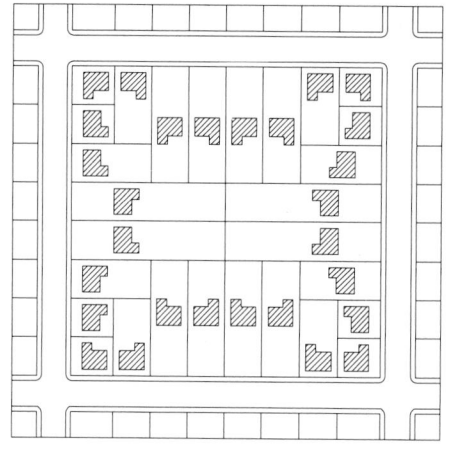

1. SQUARE BLOCK

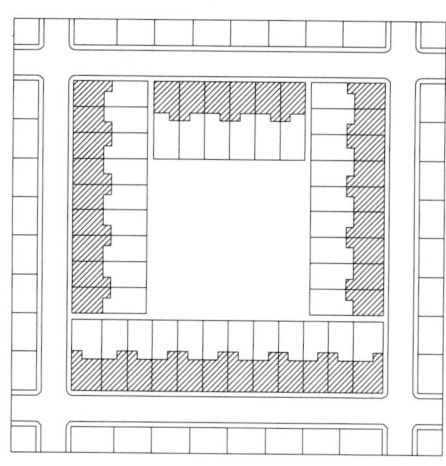

2. SQUARE BLOCK

THE ORGANIC BLOCK

This type is characterized by its irregularity; its variations are unlimited. The original organic block was the subdivision of residual land between well-worn paths (Fig. 3). It was later rationalized by Olmsted and Unwin to achieve a controllable, picturesque effect and to negotiate sloping terrain gracefully. The naturalistic block, despite its variety, generates certain recurring conditions that must be resolved by sophisticated platting. At shallow curves, it is desirable to have the facades follow the frontage smoothly. This is achieved by keeping the side lot lines perpendicular to the frontage line (Fig. 4-1). At the same time it is important for the rear lot line to be wide enough to permit vehicular access (Fig. 4-2). At sharper curves, it is desirable to have the axis of a single lot bisect the acute angle (Fig. 4-3). In the event of excessive block depth, it is possible to colonize the interior of the block by means of a close (Fig. 4-4).

3. ORGANIC BLOCK

4. ORGANIC BLOCK

THE ELONGATED BLOCK

The elongated block overcomes some of the drawbacks of the square block. More efficient and more standardized, elongated blocks provide economical double-loaded alleys, with short utility runs, to eliminate the uncontrollable variable of lot depth and maintain the option of altering lot width. By adjusting the block length, it is possible to reduce cross streets toward rural edges or to add them at urban centers. This adjustment alters the pedestrian permeability of the grid and controls the ratio of street parking to building capacity. The elongated block can "bend" somewhat along its length, giving it a limited ability to shape space and negotiate slopes (Fig. 6).

Unlike the square block, the elongated block provides two distinct types of frontage. Residential buildings are placed on the quieter sides of the block (Fig. 5-1). Commercial buildings can be set on the short end of the block, platted to face the busy street; the amount of parking behind these properties is controlled by the variable depth (Fig. 5-2).

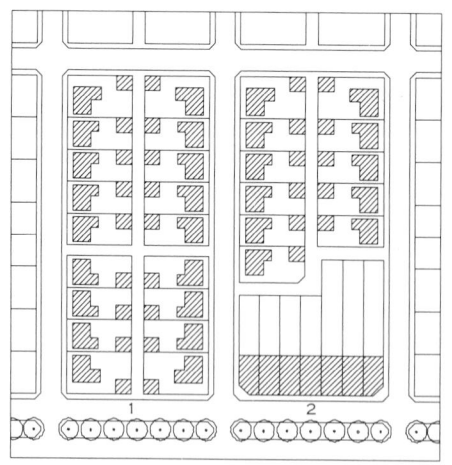

5. ELONGATED BLOCK

6. ELONGATED BLOCK

Gary Greenan, Andres Duany, Elizabeth Plater-Zyberk, Kamal Zaharin, Iskandar Shafie; Miami, Florida
The Cintas Foundation

1   SITE, COMMUNITY, AND URBAN PLANNING

GENERAL
Public open space provides orientation, hierarchy, and communal structure to a neighborhood. The specialized open spaces shown here are derived from the elongated block types. They can also be adjusted to fit both square and organic block types.

LANE
Children often make lanes behind houses into informal playgrounds. The paved surface in front of garages is convenient for ball games. Lanes are particularly successful when they are designed to eliminate through traffic (right). Garage apartments provide supervision.

PLAYGROUND
Playgrounds can be easily extracted from any block by assigning one or several lots to this use. There should be a playground within 500 ft of every residence. The playground should provide both sunny and shaded play areas, as well as an open shelter with benches for parents. Playgrounds must be fenced, lockable, and lit, if they are not to become a nuisance at night.

NURSERY
A nursery can be inserted in the middle of a block, away from major thoroughfares. It requires a limited amount of parking but substantial vehicular drop-off space. The attached playground should be securely fenced and have both sunny and shaded areas. Children's games may be noisy, so it is advisable to locate nurseries where adjacent houses are buffered by outbuildings.

CLOSE
A close is a space shared by buildings inside the block. It may be pedestrian, or it may have a roadway loop around a green area. Its minimum width must coincide with emergency vehicle turning standards. The close is a superior alternative to the cul-de-sac, as the focus is a green rather than pavement. It is especially recommended for communal subgroups such as cohousing or assisted-living cottages. The close provides additional frontage for deep square and organic blocks.

ATTACHED SQUARES
Squares are green spaces that provide settings for civic buildings and monuments, which are located at the center or edge of the square. Buildings play a part, but the space is largely defined by formal tree planting. Squares should be maintained to a higher standard than playgrounds and parks.

DETACHED SQUARES
Squares detached on all sides by roads are particularly formal. Since adjacent buildings provide much of the population that uses a public space, detached squares are less likely to be used than other types. This separation also limits the amount of natural security provided by adjacent windows. The detached square remains appropriate as a means to symbolically enhance important places or institutions.

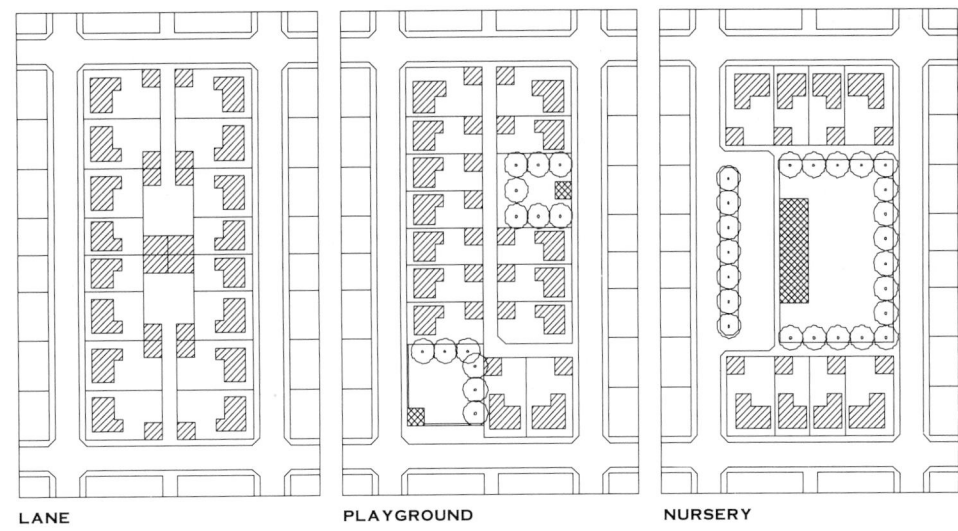

LANE PLAYGROUND NURSERY

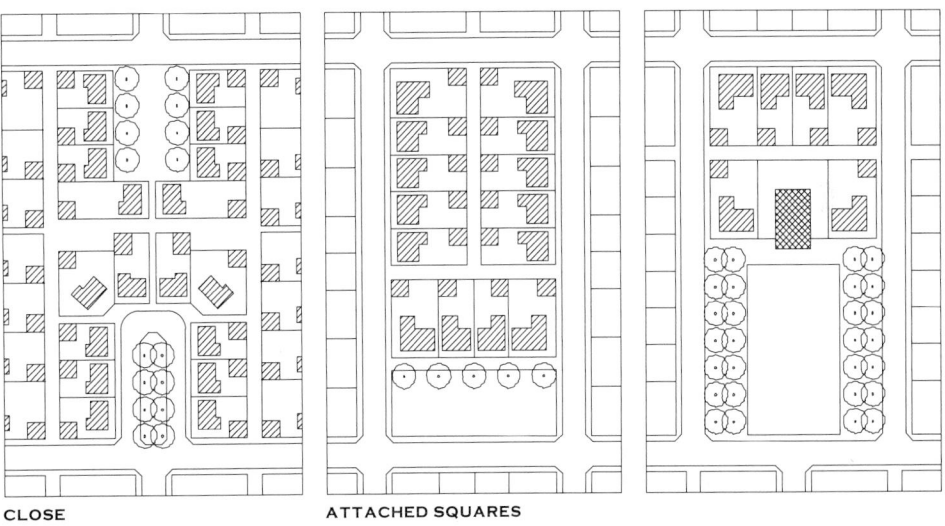

CLOSE ATTACHED SQUARES

OPEN SPACE TYPES

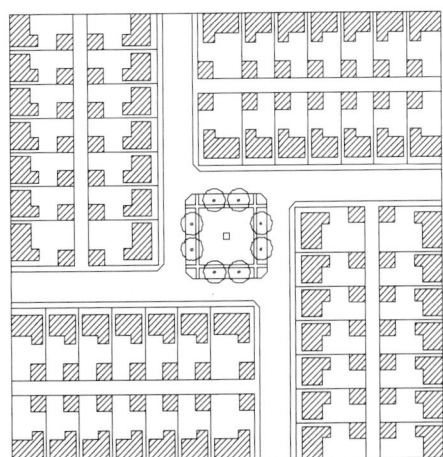 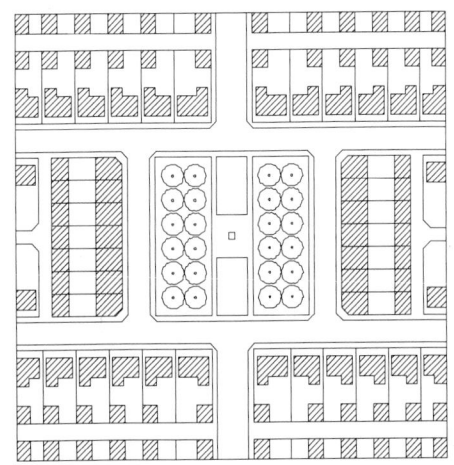 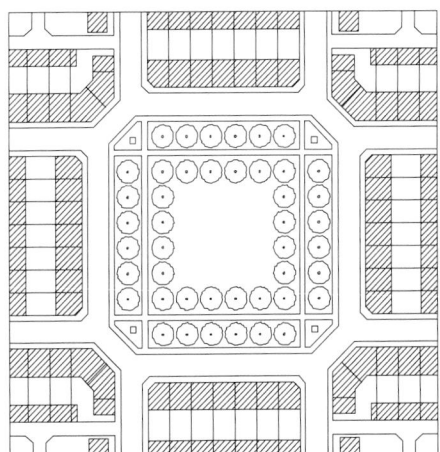

OPEN SPACE TYPES—DETACHED SQUARES

Gary Greenan, Andres Duany, Elizabeth Plater-Zyberk, Kamal Zaharin, Iskandar Shafie; Miami, Florida
The Cintas Foundation

SITE, COMMUNITY, AND URBAN PLANNING 1

MARKET PLAZA

Plazas are public spaces that are primarily paved rather than green. They can sustain very intense use by crowds and even by vehicles. Parking lots should be designed as plazas that happen to have cars on them, rather than as single-purpose areas. A smaller shopping center can be transformed into a town center if it has been designed so it can be seamlessly attached to the block system and detailed as a plaza.

CIVIC PLAZA

Civic buildings are often no larger than the private ones that surround them, and their legibility as more important buildings cannot depend solely on architectural expression. Their setting within the block system must communicate their elevated status. Sites on squares or at the terminations of avenues are ideal but not always available. Thus the most dependable technique is to organize and detail the parking areas of civic buildings as plazas.

GREEN

The green is an urban, naturalistic open space. Like the square, it is small, civic, and surrounded by buildings. Unlike the square, it is informally planted and may have an irregular topography. Greens are usually landscaped with trees at the edges and sunny lawns at the center. Greens should contain no structures other than benches, pavilions, and memorials; paths are optional.

PARK

Parks are naturalistic open spaces, like greens, but larger and less tended. They are most successful when created from virgin woodland. Parks have grassy areas only periodically. A knoll or a pond can be used as an important organizing feature. Parks exist within the urban fabric of large cities, but their inherent size usually puts them at the edges of towns and villages. Parks may be edged by public drives or by houses on very large lots, as long as connections to public paths occur at every block.

BUFFER

The buffer has the basic elements of a green, with the added purpose of buffering the impact of traffic from a highway or boulevard. Shown is a small lot development fronting a green. On the opposite side are larger lots on which houses are placed further back from the roadway edge as another buffer technique.

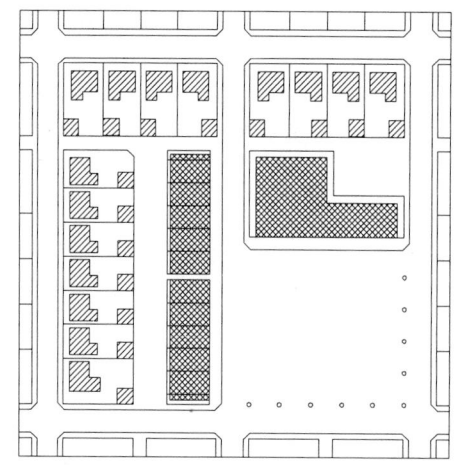

MARKET PLAZA

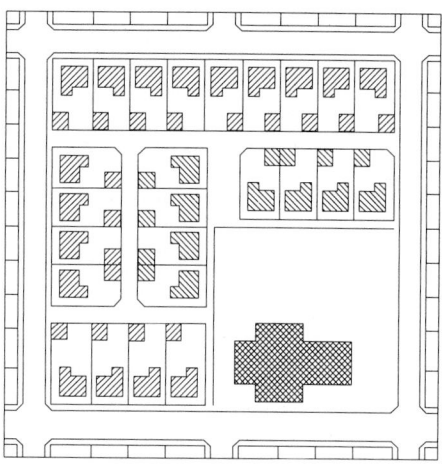

CIVIC PLAZA

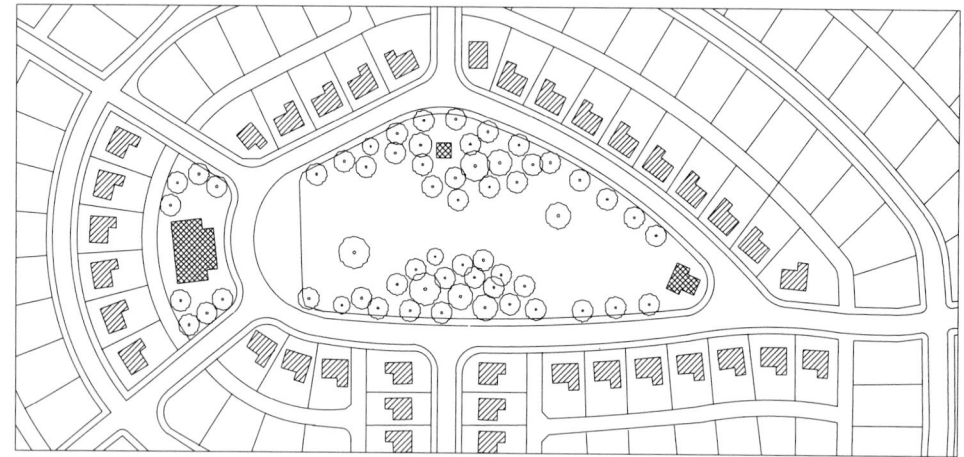

GREEN

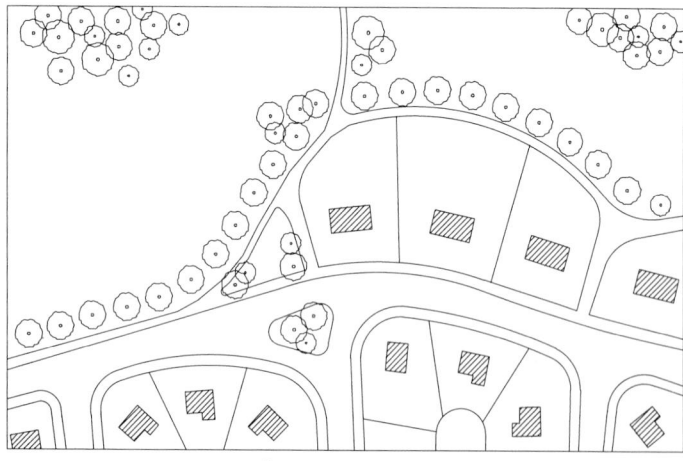

PARK

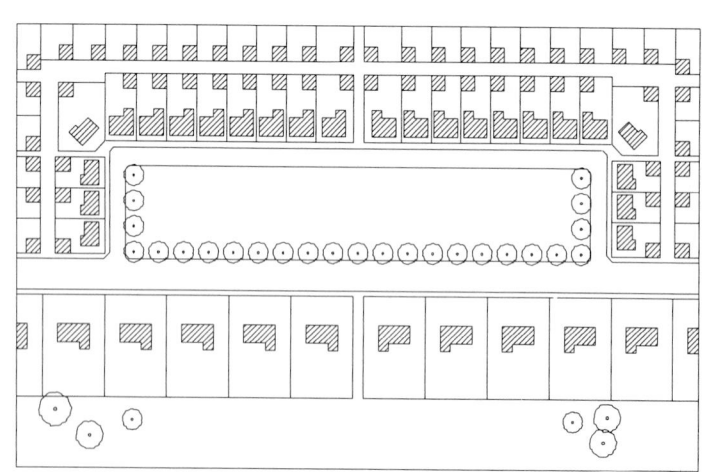

BUFFER

Gary Greenan, Andres Duany, Elizabeth Plater-Zyberk, Kamal Zaharin, Iskandar Shafie; Miami, Florida
The Cintas Foundation

1 SITE, COMMUNITY, AND URBAN PLANNING

GENERAL

The traditional increment for platting lots in North America has been the 50-ft width. This subdivision dimension was efficient for many years, creating 25-ft rowhouse and shopfront lots, as well as 50-, 75-, and 100-ft lots suitable for houses. However, the advent of the automobile added a set of dimensional constraints that required new platting standards. The 50-ft width is wasteful, since the basic increment of efficient parking is the double row at 64 ft.

The 64-ft increment, when divided by four, provides the absolute minimum rowhouse lot of 16 ft, which allows one car to be parked with additional room for pedestrian passage. The minimum side yard lot is 32 ft. The minimum perimeter yard lot is 48 ft. The 64-ft lot efficiently provides for the high parking requirement of shopfronts, apartments, and office buildings.

The platting module of 16 ft corresponds to the traditional measure of the rod. Platting in rods, without knowing what building types will occupy the lots, maintains flexibility and ensures maximum density through parking efficiency.

Four building types accommodate the common residential, retail, and workplace uses of urban life. Some buildings, however, cannot be categorized typologically. Buildings dedicated to manufacturing and transportation may be distorted by large-scale mechanical trajectories. Civic buildings, which must express the aspirations of the institutions they embody, should also be exempt from the discipline of type.

COURTYARD BUILDING

This type of building occupies all or most of the edges of its lot and defines one or more private spaces internally. This is the most urban of types as it is able to completely shield the private realm from the public realm. It is common in hot climates, but its attributes are useful everywhere. Because of its ability to accommodate incompatible activities in close proximity, it is recommended for workshops, hotels, and schools. The high security the boundary provides is useful for recolonizing crime-prone urban cores.

SIDE YARD BUILDING

This type of building occupies one side of the lot, with the primary open space on the other side. The view of the side yard on the street front makes this building type appear freestanding, so it may be interspersed with perimeter yard buildings in less urban locations. If the adjacent building is also a side yard type with a blank party wall, the open space can be quite private. This type permits systematic climatic orientation, with the long side yard elevation facing the sun or the breeze.

REAR YARD BUILDING

This type of building occupies the front of its lot, full width, leaving the rear portion as a private space. This is a relatively urban type appropriate for neighborhood and town centers. The building facade defines the edge of the public space, while the rear elevation may reflect different functional purposes. In its residential form, this type is represented by the rowhouse with a rear garden and outbuilding. In its commercial form, the depth of the rear yard can contain substantial parking for retail and office uses.

PERIMETER YARD BUILDING

This building stands free on its lot, with substantial front and rear yards and smaller side yards. It is the least urban of the types, so it is usually assigned to areas away from neighborhood and town centers. This building type is usually residential, but when parking is contained within the rear yard it lends itself to limited office and boarding uses. The rear yard can be secured for privacy by fences and a well-placed outbuilding. The front yard is intended to be semipublic and visually continuous with the yards of neighbors. The illusion of continuity is usually degraded when garage fronts are aligned with the facades, as cars seldom pull in beyond the driveway. To avoid a landscape of parked cars, garages should be set back a minimum of one car's length from the facade or entered sideways through a walled forecourt.

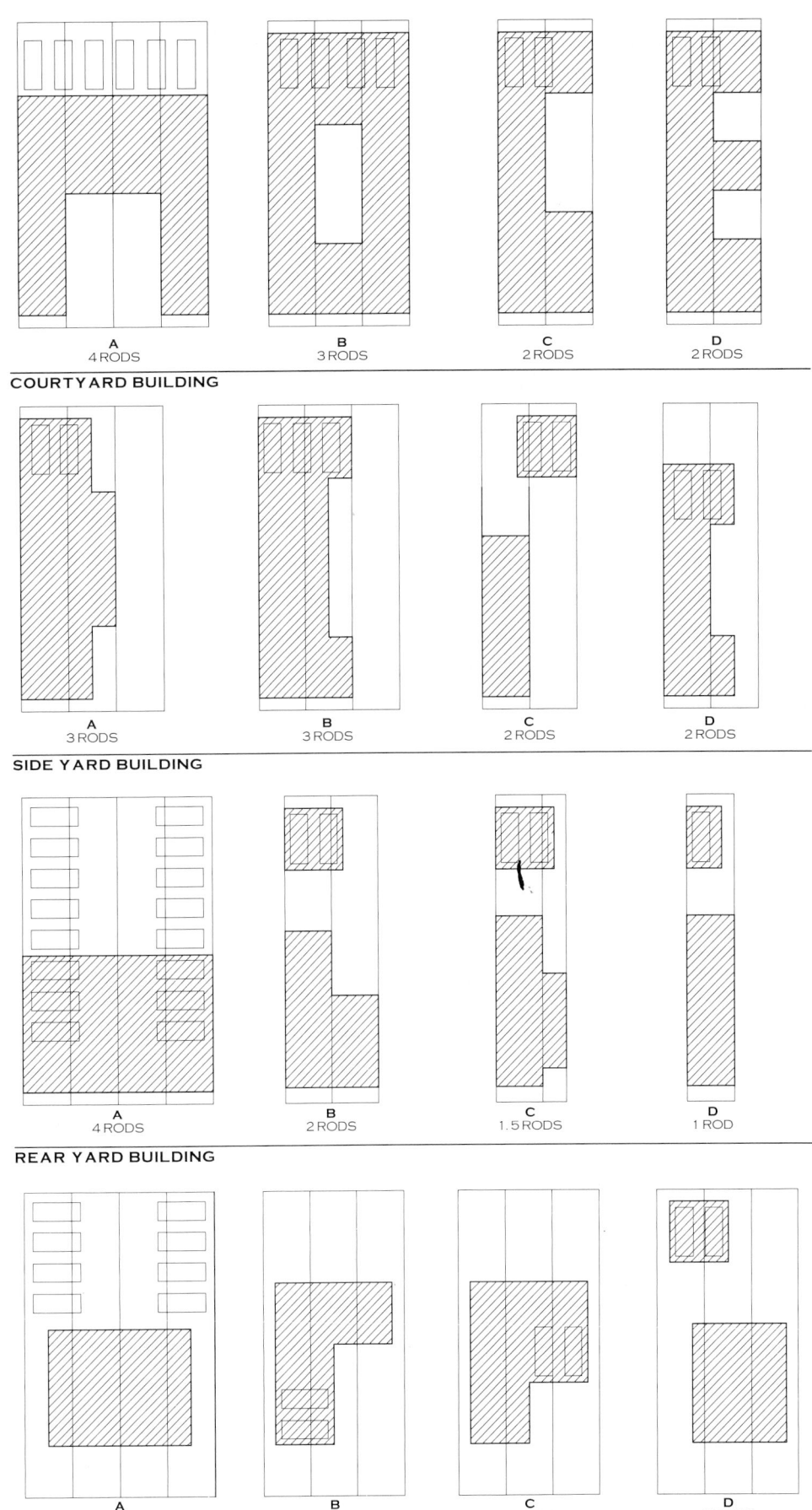

COURTYARD BUILDING

A — 4 RODS
B — 3 RODS
C — 2 RODS
D — 2 RODS

SIDE YARD BUILDING

A — 3 RODS
B — 3 RODS
C — 2 RODS
D — 2 RODS

REAR YARD BUILDING

A — 4 RODS
B — 2 RODS
C — 1.5 RODS
D — 1 ROD

PERIMETER YARD BUILDING

A — 4 RODS
B — 3 RODS
C — 3 RODS
D — 3 RODS

Gary Greenan, Andres Duany, Elizabeth Plater-Zyberk, Kamal Zaharin, Iskandar Shafie; Miami, Florida
The Cintas Foundation

GENERAL

Building delineates public space in an urban setting. Successful spatial definition is achieved when bounding buildings are aligned in a disciplined manner and the defined space does not exceed a certain height-to-width ratio.

Alignment occurs when building facades cooperate to delineate the public space, as walls form a room. Urban building articulation takes place primarily in the vertical plane or facade. If appendages such as porches, balconies, bay windows, and loggias do not obliterate the primary surface of the facade, they do not destroy alignment.

The height-to-width ratio of the space generates spatial enclosure, which is related to the physiology of the human eye. If the width of a public space is such that the cone of vision encompasses less street wall than sky opening, the degree of spatial enclosure is slight. The ratio of 1 increment of height to 6 of width is the absolute minimum, with 1 to 3 being an effective minimum if a sense of spatial enclosure is to result. As a general rule, the tighter the ratio, the stronger the sense of place and, often, the higher the real estate value. Spatial enclosure is particularly important for shopping streets that must compete with shopping malls, which provide very effective spatial definition. In the absence of spatial definition by facades, disciplined tree planting is an alternative. Trees aligned for spatial enclosure are necessary on thoroughfares that have substantial front yards.

NOMENCLATURE

THE FRONTAGE LINE

The lot boundary that coincides with a public thoroughfare or public space. The frontage line may be designed independently of the thoroughfare, to create a specific sense of place.

FACADE

The vertical surface of a building set along a frontage line. The elevation is the vertical surface set along any other boundary line. Facades are subject to control by building height, setback lines, recess lines, and transition lines. Elevations are only subject to building height and setback lines.

SETBACK

The mandatory distance between a frontage line and a facade or a lot line and an elevation

BUILDING HEIGHT

The defined limit to the vertical extent of a building. The building height should be stated as a number of stories, rather than a prescribed dimension. This prevents the compression of internal ceiling heights. Height may be determined by density and view and not by the requirements of spatial definition, which are addressed by the recess line.

RECESS LINE

A line prescribed for the full width of the facade, above which the facade is set back. The recess line effectively defines the enclosure of public space. Its location is determined by the desired height-to-width ratio of that space, compatibility with the average height of existing buildings, or provision for daylighting at the street level.

TRANSITION LINE

A line prescribed for the full width of the facade, expressed by a variation of material or by a limited projection such as a cornice or a balcony. The transition line divides the facade, permitting shopfronts and signage to vary over time without destroying the overall composition.

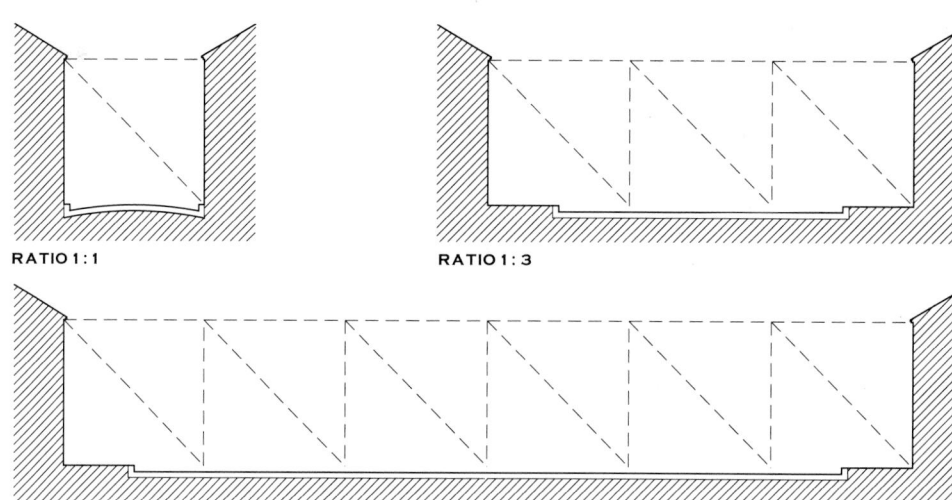

RATIO 1 : 1   RATIO 1 : 3

RATIO 1 : 6

PROPORTIONS OF BUILDING HEIGHT TO PUBLIC SPACE

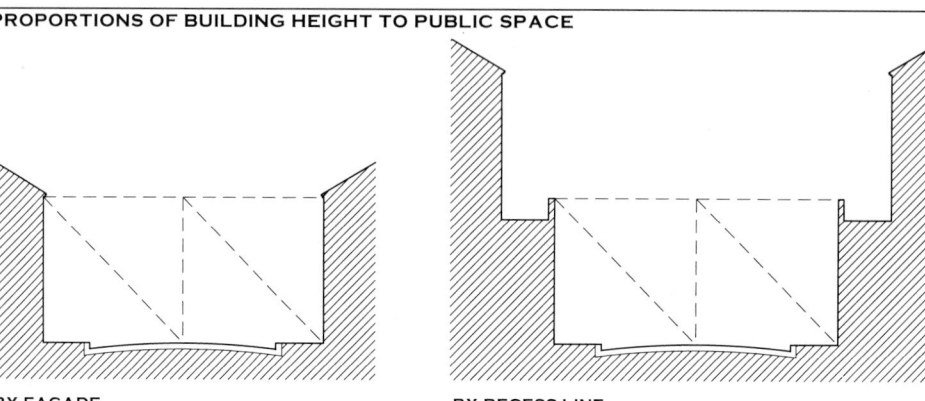

BY FACADE   BY RECESS LINE

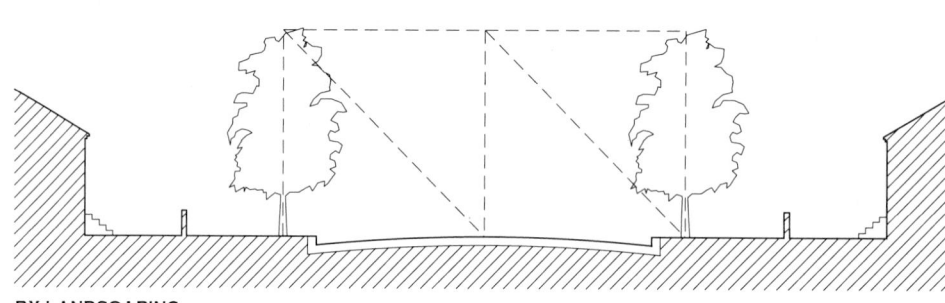

BY LANDSCAPING

TECHNIQUES OF DELINEATING PUBLIC SPACE

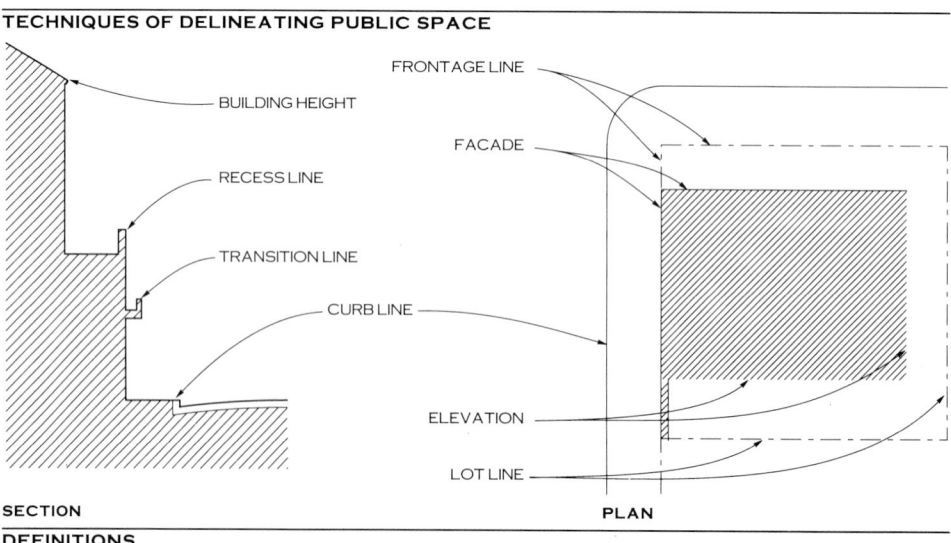

BUILDING HEIGHT

RECESS LINE

TRANSITION LINE

CURB LINE

FRONTAGE LINE

FACADE

ELEVATION

LOT LINE

SECTION   PLAN

DEFINITIONS

Gary Greenan, Andres Duany, Elizabeth Plater-Zyberk, Kamal Zaharin, Iskandar Shafie; Miami, Florida
The Cintas Foundation

SITE, COMMUNITY, AND URBAN PLANNING

GENERAL

Building type is independent of frontage type. For example, a courtyard building may have an arcade, a shopfront, a stoop, or a porch as its frontage type. Frontages can be ranked from most urban to most rural.

ARCADE

The facade overlaps the sidewalk, while the storefront remains set back. This type is excellent for retail use, but only when the sidewalk is fully absorbed so the pedestrian cannot bypass the arcade. An easement for public use of private property is required.

SHOPFRONT

The facade is aligned directly on the frontage line, with the entrance at grade. This type is conventional for sidewalk retail. It is often equipped with an awning or a porch. A transition line should separate the signage from the facade above. The absence of a setback and elevation from the sidewalk prevents residential use on the ground floor, although it is appropriate above.

STOOP

The facade is aligned directly on the frontage line, with the first floor elevated to achieve some privacy for the windows. This type is suitable for residential uses such as rowhouses and apartment buildings. An easement may be necessary to accommodate the encroaching stoop. This type may be interspersed with the shopfront.

FORECOURT

The facade is set back and replaced by a low wall at the frontage line. The forecourt thus created is suitable for gardens, vehicular drop-offs, and workshop loading and storage. It should be used sparingly and in conjunction with the shopfront and stoop types, as a continuous blind wall is boring and unsafe for pedestrians. Tree canopies within the forecourt should overhang the sidewalk.

DOORYARD

The facade is set back from the frontage line, with an elevated garden or terrace between. This type can effectively buffer residential quarters from the sidewalk, while removing the yard from public use. The terrace, when roofed, is suitable for restaurants and cafes, as the eye level of the sitter is level with that of passersby.

PORCH AND FENCE

With an encroaching habitable porch, the facade is set back substantially from the frontage line. The porch should be within a conversational distance of the sidewalk. A fence at the frontage line marks the boundary of the yard.

FRONT LAWN

The facade is set back substantially from the frontage line. The front lawn this creates should be unfenced and visually continuous with adjacent yards. The ideal is to simulate buildings sitting in a rural landscape. A front porch is usually not appropriate, since no social interaction with the street is possible at such a distance. The large setback can provide a buffer from heavy traffic, so this type is sometimes found on boulevards.

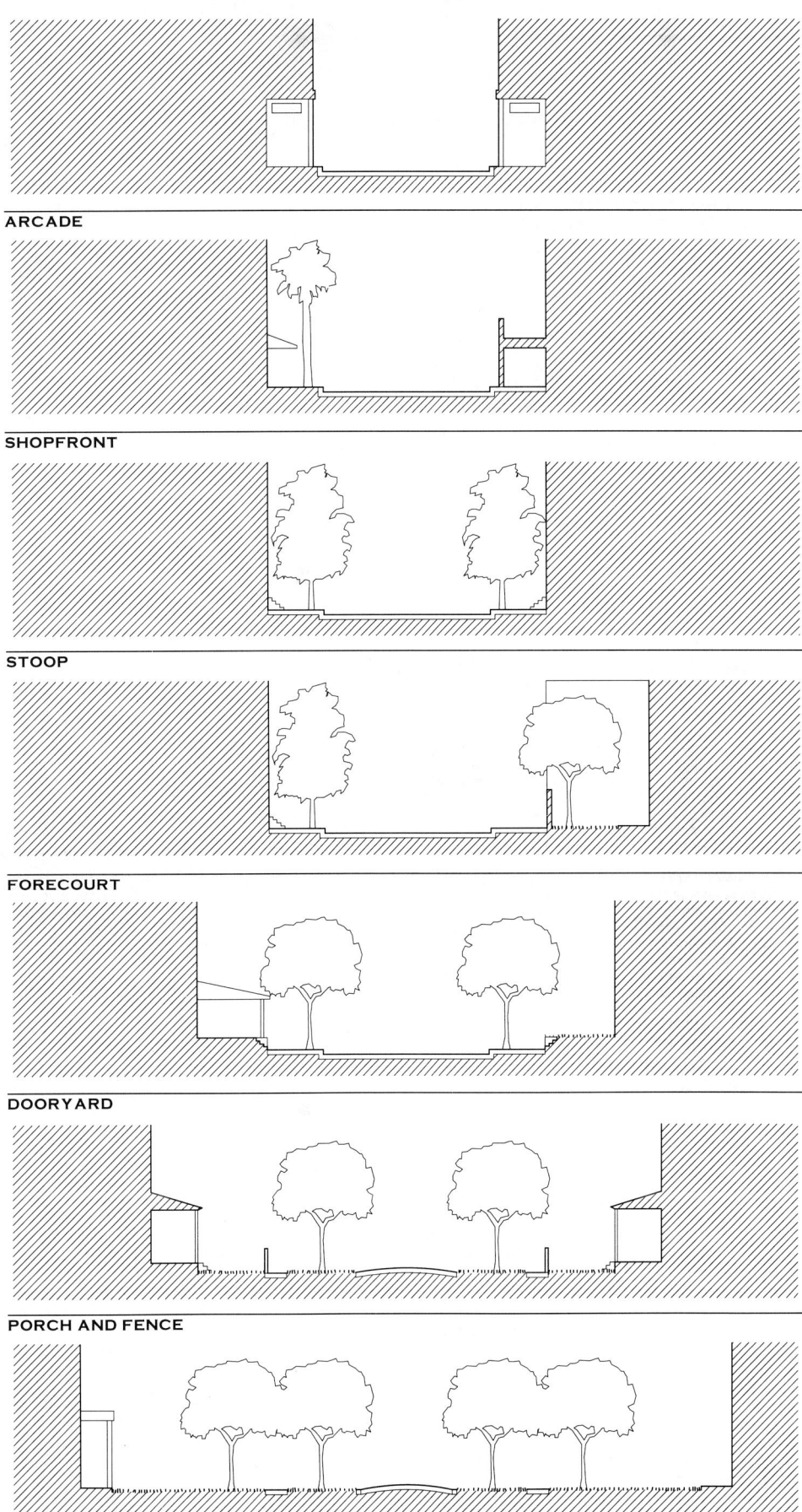

ARCADE

SHOPFRONT

STOOP

FORECOURT

DOORYARD

PORCH AND FENCE

FRONT LAWN

Gary Greenan, Andres Duany, Elizabeth Plater-Zyberk, Kamal Zaharin, Iskandar Shafie; Miami, Florida
The Cintas Foundation

SITE, COMMUNITY, AND URBAN PLANNING   1

GENERAL

The urban landscape is a set of interdependent elements that creates a controlled sense of place. It includes thoroughfare type, building type, frontage type, and the form and disposition of landscape.

Public landscaping plays many roles above and beyond that of ornamentation:

1. To correct inadequacies of spatial definition caused by building frontages. Planting steady rows of trees at the edges usually reduces the height-to-width ratio of the street space. Grids of trees are used to fill gaps left by unbuilt lots and surface parking.
2. To adjust the microclimate by providing the appropriate level of shade or sun for buildings and sidewalks. For thoroughfares running east-west, this may involve the use of asymmetrical planting.
3. To support the intended urban or rural character of the public space. Selecting appropriate species and varying the species planted, as well as the regularity of their disposition, can alter the landscape significantly.
4. To create a pleasing visual composition, being careful to mask the aesthetic failure of certain buildings as well as to reveal the successes. Consider seasonal changes of each species.
5. To create a harmonious whole of specific character by coordinating public and private plantings. Selection should vary, to ensure resistance to pests, but not result in an incoherent collection of specimens. Native species should predominate to reduce maintenance, with an emphasis on species that support wildlife compatible with human settlement.

RURAL ROAD

This type is appropriate for buildings at the edges of the neighborhood and along parks and greenbelts. There is no public planting line. The tree species should be episodic, but in coherent clusters. There are no curbs; the drainage is by open swale. Bicycle paths may be paved in asphalt.

RESIDENTIAL ROAD

This type is appropriate for houses outside of neighborhood centers. Since the frontage usually includes a substantial setback, the tree canopy may be quite wide. The rural aspect may be supported by planting several species in imperfect alignment. Roads are detailed with open swales, and, where possible, drainage is through percolation.

RESIDENTIAL STREET

This type is appropriate for residential buildings at neighborhood and town centers. Trees are in continuous planting strips, since the sidewalk does not require unusual width. Plant a single species of tree in steady alignment. A thin, vertical canopy is necessary to avoid nearby building facades. This type is dimensionally interchangeable with the commercial street type and may alternate in correspondence to the building facade. Streets are detailed with raised curbs and closed storm drainage.

COMMERCIAL STREET

This type is appropriate for commercial buildings at neighborhood and town centers. Trees are confined by individual planting areas, creating a sidewalk of maximum width with areas accommodating street furniture. Plant a single species of tree in steady alignment. Clear trunks and high canopies are necessary to avoid interference with shopfront signage and awnings. Streets are detailed with raised curbs with closed storm drainage.

AVENUE

This type is appropriate for approaches to civic buildings. The general principle is a thoroughfare of limited length, with a substantial planted median. At town centers, the median may be wide enough to hold monuments and even buildings. In residential areas, the median may be planted naturalistically to become a parkway or green.

BOULEVARD

This type is appropriate for high-capacity thoroughfares at neighborhood edges. The detailing is similar to that of a commercial street. The effect of the medians is to segregate the slower traffic and parking activity, at the edges, from through traffic, at the center.

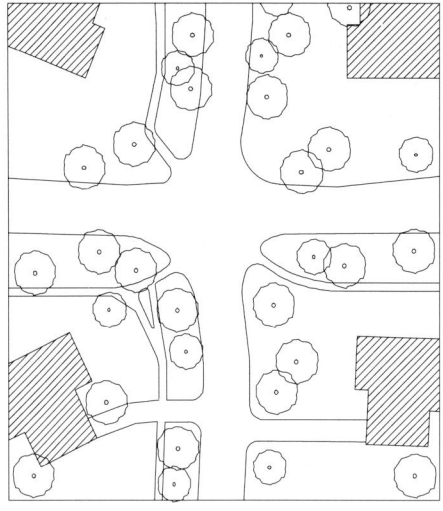

RURAL ROAD

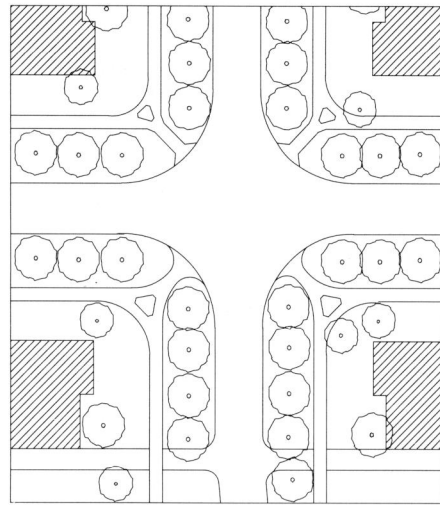

RESIDENTIAL ROAD

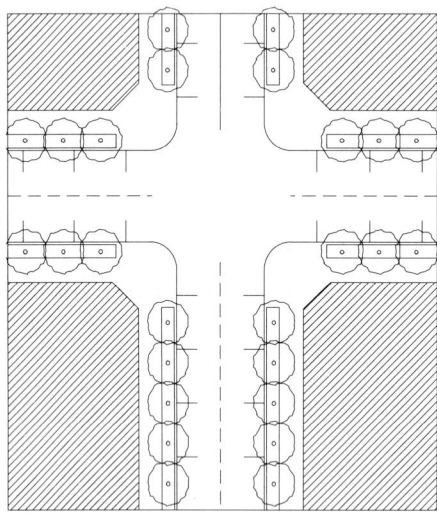

RESIDENTIAL STREET

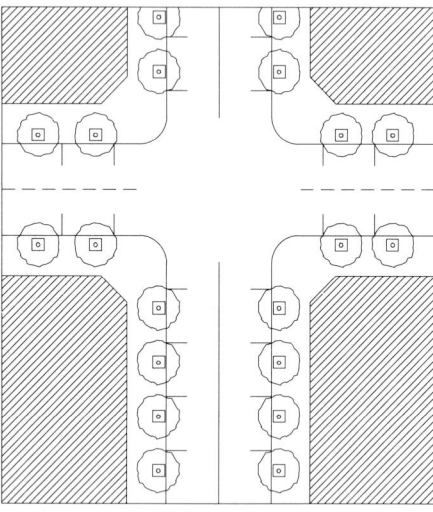

COMMERCIAL STREET

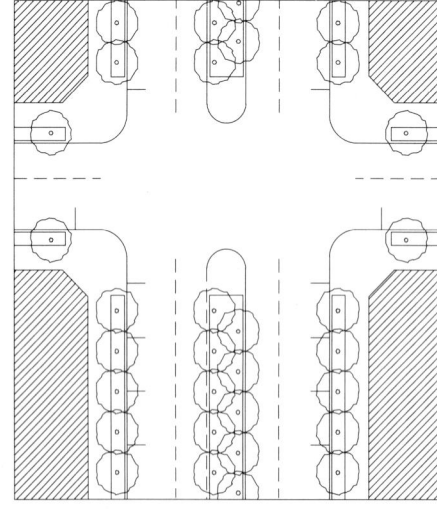

AVENUE

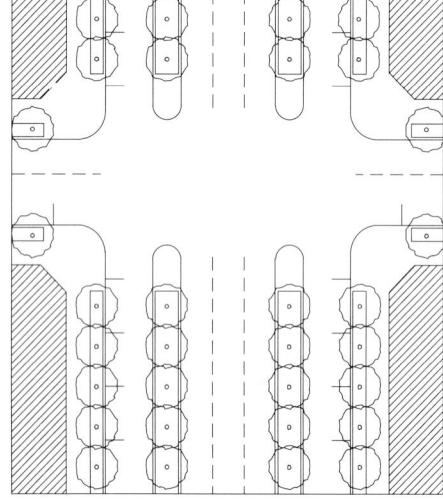

BOULEVARD

Gary Greenan, Andres Duany, Elizabeth Plater-Zyberk, Kamal Zaharin, Iskandar Shafie; Miami, Florida
The Cintas Foundation

1 SITE, COMMUNITY, AND URBAN PLANNING

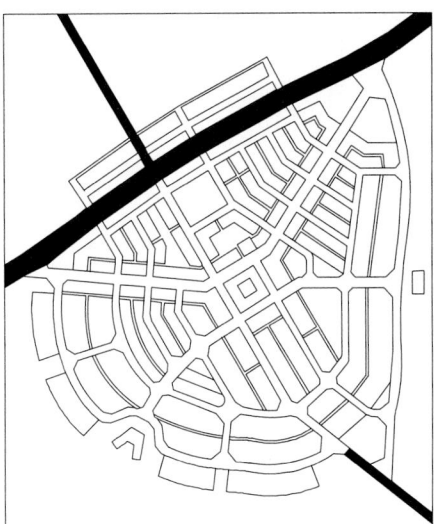

HIGHWAYS

DRIVES

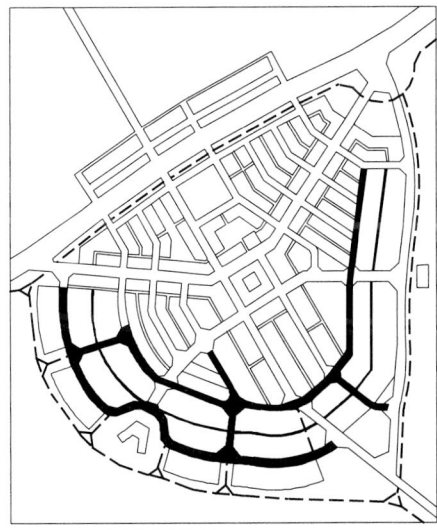

ROADS, LANES, PATHS

MORE RURAL

GENERAL

Thoroughfares are endowed with two attributes: capacity and character. Capacity refers to the number of vehicles that can move safely through a segment within a given time. It is physically manifested by the number of lanes and their width and by the centerline radius, the curb radius, and the super elevation of the pavement. Character refers to a thoroughfare's suitability for pedestrian activities and a variety of building types. Character is physically manifested by the thoroughfare's associated building, frontage, and landscape types and sidewalk width.

Conventional traffic engineering practice uses terms such as "collector" and "arterial," which denote only capacity. This is too simplistic and tends to create an environment inhospitable for pedestrians. The following nomenclature more adequately describes the combination of capacity and character necessary to create true urbanism.

NOMENCLATURE

HIGHWAY: A long-distance, medium speed vehicular corridor that traverses open country. A highway should be relatively free of intersections, driveways, and adjacent buildings; otherwise it becomes a strip, which interferes with traffic flow. (Related terms include expressway, a high speed highway with intersections replaced by grade separation, and parkway, a highway designed with naturalistic landscaping, partially accommodated within a wide and varying median.

BOULEVARD: A long-distance, medium speed vehicular corridor that traverses an urbanized area. It is usually lined by parallel parking, wide sidewalks, or side medians planted with trees. Buildings uniformly line the edges.

AVENUE: A short-distance, medium speed connector that traverses an urban area. Unlike a boulevard, its axis is terminated by a civic building or monument. An avenue may be conceived as an extremely elongated square. (A related term is allée, a rural avenue spatially defined by trees aligned on either side but devoid of buildings except at the terminus.)

DRIVE: An edge between an urban and a natural condition, usually along a waterfront, park, or promontory. One side of the drive has the urban character of a boulevard, with sidewalk and buildings, while the other has the qualities of a parkway, with naturalistic planting and rural detailing.

STREET: A small-scale, low speed local connector. Streets provide frontage for high-density buildings such as offices, shops, apartment buildings, and rowhouses. A street is urban in character, with raised curbs, closed drainage, wide sidewalks, parallel parking, trees in individual planting areas, and buildings aligned on short setbacks.

ROAD: A small-scale, low speed connector. Roads provide frontage for low-density buildings such as houses. A road tends to be rural in character with open curbs, optional parking, continuous planting, narrow sidewalks, and buildings set well back. The rural road has no curbs and is lined by pathways, irregular tree planting, and uncoordinated building setbacks.

ALLEY: A narrow access route servicing the rear of buildings on a street. Alleys have no sidewalks, landscaping, or building setbacks. Alleys are used by trucks and must accommodate dumpsters. They are usually paved to their edges, with center drainage via an inverted crown.

LANE: A narrow access route behind houses on a road. Lanes are rural in character, with a narrow strip of paving at the center or no paving. While lanes may not be necessary with front-loaded garages, they are still useful for accommodating utility runs, enhancing the privacy of rear yards, and providing play areas for children.

PASSAGE: A very narrow, pedestrian-only connector cutting between buildings. Passages provide shortcuts through long blocks or connect rear parking areas with street frontages. Passages may be roofed over and lined by shopfronts.

PATH: A very narrow pedestrian and bicycle connector traversing a park or the open country. Paths should emerge from the sidewalk network. Bicycle paths are necessary along highways but are not required to supplement boulevards, streets, and roads, where slower traffic allows sharing of the vehicular lanes.

BOULEVARDS

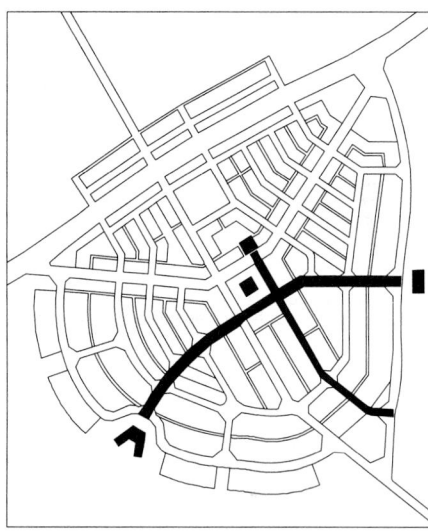

AVENUES

STREETS, ALLEYS, PASSAGES

MORE URBAN

Gary Greenan, Andres Duany, Elizabeth Plater-Zyberk, Kamal Zaharin, Iskandar Shafie; Miami, Florida
The Cintas Foundation

SITE, COMMUNITY, AND URBAN PLANNING   1

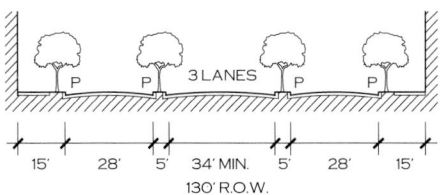

BOULEVARD

15'   28'   5'   34' MIN.   5'   28'   15'
130' R.O.W.

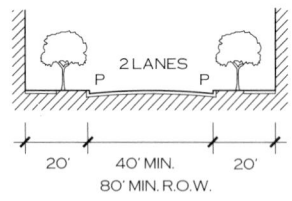

MAIN STREET

20'   40' MIN.   20'
80' MIN. R.O.W.

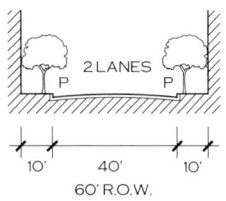

STREET

10'   40'   10'
60' R.O.W.

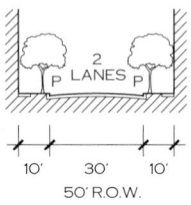

MINOR STREET

10'   30'   10'
50' R.O.W.

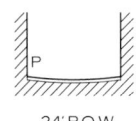

ALLEY

24' R.O.W.

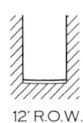

PASSAGE

12' R.O.W.

MORE URBAN

GENERAL

Capacity and character are combined and adjusted to achieve a complete series of useful thoroughfare types. The series is best regarded in pairs: keeping the right-of-way width (R.O.W) constant, each pair illustrates one type suitable in two ways, one for a relatively rural condition and another suitable for a more urban condition.

BOULEVARD		HIGHWAY
25-50 MPH	DESIGN SPEED	35-55 MPH
90 FT	MIN. CENTERLINE RADIUS	165-800 FT
15 FT	CURB RETURN RADIUS	35 FT
30 SEC	PEDESTRIAN CROSS TIME	N/A
ALWAYS	ON-STREET PARKING	NEVER
CLOSED	DRAINAGE	OPEN

MAIN STREET		AVENUE
20-25 MPH	DESIGN SPEED	25-35 MPH
90 FT	MIN. CENTERLINE RADIUS	165 FT
15 FT	CURB RETURN RADIUS	25 FT
12 SEC	PEDESTRIAN CROSS TIME	15 SEC
ALWAYS	ON-STREET PARKING	ALWAYS*
CLOSED	DRAINAGE	OPEN/ CLOSED

STREET		ROAD
20-25 MPH	DESIGN SPEED	25-35 MPH
90 FT	MIN. CENTERLINE RADIUS	165 FT
15 FT	CURB RETURN RADIUS	25 FT
12 SEC	PEDESTRIAN CROSS TIME	8.5 SEC
ALWAYS	ON-STREET PARKING	USUALLY*
CLOSED	DRAINAGE	OPEN/ CLOSED

MINOR STREET		RURAL ROAD
20-25 MPH	DESIGN SPEED	25-35 MPH
90 FT	MIN. CENTERLINE RADIUS	165 FT
15 FT	CURB RETURN RADIUS	20 FT
8.5 SEC	PEDESTRIAN CROSS TIME	13 SEC
ALWAYS*	ON-STREET PARKING	NEVER
CLOSED	DRAINAGE	OPEN

ALLEY		LANE
N/A	DESIGN SPEED	N/A
N/A	MIN. CENTERLINE RADIUS	N/A
5 FT	CURB RETURN RADIUS	20 FT
6.5 SEC	PEDESTRIAN CROSS TIME	3.5 SEC
USUALLY*	ON-STREET PARKING	USUALLY
CLOSED	DRAINAGE	OPEN

PASSAGE		PATH
N/A	DESIGN SPEED	N/A
N/A	MIN. CENTERLINE RADIUS	40 FT
N/A	CURB RETURN RADIUS	5 FT
4.5 SEC	PEDESTRIAN CROSS TIME	4.5 SEC
NEVER	ON-STREET PARKING	NEVER
CLOSED	DRAINAGE	OPEN

* Not striped

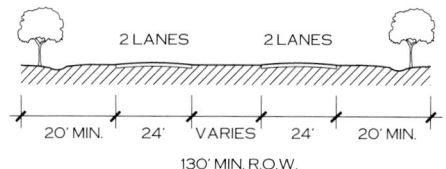

HIGHWAY

20' MIN.   24'   VARIES   24'   20' MIN.
130' MIN. R.O.W.

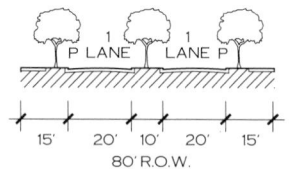

AVENUE

15'   20'   10'   20'   15'
80' R.O.W.

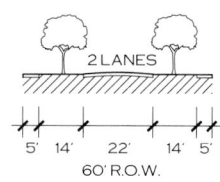

ROAD

5'   14'   22'   14'   5'
60' R.O.W.

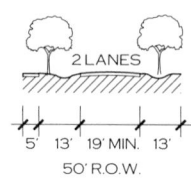

RURAL ROAD

5'   13'   19' MIN.   13'
50' R.O.W.

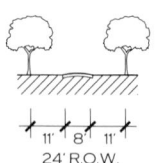

LANE

11'   8'   11'
24' R.O.W.

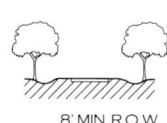

PATH

8' MIN. R.O.W.

MORE RURAL

Chester Chellman, P.E.; Ossipee, New Hampshire
Gary Greenan, Andres Duany, Elizabeth Plater-Zyberk, Kamal Zaharin, Iskandar Shafie; Miami, Florida
The Cintas Foundation

1   SITE, COMMUNITY, AND URBAN PLANNING

INTRODUCTION

The traditional neighborhood development (TND) ordinance produces compact, mixed-use, pedestrian friendly communities. It can be incorporated in municipal zoning ordinances as an overlay or as a separate district. It is intended to ensure the following conventions:

Traditional neighborhoods share the following characteristics:

1. The neighborhood's area is limited to what can be traversed in a 10-minute walk.
2. Residences, shops, workplaces, and civic buildings are located in close proximity.
3. A hierarchy of streets serves the pedestrian and the automobile equitably.
4. Physically defined squares and parks provide places for formal social activity and recreation.
5. Private buildings form a clear edge, delineating the street space.
6. Civic buildings reinforce the identity of the neighborhood, providing places of assembly for social, cultural, and religious activities.

Traditional neighborhoods pursue certain social objectives:

1. To provide the elderly and the young with independence of movement by locating most daily activities within walking distance
2. To minimize traffic congestion and limit road construction by reducing the number and length of automobile trips
3. To make public transit a viable alternative to the automobile by organizing appropriate building densities
4. To help citizens come to know each other and to watch over their collective security by providing public spaces such as streets and squares
5. To integrate age and economic classes and form the bonds of an authentic community by providing a full range of housing types and workplaces
6. To encourage communal initiatives and support the balanced evolution of society by providing suitable civic buildings

SPECIAL DEFINITIONS

Terms used in a TND ordinance may differ in meaning from their use in conventional zoning ordinances:

ARTISANAL USE: Premises used for the manufacture and sale of items that are made employing only handwork and/or table-mounted electrical tools and creating no adverse impact beyond its lot.

BLOCK: The aggregate of lots and alleys circumscribed by public use tracts, generally streets.

BUILDING HEIGHT: The height measured in stories. Attics and raised basements do not count against building height limitations.

CITIZENS' ASSOCIATION: The organization of owners of lots and buildings associated under articles. The articles shall reference an approved master plan; set standards for building location, construction, and maintenance; provide for maintenance on public tracts; and provide for the construction of new civic buildings by an ongoing special assessment.

FACADE: The building wall parallel to a frontage line.

FRONTAGE LINE: The lot line that coincides with a street tract.

GREEN EDGE: A continuous open area surrounding the neighborhood proper. The area shall be preserved in perpetuity as a natural area, golf course, or growing or playing fields, or it shall be subdivided into house lots no smaller than 20 acres each.

LIMITED LODGING: Residential premises providing no more than eight rooms for short-term letting and food services before noon only.

LIMITED OFFICE: Residential premises used for business or professional services, employing no more than four full-time employees, one of whom must be the owner.

LOT: A separately platted portion of land held privately.

PUBLIC
CIVIC
COMMERCIAL
HIGH RESIDENTIAL
LOW RESIDENTIAL
WORKPLACE

TND LAND ALLOCATION

MEETING HALL: A building designed for public assembly, containing at least one room with an area equivalent to 10 sq ft per dwelling, or 1300 sq ft, whichever is greater.

NEIGHBORHOOD PROPER: The built-up area of a TND, including blocks, streets, and squares but excluding green edges.

OUTBUILDING: A separate building, additional to a principal building, contiguous with the rear lot line, having at most two stories and a maximum habitable area of 450 sq ft. Outbuildings may be residential retail units. Outbuildings are exempt from building cover restrictions or unit counts.

PARK: A public tract naturalistically landscaped, not more than 10% paved, and surrounded by lots on no more than 50% of its perimeter.

PROHIBITED USES: Uses not permitted in the standard zoning ordinance, as well as automatic food, drink, and newspaper vending machines and any commercial use that encourages patrons to remain in their automobiles while receiving goods or services (except service stations).

SHARED PARKING: A parking place where day/night or weekday/holiday schedules allow the use of parking spaces by more than one user, resulting in a 25% reduction of the required spaces.

SQUARE: A public tract, spatially defined by surrounding buildings, with frontage on streets on at least two sides. Commercial uses shall be permitted on all surrounding lots.

STORY: A habitable level within a building no more than 14 ft in height from floor to ceiling.

STREET LAMPS: A light standard between 10 and 16 ft in height equipped with an incandescent or metal halide light source.

STREET TREE: A deciduous tree that resists root pressure and is of proven viability, in the region with no less than 4-in. caliper and 8-ft clear trunk at the time of planting.

STREET VISTA: The view, framed by buildings, at the termination of the axis of a thoroughfare.

TRACT: A separately platted portion of land held in common, such as a thoroughfare, a square, or a park.

Gary Greenan, Andres Duany, Elizabeth Plater-Zyberk, Kamal Zaharin, Iskandar Shafie; Miami, Florida
The Cintas Foundation

GUIDELINES FOR TRADITIONAL NEIGHBORHOOD DESIGN

LAND USE	LAND ALLOCATION	LOTS AND BUILDINGS	STREETS AND PARKING
A1.GENERAL: (a) The TND shall be available as an overlay option for land development in all land use and zoning categories except industrial. (b) A TND requires a minimum parcel of 40 contiguous acres and a maximum of 200 acres. Larger parcels shall be developed as multiple neighborhoods with each individually subject to the provisions of the TND.	B1.GENERAL: (a) Similar land use categories face across streets; dissimilar categories abut at rear lot lines. (b) The average perimeter of all blocks within the neighborhood does not exceed 1300 ft. For block faces longer than 500 ft, an alley or pedestrian path provides through access.	C1.GENERAL: (a) All lots share a frontage line with a street or square. (b) The main entrances of all buildings except outbuildings are on a street or square. (c) Stoops, open colonnades, and open porches may encroach into the front setback. (d) The sides of buildings at corner lots are similar to their fronts.	D1.GENERAL: (a) All streets terminate at other streets. (b) Streetlights are provided along all thoroughfares at 35- to 50-ft intervals. (c) On-street parking is allowed on all local streets. (d) Parking lots are located behind or beside building facades. (e) Parking lots and garages are not adjacent to street intersections, civic use lots, or squares and do not occupy lots that terminate a vista. (f) Shared parking reduces local parking requirements.
A2.PUBLIC: (a) Includes streets, squares, parks, playgrounds, and the like. (b) Civic use lots may be placed within tracts designated for public use. (c) Large-scale recreational uses such as golf courses, schoolyards, and multiple game fields are located only at the edge of the neighborhood.	B2.PUBLIC: (a) A minimum of 5% of the neighborhood area or 3 acres (whichever is greater) is permanently allocated to public use. (b) Each neighborhood contains at least one square, not less than one acre in size, close to the center. (c) No portion of the neighborhood is more than 2000 ft from the square. (d) At least half the perimeter of squares, parks, and waterfronts face streets. (e) At least a quarter of the perimeter of waterfronts, golf courses, greenbelts, and other natural amenities face streets.	C2.PUBLIC: (a) Balconies and open colonnades are permitted to encroach up to 5 ft into thoroughfares and other tracts. Such encroachments shall be protected by easements.	D2.PUBLIC: (a) Parking shared between public and private uses is encouraged.
A3.CIVIC: (a) Contains community buildings such as meeting halls, libraries, post offices, schools, child care centers, clubhouses, religious buildings, recreational facilities, museums, cultural societies, visual and performance arts buildings, municipal buildings, and the like.	B3.CIVIC: (a) A minimum of 2% of the neighborhood area is reserved for civic use. (b) Civic lots are within or adjacent to squares and parks or on a lot terminating a street vista. (c) Each neighborhood has a minimum of one meeting hall and one child care facility.	C3.CIVIC: (a) Civic buildings have no height or setback limitations.	D3.CIVIC: (a) The majority (75%) of the off-street parking for civic structures is behind the buildings.
A4.COMMERCIAL: (a) Contains buildings primarily for business uses, such as retail, entertainment, restaurant, club, office, residential, lodging, artisanal, medical, etc. (b) At least 25% of the building area is designated for residential use.	B4.COMMERCIAL: (a) A minimum of 2% and a maximum of 30% of the neighborhood area is designated for commercial use. (b) Commercial lots have a maximum frontage of 32 ft. (c) A maximum of four lots may be consolidated to construct a single building.	C4.COMMERCIAL: (a) Buildings are built out to a minimum of 80% of their frontage at the frontage line. (b) Buildings have no required setback from the side lot lines. (c) Buildings do not exceed four stories in height and are no less than two stories in height. When fronting a square, buildings are no less than three stories in height. (d) Building coverage does not exceed 70% of the lot area.	D4.COMMERCIAL: (a) Lots front streets no more than four lanes wide; parallel parking and sidewalks minimum 15 ft wide. (b) Rear lot lines coincide with an alley. (c) Streets have curbs with a radius at intersections of 5 to 15 ft. (d) Street trees are aligned on both sides of the street at 35- to 50-ft intervals; when open colonnades are provided, no street trees are necessary. (e) The majority (75%) of the off-street parking is behind the buildings.
A5.HIGH RESIDENTIAL: (a) Contains buildings for residential use, limited office use, cafes, retail, lodging, and artisanal uses. (b) All of the building area above the ground floor is designated for residential use. (c) Outbuildings are permitted.	B5.HIGH RESIDENTIAL: (a) A minimum of 20% and a maximum of 60% of the neighborhood area is designated for high residential use. (b) High residential lots have a maximum frontage of 16 ft. (c) A maximum of eight lots may be consolidated for the purpose of constructing a single building containing one or more residential units.	C5.HIGH RESIDENTIAL: (a) Buildings are built out to a minimum of 70% of their frontage, at a continuous alignment no further than 10 ft from the frontage line. (b) Buildings have no required setback from side lot lines. (c) Buildings do not exceed four stories in height and, when fronting a square, are no less than three stories in height. (d) Building coverage does not exceed 50% of the lot area.	D5.HIGH RESIDENTIAL: (a) Lots front streets no more than three lanes wide, with parallel parking and sidewalks minimum 15 ft wide. (b) Street trees are aligned both sides of streets at 35- to 50-ft intervals. (c) Rear lot lines coincide with an alley. (d) All off-street parking is behind the buildings.
A6.LOW RESIDENTIAL: (a) Contains buildings for residential uses, including art studios, limited offices, limited lodging, and the like. (b) All of the building area above the ground floor is designated for residential use. (c) Outbuildings are permitted.	B6.LOW RESIDENTIAL: (a) A maximum of 60% of the neighborhood area is designated for low residential use. (b) Lots have a maximum frontage of 64 ft. (c) A maximum of two lots may be consolidated for the purpose of constructing a single building.	C6.LOW RESIDENTIAL: (a) Buildings are built out to a minimum of 40% of their frontage at a continuous alignment no further than 30 ft from the frontage line. (b) Side setbacks are no less than 10 ft in aggregate and may be allocated to one side. Buildings are set back no less than 20 ft from the rear lot line. Outbuildings have no required setback. (c) Buildings do not exceed three stories in height. (d) Building coverage does not exceed 50% of the lot area.	D6.LOW RESIDENTIAL: (a) Lots front roads no more than two lanes wide with optional parallel parking and sidewalks minimum 6 ft wide. (b) Street trees are installed on both sides of the street at no more than 50-ft intervals. (c) Rear lot lines may coincide with an alley. (d) All off-street parking is to the side or rear of the building. Where access is through the frontage, garages or carports are located a minimum of 20 ft behind the facade.
A7.WORKPLACE: (a) Contains buildings for uses such as corporate office, light industry, artisanal, warehousing, automotive, and the like.	B7.WORKPLACE: (a) A minimum of 2% and a maximum of 30% of the neighborhood area is designated for workplace use. (b) Lots have a maximum frontage of 64 ft. (c) A maximum of four lots may be consolidated for the purpose of constructing a single building.	C7.WORKPLACE: (a) Buildings are built out to a minimum of 70% of their frontage at a continuous alignment no further than 10 ft from the frontage line. (b) Buildings have no setbacks from side or rear lot lines. (c) Buildings do not exceed three stories in height. (d) Building coverage does not exceed 70% of the lot area. (e) Lots are separated from other use types at the side and rear lot lines by a wall of between 3 and 8 ft high.	D7.WORKPLACE: (a) Lots front streets as wide as necessary to accommodate truck traffic. (b) Street trees are aligned on both sides of the street at 35- to 50-ft intervals. (c) Rear lot lines coincide with an alley. (d) All off-street parking is to the side or rear of the building.

Gary Greenan, Andres Duany, Elizabeth Plater-Zyberk, Kamal Zaharin, Iskandar Shafie; Miami, Florida
The Cintas Foundation

SITE, COMMUNITY, AND URBAN PLANNING

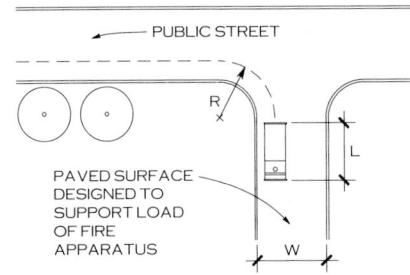

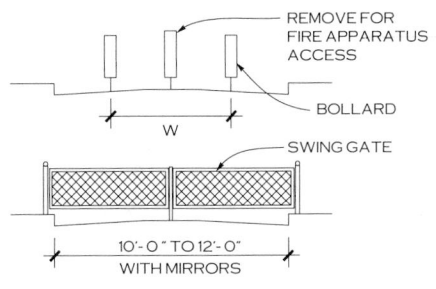

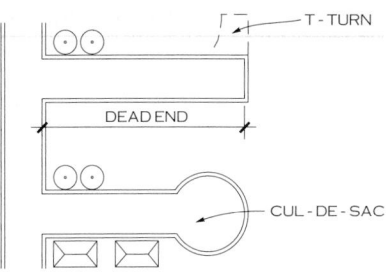

FIRE APPARATUS ACCESS

Fire apparatus (i.e., pumpers, ladder trucks, tankers) should have unobstructed access to buildings. Check with local fire department for apparatus turning radius (R), length (L), and other operating characteristics. Support systems embedded in lawn areas adjacent to the building are acceptable.

RESTRICTED AREAS

Buildings constructed near cliffs or steep slopes should not restrict access by fire apparatus to only one side of the building. Grades greater than 10% make operation of fire apparatus difficult and dangerous. Avoid parking decks abutted to buildings. Consider pedestrian bridge overs instead.

FIRE DEPARTMENT RESPONSE TIME FACTOR

Site planning factors that determine response time are street accessibility (curbs, radii, bollards, T-turns, culs-de-sac, street and site slopes, street furniture and architectural obstructions, driveway widths), accessibility for firefighting (fire hydrant and standpipe connection layouts, outdoor lighting, identifying signs), and location (city, town, village, farm). Check with local codes, fire codes, and fire department for area regulations.

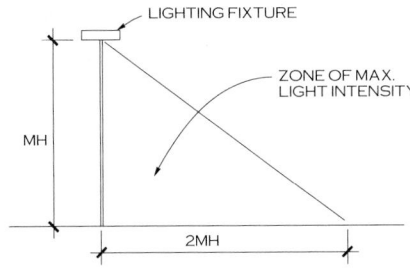

OUTDOOR LIGHTING

Streets that are properly lighted enable fire fighters to locate hydrants quickly and to position apparatus at night. Avoid layouts that place hydrants and standpipe connections in shadows. In some situations, lighting fixtures can be integrated into exterior of buildings. All buildings should have a street address number on or near the main entrance.

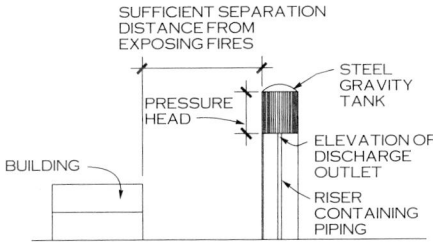

GRAVITY TANK

Gravity tanks can provide a reliable source of pressure to building standpipe or sprinkler systems. Available pressure head increased by 0.434 psi/ft increase of water above tank discharge outlet. Tank capacity in gallons depends on fire hazard, water supply, and other factors. Tanks require periodic maintenance and protection against freezing during cold weather. Locations subject to seismic forces or high winds require special consideration. Gravity tanks also can be integrated within building design.

ACCESS OBSTRUCTIONS

Bollards used for traffic control and fences for security should allow sufficient open road width (W) for access by fire apparatus. Bollards and gates can be secured by standard fire department keyed locks (check with department having jurisdiction).

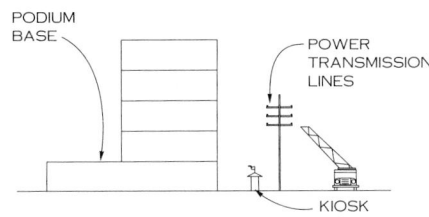

STREET FURNITURE AND ARCHITECTURAL OBSTRUCTIONS

Utility poles can obstruct use of aerial ladders for rescue and fire suppression operations. Kiosks, outdoor sculpture, fountains, newspaper boxes, and the like can also seriously impede fire fighting operations. Wide podium bases can prevent ladder access to the upper stories of buildings. Canopies and other nonstructural building components can also prevent fire apparatus operations close to buildings.

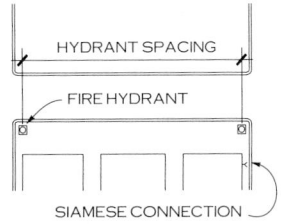

FIRE HYDRANT AND STANDPIPE CONNECTION LAYOUT

Locate fire hydrants at street intersections and at intermediate points along roads so that spacing between hydrants does not exceed capability of local fire jurisdiction. Hydrants should be placed 2 to 10 ft from curb lines. Siamese connections for standpipes should be visible, marked conspicuously, and be adjacent to the principal vehicle access point to allow rapid connection by fire fighters to the pumping engine.

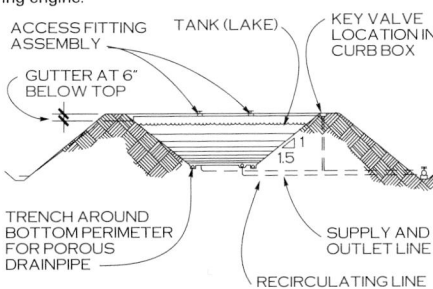

ON-SITE LAKES

Man-made and natural on-site lakes are used for private fire fighting in suburbs, on farms, and at resorts. A piped supply system to a dry hydrant is preferred for its quantity, flexibility, better maintenance, and accessibility. Man-made lakes with reservoir liners can be berm-supported or sunk in the ground. Lakes and ponds are natural water supplies dependent on the environment. See local codes, fire codes, and fire departments for on-site lake regulations.

DRIVEWAY LAYOUTS

Long dead ends (greater than 150 ft) can cause time consuming, hazardous backup maneuvers. Use t-turns, culs-de-sac, and curved driveway layouts to allow unimpeded access to buildings.

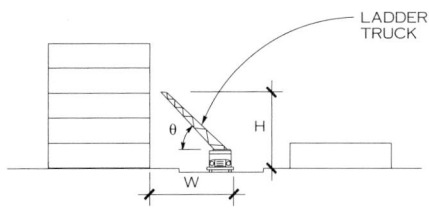

DRIVEWAY WIDTHS

For full extension of aerial ladders at a safe climbing angle (θ), sufficient driveway width (W) is required. Estimate the required width in feet by: $W = (H-6) \cot\theta + 4$, where preferred climbing angles are 60 to 80°. Check with local fire department for aerial apparatus operating requirements, including width of aerial device with stabilizing outriggers extended.

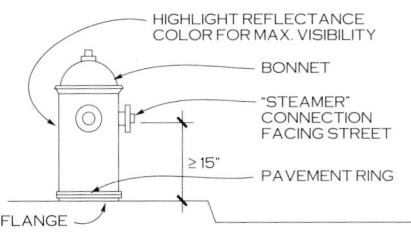

FIRE HYDRANT PLACEMENT

Fire hose connections should be at least 15 in. above grade. Do not bury hydrants or locate them behind shrubs or other visual barriers. Avoid locations where runoff water and snow can accumulate. Bollards and fences used to protect hydrants from vehicular traffic must not obstruct fire fighters' access to hose connections. "Steamer" connection should usually face the side of arriving fire apparatus.

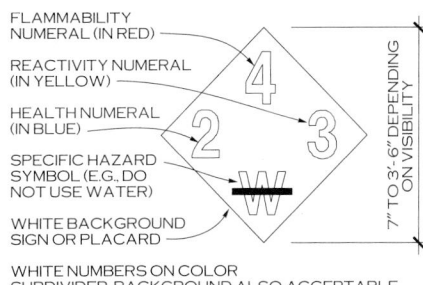

NFPA 704 DIAMOND SYMBOLS

Standard diamond symbols provide information fire fighters need to avoid injury from hazardous building contents. zero (0) is the lowest degree of hazard, 4 is highest. Locate symbols near building entrances. Correct spatial arrangement for two kinds of diamond symbols are shown. Consider integrating symbols with overall graphics design of building. (Refer to "Identification of the Fire Hazards of Materials," NFPA No. 704, available from the National Fire Protection Association.)

D. L. Collins and M. David Egan, P. E., College of Architecture, Clemson University; Clemson, South Carolina
Nicholas A. Phillips, AIA; Lockwood Greene; New York, New York

SITE, COMMUNITY, AND URBAN PLANNING   1

FLOOD DAMAGE MANAGEMENT

Flood hazards are caused by building in flood-prone areas. Floods cannot be prevented, but the damage they wreak on man-made properties can be managed, either by altering the flood potential of an area or by avoiding construction in locations subject to flooding. Historically, flood damage management in the United States has focused on the former management technique, attempting to divert floods with structural flood controls–dams, levees, and channel modifications. However, such flood control measures have proved unsatisfactory over time.

Structural flood control projects have tended to encourage development in high hazard areas, often without appropriate land use planning. When a storm exceeds or violates the design parameters of a flood control structure, the damage that results from a flood can exceed what would have occurred if the structure had not been built. For example, floodplain invasion often occurs where levees have been built with the intention of reducing damage to agriculture. Although in some regions levees have reduced the number of high-frequency floods, in general they cause conditions favorable for their own failure by altering erosion patterns and increasing stages.

Recognition of the cost of development in high-risk areas, the uneven distribution of flood hazards on the landscape, and the natural and beneficial values of floodplains have led to more common adoption of nonstructural flood hazard management techniques. In particular, land use management and modified building practices are finding widespread acceptance.

Information on flood damage management and floodplain and wetland conservation is available from the Federal Emergency Management Agency (FEMA), the Natural Hazards Research Applications and Information Center, the U.S. Army Corps of Engineers, the Environmental Protection Agency, the National Park Service, and state and local agencies.

FLOOD HAZARDS

Most flood damage is caused by weather conditions such as hurricanes, fronts associated with midlatitude cyclones, thunderstorms, and melting snow packs. These conditions interact wtih surface features such as floodplains, coasts, wetlands, and alluvial fans, resulting in floods, mudslides, and erosion. Geologic phenomena such as earthquakes may also trigger floods.

Weather and climate information is available from the National Climate Data Center, regional climate research centers, and state climatology offices. Geologic and hydrologic information is available from the U.S. Geological Survey and state geological and geographical surveys.

FLOOD-PRONE AREAS

FLOODPLAIN: The relatively flat area within which a river moves and upon which it regularly overflows.

Rivers typically meander over their floodplains, eroding the cutbank and redepositing sediments in accretion zones such as point bars, meander belts, and natural levees. Channel shifting may be extreme in alluvial fans. Coastal floodplains, which include barrier islands, shores, and wetlands, have the same relationship to the sea that riverine floodplains have to rivers.

WETLANDS: areas characterized by frequent flooding or soil saturation, hydrophytic vegetation (vegetation adapted to survival in saturated areas), and hydric soils (soil whose chemical composition reflects saturation). Wetlands are often found in floodplains but are more restrictively defined.

FLOOD TYPES

Floods may be classified by their locations or physical characteristics.

RIVERINE FLOOD: great overflows of water from a river channel onto a floodplain caused by precipitation over large areas, melting snow, or both. Over-bank flow is a normal geophysical event that occurs on average every two years for most rivers.

HEADWATER FLOOD: a riverine flood that results from precipitation directly in a basin.

BACKWATER FLOOD: a riverine flood caused by high stages on downstream outlets, which prevent drainage from tributary basins or even reverse the flow.

COASTAL FLOOD: overflows onto coastal lands bordering an ocean, estuary, or lake. Coastal floods are caused by tsunamis (seismic sea waves), hurricanes, and northeasters.

FLASH FLOOD: a local flood of great volume and short duration. Flash floods differ from riverine floods in extent and duration. Flash floods generally result from a torrential rain or "cloudburst" covering a relatively small drainage area. Flash floods may also result from the failure of a dam or sudden breakup of an ice jamb.

FLOOD RISKS

Flood risk is usually expressed as the estimated annual frequency with which a flood equals or exceeds a specified magnitude. The flood risk for a future period of time is the joint probability of the occurrence of the annual flood risk. For example, if a house is situated at the "100-year flood" elevation (1% annual exceedance frequency), then its flood risk for a 30-year period is 26% or approximately a one in four chance it will be flooded to the specified depth or greater.

STANDARD PROJECTED FLOOD (SPF): a flood that may be expected from the most severe combination of meteorological and hydrological conditions characteristic of the geographic area in which the drainage basin is located, excluding extremely rare combinations.

SPFs are used in designing dams and other facilities with high damage potential.

PROBABLE MAXIMUM FLOOD (PMF): the most severe flood that may be expected from a combination of the most critical meteorological and hydrological conditions reasonably possible in a drainage basin. (This term is not a statistical concept.)

PMFs are used in designing high-risk flood protection works and in siting structures and facilities that must be subject to almost no risk of flooding.

LAND USE IN FLOOD ZONES

Land use management is the most effective method of managing flood damage. State control of land use in hazardous areas, authorized by the police-powers clause of the U.S. Constitution, is usually delegated to local planning and zoning boards. Local, state, and federal governments also regulate ecosystems essential for flood damage management, such as wetlands, coastal dunes, and mangrove stands. Land use management often includes setback regulations, which attempt to limit flood-related erosion damage. Regardless of regulations imposed by the government, developers should evaluate building sites for their intrinsic suitability for the intended use.

The National Flood Insurance Program (NFIP) requires that participating local governments adopt minimum floodplain management plans based on data provided by the federal insurance administrator. The NFIP does not require local governments to adopt land use or transportation plans that require preferential development of hazard-free areas or prohibit development of land in high-hazard areas. New construction in coastal zones is required to be located landward of the reach of the mean high tide. Local land use

and development or floodplain management plans that are more stringent than NFIP requirements supersede NFIP requirements. The NFIP divides riverine floodplains into floodway and floodway fringes for land use management. Coastal floodplains are divided into coastal high-hazard areas and coastal fringes. Land uses in these areas should always be verified with local agencies.

FLOODWAYS

Floodways include the channel of a watercourse and those portions of the adjoining floodplain required to permit the passage of a flood of specified magnitude at no more than a specified level above natural conditions. The NFIP requires floodways to be large enough to accommodate floods with a 1% annual exceedance frequency (100-year flood) without causing an increase in water levels of more than a specified amount (1 ft in most areas). Some localities object to the acceptability of increased flood levels this NFIP requirement implies. Instead, they define the floodway as the area inundated by floods with a 4% annual exceedance frequency (25-year flood).

Uses permitted in a floodway are those with low flood damage potential that do not obstruct flood flows or require structures, fill, or storage of materials or equipment. Fill is prohibited, and most structures are strongly discouraged. The following uses are generally permitted:

FUNCTIONALLY DEPENDENT USES: facilities and structures that must be located close to water in order to function, such as docking and port facilities and shipbuilding and repair facilities. Water supply and sanitary sewage treatment plants must be floodproofed if they must be located adjacent to bodies of water.

AGRICULTURAL USES: general farming, pasture, outdoor plant nurseries, horticulture, viticulture, truck farming, forestry, sod farming, and wild crop harvesting.

RECREATIONAL USES: golf courses, tennis courts, driving ranges, archery ranges, picnic grounds, boat launching ramps, swimming areas, parks, wildlife and nature preserves, game farms, fish hatcheries, shooting preserves, target ranges, trap and skeet ranges, hunting and fishing areas, and hiking and horseback riding trails.

INCIDENTAL INDUSTRIAL-COMMERCIAL USES: loading areas, parking areas, and airport landing strips (except in flash flood areas).

INCIDENTAL RESIDENTIAL USES: lawns, gardens, parking areas, and play areas.

FLOODWAY FRINGES

Floodway fringes are the portion of the regulatory floodplain outside of the floodway. Floodway fringes are treated as storage area for flood waters. Where permitted, property owners on each side of the floodplain may obstruct flood flows equally.

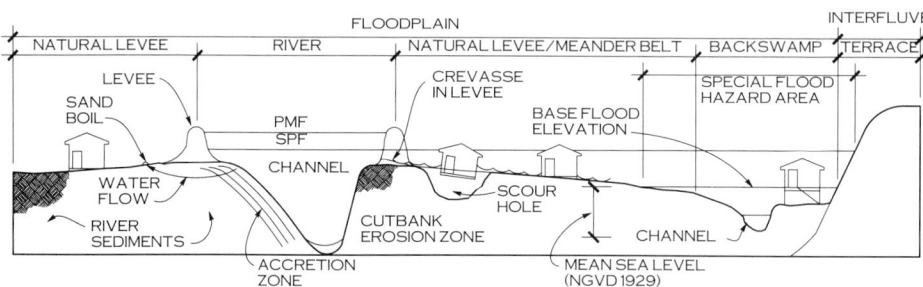

INVERTED RIVER VALLEY

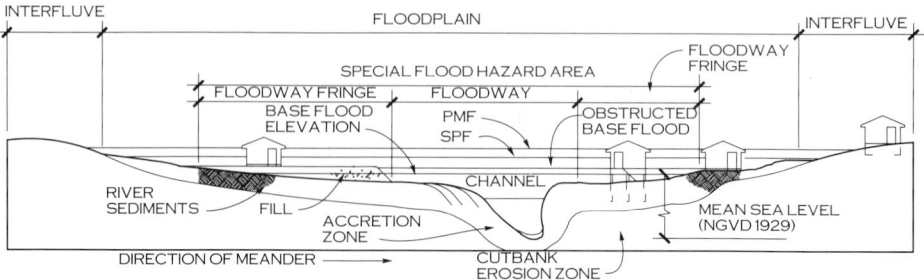

V-SHAPED RIVER VALLEY

Mattie Fincher Coxe; Baton Rouge, Louisiana

Uses permitted in floodway fringes include those permitted in floodways and elevated or otherwise flood-proofed structures. Prohibited or strongly discouraged uses include facilities for storing materials that are toxic or flammable or explosive in water, vital facilities such as hospitals and civil defense or rescue facilities, and facilities that are difficult to evacuate, such as nursing homes and prisons.

FLOOD INSURANCE RATE ZONES

The NFIP is a program intended to reduce federal expenditures for flood disaster relief. It provides flood damage insurance as an incentive for communities to adopt floodplain management regulations, especially those governing floodplain obstructions and building practices in floodplains. NFIP minimum standards require a low level of flood damage management based on historic conditions.

States and localities may establish standards higher than NFIP's, in which case these supersede NFIP standards. For example, other governments may control land use in hazardous areas, regulate runoff, have freeboard requirements, or base regulatory flood elevations on historic floods that exceeded the base flood or on the projected effects of future development. The NFIP Community Rating System provides insurance rate reductions as an incentive to adopt higher standards.

The NFIP bases Flood Insurance Rate Zones on the frequency of flooding and the presence of storm surge and waves. Local governments are typically required to regulate building practices in A and V zones as a condition of eligibility for flood insurance.

The most important requirement in A and V zones is that the first floor of new buildings be built equal to or higher than the base flood level, which has a 1% chance of being equaled or exceeded in any given year (100-year flood). The base flood is the still water height for riverine floods. For the Atlantic Coast and the Gulf of Mexico, the base flood includes storm surge plus wave crest height because of northeasters and hurricanes. The base flood for the Pacific Coast includes astronomical tides plus wave run-up caused by tropical cyclones and tsunamis. For major lakes, the base flood includes seiche (sloshing because of wind, seismic activity, and storm surge). The base flood elevation (BFE) is the height of the base flood in reference to mean sea level as defined by the National Geodetic Vertical Datum of 1929 (NGVD 1929).

Local communities may adopt regulatory flood datums (RFD) in place of base flood elevations. RFDs are the base flood plus a freeboard, a factor of safety expressed in feet and used to compensate for uncertainties that could contribute to greater flood height than that computed for a base flood. Freeboard allows for hazards excluded from consideration in figuring the base flood and uncertainties in analysis, design, and construction. Severe structural subsidence, increases in floods because of obstructions in the floodplain, urban runoff, or normal climatic variability, as well as long-term increases in sea level and storms, are often excluded from consideration in determining base flood levels. Urban conditions, low accuracy base maps, and unplanned development are other common sources of uncertainty that justify freeboard.

Some communities require up to a 3-ft freeboard to compensate for inaccurate flood insurance rate maps (FIRMs). The margin of error of base maps may be estimated as plus or minus one-half of the contour interval. Most FIRMs are developed from maps with a contour interval of 5 ft, and a margin of error of −2 1/2 ft. Field survey maps with a contour interval of 2 ft or less are used in some communities; the smaller interval reduces the uncertainty of the risk and the need for freeboard.

The NFIP classifies land either as special flood hazard areas (SFHA)—high-frequency flood, flood-related erosion, and mudslide zones—or low-risk and undetermined flood hazard zones. Zone names that include actuarial risk factors, such as A1-A30 and V1-V30, are being replaced by AE and VE designations with flood depths.

A ZONES (A, AE, A1-A30, AO, AH, AR, A99)

Zones A and AE (formerly A1-A30) are high-risk riverine areas susceptible to inundation by the still-water base flood. AO zones are areas of shallow flooding (1 to 3 ft) without defined channels, usually sheet flow on sloping terrain. AH zones indicate shallow flooding, usually with water ponding. AR zones are areas in which structural flood protection is deficient. A99 zones are areas in which structural flood protection systems are near completion.

The finished floor of the lowest habitable level of residences, usually including basements, must be elevated to the base flood elevation in zone A. Flood-resistant residential

basements are permitted only in communities that meet special NFIP flood criteria and adopt special local standards for their design and construction. Commercial structures must be elevated or otherwise floodproofed to the BFE.

B ZONES

B zones indicate areas subject to inundation by floods with an annual exceedance frequency greater than the base flood with less than a 0.2% annual exceedance frequency (500-year flood). B-zone designations are not used on recent FIRMs because of the lack of statistical validity of most estimates of 500-year floods and the false perception that they are generally safe. On some maps B zones are shown as shaded X zones.

C ZONES

C zones, including all areas that are not in zones A, B, or V, are not necessarily flood free. They may include low-risk interfluvial regions (areas of a watershed above the natural floodplain), moderate-risk floodplain between the interfluve and the regulatory floodplain, areas with localized nonriverine flooding, high-risk areas with small contributing drainage areas, and floodplains with structural flood protection that may be subject to low frequency catastrophic floods.

D ZONES

D zones are areas of possible but undetermined flood hazard.

X ZONES

X zones include all areas not in zones A or V, combining B and C zones found on older maps. On some maps, X zones that were formerly B zones and X zones within levee systems are shaded.

V ZONES (V, VE, V1-V30, VO)

Velocity zones V and VE (formerly V1-V30) are coastal high hazard areas identified as susceptible to inundation by the base flood, including storm surges with high velocity waves greater than 3 ft. Generally, zone V indicates the inland extent of a 3-ft breaking wave, where the still-water depth during the 100-year flood decreases to less than 4 ft. VO zones are proposed alluvial fan zones with high velocity shallow flow (1 to 3 ft) and unpredictable flow paths.

Elevation and structural requirements are most stringent in coastal high hazard areas. Fill below buildings is prohibited. If construction is permitted by the local government, the lowest horizontal structural member of the lowest habitable floor must be built above the base flood elevation. Rigid frames or semirigid frames with grade beams can re-

sist the impact of storm surge and waves. Semirigid frames without grade beams should be used only in areas not subject to potential scour. Freestanding pole structures are unsafe; large rotations develop at moment connections, causing deflection of pilings under sustained lateral loads that can lead to collapse.

Destruction of coastal dunes and wetlands dramatically increases the inland reach of storm surge and waves and increases the severity of flood damage. Buildings may be destroyed if dunes and wetlands are inadequately protected, even if they conform to legal building requirements.

E AND M ZONES (E, M)

E zones are areas adjoining the shore of a lake or other body of water that are likely to suffer flood-related erosion. M zones are areas with land surfaces and slopes of unconsolidated material in which the history, geology, and climate indicate a potential for mudflow. Setbacks and special building requirements are used in E and M zones.

SOURCES

Coastal Construction Manual (FEMA-55). Dames & Moore and Bliss & Nyitray, Inc., 1986.

Elevated Residential Structures (FEMA)-54). Washington, D.C.: American Institute of Architects, 1984.

Elevating to the Wave Crest Level: A Benefit: Cost Analysis (FIA-6), Shaeffer & Roland, Inc., 1980.

Federal Emergency Management Agency. *Answers to Questions About the National Flood Insurance Program* (FIA-2)., Washington, D.C.: FEMA.

Federal Emergency Management Agency. *The Floodway: A Guide for Community Permit Officials.* Community Assistance Series No. 4. Washington, D.C.: FEMA.

Flood Loss Reduction Associates. *Floodplain Management Handbook.* U.S. Water Resources Council, 1981.

Floodproofing Nonresidential Structures (FEMA)-102). Booker Associates, Inc., 1986.

Hayes, W. W., ed. *Facing Geologic and Hydrologic Hazards: Earth-Science Considerations.* Washington, D.C.: U.S. Geological Survey, 1981.

Permit Officials' Handbook for the National Flood Insurance Program. 3rd ed. Baton Rouge Louisiana Department of Transportation and Development, 1993.

GENERAL LIMITS OF FLOODPROOFING

METHOD	DEPTH	VELOCITY	WARNING REQUIREMENTS
Levees	4-7'	< 1 0'/sec	Advance warning required for installation of floodgates in openings
Floodwalls	4-7'	< 12'/sec	
Closures (24 hr maximum)	4-8'	< 8'/sec	5-8 hr advance warning required for installation of closures
Fill	10'+	< 1 0'/sec	Evacuation time required unless fill connects to higher ground
Piles, piers, and columns	10-12'	< 8'/sec	Adequate evacuation time required

NOTE

Information presented is general and warrants caution. Time available for warning may be severely limited by a flood's rate of rise.

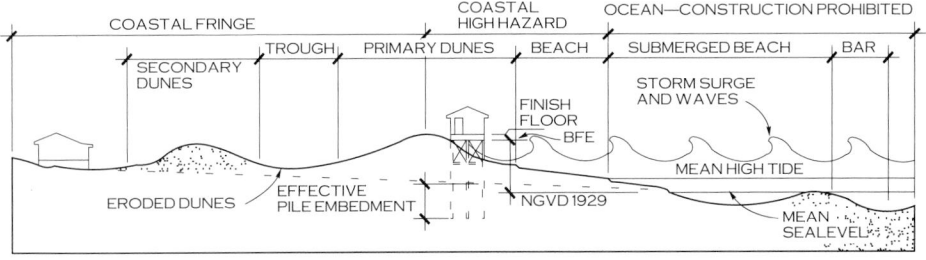

COASTAL DUNES AND BEACHES

Mattie Fincher Coxe; Baton Rouge, Louisiana

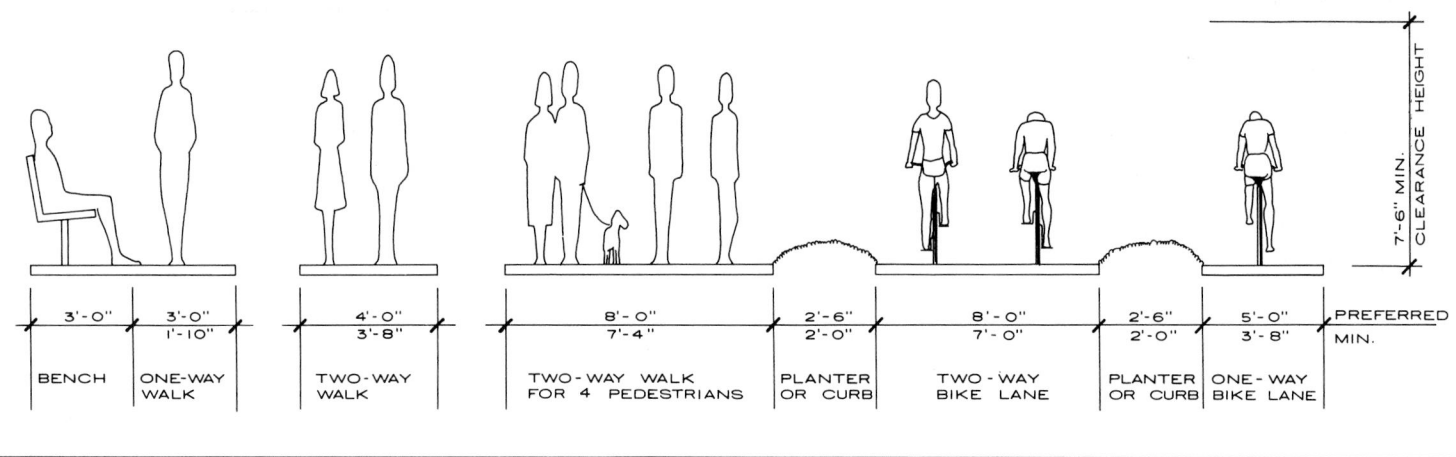

WALK AND BIKE LANE WIDTHS

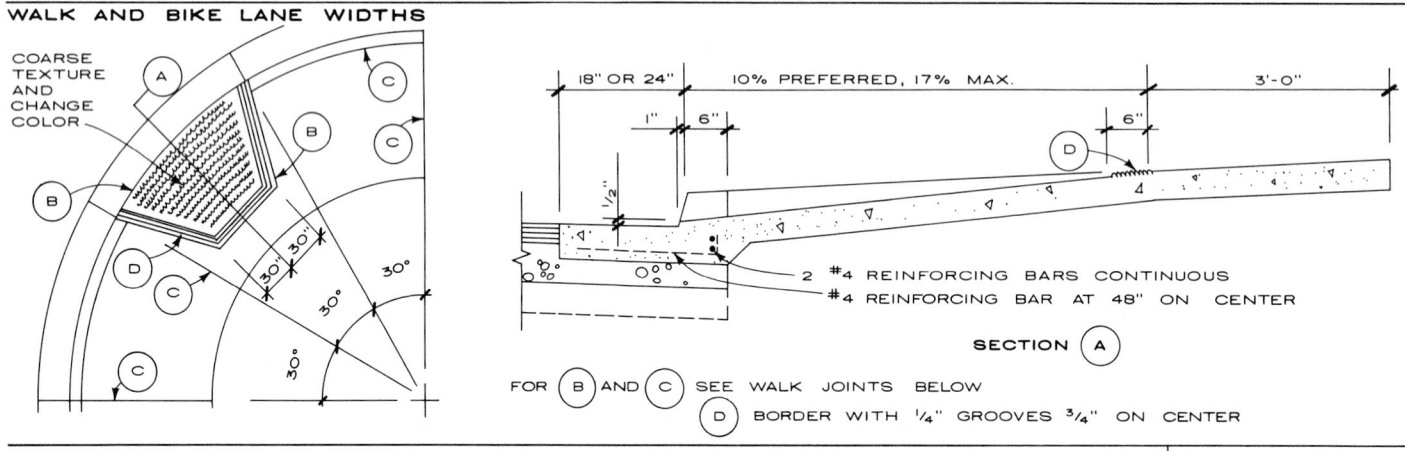

COARSE TEXTURE AND CHANGE COLOR

FOR (B) AND (C) SEE WALK JOINTS BELOW

(D) BORDER WITH ¼" GROOVES ¾" ON CENTER

18" OR 24"   10% PREFERRED, 17% MAX.   3'-0"

2 #4 REINFORCING BARS CONTINUOUS
#4 REINFORCING BAR AT 48" ON CENTER

SECTION (A)

WHEELCHAIR RAMP AT CURB
(ROUND CURB SHOWN IN PLAN.
SECTION TYPICAL FOR ANY CURB)

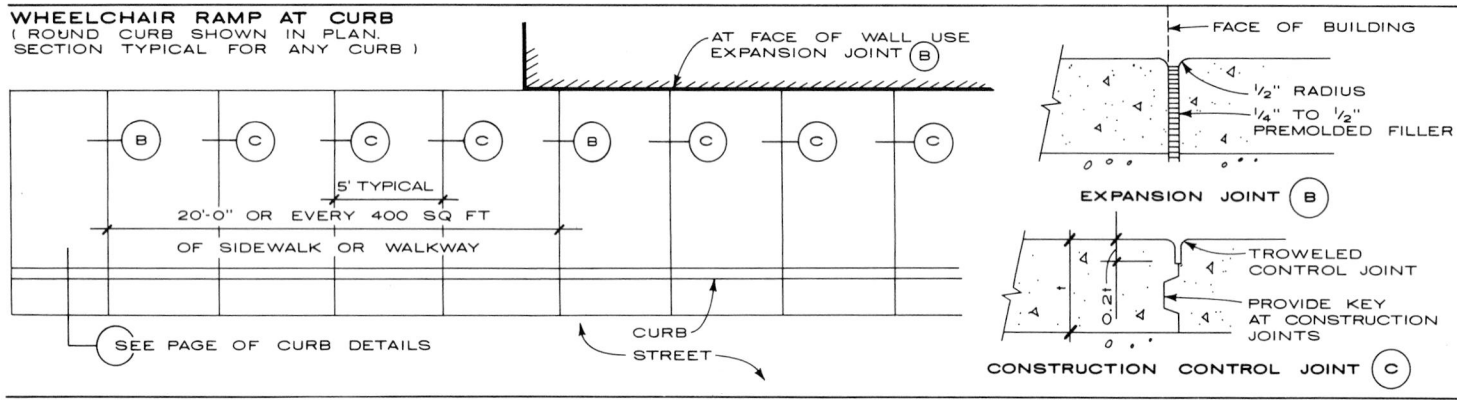

5' TYPICAL
20'-0" OR EVERY 400 SQ FT
OF SIDEWALK OR WALKWAY

SEE PAGE OF CURB DETAILS

CURB
STREET

AT FACE OF WALL USE
EXPANSION JOINT (B)

FACE OF BUILDING
½" RADIUS
¼" TO ½"
PREMOLDED FILLER

EXPANSION JOINT (B)

TROWELED CONTROL JOINT
PROVIDE KEY AT CONSTRUCTION JOINTS

CONSTRUCTION CONTROL JOINT (C)

WALK AND CURB JOINTS

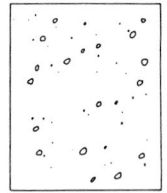

ROCK SALT

Spread on troweled surface and press in. Wash salt away after concrete hardens. Protect planting.

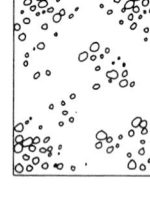

EXPOSED AGGREGATE

Seed aggregate uniformly onto surface. Embed by tamping. After setup, brush lightly and clean with spray. If using aggregate mix, trowel and expose by washing fines or use a retarder.

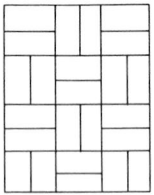

PRESSED OR STAMPED

Stock patterns are available. Use integral or dry shake colors. Joints may be filled with mortar.

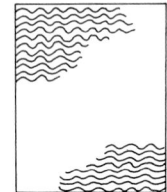

BROOM SURFACE

Use stiff bristle for coarse texture. Use soft bristle on steel troweled surface for fine texture.

TROWELED

Use wood float for coarse texture. Use steel float for fine texture.

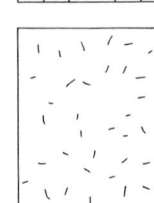

NONSLIP

Apply silicon carbide (sparkling) or aluminum oxide at ¼ to ½ psf; trowel lightly.

WALK SURFACES AND TEXTURES

William T. Mahan, AIA; Santa Barbara, California

DESIGN CONSIDERATIONS

1. Design storm drain system to shed water away from curb ramps.
2. Detectable warnings identify potentially hazardous conditions to persons with visual impairments. Because curb ramps take away the curb, the traditional warning that one is approaching a street, detectable warnings are required where the transition between sidewalk and street is smooth. Warnings may be required at all curb ramps.
3. Dimensions shown are for new construction. For alterations where these dimensions are impractical, review the Americans with Disabilities Act Accessibility Guidelines (ADAAG) for less strict dimensions.

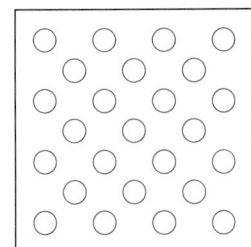

DETECTABLE WARNING DEVICE

NOTE

ADAAG standardizes detectable warnings as raised truncated domes with a nominal 0.9 in. diameter, 0.2 in. height, and nominal 2.35 in. on center which must contrast visually with adjoining surfaces. Verify requirements prior to use.

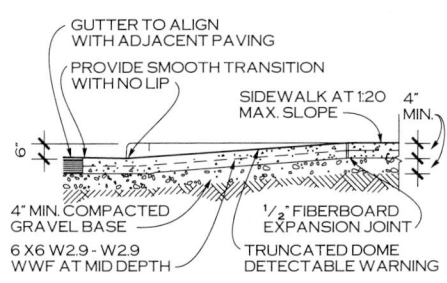

CURB RAMP SECTION

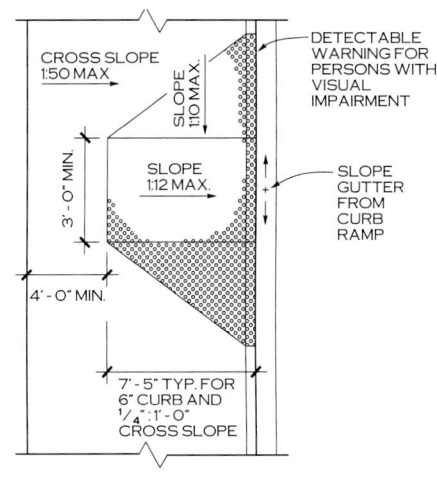

TYPE E

NOTE

If 4 ft 0 in. minimum cannot be met, the 1:10 slope is then 1:12 maximum.

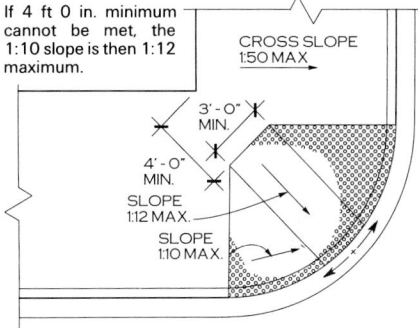

TYPE F

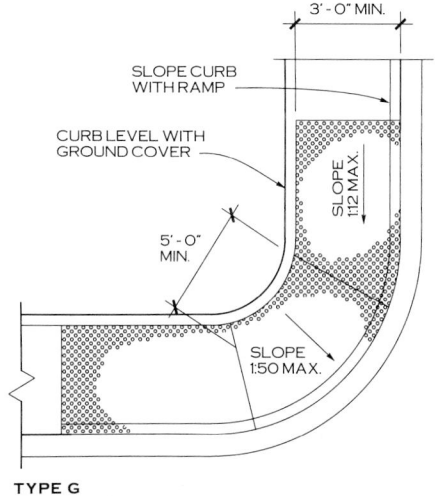

TYPE G

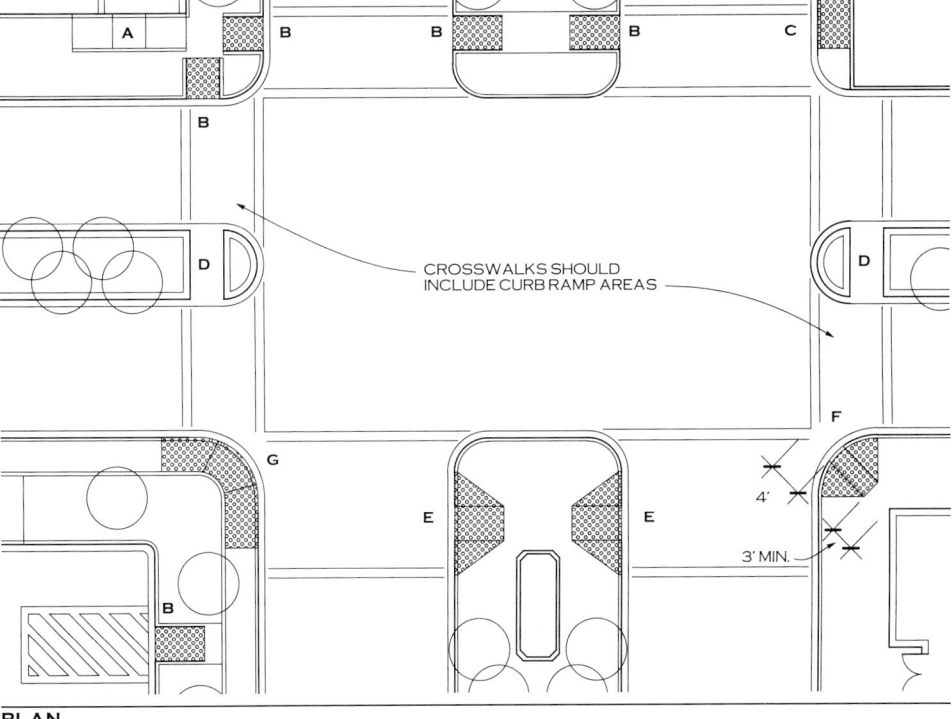

CROSSWALKS SHOULD INCLUDE CURB RAMP AREAS

PLAN

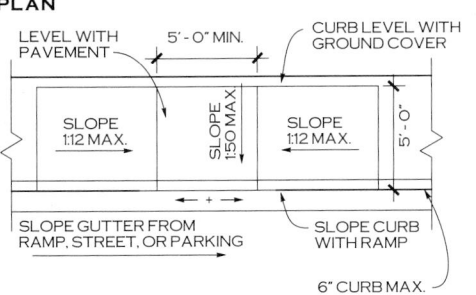

TYPE A

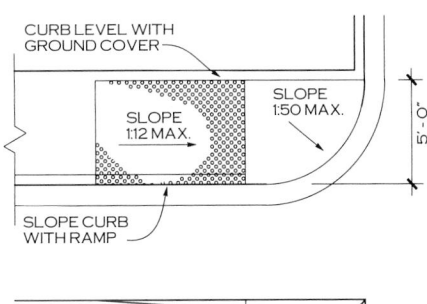

TYPE C

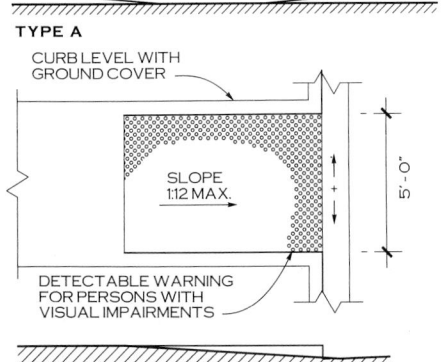

TYPE B

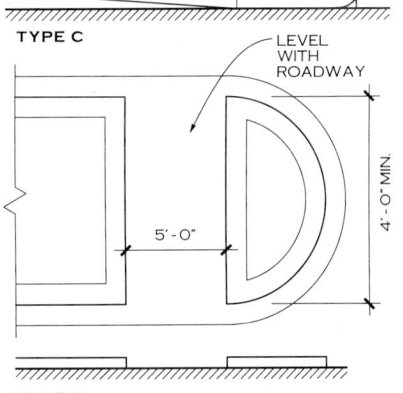

TYPE D

CURB RAMP TYPES

Mark J. Mazz, AIA; CEA, Inc.; Hyattsville, Maryland

NOTE

Each design vehicle in Groups I, II, III, IV, and V represents a composite of the critical dimensions of the real vehicles within each group below. Parking lot dimensions on the parking lot development page are based on these groups and dimensions. For parking purposes, both compact and midsize vehicles are in Group II. Turning dimensions R, R1, and C are shown on the private roads page.

DESIGN VEHICLE

GROUP I		SUBCOMPACTS
L	Length	11'-7" to 14'-8"
W	Width	5'-1" to 5'-8"
H	Height	4'-2" to 4'-7"
WB	Wheelbase	7'-1" to 8'-7"
OF	Overhang front	2'-6"
OR	Overhang rear	3'-9"
OS	Overhang sides	0'-7"
GW	Gross Weight	1620# to 3180#

GROUP II		COMPACTS
L	Length	13'-10" to 15'-4"
W	Width	5'-6" to 5'-8"
H	Height	4'-4" to 4'-8"
WB	Wheelbase	8'-1" to 8'-9"
OF	Overhang front	2'-8"
OR	Overhang rear	4'-3"
OS	Overhang sides	0'-8"
GW	Gross Weight	2300# to 3100#

GROUP III		MIDSIZE
L	Length	15'-0" to 16'-8"
W	Width	5'-7" to 6'-0"
H	Height	4'-2" to 4'-9"
WB	Wheelbase	8'-4" to 9'-5"
OF	Overhang front	2'-10"
OR	Overhang rear	4'-4"
OS	Overhang sides	0'-9"
GW	Gross Weight	2740# to 4000#

GROUP IV		LARGE CARS
L	Length	15'-2" to 18'-5"
W	Width	5'-8" to 6'-8"
H	Height	4'-7" to 5'-0"
WB	Wheelbase	8'-9" to 10'-1"
OF	Overhang front	2'-11"
OR	Overhang rear	4'-5"
OS	Overhang sides	0'-9"
GW	Gross Weight	3200# to 5300#

GROUP V		LARGE PICK-UP
L	Length	15'-10" to 20'-2"
W	Width	6'-5" to 6'-9"
H	Height	5'-9" to 6'-4"
WB	Wheelbase	9'-7" to 14'-0"
OF	Overhang front	2'-10"
OR	Overhang rear	4'-4"
OS	Overhang sides	0'-9"
GW	Gross Weight	3600# to 3700#

LARGE VEHICLE DIMENSIONS*

VEHICLE	(L) LENGTH	(W) WIDTH	(H) HEIGHT	(OR) OVERHANG REAR
Intercity bus	45'-0"	9'-0"	9'-0"	10'-1"
City bus	40'-0"	8'-6"	8'-6"	8'-0"
School bus	39'-6"	8'-0"	8'-6"	12'-8"
Ambulance	20'-10¼"	6'-11"	10'-0"	5'-4"
Paramedic van	21'-6"	8'-0"	6'-6"	4'-0"
Hearse	19'-8"	6'-8"	9'-3"	5'-4"
Airport limousine	22'-5¾"	6'-4"	5'-0"	3'-11"
Trash truck	28'-2"	8'-0"	11'-0"	6'-0"
U.P.S. truck	26'-3"	7'-11"	10'-8"	8'-5"
Fire truck	32'-0"	8'-0"	9'-8"	10'-0"

*Exact sizes of large vehicles may vary
For truck and trailer information, see pages on truck and trailer sizes.

Harold C. Munger, FAIA; Munger Munger + Associates Architects, Inc.; Toledo, Ohio
William T. Mahan, AIA; Santa Barbara, California

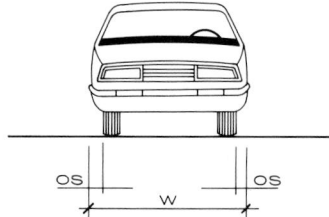

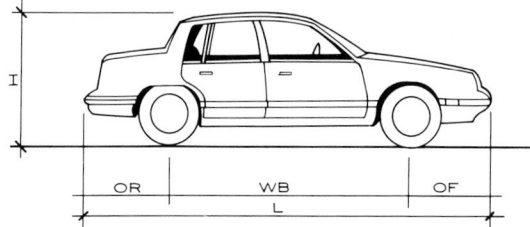

NOTE

Angles shown below may vary depending on speed, load, tire pressure, and condition of shock absorbers.

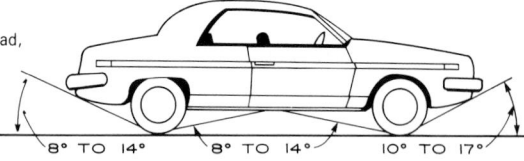

8° TO 14°   8° TO 14°   10° TO 17°

NOTE

Composite vehicle is shown with maximum wheelbase, front overhang, and rear overhang.

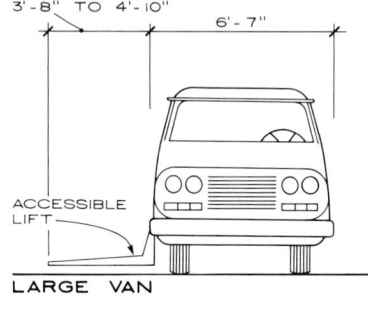

3'-8" TO 4'-10"   6'-7"

ACCESSIBLE LIFT

LARGE VAN

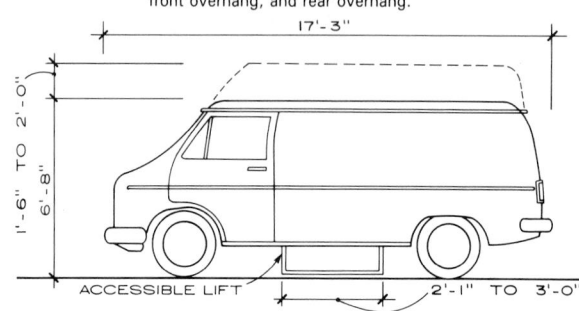

17'-3"

1'-6" TO 2'-0"   6'-8"

ACCESSIBLE LIFT   2'-1" TO 3'-0"

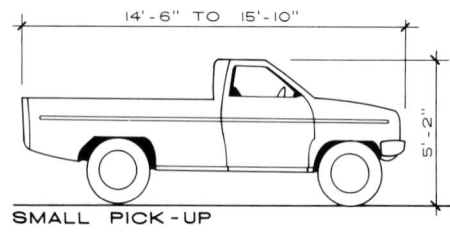

14'-6" TO 15'-10"

5'-2"

SMALL PICK-UP

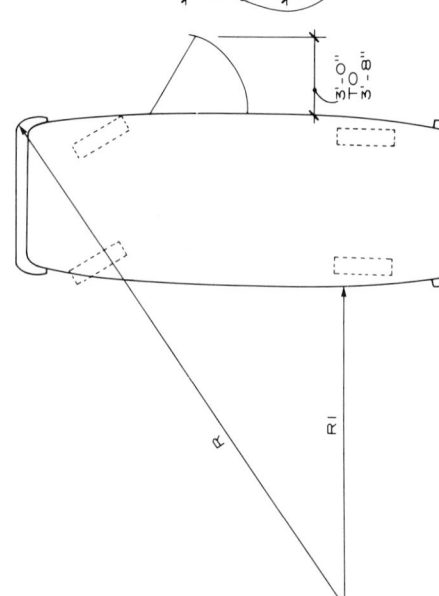

3'-0" 3'-8"

R   R1

NOTE

For dimensions R and R1 see page on private roads. Accessible parking areas typically require 20 ft x 12 ft.

For further parking information, see pages on parking lot development and parking garages.

See local codes and standards for parking requirements, size, and quantity of parking spaces and number of spaces required for persons with disabilities.

1   AUTOMOBILES, ROADS, AND PARKING

GENERAL NOTES

Examples shown are for easy driving at moderate speed. See the preceding page for vehicle dimensions (L, W, and OR). The "U" drive shown below illustrates a procedure for designating any drive configuration, given the vehicle's dimensions and turning radii. The T (tangent) dimensions given here are approximate minimums only and may vary with the driver's ability and speed.

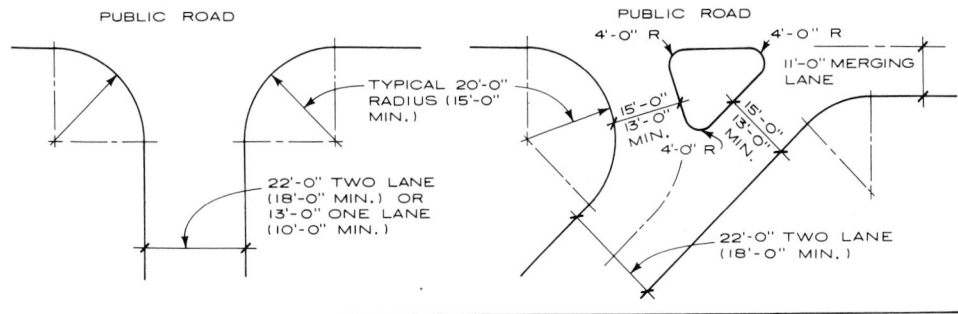

PRIVATE ROADS INTERSECTING PUBLIC ROADS

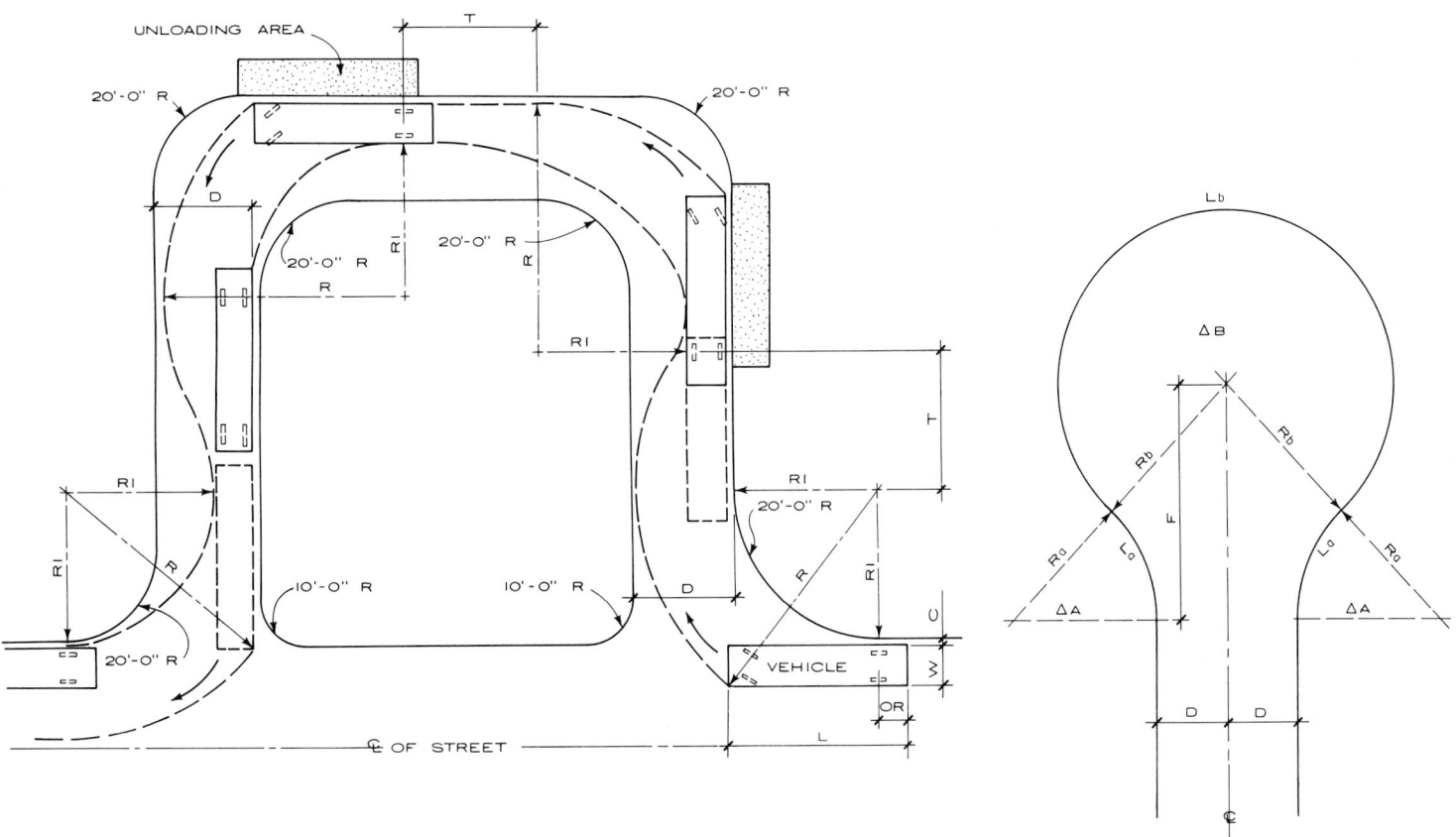

"U" DRIVE AND VEHICLE TURNING DIMENSIONS

VEHICLE	R	RI	T	D	C
Small car	19'-10''	10'-9''	12'-0''	10'-0'	6''
Compact car	21'-6''	11'-10''	15'-0''	10'-10''	7''
Standard car	22'-5''	12'-7''	15'-0''	11'-2''	8''
Large car	23'-0''	12'-7''	15'-0''	12'-0''	9''
Intercity bus*	55'-0''	33'-0''	30'-0''	22'-6''	1'-0''
City bus	53'-6''	33'-0''	30'-0''	22'-6''	1'-0''
School bus	43'-6''	26'-0''	30'-0''	19'-5''	1'-0''
Ambulance	30'-0''	18'-9''	25'-0''	13'-3''	1'-0''
Paramedic van	25'-0''	14'-0''	25'-0''	13'-0''	1'-0''
Hearse	30'-0''	18'-9''	20'-0''	13'-3''	1'-0''
Airport limousine	28'-3''	15'-1½''	20'-0''	15'-1½''	1'-0''
Trash truck†	32'-0''	18'-0''	20'-0''	16'-0''	1'-0''
U.P.S. truck	28'-0''	16'-0''	20'-0''	14'-0''	1'-0''
Fire truck	48'-0''	34'-4'	30'-0''	15'-8''	1'-0''

*Headroom = 14'.
†Headroom = 15'.

William T. Mahan, AIA; Santa Barbara, California

CUL-DE-SAC

	SMALL	LARGE
O	16'-0''	22'-0''
F	50'-11''	87'-3''
A	46.71°	35.58°
B	273.42°	251.15°
Ra	32'-0''	100'-0''
Rb	38'-0''	50'-0''
La	26'-1''	61'-8''
Lb	181'-4''	219'-2''

NOTE: R values for vehicles intended to use these culs-de-sac should not exceed Rb.

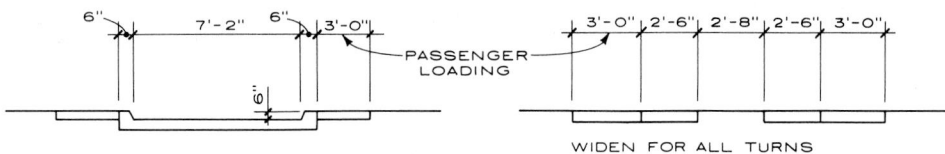

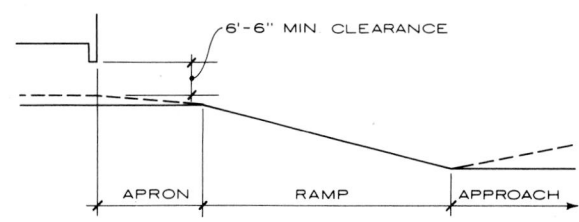

CONCRETE RUNWAYS TO GARAGE

RAMP	APPROACH	APRON
4%	0% to 4%	0% to 2%
5%	0% to 3%	0% to 2%
6%	0% to 2%	0% to 2%
7%	0% to 1%	0% to 1%
8%	0%	0%

ROAD TO GARAGE RAMPS

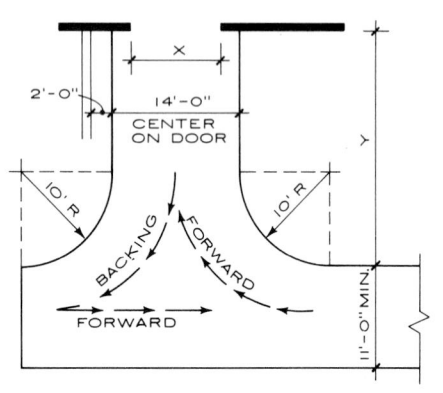

90° IN—BACK OUT (1 CAR)

X	8'-9"	9'-0"	10'-0"	11'-0"	12'-0"
Y	25'-0"	24'-6"	23'-8"	23'-0"	22'-0"

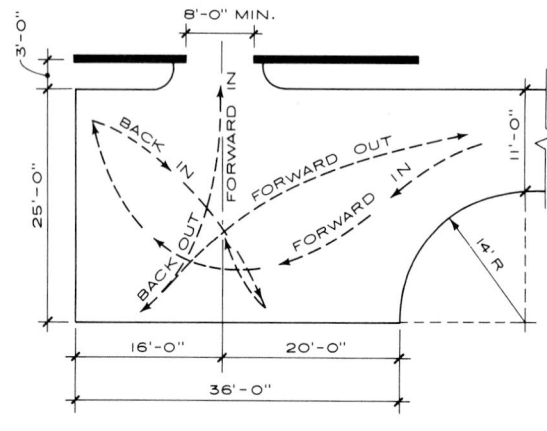

NOTE

Three maneuver entrance for single car garage. Employ only when space limitations demand use. Dimensioned for large car.

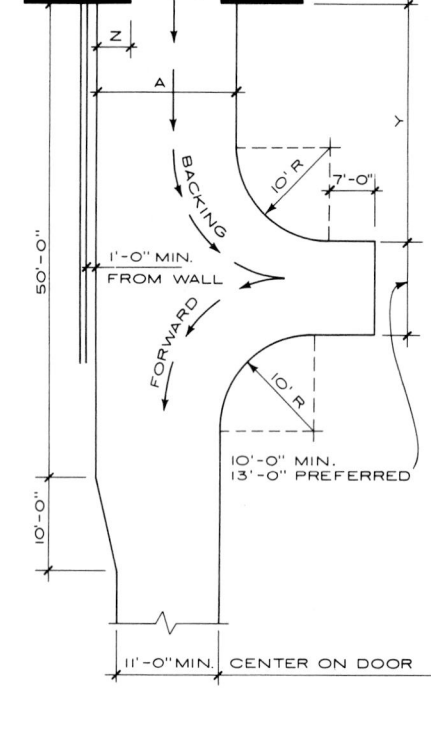

STRAIGHT IN—BACK OUT

X	9'-0"	10'-0"	12'-0"	16'-0"
Y	26'-0"	25'-0"	23'-6"	24'-0"
Z	3'-4"	3'-1"	2'-0"	3'-0"
A	14'-4"	14'-5"	14'-8"	20'-0"

PRIVATE DRIVEWAYS TO GARAGES

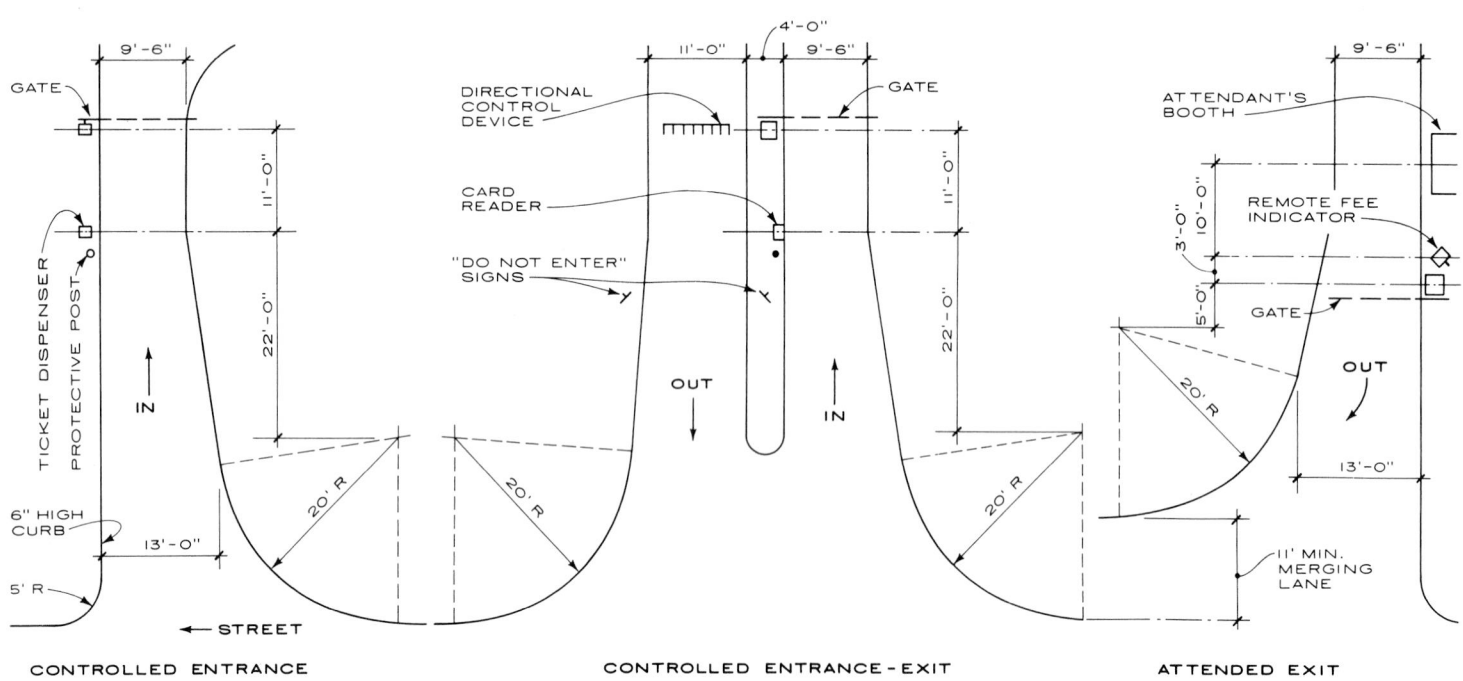

CONTROLLED ENTRANCE   CONTROLLED ENTRANCE-EXIT   ATTENDED EXIT

DRIVEWAYS FOR PARKING FACILITIES

William T. Mahan, AIA; Santa Barbara, California

1   AUTOMOBILES, ROADS, AND PARKING

NOTE: Small car dimensions should be used only in lots designated for small cars or with entrance controls that admit only small cars. Placing small car stalls into a standard car layout is not recommended. Standard car parking dimensions will accommodate all normal passenger vehicles. Large car parking dimensions make parking easier and faster and are recommended for luxury, a high turnover, and use by the elderly. When the parking angle is 60° or less, it may be necessary to add 3 to 6 ft to the bay width to provide aisle space for pedestrians walking to and from their parked cars. Local zoning laws should be reviewed before proceeding.

RECOMMENDED RANGE OF STALL WIDTHS (SW)

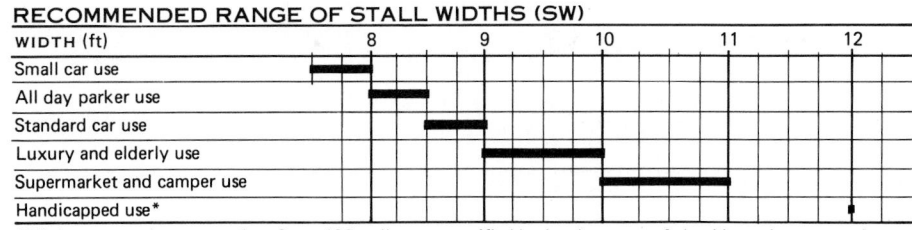

WIDTH (ft) 8 9 10 11 12
- Small car use
- All day parker use
- Standard car use
- Luxury and elderly use
- Supermarket and camper use
- Handicapped use*

*Minimum requirements = 1 or 2 per 100 stalls or as specified by local, state, or federal law; place convenient to destination.

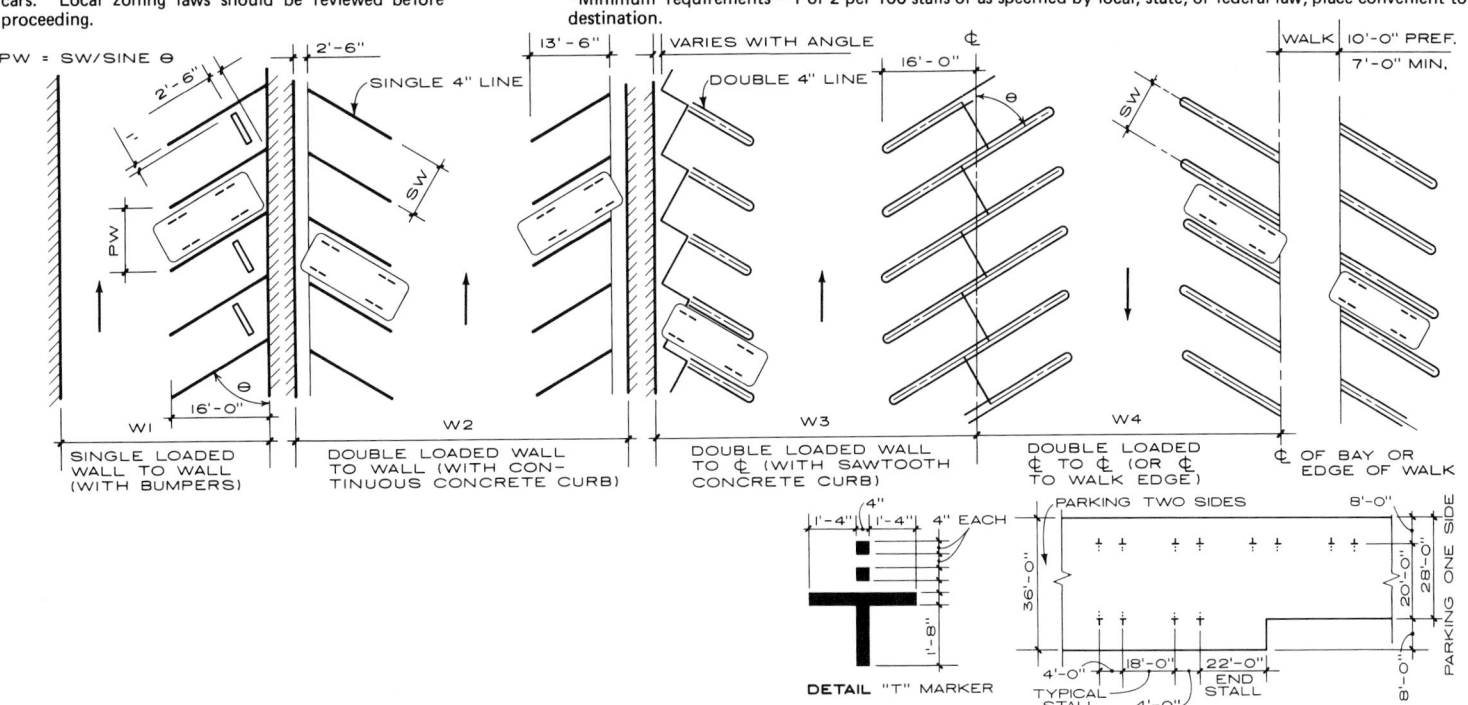

$PW = SW/\text{sine }\theta$

SINGLE LOADED WALL TO WALL (WITH BUMPERS) — W1

DOUBLE LOADED WALL TO WALL (WITH CONTINUOUS CONCRETE CURB) — W2

DOUBLE LOADED WALL TO ₵ (WITH SAWTOOTH CONCRETE CURB) — W3

DOUBLE LOADED ₵ TO ₵ (OR ₵ TO WALK EDGE) — W4

₵ OF BAY OR EDGE OF WALK

DETAIL "T" MARKER

PARALLEL PARKING STALLS AND "T" MARKER DETAIL

PARKING DIMENSIONS IN FEET AND INCHES

θ ANGLE OF PARK

	SW	W	45°	50°	55°	60°	65°	70°	75°	80°	85°	90°
Group I: small cars	8'-0"	1	25'-9"	26'-6"	27'-2"	29'-4"	31'-9"	34'-0"	36'-2"	38'-2"	40'-0"	41'-9"
		2	40'-10"	42'-0"	43'-1"	45'-8"	48'-2"	50'-6"	52'-7"	54'-4"	55'-11"	57'-2"
		3	38'-9"	40'-2"	41'-5"	44'-2"	47'-0"	49'-6"	51'-10"	53'-10"	55'-8"	57'-2"
		4	36'-8"	38'-3"	39'-9"	42'-9"	45'-9"	48'-6"	51'-1"	53'-4"	55'-5"	57'-2"
Group II: standard cars	8'-6"	1	32'-0"	32'-11"	34'-2"	36'-2"	38'-5"	41'-0"	43'-6"	45'-6"	46'-11"	48'-0"
		2	49'-10"	51'-9"	53'-10"	56'-0"	58'-4"	60'-2"	62'-0"	63'-6"	64'-9"	66'-0"
		3	47'-8"	49'-4"	51'-6"	54'-0"	56'-6"	59'-0"	61'-2"	63'-0"	64'-6"	66'-0"
		4	45'-2"	46'-10"	49'-0"	51'-8"	54'-6"	57'-10"	60'-0"	62'-6"	64'-3"	66'-0"
	9'-0"	1	32'-0"	32'-9"	34'-0"	35'-4"	37'-6"	39'-8"	42'-0"	44'-4"	46'-2"	48'-0"
		2	49'-4"	51'-0"	53'-2"	55'-6"	57'-10"	60'-0"	61'-10"	63'-4"	64'-9"	66'-0"
		3	46'-4"	48'-10"	51'-4"	53'-10"	56'-0"	58'-8"	61'-0"	63'-0"	64'-6"	66'-0"
		4	44'-8"	46'-6"	49'-0"	51'-6"	54'-0"	57'-0"	59'-8"	62'-0"	64'-2"	66'-0"
	9'-6"	1	32'-0"	32'-8"	34'-0"	35'-0"	36'-10"	38'-10"	41'-6"	43'-8"	46'-0"	48'-0"
		2	49'-2"	50'-6"	51'-10"	53'-6"	55'-4"	58'-0"	60'-6"	62'-8"	64'-6"	65'-11"
		3	47'-0"	48'-2"	49'-10"	51'-6"	53'-11"	57'-0"	59'-8"	62'-0"	64'-3"	65'-11"
		4	44'-8"	45'-10"	47'-6"	49'-10"	52'-6"	55'-9"	58'-9"	61'-6"	63'-10"	65'-11"
Group III: large cars	9'-0"	1	32'-7"	33'-0"	34'-0"	35'-11"	38'-3"	40'-11"	43'-6"	45'-5"	46'-9"	48'-0"
		2	50'-2"	51'-2"	53'-3"	55'-4"	58'-0"	60'-4"	62'-9"	64'-3"	65'-5"	66'-0"
		3	47'-9"	49'-1"	52'-3"	53'-8"	56'-2"	59'-2"	61'-11"	63'-9"	65'-2"	66'-0"
		4	45'-5"	46'-11"	49'-0"	51'-8"	54'-9"	58'-0"	61'-0"	63'-2"	64'-10"	66'-0"
	9'-6"	1	32'-4"	32'-8"	33'-10"	34'-11"	37'-2"	39'-11"	42'-5"	45'-0"	46'-6"	48'-0"
		2	49'-11"	50'-11"	52'-2"	54'-0"	56'-6"	59'-3"	61'-9"	63'-4"	64'-8"	66'-0"
		3	47'-7"	48'-9"	50'-2"	52'-4"	55'-1"	58'-4"	60'-11"	62'-10"	64'-6"	66'-0"
		4	45'-3"	46'-8"	48'-5"	50'-8"	53'-8"	57'-0"	59'-10"	62'-2"	64'-1"	66'-0"
	10'-0"	1	32'-4"	32'-8"	33'-10"	34'-11"	37'-2"	39'-11"	42'-5"	45'-0"	46'-6"	48'-0"
		2	49'-11"	50'-11"	52'-2"	54'-0"	56'-6"	59'-3"	61'-9"	62'-10"	64'-8"	66'-0"
		3	47'-7"	48'-9"	50'-2"	52'-4"	55'-1"	58'-4"	60'-11"	62'-2"	64'-6"	66'-0"
		4	45'-3"	46'-8"	48'-5"	50'-8"	53'-8"	57'-0"	59'-10"	62'-2"	64'-1"	66'-0"

NOTE: θ angles greater than 70° have aisle widths wide enough for two-way travel.

William T. Mahan, AIA; Santa Barbara, California
Frederick J. Gaylord, AIA; McClellan/Cruz/Gaylord & Associates; Pasadena, California

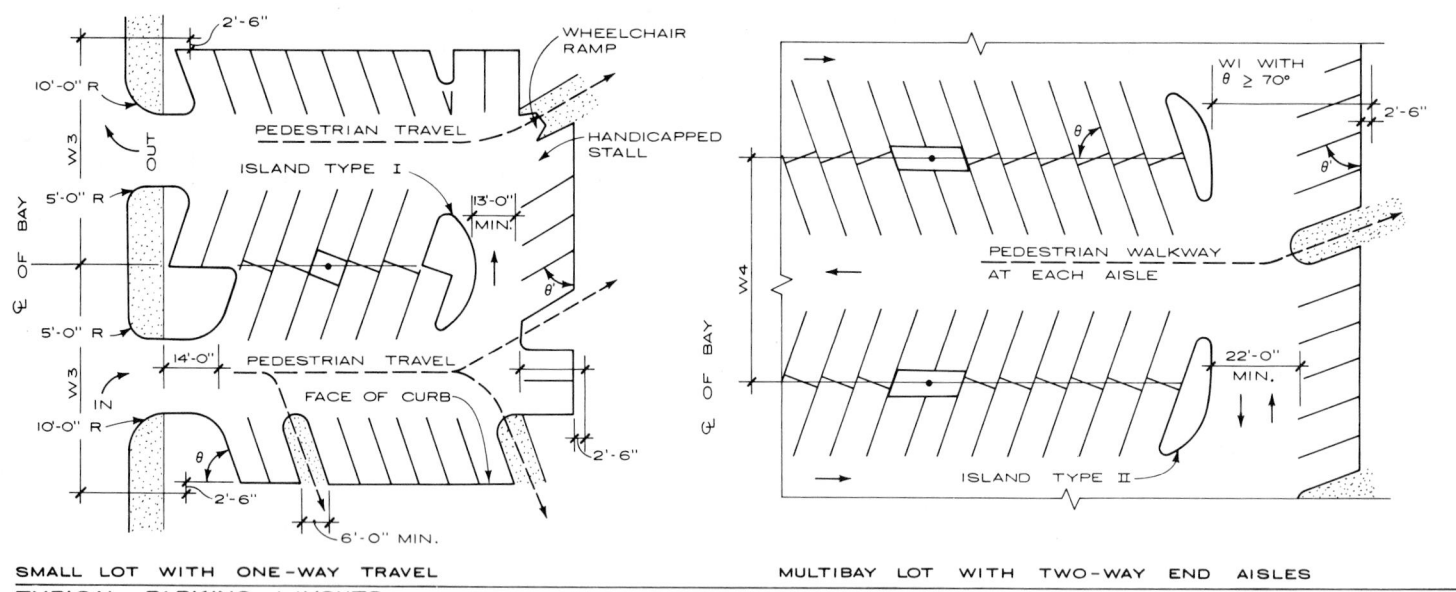

SMALL LOT WITH ONE-WAY TRAVEL

MULTIBAY LOT WITH TWO-WAY END AISLES

TYPICAL PARKING LAYOUTS

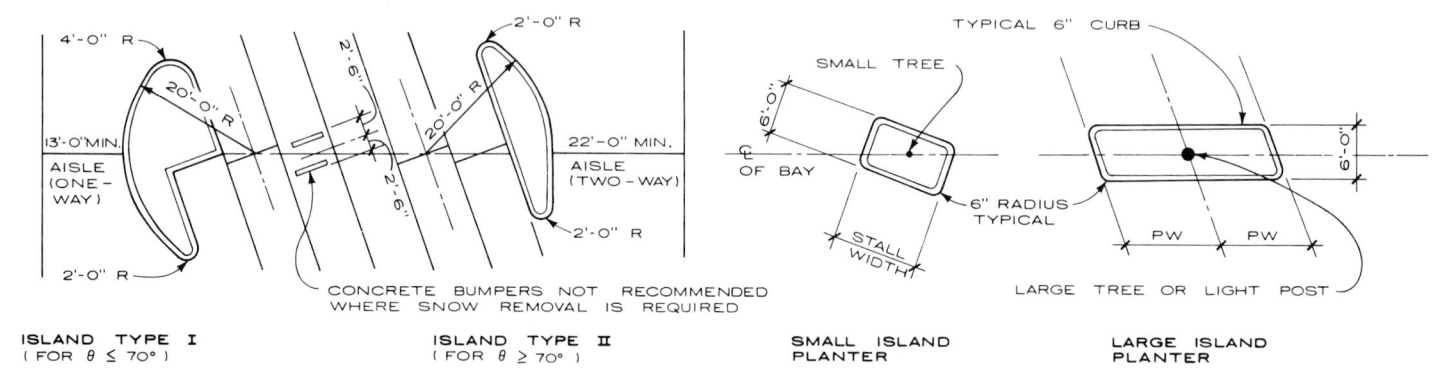

ISLAND TYPE I
(FOR $\theta \leq 70°$)

ISLAND TYPE II
(FOR $\theta \geq 70°$)

SMALL ISLAND
PLANTER

LARGE ISLAND
PLANTER

TYPICAL PLANTER ISLANDS

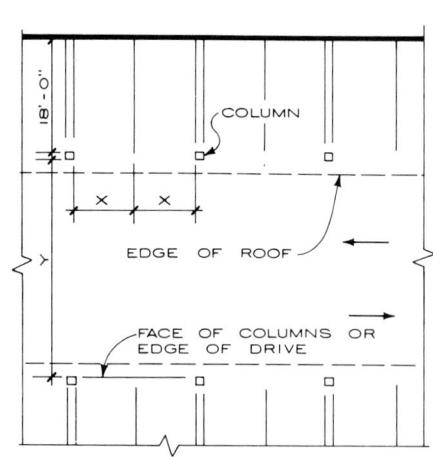

TWO STALL 90° APARTMENT CARPORTS

X	9'-0"	10'-0"	11'-0"	12'-0"
Y	35'-0"	34'-0"	33'-0"	32'-0"

ANGLE PARKING WITH 3 STALLS PER COLUMN

θ	PW	PW'	W2	E	A	B	AREA/STALL
60°	10'-5"	13'-0"	55'-0"	18'-0"	19'-0"	33'-10"	310 sq ft
70°	9'-7"	11'-1"	59'-10"	18'-0"	23'-10"	30'-3"	302 sq ft
80°	9'-1"	10'-2"	63'-4"	18'-0"	27'-4"	28'-4"	300 sq ft

PARKING LAYOUTS WITH COLUMNS

William T. Mahan, AIA; Santa Barbara, California
Frederick J. Gaylord, AIA; McClellan/Cruz/Gaylord & Associates; Pasadena, California

1   **AUTOMOBILES, ROADS, AND PARKING**

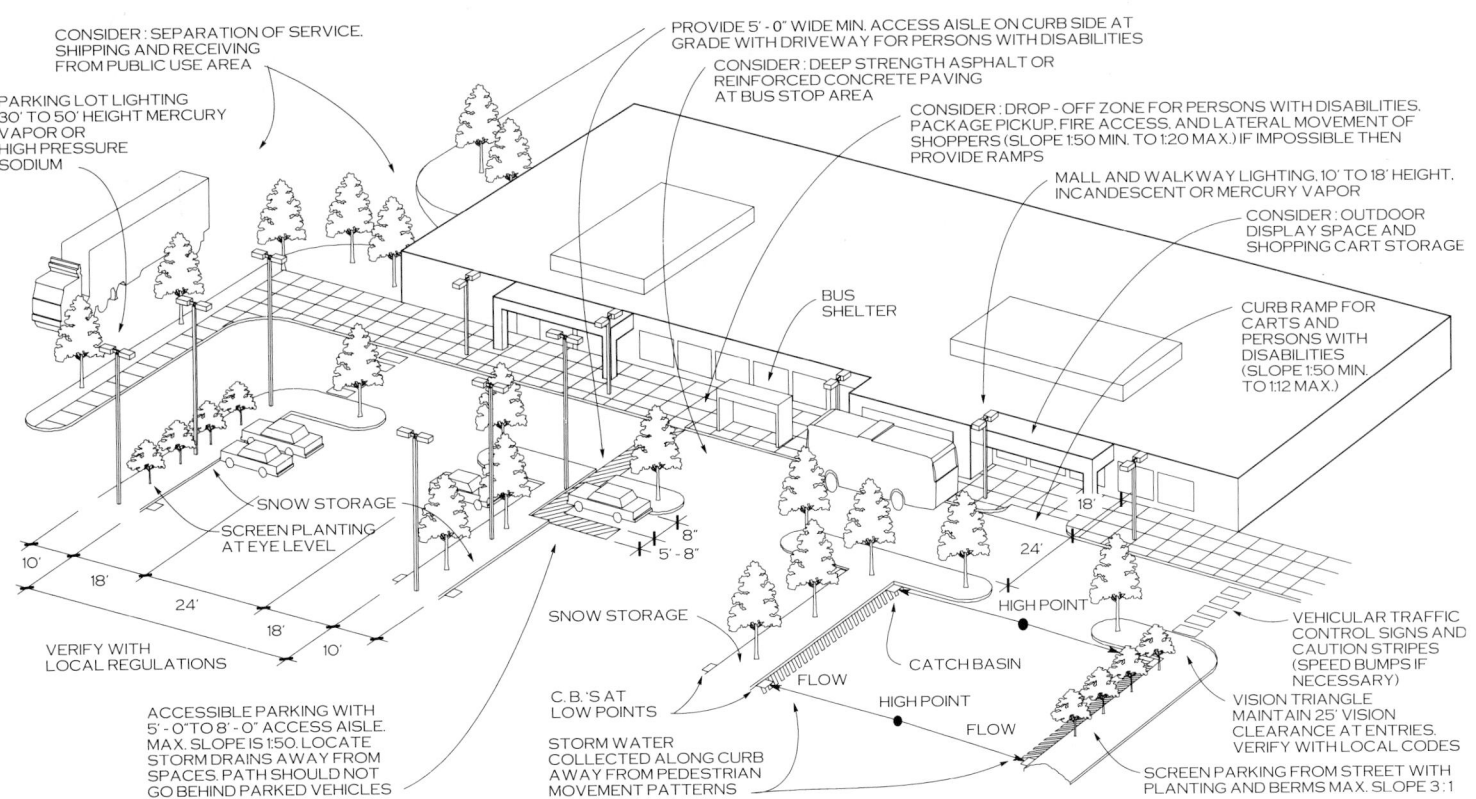

CONSIDER: SEPARATION OF SERVICE. SHIPPING AND RECEIVING FROM PUBLIC USE AREA

PARKING LOT LIGHTING 30' TO 50' HEIGHT MERCURY VAPOR OR HIGH PRESSURE SODIUM

PROVIDE 5'-0" WIDE MIN. ACCESS AISLE ON CURB SIDE AT GRADE WITH DRIVEWAY FOR PERSONS WITH DISABILITIES

CONSIDER: DEEP STRENGTH ASPHALT OR REINFORCED CONCRETE PAVING AT BUS STOP AREA

CONSIDER: DROP-OFF ZONE FOR PERSONS WITH DISABILITIES. PACKAGE PICKUP, FIRE ACCESS, AND LATERAL MOVEMENT OF SHOPPERS (SLOPE 1:50 MIN. TO 1:20 MAX.) IF IMPOSSIBLE THEN PROVIDE RAMPS

MALL AND WALKWAY LIGHTING. 10' TO 18' HEIGHT, INCANDESCENT OR MERCURY VAPOR

CONSIDER: OUTDOOR DISPLAY SPACE AND SHOPPING CART STORAGE

CURB RAMP FOR CARTS AND PERSONS WITH DISABILITIES (SLOPE 1:50 MIN. TO 1:12 MAX.)

BUS SHELTER

SNOW STORAGE

SCREEN PLANTING AT EYE LEVEL

10' 18' 24' 18' 10'

VERIFY WITH LOCAL REGULATIONS

ACCESSIBLE PARKING WITH 5'-0" TO 8'-0" ACCESS AISLE. MAX. SLOPE IS 1:50. LOCATE STORM DRAINS AWAY FROM SPACES. PATH SHOULD NOT GO BEHIND PARKED VEHICLES

SNOW STORAGE

C.B.'S AT LOW POINTS

STORM WATER COLLECTED ALONG CURB AWAY FROM PEDESTRIAN MOVEMENT PATTERNS

8" 5'-8"

FLOW

CATCH BASIN

HIGH POINT

HIGH POINT

FLOW

18' 24'

VEHICULAR TRAFFIC CONTROL SIGNS AND CAUTION STRIPES (SPEED BUMPS IF NECESSARY)

VISION TRIANGLE MAINTAIN 25' VISION CLEARANCE AT ENTRIES. VERIFY WITH LOCAL CODES

SCREEN PARKING FROM STREET WITH PLANTING AND BERMS MAX. SLOPE 3:1

DESIGN GUIDELINES

1. Determine an efficient means of laying out the parking lot (see vehicle and parking space dimension data in chapter 1). A smaller paved area costs less to build and maintain, walking distance from car to building is reduced, water runoff problems are lessened, and more space may be available for site landscaping.

2. Provide safe and coherent site circulation routes.

3. Provide for fire rescue and mass transit access. Consult local requirements.

4. Parking lots should provide direct and easy access for people walking between their vehicles and the building entrances. Pedestrians usually walk in the aisles behind parked vehicles; aisles perpendicular to the building face allow pedestrians to walk to and from the building without squeezing between parked cars. Walking areas should be graded to prevent standing water.

5. Accessible design is now mandatory, requiring designated parking spaces and curb ramps near building entrances.

6. In areas that receive significant snowfall, space should be provided for the deposit of plowed snow which may take a considerable amount of time to melt.

7. Minimum vertical clearance for van parking is 8 ft 2 in.; clearance for a drop-off area is 9 ft 2 in.

8. Wherever possible, integrate small groups of parking spaces with landscaping.

LANDSCAPING

The use of plants in parking areas can help relieve the visually overwhelming scale of large parking lots. To maximize the impact of landscaping, consider the screening capabilities of plants. Low branching, densely foliated trees and shrubs can soften the visual impact of large parking areas. High branching canopy trees do not create a visual screen at eye level but do provide shade. When possible, create islands large enough to accommodate a mixture of canopy trees, flowering trees, evergreen trees, shrubs and flowers. Consider the use of evergreens and avoid plants that drop fruit or sap.

NUMBER OF REQUIRED ACCESSIBLE PARKING SPACES (PER ADAAG)

TOTAL PARKING SPACES	VANS	CARS	TOTAL ACCESSIBLE
1 - 25	1	0	1
26 - 50	1	1	2
51 - 75	1	2	3
76 - 100	1	3	4
101 - 150	1	4	5
151 - 200	1	5	6
201 - 300	1	6	7
301 - 400	1	7	8
401 - 500	2	7	9
501 - 800	2	2%, less 2 van	2% min.
801 - 1,000	3	2%, less 3 van	2% min.
1,001 and over	0.125% + 1	1% + 10, less vans	20 + 1 for each 100 over 1,000

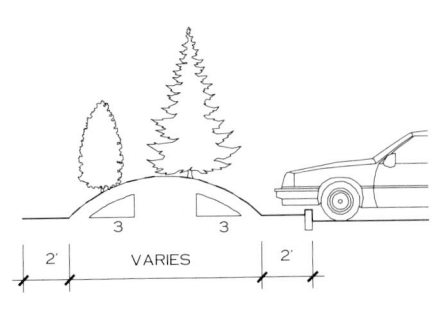

3   3

2'   VARIES   2'

BERM SECTION

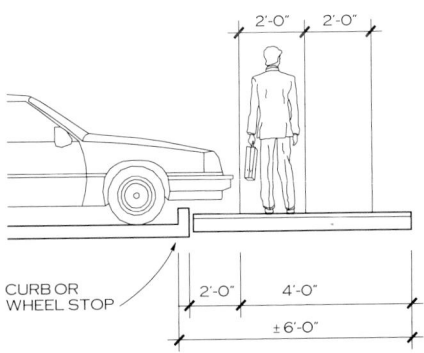

2'-0"   2'-0"

CURB OR WHEEL STOP

2'-0"   4'-0"

±6'-0"

AUTOMOBILE OVERHANG REQUIREMENT

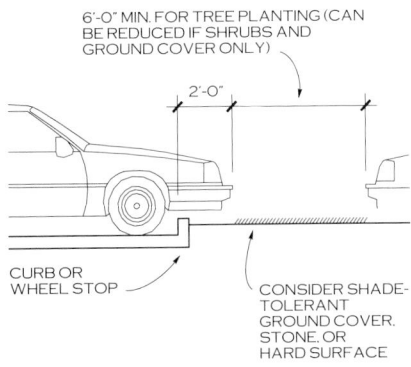

6'-0" MIN. FOR TREE PLANTING (CAN BE REDUCED IF SHRUBS AND GROUND COVER ONLY)

2'-0"

CURB OR WHEEL STOP

CONSIDER SHADE-TOLERANT GROUND COVER. STONE, OR HARD SURFACE

OVERHANG IN PLANTING AREA

Johnson, Johnson & Roy; Ann Arbor, Michigan
Mark J. Mazz, AIA; CEA, Inc.; Hyattsville, Maryland

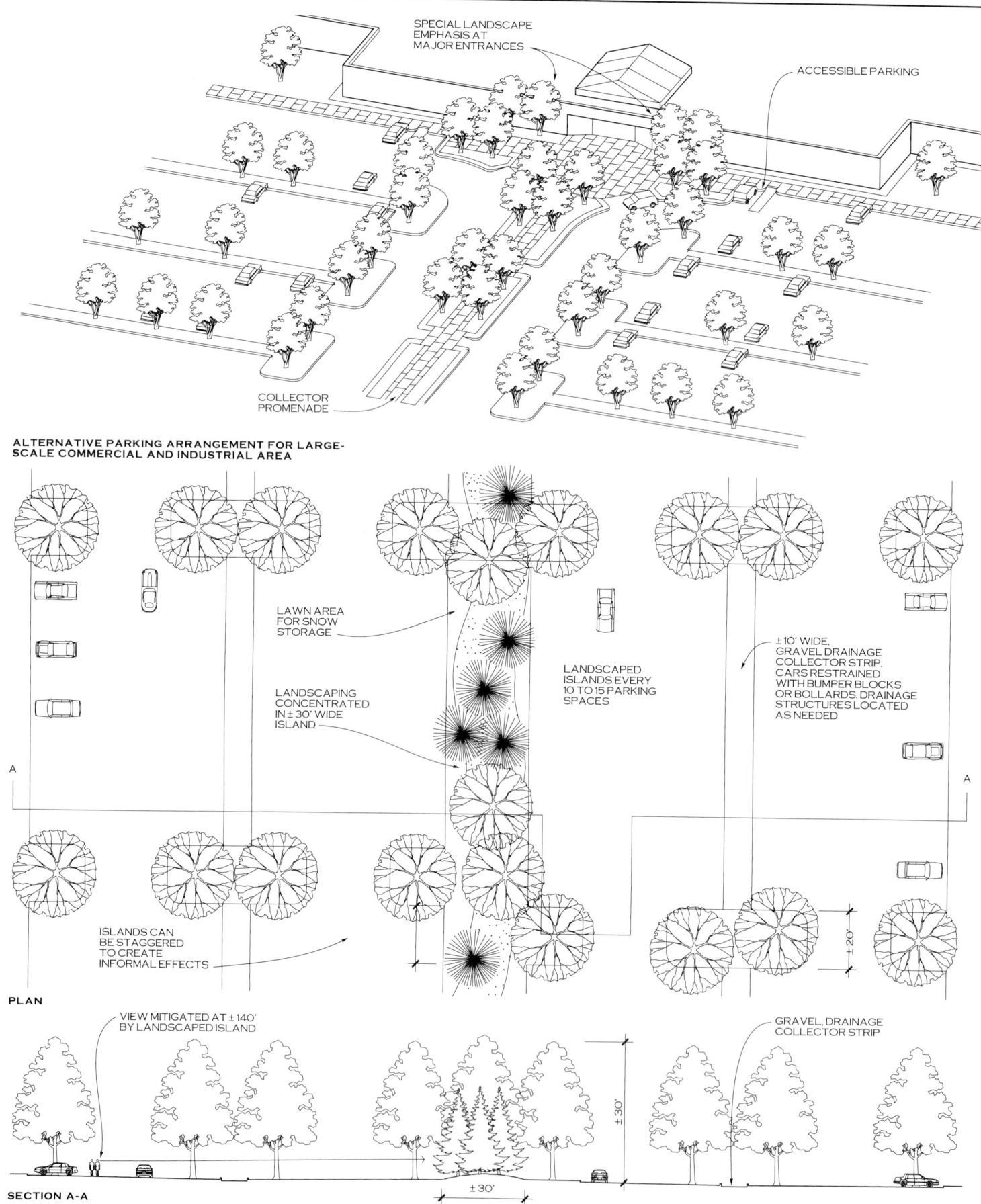

SPECIAL LANDSCAPE
EMPHASIS AT
MAJOR ENTRANCES

ACCESSIBLE PARKING

COLLECTOR
PROMENADE

ALTERNATIVE PARKING ARRANGEMENT FOR LARGE-
SCALE COMMERCIAL AND INDUSTRIAL AREA

LAWN AREA
FOR SNOW
STORAGE

LANDSCAPING
CONCENTRATED
IN ± 30' WIDE
ISLAND

LANDSCAPED
ISLANDS EVERY
10 TO 15 PARKING
SPACES

± 10' WIDE,
GRAVEL DRAINAGE
COLLECTOR STRIP.
CARS RESTRAINED
WITH BUMPER BLOCKS
OR BOLLARDS. DRAINAGE
STRUCTURES LOCATED
AS NEEDED

A   A

ISLANDS CAN
BE STAGGERED
TO CREATE
INFORMAL EFFECTS

± 20'

PLAN

VIEW MITIGATED AT ± 140'
BY LANDSCAPED ISLAND

GRAVEL, DRAINAGE
COLLECTOR STRIP

± 30'

± 30'

SECTION A-A

CONCENTRATED PLANTING FOR LARGE PARKING AREAS

Johnson, Johnson & Roy; Ann Arbor, Michigan
Mark J. Mazz, AIA; CEA, Inc.; Hyattsville, Maryland

1   AUTOMOBILES, ROADS, AND PARKING

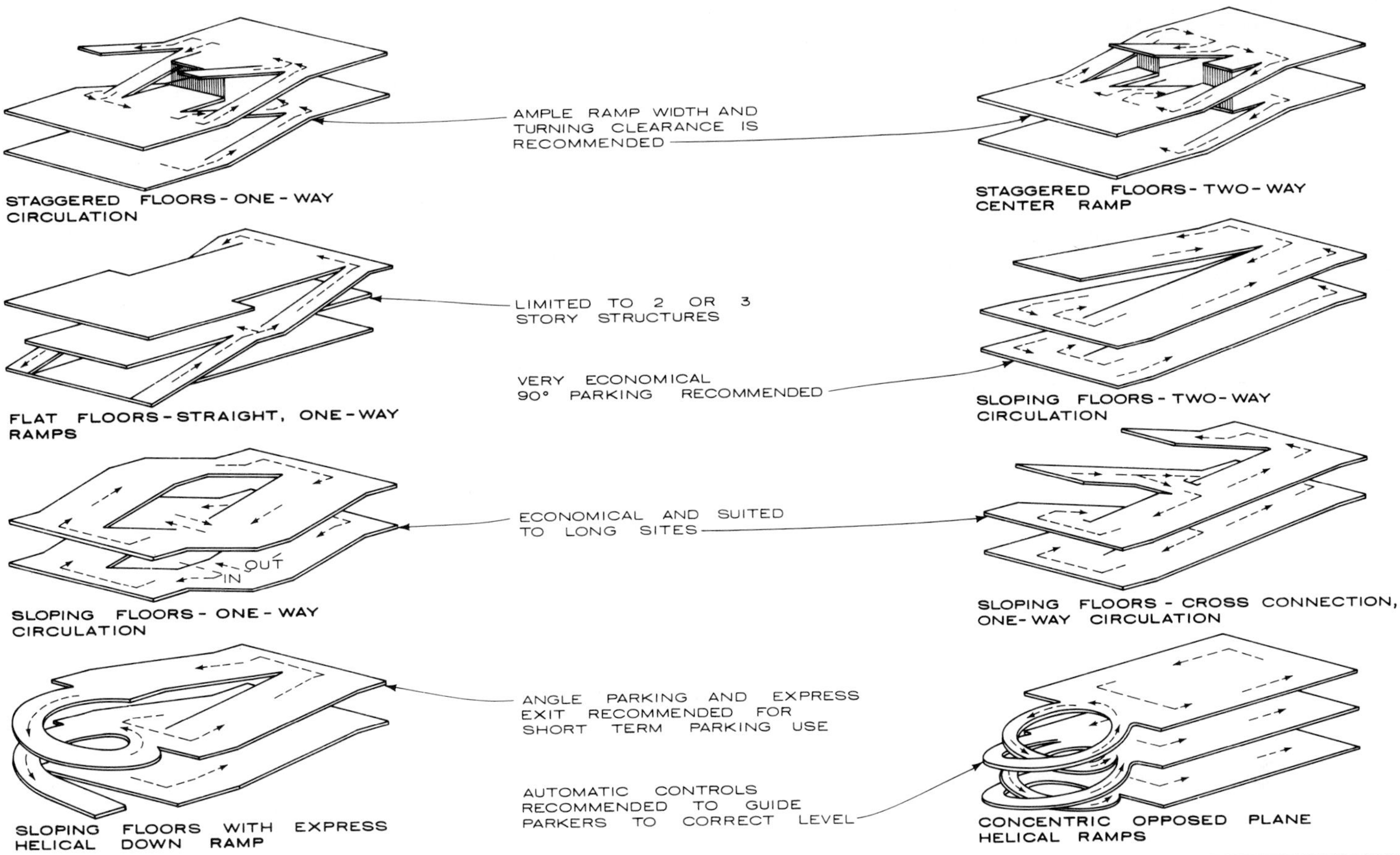

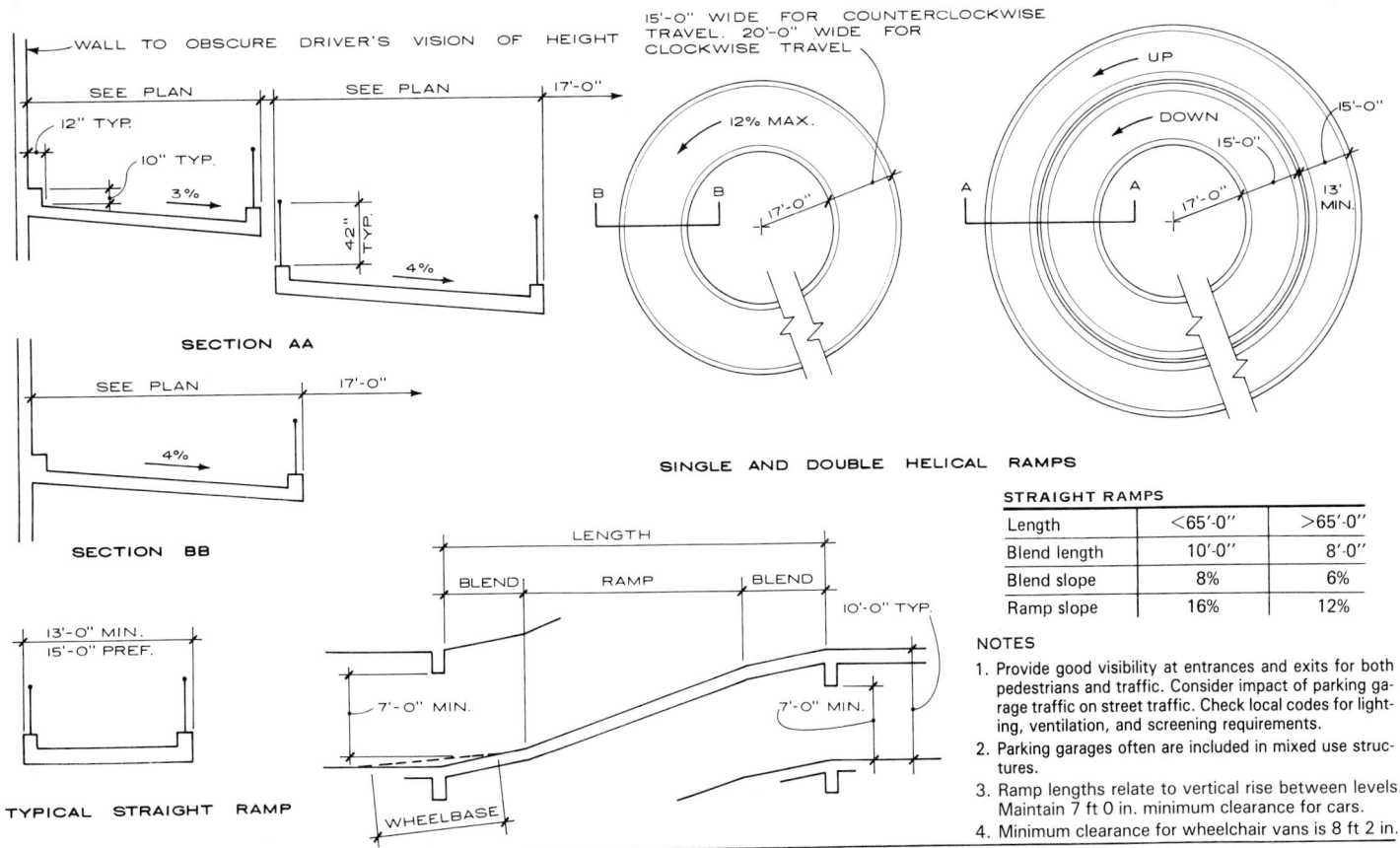

STAGGERED FLOORS-ONE-WAY
CIRCULATION

STAGGERED FLOORS-TWO-WAY
CENTER RAMP

AMPLE RAMP WIDTH AND
TURNING CLEARANCE IS
RECOMMENDED

FLAT FLOORS-STRAIGHT, ONE-WAY
RAMPS

LIMITED TO 2 OR 3
STORY STRUCTURES

VERY ECONOMICAL
90° PARKING RECOMMENDED

SLOPING FLOORS-TWO-WAY
CIRCULATION

SLOPING FLOORS-ONE-WAY
CIRCULATION

OUT
IN

ECONOMICAL AND SUITED
TO LONG SITES

SLOPING FLOORS-CROSS CONNECTION,
ONE-WAY CIRCULATION

SLOPING FLOORS WITH EXPRESS
HELICAL DOWN RAMP

ANGLE PARKING AND EXPRESS
EXIT RECOMMENDED FOR
SHORT TERM PARKING USE

AUTOMATIC CONTROLS
RECOMMENDED TO GUIDE
PARKERS TO CORRECT LEVEL

CONCENTRIC OPPOSED PLANE
HELICAL RAMPS

TYPICAL RAMP SYSTEMS

WALL TO OBSCURE DRIVER'S VISION OF HEIGHT

SEE PLAN   SEE PLAN   17'-0"

12" TYP.

10" TYP.

3%

42" TYP.

4%

SECTION AA

SEE PLAN   17'-0"

4%

SECTION BB

13'-0" MIN.
15'-0" PREF.

7'-0" MIN.

TYPICAL STRAIGHT RAMP

15'-0" WIDE FOR COUNTERCLOCKWISE
TRAVEL. 20'-0" WIDE FOR
CLOCKWISE TRAVEL

12% MAX.

B   B   17'-0"

UP

DOWN
15'-0"
15'-0"

15'-0"

13' MIN.

A   A   17'-0"

SINGLE AND DOUBLE HELICAL RAMPS

LENGTH

BLEND   RAMP   BLEND

10'-0" TYP.

7'-0" MIN.   7'-0" MIN.

WHEELBASE

STRAIGHT RAMPS

Length	<65'-0"	>65'-0"
Blend length	10'-0"	8'-0"
Blend slope	8%	6%
Ramp slope	16%	12%

NOTES

1. Provide good visibility at entrances and exits for both pedestrians and traffic. Consider impact of parking garage traffic on street traffic. Check local codes for lighting, ventilation, and screening requirements.
2. Parking garages often are included in mixed use structures.
3. Ramp lengths relate to vertical rise between levels. Maintain 7 ft 0 in. minimum clearance for cars.
4. Minimum clearance for wheelchair vans is 8 ft 2 in.

TYPICAL RAMP DETAILS

William T. Mahan, AIA; Santa Barbara, California

AUTOMOBILES, ROADS, AND PARKING   1

TRIPLE SEMITRAILER AND TRACTOR

MAXIMUM ALLOWABLE LENGTH
NOT PERMITTED, EXCEPT IN THOSE STATES
LISTED BELOW

UNIT	STATE
90'-0"	AK
(each trailer 27'-0")	AZ
105'-0"	CO
105'-0"	ID
105'-0"	NV
105'-0"	OR
105'-0"	UT
65'-0"	IN
110'-0"	ND

DOUBLE SEMITRAILER AND TRACTOR

MAXIMUM ALLOWABLE LENGTH

UNIT	EACH TRAILER	STATE
60'-0"	28'-0"	GA, SC, VT, VA
61'-0"	—	UT
65'-0"	30'-0"	LA
65'-0"	28'-6"	MA, MN, NY, TX
65'-0"	28'-0"	DE, HI, MD, MO, NM, PA
65'-0"	—	ME, NB
70'-0"	28'-0"	CO, OK
75'-0"	28'-6"	CA, MT
75'-0"	28'-0"	ND
75'-0"	—	AK, OR
80'-0"	28'-6"	SD
85'-0"	—	WY
105'-0"	—	ID
—	30'-0"	MS
—	28'-6"	AL, AZ, IN, IA, KS, MI, TN, WI
—	28'-0"	AK, CT, DC, FL, KY, NH, NJ, NC, WV
—	27'-6"	RI
—	—	IL, NV, OH, WA

SEMITRAILER AND TRACTOR

MAXIMUM ALLOWABLE LENGTH

UNIT	EACH TRAILER	STATE
55'-0"	53'-0"	DC
55'-0"	48'-0"	MD
60'-0"	53'-0"	DE, WI
60'-0"	48'-0"	GA, NC, SC, VA, WV
60'-0"	45'-0"	MA, NY
60'-0"	—	MO, OR, VT
65'-0"	57'-0"	TX
65'-0"	53'-0"	OK
65'-0"	50'-0"	LA
65'-0"	48'-0"	HI, ME
65'-0"	—	CA, MN, NM, PA
70'-0"	48'-0"	AK
70'-0"	—	CO, NV
75'-0"	48'-0"	ID, MT
75'-0"	—	ND
80'-0"	53'-0"	SD
85'-0"	60'-0"	WY
—	53'-0"	NB, OH, IL, IN, IA, KS, KY
—	51'-0"	AZ
—	50'-0"	AL, MI, MS
—	48'-0"	AR, CT, FL, NH, NJ, RI, UT, WA
—	—	TN

STRAIGHT BODY TRUCKS

MAXIMUM ALLOWABLE LENGTH

UNIT	STATE
40'-0"	In all states, except those listed below
35'-0"	FL, KY, MA, NH, NJ, NY, NC, SC, WV
36'-0"	IN
42'-0"	IL
42'-6"	KS
45'-0"	LA, ME, SD, TX, UT
50'-0"	ND
60'-0"	CT, GA, VT, WY

Robert H. Lorenz, AIA; Preston Trucking Company, Inc.; Preston, Maryland
The Operations Council, American Trucking Association; Washington, D.C.

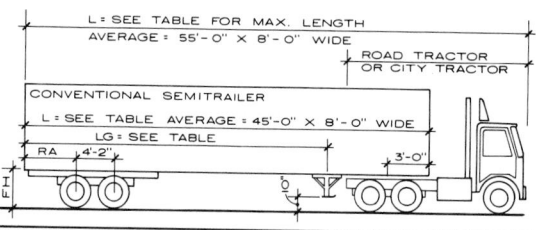

DOUBLE SEMITRAILER AND CITY TRACTOR

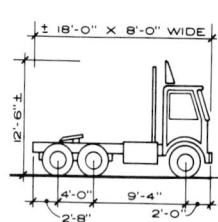

CITY TRACTOR

SEMITRAILER AND ROAD TRACTOR
TIRE SIZE APPROX. 41" ± DIA. X 10" ± WIDE

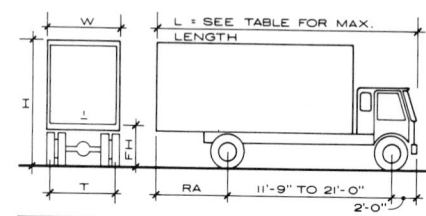

ROAD TRACTOR

VEHICLE HEIGHT

MAXIMUM ALLOWABLE

TOTAL HEIGHT	STATE
13'-6"	In all states, except those listed below
13'-0"	FL
14'-0"	CA, ID, ME, NV, ND, OR, UT, WA, WY
14'-6"	CO, NB

VEHICLE WIDTH

MAXIMUM ALLOWABLE

TOTAL WIDTH	STATE
8'-6"	In all states, except those listed below
8'-0"	DE, DC, FL, IL, IA, KY, LA, MI, MO, NY, NC, PA, SC, TN, VA, WV

NOTE: Width is 8'-0" or 8'-6" according to state. Length and area restrictions vary with each state and locale. Verify exact dimensions and restrictions.

STRAIGHT BODY TRUCK

AVERAGE SEMITRAILER DIMENSIONS

	LENGTH (L)			
	27'-0"	40'-0"	45'-0"	REFRIG. 40'-0"
Floor height (FH)	4'-2"	4'-2"	4'-2"	4'-9"
Rear axle (RA)	3'-0"	5'-2"	5'-10"	4'-5"
Landing gear (LG)	19'-0"	30'-0"	34'-6"	29'-5"
Cubic feet (CU)	1564±	2327±	2620±	2113±

AVERAGE DIMENSIONS OF VEHICLES

	TYPE OF VEHICLES		
	DOUBLE SEMITRAILER	CONVENTIONAL SEMITRAILER	STRAIGHT BODY TRUCK
Length (L)	70'-0"	55'-0"	17'-0" to 40'-0"
Width (W)	8'-0"	8'-0"	8'-0"
Height (H)	13'-6"	13'-6"	13'-6"
Floor Height (FH)	4'-0" to 4'-6"	4'-0" to 4'-4"	3'-0" to 4'-0"
Track (T)	6'-6"	6'-6"	5'-10"
Rear Axle (RA)	3'-0" to 4'-0"	4'-0" to 12'-0"	2'-3" to 12'-0"

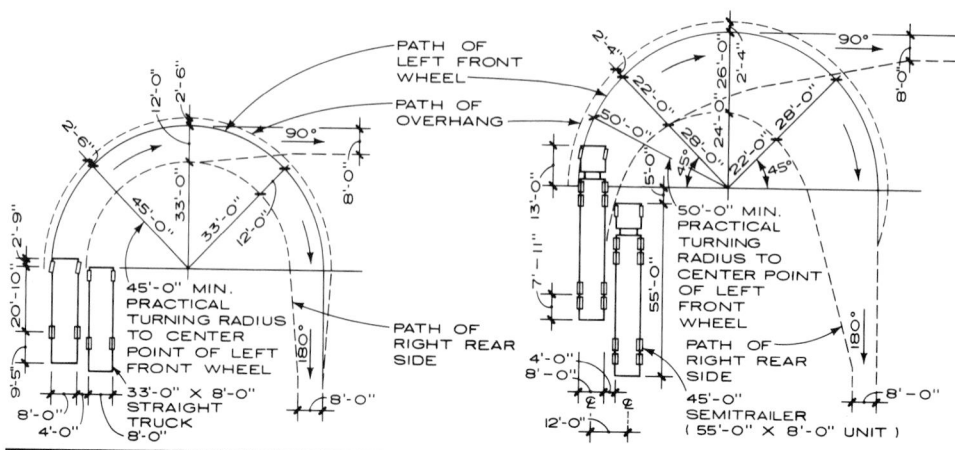

33'-0" STRAIGHT BODY TRUCK MINIMUM PRACTICAL TURNING RADIUS OF 45'-0"

55'-0" SEMITRAILER AND TRACTOR COMBINATION MINIMUM PRACTICAL TURNING RADIUS OF 50'-0"

1   **TRUCKS, TRAINS, AND BOATS**

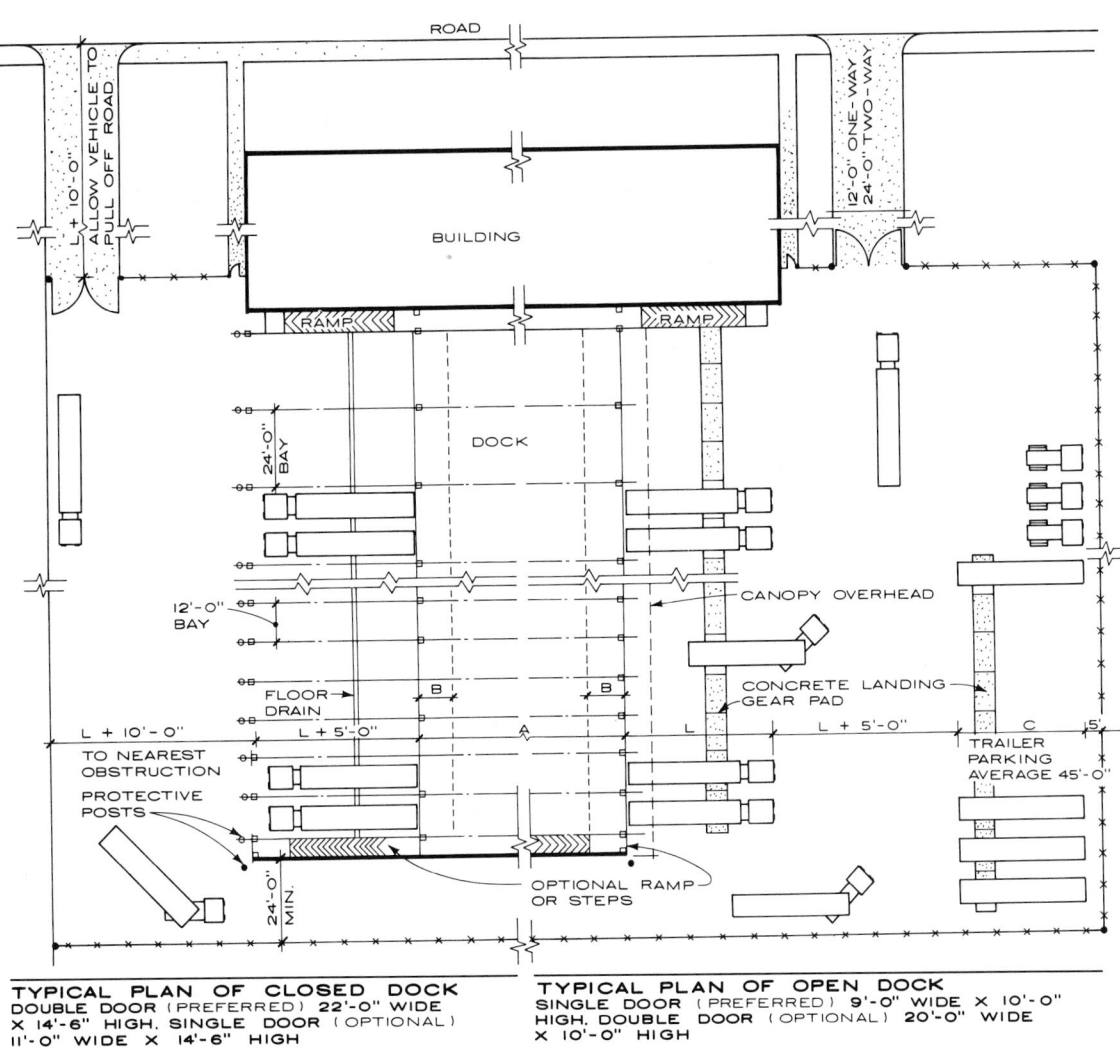

ROAD

BUILDING

DOCK

CANOPY OVERHEAD

CONCRETE LANDING GEAR PAD

TRAILER PARKING AVERAGE 45'-0"

FLOOR DRAIN

TO NEAREST OBSTRUCTION

PROTECTIVE POSTS

OPTIONAL RAMP OR STEPS

TYPICAL PLAN OF CLOSED DOCK
DOUBLE DOOR (PREFERRED) 22'-0" WIDE × 14'-6" HIGH. SINGLE DOOR (OPTIONAL) 11'-0" WIDE × 14'-6" HIGH

TYPICAL PLAN OF OPEN DOCK
SINGLE DOOR (PREFERRED) 9'-0" WIDE × 10'-0" HIGH. DOUBLE DOOR (OPTIONAL) 20'-0" WIDE × 10'-0" HIGH

NOTES

1. Allow for off-street employee and driver parking.
2. Entrances and exits should be of reinforced concrete when excessive twisting and turning of vehicles are expected.
3. Average gate (swing or slide) 30 ft 0 in. wide for two-way traffic. People gate 5 ft 0 in. wide with concrete walkway 4 ft 0 in. to 6 ft 0 in. wide.
4. For yard security use a 6 ft 0 in. high chain link fence with barbed wire on top.
5. On-site fueling facilities are desirable for road units.
6. Provide general yard lighting from fixtures mounted on building or on 24 ft 0 in. high minimum poles at fence line. Mercury vapor or high pressure sodium preferred.
7. Tractor parking requires 12 ft 0 in. wide × 20 ft 0 in. long slot minimum. Provide motor heater outlets for diesel engines in cold climates.
8. Trailer parking requires 10 ft 0 in. wide slot minimum. Provide 10 ft 0 in. wide concrete pad for landing gear. Score concrete at 12 ft 0 in. o.c. to aid in correct spotting of trailer.
9. 4 ft 0 in. wide minimum concrete ramp from dock to grade. Slopes of 3 to 15% (10% average), score surface for traction.
10. Vehicles should circulate in a counter-clockwise direction, making left hand turns, permitting driver to see rear of unit when backing into dock.
11. Double trailers are backed into dock separately.

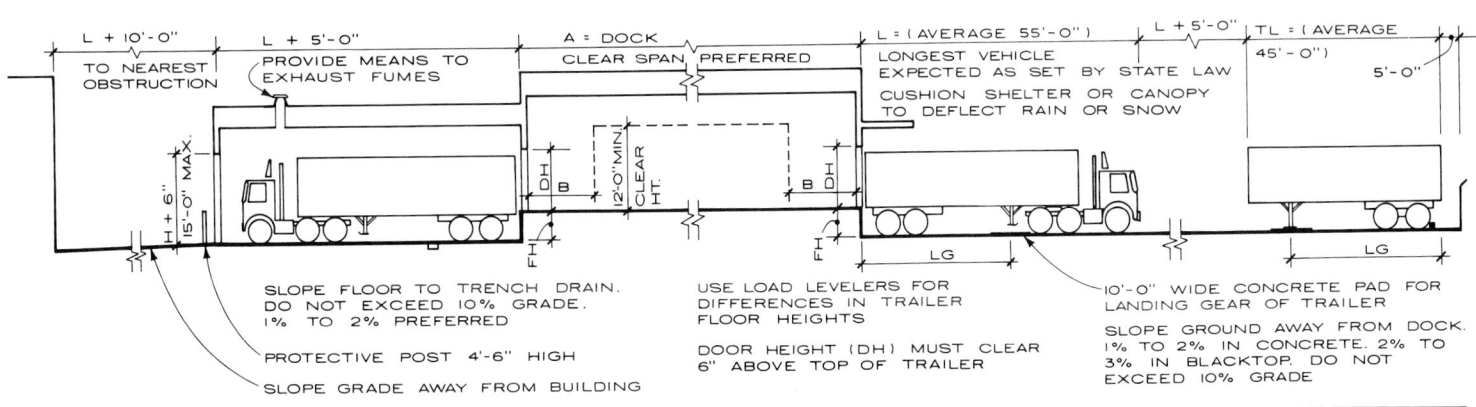

PROVIDE MEANS TO EXHAUST FUMES

A = DOCK CLEAR SPAN PREFERRED

L = (AVERAGE 55'-0") LONGEST VEHICLE EXPECTED AS SET BY STATE LAW

CUSHION SHELTER OR CANOPY TO DEFLECT RAIN OR SNOW

TO NEAREST OBSTRUCTION

SLOPE FLOOR TO TRENCH DRAIN. DO NOT EXCEED 10% GRADE. 1% TO 2% PREFERRED

PROTECTIVE POST 4'-6" HIGH

SLOPE GRADE AWAY FROM BUILDING

USE LOAD LEVELERS FOR DIFFERENCES IN TRAILER FLOOR HEIGHTS

DOOR HEIGHT (DH) MUST CLEAR 6" ABOVE TOP OF TRAILER

10'-0" WIDE CONCRETE PAD FOR LANDING GEAR OF TRAILER

SLOPE GROUND AWAY FROM DOCK. 1% TO 2% IN CONCRETE. 2% TO 3% IN BLACKTOP. DO NOT EXCEED 10% GRADE

TYPICAL SECTION OF CLOSED DOCK

TYPICAL SECTION OF OPEN DOCK

AVERAGE VEHICLE DIMENSIONS

LENGTH OF VEHICLE (L)	FLOOR HEIGHT (FH)	VEHICLE HEIGHT (H)
60 ft tractor trailer	4'-0" to 4'-6"	14'-0"
45 ft trailer	4'-0" to 4'-2"	13'-6"
40 ft straight body	3'-8" to 4'-2"	13'-6"
18 ft van	2'-0" to 2'-8"	7'-0"

NOTE: Refer to other pages for truck and trailer sizes.

AVERAGE WIDTHS OF DOCKS

TYPE OF OPERATION	TWO-WHEEL HAND TRUCK	FOUR-WHEEL HAND TRUCK	FORKLIFT TRUCK	DRAGLINE	AUTO SPUR DRAGLINE
Dock width (A)	50'-0"	60'-0"	60'-0" to 70'-0"	80'-0"	120'-0" to 140'-0"
Work aisle (B)	6'-0"	10'-0"	15'-0"	10'-0" to 15'-0"	10'-0" to 15'-0"

Robert H. Lorenz, AIA; Preston Trucking Company, Inc.; Preston, Maryland
The Operations Council, American Trucking Association; Washington, D.C.

TRUCKS, TRAINS, AND BOATS

1

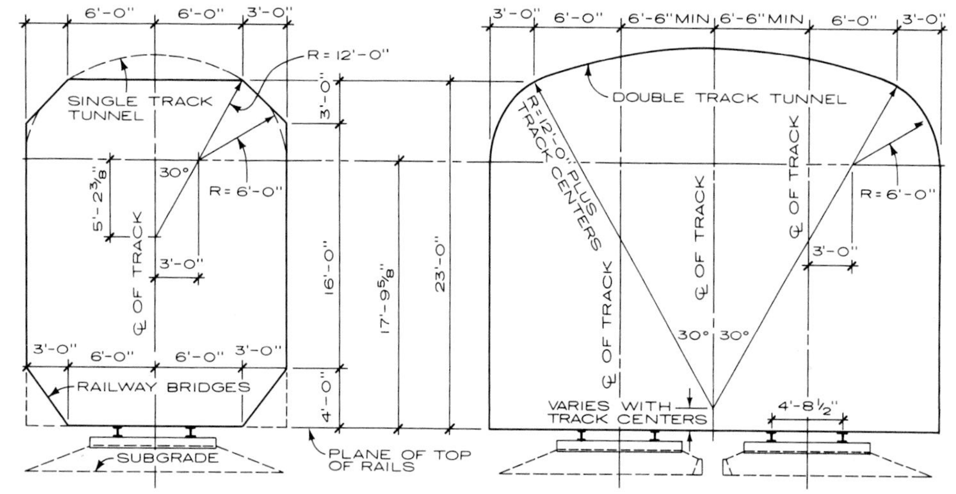

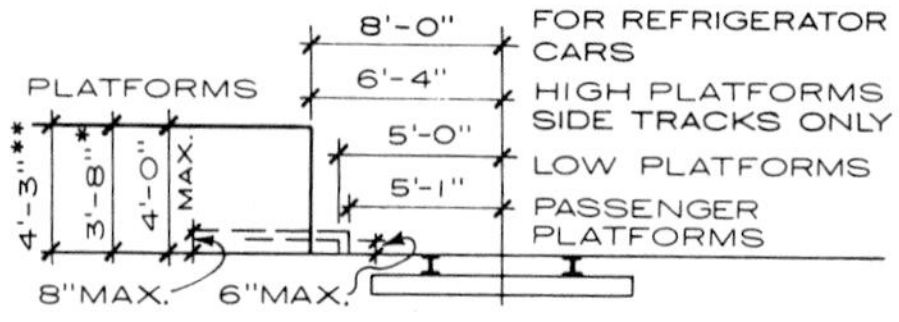

RAILWAY CLEARANCES

SINGLE TRACK TUNNEL

R = 12'-0"
R = 6'-0"
30°

RAILWAY BRIDGES

SUBGRADE

PLANE OF TOP OF RAILS

DOUBLE TRACK TUNNEL

R = 12'-0" PLUS TRACK CENTERS

R = 6'-0"

30° 30°

VARIES WITH TRACK CENTERS

4'-8½"

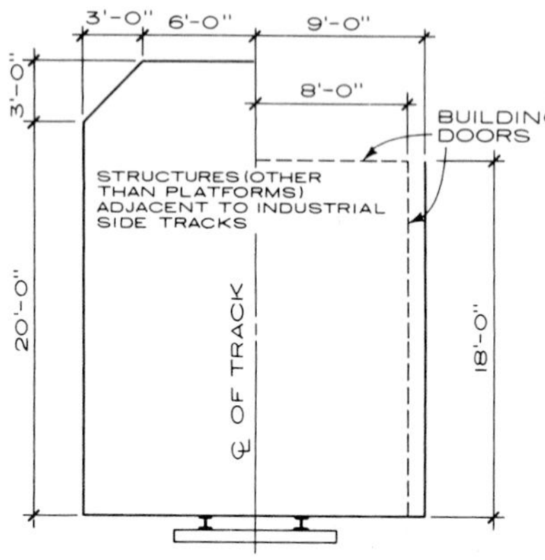

STRUCTURES (OTHER THAN PLATFORMS) ADJACENT TO INDUSTRIAL SIDE TRACKS

BUILDING DOORS

PLATFORMS

8'-0"   FOR REFRIGERATOR CARS
6'-4"   HIGH PLATFORMS SIDE TRACKS ONLY
5'-0"   LOW PLATFORMS
5'-1"   PASSENGER PLATFORMS

8" MAX.   6" MAX.

*RECOMMENDED HEIGHT FOR AVERAGE CAR
**STANDARD HEIGHT FOR PASSENGER CAR

NOTE

The 6 ft 4 in. dimension will accommodate cars with either flush sliding doors or plug doors. Cars with hinged double doors require full clearance of 8 ft. Where 6 ft 4 in. platform is used, full clearance should be provided on opposite side, except inside buildings. (Several states allow a platform height of 4 ft 6 in. for refrigerator cars only, if the full lateral clearance of 8 ft is provided.)

NOTES

1. Given clearances are the recommended minimums of the American Railway Engineering Association. Actual requirements vary from state to state.
2. Clearances shown are for the tangent track and new construction. Clearances for reconstruction work or for alteration are dependent on existing physical conditions and, where reasonably possible, should be improved to meet the requirements for new construction.
3. On curved track, the lateral clearances each side of track center line shall be increased 1½ in. per degree of curvature.
4. Common state requirement for lateral clearance of poles is 8 ft 6 in. (varies from 8 to 12 ft).
5. Standard American railroad gauge of 4 ft 8½ in. is measured between the inner faces of the rails.

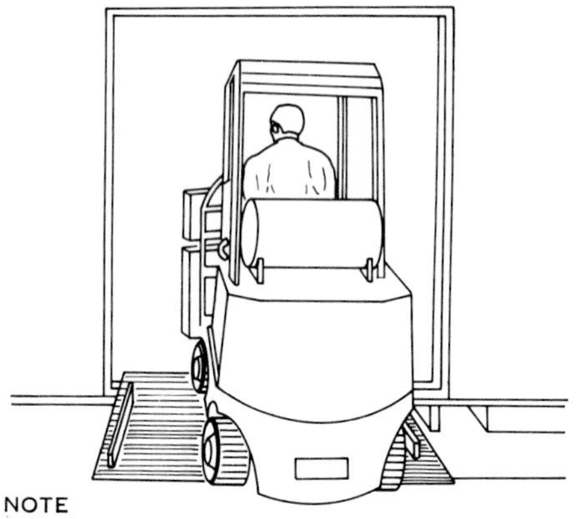

RAIL DOCK RAMPS

NOTE

Ramp travels laterally on rail mounted to edge of dock for positioning to rail car opening. It adjusts above and below dock level and locks to the rail when in the lowered position. Self-stores in vertical position when not in use. Available in varying lengths and widths.

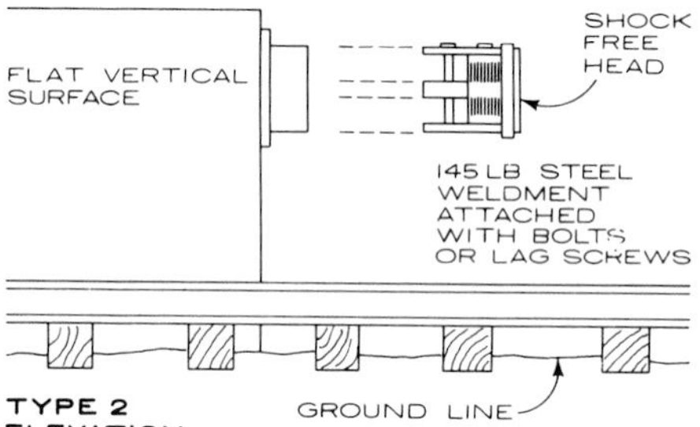

SHOCK FREE HEAD

FLAT VERTICAL SURFACE

145 LB STEEL WELDMENT ATTACHED WITH BOLTS OR LAG SCREWS

TYPE 2 ELEVATION   GROUND LINE

TYPICAL BUMPING POSTS

PLAN

2½" TO 7½"
Ç OF TRACK

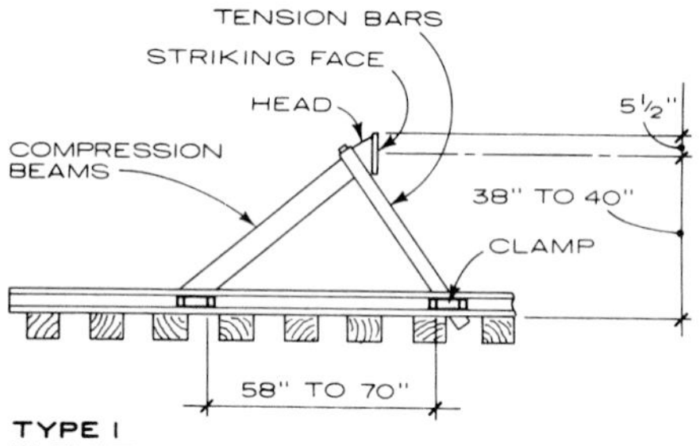

TENSION BARS
STRIKING FACE
HEAD
COMPRESSION BEAMS
CLAMP

5½"
38" TO 40"
58" TO 70"

TYPE 1 ELEVATION

TYPICAL RAILROAD CAR TYPES AND SIZES (ACTUAL CAR SIZES VARY GREATLY EVEN AMONG LIKE CAR TYPES)

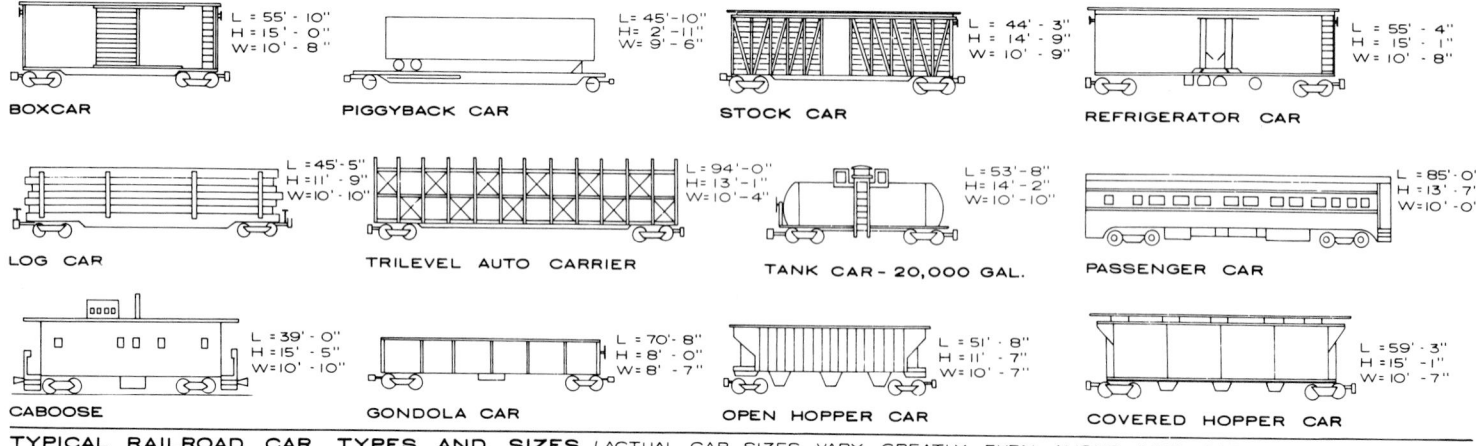

BOXCAR
L = 55'-10"
H = 15'-0"
W = 10'-8"

PIGGYBACK CAR
L = 45'-10"
H = 2'-11"
W = 9'-6"

STOCK CAR
L = 44'-3"
H = 14'-9"
W = 10'-9"

REFRIGERATOR CAR
L = 55'-4"
H = 15'-1"
W = 10'-8"

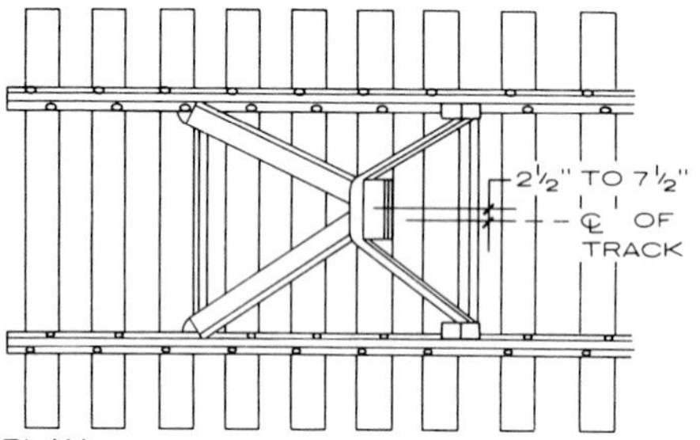

LOG CAR
L = 45'-5"
H = 11'-9"
W = 10'-4"

TRILEVEL AUTO CARRIER
L = 94'-0"
H = 13'-1"
W = 10'-4"

TANK CAR - 20,000 GAL.
L = 53'-8"
H = 14'-2"
W = 10'-10"

PASSENGER CAR
L = 85'-0"
H = 13'-7"
W = 10'-0"

CABOOSE
L = 39'-0"
H = 15'-5"
W = 10'-10"

GONDOLA CAR
L = 70'-8"
H = 8'-0"
W = 8'-7"

OPEN HOPPER CAR
L = 51'-8"
H = 11'-7"
W = 10'-7"

COVERED HOPPER CAR
L = 59'-3"
H = 15'-1"
W = 10'-7"

Ed Hesner; Rasmussen & Hobbs Architects; Tacoma, Washington
N. Claiborne Porter Jr., AIA; Anchorage, Alaska

1 TRUCKS, TRAINS, AND BOATS

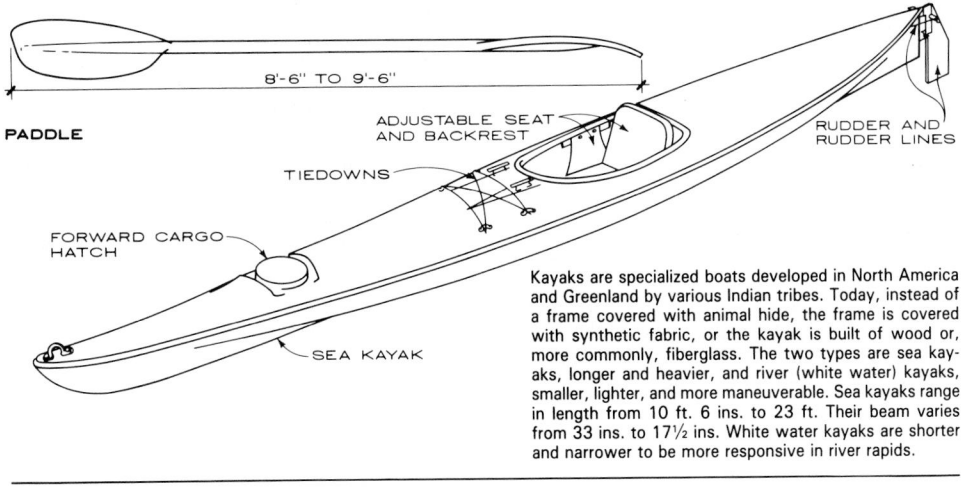

PADDLE

8'-6" TO 9'-6"

ADJUSTABLE SEAT
AND BACKREST

RUDDER AND
RUDDER LINES

TIEDOWNS

FORWARD CARGO
HATCH

SEA KAYAK

Kayaks are specialized boats developed in North America and Greenland by various Indian tribes. Today, instead of a frame covered with animal hide, the frame is covered with synthetic fabric, or the kayak is built of wood or, more commonly, fiberglass. The two types are sea kayaks, longer and heavier, and river (white water) kayaks, smaller, lighter, and more maneuverable. Sea kayaks range in length from 10 ft. 6 ins. to 23 ft. Their beam varies from 33 ins. to 17½ ins. White water kayaks are shorter and narrower to be more responsive in river rapids.

KAYAK

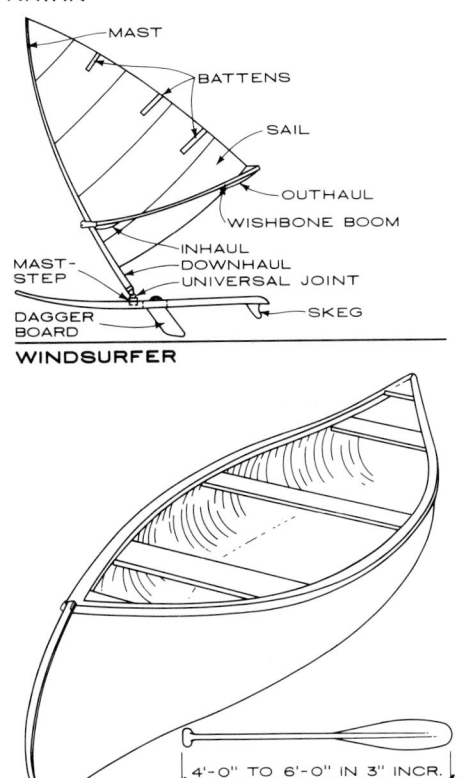

MAST

BATTENS

SAIL

OUTHAUL

WISHBONE BOOM

INHAUL
DOWNHAUL
UNIVERSAL JOINT

MAST-
STEP

DAGGER
BOARD

SKEG

WINDSURFER

PADDLE

4'-0" TO 6'-0" IN 3" INCR.

CANOE

Canoes have shallow draft, and they range in length from 12 ft. to 35 ft. They can be paddled, sailed, or motored, and they can be loaded with equipment. They are constructed of wood, fiberglass, or aluminum.

SLIDING SEAT

OARLOCK

SECTION

OARLOCK

RIGGER

WASHBOARD

SLIDING SEAT

ROWING SHELL

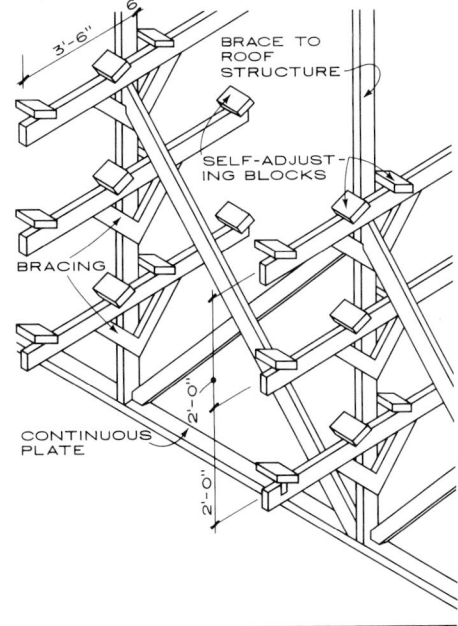

3'-6"

6"

BRACE TO
ROOF
STRUCTURE

SELF-ADJUST-
ING BLOCKS

BRACING

2'-0"

2'-0"

CONTINUOUS
PLATE

ROWING SHELL STORAGE RACK

Storage for rowing shells requires: two racks 8 feet apart for single and double; three racks 8 feet apart for eight-oared. Shells used daily should not be stored higher than 6 ft. Storage racks can be adapted easily to hold kayaks or canoes by adjusting the spacing between racks and the height between horizontal members.

Racing shells, built primarily of carbon fiber or plastic, are narrow and unstable in the water. There are two rowing styles: sweep rowing, where oarsmen work one oar with both hands; and sculling, where each oarsman works two oars, one in each hand. Sweeps are 12 ft. to 13 ft. long; sculling oars are 9 ft. 6 ins. to 10 ft. long.

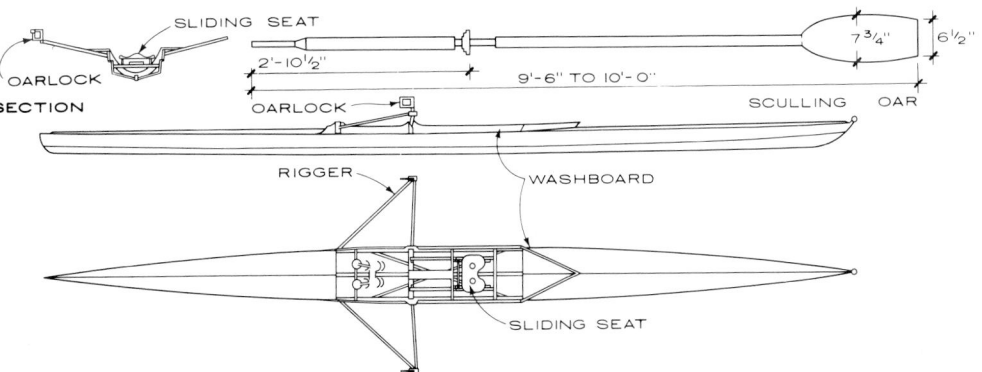

2'-10½"

9'-6" TO 10'-0"

7¾"

6½"

SCULLING   OAR

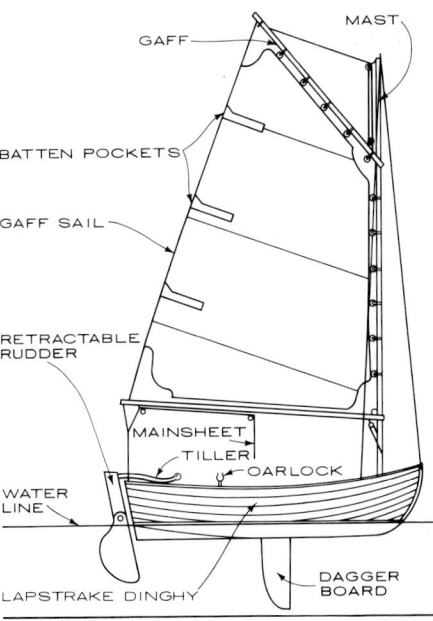

GAFF

MAST

BATTEN POCKETS

GAFF SAIL

RETRACTABLE
RUDDER

MAINSHEET

TILLER

OARLOCK

WATER
LINE

LAPSTRAKE DINGHY

DAGGER
BOARD

DINGHIES

Dinghies are small boats used as auxiliaries to larger craft. They also can be sailed and raced on their own. They vary in length from 6 ft. to 16 ft., and they are 2 ft. 10 ins. to 5 ft. 6 ins. in beam. They are constructed of wood or fiberglass, and they can be rigged for sail, rowing, or motoring.

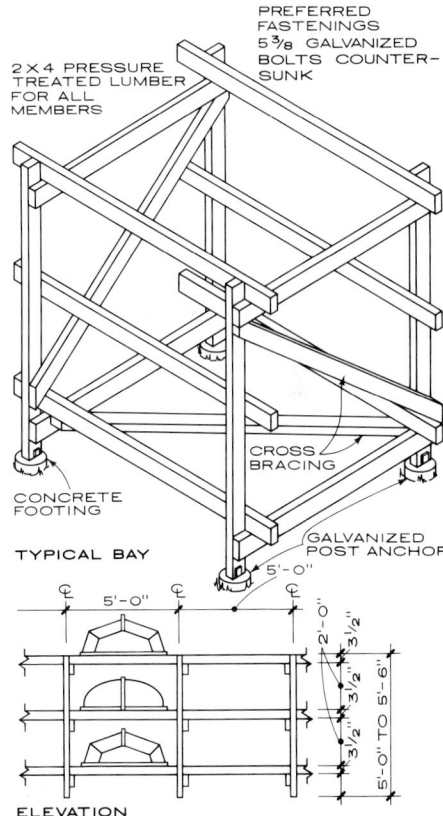

PREFERRED
FASTENINGS
5⅜ GALVANIZED
BOLTS COUNTER-
SUNK

2 X 4 PRESSURE
TREATED LUMBER
FOR ALL
MEMBERS

CROSS
BRACING

CONCRETE
FOOTING

GALVANIZED
POST ANCHOR

TYPICAL BAY

5'-0"

5'-0"

5'-0"

2'-0"

3½"

3½"

3½"

3½"

5'-0" TO 5'-6"

ELEVATION

DINGHY STORAGE RACK

Dinghy racks store the small boats year round, and should be weather-treated. The rack members are fastened with countersunk bolts to avoid damaging dinghies. Racks must be able to support the weight of the boats and anyone climbing on the racks.

Timothy B. McDonald; Washington, D.C.

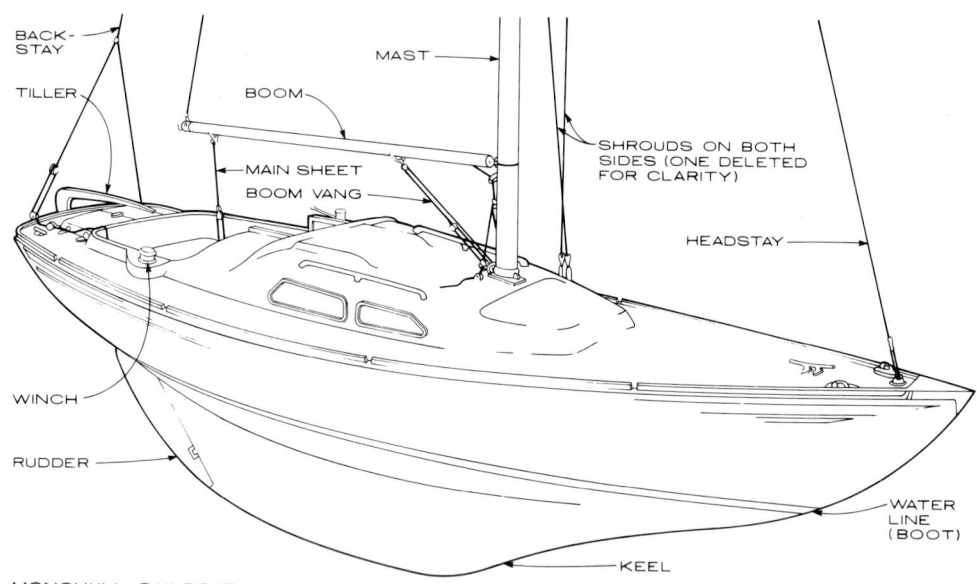

MONOHULL SAILBOAT

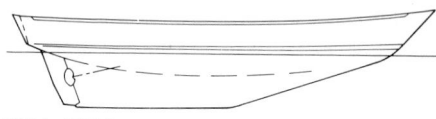

FULL KEEL

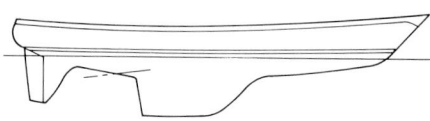

FIN KEEL

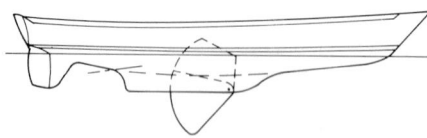

FIN KEEL/CENTER BOARD

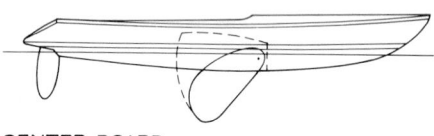

CENTER BOARD

MONOHULL -
BASIC UNDERWATER HULL SHAPES

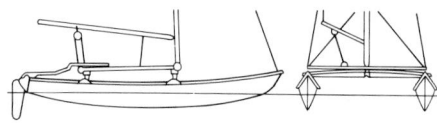

MULTIHULL

CATBOAT RIG

Traditionally puts a lot of sail area on one short mast, as shown here, which is stepped far forward in the boat.

SLOOP

Design with two basic sails, mainsail and headsail; the latter, called a "fractional rig," is set either to the mast-head or some distance below the masthead.

CUTTER

Like the sloop, a cutter rig has one mast carrying two headsails instead of one. The inner sail is the fore-stay sail and the outer sail is the jib.

YAWL

Unlike the sloop or cutter, the yawl is a two masted rig consisting of a mainmast and a mizzen mast that is stepped abaft (behind) the rudder post. The mizzen sail is much smaller than the main sail.

KETCH

Like the yawl, the ketch is also a two-masted rig; however, the mizzen mast is stepped forward of the rudder post and is larger than the yawl's mizzen. This placement dictates a smaller mainsail.

SCHOONER

Usually two-masted but can be three-masted. Commonly the foremast is the shorter of the two, and may be gaff or marconi rigged or at times a combination of both.

A combination of mast and rigging placement (where the mast is stepped), along with size, type and number of sails, make up the main differences in sailboat rigs. Today the most common is the marconi rig distinguished by a triangular mainsail, but it is not unusual for boats to be rigged with a traditional gaff, which is a four-sided sail that hangs from a spar called a gaff. In some instances marconi and gaff rigs are used together as shown on the schooner below.

Headsails are triangular sails set ahead of the mast. Basic headsails are the jib, working jib, staysail, and genoa. The working jib, unlike other jibs, does not overlap the mast and is often attached to a boom for easier control. Jibs and genoas do overlap the mast and mainsail. The fore-staysail is combined with the jib to create a double-head-sail and is used primarily on cutters and schooners.

Spinnakers, usually the largest sail set before the mast, come in several different shapes and sizes according to use.

DEFINITIONS

1. Length overall—LOA—boat's greatest length excluding bowsprits rudder or other extensions.
2. Length of water line—LWL—boat's greatest length at the water level excluding extensions such as rudders.
3. Beam—boat's maximum breadth.
4. Draft—distance from the waterline to the bottom of the boat's keel determining the least depth of water the boat can operate in: i.e., the amount it draws.
5. Displacement—weight of the water that the boat displaces.

NOTES FOR BASIC RIGS

LATEEN

Ancestor of the fore and aft rigs shown here. It dates back thousands of years and is still used in many parts of the world.

EXAMPLES

	LOA	LWL	BEAM		DRAFT	
FULL KEEL BOATS						
Folkboat	25'-10"	19'-10"	7'-4"		3'-11"	
Cape Dory 45	45'-3"	33'-6"	13'-0"		6'-3"	
FIN KEEL BOATS						
Tartan 28	28'-3"	23'-3"	9'-10"		4'-11"	
O'Day 35	35'-0"	28'-9"	11'-3"		5'-7"	
FIN/CENTERBOARD				UP		DOWN
Cape Dory (270)	27'-3"	20'-9"	9'-5"	3'-0"		7'-0"
Tartan 37	37'-3"	28'-6"	11'-9"	4'-2"		7'-9"
CENTERBOARD				UP		DOWN
Sunfish	13'-10"	13'-10"	4'-1/2"	3"		2'-8"
Laser	13'-10"	12'-6"	4'-6"	6"		2'-8"
El Toro	8'-0"	7'-0"	3'-10"	3"		1'-10"
MULTIHULLS						
Hobie 16	16'-7"	15'-9"	7'-11"		10"	

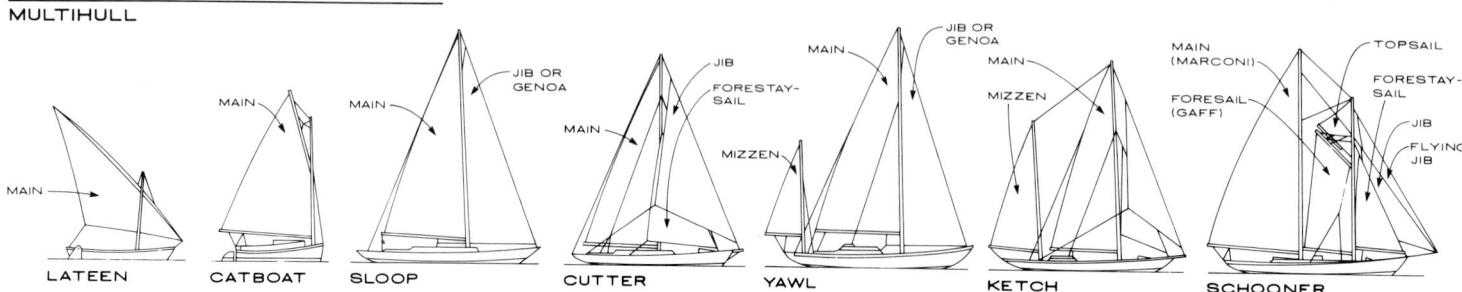

BASIC BOAT RIGS

Timothy B. McDonald; Washington, D.C.

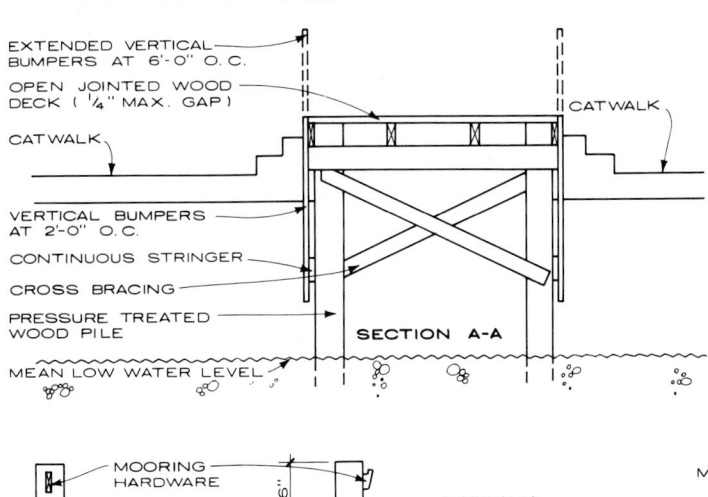

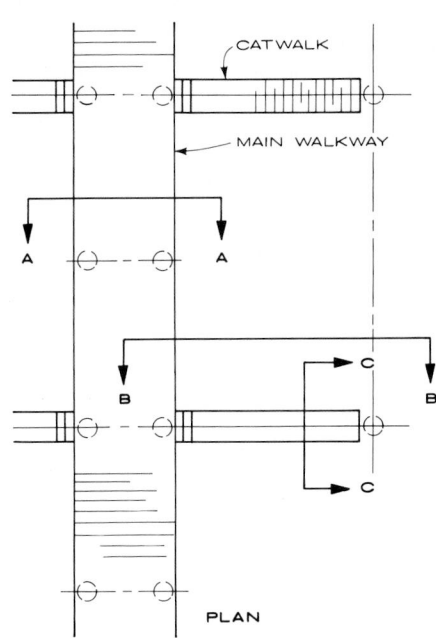

EXTENDED VERTICAL BUMPERS AT 6'-0" O.C.
OPEN JOINTED WOOD DECK (¼" MAX. GAP)
CATWALK
VERTICAL BUMPERS AT 2'-0" O.C.
CONTINUOUS STRINGER
CROSS BRACING
PRESSURE TREATED WOOD PILE
MEAN LOW WATER LEVEL
CATWALK
SECTION A-A

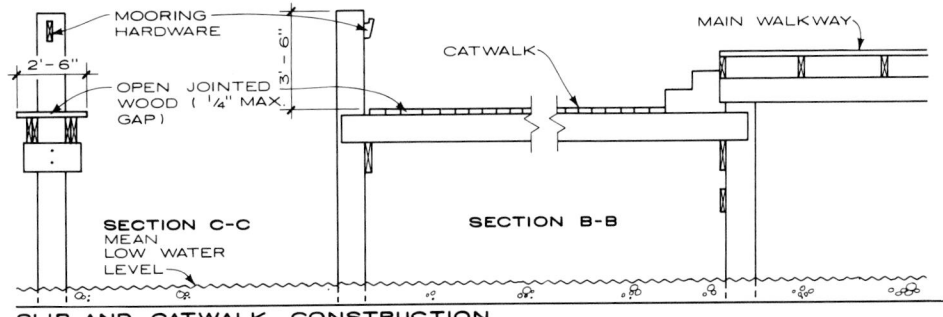

MOORING HARDWARE
2'-6"
3'-6"
OPEN JOINTED WOOD (¼" MAX. GAP)
CATWALK
MAIN WALKWAY
SECTION C-C
MEAN LOW WATER LEVEL
SECTION B-B

SLIP AND CATWALK CONSTRUCTION

PLAN

GENERAL NOTES

1. Wood marine construction must be pressure treated with a preservative. Wood preservatives for use in marine applications fall into two general categories, creosote and waterborne. To select a specific preservative from within these categories, the decaying agents must be identified. A preservative may then be chosen based on the recommendations of the American Wood Preservers Institute.
2. Waterborne preservatives are recommended for decks because creosote stains shoes and bare feet.
3. The preservatives selected should be approved by the Environmental Protection Agency.
4. Dock height above water is determined by average deck levels and probable water level. Maintain a 12 in. minimum dimension between water and deck. Floating docks may be required in tidal waters. Consult manufacturer for construction information.
5. Cross bracing should be minimized to avoid entanglement of swimmers.

LAUNCHING RAMPS

1. Launching ramps are for sheltered waters only.
2. A catwalk may be provided alongside the ramp.
3. Floating ramps may be required in tidal waters.

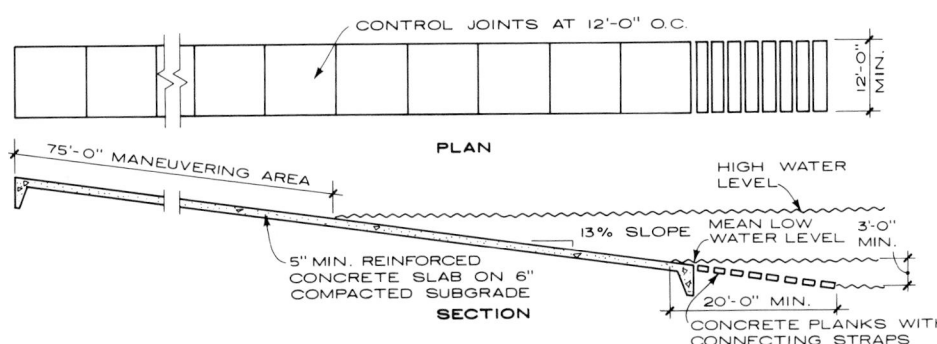

CONTROL JOINTS AT 12'-0" O.C.
12'-0" MIN.
PLAN
75'-0" MANEUVERING AREA
HIGH WATER LEVEL
13% SLOPE
MEAN LOW WATER LEVEL
3'-0" MIN.
5" MIN. REINFORCED CONCRETE SLAB ON 6" COMPACTED SUBGRADE
SECTION
20'-0" MIN.
CONCRETE PLANKS WITH CONNECTING STRAPS

BOAT LAUNCHING RAMP

TABLE OF DIMENSIONS FOR SLIPS AND CATWALKS TO BE USED WITH PLAN DIAGRAM

LENGTH GROUP FOR BOAT	BEAM TO BE PROVIDED FOR	MIN. CLEAR WIDTH OF SLIP	GROSS SLIP WIDTH TYPE A	GROSS SLIP WIDTH TYPE B	GROSS SLIP WIDTH TYPE C	1ST CATWALK SPAN LENGTH D	2ND CATWALK SPAN LENGTH E	3RD CATWALK SPAN LENGTH F	DISTANCE G TO ANCHOR PILE
Up to 14'	6'-7"	8'-10"	10'-9"	10'-6"	11'-2"	12'-0"			17'-0"
Over 14' to 16'	7'-4"	9'-8"	11'-7"	11'-4"	12'-0"	12'-0"			19'-0"
Over 16' to 18'	8'-0"	10'-5"	12'-4"	12'-1"	12'-9"	14'-0"			21'-0"
Over 18' to 20'	8'-7"	11'-1"	13'-0"	12'-9"	13'-5"	8'-0"	8'-0"		23'-0"
Over 20' to 22'	9'-3"	11'-9"	13'-8"	13'-5"	14'-1"	10'-0"	8'-0"		25'-0"
Over 22' to 25'	10'-3"	13'-1"	15'-0"	14'-9"	15'-5"	10'-0"	8'-0"		28'-0"
Over 25' to 30'	11'-3"	14'-3"	16'-2"	15'-11"	16'-7"	10'-0"	10'-0"		33'-0"
Over 30' to 35'	12'-3"	15'-8"	17'-7"	17'-4"	18'-0"	12'-0"	10'-0"		38'-0"
Over 35' to 40'	13'-3"	16'-11"	18'-10"	18'-7"	19'-3"	12'-0"	12'-0"		43'-0"
Over 40' to 45'	14'-1"	17'-11"	19'-10"	19'-7"	20'-3"	14'-0"	12'-0"		48'-0"
Over 45' to 50'	14'-11"	19'-0"	20'-11"	20'-8"	21'-4"	9'-0"	9'-0"	10'-0"	53'-0"
Over 50' to 60'	16'-6"	21'-0"	22'-11"	22'-8"	23'-4"	11'-0"	11'-0"	12'-0"	63'-0"
Over 60' to 70'	18'-1"	23'-0"	26'-8"	24'-8"	25'-4"	11'-0"	11'-0"	12'-0"	73'-0"
Over 70' to 80'	19'-9"	24'-11"	28'-7"	26'-7"	26'-3"	11'-0"	11'-0"	12'-0"	83'-0"

David E. Rose; Rossen/Neumann Associates; Southfield, Michigan

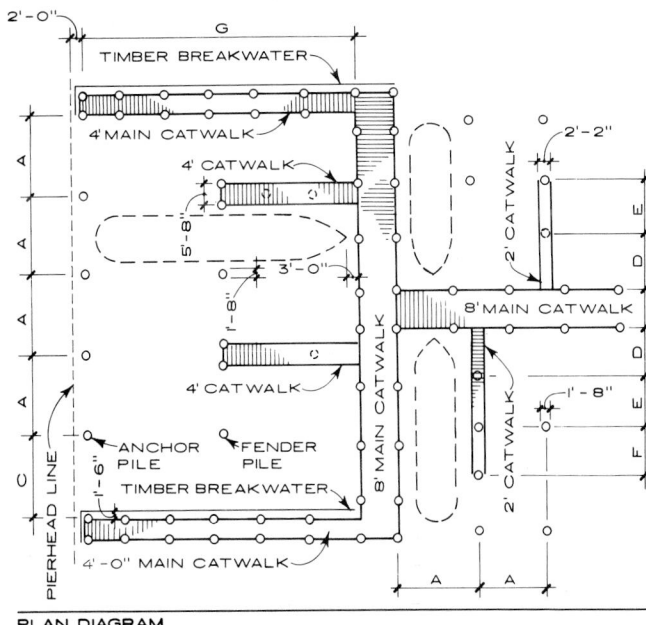

2'-0"
G
TIMBER BREAKWATER
4' MAIN CATWALK
4' CATWALK
CATWALK
2'-2"
5'-8"
3'-0"
1'-8"
8' MAIN CATWALK
4' CATWALK
ANCHOR PILE
FENDER PILE
TIMBER BREAKWATER
PIERHEAD LINE
8' MAIN CATWALK
2' CATWALK
1'-8"
1'-6"
4'-0" MAIN CATWALK

PLAN DIAGRAM

TRUCKS, TRAINS, AND BOATS

1

GENERAL

Classical architecture is based on five distinct and formalized systems of columns and horizontal supports, called the orders. A proportional system in which the parts and divisions of each order, measured in multiples or divisions of the diameter of the lowest part of the relevant tapered column shaft, distinguishes each unique order.

NOTE

A parallel comparison based on Vignola proportions in terms of a constant lower diameter.

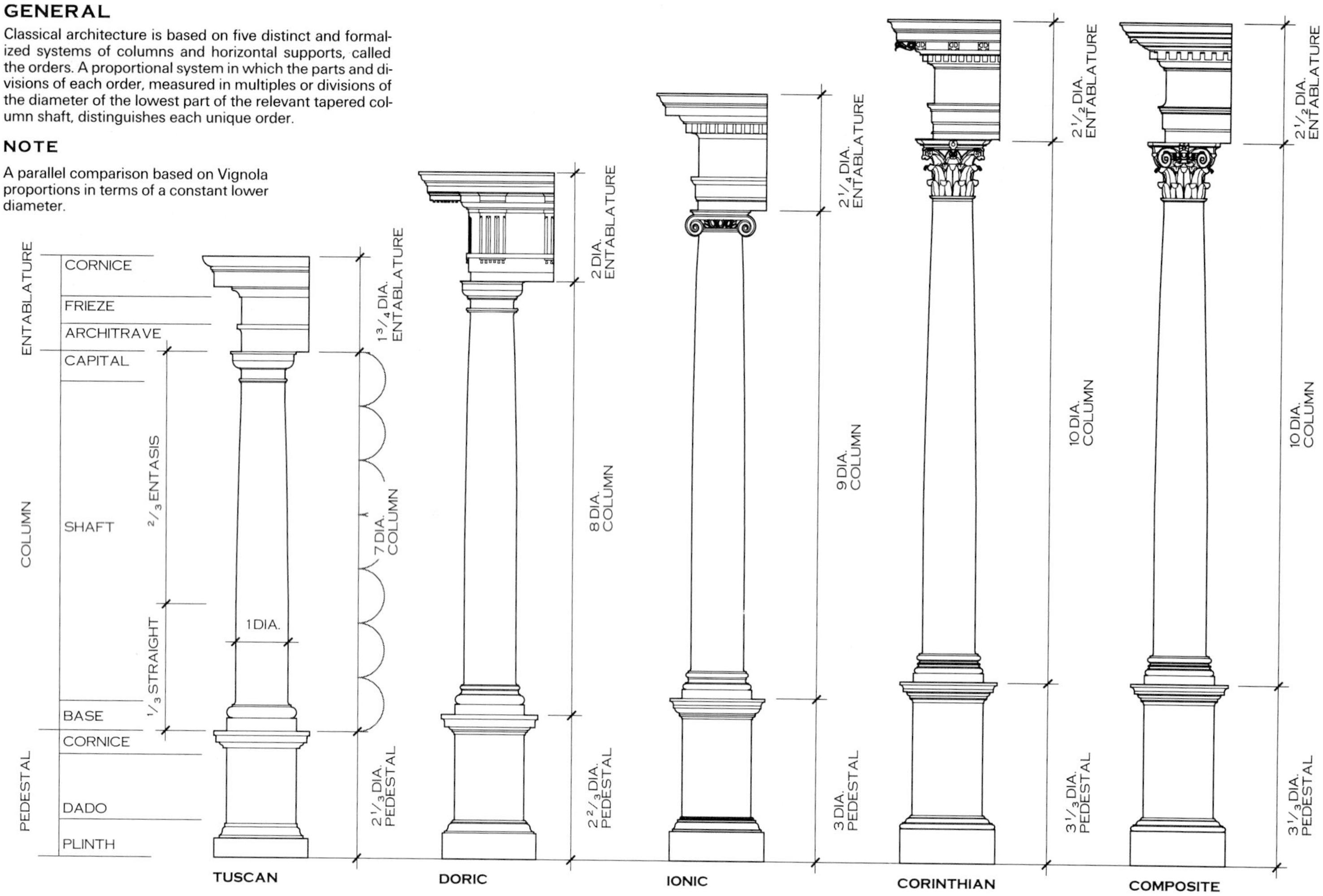

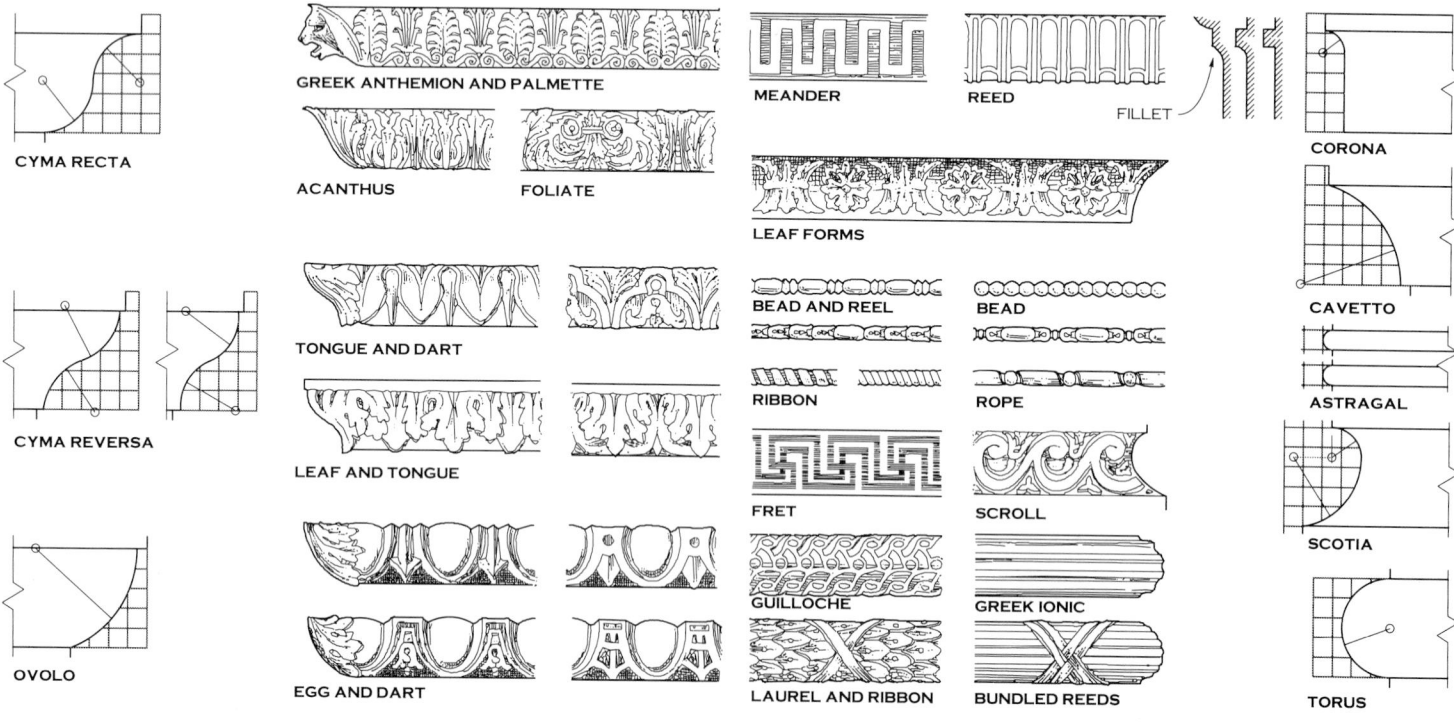

ENTABLATURE
- CORNICE
- FRIEZE
- ARCHITRAVE
- CAPITAL

COLUMN
- SHAFT

BASE

PEDESTAL
- CORNICE
- DADO
- PLINTH

1 DIA.

²/₃ ENTASIS

¹/₃ STRAIGHT

TUSCAN — 1 DIA.
1³/₄ DIA. ENTABLATURE
7 DIA. COLUMN
2¹/₃ DIA. PEDESTAL

DORIC
2 DIA. ENTABLATURE
8 DIA. COLUMN
2²/₃ DIA. PEDESTAL

IONIC
2¹/₄ DIA. ENTABLATURE
9 DIA. COLUMN
3 DIA. PEDESTAL

CORINTHIAN
2¹/₂ DIA. ENTABLATURE
10 DIA. COLUMN
3¹/₃ DIA. PEDESTAL

COMPOSITE
2¹/₂ DIA. ENTABLATURE
10 DIA. COLUMN
3¹/₃ DIA. PEDESTAL

THE FIVE CLASSICAL ORDERS — RENAISSANCE PROPORTIONS

CYMA RECTA

GREEK ANTHEMION AND PALMETTE

ACANTHUS   FOLIATE

MEANDER   REED   FILLET   CORONA

LEAF FORMS

CYMA REVERSA

TONGUE AND DART

LEAF AND TONGUE

BEAD AND REEL   BEAD   CAVETTO

RIBBON   ROPE   ASTRAGAL

FRET   SCROLL

OVOLO

EGG AND DART

GUILLOCHE   GREEK IONIC   SCOTIA

LAUREL AND RIBBON   BUNDLED REEDS   TORUS

MOLDINGS — TYPES, PATTERNS, AND DECORATIONS

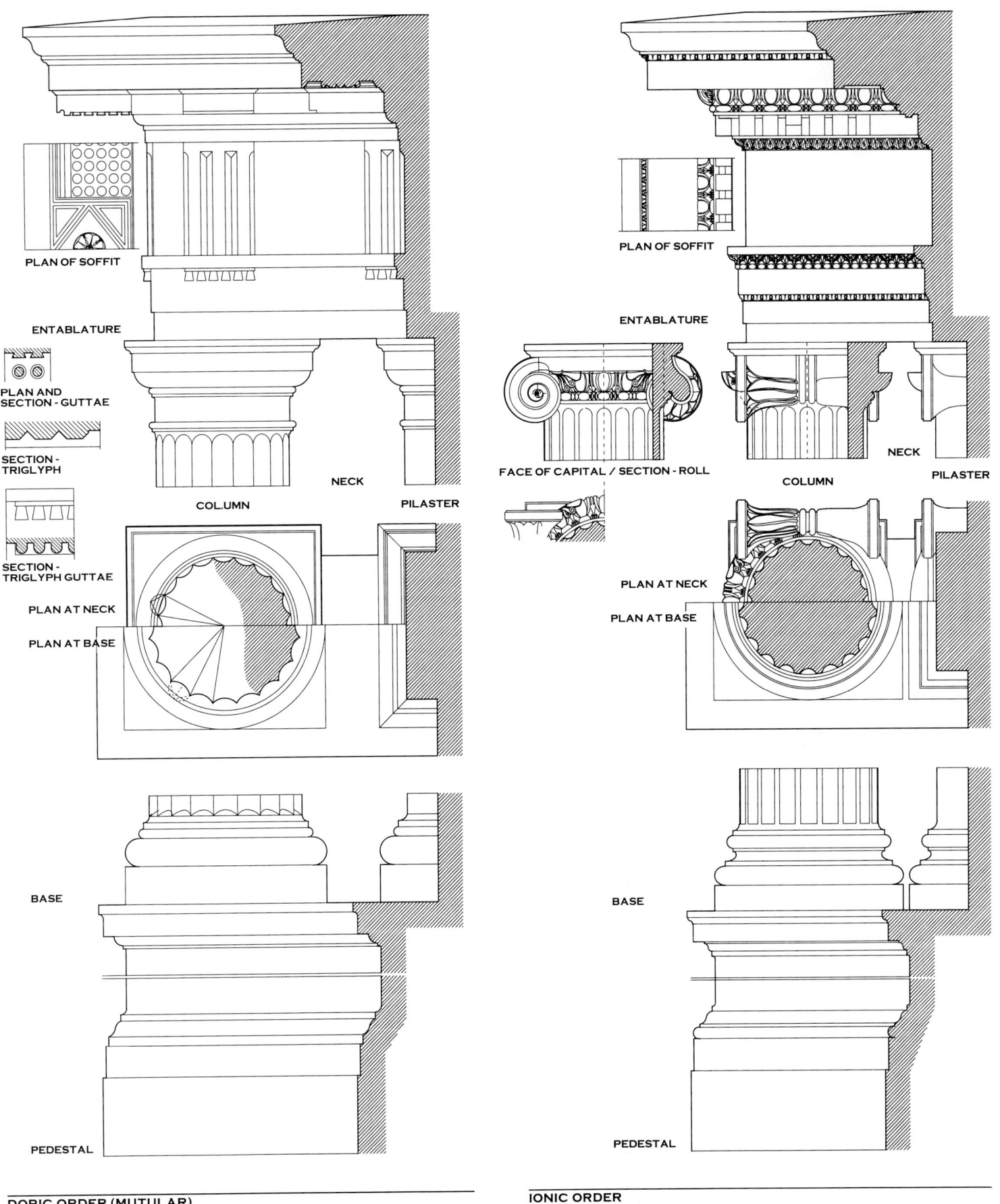

PLAN OF SOFFIT

ENTABLATURE

PLAN AND
SECTION - GUTTAE

SECTION -
TRIGLYPH

SECTION -
TRIGLYPH GUTTAE

PLAN AT NECK

PLAN AT BASE

NECK

COLUMN

PILASTER

BASE

PEDESTAL

DORIC ORDER (MUTULAR)

PLAN OF SOFFIT

ENTABLATURE

FACE OF CAPITAL / SECTION - ROLL

NECK

PLAN AT NECK

PLAN AT BASE

COLUMN

PILASTER

BASE

PEDESTAL

IONIC ORDER

CLASSICAL ARCHITECTURE 1

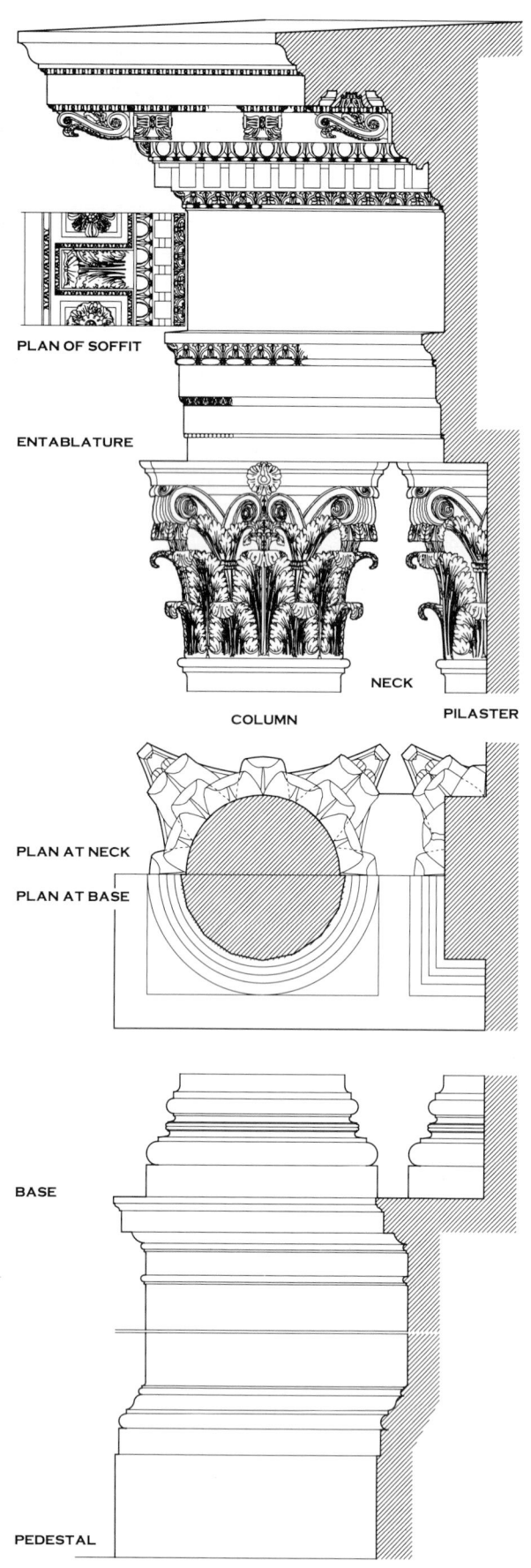

PLAN OF SOFFIT

ENTABLATURE

NECK

COLUMN   PILASTER

PLAN AT NECK

PLAN AT BASE

BASE

PEDESTAL

CORINTHIAN ORDER

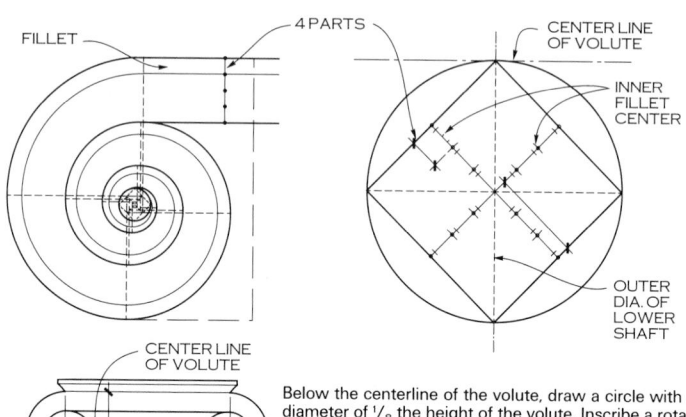

TRUE
RAKING
SECTION

SECTION
AT RETURN

HORIZONTAL
SECTION

RETURN
OF RAKE

ANY NUMBER OF
APPROXIMATELY
EQUAL PARTS

RAKING MOLDINGS

FILLET

4 PARTS

CENTER LINE
OF VOLUTE

INNER
FILLET
CENTER

OUTER
DIA. OF
LOWER
SHAFT

CENTER LINE
OF VOLUTE

DIA. OF LOWER
PART OF SHAFT

Below the centerline of the volute, draw a circle with a diameter of $1/_8$ the height of the volute. Inscribe a rotated, quartered square within this circle or "eye." The sixth points of the centerline of this square give the centers for a series of diminishing arcs. From center 1 draw arc 1, from center 2, arc 2, etc. Successive arcs meet at a line defined by their centers. The inner line of the fillet is gained by repeating the process using the secondary centers shown below.

CONSTRUCTING A VOLUTE

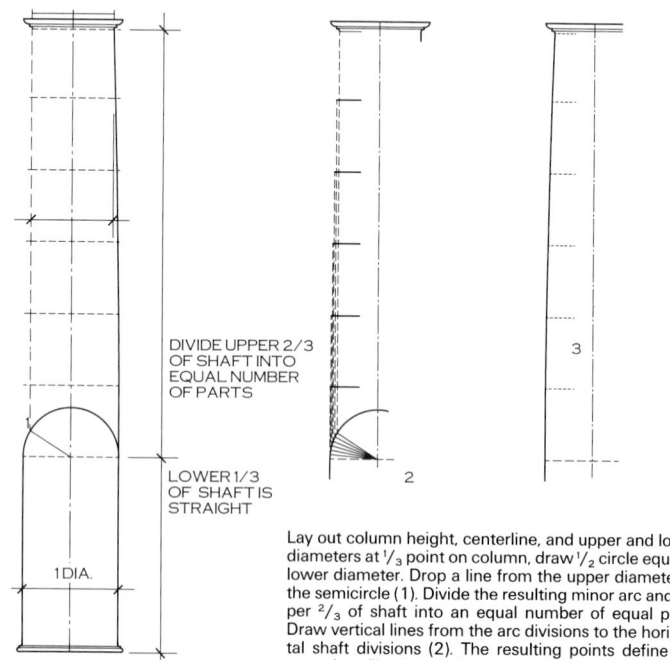

DIVIDE UPPER 2/3
OF SHAFT INTO
EQUAL NUMBER
OF PARTS

LOWER 1/3
OF SHAFT IS
STRAIGHT

1 DIA.

3

2

Lay out column height, centerline, and upper and lower diameters at $1/_3$ point on column, draw $1/_2$ circle equal to lower diameter. Drop a line from the upper diameter to the semicircle (1). Divide the resulting minor arc and upper $2/_3$ of shaft into an equal number of equal parts. Draw vertical lines from the arc divisions to the horizontal shaft divisions (2). The resulting points define the curved profile of the column shaft (3).

ENTASIS

1

CLASSICAL ARCHITECTURE

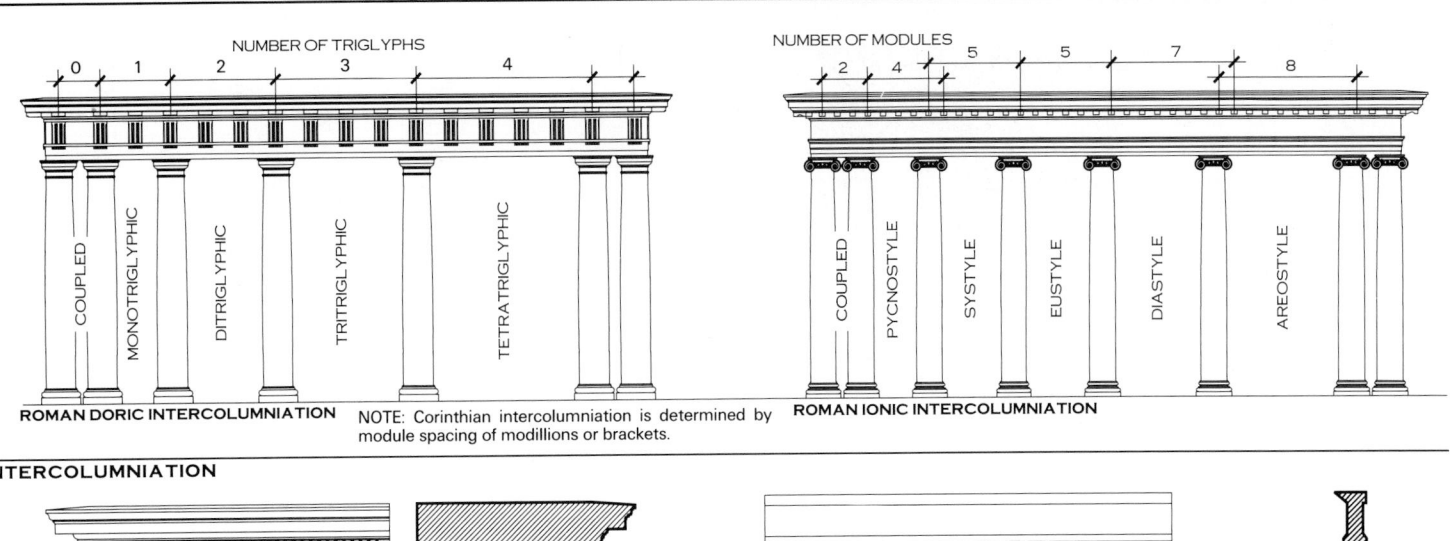

NUMBER OF TRIGLYPHS

0   1   2   3   4

COUPLED / MONOTRIGLYPHIC / DITRIGLYPHIC / TRITRIGLYPHIC / TETRATRIGLYPHIC

ROMAN DORIC INTERCOLUMNIATION

NUMBER OF MODULES

2   4   5   5   7   8

COUPLED / PYCNOSTYLE / SYSTYLE / EUSTYLE / DIASTYLE / AREOSTYLE

ROMAN IONIC INTERCOLUMNIATION

NOTE: Corinthian intercolumniation is determined by module spacing of modillions or brackets.

INTERCOLUMNIATION

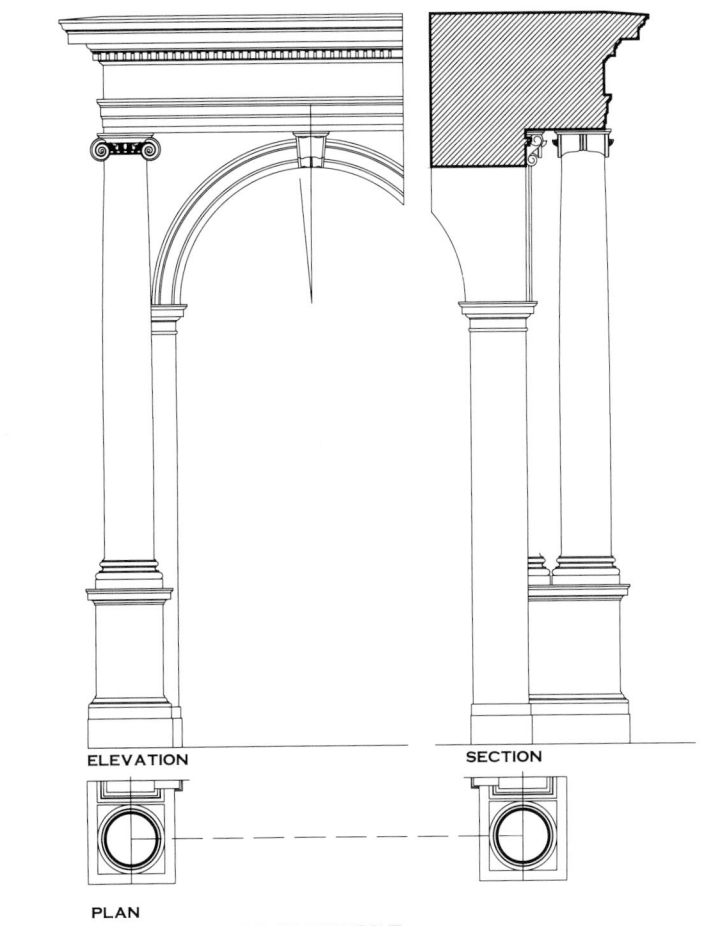

ELEVATION   SECTION

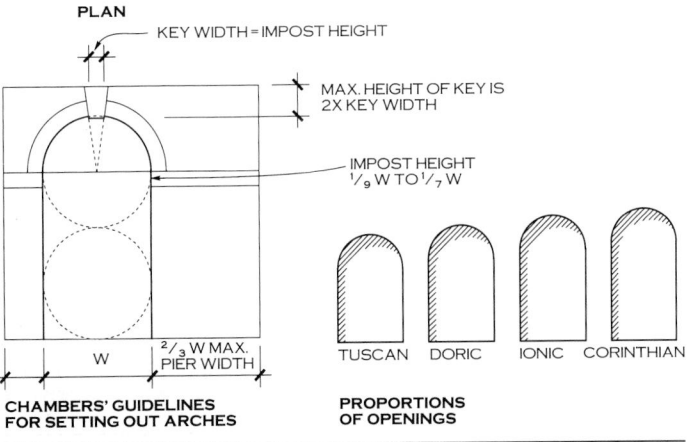

PLAN

KEY WIDTH = IMPOST HEIGHT

MAX. HEIGHT OF KEY IS 2X KEY WIDTH

IMPOST HEIGHT $\frac{1}{9}$ W TO $\frac{1}{7}$ W

W $\frac{2}{3}$ W MAX. PIER WIDTH

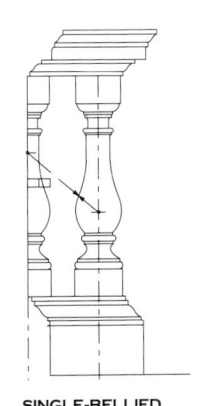

TUSCAN   DORIC   IONIC   CORINTHIAN

CHAMBERS' GUIDELINES FOR SETTING OUT ARCHES

PROPORTIONS OF OPENINGS

ARCHED DOORWAY

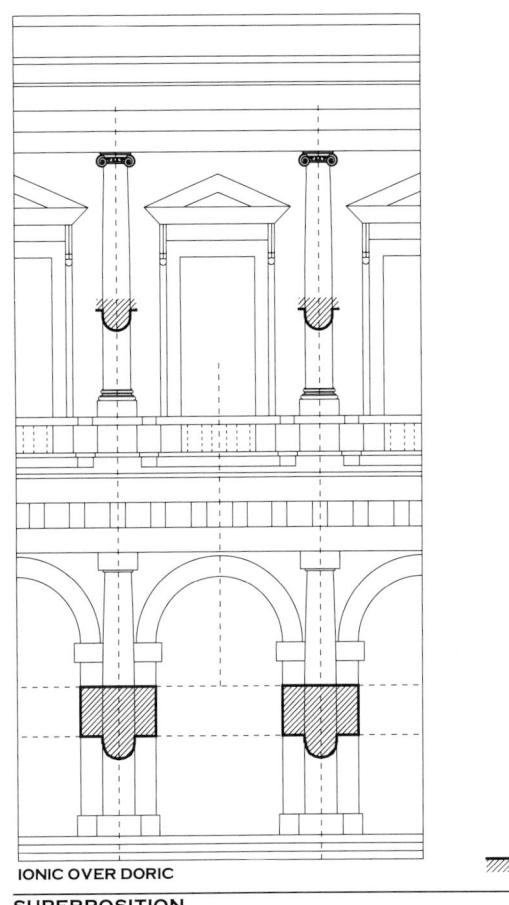

IONIC OVER DORIC

SUPERPOSITION

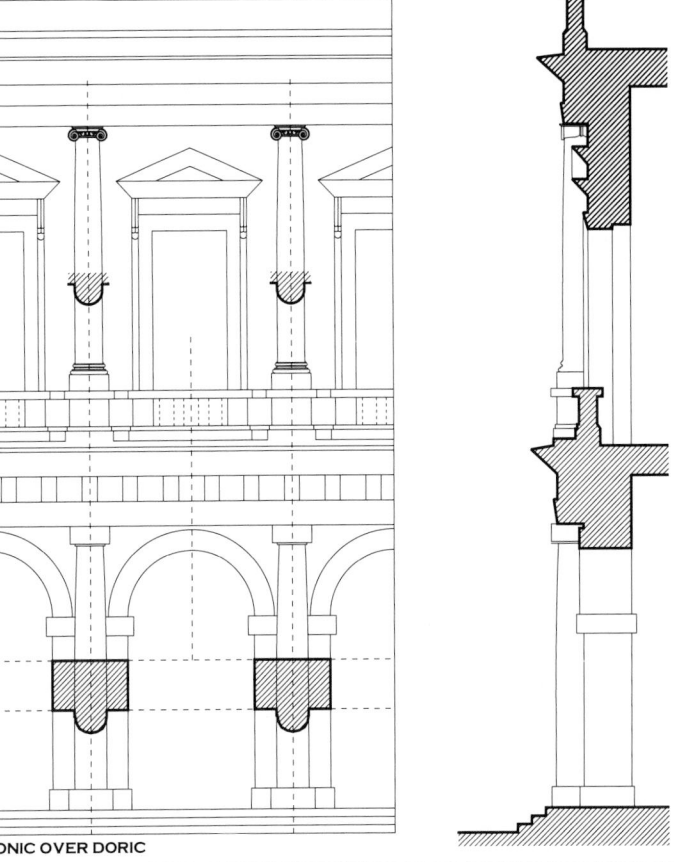

NOTE

Balustrades are often used purely ornamentally to infill arched openings or as a termination above an order. For this use, a height of about four-fifths of the entablature gives the correct proportion in terms of the cohesion of the order. However, it is perhaps unwise to depart too far from the practical dimension of 3 ft 0 in because doing so imparts a false impression of the size of the order. In such cases it is better to find another type of ornament.

SINGLE-BELLIED   DOUBLE-BELLIED

BALUSTRADES

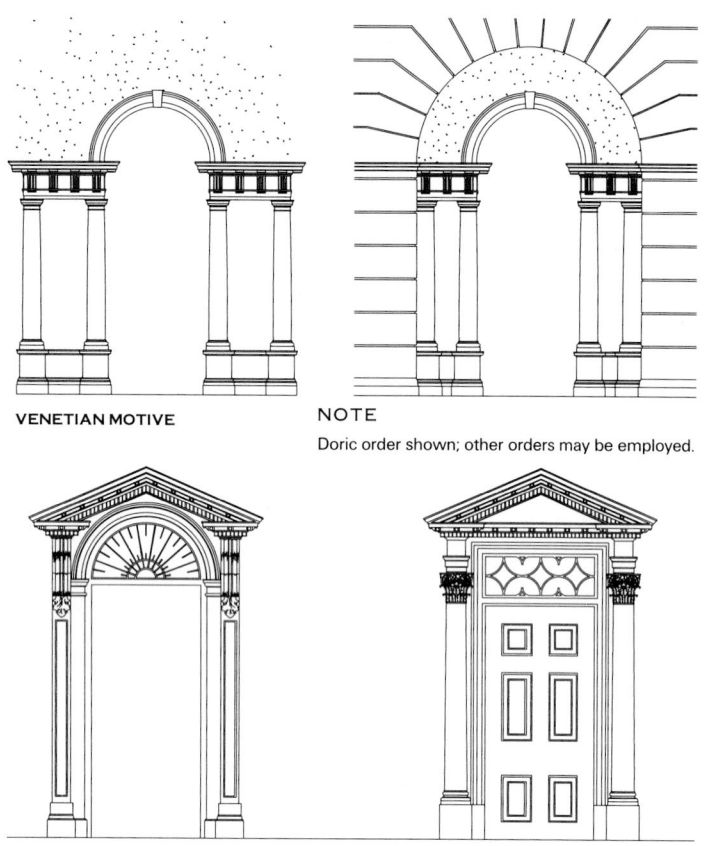

VENETIAN MOTIVE

NOTE

Doric order shown; other orders may be employed.

DOORS

1:1

1: √2

1: √3

1:2

WINDOWS

SEGMENTAL

BROKEN SEGMENTAL

VARIOUS RAKED CORNICES

SEMICIRCULAR

BROKEN CORNICE

ORNAMENTAL

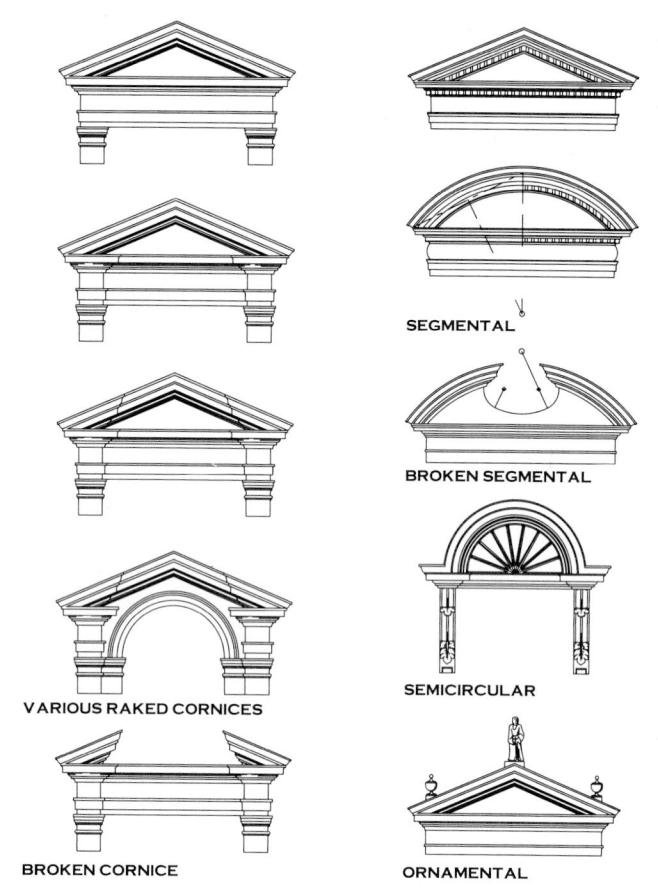

PEDIMENTS

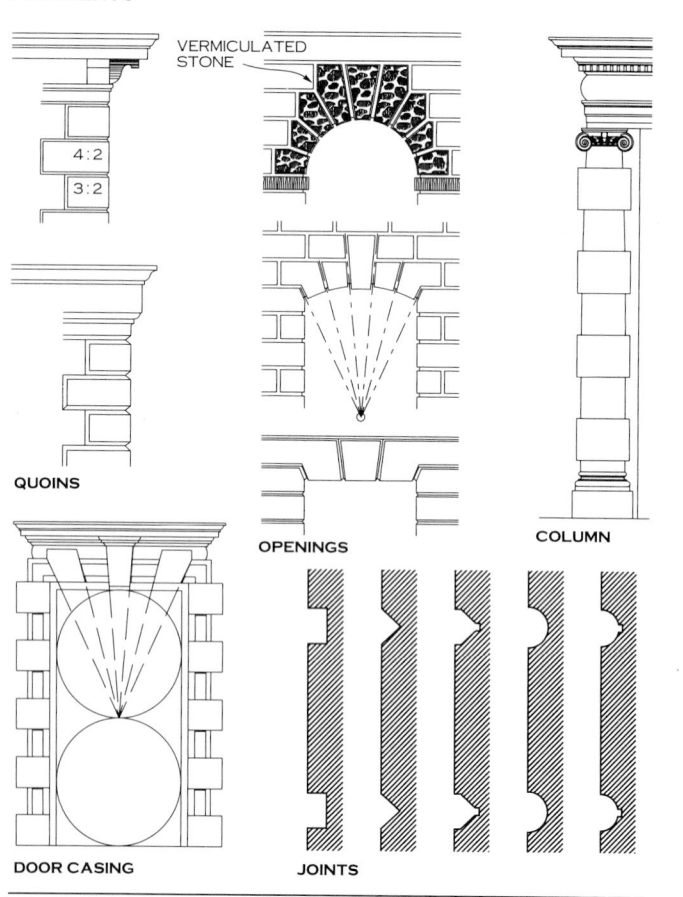

VERMICULATED STONE

4:2

3:2

QUOINS

OPENINGS

COLUMN

DOOR CASING

JOINTS

RUSTICATION

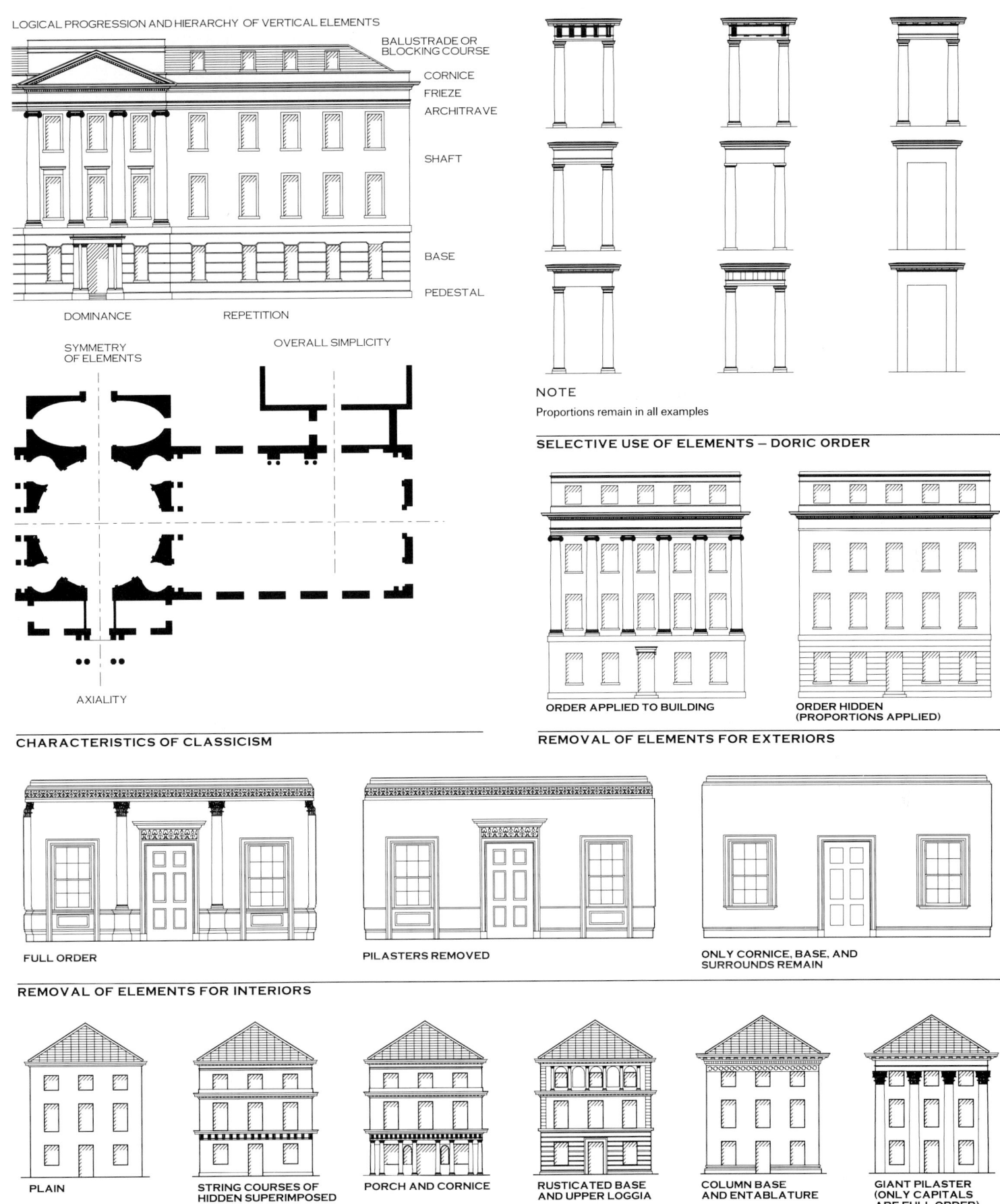

LOGICAL PROGRESSION AND HIERARCHY OF VERTICAL ELEMENTS

BALUSTRADE OR
BLOCKING COURSE

CORNICE
FRIEZE
ARCHITRAVE

SHAFT

BASE

PEDESTAL

DOMINANCE   REPETITION

SYMMETRY
OF ELEMENTS

OVERALL SIMPLICITY

AXIALITY

CHARACTERISTICS OF CLASSICISM

NOTE

Proportions remain in all examples

SELECTIVE USE OF ELEMENTS — DORIC ORDER

ORDER APPLIED TO BUILDING

ORDER HIDDEN
(PROPORTIONS APPLIED)

REMOVAL OF ELEMENTS FOR EXTERIORS

FULL ORDER

PILASTERS REMOVED

ONLY CORNICE, BASE, AND
SURROUNDS REMAIN

REMOVAL OF ELEMENTS FOR INTERIORS

PLAIN

STRING COURSES OF
HIDDEN SUPERIMPOSED
ORDERS

PORCH AND CORNICE

RUSTICATED BASE
AND UPPER LOGGIA

COLUMN BASE
AND ENTABLATURE

GIANT PILASTER
(ONLY CAPITALS
ARE FULL ORDER)

ADDING CLASSICAL ELEMENTS

ARCHITECTURAL AREA OF BUILDINGS

The architectural area of a building is the sum of the areas of the floors, measured horizontally in plan to the exterior faces of perimeter walls or to the center-line of walls separating buildings. Included are areas occupied by partitions, columns, stairwells, elevator shafts, duct shafts, elevator rooms, pipe spaces, mechanical penthouses, and similar spaces having a headroom of 6 ft and over. Areas of sloping surfaces, such as staircases, bleachers, and tiered terraces, should be measured horizontally in plan. Auditoriums, swimming pools, gymnasiums, foyers, and similar spaces extending through two or more floors should be measured once only, taking the largest area in plan at any level.

Mechanical penthouse rooms, pipe spaces, bulkheads, and similar spaces having a headroom less than 6 ft and balconies projecting beyond exterior walls, covered terraces and walkways, porches, and similar spaces shall have the architectural area multiplied by 0.50 in calculating the building gross area.

Exterior staircases and fire escapes, exterior steps, patios, terraces, open courtyards and lightwells, roof overhangs, cornices and chimneys, unfinished roof and attic areas, pipe trenches, and similar spaces are excluded from the architectural area calculations. Interstitial space in health care facilities is also excluded.

ARCHITECTURAL VOLUME OF BUILDINGS

The architectural volume of a building is the sum of the products of the areas defined in the architectural area times the height from the underside of the lowest floor construction to the average height of the surface of the finished roof above, for the various parts of the building. Included in the architectural volume is the actual space enclosed within the outer surfaces of the exterior or outer walls and contained between the outside of the roof and the bottom of the lowest floor, taken in full: bays, oriels, dormers; penthouses, chimneys; walk tunnels; enclosed porches and balconies, including screened areas.

The following volumes are multiplied by 0.50 in calculating the architectural volume of a building; nonenclosed porches, if recessed into the building and without enclosing sash or screens; nonenclosed porches built as an extension to the building and without sash or screen; areaways and pipe tunnels; and patio areas that have building walls extended on two sides, roof over, and paved surfacing.

Excluded from the architectural volume are outside steps, terraces, courts, garden walls; light shafts, parapets, cornices, roof overhangs; footings, deep foundations, piling cassions, special foundations, and similar features.

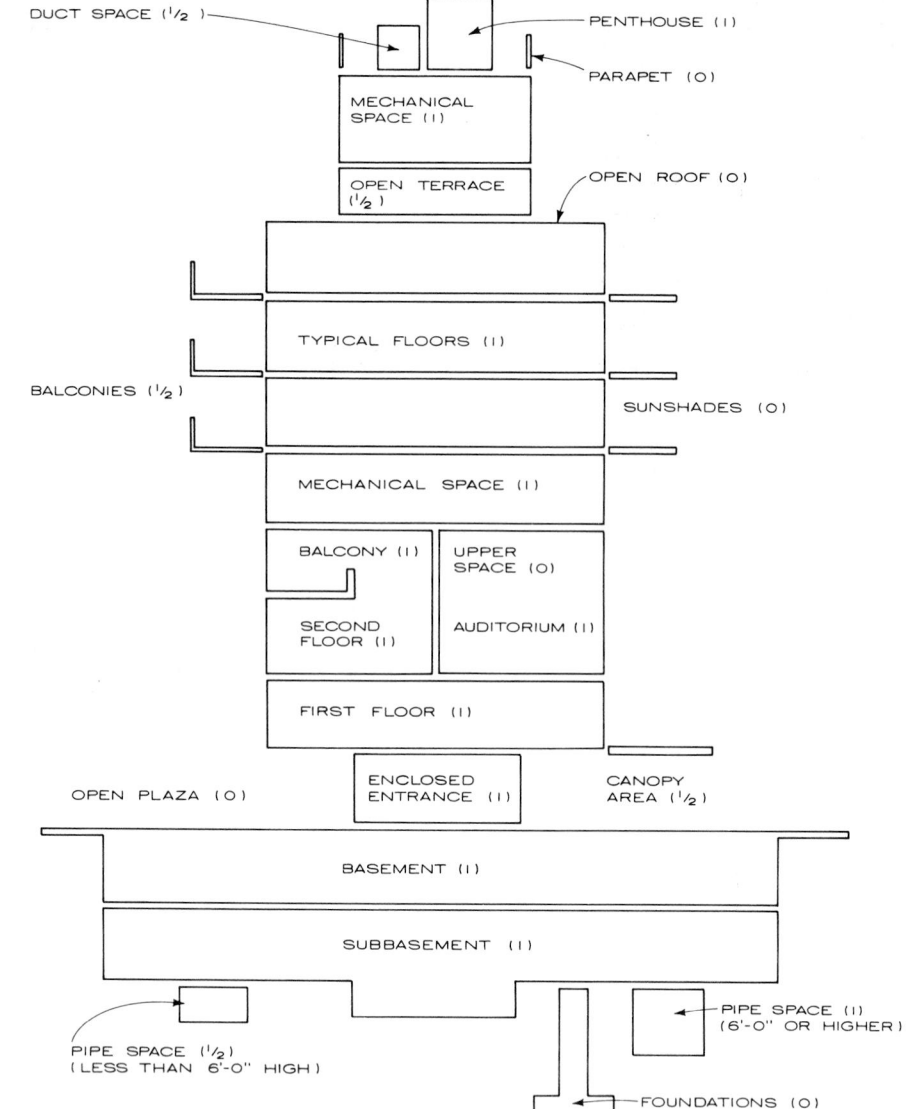

ARCHITECTURAL AREA DIAGRAM

NET ASSIGNABLE AREA

The net assignable area is that portion of the area which is available for assignment to an occupant, including every type of space usable by the occupant.

The net assignable area should be measured from the predominant inside finish of enclosing walls in the categories defined below. Areas occupied by exterior walls, partitions, internal structural, or party walls are to be excluded from the groups and are to be included under "construction area."

1. "NET ASSIGNABLE AREA": Total area of all enclosed spaces fulfilling the main functional requirements of the building for occupant use, including custodial and service areas such as guard rooms, workshops, locker rooms, janitors' closets, storerooms, and the total area of all toilet and washroom facilities.
2. "CIRCULATION AREA": Total area of all enclosed spaces which is required for physical access to subdivisions of space such as corridors, elevator shafts, escalators, fire towers or stairs, stairwells, elevator entrances, public lobbies, and public vestibules.
3. "MECHANICAL AREA": Total area of all enclosed spaces designed to house mechanical and electrical equipment and utility services such as mechanical and electrical equipment rooms, duct shafts, boiler rooms, fuel rooms, and mechanical service shafts.
4. "CONSTRUCTION AREA": The area occupied by exterior walls, partitions, structure, and so on.
5. "GROSS FLOOR OR ARCHITECTURAL AREA": The sum of areas 1, 2, 3, and 4 plus the area of all factored non- and semienclosed areas equal the gross floor area or architectural area of a building.

In commercial buildings constructed for leasing, net areas are to be measured in accordance with the "Standard Method of Floor Measurement," as set by the Building Owners and Managers Association (BOMA).

The net rentable area for offices is to be measured from the inside finish of permanent outer building walls, to the office or occupancy side of corridors and/or other permanent partitions, and to the center of partitions that separate the premises from adjoining rentable areas. No deductions are to be made for columns and projections necessary to the building.

The net rentable area for stores is to be measured from the building line in case of street frontages and from the inside finish of other outer building walls, corridor, and permanent partitions and to the center of partitions that separate the premises from adjoining rentable areas. No deductions are to be made for vestibules inside the building line or for columns and projections necessary to the building. No addition is to be made for projecting bay windows.

If a single occupant is to occupy the total floor in either the office or store categories, the net rentable area would include the accessory area for that floor of corridors, elevator lobbies, toilets, janitors' closets, electrical and telephone closets, air-conditioning rooms and fan rooms, and similar spaces.

The net rentable area for apartments is to be measured from the inside face of exterior walls, and all enclosing walls of the unit.

NOTE

Various governmental agencies have their own methods of calculating the net assignable area of buildings. They should be investigated if federal authority or funding apply to a project. Also, various building codes provide their own definitions of net and gross areas of building for use in quantifying requirements.

T. Edward Thomas, AIA; Hansen Lind Meyer, Inc.; Orlando, Florida

INTRODUCTION

A construction cost estimate is an approximation of the probable costs of a project. Construction cost estimates are used for various purposes by all of the people involved in the construction process. The type of estimate prepared depends upon the information available, the time available, and the intended use of the estimate. The accuracy of an estimate depends upon all of these same items plus the estimator's knowledge and experience.

At the conceptual stage of a project, the information available is minimal. There are no detailed plans and specifications, and only the basic requirements are known. An order of magnitude estimate can be produced based on a cost per usable unit of occupancy. If an approximate size of the building is known, in either floor space or volume, a square foot or cubic foot estimate can be calculated. Both of these types of estimates are generally used during the schematic phase of the construction process.

As more information becomes available, and construction documentation progresses, an assemblies, or systems, estimate can be produced during the design development phase of the process. An assemblies estimate is based on the major building systems or components of construction.

When a complete set of construction documents is produced, a very detailed unit price estimate can be obtained. This is the most accurate type of estimate, but is also very exacting and time-consuming. It requires a breakdown of all elements that go into the building process and knowledge of the associated costs for all material, labor, and equipment.

PURPOSE

The cost data shown here are designed to provide reliable total costs of construction for typical building structures when only minimum dimensions, specifications, and technical data are available. It is specifically useful in the conceptual or planning stage for preparing preliminary estimates that can be supported and developed into complete estimates for construction.

It is especially useful for preparing capital expenditure budgets and rapid estimating of replacement costs.

CONSIDERATIONS

Due to the almost limitless variation of building designs and combinations of construction methods and materials, the "typical building" costs shown on these pages must be used with discretion.

By definition, a square foot estimate, due to the short time and limited amount of detail required, involves a relatively lower degree of accuracy than a more detailed unit price based estimate. The accuracy of an estimate will increase as the project is defined in more detailed components. The user should examine closely and compare the specific requirements of the project being estimated with the components included in these models. Any differences should be accounted for in the estimate.

The costs for the various building models do not include site work beyond the typical building perimeter.

In many building projects, there may be factors that increase or decrease the cost beyond the range shown in the following tables. Some of these factors are:

1. Substitution of building materials or systems for those used in the model.
2. Custom designed finishes, fixtures, and equipment.
3. Special structural requirements (allowance for high winds or earthquakes, future expansion, long spans, or unusual shapes).
4. Special foundations and substructures to compensate for unusual soil conditions.
5. Inclusion of typical "owner supplied" equipment in the building cost (special testing and monitoring equipment for hospitals, kitchen equipment for hotels, offices that have cafeteria accommodations for employees, etc.).
6. An abnormal shortage of labor or materials.
7. Isolated building site or rough terrain that would affect the transportation of personnel, material, or equipment.
8. Unusual climatic conditions during construction.

For maximum accuracy, these factors should be considered each time a structure is evaluated.

If greater accuracy is required than these numbers can provide, an assemblies or unit price based estimate is recommended.

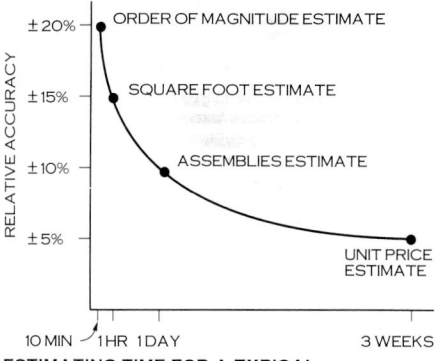

ESTIMATING TIME FOR A TYPICAL $2 TO 5 MILLION BUILDING

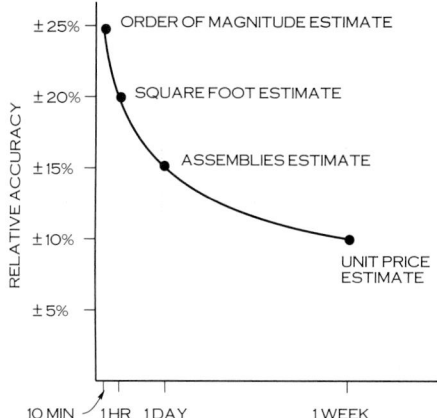

ESTIMATING TIME FOR A TYPICAL $500,000 REMODELING PROJECT

ESTIMATING TIME VERSUS ACCURACY

APARTMENT (1 TO 3 STORY WITH 10 FEET FLOOR TO FLOOR)

AREA IN SQUARE FEET		8,000	12,000	15,000	19,000	22,500	25,000	29,000	32,000	36,000
PERIMETER IN LINEAR FEET		213	280	330	350	400	433	442	480	520
EXTERIOR WALL	STRUCTURAL FRAME	COST PER SQUARE FOOT								
Face brick with concrete block backup	Wood joists	85.25	76.00	72.25	67.10	65.20	64.20	61.60	60.90	59.90
	Steel joists	85.10	76.30	72.80	68.15	66.40	65.40	63.10	62.50	61.55
Stucco on concrete block	Wood joists	75.00	66.75	63.40	59.30	57.65	56.70	54.75	54.15	53.30
	Steel joists	79.80	71.50	68.15	64.00	62.30	61.40	59.40	58.75	57.95
Wood siding	Wood frame	73.45	65.40	62.15	58.25	56.60	55.75	53.90	53.30	52.50
Brick veneer	Backup wood frame	78.55	69.80	66.30	61.70	59.95	58.95	56.65	56.05	55.10
ADDITIONS OR DEDUCTIONS	COST PER									
Perimeter adjacent	100 linear feet	10.35	6.90	5.55	4.35	3.75	3.30	2.85	2.60	2.35
Story height adjacent	Foot	1.95	1.70	1.60	1.30	1.35	1.25	1.10	1.10	1.05
Basement	Square foot of area	17.20	17.20	17.20	17.20	17.20	17.20	17.20	17.20	17.20

COLLEGE, DORMITORY (4 TO 8 STORY WITH 12 FEET FLOOR TO FLOOR)

AREA IN SQUARE FEET		50,000	70,000	90,000	100,000	110,000	130,000	150,000	170,000	190,000
PERIMETER IN LINEAR FEET		372	461	550	533	566	633	650	703	756
EXTERIOR WALL	STRUCTURAL FRAME	COST PER SQUARE FOOT								
Face brick with concrete block backup	Reinforced concrete	71.30	69.20	68.05	66.65	66.20	65.60	64.60	64.15	63.85
	Steel	76.70	74.60	73.45	72.05	71.60	71.00	70.00	69.55	69.25
Decorative concrete block	Reinforced concrete	67.45	65.75	64.85	63.85	63.50	63.05	62.30	62.00	61.75
	Steel	72.85	71.20	70.30	69.30	68.95	68.50	67.75	67.40	67.15
Precast concrete panels with exposed aggregate	Reinforced concrete	71.90	69.75	68.55	67.10	66.60	66.00	64.95	64.50	64.15
	Steel	77.25	75.10	73.90	72.45	71.95	71.35	70.30	69.85	69.55
ADDITIONS OR DEDUCTIONS	COST PER									
Perimeter adjacent	100 linear feet	3.35	2.40	1.90	1.65	1.55	1.30	1.10	1.00	0.85
Story height adjacent	Foot	0.95	0.85	0.80	0.70	0.65	0.60	0.55	0.55	0.50
Basement	Square foot of area	17.45	17.45	17.45	17.45	17.45	17.45	17.45	17.45	17.45

By permission of R. S. Means Company, Inc.; Kingston, Massachusetts, from Means Square Foot Costs, 1992

HIGH SCHOOL (2 TO 3 STORY WITH 12 FEET FLOOR TO FLOOR)

AREA IN SQUARE FEET PERIMETER IN LINEAR FEET		50,000 816	70,000 1,083	90,000 1,100	110,000 1,300	130,000 1,290	150,000 1,450	170,000 1,433	190,000 1,566	210,000 1,700
EXTERIOR WALL	STRUCTURAL FRAME	COST PER SQUARE FOOT								
Face brick with concrete block backup	Steel	61.25	59.70	56.75	56.10	54.40	54.05	53.00	52.80	52.60
	Reinforced concrete	63.85	62.35	59.50	58.90	57.25	56.90	55.90	55.65	55.50
Decorative concrete block	Steel	58.65	57.30	54.85	54.30	52.90	52.65	51.75	51.55	51.40
	Reinforced concrete	61.65	60.30	57.85	57.30	55.95	55.65	54.75	54.55	54.40
Limestone with concrete block backup	Steel	65.75	64.00	60.20	59.45	57.25	56.85	55.45	55.15	54.90
	Reinforced concrete	69.15	67.45	63.60	62.85	60.65	60.25	58.85	58.55	58.30
ADDITIONS OR DEDUCTIONS	COST PER									
Perimeter adjacent	100 linear feet	1.55	1.10	0.85	0.65	0.60	0.55	0.45	0.40	0.30
Story height adjacent	Foot	0.90	0.80	0.65	0.65	0.55	0.55	0.45	0.40	0.40
Basement	Square foot	17.25	17.25	17.25	17.25	17.25	17.25	17.25	17.25	17.25

HOSPITAL (4 TO 8 STORY WITH 12 FEET FLOOR TO FLOOR)

AREA IN SQUARE FEET PERIMETER IN LINEAR FEET		100,000 594	125,000 705	150,000 816	175,000 783	200,000 866	225,000 950	250,000 1,033	275,000 1,116	300,000 1,200
EXTERIOR WALL	STRUCTURAL FRAME	COST PER SQUARE FOOT								
Face brick with structural facing tile	Steel	98.95	97.45	96.40	94.00	93.35	92.90	92.45	92.15	91.90
	Reinforced concrete	102.60	101.10	100.05	97.65	97.00	96.55	96.10	95.80	95.55
Face brick with concrete block backup	Steel	96.95	95.55	94.55	92.50	91.90	91.45	91.10	90.80	90.60
	Reinforced concrete	100.60	99.20	98.20	96.15	95.50	95.10	94.70	94.45	94.20
Precast concrete panels with exposed aggregate	Steel	97.00	95.60	94.65	92.65	92.05	91.65	91.25	91.00	90.80
	Reinforced concrete	100.10	98.70	97.75	95.80	95.15	94.75	94.35	94.10	93.90
ADDITIONS OR DEDUCTIONS	COST PER									
Perimeter adjacent	100 linear feet	2.05	1.65	1.65	1.15	1.05	0.90	0.85	0.80	0.65
Story height adjacent	Foot	0.95	0.90	0.90	0.75	0.70	0.65	0.70	0.65	0.65
Basement	Square foot	18.55	18.55	18.55	18.55	18.55	18.55	18.55	18.55	18.55

HOTEL (8 TO 24 STORY WITH 10 FEET FLOOR TO FLOOR)

AREA IN SQUARE FEET PERIMETER IN LINEAR FEET		140,000 403	243,000 587	346,000 672	450,000 800	552,000 935	655,000 1,073	760,000 1,213	860,000 1,195	965,000 1,312
EXTERIOR WALL	STRUCTURAL FRAME	COST PER SQUARE FOOT								
Face brick with concrete block backup	Steel	75.60	72.10	69.55	68.55	68.00	67.60	67.35	66.40	66.25
	Reinforced concrete	77.75	74.25	71.70	70.70	70.15	69.75	69.50	68.60	68.40
Face brick veneer on steel studs	Steel	74.80	71.40	69.00	68.05	67.50	67.15	66.90	66.05	65.85
	Reinforced concrete	77.25	73.85	71.45	70.50	69.95	69.55	69.30	68.50	68.30
Glass and metal curtain walls	Steel	82.70	78.05	75.25	74.00	73.30	72.85	72.45	71.65	71.40
	Reinforced concrete	85.15	80.50	77.70	76.45	75.75	75.25	74.90	74.10	73.85
ADDITIONS OR DEDUCTIONS	COST PER									
Perimeter adjacent	100 linear feet	2.80	1.60	1.15	0.85	0.70	0.60	0.50	0.50	0.40
Story height adjacent	Foot	1.10	0.90	0.75	0.70	0.65	0.65	0.60	0.55	0.50
Basement	Square foot	17.85	17.85	17.85	17.85	17.85	17.85	17.85	17.85	17.85

OFFICE BUILDING (2 TO 4 STORY WITH 12 FEET FLOOR TO FLOOR)

AREA IN SQUARE FEET PERIMETER IN LINEAR FEET		10,000 246	22,000 393	34,000 443	46,000 543	58,000 562	63,000 590	68,000 603	73,000 624	78,000 645
EXTERIOR WALL	STRUCTURAL FRAME	COST PER SQUARE FOOT								
Face brick with concrete block backup	Wood joists	77.05	65.85	59.95	58.10	55.70	55.30	54.70	54.30	53.95
	Steel joists	81.80	70.60	64.65	62.85	60.45	60.05	59.45	59.05	58.70
Glass and metal curtain walls	Steel	81.95	71.15	65.55	63.75	61.50	61.10	60.55	60.20	59.85
	Reinforced concrete	84.10	73.35	67.70	65.95	63.70	63.30	62.75	62.40	62.05
Wood siding	Wood	69.05	60.05	55.70	54.25	52.55	52.25	51.85	51.55	51.25
Brick veneer	Wood	73.65	63.40	58.10	56.45	54.35	53.95	53.50	53.15	52.80
ADDITIONS OR DEDUCTIONS	COST PER									
Perimeter adjacent	100 linear feet	9.40	4.30	2.75	2.05	1.60	1.45	1.40	1.30	1.25
Story height adjacent	Foot	1.70	1.25	0.85	0.80	0.65	0.60	0.65	0.60	0.60
Basement	Square foot	17.20	17.20	17.20	17.20	17.20	17.20	17.20	17.20	17.20

By permission of R. S. Means Company, Inc.; Kingston, Massachusetts, from Means Square Foot Costs, 1992

 AREA CALCULATION AND COST ESTIMATING

WAREHOUSE (24 FEET FLOOR TO FLOOR)

AREA IN SQUARE FEET PERIMETER IN LINEAR FEET		10,000 410	15,000 500	20,000 600	25,000 700	30,000 700	35,000 766	40,000 833	50,000 966	60,000 1,000
EXTERIOR WALL	STRUCTURAL FRAME	COST PER SQUARE FOOT								
Brick with concrete block backup	Steel	62.95	56.45	53.50	51.75	48.45	47.25	46.45	45.25	43.40
	Bearing walls	62.45	55.80	52.75	50.95	47.65	46.40	45.55	44.35	42.45
Concrete block	Steel	51.20	46.85	44.85	43.65	41.70	40.95	40.40	39.65	38.55
	Bearing walls	50.45	46.05	44.00	42.80	40.80	40.05	39.50	38.70	37.60
Galvanized steel siding	Steel	52.95	48.85	46.95	45.80	44.00	43.30	42.75	42.05	41.10
Metal sandwich panels	Steel	52.90	48.25	46.10	44.80	42.70	41.85	41.25	40.45	39.25
ADDITIONS OR DEDUCTIONS	COST PER									
Perimeter adjacent	100 linear feet	6.30	4.20	3.15	2.50	2.10	1.85	1.60	1.30	1.05
Story height adjacent	Foot	0.85	0.70	0.65	0.60	0.50	0.50	0.45	0.40	0.35
Basement	Square foot	13.80	13.80	13.80	13.80	13.80	13.80	13.80	13.80	13.80

PARKING GARAGE (10 FEET FLOOR TO FLOOR)

AREA IN SQUARE FEET PERIMETER IN LINEAR FEET		85,000 529	115,000 638	145,000 723	175,000 823	205,000 923	235,000 951	265,000 1,037	295,000 1,057	325,000 1,132
EXTERIOR WALL	STRUCTURAL FRAME	COST PER SQUARE FOOT								
Face brick with concrete	Steel	28.45	27.85	27.45	27.20	27.05	26.75	26.65	26.40	26.35
block backup	Reinforced concrete	25.05	24.50	24.05	23.85	23.65	23.35	23.25	23.00	22.95
Precast concrete	Steel	29.35	28.75	28.25	28.00	27.80	27.50	27.35	27.10	27.00
	Reinforced concrete	25.60	24.95	24.50	24.25	24.05	23.70	23.60	23.35	23.25
Reinforced concrete	Steel	28.20	27.70	27.35	27.15	27.05	26.75	26.70	26.50	26.45
	Reinforced concrete	24.25	23.80	23.45	23.25	23.10	22.85	22.75	22.55	22.50
ADDITIONS OR DEDUCTIONS	COST PER									
Perimeter adjacent	100 linear feet	0.75	0.60	0.45	0.40	0.30	0.30	0.25	0.20	0.20
Story height adjacent	Foot	0.25	0.25	0.20	0.20	0.20	0.15	0.15	0.15	0.10

LOCATION FACTORS

STATE/PROVINCE	FACTOR
Alabama	0.82
Alaska	1.25
Arizona	0.90
Arkansas	0.83
California	1.14
Colorado	0.91
Connecticut	0.98
Delaware	1.01
District of Columbia	0.96
Florida	0.85
Georgia	0.85
Hawaii	1.18
Idaho	0.95
Illinois	0.97
Indiana	0.96
Iowa	0.86
Kansas	0.86
Kentucky	0.90
Louisiana	0.84
Maine	0.88
Maryland	0.98
Massachusetts	1.06
Michigan	0.95
Minnesota	0.93
Mississippi	0.80
Missouri	0.96
Montana	0.91
Nebraska	0.83
Nevada	1.02
New Hampshire	0.88
New Jersey	1.07
New Mexico	0.88
New York	1.16

STATE/PROVINCE	FACTOR
North Carolina	0.79
North Dakota	0.87
Ohio	0.97
Oklahoma	0.86
Oregon	0.98
Pennsylvania	1.00
Rhode Island	0.99
South Carolina	0.79
South Dakota	0.80
Tennessee	0.85
Texas	0.85
Utah	0.89
Vermont	0.86
Virginia	0.87
Washington	1.00
West Virginia	0.98
Wisconsin	0.93
Wyoming	0.86
Alberta	1.02
British Columbia	1.09
Manitoba	1.03
New Brunswick	0.94
Newfoundland	0.96
Nova Scotia	0.95
Ontario	1.12
Prince Edward Island	0.98
Quebec	1.04
Saskatchewan	1.08

NOTES

Costs shown here are based on national averages for materials and installation. To adjust these costs to a specific location, simply multiply the base cost by the factor for that city. Canadian factors reflect Canadian currency.

ESTIMATING GUIDELINES

Here are a few suggestions to the estimator to perform conceptual estimating in a logical, easy to check, and thorough manner.

1. The estimator should analyze all available job data: calculating the square footage and perimeter, the number of stories and story height, general types of construction used, and any special requirements.

2. Use preprinted or computer generated forms for orderly sequence of dimensions and locations and general organization of information.

3. Use printed, rather than measured, dimensions where given, and be consistent in listing dimensions: for example, length x width x height.

4. It may be necessary to list items called for as alternates or modifications to make the job complete.

5. Include items such as the architectural fees and percentages for construction contingencies.

6. When using published cost data, make the appropriate adjustments for the project location based on construction cost indexes.

Organizing and being consistent in your estimating procedures will minimize confusion and simplify checking to insure against omissions and duplications.

By permission of R. S. Means Company, Inc.; Kingston, Massachusetts, from Means Square Foot Costs, 1992

GENERAL

Life-cycle costing (LCC) is a method for evaluating all relevant costs over time of alternative building designs, systems, components, materials, or practices. The LCC method takes into account first costs, including the cost of planning, design, purchase, and installation; future costs, including costs of fuel, operation, maintenance, repair, and replacement; and any resale or salvage value recovered during or at the end of the time period examined.

TIME ADJUSTMENTS

Adjustments to place all dollar values on a comparable time basis are necessary for the valid assessment of a project's life-cycle costs. Time adjustments are necessary because receiving or expending a dollar in the future is not the same as receiving or expending a dollar today. Currency's purchasing power may fall over time because of inflation, and money in hand may be invested productively to earn a return over time, apart from inflation. Because of inflation and the productive earning potential of resources in hand, investors usually prefer to delay payments of costs or debts and to hasten receipts. The adjustment for time can be accomplished by converting all costs and resale or salvage values to "present values," as though they were all to be incurred today, or to "annual values," as though they were all spread out over a given time in even, annual installments. This time adjustment, often called "discounting cash flows," is accomplished by using "discount formulas" or by multiplying dollar amounts by special "discount factors" calculated from the formulas. The most frequently used discount formulas for evaluating building projects are described below. The following notation is used:

P = present value
F = future value
A = annual value
A_0 = initial value of a periodic amount
D = discount rate
N = number of periods
E = price escalation rate

D is the minimum rate of return the investor is willing to accept and is based on the yield available on the next best investment opportunity of comparable risk. The values of D, F, and E specified in the discount operations below can be expressed in either of two ways: including or excluding projected general price inflation/deflation. It is essential, however, that they all be treated consistently within a given LCC analysis. If general price inflation/deflation is included, the analysis is said to be in "current dollars"; if it is excluded, the analysis is said to be in "constant dollars." Both approaches result in the same LCC results.

SINGLE PRESENT WORTH

The single present worth (SPW) formula is used to find the present value of a future amount, such as the value today of a future replacement cost.

SPW (single present worth) $P = F (1 + D)^N$

UNIFORM PRESENT WORTH

The uniform present worth (UPW) formula is used to find the present value of a series of uniform annual amounts, such as the value today of the costs of future yearly routine maintenance.

UPW (uniform present worth) $P = A \left[\dfrac{(1 + D)^N - 1}{D(1 + D)^N} \right]$

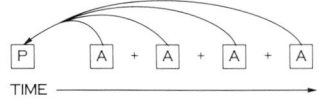

MODIFIED UNIFORM PRESENT WORTH

A modified version of the uniform present worth formula (here designated UPW*) is used to find the present value of an initial value of a periodic amount (A_0) escalating at a constant annual rate (E), such as the value today of future yearly energy costs, when energy prices are expected to escalate at a given rate.

UPW* (uniform present worth-modified)

$$P = A_0 \left[\left[\frac{1 + E}{D - E} \right] \left[1 - \left[\frac{1 + E}{1 + D} \right]^N \right] \right]$$

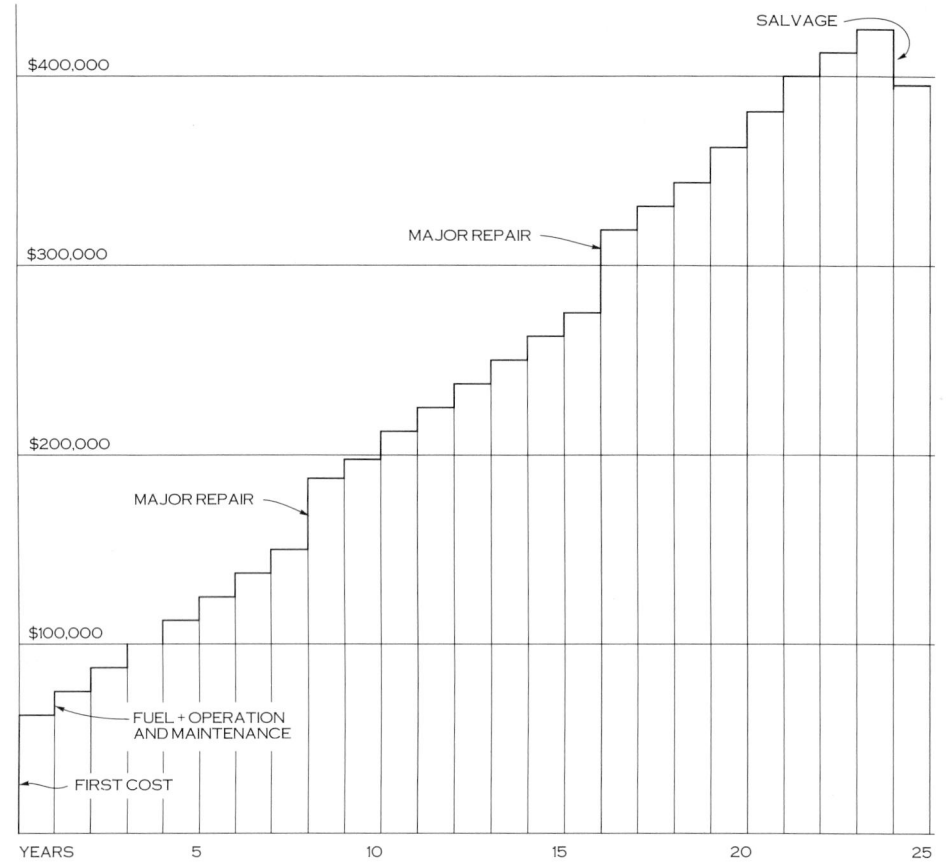

CUMULATIVE COSTS

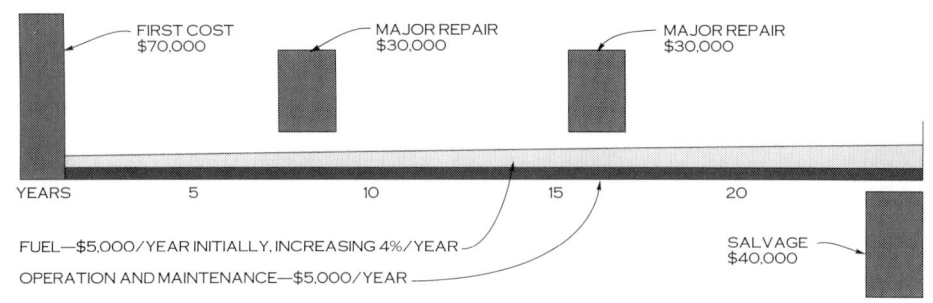

FIRST COST $70,000   MAJOR REPAIR $30,000   MAJOR REPAIR $30,000

FUEL—$5,000/YEAR INITIALLY, INCREASING 4%/YEAR
OPERATION AND MAINTENANCE—$5,000/YEAR

SALVAGE $40,000

YEARLY COSTS

UNIFORM CAPITAL RECOVERY

The uniform capital recovery (UCR) formula is used to find the annual value of a present value amount. It can be used to amortize a loan, i.e., to determine how much it would be necessary to pay each year in order to pay off a loan made today at a given rate of interest for a given period of time.

UCR (uniform capital recovery) $A = P \left[\dfrac{D(1 + D)^N}{(1 + D)^N - 1} \right]$

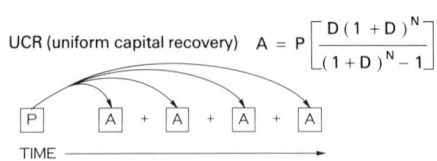

NOTE

The discount factors for each of these discounting formulas have been precalculated for a range of discount rates and time periods and put into tables to facilitate their use. These tables can be found in most engineering economics textbooks. A table of discount factors for a 10% discount rate is shown opposite.

LIFE-CYCLE COST FORMULA

To find the total life-cycle cost of a project, sum the present values (or, alternatively, the annual values) of each kind of cost and subtract the present values (or annual values) of any positive cash flows such as resale values. Thus, where all dollar amounts are adjusted by discounting to either present values or annual values, the following formula applies:

Life-cycle cost = first costs + maintenance and repair
+ energy + replacement − salvage value

APPLICATIONS

Alternative projects may be compared by computing the life-cycle costs for each project using the formula above and seeing which is lower.

The LCC method can be applied to many different kinds of building problems when the focus is on determining the least-cost alternative for achieving a given level of performance.

For example, it can be used to compare the long-run costs of two building designs; to determine the expected dollar savings of retrofitting a building for energy conservation or the least expensive way of reaching a targeted energy budget for a building; to select the most economical floor coverings and furnishings; or to determine the optimal size of a solar energy system.

In addition to the life-cycle formula shown above, there are other closely related methods of combining present or annual values to measure a project's economic performance over time, such as net benefits or net savings, benefit-to-cost or savings-to-investment ratio, internal rate of return or overall rate of return; and discounted time to payback methods.

Harold E. Marshall and Rosalie Ruegg, economists; Porter Driscoll, AIA, Architect; National Institute of Standards and Technology

SAMPLE LCC PROBLEM

Determine for a public office building the present value of costs that will occur during the life of a component so it can be compared with the value of costs for an alternative component that serves the same purpose.

ASSUMPTIONS

Component life (for both)	25 years
Discount rate	10%
Fuel price increases in excess of inflation (i.e., excluding inflation)	4%
First cost of component	$70,000
Repairs to component at 8th and 16th years (constant dollars)	$30,000/repair
Operations and maintenance (constant dollars)	$5,000/year
Annual cost of fuel at onset	$5,000

NOTE

When financing costs and tax effects are relevant, they should be incorporated into LCC analysis. For this public building they are not relevant.

SOLUTION

1. Calculate present value of equipment by converting all equipment costs (first cost, two major repair costs, and salvage value) to present values and combining them. (Since the first cost occurs in the present, no change is made to the $70,000 sum.)

   The first major repair, estimated to occur 8 years in the future, is discounted at the rate of 10% back to the present using the SPW factor (see Discount Factor Chart, column 2) for 8 years at 10%, 0.4665. Therefore, PV = $30,000 x 0.4665 = $13,995.

   The second major repair is discounted 16 years back to the present in a similar manner. The SPW factor for 16 years at 10% = 0.2176. Therefore, PV = $30,000 x 0.2176 = $6,528. These two present values are added to the first cost of the component.

   The $40,000 to be realized from salvage at the end of the 25-year period is discounted back to the present in the same manner. The SPW factor for 25 years, at 10% = 0.0923. Therefore, PV = $40,000 x 0.0923 = $3,692. Since this sum is income, not expense, it must be subtracted from the sum of the other present values as indicated.

   Thus, the present value of equipment is determined to be $86,831.

2. Establish present value of operation and maintenance costs and fuel costs. Operation and maintenance costs are estimated to be equal amounts that occur yearly during the component life and are converted to present value using the UPW factor (column 3) for 25 years at 10%, 9.0770. Therefore PV = $5,000 x 9.0770 = $45,385. Annual fuel costs are estimated to be $5,000 initially and are projected to increase at the rate of 4% per year higher than general price inflation. These costs are converted to present value using the modified UPW* factor (column 4) for 25 years at 10%, 13.0686. Therefore, PV = $5,000 x 13.0686 = $65,343. These two present values are added to the present value of equipment costs as shown in the Total Present Value chart.

3. Total life-cycle cost in present value dollars is the sum of the present value of equipment, operation and maintenance, and fuel costs, which equals $197,559. The present value of equipment, operation and maintenance, and fuel costs of other components that serve the same purpose can be computed over the same period of time and compared to these figures to determine the best economic value.

REFERENCES

1. Rosalie T. Ruegg and Harold E. Marshall, *Building Economics: Theory and Practice* (New York: Van Nostrand, Reinhold, 1990).

2. Harold E. Marshall and Rosalie T. Ruegg, "Life-cycle Costing Guide for Energy Conservation in Buildings" in *Energy Conservation through Building Design*, ed. Donald Watson (New York: McGraw-Hill, 1979).

3. "Simplified Energy Design Economics," NBS special publication 544, Center for Building Technology, National Bureau of Standards, Washington, D.C., 1980.

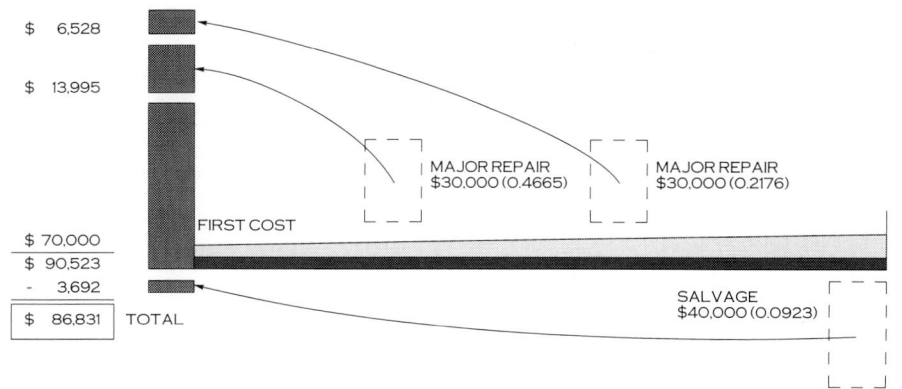

$ 6,528	
$ 13,995	
$ 70,000	FIRST COST
$ 90,523	
- 3,692	
$ 86,831	TOTAL

MAJOR REPAIR $30,000 (0.4665)
MAJOR REPAIR $30,000 (0.2176)
SALVAGE $40,000 (0.0923)

PRESENT VALUE OF EQUIPMENT

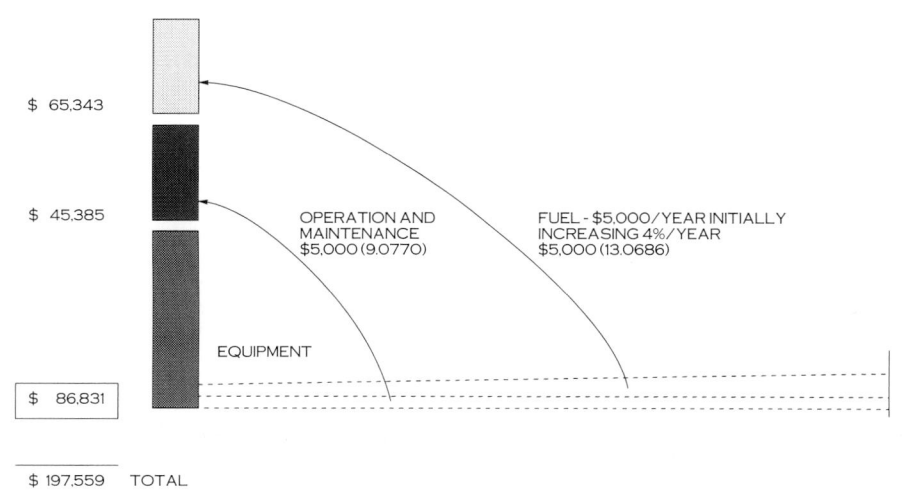

$ 65,343	
$ 45,385	
	EQUIPMENT
$ 86,831	
$ 197,559	TOTAL

OPERATION AND MAINTENANCE $5,000 (9.0770)
FUEL - $5,000/YEAR INITIALLY INCREASING 4%/YEAR $5,000 (13.0686)

TOTAL PRESENT VALUE

DISCOUNT FACTORS (BASED ON 10% DISCOUNT RATE)

1. YEARS	2. SPW	3. UPW	4. UPW* (4% PRICE ESCALATION)	5. UCR
1	0.9091	0.909	0.9455	1.100 00
2	0.8264	1.736	1.8393	0.576 19
3	0.7513	2.487	2.6844	0.402 11
4	0.6830	3.170	3.4834	0.315 47
5	0.6209	3.791	4.2388	0.263 80
6	0.5645	4.355	4.9531	0.229 61
7	0.5132	4.868	5.6284	0.205 41
8	0.4665	5.335	6.2669	0.187 44
9	0.4241	5.759	6.8705	0.173 64
10	0.3855	6.144	7.4411	0.162 75
11	0.3505	6.495	7.9807	0.153 96
12	0.3186	6.814	8.4909	0.146 76
13	0.2897	7.103	8.9733	0.140 78
14	0.2633	7.367	9.4293	0.135 75
15	0.2394	7.606	9.8604	0.131 47
16	0.2176	7.824	10.2680	0.127 82
17	0.1978	8.022	10.6535	0.124 66
18	0.1799	8.201	11.0177	0.121 93
19	0.1635	8.365	11.3622	0.119 55
20	0.1486	8.514	11.6878	0.117 46
21	0.1351	8.649	11.9957	0.115 62
22	0.1228	8.772	12.2870	0.144 01
23	0.1117	8.883	12.5623	0.112 57
24	0.1015	8.985	12.8225	0.111 30
25	0.0923	9.077	13.0686	0.110 17

Harold E. Marshall and Rosalie Ruegg, economists; Porter Driscoll, AIA, Architect; National Institute of Standards and Technology

AREA CALCULATION AND COST ESTIMATING   1

GENERAL

Allen, Edward. *Fundamentals of Building Construction*. 2nd ed. New York: John Wiley & Sons, 1990.
Allen, Edward, and Joseph Iano. The Architect's Studio Companion. New York: John Wiley & Sons, 1989.

UNIVERSAL ACCESSIBILITY

Americans with Disabilities Act Information Office
U.S. Department of Justice
Civil Rights Division
P.O. Box 66738
Washington, DC 20035-998
Tel: (202) 514-0301

The Center for Accessible Housing (CAH)
School of Design
North Carolina State University
P.O. Box 8613
Raleigh, NC 27695-8613
Tel: (919) 515-3082
Fax:(919) 515-3023

Fair Housing Information Clearinghouse
P.O. Box 6091
Rockville, Maryland 20850
Tel: (800) 343-3442 (V) or
Tel: (800) 877-8339 (TDD)

REFERENCES

ADA Compliance Guidebook: A Checklist for Your Building. Washington, D.C.: Building Owners and Managers Association International, 1991. [202/408-2662]
Americans with Disabilities Act Accessiblity Guidelines Checklist for Buildings and Facilities (ADAAG). ADA Information Office, 1991.

EGRESS PLANNING/SAFETY DESIGN

American Society of Safety Engineers
1800 East Oakton
Des Plaines, IL 60018-2187
Tel: (708) 692-4121
Fax:(708) 296-3769

National Fire Protection Association
P.O. Box 9101
1 Batterymarch Park
Quincy, MA 02269-9101
Tel: (617) 770-3000
Fax:(617) 770-0700

Occupational Safety and Health Administration (OSHA)
200 Constitution Avenue
Washington, DC 20210
Tel: (202) 219-8148

REFERENCES

Factory Mutual. *Loss Prevention Data Books for Architects and Engineers*. [looseleaf binders, periodic updates]
Lathrop, J., ed. *Life Safety Code Handbook*. Quincy, Mass.: NFPA, 1991.
National Fire Protection Association. *Fire Protection Handbook*. 17th ed. Quincy, Mass.: NFPA, 1991.

BUILDING SYSTEMS

Building Systems Institute
1300 Sumner Avenue
Cleveland, OH 44115-2180
Tel: (216) 241-7333
Fax:(216) 241-0105

REFERENCES

Rush, Richard D., ed. *The Building Systems Integration Handbook*. New York: J. Wiley & Sons, 1986.

SEISMIC DESIGN

Building Seismic Safety Council (BSSC)
National Institute of Building Sciences
1201 L Street N.W., 4th Floor
Washington, DC 20005
Tel: (202) 289-7800
Fax:(202) 289-1092

Federal Emergency Management Agency (FEMA)
Federal Center Plaza
500 C Street, SW
Washington, DC 20472
Tel: (202) 646-2500

REFERENCES

Arnold, C., and R. Reitherman. *Building Configuration and Seismic Design*. New York: J. Wiley & Sons, 1982.
Lagorio, H. *An Architect's Guide to Nonstructural Seismic Hazards*. New York: J. Wiley & Sons, 1990.

LIGHTING DESIGN

Illuminating Engineering Society of North America (IES)
120 Wall Street, 17th Floor
New York, NY 10005
Tel: (212) 248-5000
Fax:(212) 248-5017

International Association of Lighting Designers (IALD)
18 E 16th St., Suite 208
New York, NY 10003
Tel: (212) 206-1281
Fax:(212) 206-1327

REFERENCES

Kaufman, John E., ed. *Illuminating Engineering Society Handbook*, reference vol. Illuminating Engineering Society (IES), 1981 and 1984.

ACOUSTICAL DESIGN

Acoustical Society of America (ASA)
500 Sunnyside Blvd.
Woodbury, NY 11797
Tel: (516) 576-2360

National Council of Acoustical Consultants (NCAC)
66 Morris Avenue, Suite 1A
Springfield, NJ 07081-1409
Tel: (201) 564-5859
Fax:(201) 564-7480

REFERENCES

Burris-Meyer, H.G. *Acoustics for the Architect*. New York: Van Nostrand Reinhold.

BUILDING SECURITY

National Burglar and Fire Alarm Association
7101 Wisconsin Avenue, Suite 901
Bethesda, MD 20814-4805
Tel: (301) 907-3202
Fax:(301) 907-7897

National Crime Prevention Institute (NCPI)
University of Louisville
Brigman Hall, Room 102A
Louisville, Kentucky 40292-0001
Tel: (502) 852-6987
Fax:(502) 852-6990

SITE, COMMUNITY, AND URBAN PLANNING

American Institute of Certified Planners/
    American Planning Association (AICP/APA)
1776 Massachusetts Avenue, NW, Suite 300
Washington, DC 20036
Tel: (202) 872-0611
Fax:(202) 872-0643

American Planning Association
1776 Massachusetts Avenue, NW
Washington, DC 20036
Tel: (202) 872-0611

American Society of Consulting Planners
c/o Dennis Larkin, WBDC Group
31050 Telegraph Road, Suite 340
Bingham Farms, MI 48025
Tel:(313) 642-3999

Urban Land Institute
625 Indiana Avenue, NW
Washington, DC 20004-2930
Tel: (202) 624-7000
Fax:(202) 624-7140

FLOOD DAMAGE CONTROL

REFERENCES

AIA Research Corporation. *Design Guidelines for Flood Damage Reduction*. Washington, D.C.: U.S. Government Printing Office, 1981.

AUTOMOBILES, ROADS, AND PARKING

National Parking Association
1112 16th Street, NW, Suite 300
Washington, DC 20036
Tel: (202) 296-4336
Fax:(202) 331-8523

AREA CALCULATION AND COST ESTIMATING

American Association of Certified Appraisers
800 Compton Road, #10
Cincinnati, OH 45231
Tel: (513) 729-1400
Fax:(513) 729-1401

American Association of Cost Engineers
P.O. Box 1557
209 Prairie Ave.
Morgantown, WV 26507-1557
Tel: (304) 296-8444
Fax:(304) 291-5728

American Society of Professional Estimators
11141 Georgia Avenue, Suite 412
Wheaton, MD 20902
Tel: (301) 929-8848
Fax:(301) 929-0231

REFERENCES

Means Building Construction Cost Data Book. Kingston, Mass.: R.S. Means Company. [617/585-7880]

GOVERNMENT SERVICES

Department of Housing and Urban Development
451 Seventh Street, SW
Washington, DC 20410
Tel: (202) 708-1112

Environmental Protection Agency
401 M Street, SW
Washington, DC 20460
Tel: (202) 260-2090

Office of Urban Rehabilitation
Department of Housing and Urban Development
451 Seventh Street, SW
Washington, DC 20410
Tel: (202) 708-1422

REGULATORY AND RELATED ORGANIZATIONS

American National Standards Institute (ANSI)
11 West 42nd Street, 13th Floor
New York, NY 10036-8002
Tel: (212) 642-4900
Fax:(212) 398-0023

American Society for Testing and Materials (ASTM)
1916 Race St.
Philadelphia, PA 19103-1187
Tel: (215) 299-5400
Fax:(215) 977-9679

Building Officials and Code Administrators
    International (BOCA)
4051 W. Flossmoor Rd.
Country Club Hills, IL 60478-5795
Tel: (708) 799-2300
Fax:(708) 799-4981

Construction Specifications Institute, Inc.
601 Madison Street
Alexandria, VA 22314
Tel: (703) 684-0300

International Conference of Building Officials (ICBO)
5360 S. Workman Mill Road
Whittier, CA 90601-2298
Tel: (310) 699-0541
Fax:(310) 692-3853

National Conference of States on Building Codes
    and Standards (NCSBCS)
505 Huntmar Park Drive, Suite 210
Herndon, VA 22070
Tel: (800) 362-2633 or (703) 437-0100
Fax:(703) 481-3596

Southern Building Code Congress
    International, Inc. (SBCCI)
900 Montclair Road
Birmingham, AL 35213-1206
Tel: (205) 591-1853
Fax:(205) 591-1853

CHAPTER

2

SITEWORK

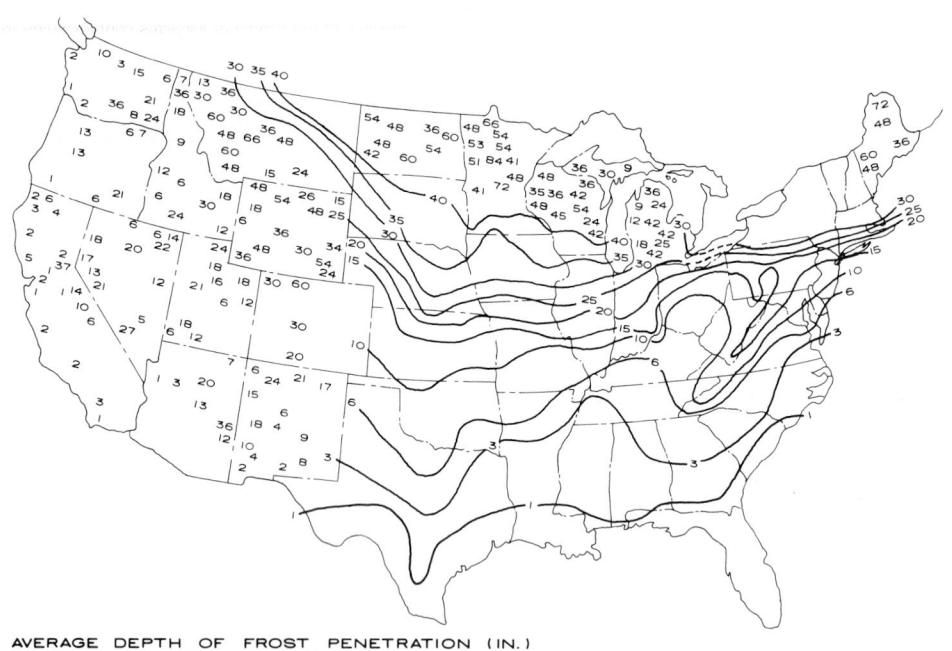

AVERAGE DEPTH OF FROST PENETRATION (IN.)
SOURCE: U.S. DEPT. OF COMMERCE WEATHER BUREAU

PRELIMINARY SUBSURFACE INFORMATION

A. Collect available information for soil, rock, and water conditions, including the following:
  1. Topographic and aerial mapping.
  2. Geological survey maps and publications.
  3. Local knowledge (history of site development, experience of nearby structures, flooding, subsidence, etc.).
  4. Existing subsurface data (boreholes, well records, water soundings).
  5. Reconnaissance site survey.
  6. Previous studies.
B. Evaluate available information for site acceptability. If available data are insufficient, consult a geotechnical engineer to perform a limited subsurface investigation to gather basic information.
C. Consult geotechnical engineer for potential foundation performance at each site as part of the selection process.

DETAILED SUBSURFACE INFORMATION

After selection of a potential site a subsurface and laboratory test investigation should be carried out by a qualified geotechnical engineer before design is undertaken.

The investigation should provide an adequate understanding of the subsurface conditions and the information should be assessed to determine potential foundation behavior.

The engineer should evaluate alternative foundation methods and techniques in conjunction with the architect.

The engineer or architect should provide inspection during construction to ensure that material and construction procedures are as specified and to evaluate unexpected soil, rock, or groundwater conditions that may be exposed by excavations.

SOIL TYPES AND THEIR PROPERTIES

DIVISION	LETTER	HATCH-ING	COLOR	SOIL DESCRIPTION	VALUE AS A FOUNDATION MATERIAL	FROST ACTION	DRAINAGE
Gravel and gravelly soils	GW		Red	Well-graded gravel, or gravel-sand mixture, little or no fines	Excellent	None	Excellent
	GP		Red	Poorly graded gravel, or gravel-sand mixtures, little or no fines	Good	None	Excellent
	GM		Yellow	Silty gravels, gravel-sand-silt mixtures	Good	Slight	Poor
	GC		Yellow	Clayey-gravels, gravel-clay-sand mixtures	Good	Slight	Poor
Sand and sandy soils	SW		Red	Well-graded sands, or gravelly sands, little or no fines	Good	None	Excellent
	SP		Red	Poorly graded sands, or gravelly sands, little or no fines	Fair	None	Excellent
	SM		Yellow	Silty sands, sand-silt mixtures	Fair	Slight	Fair
	SC		Yellow	Clayey sands, sand-clay mixtures	Fair	Medium	Poor
Silts and clays LL < 50	ML		Green	Inorganic silts, rock flour, silty or clayey fine sands, or clayey silts with slight plasticity	Fair	Very high	Poor
	CL		Green	Inorganic clays of low to medium plasticity, gravelly clays, silty clays, lean clays	Fair	Medium	Impervious
	OL		Green	Organic silt-clays of low plasticity	Poor	High	Impervious
Silts and clays LL > 50	MH		Blue	Inorganic silts, micaceous or diatomaceous fine sandy or silty soils, elastic silts	Poor	Very high	Poor
	CH		Blue	Inorganic clays of high plasticity, fat clays	Very poor	Medium	Impervious
	OH		Blue	Organic clays of medium to high plasticity, organic silts	Very poor	Medium	Impervious
Highly organic soils	Pt		Orange	Peat and other highly organic soils	Not suitable	Slight	Poor

NOTES
1. Consult geotechnical engineers and local building codes for allowable soil bearing capacities.
2. LL indicates liquid limit.

Mueser Rutledge Consulting Engineers; New York, New York

2   SUBSURFACE INVESTIGATION

ASBESTOS AND ITS EFFECTS

Asbestos is the term used for six naturally occurring fibrous minerals. Three of these, chrysotile, amosite, and crocidilite, have been used in a variety of building products since about 1900, and most extensively from about 1940 through the mid-1970s. The value of asbestos stems from its resistance to burning and corrosion and its thermal insulation properties.

The government has determined that asbestos fibers can cause serious health problems. Three specific diseases, asbestosis (a fibrous scarring of the lungs), lung cancer, and mesothelioma (a cancer of the lining of the chest or abdominal cavity), have been linked to exposure to asbestos fibers. Most of the serious health problems are believed to have resulted from very high levels of asbestos fibers in the air. Because of the seriousness of these diseases, prevention technologies have been sought by government and industry alike. Recently, because of the cost and difficulty of safely removing asbestos, emphasis has been given to managing asbestos-containing building materials in place.

Although the government acknowledges there is insufficient information about health effects resulting from low-level asbestos exposure, it has determined that the health and safety of construction and building maintenance workers may be at risk because of possible periodic exposure to elevated levels of asbestos fibers on the job. In response to questions about how hazardous asbestos is, the U.S. Environmental Protection Agency developed the following five facts:

1. Although asbestos is hazardous, the risk of asbestos-related disease depends upon exposure to airborne asbestos fibers.
2. Based on available data, the average airborne asbestos levels in buildings seem to be very low. Accordingly, the health risk to most building occupants also appears to be very low.
3. Removal is often not a building owner's best course of action to reduce asbestos exposure. In fact, improper removal can create a dangerous situation where none previously existed.
4. EPA only requires asbestos removal in order to prevent significant exposure to airborne asbestos fibers during building demolition or renovation activities.
5. EPA recommends a proactive, in-place management program whenever asbestos-containing material is discovered.

Asbestos-containing materials (ACM) in buildings are usually defined as materials containing one percent or more asbestos. ACM are often organized in the categories of surface-applied ACM, thermal system insulation ACM (TSI), and miscellaneous ACM. Some, but not necessarily all, materials that may contain asbestos are shown in the accompanying diagram. This information and other lists of suspect ACM should not be used as the basis for determining whether or not actual materials contain asbestos or for their location in buildings.

APPLICABLE LAWS AND REGULATIONS

Primary federal asbestos regulations include the EPA's National Emission Standards for Hazardous Air Pollutants (NESHAP), 40 CFR 61 Subpart M; the Occupational Safety and Health Administration's (OSHA) Construction Industry Asbestos Standard, 29 CFR 1926.58; the EPA's Asbestos Abatement Projects; Worker Protection, Final Rule, 40 CFR 763 Subpart G; and the EPA's Asbestos Hazard Emergency Response Act (AHERA), Asbestos-Containing Materials In Schools; Final Rule and Notice, 40 CFR 763 Subpart E. These and other federal asbestos related regulations are listed in EPA's Green Book. The general scope of the above regulations is summarized below; however, those involved in asbestos work should obtain and must follow applicable regulations.

The NESHAP usually requires friable ACM (materials that can be crumbled by hand pressure) to be removed before a building is demolished and, depending on their extent, may require their removal before renovation. Typically, friable asbestos-containing materials must be wetted during removal. Certain notifications may also be required of the owner.

OSHA's Construction Industry Standard applies to all private sector workers and public sector workers in states with an OSHA state plan. It covers general construction, abatement, and operations and maintenance (O&M) workers. When employees are exposed to asbestos fiber levels defined in the rule, such actions as the use of respirators, engineering controls, protective clothing, medical surveillance, and establishing regulated areas may be required. Compliance with the rule's requirements is primarily the employer's responsibility. OSHA is considering a substantial number of changes to this rule.

EPA's Worker Protection Rule is similar to the OSHA rule. It covers certain state and local government employees involved in abatement work who are not covered under the OSHA rule, but it does not cover workers involved in building O&M activities.

The AHERA rule requires inspection, the development of comprehensive management plans, and the selection of responses to deal with asbestos hazards in public and private primary and secondary schools.

In addition to pertinent federal regulations, many states and localities have issued asbestos-related laws and regulations. These requirements may conflict with one another or other laws and regulations applicable to buildings, and it may be difficult to interpret how some of the rules apply to specific projects. Due to these complexities, a body of design and environmental professionals and contractors who specialize in asbestos abatement work has developed over the past decade.

A PLAN OF ACTION

An owners' plans (continued use, renovation, sale, lease, demolition, expansion, etc.) for buildings that contain ACM are fundamental to selecting the best ways to deal with the building's ACM, both in complying with applicable laws and regulations and in cost-effective facility operation and management. The following primary steps, typically carried out for the owner by qualified and experienced specialists, are intended to assist owners in dealing with ACM in buildings. Fundamental tasks for obtaining accurate and complete information about the ACM include:

1. Review building design, construction, alteration, and repair records, including as-built drawings, specifications, shop drawings, other submittals, purchase orders, and the like.
2. Conduct visual inspections to locate and document potential ACM, its extent, condition, potential for being disturbed during construction or building O&M work, and other characteristics.
3. Laboratory analysis of samples is the only accurate way to determine whether a material contains asbestos, and the amount and type. Lab results should be correlated with data collected in the visual inspection. See EPA's Purple Book.

Those conducting visual inspections and collecting bulk samples of potential ACM may be exposed to asbestos fibers. Their employers are responsible for compliance with applicable regulations.

The owner uses the building survey to select the appropriate actions to deal with the building's ACM. Primary options include:

1. ACM removal
2. Enclosing, encasing, or encapsulating the ACM
3. Specialized O&M procedures.

If friable ACM are found and they will be disturbed during construction (including by demolition), depending on the quantities and condition of the material present, the NESHAP requirements probably apply. If nonfriable ACM such as resilient flooring are not likely to be rendered friable by construction activities, they probably will not trigger action under the NESHAP, but it is wise to seek a decision by EPA's regional asbestos coordinator, and to check whether OSHA and other laws and regulations apply.

SECURING QUALIFIED ASSISTANCE

Because single-source professional services for asbestos abatement are difficult to find, many owners assemble a "design team" comprised of several specialty consultants. A prime consultant may be assigned coordination responsibility. The team may include abatement designers, industrial hygienists, a project monitor, and architects and engineers. Primary qualifications to consider for selecting design team members include: the firm's history, similar work experience, references, training, certification, accreditation, licensure, technical staff, financial resources, and history of complaints and settlements.

When evaluating abatement contractors, primary considerations include: experience with similar projects; references; training; certification/accreditation; licensure; staff, especially supervisors; respiratory protection; hazard communication, and medical surveillance programs; bonding capacity and credit worthiness; and history of complaints and settlements.

Asbestos abatement projects focus on protecting workers and preventing the spread of asbestos contamination to other parts of the building or outside the building. This is the contractor's responsibility in accordance with the contract and applicable laws and regulations. Systems designed to protect workers' safety and prevent contamination can fail quickly and without warning. Continuous on-site monitoring of the work helps avoid such failures and fosters corrective action if they occur. For guidance in selecting surveyors/inspectors, designers, project monitors, and contractors, see the introduction to NIBS' Asbestos Guide Specifications.

THE ARCHITECT'S ROLE

In designing alterations to a facility that contains ACM, one of the often-neglected responsibilities is coordinating the asbestos abatement work with the alteration work. Often contract documents for abatement are not properly organized and coordinated. This may stem from environmental consultants' lack of training and experience in assembling complete and comprehensive sets of contract documents. NIBS' Asbestos Guide Specifications are designed to be used in conjunction with commercially available guide specification systems like the American Institute of Architects' Masterspec. It also stresses the importance of preparing complete and well-coordinated contract documents, including the use of standard contract documents and guides like those published by the AIA.

The selection of materials to replace ACM fireproofing on structural members or ACM fire separation assemblies is an important design consideration that is usually included in the renovation contract, but for buildings which must remain partially occupied during the work, temporary provisions may be necessary.

SPECIALIZED ASBESTOS ABATEMENT SYSTEMS AND PROCEDURES

The following are some of the major systems and procedures used on asbestos abatement projects:

Pressure Differential Containment System: A system designed to maintain lower air pressure in the work area than in adjacent areas. This can be achieved by exhausting air from the work area through high efficiency particulate air (HEPA) filters that remove asbestos fibers from the air. This prevents the spread of airborne asbestos fibers beyond the work area. When the air pressure in the work area is lower than in the surrounding areas, air movement is from outside to inside the work area. This is also called a negative pressure system.

Exposure Monitoring: OSHA rules require employers to monitor workers' exposures to fiber levels to ensure adequate protection. Initial monitoring is required to determine the exposure levels at which workers need to be protected. Periodic monitoring is required to determine if this exposure changes.

Respiratory Protection Systems: There are two categories of respirators for asbestos abatement work: air purifying (filtering) respirators and atmosphere supplying respirators. OSHA requires that respirators be used whenever engineering controls and work practices cannot keep airborne fiber levels below the permissible exposure level (PEL). The respirator must be able to reduce the fiber level inside the face piece to the PEL or below.

1. The two types of air purifying respirators are negative pressure air purifying respirators and powered air purifying respirators (PAPR).

Negative pressure respirators draw air from outside the respirator through HEPA filters into the respirator by the inhalation of the worker. Exhaled air escapes through a one-way exhaust valve. A fault in the respirator's fit to the worker's face will allow contaminated air to be inhaled.

Powered air purifying respirators use battery powered fans to pump air through a HEPA filter into the face piece. They positively pressurize the air inside the respirator so failures in the face-piece seal will result in filtered air leaking out of the respirator rather than contaminated air leaking in.

2. The two types of atmosphere supplying respirators are supplied air (Type-C) respirators and self-contained breathing apparatus (SCBA).

Atmosphere supplying respirators provide clean air from outside the work area which is carried by a flexible hose to the workers. Type C systems can restrict workers' movements and the hoses can be tripping hazards.

SCBA systems, which contain compressed air in tanks, are well suited to difficult-to- access work areas where the use of hoses is difficult. However, the limited air supply and the heavy tank can be disadvantages.

David A. Harris, FAIA; National Institute of Building Sciences; Washington, D.C.

Primary and Secondary Barrier Systems: To protect exist-ing finishes and adjacent areas from damage during abate-ment work, sheet-plastic coverings or strippable coatings (primary barrier) are installed on walls and floors of the as-bestos abatement work area in combination with a second sheet plastic drop-cloth layer (secondary barrier).

COST CONSIDERATIONS

Costs of asbestos-related services are hard to predict and can vary greatly. The following is for general guidance only. Cost estimates for specific projects should be obtained from qualified specialists.

Asbestos survey and laboratory analysis services costs can range from about 30 cents to $1.30 or more per square meter of floor area (3 to 12 cents per sq ft). Factors influ-encing these unit costs include the region of the country, accessibility of suspected ACM, work schedule, building type, owner's requirements (number of samples to be tak-en, etc.), and size of the building. Typically, survey/inspec-tion costs are highest in industrial buildings and lowest in general building types. School buildings covered by AHERA are in between.

Mid-range costs for asbestos removal work in typical in-stallations can be organized into the following categories for common ACM:

ASBESTOS REMOVAL COSTS

Fireproofing	$12.50 - $35 per square foot $135 - $374 per square meter
Acoustical plaster	$8.50 - $17 per square foot $90 - $180 per square meter
Thermal system pipe insulation	$12 - $22 per foot $40 - $72 per meter
Insulation on pipe joints	$15 - $28 each

Asbestos abatement costs vary due to factors similar to those for survey and laboratory analysis costs, plus regula-tions, project size, availability of disposal sites, time of year (school work is typically scheduled during summer), whether or not the building will be occupied during the work (may require work at night and on weekends), the ACM's accessibility (height above the floor, restricted ac-cess, etc.), temperature of work area and substrate, and building's height. These cost ranges do not include re-placement materials for building systems and materials re-moved to gain access to the ACM. Encapsulation, encasement, enclosure, and other abatement actions may be used based on life-cycle cost considerations. The cost of these methods vary based on considerations similar to re-moval.

Decisions to remove ACM, use other abatement options, start an O&M program, or combinations of these options should be made with complete and accurate information about the facility's ACM. With the exception of statutory and regulatory requirements, decisions about cost, liabili-ty, market issues, and other factors are the owner's prerog-ative.

REFERENCES

The EPA has produced many guidance documents on as-bestos in buildings. Some of the most pertinent are:

Guidance for Controlling Asbestos-Containing Materials in Buildings (Purple Book), EPA 560/5-85-024

A Guide to Respiratory Protection for the Asbestos Abate-ment Industry (White Book), EPA-560-OPTS-86-001

Managing Asbestos In Place, A Building Owner's Guide to Operations and Maintenance Programs for Asbestos- Con-taining Materials (Green Book), EPA 20T-2003

EPA maintains an asbestos information "hot line" and pub-lications ordering number, (202) 554-1404. For school-related asbestos information, call (800) 835-6700.

The National Institute of Building Sciences (NIBS), Wash-ington, D.C. (202) 289-7800.

Asbestos Abatement and Management in Buildings: Mod-el Guide Specifications, 2nd ed., August 1988. New sec-tions on asbestos-containing resilient flooring and a new introduction and instructions for use section will be pub-lished in early 1992.

In 1992, NIBS will publish a detailed operations and main-tenance (O&M) guidance manual for work practices involv-ing ACM in buildings.

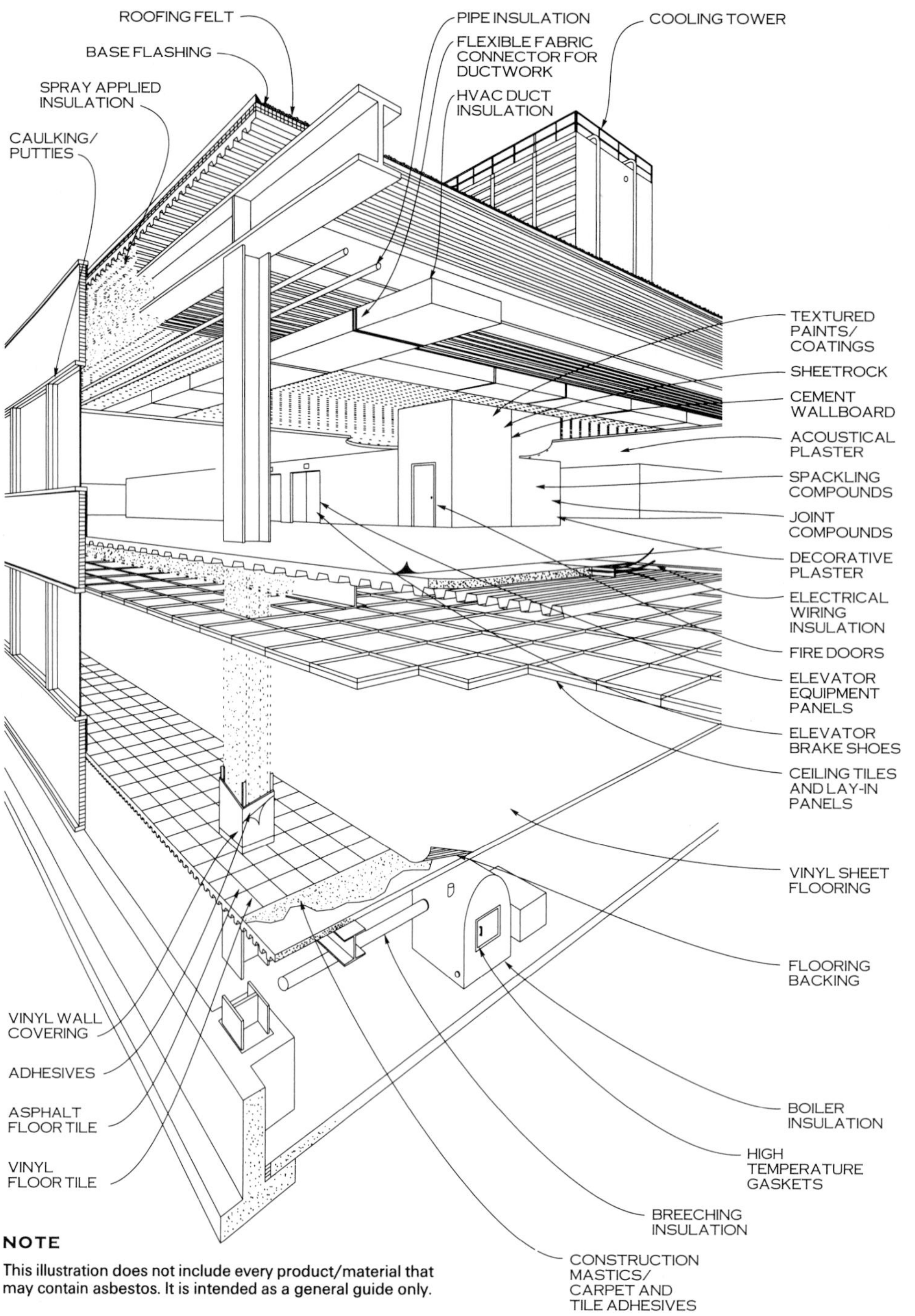

TYPICAL LOCATION OF ASBESTOS-CONTAINING MATERIALS

Labels on illustration: ROOFING FELT, BASE FLASHING, SPRAY APPLIED INSULATION, CAULKING/PUTTIES, PIPE INSULATION, COOLING TOWER, FLEXIBLE FABRIC CONNECTOR FOR DUCTWORK, HVAC DUCT INSULATION, TEXTURED PAINTS/COATINGS, SHEETROCK, CEMENT WALLBOARD, ACOUSTICAL PLASTER, SPACKLING COMPOUNDS, JOINT COMPOUNDS, DECORATIVE PLASTER, ELECTRICAL WIRING INSULATION, FIRE DOORS, ELEVATOR EQUIPMENT PANELS, ELEVATOR BRAKE SHOES, CEILING TILES AND LAY-IN PANELS, VINYL SHEET FLOORING, FLOORING BACKING, BOILER INSULATION, HIGH TEMPERATURE GASKETS, BREECHING INSULATION, CONSTRUCTION MASTICS/CARPET AND TILE ADHESIVES, VINYL WALL COVERING, ADHESIVES, ASPHALT FLOOR TILE, VINYL FLOOR TILE

NOTE

This illustration does not include every product/material that may contain asbestos. It is intended as a general guide only.

OTHER SOURCES:

State Asbestos Programs Related to Asbestos Hazard Emergency Response Act: A Survey Update of State Laws and Regulations, National Conference of State Legisla-tures, Denver, Colorado (303) 830-2200.

Recommended Work Practices for the Removal of Resi-lient Floor Coverings, Resilient Floor Covering Institute, Rockville, Maryland (301) 340-8580.

The Asbestos Regulatory Directory, National Asbestos Council–Environmental Information Association, Atlanta, Georgia (404) 633-2622.

U.S. Federal Asbestos Regulations 1991, Asbestos Infor-mation Association, Arlington, Virginia (703) 979-1150.

NOTE

The text has been compiled from a variety of public and pri-vate sources. Its purpose is to provide summary informa-tion on asbestos in buildings, not to provide complete and comprehensive information on the subject. The author has made reasonable efforts to provide accurate information, but does not warrant it or assume any responsibility for its accuracy, completeness, or fitness for the reader's pur-pose. There are many other laws, rules, standards, guides, and other sources on asbestos in buildings in addition to those listed herein. Citations herein do not imply endorse-ment. The information is not necessarily the opinion of the National Institute of Building Sciences.

David A. Harris, FAIA; National Institute of Building Sciences; Washington, D.C.

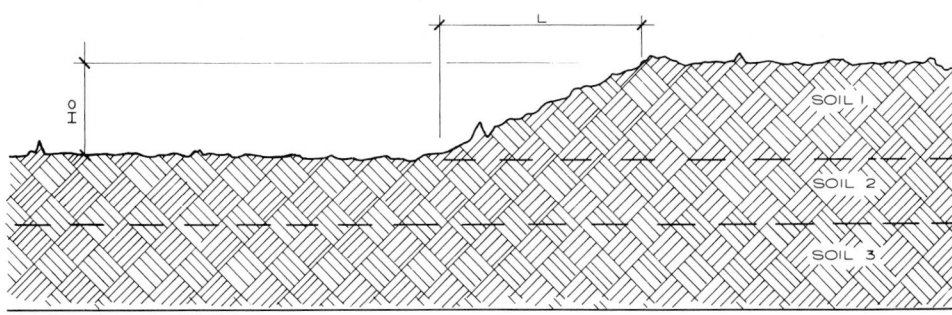

OPEN EXCAVATION

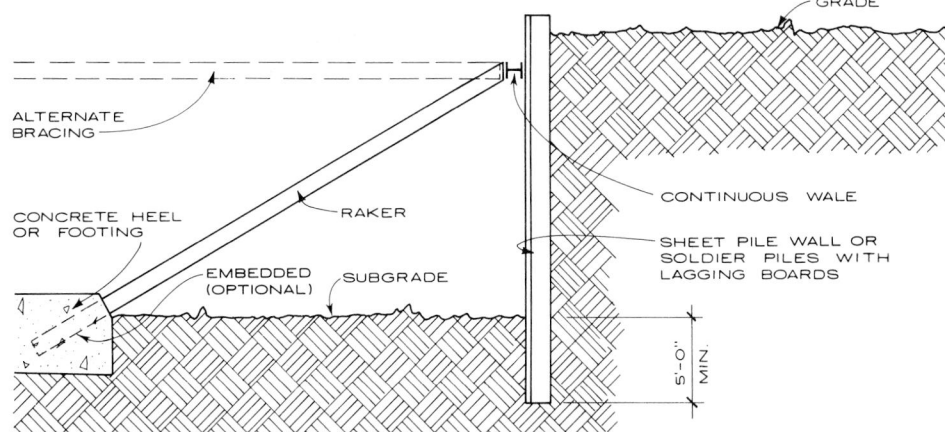

BRACED EXCAVATION USING RAKERS

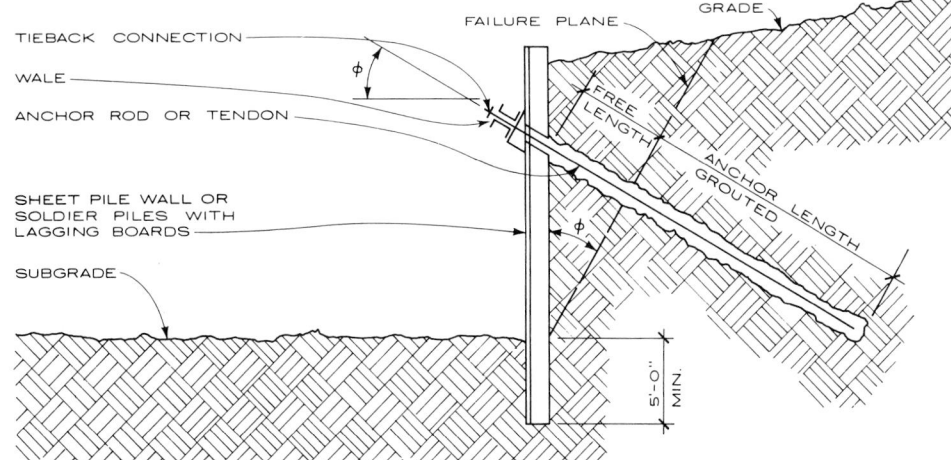

BRACED EXCAVATION USING EARTH ANCHORS

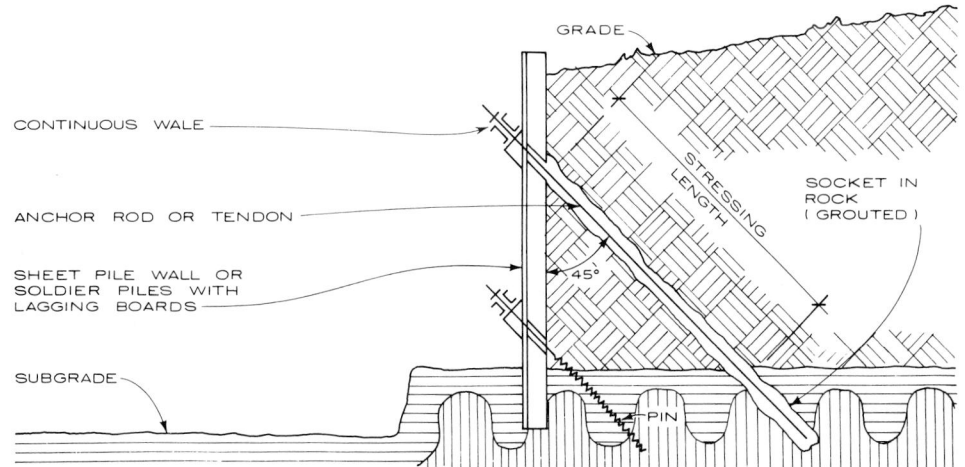

BRACED EXCAVATION USING ROCK ANCHORS

Mueser Rutledge Consulting Engineers; New York, New York

EMBANKMENT STABILITY
CONSULT FOUNDATION ENGINEER

SOIL TYPES			$L/_{HO}$	REMARKS
S1	S2	S3		
Fill	Rock		>1.5	Check sliding of S1
Soft clay	Hard clay	Rock	>1.0	Check sliding of S1
Sand	Soft clay	Hard clay	>1.5	Check lateral displacement of S2
Sand	Sand	Hard clay	>1.5	
Hard clay	Soft clay	Sand	<1.0	Check lateral displacement of S2

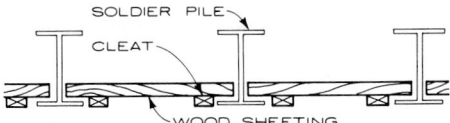

TIMBER LAGGING

TIMBER SHEETING

STEEL SHEETING

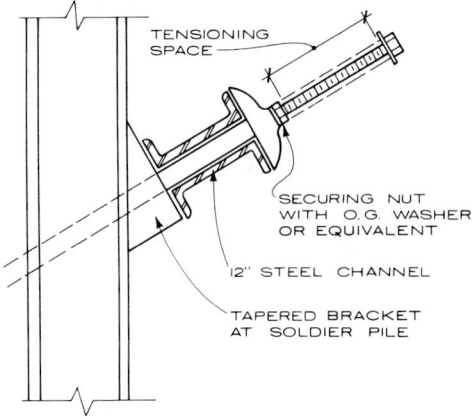

CHANNEL WALER DETAIL

NOTES

1. For shallow depths of excavation cantilever sheeting may be used, if driven to sufficient depth.
2. For deep excavations, several tiers of bracing may be necessary.
3. If subgrade of excavation is used for installation of spreadfootings or mats, proper dewatering procedures may be required to avoid disturbance of bearing level.
4. At times it may be possible to improve the bearing stratum by excavation of compressible materials and their replacement with compacted granular backfill.
5. For evaluation of problems encountered with sheeting and shoring, a foundation engineer should be consulted.
6. Local codes and OSHA regulations must be considered.
7. Proximity of utilities and other structures must be considered in design.

Embankment stabilization is required where extremely steep slopes exist that are subject to heavy storm water runoff. The need for mechanical stabilization can be reduced by intercepting the runoff, or slowing the velocity of the runoff down the slope. Diversions are desirable at the tops of slopes to intercept the runoff. Slopes can be shelved or terraced to reduce the velocity of runoff to the point where a major erosion hazard is avoided. Use an armored channel or slope drain if concentrated runoff down a slope must be controlled.

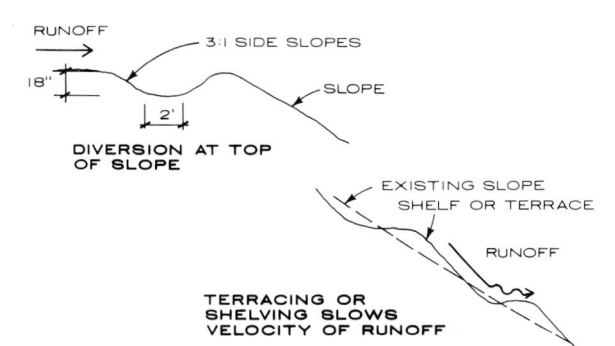

RUNOFF → 3:1 SIDE SLOPES / SLOPE
18"
2'
DIVERSION AT TOP OF SLOPE

EXISTING SLOPE / SHELF OR TERRACE
RUNOFF
TERRACING OR SHELVING SLOWS VELOCITY OF RUNOFF

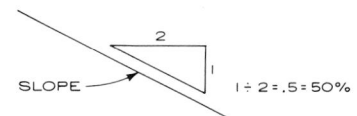

2
SLOPE   1 ÷ 2 = .5 = 50%

SOIL	GRADIENT	RATIO
Dry sand	33%	3:1
Loam	40%	2.5:1
Compacted clay	80%	1.25:1
Saturated clay	20%	5:1

MAX. GRADIENTS FOR BARE SOILS

SLOPE STABILIZATION WITH RIPRAP

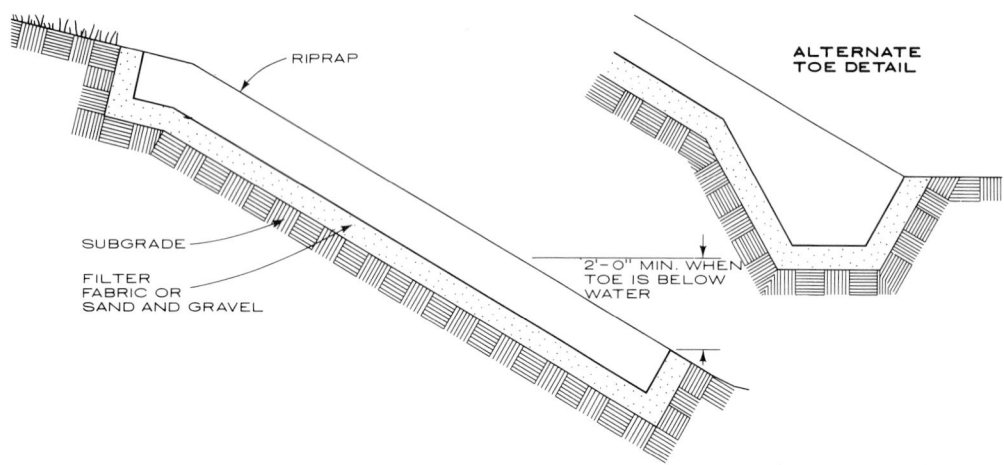

RIPRAP

ALTERNATE TOE DETAIL

SUBGRADE

FILTER FABRIC OR SAND AND GRAVEL

2'-0" MIN. WHEN TOE IS BELOW WATER

NOTE

A number of mechanical embankment stabilization materials are illustrated. Two important features all methods have in common are

1. Embedment of the toe and lateral limits to prevent undercutting and outflanking, and
2. Use of a granular or fabric filter to protect the soil beneath the protective layer from the effects of flowing water or exiting groundwater.

RIPRAP EMBANKMENT WITH ALTERNATE TOE

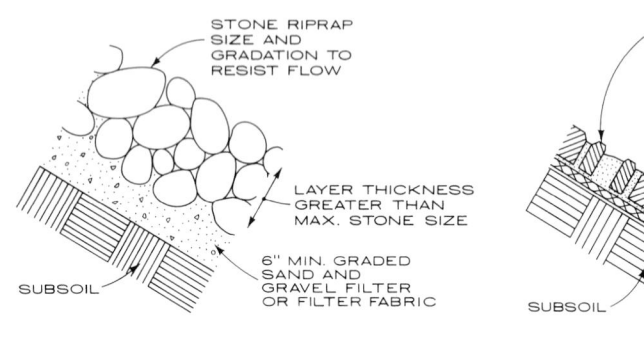

STONE RIPRAP SIZE AND GRADATION TO RESIST FLOW

LAYER THICKNESS GREATER THAN MAX. STONE SIZE

6" MIN. GRADED SAND AND GRAVEL FILTER OR FILTER FABRIC

SUBSOIL

STONE

PRECAST CONCRETE RIPRAP INTERLOCKING GRID SYSTEM

FILL OPEN CELLS AND JOINT WITH SHARP SAND OR EARTH FOR SEEDING

FILTER FABRIC AND/OR GRADED FILTER MATERIAL

SUBSOIL

PRECAST CONCRETE

FABRIC FORMED REVETMENT (ANCHOR AT TOP OF SLOPE)

REINFORCING STEEL CABLES (OPTIONAL)

FILLED WITH A PUMPABLE SAND/CEMENT GROUT

FILTER FABRIC

SUBSOIL

FABRIC FORMED REVETMENTS

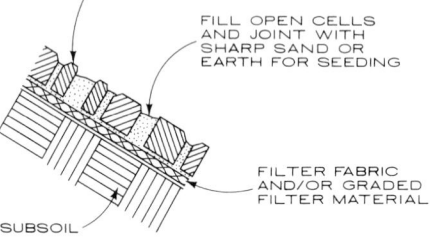

FILTER FABRIC AND/OR GRADED FILTER MATERIAL

STEEP STACKING METHOD

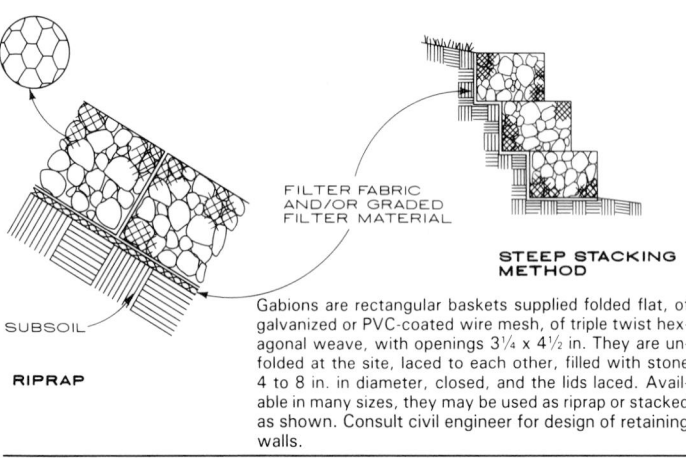

SUBSOIL

RIPRAP

Gabions are rectangular baskets supplied folded flat, of galvanized or PVC-coated wire mesh, of triple twist hexagonal weave, with openings 3¼ x 4½ in. They are unfolded at the site, laced to each other, filled with stone 4 to 8 in. in diameter, closed, and the lids laced. Available in many sizes, they may be used as riprap or stacked as shown. Consult civil engineer for design of retaining walls.

GABION

DIVERSION AT TOP OF SLOPE

TOP OF SLOPE

Slope drain channels may be constructed of 4 in. thick concrete mortared riprap, or 2½ in. deep asphalt. Anchored sod may be used if channel slope does not exceed 3:1 slope and minimal flows are expected. Channel dimensions should accommodate expected runoff. Consult civil engineer for calculations and design of runoff channels.

SLOPE DRAIN

Derek Martin, FAIA; Pittsburgh, Pennsylvania
John M. Beckett, Beckett & Raeder, Inc.; Ann Arbor, Michigan
James E. Sekela, PE; United States Army Corps of Engineers; Pittsburgh, Pennsylvania

 RETAINING WALLS

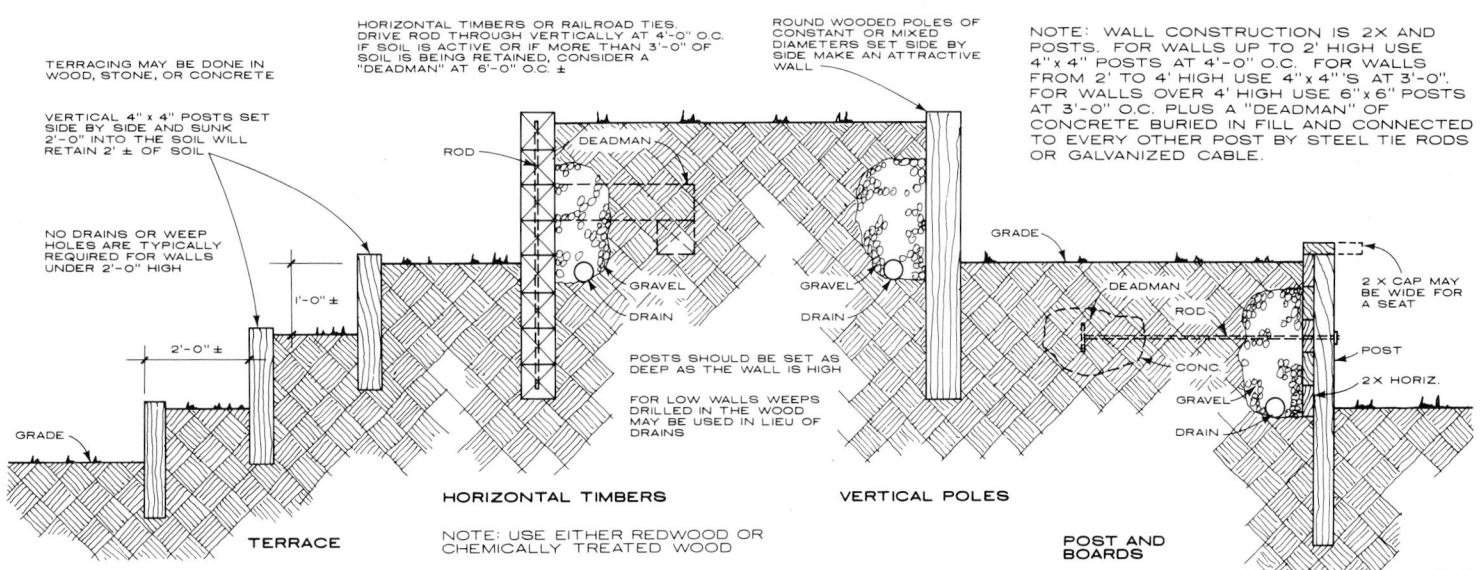

TERRACING MAY BE DONE IN WOOD, STONE, OR CONCRETE

VERTICAL 4" x 4" POSTS SET SIDE BY SIDE AND SUNK 2'-0" INTO THE SOIL WILL RETAIN 2' ± OF SOIL

NO DRAINS OR WEEP HOLES ARE TYPICALLY REQUIRED FOR WALLS UNDER 2'-0" HIGH

GRADE

1'-0" ±

2'-0" ±

HORIZONTAL TIMBERS OR RAILROAD TIES. DRIVE ROD THROUGH VERTICALLY AT 4'-0" O.C. IF SOIL IS ACTIVE OR IF MORE THAN 3'-0" OF SOIL IS BEING RETAINED, CONSIDER A "DEADMAN" AT 6'-0" O.C. ±

ROUND WOODED POLES OF CONSTANT OR MIXED DIAMETERS SET SIDE BY SIDE MAKE AN ATTRACTIVE WALL

ROD

DEADMAN

GRAVEL

GRAVEL

DRAIN

DRAIN

POSTS SHOULD BE SET AS DEEP AS THE WALL IS HIGH

FOR LOW WALLS WEEPS DRILLED IN THE WOOD MAY BE USED IN LIEU OF DRAINS

NOTE: WALL CONSTRUCTION IS 2X AND POSTS. FOR WALLS UP TO 2' HIGH USE 4" x 4" POSTS AT 4'-0" O.C. FOR WALLS FROM 2' TO 4' HIGH USE 4"x 4"'S AT 3'-0". FOR WALLS OVER 4' HIGH USE 6"x 6" POSTS AT 3'-0" O.C. PLUS A "DEADMAN" OF CONCRETE BURIED IN FILL AND CONNECTED TO EVERY OTHER POST BY STEEL TIE RODS OR GALVANIZED CABLE.

GRADE

DEADMAN

ROD

CONC.

GRAVEL

DRAIN

2 X CAP MAY BE WIDE FOR A SEAT

POST

2 X HORIZ.

TERRACE

HORIZONTAL TIMBERS

NOTE: USE EITHER REDWOOD OR CHEMICALLY TREATED WOOD

VERTICAL POLES

POST AND BOARDS

WOOD APPLICATIONS

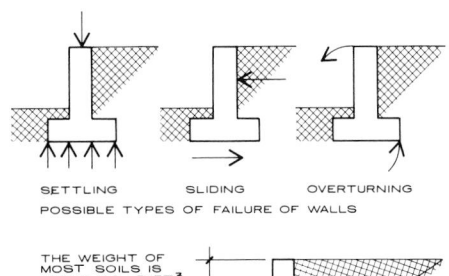

SETTLING   SLIDING   OVERTURNING

POSSIBLE TYPES OF FAILURE OF WALLS

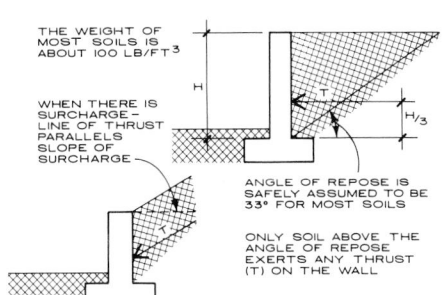

THE WEIGHT OF MOST SOILS IS ABOUT 100 LB/FT³

WHEN THERE IS SURCHARGE – LINE OF THRUST PARALLELS SLOPE OF SURCHARGE

ANGLE OF REPOSE IS SAFELY ASSUMED TO BE 33° FOR MOST SOILS

ONLY SOIL ABOVE THE ANGLE OF REPOSE EXERTS ANY THRUST (T) ON THE WALL

GENERAL RELATIONSHIPS

SLIDING

The thrust on the wall must be resisted. The resisting force is the weight of the wall times the coefficient of soil friction. Use a safety factor of 1.5. Therefore:

$$W(C.F.) \geq 1.5T$$

Average coefficients:

Gravel	0.6
Silt/dry clay	0.5
Sand	0.4
Wet clay	0.3

OVERTURNING

The overturning moment equals T(H/3). This is resisted by the resisting moment. For symmetrical sections, resisting moment equals W times (width of base/2). Use a safety factor of 2.0. Therefore:

$$M_R \geq 2(M_0)$$

SETTLING

Soil bearing value must resist vertical force. For symmetrical sections that force is W (or W')/bearing area. Use a safety factor of 1.5. Therefore:

$$S.B. \geq 1.5(W/A)$$

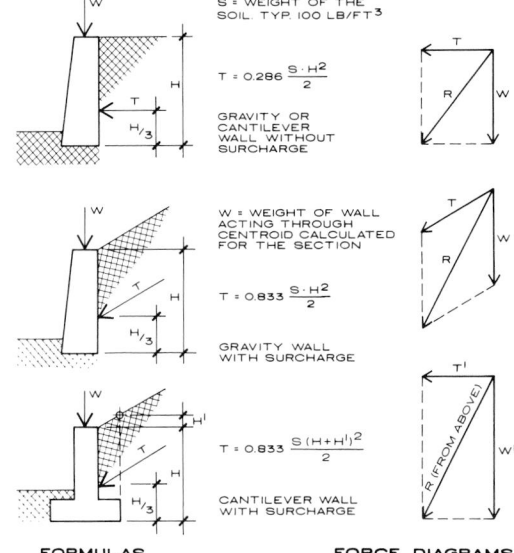

S = WEIGHT OF THE SOIL. TYP. 100 LB/FT³

$$T = 0.286 \frac{S \cdot H^2}{2}$$

GRAVITY OR CANTILEVER WALL WITHOUT SURCHARGE

W = WEIGHT OF WALL ACTING THROUGH CENTROID CALCULATED FOR THE SECTION

$$T = 0.833 \frac{S \cdot H^2}{2}$$

GRAVITY WALL WITH SURCHARGE

$$T = 0.833 \frac{S(H+H')^2}{2}$$

CANTILEVER WALL WITH SURCHARGE

FORMULAS

FORCE DIAGRAMS

STRUCTURAL DESIGN CONSIDERATIONS

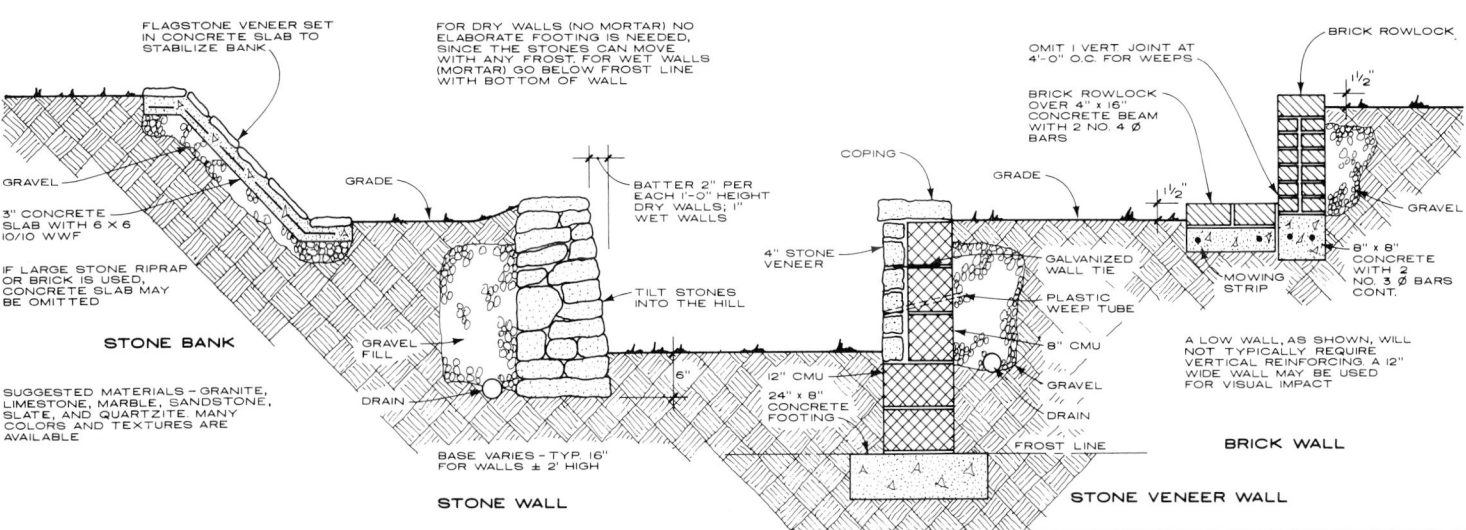

FLAGSTONE VENEER SET IN CONCRETE SLAB TO STABILIZE BANK

GRAVEL

3" CONCRETE SLAB WITH 6 x 6 10/10 WWF

IF LARGE STONE RIPRAP OR BRICK IS USED, CONCRETE SLAB MAY BE OMITTED

STONE BANK

SUGGESTED MATERIALS – GRANITE, LIMESTONE, MARBLE, SANDSTONE, SLATE, AND QUARTZITE. MANY COLORS AND TEXTURES ARE AVAILABLE

FOR DRY WALLS (NO MORTAR) NO ELABORATE FOOTING IS NEEDED, SINCE THE STONES CAN MOVE WITH ANY FROST. FOR WET WALLS (MORTAR) GO BELOW FROST LINE WITH BOTTOM OF WALL

GRADE

BATTER 2" PER EACH (1'-0") HEIGHT DRY WALLS; 1" WET WALLS

TILT STONES INTO THE HILL

GRAVEL FILL

DRAIN

6"

BASE VARIES - TYP. 16" FOR WALLS ± 2' HIGH

STONE WALL

COPING

4" STONE VENEER

12" CMU

24" x 8" CONCRETE FOOTING

OMIT 1 VERT JOINT AT 4'-0" O.C. FOR WEEPS

BRICK ROWLOCK OVER 4" x 16" CONCRETE BEAM WITH 2 NO. 4 Ø BARS

GRADE

GALVANIZED WALL TIE

PLASTIC WEEP TUBE

8" CMU

GRAVEL

DRAIN

FROST LINE

STONE VENEER WALL

BRICK ROWLOCK

1½"

1½"

MOWING STRIP

GRAVEL

8" x 8" CONCRETE WITH 2 NO. 3 Ø BARS CONT.

A LOW WALL, AS SHOWN, WILL NOT TYPICALLY REQUIRE VERTICAL REINFORCING. A 12" WIDE WALL MAY BE USED FOR VISUAL IMPACT

BRICK WALL

STONE AND MASONRY APPLICATIONS

Charles R. Heuer, FAIA; Covenants; Somerville, Massachusetts

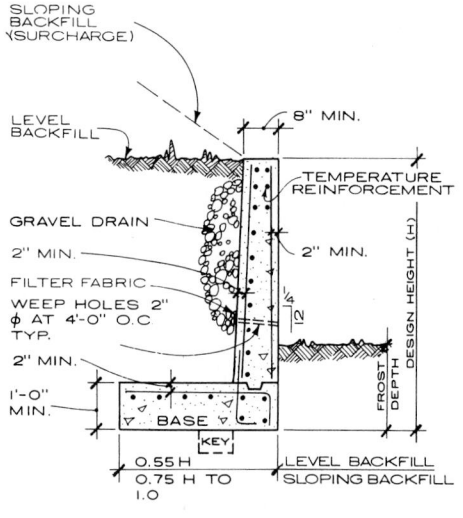

Place base below frost line. Dimensions are approximate.

L-TYPE RETAINING WALLS

Soil pressure at toe equals 0.2 times the height in kips per square foot. Dimensions are preliminary.

GRAVITY RETAINING WALL

VERTICAL CONTROL JOINT

VERTICAL EXPANSION JOINT

RETAINING WALL JOINTS

NOTES

Provide control and/or construction joints in concrete retaining walls about every 25 ft and expansion joints about every fourth control and/or construction joint. Coated dowels should be used if average wall height on either side of a joint is different.

Consult with a structural engineer for final design of concrete retaining walls. An engineer's seal may be required for final design approval by local code officials.

Use temperature bars if wall is more than 10 in. thick.

Keys shown dashed may be required to prevent sliding in high walls and those on moist clay.

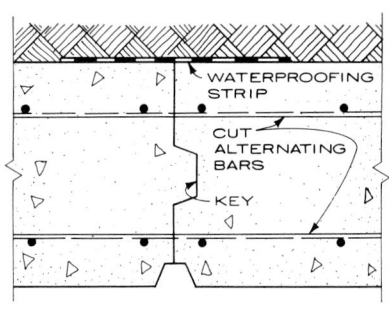

PRELIMINARY DIMENSIONS

BACKFILL SLOPING ϕ = 29° 45' (1¾:1) APPROXIMATE CONCRETE DIMENSIONS					BACKFILL LEVEL—NO SURCHARGE APPROXIMATE CONCRETE DIMENSIONS				
HEIGHT OF WALL H (FT)	WIDTH OF BASE B (FT)	WIDTH OF WALL a (FT)	HEEL b (FT)	TOE c (FT)	HEIGHT OF WALL H (FT)	WIDTH OF BASE B (FT)	WIDTH OF WALL a (FT)	HEEL b (FT)	TOE c (FT)
3	2'-8''	0'-9''	1'-5''	0'-6''	3	2'-1''	0'-8''	1'-0''	0'-5''
4	3'-5''	0'-9''	2'-0''	0'-8''	4	2'-8''	0'-8''	1'-7''	0'-5''
5	4'-6''	0'-10''	2'-6''	1'-2''	5	3'-3''	0'-8''	2'-2''	0'-5''
6	5'-4''	0'-10''	2'-11''	1'-7''	6	3'-9''	0'-8''	2'-5''	0'-8''
7	6'-3''	0'-10''	3'-5''	2'-0''	7	4'-2''	0'-8''	2'-6''	1'-0''
8	7'-0''	1'-0''	3'-8''	2'-4''	8	4'-8''	1'-0''	2'-8''	1'-0''
9	7'-6''	1'-0''	4'-2''	2'-4''	9	5'-2''	1'-0''	3'-2''	1'-0''
10	8'-6''	1'-0''	4'-9''	2'-9''	10	5'-9''	1'-0''	3'-7''	1'-2''
11	11'-0''	1'-1''	7'-2''	2'-9''	11	6'-7''	1'-1''	4'-1''	1'-5''
12	12'-0''	1'-2''	7'-10''	3'-0''	12	7'-3''	1'-2''	4'-7''	1'-6''
13	13'-0''	1'-4''	8'-5''	3'-3''	13	7'-10''	1'-2''	5'-0''	1'-8''
14	14'-0''	1'-5''	9'-1''	3'-6''	14	8'-5''	1'-3''	5'-5''	1'-9''
15	15'-0''	1'-6''	9'-9''	3'-9''	15	9'-0''	1'-4''	5'-9''	1'-11''
16	16'-0''	1'-7''	10'-5''	4'-0''	16	9'-7''	1'-5''	6'-2''	2'-0''
17	17'-0''	1'-8''	11'-1''	4'-3''	17	10'-3''	1'-6''	6'-7''	2'-2''
18	18'-0''	1'-10''	11'-8''	4'-6''	18	10'-10''	1'-6''	7'-1''	2'-3''
19	19'-0''	1'-11''	12'-4''	4'-9''	19	11'-5''	1'-7''	7'-5''	2'-5''
20	20'-0''	2'-0''	13'-0''	5'-0''	20	12'-0''	1'-8''	7'-10''	2'-6''
21	21'-0''	2'-2''	13'-7''	5'-3''	21	12'-7''	1'-9''	8'-2''	2'-8''
22	22'-0''	2'-4''	14'-4''	5'-4''	22	13'-3''	1'-11''	8'-7''	2'-9''

T-TYPE RETAINING WALLS

Kenneth D. Franch, AIA, PE; Phillips Swager Associates, Inc.; Dallas, Texas
Neubaur Sohn, Engineers; Washington, D.C.

DIMENSIONS AND REINFORCEMENT

WALL	H	B	T	A	"V" BARS	"F" BARS
8''	3' 4''	2' 4''	9''	8''	#3 @ 32''	#3 @ 27''
	4' 0''	2' 9''	9''	10''	#4 @ 32''	#3 @ 27''
	4' 8''	3' 4''	10''	12''	#5 @ 32''	#3 @ 27''
	5' 4''	3' 8''	10''	14''	#4 @ 16''	#4 @ 30''
	6' 0''	4' 2''	12''	16''	#6 @ 24''	#4 @ 25''
12''	5' 4''	3' 8''	10''	14''	#4 @ 24''	#3 @ 25''
	6' 0''	4' 2''	12''	15''	#4 @ 16''	#4 @ 30''
	6' 8''	4' 6''	12''	16''	#6 @ 24''	#4 @ 22''
	7' 4''	4' 10''	12''	18''	#5 @ 16''	#5 @ 26''
	8' 0''	5' 4''	12''	20''	#7 @ 24''	#5 @ 21''
	8' 8''	5' 10''	14''	22''	#6 @ 8''	#6 @ 26''
	9' 4''	6' 2''	14''	24''	#8 @ 8''	#6 @ 21''

NOTE: See General Notes for design parameters.

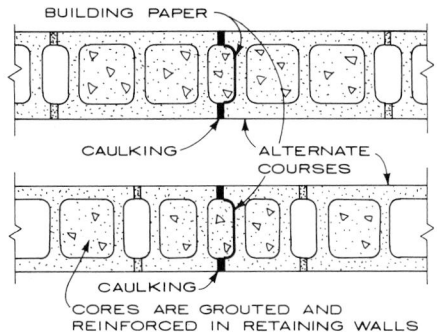

SHEAR - RESISTING CONTROL JOINT

NOTE

Long retaining walls should be broken into panels 20 ft. to 30 ft. long by vertical control joints designed to resist shear and other lateral forces while permitting longitudinal movement.

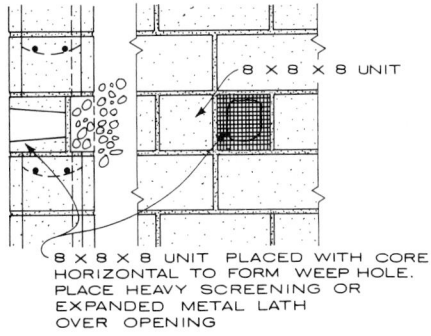

8 X 8 X 8 UNIT PLACED WITH CORE HORIZONTAL TO FORM WEEP HOLE. PLACE HEAVY SCREENING OR EXPANDED METAL LATH OVER OPENING

ALTERNATE WEEP HOLE DETAIL

NOTE

Four inch diameter weepholes located at 5 to 10 ft spacing along the base of the wall should be sufficient. Place about 1 cu ft of gravel or crushed stone around the intake of each weephole.

GENERAL NOTES

1. Materials and construction practices for concrete masonry retaining walls should comply with "Building Code Requirements for Concrete Masonry Structures (ACI 531)."

2. Use fine grout where grout space is less than 3 in. in least dimension. Use coarse grout where the least dimension of the grout space is 3 in. or more.

3. Steel reinforcement should be clean, free from harmful rust, and in compliance with applicable ASTM standards for deformed bars and steel wire.

4. Alternate vertical bars may be stopped at wall midheight. Vertical reinforcement usually is secured in

place after the masonry work has been completed and before grouting.

5. Designs herein are based on an assumed soil weight (vertical pressure) of 100 pcf. Horizontal pressure is based on an equivalent fluid weight for the soil of 45 pcf.

6. Walls shown are designed with a safety factor against overturning of not less than 2 and a safety factor against horizontal sliding of not less than 1.5. Computations in the table for wall heights are based on level backfill. One method of providing for additional loads due to sloping backfill or surface loads is to consider them as an additional depth of soil, that is, an extra load of 300 psf can be treated as 3 ft. of extra soil weighing 100 psf.

7. Top of masonry retaining walls should be capped or otherwise protected to prevent entry of water into unfilled hollow cells and spaces. If bond beams are used, steel is placed in the beams as the wall is constructed. Horizontal joint reinforcement may be

placed in each joint (8 in. o.c.) and the bond beams omitted.

8. Allow 24 hours for masonry to set before grouting. Pour grout in 4 ft. layers, 1 hour between each pour. Break long walls into panels of 20 ft. to 30 ft. in length with vertical control joints. Allow 7 days for finished wall to set before backfilling. Prevent water from accumulating behind wall by means of 4 in. diameter weepholes at 5 ft. to 10 ft. spacing (with screen and graded stone) or by a continuous drain with felt-covered open joints combined with waterproofing.

9. Where backfill height exceeds 6 ft., provide a key under the footing base to resist the wall's tendency to slide horizontally.

10. Heavy equipment used in backfilling should not approach closer to the top of the wall than a distance equal to the height of the wall.

11. A structural engineer should be consulted for final design.

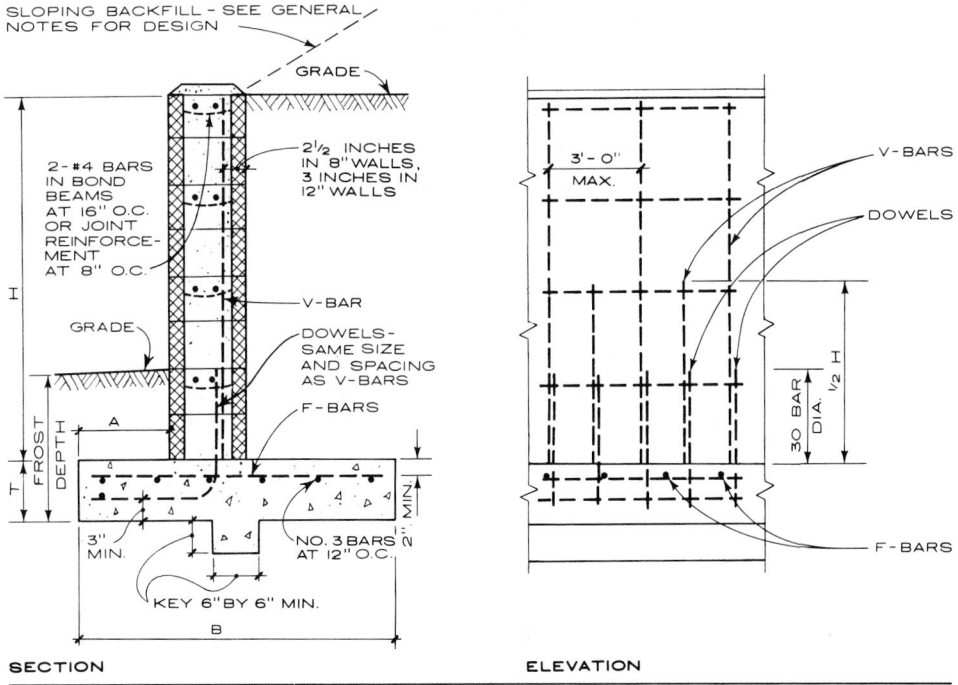

SECTION   **ELEVATION**

TYPICAL CANTILEVER RETAINING WALL

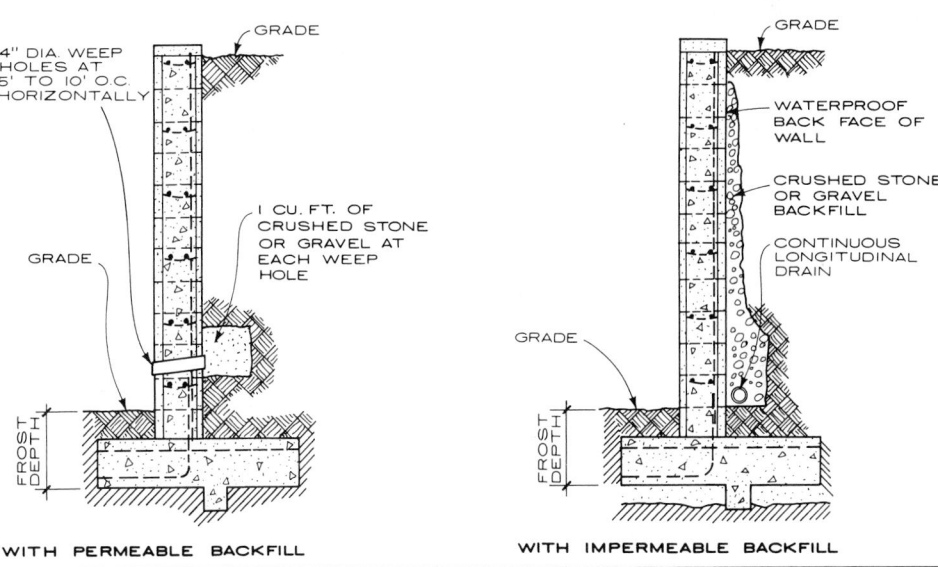

WITH PERMEABLE BACKFILL   **WITH IMPERMEABLE BACKFILL**

DRAINAGE DETAILS FOR VARYING SOIL CONDITIONS

Kenneth D. Franch, AIA, PE; Phillips Swager Associates, Inc.; Dallas, Texas
Stephen J. Zipp, AIA; Wilkes and Faulkner Associates; Washington, D.C.

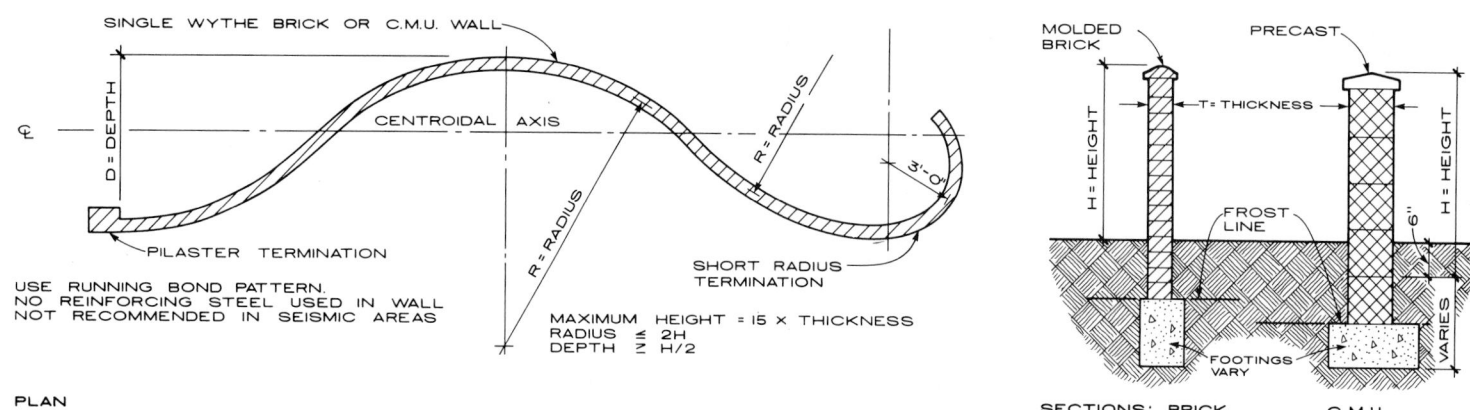

SINGLE WYTHE BRICK OR C.M.U. WALL

CENTROIDAL AXIS

D = DEPTH

R = RADIUS

R = RADIUS

R = RADIUS

3'-0"

SHORT RADIUS TERMINATION

PILASTER TERMINATION

USE RUNNING BOND PATTERN.
NO REINFORCING STEEL USED IN WALL
NOT RECOMMENDED IN SEISMIC AREAS

MAXIMUM HEIGHT = 15 × THICKNESS
RADIUS ≤ 2H
DEPTH ≥ H/2

PLAN
SERPENTINE GARDEN WALLS

MOLDED BRICK   PRECAST

H = HEIGHT   T = THICKNESS   H = HEIGHT

FROST LINE

6"

FOOTINGS VARY   VARIES

SECTIONS: BRICK   C.M.U.

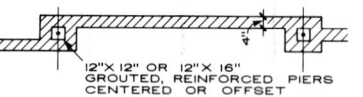

12"× 12" OR 12"× 16"
GROUTED, REINFORCED PIERS
CENTERED OR OFFSET

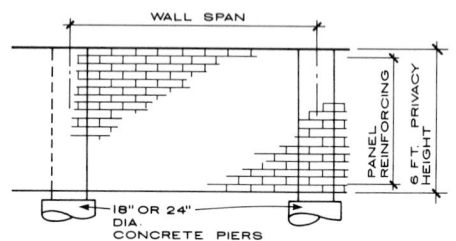

WALL SPAN

PANEL REINFORCING

6 FT. PRIVACY HEIGHT

18" OR 24" DIA. CONCRETE PIERS

REINFORCED WALLS
PIER AND PANEL GARDEN WALLS

PANEL WALL REINFORCING STEEL

WALL SPAN (FT.)	VERTICAL SPACING* (IN.)								
	WIND LOAD 10 PSF			WIND LOAD 15 PSF			WIND LOAD 20 PSF		
	A	B	C	A	B	C	A	B	C
8	45	30	19	30	20	12	23	15	9.5
10	29	19	12	19	12	8.0	14	10	6.0
12	20	13	8.5	13	9.0	5.5	10	7.0	4.0
14	15	10	6.5	10	6.5	4.0	7.5	5.0	3.0
16	11	7.5	5.0	7.5	5.0	3.0	6.0	4.0	2.5

*A, two #2 bars; B, two 3/16 in. diameter wires; C, two 9-gauge wires.
NOTE: Wall spans between piers, no footing.

T = THICKNESS

L = LENGTH

NON-REINFORCED WALLS L/T RATIO

WIND PRESSURE (P.S.F.)	MAXIMUM LENGTH/THICKNESS RATIO
5	35
10	25
15	20
20	18
25	16
30	14
35	13
40	12

NON-REINFORCED WALLS WITH CONTINUOUS FOOTINGS

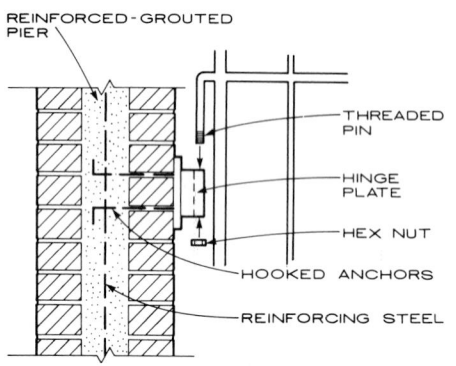

REINFORCED-GROUTED PIER

THREADED PIN

HINGE PLATE

HEX NUT

HOOKED ANCHORS

REINFORCING STEEL

HINGE DETAIL
IRON GARDEN GATE

ANALYSIS OF SECTIONS

M_o = OVERTURNING MOMENT

M_r = RESISTING MOMENT

W = WEIGHT OF WALL AND FOOTING (LB.)

P = WIND LOAD (LB./FT.²) (FROM CODE)

$M_o = PL_1$ $M_r = WL_2$

FOR STABILITY $M_r \geq M_o$;

IF NOT, REDESIGN

CANTILEVER FOOTINGS ARE OFTEN USED AT PROPERTY LINES OR TO INCREASE RESISTANCE TO OVERTURNING. BE SURE TO CHECK FOR WIND FROM EITHER DIRECTION

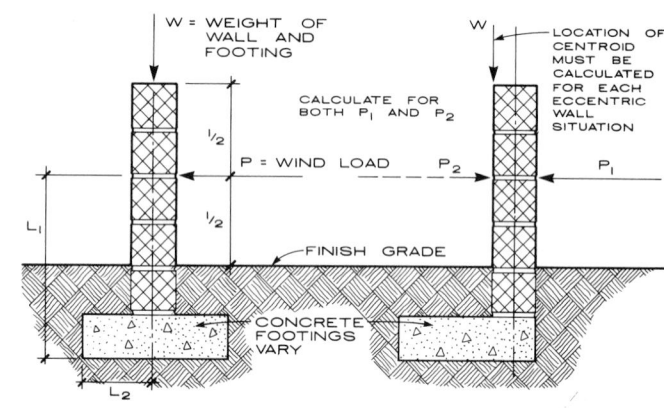

W = WEIGHT OF WALL AND FOOTING

LOCATION OF CENTROID MUST BE CALCULATED FOR EACH ECCENTRIC WALL SITUATION

CALCULATE FOR BOTH P_1 AND P_2

1/2

1/2

L_1

P = WIND LOAD P_2 P_1

FINISH GRADE

CONCRETE FOOTINGS VARY

L_2

SYMMETRICAL   CANTILEVER/ECCENTRIC

HORIZONTAL LOADING - FREESTANDING WALLS

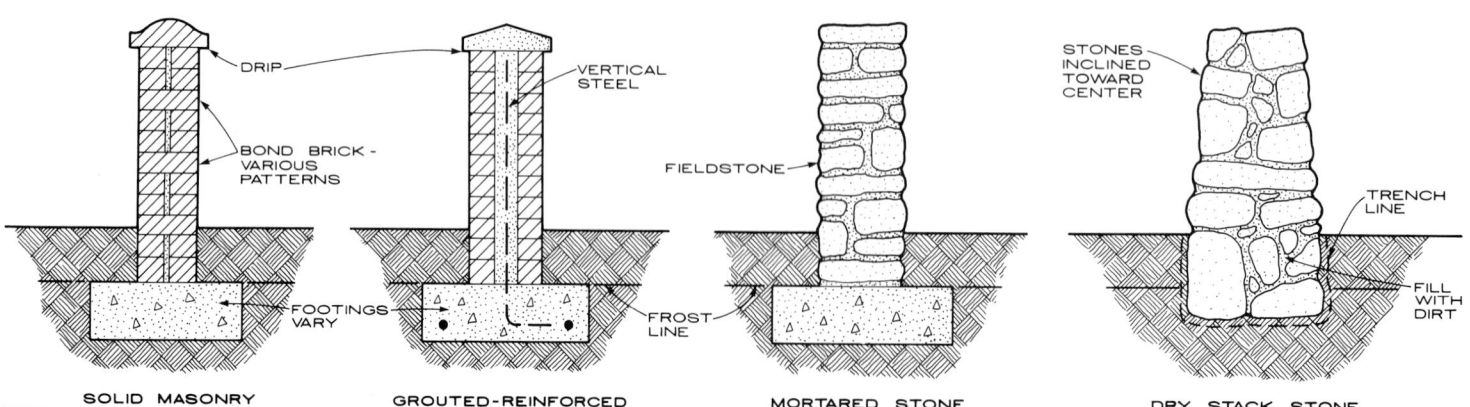

DRIP

BOND BRICK - VARIOUS PATTERNS

VERTICAL STEEL

STONES INCLINED TOWARD CENTER

FIELDSTONE

TRENCH LINE

FOOTINGS VARY

FROST LINE

FILL WITH DIRT

SOLID MASONRY   GROUTED-REINFORCED   MORTARED STONE   DRY STACK STONE

FREESTANDING WALL TYPES

Christine Beall, R.A., CCS; Austin, Texas
Charles R. Heuer, FAIA; Covenants; Somerville, Massachusetts

2   **RETAINING WALLS**

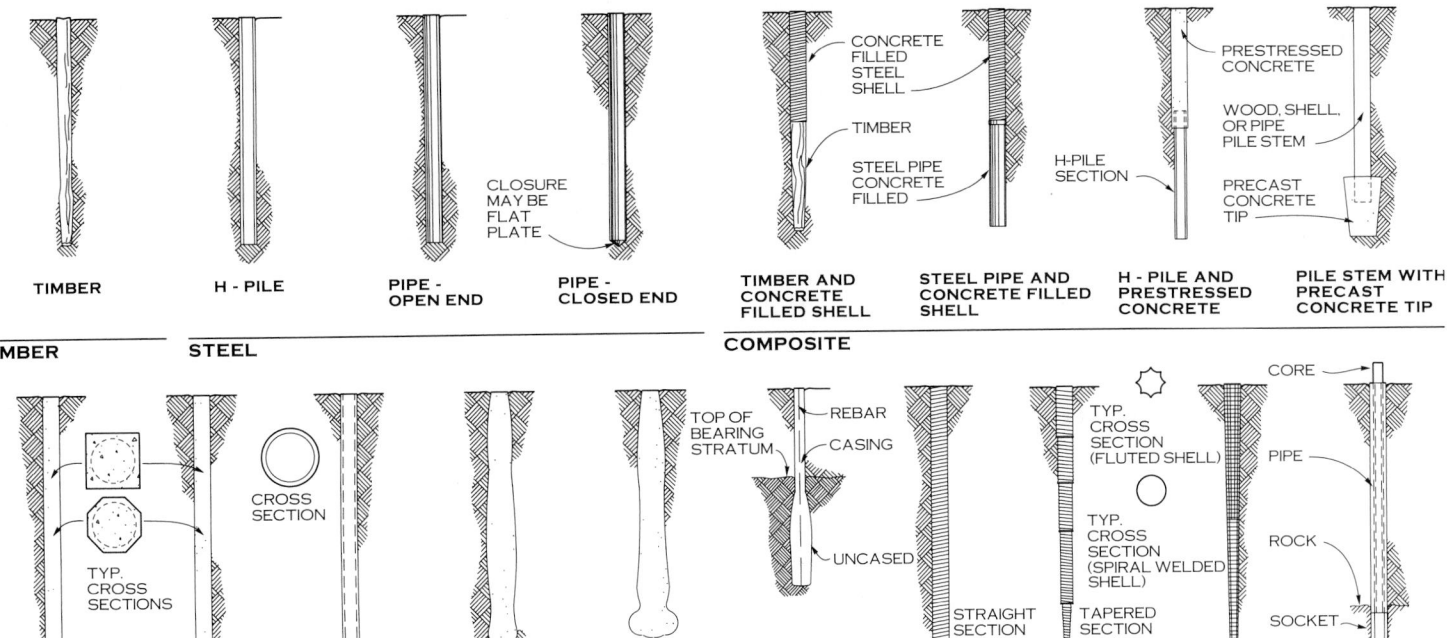

TIMBER   **STEEL**   **COMPOSITE**

CONCRETE

NOTES

1. A mandrel is a member inserted into a hollow pile to reinforce the pile shell while it is driven into the ground.

2. Timber piles must be treated with wood preservative when any portion is above the groundwater table.

3. Uncased piles smaller than 30 inches should be installed using a continuous flight hollow stem auger with grout injected under pressure. Alternatively, a heavy wall casing is used to compact zero slump concrete to enlarge the base of the pile and assure pile continuity.

4. Uncased piers 30 inches in diameter and larger are installed using various types of augers and may be enlarged at the base using a belling tool in some soils. Refer to ACI 336.1 and ACI 336.3.

GENERAL PILE DATA

PILE TYPE	MAXIMUM LENGTH (FT)	OPTIMUM LENGTH (FT)	SIZE (IN.)	MAXIMUM CAPACITY (TONS)	OPTIMUM LOAD RANGE (TONS)	USUAL SPACING
TIMBER						
Timber	110	45 - 65	5 - 10 tip 12 - 20 butt	40	15 - 25	2'- 6" to 3'- 0"
STEEL						
H -pile	250	40 - 150	8 - 14	200	50 - 200	2'- 6" to 3'- 6"
Pipe—open end concrete filled	200	40 - 120	7 - 36	250	50 - 200	3'- 0 "to 4'- 0 "
Pipe—closed end concrete filled	200	30 - 80	10 - 30	200	50 - 70	3'- 0 "to 4'- 0 "
Shell—mandrel concrete filled straight or taper	100	40 - 80	8 - 18	75	40 - 60	3'- 0 "to 3'- 6 "
Shell—no mandrel concrete filled	150	30 - 80	8 - 18	80	30 - 60	3'- 0 "to 3'- 6 "
Drilled-in caisson concrete filled	250	60 - 120	24 - 48	3,500	1,000 - 2,000	6'- 0 "to 8'- 0 "
CONCRETE						
Precast	100	40 - 50	10 - 24	100	40 - 60	3'- 0 "
Prestressed	270	60 - 80	10 - 24	200	100 - 150	3'- 0 "to 3'- 6 "
Cylinder pile	220	60 - 80	36 - 54	500	250 - 400	6'- 0 "to 9'- 0 "
Uncased or drilled piles or piers	120	10 - 50	12 - 120	500	30 - 200	3'- 0 "to 8'- 0 "
Uncased with enlarged base	120	25 - 50	14 - 20	150	40 - 100	6'- 0 "
Minipiles	200	25 - 70	2.5 - 7	100	5 - 40	2'- 0 "to 4'- 0"
COMPOSITE						
Concrete – timber	150	60 - 100	5 - 10 tip 12 - 20 butt	40	15 - 25	3'- 0 "to 3'- 6 "
Concrete – pipe	180	60 - 120	10 - 23	150	40 - 80	3'- 0 "to 4'- 0"
Prestressed concrete H - pile	200	100 - 150	20 - 24	200	120 - 150	3'- 6 "to 4'- 0 "
Precast concrete tip	80	40	13 - 35 tip 19 - 41 butt	180	30 - 150	4'- 6 "

NOTE

Applicable material specifications Concrete-ACI 318; Timber-ASTM D25: Structural Sections ASTM A36, A572, and A690. For selection of type of pile, consult a foundation engineer.

Mueser Rutledge Consulting Engineers; New York, New York

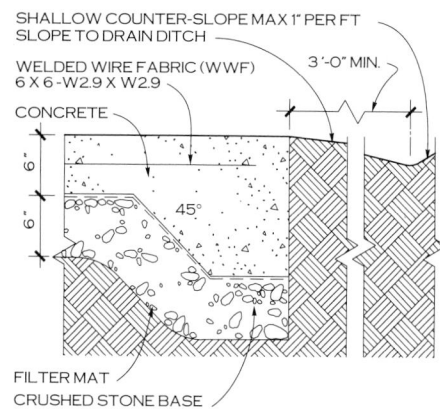

CONCRETE PAVING WITHOUT CURB

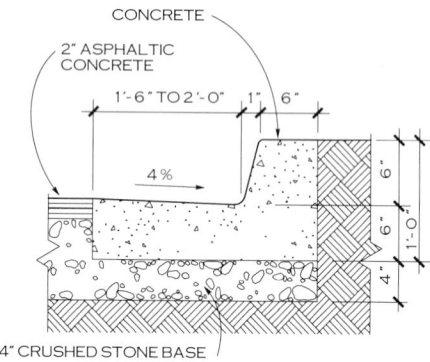

CONCRETE CURB AND GUTTER

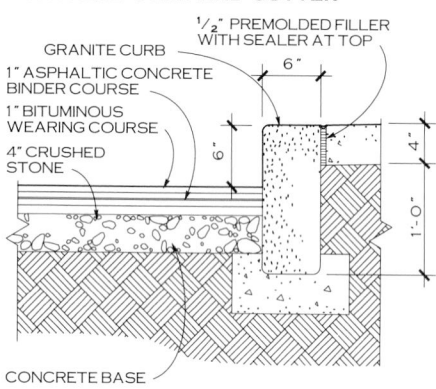

ASPHALT PAVING WITH STONE CURB

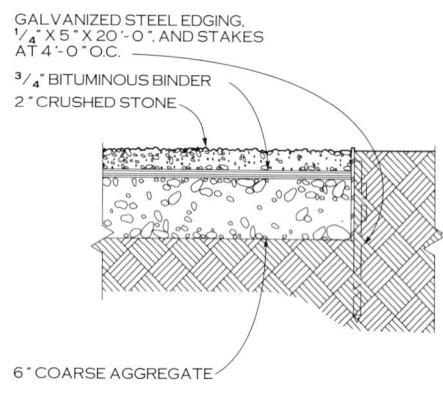

CRUSHED STONE PAVING WITH METAL EDGE

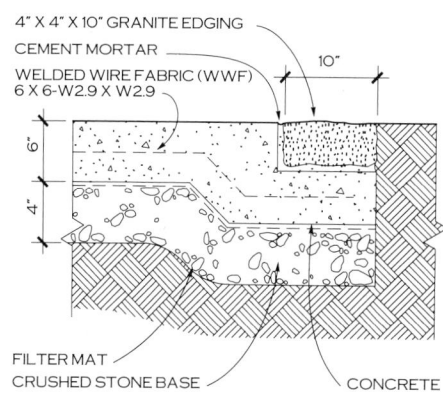

GRANITE EDGING

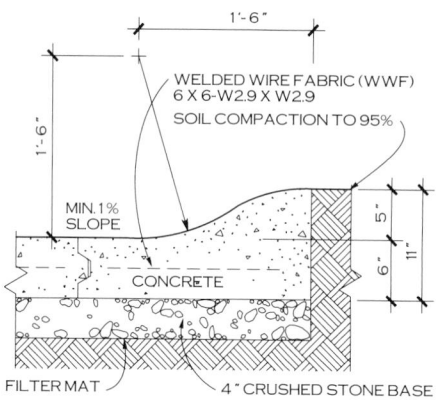

MOUNTABLE CONCRETE CURB

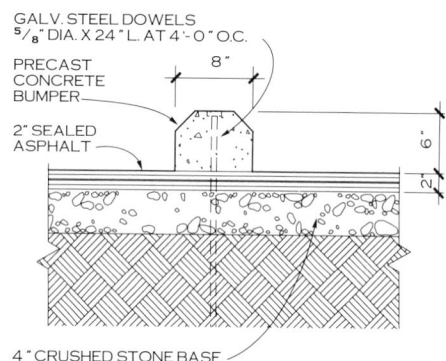

ASPHALT PAVING WITH PRECAST CONCRETE BUMPER

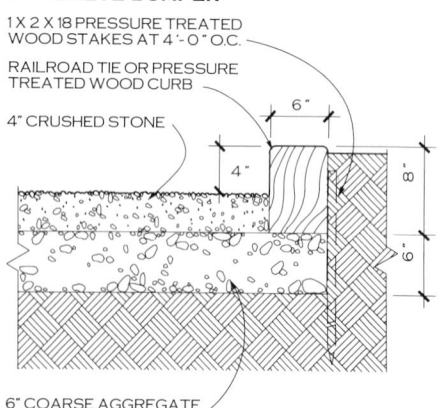

CRUSHED STONE PAVING WITH TIMBER CURB

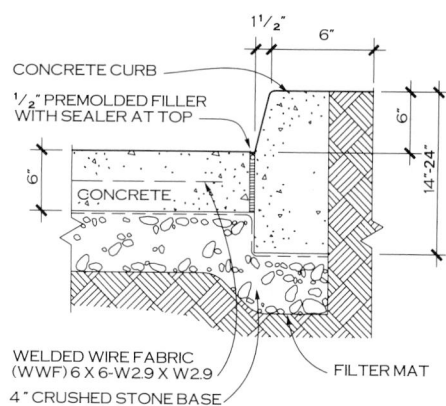

SEPARATE CONCRETE CURB

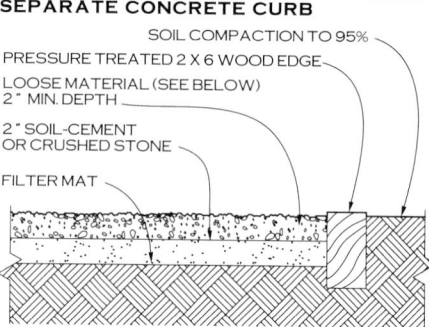

LOOSE MATERIAL SIZES
WOOD CHIPS – 1"
CRUSHED STONE – 1/2" - 3/4"
PEA GRAVEL

LOOSE MATERIAL PAVING (WOOD EDGE)

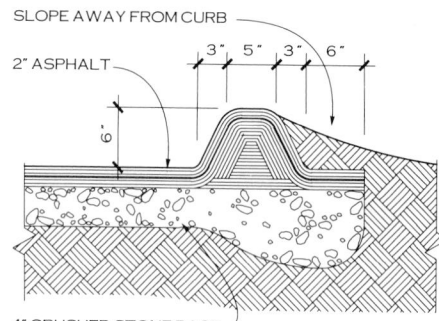

NOTE

Not recommended as a wheel stop.

ASPHALT PAVING AND CURB

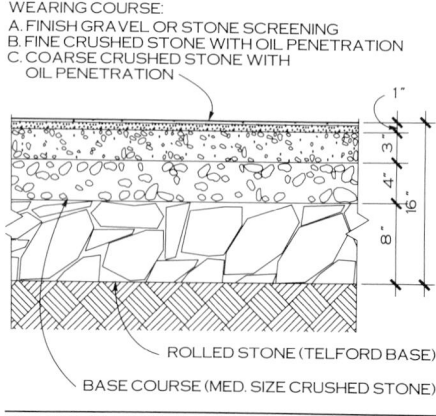

CRUSHED STONE MACADAM PAVING

Charles A. Szoradi, AIA; Washington, D.C.
Francisco Menendez; Washington, D.C.

2 **PAVING AND SURFACING**

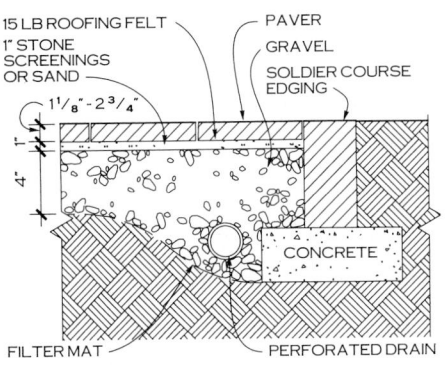

BRICK, CLAY TILE, OR ASPHALT BLOCK PAVERS OVER GRAVEL BASE

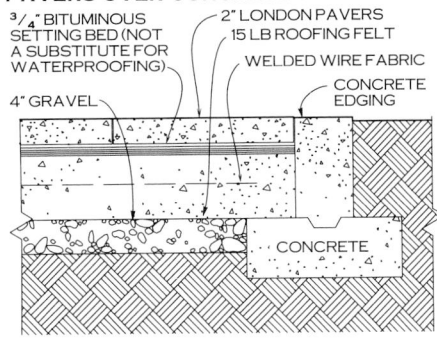

BRICK, CLAY TILE, OR ASPHALT BLOCK PAVERS OVER CONCRETE BASE

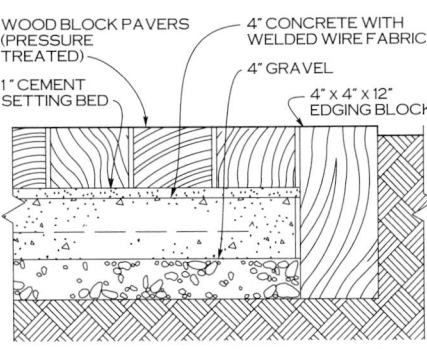

WOODBLOCK PAVERS OVER CONCRETE BASE

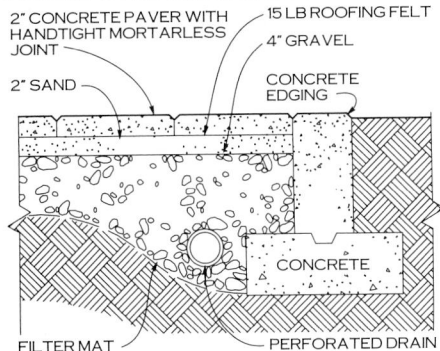

CONCRETE PAVERS OR LONDON WALKS OVER GRAVEL BASE

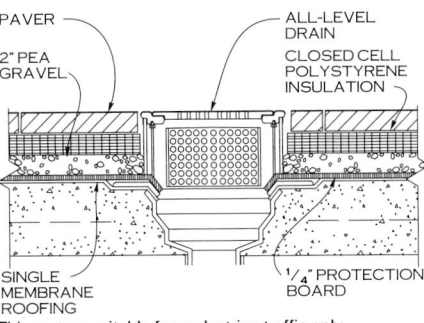

This system suitable for pedestrian traffic only.

CONCRETE PAVERS OR LONDON WALKS OVER CONCRETE BASE

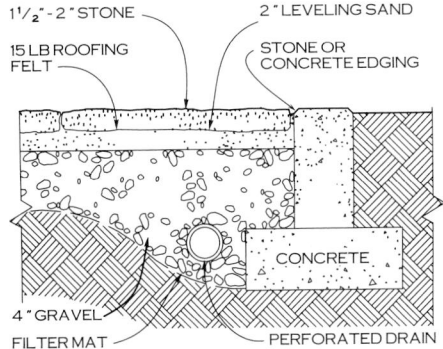

CUT STONE PAVERS OVER SAND AND GRAVEL BASE

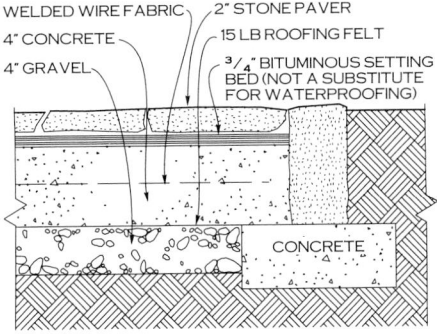

SLATE PAVERS OVER CONCRETE BASE

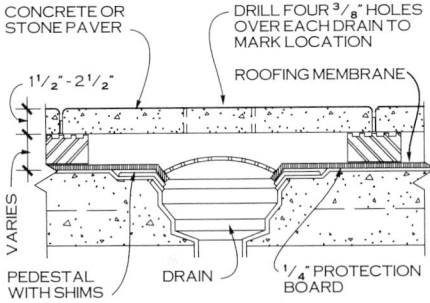

BRICK IS CLAY TILE, ASPHALT BLOCK, CONCRETE, OR STONE PAVERS OVER SUSPENDED BASE

Finish surface: level, joints acting as drains.
Drainage surface: slope to drain $1/8$" – $1/4$" per ft.

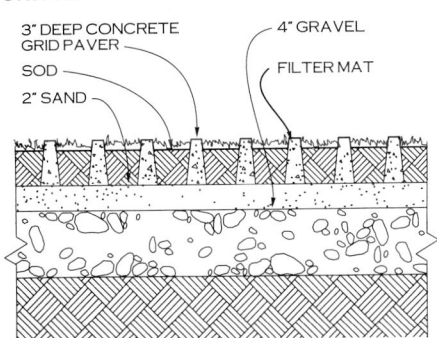

This preformed lattice unit grids are used for storm runoff control, pathways, parking areas, and soil conservation.

GRID PAVING BLOCKS OVER GRAVEL BASE

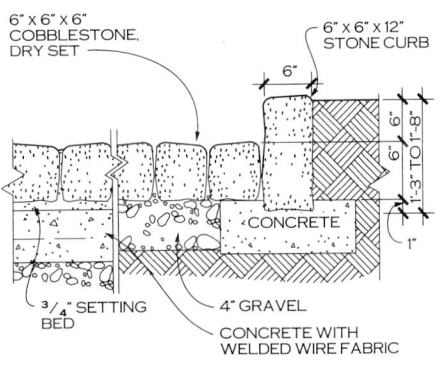

COBBLESTONE PAVERS OVER CONCRETE OR GRAVEL BASE

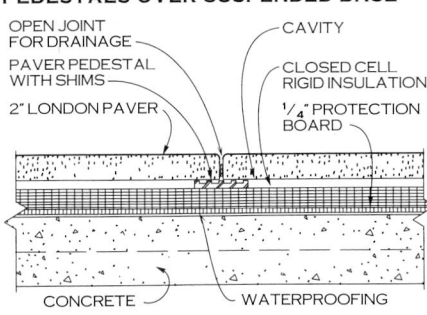

This system is suitable for pedestrian traffic only. Rigid insulation shall be suitable to carry pedestrian loads.

CONCRETE OR CUT STONE PAVER ON PEDESTALS OVER SUSPENDED BASE

LONDON PAVERS ON PEDESTALS OVER SUSPENDED BASE AND CAVITY

NOTES

1. Drainpipes may be omitted at well-drained areas.
2. Provide positive outflow for drainpipes.
3. Do not use unsatisfactory soil (expanding organic).
4. Satisfactory soil shall be compacted to 95%.

Charles A. Szoradi, AIA; Washington, D.C.

5. Flexible and suspended bases shown are for light duty traffic.
6. Handtight paving joints are preferred over mortar joints. Where mortar joints are required and freezing and thawing are frequent, use latex modified mortar.

7. Concrete footing for edging: 10 to 14 in. wide; 6 to 8 in. deep. Bottom of footing is placed preferably at freezing depth.
8. If freezing, depth is deeper than bottom of footing; provide 4 in. gravel under footing.

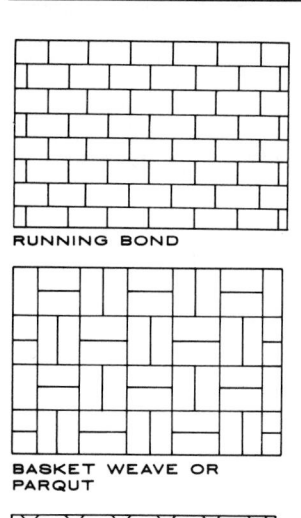
RUNNING BOND

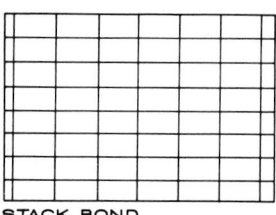
STACK BOND

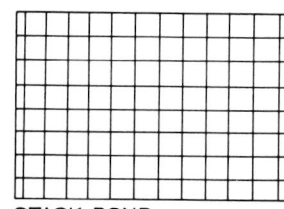
STACK BOND

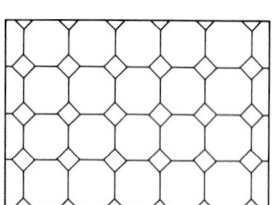
BASKET WEAVE OR PARQUT

HERRINGBONE

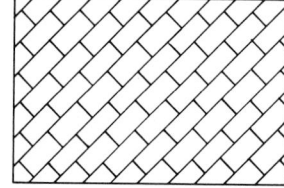
DIAGONAL RUNNING BOND

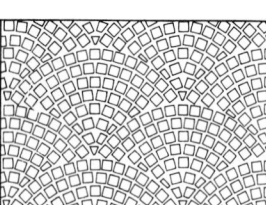
OCTAGON AND DOT

ROMAN COBBLE

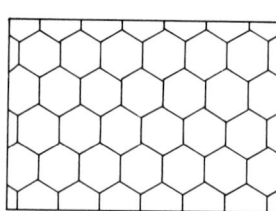
HEXAGON

UNIT PAVERS

TYPICAL UNIT PAVER TYPES AND NOMINAL SIZES

BRICK PAVERS: 4 in. x 4 in., 4 in. x 8 in., 4 in. x 12 in.; ½ in. to 2¼ in. thick.

PRESSED CONCRETE BRICKS: 4 in. x 8 in., 2½ in. to 3 in. thick.

PRESSED CONCRETE PAVERS: 12 in. x 12 in., 12 in. x 24 in., 18 in. x 18 in., 18 in. x 24 in., 24 in. x 24 in., 24 in. x 30 in., 24 in. x 36 in., 30 in. x 30 in., 36 in. x 36 in.; 1½ in. to 3 in. thick.

ASPHALT PAVERS: 5 in. x 12 in., 6 in. x 6 in., 6 in. x 12 in., 8 in. x 8 in., 8 in. hexagonal, 1¼ in. to 3 in. thick.

NOTES
1. Face brick, marble, and granite sometimes are used for paving.
2. See index for tile paver sizes and shapes.
3. Paving patterns shown often are rotated 45° for diagonal patterns.
4. Maximum 3 percent absorption for brick applications subject to vehicular traffic.
5. For pressed concrete and asphalt pavers subject to vehicular traffic, use 3 in. thickness.
6. Use modular size for brick paver patterns other than running and stack bond set with mortar joints. Use full size when set without mortar joints.

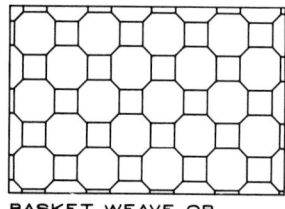
BASKET WEAVE OR PARQUET

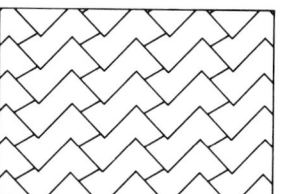
DIAGONAL RUNNING BOND

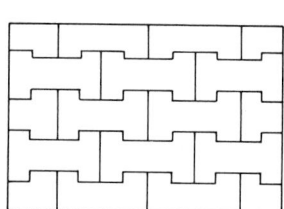
RUNNING BOND

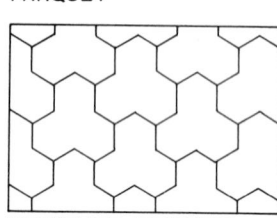
COMBINED HEXAGON

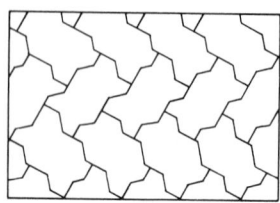
HERRINGBONE

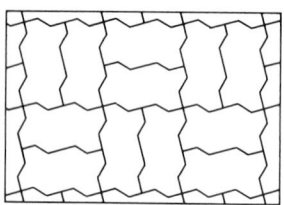
BASKET WEAVE

INTERLOCKING PAVERS

NOTES
1. Interlocking pavers are available in concrete, hydraulically pressed concrete, asphalt, and brick, and in different weight classifications, compressive strengths, surface textures, finishes, and colors. Consult local suppliers for availability.
2. Subject to manufacturer's recommendations and local code requirements, interlocking concrete pavers may be used in areas subject to heavy vehicle loads at 30 to 40 mph speeds.
3. Continuous curb or other edge restraint is required to anchor pavers in applications subject to vehicular traffic.
4. Concrete interlocking paver sizes are based on metric dimensions. Dimensions indicated are to nearest ⅛ in.
5. Where paver shape permits, herringbone pattern is recommended for paving subject to vehicular traffic.
6. Portions have been adapted, with permission, from ASTM C 939.

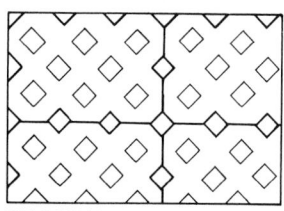
DIAGONAL SQUARES

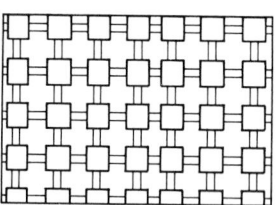
RUNNING SQUARES

RINGS

GRASS PAVERS

NOTES
1. Appearance of grass pavers when voids are filled are shown by stipple to the right of the cut line. Voids may be filled with grass, a variety of ground cover, or gravel.
2. Grass pavers may be used to control erosion.
3. Herringbone pattern is recommended for concrete grass pavers subject to vehicular traffic.
4. Grass rings are available with close ring spacing for pedestrian use or wide ring spacing for vehicular use.

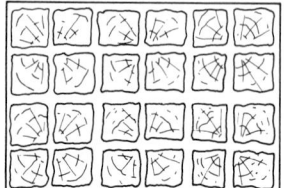
STACK BOND

RANDOM

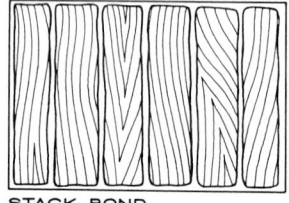
STACK BOND

BASKET WEAVE OR PARQUET

WOOD PAVERS

Jeffrey R. Vandevoort; Talbott Wilson Associates, Inc.; Houston, Texas
John Ray Hoke, Jr., FAIA; Washington, D.C.

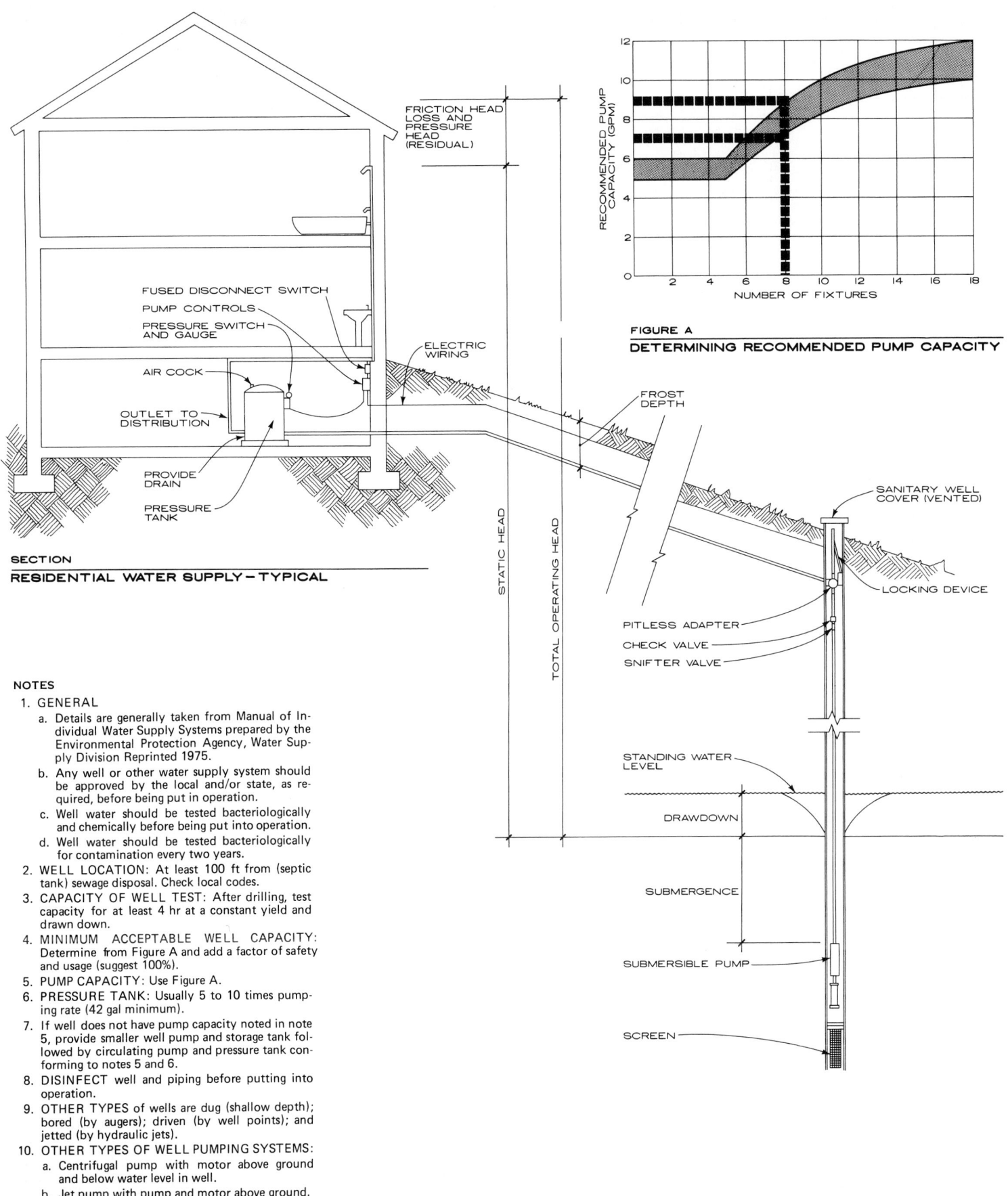

FRICTION HEAD
LOSS AND
PRESSURE
HEAD
(RESIDUAL)

FUSED DISCONNECT SWITCH
PUMP CONTROLS
PRESSURE SWITCH
AND GAUGE
AIR COCK
OUTLET TO
DISTRIBUTION
PROVIDE
DRAIN
PRESSURE
TANK
ELECTRIC
WIRING

SECTION
RESIDENTIAL WATER SUPPLY — TYPICAL

RECOMMENDED PUMP CAPACITY (GPM)
NUMBER OF FIXTURES

FIGURE A
DETERMINING RECOMMENDED PUMP CAPACITY

FROST
DEPTH

STATIC HEAD
TOTAL OPERATING HEAD

SANITARY WELL
COVER (VENTED)
LOCKING DEVICE
PITLESS ADAPTER
CHECK VALVE
SNIFTER VALVE
STANDING WATER
LEVEL
DRAWDOWN
SUBMERGENCE
SUBMERSIBLE PUMP
SCREEN

NOTES

1. GENERAL
   a. Details are generally taken from Manual of Individual Water Supply Systems prepared by the Environmental Protection Agency, Water Supply Division Reprinted 1975.
   b. Any well or other water supply system should be approved by the local and/or state, as required, before being put in operation.
   c. Well water should be tested bacteriologically and chemically before being put into operation.
   d. Well water should be tested bacteriologically for contamination every two years.

2. WELL LOCATION: At least 100 ft from (septic tank) sewage disposal. Check local codes.

3. CAPACITY OF WELL TEST: After drilling, test capacity for at least 4 hr at a constant yield and drawn down.

4. MINIMUM ACCEPTABLE WELL CAPACITY: Determine from Figure A and add a factor of safety and usage (suggest 100%).

5. PUMP CAPACITY: Use Figure A.

6. PRESSURE TANK: Usually 5 to 10 times pumping rate (42 gal minimum).

7. If well does not have pump capacity noted in note 5, provide smaller well pump and storage tank followed by circulating pump and pressure tank conforming to notes 5 and 6.

8. DISINFECT well and piping before putting into operation.

9. OTHER TYPES of wells are dug (shallow depth); bored (by augers); driven (by well points); and jetted (by hydraulic jets).

10. OTHER TYPES OF WELL PUMPING SYSTEMS:
    a. Centrifugal pump with motor above ground and below water level in well.
    b. Jet pump with pump and motor above ground.
    c. Direct or reciprocating pumps in the well with motor above ground.

FIGURE B
DRILLED WELL — SECTION

Jack L. Staunton, PE; Staunton and Freeman, Consulting Engineers; New York, New York

WATER DISTRIBUTION   2

GENERAL NOTES

Seepage and runoff each require special engineering designs to protect against potential water damage. Drainage systems intercept and dispose of the water flow to prevent inordinate damage to an area or facility from seepage and direct runoff.

Subsurface drainage systems are designed to lower the natural water table, to intercept underground flow, and to dispose of infiltration percolating down through soils from surface sources. These systems typically are used under floors, around foundations, in planters, and under athletic fields and courts. Each system must be provided with a positive outfall either by pumped discharge or gravity drain above expected high water levels.

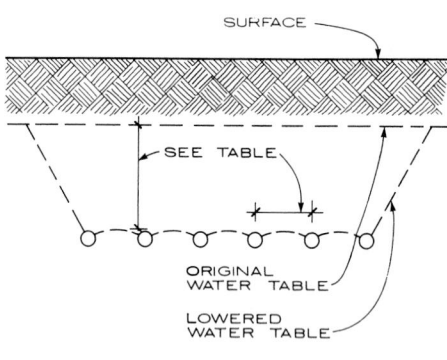

SECTION

Drain layout varies to meet need. May be grid, parallel, herringbone, or random pattern to fit topography.

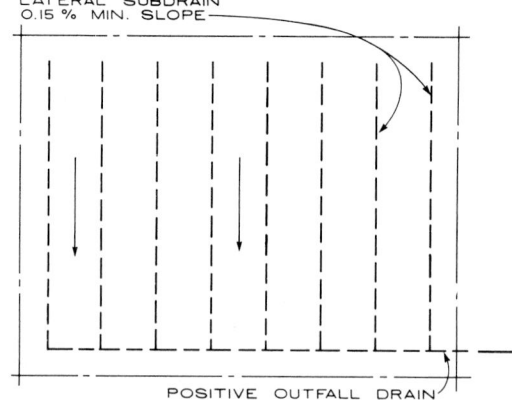

PLAN

Depths indicated in table below are minimum range. Greater depths may be required to prevent frost heave in colder climates or where soils have a high capillarity.

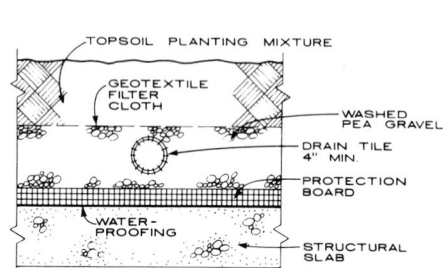

FOOTING DRAIN

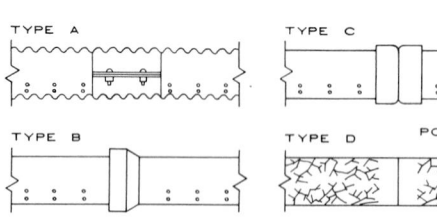

DRAINPIPES

DRAIN TYPE	MATERIAL	JOINT
A	Corrugated metal Flexible plastic	Collars
B	Concrete Clay tile	Bell and spigot
C	Rigid plastic	Sleeve socket
D	Porous concrete	Tongue and groove

SUBSURFACE DRAINPIPES IN GENERAL USE

TYPICAL SECTION

If perforated drain is used, it should be installed with the holes facing down.

When used to intercept sidehill seepage, the bottom of the trench should be cut into underlying impervious material a minimum of 6 in.

DEPTH AND SPACING OF SUBDRAINS RECOMMENDED FOR VARIOUS SOIL CLASSES

SOIL CLASSES	PERCENTAGE OF SOIL SEPARATES			DEPTH OF BOTTOM OF DRAIN (FT)	DISTANCE BETWEEN SUBDRAINS (FT)
	SAND	SILT	CLAY		
Sand	80–100	0–20	0–20	3–4 / 2–3	150–300 / 100–150
Sandy loam	50–80	0–50	0–20	3–4 / 2–3	100–150 / 85–100
Loam	30–50	30–50	0–20	3–4 / 2–3	85–100 / 75–85
Silt loam	0–50	50–100	0–20	3–4 / 2–3	75–85 / 65–75
Sandy clay loam	50–80	0–30	20–30	3–4 / 2–3	65–75 / 55–65
Clay loam	20–50	20–50	20–30	3–4 / 2–3	55–65 / 45–55
Silty clay loam	0–30	50–80	20–30	3–4 / 2–3	45–55 / 40–45
Sandy clay	50–70	0–20	30–50	3–4 / 2–3	40–45 / 35–40
Silty clay	0–20	50–70	30–50	3–4 / 2–3	35–40 / 30–35
Clay	0–50	0–50	30–100	3–4 / 2–3	30–35 / 25–30

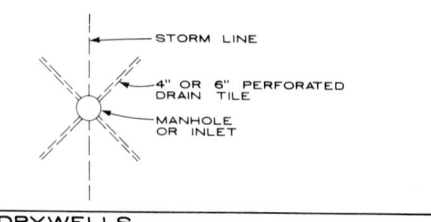

PLANTER DRAIN

DRYWELLS

The effectiveness of drywells is in direct proportion to the porosity of surrounding soils. They should be used only for draining small areas. Extended periods of rainfall runoff cannot be absorbed at the considerably lower percolation rates of most soils. Receiving soils are saturated, rendering the system unworkable. Well is refilled prior to draining completely. Careful design is required to provide the right system for a given soil type.

Harold C. Munger, FAIA; Munger Munger + Associates Architects, Inc.; Toledo, Ohio
Kurt N. Pronske, PE; Reston, Virginia

SURFACE DRAINAGE SYSTEMS: Designed to collect and dispose of rainfall runoff. There are two basic types. One, a ditch/swale and culvert, or open system, is generally used in less densely populated and more open areas where natural surfaces predominate. In urbanized areas where much of the land is overbuilt, the second type is used—the pipe, inlet/catchbasin and manhole, or closed system. Combinations of the two are quite common where terrain and density dictate.

Note that slopes, grates, swales, etc. must be laid out without restricting accessible routes for persons with disabilities.

GENERAL NOTES

1. Lay out grades to allow safe flow away from building if drains becomes blocked.
2. It is generally more economical to keep water on surface as long as possible.
3. Consider the possibility of ice forming on surface when determining slopes for vehicles and pedestrians.
4. Determine which design criteria are set by code or governmental agency, such as intensity and duration of rain storm and allowable runoff.
5. Formulas given are for approximation only. Consult qualified engineer to design the system.

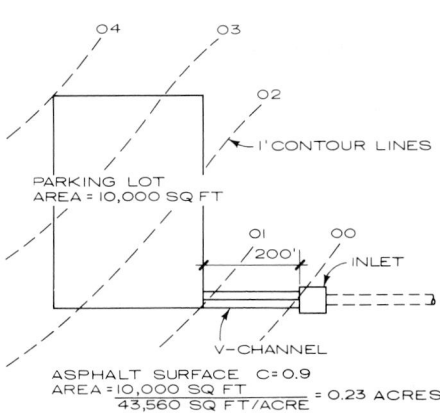

ASPHALT SURFACE C=0.9
$$\frac{\text{AREA} = 10{,}000 \text{ SQ FT}}{43{,}560 \text{ SQ FT/ACRE}} = 0.23 \text{ ACRES}$$

SITE PLAN—EXAMPLE

RATIONAL FORMULA: Simplified method of calculation for areas of less than 100 acres.

Q = CIA
Q = Flow (cu ft/sec)
C = From table (Approximate Values for C)
I = Intensity (in./hr)
   Obtain from local code requirements
A = Area of site (acres)

EXAMPLE: Assume local code requires I = 5 in./hr

Q = CIA
Q = 0.9(5)0.23
  = 1.04 cu ft/sec
  = Approximate volume of water entering the V-channel per second from the parking lot

APPROXIMATE METHOD FOR CALCULATING RUNOFF

APPROXIMATE VALUES FOR C

Roofs	0.95–1.00
Pavement	0.90–1.00
Roads	0.30–0.90
Bare soil	
Sand	0.20–0.40
Clay	0.30–0.75
Grass	0.15–0.60
Developed land	
Commercial	0.60–0.75
High-density residential	0.50–0.65
Low-density residential	0.30–0.55

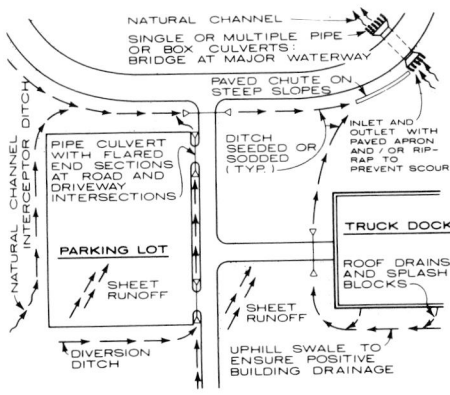

OPEN SYSTEM

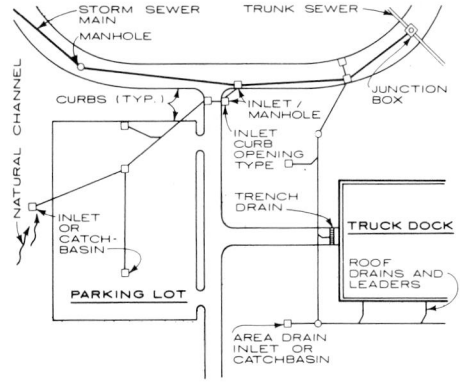

CLOSED SYSTEM

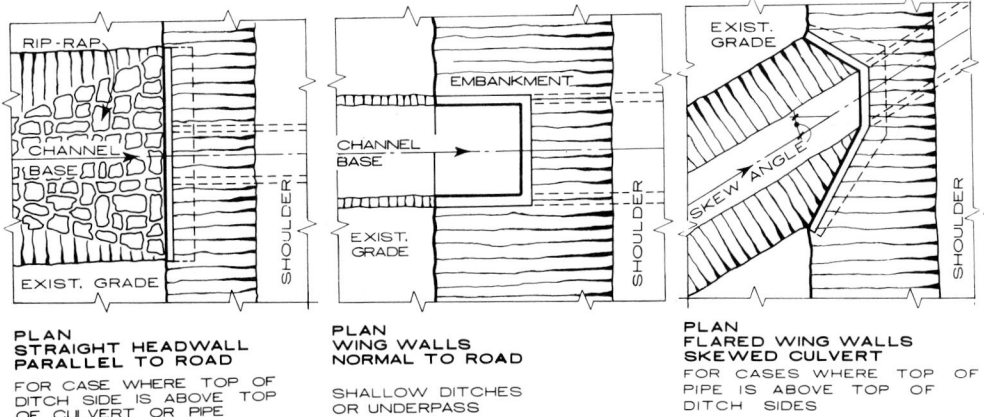

PLAN
STRAIGHT HEADWALL PARALLEL TO ROAD

FOR CASE WHERE TOP OF DITCH SIDE IS ABOVE TOP OF CULVERT OR PIPE

PLAN
WING WALLS NORMAL TO ROAD

SHALLOW DITCHES OR UNDERPASS

PLAN
FLARED WING WALLS SKEWED CULVERT

FOR CASES WHERE TOP OF PIPE IS ABOVE TOP OF DITCH SIDES

HEADWALL DESIGN AS CONTROLLED BY TOPOGRAPHY

MANNING FORMULA

$$V = \left(\frac{1.486}{n}\right) r^{0.67} S^{0.5}$$

= Velocity (ft/sec)
n = From table (n Values for Manning Formula)
r = Hydraulic radius
  See Channel Properties for derivation of r
S = Slope $\left(\dfrac{\text{drop in ft}}{\text{length in ft}}\right)$

EXAMPLE: Assume concrete V-channel

W = 2 ft
h = 0.5 ft
S = 0.005 $\left(\dfrac{1 \text{ ft}}{200 \text{ ft}}\right.$ see site plan—example$\left.\right)$
r = 0.37 (calculated using V-channel properties)
$V = \left(\dfrac{1.486}{0.015}\right)(0.37)^{0.67}(0.005)^{0.5}$
  = 2.6 ft/sec (see runoff velocity table)

CHECK FLOW

Q = Va (a from Channel Properties)
  = 2.6 (0.5) = 1.3 cu ft/sec
  1.04 cu ft/sec required from example above using the Rational Formula; therefore, flow is OK.

n VALUES FOR MANNING FORMULA

CHANNEL SURFACE	n
Cast iron	0.012
Corrugated steel	0.032
Clay tile	0.014
Cement grout	0.013
Concrete	0.015
Earth ditch	0.023
Cut rock channel	0.033
Winding channel	0.025

NOTES

1. Determine velocity with Manning formula.
2. Check flow with formula Q = Va
   a = Cross-sectional area of water in sq ft.
3. For a given Q, adjust channel shape, size, and/or slope to obtain desired velocity (noneroding for earth and grass ditches, etc.)

APPROXIMATE METHOD FOR SIZING CHANNELS

a = Wh
p = 2h + W
$r = \dfrac{Wh}{2h + W}$

a = eh
$p = 2(e^2 + h^2)^{1/2}$
$r = \dfrac{eh}{2(e^2 + h^2)^{1/2}}$

a = h(W_2 + e)
$p = W_2 + 2(e^2 + h^2)^{1/2}$
$r = \dfrac{h(W_2 + e)}{W_2 + 2(e^2 + h^2)^{1/2}}$

$a = \pi h^2/2$
$p = \pi h$
$r = \dfrac{2}{h}$

a = AREA OF WATER SECTION
p = WETTED PERIMETER
r = a/p = HYDRAULIC RADIUS

CHANNEL PROPERTIES

Fred W. Hegel, AIA; Denver, Colorado

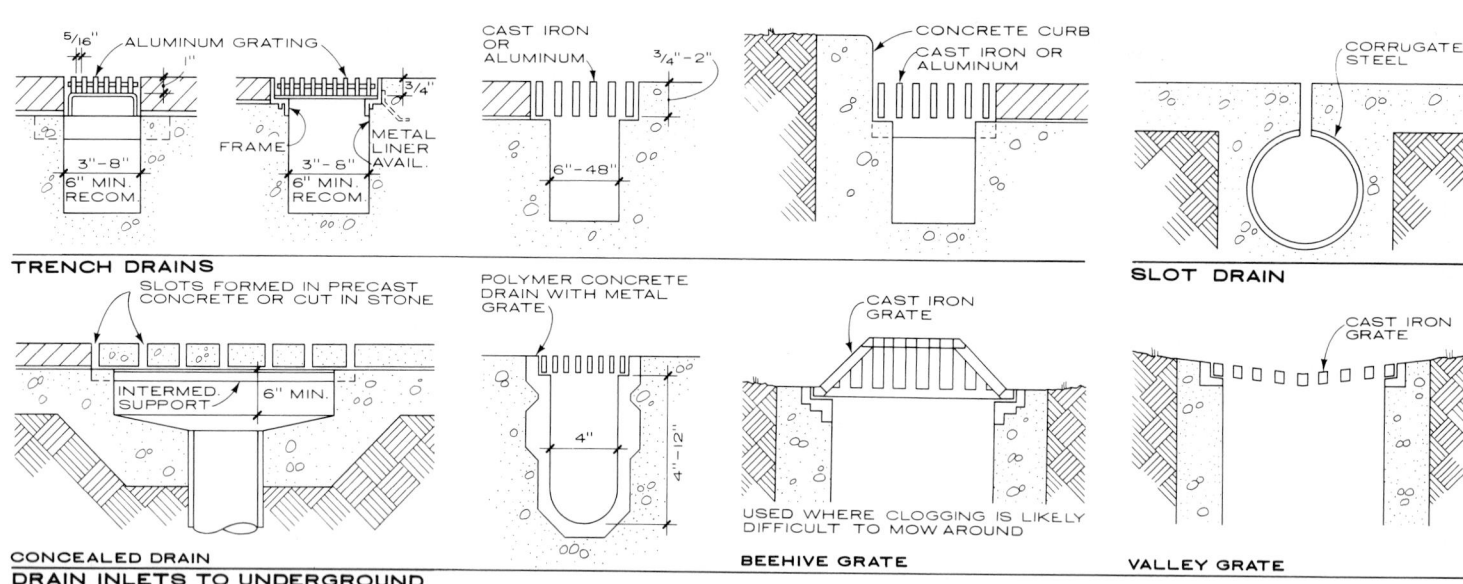

TRENCH DRAINS

SLOT DRAIN

DRAIN INLETS TO UNDERGROUND SYSTEM

CONCEALED DRAIN

BEEHIVE GRATE

VALLEY GRATE

USED WHERE CLOGGING IS LIKELY DIFFICULT TO MOW AROUND

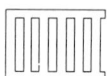 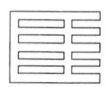   

USE GRATING DESIGNED FOR EXTERIOR USE AND CORRECT WHEEL LOAD
NOTE: SOME GRATES DESIGNED FOR BICYCLE TIRES

GRATING DESIGNS—STANDARD

GRATE SIZING

Most gratings are oversized to prevent a buildup of water. See manufacturers' catalogs for free area.

Formula shown for sizing gratings is based on a given allowable depth of water (d) over the grating.

$$Q = .66 \, CA \, (64.4 \, d)^{.5}$$

A = Free area (square feet)
d = Allowable depth of water above grate (feet)
C = Orifice coefficient
   .6 for square edges
   .8 for round edges
.66 = Clogging factor

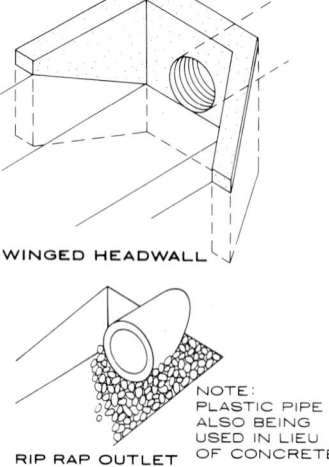

SADDLE HEADWALL

STRAIGHT HEADWALL

WINGED HEADWALL

STRAIGHT ENDWALL

RIP RAP OUTLET

NOTE: PLASTIC PIPE ALSO BEING USED IN LIEU OF CONCRETE.

PLAN
PRECAST CONCRETE END SECTION

PLAN
CORRUGATED STEEL END SECTION

HEADWALLS AND ENDWALLS

Fred W. Hegel, AIA; Denver, Colorado

CHECK DAMS USED WHERE CHANNEL SLOPE AND VELOCITY WILL CAUSE EROSION

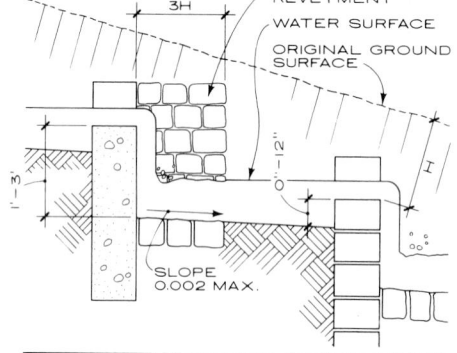

RIPRAP REVETMENT
WATER SURFACE
ORIGINAL GROUND SURFACE

SLOPE 0.002 MAX.

CHECK DAMS

DETENTION

Check with local code requirements for control of storm water and quality of runoff from sites. Many require runoff to be maintained at predevelopment rates. This is accomplished with a detention facility upstream of a controlled outlet structure. The detention basin may be a structure or a paved or grass basin. If soil types permit, seepage may be used to dispose of runoff accumulated in a grass basin. The volume of detention required can be approximated by the following formula:

AMOUNT OF DETENTION:

$$Vol. = (C_{dev.} - C_{hist.})AD$$

D = Design storm depth (inches)
A = Area site (acres)
$C_{dev.}$ = C from table for developed land
$C_{hist.}$ = C from table for land prior to development

SLOPES

DESCRIPTION	MIN. %	MAX. %	REC. %
Grass (mowed)	1	25	1.5–10
(athletic field)	.5	2	1
Walks (Long.)	.5	12*	1.5
(Transv.)	1	4	1–2
Streets (Long.)	.5	20	1–10
Parking	1	5	2–3
Channels			
Grass swale	1	8	1.5–2
Paved swale	.5	12	4–6

*8.3% max. for handicapped

RUN-OFF VELOCITY

VELOCITIES CHANNEL	MIN. FT/SEC	MAX. FT/SEC
Grass	2	4
Concrete	2	10
Gravel	2	3
Asphalt	2	7.5
Sand	.5	1.5

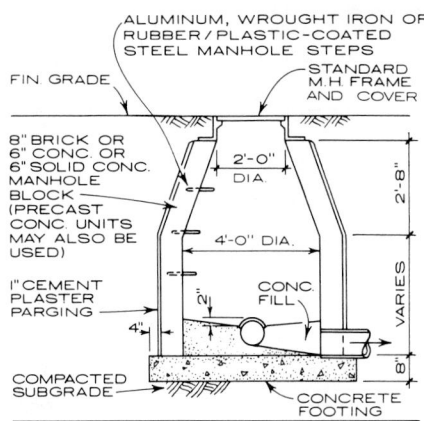

COMBINED OR SANITARY SEWER MANHOLE

NOTES

1. Parging may be omitted in construction of storm sewer manholes.
2. Brick and block walls to be as shown for manholes up to 12 ft deep. For that part of manhole deeper than 12 ft, brick and block walls shall be 12 in. thick. Manholes over 12 ft deep shall have a 12 in. thick base.

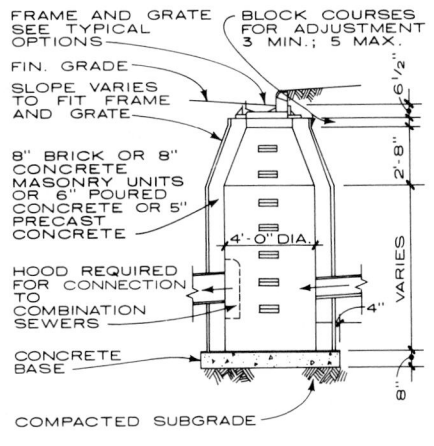

CATCH BASIN

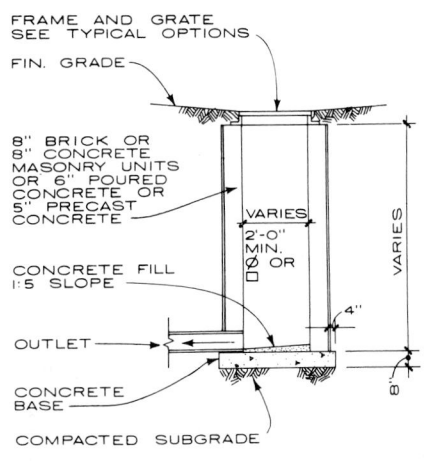

INLET

Kurt N. Pronske, PE; Reston, Virginia

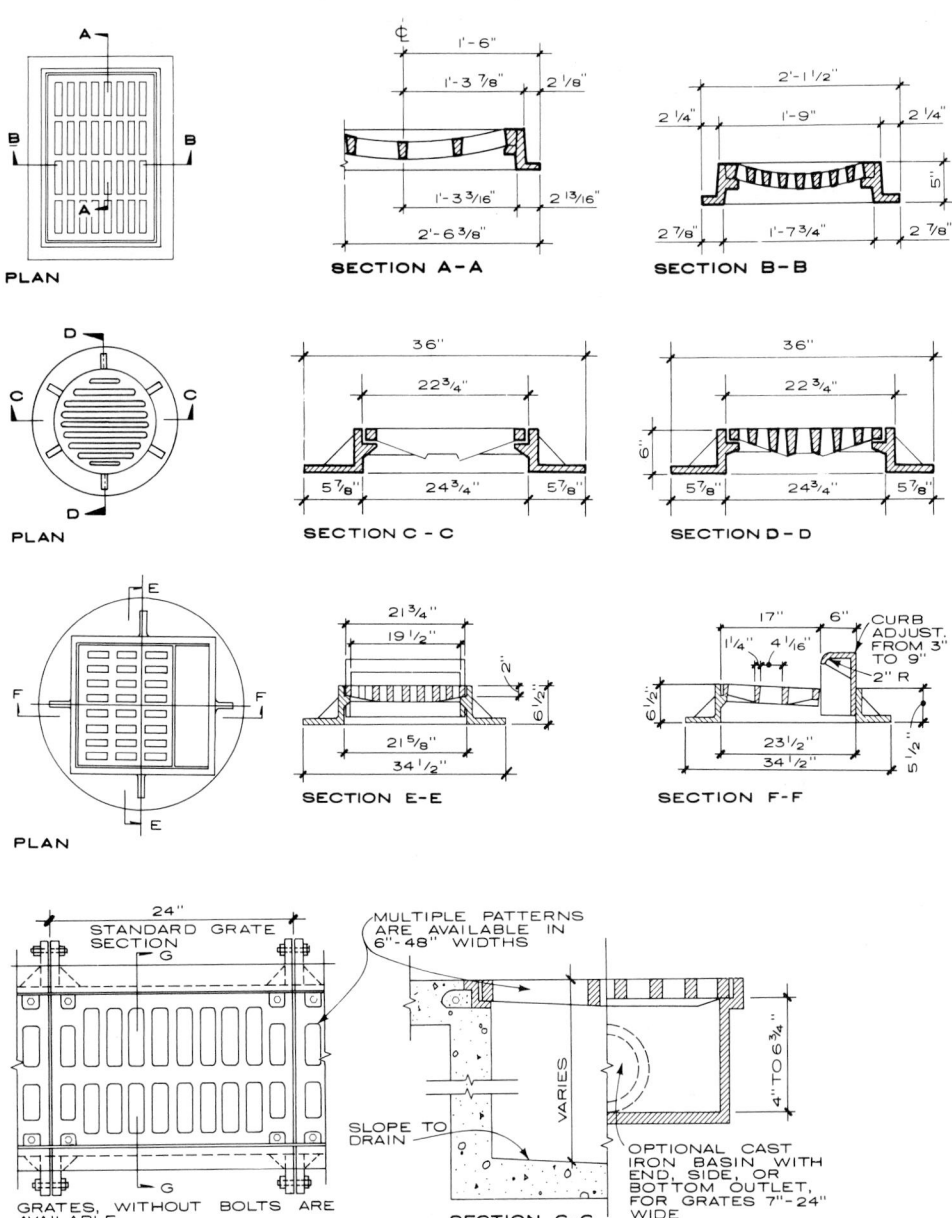

TYPICAL FRAMES AND GRATES

NOTES

1. A great number of standard shapes and sizes of frames and grates are available. They are constructed of cast or ductile iron for light or heavy duty loading conditions. The available shapes are shown above: round, rectangular or square, and linear. In addition, grates may be flat, concave, or convex. Manufacturers' catalogs and local foundries should be consulted for the full range of castings.

2. Drainage structures with grated openings should be located on the periphery of traveled ways or beyond to minimize their contact with pedestrian or vehicular traffic. Grates that will be susceptible to foot or narrow wheel contact must be so constructed as to prevent penetration by heels, crutch and cane tips, and slim tires, but still serve to provide sufficient drainage. This can be done by reducing the size of each unit opening and increasing the overall size or number of grates. Where only narrow wheel use is expected, slotted gratings can be used if the slots are oriented transversely to the direction of traffic.

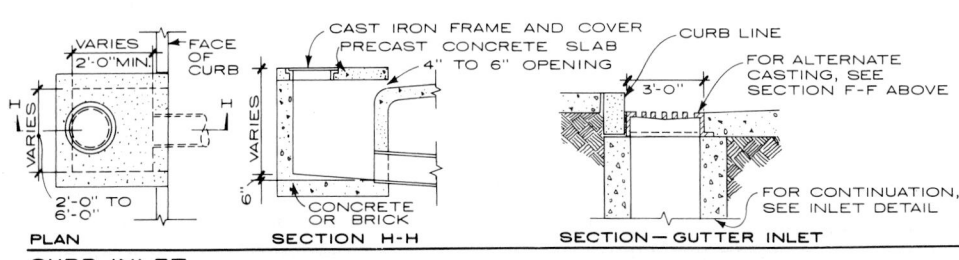

CURB INLET

GENERAL

When a public sewer system is not available to treat and dispose of a building's sewage wastes, a private sewage system is required. The most common system used today is the septic tank. This simple mechanical system treats waste water through anaerobic (not dependent on oxygen) bacteria digesting human waste into a thick sludge, which settles to the bottom and is periodically pumped out. The solid sludge is taken and dumped into the sewer system of a modern treatment plant where it is dried and hauled away to a special landfill dump. Only water—the effluent—is treated and returned to the soil through a leach field. This water, about 70% purified by the septic tank, is further purified by aerobic (dependent on oxygen) bacteria in the leach field.

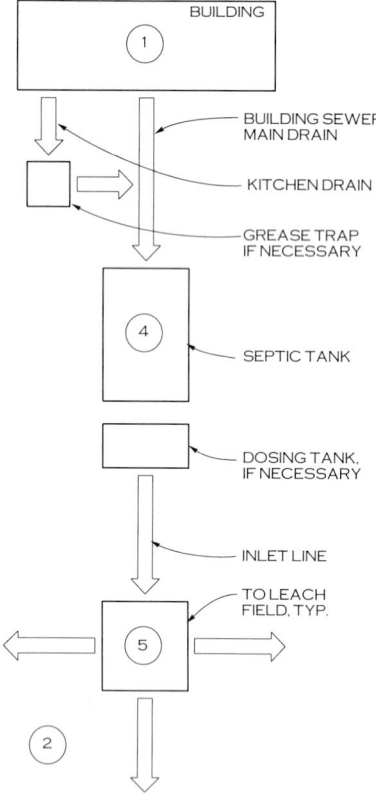

The following is a procedure for planning a private sewage disposal system:

1. Determine quantity of sewage flow (see Table A).
2. Soil and topography study.
   a. Determine type and permeability of soil; make a percolation test (see Table B).
   b. Examine site topography to help choose proper effluent disposal system.
   c. Determine elevation of watertable (groundwater).
   d. Determine proximity of wells and streams (see Table C).
3. Determine requirements of local codes.
4. Design septic tank (see Septic Tank Volume Determination).
5. Choose and layout an effluent disposal system.

NOTES

1. Since various health environmental departments have other standards, consult with them before preparing final designs.
2. Since a septic system is naturally gravity fed, when below-grade toilet fixtures are present a lift pump (which pumps sewage up and out to the septic tank) is needed.
3. Groundwater level shall be at least 2 ft below any effluent disposal system.
4. Package sewage treatment plants are recommended for flows greater than 3500 gallons/day when adequate percolation is not possible.
5. Septic tank and disposal system shall be at least 100 feet from shallow wells and 50 feet from deep wells.

L. James Cooke, Jr., PE; Department of Veterans Affairs; Washington, D.C.

TABLE A. QUANTITIES OF SEWAGE FLOWS

TYPE OF ESTABLISHMENT	GALLONS PER PERSON PER DAY
Airports (per passenger)	5
Bathhouses and swimming pools	10
Camps	
Campground with comfort station	35
Day camps (no meals served)	15
Resort camp (night and day) with limited plumbing	50
Cottages and small dwelling with seasonal occupancy[1]	50
Country clubs (per resident member)	100
Country clubs (per nonresident member)	25
Dwellings	
Boardinghouse[1]	50
Multiple family dwellings (apartment)	60
Single family dwellings[1]	75
Factories (gallons per person, per shift, exclusive of industry wastes)	35
Hospitals (per bed space)	240
Hotels with private baths (2 persons/ room)[2]	60
Institutions other than hospitals (per bed)	100
Laundries, self-service (gallons per wash, i.e., per customer)	50
Mobile home parks (per space)	250
Picnic parks (toilet wastes only, per person)	5
Picnic parks with bathhouses, showers, and flush toilets	10
Restaurants (toilets and kitchen wastes per patron)	10
Restaurants (kitchen wastes/meal served)	3
Restaurants (additional for bars and cocktail lounges)	2
Schools	
Boarding	100
Day, with gym, cafeteria, and showers	25
Service station (per vehicle served)	10
Theaters	
Movie (per auditorium seat)	5
Drive-in (per car space)	5
Travel trailer parks with individual water and sewer hookups	100
Workers	
Day, at schools and offices (per shift)	15

NOTES

1. Two people per bedroom.
2. Use also for motel.

TABLE C. EFFLUENT DISPOSAL SYSTEM LOCATION

MINIMUM DISTANCES (FEET)

FROM TANK	TO LEACH FIELD	TO SEPTIC
Wells (shallow)	100	100
Wells (deep)	50	50
Streams	25	50
Building	10	20
Property line	10	10

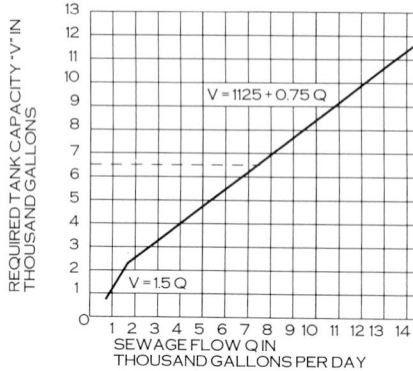

SEPTIC TANK VOLUME DETERMINATION

TABLE B.   ALLOWABLE RATE OF SEWAGE APPLICATION TO A SOIL ABSORPTION SYSTEM

PERCOLATION RATE—TIME (MIN) FOR WATER TO FALL 1 IN.	MAXIMUM RATE OF SEWAGE APPLICATION (GAL/SQ FT/DAY) FOR ABSORPTION TRENCHES,[1] SEEPAGE BEDS, AND SEEPAGE PITS[2]
1 or less	5.0
2	3.5
3	2.9
4	2.5
5	2.2
10	1.6
15	1.3
30	0.9
45 [3]	0.8
60 [3,4]	0.6

NOTES

1. Absorption area for drainage field is figured as trench bottom width and length and 12 in. of side wall and includes a statistical allowance for vertical sidewall area.
2. Absorption area for seepage pits is effective sidewall area.
3. Over 30 is unsuitable for seepage pits.
4. Over 60 is unsuitable for absorption systems. If permissible, use sand filtration system. For subsurface sand filters use 1.15 gal/sq ft/day.

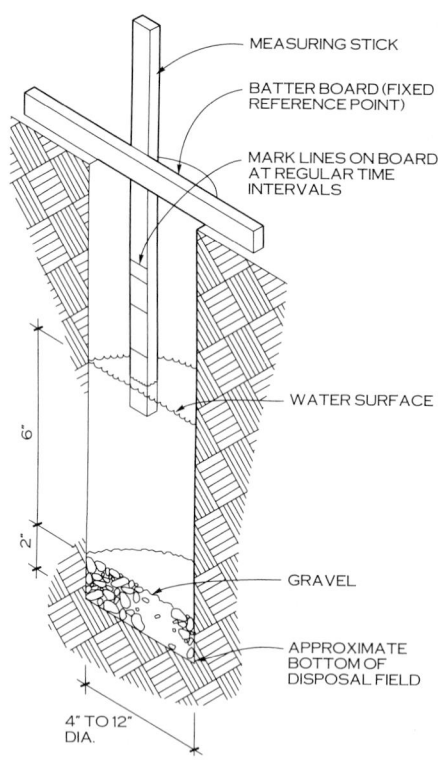

PROCEDURE

First soak hole by filling at least 12 in. over gravel with water and continue to refill with water so that hole is soaked for 24 hours. After 24 hours adjust the depth of water over the gravel to approximately 6 in. Now measure the drop in water level over a 30 minute period.

1. The location and elevation of the test hole are approximately the same as disposal field.
2. This test is recommended by the Environmental Protection Agency; check local requirements for other test conditions.

PERCOLATION TESTS

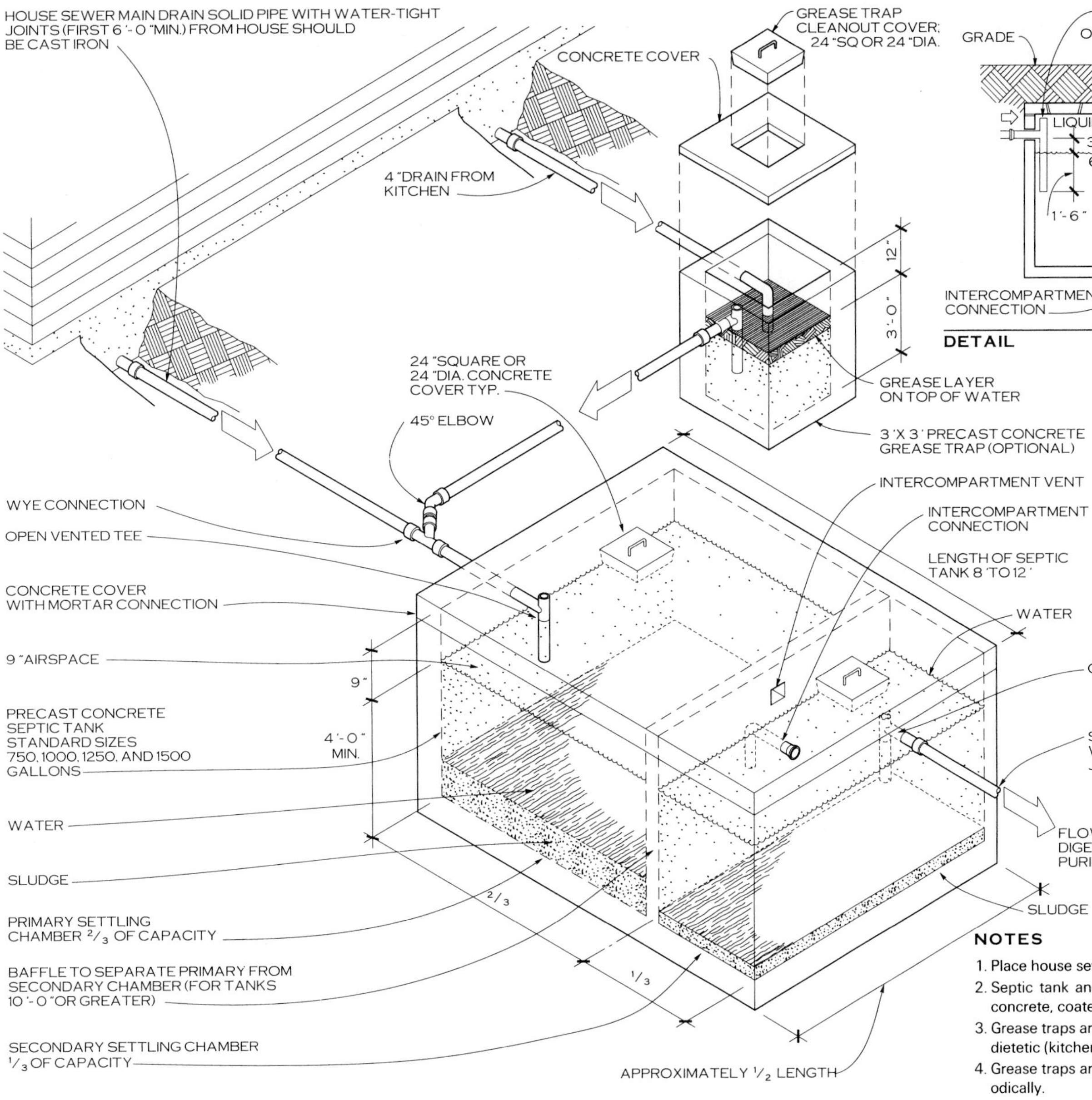

HOUSE SEWER MAIN DRAIN SOLID PIPE WITH WATER-TIGHT JOINTS (FIRST 6'-0"MIN.) FROM HOUSE SHOULD BE CAST IRON

GREASE TRAP CLEANOUT COVER; 24"SQ OR 24"DIA.

CONCRETE COVER

4"DRAIN FROM KITCHEN

GRADE

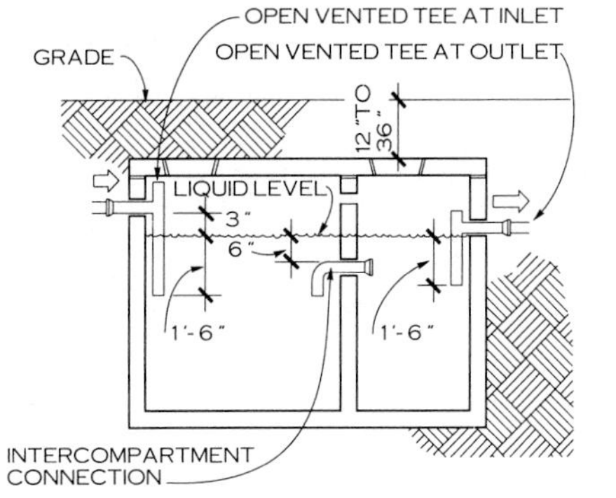

OPEN VENTED TEE AT INLET
OPEN VENTED TEE AT OUTLET

12"TO 36"

LIQUID LEVEL

3"

6"

1'-6"

1'-6"

INTERCOMPARTMENT CONNECTION

DETAIL

12"

3'-0"

24"SQUARE OR 24"DIA. CONCRETE COVER TYP.

45° ELBOW

GREASE LAYER ON TOP OF WATER

3'X 3' PRECAST CONCRETE GREASE TRAP (OPTIONAL)

WYE CONNECTION

OPEN VENTED TEE

CONCRETE COVER WITH MORTAR CONNECTION

9"AIRSPACE

9"

PRECAST CONCRETE SEPTIC TANK STANDARD SIZES 750, 1000, 1250, AND 1500 GALLONS

4'-0" MIN.

WATER

SLUDGE

PRIMARY SETTLING CHAMBER 2/3 OF CAPACITY

BAFFLE TO SEPARATE PRIMARY FROM SECONDARY CHAMBER (FOR TANKS 10'-0"OR GREATER)

SECONDARY SETTLING CHAMBER 1/3 OF CAPACITY

2/3

1/3

APPROXIMATELY 1/2 LENGTH

INTERCOMPARTMENT VENT

INTERCOMPARTMENT CONNECTION

LENGTH OF SEPTIC TANK 8'TO 12'

WATER

OPEN VENTED TEE

SOLID OUTLET PIPE WITH WATER-TIGHT JOINTS

FLOW OF CLARIFIED AND DIGESTED EFFLUENT (ABOUT 70% PURIFIED) TO DISPOSAL SYSTEM

SLUDGE

NOTES

1. Place house sewer below frost line.
2. Septic tank and grease traps are also made from concrete, coated steel, or thick-walled fiberglass.
3. Grease traps are not required unless there is a large dietetic (kitchen disposal) discharge.
4. Grease traps are only to be used if cleaned out periodically.

SEPTIC TANK

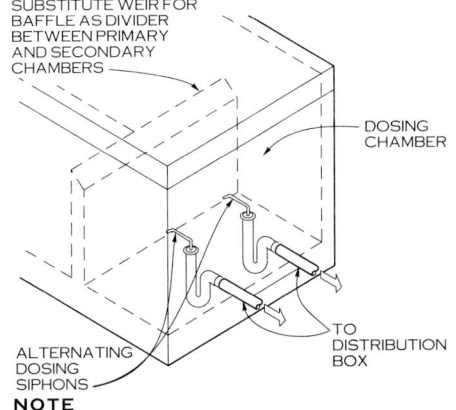

SUBSTITUTE WEIR FOR BAFFLE AS DIVIDER BETWEEN PRIMARY AND SECONDARY CHAMBERS

DOSING CHAMBER

TO DISTRIBUTION BOX

ALTERNATING DOSING SIPHONS

NOTE

Used primarily in larger (e.g., commercial) capacity situations that have large leach fields, effluent is collected in specific amounts, 500 to 1000 gallons at a time. Then it is released quickly to the distribution box in order to flood the leach field intermittently and evenly. Also used in conjunction with sand filter disposal systems.

DOSING OR SIPHON CHAMBER

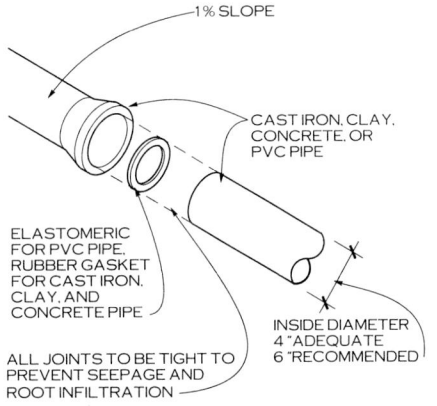

1% SLOPE

CAST IRON, CLAY, CONCRETE, OR PVC PIPE

ELASTOMERIC FOR PVC PIPE, RUBBER GASKET FOR CAST IRON, CLAY, AND CONCRETE PIPE

INSIDE DIAMETER 4"ADEQUATE 6"RECOMMENDED

ALL JOINTS TO BE TIGHT TO PREVENT SEEPAGE AND ROOT INFILTRATION

NOTE

Use cast iron or PVC pipe at first 6 ft minimum from house for main drain (inlet); areas near wells or other natural water supplies; areas near trees or shrubs that may cause root stoppage in clay pipes.

SOLID DRAIN AND OUTLET PIPE

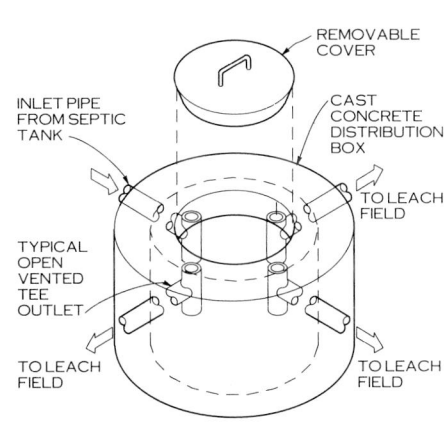

REMOVABLE COVER

INLET PIPE FROM SEPTIC TANK

CAST CONCRETE DISTRIBUTION BOX

TO LEACH FIELD

TYPICAL OPEN VENTED TEE OUTLET

TO LEACH FIELD

TO LEACH FIELD

NOTE

Purpose is to distribute effluent from septic tank equally to each leach line and thereby to the whole leach field.

DISTRIBUTION BOX

L. James Cooke, Jr., PE; Department of Veterans Affairs; Washington, D.C.

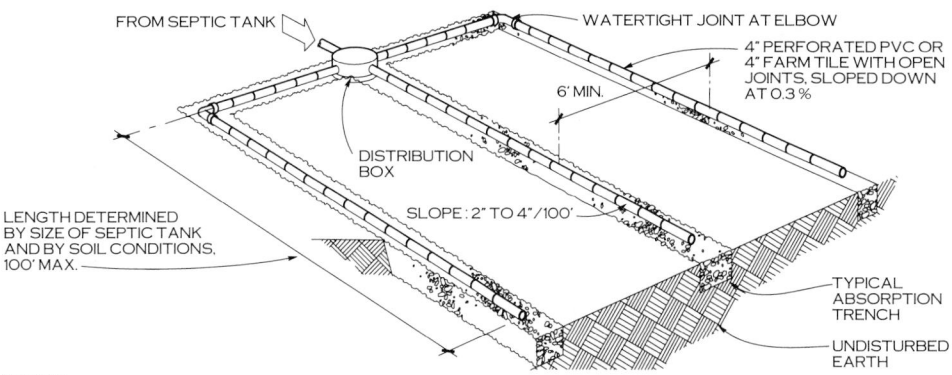

NOTE

A leach field or seepage bed replaces the typical absorption trench with an entirely excavated leach field filled with gravel. This type of installation requires more gravel but allows freer lateral movement for effluent and better aerobic breakdown and is often cheaper and faster to build.

OPEN-ENDED LEACH LINES LAYOUT (SLIGHTLY SLOPED GRADE)

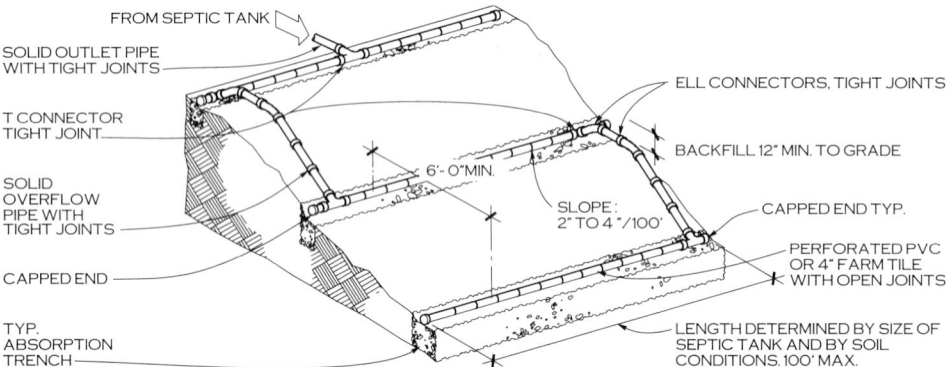

INTERCONNECTED (SERIAL) LEACH LINES LAYOUT (FLAT GRADE)

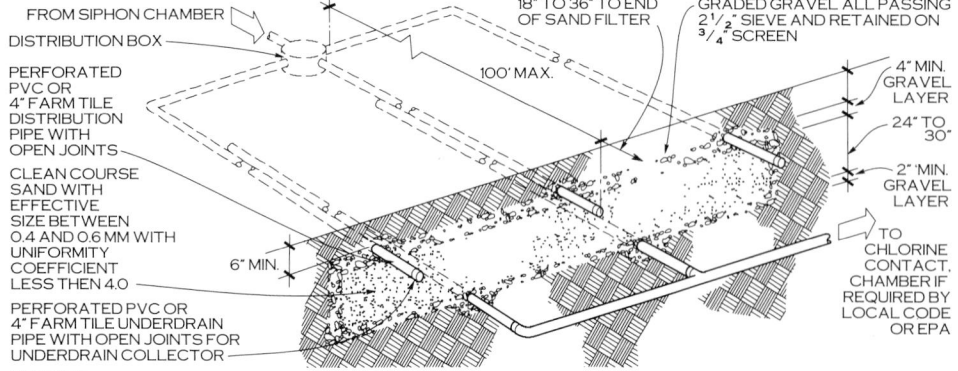

INTERCONNECTED (SERIAL) LEACH LINES LAYOUT (HIGHLY SLOPED GRADE)

NOTES

1. Due to cost, sand filters should be used only where other systems are not feasible, such as the soil having a percolation rate of 1 in. in 30 minutes or above.
2. Use this system in conjunction with a siphon chamber.

SAND FILTER LAYOUT

L. James Cooke, Jr., PE; Department of Veteran Affairs; Washington, D.C.

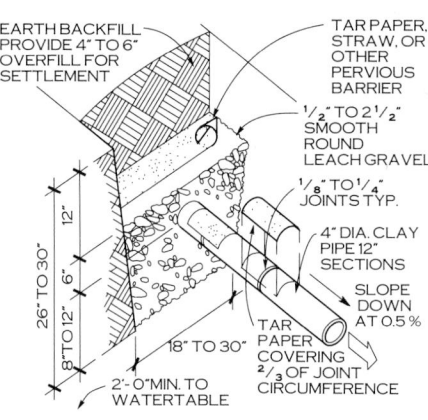

NOTE

Perforated PVC may be used in place of farm tile.

ABSORPTION TRENCH DETAIL

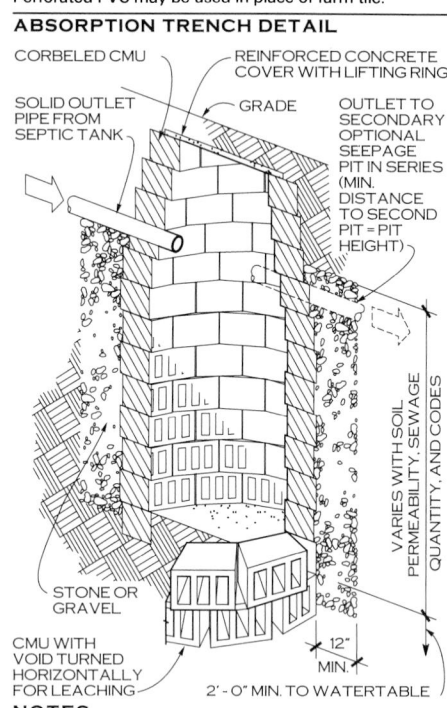

NOTES

1. Seepage pits may be made from precast concrete with slots for leaching.
2. For proper installation, soil must be absorbent.

SEEPAGE PIT

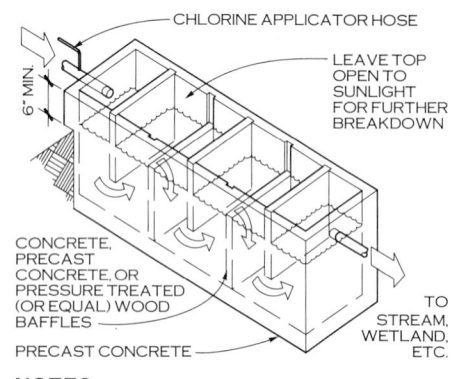

NOTES

1. Local codes may require use of chlorine contact chamber to further treat effluent that may run too closely to wetlands, streams, etc. Use with sand filter system.
2. Provide 20 minutes of detention at average flow. Minimum size is 50 gallons.

CHLORINE CONTACT CHAMBER

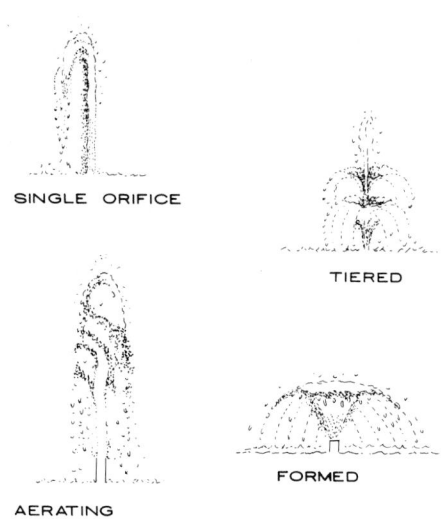

SINGLE ORIFICE

TIERED

AERATING

FORMED

GENERAL JET TYPES

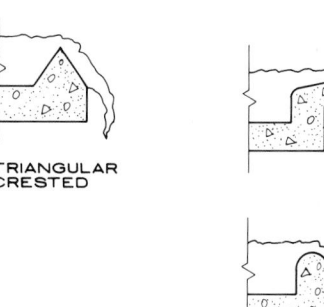

TRIANGULAR
CRESTED

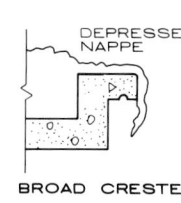

DEPRESSED
NAPPE

BROAD CRESTED

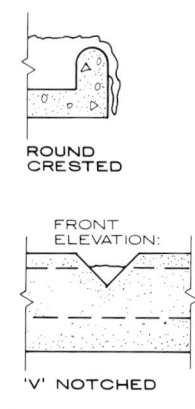

ROUND
CRESTED

FRONT
ELEVATION:

'V' NOTCHED

WEIR SECTIONS

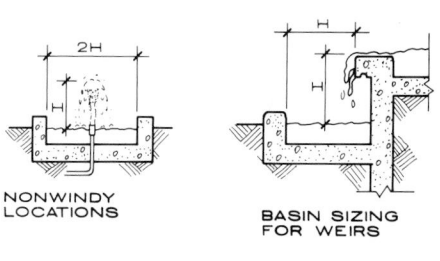

NONWINDY
LOCATIONS

BASIN SIZING
FOR WEIRS

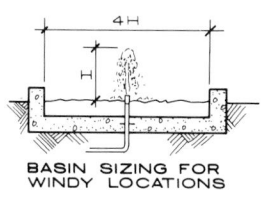

BASIN SIZING FOR
WINDY LOCATIONS

BASIN SIZING FOR FOUNTAINS

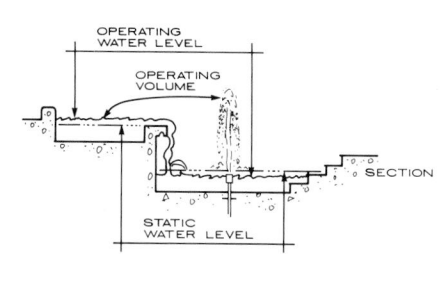

OPERATING
WATER LEVEL

OPERATING
VOLUME

SECTION

STATIC
WATER LEVEL

$$\frac{\text{CIRCULATING VOLUME (CU FT)}}{\text{BASIN AREA (SQ FT)}} = \begin{matrix}\text{DIFFERENCE BETWEEN}\\\text{STATIC AND}\\\text{OPERATING LEVELS}\\\text{(IN.)}\end{matrix}$$

STATIC AND OPERATING LEVELS OF FOUNTAINS

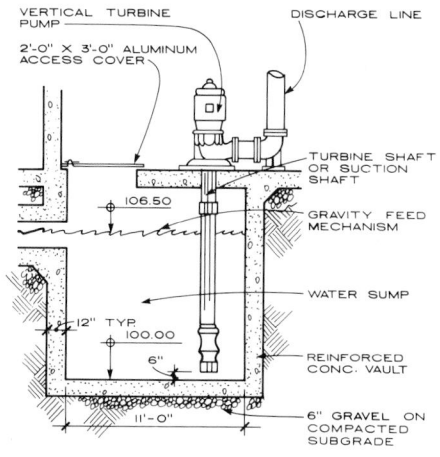

VERTICAL TURBINE
PUMP

2'-0" X 3'-0" ALUMINUM
ACCESS COVER

DISCHARGE LINE

TURBINE SHAFT
OR SUCTION
SHAFT

106.50

GRAVITY FEED
MECHANISM

12" TYP.
100.00

WATER SUMP

6"

REINFORCED
CONC. VAULT

11'-0"

6" GRAVEL ON
COMPACTED
SUBGRADE

VERTICAL TURBINE PUMP

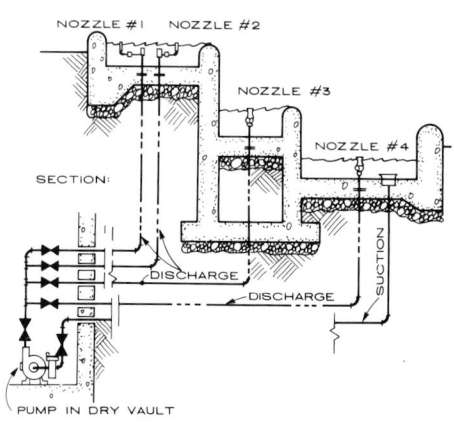

NOZZLE #1   NOZZLE #2

NOZZLE #3

SECTION:

NOZZLE #4

DISCHARGE

DISCHARGE

SUCTION

PUMP IN DRY VAULT

PIPE SCHEMATIC — DRY CENTRIFUGAL PUMP

PURPOSE

Fountains can provide the following site considerations or program elements:

1. Recreation
2. An altered environment to increase comfort
3. Image
4. Visual focal point
5. An activities focal point
6. To frame views
7. Acoustical control

FORMS

1. Held water in pools and ponds. Form and reflectivity are design considerations.
2. Falling water. The effect depends on water velocity, water volume, container surface, or the edge over or through which the water is moving.
3. Flowing water. The visual effect of the same volume of flowing water can be changed by narrowing or widening a channel, by placing objects in its path, by changing the direction of the flow, and by changing the slope and roughness of the bottom and sides.
4. Jets. An effect derived by forcing water into the air to create a pattern. Jet types include single orifice nozzles, tiered jets, aerated nozzles, and formed jets. A wide variety of forms, patterns, and types is available.
5. Surge. An effect created by a contrast between relatively quiet water and a surge (a wave or a splash),

made by quickly adding water, by raising or lowering an object in the water, by moving an object back and forth through the water, or by introducing strong air currents.

OVERALL DESIGN CONSIDERATIONS

1. Scale. Size of the water feature in context to the surroundings.
2. Basin sizing: Width—consider fountain height and prevailing winds. Depth—consider weight (1 cu ft water = 62.366 lb). Safety—consider children playing near or in the pool. Cover—allow space for lights, nozzles, and pumps. Local codes may classify basins of a certain depth as swimming pools. Nozzle spray may be cushioned to prevent excessive surge.
3. Bottom appearance is important when clear water is maintained. It can be enhanced by patterns, colors, materials, three-dimensional objects, or textures. Dark bottoms increase reflectivity.
4. Edges or copings. In designing the water's edge, consider the difference between the operating water level and the static water level. Loosely defined edges (as in a pond) make movement into the water possible both visually and physically. Clearly defined edges (as in a basin) use copings to delineate the water's edge.
5. Lips and weirs—A lip is an edge over which flowing water falls. A weir is a dam in the water to divert the water flow or to raise the water level. If volume and velocity are insufficient to break the surface tension, a reglet on the underside of the edge may overcome this problem.

MATERIAL SELECTION CRITERIA

1. Waterproof
2. Crack resistant
3. Weather resistant, durable
4. Stain resistant
5. Workable material appropriate for intended effect

GENERATION OF WATER PRESSURE

1. Elevated dam structures, used in early fountains, are not feasible today.
2. Submersible pumps, used for low volume fountains only, are easy to install and require short pipe runs. The pump must be covered with water to operate correctly; it may be damaged if the water level drops. Vandalism can be a problem. Motors range from $1/20$ to 1 horsepower.
3. Dry centrifugal pumps are used most commonly for larger water features. Motors range from $1/4$ to 100 horsepower. The assembly consists of a pump, electric motor, suction line, and discharge line. The pump and motor are located in an isolated dry vault.
4. Vertical turbine pumps usually are more energy efficient than pumps with suction lines because the pump uses no energy to move the water to the pump. Water flows to the pump by gravity and thus reduces the amount of work exerted by the pump. The assembly consists of a pump and motor, a water sump in the equipment vault, a gravity feed mechanism to the pump, and a discharge line.

Barry R. Thalden, AIA; Thalden Corporation; St. Louis, Missouri

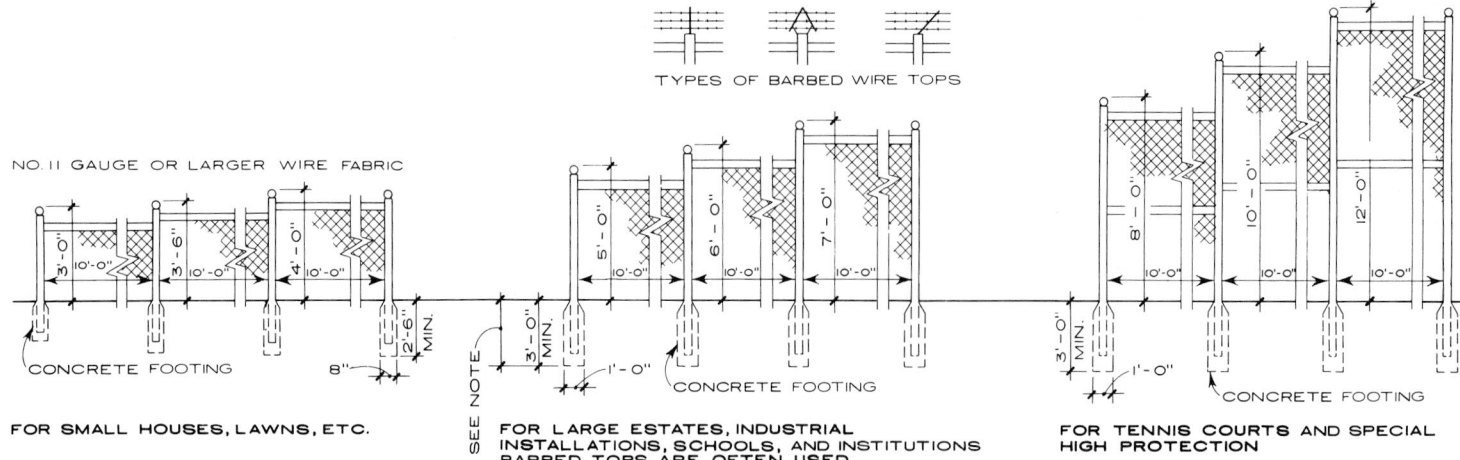

TYPES OF BARBED WIRE TOPS

NO. 11 GAUGE OR LARGER WIRE FABRIC

CONCRETE FOOTING   8"

FOR SMALL HOUSES, LAWNS, ETC.

SEE NOTE

CONCRETE FOOTING

FOR LARGE ESTATES, INDUSTRIAL INSTALLATIONS, SCHOOLS, AND INSTITUTIONS BARBED TOPS ARE OFTEN USED

CONCRETE FOOTING

FOR TENNIS COURTS AND SPECIAL HIGH PROTECTION

HEIGHTS OF FENCES FOR VARIOUS USES

See note at right for depth of concrete footings.

MATERIALS

SIZES GIVEN ARE NOT STANDARD BUT REPRESENT THE AVERAGE SIZES USED

Wire gauge	Usually No. 11 or No. 9 W & M. For specially rugged use use No. 6. For tennis courts usually No. 11
Wire mesh	Usually 2". For tennis courts usually $1^5/_8$" or $1^1/_4$" of chain link steel hot dip galvanized after weaving. Top and bottom salvage may be barbed or knuckled
Corner and end posts	For lawn fences usually 2" O.D. For estate fences 2" for low and $2^1/_2$" for medium and 3" O.D. for heavy or high For tennis courts 3" O.D.
Line or intermediate posts	For lawn $1^3/_8$" or 2" O.D. round For estate etc. 2", $2^1/_4$", $2^1/_2$" H or I sections For tennis courts $2^1/_2$" round O.D. or $2^1/_4$" H or I sections
Gate posts	The same or next size larger than the corner posts. Footings for gate posts 3'-6" deep
Top rails	$1^5/_8$" O.D. except some lawn fence may be $1^3/_8$" O.D.
Middle rails	On 12'-0" fence same as top rail
Gates	Single or double any width desired. Accessible routes require clear opening width of 32" min. and 18" latch-side clearance; latches must be accessible.
Post spacing	Line posts 10'-0" O.C., 8'-0" O.C. may be used on heavy construction

O.D. = outside diameter.

POST SIZES FOR HEAVY DUTY GATES

A.S.A. SCHEDULE 40 PIPE SIZES	SWING GATE OPENINGS	
	SINGLE GATE	DOUBLE GATE
$2^1/_2$"	To 6'-0"	Up to 12'-0"
$3^1/_2$"	Over 6' to 18'	Over 12' to 26'
6"	Over 13' to 18'	Over 26' to 36'
8"	Over 18' to 32'	Over 36' to 64'

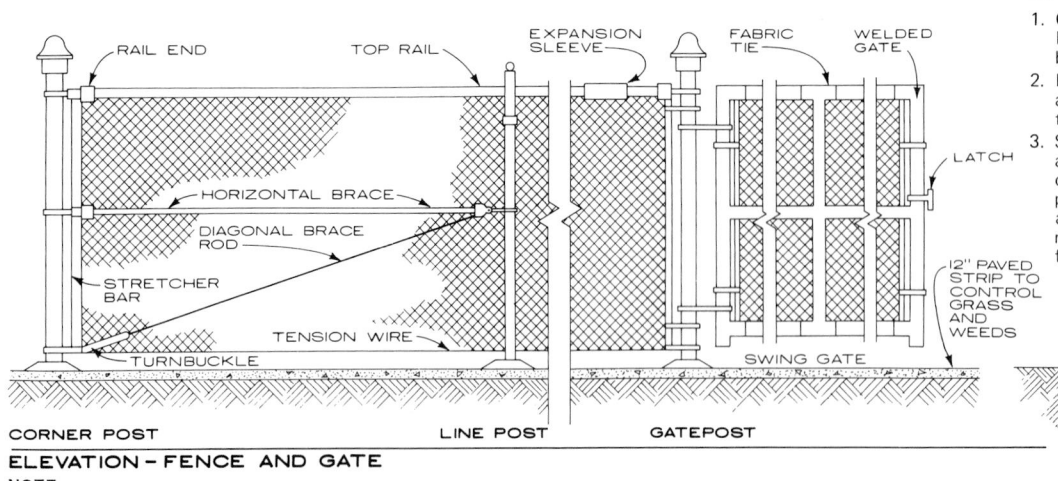

ELEVATION – FENCE AND GATE

NOTE

For fences 5 ft 0 in. and taller a horizontal or diagonal brace, or both, is used for greater stability. Post spacing should be equidistant and should not exceed 10 ft 0 in. o.c.

Charles Driesen; Ewing Cole Erdman & Eubank; Philadelphia, Pennsylvania

CONCRETE FOOTING

Bottom of concrete footing to be set below frost line (see local code). Concrete footing sizes shown are the recommended minimum; they should be redesigned for conditions where soil is poor.

TYPES OF WIRE FABRIC MESH

VINYL-COATED: Suitable for residential, commercial, or industrial applications.
Mesh sizes: 1, $1^1/_4$, $1^1/_2$, $1^3/_4$, and 2 in.
Gauge sizes: 11, 9, 6, and 3.

REDWOOD SLATS

Used for visual privacy and appearance. Suitable for homes, swimming pools, and gardens.
Mesh size: $3^1/_2$ x 5 in.
Gauge size: 9.

1. PREGALVANIZED: Should be restricted to such residential applications as residential perimeter fencing, swimming pool enclosures, private tennis courts, dog kennels, and interior industrial storage.
   Mesh sizes: $1^1/_2$, $1^3/_4$, and 2 in. Gauge sizes: 13, 11, and 9.

2. HOT DIPPED GALVANIZED: Suitable for highway enclosures, institutional security fencing, highway bridge enclosures, exterior industrial security fences, parking lot enclosures, recreational applications, and any other environment where resistance to abuse and severe climatic conditions exist.
   Mesh sizes: $1^1/_2$, $2^3/_4$, and 2 in. Gauge sizes: 9 and 6.

COATINGS

Protective coatings used on fencing, such as zinc and aluminum. Various decorative coatings can be applied including vinyl bonded and organic coatings available from most manufacturers.

SPECIAL FENCING

1. ORNAMENTAL: Vertical struts only—no chain link fabric required. Ideal for landscape or as barrier fence.

2. ELEPHANT FENCE: This fence can actually stop an elephant, hold back a rock slide, or bring a small truck to a halt. Size: 3 gauges x 2-in. mesh.

3. SECURITY FENCE: This fabric is nonclimbable and cannot be penetrated by gun muzzles, knives, or other weapons. Suitable as security barrier for police stations, prisons, reformatories, hospitals, and mental institutions. Mesh size: $3/_8$ in. for maximum security, $1/_2$ in. for high security, $5/_8$ in. for supersecurity, and 1 in. for standard security.

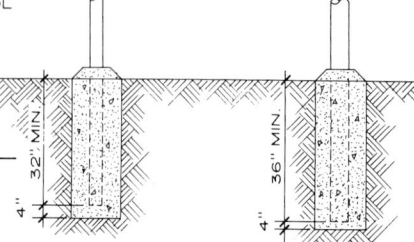

LINE POST   CORNER AND GATEPOST

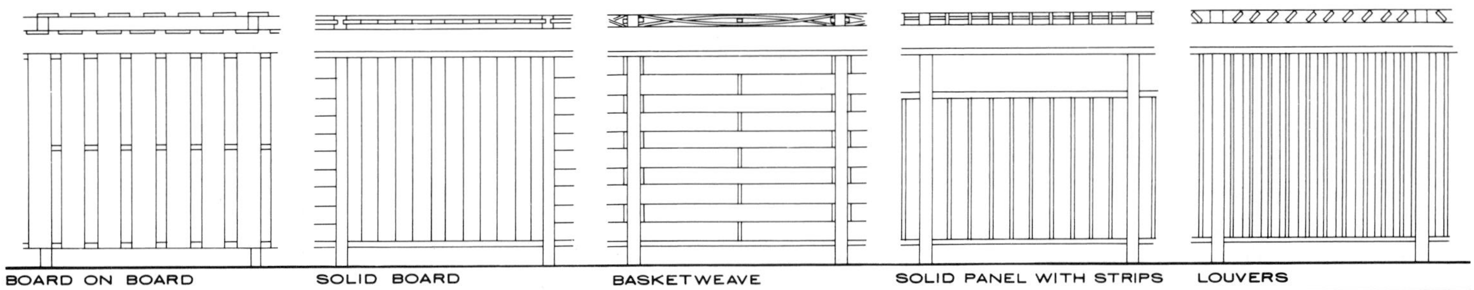

BOARD ON BOARD   SOLID BOARD   BASKETWEAVE   SOLID PANEL WITH STRIPS   LOUVERS

SOLID FENCE TYPES

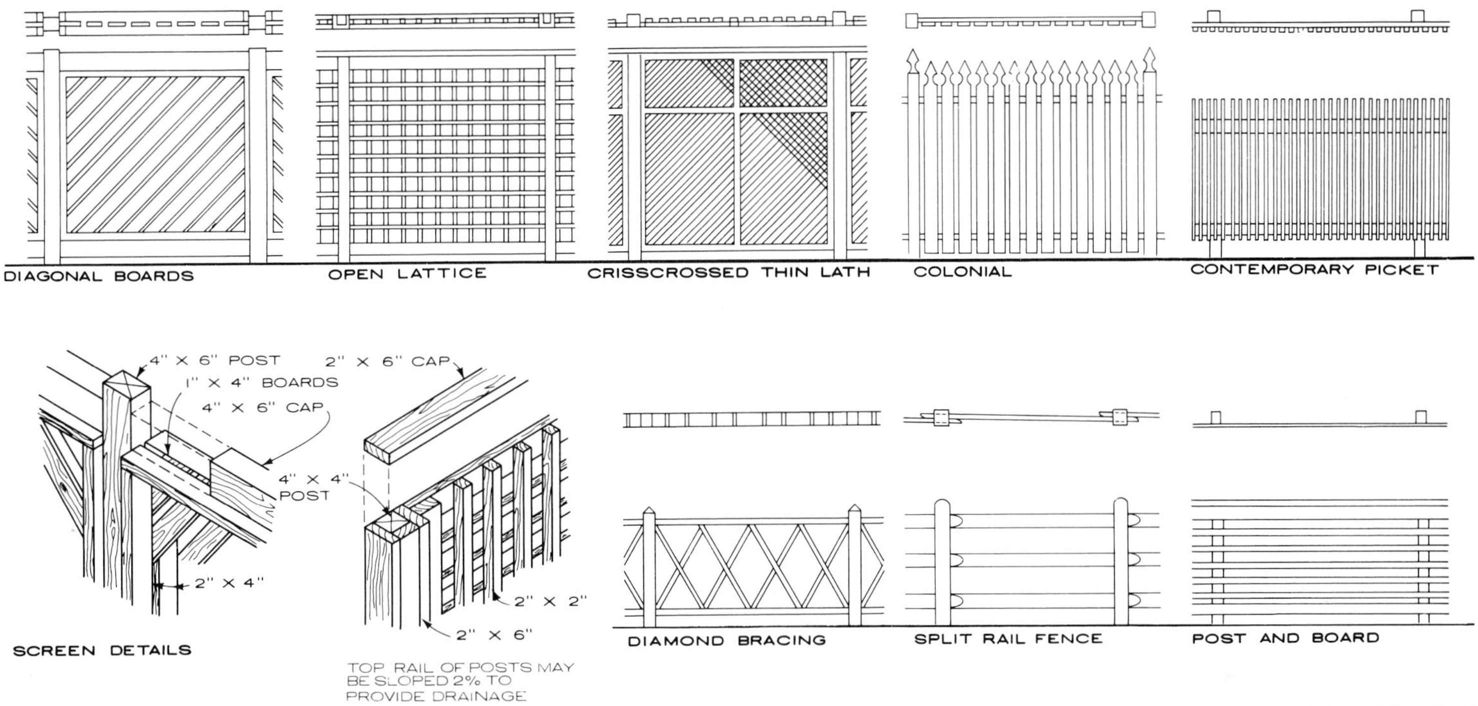

DIAGONAL BOARDS   OPEN LATTICE   CRISSCROSSED THIN LATH   COLONIAL   CONTEMPORARY PICKET

4" X 6" POST   2" X 6" CAP
1" X 4" BOARDS
4" X 6" CAP
4" X 4" POST
2" X 4"
2" X 2"
2" X 6"

SCREEN DETAILS

TOP RAIL OF POSTS MAY
BE SLOPED 2% TO
PROVIDE DRAINAGE

DIAMOND BRACING   SPLIT RAIL FENCE   POST AND BOARD

TRANSPARENT FENCES AND SCREENS

6' TO 9' MAX.
CHECK ZONING CODE
POSTS AT GATE 1 SIZE LARGER THAN TYPICAL
2" X 4"
3'-6" TO 6'-0"
4" X 4" OR 4" X 6"
TENSION BRACING OR COMPRESSION BRACING

TYPICAL FENCE DIMENSIONS

WOOD POST
COMPACTED FILL
WOOD CLEATS
FROST LINE
GRAVEL
ROCKS FOR STABILITY
FROST LINE

TAR SEAL
CONCRETE
WOOD POST
U-SHAPED METAL POST BASE
METAL DOWELS
FROST LINE
GRAVEL
CONCRETE
RECOMMENDED FOR DURABILITY

FOOTING DETAILS

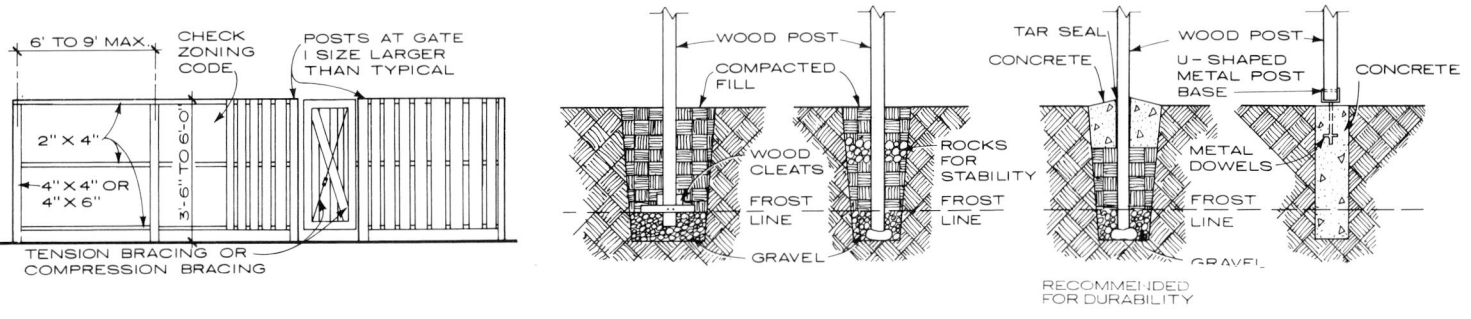

NOTES

When selecting a wood fence pattern, consider:

1. Site topography and prevailing wind conditions;
2. Architectural style of surrounding buildings and adjacent land use;
3. Required fence height and size of the property to be enclosed.

PURPOSE

Wood fences are used for security, privacy, and screening of outdoor spaces. Picket fences 3 ft. or 4 ft. high keep small children or small dogs in the yard. Board-on-board fences, by standards built taller, provide greater wind and view barriers. Acoustical fences are built to keep out sound and wind, and to provide privacy. Open lattice or louvered fences, usually a minimum of 4 ft. high with self-closing gates and latches, are used for swimming pool enclosures. A semitransparent wood screen often is used to enclose an outdoor room to avoid totally obstructing the view or restricting natural ventilation. Long, open fence patterns are used best at the property line to define boundaries or limit access to a site.

FASTENERS

Fasteners should be of noncorrosive aluminum alloy or stainless steel. Top quality, hot dipped galvanized steel is acceptable. Metal flanges, cleats, bolts, and screws are better than common nails.

Pressure-treated wood commonly is used for fencing. Certain species of nontreated woods, such as cedar and redwood heart, also are suitable. Refer to pages on wood uses in Chapter 6 for further information. Natural, stain, and paint finishes may be used.

Charles R. Heuer, FAIA; Covenants; Somerville, Massachusetts

SITE IMPROVEMENTS 2

CONSIDERATIONS

The following factors must be considered when installing or renovating outdoor lighting systems:

1. In general, overhead lighting is more efficient and economical than low level lighting.
2. Fixtures should provide an overlapping pattern of light at a height of about 7 ft.
3. Lighting levels should respond to site hazards such as steps, ramps, and steep embankments.
4. Posts and standards should be placed so that they do not create hazards for pedestrians or vehicles.

NOTES

1. Because of their effect on light distribution, trees and shrubs at present height and growth potential should be considered in a lighting layout.
2. It is recommended to use manufacturer-provided lighting templates sized for fixture type, wattage, pole height, and layout scale.
3. Color rendition should be considered when selecting light source. When possible, colors should be selected under proposed light source.
4. Light pollution to areas other than those to be illuminated should be avoided.

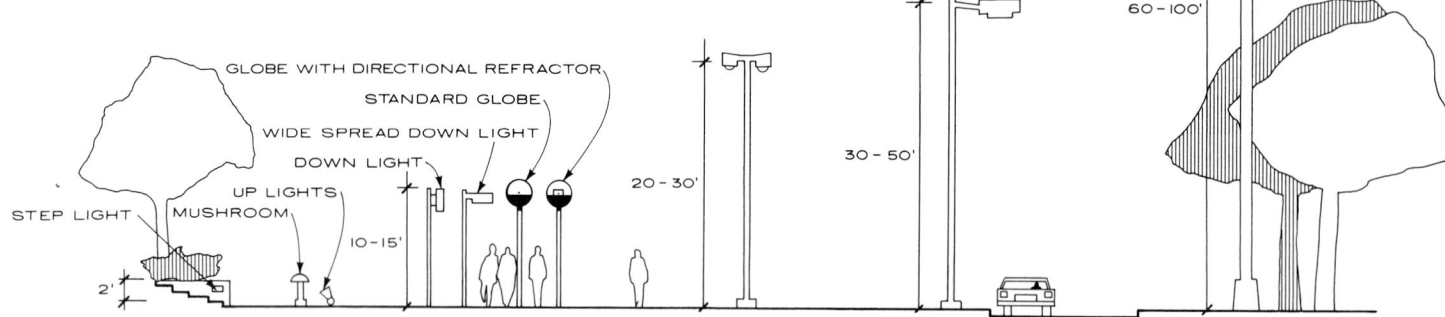

LOW LEVEL LIGHTING

1. Heights below eye level.
2. Very finite patterns with low wattage capabilities.
3. Incandescent, fluorescent, and high-pressure sodium, 5 to 150 watt lamps.
4. Lowest maintenance requirements, but highly susceptible to vandals.

MALL AND WALKWAY LIGHTING

1. 10 ft. to 15 ft. heights average for multiuse areas. Wide variety of fixtures and light patterns.
2. Mercury, metal halide, or high-pressure sodium, 70 to 250 watt lamps.
3. Susceptible to vandals.

SPECIAL PURPOSE LIGHTING

1. 20 ft. to 30 ft. heights average.
2. Recreational, commercial, residential, industrial.
3. Mercury, metal halide, or high-pressure sodium, 200 to 400 watt lamps.
4. Fixtures maintained by gantry.

PARKING AND ROADWAY LIGHTING

1. 30 ft. to 50 ft. heights average.
2. Large recreational, commercial, industrial areas, highways.
3. Mercury, metal halide, or high-pressure sodium, 400 to 1000 watt lamps.
4. Fixtures maintained by gantry.

HIGH MASTLIGHTING

1. 60 ft. to 100 ft. heights average.
2. Large areas—parking, recreational, highway interchanges.
3. Metal halide or high-pressure sodium, 1000 watt lamps.
4. Fixtures must lower for maintenance.

DEFINITIONS

A lumen is a unit used for measuring the amount of light energy given off by a light source. A footcandle is a unit used for measuring the amount of illumination on a surface. The amount of usable light from any given source is partially determined by the source's angle of incidence and the distance to the illuminated surface. See Chapter 1 on illumination.

NOTE

All exterior installations must be provided with ground fault interruption circuit.

RECOMMENDED LIGHTING LEVELS IN FOOTCANDLES

	COMMER-CIAL	INTERME-DIATE	RESIDEN-TIAL
PEDESTRIAN AREAS			
Sidewalks	0.9	0.6	0.2
Pedestrian ways	2.0	1.0	0.5
VEHICULAR ROADS			
Freeway*	0.6	0.6	0.6
Major road and expressway*	2.0	1.4	1.0
Collector road	1.2	0.9	0.6
Local road	0.9	0.6	0.4
Alleys	0.6	0.4	0.2
PARKING AREAS			
Self-parking	1.0	—	—
Attendant parking	2.0	—	—
Security problem area	—	—	5.0
Minimum for television viewing of important interdiction areas	10.0	10.0	10.0
BUILDING AREAS			
Entrances	5.0	—	—
General grounds	1.0	—	—

*Both mainline and ramps.

Johnson, Johnson & Roy; Ann Arbor, Michigan
Tomblinson Harburn Associates; Flint, Michigan

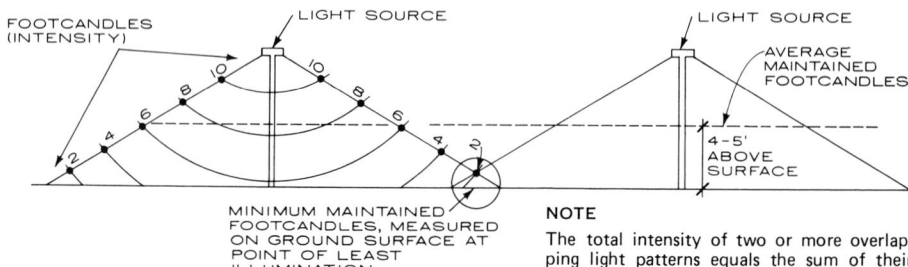

MEASURING LIGHT INTENSITY IN FOOTCANDLES

NOTE

The total intensity of two or more overlapping light patterns equals the sum of their individual intensities.

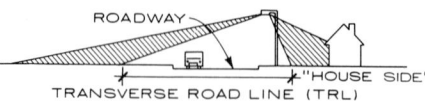

1. CUTOFF means that maximum of 10 percent of light source lumens fall outside of TRL area.
2. SEMICUTOFF means that maximum of 30 percent of light source lumens fall outside of the TRL area.
3. NONCUTOFF means that no control limitations exist.

CUTOFF TERMINOLOGY
(NOTE: "CUTOFF" IS MEASURED ALONG TRL.)

NOTE

Degree of cutoff is determined by one of the following:

(a) design of fixture housing
(b) incorporation of prismatic lens over light source
(c) addition of shield to fixture on "house side"

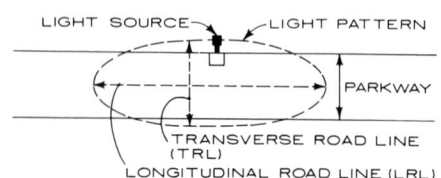

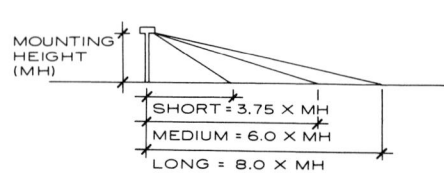

TYPES OF DISTRIBUTION
(NOTE: DISTRIBUTION IS MEASURED ALONG LRL)

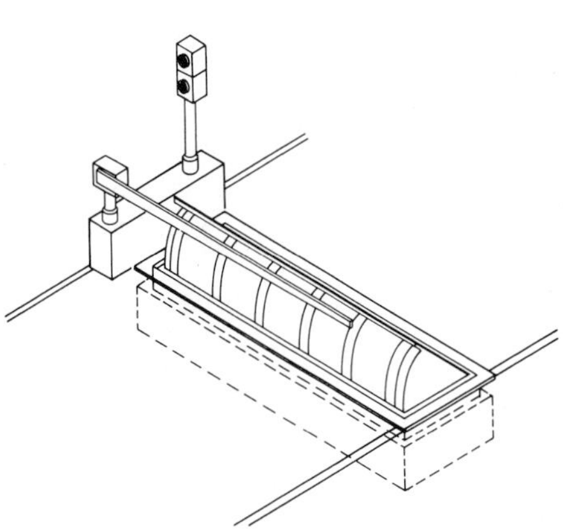

RETRACTABLE BARRIER

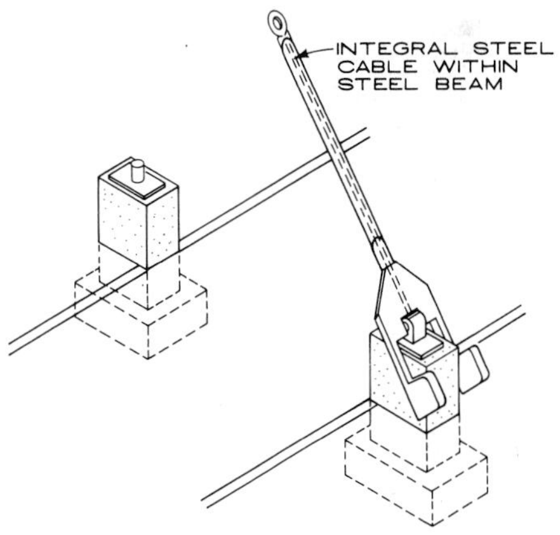

CABLE CRASH BEAM
INTEGRAL STEEL CABLE WITHIN STEEL BEAM

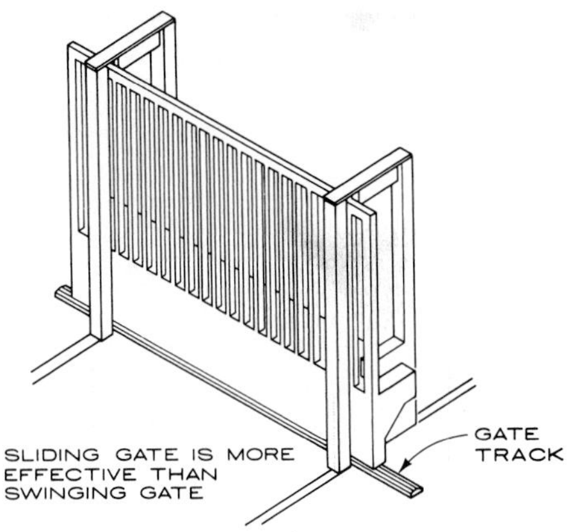

SLIDING CRASH GATE
SLIDING GATE IS MORE EFFECTIVE THAN SWINGING GATE
GATE TRACK

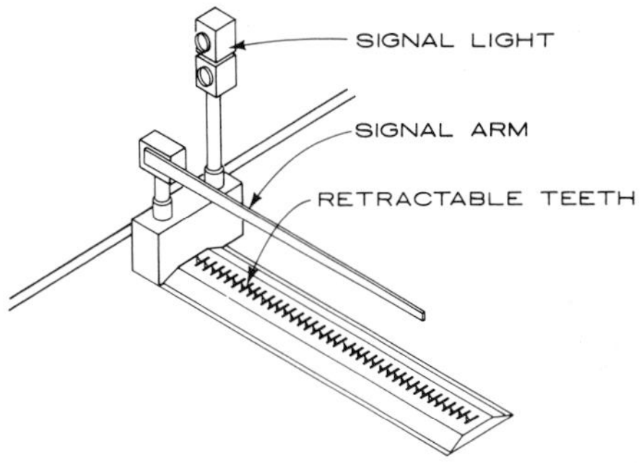

TRAFFIC CONTROLLER
SIGNAL LIGHT
SIGNAL ARM
RETRACTABLE TEETH

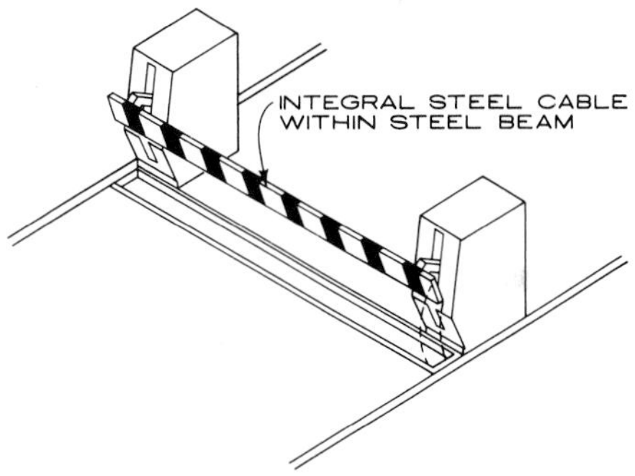

LIFT CRASH GATE
INTEGRAL STEEL CABLE WITHIN STEEL BEAM

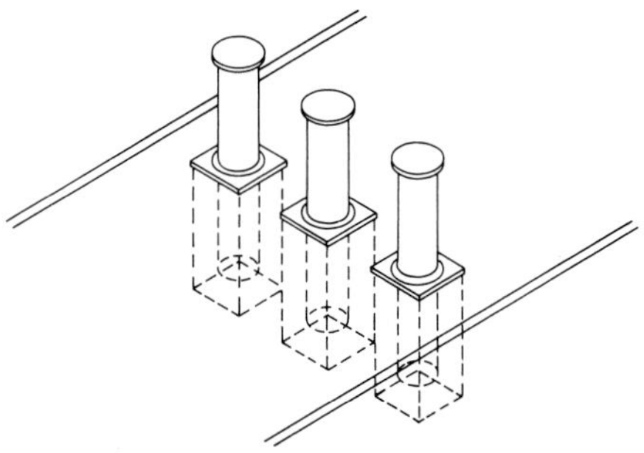

RETRACTABLE BOLLARDS

MECHANICAL BARRIERS

VEHICLE BARRIERS

1. Active barriers at access/egress points in high security areas should be fully engaged until vehicle is cleared for passage. A visible signal light or drop arm should indicate the barrier's status to approaching vehicles. Operating time should not exceed 3–4 sec. The barrier system must maintain its position, preventing access in case of power failure, be capable of manual operation, and should be connected to emergency power. Remote controls should include a status indicator.

2. Passive vehicle barriers (walls, bollards, planters, trench/berms, and ponds) can enhance site design and be inexpensive, low-maintenance vehicle barriers.

3. Concrete bollards and walls require heavy reinforcement tied into massive continuously reinforced concrete footings.

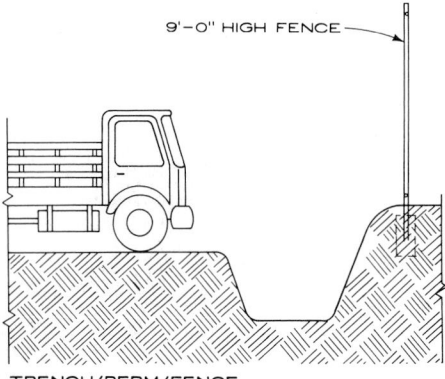

TRENCH/BERM/FENCE
9'-0" HIGH FENCE

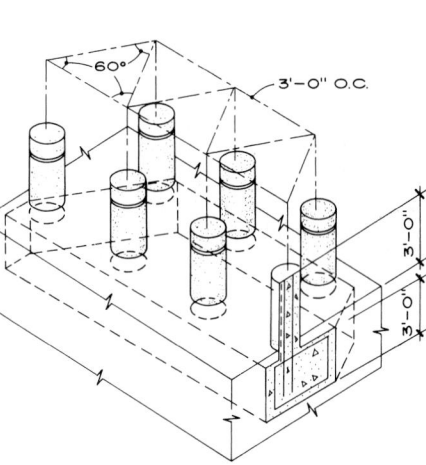

CONCRETE BOLLARDS WITH CONTINUOUS FOOTING
60°   3'-0" O.C.   3'-0"   3'-0"

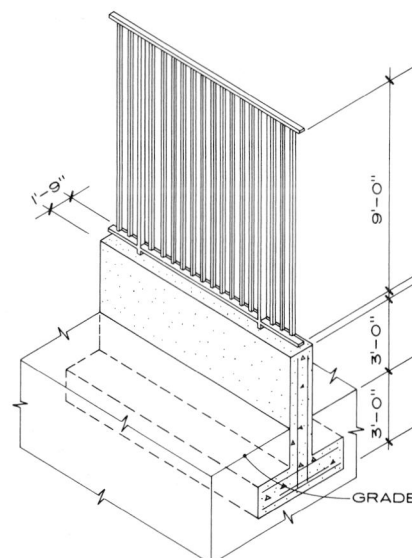
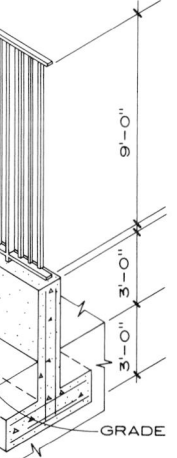

FENCE ON BARRIER WALL
1'-9"   9'-0"   3'-0"   3'-0"   GRADE

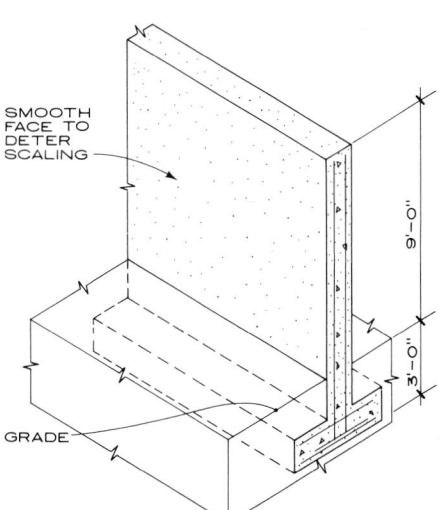

CONCRETE BARRIER WALL
SMOOTH FACE TO DETER SCALING   9'-0"   3'-0"   GRADE

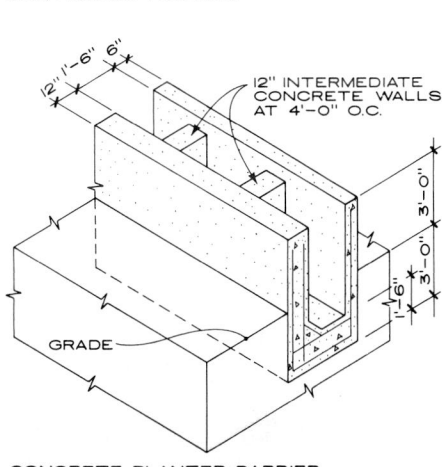

CONCRETE PLANTER BARRIER
12" 1'-6" 6"   12" INTERMEDIATE CONCRETE WALLS AT 4'-0" O.C.   3'-0"   6"   3'-0"   GRADE

FIXED BARRIERS

Edwin Daly, AIA, and Ellen Delaney; Joseph Handwerger, Architects; Washington, D.C.
William G. Miner, AIA; Washington, D.C.

SITE IMPROVEMENTS 2

INTRODUCTION

Playing is vital to the physical, emotional, and social growth of children. To encourage healthy growth, the play environment must challenge children at their level of development yet reassure them as they investigate their physical limits. Each stage of development results in different types and levels of interaction and activity. The outdoor play environment becomes increasingly important as the boundaries of the child's world stretch beyond the home and primary care. Play equipment should be selected and designed to attract, fascinate, and sustain the interest of the age groups who will use it, while promoting agility, strength, and balance.

Playing may consist of imitation, role play, and fantasy play, as well as more active pursuits. Space and equipment must be provided to encourage jumping, climbing, swinging, sliding, crawling, hanging, running, building, sitting, and meeting. Designs should provide opportunities for children to be imaginative and to interact socially. Think of the equipment as a flexible, three-dimensional system that allows children to move in every direction and challenges them with a consistently changing space.

Three age groups must be considered in designing playgrounds. Toddlers (3 to 5 years) should be separated from older children by a fence they can see through. This makes it easier for caregivers to supervise the younger children but allows the toddlers to feel part of things. Early elementary (6 to 9 years) and late elementary (9 to 12 years) children have traditionally been separated, but another option is to design equipment that has several levels of difficulty, allowing use by both groups.

Most traditional play equipment is designed to stand alone as single units, although these may be linked together. Where space or other conditions limit the scope of development, such equipment is useful. However, because a child's play activity tends to proceed in a continuous flow, integrated play areas have proved more successful than arrangements of individual items. Combining several materials, colors, and textures also makes the play space more inviting. A variety of options is available to the designer in both custom and manufactured products.

DESIGN SUGGESTIONS

The design of a playground should meet the needs and sustain the interest of the children who will use the site. Using nonrepetitive elements and semitransparent features creates mystery and surprise. Dynamic, movable components allow more creative opportunities for children, and a variety of textures stimulates the sense of touch. Children never tire of playing with sand and water. Manufacturers offer a wide variety of water features for the playground, including wading pools and fountains. Water elements also encourage adult interaction. Space for congregating can be provided as semienclosed refuge or open areas. Bridges add interest to equipment and can provide connections between structures; they also create more climbing and refuge space. In addition to traditional plank bridges, there are arched, rope, suspension, or tire bridges. Suspension bridges may be designed to meet specifications provided in the Americans with Disabilities Act (ADA).

If a theme such as a ship, castle, or fort is incorporated in the playground, the equipment will automatically encourage the child's imagination. However, don't replicate these themes too closely. Leave most of the creation to the child.

Adults should not be separated from the play area. Ample seating should be provided, and the equipment should be interesting to adults, too, since their presence gives security, instruction, and approval.

Practical concerns should be taken into account in designing a playground: how does the equipment appear from the surrounding area? What are the views from the site? How much noise will travel to and from the playground? The design should consider the time of day the equipment will be used and be suitable for use all year. Drainage is important, especially around swings and berms, and shade is especially desirable over metal slides.

SAFETY AND MATERIALS

No playground is completely safe. The potential for accidents is inherent in the element of risk involved in most play. Nonetheless, playground equipment should provide challenging activities in the safest way possible.

Round, square, and rectangular timber should be pine or fir (oak warps, redwood splinters). Color should be in the form of stain, not paint, and all edges should be beveled or rounded. Steel pipe, sheets, chain, and drums can be vinyl coated. Chain, rope, and tires are available in plastic. Use of concrete and stone should be kept to a minimum. Hardware should be galvanized, and joints and connections covered or recessed.

Most important, a bed of absorbing ground cover, such as pine bark or wood chips (12 in. deep), pea gravel (10 in. deep), or sand (10 in. deep), should be installed beneath the equipment. Hardwood chips and rubberized surfacing are easier for persons with disabilities to travel over. Asphalt, packed dirt, and exposed concrete are not acceptable play surfaces.

A safety zone of at least 4 ft should surround the entire play area, with 7 ft in front of slides, 9 ft in front of swings, and 4 to 5 ft on the sides of the swings. Allow 65 to 70 sq ft of play space per child.

EQUIPMENT FOR CHILDREN WITH DISABILITIES

The ADA has raised a new understanding of the need to include children with disabilities in play activity wherever possible. Several elements will encourage the participation of children with disabilities. Bump stairs, transfer platforms, accessible suspension bridges, and slides (provided there is enough traction), as well as components that can be manipulated from a wheelchair, are all useful. Many persons with disabilities have some upper-body mobility, and horizontal ladders and rings can help children strengthen the upper body. Ramps and handrails should be used wherever possible.

MANUFACTURED VERSUS CUSTOM EQUIPMENT

Manufacturers of playground equipment offer products in timber, plastic, or powder-coated steel. Available as either individual items or in predesigned arrangements, these products are durable and easy to install and offer a variety of accessories. Because they are designed as modular units, they can be used to create a limitless number of compositions and can be expanded at a later date. Some have no need for foundations. All products must conform to the Consumer Product Safety Code.

Custom-designed equipment has the advantage of being site and situation specific. In addition, the manipulation of landforms by the designer can result in a much more interesting and creative site. Most of the materials used by manufacturers are readily available to designers, making custom design of equipment an affordable option.

GROWTH AND DEVELOPMENT

NOTES

Two methods of expanding the capabilities of an integrated playground are:

1. LINKING OF EQUIPMENT: Connecting activity centers with links that are in themselves play structures, thus multiplying the possible uses of all of the structures involved.
2. JUXTAPOSITIONING EQUIPMENT: Placing units close enough together to generate interaction from one to the other; also increases the play potential and interest of the area.

Andrew Sumners; University Park, Maryland

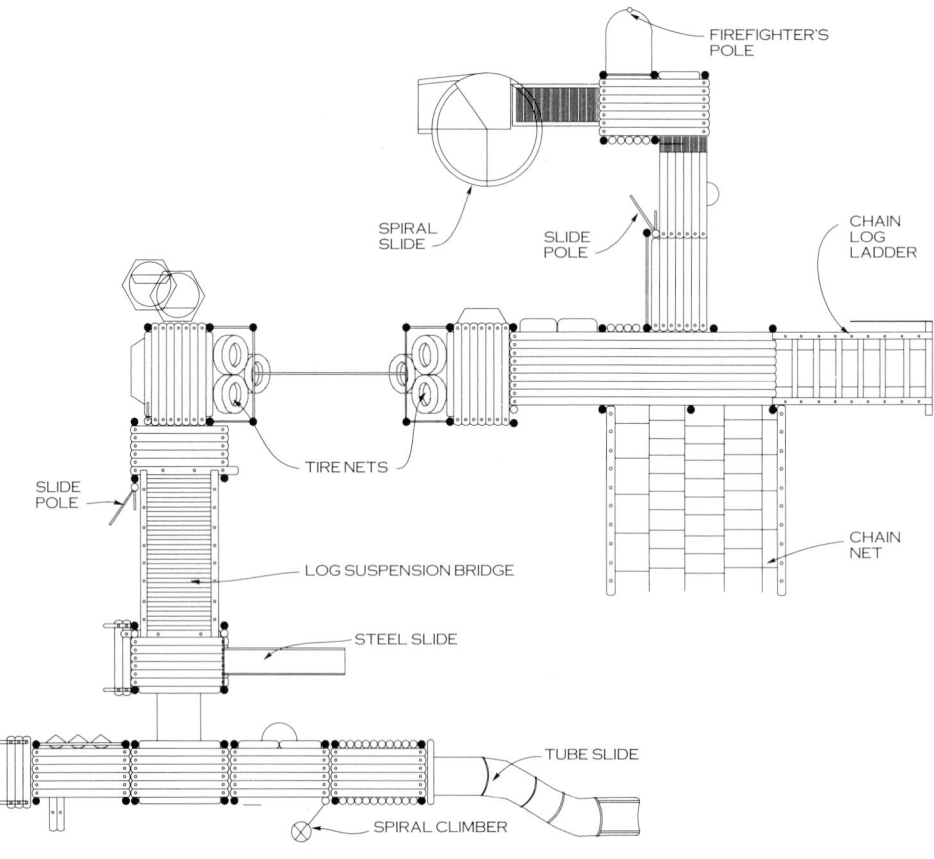

INTEGRATED PLAY AREA

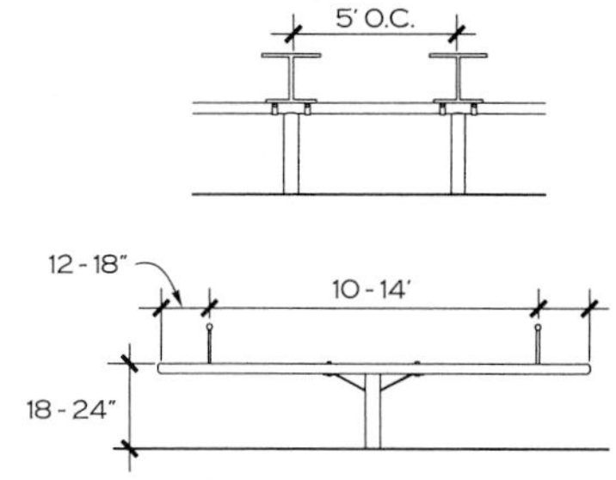

SEESAW

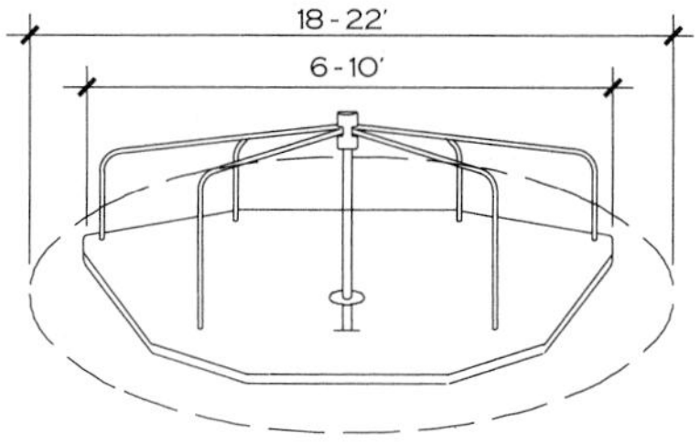

5' O.C.

12 - 18"

10 - 14'

18 - 24"

CAROUSEL

18 - 22'

6 - 10'

SINGLE UNIT COMPONENTS

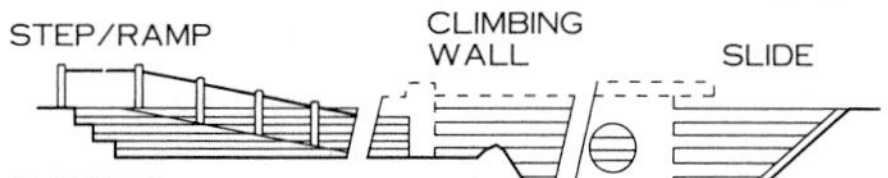

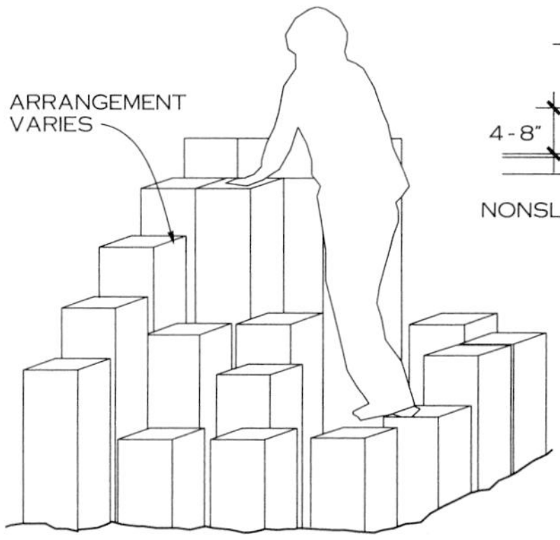

ARRANGEMENT
VARIES

STEPPED POSTS

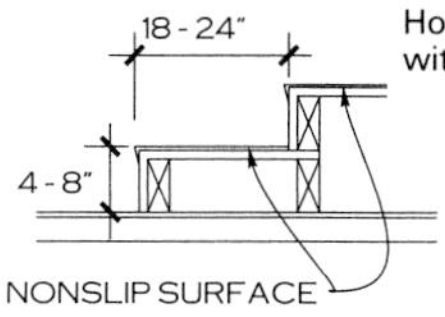

18 - 24"

4 - 8"

NONSLIP SURFACE

**BUMP STAIR
(ACCESSIBLE
AND TODDLERS)**

HAND LOOP

2 3/8" COATED
STEEL PIPE OR
GALVANIZED

1 5/16" COATED
STEEL PIPE OR
GALVANIZED
RUNG

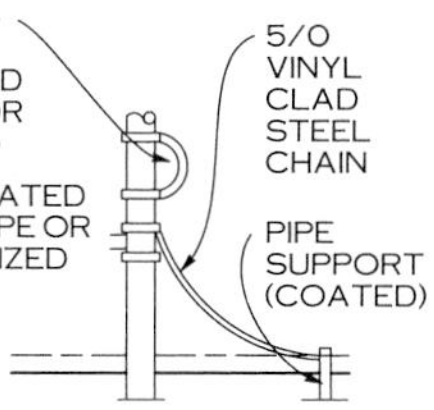

5/0
VINYL
CLAD
STEEL
CHAIN

PIPE
SUPPORT
(COATED)

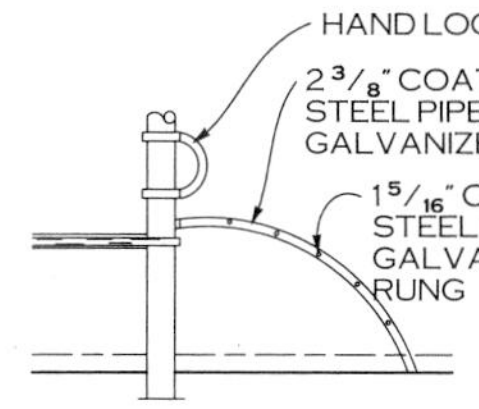

ARCH CLIMBER   ### CHAIN LADDER

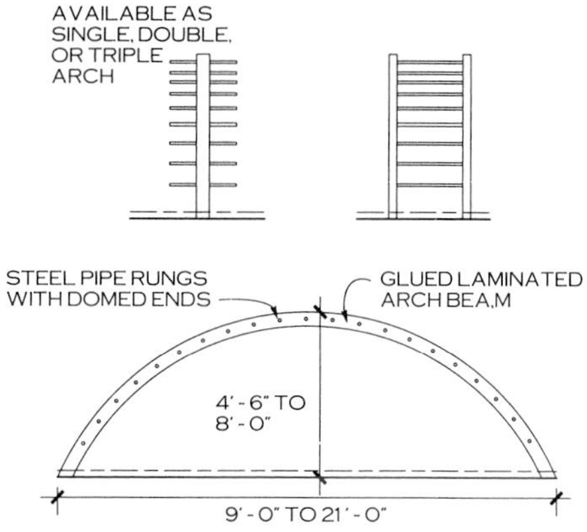

CLIMBERS AND LADDERS

NOTE

Optional seats for standard swing include full or partial bucket
seats, flat molded rubber seats, and molded contour chair seats.

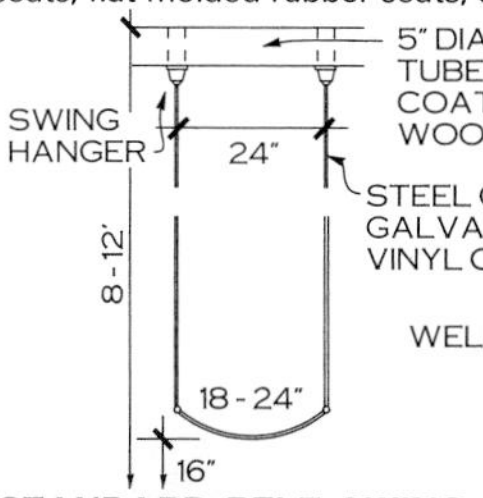

SWING
HANGER

24"

8 - 12'

18 - 24"

16"

5" DIA. STEEL
TUBE (POWDER
COATED) OR
WOOD BEAM

STEEL CHAIN -
GALVANIZED OR
VINYL COATED

WELDED

20"

STANDARD BELT SWING

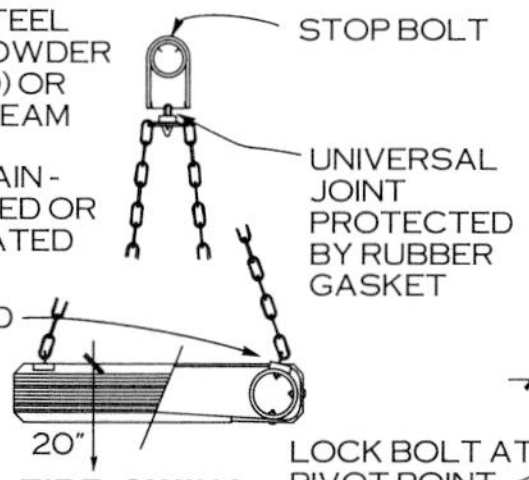

STOP BOLT

UNIVERSAL
JOINT
PROTECTED
BY RUBBER
GASKET

LOCK BOLT AT
PIVOT POINT

TIRE SWING

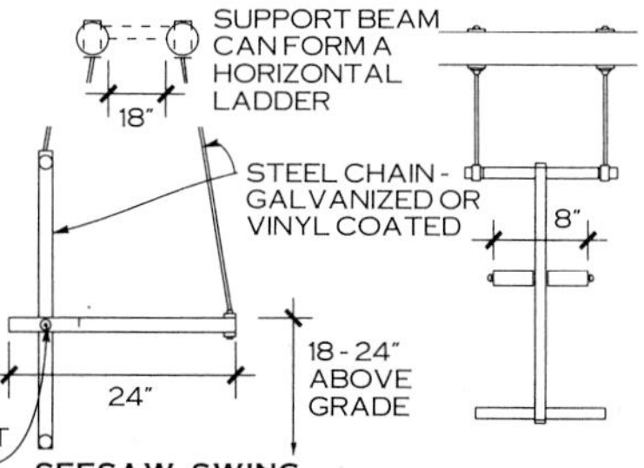

SUPPORT BEAM
CAN FORM A
HORIZONTAL
LADDER

18"

STEEL CHAIN -
GALVANIZED OR
VINYL COATED

24"

18 - 24"
ABOVE
GRADE

8"

SEESAW SWING

SWINGS

SMALL CHILDREN   OLDER CHILDREN

STEP/RAMP

CLIMBING
WALL

SLIDE

NOTES

1. Slopes are used for running, sliding,
climbing, jumping, and rolling.
2. Slopes greater than 2:1 must be
stabilized with concrete, stone,
timber, etc.

LANDFORMS
MAY DEFINE
PLAY AREAS
AND SEPARATE
ZONES

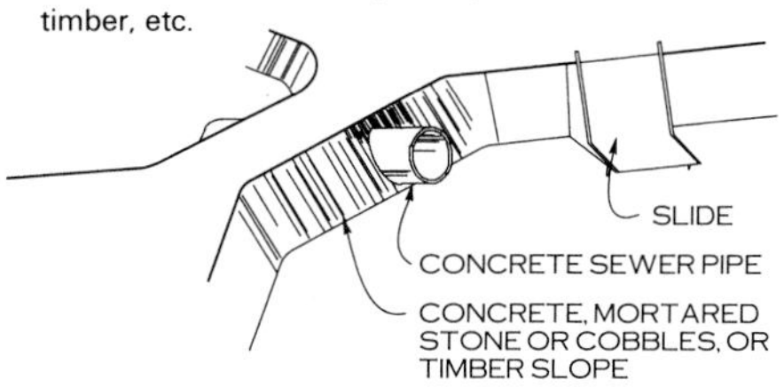

SLIDE

CONCRETE SEWER PIPE

CONCRETE, MORTARED
STONE OR COBBLES, OR
TIMBER SLOPE

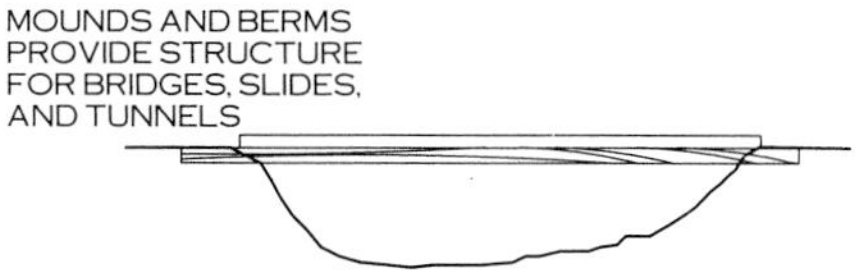

MOUNDS AND BERMS
PROVIDE STRUCTURE
FOR BRIDGES, SLIDES,
AND TUNNELS

LANDFORMS

NOTE

Horizontal ladders build strength in disabled children
with upper mobility: place at 48 to 54 in. in height.

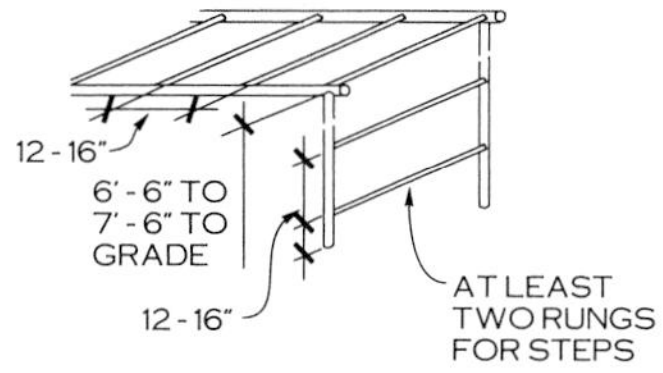

12 - 16"

6' - 6" TO
7' - 6" TO
GRADE

12 - 16"

AT LEAST
TWO RUNGS
FOR STEPS

HORIZONTAL LADDER

AVAILABLE AS
SINGLE, DOUBLE,
OR TRIPLE
ARCH

STEEL PIPE RUNGS
WITH DOMED ENDS

GLUED LAMINATED
ARCH BEA,M

4' - 6" TO
8' - 0"

9' - 0" TO 21' - 0"

ARCH LADDER

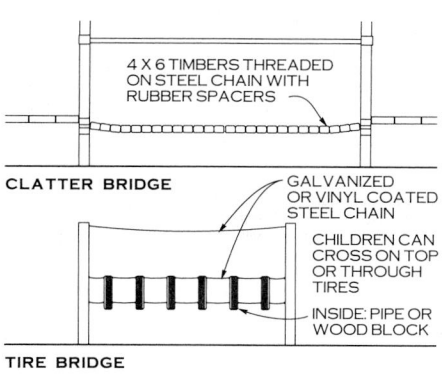

4 X 6 TIMBERS THREADED
ON STEEL CHAIN WITH
RUBBER SPACERS

CLATTER BRIDGE

GALVANIZED
OR VINYL COATED
STEEL CHAIN

CHILDREN CAN
CROSS ON TOP
OR THROUGH
TIRES

INSIDE: PIPE OR
WOOD BLOCK

TIRE BRIDGE

BRIDGES

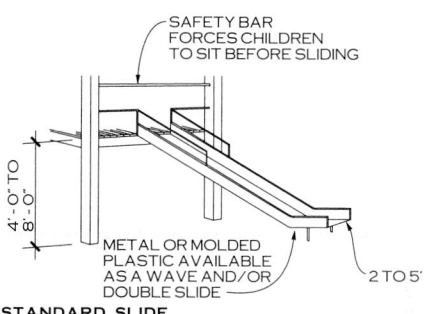

SAFETY BAR
FORCES CHILDREN
TO SIT BEFORE SLIDING

4' - 0" TO
8' - 0"

METAL OR MOLDED
PLASTIC AVAILABLE
AS A WAVE AND/OR
DOUBLE SLIDE

2 TO 5'

STANDARD SLIDE

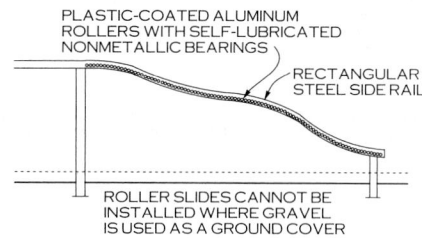

PLASTIC-COATED ALUMINUM
ROLLERS WITH SELF-LUBRICATED
NONMETALLIC BEARINGS

RECTANGULAR
STEEL SIDE RAIL

ROLLER SLIDES CANNOT BE
INSTALLED WHERE GRAVEL
IS USED AS A GROUND COVER

ROLLER SLIDE

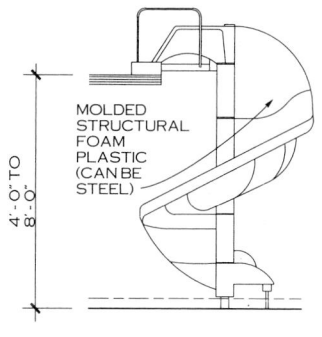

4' - 0" TO
8' - 0"

MOLDED
STRUCTURAL
FOAM
PLASTIC
(CAN BE
STEEL)

SPIRAL SLIDE

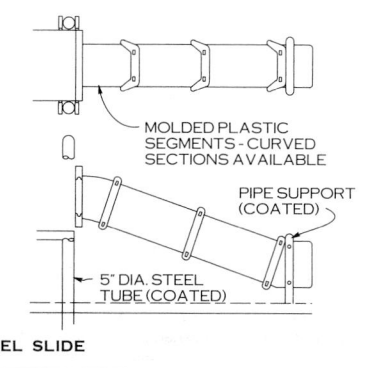

MOLDED PLASTIC
SEGMENTS - CURVED
SECTIONS AVAILABLE

PIPE SUPPORT
(COATED)

5" DIA. STEEL
TUBE (COATED)

TUNNEL SLIDE

SLIDES

Andrew Sumners; University Park, Maryland

SITE IMPROVEMENTS   2

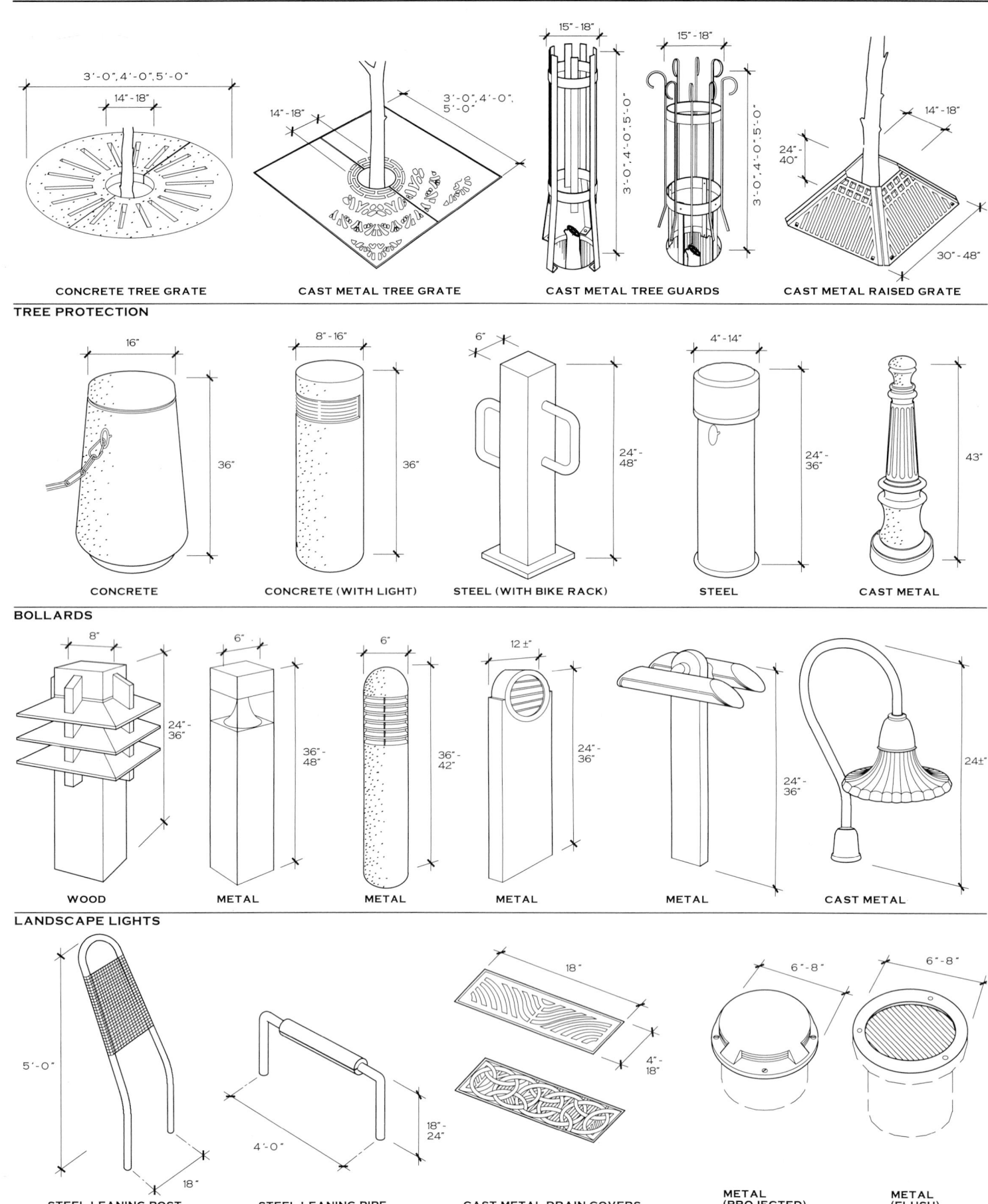

CONCRETE TREE GRATE   CAST METAL TREE GRATE   CAST METAL TREE GUARDS   CAST METAL RAISED GRATE

TREE PROTECTION

CONCRETE   CONCRETE (WITH LIGHT)   STEEL (WITH BIKE RACK)   STEEL   CAST METAL

BOLLARDS

WOOD   METAL   METAL   METAL   METAL   CAST METAL

LANDSCAPE LIGHTS

STEEL LEANING POST   STEEL LEANING PIPE   CAST METAL DRAIN COVERS

MISCELLANEOUS

METAL (PROJECTED)   METAL (FLUSH)

DRIVE / WALKOVER LIGHTS

Richard J. Vitullo, AIA; Oak Leaf Studio; Crownsville, Maryland

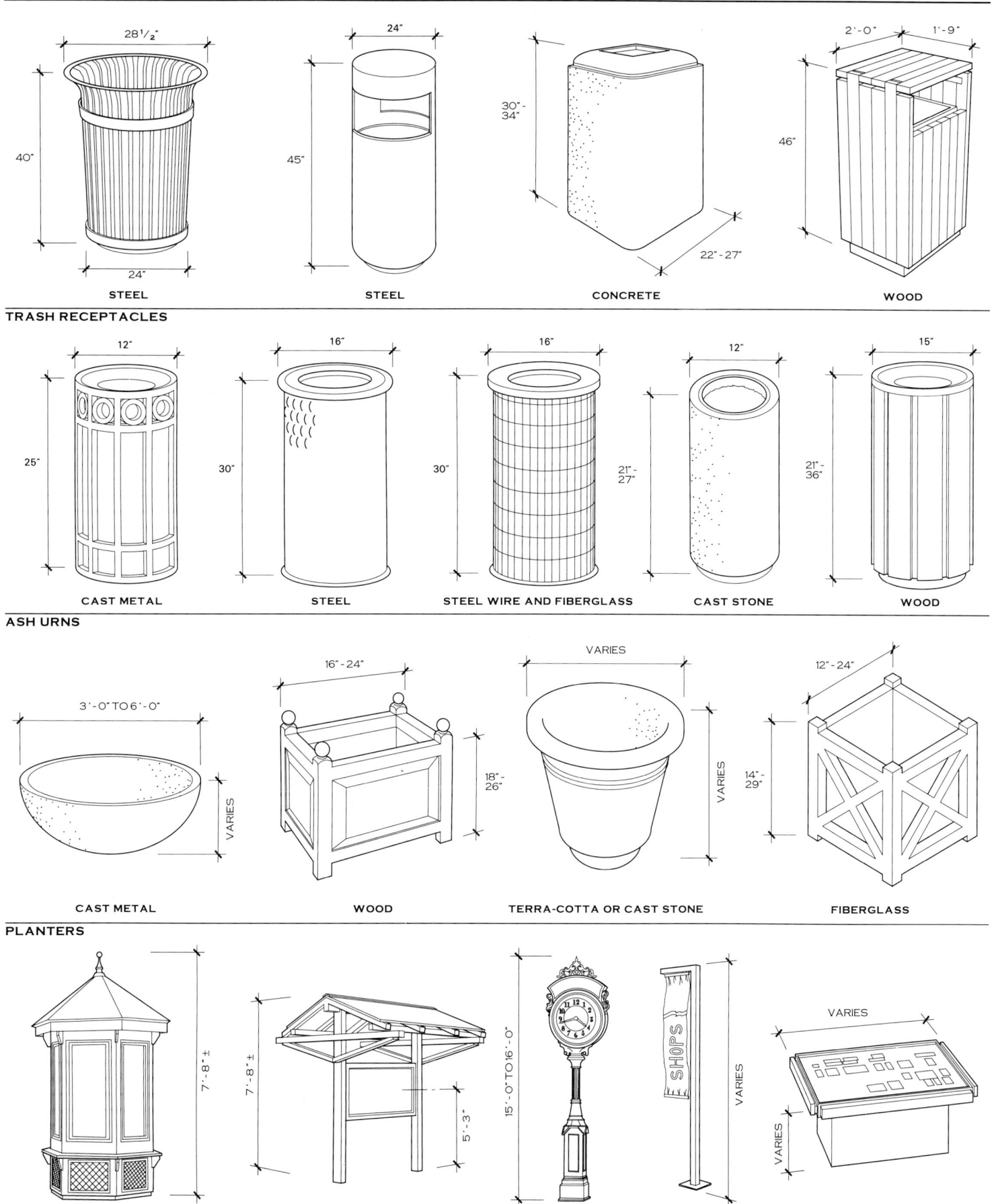

28¹/₂"

40"

24"

STEEL

24"

45"

STEEL

30"–34"

22"–27"

CONCRETE

2'-0"   1'-9"

46"

WOOD

TRASH RECEPTACLES

12"

25"

CAST METAL

16"

30"

STEEL

16"

30"

STEEL WIRE AND FIBERGLASS

12"

21"–27"

CAST STONE

15"

21"–36"

WOOD

ASH URNS

3'-0" TO 6'-0"

VARIES

CAST METAL

16"–24"

18"–26"

WOOD

VARIES

VARIES

TERRA-COTTA OR CAST STONE

12"–24"

14"–29"

FIBERGLASS

PLANTERS

7'-8"±

KIOSK

7'-8"±

5'-3"

MESSAGE BOARD

15'-0" TO 16'-0"

SHOPS

CLOCK   **BANNER AND POLE**

VARIES

VARIES

DIRECTORY

INFORMATION-RELATED FURNISHINGS

Richard J. Vitullo, AIA; Oak Leaf Studio; Crownsville, Maryland

SITE IMPROVEMENTS   2

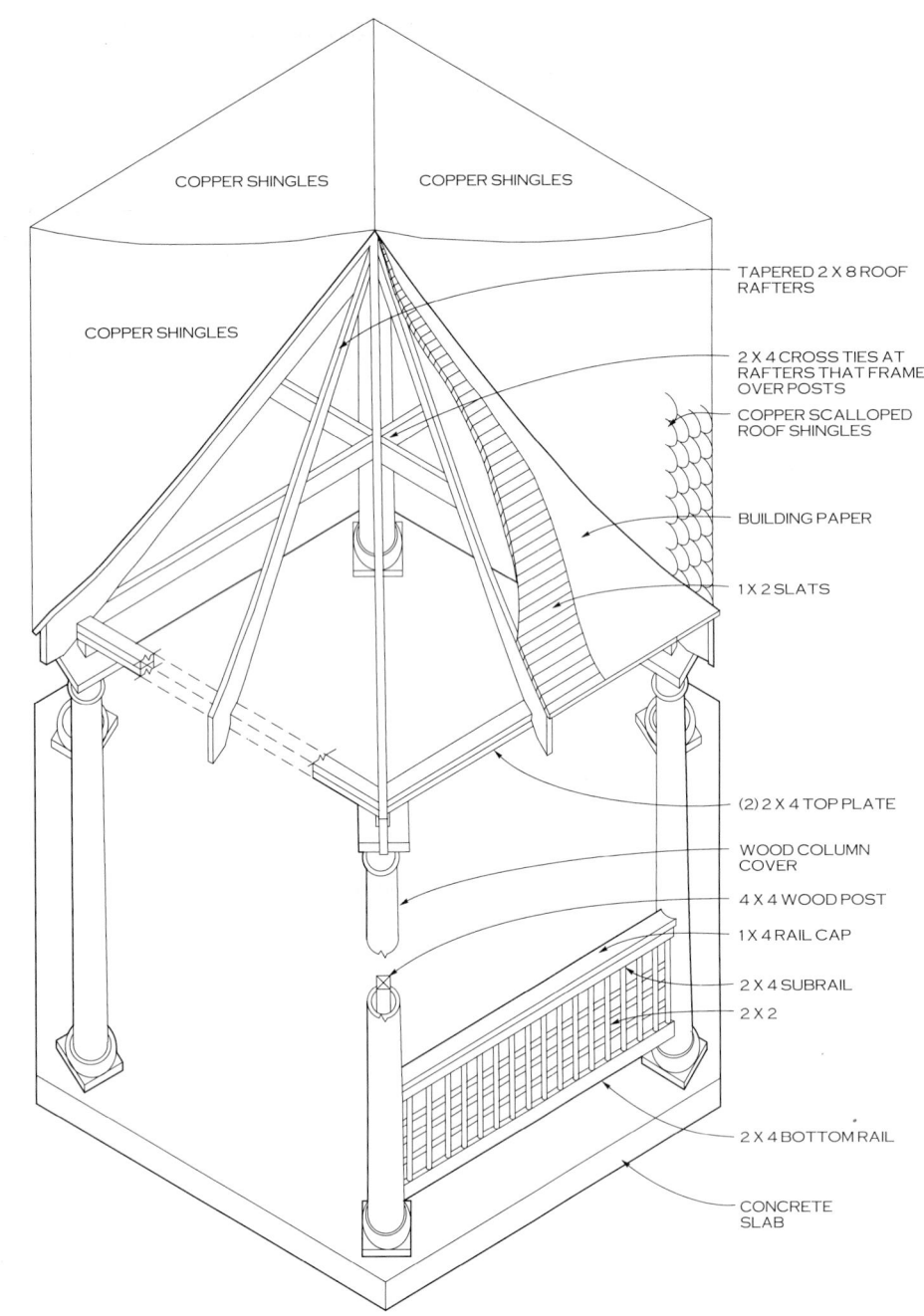

COPPER SHINGLES   COPPER SHINGLES

COPPER SHINGLES

TAPERED 2 X 8 ROOF
RAFTERS

2 X 4 CROSS TIES AT
RAFTERS THAT FRAME
OVER POSTS

COPPER SCALLOPED
ROOF SHINGLES

BUILDING PAPER

1 X 2 SLATS

(2) 2 X 4 TOP PLATE

WOOD COLUMN
COVER

4 X 4 WOOD POST

1 X 4 RAIL CAP

2 X 4 SUBRAIL

2 X 2

2 X 4 BOTTOM RAIL

CONCRETE
SLAB

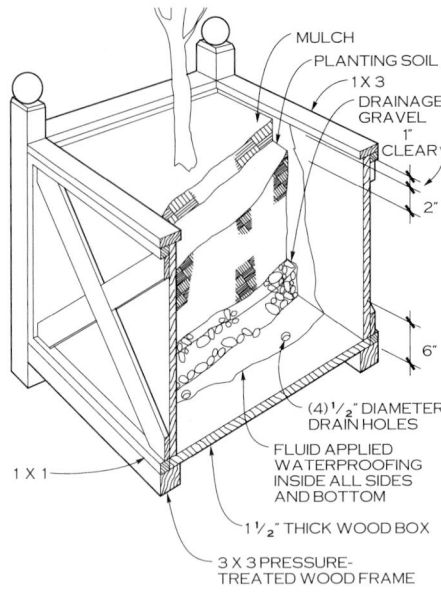

MULCH
PLANTING SOIL
1 X 3
DRAINAGE
GRAVEL
1"
CLEAR
2"
6"
(4) 1/2" DIAMETER
DRAIN HOLES
FLUID APPLIED
WATERPROOFING
INSIDE ALL SIDES
AND BOTTOM
1 X 1
1 1/2" THICK WOOD BOX
3 X 3 PRESSURE-
TREATED WOOD FRAME

WOOD PLANTER

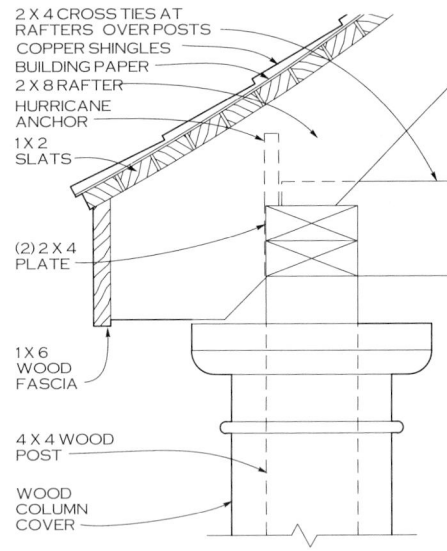

2 X 4 CROSS TIES AT
RAFTERS OVER POSTS
COPPER SHINGLES
BUILDING PAPER
2 X 8 RAFTER
HURRICANE
ANCHOR
1 X 2
SLATS
(2) 2 X 4
PLATE
1 X 6
WOOD
FASCIA
4 X 4 WOOD
POST
WOOD
COLUMN
COVER

GAZEBO DETAIL

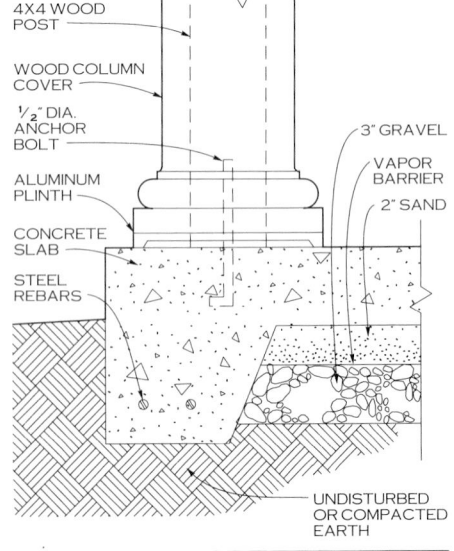

4 X 4 WOOD
POST
WOOD COLUMN
COVER
1/2" DIA.
ANCHOR
BOLT
ALUMINUM
PLINTH
CONCRETE
SLAB
STEEL
REBARS
3" GRAVEL
VAPOR
BARRIER
2" SAND
UNDISTURBED
OR COMPACTED
EARTH

GAZEBO DETAIL

GAZEBO

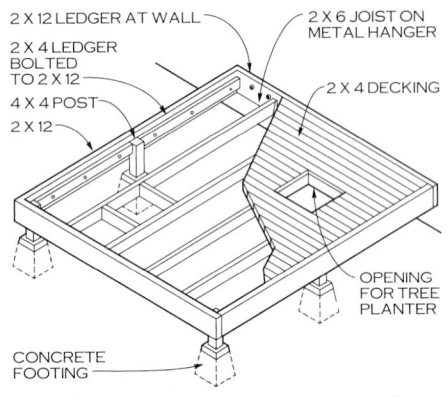

2 X 12 LEDGER AT WALL
2 X 4 LEDGER
BOLTED
TO 2 X 12
4 X 4 POST
2 X 12
2 X 6 JOIST ON
METAL HANGER
2 X 4 DECKING
OPENING
FOR TREE
PLANTER
CONCRETE
FOOTING

WOOD DECK PLATFORM

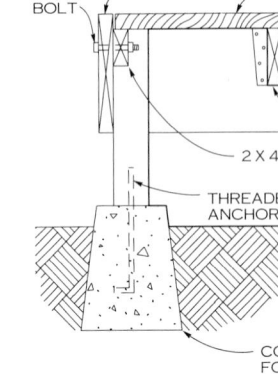

3/8" X 6"
BOLT
2 X 12
2 X 4 DECKING
2 X 6 ON METAL
HANGER
2 X 4 LEDGER
THREADED
ANCHOR BOLT
CONCRETE
FOOTING

PLATFORM FOOTING DETAIL

Gary Greenan; Miami, Florida
Richard J. Vitullo, AIA; Oak Leaf Studio; Crownsville, Maryland

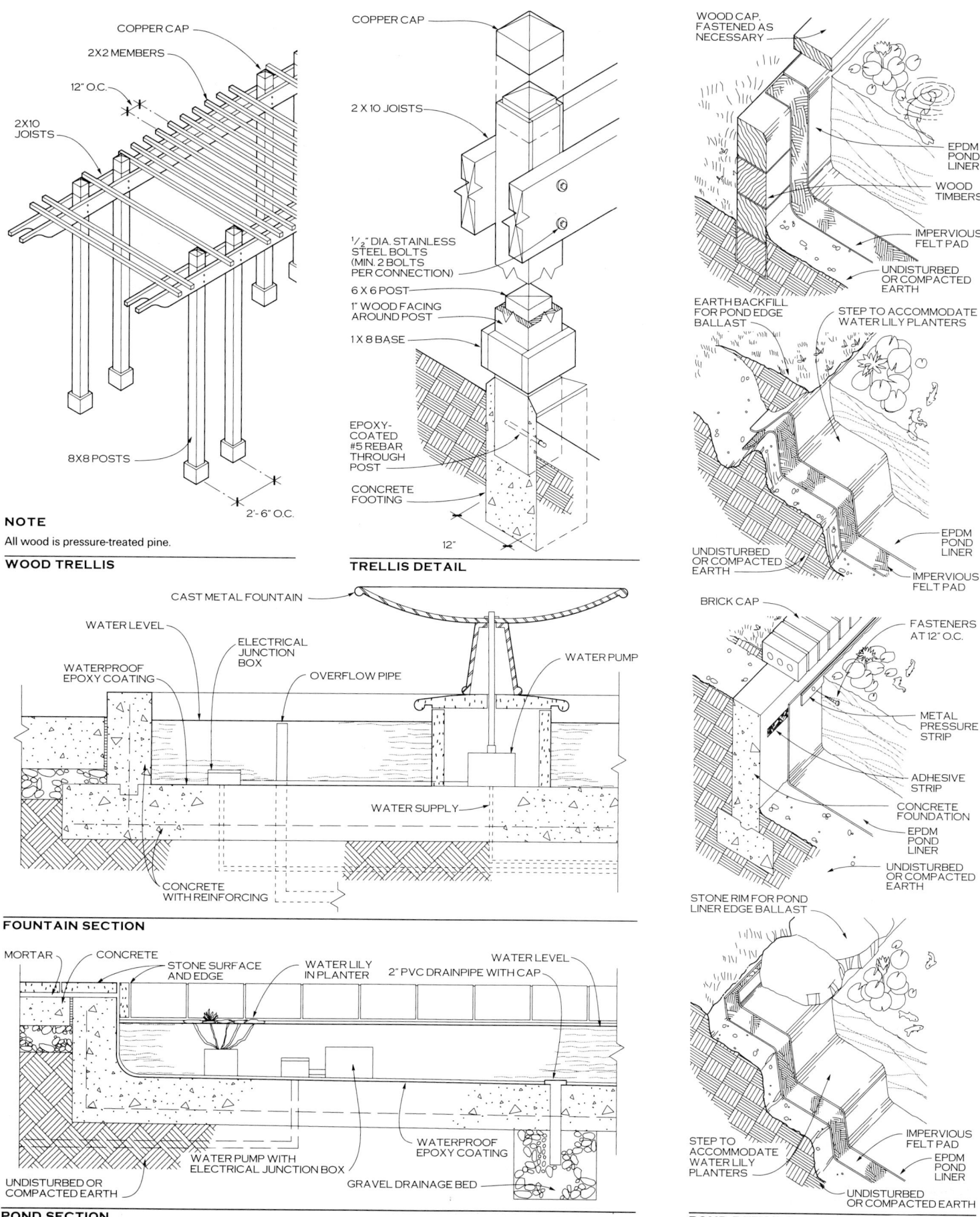

WOOD TRELLIS

COPPER CAP

2X2 MEMBERS

12" O.C.

2X10 JOISTS

8X8 POSTS

2'-6" O.C.

NOTE

All wood is pressure-treated pine.

TRELLIS DETAIL

COPPER CAP

2 X 10 JOISTS

1/2" DIA. STAINLESS STEEL BOLTS (MIN. 2 BOLTS PER CONNECTION)

6 X 6 POST

1" WOOD FACING AROUND POST

1 X 8 BASE

EPOXY-COATED #5 REBAR THROUGH POST

CONCRETE FOOTING

12"

FOUNTAIN SECTION

CAST METAL FOUNTAIN

WATER LEVEL

WATERPROOF EPOXY COATING

ELECTRICAL JUNCTION BOX

OVERFLOW PIPE

WATER PUMP

WATER SUPPLY

CONCRETE WITH REINFORCING

POND SECTION

MORTAR

CONCRETE

STONE SURFACE AND EDGE

WATER LILY IN PLANTER

WATER LEVEL

2" PVC DRAINPIPE WITH CAP

WATER PUMP WITH ELECTRICAL JUNCTION BOX

WATERPROOF EPOXY COATING

GRAVEL DRAINAGE BED

UNDISTURBED OR COMPACTED EARTH

POND DETAILS

WOOD CAP, FASTENED AS NECESSARY

EPDM POND LINER

WOOD TIMBERS

IMPERVIOUS FELT PAD

UNDISTURBED OR COMPACTED EARTH

EARTH BACKFILL FOR POND EDGE BALLAST

STEP TO ACCOMMODATE WATER LILY PLANTERS

EPDM POND LINER

UNDISTURBED OR COMPACTED EARTH

IMPERVIOUS FELT PAD

BRICK CAP

FASTENERS AT 12" O.C.

METAL PRESSURE STRIP

ADHESIVE STRIP

CONCRETE FOUNDATION

EPDM POND LINER

UNDISTURBED OR COMPACTED EARTH

STONE RIM FOR POND LINER EDGE BALLAST

STEP TO ACCOMMODATE WATER LILY PLANTERS

IMPERVIOUS FELT PAD

EPDM POND LINER

UNDISTURBED OR COMPACTED EARTH

Gary Greenan; Miami, Florida

Richard J. Vitullo, AIA; Oak Leaf Studio; Crownsville, Maryland

SITE IMPROVEMENTS 2

NOTES

Following are several factors to consider regarding the function and environmental regulatory effects of trees:

1. The physical environment of the site:
   Soil conditions (acidity, porosity)
   Amount and intensity of sunlight and precipitation
   Seasonal temperature range
   Site location and topography related to cold winds and cooling breezes
2. The design needs of the project:
   Directing pedestrian or vehicle movement
   Framing vistas and screening objectionable views
   Modifying the microclimate of the site
   Conserving energy (heating, cooling, lighting)
   Defining and shaping exterior space
3. The design character of trees:
   Deciduous (effects change with seasons)
   Conifers (effects remain relatively constant)
   Height and mass over time as the tree matures
   Shape (columnar, conical, spherical, spreading)
   Inherent color and texture (coarse, medium, fine)
   Growth habits (slow to fast)

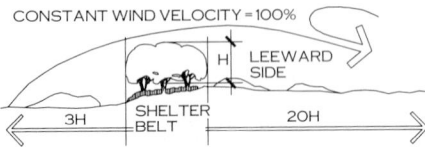

Protection is directly related to shelter belt height and density.

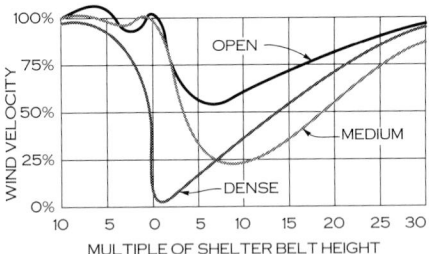

WIND PROTECTION

Shelter belt wind protection has the following effects:
1. Reduces evaporation at ground level
2. Increases relative humidity
3. Lowers temperature in summer
4. Reduces heat loss in winter
5. Reduces blowing dust and drifting snow

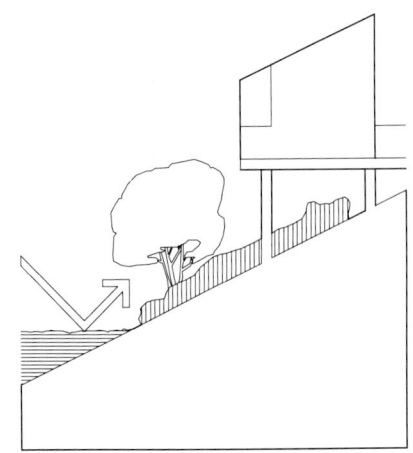

GLARE PROTECTION

The sun's vertical angle changes seasonally; therefore, the area subject to the glare of reflected sunlight varies. Plants of various heights screen glare from adjacent surfaces (water, paving, glass, and building surfaces).

A.E. Bye and Associates, Landscape Architects; Old Greenwich, Connecticut
Robin Roberts; Washington, D.C.

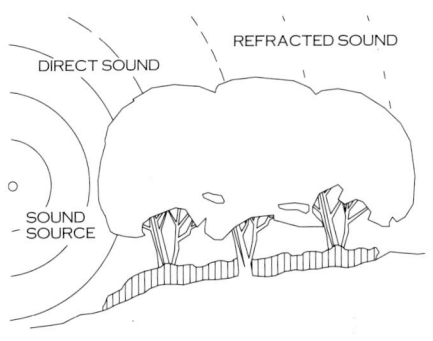

SOUND ATTENUATION

A combination of deciduous and evergreen plants reduces sound more effectively than deciduous plants alone. Planting on earth mounds increases the attenuating effects of the buffer.

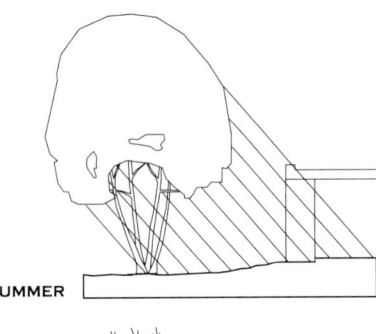

SUMMER

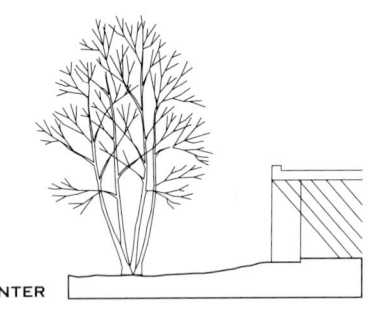

WINTER

RADIATION PROTECTION

In summer deciduous plants obstruct or filter the sun's strong radiation, thus cooling the area beneath them. In winter the sun penetrates through.

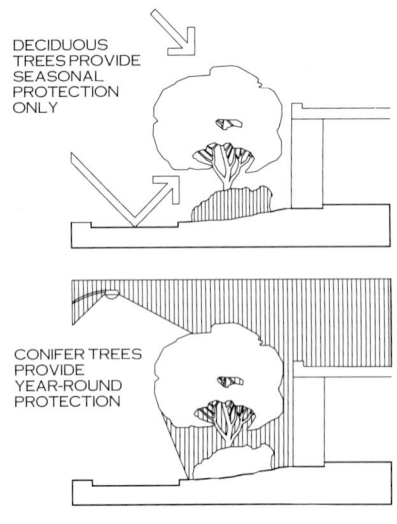

GLARE PROTECTION

Glare and reflection from sunlight and/or artificial sources can be screened or blocked by plants of various height and placement.

CROWN: HEAD OF FOLIAGE OF TREE

LEAVES: FOLIAGE UNIT OF TREE THAT FUNCTIONS PRIMARILY IN FOOD MANUFACTURING BY PHOTOSYNTHESIS

ROOTS: ANCHOR THE TREE AND HELP HOLD THE SOIL AGAINST EROSION

ROOT HAIRS: ABSORB MINERALS FROM THE SOIL MOISTURE AND SEND THEM AS NUTRIENT SALTS IN THE THE SAPWOOD TO THE LEAVES

HEARTWOOD: NONLIVING CENTRAL PART OF TREE GIVING STRENGTH AND STABILITY

ANNUAL RINGS: REVEAL AGE OF TREE BY SHOWING YEARLY GROWTH

OUTER BARK: AGED INNER BARK THAT PROTECTS TREE FROM DESSICATION AND INJURY

INNER BARK (PHLOEM): CARRIES FOOD FROM LEAVES TO BRANCHES, TRUNK, AND ROOTS

SAPWOOD (XYLEM): CARRIES NUTRIENTS AND WATER TO LEAVES FROM ROOTS

CAMBIUM: LAYER BETWEEN AND PHLOEM WHERE CELL ADDING GROWTH OCCURS, NEW SAPWOOD TO INSIDE AND NEW INNER BARK OUTSIDE

PHYSICAL CHARACTERISTICS

Particular matter trapped on the leaves is washed to the ground during a rainfall. Gaseous and other pollutants are assimilated in the leaves.

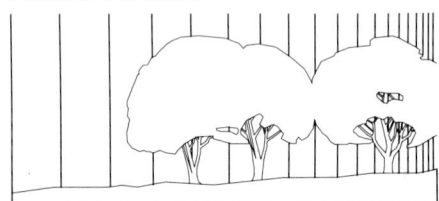

Fumes and odors can be mechanically masked by fragrant plants and chemically metabolized in the photosynthetic process.

AIR FILTRATION

Large masses of plants physically and chemically filter and deodorize the air to reduce air pollution.

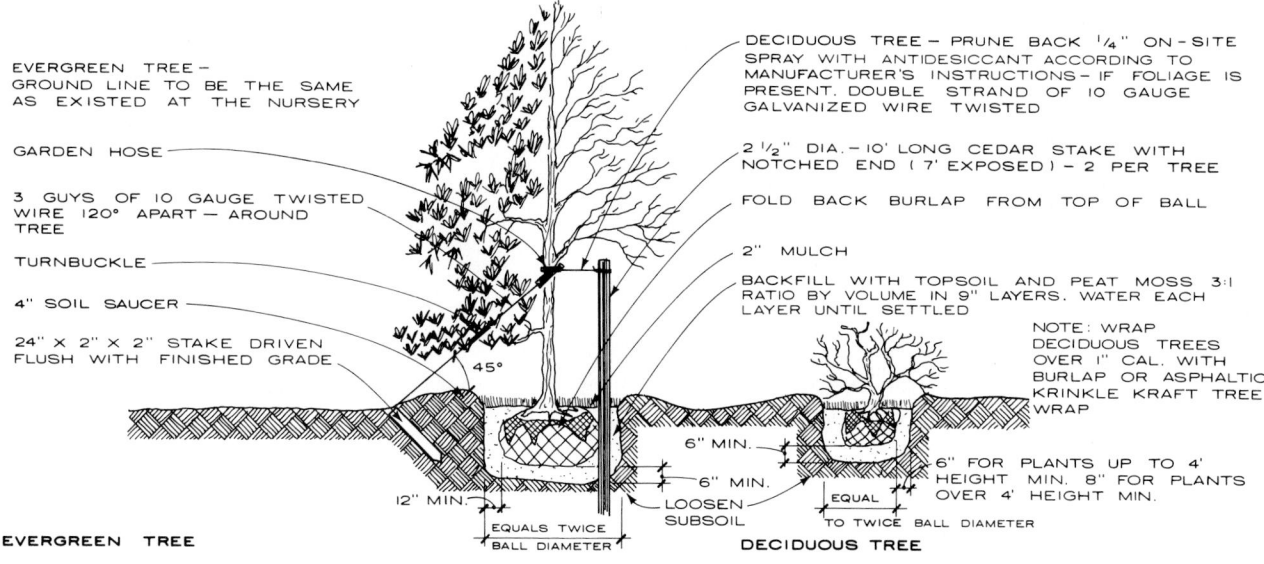

EVERGREEN TREE —
GROUND LINE TO BE THE SAME
AS EXISTED AT THE NURSERY

GARDEN HOSE

3 GUYS OF 10 GAUGE TWISTED
WIRE 120° APART — AROUND
TREE

TURNBUCKLE

4" SOIL SAUCER

24" X 2" X 2" STAKE DRIVEN
FLUSH WITH FINISHED GRADE

45°

EVERGREEN TREE

12" MIN.

EQUALS TWICE
BALL DIAMETER

6" MIN.
6" MIN.
LOOSEN
SUBSOIL

DECIDUOUS TREE — PRUNE BACK ¼" ON-SITE
SPRAY WITH ANTIDESICCANT ACCORDING TO
MANUFACTURER'S INSTRUCTIONS — IF FOLIAGE IS
PRESENT. DOUBLE STRAND OF 10 GAUGE
GALVANIZED WIRE TWISTED

2½" DIA. — 10' LONG CEDAR STAKE WITH
NOTCHED END (7' EXPOSED) — 2 PER TREE

FOLD BACK BURLAP FROM TOP OF BALL

2" MULCH

BACKFILL WITH TOPSOIL AND PEAT MOSS 3:1
RATIO BY VOLUME IN 9" LAYERS. WATER EACH
LAYER UNTIL SETTLED

NOTE: WRAP
DECIDUOUS TREES
OVER 1" CAL. WITH
BURLAP OR ASPHALTIC
KRINKLE KRAFT TREE
WRAP

6" FOR PLANTS UP TO 4'
HEIGHT MIN. 8" FOR PLANTS
OVER 4' HEIGHT MIN.

EQUAL
TO TWICE BALL DIAMETER

DECIDUOUS TREE

PLANTING DETAILS — TREES AND SHRUBS

SHRUBS AND MINOR TREES BALLED AND BURLAPPED

HEIGHT RANGE (FT)	MINIMUM BALL DIAMETER (IN.)	MINIMUM BALL DEPTH (IN.)
1½–2	10	8
2–3	12	9
3–4	13	10
4–5	15	11
5–6	16	12
6–7	18	13
7–8	20	14
8–9	22	15
9–10	24	16
10–12	26	17

NOTE: Ball sizes should always be of a diameter to
encompass the fibrous and feeding root system
necessary for the full recovery of the plant.

STANDARD SHADE TREES—BALLED AND BURLAPPED

CALIPER* (IN.)	HEIGHT RANGE (FT)	MAXIMUM HEIGHTS (FT)	MINIMUM BALL DIAMETER (IN.)	MINIMUM BALL DEPTH (IN.)
½–¾	5–6	8	12	9
¾–1	6–8	10	14	10
1–1¼	7–9	11	16	12
1¼–1½	8–10	12	18	13
1½–1¾	10–12	14	20	14
1¾–2	10–12	14	22	15
2–2½	12–14	16	24	16
2½–3	12–14	16	28	19
3–3½	14–16	18	32	20
3½–4	14–16	18	36	22
4–5	16–18	22	44	26
5–6	18 and up	26	48	29

*Caliper indicates the diameter of the trunk taken 6 in. above the ground level
up to and including 4 in. caliper size and 12 in. above the ground level for
larger sizes.

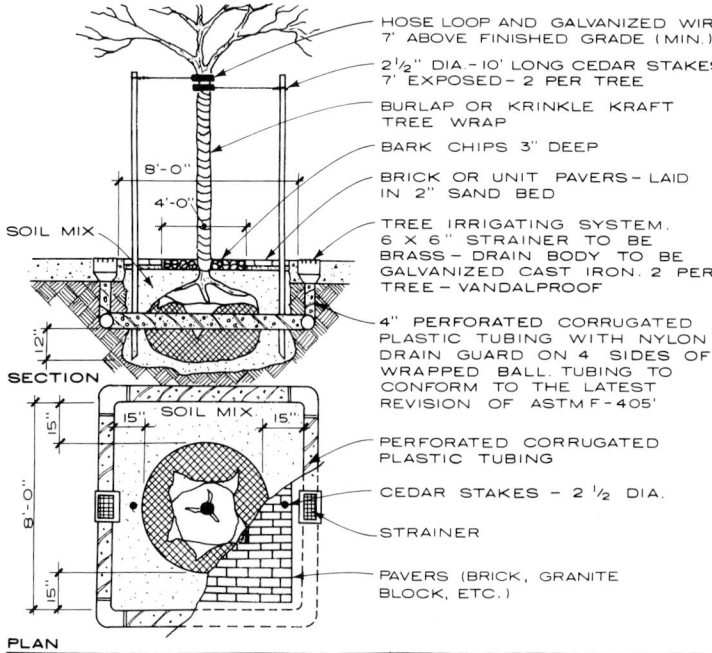

HOSE LOOP AND GALVANIZED WIRE
7' ABOVE FINISHED GRADE (MIN.)

2½" DIA.— 10' LONG CEDAR STAKES
7' EXPOSED — 2 PER TREE

BURLAP OR KRINKLE KRAFT
TREE WRAP

BARK CHIPS 3" DEEP

BRICK OR UNIT PAVERS — LAID
IN 2" SAND BED

TREE IRRIGATING SYSTEM.
6 X 6" STRAINER TO BE
BRASS — DRAIN BODY TO BE
GALVANIZED CAST IRON. 2 PER
TREE — VANDALPROOF

4" PERFORATED CORRUGATED
PLASTIC TUBING WITH NYLON
DRAIN GUARD ON 4 SIDES OF
WRAPPED BALL. TUBING TO
CONFORM TO THE LATEST
REVISION OF ASTM F-405'

PERFORATED CORRUGATED
PLASTIC TUBING

CEDAR STAKES — 2½ DIA.

STRAINER

PAVERS (BRICK, GRANITE
BLOCK, ETC.)

SOIL MIX
8'-0"
4'-0"
12"
SECTION

SOIL MIX
15"   15"
15"
8'-0"
15"
PLAN

PLANTING DETAIL — TREE IN PAVING

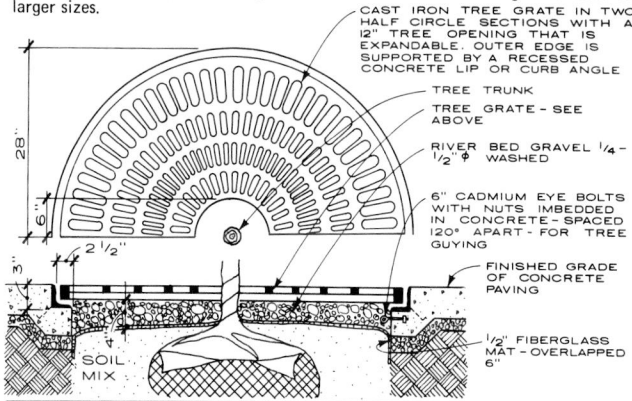

CAST IRON TREE GRATE IN TWO
HALF CIRCLE SECTIONS WITH A
12" TREE OPENING THAT IS
EXPANDABLE. OUTER EDGE IS
SUPPORTED BY A RECESSED
CONCRETE LIP OR CURB ANGLE

TREE TRUNK

TREE GRATE — SEE
ABOVE

RIVER BED GRAVEL ¼–
½ ⌀ WASHED

6" CADMIUM EYE BOLTS
WITH NUTS IMBEDDED
IN CONCRETE — SPACED
120° APART — FOR TREE
GUYING

FINISHED GRADE
OF CONCRETE
PAVING

½" FIBERGLASS
MAT — OVERLAPPED
6"

SOIL
MIX

28"
6"
2½"
3"

TREE GRATE DETAIL

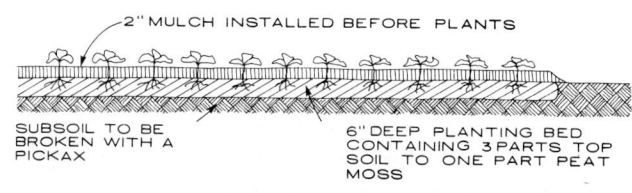

2" MULCH INSTALLED BEFORE PLANTS

SUBSOIL TO BE
BROKEN WITH A
PICKAX

6" DEEP PLANTING BED
CONTAINING 3 PARTS TOP
SOIL TO ONE PART PEAT
MOSS

GROUND COVER PLANTING DETAIL
NOTE: GROUND COVERS SHOULD BE POT OR CONTAINER GROWN

A.E. Bye and Associates, Landscape Architects; Old Greenwich, Connecticut

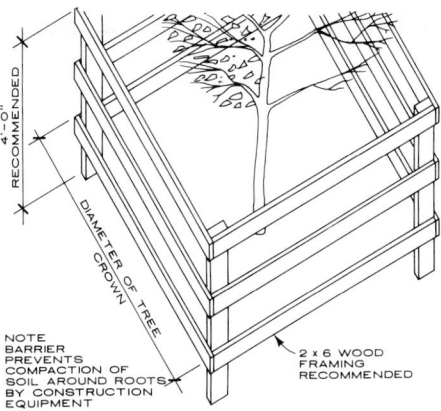

TREE PROTECTION BARRIER

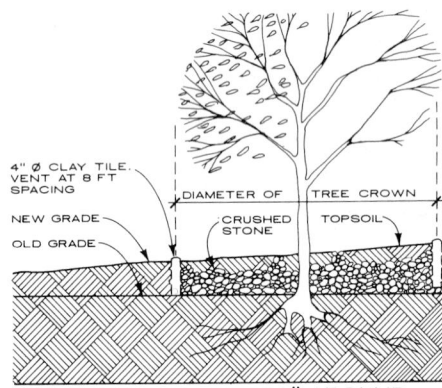

FILLING LESS THAN 30" AROUND EXISTING TREE

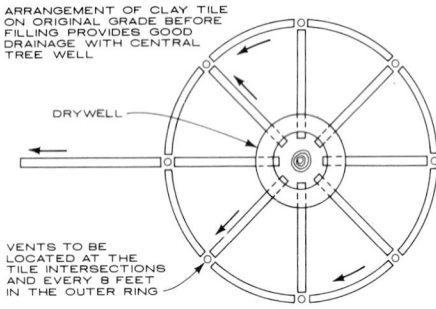

PLAN
FILLING OVER 30" AROUND EXISTING TREE

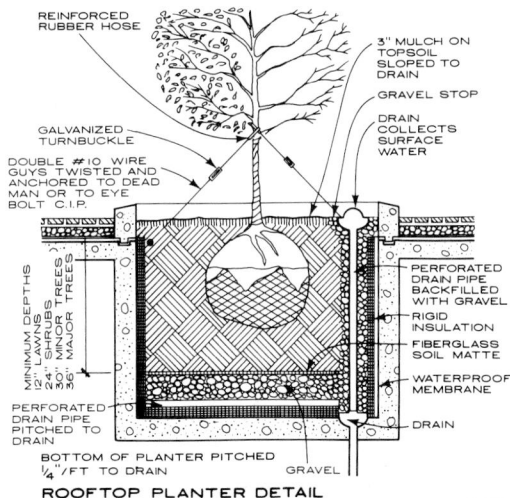

ROOFTOP PLANTER DETAIL
PLANTING ON STRUCTURES

TREE TRUNK PROTECTION

CUTTING AROUND EXISTING TREES

Extreme care should be taken not to compact the earth within the crown of the tree. Compaction can cause severe root damage and reduce the air and water holding capacity of the soil.

If no surrounding barrier is provided, care should be taken not to operate equipment or store materials within the crown spread of the tree. If this area should be compacted, it would be necessary to aerate the soil thoroughly in the root zone immediately following construction. Certain tree species are severely affected by manipulation of the water table, and great care should be exercised to minimize this condition.

SPECIAL USE OF TREES

Trees for special uses should be branched or pruned naturally according to type. Where a form of growth is desired that is not in accordance with a natural growth habit, this form should be specified. For example:

1. BUSH FORM: Trees that start to branch close to the ground in the manner of a shrub.
2. CLUMPS: Trees with three or more main stems starting from the ground.
3. CUT BACK OR SHEARED: Trees that have been pruned back so as to multiply the branching structure and to develop a more formal structure.
4. ESPALIER: Trees pruned and trained to grow flat against a building or trellis, usually in a predetermined pattern or design.
5. PLEACHING: A technique of severe pruning, usually applied to a row or bosque of trees to produce a geometrically formal or clipped hedgelike effect.
6. POLLARDING: The technique in which annual severe pruning of certain species of trees serves to produce abundant vigorous growth the following year.
7. TOPIARY: Trees sheared or trimmed closely in a formal geometric pattern, or sculptural shapes frequently resembling animals or flowers.

SELECTING PLANTS FOR ROOFTOPS

WIND TOLERANCE

Higher elevations and exposure to wind can cause defoliation and increased transpiration rate. High parapet walls with louvers screen wind velocity and provide shelter for plants.

HIGH EVAPORATION RATE

Drying effects of wind and sun on soil around planter reduce available soil moisture rapidly. Irrigation, mulches, moisture holding soil additives (perlite, vermiculite and peat moss), and insulation assist in reducing this moisture loss.

RAPID SOIL TEMPERATURE FLUCTUATION

The conduction capacity of planter materials tends to produce a broad range of soil temperatures. Certain plant species suffer severe root damage because of cold or heat. Use of rigid insulation lining planter alleviates this condition.

UNDERGROUND UTILITIES NEAR EXISTING TREES

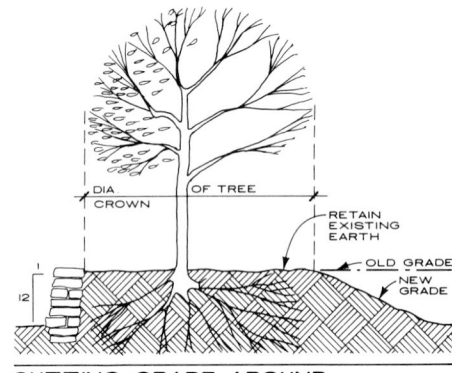

FILLING GRADE AROUND EXISTING TREE

CUTTING GRADE AROUND EXISTING TREE

TOPSOIL

Topsoil in planters should be improved to provide the optimum growing condition. A general formula would add fertilizer (as per soil testing) plus 1 part peat moss or vermiculite (high water holding capacity) to 3 parts topsoil. More specific requirements for certain varieties of plants or grasses should be considered.

ROOT CAPACITY

Plant species should be carefully selected to adapt to the size of the plant bed. If species with shallow fibrous roots are used instead of species with a tap root system consult with nurseryman. Consider the ultimate maturity of the plant species in sizing planter.

Jim E. Miller and David W. Wheeler; Saratoga Associates; Saratoga Springs, New York
William Cook; Lawrence Cook Associates, P.C. Architects; Falls Church, Virginia
Connecticut Coastal Management Program

INTRODUCTION

The selection of plant species for specific locations should be the culmination of a deductive analytical process. Site and plant characteristics, design criteria and intent, and plant growth and maintenance considerations are integral to the selection process.

Following is a list of site analysis determinants and potential program criteria for ornamental landscaping:

SITE ANALYSIS

1. Soils: Factors may include mechanical and/or physical properties, pH levels, and permeability.

2. Climate: Factors may include regional temperature variations, annual rainfall, microclimates created by structures, large bodies of water or other plantings, and prevailing winds.

3. Slope: Factors may include steepness, erodibility, and orientation to the sun.

4. Hydrology: Factors may include natural drainage patterns, water table levels, erosion potential, seasonal flooding, and drought-prone areas.

PROGRAM CRITERIA

1. Vistas and views: Factors may include providing framed glimpses of points of interest or maintaining open views to distant elements.

2. Screen: Factors may include masking on-site elements or adjacent land uses.

3. Shelter: Factors may include shading terraces or structures in summer or providing wind breaks for winter winds.

4. Habitat: Factors may include fruit-bearing plants as food and/or other trees and shrubs to shelter wildlife.

5. Color: Factors may include seasonal leaf change, bark or branching characteristics, leaf color or finish, fruit or flower color.

6. Scent: Factors may include flower, fruit, or foliage near windows, terraces, or entrances.

CANOPY: Typically large trees and shrubs, deciduous or evergreen, that provide structure, define space, or provide enclosure.

UNDERSTORY: Typically smaller trees, deciduous or evergreen, that provide special qualities such as fruiting, flowering, texture, and transition

GROUND COVER: Typically low growing plants but should include herbaceous material (perennials, grasses, etc.) and low, medium, and tall shrubs. These plantings add depth and dimension, in mass or as random accents.

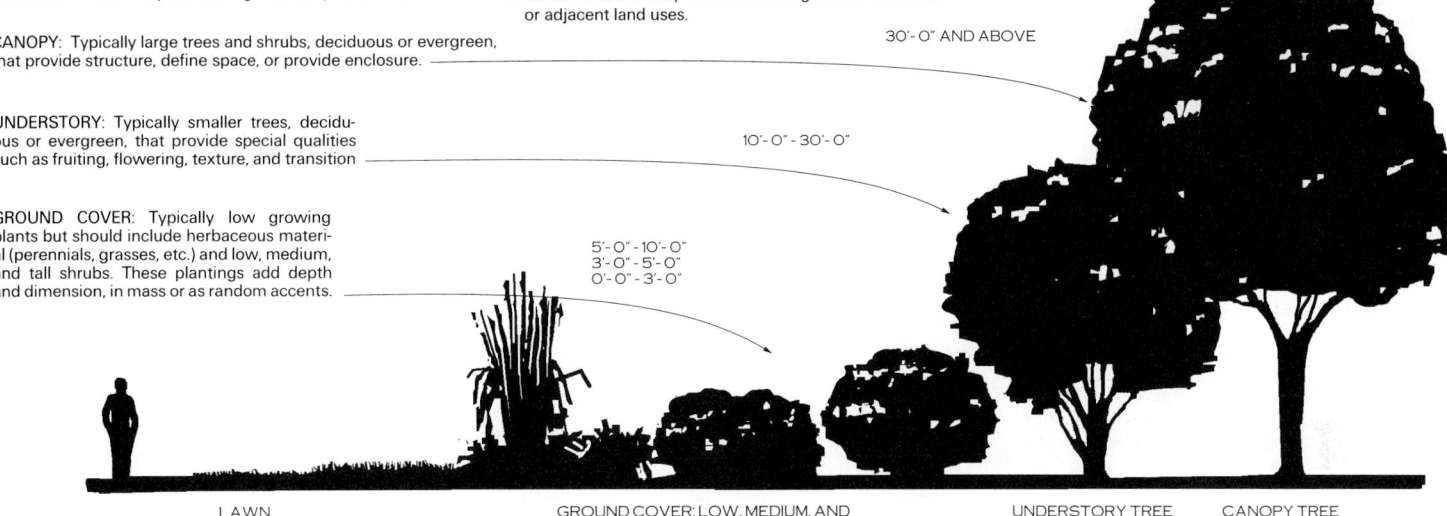

30'- 0" AND ABOVE

10'- 0" - 30'- 0"

5'- 0" - 10'- 0"
3'- 0" - 5'- 0"
0'- 0" - 3'- 0"

LAWN   GROUND COVER; LOW, MEDIUM, AND TALL SHRUBS; HERBACEOUS PLANTS   UNDERSTORY TREE   CANOPY TREE

NOTE
Plant selection is often a function of scale, both in terms of plant height and bed depth. Site constraints and/or program criteria often set the perimeters of scale.

PLANTS AND SCALE

ISSUES FOR URBAN GARDENS

1. CODES: State, region, or city restrictions and setback requirements regarding height and/or type of planting

2. SPATIAL LIMITATIONS: Issues relating to current size constraints and future growth

3. MICROCLIMATES: Factors relating to on-site structures or other plantings

4. WATER: Issues regarding current water needs and potential availability for irrigation

5. SOIL: Issues of compaction, nutrient availability, and content

6. EXISTING CONDITIONS: Issues relating to the protection of existing plantings and erosion and surface runoff during construction

REFERENCES

Dirr, Michael A. *Manual of Woody Landscape Plants.* Stipes Publishing Company.

Hightshoe, Gary L. *Native Trees, Shrubs and Vines for Urban and Rural America.* Van Nostrand Reinhold.

Oehme, Wolfgang, James van Sweden, and Susan Radenmacher Frey. *Bold Romantic Gardens.* Acropolis Books.

Simonds, John Ormsbee. *Landscape Architecture.* McGraw-Hill.

NOTE
Plants can be specified by a number of distinct characteristics: color, size, texture, and shape. Shape often sets the tone for the overall design or can result from spatial constraints. A common example of shape is the distinct form of the American elm.

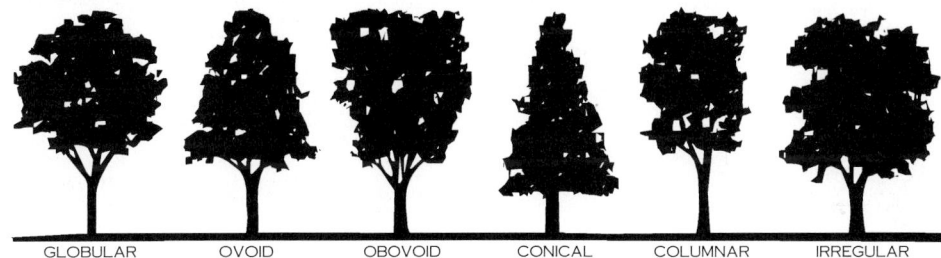

GLOBULAR   OVOID   OBOVOID   CONICAL   COLUMNAR   IRREGULAR

BASIC PLANT SHAPE CHARACTERISTICS

INITIAL PLANTING: Each plant retains individual qualities; herbaceous plantings show the quickest gowth, followed by shrubs and trees.

GROWTH RATE

INTERMEDIATE YEARS: Ground covers, herbaceous plants, and shrubs mature and blend. Trees begin to fill out and mature form becomes apparent.

MATURITY: Trees continue to mature, while shrubs and herbaceous plants continue to fill out or may need to be replanted.

Oehme, van Sweden & Associates, Inc.; Washington, D.C.

SOIL MECHANICS

The Association of Engineering Firms
    Practicing in the Geosciences (ASFE)
8811 Colesville Rd
Suite G106
Silver Spring, MD 20910
Tel: (301) 565-2733

Deep Foundations Institute (DFI)
Box 281
Sparta, NJ 07871
Tel: (201) 729-9679

Underground Space Center (UGSC)
University of Minnesota
500 Pillsbury Drive SE
Minneapolis, MN 55455
Tel: (612) 624-0066

US National Society for the International Society
    of Soil Mechanics and Foundation Engineering
(USNS/ISSMFE)
c/o Professor Harvey E. Wahls
CE Department, Box 7908
North Carolina State University
Raleigh, NC 27695
Tel: (919) 737-7244

REFERENCES

Bowles, Joseph E. *Foundation Analysis and Design.* New
    York: McGraw-Hill, 1982.
Duncan, Chester I. *Soils and Foundations for Architects
    and Engineers.* New York: Van Nostrand Reinhold,
    1992.
Excavating, Backfilling, & Compacting, SpecGUIDE
    G02220. Construction Specifications Institute, 1987.
Hayes, W. W. *Facing Geological and Hydrologic Hazards:
    Earth Science Considerations.* U.S. Geological Survey.
"Introduction to Lateral Pressure," Ch. 7.2 in *Building Foun-
    dation Design Handbook.* Underground Space Center,
    1988.
Landphair, H., and J. Motloch. *Site Reconnaissance and
    Engineering.* Elsevier, 1985.
PCA Soil Primer, EB007. Portland Cement Association,
    1992.
Schroeder, W. L. *Soils in Construction.* New York: J. Wiley
    & Sons, 1984.
Soil Preparation, SpecGUIDE G02100, Construction Spec-
    ifications Insitute, 1987.
Stamatopoulos, Aris C., and P. C. Kofzias. *Soil Improve-
    ment by Preloading.* New York: Wiley, 1985.
Truit, Marcus M. *Soil Mechanics Technology.* Englewood
    Cliffs, N.J.: Prentice-Hall, 1993.
Zeevaert, Leonardo. *Foundation Engineering for Different
    Subsoil Conditions.* New York: Van Nostrand Rein-
    hold, 1983.

DEMOLITION

Asbestos Information Association of North America
1745 Jefferson Davis Highway
Suite 509
Arlington, VA 22202
Tel: (703) 979-1150
Fax:(703) 979-1152

Toxic Substance Control Act
Toxic Materials Information Hotline
    Tel: (202) 554-1404

REFERENCES

Demolition, SpecGUIDE G02050, CSI, 1989.
National Association of Home Builders and Association of
    the Wall and Ceiling Industries, International. *Asbes-
    tos Handbook for Remodeling: How to Protect Your
    Business and Your Health.* Washington, D.C.: National
    Association of Home Builders, 1989.
Pielert, J. H. and Robert C. Mathey. *Guidelines for Assess-
    ment and Abatement of Asbestos.* Washington, D.C.:
    U.S. Department of Commerce, National Bureau of
    Standards, 1983.

PAVING AND SURFACING

Asphalt Institute
P.O. Box 14052
Research Park Drive
Lexington, KY 40512-4052
Tel: (606) 288-4960
Fax:(606) 288-4999

Concrete Paver Institute/National
    Concrete Masonry Association (CPI/NCMA)
2302 Horse Pen Road
Herndon, VA 22071
Tel: (703) 713-1900
Fax:(703) 713-1910

WATER, SEWERAGE, AND DRAINAGE

American Concrete Pipe Association
8300 Boone Blvd., Suite 400
Vienna, VA 22182
Tel: (703) 821-1990
Fax:(703) 821-3054

Cast Iron Soil Pipe Institute
5959 Shallow Ford Road
Suite 419
Chattanooga, TN 37421
Tel: (615) 892-0137
Fax:(615) 892-0817

REFERENCES

Cedergren, Harry R. *Seepage, Drainage, and Flow Nets.*
    New York: Wiley, 1977.
"Subdrainage," Ch. 8 in *Building Foundation Design Hand-
    book.* Underground Space Center, 1988.

SITE IMPROVEMENTS

American Society of Civil Engineers (ASCE)
345 E. 47th St.
New York, NY 10017
Tel: (212) 705-7722

Urban Land Institute (ULI)
625 Indiana Ave, N.W.
Suite 400
Washington, DC 20004
Tel: (800) 321-5011
Fax:(202) 624-7140

REFERENCES

Aurand, C. Douglas. *Fountains and Pools.* PDA Publishers
    Corporation.
"Brick Floors and Pavements." *Technical Notes on Brick
    Construction* 14, 14A, 14B. Brick Institute of America.
Lynch, Kevin. *Site Planning,* 3rd ed. MIT Press, 1984.
Parker, H., J. MacGuire, and J. Ambrose. *Simplified Site
    Engineering.* 2nd ed. New York: J. Wiley & Sons,
    1991.
Spirn, Anne Whiston. *The Granite Garden: Urban Nature
    and Human Design.* Basic Books, Inc., 1984.

LANDSCAPING

American Association of Nurserymen
1250 I Street, N.W.
Suite 500
Washington, DC 20005
Tel: (202) 789-2900
Fax:(202) 789-1893

American Society of Civil Engineers (ASCE)
345 East 47th Street
New York, NY 10017
Tel: (212) 705-7496
Fax:(212) 980-4681

American Society of Golf Course Architects (ASGCA)
221 North LaSalle Street, 35th Floor
Chicago, IL, 60601
Tel: (312) 372-7090

American Society of Landscape Architects (ASLA)
4401 Connecticut Ave., NW, 5th Floor
Washington, DC 20008
Tel: (800) 787-2665
  or (202) 686-2752
Fax:(202) 686-1001

Associated Landscape Contractors of America
405 N. Washington Street, Suite 104
Falls Church, VA 22046
Tel: (703) 241-4004
Fax:(703) 532-0463

Canadian Society of Landscape Architects (CSLA)
1339 15th Avenue, SW, unit 310
Calgary
Alberta, Canada T3C 3V3
Tel: (613) 232-6342

Concrete Paver Institute (CPI)
NCMA
2302 Horse Pen Rd.
Herndon, VA 22071-3406
Tel: (703) 713-1900

Council of Landscape
    Architecture Registration Boards
12700 Fair Lakes Circle, Suite 110
Fairfax, VA 22033-4905
Tel: (703) 818-1300
Fax:(703) 818-1309

National Landscape Association
1250 Eye Street, NW, Suite 500
Washington, DC 20005
Tel: (202) 789-2900

REFERENCES

Austin, Richard L. *Designing the Natural Landscape.* New
    York: Van Nostrand Reinhold, 1984.
DeChiara. *Time-Saver Standards for Site Planning.*
    McGraw-Hill, 1984.
Handbook of Landscape Architectural Construction.
    American Society of Landscape Architects (ASLA).
Ingels, Jack E. *Landscape Book.* New York: Van Nostrand
    Reinhold, 1983.
Lowry, W. P. *Atmospheric Ecology for Designers and Plan-
    ners.* Van Nostrand Reinhold, 1991.
Handbook of Landscape Architectural Construction. Land-
    scape Architecture Bookstore, 1976.
Harris, Charles W., and N. T. Dines. *Time-Saver Standards
    for Landscape Architecture.* McGraw-Hill, 1988.
Jewell, Linda. *Landscape Architecture.* American Society
    of Landscape Architects Publication Board, 1982.
Landphair, Harlow C., and Fred Klatt, Jr. *Landscape Archi-
    tecture Construction.* Elsevier Science Publishing Co.,
    Inc., 1979.
Levin, A. *Hillside Building: Design and Construction.* Arts +
    Architecture Press, 1991.
McCulley, E. Byron, and Jot D. Carpenter. *Handbook of
    Landscape Architectural Construction.* Landscape Ar-
    chitecture Foundation, Inc.
Munsun, Albe E. *Design for Landscape Architects.*
    McGraw-Hill, 1984.
Seelye, Elwyn E. *Data Book for Civil Engineers,* vol. 1: De-
    sign. New York: J. Wiley & Sons, 1945.
Untermann, R. *Grade Easy.* Landscape Architecture Book-
    store, 1973.

RELATED JOURNALS

Landscape Architecture
American Society of Landscape Architects
4401 Connecticut Avenue, NW
Washington, DC 20008-2302
Tel: (202) 686-2752

Landscape Journal
Council of Education in Landscape Architecture
University of Illinois
214 Mumford Hall
1301 W. Gregory Drive
Urbana, IL 60606
Tel: (217) 333-0175

Urban Land Magazine
Urban Land Institute
625 Indiana Avenue, NW
Suite 400
Washington, DC 20004
Tel: (202) 624-7000

CHAPTER

3

CONCRETE

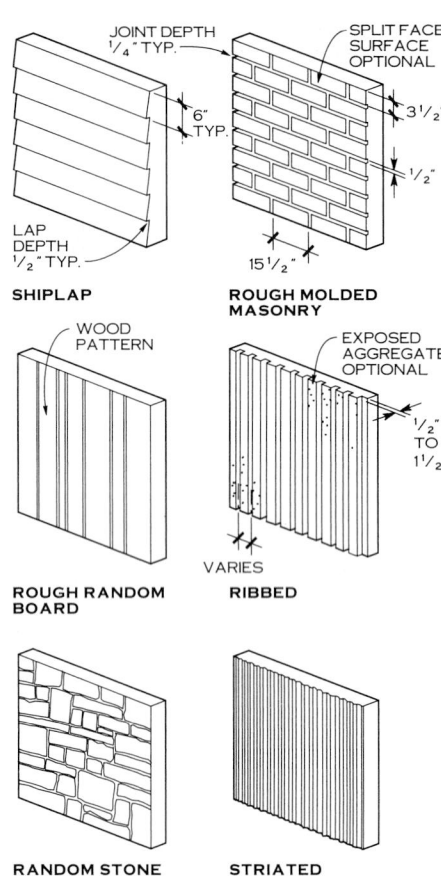

SHIPLAP

ROUGH MOLDED MASONRY

ROUGH RANDOM BOARD

RIBBED

RANDOM STONE

STRIATED

TYPICAL FORM PATTERNS

NOTE

Standard sheet sizes for reusable plastic form liners are 4 x 8 ft and 4 x 10 ft. Choose a textured concrete surface instead of trying to get a perfectly smooth finish. A great variety of rigid and elastometric patterned form liners is available to produce concrete surfaces with ribbed, jointed, or wood textures. The texture and resulting shadow patterns conceal minor color variations or damage that would be conspicuous and unacceptable on a smooth surface. Use rustication strips or broad reveals at joints in textured liners to simplify form assembly work.

REUSABLE PLASTIC FORM LINERS

GENERAL NOTES

Formwork costs are a substantial part of the total cost of putting concrete in place—anywhere from 35 to 60%. Thus, by developing design elements and details that simplify or standardize form requirements, the architect can help contain overall costs.

1. REUSE FORMS. This is crucial to economy of construction. The designer can facilitate form reuse by standardizing the dimensions of windows, columns, beams, and footings, using as few different sizes of each as possible. Where columns must change size, hold one dimension, such as width, constant while varying the depth. This enables at least half of the form panels to be used many times. Repeat the same floor and column layout from bay-to-bay each floor and from floor-to-floor. This improves labor productivity and permits reuse of many forms.

2. USE A PRECONSTRUCTION MOCKUP. Since formwork quality determines the appearance of architectural concrete, it is also cost effective for architect and builder to agree on the location and desired, appearance of architectural surfaces *before* any of the exposed concrete work begins. Specify a full-scale preconstruction mockup to help achieve this and to avoid postconstruction disagreements.

3. HANDLE FORMS IN LARGE PANELS. This also reduces construction costs. Wherever possible, make uninterrupted formed areas the same size. Increasing the size of such areas enables the builder to combine form panels into gangs for efficient crane use.

4. SIMPLIFY DESIGN DETAILS. Intricacies and irregularities cost more and often do not add proportionately to the aesthetic effect.

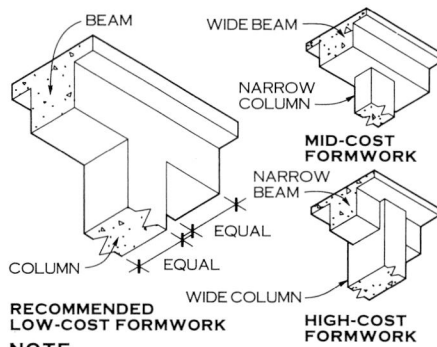

RECOMMENDED LOW-COST FORMWORK

MID-COST FORMWORK

HIGH-COST FORMWORK

NOTE

In general, the least costly design to form involves making the columns the same width or narrower than the beams they support, since the beam form can be erected in a continuous line. The mid-cost formwork design costs more because the beam bottom forms must be cut to fit around the column tops. The high-cost formwork design is the most expensive because the beam forms must be fitted into pockets on both sides of the column forms.

BEAM-TO-COLUMN FORMWORK ECONOMIES

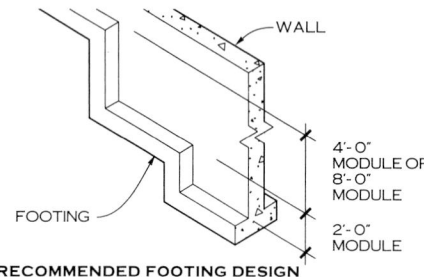

RECOMMENDED FOOTING DESIGN

NOTE

When stepped footings are required, use fewer steps and design them to standard lumber and plywood dimensions or modular divisions of these dimensions. Example: Use 2-ft, 4-ft, or 8ft dimensions, as these are standard divisions of 4 x 8 ft plywood, as well as divisions of 8-ft or 10-ft standard lumber lengths.

WALL FOOTINGS

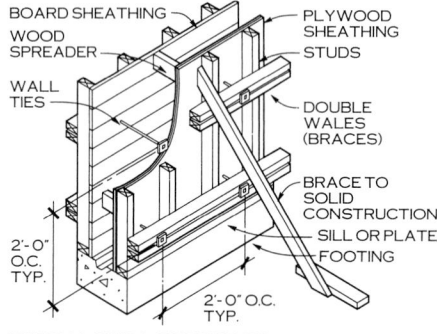

TYPICAL WALL FORMWORK

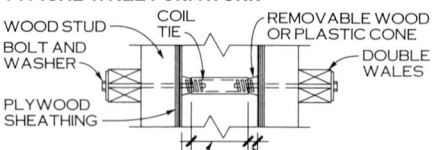

SECTION AT WALL TIE

NOTE

Installing and removing ties and patching tie holes are some of the most labor-intensive operations in forming walls. Also, getting a durable, inconspicuous patch often proves difficult. Avoid this problem by specifying smooth cone fittings at the tie ends, then leaving the resulting uniform tie holes exposed. Space tie holes 2 ft on center in most work, but be ready to consider a builder's proposal for wider spacing to reduce the total number of ties.

FORM TIE PATTERN

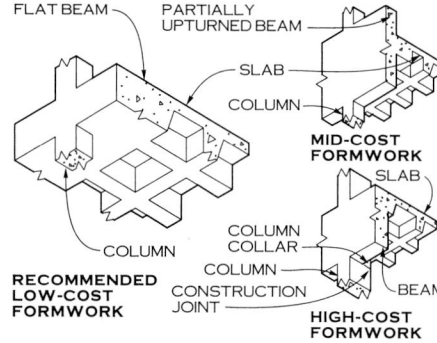

RECOMMENDED LOW-COST FORMWORK

MID-COST FORMWORK

HIGH-COST FORMWORK

NOTE

Flat beams designed to be equal in depth to the floor assembly are the least costly, since they most efficiently accommodate flying form construction. Deeper, narrower beams cost more, as they limit the efficient use of flying forms. If deeper beams are needed, costs can be controlled by designing the beam to be the same thickness as the column depth and at least partially upturned. The most costly option is designing a column thicker than the beam, since this requires a column collar with construction joint.

SPANDREL BEAM FORMWORK ECONOMIES

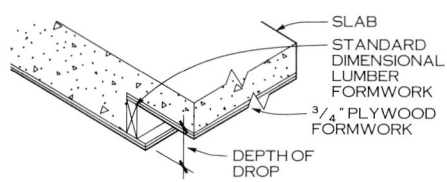

SLAB FORMWORK

NOTE

If you adapt design elements to the modular sizes of formwork lumber and plywood, dimensioning parts of the structure to fit the modules, you can save the expense of custom formwork. For example, you can save the waste and time of sawing and piecing together the edge form if you make the depth of the drop in a slab equal to the actual size of standard lumber plus 3/4 in. for the plywood's thickness.

STANDARD LUMBER FORMS

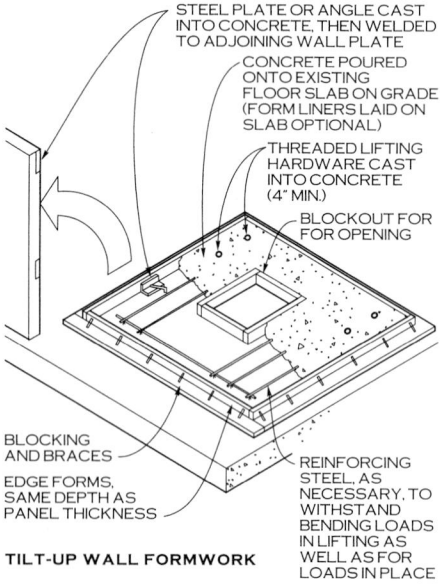

TILT-UP WALL FORMWORK

NOTE

With tilt-up construction, walls are cast on top of the completed floor slab, which must be level, smoothly finished, and treated with a bond breaking agent to permit easy separation. The slab is then tilted or lifted into vertical position and fastened to the adjoining wall piece. This method reduces formwork and labor to a minimum since the floor slab itself serves as the casting bed or bottom form.

TILT-UP WALLS

M. K. Hurd; Engineered Publications; Farmington Hills, Michigan

 CONCRETE FORMWORK

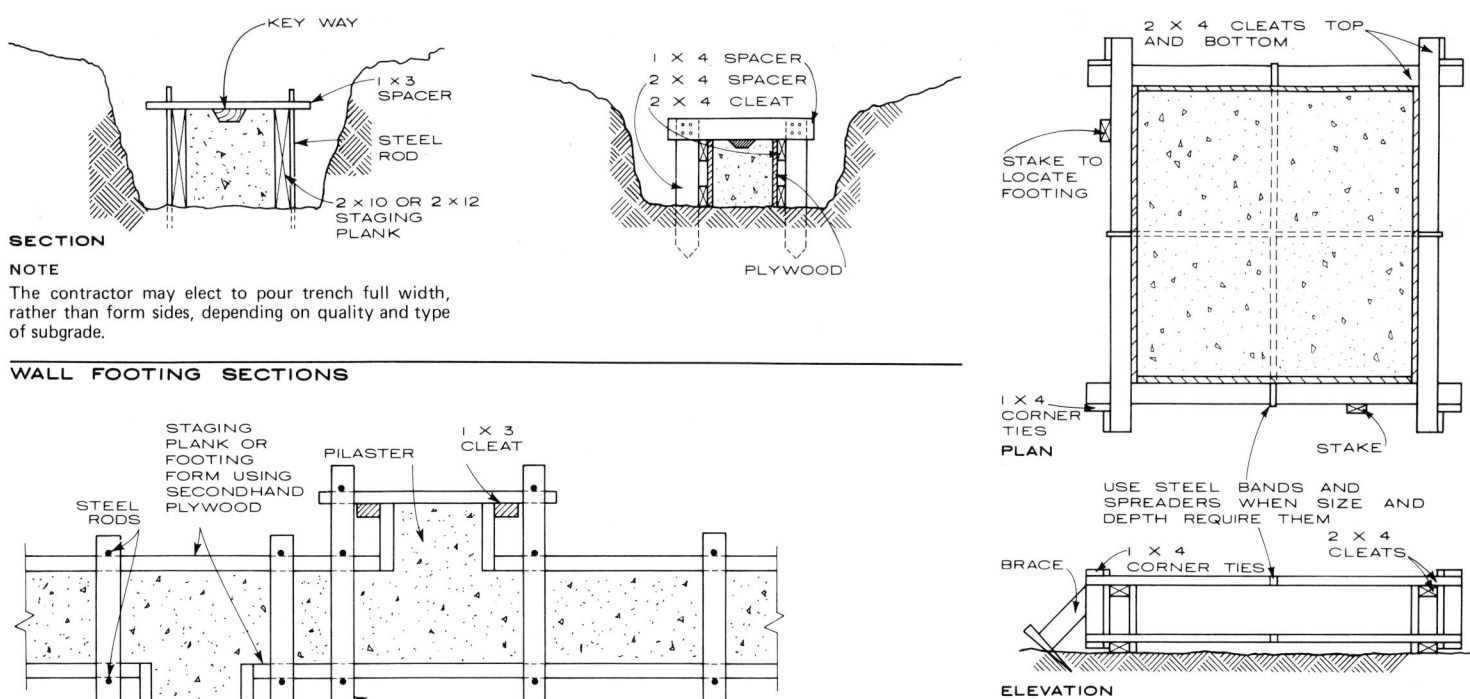

KEY WAY

1 X 3 SPACER

STEEL ROD

2 X 10 OR 2 X 12 STAGING PLANK

SECTION

NOTE

The contractor may elect to pour trench full width, rather than form sides, depending on quality and type of subgrade.

WALL FOOTING SECTIONS

1 X 4 SPACER
2 X 4 SPACER
2 X 4 CLEAT

PLYWOOD

2 X 4 CLEATS TOP AND BOTTOM

STAKE TO LOCATE FOOTING

1 X 4 CORNER TIES

PLAN

STAKE

USE STEEL BANDS AND SPREADERS WHEN SIZE AND DEPTH REQUIRE THEM

BRACE

1 X 4 CORNER TIES

2 X 4 CLEATS

ELEVATION
COLUMN FOOTINGS

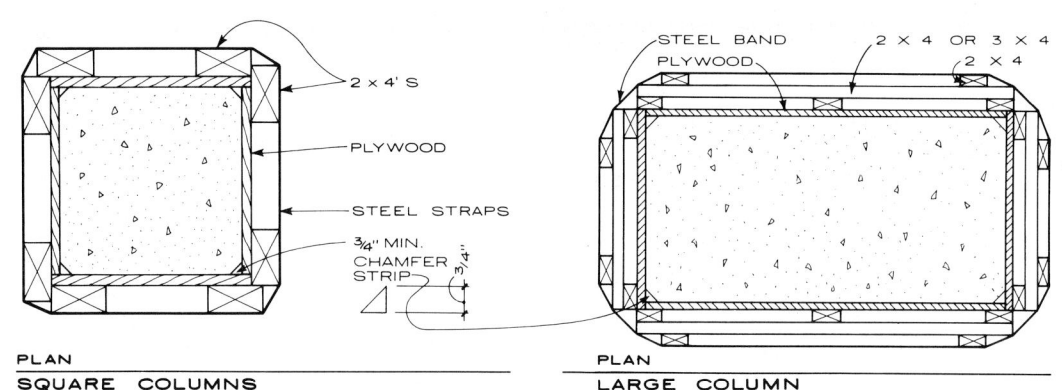

STAGING PLANK OR FOOTING FORM USING SECONDHAND PLYWOOD

STEEL RODS

PILASTER

1 X 3 CLEAT

SPACERS

PLAN OF WALL FOOTINGS

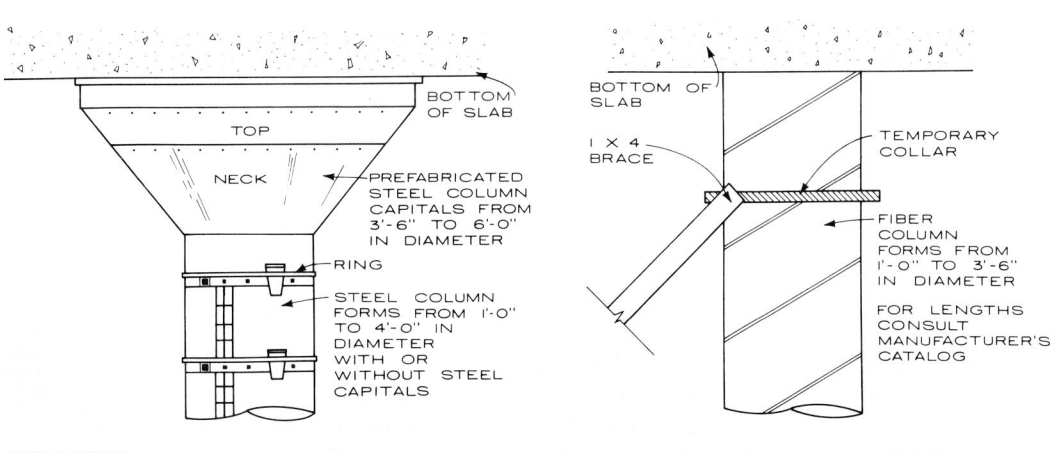

2 X 4'S

PLYWOOD

STEEL STRAPS

3/4" MIN. CHAMFER STRIP

PLAN
SQUARE COLUMNS

STEEL BAND
PLYWOOD

2 X 4 OR 3 X 4
2 X 4

PLAN
LARGE COLUMN

NOTE

Height of column will change thickness and spaces of steel bands. Consult manufacturers' catalogs. Selection of sheathing (or plywood), type of column clamps (job built or patented metal types), and their spacing will depend on column height, rate of concrete pour (ft/hr), and concrete temperature (°F), as well as on whether the concrete is to be vibrated during pour. Consult design guides for correct selection of materials to ensure safe column forms.

It is recommended that chamfer strips be used at all outside corners to reduce damage to concrete when forms are removed.

BOTTOM OF SLAB

TOP

NECK

PREFABRICATED STEEL COLUMN CAPITALS FROM 3'-6" TO 6'-0" IN DIAMETER

RING

STEEL COLUMN FORMS FROM 1'-0" TO 4'-0" IN DIAMETER WITH OR WITHOUT STEEL CAPITALS

ELEVATIONS
ROUND COLUMNS

BOTTOM OF SLAB

1 X 4 BRACE

TEMPORARY COLLAR

FIBER COLUMN FORMS FROM 1'-0" TO 3'-6" IN DIAMETER

FOR LENGTHS CONSULT MANUFACTURER'S CATALOG

HINGE OR FIXED CORNER

BOARD OR 1 X 4

SHEATHING OR PLYWOOD

ADJUSTABLE CORNER, I.E., PATENTED LOCK OR DROP PINNED

PLAN
TYPICAL PATENTED COLUMN CLAMP

Tucker Concrete Form Co.; Malden, Massachusetts

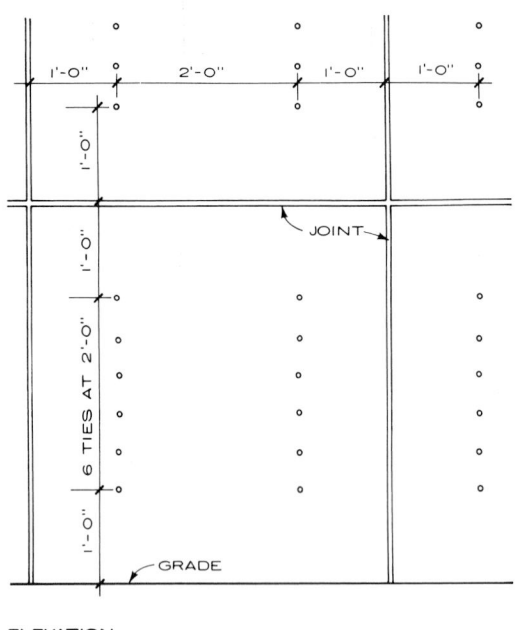

ELEVATION
EXPOSED CONCRETE WITH
RUSTICATION STRIP (IF DESIRED)

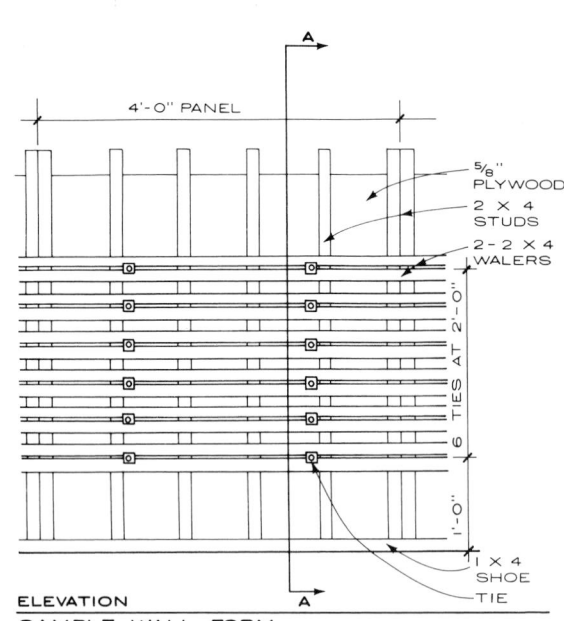

ELEVATION
SAMPLE WALL FORM

Mortar-tight forms are required for architectural exposed concrete. Consult manufacturers' literature on the proper use of metal forms or plywood forms with metal frames.

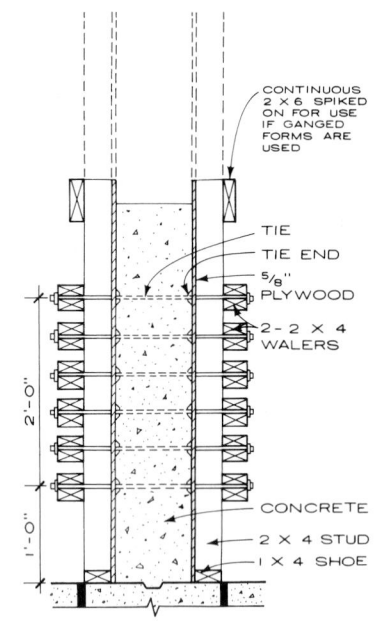

SECTION A–A

The section above will change if there are any variations in the thickness of plywood used, the type and strength of ties, or the size of studs and walers.

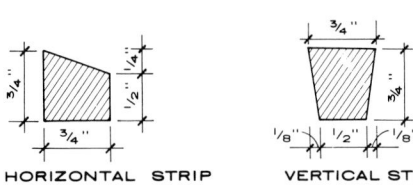

HORIZONTAL STRIP **VERTICAL STRIP**

RUSTICATION STRIPS

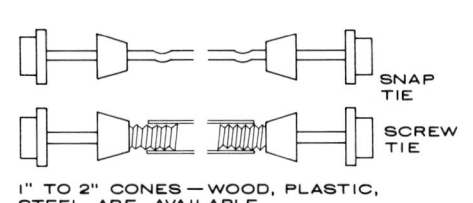

1" TO 2" CONES — WOOD, PLASTIC, STEEL ARE AVAILABLE

TYPICAL TIES

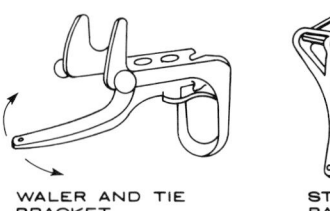

WALER AND TIE BRACKET **STRONG-BACK CAM**

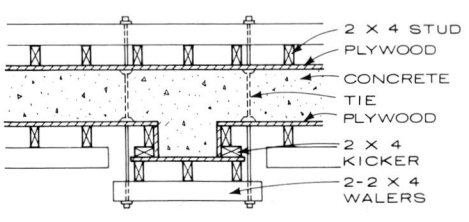

PLAN
SMALL PILASTER

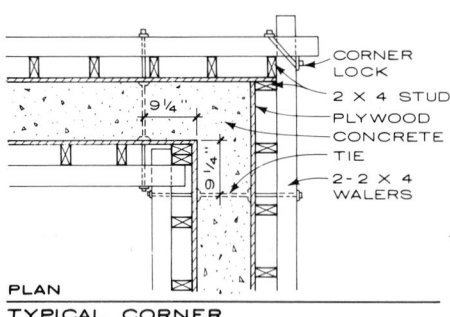

PLAN
TYPICAL CORNER

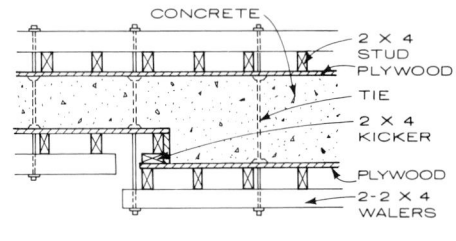

PLAN
TYPICAL WALL WITH OFFSET

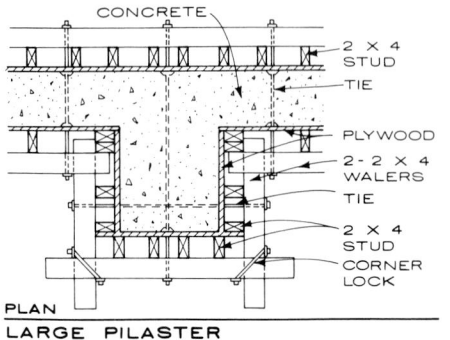

PLAN
LARGE PILASTER

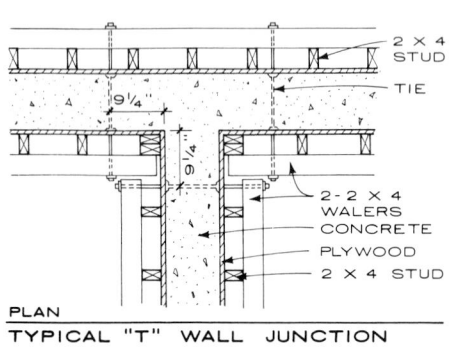

PLAN
TYPICAL "T" WALL JUNCTION

FORM DESIGN NOTES

1. Pressure depends on rate of pour (ft/hr) and concrete temperature (°F). Vibration of concrete is also a factor in form pressure.
2. Provide cleanout doors at bottom of wall forms.
3. Various types of form ties are on the market. Some are not suitable for architectural concrete work, i.e., they cannot be withdrawn from the concrete.
4. Various plastic cones 1½ in. in diameter and ½ in. deep can be used and the holes are left ungrouted to form a type of architectural feature.
5. Consult manufacturers' catalogs for form design and tie strength information.

Tucker Concrete Form Co.; Malden, Massachusetts

3 **CONCRETE FORMWORK**

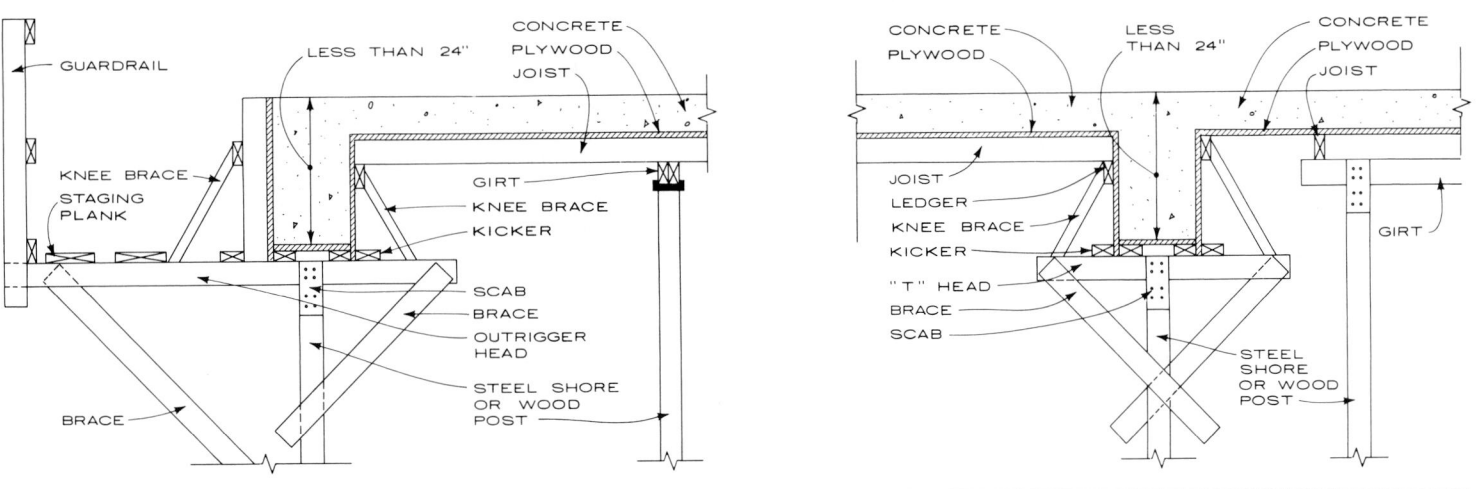

TYPICAL SLAB AND SHALLOW BEAM FORMING

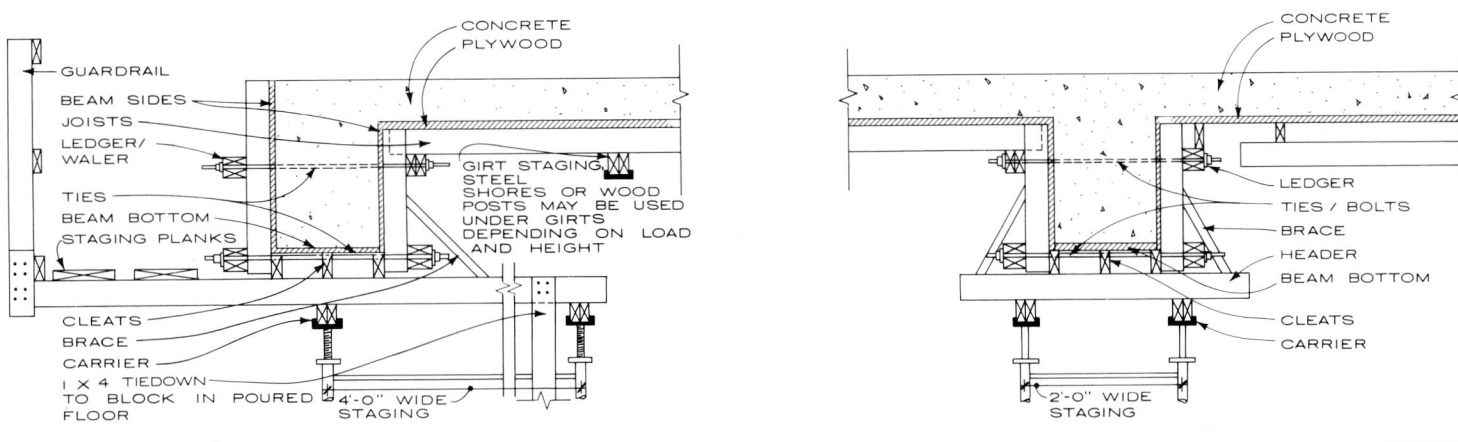

TYPICAL SLAB AND HEAVY BEAM FORMING

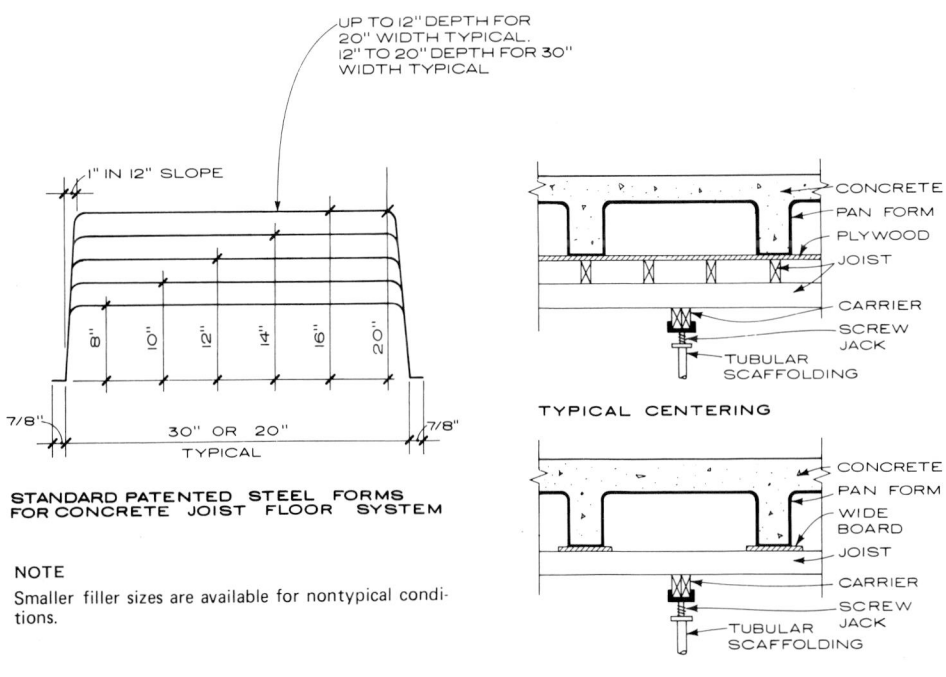

STANDARD PATENTED STEEL FORMS FOR CONCRETE JOIST FLOOR SYSTEM

NOTE
Smaller filler sizes are available for nontypical conditions.

TYPICAL CENTERING

ALTERNATE SYSTEM

NOTES

1. Staging, steel shores, or wood posts may be used under girts depending on loads and height requirements.

2. For flat slabs of flat plate forming, metal "flying forms" are commonly used.

3. Patented steel forms or fillers are also available for nontypical conditions on special order. See manufacturer's catalogs. Fiber forms, too, are on the market in similar sizes. Plywood deck is required for forming.

4. Plywood is usually ⁵/₈" minimum thickness, Exposure 1.

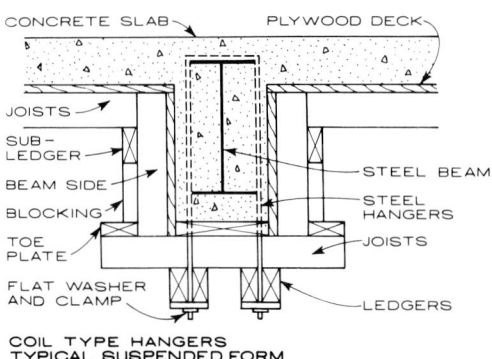

COIL TYPE HANGERS
TYPICAL SUSPENDED FORM

Tucker Concrete Form Co.; Malden, Massachusetts

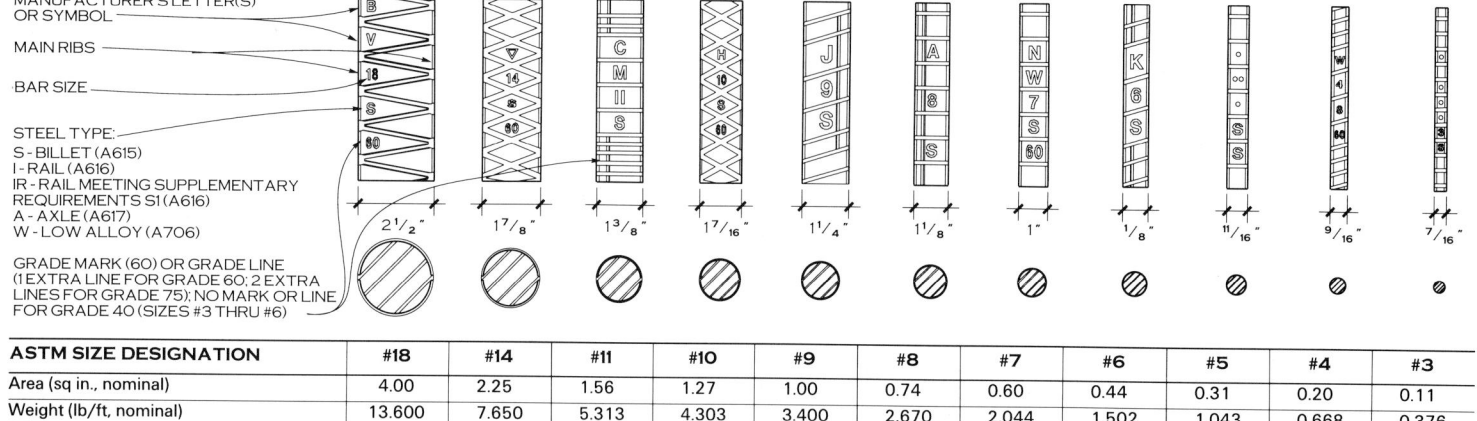

MANUFACTURER'S LETTER(S) OR SYMBOL

MAIN RIBS

BAR SIZE

STEEL TYPE:
S - BILLET (A615)
I - RAIL (A616)
IR - RAIL MEETING SUPPLEMENTARY
REQUIREMENTS S1 (A616)
A - AXLE (A617)
W - LOW ALLOY (A706)

GRADE MARK (60) OR GRADE LINE
(1 EXTRA LINE FOR GRADE 60; 2 EXTRA
LINES FOR GRADE 75); NO MARK OR LINE
FOR GRADE 40 (SIZES #3 THRU #6)

ASTM SIZE DESIGNATION	#18	#14	#11	#10	#9	#8	#7	#6	#5	#4	#3
Area (sq in., nominal)	4.00	2.25	1.56	1.27	1.00	0.74	0.60	0.44	0.31	0.20	0.11
Weight (lb/ft, nominal)	13.600	7.650	5.313	4.303	3.400	2.670	2.044	1.502	1.043	0.668	0.376
Diameter (in., nominal)	2.257	1.693	1.410	1.270	1.128	1.000	0.875	0.750	0.625	0.500	0.375

ASTM STANDARD REINFORCING BAR SIZES

GENERAL

Steel reinforcement for concrete consists of reinforcing bars and welded wire fabric. Bars are manufactured by hot-roll process as round rods with lugs, or deformations, which inhibit longitudinal movement of the bar in the surrounding concrete. Bar sizes are indicated by numbers. For sizes #3 through #8, they are the number of eighths of an inch in the nominal diameter of the bars. Sizes #9 through #11 are round and correspond to the former 1 in., 1$\frac{1}{8}$ in., and 1$\frac{1}{4}$ in. square sizes. Sizes #14 and #18 correspond to the former 1$\frac{1}{2}$ in. and 2 in. square sizes respectively. The nominal diameter of a deformed bar is equal to the actual diameter of a plain bar with the same weight per foot as the deformed bar. Epoxy-coated and zinc-coated (galvanized) reinforcing bars are used when corrosion protection is needed. In some instances, a fiber-reinforced plastic (FRP) rebar has been used for concrete reinforcement because of its high tensile strength and light weight, corrosion resistant and dielectric (nonconductive) properties. It is manufactured in the same sizes as steel rebars and also has deformations on its surface. Consult manufacturers for further information.

Welded wire fabric is used in thin slabs, shells, and other designs where the available space is too limited to give proper cover and clearance to deformed bars. Welded wire fabric, also called mesh, consists of cold drawn wire (smooth or deformed) in orthogonal patterns and is resistance welded at all intersections.

Wires in the form of individual wire or group of wires are used in the fabrication of prestressed concrete.

STRUCTURAL CONCRETE REINFORCEMENT SHRINKAGE

REINFORCEMENT		% OF CROSS SECTIONAL AREA OF CONCRETE, ONE WAY
GRADE	TYPE	
40/50	Deformed bars	0.20
—	Welded wire fabric	0.18
60	Deformed bars	0.18

STANDARD STEEL WIRE SIZES AND GAUGES

SMOOTH WIRE NUMBER	DEFORMED WIRE NUMBER	ASW GAUGE NUMBER	FRACTIONAL DIA., IN.. (NOM.)	DECIMAL DIA., IN (NOM.)	AREA (SQ. IN.)	WEIGHT (LB/ LIN. FT)
W20	D20	—	$\frac{1}{2}$	.505	.200	.680
—	—	7/0	$\frac{31}{64}$	.490	.189	.642
W18	D18	—	$\frac{15}{32}$	.479	.180	.612
—	—	6/0	$\frac{5}{32}$	.462	.168	.571
W16	D16	—	$\frac{29}{64}$	.451	.160	.544
—	—	5/0	$\frac{7}{16}$	.431	.146	.496
W14	D14	—	$\frac{13}{32}$	.422	.140	.476
—	—	4/0	$\frac{13}{32}$	.394	.122	.415
W12	D12	—	$\frac{25}{64}$	.391	.120	.408
W11	D11	—	$\frac{3}{8}$	.374	.110	.374
W10.5	—	—	$\frac{3}{8}$	.366	.105	.357
—	—	3/0	$\frac{23}{64}$	.363	.103	.350
W10	D10	—	$\frac{23}{64}$	.357	.100	.340
W9.5	—	—	$\frac{11}{32}$	.348	.095	.323
W9	D9	—	$\frac{11}{32}$	.338	.090	.306
—	—	2/0	$\frac{11}{32}$	.331	.086	.292
W8.5	—	—	$\frac{21}{64}$	.329	.085	.289
W8	D8	—	$\frac{21}{64}$	.319	.080	.272
W7.5	—	—	$\frac{5}{16}$	.309	.075	.255
—	—	1/0	$\frac{5}{16}$	.307	.074	.251
W7	D7	—	$\frac{19}{64}$	.299	.070	.238
W6.5	—	—	$\frac{19}{64}$	.288	.065	.221
—	—	1	$\frac{19}{64}$	.283	.063	.214
W6	D6	—	$\frac{9}{32}$	.276	.060	.204
W5.5	—	—	$\frac{17}{64}$	.265	.055	.187
—	—	2	$\frac{17}{64}$	.263	.054	.183
W5	D5	—	$\frac{1}{4}$	.252	.050	.170
—	—	3	$\frac{15}{64}$	.244	.047	.160
W4.5	—	—	$\frac{15}{64}$	.239	.045	.153
W4	D4	4	$\frac{7}{32}$	.226	.040	.136
W3.5	—	—	$\frac{7}{32}$	.211	.035	.119
—	—	5	$\frac{13}{64}$	.207	.034	.115
W3	—	—	$\frac{3}{16}+$	.195	.030	.102
W2.9	—	6	$\frac{3}{16}+$	.192	.029	.098
W2.5	—	—	$\frac{3}{16}$	.178	.025	.085
W2.1	—	7	$\frac{11}{64}$	.162	.021	.071
W2	—	8	$\frac{5}{32}$	.160	.020	.068
—	—	—	$\frac{5}{32}$	.148	.017	.058
W1.4	—	9	$\frac{9}{64}$	.124	.014	.048

COMMON STOCK STYLES OF WELDED WIRE FABRIC

NEW DESIGNATION (W-NUMBER)	OLD DESIGNATION (WIRE GAUGE)	STEEL AREA (IN./FT²)		WEIGHT (LB/100 SQ FT)
		LONG.	TRANS.	
SHEETS + ROLLS				
6 x 6 - W1.4 x W1.4	6 x 6 - 10 x 10	.028	.028	21
6 x 6 - W2.0 x W2.0	6 x 6 - 8 x 8	.040	.040	29
6 x 6 - W2.9 x W2.9	6 x 6 - 6 x 6	.058	.058	42
6 x 6 - W4.0 x W4.0	6 x 6 - 4 x 4	.080	.080	58
4 x 4 - W1.4 x W1.4	4 x 4 - 10 x 10	.042	.042	31
4 x 4 - W2.0 x W2.0	4 x 4 - 8 x 8	.060	.060	43
4 x 4 - W2.9 x W2.9	4 x 4 - 6 x 6	.087	.087	62
4 x 4 - W4.0 x W4.0	4 x 4 - 4 x 4	.120	.120	85

Spacing   Wire Size

6 x 12 - W16 x W8

LONGITUDINAL WIRE   TRANSVERSE WIRE

METHOD OF DESIGNATION FOR WELDED WIRE FABRIC

REINFORCING STEEL GRADES AND STRENGTHS

ASTM SPEC	MIN. YIELD STRENGTH (PSI)	MIN. TENSILE STRENGTH (PSI)	STEEL TYPE
Billet steel ASTM A-615			
Grade - 40	40,000	70,000	
Grade - 60	60,000	90,000	S
Grade - 75	75,000	100,000	
Rail steel ASTM A - 616			
Grade - 50	50,000	80,000	R
Grade - 60	60,000	90,000	
Axle steel ASTM A - 617			
Grade - 40	40,000	70,000	A
Grade - 60	60,000	90,000	
Low-Alloy ASTM A706			
Grade - 60	60,000	80,000	W
Deformed wire ASTM A - 496			
Welded fabric	70,000	80,000	-
Cold drawn wire ASTM A -82			
Welded fabric < W 1.2	56,000	70,000	-
Size ≥ W 1.2	65,000	75,000	

Concrete Reinforcing Steel Institute; Schaumburg, Illinois

CONCRETE REINFORCEMENT

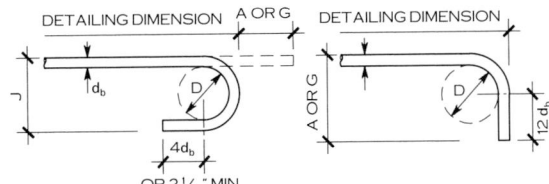

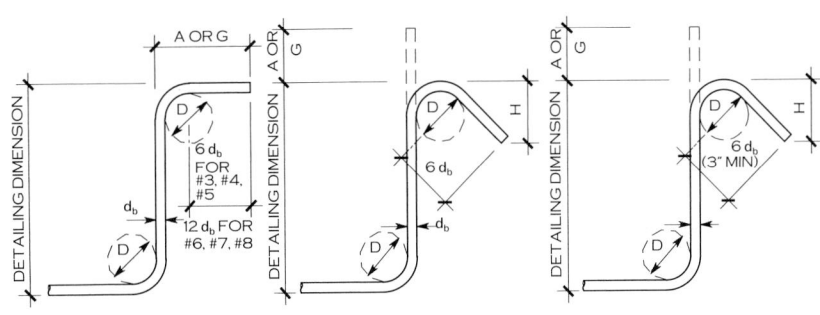

STANDARD HOOK

BAR SIZE	180° HOOK			90° HOOK	
	A OR G	J	D	A OR G	D
#3	5"	3"	2 1/4"	6"	2 1/4"
#4	6"	4"	3"	8"	3"
#5	7"	5"	3 3/4"	10"	3 3/4"
#6	8"	6"	4 1/2"	12"	4 1/2"
#7	10"	7"	5 1/4"	14"	5 1/4"
#8	11"	8"	6"	16"	6"
#9	15"	11 3/4"	9 1/2"	19"	9 1/2"
#10	17"	13 1/4"	10 3/4"	22"	10 3/4"
#11	19"	14 3/4"	12"	24"	12"
#14	27"	21 3/4"	18 1/4"	31"	18 1/4"
#18	36"	28 1/2"	24"	41"	24"

STANDARD REINFORCING BAR HOOK DETAILS

STIRRUP HOOKS AND TIES

BAR SIZE	90° HOOK/TIE		135° HOOK/TIE			135° SEISMIC HOOK/TIE		
	A OR G	D	A OR G	D	H	A OR G	D	H
#3	4"	1 1/2"	4"	1 1/2"	2 1/2"	4 1/4"	1 1/2"	3"
#4	4 1/2"	2"	4 1/2"	2"	3"	4 1/2"	2"	3"
#5	6"	2 1/2"	5 1/2"	2 1/2"	3 3/4"	5 1/2"	2 1/2"	3 3/4"
#6	12"	4 1/2"	7 3/4"	4 1/2"	4 1/2"	7 3/4"	4 1/2"	4 1/2"
#7	14"	5 1/4"	9"	5 1/4"	5 1/4"	9"	5 1/4"	5 1/4"
#8	16"	6"	10 1/4"	6"	6"	10 1/4"	6"	6"

COMPRESSION LAP SPLICES AND ANCHORAGES FOR REINFORCING BARS

STEEL GRADE (FY-KSI)	CONCRETE COMPRESSION STRENGTH (F'c)	LAP SPLICE IN $d_b \geq 12$ IN.	DOWELS, IN d_b (8 IN. MIN.)
40	3000	20	15
	4000	20	13
	5000	20	12
50	3000	25	18
	4000	25	16
	5000	25	15
60	3000	30	22
	4000	30	19
	5000	30	18
75	3000	44	28
	4000	44	24
	5000	44	23

NOTES

1. d_b = reinforcing bar diameter.
2. Reinforcing bars #14 and #18 may not be used in lap splices except when lapped to #11 bars or smaller. To find the lap dimension, take the larger figure of either 22 d_b of the larger bar or 30 d_b of the smaller bar.
3. Consult Concrete Reinforcing Steel Institute (CRSI) for tension splices and anchorages.

TENSION LAP SPLICES AND ANCHORAGE F'c = 3000 PSI, NORMAL WEIGHT

BAR SIZE	LAP CLASS	TOP BARS CATEGORY						OTHER BARS CATEGORY					
		1	2	3	4	5	6	1	2	3	4	5	6
#3	A	16	16	16	16	16	16	13	13	13	13	13	13
	B	21	21	21	21	21	21	16	16	16	16	16	16
#4	A	23	22	22	22	22	22	18	17	17	17	17	17
	B	30	28	28	28	28	28	23	22	22	22	22	22
#5	A	36	29	27	27	27	27	27	22	21	21	21	21
	B	46	37	35	35	35	35	36	29	27	27	27	27
#6	A	50	40	35	32	32	32	39	31	27	25	25	25
	B	65	52	46	42	42	42	50	40	35	32	32	32
#7	A	69	55	48	39	38	38	53	42	37	30	29	29
	B	89	71	63	50	49	49	69	55	48	39	38	38
#8	A	90	72	63	51	45	43	70	56	49	39	35	33
	B	117	94	82	66	59	56	90	72	63	51	45	43
#9	A	114	91	80	64	57	48	88	70	62	49	44	37
	B	148	119	104	83	74	63	114	91	80	64	57	48
#10	A	145	116	102	81	73	58	112	89	78	63	56	45
	B	188	151	132	106	94	76	145	116	102	81	73	58
#11	A	178	142	125	100	89	71	137	110	96	77	69	55
	B	231	185	162	130	116	93	178	142	125	100	89	71
#14	N/A	242	242	170	170	121	121	187	187	131	131	93	93
#18	N/A	356	356	250	250	178	178	274	274	192	192	137	137

NOTES

1. Lap splice lengths are multiples of tension development lengths; Class A = 1.0 l_D, Class B = 1.3 l_D" (ACI 12.15.1) Values of l_D for bars in beams or columns are based on transverse reinforcement meeting minimum requirements for stirrups in ACI 11.5.4 and 11.5.5.3, or meeting tie requirements in ACI 7.10.5; and are based on minimum cover specified in ACI 7.7.1.
2. Conditions that require Category 1 or Category 2 lap splice lengths should be avoided if at all possible for the larger bar sizes. These inordinately long lengths present possible construction problems due to placing, congestion, etc. Options available in trying to avoid Category 1 or 2 conditions include:
   a. Increasing the concrete cover to more than one bar diameter and/or increase the bar c.-c. spacing to more than three bar diameters.
   b. Utilizing the A_{TR} allowance in ACI 12.2.3 (b) for beams or columns. Note that if ties or stirrups meet the minimum A_{TR} requirement, Category 1 lengths are reduced to Category 5 lengths and Category 2 lengths are reduced to Category 6 lengths.
3. The ACI 318-89 code does not allow lap splices of #14 or #18 bars. The values tabulated for those bar sizes are the tension development lengths.
4. Top bars are horizontal bars with more than 12 in. of concrete cast below the bars.
5. #11 and smaller edge bars with c.-c. spacing not less than 6d_b are assumed to have a side cover not less than 2.5d_b. Otherwise, Category 5 applies rather than Category 6.
6. For lightweight aggregate, multiply the values above by 1.3.
7. For epoxy-coated reinforcing bars, multiply the values above by one of the following factors:
   a. Cover < 3d_b or c.-c. spacing < 7d_b multiply top bars by 1.31 and all other bars by 1.50.
   b. Cover > 3d_b and c.-c. spacing > 7d_b multiply top bars and all other bars by 1.20.
8. See CRSI's *Reinforcement: Anchorages, Lap Splices and Connections* manual for tables of tension development and lap splices for other concrete strengths and epoxy-coated rebars.

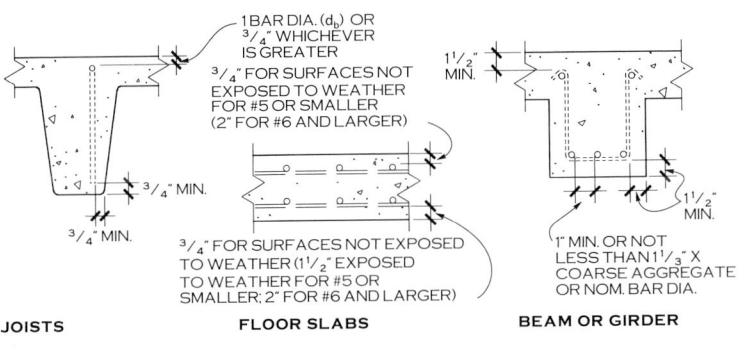

JOISTS   FLOOR SLABS   BEAM OR GIRDER

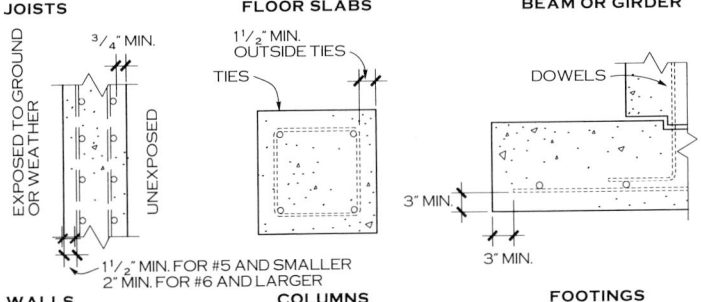

WALLS   COLUMNS   FOOTINGS

PROTECTION FOR REINFORCEMENT

Concrete Reinforcing Steel Institute; Schaumburg, Illinois

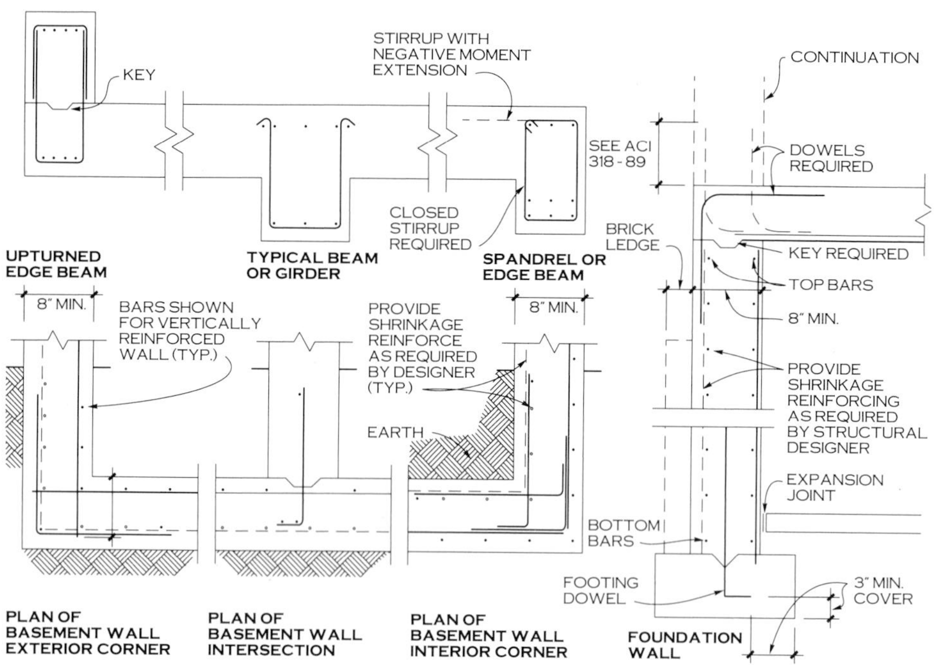

KEY

STIRRUP WITH NEGATIVE MOMENT EXTENSION

CONTINUATION

DOWELS REQUIRED

SEE ACI 318 - 89

CLOSED STIRRUP REQUIRED

BRICK LEDGE

KEY REQUIRED

TOP BARS

8" MIN.

UPTURNED EDGE BEAM

TYPICAL BEAM OR GIRDER

SPANDREL OR EDGE BEAM

8" MIN.

BARS SHOWN FOR VERTICALLY REINFORCED WALL (TYP.)

PROVIDE SHRINKAGE REINFORCE AS REQUIRED BY DESIGNER (TYP.)

8" MIN.

PROVIDE SHRINKAGE REINFORCING AS REQUIRED BY STRUCTURAL DESIGNER

EARTH

EXPANSION JOINT

BOTTOM BARS

FOOTING DOWEL

3" MIN. COVER

FOUNDATION WALL

PLAN OF BASEMENT WALL EXTERIOR CORNER

PLAN OF BASEMENT WALL INTERSECTION

PLAN OF BASEMENT WALL INTERIOR CORNER

REINFORCING DETAILS

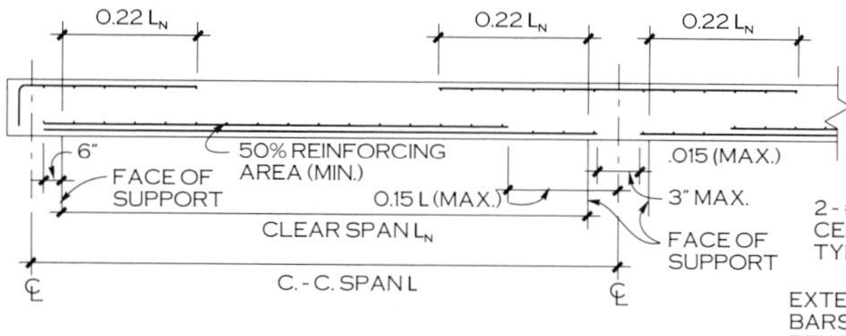

$0.22 L_N$ $0.22 L_N$ $0.22 L_N$

6"   50% REINFORCING AREA (MIN.)

FACE OF SUPPORT

$0.15 L$ (MAX.)

CLEAR SPAN L_N

.015 (MAX.)

3" MAX.

FACE OF SUPPORT

C.- C. SPAN L

FLAT PLATE CONSTRUCTION — MIDDLE STRIP

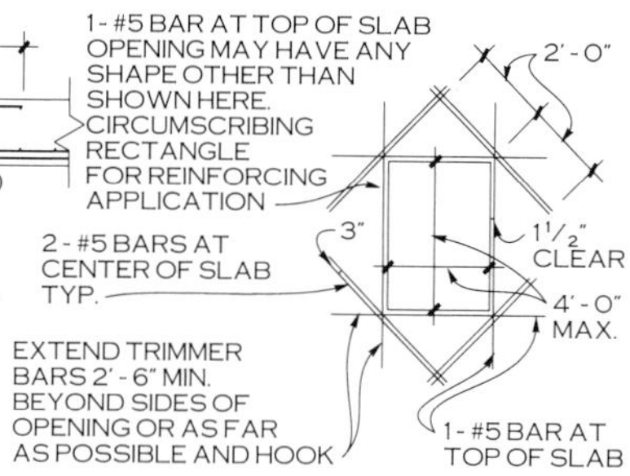

1- #5 BAR AT TOP OF SLAB OPENING MAY HAVE ANY SHAPE OTHER THAN SHOWN HERE. CIRCUMSCRIBING RECTANGLE FOR REINFORCING APPLICATION.

2' - 0"

2 - #5 BARS AT CENTER OF SLAB TYP.

3"

$1\frac{1}{2}$" CLEAR

4' - 0" MAX.

EXTEND TRIMMER BARS 2' - 6" MIN. BEYOND SIDES OF OPENING OR AS FAR AS POSSIBLE AND HOOK

1 - #5 BAR AT TOP OF SLAB

NOTES

1. Provide extra bars (not shown) parallel to sides of openings, equal to areas of interrupted slab bars. Extend full length of span or to top bars as applicable.

2. This detail is typical at openings up to 4 ft maximum dimensions except as otherwise shown.

3. Circular openings less than 18 in. diameter require no reinforcing.

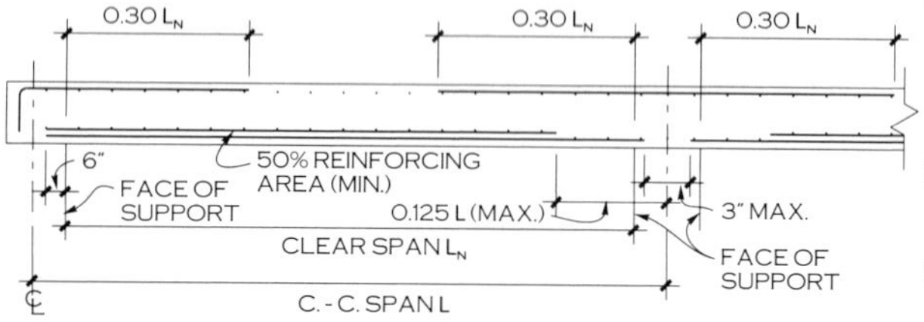

$0.30 L_N$ $0.30 L_N$ $0.30 L_N$

6"   50% REINFORCING AREA (MIN.)

FACE OF SUPPORT

$0.125 L$ (MAX.)

CLEAR SPAN L_N

3" MAX.

FACE OF SUPPORT

C.- C. SPAN L

FLAT PLATE CONSTRUCTION — COLUMN STRIP

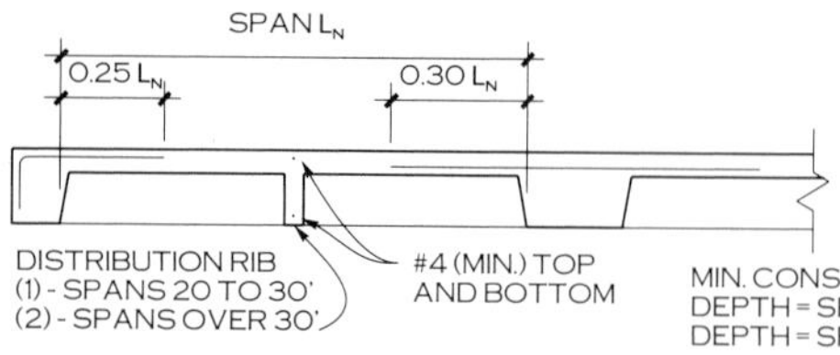

OPENING IN SLAB OR WALL

SPAN L_N

$0.25 L_N$ $0.30 L_N$

DISTRIBUTION RIB
(1) - SPANS 20 TO 30'
(2) - SPANS OVER 30'

#4 (MIN.) TOP AND BOTTOM

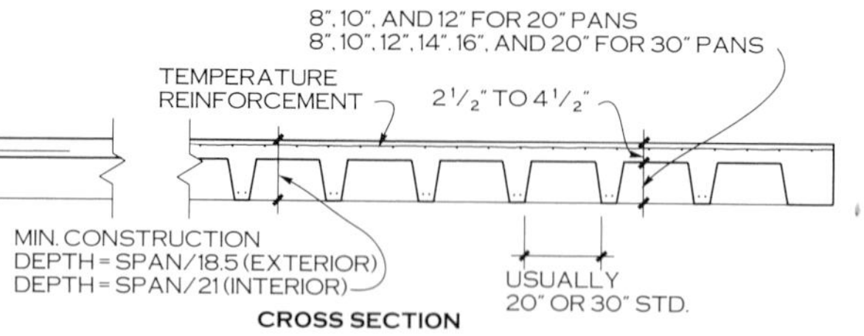

8", 10", AND 12" FOR 20" PANS
8", 10", 12", 14", 16", AND 20" FOR 30" PANS

TEMPERATURE REINFORCEMENT

$2\frac{1}{2}$" TO $4\frac{1}{2}$"

MIN. CONSTRUCTION DEPTH = SPAN/18.5 (EXTERIOR)
DEPTH = SPAN/21 (INTERIOR)

USUALLY 20" OR 30" STD.

CROSS SECTION

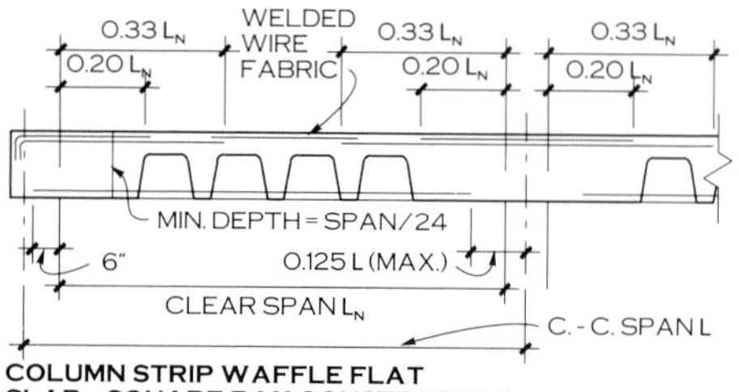

8", 10", 12", 14", AND 16" DEEP PANS - 19" SQ. DOMES
8", 10", 12", 14", 16", AND 20" DEEP PANS - 30" SQ. DOMES

LONGITUDINAL SECTION—ONE WAY CONCRETE JOIST CONSTRUCTION

$0.33 L_N$ $0.33 L_N$ $0.33 L_N$

$0.20 L_N$ $0.20 L_N$ $0.20 L_N$

WELDED WIRE FABRIC

MIN. DEPTH = SPAN/24

6" $0.125 L$ (MAX.)

CLEAR SPAN L_N

C.- C. SPAN L

COLUMN STRIP WAFFLE FLAT SLAB—SQUARE BAY CONSTRUCTION

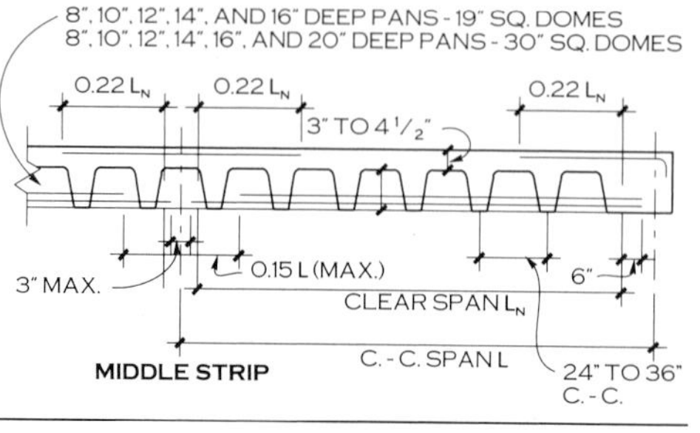

$0.22 L_N$ $0.22 L_N$ $0.22 L_N$

3" TO $4\frac{1}{2}$"

3" MAX.

$0.15 L$ (MAX.)

CLEAR SPAN L_N

6"

C.- C. SPAN L

24" TO 36" C.- C.

MIDDLE STRIP

CONCRETE FLOOR SYSTEMS

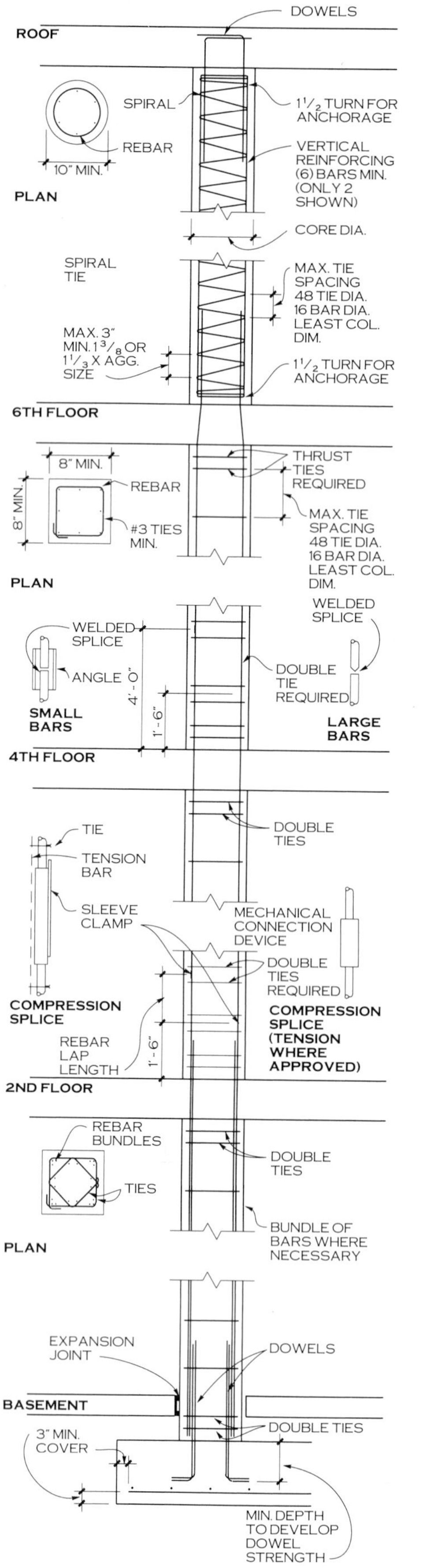

DOWELS

ROOF

SPIRAL

REBAR

10" MIN.

PLAN

$1\frac{1}{2}$ TURN FOR ANCHORAGE

VERTICAL REINFORCING (6) BARS MIN. (ONLY 2 SHOWN)

CORE DIA.

SPIRAL TIE

MAX. 3" MIN. $1\frac{3}{8}$ OR $1\frac{1}{3}$ X AGG. SIZE

MAX. TIE SPACING 48 TIE DIA. 16 BAR DIA. LEAST COL. DIM.

$1\frac{1}{2}$ TURN FOR ANCHORAGE

6TH FLOOR

8" MIN.

8" MIN.

REBAR

#3 TIES MIN.

PLAN

THRUST TIES REQUIRED

MAX. TIE SPACING 48 TIE DIA. 16 BAR DIA. LEAST COL. DIM.

WELDED SPLICE

WELDED SPLICE

ANGLE

DOUBLE TIE REQUIRED

SMALL BARS

4' - 0"

1' - 6"

LARGE BARS

4TH FLOOR

TIE

TENSION BAR

SLEEVE CLAMP

DOUBLE TIES

MECHANICAL CONNECTION DEVICE

DOUBLE TIES REQUIRED

COMPRESSION SPLICE

REBAR LAP LENGTH

COMPRESSION SPLICE (TENSION WHERE APPROVED)

1' - 6"

2ND FLOOR

REBAR BUNDLES

TIES

DOUBLE TIES

PLAN

BUNDLE OF BARS WHERE NECESSARY

EXPANSION JOINT

DOWELS

BASEMENT

3" MIN. COVER

DOUBLE TIES

MIN. DEPTH TO DEVELOP DOWEL STRENGTH

COLUMN REINFORCEMENT

Anthony L. Felder; Concrete Reinforcing Steel Institute; Schaumburg, Illinois
Kenneth D. Franch, AIA, PE; Phillips Swager Associates, Inc.; Dallas, Texas

CONCRETE REINFORCEMENT

CAST-IN-PLACE CONCRETE CONSTRUCTION; PRELIMINARY DATA

REINFORCED CONCRETE

Reinforced concrete consists of concrete and reinforcing steel; the concrete resists the compressive stresses and the reinforcing steel resists the tensile stresses.

Concrete is a mixture of hydraulic cement (usually portland cement), aggregate, admixtures, and water. The concrete strength develops by the hydration of the portland cement, which binds the aggregate together.

TYPES OF CEMENT

Five types of portland cement are manufactured to meet ASTM standards.

Type I is a general purpose cement for all uses. It is the most commonly used type.

Type II cement provides moderate protection from sulfate attack for concrete in drainage structures and a lower heat of hydration for concrete use in heavy retaining walls, piers, and abutments where heat buildup in the concrete can cause problems.

Type III cement provides high strengths at an early age, a week or less. Type III is used when rapid removal of forms is desired and in cold weather to reduce time of controlled curing conditions.

Type IV cement has a low heat of hydration and is used for massive concrete structures such as gravity dams.

Type V cement is sulfate-resisting cement for use where the soil and groundwater have a high sulfate content.

Pozzolans such as fly ash can be used to reduce the amount of cement in a concrete mix. Fly ash is a powdery residue resulting from combustion in coal-fired electric generating plants. It reacts chemically with calcium hydroxide produced by hydration to form cementitious compounds. Fly ash usually replaces no more than 20% of the cement required by weight.

ADMIXTURES

Admixtures are various compounds, other than cement, water, and aggregates, added to a mixture to modify the fresh or hardened properties of concrete.

Air entraining admixtures disperse small air bubbles in the concrete, which improves the concrete's resistance to freezing and thawing and to scaling by deicing chemicals. Recommended total air contents are shown in Table 1 for different exposure conditions and for maximum size of aggregate.

TABLE 1. RECOMMENDED AIR CONTENT PERCENTAGE

NOMINAL MAXIMUM SIZE OF COARSE AGGREGATE (IN.)	EXPOSURE	
	MILD	EXTREME
3/8 (10 mm)	4.5	7.5
1/2 (13 mm)	4.0	6.0
3/4 (19 mm)	3.5	6.0
1 (25 mm)	3.0	6.0
1 1/2 (40 mm)	2.5	5.5
2 (50 mm)	2.0	5.0
3 (75 mm)	1.5	4.5

TABLE 2. RECOMMENDED SLUMPS FOR VARIOUS TYPES OF CONSTRUCTION

CONCRETE CONSTRUCTION	SLUMP (IN.)	
	MAXIMUM*	MINIMUM
Reinforced foundation walls and footings	3	1
Plain footings, caissons, and substructure walls	3	1
Beams and reinforced walls	4	1
Building columns	4	1
Pavements and slabs	3	1
Mass concrete	2	1

*May be increased 1 in. for consolidation by hand methods such as rodding and spading.

Quentin L. Reutershan, AIA, Architect; Potsdam, New York
Gordon B. Batson, P.E.; Potsdam, New York
Bob Cotton; W.E. Simpson Company Inc.; San Antonio, Texas

Water reducing admixtures reduce the quantity of mixing water needed for a given consistency. Admixtures may delay the set time, and they also may entrain air.

Other admixtures are used to retard or to accelerate the set of concrete. Some accelerating admixtures contain chlorides that can cause corrosion of the reinforcing steel; therefore, they should be used with caution and only for very specific purposes. Some water reducing and accelerating admixtures may increase dry shrinkage.

Superplasticizers are high-range water reducers that can greatly affect the slump and strength of concrete. When used in concrete with normal water-cement ratios, they produce a high slump, flowable concrete that is easily placed. When used to reduce the water-cement ratio, the slump is not affected, but significantly higher than normal strengths are attained. When used to produce flowable concrete, the plasticizer's effect has a limited timespan.

AGGREGATES

The aggregate portion of a concrete mix is divided into fine and coarse aggregates. The fine aggregate generally is sand of particles less than 3/8 in. large. The coarse aggregate is crushed rock or gravel. Concrete weighs 135 pcf to 165 pcf. Lightweight aggregate is manufactured from expanded shale, slate, clay, or slag, and the concrete weighs from 85 pcf to 115 pcf.

Normal weight aggregates must meet ASTM Specification C33. Lightweight aggregates must meet ASTM Specification C330.

The aggregate represents 60 percent to 80 percent of the concrete volume, and the gradation (range of particle sizes) affects the amount of cement and water required in the mix, the physical properties during placing and finishing, and the compressive strength. Aggregates should be clean, hard, strong, and free of surface materials.

REINFORCING STEEL

Reinforcing steel, manufactured as round rods with raised deformations for adhesion and resistance to slip in the concrete, is available in several grades (yield strengths) and diameters manufactured in ASTM standards. Commonly used reinforcing steels have a yield strength of 60,000 psi available in sizes from #3 to #18, the size being the diameter in eighths of an inch. Reinforcing rods having a yield strength of 40,000 psi also are available in the smaller bar sizes. Reinforcing steel with a yield strength of 75,000 psi is available in sizes #11, #14, and #18. ACI 318 allows the grades of steel and yield strengths shown in Table 3; all bar sizes are not available in every grade of steel shown in the table.

Galvanized and epoxy coated rebars may be required for reinforced concrete in aggressive (corrosive) envi-

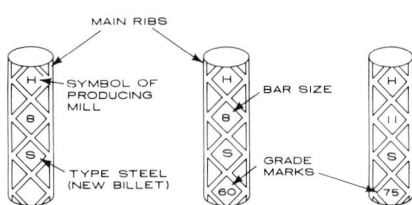

NUMBER SYSTEM – GRADE MARKS

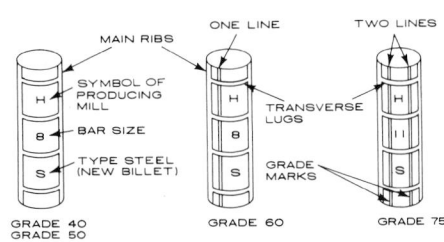

LINE SYSTEM – GRADE MARKS

FIGURE 1. REINFORCING BAR IDENTIFICATION

---

ronments such as parking structures and bridge decks where deicing agents are used.

SLUMP TEST

The ASTM standard slump cone test is to determine only the consistency among batches of concrete of the same mix design; it should not be used to compare mixes of greatly different mix proportions. A slump test mold is a funnel-shaped sheet metal form. The slump mold is filled from the top in three levels, each level being tamped 25 times with a 5/8 in. diameter rod. The mold is removed slowly, allowing the concrete to slump down from its original height. The difference from the top of the mold to the top of the slumped concrete is the slump. There is no "right" slump consistency for all concrete work. It can vary from 1 in. to 6 in., depending on the specific requirements of the job. Table 2 lists typical slumps for various types of construction.

Workability is the ease or difficulty of placing, consolidating, and finishing the concrete. Concrete should be workable, but it should not segregate or bleed excessively before finishing.

CYLINDER TEST

A major problem with concrete tests is that the most important data, the compressive strength, cannot be determined until after curing has begun. This occasionally has caused the removal of deficient concrete several weeks after it was placed. A standard compression test is made in accordance with ASTM C39 by placing three layers of concrete in a cardboard cylinder 6 in. in diameter and 12 in. high. Each layer is rodded 25 times with a 5/8 in. diameter steel rod. The cylinder should be protected from damage but placed in the same temperature and humidity environment as the concrete from which the sample was obtained. At the end of the test curing time, usually 7 to 28 days, the concrete cylinder is removed from its form and tested in compression. The load at which the cylinder fails in compression is registered on a gauge in pounds, and the strength of the concrete is calculated in pounds per square inch.

PLACING CONCRETE

Concrete should be placed as near its final position as possible, and it should not be moved horizontally in forms because segregation of the mortar from the coarser material may occur. Concrete should be placed in horizontal layers of uniform thickness, each layer being thoroughly consolidated before the next layer is positioned.

Consolidation of concrete can be achieved either by hand tamping and rodding or by mechanical internal or external vibration. The frequency and amplitude of an internal mechanical vibration should be appropriate for the plastic properties (stiffness or slump) and space in the forms to prevent segregation of the concrete during placing. External vibration can be accomplished by surface vibration for thin sections (slabs) that cannot be consolidated practically by internal vibration. Surface vibrators may be used directly on the surface of slab or with plates attached to the concrete form stiffeners. External vibration must be done for a longer time (1 to 2 min.) than for internal vibration (5 to 15 sec.) to achieve the same consolidation.

TABLE 3. REINFORCING STEEL GRADES AND STRENGTH

ASTM SPEC	YIELD STRENGTH (PSI)	ULTIMATE STRENGTH (PSI)	STEEL GRADE MARK
ASTM A-615			
Grade 40	40,000	70,000	
Grade 60	60,000	90,000	S
Grade 75	75,000	100,000	
ASTM A-616			
Grade 50	50,000	80,000	
Grade 60	60,000	90,000	R
ASTM A-617			
Grade 40	40,000	70,000	
Grade 60	60,000	90,000	A
ASTM A-706	60,000	80,000	W
Deformed wire ASTM A-496 Size D-1 to D-31	75,000	85,000	
Cold drawn wire ASTM A-82 Size WD.5 to W-31	70,000	80,000	

PROPERTIES OF CONCRETE

Concrete design strength generally is stated as a minimum compressive strength at 28 days of age for concrete in various structural elements. The normal 28-day compressive strength for commercial-ready mix concrete is 3,000 psi to 4,000 psi; however, higher strengths of 5,000 psi to 7,000 psi generally are required for pre- or post-tensioned concrete. Higher concrete design strengths of 10,000 to 12,000 psi have been used for columns in high-rise buildings, and a design strength of 20,000 psi has been used for concrete columns confined in a steel tube or pipe. These very high design strength concretes require close coordination among the concrete mix vendor, contractor, and concrete inspection service. Tests on very high strength concrete are usually based on 56- or 90-day tests using 4 x 8 in. rather than 6 x 12 in. cylinders. The test cylinders ends may have to be machined or ground parallel and flat for satisfactory strength tests.

A typical design mix for 3,000 psi concrete would have 517 lb. of cement (5½ sacks), 1,300 lb. of sand, 1,800 lb. of gravel, and 34 gal. of water (6.2 gal. per sack), which would yield one cu. yd. of concrete, the standard unit of measure.

Compressive strength depends primarily on the type of cement, water-cement ratio, and aggregate quality; the most important is the water-cement ratio. The lower the water-cement ratio, the greater the compressive strength for workable mixes.

Concrete gains strength by hydration, a chemical reaction independent of drying, when water, cement, and aggregate are mixed. Concrete does not require air to cure; it sets up under water (thus the term "hydraulic cement"). Concrete sets or becomes firm within hours after it has been mixed, but curing, the process of attaining strength, takes considerably longer. For 28-day design strengths less than 10,000 psi, most of the strength is achieved in a few days; approximately 50% is reached in three days and 70% is reached in seven days. The remaining 30% occurs at a much slower rate during the last 21 days, and the strength normally continues to increase beyond the 28-day strength. Concrete design strength in excess of 12,000 psi may require 56 or 90 days before compression test cylinders achieve the design strength.

CURING AND PROTECTION

Two physical conditions profoundly affect concrete's final compressive strength and curing: temperature and the rate at which water used in mixing is allowed to leave the concrete. Optimum temperature for curing concrete is 73°F (22.8°C). Any great variance from this mark reduces its compressive strength. Freezing concrete during curing greatly reduces the compressive strength and its weather resistance.

Proper curing is essential to obtain design strength. Moisture, at temperatures above 50°F, must be available for hydration, and the concrete must be protected against temperatures below 40°F during early curing. The longer the water is in the concrete, the longer the reaction takes place; hence, the stronger it becomes.

Moisture conditions can be maintained by spreading wet coverings of burlap or mats, waterproof paper, or plastic sheets over the concrete; by placing plastic sheets on the ground before the slab is poured; by spraying liquid curing compound on the surface of fresh concrete; and by leaving the concrete in forms longer.

HOT AND COLD WEATHER CONSTRUCTION

Additional precautions are needed in hot and cold weather to ensure proper curing of the concrete. High temperatures accelerate hardening. More water is needed to maintain the mix consistency; more cement is required to prevent reduced strength from the added water. Chilled water or ice reduces the temperature of the aggregates, and admixtures can retard the initial set. Temperatures ranging from 75°F to 90°F are hot weather construction conditions. Hot, dry conditions also cause problems in finishing newly placed concrete. High temperatures lead to rapid drying, resulting in shrinkage cracks. Special care in finishing and curing must be taken to achieve a good quality finish.

In cold weather the concrete must be heated to above 40°F during placing and early curing, the first 7 days. Protection against freezing may be necessary for up to 2 weeks. This is accomplished by covering the concrete with plastic sheets and heating the interior space with a portable heater. Concrete floors should be protected from carbon dioxide by using specially vented heaters that conduct the exhaust away from the concrete. The time the concrete must be protected can be reduced by using Type III and IIIA cement; a low water-cement ratio; accelerator admixtures; and steam curing. Concrete never should be placed directly on frozen ground. Fresh concrete that has frozen during curing should be removed and replaced because frozen concrete containing ice crystals has very little strength.

PROPORTION OF STRUCTURAL ELEMENTS

Rules of thumb for approximating proportions of solid rectangular beams and slabs are one inch of depth for each foot of span, and the beam width is about two-thirds the depth. The area of steel varies from 1 percent to 2 percent of cross-sectional area of the beam and less than 1 percent for slabs. Columns usually have higher steel percentages than beams. The maximum for columns is 8 percent of the cross-sectional area; however, common range is 3 percent to 6 percent.

DEFLECTIONS

Deflection of a reinforced concrete member is affected by shrinkage, duration of sustained loads, and creep. Creep is the continuous deformation of the concrete due to sustained loads. Creep and shrinkage may increase the initial (instantaneous) deflection by a factor of two in five years under sustained loads. The ACI-318 sets minimum length-to-depth ratios for concrete members as shown on Table 6. When members meet or exceed these minimums, deflections usually will not be a problem, and they do not need to be calculated.

FORMWORK

Forming costs can account for 30 percent to 50 percent of a concrete structure. Economy can be gained through the repetitive use of forms. Usually it is cheaper to use one column size rather than to vary column sizes.

In sizing individual floor members, usually it is more economical to use wider girders that are the same depths as the joists or beams they support than to use narrow, deeper girders. Wall pilasters, lugs, and openings should be kept to a minimum since their use increases forming costs. All members should be sized so that readily available standard forms can be used instead of custom job-built forms.

SHORING

Floor framing forms are supported by temporary columns and bracing called shoring. Concrete must be cured for a minimum time or reach a specified percentage of its design strength before shores and forms can be removed. Reshoring is normally required for several floors if the cycle time for formwork is to be minimized.

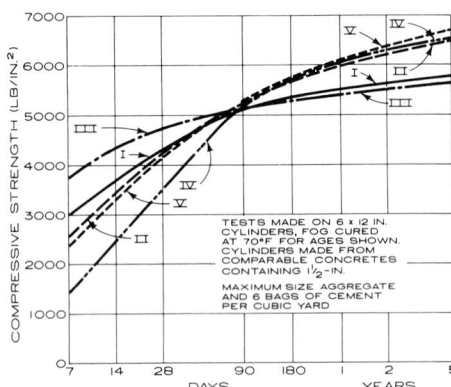

FIGURE 2. RATES OF STRENGTH DEVELOPMENT FOR CONCRETE MADE WITH VARIOUS TYPES OF CEMENT

TABLE 4. MAXIMUM WATER-CEMENT RATIOS FOR VARIOUS EXPOSURE CONDITIONS

EXPOSURE CONDITION	NORMAL WEIGHT CONCRETE, ABSOLUTE WATER-CEMENT RATIO BY WEIGHT
Concrete protected from exposure to freezing and thawing or application of deicer chemicals	Select water-cement ratio on basis of strength, workability, and finishing needs
Watertight concrete* In fresh water In seawater	0.50 0.45
Frost resistant concrete* Thin sections; any section with less than 2-in. cover over reinforcement and any concrete exposed to deicing salts	0.45
All other structures	0.50
Exposure to sulfates* Moderate Severe	0.50 0.45
Placing concrete under water	Not less than 650 lb of cement per cubic yard (386 kg/m³)
Floors on grade	Select water-cement ratio for strength, plus minimum cement requirements

*Contain entrained air within the limits of Table 1.

Bob Cotton; W.E. Simpson Company Inc.; San Antonio, Texas
Quentin L. Reutershan, AIA, Architect; Potsdam, New York
Gordon B. Batson, P.E.; Potsdam, New York

TABLE 5. MAXIMUM PERMISSIBLE WATER-CEMENT RATIOS FOR CONCRETE WHEN STRENGTH DATA FROM TRIAL BATCHES OR FIELD EXPERIENCE ARE NOT AVAILABLE

SPECIFIED COMPRESSIVE STRENGTH F'_c (PSI*)	MAXIMUM ABSOLUTE PERMISSIBLE WATER-CEMENT RATIO, BY WEIGHT	
	NON-AIR ENTRAINED CONCRETE	AIR ENTRAINED CONCRETE
2500	0.67	0.54
3000	0.58	0.46
3500	0.51	0.40
4000	0.44	0.35
4500	0.38	†
5000	†	†

NOTE: 1000 psi ≃ 7 MPa.
*28-day strength. With most materials, the water-cement ratios shown will provide average strengths greater than required.
†For strengths above 4500 psi (non-air entrained concrete) and 4000 psi (air entrained concrete), proportions should be established by the trial batch method.

TABLE 6. MINIMUM THICKNESS OF NON-PRESTRESSED BEAMS OR ONE WAY SLABS

	SIMPLY SUPPORTED	ONE END CONT.	BOTH ENDS CONT.	CANTILEVER
Solid One-Way Slabs	ℓ/20	ℓ/24	ℓ/28	ℓ/10
Beams or Ribbed One-Way Slabs	ℓ/16	ℓ/18.5	ℓ/21	ℓ/8

NOTE

Span length, l, is in inches. Values given are for members with normal weight concrete and Grade 60 reinforcement in construction not supporting or attached to partitions or other construction likely to be damaged by large deflection. For additional information, reference should be made to the American Concrete Institute Building Requirements for Reinforced Concrete (ACI 318).

CAST-IN-PLACE CONCRETE

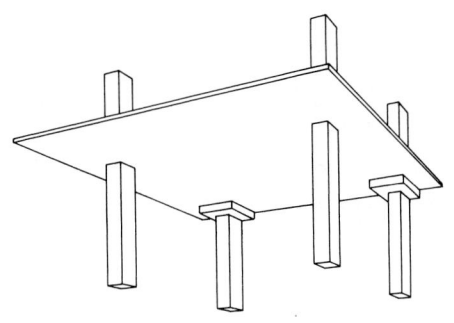

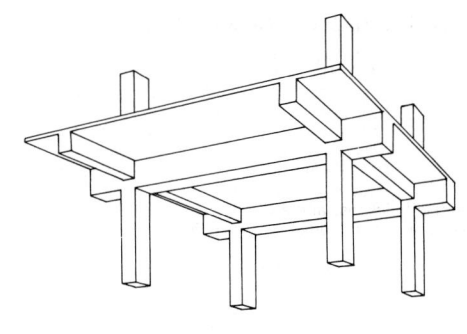

FLAT SLABS TO HAVE DROP
PANELS OR COLUMN CAPITALS.
FOR SUPERIMPOSED LOADS
OVER 100 PSF, USE BOTH DROP
PANELS AND COLUMN CAPITALS

FLAT PLATE

FLAT SLAB WITHOUT BEAMS

FLAT SLAB WITH BEAMS

IF REQUIRED, USE
TAPERED PANS AT GIRDER TO
RESIST SHEAR FORCES

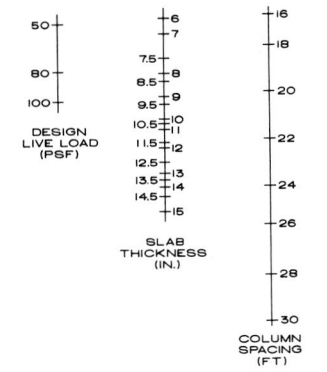

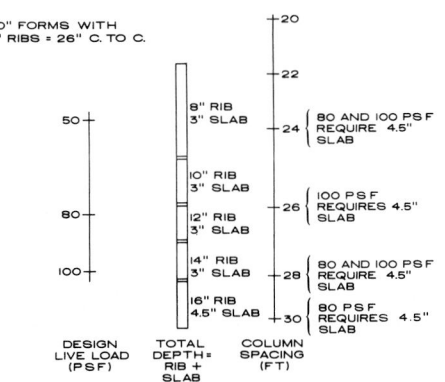

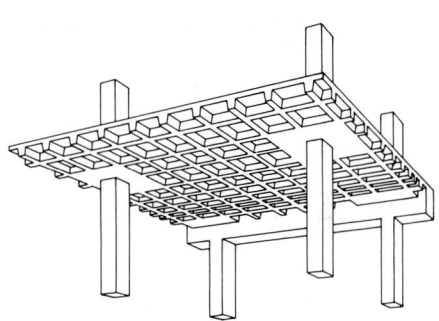

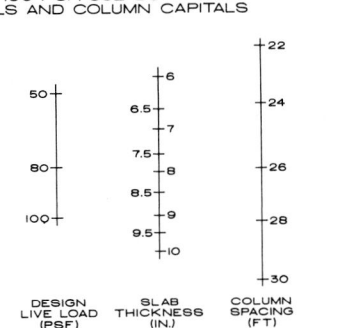

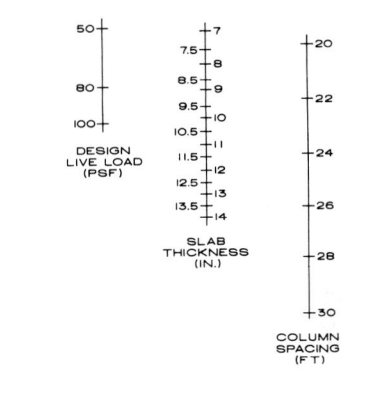

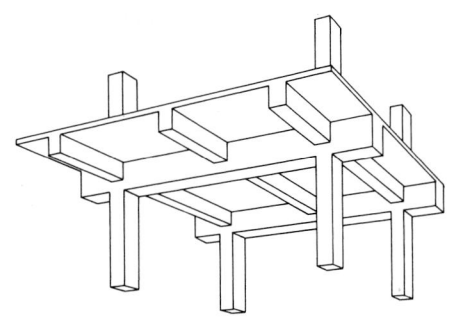

20" FORMS WITH
6" RIBS = 26" C. TO C.

19" x 19" FORMS WITH
5" RIBS = 24" C. TO C.

ONE-WAY SLAB WITH BEAMS (SPAN = ½ THE COLUMN SPACING)

ONE-WAY JOISTS WITH BEAMS (METAL PAN CONSTRUCTION)

TWO-WAY JOISTS WITHOUT BEAMS (WAFFLE FLAT PLATE CONSTRUCTION)

GENERAL NOTES

To use bar graphs, lay straight edge across chart and line up with design live load required on left bar and with selected column spacing on right bar. Slab thickness required is indicated where straight edge intersects center bar.

The examples above are all calculated by the ultimate design strength method around the following parameters:

1. Concrete strength of 4000 psi at 28 days.
2. Steel reinforcing strength of 60,000 psi.
3. Steel to concrete ratio of minimum steel.

The information represented on this page is intended to be used as a preliminary design guide only and not to replace complete analysis and calculation of each project condition by a licensed professional engineer.

Killebrew/Rucker/Associates, Inc., Architects/Planners/Engineers; Wichita Falls, Texas

CAST-IN-PLACE CONCRETE 3

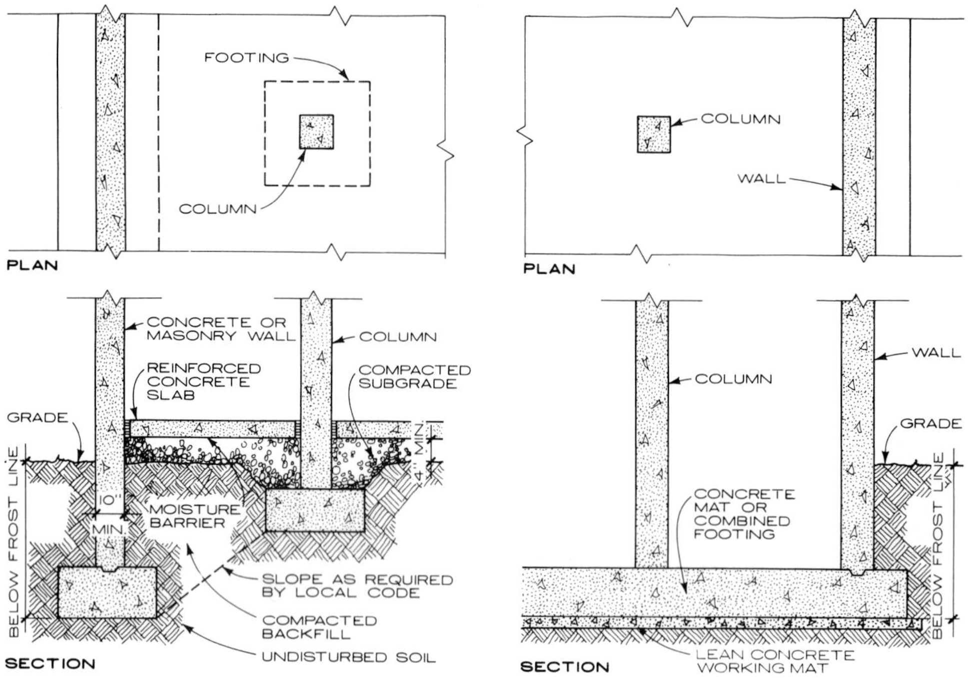

SPREAD FOOTINGS

PLAN

FOOTING
COLUMN

SECTION

GRADE
CONCRETE OR MASONRY WALL
REINFORCED CONCRETE SLAB
COLUMN
COMPACTED SUBGRADE
BELOW FROST LINE
10" MIN.
MOISTURE BARRIER
SLOPE AS REQUIRED BY LOCAL CODE
COMPACTED BACKFILL
UNDISTURBED SOIL

PLAN

COLUMN
WALL

SECTION

COLUMN
WALL
GRADE
CONCRETE MAT OR COMBINED FOOTING
BELOW FROST LINE
LEAN CONCRETE WORKING MAT

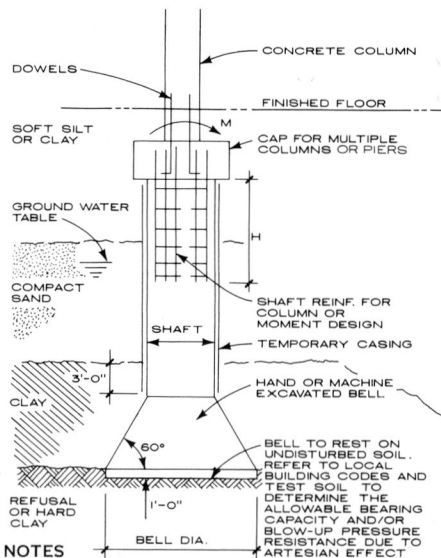

BELL PIER FOUNDATION

DOWELS
CONCRETE COLUMN
FINISHED FLOOR
SOFT SILT OR CLAY
M
CAP FOR MULTIPLE COLUMNS OR PIERS
GROUND WATER TABLE
H
COMPACT SAND
SHAFT
SHAFT REINF. FOR COLUMN OR MOMENT DESIGN
TEMPORARY CASING
3'-0"
CLAY
HAND OR MACHINE EXCAVATED BELL
60°
BELL TO REST ON UNDISTURBED SOIL. REFER TO LOCAL BUILDING CODES AND TEST SOIL TO DETERMINE THE ALLOWABLE BEARING CAPACITY AND/OR BLOW-UP PRESSURE RESISTANCE DUE TO ARTESIAN EFFECT
REFUSAL OR HARD CLAY
1'-0"
BELL DIA.

NOTES

1. H is a function of the passive resistance of the soil, generated by the moment applied to the pier cap.
2. Piers may be used under grade beams or concrete walls. For very heavy loads, pier foundations may be more economical than piles.

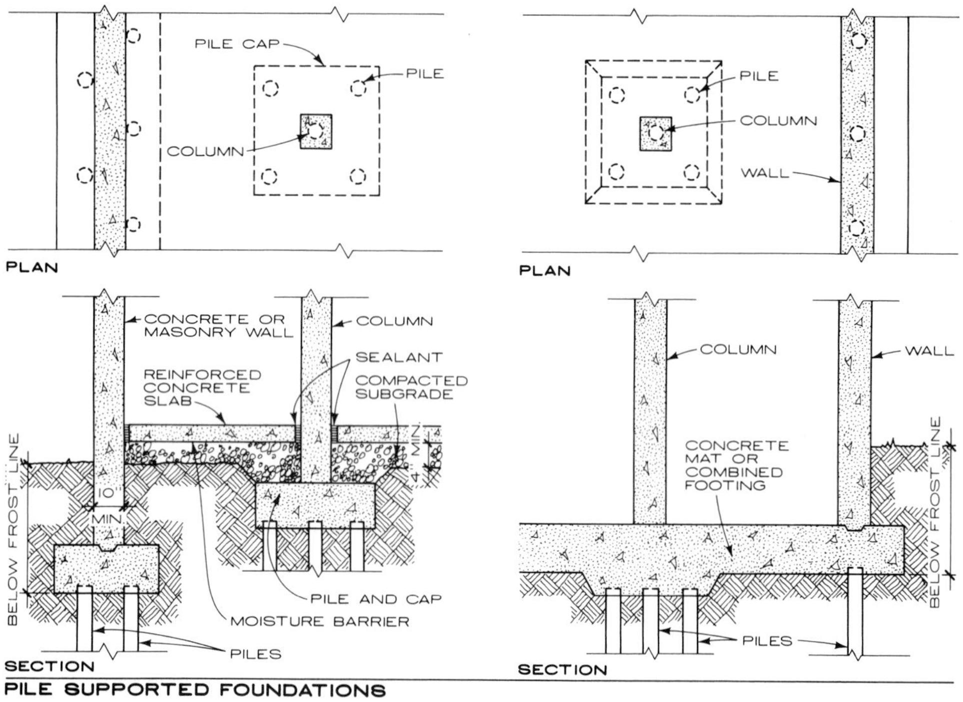

PILE SUPPORTED FOUNDATIONS

PLAN

PILE CAP
PILE
COLUMN

SECTION

CONCRETE OR MASONRY WALL
REINFORCED CONCRETE SLAB
COLUMN
SEALANT
COMPACTED SUBGRADE
BELOW FROST LINE
10" MIN.
PILE AND CAP
MOISTURE BARRIER
PILES

PLAN

PILE
COLUMN
WALL

SECTION

COLUMN
WALL
CONCRETE MAT OR COMBINED FOOTING
BELOW FROST LINE
PILES

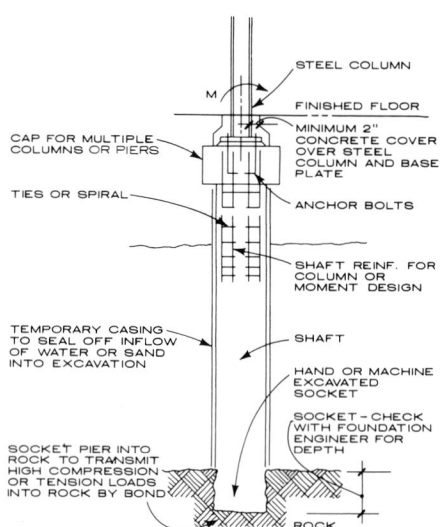

SOCKET PIER FOUNDATION

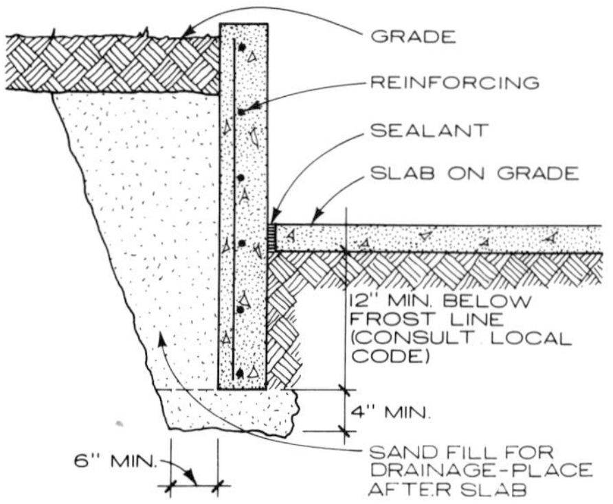

STEEL COLUMN
M
FINISHED FLOOR
MINIMUM 2" CONCRETE COVER OVER STEEL COLUMN AND BASE PLATE
CAP FOR MULTIPLE COLUMNS OR PIERS
ANCHOR BOLTS
TIES OR SPIRAL
SHAFT REINF. FOR COLUMN OR MOMENT DESIGN
TEMPORARY CASING TO SEAL OFF INFLOW OF WATER OR SAND INTO EXCAVATION
SHAFT
HAND OR MACHINE EXCAVATED SOCKET
SOCKET – CHECK WITH FOUNDATION ENGINEER FOR DEPTH
SOCKET PIER INTO ROCK TO TRANSMIT HIGH COMPRESSION OR TENSION LOADS INTO ROCK BY BOND
ROCK

NOTES

1. Pier shaft should be poured in the dry if possible, but tremie pours can be used with appropriate control.
2. Grout bottom of shaft against artesian water or sulphur gas intrusion into the excavation.

AREAWAY WALL

GRADE
REINFORCING
SEALANT
SLAB ON GRADE
12" MIN. BELOW FROST LINE (CONSULT LOCAL CODE)
4" MIN.
6" MIN.
SAND FILL FOR DRAINAGE-PLACE AFTER SLAB

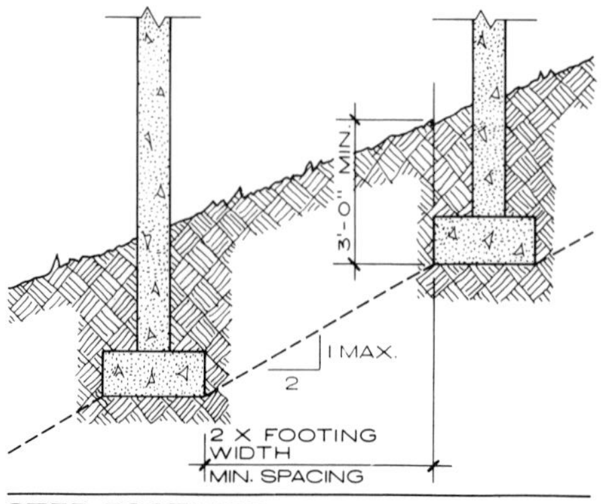

STEP FOOTINGS
MAX. STEEPNESS: 2 HORIZONTAL TO 1 VERTICAL

3'-0" MIN.
1 MAX.
2
2 X FOOTING WIDTH
MIN. SPACING

STEP FOOTING (FOR CONTINUOUS WALL)
MAX. STEEPNESS: 2 HORIZONTAL TO 1 VERTICAL

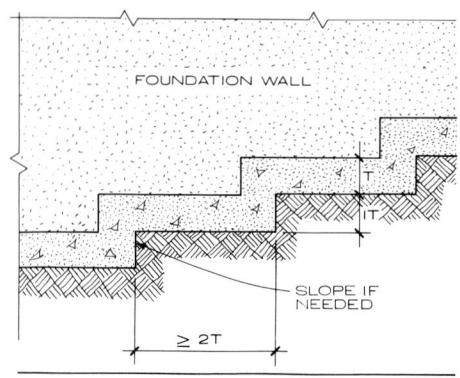

FOUNDATION WALL
T
T
SLOPE IF NEEDED
≥ 2T

Mueser Rutledge Consulting Engineers; New York, New York

CAST-IN-PLACE CONCRETE

GENERAL

Factors to consider in the design and construction of all slabs on grade include the intended use of the slab or slab section, the condition and preparation of a uniform subgrade, quality of concrete, adequacy of structural capacity, type and spacing of joints, finishing, curing, and application of special surfaces. The subgrade support must be reasonably uniform and the upper portion of the subgrade (called the base) should be of uniform material and density. Both should be properly compacted. A thin layer of compactable granular fill may be placed immediately beneath the slab to act as a percolation barrier.

Wear resistance (abrasion) is directly related to the condition of the top portion of the concrete slab. Surface hardness and abrasion resistance may be provided by special additives or hardeners to the surface. The quality of the overall concrete slab will be enhanced by proper water-to-cement ratio, reasonable slump limits, and well-graded aggregates with the maximum size of the coarse aggregate as large as placing will permit. Exterior concrete subjected to freeze-thaw cycles should have 4 to 7% entrained air.

Reinforcement in concrete slabs is unnecessary where frequent joint spacings are used. Where less frequent joint spacings are used, reinforcement is placed in the slab, at or above the mid-depth (generally $1/3$ down from the top surface) to act as crack control. Common contraction joint spacing is 15 to 25 ft, depending on the thickness of the slab and the construction type. Checkerboard placement of slabs is no longer recommended by American Concrete Institute (ACI) 302.1 "Guide for floor and slab construction," where strip placement of slabs is recommended for large areas.

Three types of joints are recommended:

1. ISOLATION JOINTS (also called expansion joints): Allow movement between slab and fixed parts of the building such as columns, walls, and machinery bases.
2. CONTRACTION JOINTS (also called control joints): Induce cracking at preselected locations.
3. CONSTRUCTION JOINTS: Provide stopping places during floor construction. Construction joints also function as control and isolation joints.

Sawcut control joints should be made as early as is practical after finishing the slab and should be filled in areas with wet conditions, hygienic and dust control requirements, or considerable traffic by hard wheel vehicles, such as forklifts. A semirigid filler Shore Hardness "A" of at least 80 should be used in joints supporting forklift traffic.

Concrete floor slabs are monolithically finished as a general procedure by floating and troweling to a smooth and dense top surface finish. ACI 302 provides specific guidance for appropriate finishing procedures to control the achievable floor flatness. ACI 302, ACI 360, and ACI 117 provide guidance for flatness selection and the techniques by which flatness and levelness are produced and measured. Two systems are used. The preferred method of measuring flatness and levelness (documented in ACI 302 and ACI 117) is the F-Number System. Special finishes are available to improve appearance as well as surface properties. These include sprinkled (shake) finishes or high-strength toppings, either as monolithic or separate (two-stage floor) surfaces. Where propagation of water vapor is undesirable, a waterproof vapor barrier, with permeance not to exceed 0.20 perms, can be used.

THICKNESS DESIGN

In general, the controlling loading to a slab on grade is the heaviest concentrated loading that it will carry. This is frequently the axle loading of an industrial lift truck, or the set post loadings from heavy rack storage shelves. The concrete slab thickness required will depend on the loading itself, the modulus of rupture of the concrete (usually based on the compressive strength of the concrete), the selected factor of safety used in the design, and the modulus of subgrade reaction (k) of the soil support system (subgrade). Procedures and examples are shown in ACI 360, ACI 330, and ACI 302. Class 1, 2, and 3 floors should be no thinner than 4 or 5 inches. Loading and usage frequently require floors thicker than 6 inches.

DOWEL SIZE AND SPACING (IN.)

SLAB DEPTH	DOWEL DIA.	TOTAL DOWEL LENGTH	DOWEL SPACING CENTER TO CENTER
5 - 6	$3/4$	16	12
7 - 8	1	18	12
9 - 10	$1 1/4$	18	12

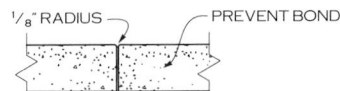

BUTT JOINT CONSTRUCTION JOINT

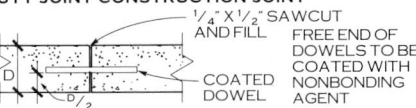

BUTT TYPE CONSTRUCTION JOINT WITH DOWELS

SAWED OR PREMOLDED CONTRACTION JOINT

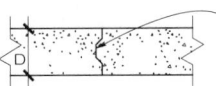

TONGUE AND GROOVE JOINT

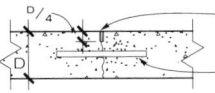

CONTRACTION JOINT WITH DOWELS

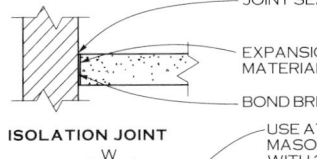

ISOLATION JOINT

THICKENED SLAB

TYPICAL DETAILS

CLASSIFICATION OF CONCRETE SLABS ON GRADE

CLASS	RECOMMENDED SLUMP (IN.)	RECOMMENDED 28-DAY COMPRESSIVE STRENGTH (PSI)	USUAL TRAFFIC	USE	SPECIAL CONSIDERATIONS	CONCRETE FINISHING TECHNIQUE
1	5	3000	Light foot	Residential surfaces; mainly with floor coverings	Grade for drainage; level slabs suitable for applied coverings; curing	Single troweling
2	5	3500	Foot	Offices and churches; usually with floor covering	Surface tolerance (including elevated slabs); nonslip aggregates in specific areas	Single troweling; nonslip finish where required
				Decorative	Colored mineral aggregate; hardener or exposed aggregate; artistic joint layout	As required
3	5	3500	Foot and pneumatic wheel	Exterior walks, driveways, garage floors, and sidewalks	Grade for drainage; proper air content; curing	Float, trowel, or broom finish
4	5	4000	Foot and light vehicular traffic	Institutional and commercial	Level slab suitable for applied coverings; nonslip aggregate for specific areas and curing	Normal steel trowel finish
5	4	4000	Industrial vehicular traffic—pneumatic wheel	Light-duty industrial floors for manufacturing, processing, and warehousing	Good uniform subgrade; surface tolerance; joint layout; abrasion resistance; curing	Hard steel trowel finish
6	4	4500	Industrial vehicular traffic—hard wheels	Industrial floors subject to heavy traffic; may be subject to impact loads	Good uniform subgrade; surface tolerance; joint layout; load transfer; abrasion resistance; curing	Special metallic or mineral aggregate; repeated hard steel troweling
7	4	Base 3500	Industrial vehicular traffic—hard wheels	Bonded two-course floors subject to heavy traffic and impact	Base slab—Good uniform subgrade; reinforcement; joint layout; level surface; curing Topping—Composed of well-graded all-mineral or all-metallic aggregate; Mineral or metallic aggregate applied to high-strength plain topping to toughen; surface tolerance; curing	Clean-textured surface suitable for subsequent bonded topping Special power floats with repeated steel trowelings
8	2	Topping 5000 - 8000	As in classes 4, 5, and 6	Unbonded toppings—Freezer floors on insulation, on old floors, or where construction schedule dictates	Bond breaker on old surface; mesh reinforcement; minimum thickness 3"(nominal 75mm) abrasion resistance, and curing	Hard steel trowel finish
9	5	4000 or higher	Superflat or critical surface tolerance required. Special materials-handling vehicles or robotics requiring specific tolerances	Narrow-aisle, high-bay warehouses; television studios	Varying concrete quality requirements. Shake-on hardeners cannot be used unless special application and great care are employed. Proper joint arrangement	Strictly follow finishing techniques as indicated in section 7.15 of ACI 302

Boyd C. Ringo; Cincinnati, Ohio

CAST-IN-PLACE CONCRETE

3

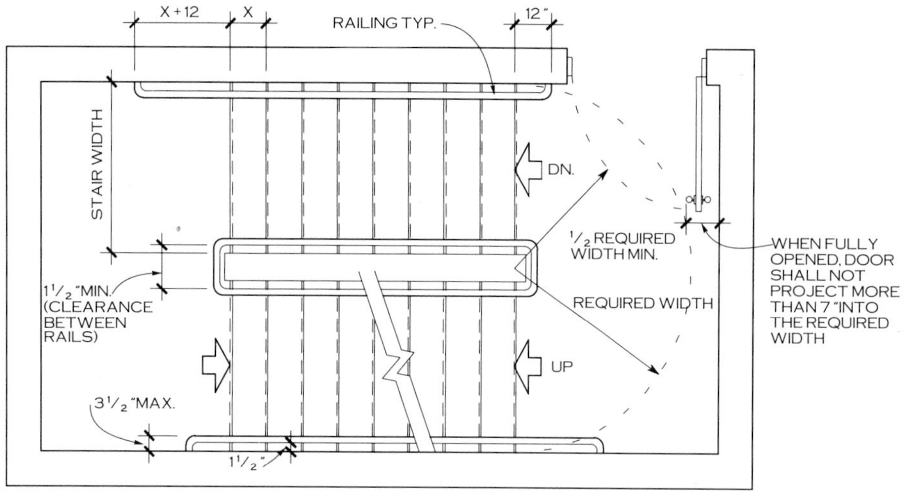

PLAN

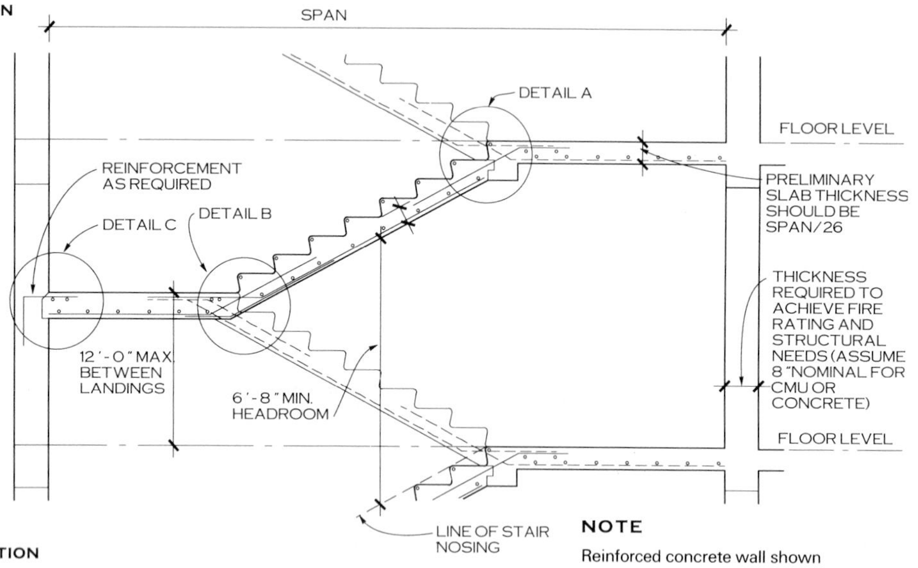

X + 12   X   RAILING TYP.   12"

STAIR WIDTH

DN.

1/2 REQUIRED WIDTH MIN.

REQUIRED WIDTH

UP

1 1/2" MIN. (CLEARANCE BETWEEN RAILS)

3 1/2" MAX.

1 1/2"

WHEN FULLY OPENED, DOOR SHALL NOT PROJECT MORE THAN 7" INTO THE REQUIRED WIDTH

SECTION

SPAN

DETAIL A

FLOOR LEVEL

REINFORCEMENT AS REQUIRED

DETAIL C   DETAIL B

12'-0" MAX BETWEEN LANDINGS

6'-8" MIN. HEADROOM

LINE OF STAIR NOSING

PRELIMINARY SLAB THICKNESS SHOULD BE SPAN/26

THICKNESS REQUIRED TO ACHIEVE FIRE RATING AND STRUCTURAL NEEDS (ASSUME 8" NOMINAL FOR CMU OR CONCRETE)

FLOOR LEVEL

NOTE

Reinforced concrete wall shown

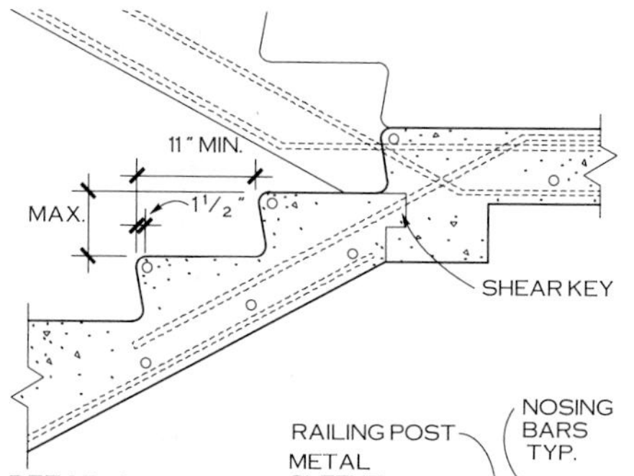

DETAIL A

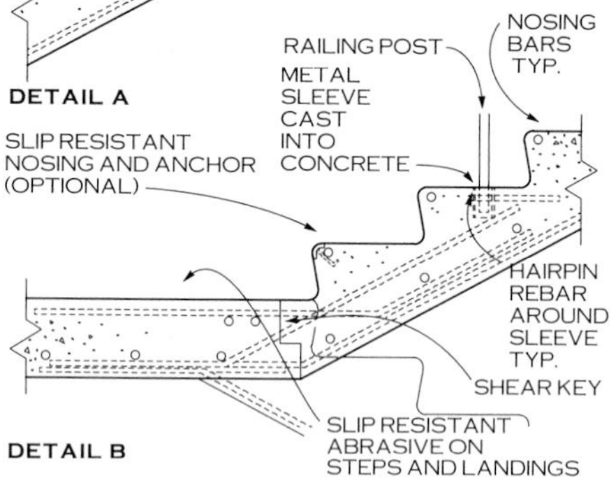

11" MIN.

MAX.   1 1/2"

SHEAR KEY

DETAIL B

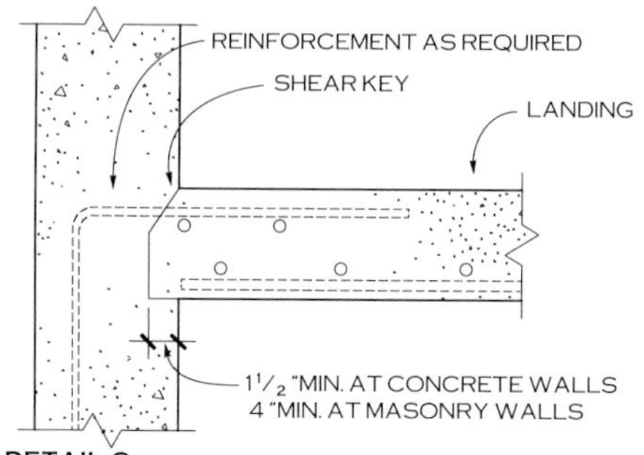

NOSING BARS TYP.

RAILING POST

METAL SLEEVE CAST INTO CONCRETE

SLIP RESISTANT NOSING AND ANCHOR (OPTIONAL)

HAIRPIN REBAR AROUND SLEEVE TYP.

SHEAR KEY

SLIP RESISTANT ABRASIVE ON STEPS AND LANDINGS

DETAIL C

REINFORCEMENT AS REQUIRED

SHEAR KEY

LANDING

1 1/2" MIN. AT CONCRETE WALLS
4" MIN. AT MASONRY WALLS

NOTES

1. Structural engineer to determine reinforcement specifications and specific placement in stairs.
2. Check codes for dimensions and clearances for accessibility standards.

U-TYPE CONCRETE STAIRS

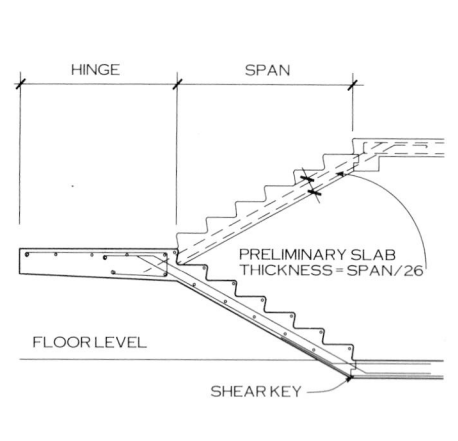

HINGE   SPAN

PRELIMINARY SLAB THICKNESS = SPAN/26

FLOOR LEVEL

SHEAR KEY

NOTE

Extend hinge only as required by stair width, unless otherwise permitted by structural engineer.

FREESTANDING CONCRETE STAIR

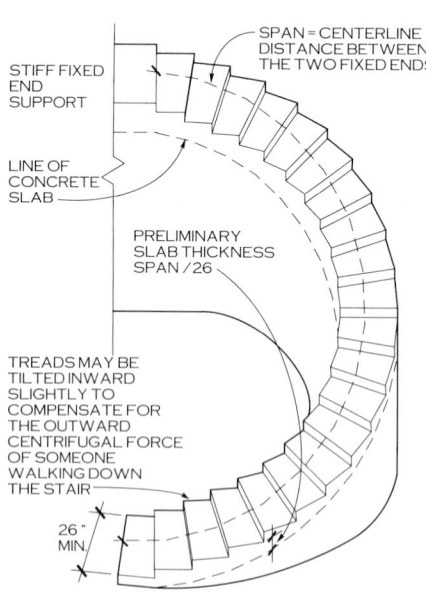

SPAN = CENTERLINE DISTANCE BETWEEN THE TWO FIXED ENDS

STIFF FIXED END SUPPORT

LINE OF CONCRETE SLAB

PRELIMINARY SLAB THICKNESS SPAN/26

TREADS MAY BE TILTED INWARD SLIGHTLY TO COMPENSATE FOR THE OUTWARD CENTRIFUGAL FORCE OF SOMEONE WALKING DOWN THE STAIR

26" MIN.

NOTE

Use of helicoidal concrete stairs depends on very stiff fixed end support and small support deflection.

HELICOIDAL CONCRETE STAIR

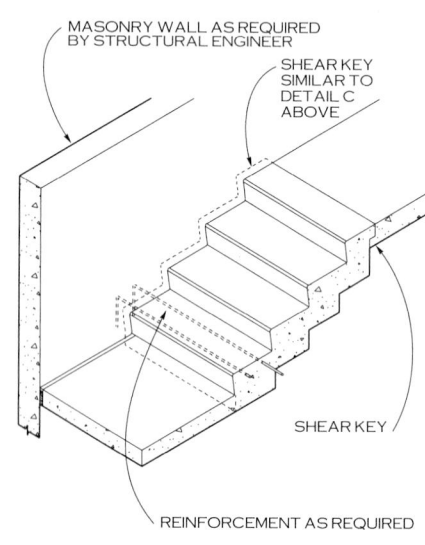

MASONRY WALL AS REQUIRED BY STRUCTURAL ENGINEER

SHEAR KEY SIMILAR TO DETAIL C ABOVE

SHEAR KEY

REINFORCEMENT AS REQUIRED

NOTE

Reinforcement must develop full bond in masonry walls and have full development length in concrete walls.

CANTILEVER CONCRETE STAIR

Krommenhoek/McKeown and Associates; San Diego, California
Karlsberger and Companies; Columbus, Ohio

CAST-IN-PLACE CONCRETE

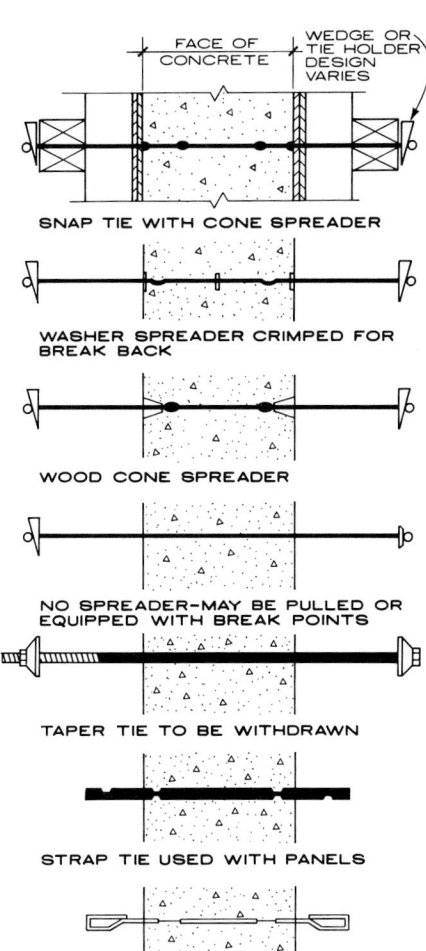

SNAP TIE WITH CONE SPREADER

WASHER SPREADER CRIMPED FOR BREAK BACK

WOOD CONE SPREADER

NO SPREADER—MAY BE PULLED OR EQUIPPED WITH BREAK POINTS

TAPER TIE TO BE WITHDRAWN

STRAP TIE USED WITH PANELS

LOOP END TIE USED WITH PANELS

TYPICAL SINGLE MEMBER TIES

CONCRETE SURFACES—GENERAL

The variety of architectural finishes is as extensive as the cost and effort expended to achieve them. There are three basic ways to improve or change the appearance of concrete:

1. Changing materials, that is, using a colored matrix and exposed aggregates.
2. Changing the mold or form by such means as a form liner.
3. By treating or tooling the concrete surface in the final stages of hardening.

The aim is to obtain maximum benefit from one of three features—color, texture, and pattern—all of which are interrelated. Color is the easiest method of changing the appearance of concrete. It should not be used on a plain concrete surface with a series of panels, since color matches are difficult to achieve. The exception is possible when white cement is used, usually as a base for the pigment to help reduce changes of color variation. Since white cement is expensive, many effects are tried with gray cement to avoid an entire plain surface. Colored concrete is most effective when it is used with an exposed aggregate finish.

FORM LINERS

1. Sandblasted Douglas fir or long leaf yellow pine dressed one side away from the concrete surface.
2. Flexible steel strip formwork adapted to curved surfaces (Schwellmer System).
3. Resin coated, striated, or sandblasted plywood.
4. Rubber mats.
5. Thermoplastic sheets with high gloss or texture laid over stone, for example.
6. Formed plastics.
7. Plaster of Paris molds for sculptured work.
8. Clay (sculpturing and staining concrete).
9. Hardboard (screen side).

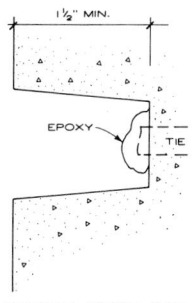 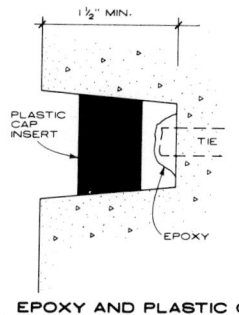 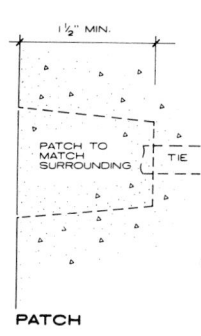

EPOXY OVER TIE   EPOXY AND PLASTIC CAP   PATCH

TIE HOLE TREATMENT OPTIONS

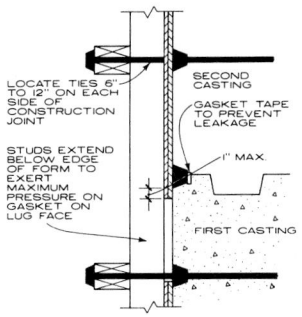

TYPICAL CONSTRUCTION JOINT

10. Standard steel forms.
11. Wood boarding and reversed battens.
12. Square-edged lumber dressed one side.
13. Resawn wood boards.

RELEASE AGENTS

1. Oils, petroleum based, used on wood, concrete, and steel forms.
2. Soft soaps.
3. Talcum.
4. Whitewash used on wood with tannin in conjunction with oils.
5. Calcium stearate powder.
6. Silicones used on steel forms.
7. Plastics used on wood forms.
8. Lacquers used on plywood and plaster forms.
9. Resins used on plywood forms.
10. Sodium silicate.
11. Membrane used over any form.
12. Grease used on plaster forms.
13. Epoxy resin plastic used on plywood.

CATEGORIES OF COMMON AGGREGATE

1. QUARTZ: Clear, white, rose.
2. MARBLE: Green, yellow, red, pink, blue, gray, white, black.
3. GRANITE: Pink, gray, black, white.
4. CERAMIC: Full range.
5. VITREOUS/GLASS: Full range.

CRITICAL FACTORS AFFECTING SURFACES

DESIGN DRAWINGS should show form details, including openings, control joints, construction joints, expansion joints, and other important specifics.

1. CEMENT: Types and brands.
2. AGGREGATES: Sources of coarse and fine aggregates.
3. TECHNIQUES: Uniformity in mixing and placing.
4. FORMS: Closure techniques or concealing joints in formwork materials.
5. SLUMP CONTROL: Ensure compliance with design.
6. CURING METHODS: Ensure compliance with design.

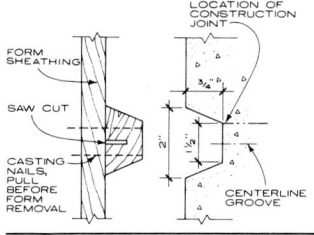

RUSTICATION AT CONSTRUCTION JOINT

TIES

A concrete tie is a tensile unit adapted to hold concrete forms secure against the lateral pressure of unhardened concrete. Two general types of concrete ties exist:

1. Continuous single member where the tensile unit is a single piece and the holding device engages the tensile unit against the exterior of the form. Standard types: working load = 2500 to 5000 lb.
2. Internal disconnecting where the tensile unit has an inner part with threaded connections to removable external members, which have suitable devices of securing them against the outside of the form. Working load = 6000 to 36,000 lb.

GUIDELINES FOR PATCHING

1. Design the patch mix to match the original, with small amount of white cement; may eliminate coarse aggregate or hand place it. Trial and error is the only reliable match method.
2. Saturate area with water and apply bonding agent to base of hole and to water of patch mix.
3. Pack patch mix to density of original.
4. Place exposed aggregate by hand.
5. Bristle brush after setup to match existing material.
6. Moist cure to prevent shrinking.
7. Use form or finish to match original.

CHECKLIST IN PLANNING FOR ARCHITECTURAL CONCRETE PLACING TECHNIQUES:

Pumping vs. bottom drop or other type of bucket.

1. FORMING SYSTEM: Evaluate whether architectural concrete forms can also be used for structural concrete.
2. SHOP DRAWINGS: Determine form quality and steel placement.
3. VIBRATORS: Verify that proper size, frequency, and power are used.
4. RELEASE AGENTS: Consider form material, color impact of agents, and possible use throughout job.
5. CURING COMPOUND: Determine how fast it wears off.
6. SAMPLES: Require approval of forms and finishes. Field mock-up is advised to evaluate appearance of panel and quality of workmanship.

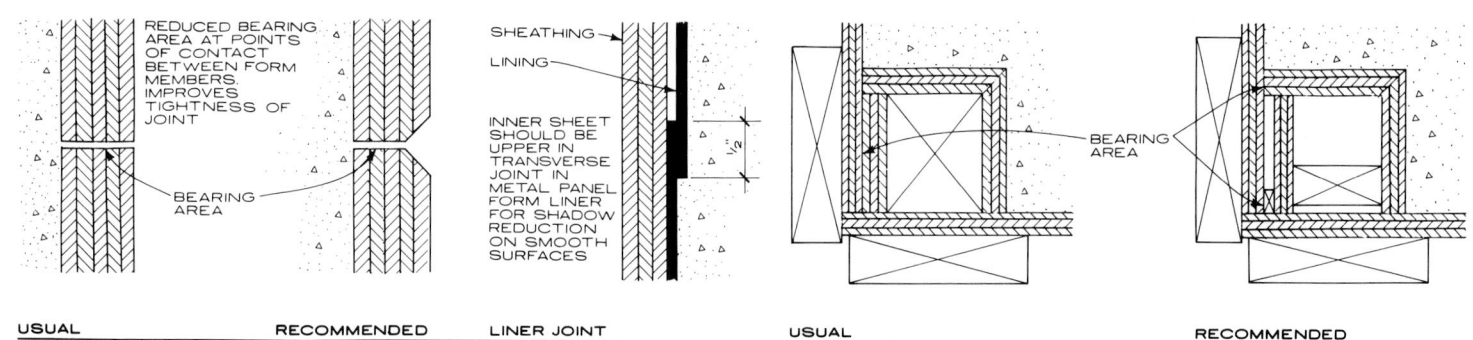

| USUAL | RECOMMENDED | LINER JOINT | USUAL | RECOMMENDED |

FORM JOINTS

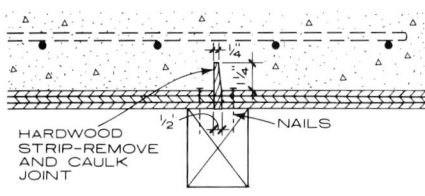

RUBBER FORM INSERT

WOOD FORM INSERT

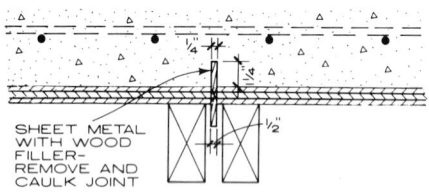

SHEET METAL FORM INSERT

CONTROL JOINTS

RUSTICATION (PREFERRED)

TAPED (MEDIUM LIGHT BLAST)

EPOXY ON 45° CUT

GASKETED

TONGUE AND GROOVED

SPLINED

IMPERVIOUS LINER (1/4" TO 3/8")

SHIPLAP

PLYWOOD BUTT JOINTS FOR EXPOSED AGGREGATE FINISHES

CATEGORIES OF ARCHITECTURAL CONCRETE SURFACES

CATEGORY	FINISH	COLOR	FORMS	CRITICAL DETAILS
1. As cast	Remains as is after form removal—usually board marks or wood grain	Cement first influence, fine aggregate second influence	Plastic best All others • Wire-brushed plywood • Sandblasted plywood • Exposed-grain plywood • Unfinished sheathing lumber • Ammonia sprayed wood • Tongue-and-groove bands spaced	Slump = 2½'' to 3½'' Joinery of forms Proper release agent Point form joints to avoid marks
2. Abrasive blasted surfaces A. Brush blast	Uniform scour cleaning	Cement plus fine aggregate have equal influence	All smooth	Scouring after 7 days Slump = 2½'' to 3½''
B. Light blast	Sandblast to expose fine and some coarse aggregate	Fine aggregate primary coarse aggregate plus cement secondary	All smooth	10% more coarse aggregate Slump = 2½'' to 3½'' Blasting between 7 and 45 days
C. Medium exposed aggregate	Sandblasted to expose coarse aggregate	Coarse aggregate	All smooth	Higher than normal coarse aggregate Slump = 2'' to 3'' Blast before 7 days
D. Heavy exposed aggregate	Sandblasted to expose coarse aggregate 80% viable	Coarse aggregate	All smooth	Special mix coarse aggregate Slump = 0'' to 2'' Blast within 24 hours Use high frequency vibrator
3. Chemical retardation of surface set	Chemicals expose aggregate Aggregate can be adhered to surface	Coarse aggregate and cement	All smooth, glass fiber best	Chemical Grade determines etch depth Stripping scheduled to prevent long drying between stripping and washoff
4. Mechanically fractured surfaces, scaling, bush hammering, jackhammering, tooling	Varied	Cement, fine and coarse Aggregate	Textured	Aggregate particles ⅜'' for scaling and tooling Aggregate particles
5. Combination/fluted	Striated/abrasive blasted/irregular pattern Corrugated/abrasive Vertical rusticated/abrasive blasted Reeded and bush hammered Reeded and hammered Reeded and chiseled	The shallower the surface, the more influence aggregate fines and cement have	Wood or rubber strips, corrugated sheet metal or glass fiber	Depends on type of finish desired Wood fluke kerfed and nailed loosely

D. Neil Rankins; SHWC, Inc.; Dallas, Texas

CAST-IN-PLACE CONCRETE

GENERAL CONSIDERATIONS

1. Concrete strength is usually 5000 psi at 28 days and at least 3,000 psi at time of prestressing. Use hardrock aggregate or lightweight concrete. Low slump controlled mix is required to reduce shrinkage. Shrinkage after prestressing decreases prestress strength gains.

2. Post-tensioning systems can be divided into three categories depending on whether the tendon is wire, strand, or bar. Wire systems use 0.25 in. diameter wires that have a minimum strength of 240,000 psi and are usually cut to length in the shop. Strand systems use tendons, made of seven wires wrapped together, that have a minimum strength of 270,000 psi and are cut in the field. Bar systems use bars ranging in diameter from $5/8$ to $1^3/8$ in. diameter, with a minimum strength of 145,000 psi; they may be smooth or deformed. The system used determines the type of anchorage used, which in turn affects the size of blockout required, in the edge of slab or beam, for the anchorage to be recessed.

3. Grease and wrap tendons, or place in conduits to reduce frictional losses during stressing operations. Limit length of continuous tendons to about 10 ft if stressed from one end. Long tendons require simultaneous stressing from both ends to reduce friction loss. Tendons may be grouted after stressing or left unbonded. Bonded tendons have structural advantages that are more important for beams and primary structural members.

4. Minimum average prestress (net prestress force per area of concrete) = 150 to 250 psi for flat plates, 200 to 500 psi for beams. Exceeding these values by much causes excessive prestress losses because of creep.

5. Field inspection of post-tensioned concrete is critical to ensure proper size and location of tendons and to monitor the tendon stress. Check tendon stress by measuring elongation of the tendon, and by monitoring gauge pressures on the stressing jack.

6. Make provisions for the shortening of post-tensioned beams and slabs caused by elastic compression, shrinkage, and creep. After the post-tensioning is complete, build shearwalls, curtain walls, or other stiff elements that adjoin post-tensioned members and isolate them with an expansion joint. Otherwise, additional post-tensioning force will be required to overcome the stiffness of the walls and prevent cracking.

7. Fire tests have been conducted on prestressed beam and slab assemblies according to ASTM E119 test procedures; they compare favorably with conventionally reinforced concrete. There is little difference between beams using grouted tendons and those using ungrouted tendons.

8. References for further study:

   Post-Tensioning Institute, "Post-Tensioning Manual."

   Prestressed Concrete Institute, "Design Handbook for Precast and Prestressed Concrete."

   Lin, T.Y., "Design of Prestressed Concrete Structures."

   American Concrete Institute, "Building Code Requirements for Reinforced Concrete" (ACI-318-83).

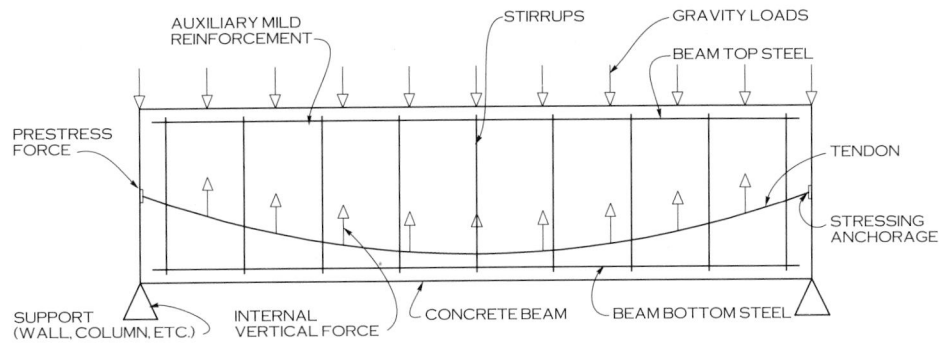

PRESTRESSED OR POST-TENSIONED BEAM

NOTES FOR DIAGRAM ABOVE

1. Prestressing force compresses entire cross-section of the beam, thereby reducing unwanted tension cracks.

2. Permanent tension is introduced into tendon and "locked in" with the stressing anchorage in one of two ways. The principle in both cases is the same. In prestressed concrete, the tendon is elongated in a stressing bed before the concrete is poured. In post-tensioned concrete, the tendon is elongated after concrete has been poured and allowed to cure by means of hydraulic jacks pushing against the beam itself. Post-tensioned beams permit casting at the site for members too large or heavy for transporting from factory to site.

3. Internal vertical forces within the beam are created by applying tension on the tendon, making the tendon begin to "straighten out." The tension reduces downward beam deflection and allows shallower beams and longer spans than in conventionally reinforced beams.

4. Auxiliary mild reinforcement provides additional strength, controls cracking, and produces more ductile behavior.

5. Use stirrups to provide additional shear strength in the beam and to support the tendons and longitudinal mild reinforcement. Stirrups should be open at the top to allow the reinforcing to be placed before the tendon is installed. After the tendons are placed, "hairpins" that close the stirrups may be used when required.

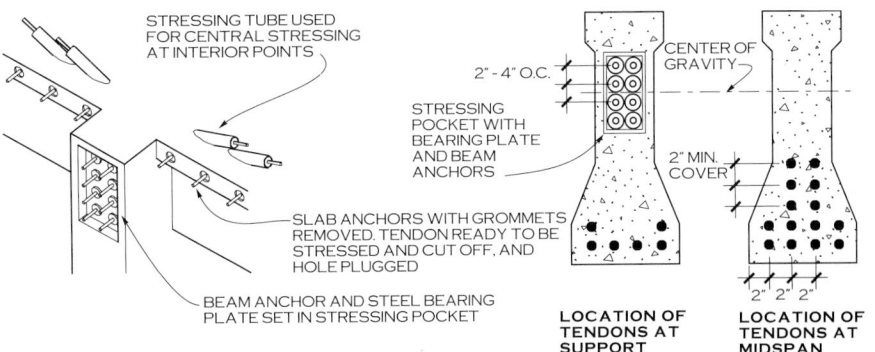

PRESTRESSED BEAM

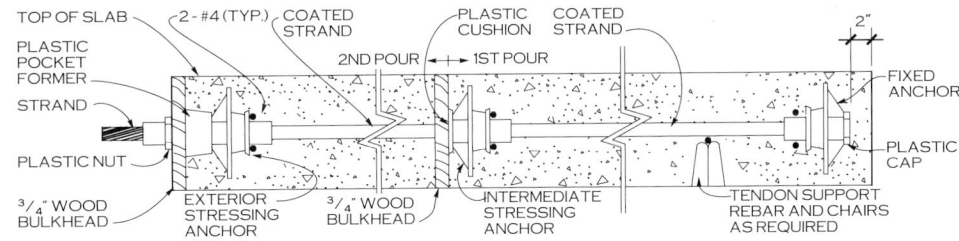

UNBONDED SINGLE STRAND TENDON INSTALLATION AT SLAB

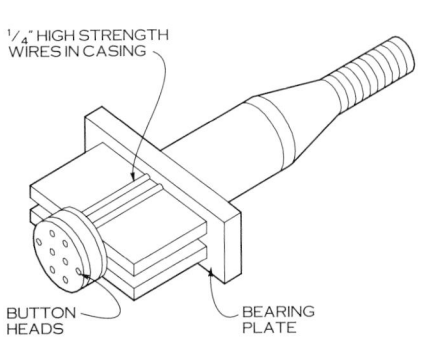

8 WIRE BBRV POST-TENSIONING ANCHOR (GROUTED)

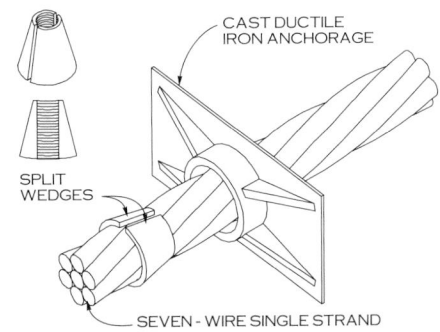

SINGLE STRAND TENDON ANCHORAGE (UNBONDED)

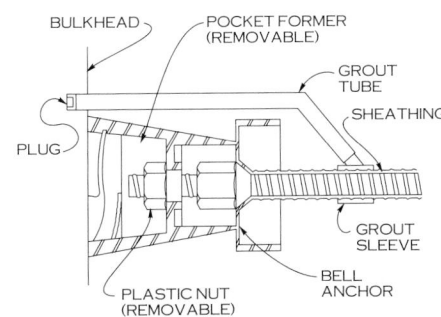

THREAD BAR ANCHORAGE (GROUTED)

Leo A. Daly, Planning/Architecture/Engineering/Interiors; Omaha, Nebraska

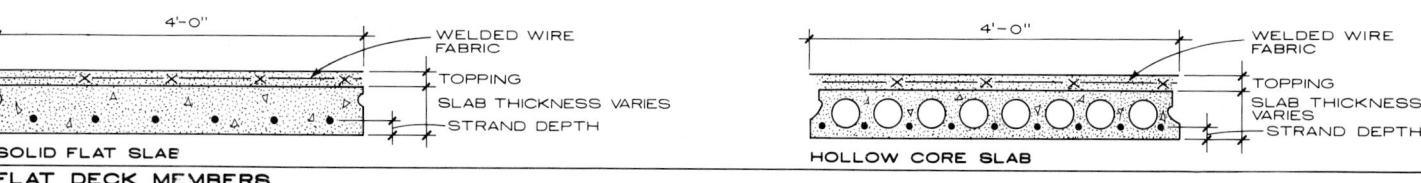

SOLID FLAT SLAB — WELDED WIRE FABRIC / TOPPING / SLAB THICKNESS VARIES / STRAND DEPTH

HOLLOW CORE SLAB — WELDED WIRE FABRIC / TOPPING / SLAB THICKNESS VARIES / STRAND DEPTH

FLAT DECK MEMBERS

TABLE 1 ✱
SAFE SUPERIMPOSED SERVICE LOADS (PSF) FOR SOLID FLAT SLABS (4 FT WIDTH)

SLAB THICKNESS (IN.)	SLAB DESIGNATION	TOPPING THICKNESS (IN.)	SPAN (FT)															
			11	12	13	14	15	16	17	18	19	20	21	22	23	24	25
4" (STRAND DESIGNATION CODE: 58-S)	FS4	NONE	212	180	154	127	104	86	70								
	FS4+2	2			274	214	166	127	95								
6" (STRAND DESIGNATION CODE: 78-S)	FS6	NONE	320	287	257	236	213	196	183	168	155	144	134	126	109	94	81
	FS6+2	2					298	273	252	231	216	199	185	169	140	115	93
8" (STRAND DESIGNATION CODE: 68-S)	FS8	NONE				318	291	266	245	227	209	196	181	169	155	136	119
	FS8+2	2								304	283	261	245	225	197	167	140

TABLE 2 ✱
SAFE SUPERIMPOSED SERVICE LOADS (PSF) FOR HOLLOW CORE SLABS (4 FT WIDTH)

SLAB THICKNESS (IN.)	SLAB DESIGNATION	TOPPING THICKNESS (IN.)	SPAN (FT)														
			12	14	16	18	20	22	24	26	28	30	32	34	36	38	40
6" (STRAND DESIGNATION CODE: 66-S)	4HC6	NONE	257	197	154	113	84	63	47								
	4HC6+2	2		278	215	153	102	65									
8" (STRAND DESIGNATION CODE: 58-S)	4HC8	NONE					275	221	175	140	112	91	73	59			
	4HC8+2	2						273	215	170	136	108	84	60			
10" (STRAND DESIGNATION CODE: 78-S)	4HC10	NONE					298	264	237	214	192	160	134	113	95	80	67
	4HC10+2	2						278	250	218	181	150	125	103	85	67	
12" (STRAND DESIGNATION CODE: 68-S)	4HC12	NONE								182	165	150	120	109	92	78	
	4HC12+2	2							249	224	200	183	164	137	114	95	78

LOAD TABLES FOR FLAT DECK MEMBERS

✱NOTE: 1. NORMAL WEIGHT (150 PCF) CONCRETE SLAB AND TOPPING
2. SLABS f_c = 5000 PSI
3. STRAND DESIGNATION CODE
7 8 - S
└ STRAIGHT
└ DIAMETER OF STRANDS IN 16THS
└ NUMBER OF STRANDS

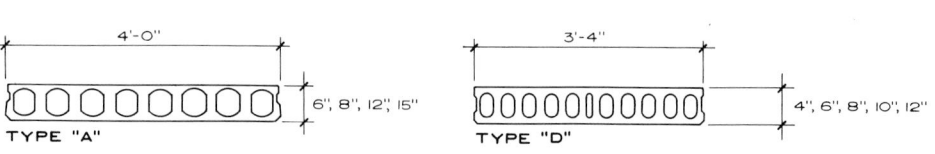

TYPE "A"   4'-0"   6", 8", 12", 15"

TYPE "D"   3'-4"   4", 6", 8", 10", 12"

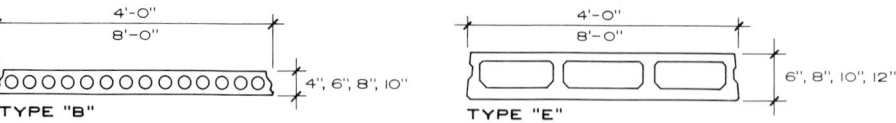

TYPE "B"   4'-0" / 8'-0"   4", 6", 8", 10"

TYPE "E"   4'-0" / 8'-0"   6", 8", 10", 12"

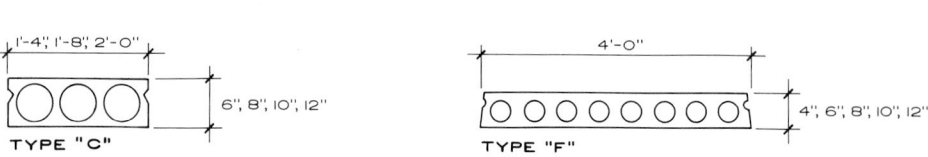

TYPE "C"   1'-4", 1'-8", 2'-0"   6", 8", 10", 12"

TYPE "F"   4'-0"   4", 6", 8", 10", 12"

HOLLOW CORE SLAB TYPES
ALL SECTIONS ARE NOT AVAILABLE FROM ALL PRODUCERS
CHECK AVAILABILITY WITH LOCAL MANUFACTURERS

NOTES

1. Normal weight (150 pcf) or lightweight concrete (115 pcf) is used in standard slab construction. Topping concrete is usually normal weight concrete with a cylinder strength of 3000 psi. All units are prestressed with strand release when concrete strength is 3500 psi.

2. Strands are available in various sizes and strengths according to individual manufacturers. Strand placement may vary, which will change load capacity, camber values, and fire resistance. Contact the local supplier for strand placement and allowable loading.

3. Camber will vary substantially depending on slab design, span, and loading. Nonstructural components attached to members may be affected by camber variations. Calculations of topping quantities should recognize camber variations.

4. Safe superimposed service loads include a dead load of 10 psf for untopped concrete and 15 psf for topped concrete. The remainder is live load.

5. Smooth or textured soffits may be available in some types; check with the supplier.

Bruce Lambert, AIA; Columbia, South Carolina

PRECAST CONCRETE

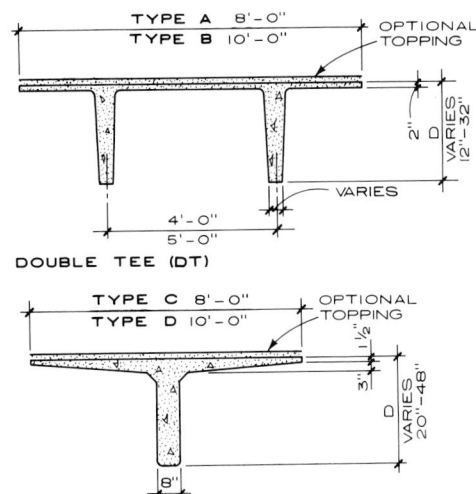

DOUBLE TEE (DT)

SINGLE TEE (ST)

STRAND PATTERN DESIGNATION

208·D1
- NO. OF STRANDS (20)
- S=STRAIGHT D=DEPRESSED
- NO. OF DEPRESSION POINTS
- DIAMETER OF STRAND IN 16THS

TOPPING CONCRETE = 3000 PSI, 150 LB./CU. FT. f'c = 5000 PSI FOR NORMAL OR LIGHTWEIGHT DECK

NOTES

1. Safe loads shown indicate dead load of 10 psf for untopped members and 15 psf for topped members. Remainder is live load.
2. Designers should contact the manufacturers in the geographic area of the proposed structure to determine availability, exact dimensions, and load tables for various sections.
3. Camber should be checked for its effect on nonstructural members (i.e., partitions, folding doors, etc.), which should be placed with adequate allowance for error. Calculations of topping quantities should also recognize camber variations.
4. Normal weight concrete is assumed to be 150 lb/cu ft; lightweight concrete is assumed to be 115 lb/cu ft.

STEMMED DECK MEMBERS
SEE CHART FOR APPROXIMATE MAX. SPANS

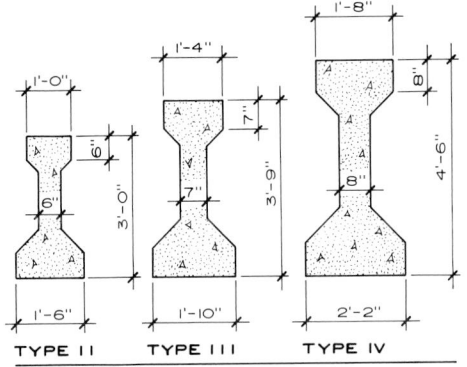

TYPE II   TYPE III   TYPE IV

AASHTO GIRDERS

TABLE OF SAFE SUPERIMPOSED SERVICE LOAD* (PLF) FOR AASHTO GIRDER

DESIG- NATION	NO. OF STRANDS	SPAN (FT)						
		36	40	44	48	52	56	60
Type II	14	3520	2785	2241	1826			
Type III	22	7231	5757	4667	3837	3192	2679	2266
Type IV	32		9848	7996	6588	5492	4622	3920

APPROXIMATE MAXIMUM SPAN FOR STEMMED DECK SECTIONS

DECK TYPE	DEPTH D (IN.)	CONCRETE WEIGHT	DESIGNATION	TOPPING DEPTH (IN.)	STRAND DESIGNATION	MAX. SPAN (FT)	SAFE LOAD (PSF)
A	12	Normal weight	8DT12	0	88·D1	40	40
			8DT12 + 2	2	68·D1	34	39
		Lightweight	8LDT12	0	68·D1	40	35
			8LDT12 + 2	2	68·D1	36	36
A	18	Normal weight	8DT18	0	108·D1	58	34
			8DT18 + 2	2	88·D1	46	48
		Lightweight	8LDT18	0	108·D1	60	37
			8LDT18 + 2	2	88·D1	50	39
A	24	Normal weight	8DT24	0	148·D1	74	38
			8DT24 + 2	2	128·D1	60	56
		Lightweight	8LDT24	0	148·D1	80	35
			8LDT24 + 2	2	108·D1	62	44
A	32	Normal weight	8DT32	0	228·D1	88	56
			8DT32 + 2	2	208·D1	76	76
		Lightweight	8LDT32	0	228·D1	100	41
			8LDT32 + 2	2	208·D1	82	67
B	32	Normal weight	10DT32	0	228·D1	86	49
			10DT32 + 2	2	208·D1	74	62
		Lightweight	10LDT32	0	228·D1	98	35
			10LDT32 + 2	2	208·D1	78	59
C	36	Normal weight	8ST36	0	228·D1	100	44
			8ST36 + 2	2″	188·D1	82	61
		Lightweight	8LST36	0	228·D1	110	38
			8LST36 + 2	2	168·D1	86	50
D	48	Normal weight	10ST48	0	248·D1	112	42
		Lightweight	10LST48	0	248·D1	120	41

TABLE OF SAFE SUPERIMPOSED SERVICE LOAD* (PLF) FOR PRECAST BEAM SECTIONS

TYPE	DESIGNATION	NO. STRAND	H (IN.)	H1/H2 (IN.)	18	22	26	30	34	38	42	46	50
RECTANGULAR BEAM	12RB24	10	24		6726	4413	3083	2248	1684	1288	1000		
	12RB32	13	32			7858	5524	4059	3080	2394	1894	1519	1230
	16RB24	13	24		8847	5803	4052	2954	2220	1705	1330		
	16RB32	18	32			7434	5464	4147	3224	2549	2036	1642	
	16RB40	22	40				8647	6599	5163	4117	3332	2728	
L-SHAPED BEAM	18LB20	9	20	12/8	5068	3303	2288	1650	1218				
	18LB28	12	28	16/12		6578	4600	3360	2531	1949	1524	1200	
	18LB36	16	36	24/12		7903	5807	4405	3422	2706	2168	1755	
	18LB44	19	44	28/16			8729	6666	5219	4166	3370	2752	
	18LB52	23	52	36/16			9538	7486	5992	4871	4007		
	18LB60	27	60	44/16						8116	6630	5481	
INVERTED TEE BEAM	24IT20	9	20	12/8	5376	3494	2412	1726	1266				
	24IT28	13	28	16/12		6951	4848	3529	2648	2030			
	24IT36	16	36	24/12			8337	6127	4644	3598	2836	2265	1825
	24IT44	20	44	28/16				9300	7075	5514	4378	3525	2868
	24IT52	24	52	36/16						7916	6326	5132	4213
	24IT60	28	60	44/16							8616	7025	5800

*Safe loads shown indicate 50% dead load and 50% live load; 800 psi top tension has been allowed, therefore additional top reinforcement is required.

Bruce Lambert, AIA; Columbia, South Carolina

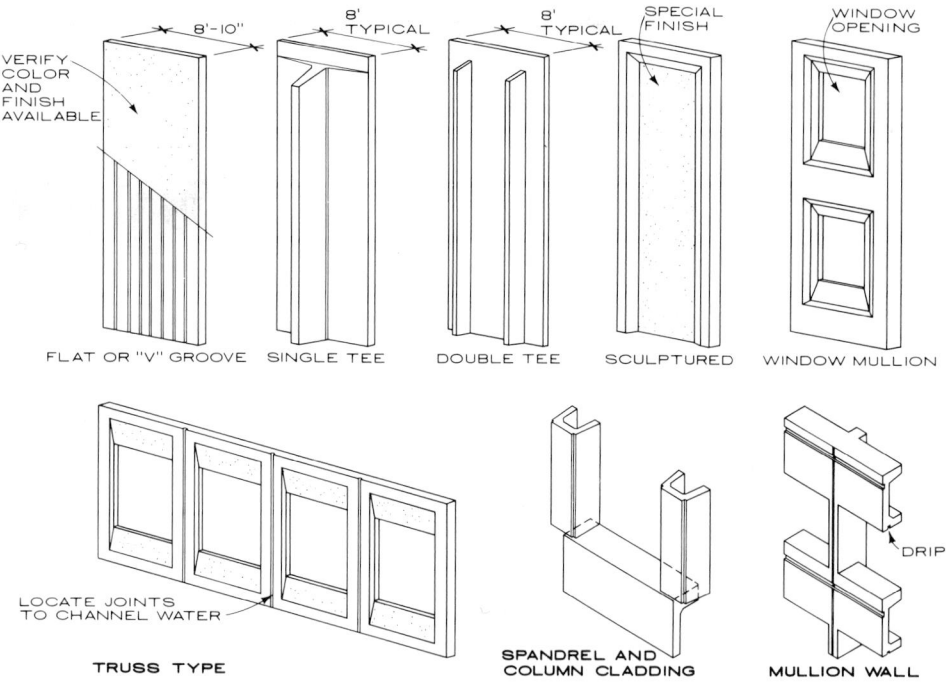

VERIFY COLOR AND FINISH AVAILABLE

8'-10"
8' TYPICAL
8' TYPICAL
SPECIAL FINISH
WINDOW OPENING

FLAT OR "V" GROOVE   SINGLE TEE   DOUBLE TEE   SCULPTURED   WINDOW MULLION

LOCATE JOINTS TO CHANNEL WATER

DRIP

TRUSS TYPE   SPANDREL AND COLUMN CLADDING   MULLION WALL

PANEL VARIATIONS

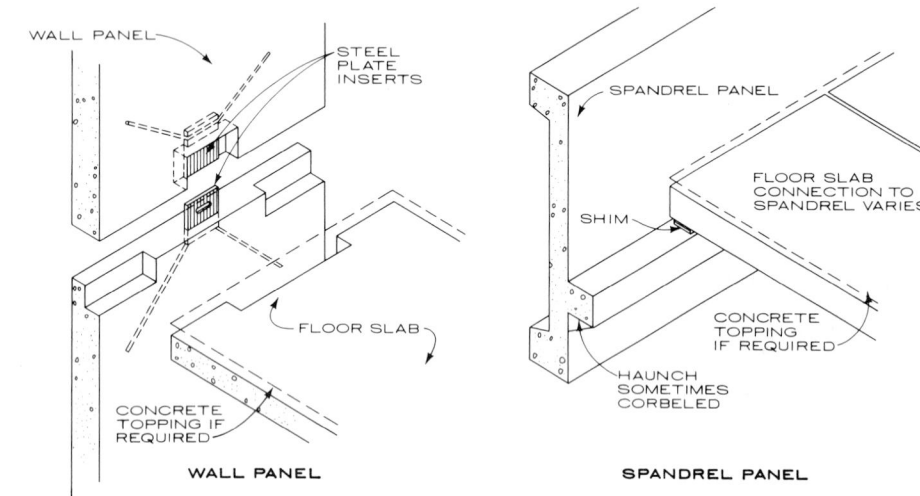

WALL PANEL
STEEL PLATE INSERTS
FLOOR SLAB
CONCRETE TOPPING IF REQUIRED

SPANDREL PANEL
SHIM
FLOOR SLAB CONNECTION TO SPANDREL VARIES
CONCRETE TOPPING IF REQUIRED
HAUNCH SOMETIMES CORBELED

WALL PANEL   SPANDREL PANEL

BEARING PANEL CONDITIONS

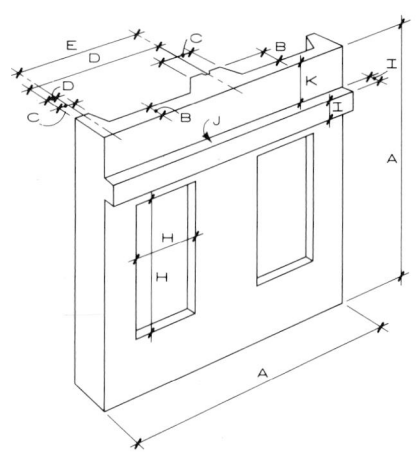

A. Overall height and width measured at face adjacent to mold at time of casting or neutral axis of ribbed member:
   10 ft or under: $\pm \frac{1}{8}$ in.
   10 ft to 20 ft: $\pm \frac{1}{8}$ in. to $\pm \frac{3}{16}$ in.
   20 ft to 30 ft: $\pm \frac{1}{8}$ in. to $\pm \frac{1}{4}$ in.
   Above 30 ft: $\pm \frac{1}{4}$ in.
B. Thickness, total or flange: $\frac{1}{4}$ in. to $\frac{1}{8}$ in.
C. Rib thickness: $\pm \frac{1}{8}$ in.
D. Rib to edge of flange: $\pm \frac{1}{8}$ in.
E. Distance between ribs: $\pm \frac{1}{8}$ in.
F. Angular deviation of plane of side mold: $\frac{1}{32}$ in. per 3 in. of depth or $\frac{1}{16}$ in. total, whichever is greater
G. Deviation from square or designated skew (difference in length of the two diagonal measurements): $\frac{1}{8}$ in. per 6 ft or $\frac{1}{4}$ in. total, whichever is greater
H. Length and width of blockouts and openings with one unit: $\pm \frac{1}{4}$ in.
I. Depth and width of haunches: $\pm \frac{1}{4}$ in.
J. Haunch-bearing surface deviation from specified plane: $\frac{1}{8}$ in.
K. Difference in relative position of adjacent haunch-bearing surfaces from specified relative position: $\frac{1}{4}$ in.

All other tolerances not defined above: $\pm \frac{1}{8}$ in.

DIMENSIONAL TOLERANCES FOR FLAT AND VERTICAL RIBBED WALL PANELS

Bruce Lambert, AIA; Columbia, South Carolina

WALL PANELS

Carefully distinguish between the more specialized architectural wall panel and the structural wall panel which is a derivative of floor systems. Always work with manufacturers early in the design process. Careful attention must be given to manufacturing and joint tolerances during design. Thoroughly examine joint sealants for adhesion and expected joint movement.

FINISHES

Form liner molds provide a wide variety of smooth and textured finishes. Finishes after casting but prior to hardening include exposed aggregate, broom, trowel, screed, float, or stippled. After hardening finishes include acid etching, sandblasting, honed, polished, or hammered rib.

COLORS

Select a color range, as complete uniformity cannot be guaranteed. White cement offers the best color uniformity; gray cement is subject to color variations even when supplied from one source. Pigments require high-quality manufacturing and curing standards. Fine aggregate color requires control of the mixture graduation; coarse aggregate color should be chosen for durability and appearance.

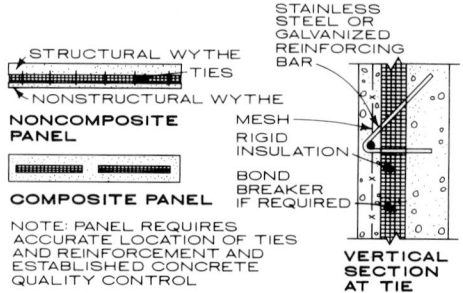

STRUCTURAL WYTHE
TIES
NONSTRUCTURAL WYTHE
NONCOMPOSITE PANEL
COMPOSITE PANEL
STAINLESS STEEL OR GALVANIZED REINFORCING BAR
MESH
RIGID INSULATION
BOND BREAKER IF REQUIRED
VERTICAL SECTION AT TIE

NOTE: PANEL REQUIRES ACCURATE LOCATION OF TIES AND REINFORCEMENT AND ESTABLISHED CONCRETE QUALITY CONTROL

SANDWICH WALL CONSTRUCTION

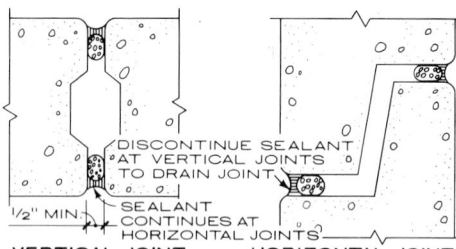

DISCONTINUE SEALANT AT VERTICAL JOINTS TO DRAIN JOINT
SEALANT CONTINUES AT HORIZONTAL JOINTS
$\frac{1}{2}$" MIN.

VERTICAL JOINT   HORIZONTAL JOINT

TWO-STAGE SEALANT JOINTS

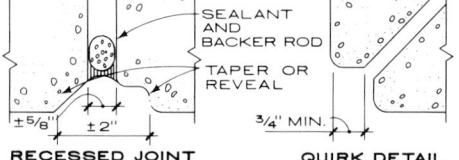

SEALANT AND BACKER ROD
TAPER OR REVEAL
$\pm \frac{5}{8}$" ± 2"
$\frac{3}{4}$" MIN.

RECESSED JOINT   QUIRK DETAIL

JOINT DETAILS

JOINT TAPER: $\frac{1}{40}$ IN. PER FT LENGTH (MAX. LENGTH OF TAPERING IN ONE DIRECTION OF 10 FT)

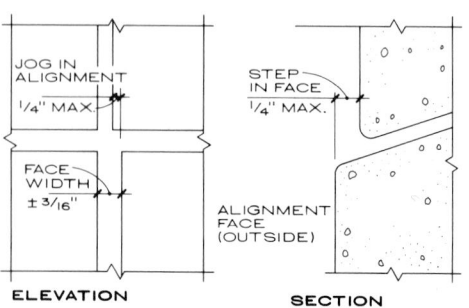

JOG IN ALIGNMENT
$\frac{1}{4}$" MAX.
FACE WIDTH $\pm \frac{3}{16}$"

STEP IN FACE
$\frac{1}{4}$" MAX.
ALIGNMENT FACE (OUTSIDE)

ELEVATION   SECTION THROUGH FACE

JOINT TOLERANCES

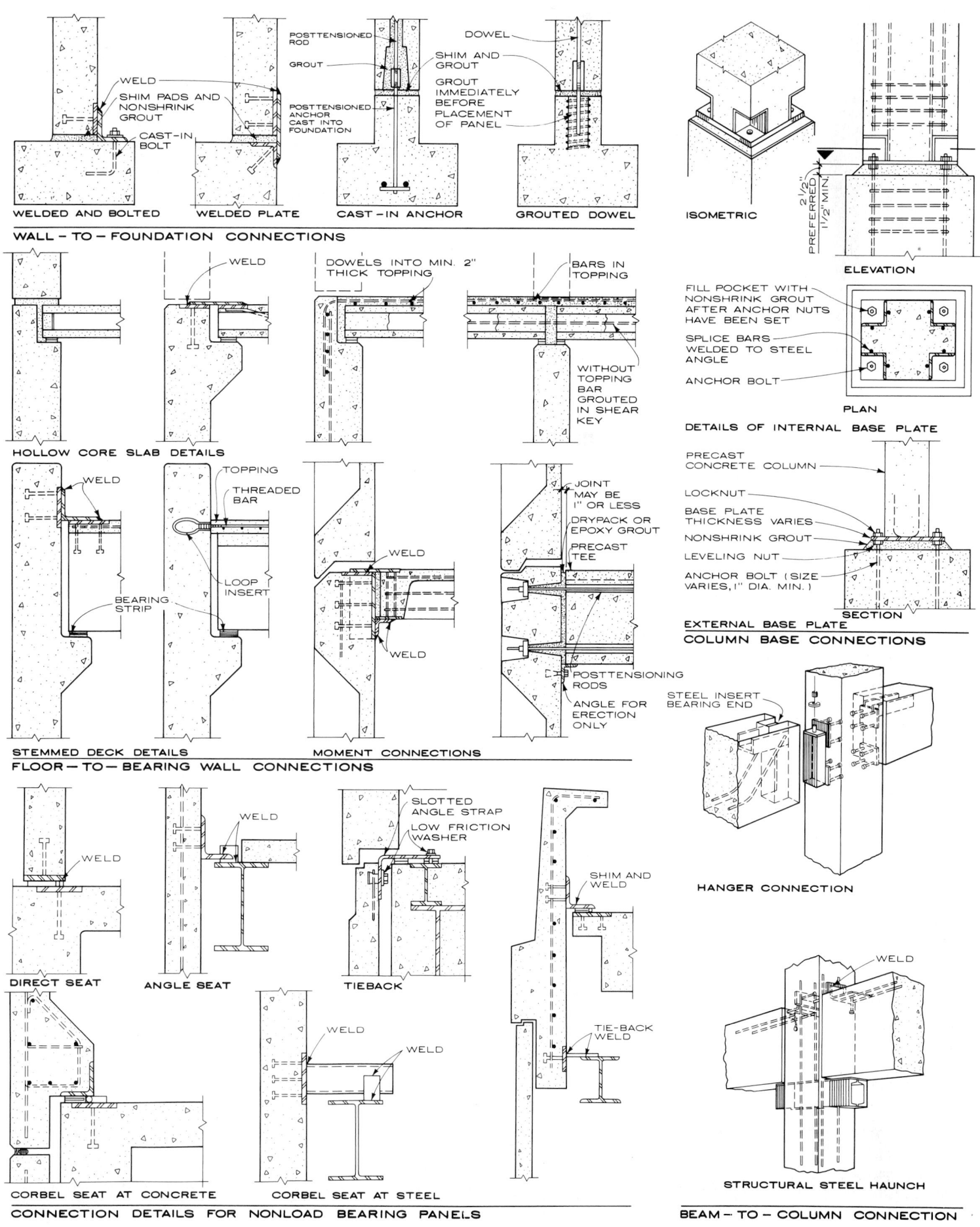

WELD
SHIM PADS AND NONSHRINK GROUT
CAST-IN BOLT

WELDED AND BOLTED

WELDED PLATE

POSTTENSIONED ROD
GROUT
POSTTENSIONED ANCHOR CAST INTO FOUNDATION

CAST-IN ANCHOR

DOWEL
SHIM AND GROUT
GROUT IMMEDIATELY BEFORE PLACEMENT OF PANEL

GROUTED DOWEL

WALL-TO-FOUNDATION CONNECTIONS

WELD

DOWELS INTO MIN. 2" THICK TOPPING

BARS IN TOPPING

WITHOUT TOPPING BAR GROUTED IN SHEAR KEY

HOLLOW CORE SLAB DETAILS

WELD

TOPPING
THREADED BAR
LOOP INSERT
BEARING STRIP

WELD
WELD

JOINT MAY BE 1" OR LESS
DRYPACK OR EPOXY GROUT
PRECAST TEE
POSTTENSIONING RODS
ANGLE FOR ERECTION ONLY

STEMMED DECK DETAILS

MOMENT CONNECTIONS

FLOOR-TO-BEARING WALL CONNECTIONS

WELD

DIRECT SEAT

WELD

ANGLE SEAT

SLOTTED ANGLE STRAP
LOW FRICTION WASHER

TIEBACK

SHIM AND WELD

TIE-BACK WELD

WELD

CORBEL SEAT AT CONCRETE

WELD
WELD

CORBEL SEAT AT STEEL

CONNECTION DETAILS FOR NONLOAD BEARING PANELS

Bruce Lambert, AIA; Columbia, South Carolina

ISOMETRIC

2½" PREFERRED
1½" MIN.

ELEVATION

FILL POCKET WITH NONSHRINK GROUT AFTER ANCHOR NUTS HAVE BEEN SET
SPLICE BARS WELDED TO STEEL ANGLE
ANCHOR BOLT

PLAN

DETAILS OF INTERNAL BASE PLATE

PRECAST CONCRETE COLUMN
LOCKNUT
BASE PLATE THICKNESS VARIES
NONSHRINK GROUT
LEVELING NUT
ANCHOR BOLT (SIZE VARIES, 1" DIA. MIN.)

SECTION

EXTERNAL BASE PLATE

COLUMN BASE CONNECTIONS

STEEL INSERT BEARING END

HANGER CONNECTION

WELD

STRUCTURAL STEEL HAUNCH

BEAM-TO-COLUMN CONNECTION

GENERAL

A glass fiber reinforced concrete (GFRC) panel consists, typically, of 5% by weight (of total mix) of alkali resistant glass fibers that are chopped and sprayed onto a mold with a portland cement/sand slurry. The thin-walled single skin panels have a typical GFRC backing thickness between $1/2$ to $5/8$ in., not including the exposed aggregate face mix or veneer finish, when used. However, design requirements or panel size may call for a thicker panel section or the use of stiffeners. In no case should the minimum thickness of the panel be less than $1/2$ in.

These cladding panels are capable of accepting and transferring wind and self-weight and their own inertial seismic loads to the building's load-resisting system, but are not considered vertical load-bearing components or a part of the lateral load-resisting system. Panels can be designed to provide a 2-hour fire resistance rating.

Panels will generally weigh from 10 to 25 psf depending on surface finish, panel size and shape, and arrangement of support steel framework.

A wide range of surface finishes, similar to precast concrete, may be achieved by using a concrete face mix and exposing the decorative aggregates using integral color, white cement, textured or featured finishes, or by using veneer-facings.

Properly designed panels with appropriate configurations and control (skin) joints have been made up to 30 ft. Shape possibilities are inherent in the manufacturing process. The designer can choose from deep reveals to complex rectilinear and curvilinear shapes, such as short radius curves, wide sweeping arcs, or 90-degree angles.

Unless the panel has a functionally strengthening shape, GFRC properties dictate the use of stiffeners on panels of any appreciable size. Stiffeners commonly used include prefabricated, plant attached, cold formed steel studs (the most economical and preferred method); upstanding, single skin ribs formed on the back of the panel; and integral ribs formed on the back of the panel by spraying over hidden rib formers, such as expanded polystyrene strips. Each of these methods reinforces and stiffens the GFRC skin and provides a means for connecting the panel to the supporting structure. In addition, the steel panel frame provides a support for attaching furring channels for drywall, as well as the window frame, and provides a cavity for installing insulation and electrical, mechanical, and telephone conduits.

For design information, refer to PCI Recommended Practice for Glass Fiber Reinforced Concrete Panels.

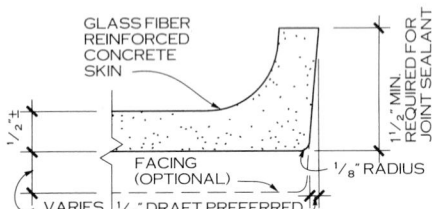

TYPICAL EDGE

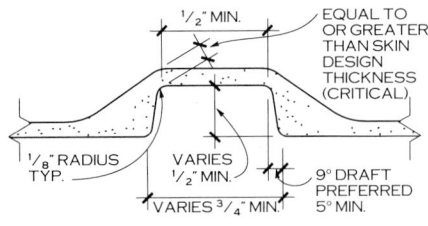

REVEAL OR FALSE JOINT

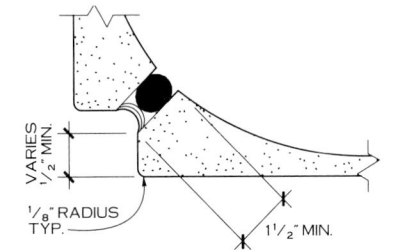

QUIRK MITER

Precast/Prestressed Concrete Institute; Chicago, Illinois

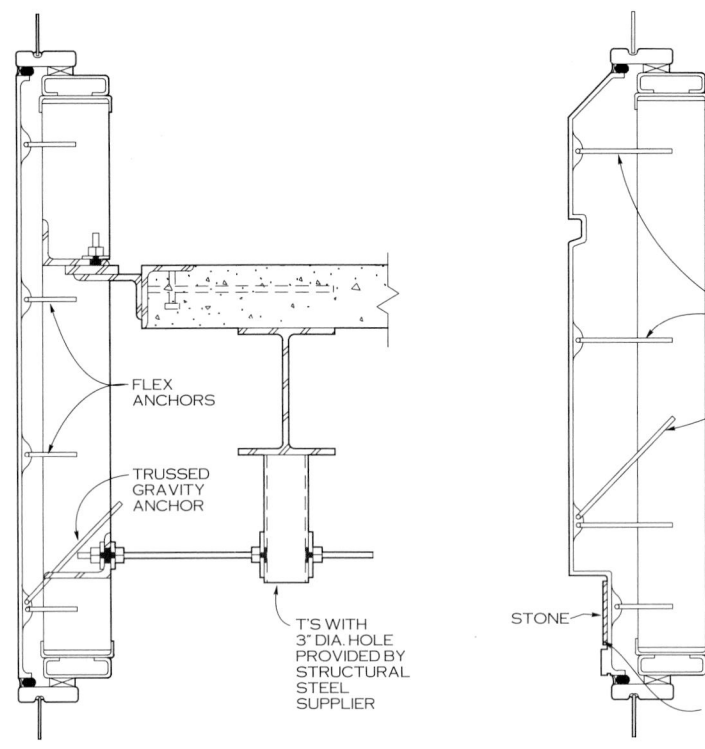

SPANDREL PANEL CONNECTIONS

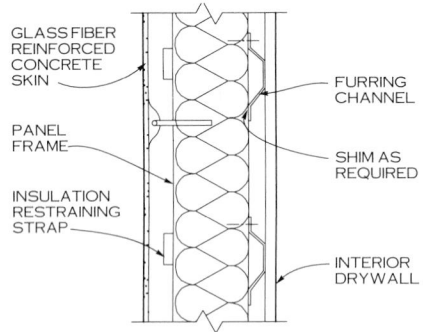

INTERIOR DRYWALL ATTACHMENT

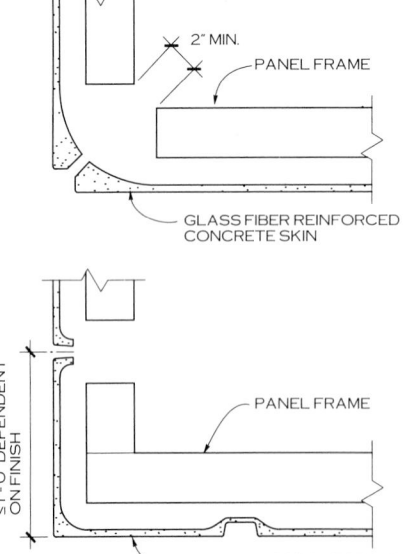

PANEL CORNER DETAILS

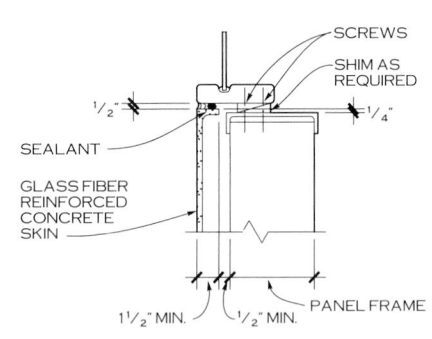

WINDOW FRAME TO STEEL PANEL FRAME ATTACHMENT

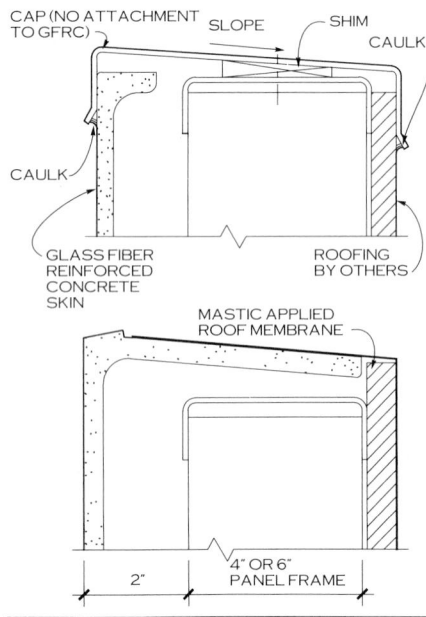

PARAPET DETAILS

GENERAL

Tilt-up concrete construction is a fast and economical method of enclosing a building with durable, load-bearing walls. Tilt-up concrete panels may be site made or factory produced. When cast on site, the building's floor slab may be used as a casting bed. Wood formwork is typically used to define the edges, reveals, details, and openings in the panel. Once the concrete has reached sufficient strength, the panels are lifted, or "tilted up," by crane and placed on isolated footings where they are braced until they are attached to the interior structural framing system.

DESIGN

Panel thickness varies from $5\frac{1}{2}$ to $11\frac{1}{4}$ in. depending on height, loads, span, depth of reveals, surface finish, local codes, and construction practices. Full-height panel widths of 15 ft and weights of 30,000–50,000 lb are typical. Spans of 30 ft are common for spandrel panels, as are cantilevers of 10–15 ft. Panels are designed structurally to resist lifting stresses, which frequently exceed in-place loads. Floor slab design must accommodate panel and crane loads.

FINISH

Most of the finishes used for factory precast concrete are possible in tilt-up construction. Panels can be cast either facedown or faceup, depending on desired finish and formwork methods. The facedown method, however, is usually easier to erect. Casting method, finish desired, and available aggregates will affect concrete mix design. Control of the concrete mix design and placement of the concrete in the forms are more difficult than with factory cast units. Discoloration occurs if cracks and joints in the casting are not sealed. Commonly used finishes are as follows:

Sandblast (light, medium, or heavy exposure)
Fractured (similar to bushhammered)
Form liner (metal deck, plastic, fiberglass, EPS)
Paint (usually textured)
Brick or tile veneer
Aggregate (cast facedown in sand bed)

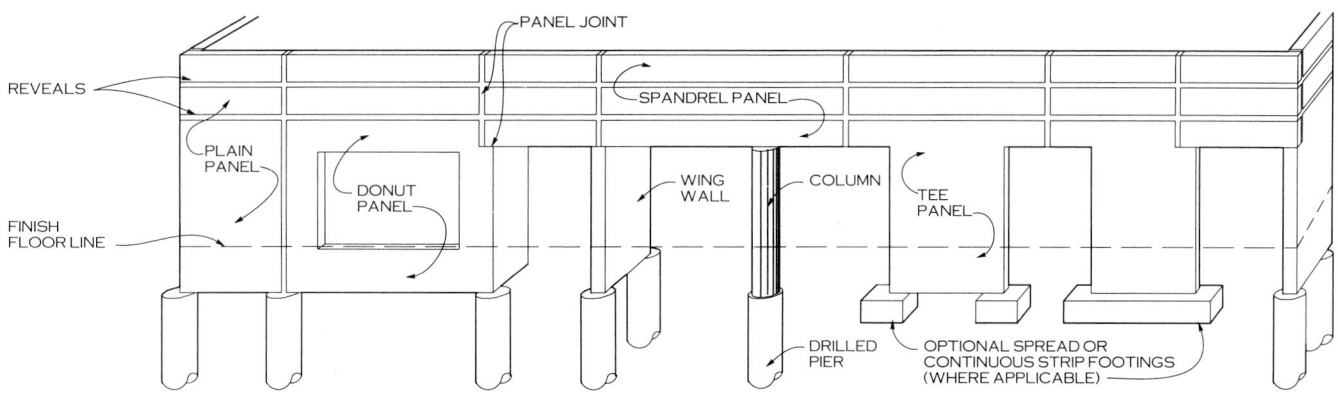

PANEL TYPES

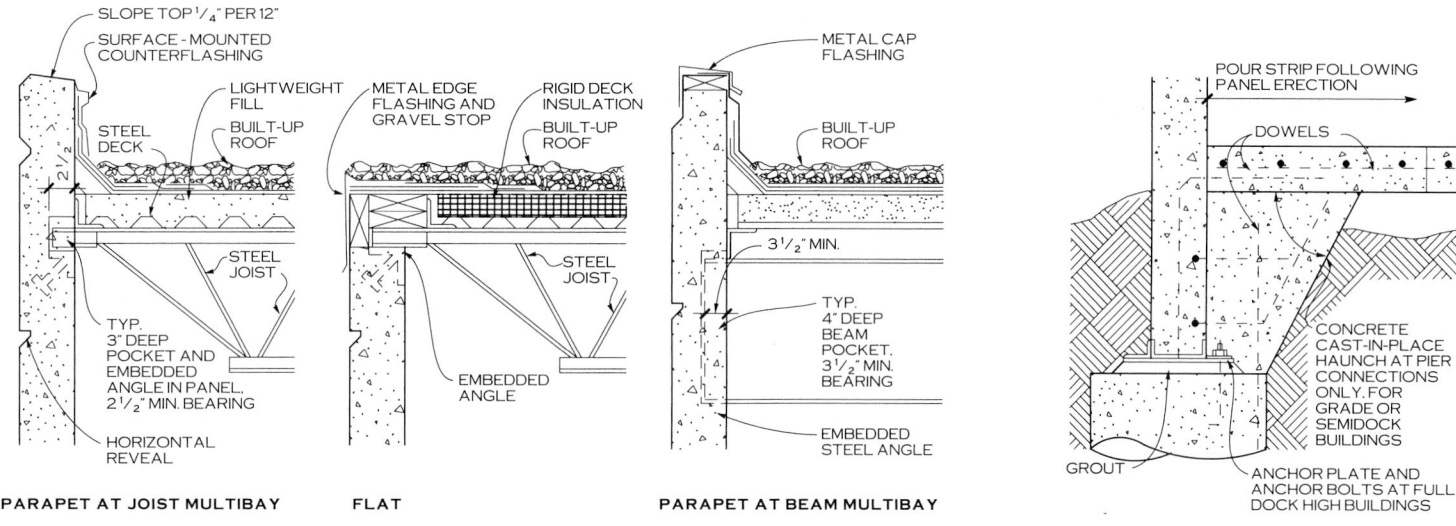

PARAPET AT JOIST MULTIBAY   FLAT   PARAPET AT BEAM MULTIBAY

LOAD-BEARING PANEL CONNECTIONS AT ROOF

PIER CONNECTION

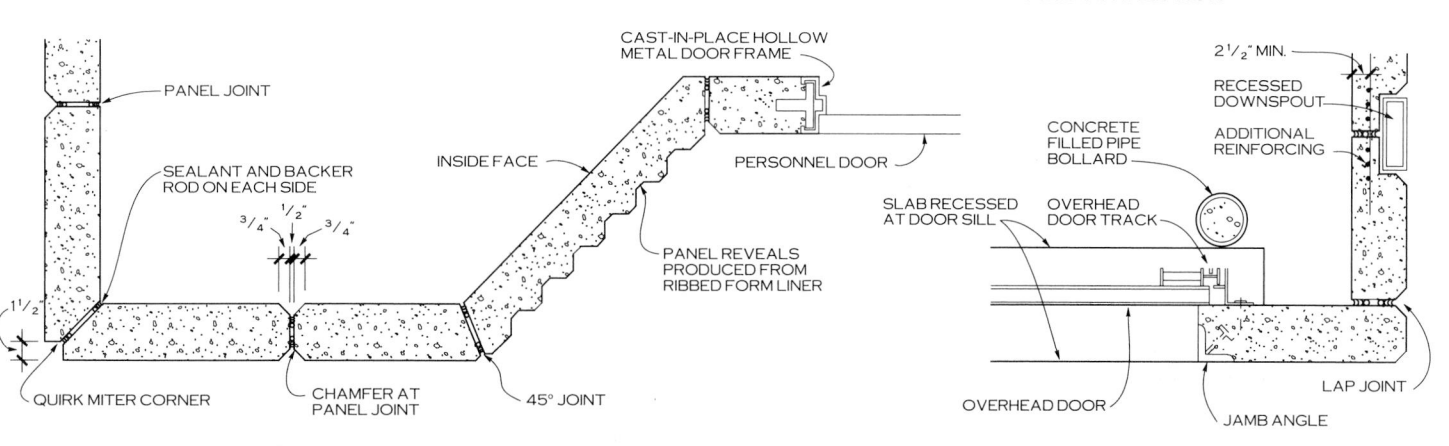

PANEL DETAILS

Harry Gendel Architects; Houston, Texas
Haynes Whaley Associates, Structural Engineers; Houston, Texas and Reston, Virginia

GENERAL

American Cement Alliance (ACA)
1212 New York Avenue, N.W., Suite 500
Washington, DC 20005-3987
Tel: (202) 408-9494
Fax:(202) 408-9392

American Concrete Institute (ACI)
22400 W. Seven Mile Road
P.O. Box 19150
Detroit, MI 48219-1849
Tel: (313) 532-2600
Fax:(313) 538-0655

American Society for Concrete Construction (ASCC)
P.O. Box 19307
Detroit, MI 48219
Tel: (313) 532-2753

Concrete Sawing and Drilling Association (CSDA)
4900 Blazer Parkway
Dublin, OH 43017
Tel: (614) 766-3656
Fax:(614) 766-3605

Flexicore Manufacturers Association (FMA)
P.O. Box 24409
Huber Heights, OH 45424
Tel: (513) 879-5775

International Association of Concrete Repair Specialists
P.O. Box 17402, Dulles International Airport
Washington, DC 20011
Tel: (703) 260-0009
Fax:(703) 661-8013

National Stone Association (NSA)
1415 Elliot Place, N.W.
Washington, D.C. 20007
Tel: (202) 342-1100
Fax:(202) 342-0702

Portland Cement Association (PCA)
5420 Old Orchard Road
Skokie, IL 60077-1083
Tel: (708) 966-6200
Fax:(708) 966-9781

REFERENCES

Annual Book of ASTM Standards. Philadelphia: American Society for Testing and Materials.

Architectural Concrete-Design and Construction Practices. Aberdeen Group, 1982.

Basic Building Code. Country Club Hills, Ill.: Building Officials and Code Administrators International (BOCA).

Bazant, Z. P., and F. H. Wittmann. *Creep and Shrinkage in Concrete Structures*. New York: J. Wiley & Sons, 1982.

Concrete Construction Magazine. [monthly since 1956]

Concrete Energy Conservation Guidelines. Skokie, Ill.: Portland Cement Association, 1980.

Concrete International: Design & Construction. Detroit: American Concrete Institute. [monthly since 1979]

The Construction Specifier. [monthly publication of the Contruction Specifications Institute, Alexandria, Va.]

Design and Control of Concrete Mixtures. 12th ed. Skokie, Ill.: Portland Cement Association, 1979.

FIP Manual of Lightweight Aggregate Concrete. New York: Halstead Press Division, J. Wiley & Sons, 1983.

Guide for Concrete Floor and Slab Construction, 302.1R, Detroit: American Concrete Institute, 1989.

"Guide for Structural Lightweight Aggregate Concrete," Report 213. American Concrete Institute, 1987.

Journal of the American Concrete Institute. [monthly]

Komendant, A. E. *Practical Structural Analysis for Architectural Engineering*. Englewood Cliffs, N.J.: Prentice-Hall, 1987.

Libby, J. R. *Modern Pressed Concrete: Design Principles and Construction Methods*, 3rd ed. New York: Van Nostrand Reinhold, 1984.

Lightweight Concrete Information Sheets. Rockville, Md.: Expanded Shale Clay and Slate Institute, Jan. 1986-Mar. 1987.

Neville, A. M., and M. Chatterton. *New Concrete Technologies and Building Design*. New York: J. Wiley, 1980.

Principles of Quality Concrete, Skokie, Ill.: Portland Cement Association, 1975.

Ropke, J. C. *Concrete Problems: Causes and Cures*. New York: McGraw-Hill, 1982.

CONCRETE FORMWORK

REFERENCES

Concrete Forming, V345Q. American Plywood Association, 1990.

Concrete Formwork, SpecGuide G03100. Construction Specifications Institute, 1986.

Formwork for Concrete, SP-4. Detroit: American Concrete Institute, 1989.

Hurd, M. K. *Formwork for Concrete*, 4th ed. American Concrete Institute, 1985.

CONCRETE REINFORCEMENT

American Welding Society, Inc. (AWS)
550 LeJeune Road, P.O. Box 351040
Miami, FL 33135
Tel: (305) 443-9353

Concrete Reinforcing Steel Institute (CRSI)
933 N. Plum Grove Road
Schaumburg, IL 60173-4758
Tel: (708) 517-1200
Fax:(708) 517-1206

Reinforced Concrete Research Council
University of Illinois at Urbana-Champaign
Newmark Civil Engineering Lab
205 North Mathews
Urbana, IL 61801
Tel: (217) 333-7384

Wire Reinforcement Institute (WRI)
1101 Connecticut Ave., N.W., Suite 700
Washington, DC 20036-4303
Tel: (202) 429-5125
Fax:(202) 223-4579

REFERENCES

ACI Committee 318. *Building Code Requirements for Reinforced Concrete*. Detroit: American Concrete Institute.

Anchorage to Concrete, SP-1 03. American Concrete Institute, 1987.

Anchors in Concrete—Design and Behavior, SP-130. American Concrete Institute, 1992.

Concrete Reinforcement, SpecGUIDE G03200, Construction Specifications Institute, 1989.

Concrete Reinforcement. Wire Reinforcement Institute, 1983.

Fiber Reinforced Concrete, SP039. Portland Cement Association, 1991.

Guide to Design of Anchor Bolts and Other Steel Embedments, AB-8 1. American Concrete Institute, 1981.

Manual of Standard Practice. Concrete Reinforcing Steel Institute, 1990.

Nawy, Edward. *Simplified Reinforced Concrete*. Englewood Cliffs, N.J.: Prentice-Hall, 1986.

Recommended Practice for Glass Fiber Reinforced Concrete Panels. Chicago: Prestressed Concrete Institute.

State-of-the-Art Report on Anchorage to Concrete, 355.1R. American Concrete Institute, 1991.

CAST-IN-PLACE CONCRETE

National Ready-Mixed Concrete Association (NRMCA)
900 Spring Street
Silver Spring, MD 20910
Tel: (301) 587-1400
Fax:(301) 585-4219

REFERENCES

Architectural Concrete–Design and Construction Practices. Aberdeen Group, 1982.

Cast-in-Place Concrete, SpecGUIDE G03300. Construction Specifications Institute, 1989.

Cold Weather Concreting, 306R. American Concrete Institute, 1988.

Color and Texture in Architectural Concrete, SP021. Portland Cement Association, 1980.

Concrete Floor System: Guide to Estimating and Economizing, SP041. Portland Cement Association, 1991.

Bushhammering of Concrete Structures, ISO51. Portland Cement Association, 1987.

Guide to Cast-in-Place Architectural Concrete Practice, 303R, American Concrete Institute, 1982, 30 pp.

Guide for Cast-in-Place Low-Density Concrete, 523.1R. American Concrete Institute, 1986.

Guide for Concrete Floor and Slab Construction, 302.1R. American Concrete Institute, 1989.

Guide to Residential Cast-in-Place Concrete Construction, 332R. American Concrete Institute, 1984.

Hot Weather Concreting, 305R-9 1. American Concrete Institute, 199 1.

Residential Concrete. National Association of Home Builders Bookstore, 1983.

Shilstone, J. "Architectural Concrete Contract Documents." *Concrete International* (ACI), Nov 1985.

Shilstone, J. M. "Cast-in-Place Architectural Concrete," Monograph 03M350. Construct. Specif. Inst., 1974.

Shotcrete, Compilation 18. Amer. Concrete Inst., 1992.

Special Concrete Finishes, SpecGUIDE G3350. Construction Specifications Institute, 1988.

Standard Practice for Curing Concrete, 308. American Concrete Institute, 1992.

Troubleshooting Site-Cast Architectural Concrete Problems. Aberdeen Group.

PRECAST CONCRETE

Architectural Precast Association (APA)
1850 Lee Road, Suite 230
Winter Park, FL 32789
Tel: (407) 740-7201

National Precast Concrete Association (NPCA)
10333 N. Meridian Street, Suite 272
Indianapolis, IN 46290
Tel: (317) 571-9500
Fax:(317) 571-0041

Post-Tensioning Institute (PTI)
1717 West Nothern Avenue, Suite 114
Phoenix, AZ 85021
Tel: (602) 870-7540
Fax:(602) 870-7541

Precast/Prestressed Concrete Institute (PCI)
175 West Jackson Blvd.
Chicago, IL 60604
Tel: (312) 786-0300
Fax:(312) 786-0353

Tilt-Up Concrete Association (TCA)
121$^1/_2$ First Street West
Mount Vernon, IA 52314
Tel: (319) 895-6911

REFERENCES

Architectural Precast Concrete. Chicago: Prestressed Concrete Institute.

Architectural Precast Concrete. PCI, 1989.

Architectural Precast Concrete—Plant Cast, SpecGUIDE G03450. Construction Specifications Institute, 1992.

Architectural Precast Joint Details. Prestr. Concrete Inst.

Connections for Tilt-Up Wall Construction, EB110. Portland Cement Association, 1987.

Design Handbook for Precast and Prestressed Concrete, 3rd ed. Prestressed Concrete Institute, 1985.

Guide for Low Density Precast Concrete Floor, Roof and Wall Units, 523.2R. Amer. Concrete Inst., 1982.

Guide Specifications for Architectural Precast Concrete. Prestressed Concrete Institute.

Guide Specifications for Precast, Prestressed Concrete Construction for Buildings. Prestressed Concrete Inst.

Journal of the Precast/Prestressed Concrete Institute. [bimonthly]

Lin, T. Y., and N. H. Burns. *Design of Prestressed Concrete Structures*. New York: J. Wiley & Sons.

Load-Bearing Architectural Wall Panels. Prestressed Concrete Institute.

Manual for Quality Control for Plants and Production of Architectural Precast Concrete Products. Prestressed Concrete Institute.

Manual for Structural Design of Architectural Precast Concrete. Prestressed Concrete Institute.

Nelson, Arthur. *Design of Prestressed Concrete*. New York: J. Wiley & Sons, 1978.

Post-Tensioning Manual. Phoenix: Post-Tensioning Inst.

Sheppard, D. A. and W. R. Phillips. Plant-Cast Precast and Prestressed Concrete: A Design Guide. New York: McGraw-Hill, 1989.

Tilt-Up Concrete Buildings, PA079, Portland Cement Association, 1989, 16 pp.

Tilt-Up Load Bearing Walls, EB074, PCA, 1979, 28 pp.

CHAPTER

MASONRY

INTRODUCTION

Masonry systems considered in Division 4, Masonry, consist of clay masonry, both brick and clay tile; concrete masonry, both brick and concrete masonry units; glass block; terra-cotta; adobe; and stonework. Masonry construction dates from prehistoric times but has been continually improved, engineered, and enhanced to meet design requirements yet be more economical. Most masonry systems are made up of relatively small building units, maximizing design versatility and providing opportunities to achieve an appropriate scale. Systems are usually erected on site, but they may be prefabricated. The colors and architectural finishes available in masonry construction are almost limitless.

Masonry systems are durable, weather resistant construction systems that may be structural, provide fire protection and thermal comfort, resist sound penetration, and reduce noise levels. Systems may be designed as load bearing elements, such as walls, piers, columns, and pilasters, as well as beams, lintels, or arches. Typically erected at a rate of about one floor per week, such load bearing construction systems are extremely economical. Masonry can be used for virtually all residential, commercial, industrial, institutional, and other building applications.

Masonry construction usually comprises relatively small building units, maximizing design versatility. Stone masonry units may be natural, cut, or polished. Manufactured masonry units are made of clay, shale, concrete, or glass and may be solid or hollow. Solid masonry units have void areas of less than 25% in every plane parallel to the bedding surface. Thus solid masonry units typically are cored or contain cells or cavities. Solid units can also contain frogs, i.e., indented panels in the bedding surface. Cores and frogs reduce weight, provide a mechanical bond for mortar, and aid in the manufacturing and shipping processes. If 100% solid units are required, they must be specified as 100% solid. Hollow masonry units have void areas in excess of 25% in every plane parallel to the bedding surface. The voids, typically called cells, are large enough to be filled with grout and reinforcing bars.

Masonry construction is typically in the form of single wythe or multi-wythe cavity wall construction or masonry veneer over a structural backup. The walls are typically categorized as either barrier type or drainage type. Barrier walls depend on a water-resistant, continuous layer within the wall system to resist water penetration. The barrier may be a continuous grout space, fully grouted hollow units, or an exterior coating. Single wythe and multi-wythe walls are typically designed, detailed, and constructed as barrier-type walls. Veneers and cavity walls are drainage-type walls. A single wythe wall may also perform as a drainage-type wall. In drainage-type walls, water that might penetrate the exterior wythe or face shell of the masonry system drains down the back side of the exterior wythe, where it is collected on flashing and channeled to the exterior through weep holes.

Manufactured clay masonry units are typically formed in rectangular prisms by a molding or extrusion process and hardened by heating, usually in excess of 1600° F. Adobe units, however, are fired or cured at very low temperatures and are often air or sun dried. Adobe units tend to gain strength from emulsifiers or other binders. Concrete masonry units are molded using zero-slump concrete and cured with hot water ranging from 100° F hot-water mist to pressurized steam hotter than 350° F. The temperatures and pressures for curing vary with the manufacturing processes and materials.

PROPERTIES OF MASONRY WALLS

WALL TYPE #1
6-in. hollow clay masonry ($5^5/_8$ in.), 67% solid, 130 pcf density

WALL TYPE #2
8-in. hollow concrete masonry ($7^5/_8$ in.), 53% solid, 135 pcf density

WALL TYPE #3
8-in. fully grouted concrete masonry ($7^5/_8$ in.), 53% solid, 135 pcf density for concrete and grout

WALL TYPE #4
4-in. solid clay masonry and 4-in. hollow concrete masonry with full collar joint ($3^5/_8 - ^3/_4 - 3^5/_8$); concrete masonry is 64% solid; 135 pcf density for clay masonry, collar joint grout, and concrete masonry

WALL TYPE #5
4-in. solid clay masonry and 4-in. solid concrete masonry with nominal 2-in. grout space ($3^5/_8 - 2^3/_4 - 3^5/_8$); concrete masonry is 64% solid; 135 pcf density for collar joint grout and concrete masonry; 130 pcf density for clay masonry

WALL TYPE #6
4-in. solid clay masonry and 6-in. hollow concrete masonry with nominal 2-in. cavity ($3^5/_8 - 2^3/_4 - 5^5/_8$); concrete masonry is 64% solid; 135 pcf density for clay masonry, collar joint grout, and concrete masonry

WALL TYPE #7
4-in. solid clay masonry ($3^5/_8$ in.), 135 pcf density with lightweight framing. Wood framing system consists of 2 x 4 studs at 16 in. o.c. with R-13 batt insulation between the studs, $^1/_2$ in. interior gypsum wallboard, and $^1/_2$ in. exterior fiberboard sheathing. There is a nominal 1-in. air space between the masonry and the exterior fiberboard. Steel framing system consists of 6-in. 18-gauge steel studs at 24 in. o.c. with R-19 batt insulation between the studs and $^1/_2$ in. interior and exterior grade gypsum wallboard. The air space between the masonry and the backup is 2 in.

FIRE RESISTANCE

Fire-safe building design is a balanced approach that includes compartmentation (fire containment), automatic detection, and automatic suppression. These are the three essential components of what is called synergistic design, in which each component works in combination to mitigate fire losses. Noncombustible masonry walls do not contribute to the fuel load, nor are they consumed by fire. They remain intact to provide continued protection throughout the duration of a fire. Masonry may be used to provide fire protection for structural steel elements. The use of noncombustible masonry for fire containment and protective cover can reduce fire insurance premiums.

THERMAL PERFORMANCE

Energy efficiency can be easily achieved with masonry construction. Masonry wall systems accommodate interior insulation, integral insulation, or exterior insulation for maximum design flexibility. Interior insulation is typically fibrous batt or rigid board insulation placed between light framing (studs and furring). Integral insulation can be granular or foamed-in-place insulation or rigid polystyrene inserts. Exterior insulation is typically rigid board fastened to the masonry and covered with a weather resistant coating.

Thermal mass is an additional benefit that contributes to the thermal performance of the masonry wall system. Thermal mass is effectively used to shift peak energy loads to off-peak hours. The benefits of thermal mass are primarily a function of climate, insulation position, and heat capacity of the wall. Because thermal mass improves building energy efficiency, masonry walls usually require less insulation than lighter frame walls. The thermal mass benefits of masonry are recognized in the design standards of the American Society of Heating, Refrigerating, and Air-Conditioning Engineers and the Council of American Building Official's model energy codes.

In passive solar buildings, masonry is an ideal storage medium for solar heat collected through the windows.

ACOUSTIC PERFORMANCE

Masonry is one of the most effective materials for controlling sound. The excellent sound insulation offered by the mass of masonry is expressed in terms of sound transmission class (STC) ratings. The discontinuity of cavity walls further increases the STC rating. Rough textured units disperse sound waves, increasing the noise reduction coefficient of the wall. Special sound-absorbing units containing metal baffles or fibrous inserts are also used.

STRUCTURAL PERFORMANCE

Masonry provides excellent structural performance in resisting both vertical and lateral loads. The inherent strength and stiffness of the load bearing masonry system limits both structural and nonstructural damage even under extreme loading events. Structural design of masonry is based on the ACI 530/ASCE 5/TMS 402 code or the provisions of building codes.

There are three basic structural design methods in masonry construction: empirical design, unreinforced allowable stress design, and reinforced allowable stress design. In addition, limit states design (strength design) is recognized and under development.

Empirical design—Empirical design is based on traditional design procedures, using prescriptive criteria. This method of design is permitted in areas with moderate to low wind and seismic risk. Preliminary wall thicknesses are typically based on lateral support requirements. Compliance with additional empirical criteria is also required.

Unreinforced allowable stress design—Unreinforced allowable stress design is a rational method of design based on the compressive and flexural strength of the masonry.

Reinforced allowable stress design—Reinforced allowable stress design is a rational design method based on the compressive strength of the masonry and the tensile strength of the reinforcement; it ignores the flexural strength of masonry.

ECONOMY

Masonry construction can be inexpensive. Its life-cycle cost is very good based on its relatively long life and low maintenance and energy costs. The variety of units, colors, sizes, textures, finishes, and shapes available with masonry construction also make it economical.

WALL WEIGHT (LB/SQ FT)

WALL TYPE	TYPE 1	TYPE 2	TYPE 3	TYPE 4	TYPE 5	TYPE 6	TYPE 7
130 pcf clay masonry	41	—	—	—	—	—	47
105 pcf concrete	—	35	76	92	68	—	—
125 pcf concrete	—	42	82	96	73	—	—
135 pcf concrete	—	45	85	98	76	—	—

*Grout is assumed to weigh 135 pcf.

CALCULATED FIRE RESISTANCE (HOURS)

WALL TYPE	TYPE 1	TYPE 2	TYPE 3	TYPE 4	TYPE 5	TYPE 6	TYPE 7
Clay masonry	1.25	—	—	—	—	—	2.00
Concrete masonry aggregates							
Calcareous or siliceous gravel	—	1.86	4.0*	4.0*	4.0*	4.0*	—
Limestone cinders or slag	—	2.04	4.0*	4.0*	4.0*	4.0*	—
Expanded clay, shale, or slate	—	2.55	4.0*	4.0*	4.0*	4.0*	—
Expanded slag or pumice	—	3.04	4.0*	4.0*	4.0*	4.0*	—

*Calculated fire resistance ratings exceed 4.0 hours, but 4.0 hours is the maximum rating.

Brian E. Trimble; Brick Institute of America; Reston, Virginia

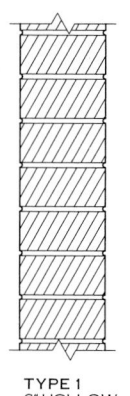
TYPE 1
6" HOLLOW
BRICK

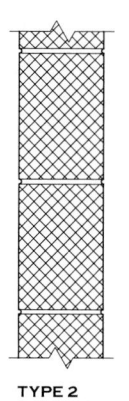
TYPE 2
8" HOLLOW CONCRETE
MASONRY

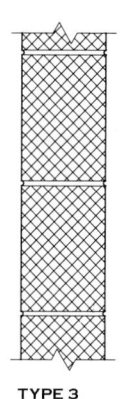
TYPE 3
8" FULLY GROUTED
CONCRETE MASONRY

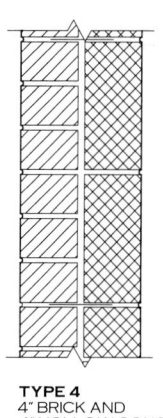
TYPE 4
4" BRICK AND
4" HOLLOW CONCRETE
MASONRY

MASONRY WALL SECTIONS

CALCULATED MAXIMUM VERTICAL SPAN

WIND OR SEISMIC LATERAL LOAD (PSF)	WALL WIDTH (IN.)				
	4	6	8	10	12
UNREINFORCED CONCRETE MASONRY[1]					
10	—	—	13'	16'	18'
15	—	—	10'	12'	15'
20	—	—	9'	11'	12'
25	—	—	8'	10'	11'
CLAY UNIT MASONRY[2]					
10	8'	7'	11'	—	—
15	6'	7'	9'	—	—
20.	6'	6'	8'	—	—
25	5'	5'	7'	—	—

NOTES

1. Based on Type S mortar and hollow concrete masonry units.
2. Based on Type S mortar and solid 4 in. and hollow 6 in. and 8 in. clay units.

THERMAL RESISTANCE [(HR·°F· SQ FT)/BTU]

WALL TYPE	TYPE 1	TYPE 2	TYPE 3	TYPE 4	TYPE 5	TYPE 6	TYPE 7
Empty	1.78	2.08	1.87	3.15	3.55	4.17	—
Filled with perlite	—	3.88	—	—	—	11.81	—
Filled with vermiculite	2.37	3.98	—	—	—	9.44	—
2 in. extruded polystyrene	—	—	—	—	—	14.17	—
2 in. polyisocyanurate	—	—	—	—	—	18.57	—
Wood studs with R-13 batt	—	—	—	—	—	15.00	—
Steel studs with R-19 batt	—	—	—	—	—	11.76	—

NOTE

Thermal resistance and conductance include air films. The interior air film is taken to have a thermal resistance of 0.68, and the exterior air film is taken to have a thermal resistance of 0.17. Concrete is taken as 135 pcf concrete. Lighter concrete provides significantly higher R-values.

HEAT CAPACITY [BTU/(SQ FT ·°F)]

WALL TYPE	TYPE 1	TYPE 2	TYPE 3	TYPE 4	TYPE 5	TYPE 6	TYPE 7
Entire wall system	8.97	9.32	9.52	18.01	14.46	14.49	16.54
Interior wythe only	—	—	—	—	—	—	7.57

THERMAL CONDUCTANCE [BTU/(HR·°F· SQ FT)]

WALL TYPE	TYPE 1	TYPE 2	TYPE 3	TYPE 4	TYPE 5	TYPE 6	TYPE 7
Empty	0.562	0.481	0.535	0.317	0.282	0.240	—
Filled with perlite	—	0.258	—	—	—	0.085	—
Filled with vermiculite	0.422	0.251	—	—	—	0.106	—
2 in. extruded polystyrene	—	—	—	—	—	0.071	—
2 in. polyisocyanurate	—	—	—	—	—	0.054	—
Wood studs with R-13 batt	—	—	—	—	—	—	0.067
Steel studs with R-19 batt	—	—	—	—	—	—	0.085

NOTE

Thermal resistance and conductance include air films. The interior air film is taken to have a thermal resistance of 0.68, and the exterior air film is taken to have a thermal resistance of 0.17. Concrete is taken as 135 pcf concrete. Lighter concrete provides significantly higher R-values.

SOUND TRANSMISSION CLASS RATING

WALL TYPE	TYPE 1	TYPE 2	TYPE 3	TYPE 4	TYPE 5	TYPE 6	TYPE 7
130 pcf clay masonry	49	45	—	—	—	—	56
105 pcf concrete	—	47	55	54	57	55	—
125 pcf concrete	—	49	56	54	57	56	—
135 pcf concrete	—	50	56	55	58	57	—

MAXIMUM DISTANCE TO LATERAL SUPPORTS (FT)

WALL TYPE	TYPE 1	TYPE 2	TYPE 3	TYPE 4	TYPE 5	TYPE 6	TYPE 7
Bearing Walls	6.0	8.4	11.4	12.7	12.0	16.7	10.9
Non-bearing walls							
Exterior	5.4	8.4	11.4	11.4	12.0	15.0	10.9
Interior	10.8	16.8	22.8	22.8	24.0	30.0	21.8

Brian E. Trimble; Brick Institute of America; Reston, Virginia

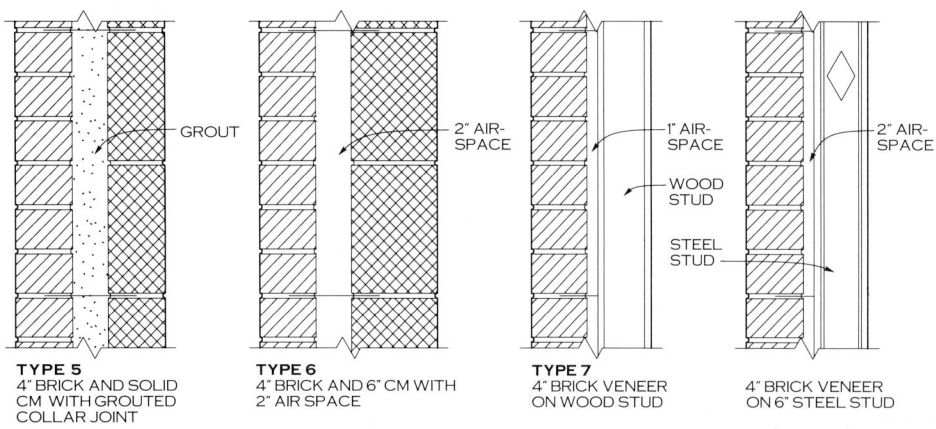

TYPE 5
4" BRICK AND SOLID
CM WITH GROUTED
COLLAR JOINT

TYPE 6
4" BRICK AND 6" CM WITH
2" AIR SPACE

TYPE 7
4" BRICK VENEER
ON WOOD STUD

4" BRICK VENEER
ON 6" STEEL STUD

MASONRY WALL SECTIONS

QUANTITIES PER 100 SQ FT OF WALL SURFACE AREA

MASONRY TYPE	SIZE OF UNIT (IN.)	QTY.
Standard brick	$3^5/_8 \times 2^1/_4 \times 8$	644
Modular brick	$3^5/_8 \times 2^1/_4 \times 7^5/_8$	675
Closure brick	$3^5/_8 \times 3^5/_8 \times 7^5/_8$	450
Utility brick	$3^5/_8 \times 3^5/_8 \times 11^5/_8$	300
CMU	any* $\times 7^5/_8 \times 15^5/_8$	113
CMU	any* $\times 4^5/_8 \times 15^5/_8$	225

*Typical thicknesses of units are $3^5/_8$, $5^5/_8$, $7^5/_8$, $9^5/_8$, and $11^5/_8$ in.

ALLOWABLE COMPRESSION OF WALL LENGTH (LB/IN)

WALL TYPE	TYPE 1	TYPE 2	TYPE 3	TYPE 4	TYPE 5	TYPE 6	TYPE 7
Type M or S mortar	785	875	875	875	1150	690	N/A
Type N mortar	675	760	760	760	1000	645	N/A

NOTE

Compressive strength of clay masonry units is assumed to be 8000 psi, and hollow clay masonry units are assumed to be 67% solid. The compressive strength of concrete masonry units is assumed to be 1500 psi, and hollow units are assumed to be 64% solid in 4 in., 57% solid in 6 in., and 53% solid in 8 in.

DESIGN INFORMATION

FLEXURAL TENSION (PSI)	TYPE 1	TYPE 2	TYPE 3	TYPE 4	TYPE 5	TYPE 6	TYPE 7
Normal to bed joints							
Portland cement-lime mortar							
Type M or S	25	25	68	25	25	25	N/A
Type N	19	19	58	19	19	19	N/A
Masonry cement mortar or air-entrained portland cement-lime mortar							
Type M or S	15	15	41	15	15	15	N/A
Type N	9	9	26	9	9	9	N/A
Parallel to bed joints in running bond							
Portland cement - lime mortar							
Type M or S	50	50	80	50	50	50	N/A
Type N	38	38	60	38	38	38	N/A
Masonry cement mortar or air-entrained portland cement-lime mortar							
Type M or S	30	30	48	30	30	30	N/A
Type N	19	19	30	19	19	19	N/A

NOTE

The flexural strength of the masonry is neglected in reinforced masonry design.

TYPICAL REINFORCING SCHEDULE FOR 8 IN. CONCRETE MASONRY WALLS (REINFORCING BAR SIZE—SPACING)

WALL HEIGHT (FT)	WIND OR SEISMIC LATERAL LOAD (PSF)					
	10	15	20	25	30	35
8	#4 - 48	#4 - 48	#4 - 48	#4 - 48	#4 - 48	#4 - 48
12	#4 - 48	#4 - 48	#4 - 48	#4 - 40	#4 - 32	#4 - 48
16	#4 - 48	#4 - 48	#4 - 32	#4 - 24	#4 - 16	#4 - 16
20	#4 - 48	#4 - 24	#4 - 16	#4 - 16	#6 - 16	#5 - 08
24	#4 - 32	#4 - 16	#5 - 16	#5 - 08	see note 1	see note 1

TYPICAL REINFORCING SCHEDULE FOR GROUTED 6 IN. CLAY MASONRY UNIT WALLS (REINFORCING BAR SIZE—SPACING)

WALL HEIGHT (FT)	WIND OR SEISMIC LATERAL LOAD (PSF)					
	10	15	20	25	30	35
8	#4 - 48	#4 - 48	#4 - 48	#4 - 48	#4 - 48	#4 - 48
12	#4 - 48	#4 - 48	#4 - 36	#4 - 30	#4 - 24	#5 - 30
16	#4 - 36	#4 - 24	#5 - 30	#6 - 30	#6 - 30	#5 - 16
20	#5 - 36	#5 - 24	#6 - 24	#6 - 18	#6 - 18	#6 - 12
24	#5 - 24	#5 - 18	#6 - 18	see note 1	see note 1	see note 1

NOTES

1. Increased wall width or two layers of reinforcement required.
2. $f'_m = 3000$ psi, $f_y = 40,000$ psi

Brian E. Trimble; Brick Institute of America; Reston, Virginia

MASONRY CONSTRUCTION

INTRODUCTION

Mortar and grout are the cementitious bonding agents that integrate masonry units into masonry assemblages. Because concrete, masonry mortar, and grout contain the same principal ingredients, some designers assume what is good practice for one will also be good practice for another. In reality, the three materials differ in proportions, working consistencies, methods of placement, and structural performance.

Mortar and grout structurally bind masonry units together, whereas concrete is usually itself a structural material. One of the most important functions of concrete elements is to carry load, whereas the principal function of mortar and grout is to develop a complete, strong, and durable bond with masonry units. Concrete is poured into nonabsorbent forms with a minimum amount of water. Mortar and grout are placed, with much more water, between absorptive forms (masonry units). The water/cement ratio, as mixed, is very important in concrete work, but it is less important in working with mortar or grout for brick masonry. When mortar or grout is placed with masonry units, the water/cement ratio rapidly decreases because of the bricks' absorbency. It is important to distinguish between the requirements for concrete, masonry mortar, and grout.

ASTM SPECIFICATIONS

ASTM C 270—MORTAR FOR UNIT MASONRY

This standard specification covers four types of mortar in each of two methods: proportion specifications and property specifications. When specifying a particular mortar type, either the proportion or the property requirements should be given, but not both. When neither proportion nor property specifications are specified, the proportion specification is mandated. Table 1 shows the proportion requirements for types M, S, N, and O mortars.

Mortar conforming to the property specifications must be established by tests of laboratory prepared mortar, which should be mixed from the mortar materials to be used in the masonry structure. Table 2 provides the property requirements for types M, S, N, and O mortars.

Although ASTM C 270 uses the same letters to designate mortar type under both the proportion and property specifications, the properties of these mortar types are not equivalent. A mortar mixed to the type N proportion specification will have a laboratory prepared compressive strength significantly higher than that of a type N mortar required by the property specifications. Mortars may be made with either portland cement or masonry cement.

ASTM C 476—GROUT FOR MASONRY

This is the standard specification governing grout for reinforced and nonreinforced masonry assemblies. Two types of grout, fine and coarse, are specified by proportions of ingredients. Both types should be proportioned within the limits given in Table 5.

Grout consists of cementitious materials and aggregate thoroughly mixed with sufficient water to attain the desired consistency. Grout should be wet enough to pour without segregation of the constituents. Grout can be used to bond two wythes of masonry, to provide additional material to resist load, or to bond steel reinforcement to masonry so the two materials exert common action under load.

MATERIALS

PORTLAND CEMENT

Portland cement, a hydraulic cement, is the principal cementitious ingredient of mortar and grout. Three types of portland cement covered by ASTM C 150—Standard Specification for Portland Cement are recommended:

Type I: For general use when the special properties of Types II and III are not required

Type II: For use when moderate sulfate resistance or moderate heat of hydration is desired

Type III: For use when high early strength is desired

The allowable stresses for the structural design of brick masonry are based on the results of tests in which only portland cements were used. The use of blended hydraulic cements and natural cements is not recommended unless the strength of the masonry is first established by appropriate tests. For nonstructural masonry, such cements may be substituted for regular portland cement without testing.

HYDRATED LIME

Hydrated lime, a dry powder, is made by adding water to quicklime, thus converting the calcium oxide into calcium hydroxide. Hydrated lime can be used without extra preparation and thus is more convenient to use than quicklime.

ASTM C 207—Hydrated Lime for Masonry Purposes is available in four types: S, SA, N, and NA. Because unhydrated oxides and plasticity are not controlled in types N or NA, only type S hydrated lime should be used for masonry mortar and grout.

MASONRY CEMENT

These proprietary mortar mixes are widely used in mortar because of their convenience and good workability. Masonry cements, however, should not be used in grout. The requirements for masonry cement are covered in ASTM C 91—Standard Specification for Masonry Cement. Masonry cements are prepackaged as types M, S, or N mortar mixes. Most building codes have lower allowable stresses when masonry cements are used.

AGGREGATE

Either natural or manufactured aggregate may be used. Gradation limits are given in ASTM C 144 and C 404 for aggregate used in mortar and grout. Only fine aggregate may be used in mortar; fine and coarse aggregate may be used in grout. Gradation can be easily altered by adding fine or coarse sands. Only clean sand is recommended for use in masonry mortar and grout.

WATER

Clean, potable water that is free of deleterious acids, alkalies, or organic materials is suitable for masonry mortar and grout.

COLOR AND OTHER ADMIXTURES

Many different types of admixtures can be added to mortar grouts. Admixtures are used in mortar to provide color, enhance workability, reduce water penetration, accelerate curing, and substitute for conventional materials. Admixtures are used in grout to increase fluidity, accelerate curing, and decrease shrinkage. Admixtures must be used with extreme caution so the performance of the masonry is not affected. Admixtures containing chlorides should never be used because they tend to corrode metal.

Air entrainment has the detrimental effect of reducing the bond between mortar and masonry units or reinforcement. The use of air-entraining portland cements (types IA, IIA, or IIIA) and air-entrained lime (types SA and NA) for masonry mortar and grout may not be appropriate. Two different air-entraining agents should not be used in the same mortar or grout. Air-entraining admixtures should not be used in structural masonry. Building codes mandate lower allowable flexural tension stresses if air-entrained cements or lime are used in mortar.

TABLE 1: PROPORTION REQUIREMENTS FOR MASONRY MORTARS*

MORTAR	TYPE	PORTLAND CEMENT OR BLENDED CEMENT	MASONRY CEMENT M	MASONRY CEMENT S	MASONRY CEMENT N	HYDRATED LIME OR LIME PUTTY	AGGREGATE RATIO (MEASURED IN DAMP, LOOSE CONDITIONS)
Cement-lime	M	1	—	—	—	$1/4$	
	S	1	—	—	—	over $1/4$ to $1/2$	
	N	1	—	—	—	over $1/2$ to $1\,1/4$	Not less than $2\,1/4$ and not more than 3 times the sum of the separate volumes of cementitious materials.
	O	1	—	—	—	over $1\,1/4$ to $2\,1/2$	
Masonry cement	M	1	—	—	1	—	
	M	—	1	—	—	—	
	S	$1/2$	—	—	1	—	
	S	—	—	1	—	—	
	N	—	—	—	1	—	
	O	—	—	—	1	—	

NOTE

* Two air-entraining materials shall not be combined in mortar.

TABLE 2: MORTAR PROPERTY SPECIFICATION REQUIREMENTS[1]

MORTAR	TYPE	AVERAGE COMPRESSIVE STRENGTH AT 28 DAYS MIN. PSI (MPA)	WATER RETENTION MINIMUM %	AIR CONTENT MAXIMUM %	AGGREGATE RATIO (MEASURED IN DAMP, LOOSE CONDITIONS)
Cement-lime	M	2500 (17.2)	75	12	
	S	1800 (12.4)	75	12	
	N	750 (5.2)	75	14[2]	
	O	350 (2.4)	75	14[2]	Not less than $2\,1/4$ and not more than $3\,1/2$ times the sum of the separate volumes of cementitious materials.
Masonry cement	M	2500 (17.2)	75	See note 3	
	S	1800 (12.4)	75	See note 3	
	N	750 (5.2)	75	See note 3	
	O	350 (2.4)	75	See note 3	

NOTES

1. Laboratory prepared mortar only.
2. When structural reinforcement is incorporated in cement-lime mortar, the maximum air content is 12%.

TABLE 3: GUIDE FOR THE SELECTION OF MASONRY MORTAR[1]

LOCATION	BUILDING SEGMENT	MORTAR TYPE RECOMMENDED	MORTAR TYPE ALTERNATIVE
Exterior, above grade	Load bearing wall	N	S or M
	Non-load bearing wall	O[2]	N or S
	Parapet wall	N	S
Exterior, at or below grade	Foundation wall, retaining wall, manholes, sewers, pavements, walks, and patios	S[3]	M or N[3]
Interior	Load bearing wall	N	S or M
	Non-bearing partitions	O	N

NOTES

1. This table does not include many specialized mortar uses, such as chimney reinforced masonry and acid-resistant mortar.
2. Type O mortar is recommended for use where the masonry is unlikely to be frozen when saturated, or unlikely to be subjected to high winds or other significant lateral loads. Types N or S mortar should be used in other cases.
3. Masonry exposed to weather in a nominally horizontal surface is extremely vulnerable to weathering. Mortar for such masonry should be selected with due caution.

Grace S. Lee; Rippeteau Architects, PC; Washington, D.C.
Brian E. Trimble; Brick Institute of America; Reston, Virginia
Stephen S. Szoke, P.E.; National Concrete Masonry Association; Herndon, Virginia

RECOMMENDED TYPES
MORTAR

No single type of mortar is best suited for all purposes, but there are several rules for selecting mortar type. Never use a mortar that is stronger in compression than needed by the structural requirements. Always select the mortar weakest in compression that is consistent with the performance requirements of the project. However, this guideline should be coupled with good engineering judgment; for example, it would be uneconomical and unwise to change mortar types in various parts of a structure. If mortar is used with reinforcement in a collar joint or in a cell of a hollow unit, then the air content must be less than 12% for portland cement–lime mortars and 18% for masonry cements. The use of mortar is recommended only in unreinforced collar joints of ³/₄ in. (19 mm) or less.

Following are the recommended uses for different types of mortar:

Type N mortar: A medium strength mortar suitable for general use in exposed masonry above grade and recommended specifically where high compressive or transverse masonry strengths are not required.

Type S mortar: A high strength mortar suitable for general use and specifically for circumstances where high transverse strength of masonry is desired; for reinforced masonry, where mortar bonds the facing and backing; and for areas subject to winds greater than 80 mph (130 kph).

Type M mortar: A high strength mortar suitable for general use and recommended specifically for masonry below grade or in contact with earth, such as foundations, retaining walls, or paving.

Type O mortar: A low strength mortar suitable for use in non-load bearing applications in walls of low axial compressive strength and where masonry is not subject to severe weathering.

TABLE 5: GROUT PROPORTIONS BY VOLUME

TYPE	PARTS BY VOLUME OF PORTLAND CEMENT OR BLENDED CEMENT	PARTS BY VOLUME OF HYDRATED LIME OR LIME PUTTY	AGGREGATE (MEASURED IN A DAMP, LOOSE CONDITION)	
			FINE	COARSE
Fine grout	1	0 - ¹/₁₀	2 ¹/₄ - 3 times the sum of the volumes of cementitious materials	—
Coarse grout	1	0 - ¹/₁₀	2 ¹/₄ - 3 times the sum of the volumes of cementitious materials	1 - 2 times the sum of the volumes of cementitious materials

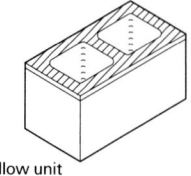
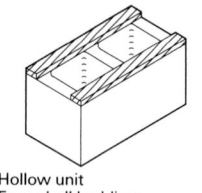

Brick more than 75% solid
Net area equals gross area
Full mortar bedding

Hollow unit
Full mortar bedding
(requires alignment of crosswebs)

Hollow unit
Face shell bedding

NET CROSS-SECTIONAL AREA

GROUT

Grout should be mixed thoroughly in a plastic mix suitable for placement without separation of the constituents. Add enough water to achieve a slump of 8 to 11 in. (200 to 275 mm). The compressive strength of the grout should match that of the brick masonry but must have a minimum compressive strength of 2000 psi (13.9 MPa).

Fine grout: Can be used for grouting interior vertical spaces between two wythes of masonry or aligned, unobstructed vertical spaces in hollow masonry units. See Table 4 for grout space requirements.

Coarse grout: May be used when the grout space exceeds 2 in. (50 mm) in width. If the minimum grout space dimension exceeds 6 in. (150 mm), a larger aggregate size may be specified.

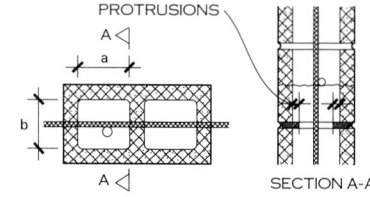

a > Minimum grout space dimension

b > Minimum grout space dimension plus horizontal bar diameter plus horizontal protrusions (see table)

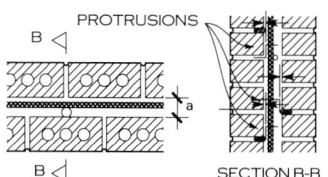

a > Minimum grout space dimension plus horizontal bar diameter plus horizontal protrusions (see table)

GROUT SPACE REQUIREMENTS

TABLE 4: GROUT SPACING REQUIREMENTS

SPECIFIED GROUT TYPE	MAXIMUM GROUT POUR HEIGHT (FT)	MINIMUM WIDTH OF GROUT SPACE (IN.)	MINIMUM GROUT SPACE DIMENSIONS FOR GROUTING CELLS OF HOLLOW UNITS (IN. X IN.)
Fine	1	³/₄	1 ¹/₂ x 2
	5	2	2 x 3
	12	2 ¹/₂	2 ¹/₂ x 3
	24	3	3 x 3
Coarse	1	1 ¹/₂	1 ¹/₂ x 3
	5	2	2 ¹/₂ x 3
	12	2 ¹/₂	3 x 3
	24	3	3 x 4

NOTES

1. Grout space dimension is the clear dimension between any masonry protrusion and shall be increased by the diameters of the horizontal bars within the cross section of the grout space.
2. Area of vertical reinforcement should not exceed 6% of the area of the grout space.

TYPES OF JOINTS

Mortar serves multiple functions:

1. Joins and seals masonry, allowing for dimensional variations in masonry units.
2. Affects overall appearance of wall color, texture, and patterns.
3. Bonds reinforcing steel to masonry, creating composite assembly.

MORTAR JOINT FINISH METHODS

1. Troweled: Excess mortar is struck off. The trowel is the only tool used for shaping and finishing.
2. Tooled: A special tool is used to compress and shape mortar in the joint.

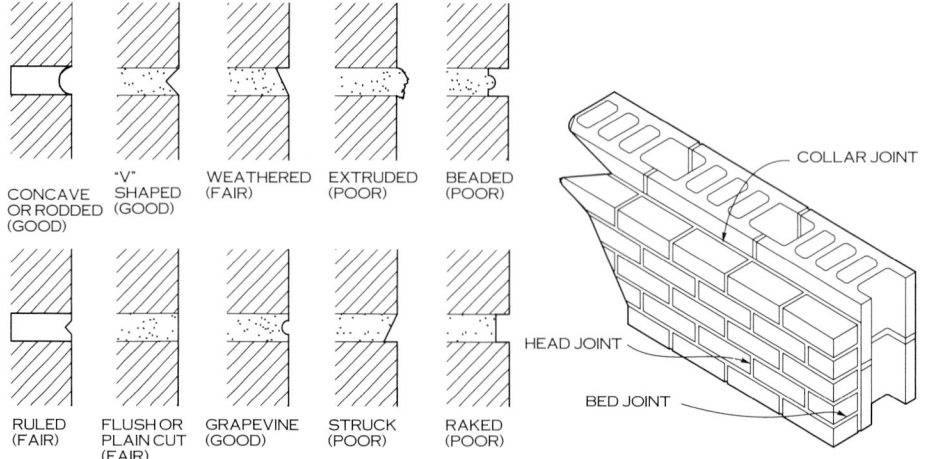

CONCAVE OR RODDED (GOOD)   "V" SHAPED (GOOD)   WEATHERED (FAIR)   EXTRUDED (POOR)   BEADED (POOR)

RULED (FAIR)   FLUSH OR PLAIN CUT (FAIR)   GRAPEVINE (GOOD)   STRUCK (POOR)   RAKED (POOR)

TYPES OF JOINTS (WEATHERABILITY)

COLLAR JOINT

HEAD JOINT

BED JOINT

TERMS APPLIED TO JOINTS

MORTAR JOINTS

Grace S. Lee; Rippeteau Architects, PC; Washington, D.C.
Brian E. Trimble; Brick Institute of America; Reston, Virginia
Stephen S. Szoke, P.E.; National Concrete Masonry Association; Herndon, Virginia

MORTAR AND MASONRY GROUT

GENERAL

Masonry construction has not always required the inclusion of metal elements. Historically, composite masonry construction consisted of multiple wythes of masonry bonded together by headers. However, contemporary masonry walls require ties between the inner and outer wythes, which are then anchored to the structural frame. Many people use the terms *wall tie* and *anchor* interchangeably, but in practice the term *tie* refers to combining a wythe of masonry to its backing system, while *anchor* refers to a component that secures structural elements to a structural support. A fastener is a device used to attach nonstructural elements to masonry. Anchors and ties with flexible components can accommodate differential movement between the structural frame and the masonry wall by allowing for in-plane movement.

CORROSION PROTECTION

The durability of any metal accessory is usually based on its ability to resist corrosion. Since masonry walls are often subject to moisture, metal items must be protected, either by galvanizing them or by use of corrosion resistant metals. The following ASTM standards apply to corrosion protection of carbon steel metal accessories based on their location and the size of the piece:

1. ASTM A 641–Mill galvanizing: joint reinforcement, interior
2. ASTM A 153–Hot-dip galvanized: joint reinforcement, wire ties, and wire anchors, exterior or moist interior
3. ASTM A 153–Hot-dip galvanized: sheet metal ties, exterior or moist interior
4. ASTM A 525–sheet metal ties, interior
5. ASTM A 123 or A 153–steel plates and bars

Corrosion protection is also provided by stainless steel anchors and ties conforming to ASTM A 167, Type 304.

ANCHORS AND REINFORCEMENT

Selection of anchors and reinforcement is determined by the relationship of the masonry element to the structural support. Reinforcing bars may be placed horizontally or vertically in masonry. The reinforcement may be placed in the cores or cells of masonry units or between wythes of masonry. The use of dovetail slots welded on steel or concrete columns requires coordination during the steel or concrete fabrication stage. The type of anchor specified, including its size, diameter, and type, should be called out on the contract documents.

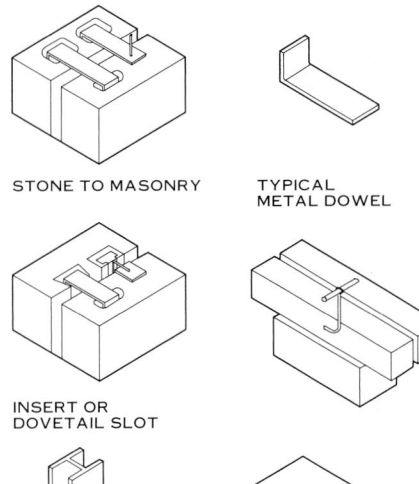

STONE TO MASONRY

TYPICAL METAL DOWEL

INSERT OR DOVETAIL SLOT

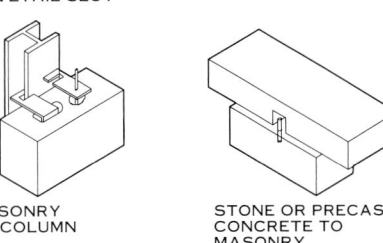

MASONRY TO COLUMN

STONE OR PRECAST CONCRETE TO MASONRY

ANCHOR DETAILS

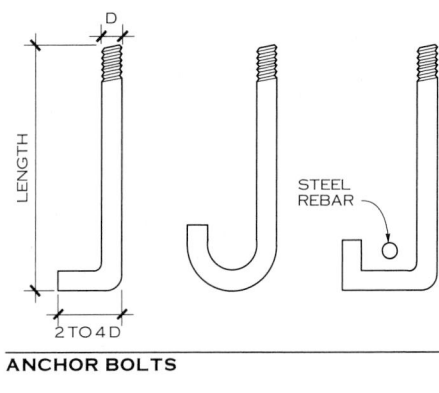

ANCHOR BOLTS

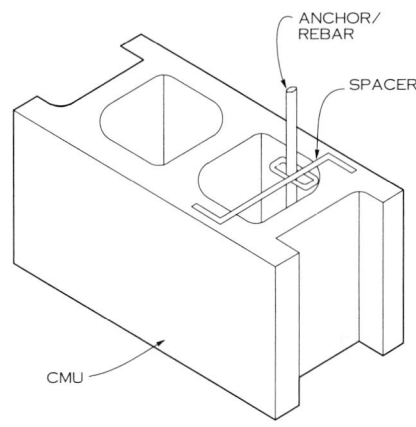

ANCHOR/ REBAR

SPACER

CMU

ANCHOR BOLT/REINFORCING BAR SPACERS

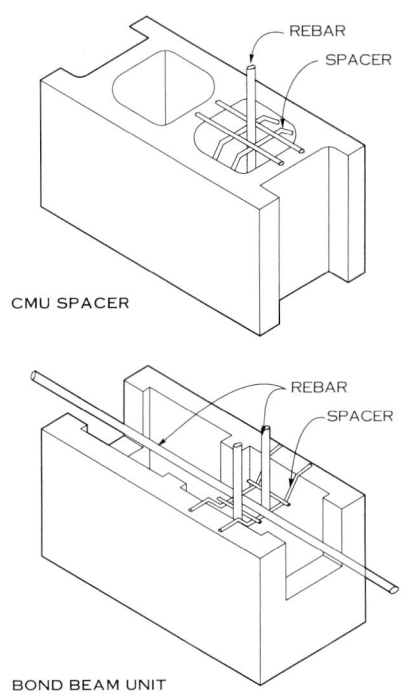

REBAR
SPACER

CMU SPACER

REBAR
SPACER

BOND BEAM UNIT

REBAR SPACERS

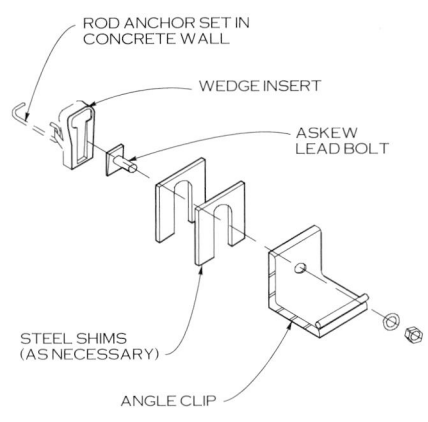

ROD ANCHOR SET IN CONCRETE WALL

WEDGE INSERT

ASKEW LEAD BOLT

STEEL SHIMS (AS NECESSARY)

ANGLE CLIP

ANGLE CLIP ANCHOR

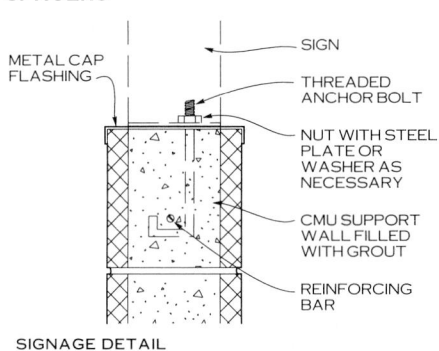

SIGN
METAL CAP FLASHING
THREADED ANCHOR BOLT
NUT WITH STEEL PLATE OR WASHER AS NECESSARY
CMU SUPPORT WALL FILLED WITH GROUT
REINFORCING BAR

SIGNAGE DETAIL

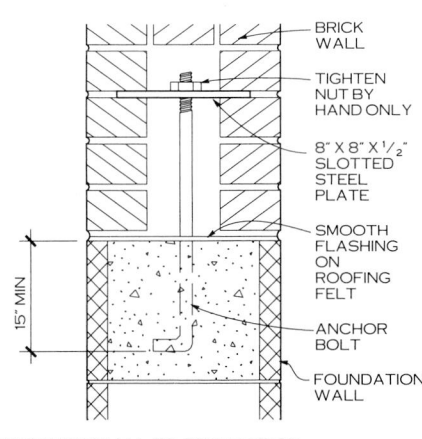

BRICK WALL
TIGHTEN NUT BY HAND ONLY
8" X 8" X 1/2" SLOTTED STEEL PLATE
SMOOTH FLASHING ON ROOFING FELT
ANCHOR BOLT
FOUNDATION WALL

15" MIN

MASONRY WALL TO FOUNDATION ANCHORAGE DETAIL

ANCHOR BOLT DETAILS

TIE SPACING RECOMMENDATIONS*

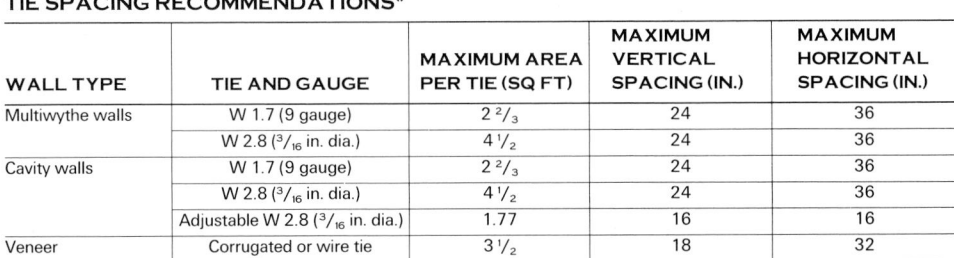

WALL TYPE	TIE AND GAUGE	MAXIMUM AREA PER TIE (SQ FT)	MAXIMUM VERTICAL SPACING (IN.)	MAXIMUM HORIZONTAL SPACING (IN.)
Multiwythe walls	W 1.7 (9 gauge)	2 2/3	24	36
	W 2.8 (3/16 in. dia.)	4 1/2	24	36
Cavity walls	W 1.7 (9 gauge)	2 2/3	24	36
	W 2.8 (3/16 in. dia.)	4 1/2	24	36
	Adjustable W 2.8 (3/16 in. dia.)	1.77	16	16
Veneer	Corrugated or wire tie	3 1/2	18	32

NOTE

* Masonry laid in running bond. Consult applicable building code for special bond patterns such as stack bond.

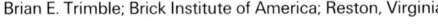

Brian E. Trimble; Brick Institute of America; Reston, Virginia

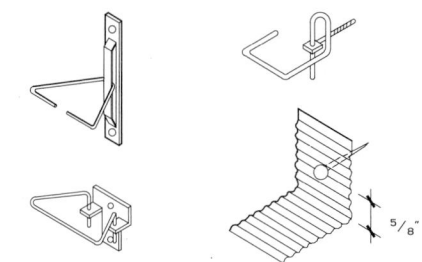

ADJUSTABLE UNIT TIES—STUD

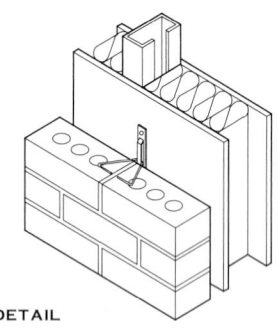

TIE DETAIL

NOTE

Differential movement must always be accounted for in stud-backed wall systems with adjustable ties.

ADJUSTABLE UNIT TIE FOR STEEL STUD BACKUP

UNIT TIES—STEEL FRAME   WELD-ON TYPE CHANNEL SLOT (ANCHOR SHOWN)

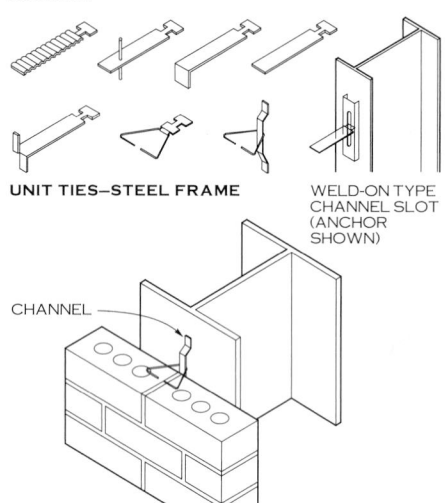

TIE DETAIL

ADJUSTABLE UNIT TIE—STEEL FRAME BACKUP

UNIT TIES—CONCRETE

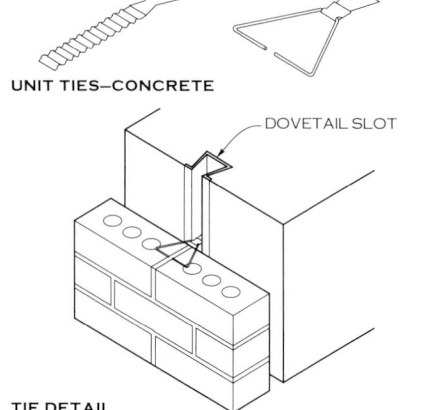

TIE DETAIL

ADJUSTABLE UNIT TIE FOR CONCRETE FRAME BACKUP

Brian E. Trimble; Brick Institute of America; Reston, Virginia

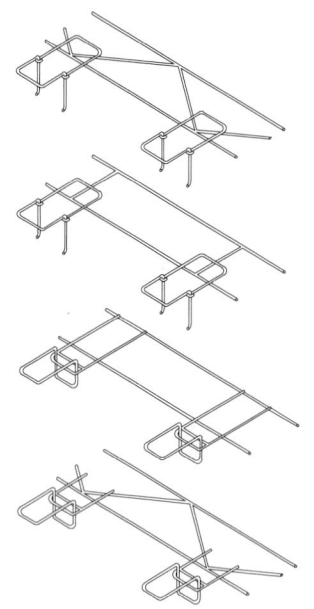

ADJUSTABLE JOINT REINFORCEMENT

TRUSS TYPE   LONGITUDINAL WIRE LADDER TYPE   LONGITUDINAL TRUSS TYPE

JOINT REINFORCEMENT FOR MASONRY BACKUP

UNIT TIES—MASONRY

ADJUSTABLE UNIT TIES—MASONRY

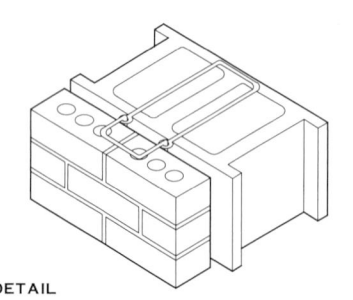

TIE DETAIL

NOTES

1. Z ties can be used only with solid masonry veneer units.
2. Tie must extend a minimum of $1\frac{1}{2}$ in. onto solid masonry units and be fully embedded in mortar on the outer face shell of hollow masonry units.

UNIT TIE FOR MASONRY BACKUP

MASONRY TIES

Wall ties perform one or more functions: they provide a connection, transfer lateral loads, permit in-plane movement to accommodate differential movements, and may act as horizontal structural reinforcement. As shown on this page, wall ties include unit ties, joint reinforcement, adjustable unit ties, and adjustable joint reinforcement. Wall tie spacing is listed in a table on the AGS page on Anchorage and Reinforcement. The ties should be staggered in alternate rows, and only one row of ties should be located in the same bed joint to allow proper embedment in the mortar.

In wall construction in which masonry wythes are built up together and the joints align, a single piece is laid over both wythes. Where one wythe of masonry is laid up before the other wythe or when joints do not align, adjustable ties may be necessary. Adjustable ties are advantageous for several reasons: (1) interior wythes can be constructed before the exterior wythe, allowing the structure to be enclosed faster; (2) the risk of damage to the ties when the exterior wythe is constructed is reduced; (3) adjustable ties can more readily accommodate construction tolerances; and (4) adjustable ties can accommodate larger differential movements. However, adjustable ties must be installed properly or the tie may be rendered useless. Location of the first piece is critical since the second piece must engage the first and be properly embedded in the exterior wythe. Large eccentricities may occur between the two pieces, which would result in less strength and stiffness than anticipated.

RECOMMENDED MINIMUM TIE DIAMETERS AND GAUGES

TIE SYSTEM	MINIMUM SPECIFIED DIMENSION*	
	DIAMETER (IN.)	GAUGE
Standard Ties		
Unit		
Rectangular and "Z"	$3/16$	–
Corrugated	–	22
Joint reinforcement		
Ladder and truss	–	9
Tab	–	9
Adjustable Ties		
Unit		
Rectangular and "Z"	$3/16$	–
Dovetail/channel slot		
Wire	$3/16$	–
Corrugated	–	16
Connectior slot	–	22
Slotted plate		
Wire	$3/16$	–
Slot plate	–	14
Backer plate	–	14
Joint reinforcement		
Standard section	–	9
Tabs	$3/16$	–

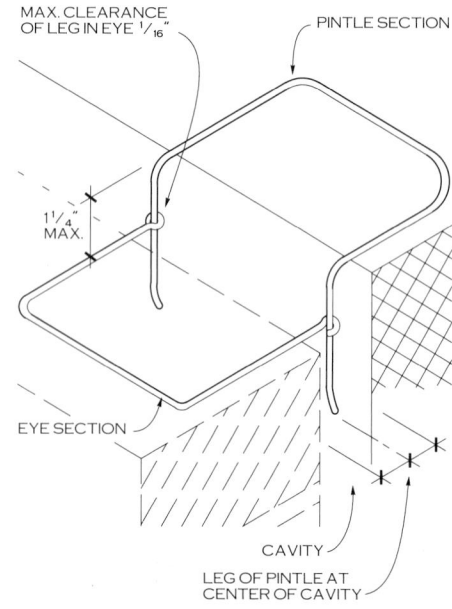

MAX. CLEARANCE OF LEG IN EYE $1/16$"   PINTLE SECTION

$1\frac{1}{4}$" MAX.

EYE SECTION

CAVITY

LEG OF PINTLE AT CENTER OF CAVITY

TYPICAL ADJUSTABLE UNIT TIE

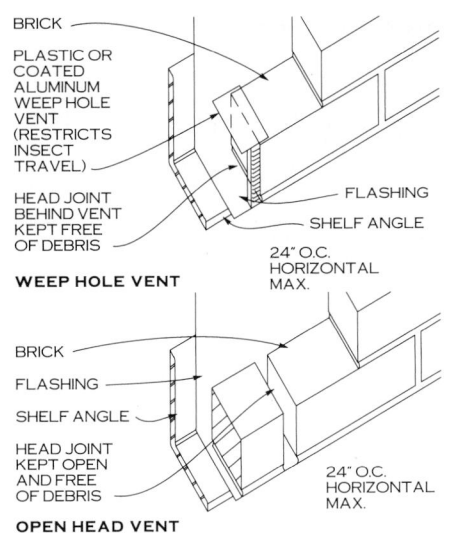

WEEP HOLE VENT
- BRICK
- PLASTIC OR COATED ALUMINUM WEEP HOLE VENT (RESTRICTS INSECT TRAVEL)
- HEAD JOINT BEHIND VENT KEPT FREE OF DEBRIS
- FLASHING
- SHELF ANGLE
- 24" O.C. HORIZONTAL MAX.

OPEN HEAD VENT
- BRICK
- FLASHING
- SHELF ANGLE
- HEAD JOINT KEPT OPEN AND FREE OF DEBRIS
- 24" O.C. HORIZONTAL MAX.

WEEP HOLE DETAILS

BRICK OR BLOCK VENT
- CMU
- CAST ALUMINUM BLOCK VENT
- WATER STOP
- INSECT SCREEN
- DRIP EDGE

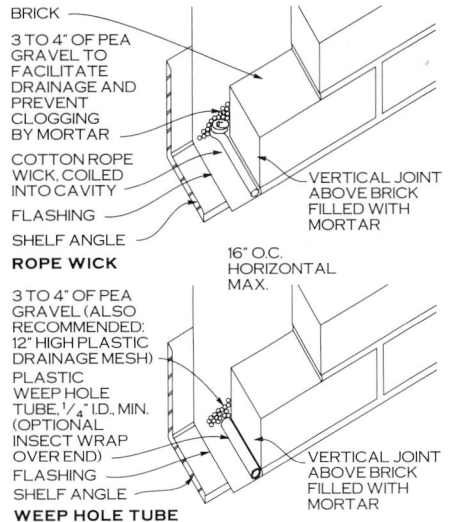

ROPE WICK
- BRICK
- 3 TO 4" OF PEA GRAVEL TO FACILITATE DRAINAGE AND PREVENT CLOGGING BY MORTAR
- COTTON ROPE WICK, COILED INTO CAVITY
- FLASHING
- SHELF ANGLE
- VERTICAL JOINT ABOVE BRICK FILLED WITH MORTAR
- 16" O.C. HORIZONTAL MAX.

WEEP HOLE TUBE
- 3 TO 4" OF PEA GRAVEL (ALSO RECOMMENDED: 12" HIGH PLASTIC DRAINAGE MESH)
- PLASTIC WEEP HOLE TUBE, $\frac{1}{4}$" I.D. MIN. (OPTIONAL INSECT WRAP OVER END)
- FLASHING
- SHELF ANGLE
- VERTICAL JOINT ABOVE BRICK FILLED WITH MORTAR

WEEP HOLE DETAILS

WEEP HOLES AND VENTS

With proper design and installation, weep holes and vents discharge water and moisture as vapor in wall cavities and must always be used with flashing. When vents are located at the bottom of the wall, directly above flashing and in conjunction with small openings at the top of the cavity, the void is vented, allowing moisture removal from the wall. The type of weep hole chosen is not critical as long as it is properly sized and spaced at the required locations. Weep holes are sometimes created by placing greased or oiled tubes or coils into the mortar and then extracting them when the mortar is ready to be tooled. For CMUs under adverse weather conditions, it may be necessary to install weep holes at the base of the first course at all open cores, as well as at the head joints for wall cavity venting. Weep holes should never be located below grade and should be small enough to keep out rodents.

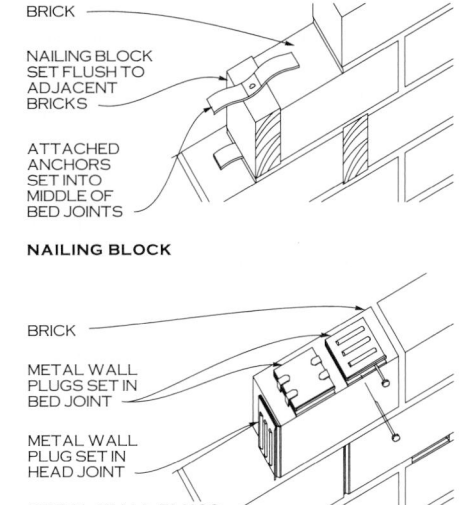

NAILING BLOCK
- BRICK
- NAILING BLOCK SET FLUSH TO ADJACENT BRICKS
- ATTACHED ANCHORS SET INTO MIDDLE OF BED JOINTS

METAL WALL PLUGS
- BRICK
- METAL WALL PLUGS SET IN BED JOINT
- METAL WALL PLUG SET IN HEAD JOINT

NAILING RECEIVERS (SET IN MASONRY)

NAILING BLOCKS AND WALL PLUGS

The procedure for attaching other materials, fixtures, and the like to brick masonry is relatively simple and can be executed either during or after construction. Postconstruction fasteners, such as lag bolts and shields, are commonly used because of their flexibility in placement. However, when the precise location of the fastener is determined, nailing blocks and metal wall plugs are an acceptable means of attachment to brick masonry. They are placed in mortar joints as the bricks are laid.

Wood nailing block should be of seasoned softwood to prevent shrinkage and be treated to inhibit deterioration. They should only be placed in the head joint. Metal wall plugs are made of galvanized metal and may contain wooden or fiber inserts. Such plugs may be placed in either the head or bed joints of masonry.

GALVANIC CORROSION (ELECTROLYSIS) POTENTIAL BETWEEN COMMON FLASHING MATERIALS AND SELECTED CONSTRUCTION MATERIALS

FLASHING MATERIALS \ CONSTRUCTION MATERIALS	COPPER	ALUMINUM	STAINLESS STEEL	GALVANIZED STEEL	ZINC	LEAD	BRASS	BRONZE	MONEL	UNCURED MORTAR OR CEMENT	WOODS WITH ACID (REDWOOD AND RED CEDAR)	IRON/STEEL
Copper		●	●	◍	●	◍	◍	◍	◍	○	○	●
Aluminum			○	○	○	◍	●	●	○	●	●	◍
Stainless steel				◍	◍	●	●	●	◍	○	○	◍
Galvanized steel					○	○	◍	◍	◍	○	◍	◍
Zinc alloy						○	●	●	◍	○	◍	●
Lead							◍	●	◍	●	○	○

NOTES

1. ● Galvanic action will occur, hence direct contact should be avoided.
   ◍ Galvanic action may occur under certain circumstances and/or over a period of time.
   ○ Galvanic action is insignificant; metals may come into direct contact under normal circumstances.
2. Galvanic corrosion is apt to occur when water runoff from one material comes in contact with a potentially reactive material.

ASTM STANDARD REINFORCING BARS FOR MASONRY

BAR SIZE DESIGNATION	WEIGHT (LB/FT)	NOMINAL DIMENSIONS – ROUND SECTIONS		
		DIAMETER (IN.)	CROSS-SECTIONAL AREA (SQ IN.)	PERIMETER (IN.)
#3	0.376	0.375	0.11	1.178
#4	0.668	0.500	0.20	1.571
#5	1.043	0.625	0.31	1.963
#6	1.502	0.750	0.44	2.356
#7	2.044	0.875	0.60	2.749
#8	2.670	1.000	0.79	3.142
#9	3.400	1.128	1.00	3.544
#10	4.303	1.270	1.27	3.990
#11*	5.313	1.410	1.56	4.430

* Bar sizes larger than #11 are not permitted in masonry work.

Grace S. Lee and A. Harris Lokmanhakim, AIA; Rippeteau Architects, PC; Washington, D.C.
Brian E. Trimble; Brick Institute of America; Reston, Virginia
Stephen S. Szoke, P.E.; National Concrete Masonry Association; Herndon, Virginia

INTRODUCTION

The various materials and elements used to construct a building are in constant motion. All building materials change in volume in response to internal or external stimuli, such as temperature changes, moisture expansion, and elastic deformation due to loads or creep. Restraining such movements may cause stresses within the building elements, which in turn may result in cracks.

To avoid cracks, the building design should minimize volume change, prevent movement, or accommodate differential movement between materials and assemblies. A system of movement joints can prevent cracks and the problems they cause. Movement joints can be designed by estimating the magnitude of the several types of movements that may occur in masonry and other building materials.

MOVEMENTS OF CONSTRUCTION MATERIALS

The design and construction of most buildings do not allow precise prediction of movements of building elements. Volume changes depend on material properties and are highly variable. Age of material and temperature at installation also influence expected movement. When mean values of material properties are used in design, the actual movement may be underestimated or overestimated. Designers should use discretion when selecting the applicable values. The types of movement affecting various building materials are indicated in the table.

MOVEMENT JOINTS

There are various types of movement joints in buildings: expansion joints, control joints, building expansion joints, and construction joints. Each type of movement joint is designed to perform a specific task and should not be used interchangeably.

Expansion joints are used to separate brick masonry into segments to prevent cracking from changes in temperature, moisture expansion, elastic deformation due to loads, and shrinkage and creep in concrete framed buildings. Expansion joints may be horizontal or vertical. They are formed of elastomeric materials placed in a continuous, unobstructed opening through the brick wythe. This construction allows the joints to close if the size of the brickwork increases. Expansion joints must be located so the structural integrity of the brick masonry is not compromised. In some cases expansion joints are necessary in concrete masonry walls. Architects often designate these joints as control joints.

Control joints are used in concrete or concrete masonry to create a plane of weakness that, used in conjunction with reinforcement or joint reinforcement, controls the location of cracks caused by volume changes resulting from shrinkage and creep. A control joint, usually vertical and formed of inelastic materials, will open rather than close. Control joints must be located so the structural integrity of the concrete masonry wall is not affected.

A building expansion (isolation) joint is used to separate a building into discrete structural sections so that stresses developed in one section will not affect the integrity of the entire structure. The isolation joint is a through-the-building joint, including the roof assembly.

A construction (cold) joint is used primarily in concrete construction when construction work is interrupted. Construction joints are located where they will least impair the strength of the structure.

SPACING OF EXPANSION AND CONTROL JOINTS

No single recommendation on the positioning and spacing of expansion and control joints can be applicable to all structures. Each building should be analyzed to determine the extent of movement expected within that particular structure. Provisions should be made to accommodate these movements and their associated stresses with a series of expansion and control joints.

Generally, spacing of expansion joints is determined by considering the amount of expected wall movement and the size of compressibility of the expansion joint and expansion joint materials. Expansion joints are often sized to resemble a mortar joint, usually $3/8$ in. (10 mm) to $1/2$ in. (13 mm). The maximum size of the expansion joint may depend on the sealant capabilities. Extensibility of highly elastic expansion joint materials is typically in the range of 25 to 50%. Compressibility of backing materials can range up to 75%.

Expansion and control joints do not have to be aligned in cavity walls; however, they should be aligned in multi-wythe walls.

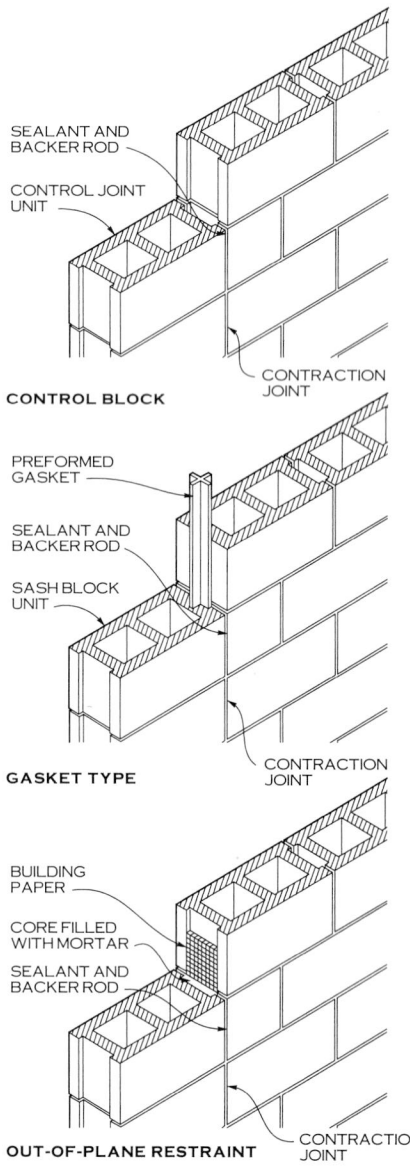

CONTROL BLOCK

GASKET TYPE

OUT-OF-PLANE RESTRAINT

CONTROL JOINTS

TYPES OF MOVEMENT OF BUILDING MATERIALS

BUILDING MATERIAL	THERMAL	REVERSIBLE MOISTURE	IRREVERSIBLE MOISTURE	ELASTIC DEFORMATION	CREEP
Brick masonry	x	—	x	x	x
Concrete masonry	x	x	—	x	x
Concrete	x	x	—	x	x
Steel	x	—	—	x	—
Wood	x	x	—	x	x

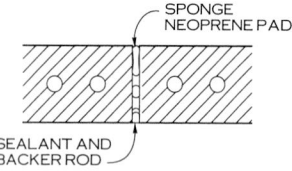

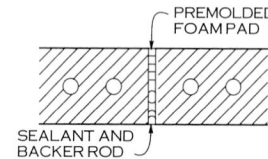

VERTICAL EXPANSION JOINTS

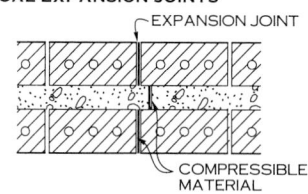

GROUTED MULTIPLE WYTHE MASONRY

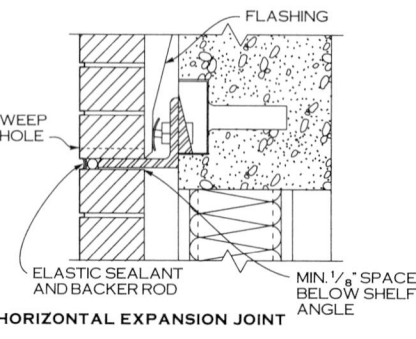

HORIZONTAL EXPANSION JOINT

EXPANSION JOINTS

CONTROL JOINT SPACING FOR MOISTURE CONTROLLED, TYPE 1 CONCRETE MASONRY UNITS

RECOMMENDED SPACING OF CONTROL JOINTS	VERTICAL SPACING OF JOINT REINFORCEMENT			
	NONE	24"	16"	8"
Expressed as ratio of panel length to height (L/H)	2	2½	3	4
Panel length (L) not to exceed (regardless of height [H])	40'	45'	50'	60'

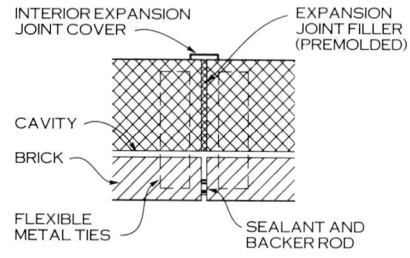

EXPANSION JOINT AT MASONRY CAVITY WALL

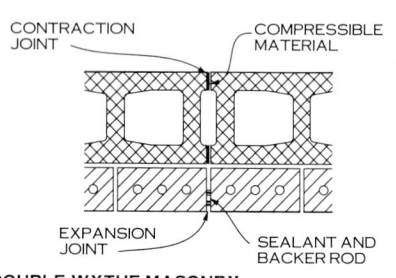

DOUBLE WYTHE MASONRY

EXPANSION AND CONTROL JOINTS

Grace S. Lee; Rippeteau Architects, PC; Washington, D.C.
Brian E. Trimble; Brick Institute of America; Reston, Virginia
Stephen S. Szoke. P.E.; National Concrete Masonry Association; Herndon, Virginia

MASONRY ACCESSORIES

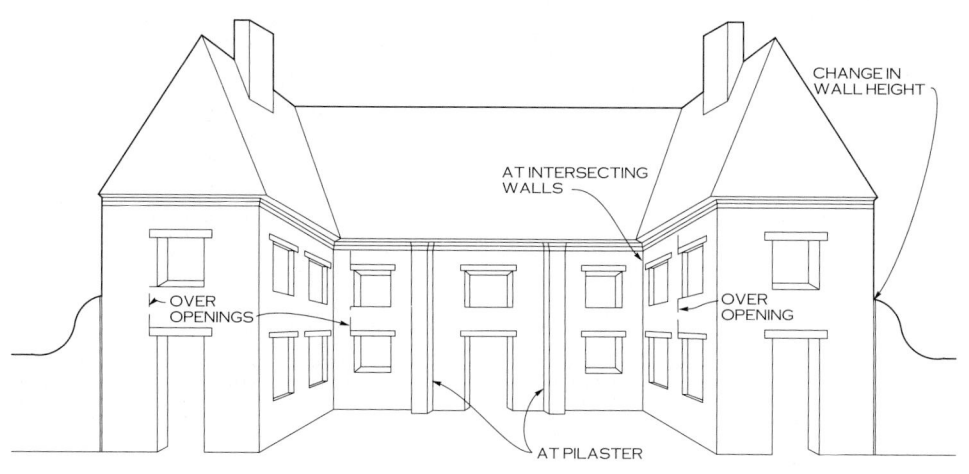

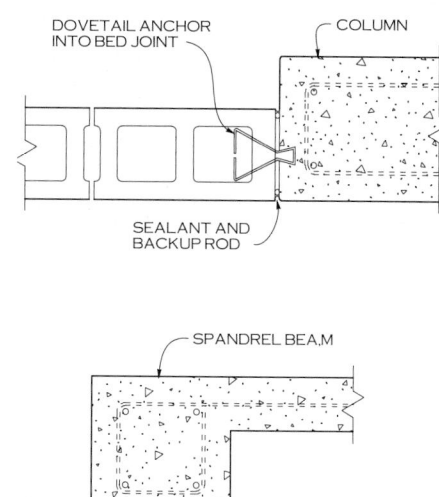

RULES OF THUMB FOR LOCATING CONTROL JOINTS

1. Spacing between joints should not exceed 60 ft (see table on preceding page).
2. Locate control joints at intersecting walls.
3. Locate control joints at changes in wall height.
4. Locate control joints at changes in wall thickness.

5. Locate control joints at openings (each side if opening is more than 6 ft wide).
6. Locate control joints in walls where control joints occur in floors or roofs bearing on the walls.
7. Locate control joints in walls where control joints occur in the foundation or floors on which the walls are bearing.

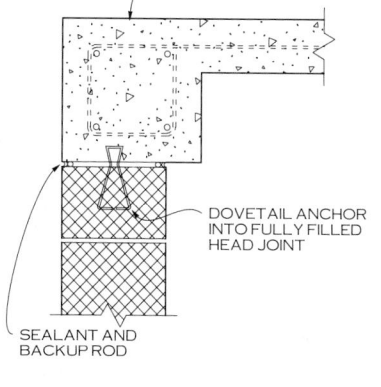

CONTROL JOINT LOCATIONS

CONTROL JOINT AT COLUMN

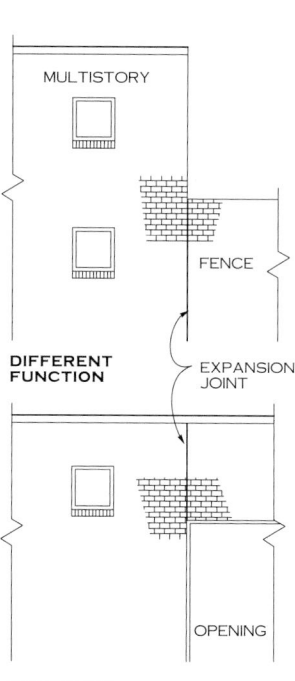

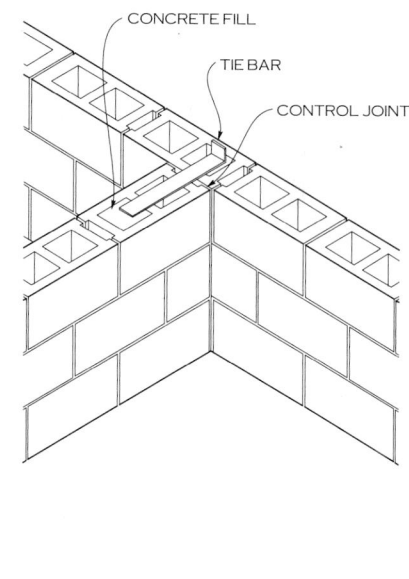

RULES OF THUMB FOR LOCATING EXPANSION JOINTS

1. Spacing between joints not to exceed 30 ft.
2. Locate expansion joints within 10 ft of one side of a corner.
3. Locate expansion joints at wall offsets.
4. Locate expansion joints at changes in wall height.
5. Locate expansion joints directly below shelf angles.

CONTROL JOINT AT WALL INTERSECTION

EXPANSION JOINT LOCATIONS

Grace S. Lee; Rippeteau Architects, PC; Washington, D.C.
Brian E. Trimble; Brick Institute of America; Reston, Virginia
Stephen S. Szoke, P.E.; National Concrete Masonry Association; Herndon, Virginia

PURPOSE

Flashing in masonry construction is necessary to collect moisture that enters the wall system and to channel it to the exterior though weep holes. Moisture manifests itself in masonry walls through condensation, penetration of wind-driven rains, failed sealant joints, interfaces with other components, or other components themselves, such as windows or roofs.

There are two types of flashing. Exposed flashings can be applied to all masonry construction, while use of embedded flashing is usually limited to drainage-type walls. Masonry is a durable, long-lasting construction material. Thus, the flashing materials selected should also be durable and have a long life, especially embedded flashing materials, which are difficult to replace.

MATERIALS

Flashing may be made of sheet metal (copper, lead, stainless steel, galvanized steel, or aluminum), plastic, or composite materials (usually paper-backed, coated, metallic sheet, or fibrous glass mesh). When selecting flashing materials, be careful to avoid choosing a material that would have cathodic reactions with mortar, other metals, or other construction materials. The thickness of the flashing material specified should take into account the span between embedment, bends, or connections. Copper may cause a patina, which may be desirable. Lead and galvanized metal

may result in some white staining, but this may be minimal if coated materials are used. Aluminum should be selected as an embedded flashing only if it is properly coated, so that it will not react with the mortar. Polyethylene should not be used as flashing unless it has been chemically stabilized so it will not deteriorate when exposed to sunlight (ultraviolet radiation). Asphalt-impregnated building paper (building felt) is not an acceptable flashing material. Adhered flashings must be held back from the face of the wall to avoid deterioration and staining caused by high temperatures.

INSTALLATION

Embedded flashing is typically used in drainage walls at the base, above all openings, at sills and shelf angles, and under copings. Continuous embedded flashing should be lapped at least 6 in. and sealed with an appropriate sealer. Discontinuous flashing should have the ends turned up at least 1 in. to form a dam. Dams prevent water collected on the flashing from draining off the ends of the flashing back into the wall system or into framing or mullions.

Embedded flashing should extend at least 8 in. vertically within the wall system; it should extend at least 1$^1/_2$ in. into the interior wythe and through the exterior wythe at least $^1/_4$ in. to form a drip. The drip minimizes possible staining. Sometimes, it may be necessary to avoid the drip, as with rough textured units and ribbed, scored, or fluted masonry units. The flashing must be carefully brought to the surface

of the recessed portion of the masonry. Plastic flashing is often exposed and cut off flush with the face of the masonry. If the flashing is recessed and does not reach the surface, water collected on it may be channeled by mortar under the flashing and back into the wall system.

Weep holes are required in the head joints of the course of masonry immediately above all embedded flashing. weep holes may be open head joints, holes formed with nylon rope or oiled rods, plastic or metal tubes, fibrous rope, or cotton sash cord. Open head joints are often fitted with vents or screens to keep out insects or rodents. Formed weep holes should have a minimum diameter of $^1/_4$ in.; tubes used for weep holes should have a minimum inside diameter of $^1/_4$ in. Weep holes are preferred as open head joints occurring no more than 32 in. on center, although in brick masonry it is generally recommended that they be spaced no more than 24 in. on center. If cord or rope is used, the material should be at least 16 in. long. Weep holes other than open head joints should be spaced no more than 16 in. on center.

Drainage within the wall system is critical for proper performance. Placing two to six inches of gravel or drainage material immediately above embedded flashing will help ensure proper drainage within the wall and effective channeling of water to the weep holes. The drainage material or pea gravel will act as a drainage field within the wall system and help keep mortar droppings from clogging the weep holes.

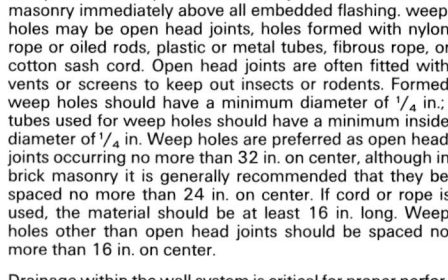

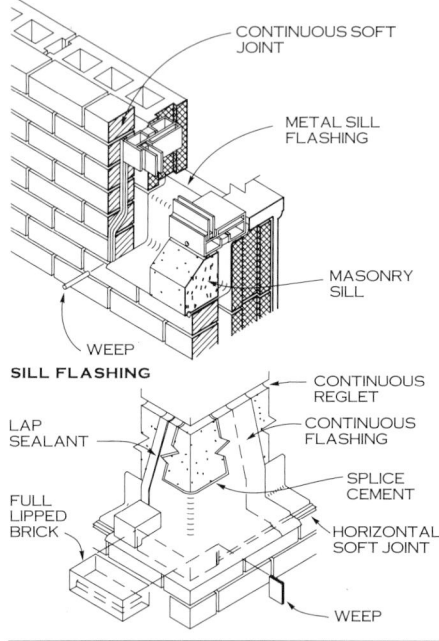

SILL FLASHING

OUTSIDE CORNER FLASHING

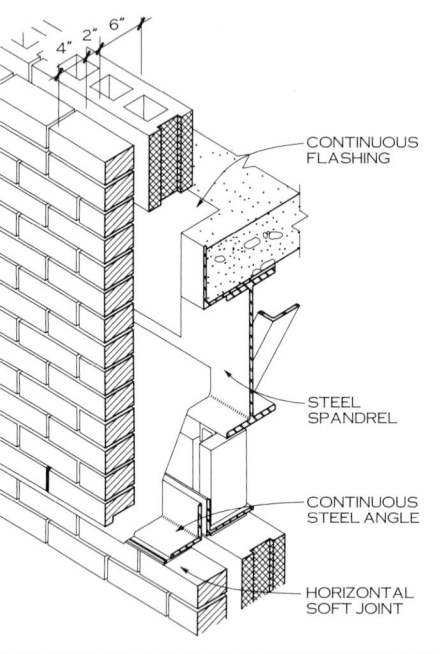

CAVITY WALL FLASHING

CAVITY WALL FLASHING

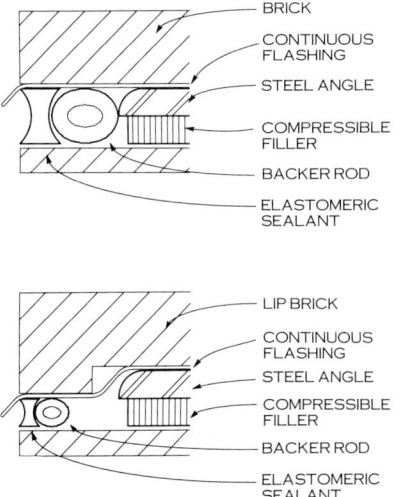

HORIZONTAL SOFT JOINT

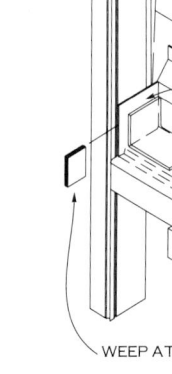

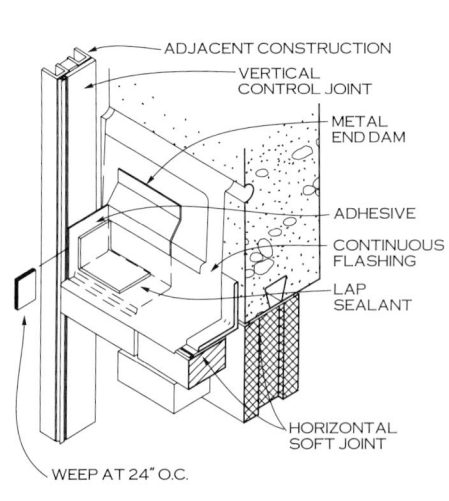

END DAM

HORIZONTAL SOFT JOINT AND
VERTICAL CONTROL JOINT

Theodore D. Sherman, AIA; Lev Zetlin Associates, Engineers and Designers; New York, New York
Brian E. Trimble, E.I.T.; Brick Institute of America; Reston, Virginia

 MASONRY ACCESSORIES

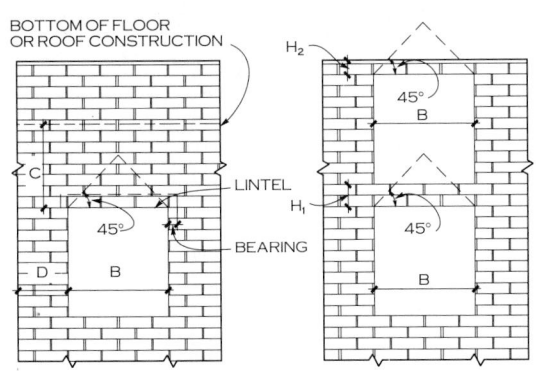

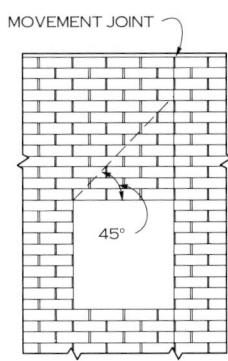

Simple lintel with arch action carries wall load only in triangle above opening: C ≥ B and D ≥ B

Simple lintel without arch action carries less wall load than triangle above opening: H₁ or H₂ < 0.6B

Lintel with uniform floor load carries both wall and floor loads in rectangle above opening: C < B

Lintel with concentrated load carries wall and portion of concentrated load distributed along length B₂.

Lintels at movement joints require special design considerations.

LINTEL LOADING CONDITIONS (CONSULT STRUCTURAL HANDBOOK FOR DESIGN FORMULAS)

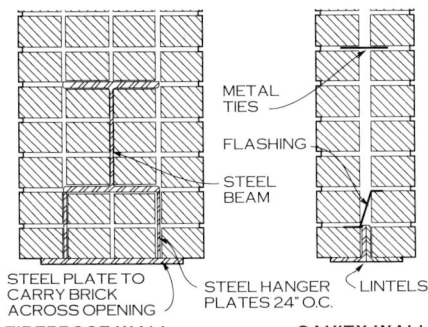

FIREPROOF WALL   **CAVITY WALL**

NOTE

Fireproof lintel for long spans. All steel members to be designed by structural engineer. Flashing details must be designed to suit job condition.

STEEL LINTEL DETAILS

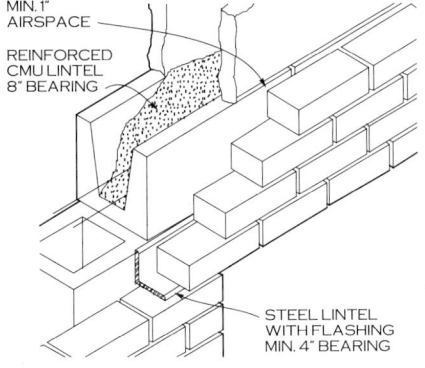

MASONRY LINTEL DETAIL

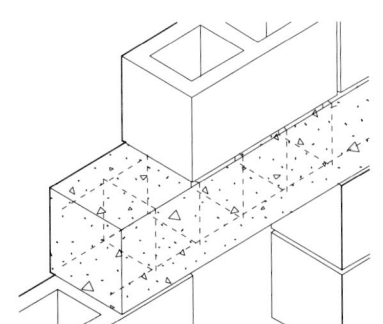

PRECAST CONCRETE LINTEL DETAIL

Grace S. Lee; Rippeteau Architects, PC; Washington, D.C.
Brian E. Trimble; Brick Institute of America; Reston, Virginia
Stephen S. Szoke, P.E.; National Concrete Masonry Association; Herndon, Virginia

ALLOWABLE UNIFORM SUPERIMPOSED LOAD (IN LB) PER LINEAR FOOT FOR STEEL ANGLE LINTELS

HORIZONTAL LEG	ANGLE SIZE	WEIGHT PER FT (LB)	SPAN (FT) (CENTER TO CENTER OF REQUIRED BEARING)									
			3	4	5	6	7	8	9	10	11	12
3 1/2	3 x 3 1/2 x 1/4	5.4	956	517	262	149	91	59				
	x 5/16	6.6	1166	637	323	184	113	73				
	3 1/2 x 3 1/2 x 1/4	5.8	1281	718	406	232	144	94	65			
	x 5/16	7.2	1589	891	507	290	179	118	80			
	4 x 3 1/2 x 1/4	6.2	1622	910	580	338	210	139	95	68		
	x 5/16	7.7	2110	1184	734	421	262	173	119	85	62	
	x 3/8	9.1	2434	1365	855	490	305	201	138	98	71	
	x 7/16	10.6	2760	1548	978	561	349	230	158	113	82	60
	5 x 3 1/2 x 1/4	7.0	2600	1460	932	636	398	264	184	132	97	73
	x 5/16	8.7	3087	1733	1106	765	486	323	224	161	119	89
	x 7/16	12.0	4224	2371	1513	1047	655	435	302	217	160	120
	6 x 3 1/2 x 1/4	7.9	3577	2009	1283	888	650	439	306	221	164	124
	x 5/16	9.8	4390	2465	1574	1090	798	538	375	271	201	151
	x 3/8	11.7	5200	2922	1865	1291	945	636	443	320	237	179

NOTE

Allowable loads to the left of the heavy line are governed by moment, and to the right by deflection. F_v = 36,000 psi. Maximum deflection 1/700. Consult structural engineer for long spans.

REQUIRED REINFORCING FOR SIMPLY SUPPORTED REINFORCED CONCRETE MASONRY LINTELS

TYPE OF LOAD	LINTEL SECTION NOMINAL SIZE (IN.)	REQUIRED REINFORCING CLEAR SPAN							
		3'-4"	4'-0"	4'-8"	5'-4"	6'-0"	6'-8"	7'-4"	8'-0"
Wall loads	6 x8	1 - #3	1 - #4	1 - #4	2 - #4	2 - #5			
	6 x 16					1 - #4	1 - #4	1 - #4	1 - #4
Floor and roof loads	6 x 16	1 - #4	1 - #4	2 - #3	1 - #5	2 - #4	2 - #4	2 - #5	2 - #5
Wall loads	8 x8	1 - #3	2 - #3	2 - #3	2 - #4	2 - #4	2 - #5	2 - #6	
	8 x 16							2 - #5	2 - #5
Floor and roof loads	8 x8	2 - #4							
	8 x 16	2 - #3	2 - #3	2 - #3	2 - #4	2 - #4	2 - #4	2 - #5	2 - #5

NOTES

1. Includes weight of lintel
2. Wall loads assumed to be 300 lb per linear ft
3. Floor and roof loads including wall loads assumed to be 1000 lb/linear ft
4. 8 in. lintels assumed to weigh 50 lb/ft
5. 16 in. lintels assumed to weigh 100 lb/ft

MAXIMUM DESIGN LOADS FOR PRECAST CONCRETE LINTELS (LB/LINEAR FT)

REINFORCEMENT	CLEAR SPAN											
	3'-4"	4'-0"	4'-8"	5'-4"	6'-0"	6'-8"	7'-4"	8'-0"	8'-8"	9'-4"	10'-0"	10'-8"
2 - #3	1585	1150	850	625	475	365	285	225	180	145	115	90
2 - #4	1855	1300	910	665	500	380	300	235	185	150	120	95
2 - #5	1825	1410	1005	725	535	410	315	250	195	155	125	100

NOTE

Lintel properties: width = 7 5/8 in., height = 7 5/8 in., weight = 60 lb/linear ft, f'c = 2500 psi

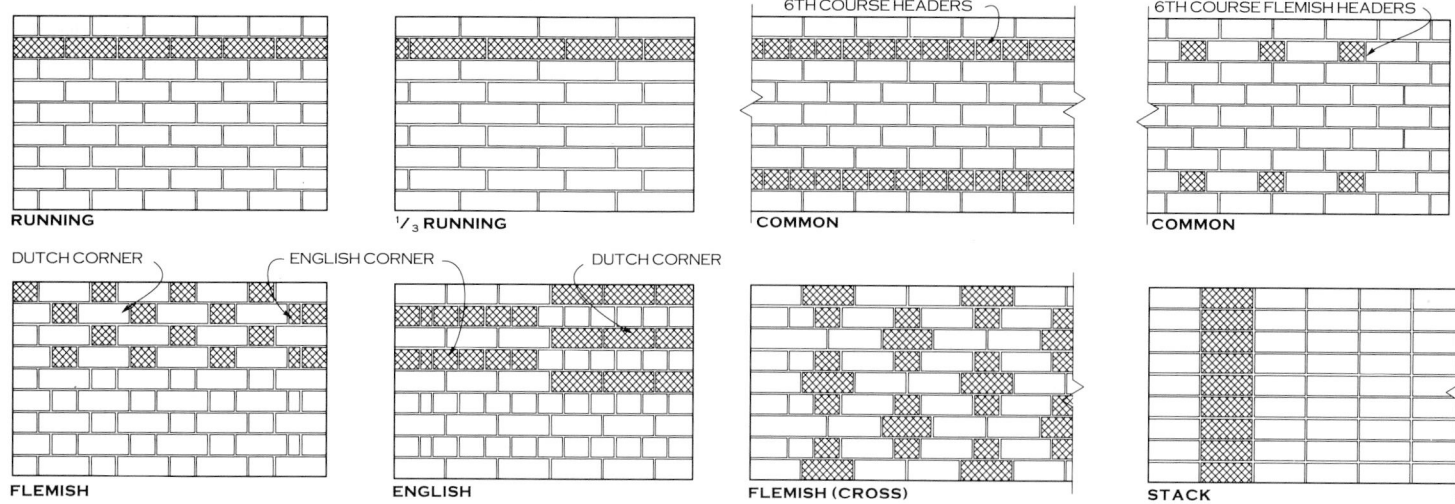

RUNNING   ¹/₃ RUNNING   COMMON (6TH COURSE HEADERS)   COMMON (6TH COURSE FLEMISH HEADERS)

FLEMISH (DUTCH CORNER, ENGLISH CORNER)   ENGLISH (DUTCH CORNER)   FLEMISH (CROSS)   STACK

BRICK BONDS

When a circular masonry wall is to be laid up in running bond, the projections of the corners of units beyond the face of the units on the courses above and below may need to be limited for aesthetic reasons. Generally, projections of approximately ¹/₈ in. for nominal 8 in. long units and ¹/₄ in. for nominal 16 in. long units are acceptable. If the wall surface is to be stuccoed or otherwise covered, projections of ¹/₂ to ³/₄ in. may not be objectionable. However, if it is desirable to obtain a smooth appearance for the curve or limit the shadows created by the projected corners, the projections should not exceed those indicated above. Projections of less than ¹/₈ in. are usually impractical because of construction tolerances.

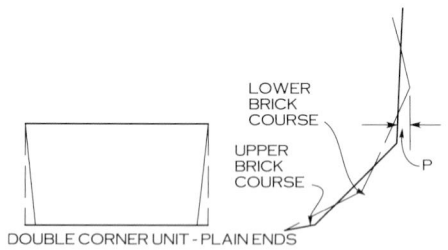

LOWER BRICK COURSE

UPPER BRICK COURSE

P

DOUBLE CORNER UNIT - PLAIN ENDS

RADIAL WALLS AND BRICK PROJECTIONS

MINIMUM RADII OF MASONRY

NOMINAL LENGTH	NOMINAL WIDTH (IN.)	³/₈ IN. EXTERIOR MORTAR JOINT			¹/₂ IN. EXTERIOR MORTAR JOINT		
		RADIUS OF WALL	NUMBER OF UNITS IN 360° WALL	PROJECTION OF UNIT (IN.)	RADIUS OF WALL	NUMBER OF UNITS IN 360° WALL	PROJECTION OF UNIT (IN.)
8 in. (uncut)	4	9'-9"	92	¹/₁₆	6'-6"	61	³/₃₂
	8	20'-4"	192	¹/₃₂	13'-7"	126	¹/₁₆
	12	31'-1"	293	¹/₃₂	20'-8"	195	¹/₃₂
16 in. (uncut)	4	19'-6"	92	¹/₈	13'-1"	61	⁷/₃₂
	8	40'-9"	192	¹/₁₆	27'-5"	128	³/₃₂
	12	62'-2"	293	¹/₁₆	41'-9"	195	¹/₁₆
8 in. (³/₄ in., cuts interior face, both ends)	4	1'-6"	14	⁷/₁₆	1'-4"	13	¹/₂
	8	8'-0"	26	⁷/₃₂	2'-9"	26	¹/₄
	12	4'-6"	42	⁵/₃₂	4'-3"	40	⁵/₃₂
16 in. (³/₄ in., cuts interior face, both ends)	4	2'-11"	14	⁷/₈	2'-9"	13	¹⁵/₁₆
	8	5'-11"	26	⁷/₁₆	5'-7"	26	¹/₂
	12	8'-11"	42	⁵/₁₆	8'-6"	40	⁵/₁₆

NOTE

Interior mortar joints maintained at approximately ¹/₈ in.

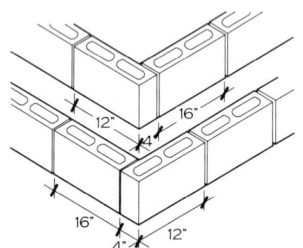

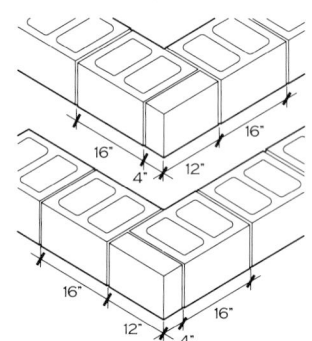

4 IN. WALL TO 4 IN. WALL

12 IN. WALL TO 12 IN. WALL

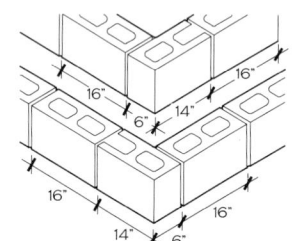
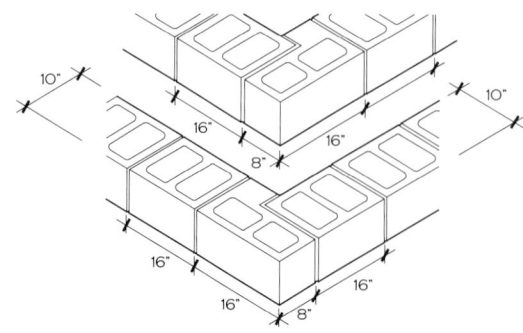

6 IN. WALL TO 6 IN. WALL

10 IN. WALL TO 10 IN. WALL

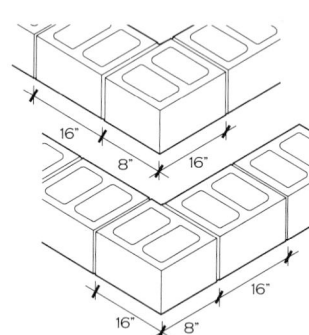
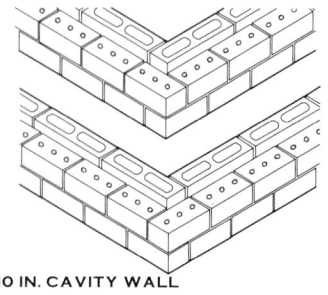

8 IN. WALL TO 8 IN. WALL

10 IN. CAVITY WALL

CORNER LAYOUT SHOWING ALTERNATING COURSES

A. Harris Lokmanhakim, AIA; Rippeteau Architects, PC; Washington, D.C.
Stephen S. Szoke, P.E.; National Concrete Masonry Association; Herndon, Virginia
Brian E. Trimble.; Brick Institute of America; Reston, Virginia

BRICK AND TILE CLASSIFICATION

Brick and tile are classified according to the specific location where they are used. Standard specifications have been developed to produce uniform requirements for brick. The American Society for Testing and Materials (ASTM) publishes the most widely accepted standards on brick. Standard specifications include strength, durability, and aesthetic requirements.

CLASSIFICATIONS

TYPE OF BRICK UNIT	ASTM DESIGNATION
Building brick	C 62
Facing brick	C 216
Hollow brick	C 652
Paving brick	C 902
Ceramic glazed brick	C 126
Thin brick veneer units	C 1088
Sewer and manhole brick	C 32
Chemical resistant brick	C 279
Industrial floor brick	C 410

TYPE OF TILE UNIT	
Structural clay load bearing tile	C 34
Structural clay non-load bearing tile	C 56
Structural clay facing tile	C 212
Structural clay non-load bearing screen tile	C 530
Ceramic glazed tile	C 126

GENERAL REQUIREMENTS

Terms used in each standard for classification may include exposure, appearance, physical properties, efflorescence, dimensional tolerances, distortion, chipping, core, and frogs. Bricks can be classified by use, grade, type, and/or class in most specifications. All options should be specified, as each ASTM standard has minimum requirements for grade and type that apply automatically if an option is omitted. If the desired requirements are not specified, a delivery may contain bricks unsuitable for the intended use.

EXPOSURE

Specific grades of brick are required to accommodate the various climates found in the United States and the differ-ent applications in which brick can be used. Bricks must meet a grade of SW, MW, or NW based on the weathering index and the exposure they will receive. The weathering index is the product of the average annual number of freezing cycle days and the average annual winter rainfall in inches (see map below). The exposure is related to whether the brick is used on a vertical or horizontal surface and whether the unit will be in contact with the earth (see table 3). A higher weathering index or a more severe exposure will require face brick to meet the SW requirements. The grade is typically based on physical properties of the brick. The grades for each specification are listed in table 2.

TABLE 2: GRADE REQUIREMENTS FOR FACE EXPOSURES*

	WEATHERING INDEX	
EXPOSURE	LESS THAN 50	50 AND GREATER
In vertical surfaces:		
In contact with earth	MW	SW
Not in contact with earth	MW	SW
In other than vertical surfaces:		
In contact with earth	SW	SW
Not in contact with earth	MW	SW

*See map below.

TABLE 3: EXPOSURE

ASTM STANDARD	MORE SEVERE EXPOSURE	LESS SEVERE EXPOSURE	
C 62 Grade	SW	MW	NW
C 216 Grade	SW	MW	
C 652 Grade	SW	MW	
C 902 Grade	SX	MX	NX
C 126[1]	—	—	
C1088 Grade	Exterior	Interior	
C 32 sewer[2]	SS	SM	—
Grade manhole	MS	MM	—

NOTES

1. No requirements for durability.
2. Based on durability and abrasion.

APPEARANCE

Brick types are related to the appearance of the unit, and specifically to limits on dimensional tolerances, distortion tolerances, and chippage. The brick type can be selected depending on whether a high degree of precision is necessary, a wider range of color or size is permitted, or a characteristic architectural effect is desired. The types of brick for each specification are listed in table 4.

TABLE 4: APPEARANCE

ASTM STANDARD	TIGHTER TOLERANCES		LOOSER TOLERANCES	
C 62	None			
C 216 Type	FBX		FBS	FBA
C 652 Type	HBX	HBS	HBB	HBA
C 902 application	PX		PS	PA
C 126 Grade	S		SS	—
C1088 Type	TBX		TBS	TBA
C 32 sewer	None			
manhole	None			

AESTHETICS AND SHAPES

Brick is readily available in many sizes, colors, textures, and shapes, all adaptable for virtually any style or expression. Brick's small module can be related to the scale of the wall, and its sizes can be combined to create different appearances and patterns. Sizes available are shown in table 1.

When specifying the size of units, dimensions should be listed in the following order: width by thickness by length. The size of the brick influences cost because larger units require fewer bricks, normally resulting in less labor. Specially shaped bricks are available to add interest to a wall, including water table bricks, radials, caps, copings, corners, and others. Consult the manufacturer for specific sizes and availability.

CORNER BRICK

RADIAL BRICK

COVE WATER TABLE

BULLNOSE WATER TABLE

BRICK SHAPES

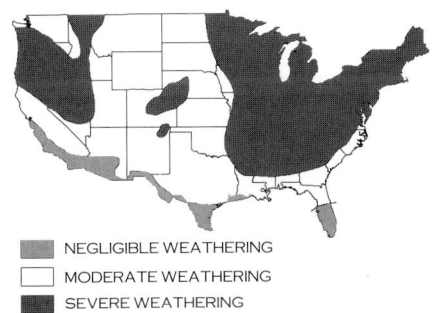

NEGLIGIBLE WEATHERING
MODERATE WEATHERING
SEVERE WEATHERING

U.S. WEATHERING INDEXES

TABLE 1: STANDARD NOMENCLATURE FOR BRICK SIZES

MODULAR BRICK SIZES

UNIT DESIGNATION	NOMINAL DIMENSIONS (IN.)			JOINT THICKNESS[1] (IN.)	SPECIFIED DIMENSIONS[2] (IN.)			VERTICAL COURSING
	W	H	D		W	H	L	
Modular	4	2²/₃	8	³/₈ ¹/₂	3⁵/₈ 3¹/₂	2¹/₄ 2¹/₄	7⁵/₈ 7¹/₂	3C = 8 in.
Engineer modular	4	3¹/₅	8	³/₈ ¹/₂	3⁵/₈ 3¹/₂	2³/₄ 2¹³/₁₆	7⁵/₈ 7¹/₂	5C = 16 in.
Closure modular	4	4	8	³/₈ ¹/₂	3⁵/₈ 3¹/₂	3⁵/₈ 3¹/₂	7⁵/₈ 7¹/₂	1C = 4 in.
Roman	4	2	12	³/₈ ¹/₂	3⁵/₈ 3¹/₂	1⁵/₈ 1¹/₂	11⁵/₈ 11¹/₂	2C = 4 in.
Norman	4	2²/₃	12	³/₈ ¹/₂	3⁵/₈ 3¹/₂	2¹/₄ 2¹/₄	11⁵/₈ 11¹/₂	3C = 8 in.
Engineer norman	4	3¹/₅	12	³/₈ ¹/₂	3⁵/₈ 3¹/₂	2³/₄ 2¹³/₁₆	11⁵/₈ 11¹/₂	5C = 16 in.
Utility	4	4	12	³/₈ ¹/₂	3⁵/₈ 3¹/₂	3⁵/₈ 3¹/₂	11⁵/₈ 11¹/₂	1C = 4 in.

NONMODULAR BRICK SIZES

Standard				³/₈ ¹/₂	3⁵/₈ 3¹/₂	2¹/₄	8	3C = 8 in.
Engineer standard				³/₈ ¹/₂	3⁵/₈ 3¹/₂	2³/₄ 2¹³/₁₆	8	5C = 16 in.
Closure standard				³/₈ ¹/₂	3⁵/₈ 3¹/₂	3⁵/₈ 3¹/₂	8	1C = 4 in.
King				³/₈	3 2³/₄	2³/₄ 2⁵/₈	9⁵/₈ 9⁵/₈	5C = 16 in.
Queen				³/₈	3 2³/₄	2³/₄ 2³/₄	8 8	5C = 16 in.

NOTES

1. Common joint sizes used with length and width dimensions. Actual joint thicknesses vary between bed joints and head joints.
2. Specified dimensions may vary within this range among manufacturers.

Grace S. Lee; Rippeteau Architects, PC; Washington, D.C.
Stephen S. Szoke, P.E.; National Concrete Masonry Association; Herndon, Virginia
Brian E. Trimble; Brick Institute of America; Reston, Virginia

GENERAL

Concrete masonry units (CMU) conform to ASTM standard specifications. The most common concrete masonry units used in building construction are load bearing units and concrete brick. Non-load bearing units may be specified for partitions and are commonly used for fire protection of steel columns and fire-rated partitions.

Type I or moisture-controlled units are specified to obtain a uniform degree of volume change due to moisture loss in a particular climate. The specification of Type I units facilitates the location of control joints. Type II or non-moisture controlled units may be more economical but will typically require closer spacing of control joints.

In addition to type, concrete bricks are specified by grade. Grade N is intended for use as architectural veneer and facing units in exterior walls and for use when high strength and resistance to moisture penetration and severe frost action are desired. Grade S is intended for general masonry where moderate strength and resistance to frost action and moisture penetration are required.

Concrete masonry units are available in a variety of colors, sizes, textures, configurations, and weights to accommodate design, detailing, and construction. Colors are now provided with lightfast metallic oxide pigments conforming to ASTM C 979. The textures may be smooth, ground, split, ribbed, or otherwise prepared to maximize design versatility. Smooth finishes and more color options are available with prefaced, "integral glazed" concrete masonry units.

Concrete masonry units are specified as width by height by length. The nominal dimensions are usually $3/_8$ in. larger than the actual unit dimensions. The most common nominal widths of concrete masonry units are 4 in., 6 in., 8 in., 10 in., and 12 in. The nominal heights are mostly 8 in. and 4 in., except concrete bricks are typically $2 \, 2/_3$ in. high. The nominal lengths are usually 16 or 18 in. Concrete brick length is usually 8 in. but is often 12 in. Lengths may be 18 or 24 in. in some regions. These longer lengths are usually more economical for placement.

VOLUMETRIC CHARACTERISTICS OF TYPICAL HOLLOW CONCRETE MASONRY UNITS ($7\,5/_8$ X $15\,5/_8$ IN.)

WIDTH (IN.)	GROSS VOLUME, CU IN. (CU FT)	MINIMUM THICKNESS SHELL (IN.)	MINIMUM THICKNESS WEB (IN.)	2 CORE UNITS PERCENT SOLID VOLUME	2 CORE UNITS EQUIVALENT SOLID THICKNESS (IN.)
$3\,5/_8$	432 (0.25)	0.75	0.75	64	2.32
		1.00	1.00	73	2.66
$5\,5/_8$	670 (0.388)	1.00	1.00	57	3.21
		1.12	1.00	61	3.43
		1.25	1.00	64	3.60
		1.37	1.12	68	3.82
$7\,5/_8$	908 (0.526)	1.25	1.00	53	4.04
		1.37	1.12	57	4.35
		1.50	1.12	59	4.50
$9\,5/_8$	1145 (0.664)	1.25	1.12	48	4.62
		1.37	1.12	51	4.91
		1.50	1.25	54	5.20
$11\,5/_8$	1385 (0.803)	1.25	1.12	44	5.12
		1.37	1.12	46	5.35
		1.50	1.25	49	5.70
		1.75	1.25	52	6.05

The weight of the units also varies. Depending on the aggregate used, concrete masonry units are typically made using concretes with densities ranging from 85 to 140 pcf. The lighter units tend to provide more fire resistance and have an improved noise reduction coefficient, and they often are more economical to place in the wall. Heavier units tend to provide increased compressive strength, better resistance to sound penetration, higher water penetration resistance, and greater thermal storage capabilities.

ASTM STANDARD SPECIFICATIONS

C 55—Concrete Brick

C 73—Calcium Silicate Face Brick (sand-lime brick)

C 90—Load Bearing Concrete Masonry Units

C 129—Non-load Bearing Concrete Masonry Units

C 139—Concrete Masonry Units for the Construction of Catch Basins and Manholes

C 744—Prefaced Concrete and Calcium Silicate Masonry Units

C 936—Solid Concrete Interlocking Paving Units

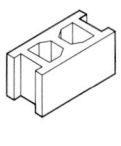
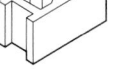
STRETCHER

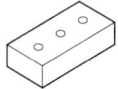
CORED

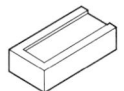
FROGGED

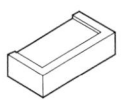
FROG OPEN IN REAR

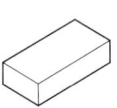
100% SOLID

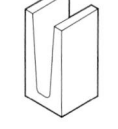
LINTEL

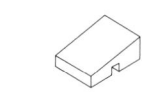
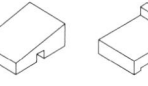
SILL

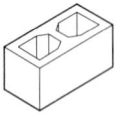
CORNER

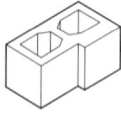
CORNER RETURN

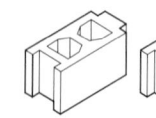
CONTROL JOINT

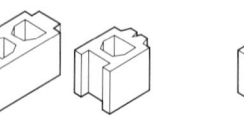

HEADER

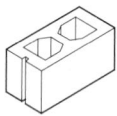
SASH

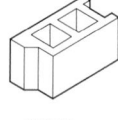
JAMB

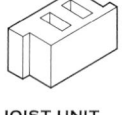
JOIST UNIT

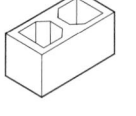
CLEANOUT UNIT

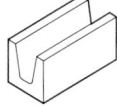

BOND BEAMS

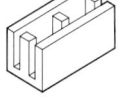
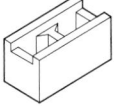
A-BLOCK BOND BEAM

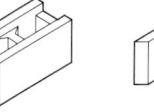
H-BLOCK BOND BEAM

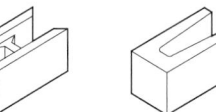
U-BLOCK - OPEN-END UNITS

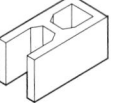
A-BLOCK

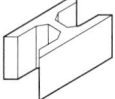

H-BLOCK

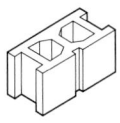
8 X 8 SCORED FACE

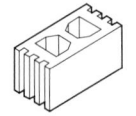
SPLIT FACE

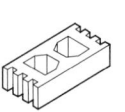
RIBBED OR SCORED

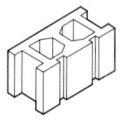
SPLIT RIBBED

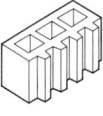
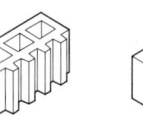
FLUTED

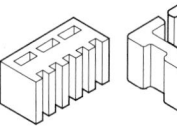
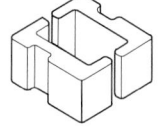
COLUMN

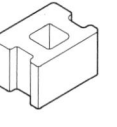
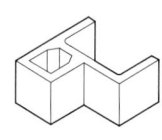
PILASTER INSERT

RIGID INSULATION

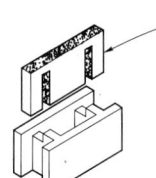
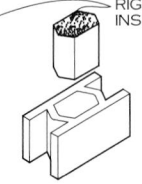
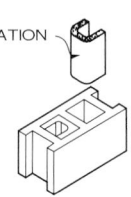
INSULATED BLOCKS

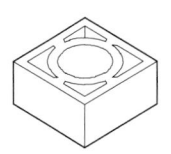
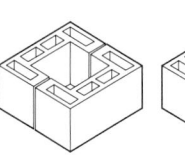
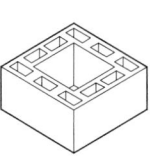
CHIMNEY UNITS

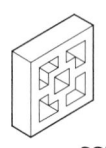

SCREEN

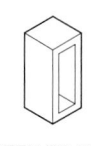
SCREEN OR VENT

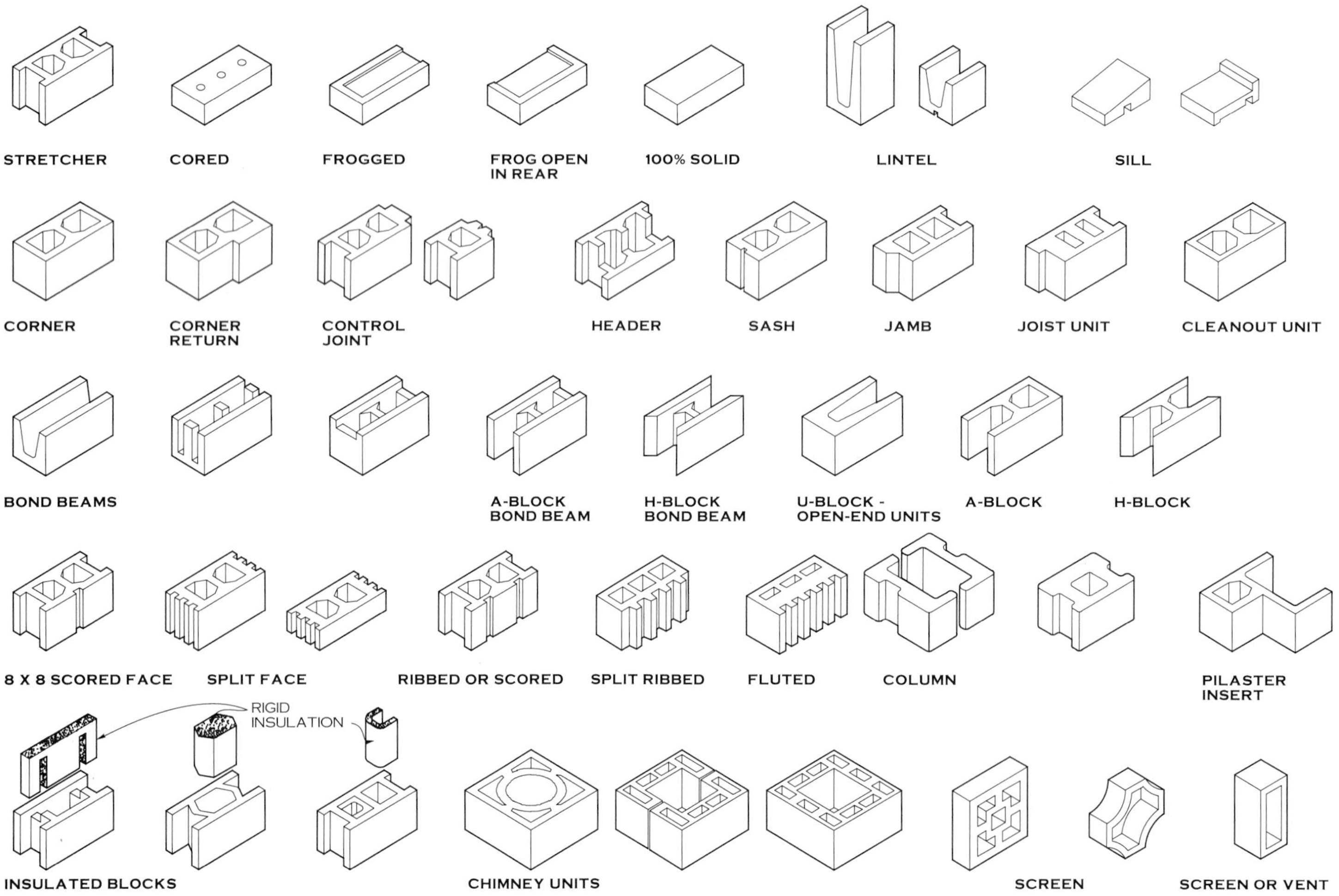

TYPICAL CONCRETE MASONRY UNIT SHAPES

Stephen S. Szoke, P.E.; National Concrete Masonry Association; Herndon, Virginia
Grace S. Lee; Rippeteau Architects, PC; Washington, D.C.

GENERAL

Masonry walls have long served as foundations for structures. Today, most masonry foundation walls consist of single wythe, hollow or solid masonry unit construction, depending on the required bearing capacity. The wall systems may be used as perimeter walls for slab-on-grade construction or to form crawl spaces or basements. The walls are reinforced as necessary to resist lateral loads. Generally, such reinforcement should be held as close to the interior face shell as possible, to provide the maximum tensile strength most economically.

Foundation systems, especially basement walls, need to do more than simply support the structure. They must protect against heat, insect infestation (particularly termites), fire, and penetration of water and soil gas.

Thermal protection may be provided with interior furring and batts or rigid board insulation, an exterior rigid board insulation and protection system, or with integral insulation strategies. The latter include foamed-in-place insulation, granular fill insulations, and premolded polystyrene inserts. Use of interior and exterior insulation rather than premolded inserts allows reinforcing steel to be installed more easily.

Optimal insect protection can be achieved using interior or integral insulation and a termite shield. Metal flashing materials often perform well as termite shields. For exterior insulation strategies in locations where termites are a concern, the termite shield must extend over the exterior insulation.

Waterproofing and dampproofing are specified by building codes, as discussed in chapter 7. Generally, waterproofing makes the foundation or basement wall resistant to air infiltration and thereby resistant to soil gases such as radon. Typical waterproofing consists of a minimum $3/4$ in. coat of cement stucco parging and an appropriate liquid-applied membrane, but some liquid-applied membranes alone or combined with built-up membranes are acceptable. Surface-bonding mortar mixes are also effective for resisting water and soil-gas penetration. A good perimeter drainage system in contact with open air or connected to a sump pit should be used for effective drainage.

If radon is a major concern, the top course of the masonry and the course of masonry at or below the slab should be constructed of 100% solid units or hollow units fully filled with grout. French drains (drainage channels at the interfaces of foundation walls and floor slabs), which often are used to collect and drain condensation moisture in basements, should be avoided in areas where soil-gas entry is a concern.

Architectural masonry units may be used to improve the appearance of foundation walls, often in the above-grade portion of the walls. Masonry units with architectural finishes facing the interior can be used for economical construction of finished basement space.

Masonry easily accommodates any floor plan, and returns and corners increase the structural performance of the wall for lateral load resistance. Returns and corners that support porches, fireplaces, and the like may also serve as wine cellars. Returns for window wells permit an increase in daylighting, making below-grade areas more attractive as habitable space.

THICKNESS OF FOUNDATION WALLS

FOUNDATION WALL CONSTRUCTION	NOMINAL THICKNESS (IN.)	MAXIMUM DEPTH OF UNBALANCED FILL (FT)
Masonry of hollow units, ungrouted	8	5
	10	6
	12	7
Masonry of solid units	8	5
	10	7
	12	7
Masonry of hollow or solid units, fully grouted	8	7
	10	8
	12	8

NOTE

Drainage must be provided on surface and below grade to remove ground water from foundation wall. The backfill must be granular and soil conditions nonexpansive.

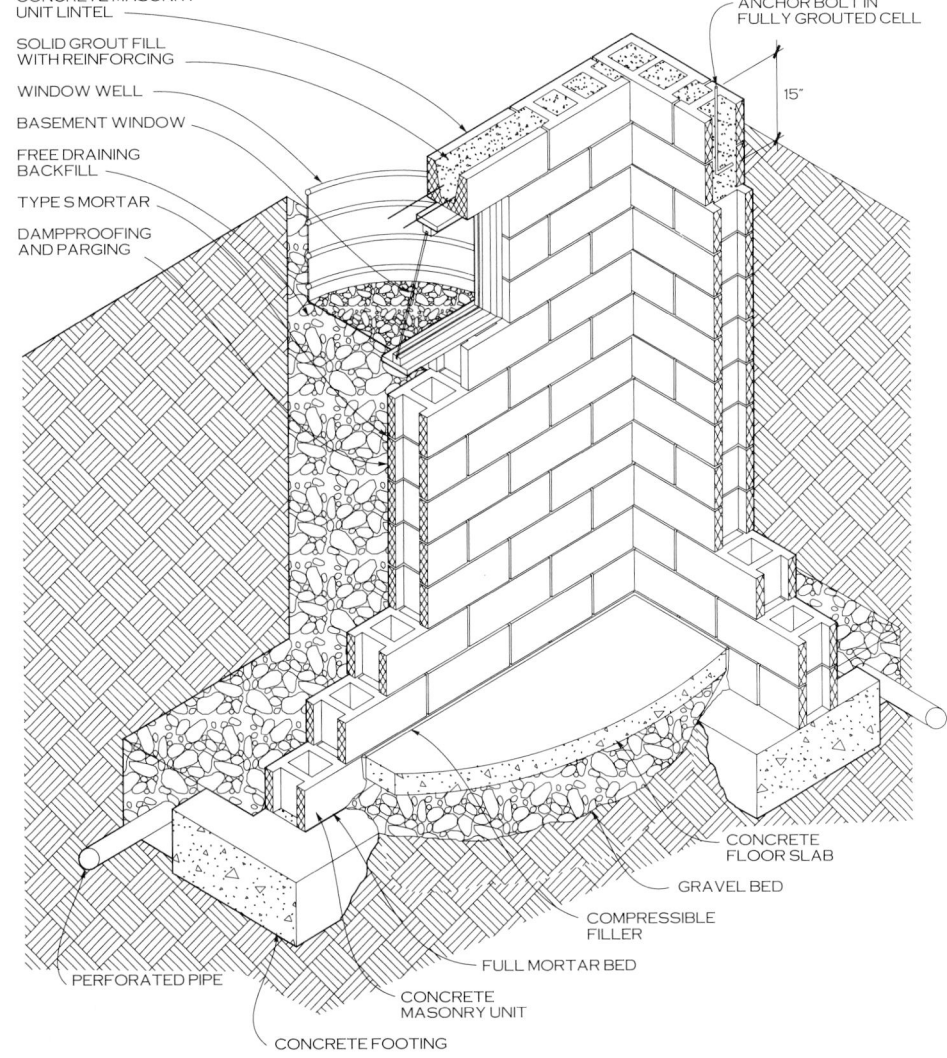

CONCRETE MASONRY UNIT LINTEL
SOLID GROUT FILL WITH REINFORCING
WINDOW WELL
BASEMENT WINDOW
FREE DRAINING BACKFILL
TYPE S MORTAR
DAMPPROOFING AND PARGING
ANCHOR BOLT IN FULLY GROUTED CELL
15"
CONCRETE FLOOR SLAB
GRAVEL BED
COMPRESSIBLE FILLER
FULL MORTAR BED
CONCRETE MASONRY UNIT
PERFORATED PIPE
CONCRETE FOOTING

TYPICAL FOUNDATION WALL

Grace S. Lee; Rippeteau Architects, PC; Washington, D.C.
Stephen S. Szoke, P.E.; National Concrete Masonry Association; Herndon, Virginia

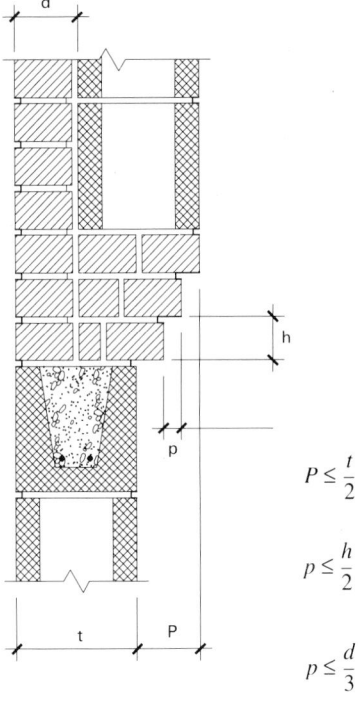

$$P \leq \frac{t}{2}$$

$$p \leq \frac{h}{2}$$

$$p \leq \frac{d}{3}$$

Where:

P = allowable total horizontal projection of corbeling

p = allowable projection of one unit

t = nominal wall thickness (actual thickness plus the thickness of one mortar joint)

h = nominal unit height (actual height plus the thickness of one mortar joint)

d = nominal unit bed depth (actual bed depth plus the thickness of one mortar joint)

NOTE

Corbeling is used to increase wall thickness to suit bearing requirements above foundation. Corbeling may be equal on both sides of the wall.

LIMITATIONS ON CORBELING

UNIT MASONRY

NOTE

S = spacing of vertical reinforcing bars

B = bar size

H = height of backfill

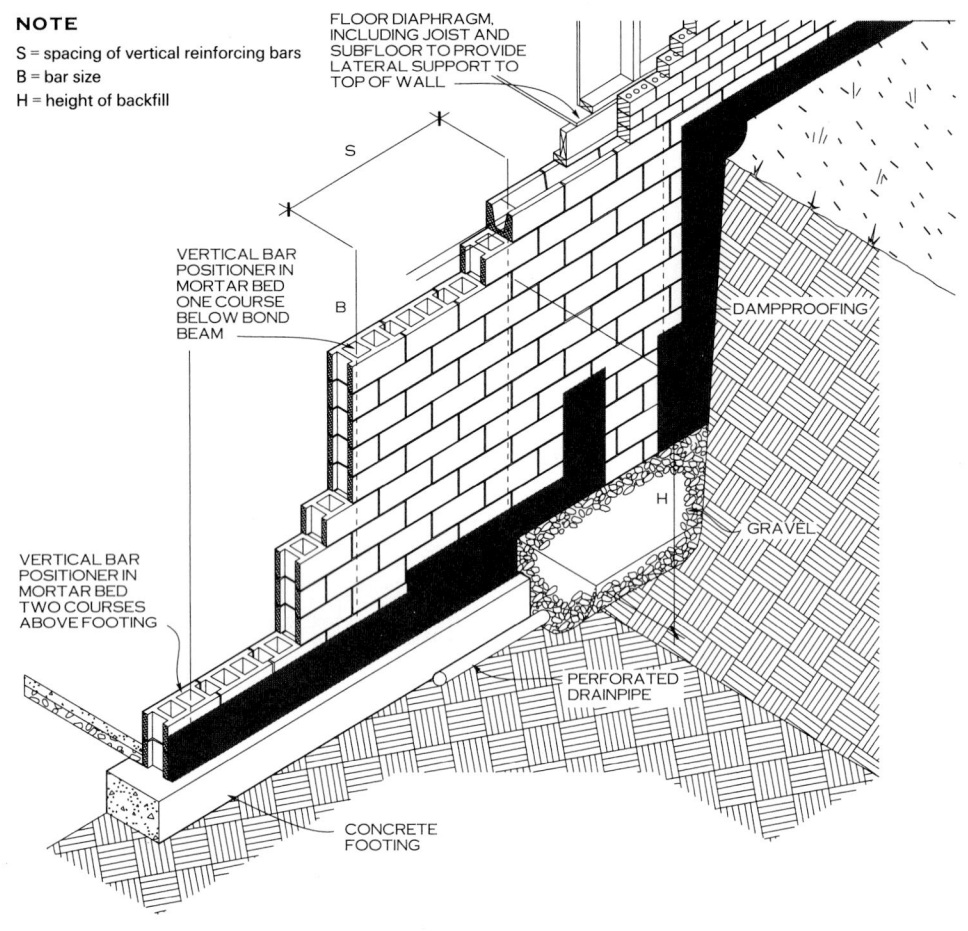

FLOOR DIAPHRAGM, INCLUDING JOIST AND SUBFLOOR TO PROVIDE LATERAL SUPPORT TO TOP OF WALL

VERTICAL BAR POSITIONER IN MORTAR BED ONE COURSE BELOW BOND BEAM

VERTICAL BAR POSITIONER IN MORTAR BED TWO COURSES ABOVE FOOTING

DAMPPROOFING

GRAVEL

PERFORATED DRAINPIPE

CONCRETE FOOTING

FOUNDATION WALL REINFORCEMENT

VERTICAL REINFORCEMENT

BAR SIZE AND MAXIMUM BAR SPACING

	HEIGHT OF BACKFILL, H				
	8'	7'	6'	5'	4'
Bar size, B	#6	#6	#5	#5	#4
Spacing, S	48"	56"	64"	72"	72"

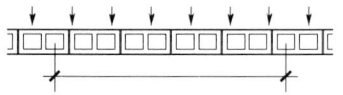

HORIZONTAL JOINT REINFORCEMENT

MORTAR JOINT	HEIGHT OF BACKFILL, H				
	8'	7'	6'	5'	4'
13	—	—	—	—	—
12	—	—	—	—	—
11	8 ga.	9 ga.	9 ga.	9 ga.	9 ga.
10	—	—	—	—	—
9	8 ga.	9 ga.	9 ga.	9 ga.	—
8	—	—	—	—	9 ga.
7	8 ga.	9 ga.	9 ga.	9 ga.	—
6	—	—	—	—	—
5	8 ga.	9 ga.	9 ga.	9 ga.	—
4		9 ga.	9 ga.	9 ga.	9 ga.
3	8 ga.	9 ga.	9 ga.	9 ga.	9 ga.
2	—	—	—	—	
1	—	—	—	—	

NOTES

1. The empirical design method of the Building Code Requirements for Masonry Structures, ACI 530/ASCE 5, chapter 9, allows up to 5 ft of backfill on an 8 in. nonreinforced concrete masonry wall.

2. As an alternate, 9 gauge joint reinforcement placed in joints numbers 3, 4, 5, 7, 8, and 11 may be used.

VERTICAL REINFORCEMENT SPACING

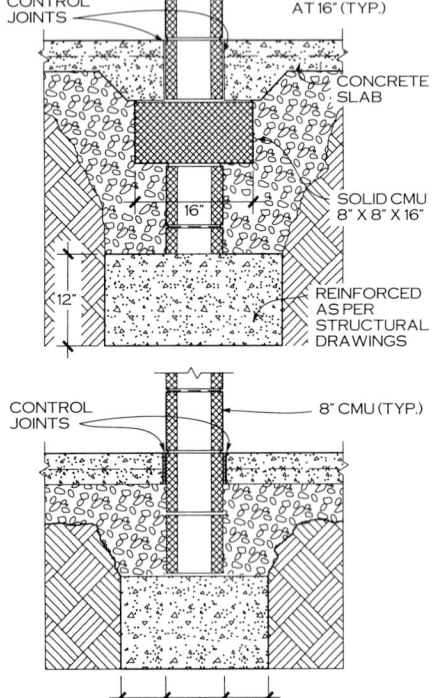

8" CMU (TYP.)

CONTROL JOINTS

JOINT REINFORCEMENT AT 16" (TYP.)

CONCRETE SLAB

SOLID CMU 8" X 8" X 16"

REINFORCED AS PER STRUCTURAL DRAWINGS

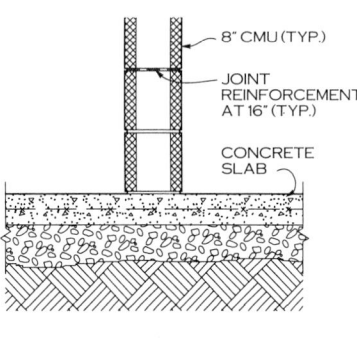

8" CMU (TYP.)

JOINT REINFORCEMENT AT 16" (TYP.)

CONCRETE SLAB

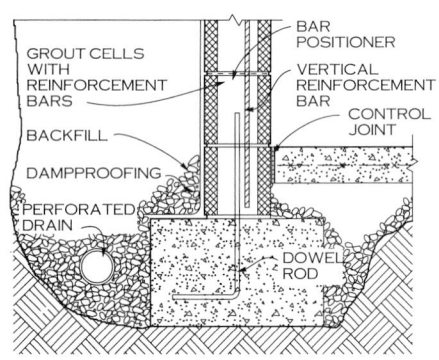

BAR POSITIONER

GROUT CELLS WITH REINFORCEMENT BARS

VERTICAL REINFORCEMENT BAR

BACKFILL

CONTROL JOINT

DAMPPROOFING

PERFORATED DRAIN

DOWEL ROD

CONTROL JOINTS

8" CMU (TYP.)

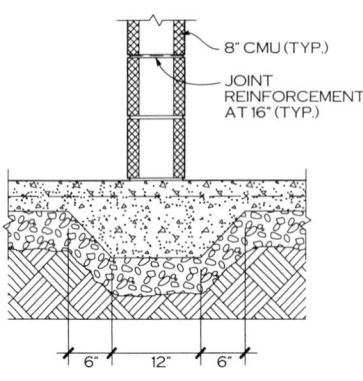

8" CMU (TYP.)

JOINT REINFORCEMENT AT 16" (TYP.)

DOWELED FOOTING DETAIL

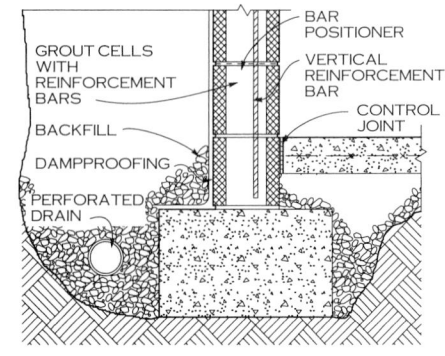

GROUT CELLS WITH REINFORCEMENT BARS

BAR POSITIONER

VERTICAL REINFORCEMENT BAR

BACKFILL

CONTROL JOINT

DAMPPROOFING

PERFORATED DRAIN

WALL FOUNDATION FOR INTERIOR BEARING WALLS

WALL FOUNDATION FOR NON-BEARING OR BEARING INTERIOR WALLS

REINFORCED FOUNDATION WALL DETAIL

Grace S. Lee; Rippeteau Architects, PC; Washington, D.C.

Stephen S. Szoke, P.E.; National Concrete Masonry Association; Herndon, Virginia

UNIT MASONRY

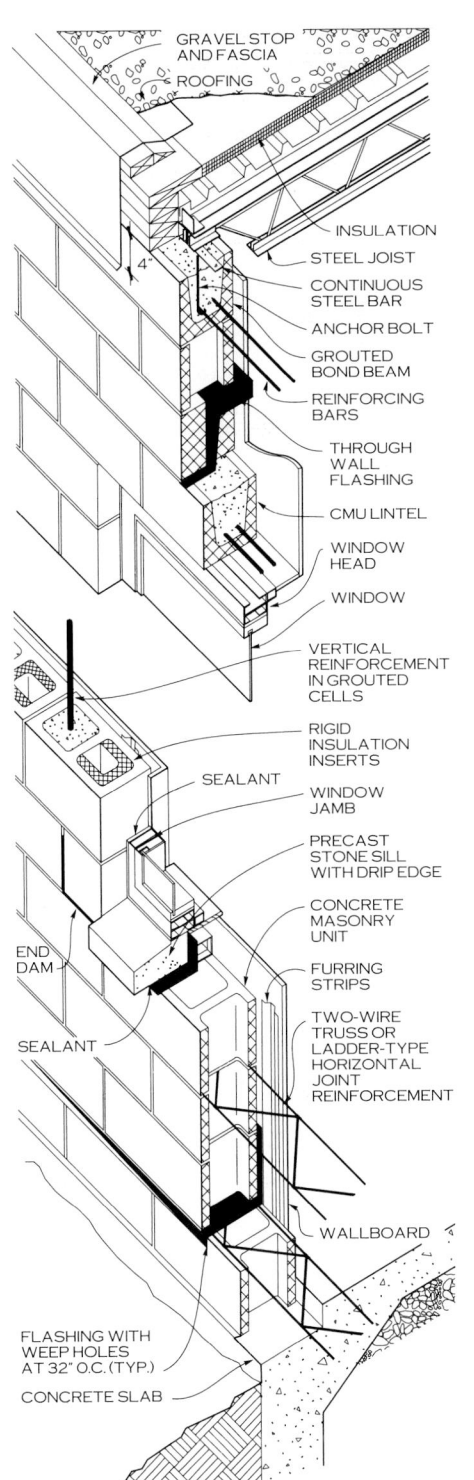

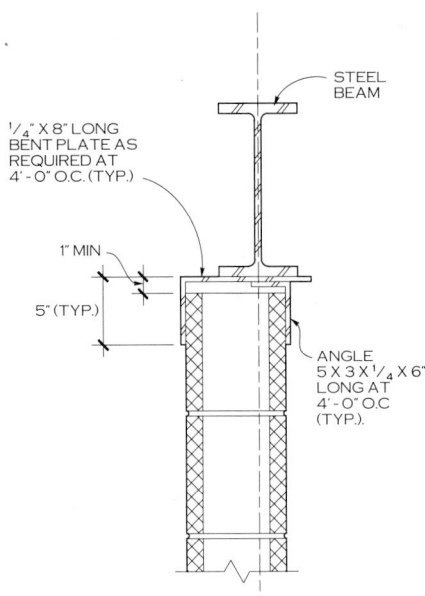

HORIZONTAL SUPPORT FOR NON-LOAD BEARING WALLS — STEEL FRAME

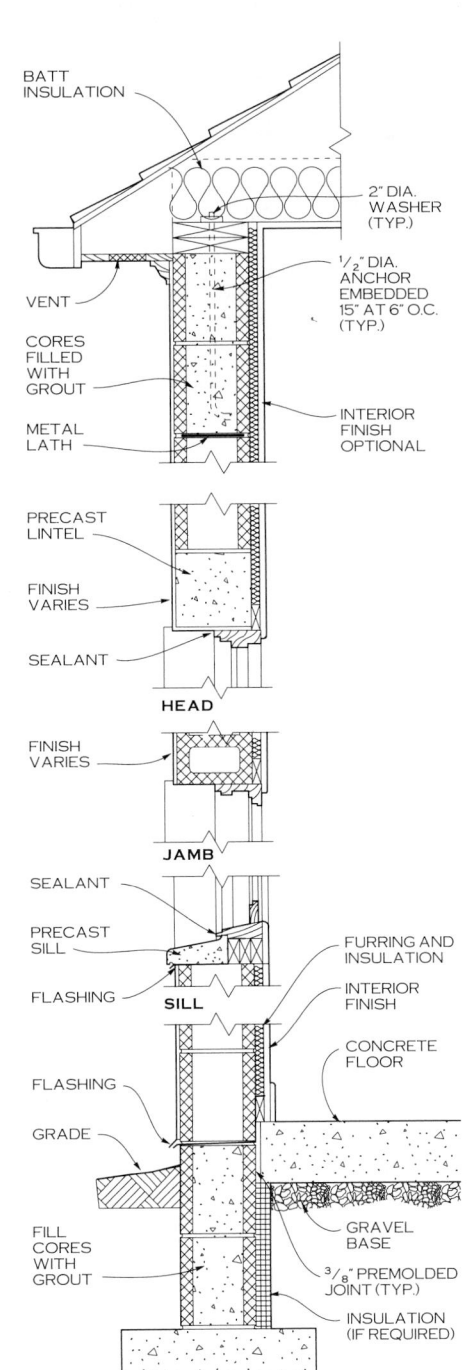

HEAD

JAMB

SILL

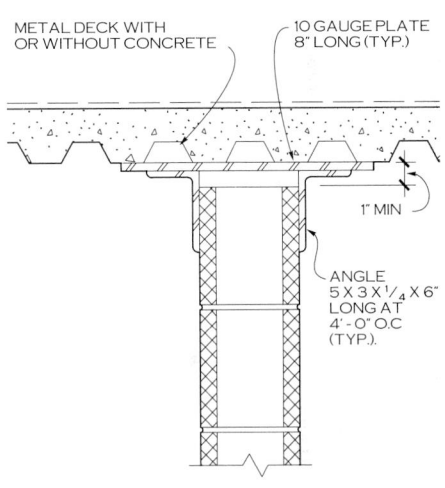

HORIZONTAL SUPPORT FOR NON-LOAD BEARING WALLS — METAL DECK

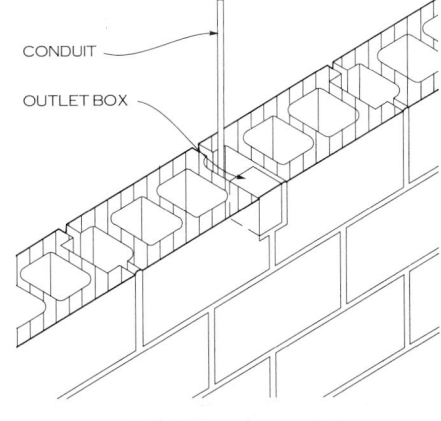

ELECTRICAL OUTLET BOX IN CMU WALL

SINGLE WYTHE MASONRY WALL WITH STEEL FRAME

SINGLE WYTHE MASONRY WALL WITH WOOD FRAME

SINGLE WYTHE MASONRY

Single wythe masonry wall construction is common for many applications, both load bearing and non-load bearing and interior and exterior walls. These systems are frequently used as interior partitions for fire protection.

Exterior single wythe walls may be integrally insulated with granular fill insulation, foamed-in-place insulation, or site installed or factory installed molded polystyrene inserts. Single wythe walls may also be insulated on the interior or exterior. The insulation may be adhered or mechanically fastened directly to the masonry, or it may be installed in conjunction with conventional furring or studding systems. The benefits of thermal mass are generally optimized with integral and exterior insulation strategies.

When single wythe walls are used as exterior walls and a high degree of water penetration resistance is required, the use of integral water repellents; exterior coatings, sealers, or finishes; or both may be required for concrete masonry construction. Clay masonry does not require these treatments.

Grace S. Lee; Rippeteau Architects, PC; Washington, D.C.
Stephen S. Szoke, P.E.; National Concrete Masonry Association; Herndon, Virginia
Brian E. Trimble; Brick Institute of America; Reston, Virginia

UNIT MASONRY

GENERAL

Design of multistory bearing wall buildings is based on combined structural action of the floor and roof system with the masonry walls. Floors carry the vertical loads and, acting as diaphragms, also distribute lateral loads to the walls. In masonry bearing wall buildings, lateral forces from winds or earthquakes are usually resisted by shear walls parallel to the direction of the lateral force. By their shearing and flexural resistance, these walls transfer lateral forces to the foundation.

The action of roof and floor diaphragms affects the distribution of lateral forces to the shear walls. Diaphragms are classified into three groups: rigid, semirigid (or semiflexible), and flexible. In design, the rigid diaphragm is assumed to distribute horizontal forces to vertical shear walls in proportion to their relative rigidities (longer or thicker walls being more rigid than shorter or thinner walls). More complex design approaches may consider the diaphragms to be semirigid or flexible. The distribution of loads in these more complex designs is similar to continuous beam design and design based on tributary areas, respectively.

For the diaphragms to be effective, there must be adequate connections between the roof and floor systems and the masonry walls. In many instances, adequate connection is achieved with the walls supported on masonry bond beams. Horizontal members (roofs and floors) are often connected to the walls with reinforcing steel. Adequate connections may be reinforcing steel into bond beams or may be coordinated with the masonry wall reinforcement. Connections will vary with the requirement to resist loads.

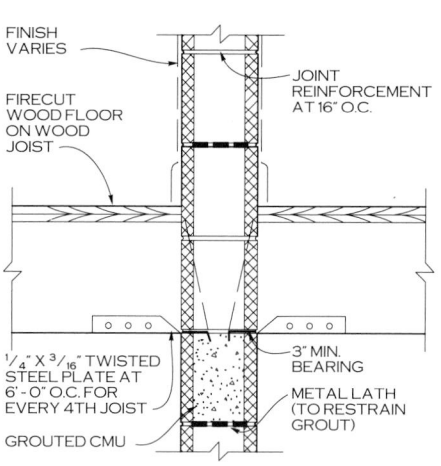

CMU WALL TO WOOD JOIST ANCHORAGE

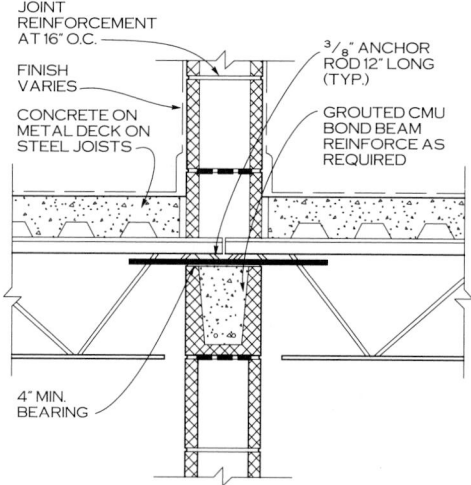

CMU WALL TO STEEL JOIST ANCHORAGE

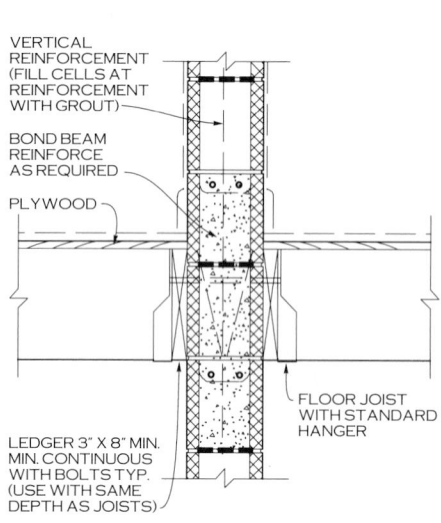

INTERIOR WALL TO JOIST ANCHORAGE

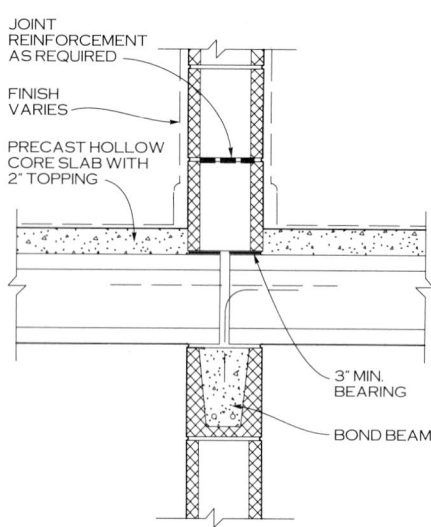

CMU WALL TO CONCRETE JOIST ANCHORAGE

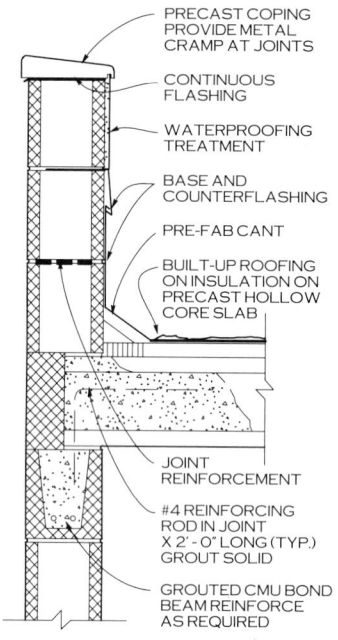

CMU PARAPET TO CONCRETE ROOF ANCHORAGE

WALL ANCHORAGE DETAILS

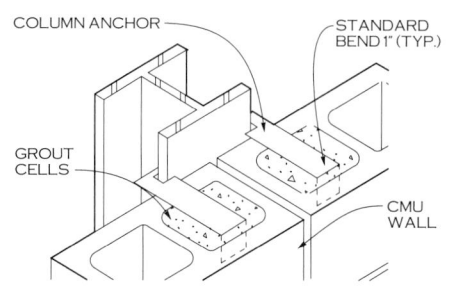

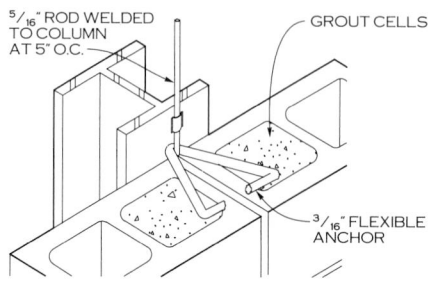

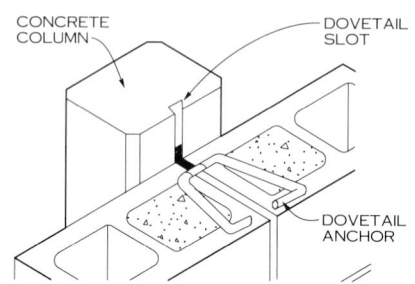

WALL TO COLUMN ANCHORAGE DETAILS

Grace S. Lee; Rippeteau Architects, PC; Washington, D.C.
Stephen S. Szoke, P.E.; National Concrete Masonry Association; Herndon, Virginia
Brian E. Trimble; Brick Institute of America; Reston, Virginia

 UNIT MASONRY

REINFORCEMENT

In many applications, single wythe walls are reinforced. The term *partially reinforced* is erroneous. Reinforcement schedules are designed for a particular application, and all the required reinforcement is necessary.

Walls are often partially grouted, that is, only the cells or cavities of the wall containing reinforcement are grouted. When walls are partially grouted, special units or construction fabric are used for vertical containment of the grout. Horizontal containment is usually provided by mortaring the webs of the masonry units. When steel placement is frequent, it may become economical or necessary to fully grout the walls.

Structural components of a building using reinforced masonry combine the tensile strength of reinforcement with the compressive strength of the masonry to resist design loads. Walls, columns, pilasters, and beams are designed to resist dead, live, wind, seismic, and lateral earth pressures using reinforced masonry. The benefits of incorporating reinforcement are improved ductility, structural integrity, and resistance to flexural and shear stresses. Reinforced masonry walls are extensively used for warehouses, institutional buildings, retaining walls, shear walls, basement walls, and load bearing walls, particularly in multistory hotels and apartment buildings. Reinforced masonry provides economical construction, especially when a high degree of resistance to lateral loads is necessary.

Seismic performance categories A and B require no special provisions. In many instances, the wind loads will govern the minimum reinforcing levels in seismic performance category C and above.

For designs in seismic performance category C, vertical reinforcement of at least 0.20 in. in cross-sectional areas shall be provided continuously from support to support at each corner, at each side of each opening, and at the ends of walls. Horizontal reinforcement of not less than 0.20 in. shall be provided at the bottom and top of all openings and extend not less than 24 in. nor less than 40 bar diameters past the opening. Horizontal reinforcement should be installed continuously at structurally connected roof and floor levels, at the tops of walls, and at the bottom of the wall or at the top of the foundation; maximum spacing is 10 ft unless uniformly distributed joint reinforcement is provided.

For designs in seismic performance categories D and E, walls shall be reinforced both vertically and horizontally. Requirements in addition to those for seismic performance category C include that spacing shall not exceed 4 ft, except for designs using moment resisting space frames, where the spacing of principal reinforcement shall not exceed 2 ft. Also, the diameter of the reinforcement shall not be less than $3/8$ in., except for joint reinforcement.

STANDARD MATERIALS SELECTION FOR REINFORCED MASONRY

MASONRY UNITS		MORTAR AND GROUT		REINFORCEMENT	
ASTM C 90	Load bearing Concrete Masonry Units	ASTM C 270	Mortar for Unit Masonry Construction	ASTM A 82	Steel Wire, Plain
ASTM C 216	Facing Brick (solid masonry units made from clay or shales)	ASTM C 476	Grout for Masonry	ASTM A 615	Deformed and Plain Billet-Steel Bars
ASTM C 652	Hollow Brick (hollow masonry units made from clay or shale)			ASTM A 616	Rail-Steel Deformed and Plain Bars
				ASTM A 706	Low-Alloy Steel Deformed Bars
				UBC 24-15	Joint Reinforcement for Masonry

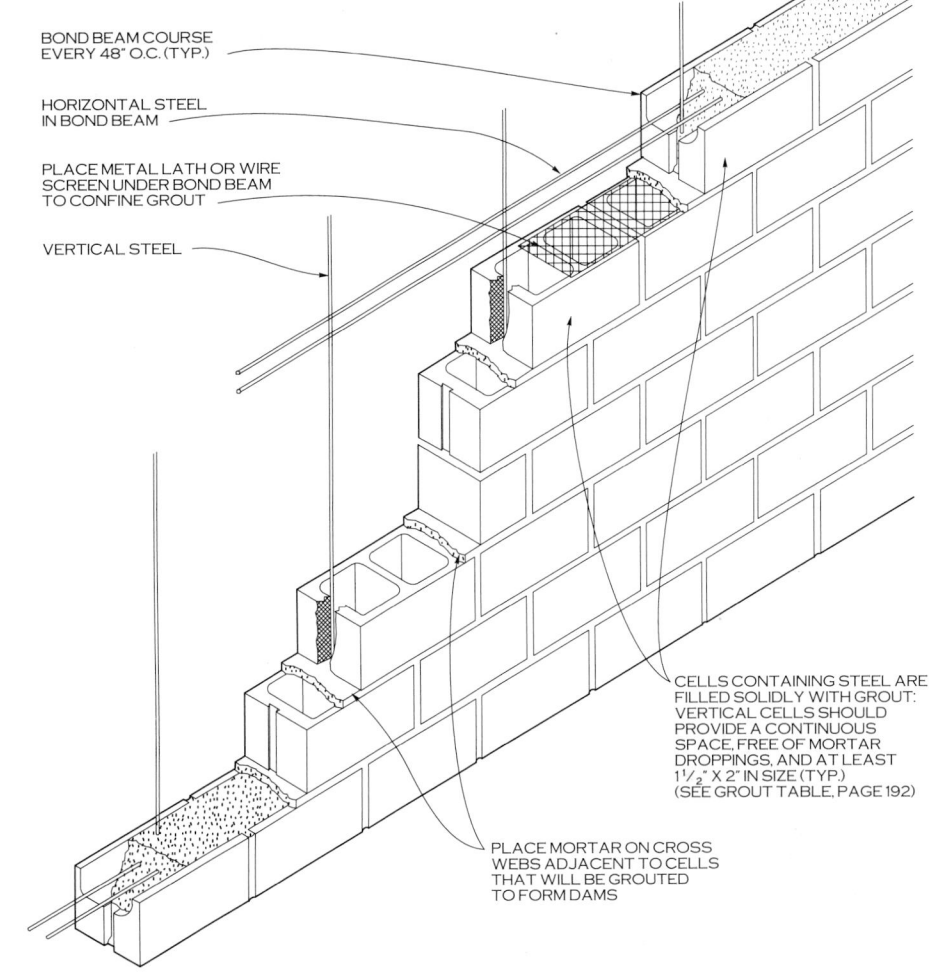

BOND BEAM COURSE EVERY 48" O.C. (TYP.)

HORIZONTAL STEEL IN BOND BEAM

PLACE METAL LATH OR WIRE SCREEN UNDER BOND BEAM TO CONFINE GROUT

VERTICAL STEEL

CELLS CONTAINING STEEL ARE FILLED SOLIDLY WITH GROUT: VERTICAL CELLS SHOULD PROVIDE A CONTINUOUS SPACE, FREE OF MORTAR DROPPINGS, AND AT LEAST $1\frac{1}{2}$" X 2" IN SIZE (TYP.) (SEE GROUT TABLE, PAGE 192)

PLACE MORTAR ON CROSS WEBS ADJACENT TO CELLS THAT WILL BE GROUTED TO FORM DAMS

METHODS OF REINFORCING

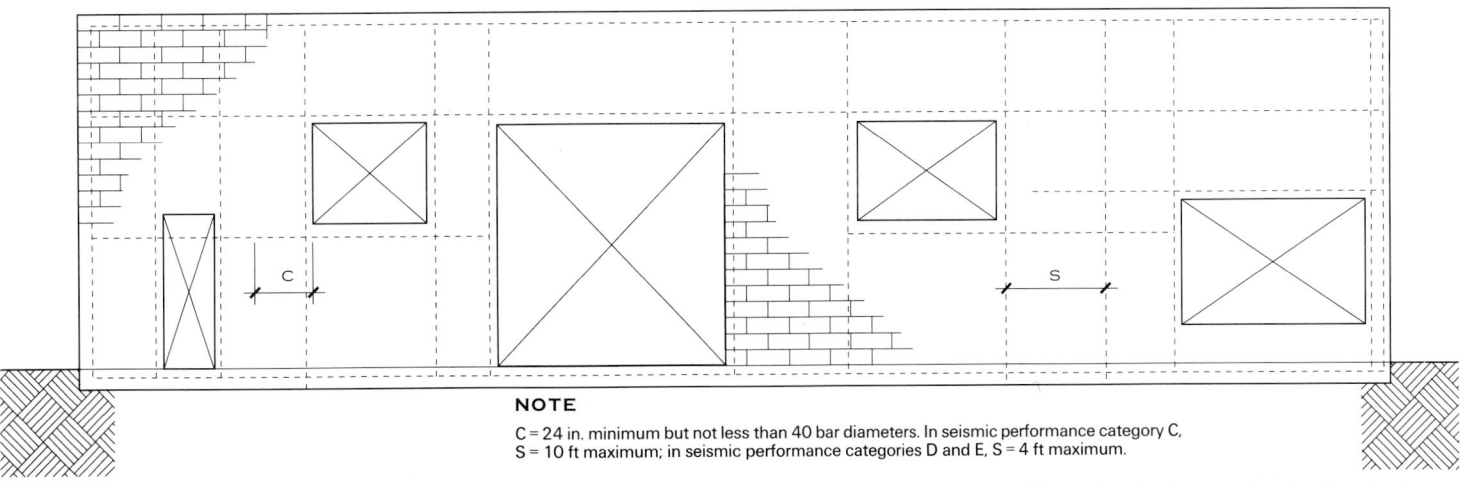

NOTE

C = 24 in. minimum but not less than 40 bar diameters. In seismic performance category C,
S = 10 ft maximum; in seismic performance categories D and E, S = 4 ft maximum.

REINFORCED LOAD BEARING BRICK OR CMU WALLS

Grace S. Lee; Rippeteau Architects, PC; Washington, D.C.
Stephen S. Szoke, P.E.; National Concrete Masonry Association; Herndon, Virginia
Brian E. Trimble ; Brick Institute of America; Reston, Virginia

MULTI-WYTHE MASONRY

Multi-wythe masonry construction is common for many applications, both load bearing and non-load bearing and for interior and exterior walls. These systems are frequently used as exterior walls or other applications when exposed architectural masonry units are required on one or both sides of the masonry. Such walls are constructed with full collar joints between wythes of masonry. The most common multi-wythe wall is the composite wall, which consists of a clay brick wythe and a concrete masonry wythe with a 3/4 in. collar joint, and brick headers or anchors. The collar joint is often difficult to fill and may be filled by parging the backup or by grouting. Generally the method of filling the joint should not be specified. The mason should be permitted to use the method that is most ef-

fective based on the talent available, the wall configuration, and the construction sequence. Often a single wythe of the wall might be reinforced. See the section on single wythe walls for a discussion of reinforced masonry. In multi-wythe construction the collar joint may contain reinforcement. If this is so, the collar joint width must be increased to provide adequate coverage for the reinforcement. The diameter of the reinforcement should not exceed half the collar joint thickness. When fine grout is used there must be at least 1/4 in. between the reinforcement and the masonry. When coarse grout is used, the space must be at least 1/2 in.

Multi-wythe walls may be constructed as partially grouted walls, using cavity wall or multi-wythe wall construction.

For this type of wall, the grout is contained horizontally with building fabric and vertically with dams. The dams are typically masonry units placed within the cavity. In partially grouted hollow wall construction, flashing may be necessary at horizontal interruptions in the cavity.

Insulation for exterior walls may be integral in a wythe of masonry or may be on the exterior of the wall, but it is usually on the interior. The insulation may be adhered or mechanically fastened directly to the masonry, or the insulation system may be part of a conventional furring or studding system. The benefits of thermal mass are generally optimized with integral and exterior insulation strategies.

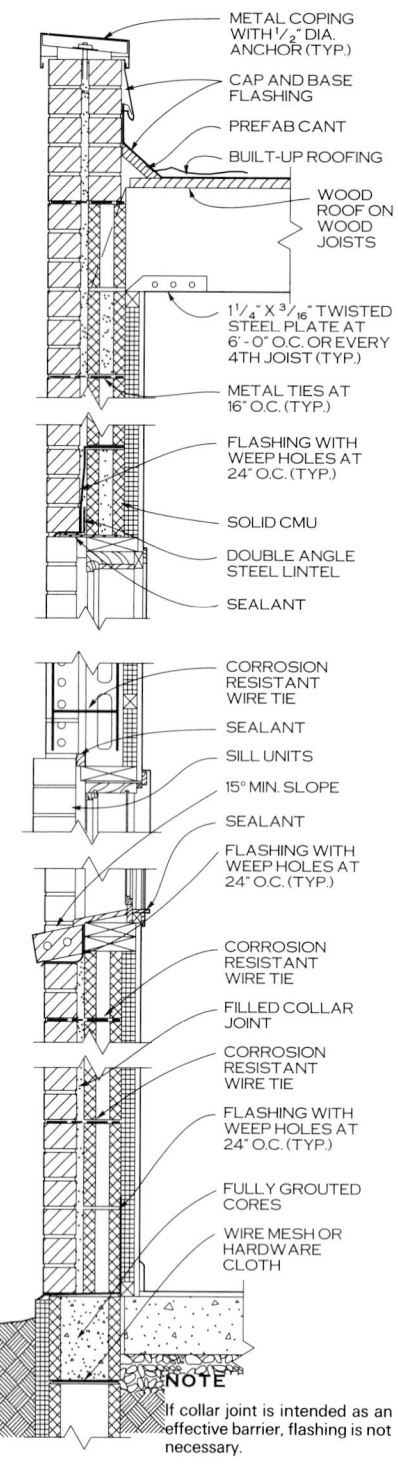

MULTI-WYTHE MASONRY WALL

ALTERNATE MULTI-WYTHE WALL SECTION

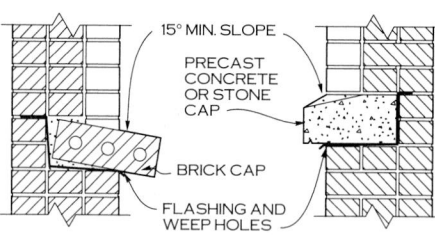

RECESS AND SILL DETAILS IN BRICK WALLS

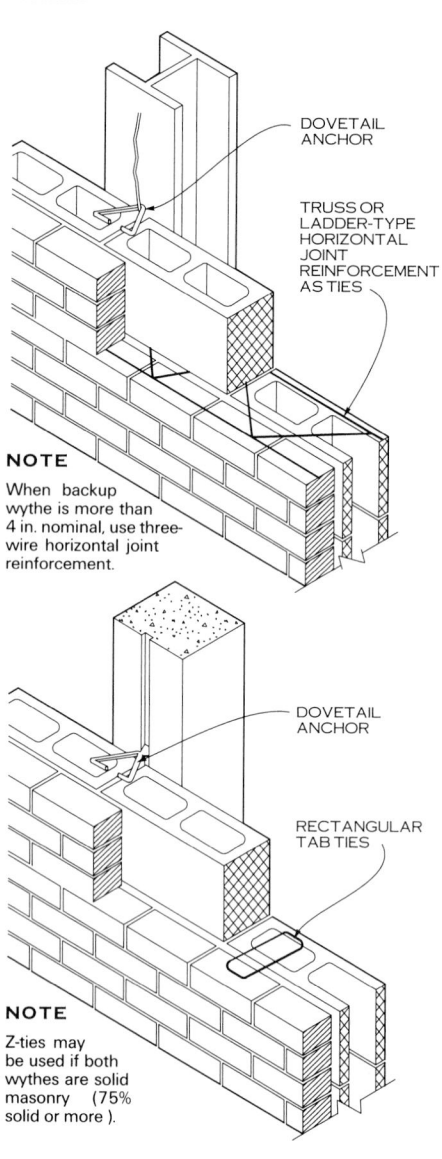

NOTE

When backup wythe is more than 4 in. nominal, use three-wire horizontal joint reinforcement.

NOTE

Z-ties may be used if both wythes are solid masonry (75% solid or more).

STEEL AND CONCRETE COLUMN ANCHORAGE

Grace S. Lee; Rippeteau Architects, PC; Washington, D.C.
Stephen S. Szoke, P.E.; National Concrete Masonry Association; Herndon, Virginia
Brian E. Trimble; Brick Institute of America; Reston, Virginia

 UNIT MASONRY

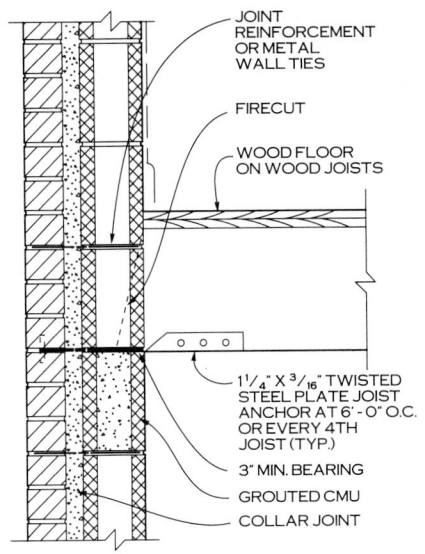

WALL TO WOOD JOIST ANCHORAGE

- JOINT REINFORCEMENT OR METAL WALL TIES
- FIRECUT
- WOOD FLOOR ON WOOD JOISTS
- 1 1/4" X 3/16" TWISTED STEEL PLATE JOIST ANCHOR AT 6'-0" O.C. OR EVERY 4TH JOIST (TYP.)
- 3" MIN. BEARING
- GROUTED CMU
- COLLAR JOINT

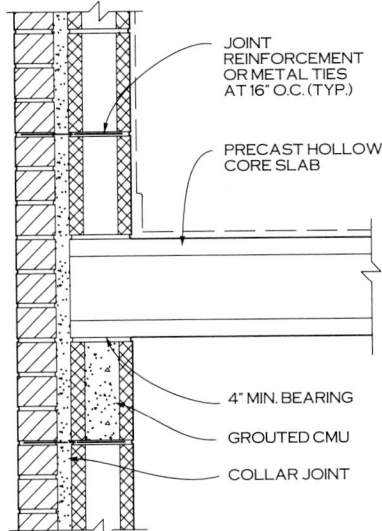

WALL TO CONCRETE JOIST ANCHORAGE

- JOINT REINFORCEMENT OR METAL TIES AT 16" O.C. (TYP.)
- PRECAST HOLLOW CORE SLAB
- 4" MIN. BEARING
- GROUTED CMU
- COLLAR JOINT

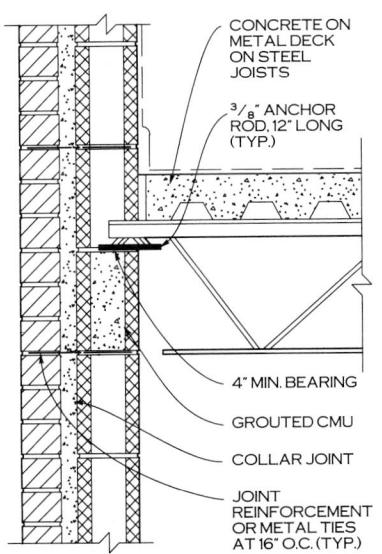

WALL TO STEEL JOIST ANCHORAGE

- CONCRETE ON METAL DECK ON STEEL JOISTS
- 3/8" ANCHOR ROD, 12" LONG (TYP.)
- 4" MIN. BEARING
- GROUTED CMU
- COLLAR JOINT
- JOINT REINFORCEMENT OR METAL TIES AT 16" O.C. (TYP.)

Grace S. Lee; Rippeteau Architects, PC; Washington, D.C.
Stephen S. Szoke, P.E.; National Concrete Masonry Association; Herndon, Virginia
Brian E. Trimble; Brick Institute of America; Reston, Virginia

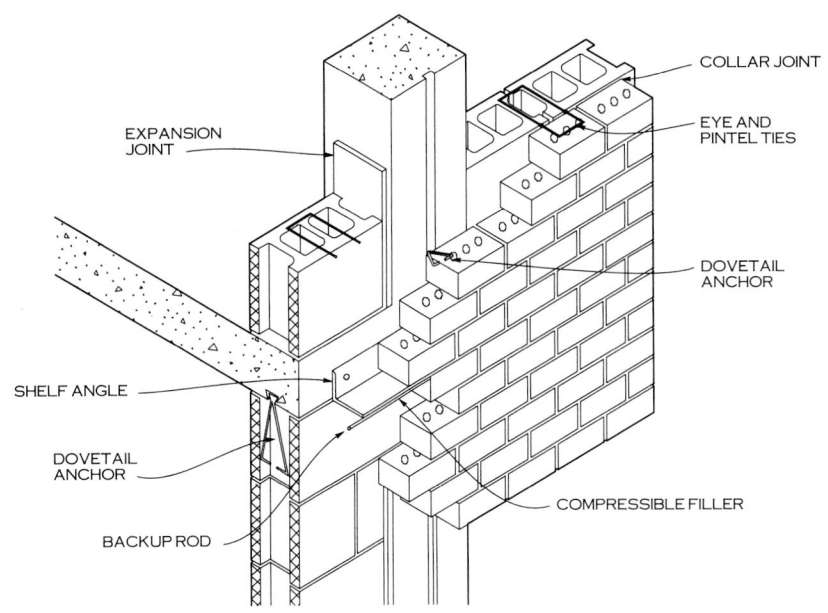

- EXPANSION JOINT
- COLLAR JOINT
- EYE AND PINTEL TIES
- DOVETAIL ANCHOR
- SHELF ANGLE
- DOVETAIL ANCHOR
- BACKUP ROD
- COMPRESSIBLE FILLER

CONCRETE BEAM AND COLUMN ANCHORAGE DETAIL

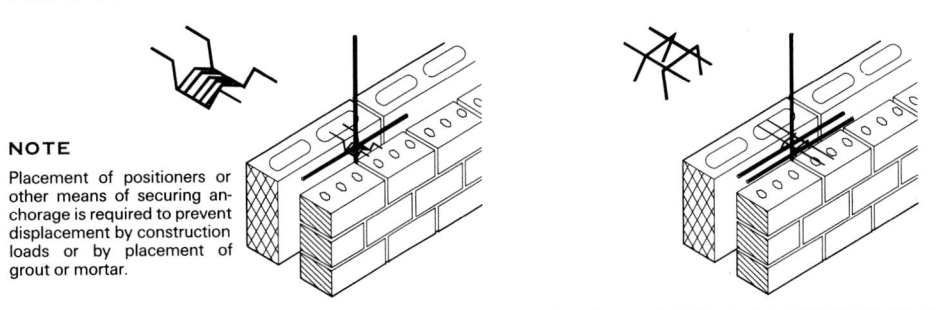

NOTE
Placement of positioners or other means of securing anchorage is required to prevent displacement by construction loads or by placement of grout or mortar.

TYPICAL REBAR POSITIONERS

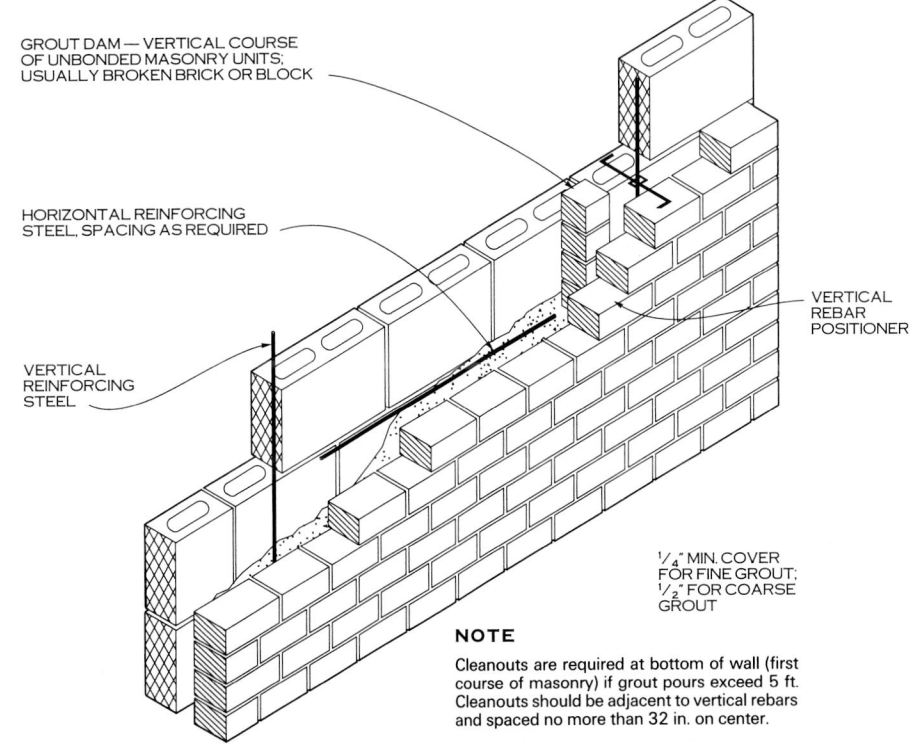

- GROUT DAM — VERTICAL COURSE OF UNBONDED MASONRY UNITS; USUALLY BROKEN BRICK OR BLOCK
- HORIZONTAL REINFORCING STEEL, SPACING AS REQUIRED
- VERTICAL REINFORCING STEEL
- VERTICAL REBAR POSITIONER
- 1/4" MIN. COVER FOR FINE GROUT; 1/2" FOR COARSE GROUT

NOTE
Cleanouts are required at bottom of wall (first course of masonry) if grout pours exceed 5 ft. Cleanouts should be adjacent to vertical rebars and spaced no more than 32 in. on center.

GROUTED HOLLOW WALL

UNIT MASONRY 4

GENERAL

Cavity walls consist of two wythes of masonry separated by at least a 2 in. airspace. The airspace may be increased to 4 1/2 in. with only minor increases in tie size and or spacing. If the cavity is to be more than 4 1/2 in., the wall system should be appropriately engineered. Either or both wythes of the wall system may be load bearing.

The cavity wall is a drainage-type wall that provides excellent resistance to water penetration. The mass and discontinuity of construction provided by the metal ties result in optimal sound penetration resistance. The calculated fire resistance of cavity walls usually exceeds 4 hours. Interior and exterior wythes may be considered as thermal mass for specific thermal requirements. Either or both wythes may be used to provide the desired architectural finishes, interior or exterior. For these reasons, the masonry cavity wall is generally preferred.

When the cavity wall is selected because of its thermal performance, generally only the interior wythe is load bearing. This construction permits the insulation layer to be continuous within the wall and pass the slabs, minimizing thermal bridges. The insulation may be granular fill or rigid board insulation. If rigid board insulation is selected, there must be a nominal 1 in. airspace between the back of the exterior wythe and the exterior surface of the insulation board. The insulation board may be held in place with the wall ties. Two-piece adjustable ties serve well for this application. Seams in the insulation should be made with tongue-and-groove joints, shiplapped, or sealed with tape. If the ties selected are not appropriate for holding the insulation against the backup wythe, then the rigid board insulation should be adhered or mechanically fastened to the backup. If granular fill is used, it is necessary to select weep hole systems that will permit drainage but keep the granular fill within the wall system. Typical cavity walls may contain 2 to 4 1/2 in. of granular fill insulation or 3 1/2 in. of rigid board insulation.

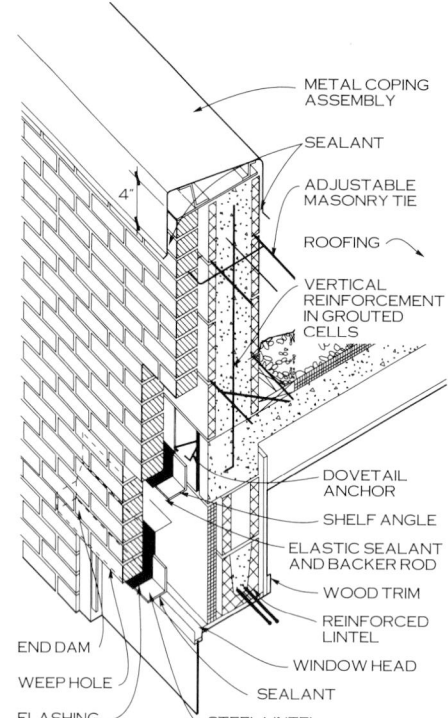

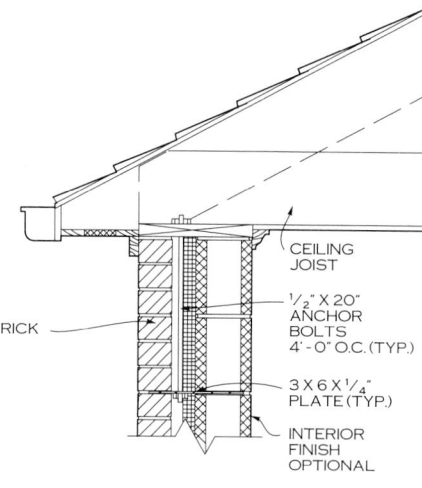

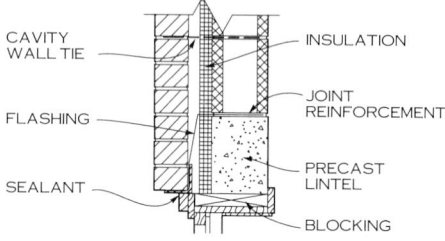

HEAD

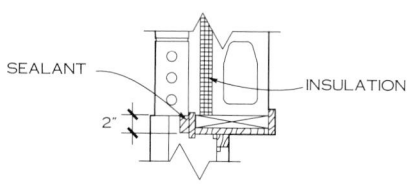

JAMB

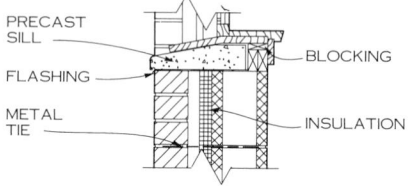

SILL

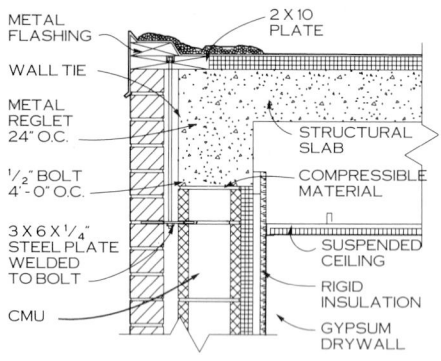

ALTERNATE ROOF DETAIL

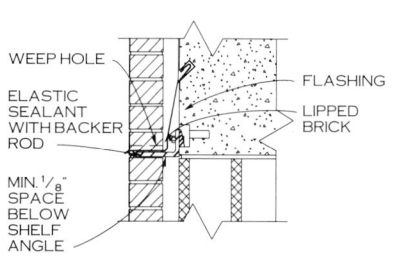

ALTERNATE EXPANSION JOINT DETAIL

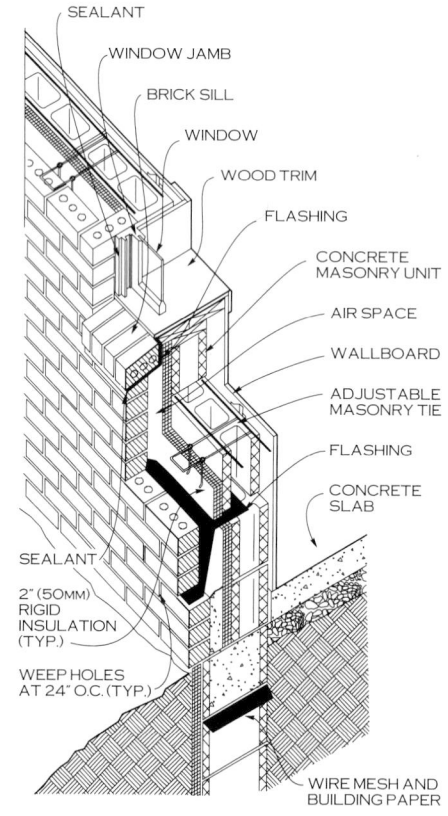

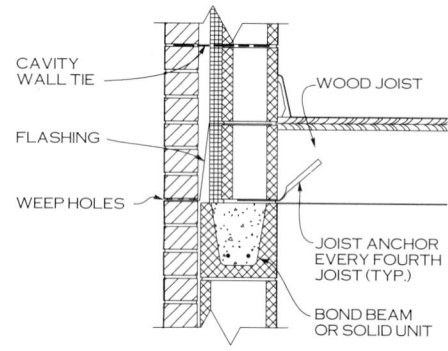

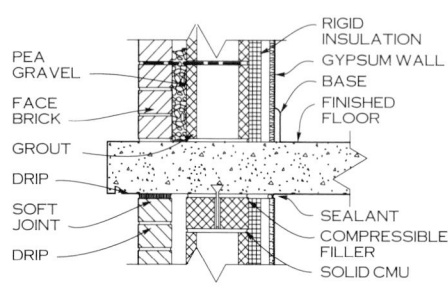

EXPOSED SLAB DETAIL

BRICK AND CMU CAVITY WALL

ALTERNATE BRICK AND CMU CAVITY WALL SECTION

Grace S. Lee and A. Harris Lokmanhakim, AIA; Rippeteau Architects, PC; Washington, D.C.
Stephen S. Szoke, P.E.; National Concrete Masonry Association; Herndon, Virginia
Brian E. Trimble; Brick Institute of America; Reston, Virginia

UNIT MASONRY

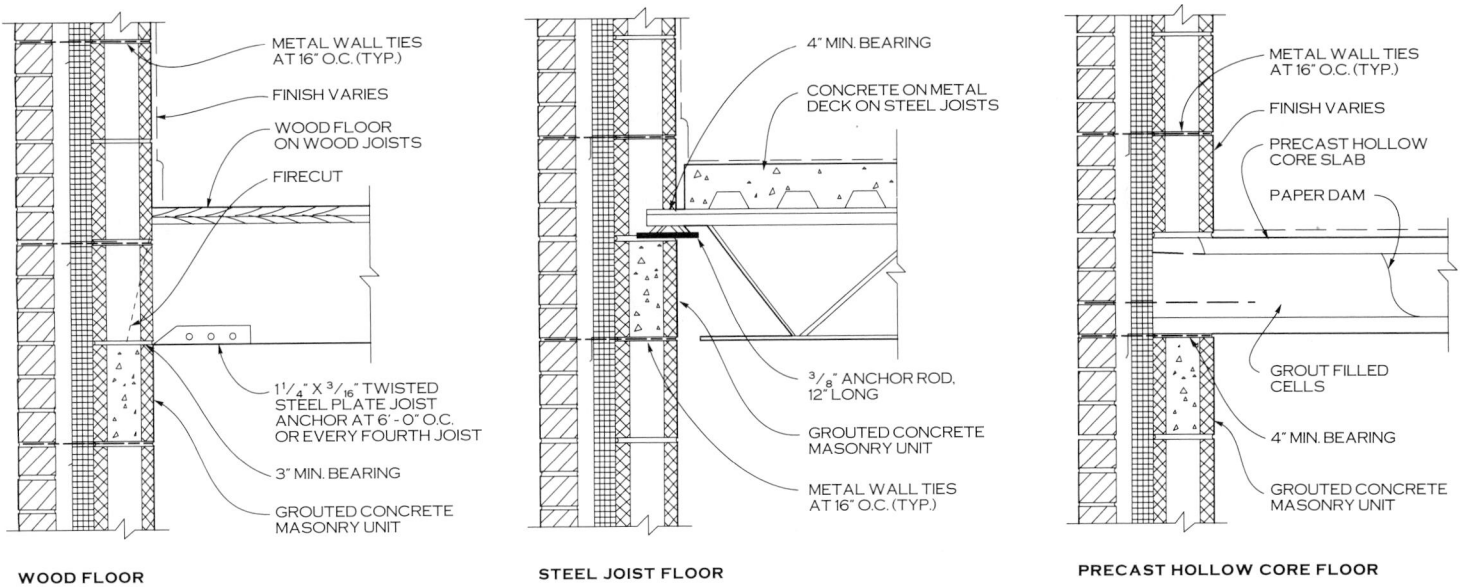

WOOD FLOOR

- METAL WALL TIES AT 16" O.C. (TYP.)
- FINISH VARIES
- WOOD FLOOR ON WOOD JOISTS
- FIRECUT
- 1¼" X 3/16" TWISTED STEEL PLATE JOIST ANCHOR AT 6'-0" O.C. OR EVERY FOURTH JOIST
- 3" MIN. BEARING
- GROUTED CONCRETE MASONRY UNIT

STEEL JOIST FLOOR

- 4" MIN. BEARING
- CONCRETE ON METAL DECK ON STEEL JOISTS
- 3/8" ANCHOR ROD, 12" LONG
- GROUTED CONCRETE MASONRY UNIT
- METAL WALL TIES AT 16" O.C. (TYP.)

PRECAST HOLLOW CORE FLOOR

- METAL WALL TIES AT 16" O.C. (TYP.)
- FINISH VARIES
- PRECAST HOLLOW CORE SLAB
- PAPER DAM
- GROUT FILLED CELLS
- 4" MIN. BEARING
- GROUTED CONCRETE MASONRY UNIT

WALL TO FLOOR ANCHORAGE AT CAVITY WALLS

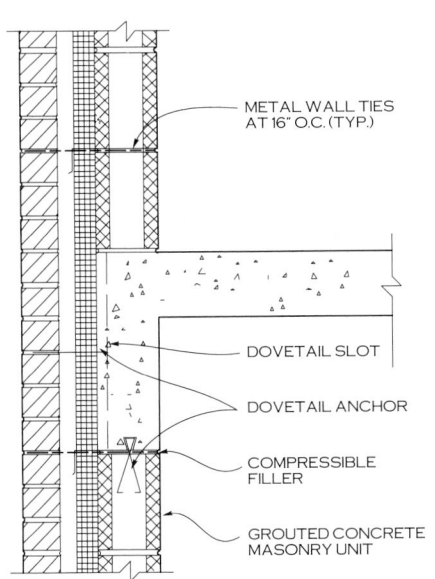

SPANDREL DETAIL

- METAL WALL TIES AT 16" O.C. (TYP.)
- DOVETAIL SLOT
- DOVETAIL ANCHOR
- COMPRESSIBLE FILLER
- GROUTED CONCRETE MASONRY UNIT

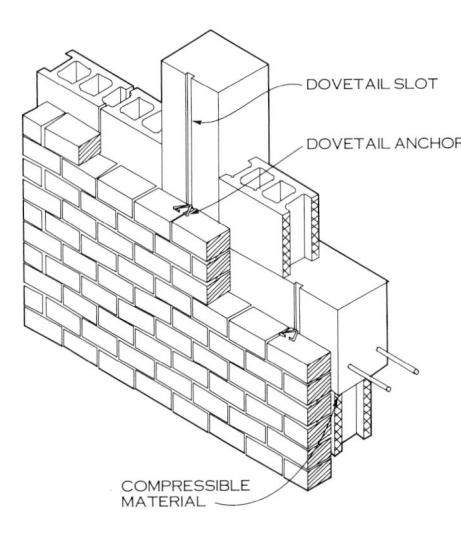

- DOVETAIL SLOT
- DOVETAIL ANCHOR
- COMPRESSIBLE MATERIAL

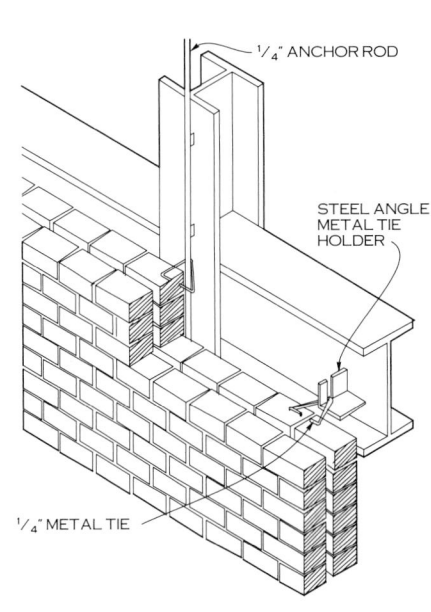

- ¼" ANCHOR ROD
- STEEL ANGLE METAL TIE HOLDER
- ¼" METAL TIE

COLUMN AND BEAM ANCHORAGE DETAILS

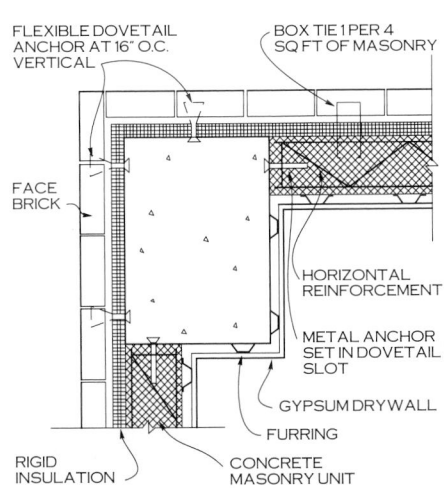

DOVETAIL ANCHORS AT CORNER

- FLEXIBLE DOVETAIL ANCHOR AT 16" O.C. VERTICAL
- BOX TIE 1 PER 4 SQ FT OF MASONRY
- FACE BRICK
- HORIZONTAL REINFORCEMENT
- METAL ANCHOR SET IN DOVETAIL SLOT
- GYPSUM DRYWALL
- FURRING
- RIGID INSULATION
- CONCRETE MASONRY UNIT

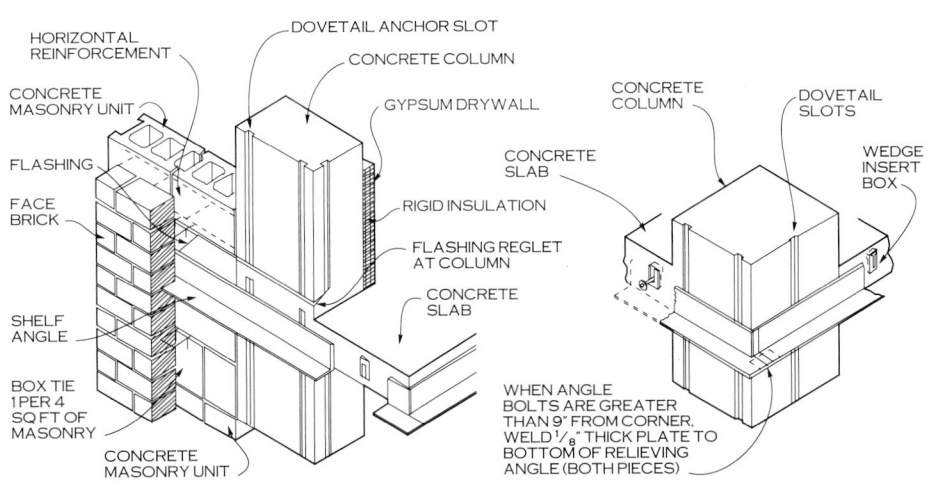

SHELF ANGLE AT CORNER COLUMN

- HORIZONTAL REINFORCEMENT
- CONCRETE MASONRY UNIT
- FLASHING
- FACE BRICK
- SHELF ANGLE
- BOX TIE 1 PER 4 SQ FT OF MASONRY
- CONCRETE MASONRY UNIT
- DOVETAIL ANCHOR SLOT
- CONCRETE COLUMN
- GYPSUM DRYWALL
- RIGID INSULATION
- FLASHING REGLET AT COLUMN
- CONCRETE SLAB
- CONCRETE SLAB
- CONCRETE COLUMN
- DOVETAIL SLOTS
- WEDGE INSERT BOX
- WHEN ANGLE BOLTS ARE GREATER THAN 9" FROM CORNER, WELD 1/8" THICK PLATE TO BOTTOM OF RELIEVING ANGLE (BOTH PIECES)

Grace S. Lee; Rippeteau Architects, PC; Washington, D.C.
Stephen S. Szoke, P.E.; National Concrete Masonry Association; Herndon, Virginia
Brian E. Trimble; Brick Institute of America; Reston, Virginia

Cavity Walls

212

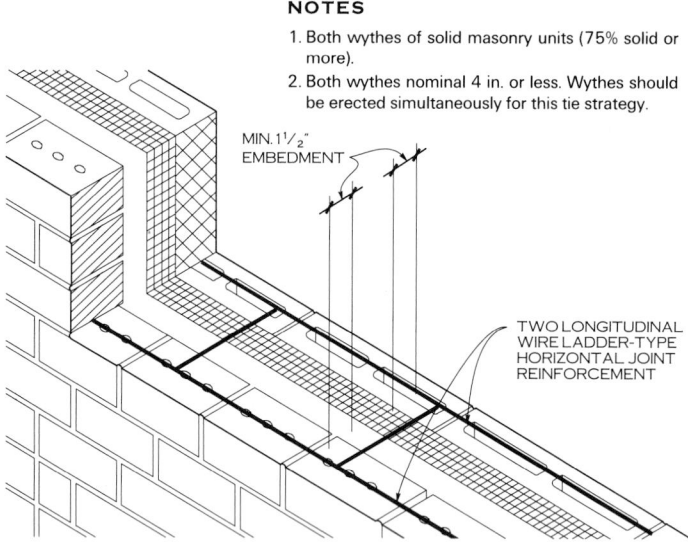

NOTES

1. Both wythes of solid masonry units (75% solid or more).
2. Both wythes nominal 4 in. or less. Wythes should be erected simultaneously for this tie strategy.

MIN. 1¹⁄₂" EMBEDMENT

TWO LONGITUDINAL WIRE LADDER-TYPE HORIZONTAL JOINT REINFORCEMENT

LADDER-TYPE HORIZONTAL JOINT REINFORCEMENT AS TIES FOR 4 IN. WYTHES OR LESS

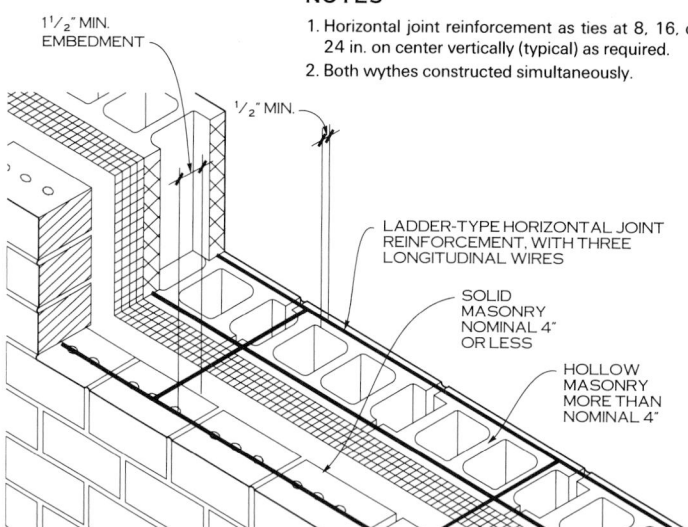

1¹⁄₂" MIN. EMBEDMENT

¹⁄₂" MIN.

NOTES

1. Horizontal joint reinforcement as ties at 8, 16, or 24 in. on center vertically (typical) as required.
2. Both wythes constructed simultaneously.

LADDER-TYPE HORIZONTAL JOINT REINFORCEMENT, WITH THREE LONGITUDINAL WIRES

SOLID MASONRY NOMINAL 4" OR LESS

HOLLOW MASONRY MORE THAN NOMINAL 4"

LADDER-TYPE HORIZONTAL JOINT REINFORCEMENT AS TIES FOR MORE THAN 4 IN. WYTHES

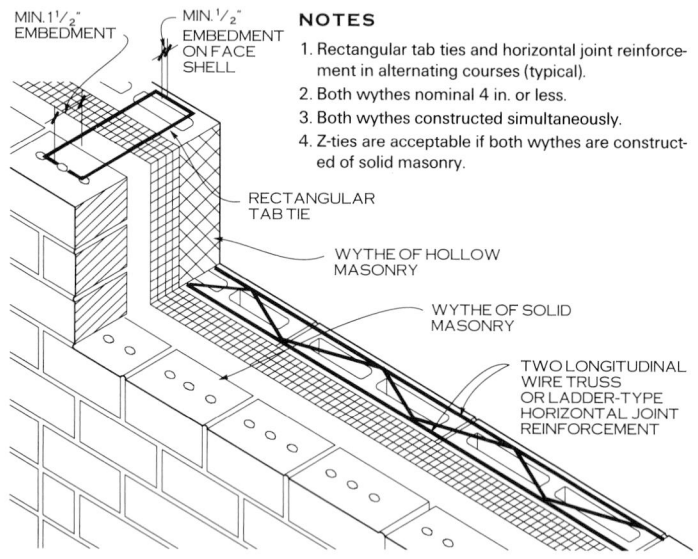

MIN. 1¹⁄₂" EMBEDMENT

MIN. ¹⁄₂" EMBEDMENT ON FACE SHELL

NOTES

1. Rectangular tab ties and horizontal joint reinforcement in alternating courses (typical).
2. Both wythes nominal 4 in. or less.
3. Both wythes constructed simultaneously.
4. Z-ties are acceptable if both wythes are constructed of solid masonry.

RECTANGULAR TAB TIE

WYTHE OF HOLLOW MASONRY

WYTHE OF SOLID MASONRY

TWO LONGITUDINAL WIRE TRUSS OR LADDER-TYPE HORIZONTAL JOINT REINFORCEMENT

RECTANGULAR TAB TIES FOR 4 IN. WYTHES OR LESS

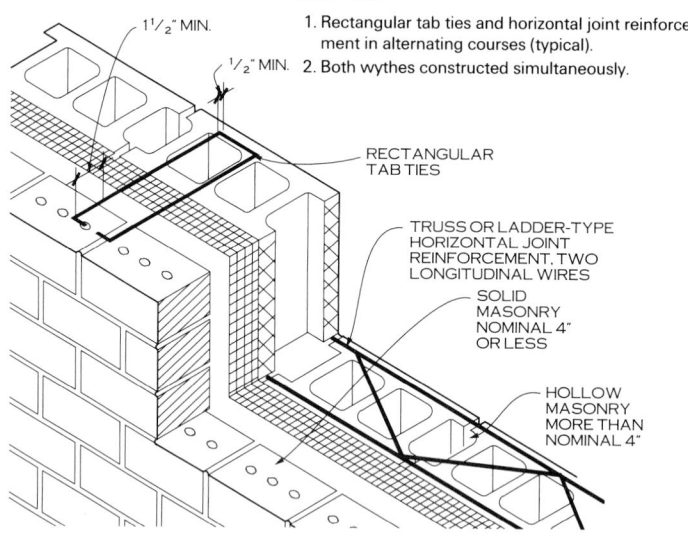

1¹⁄₂" MIN.

¹⁄₂" MIN.

NOTES

1. Rectangular tab ties and horizontal joint reinforcement in alternating courses (typical).
2. Both wythes constructed simultaneously.

RECTANGULAR TAB TIES

TRUSS OR LADDER-TYPE HORIZONTAL JOINT REINFORCEMENT, TWO LONGITUDINAL WIRES

SOLID MASONRY NOMINAL 4" OR LESS

HOLLOW MASONRY MORE THAN NOMINAL 4"

RECTANGULAR TAB TIES FOR MORE THAN 4 IN. WYTHES

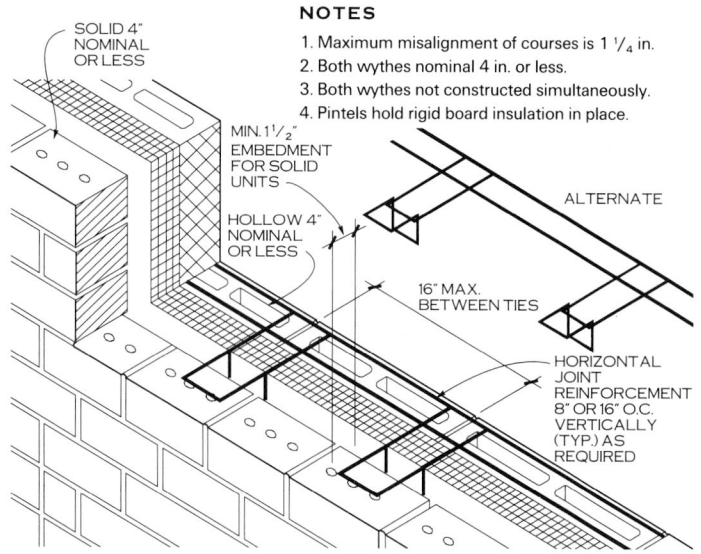

SOLID 4" NOMINAL OR LESS

MIN. 1¹⁄₂" EMBEDMENT FOR SOLID UNITS

HOLLOW 4" NOMINAL OR LESS

NOTES

1. Maximum misalignment of courses is 1¹⁄₄ in.
2. Both wythes nominal 4 in. or less.
3. Both wythes not constructed simultaneously.
4. Pintels hold rigid board insulation in place.

ALTERNATE

16" MAX. BETWEEN TIES

HORIZONTAL JOINT REINFORCEMENT 8" OR 16" O.C. VERTICALLY (TYP.) AS REQUIRED

ADJUSTABLE TIES FOR 4 IN. WYTHES OR LESS

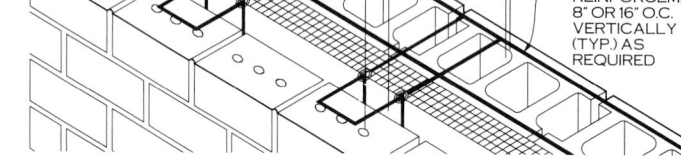

SOLID MASONRY NOMINAL 4" OR LESS

HOLLOW MASONRY MORE THAN NOMINAL 4"

NOTES

1. Maximum misalignment of courses is 1¹⁄₄ in.
2. Both wythes not constructed simultaneously.
3. Pintels hold rigid board insulation in place.

ALTERNATE

EYE AND PINTEL TIES

16" MAX. BETWEEN TIES

1¹⁄₂" MIN.

¹⁄₂" MIN.

HORIZONTAL JOINT REINFORCEMENT 8" OR 16" O.C. VERTICALLY (TYP.) AS REQUIRED

ADJUSTABLE TIES FOR MORE THAN 4 IN. WYTHES

Grace S. Lee; Rippeteau Architects, PC; Washington, D.C.
Stephen S. Szoke, P.E.; National Concrete Masonry Association; Herndon, Virginia
Brian E. Trimble; Brick Institute of America; Reston, Virginia

 UNIT MASONRY

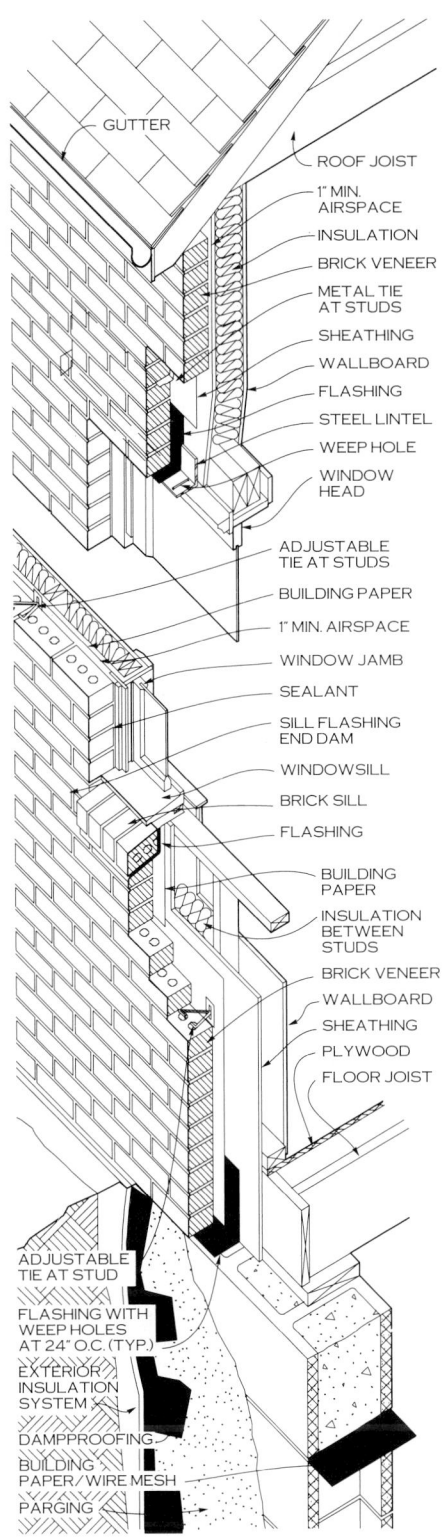

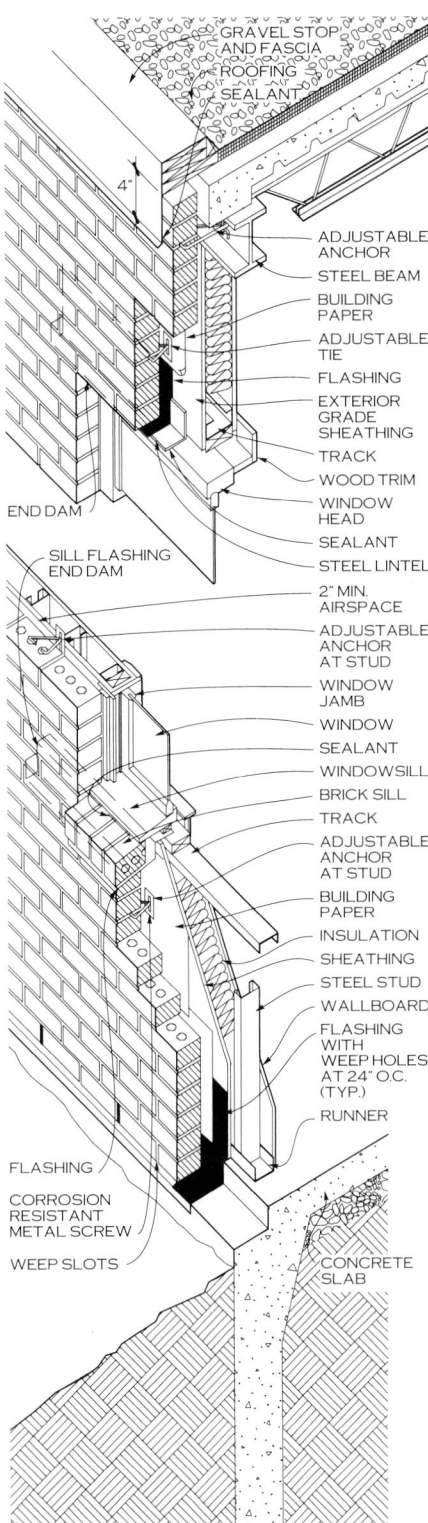

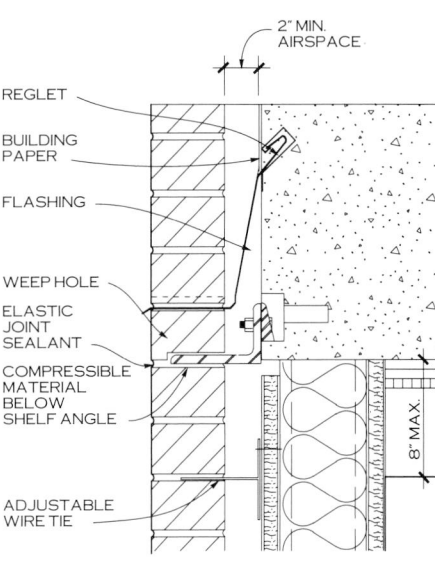

SHELF ANGLE DETAIL

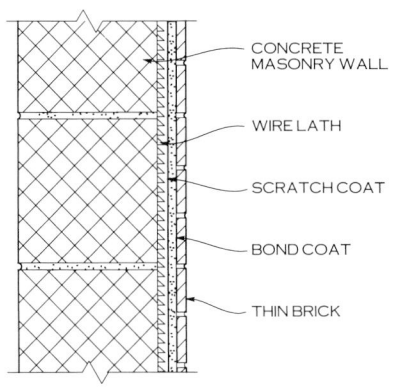

THIN BRICK VENEER ON CMU

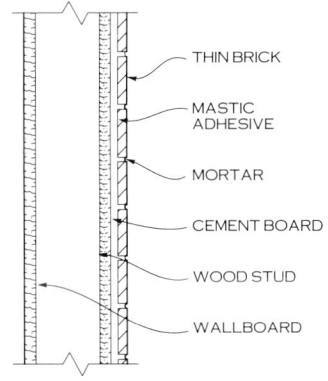

THIN BRICK VENEER ON WOOD FRAME

BRICK VENEER ON WOOD STUD BACKUP

ANCHORED VENEERS

Masonry veneers provide an aesthetic, durable, noncombustible, weather resistant finish for structural masonry or light framing construction. The inherent mass of the veneer provides increased thermal performance, sound penetration resistance, and fire resistance. Anchored veneers typically consist of nominal 3 or 4 in. wythes of masonry tied to a backing system. Veneers are not intended to support any loads other than their own weight. All lateral loads are intended to be transferred to the backing system. Empirical design permits the construction of masonry veneers with a nominal thickness of 4 in. to heights of three stories,

BRICK VENEER ON STEEL STUD BACKUP

30 ft at the plate and 38 ft at the gables. For veneers with a nominal thickness of 3 in., the height is limited to two stories, 20 ft at the plate and 28 ft at the gable. For building heights greater than two stories, the brick veneer must be supported by a shelf angle at every floor.

Veneers are drainage-type walls. Although a nominal 1 in. airspace is acceptable for drainage in most low-rise, residential applications, a minimum 2 in. airspace between the back of the masonry and the exterior surface of the backing or exterior sheathing is recommended for masonry veneers in mid-rise and high-rise construction.

ADHERED VENEERS

Thin brick veneer, also referred to as adhered veneer, is an application of thin brick veneer units—between $1/2$ to $1 3/4$ in. thick—on a backing system. Adhered veneer relies on the bonding agent between the thin brick units and the backup substrate. This construction may be classified as either thin bed set or thick bed set. The thin brick can be adhered to a stud backing, attached to a concrete masonry backing, cast into a concrete panel, or laid into a preformed modular panel. Thin brick panels can be prefabricated or laid in place, depending on the size or intricacies of the project.

Grace S. Lee; Rippeteau Architects, PC; Washington, D.C.
Brian E. Trimble; Brick Institute of America; Reston, Virginia

UNIT MASONRY

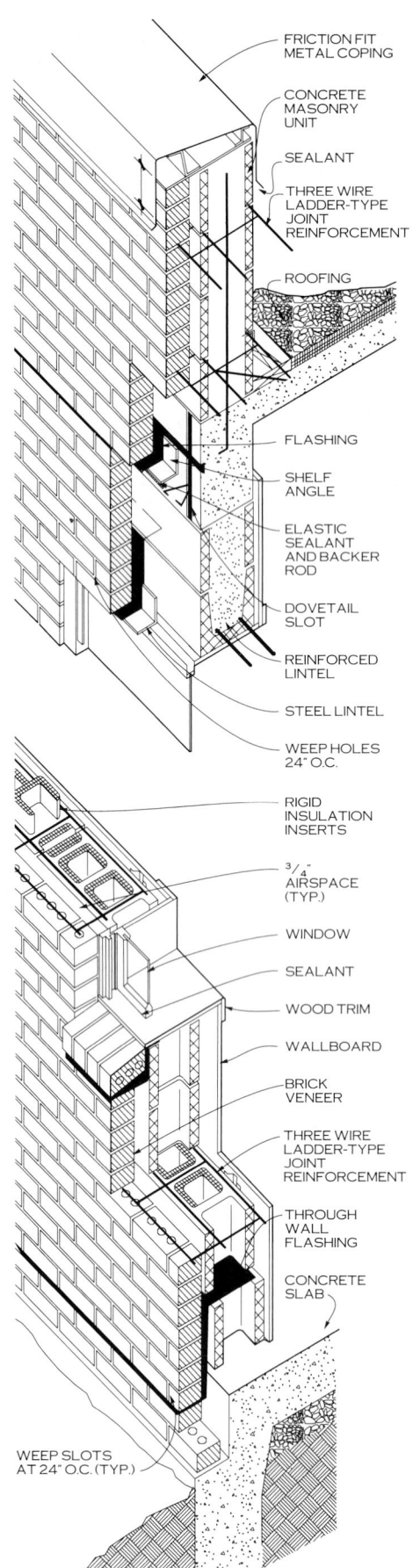

FRICTION FIT
METAL COPING

CONCRETE
MASONRY
UNIT

SEALANT

THREE WIRE
LADDER-TYPE
JOINT
REINFORCEMENT

ROOFING

FLASHING

SHELF
ANGLE

ELASTIC
SEALANT
AND BACKER
ROD

DOVETAIL
SLOT

REINFORCED
LINTEL

STEEL LINTEL

WEEP HOLES
24" O.C.

RIGID
INSULATION
INSERTS

$3/_4$"
AIRSPACE
(TYP.)

WINDOW

SEALANT

WOOD TRIM

WALLBOARD

BRICK
VENEER

THREE WIRE
LADDER-TYPE
JOINT
REINFORCEMENT

THROUGH
WALL
FLASHING

CONCRETE
SLAB

WEEP SLOTS
AT 24" O.C. (TYP.)

**BRICK VENEER ON CONCRETE MASONRY
UNIT BACK-UP**

Grace S. Lee; Rippeteau Architects, PC; Washington, D.C.
Brian E. Trimble; Brick Institute of America; Reston, Virginia

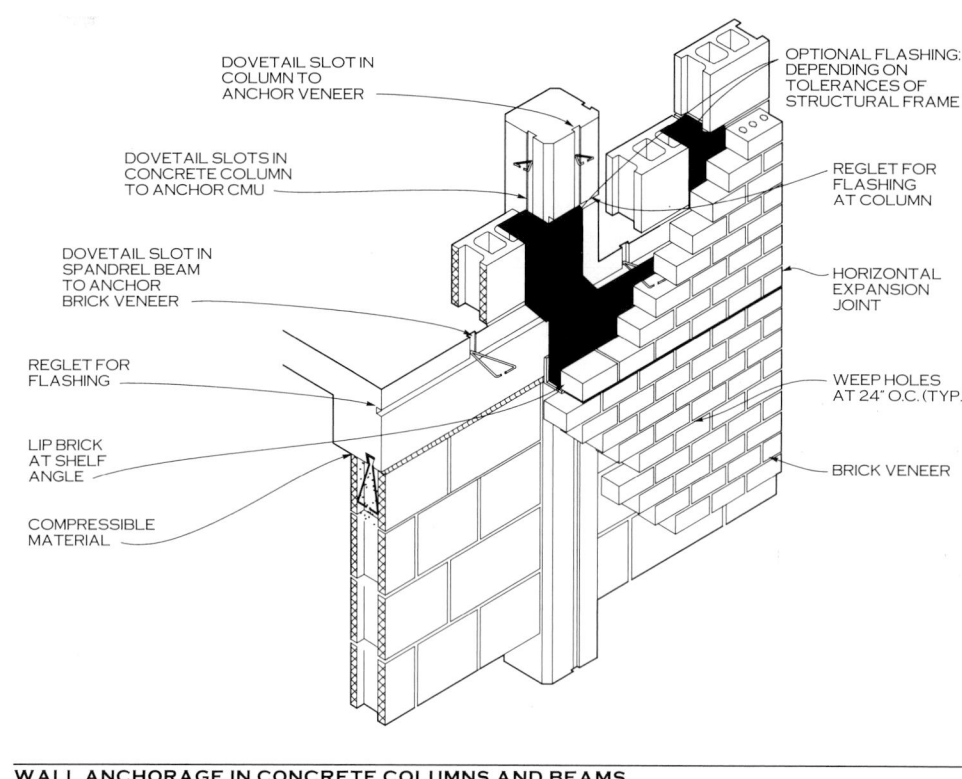

DOVETAIL SLOT IN
COLUMN TO
ANCHOR VENEER

OPTIONAL FLASHING:
DEPENDING ON
TOLERANCES OF
STRUCTURAL FRAME

DOVETAIL SLOTS IN
CONCRETE COLUMN
TO ANCHOR CMU

REGLET FOR
FLASHING
AT COLUMN

DOVETAIL SLOT IN
SPANDREL BEAM
TO ANCHOR
BRICK VENEER

HORIZONTAL
EXPANSION
JOINT

REGLET FOR
FLASHING

WEEP HOLES
AT 24" O.C. (TYP.)

LIP BRICK
AT SHELF
ANGLE

BRICK VENEER

COMPRESSIBLE
MATERIAL

WALL ANCHORAGE IN CONCRETE COLUMNS AND BEAMS

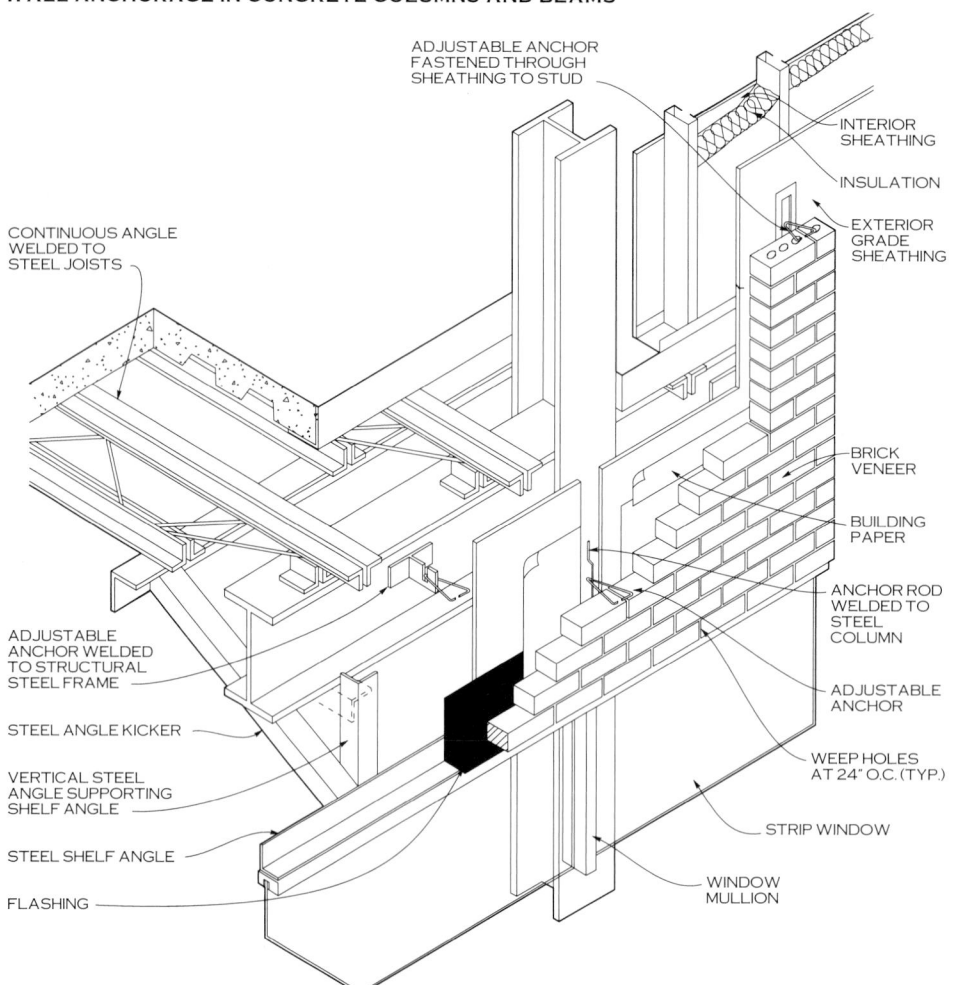

ADJUSTABLE ANCHOR
FASTENED THROUGH
SHEATHING TO STUD

INTERIOR
SHEATHING

INSULATION

CONTINUOUS ANGLE
WELDED TO
STEEL JOISTS

EXTERIOR
GRADE
SHEATHING

BRICK
VENEER

BUILDING
PAPER

ADJUSTABLE
ANCHOR WELDED
TO STRUCTURAL
STEEL FRAME

ANCHOR ROD
WELDED TO
STEEL
COLUMN

STEEL ANGLE KICKER

ADJUSTABLE
ANCHOR

VERTICAL STEEL
ANGLE SUPPORTING
SHELF ANGLE

WEEP HOLES
AT 24" O.C. (TYP.)

STEEL SHELF ANGLE

STRIP WINDOW

FLASHING

WINDOW
MULLION

WALL ANCHORAGE IN STEEL COLUMNS AND BEAMS

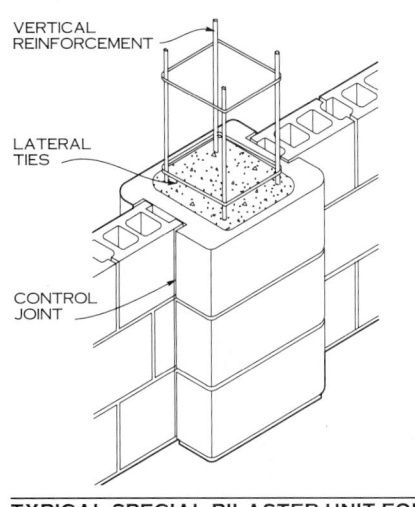

TYPICAL SPECIAL PILASTER UNIT FOR USE WITH CONTROL JOINTS

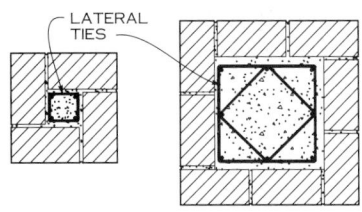

12 IN. SQUARE BRICK COLUMN

20 IN. SQUARE BRICK COLUMN

REINFORCED COLUMNS

REINFORCED BRICK MASONRY COLUMN

BRICK CURTAIN WALL AND PANEL WALL REINFORCEMENT

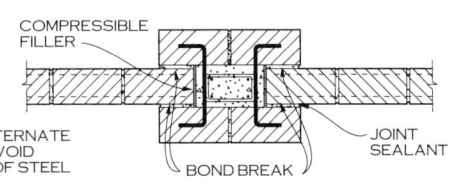

TIES EMBEDDED ON MORTAR JOINTS

ALTERNATE COURSES

TIES EMBEDDED ON MORTAR JOINTS

ALTERNATE COURSES

$\frac{1}{4}$" DIA. BARS BENT IN FORM OF U, GREASED LEGS AND SPACED 16" O.C.

TYPICAL PILASTER LAYOUTS

COMPRESSIBLE FILLER

JOINT SEALANT

BOND BREAK

REINFORCED BRICK MASONRY PILASTER

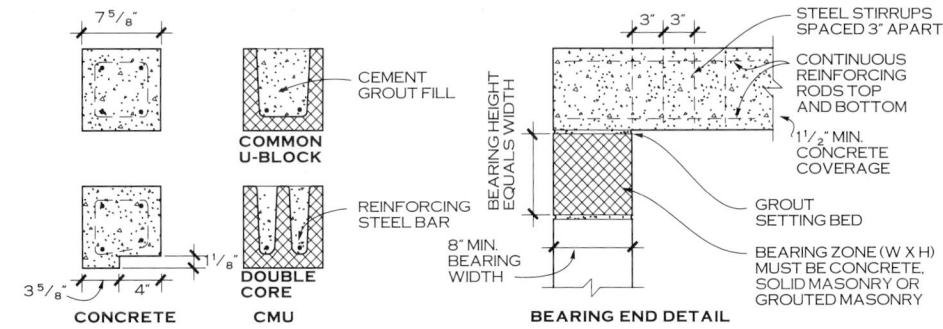

COMMON U-BLOCK

CEMENT GROUT FILL

REINFORCING STEEL BAR

CONCRETE

DOUBLE CORE

CMU

STEEL STIRRUPS SPACED 3" APART

CONTINUOUS REINFORCING RODS TOP AND BOTTOM

$1\frac{1}{2}$" MIN. CONCRETE COVERAGE

GROUT SETTING BED

BEARING ZONE (W X H) MUST BE CONCRETE, SOLID MASONRY OR GROUTED MASONRY

8" MIN. BEARING WIDTH

BEARING HEIGHT EQUALS WIDTH

BEARING END DETAIL

PRECAST CONCRETE AND CMU BEAMS OR LINTELS

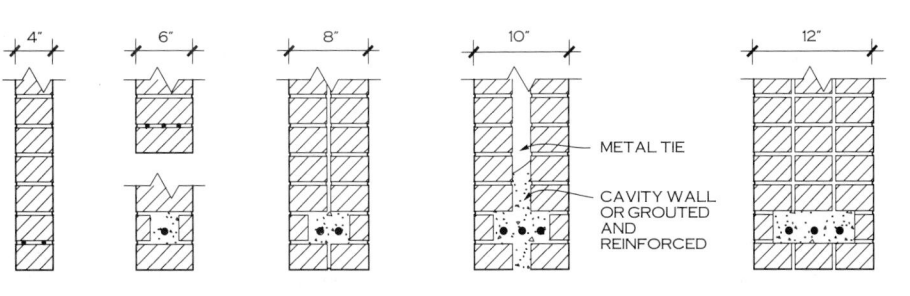

METAL TIE

CAVITY WALL OR GROUTED AND REINFORCED

REINFORCED BRICK BEAMS OR LINTELS

Grace S. Lee; Rippeteau Architects, PC; Washington, D.C.
Brian E. Trimble; Brick Institute of America; Reston, Virginia; S
Stephen S. Szoke, P.E.; National Concrete Masonry Association; Herndon, Virginia

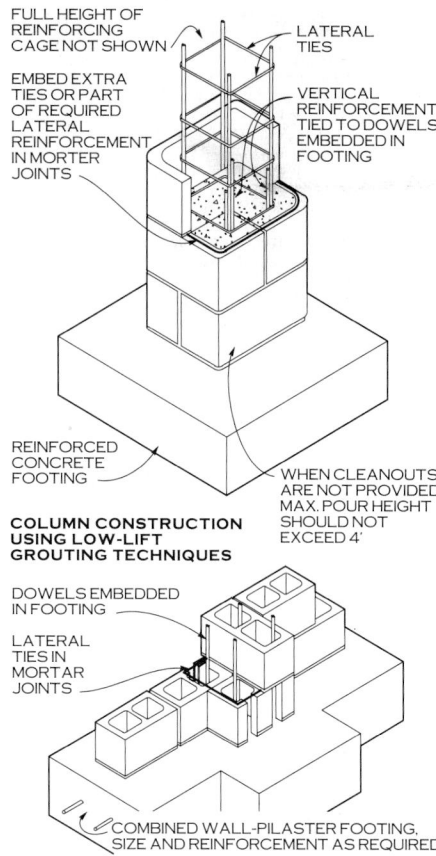

FULL HEIGHT OF REINFORCING CAGE NOT SHOWN

LATERAL TIES

EMBED EXTRA TIES OR PART OF REQUIRED LATERAL REINFORCEMENT IN MORTER JOINTS

VERTICAL REINFORCEMENT TIED TO DOWELS EMBEDDED IN FOOTING

REINFORCED CONCRETE FOOTING

WHEN CLEANOUTS ARE NOT PROVIDED MAX. POUR HEIGHT SHOULD NOT EXCEED 4'

COLUMN CONSTRUCTION USING LOW-LIFT GROUTING TECHNIQUES

DOWELS EMBEDDED IN FOOTING

LATERAL TIES IN MORTAR JOINTS

COMBINED WALL-PILASTER FOOTING, SIZE AND REINFORCEMENT AS REQUIRED

PILASTER CONSTRUCTION USING LOW-LIFT GROUTING TECHNIQUES
NOTE

Cut block in first course before laying to form cleanout openings at base of cells to be filled. Remove all mortar droppings, set and inspect vertical reinforcement, and form over opening before filling with grout or concrete. When cleanouts are not provided maximum pour should not exceed 4 ft.

COLUMN AND PILASTER CONSTRUCTION

NUMBER AND SIZE OF REBARS REQUIRED

LINTEL TYPE	CLEAR SPAN (MAX.)	8" BRICK WALL (80 LB/ SQ FT)	8" CMU WALL (50 LB/ SQ FT)
Reinforced concrete ($7\frac{5}{8}$" square section)	4'- 0"	4 - #3	4 - #3
	6'- 0"	4 - #4	4 - #3
	8'- 0"	4 - #5	4 - #4
Concrete masonry unit ($7\frac{5}{8}$" square section) nominal 8 x 8 x 16 unit	4'- 0"	2 - #4	2 - #3
	6'- 0"	2 - #5	2 - #4
	8'- 0"	2 - #6	2 - #5

NOTES

1. For precast concrete and reinforced concrete masonry unit lintels with no superimposed loads.

2. fc' = 3000 psi concrete and grout; fy = 60,000 psi

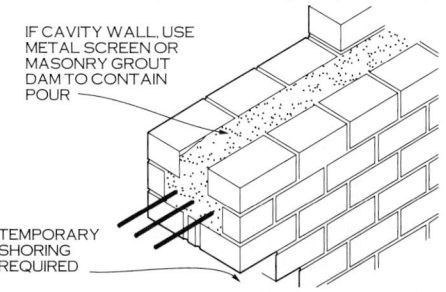

IF CAVITY WALL, USE METAL SCREEN OR MASONRY GROUT DAM TO CONTAIN POUR

TEMPORARY SHORING REQUIRED

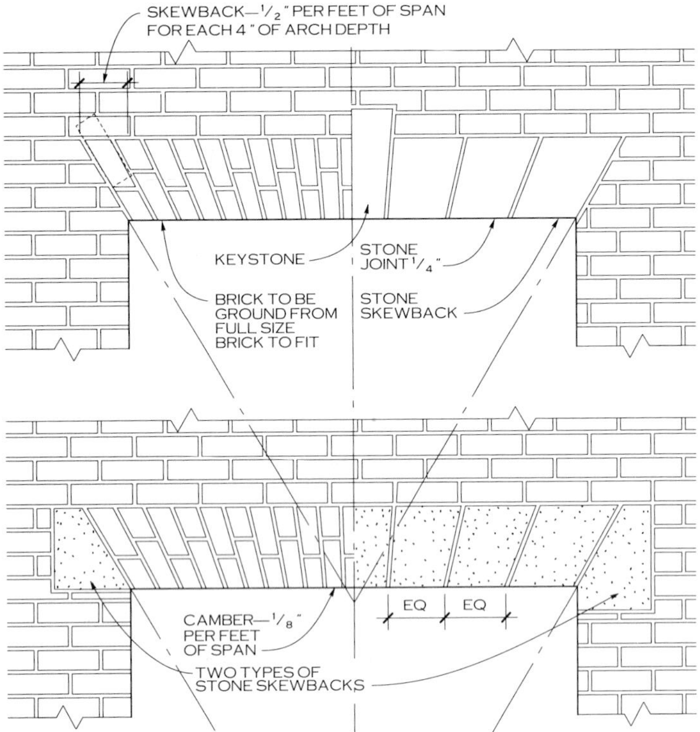

SKEWBACK—1/2" PER FEET OF SPAN
FOR EACH 4" OF ARCH DEPTH

KEYSTONE

STONE JOINT 1/4"

BRICK TO BE GROUND FROM FULL SIZE BRICK TO FIT

STONE SKEWBACK

CAMBER—1/8" PER FEET OF SPAN

EQ EQ

TWO TYPES OF STONE SKEWBACKS

TYPES OF JACK ARCHES

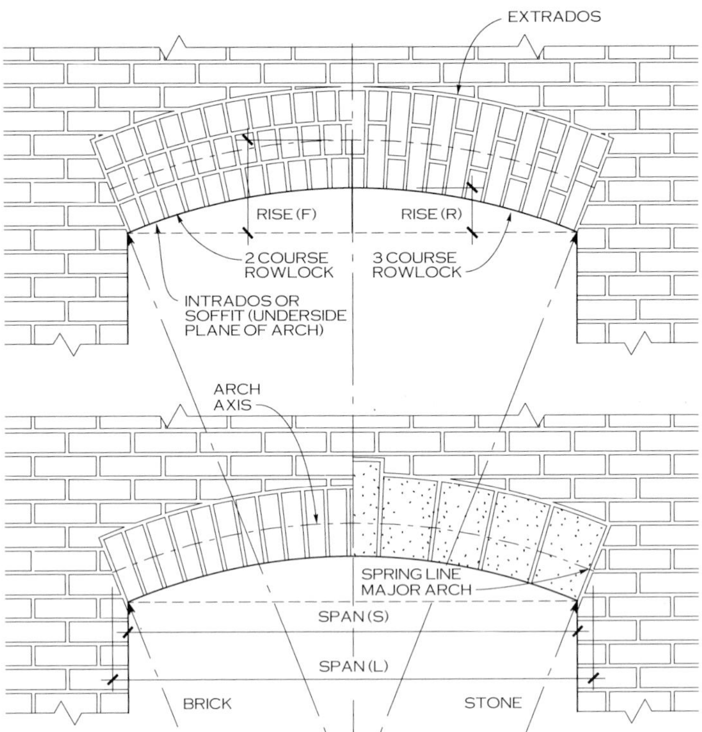

EXTRADOS

RISE (F)   RISE (R)

2 COURSE ROWLOCK   3 COURSE ROWLOCK

INTRADOS OR SOFFIT (UNDERSIDE PLANE OF ARCH)

ARCH AXIS

SPRING LINE MAJOR ARCH

SPAN (S)

SPAN (L)

BRICK   STONE

TYPES OF SEGMENTAL ARCHES

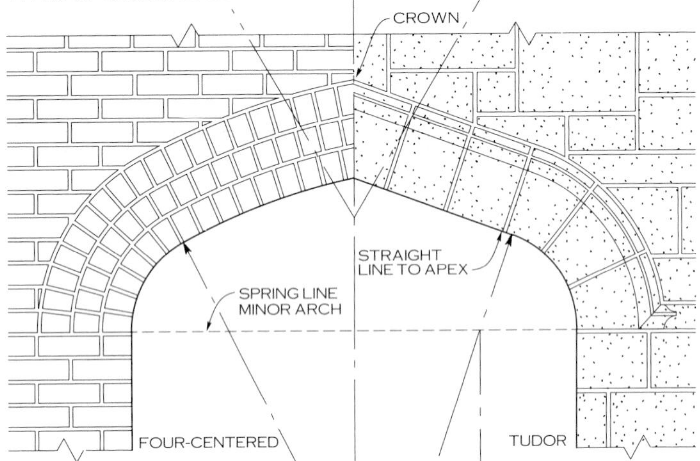

CROWN

STRAIGHT LINE TO APEX

SPRING LINE MINOR ARCH

FOUR-CENTERED   **TUDOR**

FOUR-CENTERED AND TUDOR

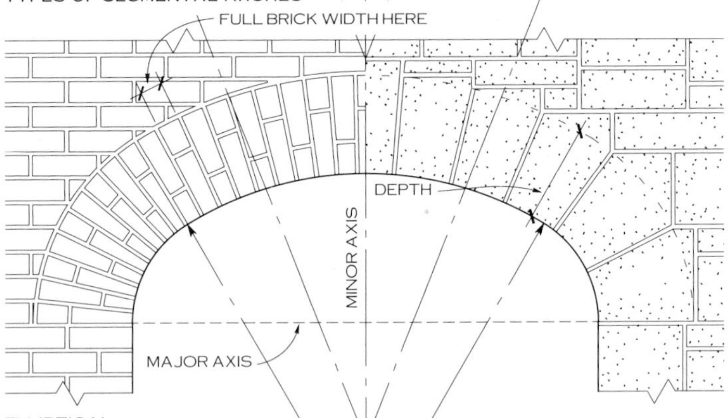

FULL BRICK WIDTH HERE

DEPTH

MINOR AXIS

MAJOR AXIS

ELLIPTICAL

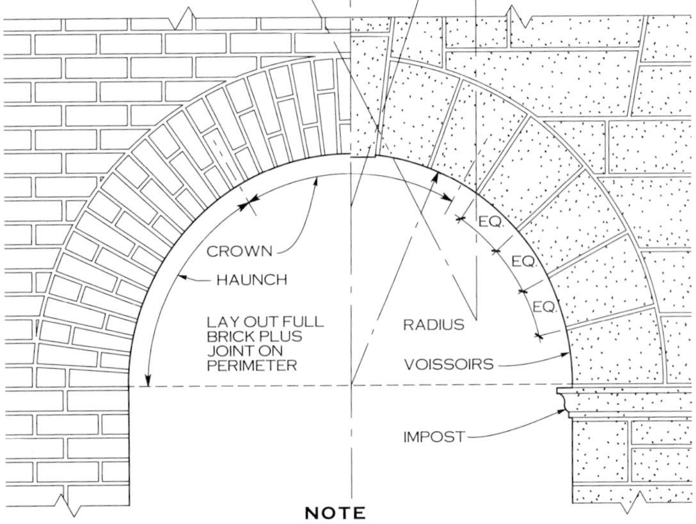

CROWN

HAUNCH

LAY OUT FULL BRICK PLUS JOINT ON PERIMETER

RADIUS

EQ

EQ

EQ

VOISSOIRS

IMPOST

ROMAN OR SEMICIRCULAR

NOTE

Walls, piers, or abutments adjacent to masonry must be of sufficient strength to resist horizontal thrusts.

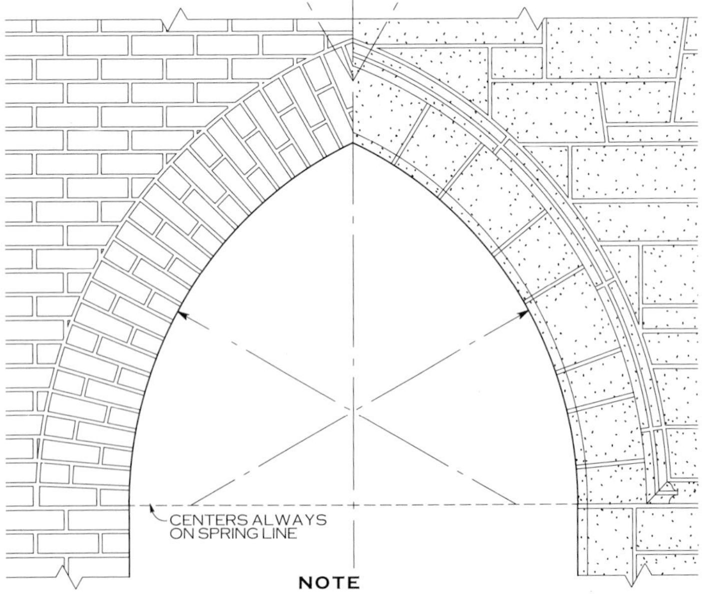

CENTERS ALWAYS ON SPRING LINE

GOTHIC

NOTE

Arch is called pointed when radii are equal to span and is called lancet when radii are greater than span.

Charles George Ramsey, AIA and Harold Reeve Sleeper, FAIA; New York, New York

4   **UNIT MASONRY**

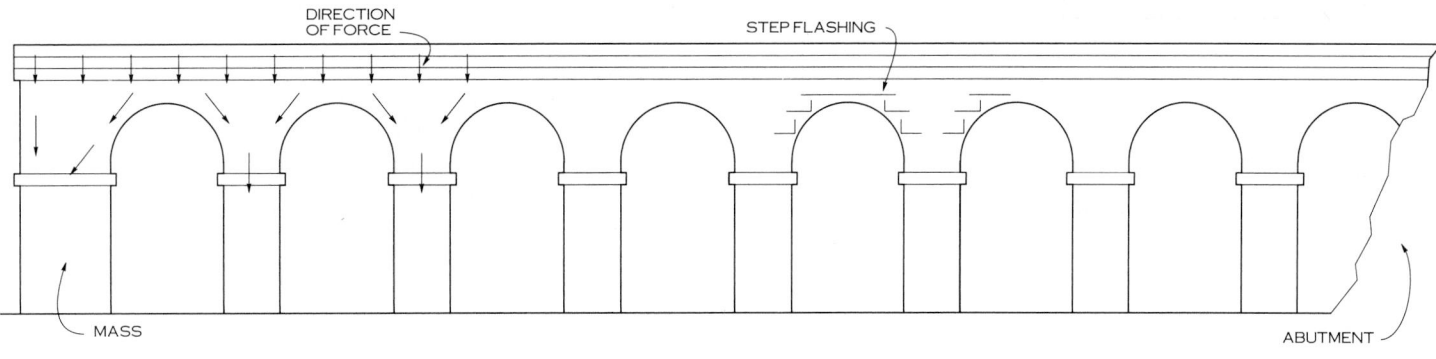

PRINCIPLES OF ARCH CONSTRUCTION

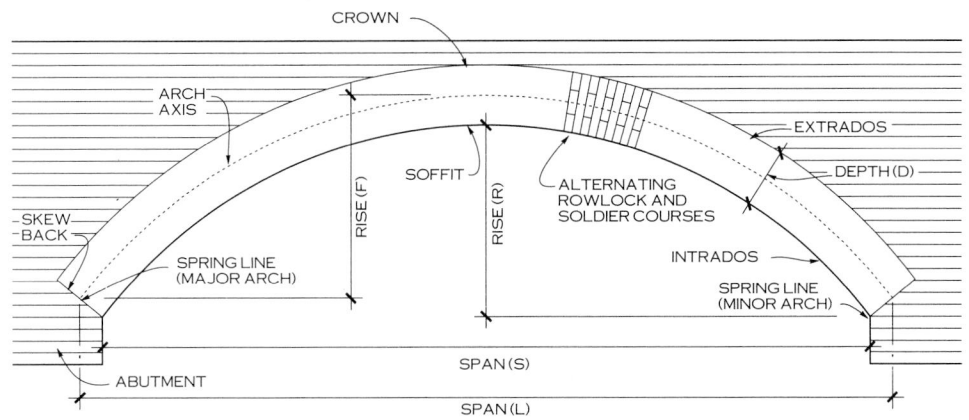

ARCH TERMINOLOGY

GENERAL

The arch shape has appealed to architects and builders since it was first used by the Babylonians. From the arch came other, similar shapes such as the vault and the dome. Because arches are required to resist mainly compressive forces, they are well suited to masonry construction. Architect Louis Kahn is said to have asked a brick, "What form do you want to be?" The brick replied, "An arch."

As illustrated on the preceding page, arch forms are numerous. Arches can be classified based on span length: the minor arch has a span less than or equal to 6 ft; the major arch has a span greater than 6 ft.

The arch is one of the most economical structural shapes. In essence, it is simply a curved beam. All forces in it are transmitted to the abutments. The arch can be a single wythe or several feet thick, as in the case of a vault. Arches may be used as building elements or in bridges or other structures. The true arch does not require any reinforcement if it is designed properly, and it can provide structure, fireproofing, and beauty all in one.

Masonry arches derive their strength from their shape, their material properties, and the size of their abutments. The two classical ways of approaching arch design are the line-of-thrust theory and the plastic theory. The former theory has been used for centuries and is known as the middle-third rule. According to this rule, the line of thrust of the arch must lie within the middle third of the arch's cross section for equilibrium. Graphic methods have been developed to determine the stability of an arch based on this theory. The plastic theory, on the other hand, requires rigorous calculations to develop the limits of the arch. Information on arch design is available in the Brick Institute of America's *Technical Notes* 31 Series.

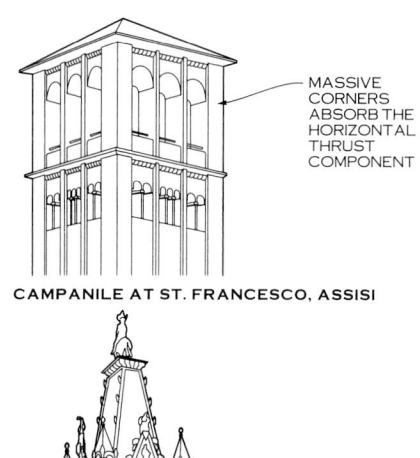

CAMPANILE AT ST. FRANCESCO, ASSISI

MASSIVE CORNERS ABSORB THE HORIZONTAL THRUST COMPONENT

IRON TIES IN TENSION ABSORB THE HORIZONTAL THRUST COMPONENT

TOMB OF THE SCALIGERS, VERONA

HISTORICAL REFERENCES

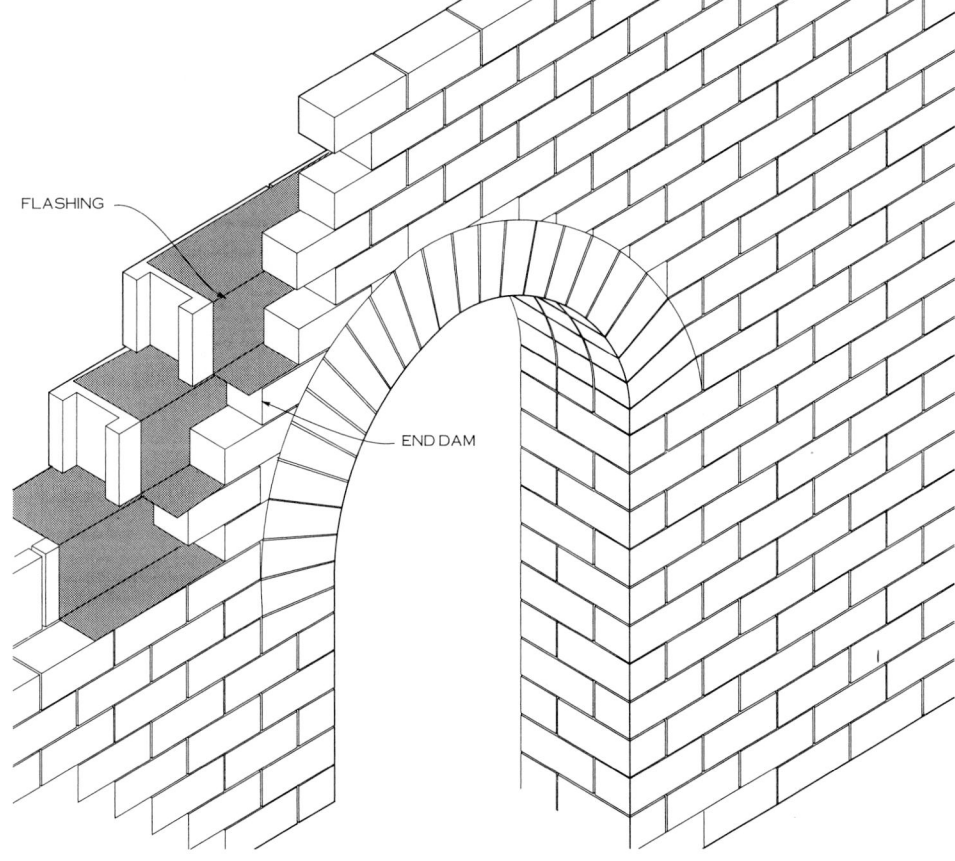

STEP FLASHING DETAIL

Grace S. Lee; Rippeteau Architects, PC; Washington, D.C.
Brian E. Trimble; Brick Institute of America; Reston, Virginia

GENERAL

The fireplace and chimney are usually large elements in residences, but their scale can be adapted to any architectural style. The purpose of the residential fireplace has changed over the years from heating to decoration. However, increasing public interest in renewable forms of energy has instigated a new demand for fireplaces for heating homes. Fireplace design and construction are governed by building and mechanical codes. The internal diagram of a working fireplace shows the several required parts and their vertical organization. Each part is illustrated on succeeding pages.

The main function of the fireplace and chimney is to sustain combustion and carry smoke away safely. Their design is based on empirical data proven with years of safe performance. The charts on the following pages show the appropriate sizes of fireplace and chimney elements. One of the most important design decisions is the location of the fireplace. To prevent heat loss to the exterior, it is best to locate a fireplace at the center of the house. Again to improve performance, a fireplace should not be located opposite an outside door or near an open stairway leading to an upper floor, a forced air furnace, or a return air register. Combustion can be improved by providing a measured supply of outside air, independent of room air, to the fireplace. This is done by installing an air duct from the exterior of the house to the fireplace. The chimney must be properly sized to carry the combustion products away. Two factors primarily affect the chimney draft: size of the fireplace opening and height of the chimney. The figure on the following page should be used to size the flue accurately based on these factors.

Several distinct types of fireplaces are currently used in residential applications. Single-face fireplace styles are the most popular and include the conventional fireplace, the Rumford fireplace, the Rosin fireplace, and air circulating fireplaces. Multiface fireplaces are also popular and include the see-through fireplace, the corner fireplace, and the freestanding fireplace. The masonry heater, or masonry stove, is a specialized type of fireplace and is the most efficient of all these types.

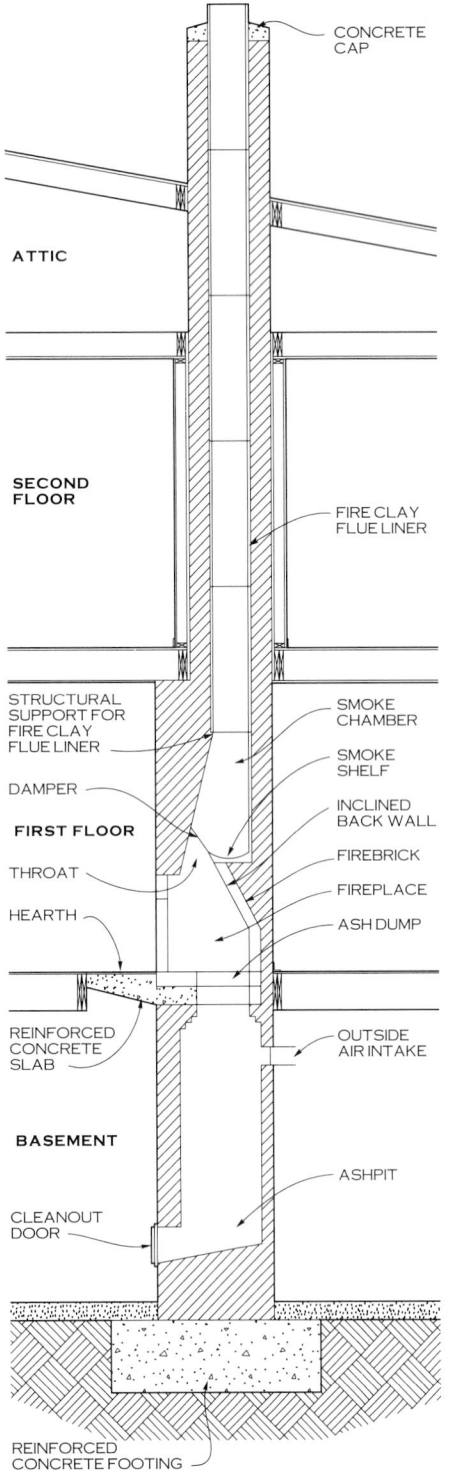

SECTION

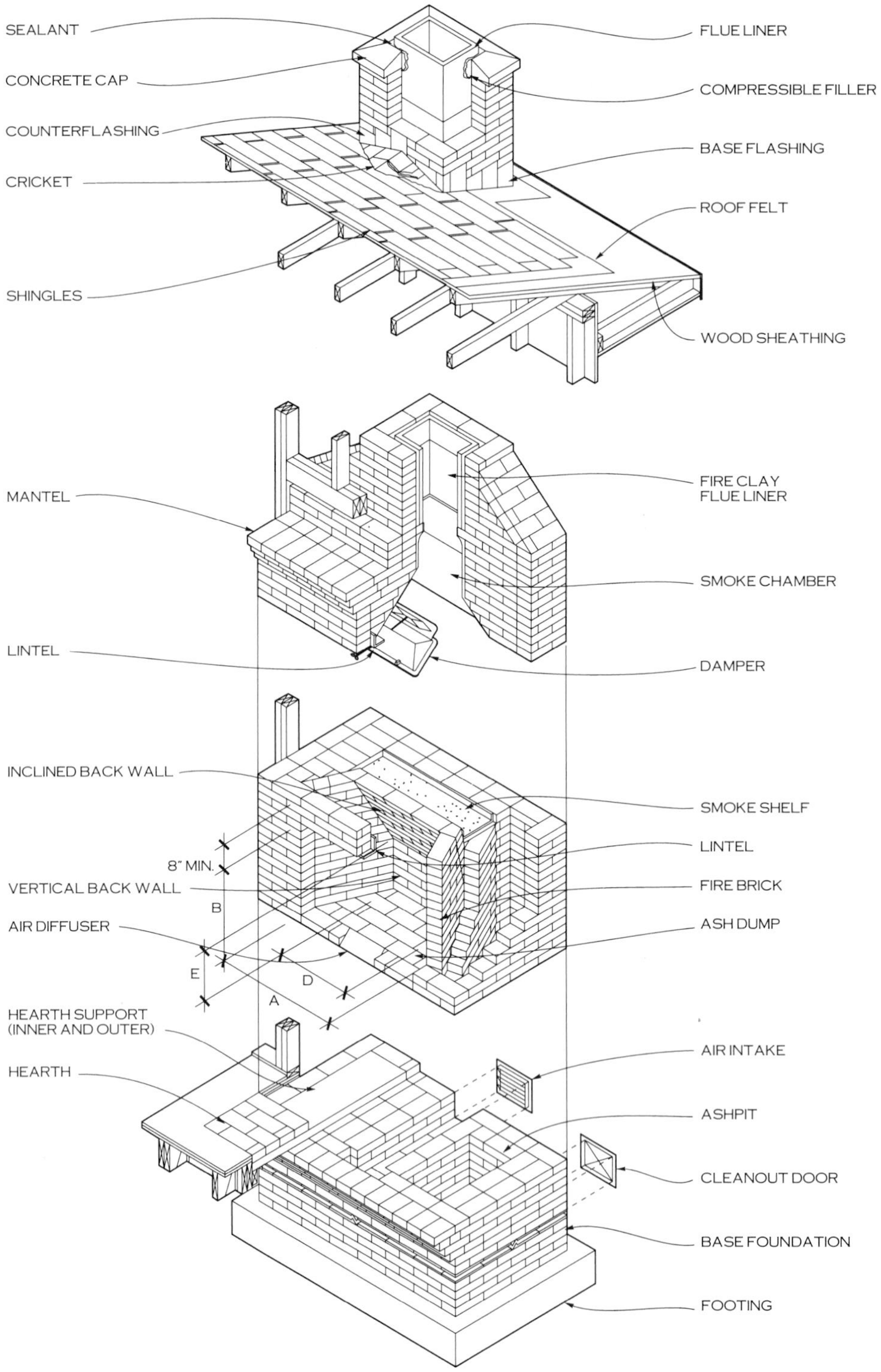

Labels (section diagram, left):
CONCRETE CAP · ATTIC · SECOND FLOOR · FIRE CLAY FLUE LINER · STRUCTURAL SUPPORT FOR FIRE CLAY FLUE LINER · SMOKE CHAMBER · SMOKE SHELF · DAMPER · INCLINED BACK WALL · FIRST FLOOR · FIREBRICK · THROAT · FIREPLACE · HEARTH · ASH DUMP · REINFORCED CONCRETE SLAB · OUTSIDE AIR INTAKE · BASEMENT · ASHPIT · CLEANOUT DOOR · REINFORCED CONCRETE FOOTING

ISOMETRIC

Labels (isometric diagrams, right):
SEALANT · CONCRETE CAP · COUNTERFLASHING · CRICKET · SHINGLES · FLUE LINER · COMPRESSIBLE FILLER · BASE FLASHING · ROOF FELT · WOOD SHEATHING · MANTEL · LINTEL · FIRE CLAY FLUE LINER · SMOKE CHAMBER · DAMPER · INCLINED BACK WALL · VERTICAL BACK WALL · AIR DIFFUSER · 8" MIN. · B · E · D · A · HEARTH SUPPORT (INNER AND OUTER) · HEARTH · SMOKE SHELF · LINTEL · FIRE BRICK · ASH DUMP · AIR INTAKE · ASHPIT · CLEANOUT DOOR · BASE FOUNDATION · FOOTING

Brian E. Trimble; Brick Institute of America; Reston, Virginia
Grace S. Lee; Rippeteau Architects, PC; Washington, D.C.

4 **UNIT MASONRY**

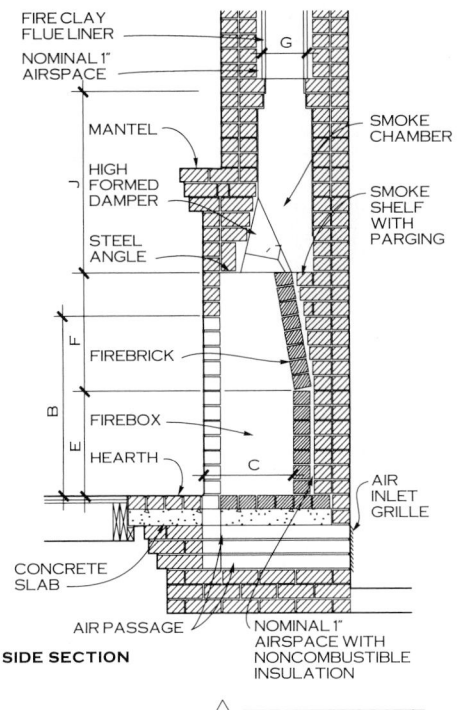

SIDE SECTION

Labels: FIRE CLAY FLUE LINER, NOMINAL 1" AIRSPACE, MANTEL, HIGH FORMED DAMPER, STEEL ANGLE, FIREBRICK, FIREBOX, HEARTH, CONCRETE SLAB, AIR PASSAGE, G, SMOKE CHAMBER, SMOKE SHELF WITH PARGING, AIR INLET GRILLE, NOMINAL 1" AIRSPACE WITH NONCOMBUSTIBLE INSULATION

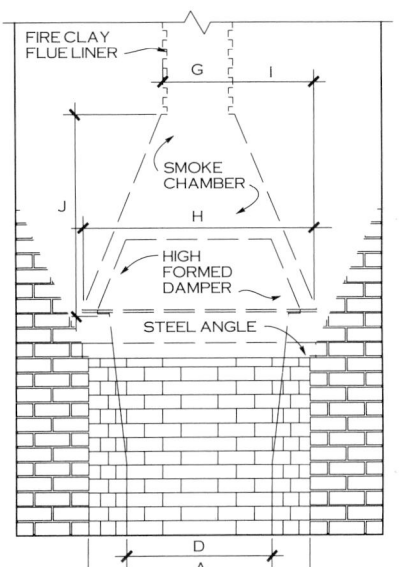

FRONT ELEVATION

Labels: FIRE CLAY FLUE LINER, G, I, J, SMOKE CHAMBER, HIGH FORMED DAMPER, H, STEEL ANGLE, D, A

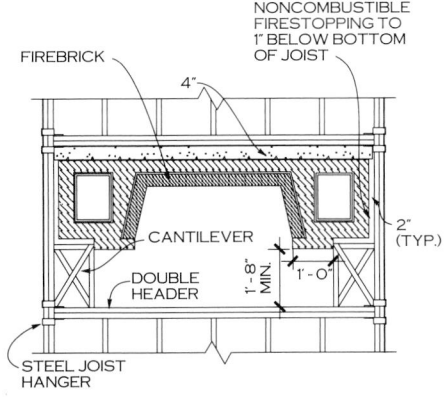

FLOOR FRAMING AT FIREPLACE

CONVENTIONAL FIREPLACE

Labels: FIREBRICK, 4", NONCOMBUSTIBLE FIRESTOPPING TO 1" BELOW BOTTOM OF JOIST, CANTILEVER, 1'-8" MIN., 1'-0", 2" (TYP.), DOUBLE HEADER, STEEL JOIST HANGER

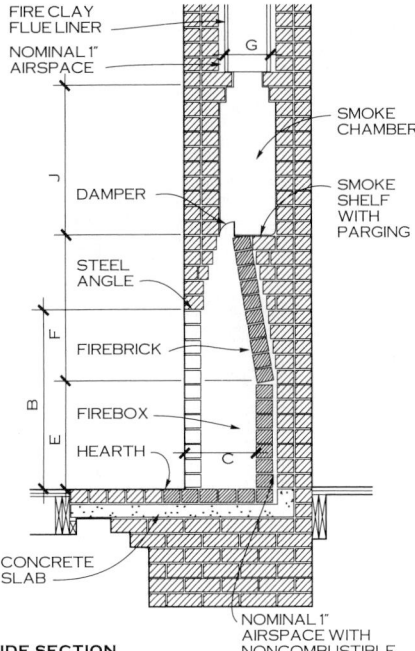

SIDE SECTION

Labels: FIRE CLAY FLUE LINER, NOMINAL 1" AIRSPACE, DAMPER, STEEL ANGLE, FIREBRICK, FIREBOX, HEARTH, CONCRETE SLAB, G, SMOKE CHAMBER, SMOKE SHELF WITH PARGING, NOMINAL 1" AIRSPACE WITH NONCOMBUSTIBLE INSULATION

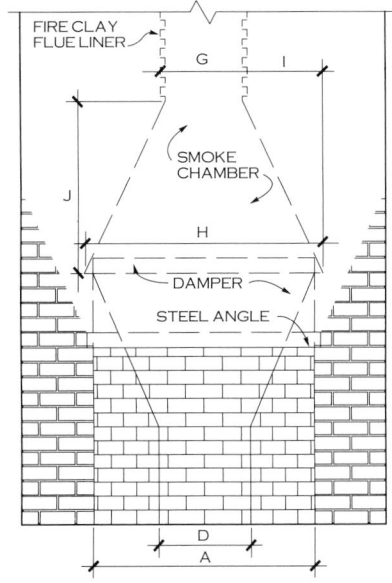

FRONT ELEVATION

Labels: FIRE CLAY FLUE LINER, G, I, J, SMOKE CHAMBER, H, DAMPER, STEEL ANGLE, D, A

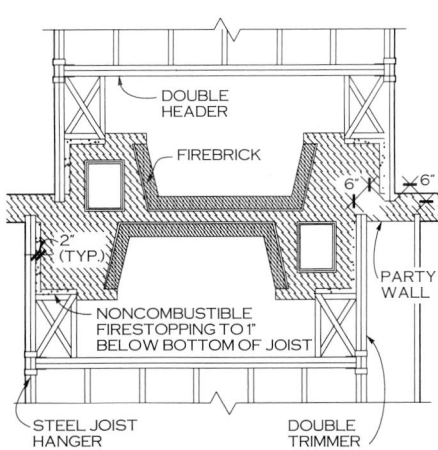

FIREPLACES BACK TO BACK IN PARTY WALL

RUMFORD FIREPLACE

Labels: DOUBLE HEADER, FIREBRICK, 6", 6", 2" (TYP.), NONCOMBUSTIBLE FIRESTOPPING TO 1" BELOW BOTTOM OF JOIST, PARTY WALL, STEEL JOIST HANGER, DOUBLE TRIMMER

Grace S. Lee; Rippeteau Architects, PC; Washington, D.C.

CONVENTIONAL FIREPLACES

The design of single-face fireplaces has been well documented, resulting in the development of a reasonably accurate set of design dimensions for fireplace openings, dampers, and flue liners.

Single-face fireplaces can be efficient radiant heaters. The amount of heat radiated and reflected into the room is directly proportional to the masonry surface area exposed to the fire. The Rumford fireplace is a variation of the single-face fireplace with a shallow firebox, a high throat, and widely splayed sides, all features that contribute to optimal direct radiant heating.

In addition, the energy efficiency of new fireplaces can be improved by following these recommendations:

1. Locate the fireplace on the interior of the house.
2. Supply outside air for combustion and maintenance of positive room pressure.
3. Provide glass fireplace screens to prevent unwanted air infiltration when the fireplace is not in use.

CONVENTIONAL SINGLE-FACE FIREPLACE DIMENSIONS* (IN.)

FINISHED FIREPLACE OPENING						ROUGH BRICKWORK		
A	B	C	D	E	F	H	I	J
24	24	16	11	14	18	32	10	19
26	24	16	13	14	18	34	11	21
28	24	16	15	14	18	36	12	21
30	29	16	17	14	23	38	13	24
32	29	16	19	14	23	40	14	24
36	29	16	23	14	23	44	16	27
40	29	16	27	14	23	48	16	29
42	32	16	29	16	24	50	17	32
48	32	18	33	16	24	56	20	37
54	37	20	37	16	29	68	26	45
60	37	22	42	16	29	72	26	45
60	40	22	42	18	30	72	26	45
72	40	22	54	18	30	84	32	56
84	40	24	64	18	30	96	36	61
96	40	24	76	18	30	108	42	75

NOTE

* Determine flue liner dimensions, G. Dimensions are equal to the outside dimensions of the flue liner plus at least 1 in. (25 mm).

RUMFORD SINGLE-FACE FIREPLACE DIMENSIONS* (IN.)

FINISHED FIREPLACE OPENING						ROUGH BRICKWORK		
A	B	C	D	E	F	H	I	J
36	32	16	16	16	28	44	14	27
40	32	16	16	16	28	48	16	29
40	37	16	16	16	33	48	16	29
40	40	20	20	20	32	48	16	29
48	37	16	16	20	33	56	18	36
48	40	20	20	20	32	56	18	36
48	48	20	20	20	40	56	18	36
54	40	20	20	20	32	66	23	45
54	48	20	20	20	40	66	23	45
54	54	20	20	20	46	66	21	42
60	48	20	20	20	40	72	24	45

NOTE

* Determine flue liner dimensions, G. Dimensions are equal to the outside dimensions of the flue liner plus at least 1 in. (25 mm) for airspace surrounding flue liner.

INTRODUCTION

In North America brick masonry heaters or masonry stoves are adapted from those used in northern and eastern Europe, which were used for cooking as well as heating. Masonry heaters make use of two basic principles to obtain high combustion and heating efficiencies–controlled air intake to the combustion chamber/firebox and a heat exchange system of baffled chambers through which hot combustion gases are circulated. Such heaters are efficient, clean burning devices.

Masonry heaters come in a wide variety of shapes and sizes. The size and layout of the house, the climate, and the needs of the homeowner are all considered in the design of a masonry heater. For optimum performance, however, it should be located near the center of the house. Masonry heaters may be custom built on-site or assembled from prefabricated components. Modern masonry heaters may incorporate fire viewing, bake ovens, stoves, and warming benches.

FINNISH MASONRY HEATERS

Finnish or contraflow heaters are so called because heated air is forced from the top of the smoke chamber down through the baffles on the sides of the heater, while room air rises by convection along the exterior surfaces of the masonry. This construction allows for even heating of the masonry and efficient radiant heating of the room. The baffles converge below the firebox and open out to the flue at the base of the chimney.

RUSSIAN MASONRY HEATERS

Russian heaters are typically deep with a small opening to the firebox and above it a system of either vertically or horizontally aligned baffles, which replace the smoke chamber. After circulating through the baffle system, exhaust gases pass directly into the flue. There is no decided advantage to either baffle alignment, though the horizontal system is easier to construct. Cleanouts are optional on either system, but are recommended to observe creosote or ash buildup.

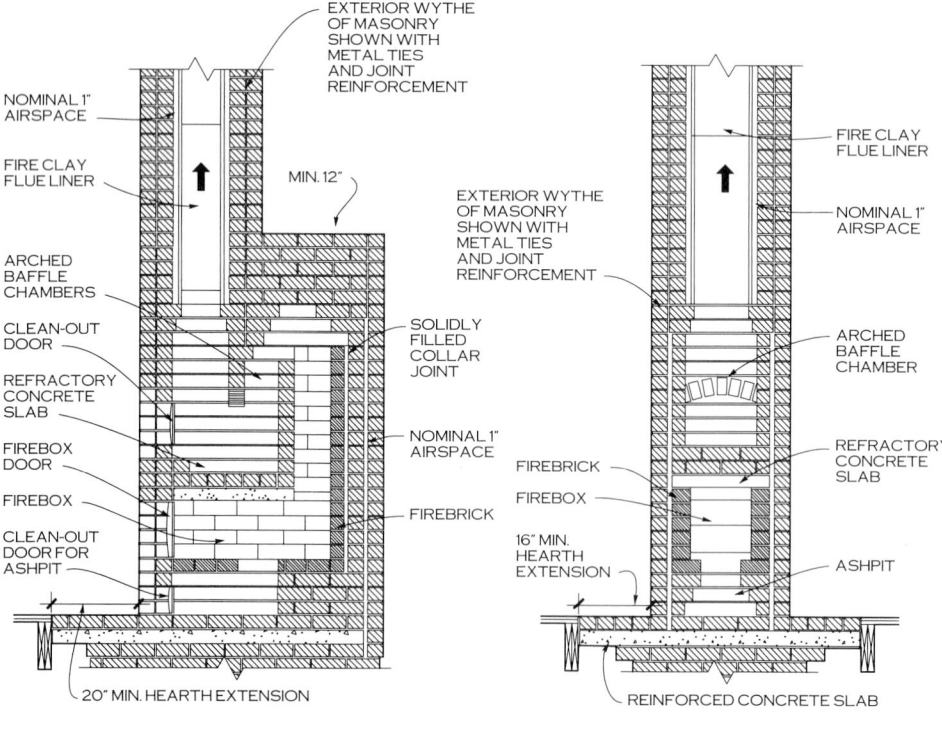

FINNISH MASONRY STOVE

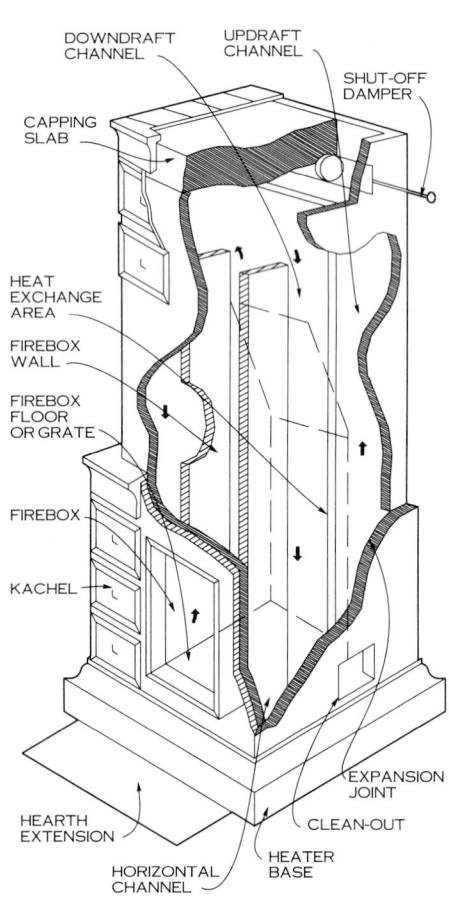

KAKELUGN

Timothy B. McDonald; Washington, D.C.
Brian E. Trimble; Brick Institute of America; Reston, Virginia

RUSSIAN MASONRY STOVE

 UNIT MASONRY

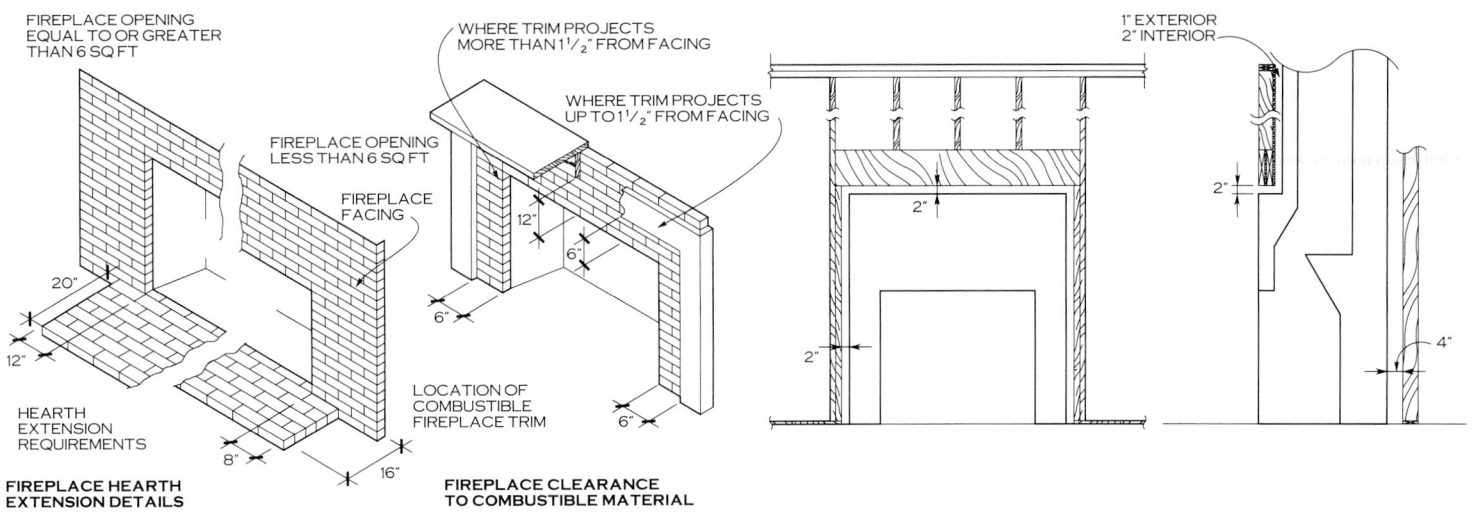

FIREPLACE HEARTH EXTENSION DETAILS

FIREPLACE CLEARANCE TO COMBUSTIBLE MATERIAL

FIREPLACE CLEARANCES

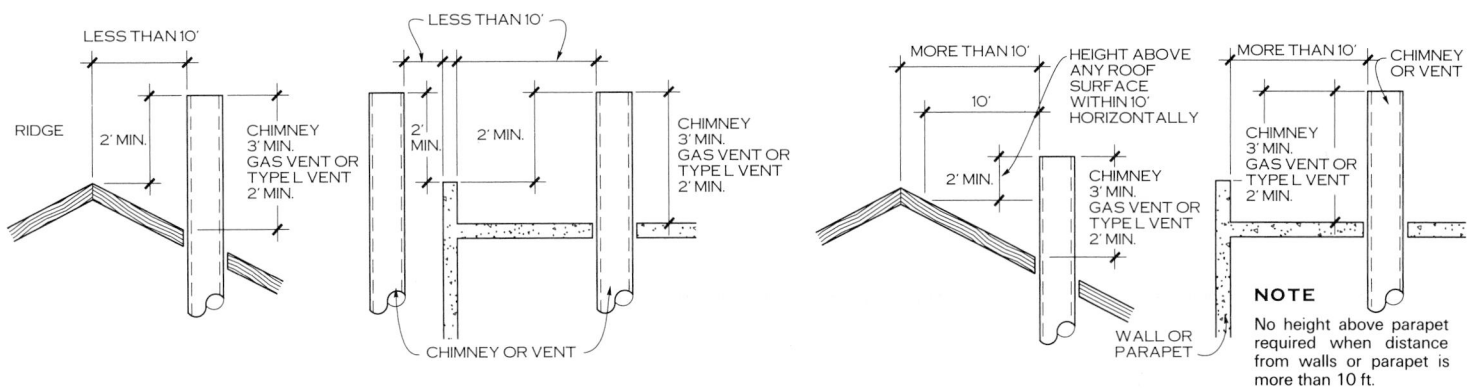

TERMINATION LESS THAN 10 FT FROM RIDGE, WALL, OR PARAPET

TERMINATION MORE THAN 10 FT FROM RIDGE, WALL, OR PARAPET

NOTE
No height above parapet required when distance from walls or parapet is more than 10 ft.

CHIMNEY CLEARANCES

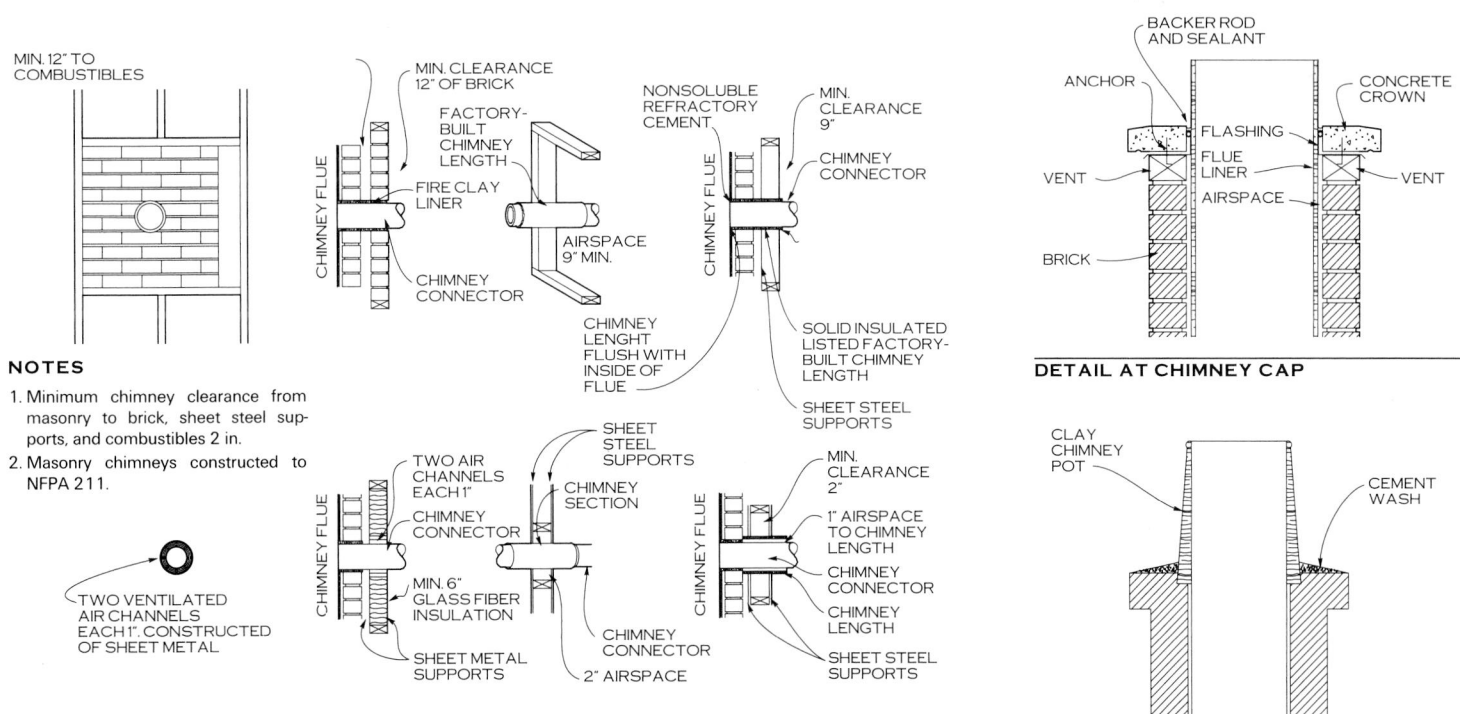

NOTES

1. Minimum chimney clearance from masonry to brick, sheet steel supports, and combustibles 2 in.
2. Masonry chimneys constructed to NFPA 211.

TWO VENTILATED AIR CHANNELS EACH 1". CONSTRUCTED OF SHEET METAL

CHIMNEY CONNECTOR SYSTEMS AND CLEARANCES FROM COMBUSTIBLE WALLS

DETAIL AT CHIMNEY CAP

CHIMNEY POT

Grace S. Lee; Rippeteau Architects, PC; Washington, D.C.
Brian E. Trimble; Brick Institute of America; Reston, Virginia

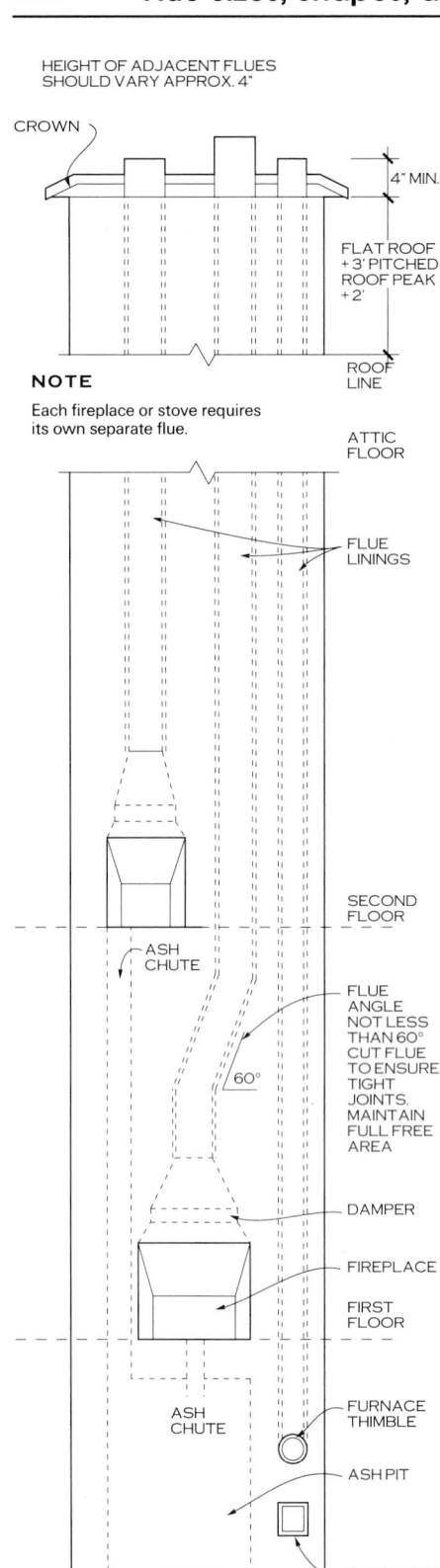

HEIGHT OF ADJACENT FLUES SHOULD VARY APPROX. 4"

CROWN

4" MIN.

FLAT ROOF + 3' PITCHED ROOF PEAK + 2'

ROOF LINE

NOTE

Each fireplace or stove requires its own separate flue.

ATTIC FLOOR

FLUE LININGS

SECOND FLOOR

ASH CHUTE

FLUE ANGLE NOT LESS THAN 60° CUT FLUE TO ENSURE TIGHT JOINTS. MAINTAIN FULL FREE AREA

60°

DAMPER

FIREPLACE

FIRST FLOOR

ASH CHUTE

FURNACE THIMBLE

ASH PIT

CLEANOUT DOORS

2" (TYP.)

BASEMENT

TYPICAL RESIDENTIAL CHIMNEY

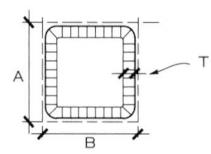

RECTANGULAR FLUE LINING (STANDARD)

AREA (SQ IN.)	A	B	T
51	8 1/2"	8 1/2"	3/4"
79	8 1/2"	13"	7/8"
108	8 1/2"	18"	1"
125	13"	13"	7/8"
168	13"	17 3/4"	1"
232	17 3/4"	17 3/4"	1 1/4"
279	20"	20"	1 3/8"
338	20"	24"	1 1/2"
420	24"	24"	1 5/8"

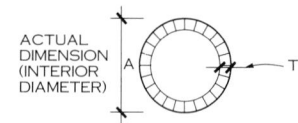

RECTANGULAR FLUE LINING (MODULAR)

AREA (SQ IN.)	A	B	T
57	7 1/2"	11 1/2"	3/4"
87	11 1/2"	11 1/2"	7/8"
120	11 1/2"	15 1/2"	1"
162	15 1/2"	15 1/2"	1 1/8"
208	15 1/2"	19 1/2"	1 1/4"
262	19 1/2"	19 1/2"	1 3/8"
320	19 1/2"	23 1/2"	1 1/2"
385	23 1/2"	23 1/2"	1 5/8"

ACTUAL DIMENSION (INTERIOR DIAMETER)

ROUND FLUE LINING

AREA (SQ IN.)	A	T	LENGTH
47	8"	3/4"	2'-0"
74.5	10"	7/8"	2'-0"
108	12"	1"	2'-0"
171	15"	1 1/8"	2'-0"
240	18"	1 1/4"	2'-0"
298	20"	1 3/8"	2'-0"
433	24"	1 5/8"	2'-0"

CLAY FLUE LININGS

NOTES

1. Availability of specific clay flue liners varies according to location. Generally, round flue liners used in construction with reinforcing bars are available in the western states, while rectangular flue liners are commonly found throughout the eastern states. Check with local manufacturers for available types and sizes.

2. Nominal flue size for round flues is interior diameter; nominal flue sizes for standard rectangular flues are the exterior dimensions and, for modular flue linings, the outside dimensions plus 1/2 in.

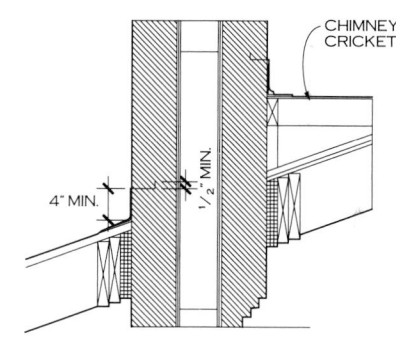

CHIMNEY CRICKET

1/2" MIN.

4" MIN.

INSULATION OF WOOD FRAMING MEMBERS AT A CHIMNEY

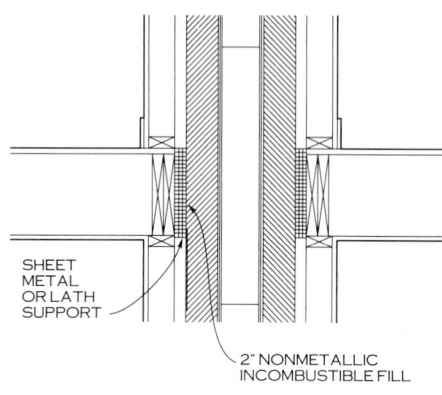

SHEET METAL OR LATH SUPPORT

2" NONMETALLIC INCOMBUSTIBLE FILL

BRICK CHIMNEY CONCEALED BEHIND STUD WALL

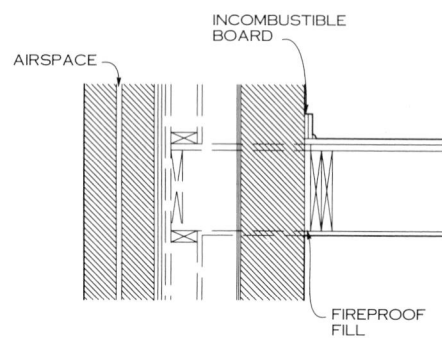

INCOMBUSTIBLE BOARD

AIRSPACE

FIREPROOF FILL

BRICK CHIMNEY EXPOSED

CHIMNEY FRAMING AND INSULATION

3. Areas shown are net minimum inside areas.

4. All flue liners are generally available in 2 ft lengths.

5. Fireplace flue sizes can be approximated using the following rules of thumb: One-tenth the area of fireplace opening recommended; one-eighth the area of opening recommended if chimney is higher than 20 ft and rectangular flues are used; one-twelfth the area is minimum required; verify with local codes.

 UNIT MASONRY

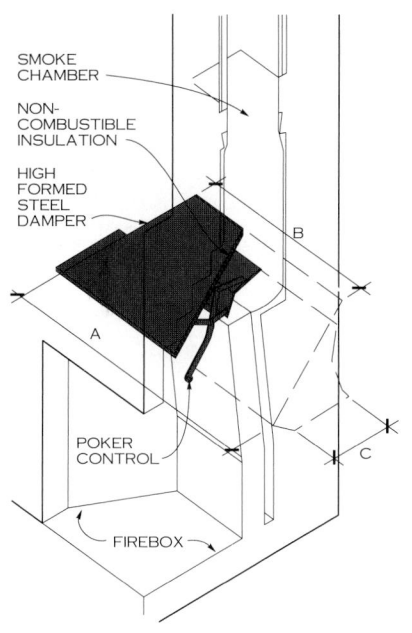

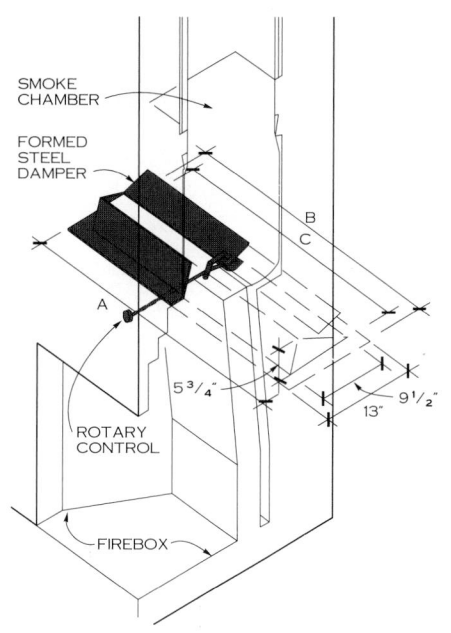

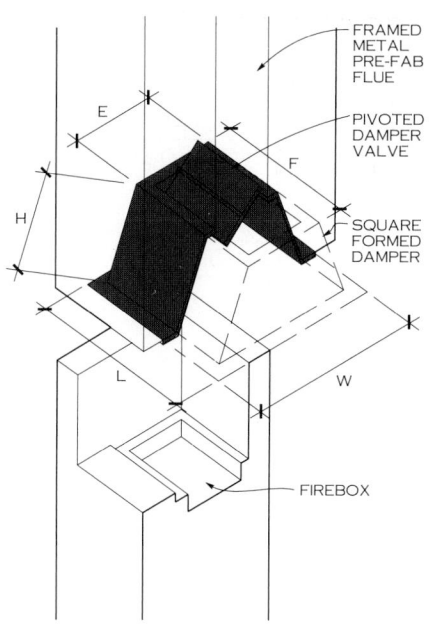

HIGH FORMED DAMPER (IN.)

A	B	C
32	15 1/4	9 3/4
36	19 1/4	9 3/4
40	23 1/4	9 3/4
44	27 1/4	9 3/4
48	31 1/4	9 3/4

HIGH FORMED DAMPERS provide correct ratio of throat-to-fireplace opening with an optional preformed smoke shelf, which can reduce material and labor requirements. They are useful for both single and multiple opening fireplaces.

FORMED DAMPER (IN.)

WIDTH OF OPENING	DAMPER DIMENSIONS (IN.)		
	A	B	C
24 to 26	28 1/4	26 3/4	24
27 to 30	32 1/4	30 3/4	28
31 to 34	36 1/4	34 3/4	32
35 to 38	40 1/4	38 3/4	36
39 to 42	44 1/4	42 3/4	40
43 to 46	48 1/4	46 3/4	44
47 to 50	52 1/4	50 3/4	48

FORMED STEEL DAMPERS are designed to provide the correct ratio of throat-to-fireplace opening, producing maximum draft. These dampers are equipped with poker type control and are easily installed.

SQUARE FORMED DAMPER (IN.)

TOP OUTLET			OVERALL SIZE	
E	F	H	L	W
17	17	17	41	27
17	17	25	45	27
17	23	25	49	27

SQUARE FORMED DAMPERS have high sloping sides that promote even draw on all sides of multiple opening fireplaces. They are properly proportioned for a strong draft and smokefree operation.

FORMED STEEL DAMPERS

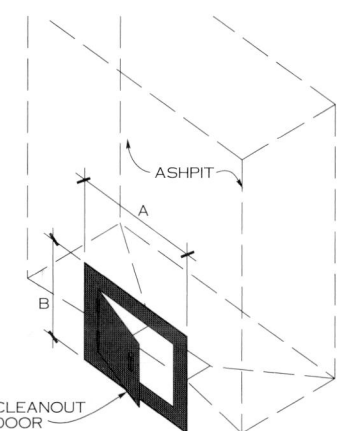

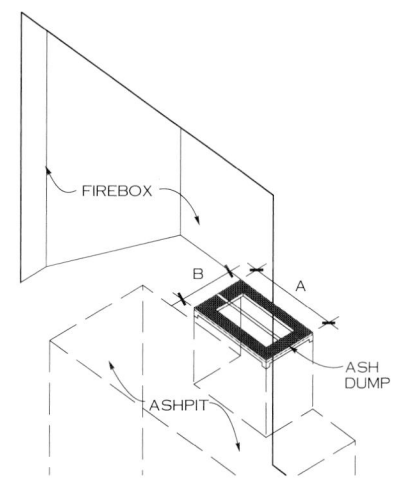

NOTES

1. Locate bottom of damper minimum 6 to 8 in. from top of fireplace opening.
2. Mineral wool blanket allows for expansion of metal damper walls.
3. Dampers are available in heavy gauge steel or cast iron. Check with local suppliers for specific forms and sizes.
4. A cord of wood consists of 128 cu ft or a stack 4 ft high and 8 ft wide, with logs 4 ft long.
5. A face cord of wood consists of 64 cu ft or a stack 4 ft high and 8 ft wide, with logs 2 ft long.
6. Logs are cut to lengths of 1 ft 4 in., 2 ft 0 in., 2 ft 6 in., and 4 ft. Allow 3 in. minimum clearance between logs and each side of fireplace.

DOOR DIMENSIONS (IN.)

A	B
6	8
8	8, 10
10	10, 12
12	8, 10, 12, 16, 18

CLEANOUT OR ASHPIT DOOR

DUMP DIMENSIONS (IN.)

A	3 1/2	4 1/2	7
B	7	9	10

NOTE

Ash dumps and cleanout doors are available in heavy gauge steel or cast iron. See local manufacturers for available types and sizes.

ASH DUMP

Timothy B. McDonald; Washington, D.C.

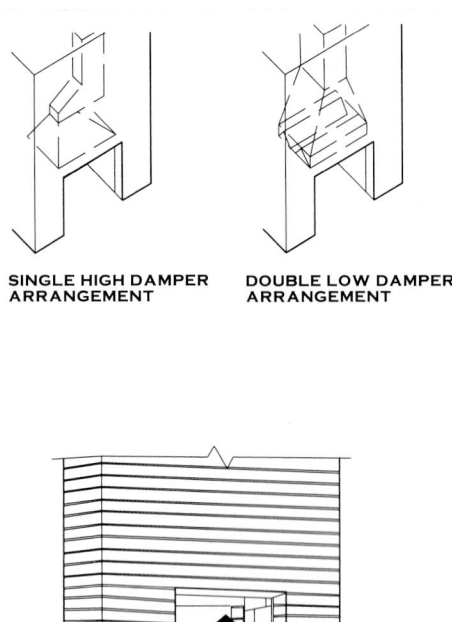

SINGLE HIGH DAMPER ARRANGEMENT **DOUBLE LOW DAMPER ARRANGEMENT**

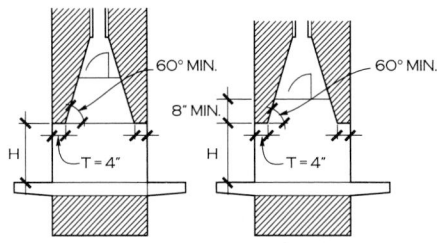

SECTION A   **SECTION B**

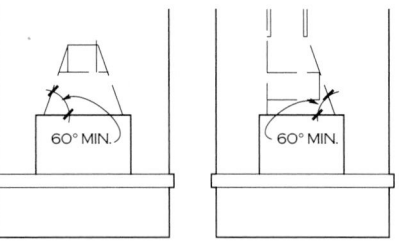

ELEVATION A   **ELEVATION B**

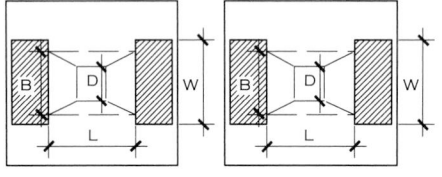

PLAN A   **PLAN B**

NOTE

Fireplace must be located and designed to allow proper updraft through both openings. Do not place an exterior door opposite the fireplace on either side. Such doors may cause cross drafts through the fireplace.

FIREPLACE OPEN FRONT AND SIDE

FIREPLACE OPEN FRONT AND BACK

H = Height from top of hearth to bottom of facing.

B = (depth of burning area) $\frac{5}{8}$ H minus 8 in., but never less than 16 in.

W = (width of fireplace) B + 2T.

D = (damper at bottom of flue, see Section A) equal to free area of flue.

D = (damper closer to fire, see Section B) equal to twice the free area of flue. Set damper a minimum of 8 in. from bottom of smoke chamber. Open damper should extend entire length of smoke chamber.

TYPICAL FIREPLACE DIMENSIONS

L	H	B	FLUE
28	24	16	13 x 13
30	28	16	13 x 18
36	30	17	18 x 18
48	32	19	20 x 24
54	36	22	24 x 24

NOTE

W should not be less than 24 in.

NOTE

Modified open corner version can solve cross draft problems. Fireplace design is similar to basic front-open type.

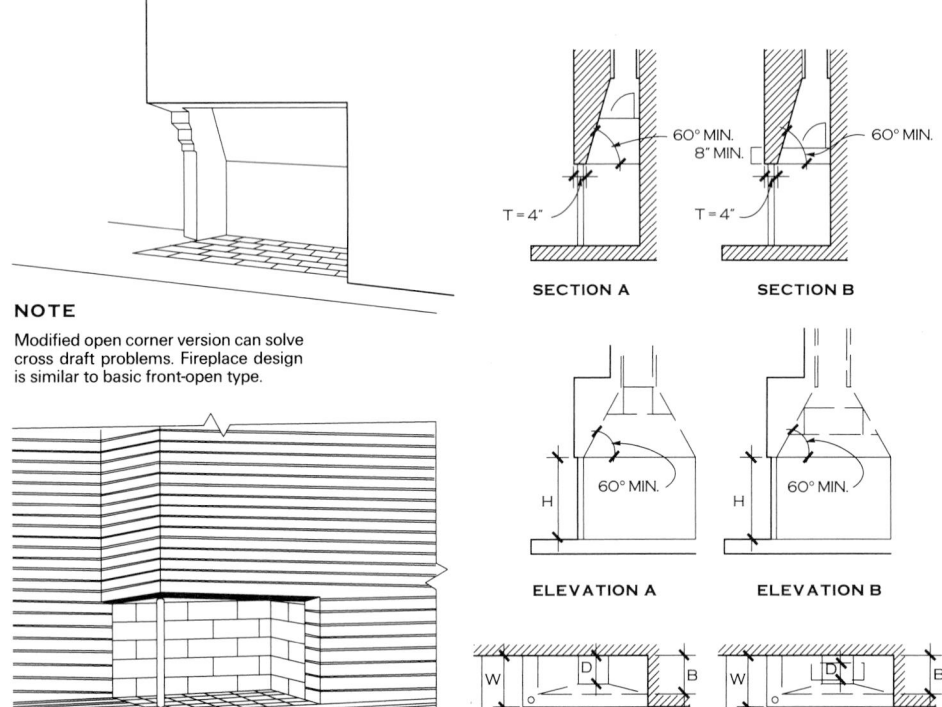

SECTION A   **SECTION B**

ELEVATION A   **ELEVATION B**

PLAN A   **PLAN B**

NOTE

Fireplace shown as part of massive wall. open corner supported by pipe column.

FIREPLACE OPEN FRONT AND SIDE

FIREPLACE OPEN FRONT AND SIDE

H = Height from top of hearth to bottom of facing.

B = (depth of burning area) $\frac{2}{3}$ H minus 4 in.

W = (width of fireplace) B + T.

D = (damper at bottom of flue, see Section A) equal to twice the free area of flue. Set damper a minimum of 8 in. from bottom of smoke chamber.

TYPICAL FIREPLACE DIMENSIONS

L	H	B	FLUE
28	24	16	12 x 12
30	28	18	13 x 18
36	30	20	13 x 18
48	32	22	18 x 18

Darrel Downing Rippeteau, AIA, Architect; Washington, D.C.

UNIT MASONRY

GENERAL

Structural clay facing tile is chosen as an attractive and durable wall system in many specialized applications, especially when maintenance and resistance to vandalism are considered. Applications include walls and partitions in correctional facilities, schools, public buildings, and food processing facilities. Structural clay tile can be glazed or unglazed, load bearing or non-load bearing, and behaves similarly to brick. Structural clay tile is manufactured in many sizes and shapes. Numbers and letters shown on the units in the figures indicate the standard shape classifications of structural clay tile used by manufacturers.

WALL SECTIONS AND PROPERTIES

WALL TYPE NUMBER		1	2	3	4	5
Allowable load (lb/linear ft)	Types M and S mortar			9660	9660	12390
	Type N mortar			8280	8280	10620
Material quantity (per 100 sq ft)	Mortar (cu ft) 25% waste added	2.19	2.19	3.36	3.36[2]	6.97
	Facing tile 2% waste added	230	230	230	230	230
	Brick 5% waste added					709
U values (BTU/sq ft · hr · °F)	Unplastered partition	0.40	0.40	0.35	0.34	
	Exterior wall					0.30
	With 2 in. insulation					0.08
Lateral support spacing required (ft)	Non-load bearing	12	12	18	18	24
	Load bearing			9	9	12
Wall weight	Unplastered	30	30	41	47	67
Sound resistance (dB)	Unplastered	45	45	47	48	54
Fire resistance (hr)	Regular coring	See note 1	See note 1	1	2	3
	Fire rated coring	1	1	2	3	4

NOTES

1. $^{3}/_{4}$ in. plaster on back of these units will produce 1 hour fire rating.
2. If collar joint is filled, add 2.6 cu ft per 100 sq ft of wall.

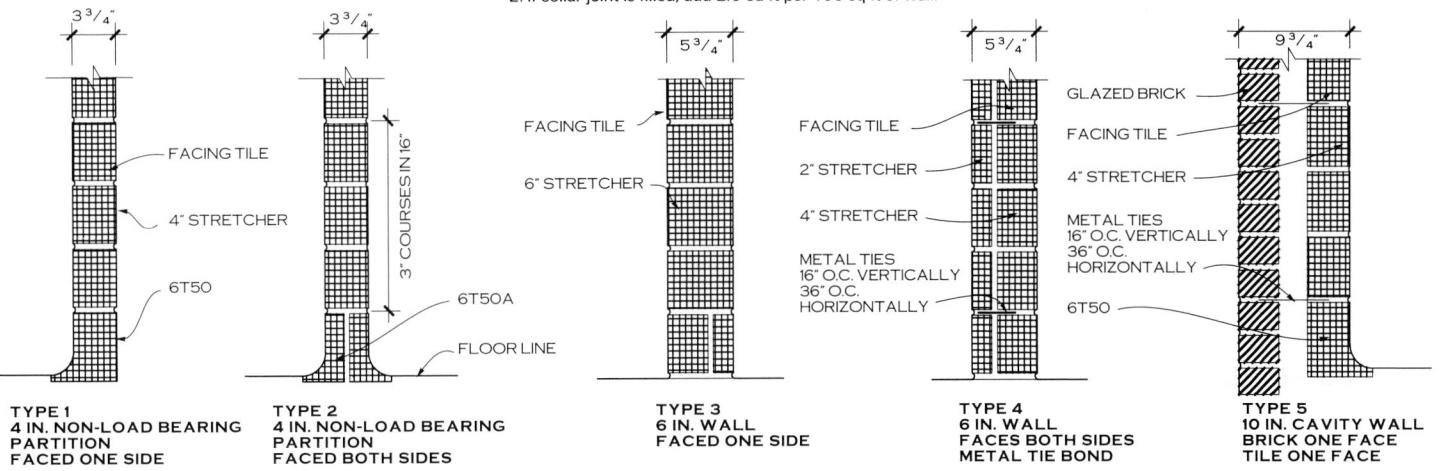

TYPE 1
4 IN. NON-LOAD BEARING PARTITION FACED ONE SIDE

TYPE 2
4 IN. NON-LOAD BEARING PARTITION FACED BOTH SIDES

TYPE 3
6 IN. WALL FACED ONE SIDE

TYPE 4
6 IN. WALL FACES BOTH SIDES METAL TIE BOND

TYPE 5
10 IN. CAVITY WALL BRICK ONE FACE TILE ONE FACE

SECTION

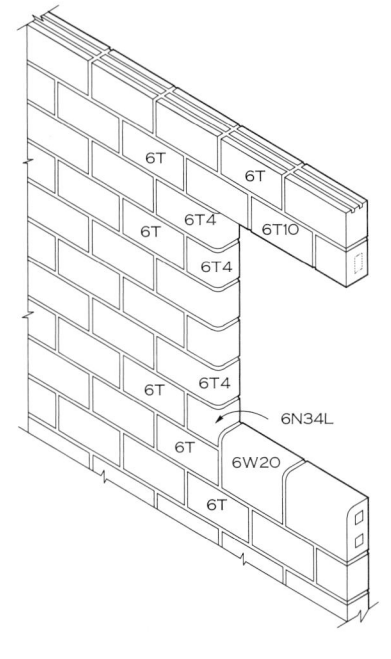

4 IN. SINGLE-FACED WALL WITH BULLNOSE SILL AND JAMB; SQUARE LINTEL RUNNING BOND

SECTION

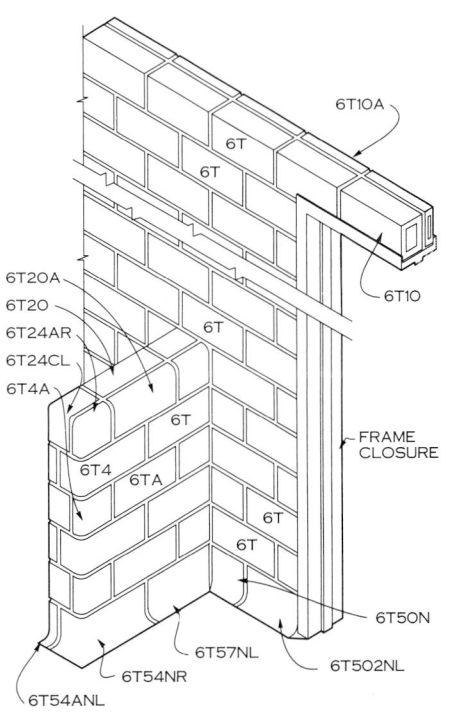

6 IN. DOUBLE-FACED WING WALL BONDED TO MAIN WALL WITH TYPICAL BUTT JOINTS

SECTION

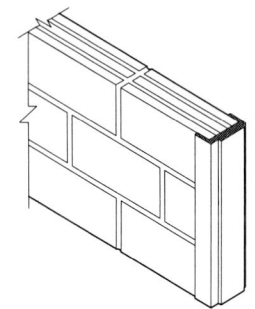

4 IN. WALL

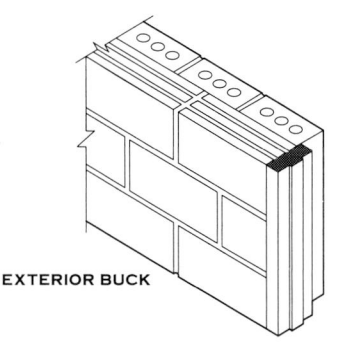

EXTERIOR BUCK

FRAME FITTINGS

Grace S. Lee; Rippeteau Architects, PC; Washington, D.C.
Facing Tile Institute; Washington, D.C.

TERRA-COTTA

Terra-cotta is a high grade of weathered or aged clay, which, when mixed with sand or with pulverized fired clay, can be molded to a hardness and compactness not obtainable with other materials. Used extensively until the 1930s, terra-cotta has been largely replaced with ceramic veneer.

Terra-cotta was usually hollow cast in blocks, open to the back to reveal internal webbing.

Ceramic veneer is not hollow cast but is a veneer of glazed ceramic tile that is ribbed on the back. It is frequently attached to metal ties that are anchored to the building.

Other types of terra-cotta are:

1. Brownstone terra-cotta. A dark red or brown block, which is hollow cast. Used extensively in the mid- to late-19th century.
2. Fireproof construction terra-cotta. Inexpensive and lightweight, these rough-finished hollow building blocks span beams. The blocks are available but not used widely today.
3. Glazed architectural terra-cotta. Hollow units were hand cast in molds or carved in clay and heavily glazed. Sometimes called architectural ceramics, this terra-cotta type was used until the 1930s.

NOTES

Ceramic veneer can be anchored or adhered to masonry.

The ceramic veneer manufacturer should provide scale shop drawings as detailed from the architect's drawings. To be used for setting, the shop drawings should indicate all dimensions and sizes of joints, and all anchors, hangers, expansion, and control or pressure-relieving joints.

Nonferrous metal anchors should be embedded in the masonry and encased for protection from corrosion.

The minimum thickness of anchored-type ceramic veneer, exclusive of ribs, should be 1 in.

Ceramic veneer should be set true to line in setting mortar. Spaces between anchored ceramic veneer and backing walls should be filled with grout: spaces $3/4$ in. or more in width with pea gravel and spaces $3/4$ in. with mortar.

The minimum thickness of adhesion-type ceramic veneer, including ribs, should be $1/4$ in. with ribbed or scored backs.

An evenly spread coat of neat portland cement and water should be applied to the wall and the entire back of the ceramic veneer panel about to be set. Then one half of the setting mortar coat should be immediately applied on the chosen wall area and the other on the ceramic veneer piece's entire back. Tap the piece into place on the wall to completely fill all voids, with the total thickness of the mortar averaging $3/4$ in. There should be some excess mortar forced out at the joints and edge of the ceramic veneer.

MOLD-PRESSED CERAMIC VENEER

The minimum thickness of the exposed faces of mold-pressed ceramic veneer is 1 in. Backs of special shapes should be open and ribbed.

For placement, turn all units bottom-side up and fill solidly with grout filler for mold-pressed ceramic veneer. When the fill has set sufficiently to permit handling, set the units.

When applied to soffits, each piece of ceramic veneer, in addition to the usual centers and wooden wedges, shall be supported by bent and vertical wooden shores. A constant upward pressure is needed until the mortar coat has set.

Adhesion can be tested with a 1 x 1 x 4 in. vitrified test bar. First dissolve vinyl acetate in methyl iso-butyl ketone. Apply to the ceramic veneer surface and test bar. The adhesive is heated by means of an infrared lamp until bubbling ceases. Press the two surfaces together until cool. Then knock or pry off test bar.

TERRA-COTTA VENEER PRECAST PANEL

Terra-cotta precast panels have a keyback design, which allows each piece to easily become an integral part of the precast unit through a mechanical bond. No fasteners are needed.

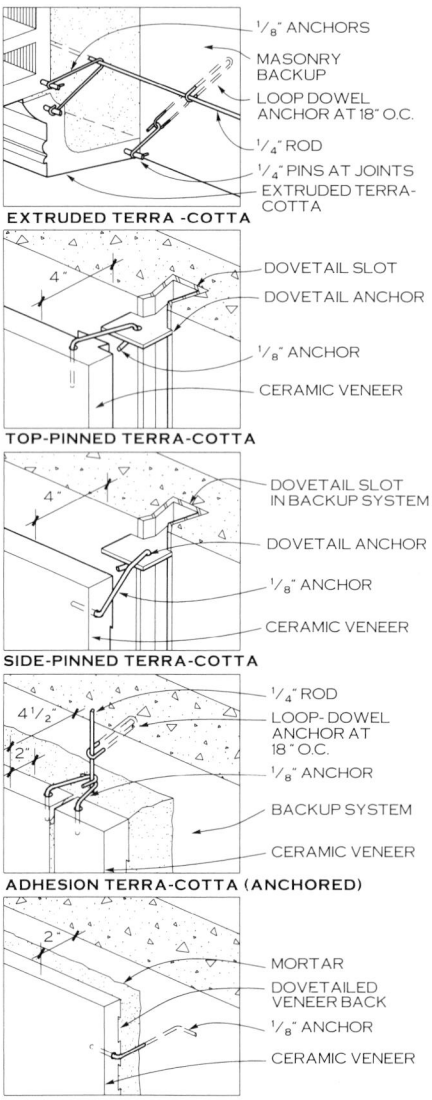

TYPICAL CORNICE

TYPICAL BASE
NOTE

Design of Best Products Corporation

TERRA-COTTA WALL SECTION

Eric K. Beach; Rippeteau Architects, PC; Washington, D.C.

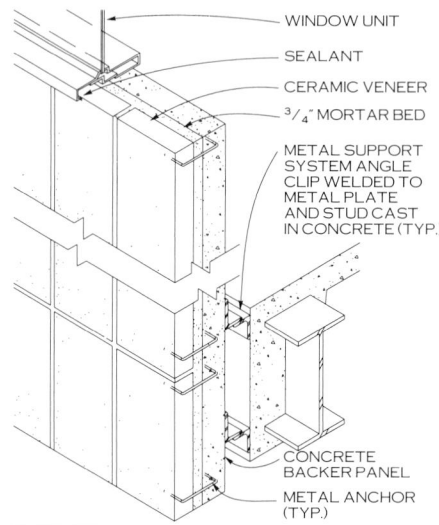

EXTRUDED TERRA-COTTA

TOP-PINNED TERRA-COTTA

SIDE-PINNED TERRA-COTTA

ADHESION TERRA-COTTA (ANCHORED)

ADHESION TERRA-COTTA (ANCHORED)

ANCHORING SYSTEMS

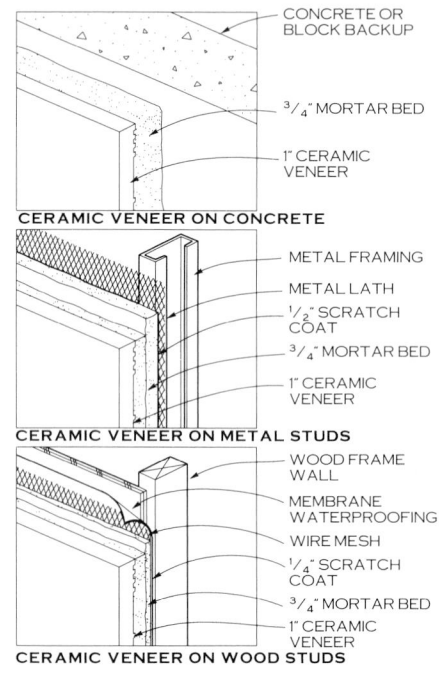

TERRA-COTTA PRECAST PANEL

CERAMIC VENEER ON CONCRETE

CERAMIC VENEER ON METAL STUDS

CERAMIC VENEER ON WOOD STUDS

GROUT-ADHERED CERAMIC VENEER

GENERAL

Glass block is a diverse building material whose many applications exhibit its multifaceted characteristics. The varying forms of glass block — type, thickness, size, shape, and patterns — along with the methods of installation can combine to create unique design solutions. Applications range from entire facades, windows, interior dividers, and partitions to skylights, floors, walkways, and stairways. In all applications, glass block units permit the control of light, both natural and artificial, for function or drama. Glass block also allows for control of thermal transmission, noise, dust, and drafts. With the use of thick-faced glass block or solid 3 in. bullet-resistant block, security can also be achieved.

MORTAR

An optimum mortar mix for installing glass block units is 1 part portland cement, $1/2$ part lime, and 4 parts sand.

The table below gives the number of glass block that can be installed with a mortar batch consisting of:
- 1.0 cu ft (1 bag/94 lb) portland cement
- 0.5 cu ft (20 lb) lime
- 4.0 cu ft (320 lb) sand

GLASS BLOCK/MORTAR BATCH

SERIES	BLOCK SIZE[1]	BLOCK NUMBER[2]
Regular	4 x 8	350
	6 x 6	350
	8 x 8	260
	12 x 12	190
Thin	4 x 8	450
	6 x 6	450
	8 x 8	335

NOTES

1. Includes 15% waste
2. Based on a $1/4$ in. exposed joint

SOUND TRANSMISSION[1]

STC[2]	SIZE	PATTERN	ASSEMBLY CONSTRUCTION
31	8" x 8" x 3"	All patterns	Silicone system
37[3]	8" x 8" x 4"	All patterns	Mortar
40	8" x 8" x 4" with LX fibrous filter	All patterns	Mortar
50	8" x 8" x 4" thick faced block	Thick block	Mortar
53	8" x 8" x 3" solid units	Solid block	Mortar

NOTES

1. Tested in accordance with ASTM E90-90 "... Measurement of Airborne Sound Transmission Loss..."
2. STC rating value in accordance with ASTM E413-87 "Classification for Rating Sound Insulation."
3. Test method and STC rating value in accordance with ASTM E90-81 and ASTM E413-73 accordingly.

THERMAL PERFORMANCE/LIGHT TRANSMISSION[1,3]

BLOCK TYPE	HEAT TRANSMISSION[2] U-VALUE (BTU/HR FT[2] °F)	THERMAL RESISTANCE[2] R-VALUE (HR FT[2] °F/BTU)	THERMAL EXPANSION COEFFICIENT (/°F)	VISIBLE LIGHT TRANSMISSION (%)	SHADING COEFFICIENT[4]
Regular series	0.51 (0.48 with "LX")	1.96 (2.08 with "LX")	47 x 10[7]	75	0.65
Solar reflective	0.51	1.96	47 x 10[7]	5 - 20	0.20 - 0.25
Thin series	0.57 (0.54 with "LX")	1.75 (1.85 with "LX")	47 x 10[7]	75	0.65
Solid	0.87	1.15	47 x 10[7]	80	
Flat sheet glass	1.04	0.96	47 x 10[7]	90	1.00

NOTES

1. Values equal ± 5%.
2. Winter night values.
3. To calculate instantaneous heat gain through glass block panels, see ASHRAE Handbook of Fundamentals, 1985, section 22.41.B.
4. Based on 8 in. square units: ratio of heat gain through glass block panels vs. that through a single light of double strength sheet glass under specific conditions.

Grace S. Lee; Rippeteau Architects, PC; Washington, D.C.

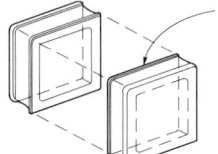

PATTERNS OCCUR ON THE INTERIOR SURFACE PRIOR TO FUSING

The basic glass block unit is made of two halves fused together with a partial vacuum inside. Faces may be clear, figured, or with integral relief forms.

Glass block is available in thicknesses ranging from a minimum of 3 in. for solid units to a maximum of 4 in. (nominal) for hollow units. Metric thicknesses range from 76 to 98 mm.

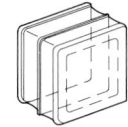 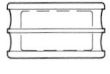

SQUARE

$4\,1/2$ in. x $4\,1/2$ in.
6 in. x 6 in. ($5\,3/4$ in. x $5\,3/4$ in. actual)
$7\,1/2$ in. x $7\,1/2$ in.
8 in. x 8 in. ($7\,3/4$ in. x $7\,3/4$ in. actual)
$9\,1/2$ in. x $9\,1/2$ in.
12 in. x 12 in. ($11\,3/4$ in. x $11\,3/4$ in. actual)

115 mm x 115 mm
190 mm x 190 mm
240 mm x 240 mm
300 mm x 300 mm

Metric sizes are available from foreign manufacturers through distributors in the United States.

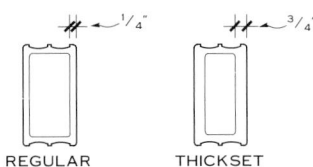

REGULAR   THICKSET

Some manufacturers provide thick blocks for critical applications where a thick-faced, heavier glass block is needed. These blocks have a superior sound transmission rating properties. Their faces are three times as thick as regular units.

THICK BLOCK

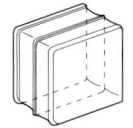 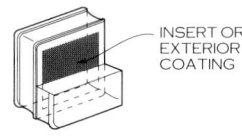

INSERT OR EXTERIOR COATING

Solid glass block units (glass bricks) are impact resistant and allow through vision.

Solar control units have either inserts or exterior coatings to reduce heat gain. Coated units require periodic cleaning to remove alkali and metal ions that can harm the surface coating. Edge drips are required to prevent moisture rundown on the surface.

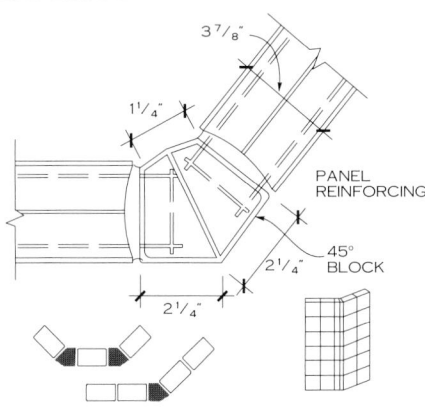

EXPANSION STRIP

2" MAX.
4" MAX.

End block units have a rounded, finished surface on one edge. They may be used to end interior partitions or walls as well as space dividers when installed horizontally.

END BLOCK

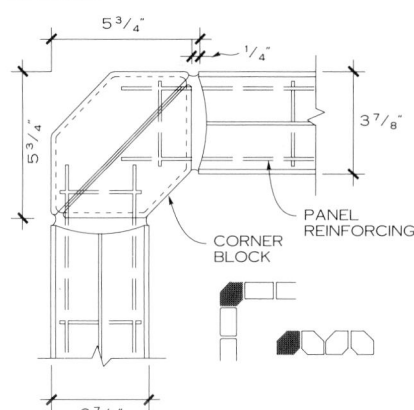

$3\,7/8$"
$1\,1/4$"
PANEL REINFORCING
45° BLOCK
$2\,1/4$"
$2\,1/4$"

45° BLOCK

$5\,3/4$"
$1/4$"
$5\,3/4$
$3\,7/8$"
PANEL REINFORCING
CORNER BLOCK
$3\,7/8$"

CORNER BLOCK

A few manufacturers have special shapes to execute corner designs. These units also may be placed together for varying patterns and forms.

SPECIAL SHAPES (CORNERS)

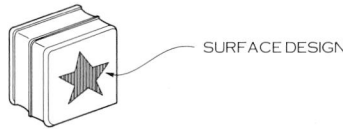

SURFACE DESIGN

Surface decoration may be achieved with fused-on ceramic, etching, or sandblasting. Glass block units may be split or shipped in halves in order to apply some decoration to the inside. Blocks then must be resealed. Resealed blocks will not perform the same under various stresses as factory sealed units. Placement in walls or panels should be limited to areas receiving minimum loading.

MAXIMUM PANEL DIMENSIONS

PERIMETER SUPPORT METHOD	REGULAR SERIES			THIN SERIES		
	AREA (SQ FT)	HEIGHT (FT)	WIDTH (FT)	AREA (SQ FT)	HEIGHT (FT)	WIDTH (FT)
EXTERIOR						
Channel type restraint	144	20	25	85	10	25
Panel anchors	144	20	25	85	10	25
Channels or panel anchors with intermediate stiffener	250	20	25	150	20	25
INTERIOR						
Channel type restraint	250	20	25	150	20	25
Panel anchors	250	20	25	150	20	25

NOTE

Maximum exterior panel sizes are based on a design wind load of 20 lb/sq ft with a 2.7 safety factor.

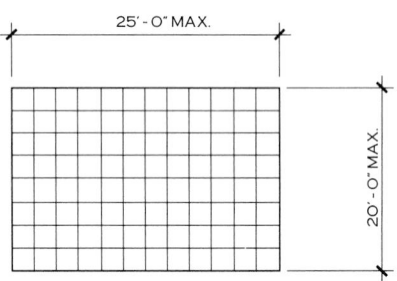

ELEVATION

NOTES

1. Area of exterior unbraced panel should not exceed 144 sq ft.
2. Area of interior unbraced panel should not exceed 250 sq ft.
3. Panels are designed to be mortared at sill, with head and jambs providing for movement and settling. Deflection of lintel at head should be anticipated.
4. Consult manufacturers for specific design limitations of glass block panels. Thickness of block used also determines maximum panel size.

NUMBER OF BLOCKS FOR 100 SQ FT PANEL

BLOCK SIZE (NOMINAL)	6"	8"	12"
Number of blocks	400	225	100

GLASS BLOCK PANELS

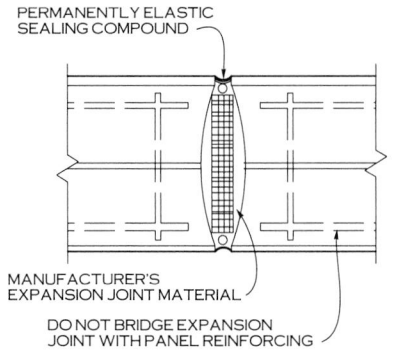

NOTE

Expansion joints should be installed at every change of direction of a multicurved wall, at points of curved wall intersection with straight walls, and at center of curvature in excess of 90 degrees.

GLASS BLOCK EXPANSION JOINT

Grace S. Lee; Rippeteau Architects, PC; Washington, D.C.

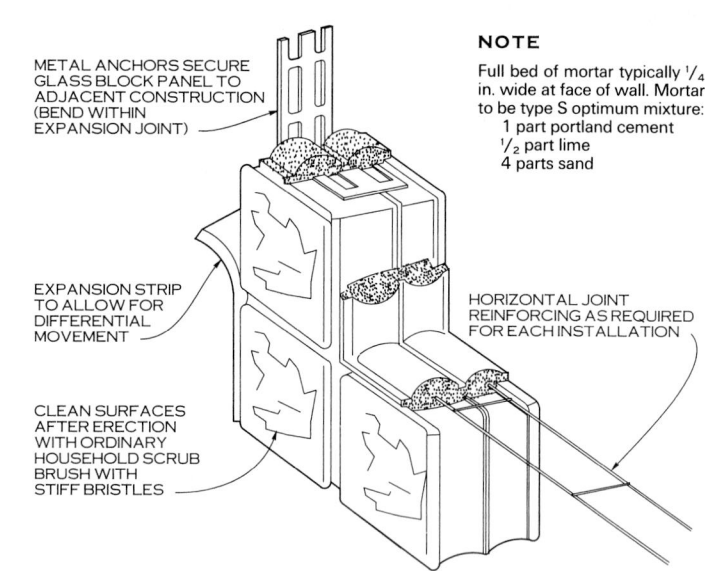

GLASS BLOCK PANEL COMPONENTS

NOTE

Full bed of mortar typically $1/4$ in. wide at face of wall. Mortar to be type S optimum mixture:
1 part portland cement
$1/2$ part lime
4 parts sand

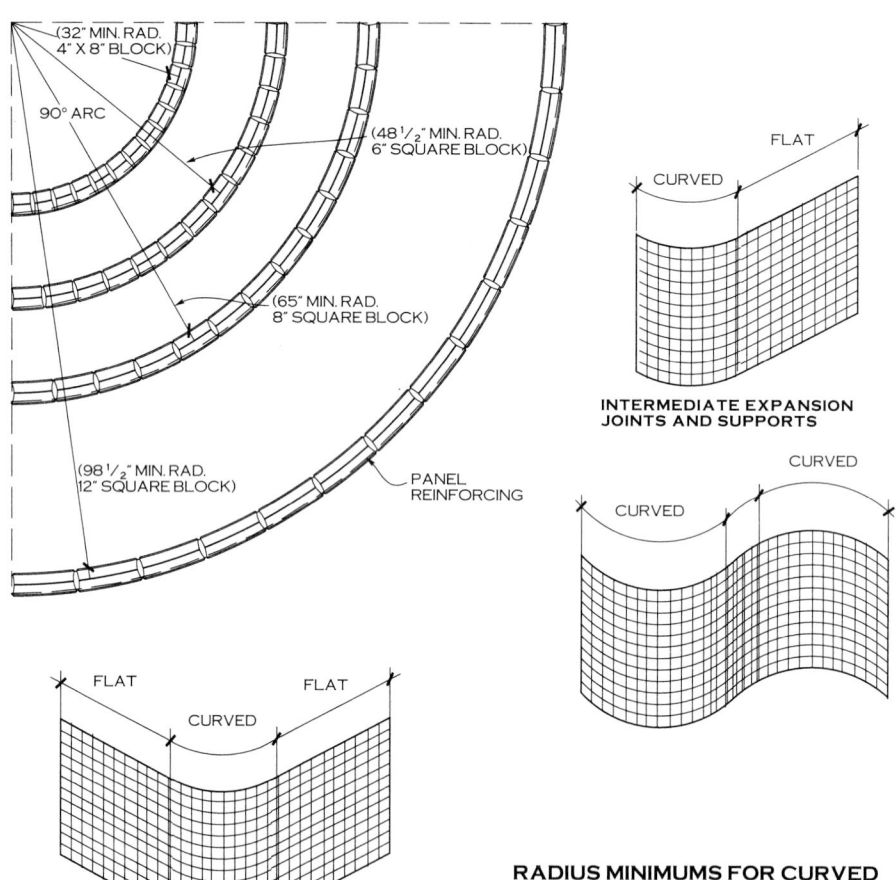

INTERMEDIATE EXPANSION JOINTS AND SUPPORTS

NOTES

1. It is suggested that curved areas be separated from flat areas by intermediate expansion joints and supports, as indicated in these drawings.
2. When straight, ladder-type reinforcing is used on curved walls, the innermost parallel wire may be cut periodically and bent to accommodate the curvature of the wall.

CURVED PANEL CONSTRUCTION

RADIUS MINIMUMS FOR CURVED PANEL CONSTRUCTION

BLOCK SIZE	INSIDE RADIUS (IN.)	NUMBER OF BLOCKS IN 90° ARC	JOINT THICKNESS (IN.)	
			INSIDE	OUTSIDE
4" x 8"	32	13	$1/8$	$5/8$
6" x 6"	$48\,1/2$	13	$1/8$	$5/8$
8" x 8"	65	13	$1/8$	$5/8$
12" x 12"	$98\,1/2$	13	$1/8$	$5/8$

TYPICAL SUPPORT DESIGN CRITERIA

When specifying supports and shelf angles, the installed weight and deflection limitation of the glass block should be taken into account. Local building codes should be checked for any limits on panel sizes or installation details.

INSTALLED WEIGHT OF GLASS BLOCK

TYPE OF UNIT	INSTALLED WEIGHT (LB/SQ FT)
Regular	20
Thin	16
Thick	26
Solid	38

DEFLECTION LIMITATIONS

Maximum deflection of structural members supporting glass block panels shall not exceed:

$$\frac{L}{600}$$

Where L = distance between vertical supports

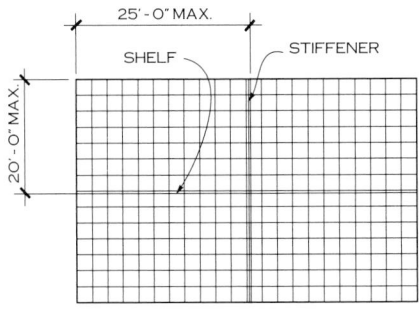

ELEVATION

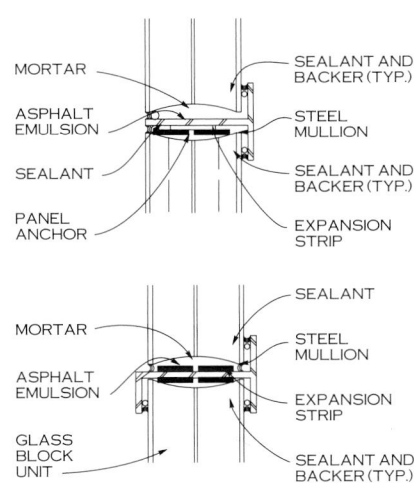

SHELF ANGLES IN MULTIPLE VERTICAL PANELS

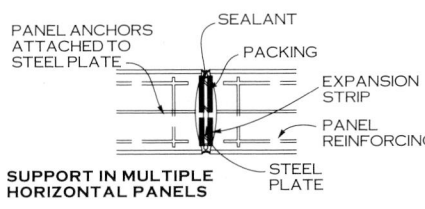

SUPPORT IN MULTIPLE HORIZONTAL PANELS

NOTE

Panels with an expansion joint stiffener incorporating a concealed vertical plate should be limited to 10 ft maximum height.

SECTIONS AT SUPPORTS

Grace S. Lee; Rippeteau Architects, PC; Washington, D.C.

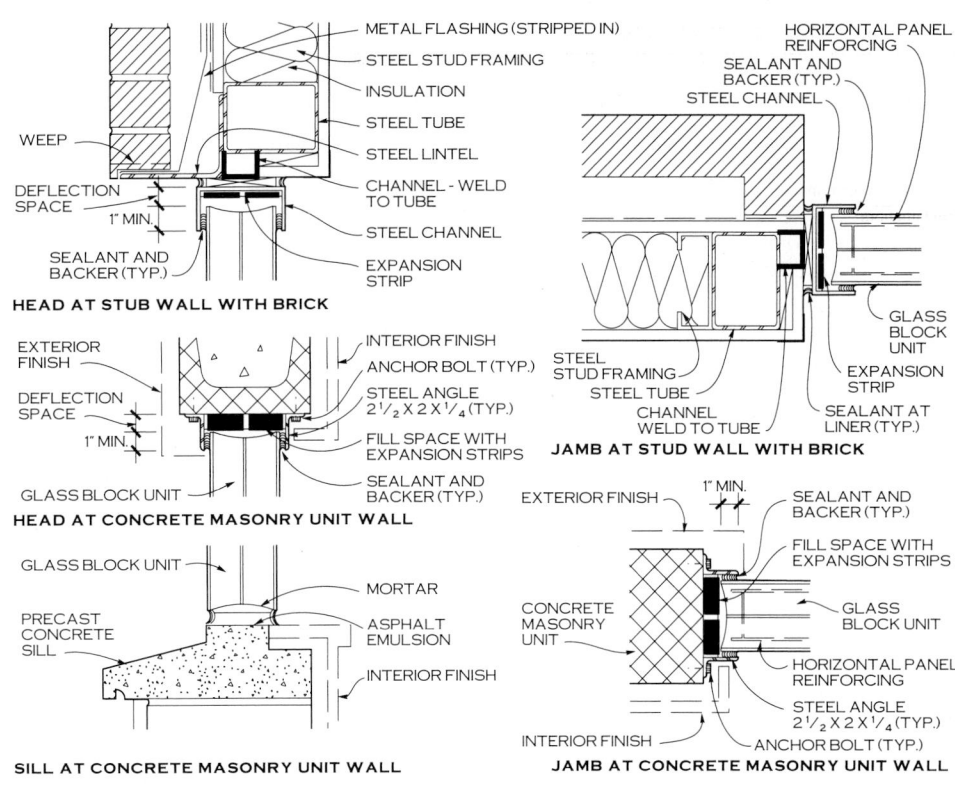

HEAD AT STUB WALL WITH BRICK

HEAD AT CONCRETE MASONRY UNIT WALL

SILL AT CONCRETE MASONRY UNIT WALL

JAMB AT STUD WALL WITH BRICK

JAMB AT CONCRETE MASONRY UNIT WALL

EXTERIOR CONNECTION DETAILS

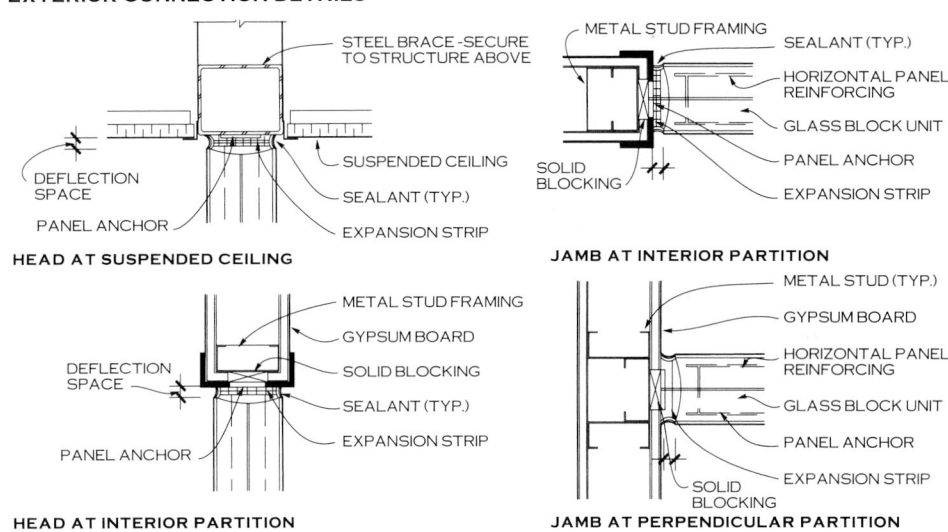

HEAD AT SUSPENDED CEILING

JAMB AT INTERIOR PARTITION

HEAD AT INTERIOR PARTITION

JAMB AT PERPENDICULAR PARTITION

INTERIOR CONNECTION DETAILS

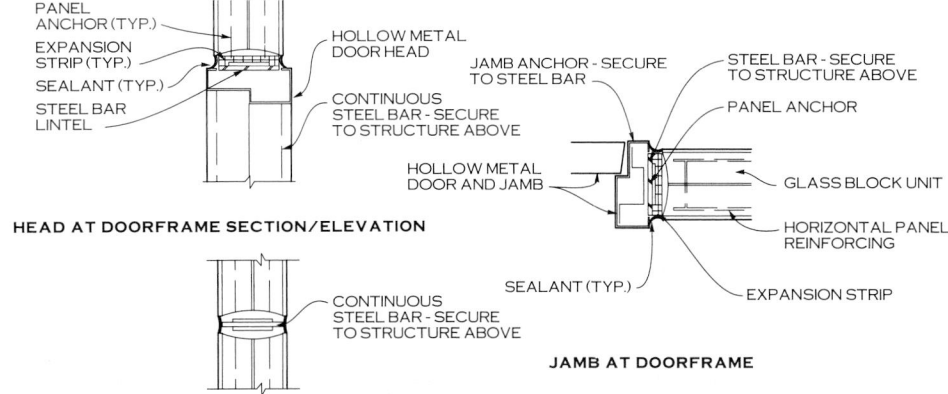

HEAD AT DOORFRAME SECTION/ELEVATION

JAMB AT DOORFRAME

HEAD AT DOORFRAME PLAN (JOINT ABOVE JAMB)

DOORFRAME DETAILS

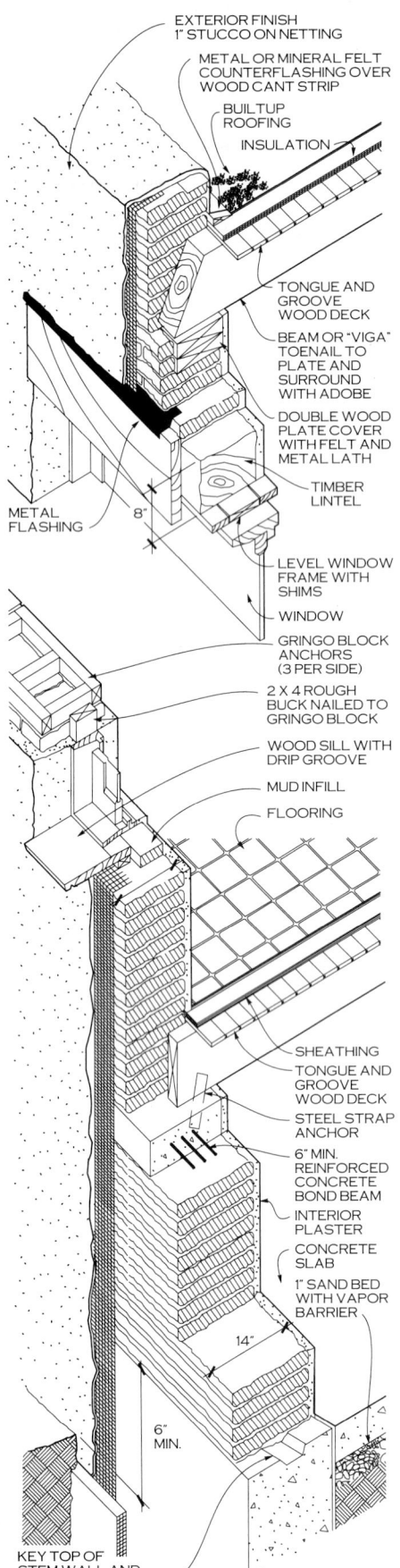

EXTERIOR FINISH 1" STUCCO ON NETTING

METAL OR MINERAL FELT COUNTERFLASHING OVER WOOD CANT STRIP

BUILT UP ROOFING

INSULATION

TONGUE AND GROOVE WOOD DECK

BEAM OR "VIGA" TOENAIL TO PLATE AND SURROUND WITH ADOBE

DOUBLE WOOD PLATE COVER WITH FELT AND METAL LATH

METAL FLASHING   8"

TIMBER LINTEL

LEVEL WINDOW FRAME WITH SHIMS

WINDOW

GRINGO BLOCK ANCHORS (3 PER SIDE)

2 X 4 ROUGH BUCK NAILED TO GRINGO BLOCK

WOOD SILL WITH DRIP GROOVE

MUD INFILL

FLOORING

SHEATHING

TONGUE AND GROOVE WOOD DECK

STEEL STRAP ANCHOR

6" MIN. REINFORCED CONCRETE BOND BEAM

INTERIOR PLASTER

CONCRETE SLAB

1" SAND BED WITH VAPOR BARRIER

14"

6" MIN.

KEY TOP OF STEM WALL AND WATERPROOFING

ADOBE WALL SECTION

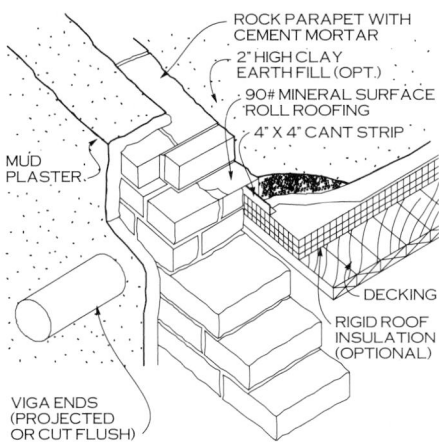

ROCK PARAPET WITH CEMENT MORTAR

2" HIGH CLAY EARTH FILL (OPT.)

90# MINERAL SURFACE ROLL ROOFING

4" X 4" CANT STRIP

MUD PLASTER

DECKING

RIGID ROOF INSULATION (OPTIONAL)

VIGA ENDS (PROJECTED OR CUT FLUSH)

TYPICAL PARAPET WITH EXTENDED VIGAS

ADOBE WALL CONSTRUCTION

The strength of an adobe wall lies in its mass and homogeneous nature: the same material, mud, is used for both bricks and mortar. In fact, reinforcing bars or anchor bolts may actually weaken joints. Sun-dried bricks are best made near the point of use. Because each locale has its own traditions and manufacturers, the uniform properties of the bricks can vary widely. Larger sizes of great weight add to the labor cost. Minimum bonding distance is approximately 4 in.

An international use standard for adobe wall thickness-height ratio is approximately 1:10. One-story walls should be 12 in. thick in Arizona and 10 in. in New Mexico and should not exceed 12 ft in height. Two-story walls should be 18 in. thick at the first floor and 12 in. at the second and not exceed 22 ft in height.

The most important detail consideration is preventing water from flowing on mud surfaces. Rising damp is of no consequence if the site immediately adjacent is well drained and moisture is not trapped by waterproofing materials. Unstabilized mud brick or plaster (without the addition of waterproofing compounds) bonds well to itself and to wood without normal lathing reinforcement. Rain erosion

of unstabilized mud surfaces will approximate only 1 in. in 20 years in rainfall areas of 10 to 25 in. per year. Monolithic slab/foundations are not desirable with mud adobe because during construction rainwater may collect on the slab and damage lower courses.

Effective U-values for insulation are more significant than the ASHRAE "steady-state" values in common use. The effective values take into account thermal mass, storage, insulation gains in various climate zones, wall compass orientation, and color.

"Burned adobe," a low-fired brick, should be dealt with in the manner normal for brick masonry. Its use is not recommended in climate zones where high daily temperature fluctuations can cause severe freeze-thaw cycle damage. Mud bricks can be stabilized (waterproofed) by the addition of cement, asphalt emulsion, or other compounds. However, these materials often do not bond well with themselves in repeated layers and may accelerate the deterioration at the point of contact with the mud material.

NOTES

Sun-dried mud bricks may be made simply of mud or stabilized with additives. Proportions for the mud mixture of sand, silt, and clay normally are not critical. Gravel and small stones can also be added, up to 50% of the volume.

Adobe is approved by local building officials in areas where it is traditional or familiar to builders and construction officials. Some building codes may require additional thicknesses and reinforcement of concrete bond beams. Pitched roof structures may be anchored by normal attachment to the bond beams, as shown.

For nailing anchors, use wood adobes ("Gringo blocks"), either solid or made of scrap lumber, laid up with the wall where door and window jambs may require attachment. Nails will not hold permanently in adobe bricks unless secured with plaster or other material. Make later attachments by driving wooden triple wedges into a pilot hole. Channels for wiring, pipes, and decorative features may be easily cut in the wall after it is in place.

ENERGY

Earth-wall buildings can be manufactured and built with a minimum investment of energy and are low-cost alternative building systems.

ECOLOGY

All over the world, the supply of earth for buildings is limitless. If neglected, buildings made from earthen material recycle themselves naturally. They are prime examples of ecologically friendly structures.

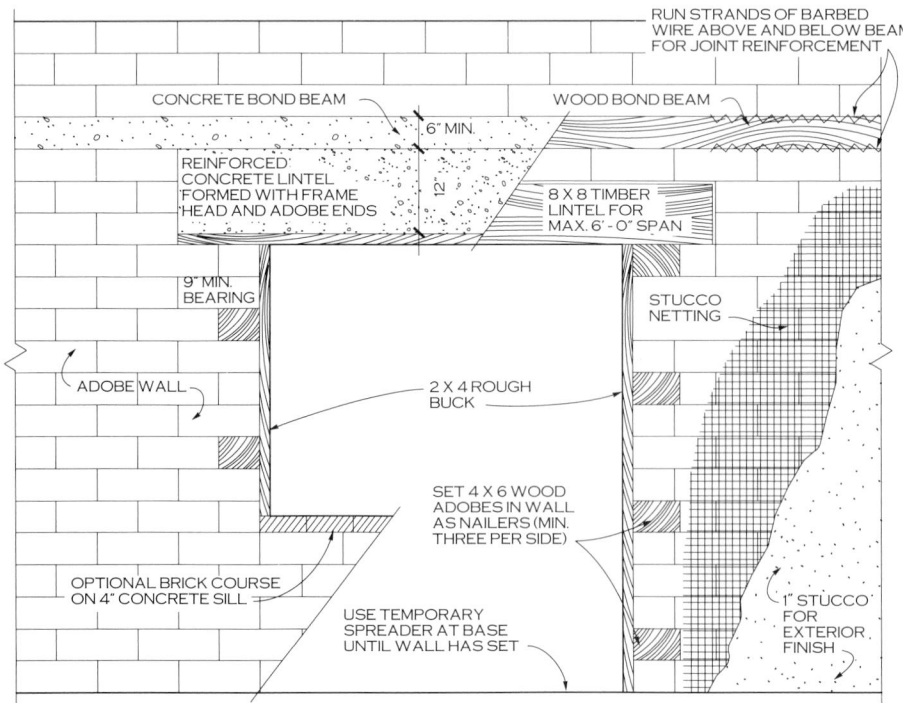

RUN STRANDS OF BARBED WIRE ABOVE AND BELOW BEAM FOR JOINT REINFORCEMENT

CONCRETE BOND BEAM

WOOD BOND BEAM

6" MIN.

REINFORCED CONCRETE LINTEL FORMED WITH FRAME HEAD AND ADOBE ENDS

8 X 8 TIMBER LINTEL FOR MAX. 6'-0" SPAN

9" MIN. BEARING

STUCCO NETTING

ADOBE WALL

2 X 4 ROUGH BUCK

SET 4 X 6 WOOD ADOBES IN WALL AS NAILERS (MIN. THREE PER SIDE)

OPTIONAL BRICK COURSE ON 4" CONCRETE SILL

USE TEMPORARY SPREADER AT BASE UNTIL WALL HAS SET

1" STUCCO FOR EXTERIOR FINISH

ELEVATION OF TYPICAL FRAMED OPENINGS

Grace S. Lee and A. Harris Lokmanhakim, AIA; Rippeteau Architects, PC; Washington, D.C.
P. G. McHenry, Jr., AIA; Albuquerque, New Mexico

 ADOBE UNIT MASONRY

GENERAL

Natural stone is used in building as a facing, veneer, and decoration. The major factors affecting the suitability and use of stone fall under two broad, but overlapping categories: physical and structural properties and aesthetic qualities. The three factors of building stone that most influence their selection by architects for aesthetic reasons are pattern, texture, and color. Consideration also should be given to costs, availability, weathering characteristics, physical properties, and size and thickness limitations.

Stone patterns are highly varied, and they provide special features that make building stone a unique material. Texture is varied, ranging from coarse fragments to fine grains and crystalline structures. Texture also varies with the hardness of minerals composing the stone. To accurately compare stone colors, the rock color chart published by the Geological Society of America (Boulder, CO) is recommended. Samples also may be used to establish acceptable color ranges for a particular installation.

Pattern, texture, and color all are affected by how the stone is fabricated and finished. Granites tend to hold their color and pattern, while limestone color and pattern changes with exposure. Textures may range from rough and flamed finishes to honed or polished surfaces. The harder the stone, the better it takes and holds a polish.

The three rock classes are igneous, sedimentary, and metamorphic. Common construction stones are marketed under the names given in the table below, although specialty stones such as soapstone and serpentine also are available. Each stone has various commercial grades. Limestone grades are A, statuary; B, select; C, standard; D, rustic; E, variegated; and F, old Gothic. Marble is graded A, B, C, or D on the basis of working qualities, uniformity, and flaws and imperfections.

PHYSICAL PROPERTIES OF STONE

The physical characteristics of a particular stone must be suitable for its intended use. It is important to determine the physical properties of the actual stone being used rather than using values from a generic table, which can be very misleading. Considerations of the physical properties of the stone being selected include modulus of rupture, shear strength, coefficient of expansion, permanent irreversible growth and change in shape, creep deflection, compressive strength, modulus of elasticity, moisture resistance, and weatherability. Epoxy adhesives, often used with stone, are affected by cleanliness of surfaces to be bonded and ambient temperature. Curing time increases with cold temperatures and decreases with warmer temperatures.

FABRICATION AND INSTALLATION

With the introduction of new systems of fabrication and installation and recent developments in the design and detailing of stone cutting, support, and anchorage, costs are better controlled. Correct design of joints, selection of mortars, and use of sealants affect the quality and durability of installation. Adequate design and detailing of the anchorage of each piece of stone are required. The size and thickness of the stone should be established based on physical properties of the stone, its method of anchorage, and the loads it must resist. Appropriate safety factors should be developed based on the variability of the stone properties as well as other considerations such as imperfect workmanship, method of support and anchorage, and degree of exposure of the cladding installation. Relieving angles for stone support and anchorage may be necessary to preclude unacceptable loading of the stone. The stone should be protected from staining and breakage during shipment, delivery, and installation.

Since stone cladding design and detailing vary with type of stone and installation, the designer should consult stone suppliers, stone-setting specialty contractors, industry standards (such as ASTM), and other publications to help select and implement a stone cladding system. Resource information is available in publications such as the Indiana Limestone Institute's *Indiana Limestone Handbook* and the Marble Institute of America's *Dimensioned Stone*, (vol. 3).

STONE CLASSIFIED ACCORDING TO QUALITIES AFFECTING USE

CLASS	COLOR	TEXTURE	SPECIAL FEATURES	PARTING	HARDNESS	CHIEF USES
Sandstone	Very light buff to light chocolate brown or brick red; may tarnish to brown	Granular, showing sand grains, cemented together	Ripple marks; oblique color bands ("cross bedding")	Bedding planes; also fractures transverse to beds	Fairly hard if well cemented	General; walls; building; flagstone
Limestone	White, light gray to light buff	Fine to crystalline; may have fossils	May show fossils	Parallel to beds; also fractures across beds	Fairly soft; steel easily scratches	All building uses
Marble	Highly varied: snow white to black; also blue-gray and light to dark olive green; also pinkish	Finely granular to very coarsely crystalline showing flat-sided crystals	May show veins of different colors or angular rock pieces or fossils	Usually not along beds but may have irregular fractures	Slightly harder than limestone	May be used for building stone but usually in decorative panels
Granite (light igneous rock)	Almost white to pink-and-white or gray-and-white	Usually coarsely crystalline; crystals may be varicolored; may be fine grained	May be banded with pink, white, or gray streaks and veins	Not necessarily any regular parting but fractures irregularly	Harder than limestone and marble; keeps cut shape well	Building stone, but also in paneling if attractively colored
Dark igneous rock	Gray, dark olive green to black; Laurvikite is beautifully crystalline	Usually coarsely crystalline if quarried but may be fine grained	May be banded with lighter and darker gray bands and veins	Not necessarily any regular parting but may fracture irregularly	About like granite; retains cut shape well	Building stone, but also used in panels if nicely banded or crystalline
Lavas	Varies: pink, purple, black; if usable, rarely almost white	Fine grained; may have pores locally	Note rare porosity	Not necessarily any regular parting, as a rule, but some have parallel fractures	About as strong as granite; if light colored, usually softer	Good foundation and building stone; not decorative
Quartzite	Variable: white, buff, red, or brown	Dense, almost glassy ideally	Very resistant to weather and impact	Usually no special parting	Very hard if well cemented, as usually the case	Excellent for building but hard to "shape"
Slate	Grayish-green, brick red, or dark brown, usually gray; may be banded	Finely crystalline; flat crystals give slaty facture	Some slate have color-fading with age	Splits along slate surface, often crossing color bands	Softer than granite or quartzite; scratches easily	Roofing; blackboards; paving
Gneiss	Usually gray with some pink, white, or light gray bands	Crystalline, like granite, often with glassy bands (veins)	Banding is decorative; some bands very weak, however	No special parting; tends to break along banding	About like granite	Used for buildings; also may be decorative if banded

PHYSICAL PROPERTIES OF REPRESENTATIVE STONES

PHYSICAL PROPERTY	IGNEOUS ROCK		SEDIMENTARY ROCK		METAMORPHIC ROCK	
	GRANITE	TRAPROCK	LIMESTONE	SANDSTONE	MARBLE	SLATE
Compressive — ultimate strength (psi)	15,000 – 30,000	20,000	4000 – 20,000	3000 – 20,000	10,000 – 23,000	10,000 – 15,000
Compressive — allowable working strength (psi)	800 – 1500		500 – 1000	400 – 700	500 – 900	1000
Shear — ultimate stress (psi)	1800 – 2700		1000 – 2000	1200 – 2500	900 – 1700	
Shear — allowable working stress (psi)	200		200	150	150	
Tension — allowable working stress (psi)	150		125	75	125	
Weight (psf)	156 – 170	180 – 185	147 – 170	135 – 155	165 – 178	170 – 180
Specific gravity	2.4 – 2.7	2.96	2.1 – 2.8	2.0 – 2.6	2.4 – 2.8	2.7 – 2.8
Absorption of water (percentage by weight)	0.13%		2.63%	4.16%	0.33%	0.23%
Modulus of elasticity (psi)	6 – 10,000,000	12,000,000	4 – 14,000,000	1 – 7,500,000	4 – 13,500,000	12,000,000
Coefficient of expansion (psf)	0.0000040		0.0000045	0.0000055	0.0000045	0.0000058

NOTE

Particular stones may vary greatly from average properties shown in table. A particular stone's physical properties, as well as its allowable working values, always should be developed for each particular application.

The McGuire & Shook Corporation; Indianapolis, Indiana
Christine Beall, RA, CCS; Austin, Texas

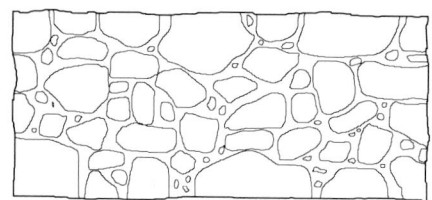

UNCOURSED FIELDSTONE PATTERN

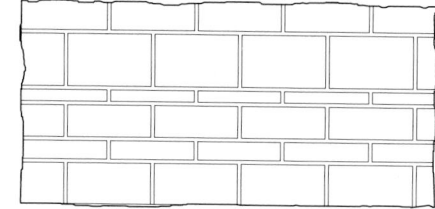

COURSED ASHLAR – RUNNING BOND

ONE-HEIGHT PATTERN (SINGLE RISE)

UNCOURSED LEDGE ROCK PATTERN

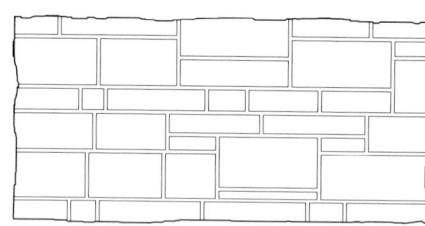

RANDOM COURSED ASHLAR

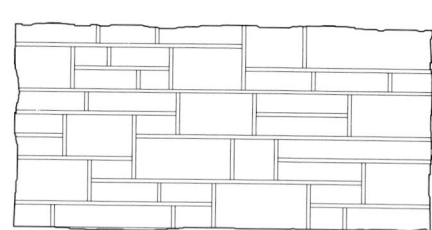

TWO-HEIGHT PATTERN (40% AT 2¹⁄₄ IN.; 60% AT 5 IN.)

UNCOURSED ROUGHLY SQUARE PATTERN

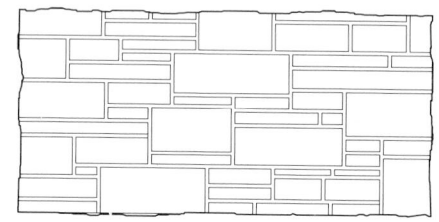

RANDOM BROKEN COURSED ASHLAR

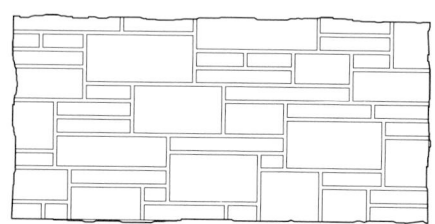

THREE - HEIGHT PATTERN (15% AT 2¹⁄₄ IN.; 40% AT 5 IN.; 45% AT 7³⁄₄ IN.)

RUBBLE STONE MASONRY PATTERNS – ELEVATIONS

SPLIT STONE MASONRY PATTERNS – ELEVATIONS

SPLIT STONE MASONRY HEIGHT PATTERNS – ELEVATIONS

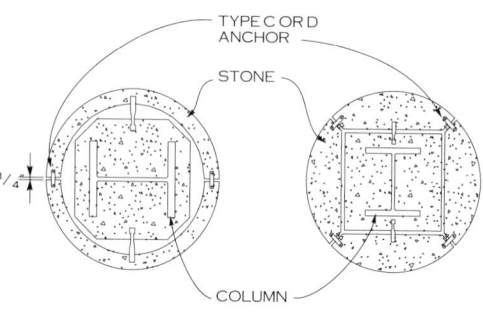

TYPE A OR B ANCHOR

STONE

COLUMN

SQUARE COLUMNS

TYPE C OR D ANCHOR

STONE

¹⁄₄

COLUMN

ROUND/QUADRANT COLUMNS

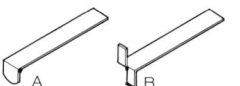

A   B

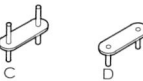

C   D

STONE TO STRUCTURE   STONE TO STONE

ANCHORS

NOTES

1. A course is a horizontal row of stone. Bond pattern is described by the horizontal arrangement of vertical joints. (See also Brickwork.) Structural bond refers to the physical tying together of load bearing and veneer portions of a composite wall. Structural bond can be accomplished with metal ties or with stone units set as headers into the backup.

2. Ashlar masonry is composed of squared-off building stone units of various sizes. Cut ashlar is dressed to specific design dimensions at the mill. Ashlar is often used in random lengths and heights, with jointing worked out on the job.

3. All ties and anchors must be made of noncorrosive material. Chromium-nickel stainless steel types 302 and 304 and eraydo alloy zinc are the most resistant to corrosion and staining. Use stainless steel type 316 in highly corrosive environments (polluted or near the sea). Copper, brass, and bronze will stain under some conditions. Local building codes often govern the types of metal that may be used for some stone anchors.

4. Nonstaining cement mortar should be used on porous and light colored stones. At all corners use extra ties and when possible, larger stones. Joints for rough work are usually ¹⁄₂ to 1¹⁄₂ in. and ³⁄₈ to ³⁄₄ in. for ashlar. Prevent electrochemical reaction between different metals combined in the same assembly by properly isolating or coating them.

INSTALLATION DETAILS

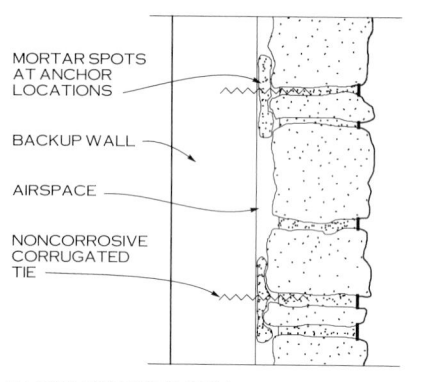

MORTAR SPOTS AT ANCHOR LOCATIONS

BACKUP WALL

AIRSPACE

NONCORROSIVE CORRUGATED TIE

CAVITY VENEERED WALL

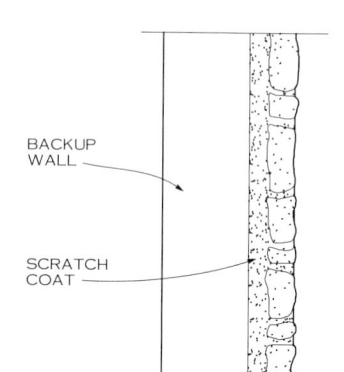

BACKUP WALL

SCRATCH COAT

THIN VENEERED WALL (INTERIOR ONLY)

TYPICAL WALL SECTIONS

George M. Whiteside, III, AIA and James D. Lloyd; Kennett Square, Pennsylvania
Building Stone Institute; New York, New York
Alexander Keyes; Rippeteau Architects, PC; Washington, D.C.

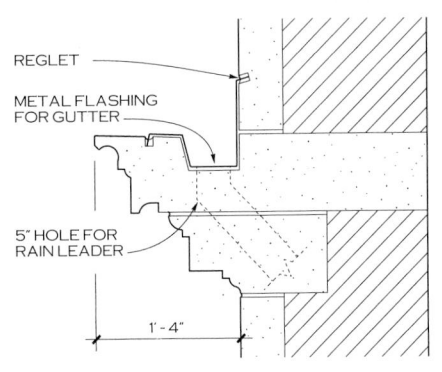

CORNICE WITH BUILT-IN GUTTER

REGLET

METAL FLASHING FOR GUTTER

5" HOLE FOR RAIN LEADER

1'- 4"

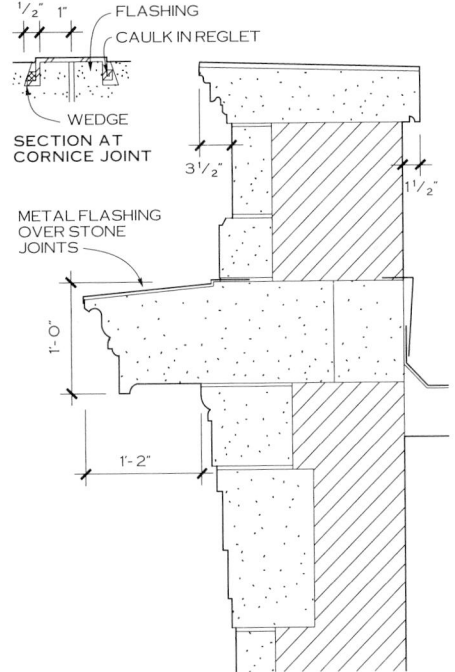

½" 1"
FLASHING
CAULK IN REGLET
WEDGE

SECTION AT CORNICE JOINT

3½"   1½"

METAL FLASHING OVER STONE JOINTS

1'-0"

1'- 2"

CORNICE WITH SEPARATE PARAPET

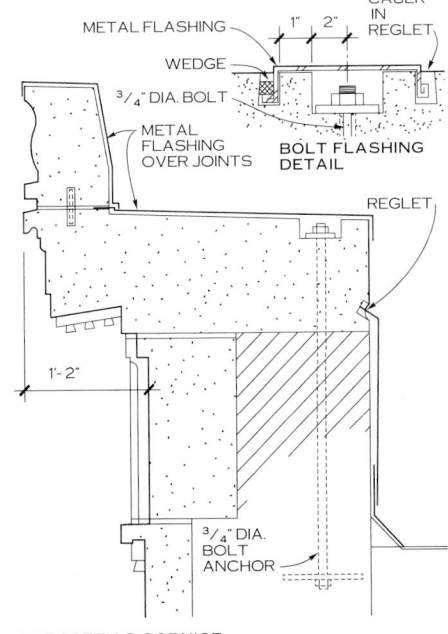

METAL FLASHING

CAULK IN REGLET

1"   2"

WEDGE

¾" DIA. BOLT

METAL FLASHING OVER JOINTS

BOLT FLASHING DETAIL

REGLET

1'- 2"

¾" DIA. BOLT ANCHOR

PARAPET AS CORNICE

STONE PARAPET DETAILS

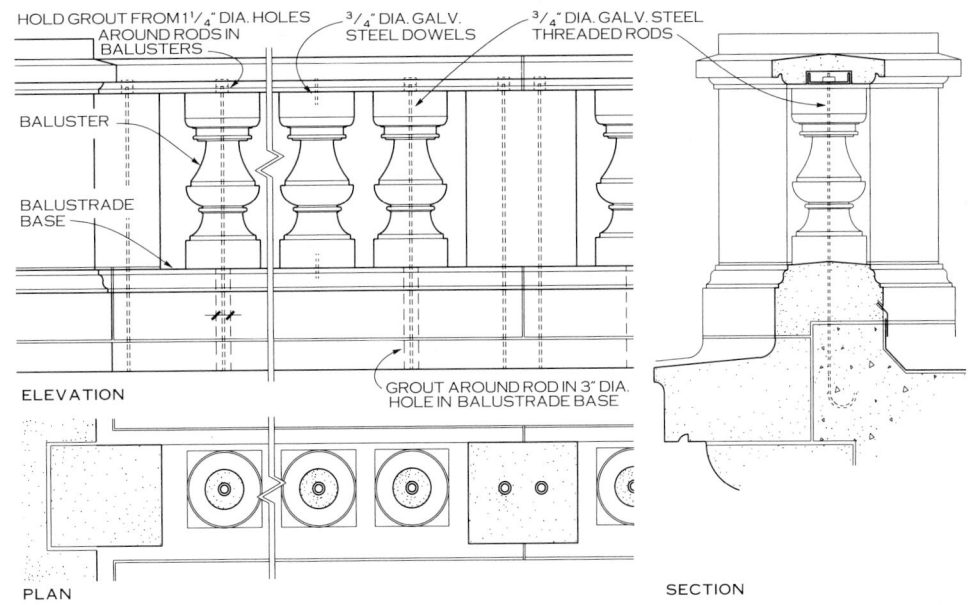

HOLD GROUT FROM 1¼" DIA. HOLES AROUND RODS IN BALUSTERS

¾" DIA. GALV. STEEL DOWELS

¾" DIA. GALV. STEEL THREADED RODS

BALUSTER

BALUSTRADE BASE

ELEVATION

GROUT AROUND ROD IN 3" DIA. HOLE IN BALUSTRADE BASE

PLAN

SECTION

STONE BALUSTRADE

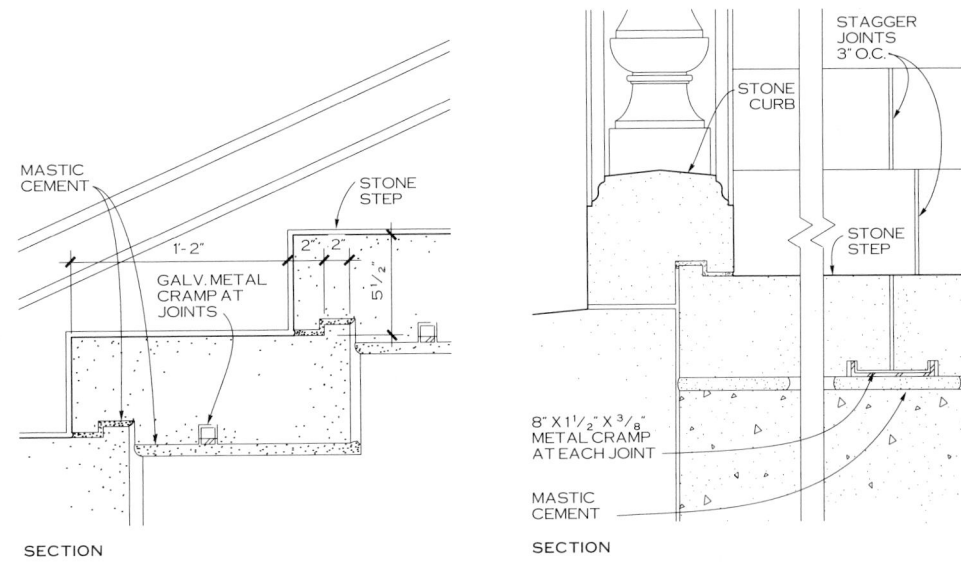

MASTIC CEMENT

STONE STEP

1'- 2"   2" 2"

GALV. METAL CRAMP AT JOINTS

5½"

SECTION

STAGGER JOINTS 3" O.C.

STONE CURB

STONE STEP

8" X 1½" X ⅜" METAL CRAMP AT EACH JOINT

MASTIC CEMENT

SECTION

STONE STEPS AND CURBS

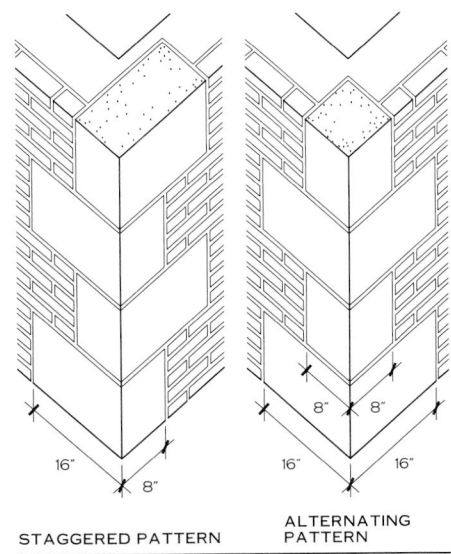

STAGGERED PATTERN

16"   8"

ALTERNATING PATTERN

16"   16"

8"   8"

STONE QUOIN IN BRICK WALL

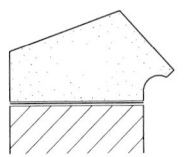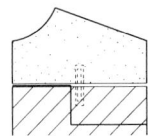

NOTE

Dowel between stone pieces allows flat interrupted flashing. Dowel set vertically is typical for stepped flashing (min. 2 dowels per stone).

GOTHIC-TYPE STONE COPINGS, INSIDE WASH

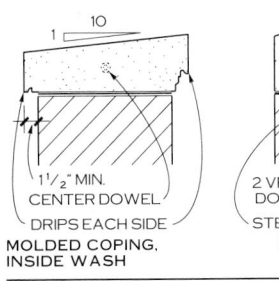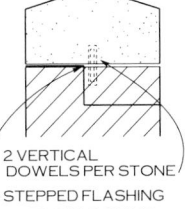

1   10

1½" MIN. CENTER DOWEL

DRIPS EACH SIDE

MOLDED COPING, INSIDE WASH

2 VERTICAL DOWELS PER STONE

STEPPED FLASHING

PLAIN COPING

STONE COPINGS

Richard J. Vitullo, AIA; Oak Leaf Studio; Crownsville, Maryland

STONE   4

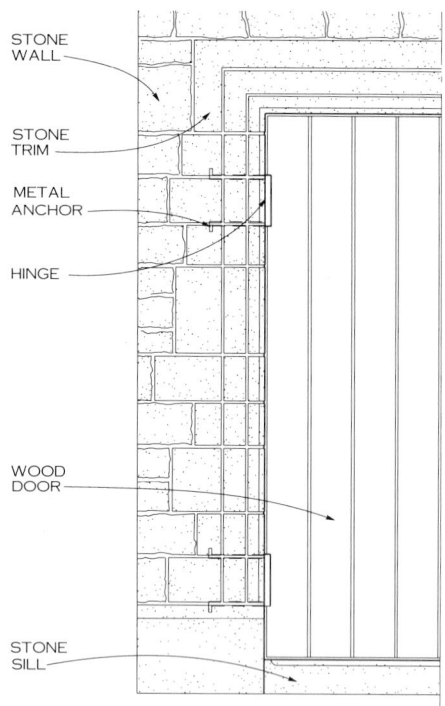

ELEVATION—WOOD DOOR IN STONE WALL

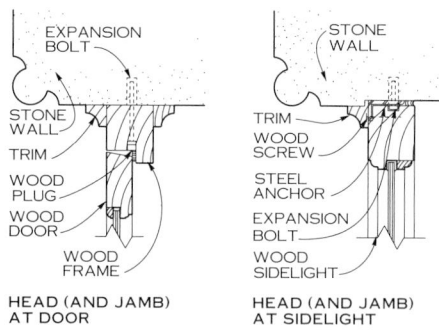

HEAD (AND JAMB) AT DOOR   **HEAD (AND JAMB) AT SIDELIGHT**

WOOD FRAME DETAILS

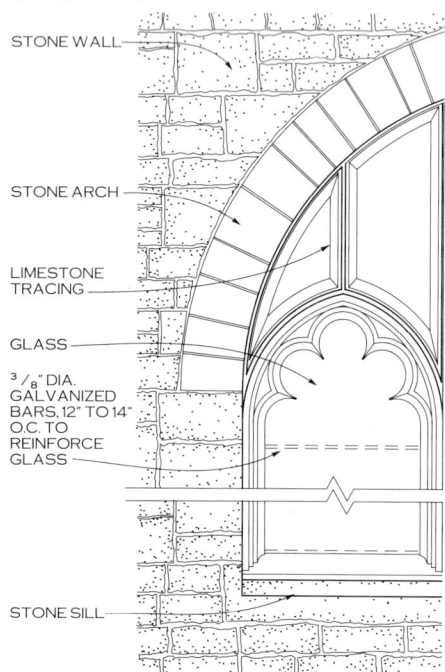

ELEVATION—WINDOW IN STONE WALL

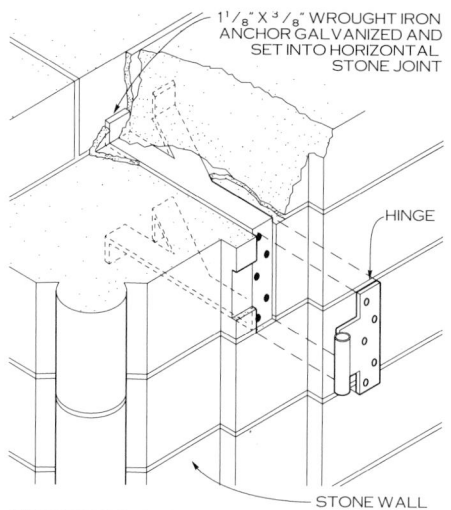

HINGE DETAIL SHOWING STONE ANCHOR

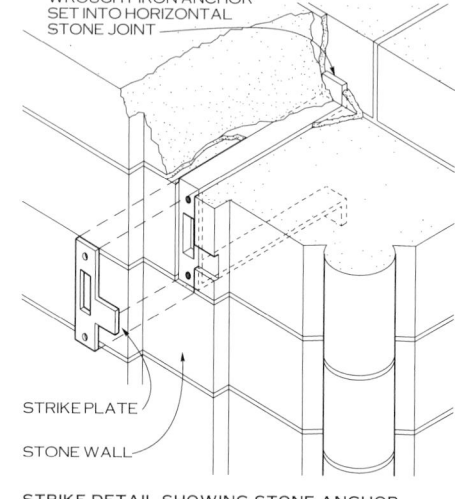

STRIKE DETAIL SHOWING STONE ANCHOR

CONCEALED ANCHOR DOOR DETAILS

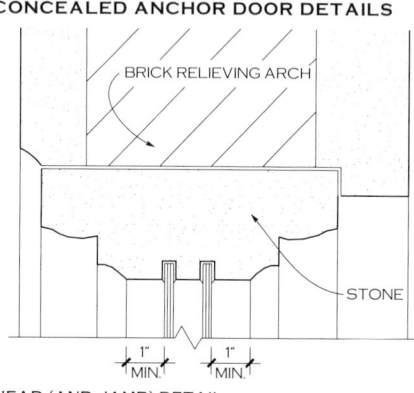

HEAD (AND JAMB) DETAIL

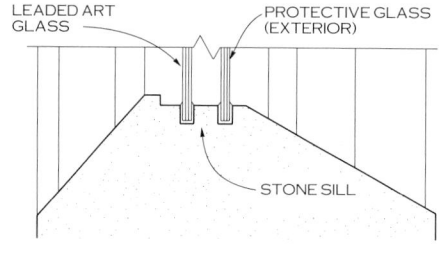

SILL DETAIL

SECTION A—WINDOW IN STONE WALL

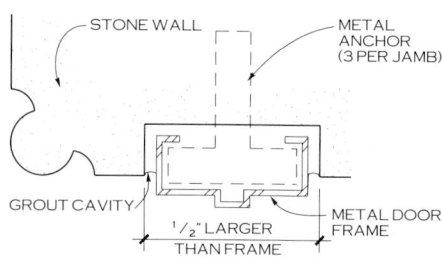

HOLLOW METAL FRAME

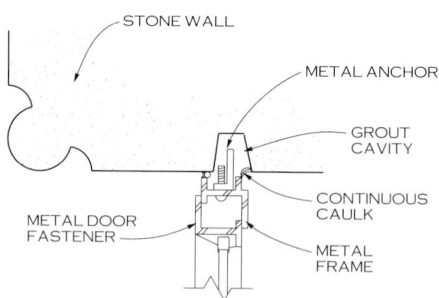

HEAD AND JAMB DETAILS AT STONE WALL

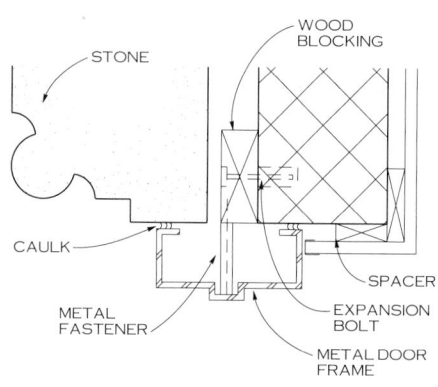

HEAD AND JAMB DETAILS AT CAVITY WALL

ALTERNATE METAL FRAME DETAILS

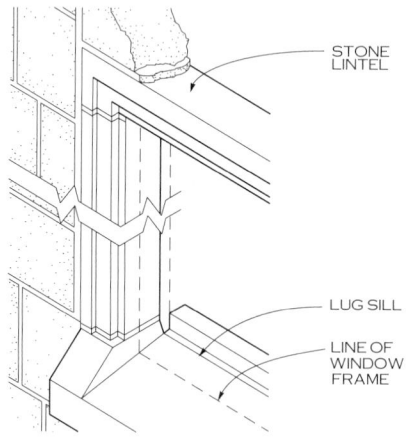

STONE LUG SILL AND LINTEL DETAIL

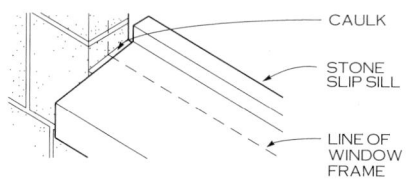

STONE SLIP SILL DETAIL

ALTERNATE STONE TRIM DETAILS

Richard J. Vitullo, AIA; Oak Leaf Studio; Crownsville, Maryland

 STONE

NOTES

Use of the steel stud support system as shown requires an architect or engineer to develop adequate and realistic performance criteria, including thorough consideration of the long-term durability and corrosion resistance of light gauge members, mechanical fasteners, and other system components; provisions for adequate thermal movement; development of adequate system strength and stiffness; recognition of the structural interaction between the stone support system; and consideration of vapor retarders and flashing to control moisture migration. It also is important that adequate provisions be developed to ensure quality workmanship necessary to implement the system and to achieve the expected quality and durability.

The stone thickness depicted is a minimum of $1\frac{1}{2}$ in. Thicker stone materials can use the same type of support system; however, engineering analyses of the system will be necessary to ensure proper performance and compliance with recommended design practices.

Design criteria for stone anchorage must include consideration of the particular stone's average as well as lowest strength values for safety, particularly at anchorage points. The proposed stone should be tested for adequate design properties and values. Stone anchorage size and location depend on establishing the particular stone's strength values, natural faults, and other properties; the stone's thickness and supported area; the expected lateral as well as gravity loading; and the amount of thermal movement to be accommodated.

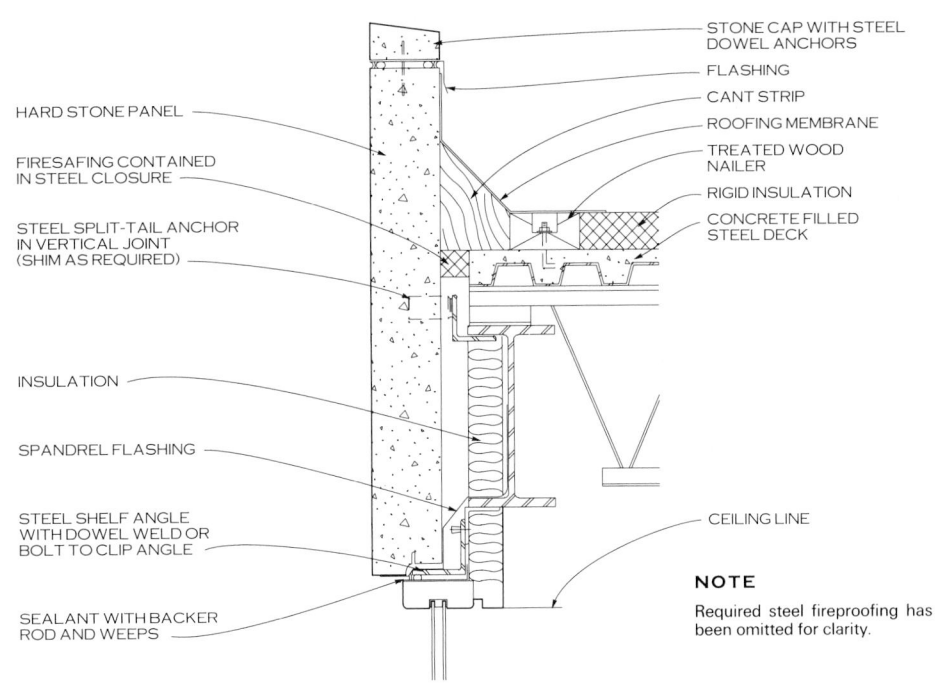

SECTION THROUGH ROOF PARAPET AT HARD STONE PANEL

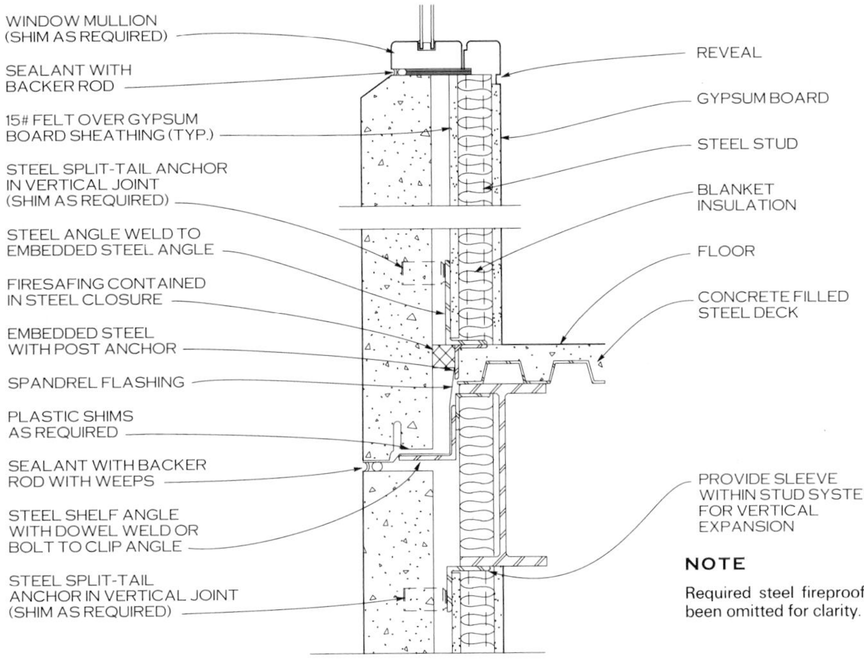

Labels (top diagram):
STONE CAP WITH STEEL DOWEL ANCHORS
FLASHING
CANT STRIP
ROOFING MEMBRANE
TREATED WOOD NAILER
RIGID INSULATION
CONCRETE FILLED STEEL DECK
HARD STONE PANEL
FIRESAFING CONTAINED IN STEEL CLOSURE
STEEL SPLIT-TAIL ANCHOR IN VERTICAL JOINT (SHIM AS REQUIRED)
INSULATION
SPANDREL FLASHING
STEEL SHELF ANGLE WITH DOWEL WELD OR BOLT TO CLIP ANGLE
SEALANT WITH BACKER ROD AND WEEPS
CEILING LINE

NOTE
Required steel fireproofing has been omitted for clarity.

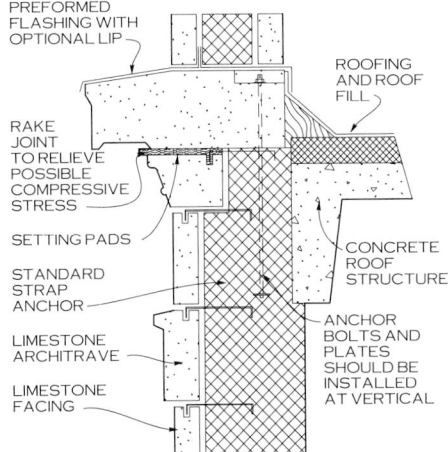

WALL SECTION

Labels:
PREFORMED FLASHING WITH OPTIONAL LIP
ROOFING AND ROOF FILL
RAKE JOINT TO RELIEVE POSSIBLE COMPRESSIVE STRESS
SETTING PADS
STANDARD STRAP ANCHOR
CONCRETE ROOF STRUCTURE
LIMESTONE ARCHITRAVE
ANCHOR BOLTS AND PLATES SHOULD BE INSTALLED AT VERTICAL
LIMESTONE FACING

Shown here is the most common method of anchoring a cornice, which has a projection large enough to be balanced in the wall.

The bed joint immediately below the heavy cornice is open far enough back to remove any compressive stress that would have a tendency to break off stone below.

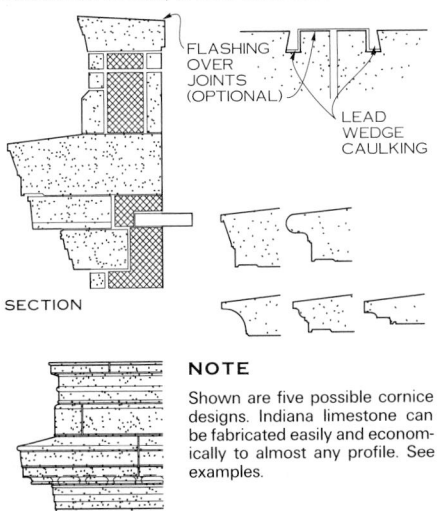

Labels:
FLASHING OVER JOINTS (OPTIONAL)
LEAD WEDGE CAULKING

SECTION

ELEVATION

NOTE
Shown are five possible cornice designs. Indiana limestone can be fabricated easily and economically to almost any profile. See examples.

TRADITIONAL CORNICES

The Specter Group; North Hills, New York

SECTION THROUGH HARD STONE PANEL AT WINDOW WALL

Labels (middle diagram):
WINDOW MULLION (SHIM AS REQUIRED)
SEALANT WITH BACKER ROD
15# FELT OVER GYPSUM BOARD SHEATHING (TYP.)
STEEL SPLIT-TAIL ANCHOR IN VERTICAL JOINT (SHIM AS REQUIRED)
STEEL ANGLE WELD TO EMBEDDED STEEL ANGLE
FIRESAFING CONTAINED IN STEEL CLOSURE
EMBEDDED STEEL WITH POST ANCHOR
SPANDREL FLASHING
PLASTIC SHIMS AS REQUIRED
SEALANT WITH BACKER ROD WITH WEEPS
STEEL SHELF ANGLE WITH DOWEL WELD OR BOLT TO CLIP ANGLE
STEEL SPLIT-TAIL ANCHOR IN VERTICAL JOINT (SHIM AS REQUIRED)
REVEAL
GYPSUM BOARD
STEEL STUD
BLANKET INSULATION
FLOOR
CONCRETE FILLED STEEL DECK
PROVIDE SLEEVE WITHIN STUD SYSTEM FOR VERTICAL EXPANSION

NOTE
Required steel fireproofing has been omitted for clarity.

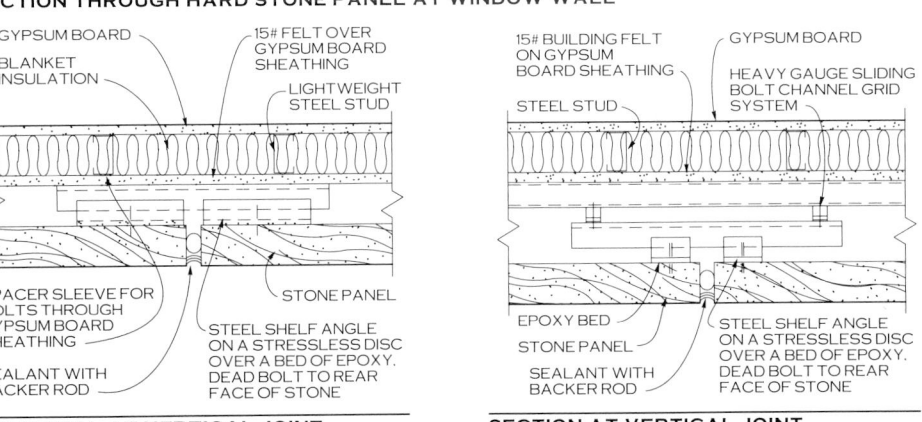

SECTIONAL AT VERTICAL JOINT

Labels:
GYPSUM BOARD
BLANKET INSULATION
15# FELT OVER GYPSUM BOARD SHEATHING
LIGHTWEIGHT STEEL STUD
SPACER SLEEVE FOR BOLTS THROUGH GYPSUM BOARD SHEATHING
STONE PANEL
STEEL SHELF ANGLE ON A STRESSLESS DISC OVER A BED OF EPOXY. DEAD BOLT TO REAR FACE OF STONE
SEALANT WITH BACKER ROD

SECTION AT VERTICAL JOINT

Labels:
15# BUILDING FELT ON GYPSUM BOARD SHEATHING
GYPSUM BOARD
HEAVY GAUGE SLIDING BOLT CHANNEL GRID SYSTEM
STEEL STUD
EPOXY BED
STONE PANEL
SEALANT WITH BACKER ROD
STEEL SHELF ANGLE ON A STRESSLESS DISC OVER A BED OF EPOXY. DEAD BOLT TO REAR FACE OF STONE

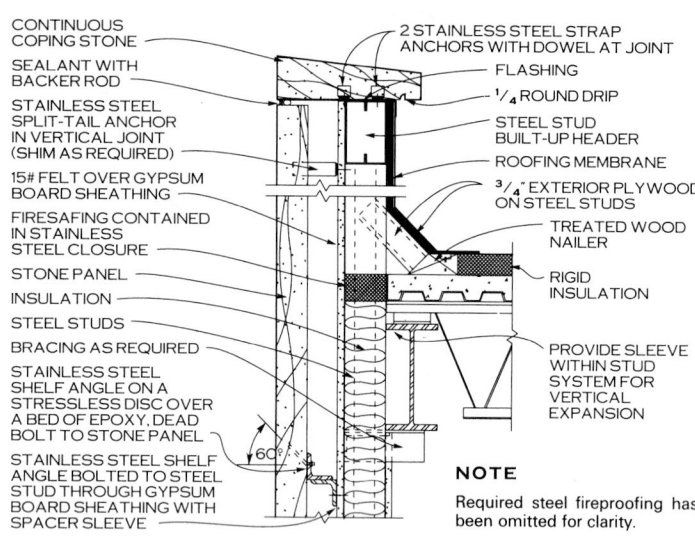

CONTINUOUS COPING STONE

SEALANT WITH BACKER ROD

STAINLESS STEEL SPLIT-TAIL ANCHOR IN VERTICAL JOINT (SHIM AS REQUIRED)

15# FELT OVER GYPSUM BOARD SHEATHING

FIRESAFING CONTAINED IN STAINLESS STEEL CLOSURE

STONE PANEL

INSULATION

STEEL STUDS

BRACING AS REQUIRED

STAINLESS STEEL SHELF ANGLE ON A STRESSLESS DISC OVER A BED OF EPOXY, DEAD BOLT TO STONE PANEL

STAINLESS STEEL SHELF ANGLE BOLTED TO STEEL STUD THROUGH GYPSUM BOARD SHEATHING WITH SPACER SLEEVE

2 STAINLESS STEEL STRAP ANCHORS WITH DOWEL AT JOINT

FLASHING

1/4 ROUND DRIP

STEEL STUD BUILT-UP HEADER

ROOFING MEMBRANE

3/4" EXTERIOR PLYWOOD ON STEEL STUDS

TREATED WOOD NAILER

RIGID INSULATION

PROVIDE SLEEVE WITHIN STUD SYSTEM FOR VERTICAL EXPANSION

NOTE

Required steel fireproofing has been omitted for clarity.

SECTION AT ROOF PARAPET AND WINDOWLESS WALL

SEALANT WITH BACKER ROD

STONE SILL

STAINLESS STEEL STRAP ANCHOR WITH 2 DOWELS AT JOINT

FLASHING

SEALANT WITH BACKER ROD

STAINLESS STEEL SPLIT-TAIL ANCHOR IN VERTICAL JOINT (SHIM AS REQUIRED)

15# FELT OVER GYPSUM BOARD SHEATHING (TYP.)

STONE PANEL

FIRESAFING CONTAINED IN STAINLESS STEEL CLOSURE

STAINLESS STEEL SHELF ANGLE ON A STRESSLESS DISC OVER A BED OF EPOXY, DEAD BOLT TO STONE PANEL

PLASTIC SHIMS

STAINLESS STEEL SPLIT-TAIL ANCHOR IN VERTICAL JOINT (SHIM AS REQUIRED)

DRIP

SEALANT WITH BACKER ROD AND WEEPS

WINDOW HEAD FLASHING

WINDOW HEAD MULLION

GYPSUM BOARD

STEEL STUDS

INSULATION

FLOOR

STAINLESS STEEL SHELF ANGLE BOLTED TO STEEL STUD THOUGH GYPSUM BOARD SHEATHING WITH SPACER SLEEVE

PROVIDE SLEEVE WITHIN STUD SYSTEM FOR VERTICAL EXPANSION

BRACING AS REQUIRED

INSULATION

STEEL STUD

EPOXY-FASTENED STONE RETURN WITH DOWEL (FACTORY FABRICATED)

STEEL STUD BUILT-UP HEADER

CEILING LINE

NOTE

Required steel fireproofing has been omitted for clarity.

STONE SPANDREL AT WINDOW HEAD AND SILL

STONE PANEL

15# FELT OVER GYPSUM BOARD SHEATHING

STAINLESS STEEL SPLIT-TAIL ANCHOR IN VERTICAL JOINT (SHIM AS REQUIRED)

FLASHING OVER CONCRETE SLAB

WEEP HOLE THROUGH

PLASTIC SHIMS AS REQUIRED

INSULATION

STEEL STUDS

GYPSUM BOARD

FLOOR

STONE SPANDREL AT GRADE

The Spector Group; North Hills, New York

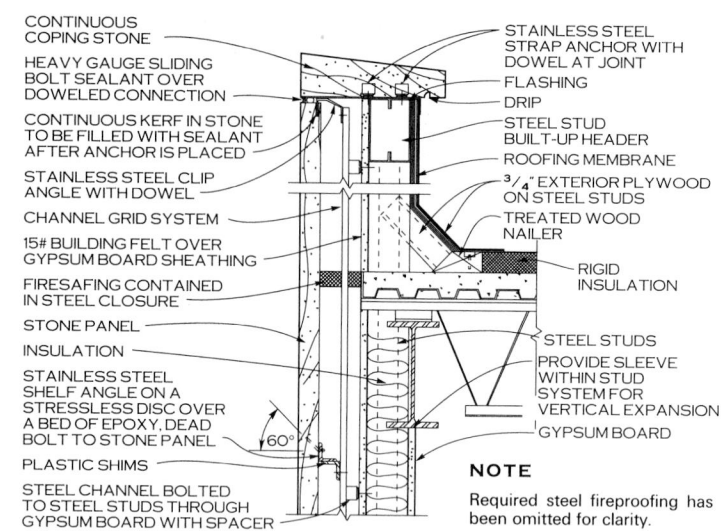

CONTINUOUS COPING STONE

HEAVY GAUGE SLIDING BOLT SEALANT OVER DOWELED CONNECTION

CONTINUOUS KERF IN STONE TO BE FILLED WITH SEALANT AFTER ANCHOR IS PLACED

STAINLESS STEEL CLIP ANGLE WITH DOWEL

CHANNEL GRID SYSTEM

15# FELT OVER GYPSUM BOARD SHEATHING

FIRESAFING CONTAINED IN STEEL CLOSURE

STONE PANEL

INSULATION

STAINLESS STEEL SHELF ANGLE ON A STRESSLESS DISC OVER A BED OF EPOXY, DEAD BOLT TO STONE PANEL

PLASTIC SHIMS

STEEL CHANNEL BOLTED TO STEEL STUDS THROUGH GYPSUM BOARD WITH SPACER

STAINLESS STEEL STRAP ANCHOR WITH DOWEL AT JOINT

FLASHING

DRIP

STEEL STUD BUILT-UP HEADER

ROOFING MEMBRANE

3/4" EXTERIOR PLYWOOD ON STEEL STUDS

TREATED WOOD NAILER

RIGID INSULATION

STEEL STUDS

PROVIDE SLEEVE WITHIN STUD SYSTEM FOR VERTICAL EXPANSION

GYPSUM BOARD

NOTE

Required steel fireproofing has been omitted for clarity.

SECTION AT ROOF PARAPET AND WINDOWLESS WALL

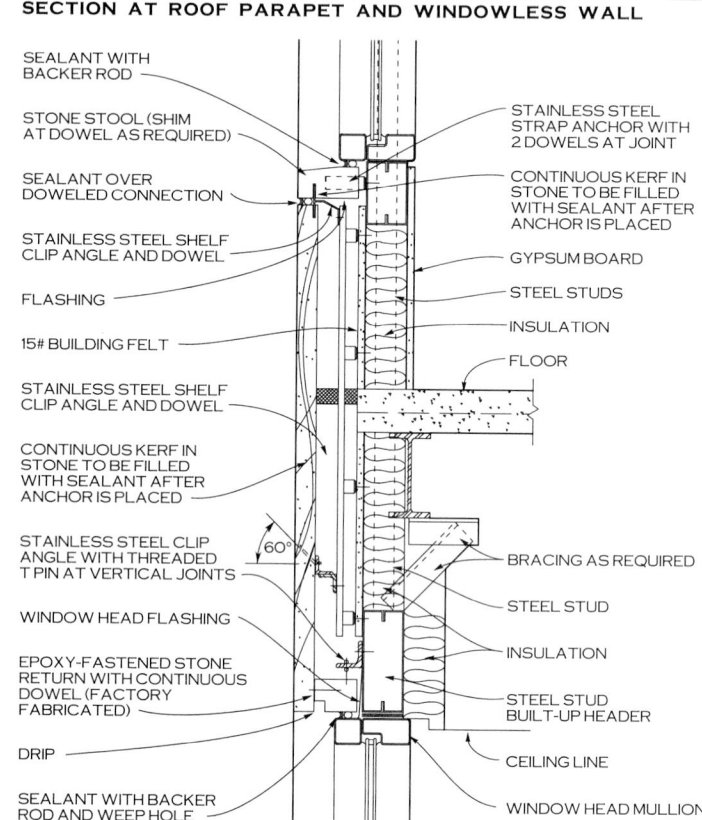

SEALANT WITH BACKER ROD

STONE STOOL (SHIM AT DOWEL AS REQUIRED)

SEALANT OVER DOWELED CONNECTION

STAINLESS STEEL SHELF CLIP ANGLE AND DOWEL

FLASHING

15# BUILDING FELT

STAINLESS STEEL SHELF CLIP ANGLE AND DOWEL

CONTINUOUS KERF IN STONE TO BE FILLED WITH SEALANT AFTER ANCHOR IS PLACED

STAINLESS STEEL CLIP ANGLE WITH THREADED T PIN AT VERTICAL JOINTS

WINDOW HEAD FLASHING

EPOXY-FASTENED STONE RETURN WITH CONTINUOUS DOWEL (FACTORY FABRICATED)

DRIP

SEALANT WITH BACKER ROD AND WEEP HOLE

STAINLESS STEEL STRAP ANCHOR WITH 2 DOWELS AT JOINT

CONTINUOUS KERF IN STONE TO BE FILLED WITH SEALANT AFTER ANCHOR IS PLACED

GYPSUM BOARD

STEEL STUDS

INSULATION

FLOOR

BRACING AS REQUIRED

STEEL STUD

INSULATION

STEEL STUD BUILT-UP HEADER

CEILING LINE

WINDOW HEAD MULLION

STONE SPANDREL AT WINDOW HEAD AND SILL

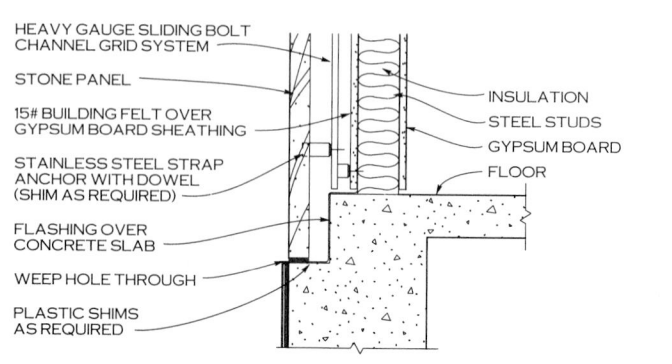

HEAVY GAUGE SLIDING BOLT CHANNEL GRID SYSTEM

STONE PANEL

15# BUILDING FELT OVER GYPSUM BOARD SHEATHING

STAINLESS STEEL STRAP ANCHOR WITH DOWEL (SHIM AS REQUIRED)

FLASHING OVER CONCRETE SLAB

WEEP HOLE THROUGH

PLASTIC SHIMS AS REQUIRED

INSULATION

STEEL STUDS

GYPSUM BOARD

FLOOR

STONE SPANDREL AT GRADE

NOTES

1. Throughout this section, flashing, sealants, and other ancillary materials necessary for sound weatherproof construction sometimes have been omitted for clarity. See flashing and sealant details elsewhere.
2. Allow for tolerances by including correct shimming to prevent installation problems or performance failure.
3. All stone anchors embedded in or in contact with stone shall be stainless steel type 300 series.
4. Stone support or anchor systems should be designed by an architect or engineer experienced in stone cladding design and construction.

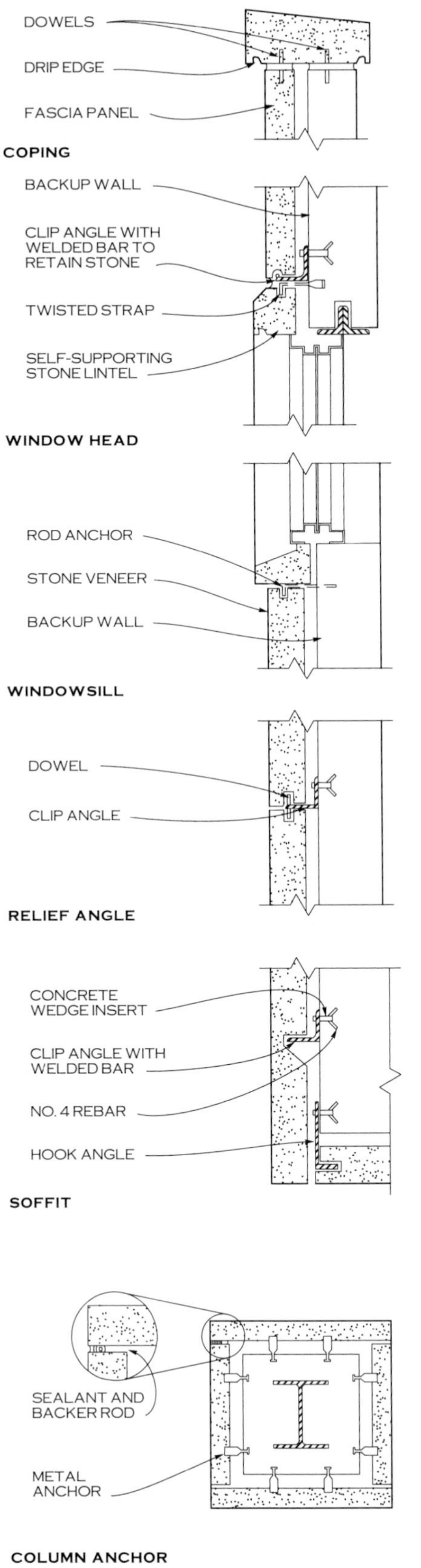

COPING
— DOWELS
— DRIP EDGE
— FASCIA PANEL

COPING
— BACKUP WALL
— CLIP ANGLE WITH WELDED BAR TO RETAIN STONE
— TWISTED STRAP
— SELF-SUPPORTING STONE LINTEL

WINDOW HEAD
— ROD ANCHOR
— STONE VENEER
— BACKUP WALL

WINDOW SILL
— DOWEL
— CLIP ANGLE

RELIEF ANGLE
— CONCRETE WEDGE INSERT
— CLIP ANGLE WITH WELDED BAR
— NO. 4 REBAR
— HOOK ANGLE

SOFFIT
— SEALANT AND BACKER ROD
— METAL ANCHOR

COLUMN ANCHOR

STONE VENEER ON CONCRETE WITH MASONRY BACKUP

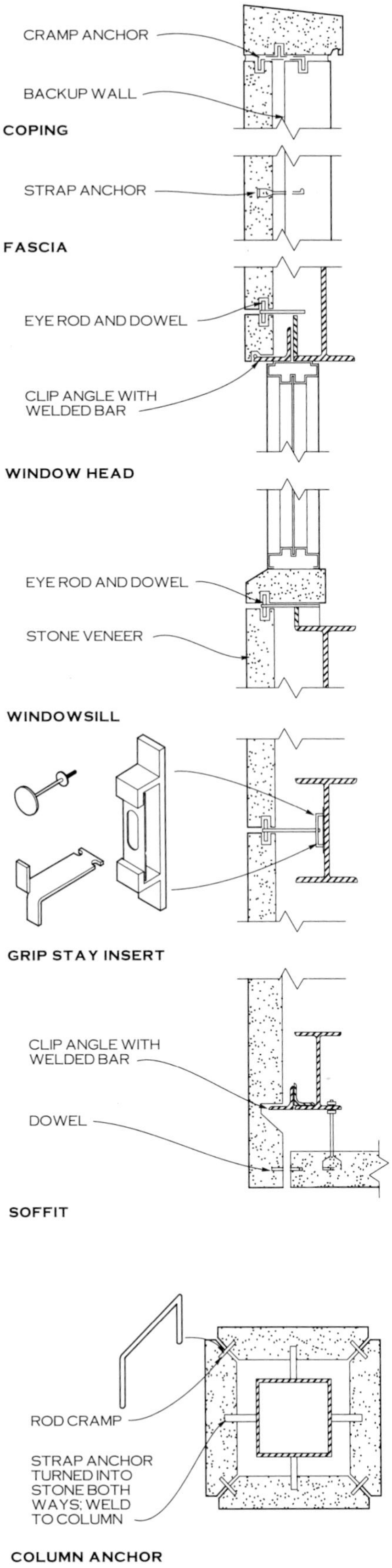

— CRAMP ANCHOR
— BACKUP WALL

COPING
— STRAP ANCHOR

FASCIA
— EYE ROD AND DOWEL
— CLIP ANGLE WITH WELDED BAR

WINDOW HEAD
— EYE ROD AND DOWEL
— STONE VENEER

WINDOW SILL

GRIP STAY INSERT
— CLIP ANGLE WITH WELDED BAR
— DOWEL

SOFFIT
— ROD CRAMP
— STRAP ANCHOR TURNED INTO STONE BOTH WAYS; WELD TO COLUMN

COLUMN ANCHOR

STONE VENEER ON STEEL FRAME

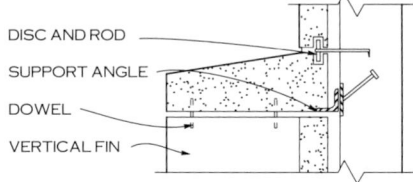
— DISC AND ROD
— SUPPORT ANGLE
— DOWEL
— VERTICAL FIN

SUN SCREEN

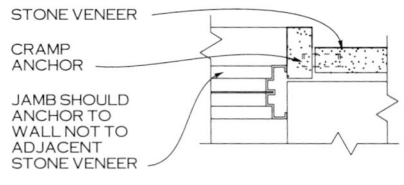
— STONE VENEER
— CRAMP ANCHOR
— JAMB SHOULD ANCHOR TO WALL NOT TO ADJACENT STONE VENEER

WINDOW JAMB

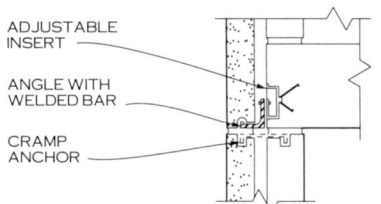
— ADJUSTABLE INSERT
— ANGLE WITH WELDED BAR
— CRAMP ANCHOR

RELIEF ANGLE

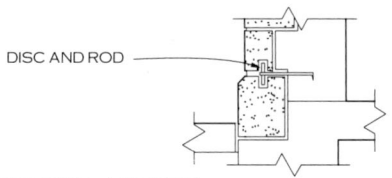
— DISC AND ROD

BOND WALL AND BASE

STONE VENEER DETAILS: OPTIONS

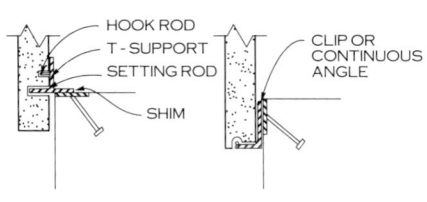
— HOOK ROD
— T-SUPPORT
— SETTING ROD
— SHIM
— CLIP OR CONTINUOUS ANGLE

HOOK ROD ANCHOR   **ANGLE WITH WELDED BAR**

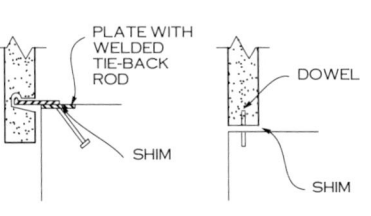
— PLATE WITH WELDED TIE-BACK ROD
— SHIM
— DOWEL
— SHIM

PLATE WITH WELDED BAR   **DOWEL PIN CONNECTION**

BASE DETAILS

George M. Whiteside, III, AIA, and James D. Lloyd; Kennett Square, Pennsylvania
Building Stone Institute; New York, New York
Alexander Keyes; Rippeteau Architects, PC; Washington, D.C.

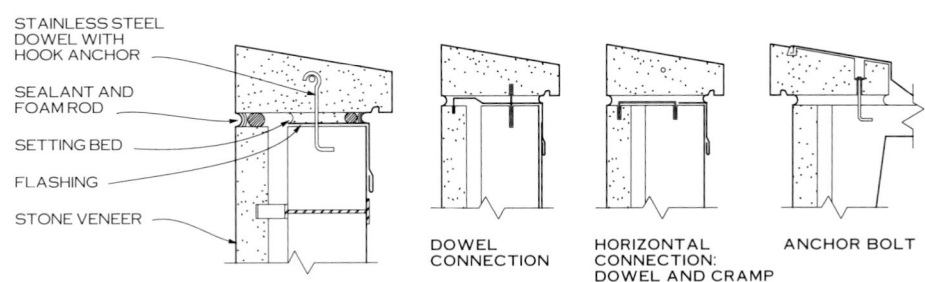

DOWEL CONNECTION

HORIZONTAL CONNECTION: DOWEL AND CRAMP

ANCHOR BOLT

ANCHORAGE DIMENSIONS

Standard flat stock anchors are made of strap 1 and 1¼ in. wide by ⅛, ³⁄₁₆, and ¼ in. thick. Lengths vary up to 6, 8, 10, and 12 in. Dovetail anchors are usually 4¼ in. overall with 3½ in. projection for face of concrete. Bends are ¾, 1, and 1¼ in.

Round stock anchors are made from stock of any diameter; ¼ and ⅜ in. are most common for rods; ⅛ in. (#11 ga.) through ³⁄₁₆ in. (#6 ga.) for wire anchors; and ¼ and ⅜ in. are most common for dowels. Dowel lengths are usually 2 to 6 in.

NOTES

1. Refer to page on 3 in. stone veneer for additional anchorage information.
2. Allow for tolerances by including correct shimming to prevent installation fitting problems or performance failure.
3. Stone anchorage systems should be designed by a professional engineer experienced in stone cladding design.
4. Sizes may differ widely from the standard sizes listed here.
5. Specify stainless steel.

COPINGS

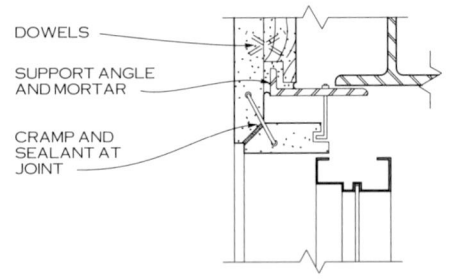

HEAD (JAMB SIMILAR)

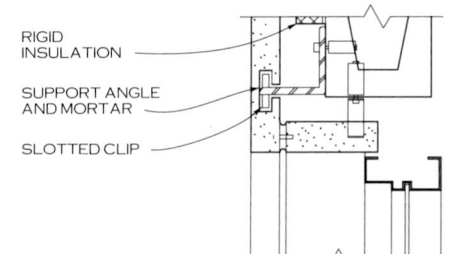

HEAD (JAMB SIMILAR)

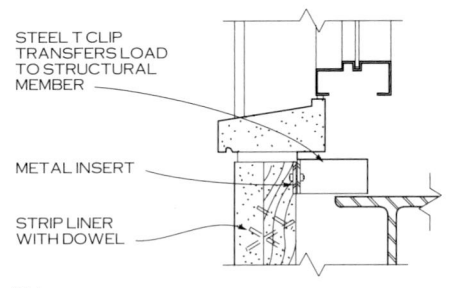

SILL

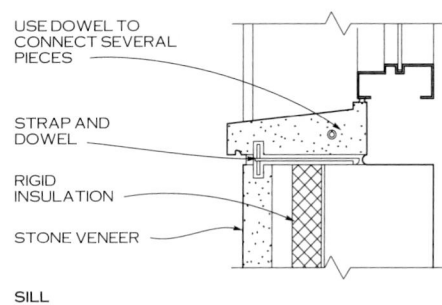

SILL

WINDOW DETAILS

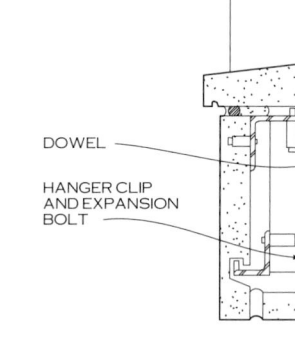

SILL DETAIL

RELIEF ANGLE SUPPORTS

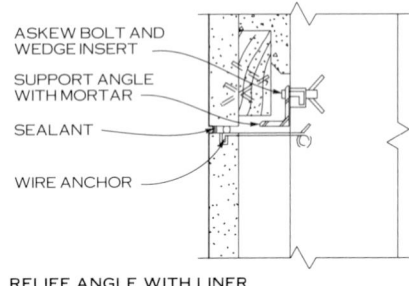

RELIEF ANGLE WITH LINER

ANGLE SUPPORT WITH SHEAR RESISTANCE

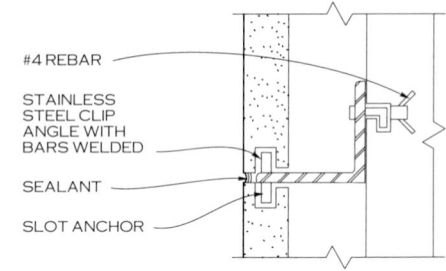

EXPANSION JOINT DETAIL

CORNER DETAILS

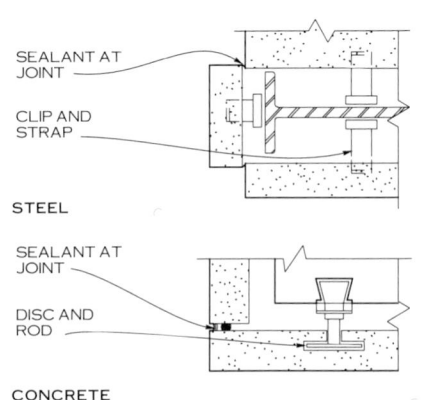

STEEL

CONCRETE

BASE DETAILS

NOTE

It is recommended that water repellent treatment be provided at the sidewalk.

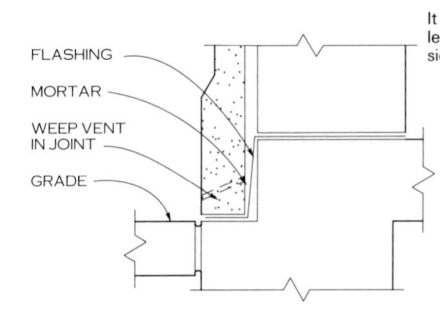

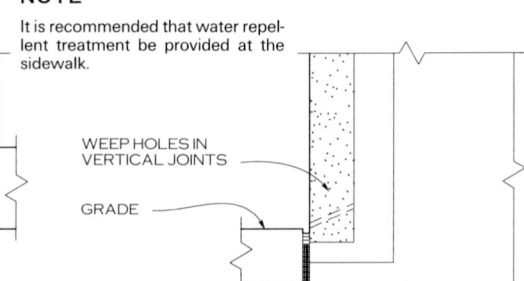

George M. Whiteside, III, AIA, and James D. Lloyd; Kennett Square, Pennsylvania
Building Stone Institute; New York, New York
Alexander Keyes; Rippeteau Architects, PC; Washington, D.C.

 STONE

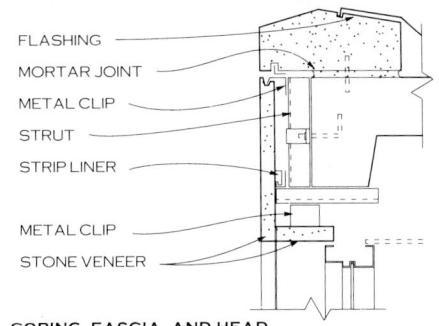

FLASHING
MORTAR JOINT
METAL CLIP
STRUT
STRIP LINER
METAL CLIP
STONE VENEER

COPING, FASCIA, AND HEAD

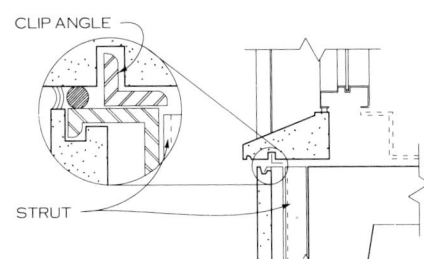

CLIP ANGLE

STRUT

SILL DETAIL

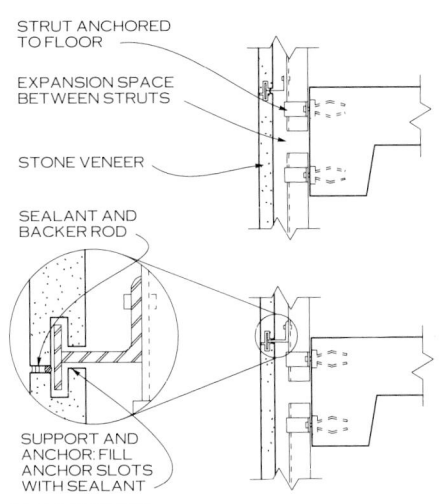

STRUT ANCHORED TO FLOOR
EXPANSION SPACE BETWEEN STRUTS
STONE VENEER

SEALANT AND BACKER ROD

SUPPORT AND ANCHOR: FILL ANCHOR SLOTS WITH SEALANT

WALL SECTION

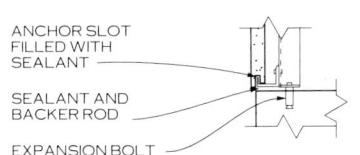

ANCHOR SLOT FILLED WITH SEALANT
SEALANT AND BACKER ROD
EXPANSION BOLT

BASE OR STARTER SUPPORT

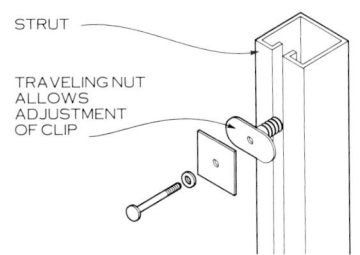

STRUT

TRAVELING NUT ALLOWS ADJUSTMENT OF CLIP

CLIP ANCHORING SYSTEM

GRID STRUT SYSTEM - CONCRETE FRAME

George M. Whiteside, III, AIA, and James D. Lloyd; Kennett Square, Pennsylvania
Building Stone Institute; New York, New York
Alexander Keyes; Rippeteau Architects, PC; Washington, D.C.

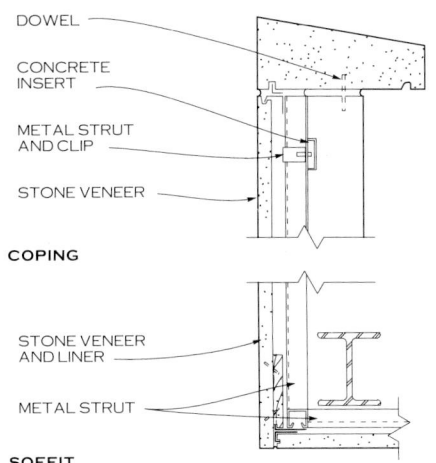

DOWEL
CONCRETE INSERT
METAL STRUT AND CLIP
STONE VENEER

COPING

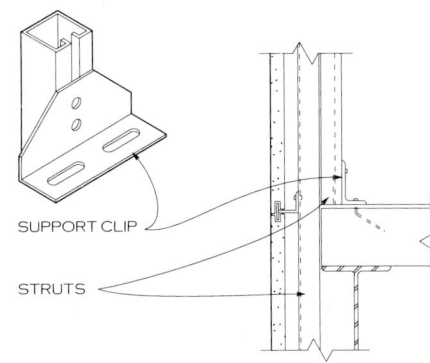

STONE VENEER AND LINER
METAL STRUT

SOFFIT

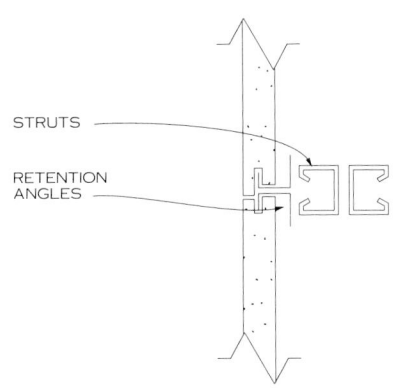

SUPPORT CLIP

STRUTS

SHEAR WALL SUPPORT

STRUTS
RETENTION ANGLES

SHEAR WALL SIDE RETENTION (PLAN)

GRID STRUT SYSTEM - METAL FRAME

GRID ANCHOR SPACING AND STRUT SIZE — MARBLE

MAXIMUM SPACING		ANCHOR	STRUT SIZE
7/8" THICK	1 1/4" THICK		WIDTH, DEPTH, AND SHAPE
4'-0"	4'-0"		1 5/8" x 1 5/8"
7'-0"	6'-0"		1 5/8" x 2 7/16"
10'-0"	9'-0"		1 5/8" x 3 1/4"
15'-0"	13'-0"		1 5/8" x 4 7/8"

NOTES
1. "X" = dimension between strut and outside face of stone.
2. "X" = 1 5/8" for 7/8" marble.
3. "X" = 1 3/4" for 1 1/4" marble.

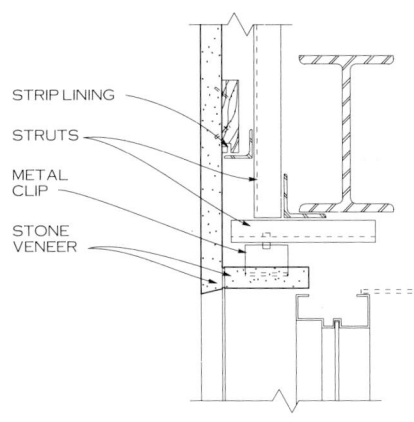

STRIP LINING
STRUTS
METAL CLIP
STONE VENEER

FASCIA AND WINDOW HEAD

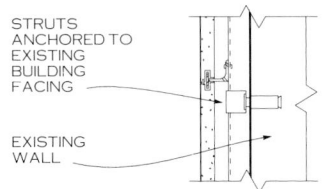

STRUTS ANCHORED TO EXISTING BUILDING FACING
EXISTING WALL

CONNECTION TO EXISTING FACING

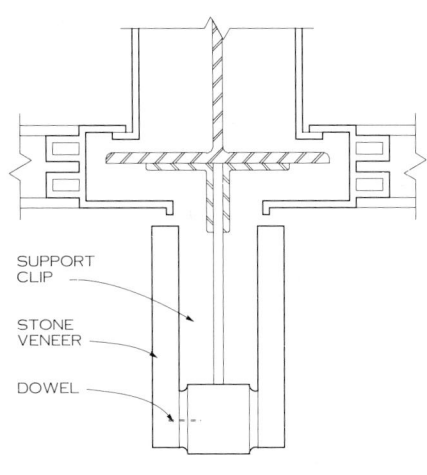

SUPPORT CLIP
STONE VENEER
DOWEL

PLAN

COLUMN RETURN

NOTES
1. Engineering design of all supports for this type of construction is essential.
2. Grid strut spacing is subject to engineering design.

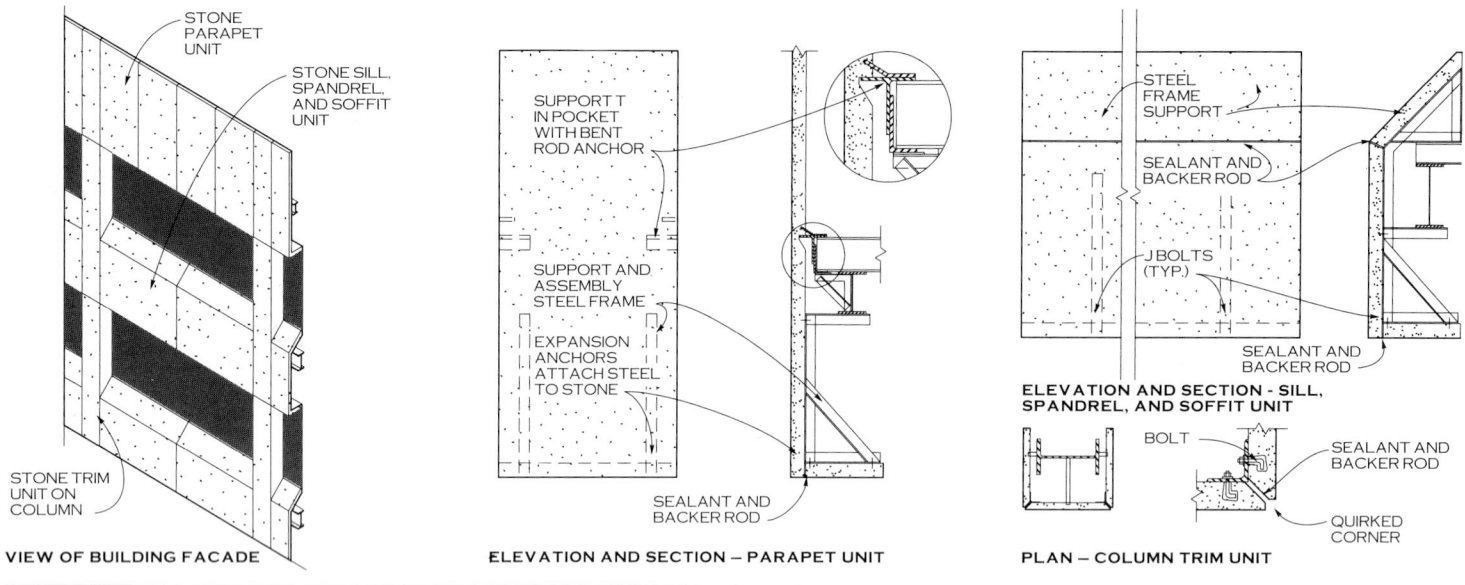

VIEW OF BUILDING FACADE

- STONE PARAPET UNIT
- STONE SILL, SPANDREL, AND SOFFIT UNIT
- STONE TRIM UNIT ON COLUMN

ELEVATION AND SECTION – PARAPET UNIT

- SUPPORT T IN POCKET WITH BENT ROD ANCHOR
- SUPPORT AND ASSEMBLY STEEL FRAME
- EXPANSION ANCHORS ATTACH STEEL TO STONE
- SEALANT AND BACKER ROD

ELEVATION AND SECTION - SILL, SPANDREL, AND SOFFIT UNIT

- STEEL FRAME SUPPORT
- SEALANT AND BACKER ROD
- J BOLTS (TYP.)
- SEALANT AND BACKER ROD

PLAN – COLUMN TRIM UNIT

- BOLT
- SEALANT AND BACKER ROD
- QUIRKED CORNER

PREASSEMBLED STONE UNIT WITH EPOXY ON STEEL FRAME

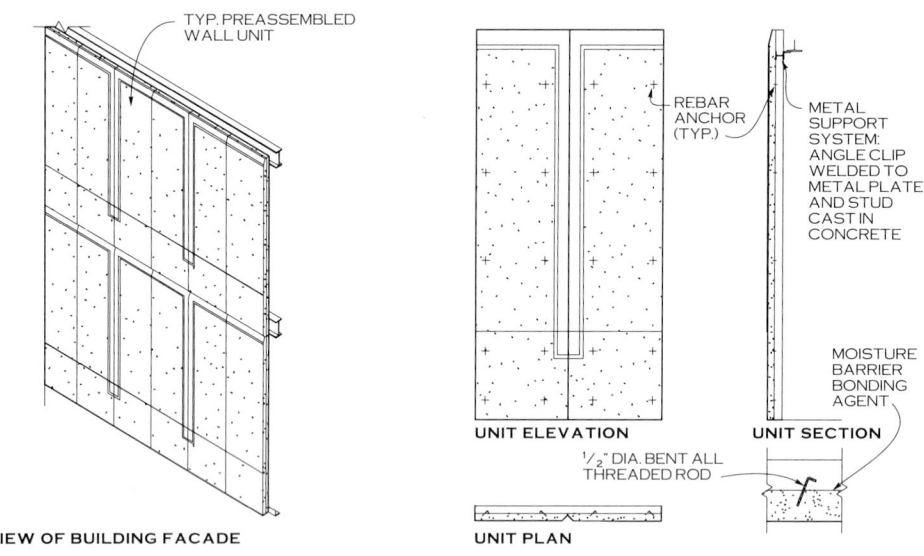

VIEW OF BUILDING FACADE

- TYP. PREASSEMBLED WALL UNIT

UNIT ELEVATION

- REBAR ANCHOR (TYP.)

UNIT SECTION

- METAL SUPPORT SYSTEM: ANGLE CLIP WELDED TO METAL PLATE AND STUD CAST IN CONCRETE
- MOISTURE BARRIER BONDING AGENT

UNIT PLAN

- 1/2" DIA. BENT ALL THREADED ROD

STONE UNIT PRECAST WITH CONCRETE BACKUP

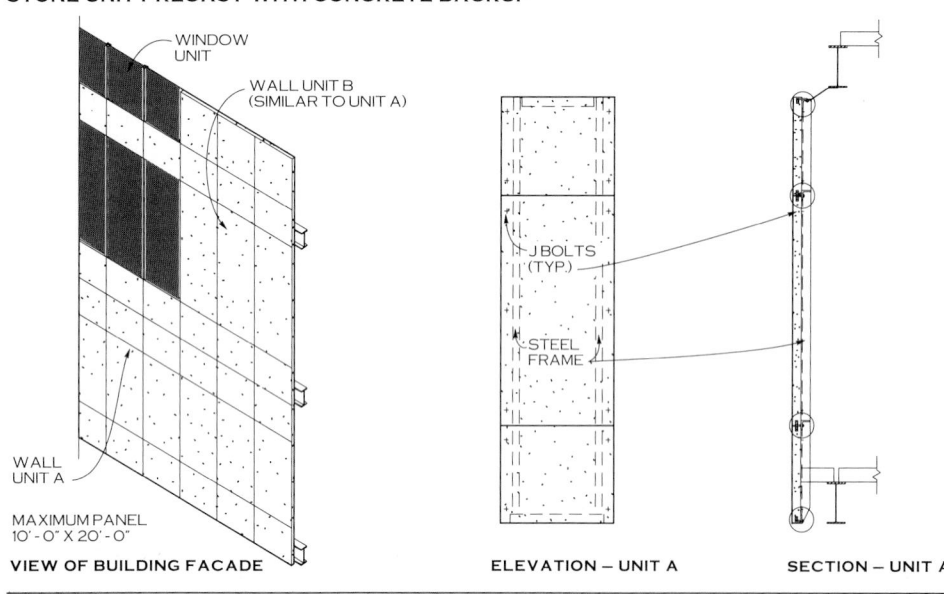

VIEW OF BUILDING FACADE

- WINDOW UNIT
- WALL UNIT B (SIMILAR TO UNIT A)
- WALL UNIT A
- MAXIMUM PANEL 10' - 0" X 20' - 0"

ELEVATION – UNIT A

- J BOLTS (TYP.)
- STEEL FRAME

SECTION – UNIT A

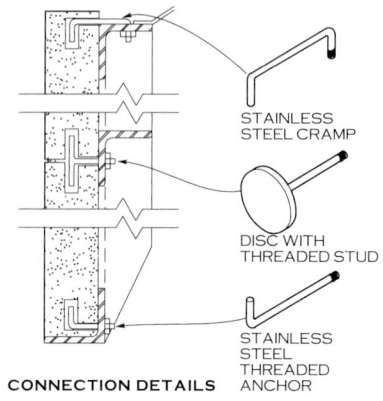

CONNECTION DETAILS

- STAINLESS STEEL CRAMP
- DISC WITH THREADED STUD
- STAINLESS STEEL THREADED ANCHOR

PREASSEMBLED STONE UNIT ON STEEL FRAME

PREASSEMBLED PANELS

Preassembled stone panel technology offers savings in on-site labor and accurate component stone unit joining.

Shipping and erection stresses on the stone panels and stone anchorage system to the preassembled units should be evaluated.

Design of sealant joints between preassembled units should include at least the following: thermal movement, fabrication and erection tolerances, irreversible material growth or shrinkage, and sealant movement potential.

STONE ON STEEL FRAME WITH EPOXY JOINTS

Stone units are mounted in a steel frame plus expansion anchors and dowel pins (as recommended by manufacturer). Joints in stone are epoxied and held to approximately 1/8 in. when finished for delivery. All stones in the assembly are anchored as a unit to the structure. Preassembled unit installation reduces individual leveling, plumbing, and aligning, and on-site joint sealing is not as extensive as with individual stone panels.

COMPOSITE ASSEMBLIES OF STONE AND CONCRETE

Stone units are bonded to reinforced precast concrete panels with bent stainless steel anchors. A moisture barrier and a bonding agent are installed between the stone and concrete in conditions where concrete alkali slats may stain stone units.

STONE AND STEEL ASSEMBLIES WITH SEALANT JOINTS

Stone units are shimmed and anchored to a steel frame using standard stone connecting hardware. Joints may be sealed on site, along with joints between assemblies.

George M. Whiteside, III, AIA, and James D. Lloyd; Kennett Square, Pennsylvania
Building Stone Institute; New York, New York
Alexander Keyes; Rippeteau Architects, PC; Washington, DC

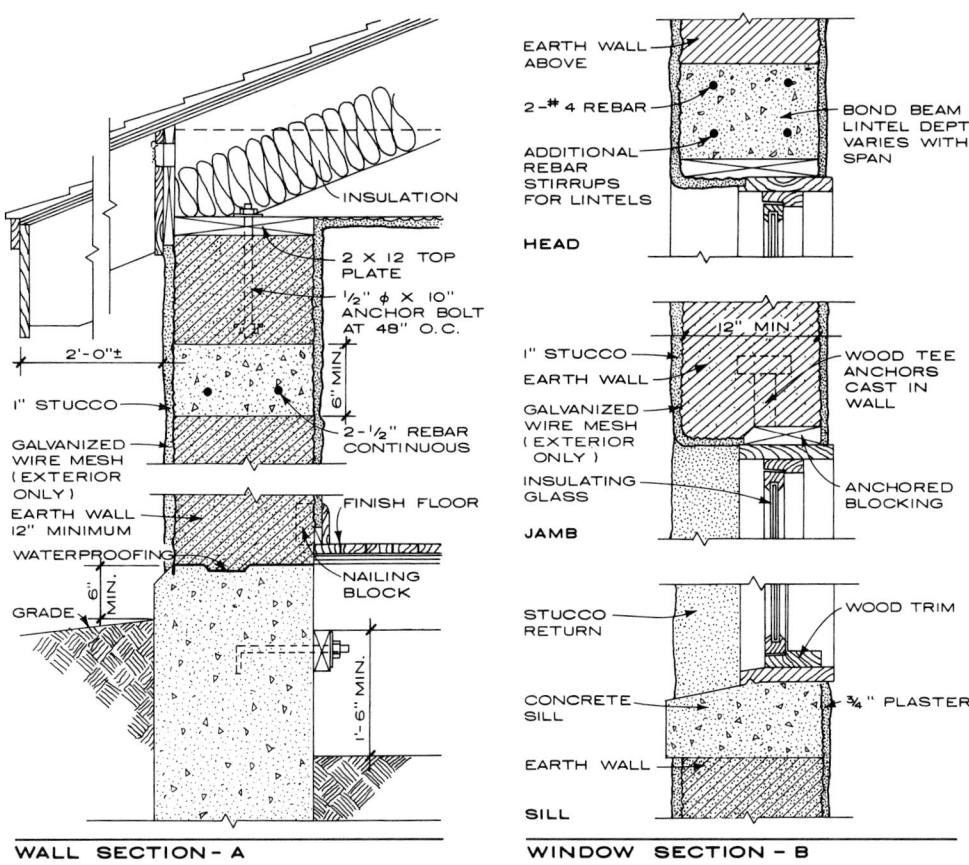

WALL SECTION - A

EARTH WALL ABOVE

2 - #4 REBAR

ADDITIONAL REBAR STIRRUPS FOR LINTELS

BOND BEAM LINTEL DEPTH VARIES WITH SPAN

HEAD

1" STUCCO
EARTH WALL
GALVANIZED WIRE MESH (EXTERIOR ONLY)
INSULATING GLASS

12" MIN.

WOOD TEE ANCHORS CAST IN WALL

ANCHORED BLOCKING

JAMB

STUCCO RETURN

CONCRETE SILL

EARTH WALL

WOOD TRIM

¾" PLASTER

SILL

WINDOW SECTION - B

NOTES

1. Rammed earth wall construction is an old technique used effectively in many parts of the world. The basic material is earth, with allowable proportions of clay, silt, and aggregate, commonly found almost everywhere. The soil in most locations has naturally usable proportions that do not require further tempering. The ideal soil mixture will have less than 50% clay and silt, and a maximum aggregate size of ¼ in. The solid is dampened to a moisture content of approximately 10% by weight, of dry soil. Saltwater should not be used under any circumstances.

2. The walls are constructed by the use of slip forms, (24 to 36 in. high x 8 to 12 ft long) placed level and secure. The forms are filled with damp (not wet) earth in 4 in. lifts. Each lift is rammed with a tamper until full compaction is reached. The tamp should be flat, approximately 6 x 6 in., weighing 18 to 25 lb, tamped by hand or mechanically. Full compaction can be determined by a ringing sound when the tamp compacts the fill. When the form is full and compacted, it is moved to a new location and secured and the process is repeated. The corners should be placed first, with special corner forms. When the full circumference is completed, the next course is started. The form heights (courses) are best coordinated with heights of window and door lintels. Form replacement can begin as soon as compaction is reached, without further drying.

3. Exterior wall thickness should be a minimum of 12 in. for one story, 18 in. to support a second story, and interior walls of not less than 9 in. Wall thickness can be increased as appropriate to the design. Basic rammed earth walls have many of the same characteristics of sundried adobe. The insulation value of the walls is not as great as more efficient insulating materials, but will provide thermal mass for heat storage, sound control, and other benefits.

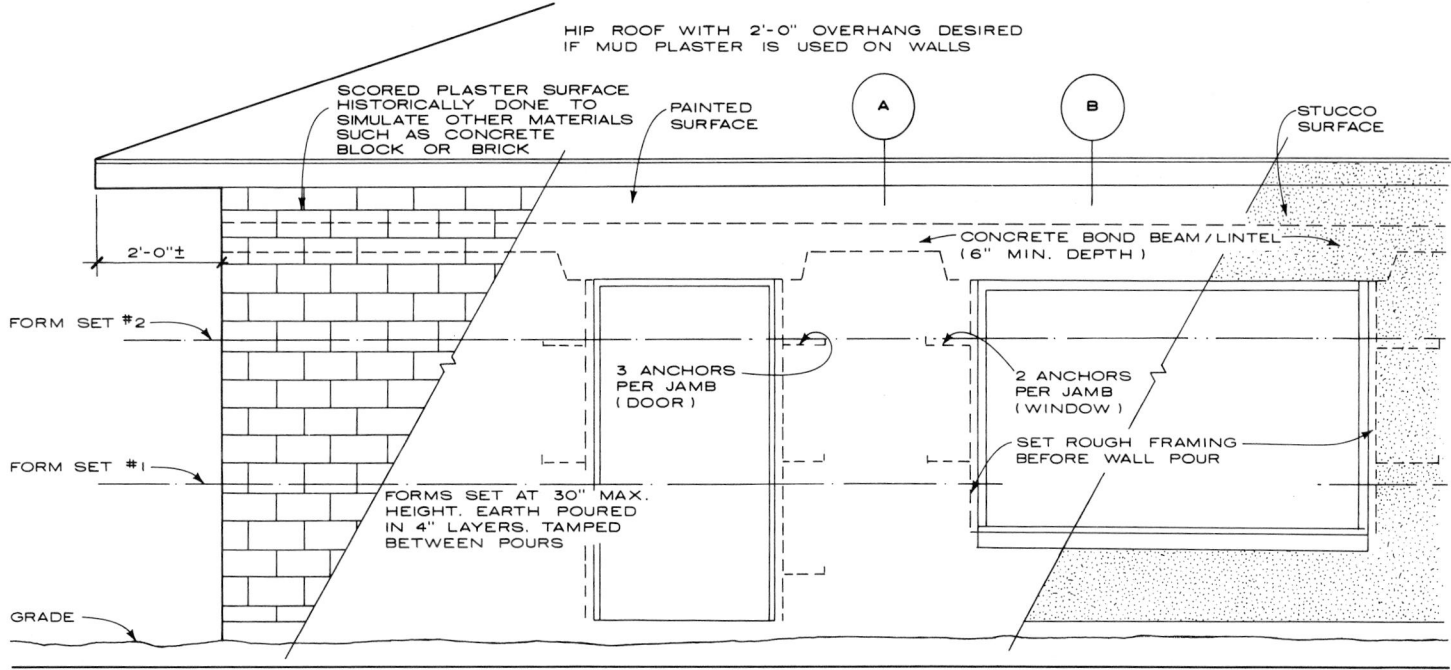

ELEVATION

NOTES

1. Foundations are normally conventional spread footings of sufficient width to support the heavy (3000 # per lin ft) walls. The foundation wall should be of a waterproof material, topped with a vapor barrier to prevent capillary moisture rise. Attachment anchors in the form of wood tees or plugs are placed in the wall as it is erected, in the positions required to secure window and door frames. A continuous steel reinforced concrete beam (6 in. thick) is placed as a continuous lintel beam to support walls above the openings.

2. A top plate of wood is secured by means of anchor bolts cast in the top of the walls. The plate provides load distribution and an attachment point for the roof structure. Interior and exterior walls can be finished by the application of conventional stucco or plaster. Simpler treatment can be achieved by smoothing or texturing the earth wall with a sponge rubber float, wet burlap, or sheepskin, and painting it. Sealing and preparation of the surface before painting is the same as for plaster. If waterproof stucco is not used, roof overhangs should be of sufficient width to protect the walls from rain erosion.

P. G. McHenry, Jr., AIA; Albuquerque, New Mexico

MASONRY CONSTRUCTION

Brick Institute of America (BIA)
11490 Commerce Park Drive, Suite 300
Reston, VA 22091-1525
Tel: (703) 620-0010
Fax:(703) 620-3928

International Masonry Institute (IMI)
823 15th Street, NW, Suite 1001
Washington, DC 20005
Tel: (202) 783-3908
Fax:(202)783-0433

Mason Contractors Association of America
1550 Spring Road, #320
Oakbrook, IL 60521
Tel: (708) 782-6767
Fax:(708) 782-6786

Masonry Heater Association of North America
11490 Commerce Park Drive
Reston, VA 22091-1525
Tel: (703) 620-3171

Masonry Institute of America (MIA)
2550 Beverly Blvd.
Los Angeles, CA 90057-1085
Tel: (213) 388-0472
Fax:(213) 389-7514

The Masonry Society (TMS)
2619 Spruce Street
Boulder, CO 80302
Tel: (303) 939-9700
Fax:(303) 444-3239

National Concrete Masonry Association (NCMA)
2302 Horse Pen Road
Herndon, VA 22071
Tel: (703) 713-1900
Fax:(703) 713-1900

National Lime Association (NLA)
200 North Glebe Road, Suite 800
Arlington, VA 22203
Tel: (703) 243-LIME
Fax:(703) 243-5489

REFERENCES

Ambrose, James E. *Simplified Design of Masonry Structures.* New York: J. Wiley & Sons, 1991.

Amrhein, J. *Residential Masonry Fireplace and Chimney Handbook.* Masonry Institute of America, 1989.

ASTM Standards on Masonry, compilation. American Society for Testing and Materials, 1990.

Beall, Christine. *Masonry Design and Detailing: for Architects, Engineers, and Builders.* Englewood Cliffs, N.J.: Prentice-Hall, 1984.

Building Code Requirements for Masonry Structures and Specifications, ACI 530-88. American Concrete Institute, 1989.

Davison, J. *Rain Penetraiton and Design Detail for Masonry Walls,* BPN 13. NRCC, 1979.

Gage, Michael J., and Tom Kirkbride. *Design in Blockwork.* London: Architecture Press, 1980.

Kreh, T. H. *Advanced Masonry Skills.* Albany, N.Y.: Delmar Publishers, 1983.

Masonry: Components to Assemblages, STP 1063. American Society for Testing and Materials, 1990.

Masonry Designer's Guide, TMS. Council for Masonry Research, 1992.

The Masonry Journal, Masonry Society. [semiannual]

Masonry Structures: Behavior and Design. Brick Institute of America and National Concrete Masonry Association, 1993.

A Manual of Facts on Concrete Masonry, TB-1. NCMA-TEK series. National Concrete Masonry Association. [subscription series binder, regularly updated]

Newman, Morton. *Structural Details for Masonry Construction.* ed. by Jeremy Robinson. N.Y.: McGraw-Hill, 1988.

Panarese, W., et al. *Concrete Masonry Handbook for Architects, Engineers, Builders,* EB008. Portland Cement Association, 1991.

Principles of Brick Masonry. Brick Inst. of America, 1989.

Redstone, Louis G. *Masonry in Architecture.* New York: McGraw-Hill, 1984.

The Reference Manual: Specifications for Masonry Structures with ASTM References, ACI 530.1/ASCE 6-88, SP-115. American Concrete Institute, 1989.

Technical Notes on Brick Construction. Brick Inst. of America. [subscription series binder, regularly updated]

MORTAR AND GROUT

Portland Cement Association (PCA)
5420 Old Orchard Road
Skokie, IL 60077-1083
Tel: (708) 966-6200
Fax:(708) 966-9781

REFERENCES

How to Specify and Use Mortar. Aberdeen Group, 1990.

Masonry and Cement Mortars, IS181. Portland Cement Association, 1988.

Masonry Mortar Technical Note Series, various dates. National Lime Association.

Mortar and Masonry Grout, SpecGUIDE G04100. Construction Specifications Institute, 1991.

Mortars for Masonry Walls, IS040, Portland Cement Association, 1987.

UNIT MASONRY

National Association of Brick Distributors (NABD)
1600 Spring Hill Road, #305
Vienna, VA 22182
Tel: (703) 749-6223
Fax:(703) 749-6277

REFERENCES

Amrhein, J. *Masonry Veneer.* Masonry Institute of America, 1987.

Amrhein, J., and M. Merrigan. *Reinforced Concrete Masonry Construction Inspector's Handbook.* Masonry Institue of America, 1989.

"Brick Institute Recommendations." *P/A* (Feb. 1992), pp. 117-18.

Brick Unit Masonry, SpecGUIDE G04211, Construction Specifications Institute, 1989.

Concrete Masonry Design Tables, Non-Reinforced, TR-83, National Concrete Masonry Association.

Concrete Masonry Design Tables, Reinforced, TR-84, National Concrete Masonry Association.

Concrete Unit Masonry, SpecGUIDE G04220, Construction Specifications Institute (CSI),1988.

Glass Unit Masonry, SpecGUIDE G04270, CSI,1988.

ADOBE UNIT MASONRY
REFERENCES

Clifton, James R. *Preservation of Historic Adobe Structures: A Status Report.* Washington, D.C.: National Bureau of Standards, 1977, 30 p., ill.

Southwick, Marcia. *Building with Adobe.* Chicago: Sage Books, 1974.

Wolfskill, Lyle A. *Handbook for Building Homes of Earth.* College Station, Texas, 1963.

STONE

Allied Stone Industries (ASI)
P.O. Box 360747
Columbus, OH 43236-0747
Tel: (614) 228-5489

Building Stone Institute (BSI)
P.O. Box 3507
Purdys, NY 10578
Tel: (914) 232-5725
Fax:(914) 232-5259

Cast Stone Institute (CastSI)
1850 Lee Road, Suite 230
Winter Park, FL 32789-2106
Tel: (407) 740-7721
Fax:(407) 740-5321

Cultured Marble Institute
International Cast Polymer Association
1735 North Lynn Street, Suite 950
Arlington, VA 22209
Tel: (703) 276-2644
Fax:(703) 524-2303

Indiana Limestone Institute of America (ILIA)
Stone City Bank Building, Suite 400
Bedford, IN 47421
Tel: (812) 275-4426
Fax:(812) 279-8682

Italian Marble Center (IMC)
Italian Trade Commission
499 Park Avenue
New York, NY 10022
Tel: (212) 980-1500

Marble Institute of America
33505 State Street
Farmington, MI 48335
Tel: (810) 476-5558
Fax:(810) 476-1630

National Stone Association (NSA)
1415 Elliot Place, NW
Washington, DC 20007
Tel: (202) 342-1100
Fax:(202) 342-0702

Pulverized Limestone Association
see National Stone Association

REFERENCES

Amrhein, J., and M. Merrigan. *Marble and Stone Slab Veneer.* Marble Institute of America, 1989.

Dimension Stone Design Manual #4. Marble Institute of America, 1991. [looseleaf binder]

Dimension Stones of the World, vol. 1. Masonry Institute of America, 1990.

Donaldson, B., ed. *New Stone Technology, Design and Construction for Exterior Wall Systems,* STP 996. American Society for Testing and Materials, 1988.

Indiana Limestone Handbook. Indiana Limestone Institute of America, 1985.

Marble from Italy. Italian Marble Center.

"Quality from the Quarry." *P/A* (Aug. 1991), pp. 45-47.

Stone, SpecGUIDE G04400. Construction Specifications Institute, 1987.

MASONRY RESTORATION AND CLEANING

International Association of Stone
Restoration & Conservation (IASRC)
36 W. Gay Street, Suite 304
Columbus, OH 43215
Tel:(614) 461-5852

Sealant, Waterproofing, and Restoration Institute (SWRI)
3101 Broadway #585
Kansas City, MO 64111
Tel: (816) 561-8230
Fax:(816) 561-7765

REFERENCES

"Cleaning Brick Masonry." *Technical Notes on Brick Construction,* no. 20. Brick Inst. of Amer., 1990.

Cleaning New Masonry, Monograph 04M511. Construction Specifications Institute, 1987.

Clifton, J., ed. *Cleaning Stone and Masonry,* STP 935. American Society for Testing and Materials, 1986.

Exterior Masonry Restorative Cleaning, Monograph 04M521. Construction Specifications Institute, 1987.

Glossary of Historic Masonry Deterioration Problems and Preservation Treatments. National Park Service, 1988. [#024-005-01035-1, US GPO]

Grimmer, Anne E. *Keeping It Clean: Removing Exterior Dirt, Paint, Stains, and Graffiti from Historic Masonry Buildings.* Washington, D.C.: National Park Service, Preservation Assistance Division, 1988.

Hutchens, Nigel. *Restoring Houses of Brick and Stone.* New York: Van Nostrand Reinhold., 1982.

London, Mark. *Masonry: How to Care for Old and Historic Brick and Stone.* Respectful Rehabilitation Series. Washington, D.C.: Preservation Press, 1988.

Mack, Robert C. *Cleaning and Waterproof Coating of Masonry Buildings.* National Park Service, Preservation Assistance Div., Technical Preservation Services, 1975.

Masonry Repointing, Monograph 04M502, Construction Specifications Institute, 1990.

Moisture Resistance of Brick Masonry Maintenance, 7F. Brick Institute of America, 1987.

"The Preservation of Historic Glazed Architectural Terra Cotta," Preservation Brief 7. National Park Service, 1979. [#024-005-00883-7]

CHAPTER
5
METALS

TYPES OF METALS

There are two general types of metals, ferrous and nonferrous. Ferrous metals contain iron, nonferrous do not.

FERROUS METALS

Iron, which contains no trace amount of carbon, is soft, ductile, easily worked, oxidizes rapidly, but is susceptible to most acids. It is the main element in steel.

Cast iron and gray cast iron both are brittle metals with high compressive strength and capacity to absorb vibration, which makes them ideal for gratings, stair components and manhole covers. Neither should be hammered or beaten because they lack ductility. Both are relatively corrosion resistant.

Malleable iron, often used for the same purposes, is a low carbon iron that is cast, reheated and slowly cooled, or annealed, to improve its workability.

Wrought iron is soft, corrosion and fatigue resistant, and machinable. It is easily worked, making it ideal for railings, grilles, fences, screens, and various types of ornamental work. It often is cast or worked into bars, sheets or pipes. Because of its corrosion resistance, wrought iron until recently was used for below grade applications. Other metals are now preferred.

Steel is iron with low to medium amounts of carbon; carbon content is the measure used to categorize carbon steel. Greater carbon content increases strength and hardness but reduces ductility and welding capability. Its corrosion resistance is increased when a finish such as galvanizing or an organic coating is applied. Some architectural uses are as structural shapes, castings, studs, joists, fasteners, wall grilles, and ceiling suspension grids.

Steel alloys are produced when other elements are combined with carbon steel to modify steel properties. For example, high strength, low alloy steels (HSLA) improve corrosion resistance and are chosen where weight is a consideration and high strength is required. They are used infrequently in architectural applications because water runoff tends to stain adjacent materials. Below are a number of modifying alloy elements:

1. Aluminum for surface hardening.
2. Chromium for corrosion resistance.
3. Copper for resistance to atmospheric corrosion.
4. Manganese in small amounts for hardening; in larger amounts for wear resistance.
5. Molybdenum, combined with other alloying metals such as chromium and nickel, to increase corrosion resistance and to raise tensile strength without reducing ductility.
6. Nickel to increase tensile strength without reducing ductility; in high concentrations, to improve corrosion resistance.
7. Silicon to strengthen low-alloy steels and improve oxidation resistance; in larger amounts to provide hard, brittle castings resistant to corrosive chemicals.
8. Sulfur for free machining, especially in mild steels.
9. Titanium to prevent intergranular corrosion of stainless steels.
10. Tungsten, vanadium, and cobalt for hardness and abrasion resistance.

Stainless steel contains a minimum of 11.5 percent chromium. Nickel is added to boost atmospheric corrosion resistance. Where maximum corrosion resistance is required, such as resistance to pitting by sea water, molybdenum is added. Stainless steel is used in construction for flashing, coping, fasciae, wall panels, floor plates, gratings, handrails, hardware, fasteners and anchors.

NONFERROUS METALS

Nonferrous metals (those containing no iron) used in construction are:

Aluminum: High-purity aluminum is soft and ductile, highly corrosion resistant, but lacking in strength. Aluminum alloys are identified by numbers that distinguish each by its relative properties. For example, the identification number of pure aluminum is 1100. The manganese-based aluminum alloy, 3003, is used for roofing, sheet metal, siding, and conduit.

Lead: Extremely dense metal, easily worked, and corrosion resistant. Alloys are added to improve its properties

such as hardness and strength. Lead is used for waterproofing, sound and vibration isolation, and radiation shielding. It can be combined with a tin alloy to plate iron or steel, commonly called "terneplate." Care should be taken where and how lead is used because lead vapors or dust are toxic if ingested.

Zinc, although corrosion resistant in water and air, is brittle and low in strength. Its major use is in galvanizing (dipping hot iron or steel in molten zinc), but it also is used for roofing, flashing, hardware, die casting and as an alloying element.

Chromium and nickel also are used primarily as alloying elements; however, both can take a bright polish and do not tarnish in air, making them ideal for use in plating.

Monel, a nickel-copper alloy, most commonly is used to make fasteners and anchors, and is excellent where high corrosion resistance is required.

Copper is resistant to corrosion, impact and fatigue, yet it is ductile. It is used primarily in construction as electrical wiring, roofing, flashing, and piping.

Bronze originally was a copper-tin alloy; however, today copper is alloyed with various elements such as aluminum or silicon. In fact, the term "bronze" seldom is used without a modifying adjective giving the name of at least one of its alloying components, such as phosphor bronze, a copper-tin-phosphorus alloy, or leaded phosphor bronze composed of copper-lead-tin and phosphorus; aluminum bronze containing copper and aluminum; and silicon bronze, a copper-silicon alloy.

Brass is copper with zinc as its principal alloying element; however, some types of brass alloys often are called bronze even though they are not. Some nonbronze, brass alloys are: commercial bronze, 90 percent copper, 10 percent zinc; naval brass, 60 percent copper, 29 percent zinc, one percent tin; and manganese bronze, 58 percent copper, 39 percent zinc, one percent tin and iron. When a metal is identified as bronze, the alloy cannot contain zinc or nickel; if it does, it probably is brass. Architectural and commercial bronze are really brass, and are used for doors, windows, door and window frames, railings, trim and grilles and for finish hardware.

THE GALVANIC SERIES

Anode (least noble)	Magnesium, magnesium alloys
	Zinc
+	Aluminum 1100
	Cadmium
	Aluminum 2024-T4
	Steel or Iron, Cast iron
	Chromium iron (active)
	Ni-Resist
	Type 304, 316 stainless (active)
	Hastelloy "C"
	Lead, Tin
electric current flows from positive (+) to negative (−)	Nickel (Inconel) (active)
	Hastelloy "B"
	Brasses, Copper, Bronzes, Copper-Nickel alloys, Monel
	Silver solder
	Nickel (Inconel) (passive)
	Chromium iron (passive)
	Type 304, 316 stainless (passive)
−	Silver
	Titanium
Cathode (most noble)	Graphite, Gold, Platinum

CORROSION TO METALS

Galvanic action, or corrosion, occurs between dissimilar metals or metals and other materials when sufficient moisture is present to carry an electrical current. The galvanic series, a list of metals arranged in order from "least noble, most reactive to corrosion" to "most noble, least reactive to corrosion," is a good indicator of corrosion susceptibility due to galvanic action. The farther apart two metals are on the list, the greater the deterioration of the least noble one.

Metal deterioration also occurs when metals come in contact with chemically active materials, particularly when moisture is present. For example, aluminum in direct contact with concrete or mortar corrodes, or steel in contact with certain types of treated wood corrodes.

Other types of corrosion are pitting and concentration cell corrosion. Pitting corrosion occurs when particles or bubbles of gas are deposited on a metal surface. Oxygen deficiency under the deposit sets up anodic areas causing pitting. Concentration cell corrosion is similar to galvanic corrosion; the difference is in electrolytes. Concentration cell corrosion may be produced by differences in ion concentration, oxygen concentration, or foreign matter adhering to the surface.

FABRICATION ON METALS

Fabrication is a process applied to metal to obtain a shape. Following are various types of fabrication.

Rolling hot or cold metal between rollers under pressure produces most of the primary shapes available. The metal's temperature determines the properties of the end product. This method is applicable to most metals except iron.

In the extruding process metal is pushed under pressure through a die orifice producing various complex shapes limited only by the size or capability of the die. This process is applicable to all metals except iron.

Casting is a process in which molten metal is poured into molds and allowed to solidify into the shape of the mold. Casting is applicable to aluminum, copper, iron, steel, bronze, and other metals; however, surface quality and physical characteristics are affected by metal type, casting technique, and the molten metal's temperature.

In the drawing process either hot or cold metal is pulled through dies that alter or reduce its cross-sectional shape to attain three-dimensional shapes. Common extrusions are sheets, tubes, pipes, rods, bars, and wires. Drawing is applicable to all metals except iron.

Forging is a process of hammering or pressing hot or cold metal to a desired shape. It usually improves the strength and surface characteristics of the metal. Forging is applicable to aluminum, copper and steel.

Forming shapes metals by mechanical operations, excluding machining.

Bending produces curved shapes, and generally is applied to tubes, rods, and extrusions.

Brake forming, usually applied to plates or metal sheets, is a process of successive pressings to achieve specific shapes.

In the spinning process metal is shaped with tools while it is spun on an axis.

Embossing and coining are processes usually performed on flat shapes to achieve textured or raised patterns.

Blanking is shearing, sawing or cutting metal sheets with a punch press to achieve an outline.

Perforating is achieved by punching or drilling holes usually in flat shapes.

Piercing is a process that punches holes through metal without removing any of the metal.

Welding is the fusion of metals above the molten point with or without the aid of a metal filler. Gas welding is the most portable and economical. It can be used on site. The heat for fusion is provided by a torch using oxygen and acetylene gases.

Shielded metal arc welding, sometimes called manual, hand, or stick welding, can be performed in the shop or the field. An electric arc between a coated metal electrode and the components to be welded heat them both to a point where a molten pool forms on the surface of the components. As the arc is moved along the joint between the components, the pool solidifies, forming a homogeneous weld.

Gas metal arc welding also can be done on site or in a shop; however, provisions must be made on a job site to screen from any winds. This process uses an uncoated solid wire electrode and a stream of gas to provide shielding for the arc and welded metal. Several other types of welding are confined to the shop. Further information on welding is available from the American Welding Society.

FINISHES, MECHANICAL AND CHEMICAL

An as-fabricated finish is the texture and surface appearance given to a metal by the fabrication process.

A brightened finish is produced by electrolytic brightening or dipping the metal in acid solutions.

A buffed finish is produced by successive polishing and buffing operations using fine abrasives, lubricants, and soft fabric wheels.

A chemical finish produces a physical change on the metal's surface depending on the type of metal and chemical used.

Directional textured finishes have a smooth satiny sheen produced by making tiny parallel scratches on the metal surface using a belt or wheel and fine abrasive, or by hand rubbing with steel wool. Non-directional textured finishes are produced by blasting the metal under controlled conditions with sand, glass beads, or metal shot.

An etched finish produces a matte, frosted surface with varying degrees of roughness by treating the metal with an acid or alkaline solution.

Metallic finishes are created by applying one metal to another by electrolysis, hot dipping, electroplating, or other techniques.

Galvanizing is an example of metal coating where zinc is applied to steel. Zinc may be applied by electrolysis, peening, hot zinc spray, hot dip or paint. Hot dip galvanizing is used for nails, nuts and bolts, and structural members. Thickness of the zinc coating may be varied depending on the corrosive nature of the atmosphere at the place of use. Galvanized steel may be painted with special formulated coatings to substantially extend the life of the galvanized coating.

Patterned finishes, mechanically produced, are available in various textures and designs. They are produced by passing an as-fabricated sheet either between two machine matched-design rollers, embossing patterns on both sides of the sheet, or between a smooth roll and a design roll, embossing or coining on one side of the sheet only.

APPLIED COATINGS

Applied coatings are surface coverings over metal. They may be inorganic, such as porcelain enamel, or organic, like most commonly used fluorocarbons. Both can be applied over suitable primers (although not always necessary) for added corrosion resistance and to improve adhesion. Generally they are applied and baked on at the factory. Air-dry formulas usually are available for touch-ups.

Fluorocarbons generally are based on resins and are applied over primers such as epoxy-zinc chromate primers. They are available in a wide range of colors and in low to medium ranges of gloss.

Siliconized polymers, a combination of organic polymers and silicone intermediates, are applied in combination with a primer or alone. They are available in a wide range of colors and low to high gloss. The silicone extends gloss retention and improves resistance to color change and weathering. The two principal types are siliconized acrylic and siliconized polyester.

Plastisols are the top coat of a two-coat system. They require a special primer to bond to the metal surface. The top coat thickness can vary from 3 mils to 15 mils.

Conversion coatings for aluminum are amorphous chrome phosphate; for steel, a phosphate or various strong salt solutions generally is used.

Vitreous coatings are composed of inorganic glossy materials such as porcelain enamels. They are one of the hardest and most durable finishes, but they are brittle. Deformation of metal may cause cracking and spalling. These coatings are available in a wide range of colors and finishes from matte to high gloss.

Anodic finishes for coating aluminum consist of a mechanical finish, then a preanodic treatment to remove all foreign matter, and finally an oxide coating. Aluminum alloys must be suitable for anodizing. Fabrication, such as welding, can show when anodized.

REPRESENTATIVE ARCHITECTURAL USES AND COMPARATIVE PROPERTIES OF COATINGS

BINDER TYPE	TYPICAL USES	APPLICATION SHOP	APPLICATION FIELD	COST	OUT-DOOR LIFE (YEARS)	COLOR STABLE, EX-TERIOR	GLOSS RETEN-TION, EX-TERIOR	STAIN RESIS-TANCE	WEATHER RESIS-TANCE	ABRA-SION AND IM-PACT RESIS-TANCE	FLEXI-BILITY	WATER-REDU-CIBLE AVAIL-ABLE	CLEAR AVAIL-ABLE	WELD-ABLE AS PRIMER
Acrylics— Solvent reducible	Residential siding and similar products; cabinets and implements; clear top coats	yes	no	M	10	yes	G	F	G	G	G	—	yes	yes*
Water reducible: air dried		yes	yes	M	5–10	yes	F	F	G	G	G	yes	yes	yes*
baked		yes	no	M	15–20	yes	G–E	F	G–E	G	G	yes	yes	yes*
Alkyds	Exterior primers and enamels	yes	yes	L–M	5–9	no	G	F	F	F	F–G	yes	yes	yes*
Cellulose Acetate Butyrate	Decorative high gloss finishes	yes	no	M	NA	yes	G	F	G	G	G	no	yes	no
Chlorinated rubber	Corrosion-resistant paints; swimming pool coatings; protection of dissimilar metals	yes	yes	M	10	yes	F	F	G	G	G	no	no	no
Chloro-sulfonated polyethylene	Paints for piping, tanks, valves, etc.	yes	yes	VH	15	yes	NA	F	E	F–G	E	no	no	no
Epoxy	Moisture- and alkali-resistant coatings; nondecorative interior uses requiring high chemical resistance	yes	yes	H–VH	15–20	no	P	G	G–E	E	G	no	no	yes*
Fluorocarbons	High performance exterior coatings; industrial siding; curtain walls	yes	no	VH	20+	yes	E	E	E	E	G	no	no	no
Phenol formaldehyde	Chemical- and moisture-resistant coatings	yes	yes	M	10	no	F	F	G–E	G–E	G	no	yes	yes*
Polyester	Cabinets and furniture; ceiling tile; piping	yes	yes	H	15	some versions	G–E	G–E	G–E	G	G–E	yes	yes	no
Polyvinyl chloride	Residential siding; rain-carrying equipment; metal wall tile; base-board heating covers, etc. Plasti-sols: industrial siding; curtain walls	yes	yes	H	15	yes	G	F	G–E	G	G–E	yes	no	yes*
Silicates (inorganic)	Corrosion-inhibitive primers; solvent-resistant coatings	yes	yes	H	NA	NA	NA	NA	NA	G	G	no	no	yes
Silicone-modified polymers	High performance exterior coatings; industrial siding; curtain walls	yes	yes	H–VH	15–20	yes	G–E	G	G–E	G–E	G	yes	no	no
Urethane (aliphatic-cured)	Heavy duty coatings for stain, chemical, abrasion, and corrosion resistance	yes	yes	VH	20+	some versions	E	G–E	G–E	G–E	E	yes	yes	yes*

KEY: L = Low; M = Moderate; H = High; VH = Very High; NA = not applicable or not available; P = Poor; F = Fair; G = Good; E = Excellent   *For light welding only

STRUCTURAL WELDING

Structural welds can be made with hundreds of different welding processes. The most common are forms of shielded metal arc and oxyfuel gas welding. These processes are designed for the specific welding conditions: type of metal, structural requirements, weld position, and joint specifications. Normally, however, the designer does not specify the process which is to be used to make a welded joint. The designer specifies the type and size of weld needed for the specific joint and leaves the details of how the joint is to be made up to the fabricator.

The two most important types of structural welds are fillet welds and groove welds. They are the most useful in structural applications. Back welds are used in conjunction with single groove welds to complete the weld penetration. Plug, slot, and flare welds are of secondary importance and are limited in application.

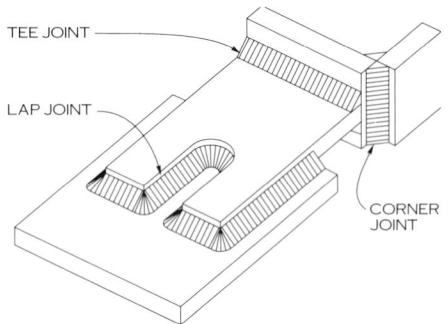

FILLET WELD JOINTS

With a triangular cross section, fillet welds join two surfaces approximately at right angles to each other in lap, tee, and corner joints. They are also used with groove welds as reinforcements in corner joints.

FILLET WELDS

Groove welds are welds made in a groove between adjacent ends, edges, or surfaces of two parts to be joined in a butt, tee, or corner joint.

The edge or ends of parts to be groove welded are usually prepared by flame cutting, arc air gouging, or edge planing to provide square, vee, bevel, U-, or J-shaped grooves that are straight and true to dimension. The preparation is done to ensure that the base metal is welded evenly completely through the joint. With thicker metal it is also done to open up the joint area for welding. Relatively thin material may be groove welded with square cut edges.

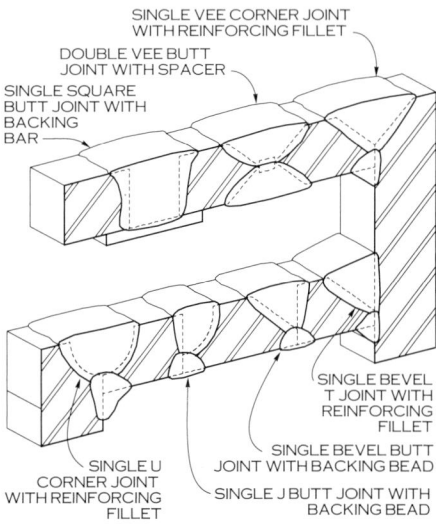

EXAMPLES OF COMPLETE PENETRATION GROOVE WELDS

The two types of groove welds are complete penetration and partial penetration. A complete penetration weld is one that achieves fusion of weld and base metal throughout the depth of the joint. It is made by welding from both sides of the joint, from one side to a backing bar, or back welding the first weld.

GROOVE WELDS

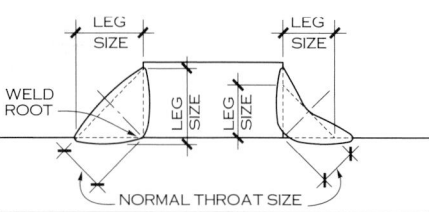

FILLET WELD NOMENCLATURE

The model cross section of a fillet weld is a right triangle with equal legs. The leg size designates the effective size of the weld. The length of a fillet weld is the distance from end-to-end of the full size fillet, measured parallel to its root line. For curved fillet welds the effective length is equal to the throat length, measured along a line bisecting the throat area.

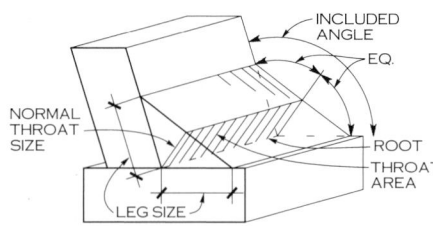

The cross section of a fillet weld may differ from the right triangle model in several ways. The included angle of the weld may vary from 60° to 135°, or unequal leg welds may be employed. When unequal leg welds are used, the use of the normal throat size as the effective size in weld strength calculations will, in most cases, be conservative. However, when the included angle of weld deposit is substantially greater than 90°, the effective throat size should be determined from the actual dimensions of the weld according to American Welding Society specifications.

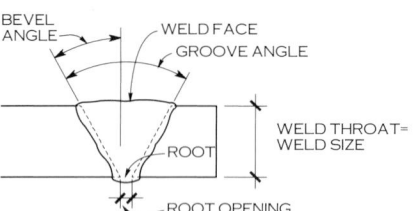

FULL PENETRATION GROOVE WELD NOMENCLATURE

Except where backing bars are employed, specifications require that the weld roots generally must be chipped or gouged to sound metal before making the second weld. For purposes of stress computation, the throat dimension of a full penetration groove weld is considered to be the full thickness of the thinner part joined, exclusive of weld reinforcement, such as backing bars.

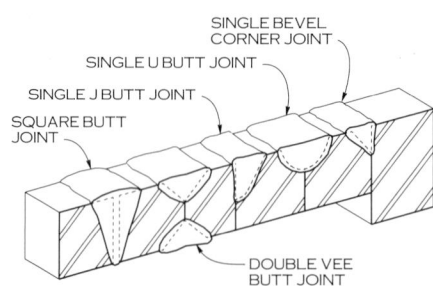

EXAMPLES OF PARTIAL PENETRATION GROOVE WELDS

Partial penetration groove welds are employed when stresses to be transferred do not require full penetration, or when welding must be done from one side of a joint only and it is not possible to use backing bars or to gouge weld roots for back welds. The application of partial penetration groove welds is governed by specifications and may limit the effective throat thickness or the thickness of the material on which they are to be used.

JOINT PREQUALIFICATION

Welded joints that conform to all American Welding Society code and specification provisions for design, material, and workmanship are prequalified joints. There are a variety of specific fillet and groove welded joints that meet most structural work requirements and are recommended for general use in buildings and bridges. Joints that are not prequalified under the AWS code are required to be qualified by tests as prescribed by the code.

For quick reference and more advanced consideration, the prequalified joints are shown in AWS "Structural Welding Code–Steel."

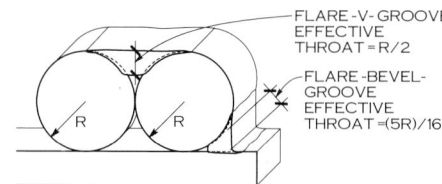

FLARE WELD NOMENCLATURE

Flare welds are special cases of groove welds in which the groove surface of one or both parts of a joint is convex. This convexity may be the result of edge preparation, but more often one or both components consists of a round rod or rounded shape. Complete penetration in a flare weld is usually difficult to achieve and the quality of the weld is difficult to control; therefore, design values should be applied conservatively and special considerations need to be taken in certain instances.

FLARE WELDS

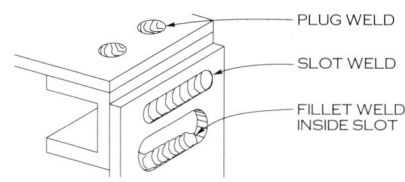

PLUG AND SLOT WELDS

Plug and slot welds are used in lap joints to transmit shear loads, prevent buckling of lapped parts, or join component parts of built-up members. Round holes or slots are punched or otherwise formed in one component of the joint before assembly. With parts in position, weld metal is deposited in the openings, which may be partially or completely filled, depending on the thickness of the punched material. AWS "Structural Welding Code–Steel" should be consulted for allowable proportion and spacing of holes and slots and the depth of welds.

It is necessary to distinguish between plug or slot welds and fillet welds placed around the inside of a hole or slot. Fillet welds in a slot are easier to make and inspect and are usually preferred over fillet welds in round holes or plug and slot welds.

PLUG AND SLOT WELDS

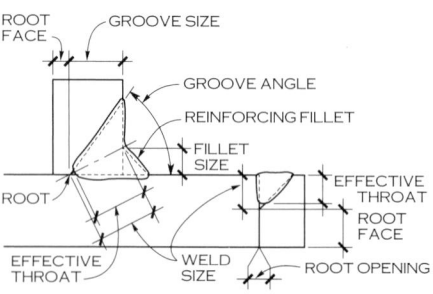

PARTIAL PENETRATION GROOVE WELD NOMENCLATURE

Edge preparation of base material for partial penetration welds is similar to that for full penetration groove welds, but it usually covers less than the full thickness. The effective throat thickness and, hence, the weld strength of partial penetration groove welds is normally limited to less than the full joint thickness.

The use of partial penetration welds is subject to AWS code and other specification provisions. These are more restrictive in bridge specifications than in building codes.

BASIC WELDING SYMBOLS

The three basic parts needed to form a welding symbol are: an arrow pointing to the joint, a reference line upon which the dimensional data are placed, and a weld device symbol indicating the weld type required. The tail of the welding symbol is only necessary to indicate additional data, such as specification, process, or detail references.

The arrow indicates the joint where the weld is to be made. The basic weld device symbol or device indicates the type of weld to be made, for example: fillet, U-groove, bevel, or plug. The position of the basic weld symbol or device indicates which side of the joint is to be welded. The bottom side of the reference line is designated as the arrow side, meaning any welding operation shown on this side of the reference line is to be performed on the same side of the joint as the arrow. When an operation is shown on the top side of the reference line it is to be performed on the joint side opposite the arrow.

The weld dimensions, size, length, pitch, etc., are placed on the reference line next to the weld device. These dimensions read from left to right regardless of which side the arrow is on.

FILLET WELDS

The dimensions needed for fillet welds are weld size and length and, for intermittent fillet welds, pitch. The weld size is equal to the weld leg size, assuming that the legs are equal. In the rare instance that the legs are not equal, the size is not given in the welding symbol but instead the weld legs are dimensioned in the drawing to avoid confusion. If there is a typical weld size for a particular drawing, the size may be noted in the notes and left off of the symbol. If the joint is to be welded on both sides, then both sides must be dimensioned, even if they are the same.

If the length of a fillet weld is omitted, it is understood to mean that the weld is to extend the full distance between abrupt changes in the part of the joint outline specified by the weld symbol arrow. If the same size fillet is required for the full length of all sides of a particular joint, regardless of abrupt changes in its direction, the weld-all-around symbol can be used to simplify the drawing.

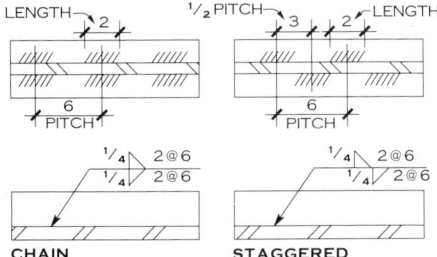

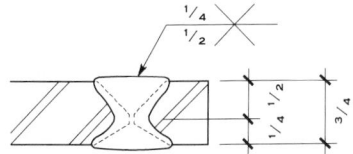

CHAIN   STAGGERED

INTERMITTENT FILLET WELDS

Pitch is used with intermittent fillet welds to give the center to center dimensions between welded sections. When using pitch, length is the dimension of the individual weld sections.

COMPLETE PENETRATION GROOVE WELDS

When detailing complete penetration groove welds the dimensions usually include the weld size, root opening, the groove angle for vee, bevel, J, and U welds, and the groove radii for J and U welds. The length of groove welds is not given, because the welds are accepted to go from end to end of pieces welded. Any deviation from this requires additional detailing.

UNSYMMETRICAL GROOVE WELD CALLOUT

Normally the weld size of a complete joint penetration groove weld is understood to be the full thickness of the thinner metal connected, and its dimension need not be shown on the welding symbol. However, if the preparation of a double groove weld is not symmetrical, the size of each side of the weld must be shown.

The root opening is shown near the root of the groove device. The groove angle is to be shown within the groove

BASIC WELD DEVICE SYMBOLS

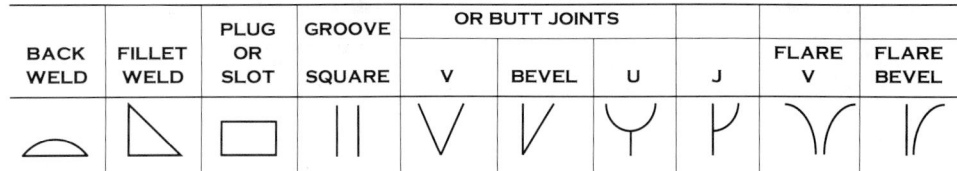

BACK WELD	FILLET WELD	PLUG OR SLOT	GROOVE	OR BUTT JOINTS					FLARE V	FLARE BEVEL
			SQUARE	V	BEVEL	U	J			

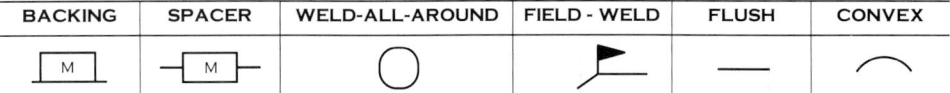

SUPPLEMENTARY WELD SYMBOLS

BACKING	SPACER	WELD-ALL-AROUND	FIELD - WELD	FLUSH	CONVEX

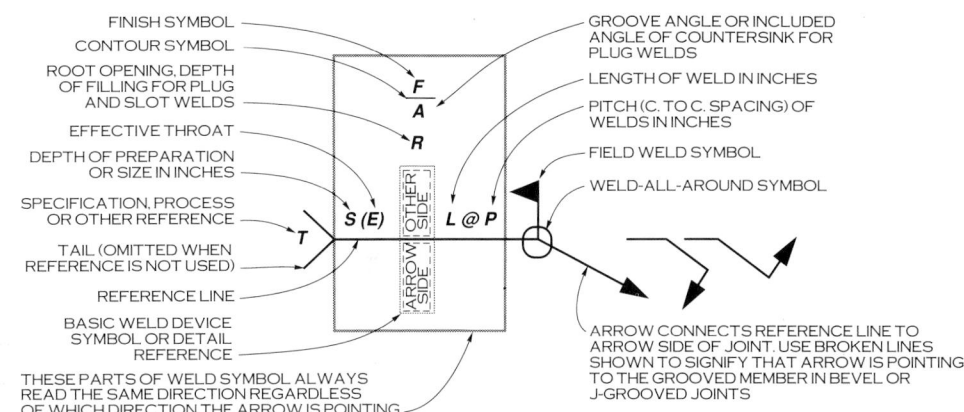

NOTE: For additional basic and supplementary weld symbols, see the American Welding Society A2.4-79.

STANDARD LOCATION OF ELEMENTS OF A WELDING SYMBOL

NOTES

1. Size, weld symbol, length of weld, and spacing must read in that order from left to right along the reference line. Neither orientation of reference line nor location of the arrow alters this rule.
2. The perpendicular leg of △ ⋁ ⊬ ⌒ weld symbols must be at left.
3. Arrow and other side welds are of the same size unless otherwise shown. Dimensions of fillet welds must be shown on both the arrow side and the other side symbol.
4. The point of the field weld symbol must point toward the tail
5. Symbols apply between abrupt changes in direction of welding unless governed by the "all-around" symbol or otherwise dimensioned.
6. These symbols do not explicitly provide for the case that frequently occurs in structural work, where duplicate material (such as stiffeners) occurs on the far side of a web or gusset plate. The fabricating industry has adopted the following convention: when the billing of the detail material discloses the existence of a member on the far side as well as on the near side, the welding shown for the near side shall be duplicated on the far side.

STANDARD LOCATION OF ELEMENTS OF A WELDING SYMBOL

faces of the device and above the root opening. The angle is understood to be the total, or included, angle of the groove.

There is no provision for dimensioning radii of U and J groove welds in the AWS welding symbol. This is usually covered by the fabricator's standard weld proportions, with reference to AWS prequalified joints. If not, it must be shown by note or sketch in the drawing.

PARTIAL PENETRATION GROOVE WELDS

Partial penetration groove welds require all of the same dimensions as complete penetration groove welds, plus two additional dimensions: effective throat and weld size. With partial penetration groove welds, the weld preparation usually is less than the thickness of the material being welded. Because of this the weld size must always be

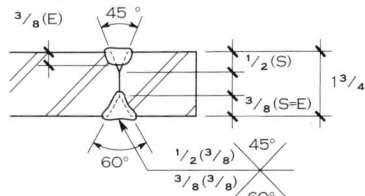

PARTIAL PENETRATION GROOVE WELD CALLOUT

given. The effective throat must also be given because it can vary from the weld size due to welding process, welding position, or the groove angle used. Depending on these factors, the depth of weld deposit, or the effective throat, can be less than the depth of the groove, or weld size.

Partial penetration groove welds can be used as intermittent welds. Consideration must be given to the transition at the beginning and end of the weld. Therefore, contract design drawings should only specify the effective weld length and the required effective throat. The shop drawings should then show the groove depth and geometry that will provide for the required effective throat.

PLUG AND SLOT WELDS

The size for plug welds specifies the diameter of the punched hole. For slot welds the size includes the width and length of the slot. Plug and slot welds will be completely filled unless the depth of the filling is shown inside the weld symbol. Slot welds are noted by detail references in the tail that refer to dimensioned sketches of the slot for clarity. The arrow and other side indicates which side of the joint is to be punched. The flush weld symbol is used if the top of the weld is to be leveled off.

CONTOUR SYMBOLS

The flush and convex symbols are used to modify the shape of the weld face. The contour symbols are placed over the weld device. Almost all of the basic weld symbols can be combined with each other and with the spacer, backing bar, back weld, and contour symbols to create many different welds.

STRUCTURAL ECONOMY—STEEL FRAMING

The most commonly used strength grade of structural steel is 36,000 psi yield strength (ASTM A36). For heavily loaded members such as columns, girders, or trusses where buckling, lateral stability, deflection, or vibration does not control member selection, higher yield strength steels may be economically utilized. A 50,000 psi yield strength is most frequently used among high strength, low alloy steels.

The Manual of Steel Construction of the AISC contains column and beam load tables for both 36,000 and 50,000 psi yield strengths.

High strength, low alloy steels are available in several grades, and some possess superior corrosion resistance to such a degree that they are classified as "weathering steel." Table 1 contains data for several ASTM alloys used for structural members.

TABLE 1   STRUCTURAL STEEL DATA

ATSM DESIGNATION	STRENGTH GRADES (KSI)	ATMOSPHERIC CORROSION RESISTANCE	REMARKS
A572	42, 45, 50, 55, 60, 65	Same as carbon steel	Most commonly used of low alloy steels
A441	40, 42, 46, 50	Twice the resistance of carbon steel	Primarily for welded structures—not frequently used
A242	42, 46, 50*	5 to 8 times the resistance of carbon steel	Used exposed as "weathering steel" or painted
A588	42, 46, 50*	4 times the resistance of carbon steel	Used exposed as "weathering steel" or painted

*50 KSI normally provided, but reduced for thicker material.

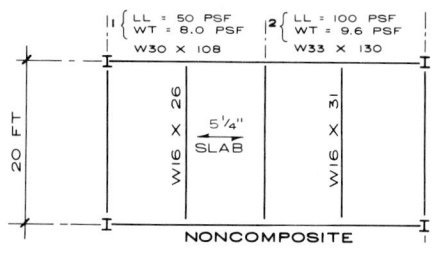

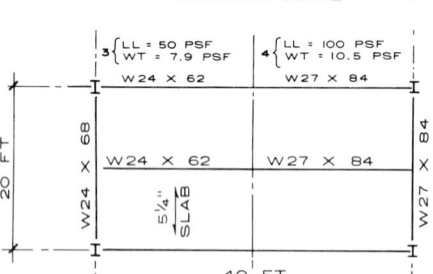

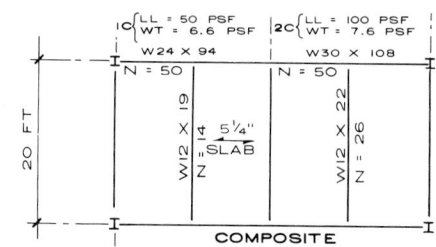

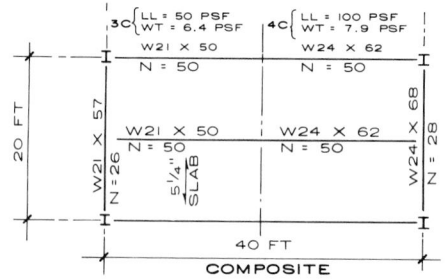

TABLE 2   ALTERNATE FRAMING

	SHORT BEAMS, LONG GIRDERS				LONG BEAMS, SHORT GIRDERS			
	LL = 50 PSF		LL = 100 PSF		LL = 50 PSF		LL = 100 PSF	
	1	1C	2	2C	3	3C	4	4C
Girder depth	30"	24"	33"	30"	24"	21"	27"	24"
Steel weight per bay (lb)	6400	5280	7680	6080	6320	5140	8400	6320
Weight ratio— Noncomposite : composite	1.21 : 1		1.26 : 1		1.23 : 1		1.33 : 1	
No. shear studs	0	106	0	154	0	126	0	128
Cost ratio (see Note 5)	1.16 : 1		1.19 : 1		1.16 : 1		1.27 : 1	

NOTES

1. Floor slab: 5¼ in. total thickness—3¼ in. lightweight concrete over 2 in. composite metal deck, all schemes. This provides a 2 hr fire rating without spraying the deck.
2. Additional dead load allowance for finishes, etc.: 30 psf, all schemes.
3. All steel ASTM A36.
4. Shear studs: ¾ in. dia. x 3½ in. long. N = 50 indicates total number of studs per beam.
5. The cost ratio between noncomposite and composite floor steel is approximately 95% of the weight ratio. The cost of studs accounts for the difference.
6. Vibration of floor beams should be analyzed.

Walter D. Shapiro, PE; Tor, Shapiro & Associates; New York, New York

 STRUCTURAL METAL FRAMING

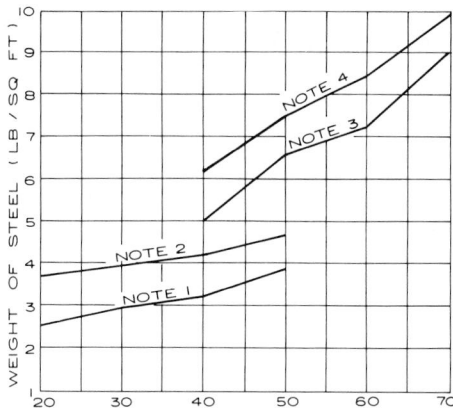

Figure above shows approximate weight of noncomposite structural steel floor or roof framing versus bay size.

NOTES

1. Roof of 15 ft high one-story structure, H-series open web joists on continuous A36 girders (weight of A36 columns included). Joist span = 30 ft.
2. Same as (1) except that joist span = 45 ft.
3. Typical level of five-story garage, V-50 steel throughout (weight of columns included) bay width = 20 ft.
4. Same as (3) except that bay width = 30 ft.

NOTES

The weight of structural steel per square foot of floor area increases with bay size, as does the depth of the structure. Cost of structural steel may not rise as rapidly as weight if savings can be realized by reducing the number of pieces to be fabricated and erected. Improved space utilization afforded by larger bay sizes is offset by increases in wall area and building volume resulting from increased structure depth.

Steel frame economy can be improved by incorporating as many of these cost reducing factors into the structure layout and design as architectural requirements permit:

1. Keep columns in line in both directions and avoid offsets or omission of columns.
2. Design for maximum repetition of member sizes within each level and from floor to floor.
3. Reduce the number of beams and girders per level to reduce fabrication and erection time and cost.
4. Maximize the use of simple beam connections by bracing the structure at a limited number of moment resisting bents or by the most efficient method, cross-bracing.
5. Utilize high strength steels for columns and floor members where studies indicate that cost can be reduced while meeting other design parameters.
6. Use composite design, but consider effect of in-slab electric raceways or other discontinuities.
7. Consider open web steel joists, especially for large roofs of one-story structures, and for floor framing in many applications.

An analysis of alternate framing schemes for a 20 x 40 ft interior floor bay appears in Table 2.

One constant relationship that may be noted in the analysis is the decrease in girder depth when using long beams and short girders. The weight of steel for roofs or lightly loaded floors is generally least when long beams and short girders are used. For heavier loadings long girders and short filler beams should result in less steel weight. The most economical framing type (composite, noncomposite, continuous, simple spans, etc.) and arrangement must be determined for each structure, considering such factors as structure depth, building volume, wall area, mechanical system requirements, deflection or vibration limitations, wind or seismic load interaction between floor system and columns or shear walls.

MAXIMUM ALLOWABLE FORM LOAD (KIPS) FOR BEAMS LATERALLY SUPPORTED—ASTM A-36 STEEL*

LENGTH (FT)	DEPTH† WEIGHT →	w6			w8								w10								w12							M14	w14		
		9	12	16	10	12	15	18	21	24	28	31	12	15	17	19	22	26	30	33	14	16	19	22	26	30	35	40	18	22	26
6		15	20	27	21	27	32	41	49	56	65	73	29	37	43	50	62	74	86	93	40	46	57	68	89	103	122	138	56	77	94
8		11	15	20	16	20	24	30	36	42	49	55	22	28	32	38	46	56	65	70	30	34	43	51	67	77	91	104	42	58	71
10		9	12	16	13	16	19	24	29	33	39	44	17	22	26	30	37	45	52	56	24	27	34	41	53	62	73	83	34	46	57
12		7	10	14	10	13	16	20	24	28	32	37	15	18	22	25	31	37	43	47	20	23	28	34	45	52	61	69	28	39	47
14					9	11	14	17	21	24	28	31	12	16	19	22	27	32	37	40	17	20	24	29	38	44	52	59	24	33	40
16					8	10	12	15	18	21	24	28	11	14	16	19	23	28	32	35	15	17	21	25	33	39	46	52	21	29	35
18													10	12	14	17	21	25	29	31	13	15	19	23	30	34	41	46	19	26	31
20													9	11	13	15	19	22	26	28	12	14	17	20	27	31	37	42	17	23	28
22																					11	12	16	18	24	28	33	38	15	21	26
24																					10	11	14	17	22	26	30	35	14	19	24

NOTE: Verify lateral support with structural engineering consultant.

*For capacity of beams that are not shown see "AISC Manual of Steel Construction."
†Depth = steel designation (in.); weight = lb/ft; Kip = 1000 lb.

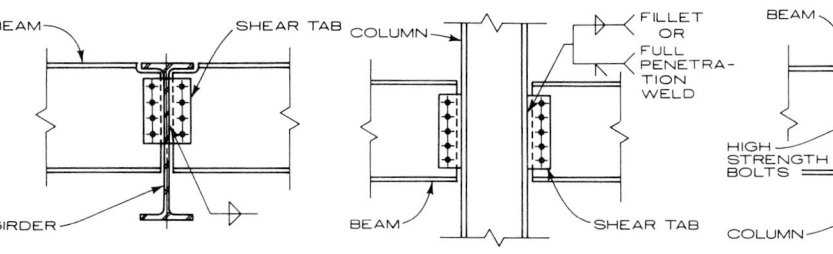

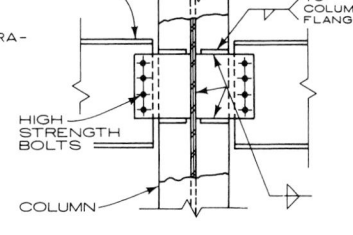

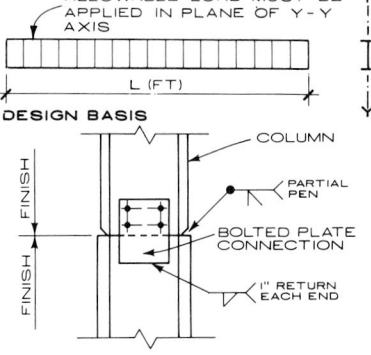

ALLOWABLE LOAD MUST BE APPLIED IN PLANE OF Y-Y AXIS

DESIGN BASIS

SHEAR CONNECTION BEAM TO GIRDER
SHOP WELDED TAB FIELD HIGH STRENGTH BOLTED

NONMOMENT CONNECTION BEAM TO COLUMN FLANGE
SHOP WELDED TAB FIELD H.S. BOLTED

NONMOMENT CONNECTION BEAM TO COLUMN WEB
SHOP WELD TAB TO COLUMN WEB AND PLATES FIELD H.S. BOLTED

COLUMN SPLICE FLANGE AND WEB
WEB-FIELD H.S. BOLTED FLANGE-PARTIAL PENETRATION

MAXIMUM ALLOWABLE CONCENTRIC LOAD (KIPS) FOR COLUMNS
ASTM A-36 STEEL (W SHAPES AND PIPE) A-46 STEEL (TUBING)

DESIGNATION	*	6	7	8	9	10	11	12	13	14	15	16	17	18	19	20	22	24
W4	13	62	57	52	46	39	33	28	24	20	18	16						
	15	81	78	75	71	67	62	58	53	48	43	38	33	30	27	24	20	17
W6	20	109	105	100	95	90	85	79	73	67	60	54	47	42	38	34	28	24
	25	136	131	126	120	114	107	100	93	85	77	69	61	54	49	44	36	31
	24	133	129	124	118	113	107	101	95	88	81	74	66	59	53	48	39	33
W8	28	155	150	144	138	132	125	118	111	103	95	87	78	69	62	56	46	39
	31	178	174	170	165	160	154	149	143	137	131	124	117	110	103	95	80	67
pipe 3″ 3.5″ OD	0.216	38	36	34	31	28	25	22	19	16	14	12	11	10	9			
	0.300	52	48	45	41	37	33	28	24	21	18	16	14	12	11			
	0.600	91	84	77	69	60	51	43	37	32	28	24	22					
pipe 3½″ 4″ OD	0.226	48	46	44	41	38	35	32	29	25	22	19	17	15	14	12	10	
	0.318	66	63	59	55	51	47	43	38	33	29	25	23	20	18	16		
pipe 4″ 4½″ OD	0.237	59	57	54	52	49	46	43	40	36	33	29	26	23	21	19	15	13
	0.337	81	78	75	71	67	63	59	54	49	44	39	35	31	28	25	21	17
	0.674	147	140	133	126	118	109	100	91	81	70	62	55	49	44	40	33	
pipe 5″ 5.563″ OD	0.258	83	81	78	76	73	71	68	65	61	58	55	51	47	43	39	32	27
	0.375	118	114	111	107	103	99	95	91	86	81	76	70	65	59	54	44	37
	0.750	216	209	202	195	187	178	170	160	151	141	130	119	108	97	87	72	61
pipe 6″ 6.625″ OD	0.280	110	108	106	103	101	98	95	92	89	86	82	79	75	71	67	59	51
	0.432	166	162	159	155	151	146	142	137	132	127	122	117	111	105	99	86	73
	0.864	306	299	292	284	275	266	257	247	237	227	216	205	193	181	168	142	119
TS 4 x 4	0.250	83	79	75	70	65	60	55	49	43	38	33	29	26	24	21	18	15
TS 5 x 5	0.250	111	108	104	100	96	92	87	82	77	72	66	60	54	49	44	36	31
TS 6 x 6	0.250	140	137	133	130	126	122	117	113	108	104	99	94	88	83	77	65	55
TS 5 x 3	0.250	76	70	64	58	51	43	36	31	27	23	20	18	16	15			
TS 6 x 4	0.250	107	103	98	92	87	81	75	68	61	54	48	42	38	34	30	25	21
TS 8 x 4	0.250	132	126	120	114	108	101	94	86	79	70	62	55	49	40	33		

NOTE: For additional columns and actual dimensions of tubing see "AISC Manual of Steel Construction."

*Weight per foot for w columns. Wall thickness for tubing. KIP = 1000 lb; K = effective length factor (verify with structural engineering consultant).

All data on this page derived from "AISC Manual of Steel Construction 8th edition."

Thompson & Czark; Hempstead, New York

W SHAPES—DIMENSIONS FOR DETAILING

Designation	Depth d (in.)	Flange Width b_f (in.)	Flange Thickness t_f (in.)	Web Thickness t_w (in.)
W36 x 300	36 3/4	16 5/8	1 11/16	15/16
x 280	36 1/2	16 5/8	1 9/16	7/8
x 260	36 1/4	16 1/2	1 7/16	13/16
x 245	36 1/8	16 1/2	1 3/8	13/16
x 230	35 7/8	16 1/2	1 1/4	3/4
W36 x 210	36 3/4	12 1/8	1 3/8	13/16
x 194	36 1/2	12 1/8	1 1/4	3/4
x 182	36 3/8	12 1/8	1 3/16	3/4
x 170	36 1/8	12	1 1/8	11/16
x 160	36	12	1	5/8
x 150	35 7/8	12	15/16	5/8
x 135	35 1/2	12	13/16	5/8
W33 x 241	34 1/8	15 7/8	1 3/8	13/16
x 221	33 7/8	15 3/4	1 1/4	3/4
x 201	33 5/8	15 3/4	1 1/8	11/16
W33 x 152	33 1/2	11 5/8	1 1/16	5/8
x 141	33 1/4	11 1/2	15/16	5/8
x 130	33 1/8	11 1/2	7/8	9/16
x 118	32 7/8	11 1/2	3/4	9/16
W30 x 211	31	15 1/8	1 5/16	3/4
x 191	30 5/8	15	1 3/16	11/16
x 173	30 1/2	15	1 1/16	5/8
W30 x 132	30 1/4	10 1/2	1	5/8
x 124	30 1/8	10 1/2	15/16	9/16
x 116	30	10 1/2	7/8	9/16
x 108	29 7/8	10 1/2	3/4	9/16
x 99	29 5/8	10 1/2	11/16	1/2
W27 x 178	27 3/4	14 1/8	1 3/16	3/4
x 161	27 5/8	14	1 1/16	11/16
x 146	27 3/8	14	1	5/8
W27 x 114	27 1/4	10 1/8	15/16	9/16
x 102	27 1/8	10	13/16	1/2
x 94	26 7/8	10	3/4	1/2
x 84	26 3/4	10	5/8	7/16
W24 x 162	25	13	1 1/4	11/16
x 146	24 3/4	12 7/8	1 1/16	5/8
x 131	24 1/2	12 7/8	15/16	5/8
x 117	24 1/4	12 3/4	7/8	9/16
x 104	24	12 3/4	3/4	1/2
W24 x 94	24 1/4	9 1/8	7/8	1/2
x 84	24 1/8	9	3/4	1/2
x 76	23 7/8	9	11/16	7/16
x 68	23 3/4	9	9/16	7/16
W24 x 62	23 3/4	7	9/16	7/16
x 55	23 5/8	7	1/2	3/8
W21 x 147	22	12 1/2	1 1/8	3/4
x 132	21 7/8	12 1/2	1 1/16	5/8
x 122	21 5/8	12 3/8	15/16	5/8
x 111	21 1/2	12 3/8	7/8	9/16
x 101	21 3/8	12 1/4	13/16	1/2
W21 x 93	21 5/8	8 3/8	15/16	9/16
x 83	21 3/8	8 3/8	13/16	1/2
x 73	21 1/4	8 1/4	3/4	7/16
x 68	21 1/8	8 1/4	11/16	7/16
x 62	21	8 1/4	5/8	3/8
W21 x 57	21	6 1/2	5/8	3/8
x 50	20 7/8	6 1/2	9/16	3/8
x 44	20 5/8	6 1/2	7/16	3/8
W18 x 119	19	11 1/4	1 1/16	5/8
x 106	18 3/4	11 1/4	15/16	9/16
x 97	18 5/8	11 1/8	7/8	9/16
x 86	18 3/8	11 1/8	3/4	1/2
x 76	18 1/4	11	11/16	7/16
W18 x 71	18 1/2	7 5/8	13/16	1/2
x 65	18 3/8	7 5/8	3/4	7/16
x 60	18 1/4	7 1/2	11/16	7/16
x 55	18 1/8	7 1/2	5/8	3/8
x 50	18	7 1/2	9/16	3/8
W18 x 46	18	6	5/8	3/8
x 40	17 7/8	6	1/2	5/16
x 35	17 3/4	6	7/16	5/16
W16 x 100	17	10 3/8	1	9/16
x 89	16 3/4	10 3/8	7/8	1/2
x 77	16 1/2	10 1/4	3/4	7/16
x 67	16 3/8	10 1/4	11/16	3/8
W16 x 57	16 3/8	7 1/8	11/16	7/16
x 50	16 1/4	7 1/8	5/8	3/8
x 45	16 1/8	7	9/16	3/8
x 40	16	7	1/2	5/16
x 36	15 7/8	7	7/16	5/16
W16 x 31	15 7/8	5 1/2	7/16	1/4
x 26	15 3/4	5 1/2	3/8	1/4
W14 x 730	22 3/8	17 7/8	4 15/16	3 1/16
x 665	21 5/8	17 5/8	4 1/2	2 13/16
x 605	20 7/8	17 3/8	4 3/16	2 5/8
x 550	20 1/4	17 1/4	3 13/16	2 3/8
x 500	19 5/8	17	3 1/2	2 3/16
x 455	19	16 7/8	3 3/16	2
W14 x 426	18 5/8	16 3/4	3 1/16	1 7/8
x 398	18 1/4	16 5/8	2 7/8	1 3/4
x 370	17 7/8	16 1/2	2 11/16	1 5/8
x 342	17 1/2	16 3/8	2 1/2	1 9/16
x 311	17 1/8	16 1/4	2 1/4	1 7/16
x 283	16 3/4	16 1/8	2 1/16	1 5/16
x 257	16 3/8	16	1 7/8	1 3/16
x 233	16	15 7/8	1 3/4	1 1/16
x 211	15 3/4	15 3/4	1 9/16	1
x 193	15 1/2	15 3/4	1 7/16	7/8
x 176	15 1/4	15 5/8	1 5/16	13/16
x 159	15	15 5/8	1 3/16	3/4
x 145	14 3/4	15 1/2	1 1/16	11/16
W14 x 132	14 5/8	14 3/4	1	5/8
x 120	14 1/2	14 5/8	15/16	9/16
x 109	14 3/8	14 5/8	7/8	1/2
x 99	14 1/8	14 5/8	3/4	1/2
x 90	14	14 1/2	11/16	7/16
W14 x 82	14 1/4	10 1/8	7/8	1/2
x 74	14 1/8	10 1/8	13/16	7/16
x 68	14	10	3/4	7/16
x 61	13 7/8	10	5/8	3/8
W14 x 53	13 7/8	8	11/16	3/8
x 48	13 3/4	8	5/8	5/16
x 43	13 5/8	8	1/2	5/16
W14 x 38	14 1/8	6 3/4	1/2	5/16
x 34	14	6 3/4	7/16	5/16
x 30	13 7/8	6 3/4	3/8	1/4
W14 x 26	13 7/8	5	7/16	1/4
x 22	13 3/4	5	5/16	1/4
W12 x 336	16 7/8	13 3/8	2 15/16	1 3/4
x 305	16 3/8	13 1/4	2 11/16	1 5/8
x 279	15 7/8	13 1/8	2 1/2	1 1/2
x 252	15 3/8	13	2 1/4	1 3/8
x 230	15	12 7/8	2 1/16	1 5/16
x 210	14 3/4	12 3/4	1 7/8	1 3/16
W12 x 190	14 3/8	12 5/8	1 3/4	1 1/16
x 170	14	12 5/8	1 9/16	15/16
x 152	13 3/4	12 1/2	1 3/8	7/8
x 136	13 3/8	12 3/8	1 1/4	13/16
x 120	13 1/8	12 3/8	1 1/8	11/16
x 106	12 7/8	12 1/4	1	5/8
x 96	12 3/4	12 1/8	7/8	9/16
x 87	12 1/2	12 1/8	13/16	1/2
x 79	12 3/8	12 1/8	3/4	1/2
x 72	12 1/4	12	11/16	7/16
x 65	12 1/8	12	5/8	3/8
W12 x 58	12 1/4	10	5/8	3/8
x 53	12	10	9/16	3/8
W12 x 50	12 1/4	8 1/8	3/8	5/8
x 45	12	8	5/16	9/16
x 40	12	8	5/16	1/2
W12 x 35	12 1/2	6 1/2	5/16	1/2
x 30	12 3/8	6 1/2	1/4	7/16
x 26	12 1/4	6 1/2	1/4	3/8
W12 x 22	12 1/4	4	7/16	1/4
x 19	12 1/8	4	3/8	1/4
x 16	12	4	1/4	1/4
x 14	11 7/8	4	1/4	3/16
W10 x 112	11 3/8	10 3/8	1 1/4	3/4
x 100	11 1/8	10 3/8	1 1/8	11/16
x 88	10 7/8	10 1/4	1	5/8
x 77	10 5/8	10 1/4	7/8	1/2
x 68	10 3/8	10 1/8	3/4	1/2
x 60	10 1/4	10 1/8	11/16	7/16
x 54	10 1/8	10	5/8	3/8
x 49	10	10	9/16	5/16
W10 x 45	10 1/8	8	5/8	3/8
x 39	9 7/8	8	1/2	5/16
x 33	9 3/4	8	7/16	5/16
W10 x 30	10 1/2	5 3/4	1/2	5/16
x 26	10 3/8	5 3/4	7/16	1/4
x 22	10 1/8	5 3/4	3/8	1/4
W10 x 19	10 1/4	4	3/8	1/4
x 17	10 1/8	4	5/16	1/4
x 15	10	4	1/4	1/4
x 12	9 7/8	4	3/16	3/16
W8 x 67	9	8 1/4	15/16	9/16
x 58	8 3/4	8 1/4	13/16	1/2
x 48	8 1/2	8 1/8	11/16	3/8
x 40	8 1/4	8 1/8	9/16	3/8
x 35	8 1/8	8	1/2	5/16
x 31	8	8	7/16	5/16
W8 x 28	8	6 1/2	7/16	5/16
x 24	7 7/8	6 1/2	3/8	1/4
W8 x 21	8 1/4	5 1/4	3/8	1/4
x 18	8 1/8	5 1/4	5/16	1/4
W8 x 15	8 1/8	4	5/16	1/4
x 13	8	4	1/4	1/4
x 10	7 7/8	4	3/16	3/16
W6 x 25	6 3/8	6 1/8	7/16	5/16
x 20	6 1/4	6	3/8	1/4
x 15	6	6	1/4	1/4
W6 x 16	6 1/4	4	3/8	1/4
x 12	6	4	1/4	1/4
x 9	5 7/8	4	3/16	3/16
W5 x 19	5 1/8	5	7/16	1/4
x 16	5	5	3/8	1/4
W4 x 13	4 1/8	4	3/8	1/4

M SHAPES—DIMENSIONS FOR DETAILING

Designation	Depth d (in.)	Flange Width b_f (in.)	Flange Thickness t_f (in.)	Web Thickness t_w (in.)
M 14 x 17.2	14	4	1/4	3/16
M 12 x 11.8	12	3 1/8	1/4	3/16
M 10 x 29.1	9 7/8	5 7/8	3/8	7/16
x 22.9	9 7/8	5 3/4	3/8	1/4
M 10 x 9	10	2 3/4	3/16	3/16
M 8 x 37.7	8 1/8	8	1/2	3/8
x 34.3	8	8	7/16	3/8
x 32.6	8	8	7/16	5/16
M 8 x 22.5	8	5 3/8	3/8	3/8
x 18.5	8	5 1/4	3/8	1/4
M 8 x 6.5	8	2 1/4	3/16	1/8
M 7 x 5.5	7	2 1/8	3/16	1/8
M 6 x 33.75	6 1/4	6 1/8	5/8	1/2
x 22.5	6	6	3/8	3/8
x 20	6	6	3/8	1/4
M 6 x 4.4	6	1 7/8	3/16	1/8
M 5 x 18.9	5	5	7/16	5/16
M 4 x 16.3	4 1/4	4	1/2	5/16
x 13.8	4	4	3/8	5/16
x 13	4	4	3/8	1/4

S SHAPES— DIMENSIONS FOR DETAILING

DESIGNA-TION	DEPTH d (IN.)	FLANGE WIDTH b_f (IN.)	FLANGE AVERAGE THICKNESS t_f (IN.)	WEB THICKNESS t_w (IN.)
S 24 x 120	24	8	$1\frac{1}{8}$	$\frac{13}{16}$
x 105.9	24	$7\frac{7}{8}$	$1\frac{1}{8}$	$\frac{5}{8}$
S 24 x 100	24	$7\frac{1}{4}$	$\frac{7}{8}$	$\frac{3}{4}$
x 90	24	$7\frac{1}{8}$	$\frac{7}{8}$	$\frac{5}{8}$
x 79.9	24	7	$\frac{7}{8}$	$\frac{1}{2}$
S 20 x 95	20	$7\frac{1}{4}$	$\frac{15}{16}$	$\frac{13}{16}$
x 85	20	7	$\frac{15}{16}$	$\frac{5}{8}$
S 20 x 75	20	$6\frac{3}{8}$	$\frac{13}{16}$	$\frac{5}{8}$
x 65.4	20	$6\frac{1}{4}$	$\frac{13}{16}$	$\frac{1}{2}$
S 18 x 70	18	$6\frac{1}{4}$	$\frac{11}{16}$	$\frac{11}{16}$
x 54.7	18	6	$\frac{11}{16}$	$\frac{7}{16}$
S 15 x 50	15	$5\frac{5}{8}$	$\frac{5}{8}$	$\frac{9}{16}$
x 42.9	15	$5\frac{1}{2}$	$\frac{5}{8}$	$\frac{7}{16}$
S 12 x 50	12	$5\frac{1}{2}$	$\frac{11}{16}$	$\frac{11}{16}$
x 40.8	12	$5\frac{1}{4}$	$\frac{11}{16}$	$\frac{7}{16}$
S 12 x 35	12	$5\frac{1}{8}$	$\frac{9}{16}$	$\frac{7}{16}$
x 31.8	12	5	$\frac{9}{16}$	$\frac{3}{8}$
S 10 x 35	10	5	$\frac{1}{2}$	$\frac{5}{8}$
x 25.4	10	$4\frac{5}{8}$	$\frac{1}{2}$	$\frac{5}{16}$
S 8 x 23	8	$4\frac{1}{8}$	$\frac{7}{16}$	$\frac{7}{16}$
x 18.4	8	4	$\frac{7}{16}$	$\frac{1}{4}$
S 7 x 20	7	$3\frac{7}{8}$	$\frac{3}{8}$	$\frac{7}{16}$
x 15.3	7	$3\frac{5}{8}$	$\frac{3}{8}$	$\frac{1}{4}$
S 6 x 17.25	6	$3\frac{5}{8}$	$\frac{3}{8}$	$\frac{7}{16}$
x 12.5	6	$3\frac{5}{8}$	$\frac{3}{8}$	$\frac{1}{4}$
S 5 x 14.75	5	$3\frac{1}{4}$	$\frac{5}{16}$	$\frac{1}{2}$
x 10	5	3	$\frac{5}{16}$	$\frac{3}{16}$
S 4 x 9.5	4	$2\frac{3}{4}$	$\frac{5}{16}$	$\frac{5}{16}$
x 7.7	4	$2\frac{5}{8}$	$\frac{5}{16}$	$\frac{3}{16}$
S 3 x 7.5	3	$2\frac{1}{2}$	$\frac{1}{4}$	$\frac{3}{8}$
x 5.7	3	$2\frac{3}{8}$	$\frac{1}{4}$	$\frac{3}{16}$

HP SHAPES— DIMENSIONS FOR DETAILING

DESIGNA-TION	DEPTH d (IN.)	FLANGE WIDTH b_f (IN.)	FLANGE AVERAGE THICKNESS t_f (IN.)	WEB THICKNESS t_w (IN.)
HP14 x 117	$14\frac{1}{4}$	$14\frac{7}{8}$	$\frac{13}{16}$	$\frac{13}{16}$
x 102	14	$14\frac{3}{4}$	$\frac{11}{16}$	$\frac{11}{16}$
x 89	$13\frac{7}{8}$	$14\frac{3}{4}$	$\frac{5}{8}$	$\frac{5}{8}$
x 73	$13\frac{5}{8}$	$14\frac{5}{8}$	$\frac{1}{2}$	$\frac{1}{2}$
HP12 x 74	$12\frac{1}{8}$	$12\frac{1}{8}$	$\frac{5}{8}$	$\frac{5}{8}$
x 53	$11\frac{3}{4}$	12	$\frac{7}{16}$	$\frac{7}{16}$
HP10 x 57	10	$10\frac{1}{4}$	$\frac{9}{16}$	$\frac{9}{16}$
x 42	$9\frac{3}{4}$	$10\frac{1}{8}$	$\frac{7}{16}$	$\frac{7}{16}$
HP8 x 36	8	$8\frac{1}{8}$	$\frac{7}{16}$	$\frac{7}{16}$

AMERICAN STANDARD CHANNELS

DESIGNATION	DEPTH d	FLANGE WIDTH b_f	FLANGE AVERAGE THICKNESS t_f	WEB THICKNESS t_w
C 15 x 50	15	$3\frac{3}{4}$	$\frac{5}{8}$	$\frac{11}{16}$
x 40	15	$3\frac{1}{2}$	$\frac{5}{8}$	$\frac{1}{2}$
x 33.9	15	$3\frac{3}{8}$	$\frac{5}{8}$	$\frac{3}{8}$
C 12 x 30	12	$3\frac{1}{8}$	$\frac{1}{2}$	$\frac{1}{2}$
x 25	12	3	$\frac{1}{2}$	$\frac{3}{8}$
x 20.7	12	3	$\frac{1}{2}$	$\frac{5}{16}$
C 10 x 30	10	3	$\frac{7}{16}$	$\frac{11}{16}$
x 25	10	$2\frac{7}{8}$	$\frac{7}{16}$	$\frac{1}{2}$
x 20	10	$2\frac{3}{4}$	$\frac{7}{16}$	$\frac{3}{8}$
x 15.3	10	$2\frac{5}{8}$	$\frac{7}{16}$	$\frac{1}{4}$
C 9 x 20	9	$2\frac{5}{8}$	$\frac{7}{16}$	$\frac{7}{16}$
x 15	9	$2\frac{1}{2}$	$\frac{7}{16}$	$\frac{5}{16}$
x 13.4	9	$2\frac{3}{8}$	$\frac{7}{16}$	$\frac{1}{4}$
C 8 x 18.75	8	$2\frac{1}{2}$	$\frac{3}{8}$	$\frac{1}{2}$
x 13.75	8	$2\frac{3}{8}$	$\frac{3}{8}$	$\frac{5}{16}$
x 11.5	8	$2\frac{1}{4}$	$\frac{3}{8}$	$\frac{1}{4}$
C 7 x 14.75	7	$2\frac{1}{4}$	$\frac{3}{8}$	$\frac{7}{16}$
x 12.25	7	$2\frac{1}{4}$	$\frac{3}{8}$	$\frac{5}{16}$
x 9.8	7	$2\frac{1}{8}$	$\frac{3}{8}$	$\frac{1}{4}$
C 6 x 13	6	$2\frac{1}{8}$	$\frac{5}{16}$	$\frac{7}{16}$
x 10.5	6	2	$\frac{5}{16}$	$\frac{5}{16}$
x 8.2	6	$1\frac{7}{8}$	$\frac{5}{16}$	$\frac{3}{16}$
C 5 x 9	5	$1\frac{7}{8}$	$\frac{5}{16}$	$\frac{5}{16}$
x 6.7	5	$1\frac{3}{4}$	$\frac{5}{16}$	$\frac{3}{16}$
C 4 x 7.25	4	$1\frac{3}{4}$	$\frac{5}{16}$	$\frac{5}{16}$
x 5.4	4	$1\frac{5}{8}$	$\frac{5}{16}$	$\frac{3}{16}$
C 3 x 6	3	$1\frac{5}{8}$	$\frac{1}{4}$	$\frac{3}{8}$
x 5	3	$1\frac{1}{2}$	$\frac{1}{4}$	$\frac{1}{4}$
x 4.1	3	$1\frac{3}{8}$	$\frac{1}{4}$	$\frac{3}{16}$

MISCELLANEOUS CHANNELS— DIMENSIONS FOR DETAILING

DESIG-NATION	DEPTH d (IN.)	FLANGE WIDTH b_f (IN.)	FLANGE AVERAGE THICKNESS t_f (IN.)	WEB THICKNESS t_w (IN.)
MC 18 x 58	18	$4\frac{1}{4}$	$\frac{11}{16}$	$\frac{5}{8}$
x 51.9	18	$4\frac{1}{8}$	$\frac{5}{8}$	$\frac{5}{8}$
x 45.8	18	4	$\frac{1}{2}$	$\frac{5}{8}$
x 42.7	18	4	$\frac{7}{16}$	$\frac{5}{8}$
MC 13 x 50	13	$4\frac{3}{8}$	$\frac{13}{16}$	$\frac{5}{8}$
x 40	13	$4\frac{1}{8}$	$\frac{9}{16}$	$\frac{5}{8}$
x 35	13	$4\frac{1}{8}$	$\frac{7}{16}$	$\frac{5}{8}$
x 31.8	13	4	$\frac{3}{8}$	$\frac{5}{8}$
MC 12 x 50	12	$4\frac{1}{8}$	$\frac{13}{16}$	$\frac{11}{16}$
x 45	12	4	$\frac{11}{16}$	$\frac{11}{16}$
x 40	12	$3\frac{7}{8}$	$\frac{9}{16}$	$\frac{11}{16}$
x 35	12	$3\frac{3}{4}$	$\frac{7}{16}$	$\frac{11}{16}$
MC 12 x 37	12	$3\frac{5}{8}$	$\frac{5}{8}$	$\frac{5}{8}$
x 32.9	12	$3\frac{1}{2}$	$\frac{1}{2}$	$\frac{5}{8}$
x 30.9	12	$3\frac{1}{2}$	$\frac{7}{16}$	$\frac{5}{8}$
MC 12 x 10.6	12	$1\frac{1}{2}$	$\frac{3}{16}$	$\frac{5}{16}$
MC 10 x 41.1	10	$4\frac{3}{8}$	$\frac{13}{16}$	$\frac{9}{16}$
x 33.6	10	$4\frac{1}{8}$	$\frac{9}{16}$	$\frac{9}{16}$
x 28.5	10	4	$\frac{7}{16}$	$\frac{9}{16}$
MC 10 x 28.3	10	$3\frac{1}{2}$	$\frac{1}{2}$	$\frac{9}{16}$
x 25.3	10	$3\frac{1}{2}$	$\frac{7}{16}$	$\frac{1}{2}$
x 24.9	10	$3\frac{3}{8}$	$\frac{3}{8}$	$\frac{9}{16}$
x 21.9	10	$3\frac{1}{2}$	$\frac{5}{16}$	$\frac{1}{2}$
MC 10 x 8.4	10	$1\frac{1}{2}$	$\frac{3}{16}$	$\frac{1}{4}$
MC 10 x 6.5	10	$1\frac{1}{8}$	$\frac{1}{8}$	$\frac{3}{16}$
MC 9 x 25.4	9	$3\frac{1}{2}$	$\frac{9}{16}$	$\frac{7}{16}$
9 x 23.9	9	$3\frac{1}{2}$	$\frac{9}{16}$	$\frac{3}{8}$
MC 8 x 22.8	8	$3\frac{1}{2}$	$\frac{1}{2}$	$\frac{7}{16}$
x 21.4	8	$3\frac{1}{2}$	$\frac{1}{2}$	$\frac{3}{8}$
MC 8 x 20	8	3	$\frac{1}{2}$	$\frac{3}{8}$
x 18.7	8	3	$\frac{1}{2}$	$\frac{5}{16}$
MC 8 x 8.5	8	$1\frac{7}{8}$	$\frac{5}{16}$	$\frac{3}{16}$
MC 7 x 22.7	7	$3\frac{5}{8}$	$\frac{1}{2}$	$\frac{1}{2}$
x 19.1	7	$3\frac{1}{2}$	$\frac{1}{2}$	$\frac{3}{8}$
MC 7 x 17.6	7	3	$\frac{1}{2}$	$\frac{3}{8}$
MC 6 x 18	6	$3\frac{1}{2}$	$\frac{1}{2}$	$\frac{3}{8}$
x 15.3	6	$3\frac{1}{2}$	$\frac{3}{8}$	$\frac{5}{16}$
MC 6 x 16.3	6	3	$\frac{1}{2}$	$\frac{3}{8}$
x 15.1	6	3	$\frac{1}{2}$	$\frac{5}{16}$
MC 6 x 12	6	$2\frac{1}{2}$	$\frac{3}{8}$	$\frac{5}{16}$

ANGLES (EQUAL LEGS)— DIMENSIONS FOR DETAILING

SIZE AND THICKNESS (IN.)	SIZE AND THICKNESS (IN.)
L 8 x 8 x $1\frac{1}{8}$	L $3\frac{1}{2}$ x $3\frac{1}{2}$ x $\frac{1}{2}$
1	$\frac{7}{16}$
$\frac{7}{8}$	$\frac{3}{8}$
$\frac{3}{4}$	$\frac{5}{16}$
$\frac{5}{8}$	$\frac{1}{4}$
$\frac{9}{16}$	
$\frac{1}{2}$	L 3 x 3 x $\frac{1}{2}$
L 6 x 6 x 1	$\frac{7}{16}$
$\frac{7}{8}$	$\frac{3}{8}$
$\frac{3}{4}$	$\frac{5}{16}$
$\frac{5}{8}$	$\frac{1}{4}$
$\frac{9}{16}$	$\frac{3}{16}$
$\frac{1}{2}$	L $2\frac{1}{2}$ x $2\frac{1}{2}$ x $\frac{1}{2}$
$\frac{7}{16}$	$\frac{3}{8}$
$\frac{3}{8}$	$\frac{5}{16}$
$\frac{5}{16}$	$\frac{1}{4}$
	$\frac{3}{16}$
L 5 x 5 x $\frac{7}{8}$	L 2 x 2 x $\frac{3}{8}$
$\frac{3}{4}$	$\frac{5}{16}$
$\frac{5}{8}$	$\frac{1}{4}$
$\frac{1}{2}$	$\frac{3}{16}$
$\frac{7}{16}$	$\frac{1}{8}$
$\frac{3}{8}$	
$\frac{5}{16}$	L $1\frac{3}{4}$ x $1\frac{3}{4}$ x $\frac{1}{4}$
L 4 x 4 x $\frac{3}{4}$	$\frac{3}{16}$
$\frac{5}{8}$	$\frac{1}{8}$
$\frac{1}{2}$	L $1\frac{1}{2}$ x $1\frac{1}{2}$ x $\frac{1}{4}$
$\frac{7}{16}$	$\frac{3}{16}$
$\frac{3}{8}$	$\frac{5}{32}$
$\frac{5}{16}$	$\frac{1}{8}$
$\frac{1}{4}$	L $1\frac{1}{4}$ x $1\frac{1}{4}$ x $\frac{1}{4}$
	$\frac{3}{16}$
	$\frac{1}{8}$
	L 1 x 1 x $\frac{1}{4}$
	$\frac{3}{16}$
	$\frac{1}{8}$

ANGLES (UNEQUAL LEGS)—DIMENSIONS FOR DETAILING

SIZE AND THICKNESS (IN.)	SIZE AND THICKNESS (IN.)	SIZE AND THICKNESS (IN.)	SIZE AND THICKNESS (IN.)
L 9 x 4 x 1	L 6 x 4 x $\frac{7}{8}$	L 4 x $3\frac{1}{2}$ x $\frac{5}{8}$	L 3 x 2 x $\frac{1}{2}$
$\frac{7}{8}$	$\frac{3}{4}$	$\frac{1}{2}$	$\frac{7}{16}$
$\frac{3}{4}$	$\frac{5}{8}$	$\frac{7}{16}$	$\frac{3}{8}$
$\frac{5}{8}$	$\frac{9}{16}$	$\frac{3}{8}$	$\frac{5}{16}$
$\frac{9}{16}$	$\frac{1}{2}$	$\frac{5}{16}$	$\frac{1}{4}$
$\frac{1}{2}$	$\frac{7}{16}$	$\frac{1}{4}$	$\frac{3}{16}$
	$\frac{3}{8}$		
L 8 x 6 x 1	$\frac{5}{16}$	L 4 x 3 x $\frac{5}{8}$	L $2\frac{1}{2}$ x 2 x $\frac{3}{8}$
$\frac{7}{8}$	$\frac{1}{4}$	$\frac{1}{2}$	$\frac{5}{16}$
$\frac{3}{4}$		$\frac{7}{16}$	$\frac{1}{4}$
$\frac{5}{8}$	L 6 x $3\frac{1}{2}$ x $\frac{1}{2}$	$\frac{3}{8}$	$\frac{3}{16}$
$\frac{9}{16}$	$\frac{3}{8}$	$\frac{5}{16}$	
$\frac{1}{2}$	$\frac{5}{16}$		L $2\frac{1}{2}$ x $1\frac{1}{2}$ x $\frac{5}{16}$
$\frac{7}{16}$	$\frac{1}{4}$	L $3\frac{1}{2}$ x 3 x $\frac{1}{2}$	$\frac{1}{4}$
		$\frac{7}{16}$	$\frac{3}{16}$
L 8 x 4 x 1	L 5 x $3\frac{1}{2}$ x $\frac{3}{4}$	$\frac{3}{8}$	
$\frac{7}{8}$	$\frac{5}{8}$	$\frac{5}{16}$	L 2 x $1\frac{1}{2}$ x $\frac{1}{4}$
$\frac{3}{4}$	$\frac{1}{2}$	$\frac{1}{4}$	$\frac{3}{16}$
$\frac{5}{8}$	$\frac{7}{16}$		$\frac{1}{8}$
$\frac{9}{16}$	$\frac{3}{8}$	L $3\frac{1}{2}$ x $2\frac{1}{2}$ x $\frac{1}{2}$	
$\frac{1}{2}$	$\frac{5}{16}$	$\frac{7}{16}$	L 2 x $1\frac{1}{4}$ x $\frac{1}{4}$
$\frac{7}{16}$	$\frac{1}{4}$	$\frac{3}{8}$	$\frac{3}{16}$
		$\frac{5}{16}$	$\frac{1}{8}$
L 7 x 4 x $\frac{7}{8}$	L 5 x 3 x $\frac{1}{2}$	$\frac{1}{4}$	
$\frac{3}{4}$	$\frac{7}{16}$		L $1\frac{3}{4}$ x $1\frac{1}{4}$ x $\frac{1}{4}$
$\frac{5}{8}$	$\frac{3}{8}$	L 3 x $2\frac{1}{2}$ x $\frac{1}{2}$	$\frac{3}{16}$
$\frac{9}{16}$	$\frac{5}{16}$	$\frac{7}{16}$	$\frac{1}{8}$
$\frac{1}{2}$	$\frac{1}{4}$	$\frac{3}{8}$	
$\frac{7}{16}$		$\frac{5}{16}$	
$\frac{3}{8}$		$\frac{1}{4}$	
		$\frac{3}{16}$	

STRUCTURAL TEES CUT FROM W SHAPES—DIMENSIONS FOR DETAILING

DESIGNATION	DEPTH OF SECTION d (IN.)	FLANGE WIDTH b_f (IN.)	FLANGE AVERAGE THICKNESS t_f (IN.)	STEM THICKNESS t_w (IN.)
WT18 x 150	18.370	16.655	1.680	0.945
x 140	18.260	16.595	1.570	0.885
x 130	18.130	16.550	1.440	0.840
x 122.5	18.040	16.510	1.350	0.800
x 115	17.950	16.470	1.260	0.760
WT18 x 105	18.345	12.180	1.360	0.830
x 97	18.245	12.115	1.260	0.765
x 91	18.165	12.075	1.180	0.725
x 85	18.085	12.030	1.100	0.680
x 80	18.005	12.000	1.020	0.650
x 75	17.925	11.975	0.940	0.625
x 67.5	17.775	11.950	0.790	0.600
WT16.5 x 120.5	17.090	15.860	1.400	0.830
x 110.5	16.965	15.805	1.275	0.775
x 100.5	16.840	15.745	1.150	0.715
WT16.5 x 76	16.745	11.565	1.055	0.635
x 70.5	16.650	11.535	0.960	0.605
x 65	16.545	11.510	0.855	0.580
x 59	16.430	11.480	0.740	0.550
WT15 x 105.5	15.470	15.105	1.315	0.775
x 95.5	15.340	15.040	1.185	0.710
x 86.5	15.220	14.985	1.065	0.655
WT15 x 66	15.155	10.545	1.000	0.615
x 62	15.085	10.515	0.930	0.585
x 58	15.005	10.495	0.850	0.565
x 54	14.915	10.475	0.760	0.545
x 49.5	14.825	10.450	0.670	0.520
WT13.5 x 89	13.905	14.085	1.190	0.725
x 80.5	13.795	14.020	1.080	0.660
x 73	13.690	13.965	0.975	0.605
WT13.5 x 57	13.645	10.070	0.930	0.570
x 51	13.545	10.015	0.830	0.515
x 47	13.460	9.990	0.745	0.490
x 42	13.355	9.960	0.640	0.460
WT12 x 81	12.500	12.955	1.220	0.705
x 73	12.370	12.900	1.090	0.650
x 65.5	12.240	12.855	0.960	0.605
x 58.5	12.130	12.800	0.850	0.550
x 52	12.030	12.750	0.750	0.500
WT12 x 47	12.155	9.065	0.875	0.515
x 42	12.050	9.020	0.770	0.470
x 38	11.960	8.990	0.680	0.440
x 34	11.865	8.965	0.585	0.415
WT12 x 31	11.870	7.040	0.590	0.430
x 27.5	11.785	7.005	0.505	0.395
WT10.5 x 73.5	11.030	12.510	1.150	0.720
x 66	10.915	12.440	1.035	0.650
x 61	10.840	12.390	0.960	0.600
x 55.5	10.755	12.340	0.875	0.550
x 50.5	10.680	12.290	0.800	0.500
WT10.5 x 46.5	10.810	8.420	0.930	0.580
x 41.5	10.715	8.355	0.835	0.515
x 36.5	10.620	8.295	0.740	0.455
x 34	10.565	8.270	0.685	0.430
x 31	10.495	8.240	0.615	0.400
WT10.5 x 28.5	10.530	6.555	0.650	0.405
x 25	10.415	6.530	0.535	0.380
x 22	10.330	6.500	0.450	0.350
WT9 x 59.5	9.485	11.265	1.060	0.655
x 53	9.365	11.200	0.940	0.590
x 48.5	9.295	11.145	0.870	0.535
x 43	9.195	11.090	0.770	0.480
x 38	9.105	11.035	0.680	0.425
WT9 x 35.5	9.235	7.635	0.810	0.495
x 32.5	9.175	7.590	0.750	0.450
x 30	9.120	7.555	0.695	0.415
x 27.5	9.055	7.530	0.630	0.390
x 25	8.995	7.495	0.570	0.355
WT9 x 23	9.030	6.060	0.605	0.360
x 20	8.950	6.015	0.525	0.315
x 17.5	8.850	6.000	0.425	0.300
WT8 x 50	8.485	10.425	0.985	0.585
x 44.5	8.375	10.365	0.875	0.525
x 38.5	8.260	10.295	0.760	0.455
x 33.5	8.165	10.235	0.665	0.395
WT8 x 28.5	8.215	7.120	0.715	0.430
x 25	8.130	7.070	0.630	0.380
x 22.5	8.065	7.035	0.565	0.345
x 20	8.005	6.995	0.505	0.305
x 18	7.930	6.985	0.430	0.295
WT8 x 15.5	7.940	5.525	0.440	0.275
x 13	7.845	5.500	0.345	0.250
WT7 x 365	11.210	17.890	4.910	3.070
x 332.5	10.820	17.650	4.520	2.830
x 302.5	10.460	17.415	4.160	2.595
x 275	10.120	17.200	3.820	2.380
x 250	9.800	17.010	3.500	2.190
x 227.5	9.510	16.835	3.210	2.015
WT7 x 213	9.335	16.695	3.035	1.875
x 199	9.145	16.590	2.845	1.770
x 185	8.960	16.475	2.660	1.655
x 171	8.770	16.360	2.470	1.540
x 155.5	8.560	16.230	2.260	1.410
x 141.5	8.370	16.110	2.070	1.290
x 128.5	8.190	15.995	1.890	1.175
x 116.5	8.020	15.890	1.720	1.070
x 105.5	7.860	15.800	1.560	0.980
x 96.5	7.740	15.710	1.440	0.890
x 88	7.610	15.650	1.310	0.830
x 79.5	7.490	15.565	1.190	0.745
x 72.5	7.390	15.500	1.090	0.680
WT7 x 66	7.330	14.725	1.030	0.645
x 60	7.240	14.670	0.940	0.590
x 54.5	7.160	14.605	0.860	0.525
x 49.5	7.080	14.565	0.780	0.485
x 45	7.010	14.520	0.710	0.440
WT7 x 41	7.155	10.130	0.855	0.510
x 37	7.085	10.070	0.785	0.450
x 34	7.020	10.035	0.720	0.415
x 30.5	6.945	9.995	0.645	0.375
WT7 x 26.5	6.960	8.060	0.660	0.370
x 24	6.895	8.030	0.595	0.340
x 21.5	6.830	7.995	0.530	0.305
WT7 x 19	7.050	6.770	0.515	0.310
x 17	6.990	6.745	0.455	0.285
x 15	6.920	6.730	0.385	0.270
WT7 x 13	6.955	5.025	0.420	0.255
x 11	6.870	5.000	0.335	0.230
WT6 x 95	7.190	12.670	1.735	1.060
x 85	7.015	12.570	1.560	0.960
x 76	6.855	12.480	1.400	0.870
x 68	6.705	12.400	1.250	0.790
x 60	6.560	12.320	1.105	0.710
x 53	6.445	12.220	0.990	0.610
x 48	6.355	12.160	0.900	0.550
x 43.5	6.265	12.125	0.810	0.515
x 39.5	6.190	12.080	0.735	0.470
x 36	6.125	12.040	0.670	0.430
x 32.5	6.060	12.000	0.605	0.390
WT6 x 29	6.095	10.010	0.640	0.360
x 26.5	6.030	9.995	0.575	0.345
WT6 x 25	6.095	8.080	0.640	0.370
x 22.5	6.030	8.045	0.575	0.335
x 20	5.970	8.005	0.515	0.295
WT6 x 17.5	6.250	6.560	0.520	0.300
x 15	6.170	6.520	0.440	0.260
x 13	6.110	6.490	0.380	0.230
WT6 x 11	6.155	4.030	0.425	0.260
x 9.5	6.080	4.005	0.350	0.235
x 8	5.995	3.990	0.265	0.220
x 7	5.955	3.970	0.225	0.200
WT5 x 56	5.680	10.415	1.250	0.755
x 50	5.550	10.340	1.120	0.680
x 44	5.420	10.265	0.990	0.605
x 38.5	5.300	10.190	0.870	0.530
x 34	5.200	10.130	0.770	0.470
x 30	5.110	10.080	0.680	0.420
x 27	5.045	10.030	0.615	0.370
x 24.5	4.990	10.000	0.560	0.340
WT5 x 22.5	5.050	8.020	0.620	0.350
x 19.5	4.960	7.985	0.530	0.315
x 16.5	4.865	7.960	0.435	0.290
WT5 x 15	5.235	5.810	0.510	0.300
x 13	5.165	5.770	0.440	0.260
x 11	5.085	5.750	0.360	0.240
WT5 x 9.5	5.120	4.020	0.395	0.250
x 8.5	5.055	4.010	0.330	0.240
x 7.5	4.995	4.000	0.270	0.230
x 6	4.935	3.960	0.210	0.190
WT4 x 33.5	4.500	8.280	0.935	0.570
x 29	4.375	8.220	0.810	0.510
x 24	4.250	8.110	0.685	0.400
x 20	4.125	8.070	0.560	0.360
x 17.5	4.060	8.020	0.495	0.310
x 15.5	4.000	7.995	0.435	0.285
WT4 x 14	4.030	6.535	0.465	0.285
x 12	3.965	6.495	0.400	0.245
WT4 x 10.5	4.140	5.270	0.400	0.250
x 9	4.070	5.250	0.330	0.230
WT4 x 7.5	4.055	4.015	0.315	0.245
x 6.5	3.995	4.000	0.255	0.230
x 5	3.945	3.940	0.205	0.170
WT3 x 12.5	3.190	6.080	0.455	0.320
x 10	3.100	6.020	0.365	0.260
x 7.5	2.995	5.990	0.260	0.230
WT3 x 8	3.140	4.030	0.405	0.260
x 6	3.015	4.000	0.280	0.230
x 4.5	2.950	3.940	0.215	0.170

STRUCTURAL TEES CUT FROM S SHAPES—DIMENSIONS FOR DETAILING

DESIGNATION	DEPTH OF SECTION d (IN.)	FLANGE WIDTH b_f (IN.)	FLANGE AVERAGE THICKNESS t_f (IN.)	STEM THICKNESS t_w (IN.)
ST12 x 60	12.00	8.048	1.102	0.798
x 52.95	12.00	7.875	1.102	0.625
ST12 x 50	12.00	7.247	0.871	0.747
x 45	12.00	7.124	0.871	0.624
x 39.95	12.00	7.001	0.871	0.501
ST10 x 47.5	10.00	7.200	0.916	0.800
x 42.5	10.00	7.053	0.916	0.653
ST10 x 37.5	10.00	6.391	0.789	0.641
x 32.7	10.00	6.250	0.789	0.500
ST9 x 35	9.00	6.251	0.691	0.711
x 27.35	9.00	6.001	0.691	0.461
ST7.5 x 25	7.50	5.640	0.622	0.550
x 21.45	7.50	5.501	0.622	0.411
ST6 x 25	6.00	5.477	0.659	0.687
x 20.4	6.00	5.252	0.659	0.462
ST6 x 17.5	6.00	5.078	0.544	0.428
x 15.9	6.00	5.000	0.544	0.350
ST5 x 17.5	5.00	4.944	0.491	0.594
x 12.7	5.00	4.661	0.491	0.311
ST4 x 11.5	4.00	4.171	0.425	0.441
x 9.2	4.00	4.001	0.425	0.271
ST3.5 x 10	3.50	3.860	0.392	0.450
x 7.65	3.50	3.662	0.392	0.252
ST3 x 8.625	3.00	3.565	0.359	0.465
x 6.25	3.00	3.332	0.359	0.232
ST2.5 x 7.375	2.50	3.284	0.326	0.494
x 5	2.50	3.004	0.326	0.214
ST2 x 4.75	2.00	2.796	0.293	0.326
x 3.85	2.00	2.663	0.293	0.193
ST1.5 x 3.75	1.50	2.509	0.260	0.349
x 2.85	1.50	2.330	0.260	0.170

MOMENT-RESISTING FRAME

A moment-resisting frame's lateral stability and resistance to wind and seismic forces depend on a fixed connection of beams and columns. A moment-resisting connection is achieved when the top and bottom flanges of each beam are welded to the flanges of the connecting columns with full-depth welds. By directly welding the beam web to the column flange, the beam's horizontal reaction to wind forces is transferred to the column. (A connection using web angles and high-strength bolts is also permitted.) The building's floors are designed to act as diaphragms that connect all of the columns and beams, enabling the building to re-act as a unit.

Moment-resisting frames are uneconomical in tall steel buildings because the larger lateral forces in such buildings can be handled more efficiently by compression and tension diagonal members, as found in braced frames. To save costs, often the upper stories of a braced frame building use moment-resisting beam-column connections to resist wind loads.

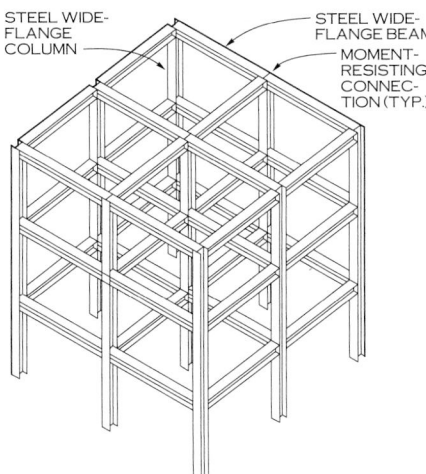

MOMENT-RESISTING STEEL FRAME

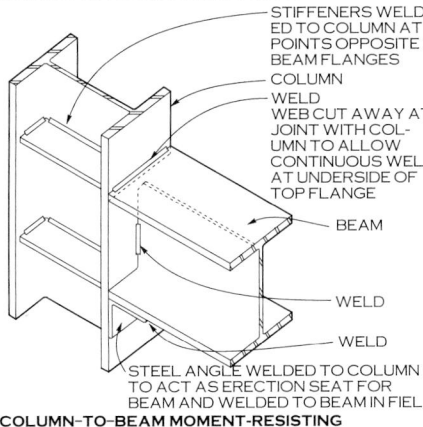

COLUMN-TO-BEAM MOMENT-RESISTING CONNECTION

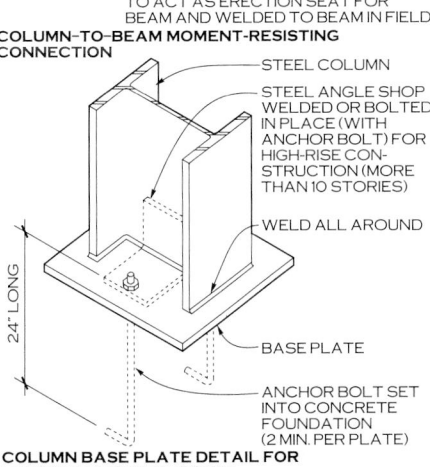

COLUMN BASE PLATE DETAIL FOR LOW-RISE CONSTRUCTION

MOMENT-RESISTING FRAME

RIGID FRAME

Rigid frame construction combines columns and a beam or girder welded together to make a rigid connection. Such a frame can carry vertical loads and resist horizontal forces, either wind or seismic. Rigid frame buildings are usually single story and are available with provisions for cranes, balconies, and mezzanines. The roofs are generally sloped, which permits the use of combined roof decks and water-proofing systems; the slope varies but is usually at least 1 in 12.

Because they span fairly long distances relatively cheaply (widths range between 30 and 130 ft), rigid frame structures are used for recreational buildings; warehouses; light industrial buildings; and commercial buildings, such as supermarkets, automobile dealer showrooms, and garages. Bay sizes are usually 20 to 24 ft but may be extended to 30 ft. The roof profile is most often configured as a symmetrical gable, but such a profile is not a structural necessity. Roofs and side walls are usually covered with 26-gauge colored steel siding; insulation options vary. Some manufacturers offer precast concrete and masonry siding. Pre-engineered buildings most often use rigid frames for roof and wall supports.

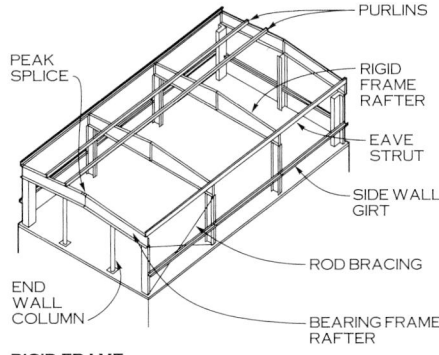

RIGID FRAME

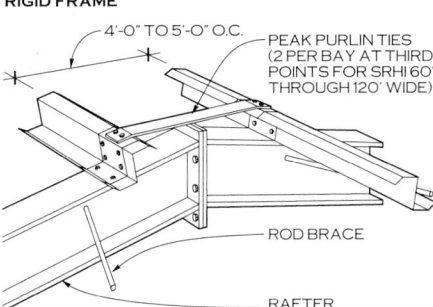

RIDGE DETAIL

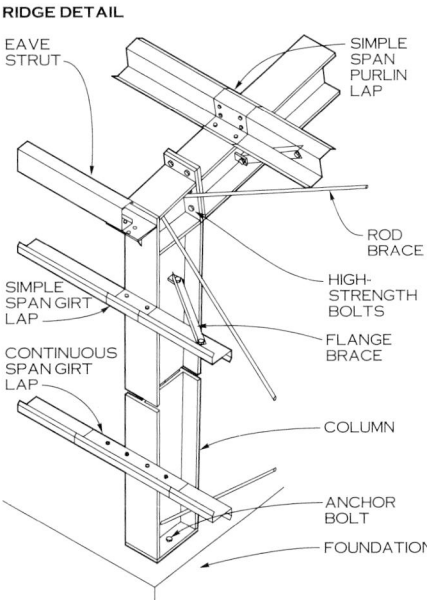

RAFTER-TO-COLUMN DETAIL

RIGID FRAME

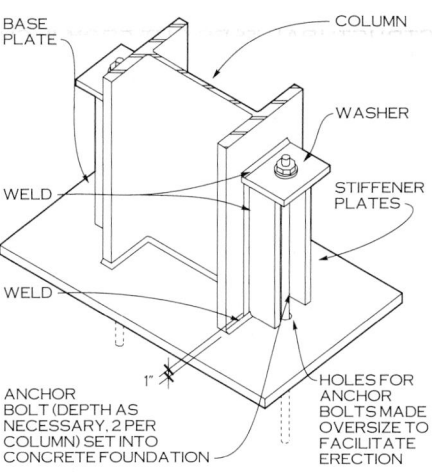

TYPICAL SEISMIC FOUNDATION CONNECTION

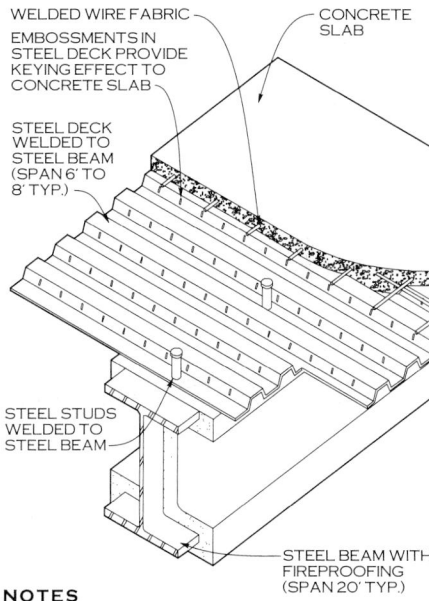

NOTES

1. For nonfire-rated ceiling situations
2. Typically used for heavy loads; noncomposite floor system for light loads

COMPOSITE FLOOR AND BEAM SYSTEM

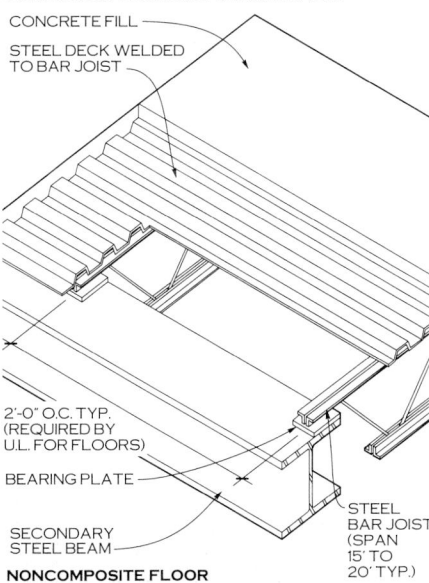

TYPICAL FLOOR SYSTEMS

Donald J. Neubauer, P.E.; Neubauer - Sohn, Consulting Engineers; Potomac, Maryland
Richard J. Vitullo, AIA; Oak Leaf Studio; Crownsville, Maryland

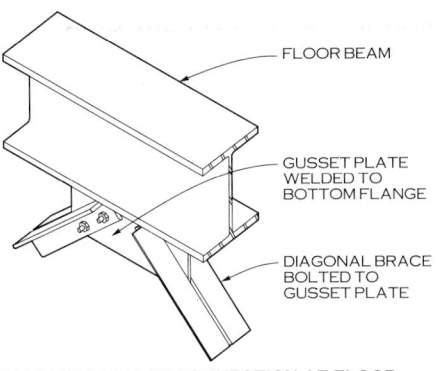

DIAGONAL BRACE CONNECTION AT FLOOR BEAM—INTERMEDIATE (MIDSPAN)

- FLOOR BEAM
- GUSSET PLATE WELDED TO BOTTOM FLANGE
- DIAGONAL BRACE BOLTED TO GUSSET PLATE

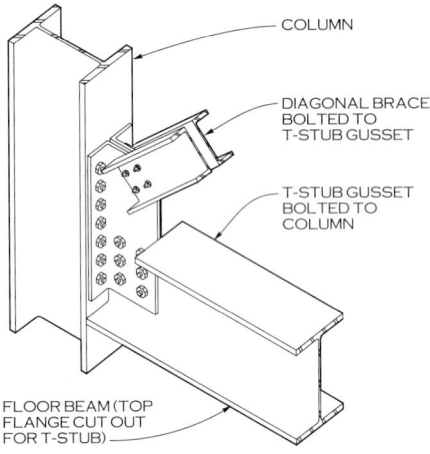

DIAGONAL BRACE CONNECTION AT FLOOR BEAM—END

- COLUMN
- DIAGONAL BRACE BOLTED TO T-STUB GUSSET
- T-STUB GUSSET BOLTED TO COLUMN
- FLOOR BEAM (TOP FLANGE CUT OUT FOR T-STUB)

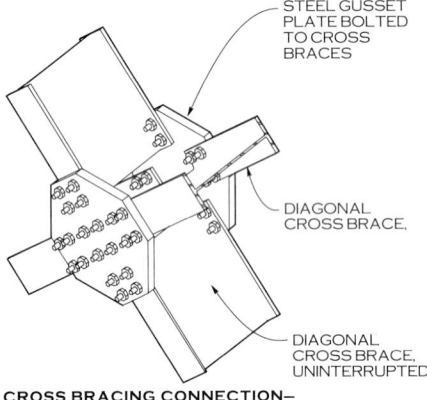

CROSS BRACING CONNECTION—INTERMEDIATE

- STEEL GUSSET PLATE BOLTED TO CROSS BRACES
- DIAGONAL CROSS BRACE,
- DIAGONAL CROSS BRACE, UNINTERRUPTED

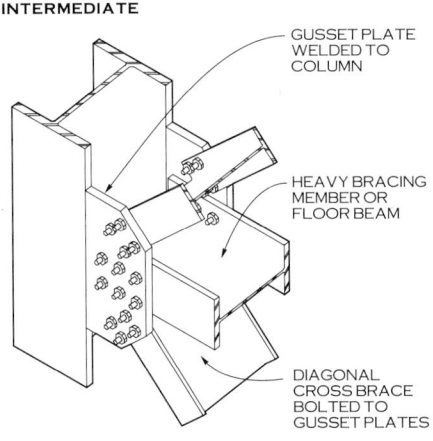

CROSS BRACING CONNECTION—END

- GUSSET PLATE WELDED TO COLUMN
- HEAVY BRACING MEMBER OR FLOOR BEAM
- DIAGONAL CROSS BRACE BOLTED TO GUSSET PLATES

VERTICAL BRACING DETAILS

FRAMED TUBE

In the framed tube system, structural steel members form the load bearing exterior perimeter wall; this wall is designed so the entire building becomes, in effect, a structural steel tube. The tubular strength is achieved in two ways: the exterior columns are spaced closely together, perhaps 6 ft on center, and connected to spandrel beams; the structure is stiffened by the floors to form a torsionally rigid tube. The spandrel beams are generally very deep, in units of feet as opposed to inches. The columns and spandrel beams are welded together to create a moment-resisting connection. Often this system is referred to as a pierced tube, the pierced areas being the window openings.

The framed tube system is most economical for very tall buildings. The World Trade Center Towers in New York and the Sears Tower in Chicago are the most conspicuous examples. Systems like that at the Sears Tower, a combination of nine framed tubes in a 3 by 3 array, are sometimes called bundled tubes.

BRACED CORE

In the braced core system, walls around elevator shafts and stairwells are designed to act as vertical trusses that cantilever up from the foundation. The chords of each truss are building columns; the floor beams act as ties. Diagonals placed in a K pattern (occasionally in an X pattern) complete the truss. A system employing knee braces is used in seismic areas because of its greater ability to dissipate earthquake energy. Braced core systems can be used efficiently in single-story buildings as well as in buildings over 50 stories.

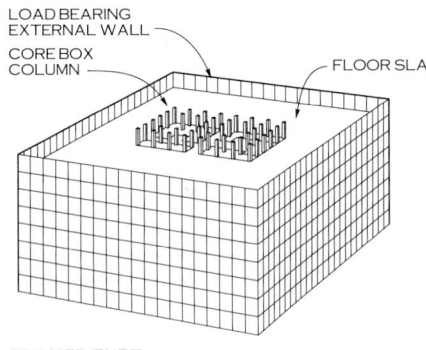

- LOAD BEARING EXTERNAL WALL
- CORE BOX COLUMN
- FLOOR SLAB

FRAMED TUBE

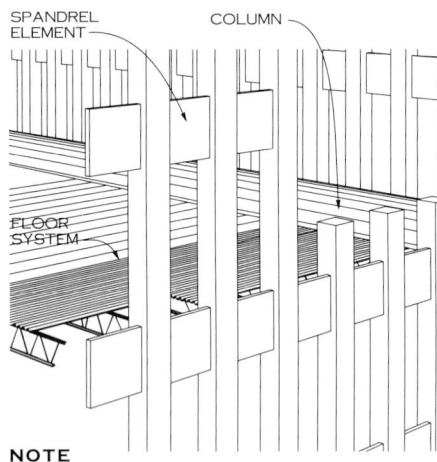

- SPANDREL ELEMENT
- COLUMN
- FLOOR SYSTEM

NOTE

External wall units typically staggered in one-story heights

PERIMETER WALL DETAIL

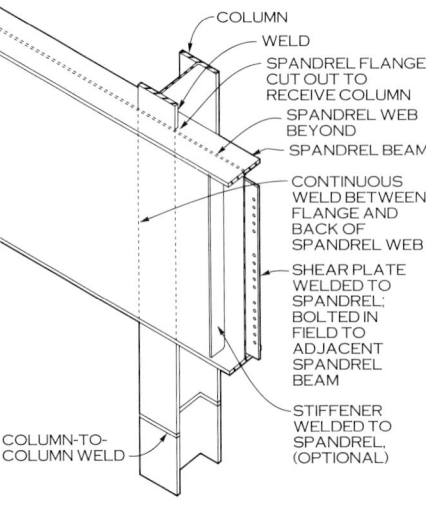

- COLUMN
- WELD
- SPANDREL FLANGE CUT OUT TO RECEIVE COLUMN
- SPANDREL WEB BEYOND
- SPANDREL BEAM
- CONTINUOUS WELD BETWEEN FLANGE AND BACK OF SPANDREL WEB
- SHEAR PLATE WELDED TO SPANDREL; BOLTED IN FIELD TO ADJACENT SPANDREL BEAM
- STIFFENER WELDED TO SPANDREL. (OPTIONAL)
- COLUMN-TO-COLUMN WELD

SPANDREL AND COLUMN DETAILS

FRAMED TUBE

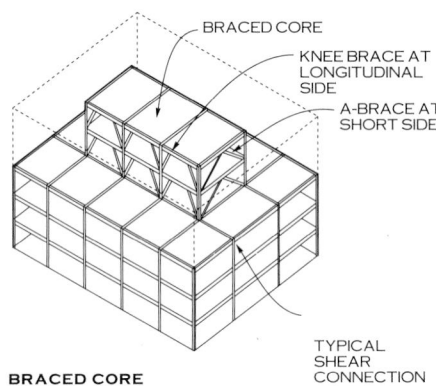

- BRACED CORE
- KNEE BRACE AT LONGITUDINAL SIDE
- A-BRACE AT SHORT SIDE
- TYPICAL SHEAR CONNECTION

BRACED CORE

NOTE

Bracing design to be determined by structural engineer based on specific loading configurations

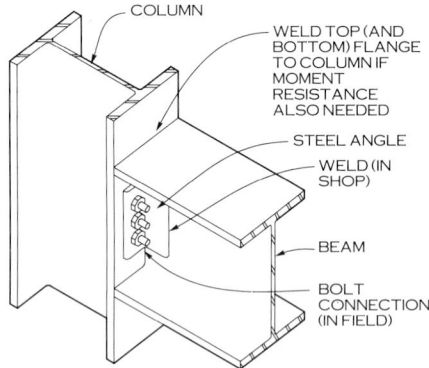

- COLUMN
- WELD TOP (AND BOTTOM) FLANGE TO COLUMN IF MOMENT RESISTANCE ALSO NEEDED
- STEEL ANGLE
- WELD (IN SHOP)
- BEAM
- BOLT CONNECTION (IN FIELD)

COLUMN-TO-BEAM SHEAR CONNECTION

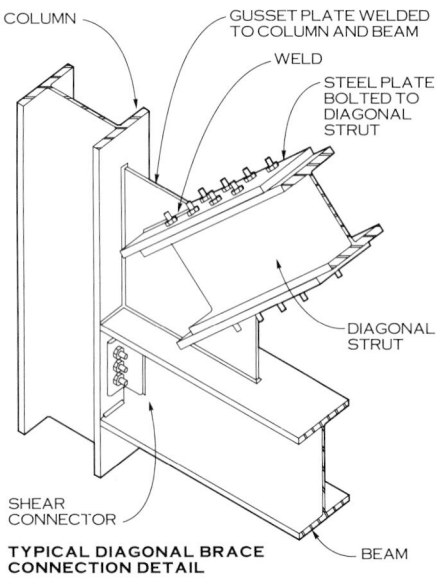

- COLUMN
- GUSSET PLATE WELDED TO COLUMN AND BEAM
- WELD
- STEEL PLATE BOLTED TO DIAGONAL STRUT
- DIAGONAL STRUT
- SHEAR CONNECTOR
- BEAM

TYPICAL DIAGONAL BRACE CONNECTION DETAIL

BRACED CORE

Donald J. Neubauer, P.E.; Neubauer - Sohn, Consulting Engineers; Potomac, Maryland
Richard Vitullo, AIA; Oak Leaf Studio; Crownsville, Maryland

STRUCTURAL METAL FRAMING

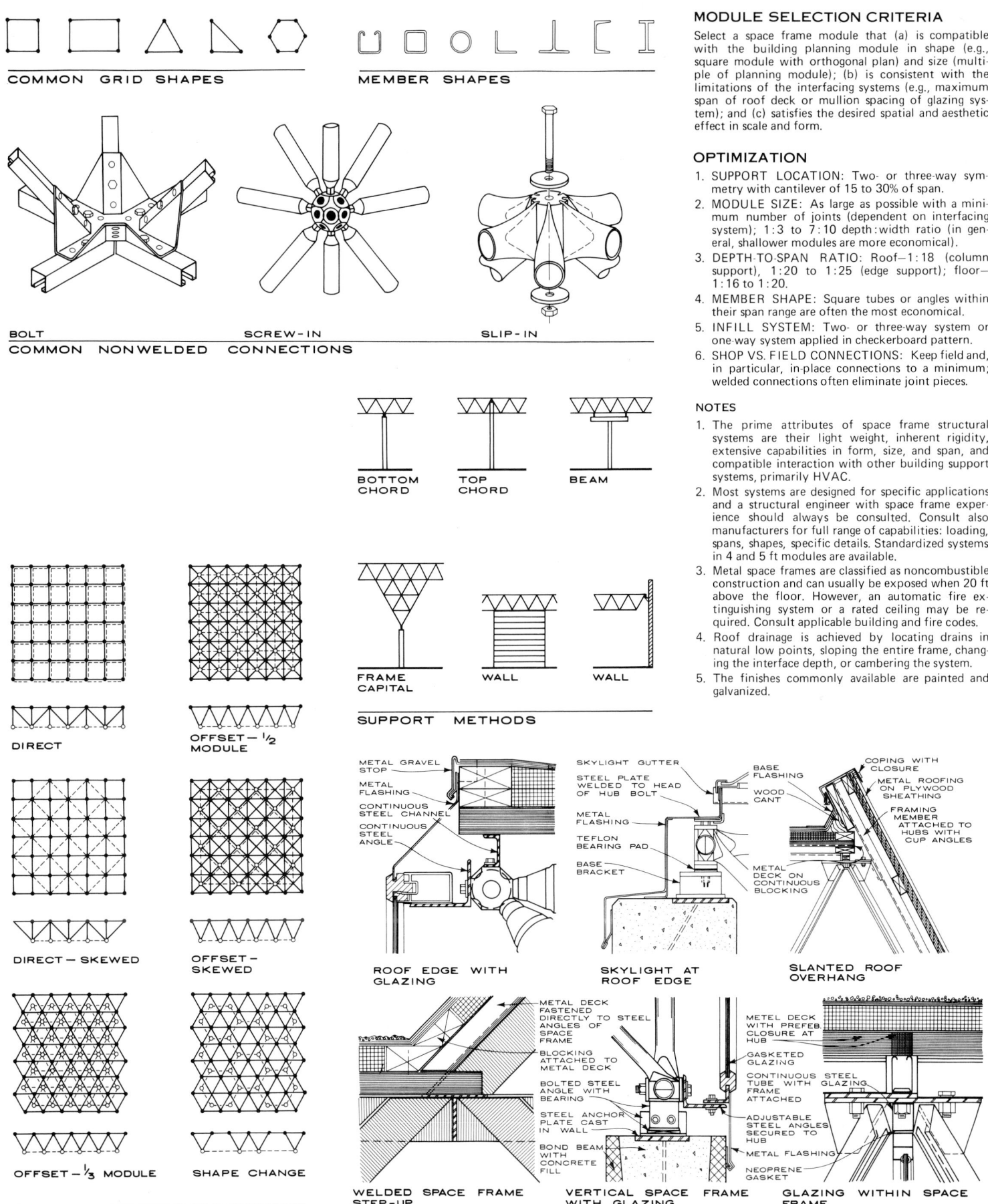

COMMON GRID SHAPES

MEMBER SHAPES

BOLT   SCREW-IN   SLIP-IN
COMMON NONWELDED CONNECTIONS

BOTTOM CHORD   TOP CHORD   BEAM

FRAME CAPITAL   WALL   WALL
SUPPORT METHODS

DIRECT   OFFSET—1/2 MODULE

DIRECT—SKEWED   OFFSET—SKEWED

OFFSET—1/3 MODULE   SHAPE CHANGE
COMMON PATTERNS

ROOF EDGE WITH GLAZING   SKYLIGHT AT ROOF EDGE   SLANTED ROOF OVERHANG

WELDED SPACE FRAME STEP-UP   VERTICAL SPACE FRAME WITH GLAZING   GLAZING WITHIN SPACE FRAME
DETAILS

MODULE SELECTION CRITERIA

Select a space frame module that (a) is compatible with the building planning module in shape (e.g., square module with orthogonal plan) and size (multiple of planning module); (b) is consistent with the limitations of the interfacing systems (e.g., maximum span of roof deck or mullion spacing of glazing system); and (c) satisfies the desired spatial and aesthetic effect in scale and form.

OPTIMIZATION

1. SUPPORT LOCATION: Two- or three-way symmetry with cantilever of 15 to 30% of span.
2. MODULE SIZE: As large as possible with a minimum number of joints (dependent on interfacing system); 1:3 to 7:10 depth:width ratio (in general, shallower modules are more economical).
3. DEPTH-TO-SPAN RATIO: Roof—1:18 (column support), 1:20 to 1:25 (edge support); floor—1:16 to 1:20.
4. MEMBER SHAPE: Square tubes or angles within their span range are often the most economical.
5. INFILL SYSTEM: Two- or three-way system or one-way system applied in checkerboard pattern.
6. SHOP VS. FIELD CONNECTIONS: Keep field and, in particular, in-place connections to a minimum; welded connections often eliminate joint pieces.

NOTES

1. The prime attributes of space frame structural systems are their light weight, inherent rigidity, extensive capabilities in form, size, and span, and compatible interaction with other building support systems, primarily HVAC.
2. Most systems are designed for specific applications and a structural engineer with space frame experience should always be consulted. Consult also manufacturers for full range of capabilities: loading, spans, shapes, specific details. Standardized systems in 4 and 5 ft modules are available.
3. Metal space frames are classified as noncombustible construction and can usually be exposed when 20 ft above the floor. However, an automatic fire extinguishing system or a rated ceiling may be required. Consult applicable building and fire codes.
4. Roof drainage is achieved by locating drains in natural low points, sloping the entire frame, changing the interface depth, or cambering the system.
5. The finishes commonly available are painted and galvanized.

Steven W. Henkelman, R.A.; Cope, Linder, Walmsley; Philadelphia, Pennsylvania

STRUCTURAL METAL FRAMING

5

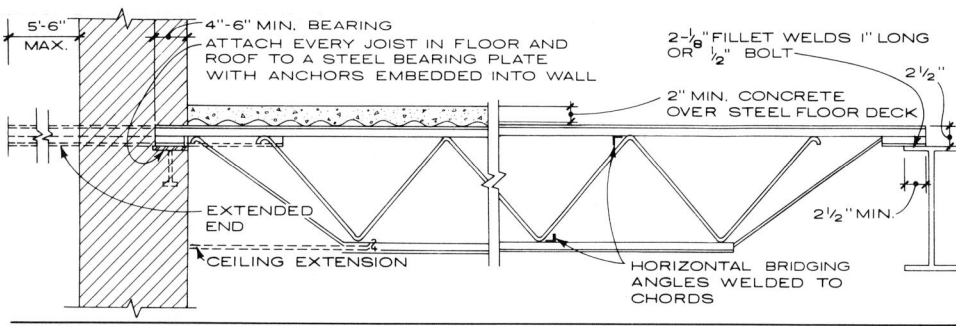

SECTION THROUGH JOIST BEARING

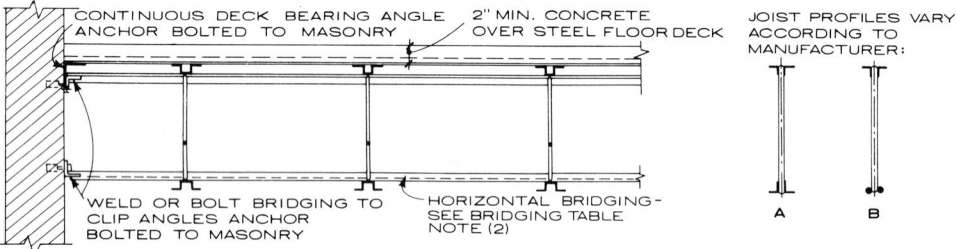

SECTION THROUGH JOISTS

NOTES

The following information applies to both open web and long span steel joists.

JOIST DESIGNATION:

```
25  K  10  ← Chord
              Type of steel
              K-series joist
              Nominal depth (in.)
```

For greater economy, the K-series joist replaced the H-series joist in 1986.

1. ROOF CONSTRUCTION: Joists are usually covered by steel deck topped with either rigid insulation board or lightweight concrete fill and built-up felt and gravel roof or single-ply roofing with ballast. Plywood, poured gypsum, or structural wood fiber deck systems can also be used with built-up roof.

2. CEILINGS: Ceiling supports can be suspended from or mounted directly to bottom chords of joists, although suspended systems are recommended because of dimensional variations in actual joist depths.

3. FLOOR CONSTRUCTION: Joists usually covered by $2\frac{1}{2}$ to 3 in. concrete on steel decking. Concrete thickness may be increased for electrical conduit or electrical/communications raceways. Precast concrete, gypsum planks, or plywood can also be used for the floor system.

4. VIBRATION: Objectionable vibrations can occur in open web joist and $2\frac{1}{2}$ in. concrete slab designs for open floor areas at spans between 24 and 40 ft, especially at 28 ft. When a floor area cannot have partitions, objectionable vibrations can be prevented or reduced by increasing slab thickness, joist spacing, or floor spans. Attention should also be given to support framing beams which can magnify a vibration problem.

5. OPENINGS IN FLOOR OR ROOF SYSTEMS: Small openings between joists are framed with angles or channel supported on the adjoining two joists. Larger openings necessitating interruption of joists are framed with steel angle or channel headers spanning between the adjoining two joists. The interrupted joists bear on the headers.

6. ROOF DRAINAGE: Roof drainage should be carefully considered on level or near level roofs especially with parapet walls. Roof insulation can be sloped, joists can be sloped or obtained with sloping top chords in one or both directions, and overflow scuppers should be provided in parapet walls. If roof slope is less than $\frac{1}{4}$ in. per foot, ponding of water may occur.

PRELIMINARY JOIST SELECTION: The tables below are not to be used for final joist design but are intended as an aid in speeding selection of steel joists for preliminary design and planning. The final design must be a separate and thorough process, involving a complete investigation of the pertinent conditions. This page is not for that purpose. Consult structural engineer.

EXAMPLE: Assume a particular clear span. By assuming a joist spacing and estimating the total load a joist can immediately be selected from the table. Then proceed with preliminary design studies.

NOTES

1. Total safe load = live load + dead load. Dead load includes weight of joist. For dead loads and recommended live loads, see pages on weights of materials. Local codes will govern.

2. Span not to exceed a depth 24 times that of a nominal joist.

3. For more detailed information refer to standard specifications and load tables adopted by the Steel Joist Institute.

NUMBER OF ROWS OF BRIDGING (FT)
DISTANCES ARE CLEAR SPAN DIMENSIONS

CHORD SIZE[1]	1 ROW	2 ROWS	3 ROWS	4 ROWS[2]	5 ROWS[2]
#1	Up to 16	16–24	24–28	—	—
#2	Up to 17	17–25	25–32	—	—
#3	Up to 18	18–28	28–38	38–40	—
#4	Up to 19	19–28	28–38	38–48	—
#5	Up to 19	19–29	29–39	39–50	50–52
#6	Up to 19	19–29	29–39	39–51	51–56
#7	Up to 20	20–33	33–45	45–58	58–60
#8	Up to 20	20–33	33–45	45–58	58–60
#9	Up to 20	20–33	33–46	46–59	59–60
#10	Up to 20	20–37	37–51	51–60	
#11	Up to 20	20–38	38–53	53–60	
#12	Up to 20	20–39	39–53	53–60	

1. Last digit(s) of joist designation shown in load table below.
2. Where four or five rows of bridging are required, a row nearest the midspan of the joist shall be diagonal bridging with bolted connections at chords and intersections.

SELECTED LOAD TABLES: K SERIES—TOTAL SAFE UNIFORMLY DISTRIBUTED LOAD (LB/FT)

JOIST DESIGNATION		8	12	16	20	24	28	32	36	42	48	54	60
K SERIES f_s = 30,000 psi	8K1	550	444	246									
	10K1		550	313	199								
	12K3		550	476	302	208							
	14K4			550	428	295	216						
	16K5			550	550	384	281	214					
	18K6				550	473	346	264	208				
	20K7				550	550	430	328	259				
	22K9					550	550	436	344	252			
	24K9					550	550	478	377	276	211		
	26K10						550	549	486	356	272		
	28K10						550	549	487	384	294	232	
	30K11							549	487	417	362	285	231
	30K12							549	487	417	365	324	262

Note: Number preceding letter is joist depth; 14K4 is 14 in. deep.

Kenneth D. Franch, AIA, PE; Phillips Swager Associates, Inc.; Dallas, Texas
Setter, Leach & Lindstrom, Inc.; Minneapolis, Minnesota

METAL JOISTS

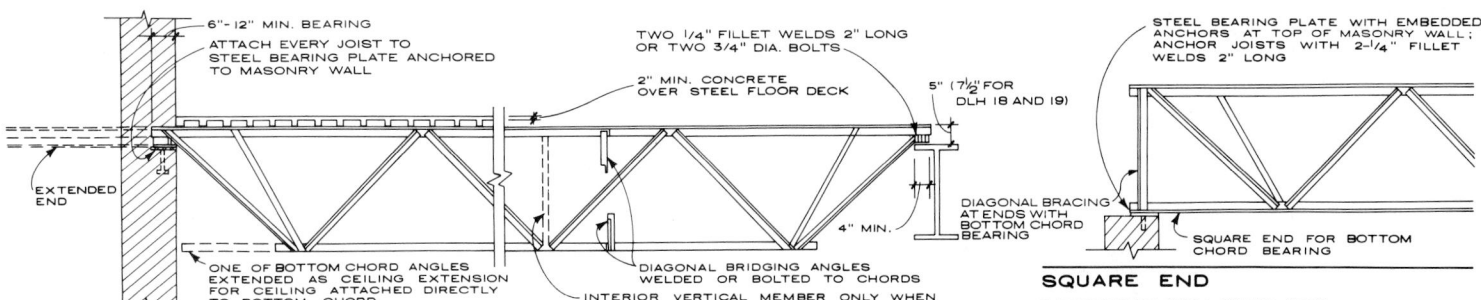

SECTION THROUGH JOIST BEARING

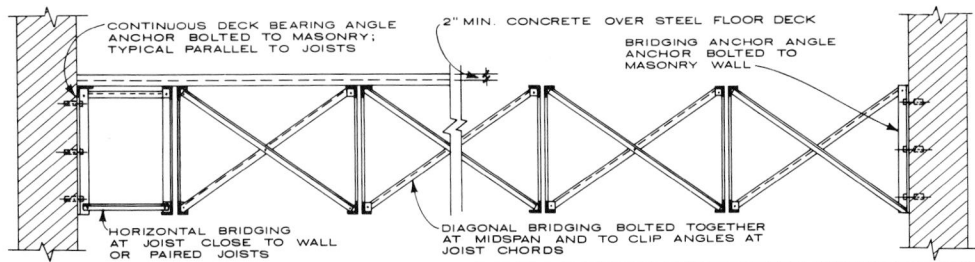

SECTION THROUGH JOISTS

SQUARE END
BRIDGING SPACING (FT)

LH CHORD SIZE†	MAXIMUM SPACING (FT)
02–09	11
10–14	16
15–17	21

DLH CHORD SIZE†	MAXIMUM SPACING (FT)
10	14
11–14	16
15–17	21
18–19	26

NOTE: For spans up to 40 ft, welded horizontal bridging may be used. For spans of 40 to 60 ft, welded horizontal bridging may be used, but one row nearest the midspan shall be bolted diagonal bridging. For spans over 60 ft, bolted diagonal bridging shall be used.

PRELIMINARY JOIST SELECTION

The tables below are not to be used for final joist design but are intended as an aid in speeding selection of steel joists for preliminary design and planning.

The final design must be a separate thorough process, involving a complete investigation of the pertinent conditions. This page is not for that purpose. Consult a structural engineer.

EXAMPLE

Assume a particular clear span. By assuming a joist spacing and estimating the total load a joist can immediately be selected from the table. Then proceed with preliminary design studies.

NOTES

1. Total safe load = live load + dead load. Dead load includes weight of joist. For dead loads and recommended live loads, see pages on weights of materials. Local codes will govern.
2. Span not to exceed 24 times depth of a nominal joist for roofs; 20 times depth for floors.
3. For more detailed information refer to standard specifications and load tables adopted by the Steel Joist Institute.

FIRE RESISTANCE RATINGS

TIME (HR)	FLOOR ASSEMBLIES	TIME (HR)	ROOF ASSEMBLIES
1 or 1½	2" reinforced concrete, listed ½" (⅝" for 1½ hr) acoustical tile ceiling, concealed ceiling grid suspended from joists	1	Built-up roofing on 2" structural wood fiber units, listed ¾" acoustical ceiling tiles, concealed ceiling grid suspended from joists
	2" reinforced concrete, listed ½" acoustical board ceiling, listed exposed ceiling grid suspended from joists		Built-up roofing and insulation on 26 gauge min. steel deck, listed ⅝" acoustical ceiling boards, listed exposed ceiling grid suspended from joists
	2" reinforced concrete, listed ½" gypsum board ceiling fastened to joists		Built-up roofing over 2" vermiculite on centering, listed ½" acoustical ceiling boards, listed exposed ceiling grid suspended from joists
2	2½" reinforced concrete, listed ⅝" acoustical tile ceiling, listed concealed ceiling grid suspended from joists		
	2½" reinforced concrete, listed ½" acoustical board ceiling, listed exposed ceiling grid suspended from joists	2	Built-up roofing on 2" listed gypsum building units, listed ⅝" acoustical ceiling boards, listed exposed ceiling grid suspended from joists
	2" reinforced concrete, listed ⅝" gypsum board ceiling fastened to joists		Built-up roofing on 22 gauge minimum steel deck, suspended ⅞" metal lath and plaster ceiling
	2½" reinforced concrete, listed ½" gypsum board ceiling fastened to joists		

NOTE: Listed by Underwriters Laboratories or Factory Mutual approved, as appropriate. Ratings are the result of tests made in accordance with ASTM Standard E 119. A more complete list can be obtained from the SJI Technical Digest concerning the design of fire resistive assemblies with steel joists.

SELECTED LOAD TABLES: LH AND DLH SERIES—TOTAL SAFE UNIFORMLY DISTRIBUTED LOAD (LB/FT)

JOIST DESIGNATION		28	32	36	42	48	54	60	66	72	78	84	90	96
LH Series f_s = 30,000 psi	18LH05	581	448	355										
	20LH06	723	560	444										
	24LH07			588	446	343								
	28LH09				639	499	401							
	32LH10						478	389						
	36LH11							451	378	322				
	40LH12								472	402	346			
	44LH13										423	369		
	48LH14											444	390	346

		90	96	102	108	114	120	126	132	138	144			
DLH Series f_s = 30,000 psi	52DLH13	433	381	338										
	56DLH14			411	368									
	60DLH15				442	398	361							
	64DLH16					466	421	382						
	68DLH17							460	420					
	72DLH18								505	463	426			

NOTE: Number preceding letter is joist depth; 32LH10 is 32 in. deep.

Setter, Leach & Lindstrom, Inc.; Minneapolis, Minnesota

EXAMPLES OF THE MANY TYPES OF DECK AVAILABLE (SEE TABLES)

1. Roof deck.
2. Floor deck (noncomposite).
3. Composite floor deck interacting with concrete.
4. Permanent forms for self-supporting concrete slabs.
5. Cellular deck (composite or noncomposite).
6. Acoustical roof deck.
7. Acoustic cellular deck (composite or non-composite).
8. Electric raceway cellular deck.
9. Prevented roof deck (used with lightweight insulating concrete fill).

All metal floor and roof decks must be secured to all supports, generally by means of "puddle welds" made through the deck to supporting steel. Steel sheet lighter than 22 gauge (0.0295 in. thick) should be secured by use of welding washers (see illustration).

Shear studs welded through floor deck also serve to secure the deck to supporting steel. Power actuated and pneumatically driven fasteners may also be used in certain applications.

Side laps between adjacent sheets of deck must be secured by button-punching standing seams, welding, or screws, in accordance with manufacturer's recommendations.

Decks used as lateral diaphragms must be welded to steel supports around their entire perimeter to ensure development of diaphragm action. More stringent requirements may govern the size and/or spacing of attachments to supports and side lap fasteners or welds.

Roof deck selection must take into consideration construction and maintenance loads as well as the capacity to support uniformly distributed live loads. Consult current Steel Deck Institute recommendations and Factory Mutual requirements.

Floor deck loadings are virtually unlimited in scope, ranging from light residential and institutional loads to heavy duty industrial floors utilizing composite deck with slabs up to 24 in. thick. The designer can select the deck type, depth, and gauge most suitable for the application.

Fire resistance ratings for roof deck assemblies are published by Underwriters Laboratories and Factory Mutual. Ratings of 1 to 2 hr are achieved with spray-on insulation: a 1 hr rating with suspended acoustical ceiling and a 2 hr rating with a metal lath and plaster ceiling.

Floor deck assembly fire resistive ratings are available both with and without spray-applied fireproofing, and with regular weight or lightweight concrete fill. From 1 to 3 hr ratings are possible using only concrete fill—consult Underwriters Laboratory Fire Resistance Index for assembly ratings.

Consult manufacturer's literature and technical representatives for additional information. Consult "Steel Deck Institute Design Manual for Floor Decks and Roof Decks" and "Tentative Recommendations for the Design of Steel Deck Diaphragms" by the Steel Deck Institute.

ADVANTAGES OF METAL ROOF DECKS

1. High strength-to-weight ratio reduces roof dead load.
2. Can be erected in most weather conditions.
3. Variety of depths and rib patterns available.
4. Acoustical treatment is possible.
5. Serve as base for insulation and roofing.
6. Fire ratings can be obtained with standard assemblies.
7. Provide lateral diaphragm.
8. Can be erected quickly.
9. Can be erected economically.

The use of vapor barriers on metal deck roofs is not customary for normal building occupancies. For high relative humidity exposure a vapor barrier may be provided as part of the roofing system, but the user should be aware of the great difficulties encountered in installing a vapor barrier on metal deck. Punctures of the vapor barrier over valleys might reduce or negate entirely the effectiveness of the vapor barrier.

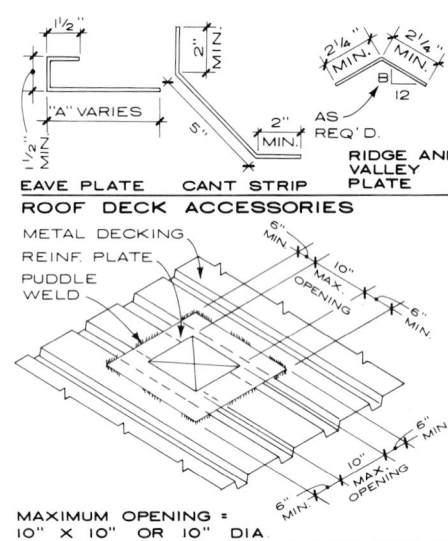

ROOF DECK ACCESSORIES

REINFORCING PLATE

Small openings (up to 6 x 6 in. or 6 in. dia.) may usually be cut in roof or floor deck without reinforcing the deck. Openings up to 10 x 10 in. or 10 in. dia. require reinforcing of the deck by either welding a reinforcing plate to the deck all around the opening, or by providing channel shaped headers and/or supplementary reinforcing parallel to the deck span. Reinforcing plates should be 14 gauge sheets with a minimum projection of 6 in. beyond all sides of the opening, and they should be welded to each cell of the deck.

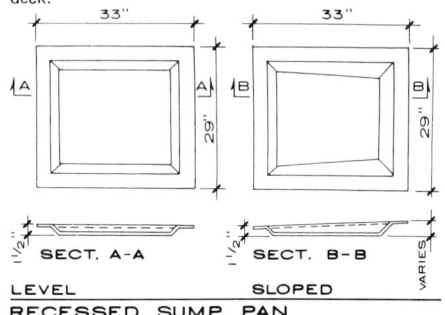

RECESSED SUMP PAN

Preformed recessed sump pans are available from deck manufacturers for use at roof drains.

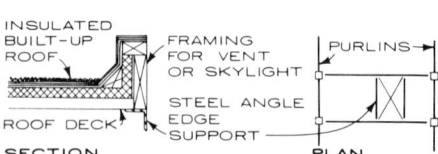

FRAMED OPENING

Larger openings should be framed with supplementary steel members so that all free edges of deck are supported.

Roof-mounted mechanical equipment should not be placed directly on metal roof deck. Equipment on built-up or prefabricated curbs should be supported directly on main and supplementary structural members and the deck must also be supported along all free edges (see illustration). Heavy items such as cooling towers which must be elevated should be supported by posts extending through pitch pockets directly onto structural members below the deck. Openings through the deck may be handled as previously discussed.

ROOF DECK (ACOUSTICAL ROOF DECKS ARE AVAILABLE IN MANY OF THESE PROFILES—CONSULT MANUFACTURERS)

TYPICAL EXAMPLES	ECONOMICAL SPANS	USUAL WIDTH	MAX. LENGTH AVAILABLE
1½" NARROW RIB	4'-6'	24"-36"	36'-42'
1½" INTERMEDIATE RIB	5'-7'	24"-36"	40'-42'
1½" WIDE RIB	6'-9'	24"-30"	32'-42'
(3" profile)	8'-16'	24"	40'
(4½" profile)	15'-18'	12"	32'
(1½" profile)	7'-11'	24"	32'
(3/16" profile)	10'-20'	24"	40'
(7½" profile)	12'-30'	12"	40'-42'
(7½" profile)	13'-33'	24"	40'

Walter D. Shapiro, PE; Tor, Shapiro & Associates; New York, New York

5 METAL DECKING

FLOOR DECK – COMPOSITE WITH CONCRETE FILL

TYPICAL EXAMPLES	ECONOMICAL SPANS	USUAL WIDTH	MAX. LENGTH AVAILABLE
1 1/2"	4' – 9'	30"	36'
2"	8' – 12'	30"	40' – 45'
3"	8' – 15'	24"	40'
7 1/2" 6" 4 1/2" 3" 2"	8' – 24'	12"	40'

FLOOR DECK – COMPOSITE CELLULAR (ACOUSTIC DECK AVAILABLE IN SOME PROFILES; CONSULT MANUFACTURERS)

	ECONOMICAL SPANS	USUAL WIDTH	MAX. LENGTH AVAILABLE
1 1/2" 6"	6' – 12'	24"	40'
1 5/8"	6' – 12'	24"	40'
2"	6' – 12'	30"	36' – 45'
3"	10' – 16'	24"	40'
7 1/2" 6" 4 1/2" 3"	8' – 24'	24"	40'

CORRUGATED FORMS FOR CONCRETE SLABS – NONCOMPOSITE

	ECONOMICAL SPANS	USUAL WIDTH	MAX. LENGTH AVAILABLE
1/2"	1' – 2'	96"	2' – 6'
9/16"	1' 6" – 3'	30"	40'
15/16"	3' – 5'	29"	40'
1" 4"	3' – 5'	28"	30' – 40'
1 5/16" 4 1/2"	4' – 9'	27"	30' – 40'
2" 6"	7' – 12'	24"	30' – 40'

Walter D. Shapiro, PE; Tor, Shapiro & Associates; New York, New York

ADVANTAGES OF METAL FLOOR DECKS:

1. Provide a working platform, eliminating temporary wood planking in highrise use.
2. Composite decks provide positive reinforcement for concrete slabs.
3. Noncomposite and composite decks serve as forms for concrete, eliminate forming and stripping.
4. Fire ratings can be achieved without spray-on fireproofing or rated ceilings.
5. Acoustical treatment is possible.
6. Electric raceways may be built into floor slab.
7. Economical floor assemblies.

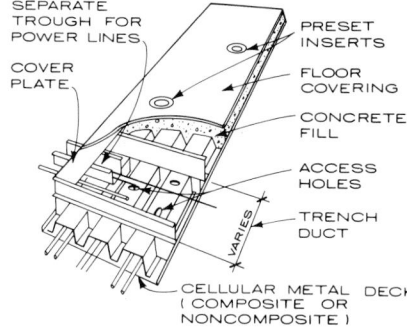

ELECTRICAL TRENCH DUCT

Electric raceways may be built into floor slabs by use of cellular deck or special units that are blended with plain deck. Two-way distribution is achieved by use of trench ducts that sit astride the cellular units at right angles. Use of trench ducts with composite floor deck may reduce or eliminate entirely the effectiveness of composite action at the trench duct. This is also true for composite action between steel floor beams and concrete fill. Trench duct locations must be taken into account in deciding whether composite action is possible.

Openings in composite deck may be blocked out on top of the deck and the deck can be burned out after the concrete has set and become self-supporting. Reinforcing bars can be added alongside openings to replace positive moment deck steel area lost at openings.

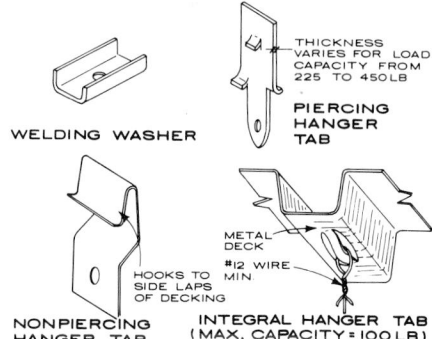

DECKING ATTACHMENTS

A convenient and economical means for supporting lightweight acoustical ceilings is by attaching suspension system to hanger tabs at side laps, piercing tabs driven through deck, or prepunched tabs in roof deck (see illustrations above). These tabs and metal decks must not be used to support plaster ceilings, piping, ductwork, electric equipment, or other heavy loads. Such elements must be supported directly from structural joists, beams, girders, and so on, or from supplementary subframing, and not from metal deck.

ALLOWABLE LOADS FOR SIMPLE SPAN STEEL "C" JOISTS (LB/LINEAR FOOT) MADE OF 40 KSI MATERIAL

SPAN	SECTION (DEPTH/GAUGE)	SINGLE MEMBER		DOUBLE MEMBER	
		TOTAL ALLOWABLE LOAD	ALLOWABLE LIVE LOAD	TOTAL ALLOWABLE LOAD	ALLOWABLE LIVE LOAD
8'	6"/18	201	189	402*	378
	6"/16	245	230	490	460
	6"/14	301	283	602	566
	8"/18	295	295	590*	590
	8"/16	359	359	718*	718
	8"/14	442	442	884*	884
	10"/16	506	506	1012*	1012
	10"/14	627	627	1254*	1254
10'	6"/18	129	97	258	194
	6"/16	157	118	314	236
	6"/14	193	144	386	288
	8"/18	188	186	376*	372
	8"/16	230	228	460*	456
	8"/14	283	280	566	560
	10"/16	326	326	652*	652
	10"/14	401	401	802*	802
12'	6"/18	89	56	178	112
	6"/16	109	68	218	136
	6"/14	134	83	268	166
	8"/18	131	108	262*	216
	8"/16	159	131	318	262
	8"/14	196	162	392	324
	10"/16	226	226	452*	452
	10"/14	278	278	556*	556
14'	6"/18	65	35	130	70
	6"/16	80	43	160	86
	6"/14	98	52	196	204
	8"/18	96	68	192	136
	8"/16	117	83	234	166
	8"/14	144	102	288	204
	10"/16	166	150	332*	300
	10"/14	204	184	408	368
16'	6"/18	50	23	100	46
	6"/16	61	28	122	56
	6"/14	75	35	150	70
	8"/18	73	45	146	90
	8"/16	89	55	178	110
	8"/14	110	68	220	136
	10"/16	127	100	254	200
	10"/14	156	123	312	246
18'	8"/18	58	32	116	64
	8"/16	71	39	142	78
	8"/14	87	48	174	96
	10"/16	100	70	200	140
	10"/14	123	86	246	172
20'	8"/18	47	23	94	46
	8"/16	57	28	114	56
	8"/14	70	35	140	70
	10"/16	81	51	162	102
	10"/14	100	63	200	126
22'	8"/18	39	17	78	34
	8"/16	47	21	94	42
	8"/14	58	26	116	52
	10"/16	67	38	134	76
	10"/14	82	47	164	94
24'	10"/16	56	29	112	58
	10"/14	69	36	138	72

NOTES

The tables on this page are not to be used for final design.
They are intended to serve only as aids in the preliminary selection of members.
Consult appropriate manufacturers' literature for final and/or additional information.
*Ends of members require additional reinforcing, such as by end clips.

Ed Hesner; Rasmussen & Hobbs Architects; Tacoma, Washington

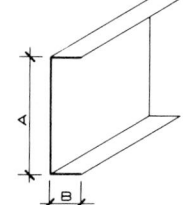 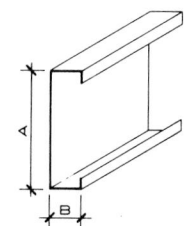 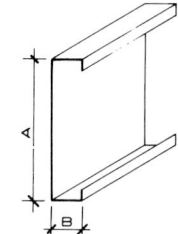

CHANNEL STUDS		"C" STUDS		"C" JOISTS	
A	B	A	B	A	B
2½"	1"	2½"	1¼"	5½"	1⅞"
3¼"	1⅜"	3"	1⅜"	6"	1⅝"
3⅝"		3⅝"	1½"	7¼"	1¾"
4"		3¼"	1⅝"	8"	2"
6"		3½"		9¼"	2½"
		4"		10"	
		5½"		12"	
		6"			
		7½"			
		8"			

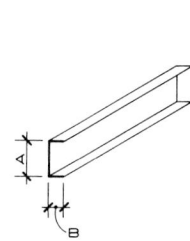 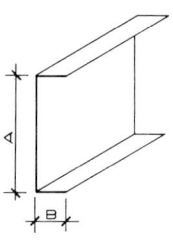 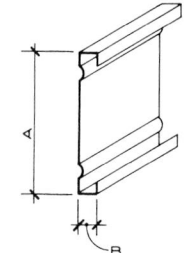

FURRING CHANNEL		"C" JOIST CLOSURE		NESTABLE JOIST	
A	B	A	B	A	B
¾"	½"	5½"	1¼"	7¼"	1¾"
1½"	17/32"	6"		7½"	
		7¼"		8"	
		8"		9¼"	
		9¼"		9½"	
		10"		11½"	
		12"		13½"	

Normally available in all joist sizes

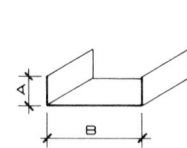 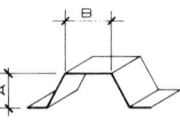 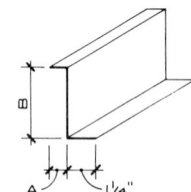

RUNNER CHANNEL		FURRING HAT CHANNEL		"Z" FURRING	
A	B	A	B	A	B
¾"	2 11/16"	⅞"	1⅜"	¾"	1"
1"	3 13/16"	1½"	1¼"		1½"
1⅜"	3 7/16"				2"
1¼"	4 3/16"				3"
1½"	6 3/16"				
1¾"	8 3/16"				
3½"					

LIGHT GAUGE FRAMING MEMBERS
MEMBERS AVAILABLE IN 14, 16, 18, 20 & 22 GAUGE MATERIAL

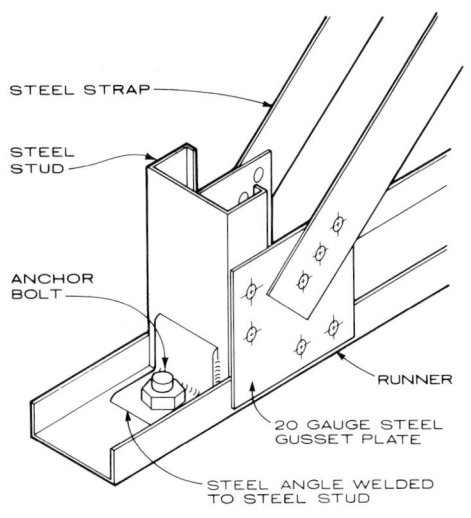

DIAGONAL STEEL STRAPPING

DIAGONAL STEEL STRAPPING

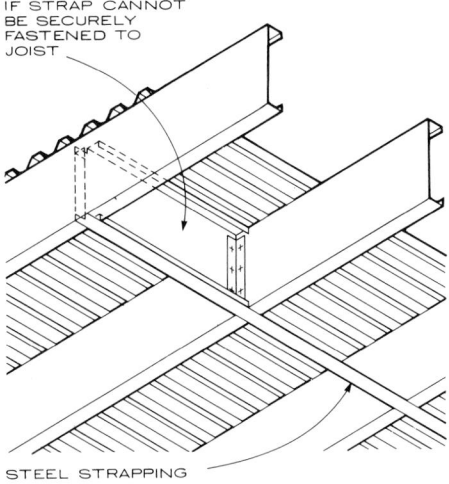

JOIST BRACING

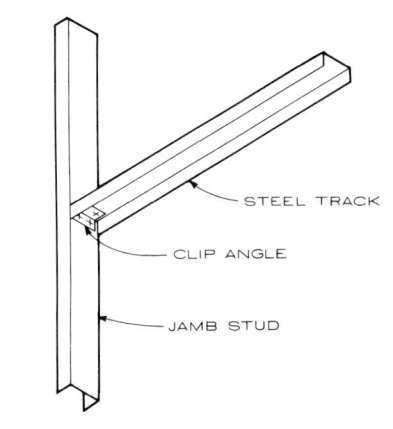

SILL ATTACHMENT

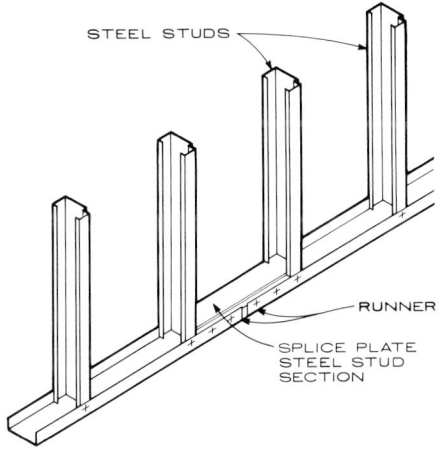

RUNNER SPLICE

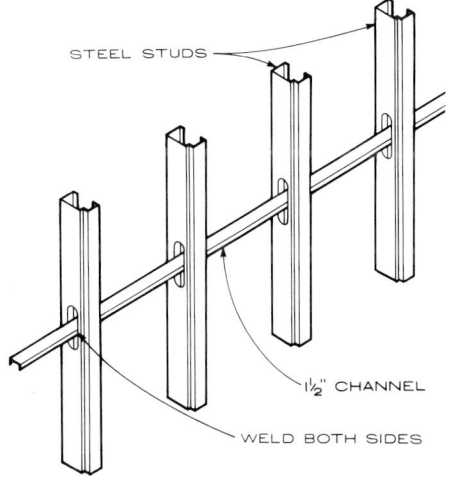

HORIZONTAL BRACING

LIMITING HEIGHT TABLES FOR INTERIOR PARTITIONS AND CHASE WALL PARTITIONS

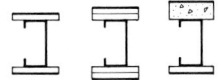

LIMITING HEIGHTS 25 GAUGE STEEL STUD ASSEMBLIES

STUD WIDTH	STUD SPACING	ALLOW. DEFL.	PARTITION ONE LAYER	PARTITION TWO LAYERS	FURRING ONE LAYER
1 5/8"	16"	1/120	10'9"f	10'9"d	10'3"d
		1/240	9'6"d	10'6"d	8'3"d
	24"	1/120	8'9"f	8'9"f	8'9"f
		1/240	8'3"d	8'9"f	7'3"d
2 1/2"	16"	1/120	14'3"f	14'3"f	14'0"d
		1/240	12'6"d	13'6"d	11'0"d
	24"	1/120	11'6"f	11'6"f	11'6"f
		1/240	10'9"f	11'6"f	9'9"d
3 5/8"	16"	1/120	18'3"f	18'3"f	18'3"f
		1/240	16'0"d	17'0"d	14'6"d
	24"	1/120	15'0"f	15'0"f	15'0"f
		1/240	14'0"d	14'9"d	12'9"d
4"	16"	1/120	19'6"f	19'6"f	19'6"f
		1/240	17'3"d	18'3"d	15'9"d
	24"	1/120	16'0"f	16'0"f	16'0"f
		1/240	15'0"d	15'9"d	13'9"d
6"	16"	1/120	26'0"f	26'0"f	26'0"f
		1/240	23'0"d	24'0"d	21'6"d
	24"	1/120	21'3"f	21'3"f	21'3"f
		1/240	20'3"d	21'0"d	18'9"d

20 GAUGE STEEL STUDS ASSEMBLIES

STUD WIDTH	STUD SPACING	ALLOW. DEFL.	PARTITION ONE LAYER	PARTITION TWO LAYERS	FURRING ONE LAYER
2 1/2"	16"	1/120	17'9"f	18'6"d	16'6"d
		1/240	14'0"d	14'9"d	13'0"d
	24"	1/120	15'6"d	16'3"f	14'6"d
		1/240	12'3"d	13'0"d	11'6"d
3 5/8"	16"	1/120	23'0"d	24'0"d	21'9"d
		1/240	18'3"d	19'0"d	17'3"d
	24"	1/120	20'0"d	20'9"f	19'0"d
		1/240	16'0"d	16'6"d	15'0"d
4"	16"	1/120	24'9"d	25'9"d	23'6"d
		1/240	19'6"d	20'3"d	18'9"d
	24"	1/120	21'6"d	22'0"f	20'6"d
		1/240	17'3"d	17'9"d	16'3"d
6"	16"	1/120	33'6"d	34'6"d	32'3"d
		1/240	26'6"d	27'6"d	25'6"d
	24"	1/120	29'3"d	29'6"f	28'0"d
		1/240	23'3"d	24'0"d	22'3"d

LIMITING HEIGHT 25 GAUGE CHASE WALL PARTITIONS

STUD WIDTH	STUD SPACING	ALLOW. DEFL.	PARTITION ONE LAYER	PARTITION TWO LAYERS	FURRING ONE LAYER
1 5/8"	16"	1/120	15'3"f	15'3"f	
		1/240	13'3"d	14'6"d	
	24"	1/120	12'6"f	12'6"f	
		1/240	11'6"d	12'6"f	
2 1/2"	16"	1/120	20'3"f	20'3"f	
		1/240	17'6"d	19'0"d	
	24"	1/120	16'6"f	16'6"f	
		1/240	15'6"d	16'6"f	
3 5/8"	16"	1/120	25'9"f	25'9"f	
		1/240	22'9"d	24'3"d	
	24"	1/120	21'0"d	21'0"f	
		1/240	19'9"d	21'0"f	
2 1/2"*	16"	1/120	24'3"d	25'9"d	
		1/240	19'3"d	20'6"d	
	24"	1/120	21'3"d	22'6"d	
		1/240	17'0"d	18'0"d	

NOTE

1. Limiting height for 1/2 in. or 5/8 in. thick panels and 5 psf uniform load perpendicular to partition or furring. Use one-layer heights for unbalanced assemblies. Limiting criteria: d-deflection, f-bending stress. Consult local code authority for limiting criteria.

* 20 Gauge chase wall partitions

Timothy B. McDonald; Washington, D.C.

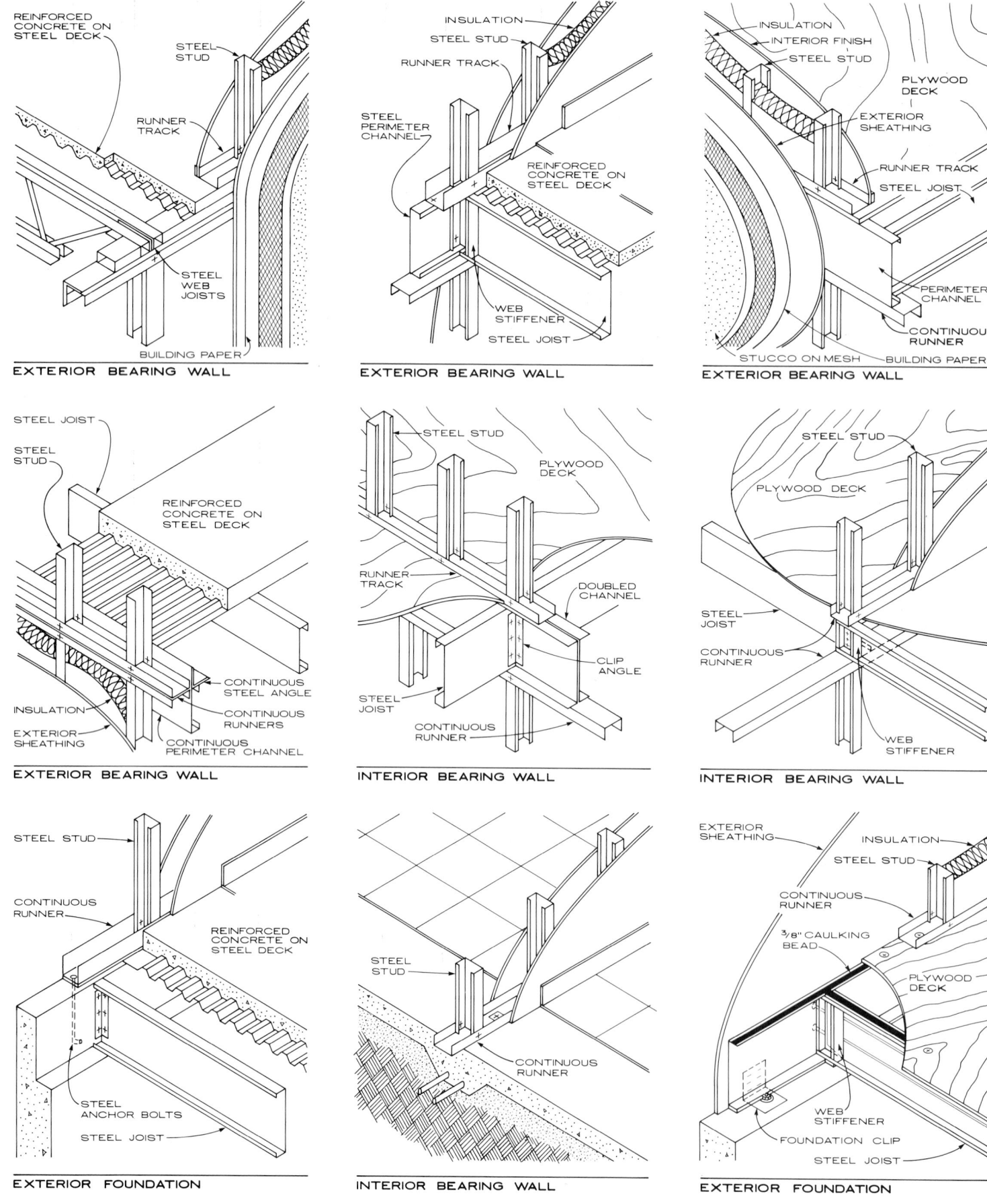

REINFORCED CONCRETE ON STEEL DECK
STEEL STUD
RUNNER TRACK
STEEL WEB JOISTS
BUILDING PAPER

EXTERIOR BEARING WALL

INSULATION
STEEL STUD
RUNNER TRACK
STEEL PERIMETER CHANNEL
REINFORCED CONCRETE ON STEEL DECK
WEB STIFFENER
STEEL JOIST

EXTERIOR BEARING WALL

INSULATION
INTERIOR FINISH
STEEL STUD
PLYWOOD DECK
EXTERIOR SHEATHING
RUNNER TRACK
STEEL JOIST
PERIMETER CHANNEL
CONTINUOUS RUNNER
STUCCO ON MESH
BUILDING PAPER

EXTERIOR BEARING WALL

STEEL JOIST
STEEL STUD
REINFORCED CONCRETE ON STEEL DECK
CONTINUOUS STEEL ANGLE
CONTINUOUS RUNNERS
INSULATION
EXTERIOR SHEATHING
CONTINUOUS PERIMETER CHANNEL

EXTERIOR BEARING WALL

STEEL STUD
PLYWOOD DECK
RUNNER TRACK
DOUBLED CHANNEL
CLIP ANGLE
STEEL JOIST
CONTINUOUS RUNNER

INTERIOR BEARING WALL

STEEL STUD
PLYWOOD DECK
STEEL JOIST
CONTINUOUS RUNNER
WEB STIFFENER

INTERIOR BEARING WALL

STEEL STUD
CONTINUOUS RUNNER
REINFORCED CONCRETE ON STEEL DECK
STEEL ANCHOR BOLTS
STEEL JOIST

EXTERIOR FOUNDATION

STEEL STUD
CONTINUOUS RUNNER

INTERIOR BEARING WALL

EXTERIOR SHEATHING
INSULATION
STEEL STUD
CONTINUOUS RUNNER
3/8" CAULKING BEAD
PLYWOOD DECK
WEB STIFFENER
FOUNDATION CLIP
STEEL JOIST

EXTERIOR FOUNDATION

Timothy B. McDonald; Washington, D.C.

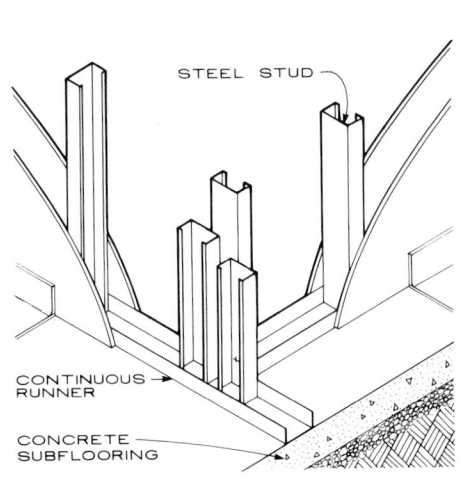

PARTITION INTERSECTION

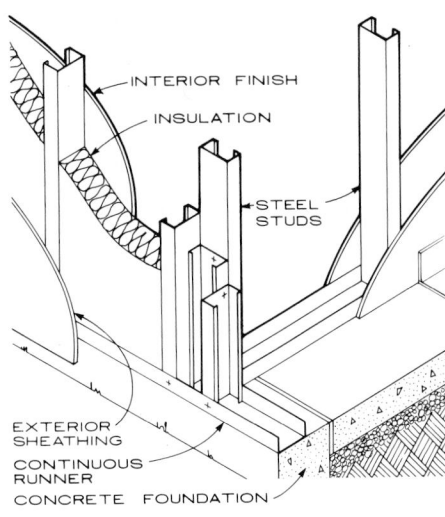

PARTITION/EXTERIOR WALL

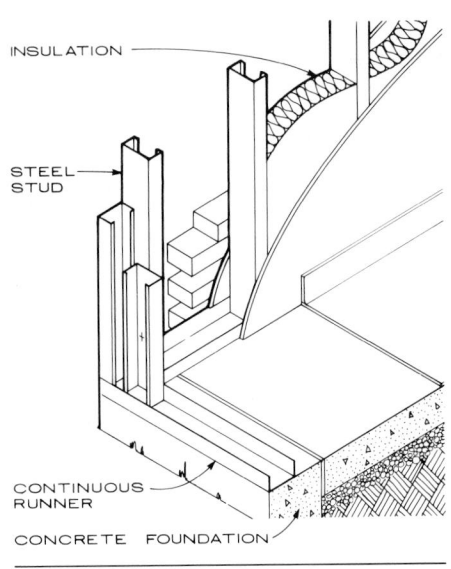

EXTERIOR CORNER

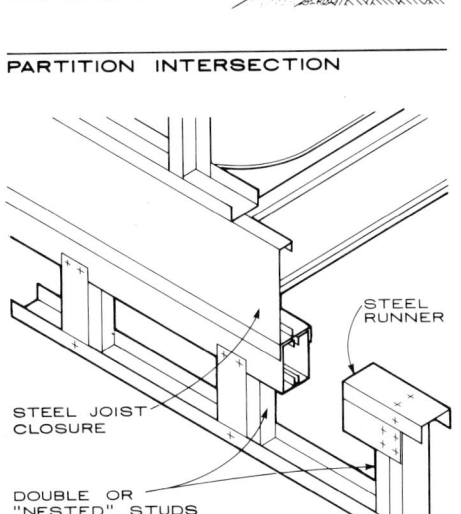

TWO MEMBER LINTEL

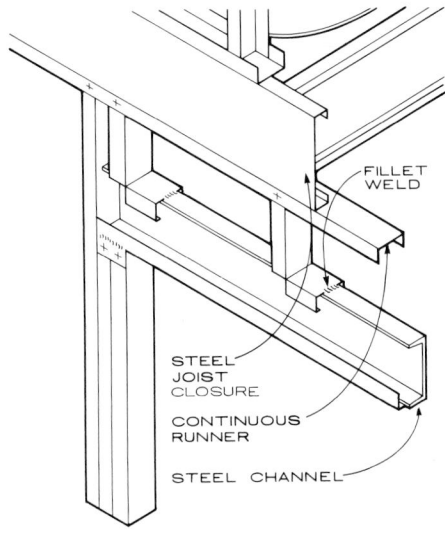

LONG SPAN LINTEL

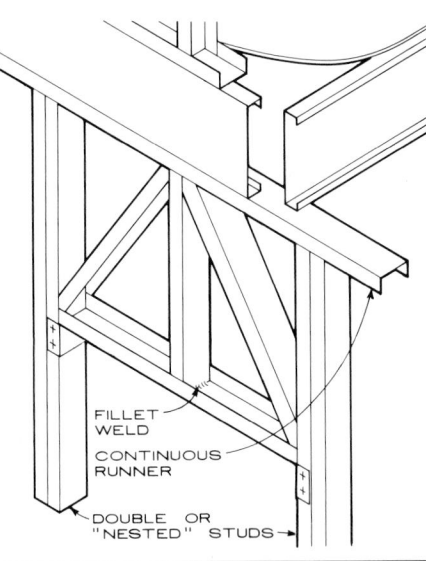

TRUSSED HEADER

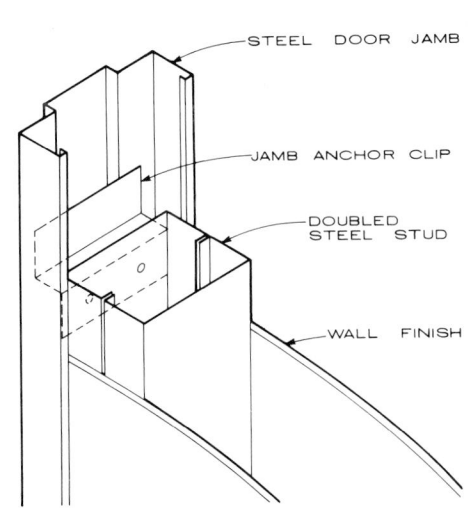

STUD-TO-DOOR BUCK

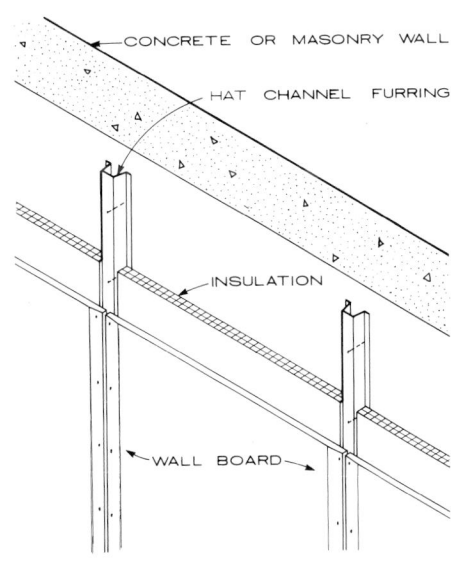

FURRING

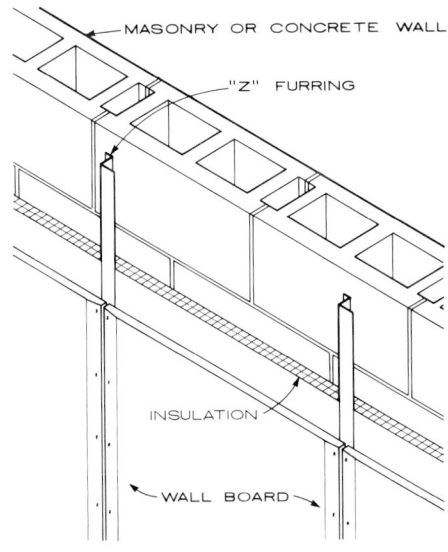

FURRING

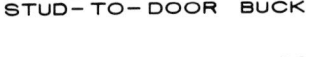
Timothy B. McDonald; Washington, D.C.

NOTE
The following tables show sizes and shapes usually stocked or readily available. Manufacturers' data should be checked for availability of sizes other than those in these tables. Where necessary, and where extra cost is warranted, other sections may be produced by welding, cutting, or other methods.

STEEL CHANNEL

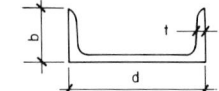

STEEL CHANNELS—BAR SIZE (IN.)

d x b x t	d x b x t	d x b x t
3/4 x 5/16 x 1/8	1 1/4 x 1/2 x 1/8	2 x 9/16 x 3/16
3/4 x 3/8 x 1/8	1 1/2 x 1/2 x 1/8	2 x 5/8 x 1/4
7/8 x 3/8 x 1/8	1 1/2 x 9/16 x 3/16	2 x 1 x 1/8
7/8 x 7/16 x 1/8	1 1/2 x 3/4 x 1/8	2 x 1 x 3/16
1 x 3/8 x 1/8	1 1/2 x 1 1/2 x 3/16	2 1/2 x 5/8 x 3/16
1 x 1/2 x 1/8	1 3/4 x 1/2 x 3/16	
1 1/8 x 9/16 x 3/16	2 x 1/2 x 1/8	

NOTE: For structural channel sizes (d = 3 in. and larger) see Dimensions of Channel Shapes in this chapter.

STEEL TEES

STEEL TEES—BAR SIZE (IN.)

b x d x t	b x d x t	b x d x t
3/4 x 3/4 x 1/8	1 1/2 x 1 1/2 x 3/16	2 x 2 x 5/16
1 x 1 x 1/8	1 1/2 x 1 1/2 x 1/4	2 1/4 x 2 1/4 x 1/4
1 x 1 x 3/16	1 3/4 x 1 3/4 x 3/16	2 1/2 x 2 1/4 x 1/4
1 1/4 x 1 1/4 x 1/8	1 3/4 x 1 3/4 x 1/4	2 1/2 x 2 1/2 x 5/16
1 1/4 x 1 1/4 x 3/16	2 x 1 1/2 x 1/4	2 1/2 x 2 1/2 x 3/8
1 1/4 x 1 1/4 x 1/4	2 x 2 x 1/4	

STRUCTURAL

3 x 2 1/2 x 5/16	3 x 3 x 3/8	4 x 4 x 1/2
3 x 3 x 5/16	4 x 3 x 3/8	5 x 3 1/8 x 1/2

ALUMINUM ANGLE STRUCTURAL

ALUMINUM ANGLES—STRUCTURAL—EQUAL LEGS (IN.)

SIZE x t	SIZE x t	SIZE x t
3/4 x 3/4 x 1/8, 1/16	2 x 2 x 3/16, 1/8	3 1/2 x 3 1/2 x 1/4
1 x 1 x 1/8, 1/16,	2 x 2 x 1/4	3 1/2 x 3 1/2 x 3/8
1 x 1 x 3/16	2 x 2 x 5/16	3 1/2 x 3 1/2 x 1/2
1 x 1 x 1/4	2 x 2 x 3/8	4 x 4 x 1/4
1 1/4 x 1 1/4 x 1/8	2 1/2 x 2 1/2 x 1/8	4 x 4 x 5/16
1 1/4 x 1 1/4 x 3/16	2 1/2 x 2 1/2 x 3/16	4 x 4 x 3/8
1 1/4 x 1 1/4 x 1/4	2 1/2 x 2 1/2 x 1/4	4 x 4 x 1/2
1 1/2 x 1 1/2 x 1/8	2 1/2 x 2 1/2 x 5/16	4 x 4 x 3/4
1 1/2 x 1 1/2 x 3/16	2 1/2 x 2 1/2 x 3/8	5 x 5 x 3/8
1 1/2 x 1 1/2 x 1/4	3 x 3 x 3/16	5 x 5 x 1/2
1 3/4 x 1 3/4 x 1/8	3 x 3 x 1/4	6 x 6 x 3/8
1 3/4 x 1 3/4 x 3/16	3 x 3 x 5/16	6 x 6 x 1/2
1 3/4 x 1 3/4 x 1/4	3 x 3 x 3/8	8 x 8 x 1/2
2 x 2 x 1/8	3 x 3 x 1/2	

UNEQUAL LEGS (IN.)

1 1/2 x 1 1/4 x 1/8	2 1/2 x 2 x 5/16	4 x 3 x 1/2
1 1/2 x 1 1/4 x 3/16	2 1/2 x 2 x 3/8	5 x 3 x 3/8
1 1/2 x 1 1/4 x 1/4	3 x 2 x 3/16	5 x 3 x 1/2
1 3/4 x 1 1/4 x 1/8	3 x 2 x 1/4	5 x 3 1/2 x 5/16
1 3/4 x 1 1/4 x 3/16	3 x 2 x 3/8	5 x 3 1/2 x 3/8
1 3/4 x 1 1/4 x 1/4	3 x 2 1/2 x 1/4	5 x 3 1/2 x 1/2
2 x 1 1/2 x 1/8	3 x 2 1/2 x 3/8	6 x 3 1/2 x 5/16
2 x 1 1/2 x 3/16	3 1/2 x 2 1/2 x 1/4	6 x 3 1/2 x 1/2
2 x 1 1/2 x 1/4	3 1/2 x 2 1/2 x 3/8	6 x 4 x 3/8
2 1/2 x 1 1/2 x 1/4	3 1/2 x 3 x 1/4	6 x 4 x 1/2
2 1/2 x 2 x 3/16	4 x 3 x 1/4	6 x 4 x 5/8
2 1/2 x 2 x 1/4	4 x 3 x 3/8	8 x 6 x 3/4

STEEL ANGLES UNEQUAL LEGS

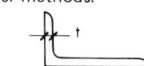

STEEL ANGLES—UNEQUAL LEGS—BAR SIZE (IN.)

SIZE x t	SIZE x t	SIZE x t
1 x 5/8 x 1/8	1 3/4 x 1 1/4 x 1/4	2 1/2 x 1 1/2 x 3/16
1 x 3/4 x 1/8	2 x 1 1/4 x 3/16	2 1/2 x 1 1/2 x 1/4
1 3/8 x 7/8 x 1/8	2 x 1 1/4 x 1/4, 3/16	2 1/2 x 1 1/2 x 5/16
1 3/8 x 7/8 x 3/16	2 x 1 1/2 x 1/8	2 1/2 x 2 x 3/16
1 1/2 x 1 1/4 x 3/16	2 x 1 1/2 x 3/16	2 1/2 x 2 x 1/4
1 3/4 x 1 1/4 x 1/8	2 x 1 1/2 x 1/4	2 1/2 x 2 x 5/16
1 3/4 x 1 1/4 x 3/16	2 1/4 x 1 1/2 x 3/16	2 1/2 x 2 x 3/8

NOTE: For structural angle sizes (3 x 2 x 3/16 in. and larger) see Dimensions of Angle Shapes in this chapter.

STEEL ZEES

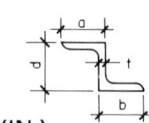

STEEL ZEES—BAR SIZE (IN.)

d x a x b x t	d x a x b x t
1 x 1/2 x 5/8 x 1/8	1 3/8 x 3/4 x 13/16 x 1/8
1 3/16 x 5/8 x 3/4 x 1/8	1 3/4 x 1 1/4 x 3/4 x 3/16

STRUCTURAL

3 x 2 11/16 x 2 11/16 x 1/4	4 1/8 x 3 3/16 x 3 3/16 x 3/8
3 x 2 11/16 x 2 11/16 x 3/8	5 x 3 1/4 x 3 1/4 x 5/16
3 x 2 11/16 x 2 11/16 x 1/2	5 x 3 1/4 x 3 1/4 x 1/2
4 x 3 1/16 x 3 1/16 x 1/4	5 1/16 x 3 5/16 x 3 5/16 x 3/8
4 1/16 x 3 1/8 x 3 1/8 x 5/16	6 x 3 1/2 x 3 1/2 x 3/8

ALUMINUM ANGLE SQUARE CORNERS

ALUMINUM ANGLES—SQUARE CORNERS—EQUAL LEGS (IN.)

SIZE x t	SIZE x t	SIZE x t
1/2 x 1/2 x 1/16	1 1/4 x 1 1/4 x 1/4	2 1/2 x 2 1/2 x 3/16, 1/4
1/2 x 1/2 x 1/8	1 1/2 x 1 1/2 x 1/8	3 x 3 x 1/8
5/8 x 5/8 x 1/8	1 1/2 x 1 1/2 x 3/16	3 x 3 x 3/16, 1/4
3/4 x 3/4 x 1/16, 1/8	1 1/2 x 1 1/2 x 1/4	3 x 3 x 5/16, 3/8, 1/2
1 x 1 x 1/8	1 3/4 x 1 3/4 x 3/16, 1/4	3 1/2 x 3 1/2 x 1/4
1 x 1 x 3/16	2 x 2 x 1/8	3 1/2 x 3 1/2 x 3/8
1 x 1 x 1/4	2 x 2 x 3/16, 1/8	3 1/2 x 3 1/2 x 1/2
1 1/8 x 1 1/8 x 3/16	2 x 2 x 1/4, 5/16, 3/8	4 x 4 x 1/4, 3/8, 1/2
1 1/4 x 1 1/4 x 1/8	2 1/2 x 2 1/2 x 1/8	6 x 6 x 3/8, 1/2

UNEQUAL LEGS (IN.)

SIZE x t	SIZE x t	SIZE x t
3/4 x 3/8 x 3/32	2 x 3/4 x 1/8	3 1/2 x 2 x 1/8
1 x 1/2 x 1/8	2 x 1 x 1/8	3 1/2 x 2 1/2 x 1/8
1 x 3/4 x 1/8	2 x 1 x 3/16	3 1/2 x 3 x 1/8
1 1/4 x 1/2 x 1/8	2 x 1 1/2 x 1/8	4 x 2 x 1/8
1 1/2 x 1/2 x 1/8	2 1/2 x 1 x 1/8	4 x 3 x 1/8
1 1/2 x 3/4 x 1/8	2 1/2 x 1 1/2 x 1/8	5 x 3 x 1/8
1 1/2 x 1 x 1/8	2 1/2 x 2 x 1/8	5 x 4 x 1/8
1 3/4 x 1 x 1/8	3 x 1 x 1/8	5 1/4 x 2 1/4 x 1/8
1 3/4 x 1 1/2 x 1/8	3 x 2 x 1/8	
2 x 1/2 x 1/8	3 1/2 x 1 1/4 x 1/8	

ALUMINUM ZEES SQUARE CORNERS

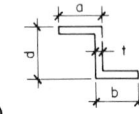

ALUMINUM ZEES—SQUARE CORNERS (IN.)

d x a x b x t	d x a x b x t
1/2 x 1/2 x 1/2 x 3/32	1 x 1 1/8 x 1 1/8 x 1/8
3/4 x 3/4 x 3/4 x 1/8	1 x 5/8 x 7/8 x 1/8
7/8 x 3/4 x 3/4 x 1/8	

STEEL ANGLES EQUAL LEGS

STEEL ANGLES—EQUAL LEGS—BAR SIZE (IN.)

SIZE x t	SIZE x t	SIZE x t
1/2 x 1/2 x 1/8	1 1/4 x 1 1/4 x 3/16	2 x 2 x 3/16
5/8 x 5/8 x 1/8	1 1/4 x 1 1/4 x 1/4	2 x 2 x 1/4
3/4 x 3/4 x 1/8	1 1/2 x 1 1/2 x 1/8	2 x 2 x 5/16
7/8 x 7/8 x 1/8	1 1/2 x 1 1/2 x 3/16	2 x 2 x 3/8
1 x 1 x 1/8	1 1/2 x 1 1/2 x 3/8	2 1/2 x 2 1/2 x 3/16
1 x 1 x 3/16	1 3/4 x 1 3/4 x 1/8	2 1/2 x 2 1/2 x 1/4
1 x 1 x 1/4	1 3/4 x 1 3/4 x 3/16	2 1/2 x 2 1/2 x 5/16
1 1/8 x 1 1/8 x 1/8	1 3/4 x 1 3/4 x 1/4	2 1/2 x 2 1/2 x 3/8
1 1/4 x 1 1/4 x 1/8	2 x 2 x 1/8	2 1/2 x 2 1/2 x 1/2

NOTE: For structural angle sizes (3 x 3 x 3/16 in. and larger) see Dimensions of Angle Shapes in this chapter.

ALUMINUM CHANNEL SQUARE CORNERS

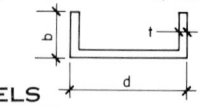

ALUMINUM CHANNELS—SQUARE CORNERS (IN.)

d x b x t	d x b x t	d x b x t
3/8 x 3/8 x 7/64	1 1/4 x 3/4 x 1/8	2 1/2 x 3/4 x 1/8
1/2 x 3/8 x 1/8	1 1/4 x 1 1/4 x 1/8	2 1/2 x 1 1/2 x 1/8
1/2 x 1/2 x 3/32	1 1/2 x 1/2 x 1/8	2 1/2 x 2 1/2 x 1/8
1/2 x 1/2 x 1/8	1 1/2 x 5/8 x 1/8	3 x 1/2 x 1/8
5/8 x 5/8 x 1/8	1 1/2 x 3/4 x 1/8	3 x 1 x 1/8
5/8 x 1 x 1/8	1 1/2 x 1 x 1/8	3 x 2 x 1/8
3/4 x 3/8 x 1/8	1 1/2 x 1 1/2 x 1/8	3 x 3 x 1/8
3/4 x 1/2 x 1/8	1 3/4 x 1/2 x 1/8	4 x 1 1/2 x 1/8
3/4 x 3/4 x 1/8	1 3/4 x 3/4 x 1/8	4 1/2 x 2 x 1/8
1 x 1/2 x 1/8	1 3/4 x 1 x 1/8	5 x 2 x 3/16
1 x 3/4 x 1/8	2 x 1/2 x 1/8	
1 x 1 x 1/8	2 x 1 x 1/8	
1 1/4 x 1/2 x 1/8	2 x 2 x 1/8	
1 1/4 x 5/8 x 1/8	2 1/4 x 7/8 x 1/8	

NOTE: For aluminum channels in American Standard sizes and Aluminum Association Standard sizes, see Dimensions of Channel Shapes in this chapter.

ALUMINUM TEES SQUARE CORNERS

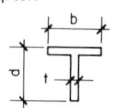

ALUMINUM TEES—SQUARE CORNERS (IN.)

b x d x t	b x d x t	b x d x t
3/4 x 3/4 x 1/8	1 1/8 x 1/2 x 3/8	2 x 3/4 x 1/8
3/4 x 1 1/4 x 1/8	1 1/8 x 1 1/8 x 1/8	2 x 2 x 3/16
1 x 3/4 x 1/8	1 1/4 x 7/8 x 1/8	
1 x 1 x 1/8	1 1/2 x 1 1/2 x 1/8	

ALUMINUM TEES SQUARE CORNERS

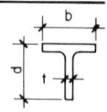

STRUCTURAL (IN.)

1 1/2 x 1 1/2 x 1/4	2 1/4 x 2 1/4 x 1/4	4 x 4 x 3/8
2 x 2 x 1/4	3 x 3 x 3/8	

STAINLESS STEEL ANGLES

STAINLESS STEEL ANGLES (IN.)

SIZE x t	SIZE x t	SIZE x t
3/4 x 3/4 x 1/8	1 1/2 x 1 1/2 x 3/16	2 1/2 x 2 1/2 x 1/4
1 x 1 x 1/8	1 1/2 x 1 1/2 x 1/4	3 x 3 x 1/4
1 x 1 x 3/16	2 x 2 x 1/8	3 x 3 x 5/16
1 1/4 x 1 1/4 x 1/8	2 x 2 x 3/16	3 x 3 x 3/8
1 1/4 x 1 1/4 x 3/16	2 x 2 x 1/4	
1 1/2 x 1 1/2 x 1/8	2 1/2 x 2 1/2 x 3/16	

HMC Group; Ontario, California

RECTANGULAR TUBING - STEEL

SIZE (IN.)	T = WALL THICKNESS (BW GAUGE OR IN.)						
1 x $^1/_2$	16						
1$^1/_2$ x $^3/_4$	14	14	11				
1$^1/_2$ x 1	16	14	11				
2 x 1	16	15	14	11			
2 x 1$^1/_4$	14						
2 x 1$^1/_2$	14	11					
2$^1/_2$ x 1	14						
2$^1/_2$ x 1$^1/_4$	14						
2$^1/_2$ x 1$^1/_2$	14	11	$^1/_8$"	$^3/_{16}$"	$^1/_4$"		
3 x 1	14	11					
3 x 1$^1/_2$	14	12	11	$^1/_8$"	$^3/_{16}$"		
3 x 2	14	11	$^1/_8$"	7	$^3/_{16}$"	$^1/_4$"	$^5/_{16}$"
4 x 2	14	11	$^1/_8$"	7	$^3/_{16}$"	$^1/_4$"	$^5/_{16}$"
4 x 2$^1/_2$	$^1/_8$"						
4 x 3	$^1/_8$"	7	$^3/_{16}$"	$^1/_4$"	$^5/_{16}$"		
5 x 2	7	$^3/_{16}$"	$^1/_4$"	$^5/_{16}$"			
5 x 2$^1/_2$	$^1/_8$"	$^3/_{16}$"					
5 x 3	7	$^3/_{16}$"	$^1/_4$"	$^5/_{16}$"	$^3/_8$"	$^1/_2$"	
6 x 2	7	$^3/_{16}$"	$^1/_4$"	$^5/_{16}$"			
6 x 3	7	$^3/_{16}$"	$^1/_4$"	$^5/_{16}$"	$^3/_8$"	$^1/_2$"	
6 x 4	7	$^3/_{16}$"	$^1/_4$"	$^5/_{16}$"	$^3/_8$"	$^1/_2$"	
7 x 3	$^3/_8$"						
7 x 4	$^3/_{16}$"	$^1/_4$"	$^3/_8$"				
7 x 5	0.135"	7	$^3/_{16}$"	$^1/_4$"	$^3/_8$"	$^1/_2$"	
8 x 2	7	$^3/_{16}$"	$^1/_4$"	$^5/_{16}$"	$^3/_8$"		
8 x 3	$^3/_{16}$"	$^1/_4$"	$^3/_8$"	$^1/_2$"			
8 x 4	7	$^3/_{16}$"	$^1/_4$"	$^5/_{16}$"	$^3/_8$"	$^1/_2$"	
8 x 6	7	$^3/_{16}$"	$^1/_4$"	$^5/_{16}$"	$^3/_8$"	$^1/_2$"	
9 x 5	$^3/_8$"						
9 x 7	$^1/_4$"	$^5/_{16}$"					
10 x 2	$^3/_{16}$"	$^1/_4$"					
10 x 4	7	$^3/_{16}$"	$^1/_4$"	$^3/_8$"	$^1/_2$"		
10 x 5	$^1/_4$"						
10 x 6	$^1/_4$"	$^5/_{16}$"	$^3/_8$"	$^1/_2$"			
10 x 8	$^1/_4$"	$^3/_8$"	$^1/_2$"				
12 x 2	$^3/_{16}$"						
12 x 4	7	$^1/_4$"	$^3/_8$"	$^1/_2$"			
12 x 6	$^1/_4$"	$^3/_8$"	$^1/_2$"				
12 x 8	$^1/_4$"	$^3/_8$"	$^1/_2$"				

ALUMINUM

SIZE	T
1 x 1$^1/_2$	0.125"
1 x 2	0.125"
1$^1/_2$ x 2	0.125"
1$^1/_2$ x 2$^1/_2$	0.125"
1$^1/_2$ x 3	0.125"
1$^3/_4$ x 2$^1/_4$	0.125"
1$^3/_4$ x 3	0.125"
1$^3/_4$ x 3$^1/_2$	0.125"
1$^3/_4$ x 4	0.125"
1$^3/_4$ x 4$^1/_2$	0.125"
1$^3/_4$ x 5	0.125"
2 x 3	0.125"
2 x 4	0.125"
2 x 5	0.125"
2 x 6	0.125"
2 x 8	0.125"

STAINLESS STEEL

SIZE			
1 x 1$^1/_2$	11		
1 x 2	11		
2 x 3	11	7	
2 x 4	11	7	$^1/_4$"

STEEL   ALUMINUM

RECTANGULAR AND SQUARE TUBING

HMC Group; Ontario, California

RECTANGULAR ALUMINUM TUBING (IN.)

SIZE x T	SIZE x T	SIZE x T
1$^1/_2$ x 1$^1/_2$ x $^1/_8$	1$^3/_4$ x 2$^1/_4$ x $^1/_8$	2 x 3 x $^1/_8$
1 x 2 x $^1/_8$	1$^3/_4$ x 3 x $^1/_8$	2 x 4 x $^1/_8$
1$^1/_2$ x 2 x $^1/_8$	1$^3/_4$ x 3$^1/_2$ x $^1/_8$	2 x 5 x $^1/_8$
1$^1/_2$ x 2$^1/_2$ x $^1/_8$	1$^3/_4$ x 4 x $^1/_8$	2 x 6 x $^1/_8$
	1$^3/_4$ x 4$^1/_2$ x $^1/_8$	3 x 5 x $^1/_8$
	1$^3/_4$ x 5 x $^1/_8$	3 x 5 x $^1/_8$

SQUARE ALUMINUM TUBING (IN.)

SIZE x T	SIZE x T	SIZE x T
$^1/_2$ x $^1/_2$ x $^1/_{16}$	1$^1/_4$ x 1$^1/_4$ x $^1/_8$	2 x 2 x $^1/_8$
$^5/_8$ x $^5/_8$ x $^1/_{16}$	1$^1/_4$ x 1$^1/_4$ x $^1/_8$	2$^1/_2$ x 2$^1/_2$ x $^1/_8$
$^3/_4$ x $^3/_4$ x $^1/_8$	1$^1/_2$ x 1$^1/_2$ x $^5/_{64}$	3 x 3 x $^1/_8$
$^3/_4$ x $^3/_4$ x $^1/_8$	1$^1/_2$ x 1$^1/_2$ x $^1/_8$	4 x 4 x $^1/_8$
1 x 1 x $^1/_{16}$	1$^3/_4$ x 1$^3/_4$ x $^1/_8$	
1 x 1 x $^1/_8$		

NOTE

Rectangular and square tubing with sharp corners is usually used for miscellaneous architectural metalwork.

ROUND TUBING - COPPER

SIZE (IN.) NOMINAL INSIDE DIA.	OUTSIDE DIA. (BW GAUGE)	INSIDE DIAMETER (BW GAUGE)			
		TYPE K	TYPE L	TYPE M	TYPE DMV
$^1/_4$	0.375	0.305	0.315		
$^1/_2$	0.625	0.527	0.545	0.569	
$^3/_4$	0.875	0.745	0.785	0.811	
1	1.125	0.995	1.025	1.055	
1$^1/_2$	1.625	1.481	1.505	1.527	1.541
2	2.125	1.959	1.985	2.009	2.041
4	4.125	3.857	3.905	3.935	4.009

NOTES

Round tubing, usually manufactured for mechanical purposes, is used for architectural metalwork to supplement round pipe. Round tubing is measured by the outside diameter and the wall thickness by gauge, fractions, or decimals of an inch. Round tubing is used where a high grade finish is required and exact diameters are necessary.

Round tubing is available in steel, aluminum, copper, stainless steel, and other metals. Individual manufacturers' catalogs should be consulted for availability of materials and sizes.

SQUARE TUBING - STEEL

SIZE (IN.)	WALL THICKNESS (BW GAUGE OR IN.)													
$^1/_2$ x $^1/_2$	20	18	0.063	16									
$^5/_8$ x $^5/_8$	20	18	16										
$^3/_4$ x $^3/_4$	20	18	0.063	16	14	11							
$^7/_8$ x $^7/_8$	18	16	14										
1 x 1	20	18	0.063	16	15	0.073	14	13	12	11			
1$^1/_8$ x 1$^1/_8$	18	16											
1$^1/_4$ x 1$^1/_4$	18	0.063	16	15	14	13	12	11	0.135	$^3/_{16}$"			
1$^1/_2$ x 1$^1/_2$	18	0.063	16	15	14	13	12	11	0.145	$^3/_{16}$"	$^1/_4$"		
1$^3/_4$ x 1$^3/_4$	16	14	11										
2 x 2	18	0.063	16	15	14	13	12	11	$^1/_8$"	10	7	$^3/_{16}$"	$^1/_4$"
2$^1/_4$ x 2$^1/_4$	16												
2$^1/_2$ x 2$^1/_2$	14	11	$^1/_8$"	10	7	$^3/_{16}$"	$^1/_4$"						
3 x 3	14	11	$^1/_8$"	7	$^3/_{16}$"	$^1/_4$"	$^5/_{16}$"	$^3/_8$"					
3$^1/_2$ x 3$^1/_2$	$^1/_8$"	7	$^3/_{16}$"	$^1/_4$"	$^5/_{16}$"								
4 x 4	11	$^1/_8$"	7	$^3/_{16}$"	$^1/_4$"	$^5/_{16}$"	$^3/_8$"	$^1/_2$"					
4$^1/_2$ x 4$^1/_2$	$^3/_{16}$"	$^1/_4$"											
5 x 5	$^1/_8$"	7	$^3/_{16}$"	$^1/_4$"	$^5/_{16}$"	$^3/_8$"	$^1/_2$"						
6 x 6	7	$^3/_{16}$"	$^1/_4$"	$^5/_{16}$"	$^3/_8$"	$^1/_2$"							
7 x 7	$^3/_{16}$"	$^1/_4$"	$^3/_8$"	$^1/_2$"									
8 x 8	7	$^3/_{16}$"	$^1/_4$"	$^5/_{16}$"	$^3/_8$"	$^1/_2$"	$^5/_8$"						
10 x 10	$^1/_4$"	$^5/_{16}$"	$^3/_8$"	$^1/_2$"	$^5/_8$"								
12 x 12	$^1/_4$"	$^3/_8$"	$^1/_2$"										
14 x 14	$^1/_2$"												
16 x 16	$^1/_2$"												

SIZE (IN.)	WALL THICKNESS (BW GAUGE OR IN.)				
	Aluminum (in.)				
$^3/_4$ x $^3/_4$	0.125				
1 x 1	0.125				
1$^1/_4$ x 1$^1/_4$	0.125				
1$^1/_2$ x 1$^1/_2$	0.125				
1$^3/_4$ x 1$^3/_4$	0.125				
2 x 2	0.125	0.250			
2$^1/_2$ x 2$^1/_2$	0.125				
3 x 3	0.125	0.250			
4 x 49	0.250				
	Stainless Steel				
1 x 1	18	16	11		
1$^1/_4$ x 1$^1/_4$	16	14	11		
1$^1/_2$ x 1$^1/_2$	16	14	11		
2 x 2	16	14	11	7	$^1/_4$"
2$^1/_2$ x 2$^1/_2$	11				
3 x 3	11	14	7	$^1/_4$"	
4 x 4	11	7	$^1/_4$"		

ROUND PIPE - STEEL

SIZE (IN.) NOMINAL INSIDE DIA.	OUTSIDE DIA. (BW GAUGE)	INSIDE DIAMETER (BW GAUGE)		
		STD.	EXTRA STRONG	DOUBLE EXTRA STRONG
$^1/_8$	0.405	0.269	0.215	
$^1/_4$	0.540	0.364	0.302	
$^3/_8$	0.675	0.493	0.423	
$^1/_2$	0.840	0.622	0.546	
$^3/_4$	1.050	0.824	0.742	
1	1.315	1.049	0.957	
1$^1/_4$	1.660	1.380	1.278	
1$^1/_2$	1.900	1.610	1.500	
2	2.375	2.067	1.939	1.503
2$^1/_2$	2.875	2.469	2.323	1.771
3	3.500	3.068	2.900	2.300
3$^1/_2$	4.000	3.548	3.364	
4	4.500	4.026	3.826	3.152
5	5.563	5.047	4.813	4.063
6	6.625	6.065	5.761	4.897
8	8.625	7.981	7.625	6.875
10	10.750	10.020	9.750	
12	12.750	12.000	11.750	

NOTE

Round pipe is made primarily in three weights: standard, extra strong (or extra heavy), and double extra strong (or double extra heavy). Outside diameters of the three weights of pipe in each size are always the same: extra wall thickness is always on the inside and therefore reduces the inside diameter of the heavier pipe. All sizes are specified by what is known as the "nominal inside diameter."

Round pipe is also available in aluminum and stainless steel. Individual manufacturers' catalogs should be consulted for sizes.

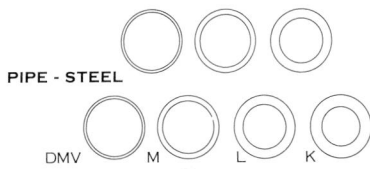

PIPE - STEEL

DMV   M   L   K

TUBING - COPPER

ROUND TUBING AND PIPE

GENERAL

Lally columns are prefabricated structural units that consist of a load-bearing steel column, filled with concrete. This creates a column with increased load-bearing capacity in a space no larger than a standard column. Fireproof lally columns have a thin steel shell and a layer of insulating material between the shell and the structural steel. Fire ratings range from two to four hours depending on the thickness of the insulating material. The protective steel shell allows fireproof lally columns to be left exposed in either interior or exterior applications.

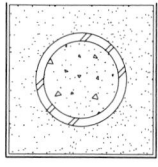
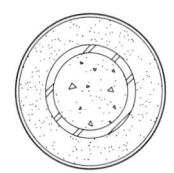
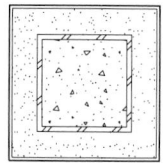
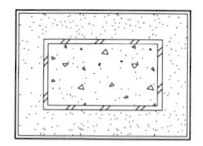

TYPICAL LALLY COLUMN SHAPES

CONCRETE FILLED STEEL TUBING

| OUTER DIMENSION OF TUBING | WALL THICK-NESS | WEIGHT PER FT | ALLOWABLE SAFE LOADS IN KIPS EFFECTIVE LENGTH IN FEET KL WITH RESPECT TO RADIUS OF GYRATION | | | | | | | | | | U.L. RATED/ FIRE-PROOFED COLUMN SQUARE SHELL SIZES (IN.) | | |
			6	8	10	12	14	16	18	20	22	24	2 HR.	3 HR.	4 HR.
3 x 3	$1/4$	15	62	53	40								6 x 6	7 x 7	8 x 8
3½ x 3½	$1/4$	20	77	68	55	42							6 x 6	7 x 7	8 x 8
4 x 4	$1/4$	25	98	89	78	65	51	40					6 x 6	7 x 7	8 x 8
	$3/8$	28	132	119	102	85	64								
5 x 5	$1/4$	36	137	128	118	107	94	80	64						
	$3/8$	40	185	172	158	141	124	103	82				7 x 7	8 x 8	9 x 9
	$1/3$	44	229	212	194	173	150	124							
6 x 6	$1/4$	49	178	169	160	150	138	125	110	95	79				
	$3/8$	55	241	228	215	200	183	165	145	124	101		8 x 8	9 x 9	10 x 10
	$1/2$	60	299	283	267	248	226	204	177	151					
7 x 7	$1/4$	65	221	213	204	194	183	171	158	143	128	111			
	$3/8$	72	297	285	273	259	243	227	208	189	168	146	9 x 9	10 x 10	11 x 11
	$1/2$	78	369	354	337	320	301	279	255	230	204	176			
8 x 8	$1/4$	82	266	259	251	240	231	218	206	193	178	163			
	$3/8$	90	357	346	334	321	306	291	272	254	236	215	10 x 10	11 x 11	12 x 12
	$1/2$	98	440	427	412	395	377	355	334	311	286	259			
10 x 10	$1/4$	122	364	357	349	340	330	320	308	296	282	267			
	$3/8$	132	482	471	460	448	435	419	404	388	369	350	12 x 12	13 x 13	14 x 14
	$1/2$	142	592	579	566	550	533	515	495	474	453	428			

NOTE

Load table based on F_y = 46 ksi

CONCRETE FILLED STEEL PIPE

| OUTER DIAMETER OF PIPE (IN.) | WALL THICKNESS | WEIGHT PER FT | ALLOWABLE SAFE LOADS IN KIPS EFFECTIVE LENGTH IN FEET KL WITH RESPECT TO RADIUS OF GYRATION | | | | | | | | | | | U.L.-RATED FIREPROOFED COLUMNS SQUARE SHELL SIZES (IN.) | | | ROUND SHELL SIZES (IN.) | | |
			6	8	10	12	14	16	18	20	22	24	26	2 HR.	3 HR.	4 HR.	2 HR.	3 HR.	4 HR.
3	.216	15	45	40	32									6 x 6	7 x 7	8 x 8	6 ⅝	6 ⅝	8 ⅝
	.300	17	58	49	39														
	.600	23	94	79	60														
4	.226	20	58	53	45	36								6 x 6	7 x 7	9 x 9	6 ⅝	8 ⅝	8 ⅝
	.318	22	75	66	56	46													
4 ½	.237	24	73	66	59	51	41							7 x 7	8 x 8	9 x 9	6 ⅝	8 ⅝	8 ⅝
	.337	27	93	86	76	65	52												
	.674	36	155	139	122	102													
5 ½	.258	36	106	99	92	85	75	66	54					8 x 8	9 x 9	10 x 10	8 ⅝	8 ⅝	10 ¾
	.375	39	139	130	120	110	98	84	69										
	.750	52	230	215	198	178	156	132											
6 ⅝	.280	49	144	139	132	123	114	104	93	81	68			9 x 9	10 x 10	11 x 11	8 ⅝	10 ¾	10 ¾
	.432	56	197	188	178	166	153	140	125	109									
	.864	73	327	312	293	272	249	225	198	169									
8 ⅝	.322	81	232	225	218	210	201	190	179	167	154	141	127	11 x 11	12 x 12	13 x 13	10¾	12 ¾	12 ¾
	.500	91	314	305	295	283	270	257	242	226	209	191	171						
	.875	111	475	460	444	425	404	383	359	334	307	278	248						
10 ¾	.365	123	342	336	328	320	311	300	289	277	264	251	237	13 x 13	14 x 14	15 x 15	14	14	16
	.500	133	423	415	406	394	383	370	356	342	326	309	291						
12 ¾	.375	169	442	437	429	421	412	402	391	380	368	355	341	15 x 15	16 x 16	17 x 17	16	16	18
	.500	178	534	526	517	507	496	484	470	457	442	426	409						

NOTE

Load table based on F_y = 46 ksi

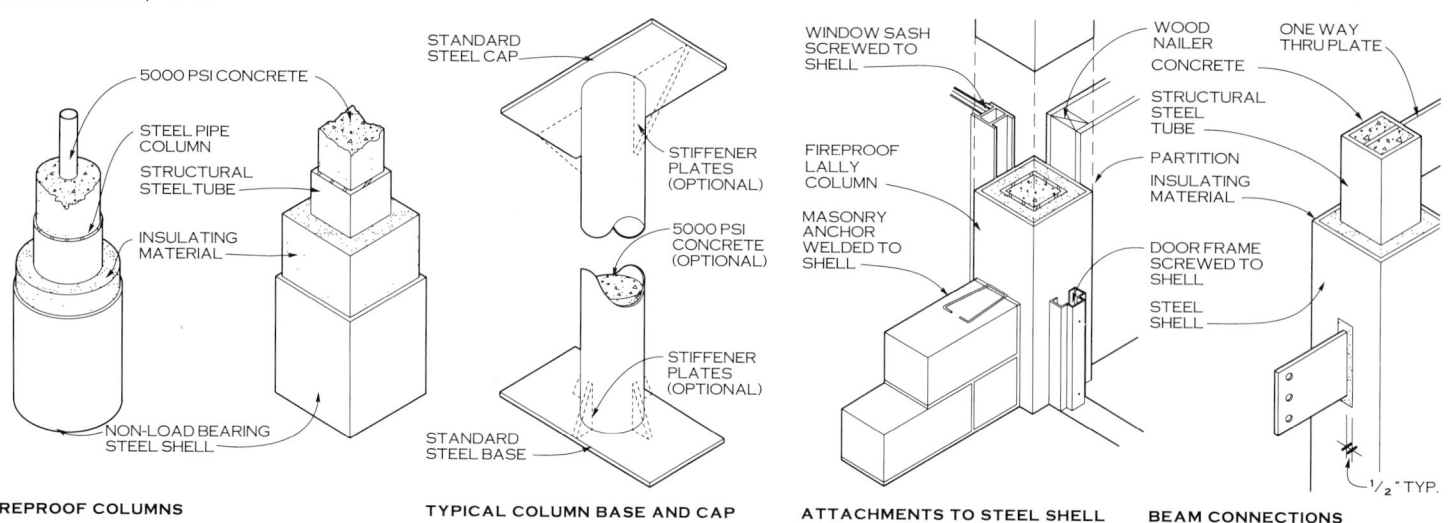

FIREPROOF COLUMNS — 5000 PSI CONCRETE; STEEL PIPE COLUMN; STRUCTURAL STEEL TUBE; INSULATING MATERIAL; NON-LOAD BEARING STEEL SHELL

TYPICAL COLUMN BASE AND CAP — STANDARD STEEL CAP; STIFFENER PLATES (OPTIONAL); 5000 PSI CONCRETE (OPTIONAL); STIFFENER PLATES (OPTIONAL); STANDARD STEEL BASE

ATTACHMENTS TO STEEL SHELL — WINDOW SASH SCREWED TO SHELL; FIREPROOF LALLY COLUMN; MASONRY ANCHOR WELDED TO SHELL; WOOD NAILER; CONCRETE; PARTITION; INSULATING MATERIAL; DOOR FRAME SCREWED TO SHELL; STEEL SHELL

BEAM CONNECTIONS — ONE WAY THRU PLATE; STRUCTURAL STEEL TUBE; ½" TYP.

TYPICAL LALLY COLUMN ASSEMBLIES

Eric Gastier; Alexandria, Virginia

METAL FABRICATIONS

GUIDELINES

1. Width of stair:
   a. Dwelling stairs: minimum 36 in. treads
   b. Public exit stairs: minimum 44 in. treads
   c. Rescue assistance area (ADA): 48 in. between hand-rails.
2. Treads:
   a. Minimum 11 in. nosing to nosing
   b. Uniform width within one flight.
3. Risers:
   a. Minimum 4 in.; maximum 7 in.
   b. Uniform height within one flight.
4. Nosing: maximum $1 \frac{1}{2}$ in. with 60° under nosing; maximum $\frac{1}{2}$ in. radius at edge.
5. Stair rails:
   a. Height in dwellings: 36 in.
   b. Height in exit stairs: 42 in.
   c. The various members of the railing system shall be arranged so that a sphere 4 in. in diameter cannot be passed through (some building codes allow greater spacing).

d. The members should be arranged to discourage climbing.
e. Concentrated load nonconcurrently applied at the top rail shall be 200 lbf in horizontal and vertical downward direction. The test loads are applicable for railings with supports not more the 8 ft apart.
5. Handrails:
   a. Required on both sides for ADA.
   b. Height: 34 to 38 in.
   c. Grip surface: $1 \frac{1}{4}$ to $1 \frac{1}{2}$ in.
   d. Clearance at wall: $1 \frac{1}{2}$ in.
   e. Projecting or recessed
   f. Extension at top of run: 12 in.
   g. Extension at bottom of run: 12 in. plus width of tread.
   h. When a guardrail of more than 38 in. height is used, a separate handrail shall be installed (ASTM).
   i. Nothing should interrupt the continuous sliding of hands.
6. Regulators and standards: building codes, ADA, ASTM, ANSI, and OSHA

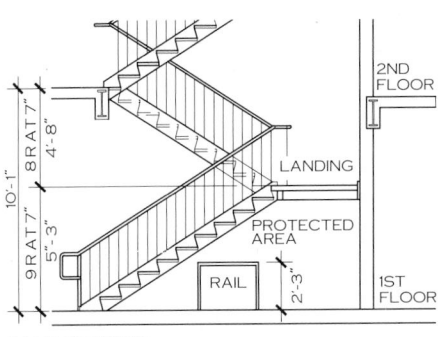

STAIR SECTION

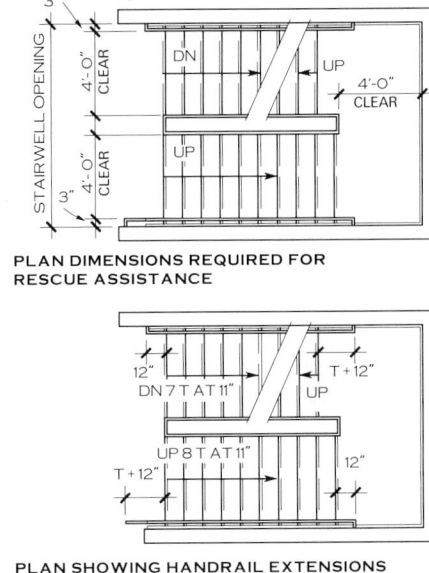

PLAN DIMENSIONS REQUIRED FOR RESCUE ASSISTANCE

PLAN SHOWING HANDRAIL EXTENSIONS

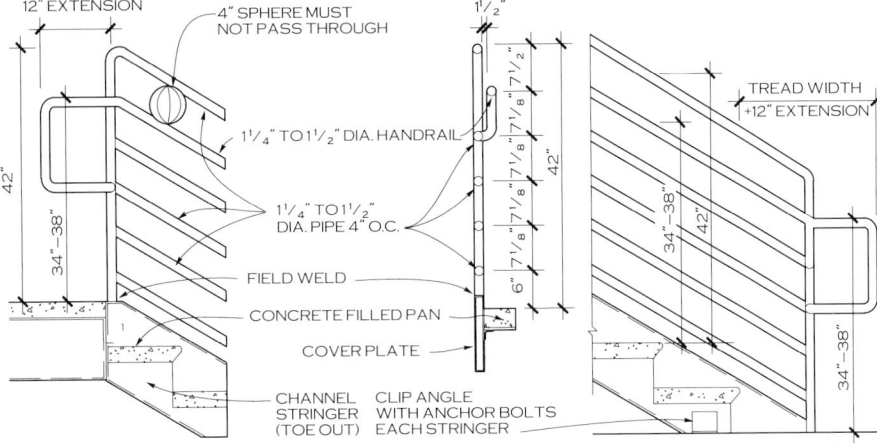

STEEL STAIR RAILS

NOSING OF CLOSELY SPACED BARS, ANGLE ENDS

CHECKER PLATE NOSING, BAR END PLATES

NOSING OF ANGLE AND ABRASIVE STRIP AND BAR ENDS

FLOOR PLATE NOSING, BAR END PLATES

HEAVY FRONT AND BACK BEARING BARS AND BAR END PLATES

PLATE TYPE

TREADS

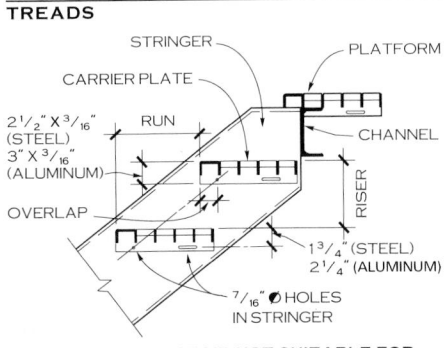

STAIR NOT SUITABLE FOR PERSONS WITH DISABILITIES

INDUSTRIAL AND SERVICE STAIRS

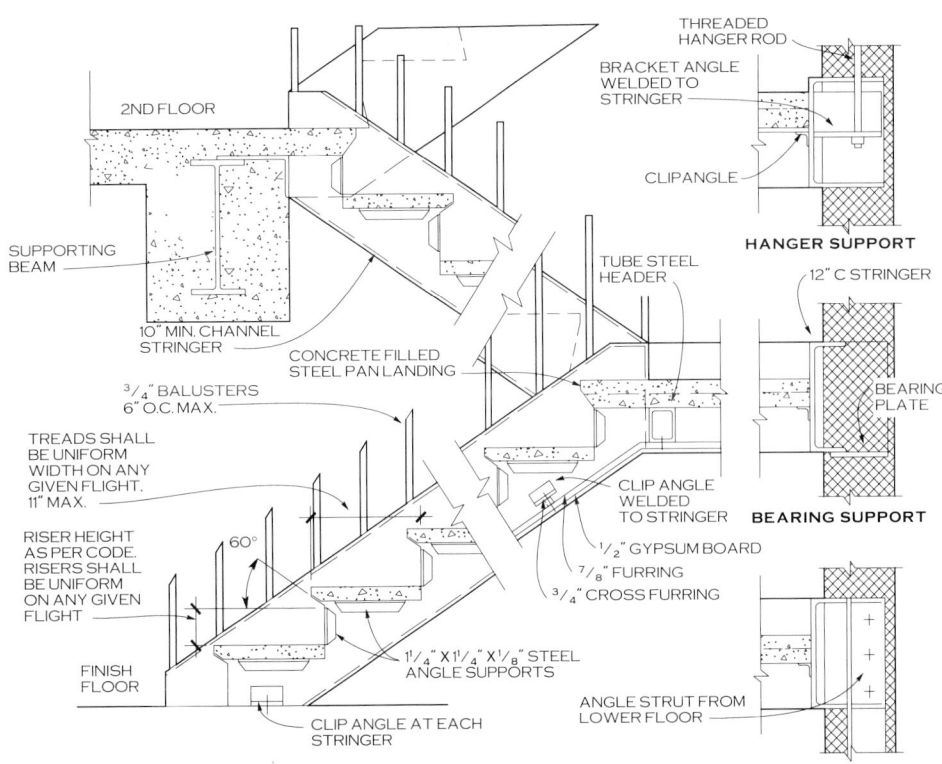

PAN TYPE STAIR CONSTRUCTION

John D. Harvey, AIA; Wheatley Associates; Charlotte, North Carolina
Charles A. Szoradi, AIA, Architect; Washington, D.C.

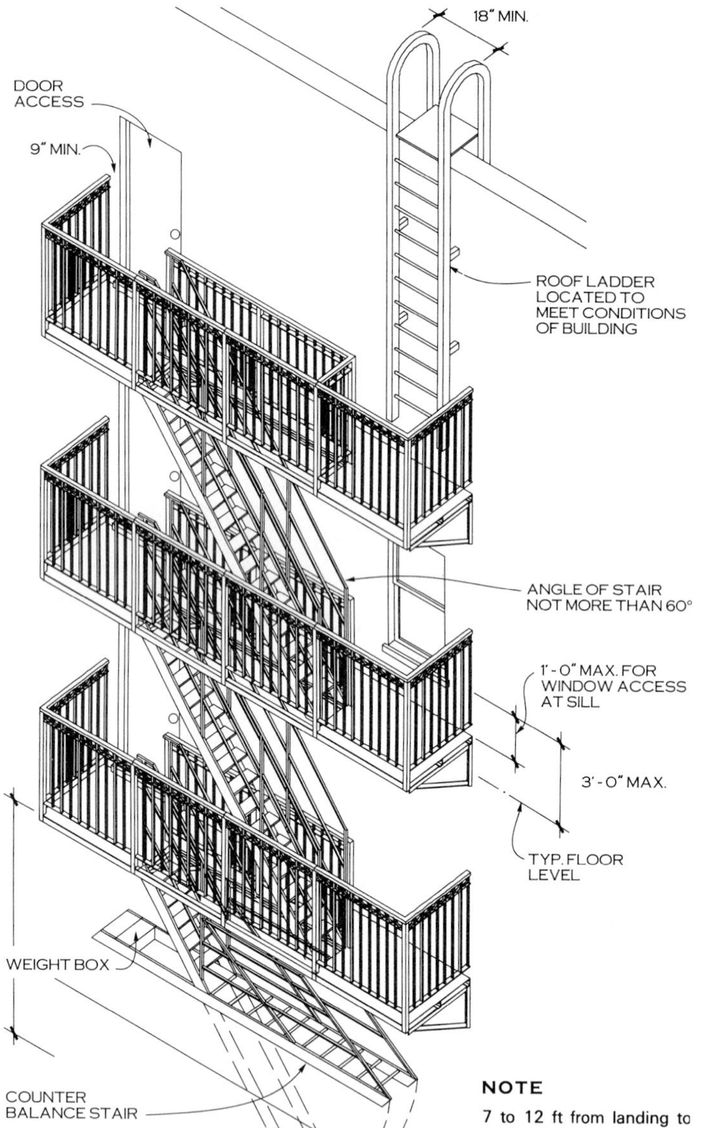

18" MIN.

DOOR ACCESS

9" MIN.

ROOF LADDER LOCATED TO MEET CONDITIONS OF BUILDING

ANGLE OF STAIR NOT MORE THAN 60°

1'-0" MAX. FOR WINDOW ACCESS AT SILL

3'-0" MAX.

TYP. FLOOR LEVEL

WEIGHT BOX

COUNTER BALANCE STAIR

NOTE

Clear access must be provided to streets, alleys, or other public ways without any obstruction.

FIRE ESCAPE

NOTE

7 to 12 ft from landing to grade at front of building (12 ft minimum at alleys or thoroughfares less than 30 ft wide).

6"

MOUNTING BRACKETS

HANDLE FOR LADDER RETRACTION AT EACH ACCESS POINT

5'-0" RECOMMENDED

1'-3"

CHECK LOCAL CODES

FLOOR LEVEL

RETRACTABLE LATERAL GUARDRAIL

CLOSED POSITION   OPEN POSITION

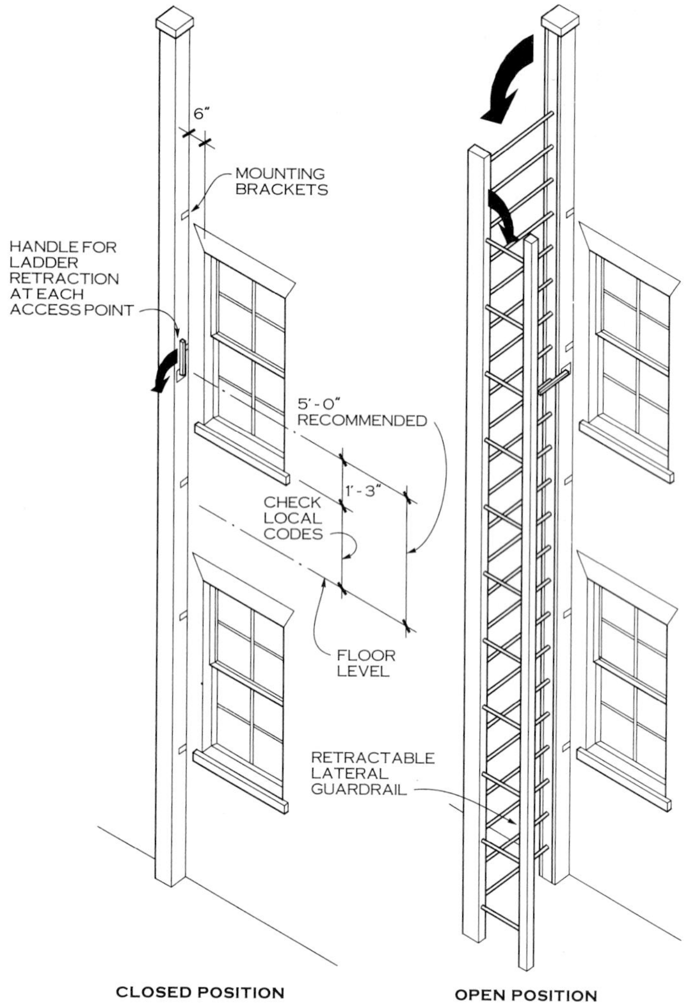

RETRACTABLE ESCAPE LADDER

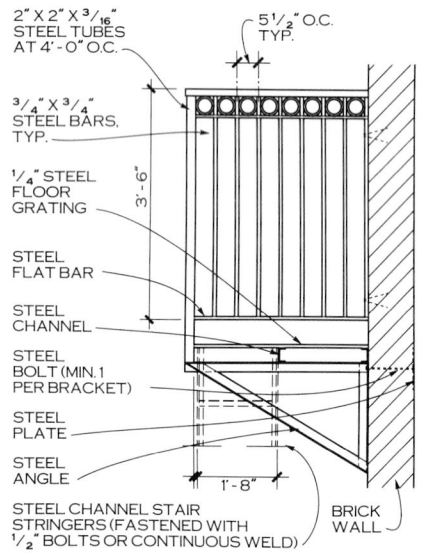

2" X 2" X 3/16" STEEL TUBES AT 4'-0" O.C.

5 1/2" O.C. TYP.

3/4" X 3/4" STEEL BARS, TYP.

1/4" STEEL FLOOR GRATING

3'-6"

STEEL FLAT BAR

STEEL CHANNEL

STEEL BOLT (MIN. 1 PER BRACKET)

STEEL PLATE

STEEL ANGLE

1'-8"

STEEL CHANNEL STAIR STRINGERS (FASTENED WITH 1/2" BOLTS OR CONTINUOUS WELD)

BRICK WALL

ELEVATION - FIRE ESCAPE

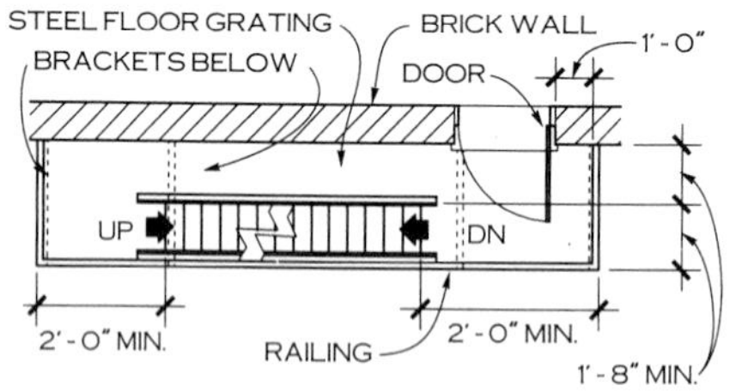

STEEL FLOOR GRATING   BRICK WALL

BRACKETS BELOW   DOOR   1'-0"

UP   DN

2'-0" MIN.   RAILING   2'-0" MIN.   1'-8" MIN.

PLAN - FIRE ESCAPE

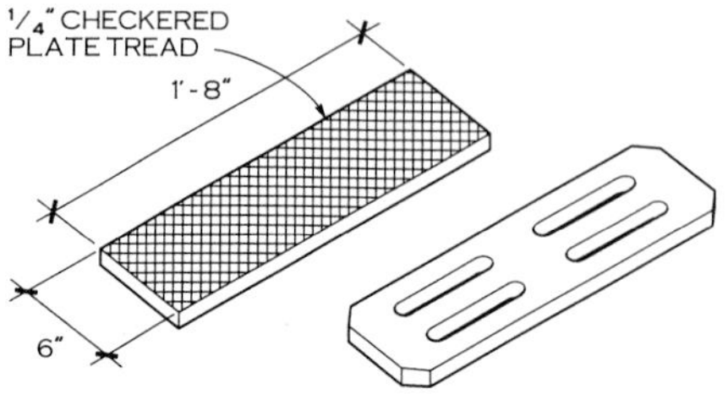

1/4" CHECKERED PLATE TREAD

1'-8"

6"

TYPICAL STAIR TREADS

FIRE ESCAPE NOTES

1. In general, exterior fire escapes are not permitted as any part of the required means of egress for new buildings, but may be continued as a component in the means of egress in existing buildings. New fire escapes for existing buildings are permitted only where exterior stairs cannot be utilized due to lot lines that limit stair size or due to sidewalks, alleys, or streets at grade level. Access by windows is generally not permitted.

2. For other specific requirements, refer to applicable national and local building codes.

3. For standards for fire escapes as well as for stairs and means of egress, consult ANSI 117.1, OSHA, and NFPA 1010 (Life Safety Code).

4. Since fire escapes are mounted outside of the building envelope, consideration must be given to exterior lighting provided on the building itself or general street lighting that would illuminate it.

5. Standard fire escapes are typically designed to support a live load of 100 lb/sq ft; stair treads shall be designed to support a concentrated live load of 250 lb at any point.

ESCAPE LADDER NOTES

1. Located adjacent to windows or balconies, the retractable aluminum escape ladder is used solely for emergency exit, rescue, or supplemental escape route. Also provides access to mechanical equipment or other secured spaces. Not to be used as any component in the means of egress.

2. Consult manufacturer for mounting details. Refer to national and local building codes for specific requirements concerning access opening types, sill heights, clearances, and maximum installation heights allowed. In some instances, a balcony may be used at any level to access the ladder.

Richard J. Vitullo, AIA; Oak Leaf Studio; Crownsville, Maryland
Jomy Safety Ladder Company, Inc.; Boulder, Colorado

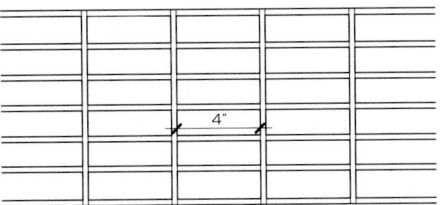

WITH SPACER BARS WELDED 4″ O.C.
NOTE

Constructed of flat bearing bars of steel or aluminum I-bars, with space bars at right angles. Space bars may be square, rectangular, or of another shape. Spacer bars are connected to bearing bars by pressing them into prepared

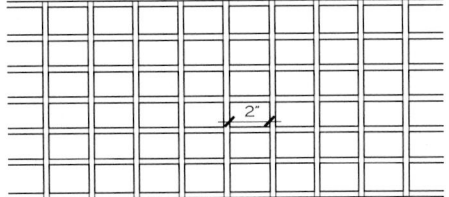

WITH SPACER BARS WELDED 2″ O.C.

slots or by welding. They have open ends or ends banded with flat bars about the same size as welded bearing bars. Standard bar spacings are $^{15}/_{16}$ and $1^3/_{16}$ in.

RECTANGULAR BAR GRATING (WELDED OR PRESSURE LOCKED)

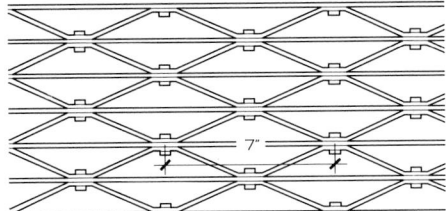

WITH SPACER BARS RIVETED APPROX. 7″ O.C.
USED FOR AVERAGE INSTALLATION
NOTE

Flat bearing bars are made of steel or aluminum, and continuous bent spacer or reticulate bars are riveted to the bearing bars. Usually they have open ends or ends that are banded with flat bars of the same size as bearing bars, welded across the ends. Normal spacing of bars: $^3/_4$, $1^1/_8$,

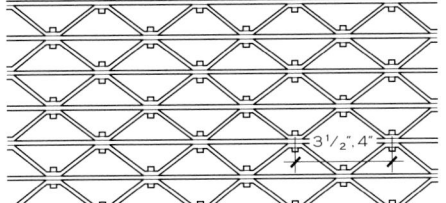

WITH SPACER BARS RIVETED $3^1/_2$″ OR 4″
USED FOR HEAVY TRAFFIC AND WHERE WHEELED EQUIPMENT IS USED

or $2^5/_{16}$ in. Many bar gratings cannot be used in areas of public pedestrian traffic (openings are too big for crutches, canes, pogo sticks, women's shoes, etc.). Close mesh grating ($^1/_4$ in.) is available in steel and aluminum for use in pedestrian traffic areas.

RETICULATED GRATING (RIVETED)

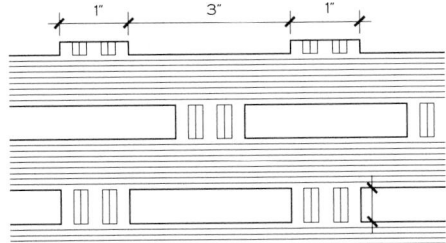

PLAN
NOTE

Grating is extruded from aluminum alloy in one piece with integral I-beam ribs and can have a natural finish or be an-

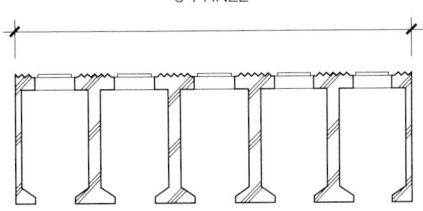

SECTION

odized. Top of surface may be solid or punched. Standard panel width is 6 in.

ALUMINUM PLANK GRATING

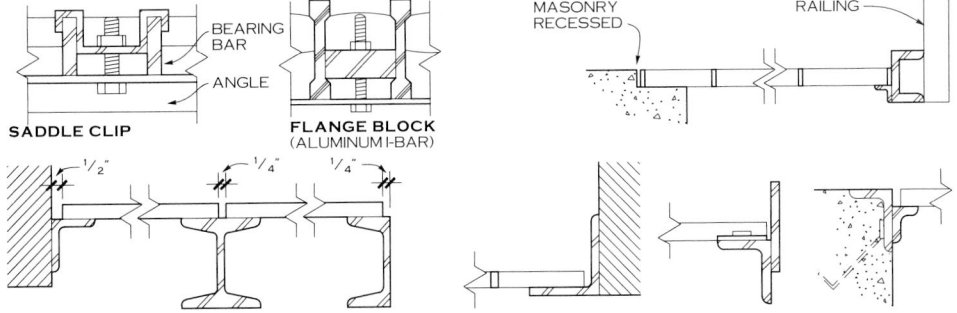

STANDARD ERECTION CLEARANCES
USUALLY ATTACHED BY WELDING, WHERE SUPPORT AND GRATE ARE CONSTRUCTED AS A UNIT
FIXED OR LOOSE GRATINGS—TYPICAL DETAILS

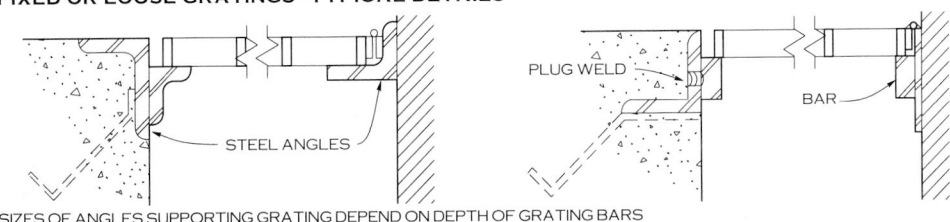

SIZES OF ANGLES SUPPORTING GRATING DEPEND ON DEPTH OF GRATING BARS
HINGED GRATINGS—TYPICAL DETAILS

Charles F. D. Egbert, AIA; Washington, D.C.
Vicente Cordero, AIA; Arlington, Virginia

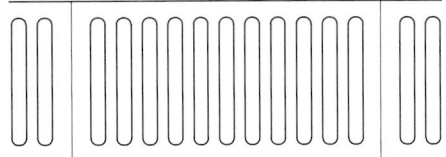
STANDARD DOUBLE-SLOT GRATING

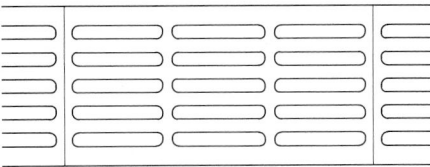
STANDARD SINGLE-SLOT GRATING

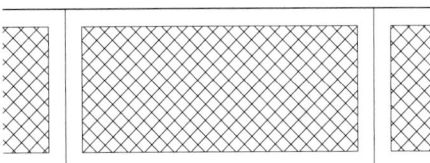
TRIPLE-SLOT GRATING
SLOTS PARALLEL TO FRAME

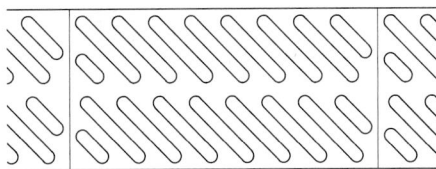
SOLID COVER

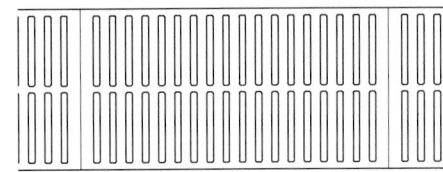
WHEELCHAIR/BICYCLE GRATING

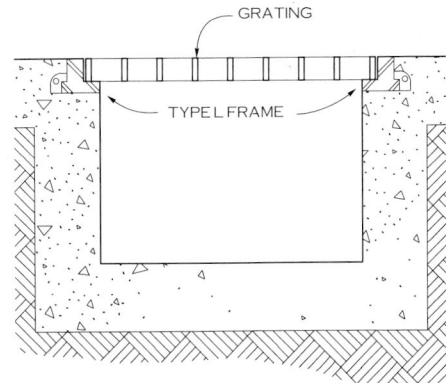
PEDESTRIAN GRATING
NOTE

Grates made of gray cast iron, ductile cast iron, or cast aluminum
STANDARD GRATE DESIGNS

SECTION
TRENCH GRATINGS—FRAME DETAIL

NOTES

1. Follow all local code requirements for ramp design, rail diameter, and rail clearances; also see ASTM, ANSI, ADA, and OSHA requirements.
2. Verify allowable design stresses of rails, posts, and panels.
3. Verify the structural value of fasteners and anchorage to building structure for both vertical and lateral forces.
4. ASTM E-985 requirements:

   GUARDRAILS - Protect occupants at or near the outer edge of a ramp, landing, platform, balcony, or accessible roof. Railing systems usually are not provided where the vertical distance between adjacent levels is 24 in. or less. Railing members should be arranged to discourage climbing. Provide 4 in. high toeboards where tools or other objects could be dislodged. Concentrated load nonconcurrently applied at the top rail shall be 200 lb/ft in the horizontal and vertical direction. The test loads are applicable for railings with supports not more than 8 ft apart.

   HANDRAILS - Corridors, ramps, and walkways having a slope at least 1 in 20 shall have handrails. When a guardrail of more than 38 in. height is used, a separate handrail shall be installed. Nothing should interrupt the continuous sliding of hands. The ends of the handrail shall be returned to walls or arranged to avoid projecting rail ends.

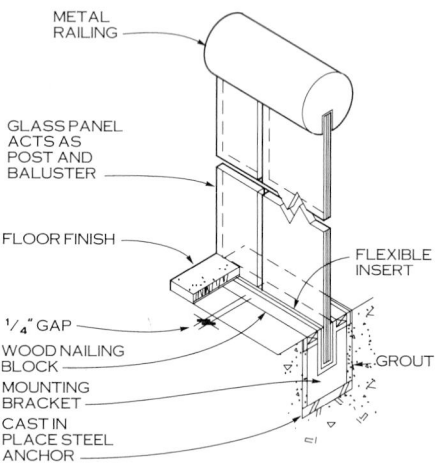

FLUSH MOUNTED GLASS RAIL SYSTEM

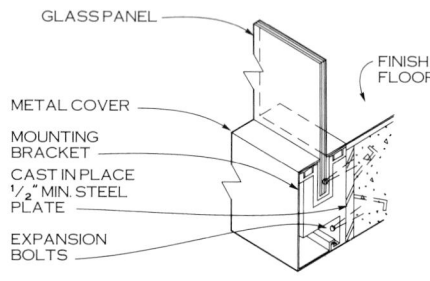

SIDE MOUNTED GLASS PANEL

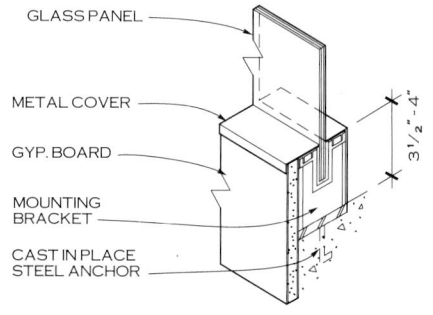

SURFACE MOUNTED GLASS PANEL

Richard J. Vitullo, AIA; Oak Leaf Studio; Crownsville, Maryland

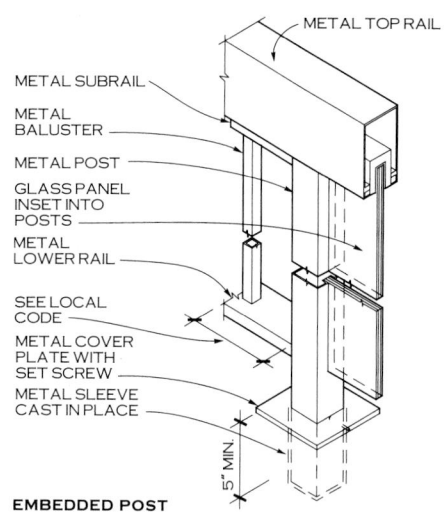

EMBEDDED POST

METAL POST AND RAIL

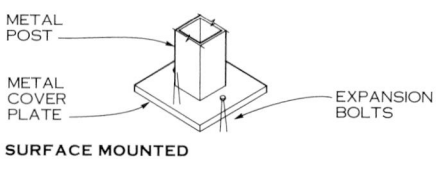

SURFACE MOUNTED

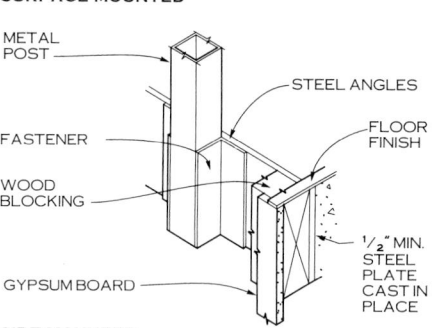

SIDE MOUNTED

POST MOUNTING

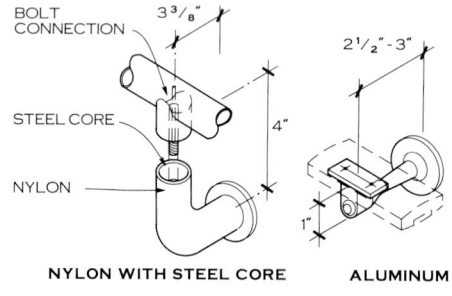

NYLON WITH STEEL CORE   ALUMINUM   BRONZE   STAINLESS STEEL

WALL BRACKETS

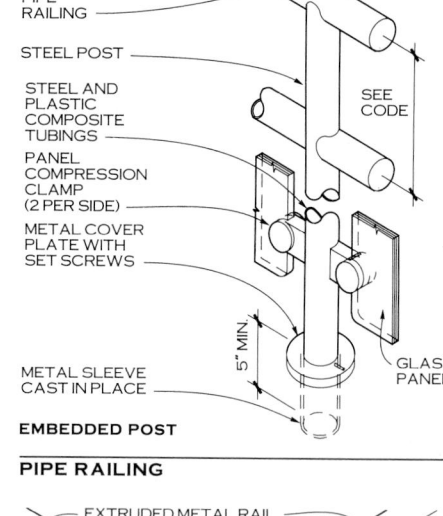

EMBEDDED POST

PIPE RAILING

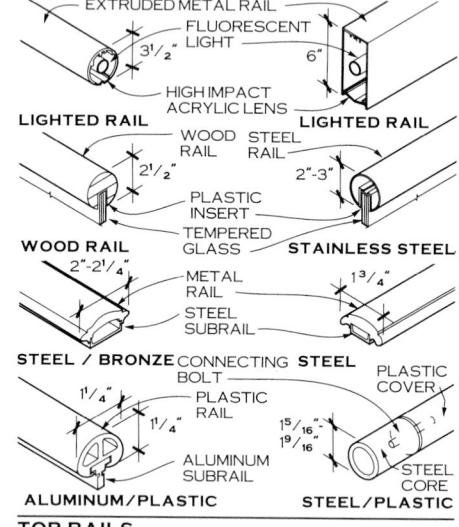

LIGHTED RAIL   LIGHTED RAIL

WOOD RAIL   STAINLESS STEEL

STEEL / BRONZE   STEEL

ALUMINUM/PLASTIC   STEEL/PLASTIC

TOP RAILS

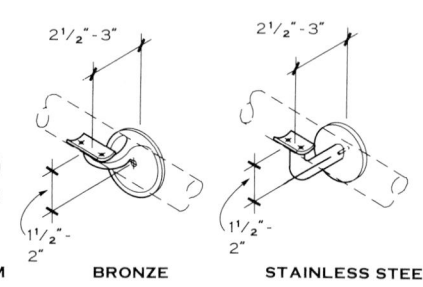

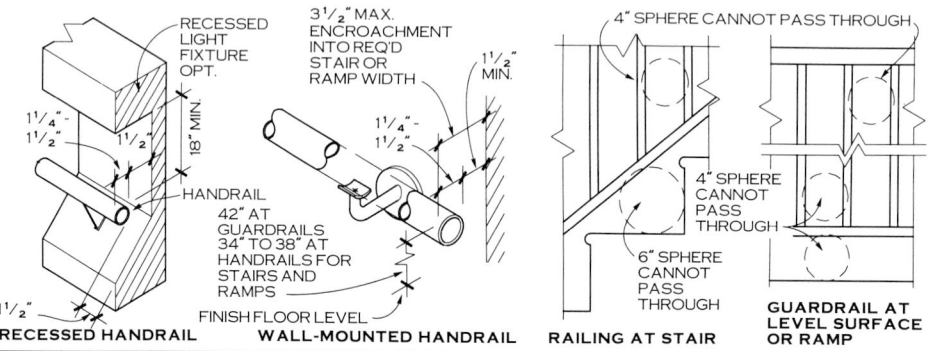

RECESSED HANDRAIL   WALL-MOUNTED HANDRAIL   RAILING AT STAIR   GUARDRAIL AT LEVEL SURFACE OR RAMP

ACCESSIBLE HANDRAILS/GUARDRAILS DIMENSIONS

NOTES

1. A large selection of prefabricated assemblies to cover interior expansion joints is available from various manufacturers to satisfy most joint and finish conditions.
2. Fire-rated barrier-type inserts are available and applicable to most assemblies.
3. Expansion joint covers that will respond to differential movement, both laterally and horizontally, should be provided at joints in structures located where seismic action (earth tremors and quakes) may be expected or where differential settlement is anticipated.

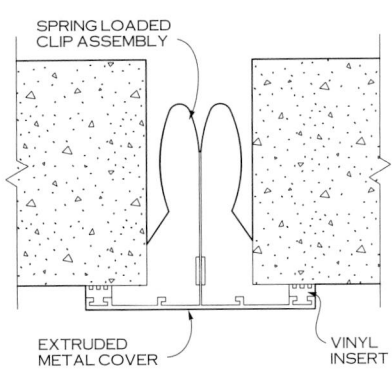

AT WALL OR CEILING

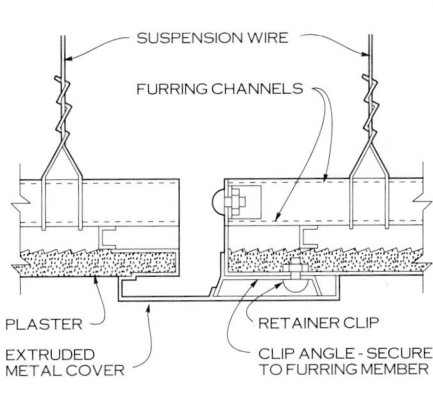

AT SUSPENDED CEILING

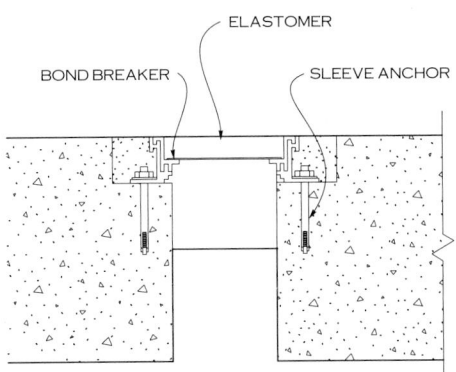

ELASTOMERIC JOINT COVER (REMOVABLE)

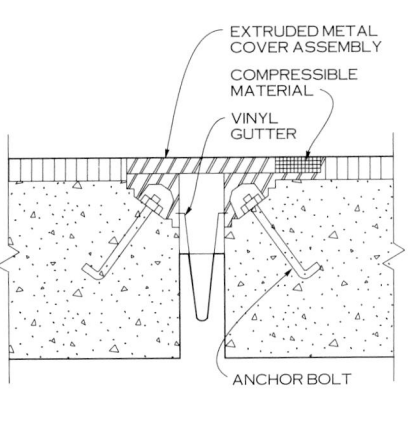

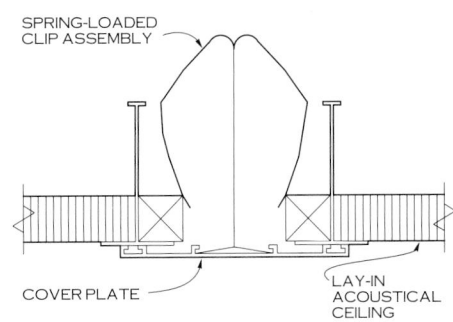

SUSPENDED ACOUSTICAL CEILING

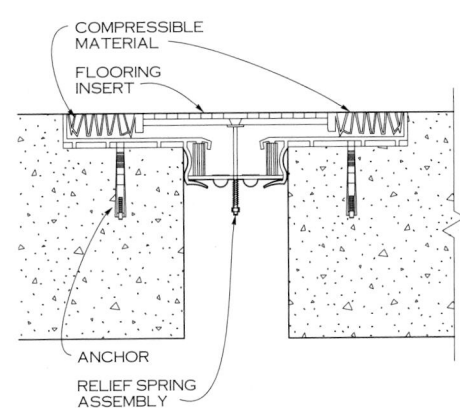

SEISMIC FLOOR JOINT COVER FOR JOINTS UP TO 24 IN.

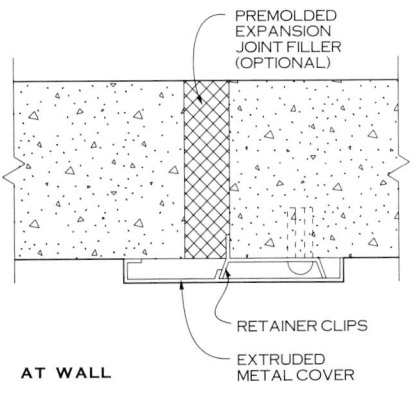

AT FLOOR

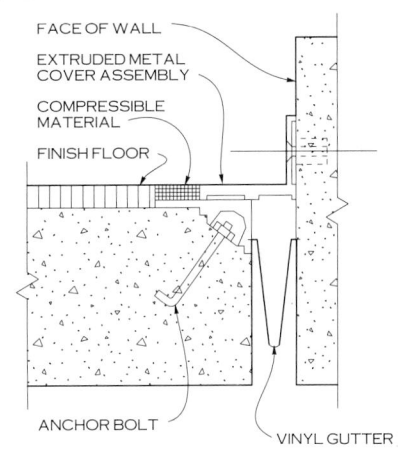

AT FLOOR AND WALL

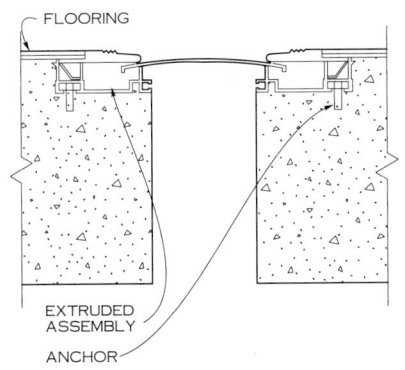

SEISMIC FLOOR JOINT COVER FOR JOINTS UP TO 8 IN.

AT WALL

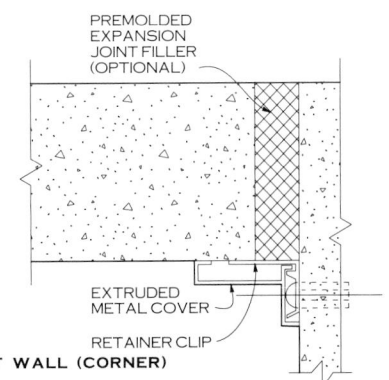

AT WALL (CORNER)

PREFABRICATED INTERIOR EXPANSION JOINT COVERS

J. N. Pease Associates, Charlotte, North Carolina

METAL MATERIALS

Aluminum Association Inc.
900 19th Street, NW, #300
Washington, DC 20006-2168
Tel: (202) 862-5100
Fax:(202) 862-5164

American Institute of Steel Construction, Inc.
1 East Wacker Drive, Suite 3100
Chicago, IL 60601-2001
Tel: (312) 670-2400
Fax:(312) 670-5403

American Iron & Steel Institute
1101 17th Street, NW, Suite 1300
Washington, DC 20036
Tel: (202) 452-7100
Fax:(202) 463-6573

Cold Finished Steel Bar Institute (CFSBI)
700 14th Street, NW, Suite 900
Washington, DC 20005
Tel: (202) 508-1030
Fax:(202) 508-1010

Copper Development Association (CDA)
260 Madison Avenue
New York, NY 10016-2401
Tel: (212) 251-7200
Fax:(212) 251-7234

Industrial Perforators Association
710 North Plankinton Avenue
Milwaukee, WI 53203
Tel: (414) 271-2263
Fax:(414) 271-5154

International Copper Association, Ltd.
260 Madison Avenue, 16th Floor
New York, NY 10016
Tel: (212) 251-7240
Fax:(212) 251-7245

The Materials Properties Council
345 East 47th Street, 14th Floor
New York, NY 10017
Tel: (212) 705-7693
Fax:(212) 752-4929

Metal Building Manufacturers Association
1300 Sumner Avenue
Cleveland, OH 44115-2851
Tel: (216) 241-7333

National Association of
    Architectural Metal Manufacturers (NAAMM)
600 South Federal, Suite 400
Chicago, IL 60605
Tel: (312) 922-6222

Nickel Development Institute (NDI)
214 King Street West, Suite 510
Toronto, ON
Canada M5H 2S6
Tel: (416) 591-7999

REFERENCES

Aluminum Standards and Data. Aluminum Association.

Architectural Metal Handbook. National Association of Architectural Metal Manufacturers.

Cowan, H., and P. Smith. "Metals," Chapter 2. *Handbook of Architectural Technology.* V.N. Reinhold, 1991.

Degradation of Metals in the Atmosphere, STP 965. American Society for Testing and Materials, 1988.

Gayle, M., and D. W. Look. *Metals in America's Historic Buildings: Uses and Preservation Treatments.* National Technical Information Svc., 1980. [#PB90-20629]

Lead as a Modern Design Material. Lead Industries Association.

Metals in Construction. Iron and Steel Industrial Promotion Fund of New York. [(212) 697-5553]

Simmons, H. L. *Repairing and Extending Nonstructural Metals.* Van Nostrand Reinhold, 1990.

METAL FINISHES AND COATINGS

American Galvanizers Association
12200 East Iliff Avenue, Suite 204
Aurora, CO 80014
Tel: (303) 750-2900

Architectural Anodizers Council (AAC)
1000 North Rand , Suite 214
Wauconda, IL 60084
Tel: (708) 526-2010
Fax:(708) 526-3993

Metal Treating Institute
302 3rd Street, Suite 1
Neptune Beach, FL 32266
Tel: (904) 249-0448
Fax:(904) 249-0959

Steel Structures Painting Council (SSPC)
4516 Henry Street, Suite 301
Pittsburgh, PA 15213-3728
Tel: (412) 687-1113
Fax:(412) 687-1153

REFERENCES

Anodic Finishes/Painted Aluminum, AFPA-91. American Architectural Manufacturers Association, 1991.

Anodized Aluminum Color Standards, Architectural Anodizers Council (AAC), 1991.

Architectural Finishes for Aluminum, Monograph 05M031. Construction Specifications Institute, 1990.

"Finishes for Aluminum Curtain Walls," vol. 8. *Aluminum Curtain Wall Design Guide Manual.* American Architectural Manufacturers Association.

Metal Finishes Manual. National Association of Metal Manufacturers, 1988.

Steel Structures Painting Manual, 2 vols. Steel Structures Painting Council.

METAL FASTENING

American Welding Society
550 N.W. LeJeune Road
P.O. Box 351040
Miami, FL 33135
Tel: (305) 443-9353
Fax:(305) 443-7559

Welding Research Council
345 E. 47th Street, Rm. 1301
New York, NY 10017
Tel: (212) 705-7956
Fax:(212) 371-9622

REFERENCES

Parmley, R. "Structural Steel Connections," Section 9. *Standard Handbook of Fastening and Joining.* McGraw-Hill, 1989.

Welding Handbook. American Welding Society.

METAL JOISTS

Steel Joist Institute
1205 48th Avenue, North
    Suite A
Myrtle Beach, SC 29577
Tel: (803) 449-0487

REFERENCES

Catalog of Standard Specifications, Load Tables, and Weight Tables for Steel Joists. Steel Joist Institute, 1992.

Steel Joists, SpecGUIDE G05210, CSI, 1988.

Structural Design of Steel Joist Roofs to Resist Uplift Loads. Steel Joist Institute.

METAL DECKING

Steel Deck Institute
P.O. Box 9506
Canton, OH 44711
Tel: (216) 493-7886

REFERENCES

Corrosion Protection for New Steel Roof Decks. Bulletin 15-91. National Roofing Contractors Association, 1991.

Design Manual for Floor Decks and Roof Decks. Steel Deck Institute.

Steel Decking, SpecGUIDE, G05310. Construction Specifications Institute, 1986.

Steel Deck Institute Design Manual. Steel Deck Institute, 1992.

STRUCTURAL METAL FRAMING

American Institute for
    Hollow Structural Sections (AIHSS)
8500 Station Street, Suite 220
Mentor, OH 44060
Tel: (412) 221-8880

Metal Lath/Steel Framing
    Association Division of NAAMM (ML/SFA)
600 S. Federal Street, Suite 400
Chicago, IL 60605
Tel: (312) 922-6222

REFERENCES

Detailing for Steel Construction. American Instiute of Steel Construction (AISC), 1983.

Lightweight Steel Framing Systems Manual. National Association of Architectural Metal Manufacturers, 1987.

Manual of Steel Construction, 9th ed. AISC, 1989.

Newman, M. *Structural Details for Steel Construction.* McGraw-Hill, 1988.

Parker, H. *Simplified Design of Steel Structures.* New York: J. Wiley & Sons, 1990.

Structural Aluminum, SpecGUIDE G05140. Construction Specifications Institute (CSI), 1988.

Structural Steel, SpecGUIDE G05120. CSI, 1987.

METAL FABRICATIONS

Lead Industries Association (LIA)
295 Madison Ave
New York, NY 10017
Tel: (212) 578-4750
Fax:(212) 684-7714

Sheet Metal and Air Conditioning
    Contractors National Association (SMACNA)
4201 Lafayette Center Drive
Chantilly, VA 22021-1209
Tel: (703) 803-2980
Fax:(703) 803-3732

REFERENCES

Architectural Sheet Metal Manual. Sheet Metal and Air Conditioning Contractors National Association, 1987.

Copper and Common Sense. Rome, N.Y.: Revere Copper Products, 1982. [(315) 338-2022]

Metal Stairs Manual, 5th ed. National Association of Architectural Metal Manufacturers, 1992.

ORNAMENTAL METAL

Brass and Bronze Ingot Manufacturers
300 W. Washington, Rm 1500
Chicago, IL 60606
Tel: (312) 236-2715

National Institute of Steel Detailing
300 South Harbor Blvd., Suite 500
Anaheim, CA 92805
Tel: (714) 776-3200

National Ornamental and
    Miscellaneous Metals Association (NOMMA)
804-10 Main Street, Suite E
Forest Park, GA 30050
Tel: (404) 363-4009
Fax:(404) 366-1852

REFERENCES

Glossary of Architectural Metal Terms for Stairs and Railings. National Ornamental and Miscellaneous Metals Association (NOMMA).

Pipe Railing Manual. National Association of Architectural Metal Manufacturers, 1985.

Ornamental Metal, SpecGUIDE G05700. Construction Specifications Institute, 1989.

Metal Rail Manual. NOMMA.

RELATED JOURNALS

Construction Specifier
601 Madison Street
Alexandria, VA 22314
Tel: (703) 684-0300
Fax:(703) 684-0465

Metal Architecture
123 N. Poplar Street
Fostoria, OH 44830
Tel: (419) 435-8571
Fax:(419) 435-0863

Ornamental and Miscellaneous Metal Fabricator
National Ornamental and
    Miscellaneous Metals Association
804-10 Main Street, Suite E
Forest Park, GA 30050
Tel: (404) 363-4009

CHAPTER

WOOD AND PLASTICS

WOOD AS A CONSTRUCTION MATERIAL

Approximately nine of every ten buildings constructed in the United States each year are framed with wood, including most single-family and multifamily residences and a large percentage of commercial, institutional, and public buildings. Wood is favored as both a structural material and a finish material for its economy, architectural flexibility, and visual qualities. Many contractors know how to build with it: most wood members can be handled by small work crews without special lifting equipment; cutting and fastening can be accomplished on-site with hand or portable power tools; and the skills needed for wood construction are easily learned. Yet wood is one of the most difficult materials for the designer to master, because it is virtually the only building material that is vegetable rather than mineral. With this vegetable origin comes a host of idiosyncrasies relating to directional properties, strength, stiffness, grain patterns, shrinkage, distortion, decay, insect damage, and fire.

Today most wood comes from younger forests, with trees smaller than those typically harvested a few decades ago. Large solid timbers are becoming increasingly hard to obtain, and the general quality of lumber is declining. As a result we are becoming more and more dependent on manufactured wood products such as laminated wood, veneer-based lumber, oriented-strand lumber, and manufactured wood I-joists and trusses. These products tend to be straighter, stronger, stiffer, less prone to distortion, and more economical of trees than conventional solid lumber, but they are not always suitable for display in a building.

WOOD AS A STRUCTURAL MATERIAL

On the basis of performance per unit weight, typical construction lumber is at least as strong and stiff as structural steel. Because of its microstructure of longitudinal cells, wood has different structural properties in its two principal directions. Parallel to the grain, wood is strong and stiff; perpendicular to grain, it is weak and deformable. Fasteners that act in a direction parallel to grain can transmit considerably more force than those that act perpendicular to grain. The strength of wood varies with the duration of the load: For short-term loads such as snow, wind, and impact, allowable stress values are increased by 15% to 100% over those allowed for normal-term loads. Under very long term loading, however, wood has a tendency to creep, and reduced stress values must be used.

WOOD AS A FINISH MATERIAL

Wood is used as a finish material in buildings of every kind. Limited quantities of wood finish may be used even in the most fire-resistant types of construction. With proper protection from water and sunlight, wood can serve as a durable exterior material for cladding, trim, and even roofing. For interior finishes, despite recent concerns regarding the depletion of rare or old-growth woods, woods of many types remain commonly available in solid or veneer form, exhibiting great variety in hardness, grain figure, color, suitability for different finishes, and cost. Finish woods are readily available in many preformed shapes and are also easily shaped and cut in the field. Wood may be finished with clear or opaque coatings, or it may serve as a base for applied plastic laminates.

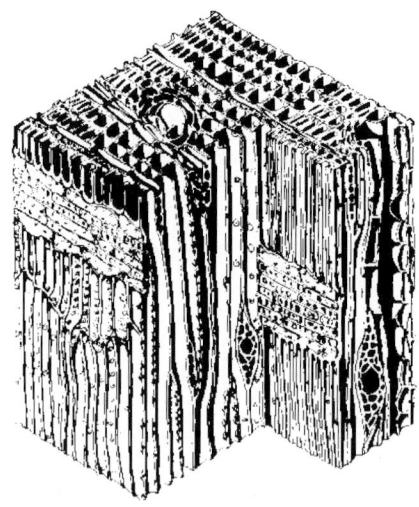

CELL STRUCTURE OF A SOFTWOOD

TYPES OF WOOD CONSTRUCTION

Building codes categorize wood construction as two distinct types. *Heavy-timber construction,* consisting of exposed columns, girders, beams, and decking large enough to be slow to catch fire and burn, is permitted for use in relatively large buildings across a broad spectrum of uses. *Wood light-frame construction* is made up of nominal 2 in. (38 mm) framing members that are spaced closely together and normally concealed by interior finish materials such as plaster, gypsum board, or wood paneling. Because such construction is less resistant to fire than heavy-timber construction, building codes limit the heights and areas of light-frame buildings. (Three stories are the maximum generally permitted in residential light-frame buildings, or four stories if an approved sprinkler system is installed.) Heavy-timber buildings are engineered in accordance with the *National Design Specification for Wood Construction.* Most wood light-frame engineering can be done by reading values from tables in the *CABO One and Two Family Dwelling Code,* which has been widely adopted by states and municipalities.

Because of its large member dimensions and spans, heavy-timber construction is best suited to buildings with regular, repetitive bays. Light-frame construction, with its small members and close member spacings, adapts readily to even the most intricate spaces and architectural forms.

LUMBER PRODUCTION

Commercially marketed lumber includes trees of dozens of species, roughly divided into softwoods, which are the evergreen species, and hardwoods, those species that drop their leaves in the fall. Nearly all framing lumber comes from the comparatively plentiful softwoods. Hardwoods, with their greater range of colors and grain figures, are used primarily for interior finishes, flooring, cabinets, and furniture.

Seen under a low-power magnifier, wood is made up primarily of hollow tubular cells of cellulose that run parallel to the long axis of the tree trunk. When the tree is harvested, both the hollows and the walls of these tubes are full of watery sap. The tree is sawed into rough lumber while in this saturated or "green" condition. Green framing lumber, either unsurfaced (rough) or surfaced (planed), is commonly used in geographic areas relatively close to lumber mills, where its increased shipping weight is not a large price factor. Lumber that will be shipped greater distances, and all finish lumber, is "seasoned" (dried of much of its sap), either by stacking it in the open air for a period of months or, more commonly, by heating it in a kiln for a period of days. During seasoning, the sap evaporates first from the hollows of the tubes, and then from the cellulose walls of the tubes, causing the lumber to shrink. By the time the lumber leaves the kiln, it is considerably smaller. Further shrinkage usually occurs after the lumber has been incorporated into the building, as the moisture content in the wood comes gradually into equilibrium with the moisture content of the surrounding air, in the range of 11% to 15% of the dry weight of the wood. Wood absorbs moisture during damp weather and gives it off during dry weather in a never-ending cycle of swelling and shrinking, a fact that must be taken into account when detailing wood components of buildings.

Most lumber is surfaced after seasoning to reduce it to its final dimensions and give it smooth faces. Edges are rounded to make the lumber easier and safer to handle.

LUMBER GRADING

Because it is a natural product, wood is highly variable in appearance and structural properties. Consequently, elaborate systems of grading have been established to indicate the quality of each piece of lumber. Within each species of wood there are two grading systems, one based on structural strength and stiffness, the other based on appearance. Appearance is graded visually. Structural grading is done either visually, based on the sizes and positions of knots and other defects, or by machines that flex each piece of lumber and measure its structural properties directly.

Strength and stiffness values for wood are tabulated later in this chapter. They vary considerably from one species and grade to another; when engineering a wood structure, it is necessary to know what species and grade will be specified. If in doubt, structural calculations should be based on the weakest species and grade locally available.

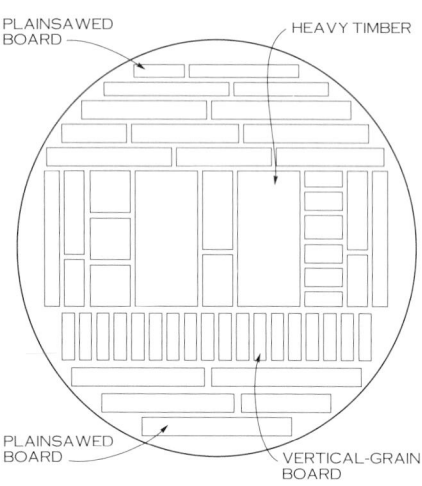

PLAINSAWED BOARD

HEAVY TIMBER

PLAINSAWED BOARD

VERTICAL-GRAIN BOARD

TYPICAL SAWING OF A LARGE LOG

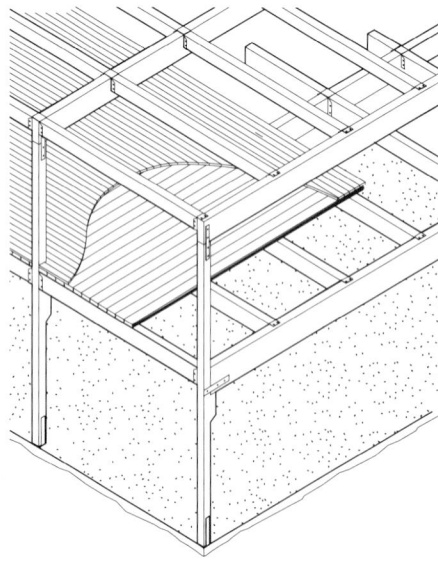

HEAVY-TIMBER CONSTRUCTION

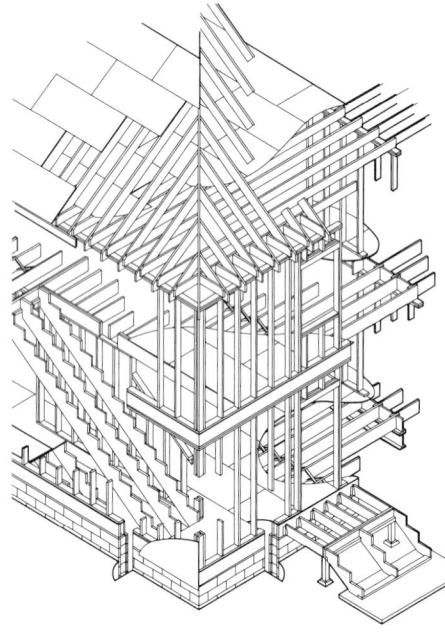

WOOD LIGHT-FRAME CONSTRUCTION

Edward Allen, AIA; South Natick, Massachusetts
Joseph Iano, Architect; Boston, Massachusetts

 WOOD FRAME DESIGN

JOINING WOOD

Nailing is the most common method of joining light structural members. Nails are inexpensive to buy and install and may be driven by hand or by a pneumatic gun. When applied in proper size, number, and spacing, they form a strong, resilient joint. Sheet metal straps, anchors, and brackets can be nailed to connections where greater resistance to tension or shear is necessary. Detailed nailing requirements for light-frame construction are included in building codes. Heavy-timber construction typically relies on bolts and lag screws, together with fabricated metal connecting devices.

In finish wood construction, nearly headless finish nails are used for improved appearance. Screws, concealed or embedded fasteners, splines, and fitted and glued joints provide greater mechanical stiffness and optimal appearance. Standards for finish joinery based on appearance and cost have been established for cabinet construction by the Architectural Woodwork Institute.

DECAY AND INSECTS

Wood provides food and habitat to various insects and decay-causing fungi. For the most part, decay and insect attack can be avoided by detailing the building in such a way that wood remains dry at all times. Wood components should be kept at least 6 in. (150 mm) away from the soil. Details that trap and hold moisture, such as connections in exterior decks and railings, should be avoided unless preservative treated wood or decay-resistant species such as redwood, cedar, or cypress are used.

FIRE

Wood burns easily, giving off highly toxic combustion products, so it is important to design wooden buildings for fire safety. Following the height and area restrictions of the building codes, along with code provisions for easy egress from wooden buildings, is a first step. Smoke and heat alarms are essential in wooden residential buildings. Heavy-timber buildings have a natural resistance to fire because their massive timbers are slow to catch fire and burn as compared to the smaller framing members in light-frame construction. Wood light-frame buildings have internal hollow passages that encourage the spread of fire; these must be closed off at each floor by wood blocking or by the floor platform framing. Light-frame buildings are generally finished with interior surfaces of gypsum plaster or gypsum wallboard, which are highly resistant to fire.

MOISTURE MOVEMENT IN WOOD

The drying shrinkage of wood is not uniform. Wood shrinks very little along the length of the grain. It shrinks considerably in the radial direction of a cylindrical log, and it shrinks even more in the tangential direction of the log than in the radial, as shown in the accompanying graph. One consequence of the difference between the radial and tangential shrinkage is that radial splits called *checks* form inevitably during seasoning, especially in lumber of large dimension. Another consequence is that pieces of lumber distort noticeably in accordance with their original positions in the tree trunk. For pieces of lumber that must stay flat, such as flooring, outdoor decking, base-boards, casings, and paneling, vertical-grain lumber, which is sawed so the annual growth rings are more or less perpendicular to the broad face of the board, is often specified. One particular sawing pattern that produces vertical-grain lumber is called *quartersawing*. For ordinary framing, seasoning distortions are of little consequence, so plainsawed boards are used.

A number of accepted wood detailing practices have been developed in response to the large amounts of moisture movement that occur in wood and the distortions that result from the differences in the rates of shrinkage along the three axes of the grain. In applying wood siding, it is necessary to use nailing patterns that do not restrain the cross-grain seasonal shrinking and swelling of the wood. Horizontal bevel siding is nailed in such a way that each board is fastened by one row of nails only, creating a sliding joint at each overlapping edge to allow for movement. Tongue and groove siding boards are nailed at the tongue edge only, the other edge being restrained by the tongue of the adjacent board sliding freely in its groove. Vertical board-and-batten siding is nailed only at the centers of the boards and battens, allowing for free expansion and contraction of the wood.

Because the shrinkage of wood is so much greater in the tangential direction than in the radial, plainsawed boards tend to cup noticeably in a direction opposite to the curvature of the annual rings. Plainsawed decking and flooring should be laid with the "bark side" of each board facing down to reduce the raising of edges. On outdoor decks, this practice will also minimize puddling of water on the boards. Vertical-grain flooring and deck boards are preferable to plainsawed boards, not only because their tighter grain pattern wears better underfoot.

Broad interior finish pieces are frequently given a relieved back, a hidden groove or grooves that reduce the effective thickness of the piece, thus reducing the tendency of the piece to cup. Many stock millwork patterns include relieved backs. Boards may be relieved on-site by cutting multiple grooves on a table saw. Cupping can also be minimized by back priming, painting the back surface of each piece a day or more before installation. After the piece has been installed and the exposed side has been painted or varnished, the back priming causes the back side to absorb and give off moisture at about the same rate as the exposed side, minimizing distortions.

REFERENCES

American Forest and Paper Association, *National Design Specification for Wood Construction*. Washington, D.C., 1991.

American Wood Council, *Code-Conforming Wood Design*. Washington, D.C.

Architectural Woodwork Institute, *Architectural Woodwork Quality Standards*. Arlington, Va., 1988.

Breyer, Donald E. *Design of Wood Structures*. New York: McGraw-Hill, 1980.

Council of American Building Officials, *CABO One and Two Family Dwelling Code*. Falls Church, Va., 1992.

Goetz, Karl-Heinz, et al. *Timber Design Construction Sourcebook*. New York: McGraw-Hill, 1989.

Hoadley, R. Bruce. *Understanding Wood*. Newtown, Conn.: Taunton Press, 1980.

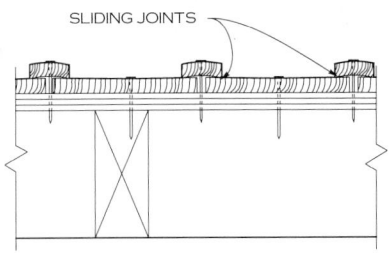

SLIDING JOINTS IN BOARD-AND-BATTEN SIDING

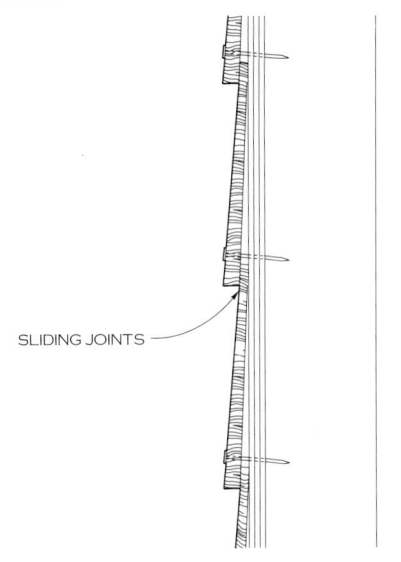

SLIDING JOINTS IN HORIZONTAL WOOD SIDING

CORRECT: BARK SIDE DOWN

INCORRECT: BARK SIDE UP

SHRINKAGE DISTORTION OF PLAINSAWED DECKING

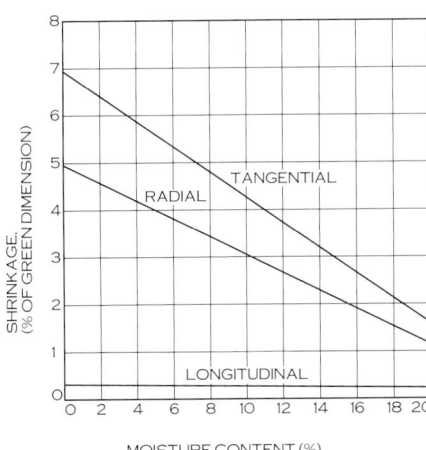

MOISTURE SHRINKAGE OF A TYPICAL SOFTWOOD

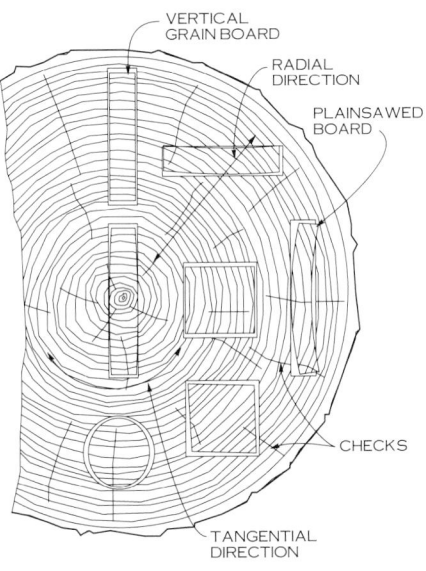

SHRINKAGE DISTORTIONS BY POSITION IN LOG

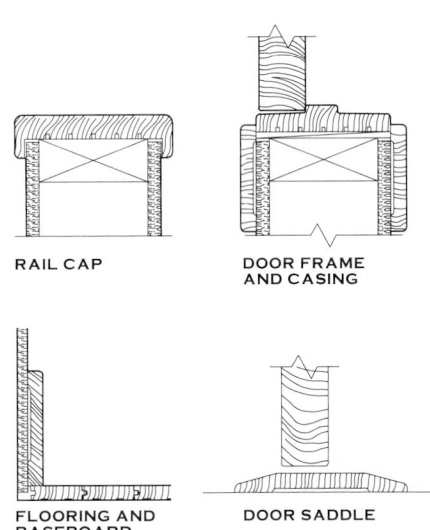

TYPICAL RELIEVED BACKS IN FLAT MILLWORK

Edward Allen, AIA; South Natick, Massachusetts
Joseph Iano, Architect; Boston, Massachusetts

WOOD FRAME DESIGN

DESIGN CRITERIA

STRENGTH: Live load of 30 psf plus dead load of 10 psf determines the required fiber stress value.
DEFLECTION: For 30 psf live load. Limited to span in inches divided by 360.

FLOOR JOISTS—30 LB LIVE LOAD

ALL ROOMS USED FOR SLEEPING AREAS AND ATTIC FLOORS

JOIST (IN.)		MODULUS OF ELASTICITY, E, IN 1,000,000 PSI														
SIZE	SPACING	0.5	0.6	0.7	0.8	0.9	1.0	1.1	1.2	1.3	1.4	1.5	1.6	1.7	1.8	1.9
2 x 6	12	8-0 510	8-6 570	8-11 640	9-4 700	9-9 750	10-1 810	10-5 860	10-9 910	11-0 960	11-3 1010	11-7 1060	11-10 1100	12-0 1150	12-3 1200	12-6 1240
	16	7-3 560	7-9 630	8-2 700	8-6 770	8-10 830	9-2 890	9-6 950	9-9 1000	10-0 1060	10-3 1110	10-6 1160	10-9 1220	10-11 1270	11-2 1320	11-4 1360
	24	6-4 640	6-9 720	7-1 800	7-5 880	7-9 950	8-0 1020	8-3 1080	8-6 1150	8-9 1210	8-11 1270	9-2 1330	9-4 1390	9-7 1450	9-9 1510	9-11 1560
2 x 8	12	10-7 510	11-3 570	11-10 640	12-4 700	12-10 750	13-4 810	13-9 860	14-2 910	14-6 960	14-11 1010	15-3 1060	15-7 1100	15-10 1150	16-2 1200	16-6 1240
	16	9-7 560	10-2 630	10-9 700	11-13 770	11-8 830	12-1 890	12-6 950	12-10 1000	13-2 1060	13-6 1110	13-10 1160	14-2 1220	14-5 1270	14-8 1320	15-0 1360
	24	8-5 640	8-11 720	9-4 800	9-10 880	10-2 950	10-7 1020	10-11 1080	11-3 1150	11-6 1210	11-10 1270	12-1 1330	12-4 1390	12-7 1450	12-10 1510	13-1 1560
2 x 10	12	13-6 510	14-4 570	15-1 640	15-9 700	16-5 750	17-0 810	17-6 860	18-0 910	18-6 960	19-0 1010	19-5 1060	19-10 1100	20-3 1150	20-8 1200	21-0 1240
	16	12-3 560	13-0 630	13-8 700	14-4 770	14-11 830	15-5 890	15-11 950	16-5 1000	16-10 1060	17-3 1110	17-8 1160	18-0 1220	18-5 1270	18-9 1320	19-1 1360
	24	10-8 640	11-4 720	11-11 800	12-6 880	13-0 950	13-6 1020	13-11 1080	14-4 1150	14-8 1210	15-1 1270	15-5 1330	15-9 1390	16-1 1450	16-5 1510	16-8 1560
2 x 12	12	16-5 510	17-5 570	18-4 640	19-2 700	19-11 750	20-8 810	21-4 860	21-11 910	22-6 960	23-1 1010	23-7 1060	24-2 1100	24-8 1150	25-1 1200	25-7 1240
	16	14-11 560	15-10 630	16-8 700	17-5 770	18-1 830	18-9 890	19-4 950	19-11 1000	20-6 1060	21-0 1110	21-6 1160	21-11 1220	22-5 1270	22-10 1320	23-3 1360
	24	13-0 640	13-10 720	14-7 800	15-2 880	15-10 950	16-5 1020	16-11 1080	17-5 1150	17-11 1210	18-4 1270	18-9 1330	19-2 1390	19-7 1450	19-11 1510	20-3 1560

NOTE: The required extreme fiber stress in bending, F_b, in psi is shown below each span.

DESIGN CRITERIA

STRENGTH: Live load of 40 psf plus dead load of 10 psf determines the required fiber stress value.
DEFLECTION: For 40 psf live load. Limited to span in inches divided by 360.

FLOOR JOISTS—40 LB LIVE LOAD

ALL ROOMS EXCEPT THOSE USED FOR SLEEPING AREAS AND ATTIC FLOORS

JOIST (IN.)		MODULUS OF ELASTICITY, E, IN 1,000,000 PSI														
SIZE	SPACING	0.5	0.6	0.7	0.8	0.9	1.0	1.1	1.2	1.3	1.4	1.5	1.6	1.7	1.8	1.9
2 x 6	12	7-3 520	7-9 590	8-2 660	8-6 720	8-10 780	9-2 830	9-6 890	9-9 940	10-0 990	10-3 1040	10-6 1090	10-9 1140	10-11 1190	11-2 1230	11-4 1280
	16	6-7 580	7-0 650	7-5 720	7-9 790	8-0 860	8-4 920	8-7 980	8-10 1040	9-1 1090	9-4 1150	9-6 1200	9-9 1250	9-11 1310	10-2 1360	10-4 1410
	24	5-9 660	6-2 750	6-6 830	6-9 900	7-0 980	7-3 1050	7-6 1120	7-9 1190	7-11 1250	8-2 1310	8-4 1380	8-6 1440	8-8 1500	8-10 1550	9-0 1610
2 x 8	12	9-7 520	10-2 590	10-9 660	11-3 720	11-8 780	12-1 830	12-6 890	12-10 940	13-2 990	13-6 1040	13-10 1090	14-2 1140	14-5 1190	14-8 1230	15-0 1280
	16	8-9 580	9-3 650	9-9 720	10-2 790	10-7 850	11-0 920	11-4 980	11-8 1040	12-0 1090	12-3 1150	12-7 1200	12-10 1250	13-1 1310	13-4 1360	13-7 1410
	24	7-7 660	8-1 750	8-6 830	8-11 900	9-3 980	9-7 1050	9-11 1120	10-2 1190	10-6 1250	10-9 1310	11-0 1380	11-3 1440	11-5 1500	11-8 1550	11-11 1610
2 x 10	12	12-3 520	13-0 590	13-8 660	14-4 720	14-11 780	15-5 830	15-11 890	16-5 940	16-10 990	17-3 1040	17-8 1090	18-0 1140	18-5 1190	18-9 1230	19-1 1280
	16	11-1 580	11-10 650	12-5 720	13-0 790	13-6 850	14-0 920	14-6 980	14-11 1040	15-3 1090	15-8 1150	16-0 1200	16-5 1250	16-9 1310	17-0 1360	17-4 1410
	24	9-9 660	10-4 750	10-10 830	11-4 900	11-10 980	12-3 1050	12-8 1120	13-0 1190	13-4 1250	13-8 1310	14-0 1380	14-4 1440	14-7 1500	14-11 1550	15-2 1610
2 x 12	12	14-11 520	15-10 590	16-8 660	17-5 720	18-1 780	18-9 830	19-4 890	19-11 940	20-6 990	21-0 1040	21-6 1090	21-11 1140	22-5 1190	22-10 1230	23-3 1280
	16	13-6 580	14-4 650	15-2 720	15-10 790	16-5 860	17-0 920	17-7 980	18-1 1040	18-7 1090	19-1 1150	19-6 1200	19-11 1250	20-4 1310	20-9 1360	21-1 1410
	24	11-10 660	12-7 750	13-3 830	13-10 900	14-4 980	14-11 1050	15-4 1120	15-10 1190	16-3 1250	16-8 1310	17-0 1380	17-5 1440	17-9 1500	18-1 1550	18-5 1610

NOTE: The required extreme fiber stress in bending, F_b, in psi is shown below each span.

American Forest and Paper Association; Washington, D.C.

DESIGN LOAD TABLES

GENERAL DESIGN INFORMATION

For floor construction where live loading is heavier than customarily found in residential occupancies, tabular data are provided.

The tabulated spans are based on bending strength using the live load indicated in each table heading plus a dead load of 10 psf. In calculating the required modulus of elasticity for the tabulated span, the live load only was used, since this is in accordance with established practice for design of floor joists.

SPAN

While the effective span length for an isolated beam is customarily taken as the distance from face to face

of supports plus one-half the required length of bearing at each end, it is the practice in designing joists spaced not over 24 in. apart to consider the span as the clear distance between supports.

NET SIZES OF LUMBER

Joists are customarily specified in terms of nominal sizes, but calculations to determine the allowable span and required modulus of elasticity are based on actual sizes.

DESIGN STRESSES

Unit design values for design of wood joists are given in the National Design Specification for Wood Construc-

tion, available from the American Forest & Paper Association.

ADJUSTMENT OF MODULUS OF ELASTICITY

The modulus of elasticity values listed in the span tables for joists are those required for the tabulated spans if deflection under the live load is limited to $\ell/360$. Where other deflection limits are acceptable, the tabular E values may be adjusted by multiplying them by the following factors:

For limit of $\ell/300$: 0.833
For limit of $\ell/240$: 0.667
For limit of $\ell/180$: 0.500

FLOOR JOISTS—50 LB LIVE LOAD

JOIST (IN.)		EXTREME FIBER STRESS IN BENDING, F_b (PSI)									
SIZE, SPACING		900	1000	1100	1200	1300	1400	1500	1600	1800	2000
2 x 6	12	8-8 1.063	9-2 1.246	9-7 1.437	10-0 1.637	10-5 1.846	10-10 2.063	11-3 2.289	11-7 2.521	12-3 3.007	12-11 3.522
	16	7-6 0.924	7-11 1.083	8-4 1.249	8-8 1.423	9-1 1.605	9-5 1.794	9-9 1.989	10-0 2.191	10-7 2.614	11-2 3.062
	24	6-1 0.744	6-5 0.871	6-9 1.005	7-1 1.144	7-4 1.291	7-7 1.443	7-11 1.600	8-2 1.762	8-7 2.103	9-1 2.463
2 x 8	12	11-5 1.063	12-1 1.246	12-7 1.437	13-3 1.631	13-9 1.846	14-3 2.063	14-9 2.289	15-3 2.521	16-2 3.007	17-1 3.522
	16	9-11 0.924	10-5 1.083	11-0 1.249	11-6 1.423	11-11 1.605	12-5 1.794	12-10 1.989	13-3 2.191	14-0 2.614	14-10 3.062
	24	8-1 0.744	8-6 0.871	8-11 1.005	9-4 1.144	9-8 1.291	10-1 1.443	10-5 1.600	10-9 1.762	11-5 2.103	12-0 2.463
2 x 10	12	14-7 1.063	15-5 1.246	16-2 1.437	16-10 1.637	17-6 1.846	18-2 2.063	18-10 2.289	19-5 2.521	20-7 3.007	21-9 3.522
	16	12-7 0.924	13-4 1.083	14-0 1.249	14-7 1.423	15-3 1.605	15-10 1.794	16-4 1.989	16-10 2.191	17-11 2.614	18-11 3.062
	24	10-3 0.744	10-10 0.871	11-4 1.005	11-10 1.144	12-4 1.291	12-10 1.443	13-3 1.600	13-9 1.762	14-7 2.103	15-4 2.463
2 x 12	12	17-9 1.063	18-9 1.246	19-7 1.437	20-6 1.637	21-4 1.846	22-2 2.063	22-11 2.289	23-8 2.521	25-1 3.007	26-6 3.522
	16	15-5 0.924	16-3 1.083	17-1 1.249	17-10 1.423	18-6 1.605	19-2 1.794	19-10 1.989	20-6 2.191	21-9 2.614	23-0 3.062
	24	12-6 0.744	13-2 0.871	13-10 1.005	14-5 1.144	15-0 1.291	15-7 1.443	16-2 1.600	16-7 1.762	17-8 2.103	18-10 2.463
2 x 14	12	20-11 1.063	22-1 1.246	23-2 1.437	24-2 1.637	25-2 1.846	26-1 2.063	27-0 2.289	27-11 2.521	29-7 3.007	31-2 3.522
	16	18-2 0.924	19-2 1.083	20-1 1.249	20-11 1.423	21-9 1.605	22-7 1.794	23-5 1.989	24-2 2.191	25-7 2.614	27-0 3.062
	24	14-9 0.744	15-6 0.871	16-3 1.005	17-0 1.144	17-8 1.291	18-4 1.443	19-0 1.600	19-7 1.762	20-10 2.103	22-0 2.463
3 x 6	12	11-2 1.373	11-10 1.608	12-5 1.855	12-11 2.113	13-6 2.383	14-0 2.663	14-6 2.953	14-11 3.254	15-10 3.882	16-9 4.547
	16	9-9 1.193	10-3 1.397	10-9 1.612	11-3 1.836	11-8 2.071	12-2 2.314	12-7 2.567	12-11 2.827	13-9 3.374	14-6 3.952
	24	7-11 0.960	8-4 1.124	8-9 1.297	9-2 1.478	9-6 1.666	9-10 1.862	10-2 2.065	10-6 2.275	11-2 2.714	11-9 3.179
3 x 8	12	14-9 1.373	15-7 1.608	16-4 1.855	17-1 2.113	17-9 2.383	18-5 2.663	19-1 2.953	19-9 3.254	20-11 3.882	22-1 4.547
	16	12-10 1.193	13-6 1.397	14-2 1.612	14-10 1.836	15-5 2.071	16-0 2.314	16-7 2.567	17-1 2.827	18-1 3.374	19-1 3.952
	24	10-5 0.960	11-0 1.124	11-6 1.297	12-0 1.478	12-6 1.666	13-0 1.862	13-5 2.065	13-10 2.275	14-8 2.714	15-6 3.179
3 x 10	12	18-10 1.373	19-10 1.608	20-10 1.855	21-9 2.113	22-7 2.383	23-6 2.663	24-4 2.953	25-1 3.254	26-7 3.882	28-1 4.547
	16	16-4 1.193	17-3 1.397	18-1 1.612	18-10 1.836	19-7 2.071	20-5 2.314	21-1 2.567	21-10 2.827	23-2 3.374	24-5 3.952
	24	13-3 0.960	14-0 1.124	14-8 1.297	15-4 1.478	16-0 1.666	16-7 1.862	17-2 2.065	17-8 2.275	18-9 2.714	19-10 3.179
3 x 12	12	22-11 1.373	24-2 1.608	25-4 1.855	26-5 2.113	27-6 2.383	28-7 2.663	29-7 2.953	30-7 3.254	32-5 3.882	34-2 4.547
	16	19-11 1.193	20-11 1.397	21-11 1.612	22-11 1.836	23-11 2.071	24-10 2.314	25-8 2.567	26-6 2.827	28-1 3.374	29-7 3.952
	24	16-2 0.960	17-0 1.124	17-10 1.297	18-8 1.478	19-5 1.666	20-2 1.862	20-10 2.065	21-6 2.275	22-10 2.714	24-1 3.179
3 x 14	12	27-0 1.373	28-5 1.608	29-10 1.855	31-2 2.113	32-5 2.383	33-8 2.663	34-10 2.953	36-0 3.254	38-2 3.882	40-3 4.547
	16	23-5 1.193	24-8 1.397	25-11 1.612	27-1 1.836	28-2 2.071	29-3 2.314	30-3 2.567	31-3 2.827	33-1 3.374	34-11 3.952
	24	19-0 0.960	20-0 1.124	21-0 1.297	22-0 1.478	22-11 1.666	23-9 1.862	24-7 2.065	25-5 2.275	26-11 2.714	28-4 3.179

NOTE: The required modulus of elasticity, E, in 1,000,000 psi is shown below each span, if deflection under the live load is limited to $\ell/360$.

American Forest and Paper Association; Washington, D.C.

DESIGN LOAD TABLES   6

GENERAL DESIGN INFORMATION

For floor construction where live loading is heavier than customarily found in residential occupancies, tabular data are provided.

The tabulated spans are based on bending strength using the live load indicated in each table heading plus a dead load of 10 psf. In calculating the required modulus of elasticity for the tabulated span, the live load only was used, since this is in accordance with established practice for design of floor joists.

SPAN

While the effective span length for an isolated beam is customarily taken as the distance from face to face of supports plus one-half the required length of bearing at each end, it is the practice in designing joists spaced not over 24 in. apart to consider the span as the clear distance between supports.

NET SIZES OF LUMBER

Joists are customarily specified in terms of nominal sizes, but calculations to determine the allowable span and required modulus of elasticity are based on actual sizes.

DESIGN STRESSES

Unit design values for design of wood joists are given in the National Design Specification for Wood Construc-tion, available from the American Forest & Paper Association.

ADJUSTMENT OF MODULUS OF ELASTICITY

The modulus of elasticity values listed in the span tables for joists are those required for the tabulated spans if deflection under the live load is limited to $\ell/360$. Where other deflection limits are acceptable, the tabular E values may be adjusted by multiplying them by the following factors:

For limit of $\ell/300$: 0.833
For limit of $\ell/240$: 0.667
For limit of $\ell/180$: 0.500

FLOOR JOISTS— 60 LB LIVE LOAD

JOIST (IN.) SIZE, SPACING		900	1000	1100	1200	1300	1400	1500	1600	1800	2000
2 x 6	12	8-1 / 1.012	8-6 / 1.186	8-11 / 1.368	9-3 / 1.558	9-8 / 1.757	10-0 / 1.964	10-5 / 2.179	10-9 / 2.400	11-5 / 2.863	12-0 / 3.353
	16	7-0 / 0.880	7-4 / 1.031	7-9 / 1.189	8-1 / 1.355	8-5 / 1.528	8-8 / 1.708	9-0 / 1.894	9-4 / 2.191	9-10 / 2.489	10-5 / 2.915
	24	5-8 / 0.708	6-0 / 0.829	6-4 / 0.957	6-7 / 1.089	6-10 / 1.229	7-1 / 1.374	7-4 / 1.523	7-7 / 1.677	8-0 / 2.002	8-5 / 2.345
2 x 8	12	10-7 / 1.012	11-2 / 1.186	11-9 / 1.368	12-3 / 1.558	12-9 / 1.757	13-3 / 1.964	13-8 / 2.179	14-1 / 2.400	15-0 / 2.863	15-10 / 3.353
	16	9-2 / 0.880	9-8 / 1.031	10-2 / 1.189	10-7 / 1.355	11-0 / 1.528	11-5 / 1.708	11-10 / 1.894	12-3 / 2.191	13-0 / 2.489	13-8 / 2.915
	24	7-6 / 0.708	7-11 / 0.829	8-3 / 0.957	8-7 / 1.089	9-0 / 1.229	9-4 / 1.374	9-7 / 1.523	9-11 / 1.677	10-7 / 2.002	11-2 / 2.345
2 x 10	12	13-6 / 1.012	14-3 / 1.186	14-11 / 1.368	15-7 / 1.558	16-3 / 1.757	16-10 / 1.964	17-5 / 2.179	18-0 / 2.400	19-1 / 2.863	20-2 / 3.353
	16	11-9 / 0.880	12-3 / 1.031	13-0 / 1.189	13-6 / 1.355	14-0 / 1.528	14-6 / 1.708	15-1 / 1.894	15-7 / 2.191	16-7 / 2.489	17-6 / 2.915
	24	9-6 / 0.708	10-0 / 0.829	10-6 / 0.957	11-0 / 1.089	11-6 / 1.229	11-11 / 1.374	12-4 / 1.523	12-9 / 1.677	13-6 / 2.002	14-3 / 2.345
2 x 12	12	16-6 / 1.012	17-4 / 1.186	18-2 / 1.368	19-0 / 1.558	19-9 / 1.757	20-6 / 1.964	21-3 / 2.179	21-11 / 2.400	23-3 / 2.863	24-6 / 3.353
	16	14-3 / 0.880	15-0 / 1.031	15-9 / 1.189	16-6 / 1.355	17-2 / 1.528	17-10 / 1.708	18-5 / 1.894	19-0 / 2.191	20-2 / 2.489	21-3 / 2.915
	24	11-7 / 0.708	12-3 / 0.829	12-10 / 0.957	13-5 / 1.089	13-11 / 1.229	14-5 / 1.374	14-11 / 1.523	15-5 / 1.677	16-5 / 2.002	17-5 / 2.345
2 x 14	12	19-5 / 1.012	20-5 / 1.186	21-5 / 1.368	22-4 / 1.558	23-3 / 1.757	24-2 / 1.964	25-0 / 2.179	25-10 / 2.400	27-5 / 2.863	28-11 / 3.353
	16	16-10 / 0.880	17-8 / 1.031	18-6 / 1.189	19-4 / 1.355	20-2 / 1.528	20-11 / 1.708	21-8 / 1.894	22-5 / 2.191	23-9 / 2.489	25-1 / 2.915
	24	13-8 / 0.708	14-5 / 0.829	15-1 / 0.957	15-9 / 1.089	16-5 / 1.229	17-0 / 1.374	17-7 / 1.523	18-2 / 1.677	19-3 / 2.002	20-4 / 2.345
3 x 6	12	10-4 / 1.307	10-11 / 1.531	11-6 / 1.766	12-0 / 2.012	12-6 / 2.269	13-0 / 2.535	13-5 / 2.811	13-10 / 3.098	14-8 / 3.696	15-6 / 4.329
	16	9-0 / 1.136	9-6 / 1.330	10-0 / 1.535	10-5 / 1.748	10-10 / 1.972	11-3 / 2.203	11-8 / 2.444	12-0 / 2.691	12-9 / 3.212	13-5 / 3.762
	24	7-4 / 0.914	7-9 / 1.070	8-1 / 1.235	8-5 / 1.406	8-9 / 1.586	9-1 / 1.773	9-5 / 1.966	9-9 / 2.166	10-4 / 2.584	10-11 / 3.026
3 x 8	12	13-8 / 1.307	14-5 / 1.531	15-2 / 1.766	15-10 / 2.012	16-6 / 2.269	17-1 / 2.535	17-8 / 2.811	18-3 / 3.098	19-4 / 3.696	20-5 / 4.329
	16	11-10 / 1.136	12-6 / 1.330	13-1 / 1.535	13-8 / 1.748	14-3 / 1.972	14-10 / 2.203	15-4 / 2.444	15-10 / 2.691	16-9 / 3.212	17-8 / 3.762
	24	9-7 / 0.914	10-1 / 1.070	10-7 / 1.235	11-1 / 1.406	11-7 / 1.586	12-0 / 1.773	12-5 / 1.966	12-10 / 2.166	13-7 / 2.584	14-4 / 3.026
3 x 10	12	17-5 / 1.307	18-5 / 1.531	19-4 / 1.766	20-2 / 2.012	21-0 / 2.269	21-9 / 2.535	22-7 / 2.811	23-4 / 3.098	24-9 / 3.696	26-1 / 4.329
	16	15-2 / 1.136	16-0 / 1.330	16-9 / 1.535	17-6 / 1.748	18-2 / 1.972	18-10 / 2.203	19-6 / 2.444	20-2 / 2.691	21-5 / 3.212	22-7 / 3.762
	24	12-4 / 0.914	13-0 / 1.070	13-7 / 1.235	14-2 / 1.406	14-9 / 1.586	15-4 / 1.773	15-10 / 1.966	16-4 / 2.166	17-5 / 2.584	18-4 / 3.026
3 x 12	12	21-3 / 1.307	22-4 / 1.531	23-5 / 1.766	24-6 / 2.012	25-6 / 2.269	26-6 / 2.535	27-5 / 2.811	28-4 / 3.098	30-0 / 3.696	31-7 / 4.329
	16	18-5 / 1.136	19-5 / 1.330	20-4 / 1.535	21-3 / 1.748	22-2 / 1.972	23-0 / 2.203	23-9 / 2.444	24-6 / 2.691	26-0 / 3.212	27-5 / 3.762
	24	15-0 / 0.914	15-9 / 1.070	16-6 / 1.235	17-3 / 1.406	18-0 / 1.586	18-8 / 1.773	19-4 / 1.966	20-0 / 2.166	21-2 / 2.584	22-4 / 3.036
3 x 14	12	25-0 / 1.307	26-4 / 1.531	27-7 / 1.766	28-10 / 2.012	30-1 / 2.269	31-3 / 2.535	32-4 / 2.811	33-4 / 3.098	35-4 / 3.696	37-4 / 4.329
	16	21-8 / 1.136	22-10 / 1.330	24-0 / 1.535	25-1 / 1.748	26-1 / 1.972	27-1 / 2.203	28-0 / 2.444	28-11 / 2.691	30-8 / 3.212	32-4 / 3.762
	24	17-7 / 0.914	18-7 / 1.070	19-6 / 1.235	20-4 / 1.406	21-2 / 1.586	22-0 / 1.773	22-9 / 1.966	23-6 / 2.166	24-11 / 2.584	26-3 / 3.026

Header for table: EXTREME FIBER STRESS IN BENDING, F_b (PSI)

NOTE: The required modulus of elasticity, E, in 1,000,000 psi is shown below each span, if deflection under the live load is limited to $\ell/360$.

American Forest and Paper Association; Washington, D.C.

DESIGN LOAD TABLES

GENERAL DESIGN INFORMATION

For floor construction where live loading is heavier than customarily found in residential occupancies, tabular data are provided.

The tabulated spans are based on bending strength using the live load indicated in each table heading plus a dead load of 10 psf. In calculating the required modulus of elasticity for the tabulated span, the live load only was used, since this is in accordance with established practice for design of floor joists.

SPAN

While the effective span length for an isolated beam is customarily taken as the distance from face to face

of supports plus one-half the required length of bearing at each end, it is the practice in designing joists spaced not over 24 in. apart to consider the span as the clear distance between supports.

NET SIZES OF LUMBER

Joists are customarily specified in terms of nominal sizes, but calculations to determine the allowable span and required modulus of elasticity are based on actual sizes.

DESIGN STRESSES

Unit design values for design of wood joists are given in the National Design Specification for Wood Construc-

tion, available from the American Forest & Paper Association.

ADJUSTMENT OF MODULUS OF ELASTICITY

The modulus of elasticity values listed in the span tables for joists are those required for the tabulated spans if deflection under the live load is limited to $\ell/360$. Where other deflection limits are acceptable, the tabular E values may be adjusted by multiplying them by the following factors:

For limit of $\ell/300$: 0.833
For limit of $\ell/240$: 0.667
For limit of $\ell/180$: 0.500

FLOOR JOISTS—70 LB LIVE LOAD

JOIST (IN.)		EXTREME FIBER STRESS IN BENDING, F_b (PSI)									
SIZE, SPACING		900	1000	1100	1200	1300	1400	1500	1600	1800	2000
2 x 10	12	12-8 / 0.963	13-4 / 1.133	14-0 / 1.306	14-7 / 1.488	15-2 / 1.678	15-9 / 1.875	16-4 / 2.081	16-10 / 2.292	17-11 / 2.733	18-10 / 3.201
	16	11-1 / 0.840	11-7 / 0.984	12-1 / 1.135	12-7 / 1.294	13-2 / 1.459	13-8 / 1.631	14-2 / 1.808	14-7 / 1.992	15-6 / 2.376	16-4 / 2.783
	24	8-11 / 0.676	9-5 / 0.792	9-10 / 0.914	10-3 / 1.040	10-8 / 1.174	11-1 / 1.312	11-6 / 1.454	11-11 / 1.602	12-7 / 1.912	13-3 / 2.239
2 x 12	12	15-5 / 0.963	16-3 / 1.133	17-0 / 1.306	17-9 / 1.488	18-6 / 1.678	19-2 / 1.875	19-10 / 2.081	20-6 / 2.292	21-9 / 2.733	22-11 / 3.201
	16	13-4 / 0.840	14-1 / 0.984	14-9 / 1.135	15-5 / 1.294	16-0 / 1.459	16-7 / 1.631	17-3 / 1.808	17-10 / 1.992	18-10 / 2.376	19-11 / 2.783
	24	10-10 / 0.676	11-5 / 0.792	12-0 / 0.914	12-6 / 1.040	13-0 / 1.174	13-6 / 1.312	14-0 / 1.454	14-5 / 1.602	15-4 / 1.912	16-4 / 2.239
2 x 14	12	18-2 / 0.963	19-1 / 1.133	20-0 / 1.306	20-11 / 1.488	21-9 / 1.678	22-7 / 1.875	23-5 / 2.081	24-2 / 2.292	25-7 / 2.733	27-0 / 3.201
	16	15-9 / 0.840	16-7 / 0.984	17-5 / 1.135	18-2 / 1.294	18-11 / 1.459	19-7 / 1.631	20-3 / 1.808	20-11 / 1.992	22-3 / 2.376	23-5 / 2.783
	24	12-9 / 0.676	13-6 / 0.792	14-2 / 0.914	14-9 / 1.040	15-4 / 1.174	15-11 / 1.312	16-6 / 1.454	17-0 / 1.602	18-1 / 1.912	19-1 / 2.239
3 x 8	12	12-10 / 1.248	13-6 / 1.462	14-2 / 1.686	14-9 / 1.921	15-4 / 2.166	15-11 / 2.421	16-6 / 2.684	17-1 / 2.958	18-1 / 3.529	19-1 / 4.133
	16	11-1 / 1.084	11-8 / 1.270	12-3 / 1.465	12-10 / 1.669	13-4 / 1.883	13-10 / 2.103	14-4 / 2.333	14-10 / 2.570	15-8 / 3.067	16-7 / 3.592
	24	9-0 / 0.873	9-6 / 1.022	10-0 / 1.179	10-5 / 1.344	10-10 / 1.514	11-3 / 1.693	11-8 / 1.877	12-0 / 2.068	12-9 / 2.467	13-5 / 2.900
3 x 10	12	16-4 / 1.248	17-3 / 1.462	18-1 / 1.686	18-10 / 1.921	19-7 / 2.166	20-4 / 2.421	21-1 / 2.684	21-9 / 2.958	23-1 / 3.529	24-4 / 4.133
	16	14-2 / 1.084	14-11 / 1.270	15-8 / 1.465	16-4 / 1.669	17-0 / 1.883	17-8 / 2.103	18-3 / 2.333	18-11 / 2.570	20-1 / 3.067	21-1 / 3.592
	24	11-6 / 0.873	12-2 / 1.022	12-9 / 1.179	13-3 / 1.344	13-10 / 1.514	14-4 / 1.693	14-10 / 1.877	15-4 / 2.068	16-3 / 2.467	17-2 / 2.900
3 x 12	12	19-11 / 1.248	20-11 / 1.462	21-11 / 1.686	22-11 / 1.921	23-10 / 2.166	24-9 / 2.421	25-8 / 2.684	26-6 / 2.958	28-1 / 3.529	29-7 / 4.133
	16	17-3 / 1.084	18-2 / 1.270	19-1 / 1.465	19-11 / 1.669	20-9 / 1.883	21-6 / 2.103	22-3 / 2.333	23-0 / 2.570	24-4 / 3.067	25-8 / 3.592
	24	14-0 / 0.873	14-9 / 1.022	15-6 / 1.179	16-2 / 1.344	16-10 / 1.514	17-6 / 1.693	18-1 / 1.877	18-7 / 2.068	19-9 / 2.467	20-10 / 2.900
3 x 14	12	23-4 / 1.248	24-7 / 1.462	25-10 / 1.686	27-0 / 1.921	28-1 / 2.166	29-2 / 2.421	30-2 / 2.684	31-2 / 2.958	33-1 / 3.529	34-11 / 4.133
	16	20-3 / 1.084	21-4 / 1.270	22-5 / 1.465	23-5 / 1.669	24-5 / 1.883	25-4 / 2.103	26-2 / 2.333	27-0 / 2.570	28-8 / 3.067	30-3 / 3.592
	24	16-6 / 0.873	17-4 / 1.022	18-7 / 1.179	19-0 / 1.344	19-9 / 1.514	20-6 / 1.693	21-3 / 1.877	22-0 / 2.068	23-4 / 2.467	24-7 / 2.900
4 x 8	12	15-2 / 1.490	16-0 / 1.745	16-10 / 2.015	17-7 / 2.295	18-3 / 2.588	18-11 / 2.891	19-7 / 3.207	20-3 / 3.533	21-6 / 4.217	22-7 / 4.939
	16	13-2 / 1.300	13-11 / 1.533	14-7 / 1.757	15-3 / 2.002	15-11 / 2.257	16-6 / 2.522	17-1 / 2.799	17-7 / 3.082	18-7 / 3.676	19-7 / 4.306
	24	10-9 / 1.054	11-4 / 1.234	11-11 / 1.425	12-5 / 1.625	12-11 / 1.831	13-5 / 2.046	13-11 / 2.268	14-4 / 2.500	15-2 / 2.922	16-0 / 3.492
4 x 10	12	19-5 / 1.490	20-5 / 1.745	21-5 / 2.015	22-5 / 2.295	22-4 / 2.588	24-2 / 2.891	25-0 / 3.207	25-10 / 3.533	27-5 / 4.217	28-9 / 4.939
	16	16-10 / 1.300	17-9 / 1.533	18-7 / 1.757	19-5 / 2.002	20-3 / 2.257	21-0 / 2.522	21-9 / 2.799	22-5 / 3.082	23-10 / 3.676	25-1 / 4.306
	24	13-8 / 1.054	14-5 / 1.234	15-2 / 1.425	15-10 / 1.625	16-6 / 1.831	17-1 / 2.046	17-8 / 2.268	18-3 / 2.500	19-3 / 2.922	20-5 / 3.492
4 x 12	12	23-7 / 1.490	24-10 / 1.745	26-1 / 2.015	27-3 / 2.295	28-4 / 2.588	29-5 / 2.891	30-5 / 3.207	31-5 / 3.533	33-4 / 4.217	35-2 / 4.939
	16	20-6 / 1.300	21-7 / 1.533	22-7 / 1.757	23-7 / 2.002	24-7 / 2.257	25-6 / 2.522	26-5 / 2.799	27-4 / 3.082	28-5 / 3.676	30-6 / 4.306
	24	16-8 / 1.054	17-7 / 1.234	18-5 / 1.425	19-3 / 1.625	20-1 / 1.831	20-10 / 2.046	21-6 / 2.268	22-2 / 2.500	23-6 / 2.922	24-10 / 3.492

NOTE: The required modulus of elasticity, E, in 1,000,000 psi is shown below each span, if deflection under the live load is limited to $\ell/360$.

American Forest and Paper Association; Washington, D.C.

GENERAL DESIGN INFORMATION

For floor construction where live loading is heavier than customarily found in residential occupancies, tabular data are provided.

The tabulated spans are based on bending strength using the live load indicated in each table heading plus a dead load of 10 psf. In calculating the required modulus of elasticity for the tabulated span, the live load only was used, since this is in accordance with established practice for design of floor joists.

SPAN

While the effective span length for an isolated beam is customarily taken as the distance from face to face of supports plus one-half the required length of bearing at each end, it is the practice in designing joists spaced not over 24 in. apart to consider the span as the clear distance between supports.

NET SIZES OF LUMBER

Joists are customarily specified in terms of nominal sizes, but calculations to determine the allowable span and required modulus of elasticity are based on actual sizes.

DESIGN STRESSES

Unit design values for design of wood joists are given in the National Design Specification for Wood Construc-tion, available from the American Forest & Paper Asso-ciation.

ADJUSTMENT OF MODULUS OF ELASTICITY

The modulus of elasticity values listed in the span tables for joists are those required for the tabulated spans if deflection under the live load is limited to $\ell/360$. Where other deflection limits are acceptable, the tabular E values may be adjusted by multiplying them by the following factors:

For limit of $\ell/300$: 0.833
For limit of $\ell/240$: 0.667
For limit of $\ell/180$: 0.500

FLOOR JOISTS—80 LB LIVE LOAD

JOIST (IN.)		EXTREME FIBER STRESS IN BENDING, F_b (PSI)									
SIZE, SPACING		900	1000	1100	1200	1300	1400	1500	1600	1800	2000
2 x 10	12	11-11 / 0.926	12-7 / 1.084	13-2 / 1.250	13-9 / 1.423	14-4 / 1.604	14-11 / 1.795	15-5 / 1.988	15-11 / 2.191	16-10 / 2.617	17-9 / 3.062
	16	10-4 / 0.803	10-11 / 0.941	11-5 / 1.086	11-11 / 1.236	12-5 / 1.395	12-11 / 1.561	13-4 / 1.730	13-9 / 1.903	14-7 / 2.273	15-5 / 2.662
	24	8-5 / 0.646	8-10 / 0.758	9-3 / 0.873	9-8 / 0.995	10-1 / 1.124	10-6 / 1.254	10-10 / 1.390	11-2 / 1.533	11-10 / 1.829	12-6 / 2.143
2 x 12	12	14-6 / 0.926	15-4 / 1.084	16-1 / 1.250	16-9 / 1.423	17-5 / 1.604	18-1 / 1.795	18-9 / 1.988	19-4 / 2.191	20-6 / 2.617	21-7 / 3.062
	16	12-7 / 0.803	13-3 / 0.941	13-11 / 1.089	14-6 / 1.236	15-1 / 1.395	15-8 / 1.561	16-3 / 1.730	16-9 / 1.903	17-9 / 2.273	18-9 / 2.662
	24	10-3 / 0.646	10-9 / 0.758	11-3 / 0.873	11-9 / 0.995	12-3 / 1.124	12-9 / 1.254	13-2 / 1.390	13-7 / 1.533	14-5 / 1.829	15-5 / 2.143
2 x 14	12	17-1 / 0.926	18-0 / 1.084	18-10 / 1.250	19-8 / 1.423	20-6 / 1.604	21-4 / 1.795	22-1 / 1.988	22-9 / 2.191	24-2 / 2.617	25-5 / 3.062
	16	14-10 / 0.803	15-7 / 0.941	16-4 / 1.086	17-1 / 1.236	17-10 / 1.395	18-6 / 1.561	19-2 / 1.730	19-9 / 1.903	20-11 / 2.273	22-1 / 2.662
	24	12-0 / 0.646	12-8 / 0.758	13-4 / 0.873	13-11 / 0.995	14-5 / 1.124	15-0 / 1.254	15-6 / 1.390	16-0 / 1.533	17-0 / 1.829	18-0 / 2.143
3 x 8	12	12-0 / 1.195	12-8 / 1.399	13-4 / 1.614	13-11 / 1.838	14-6 / 2.073	15-1 / 2.317	15-7 / 2.569	16-1 / 2.831	17-1 / 3.377	18-0 / 3.956
	16	10-6 / 1.038	11-0 / 1.215	11-7 / 1.402	12-1 / 1.597	12-7 / 1.802	13-1 / 2.013	13-6 / 2.233	13-11 / 2.459	14-9 / 2.935	15-7 / 3.438
	24	8-6 / 0.835	9-0 / 0.978	9-5 / 1.128	9-10 / 1.286	10-3 / 1.449	10-7 / 1.620	11-0 / 1.797	11-4 / 1.979	12-0 / 2.361	12-8 / 2.766
3 x 10	12	15-5 / 1.195	16-3 / 1.399	17-0 / 1.614	17-9 / 1.838	18-6 / 2.073	19-2 / 2.317	19-10 / 2.569	20-6 / 2.831	21-8 / 3.377	22-11 / 3.956
	16	13-4 / 1.038	14-1 / 1.215	14-9 / 1.402	15-5 / 1.597	16-0 / 1.802	16-7 / 2.013	17-3 / 2.233	17-9 / 2.459	18-10 / 2.935	19-11 / 3.438
	24	10-10 / 0.835	11-5 / 0.978	12-0 / 1.128	12-6 / 1.286	13-0 / 1.446	13-6 / 1.620	14-0 / 1.797	14-5 / 1.979	15-4 / 2.361	16-2 / 2.766
3 x 12	12	18-9 / 1.195	19-9 / 1.399	20-8 / 1.614	21-7 / 1.838	22-6 / 2.073	23-4 / 2.317	24-2 / 2.569	25-0 / 2.831	26-5 / 3.377	27-11 / 3.956
	16	16-3 / 1.038	17-1 / 1.215	17-11 / 1.402	18-9 / 1.597	19-6 / 1.802	20-3 / 2.013	20-11 / 2.233	21-7 / 2.459	22-11 / 2.935	24-2 / 3.438
	24	13-2 / 0.835	13-11 / 0.978	14-7 / 1.128	15-3 / 1.286	15-10 / 1.449	16-5 / 1.620	17-0 / 1.797	17-7 / 1.979	18-7 / 2.361	19-7 / 2.766
3 x 14	12	22-1 / 1.195	23-3 / 1.399	24-4 / 1.614	25-5 / 1.838	26-6 / 2.073	27-6 / 2.317	28-6 / 2.569	29-5 / 2.831	31-2 / 3.377	32-10 / 3.956
	16	19-2 / 1.038	20-2 / 1.215	21-2 / 1.402	22-1 / 1.597	23-0 / 1.802	23-10 / 2.013	24-8 / 2.233	25-6 / 2.459	27-1 / 2.935	28-6 / 3.438
	24	15-6 / 0.835	16-4 / 0.978	17-2 / 1.128	17-11 / 1.286	18-8 / 1.449	19-5 / 1.620	20-1 / 1.797	20-9 / 1.979	22-0 / 2.361	23-2 / 2.766
4 x 8	12	14-4 / 1.426	15-1 / 1.670	15-10 / 1.928	16-6 / 2.196	17-2 / 2.475	17-10 / 2.766	18-5 / 3.068	19-0 / 3.379	20-3 / 4.034	21-4 / 4.725
	16	12-5 / 1.243	13-1 / 1.457	13-9 / 1.681	14-4 / 1.915	14-11 / 2.159	15-6 / 2.413	16-1 / 2.677	16-7 / 2.948	17-7 / 3.516	18-6 / 4.119
	24	10-2 / 1.009	10-8 / 1.180	11-2 / 1.363	11-8 / 1.554	12-2 / 1.752	12-6 / 1.957	13-1 / 2.170	13-6 / 2.391	14-4 / 2.795	15-1 / 3.340
4 x 10	12	18-3 / 1.426	19-3 / 1.670	20-2 / 1.928	21-1 / 2.196	21-11 / 2.475	22-9 / 2.766	23-7 / 3.068	24-4 / 3.379	25-10 / 4.034	27-3 / 4.725
	16	15-10 / 1.243	16-8 / 1.457	17-6 / 1.681	18-4 / 1.915	19-1 / 2.159	19-10 / 2.413	20-6 / 2.677	21-2 / 2.948	22-5 / 3.516	23-7 / 4.119
	24	12-11 / 1.009	13-7 / 1.180	14-3 / 1.363	14-11 / 1.554	15-6 / 1.752	16-1 / 1.957	16-8 / 2.170	17-2 / 2.391	18-2 / 2.795	19-3 / 3.340
4 x 12	12	22-3 / 1.426	23-5 / 1.670	24-6 / 1.928	25-7 / 2.196	26-8 / 2.475	27-8 / 2.766	28-8 / 3.068	29-7 / 3.379	31-5 / 4.034	33-2 / 4.725
	16	19-3 / 1.243	20-4 / 1.457	21-4 / 1.681	22-3 / 1.915	23-2 / 2.159	24-1 / 2.413	24-11 / 2.677	25-9 / 2.948	27-3 / 3.516	28-9 / 4.119
	24	15-9 / 1.009	16-7 / 1.180	17-4 / 1.363	18-1 / 1.554	18-10 / 1.752	19-7 / 1.957	20-3 / 2.170	20-11 / 2.391	22-2 / 2.795	23-5 / 3.340

NOTE: The required modulus of elasticity, E, in 1,000,000 psi is shown below each span, if deflection under the live load is limited to $\ell/360$.

American Forest and Paper Association; Washington, D.C.

DESIGN LOAD TABLES

UNIT AXIAL STRESSES: SIMPLE SOLID COLUMNS— ℓ/d FROM 11 TO 30

E	F_c	11+	12	13	14	15	16	17	18	19	20	21	22	23	24	25	26	27	28	29	30
1,800,000	1500	1475	1464	1451	1434	1413	1388	1357	1320	1277	1226	1167	1098	1020	938	864	799	741	689	642	600
	1400	1380	1371	1360	1346	1329	1309	1284	1254	1218	1177	1129	1073	1010	937	864	799	741	689	642	600
	1300	1284	1277	1268	1257	1243	1227	1207	1183	1155	1121	1083	1039	988	930	864	799	741	689	642	600
	1200	1187	1182	1175	1166	1156	1142	1127	1108	1086	1060	1029	994	954	909	857	799	741	689	642	600
1,700,000	1500	1472	1460	1445	1426	1403	1374	1339	1298	1249	1192	1126	1050	964	885	816	754	700	651	606	567
	1400	1377	1368	1355	1340	1321	1298	1269	1236	1196	1150	1096	1034	963	885	816	754	700	651	606	567
	1300	1282	1274	1264	1252	1237	1218	1195	1169	1137	1100	1057	1007	950	885	816	754	700	651	606	567
	1200	1186	1180	1172	1162	1150	1135	1118	1097	1072	1043	1009	969	925	873	816	754	700	651	606	567
1,600,000	1500	1468	1455	1438	1417	1390	1358	1319	1272	1217	1153	1078	992	907	833	768	710	658	612	571	533
	1400	1374	1363	1350	1332	1311	1284	1253	1215	1170	1118	1057	987	907	833	768	710	658	612	571	533
	1300	1279	1271	1260	1246	1228	1207	1182	1152	1116	1074	1025	969	905	833	768	710	658	612	571	533
	1200	1184	1177	1168	1157	1144	1127	1107	1083	1055	1022	984	940	889	831	768	710	658	612	571	533
	1100	1087	1082	1076	1067	1057	1044	1029	1010	988	963	934	900	861	816	766	710	658	612	571	533
	1000	991	987	982	975	967	958	946	933	916	897	875	849	820	787	749	706	658	612	571	533
	900	893	890	887	882	876	869	861	851	839	825	809	790	769	744	717	686	651	612	571	533
1,500,000	1400	1371	1358	1343	1323	1298	1268	1232	1189	1138	1079	1010	930	851	781	720	666	617	574	535	500
	1300	1276	1267	1254	1238	1219	1195	1166	1131	1091	1043	987	923	851	781	720	666	617	574	535	500
	1200	1181	1174	1164	1151	1136	1117	1094	1067	1035	998	954	904	846	781	720	666	617	574	535	500
	1100	1086	1080	1072	1063	1051	1036	1019	998	973	944	911	872	828	777	720	666	617	574	535	500
	1000	989	985	979	972	963	952	939	923	905	883	858	829	795	757	714	666	617	574	535	500
	900	892	889	885	880	873	865	855	844	830	815	796	775	751	723	692	656	617	574	535	500
	800	795	792	789	786	781	775	769	761	751	740	727	712	695	676	654	629	601	570	535	500
	700	696	695	693	690	687	684	679	674	667	660	651	641	630	617	602	585	567	546	523	497
	600	598	597	595	594	592	590	587	583	579	575	569	563	556	548	538	528	516	503	488	472
1,400,000	1200	1179	1170	1159	1144	1127	1105	1079	1048	1011	968	918	860	794	729	672	621	576	536	499	467
	1100	1084	1077	1068	1057	1043	1027	1007	983	954	921	883	838	787	729	672	621	576	536	499	467
	1000	988	983	976	968	957	945	930	912	891	866	837	803	765	721	672	621	576	536	499	467
	900	891	887	883	876	869	860	849	836	820	802	781	757	729	697	661	620	576	536	499	467
	800	794	791	788	783	778	772	764	755	744	731	716	699	680	657	632	604	571	536	499	467
	700	696	694	692	689	685	681	676	670	662	654	644	633	619	604	587	568	547	523	496	467
1,300,000	1100	1081	1073	1063	1050	1034	1015	992	964	931	893	848	796	737	677	624	577	535	497	464	433
	1000	986	980	972	963	951	936	919	898	873	844	811	772	727	677	624	577	535	497	464	433
	900	890	885	880	873	864	853	841	825	807	786	762	734	701	664	623	577	535	497	464	433
	800	793	790	786	781	775	767	758	748	735	720	703	683	660	635	605	572	535	497	464	433
	700	695	693	690	687	683	678	672	665	656	647	635	622	607	589	569	547	522	495	464	433
1,200,000	1100	1078	1068	1057	1042	1023	1000	973	940	902	857	804	744	681	625	576	533	494	459	428	400
	1000	983	976	967	956	942	925	905	880	851	817	778	732	680	625	576	533	494	459	428	400
	900	888	883	876	868	858	845	830	813	791	767	738	705	667	624	576	533	494	459	428	400
	800	791	788	783	778	770	762	751	739	724	706	686	663	636	606	571	533	494	459	428	400
	700	694	692	689	685	680	674	667	659	649	637	624	608	590	570	547	521	492	459	428	400
	600	596	595	593	591	588	584	579	574	568	560	552	542	531	518	504	487	469	448	425	400
	500	498	497	496	495	493	491	488	485	481	477	472	467	460	453	444	435	424	412	399	384
	400	399	398	398	397	396	395	394	392	390	388	386	383	380	376	371	367	361	355	348	341
1,100,000	900	885	879	872	862	850	835	817	796	771	741	707	668	622	573	528	488	453	421	392	397
	800	790	786	780	773	765	754	742	727	709	689	665	637	605	569	528	488	453	421	392	397
	700	693	690	687	682	676	669	661	651	639	625	609	591	569	545	518	487	453	421	392	397
	600	596	594	592	589	585	581	575	569	562	553	543	531	518	503	485	466	444	419	392	397
	500	498	496	495	493	491	489	486	482	478	473	467	460	452	444	434	422	410	395	380	362
	400	399	398	398	397	396	394	393	391	389	386	383	380	376	371	366	360	354	346	338	329
1,000,000	700	692	688	684	678	671	663	653	641	626	610	590	568	542	513	479	444	412	383	357	333
	600	595	593	590	586	582	577	570	563	554	543	531	517	501	482	461	438	411	383	357	333
	500	497	496	494	492	490	487	483	478	473	467	460	452	442	432	420	406	391	374	354	333
	400	398	398	397	396	395	393	391	389	386	383	380	375	371	365	359	352	344	335	325	315
	300	299	299	299	298	298	297	296	295	294	293	291	290	288	285	283	280	276	273	269	264

UNIT AXIAL STRESSES: SIMPLE SOLID COLUMNS— ℓ/d FROM 30 TO 50

E	F_c	30	31	32	33	34	35	36	37	38	39	40	41	42	43	44	45	46	47	48	49	50
1,800,000	900 or more	600	562	527	496	467	441	417	394	374	355	338	321	306	292	279	267	255	244	234	225	216
1,700,000	900 or more	567	531	498	468	441	416	394	373	353	335	319	303	289	276	263	252	241	231	221	212	204
1,600,000	800 or more	533	499	469	441	415	392	370	351	332	316	300	286	272	260	248	237	227	217	208	200	192
1,500,000	800 or more	500	468	439	413	389	367	347	329	312	296	281	268	255	243	232	222	213	204	195	187	180
1,400,000	700 or more	467	437	410	386	363	343	324	307	291	276	263	250	238	227	217	207	198	190	182	175	168
1,300,000	700 or more	433	406	381	358	337	318	301	285	270	256	244	232	221	211	201	193	184	177	169	162	156
1,200,000	600 or more	400	375	352	331	311	294	278	263	249	237	225	214	204	195	186	178	170	163	156	150	144
1,100,000	600 or more	367	343	322	303	285	269	255	241	229	217	206	196	187	178	170	163	156	149	143	137	132
1,000,000	500 or more	333	312	293	275	260	245	231	219	208	197	188	178	170	162	155	148	142	136	130	125	120

NOTES

1. Obtain design values for E and F_c from the National Design Specification for Wood Construction.
2. Modify F_c for different load duration, if applicable.
3. Calculate ℓ/d where ℓ = unsupported length of column (in.) and d = applicable least actual dimension of column cross section.
4. Determine value of F_c' from table.
5. Total design load on column = cross-sectional area (sq in.) x F_c' value.

American Forest and Paper Association; Washington, D.C.

FLOOR AND ROOF BEAMS—DESIGN TABLES 20 POUNDS PSF

REQUIRED VALUES FOR FIBER STRESS IN BENDING (f) AND MODULUS OF ELASTICITY (E) FOR THE SIZES SHOWN TO SUPPORT SAFELY A LIVE LOAD OF 20 POUNDS PER SQUARE FOOT WITH A DEFLECTION LIMITATION OF $1/300$ 1 = SPAN IN INCHES.

SPAN OF BEAM	NOMINAL SIZE OF BEAM	6'-0" f	6'-0" E	7'-0" f	7'-0" E	8'-0" f	8'-0" E
10'	2-3 x 6	1070	975000	1250	1138000	1430	1300000
	1-3 x 8	1235	850000	1440	992000	1645	1133000
	2-2 x 8	1030	712000	1200	831000	1370	949000
	1-4 x 8	880	606000	1030	707000	1175	808000
	3-2 x 8	685	475000	800	554000	915	633000
	2-3 x 8	615	425000	720	496000	820	566000
	2-2 x 10	630	341000	735	398000	840	455000
11'	2-3 x 6	1295	1296000	1510	1512000	1730	1727000
	1-3 x 8	1490	1131000	1740	1320000	1990	1508000
	2-2 x 8	1245	942000	1450	1099000	1660	1256000
	1-4 x 8	1065	809000	1245	944000	1420	1078000
	3-2 x 8	830	629000	970	734000	1105	838000
	2-3 x 8	745	566000	870	660000	995	754000
	2-2 x 10	765	454000	890	530000	1020	605000
12'	2-3 x 6	1545	1682000	1800	1963000	2060	2242000
	1-3 x 8	1775	1469000	2070	1714000	2370	1958000
	2-2 x 8	1480	1225000	1725	1429000	1970	1633000
	1-4 x 8	1270	1050000	1480	1225000	1690	1400000
	3-2 x 8	985	816000	1150	952000	1315	1088000
	2-3 x 8	890	735000	1035	858000	1185	980000
	1-6 x 8	755	604000	880	705000	1005	805000
	2-2 x 10	910	590000	1060	688000	1210	786000
13'	1-3 x 8	2085	1867000	2430	2179000	2780	2489000
	2-2 x 8	1740	1556000	2025	1816000	2315	2074000
	1-4 x 8	1490	1334000	1735	1557000	1985	1778000
	3-2 x 8	1160	1037000	1350	1210000	1545	1382000
	2-3 x 8	1045	934000	1215	1090000	1390	1245000
	1-6 x 8	885	767000	1040	895000	1185	1022000
	2-2 x 10	1070	750000	1245	875000	1420	1000000
	1-3 x 10	1280	899000	1495	1049000	1710	1198000
	1-4 x 10	915	642000	1070	749000	1220	856000
14'	3-2 x 8	1340	1296000	1570	1512000	1790	1727000
	2-3 x 8	1210	1166000	1410	1361000	1610	1554000
	1-6 x 8	1025	957000	1200	1117000	1370	1276000
	1-3 x 10	1485	1124000	1730	1312000	1980	1498000
	2-2 x 10	1235	936000	1445	1092000	1650	1248000
	1-4 x 10	1060	802000	1240	936000	1415	1069000
	3-2 x 10	825	624000	965	728000	1100	832000
	2-3 x 10	740	561000	865	655000	990	748000
	1-6 x 10	640	471000	745	550000	850	628000
	4-2 x 10	620	468000	720	546000	825	624000
	2-2 x 12	835	520000	975	607000	1115	693000
15'	3-2 x 8	1540	1594000	1800	1860000	2055	2125000
	2-3 x 8	1390	1435000	1620	1675000	1850	1913000
	1-6 x 8	1180	1179000	1375	1376000	1570	1572000
	1-3 x 10	1705	1381000	1990	1612000	2270	1841000
	2-2 x 10	1420	1151000	1660	1343000	1895	1534000
	1-4 x 10	1220	986000	1420	1151000	1625	1314000
	3-2 x 10	950	767000	1105	895000	1265	1022000
	2-3 x 10	850	691000	995	806000	1135	921000
	1-6 x 10	735	580000	855	677000	980	773000
	4-2 x 10	710	576000	830	672000	945	768000
	2-2 x 12	960	640000	1120	747000	1280	853000
	1-4 x 12	825	549000	960	641000	1100	732000
16'	2-3 x 8	1580	1741000	1840	2032000	2105	2321000
	2-2 x 10	1615	1397000	1890	1630000	2155	1862000
	1-4 x 10	1385	1197000	1615	1397000	1845	1596000
	3-2 x 10	1075	931000	1260	1086000	1435	1241000
	2-3 x 10	970	839000	1130	979000	1290	1118000
	1-6 x 10	835	704000	975	821000	1130	938000
	4-2 x 10	810	699000	945	816000	1080	932000
	1-8 x 10	615	516000	715	602000	815	688000
	1-3 x 12	1310	932000	1530	1087000	1750	1242000
	2-2 x 12	1090	776000	1275	905000	1455	1034000
	1-4 x 12	935	666000	1090	777000	1250	888000
	3-2 x 12	730	518000	850	604000	970	690000

SPAN OF BEAM	NOMINAL SIZE OF BEAM	6'-0" f	6'-0" E	7'-0" f	7'-0" E	8'-0" f	8'-0" E
17'	2-2 x 10	1825	1676000	2130	1956000	2435	2234000
	1-4 x 10	1565	1437000	1825	1677000	2085	1915000
	3-2 x 10	1215	1117000	1420	1303000	1625	1489000
	2-3 x 10	1095	1005000	1280	1173000	1460	1340000
	1-6 x 10	945	844000	1100	985000	1260	1125000
	4-2 x 10	910	837000	1065	977000	1215	1116000
	1-8 x 10	690	619000	805	722000	910	825000
	1-3 x 12	1480	1117000	1725	1303000	1975	1489000
	2-2 x 12	1235	931000	1440	1086000	1645	1241000
	1-4 x 12	1060	799000	1230	932000	1410	1065000
	3-2 x 12	820	621000	960	725000	1095	828000
	2-3 x 12	740	559000	865	652000	990	745000
18'	1-4 x 10	1755	1705000	2045	1990000	2340	2273000
	3-2 x 10	1365	1326000	1590	1547000	1815	1767000
	2-3 x 10	1270	1194000	1480	1393000	1695	1592000
	1-6 x 10	1060	1001000	1235	1168000	1415	1334000
	4-2 x 10	1020	995000	1195	1161000	1365	1326000
	1-8 x 10	780	735000	910	858000	1040	980000
	1-3 x 12	1660	1327000	1935	1549000	2210	1769000
	2-2 x 12	1380	1106000	1615	1291000	1845	1474000
	1-4 x 12	1185	947000	1385	1105000	1580	1262000
	3-2 x 12	920	737000	1075	860000	1230	982000
	2-3 x 12	830	664000	970	775000	1105	885000
	1-6 x 12	720	565000	840	659000	960	753000
19'	3-2 x 10	1520	1560000	1775	1820000	2025	2079000
	2-3 x 10	1365	1404000	1595	1638000	1825	1871000
	1-6 x 10	1170	1179000	1365	1376000	1560	1572000
	4-2 x 10	1140	1170000	1330	1365000	1520	1560000
	2-4 x 10	975	1002000	1140	1169000	1300	1336000
	1-8 x 10	860	864000	1005	1008000	1145	1152000
	1-3 x 12	1850	1561000	2155	1822000	2465	2081000
	2-2 x 12	1540	1301000	1800	1518000	2055	1734000
	1-4 x 12	1320	1115000	1540	1301000	1760	1486000
	3-2 x 12	1025	867000	1200	1012000	1370	1156000
	2-3 x 12	925	780000	1080	910000	1230	1040000
	1-6 x 12	805	664000	940	775000	1070	885000
20'	3-2 x 10	1685	1820000	1965	2124000	2245	2426000
	2-3 x 10	1515	1637000	1770	1910000	2020	2182000
	1-6 x 10	1300	1374000	1515	1603000	1735	1831000
	4-2 x 10	1260	1365000	1475	1593000	1685	1819000
	2-4 x 10	1080	1170000	1265	1365000	1445	1560000
	1-8 x 10	960	1007000	1120	1175000	1280	1342000
	2-2 x 12	1705	1517000	1990	1770000	2275	2022000
	1-4 x 12	1465	1300000	1710	1517000	1950	1733000
	3-2 x 12	1140	1011000	1330	1180000	1520	1348000
	2-3 x 12	1025	910000	1195	1062000	1365	1213000
	1-6 x 12	970	775000	1130	904000	1295	1003000
	4-2 x 12	855	759000	995	886000	1135	1012000
21'	2-3 x 10	1670	1895000	1950	2211000	2225	2526000
	1-6 x 10	1430	1591000	1670	1857000	1905	2121000
	4-2 x 10	1390	1580000	1625	1844000	1855	2106000
	2-4 x 10	1195	1354000	1390	1580000	1590	1805000
	1-8 x 10	1050	1166000	1225	1361000	1400	1554000
	2-2 x 12	1880	1756000	2195	2049000	2510	2341000
	1-4 x 12	1615	1505000	1880	1756000	2150	2006000
	3-2 x 12	1255	1171000	1465	1366000	1670	1561000
	2-3 x 12	1130	1054000	1320	1230000	1505	1405000
	1-6 x 12	970	896000	1130	1046000	1295	1194000
	4-2 x 12	940	878000	1100	1025000	1255	1170000
	2-4 x 12	805	752000	940	877000	1075	1002000
22'	4-2 x 10	1525	1816000	1780	2119000	2035	2421000
	2-4 x 10	1310	1556000	1530	1816000	1745	2074000
	1-8 x 10	1160	1341000	1355	1565000	1545	1787000
	1-4 x 12	1770	1730000	2065	2019000	2360	2306000
	3-2 x 12	1375	1346000	1605	1571000	1835	1794000
	2-3 x 12	1240	1211000	1445	1413000	1655	1614000
	1-6 x 12	1080	1031000	1260	1203000	1440	1374000
	4-2 x 12	1030	1010000	1205	1179000	1375	1346000
	2-4 x 12	885	865000	1035	1009000	1180	1153000
	5-2 x 12	825	807000	965	942000	1105	1076000
	3-3 x 12	825	799000	965	932000	1105	1065000

American Forest and Paper Association; Washington, D.C.

DESIGN LOAD TABLES

FLOOR AND ROOF BEAMS—DESIGN TABLES 30 POUNDS PSF

REQUIRED VALUES FOR FIBER STRESS IN BENDING (f) AND MODULUS OF ELASTICITY (E) FOR THE SIZES SHOWN TO SUPPORT SAFELY A LIVE LOAD OF 30 POUNDS PER SQUARE FOOT WITH A DEFLECTION LIMITATION OF $1/300$ 1 = SPAN IN INCHES.

SPAN OF BEAM	NOMINAL SIZE OF BEAM	6'-0" f	6'-0" E	7'-0" f	7'-0" E	8'-0" f	8'-0" E
10'	2-3 x 6	1430	1462000	1670	1706000	1905	1948000
	1-3 x 8	1645	1275000	1920	1488000	2195	1699000
	1-4 x 8	1175	909000	1370	1061000	1565	1212000
	3-2 x 8	915	712000	1070	831000	1220	949000
	2-3 x 8	820	637000	955	743000	1095	849000
	2-4 x 8	590	455000	690	531000	785	606000
	2-2 x 10	840	511000	980	596000	1120	681000
11'	1-3 x 8	1990	1696000	2320	1979000	2655	2261000
	1-4 x 8	1420	1212000	1660	1414000	1895	1615000
	3-2 x 8	1105	942000	1290	1099000	1475	1255000
	2-3 x 8	995	849000	1160	991000	1325	1132000
	2-4 x 8	710	606000	830	707000	945	808000
	2-2 x 10	1020	680000	1190	793000	1360	906000
	1-3 x 10	1220	817000	1425	953000	1625	1089000
12'	1-4 x 8	1690	1575000	1970	1838000	2255	2099000
	3-2 x 8	1315	1224000	1535	1428000	1755	1631000
	2-3 x 8	1185	1102000	1385	1286000	1580	1469000
	2-4 x 8	845	787000	985	918000	1125	1049000
	1-6 x 8	1005	905000	1175	1056000	1340	1206000
	2-2 x 10	1210	885000	1410	1033000	1615	1180000
	3-2 x 10	810	590000	945	688000	1080	786000
	2-3 x 10	725	530000	845	618000	965	706000
13'	1-4 x 8	1985	2000000	2315	2334000	2645	2666000
	3-2 x 8	1545	1556000	1805	1816000	2060	2074000
	2-3 x 8	1390	1400000	1620	1634000	1855	1866000
	2-4 x 8	990	1001000	1155	1168000	1320	1334000
	1-6 x 8	1180	1151000	1375	1343000	1575	1534000
	2-2 x 10	1425	1125000	1665	1313000	1900	1500000
	3-2 x 10	950	750000	1110	875000	1265	1000000
	2-3 x 10	855	675000	1000	788000	1140	900000
	1-4 x 10	1220	1154000	1425	1347000	1625	1538000
14'	3-2 x 8	1790	1944000	2090	2268000	2385	2591000
	2-3 x 8	1610	1750000	1880	2042000	2145	2333000
	2-4 x 8	1150	1250000	1340	1459000	1535	1666000
	1-6 x 8	1370	1436000	1600	1676000	1825	1914000
	2-2 x 10	1650	1404000	1925	1638000	2200	1871000
	3-2 x 10	1100	935000	1285	1091000	1465	1246000
	2-3 x 10	990	841000	1155	981000	1320	1121000
	1-4 x 10	1415	1204000	1650	1405000	1885	1605000
	1-6 x 10	915	1179000	1070	1376000	1220	1572000
	2-4 x 10	705	601000	825	701000	940	801000
15'	2-4 x 8	1320	1537000	1540	1794000	1760	2049000
	1-6 x 8	1570	1767000	1830	2062000	2095	2355000
	2-2 x 10	1895	1726000	2210	2014000	2525	2301000
	3-2 x 10	1260	1151000	1470	1343000	1680	1534000
	2-3 x 10	1135	1036000	1325	1209000	1515	1381000
	1-4 x 10	1620	1479000	1890	1726000	2160	1971000
	1-6 x 10	980	870000	1145	1015000	1305	1160000
	2-4 x 10	810	740000	945	863000	1080	986000
	4-2 x 10	945	864000	1105	1008000	1260	1152000
	1-8 x 10	720	637000	840	743000	960	849000
	2-2 x 12	1280	960000	1495	1120000	1705	1280000
	1-4 x 12	1095	822000	1280	959000	1460	1096000
16'	2-2 x 10	2155	2096000	2515	2446000	2875	2794000
	3-2 x 10	1435	1396000	1675	1629000	1915	1861000
	2-3 x 10	1290	1257000	1505	1467000	1720	1675000
	1-4 x 10	1845	1796000	2155	2096000	2460	2394000
	1-6 x 10	1115	1055000	1300	1231000	1485	1406000
	2-4 x 10	925	899000	1080	1049000	1235	1198000
	4-2 x 10	1075	1047000	1255	1222000	1435	1395000
	1-8 x 10	815	774000	950	903000	1085	1032000
	2-2 x 12	1455	1164000	1700	1358000	1940	1552000
	1-4 x 12	1250	999000	1460	1166000	1665	1332000
	3-2 x 12	970	776000	1130	905000	1295	1034000
	2-3 x 12	875	699000	1020	816000	1165	932000

SPAN OF BEAM	NOMINAL SIZE OF BEAM	6'-0" f	6'-0" E	7'-0" f	7'-0" E	8'-0" f	8'-0" E
17'	3-2 x 10	1620	1676000	1890	1956000	2160	2234000
	2-3 x 10	1460	1507000	1705	1759000	1945	2009000
	1-6 x 10	1255	1265000	1465	1476000	1675	1686000
	2-4 x 10	1040	1077000	1215	1257000	1385	1435000
	4-2 x 10	1215	1256000	1420	1466000	1620	1674000
	1-8 x 10	920	927000	1075	1082000	1225	1236000
	2-2 x 12	1645	1396000	1920	1629000	2195	1861000
	1-4 x 12	1410	1197000	1645	1397000	1880	1596000
	3-2 x 12	1095	931000	1280	1086000	1460	1241000
	2-3 x 12	985	839000	1150	979000	1315	1118000
	4-2 x 12	820	699000	955	816000	1095	932000
	2-4 x 12	705	599000	820	699000	940	799000
18'	2-3 x 10	1695	1790000	1980	2089000	2260	2386000
	1-6 x 10	1415	1501000	1650	1752000	1885	2000000
	2-4 x 10	1170	1279000	1365	1492000	1560	1705000
	4-2 x 10	1360	1492000	1590	1741000	1815	1989000
	1-8 x 10	1040	1102000	1215	1286000	1385	1469000
	2-2 x 12	1840	1659000	2150	1936000	2455	2211000
	1-4 x 12	1580	1421000	1845	1658000	2105	1894000
	3-2 x 12	1230	1106000	1435	1291000	1640	1474000
	2-3 x 12	1105	995000	1290	1161000	1475	1326000
	4-2 x 12	920	829000	1075	967000	1225	1105000
	2-4 x 12	790	711000	920	830000	1055	948000
	5-2 x 12	735	664000	860	775000	980	885000
19'	1-6 x 10	1570	1767000	1830	2062000	2095	2355000
	2-4 x 10	1300	1504000	1515	1755000	1735	2005000
	4-2 x 10	1520	1755000	1775	2048000	2025	2339000
	1-8 x 10	1145	1295000	1335	1511000	1525	1726000
	1-4 x 12	1760	1672000	2055	1951000	2345	2229000
	3-2 x 12	1370	1301000	1600	1518000	1825	1734000
	2-3 x 12	1230	1170000	1435	1365000	1640	1560000
	4-2 x 12	1025	975000	1195	1138000	1365	1300000
	2-4 x 12	880	836000	1025	976000	1175	1114000
	5-2 x 12	820	780000	955	910000	1095	1040000
	1-6 x 12	1070	995000	1250	1161000	1425	1326000
	3-3 x 12	820	771000	955	900000	1095	1028000
20'	1-8 x 10	1280	1511000	1495	1763000	1705	2014000
	3-2 x 12	1520	1516000	1775	1769000	2025	2021000
	2-3 x 12	1365	1365000	1595	1593000	1820	1819000
	4-2 x 12	1025	1137000	1195	1327000	1365	1516000
	2-4 x 12	975	975000	1140	1138000	1300	1300000
	5-2 x 12	910	910000	1060	1062000	1215	1213000
	1-6 x 12	1295	1162000	1510	1356000	1725	1549000
	3-3 x 12	910	900000	1060	1050000	1215	1200000
	1-8 x 12	870	852000	1015	994000	1160	1136000
	1-10 x 12	690	672000	805	784000	920	896000
	4-3 x 12	680	682000	795	796000	905	909000
	2-3 x 14	985	836000	1150	976000	1315	1114000
21'	3-2 x 12	1670	1756000	1950	2049000	2225	2341000
	2-3 x 12	1505	1580000	1755	1844000	2005	2106000
	4-2 x 12	1255	1317000	1465	1537000	1675	1755000
	2-4 x 12	1075	1129000	1255	1317000	1435	1505000
	5-2 x 12	1005	1054000	1175	1230000	1340	1405000
	1-6 x 12	1295	1344000	1510	1568000	1725	1791000
	3-3 x 12	1005	1041000	1175	1215000	1340	1388000
	1-8 x 12	960	986000	1120	1151000	1280	1314000
	1-10 x 12	760	779000	885	909000	1015	1038000
	4-3 x 12	750	790000	875	922000	1000	1053000
	2-3 x 14	1085	967000	1265	1128000	1445	1289000
	1-6 x 14	950	832000	1110	971000	1265	1109000
22'	4-2 x 12	1375	1515000	1605	1768000	1835	2019000
	2-4 x 12	1180	1297000	1380	1513000	1575	1729000
	5-2 x 12	1100	1211000	1285	1413000	1465	1614000
	1-6 x 12	1440	1546000	1680	1804000	1920	2061000
	3-3 x 12	1100	1197000	1285	1397000	1465	1596000
	1-8 x 12	1055	1134000	1230	1323000	1405	1511000
	1-10 x 12	830	895000	970	1044000	1105	1193000
	4-3 x 12	825	909000	965	1061000	1100	1212000
	2-3 x 14	1190	1112000	1390	1298000	1585	1482000
	1-6 x 14	1045	956000	1220	1116000	1395	1274000
	3-3 x 14	795	736000	930	859000	1060	981000
	2-4 x 14	820	751000	955	1114000	1095	1001000

American Forest and Paper Association; Washington, D.C.

FLOOR AND ROOF BEAMS—DESIGN TABLES 40 POUNDS PSF

REQUIRED VALUES FOR FIBER STRESS IN BENDING (f) AND MODULUS OF ELASTICITY (E) FOR THE SIZES SHOWN TO SUPPORT SAFELY A LIVE LOAD OF 40 POUNDS PER SQUARE FOOT WITHIN A DEFLECTION LIMITATION OF 1/300 1 = SPAN IN INCHES.

SPAN OF BEAM	NOMINAL SIZE OF BEAM	MINIMUM "f" & "E" IN PSI FOR BEAMS SPACED: 6'-0" f	E	7'-0" f	E	8'-0" f	E
10'	1-3 x 8	2055	1700000	2400	1984000	2740	2266000
	2-2 x 8	1710	1417000	1995	1654000	2280	1889000
	1-4 x 8	1470	1211000	1715	1413000	1960	1614000
	1-6 x 8	875	697000	1020	813000	1165	929000
	2-2 x 10	1050	681000	1225	795000	1400	908000
	1-3 x 10	1260	819000	1470	956000	1680	1092000
	1-4 x 10	900	585000	1050	683000	1200	780000
11'	2-2 x 8	2070	1886000	2415	2201000	2760	2514000
	1-4 x 8	1775	1616000	2070	1886000	2365	2154000
	1-6 x 8	1055	929000	1230	1084000	1405	1238000
	2-2 x 10	1275	906000	1490	1057000	1700	1208000
	1-3 x 10	1525	1090000	1780	1272000	2030	1453000
	1-4 x 10	1090	779000	1270	909000	1455	1038000
	3-2 x 10	850	605000	990	706000	1135	806000
12'	1-6 x 8	1255	1206000	1465	1407000	1670	1607000
	3-2 x 8	1645	1631000	1920	1903000	2190	2174000
	2-2 x 10	1510	1180000	1760	1377000	2010	1573000
	1-3 x 10	1820	1415000	2125	1651000	2425	1886000
	1-4 x 10	1300	1010000	1515	1179000	1735	1346000
	3-2 x 10	1010	786000	1180	917000	1345	1048000
	2-3 x 10	905	706000	1055	824000	1205	941000
	1-6 x 10	785	594000	915	693000	1045	792000
	2-4 x 10	650	505000	760	589000	865	673000
13'	1-6 x 8	1475	1535000	1720	1791000	1965	2046000
	2-3 x 8	1735	1866000	2025	2178000	2315	2487000
	2-4 x 8	1235	1335000	1440	1558000	1645	1779000
	3-2 x 10	1185	1000000	1380	1167000	1580	1333000
	2-2 x 10	1780	1500000	2075	1750000	2370	2000000
	1-3 x 10	2130	1799000	2485	2099000	2840	2398000
	2-3 x 10	1070	900000	1250	1050000	1425	1200000
	1-4 x 10	1525	1537000	1780	1794000	2035	2049000
	2-4 x 10	760	642000	890	749000	1015	856000
14'	2-4 x 8	1435	1666000	1675	1944000	1915	2221000
	3-2 x 10	1375	1246000	1605	1454000	1830	1661000
	2-3 x 10	1235	1121000	1440	1308000	1645	1494000
	1-4 x 10	1770	1605000	2065	1873000	2360	2139000
	2-4 x 10	880	801000	1025	935000	1175	1068000
	3-3 x 10	825	749000	960	874000	1100	998000
	1-6 x 10	1145	1571000	1335	1833000	1525	2094000
	1-8 x 10	780	691000	910	806000	1040	921000
	4-2 x 10	1030	936000	1200	1092000	1375	1248000
	2-2 x 12	1395	1040000	1630	1214000	1860	1386000
15'	3-2 x 10	1575	1535000	1840	1791000	2100	2046000
	2-3 x 10	1420	1381000	1655	1612000	1890	1841000
	2-4 x 10	1010	986000	1175	1151000	1345	1314000
	3-3 x 10	945	921000	1100	1075000	1260	1228000
	1-6 x 10	1225	1160000	1430	1354000	1635	1546000
	1-8 x 10	900	850000	1050	992000	1200	1133000
	4-2 x 10	1180	1151000	1375	1343000	1575	1534000
	2-2 x 12	1600	1280000	1865	1494000	2130	1706000
	3-2 x 12	1065	854000	1240	997000	1420	1138000
	1-3 x 12	1920	1536000	2240	1792000	2560	2047000
	4-2 x 12	800	640000	935	747000	1065	853000
	2-3 x 12	960	767000	1120	895000	1280	1022000
16'	3-2 x 10	1795	1861000	2095	2172000	2395	2481000
	2-3 x 10	1610	1676000	1880	1956000	2145	2234000
	2-4 x 10	1155	1199000	1350	1399000	1540	1598000
	3-3 x 10	1075	1117000	1255	1303000	1435	1489000
	1-6 x 10	1395	1406000	1625	1641000	1860	1874000
	1-8 x 10	1020	1031000	1190	1203000	1360	1374000
	4-2 x 10	1345	1396000	1570	1629000	1790	1861000
	2-2 x 12	1820	1551000	2120	1810000	2425	2067000
	3-2 x 12	1210	1035000	1410	1208000	1610	1380000
	4-2 x 12	910	776000	1060	905000	1215	1034000
	5-2 x 12	730	621000	850	725000	975	828000
	2-3 x 12	1095	931000	1280	1086000	1460	1241000

SPAN OF BEAM	NOMINAL SIZE OF BEAM	MINIMUM "f" & "E" IN PSI FOR BEAMS SPACED: 6'-0" f	E	7'-0" f	E	8'-0" f	E
17'	2-3 x 10	1825	2010000	2130	2345000	2430	2679000
	2-4 x 10	1300	1436000	1520	1676000	1735	1914000
	3-3 x 10	1215	1341000	1420	1565000	1620	1787000
	1-8 x 10	1150	1236000	1340	1442000	1535	1647000
	3-2 x 12	1370	1241000	1600	1448000	1825	1654000
	4-2 x 12	1025	931000	1195	1086000	1365	1241000
	5-2 x 12	820	745000	955	869000	1095	993000
	2-3 x 12	1230	1119000	1435	1306000	1640	1492000
	3-3 x 12	820	737000	955	860000	1095	982000
	2-4 x 12	880	799000	1025	932000	1175	1065000
	1-6 x 12	1070	951000	1250	1110000	1425	1268000
	1-8 x 12	785	697000	915	813000	1045	929000
18'	2-4 x 10	1460	1705000	1705	1990000	1945	2273000
	3-3 x 10	1365	1591000	1595	1857000	1820	2121000
	1-8 x 10	1300	1470000	1515	1715000	1730	1959000
	3-2 x 12	1540	1475000	1800	1721000	2050	1966000
	4-2 x 12	1150	1105000	1340	1289000	1530	1473000
	5-2 x 12	920	885000	1075	1033000	1225	1180000
	2-3 x 12	1380	1326000	1610	1547000	1840	1767000
	3-3 x 12	920	875000	1075	1021000	1225	1166000
	2-4 x 12	990	949000	1155	1107000	1320	1265000
	1-6 x 12	1200	1129000	1400	1317000	1600	1505000
	1-8 x 12	880	829000	1025	967000	1175	1105000
	3-4 x 12	660	632000	770	737000	880	842000
19'	3-3 x 10	1520	1872000	1775	2184000	2025	2495000
	3-2 x 12	1710	1735000	1995	2025000	2280	2313000
	4-2 x 12	1280	1300000	1495	1517000	1705	1733000
	5-2 x 12	1025	1040000	1195	1214000	1365	1386000
	2-3 x 12	1540	1560000	1795	1820000	2050	2079000
	3-3 x 12	1025	1029000	1195	1201000	1365	1372000
	2-4 x 12	1100	1115000	1280	1301000	1465	1486000
	1-6 x 12	1335	1326000	1560	1547000	1780	1767000
	1-8 x 12	980	973000	1145	1135000	1305	1297000
	3-4 x 12	735	744000	860	868000	980	992000
	4-3 x 12	770	780000	900	910000	1025	1040000
	2-6 x 12	670	1329000	780	1551000	895	1771000
20'	3-2 x 12	1900	2021000	2220	2358000	2530	2694000
	4-2 x 12	1280	1516000	1495	1769000	1705	2021000
	5-2 x 12	1135	1214000	1325	1417000	1515	1618000
	3-3 x 12	1135	1200000	1325	1400000	1515	1600000
	2-4 x 12	1220	1300000	1425	1517000	1625	1733000
	1-6 x 12	1620	1550000	1890	1809000	2160	2066000
	1-8 x 12	1085	1136000	1265	1326000	1445	1514000
	3-4 x 12	810	866000	945	1011000	1080	1154000
	4-3 x 12	850	910000	990	1062000	1135	1213000
	2-6 x 12	740	775000	865	904000	985	1033000
	1-10 x 12	860	896000	1005	1046000	1145	1194000
	2-3 x 14	1230	1114000	1435	1300000	1640	1485000
21'	4-2 x 12	1570	1756000	1830	2049000	2095	2341000
	5-2 x 12	1255	1405000	1465	1640000	1675	1873000
	3-3 x 12	1255	1389000	1465	1621000	1675	1851000
	2-4 x 12	1345	1505000	1570	1756000	1795	2006000
	1-8 x 12	1200	1315000	1400	1535000	1600	1753000
	3-4 x 12	895	1004000	1045	1172000	1195	1338000
	4-3 x 12	935	1054000	1090	1230000	1245	1405000
	2-6 x 12	820	896000	955	1046000	1095	1194000
	1-10 x 12	950	1039000	1110	1212000	1265	1385000
	2-3 x 14	1355	1290000	1580	1505000	1805	1719000
	1-6 x 14	1190	1109000	1390	1294000	1585	1478000
	2-4 x 14	930	871000	1085	1016000	1240	1161000
22'	4-2 x 12	1720	2020000	2005	2357000	2295	2693000
	5-2 x 12	1375	1615000	1605	1885000	1830	2153000
	3-3 x 12	1375	1596000	1605	1862000	1830	2127000
	3-4 x 12	985	1154000	1150	1347000	1315	1538000
	4-3 x 12	1030	1211000	1200	1413000	1375	1614000
	2-6 x 12	900	1031000	1050	1203000	1200	1374000
	1-10 x 12	1035	1194000	1205	1393000	1380	1592000
	2-3 x 14	1485	1484000	1730	1732000	1980	1978000
	1-6 x 14	1305	1275000	1525	1488000	1740	1700000
	2-4 x 14	1025	1001000	1195	1168000	1365	1334000
	3-3 x 14	995	981000	1160	1145000	1325	1308000
	3-4 x 14	680	667000	795	778000	905	889000

American Forest and Paper Association; Washington, D.C.

DESIGN LOAD TABLES

CEILING JOISTS—10 LB/SQ FT LIVE LOAD (GYPSUM WALLBOARD CEILING)
No attic storage and roof slope not steeper than 3 IN 12.

MAXIMUM ALLOWABLE LENGTHS L BETWEEN SUPPORTS

JOIST SIZE (NOMINAL) (IN.)	JOIST SPACING (NOMINAL) (IN.)	SPAN L LIMITED BY DEFLECTION AND F_b IS EXTREME FIBER STRESS				
		E =	1,000,000	1,200,000	1,400,000	1,600,000
2 x 4	12	L =	10-7	11-3	11-10	12-5
		F_b =	830	930	1030	1130
	16	L =	9-8	10-3	10-9	11-3
		F_b =	910	1030	1140	1240
	24	L =	8-5	8-11	9-5	9-10
		F_b =	1040	1170	1300	1420
2 x 6	12	L =	16-8	17-8	18-8	19-6
		F_b =	830	930	1030	1130
	16	L =	15-2	16-1	16-11	17-8
		F_b =	910	1030	1140	1240
	24	L =	13-3	14-1	14-9	15-6
		F_b =	1040	1170	1300	1420
2 x 8	12	L =	21-11	23-4	24-7	25-8
		F_b =	830	930	1030	1130
	16	L =	19-11	21-2	22-4	23-4
		F_b =	910	1030	1140	1240
	24	L =	17-5	18-6	19-6	20-5
		F_b =	1040	1170	1300	1420
2 x 10	12	L =	28-0	29-9	31-4	32-9
		F_b =	830	930	1030	1130
	16	L =	25-5	27-1	28-6	29-9
		F_b =	910	1030	1140	1240
	24	L =	22-3	23-8	24-10	26-0
		F_b =	1040	1170	1300	1420

NOTE: L in feet and inches; E and F_b in pounds per square inch as shown above.

DESIGN CRITERIA

1. Maximum allowable deflection = 1/240 of span length.
2. Live load of 10 lb/sq ft plus dead load of 5 lb/sq ft determine required fiber stress value.

CEILING JOISTS—20 LB/SQ FT LIVE LOAD (GYPSUM WALLBOARD CEILING)
Limited attic storage where development of future rooms is not possible.

MAXIMUM ALLOWABLE LENGTHS L BETWEEN SUPPORTS

JOIST SIZE (NOMINAL) (IN.)	JOIST SPACING (NOMINAL) (IN.)	SPAN L LIMITED BY DEFLECTION AND F_b IS EXTREME FIBER STRESS				
		E =	1,000,000	1,200,000	1,400,000	1,600,000
2 x 4	12	L =	8-5	8-11	9-5	9-10
		F_b =	1040	1170	1300	1420
	16	L =	7-8	8-1	8-7	8-11
		F_b =	1140	1290	1430	1570
	24	L =	6-8	7-1	7-6	7-10
		F_b =	1310	1480	1640	1790
2 x 6	12	L =	13-3	14-1	14-9	15-6
		F_b =	1040	1170	1300	1420
	16	L =	12-0	12-9	13-5	14-1
		F_b =	1140	1290	1430	1570
	24	L =	10-6	11-2	11-9	12-3
		F_b =	1310	1480	1640	1790
2 x 8	12	L =	17-5	18-6	19-6	20-5
		F_b =	1040	1170	1300	1420
	16	L =	15-10	16-10	17-9	18-6
		F_b =	1140	1290	1430	1570
	24	L =	13-10	14-8	15-6	16-2
		F_b =	1310	1480	1640	1790
2 x 10	12	L =	22-3	23-8	24-10	26-0
		F_b =	1040	1170	1300	1420
	16	L =	20-2	21-6	22-7	23-8
		F_b =	1140	1290	1430	1570
	24	L =	17-8	18-9	19-9	20-8
		F_b =	1310	1480	1640	1790

NOTE: L in feet and inches; E and F_b in pounds per square inch as shown above.

DESIGN CRITERIA

1. Maximum allowable deflection = 1/240 of span length.
2. Live load of 20 lb/sq ft plus dead load of 10 lb/sq ft determine required fiber stress value.

NOTE

For rafters, design values in F_b may be greater than the design values for normal duration of load, by the following amounts:

15% for 2 months' duration, as for snow.
25% for 7 days' duration, as for construction loading.

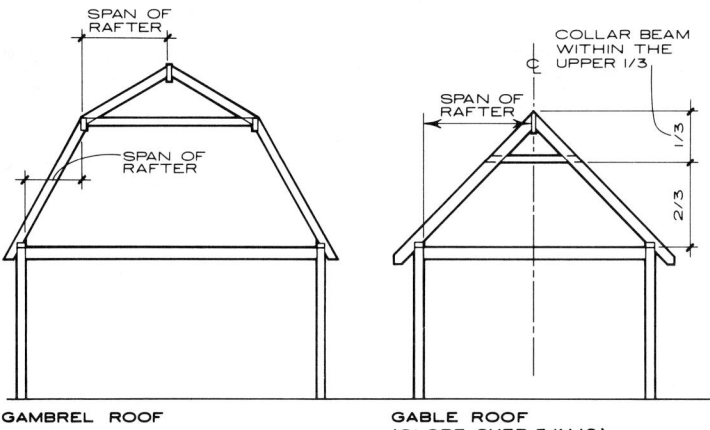

GAMBREL ROOF

GABLE ROOF (SLOPE OVER 3 IN 12)

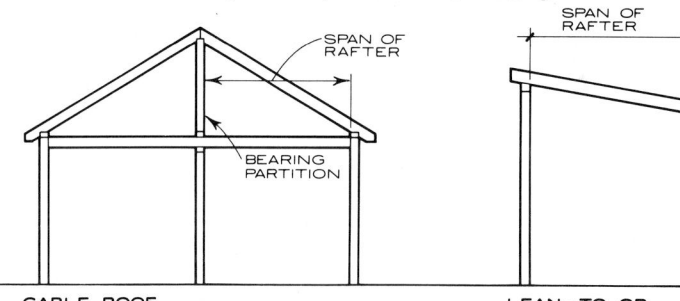

GABLE ROOF (SLOPE UNDER 3 IN 12)

LEAN-TO OR SHED ROOF

SECTION MODULUS

LUMBER SIZES (NOMINAL)	S (IN.³)
2 x 3	1.56
2 x 4	3.06
2 x 6	7.56
2 x 8	13.14
2 x 10	21.39
2 x 12	31.64
3 x 6	12.60
3 x 8	21.90
3 x 10	35.65
3 x 12	52.73
3 x 14	73.15
4 x 4	7.15
4 x 6	17.65
4 x 8	30.66
4 x 10	49.91
4 x 12	73.83

SECTION MODULUS

$$S = \frac{bd^2}{6} \quad (IN.^3)$$

b AND d ARE ACTUAL DIMENSIONS.

NOTE

(Applicable to this page and the following pages on joist and rafter sizes.)

SPANS LIMITED BY DEFLECTION: The weight of plaster itself was ignored in the assumed loads for the deflection computations, because the initial deflection from the dead load occurs before plaster sets. The influence of live loads, rather than dead loads, when the ratio of live to dead loads is relatively high, is the principal factor to be considered. Also with joisted floors, flooring and bridging serve to distribute moving or concentrated loads to adjoining members. The omission of the plaster weight in load assumption applies to deflection computations only; the full dead and live load is considered when computing for strength.

American Forest and Paper Association; Washington, D.C.

E = modulus of elasticity
F_b = extreme fiber stress in bending
L = span length between supports

LIVE LOAD ASSUMPTIONS: Uniformly distributed.

PARTITIONS: Spans shown are computed for the given live load plus the dead load and do not provide for additional loads such as partitions. Where concentrated loads are imposed the spans should be recomputed to provide for them.

DESIGN CRITERIA

STRENGTH: 15 psf dead load plus 20 psf live load determines required fiber stress.

DEFLECTION: For 20 psf live load. Limited to span in inches divided by 240.

RAFTERS: Spans are measured along the horizontal projection, and loads are considered as applied on the horizontal projection.

FLAT OR SLOPED RAFTERS—20 LB LIVE LOAD
FLAT ROOF OR CATHEDRAL CEILING WITH NO ATTIC SPACE—SUPPORTING GYPSUM WALLBOARD CEILING

RAFTER SIZE, SPACING (IN.)		EXTREME FIBER STRESS IN BENDING, F_b (PSI)														
		500	600	700	800	900	1000	1100	1200	1300	1400	1500	1600	1700	1800	1900
2 x 6	12	8-6 0.26	9-4 0.35	10-0 0.44	10-9 0.54	11-5 0.64	12-0 0.75	12-7 0.86	13-2 0.98	13-8 1.11	14-2 1.24	14-8 1.37	15-2 1.51	15-8 1.66	16-1 1.81	16-7 1.96
	16	7-4 0.23	8-1 0.30	8-8 0.38	9-4 0.46	9-10 0.55	10-5 0.65	10-11 0.75	11-5 0.85	11-10 0.96	12-4 1.07	12-9 1.19	13-2 1.31	13-7 1.44	13-11 1.56	14-4 1.70
	24	6-0 0.19	6-7 0.25	7-1 0.31	7-7 0.38	8-1 0.45	8-6 0.53	8-11 0.61	9-4 0.70	9-8 0.78	10-0 0.88	10-5 0.97	10-9 1.07	11-1 1.17	11-5 1.28	11.8 1.39
2 x 8	12	11-2 0.26	12-3 0.35	13-3 0.44	14-2 0.54	15-0 0.64	15-10 0.75	16-7 0.86	17-4 0.98	18-0 1.11	18-9 1.24	19-5 1.37	20-0 1.51	20-8 1.66	21-3 1.81	21-10 1.96
	16	9-8 0.23	10-7 0.30	11-6 0.38	12-3 0.46	13-0 0.55	13-8 0.65	14-4 0.75	15-0 0.85	15-7 0.96	16-3 1.07	16-9 1.19	17-4 1.31	17-10 1.44	18-5 1.56	18-11 1.70
	24	7-11 0.19	8-8 0.25	9-4 0.31	10-0 0.38	10-7 0.45	11-2 0.53	11-9 0.61	12-3 0.70	12-9 0.78	13-3 0.88	13-8 0.97	14-2 1.07	14-7 1.17	15-0 1.28	15-5 1.39
2 x 10	12	14-3 0.26	15-8 0.35	16-11 0.44	18-1 0.54	19-2 0.64	20-2 0.75	21-2 0.86	22-1 0.98	23-0 1.11	23-11 1.24	24-9 1.37	25-6 1.51	26-4 1.66	27-1 1.81	27.10 1.96
	16	12-4 0.23	13-6 0.30	14-8 0.38	15-8 0.46	16-7 0.55	17-6 0.65	18-4 0.75	19-2 0.85	19-11 0.96	20-8 1.07	21-5 1.19	22-1 1.31	22-10 1.44	23-5 1.56	24.1 1.70
	24	10-1 0.19	11-1 0.25	11-11 0.31	12-9 0.38	13-6 0.45	14-3 0.53	15-0 0.61	15-8 0.70	16-3 0.78	16-11 0.88	17-6 0.97	18-1 1.07	18-7 1.17	19-2 1.28	19-8 1.39
2 x 12	12	17-4 0.26	19-0 0.35	20-6 0.44	21-11 0.54	23-3 0.64	24-7 0.75	25-9 0.86	26-11 0.98	28-0 1.11	29-1 1.24	30-1 1.37	31-1 1.51	32-0 1.66	32-11 1.81	33-10 1.96
	16	15-0 0.23	16-6 0.30	17-9 0.38	19-0 0.46	20-2 0.55	21-3 0.65	22-4 0.75	23-3 0.85	24-3 0.96	25-2 1.07	26-0 1.19	26-11 1.31	27-9 1.44	28.6 1.56	29-4 1.70
	24	12-3 0.19	13-5 0.25	14-6 0.31	15-6 0.38	16-6 0.45	17-4 0.53	18-2 0.61	19-0 0.70	19-10 0.78	20-6 0.88	21-3 0.97	21-11 1.07	22-8 1.17	23-3 1.28	23-11 1.39

NOTE: The required modulus of elasticity, E, in 1,000,000 psi is shown below each span.

DESIGN CRITERIA

STRENGTH: 15 psf dead load plus 30 psf live load determines required fiber stress.

DEFLECTION: For 30 psf live load. Limited to span in inches divided by 240.

RAFTERS: Spans are measured along the horizontal projection, and loads are considered as applied on the horizontal projection.

FLAT OR SLOPED RAFTERS—30 LB LIVE LOAD
FLAT ROOF OR CATHEDRAL CEILING WITH NO ATTIC SPACE—SUPPORTING GYPSUM WALLBOARD CEILING

RAFTER SIZE, SPACING (IN.)		EXTREME FIBER STRESS IN BENDING, F_b (PSI)														
		500	600	700	800	900	1000	1100	1200	1300	1400	1500	1600	1700	1800	1900
2 x 6	12	7-6 0.27	8-2 0.36	8-10 0.45	9-6 0.55	10-0 0.66	10-7 0.77	11-1 0.89	11-7 1.01	12-1 1.14	12-6 1.28	13-0 1.41	13-5 1.56	13-10 1.71	14-2 1.86	14-7 2.02
	16	6-6 0.24	7-1 0.31	7-8 0.39	8-2 0.48	8-8 0.57	9-2 0.67	9-7 0.77	10-0 0.88	10-5 0.99	10-10 1.10	11-3 1.22	11-7 1.35	11-11 1.48	12-4 1.61	12-8 1.75
	24	5-4 0.19	5-10 0.25	6-3 0.32	6-8 0.39	7-1 0.46	7-6 0.54	7-10 0.63	8-2 0.72	8-6 0.81	8-10 0.90	9-2 1.00	9-6 1.10	9-9 1.21	10-0 1.31	10-4 1.43
2 x 8	12	9-10 0.27	10-10 0.36	11-8 0.45	12-6 0.55	13-3 0.66	13-11 0.77	14-8 0.89	15-3 1.01	15-11 1.14	16-6 1.28	17-1 1.41	17-8 1.56	18-2 1.71	18-9 1.86	19-3 2.02
	16	8-7 0.24	9-4 0.31	10-1 0.39	10-10 0.48	11-6 0.57	12-1 0.67	12-8 0.77	13-3 0.88	13-9 0.99	14-4 1.10	14-10 1.22	15-3 1.35	15-9 1.48	16-3 1.61	16-8 1.75
	24	7-0 0.19	7-8 0.25	8-3 0.32	8-10 0.39	9-4 0.46	9-10 0.54	10-4 0.63	10-10 0.72	11-3 0.81	11-8 0.90	12-1 1.00	12-6 1.10	12-10 1.21	13-3 1.31	13-7 1.43
2 x 10	12	12-7 0.27	13-9 0.36	14-11 0.45	15-11 0.55	16-11 0.66	17-10 0.77	18-8 0.89	19-6 1.01	20-4 1.14	21-1 1.28	21-10 1.41	22-6 1.56	23-3 1.71	23-11 1.86	24-6 2.02
	16	10-11 0.24	11-11 0.31	12-11 0.39	13-9 0.48	14-8 0.57	15-5 0.67	16-2 0.77	16-11 0.88	17-7 0.99	18-3 1.10	18-11 1.22	19-6 1.35	20-1 1.48	20-8 1.61	21-3 1.75
	24	8-11 0.19	9-9 0.25	10-6 0.32	11-3 0.39	11-11 0.46	12-7 0.54	13-2 0.63	13-9 0.72	14-4 0.81	14-11 0.90	15-5 1.00	15-11 1.10	16-5 1.21	16-11 1.31	17-4 1.43
2 x 12	12	15-4 0.27	16-9 0.36	18-1 0.45	19-4 0.55	20-6 0.66	21-8 0.77	22-8 0.89	23-9 1.01	24-8 1.14	25-7 1.28	26-6 1.41	27-5 1.56	28-3 1.71	29-1 1.86	29-10 2.02
	16	13-3 0.24	14-6 0.31	15-8 0.39	16-9 0.48	17-9 0.57	18-9 0.67	19-8 0.77	20-6 0.88	21-5 0.99	22-2 1.10	23-0 1.22	23-9 1.35	24-5 1.48	25-2 1.61	25-10 1.75
	24	10-10 0.19	11-10 0.25	12-10 0.32	13-8 0.39	14-6 0.46	15-4 0.54	16-1 0.63	16-9 0.72	17-5 0.81	18-1 0.90	18-9 1.00	19-4 1.10	20-0 1.21	20-6 1.31	12-1 1.43

NOTE: The required modulus of elasticity, E, in 1,000,000 psi is shown below each span.

American Forest and Paper Association; Washington, D.C.

DESIGN LOAD TABLES

DESIGN CRITERIA

STRENGTH: 10 psf dead load plus 20 psf live load determines required fiber stress.

DEFLECTION: For 20 psf live load. Limited to span in inches divided by 240.

RAFTERS: Spans are measured along the horizontal projection, and loads are considered as applied on the horizontal projection.

FLAT OR LOW SLOPE RAFTERS—20 LB LIVE LOAD
NO CEILING LOAD—SLOPE 3 IN 12 OR LESS

EXTREME FIBER STRESS IN BENDING, F_b (PSI)

RAFTER SIZE, SPACING (IN.)		500	600	700	800	900	1000	1100	1200	1300	1400	1500	1600	1700	1800	1900
2 x 6	12	9-2	10-0	10-10	11-7	12-4	13-0	13-7	14-2	14-9	15-4	15-11	16-5	16-11	17-5	17-10
		0.33	0.44	0.55	0.67	0.80	0.94	1.09	1.24	1.40	1.56	1.73	1.91	2.09	2.28	2.47
	16	7-11	8-8	9-5	10-0	10-8	11-3	11-9	12-4	12-10	13-3	13-9	14-2	14-8	15-1	15-6
		0.29	0.38	0.48	0.58	0.70	0.82	0.94	1.07	1.21	1.35	1.50	1.65	1.81	1.97	2.14
	24	6-6	7-1	7-8	8-2	8-8	9-2	9-7	10-0	10-5	10-10	11-3	11-7	11-11	12-4	12-8
		0.24	0.31	0.39	0.48	0.57	0.67	0.77	0.88	0.99	1.10	1.22	1.35	1.48	1.61	1.75
2 x 8	12	12-1	13-3	14-4	15-3	16-3	17-1	17-11	18-9	19-6	20-3	20-11	21-7	22-3	22-11	23-7
		0.33	0.44	0.55	0.67	0.80	0.94	1.09	1.24	1.40	1.56	1.73	1.91	2.09	2.28	2.47
	16	10-6	11-6	12-5	13-3	14-0	14-10	15-6	16-3	16-10	17-6	18-2	18-9	19-4	19-10	20-5
		0.29	0.38	0.48	0.58	0.70	0.82	0.94	1.07	1.21	1.35	1.50	1.65	1.81	1.97	2.14
	24	8-7	9-4	10-1	10-10	11-6	12-1	12-8	13-3	13-9	14-4	14-10	15-3	15-9	16-3	16-8
		0.24	0.31	0.39	0.48	0.57	0.67	0.77	0.88	0.99	1.10	1.22	1.35	1.48	1.61	1.75
2 x 10	12	15-5	16-11	18-3	19-6	20-8	21-10	22-10	23-11	24-10	25-10	26-8	27-7	28-5	29-3	30-1
		0.33	0.44	0.55	0.67	0.80	0.94	1.09	1.24	1.40	1.56	1.73	1.91	2.09	2.28	2.47
	16	13-4	14-8	15-10	16-11	17-11	18-11	19-10	20-8	21-6	22-4	23-2	23-11	24-7	25-4	26-0
		0.29	0.38	0.48	0.58	0.70	0.82	0.94	1.07	1.21	1.35	1.50	1.65	1.81	1.97	2.14
	24	10-11	11-11	12-11	13-9	14-8	15-5	16-2	16-11	17-7	18-3	18-11	19-6	20-1	20-8	21-3
		0.24	0.31	0.39	0.48	0.57	0.67	0.77	0.88	0.99	1.10	1.22	1.35	1.48	1.61	1.75
2 x 12	12	18-9	20-6	22-2	23-9	25-2	26-6	27-10	29-1	30-3	31-4	32-6	33-6	34-7	35-7	36-7
		0.33	0.44	0.55	0.67	0.80	0.94	1.09	1.24	1.40	1.56	1.73	1.91	2.09	2.28	2.47
	16	16-3	17-9	19-3	20-6	21-9	23-0	24-1	25-2	26-2	27-2	28-2	29-1	29-11	30-10	31-8
		0.29	0.38	0.48	0.58	0.70	0.82	0.94	1.07	1.21	1.35	1.50	1.65	1.81	1.97	2.14
	24	13-3	14-6	15-8	16-9	17-9	18-9	19-8	20-6	21-5	22-2	23-0	23-9	24-5	25-2	25-10
		0.24	0.31	0.39	0.48	0.57	0.67	0.77	0.88	0.99	1.10	1.22	1.35	1.48	1.61	1.75

NOTE: The required modulus of elasticity, E, in 1,000,000 psi is shown below each span.

DESIGN CRITERIA

STRENGTH: 10 psf dead load plus 30 psf live load determines required fiber stress.

DEFLECTION: For 30 psf live load. Limited to span in inches divided by 240.

RAFTERS: Spans are measured along the horizontal projection, and loads are considered as applied on the horizontal projection.

FLAT OR LOW SLOPE RAFTERS—30 LB LIVE LOAD
NO CEILING LOAD—SLOPE 3 IN 12 OR LESS

EXTREME FIBER STRESS IN BENDING, F_b (PSI)

RAFTER SIZE, SPACING (IN.)		500	600	700	800	900	1000	1100	1200	1300	1400	1500	1600	1700	1800	1900
2 x 6	12	7-11	8-8	9-5	10-0	10-8	11-3	11-9	12-4	12-10	13-3	13-9	14-2	14-8	15-1	15-6
		0.32	0.43	0.54	0.66	0.78	0.92	1.06	1.21	1.36	1.52	1.69	1.86	2.04	2.22	2.41
	16	6-11	7-6	8-2	8-8	9-3	9-9	10-2	10-8	11-1	11-6	11-11	12-4	12-8	13-1	13-5
		0.28	0.37	0.47	0.57	0.68	0.80	0.92	1.05	1.18	1.32	1.46	1.61	1.76	1.92	2.08
	24	5-7	6-2	6-8	7-1	7-6	7-11	8-4	8-8	9-1	9-5	9-9	10-0	10-4	10-8	10-11
		0.23	0.30	0.38	0.46	0.55	0.65	0.75	0.85	0.96	1.08	1.19	1.31	1.44	1.57	1.70
2 x 8	12	10-6	11-6	12-5	13-3	14-0	14-10	15-6	16-3	16-10	17-6	18-2	18-9	19-4	19-10	20-5
		0.32	0.43	0.54	0.66	0.78	0.92	1.06	1.21	1.36	1.52	1.69	1.86	2.04	2.22	2.41
	16	9-1	9-11	10-9	11-6	12-2	12-10	13-5	14-0	14-7	15-2	15-8	16-3	16-9	17-2	17-8
		0.28	0.37	0.47	0.57	0.68	0.80	0.92	1.05	1.18	1.32	1.46	1.61	1.76	1.92	2.08
	24	7-5	8-1	8-9	9-4	9-11	10-6	11-0	11-6	11-11	12-5	12-10	13-3	13-8	14-0	14-5
		0.23	0.30	0.38	0.46	0.55	0.65	0.75	0.85	0.96	1.08	1.19	1.31	1.44	1.57	1.70
2 x 10	12	13-4	14-8	15-10	16-11	17-11	18-11	19-10	20-8	21-6	22-4	23-2	23-11	24-7	25-4	26-0
		0.32	0.43	0.54	0.66	0.78	0.92	1.06	1.21	1.36	1.52	1.69	1.86	2.04	2.22	2.41
	16	11-7	12-8	13-8	14-8	15-6	16-4	17-2	17-11	18-8	19-4	20-0	20-8	21-4	21-11	22-6
		0.28	0.37	0.47	0.57	0.68	0.80	0.92	1.05	1.18	1.32	1.46	1.61	1.76	1.92	2.08
	24	9-5	10-4	11-2	11-11	12-8	13-4	14-0	14-8	15-3	15-10	16-4	16-11	17-5	17-11	18-5
		0.23	0.30	0.38	0.46	0.55	0.65	0.75	0.85	0.96	1.08	1.19	1.31	1.44	1.57	1.70
2 x 12	12	16-3	17-9	19-3	20-6	21-9	23-0	24-1	25-2	26-2	27-2	28-2	29-1	29-11	30-10	31-8
		0.32	0.43	0.54	0.66	0.78	0.92	1.06	1.21	1.36	1.52	1.69	1.86	2.04	2.22	2.41
	16	14-1	15-5	16-8	17-9	18-10	19-11	20-10	21-9	22-8	23-6	24-4	25-2	25-11	26-8	27-5
		0.28	0.37	0.47	0.57	0.68	0.80	0.92	1.05	1.18	1.32	1.46	1.61	1.76	1.92	2.08
	24	11-6	12-7	13-7	14-6	15-5	16-3	17-0	17-9	18-6	19-3	19-11	20-6	21-2	21-9	22-5
		0.23	0.30	0.38	0.46	0.55	0.65	0.75	0.85	0.96	1.08	1.19	1.31	1.44	1.57	1.70

NOTE: The required modulus of elasticity, E, in 1,000,000 psi is shown below each span.

American Forest and Paper Association; Washington, D.C.

DESIGN CRITERIA

STRENGTH: 15 psf dead load plus 20 psf live load determines required fiber stress.

DEFLECTION: For 20 psf live load. Limited to span in inches divided by 180.

RAFTERS: Spans are measured along the horizontal projection, and loads are considered as applied on the horizontal projection.

MEDIUM OR HIGH SLOPE RAFTERS—20 LB LIVE LOAD
HEAVY ROOF COVERING—NO CEILING LOAD—SLOPE OVER 3 IN 12

RAFTER SIZE, SPACING (IN.)		EXTREME FIBER STRESS IN BENDING, F_b (PSI)														
		500	600	700	800	900	1000	1100	1200	1300	1400	1500	1600	1700	1800	1900
2 x 4	12	5-5 / 0.20	5-11 / 0.26	6-5 / 0.33	6-10 / 0.40	7-3 / 0.48	7-8 / 0.56	8-0 / 0.65	8-4 / 0.74	8-8 / 0.83	9-0 / 0.93	9-4 / 1.03	9-8 / 1.14	9-11 / 1.24	10-3 / 1.36	10-6 / 1.47
	16	4-8 / 0.17	5-1 / 0.23	5-6 / 0.28	5-11 / 0.35	6-3 / 0.41	6-7 / 0.49	6-11 / 0.56	7-3 / 0.64	7-6 / 0.72	7-10 / 0.80	8-1 / 0.89	8-4 / 0.98	8-7 / 1.08	8-10 / 1.17	9-1 / 1.27
	24	3-10 / 0.14	4-2 / 0.18	4-6 / 0.23	4-10 / 0.28	5-1 / 0.34	5-5 / 0.40	5-8 / 0.46	5-11 / 0.52	6-2 / 0.59	6-5 / 0.66	6-7 / 0.73	6-10 / 0.80	7-0 / 0.88	7-3 / 0.96	7-5 / 1.04
2 x 6	12	8-6 / 0.20	9-4 / 0.26	10-0 / 0.33	10-9 / 0.40	11-5 / 0.48	12-0 / 0.56	12-7 / 0.65	13-2 / 0.74	13-8 / 0.83	14-2 / 0.93	14-8 / 1.03	15-2 / 1.14	15-8 / 1.24	16-1 / 1.36	16-7 / 1.47
	16	7-4 / 0.17	8-1 / 0.23	8-8 / 0.28	9-4 / 0.35	9-10 / 0.41	10-5 / 0.49	10-11 / 0.56	11-5 / 0.64	11-10 / 0.72	12-4 / 0.80	12-9 / 0.89	13-2 / 0.98	13-7 / 1.08	13-11 / 1.17	14-4 / 1.27
	24	6-0 / 0.14	6-7 / 0.18	7-1 / 0.23	7-7 / 0.28	8-1 / 0.34	8-6 / 0.40	8-11 / 0.46	9-4 / 0.52	9-8 / 0.59	10-0 / 0.66	10-5 / 0.73	10-9 / 0.80	11-1 / 0.88	11-5 / 0.96	11-8 / 1.04
2 x 8	12	11-12 / 0.20	12-3 / 0.26	13-3 / 0.33	14-2 / 0.40	15-0 / 0.48	15-10 / 0.56	16-7 / 0.65	17-4 / 0.74	18-0 / 0.83	18-9 / 0.93	19-5 / 1.03	20-0 / 1.14	20-8 / 1.24	21-3 / 1.36	21-10 / 1.47
	16	9-8 / 0.17	10-7 / 0.23	11-6 / 0.28	12-3 / 0.35	13-0 / 0.41	13-8 / 0.49	14-4 / 0.56	15-0 / 0.64	15-7 / 0.72	16-3 / 0.80	16-9 / 0.89	17-4 / 0.98	17-10 / 1.08	18-5 / 1.17	18-11 / 1.27
	24	7-11 / 0.14	8-8 / 0.18	9-4 / 0.23	10-0 / 0.28	10-7 / 0.34	11-2 / 0.40	11-9 / 0.46	12-3 / 0.52	12-9 / 0.59	13-3 / 0.66	13-8 / 0.73	14-2 / 0.80	14-7 / 0.88	15-0 / 0.96	15-5 / 1.04
2 x 10	12	14-3 / 0.20	15-8 / 0.26	16-11 / 0.33	18-1 / 0.40	19-2 / 0.48	20-2 / 0.56	21-2 / 0.65	22-1 / 0.74	23-0 / 0.83	23-11 / 0.93	24-9 / 1.03	25-6 / 1.14	26-4 / 1.24	27-1 / 1.36	27-10 / 1.47
	16	12-4 / 0.17	13-6 / 0.23	14-8 / 0.28	15-8 / 0.35	16-7 / 0.41	17-6 / 0.49	18-4 / 0.56	19-2 / 0.64	19-11 / 0.72	20-8 / 0.80	21-5 / 0.89	22-1 / 0.98	22-10 / 1.08	23-5 / 1.17	24-1 / 1.27
	24	10-1 / 0.14	11-1 / 0.18	11-11 / 0.23	12-9 / 0.28	13-6 / 0.34	14-3 / 0.40	15-0 / 0.46	15-8 / 0.52	16-3 / 0.59	16-11 / 0.66	17-6 / 0.73	18-1 / 0.80	18-7 / 0.88	19-2 / 0.96	19-8 / 1.04

NOTE: The required modulus of elasticity, E, in 1,000,000 psi is shown below each span.

DESIGN CRITERIA

STRENGTH: 15 psf dead load plus 30 psf live load determines required fiber stress.

DEFLECTION: For 30 psf live load. Limited to span in inches divided by 180.

RAFTERS: Spans are measured along the horizontal projection, and loads are considered as applied on the horizontal projection.

MEDIUM OR HIGH SLOPE RAFTERS—30 LB LIVE LOAD
HEAVY ROOF COVERING—NO CEILING LOAD—SLOPE OVER 3 IN 12

RAFTER SIZE, SPACING (IN.)		EXTREME FIBER STRESS IN BENDING, F_b (PSI)														
		500	600	700	800	900	1000	1100	1200	1300	1400	1500	1600	1700	1800	1900
2 x 4	12	4-9 / 0.20	5-3 / 0.27	5-8 / 0.34	6-0 / 0.41	6-5 / 0.49	6-9 / 0.58	7-1 / 0.67	7-5 / 0.76	7-8 / 0.86	8-0 / 0.96	8-3 / 1.06	8-6 / 1.17	8-9 / 1.28	9-0 / 1.39	9-3 / 1.51
	16	4-1 / 0.18	4-6 / 0.23	4-11 / 0.29	5-3 / 0.36	5-6 / 0.43	5-10 / 0.50	6-1 / 0.58	6-5 / 0.66	6-8 / 0.74	6-11 / 0.83	7-2 / 0.92	7-5 / 1.01	7-7 / 1.11	7-10 / 1.21	8-0 / 1.31
	24	3-4 / 0.14	3-8 / 0.19	4-0 / 0.24	4-3 / 0.29	4-6 / 0.35	4-9 / 0.41	5-0 / 0.47	5-3 / 0.54	5-5 / 0.61	5-8 / 0.68	5-10 / 0.75	6-0 / 0.83	6-3 / 0.90	6-5 / 0.99	6-7 / 1.07
2 x 6	12	7-6 / 0.20	8-2 / 0.27	8-10 / 0.34	9-6 / 0.41	10-0 / 0.49	10-7 / 0.58	11-1 / 0.67	11-7 / 0.76	12-1 / 0.86	12-6 / 0.96	13-0 / 1.06	13-5 / 1.17	13-10 / 1.28	14-2 / 1.39	14-7 / 1.51
	16	6-6 / 0.18	7-1 / 0.23	7-8 / 0.29	8-2 / 0.36	8-8 / 0.43	9-2 / 0.50	9-7 / 0.58	10-0 / 0.66	10-5 / 0.74	10-10 / 0.83	11-3 / 0.92	11-7 / 1.01	11-11 / 1.11	12-4 / 1.21	12-8 / 1.31
	24	5-4 / 0.14	5-10 / 0.19	6-3 / 0.24	6-8 / 0.29	7-1 / 0.35	7-6 / 0.41	7-10 / 0.47	8-2 / 0.54	8-6 / 0.61	8-10 / 0.68	9-2 / 0.75	9-6 / 0.83	9-9 / 0.90	10-0 / 0.99	10-4 / 1.07
2 x 8	12	9-10 / 0.20	10-10 / 0.27	11-8 / 0.34	12-6 / 0.41	13-3 / 0.49	13-11 / 0.58	14-8 / 0.67	15-3 / 0.76	15-11 / 0.86	16-6 / 0.96	17-1 / 1.06	17-8 / 1.17	18-2 / 1.28	18-9 / 1.39	19-3 / 1.51
	16	8-7 / 0.18	9-4 / 0.23	10-1 / 0.29	10-10 / 0.36	11-6 / 0.43	12-1 / 0.50	12-8 / 0.58	13-3 / 0.66	13-9 / 0.74	14-4 / 0.83	14-10 / 0.92	15-3 / 1.01	15-9 / 1.11	16-3 / 1.21	16-8 / 1.31
	24	7-0 / 0.14	7-8 / 0.19	8-3 / 0.24	8-10 / 0.29	9-4 / 0.35	9-10 / 0.41	10-4 / 0.47	10-10 / 0.54	11-3 / 0.61	11-8 / 0.68	21-1 / 0.75	12-6 / 0.83	12-10 / 0.90	13-3 / 0.99	13-7 / 1.07
2 x 10	12	12-7 / 0.20	13-9 / 0.27	14-11 / 0.34	15-11 / 0.41	16-11 / 0.49	17-10 / 0.58	18-8 / 0.67	19-6 / 0.76	20-4 / 0.86	21-1 / 0.96	21-10 / 1.06	22-6 / 1.17	23-3 / 1.28	23-11 / 1.39	24-6 / 1.51
	16	10-11 / 0.18	11-11 / 0.23	12-11 / 0.29	13-9 / 0.36	14-8 / 0.43	15-5 / 0.50	16-2 / 0.58	16-11 / 0.66	17-7 / 0.74	18-3 / 0.83	18-11 / 0.92	19-6 / 1.01	20-1 / 1.11	20-8 / 1.21	21-3 / 1.31
	24	8-11 / 0.14	9-9 / 0.19	10-6 / 0.24	11-3 / 0.29	11-11 / 0.35	12-7 / 0.41	13-2 / 0.47	13-9 / 0.54	14-4 / 0.61	14-11 / 0.68	15-5 / 0.75	15-11 / 0.83	16-5 / 0.90	16-11 / 0.99	17-4 / 1.07

NOTE: The required modulus of elasticity, E, in 1,000,000 psi is shown below each span.

American Forest and Paper Association; Washington, D.C.

DESIGN LOAD TABLES

DESIGN CRITERIA

STRENGTH: 7 psf dead load plus 20 psf live load determines required fiber stress.

DEFLECTION: For 20 psf live load. Limited to span in inches divided by 180.

RAFTERS: Spans are measured along the horizontal projection, and loads are considered as applied on the horizontal projection.

MEDIUM OR HIGH SLOPE RAFTERS—20 LB LIVE LOAD
LIGHT ROOF COVERING—NO CEILING LOAD—SLOPE OVER 3 IN 12

RAFTER SIZE, SPACING (IN.)		EXTREME FIBER STRESS IN BENDING, F_b (PSI)														
		500	600	700	800	900	1000	1100	1200	1300	1400	1500	1600	1700	1800	1900
2 x 4	12	6-2 / 0.29	6-9 / 0.38	7-3 / 0.49	7-9 / 0.59	8-3 / 0.71	8-8 / 0.83	9-1 / 0.96	9-6 / 1.06	9-11 / 1.23	10-3 / 1.37	10-8 / 1.52	11-0 / 1.68	11-4 / 1.84	11-8 / 2.00	12-0 / 2.17
	16	5-4 / 0.25	5-10 / 0.33	6-4 / 0.42	6-9 / 0.51	7-2 / 0.61	7-6 / 0.72	7-11 / 0.83	8-3 / 0.94	8-7 / 1.06	8-11 / 1.19	9-3 / 1.32	9-6 / 1.45	9-10 / 1.59	10-1 / 1.73	10-5 / 1.88
	24	4-4 / 0.21	4-9 / 0.27	5-2 / 0.34	5-6 / 0.42	5-10 / 0.50	6-2 / 0.59	6-5 / 0.68	6-9 / 0.77	7-0 / 0.87	7-3 / 0.97	7-6 / 1.08	7-9 / 1.19	8-0 / 1.30	8-3 / 1.41	8-6 / 1.53
2 x 6	12	9-8 / 0.29	10-7 / 0.38	11-5 / 0.49	12-3 / 0.59	13-0 / 0.71	13-8 / 0.83	14-4 / 0.96	15-0 / 1.09	15-7 / 1.23	16-2 / 1.37	16-9 / 1.52	17-3 / 1.68	17-10 / 1.84	18-4 / 2.00	18-10 / 2.17
	16	8-4 / 0.25	9-2 / 0.33	9-11 / 0.42	10-7 / 0.51	11-3 / 0.61	11-10 / 0.72	12-5 / 0.83	13-0 / 0.94	13-6 / 1.06	14-0 / 1.19	14-6 / 1.32	15-0 / 1.45	15-5 / 1.59	15-11 / 1.73	16-4 / 1.88
	24	6-10 / 0.21	7-6 / 0.27	8-1 / 0.34	8-8 / 0.42	9-2 / 0.50	9-8 / 0.59	10-2 / 0.68	10-7 / 0.77	11-0 / 0.87	11-5 / 0.97	11-10 / 1.08	12-3 / 1.19	12-7 / 1.30	13-0 / 1.41	13-4 / 1.53
2 x 8	12	12-9 / 0.29	13-11 / 0.38	15-1 / 0.49	16-1 / 0.59	17-1 / 0.71	18-0 / 0.83	18-11 / 0.96	19-9 / 1.09	20-6 / 1.23	21-4 / 1.37	22-1 / 1.52	22-9 / 1.68	23-6 / 1.84	24-2 / 2.00	24-10 / 2.17
	16	11-0 / 0.25	12-1 / 0.33	13-1 / 0.42	13-11 / 0.51	14-10 / 0.61	15-7 / 0.72	16-4 / 0.83	17-1 / 0.94	17-9 / 1.06	18-5 / 1.19	19-1 / 1.32	19-9 / 1.45	20-4 / 1.59	20-11 / 1.73	21-6 / 1.88
	24	9-0 / 0.21	9-10 / 0.27	10-8 / 0.34	11-5 / 0.42	12-1 / 0.50	12-9 / 0.59	13-4 / 0.68	13-11 / 0.77	14-6 / 0.87	15-1 / 0.97	15-7 / 1.08	16-1 / 1.19	16-7 / 1.30	17-1 / 1.41	17-7 / 1.53
2 x 10	12	16-3 / 0.29	17-10 / 0.38	19-3 / 0.49	20-7 / 0.59	21-10 / 0.71	23-0 / 0.83	24-1 / 0.96	25-2 / 1.09	26-2 / 1.23	27-2 / 1.37	28-2 / 1.52	29-1 / 1.68	30-0 / 1.84	30-10 / 2.00	31-8 / 2.17
	16	14-1 / 0.25	15-5 / 0.33	16-8 / 0.42	17-10 / 0.51	18-11 / 0.61	19-11 / 0.72	20-10 / 0.83	21-10 / 0.94	22-8 / 1.06	23-7 / 1.19	24-5 / 1.32	25-2 / 1.45	25-11 / 1.59	26-8 / 1.73	27-5 / 1.88
	24	11-6 / 0.21	12-7 / 0.27	13-7 / 0.34	14-6 / 0.42	15-5 / 0.50	16-3 / 0.59	17-1 / 0.68	17-10 / 0.77	18-6 / 0.87	19-3 / 0.97	19-11 / 1.08	20-7 / 1.19	21-2 / 1.30	21-10 / 1.41	22-5 / 1.53

NOTE: The required modulus of elasticity, E, in 1,000,000 psi is shown below each span.

DESIGN CRITERIA

STRENGTH: 7 psf dead load plus 30 psf live load determines required fiber stress.

DEFLECTION: For 30 psf live load. Limited to span in inches divided by 180.

RAFTERS: Spans are measured along the horizontal projection, and loads are considered as applied on the horizontal projection.

MEDIUM OR HIGH SLOPE RAFTERS—30 LB LIVE LOAD
LIGHT ROOF COVERING—NO CEILING LOAD—SLOPE OVER 3 IN 12

RAFTER SIZE, SPACING (IN.)		EXTREME FIBER STRESS IN BENDING, F_b (PSI)														
		500	600	700	800	900	1000	1100	1200	1300	1400	1500	1600	1700	1800	1900
2 x 4	12	5-3 / 0.27	5-9 / 0.36	6-3 / 0.45	6-8 / 0.55	7-1 / 0.66	7-5 / 0.77	7-9 / 0.89	8-2 / 1.02	8-6 / 1.15	8-9 / 1.28	9-1 / 1.42	9-5 / 1.57	9-8 / 1.72	10-0 / 1.87	10-3 / 2.03
	16	4-7 / 0.24	5-0 / 0.31	5-5 / 0.39	5-9 / 0.48	6-1 / 0.57	6-5 / 0.67	6-9 / 0.77	7-1 / 0.88	7-4 / 0.99	7-7 / 1.11	7-11 / 1.23	8-2 / 1.36	8-5 / 1.49	8-8 / 1.62	8-10 / 1.76
	24	3-9 / 0.19	4-1 / 0.25	4-5 / 0.32	4-8 / 0.39	5-0 / 0.47	5-3 / 0.55	5-6 / 0.63	5-9 / 0.72	6-0 / 0.81	6-3 / 0.91	6-5 / 1.01	6-8 / 1.11	6-10 / 1.21	7-1 / 1.32	7-3 / 1.43
2 x 6	12	8-3 / 0.27	9-1 / 0.36	9-9 / 0.45	10-5 / 0.55	11-1 / 0.66	11-8 / 0.77	12-3 / 0.89	12-9 / 1.02	13-4 / 1.15	13-10 / 1.28	14-4 / 1.42	14-9 / 1.57	15-3 / 1.72	15-8 / 1.87	16-1 / 2.03
	16	7-2 / 0.24	7-10 / 0.31	8-5 / 0.39	9-1 / 0.48	9-7 / 0.57	10-1 / 0.67	10-7 / 0.77	11-1 / 0.88	11-6 / 0.99	12-0 / 1.11	12-5 / 1.23	12-9 / 1.36	13-2 / 1.49	13-7 / 1.62	13-11 / 1.76
	24	5-10 / 0.19	6-5 / 0.25	6-11 / 0.32	7-5 / 0.39	7-10 / 0.47	8-3 / 0.55	8-8 / 0.63	9-1 / 0.72	9-5 / 0.81	9-9 / 0.91	10-1 / 1.01	10-5 / 1.11	10-9 / 1.21	11-1 / 1.32	11-5 / 1.43
2 x 8	12	10-11 / 0.27	11-11 / 0.36	12-10 / 0.45	13-9 / 0.55	14-7 / 0.66	15-5 / 0.77	16-2 / 0.89	16-10 / 1.02	17-7 / 1.15	18-2 / 1.28	18-10 / 1.42	19-6 / 1.57	20-1 / 1.72	20-8 / 1.87	21-3 / 2.03
	16	9-5 / 0.24	10-4 / 0.31	11-2 / 0.39	11-11 / 0.48	12-8 / 0.57	13-4 / 0.67	14-0 / 0.77	14-7 / 0.88	15-2 / 0.99	15-9 / 1.11	16-4 / 1.23	16-10 / 1.36	17-4 / 1.49	17-11 / 1.62	18-4 / 1.76
	24	7-8 / 0.19	8-5 / 0.25	9-1 / 0.32	9-9 / 0.39	10-4 / 0.47	10-11 / 0.55	11-5 / 0.63	11-11 / 0.72	12-5 / 0.81	12-10 / 0.91	13-4 / 1.01	13-9 / 1.11	14-2 / 1.21	14-7 / 1.32	15-0 / 1.43
2 x 10	12	13-11 / 0.27	15-2 / 0.36	16-5 / 0.45	17-7 / 0.55	18-7 / 0.66	19-8 / 0.77	20-7 / 0.89	21-6 / 1.02	22-5 / 1.15	23-3 / 1.28	24-1 / 1.42	24-10 / 1.57	25-7 / 1.72	26-4 / 1.87	27-1 / 2.03
	16	12-0 / 0.26	13-2 / 0.34	14-3 / 0.43	15-2 / 0.53	16-2 / 0.63	17-0 / 0.74	17-10 / 0.85	18-7 / 0.97	19-5 / 1.09	20-1 / 1.22	20-10 / 1.35	21-6 / 1.49	22-2 / 1.63	22-10 / 1.78	23-5 / 1.93
	24	9-10 / 0.19	10-9 / 0.25	11-7 / 0.32	12-5 / 0.39	13-2 / 0.47	13-11 / 0.55	14-7 / 0.63	15-2 / 0.72	15-10 / 0.81	16-5 / 0.91	17-0 / 1.01	17-7 / 1.11	18-1 / 1.21	18-7 / 1.32	19-2 / 1.43

NOTE: The required modulus of elasticity, E, in 1,000,000 psi is shown below each span.

American Forest and Paper Association; Washington, D.C.

GENERAL NOTES

1. Nails are made of many materials for diverse uses. When selecting nails, follow the recommendation of the manufacturer of the material to be fastened, as well as building codes when applicable.
2. Select nails so as to avoid galvanic action between the nail and the nailed material.
3. Select nail head size according to the strength and area of the material to be held.
4. In wood framing the correct size and number of nails must be used at any given point to withstand stress. Procedures for calculating nailed connections can be found in *National Design Specifications for Wood Construction* (Washington: National Forest Products Association [American Forest and Paper Association]).
5. Base nail selection on the type(s) of wood or other materials to be assembled, joined, or connected.
6. Nails with serrated or helically threaded shanks have increased holding power. Such nails are difficult, if not impossible, to remove without destroying the surrounding material.
7. Where nails are exposed to moisture or weather, for example, in exterior stucco lath, use nonferrous (aluminum or zinc-coated) nails.
8. Choose nails for automatic nailing equipment specifically for the equipment used. See ANSI "Safety Requirements for Power Actuated Fastening Systems" and OSHA regulations.

COMMON NAIL SIZES

LENGTH	PENNY	GAUGE	DIA. OF HEAD (IN.)	NAILS/ LB
1	2	15	$^{11}/_{64}$	847
$1^1/_4$	3	14	$^{13}/_{64}$	543
$1^1/_2$	4	$12^1/_2$	$^1/_4$	296
$1^3/_4$	5	$12^1/_2$	$^1/_4$	254
2	6	$11^1/_2$	$^{17}/_{64}$	167
$2^1/_4$	7	$11^1/_2$	$^{17}/_{64}$	150
$2^1/_2$	8	$10^1/_4$	$^9/_{32}$	101
$2^3/_4$	9	$10^1/_4$	$^9/_{32}$	92.1
3	10	9	$^5/_{16}$	66
$3^1/_4$	12	9	$^5/_{16}$	66.1
$3^1/_2$	16	8	$^{11}/_{32}$	47.4
4	20	6	$^{13}/_{32}$	29.7
$4^1/_2$	30	5	$^7/_{16}$	22.7
5	40	4	$^{15}/_{32}$	17.3
$5^1/_2$	50	3	$^1/_2$	13.5
6	60	2	$^{17}/_{32}$	10.7

Charles F. D. Egbert, AIA; Architect; Washington, D.C.

ROUGH CONSTRUCTION

NAME	SHAPE	MATERIAL	FINISH
COMMON		Steel or aluminum	Smooth
ANNULAR		Steel, hardened steel, copper, brass, bronze, silicon bronze, nickel silver, aluminum, monel, or stainless steel	Bright, hardened
HELICAL			
COMMON CUT STRIKE		Steel or iron	Bright or zinc-coated
DOUBLE-HEADED		Steel	Bright or zinc-coated
		Aluminum	Bright
SQUARE		Steel	Smooth, bright, zinc-coated
ROUND WIRE			
ANNULAR		Aluminum	Bright or hard

ROOFING

NAME	SHAPE	MATERIAL	FINISH
SIDING & SHINGLE		Steel, copper, or aluminum	Smooth, bright, zinc- or cement-coated
ROOFING (BARBED)		Steel or aluminum	
ROOFING		Steel	Bright or zinc-coated
NONLEAKING ROOFING			
SHINGLE NAIL		Steel or cut iron	Plain or zinc-coated
CUT SLATING (NONFERROUS)		Copper, muntz metal, or zinc	
GUTTER SPIKE (ROUND)		Steel	Bright or zinc-coated
GUTTER SPIKE (ANNULAR)		Copper	Bright

FINISH WORK

NAME	SHAPE	MATERIAL	FINISH
WALLBOARD		Steel or aluminum	Smooth, bright, blued, or cement-coated
FINE NAIL		Steel	Bright
LATH			Blued or cement-coated
LATH		Steel or aluminum	Smooth, bright, blued, or cement-coated
CASING OR BRAD			Bright or cement-coated
FINISHING		Steel	Smooth

MISCELLANEOUS

NAME	SHAPE	MATERIAL	FINISH
CEMENT			Smooth, bright, or oil-quenched
CEMENT (FLUTED HELICAL)			Hardened
OFFSET (LATH)		Steel	
HOOKED (LATH)			Bright, blued, or zinc-coated
STAPLE			

MACHINE BOLT ANCHORS AND SHIELDS (IN.)

BOLT DIA.	THPS PER INCH	DECIMAL EQUIV. (IN.)	SINGLE EXPANDING ANCHOR (CAULKING) A	SINGLE EXPANDING ANCHOR (CAULKING) L	SINGLE EXPANDING ANCHOR (NONCAULKING) A	SINGLE EXPANDING ANCHOR (NONCAULKING) L	MULTIPLE EXPANDING ANCHOR (PLAIN STYLE) A	MULTIPLE EXPANDING ANCHOR (PLAIN STYLE) L UNITS 2	MULTIPLE EXPANDING ANCHOR (PLAIN STYLE) L UNITS 3	MULTIPLE EXPANDING ANCHOR (THREADED STYLE) A	MULTIPLE EXPANDING ANCHOR (THREADED STYLE) L UNITS 2	MULTIPLE EXPANDING ANCHOR (THREADED STYLE) L UNITS 3	DOUBLE ACTING SHIELD A	DOUBLE ACTING SHIELD L
6	32	.138	5/16	1/2										
8	32	.164	5/16	1/2										
10	24	.190	3/8	5/8										
12	24	.216	1/2	7/8										
1/4	20	.250	1/2	7/8	1/2	1 3/8	1/2"	1 1/8		1/2	1		1/2	1 1/4
5/16	18	.312	5/8	1	5/8	1 5/8							5/8	1 1/2
3/8	16	.375	3/4	1 1/4	5/8	1 5/8	3/4	1 1/2		3/4	1 1/2		3/4	1 3/4
1/2	13	.500	7/8	1 1/2	7/8	2 1/2	1	1 3/4	2 3/8	1	1 3/4	2 1/4	7/8	2 1/4
5/8	11	.625	1 1/8	2	1	2 3/4	1 1/8	*	2 5/8	1 1/8	*	2 1/2	1	2 1/2
3/4	10	.750	1 1/4	2 1/4	1 1/4	2 7/8	1 3/8	*	3	1 3/8	*	3 1/8	1 1/4	3 1/2
7/8	9	.875					1 1/2	*	3 1/2	1 1/2	*	3 5/8	1 5/8	4"
1	8	1.00					1 5/8	*	3 7/8	1 5/8	*	3 3/4	1 3/4	4 1/4

*Use of three units in these diameters is recommended.

NOTE
1. Extension sleeve for deep setting.
2. Expansion shields and anchors shown are representative of many types, some of which may be used in single or multiple units.
3. Many are threaded for use with the head of the screw outside, some with the head inside and some types require setting tools to install.
4. In light construction plastic expansion shields are used frequently.

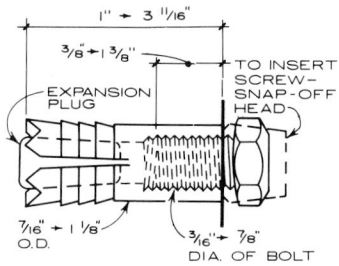

SELF-DRILLING EXPANSION ANCHOR (SNAP-OFF TYPE)

NOTE

1. Refer to manufacturers for size variations within the limits shown, and for different types of bolts.
2. The anchor is made of case hardened steel and drawn carburizing steel.

HOLLOW WALL ANCHORS

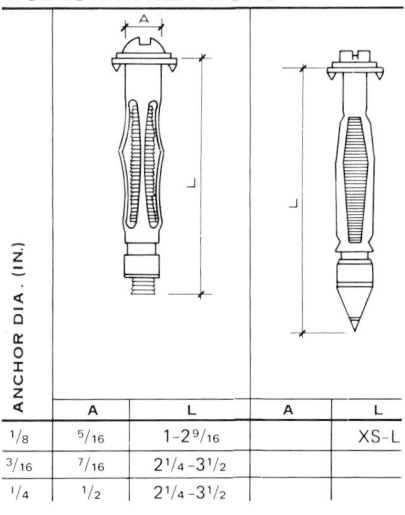

ANCHOR DIA. (IN.)	A	L	A	L
1/8	5/16	1-2 9/16		XS-L
3/16	7/16	2 1/4-3 1/2		
1/4	1/2	2 1/4-3 1/2		

SHIELDS FOR LAG BOLTS AND WOOD SCREWS (IN.)

LAG SCREW DIA. (IN.)	WOOD SCREW SIZES	DECIMAL EQUIV. (IN.)	LAG BOLT EXPANSION SHIELD A	LAG BOLT EXPANSION SHIELD L SHORT	LAG BOLT EXPANSION SHIELD L LONG	LEAD SHIELD FOR LAG BOLT OR WOOD SCREW A	LEAD SHIELD FOR LAG BOLT OR WOOD SCREW L
	6	.138				1/4	3/4-1 1/2
	8	.164				1/4	3/4-1 1/2
	10	.190				5/16	1-1 1/2
	12	.216				5/16	1-1 1/2
1/4	14	.250	1/2	1	1 1/2	5/16	1-1 1/2
	16	.268				3/8	1 1/2
	18	.294				3/8	1 1/2
5/16	20	.320	1/2	1 1/4	1 3/4	7/16	1 3/4
3/8	24	.372	5/8	1 3/4	2 1/2	7/16	1 3/4
1/2		.500	3/4	2	3		
5/8		.625	7/8	2	3 1/2		
3/4		.750	1	2	3 1/2		

ONE PIECE ANCHORS (IN.)

ANCHOR SIZE AND DRILL SIZE	DECIMAL EQUIV. (IN.)	WEDGE ANCHOR L	WEDGE ANCHOR MIN. HOLE DEPTH D	STUD ANCHOR L	STUD ANCHOR MIN. HOLE DEPTH D	SLEEVE ANCHOR L	SLEEVE ANCHOR MIN. HOLE DEPTH D	HEAD STYLE
1/4	.250	1 3/4-3 1/4	1 3/8	1 3/4-3 1/4	1 3/8	5/8-2 1/4	1/2-1 1/8	Acorn nut
5/16	.320			1 1/2-2 1/2	1 1/8			Hex nut
3/8	.375	2 1/4-5	1 3/4	2 1/4-6	1 5/8	1 7/8-3	1 1/2	''
1/2	.500	2 3/4-7	2 1/8	2 3/4-5 1/4	1 7/8	2 1/4-4	1 7/8	''
5/8	.625	3 1/2-8 1/2	2 5/8	3 3/8-7	2 3/8	2 1/4-6	2	''
3/4	.750	4 1/4-10	3 1/4	4 1/4-8 1/2	2 7/8	2 1/2-8	2 1/4-5 1/2	''
7/8	.875	6-10	3 3/4					
1	1.00	6-12	4 1/2					
1 1/4	1.25	9-12	5 1/2					

Sleeve anchors available in acorn nut, hex nut, flat head, round head, Phillips round head, and tie wire head styles.

MACHINE SCREW AND STOVE BOLT (INS.)

STOVE BOLT DIAM.	MACHINE SCREW DIAM.	ROUND HEAD	FLAT HEAD	FILLISTER HEAD	OVAL HEAD	OVEN HEAD
	2	1/8–7/8		1/8–7/8		
	3	1/8–7/8		1/8–7/8		
	4	1/8–1 1/2	40 N.C.	1/8–1 1/2		
	4	1/8–1 1/2	36 N.C.	1/8–1 1/2		1/8–3/4
1/8	5	1/8–2		1/8–2		3/8–2
	6	1/8–2		1/8–2		1/8–1
5/32	8	3/16–3		3/16–3		3/16–2
3/16	10	3/16–6		3/16–3		1/4–6
	12	1/4–3		1/4–3		
1/4	1/4	5/16–6		5/16–3		3/8–6
5/16	5/16	3/8–6		3/8–3		3/4–6
3/8	3/8	1/2–5		1/2–3		3/4–5
1/2		1–4				

Length intervals = 1/16 in. increments up to 1/2 in., 1/8 in. increments from 5/8 in. to 1 1/4 in., 1/4 in. increments from 1 1/2 in. to 3 in., 1/2 in. increments from 3 1/2 in. to 6 in.
NOTE: N.C. = Course thread

SCREW AND BOLT LENGTHS (INS.)

DIAMETER (INS.)	CAP SCREWS BUTTON HEAD	FLAT HEAD	HEXAGON HEAD	FILLISTER HEAD	BOLTS MACHINE BOLT	CARRIAGE BOLT	LAG BOLT
1/4	1/2–2 1/4		1/2–3 1/2	3/4–3	1/2–8	3/4–8	1–6
5/16	1/2–2 3/4		1/2–3 1/2	3/4–3 3/4	1/2–8	3/4–8	1–10
3/8	5/8–3		1/2–4	3/4–3 1/2	3/4–12	3/4–12	1–12
7/16	3/4–3		3/4–4	3/4–3 3/4	3/4–12	1–12	1–12
1/2	3/4–4		3/4–4 1/2	3/4–4	3/4–24	1–20	1–12
9/16	1–4		1–4 1/2	1–4	1–30	1–20	
5/8	1–4		1–5	1 1/4–4 1/2	1–30	1–20	1 1/2–16
3/4	1–4		1 1/4–5	1 1/2–4 1/2	1–30	1–20	1 1/2–16
7/8			2–6	1 3/4–5	1 1/2–30		2–16
1			2–6	2–5	1 1/2–30		2–16

Length intervals = 1/8 in. increments up to 1 in., 1/4 in. increments from 1 1/4 in. to 4 in., 1/2 in. increments from 4 1/2 in. to 6 in.

Length intervals = 1/4 in. increments up to 6 in., 1/2 in. increments from 6 1/2 in. to 12 in., 1 in. increments over 12 in.

Length intervals = 1/2 in. increments up to 8 in., 1 in. increments over 8 in.

ROUND   FLAT   OVAL   PAN   FILLISTER   TRUSS   HEX   WASHER

HEAD TYPES

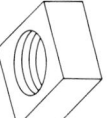  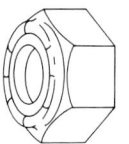 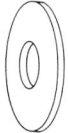  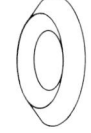

SQUARE   HEX   LOCK   FLAT   LOCK (SPRING)   COUNTERSUNK

CASTELLATED   CAP   WING   TOOTHLOCK (INTERNAL)   (EXTERNAL)

Self-locking nuts have a pin that acts as a rachet, sliding down the thread as the bolt is tightened, to prevent loosening from shock and vibration.

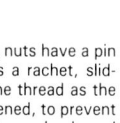

LOCK

NUTS

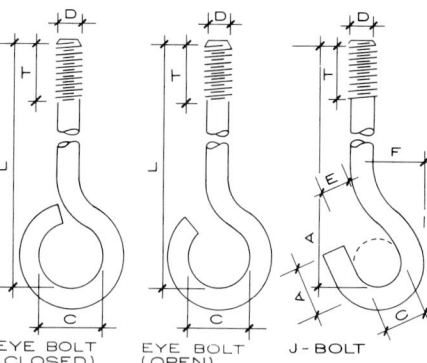

EYE BOLT (CLOSED)   EYE BOLT (OPEN)   J-BOLT

LOAD INDICATOR

WASHERS

The bolt's clamping force causes protrusions on the washer to flatten partially, closing the gap between the washer and the bolt head. Measurement of the gap indicates whether the bolt has been tightened adequately.

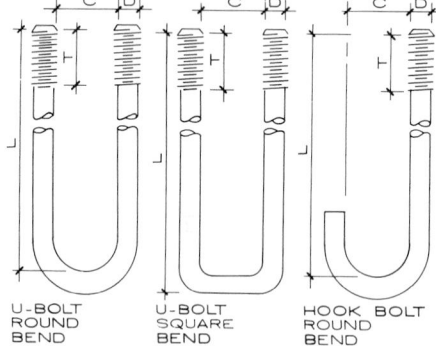

U-BOLT ROUND BEND   U-BOLT SQUARE BEND   HOOK BOLT ROUND BEND

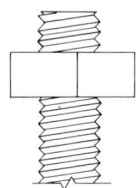

Fiberglass nuts and bolts are noncorrosive and non-conductive. Bolts are available in 3/8 in., 1/2 in., 5/8 in., 3/4 in., and 1 in. standard diameters.

FIBERGLASS NUTS AND BOLTS

High tension, stainless steel helical inserts are held in place by spring-like pressure, and they are used to salvage damaged threads. They also eliminate thread failure due to stress conditions.

HELICAL INSERTS

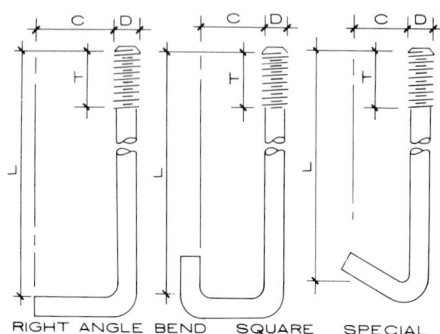

RIGHT ANGLE BEND   SQUARE BEND   SPECIAL

HOOK BOLTS

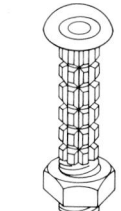

Interference body bolts are driven into reamed or drilled holes to create a joint in full bearing.

INTERFERENCE BODY BOLTS

NOTES
1. Bent bolts are specialty items made to order.
2. D = bolt diameter; C = inside opening width; T = thread length; L = inside length of bolt; A = inside depth.

Timothy B. McDonald; Washington, D.C.

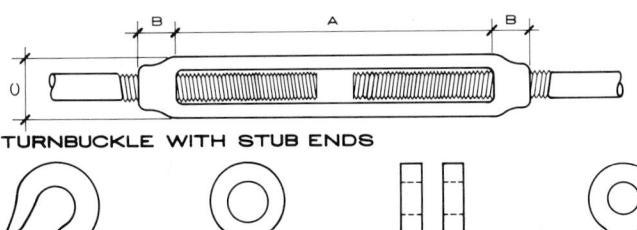

TURNBUCKLE WITH STUB ENDS

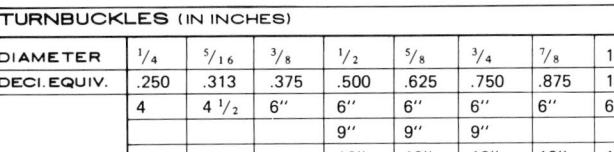

HOOK   EYE   CLEVIS

TURNBUCKLES (IN INCHES)

DIAMETER	$1/4$	$5/16$	$3/8$	$1/2$	$5/8$	$3/4$	$7/8$	1
DECI. EQUIV.	.250	.313	.375	.500	.625	.750	.875	1.00
	4	$4\,1/2$	6"	6"	6"	6"	6"	6"
				9"	9"	9"		
A				12"	12"	12"	12"	12"
B	$7/16$	$1/2$	$9/16$	$3/4$	$29/32$	$1\,1/16$	$1\,7/32$	$1\,3/8$
C	$3/4$	$7/8$	$31/32$	$1\,7/32$	$1\,1/2$	$1\,23/32$	$1\,7/8$	$2\,1/32$

DIAMETERS OVER I" AVAILABLE, NOT ALWAYS STOCKED.

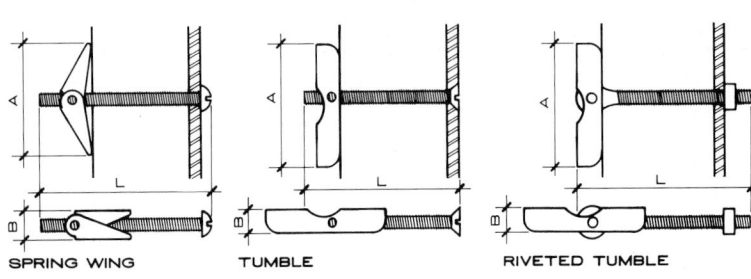

SPRING WING   TUMBLE   RIVETED TUMBLE

TOGGLE BOLTS (IN INCHES)

DIAMETER		$1/8$	$5/32$	$3/16$	$1/4$	$5/16$	$3/8$	$1/2$
DECIMAL EQUIV.		.138	.164	.190	.250	.313	.375	.500
SPRING WING	A	1.438	1.875	1.875	2.063	2.750	2.875	4.625
	B	.375	.500	.500	.688	.875	1.000	1.250
	L	$2-4$	$2\,1/2-4$	$2-6$	$2\,1/2-6$	$3-6$	$3-6$	$4-6$
TUMBLE	A	1.250	2.000	2.000	2.250	2.750	2.750	
	B	.375	.500	.500	.688	.875	.875	
	L	$2-4$	$2\,1/2-4$	$3-6$	$3-6$	$3-6$	$3-6$	
RIVETED TUMBLE	A		2.000	2.000	2.250	2.750	2.750	3.375
	B		.375	.375	.500	.625	.688	.875
	L		$2\,1/2-4$	$3-6$	$3-6$	$3-6$	$3-6$	$3-6$

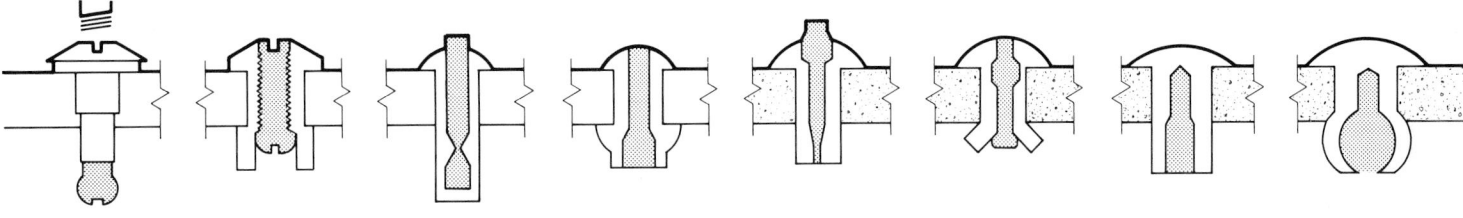

THREADED   PULL MANDREL   DRIVE PIN   CHEMICALLY EXPANDED

BLIND RIVETS FOR USE IN A JOINT THAT IS ACCESSIBLE FROM ONLY ONE SIDE

 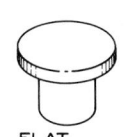  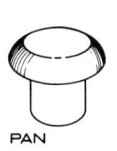 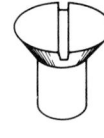 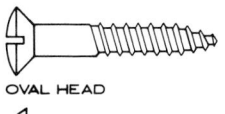

ROUND   TRUSS   FLAT   COUNTERSUNK   PAN   OVAL HEAD

RIVETS
STANDARD RIVETS AVAILABLE WITH SOLID, TUBULAR AND SPLIT SHANKS OF STEEL, BRASS, COPPER, ALUMINUM, MONEL METAL AND STAINLESS STEEL; IN DIAMETERS OF 1/8" TO 7/16" AND LENGTHS OF 3/16" TO 4 IN.

SLOTTED   ROUND HEAD

FLAT HEAD

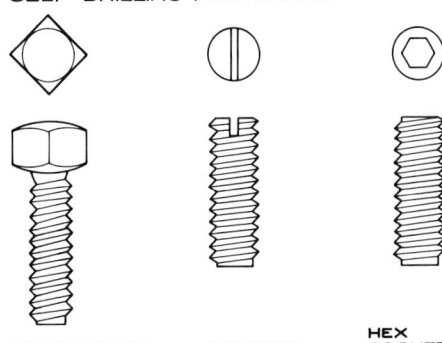

Self-drilling fasteners: used to attach metal to metal, wood, and concrete. Consult manufacturer for sizes and drilling capabilities.

SHEET METAL GIMLET POINT

Sheet metal gimlet point: hardened, self-tapping. Used in 28 gauge to 6 gauge sheet metal; aluminum, plastic, slate, etc. Usual head types.

PHILLIPS

SELF-DRILLING FASTENERS

SQUARE HEAD   SLOTTED   HEX SOCKET

Set Screws: headless with socket or slotted top; made in sizes 4 in. to 1/2 in., and in lengths 1/2 in. to 5 in. Square head sizes 1/4 in. to 1 in., and lengths 1/2 in. to 5 in.

SET SCREWS

SHEET METAL BLUNT POINT

Sheet metal blunt point: hardened, self-tapping. Used in 28 to 18 gauge sheet metal. Made in sizes 4 to 14 in usual head types.

FREARSON

THREAD CUTTING- CUTTING SLOT

Thread cutting, cutting slot: hardened. Used in metals up to 1/4 in. thick in sizes 4 in. to 5/16 in. in usual head types.

WOOD SCREWS (IN IN.)

DIA.	DECI. EQUIV.	LENGTH
0	.060	$1/4 - 3/8$
1	.073	$1/4 - 1/2$
2	.086	$1/4 - 3/4$
3	.099	$1/4 - 1$
4	.112	$1/4 - 1\,1/2$
5	.125	$3/8 - 1\,1/2$
6	.138	$3/8 - 2\,1/2$
7	.151	$3/8 - 2\,1/2$
8	.164	$3/8 - 3$
9	.177	$1/2 - 3$
10	.190	$1/2 - 3\,1/2$
11	.203	$5/8 - 3\,1/2$
12	.216	$5/8 - 4$
14	.242	$3/4 - 5$
16	.268	$1 - 5$
18	.294	$1\,1/4 - 5$
20	.320	$1\,1/2 - 5$
24	.372	$3 - 5$

SHEET METAL & THREADING SCREWS

DRIVE TYPES

Timothy B. McDonald; Washington, D.C.

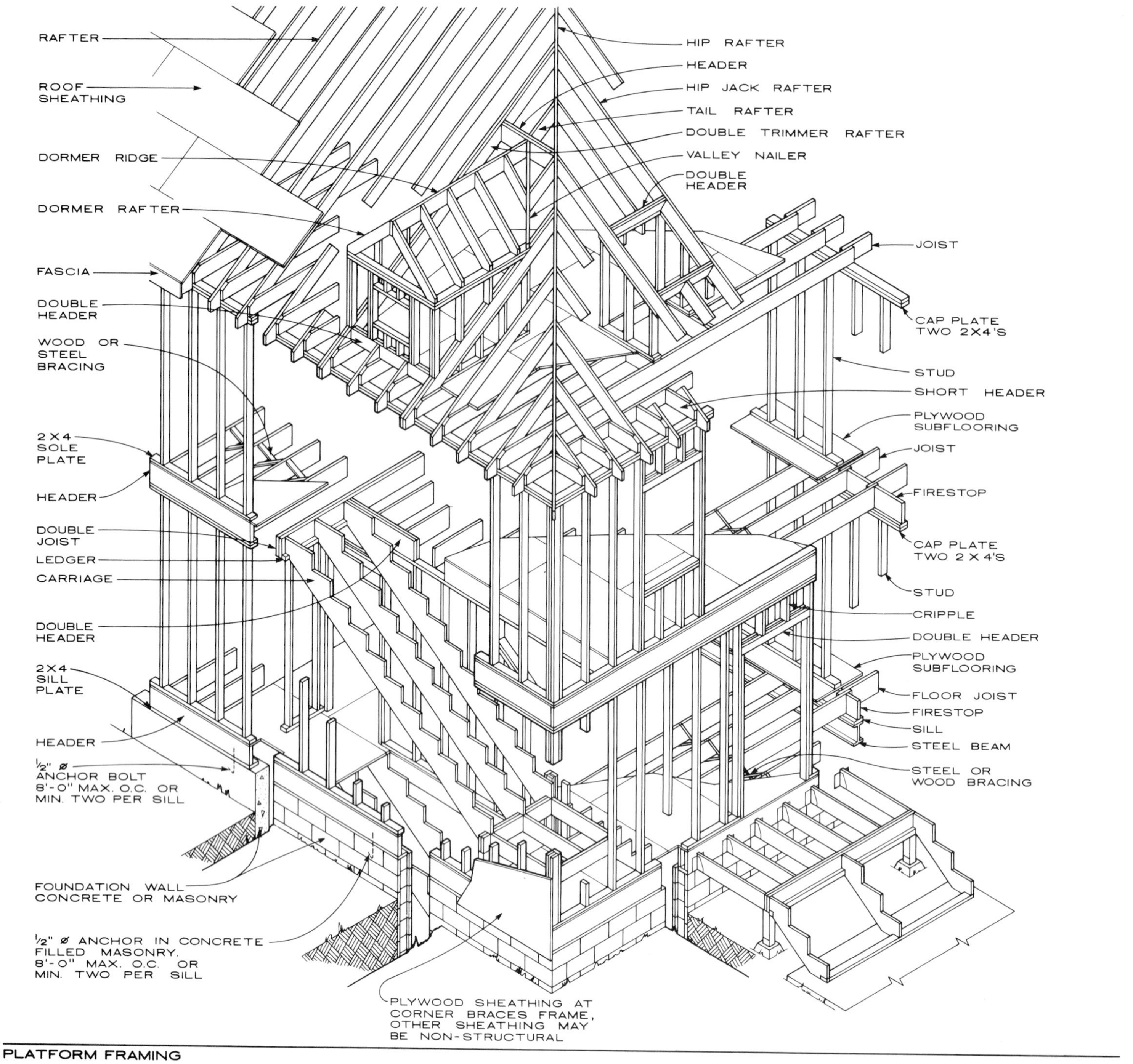

RAFTER

ROOF SHEATHING

DORMER RIDGE

DORMER RAFTER

FASCIA

DOUBLE HEADER

WOOD OR STEEL BRACING

2 X 4 SOLE PLATE

HEADER

DOUBLE JOIST

LEDGER

CARRIAGE

DOUBLE HEADER

2 X 4 SILL PLATE

HEADER

½" Ø ANCHOR BOLT 8'-0" MAX. O.C. OR MIN. TWO PER SILL

FOUNDATION WALL CONCRETE OR MASONRY

½" Ø ANCHOR IN CONCRETE FILLED MASONRY. 8'-0" MAX. O.C. OR MIN. TWO PER SILL

HIP RAFTER

HEADER

HIP JACK RAFTER

TAIL RAFTER

DOUBLE TRIMMER RAFTER

VALLEY NAILER

DOUBLE HEADER

JOIST

CAP PLATE TWO 2X4'S

STUD

SHORT HEADER

PLYWOOD SUBFLOORING

JOIST

FIRESTOP

CAP PLATE TWO 2 X 4'S

STUD

CRIPPLE

DOUBLE HEADER

PLYWOOD SUBFLOORING

FLOOR JOIST

FIRESTOP

SILL

STEEL BEAM

STEEL OR WOOD BRACING

PLYWOOD SHEATHING AT CORNER BRACES FRAME, OTHER SHEATHING MAY BE NON-STRUCTURAL

PLATFORM FRAMING

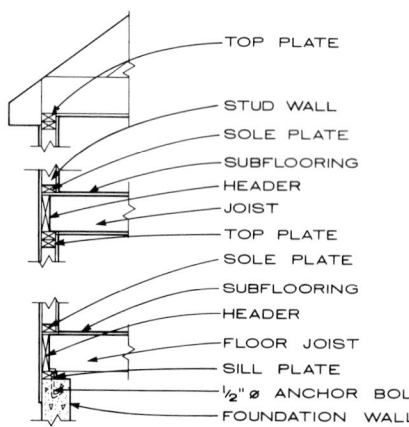

TOP PLATE

STUD WALL

SOLE PLATE

SUBFLOORING

HEADER

JOIST

TOP PLATE

SOLE PLATE

SUBFLOORING

HEADER

FLOOR JOIST

SILL PLATE

½" Ø ANCHOR BOLT

FOUNDATION WALL

Timothy B. McDonald; Washington, D.C.

NOTES

WESTERN OR PLATFORM FRAMING

Before any of the superstructure is erected, the first floor subflooring is put down making a platform on which the walls and partitions can be assembled and tilted into place. The process is repeated for each story of the building. This framing system is used frequently .

FIRESTOPPING

All concealed spaces in framing, with the exception of areas around flues and chimneys, are to be fitted with 2 in. blocking arranged to prevent drafts between spaces.

EXTERIOR WALL FRAMING

One story buildings: 2 x 4's, 16 in. or 24 in. o.c.;
  2 x 6's, 24 in. o.c.
Two and three stories: 2 x 4's, 16 in. o.c.;
  2 x 6's, 24 in. o.c.

BRACING EXTERIOR WALLS

Because floor framing and wall frames do not interlock, adequate sheathing must act as bracing and provide the necessary lateral resistance. Where required for additional stiffness or bracing, 1 x 4's may be let into outer face of studs at 45° angle secured at top, bottom, and to studs.

BRIDGING FOR FLOOR JOISTS

May be omitted when flooring is nailed adequately to joist; however, where nominal depth-to-thickness ratio of joists exceeds 6, bridging would be installed at 8 ft. 0 in. intervals. Building codes may allow omission of bridging under certain conditions.

Steel bridging is available. Some types do not require nails.

ROUGH CARPENTRY

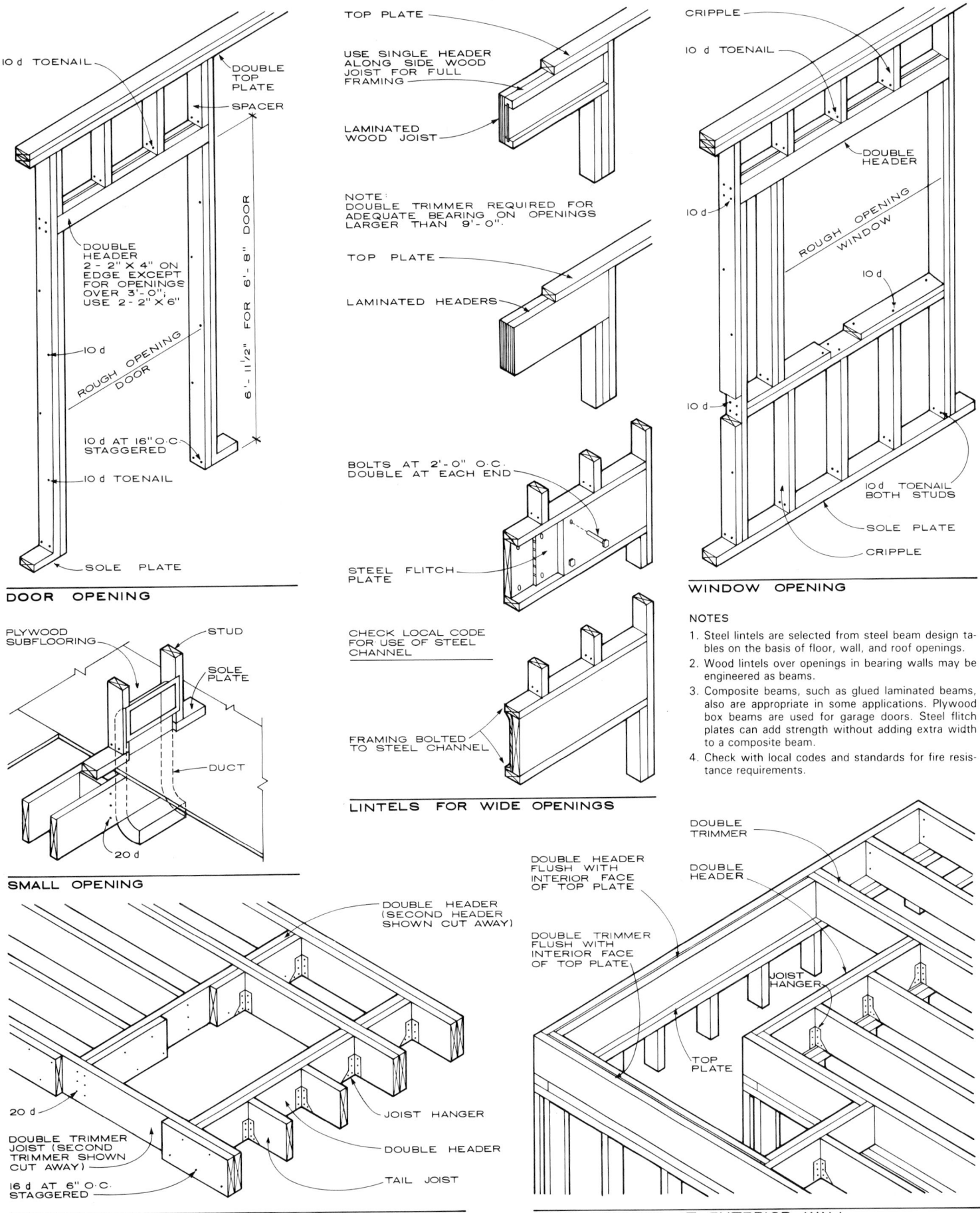

DOOR OPENING

10 d TOENAIL

DOUBLE TOP PLATE

SPACER

DOUBLE HEADER 2 - 2" X 4" ON EDGE EXCEPT FOR OPENINGS OVER 3'-0"; USE 2 - 2" X 6"

6'- 11 1/2" FOR 6'- 8" DOOR

ROUGH OPENING DOOR

10 d

10 d AT 16" O.C. STAGGERED

10 d TOENAIL

SOLE PLATE

SMALL OPENING

PLYWOOD SUBFLOORING

STUD

SOLE PLATE

DUCT

20 d

TOP PLATE

USE SINGLE HEADER ALONG SIDE WOOD JOIST FOR FULL FRAMING

LAMINATED WOOD JOIST

NOTE: DOUBLE TRIMMER REQUIRED FOR ADEQUATE BEARING ON OPENINGS LARGER THAN 9'-0".

TOP PLATE

LAMINATED HEADERS

BOLTS AT 2'-0" O.C. DOUBLE AT EACH END

STEEL FLITCH PLATE

CHECK LOCAL CODE FOR USE OF STEEL CHANNEL

FRAMING BOLTED TO STEEL CHANNEL

LINTELS FOR WIDE OPENINGS

CRIPPLE

10 d TOENAIL

DOUBLE HEADER

10 d

ROUGH OPENING WINDOW

10 d

10 d

10 d TOENAIL BOTH STUDS

SOLE PLATE

CRIPPLE

WINDOW OPENING

NOTES

1. Steel lintels are selected from steel beam design tables on the basis of floor, wall, and roof openings.
2. Wood lintels over openings in bearing walls may be engineered as beams.
3. Composite beams, such as glued laminated beams, also are appropriate in some applications. Plywood box beams are used for garage doors. Steel flitch plates can add strength without adding extra width to a composite beam.
4. Check with local codes and standards for fire resistance requirements.

LARGE OPENING REMOVED FROM BEARING WALLS

DOUBLE HEADER (SECOND HEADER SHOWN CUT AWAY)

JOIST HANGER

DOUBLE HEADER

TAIL JOIST

20 d

DOUBLE TRIMMER JOIST (SECOND TRIMMER SHOWN CUT AWAY)

16 d AT 6" O.C. STAGGERED

STAIR OPENING AT EXTERIOR WALL

DOUBLE TRIMMER

DOUBLE HEADER

DOUBLE HEADER FLUSH WITH INTERIOR FACE OF TOP PLATE

DOUBLE TRIMMER FLUSH WITH INTERIOR FACE OF TOP PLATE

JOIST HANGER

TOP PLATE

Joseph A. Wilkes, FAIA; Wilkes and Faulkner; Washington, D.C.

ROUGH CARPENTRY 6

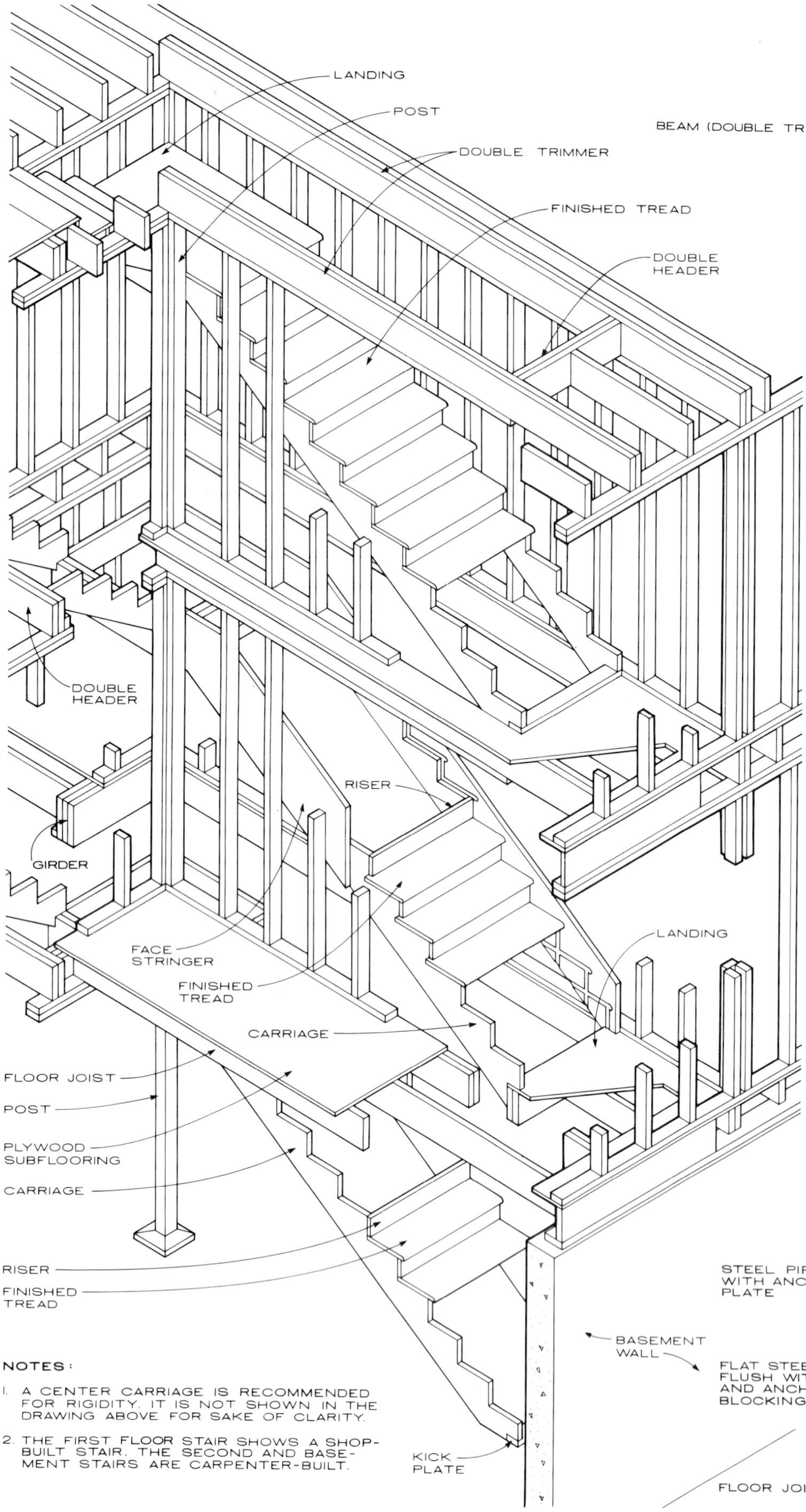

LANDING

POST

DOUBLE TRIMMER

FINISHED TREAD

DOUBLE HEADER

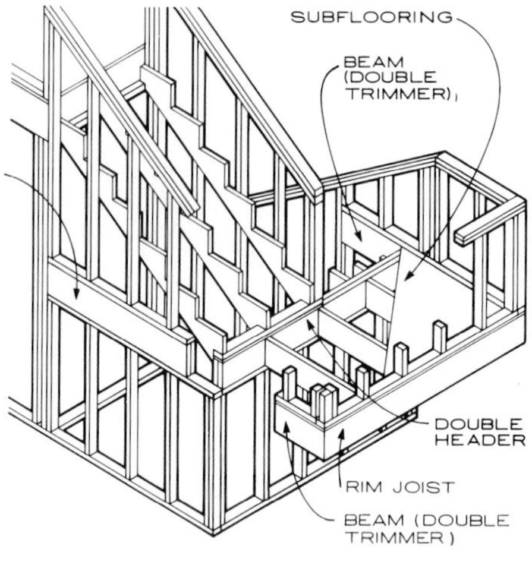

SUBFLOORING

BEAM (DOUBLE TRIMMER)

BEAM (DOUBLE TRIMMER)

DOUBLE HEADER

RIM JOIST

BEAM (DOUBLE TRIMMER)

CANTILEVERED LANDING

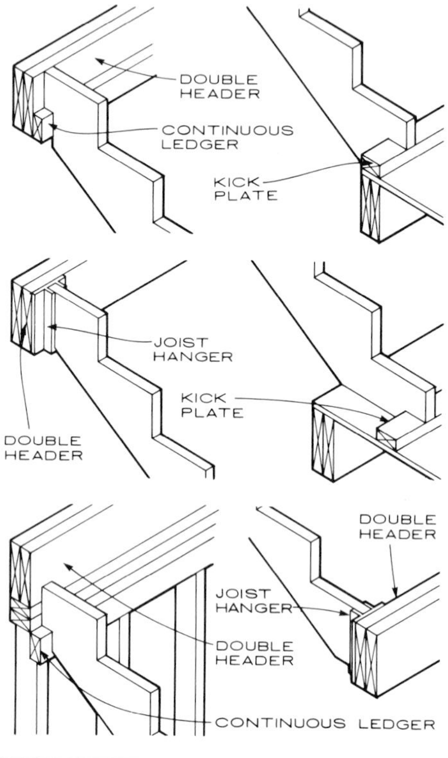

DOUBLE HEADER

DOUBLE HEADER

CONTINUOUS LEDGER

KICK PLATE

GIRDER

DOUBLE HEADER

RISER

FACE STRINGER

FINISHED TREAD

CARRIAGE

LANDING

FLOOR JOIST

POST

PLYWOOD SUBFLOORING

CARRIAGE

RISER

FINISHED TREAD

BASEMENT WALL

JOIST HANGER

KICK PLATE

DOUBLE HEADER

DOUBLE HEADER

JOIST HANGER

DOUBLE HEADER

CONTINUOUS LEDGER

STAIR DETAILS

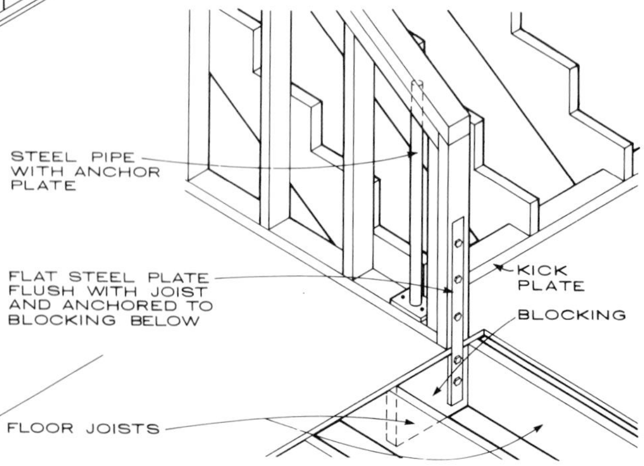

STEEL PIPE WITH ANCHOR PLATE

FLAT STEEL PLATE FLUSH WITH JOIST AND ANCHORED TO BLOCKING BELOW

KICK PLATE

BLOCKING

FLOOR JOISTS

NOTES:

1. A CENTER CARRIAGE IS RECOMMENDED FOR RIGIDITY. IT IS NOT SHOWN IN THE DRAWING ABOVE FOR SAKE OF CLARITY.

2. THE FIRST FLOOR STAIR SHOWS A SHOP-BUILT STAIR. THE SECOND AND BASE-MENT STAIRS ARE CARPENTER-BUILT.

KICK PLATE

STAIR FRAMING DETAIL

ANCHORS AT END OF SOLID RAIL

Timothy B. McDonald; Washington, D.C.

ROUGH CARPENTRY

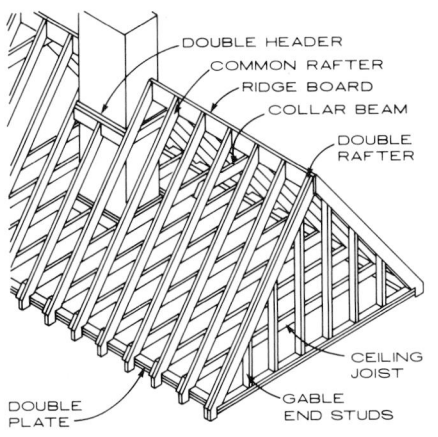

DOUBLE HEADER
COMMON RAFTER
RIDGE BOARD
COLLAR BEAM
DOUBLE RAFTER
CEILING JOIST
GABLE END STUDS
DOUBLE PLATE

GABLE ROOF

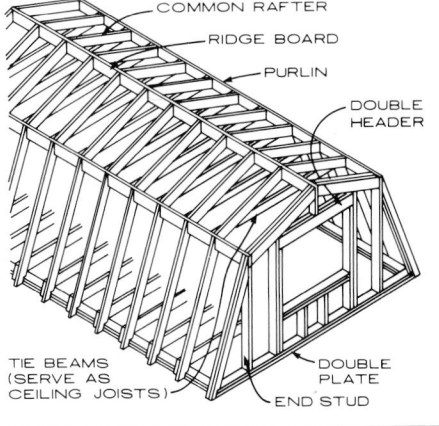

COMMON RAFTER
RIDGE BOARD
PURLIN
DOUBLE HEADER
DOUBLE PLATE
END STUD
TIE BEAMS (SERVE AS CEILING JOISTS)

GAMBREL ROOF

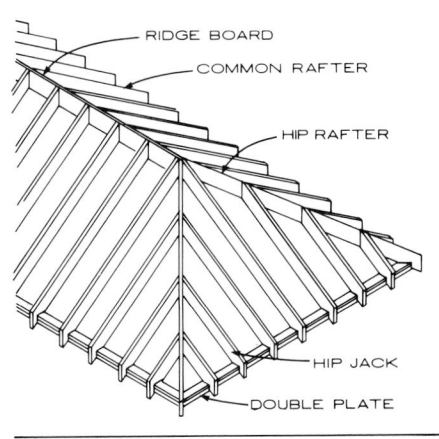

RIDGE BOARD
COMMON RAFTER
HIP RAFTER
HIP JACK
DOUBLE PLATE

HIP ROOF

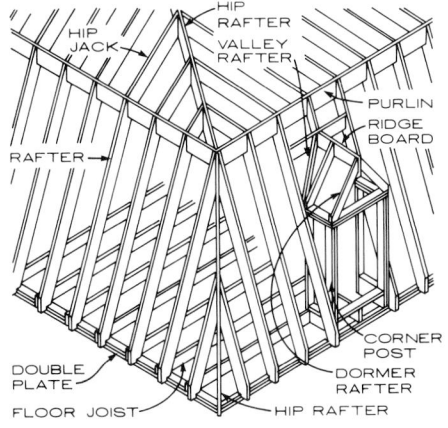

HIP RAFTER
HIP JACK
VALLEY RAFTER
PURLIN
RIDGE BOARD
RAFTER
CORNER POST
DORMER RAFTER
DOUBLE PLATE
FLOOR JOIST
HIP RAFTER

MANSARD ROOF

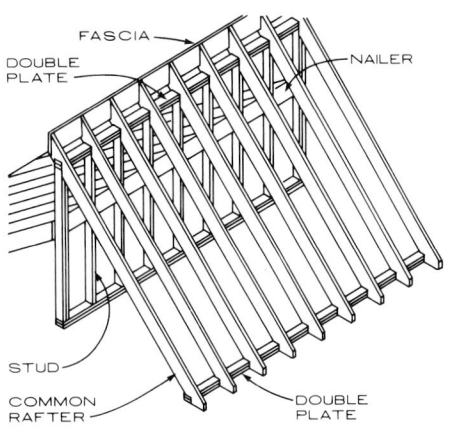

FASCIA
DOUBLE PLATE
NAILER
STUD
COMMON RAFTER
DOUBLE PLATE

SHED ROOF

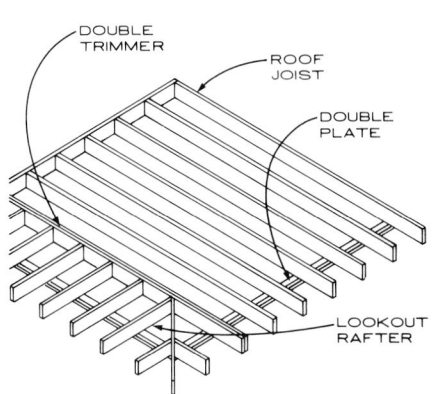

DOUBLE TRIMMER
ROOF JOIST
DOUBLE PLATE
LOOKOUT RAFTER

FLAT ROOF

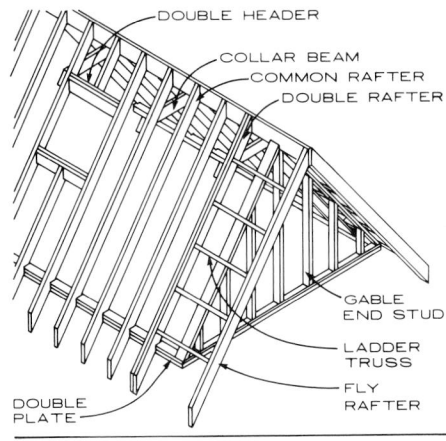

DOUBLE HEADER
COLLAR BEAM
COMMON RAFTER
DOUBLE RAFTER
GABLE END STUD
LADDER TRUSS
FLY RAFTER
DOUBLE PLATE

GABLE ROOF WITH OVERHANG

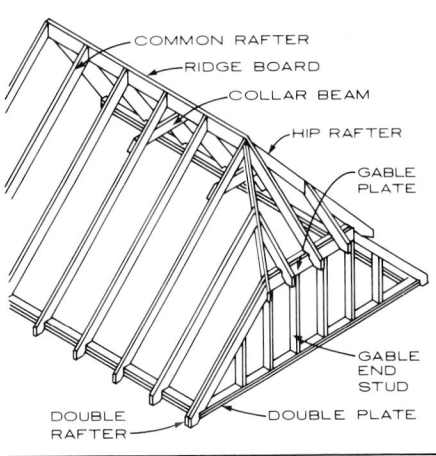

COMMON RAFTER
RIDGE BOARD
COLLAR BEAM
HIP RAFTER
GABLE PLATE
GABLE END STUD
DOUBLE RAFTER
DOUBLE PLATE

HIP GABLE ROOF

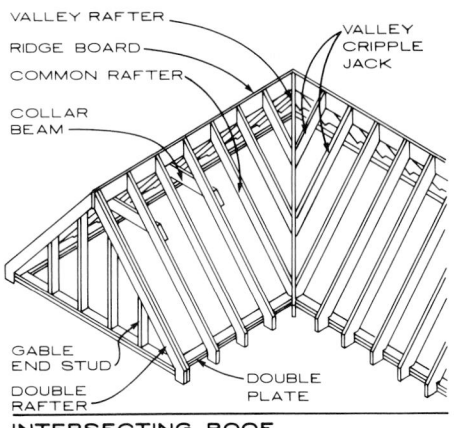

VALLEY RAFTER
RIDGE BOARD
COMMON RAFTER
COLLAR BEAM
VALLEY CRIPPLE JACK
GABLE END STUD
DOUBLE RAFTER
DOUBLE PLATE

INTERSECTING ROOF

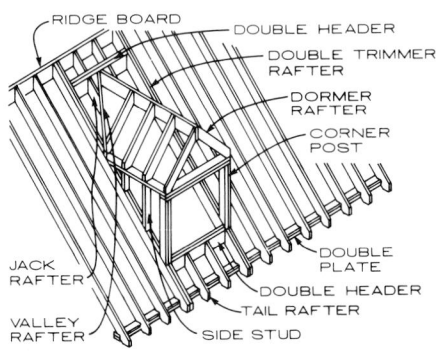

RIDGE BOARD
DOUBLE HEADER
DOUBLE TRIMMER RAFTER
DORMER RAFTER
CORNER POST
DOUBLE PLATE
DOUBLE HEADER
JACK RAFTER
TAIL RAFTER
VALLEY RAFTER
SIDE STUD

DORMER

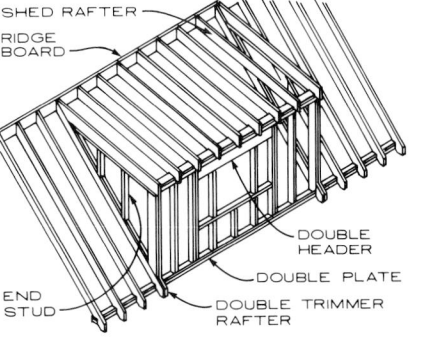

SHED RAFTER
RIDGE BOARD
DOUBLE HEADER
DOUBLE PLATE
END STUD
DOUBLE TRIMMER RAFTER

SMALL SHED DORMER

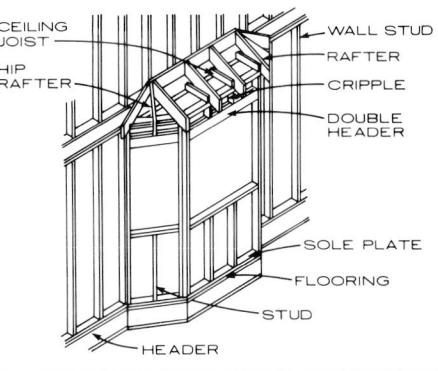

CEILING JOIST
WALL STUD
HIP RAFTER
RAFTER
CRIPPLE
DOUBLE HEADER
SOLE PLATE
FLOORING
STUD
HEADER

BAY WINDOW

Timothy B. McDonald; Washington, D.C.

ROUGH CARPENTRY   6

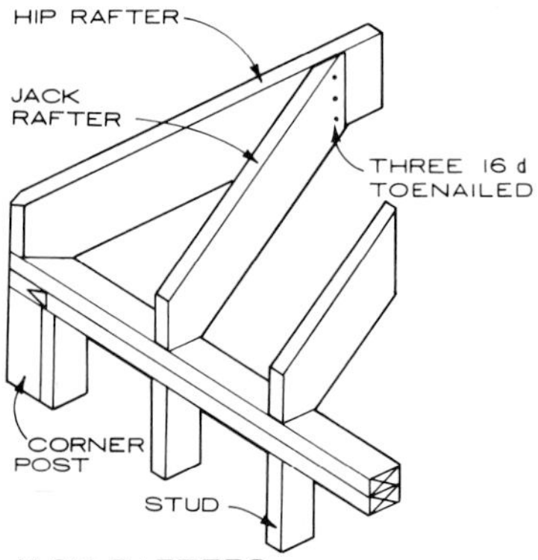

HIP RAFTER

JACK RAFTER

THREE 16 d TOENAILED

CORNER POST

STUD

JACK RAFTERS

NOTE: d = PENNY

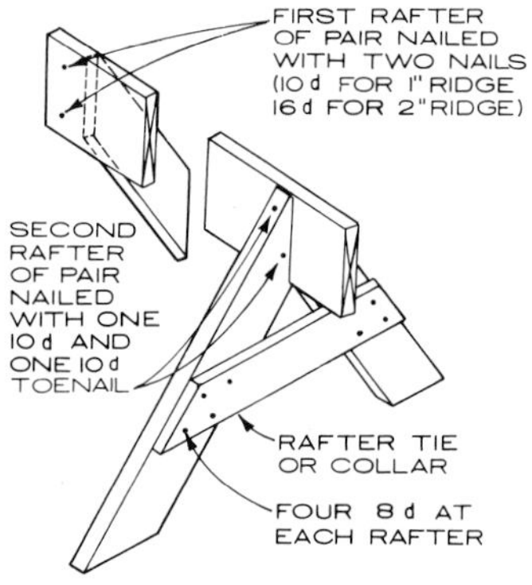

FIRST RAFTER OF PAIR NAILED WITH TWO NAILS (10 d FOR 1" RIDGE 16 d FOR 2" RIDGE)

SECOND RAFTER OF PAIR NAILED WITH ONE 10 d AND ONE 10 d TOENAIL

RAFTER TIE OR COLLAR

FOUR 8 d AT EACH RAFTER

ROOF PEAK

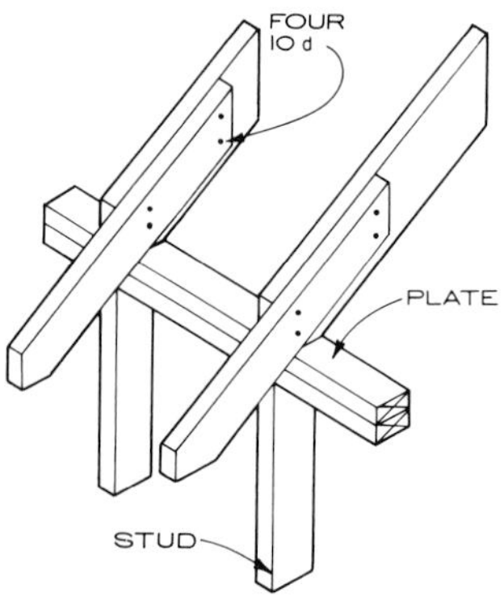

FOUR 10 d

PLATE

STUD

RAFTER ENDS

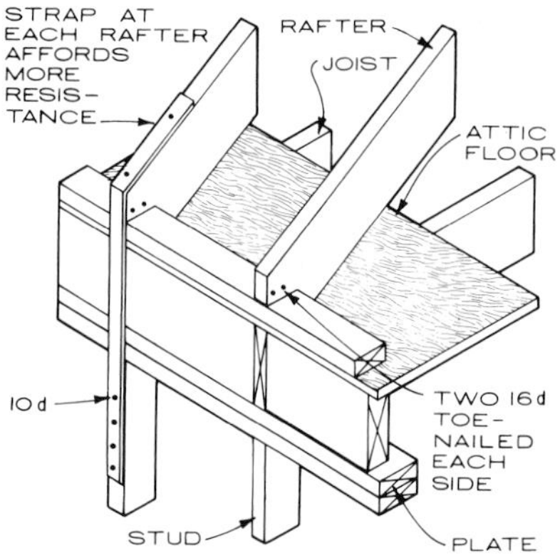

STRAP AT EACH RAFTER AFFORDS MORE RESISTANCE

RAFTER

JOIST

ATTIC FLOOR

10 d

TWO 16 d TOE-NAILED EACH SIDE

STUD

PLATE

BEVELED RAFTERS BACK-NOTCHED OVER PLATE

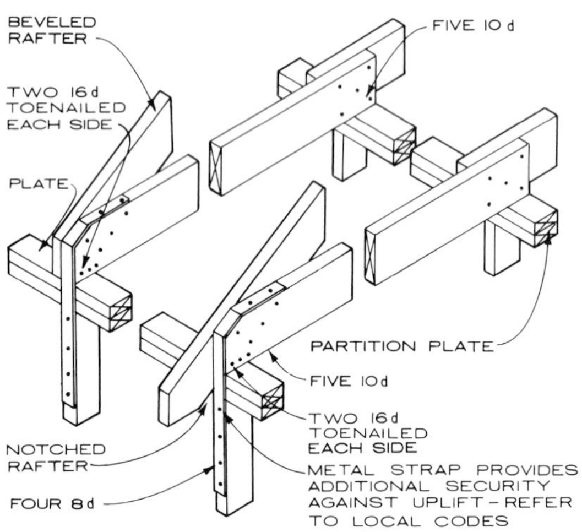

BEVELED RAFTER

TWO 16 d TOENAILED EACH SIDE

PLATE

NOTCHED RAFTER

FOUR 8 d

FIVE 10 d

PARTITION PLATE

FIVE 10 d

TWO 16 d TOENAILED EACH SIDE

METAL STRAP PROVIDES ADDITIONAL SECURITY AGAINST UPLIFT – REFER TO LOCAL CODES

RAFTERS AND CEILING JOISTS RESTING ON WALL PLATES

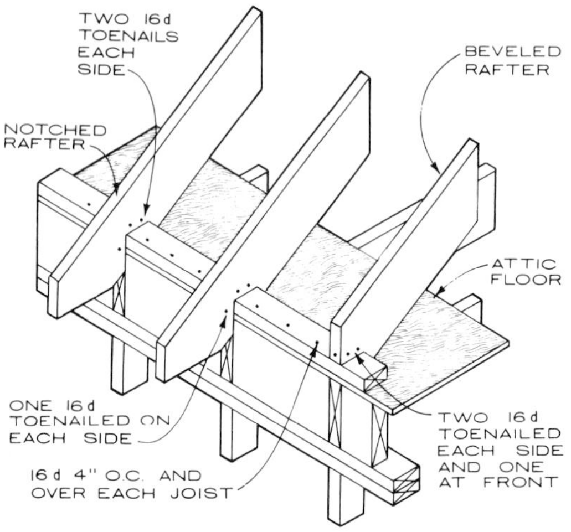

TWO 16 d TOENAILS EACH SIDE

NOTCHED RAFTER

BEVELED RAFTER

ATTIC FLOOR

ONE 16 d TOENAILED ON EACH SIDE

16 d 4" O.C. AND OVER EACH JOIST

TWO 16 d TOENAILED EACH SIDE AND ONE AT FRONT

NOTCHED OR BEVELED RAFTERS RESTING ON PLATE

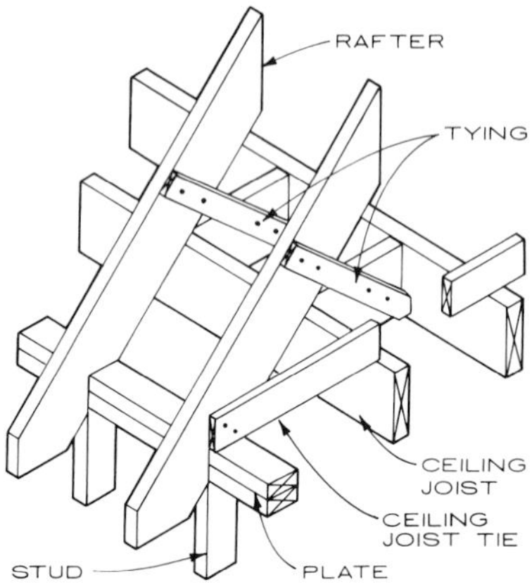

RAFTER

TYING

CEILING JOIST

CEILING JOIST TIE

STUD

PLATE

BRACING OF ROOF RAFTERS ARE AT RT. ANGLES TO JOISTS

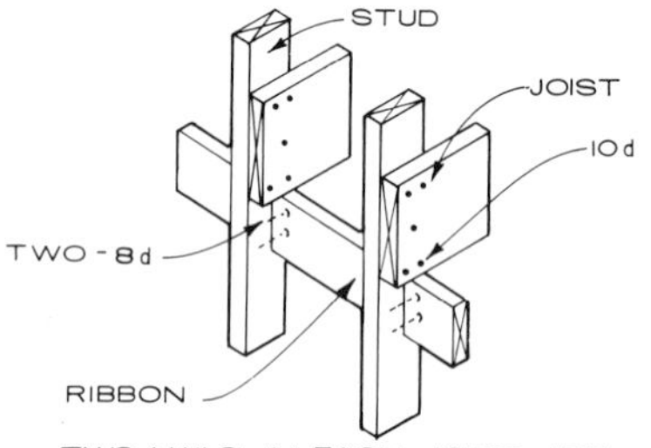

A   FILLER BLOCK

B

ONE 16 d TO FILLER BLOCK

THREE 16 d TO FILLER BLOCK

16 d STAGGERED 12" O.C. VERTICAL

THREE 16 d TO FILLER BLOCK

10 d TOE-NAILED TO SOLE

SOLE

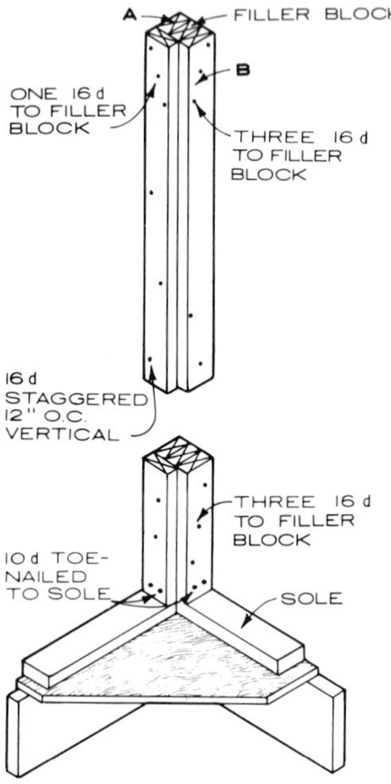

STUD A TO HAVE SAME NAILING TO FILLER BLOCK AS STUD B

CORNER POST

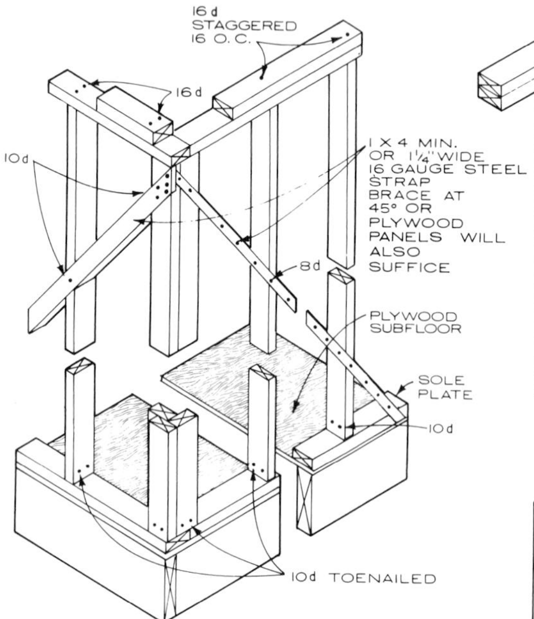

16 d STAGGERED 16 O.C.

16 d

10 d

8 d

PLYWOOD SUBFLOOR

1 X 4 MIN. OR 1¼" WIDE 16 GAUGE STEEL STRAP BRACE AT 45° OR PLYWOOD PANELS WILL ALSO SUFFICE

SOLE PLATE

10 d

10 d TOENAILED

TOP PLATE AND BRACING

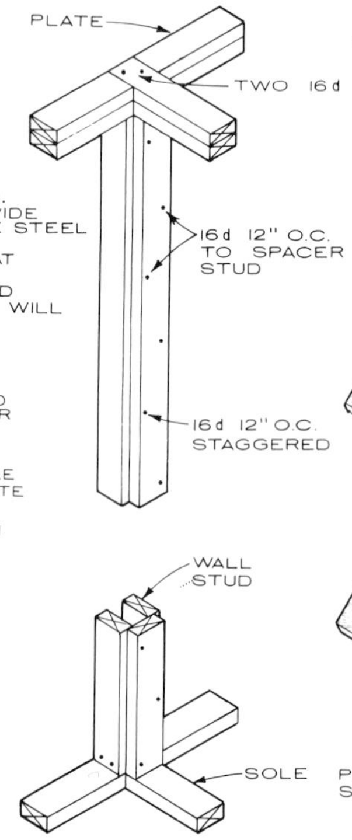

PLATE

TWO 16 d

16 d 12" O.C. TO SPACER STUD

16 d 12" O.C. STAGGERED

WALL STUD

SOLE

PARTITION TO WALL CONNECTION

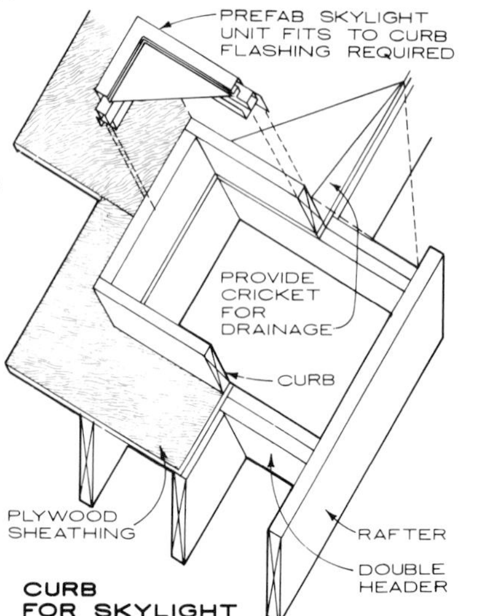

STUD

JOIST

10 d

TWO - 8 d

RIBBON

TWO NAILS IN EACH JOIST ARE SUFFICIENT IF FULL STORY ABOVE RIBBON

JOISTS BEARING ON RIBBON

PREFAB SKYLIGHT UNIT FITS TO CURB FLASHING REQUIRED

PROVIDE CRICKET FOR DRAINAGE

CURB

PLYWOOD SHEATHING

RAFTER

DOUBLE HEADER

CURB FOR SKYLIGHT

(PREFAB CURBS ALSO AVAILABLE.)

Joseph A. Wilkes, FAIA; Wilkes and Faulkner; Washington, D.C.

  ROUGH CARPENTRY

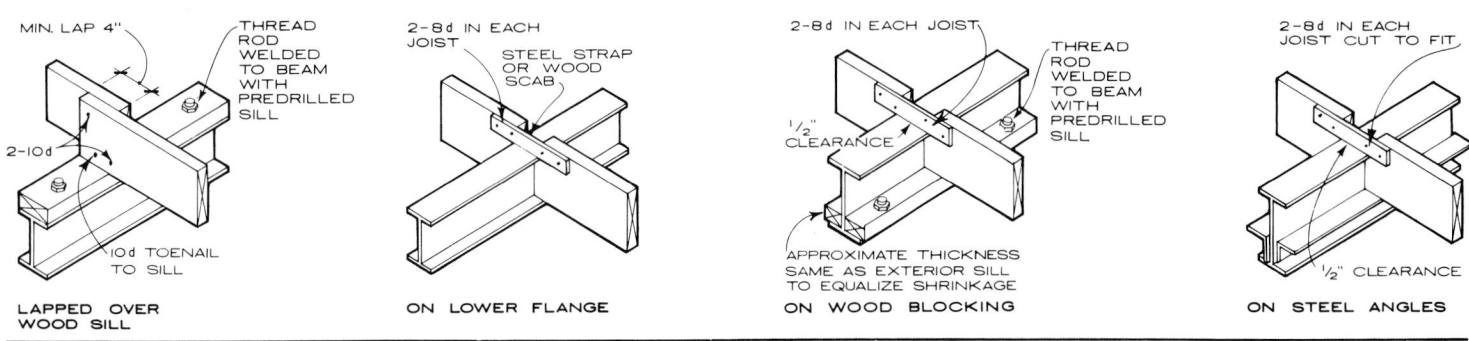

LAPPED OVER WOOD SILL

ON LOWER FLANGE

ON WOOD BLOCKING

ON STEEL ANGLES

WOOD JOISTS SUPPORTED ON STEEL GIRDERS

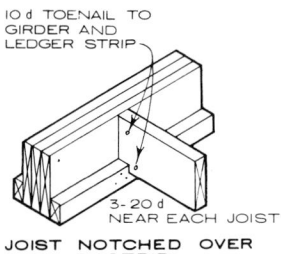

JOIST NOTCHED OVER LEDGER STRIP
NOTCHING OVER BEARING NOT RECOMMENDED

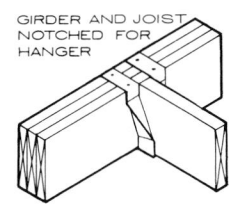

JOIST IN JOIST HANGER IRON
ALSO CALLED STIRRUP OR BRIDLE IRON

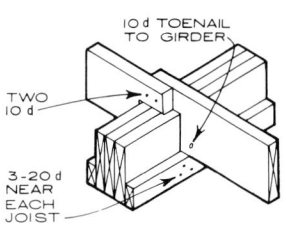

OVERLAPPING JOISTS NOTCHED OVER GIRDER
BEARING ONLY ON LEDGER, NOT ON TOP OF GIRDER

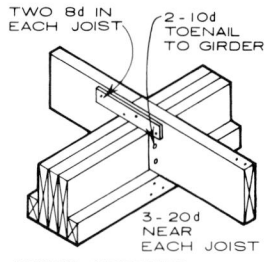

JOISTS NOTCHED OVER GIRDER
BEARING ONLY ON LEDGER, NOT ON TOP OF GIRDER

WOOD JOISTS SUPPORTED ON WOOD GIRDERS

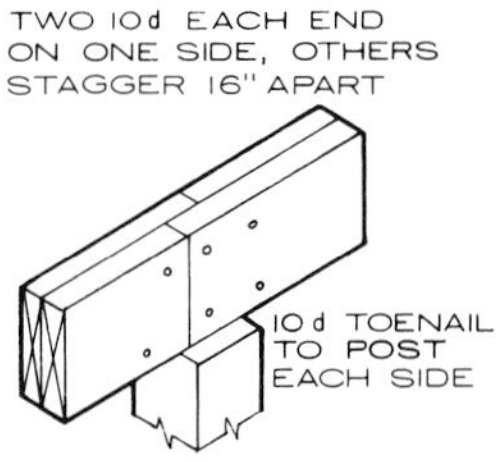

TWO PIECE GIRDER
GIRDER JOINTS ONLY AT SUPPORTS STAGGER JOINTS

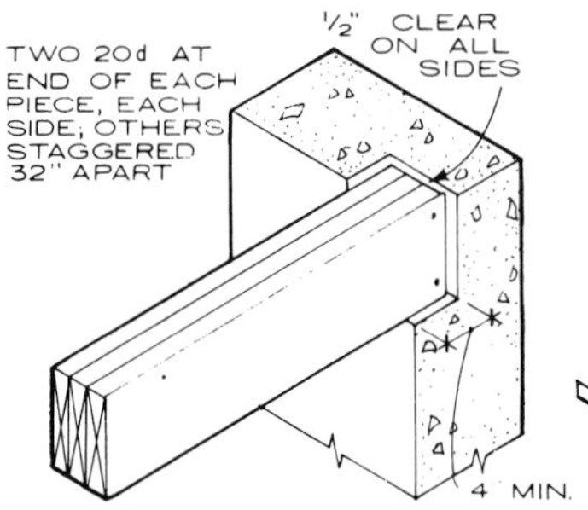

THREE PIECE GIRDER
FOR FOUR PIECE GIRDER ADD NAILS

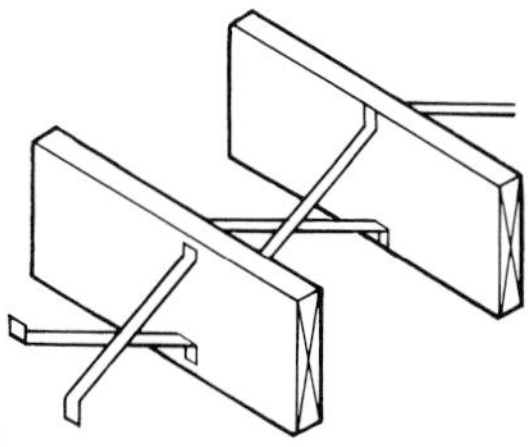

STEEL BRIDGING
SOME HAVE BUILT-IN TEETH, NEEDS NO NAILS

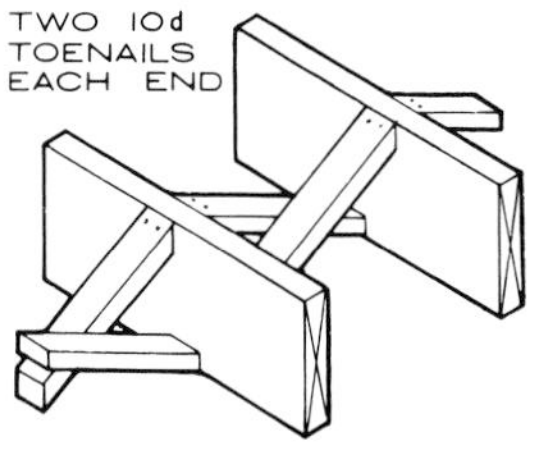

1" X 3" CROSS BRIDGING
LOWER ENDS NOT NAILED, UNTIL SUBFLOORING IS LAYED

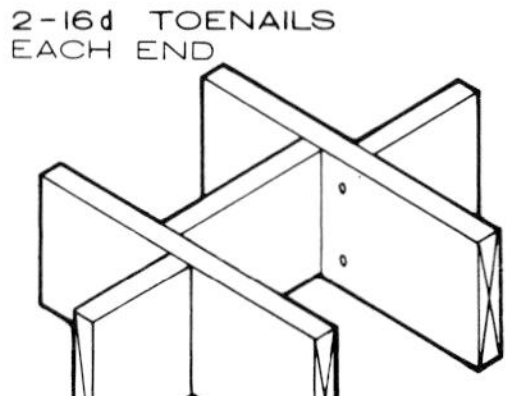

SOLID BRIDGING
USED UNDER PARTITIONS FOR HEAVY LOADING STAGGER BOARDS FOR EASE OF NAILING

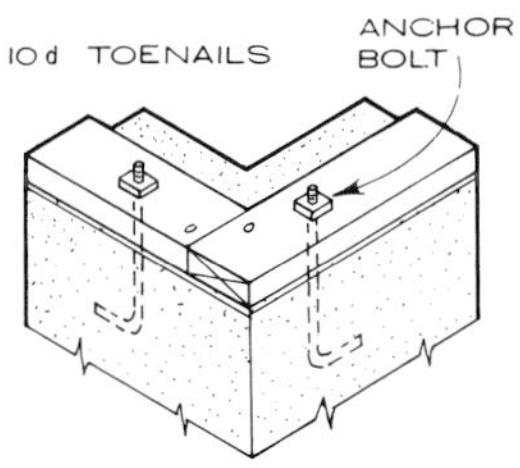

2 X 6 SILL

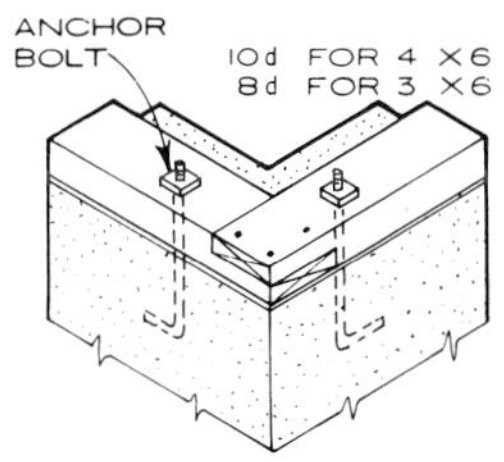

3 X 6, 4 X 6 SILL
HALVED AT CORNERS

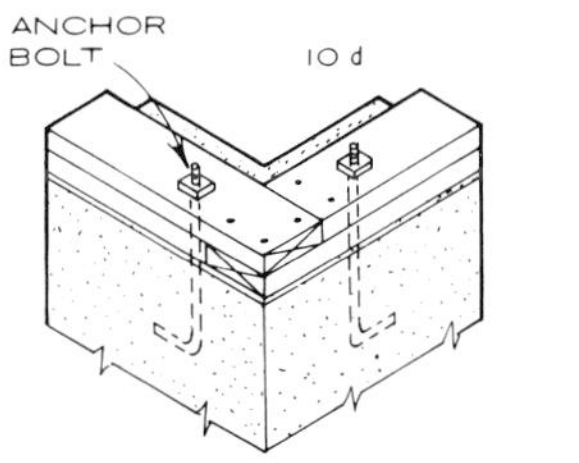

4 X 6 DOUBLE SILL
NAILS STAGGERED ALONG SILL 24" ON CENTER

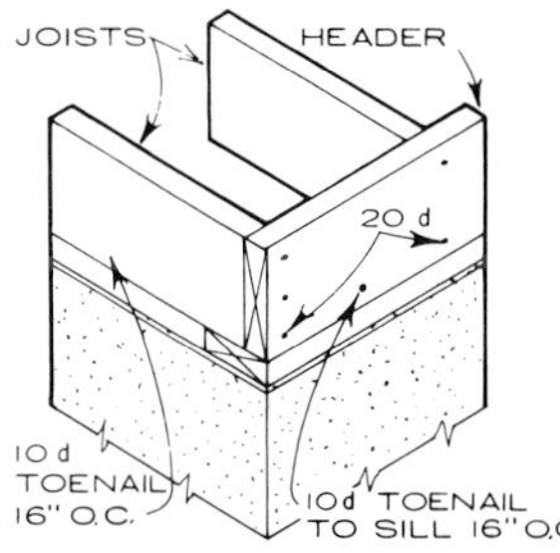

PLATFORM FRAMING
TOENAIL TO SILL NOT REQUIRED IF DIAGONAL SHEATHING USED

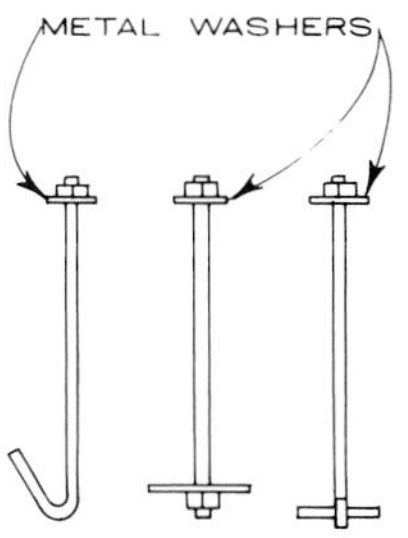

TYPES OF SILL ANCHOR BOLTS

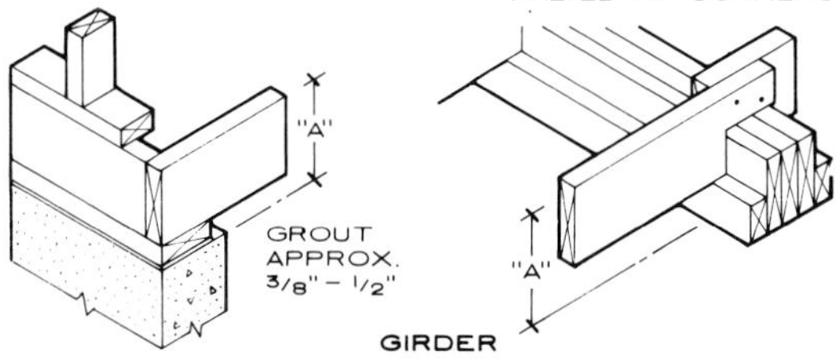

SHRINKAGE
SELECT JOIST-GIRDER DETAIL THAT HAS APPROXIMATE SAME SHRINKAGE "A" AS THE SILL DETAIL USED

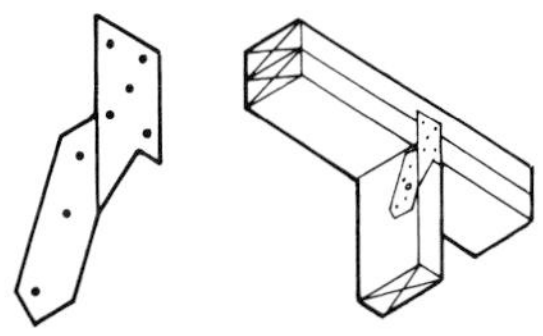

DU-AL-CLIP
METAL FRAMING DEVICES

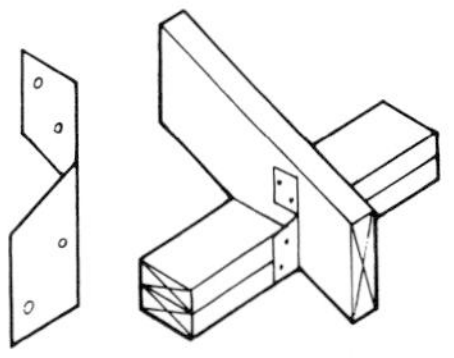

TY-DOWN ANCHOR

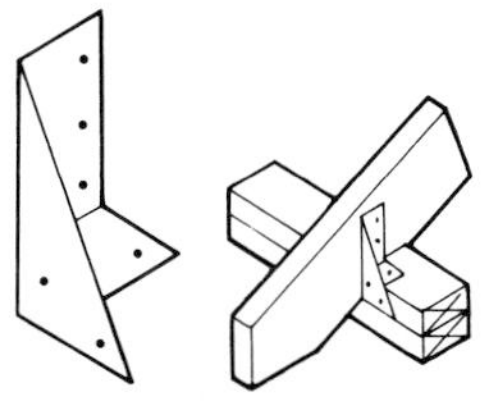

TRIP-L-GRIP
16-18 GAUGE ZINC COATED STEEL

Joseph A. Wilkes, FAIA; Wilkes and Faulkner; Washington, D.C.

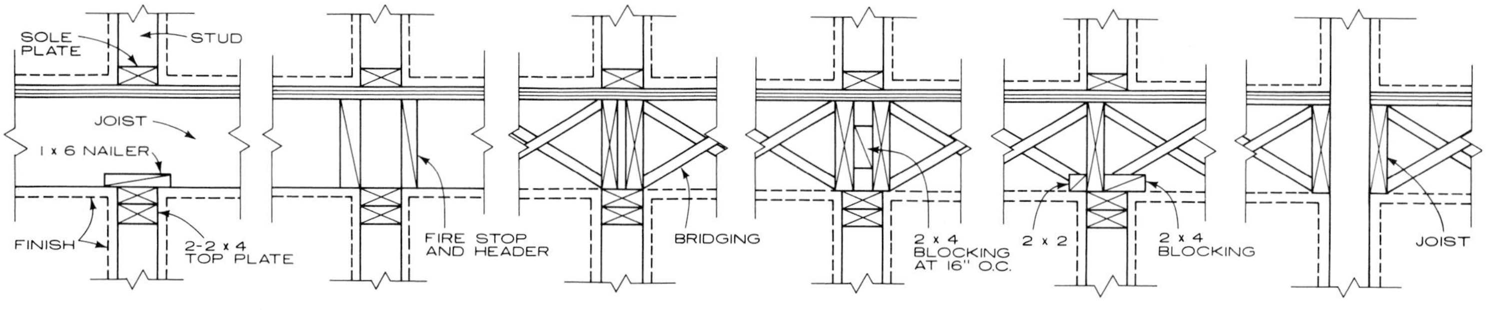

BEARING INTERIOR PARTITIONS

SOLE PLATE · STUD · JOIST · 1 x 6 NAILER · FINISH · 2-2 x 4 TOP PLATE · FIRE STOP AND HEADER · BRIDGING · 2 x 4 BLOCKING AT 16" O.C. · 2 x 2 · 2 x 4 BLOCKING · JOIST

PARTITIONS PERPENDICULAR TO JOISTS   PARTITIONS PARALLEL TO JOISTS   BALLOON AND BRACED

NONBEARING INTERIOR PARTITIONS

PLYWOOD SUBFLOOR · FINISH · STUD · JOIST · JOIST · TOP PLATE · FINISH · STUD · FINISH · 2 x 4 BLOCKING AT 16" O.C. · STUD · 1 x 6 NAILER · 2 x 6 BLOCKING AT 16" O.C. · 2 x 2 LEDGER · DOUBLE JOIST SPACE TO ALLOW FOR PIPES · 2" SOLID BRIDGING · FINISH · DOUBLE JOISTS UNDER PARTITIONS · 2 x 4 BLOCKING AT 16" O.C. · PARTITIONS BEARING BETWEEN JOISTS

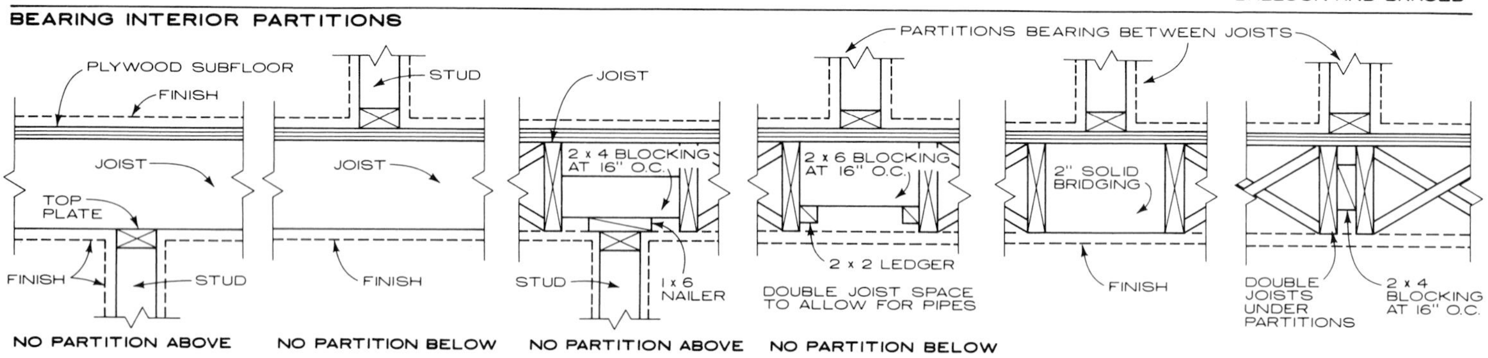

NO PARTITION ABOVE   NO PARTITION BELOW   NO PARTITION ABOVE   NO PARTITION BELOW

PARTITIONS PERPENDICULAR TO JOISTS   PARTITIONS PARALLEL TO JOISTS

2 x 4 WALL FRAMING

BLOCKING · 3-2 x 4's · 3-2 x 4's · 3-2 x 4's · 3-2 x 4's · WOOD LATH · 2 x 4 · 4 x 6 · 3-2 x 4's · 3-2 x 4's · 2-2 x 6's · 2 x 2 · 3-2 x 4's · 2 x 4 BLOCKING AT 16" O.C. · 1 x 6 · PLYWOOD SHEATHING · WALL FINISH

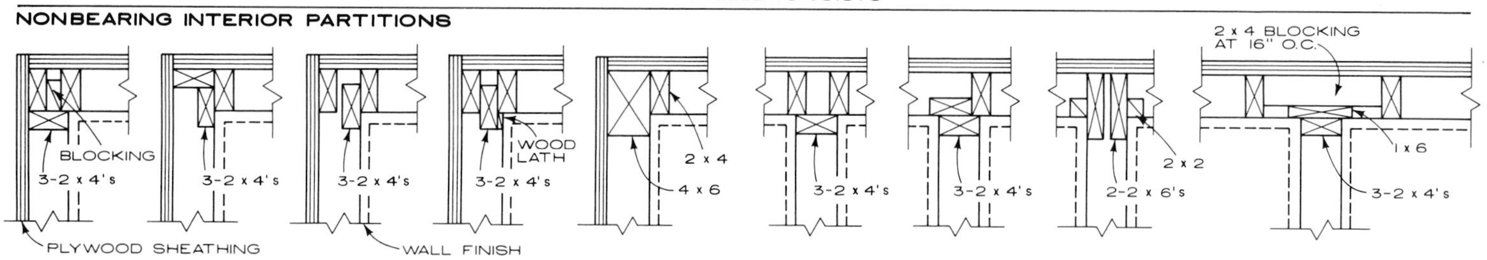

PLANS OF OUTSIDE CORNERS   PLANS OF INTERSECTING PARTITIONS

2 x 6 CORNER WALL FRAMING

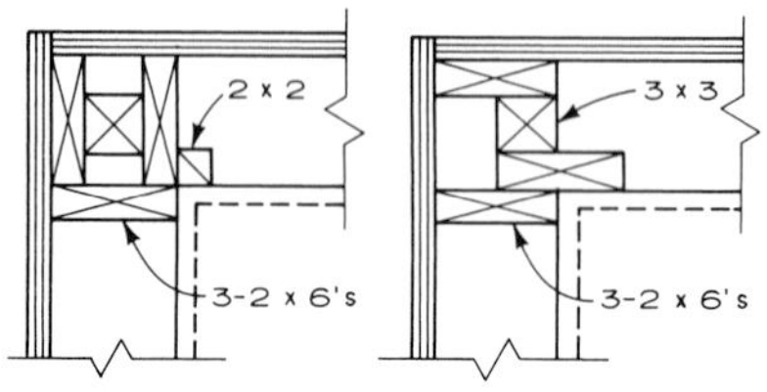

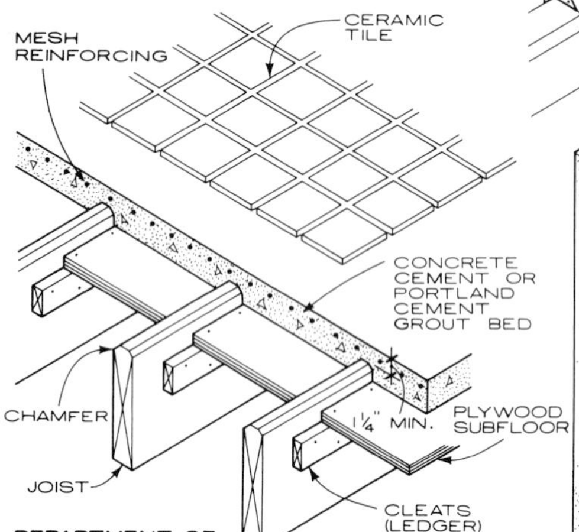

2 x 2 · 3 x 3 · 3-2 x 6's · 3-2 x 6's

PLAN

CERAMIC TILE FLOOR

MESH REINFORCING · CERAMIC TILE · CONCRETE CEMENT OR PORTLAND CEMENT GROUT BED · CHAMFER · JOIST · 1¼" MIN. · PLYWOOD SUBFLOOR · CLEATS (LEDGER)

DEPARTMENT OF AGRICULTURE HANDBOOK NO. 73 (1975)

FLOOR CANTILEVERS

DOUBLE JOIST · JOIST DIRECTION · JOIST HANGER · TAIL JOIST · STRINGER · DOUBLE STRINGER · DOUBLE JOIST · JOIST DIRECTION · JOIST · HEADER · 20 d NAIL · EXTENSION * · FOUNDATION WALL · TYPES OF CUTS IN BLOCKING. SEE NOTE · HEADER · 20 d NAIL · EXTENSION * · FOUNDATION WALL

NOTE: IF SPACE ABOVE IS TO BE HEATED, INSULATE BETWEEN JOISTS AND PROVIDE CUTS IN BLOCKING AS SHOWN

* ANY EXTENSION GREATER THAN 2'-0" MUST BE ENGINEERED

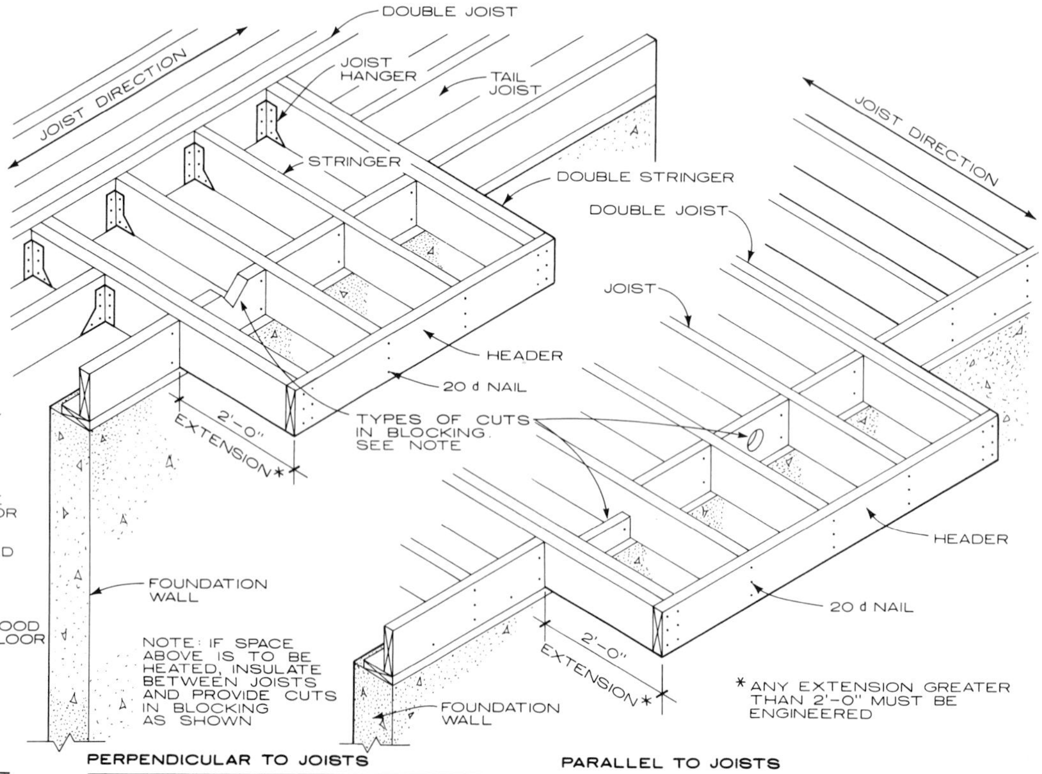

PERPENDICULAR TO JOISTS   PARALLEL TO JOISTS

John Ray Hoke, Jr., FAIA; Washington D.C.

ROUGH CARPENTRY

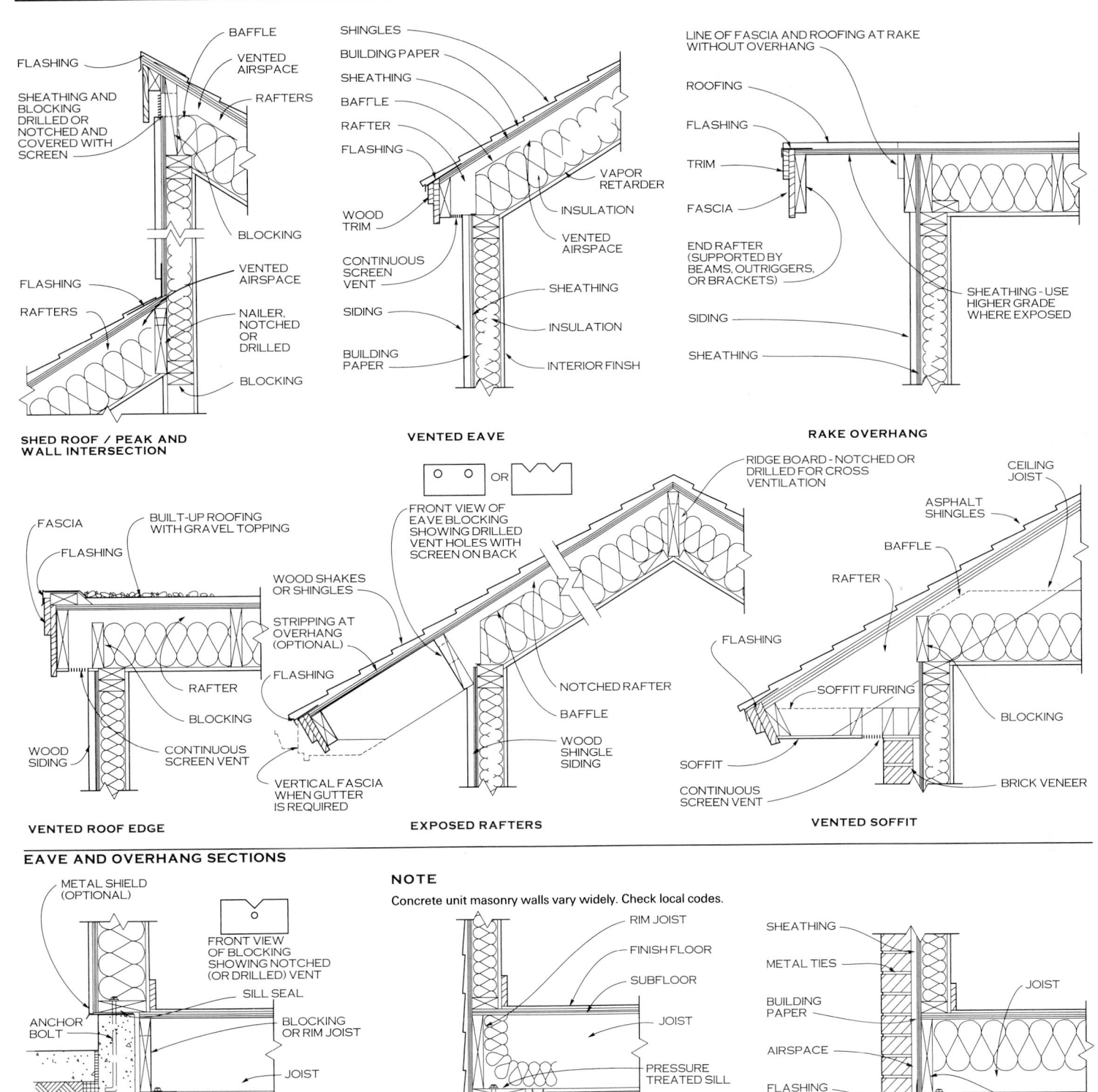

SHED ROOF / PEAK AND WALL INTERSECTION

FLASHING

SHEATHING AND BLOCKING DRILLED OR NOTCHED AND COVERED WITH SCREEN

BAFFLE

VENTED AIRSPACE

RAFTERS

BLOCKING

FLASHING

RAFTERS

VENTED AIRSPACE

NAILER, NOTCHED OR DRILLED

BLOCKING

VENTED EAVE

SHINGLES

BUILDING PAPER

SHEATHING

BAFFLE

RAFTER

FLASHING

WOOD TRIM

CONTINUOUS SCREEN VENT

SIDING

BUILDING PAPER

VAPOR RETARDER

INSULATION

VENTED AIRSPACE

SHEATHING

INSULATION

INTERIOR FINSH

RAKE OVERHANG

LINE OF FASCIA AND ROOFING AT RAKE WITHOUT OVERHANG

ROOFING

FLASHING

TRIM

FASCIA

END RAFTER (SUPPORTED BY BEAMS, OUTRIGGERS, OR BRACKETS)

SIDING

SHEATHING

SHEATHING - USE HIGHER GRADE WHERE EXPOSED

EAVE AND OVERHANG SECTIONS

VENTED ROOF EDGE

FASCIA

FLASHING

BUILT-UP ROOFING WITH GRAVEL TOPPING

RAFTER

BLOCKING

WOOD SIDING

CONTINUOUS SCREEN VENT

EXPOSED RAFTERS

○ ○ OR 〜

FRONT VIEW OF EAVE BLOCKING SHOWING DRILLED VENT HOLES WITH SCREEN ON BACK

WOOD SHAKES OR SHINGLES

STRIPPING AT OVERHANG (OPTIONAL)

FLASHING

VERTICAL FASCIA WHEN GUTTER IS REQUIRED

NOTCHED RAFTER

BAFFLE

WOOD SHINGLE SIDING

RIDGE BOARD - NOTCHED OR DRILLED FOR CROSS VENTILATION

VENTED SOFFIT

CEILING JOIST

ASPHALT SHINGLES

BAFFLE

RAFTER

FLASHING

SOFFIT FURRING

SOFFIT

CONTINUOUS SCREEN VENT

BLOCKING

BRICK VENEER

FOUNDATION WALL SECTIONS

NOTE
Concrete unit masonry walls vary widely. Check local codes.

STEPPED DETAIL/CRAWL SPACE

METAL SHIELD (OPTIONAL)

FRONT VIEW OF BLOCKING SHOWING NOTCHED (OR DRILLED) VENT

SILL SEAL

ANCHOR BOLT

BLOCKING OR RIM JOIST

JOIST

VENTED AIRSPACE

ANCHOR BOLT

RIGID INSULATION TO FOOTING

CONCRETE SKIM COAT

VAPOR RETARDER

DAMPPROOFING

10"

TYPICAL DETAIL/FINISHED BASEMENT

RIM JOIST

FINISH FLOOR

SUBFLOOR

JOIST

PRESSURE TREATED SILL

SILL SEAL

ANCHOR BOLT SET IN CONCRETE FILLED VOID

CONCRETE MASONRY UNIT

FURRING (PRESSURE TREATED)

DAMPPROOFING

RIGID INSULATION

6" MIN.

BRICK VENEER/VENTED CRAWL SPACE OR UNFINISHED BASEMENT (UNHEATED)

SHEATHING

METAL TIES

BUILDING PAPER

AIRSPACE

FLASHING

WEEP HOLE

JOIST

RIM JOIST

GROUT

ANCHOR BOLT

Ted Cameron, AIA; The Bumgardner Architects; Seattle, Washington

ROUGH CARPENTRY 6

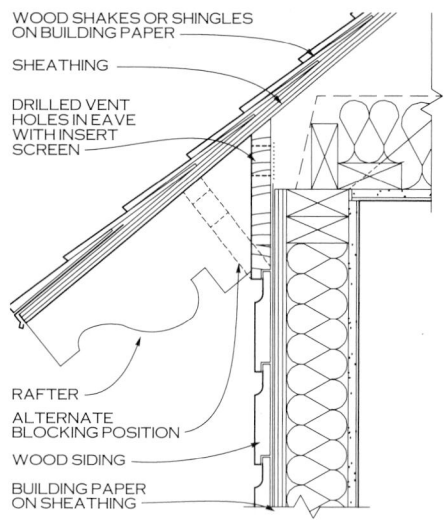

WOOD SHAKES OR SHINGLES
ON BUILDING PAPER

SHEATHING

DRILLED VENT
HOLES IN EAVE
WITH INSERT
SCREEN

RAFTER

ALTERNATE
BLOCKING POSITION

WOOD SIDING

BUILDING PAPER
ON SHEATHING

EXPOSED RAFTER END

NOTE

An eave is the lower edge of a sloping roof that projects past the face of the wall below. An overhang is a more general term for any projection out from a wall, sloping or flat. Both protect the wall below from precipitation by either throwing the water away from the wall (and foundation) or directing it into gutters and downspouts. Both also provide protection and shading for openings below.

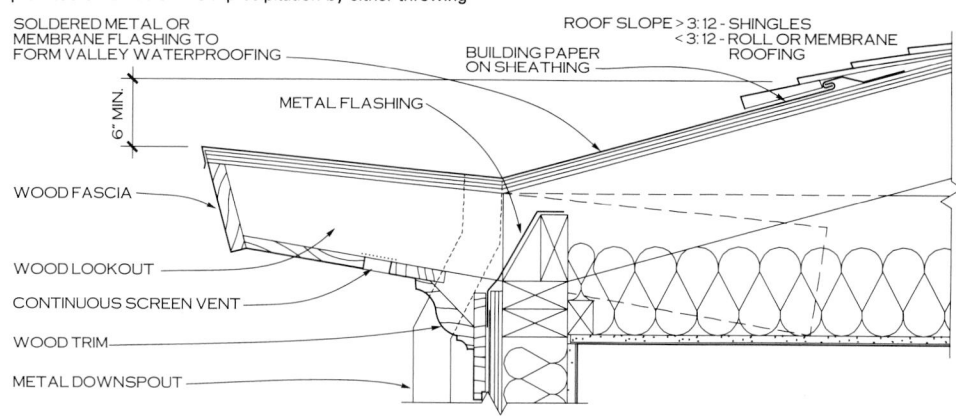

SOLDERED METAL OR
MEMBRANE FLASHING TO
FORM VALLEY WATERPROOFING

METAL FLASHING

ROOF SLOPE > 3:12 - SHINGLES
< 3:12 - ROLL OR MEMBRANE
ROOFING

BUILDING PAPER
ON SHEATHING

6" MIN.

WOOD FASCIA

WOOD LOOKOUT

CONTINUOUS SCREEN VENT

WOOD TRIM

METAL DOWNSPOUT

REVERSE SLOPE OVERHANG

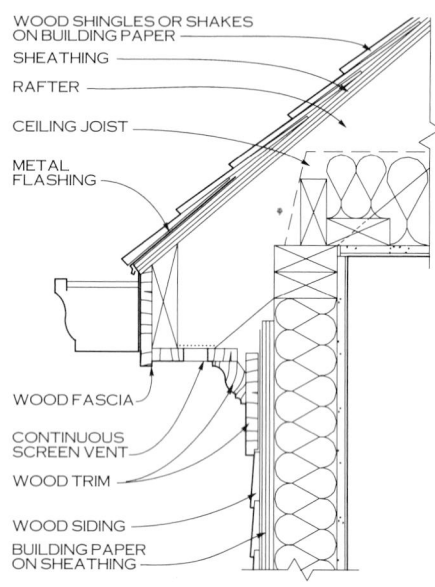

WOOD SHINGLES OR SHAKES
ON BUILDING PAPER

SHEATHING

RAFTER

CEILING JOIST

METAL
FLASHING

WOOD FASCIA

CONTINUOUS
SCREEN VENT

WOOD TRIM

WOOD SIDING

BUILDING PAPER
ON SHEATHING

EAVE AT WOOD SIDING

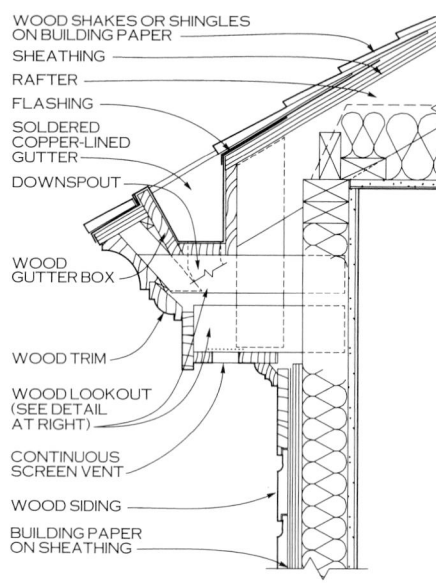

WOOD SHAKES OR SHINGLES
ON BUILDING PAPER

SHEATHING

RAFTER

FLASHING

SOLDERED
COPPER-LINED
GUTTER

DOWNSPOUT

WOOD
GUTTER BOX

WOOD TRIM

WOOD LOOKOUT
(SEE DETAIL
AT RIGHT)

CONTINUOUS
SCREEN VENT

WOOD SIDING

BUILDING PAPER
ON SHEATHING

EAVE WITH BUILT-IN GUTTER

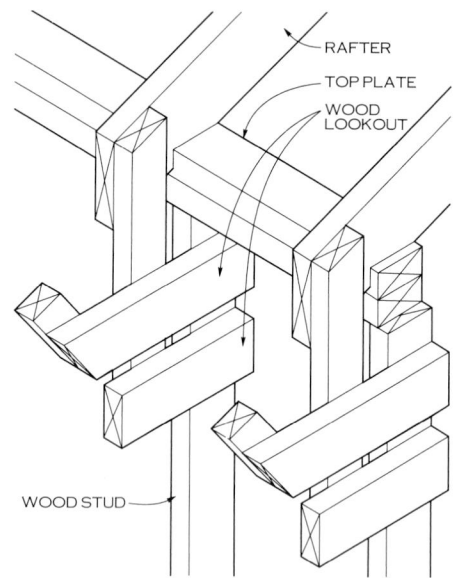

RAFTER

TOP PLATE

WOOD
LOOKOUT

WOOD STUD

CORNICE SUPPORT DETAIL

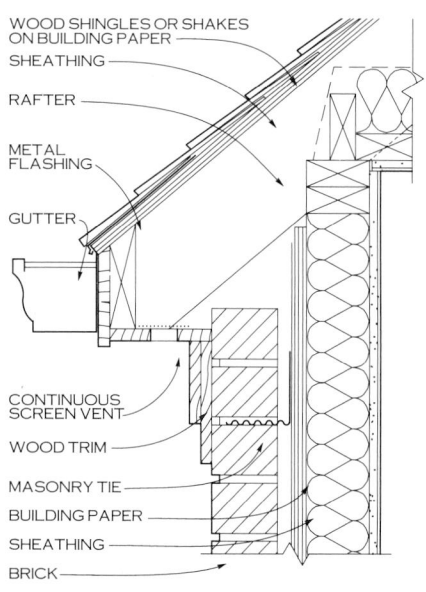

WOOD SHINGLES OR SHAKES
ON BUILDING PAPER

SHEATHING

RAFTER

METAL
FLASHING

GUTTER

CONTINUOUS
SCREEN VENT

WOOD TRIM

MASONRY TIE

BUILDING PAPER

SHEATHING

BRICK

EAVE AT BRICK VENEER

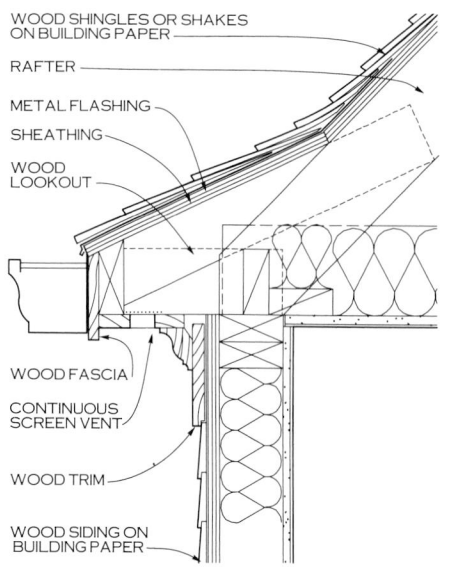

WOOD SHINGLES OR SHAKES
ON BUILDING PAPER

RAFTER

METAL FLASHING

SHEATHING

WOOD
LOOKOUT

WOOD FASCIA

CONTINUOUS
SCREEN VENT

WOOD TRIM

WOOD SIDING ON
BUILDING PAPER

PROJECTED EAVE WITH SHALLOW SLOPE

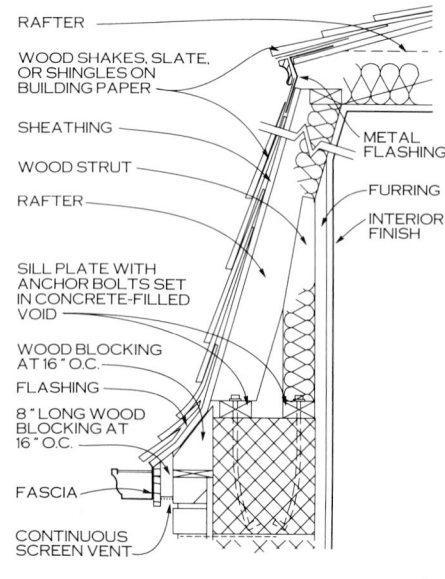

RAFTER

WOOD SHAKES, SLATE,
OR SHINGLES ON
BUILDING PAPER

SHEATHING

WOOD STRUT

RAFTER

METAL
FLASHING

FURRING

INTERIOR
FINISH

SILL PLATE WITH
ANCHOR BOLTS SET
IN CONCRETE-FILLED
VOID

WOOD BLOCKING
AT 16" O.C.

FLASHING

8" LONG WOOD
BLOCKING AT
16" O.C.

FASCIA

CONTINUOUS
SCREEN VENT

MANSARD ROOF

Richard J. Vitullo, AIA; Oak Leaf Studio; Crownsville, Maryland

 ROUGH CARPENTRY

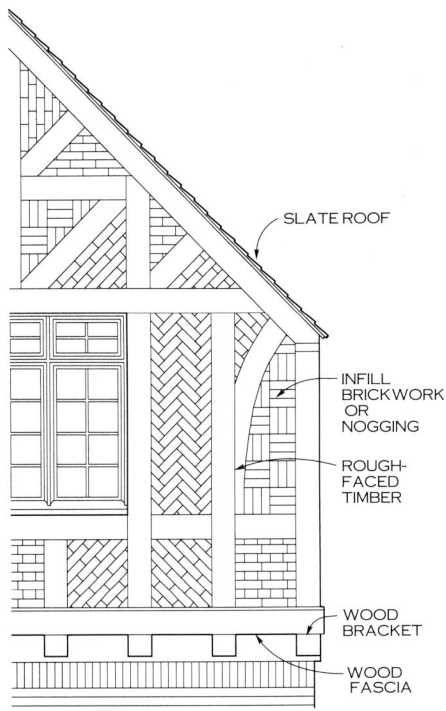

SLATE ROOF

INFILL BRICKWORK OR NOGGING

ROUGH-FACED TIMBER

WOOD BRACKET

WOOD FASCIA

GENERAL

In the 16th and 17th centuries half timber structures were built with strong timber foundations, supports, and studs. The spaces between the framework were filled in with either stone, brick, plaster, or boarding laid horizontally. Today the primary structure is wood stud or masonry backup, and the half timber construction is attached as veneer. Half timber is an inherently leaky type of wall construction in which the timbers are subject to premature decay.

NOTE

Shown are some of many brick infill panel design types.

ELEVATION – BRICK AND TIMBER

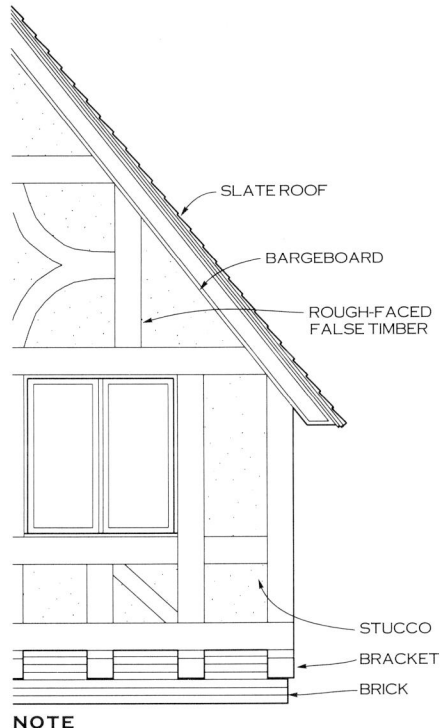

SLATE ROOF

BARGEBOARD

ROUGH-FACED FALSE TIMBER

STUCCO

BRACKET

BRICK

NOTE

To preserve historical character of half-timber construction

ELEVATION – STUCCO AND TIMBER

Richard J. Vitullo, AIA; Oak Leaf Studio; Crownsville, Maryland

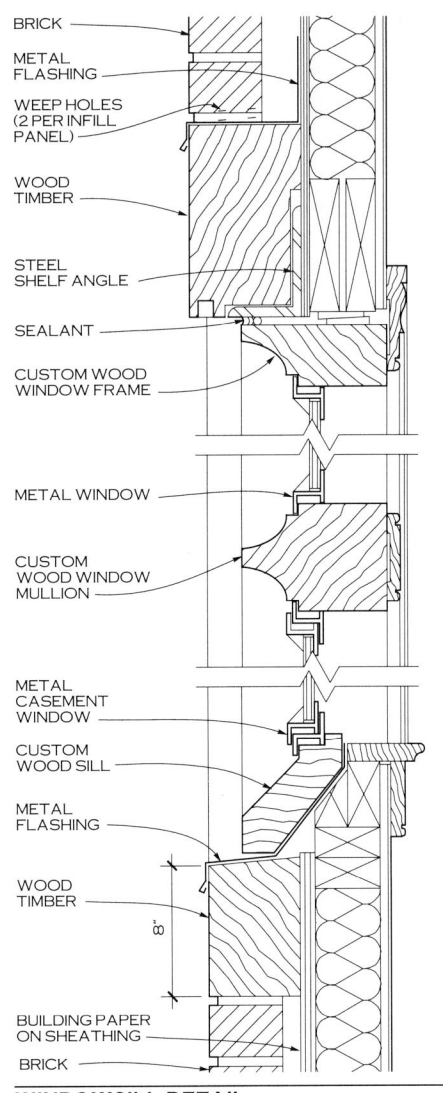

BRICK

METAL FLASHING

WEEP HOLES (2 PER INFILL PANEL)

WOOD TIMBER

STEEL SHELF ANGLE

SEALANT

CUSTOM WOOD WINDOW FRAME

METAL WINDOW

CUSTOM WOOD WINDOW MULLION

METAL CASEMENT WINDOW

CUSTOM WOOD SILL

METAL FLASHING

WOOD TIMBER

8"

BUILDING PAPER ON SHEATHING

BRICK

WINDOWSILL DETAIL

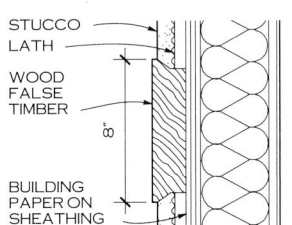

STUCCO
LATH

WOOD FALSE TIMBER

8"

BUILDING PAPER ON SHEATHING

FALSE TIMBER DETAIL

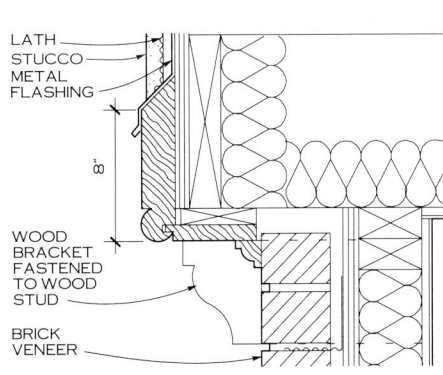

LATH
STUCCO
METAL FLASHING

8"

WOOD BRACKET FASTENED TO WOOD STUD

BRICK VENEER

OVERHANG DETAIL

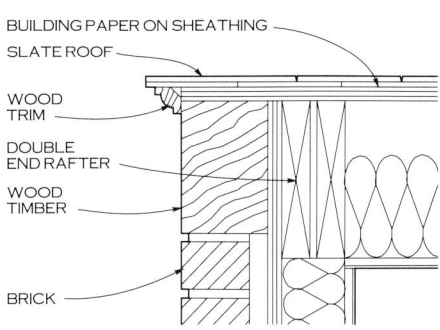

BUILDING PAPER ON SHEATHING

SLATE ROOF

WOOD TRIM

DOUBLE END RAFTER

WOOD TIMBER

BRICK

GABLE EDGE DETAIL

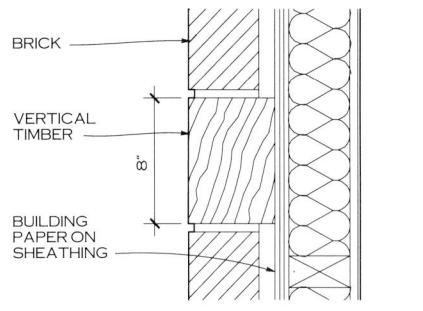

BRICK

VERTICAL TIMBER

8"

BUILDING PAPER ON SHEATHING

TIMBER DETAIL

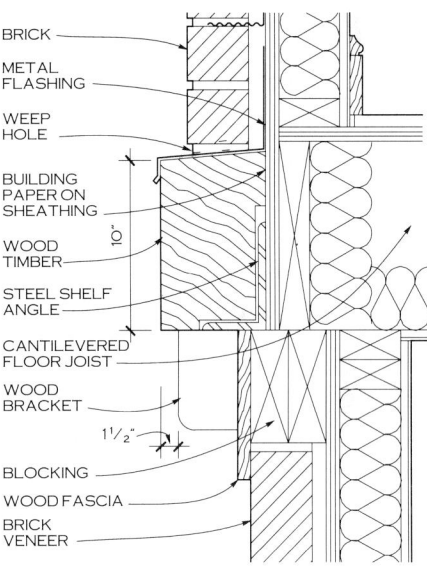

BRICK

METAL FLASHING

WEEP HOLE

BUILDING PAPER ON SHEATHING

WOOD TIMBER

10"

STEEL SHELF ANGLE

CANTILEVERED FLOOR JOIST

WOOD BRACKET

$1\frac{1}{2}$"

BLOCKING

WOOD FASCIA

BRICK VENEER

TIMBER SHELF DETAIL

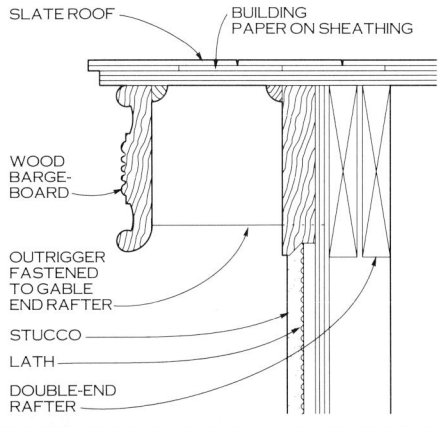

SLATE ROOF

BUILDING PAPER ON SHEATHING

WOOD BARGE-BOARD

OUTRIGGER FASTENED TO GABLE END RAFTER

STUCCO

LATH

DOUBLE-END RAFTER

BARGEBOARD DETAIL

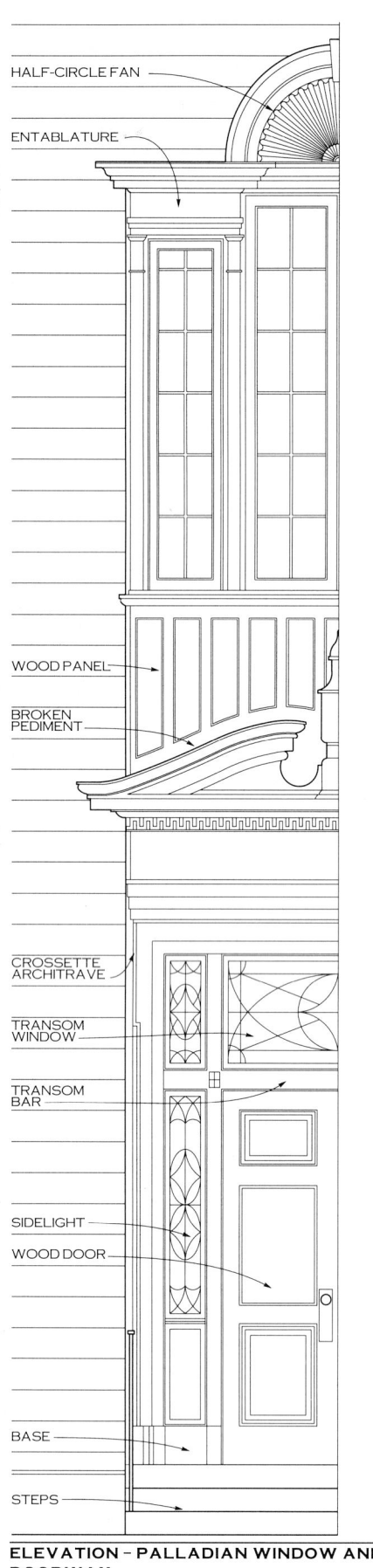

ELEVATION – PALLADIAN WINDOW AND DOORWAY

Labels on elevation (top to bottom): HALF-CIRCLE FAN; ENTABLATURE; WOOD PANEL; BROKEN PEDIMENT; CROSSETTE ARCHITRAVE; TRANSOM WINDOW; TRANSOM BAR; SIDELIGHT; WOOD DOOR; BASE; STEPS

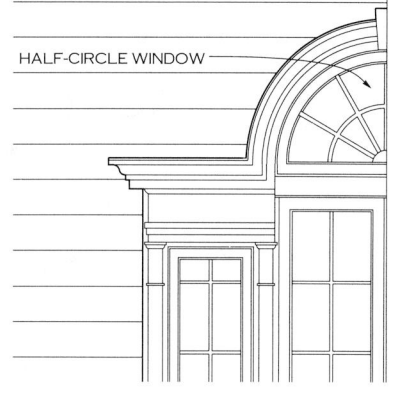

ALTERNATE ELEVATION – HALF-CIRCLE WINDOW

Label: HALF-CIRCLE WINDOW

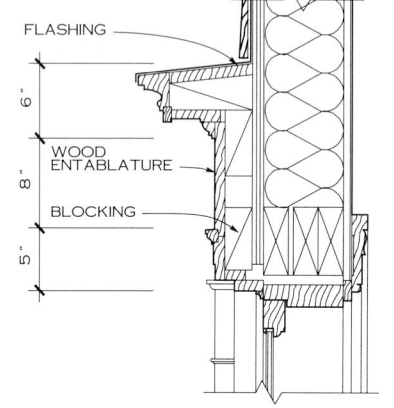

ENTABLATURE SECTION

Labels: FLASHING; WOOD ENTABLATURE; BLOCKING. Dimensions: 6"; 8"; 5"

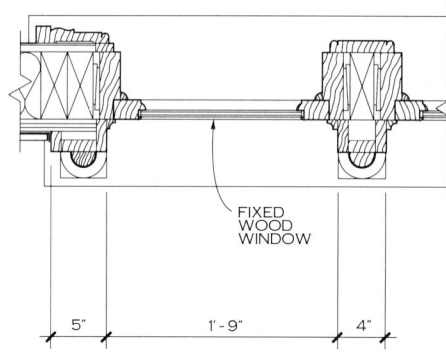

WINDOW PLAN

Label: FIXED WOOD WINDOW. Dimensions: 5"; 1'-9"; 4"

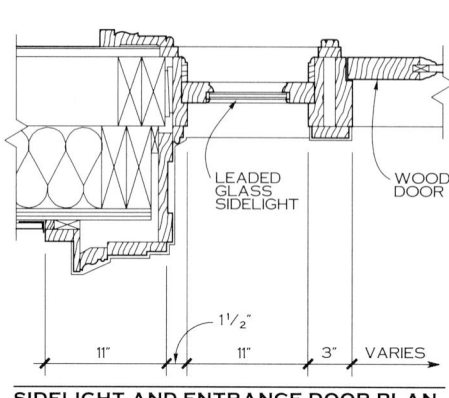

SIDELIGHT AND ENTRANCE DOOR PLAN

Labels: LEADED GLASS SIDELIGHT; WOOD DOOR. Dimensions: 11"; 1½"; 11"; 3"; VARIES

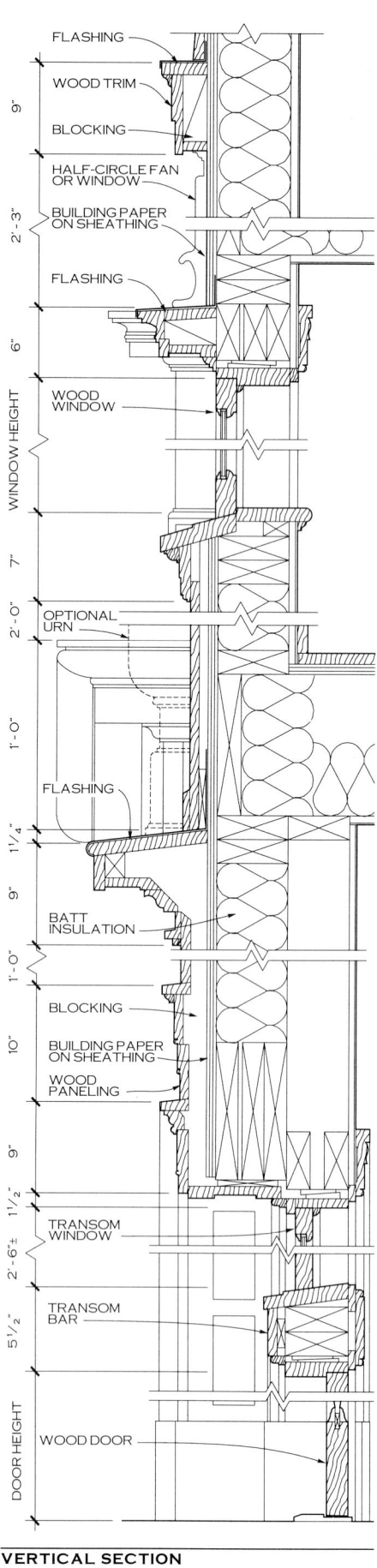

VERTICAL SECTION

Labels (top to bottom): FLASHING; WOOD TRIM; BLOCKING; HALF-CIRCLE FAN OR WINDOW; BUILDING PAPER ON SHEATHING; FLASHING; WOOD WINDOW; OPTIONAL URN; FLASHING; BATT INSULATION; BLOCKING; BUILDING PAPER ON SHEATHING; WOOD PANELING; TRANSOM WINDOW; TRANSOM BAR; WOOD DOOR

Dimensions (left side, top to bottom): 9"; 2'-3"; 6"; 7"; 2'-0"; 1'-0"; 1½"; 9"; 1'-0"; 10"; 9"; 1½"; 2'-6"±; 5½". Also: WINDOW HEIGHT; DOOR HEIGHT

Richard J. Vitullo, AIA; Oak Leaf Studio; Crownsville, Maryland

ROUGH CARPENTRY

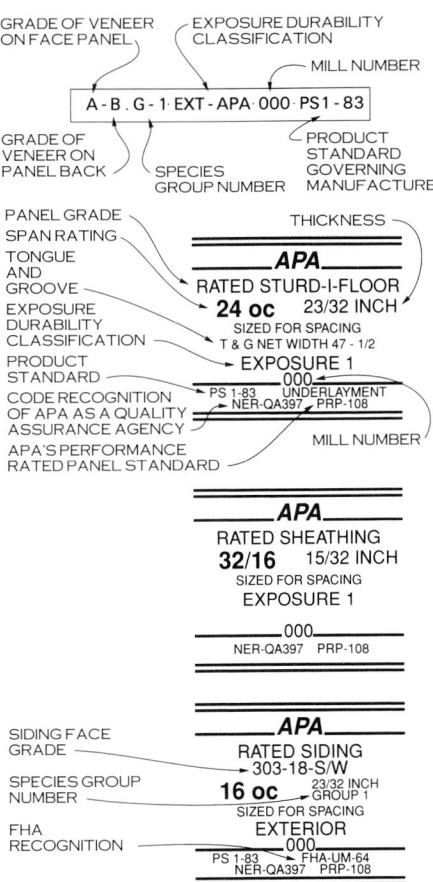

GRADE OF VENEER ON FACE PANEL

EXPOSURE DURABILITY CLASSIFICATION

MILL NUMBER

A · B · G · 1 · EXT · APA · 000 · PS1 - 83

GRADE OF VENEER ON PANEL BACK

SPECIES GROUP NUMBER

PRODUCT STANDARD GOVERNING MANUFACTURE

PANEL GRADE
SPAN RATING
TONGUE AND GROOVE
EXPOSURE DURABILITY CLASSIFICATION
PRODUCT STANDARD
CODE RECOGNITION OF APA AS A QUALITY ASSURANCE AGENCY
APA'S PERFORMANCE RATED PANEL STANDARD

THICKNESS

_____APA_____
RATED STURD-I-FLOOR
24 oc 23/32 INCH
SIZED FOR SPACING
T & G NET WIDTH 47 - 1/2
EXPOSURE 1
000
PS 1-83 UNDERLAYMENT
NER-QA397 PRP-108
MILL NUMBER

_____APA_____
RATED SHEATHING
32/16 15/32 INCH
SIZED FOR SPACING
EXPOSURE 1
000
NER-QA397 PRP-108

SIDING FACE GRADE
SPECIES GROUP NUMBER
FHA RECOGNITION

_____APA_____
RATED SIDING
303-18-S/W
16 oc 23/32 INCH
GROUP 1
SIZED FOR SPACING
EXTERIOR
000
PS 1-83 FHA-UM-64
NER-QA397 PRP-108

APA TRADEMARKS
GRADE DESIGNATIONS

Structural panel grades are generally identified in terms of the veneer grade used on the face and back of the panel (e.g., A-B, B-C, etc.) or rated by a name suggesting the panel's intended end use (e.g., APA-rated Sheathing, APA-rated Sturd-I-Floor, etc.).

VENEER GRADES

Veneer grades define veneer appearance in terms of natural unrepaired growth characteristics and the number and size of repairs allowable during manufacture. The highest quality veneer grades are N and A. The minimum grade of veneer permitted in Exterior plywood is C-grade. D-grade veneer is used only for backs and inner plies of panels intended for interior use or applications protected from exposure to permanent or severe moisture.

N— Smooth surface "natural finish" veneer. Select, all heartwood or all sapwood. Free of open defects. Allows not more than 6 repairs, wood only, per 4 x 8 panel, made parallel to grain and well matched for grain and color.

A— Smooth, paintable. Not more than 18 neatly made repairs, boat, sled, or router type, parallel to grain permitted. May be used for natural finish in less demanding applications. Synthetic repairs permitted.

B— Solid surface. Shims, circular repair plugs, and tight knots to 1 in. across grain permitted. Some minor splits and synthetic repairs permitted.

C— PLUGGED—Improved C-grade veneer with splits limited to $1/8$ in. width, knotholes and borer holes limited to $1/4$ x $1/2$ in. Admits some broken grain. Synthetic repairs permitted.

C— Tight knots to $1^1/2$ in. Knotholes to 1 in. across grain and some to $1^1/2$ in. if total width of knots and knotholes is within specified limits. Synthetic or wood repairs. Discoloration and sanding defects that do not impair strength permitted. Limited splits allowed. Stitching permitted.

D— Knots and knotholes to $2^1/2$ in. width across grain and $1/2$ in. larger within specified limits. Limited splits allowed. Stitching permitted. Limited to interior and Exposure 1 panels.

SPAN RATINGS

APA-rated Sheathing, APA-rated Sturd-I-Floor, and APA-rated Siding carry numbers in their trademarks called span ratings. These denote the maximum recommended center-to-center spacing in inches of supports for the panels in construction applications. Except for APA-rated Siding panels, the span rating in the trademark applies when the long panel dimension is across supports, unless the strength axis is otherwise identified. The span rating in the trademark of rated Siding panels applies when installed vertically.

The span rating in APA-rated Sheathing trademarks appears as two numbers separated by a slash, such as 32/16, 48/14, etc. (An exception is APA-rated Sheathing intended for use on walls only. The trademarks for these contain a single number similar to the span rating for APA-rated Siding.) The left-hand number denotes the maximum recommended spacing of supports when the panel is used for roof sheathing with the long dimension or strength axis of the panel across three or more supports. The right-hand number indicates the maximum recommended spacing of supports when the panel is used for subflooring with the long dimension or strength axis of the panel across three or more supports. A panel marked 32/16, for example, may be used for roof decking over supports 32 in. o.c. or for subflooring over supports 16 in. o.c.

The span ratings in the trademarks on APA-rated Sturd-I-Floor and Siding panels appear as a single number. APA-rated Sturd-I-Floor panels are designed specifically for single-floor (combined subfloor underlayment) applications under carpet and pad and are manufactured with span ratings of 16, 20, 24, 32, and 48 in. The span ratings for APA-rated Sturd-I-Floor panels, like those for APA-rated Sheathing, are based on application of the panel with the long dimension or strength axis across three or more supports.

APA-rated Siding is available with span ratings of 16 and 24 in. Span-rated panels and lap siding may be applied direct to studs or over nonstructural wall sheathing (Sturd-I-Wall construction), or over nailable panel or lumber sheathing (double wall construction). Panels and lap siding with a span rating of 16 in. may be applied direct to studs spaced 16 in. o.c. Panels and lap siding bearing a span rating of 24 in. may be applied direct to studs 24 in. o.c. All rated siding panels may be applied horizontally direct to studs 16 or 24 in. o.c., provided horizontal joints are blocked. When used over nailable structural sheathing, the span rating of rated siding panels refers to the maximum recommended spacing of vertical rows of nails rather than to stud spacing.

GROUP NUMBER

Plywood can be manufactured from more than 70 species of wood. These species are divided, on the basis of bending strength and stiffness, into five groups under U.S. Product Standard PS 1-83. Strongest species are in Group 1, the next strongest in Group 2, and so on. The group number that appears in the trademark on some APA trademarked panels—primarily sanded grades—is based on the species of face and back veneers. Where face and back veneers are not from the same species group, the higher group number is used, except for sanded and decorative panels $3/8$ in. thick or less. These are identified by face species because they are chosen primarily for appearance and used in applications where structural integrity is not critical. Sanded panels greater than $3/8$ in. are identified by face species if C or D grade backs are at least $1/8$ in. and are no more than one species group number larger. Some species are used widely in plywood manufacture, others rarely. Check local availability before specifying if a particular species is desired.

EXPOSURE DURABILITY

APA-trademarked panels may be produced in four exposure durability classifications—Exterior, Exposure 1, Exposure 2, and Interior. Note: All-veneer APA-rated Sheathing, Exposure 1, commonly called "CDX" in the trade, is frequently mistaken as an Exterior panel and erroneously used in applications for which it does not possess the required resistance to weather. "CDX" should only be used for applications as outlined under Exposure 1 below. For sheathing grade Panels that will be exposed permanently to the weather, specify APA-rated Sheathing Exterior (C-C Exterior under Product Standard PS1 for manufacturing).

EXTERIOR PANELS have a fully waterproof bond and are designed for applications subject to permanent exposure to the weather or to moisture.

EXPOSURE 1 PANELS have a fully waterproof bond and are designed for applications where long construction time may delay permanent protection, is provided, or where high moisture conditions may be encountered in service. Exposure 1 panels are made with the same adhesives used in Exterior panels. However, because other compositional factors may affect bond performance, only Exterior panels should be used for permanent exposure to the weather.

EXPOSURE 2 PANELS (identified as Interior type with intermediate glue under PS1) are intended for protected construction applications where only moderate delays in providing protection from moisture are expected.

INTERIOR PANELS that lack further glueline information in their trademarks are manufactured with interior glue and are intended for interior applications only.

SANDED, UNSANDED, AND TOUCH-SANDED PANELS

Panels with B-grade or better veneer faces are sanded smooth in manufacture to fulfill the requirements of their intended applications (cabinets, shelving, furniture, built-ins, etc.). APA-rated Sheathing panels are unsanded since a smooth surface is not required for their intended use. Other APA panels—Underlayment, rated Sturd-I-Floor, C-D Plugged, and C-C Plugged—require only touch-sanding for "sizing" to make the panel thickness more uniform.

Unsanded and touch-sanded panels, and panels with B-grade or better veneer on one side only, usually carry the APA trademark on the panel back. Panels with both sides of B-grade or better veneer, or with special overlaid surfaces (such as Medium Density Overlay), carry the APA trademark on the panel edge.

CLASSIFICATION

GROUP 1	GROUP 2		GROUP 3	GROUP 4	GROUP 5
Apitong	Cedar,	Hemlock,	Alder, Red	Aspen,	Basswood
Beech, American	Port	Western	Birch, Paper	Bigtooth	Poplar,
Birch,	Oxford	Maple, Black	Cedar, Alaska	Quaking	Balsam
Sweet	Cypress	Mengkulang	Fir, Subalpine	Cativo	
Yellow	Douglas	Meranti,	Hemlock,	Cedar,	
Douglas Fir No. 1[a]	Fir No. 2[a]	Red[b]	Eastern	Incense	
Kapur	Fir,	Mersawa	Maple,	Western Red	
Keruing	Balsam	Pine,	Bigleaf	Cottonwood,	
Larch, Western	California	Pond	Pine,	Eastern	
Maple, Sugar	Red	Red	Jack	Black	
Pine,	Grand	Virginia	Lodgepole	(Western	
Caribbean	Noble	Western	Ponderosa	Poplar)	
Ocote	Pacific Silver	White	Spruce	Pine,	
Pine, Southern	White	Spruce,	Redwood	Eastern	
Loblolly	Lauan,	Black	Spruce,	White	
Longleaf	Almon	Red	Engelmann	Sugar	
Shortleaf	Bagtikan	Sitka	White		
Slash	Mayapis	Sweetgum			
Tanoak	Red	Tamarack			
	Tangile	Yellow-Poplar			
	White				

NOTES

a. Douglas Fir from trees grown in the states of Washington, Oregon, California, Idaho, Montana, and Wyoming and the Canadian provinces of Alberta and British Columbia shall be classed as Douglas Fir No. 1. Douglas Fir from trees grown in the states of Nevada, Utah, Colorado, Arizona, and New Mexico shall be classed as Douglas Fir No. 2.

b. Red Meranti shall be limited to species having a specific gravity of 0.41 or more based on green volume and oven dry weight.

Bloodgood, Sharp, Buster Architects and Planners; Des Moines, Iowa
American Plywood Association; Tacoma, Washington

APA-RATED SIDING PANELS

For exterior siding, fencing, etc. Can be manufactured as conventional veneered plywood, as a composite, or as an overlaid oriented strand board siding. Both panel and lap siding available. Special surface treatment such as V-groove, shallow channel groove, deep groove (such as APA Texture 1-11), kerfed groove, brushed, rough-sawn, and texture-embossed (MDO). Span Rating (stud spacing for siding qualified for APA Sturd-I-Wall applications) and face grade classification (for veneer-faced siding) indicated in trademark Exposure Durability Classification: Exterior. Common thicknesses: $^{11}/_{32}$, $^3/_8$, $^{15}/_{32}$, $^1/_2$, $^{19}/_{32}$, $^5/_8$.

303-PLYWOOD SIDING FACE GRADES

CLASS	GRADE[1]	WOOD PATCHES	SYNTHETIC PATCHES
Special Series 303	303-OC [2,3]	Not permitted	Not permitted
	303-OL [4]	Not applicable for overlays	
	303-NR [5]	Not permitted	Not permitted
	303-SR [6]	Not permitted	Permitted as natural defect shape only
303-6	303-6-W	Limit 6	Not permitted
	303-6-S	Not permitted	Limit 6
	303-6-S/W	Limit 6 - any combination	
303-18	303-18-W	Limit 18	Not permitted
	303-18-S	Not permitted	Limit 18
	303-18-S/W	Limit 18 - any combination	
303-30	303-30-W	Limit 30	Not permitted
	303-30-S	Not permitted	Limit 30
	303-30-S/W	Limit 30 - any combination	

NOTES

1. Limitations on grade characteristics are based on 4 x 8 ft panel size. Limits on other sizes vary in proportion. All panels except 303-NR allow restricted minor repairs such as shims. These and such other face appearance characteristics as knots, knotholes, splits, etc., are limited by both size and number in accordance with panel grades, 303 OC being most restrictive and 303-30 being least. Multiple repairs are permitted only on 303-18 and 303-30 panels. Patch size is restricted on all panel grades. For additional information, including finishing recommendations, see APA Product Guide: 303 Plywood Siding, E300.
2. Check local availability.
3. "Clear"
4. "Overlaid" (e.g., Medium Density Overlay siding)
5. "Natural Rustic"
6. "Synthetic Rustic"

APA TEXTURE 1-11

Special 303-Siding panel with grooves $^1/_4$ in. deep, $^3/_8$ in. wide, spaced 4 or 8 in. o.c. Other spacings may be available on special order. Edges shiplapped. Available unsanded, textured, and other surfaces. Exposure Classification: Exterior. Thicknesses: $^{19}/_{32}$ and $^5/_8$ only.

APA SANDED AND TOUCH-SANDED PANELS [3,4,6]

APA A-A

Use where appearance of both sides is important for interior applications such as built-ins, cabinets, furniture, partitions; and exterior applications such as fences, signs, boats, shipping containers, tanks, ducts, etc. Smooth surfaces suitable for painting. Exposure Durability Classifications: Interior, Exposure 1, Exterior. Common thicknesses: $^1/_4$, $^3/_8$, $^1/_2$, $^5/_8$, $^3/_4$.[6]

APA A-B

For use where appearance of one side is less important but where two solid surfaces are necessary Exposure Durability Classifications: Interior, Exposure 1, Exterior. Common thicknesses: $^1/_4$, $^3/_8$, $^1/_2$, $^5/_8$, $^3/_4$.[6]

APA A-C

For use where appearance of only one side is important in exterior applications, e.g., soffits, fences, structural uses, boxcar and truck linings, farm buildings, tanks, trays, commercial refrigerators, etc. Exposure Durability Classification: Exterior. Common thicknesses: $^1/_4$, $^3/_8$, $^1/_2$, $^5/_8$, $^3/_4$.[6]

APA A-D

For use where appearance of only one side is important in interior applications, e.g., paneling, built-ins, shelving, partitions, etc. Exposure Durability Classifications: Interior, Exposure 1. Common thicknesses: $^1/_4$, $^3/_8$, $^1/_2$, $^5/_8$, $^3/_4$.[6]

APA B-B

Utility panels with two solid sides. Exposure Durability Classifications: Interior, Exposure 1, Exterior. Common thicknesses: $^1/_4$, $^3/_8$, $^1/_2$, $^5/_8$, $^3/_4$.[6]

APA B-C

Utility panel for farm service and work buildings, boxcar and truck linings, containers, tanks, agricultural equipment, as a base for exterior coatings and other exterior uses. Exposure Durability Classification: Exterior. Common thicknesses: $^1/_4$, $^3/_8$, $^1/_2$, $^5/_8$, $^3/_4$.[6]

APA B-D

Utility panel for backing, sides of built-ins, industry shelving, slip sheets, separator boards, bins, and other interior or protected applications. Exposure Durability Classifications: Interior, Exposure 1. Common thicknesses: $^1/_4$, $^3/_8$, $^1/_2$, $^5/_8$, $^3/_4$.[6]

APA UNDERLAYMENT

For application over structural subfloor. Provides smooth surface for application of carpet and pad and has high concentrated and impact load resistance. Touch-sanded. Exposure Durability Classifications: Interior, Exposure 1. Common thicknesses: $^3/_8$, $^1/_2$, $^{19}/_{32}$, $^5/_8$, $^{23}/_{32}$, $^3/_4$, $^{11}/_{32}$.

APA C-C PLUGGED

For use as underlayment over structural subfloor, refrigerated or controlled atmosphere storage rooms, pallet bins, tanks, truck floors, linings and other exterior applications. Touch-sanded. Exposure Durability Classification: Exterior. Common thicknesses: $^3/_8$, $^1/_2$, $^{19}/_{32}$, $^5/_8$, $^{23}/_{32}$, $^3/_4$, $^{11}/_{32}$.

APA C-D PLUGGED

For open soffits, built-ins, cable reels, walkways, separator boards, and other interior or protected applications. Not a substitute for underlayment or APA-rated Sturd-I-Floor as it lacks puncture resistance. Exposure Durability Classifications: Interior, Exposure 1. Common thicknesses: $^3/_8$, $^1/_2$, $^{19}/_{32}$, $^5/_8$, $^{23}/_{32}$, $^3/_4$.

APA SPECIALTY PANELS

APA DECORATIVE

Rough-sawn, brushed, grooved, or other faces. For paneling, interior accent walls, built-ins, counter facing, exhibit displays. Can also be made by some manufacturers in Exterior for siding, gable ends, fences, etc. Use recommendations for exterior panels vary with the particular product; check with manufacturer. Exposure Durability Classifications: Interior, Exposure 1. Exterior. Common thicknesses: $^5/_{16}$, $^3/_8$, $^1/_2$, $^5/_8$.

APA HIGH-DENSITY OVERLAY (HDO)

Has a hard semi-opaque resin-fiber overlay both sides. Abrasion-resistant. For concrete forms, cabinets, countertops, signs, tanks. Also available with skid-resistant screen-grid surface. Exposure Durability Classification: Exterior. Common thicknesses: $^3/_8$, $^1/_2$, $^5/_8$, $^3/_4$.

APA MEDIUM-DENSITY OVERLAY (MDO)

Smooth, opaque, resin-fiber overlay one or both sides. Ideal base for paint, indoors and outdoors. Available as a 303 Siding. Exposure Durability Classification: Exterior. Common thicknesses: $^{11}/_{32}$, $^3/_8$, $^1/_2$, $^5/_8$, $^3/_4$, $^{15}/_{32}$, $^{19}/_{32}$, $^{23}/_{32}$.

APA MARINE

Ideal for boat hulls. Made only with Douglas fir or western larch. Special solid-jointed core construction. Subject to special limitations on core gaps and face repairs. Also available with HDO or MDO faces. Exposure Durability Classification: Exterior. Common thicknesses: $^1/_4$, $^3/_8$, $^1/_2$, $^5/_8$, $^3/_4$.

APA B-B PLYFORM CLASS I AND II

Concrete form grades with high reuse factor. Sanded both sides and mill-oiled unless otherwise specified. Special restrictions on species. Class I panels are stiffest, strongest, and most commonly available. Also available in HDO for very smooth concrete finish, in Structural I (all plies limited to Group 1 species), and with special overlays. Exposure Durability Classification: Exterior. Common thicknesses: $^{19}/_{32}$, $^5/_8$, $^{23}/_{32}$, $^3/_4$.

APA PLYRON

Hardboard face on both sides. Faces tempered, untempered, smooth, or screened. For countertops, shelving, cabinet doors, flooring, etc. Exposure Durability Classifications: Interior, Exposure 1, Exterior. Common thicknesses: $^1/_2$, $^5/_8$, $^3/_4$.

APA PERFORMANCE-RATED PANELS [1,2]

APA-RATED SHEATHING

Specially designed for subflooring and wall and roof sheathing. Also good for broad range of other construction and industrial applications. Can be manufactured as a conventional veneered plywood, as a composite, or as a non-veneered panel. For special engineered applications, veneered panels conforming to PS1 may be required. Exposure Durability Classifications: Exterior, Exposure 1, Exposure 2. Common thicknesses: $^5/_{16}$, $^3/_8$, $^7/_{16}$, $^1/_2$, $^5/_8$, $^3/_4$, $^{15}/_{32}$, $^{19}/_{32}$, $^{23}/_{32}$.

APA STRUCTURAL I AND II RATED SHEATHING

Unsanded all-veneer PS1 plywood grades for use where strength is of maximum importance; for box beams, gusset plates, stressed-skin panels, containers, pallet bins. Structural I is more commonly available. Exposure Durability Classifications: Exterior, Exposure 1. Common thicknesses: $^5/_{16}$, $^3/_8$, $^1/_2$, $^{15}/_{32}$, $^{19}/_{32}$, $^5/_8$, $^{23}/_{32}$.

APA-RATED STURD-I-FLOOR

Specially designed as combination subfloor-underlayment. Provides smooth surface for application of carpet and pad and possesses high concentrated and load impact resistance. Can be manufactured as a nonveneered panel. Available square-edged or tongue-and-grooved. Exposure Durability Classifications: Exterior, Exposure 1, Exposure 2. Common thicknesses: $^{19}/_{32}$, $^5/_8$, $^{23}/_{32}$, $^3/_4$.

APA-RATED STURD-I-FLOOR 48 OC (2-4-1)

For combination subfloor-underlayment on 32- and 48-inch spans and for heavy timber roof construction. Manufactured only as conventional veneered plywood. Available square-edged or tongue-and-grooved. Exposure Durability Classifications: Exposure 1. Thickness: $1^1/_8$.

NOTES FOR SANDED AND PERFORMANCE-RATED PANELS

1. Specify performance-rated panels by thickness and span rating. Span ratings are based on panel strength and stiffness. Since these properties are a function of panel composition and configuration as well as thickness, the same span rating may appear on panels of different thickness. Conversely, panels of the same thickness may be marked with different span ratings.
2. All plies in Structural I panels are limited to Group 1 species. Structural II panels are seldom available.
3. Exterior sanded panels, C-C Plugged, C-D Plugged, and Underlayment grades can also be manufactured in Structural I (all plies limited to Group 1 species).
4. Some manufacturers also produce panels with premium N-grade veneer on one or both faces. Available only by special order.
5. Can also be manufactured in Structural I (all plies limited to Group 1 species).
6. Also available in $^{11}/_{32}$, $^{15}/_{32}$, $^{19}/_{32}$, $^{23}/_{32}$ in. thicknesses.

Bloodgood, Sharp, Buster Architects and Planners; Des Moines, Iowa
American Plywood Association; Tacoma, Washington

EXTERIOR TYPE PANELS

APPEARANCE (1, 3)		VENEER			THICKNESS (IN.)					
GRADE (2)	COMMON USES	F	M	B	1/4	5/16	11/32 3/8	15/32 1/2	19/32 5/8	23/32 3/4
A-A EXT APA (5)	Use where both sides are visible	A	C	A	•		•	•	•	•
A-B EXT APA (5)	Use where view of one side is less important	A	C	B	•		•	•	•	•
A-C EXT APA (5)	Use where only one side is visible	A	C	C	•		•	•	•	•
B-B EXT APA (5)	Utility panel with two solid faces	B	C	B	•		•	•	•	•
B-C EXT APA (5)	Utility panel. Also used as base for exterior coatings on walls and roofs	B	C	C	•		•	•	•	•
HDO EXT-APA (5)	High density overlay plywood has a hard, semi-opaque resin fiber overlay on both faces. Abrasion resistant. Use for concrete forms, cabinets, and countertops	A B	C	A B			•	•	•	•
MDO EXT APA (5)	Medium density overlay with smooth resin fiber overlay on one or two faces. Recommended for siding and other outdoor applications. Ideal base for paint	B	C	B C			•	•	•	•
303 SIDING EXT-APA (7)	Special surface treatment such as V-groove, channel groove, striated, brushed, rough sawn	(6)	C	C			•	•	•	
T1-11 EXT-APA (7)	Special 303 panel having grooves 1/4 in. deep, 3/8 in. wide, spaced 4 in. or 8 in. o.c. Other spacing optional. Edges shiplapped. Available unsanded, textured, and medium density overlay	A B C	C	C					•	
PLYRON EXT-APA	Hardboard faces both sides, tempered, smooth or screened	HB	C	HB				•	•	•
UNDERLAYMENT C-C PLUGGED EXT-APA (5)	For application over structural subfloor. Provides smooth surface for application of carpet and pad. Touch-sanded	C	C	C				•	•	•
C-C PLUGGED EXT-APA (5)	For refrigerated or controlled atmosphere rooms. Touch-sanded	C	C	C				•	•	•
B-B PLYFORM CLASS I and CLASS II EXT-APA (4)	Concrete form grades with high reuse factor. Sanded both sides and mill-oiled unless otherwise specified. Special restrictions on species. Also available in HDO for very smooth concrete finish	B	C	B					•	•

PERFORMANCE RATED (3)		VENEER			THICKNESS (IN.)					
GRADE	COMMON USES	F	M	B	1/4	5/16	11/32 3/8	15/32 1/2	19/32 5/8	23/32 3/4
SHEATHING EXT-APA	Exterior sheathing panel for subflooring and wall and roof sheathing, siding on service and farm buildings. Manufactured as conventional veneered plywood	C	C	C		•	•	•	•	•
STRUCTURAL I SHEATHING EXT-APA	For engineered applications in construction and industry where full exterior type panels are required. Unsanded. See Note 5 for species group requirements	C	C	C		•	•	•	•	•
STURDI-I-FLOOR EXT-APA	For combination subfloor underlayment under carpet and pad where severe moisture conditions exist, as in balcony decks. Touch-sanded and tongue and groove	C	C (11)	C					•	•

INTERIOR TYPE PANELS

APPEARANCE (1, 3)		VENEER			THICKNESS (IN.)					
GRADE (2) (12)	COMMON USES	F	M	B	1/4	5/16	11/32 3/8	15/32 1/2	19/32 5/8	23/32 3/4
N-N, N-A N-B INT-APA	Cabinet quality. For natural finish furniture. Special order items	N	C	NA B						•
N-D INT-APA	For natural finish paneling. Special orders	N	D	D	•					
A-A INT-APA	For applications where both sides are visible. Smooth face; suitable for painting	A	D	A	•		•	•	•	•
A-B INT-APA	Use where view of one side is less important but two solid surfaces are needed	A	D	B	•		•	•	•	•
A-D INT-APA	Use where only one side is visible	A	D	D	•		•	•	•	•
B-B INT-APA	Utility panel with two solid sides	B	D	B	•		•	•	•	•
B-D INT-APA	Utility panel with one solid side	B	D	D	•		•	•	•	•
Decorative panels-INT-APA	Rough sawn, brushed, grooved, or striated faces for walls and built-ins	A B C	D	D		•	•	•		
PLYRON INT-APA	Hardboard face on both sides, tempered smooth or screened for counters and doors	HB	C D	HB				•	•	•
UNDER-LAYMENT INT-APA (5)	For application over structural subfloor. Provides smooth surface for application of carpet and pad. Touch-sanded. Also available with exterior glue	C	C D	D				•	•	•
C-D PLUGGED INT-APA (5)	For built-ins, wall and ceiling tile backing, cable reels, walkways, separator boards. Not a substitute for UNDERLAYMENT or STURD-I-FLOOR as it lacks their indentation resistance. Touch-sanded. Also made with exterior glue	C	D	D				•	•	•

PERFORMANCE RATED (3, 8)		VENEER (13)			THICKNESS (IN.)					
GRADE	COMMON USES	F	M	B	1/4	5/16	3/8	15/32 1/2	19/32 5/8	23/32 3/4
SHEATHING EXP 1 and 2-APA	Commonly available with exterior glue for sheathing and subflooring. Specify Exposure 1 treated wood foundations	C	D	D		•	•	•	•	•
STRUCTURAL I SHEATHING EXP 1-APA	Unsanded structural grades where plywood strength properties are of maximum importance. Made only with exterior glue for beams, gusset plates, and stressed-skin panels	C (10)	D (10)	D (10)		•	•	•		
STURD-I-FLOOR EXP 1 and 2-APA	For combination subfloor and underlayment under carpet and pad. Specify Exposure 1 where moisture is present. Available in tongue and groove.	C	C D (11)	D					•	•
STURD-I-FLOOR 48 o.c. (2, 4, 1) EXP 1-APA (9)	Combination subfloor underlayment on 32 and 48 in. spans and for heavy timber roofs. Use in areas subject to moisture; or if construction may be delayed as in site built floors. Unsanded or touch-sanded as specified	C	C D	D						1 1/8

GENERAL NOTES

1. Sanded on both sides except where decorative or other surfaces specified.
2. Available in Group 1, 2, 3, 4, or 5 unless otherwise noted.
3. Standard 4 × 8 panel sizes; other sizes available.
4. Also available in Structural I.
5. Also available in Structural I (all plies limited to Group I species).
6. C or better for five plies; C Plugged or better for three-ply panels.
7. Stud spacing is shown on grade stamp.
8. Exposure 1 made with exterior glue, Exposure 2 with intermediate glue.
9. Made only in woods of certain species to conform to APA specifications.
10. Special improved grade for structural panels.
11. Special construction to resist indentation from concentrated loads.
12. Interior type panels with exterior glue are identified as Exposure 1.
13. Also available as nonveneer or composite panels.

Bloodgood, Sharp, Buster Architects and Planners; Des Moines, Iowa
American Plywood Association; Tacoma, Washington

SHEATHING   6

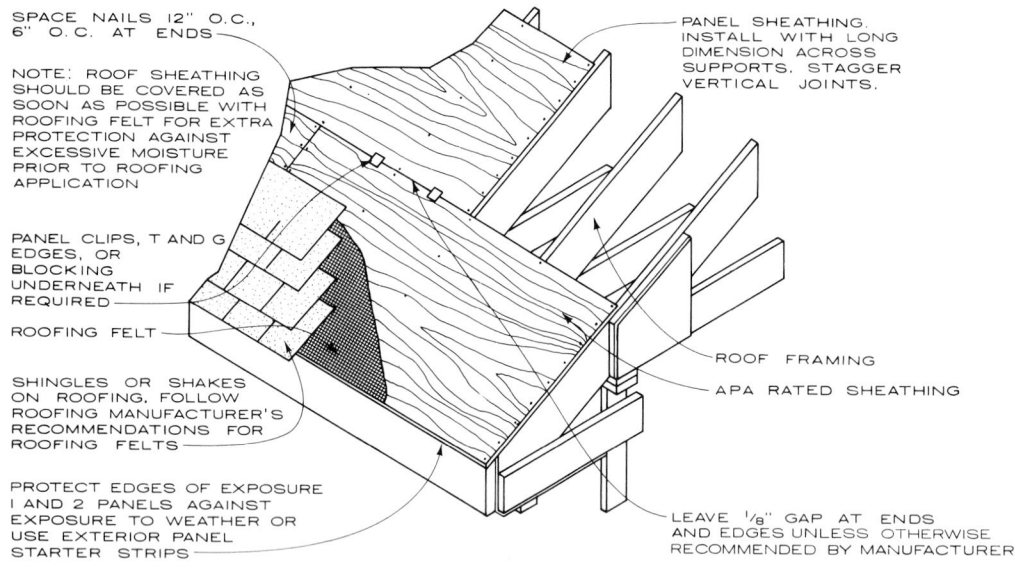

SPACE NAILS 12" O.C., 6" O.C. AT ENDS

NOTE: ROOF SHEATHING SHOULD BE COVERED AS SOON AS POSSIBLE WITH ROOFING FELT FOR EXTRA PROTECTION AGAINST EXCESSIVE MOISTURE PRIOR TO ROOFING APPLICATION

PANEL CLIPS, T AND G EDGES, OR BLOCKING UNDERNEATH IF REQUIRED

ROOFING FELT

SHINGLES OR SHAKES ON ROOFING. FOLLOW ROOFING MANUFACTURER'S RECOMMENDATIONS FOR ROOFING FELTS

PROTECT EDGES OF EXPOSURE 1 AND 2 PANELS AGAINST EXPOSURE TO WEATHER OR USE EXTERIOR PANEL STARTER STRIPS

PANEL SHEATHING. INSTALL WITH LONG DIMENSION ACROSS SUPPORTS. STAGGER VERTICAL JOINTS.

ROOF FRAMING

APA RATED SHEATHING

LEAVE 1/8" GAP AT ENDS AND EDGES UNLESS OTHERWISE RECOMMENDED BY MANUFACTURER

STRUCTURAL-USE PANEL ROOF SHEATHING

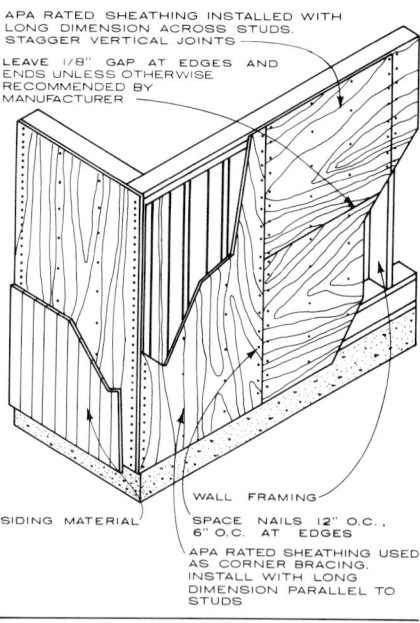

APA RATED SHEATHING INSTALLED WITH LONG DIMENSION ACROSS STUDS. STAGGER VERTICAL JOINTS.

LEAVE 1/8" GAP AT EDGES AND ENDS UNLESS OTHERWISE RECOMMENDED BY MANUFACTURER

WALL FRAMING

SIDING MATERIAL

SPACE NAILS 12" O.C., 6" O.C. AT EDGES

APA RATED SHEATHING USED AS CORNER BRACING. INSTALL WITH LONG DIMENSION PARALLEL TO STUDS

STRUCTURAL-USE PANEL WALL SHEATHING

PLYWOOD ROOF SHEATHING

Plywood grades commonly used for roof (and wall) sheathing are APA rated sheathing with span ratings. 12/0, 16/0, 20/0, 24/0, 24/16, 32/16, 40/20, 48/24; exposure durability classifications: Exterior, Exposure 1. Refer to American Plywood Association recommendations for unsupported edges.

PLYWOOD WALL SHEATHING

Common grade is same as used in roof sheathing. Refer to American Plywood Association recommendations for unsupported edges.

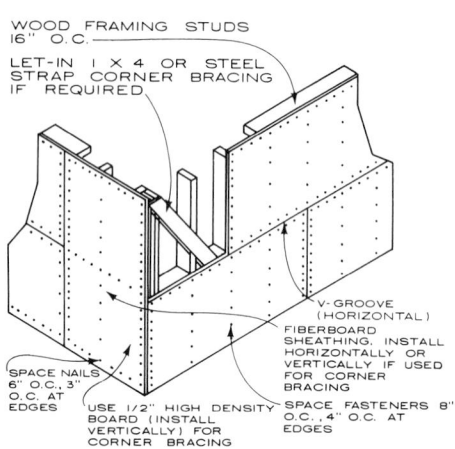

FOR HORIZONTAL SHEATHING SPACE NAILS 8" O.C. IF USED FOR CORNER BRACING SPACE NAILS 12" O.C. AND USE ADHESIVE

SPACE STUDS 24" O.C. MAX. 16" O.C. IF USED FOR CORNER BRACING

NAIL SIDING TO STUDS NOT TO GYPSUM BOARD

GYPSUM SHEATHING. INSTALL HORIZONTALLY. IF USED FOR CORNER BRACING INSTALL VERTICALLY

NOTE: REFER TO MANUFACTURER'S RECOMMENDATIONS FOR SPECIFIC INSTALLATION INSTRUCTIONS.

GYPSUM WALL SHEATHING

WOOD FRAMING STUDS 16" O.C.

LET-IN 1 X 4 OR STEEL STRAP CORNER BRACING IF REQUIRED

SPACE NAILS 6" O.C., 3" O.C. AT EDGES

USE 1/2" HIGH DENSITY BOARD (INSTALL VERTICALLY) FOR CORNER BRACING

V-GROOVE (HORIZONTAL) FIBERBOARD SHEATHING. INSTALL HORIZONTALLY OR VERTICALLY IF USED FOR CORNER BRACING

SPACE FASTENERS 8" O.C., 4" O.C. AT EDGES

FIBERBOARD SHEATHING

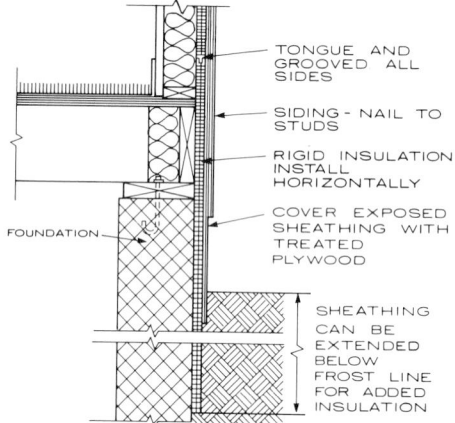

TONGUE AND GROOVED ALL SIDES

SIDING - NAIL TO STUDS

RIGID INSULATION INSTALL HORIZONTALLY

COVER EXPOSED SHEATHING WITH TREATED PLYWOOD

FOUNDATION

SHEATHING CAN BE EXTENDED BELOW FROST LINE FOR ADDED INSULATION

PLASTIC SHEATHING

GYPSUM WALL SHEATHING

Fire rated panels are available in 1/2 and 5/8 in. thicknesses. Gypsum board is not an effective vapor barrier.

FIBERBOARD SHEATHING

Also called insulation board. Can be treated or impregnated with asphalt. Available in regular or 1/2 in. high density panels.

PLASTIC SHEATHING

Can be considered an effective vapor barrier, hence wall must be effectively vented. All edges are usually tongue and groove. Some products emit toxic fumes when burned. Refer to manufacturer's specifications.

SHEATHING MATERIALS

CHARACTERISTICS	PLYWOOD	GYPSUM	FIBERBOARD	PLASTIC
Nailable base	Yes	No	Only high density	No
Vapor barrier	No	No	If asphalt treated	Yes
Insulation R value (1/2 in. thickness)	1.2	0.7	2.6	Varies with manufacturer
Corner bracing provided	Yes	Yes (see manufacturer's recommendation)	Only high density	No
Panel sizes (ft) (plastic in in.)	4 x 8, 4 x 9, 4 x 10	2 x 8, 4 x 8, 4 x 10, 4 x 12, 4 x 14	4 x 8, 4 x 9, 4 x 10, 4 x 12	16 x 96, 24 x 48, 24 x 96, 48 x 96, 48 x 108
Panel thickness (in.)	5/16, 3/8, 7/16, 15/32, 1/2, 19/32, 5/8, 23/32, 3/4, 7/8, 1, 1 1/8	1/4, 3/8, 1/2, 5/8	1/2, 25/32	1/2 to 6 (for roof)

Timothy B. McDonald; Washington, D.C.
Bloodgood, Sharp, Buster Architects and Planners; Des Moines, Iowa
American Plywood Association; Tacoma, Washington

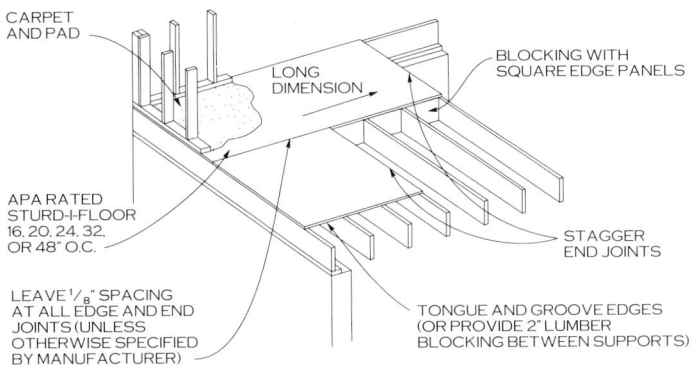

APA RATED STURD-I-FLOOR

SPAN RATING (MAXIMUM JOIST SPACING, IN.)	PANEL THICKNESS (IN.)	NAIL SIZE AND TYPE	FASTENING			
			GLUE/NAILED	NAILED ONLY	GLUE/NAILED	NAILED ONLY
			SPACING (IN.)			
			PANEL EDGE		INTERMEDIATE	
16	$^{19}/_{32}, ^5/_8, ^{21}/_{32}$	6d ring or screw shank [3]	12	6	12	12
20	$^{19}/_{32}, ^5/_8, ^{23}/_{32}, ^3/_4$	6d ring or screw shank [3]	12	6	12	12
24	$^{11}/_{16}, ^{23}/_{32}, ^3/_4$	6d ring or screw shank [3]	12	6	12	12
	$^7/_8, 1$	8d ring or screw shank [3]	12	3	12	12
48	$1^1/_8$	8d ring or screw shank [4]	6	6		

NOTES

1. For conditions not listed, see APA literature.
2. Use only APA Specification AFG-01 adhesives, properly applied. Use only solvent based glues on nonveneered panels with sealed surfaces and edges.
3. 8d common nails may be substituted if ring or screw-shank nails are not available.
4. 10d common nails may be substituted with $1^1/_8$ in. panels if supports are well seasoned.
5. Space nails 6 in. for 48 in. spans and 12 in. for 32 in. spans.

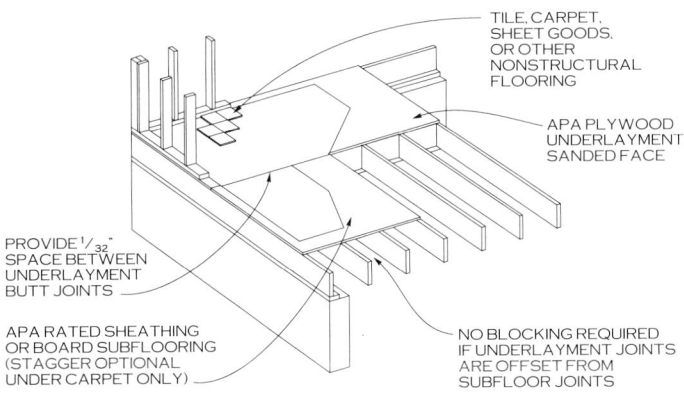

PLYWOOD UNDERLAYMENT [1]

PLYWOOD GRADES AND SPECIES GROUP	APPLICATION	MIN. PLYWOOD THICKNESS (IN.)
Groups 1, 2, 3, 4, and 5 UNDERLAYMENT INT-APA (with interior or exterior glue), or UNDERLAYMENT EXT-APA (C-C plugged) EXT	Over smooth subfloor	$^1/_4$
	Over lumber subfloor or other uneven surfaces	$^{11}/_{32}$
Same grades as above, but Group 1 only	Over lumber floor up to 4 in. wide. Face grain must be perpendicular to boards	$^1/_4$

NOTES

1. For tile, carpeting, sheet goods, or other nonstructural flooring (consult Tile Council of America for recommendations regarding ceramic tile).
2. Where floors may be subject to unusual moisture conditions, use panels with exterior glue (Exposure 1) or UNDERLAYMENT C-C Plugged EXT-APA. C-D Plugged is not an adequate substitute for underlayment grade, since it does not ensure equivalent dent resistance.
3. Recommended grades have a solid surface backed with a special inner ply construction that resists punch-through and dents from concentrated loads.

Bloodgood, Sharp, Buster Architects and Planners; Des Moines, Iowa
American Plywood Association; Tacoma, Washington

UNDERLAYMENT NAILING SCHEDULE

Use 3d ring shank nails for underlayment up to $^1/_2$ in. thickness, 4d for $^{19}/_{32}$ in. and thicker. Use 16 gauge staples, except that 18 gauge may be used with $^1/_4$ in. thick underlayment. Crown width should be $^3/_8$ in. for 16 gauge staples, $^3/_{16}$ in. for 18 gauge. Length should be sufficient to penetrate subflooring at least $^5/_8$ in. or extend completely through. Space fasteners at 3 in. along panel edges and 6 in. each way in the panel interior, except for $^{11}/_{32}$ in. or thicker underlayment applied with ring shank nails. In this case, use 6 in. spacing along edges and 8 in. spacing each way in the panel interior. Unless subfloor and joists are of thoroughly seasoned material and have remained dry during construction, countersink nail heads below surface of the underlayment just prior to laying finish floors to avoid nail popping. Space joints $^1/_{32}$ in. If thin resilient flooring is to be applied, fill and thoroughly sand joints.

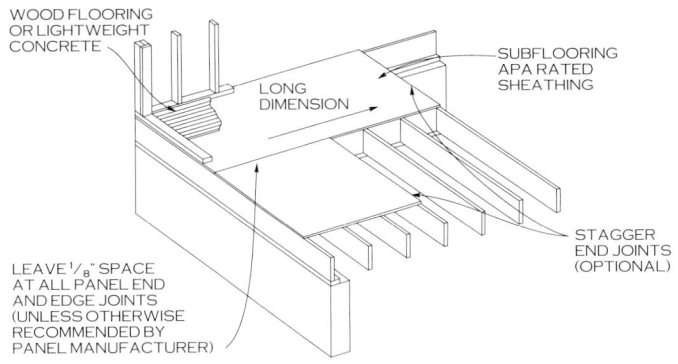

APA PANEL SUBFLOORING[1]

PANEL SPAN RATING (OR GROUP NUMBER)	PANEL THICKNESS (IN.)	MAXIMUM SPACING [2,3,5] (IN.)
24/16	$^7/_{16}, ^1/_2$	16
32/16	$^{15}/_{32}, ^1/_2, ^5/_8, ^{23}/_{32}$	16 [4]
40/20	$^{19}/_{32}, ^5/_8, ^{23}/_{32}, ^3/_4$	20 [4]
48/24	$^{23}/_{32}, ^3/_4, ^7/_8$	24
$1^1/_8$ in., Groups 1 and 2	$1^1/_8$	48

NOTES

1. Applies to APA rated sheathing grades only.
2. The spans assume plywood continuous over two or more spans with long dimension across supports.
3. In some nonresidential buildings, special conditions may require construction in excess of minimums given.
4. May be 24 in. if $^3/_4$ in. wood strip flooring is installed at right angles to joists.
5. Spans are limited to the values shown because of the possible effect of concentrated loads.

SUBFLOORING NAILING SCHEDULE

For $^7/_{16}$ in. panel, use 6d common nails at 6 in. o.c. at panel edges, 12 in. o.c. at intermediate supports. For $^{15}/_{32}$ in. to $^7/_8$ in. panels, use 8d common nails at 6 in. o.c. at panel edges, 12 in o.c. at intermediate supports. For $1^1/_8$ and $1^1/_4$ in. panels up to 48 in. span, use 10d common nails 6 in. o.c. at panel edges and 6 in. o.c. at intermediate supports.

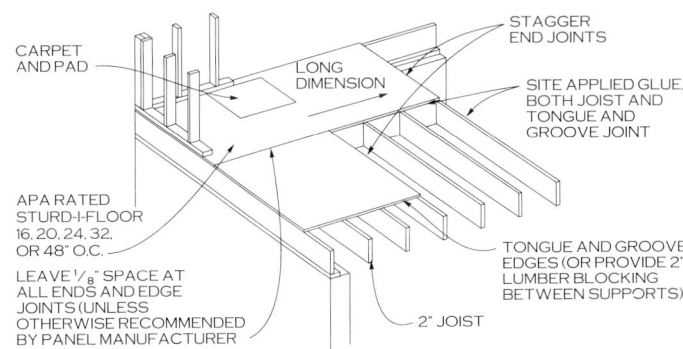

GLUED FLOOR SYSTEM

1. For complete information on glued floors, including joist span tables (based on building code criteria and lumber sizes), application sequence, and a list of recommended adhesives, contact the American Plywood Association.
2. Place APA STURD-I-FLOOR T&G across the joists with end joints staggered. Leave $^1/_8$ in. space at all end and edge joints.
3. Although tongue and groove is used more often, square edge may be used if 2 x 4 blocking is placed under panel edge joints between joists.
4. Based on live load of 40 psf, total load of 50 psf, deflection limited to 1/360 at 40 psf.
5. Glue to joists and at tongue and groove joints. If square edge panels are used, block panel edges and glue between panels and between panels and blocking.

GLUED FLOOR NAILING SCHEDULE

Panels should be secured with power driven fasteners or nailed per APA STURD-I-FLOOR table, above.

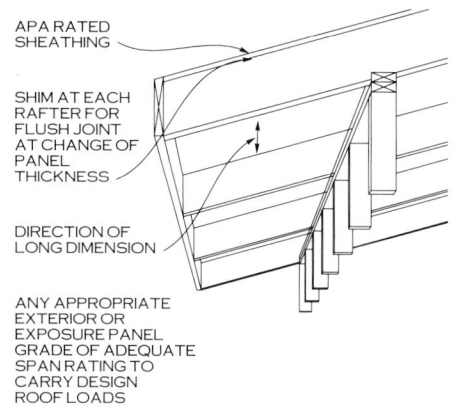

OPEN SOFFIT

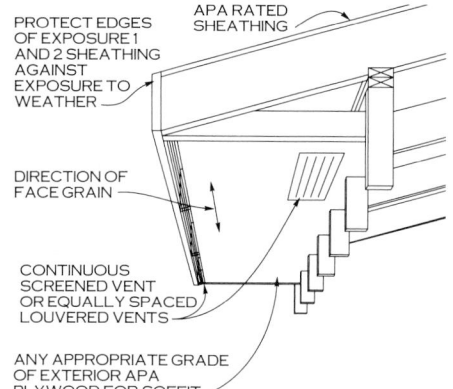

CLOSED SOFFIT

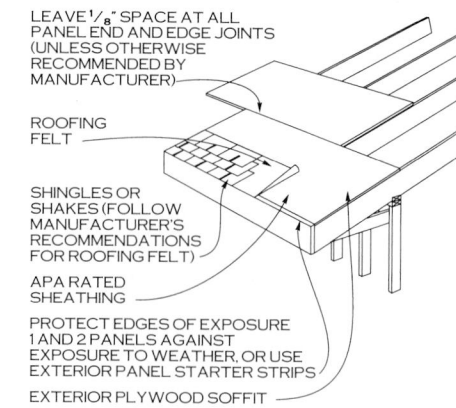

GABLE ROOF

EXTERIOR OPEN SOFFITS/COMBINED CEILING DECKING [1]

PANEL DESCRIPTIONS, MINIMUM RECOMMENDATIONS	GROUP	MAXIMUM SPAN (IN.)
$^{15}/_{32}$" APA 303 siding	1, 2, 3, 4	16
$^{15}/_{32}$" APA sanded and MDO	1, 2, 3, 4	
$^{15}/_{32}$" APA 303 siding	1	24
$^{15}/_{32}$" APA sanded and MDO	1, 2, 3	
$^{19}/_{32}$" APA 303 siding	1, 2, 3, 4	
$^{19}/_{32}$" APA sanded and MDO	1, 2, 3, 4	
$^{19}/_{32}$" APA 303 siding	1	32 [2]
$^{19}/_{32}$" APA sanded and MDO	1	
$^{23}/_{32}$" APA 303 siding	1, 2, 3, 4	
$^{23}/_{32}$" APA sanded and MDO	1, 2, 3, 4	
$1^1/_8$" APA textured	1, 2, 3, 4	48 [2]

NOTES

1. Plywood is assumed to be continuous across two or more spans with face grain across supports.
2. For spans of 32 or 48 in. in open soffit construction, provide adequate blocking, tongue and groove edges, or other support such as panel clips. Minimum loads are at least 30 psf live load, plus 10 psf dead load.

EXTERIOR CLOSED PLYWOOD SOFFITS

NOMINAL PLYWOOD THICKNESS	GROUP	MAXIMUM SPAN (IN.) ALL EDGES SUPPORTED
$^{11}/_{32}$" APA 303 Siding or APA sanded	All species groups	24
$^{15}/_{32}$" APA 303 Siding or APA sanded		32
$^{19}/_{32}$" APA 303 Siding or APA sanded		48

NOTE

Plywood is assumed to be continuous across two or more spans with face grain across supports.

NAILING SCHEDULE

For closed soffits, use nonstaining box or casing nails, 6d for $^{11}/_{32}$ in. and $^{15}/_{32}$ in. panels and 8d for $^{19}/_{32}$ in. panels. Space nails 6 in. at panel edges and 12 in. along intermediate supports for spans less than 48 in.; 6 in. at all supports for 48 in. spans.

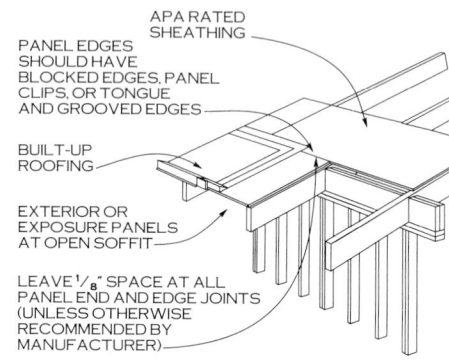

FLAT LOW-PITCHED ROOF

APA PANEL ROOF SHEATHING [1]

PANEL SPAN RATING	PANEL THICKNESS (IN.)	MAXIMUM SPAN (IN.) WITH EDGE SUPPORT	MAXIMUM SPAN (IN.) WITHOUT EDGE SUPPORT	NAIL SIZE AND TYPE	NAIL SPACING (IN.) PANEL EDGES	NAIL SPACING (IN.) INTERMEDIATE
12/0	$^5/_{16}$	12	12	6d common	6	12
16/0	$^5/_{16}, ^3/_8$	16	16			
20/0	$^5/_{16}, ^3/_8$	20	20			
24/0	$^3/_8, ^7/_{16}, ^{15}/_{32}, ^1/_2$	24	20			
24/16	$^7/_{16}, ^{15}/_{32}, ^1/_2$	24	24			
32/16	$^{15}/_{32}, ^1/_2$	32	28			
32/16	$^{19}/_{32}, ^5/_8$	32	28	8d common		
40/20	$^{19}/_{32}, ^5/_8, ^{23}/_{32}, ^3/_4, ^7/_8$	40	32			
40/24	$^{23}/_{32}, ^3/_4, ^7/_8$	48	36			

				STAPLING SPACES (IN.)		
				LEG LENGTH	PANEL EDGES	INTERMEDIATE
(see above)	$^5/_{16}$	(see above)		$1^1/_4$"	4	8
	$^3/_8$			$1^3/_8$"		
	$^7/_{16}, ^{15}/_{32}, ^1/_2$			$1^1/_2$"		

NAILING SCHEDULE

Use 6d common smooth, ring shank, or spiral thread nails for plywood $^1/_2$ in. thick or thinner and 8d for plywood to 1 in. thick. Use 8d ring shank or spiral thread or 10d common smooth for 2-4-1 and $1^1/_8$ in. panels. Space nails 6 in. at panel edges and 12 in. at intermediate supports, except for 48 in. or longer spans where nails should be spaced 6 in. at all supports.

NOTES

1. Applicable to APA rated panel sheathing.
2. All panels will support at least 30 psf live load plus 10 psf dead load at maximum span. Uniform load deflection limit is 1/180 span under live load plus dead load, or 1/240 under live load only.
3. Special conditions may require construction in excess of the given minimums.
4. Panel is assumed to be continuous across two or more spans with long dimension across supports.

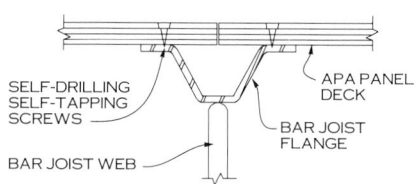

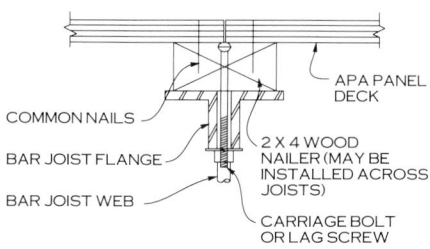

CONNECTIONS TO OPEN WEB STEEL JOIST

Bloodgood, Sharp, Buster Architects and Planners; Des Moines, Iowa
American Plywood Association; Tacoma, Washington

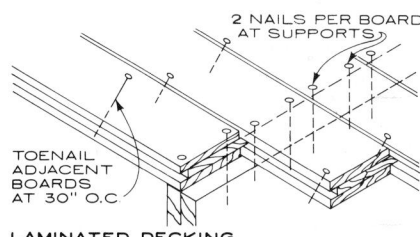

LAMINATED DECKING

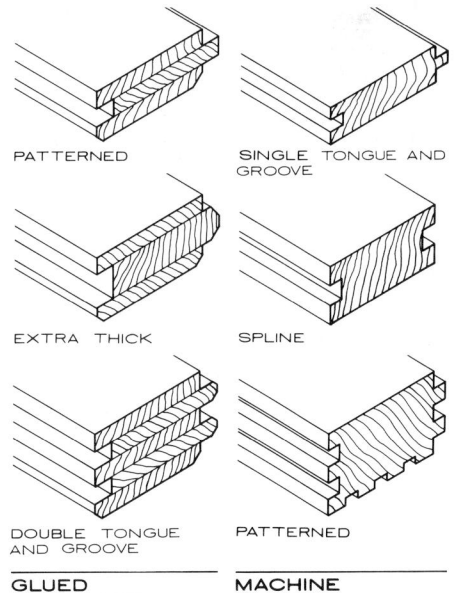

PATTERNED   SINGLE TONGUE AND GROOVE

EXTRA THICK   SPLINE

DOUBLE TONGUE AND GROOVE   PATTERNED

GLUED LAMINATED   **MACHINE SHAPED**

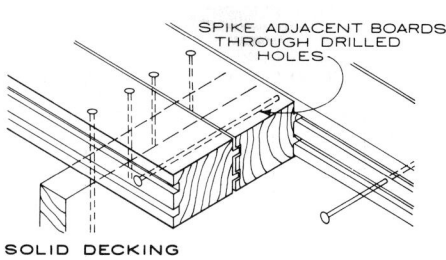

SOLID DECKING

LAMINATED SIZES (IN.)

THICKNESS		WIDTH	
NOMINAL	ACTUAL	NOMINAL	ACTUAL
3	$2^{3/16}$, $2^{1/4}$	6,8	$5^{1/4}$,7
3 STX	$2^{7/8}$		
5	$3^{21/32}$, $3^{13/16}$		

MACHINE SHAPED SIZES (IN.)

THICKNESS		WIDTH	
NOMINAL	ACTUAL	NOMINAL	ACTUAL
2	$1^{1/2}$	5,6,8,10,12	4, 5, $6^{3/4}$ $8^{3/4}$, $10^{3/4}$
3	$2^{1/2}$	6	$5^{1/4}$
4	$3^{1/2}$	6	$5^{1/4}$

WEIGHT AND INSULATION VALUES

SPECIES	DECKING THICKNESS NOMINAL IN.	DECKING WEIGHTS PSF	DECKING ONLY R
Inland Red Cedar	3	4	4.00
	3 STX	5	5.02
	5	7	6.16
Cedar Face IWP/W Fir Core & Back	3	5	3.70
	3 STX	7	4.58
	5	8	5.59
White Fir Idaho White & Ponderosa Pine	3	5	3.58
	3 STX	7	4.47
	5	9	5.48
Douglas Fir	3	6	3.08
	3 STX	8	3.81
	5	11	4.63
Southern Pine	3	7	3.05
	3 STX	9	3.69
	5	12	4.63

NOTES
1. Insulation value may be increased with added rigid insulation.
2. Use of random lengths reduces waste.

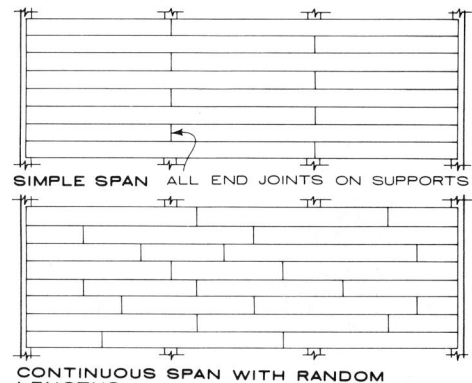

SIMPLE SPAN   ALL END JOINTS ON SUPPORTS

CONTINUOUS SPAN WITH RANDOM LENGTHS

LAMINATED DECK—ALLOWABLE UNIFORMLY DISTRIBUTED TOTAL ROOF LOADS GOVERNED BY DEFLECTION (1)

SPAN IN FEET (2)		SOUTHERN PINE—E1.8 (3) F = 2640				INLAND RED CEDAR—E1.2 (INLAND RED CEDAR FACE AND BACK) F = 1590				PONDEROSA PINE—E1.3 INLAND RED CEDAR—E1.3 (IDAHO WHITE PINE OR WHITE FIR BACK) F = 1590				IDAHO WHITE PINE—E1.5 IDAHO WHITE FIR—E1.5 F = 1850				DOUGLAS FIR/LARCH—E1.8 F = 2640			
		SIMPLE SPAN END-JOINTS OVER SUPPORTS		RANDOM LENGTH CONTINUOUS OVER THREE OR MORE SPANS		SIMPLE SPAN END-JOINTS OVER SUPPORTS		RANDOM LENGTH CONTINUOUS OVER THREE OR MORE SPANS		SIMPLE SPAN END-JOINTS OVER SUPPORTS		RANDOM LENGTH CONTINUOUS OVER THREE OR MORE SPANS		SIMPLE SPAN END-JOINTS OVER SUPPORTS		RANDOM LENGTH CONTINUOUS OVER THREE OR MORE SPANS		SIMPLE SPAN END-JOINTS OVER SUPPORTS		RANDOM LENGTH CONTINUOUS OVER THREE OR MORE SPANS	
		$1/180$ PSF	$1/240$ PSF	$1/180$ PSF	$1/240$ PSF	$1/180$ PSF	$1/240$ PSF	$1/180$ PSF	$1/240$ PSF	$1/180$ PSF	$1/240$ PSF	$1/180$ PSF	$1/240$ PSF	$1/180$ PSF	$1/240$ PSF	$1/180$ PSF	$1/240$ PSF	$1/180$ PSF	$1/240$ PSF	$1/180$ PSF	$1/240$ PSF
3 IN. NOMINAL	8	—	—	—	—	71	54	121	91	77	58	127(F)	98	89	67	151	113	107	80	181	136
	9	80	60	136	101	50	38	85	64	54	41	92	69	63	47	106	80	75	56	127	96
	10	59	44	99	74	37	27	62	46	40	30	67	50	46	34	77	58	55	41	93	70
	11	44	32	74	56	27	21	47	35	30	22	50	38	34	26	58	44	41	31	70	52
	12	33	25	57	42	21	16	36	27	23	17	39	29	26	20	45	34	32	24	54	40
	13	26	20	45	33	17	12	28	21	18	14	31	23	21	16	35	26	25	19	42	32
3 IN. STX	10	125	94	212	159	83	63	141	106	90	68	144(F)	115	104	78	168(F)	132	125	94	212	159
	11	94	70	159	119	63	47	106	79	68	51	115	86	78	59	132(F)	99	94	70	159	119
	12	72	54	122	92	48	36	82	61	52	39	88	66	60	45	102	77	72	54	122	92
	13	57	43	96	72	38	28	64	48	41	31	70	52	47	36	80	60	57	43	96	72
	14	46	34	77	58	30	23	51	39	33	25	56	42	38	28	64	48	46	34	77	58
	15	37	28	63	47	25	19	42	31	27	20	45	34	31	23	52	39	37	28	63	47
	16	31	23	52	39	20	15	34	26	22	17	37	28	25	19	43	32	31	23	52	39
	17	25	19	43	32	17	13	29	22	18	14	31	23	21	16	36	27	25	19	43	32
5 IN. NOMINAL	15	89	66	150	113	51	38	86	64	55	41	93	70	63	47	107	80				
	16	73	55	124	93	42	31	71	53	45	34	76	57	52	39	88	66				
	17	61	46	103	77	35	26	59	44	38	28	64	48	43	33	74	55				
	18	51	38	87	65	29	22	50	37	32	24	54	40	37	27	62	46				
	19	44	33	74	55	25	19	42	32	27	20	46	34	31	23	53	40				
	20	37	28	63	47	21	16	36	27	23	17	39	29	27	20	45	34				
	21	32	24	55	41	18	14	31	23	20	15	34	25	23	17	39	29				

SPAN TABLE NOTES
1. Values followed by an (f) are governed by stress. Allowable loads for floors when governed by deflection are half of those listed in the 1/180 columns.
2. Span loads shown assume compliance to layup rules. Longer spans may require specific lengths differing from the standard shipment.
3. Custom Grade 3 in. and 5 in. Southern Pine deflection values are 83% of the E1.8 values shown. 3 in. STX Southern Pine values are equal to E1.5 Idaho White Pine values except when bending governs.
4. E = Modulus of elasticity psi.
5. Information derived from data supplied by the Potlatch Corporation.

Timothy B. McDonald; Washington, D.C.

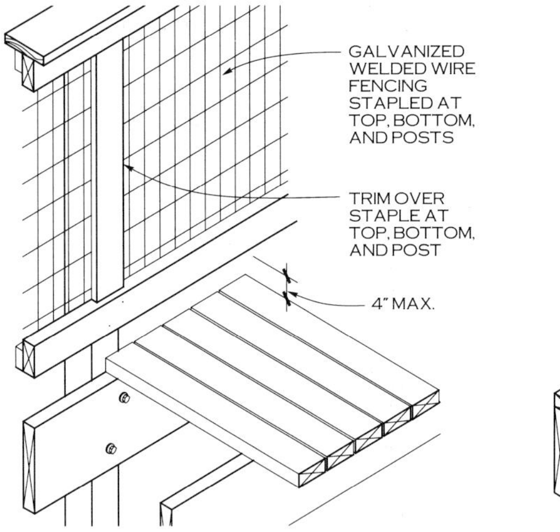

RAILINGS

GALVANIZED WELDED WIRE FENCING STAPLED AT TOP, BOTTOM, AND POSTS

TRIM OVER STAPLE AT TOP, BOTTOM, AND POST

4" MAX.

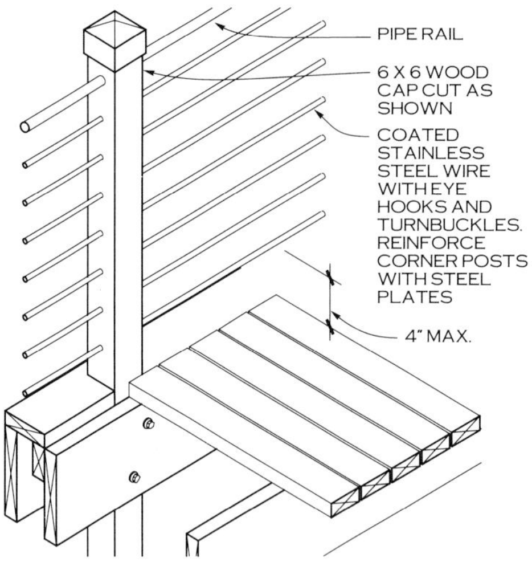

PIPE RAIL

6 X 6 WOOD CAP CUT AS SHOWN

COATED STAINLESS STEEL WIRE WITH EYE HOOKS AND TURNBUCKLES. REINFORCE CORNER POSTS WITH STEEL PLATES

4" MAX.

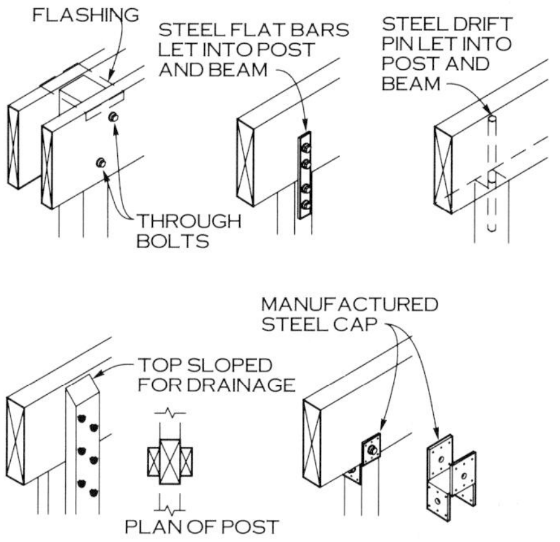

FLASHING

STEEL FLAT BARS LET INTO POST AND BEAM

STEEL DRIFT PIN LET INTO POST AND BEAM

THROUGH BOLTS

MANUFACTURED STEEL CAP

TOP SLOPED FOR DRAINAGE

PLAN OF POST

POST AND BEAM CONNECTIONS

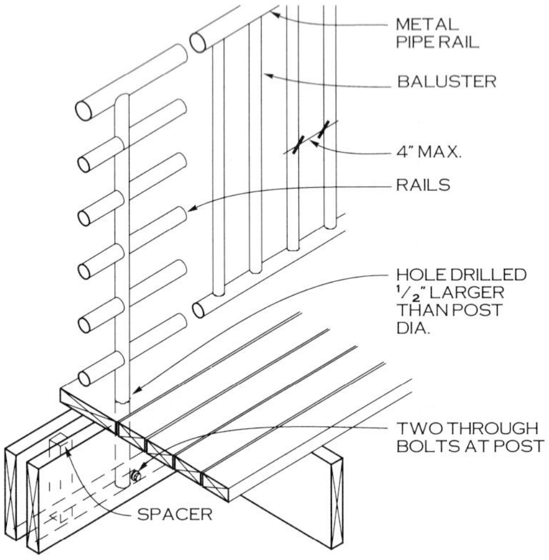

METAL PIPE RAIL

BALUSTER

4" MAX.

RAILS

HOLE DRILLED 1/2" LARGER THAN POST DIA.

TWO THROUGH BOLTS AT POST

SPACER

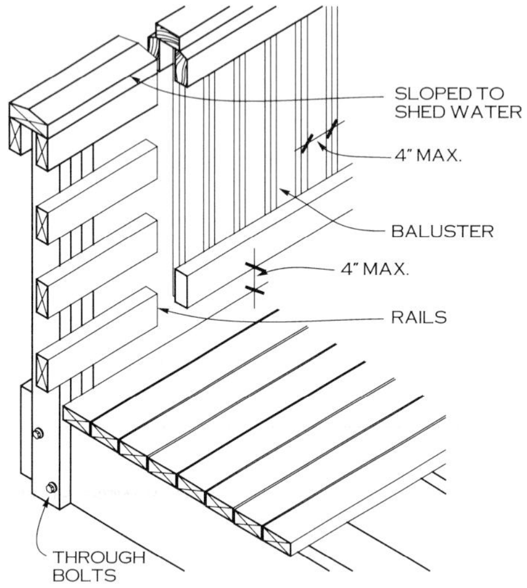

SLOPED TO SHED WATER

4" MAX.

BALUSTER

4" MAX.

RAILS

THROUGH BOLTS

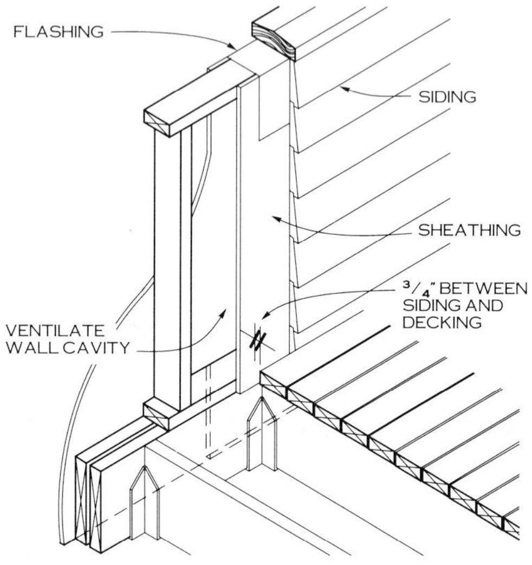

FLASHING

SIDING

SHEATHING

3/4" BETWEEN SIDING AND DECKING

VENTILATE WALL CAVITY

CONNECTIONS AT BUILDING WALL

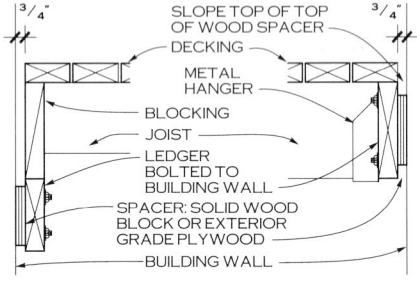

3/4"   3/4"

SLOPE TOP OF TOP OF WOOD SPACER

DECKING

METAL HANGER

BLOCKING

JOIST

LEDGER BOLTED TO BUILDING WALL

SPACER: SOLID WOOD BLOCK OR EXTERIOR GRADE PLYWOOD

BUILDING WALL

DECKING APPLICATIONS

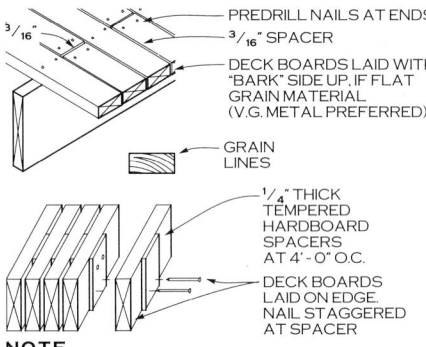

PREDRILL NAILS AT ENDS

3/16" SPACER

DECK BOARDS LAID WITH "BARK" SIDE UP, IF FLAT GRAIN MATERIAL (V.G. METAL PREFERRED)

GRAIN LINES

1/4" THICK TEMPERED HARDBOARD SPACERS AT 4'-0" O.C.

DECK BOARDS LAID ON EDGE. NAIL STAGGERED AT SPACER

NOTE

1/4" spacing not recommended for walking surfaces where high heels are anticipated.

RELATIVE COMPARISON OF VARIOUS QUALITIES OF WOOD USED IN DECK CONSTRUCTION

	DOUGLAS FIR - LARCH[4]	SOUTHERN PINE[4]	HEMLOCK FIR[1,4]	SOFT PINE[2,4]	WESTERN RED CEDAR	REDWOOD	SPRUCE	CYPRESS
Hardness	Fair	Fair	Poor	Poor	Poor	Fair	Poor	Fair
Warp resistance	Fair	Fair	Fair	Good	Good	Good	Fair	Fair
Ease of working	Poor	Fair	Fair	Good	Good	Fair	Fair	Fair
Paint holding	Poor	Poor	Poor	Good	Good	Good	Fair	Good
Stain acceptance[3]	Fair	Fair	Fair	Fair	Good	Good	Fair	Fair
Nail holding	Good	Good	Poor	Poor	Poor	Fair	Fair	Fair
Heartwood decay resistance	Fair	Fair	Poor	Poor	Good	Good	Poor	Good
Proportion of heartwood	Good	Poor	Poor	Fair	Good	Good	Poor	Good
Bending strength	Good	Good	Fair	Poor	Poor	Fair	Fair	Fair
Stiffness	Good	Good	Good	Poor	Poor	Fair	Fair	Fair
Strength as a post	Good	Good	Fair	Poor	Fair	Good	Fair	Fair
Freedom from pitch	Fair	Poor	Good	Fair	Good	Good	Good	Good

NOTES

1. Includes West Coast and eastern hemlocks.
2. Includes western and northeastern pines.
3. Categories refer to semitransparent oil base stain.
4. Use pressure preservative treated material only. All materials below deck surfaces should be pressure treated.

The Bumgardner Architects; Seattle, Washington

WOOD DECKING

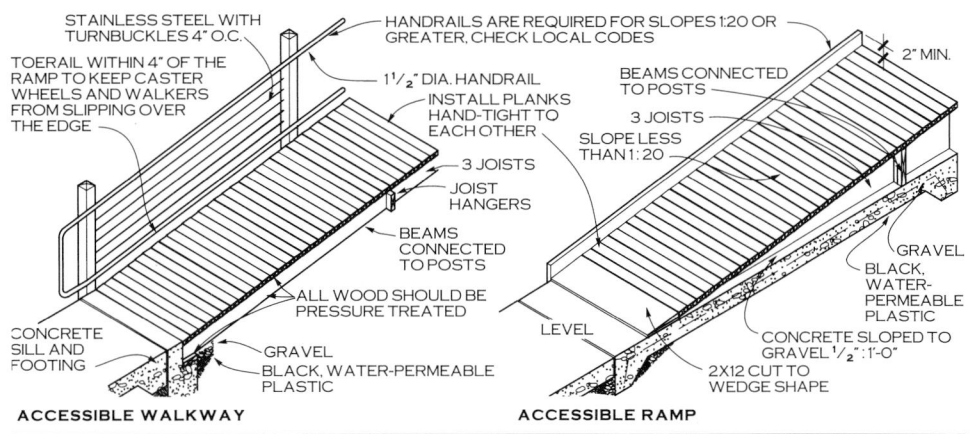

ACCESSIBLE WALKWAY

ACCESSIBLE RAMP

WALKWAYS AND RAMPS

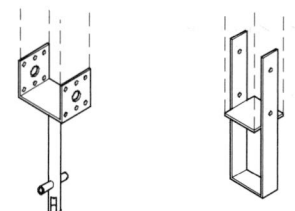

STANDARD MANUFACTURED

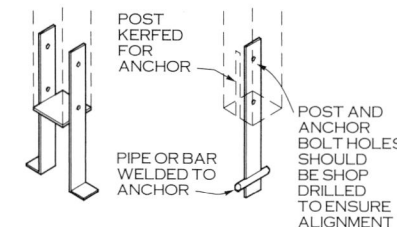

SHOP FABRICATED

LOW DECK EDGES

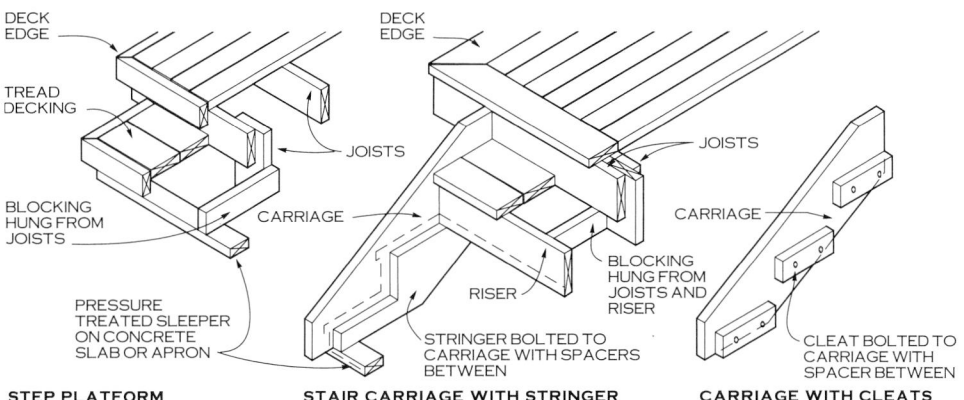

STEP PLATFORM

STAIR CARRIAGE WITH STRINGER

CARRIAGE WITH CLEATS

STEPS AND STAIRS

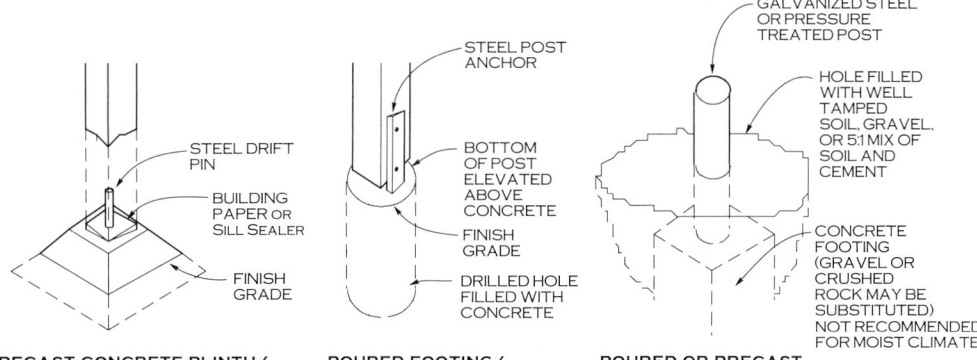

PRECAST CONCRETE PLINTH/ TREATED POST

POURED FOOTING/ TREATED POST

POURED OR PRECAST FOOTING/TREATED POST

POSTS AND FOOTINGS

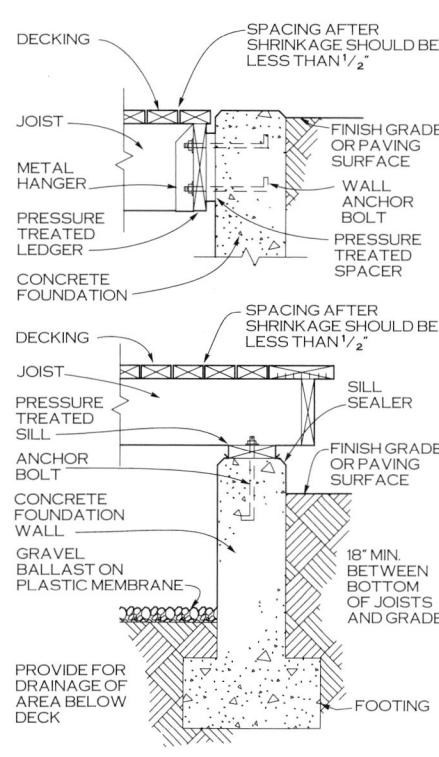

LOW DECK EDGES

FASTENERS

1. Use hot-dipped galvanized fasteners to avoid corrosion and staining.
2. To reduce board splitting by nailing: blunt nail points; predrill ($^3/_4$ of nail diameter); stagger nailing; place nails no closer to edge than one-half of board thickness.
3. Avoid end grain nailing and toenailing if possible.
4. Use flat washers under heads of lag screws and bolts, and under nuts.
5. Hot-dipped galvanized casing nails or stainless steel deck screws are best decking fasteners.
6. Plated ring shank or spiral groove shank nails are suitable for arid climates.

MOISTURE PROTECTION

1. All wood members should be protected from weather by pressure treatment or field application of preservatives, stains, or paints.
2. All wood in direct contact with soil and concrete must be pressure treated.
3. Bottoms of posts on piers should be 6 in. above grade.
4. Sterilize or cover soil with membrane to keep plant growth away from wood members so as to minimize moisture exchange.
5. Treat all ends, cuts, holes, etc. with preservative before placement.
6. Decking and flat trim boards, 2 x 6 and wider, should be kerfed on the underside with $^3/_4$ in. deep saw cuts at 1 in. o.c. to prevent cupping.
7. Avoid horizontal exposure of end grain or provide adequate protection by flashing or sealing. Avoid or minimize joint situations where moisture may be trapped by using spacers and/or flashing, caulking, sealant, or plastic roofing cement.

CONSTRUCTION

1. WOOD SELECTION: Usual requirements are good decay resistance, nonsplintering, fair stiffness, strength, hardness, and warp resistance. Selection varies according to local climate and structure.
2. BRACING: On large decks, or decks where post heights exceed 5 ft, lateral stability should be achieved with horizontal bracing (metal or wood diagonal ties on top or bottom of joists, or diagonal application of decking) in combination with vertical bracing (rigid bolted or gusseted connections at tops of posts, knee bracing, or cross bracing between posts), and/or connection to a braced building wall. Lateral stability should be checked by a structural engineer.

The Bumgardner Architects; Seattle, Washington
Mark J. Mazz, AIA; CEA, Inc.; Hyattsville, Maryland

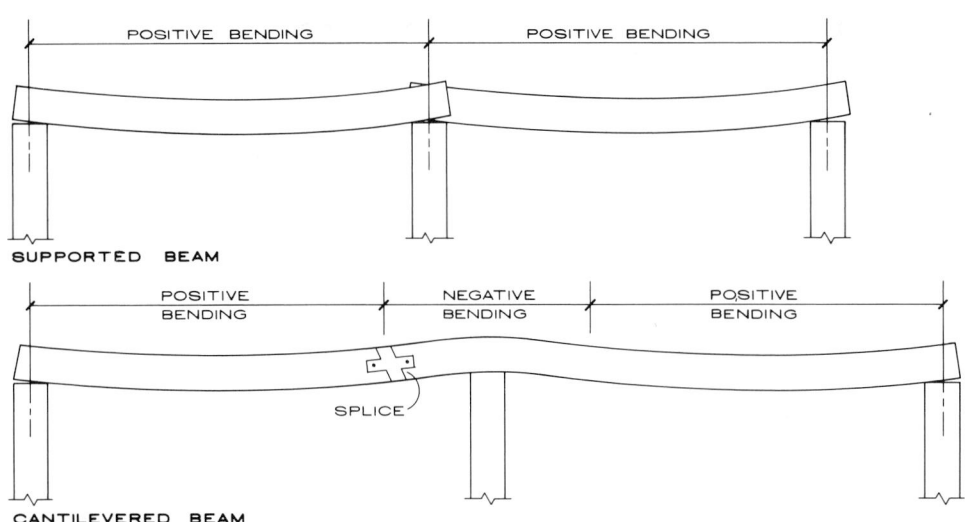

SIMPLE FRAMING: This illustration shows the "positive" or downward bending that occurs in conventional framing with simple spans.

CANTILEVERED FRAMING: This illustration shows the combination of "positive" (downward) and "negative" (upward) bending that occurs with beams spliced at quarterpoint producing supported beam and cantilevered beam. The two types of bending counterbalance each other, which produces more uniform stresses and uses material more efficiently. In-line joists simplify plywood subflooring.

MOMENT SPLICE: Compression stress is taken in bearing on the wood through a steel compression plate. Tension is taken across the splice by means of steel straps and sheer plates. Side plates and straps are used to hold sides and tops of members in position. Shear is taken by shear plates in end grain. Bolts and shear plates are used as design and construction considerations require.

SIMPLE AND CANTILEVERED FRAMING

GROOVED PLANK MOLDED SPLINE / RABBETED PLANK BATTEN INSERT / GROOVED PLANK WITH SPLINE / GROOVED PLANK WITH EXPOSED SPLINE / SQUARE EDGE / TONGUE AND GROOVE

JOINT TYPES IN EXPOSED PLANK CEILINGS

DESIGN TABLE FOR NOMINAL 2 IN. PLANK

REQUIRED VALUES FOR FIBER STRESS IN BENDING (f) AND MODULUS OF ELASTICITY (E) TO SUPPORT SAFELY A LIVE LOAD OF 20, 30, OR 40 LB/SQ FT WITHIN A DEFLECTION LIMITATION OF $\ell/240$, $\ell/300$, OR $\ell/360$.

SPAN (FT)	LIVE LOAD (PSF)	DEFLECTION LIMIT	TYPE A SINGLE SPAN f (PSI)	TYPE A E (PSI)	TYPE B DOUBLE SPAN f (PSI)	TYPE B E (PSI)	TYPE C THREE SPAN f (PSI)	TYPE C E (PSI)	TYPE D COMBINATION SINGLE AND DOUBLE SPAN f (PSI)	TYPE D E (PSI)	TYPE E RANDOM LAYUP f (PSI)	TYPE E E (PSI)
6	20	$\ell/240$	360	576,000	360	239,000	288	305,000	360	408,000	360	442,000
		$\ell/300$	360	720,000	360	299,000	288	381,000	360	509,000	360	553,000
		$\ell/360$	360	864,000	360	359,000	288	457,000	360	611,000	360	664,000
	30	$\ell/240$	480	864,000	480	359,000	384	457,000	480	611,000	480	664,000
		$\ell/300$	480	1,080,000	480	448,000	384	571,000	480	764,000	480	829,000
		$\ell/360$	480	1,296,000	480	538,000	384	685,000	480	917,000	480	995,000
	40	$\ell/240$	600	1,152,000	600	478,000	480	609,000	600	815,000	600	885,000
		$\ell/300$	600	1,440,000	600	598,000	480	762,000	600	1,019,000	600	1,106,000
		$\ell/360$	600	1,728,000	600	717,000	480	914,000	600	1,223,000	600	1,327,000
7	20	$\ell/240$	490	915,000	490	380,000	392	484,000	490	647,000	490	702,000
		$\ell/300$	490	1,143,000	490	475,000	392	605,000	490	809,000	490	878,000
		$\ell/360$	490	1,372,000	490	570,000	392	726,000	490	971,000	490	1,054,000
	30	$\ell/240$	653	1,372,000	653	570,000	522	726,000	653	971,000	653	1,054,000
		$\ell/300$	653	1,715,000	653	712,000	522	907,000	653	1,213,000	653	1,317,000
		$\ell/360$	653	2,058,000	653	854,000	522	1,088,000	653	1,456,000	653	1,581,000
	40	$\ell/240$	817	1,829,000	817	759,000	653	968,000	817	1,294,000	817	1,405,000
		$\ell/300$	817	1,187,000	817	949,000	653	1,209,000	817	1,618,000	817	1,756,000
		$\ell/360$	817	2,744,000	817	1,139,000	653	1,451,000	817	1,941,000	817	2,107,000
8	20	$\ell/240$	640	1,365,000	640	567,000	512	722,000	640	966,000	640	1,049,000
		$\ell/300$	640	1,707,000	640	708,000	512	903,000	640	1,208,000	640	1,311,000
		$\ell/360$	640	2,048,000	640	850,000	512	1,083,000	640	1,449,000	640	1,573,000
	30	$\ell/240$	853	2,048,000	853	850,000	682	1,083,000	853	1,449,000	853	1,573,000
		$\ell/300$	853	2,560,000	853	1,063,000	682	1,345,000	853	1,811,000	853	1,966,000
		$\ell/360$	853	3,072,000	853	1,275,000	682	1,625,000	853	2,174,000	853	2,359,000
	40	$\ell/240$	1,067	2,731,000	1,067	1,134,000	853	1,144,000	1,067	1,932,000	1,067	2,097,000
		$\ell/300$	1,067	3,413,000	1,067	1,417,000	853	1,805,000	1,067	2,145,000	1,067	2,621,000
		$\ell/360$	1,067	4,096,000	1,067	1,700,000	853	2,166,000	1,067	2,898,000	1,067	3,146,000

Timothy B. McDonald; Washington, D.C.

HEAVY TIMBER CONSTRUCTION

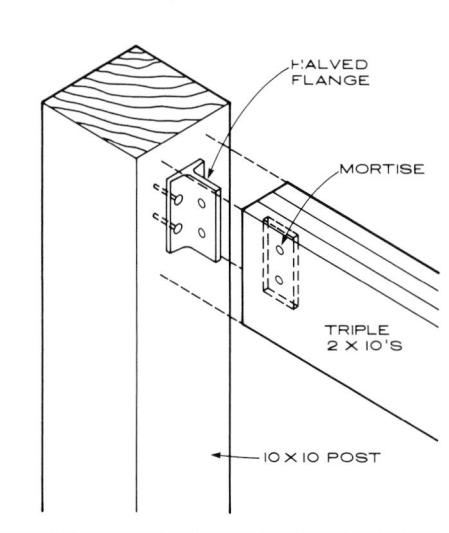

BEAM AND COLUMN CONNECTION

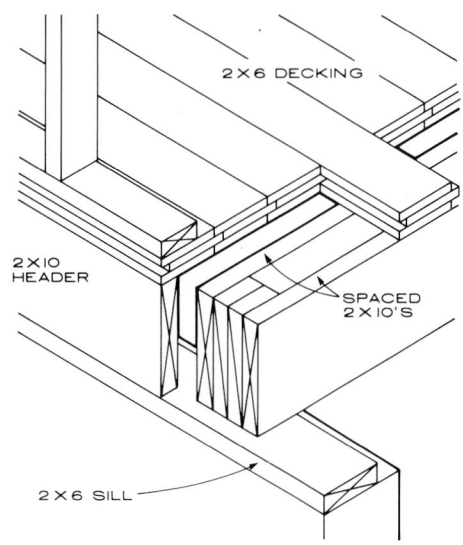

SPACED BEAM AT FOUNDATION

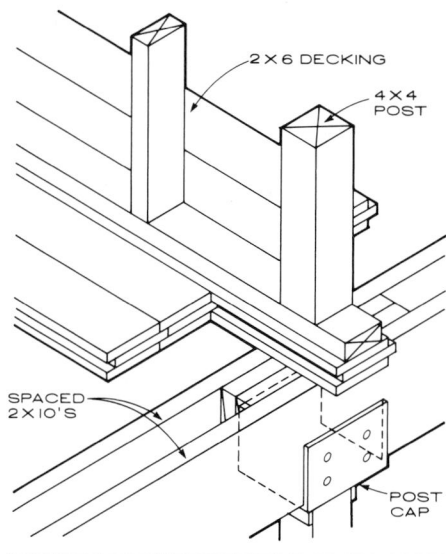

SPACED BEAM BEARING ON INTERIOR COLUMN

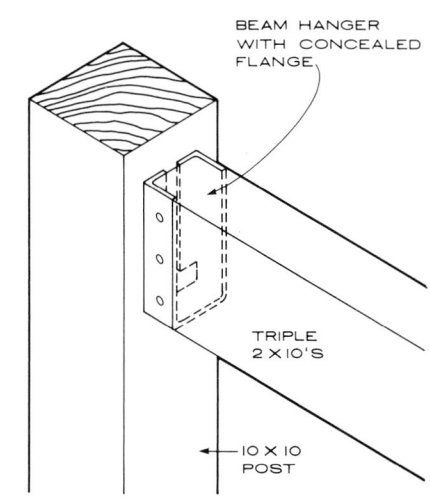

BEAM HANGER CONNECTION

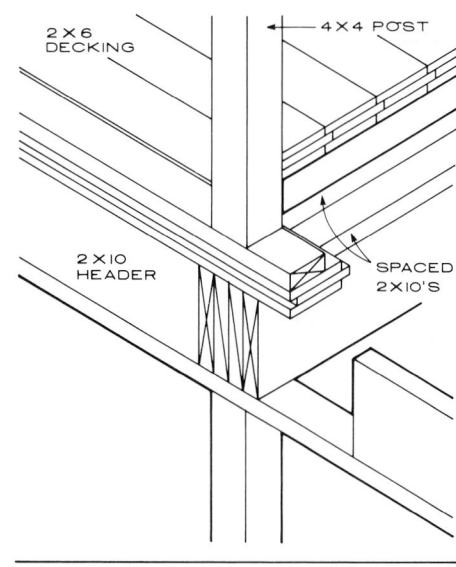

SPACED BEAM BEARING AT EXTERIOR WALL

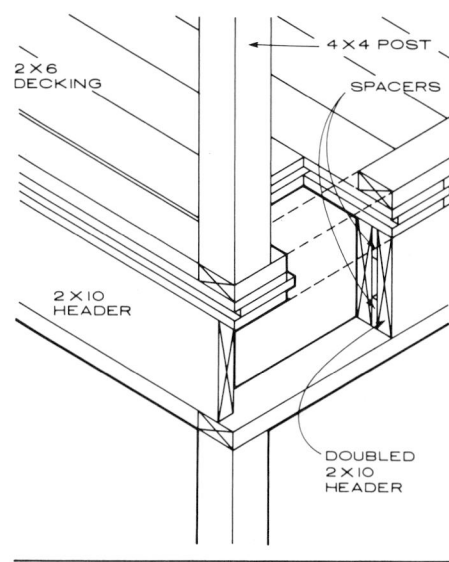

CORNER CONNECTION

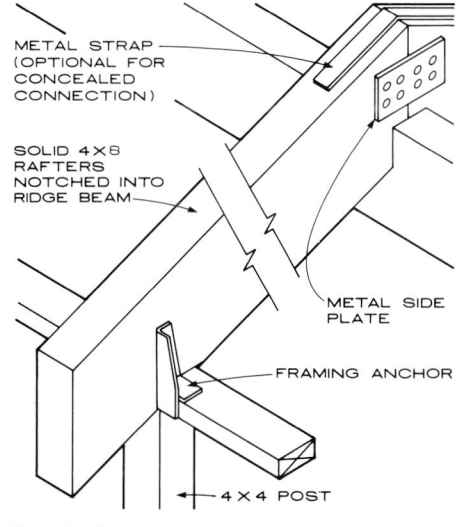

ROOF BEAM AT COLUMN AND RIDGE

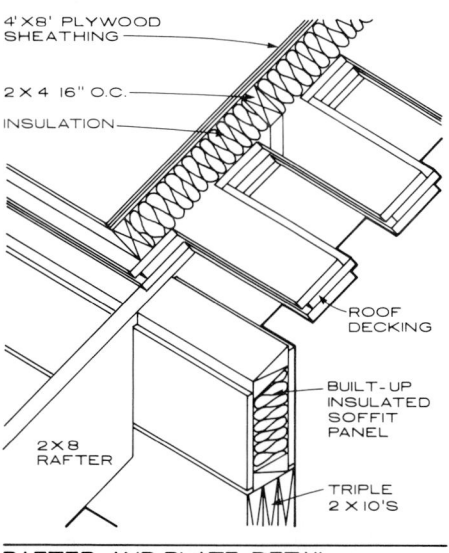

RAFTER AND PLATE DETAIL

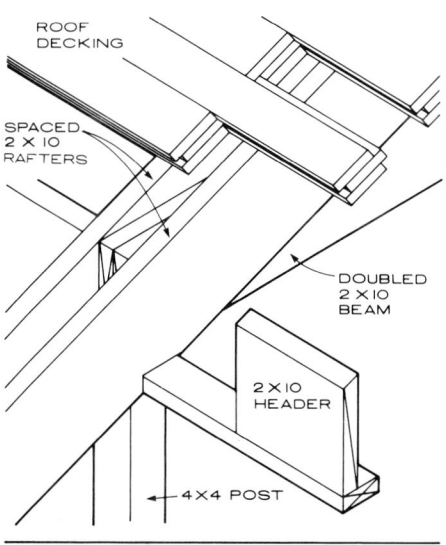

SPACED ROOF BEAM AT EXTERIOR COLUMN

Timothy B. McDonald; Washington, D.C.

HEAVY TIMBER CONSTRUCTION

6

NOTES

1. Pole embedment depth depends on soil, slope and seismic zone.
2. Cross-bracing between poles may be required to resist lateral loads if shallow embedment. Treat all exposed surfaces with approved pressure treatment.
3. Pole notching for major beams can help align beams and walls that otherwise would be out of plumb due to pole warp. Notching improves bearing of major beams but weakens poles.
4. Roofs, walls and floors should be insulated to suit local climatic conditions. Wall and soffit insulation should meet continuously at the joint. Penetration of insulation should be minimal.
5. Various siding types can be used.
6. Dapping is a U.S. carpentry term for cutting wood to receive timber connectors.

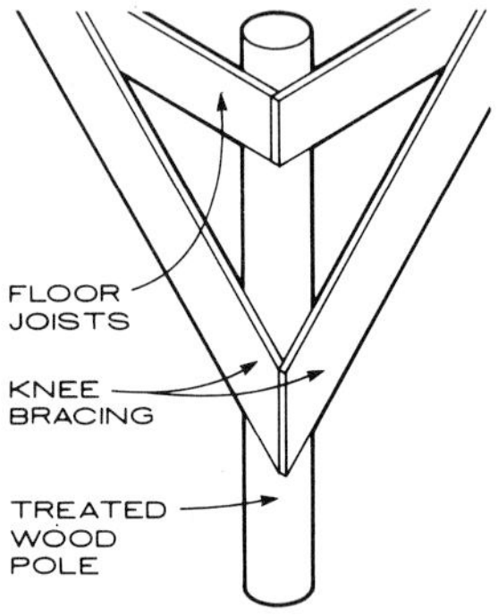

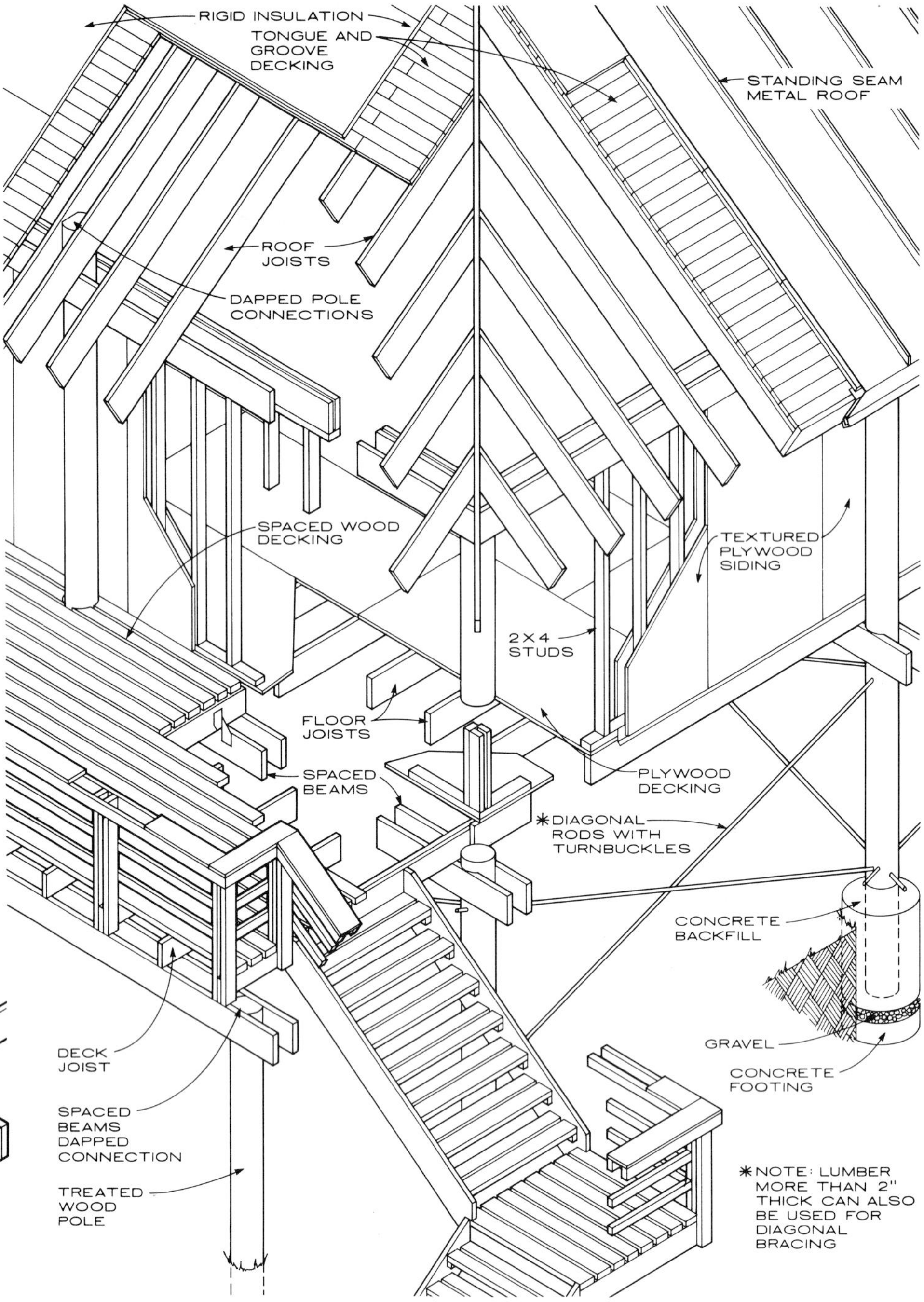

RIGID INSULATION

TONGUE AND GROOVE DECKING

STANDING SEAM METAL ROOF

ROOF JOISTS

DAPPED POLE CONNECTIONS

SPACED WOOD DECKING

TEXTURED PLYWOOD SIDING

2 X 4 STUDS

FLOOR JOISTS

SPACED BEAMS

PLYWOOD DECKING

✳DIAGONAL RODS WITH TURNBUCKLES

CONCRETE BACKFILL

GRAVEL

CONCRETE FOOTING

DECK JOIST

SPACED BEAMS DAPPED CONNECTION

TREATED WOOD POLE

✳NOTE: LUMBER MORE THAN 2" THICK CAN ALSO BE USED FOR DIAGONAL BRACING

FLOOR JOISTS

KNEE BRACING

TREATED WOOD POLE

KNEE BRACING

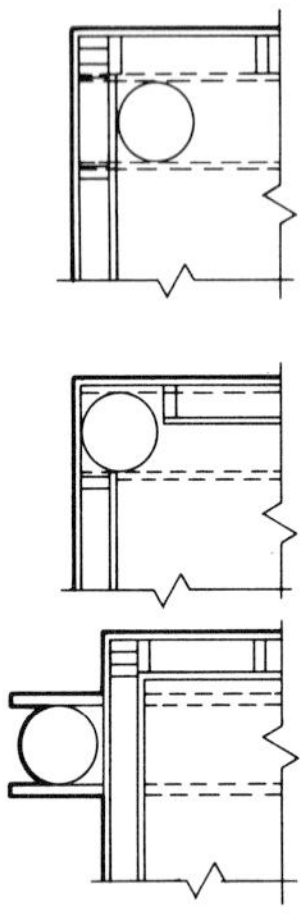

EXTERIOR WALL FRAMING OPTIONS

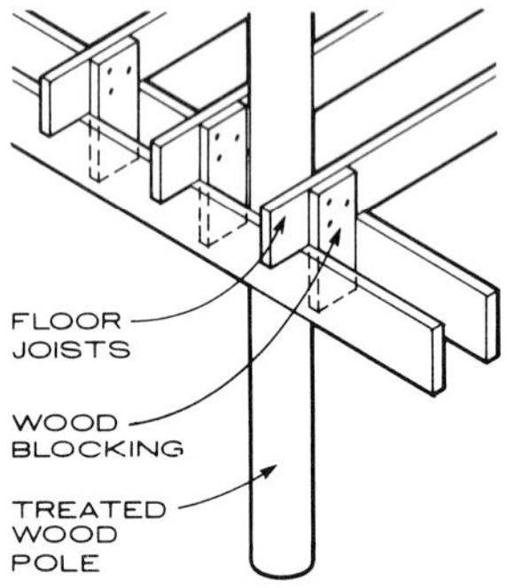

FLOOR JOISTS

WOOD BLOCKING

TREATED WOOD POLE

JOIST ANCHORS

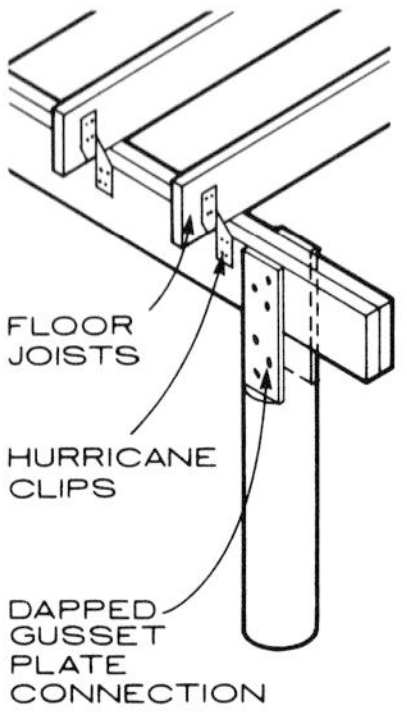

FLOOR JOISTS

HURRICANE CLIPS

DAPPED GUSSET PLATE CONNECTION

JOIST ANCHORS

ISOMETRIC OF POLE HOUSE

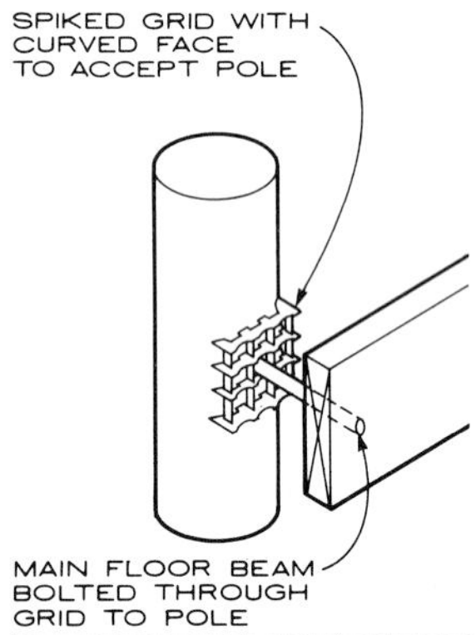

SPIKED GRID WITH CURVED FACE TO ACCEPT POLE

MAIN FLOOR BEAM BOLTED THROUGH GRID TO POLE

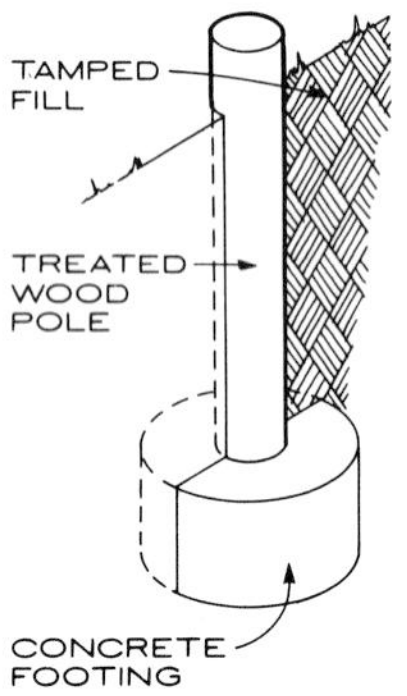

CONCRETE FOOTING

TAMPED FILL

TREATED WOOD POLE

CONCRETE FOOTING

CONCRETE FOOTING

TAMPED FILL

2'-0" MAX.

FROST LINE

12" MIN.

LAG BOLTS   GRAVEL

FOR USE IN TEMPERATE CLIMATES (FROST LINE NO DEEPER THAN 2'-0")

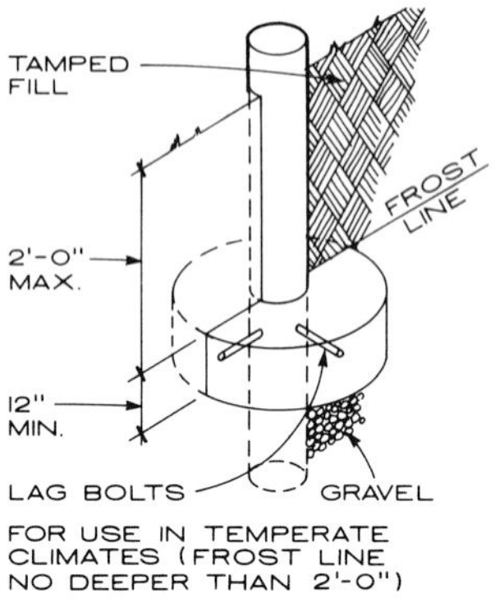

REINFORCED CONCRETE COLLAR

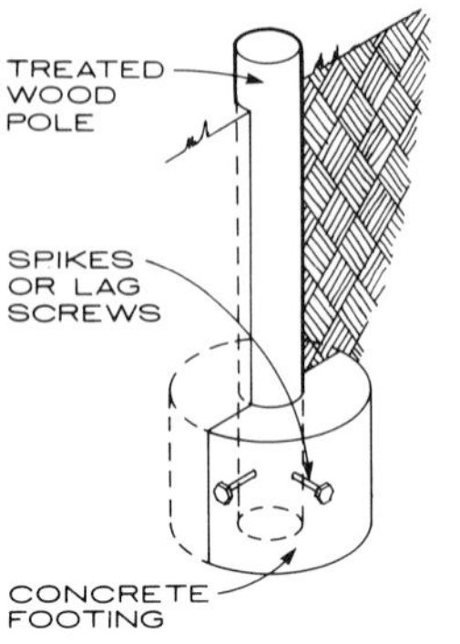

TREATED WOOD POLE

SPIKES OR LAG SCREWS

CONCRETE FOOTING

CONCRETE FOOTING WITH SPIKED ANCHORAGE

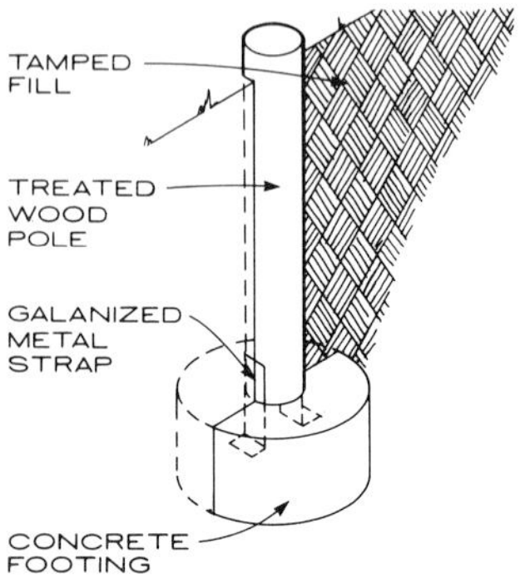

TAMPED FILL

TREATED WOOD POLE

GALANIZED METAL STRAP

CONCRETE FOOTING

CONCRETE FOOTING WITH STRAP ANCHOR

POLE CONSTRUCTION

Timothy B. McDonald; Washington, D.C.

HEAVY TIMBER CONSTRUCTION

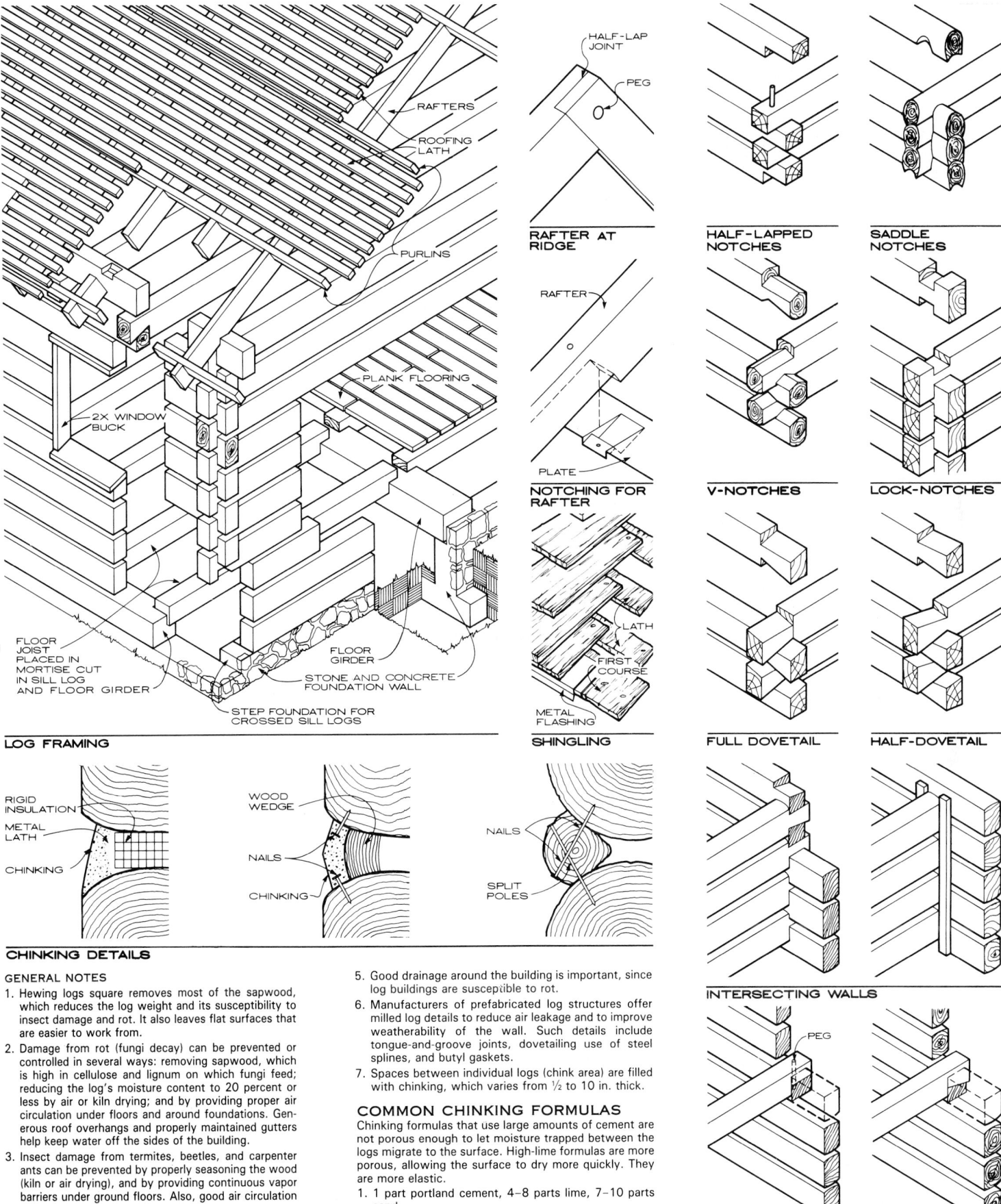

RAFTERS

ROOFING LATH

PURLINS

PLANK FLOORING

2X WINDOW BUCK

FLOOR GIRDER

FLOOR JOIST PLACED IN MORTISE CUT IN SILL LOG AND FLOOR GIRDER

STONE AND CONCRETE FOUNDATION WALL

STEP FOUNDATION FOR CROSSED SILL LOGS

LOG FRAMING

HALF-LAP JOINT

PEG

RAFTER AT RIDGE

RAFTER

PLATE

NOTCHING FOR RAFTER

LATH

FIRST COURSE

METAL FLASHING

SHINGLING

RIGID INSULATION

METAL LATH

CHINKING

WOOD WEDGE

NAILS

CHINKING

NAILS

SPLIT POLES

CHINKING DETAILS

HALF-LAPPED NOTCHES

SADDLE NOTCHES

V-NOTCHES

LOCK-NOTCHES

FULL DOVETAIL

HALF-DOVETAIL

INTERSECTING WALLS

PEG

SECOND FLOOR JOISTS

GENERAL NOTES

1. Hewing logs square removes most of the sapwood, which reduces the log weight and its susceptibility to insect damage and rot. It also leaves flat surfaces that are easier to work from.

2. Damage from rot (fungi decay) can be prevented or controlled in several ways: removing sapwood, which is high in cellulose and lignum on which fungi feed; reducing the log's moisture content to 20 percent or less by air or kiln drying; and by providing proper air circulation under floors and around foundations. Generous roof overhangs and properly maintained gutters help keep water off the sides of the building.

3. Insect damage from termites, beetles, and carpenter ants can be prevented by properly seasoning the wood (kiln or air drying), and by providing continuous vapor barriers under ground floors. Also, good air circulation can help prevent infestations.

4. Exposed interior logs must be coordinated carefully with placement of plumbing, electrical wiring, and mechanical equipment.

5. Good drainage around the building is important, since log buildings are susceptible to rot.

6. Manufacturers of prefabricated log structures offer milled log details to reduce air leakage and to improve weatherability of the wall. Such details include tongue-and-groove joints, dovetailing use of steel splines, and butyl gaskets.

7. Spaces between individual logs (chink area) are filled with chinking, which varies from $\frac{1}{2}$ to 10 in. thick.

COMMON CHINKING FORMULAS

Chinking formulas that use large amounts of cement are not porous enough to let moisture trapped between the logs migrate to the surface. High-lime formulas are more porous, allowing the surface to dry more quickly. They are more elastic.

1. 1 part portland cement, 4–8 parts lime, 7–10 parts sand.

2. $\frac{1}{4}$ part cement, 11 parts lime, 4 parts sand, $\frac{1}{8}$ part dry color, excelsior.

3. 1 part cement, 4 parts lime, 6 parts sand.

Timothy B. McDonald; Washington, D.C.

STRUCTURAL GLUED LAMINATED TIMBER

The term "structural glued laminated timber" refers to an engineered, stress-rated product made of wood laminations bonded with adhesives, with the grain approximately parallel lengthwise. Laminated pieces can be end-joined to form any length, or glued edge-to-edge to make wider pieces, or of bent pieces curved during gluing.

STANDARD DEPTHS

Dimensional lumber surfaced to $1\frac{1}{2}$ in. (38 mm) is used to laminate straight members and members that have a curvature within the bending radius limitations for the species. Boards surfaced to $\frac{3}{4}$ in. (19 mm) are recommended for laminating curved members when bending radius is too short to permit the use of dimension lumber, provided that the bending radius limitations for the species are observed. Other lamination thicknesses may be used to meet special requirements.

STANDARD WIDTHS

Nominal width	in.	3	4	6	8	10	12	14	16
Net finished width	in.	$2\frac{1}{8}$	$3\frac{1}{8}$	$5\frac{1}{8}$	$6\frac{3}{4}$*	$8\frac{3}{4}$*	$10\frac{3}{4}$*	$12\frac{1}{4}$	$14\frac{1}{4}$
	mm	57	79	130	171	222	273	311	362

* 3, 5, $8\frac{1}{2}$, and $10\frac{1}{2}$ in. for southern pine

CAMBER

Camber is curvature (circular or parabolic) made into structural glued laminated beams opposite the anticipated deflection movement. The recommended minimum camber is one and one-half times dead load deflection. After initial dead load deflection and additional plastic deformation (creep) has taken place, this usually will produce a near level floor or roof beam under dead load conditions. Additional camber or slope may insure adequate drainage of roof beams. On long-span roof beams and floor beams of multistory buildings, additional camber may be needed to counter the optical illusion of the beam sagging.

FIRE SAFETY

The self-insulating qualities of heavy timber cause a slow burning. Good structural details, elimination of concealed spaces, and use of vertical fire stops contribute to its fire performance. Heavy timber retains its strength under fire longer than unprotected metals.

Building codes generally classify glued laminated timber as heavy timber construction if certain minimum dimensional requirements are met. Codes also allow for calculation of one-hour fire ratings for exposed glued laminated timbers. See Council of American Building Officials National Evaluation Service Committee Report No. NER-250.

It is not recommended that fire-retardant treatments be applied to glued laminated timber as they do not substantially increase the fire resistance of heavy timber construction. In considering fire-retardant treatments, the reduction of strength related to type and penetration of treatment, the compatibility of treatment and adhesive, the use of special gluing procedures, the difficulty of application, and the effect on wood color and fabrication procedures must be investigated.

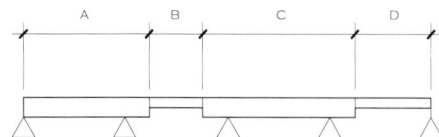

A—SINGLE CANTILEVER
B—SUSPENDED
C—DOUBLE CANTILEVER
D—SINGLE END SUSPENDED

CANTILEVERED AND CONTINUOUS SPAN

Cantilever beam systems may be composed of any of the various types and combinations of beams shown above. Cantilever systems generally permit longer spans or larger loads per size member than do simple span systems.

For economy, the negative bending moment at the support of a cantilevered beam should be equal in magnitude to the positive moment.

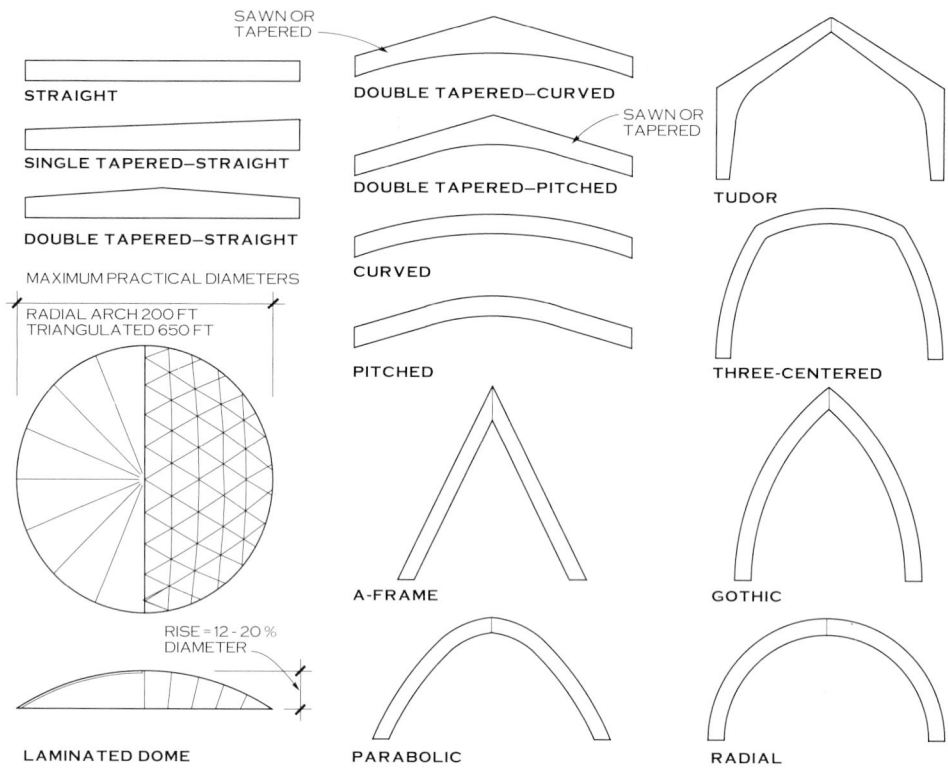

STRUCTURAL GLUED LAMINATED TIMBER SHAPES

(Shapes shown: STRAIGHT, SINGLE TAPERED—STRAIGHT, DOUBLE TAPERED—STRAIGHT, MAXIMUM PRACTICAL DIAMETERS, RADIAL ARCH 200 FT, TRIANGULATED 650 FT, RISE = 12 - 20% DIAMETER, LAMINATED DOME, DOUBLE TAPERED—CURVED, DOUBLE TAPERED—PITCHED, CURVED, PITCHED, A-FRAME, PARABOLIC, TUDOR, THREE-CENTERED, GOTHIC, RADIAL, SAWN OR TAPERED)

NOTES ON SHAPES

1. Beam names describe top and bottom surfaces of the beam. Sloped or pitched surfaces should be used on the tension side of the beam.
2. The three hinged arches and frames shown above produce horizontal reactions requiring horizontal ties or modified foundations.
3. The triangulated and the radial arch are the two basic types of stuctural glued laminated wood dome systems available. Both systems require a tension ring at the dome spring line to convert axial thrusts to vertical loads. Consideration must be given to the perimeter bond beam design since wind forces will produce loads in this member. The length of main members of the radil arch system, which must span a distance greater than half the dome diameter, limit the maximum practical dome diameter. The far smaller members of the triangulated dome result in the greater diameters. The triangulated system can be designed for five or more segments with an equal number of peripheral supports at each segment.
4. More complicated shapes may be fabricated. Contact the American Institute of Timber Construction (AITC) and the American Plywood Association (APA).

CONNECTION DESIGN

The design of connections for glued laminated timbers is similar to the design of connections for sawn lumber. Since glued laminated timbers are much larger than sawn lumber and the loads transferred also are larger, the effect of increased size should be taken into account in the design of connections. In addition to being designed for strength to transfer loads, connections also should be designed to avoid splitting of the member and to accommodate swelling and shrinking of the wood.

BEAM END CONNECTIONS

Beam end connections should be designed to carry both induced horizontal and vertical loads. Bolts or fastenings at the end of the beam should be located toward the bottom of the beam so that the effect of shrinkage between the bottom of the beam and the fastening is mimimized. Bolts or connectors located near or above the beam's neutral axis should not be used on large glued laminated beams or girders since the concentration of the tension perpendicular to grain due to restraint of shrinkage, and shear stresses acting at fasteners located in these beam areas tend to cause splitting of the member.

SUSPENDED LOADS

In cases where it is not possible for the suspending system to be carried on top of the beam, it is good practice to place the fastener above the neutral axis, particularly when other than light loading is involved or when a number of loads are to be suspended from the member. For heavy loads, a saddle detail placing loads directly on top of the beam is recommended.

Very light loads may be suspended near the bottom of a glued laminated timber. The distance above the beam bottom must exceed the specified edge distance of the fastener used.

PURLIN TO BEAM CONNECTIONS

The preferred purlin to beam connection method is to transfer the end reaction by bearing perpendicular to grain in a saddle type connection extending over the beam top.

When the end reactio of the beam or purlin is relatively small, the hanger can be fastened to the face of the girder. The bolts or connectors in the main carrying beam or girder should be placed above the neutral axis of the member, and in the supported member should be place near the bottom to avoid potential splitting.

SPLICE CONNECTIONS

At beam splice connections occurring over columns, it is important to allow for movement in the upper portions of the beam due to end rotation. Slotted connections will help to reduce the problem by allowing for some beam moavement.

CONCEALED AND PARTIALLY CONCEALED PURLIN HANGERS

Partially concealed purlin hangers are used for normal loads. Concealed hangers are appropriate for relatively light loads, as well as connections where the support plate at the base is notched into the beam, should be designed as notched beam reactions.

It is recommended that the support for the purlin be close to the bottom of the member to utilize the maximum effective area for shear. End fastenings should not include rows of bolts or other fasteners perpendicular to the grain. Glued laminated timbers, although relatively dry at the time of manufacture, may shrink when the members reach equilibrium moisture content in place. This may cause tension perpendicular to the grain and result in splitting.

Roger W. Kipp, AIA; Thomas Hodne Architects, Inc.; Minneapolis, Minnesota

ALLOWABLE UNIT STRESS RANGES FOR STRUCTURAL GLUED LAMINATED TIMBER [2] —NORMAL DURATION OF LOADING

SPECIES	EXTREME FIBER IN BENDING[3]	TENSION PARALLEL TO GRAIN	COMPRESSION PARALLEL TO GRAIN	HORIZONTAL SHEAR	COMPRESSION PERPENDICULAR TO GRAIN	MODULUS OF ELASTICITY
DRY CONDITIONS OF USE—MOISTURE CONTENT IN SERVICE LESS THAN 16%						
Douglas fir - larch	1600 TO 2400	700 TO 1300	875 TO 1750	80-165	560 TO 650	1.5 TO 1.9
Hemlock fir	1600 TO 2400	825 TO 1150	825 TO 1550	155	375 TO 500	1.4 TO 1.8
Southern pine	1600 TO 2600	650 TO 1250	950 TO 1750	90-200	560 TO 650	1.3 TO 1.9
California redwood	1600	900	1400	125	315	1.1
WET CONDITIONS OF USE FACTORS—MOISTURE CONTENT IN SERVICE 16% OR MORE (REQUIRES WET-USE ADHESIVES)						
	0.8	0.8	0.73	0.875	0.53	0.833

NOTES

1. Multiply dry-condition-of-use stress ranges by the above factors for corresponding wet-conditions-of-use value.
2. Values given are for members loaded perpendicular to wide faces of laminations. For ranges of allowable stresses for members loaded primarily as axial members or loaded parallel to the wide face of laminations, see current American Institute of Timber Construction Publication AITC 117–Design (Table 2).
3. Values shown are for the tension zones of the member.

LAMINATED FLOOR, ROOF BEAM, AND PURLIN DESIGN CHART
TYPICAL SINGLE-SPAN, SIMPLY SUPPORTED, GLUED LAMINATED BEAMS (MEMBER SIZES IN IN.)

SPAN (FT)	SPACING (FT)	TOTAL LOAD CARRYING CAPACITY (PSI)—ROOF						FLOOR BEAMS
		30 PSF	35 PSF	40 PSF	45 PSF	50 PSF	55 PSF	50 PSF
12	6	3 1/8 x 7 1/2	3 1/8 x 7 1/2	3 1/8 x 7 1/2	3 1/8 x 7 1/2	3 1/8 x 7 1/2	3 1/8 x 7 1/2	3 1/8 x 9
	8	3 1/8 x 7 1/2	3 1/8 x 7 1/2	3 1/8 x 7 1/2	3 1/8 x 9	3 1/8 x 9	3 1/8 x 9	3 1/8 x 10 1/2
	10	3 1/8 x 7 1/2	3 1/8 x 9	3 1/8 x 9	3 1/8 x 9	3 1/8 x 9	3 1/8 x 10 1/2	3 1/8 x 10 1/2
	12	3 1/8 x 9	3 1/8 x 9	3 1/8 x 9	3 1/8 x 9	3 1/8 x 10 1/2	3 1/8 x 10 1/2	3 1/8 x 12
16	8	3 1/8 x 9	3 1/8 x 10 1/2	3 1/8 x 10 1/2	3 1/8 x 10 1/2	3 1/8 x 12	3 1/8 x 12	3 1/8 x 13 1/2
	12	3 1/8 x 10 1/2	3 1/8 x 12	3 1/8 x 12	3 1/8 x 12	3 1/8 x 13 1/2	3 1/8 x 13 1/2	3 1/8 x 15
	14	3 1/8 x 12	3 1/8 x 12	3 1/8 x 13 1/2	3 1/8 x 13 1/2	3 1/8 x 15	3 1/8 x 15	3 1/8 x 15
	16	3 1/8 x 12	3 1/8 x 13 1/2	3 1/8 x 13 1/2	3 1/8 x 15	3 1/8 x 15	3 1/8 x 16 1/2	3 1/8 x 16 1/2
20	8	3 1/8 x 12	3 1/8 x 12	3 1/8 x 13 1/2	3 1/8 x 13 1/2	3 1/8 x 13 1/2	3 1/8 x 15	3 1/8 x 16 1/2
	12	3 1/8 x 13 1/2	3 1/8 x 13 1/2	3 1/8 x 15	3 1/8 x 15	3 1/8 x 16 1/2	5 1/8 x 15	5 1/8 x 15
	16	3 1/8 x 15	3 1/8 x 16 1/2	3 1/8 x 16 1/2	3 1/8 x 18	5 1/8 x 15	5 1/8 x 16 1/2	5 1/8 x 16 1/2
	20	3 1/8 x 16 1/2	3 1/8 x 18	5 1/8 x 15	5 1/8 x 16 1/2	5 1/8 x 16 1/2	5 1/8 x 18	5 1/8 x 18
24	8	3 1/8 x 13 1/2	3 1/8 x 15	3 1/8 x 15	3 1/8 x 16 1/2	3 1/8 x 16 1/2	3 1/8 x 16 1/2	5 1/8 x 16 1/2
	12	3 1/8 x 16 1/2	3 1/8 x 16 1/2	3 1/8 x 18	5 1/8 x 15	5 1/8 x 16 1/2	5 1/8 x 16 1/2	5 1/8 x 18
	16	3 1/8 x 18	5 1/8 x 16 1/2	5 1/8 x 16 1/2	5 1/8 x 18	5 1/8 x 18	5 1/8 x 19 1/2	5 1/8 x 21
	20	5 1/8 x 16 1/2	5 1/8 x 16 1/2	5 1/8 x 18	5 1/8 x 19 1/2	5 1/8 x 21	5 1/8 x 21	5 1/8 x 22 1/2
28	6	3 1/8 x 16 1/2	3 1/8 x 16 1/2	3 1/8 x 18	3 1/8 x 18	5 1/8 x 16 1/2	5 1/8 x 16 1/2	5 1/8 x 19 1/2
	8	3 1/8 x 18	5 1/8 x 16 1/2	5 1/8 x 18	5 1/8 x 18	5 1/8 x 18	5 1/8 x 19 1/2	5 1/8 x 21
	10	5 1/8 x 18	5 1/8 x 18	5 1/8 x 19 1/2	5 1/8 x 21	5 1/8 x 19 1/2	5 1/8 x 22 1/2	5 1/8 x 24
	12	5 1/8 x 18	5 1/8 x 19 1/2	5 1/8 x 21	5 1/8 x 22 1/2	5 1/8 x 21	5 1/8 x 25 1/2	5 1/8 x 25 1/2
32	8	3 1/8 x 18	5 1/8 x 16 1/2	5 1/8 x 18	5 1/8 x 18	5 1/8 x 18	5 1/8 x 19 1/2	5 1/8 x 21
	12	5 1/8 x 18	5 1/8 x 19 1/2	5 1/8 x 19 1/2	5 1/8 x 21	5 1/8 x 21	5 1/8 x 22 1/2	5 1/8 x 24
	16	5 1/8 x 19 1/2	5 1/8 x 21	5 1/8 x 22 1/2	5 1/8 x 24	5 1/8 x 25 1/2	5 1/8 x 25 1/2	5 1/8 x 27
	20	5 1/8 x 21	5 1/8 x 22 1/2	5 1/8 x 25 1/2	5 1/8 x 27	5 1/8 x 28 1/2	5 1/8 x 30	6 3/4 x 27
40	12	5 1/8 x 22 1/2	5 1/8 x 24	5 1/8 x 24	5 1/8 x 25 1/2	5 1/8 x 27	6 3/4 x 25 1/2	6 3/4 x 28 1/2
	16	5 1/8 x 24	5 1/8 x 27	5 1/8 x 28 1/2	5 1/8 x 30	6 3/4 x 28 1/2	6 3/4 x 28 1/2	6 3/4 x 31 1/2
	20	5 1/8 x 27	5 1/8 x 30	6 3/4 x 28 1/2	6 3/4 x 30	6 3/4 x 31 1/2	6 3/4 x 33	6 3/4 x 33
	24	5 1/8 x 30	6 3/4 x 28 1/2	6 3/4 x 30	6 3/4 x 33	6 3/4 x 34 1/2	6 3/4 x 36	6 3/4 x 37 1/2
48	12	5 1/8 x 27	5 1/8 x 28 1/2	5 1/8 x 30	6 3/4 x 28 1/2	6 3/4 x 28 1/2	6 3/4 x 30	6 3/4 x 33
	16	5 1/8 x 30	6 3/4 x 28 1/2	6 3/4 x 30	6 3/4 x 31 1/2	6 3/4 x 34 1/2	6 3/4 x 36	6 3/4 x 37 1/2
	20	6 3/4 x 28 1/2	6 3/4 x 31 1/2	6 3/4 x 34 1/2	6 3/4 x 36	8 3/4 x 33	8 3/4 x 36	8 3/4 x 36
	24	6 3/4 x 31 1/2	6 3/4 x 34 1/2	8 3/4 x 33	8 3/4 x 34 1/2	8 3/4 x 37 1/2	8 3/4 x 39	8 3/4 x 40 1/2

NOTES

1. Total load carrying weight capacity includes beam weight. Floor beams are designed for uniform loads of 40 psf live load and 10 psf dead load.
2. Allowable stresses: F_B = 2,400 psi (modified volume factor), F_v = 165 psi, E = 1,800,000 psi.
3. Deflection limits: roof = $1/180$, floor = $1/360$
4. Values are for preliminary design purposes only. For complete information see the American Institute of Timber Construction Timber Construction Manual.
5. AITC tables extend to members up to 40 feet in span. American Plywood Association (APA) tables extend up to 48 feet in span. The design of members of far greater span is possible using good engineering practice.

APPEARANCE GRADES

Structural glued laminated timber is produced in three appearance grades that do not modify design stresses, fabrication controls, grades of lumber used, or other provisions of the applicable standards. A textured (rough sawn) surface may be called for instead of the surfacing described. In all grades, laminations will possess the natural growth characteristics of the lumber grade.

INDUSTRIAL APPEARANCE GRADE

Void filling on lamination edges is not required. The wide face of laminations exposed to view will be free of loose knots and open knotholes. Edge joints on the wide face will not be filled. Members will be surfaced on two sides only, an occasional miss being permitted.

ARCHITECTURAL APPEARANCE GRADE

On exposed surfaces, knotholes and other voids wider than 3/4 in. (19 mm) will be dressed with clear wood inserts or a wood-tone colored filler. Inserts will be selected for similarity of the grain and color to the adjacent wood. The wide face of laminations exposed to view will be free of loose knots and open knotholes; all voids greater than 1/16 in. (2 mm) wide in edge joints on this face will be filled. Exposed faces must be surface smooth. Misses are not permitted. The corners on the wide face of laminations exposed to view will be eased. The current practice for eased edges is for a radius between 1/8 in. (3 mm) and 1/2 in. (13 mm).

PREMIUM APPEARANCE GRADE

Similar to architectural grade except that all knotholes and other voids on exposed surfaces will be replaced with wood inserts or a wood-tone colored filler. Remaining knots will be limited in size to 20% of the net face width of the lamination, with no more than two maximum size knots occurring in a 6 ft (1.8 m) length.

FINISHES

Glued laminated timber finishes include sealers, stains, and paints.

End sealers retard moisture transmission and minimize checking and normally are applied to the ends of all members.

Two types of sealers protect against soiling, control grain raising, minimize checking, and serve as a moisture retardant. Penetrating sealers provide limited protection and are used when the final finish requires staining or a natural finish. Primer and sealer coats provide maximum protection by sealing the surface of the wood but should not be specified for a natural or stained final finish. Wood color is modified by any sealer application; therefore, wood sealers followed by staining will look different from stained, untreated wood.

Roger W. Kipp, AIA; Thomas Hodne Architects, Inc.; Minneapolis, Minnesota

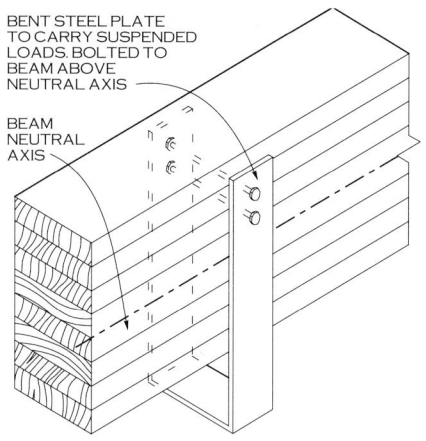

NOTE

Very light loads may be placed near bottom of beam; however, the heavier the load the higher on the beam the suspension points should be located.

BENT STEEL PLATE TO CARRY SUSPENDED LOADS. BOLTED TO BEAM ABOVE NEUTRAL AXIS

BEAM NEUTRAL AXIS

SUSPENDED LOAD—BENT PLATE ATTACHED TO SIDE

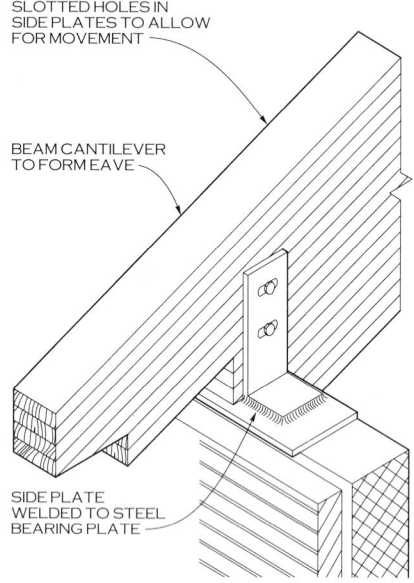

SLOTTED HOLES IN SIDE PLATES TO ALLOW FOR MOVEMENT

BEAM CANTILEVER TO FORM EAVE

SIDE PLATE WELDED TO STEEL BEARING PLATE

RAFTER TO BEARING WALL

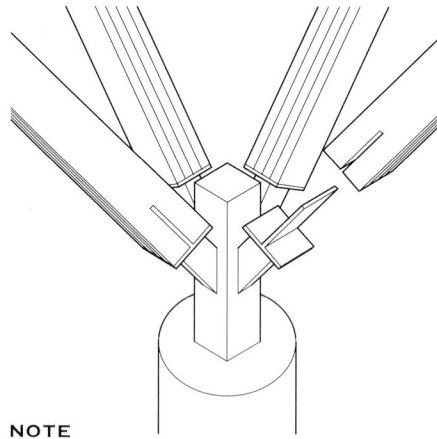

NOTE

The detail above is just one of a large variety of special connections and connection assemblies possible using structural glued laminated timber. It is critical that connections be designed carefully in accordance with good engineering practice.

SPECIAL CONNECTION

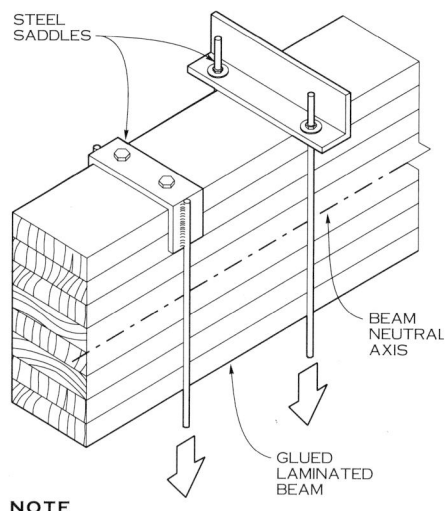

STEEL SADDLES

BEAM NEUTRAL AXIS

GLUED LAMINATED BEAM

NOTE

This detail is recommended for use with heavy loads.

SUSPENDED LOAD —SADDLE CONDITION

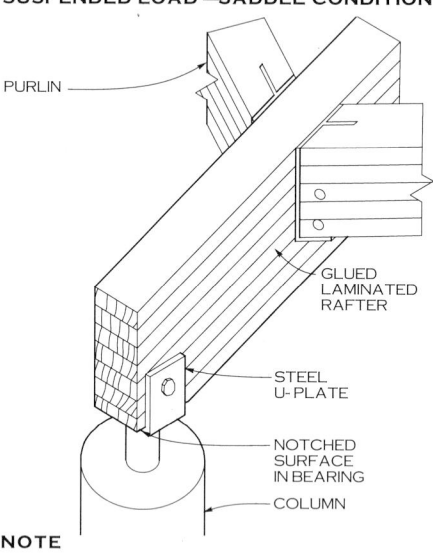

PURLIN

GLUED LAMINATED RAFTER

STEEL U-PLATE

NOTCHED SURFACE IN BEARING

COLUMN

NOTE

An abrupt notch in the end of a wood member reduces the effective shear strength of the member and may permit a more rapid migration of moisture in the lower portion of the member causing potential splitting. The shear strength of the end of the member is reduced and the exposed end grain may also result in splitting because of drying. At inclined beams, the taper cut should be loaded in bearing.

NOTCHED BEARING CONDITION

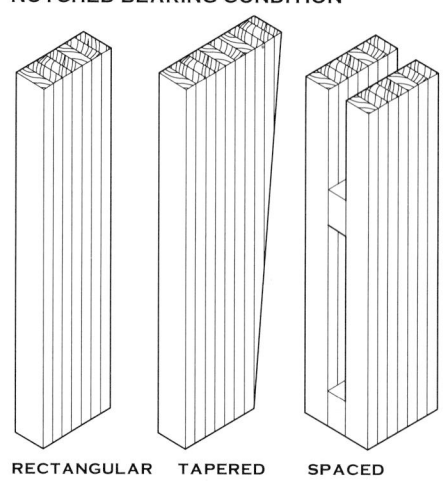

RECTANGULAR   TAPERED   SPACED

GLUED LAMINATED COLUMNS

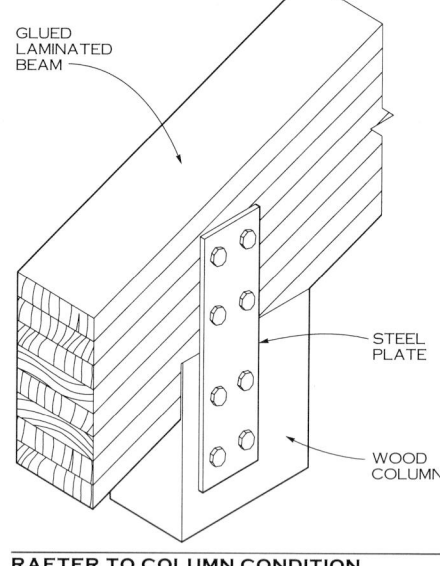

GLUED LAMINATED BEAM

STEEL PLATE

WOOD COLUMN

RAFTER TO COLUMN CONDITION

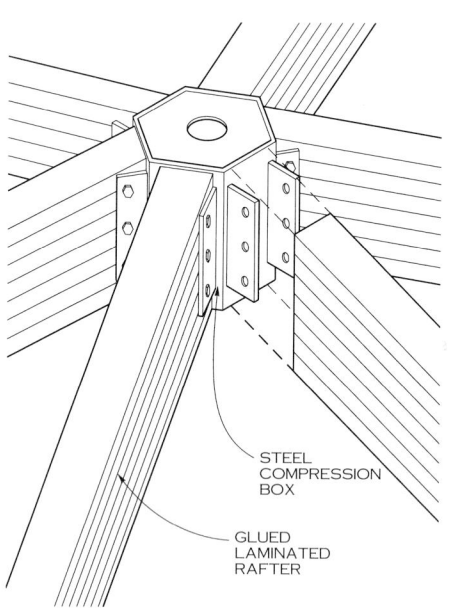

STEEL COMPRESSION BOX

GLUED LAMINATED RAFTER

STEEL COMPRESSION BOX

CONNECTION DESIGN

The design of connections for glued laminated timber and sawn timber is similar. Glued laminated timbers and their loads, however, often are much larger than sawn lumber, so the effect of increased size should be taken into account in the design.

Used to add strength to transfer loads, connections should be designed to avoid splitting and to accommodate swelling and shrinking.

GLUED LAMINATED COLUMNS

Structural glued laminated timber columns offer higher allowable stresses, controlled appearance, and the ability to fabricate variable sections. For simple rectangular columns, the slenderness ratio (the ratio of the unsupported length between points of lateral support to the least column dimension) may not exceed 50. The least dimension for tapered columns is the sum of the smaller dimension and one-third the difference between the smaller and greater dimensions. Spaced columns consist of two or more members with longitudinal axes parallel, separated at the ends and at the midpoint by blocking, and joined at the ends by shear fastenings. The members act together to carry the total column load; because of the end fixity developed, a greater slenderness ratio than allowed for solid columns is permitted.

Roger W. Kipp, AIA; Thomas Hodne Architects, Inc.; Minneapolis, Minnesota

 GLUED-LAMINATED CONSTRUCTION

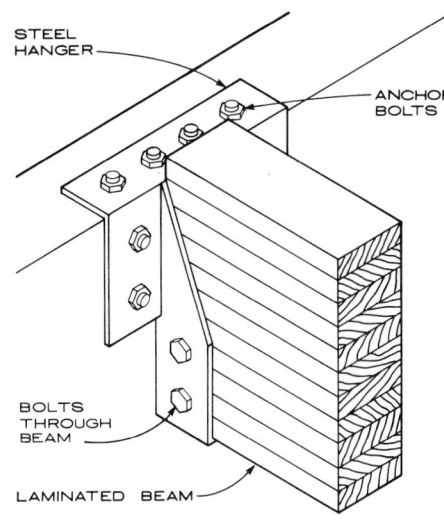

STEEL HANGER

ANCHOR BOLTS

BOLTS THROUGH BEAM

LAMINATED BEAM

BEAM HANGER

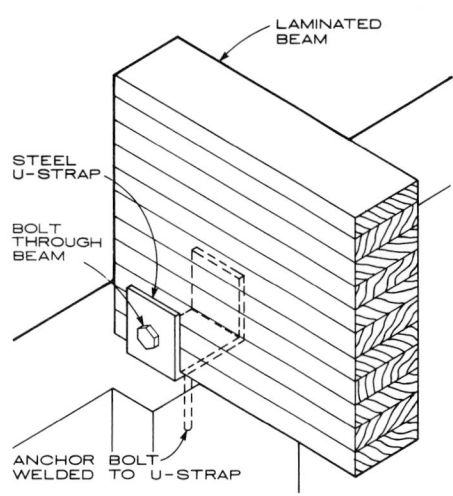

LAMINATED BEAM

STEEL U-STRAP

BOLT THROUGH BEAM

ANCHOR BOLT WELDED TO U-STRAP

BEAM ANCHOR

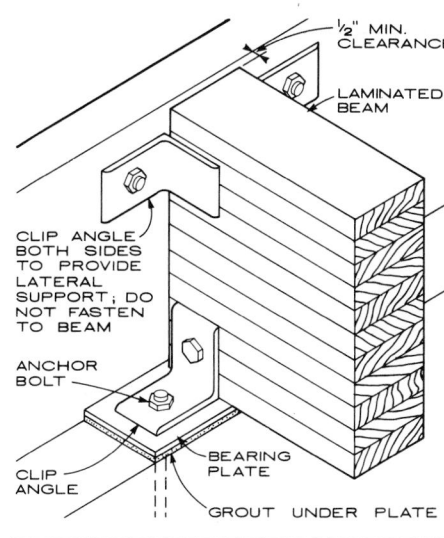

½" MIN. CLEARANCE

LAMINATED BEAM

CLIP ANGLE BOTH SIDES TO PROVIDE LATERAL SUPPORT; DO NOT FASTEN TO BEAM

ANCHOR BOLT

CLIP ANGLE

BEARING PLATE

GROUT UNDER PLATE

BEAM ANCHOR

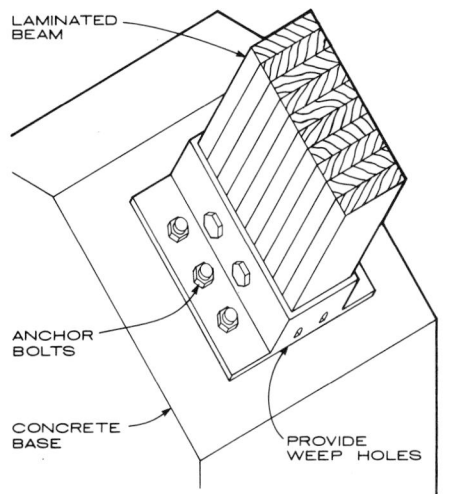

LAMINATED BEAM

ANCHOR BOLTS

CONCRETE BASE

PROVIDE WEEP HOLES

FIXED ARCH ANCHORAGE

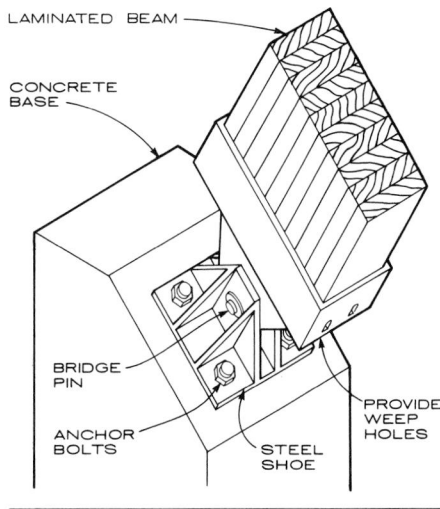

LAMINATED BEAM

CONCRETE BASE

BRIDGE PIN

ANCHOR BOLTS

STEEL SHOE

PROVIDE WEEP HOLES

TRUE HINGE ANCHORAGE FOR ARCHES

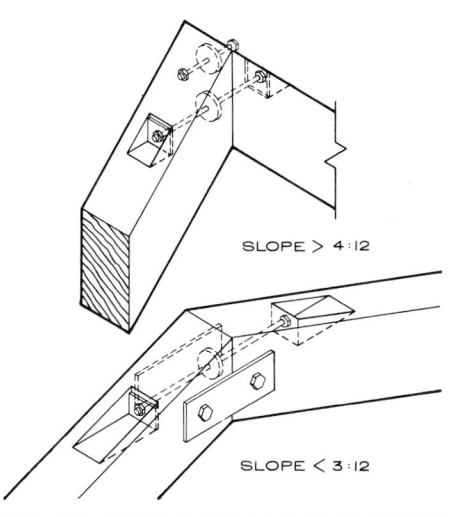

SLOPE > 4:12

SLOPE < 3:12

ARCH PEAK CONNECTION

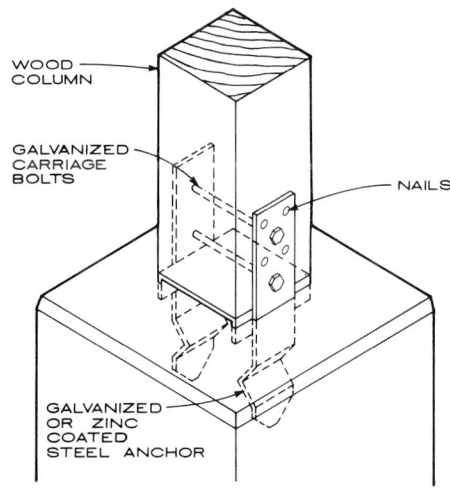

WOOD COLUMN

GALVANIZED CARRIAGE BOLTS

NAILS

GALVANIZED OR ZINC COATED STEEL ANCHOR

WET POST ANCHORAGE TO CONCRETE BASE

This detail is recommended for heavy duty use where moisture protection is desired. Anchor is set and leveled in wet concrete after screeding.

Timothy B. McDonald; Washington, D.C.

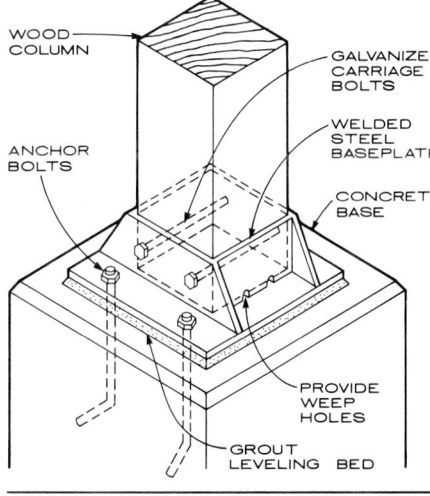

WOOD COLUMN

GALVANIZED CARRIAGE BOLTS

WELDED STEEL BASEPLATE

ANCHOR BOLTS

CONCRETE BASE

PROVIDE WEEP HOLES

GROUT LEVELING BED

WOOD COLUMN ANCHORED WITH STEEL BASEPLATE

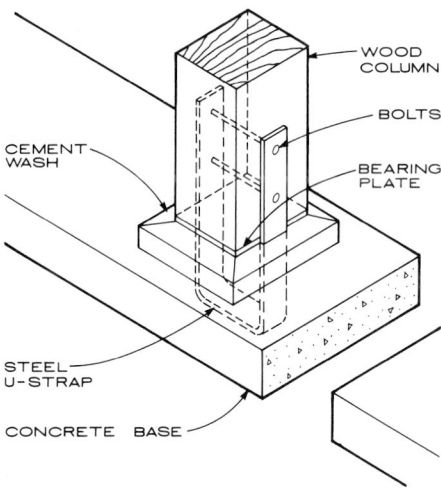

WOOD COLUMN

BOLTS

CEMENT WASH

BEARING PLATE

STEEL U-STRAP

CONCRETE BASE

U-STRAP COLUMN ANCHORAGE TO CONCRETE BASE

This detail is recommended for industrial buildings and warehouses to resist both horizontal forces and uplift. Moisture barrier is recommended. It may be used with shear plates.

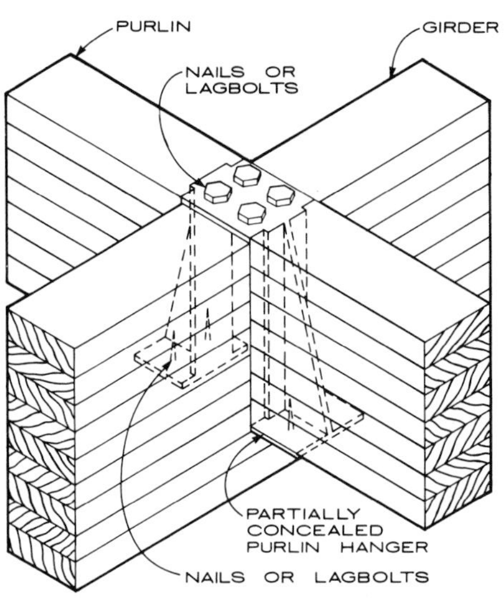

PURLIN

GIRDER

NAILS OR
LAGBOLTS

PARTIALLY
CONCEALED
PURLIN HANGER

NAILS OR LAGBOLTS

BEAM TO PURLIN CONNECTION

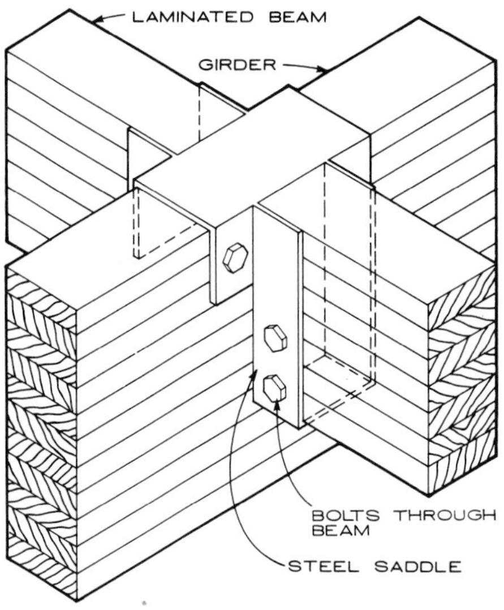

LAMINATED BEAM

GIRDER

BOLTS THROUGH
BEAM

STEEL SADDLE

BEAM TO GIRDER CONNECTION

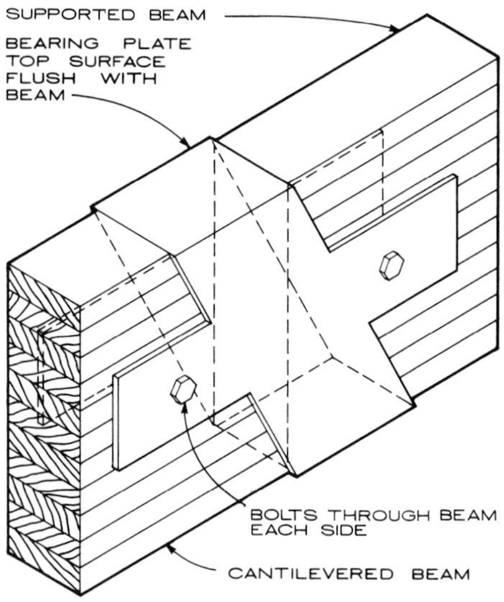

SUPPORTED BEAM

BEARING PLATE
TOP SURFACE
FLUSH WITH
BEAM

BOLTS THROUGH BEAM
EACH SIDE

CANTILEVERED BEAM

BEAM SPLICING

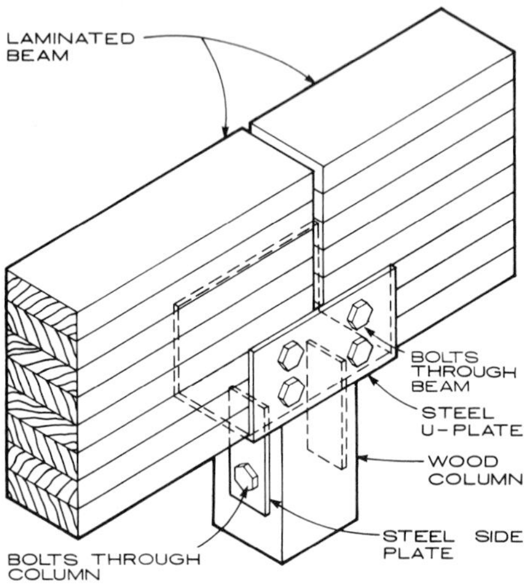

LAMINATED
BEAM

BOLTS
THROUGH
BEAM

STEEL
U-PLATE

WOOD
COLUMN

STEEL SIDE
PLATE

BOLTS THROUGH
COLUMN

BEAM TO COLUMN CONNECTION

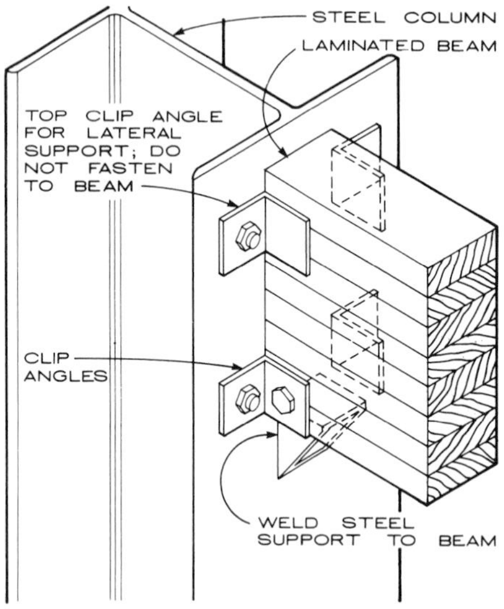

STEEL COLUMN

LAMINATED BEAM

TOP CLIP ANGLE
FOR LATERAL
SUPPORT; DO
NOT FASTEN
TO BEAM

CLIP
ANGLES

WELD STEEL
SUPPORT TO BEAM

BEAM TO COLUMN CONNECTION

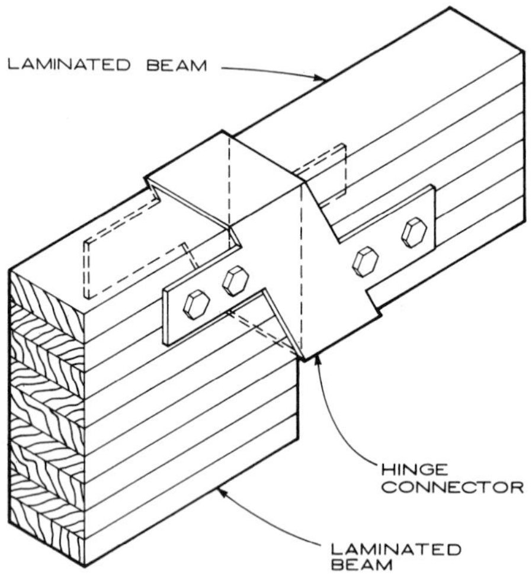

LAMINATED BEAM

HINGE
CONNECTOR

LAMINATED
BEAM

BEAM SPLICING

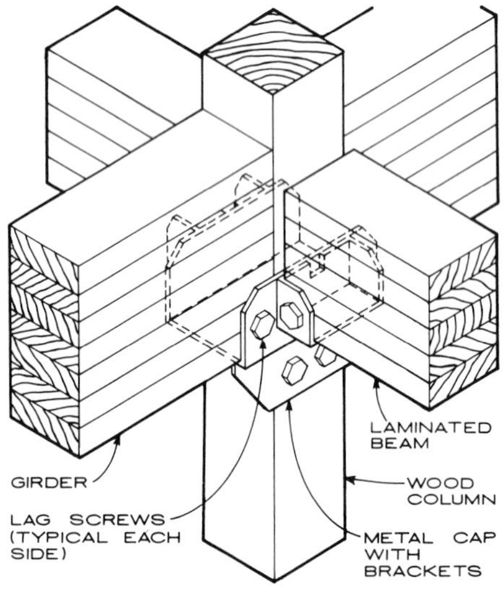

GIRDER

LAG SCREWS
(TYPICAL EACH
SIDE)

LAMINATED
BEAM

WOOD
COLUMN

METAL CAP
WITH
BRACKETS

**METAL COLUMN CAP WITH
BEAM SEATS**

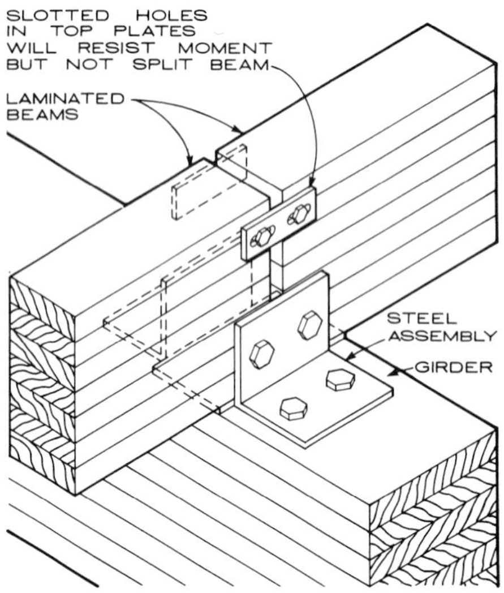

SLOTTED HOLES
IN TOP PLATES
WILL RESIST MOMENT
BUT NOT SPLIT BEAM

LAMINATED
BEAMS

STEEL
ASSEMBLY

GIRDER

BEAM CONNECTION

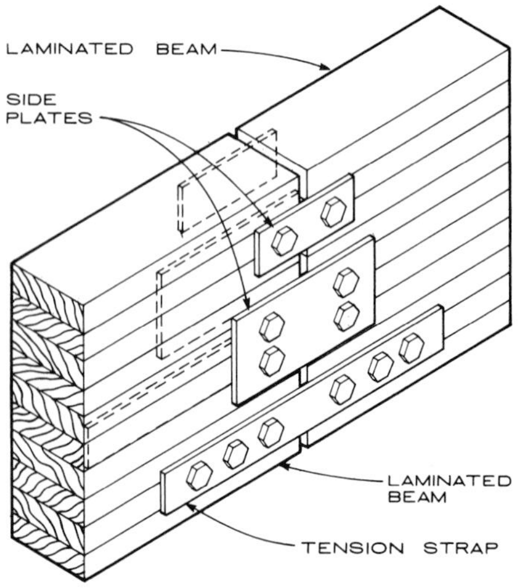

LAMINATED BEAM

SIDE
PLATES

LAMINATED
BEAM

TENSION STRAP

MOMENT SPLICING

Timothy B. McDonald; Washington, D.C.

 GLUED-LAMINATED CONSTRUCTION

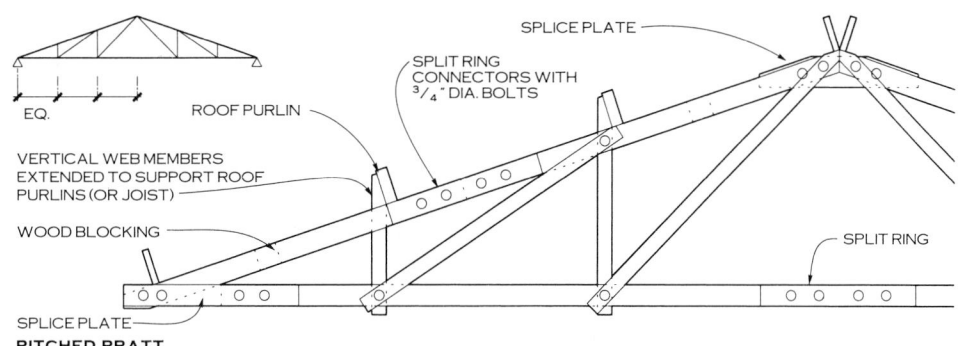

PITCHED PRATT

Labels: SPLICE PLATE · SPLIT RING CONNECTORS WITH $^3/_4$" DIA. BOLTS · ROOF PURLIN · VERTICAL WEB MEMBERS EXTENDED TO SUPPORT ROOF PURLINS (OR JOIST) · WOOD BLOCKING · SPLIT RING · SPLICE PLATE · EQ.

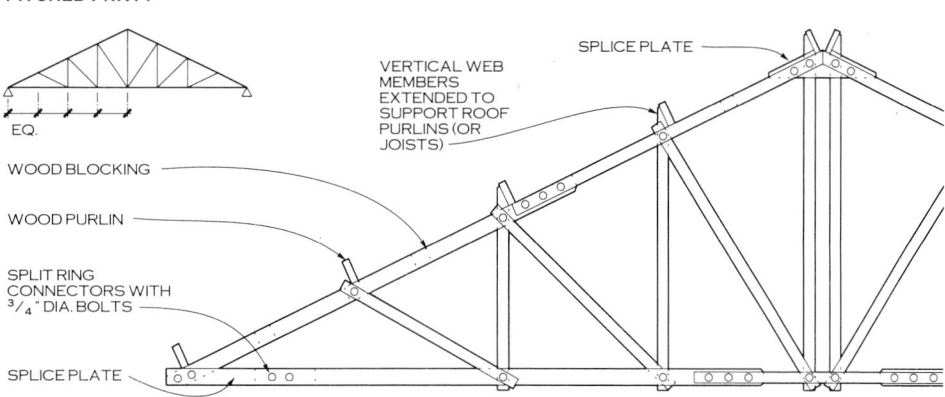

PITCHED HOWE

Labels: SPLICE PLATE · VERTICAL WEB MEMBERS EXTENDED TO SUPPORT ROOF PURLINS (OR JOISTS) · WOOD BLOCKING · WOOD PURLIN · SPLIT RING CONNECTORS WITH $^3/_4$" DIA. BOLTS · SPLICE PLATE · EQ.

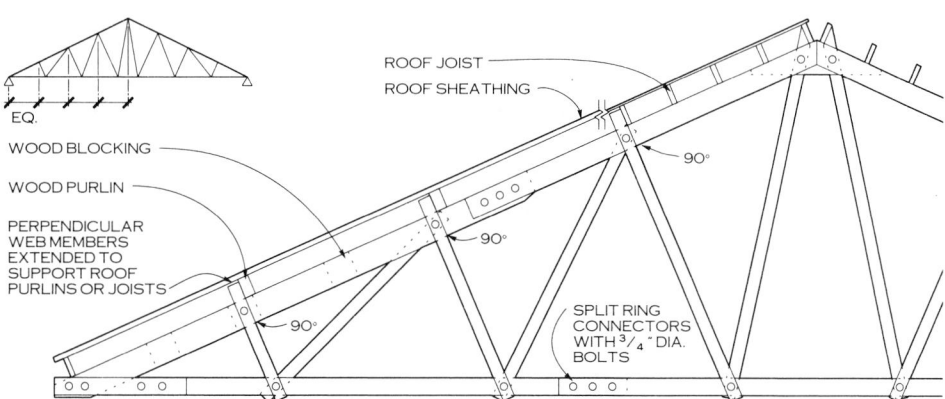

BELGIAN

Labels: ROOF JOIST · ROOF SHEATHING · 90° · 90° · 90° · SPLIT RING CONNECTORS WITH $^3/_4$" DIA. BOLTS · WOOD BLOCKING · WOOD PURLIN · PERPENDICULAR WEB MEMBERS EXTENDED TO SUPPORT ROOF PURLINS OR JOISTS · EQ.

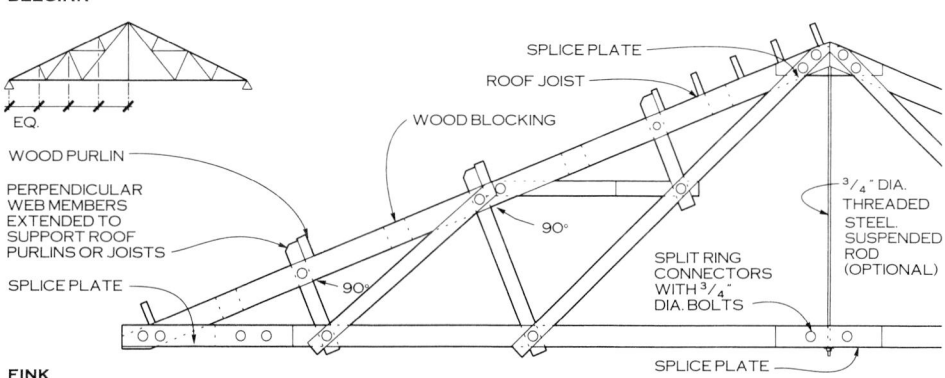

FINK

Labels: SPLICE PLATE · ROOF JOIST · WOOD BLOCKING · 90° · 90° · 90° · $^3/_4$" DIA. THREADED STEEL. SUSPENDED ROD (OPTIONAL) · SPLIT RING CONNECTORS WITH $^3/_4$" DIA. BOLTS · SPLICE PLATE · WOOD PURLIN · PERPENDICULAR WEB MEMBERS EXTENDED TO SUPPORT ROOF PURLINS OR JOISTS · SPLICE PLATE · EQ.

Pitched trusses are very economical for spans up to 70 ft (with an average spacing of 15 ft), since the member sizes are small, the joint details relatively simple, and the trusses easily fabricated.

All pitched trusses require either knee braces to columns or some other provision for lateral restraint against wind or other forces.

A typical span (l) / depth (d) ratio for the Pratt, Howe, or Belgian truss is 4 to 6, which gives a relatively normal slope of 4:12 to 6:12. Fink trusses are preferred where the slope is steep (over 7:12). Scissors trusses and other types of raised lower chord pitched roof trusses are used for special conditions where clearance or appearance requires an arched bottom chord. Consult with structural engineer to check deflection.

PITCHED TRUSSES

TECO Products; Collier, West Virginia
Richard J. Vitullo, AIA; Oak Leaf Studio; Crownsville, Maryland

GENERAL

The first wood trusses were developed for bridge design, with the kingpost truss the earliest form. It uses a primary engineering principle: a triangle will hold its shape under a load until its side members or its joints are crushed.

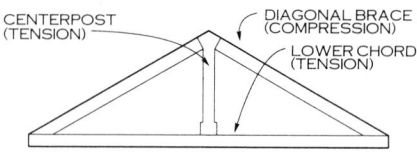

KINGPOST

Labels: CENTERPOST (TENSION) · DIAGONAL BRACE (COMPRESSION) · LOWER CHORD (TENSION)

Next came the queenpost truss, in which the peak of the kingpost was replaced by a horizontal crosspiece to allow a longer base.

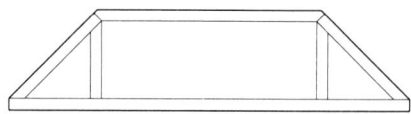

QUEENPOST

Further amplifications permitted greater flexibility to overcome different spanning challenges and to integrate various combinations of inclined wood braces, wood arches, steel tension rods, etc.

NOTES

1. A built-in camber of approximately 1 in. per 40 ft span will be introduced in the top and bottom chords during fabrication.
2. When lumber is not adequately seasoned, the trusses should be inspected periodically and adjusted, if necessary, until moisture equilibrium is reached.
3. These truss designs are meant only as a guide. To develop specific designs, including bracing and anchorage, consult a structural engineer.

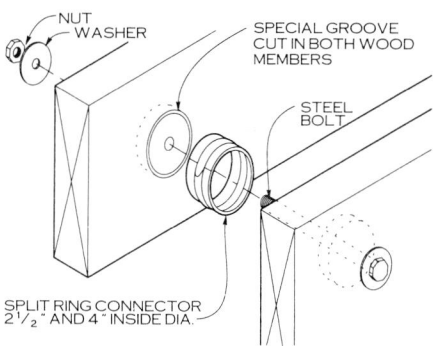

Labels: NUT · WASHER · SPECIAL GROOVE CUT IN BOTH WOOD MEMBERS · STEEL BOLT · SPLIT RING CONNECTOR $2^1/_2$" AND 4" INSIDE DIA.

SPLIT RING CONNECTOR

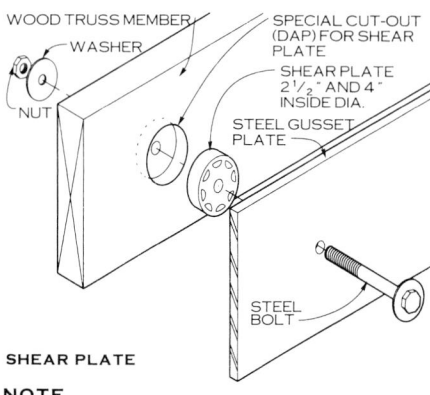

Labels: WOOD TRUSS MEMBER · WASHER · NUT · SPECIAL CUT-OUT (DAP) FOR SHEAR PLATE · SHEAR PLATE $2^1/_2$" AND 4" INSIDE DIA. · STEEL GUSSET PLATE · STEEL BOLT

SHEAR PLATE

NOTE

Shear plate connectors are commonly used to connect wood truss members to steel gusset plates but may be used to connect wood to wood.

CONNECTORS

WOOD TRUSSES 6

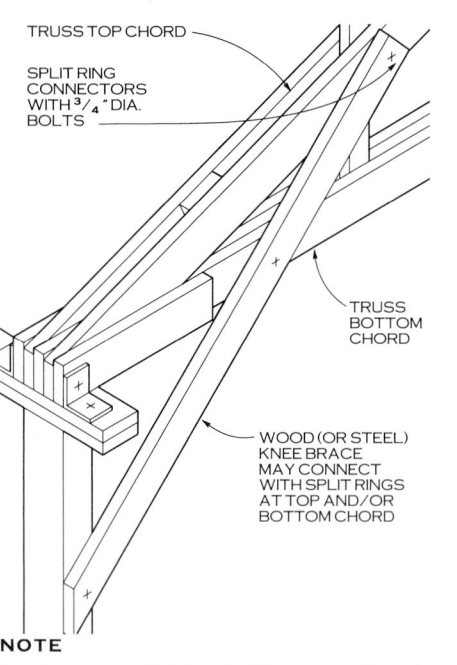

TRUSS TOP CHORD

SPLIT RING CONNECTORS WITH ³/₄" DIA. BOLTS

TRUSS BOTTOM CHORD

WOOD (OR STEEL) KNEE BRACE MAY CONNECT WITH SPLIT RINGS AT TOP AND/OR BOTTOM CHORD

NOTE

Knee braces are useful where building supports depend on truss for stability.

DETAIL—KNEE BRACE

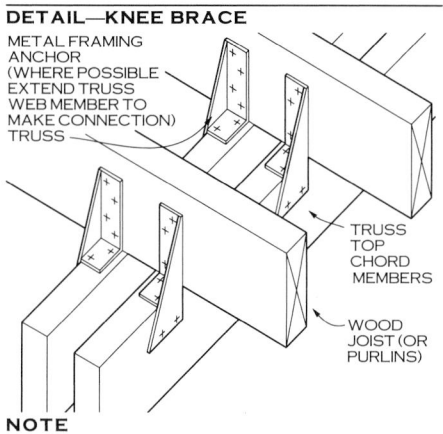

METAL FRAMING ANCHOR (WHERE POSSIBLE EXTEND TRUSS WEB MEMBER TO MAKE CONNECTION) TRUSS

TRUSS TOP CHORD MEMBERS

WOOD JOIST (OR PURLINS)

NOTE

Top chord lateral bracing is achieved by fastening roof sheathing to joists or purlins, which are securely fastened to the truss.

DETAIL—BRACE OF JOIST AND PURLIN TO TRUSS

WOOD TRUSS

VERTICAL SWAY BRACING OF STEEL RODS OR WOOD IN END SECTIONS MIN.; ONE IN MID-SPAN FOR LONG SPANS

CONTINUOUS LATERAL BRACING RUNS FULL LENGTH OF BUILDING FASTENED TO BOTTOM CHORD OR WEB MEMBERS NEAR CHORD

DETAIL—LATERAL AND VERTICAL SWAY BRACING

TECO Products; Collier, West Virginia
Richard J. Vitullo, AIA; Oak Leaf Studio; Crownsville, Maryland

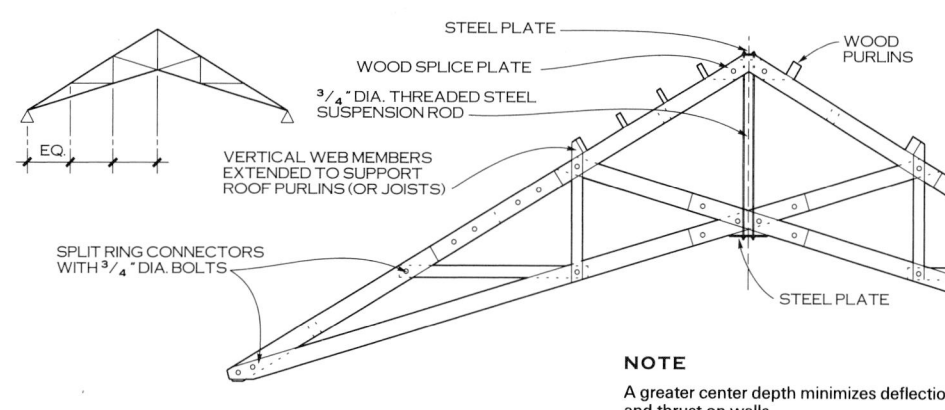

STEEL PLATE

WOOD SPLICE PLATE

³/₄" DIA. THREADED STEEL SUSPENSION ROD

VERTICAL WEB MEMBERS EXTENDED TO SUPPORT ROOF PURLINS (OR JOISTS)

WOOD PURLINS

SPLIT RING CONNECTORS WITH ³/₄" DIA. BOLTS

STEEL PLATE

NOTE

A greater center depth minimizes deflection and thrust on walls.

SCISSORS

PITCHED TRUSSES

WOOD SPLICE PLATE

WOOD PURLINS

VERTICAL WEB MEMBERS EXTENDED TO SUPPORT ROOF PURLINS (OR JOISTS)

SPLIT RING CONNECTORS WITH ³/₄" DIA. BOLTS

SEGMENTAL BOWSTRING

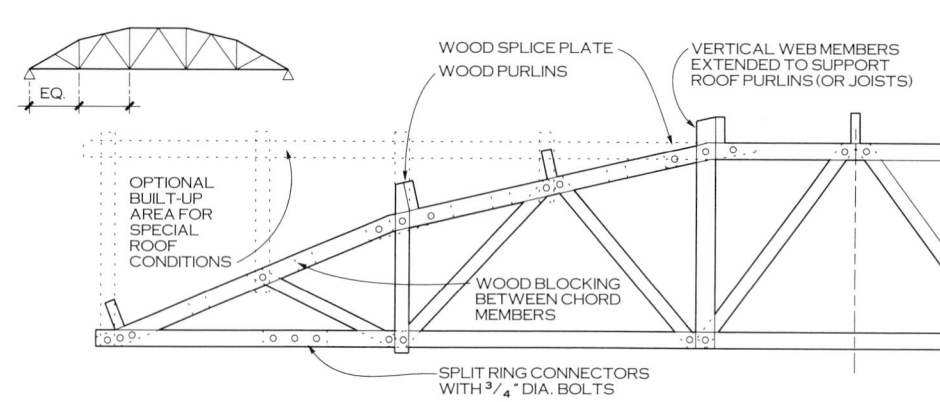

WOOD SPLICE PLATE

WOOD PURLINS

VERTICAL WEB MEMBERS EXTENDED TO SUPPORT ROOF PURLINS (OR JOISTS)

OPTIONAL BUILT-UP AREA FOR SPECIAL ROOF CONDITIONS

WOOD BLOCKING BETWEEN CHORD MEMBERS

SPLIT RING CONNECTORS WITH ³/₄" DIA. BOLTS

SEGMENTAL BOWSTRING

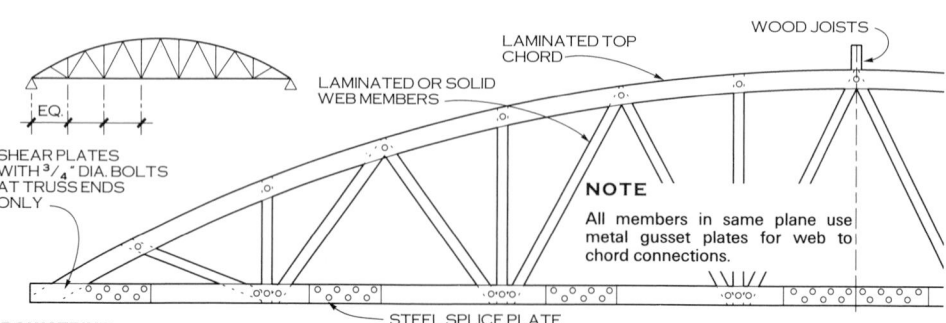

LAMINATED TOP CHORD

WOOD JOISTS

LAMINATED OR SOLID WEB MEMBERS

SHEAR PLATES WITH ³/₄" DIA. BOLTS AT TRUSS ENDS ONLY

NOTE

All members in same plane use metal gusset plates for web to chord connections.

STEEL SPLICE PLATE

BOWSTRING

Bowstring trusses are theoretically the most efficient and economical of all wood truss types for larger spans, particularly over 80 ft, although spans up to 250 ft are obtainable. Connections are simple and designed to give minimum stresses to the web members. A typical span (1)/depth (d) ratio for bowstring trusses is 6 to 8.

Connections and knee brace requirements are similar to that of pitched trusses, since lateral load forces have a similar effect on them. The bottom chord members may also be glue laminated to eliminate splices.

BOWSTRING TRUSSES

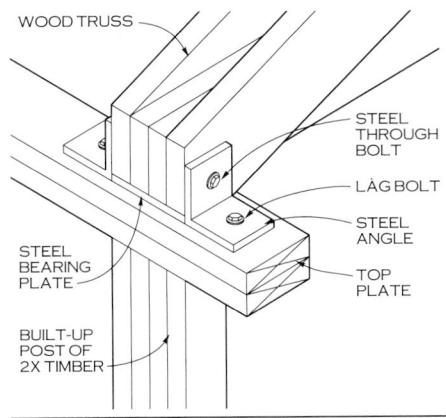

WOOD TRUSS

STEEL THROUGH BOLT

LÀG BOLT

STEEL ANGLE

STEEL BEARING PLATE

TOP PLATE

BUILT-UP POST OF 2X TIMBER

DETAIL—STEEL ANGLE BRACE TO WOOD PLATE

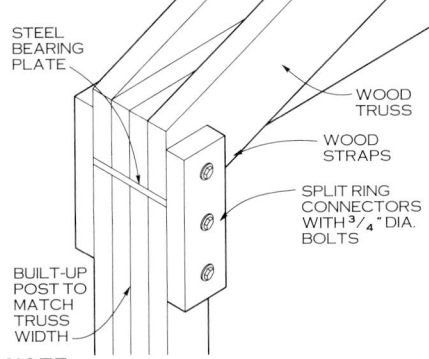

STEEL BEARING PLATE

WOOD TRUSS

WOOD STRAPS

SPLIT RING CONNECTORS WITH $3/4$" DIA. BOLTS

BUILT-UP POST TO MATCH TRUSS WIDTH

NOTE

End grain bearing of posts provides support for the truss.

DETAIL—WOOD STRAP AT WOOD COLUMN

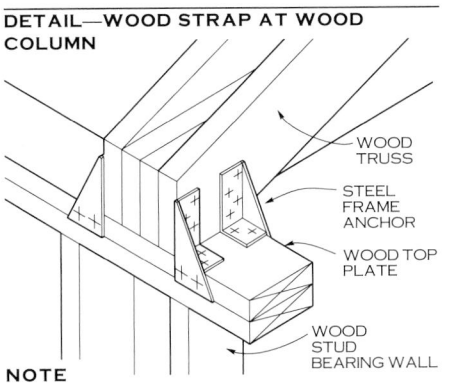

WOOD TRUSS

STEEL FRAME ANCHOR

WOOD TOP PLATE

WOOD STUD BEARING WALL

NOTE

This detail for use with light vertical and horizontal loads.

DETAIL—STEEL FRAMING ANCHOR

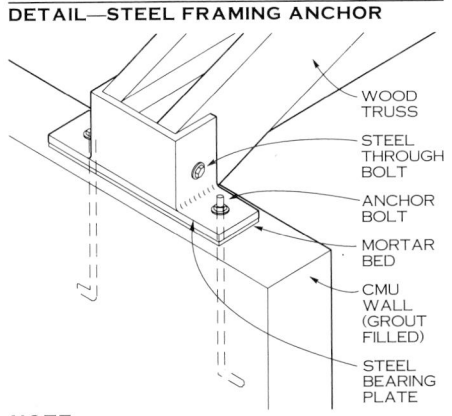

WOOD TRUSS

STEEL THROUGH BOLT

ANCHOR BOLT

MORTAR BED

CMU WALL (GROUT FILLED)

STEEL BEARING PLATE

NOTE

With scissor trusses, use slotted holes in steel to allow for thrust.

DETAIL—BEARING ON MASONRY WALL

TECO Products; Collier, West Virginia
Richard J. Vitullo, AIA; Oak Leaf Studio; Crownsville, Maryland

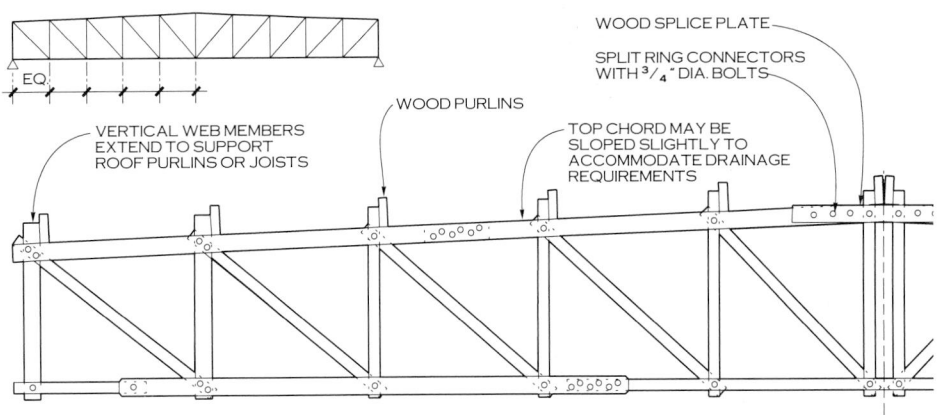

EQ

VERTICAL WEB MEMBERS EXTEND TO SUPPORT ROOF PURLINS OR JOISTS

WOOD PURLINS

WOOD SPLICE PLATE

SPLIT RING CONNECTORS WITH $3/4$" DIA. BOLTS

TOP CHORD MAY BE SLOPED SLIGHTLY TO ACCOMMODATE DRAINAGE REQUIREMENTS

FLAT PRATT

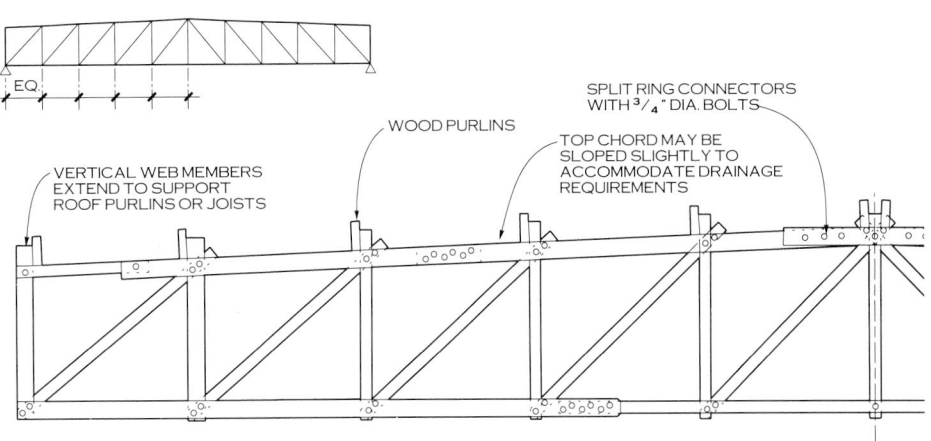

EQ

VERTICAL WEB MEMBERS EXTEND TO SUPPORT ROOF PURLINS OR JOISTS

WOOD PURLINS

SPLIT RING CONNECTORS WITH $3/4$" DIA. BOLTS

TOP CHORD MAY BE SLOPED SLIGHTLY TO ACCOMMODATE DRAINAGE REQUIREMENTS

FLAT HOWE

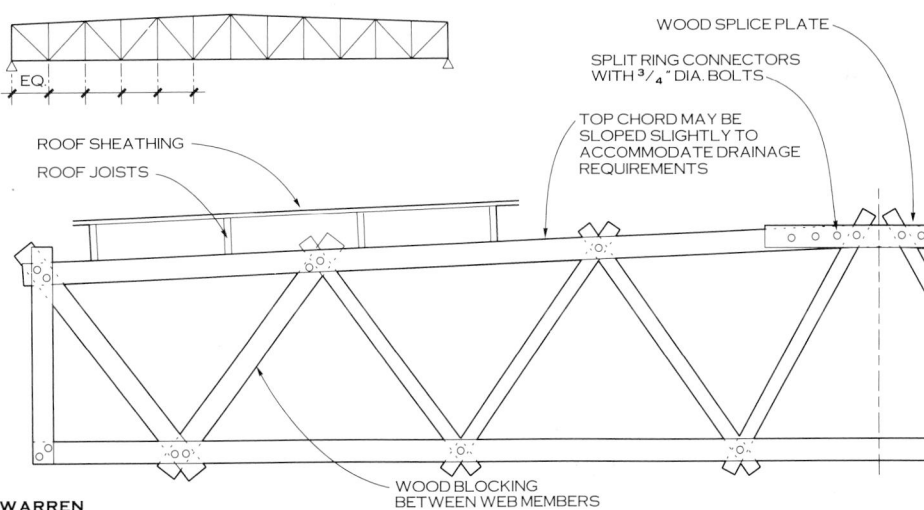

EQ

ROOF SHEATHING

ROOF JOISTS

WOOD SPLICE PLATE

SPLIT RING CONNECTORS WITH $3/4$" DIA. BOLTS

TOP CHORD MAY BE SLOPED SLIGHTLY TO ACCOMMODATE DRAINAGE REQUIREMENTS

WOOD BLOCKING BETWEEN WEB MEMBERS

WARREN

Flat trusses are generally less economical than pitched or bowstring trusses, since connections are usually more complicated and higher side walls are required. But because of their geometry, flat trusses allow the smallest roof area versus pitched or bowstring trusses for the same span. As in pitched trusses, the maximum span for flat trusses is about 70 ft.

A typical span (1)/depth (d) ratio for all types of flat trusses is generally 8 to 10.

Combinations of flat truss types are sometimes useful. For instance, a truss may be built having one-half Pratt and one-half Howe design. Warren trusses may have ends of either Pratt or Howe designs incorporated, depending on the type of support. In general, Warren trusses are used for shorter spans.

Flat trusses do not require knee braces since the upper and lower chords take the place of a lateral brace.

FLAT TRUSSES

WOOD TRUSSES 6

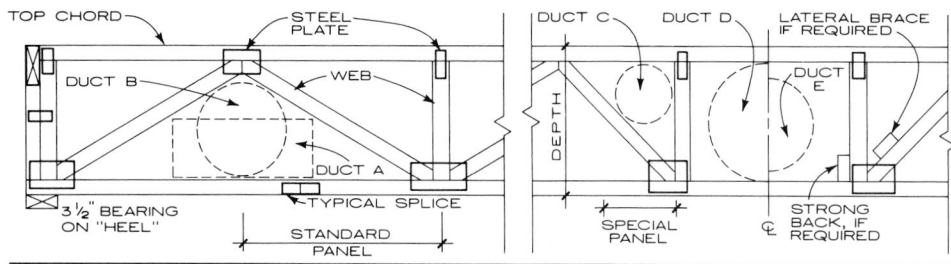

RESIDENTIAL TYPE TRUSSED FLOOR JOIST STEEL PLATE CONNECTED

DUCT SIZES

Ease of running electrical and mechanical services through framing is a major advantage of trussed joists. Most manufacturers provide a large rectangular open panel at midspan; this void will generally accommodate a trunk line.

Sizes given here are approximations. Because web size and angles vary with different brands, the designer is cautioned to verify individual sizes carefully. Note that shape E is the duct that will fit in a flat truss with double chords top and bottom.

DEPTH OF TRUSS AND SIZE OF DUCTWORK

DEPTH	12″	16″	20″	24″
SHAPE				
A	4 x 9	6 x 12	7 x 13	8 x 14
B	7″	10″	12″	14″
C	5″	7″	8″	9″
D	9″	13″	17″	21″
E	6″	10″	14″	18″

GENERAL

Monoplaner trusses are usually made up from 2 x 4 or 2 x 6 lumber. Spacing, normally 24 in. o.c., varies for special uses, especially in agriculture. Camber is designed for dead load only. Bottom chord furring generally is not required for drywall ceiling. Joints in plywood floor or roof should be staggered. Many trusses are approved by model codes, such as BOCA, ICBO, FHA, and SBC.

$$\text{CAMBER} \atop \text{(USUAL)} = \frac{L(FT)}{60}$$

BRACING

Adequate bracing of trusses is vital. Sufficient support at right angles to plane of truss must be provided to hold each truss member in its designated position. Consider bracing during design, fabrication, and erection. In addition, provide permanent bracing/anchorage as an integral part of the building. Strongbacks are often used.

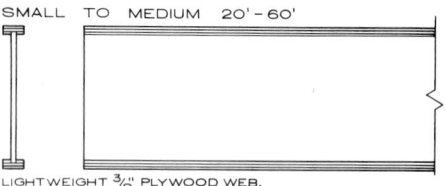

SMALL TO MEDIUM 20'-60'

LIGHTWEIGHT ³⁄₈″ PLYWOOD WEB, 2 X 3 LAMINATED FLANGE

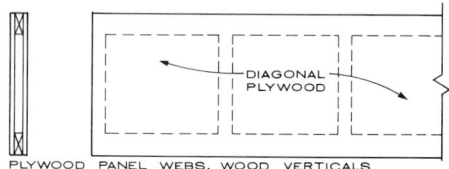

PLYWOOD PANEL WEBS, WOOD VERTICALS

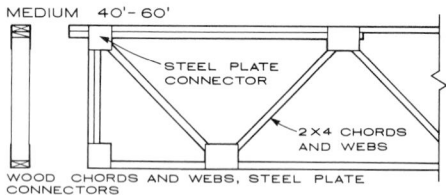

MEDIUM 40'-60'

WOOD CHORDS AND WEBS, STEEL PLATE CONNECTORS

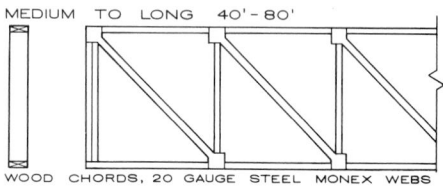

MEDIUM TO LONG 40'-80'

WOOD CHORDS, 20 GAUGE STEEL MONEX WEBS

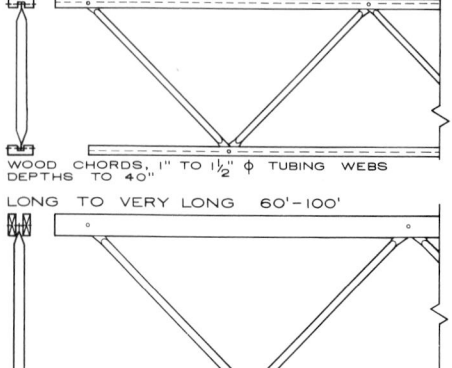

WOOD CHORDS, 1″ TO 1½″ ⌀ TUBING WEBS DEPTHS TO 40″

LONG TO VERY LONG 60'-100'

DOUBLE 2 X 6 CHORDS, 2″ ⌀ WEBS DEPTH TO 63″

TYPES OF FABRICATED TRUSSES

WOOD TRUSSED RAFTERS SPANS FOR PRELIMINARY DESIGN

	RESIDENTIAL LIVE LOADS								
	FLOORS 55 PSF Ⓐ			ROOFS 40 PSF Ⓑ		55 PSF Ⓒ		(DOUBLE CHORDS) 55 PSF Ⓒ	
	TRUSSED RAFTERS SPACING (C TO C)								
DEPTH	12″	16″	24″	16″	24″	16″	24″	16″	24″
12″	23-6	21-0	17-1	24-0	21-4	21-11	18-2		
13″	24-11	22-0	17-11						
14″	26-4	22-11	18-8	27-5	23-3	24-5	19-10		
15″	27-7	23-10	19-5						
16″	28-7	24-9	20-1	30-3	25-0	26-4	21-4	31-10	27-10
18″	30-6	26-4	21-5	32-11	26-9	28-1	22-9	35-1	30-7
20″	32-4	27-11	22-8	34-8	28-0	29-7	23-11	38-1	33-1
22″	34-0	26-9	23-11						
24″	35-8	30-10	25-0	38-3	30-11	32-7	26-4	43-10	36-7
28″				41-6	33-6	35-5	28-7	49-2	39-11
32″				44-3	35-7	37-8	30-4	52-9	42-9
36″				47-0	37-10	40-1	32-3	56-3	45-7
48″								60-0	53-3

	COMMERCIAL LIVE LOADS								
	FLOORS 80 PSF Ⓓ			100 PSF Ⓔ			120 PSF Ⓕ		
	TRUSSED RAFTERS SPACING (C TO C)								
DEPTH	12″	16″	24″	12″	16″	24″	12″	16″	24″
12″	19-0	17-3	15-1	17-3	15-8	13-7	16-0	14-7	12-4
14″	21-4	19-4	16-6	19-4	17-7	14-9	18-0	16-4	13-6
16″	23-6	21-5	17-10	21-5	19-5	15-11	19-10	17-11	14-6
18″	25-8	23-4	19-0	23-4	21-0	17-0	21-8	19-2	15-6
20″	27-8	24-10	20-2	25-2	22-3	18-0	23-4	20-3	16-5
24″	31-6	27-5	22-2	28-5	24-6	19-10	25-11	22-4	18-1
16″*	27-7	25-1	21-11	25-1	22-9	19-11	23-2	21-2	18-5
24″*	38-0	34-6	30-1	34-6	31-4	27-4	32-0	29-1	25-1
32″*	47-1	42-9	36-1	42-9	38-10	32-3	39-8	36-1	29-5

Top chord live load	40 psf	20 psf	35 psf	60 psf	80 psf	100 psf
Top chord dead load	10 psf	10 psf	10 psf	10 psf	10 psf	10 psf
Bottom chord dead load	5 psf	10 psf	10 psf	10 psf	10 psf	10 psf
Total load	Ⓐ 55 psf	Ⓑ 40 psf	Ⓒ 55 psf	Ⓓ 80 psf	Ⓔ 100 psf	Ⓕ 120 psf

NOTES

1. Spans are clear, inside to inside, for bottom chord bearing. Values shown would vary very slightly for a truss with top chord loading.
2. Spans should not exceed 24 x depth of truss.
3. Designed deflection limit under total load is ℓ/240 for roofs, ℓ/360 for residential floors, and ℓ/480 for commercial floors.
4. Roof spans include a +15% short term stress.
5. Asterisk (*) indicates that truss has double chords, top and bottom.
6. Spans shown are for only one type of lumber; in this case—#2 Southern pine, with an f_b value of 1550. Charts are available for other grades and species. Lumber and grades may be mixed in the same truss, but chord size must be identical. Repetitive member bending stress is used in this chart.

Michael Bengis, AIA; Hopatcong, New Jersey

NOTES

1. For light trusses (trussed rafters), average spacing is 2 ft. o.c., but varies up to 4 ft. o.c. The average combined dead and live loads is 45 lbs. per sq.ft. Spans, usually 20 ft. to 32 ft., can be up to 50 ft. in some applications.

2. Early in the design process, consult engineer or truss supplier for preengineered truss designs to establish the most economical and efficient truss proportions. Supplier may provide final truss engineering design.

3. Permanent and temporary erection bracing must be installed as specified to prevent failure of properly designed trusses.

4. Some locales require an engineer's stamp when prefab trusses are used. Check local codes.

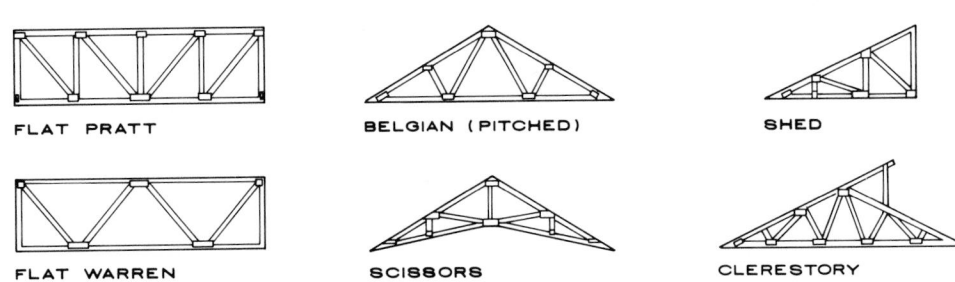

FLAT PRATT   BELGIAN (PITCHED)   SHED

FLAT WARREN   SCISSORS   CLERESTORY

TRUSS TYPES

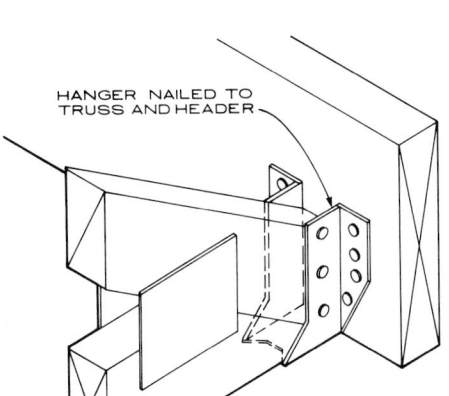

HANGER NAILED TO TRUSS AND HEADER

TRUSS HANGER (DETAIL)

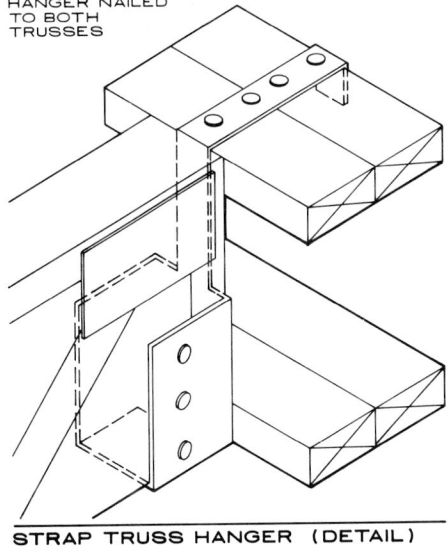

HANGER NAILED TO BOTH TRUSSES

STRAP TRUSS HANGER (DETAIL)

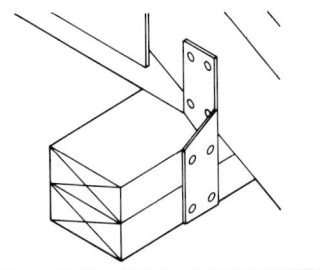

FRAMING ANCHOR (DETAIL)

Timothy B. McDonald; Washington, D.C.

PLYWOOD ROOF SHEATHING

TYPICAL ROOF TRUSS

LATERAL BRACING

WEBS

TOP CHORD

BOTTOM CHORD

CONTINUOUS BANDING TOP AND BOTTOM

PLYWOOD SUBFLOORING

TYPICAL FLOOR JOIST

TOP AND BOTTOM CHORD

CONTINUOUS BANDING

STRONGBACK

CONNECTOR PLATES

DUCTING

TOP PLATE

PROTECTIVE FLASHING

DOUBLE TRUSS BOTH ENDS

DOUBLE HEADER TRUSSES

FOUNDATION

WATERPROOF MEMBRANE

INSULATION

SILL

TRUSS FRAMING

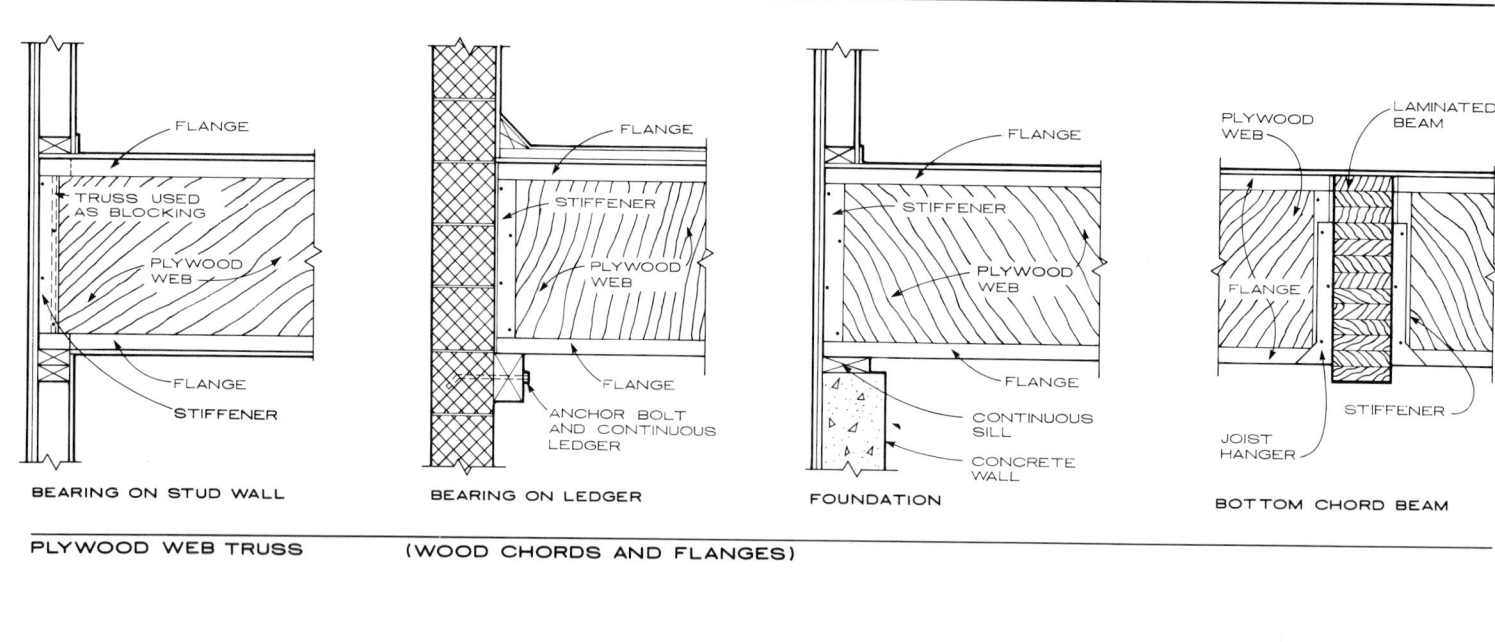

FLANGE

TRUSS USED AS BLOCKING

PLYWOOD WEB

FLANGE

STIFFENER

BEARING ON STUD WALL

FLANGE

STIFFENER

PLYWOOD WEB

FLANGE

ANCHOR BOLT AND CONTINUOUS LEDGER

BEARING ON LEDGER

FLANGE

STIFFENER

PLYWOOD WEB

FLANGE

CONTINUOUS SILL

CONCRETE WALL

FOUNDATION

PLYWOOD WEB

LAMINATED BEAM

FLANGE

JOIST HANGER

STIFFENER

BOTTOM CHORD BEAM

PLYWOOD WEB TRUSS   (WOOD CHORDS AND FLANGES)

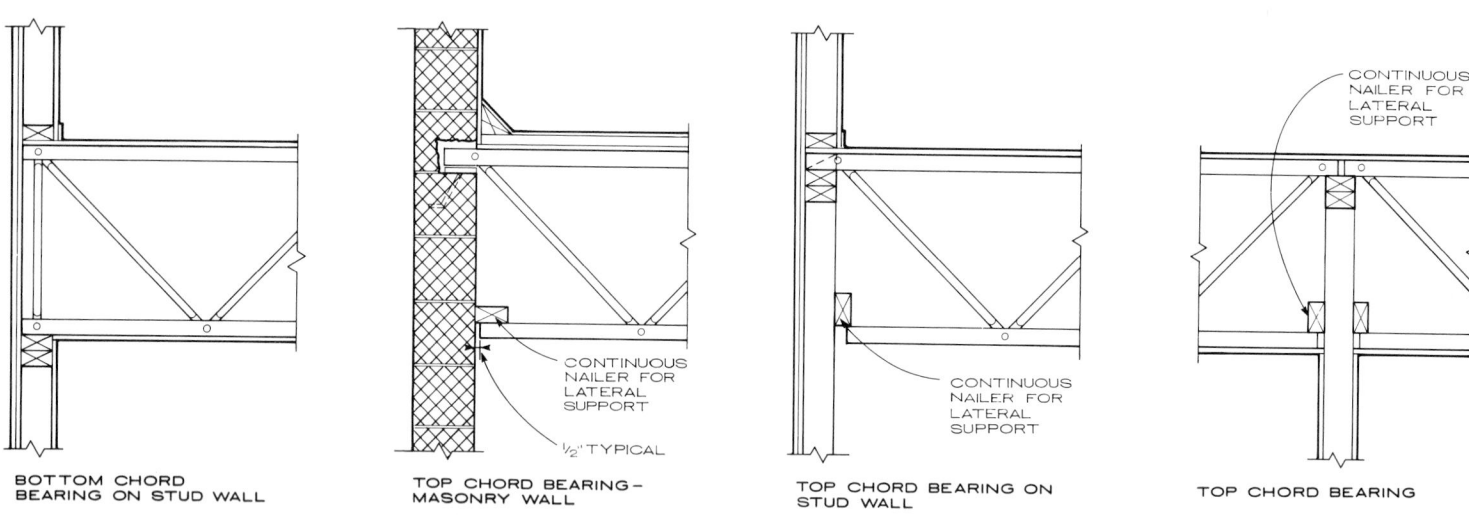

BOTTOM CHORD BEARING ON STUD WALL

CONTINUOUS NAILER FOR LATERAL SUPPORT

½" TYPICAL

TOP CHORD BEARING – MASONRY WALL

CONTINUOUS NAILER FOR LATERAL SUPPORT

TOP CHORD BEARING ON STUD WALL

CONTINUOUS NAILER FOR LATERAL SUPPORT

TOP CHORD BEARING

OPEN WEB TRUSS   (STEEL WEB WOOD CHORD)

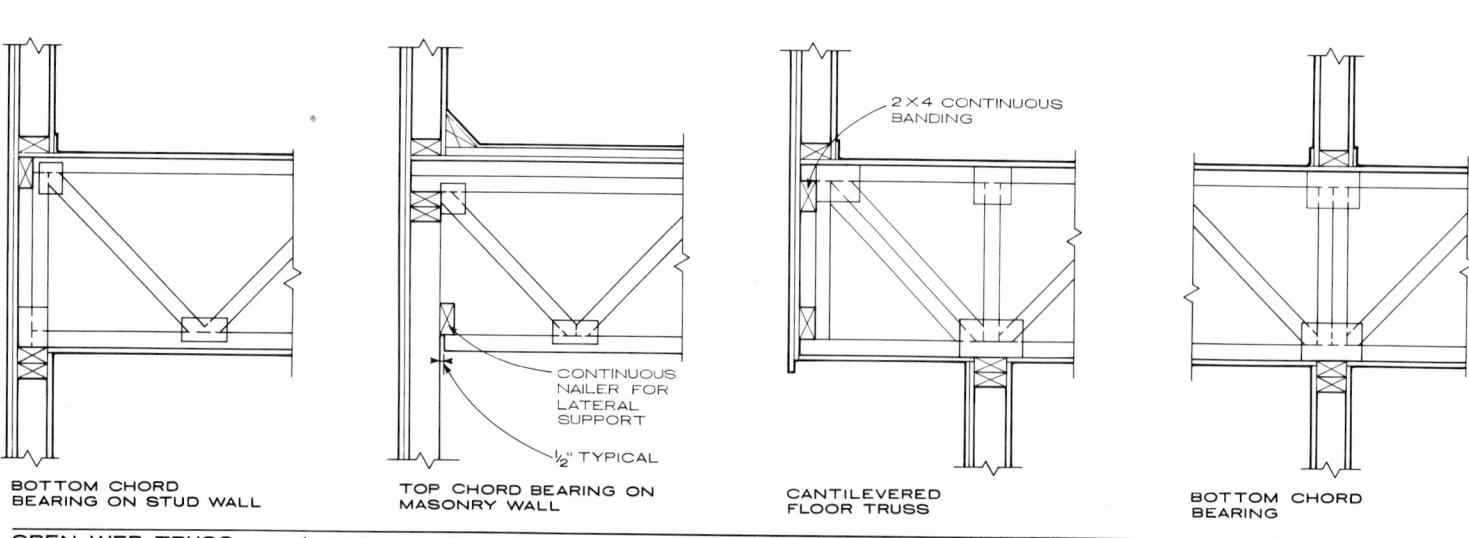

BOTTOM CHORD BEARING ON STUD WALL

CONTINUOUS NAILER FOR LATERAL SUPPORT

½" TYPICAL

TOP CHORD BEARING ON MASONRY WALL

2 X 4 CONTINUOUS BANDING

CANTILEVERED FLOOR TRUSS

BOTTOM CHORD BEARING

OPEN WEB TRUSS   (WOOD CHORDS AND WEB, METAL PLATE CONNECTORS)

Timothy B. McDonald; Washington, D.C.

WOOD TRUSSES

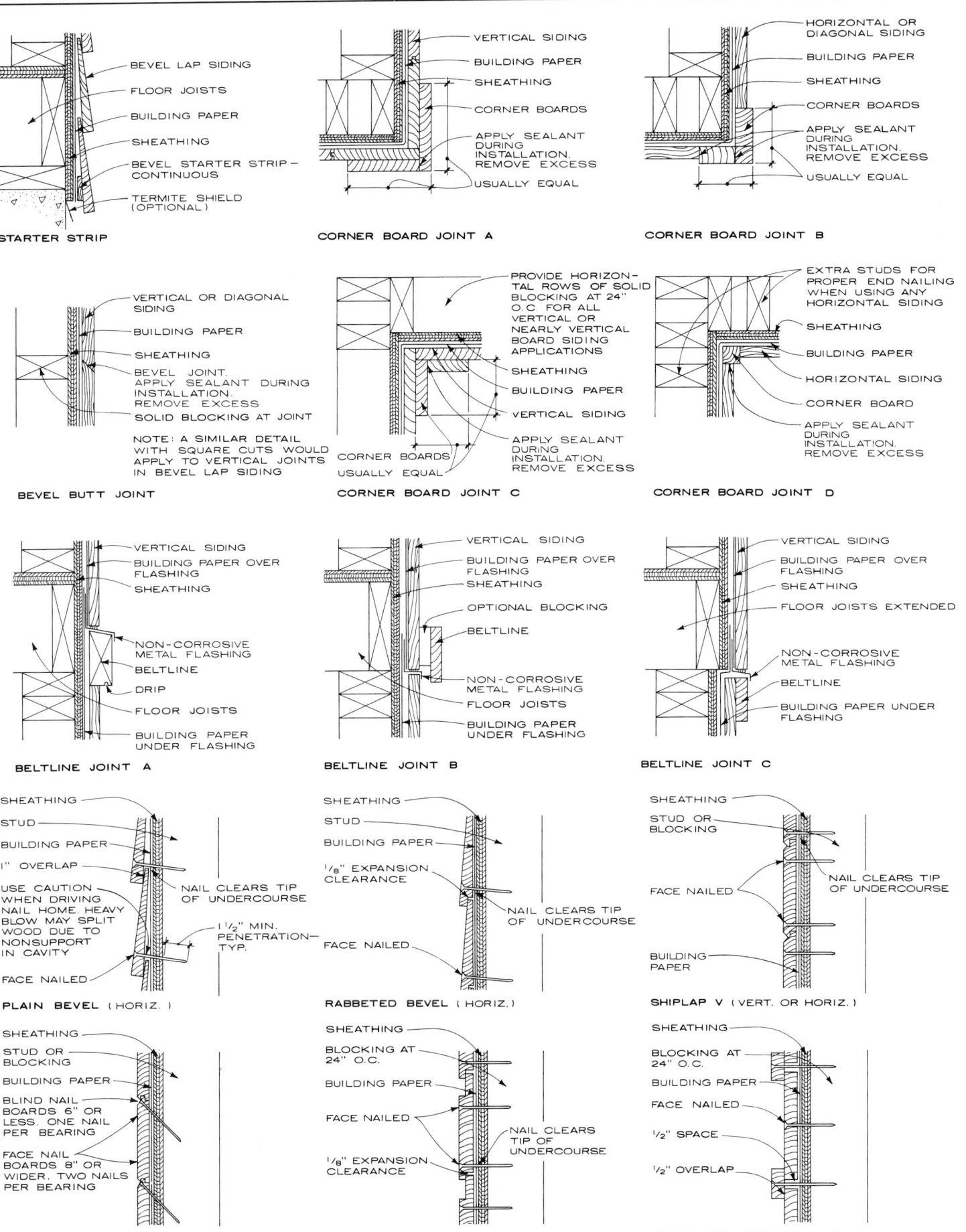

STARTER STRIP
- BEVEL LAP SIDING
- FLOOR JOISTS
- BUILDING PAPER
- SHEATHING
- BEVEL STARTER STRIP – CONTINUOUS
- TERMITE SHIELD (OPTIONAL)

CORNER BOARD JOINT A
- VERTICAL SIDING
- BUILDING PAPER
- SHEATHING
- CORNER BOARDS
- APPLY SEALANT DURING INSTALLATION. REMOVE EXCESS
- USUALLY EQUAL

CORNER BOARD JOINT B
- HORIZONTAL OR DIAGONAL SIDING
- BUILDING PAPER
- SHEATHING
- CORNER BOARDS
- APPLY SEALANT DURING INSTALLATION. REMOVE EXCESS
- USUALLY EQUAL

BEVEL BUTT JOINT
- VERTICAL OR DIAGONAL SIDING
- BUILDING PAPER
- SHEATHING
- BEVEL JOINT. APPLY SEALANT DURING INSTALLATION. REMOVE EXCESS
- SOLID BLOCKING AT JOINT

NOTE: A SIMILAR DETAIL WITH SQUARE CUTS WOULD APPLY TO VERTICAL JOINTS IN BEVEL LAP SIDING

CORNER BOARD JOINT C
- PROVIDE HORIZONTAL ROWS OF SOLID BLOCKING AT 24" O.C. FOR ALL VERTICAL OR NEARLY VERTICAL BOARD SIDING APPLICATIONS
- SHEATHING
- BUILDING PAPER
- VERTICAL SIDING
- APPLY SEALANT DURING INSTALLATION. REMOVE EXCESS
- CORNER BOARDS
- USUALLY EQUAL

CORNER BOARD JOINT D
- EXTRA STUDS FOR PROPER END NAILING WHEN USING ANY HORIZONTAL SIDING
- SHEATHING
- BUILDING PAPER
- HORIZONTAL SIDING
- CORNER BOARD
- APPLY SEALANT DURING INSTALLATION. REMOVE EXCESS

BELTLINE JOINT A
- VERTICAL SIDING
- BUILDING PAPER OVER FLASHING
- SHEATHING
- NON-CORROSIVE METAL FLASHING
- BELTLINE
- DRIP
- FLOOR JOISTS
- BUILDING PAPER UNDER FLASHING

BELTLINE JOINT B
- VERTICAL SIDING
- BUILDING PAPER OVER FLASHING
- SHEATHING
- OPTIONAL BLOCKING
- BELTLINE
- NON-CORROSIVE METAL FLASHING
- FLOOR JOISTS
- BUILDING PAPER UNDER FLASHING

BELTLINE JOINT C
- VERTICAL SIDING
- BUILDING PAPER OVER FLASHING
- SHEATHING
- FLOOR JOISTS EXTENDED
- NON-CORROSIVE METAL FLASHING
- BELTLINE
- BUILDING PAPER UNDER FLASHING

PLAIN BEVEL (HORIZ.)
- SHEATHING
- STUD
- BUILDING PAPER
- 1" OVERLAP
- USE CAUTION WHEN DRIVING NAIL HOME. HEAVY BLOW MAY SPLIT WOOD DUE TO NONSUPPORT IN CAVITY
- FACE NAILED
- NAIL CLEARS TIP OF UNDERCOURSE
- 1 1/2" MIN. PENETRATION – TYP.

RABBETED BEVEL (HORIZ.)
- SHEATHING
- STUD
- BUILDING PAPER
- 1/8" EXPANSION CLEARANCE
- NAIL CLEARS TIP OF UNDERCOURSE
- FACE NAILED

SHIPLAP V (VERT. OR HORIZ.)
- SHEATHING
- STUD OR BLOCKING
- FACE NAILED
- NAIL CLEARS TIP OF UNDERCOURSE
- BUILDING PAPER

TONGUE AND GROOVE (VERT. OR HORIZ.)
- SHEATHING
- STUD OR BLOCKING
- BUILDING PAPER
- BLIND NAIL BOARDS 6" OR LESS. ONE NAIL PER BEARING
- FACE NAIL BOARDS 8" OR WIDER. TWO NAILS PER BEARING

CHANNEL (VERT.)
- SHEATHING
- BLOCKING AT 24" O.C.
- BUILDING PAPER
- FACE NAILED
- 1/8" EXPANSION CLEARANCE
- NAIL CLEARS TIP OF UNDERCOURSE

BOARD AND BATTEN (VERT.)
- SHEATHING
- BLOCKING AT 24" O.C.
- BUILDING PAPER
- FACE NAILED
- 1/2" SPACE
- 1/2" OVERLAP

Gerald D. Graham; CTA Architects Engineers; Billings, Montana

FINISH CARPENTRY 6

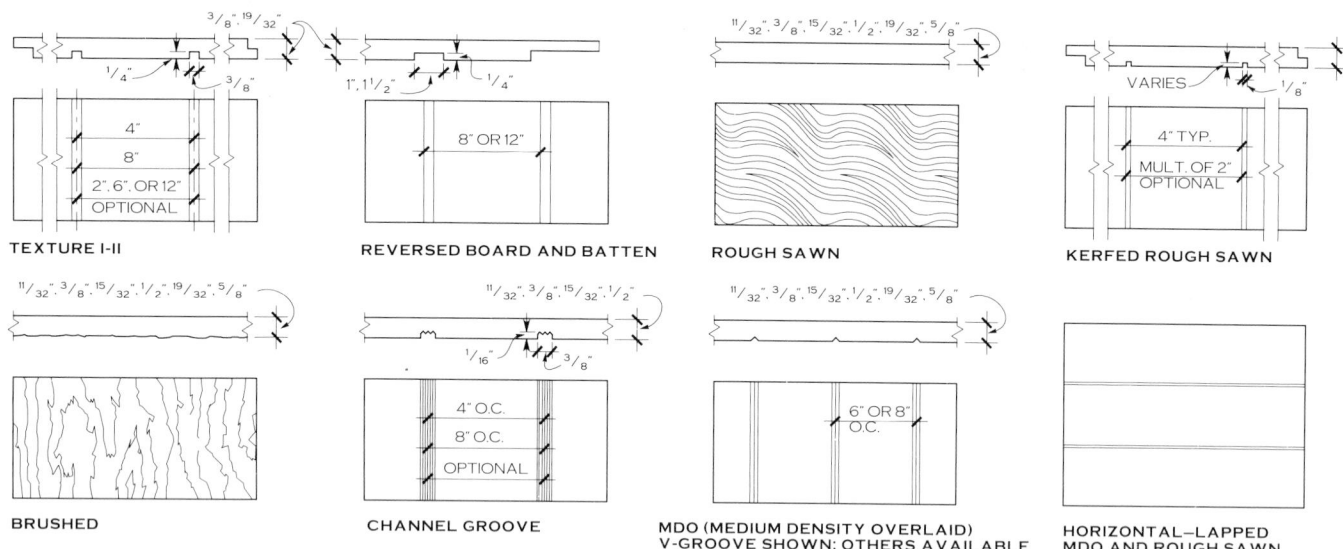

TEXTURE I-II

REVERSED BOARD AND BATTEN

ROUGH SAWN

KERFED ROUGH SAWN

BRUSHED

CHANNEL GROOVE

MDO (MEDIUM DENSITY OVERLAID)
V-GROOVE SHOWN; OTHERS AVAILABLE

HORIZONTAL—LAPPED
MDO AND ROUGH SAWN

PLYWOOD SIDING 303 AND T1-11 (303 SPECIAL)

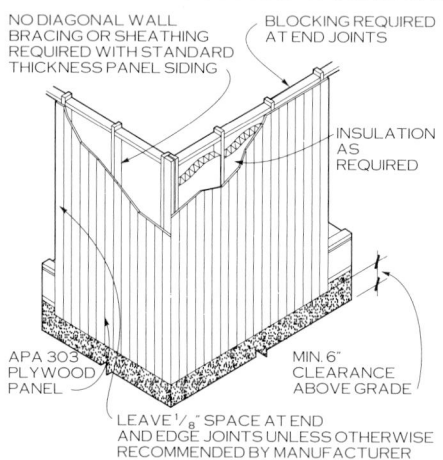

NO DIAGONAL WALL BRACING OR SHEATHING REQUIRED WITH STANDARD THICKNESS PANEL SIDING

BLOCKING REQUIRED AT END JOINTS

INSULATION AS REQUIRED

APA 303 PLYWOOD PANEL

LEAVE 1/8" SPACE AT END AND EDGE JOINTS UNLESS OTHERWISE RECOMMENDED BY MANUFACTURER

MIN. 6" CLEARANCE ABOVE GRADE

PANEL SIDING VERTICAL APPLICATION

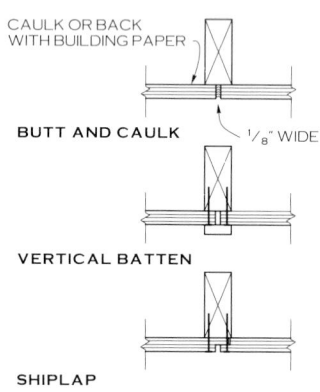

CAULK OR BACK WITH BUILDING PAPER

BUTT AND CAULK

1/8" WIDE

VERTICAL BATTEN

SHIPLAP

VERTICAL JOINTS

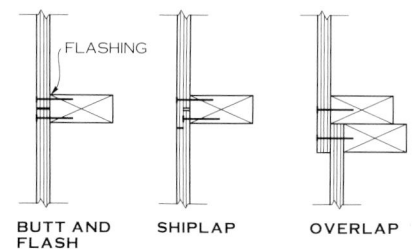

FLASHING

BUTT AND FLASH

SHIPLAP

OVERLAP

HORIZONTAL JOINTS

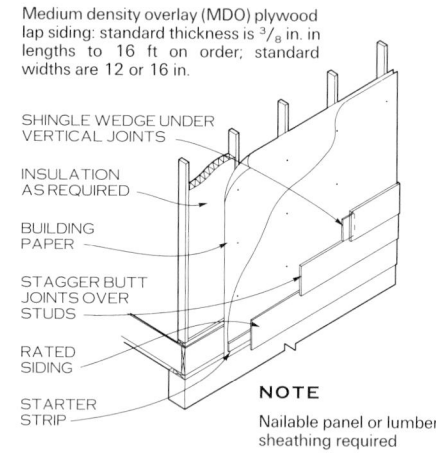

Medium density overlay (MDO) plywood lap siding: standard thickness is 3/8 in. in lengths to 16 ft on order; standard widths are 12 or 16 in.

SHINGLE WEDGE UNDER VERTICAL JOINTS

INSULATION AS REQUIRED

BUILDING PAPER

STAGGER BUTT JOINTS OVER STUDS

RATED SIDING

STARTER STRIP

NOTE

Nailable panel or lumber sheathing required

LAP SIDING APPLICATION

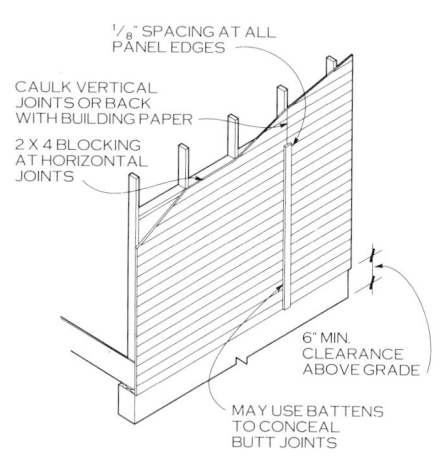

1/8" SPACING AT ALL PANEL EDGES

CAULK VERTICAL JOINTS OR BACK WITH BUILDING PAPER

2 X 4 BLOCKING AT HORIZONTAL JOINTS

6" MIN. CLEARANCE ABOVE GRADE

MAY USE BATTENS TO CONCEAL BUTT JOINTS

PANEL SIDING HORIZONTAL

APA STURD-I-WALL CONSTRUCTION RECOMMENDATIONS (SIDING DIRECT TO STUDS AND OVER NONSTRUCTURAL SHEATHING)

PANEL SIDING DESCRIPTION (ALL SPECIES GROUPS)	NOMINAL THICKNESS OR SPAN RATING (IN.)	MAX. STUD SPACING (IN.)		NAIL SIZE (USE NONSTAINING BOX, SIDING, OR CASING NAILS) [1,2]	NAIL SPACING (IN.)	
		FACE GRAIN VERTICAL	FACE GRAIN HORIZONTAL		PANEL EDGES	INTERMEDIATE
APA MDO EXT	11/32 and 3/8	16	24	6d for panels 1/2" thick or less 8d for thicker panels	6 [4]	12
	1/2 and thicker	24	24			
APA rated siding EXT	16 o.c.	16	24			
APA rated siding EXT	24 o.c. [3]	24	24			

NOTES

1. If siding is applied over sheathing thicker than 1/2 in., use next regular nail size. Use nonstaining box nails for siding installed over foam insulation sheathing.
2. Hot-dipped or hot-tumbled galvanized steel nails are recommended for most siding applications. For best performance, stainless steel nails or aluminum nails should be considered. APA tests also show that electrically or mechanically galvanized steel nails appear satisfactory when plating meets or exceeds thickness requirements of ASTM A641 Class 2 coatings and is further protected by yellow chromate coating.
3. Only panels 15/32 in. and thicker that have certain groove depths and spacing qualify for 24 in. o.c. Span Rating.
4. For braced wall sections with 11/32 in. or 3/4 in. siding applied horizontally over studs 24 in. o.c., space nails 3 in. o.c. along panel edges.

MINIMUM BENDING RADII FOR PLYWOOD PANELS

	PANEL THICKNESS (IN.)				
	1/4	3/8	1/2	5/8	3/4
Across grain (ft)	2	3	6	8	12
Parallel to grain (ft)	5	8	12	16	20

NOTE

The types of plywood recommended for exterior siding are APA grade trademarked medium density overlay (MDO), Type 303 siding or Texture 1-11 (T1-11 special 303 siding). T1-11 plywood siding is manufactured with 3/8 in. wide parallel grooves and shiplapped edges. MDO is recommended for paint finishes and is available in a variety of surfaces. 303 plywood panels are also available in a wide variety of surfaces. The most common APA plywood siding panel dimensions are 4 x 8 ft but the panels are also available in 9 and 10 ft lengths, lap siding to 16 ft.

Bloodgood, Sharp, Buster Architects and Planners; Des Moines, Iowa
American Plywood Association; Tacoma, Washington

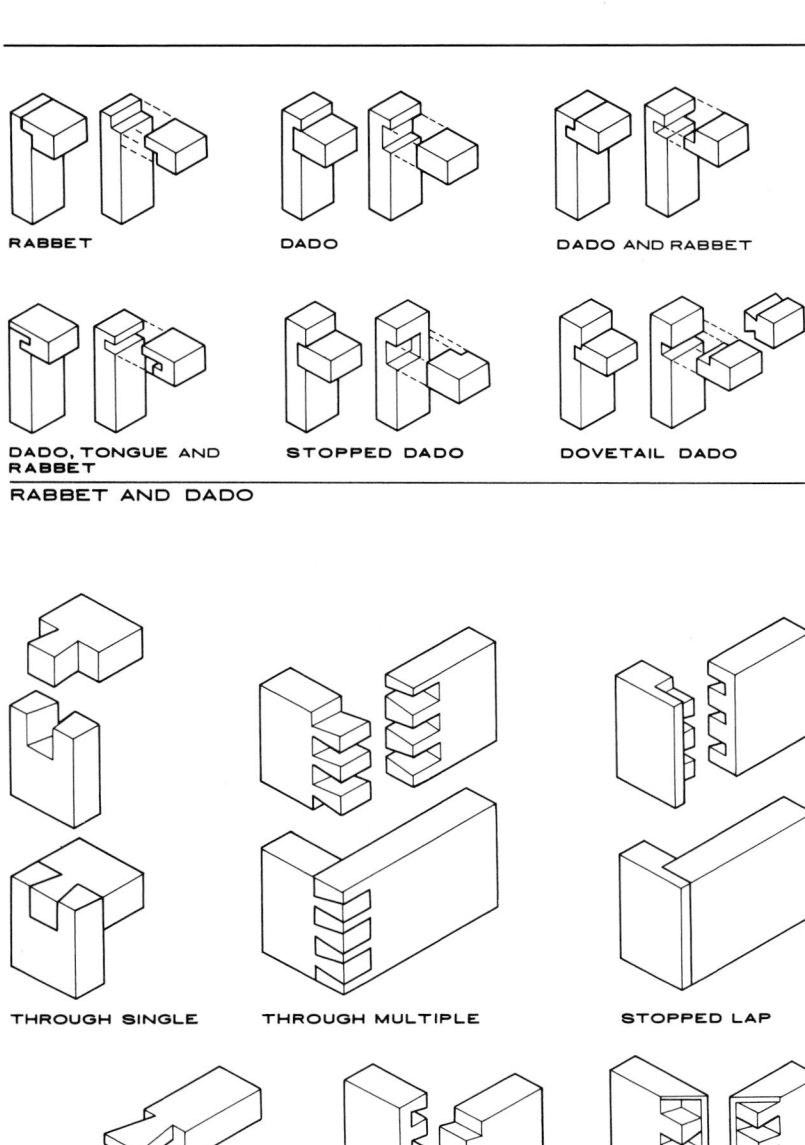

RABBET   DADO   DADO AND RABBET

DADO, TONGUE AND RABBET   STOPPED DADO   DOVETAIL DADO

RABBET AND DADO

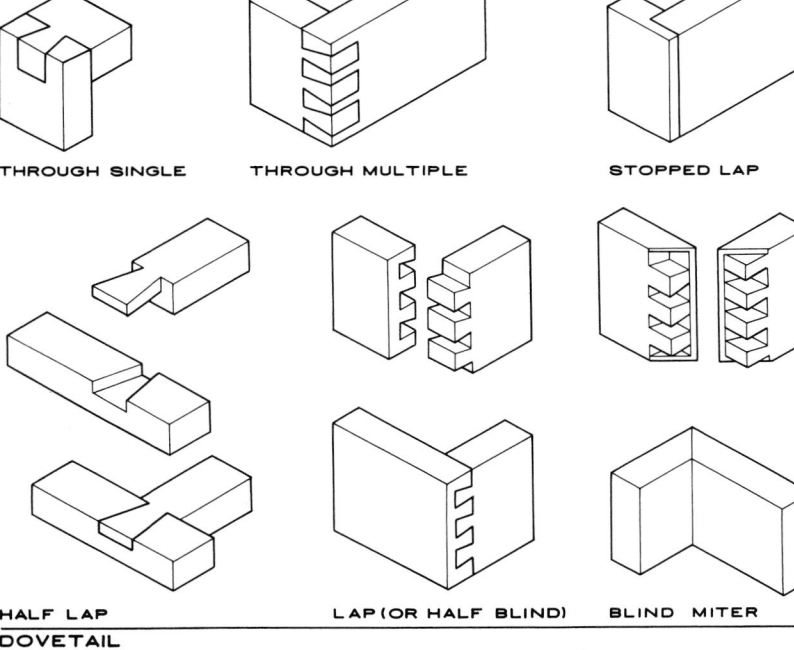

THROUGH SINGLE   THROUGH MULTIPLE   STOPPED LAP

HALF LAP   LAP (OR HALF BLIND)   BLIND MITER

DOVETAIL

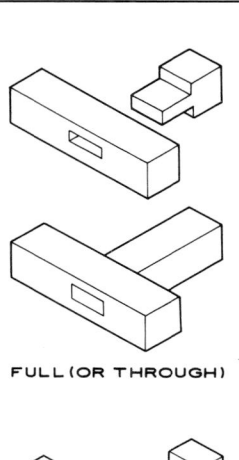

FULL (OR THROUGH)

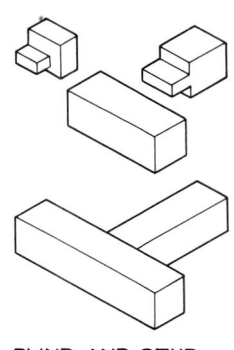

BLIND AND STUB

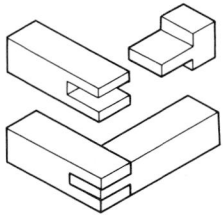

SHIP (OR OPEN)   HALF BLIND

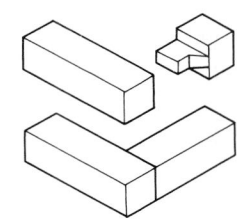

HAUNCH   HAUNCH — BLIND

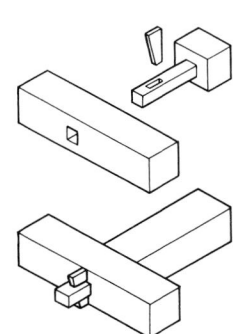

KEYED

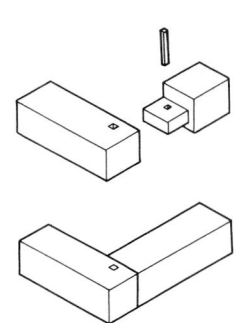

PINNED BLIND

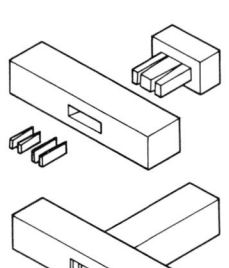

WEDGED

MORTISE AND TENON

NOTES

1. Wood joints may be grouped into three classes: (1) right angle joints, (2) end joints, and (3) edge joints.

2. End joints are used to increase the length of a wood member. By proper utilization of end joints short lengths can be used which might otherwise have been wasted.

3. Edge joints are used to increase the width of a wood member. By giving narrow widths greater use of narrow stock may result.

4. A rabbet (rebate) is a right angle cut made along a corner edge of a wood member. A dado is a rectangular groove cut across the grain of a wood member. If this groove extends along the edge or face of a wood member (being cut parallel to the grain) it is known as a plough (plow).

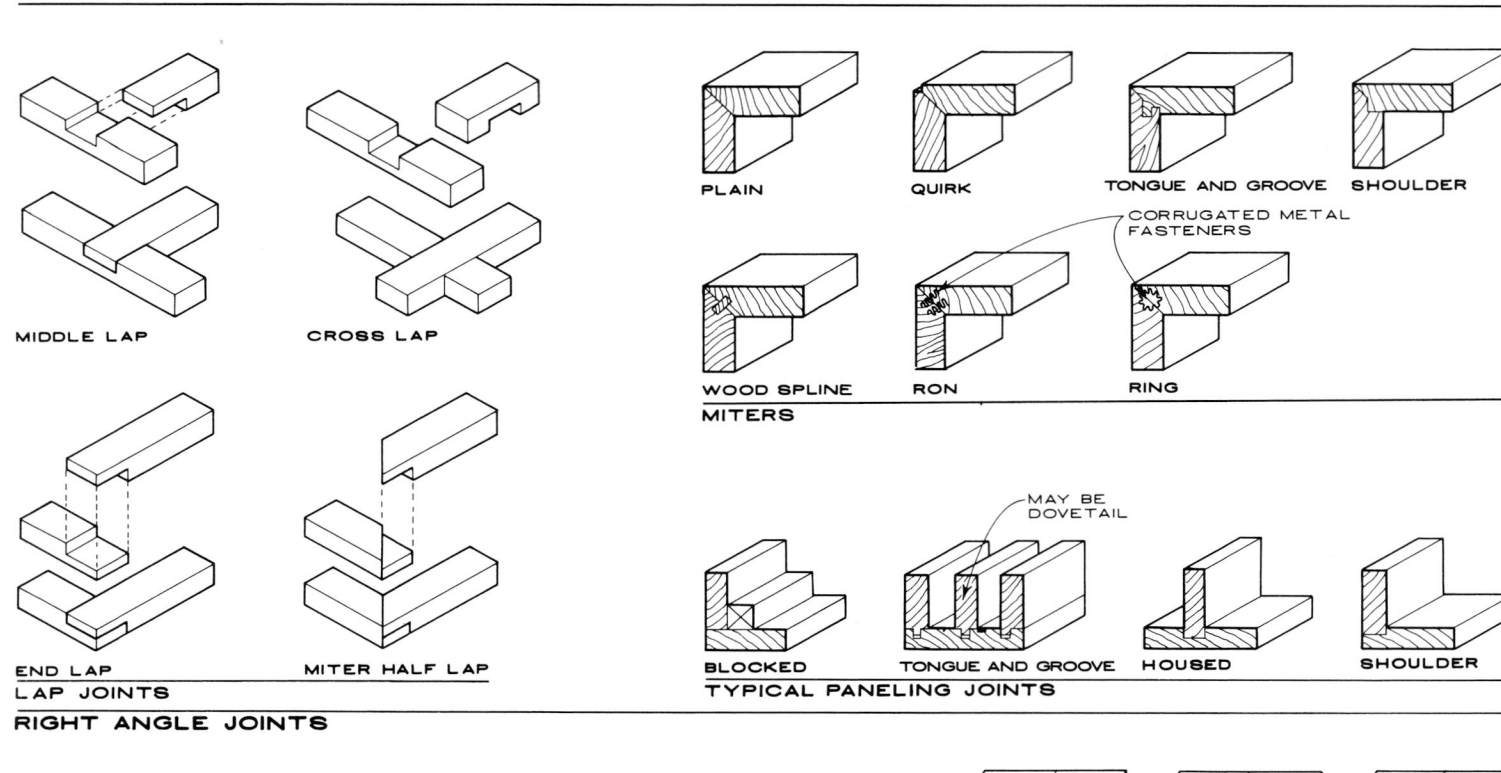

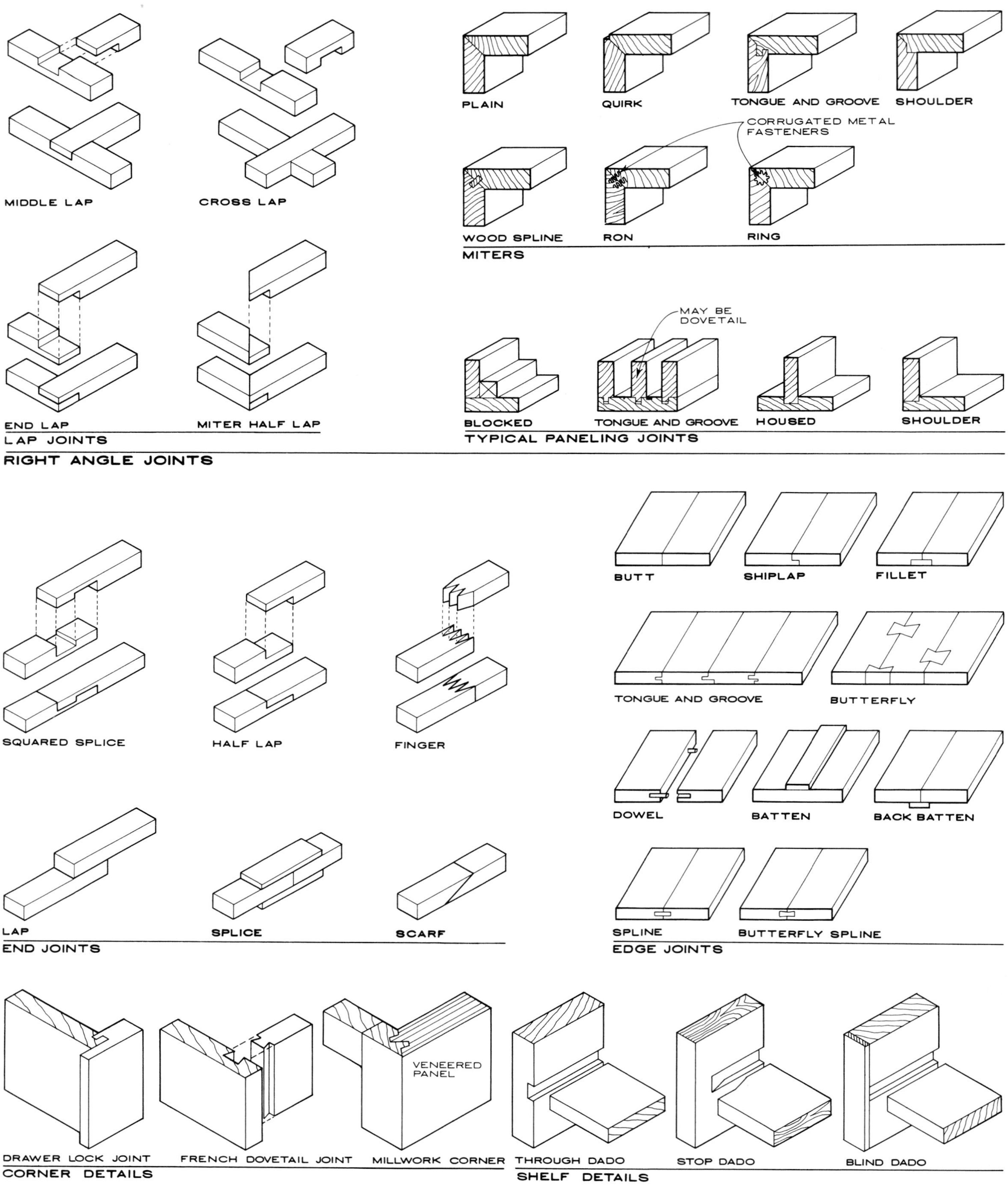

MIDDLE LAP

CROSS LAP

END LAP

MITER HALF LAP

LAP JOINTS

RIGHT ANGLE JOINTS

PLAIN

QUIRK

TONGUE AND GROOVE

SHOULDER

CORRUGATED METAL FASTENERS

WOOD SPLINE

RON

RING

MITERS

MAY BE DOVETAIL

BLOCKED

TONGUE AND GROOVE

HOUSED

SHOULDER

TYPICAL PANELING JOINTS

SQUARED SPLICE

HALF LAP

FINGER

LAP

SPLICE

SCARF

END JOINTS

BUTT

SHIPLAP

FILLET

TONGUE AND GROOVE

BUTTERFLY

DOWEL

BATTEN

BACK BATTEN

SPLINE

BUTTERFLY SPLINE

EDGE JOINTS

DRAWER LOCK JOINT

FRENCH DOVETAIL JOINT

MILLWORK CORNER

VENEERED PANEL

CORNER DETAILS

THROUGH DADO

STOP DADO

BLIND DADO

SHELF DETAILS

CABINET CLASSIFICATIONS

The Architectural Woodworking Institute classifies cabinets in three groups: economy, the lowest grade; custom, the average grade; and premium, the best grade. These details show the progression to higher quality and generally follow the AWI standards, but do not show all possible variations of cabinet details. Woodworking shops frequently set their own quality standards; thus many higher quality details can be found in lower quality work, and vice versa. Also, an architect's design may require crossover of details between the different quality groups.

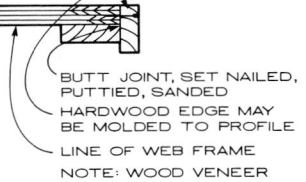

BUTT JOINT, SET NAILED, PUTTIED, SANDED
HARDWOOD EDGE MAY BE MOLDED TO PROFILE
LINE OF WEB FRAME
NOTE: WOOD VENEER
3/4" PLYWOOD SHOWN

ECONOMY GRADE

EDGE DETAIL

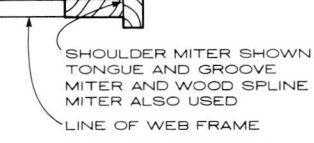

SHOULDER MITER SHOWN, TONGUE AND GROOVE MITER AND WOOD SPLINE MITER ALSO USED
LINE OF WEB FRAME
NOTE: WOOD VENEER
3/4" PLYWOOD SHOWN

CUSTOM GRADE

EDGE DETAIL

WOOD SPLINE MITER SHOWN, TONGUE AND GROOVE MITER ALSO USED
LINE OF WEB FRAME
NOTE: WOOD VENEER
3/4" PLYWOOD SHOWN

PREMIUM GRADE

EDGE DETAIL

.05" GENERAL PURPOSE PLASTIC LAMINATE SEQUENCE OF LAMINATION AT MANUFACTURER'S OPTION
3/4" PARTICLEBOARD
LINE OF WEB FRAME
NO BACK-UP SHEET REQUIRED

ECONOMY GRADE

EDGE DETAIL

.05" GENERAL PURPOSE PLASTIC LAMINATE EDGES APPLIED BEFORE TOP.
3/4" PARTICLEBOARD
.02" BACK-UP SHEET FOR UNSUPPORTED AREAS OVER 6 SQ FT

CUSTOM GRADE

EDGE DETAIL

COLOR-CORE LAMINATES SHOULD BE BUTT JOINTED; EDGES APPLIED BEFORE TOP
3/4" PLYWOOD
.02" BACK-UP SHEET FOR UNSUPPORTED AREAS OVER 4 SQ FT

PREMIUM GRADE

EDGE DETAIL

SOAPSTONE, SLATE, OR MARBLE ON THIN-SET BED
2-LAYERS 3/4" PLYWOOD

PREMIUM GRADE

STONE COUNTER

POST-FORMED PLASTIC LAMINATE

CUSTOM OR ECONOMY GRADE

POST-FORMED COUNTER

GYPSUM BOARD SOFFIT (OPTIONAL)
3/4" X 2 1/2" HARDWOOD CLEAT FASTENED TO STUDS
11 PLY PLYWOOD LIPPED DOOR WITHOUT EDGE BANDING
3/4" PLYWOOD WITH NAILED AND GLUED EDGE BAND ON FRONT
1/8"-3/16" φ HOLES FOR SHELF SUPPORTS, CONSULT MANUFACTURER FOR DIMENSIONS

1'-0" (NTS)
2"
2'-6"
2"

1'-6"
2'-0" (TYP.) 2'-6" (MAX.)
1'-0"

3'-0"
2" 4 1/2" 1/2"

2" 2 1/2"

3/4" PLYWOOD COUNTERTOP
3/4" PLYWOOD BACKSPLASH (OPTIONAL)
3/4" X 2 1/2" HARDWOOD WEB FRAME
HARDWOOD TILT STRIP
1/2" HARDWOOD DRAWER BACK
1/8" HARDBOARD DRAWER BOTTOM. 1/4" IF OVER 1'-0" WIDE
3/4" THICK HARDWOOD DRAWER SUPPORT
3/4" PLYWOOD SHELF WITH NAILED AND GLUED EDGE BAND ON FRONT
HOLES FOR SHELF SUPPORT; SPACING OPTIONAL 1" TYPICAL
11 PLY PLYWOOD LIPPED DOOR WITHOUT EDGE BANDING
2 X 4 WOOD SLEEPER AT 2'-8" O.C.

ECONOMY GRADE

SECTION THROUGH BASE AND WALL CABINETS

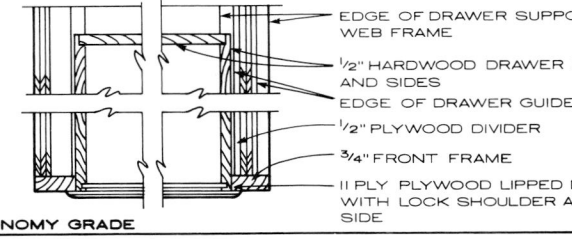

EDGE OF DRAWER SUPPORT WEB FRAME
1/2" HARDWOOD DRAWER BACK AND SIDES
EDGE OF DRAWER GUIDE
1/2" PLYWOOD DIVIDER
3/4" FRONT FRAME
11 PLY PLYWOOD LIPPED DRAWER WITH LOCK SHOULDER AT SIDE

ECONOMY GRADE

PLAN OF DRAWER (LIPPED DRAWER TYPE)

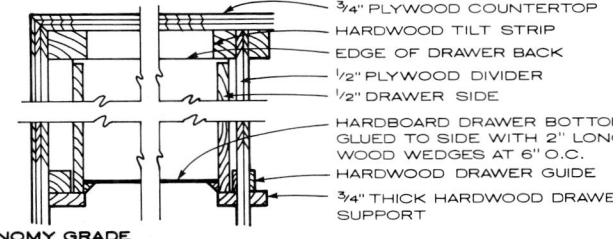

3/4" PLYWOOD COUNTERTOP
HARDWOOD TILT STRIP
EDGE OF DRAWER BACK
1/2" PLYWOOD DIVIDER
1/2" DRAWER SIDE
HARDBOARD DRAWER BOTTOM GLUED TO SIDE WITH 2" LONG WOOD WEDGES AT 6" O.C.
HARDWOOD DRAWER GUIDE
3/4" THICK HARDWOOD DRAWER SUPPORT

ECONOMY GRADE

SECTION THROUGH DRAWER

John S. Fornaro, AIA; Columbia, Virginia

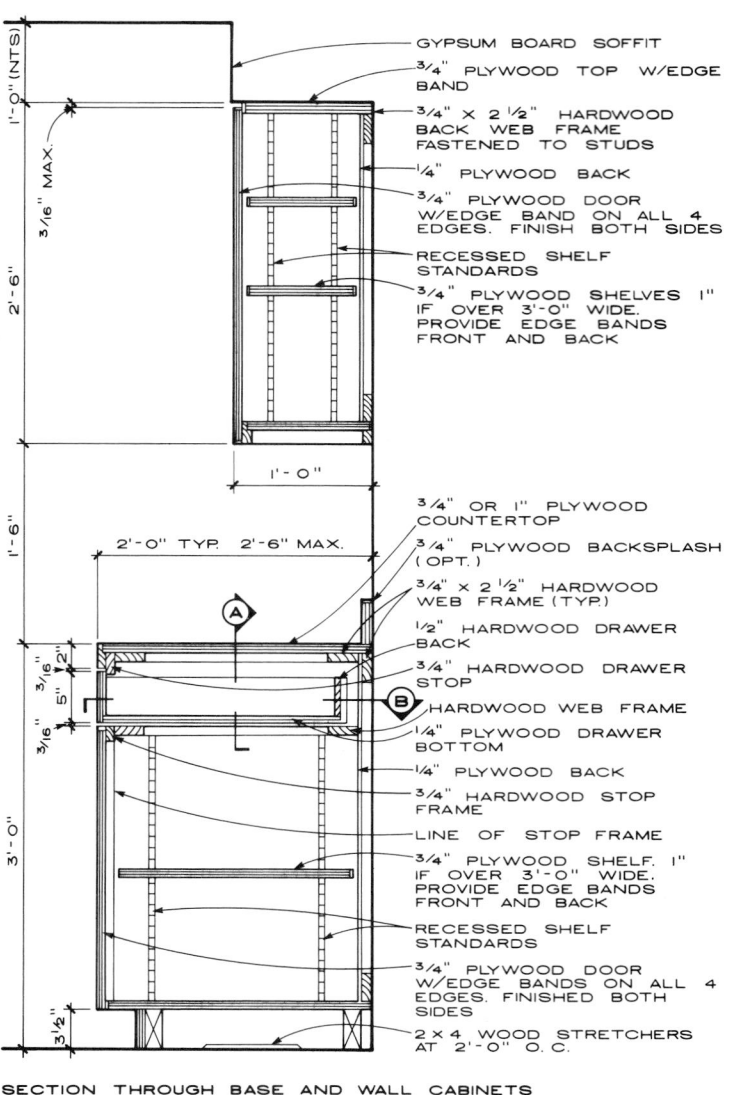

SECTION THROUGH BASE AND WALL CABINETS

Left column labels (top to bottom):
GYPSUM BOARD SOFFIT
¾" PLYWOOD TOP W/EDGE BAND
¾" × 2½" HARDWOOD BACK WEB FRAME FASTENED TO STUDS
¼" PLYWOOD BACK
¾" PLYWOOD DOOR W/EDGE BAND ON ALL 4 EDGES. FINISH BOTH SIDES
RECESSED SHELF STANDARDS
¾" PLYWOOD SHELVES 1" IF OVER 3'-0" WIDE. PROVIDE EDGE BANDS FRONT AND BACK
¾" OR 1" PLYWOOD COUNTERTOP
¾" PLYWOOD BACKSPLASH (OPT.)
¾" × 2½" HARDWOOD WEB FRAME (TYP.)
½" HARDWOOD DRAWER BACK
¾" HARDWOOD DRAWER STOP
HARDWOOD WEB FRAME
¼" PLYWOOD DRAWER BOTTOM
¼" PLYWOOD BACK
¾" HARDWOOD STOP FRAME
LINE OF STOP FRAME
¾" PLYWOOD SHELF. 1" IF OVER 3'-0" WIDE. PROVIDE EDGE BANDS FRONT AND BACK
RECESSED SHELF STANDARDS
¾" PLYWOOD DOOR W/EDGE BANDS ON ALL 4 EDGES. FINISHED BOTH SIDES
2 × 4 WOOD STRETCHERS AT 2'-0" O.C.

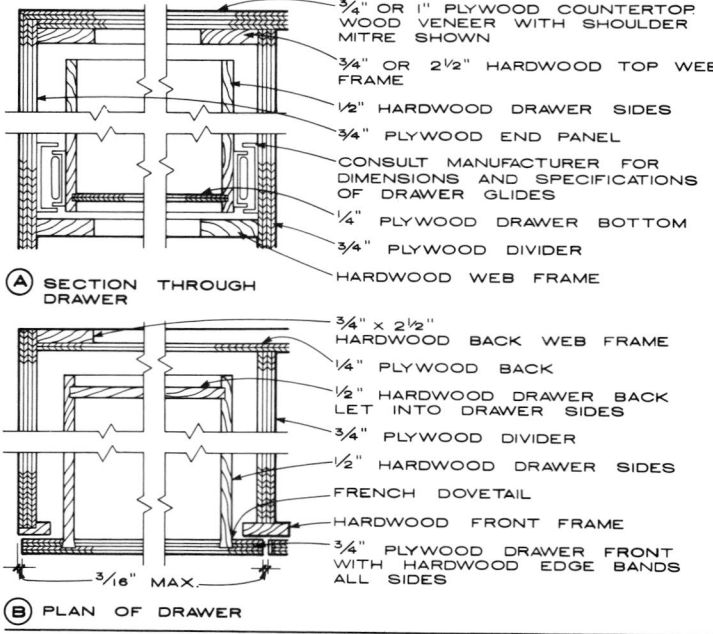

Ⓐ SECTION THROUGH DRAWER
¾" OR 1" PLYWOOD COUNTERTOP WOOD VENEER WITH SHOULDER MITRE SHOWN
¾" OR 2½" HARDWOOD TOP WEB FRAME
½" HARDWOOD DRAWER SIDES
¾" PLYWOOD END PANEL
CONSULT MANUFACTURER FOR DIMENSIONS AND SPECIFICATIONS OF DRAWER GLIDES
¼" PLYWOOD DRAWER BOTTOM
¾" PLYWOOD DIVIDER
HARDWOOD WEB FRAME

Ⓑ PLAN OF DRAWER
¾" × 2½" HARDWOOD BACK WEB FRAME
¼" PLYWOOD BACK
½" HARDWOOD DRAWER BACK LET INTO DRAWER SIDES
¾" PLYWOOD DIVIDER
½" HARDWOOD DRAWER SIDES
FRENCH DOVETAIL
HARDWOOD FRONT FRAME
¾" PLYWOOD DRAWER FRONT WITH HARDWOOD EDGE BANDS ALL SIDES

CUSTOM GRADE (FLUSH OVERLAY TYPE)

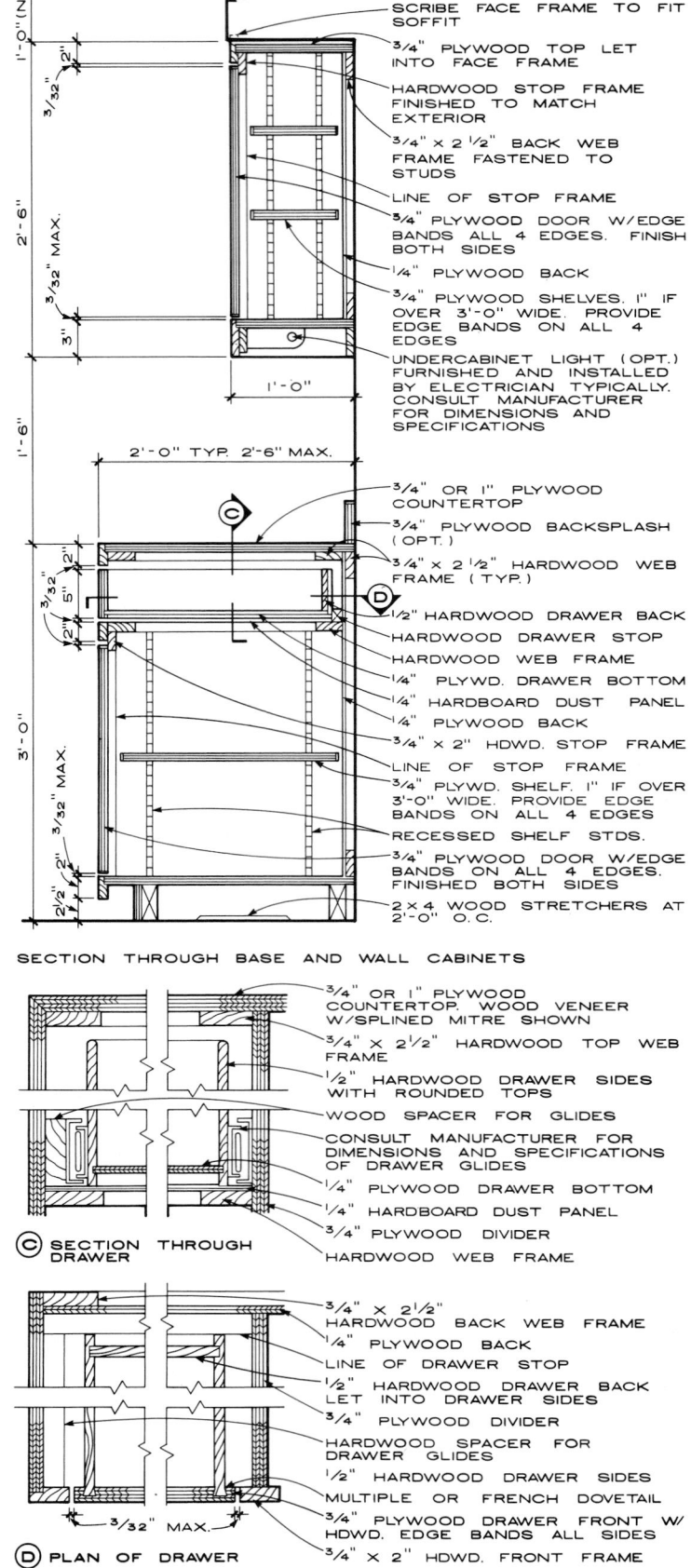

SECTION THROUGH BASE AND WALL CABINETS

Right column labels (top to bottom):
GYPSUM BOARD SOFFIT
SCRIBE FACE FRAME TO FIT SOFFIT
¾" PLYWOOD TOP LET INTO FACE FRAME
HARDWOOD STOP FRAME FINISHED TO MATCH EXTERIOR
¾" × 2½" BACK WEB FRAME FASTENED TO STUDS
LINE OF STOP FRAME
¾" PLYWOOD DOOR W/EDGE BANDS ALL 4 EDGES. FINISH BOTH SIDES
¼" PLYWOOD BACK
¾" PLYWOOD SHELVES. 1" IF OVER 3'-0" WIDE. PROVIDE EDGE BANDS ON ALL 4 EDGES
UNDERCABINET LIGHT (OPT.) FURNISHED AND INSTALLED BY ELECTRICIAN TYPICALLY. CONSULT MANUFACTURER FOR DIMENSIONS AND SPECIFICATIONS
¾" OR 1" PLYWOOD COUNTERTOP
¾" PLYWOOD BACKSPLASH (OPT.)
¾" × 2½" HARDWOOD WEB FRAME (TYP.)
½" HARDWOOD DRAWER BACK
HARDWOOD DRAWER STOP
HARDWOOD WEB FRAME
¼" PLYWD. DRAWER BOTTOM
¼" HARDBOARD DUST PANEL
¼" PLYWOOD BACK
¾" × 2" HDWD. STOP FRAME
LINE OF STOP FRAME
¾" PLYWD. SHELF. 1" IF OVER 3'-0" WIDE. PROVIDE EDGE BANDS ON ALL 4 EDGES
RECESSED SHELF STDS.
¾" PLYWOOD DOOR W/EDGE BANDS ON ALL 4 EDGES. FINISHED BOTH SIDES
2 × 4 WOOD STRETCHERS AT 2'-0" O.C.

Ⓒ SECTION THROUGH DRAWER
¾" OR 1" PLYWOOD COUNTERTOP. WOOD VENEER W/SPLINED MITRE SHOWN
¾" × 2½" HARDWOOD TOP WEB FRAME
½" HARDWOOD DRAWER SIDES WITH ROUNDED TOPS
WOOD SPACER FOR GLIDES
CONSULT MANUFACTURER FOR DIMENSIONS AND SPECIFICATIONS OF DRAWER GLIDES
¼" PLYWOOD DRAWER BOTTOM
¼" HARDBOARD DUST PANEL
¾" PLYWOOD DIVIDER
HARDWOOD WEB FRAME

Ⓓ PLAN OF DRAWER
¾" × 2½" HARDWOOD BACK WEB FRAME
¼" PLYWOOD BACK
LINE OF DRAWER STOP
½" HARDWOOD DRAWER BACK LET INTO DRAWER SIDES
¾" PLYWOOD DIVIDER
HARDWOOD SPACER FOR DRAWER GLIDES
½" HARDWOOD DRAWER SIDES
MULTIPLE OR FRENCH DOVETAIL
¾" PLYWOOD DRAWER FRONT W/ HDWD. EDGE BANDS ALL SIDES
¾" × 2" HDWD. FRONT FRAME

PREMIUM GRADE (EXPOSED FRONT FRAME TYPE)

John S. Fornaro, AIA; Columbia, Virginia

ARCHITECTURAL WOODWORK

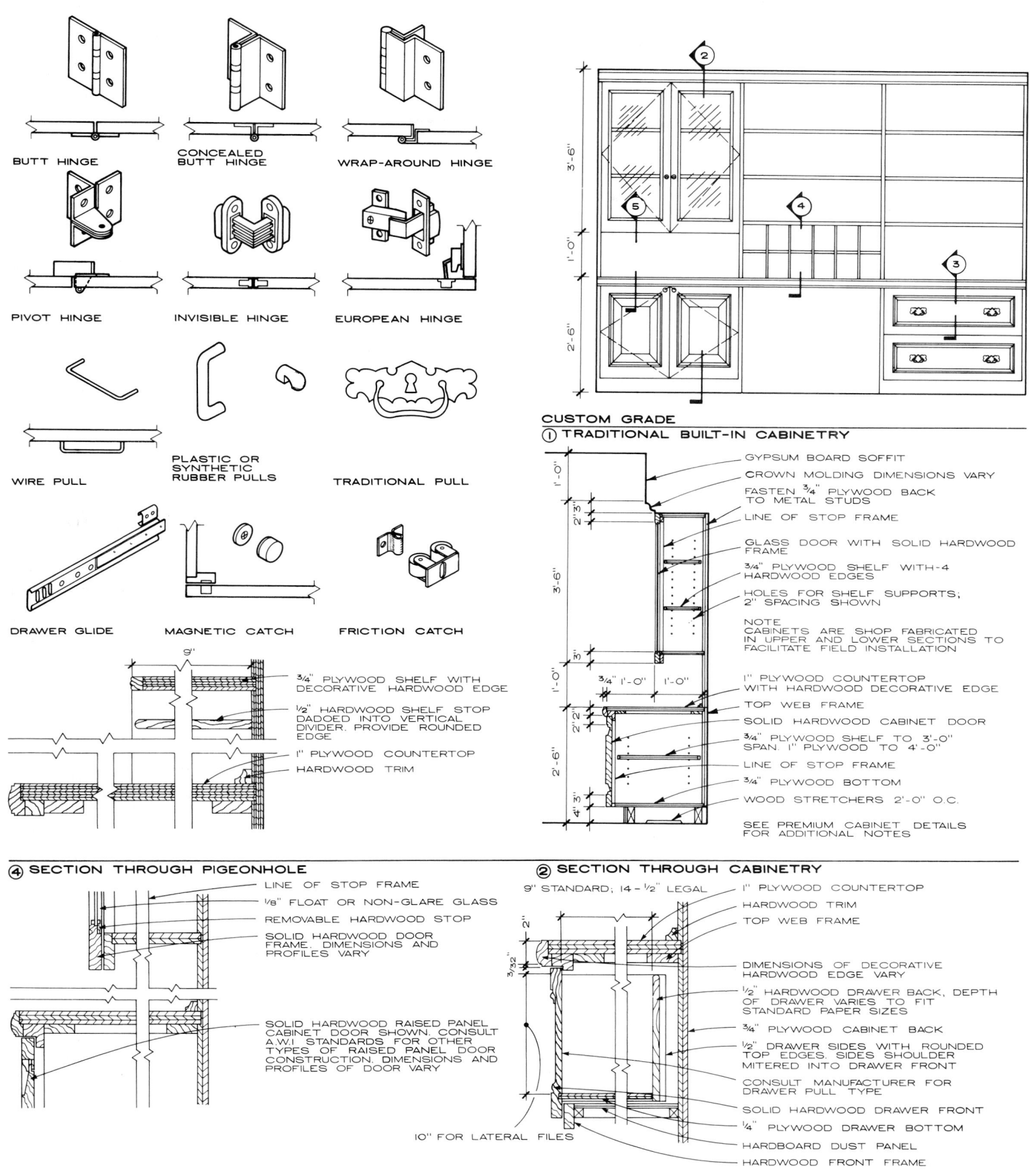

BUTT HINGE

CONCEALED
BUTT HINGE

WRAP-AROUND HINGE

PIVOT HINGE

INVISIBLE HINGE

EUROPEAN HINGE

WIRE PULL

PLASTIC OR
SYNTHETIC
RUBBER PULLS

TRADITIONAL PULL

DRAWER GLIDE

MAGNETIC CATCH

FRICTION CATCH

3/4" PLYWOOD SHELF WITH
DECORATIVE HARDWOOD EDGE

1/2" HARDWOOD SHELF STOP
DADOED INTO VERTICAL
DIVIDER. PROVIDE ROUNDED
EDGE

1" PLYWOOD COUNTERTOP

HARDWOOD TRIM

CUSTOM GRADE

① **TRADITIONAL BUILT-IN CABINETRY**

GYPSUM BOARD SOFFIT

CROWN MOLDING DIMENSIONS VARY

FASTEN 3/4" PLYWOOD BACK
TO METAL STUDS

LINE OF STOP FRAME

GLASS DOOR WITH SOLID HARDWOOD
FRAME

3/4" PLYWOOD SHELF WITH 4
HARDWOOD EDGES

HOLES FOR SHELF SUPPORTS;
2" SPACING SHOWN

NOTE
CABINETS ARE SHOP FABRICATED
IN UPPER AND LOWER SECTIONS TO
FACILITATE FIELD INSTALLATION

1" PLYWOOD COUNTERTOP
WITH HARDWOOD DECORATIVE EDGE

TOP WEB FRAME

SOLID HARDWOOD CABINET DOOR

3/4" PLYWOOD SHELF TO 3'-0"
SPAN. 1" PLYWOOD TO 4'-0"

LINE OF STOP FRAME

3/4" PLYWOOD BOTTOM

WOOD STRETCHERS 2'-0" O.C.

SEE PREMIUM CABINET DETAILS
FOR ADDITIONAL NOTES

④ **SECTION THROUGH PIGEONHOLE**

LINE OF STOP FRAME

1/8" FLOAT OR NON-GLARE GLASS

REMOVABLE HARDWOOD STOP

SOLID HARDWOOD DOOR
FRAME. DIMENSIONS AND
PROFILES VARY

SOLID HARDWOOD RAISED PANEL
CABINET DOOR SHOWN. CONSULT
A.W.I. STANDARDS FOR OTHER
TYPES OF RAISED PANEL DOOR
CONSTRUCTION. DIMENSIONS AND
PROFILES OF DOOR VARY

② **SECTION THROUGH CABINETRY**

9" STANDARD; 14-1/2" LEGAL

1" PLYWOOD COUNTERTOP

HARDWOOD TRIM

TOP WEB FRAME

DIMENSIONS OF DECORATIVE
HARDWOOD EDGE VARY

1/2" HARDWOOD DRAWER BACK, DEPTH
OF DRAWER VARIES TO FIT
STANDARD PAPER SIZES

3/4" PLYWOOD CABINET BACK

1/2" DRAWER SIDES WITH ROUNDED
TOP EDGES. SIDES SHOULDER
MITERED INTO DRAWER FRONT

CONSULT MANUFACTURER FOR
DRAWER PULL TYPE

SOLID HARDWOOD DRAWER FRONT

1/4" PLYWOOD DRAWER BOTTOM

HARDBOARD DUST PANEL

HARDWOOD FRONT FRAME

10" FOR LATERAL FILES

⑤ **SECTION THROUGH GLASS AND WOOD DOOR**

③ **SECTION THROUGH LATERAL FILE**

John S. Fornaro, AIA; Columbia, Virginia

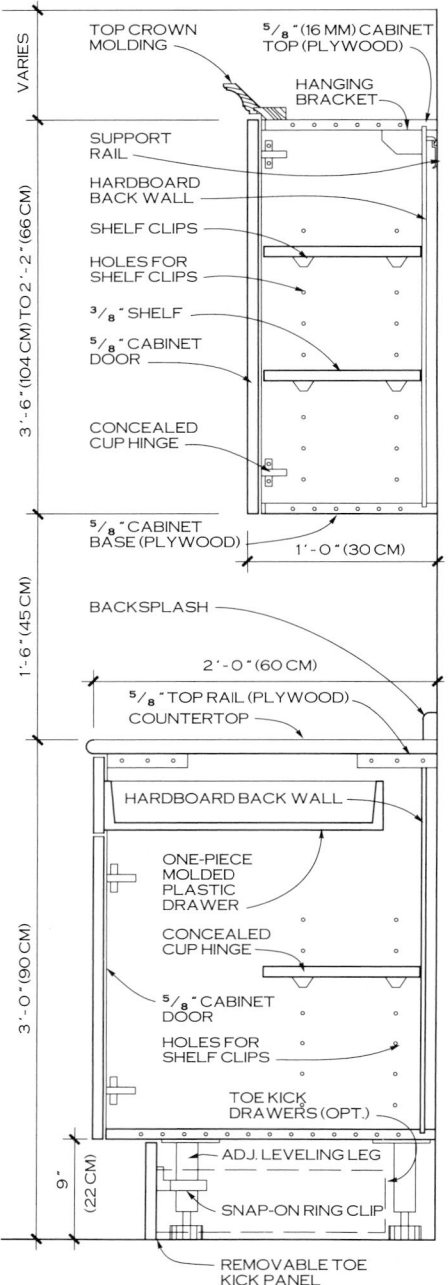

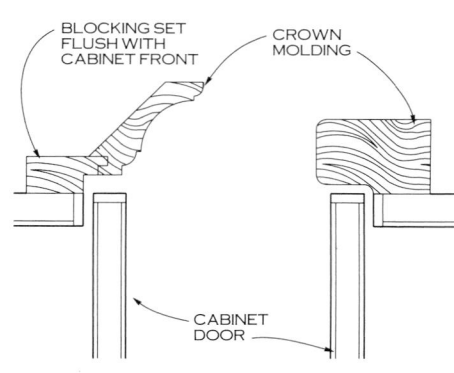

SECTION THROUGH BASE AND WALL CABINET

TOP CROWN MOLDING DETAILS

CHARACTERISTICS

The European-style kitchen cabinet system is based on the ability of the whole cabinet assembly to be easily installed, adjusted, or broken down and moved like furniture.

Wall cabinets are typically hung from a metal bracket attached at each top corner and then placed on a metal support rail attached to the finished wall. Adjustment can occur in three directions for plumb and level after the cabinet is hung; the adjustment mechanism, which is actually the back of the hanging bracket, is exposed on the inside of the cabinet. Above the cabinets, either no soffit is built, allowing over-cabinet storage, or an allowance of 3/4 in. clear is needed, so the cabinet can be lifted up and set down over the metal support rail.

The base cabinets are generally not secured to the wall or floor but are set onto metal or PVC legs, four per cabinet, which are adjustable for leveling. A removable toe kick panel allows for further adjustment to the legs or for cleaning. For island installations or peninsula cabinets, the leveling leg system should be augmented with traditional wood blocking as an anchor.

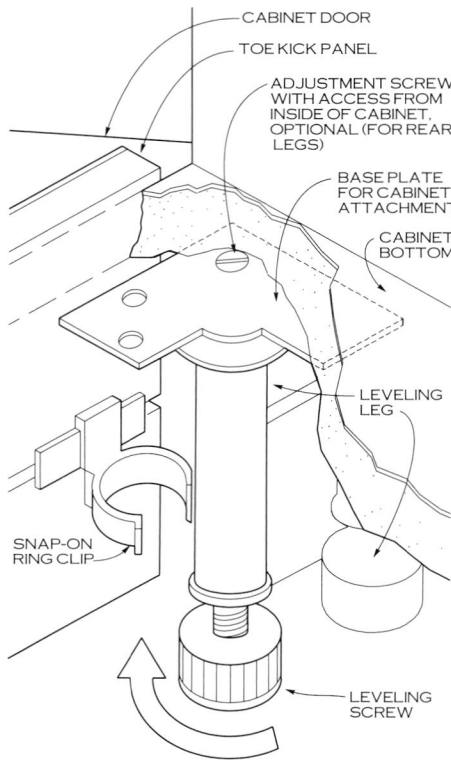

LEVELING LEG/TOE KICK PANEL

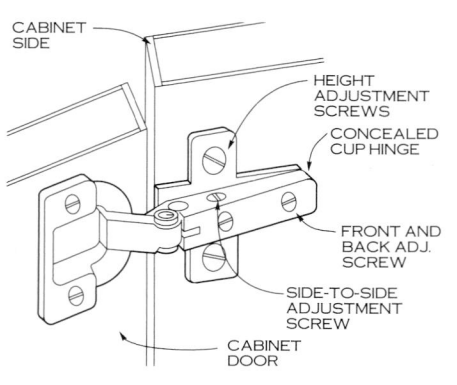

CONCEALED CUP HINGE

The construction and features of the cabinet itself differ from a typical American-style cabinet as follows:

1. The carcass is frameless and is put together by dowels running from the side panels into the top and bottom panels.
2. Sizes are based on a 32 mm module system. Dowels are drilled 32 mm apart, center posts dividing cabinets in half are 32 mm deep, shelves and carcass parts are 16 mm (1/2 module), etc.
3. Predrilled holes in the side panels accommodate shelf supports for the adjustable shelves.
4. Concealed cup hinges allow near 180° opening of cabinet doors; some varieties are also adjustable in three directions.
5. An increased toe-kick height (6 to 9 in.) can accommodate a drawer under base cabinets.

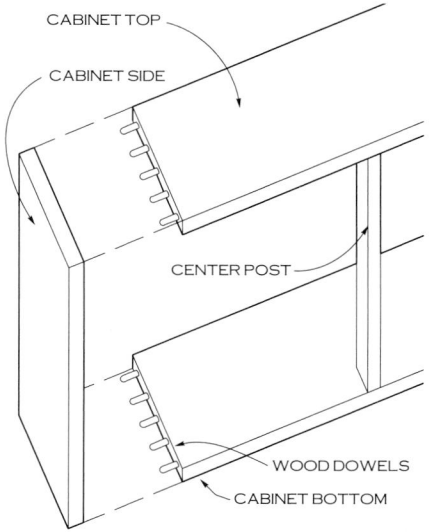

DOWELED CABINET CONSTRUCTION

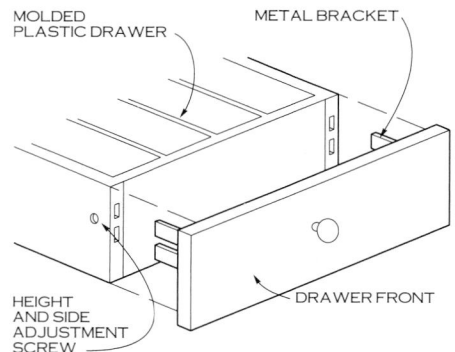

DRAWER DETAIL

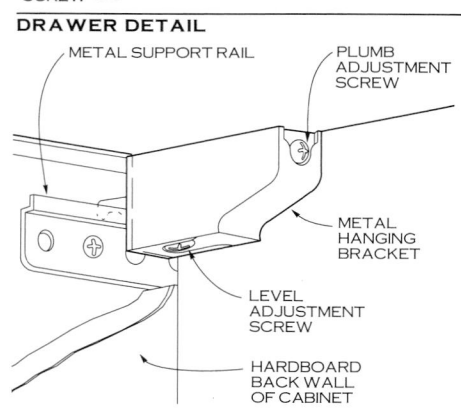

HANGING BRACKET AND RAIL DETAIL

Richard J. Vitullo, AIA; Oak Leaf Studio; Crownsville, Maryland

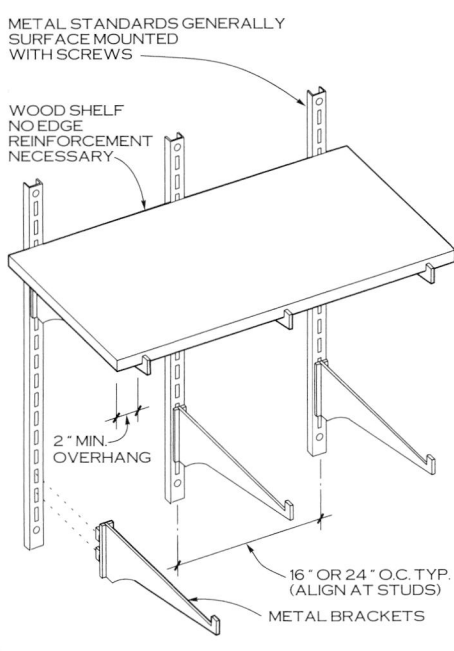

METAL STANDARDS GENERALLY SURFACE MOUNTED WITH SCREWS

WOOD SHELF NO EDGE REINFORCEMENT NECESSARY

2" MIN. OVERHANG

16" OR 24" O.C. TYP. (ALIGN AT STUDS)

METAL BRACKETS

STANDARDS AND BRACKETS SYSTEM

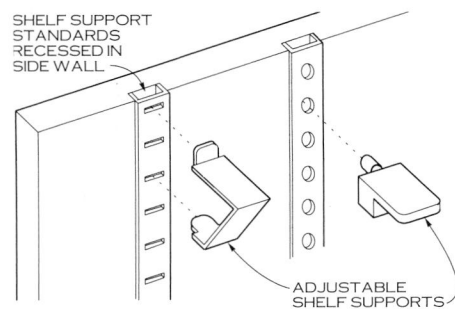

SHELF SUPPORT STANDARDS RECESSED IN SIDE WALL

ADJUSTABLE SHELF SUPPORTS

STANDARDS AND CLIP SYSTEM

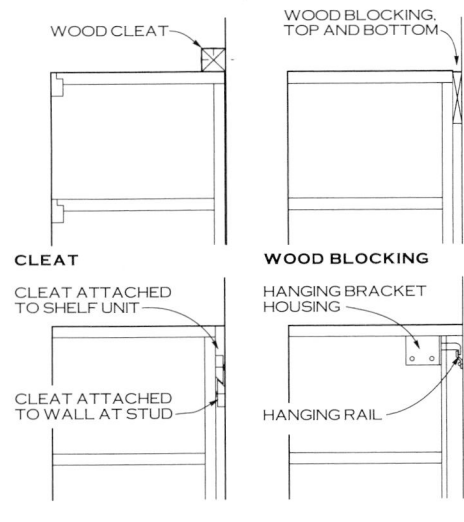

WOOD CLEAT

WOOD BLOCKING, TOP AND BOTTOM

CLEAT

WOOD BLOCKING

CLEAT ATTACHED TO SHELF UNIT

HANGING BRACKET HOUSING

CLEAT ATTACHED TO WALL AT STUD

HANGING RAIL

HANGING CLEAT

HANGING BRACKET

NOTE

All details except hanging bracket and rail must also be floor supported.

BOOKSHELF WALL ATTACHMENT

Richard J. Vitullo, AIA; Oak Leaf Studio; Crownsville, Maryland
Helmut Guenschel, Inc.; Baltimore, Maryland

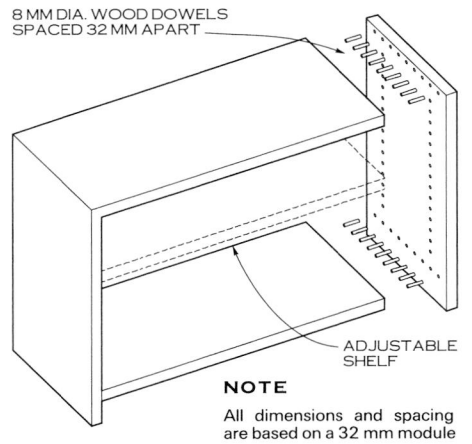

8 MM DIA. WOOD DOWELS SPACED 32 MM APART

ADJUSTABLE SHELF

NOTE

All dimensions and spacing are based on a 32 mm module

BOX FRAME DIAGRAM

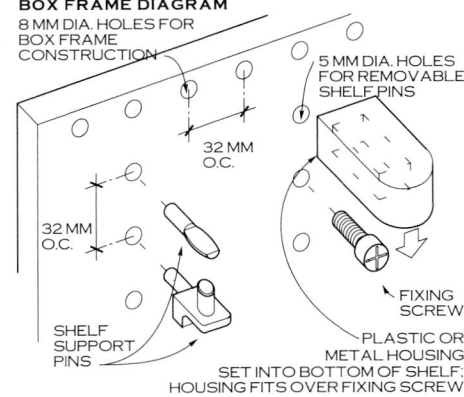

8 MM DIA. HOLES FOR BOX FRAME CONSTRUCTION

5 MM DIA. HOLES FOR REMOVABLE SHELF PINS

32 MM O.C.

32 MM O.C.

FIXING SCREW

SHELF SUPPORT PINS

PLASTIC OR METAL HOUSING SET INTO BOTTOM OF SHELF; HOUSING FITS OVER FIXING SCREW

32 MM BOX FRAME SYSTEM

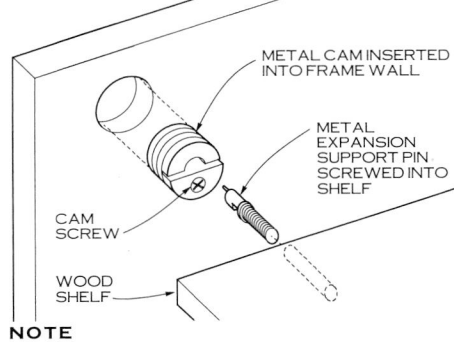

METAL CAM INSERTED INTO FRAME WALL

METAL EXPANSION SUPPORT PIN SCREWED INTO SHELF

CAM SCREW

WOOD SHELF

NOTE

This system can be hand mounted or machine inserted. A half turn of the cam screw tightens connection and prevents disassembly.

SEMI-FIXED FRAME/SHELF DETAIL

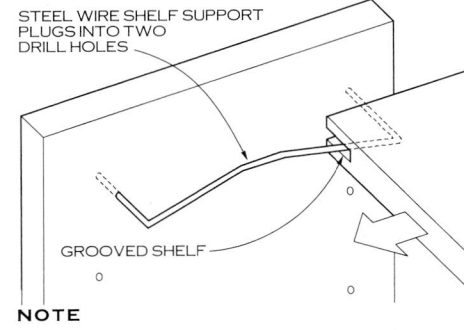

STEEL WIRE SHELF SUPPORT PLUGS INTO TWO DRILL HOLES

GROOVED SHELF

NOTE

This system can be used for horizontal shelf attachment or vertical divider support.

REMOVABLE GROOVED SHELF DETAIL

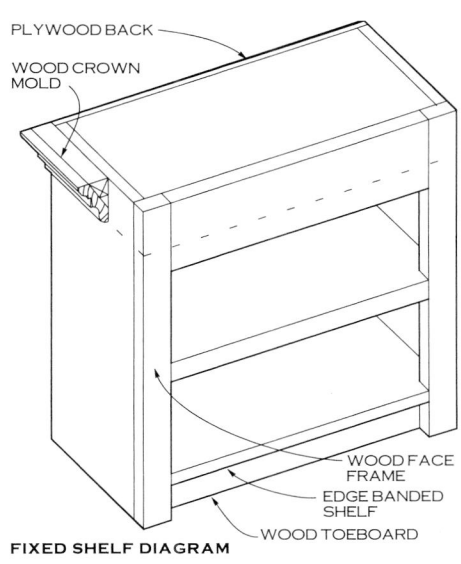

PLYWOOD BACK

WOOD CROWN MOLD

WOOD FACE FRAME

EDGE BANDED SHELF

WOOD TOEBOARD

FIXED SHELF DIAGRAM

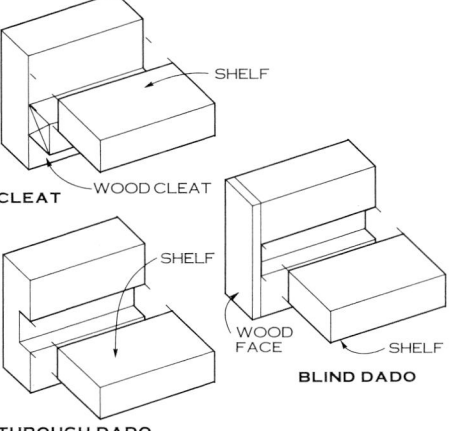

SHELF

CLEAT

WOOD CLEAT

SHELF

WOOD FACE

SHELF

BLIND DADO

THROUGH DADO
SUPPORT DETAILS AT SIDE

FIXED SHELF SYSTEM

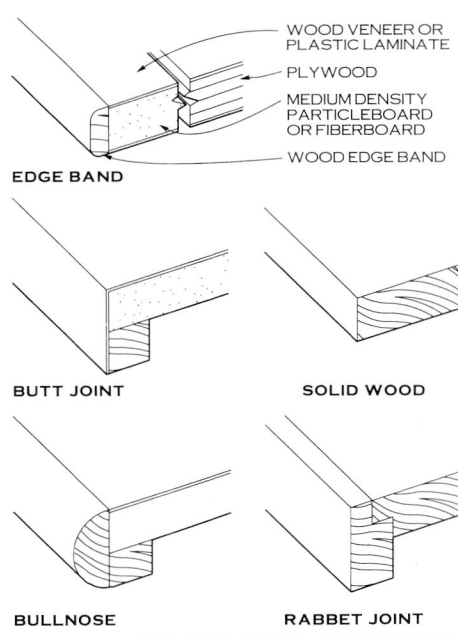

WOOD VENEER OR PLASTIC LAMINATE

PLYWOOD

MEDIUM DENSITY PARTICLEBOARD OR FIBERBOARD

WOOD EDGE BAND

EDGE BAND

BUTT JOINT

SOLID WOOD

BULLNOSE

RABBET JOINT

SHELF EDGE DETAIL

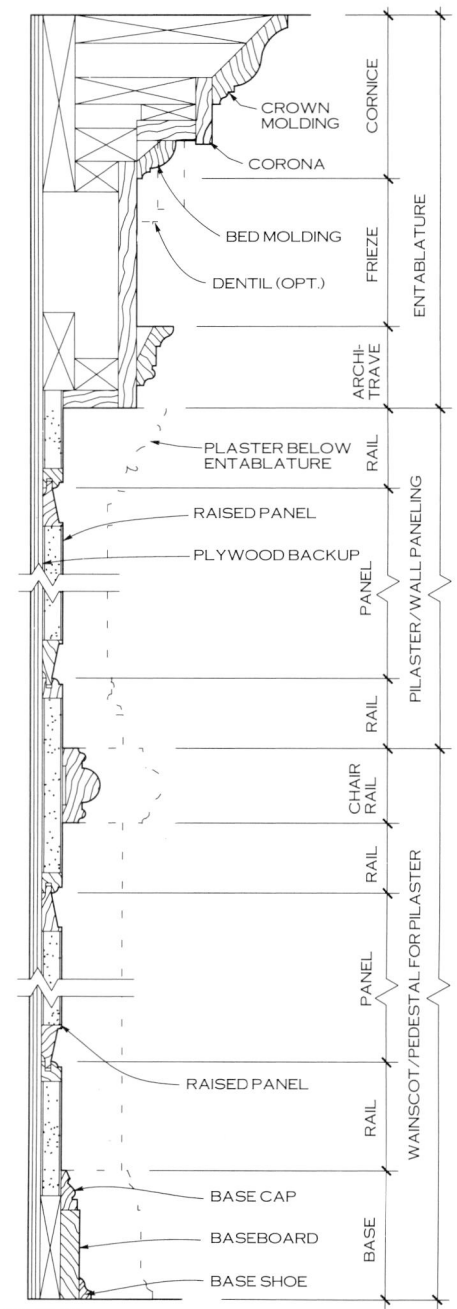

CROWN MOLDING
CORONA
BED MOLDING
DENTIL (OPT.)
PLASTER BELOW ENTABLATURE
RAISED PANEL
PLYWOOD BACKUP
RAISED PANEL
BASE CAP
BASEBOARD
BASE SHOE

CORNICE
FRIEZE
ARCHITRAVE
RAIL
PANEL
RAIL
CHAIR RAIL
RAIL
PANEL
RAIL
BASE

ENTABLATURE
PILASTER/WALL PANELING
WAINSCOT/PEDESTAL FOR PILASTER

NOTES

1. Because of its stability, plywood is preferable to solid lumber or other materials as backup.
2. To join stile to rail, mortise and tenon or dowelled joints are used. Stile to stile joints at outside corners are spline joints or lock miters; inside corners are butt jointed.

SECTION – FULL HEIGHT WALL PANEL

INTERIOR WALL PANEL DETAILS

Architectural interior paneling consists of a series of thin sheets of wood (panels) framed together by means of stouter strips of wood, vertical (stiles) and horizontal (rails), to form either a door, screen, or lining for internal walls. Paneling was first used as a wall covering in England in the 13th century. Up to the 16th century, the framing was almost as massive as half-timber construction. Then it was progressively lightened until by the middle of that century when the thickness of the framing was reduced to an inch. Today, inch thick or less panels are made from veneers over plywood or composition boards, which can be treated for fire protection. The stiles and rails are made from solid wood or veneered boards. Rim and lip moldings and other trims are almost exclusively made from solid wood.

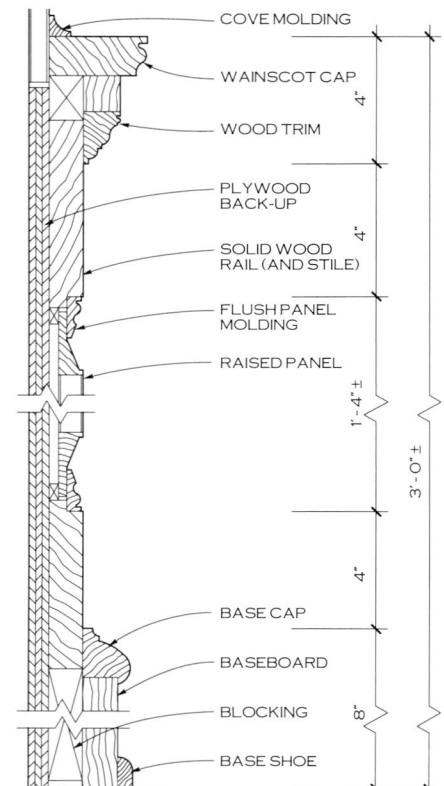

COVE MOLDING
WAINSCOT CAP
WOOD TRIM
PLYWOOD BACK-UP
SOLID WOOD RAIL (AND STILE)
FLUSH PANEL MOLDING
RAISED PANEL
BASE CAP
BASEBOARD
BLOCKING
BASE SHOE

SECTION – WAINSCOT WITH RAISED PANEL AND FLUSH MOLDING

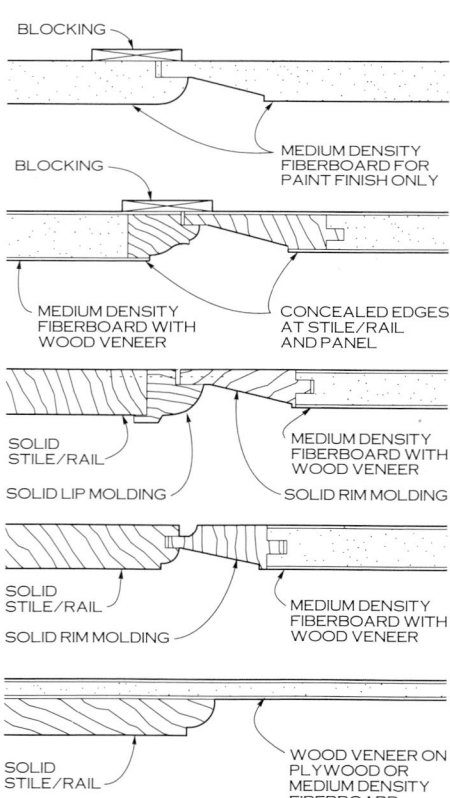

BLOCKING
BLOCKING
MEDIUM DENSITY FIBERBOARD FOR PAINT FINISH ONLY
MEDIUM DENSITY FIBERBOARD WITH WOOD VENEER
CONCEALED EDGES AT STILE/RAIL AND PANEL
SOLID STILE/RAIL
SOLID LIP MOLDING
MEDIUM DENSITY FIBERBOARD WITH WOOD VENEER
SOLID RIM MOLDING
SOLID STILE/RAIL
SOLID RIM MOLDING
MEDIUM DENSITY FIBERBOARD WITH WOOD VENEER
SOLID STILE/RAIL
WOOD VENEER ON PLYWOOD OR MEDIUM DENSITY FIBERBOARD

STILE/RAIL TO PANEL JOINERY TYPES

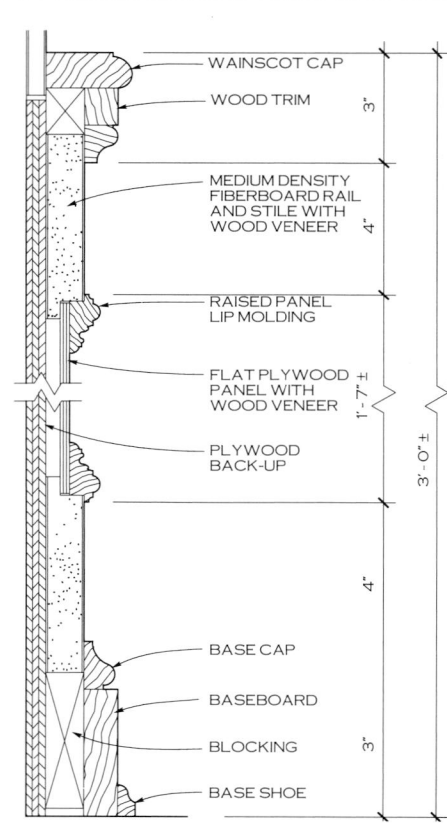

WAINSCOT CAP
WOOD TRIM
MEDIUM DENSITY FIBERBOARD RAIL AND STILE WITH WOOD VENEER
RAISED PANEL LIP MOLDING
FLAT PLYWOOD PANEL WITH WOOD VENEER
PLYWOOD BACK-UP
BASE CAP
BASEBOARD
BLOCKING
BASE SHOE

SECTION – WAINSCOT WITH FLUSH PANEL AND RAISED MOLDING

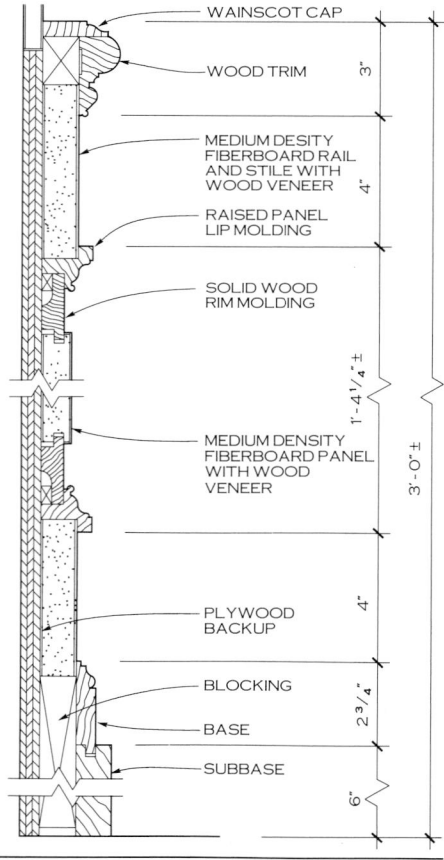

WAINSCOT CAP
WOOD TRIM
MEDIUM DESITY FIBERBOARD RAIL AND STILE WITH WOOD VENEER
RAISED PANEL LIP MOLDING
SOLID WOOD RIM MOLDING
MEDIUM DENSITY FIBERBOARD PANEL WITH WOOD VENEER
PLYWOOD BACKUP
BLOCKING
BASE
SUBBASE

SECTION – WAINSCOT WITH RAISED PANEL AND RAISED MOLDING

Richard J. Vitullo, AIA; Oak Leaf Studio; Crownsville, Maryland
Architectural Woodwork Institute; Arlington, Virginia

GUIDELINES

Construction details on this page are for shop-built stairs using Premium Grade Standards of the Architectural Woodwork Institute. Wood stairs used in private, residential applications usually are not governed by the ADA; however, wood stairs in commercial facilities and places of public accommodation must conform to ADA accessibility guidelines (ADAAG). Details on these two pages depict both alternatives.

1. Check current local building codes and regulations for requirements that may differ from the general recommendations provided here.
2. Interior stair width: 36 in. minimum.
3. Minimum headroom is 6 ft 8 in. as measured vertically from a diagonal line connecting tread nosings to the underside of the finished ceiling or stair landing directly above the stair run. Recommended headroom is 7 ft.
4. Only handrails and stair stringers may project into the required width of a stair.
   Handrail projection: $3\frac{1}{2}$ in. maximum.
   Stringer projection: $1\frac{1}{2}$ in. maximum.
   For a stair to comply with ADAAG, no projections are allowed into the minimum required stair width.
5. The width of a landing or platform should be at least as wide as the stair.
6. The maximum vertical rise of a stair between landings is 12 ft.
7. Riser height: 4 in. min. and 7 in. max.
   Tread width: 11 in. min., measured from riser to riser.
   Variation in adjacent treads or risers should not exceed $\frac{3}{16}$ in. The maximum difference allowed the tread width or riser height within a flight of stairs is $\frac{3}{8}$ in. ADAAG requires uniform treads and risers.
8. Nosings project $1\frac{1}{2}$ in. max. Check codes and ADAAG for other restrictions.
9. Height of handrail above stair nosings: 30 to 34 in.; 34 to 38 in. per ADAAG. Guardrail height at landings: 36 or 42 in.; check local code.
10. Design handrails that can be gripped easily and fit the hand. Recommended diameter is $1\frac{1}{4}$ to $1\frac{1}{2}$ in. for round handrails and a similar size for an elliptical or rounded square edge section. Handrails should be structurally designed so that both downward (vertical) and lateral (horizontal) thrust loads are considered.
11. Extensions of handrail at top and bottom of stair may affect total length of required run. Verify extensions required by local codes or ADAAG when designing a stair.
12. Refer to related stair topics in chapters 1, 3, 4, 5, and 9.

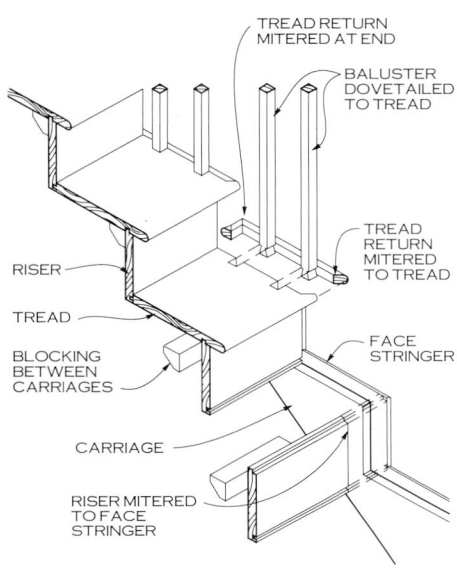

BALUSTERS AND TRIM AT FACE STRINGER

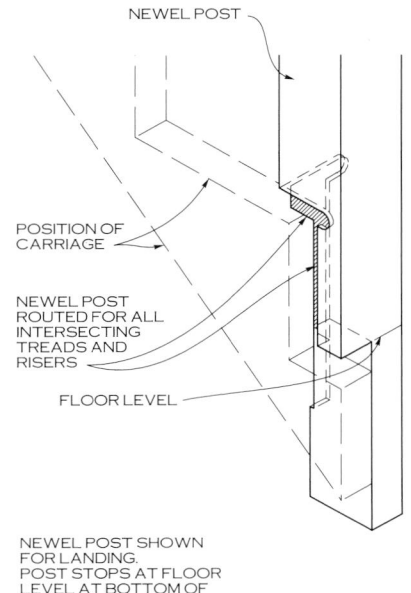

NEWEL POST

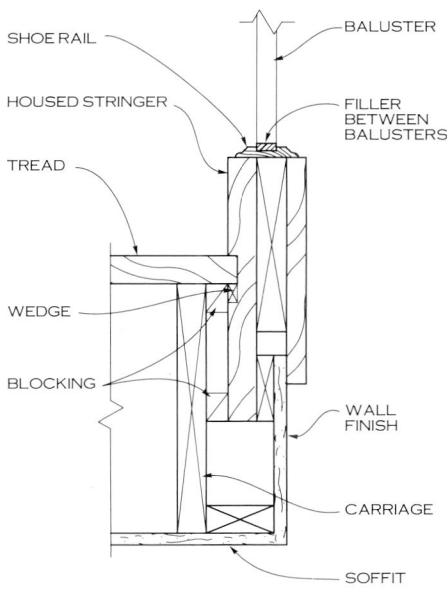

SECTION A

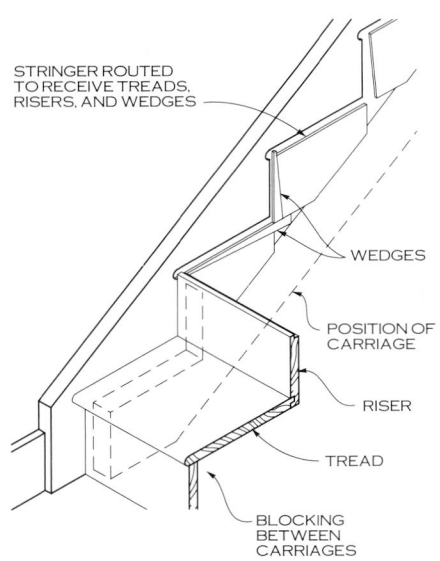

TREADS AND RISERS AT HOUSED STRINGER

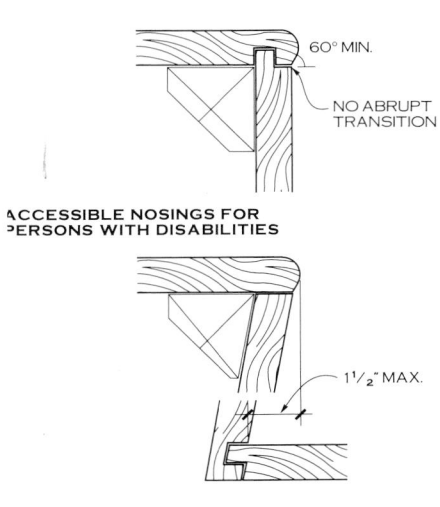

ACCESSIBLE NOSINGS

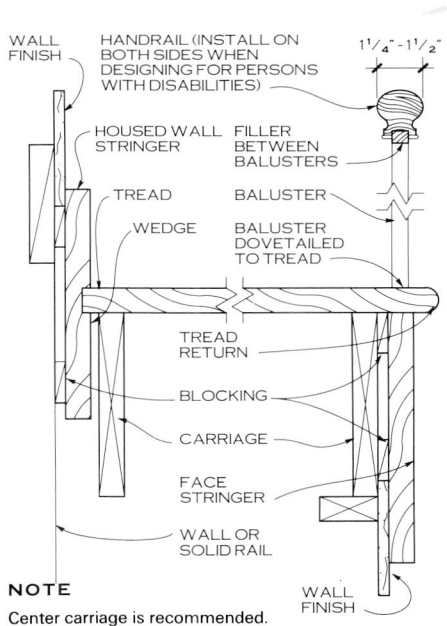

NOTE

Center carriage is recommended.

SECTION B

The Bumgardner Architects; Seattle, Washington
Janet B. Rankin, AIA; Rippeteau Architects; Washington, D.C.

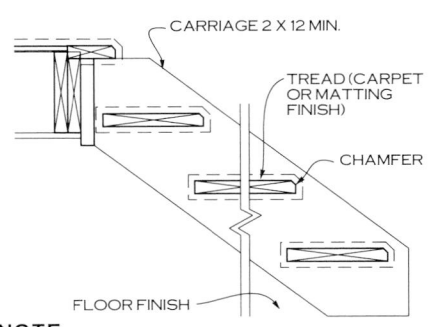

CARRIAGE 2 X 12 MIN.
TREAD (CARPET OR MATTING FINISH)
CHAMFER
FLOOR FINISH

NOTE

Open riser stairs do not comply with Americans with Disabilities Act Accessibility Guidelines.

OPEN RISER STAIR

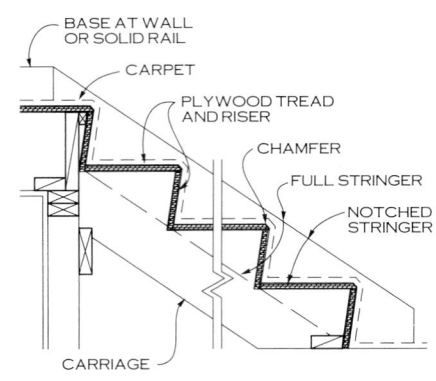

BASE AT WALL OR SOLID RAIL
CARPET
PLYWOOD TREAD AND RISER
CHAMFER
FULL STRINGER
NOTCHED STRINGER
CARRIAGE

CLOSED RISER STAIR / CARPET FINISH

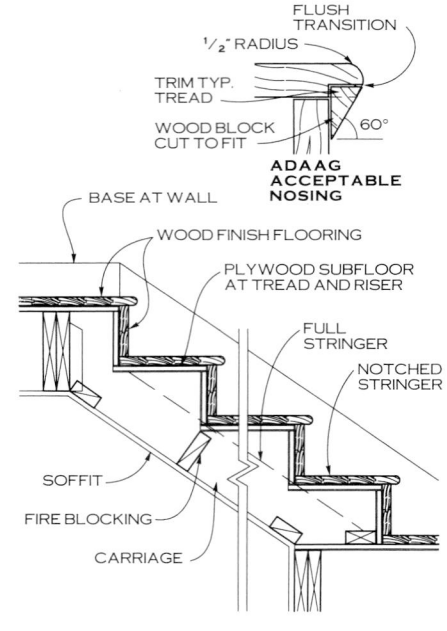

FLUSH TRANSITION
1/2" RADIUS
TRIM TYP. TREAD
WOOD BLOCK CUT TO FIT
60°
ADAAG ACCEPTABLE NOSING
BASE AT WALL
WOOD FINISH FLOORING
PLYWOOD SUBFLOOR AT TREAD AND RISER
FULL STRINGER
NOTCHED STRINGER
SOFFIT
FIRE BLOCKING
CARRIAGE

CLOSED RISER STAIR / WOOD FINISH

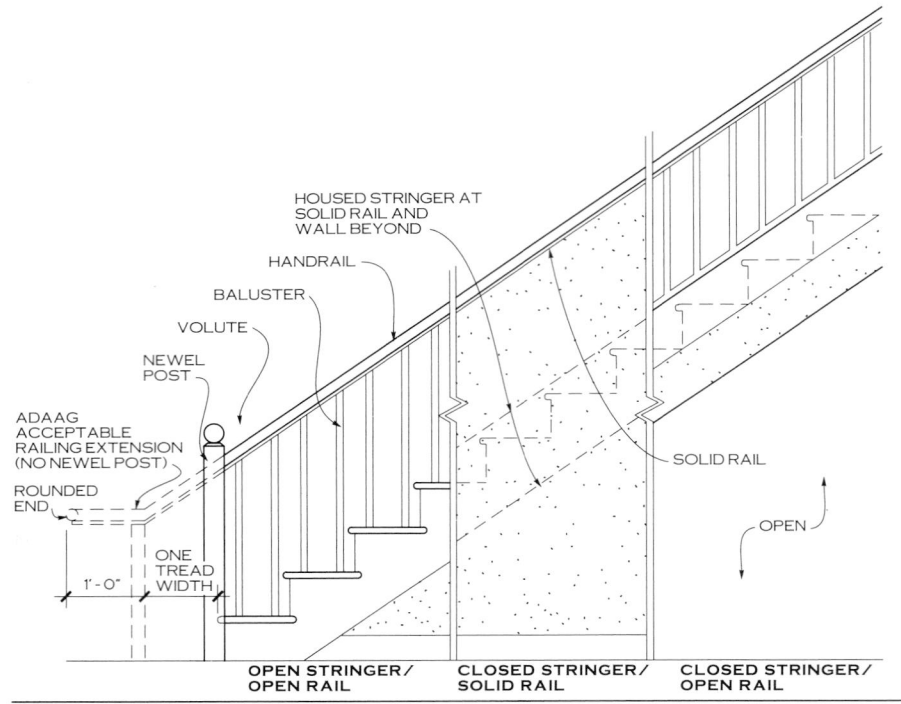

HOUSED STRINGER AT SOLID RAIL AND WALL BEYOND
HANDRAIL
BALUSTER
VOLUTE
NEWEL POST
ADAAG ACCEPTABLE RAILING EXTENSION (NO NEWEL POST)
ROUNDED END
1'-0"
ONE TREAD WIDTH
SOLID RAIL
OPEN

| OPEN STRINGER / OPEN RAIL | CLOSED STRINGER / SOLID RAIL | CLOSED STRINGER / OPEN RAIL |

ELEVATION OF FACE STRINGER

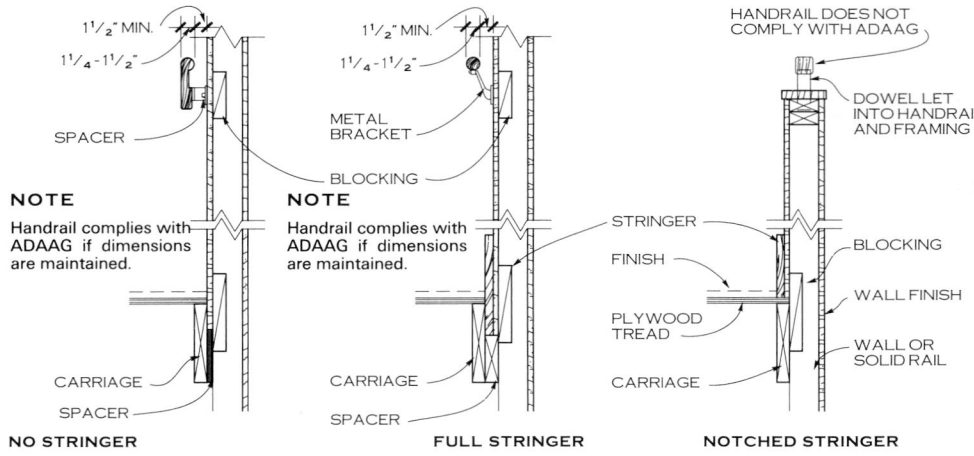

1 1/2" MIN.
1 1/4 - 1 1/2"
SPACER

NOTE
Handrail complies with ADAAG if dimensions are maintained.
CARRIAGE
SPACER
NO STRINGER

1 1/2" MIN.
1 1/4 - 1 1/2"
METAL BRACKET
BLOCKING

NOTE
Handrail complies with ADAAG if dimensions are maintained.
CARRIAGE
SPACER
FULL STRINGER

HANDRAIL DOES NOT COMPLY WITH ADAAG
DOWEL LET INTO HANDRAIL AND FRAMING
STRINGER
FINISH
PLYWOOD TREAD
CARRIAGE
BLOCKING
WALL FINISH
WALL OR SOLID RAIL
NOTCHED STRINGER

CLOSED RISER STAIRS AT WALLS AND SOLID RAILING WALLS

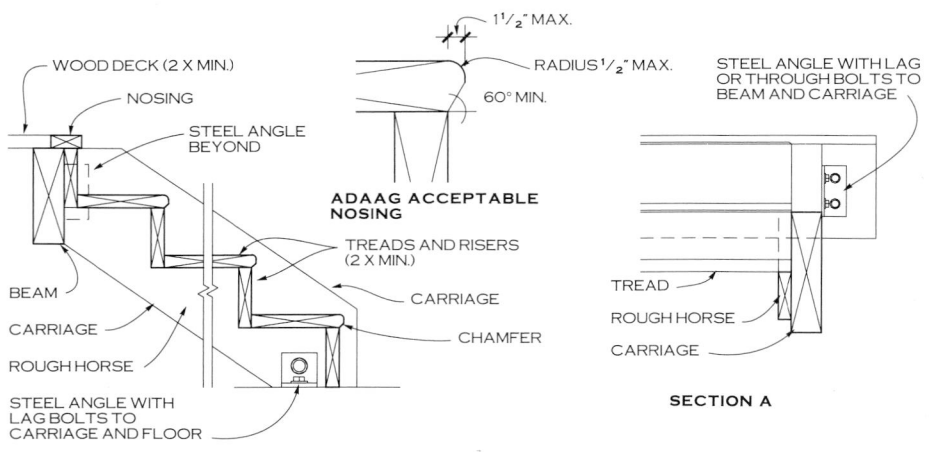

WOOD DECK (2 X MIN.)
NOSING
STEEL ANGLE BEYOND
BEAM
CARRIAGE
ROUGH HORSE
STEEL ANGLE WITH LAG BOLTS TO CARRIAGE AND FLOOR

1 1/2" MAX.
RADIUS 1/2" MAX.
60° MIN.
ADAAG ACCEPTABLE NOSING
TREADS AND RISERS (2 X MIN.)
CARRIAGE
CHAMFER

STEEL ANGLE WITH LAG OR THROUGH BOLTS TO BEAM AND CARRIAGE
TREAD
ROUGH HORSE
CARRIAGE
SECTION A

HEAVY TIMBER STAIR

The Bumgardner Architects; Seattle, Washington
Janet B. Rankin, AIA; Rippeteau Architects; Washington, D.C.

ARCHITECTURAL WOODWORK

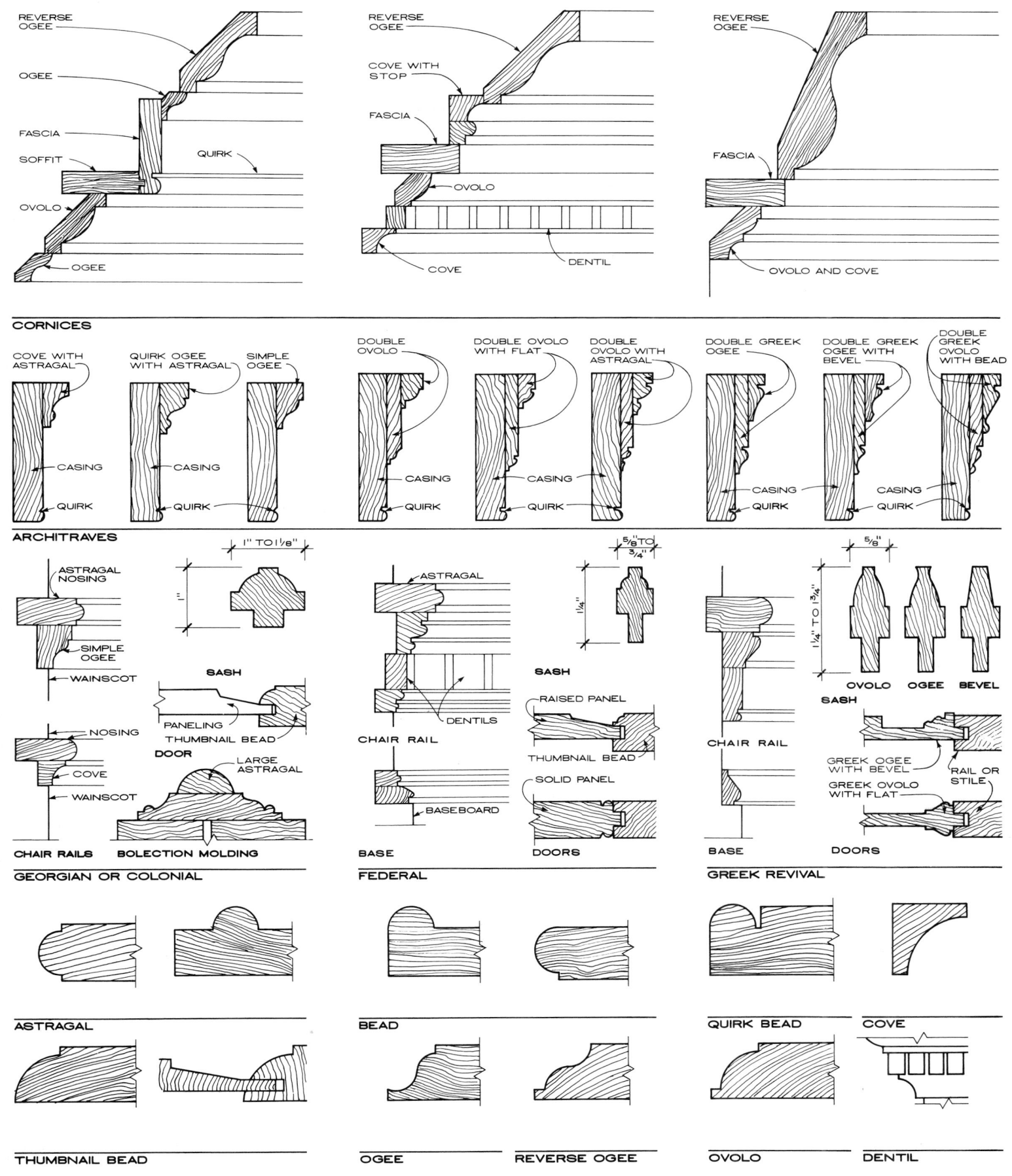

CORNICES

ARCHITRAVES

REVERSE OGEE

OGEE

FASCIA

SOFFIT

QUIRK

OVOLO

OGEE

REVERSE OGEE

COVE WITH STOP

FASCIA

OVOLO

COVE

DENTIL

REVERSE OGEE

FASCIA

OVOLO AND COVE

COVE WITH ASTRAGAL

QUIRK OGEE WITH ASTRAGAL

SIMPLE OGEE

DOUBLE OVOLO

DOUBLE OVOLO WITH FLAT

DOUBLE OVOLO WITH ASTRAGAL

DOUBLE GREEK OGEE

DOUBLE GREEK OGEE WITH BEVEL

DOUBLE GREEK OVOLO WITH BEAD

CASING

QUIRK

ASTRAGAL NOSING

SIMPLE OGEE

WAINSCOT

NOSING

COVE

WAINSCOT

1" TO 1⅛"

1"

SASH

PANELING

THUMBNAIL BEAD

DOOR

LARGE ASTRAGAL

CHAIR RAILS   BOLECTION MOLDING

GEORGIAN OR COLONIAL

ASTRAGAL

ASTRAGAL

DENTILS

CHAIR RAIL

BASE

BASEBOARD

SASH

RAISED PANEL

THUMBNAIL BEAD

SOLID PANEL

DOORS

FEDERAL

⅝" TO ¾"

1¼"

OVOLO   OGEE   BEVEL

⅝"

1¼" TO 1¾"

CHAIR RAIL

BASE

SASH

GREEK OGEE WITH BEVEL

GREEK OVOLO WITH FLAT

RAIL OR STILE

DOORS

GREEK REVIVAL

ASTRAGAL

THUMBNAIL BEAD

BEAD

OGEE   REVERSE OGEE

QUIRK BEAD

COVE

OVOLO   DENTIL

Timothy B. McDonald; Washington, D.C.

ARCHITECTURAL WOODWORK 6

STRUCTURAL PLASTICS

Structural plastic is a composite of plastic resin reinforced with one of a variety of fibers. Usually a synthetic veil is used on the surface of the part to minimize fiber projections through the surface, increae corrosion resistance, and deter ultraviolet degradation. Common reinforcement forms are as follows:

1. GLASS FIBERS for cost-effective applications

2. CARBON FIBERS for high strength applications

3. POLYESTER FIBERS for high bending applications

4. ARAMID FIBERS for security applications

There are several resins used in structural plastics, with many variations and additives for specific needs. Resins are broadly categorized into two types:

1. THERMOPLASTIC, which can be remelted

2. THERMOSET, which cannot be remelted.

Most mass produced fiber reinforced plastic (FRP) structural shapes are thermoset. There are several common resin types:

1. ISOPTHALTIC BASED RESIN

2. VINYL ESTER RESIN

3. EPOXY RESIN

Custom resin mixes are common. Color is created by adding pigment to the mix, and therefore color is throughout the shape. Other common additives are flame retardants, ultraviolet light inhibitor, catalysts , and mold releases.

The surfacing veil is an outer coating of resin to prevent water absorption and "fiber blooming," which is the eruption of reinforcing fibers through the surface of the shape.

Standard industry colors designate special characteristics of the structural shape. Standard colors are as follows:

1. OLIVE GREEN — polyester resin with no flame retardant or UV inhibitor

2. GREY — polyester resin with flame retardant and UV inhibitor

3. BEIGE — vinyl ester resin with flame retardant and UV inhibitor

GLASS - FIBER REINFORCED STRUCTURAL PLASTICS ADVANTAGES

1. LIGHT WEIGHT – 30% less than aluminum; 80% less than steel

2. CORROSION RESISTANT – will not rot; impervious to many chemicals

3. NONCONDUCTIVE – thermally and electrically a good insulator

4. NONMAGNETIC – radio frequency transparent

5. HIGH STRENGTH – stronger per pound than steel

6. DIMENSIONALLY STABLE – expands less than steel.

STRUCTURAL PLASTICS DISADVANTAGES

1. TEMPERATURE – cannot stand sustained temperatures in excess of 200° F, unless special resins are used

2. WATER ABSORPTION – shape may absorb water by wicking unless cut ends are sealed. If water is absorbed, electrical insulation qualities are reduced.

3. STIFFNESS – more elastic than steel; deflection often requires use of larger shapes

4. COST – substantially more than structural steel if assembly and life costs are ignored

5. COMBUSTIBLE – if untreated

TYPES OF STRUCTURAL PLASTICS

Fiberglass floor gratings are perhaps the most widespread structural application for plastics. The process of fabricating gratings has advanced to what is known as pultrusion, which allows for controlled placement of fiber reinforcing and shaping of the product. In pultrusion fibers are pulled through a bath of liquid resin and shaped and wrapped into specific shapes before curing. Pultrusion allows fiber reinforced plastic (FRP) shapes to be fabricated similarly to steel or aluminum structural shapes.

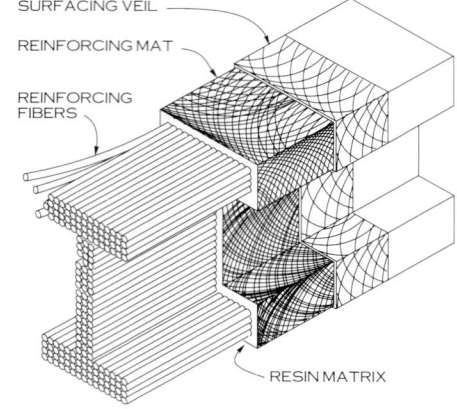

SURFACING VEIL

REINFORCING MAT

REINFORCING FIBERS

RESIN MATRIX

PULTRUDED GRATING PART

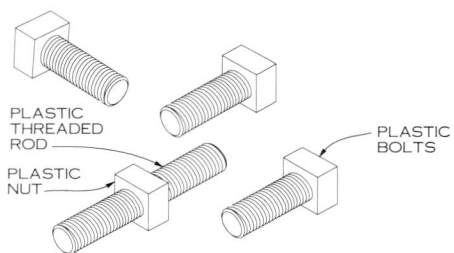

PLASTIC THREADED ROD

PLASTIC NUT

PLASTIC BOLTS

WORKABILITY

Structural plastics can be cut and shaped much like wood. Care must be taken to seal cut ends with a compatible resin equal to that used in fabrication. Connections are made with bolts or with bolts and epoxy adhesive where disassembly is not anticipated.

USES OF STRUCTURAL PLASTICS

Water applications: where structural elements are constantly exposed to water, as in off-shore drilling rigs, wastewater treatment facilities, and cooling towers.

Severe environment applications: where corrosive chemicals, caustic fumes, or electrolysis processes are used, such as chemical plants, paper mills, and mining and plating operations.

Electrical applications: where high voltage equipment is used or the potential for lightning is high.

Lightweight applications: where weight and/or ease of erection is critical, such as in exhibits, temporary structures, mezzanines.

High-tech applications: where interference with magnetic fields or radio frequency transmissions is unacceptable.

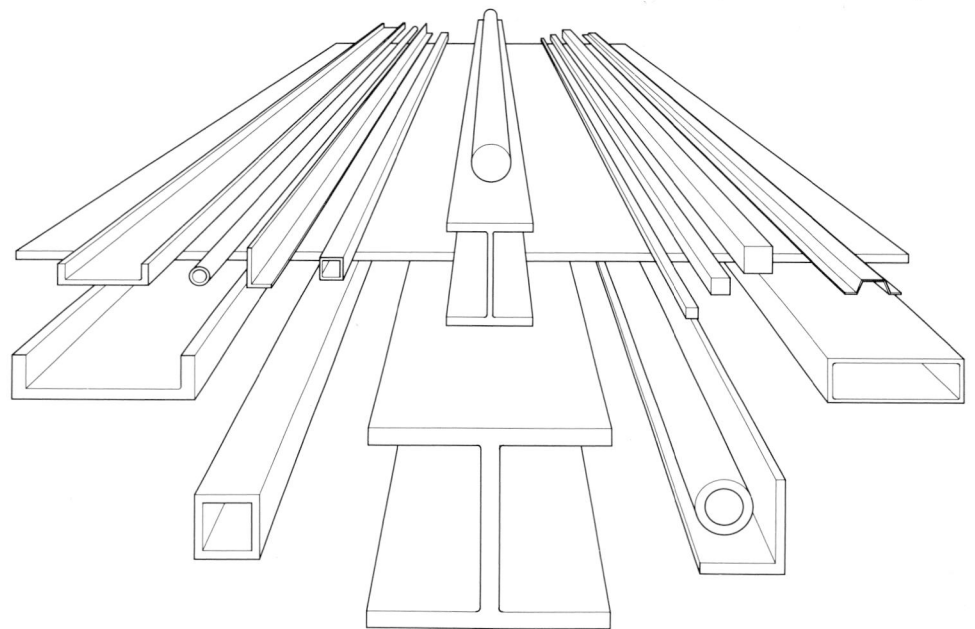

STRUCTURAL PLASTIC SHAPES

SHAPE DESIGNATION	MINIMUM SIZE		MAXIMUM SIZE	
Equal leg angles	1 x $^1/_8$	.17 lb/ft	6 x $^3/_8$	3.44 lb/ft
Channels	2 x $^9/_{16}$ x $^1/_8$	.26 lb/ft	18 x 2 x $^3/_{16}$	3.88 lb/ft
Beams	2 x 1 x $^1/_8$	.34 lb/ft	24 x 7 $^1/_2$ x $^3/_4$	16.47 lb/ft
Round tube	1 x $^1/_8$	.25 lb/ft	10 x $^3/_{16}$	4.50 lb/ft
Square tube	1 x $^1/_8$	.32 lb/ft	4 x $^1/_4$	3.08 lb/ft
Rectangular tube	2 $^1/_2$ x 1 $^5/_8$ x $^1/_8$	.75 lb/ft	9 x 11 x $^3/_4$	23.30 lb/ft
Square bar	$^1/_2$	.22 lb/ft	1 $^1/_2$	1.91 lb/ft
Rod	$^1/_4$	.043 lb/ft	2	2.69 lb/ft
Plate	$^1/_8$	1.14 lb/sq ft	1	9.27 lb/sq ft

Morrison Molded Fiber Glass Company; Bristol, Virginia
Laird Ueberroth, Architect, and Associates; McLean, Virginia

STRUCTURAL PLASTICS

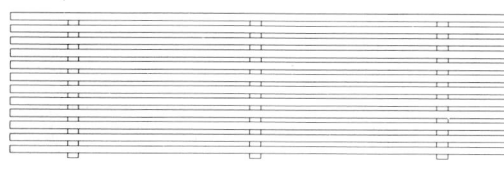

FIBERGLASS REINFORCED PLASTIC GRATINGS

Gratings and treads are one of the most common uses of structural plastics. In corrosive environments they can last up to 20 times longer than steel. Current grating designs are the fifth generation of a rapidly evolving FRP technology. Most of fiber bloom, excessive movement of components, delamination, UV degradation, and chipping problems have been solved.

Maximum panel size: 60" x 240"

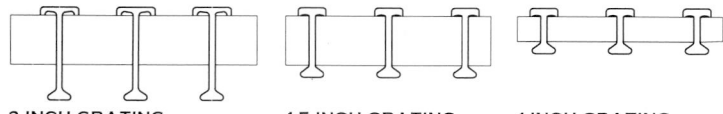

2 INCH GRATING	1.5 INCH GRATING	1 INCH GRATING

GRATING PROFILES

BAR DEPTH (IN.)	BAR CENTERS (IN.)	NO. OF BARS PER FOOT	BAR (%) OPEN AREA	APPROX. WEIGHT (LB/SQ FT)
1	1.5	8	60	2.3
1.5	1.5	8	60	3.3
2	2.0	6	50	3.1

LOAD DEFLECTION TABLE

1 INCH BEARING BARS

SPAN		LOAD/DEFLECTION									MAX. LOAD
2 FT	U	200	300	500	750	1000	1250	1500	2000	2500	2,900 lb
	Δ	.05	.08	.12	.19	.25	.31	.373	.498	.622	.721 in
	C	200	300	500	750	1000	1250	1500	2000	2500	2,900 lb
	Δ	.04	.06	.10	.15	.199	.249	.298	.398	.498	.577 in
3 FT	U	67	133	200	267	333	500	667	833		1,287 lb
	Δ	.08	.15	.23	.31	.38	.58	.77	.98		1.48 in
	C	100	200	300	400	500	750	1000	1250		1,933 lb
	Δ	.06	.12	.18	.25	.30	.46	.614	.766		1.18 in
5 FT	U	40	80	120							453 lb
	Δ	.34	.68	1.0							3.9 in
	C	100	200	300							1,018 lb
	Δ	.27	.55	.82							3.1 in

1.5 INCH BEARING BARS

SPAN		LOAD/DEFLECTION									MAX. LOAD
2 FT	U	200	300	500	750	1000	1250	1500	2000	3000	4,400 lb
	Δ	.02	.03	.05	.07	.09	.114	.138	.183	.274	.402 in
	C	200	300	500	750	1000	1250	1500	2000	3000	4,400 lb
	Δ	.02	.02	.04	.06	.07	.09	.11	.146	.219	.321 in
3 FT	U	67	133	200	267	333	500	667	833	1000	1,896 lb
	Δ	.03	.06	.09	.12	.15	.22	.23	.36	.439	.826 in
	C	100	200	300	400	500	750	1000	1250	1500	2,844 lb
	D	.02	.05	.07	.09	.11	.17	.233	.290	.349	.661 in
5 FT	U	40	80	120	160	200	300	400			608 lb
	Δ	.13	.26	.38	.51	.64	.96	1.3			1.94 in
	C	100	200	300	400	500	750	1000			1,520 lb
	Δ	.10	.20	.30	.40	.51	.77	1.02			1.55 in

2 INCH BEARING BARS

SPAN		LOAD/DEFLECTION									MAX. LOAD
2 FT	U	200	300	500	750	1000	1250	1500	2000	3000	5,667 lb
	D	.01	.02	.03	.04	.054	.067	.080	.107	.161	.303 in
	C	200	300	500	750	1000	1250	1500	2000	3000	5,667 lb
	Δ	.01	.01	.02	.03	.043	.054	.064	.086	.128	.243 in
3 FT	U	67	133	200	267	333	500	667	833	1000	2,519 lb
	Δ	.02	.04	.05	.07	.09	.13	.17	.22	.26	.654 in
	C	100	200	300	400	500	750	1000	1250	1500	3,778 lb
	Δ	.01	.03	.04	.06	.07	.10	.14	.17	.20	.524 in
5 FT	U	40	80	120	160	200	300	400	500		907 lb
	Δ	.08	.15	.23	.30	.38	.56	.75	.94		1.70 in
	C	100	200	300	400	500	750	1000	1250		2,267 lb
	Δ	.06	.12	.18	.24	.30	.45	.60	.75		1.36 in

U= Uniform load, C= Concentrated load, Δ= Deflection

Consult with structural engineer familiar with their unique properties before specifying structural plastics.

Morrison Molded Fiber Glass Company; Bristol, Virginia
Laird Ueberroth, Architect, and Associates; McLean, Virginia

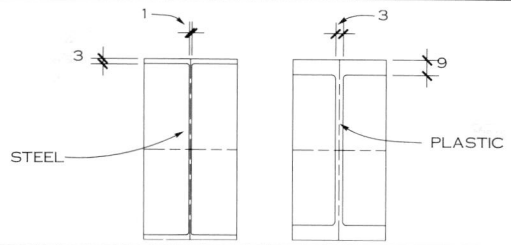

STEEL — PLASTIC

STEEL VS. PLASTIC STRUCTURAL SHAPES

FRP shapes have approximately one-fifth the weight of steel but over one-third the strength. This means an FRP shape equal in strength to a steel shape would weigh only slightly more than half the steel shape. Structural plastic shapes are generally continuously extruded (or pultruded), so length is a factor of transportability rather than fabrication. Durability is a function of the environment. Exposure to chemicals and intensity of sunlight affect the life-span of structural plastics.

FIBERGLASS REINFORCED PLASTIC WIDE FLANGE BEAM LOAD TABLE

ALLOWABLE UNIFORM LOADS IN LB/FT

W SHAPE IN.	SPAN IN FT	LATERALLY UNSUPPORTED		LATERALLY SUPPORTED DEFLECTION		
		FB'	W	L/180	L/240	L/360
6 x 6 x¹/₄	8	3761	369	303	227	152
	10	2507	158	171	128	86
	12	1823	80	105	79	52
	14	1407	45	69	51	34
8 x 8 x³/₈	8	5074	1020	884	663	442
	10	4379	724	525	394	263
	12	3150	362	333	250	167
	14	2405	203	223	167	111
10 x 10 x³/₈	12	3630	667	594	445	297
	16	2620	271	289	217	144
	20	1756	116	159	119	80
	24	1284	59	96	72	48
12 x 12 x¹/₂	16	3761	739	606	454	303
	20	2507	316	342	257	171
	24	1823	159	210	157	105
	28	1407	90	137	103	69

FIBERGLASS REINFORCED PLASTIC CHANNEL LOAD TABLE

ALLOWABLE UNIFORM LOADS IN LB/FT

C SHAPE IN.	SPAN IN FT	FB'	LATERALLY SUPPORTED DEFLECTION			
			L/150	L/180	L/240	L/360
4 x 1¹/₁₆ x¹/₈	4	164		151	113	76
	6	73	60	50	38	25
	8	41	26	22	17	11
	10	26	14	12	9	6
6 x 1⁵/₈ x¹/₄	6	411	355	296	222	148
	8	231	163	136	102	68
	10	148	87	73	55	36
	12	103	52	43	32	22
8 x 2³/₁₆ x¹/₄	8	322		307	230	153
	10	206	202	169	127	84
	12	143	122	102	76	51
	14	105	79	66	49	33
10 x 2³/₄ x¹/₂	8	1469	1223	1019	764	510
	10	940	693	578	433	289
	12	653	426	355	266	177
	14	480	279	232	174	116

Consult with structural engineer familiar with their unique properties before specifying structural plastics

STRUCTURAL PLASTICS SPECIFICATIONS

ASTM-F 1092-87	Fiberglass Handrail Specification
ASTM-D 3917	Standard Specification for Dimensional Tolerances of Thermosetting Glass-Reinforced Plastic Pultruded Shapes
ASTM-D 3918	Standard Definition of Terms Relating to Reinforced Plastic Pultruded Products
ASTM-D 3647	Standard Practice for Classifying Reinforced Plastic Pultruded Shapes According to Composition
ASTM-D 4385	Standard Practice for Classifying Visual Defects in Thermosetting Reinforced Plastic Pultruded Products
ASTM-E 84	Flame Rating
ASTM-D 635	Self Extinguishing

GENERAL

American Forest and Paper Association
(formerly National Forest Products Association)
1111 19th Street, N.W., Suite 700
Washington, DC 20036
Tel: (202) 463-2700
Fax:(202) 463-2785

American Plywood Association (APA)
7011 S. 19th St.
Tacoma, WA 98466
Tel: (206) 565-6600
Fax:(206) 565-7265

American Wood Council
National Forest Products Association (AWC/NFPA)
1250 Connecticut Ave., N.W., Suite 300
Washington, DC 20036
Tel: (202) 463-2700

California Redwood Association (CRA)
405 Enfrente Drive
Suite 200
Novato, CA 94949
Tel: (415) 382-0662
Fax:(415) 382-8531

Canadian Wood Council (CWC)
P.O. Box 88828
Seattle, WA 98138
Tel: (613) 731-7800
Fax:(206) 731-7899

Forest Products Research Society
2801 Marshall Court
Madison, WI 53705-2295
Tel: (608) 231-1361
Fax:(608) 231-2152

National Association of Home Builders (NAHB)
Home Builder Press/NAHB Bookstore
1201 14th Street, NW
Washington, DC 20005
Tel: (800) 368-5242
  or (202) 822-0200
Fax:(202) 822-0559

Northeastern Lumber
  Manufacturers Association, Inc. (NLMA)
272 Tuttle Road, P.O. Box 87A
Cumberland Center, ME 04021
Tel: (207) 829-6901
Fax:(207) 829-4293

Southern Cypress Manufacturers Association
400 Penn Center Blvd., Suite 530
Pittsburgh, PA 15235-5605
Tel: (412) 829-0770
Fax:(412) 829-0844

Southern Forest Products Association
P.O. Box 64170
Kenner, LA 70064-1700
Tel: (504) 443-4464
Fax:(504) 443-6612

Western Red Cedar Association
P.O. Box 120786
New Brighton, MN 55112
(612) 633-4334

Western Wood Products Association (WWPA)
Yeon Building
522 SW 5th Avenue
Portland, OR 97204
Tel: (503) 224-3930
Fax:(503) 224-3934

World Forest Institute (WFI)
4033 SW Canyon Road
Portland, OR 97221
Tel:(503) 228-0819
Fax:(503) 228-3624

REFERENCES

Bendtsen, B. A., and A. Freas. "Timber and Timber Products: Properties, Deterioration, Protection," Chapter 4. *Handbook of Architectural Technology.* H. Cowan, ed. Van Nostrand Reinhold, 1991.

Dost, W., and E. Botsai. *Wood: Detailing for Performance.* Mill Valley, Ca.: GRDA Publications, 1990. [(415) 388-6080]

Fine Homebuilding. Taunton Press, 63 South Main Street, Newtown, CT 06470-9957; (203) 426-8171. [bimonthly]

Hoadley, R. B. *Understanding Wood.* Taunton Press, 1980.

Journal of Light Construction, P.O Box 686, Holmes, PA 19043; (800) 345-8112. [monthly]

Manual of Wood Frame Construction, WCD6. National Forest Products Association, 1988.

National Design Specifications for Wood Construction National Forest Products Association .

Plank and Beam Framing for Residential Buildings National Forest Products Association.

Quality Standards for the Professional Remodeler, 2nd ed. National Association of Home Builders, 1991.

Small Buildings: Technology in Transition, NRCC 32333. National Research Council of Canada, 1990.

Thallon, R. *Graphic Guide to Frame Construction: Details for Builders and Designers.* Taunton Press, 1991.

Western Woods Species Book, vol. 1, Dimension Lumber; vol. 2, Selects-Finish/Commons-Boards. Western Wood Products Association (WWPA), 1985.

Western Woods Use Book, 3rd ed. WWPA, 1985.

Wilcox, W., E. Botsai, and H. Kubler. *Wood as a Building Material.* New York: J. Wiley & Sons, 1991.

Wood Handbook: Wood as an Engineering Material Agriculture Handbook 72, US GPO, 1987.

ROUGH CARPENTRY
REFERENCES

NAHB Beam Series: Wood Beams, Plywood I-Beams, Plywood Box Beams, Steel-Wood I-Beams, Flitch Plate and Steel I-Beams. Home Builder Press, 1982.

National Design Specification for Wood Construction National Forest Products Association, 1991.

Parker, H., and J. Ambrose. *Simplified Design of Structural Wood.* New York: J. Wiley & Sons, 1988.

HEAVY TIMBER CONSTRUCTION

American Institute of Timber Construction (AITC)
7012 South Revere Parkway, Suite 140
Englewood, CO 80112
Tel: (303) 792-9559
Fax:(303) 792-0669

American Lumber Standards Committee (ALSC)
P.O. Box 210
Germantown, MD 20875-0210
Tel: (301) 972-1700
Fax:(301) 540-8004

REFERENCES

American Institute of Timber Construction. *Timber Construction Manual,* 3rd ed. New York: J. Wiley & Sons, 1986.

Goetz, Hoor, Moehler, and Natterer. *Timber Design and Construction Sourcebook: A Comprehensive Guide to Methods and Practice.* McGraw-Hill, 1989.

Heavy Timber Construction Details. National Forest Products Association, 1989.

Typical Construction Details. American Institute of Timber Construction, 1984.

GLUED-LAMINATED CONSTRUCTION
REFERENCES

Laminated Timber for Industrial, Commercial, and Institutional Buildings. 1990.

Standard Specifications for Structural Glued-Laminated Timber of Softwood Species: Design, AITC-117. American Institute of Timber Construction, 1987.

WOOD TRUSSES

Wood Truss Council of America
5937 Meadowood Drive, Suite 14
Madison, WI 53711-4125
Tel: (608) 274-4489
Fax:(608) 274-3329

REFERENCES

Wood Chord Metal Truss Joists, SpecGUIDE G06151. Construction Specifications Institute, 1991.

FINISH CARPENTRY

Architectural Woodwork Institute
13924 Braddock Road
Centreville, VA 22020-8550
Tel: (703) 222-1100
Fax:(703) 222-2499

Fine Hardwood Veneer Association (FHVA)
5603 West Raymond Street, Suite O
Indianapolis, IN 46241
Tel: (317) 244-3312
Fax:(317) 244-3386

Hardwood Plywood Manufacturers Association (HPMA)
P.O. Box 2789
Reston, VA 22090-2789
Tel: (703) 435-2900
Fax:(703) 435-2537

National Hardwood Lumber Association (NHLA)
P.O. Box 34518
Memphis, TN 38184-0518
Tel: (901) 377-1818
Fax:(901) 382-6419

National Particleboard Association (NPA)
18928 Premier Court
Gaithersburg, MD 20879-1569
Tel: (301) 670-0604
Fax:(301) 840-1252

REFERENCES

Decorative Laminates for Architectural Surfacing. Architectural Woodwork Institute, 1987.

Interim Voluntary Standard for Hardwood and Decorative Plywood, HP-1. Hardwood Plywood Manufacturers Association, 1992.

Specifiers Guide to Particleboard and MDF. National Particleboard Association.

Structural Design Guide for Hardwood Plywood Hardwood Plywood Manufacturers Association, HP-SG-1986.

Wood Mouldings. Architectural Woodwork Institute, 1989.

Wood Particleboard, ANSI A208.1. National Particleboard Association, 1989.

WOOD TREATMENT

American Wood-Preservers Association
P.O. Box 286
Woodstock, MD 21163-0286
Tel: (410) 465-3169
Fax:(410) 465-3195

American Wood Preservers Institute
1945 Old Gallows Road, Suite 550
Vienna, VA 22182
Tel: (703) 893-4005
Fax:(703) 893-8492

Wood Protection Council
National Institute of Building Sciences
1201 L Street, N.W., Suite 400
Washington, DC 20005
Tel: (202) 289-7800
Fax:(202) 289-1092

REFERENCES

Dietz, Albert G. H. *Plastics in Building, Plastics for Architects and Engineers.* Cambridge, Mass.: MIT Press.

ARCHITECTURAL WOODWORK

Architectural Woodwork Institute
2310 South Walter Reed Drive
P.O. Box 1550
Centreville, VA 22020-8550
Tel: (703) 222-1100
Fax:(703) 222-2499

National Hardwood Lumber Association (NHLA)
P.O. Box 34518
Memphis, TN 38184-0518
Tel: (901) 377-1818
Fax:(901) 382-6419

STRUCTURAL PLASTICS

Plastics Institute of America (PIA)
277 Fairfield Road, Suite 101
Fairfield, NJ 07004-1932
Tel: (201) 808-5950
Fax:(201) 808-5953

Society of the Plastics Industry, Inc.
1275 K Street, N.W., #400
Washington, DC 20005
Tel: (202) 371-5200
Fax:(202) 371-1022

CHAPTER

7

THERMAL AND MOISTURE PROTECTION

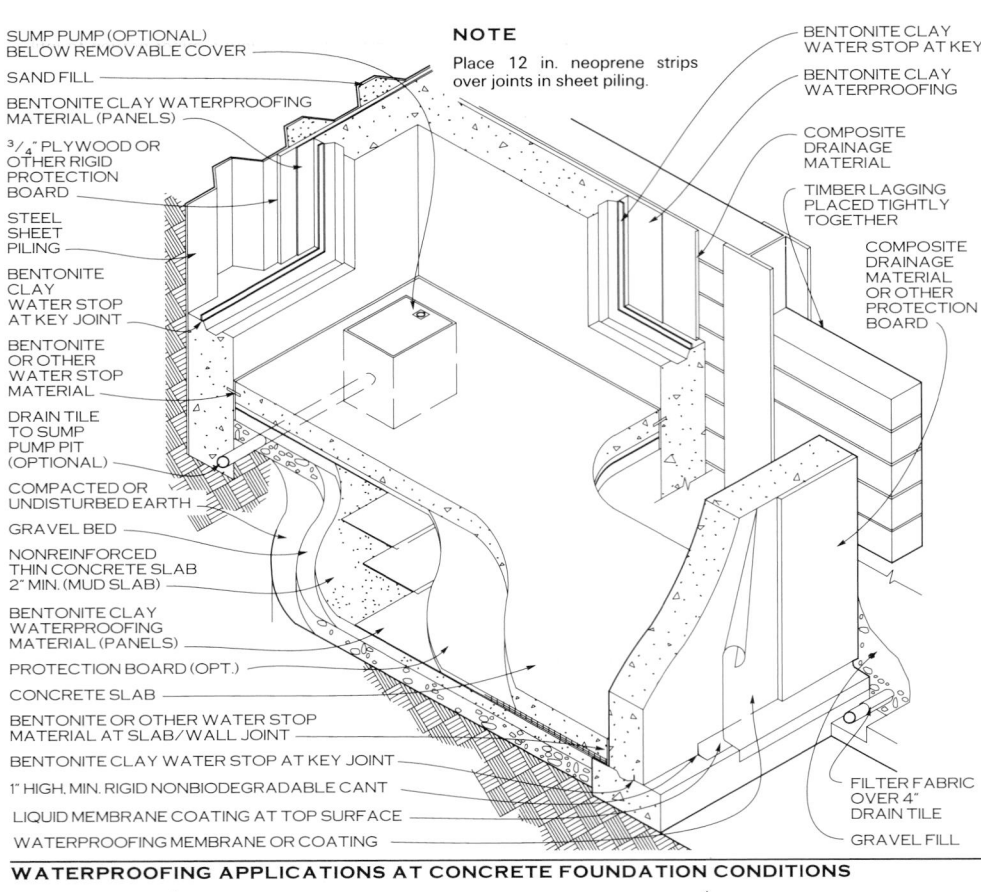

SUMP PUMP (OPTIONAL) BELOW REMOVABLE COVER
SAND FILL
BENTONITE CLAY WATERPROOFING MATERIAL (PANELS)
3/4" PLYWOOD OR OTHER RIGID PROTECTION BOARD
STEEL SHEET PILING
BENTONITE CLAY WATER STOP AT KEY JOINT
BENTONITE OR OTHER WATER STOP MATERIAL
DRAIN TILE TO SUMP PUMP PIT (OPTIONAL)
COMPACTED OR UNDISTURBED EARTH
GRAVEL BED
NONREINFORCED THIN CONCRETE SLAB 2" MIN. (MUD SLAB)
BENTONITE CLAY WATERPROOFING MATERIAL (PANELS)
PROTECTION BOARD (OPT.)
CONCRETE SLAB
BENTONITE OR OTHER WATER STOP MATERIAL AT SLAB/WALL JOINT
BENTONITE CLAY WATER STOP AT KEY JOINT
1" HIGH, MIN. RIGID NONBIODEGRADABLE CANT
LIQUID MEMBRANE COATING AT TOP SURFACE
WATERPROOFING MEMBRANE OR COATING

NOTE
Place 12 in. neoprene strips over joints in sheet piling.

BENTONITE CLAY WATER STOP AT KEY
BENTONITE CLAY WATERPROOFING
COMPOSITE DRAINAGE MATERIAL
TIMBER LAGGING PLACED TIGHTLY TOGETHER
COMPOSITE DRAINAGE MATERIAL OR OTHER PROTECTION BOARD
FILTER FABRIC OVER 4" DRAIN TILE
GRAVEL FILL

WATERPROOFING APPLICATIONS AT CONCRETE FOUNDATION CONDITIONS

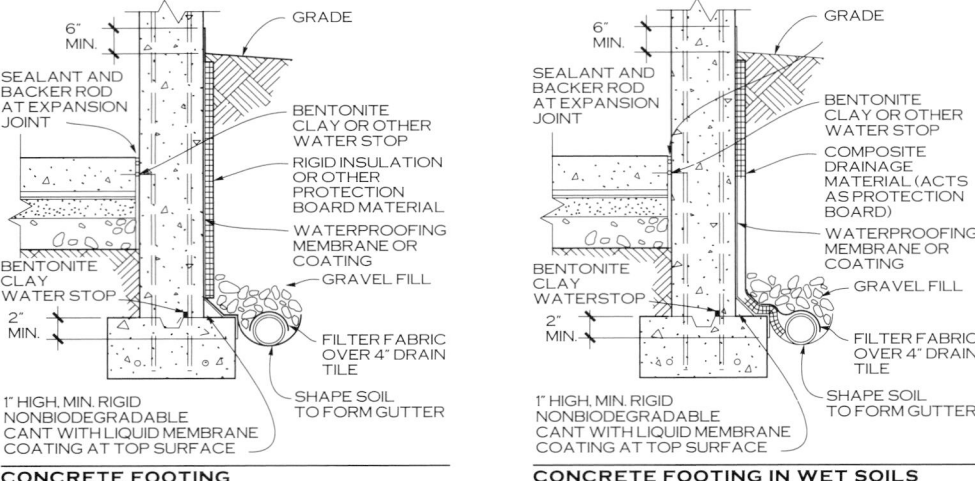

GRADE
6" MIN.
SEALANT AND BACKER ROD AT EXPANSION JOINT
BENTONITE CLAY OR OTHER WATER STOP
RIGID INSULATION OR OTHER PROTECTION BOARD MATERIAL
WATERPROOFING MEMBRANE OR COATING
GRAVEL FILL
BENTONITE CLAY WATER STOP
2" MIN.
FILTER FABRIC OVER 4" DRAIN TILE
SHAPE SOIL TO FORM GUTTER
1" HIGH, MIN. RIGID NONBIODEGRADABLE CANT WITH LIQUID MEMBRANE COATING AT TOP SURFACE

CONCRETE FOOTING

GRADE
6" MIN.
SEALANT AND BACKER ROD AT EXPANSION JOINT
BENTONITE CLAY OR OTHER WATER STOP
COMPOSITE DRAINAGE MATERIAL (ACTS AS PROTECTION BOARD)
WATERPROOFING MEMBRANE OR COATING
GRAVEL FILL
BENTONITE CLAY WATERSTOP
2" MIN.
FILTER FABRIC OVER 4" DRAIN TILE
SHAPE SOIL TO FORM GUTTER
1" HIGH, MIN. RIGID NONBIODEGRADABLE CANT WITH LIQUID MEMBRANE COATING AT TOP SURFACE

CONCRETE FOOTING IN WET SOILS

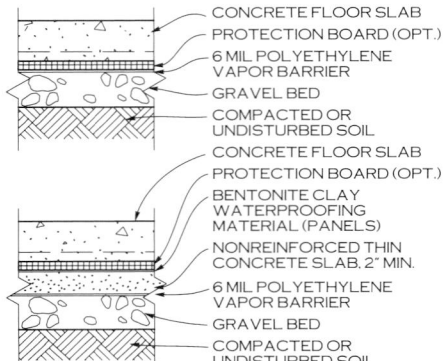

CONCRETE FLOOR SLAB
PROTECTION BOARD (OPT.)
6 MIL POLYETHYLENE VAPOR BARRIER
GRAVEL BED
COMPACTED OR UNDISTURBED SOIL

CONCRETE FLOOR SLAB
PROTECTION BOARD (OPT.)
BENTONITE CLAY WATERPROOFING MATERIAL (PANELS)
NONREINFORCED THIN CONCRETE SLAB, 2" MIN.
6 MIL POLYETHYLENE VAPOR BARRIER
GRAVEL BED
COMPACTED OR UNDISTURBED SOIL

WATERPROOFING UNDER SLAB

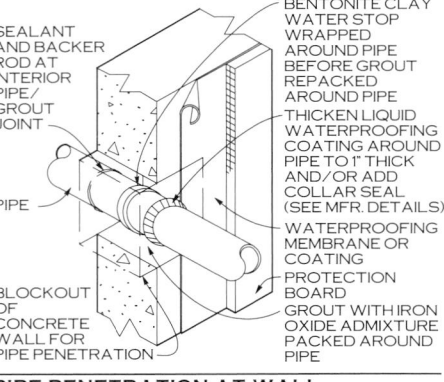

SEALANT AND BACKER ROD AT INTERIOR PIPE/GROUT JOINT
PIPE
BLOCKOUT OF CONCRETE WALL FOR PIPE PENETRATION
BENTONITE CLAY WATER STOP WRAPPED AROUND PIPE BEFORE GROUT REPACKED AROUND PIPE
THICKEN LIQUID WATERPROOFING COATING AROUND PIPE TO 1" THICK AND/OR ADD COLLAR SEAL (SEE MFR. DETAILS)
WATERPROOFING MEMBRANE OR COATING
PROTECTION BOARD
GROUT WITH IRON OXIDE ADMIXTURE PACKED AROUND PIPE

PIPE PENETRATION AT WALL

NOTES

1. Consult a soils engineer to determine soil types and groundwater levels and their effect on drainage and waterproofing methods. Consult a waterproofing specialist to determine a specific design approach for problem soils and conditions.

2. Most waterproofing materials require a stable, rigid, and level substrate. Generally, a mud slab (subslab that is nonreinforced and nonstructural) is used when the waterproofing material is placed below the structural slab and/or when a solid working surface is needed on unstable soils. When waterproofing materials are placed on top of the structural slab, a protective cover, such as another concrete slab, is required.

3. Bentonite clay waterproofing is usually manufactured in the form of corrugated cardboard panels with bentonite clay material filling the corrugation voids. When moistened, the clay swells and takes on a gel-like consistency, forming an impermeable barrier when confined. Bentonite panels may be placed over a substrate of compacted earth, sand, and pea gravel (or mud slab, for reinforced slabs greater than 6 in. thick). Since the panels swell when hydrated, pressure is exerted on adjacent construction. For slabs less than 6 in. thick, which may be adversely affected by bentonite swelling, special panels, made to accommodate the swelling, are required. A 6-mil polyethylene vapor barrier between the mud slab and gravel base will provide additional protection against water penetration. Consult with a structural engineer and the manufacturer to assure proper use and structural adequacy.

4. Protect membrane waterproofing or coatings during construction and backfilling. Protection materials include the following (select according to soil, climate, and cost requirements):

a. Composite drainage material: Recommended when water is frequently present in soils surrounding foundations. Usually made up of a rigid open-weave material, approximately 3/4 in. thick, covered on both sides by a geotextile filter fabric preventing small stones or other materials from clogging the drainage route of water inside. Typically terminated at drain tiles at the bottom of the foundation. Higher in cost than other protection board materials.

b. Rigid insulation boards: Used above frostline or if ground temperatures are low. Usually made of expanded polystyrene. Minimum thickness is 1/4 in. (when used as protection board only), up to 1 1/2 in. thick (or greater, if desired) which gives an R-8 insulating value.

c. Protection board: Used only to protect waterproofing; does not drain or insulate. Usually made of 1/8 in. asphalt-impregnated fiberboard or, as mentioned above, 1/4 in. extruded polystyrene. Least expensive.

5. Footing drains are recommended when groundwater level may rise above top of floor slab or when the foundation is subject to hydrostatic pressure after heavy rain. Composite drainage material conveys water to the drain tile, thus reducing hydrostatic pressure.

6. Special negative-side coating on interior face of foundation wall is only recommended when exterior is not accessible.

7. Bentonite clay water stop should be placed on top of footing, at vertical concrete keyed joints, and along inside edge of outermost vertical rebars before pouring the concrete wall.

8. Grout, packed around pipes penetrating the foundation, should have a mixture of iron oxide. Iron oxide chemically alters the grout to be more water-resistant.

Krommenhoek/McKeown & Associates; San Diego, California
Richard J. Vitullo, AIA; Oak leaf Studio; Crownsville, Maryland; in consultation with James B. Thompson Co.; San Marino, California

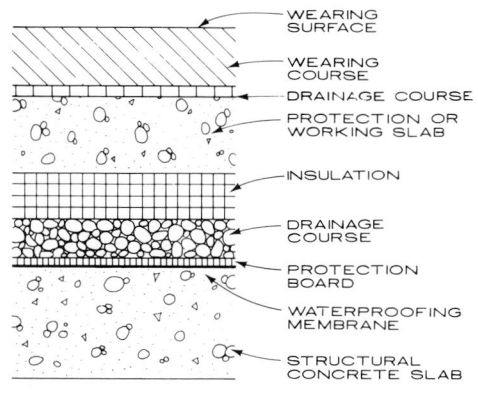

BASIC COMPONENTS OF WATERPROOFING SYSTEMS

GENERAL

The basic components, subsystems, and features for a building deck waterproofing system are the structural building deck or substrate to be waterproofed, waterproofing membrane, protection of membrane, drainage, insulation, and wearing course. See following pages for generic membrane applications.

SUBSTRATE

The substrate referred to is reinforced cast-in-place structural concrete. Precast concrete slabs pose more technical problems than cast-in-place concrete and the probability of lasting watertightness is greatly diminished and difficult to achieve because of the multitude of joints which have the capability of movement and must be treated accordingly.

The concrete used for the substrate should have a minimum density of 1762 kg/m^3 (110 lb/ft^3) and have a maximum moisture content of 8% when cured.

SLOPE FOR DRAINAGE

A monolithic concrete substrate slope of a minimum 11 mm/m (1/8 in./ft) should be maintained. Slope is best achieved with a monolithic structural slab and not with a separate concrete fill layer.

MEMBRANE

Detection of leakage can be a significant problem when the membrane is not bonded to the structural slab or when additional layers of materials separate it from the structural slab. Therefore, only membranes that can be bonded to the substrate should be used.

The membrane should be applied under dry, frost-free conditions on the surface as well as throughout the depth of the concrete slab.

When the membrane is turned up on a wall, it is preferable to terminate it above the wearing surface to eliminate the possibility of ponded surface water penetrating the wall above the membrane and running down behind it into the building.

Penetrations should be avoided wherever possible. For protection at such critical locations, pipe sleeves should be cast into the structural slab against which the membrane can be terminated by flashing onto the pipe sleeve.

Treatment at reinforced and nonreinforced joints depends on the membrane used. See following pages.

Two concepts can be considered in the detailing of expansion joints at the membrane level: the positive seal concept directly at the membrane level and the watershed concept with the seal at a higher level than the membrane. Where additional safeguards are desired, a drainage gutter under the joint could be considered. Flexible upward support of the membrane is required in each case to provide watershed-type drainage. Expansion joint details should be considered and used in accordance with their movement capability.

The positive seal concept entails a greater risk than the watershed concept, since it relies fully on positive seal joinery of materials at the membrane level, where the membrane is most vulnerable to water penetration. Since the precision required is not always attainable, this concept is best avoided.

The watershed concept, although requiring a greater height and more costly concrete forming, is superior in safeguarding against leakage, having the advantage of providing a monolithic concrete water dam at the membrane level. However, if a head of water rises to the height of the materials joinery, this concept becomes almost as vulnerable as the positive seal concept. Therefore, drainage is recommended at the membrane level.

PROTECTION BOARD

The membrane should be protected from damage throughout construction. Protection board should be applied after the membrane is installed. The proper timing of application after placement of the membrane is important and varies with the type of membrane used. Follow the manufacturer's printed instructions.

DRAINAGE SYSTEM

Drainage should be considered as a total system from the wearing surface down to the membrane, including use of multilevel drains.

Drainage at the wearing surface is generally accomplished in one of two ways: (1) by an open joint and pedestal system permitting the rainwater to penetrate rapidly down to the membrane level and subsurface drainage system; and (2) by a closed-joint system designed to remove most of the rainwater rapidly by slope

to surface drains and to allow a minor portion to infiltrate to the membrane.

A drainage course of washed, round gravel or prefabricated drainage composite should be provided above the protection board, over the membrane. This permits water to filter to the drain and provides a place where it can collect and freeze without damaging the wearing course.

INSULATION

When required, insulation should be located above the membrane, but not in direct contact with it.

PROTECTION OR WORKING SLAB

A concrete slab could be placed soon after the membrane, protection board, drainage course, and insulation, if required, have been installed. It would serve as protection for the permanent waterproofing materials and insulation below, provide a working platform for construction traffic and storage of materials (within weight limits), and provide a substantial substrate for the placement of the finish wearing course materials.

WEARING COURSE

The major requirements for the wearing course are a stable support of sufficient strength, resistance against lateral thrust, adequate drainage to avoid ponding of water, and proper treatment of joints. Under a thick-set mortar bed supporting masonry units, a prefabricated drainage composite helps resist freeze-thaw damage to the wearing course by expediting water flow down to the subsurface drainage system.

Joints in which movement is anticipated should be treated as expansion joints. Various compression seals are available that can be inserted into a formed joint under compression. Most of these, however, are not flush at the top surface and could fill up with sand or dirt.

Wet sealants are the materials most commonly used in moving joints at the wearing surface level. Dimension A is the design width dimension or the dimension at which the joint will be formed. The criterion normally used for determining this dimension with sealants capable of ± 25% movement is to multiply the maximum expected movement in one direction by 4. Generally, this is expected to be about three-fourths of the total anticipated joint movement, but if there is any doubt, multiply the total anticipated joint movement by 4. It is better to have the joint too wide than too narrow. Dimension B (sealant depth) is related to dimension A and is best established by the sealant manufacturer. Generally, B is equal to A for widths up to 13 mm (1/2 in.), 15 mm (9/16 in.) for a 16 mm (5/8 in.) width, and 16 mm (5/8 in.) for 19 mm (3/4 in.) and greater widths. This allows some tolerance for self-leveling sealants.

Reference: ASTM C 898 and C 981. Highlights of text and figures are reprinted with permission from Committee C-24 of the American Society for Testing Materials.

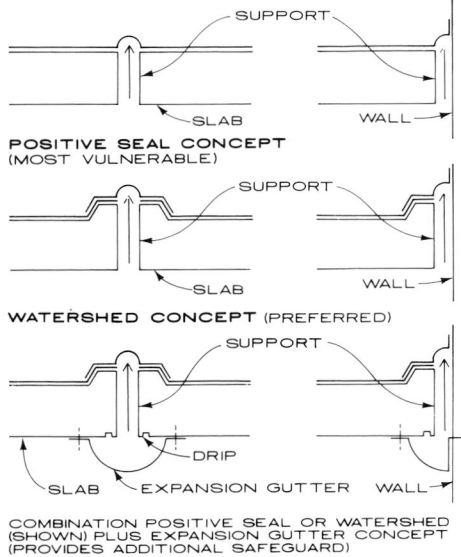

EXPANSION JOINT CONCEPTS AT MEMBRANE LEVEL

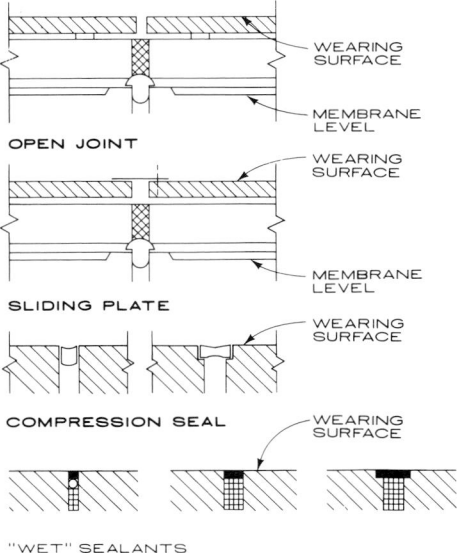

EXPANSION JOINT CONCEPTS AT WEARING SURFACE LEVEL

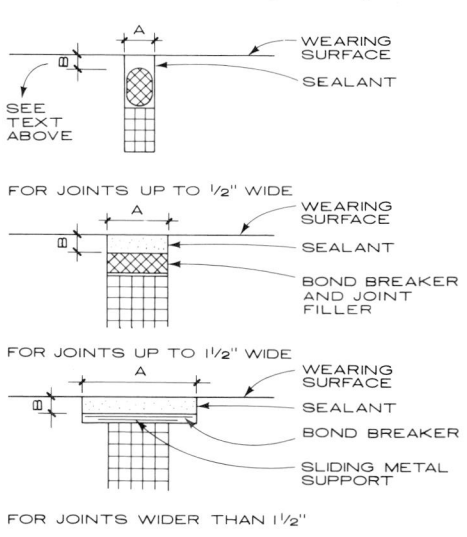

WET SEALANT DETAILS AT WEARING SURFACE

Charles J. Parise, FAIA, FASTM; Smith, Hinchman & Grylls Associates, Inc.; Detroit, Michigan

SUBSTRATE

The building deck or substrate referred to is reinforced cast-in-place structural concrete.

The structural slab should have a finish of sufficiently rough texture to provide a mechanical bond for the membrane, but not so rough to preclude achieving continuity of the membrane across the surface.

The concrete should be cured a minimum of 7 days and aged a minimum of 28 days, including curing time, before application of the bituminous membrane. Curing is accomplished chemically with moisture and should not be construed as drying. Liquid or chemical curing compounds should not be used unless approved by the manufacturer of the built-up bituminous membrane as the material may interfere with the bond of the membrane to the structural slab.

MEMBRANE

A built-up bituminous waterproofing membrane consists of components joined together and bonded to its substrate at the site. The major membrane components include primers, bitumens, reinforcements, and flashing materials.

Surfaces to receive waterproofing must be clean, dry, reasonably smooth, and free of dust, dirt, voids, cracks, laitance, or sharp projections before application of materials.

Concrete surfaces should be uniformly primed to enhance the bond between the membrane and the substrate, so as to inhibit lateral movement of water.

The number of plies of membrane reinforcement required is dependent upon the head of water and strength required by the design function of the wearing surface. Plaza deck membranes should be composed of not less than three plies. The composition of the membrane is normally of a "shingle" or "ply-on-ply" (phased) construction.

For application temperatures, follow the recommendations of the manufacturers of the membrane materials.

Over reinforced structural slab joints, one ply of 6-in.-wide membrane reinforcement should be applied before application of the bituminous membrane.

Nonreinforced joints should receive a bead of compatible sealant in a recessed joint before application of the membrane.

At expansion joints, gaskets and flexible preformed sheets are required inasmuch as bituminous membranes have little or no movement capability. Since such materials must be joined to the bituminous membrane, the watershed concept should be used.

Reinforce all intersections with walls and corners with two layers of woven fabric embedded in hot bitumen.

Flashing membranes should extend above the wearing surface and the highest possible water level and not less than 150 mm (6 in.) onto the deck membrane.

The flashing should extend over the wall dampproofing or membrane waterproofing not less than 100 mm (4 in.).

Drains must be provided with a wide metal flange or base and set slightly below the drainage level. Metal flashing for the drain, if required, and the clamping ring should be set on the membrane in bituminous plastic cement. The metal flashing should be stripped in with a minimum of two plies of membrane reinforcement and three applications of bituminous plastic cement.

Penetrations through the membrane such as conduits and pipes should be avoided whenever possible. Penetrations must be flashed to a height above the anticipated water table that may extend above the wearing surface.

The built-up bituminous membrane should be protected from damage. Protection board should be placed on the waterproofing membrane when the final mopping is being placed. It will then be adhered to the membrane.

Reference: ASTM C 981. Highlights of text and figures are reprinted with permission from ASTM Committee C-24 of the American Society for Testing and Materials.

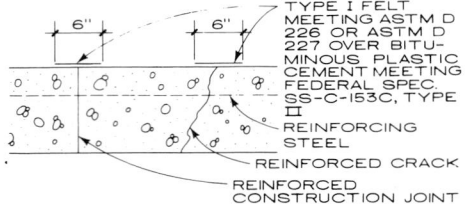

TREATMENT AT REINFORCED JOINTS

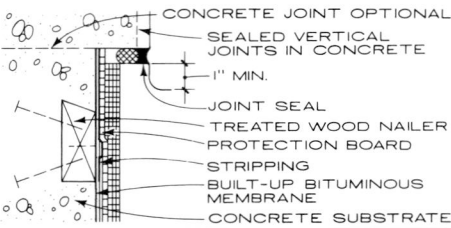

TERMINAL CONDITION ABOVE FINISH GRADE ON CONCRETE WALL

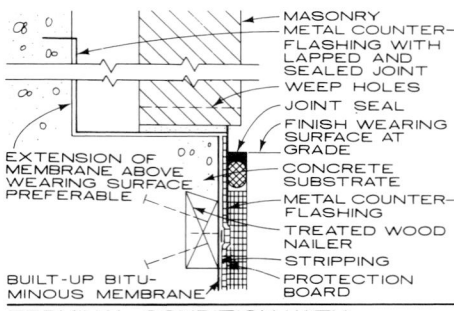

TERMINAL CONDITION WITH MASONRY ABOVE FINISH WEARING SURFACE AT GRADE

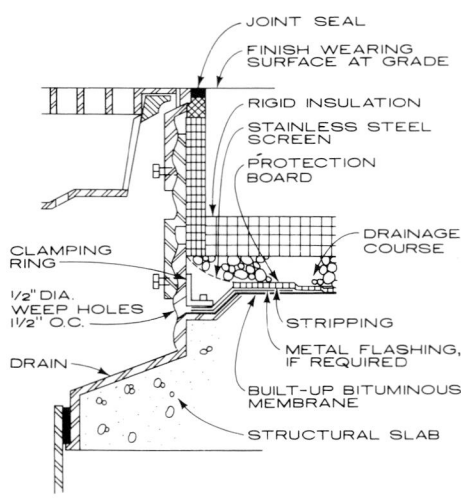

TERMINATION AT DRAIN

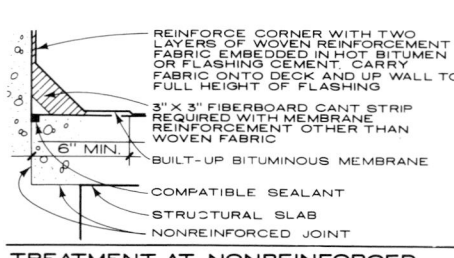

TREATMENT AT NONREINFORCED JOINTS

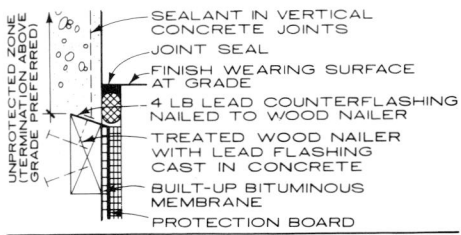

TERMINAL CONDITIONS ON CONCRETE WALL BELOW FINISH WEARING SURFACE AT GRADE

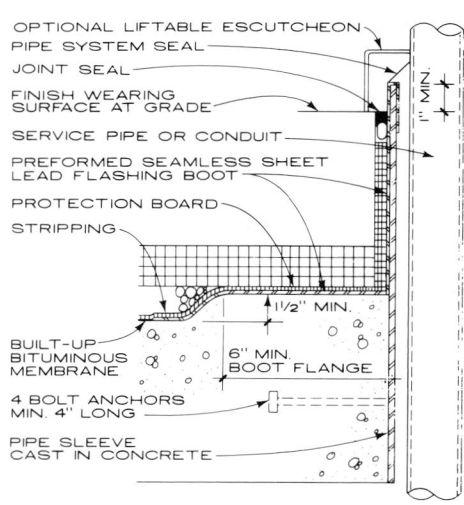

TERMINATION AT PIPE PENETRATIONS

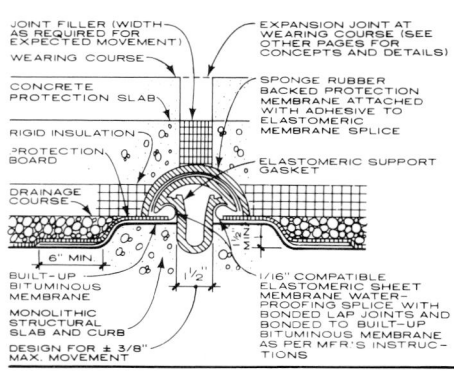

WATERSHED CONCEPT EXPANSION JOINT

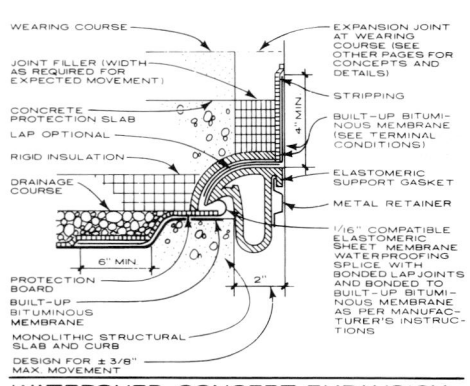

WATERSHED CONCEPT EXPANSION JOINT

Charles J. Parise, FAIA, FASTM; Smith, Hinchman & Grylls Associates, Inc.; Detroit, Michigan

SUBSTRATE

The building deck or substrate referred to is reinforced cast-in-place structural concrete.

Polymeric, latex, or other organic chemical-based admixtures or modifiers can coat the concrete particles and reduce the ability of the membrane to bond to the substrate. Admixtures should not be used in the concrete unless determined that they are acceptable for use with the membrane.

The underside of the concrete deck should not have an impermeable barrier. A metal liner or coating that forms a vapor barrier on the underside traps moisture in the concrete and destroys or prevents the adhesive bond of the membrane to the upper surface of the concrete.

The surface should be of sufficiently rough texture to provide a mechanical bond for the membrane, but not so rough as to preclude achieving continuity of the membrane of the specified thickness across the surface.

The concrete should be cured a minimum of 7 days and aged a minimum of 28 days, including curing time, before application of the liquid-applied membrane. Curing is accomplished chemically with moisture and should not be construed as drying. Liquid or chemical curing compounds should not be used unless approved by the manufacturer of the liquid-applied membrane as the material may interfere with the bond of the membrane to the structural slab.

MEMBRANE

The membrane should be applied under dry, frost-free conditions on the surface as well as throughout the depth of the concrete slab. Use manufacturer's requirements for the particular membrane.

TERMINATION ON WALLS

A liquid-applied membrane, because of its inherent adhesive properties, may be terminated flush on the wall without the use of a reglet. However, the use of a reglet in a concrete wall has the advantage of providing greater depth protection at the terminal.

TERMINATION AT DRAINS

Drains should be designed with a wide flange or base as an integral part. The drain base should be set flush with the structural slab. Vehicular supporting drains generally require additional weep holes drilled into them (see detail).

TREATMENT AT REINFORCED JOINTS

One recommended treatment of reinforced concrete joints in the structural slab is to apply a double layer of membrane over the crack. This type of detail is quite limited and implicitly relies on the membrane's crack-bridging ability. An alternative approach is to prevent the membrane from adhering to the substrate for a finite width centered on the joint or crack by means of a properly designed compatible bond-breaker tape.

TREATMENT AT NONREINFORCED JOINTS

Since the joints are not held together with reinforcing steel, some movement, however slight, should be anticipated and provided for, since the liquid-applied membrane has limited ability to take movement.

TREATMENT AT EXPANSION JOINTS

Gaskets and flexible preformed sheets lend themselves better to absorbing large amounts of movement. Since such materials, when used at an expansion joint, must be joined to the liquid-applied membrane, the watershed concept should be used.

PROTECTION BOARD

The liquid-applied membrane should be protected from damage prior to and during the remainder of deck construction. The proper timing of the application of the board is important and the manufacturer's printed instructions should be followed.

Reference: ASTM C 898. Highlights of text and figures are reprinted with permission from ASTM Committee C-24 of the American Society for Testing and Materials.

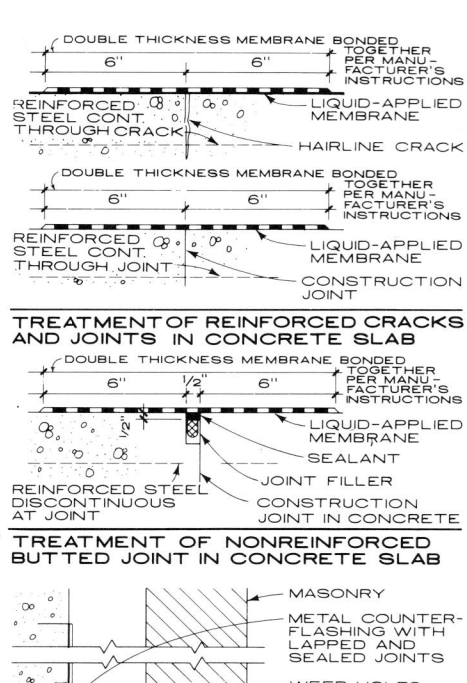

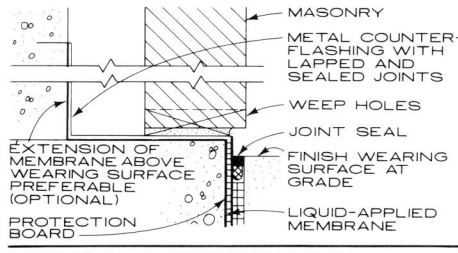

TREATMENT OF REINFORCED CRACKS AND JOINTS IN CONCRETE SLAB

TREATMENT OF NONREINFORCED BUTTED JOINT IN CONCRETE SLAB

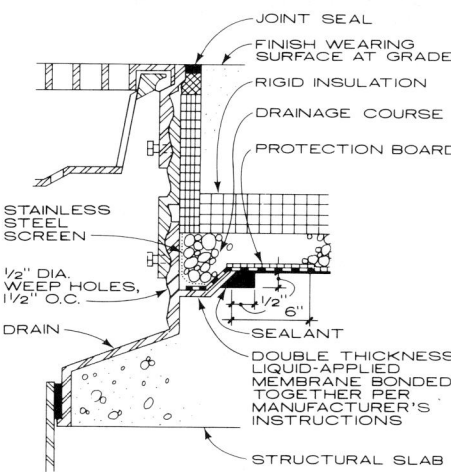

TERMINAL CONDITION WITH MASONRY ABOVE FINISH WEARING SURFACE AT GRADE

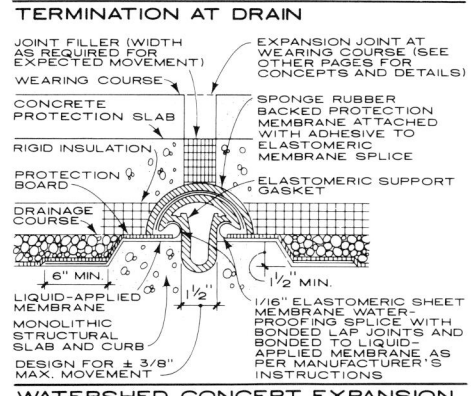

TERMINATION AT DRAIN

WATERSHED CONCEPT EXPANSION JOINT

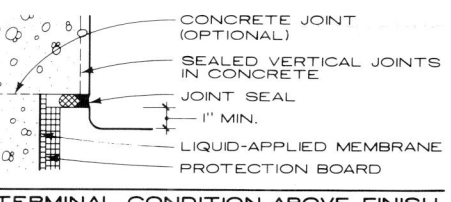

TERMINAL CONDITION ABOVE FINISH GRADE ON CONCRETE WALL

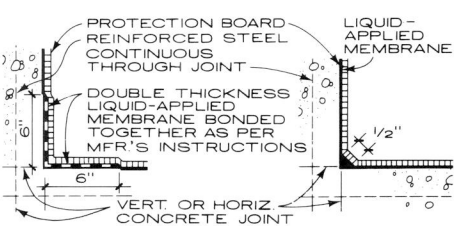

TURNUP DETAILS AT REINFORCED JOINT

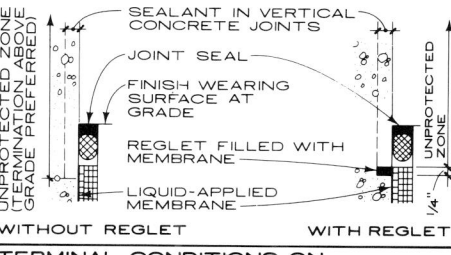

WITHOUT REGLET   WITH REGLET

TERMINAL CONDITIONS ON CONCRETE WALL BELOW FINISH WEARING SURFACE AT GRADE

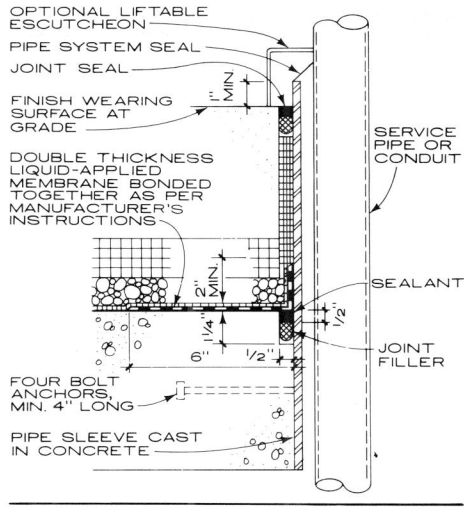

TERMINATION AT PIPE PENETRATIONS

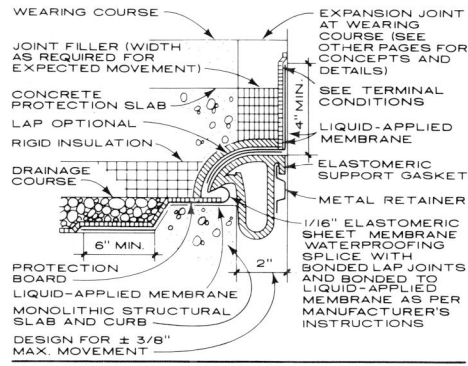

WATERSHED CONCEPT EXPANSION JOINT

Charles J. Parise, FAIA, FASTM; Smith, Hinchman & Grylls Associates, Inc.; Detroit, Michigan

GENERAL

Dampproofing or waterproofing is generally recommended for basement and foundation walls. Dampproofing may also be used for retaining walls and similar structures. Waterproofing implies the prevention of an actual flow of water through the structure. Dampproofing is intended to prevent moisture penetration by capillarity.

Water absorbed by concrete or masonry may be distributed by capillary forces through the walls until saturation occurs or evaporation balances the inflow. If there is a continuous supply of free water available on one side of a wall and evaporation is taking place on the other, there will be continuous passage of water. With adequate evaporation, moisture on the interior surface may not be present. However, if the air becomes saturated, the temperature drops, or other effects prevent sufficient evaporation, moisture may appear on the wall. When this occurs, a sealer is often applied on the interior surface, causing saturation of the foundation wall.

The appearance of moisture on the wall is not always caused by the passage of water through the wall. Dampness on interior surfaces is often mistakenly attributed to moisture penetration. In fact, it may be the result of moisture from interior air condensing on the cool interior wall surface.

Generally, the remedy is to seal the unexposed exterior surface of the wall. However, neither dampproofing nor waterproofing will prevent condensation from forming on the interior surface. For climates and conditions that are conducive to condensation, interior drainage techniques have been successfully employed to accommodate the moisture condensation on the interior surface. Use of exterior insulation or insulation within a wall system, such as preinsulated concrete masonry units, tends to keep the interior wall surface temperature warm and reduces potential condensation. Other effective measures include air circulation and dehumidification of the air in the enclosed space.

Model building codes include requirements for dampproofing and waterproofing foundation walls. Waterproofing is usually required when hydrostatic pressure conditions exist. Some codes require waterproofing on the exterior of all foundation walls enclosing habitable space. The International Conference of Building Officials Uniform Building Code, 1991 edition, calls for dampproofing of all below grade portions of foundation walls enclosing a basement. The Council of American Building Officials One and Two Family Dwelling Code, 1989 edition, requires that the exterior of all foundation walls enclosing basements be dampproofed and that foundation walls of habitable spaces located below grade be waterproofed. The Southern Building Code Congress International Standard Building Code, 1991 edition, requires waterproofing where groundwater table investigation indicates that hydrostatic pressure conditions exist; and where hydrostatic pressure conditions do not exist, dampproofing and perimeter drainage are required. The Building Officials Conference of America National Building Code, 1990 edition, requires dampproofing where hydrostatic pressure will not occur and waterproofing where hydrostatic pressure will occur.

Generally, dampproofing should be provided for all below grade walls where saturation during freezing conditions is possible. Dampproofing with adequate drainage should prevent deterioration of concrete or masonry foundation or retaining walls.

DAMP COURSES AND DAMP CHECKS

Dampproofing methods did not always include exterior wall surface coatings. Often damp cellars were used for storage and cooling, and dampproofing methods were limited to preventing water from rising by capillary action to the top of the foundation wall where its presence could damage wood portions of the structure. Damp courses were employed to prevent this continuous capillary action. A damp course is a horizontal course of dense impervious masonry units, typically slate, impervious limestone, or hard-fired clay brick. The damp course was typically located at or slightly above grade. In more recent times, this feature has been replaced with damp checks. A damp check is a continuous impervious membrane placed horizontally between courses of masonry or at the top of concrete or masonry walls. Damp checks may be formed of any material appropriate for use as embedded flashing. Liquid-applied asphalt or bituminous coatings have also demonstrated effective performance as damp checks. Damp courses and damp checks, although no longer common in foundation walls, are frequently located below copings at the roof level in chimneys and at other locations to prevent downward seepage of water, as well as to prevent the upward migration of water by capillary action.

DAMPPROOFING

Dampproof coatings are adequate in porous soils where a water head will not develop. The CABO One and Two Family Dwelling Code, 1989 edition, requires that masonry foundation walls enclosing basements be dampproofed by applying not less than $^3/_8$ inch portland cement parging from the footing to finish grade. The parging is to be covered with an approved bituminous material. The parging is not required by the code for concrete foundation walls. The SBCCI Standard Building Code, 1991 edition, provides a specific list of acceptable dampproofing materials. In addition to the $^3/_8$ inch portland cement parging with a $^1/_{16}$ inch bituminous coating, the Standard Building Code, 1991 Edition, lists

- $^1/_8$-inch bituminous coating
- $^1/_8$-inch cementitious coating
- $^1/_8$-inch surface bonding
- 40-mil acrylic latex coating
- 6-mil polyethylene or $^1/_{16}$-inch bituminous coating
- 3 lb/sq. yd. acrylic modified cement base coating

or any material or system approved for waterproofing. The BOCA National Building Code, 1990 edition, specifically permits bituminous coatings, 3 lb/sq yd acrylic modified cement, and $^1/_8$-inch surface bonding cement applied over concrete foundation walls or parged masonry foundation walls in addition to any materials permitted for waterproofing. The ICBO Uniform Building Code, 1991 edition, cites that waterproofing and dampproofing must be applied with approved methods and materials. Practice for parging consists of a $^3/_8$- to $^1/_2$-inch thick coat of portland cement and sand mix or a type M mortar mix applied in two layers of approximately equal thickness ($^3/_{16}$ to $^1/_4$ inch thick). The portland cement-sand mixture is one part portland cement by volume to two and one-half parts sand by volume. The sand should conform to ASTM C144, "Standard Specification for Aggregate for Masonry Mortar," and the portland cement should conform to ASTM C150, "Standard Specification for Portland Cement." If a Type M mortar mix is used for parging, the mixture should conform to the ingredients and proportions provided in ASTM C270, "Standard Specification for Mortar for Unit Masonry." The mortar mixture may be, in parts by volume, one part portland cement, $^1/_4$ part hydrated lime, and 3 to $3^3/_4$ parts sand; or one part Type M masonry cement and $2^1/_4$ to 3 parts sand.

To prevent masonry units from absorbing excessive amounts of water from the parge coat, the masonry surface to be coated should be cleaned and dampened (not soaked) with water immediately prior to applying the parge coat. The first coat should be roughened when partially set. This coat, referred to as a scratch coat, should be allowed to cure (usually 24 hours) and then be moistened prior to the application of the second or finish coat. The finish coat should be trowelled to form a tight, dense surface. A cove should be formed at the base of the foundation wall to prevent water from accumulating at the wall/footing juncture. The finish coat should be moist-cured for 48 hours before backfilling.

Bituminous coatings, hot or cold, may be sprayed, brushed, or trowelled on. Trowelling is the preferred method. Hot asphalt coatings tend to become brittle and crack during cooling and their emulsions are water soluble; thus these coatings are not recommended. Pitch intended for roofing applications tends to become brittle and crack with no resealing ability. Application of cement-based paints, surface bonding mortars, acrylic latex coating, and acrylic modified cement base coatings should be applied in accordance with the manufacturer's recommendations. When polyethylene is used, it should be chemically stabilized to resist degradation from exposure to the sun's ultraviolet rays.

Generally, dampproofing materials should not be applied when the ambient air temperature is below 40° F or the masonry surface is above 90° F, unless the coatings have been specially formulated for these applications.

Unless the site is located in well-drained gravel, sand, or sand-gravel soils, perimeter drainage should be provided when dampproofing is required. Foundation perimeter drains should have a slope of 0.33% (about $^3/_8$ inch per 10 feet) and discharge by gravity or mechanical means into an approved drainage system.

The perimeter drain may be constructed of crushed stone or by using drain tile or perforated pipe. Drains consisting of crushed stone should contain no more than 10% material that passes a no. 4 sieve. The drain should extend 12 inches beyond the edge of the footing. The drain should extend from a depth no less than the bottom of the floor to a height not less than 12 inches above the top of the footing. The top of the drain should be covered with a filter fabric or membrane.

When tile or pipe are used, the invert of the pipe or tile should not be higher than the floor elevation. The top of joints or perforations should be covered with an approved filter fabric or membrane. The pipe or tile should be placed on not less than two inches of crushed stone containing not more than 10% material that passes a No. 4 sieve; it should be covered with not less than six inches of the same crushed stone material. The crushed stone should extend at least 12 inches beyond the edge of the footing. The top of the crushed stone should be covered with a filter fabric or membrane.

These drainage systems, required when dampproofing is used as a water penetration resistance technique in soils other than sand and gravel, may also be used with waterproofing systems. Generally, waterproofing is only used when the groundwater is above the footer, making the drainage system of little or no benefit as it would continually fill with water. However, if the waterproofing system is employed because spaces contained by the foundation walls are intended to be habitable, or as a soil gas penetration resistance technique for conditions that would otherwise only require dampproofing, it is advisable to retain the drainage system. Waterproofing may also be employed if there is a potential for excessive movement in the foundation system. Because moisture and temperature conditions are relatively constant below grade, movements due to temperature or moisture changes are generally insignificant. However, in long spans (typically over 50 feet), the use of tensile steel in the longitudinal direction may be advisable to inhibit cracking. In masonry walls, this steel may be horizontal joint reinforcement placed vertically no more than 16 inches on center.

WATERPROOFING

Waterproofing, necessary to resist the flow of water from hydrostatic forces, makes the foundation wall system impervious to the flow of water. The CABO One and Two Family Dwelling Code, 1989 edition, requires that waterproofing be a membrane of 2-ply hot mopped felt, 6-mil polyvinylchloride, 55 lb roofing felt, or equivalent material. All laps in the membrane must be sealed and firmly affixed to the wall. Specific provisions called out in the BOCA National Building Code, 1990 edition, cite 40-mil polymer modified asphalt and 6-mil polyethylene in addition to the waterproofing systems cited in the CABO publication. The SBCCI Standard Building Code, 1991 edition, requires 3-ply instead of 2-ply hot mopped felts and, in addition to other methods or materials capable of bridging non-structural cracks, specifically permits

- 0.75 lb/sq ft bentonite clay layer
- 50-mil rubberized asphalt sheet or liquid
- 40-mil polymer modified asphalt
- 40-mil polyurethane rubber
- 20-mil single ply vulcanized rubber or thermoplastic sheet.

The ICBO Uniform Building Code, 1991 edition, refers to approved methods and materials.

Sheet membranes are usually applied in widths of 3 to 4 feet. Sheets are typically installed horizontally starting at the footing. Each successive sheet should overlap the previous sheet by at least two inches. All vertical laps in the membrane should be at least six inches. All joints should be sealed in accordance with the sheet membrane manufacturer's recommendations.

Surface bonding cements have proved to be effective waterproofing measures. Surface bonding mortar systems typically consist of glass fibers combined with portland cement and other additives. Surfaces should be dampened prior to application, and the mortar is usually trowelled on to form a $^1/_8$-inch layer with a smooth surface. On large projects, spray application of a surface bonding mortar may be more efficient.

Bentonite may be used to enhance water penetration resistance. Bentonite is a natural clay that expands 16 to 22 times its original volume when in contact with water. The clay, in its expanded state, is impervious to the penetration of any additional water. Bentonite is generally available as a fill in cardboard panels or as a spray.

Bentonite cardboard panels are nailed to the exterior wall surface. The cardboard decomposes rapidly when in contact with water, so the panels must be protected from rain until backfilling is completed. Decomposition of the cardboard permits the bentonite to expand against the masonry and the backfill to form an effective water barrier.

Spray-on bentonite consists of a mixture of bentonite and a mastic binder, which permits the mixture to adhere to the wall when sprayed. Application is usually about $^3/_8$ inch thick. Backfilling must occur before rainfall to prevent the mixture from being washed from the wall.

Brian E. Trimble, E.I.T.; Brick Institute of America; Reston, Virginia
Stephen S. Szoke, P.E.; National Concrete Masonry Association; Herndon, Virginia

All waterproofing and dampproofing membranes, liquid or sheet, should cover the wall and top of the footing. If possible, the membrane should extend about two inches down over the vertical face of the footing.

No waterproofing barrier is effective if damaged, and thus it is important to protect the barrier during installation, backfilling and from subsequent protrusions from the soil such as roots. Fiber board, roofing felt, polymer protection boards, or rigid board insulation may be used for protection. When waterproofing is to be applied to the exterior of concrete masonry walls, and the walls have full mortar joints with concave or flush joint profiles, it is not necessary to apply a parge coat before the waterproofing system or material.

SYSTEM SELECTION

Selection of a system should consider structural performance of the foundation wall, thermal protection requirements, the use of the spaces contained by the foundations walls, and the presence or lack of groundwater above the footer.

When no insulation is required or when interior insulation strategies such as furring or studs with batt or rigid board insulation are used, the waterproofing should be protected with a material or system specifically designed for that purpose. Similar provisions are necessary to protect the waterproofing if premolded insulation inserts, granular fill, or foamed in-place insulation is placed in the cores of masonry units. Exterior rigid board insulation may serve as thermal protection and as protection for the waterproofing or dampproofing. Rigid board insulation is typically rigid fibrous, expanded, or molded polystyrene, polyurethene, or polyisocyanurate boards.

When dampproofing is provided, rigid fibrous boards may also serve as a drainage system to help reduce the potential for any direct contact with water at the surface of a foundation wall. A variety of drainage board systems specifically designed for this purpose are available. The drainage board may also be used as a protection layer.

Special conditions: In some instances, it is desirable to use an interior perimeter drainage system in lieu of an exterior drainage system. These systems are employed when the drainage system is designed to accommodate the flow of water in well-draining soils and the condensation on the interior of foundation walls. These systems typically consist of a drainage system designed in the same way as one on the exterior but connected to a sump. The joint at the intersection of the foundation walls and basement floor remains open so that condensation moisture may enter the drainage system. The drainage system may be connected to the well-draining soil, a crushed stone field, or the exterior of the foundation wall by pipes through the footer or weep holes through the foundation wall. This system is not advisable when mitigation of radon or other soil gases is a major design consideration. Generally, any waterproofing technique will provide adequate resistance to soil gases.

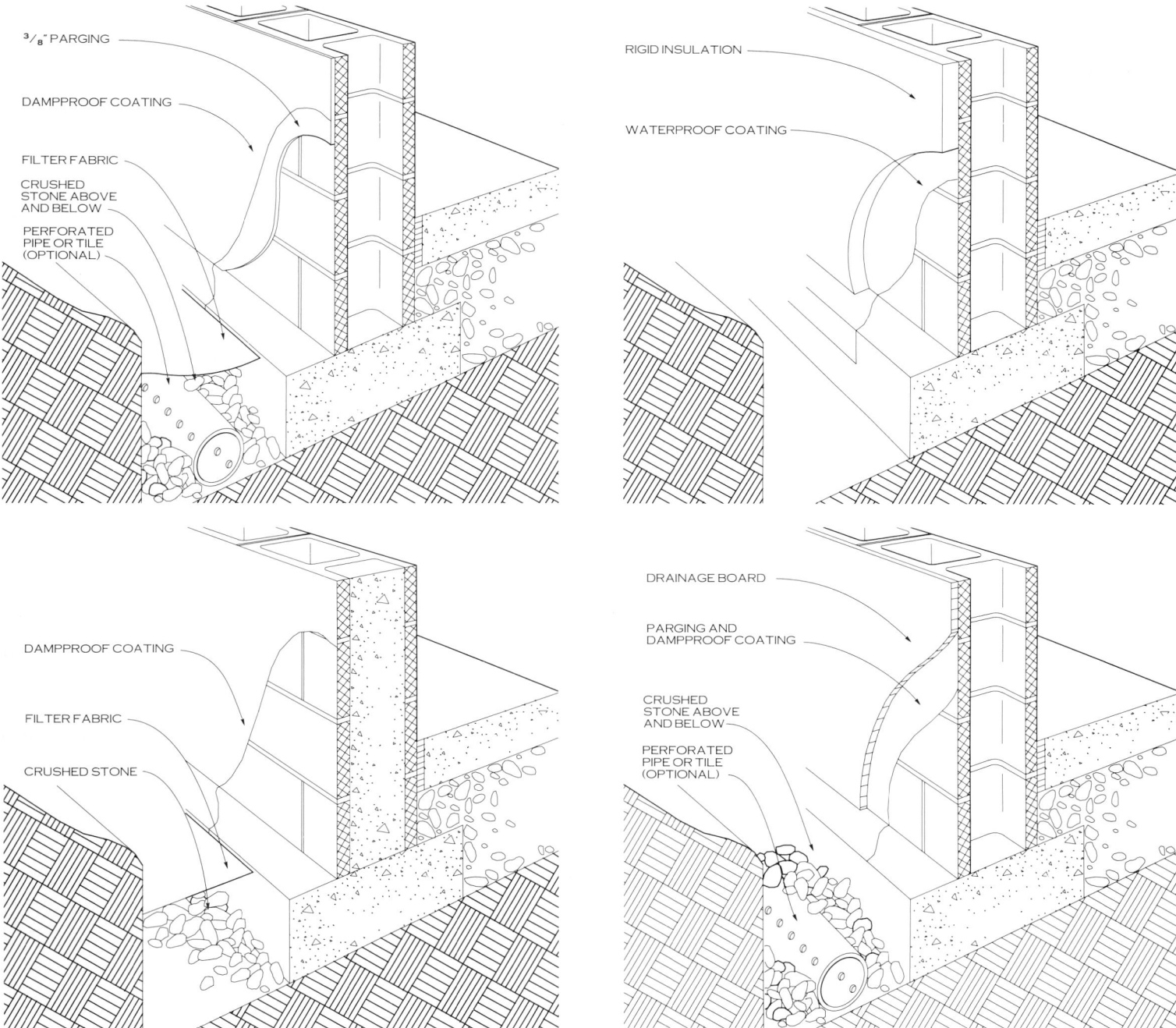

Labels (upper left): ³/₈" PARGING; DAMPPROOF COATING; FILTER FABRIC; CRUSHED STONE ABOVE AND BELOW; PERFORATED PIPE OR TILE (OPTIONAL)

Labels (upper right): RIGID INSULATION; WATERPROOF COATING

Labels (lower left): DAMPPROOF COATING; FILTER FABRIC; CRUSHED STONE

Labels (lower right): DRAINAGE BOARD; PARGING AND DAMPPROOF COATING; CRUSHED STONE ABOVE AND BELOW; PERFORATED PIPE OR TILE (OPTIONAL)

DAMPPROOFING DETAILS

Brian E. Trimble, E.I.T.; Brick Institute of America; Reston, Virginia
Stephen S. Szoke, P.E.; National Concrete Masonry Association; Herndon, Virginia

WATER VAPOR MIGRATION

Water is present as vapor in indoor and outdoor air and as absorbed moisture in many building materials. Within the range of temperatures encountered in buildings, water may exist in the liquid, vapor, or solid states. Moisture related problems may arise from changes in moisture content, from the presence of excessive moisture, or from the effects of changes of state, such as freezing within walls or deterioration of materials due to rotting or corrosion.

In the design and construction of the thermal envelope of buildings (the enclosure of desired temperatures and humidities), the behavior of moisture must be considered, particularly the change of state from vapor to liquid (condensation). Problems arise when moisture comes into contact with a relatively cold surface (temperature below the dew point), such as a window, or within outdoor walls or under-roof ceilings. Excessive condensation within indoor walls that enclose cold spaces must be considered.

While moisture moves in still air by vapor pressure differences, it is important to recognize that moisture in air is moved by the air. Consequently, the causes of air motion must be considered, especially the infiltration and exfiltration at undesirable leakage rates at windows, doors, and other penetrations through the thermal envelope of the building.

Moisture problems in residences generally occur in seasons when the outdoor temperature and vapor pressure are low and there are many indoor vapor sources. These may include cooking, laundering, bathing, breathing, and perspiration for the occupants, as well as automatic washers and dryers, dishwashers, and humidifiers. All of these sources combine to cause vapor pressure indoors to be much higher than outdoors, so that the vapor tends to migrate outward through the building envelope. Vapor cannot permeate glazed windows or metal doors, but most other building materials are permeable to some extent. Walls are particularly susceptible to this phenomenon, and such migration must be prevented or at least minimized by the use of low permeance membranes, called *vapor retarders* (formerly, *vapor barriers*). They are now called *retarders*, not *barriers*, because they do not stop moisture flow completely. A vapor retarder is a material that has a flow rating of one perm or less. (1 perm = 1 grain/hr ft - in. Hg vapor pressure difference; there is no metric perm.)

Vapor retarders should be installed as close as possible to the side of the wall through which moisture enters. Establish the side of moisture entrance in walls of controlled rooms within buildings. However, the beneficial effects of good vapor retarders are lost without adequate air barriers.

Moisture in building materials usually increases their thermal conductance significantly and unpredictably. Porous materials that become saturated with moisture lose most of their insulating capability and may not regain it when they dry out. Dust, which usually settles in airspaces, may become permanently affixed to originally reflective surfaces. Moisture migration by evaporation, vapor flow, and condensation can transport significant quantities of latent heat, particularly through fibrous insulating materials.

Positive steps should be taken to prevent migration of moisture in the form of vapor and accumulation in the form of water or ice within building components. Vapor retarders, correctly located near the source of the moisture, are an effective means of preventing such migration. Venting of moisture laden air from bathrooms, laundry rooms, and kitchens will reduce indoor vapor pressure, as will the introduction of outdoor air with low moisture content.

BUILDING SECTION ANALYSIS FOR POTENTIAL CONDENSATION

Any building section may be analyzed with simple calculations to determine where condensation might occur and what might be done in selecting materials or their method of assembly to eliminate that possibility. The section may or may not contain a vapor retarder, or it may contain an inadequate one; the building section may include cold-side materials of comparatively high resistance to the passage of vapor (which is highly undesirable). With few exceptions, the vapor resistance at or near the warm surface should be five times that of any components. The table gives permeance and permeability of building and vapor retarder materials. These values can be used in analyzing building sections by the following simple method:

- List the materials, without surface films or airspaces, in the order of their appearance in the building section, beginning with the inside surface material and working to the outside.
- Against each material list the permeance (or permeability) value from the table or a more accurate value if available from tests or manufacturers' data. Where a range is

given, select an average value or use judgment in assigning a value based on the character and potential installation method of the material proposed for use.

- Start at the top of the list and note any material that has less permeance than the materials above it on the list. At that point the possibility exists that vapor leaking through the first material may condense on the second, provided the dew point (condensation point) is reached and the movement is considerable. In that case, provide ventilation through the cold-side material or modify the design to eliminate or change the material to one of greater permeance.

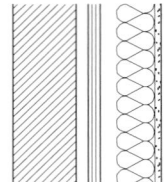

ESTIMATED PERMEANCE

GWB ($^3/_8$")	50.0
Vapor retarder	0.6 (lowest)
Insulation	29.0
Wood sheathing	2.9
4" brick veneer	1.1 (next)

EXAMPLE

In this example the vapor retarder transmits 1 grain of moisture per square foot per hour for each unit of vapor pressure difference, or one perm, and nothing else transmits less. However, since the cold brick veneer is nearly as low in permeance, it is advisable to make certain that the vapor retarder is expertly installed, with all openings at pipes and with outlet boxes or joints carefully fitted or sealed. Alternatively, the brick veneer may have open mortar joints near the top and bottom to serve both as weep holes and as vapor release openings. They will also ventilate the wall and help reduce heat gain in summer.

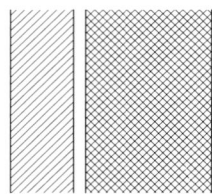

ESTIMATED PERMEANCE

GWB ($^3/_8$")	50.0
Furred space	-
8" CMU	2.4
4" brick veneer	1.1 (lowest)

EXAMPLE

Vapor (under pressure) would easily pass through the interior finish, be slowed by the concrete masonry unit, and be nearly stopped by the cold brick veneer. Unless this design is radically improved, the masonry will become saturated and may cause serious water stains or apparent "leaks" in cold weather. In addition, alternating freezing and thawing of condensation within the masonry wall can physically damage the construction.

PERMEANCE AND PERMEABILITY OF MATERIALS TO WATER VAPOR

MATERIAL	PERM IN.[5]
MATERIALS USED IN CONSTRUCTION	
Concrete (1:2:4 mix)	3.2[5]
Brick-masonry (4 in. thick)	0.8 - 1.1
Concrete masonry (8 in. cored, limestone aggregate)	2.4
Plaster on metal lath ($^3/_4$ in.)	15
Plaster on plain gypsum lath (with studs)	20
Gypsum wallboard ($^3/_8$ in. plain)	50
Structural insulating board (sheathing quality)	20 - 50[5]
Structural insulating board (interior, uncoated, $^1/_2$ in.)	50 - 90
Hardboard ($^1/_8$ in. standard)	11
Hardboard ($^1/_8$ in. tempered)	5
Built-up roofing (hot mopped)	0.0
Wood, fir sheathing, $^3/_4$ in.	2.9
Plywood (Douglas fir, exterior glue, $^1/_4$ in.)	0.7
Plywood (Douglas fir, interior glue, $^1/_4$ in.)	1.9
Acrylic, glass fiber reinforced sheet, 56 mil	0.12
Polyester, glass fiber reinforced sheet, 48 mil	0.05

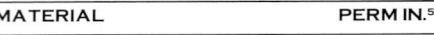

MATERIAL	PERM IN.[5]
THERMAL INSULATIONS	
Cullular glass	0.0[5]
Mineral wool, unprotected	29.0
Expanded polyurethane (R-11 blown)	0.4 -1.6[5]
Expanded polystyrene - extruded	1.2[5]
Expanded polystyrene - bead	2.0 - 5.8[5]
PLASTIC AND METAL FOILS AND FILMS[2]	
Aluminum foil (1 mil)	0.0
Polyethylene (4 mil)	0.08
Polyethylene (6 mil)	0.06
Polyethylene (8 mil)	0.04
Polyester (1 mil)	0.7
Polyvinylchloride, unplasticized (2 mil)	0.68
Polyvinylchloride, plasticized (4 mil)	0.8 -1.4
BUILDING PAPERS, FELTS, ROOFING PAPERS[3]	
Duplex sheet, asphalt laminated, aluminum foil one side (43)[4]	0.176
Saturated and coated roll roofing (326)[4]	0.24
Kraft paper and asphalt laminated, reinforced 30-120-30 (34)[4]	1.8
Asphalt-saturated, coated vapor barrier paper (43)[4]	0.6
Asphalt-saturated, not coated sheathing paper (22)[4]	20.2
15-lb asphalt felt (70)[4]	5.6
15-lb tar felt (70)[4]	18.2
Single kraft, double infused (16)[4]	42
LIQUID APPLIED COATING MATERIALS	
Paint - two coats	
Aluminum varnish on wood	0.3 - 0.5
Enamels on smooth plaster	0.5 - 1.5
Primers and sealers on interior insulation board	0.9 - 2.1
Miscellaneous primers plus one coat flat oil paint on plastic	1.6 - 3.0
Flat paint on interior insulation board	4
Water emulsion on interior insulation board	30 - 85
Paint - three coats	
Exterior paint, white lead and oil on wood siding	0.3 - 1.0
Exterior paint, white lead-zinc oxide and oil on wood	0.9
Styrene-butadiene latex coating, 2 oz/sq ft	11
Polyvinyl acetate latex coating, 4 oz/sq ft	5.5
Asphalt cutback mastic	
1/16 in. dry	0.14
3/16 in. dry	0.0
Hot melt asphalt	
2 oz/sq ft	0.5
3.5 oz/sq ft	0.1

NOTES

1. The vapor transmission rates listed will permit comparisons of materials, but selection of vapor retarder materials should be based on rates obtained from the manufacturer or from laboratory tests. The range of values shown indicates variations among mean values for materials that are similar but of different density. Values are intended for design guidance only.

2. Usually installed as vapor retarders. If used as exterior finish and elsewhere near cold side, special considerations are required.

3. Low permeance sheets used as vapor retarders. High permeance used elsewhere in construction.

4. Bases (weight in lb/500 sq ft).

5. Permeability (perm in.)

Based on data from *ASHRAE Handbook of Fundamentals*, 1984 I-P section, chapter 22.

David F. Hill; Burt Hill Kosar Rittelmann Associates; Butler, Pennsylvania
Marc A. Giaccardo; College of Architecture, Texas Tech University; Lubbock, Texas

INSULATION DEFINED

The word insulate comes from the Latin "insula," meaning island, i.e., an isolated and/or separated place or condition. An insulating material is one that isolates sources of electricity, heat, or sound energy. Building insulation should effectively isolate heat, sound or both.

Nature seeks consonance. This explains why heat (energy) moves toward cold (lack of energy). A balance and harmony is being sought. The primary concept of insulators is to resist the natural tendency of energy to flow from the source and affect the surroundings. By this definition, any material that effectively blocks, absorbs, slows down, or reflects heat and sound is a building insulator.

VAPOR AND MOISTURE

In conjunction with thermal insulators is the necessary concern for vapor retarders and barriers. Although heat energy moves in a variety of ways such as direct radiation, convection, and conduction, one primary vehicle for heat transfer is air. Air expands when it is heated and gains the capacity to hold more water vapor. When warm and moist air is cooled, it condenses and loses the capacity to hold the same amount of vapor. The water vapor condenses, dewpoint is reached, and the water vapor becomes liquid in the same manner that moisture occurs on the warm side (outer surface) of a cold glass of iced tea on a hot and humid day. Since an insulator is normally placed on the warm side of the building, closest to the interior to resist the flow of heat to cold, it follows that this is also where the greatest potential for moisture and moisture damage may occur inside the building section.

It is virtually impossible to construct a perfect vapor barrier. The word "barrier" is used in common building terminology. Construction vapor barriers are actually very effective vapor retarders made of such materials as polyethylene and various facings on insulation that do not totally stop moisture vapor transmission. When a retarder reduces the transmission of moisture to one perm or less, it may be referred to as a vapor barrier.

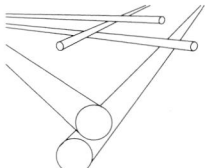 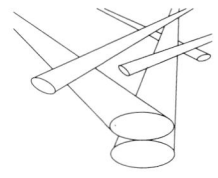

GLASS FIBERS   **CELLULOSE FIBERS**

The fibers of glass fiber insulation have firm and cylindrical cross sections that only touch at tangent points. Therefore, there is little heat transmitted by conduction. In addition, glass fibers trap a large amount of air, which increases insulation potential.

The fibers of cellulose and other blown or hand packed insulators are softer fibers that have wider contact points. This permits more heat transfer through conduction than glass fibers. These fibers also trap a large quantity of air that increases insulation value.

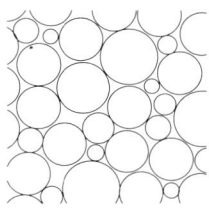 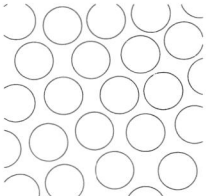

GRANULAR   **CELLULAR**

Vermiculite and perlite insulation are composed of small, rock-like, rounded granules that have small contact points that limit heat conduction. Spaces between the granules contain insulating air.

Extruded, molded, and foamed plastic insulations are cellular or honeycombed. Walls of the cells conduct heat around the cells. Cells contain a large volume of air that greatly increases insulation value.

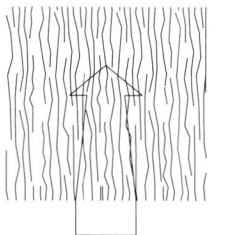 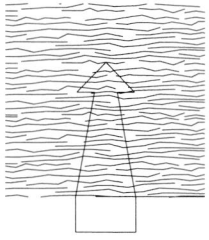

HEAT FLOW PARALLEL   **HEAT FLOW PERPENDICULAR**

If fibrous insulation is used, the direction of the fibers in relation to the direction of the heat flow will affect the rate of heat movement. Under equal conditions, fibers perpendicular to heat flow transmit heat slower than fibers parallel to heat flow.

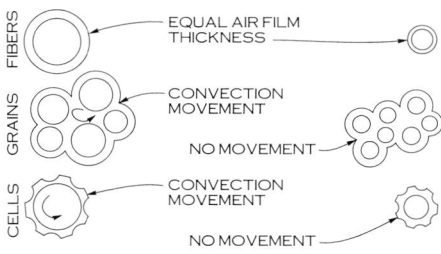

If there are many small fibers of insulation material within a given space, they provide more surface area than larger fibers in the same area. Since thickness of air films surrounding any fiber is essentially the same under still air conditions, smaller fibers provide more surface and more air. Larger fibers may leave larger gaps and paths that allow air to flow by means of convection. Granular and cellular insulation also possess air films. If the cell or space between granules is too large, convection currents can occur that will transmit heat across the space.

MATERIAL PROPERTIES OF COMMON BUILDING INSULATION

BUILDING INSULATION	DENSITY (LB/CU FT)	RESISTANCE (R) (HR/SQ FT °F BTU PER 1 IN. THICKNESS)	WATER VAPOR PERMEABILITY (PERM IN.)	WATER ABSORPTION (% BY WEIGHT)	SURFACE BURNING CHARACTERISTICS FLAME SPREAD	SMOKE DEVELOPED	TOXICITY	EFFECTS OF AGING DIMENSIONAL STABILITY	DEGRADATION DUE TO TEMPERATURE	MOISTURE	FUNGAL OR BACTERIAL GROWTH	WEATHERING	CORROSIVENESS
Glass fiber batts and blankets rigid boards	1.5–4.0 4.0–9.0	3.14 3.8–4.8	100 100	2% 10%	15–25 0–25	0–50 0–50	Some fumes if burned	None	OK below 450°F	None	None	None	None
Rock or slag wool	1.5–2.5	2.9–3.7	100	2%	0–25	0–20	None	None	600°F	Transient	None	None	None
Cellulose (loose blown)	2.0–3.0	2.8–3.7	100	15%	0–50	0–45	CO if burned	Settles 0 - 20%	Possible with long exposure	Possible with long exposure	Maybe	Possible with long exposure	Steel, aluminum, and copper
Molded polystyrene (rigid boards)	0.9–1.8	3.6–4.4	1.2–5.0	2–3%[1]	25	10–400	CO if burned	None	If above 165°F	None	None	UV degrades	None
Extruded polystyrene (rigid boards)	1.6–3.0	4.0–6.0	0.3–0.9	1–4%	25	10–400	CO if burned	None	If above 165°F	None	None	UV degrades	None
Polyurethane (rigid boards)	1.7–4.0	5.8–6.2[2]	2–3	Negligible	25–75	155–200	CO if burned	0–12% change	If above 250°F	?	None	None	None
Polyisocyanurate (rigid boards)	1.7–4.0	5.8–7.8[2]	2.5–3.0	Negligible	25	55–200	CO if burned	0–12% change	If above 250°F	?	None	None	None
Perlite (loose fill)	5–8	2.63	100	Low	0	0	None	Settles 0–10%	If above 1200°F	None	None	None	None
Vermiculite (loose fill)	4–10	2.4–3.0	100	None	0	0	None	Settles 0–10%	If above 1000°F	None	None	None	None
Phenolic (foamed-in-place or rigid boards)	2.5–4.0	4.4–8.2	1.0 for rigid	1–2% for rigid	20–50	0–35	None	None	If above 250°F	None	None	UV degrades	None

NOTES

1. By volume
2. Aged unfaced or spay applied

David F. Hill; Burt Hill Kosar Rittelmann Associates; Butler, Pennsylvania
Donald Bosserman, AIA; Saunders, Cheng & Appleton; Alexandria, Virginia

THERMAL INSULATION

Thermal insulation controls heat flow under temperatures ranging from absolute zero to 3000°F. This broad range can be subdivided into four general temperature regimes that classify applications for various types of insulation:

1. LOW TEMPERATURES: Insulation for vessels containing cryogenic materials, such as liquefied natural gas.
2. AMBIENT TEMPERATURES: Insulation for building structures.
3. MEDIUM TEMPERATURES: Insulation for tanks, pipes, and equipment in industrial process heat applications.
4. HIGH TEMPERATURES: Refractory or other specialized insulation materials used in foundry work, nuclear power facilities, the aerospace industry, and so on.

Architects and builders are generally concerned with the design and material performance of building insulations that operate within ambient temperature limits. As temperatures range much above or below ambient conditions, design and performance requirements change and must be matched with insulation materials that withstand the stress introduced by extreme temperatures, large temperature differentials, and thermal cycling.

BUILDING INSULATION—THERMAL FUNCTIONS

The two major functions of building insulations are to (1) control temperatures of inside surfaces that affect the comfort of occupants and aid or deter condensation and (2) conserve energy by reducing heat transmission through building sections that determine the energy requirements for both heating and cooling. Economics in fuel consumption can be calculated with reasonable accuracy and balanced against initial costs of insulation and the costs for heating and cooling with equipment (see figure).

ADDITIONAL FUNCTIONS

Thermal insulations may also perform several other functions:

1. Add structural strength to a wall, ceiling, or floor section.
2. Provide support for a surface finish.
3. Impede water vapor transmission.
4. Prevent or reduce damage to equipment and structure from exposure to fire and freezing conditions.
5. Reduce noise and vibration.

BASIC MATERIALS

Thermal insulation is made from the following basic materials:

1. MINERAL FIBROUS: Material such as glass, rock, slag, or asbestos that is melted and spun into thin fibers.
2. MINERAL CELLULAR: Material such as foamed glass, calcium silicate, perlite, vermiculite, foamed concrete, or ceramic.
3. ORGANIC FIBROUS: Material such as wood, cane, cotton, hair, cellulose, or synthetic fibers.
4. ORGANIC CELLULAR: Material such as cork, foamed rubber, polystyrene, or polyurethane.
5. METALLIC: Aluminum or other foils, or metallized organic reflective membranes that must face air, gas filled, or evacuated spaces.

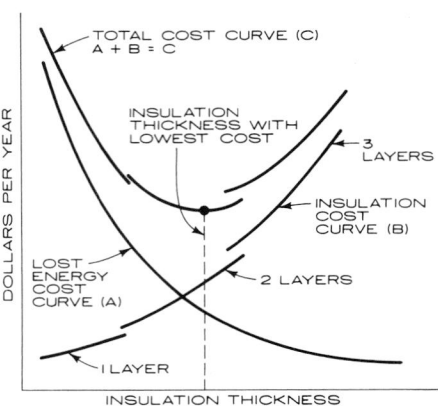

DETERMINATION OF ECONOMIC THICKNESS OF INSULATION

PHYSICAL STRUCTURE AND FORM

Thermal insulation is available in the following physical forms:

1. LOOSE FILL: Dry granules, nodules, or fibers poured or blown into place.
2. FLEXIBLE OR SEMIRIGID: Blankets and batts of wool-like material.
3. RIGID: Boards and blocks.
4. MEMBRANE: Reflective insulation.
5. SPRAY APPLIED: Mineral fiber or insulating concrete.
6. POURED-IN-PLACE: Insulating concrete.
7. FOAMED-IN-PLACE: Polyurethane, urea formaldehyde.

MECHANISMS OF HEAT TRANSFER

Heat flows through materials and space by conduction, convection, and radiation. Convection and conduction are functions of the roughness of surfaces, air movement, and the temperature difference between the air and surface. Mass insulations, by their low densities, are designed to suppress conduction and convection across their sections by the entrapment of air molecules within their structure. Convective air currents are stilled by the surrounding matrix of fibers or cells, and the chances of heat transfer by the collision of air molecules is reduced. Radiant heat transfer between objects operates independently of air currents and is controlled by the character of the surfaces (emissivity) and the temperature difference between warm objects emitting radiation and cooler objects absorbing radiation.

The resistance of these modes of heat transfer may be retarded by the elements of a building wall section.

1. OUTSIDE SURFACE FILMS: The outside surface traps a thin film of air, which resists heat flow. This film varies with wind velocity and surface roughness.
2. MATERIAL LAYERS: Each layer of material contributes to the resistance of heat flow, usually according to its density. A layer of suitable insulation is normally many times more effective in resisting heat transfer than the combination of all other materials in the section.
3. AIRSPACE: Each measurable airspace also adds to the overall resistance. Foil faced surfaces of low emissivities that form the boundaries of the airspace can further reduce the rate of radiant transfer across the space.
4. INSIDE SURFACE FILM: The inside surface of the building section also traps a thin film of air. The air film thus formed is usually thicker because of much lower air velocities.

NOTE: RECOMMENDED INSULATION ZONES FOR HEATING AND COOLING

RECOMMENDED MINIMUM THERMAL RESISTANCES (R) OF INSULATION

ZONE	CEILING	WALL	FLOOR
1	19	11	11
2	26	13	11
3	26	19	13
4	30	19	19
5	33	19	22
6	38	19	22

NOTE: The minimum insulation R values recommended for various parts of the United States as delineated on the map of insulation zones.

INSULATION ZONES

David F. Hill; Burt Hill Kosar Rittelmann Associates; Butler, Pennsylvania
Donald Bosserman, AIA; Saunders, Cheng & Appleton; Alexandria, Virginia

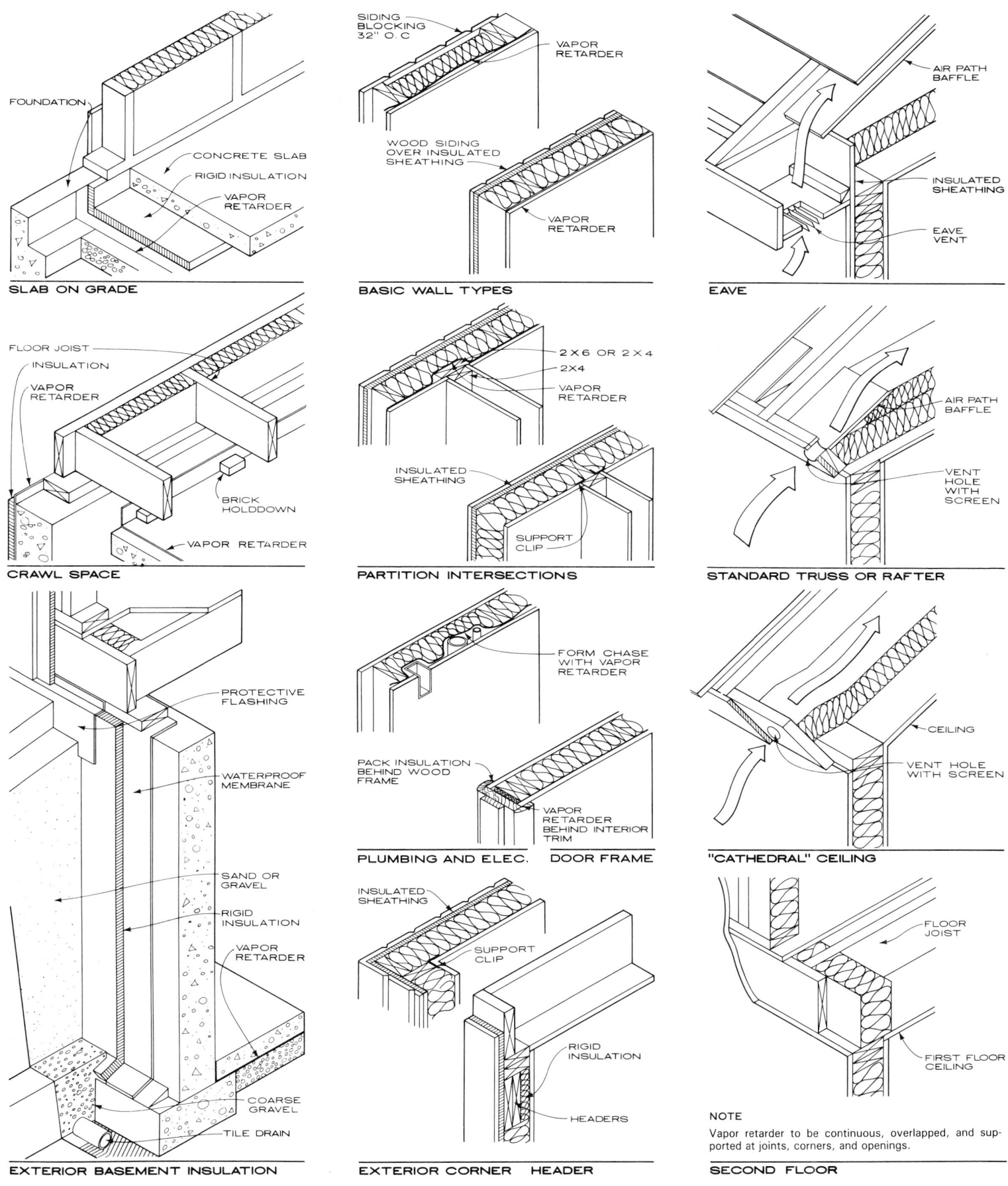

FOUNDATION

CONCRETE SLAB
RIGID INSULATION
VAPOR RETARDER

SLAB ON GRADE

FLOOR JOIST
INSULATION
VAPOR RETARDER

BRICK HOLDDOWN
VAPOR RETARDER

CRAWL SPACE

PROTECTIVE FLASHING

WATERPROOF MEMBRANE

SAND OR GRAVEL

RIGID INSULATION

VAPOR RETARDER

COARSE GRAVEL

TILE DRAIN

EXTERIOR BASEMENT INSULATION

SIDING BLOCKING 32" O.C
VAPOR RETARDER

WOOD SIDING OVER INSULATED SHEATHING

VAPOR RETARDER

BASIC WALL TYPES

2×6 OR 2×4
2×4
VAPOR RETARDER

INSULATED SHEATHING

SUPPORT CLIP

PARTITION INTERSECTIONS

FORM CHASE WITH VAPOR RETARDER

PACK INSULATION BEHIND WOOD FRAME

VAPOR RETARDER BEHIND INTERIOR TRIM

PLUMBING AND ELEC.   **DOOR FRAME**

INSULATED SHEATHING

SUPPORT CLIP

RIGID INSULATION

HEADERS

EXTERIOR CORNER   HEADER

AIR PATH BAFFLE

INSULATED SHEATHING

EAVE VENT

EAVE

AIR PATH BAFFLE

VENT HOLE WITH SCREEN

STANDARD TRUSS OR RAFTER

CEILING

VENT HOLE WITH SCREEN

"CATHEDRAL" CEILING

FLOOR JOIST

FIRST FLOOR CEILING

NOTE

Vapor retarder to be continuous, overlapped, and supported at joints, corners, and openings.

SECOND FLOOR

Timothy B. McDonald; Washington, D.C.

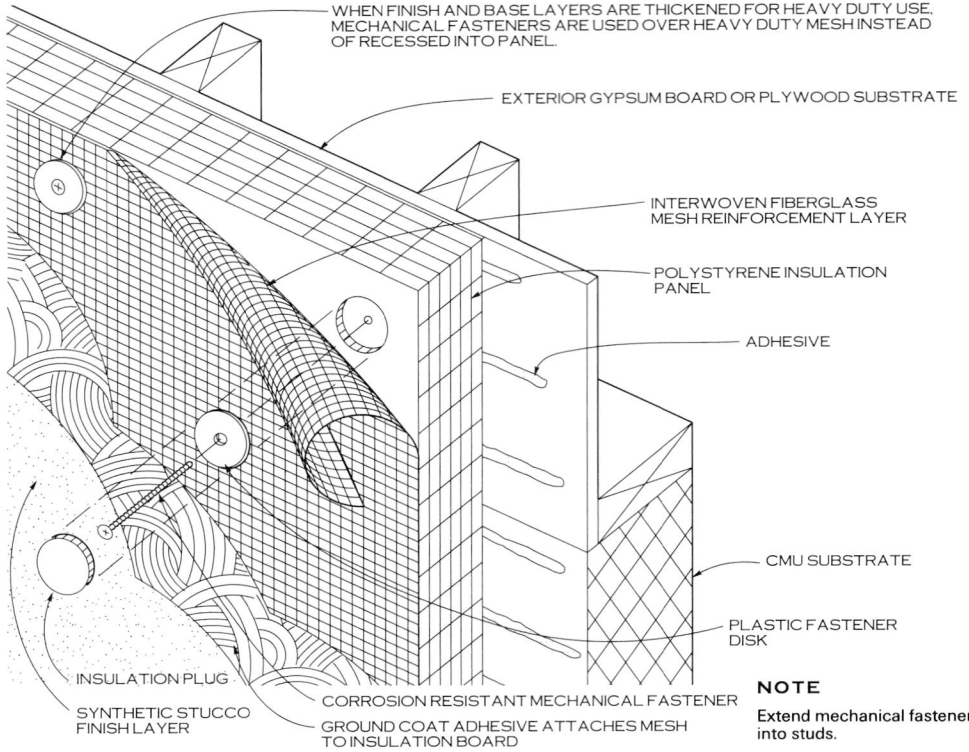

WHEN FINISH AND BASE LAYERS ARE THICKENED FOR HEAVY DUTY USE, MECHANICAL FASTENERS ARE USED OVER HEAVY DUTY MESH INSTEAD OF RECESSED INTO PANEL.

EXTERIOR GYPSUM BOARD OR PLYWOOD SUBSTRATE

INTERWOVEN FIBERGLASS MESH REINFORCEMENT LAYER

POLYSTYRENE INSULATION PANEL

ADHESIVE

CMU SUBSTRATE

PLASTIC FASTENER DISK

INSULATION PLUG

SYNTHETIC STUCCO FINISH LAYER

CORROSION RESISTANT MECHANICAL FASTENER

GROUND COAT ADHESIVE ATTACHES MESH TO INSULATION BOARD

NOTE
Extend mechanical fasteners into studs.

EXTERIOR INSULATION AND FINISH SYSTEM

GENERAL

Exterior insulation and finish systems provide an uninterrupted layer of rigid insulation that is attached by adhesives or mechanical fasteners directly onto the building substrate. A continuous fiberglass mesh layer is then applied and attached by adhesives or mechanical fasteners. A finish coat covers and seals the entire system.

NOTES

1. Insulation panels are made in varying thicknesses from 1 to 4 in., depending on the wall U-factor requirements. They come in varying sizes, generally 2 x 2 ft, 2 x 4 ft, or 2 x 8 ft, depending on manufacturer or system used. Expanded polystyrene (1 to 2 lb/cu ft) is generally used above grade; extruded polystyrene (2 to 3 lb/cu ft) is generally used below grade or in high traffic areas.
2. For areas likely to receive abuse by high impact or high traffic, a heavy duty fiberglass mesh reinforcement layer is used in addition to, or in place of, the standard mesh. Also, zinc casing beads are frequently used at finish layer edges.
3. When mechanical fasteners are used they should be installed flush with or, preferably, recessed into the insulation panel to prevent "bubbles" on the surface. When recessed, some manufacturers provide an insulation plug over the fastener to leave a continuous layer of insulation at the surface before the finish is applied.
4. For walls with damaged or brittle substrates, a mechanically fastened track system is used by some manufacturers to fasten the insulation panels to the substrate.
5. The synthetic-stucco finish layer is generally weather resistant, crack resistant, and vapor permeable and is troweled, rolled, or sprayed onto the surface over the ground coat adhesive. It is generally made from acrylic polymers with an aggregate or silica sand, quartz chips, or marble chips to give it the desired texture. Color is achieved by either tinting the finish coat with pigment or painting the surface.

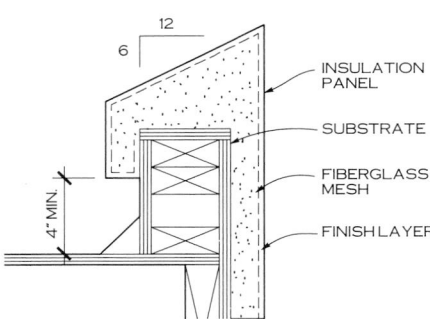

PARAPET DETAIL

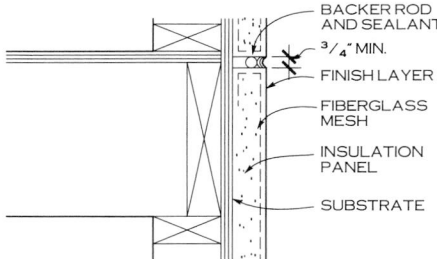

EXPANSION JOINT DETAIL AT FLOOR LEVEL

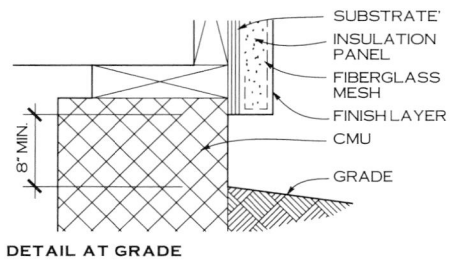

DETAIL AT GRADE

WOOD FRAME DETAILS

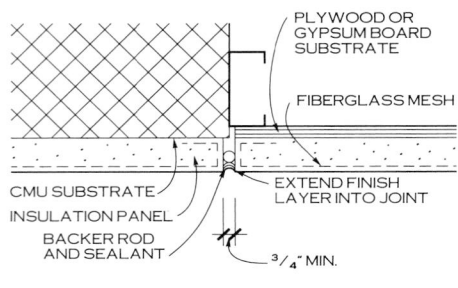

EXPANSION JOINT AT DISSIMILAR SUBSTRATES

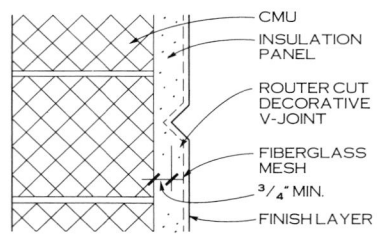

DECORATIVE JOINT

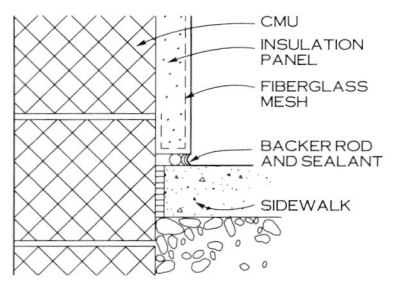

DETAIL AT SIDEWALK

MASONRY DETAILS

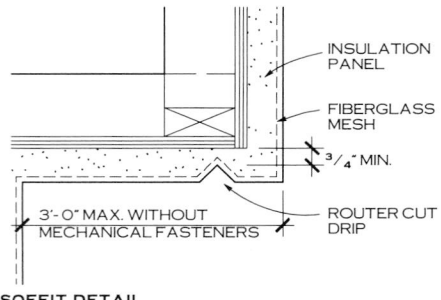

SOFFIT DETAIL

DETAIL BELOW GRADE

MISCELLANEOUS DETAILS

Richard J. Vitullo, AIA; Oak Leaf Studio; Crownsville, Maryland

UNPROTECTED STEEL

At temperatures greater than 1000°F, milled steel loses about half of its ultimate room temperature strength. Consequently, fire tests on steel beams and columns are terminated when the steel's surface temperatures reach a predetermined limit or when the applied design loading can no longer be sustained (specific alternate test procedures are given by ASTM Standard Methods E 119). Fire resistance ratings are expressed as duration in hours of fire exposure to standard temperature conditions in a test furnace (e.g., 3/4 hr, 1 hr, 2 hr, 3 hr). For further information on fire resistance tests and fire protection of steel, see the American Iron and Steel Institute's handbook series, Designing Fire Protection for Steel Beams, Columns, and Trusses.

CONCRETE ENCASEMENT

The fire resistance of steel members encased in concrete depends on the thickness of protective concrete cover, the concrete mixture, and structural restraint (i.e., method of support and method of confining thermal expansion). Lightweight aggregate concrete has better fire resistance than normal weight concrete because of its higher moisture content and higher thermal resistance to heat flow. For data on columns encased in concrete, see the National Fire Protection Association's "Fire Protection Handbook." Gunite, a mixture of cement, sand, and water, can be spray-applied but requires steel reinforcing. For exterior applications, reinforcing steel with less than 2 in. of concrete cover usually requires corrosion-resistant primers.

MASONRY ENCLOSURE

Masonry materials (brick, concrete block, gypsum block, hollow clay tile) can be used to encase steel columns. The cores (or cells), which provide openings for reinforcing, also can be filled with mortar or insulating materials such as vermiculite to increase thermal resistance to heat flow. For data on fire resistance of masonry constructions, see the National Concrete Masonry Association's "Fire Safety with Concrete Masonry."

GYPSUM MEMBRANE ENCLOSURE

Gypsum board or troweled plaster (e.g., vermiculite-gypsum, perlite-gypsum) or lath can be used to protect steel at building locations not exposed to moisture. Gypsum retards heat flow to steel by releasing chemically combined water (called "calcination") at temperatures above 180° F. To protect steel columns, gypsum board layers can be attached to steel studs by means of self-tapping screws or installed behind a galvanized or stainless steel sheet cover. For data on fire resistance of gypsum constructions, see the Gypsum Association's "Fire Resistance Design Data Manual."

MINERAL FIBER MEMBRANE ENCLOSURE

When exposed to fire, mineral fiber (made from molten rock or slag) retards heat flow to steel because of its low thermal conductivity (it can withstand temperatures above 2000°F without melting). Mineral fiber requires a protective covering when exposed to outdoor conditions or if subject to damage from accidental impact or abrasion.

SPRAY-ON CONTOUR

Spray-on applied cementitious mixtures (lightweight aggregate plasters with insulating fibers or vermiculite) or mineral fibers mixed with inorganic binders provide a thermal barrier to heat from fire. The steel surface must be clean and free of loose paint, rust, oil, and grease before spraying, and a protective primer may be required. In addition, spraying should not be scheduled during cold conditions. Lightweight spray-on contours can easily be damaged during installation of nearby gas and water pipes, air ducts, and the like, and they are subject to flaking during normal use. Pins, studs, and other mechanical fasteners can be used to secure moisture- or abrasion-resistant protective finish coatings. Applications more than 2 in. thick generally require wire mesh or lath reinforcement.

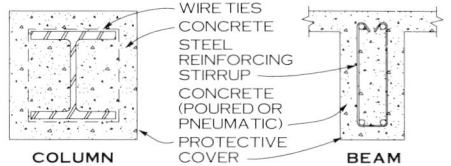

CONCRETE ENCASEMENT

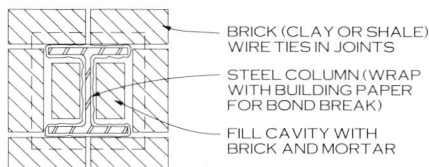

MASONRY ENCLOSURE

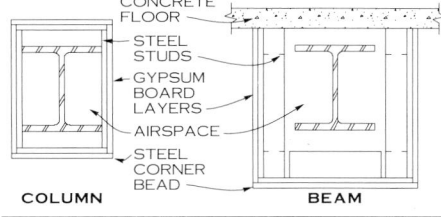

GYPSUM MEMBRANE ENCLOSURE

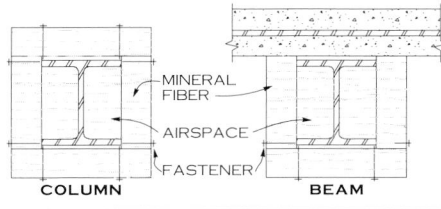

MINERAL FIBER MEMBRANE ENCLOSURE

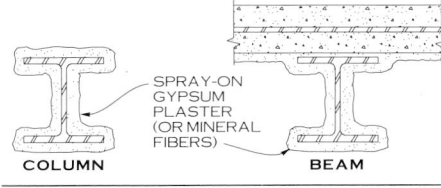

SPRAY-ON CONTOUR

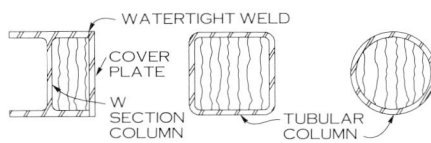

LIQUID-FILLED COLUMN

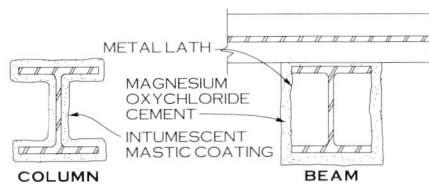

COATINGS

FLAME SHIELDS

LIQUID-FILLED COLUMNS

During a fire the liquid circulates by convection from fire floor columns, removing heat. Storage tanks or city water mains can be used to replace water converted to steam (vented by pressure relief valves or rupture discs). Pumps also may be used to avoid stagnant areas within an interconnected water circulation system of columns and piping. To prevent corrosion, use a rust inhibitor such as potassium nitrate. To prevent freezing in cold climates, use an antifreeze such as potassium carbonate. During construction, strict quality control is essential to achieve a watertight system.

COATINGS

Intumescent mastic coatings can be spray-applied like paint. When exposed to fire, the coating absorbs heat above about 300°F by expanding into a thick, lightweight thermal barrier more than about 150 times its initial thickness. This gas-filled multicellular layer retards heat flow by releasing cooling gases and blocks off oxygen supply to form a thermal barrier. Apply coatings only to steel surfaces that are free of dirt, scale, and oil. A multilayer system, consisting of intumescent mastic layers with glass fiber reinforcing between, is needed to achieve fire resistance ratings greater than 1 hr.

When exposed to heat, magnesium oxychloride cement retards heat flow to steel by releasing water of hydration at temperatures above about 570°F. Corrosion-resistant priming may be required to assure proper adhesion of magnesium oxychloride to steel surfaces. In high-intensity fires (e.g., flammable liquid or gas fires), magnesium oxychloride does not spall and the magnesium oxide residue acts as an efficient heat reflector.

FLAME SHIELDS

Steel flame shields can deflect heat and flames away from exterior structural steel members. For example, exposed exterior girders may be protected from direct flames inside the building by flame shields or thermal insulation.

DESIGN CONSIDERATIONS

1. Check prevailing building code for required fire resistance ratings of building construction type. Plan steel fire protection during the early stages of a project so it can be integrated into building design. Consult building authorities and. Insurance underwriting groups such as Industrial Risk Insurers, American Insurance Association, or Factory Mutual System may also be consulted.

2. Refer to fire resistance data based on ASTM E 119 test procedures from Underwriters Laboratories, Factory Mutual, and other nationally recognized testing laboratories.

3. In general, fire resistance of constructions with cavity airspace (e.g., walls, floor-ceiling assemblies) will be greater than similar identical weight constructions without airspace.

4. If possible, locate cavity airspace on side of construction opposite potential fire exposure.

5. For most situations, fire resistance of constructions with thermal insulation such as mineral fiber and glass fiber in cavity airspace (e.g., doors, walls) will be greater than identical constructions without cavity insulation. Be careful, however, since adding thermal insulation to suspended floor-ceiling assemblies may lower fire resistance by causing the metal suspension grid system to buckle or warp from elevated surface temperatures.

6. When plenum spaces above suspended ceilings are used for mechanical system return airflow, fire resistance of floor-ceiling assemblies will be diminished. Conversely, plenums under positive pressure from supply airflow can achieve greater fire resistances than under neutral pressure conditions (e.g., no air circulation in plenum).

7. For beams and columns, the higher the ratio of weight (e.g., pounds per unit length) to heated perimeter (i.e., surface area exposed to fire), the greater the fire resistance. Heavier members require less cover for equivalent fire resistance, since they have greater mass.

8. Beams and columns with membrane enclosure protection will have less surface area exposed to fire than identical members with spray-on contour protection. In addition, membrane enclosures (e.g., gypsum board, mineral fiber, magnesium oxychloride, or metal lath) form airspaces on both sides of W and S section webs.

M. David Egan, P.E.; College of Architecture, Clemson University; Clemson, South Carolina

FIREPROOFING AND FIRESTOPPING 7

BUILT-UP ROOFING

DECK OR SUBSTRATE	SURFACING	SLOPE (IN./FT)	BASE SHEET	PLYSHEETS	PLY BITUMEN (LB/SQ/PLY)	SURFACING BITUMEN (LB/SQ)	NOTES TO DESIGNER/SPECIFIER
Nonnailable decks or roof insulations (Consult manufacturer for approved types of roof insulation and recommendations for venting)[6]	Aggregate surface: Gravel Adhered 200 lb/sq OR Slag adhered 150 lb/sq OR White marble chips: 400 lb/sq	Inclines up to ½:12	43 lb coated base spot mopped in asphalt to deck or solid mopped in asphalt to insulation[2]	3 coal tar saturated felts (perforated)	Coal tar @ 20–40	Coal tar @ 70–75	UL Class A on most deck and insulation types[1] Requires complete surfacing daily For ponded roofs, add 4th ply of felt and double flood and double gravel surface Base flashings must be installed in flashing cement Same configuration possible on slopes of ½–3 in./ft using Type III asphalt[5]
			Organic base felts 43 lb mopped. 43 lb coated base spot mopped in asphalt to deck or solid mopped in asphalt to insulation	3 organic felts (perforated)	Type II asphalt[3] 15–40	Type I asphalt[4] @ 60	
		Inclines up to ½:12	Fiberglass base spot mopped to deck or solid mopped to insulation	3 fiberglass plysheets, ASTM D2178 Type IV	Coal tar 20–40	Coal tar @ 75	UL Class A on most deck and insulation types[1] Roofing may be left up to 6 months before surfacing For ponded roofs, add plysheet and double flood and double gravel surface Base flashings must be installed in flashing cement
				3 fiberglass plysheets[7]	Type II asphalt @ 20–40	Type I asphalt @ 60	Same configuration possible on slopes of ½–3 in./ft using Type III asphalt[5]
	Mineral surface cap sheet (72–80 lb)	¼:12[5]	Fiberglass base spot mopped to deck or solid mopped to insulation	2 fiberglass plysheets	Type III asphalt @ 20–40	Asphalt @ 25–30 for cap sheet	UL Class A, B, or C depending on deck substrate, slope, and manufacturer[1] Consult manufacturer for specific regional requirements Proper application of mineral cap sheet requires warm weather Cold process fiberglass systems also possible; consult manufacturer
	Smooth surface	¼:12[5]	Fiberglass base spot mopped to deck or solid mopped to insulation	3 fiberglass plysheets	Type II asphalt @ 20–40	Asphalt/clay emulsion @ 6 gal/sq	UL Class A, B, or C depending on deck/substrate, slope, and manufacturer[1] Consult manufacturer for specific regional requirements Reflective coatings are recommended over smooth surface systems

NOTES

1. Underwriter's Laboratories test for Fire-Hazard Classification by assembling particular constructions using specific products of stated manufacturers; consult UL or the manufacturer to verify classifications for specific roofing systems for given project conditions.
   Class A: Not readily flammable under severe fire exposure and protects roof deck to high degree.
   Class B: Not readily flammable under moderate fire exposure and protects roof deck to moderate degree.
   Class C: Not readily flammable under light fire exposure and protects roof deck to slight degree.
   Only classes A and B are fire retardant.

2. On slopes up to ½ in./ft, apply asphalt and combine with felts to comply with ASTM D312.
3. For hot climates, use Type III instead of Type II, for higher softening point.
4. For hot climates, use Type III.
5. On slopes of 1 in./ft or greater, plies should be strapped (laid parallel to slope) and back nailed to prevent slippage, and Type III or Type IV asphalt should be used; if roofing is on roof insulation, wood insulation stops/nailers should be provided.
6. Vapor retarder under roof insulation is advisable for conditions having low outdoor temperatures (below 40°F) combined with high indoor relative humidity (above 44%). Allow vapor pressure to escape from between vapor retarder and roofing membrane by use of venting base sheets, vent stacks, or other methods recommended by manufacturer.
7. Three-ply or four-ply membrane system may be used. Number of plysheets to suit system selected.

ROLL ROOFING

TYPE	DESCRIPTION	SLOPE (IN./FT) MIN.	SLOPE (IN./FT) MAX.	WEIGHT (LB/SQ)	SIZE	UNDERLAY	FASTENERS	EXPOSURE	COLOR AND TEXTURE	U.L. RATING
Asphalt Roll Roofing	Smooth surface	0	6	50	36" x 72'	ASTM D226 TYPE I OR II	Nails and cement	32"–34"	Black	C—wind or fire resistant
				86						
	Mineral surface			75–90	36" x 36'					
	Double coverage fiberglass	½	4	55–70	36" x 36'		Concealed nails; cement	17"	Various color blends	A—wind or fire resistant
	Fiberglass reinforced mineral fiber	⅛	4	75	36" x 72'				Black	B—wind or fire resistant

Walter H. Sobel, FAIA, & Associates; Chicago, Illinois
Kent Wong; Hewlett, Jamison, Atkinson & Luey; Portland, Oregon; from data furnished by A. Larry Brown; Owens/Corning Fiberglass Corporation

ROOFING TYPES, SHINGLES, AND ROOFING TILES

BUILT-UP ROOFING (CONT.)

DECK OR SUBSTRATE	SURFACING	SLOPE (IN./FT)	BASE SHEET	PLYSHEETS	PLY BITUMEN (LB/SQ/PLY)	SURFACING BITUMEN (LB/SQ)	NOTES TO DESIGNER/SPECIFIER
Wood or other nailable decking (Over wood board decks, one ply of sheathing paper should be applied under base felt next to deck) (Consult manufacturers for approved decks and fasteners)	Gravel adhered: 200 lb/sq. OR Slag adhered: 180 lb/sq. OR White marble chips: 400 lb/sq	Inclines up to ½	43 lb coated base mechanically attached	3 coal tar saturated felts (perforated)	Coal tar @ 25	Coal tar @ 75	• UL Class A on most deck types (1) • Requires complete surfacing daily • For ponded roofs, add a 4th ply of felt and double flood and double gravel surface • Base flashings must be installed in flashing cement
			43 lb organic base felt mechanically attached	3 asphalt saturated felts	Type II asphalt @ 25	Type I asphalt @ 60	• Same configuration possible on slopes of ½-3 in./ft (2) using Type III asphalt
		Inclines up to ½	Fiberglas® base mechanically attached (3)	3 fiberglass plysheets ASTM D2178 Type IV (3)	Coal tar @ 25–30	Coal tar @ 75	• UL Class A on most deck types (1) • Roofing may be left up to 6 months before surfacing • For ponded roofs, add a 3rd ply of Perma-Ply R and double flood and double gravel surface • Base flashings must be installed in flashing cement
			Fiberglas® base mechanically attached (3)	3 fiberglass plysheets ASTM D2178 Type IV (3)	Type II asphalt @ 25	Type I asphalt @ 60–70	• Same configuration possible on slopes of ½-3 in./ft (2) using Type III asphalt
	Mineral surface cap sheet (72–80 lb)	¼-12 (2)	Fiberglass base mechanically attached	2 fiberglass plysheets, ASTM D2178 Type III or IV	Asphalt @ 25	Asphalt @ 30 for cap sheet	• UL Class A, B, or C depending on deck type, slope, and manufacturer (1) • Consult manufacturer for specific regional requirements for various types of plysheets • Fiberglass roofing may be left up to 6 months before surfacing • Proper application of mineral cap sheet requires warm weather
			43 lb organic base mechanically attached	2 fiberglass plysheets, ASTM D2178 Type III or IV	Asphalt @ 30	Asphalt @ 30 for cap sheet	
	Smooth surface	¼-12 (2)	Fiberglass base mechanically attached	3 fiberglass plysheets, ASTM D2178 Type III or IV; ASTM D250 Type II	Asphalt @ 25–30	Asphalt/clay emulsion @ 6 gal/sq	• UL Class A, B, or C depending on deck type, slope, and manufacturer (1) • Consult manufacturer for specific regional requirements • Reflective coatings are recommended over smooth surface systems

SHINGLES

TYPE	DESCRIPTION	SLOPE (IN./FT) MIN.	SLOPE (IN./FT) MAX.	WEIGHT[4] (LB/SQ)[3]	SIZE	UNDERLAY	FASTENERS	EXPOSURE	COLOR AND TEXTURE	UL RATING
Asphalt Organic Felt[1,2]	3 tab	4	12	235	12″ x 36″	15 lb asphalt felt ASTM D226 D4869 Type I or II	Galvanized steel or aluminum roofing nails, or zinc-coated staples	4″–6″	Various colors; granular texture	Class C fire resistant, wind resistant
	2 tab	4	12	300	12″ x 36″					
	Random edged	4	12	345	12″ x 36″				Varied; smooth	
	No cutout	2	12	290	12″ x 36″					
	Interlocking			180	19¾″ x 20½″			—	Varied; smooth	Class C fire resistant, wind resistant
	Basketweave			245	18½″ x 20″					
Fiberglass	Random edged Laminated Overlay	4	12	300	14″ x 35⁹⁄₁₆″	15 lb asphalt felt ASTM D226 D4869 Type I or II	Galvanized steel or aluminum roofing nails, or zinc-coated staples	4″–5″	Varied; smooth	Class A fire resistant, wind resistant
	3 tab	4	12	225	12″ x 36″			5″		
	2 tab	4	12	260	12″ x 36″			5″	Varied; granular texture	
	No cutout Random edged	4	12	225	12″ x 36¼″			4″–6″	Varied; smooth	

NOTES

1. These shingles may be used on slopes down to 2 in./ft when over a two-ply felt underlayment.
2. All shingles are self-sealing.
3. A SQUARE is a term used to describe 100 sq ft of roof area.
4. ASTM D226, ASTM D3462

Walter H. Sobel, FAIA, & Associates; Chicago, Illinois
Kent Wong; Hewlett, Jamison, Atkinson & Luey; Portland, Oregon; from data furnished by A. Larry Brown; Owens/Corning Fiberglass Corporation

SHINGLES AND ROOFING TILES

TYPE	DESCRIPTION	APPLICATION	SLOPE MINIMUM (IN./FT)	WEIGHT (LB/SQ)	UNDERLAY	FASTENERS	COLOR AND TEXTURE	SIZE (IN.) L X W	BUTT THICKNESS	EXPOSURE DATA
Wood: red cedar; most types and sizes available in cypress, redwood, white cedar; shakes	Hand split and resawn	Roofs and sidewall panels for institutional, commercial, residential use	4	200–350	Open or solid sheathing 30 lb felt interlayment with shakes	Corrosion resistant nails	Natural or various stains Various textures	Length 18–24 Width random	1/2–3/4 in.	7 1/2–10 in.
	Taper split			260				Length 24 Width random	1/2 in.	10 in.
	Straight split			200–260				Length 18–24 Width random	5/8 in.	7 1/2–10 in.
	Table sawn									
Wood: red cedar; most types and sizes available in cypress, redwood, white cedar; shingles	No. 1 Blue Label No. 2 Red Label No. 3 Black Label	Roofs and sidewall panels for institutional, commercial, residential use	4	L WGT. 16 in. 144 18 in. 158 24 in. 192	Open or solid sheathing	Corrosion resistant nails	Natural or various stains Various textures	Length 16 18 24	.40 in. .45 in. .50 in.	5 in. 5 1/2 in. No. 1 grade 7 1/2 in.
	No. 4				Open sheathing shall be 1 x 4 or 1 x 6 in. boards			16 18		
	Undercoursing							16 18 Width random		5 1/2 in. 8 1/2 in. single course 14 in. double course
	No. 1 or No. 2 Rebutted-rejointed									
Clay tile	Shingle—flat	Institutional, commercial, residential	3	800–1600	One layer 30 lb or 45 lb felt over plywood	Noncorrosive copper nails	Various finishes	l w 15 x 7	3/8 in. minimum	Exposed length 6 1/2 in. Exposed width 7 in.
	Interlocking flat			800				14 x 9	7/8 in. minimum	Exposed length 11 in. Exposed width 8 1/4 in.
	French			940–1000				16 1/4 x 9	2 in.	Exposed length 13 1/8 in. Exposed width 8 1/8 in.
	Spanish		4	850				13 1/4 x 9 3/4	1/2 in.	Exposed length 10 1/2 in. Exposed width 8 1/4 in.
Concrete[1]	Shingle—flat	Institutional, commercial, residential	4	950	One layer 30 lb felt over plywood	10 penny corrosion resistant galvanized copper, or colors stainless steel box nail	Various colors	13 x 16	1 in.	3 in. overlap
	Barreled mission curved									
Slate	Commercial grade—smooth	Institutional, commercial, residential	4	700–800	One layer 30 lb asphalt saturated rag felt over plywood	Slaters hard copper wire nails cut copper, cut brass, or cut yellow metal slat nails	Blue-black	Various sizes	3/16, 1/4 in.	3 in. overlap
	Quarry—run rough			825–3600					3/8, 1/2, 3/4 in.	

NOTES

1. Specifier should ask for concrete tile freeze-thaw test.
2. Underwriters Laboratories Standard UL 580 classifies roof deck assemblies as Class 30, Class 60, and Class 90. The nominal uplift pressures and wind velocities commonly related in technical studies and literature are the following:

RATING	NOMINAL UPLIFT PRESSURE	NOMINAL WIND VELOCITY
Class 30	30 psf	100 mph
Class 60	60 psf	142 mph
Class 90	90 psf	174 mph

Consult local manufacturer or agent for roofing system rating.

3. Underwriters Laboratories classifies prepared roof covering materials as Class A, B, or C. Class A includes roof coverings that are effective against severe fire test exposure. Roof coverings of these classes are then not readily flammable and do not carry or communicate fire; afford a fairly high degree of fire protection to the roof deck; do not slip from position; possess no flying brand hazard; and do not require frequent repairs in order to maintain their fire resisting properties.

Cedar Shake and Shingle Bureau; Bellevue, Washington
Walter H. Sobel, FAIA, & Associates; Chicago, Illinois

7   **ROOFING TYPES, SHINGLES, AND ROOFING TILES**

SEAMED METAL ROOFING

TYPE	DESCRIPTION	MIN. SLOPE (IN./FT)	SIZE	THICKNESS	WEIGHT (LB/SQ)	UNDERLAY	FASTENER
Aluminum coated steel	Polyurethane insulation sandwiched between two layers of steel[1] standing seam	1/4	40'' x 32'	2 1/2''	250	None	Panels are clipped to structurals, and interlocking seams sealed
Copper coated galvanized steel	Standing seam, pan, or roll method	3	20'' x 30' max. 22'' x 30' max.	24 gauge	130	30 lb felt	Anchor clips and galvanized nails or screws
Prepainted galvanized steel	Batten seam pan method	3	24'' x 30' max.				
Zinc-copper titanium alloy	Batten or standing seam pan method	3	20'', 24'', or 28'' x 8', 10', 12', or 14'	0.027''	100	Roofing felt	Galvanized U channel or L seam support spacer with screw or nails
Terne coated stainless[2,3,5]	Standing or batten seam	3	20'', 24'', 28'', or 36'' x 96'', or 120''	0.015'' or 0.018''	89	Roofing felt and rosin paper	TCS cleats and stainless steel nails
	Flat locked seam	1/2	20'' x 28''				
Terne plate[4,6]	Batten seam	3	20'' x 120'' max.	26 gauge	62	Rosin paper	Terne cleats and roofing nails
	Standing seam	3	14'', 20''	28 gauge			
			24'' x 120'' max.	30 gauge			
	Flat locked seam (wood deck only)	1/2	14'' x 20''	28 gauge			
			20'' x 28''	30 gauge			
	Horizontal seam (wood deck only)	3 1/2	24'' x 96'' max.	26 gauge			
				28 gauge			
Painted aluminum	Standing seam	1/2	12'' x 60''-80''	0.032''	72.5	None	Anchor clips
			16'' x 60''-80''	0.040''	90.4		

NOTES

1. This is a composite section providing structural deck, insulation, and weathertight roof. U value is 0.50; class I fire rating.
2. Terne coated steel is 304 nickel-chrome stainless steel covered on both sides with terne alloy (80% lead, 20% tin).
3. Terne coated steel can be painted without special preparation of the surface.
4. Terne plate is prime copper bearing steel coated with lead-tin alloy.
5. Expansion seams must be provided on runs exceeding 30 ft where both ends are free to move or exceeding 15 ft where ends are securely fastened.
6. Terne must be shop coated or painted one coat underside and primed and painted two coats on exposed side.

METAL SHINGLES AND TILES

TYPE	DESCRIPTION	APPLICATION	SLOPE MINIMUM (IN./FT)	WEIGHT (LB/SQ)	UNDERLAY	FASTENERS	COLOR AND TEXTURE	SIZE (IN.) L X W	BUTT THICKNESS	EXPOSURE DATA
Aluminum	California mission tile	Institutional, commercial, residential	3	48	One layer 30 lb asphalt saturated rag felt over plywood	Aluminum nails, screws	Tile red Burnt red	10 1/2 x 17 5 x 14	30 gauge aluminum	2 in. overlap
	Shake—shingle	Institutional, commercial, residential	4	36-88	One layer 30 lb felt over plywood	Anchor clip nailed	Various baked enamel finishes	12 x 48	Variable up to 1 3/16 in.	12 in.
Porcelain enamel on aluminum	Individual American method	Institutional, commercial, residential	3	225	One layer 30 lb felt plus 18 in. felt strips between tile	Special sealing nails supplied with tile	Various finishes	10 x 10	Prefinish for tiles custom fabricated to fit roof	

Walter H. Sobel, FAIA, & Associates; Chicago, Illinois

CORRUGATED AND CRIMPED ROOFING

TYPE		SLOPE MIN. (IN./FT)	MAX. SPAN (IN.)	WEIGHT (LB/SQUARE)	SIZE	WEIGHT OR THICKNESS	EXPOSURE OR LAP	COLOR AND TEXTURE	FASTENER
Iron and steel or galvanized iron	2.67'' corrugations with ⅞, ¾, or ½'' depth	3	81-51[1]	Uncoated from 548 to 69. Coated from 568 to 90. Add approx. 10% for 3'' corrugations	Width 34-⅝'', 39-⅛'', length 2-45'	Gauges 18-26	31½, 36'', End lap 6'' min.	Uncoated galvanized or several colors of coatings	Corrosion resistant self-tapping screws, bolts, welded studs, power driven fasteners or nails in wood. All use neoprene washers
Protected metal (steel)[3]	Corrugated sheet 2.67'' corrugations with ¾ or ½'' depth	(4)	88-44[1]	From 244 to 147	Width 33'' length to 12'	Gauges 18-24	29-¾'' wide. End lap 6'' min.	Smooth black or several colors	Same as corrugated steel
	Mansard sheet, 6 beads per sheet				Width 30'' length to 12'				
	V-beam sheet, 5.4'' pitch and 1⅝'' deep, 5 vees per sheet			From 278 to 167					
Aluminum	Corrugated sheet, 2.67'' corrugations, ⅞'' depth	3[6,7]	77-55[1] 91-64 102-72	42 56 70	Widths 35 or 48'', length 3-39'[1]	0.024 0.032 0.040 0.050	1½'' corrugation side lap. 6'' min. end lap. 1 vee side lap[6]	Plain mill or stucco in natural and various colors of baked-on or porcelain enamel	Same as for corrugated steel, except use aluminum nails and sheet metal screws
	Curved corrugated sheet, same corrugations[5]			55.2	Width 33¾'', length 3-39'[1]	0.032			
	V-beam sheet, 4⅞'' pitch and 1⅝'' deep, top and bottom flats ¾''		130-92[1] 152-107 173-122	58.4 72.2 90.3	Width 41⅝'', length 3-39'[1]	0.032 0.040 0.050			
	Concealed clip panels (Reynolds Metals Co.)[7]			68.9 86.1 107.7	Width 13.35'', length 3-39'[1]	0.032 0.040 0.050	Width 12'', End lap 6'' min.	Stucco only; same colors as above	Clips with sheets locked at side laps
Corrugated fiberglass, wire-reinforced plastic	1¼'' corrugations, ¼'' deep	3[6,7]	40-22[2]	Approx. 40	Width 26'' (max. 50'') length 4-39'	5, 6, 8 oz/sq ft	1, 1½ or 2 corrugation side lap. 6'' min. end lap	Many colors, translucent opaque; or smooth or pebble finish.	Self-tapping screws, drive screws and nails. All with neoprene washers
	2½'' corrugations, ½'' deep		65-32[2]		Widths 26'' (max. 50'') length 4-39'	4, 5, 6, 8, 10, 12 oz/sq ft			
	4.2'' corrugations, 1¹⁄₁₆'' deep		72-50[2]		Widths 42, 50⅜'', length 4-39'	5-12 oz/sq ft			
	2.67'' corrugations, ⅞'' deep		70-42[2]		Width 50'', length 4-39'	5-12 oz/sq ft			
	5-V crimp, ½'' deep		65-32[2]		Width 26'', length 4-39'	5-8 oz/sq ft			
	5.3-V crimp, 1'' deep		84-60[2]		Width 41⅝'', 45'', length 4-39'	5-12 oz/sq ft			
Corrugated glass or plastic, nonreinforced plastic[9]	2.67'' corrugations, ⁹⁄₁₆'' deep	1	70-42[2]	Approx. 40	Width 50½'', length 8, 10, 12, 15, 20'	5-8 oz/sq ft ¼'' thick	1 corrugation side lap. 8'' min. end lap	Same as for reinforced plastic	Same as for reinforced plastic

NOTES

1. For 20 to 40 psf.
2. For 15 to 40 psf.
3. For use in chemical atmospheres. Panels are made of steel core, with both sides covered by a dry film at least 4 mils thick. The film has a special liquid resin coating, which is fused under high heat to a special corrosion resistant bond coat over chemically treated galvanized steel.
4. Corrugated and mansard sheets may be used on 4 in. min. slope with laps unsealed and on 3 in. min. slope with laps sealed. V-beam sheets may be used on 3 in. min. slope with laps unsealed and on 1½ in. min. slope with laps sealed.
5. Minimum curvature radius 18 in.
6. Use 9 in. min. side laps on slopes from 2 to 3 in. Use 6 in. min. side laps on slopes above 3 in.
7. May be used on min. ½ in. slope only when one course used on slope. When more than one slope, the min. slope is 4 in.
8. Available in General Purpose, Type I, and Fire Retardant, Type II, except Type I has 5 oz weight only.
9. Used where economy and light weight are major considerations. Corrugated glass also available with installation requiring no side lap.

INSULATION

Many roof panel systems are available with foamed-in-place insulation. Their applications are subject to temperature limitations and various building codes, however. Check codes and manufacturers' fire ratings. Certain applications of roofing systems can also be applied directly over fiberglass batts.

VAPOR BARRIERS

To control a moderate level of relative humidity in living spaces, vapor resistant membranes must be utilized:

1. To control the moisture level within the structure.
2. To prevent moisture from passing through the insulation to a cold point where it can condense into water, possibly causing structural damage or rot. Provide condensate drainage.

Walter H. Sobel, FAIA, & Associates; Chicago, Illinois

ROOFING TYPES, SHINGLES, AND ROOFING TILES

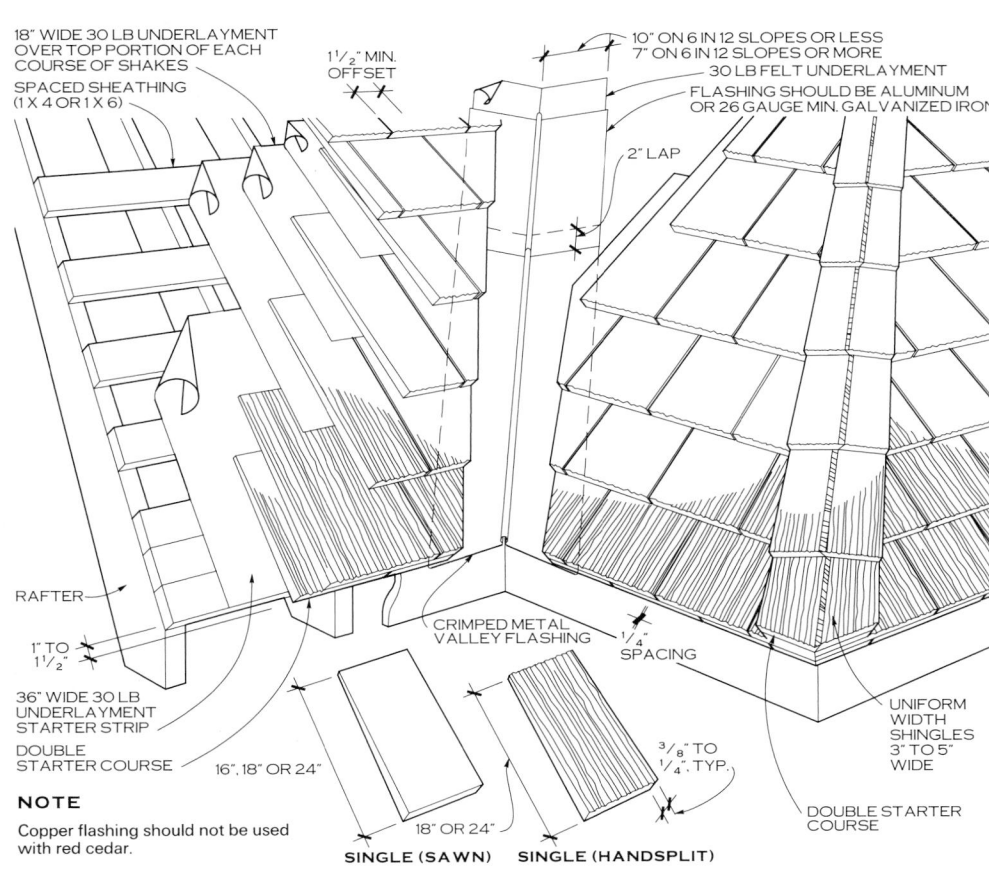

18" WIDE 30 LB UNDERLAYMENT OVER TOP PORTION OF EACH COURSE OF SHAKES

SPACED SHEATHING (1 X 4 OR 1 X 6)

1½" MIN. OFFSET

10" ON 6 IN 12 SLOPES OR LESS
7" ON 6 IN 12 SLOPES OR MORE
30 LB FELT UNDERLAYMENT
FLASHING SHOULD BE ALUMINUM OR 26 GAUGE MIN. GALVANIZED IRON

2" LAP

RAFTER

1" TO 1½"

36" WIDE 30 LB UNDERLAYMENT STARTER STRIP

DOUBLE STARTER COURSE

16", 18" OR 24"

CRIMPED METAL VALLEY FLASHING

¼" SPACING

UNIFORM WIDTH SHINGLES 3" TO 5" WIDE

DOUBLE STARTER COURSE

⅜" TO ¼", TYP.

18" OR 24"

SINGLE (SAWN)   SINGLE (HANDSPLIT)

NOTE

Copper flashing should not be used with red cedar.

RED CEDAR HANDSPLIT SHAKES

RED CEDAR HANDSPLIT SHAKES

GRADE	LENGTH AND THICKNESS	DESCRIPTION
No. 1 handsplit and resawn	15" starter-finish 18 x ½" medium 18 x ¾" heavy 24 x ⅜" 24 x ½" medium 24 x ¾" heavy	These shakes have split faces and sawn backs. Cedar logs are first cut into desired lengths. Blanks or boards of proper thickness are split and then run diagonally through a bandsaw to produce two tapered shakes from each blank.
No. 1 tapersplit	24 x ½"	Produced largely by hand, using a sharp bladed steel froe and a wooden mallet. The natural shinglelike taper is achieved by reversing the block, end-for-end, with each split.
No. 1 straight	18 x ⅜" side wall 18 x ⅜" 24 x ⅜"	Produced in the same manner as tapersplit shakes except that by splitting from the same end of the block, the shakes acquire the same thickness throughout.

RED CEDAR SHINGLES

	NO. 1 BLUE LABEL			NO. 2 RED LABEL			NO. 3 BLACK LABEL		
MAXIMUM EXPOSURE RECOMMENDED FOR ROOFS (IN.)									
ROOF PITCH	16	18	24	16	18	24	16	18	24
3 in 12 to 4 in12	3¾	4¼	5¾	3½	4	5½	3	3½	5
4 in 12 and steeper	5	5½	7½	4	4½	6½	3½	4	5½

UNDERLAYMENT AND SHEATHING

ROOFING TYPE	SHEATHING	UNDERLAYMENT	NORMAL SLOPE		LOW SLOPE	
Wood shakes and shingles	Solid or spaced	No. 30 asphalt saturated felt interlayment	4 in 12 and up	Underlayment starter course; interlayment over entire roof	3 in 12 to 4 in 12	Single layer underlayment over entire roof; interlayment over entire roof

Richard J. Vitullo, AIA; Oak Leaf Studio; Crownsville, Maryland

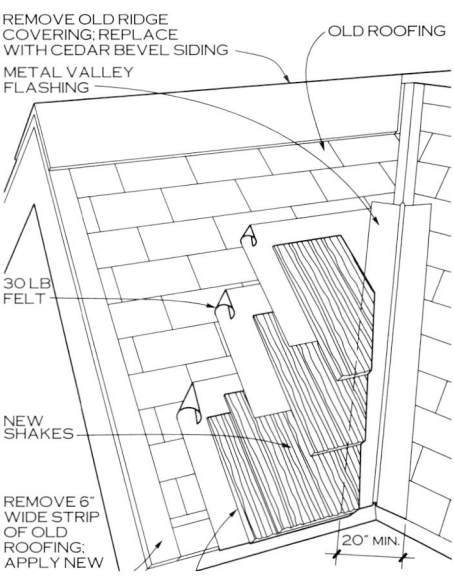

REMOVE OLD RIDGE COVERING; REPLACE WITH CEDAR BEVEL SIDING

OLD ROOFING

METAL VALLEY FLASHING

30 LB FELT

NEW SHAKES

REMOVE 6" WIDE STRIP OF OLD ROOFING; APPLY NEW

20" MIN.

NOTES

Shakes can also be applied over any existing wall or roof. Brick or other masonry requires vertical frameboards and horizontal nailing strips.

Over stucco, horizontal nailing strips are attached directly to wall. Nails should penetrate sheathing or studs. Over wood, apply shakes directly just as if on new sheathing.

WOOD SHAKES APPLIED TO EXISTING ROOF

GENERAL NOTES

1. Wood shingles and shakes are cut from wood species that are naturally resistant to water, sunlight, rot, and hail; i.e., red cedar, redwood, and tidewater red cypress. They are typically installed in the natural state, although stains, primers, and paint may be applied.

2. Nails must be hot dipped in zinc or aluminum. Nail heads should be driven flush with the surface of the shingle or shake but never into the wood.

3. Underlayment and sheathing should be designed to augment the protection provided by the shingles or shakes, depending on roof pitch and climate. A low-pitched roof subject to wind driven snow should have solid sheathing and an additional underlayment.

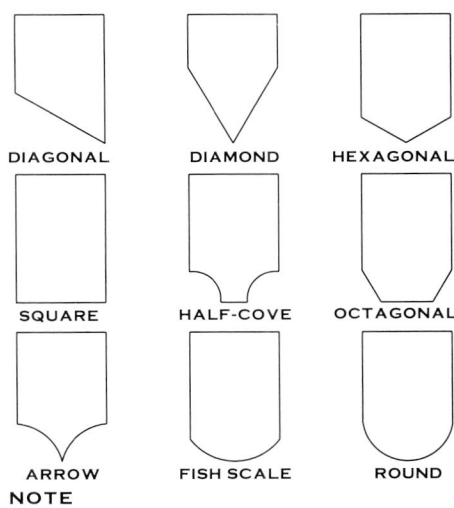

DIAGONAL   DIAMOND   HEXAGONAL

SQUARE   HALF-COVE   OCTAGONAL

ARROW   FISH SCALE   ROUND

NOTE

Fancy butt shingles are 5 in. wide and 7½ in. long, custom produced to individual orders.

FANCY BUTT RED CEDAR SHINGLE SHAPES

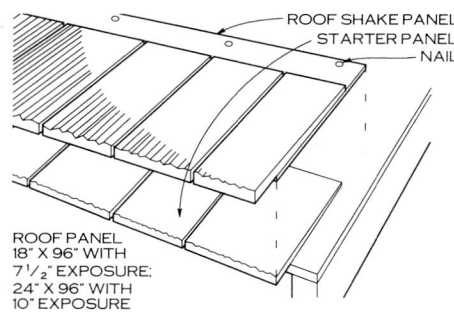

ROOF SHAKE PANEL
STARTER PANEL
NAIL

ROOF PANEL
18" X 96" WITH
7 1/2" EXPOSURE;
24" X 96" WITH
10" EXPOSURE

ROOF PANEL SYSTEM

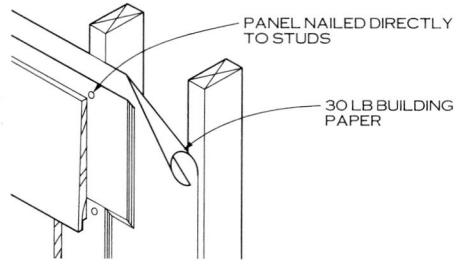

PANEL NAILED DIRECTLY
TO STUDS

30 LB BUILDING
PAPER

SIDEWALL PANEL APPLIED TO STUDS

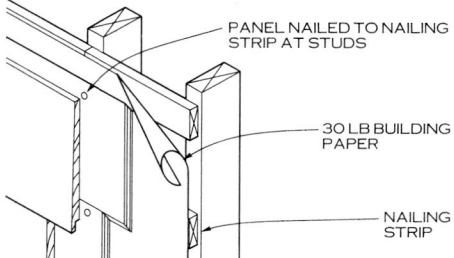

PANEL NAILED TO NAILING
STRIP AT STUDS

30 LB BUILDING
PAPER

NAILING
STRIP

SIDEWALL PANEL APPLIED TO NAILING STRIPS

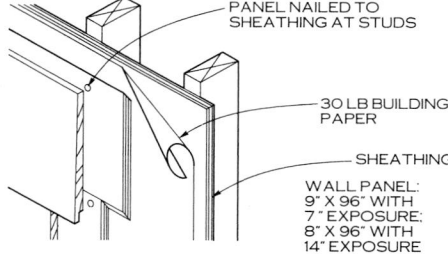

PANEL NAILED TO
SHEATHING AT STUDS

30 LB BUILDING
PAPER

SHEATHING

WALL PANEL:
9" X 96" WITH
7" EXPOSURE;
8" X 96" WITH
14" EXPOSURE

SIDEWALL PANEL APPLIED TO SHEATHING

NOTES

1. With the panel system, shakes and shingles plus sheathing go up in one operation: 8 ft roof panels have 16 handsplit shakes bonded to 6 x 1/2 in. plywood strip, which forms a solid deck when the panels are nailed. A 4 to 12 or steeper roof pitch is recommended.

2. After application of starter panels, attach panels directly to rafters. Although designed to center on 16 in. or 24 in. spacing, they may meet between rafters. Use two 6d nails at each rafter.

3. 8 ft sidewall panels are of two-ply construction:

   a. Surface layer of individual #1 grade shingles or shakes.

   b. Backup of exterior grade plywood shakes or shingles is bonded under pressure with exterior type adhesives to plywood backup.

4. Lap building paper behind panels 3 in. vertically and horizontally. Stagger joints between panels.

5. Application types are determined by local building codes.

6. Matching factory-made corners for sidewall or roof panels are available.

PANEL SYSTEMS

Richard J. Vitullo, AIA; Oak Leaf Studio; Crownsville, Maryland

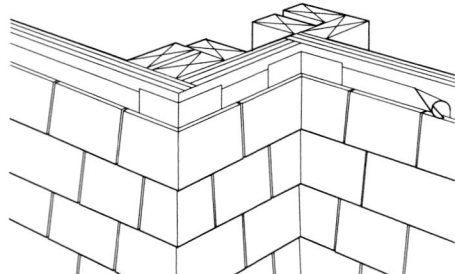

**MITERED OUTSIDE AND INSIDE CORNERS
(RECOMMENDED)**

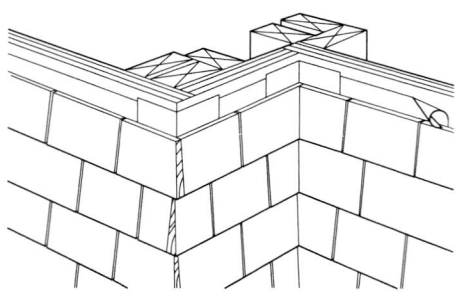

**WOVEN OUTSIDE AND INSIDE CORNERS
(MORE ECONOMICAL)**

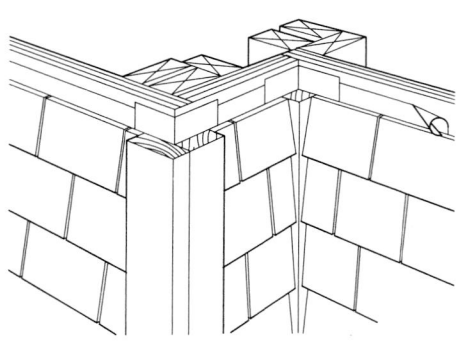

**CORNER BOARDS AT OUTSIDE AND INSIDE
CORNERS**

WOOD SHINGLES AND SHAKES FOR SIDING

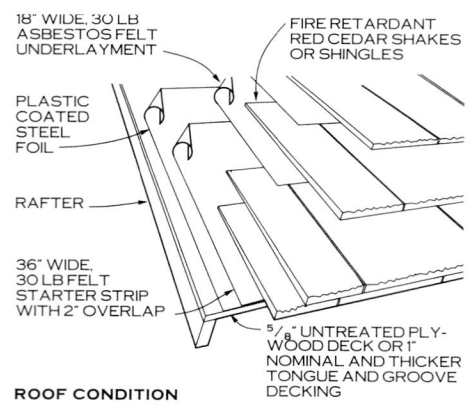

18" WIDE, 30 LB
ASBESTOS FELT
UNDERLAYMENT

FIRE RETARDANT
RED CEDAR SHAKES
OR SHINGLES

PLASTIC
COATED
STEEL
FOIL

RAFTER

36" WIDE,
30 LB FELT
STARTER STRIP
WITH 2" OVERLAP

5/8" UNTREATED PLY-
WOOD DECK OR 1"
NOMINAL AND THICKER
TONGUE AND GROOVE
DECKING

ROOF CONDITION

NOTE

In treating shakes, fire-retardant chemicals are pressure impregnated into the wood cells, and chemicals are then fixed in the wood to prevent leaching. Treatment does not alter appearance. Fire-retardant red cedar shakes are classified as Class C by UL. Class B classification by UL can be met with the addition of the deck constructed of 5/8 in. plywood with exterior glue or 1 in. nominal tongue and groove boards, overlaid with a layer of approved asbestos felt lapped 2 in. on all joints and an 18 in. wide strip of approved asbestos felt between each shake and not exposed to the weather. Decorative stains may be applied.

FIRE RATED CONSTRUCTION

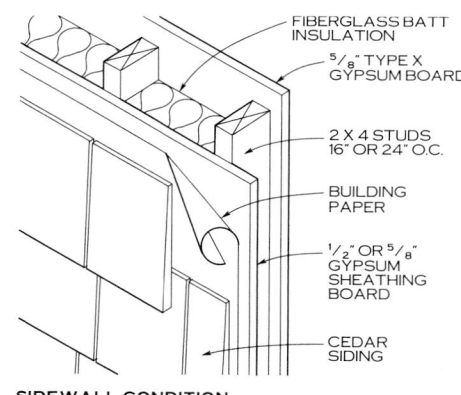

SHEATHING
BUILDING
PAPER

NAILS

DOUBLE
STARTER
COURSE

TRIPLE
STARTER
COURSE

SINGLE COURSING
APPLICATION

DOUBLE COURSING
APPLICATION
1/2"

EXPOSURE FOR SHINGLES AND SHAKES USED FOR SIDING (IN.)

LENGTH OF SHINGLES	EXPOSURE OF SHINGLES	
	SGL. COURSE	DBL. COURSE
16	6 to 7 1/2	8 to 12
18	6 to 8 1/2	9 to 14
24	8 to 11 1/2	12 to 20

NAILING: THICKNESS AND NAILS

16" long	5 butts = 2"	3d
18" long	5 butts = 2 1/4"	3d
24" long	4 butts = 2"	4d
25" to 27"	1 butt = 1/2"	5 or 6d
25" to 27"	1 butt = 5/8" to 1 1/4"	7 or 8d

SHEATHING NOTES

1. Sheathing may be strip type, solid 1 x 6 in., and diagonal type, in plywood, fiberboard, or gypsum board. Horizontal wood nailing strips (1 x 2 in.) should be used over fiberboard and gypsum sheathing. Space strips equal to shingle exposure.

2. Many finishes can be used on red cedar shakes and shingles: solid color or semitransparent ("weathering") stains, exterior latex paint with primer, wood preservative, and bleaches.

FIBERGLASS BATT
INSULATION

5/8" TYPE X
GYPSUM BOARD

2 X 4 STUDS
16" OR 24" O.C.

BUILDING
PAPER

1/2" OR 5/8"
GYPSUM
SHEATHING
BOARD

CEDAR
SIDING

SIDEWALL CONDITION

SCHEDULE OF UNDERLAYMENT

SLOPE	TYPE OF UNDERLAYMENT
Normal slope: 4 in 12 and up	Single layer of 15 lb asphalt saturated felt over entire roof
Low slope: 3 in 12 to 4 in 12	Two layers of 15 lb asphalt saturated felt over entire roof

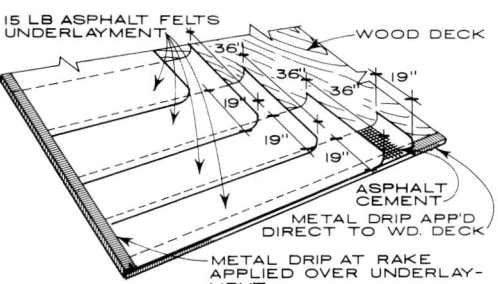

15 LB ASPHALT FELTS UNDERLAYMENT — WOOD DECK
36'
36'   36'   7'   19'
19'
19'
19'
ASPHALT CEMENT
METAL DRIP APP'D DIRECT TO WD. DECK
METAL DRIP AT RAKE APPLIED OVER UNDERLAYMENT

Use only enough nails to hold underlayment in place until shingles are laid.

APPLICATION OF UNDERLAYMENT ON LOW SLOPE ROOFS

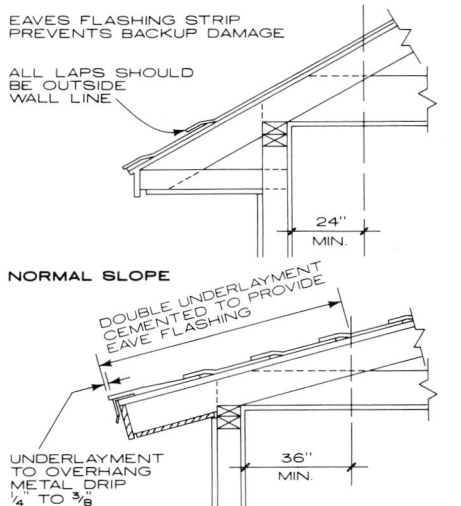

EAVES FLASHING STRIP PREVENTS BACKUP DAMAGE
ALL LAPS SHOULD BE OUTSIDE WALL LINE
24" MIN.

NORMAL SLOPE

DOUBLE UNDERLAYMENT CEMENTED TO PROVIDE EAVE FLASHING
UNDERLAYMENT TO OVERHANG METAL DRIP 1/4" TO 3/8"
36" MIN.

LOW SLOPE

EAVE FLASHING

SCHEDULE OF SHINGLE TYPES (1)

DESCRIPTION	DESIGN	MATERIAL	U.L. RATING	WEIGHT	SIZE
Three-tab square butt		Fiberglass Organic felts	A (4) C	205–225 lb/sq 235–300 lb/sq	36'' x 12''
Two-tab square butt		Fiberglass Organic felts	A (4) C	260–325 lb/sq 300 lb/sq	36'' x 12''
Laminated overlay (2)		Fiberglass Organic felts	A (3) C	300 lb/sq 330–380 lb/sq	36'' x 14''
Random edge cut		Fiberglass Organic felts	A (3) C	225–260 lb/sq 250 lb/sq	36'' x 12''

NOTE: Exposure 5'', edge lap 2''.

NOTES

1. Exposure 5 in., edge lap 2 in., for all designs.
2. More than one thickness for varying surface texture.
3. Many rated as wind resistant.
4. All rated as wind resistant.

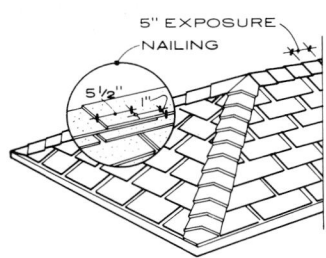

5" EXPOSURE
NAILING
5 1/2"   1"

HIP AND RIDGE

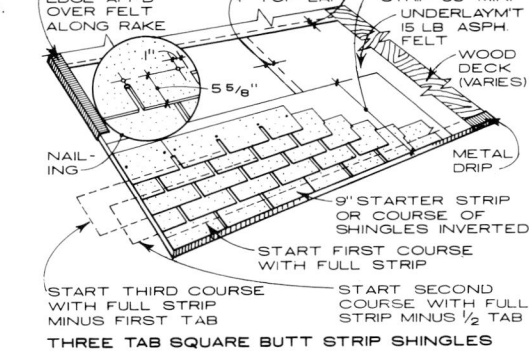

MET. DRIP EDGE APP'D OVER FELT ALONG RAKE
2" TOP LAP   4" TOP LAP
EAVES FLASH'G STRIP 36" MIN.
UNDERLAYM'T 15 LB ASPH. FELT
WOOD DECK (VARIES)
1"
5 5/8"
NAILING
METAL DRIP
9" STARTER STRIP OR COURSE OF SHINGLES INVERTED
START FIRST COURSE WITH FULL STRIP
START THIRD COURSE WITH FULL STRIP MINUS FIRST TAB
START SECOND COURSE WITH FULL STRIP MINUS 1/2 TAB

THREE TAB SQUARE BUTT STRIP SHINGLES

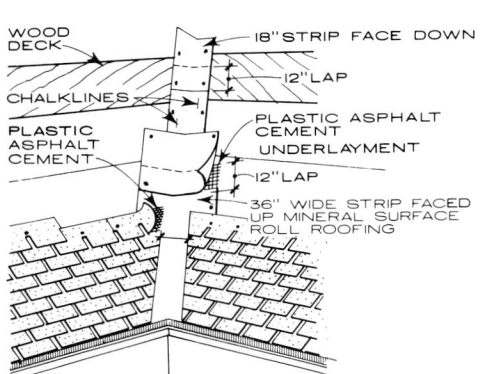

WOOD DECK
18" STRIP FACE DOWN
12" LAP
CHALKLINES
PLASTIC ASPHALT CEMENT UNDERLAYMENT
PLASTIC ASPHALT CEMENT
12" LAP
36" WIDE STRIP FACED UP MINERAL SURFACE ROLL ROOFING

OPEN VALLEY

• Valley width should be 6" wide at ridge and spread wider at the rate of 1/8"/foot downward to eave. Establish valley width using chalkline from ridge to cove.

APPLICATION DIAGRAMS

WOOD DECK
36" ROLL ROOFING AT LEAST 55 LB OR 1/16" SHEET NEOPRENE
EACH STRIP TO EXTEND AT LEAST 12" BEYOND CENTER OF VALLEY
UNDERLAYMENT
6" MIN.
EXTRA NAIL IN END OF STRIP

CLOSED VALLEY

EAVE FLASHING

Eave flashing is required wherever the January daily average temperature is 30°F or less or where there is a possibility of ice forming along the eaves.

NORMAL SLOPE—4 IN./FT OR OVER

A course of 90 lb mineral surfaced roll roofing or a course of 50 lb smooth roll roofing is installed to overhang the underlay and metal edge from 1/4 to 3/8 in. Extend up the roof far enough to cover a point at least 24 in. inside the interior wall line of the building. When the overhang requires flashing wider than 36 in., the horizontal lap joint is cemented and located on the roof deck extending beyond the exterior line of the building.

LOW SLOPE—3 TO 4 IN./FT

Cover the deck with two layers of 15# asphalt saturated felt. Begin with a 19 in. starter course laid along the eaves, followed by a 36 in. wide sheet laid even with the eaves and completely overlapping the starter course. The starter course is covered with asphalt cement. Thereafter, 36 in. sheets are laid in asphalt cement, each to overlap the preceding course 19 in., exposing 17 in. of the underlying sheet.

The plies are placed in asphalt cement to a point at least 36 in. inside the interior wall line of the building.

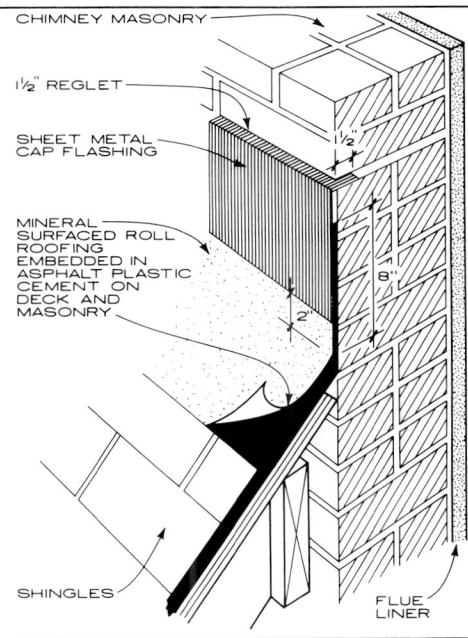

CHIMNEY MASONRY
1 1/2" REGLET
SHEET METAL CAP FLASHING
MINERAL SURFACED ROLL ROOFING EMBEDDED IN ASPHALT PLASTIC CEMENT ON DECK AND MASONRY
SHINGLES
1/2"
8"
2"
FLUE LINER

METHOD OF SECURING CAP FLASHING TO CHIMNEY MASONRY

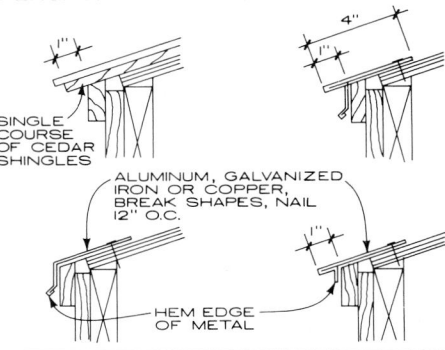

SINGLE COURSE OF CEDAR SHINGLES
1"   4"
ALUMINUM, GALVANIZED IRON OR COPPER, BREAK SHAPES, NAIL 12" O.C.
HEM EDGE OF METAL

DRIP EDGE DETAILS

SMOOTH
ANNULAR THREADED
SCREW THREADED
NAIL TYPES

NAILING OF SHINGLES RECOMMENDATION

DECK TYPE	NAIL LENGTH
1'' Wood sheathing	1 1/4''
3/8'' Plywood	7/8''
1/2'' Plywood	1''
Reroofing over asphalt shingles	1 3/4''

Robert E. Fehlberg, FAIA; CTA Architects Engineers; Billings, Montana

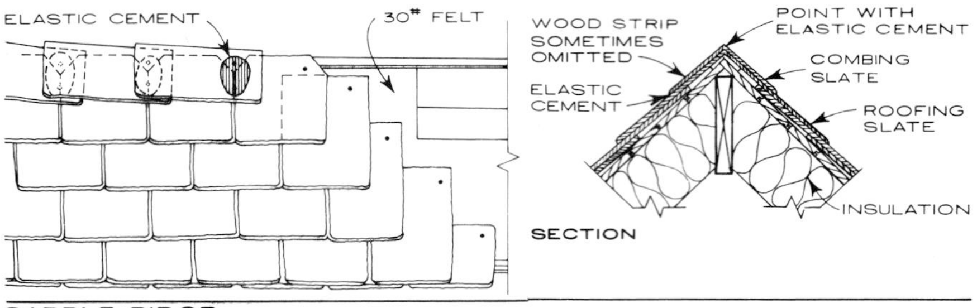

SADDLE RIDGE

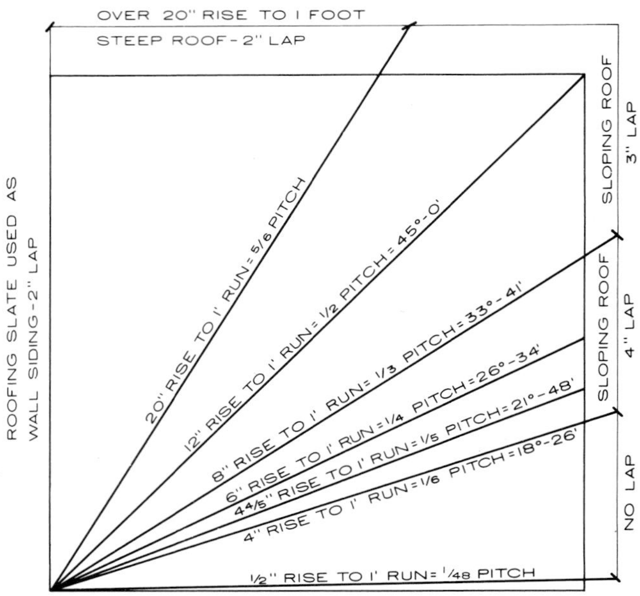

ELASTIC CEMENT
30# FELT
WOOD STRIP SOMETIMES OMITTED
ELASTIC CEMENT
POINT WITH ELASTIC CEMENT
COMBING SLATE
ROOFING SLATE
INSULATION

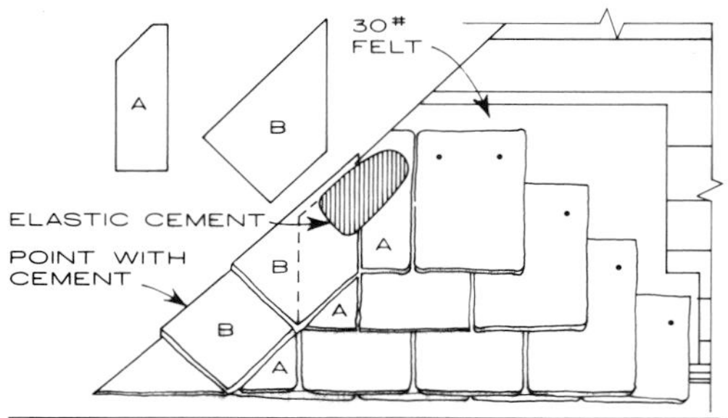

SECTION

SADDLE HIP

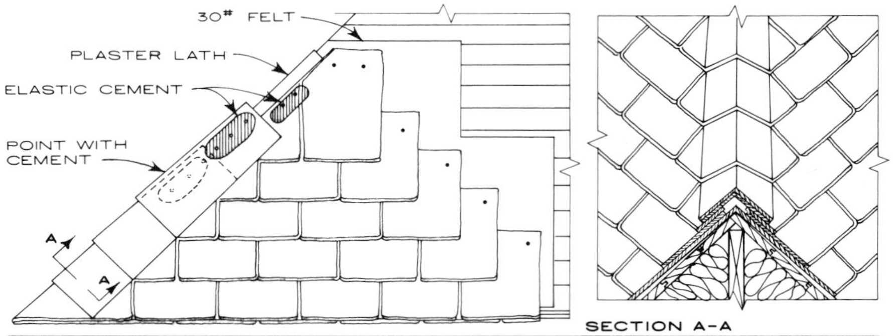

30# FELT
PLASTER LATH
ELASTIC CEMENT
POINT WITH CEMENT
A

SECTION A-A

BOSTON HIP

30# FELT
A
B
ELASTIC CEMENT
POINT WITH CEMENT
B
A
B
A

MITERED HIP

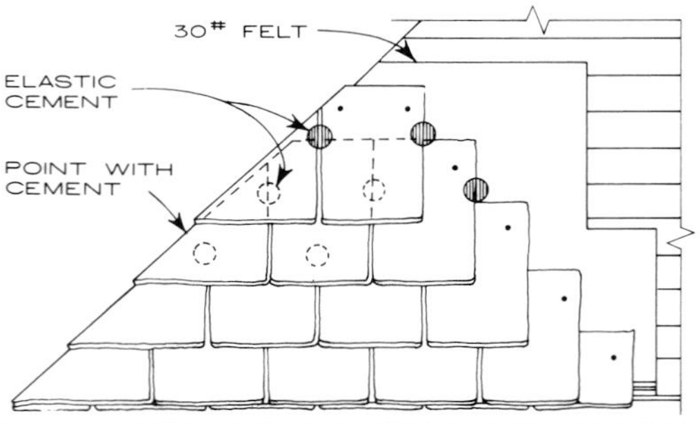

30# FELT
ELASTIC CEMENT
POINT WITH CEMENT
A

ROOFING SLATE USED AS WALL SIDING—2" LAP

STEEP ROOF—2" LAP   OVER 20" RISE TO 1 FOOT

20" RISE TO 1' RUN = 5/6 PITCH
12" RISE TO 1' RUN = 1/2 PITCH = 45°-0'
8" RISE TO 1' RUN = 1/3 PITCH = 33°-41'
6" RISE TO 1' RUN = 1/4 PITCH = 26°-34'
4 4/5" RISE TO 1' RUN = 1/5 PITCH = 21°-48'
4" RISE TO 1' RUN = 1/6 PITCH = 18°-26'

1/2" RISE TO 1' RUN = 1/48 PITCH

SLOPING ROOF   3" LAP
SLOPING ROOF   4" LAP
SLOPING ROOF   4" LAP
NO LAP

DIAGRAM OF PROPER LAP FOR RISE / RUN

GENERAL NOTES

1. COMMERCIAL STANDARD: The quarry run of $3/16$ in. thickness; includes tolerable variations above and below $3/16$ in.
2. TEXTURAL: A rough textured slate roof with uneven butts; the slates vary in thickness and size, which is generally not true of slate more than $3/8$ in. thick.
3. GRADUATED: A textural roof of large slates; more variation in thickness, size, and color.
4. A SQUARE OF ROOFING SLATE: A number of slates of any size sufficient to cover 100 ft² with a 3 in. lap. Weight per square: $3/16$ in.—800 lb; $1/4$ in.—900 lb; $3/8$ in.—1100 lb; $1/2$ in.—1700 lb; $3/4$ in.—2600 lb.
5. STANDARD NOMENCLATURE FOR SLATE COLOR: Black, blue black, mottled gray, purple, green, mottled purple and green, purple variegated, red; to be preceded by the word "Unfading" or "Weathering." Other colors and combinations are available.
6. PROPER JOINTING FOR PITCHED ROOFS: Requires a 3 in. minimum vertical overlap. Overlap varies with pitch; see graph above.
7. FELT: With Commercial Standard Slate use 30# saturated felt. With graduated roofs use 30# for $1/4$ in. slate and 45#, 50#, or 65# prepared roll roofing for heavier slate.
8. NAIL FASTENING: Use large head, slaters' hard copper wire nails, cut copper, cut brass, or cut yellow metal slating nails. Each slate punched with two nail holes. Use nails that are 1 in. longer than thickness of slate. Cover all exposed heads with elastic cement. In dry climates hot dip galvanized nails may be used.

OPEN VALLEY

TAPER 1/8" TO 1'-0" WIDEN TOWARD BOTTOM
10"
16 OZ COPPER FLASHING OR 1/16" NEOPRENE SHEET

EAVE

ROOF SHEATHING
SLATE
"UNDER-EAVE" OR STARTER SLATE
RAFTER
INSULATION
PLATE
2"
SLATE

GABLE RAKE

SLATE
SLATE
1/2" TO 1"

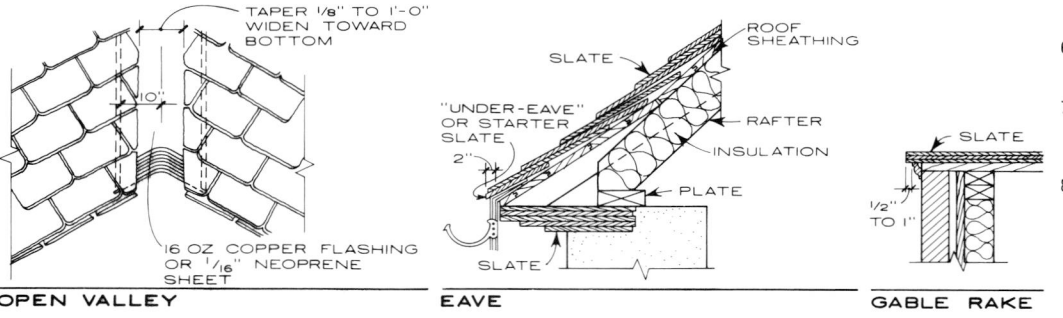

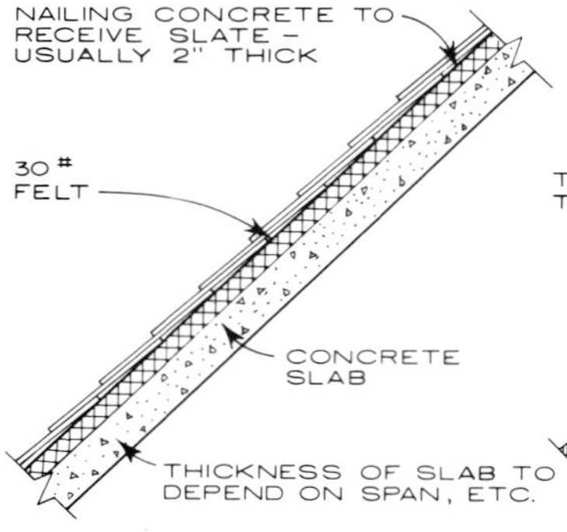

NAILING CONCRETE ON CONCRETE SLAB

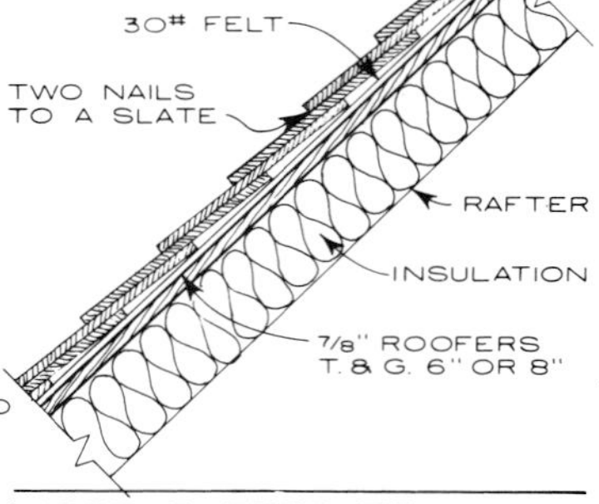

NAILING CONCRETE TO RECEIVE SLATE — USUALLY 2" THICK
30# FELT
CONCRETE SLAB
THICKNESS OF SLAB TO DEPEND ON SPAN, ETC.

WOOD RAFTER TO RECEIVE SLATE

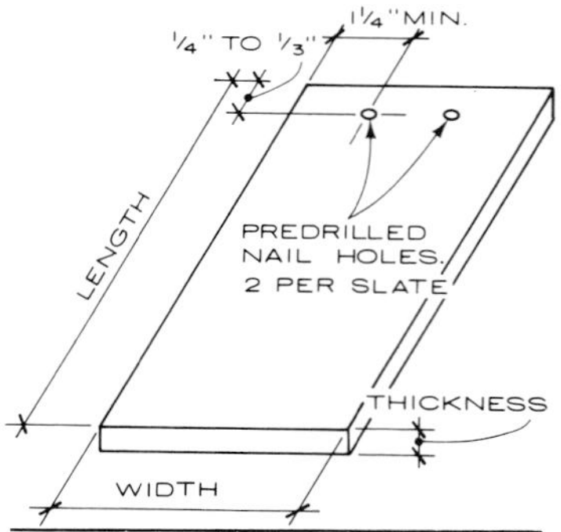

30# FELT
TWO NAILS TO A SLATE
RAFTER
INSULATION
7/8" ROOFERS T. & G. 6" OR 8"

ROOFING SLATE

1/4" TO 1/3"   1 1/4" MIN.
LENGTH
PREDRILLED NAIL HOLES, 2 PER SLATE
THICKNESS
WIDTH

STANDARD SLATE DIMENSIONS*

LENGTH (IN.)	WIDTH (IN.)
10†	6, 7, 8, 9, 10
12†	6, 7, 8, 9, 10, 12
14†	7, 8, 9, 10, 11, 12
16	8, 9, 10, 11, 12, 14
18	9, 10, 11, 12, 13, 14
20	9, 10, 11, 12, 13, 14
22	10, 11, 12, 13, 14
24	11, 12, 13, 14, 16

*The slates are split in these thicknesses: $3/16$, $1/4$, $3/8$, $1/2$, $3/4$, 1, $1 1/4$, and $1 1/2$ in.
†$1/2$ in. and larger slates are not often used in these sizes. Random widths are usually used.

Domenic F. Valente, AIA, Architect & Planner; Medford, Massachusetts

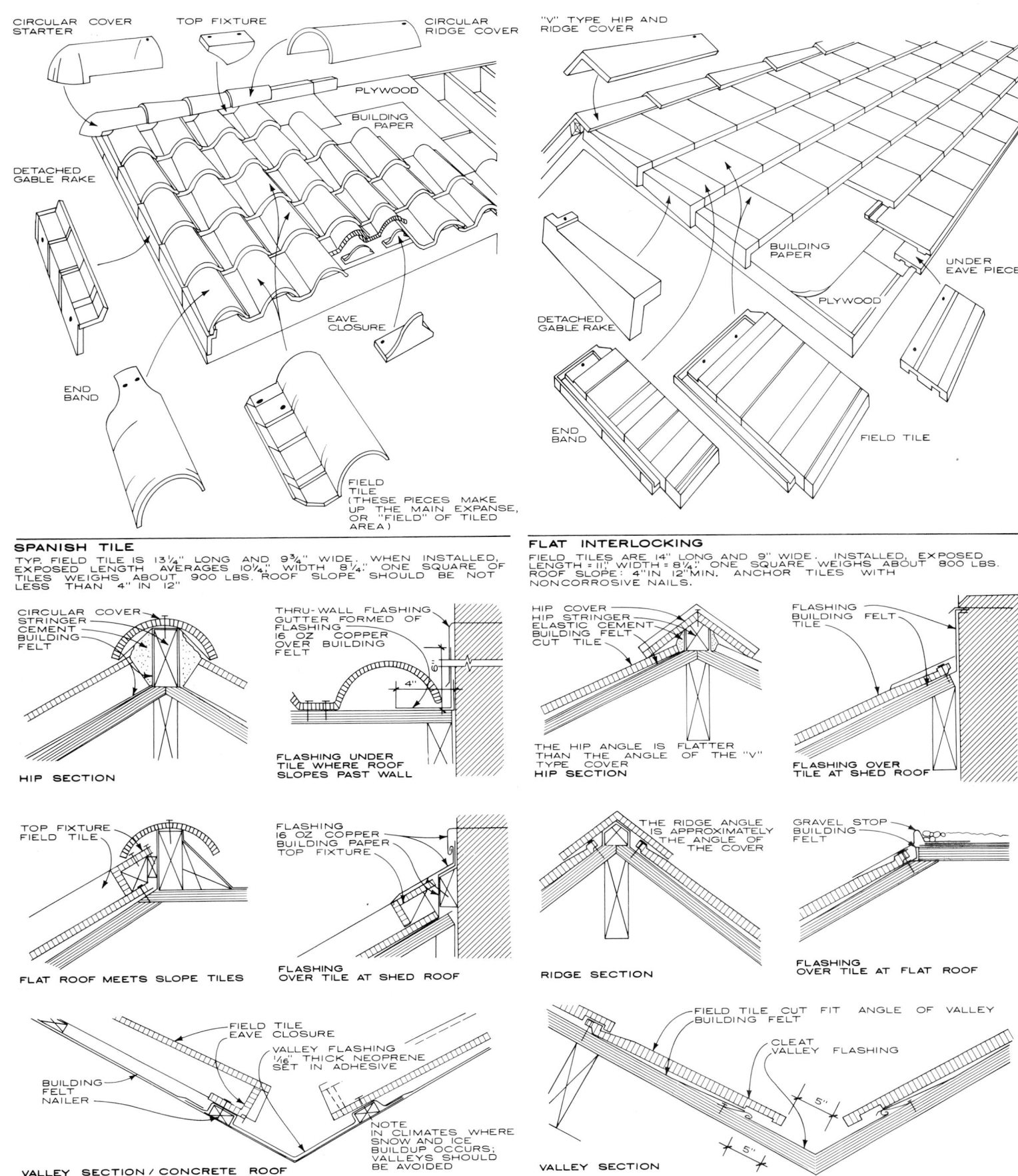

CIRCULAR COVER STARTER

TOP FIXTURE

CIRCULAR RIDGE COVER

"V" TYPE HIP AND RIDGE COVER

PLYWOOD

BUILDING PAPER

DETACHED GABLE RAKE

BUILDING PAPER

DETACHED GABLE RAKE

UNDER EAVE PIECE

PLYWOOD

EAVE CLOSURE

END BAND

END BAND

FIELD TILE

FIELD TILE (THESE PIECES MAKE UP THE MAIN EXPANSE, OR "FIELD" OF TILED AREA)

SPANISH TILE

TYP. FIELD TILE IS 13¼" LONG AND 9¾" WIDE. WHEN INSTALLED, EXPOSED LENGTH AVERAGES 10¼" WIDTH 8¼." ONE SQUARE OF TILES WEIGHS ABOUT 900 LBS. ROOF SLOPE SHOULD BE NOT LESS THAN 4" IN 12"

FLAT INTERLOCKING

FIELD TILES ARE 14" LONG AND 9" WIDE. INSTALLED, EXPOSED LENGTH = 11" WIDTH = 8¼." ONE SQUARE WEIGHS ABOUT 800 LBS. ROOF SLOPE: 4" IN 12" MIN. ANCHOR TILES WITH NONCORROSIVE NAILS.

CIRCULAR COVER STRINGER CEMENT BUILDING FELT

THRU-WALL FLASHING GUTTER FORMED OF FLASHING 16 OZ COPPER OVER BUILDING FELT

HIP COVER HIP STRINGER ELASTIC CEMENT BUILDING FELT CUT TILE

FLASHING BUILDING FELT TILE

HIP SECTION

FLASHING UNDER TILE WHERE ROOF SLOPES PAST WALL

THE HIP ANGLE IS FLATTER THAN THE ANGLE OF THE "V" TYPE COVER

HIP SECTION

FLASHING OVER TILE AT SHED ROOF

TOP FIXTURE FIELD TILE

FLASHING 16 OZ COPPER BUILDING PAPER TOP FIXTURE

THE RIDGE ANGLE IS APPROXIMATELY THE ANGLE OF THE COVER

GRAVEL STOP BUILDING FELT

FLAT ROOF MEETS SLOPE TILES

FLASHING OVER TILE AT SHED ROOF

RIDGE SECTION

FLASHING OVER TILE AT FLAT ROOF

FIELD TILE EAVE CLOSURE

VALLEY FLASHING 1/16" THICK NEOPRENE SET IN ADHESIVE

FIELD TILE CUT FIT ANGLE OF VALLEY BUILDING FELT

CLEAT VALLEY FLASHING

BUILDING FELT NAILER

NOTE IN CLIMATES WHERE SNOW AND ICE BUILDUP OCCURS; VALLEYS SHOULD BE AVOIDED

5"

VALLEY SECTION / CONCRETE ROOF

VALLEY SECTION

5"

5"

Darrel Downing Rippeteau, Architect; Washington, D.C.

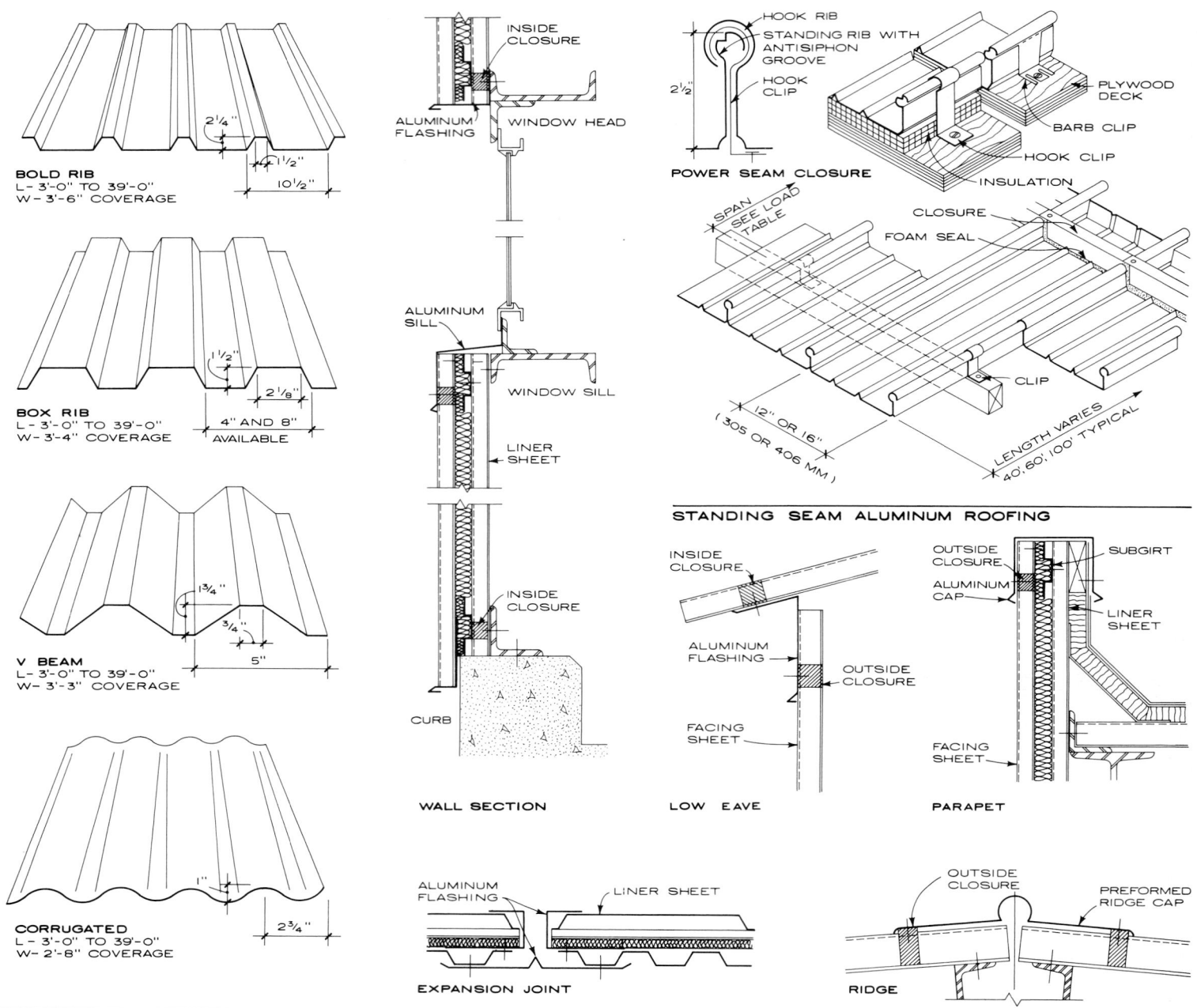

FORMED ALUMINUM ROOFING AND SIDING

NOTES

1. Endlaps for roofing and siding shall be at least 6 in. and fastened at every rib. Two fasteners may be required when designing for a negative (uplift) loading condition.
2. Minimum sidelaps shall be equal to one rib or corrugation and laid away from prevailing wind. Fasteners shall be spaced a maximum of 12 in. on center for all types of roofing and siding.
3. For roofing, fasteners shall pierce only the high corrugation. For siding, fasteners shall pierce either the high or low corrugation. Consult manufacturer for proper sheet metal fasteners and accessories.
4. Minimum slopes for sheet roofing are as follows:
   a. 1 in. depth corrugated—3 in 12.
   b. 1½ in. depth ribbed—2 in 12.
   c. 1¾ in. v-corrugated—2 in 12.
5. See page on Metal Walls for insulation details and fire rated wall assemblies.

John A. Schulte; Hellmuth, Obata & Kassabaum, Inc.; St. Louis, Missouri

MAXIMUM SPAN TABLE FOR FORMED ALUMINUM ROOFING AND SIDING (IN.)

DESIGN LOAD (PSF)	BOLD RIB		4" BOX RIB		V BEAM		CORRUGATED		STANDING SEAM	
	0.032 IN. THICK	0.040 IN. THICK	0.032 IN. THICK	0.040 IN. THICK	0.032 IN. THICK	0.040 IN. THICK	0.032 IN. THICK	0.040 IN. THICK	0.032 IN. THICK	0.040 IN. THICK
20	95	123	100	120	131	151	90	98	103	124
30	77	100	82	98	107	124	73	80	86	104
40	67	87	71	85	92	107	64	69	77	92
50	60	76	63	76	83	96	57	62	70	83

NOTE: Values are based on uniform positive (downward) and walking loads on single span only.

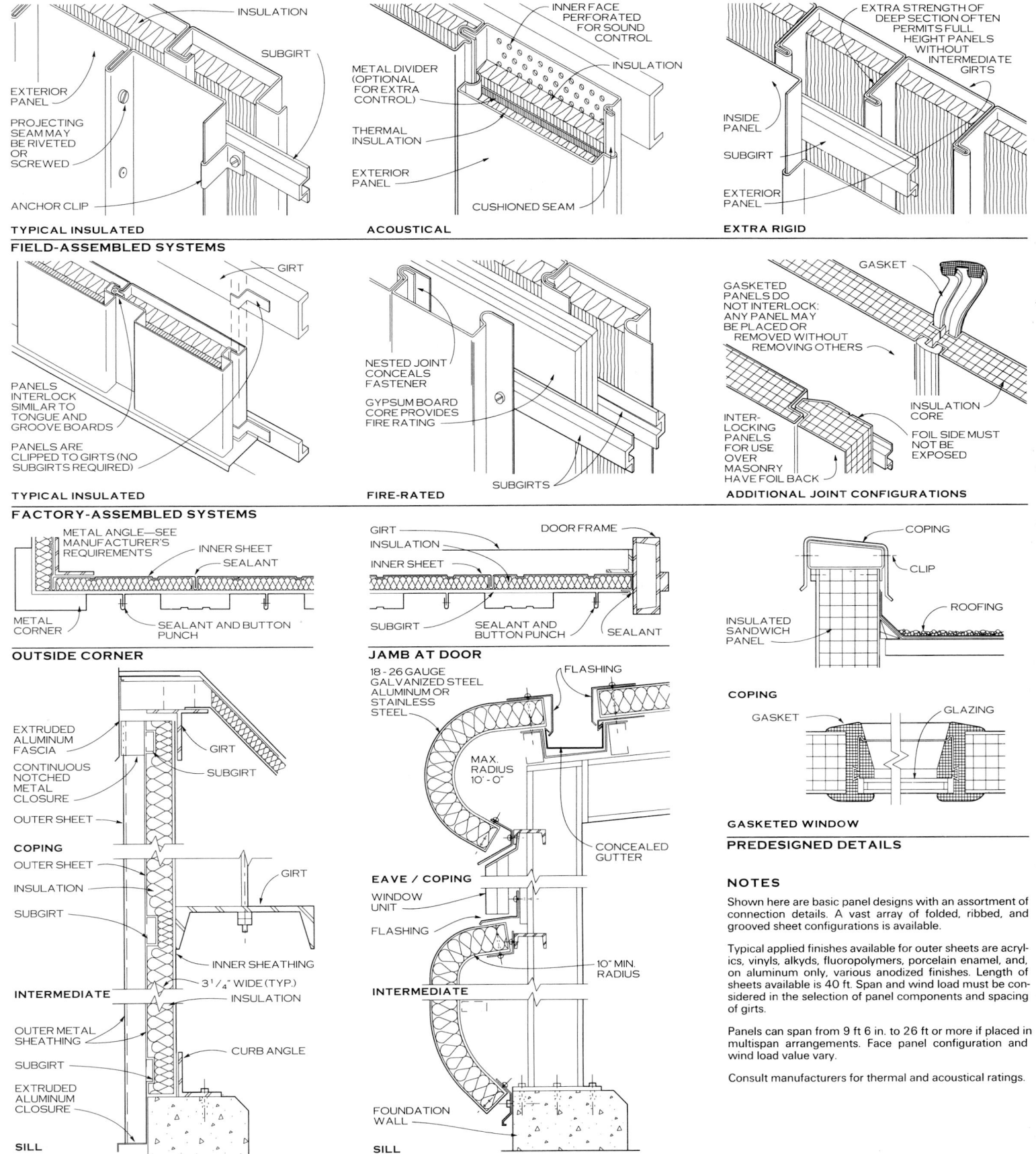

TYPICAL INSULATED

- INSULATION
- SUBGIRT
- EXTERIOR PANEL
- PROJECTING SEAM MAY BE RIVETED OR SCREWED
- ANCHOR CLIP

ACOUSTICAL

- INNER FACE PERFORATED FOR SOUND CONTROL
- INSULATION
- METAL DIVIDER (OPTIONAL FOR EXTRA CONTROL)
- THERMAL INSULATION
- EXTERIOR PANEL
- CUSHIONED SEAM

EXTRA RIGID

- EXTRA STRENGTH OF DEEP SECTION OFTEN PERMITS FULL HEIGHT PANELS WITHOUT INTERMEDIATE GIRTS
- INSIDE PANEL
- SUBGIRT
- EXTERIOR PANEL

FIELD-ASSEMBLED SYSTEMS

TYPICAL INSULATED

- GIRT
- PANELS INTERLOCK SIMILAR TO TONGUE AND GROOVE BOARDS
- PANELS ARE CLIPPED TO GIRTS (NO SUBGIRTS REQUIRED)

FIRE-RATED

- NESTED JOINT CONCEALS FASTENER
- GYPSUM BOARD CORE PROVIDES FIRE RATING
- SUBGIRTS

ADDITIONAL JOINT CONFIGURATIONS

- GASKET
- GASKETED PANELS DO NOT INTERLOCK; ANY PANEL MAY BE PLACED OR REMOVED WITHOUT REMOVING OTHERS
- INSULATION CORE
- INTERLOCKING PANELS FOR USE OVER MASONRY HAVE FOIL BACK
- FOIL SIDE MUST NOT BE EXPOSED

FACTORY-ASSEMBLED SYSTEMS

OUTSIDE CORNER

- METAL ANGLE—SEE MANUFACTURER'S REQUIREMENTS
- INNER SHEET
- SEALANT
- METAL CORNER
- SEALANT AND BUTTON PUNCH

JAMB AT DOOR

- GIRT
- INSULATION
- INNER SHEET
- DOOR FRAME
- SUBGIRT
- SEALANT AND BUTTON PUNCH
- SEALANT

COPING

- COPING
- CLIP
- ROOFING
- INSULATED SANDWICH PANEL

GASKETED WINDOW

- COPING
- GASKET
- GLAZING

PREDESIGNED DETAILS

FIELD-ASSEMBLED INSULATED METAL WALLS

- EXTRUDED ALUMINUM FASCIA
- CONTINUOUS NOTCHED METAL CLOSURE
- OUTER SHEET
- GIRT
- SUBGIRT

COPING
- OUTER SHEET
- INSULATION
- SUBGIRT
- GIRT
- INNER SHEATHING
- 3 1/4" WIDE (TYP.)
- INSULATION

INTERMEDIATE
- OUTER METAL SHEATHING
- SUBGIRT
- EXTRUDED ALUMINUM CLOSURE
- CURB ANGLE

SILL

FACTORY-FORMED, FIELD-ASSEMBLED INSULATED METAL PANELS

- 18 - 26 GAUGE GALVANIZED STEEL ALUMINUM OR STAINLESS STEEL
- FLASHING
- MAX. RADIUS 10'-0"
- CONCEALED GUTTER

EAVE / COPING
- WINDOW UNIT
- FLASHING
- 10" MIN. RADIUS

INTERMEDIATE

SILL
- FOUNDATION WALL

NOTES

Shown here are basic panel designs with an assortment of connection details. A vast array of folded, ribbed, and grooved sheet configurations is available.

Typical applied finishes available for outer sheets are acrylics, vinyls, alkyds, fluoropolymers, porcelain enamel, and, on aluminum only, various anodized finishes. Length of sheets available is 40 ft. Span and wind load must be considered in the selection of panel components and spacing of girts.

Panels can span from 9 ft 6 in. to 26 ft or more if placed in multispan arrangements. Face panel configuration and wind load value vary.

Consult manufacturers for thermal and acoustical ratings.

Eric K. Beach; Rippeteau Architects, PC; Washington, D.C.

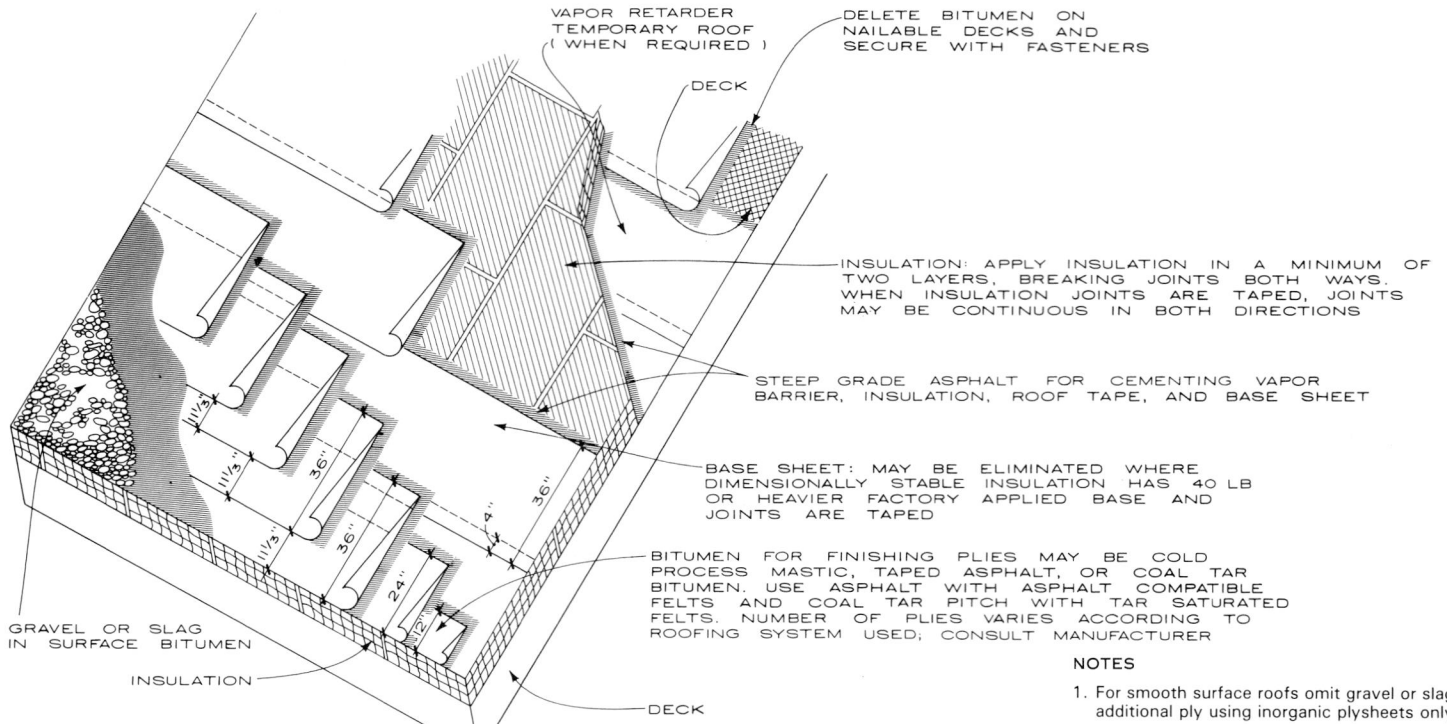

VAPOR RETARDER TEMPORARY ROOF (WHEN REQUIRED)

DELETE BITUMEN ON NAILABLE DECKS AND SECURE WITH FASTENERS

DECK

INSULATION: APPLY INSULATION IN A MINIMUM OF TWO LAYERS, BREAKING JOINTS BOTH WAYS. WHEN INSULATION JOINTS ARE TAPED, JOINTS MAY BE CONTINUOUS IN BOTH DIRECTIONS

STEEP GRADE ASPHALT FOR CEMENTING VAPOR BARRIER, INSULATION, ROOF TAPE, AND BASE SHEET

BASE SHEET: MAY BE ELIMINATED WHERE DIMENSIONALLY STABLE INSULATION HAS 40 LB OR HEAVIER FACTORY APPLIED BASE AND JOINTS ARE TAPED

BITUMEN FOR FINISHING PLIES MAY BE COLD PROCESS MASTIC, TAPED ASPHALT, OR COAL TAR BITUMEN. USE ASPHALT WITH ASPHALT COMPATIBLE FELTS AND COAL TAR PITCH WITH TAR SATURATED FELTS. NUMBER OF PLIES VARIES ACCORDING TO ROOFING SYSTEM USED; CONSULT MANUFACTURER

GRAVEL OR SLAG IN SURFACE BITUMEN

INSULATION

DECK

NOTES

1. For smooth surface roofs omit gravel or slag and add additional ply using inorganic plysheets only.
2. On slopes over 1 in./ft all felts along top edge must usually be strapped and back-nailed.
3. When vapor retarder is used, edges of felt should be turned up to a height of 2 in. above cant strip at vertical surfaces. Felts should overlap all roof edges a minimum of 6 in. before application of roofing. 6 in. of felt must be re-turned over the insulation and mopped solidly.

20 YEAR TYPE BUILT-UP ROOF OVER INSULATION

NOTES

1. Over nonnailable deck or insulation omit rosin paper and cement with asphalt. Nailing strips must be provided.
2. Minimum slope for organic felt: $\frac{1}{2}$ in./ft.
3. Minimum slope for fiberglass felt: 0 in./ft.
4. Consult manufacturer for spacing of nails for particular roofing system.

SCHEDULE OF FELT OVERLAP (INCHES)

Organic base sheet	4
Fiberglass or base sheet	2
2-ply felts/plysheets	19
3-ply felts/plysheets	$24^{2}/_{3}$
4-ply felts/plysheets	$27^{1}/_{2}$
Fiberglass mineral	3 if selvage granulated
Surface cap sheet	2 if selvage granulated

STAGGER NAILS AT 12" O.C.

NAILABLE DECK

ROSIN PAPER (OVER WOOD, EXCEPT PLYWOOD)

ASPHALT BETWEEN PLIES OF 15 LB FELT. ASPHALT TYPE (I, II, III, OR IV) DETERMINED BY ROOF SLOPE

MINERAL SURFACE ROOFING. 2" SIDE LAPS IF SELVAGE IS UNGRANULATED; 3" SIDE LAPS IF SELVAGE IS GRANULATED

STEEP GRADE ASPHALT

MINERAL SURFACE BUILT-UP ROOF

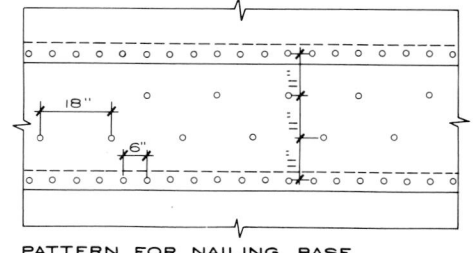

PATTERN FOR NAILING BASE SHEET OR VAPOR RETARDER OVER NAILABLE DECK

Kent Wong; Hewlett, Jamison, Atkinson & Luey; Portland, Oregon;
Developed by Angelo J. Forlidas, AIA; Charlotte, North Carolina; from data furnished by Robert M. Stafford, P.E., Consulting Engineer; Charlotte, North Carolina

NOTE

Polyvinyl chloride (PVC) is a semirigid material that requires the addition of plasticizers to fabricate a flexible roofing membrane. PVC exhibits excellent weldability for making lap joints or attaching to PVC clad metal flashing.

TYPES OF MEMBRANE

Unreinforced sheet
Sheet reinforced with fiberglass or polyester

METHOD OF MANUFACTURE

Calendering
Spread coating
Extruding

GENERAL

Single ply roofing systems are also referred to as flexible sheet roofing systems. Consult manufacturers for specific requirements regarding materials selection and installation requirements. Compatibility of materials comprising total roofing system is essential.

MATERIAL PROPERTIES

Thickness: Typically 48 and 60 mil; 45 mil minimum

Color: Typically gray; other colors available

Contaminants to avoid: Bitumen, oils, animal fats, and coal tar pitch. See manufacturer's chemical resistance list.

Minimum standards: ASTM has developed standard test methods to evaluate the materials properties of PVC roof membranes. These test results form a useful basis for comparing various PVC membranes. ASTM's standard specification establishes minimum performance criteria for tensile strength, elongation, tear resistance, heat aging, weathering, and water absorption.

INSTALLATION

General guidelines: It is recommended that all roofing materials be installed on roofs with positive slope to drainage. Check with manufacturers regarding their specific requirements.

Lap joining methods: Hot air or solvent weld

Flashing methods: Membrane or PVC coated metal

Types of preformed accessories available: Inside and outside corners; pipe stacks

Weather restrictions during installation: 0°–120°F temperature range. Substrates and welding/bonding surfaces must be dry.

Method of repair: Clean surface; hot air or solvent weld of PVC patch

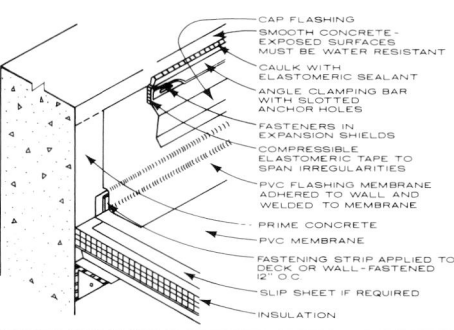

TYPICAL PARAPET FLASHING

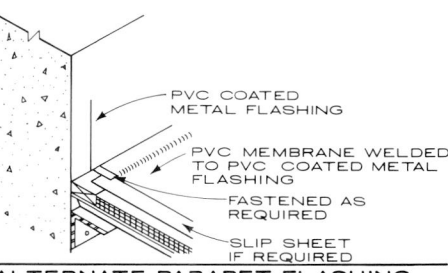

ALTERNATE PARAPET FLASHING

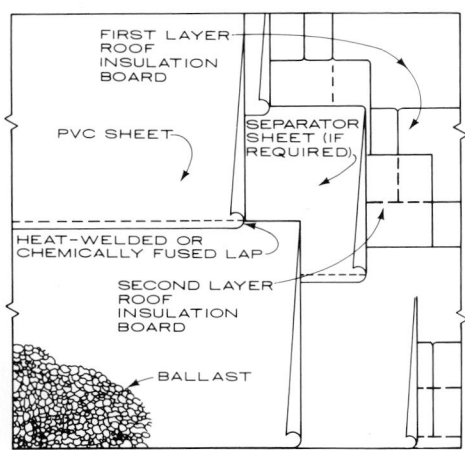

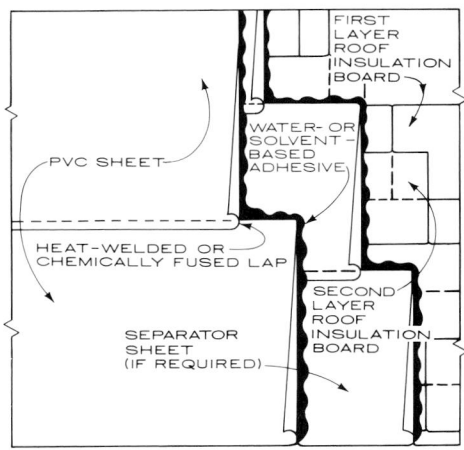

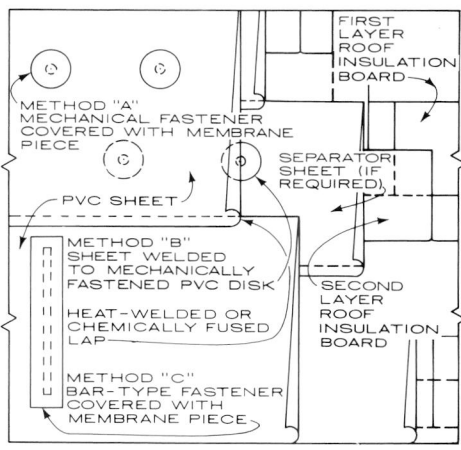

Membrane sheets are laid loose over roof insulation (also laid loose) and secured at the perimeter and around penetrations only. The membrane is then covered with a ballast of river-washed stones (typically 10 lb/sq ft) or appropriate pavers.

This system works efficiently with insulation approved by the membrane manufacturer and on roofs with a slope not exceeding 2 in 12.

LOOSE-LAID BALLASTED SHEETS

Membrane sheets are laid loose over a sloped roof deck and with the insulation on top of it. When the roof deck is dead level, tapered roof insulation is either loose laid or mechanically attached under the membrane to achieve positive slope to drainage. In either instance, a layer of insulation is placed over the membrane and held in place by one of two methods: Either a loose fabric is laid over the insulation, with a minimum of 10 lb/sq ft of ballast laid over the fabric, or insulation with an integrally bonded concrete facing is used in place of the fabric and loose ballast. Membrane manufacturers should be consulted for their approved insulation list. In this roofing system, the membrane is protected from year-round temperature extremes, direct exposure to weather, and damage from other sources. The heat gain or loss is just the same as if the insulation were installed under the membrane. Since the waterproofing membrane is placed on the warm side of the insulation, it functions as a vapor retarder. For high humidity conditions with a dead level roof deck utilizing tapered insulation, a separate vapor barrier should be placed directly beneath the tapered insulation to prevent condensation.

PROTECTED MEMBRANE SHEET

For system with no slope limitations which secures membrane to substrate with bonding adhesive and by mechanically fastening the membrane to perimeter and penetrations. System is appropriate for contoured roofs and roofs that cannot withstand weight of ballasted system.

Membrane can be directly applied to deck surface of concrete, wood surfaces, or be applied to compatible insulation that is mechanically fastened to the deck.

FULLY ADHERED SHEETS

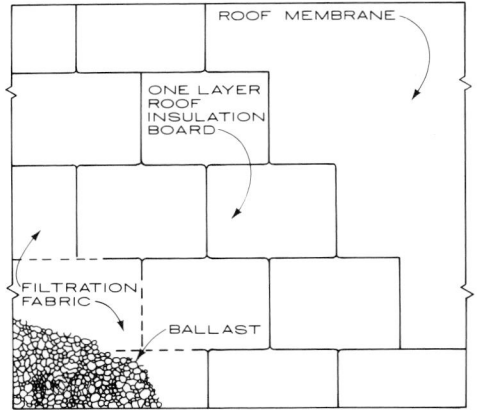

A mechanically anchored roof system is appropriate for roofs that cannot carry the additional load of ballasted roof systems. Systems are available with fasteners that penetrate the membrane or that require no membrane penetration.

The membrane is anchored to the roof using metal bars or individual clips, and it may be installed over concrete, wood, metal, or compatible insulation.

MECHANICALLY ATTACHED SHEETS

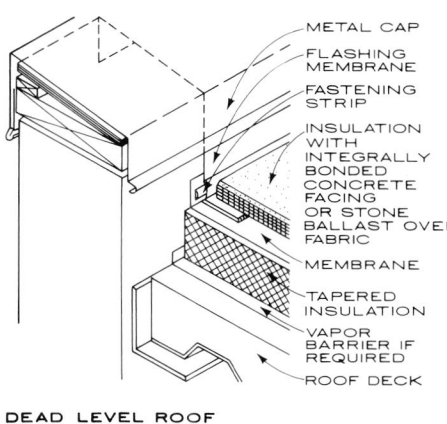

DEAD LEVEL ROOF

CTA Architects Engineers; Billings, Montana

NOTES

There are three generic installation methods for EPDM roofing:

1. Fully Adhered: Membrane roofing is rolled onto the substrate and allowed to relax. Underside is then fully coated with bonding adhesive. After both surfaces are tacky, the membrane is pressed onto the substrate with a push broom. Adjoining sheets must overlap at least 3 in., with laps spliced and cemented. Membrane is mechanically secured at perimeter and penetration edges. Flashing protects all edges, openings, and penetrations.
2. Loose Laid: Roofing in this application is laid loose over the substrate, either deck or rigid insulation, and ballasted in place. It is positioned without stretching, allowed to attain its natural shape, and adjacent sheets spliced with adjoining sheets overlapping at least 3 in. Sheets are cemented and rolled together to seal seams. The membrane is mechanically secured at perimeter and penetration edges, and flashing is installed. For ballast, a sufficient amount of river-washed gravel is laid over the membrane to provide 10 lb/sq ft of weight. As an alternate, a precast roof paver system is applied to hold the roofing membrane.
3. Mechanically Fastened: Membrane roof is directly attached to the roof deck with mechanical fasteners. The substrate is anchored to the roof deck, and the fasteners either go through both membrane and insulation or only go through the insulation and deck, with the membrane held down by retainer and cap over the base. Sealant protects against moisture.

Many EPDM membranes are field surfaced to improve resistance to weathering and fire, or to enhance appearance.

GENERAL NOTES

EPDM elastomeric roofing is synthesized from ethylene, propylene, and a small amount of diene monomer. Manufactured sheets range in thickness from 30 to 60 mils.

Advantages: EPDM roofing exhibits a high degree of resistance to ozone, ultraviolet, extreme temperature and other elements, and degradation from abrasion. It is resilient, strong, elastic, and less prone to cracking and tearing when compared to other forms of membrane roofing.

Disadvantages: Application methods, specific formulas and configurations for adhesives, fasteners, and coatings are unique with each system manufactured. Materials, design, and appropriate use vary widely. Close supervision and regular inspection by manufacturer are a requirement. Labor cost and time allotted for installation may vary.

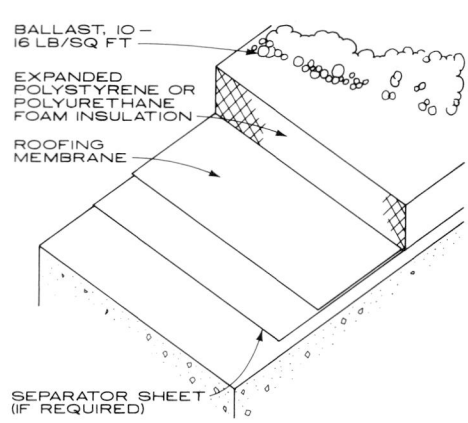

INSULATED ROOF MEMBRANE APPLICATION

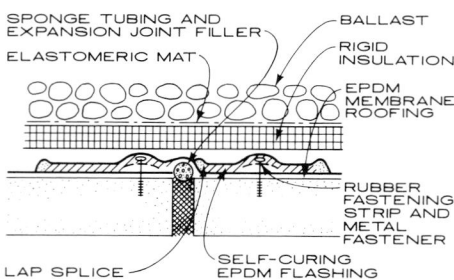

EXPANSION JOINT: INSULATED ROOF MEMBRANE BALLASTED

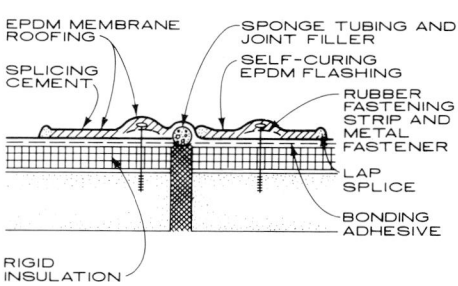

EXPANSION JOINT: FULLY ADHERED ROOF MEMBRANE

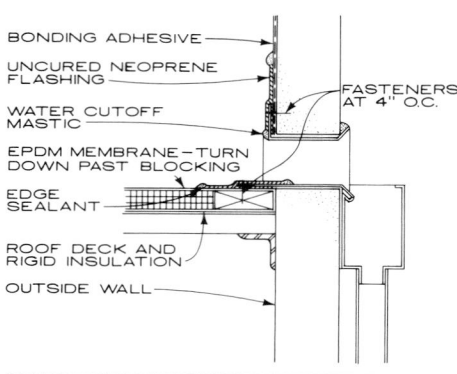

FULLY ADHERED ROOF AT PARAPET OR WALL

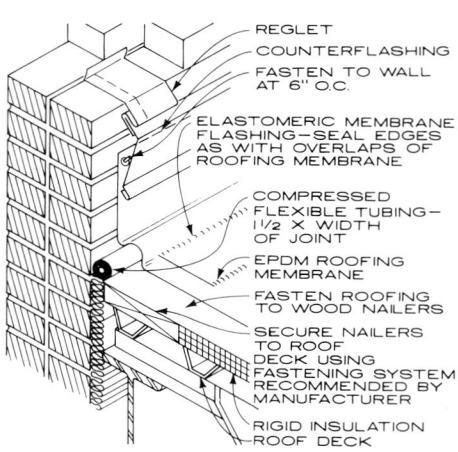

ROOF EDGE AT NONSUPPORTING WALL

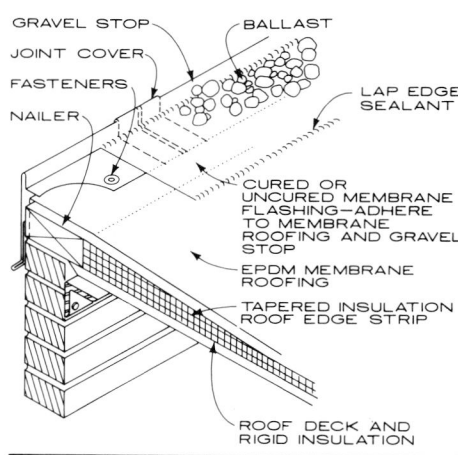

LIGHT METAL ROOF EDGE

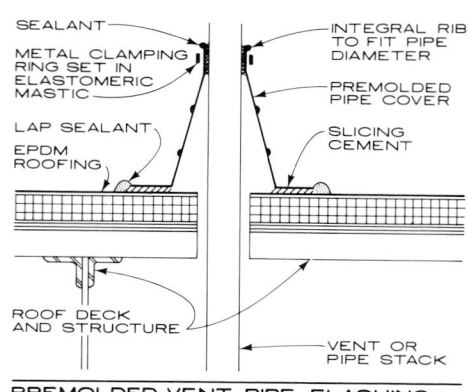

FULLY ADHERED ROOF SCUPPER

PREMOLDED VENT PIPE FLASHING

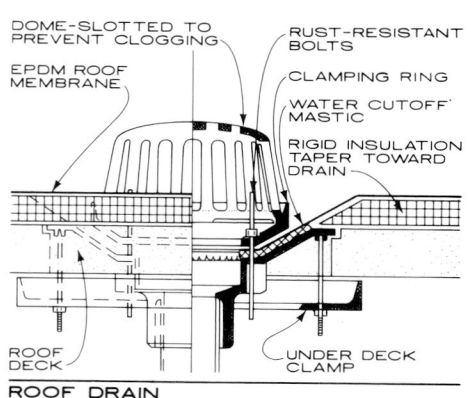

ROOF DRAIN

Catherine A. Broad; Washington, D.C.

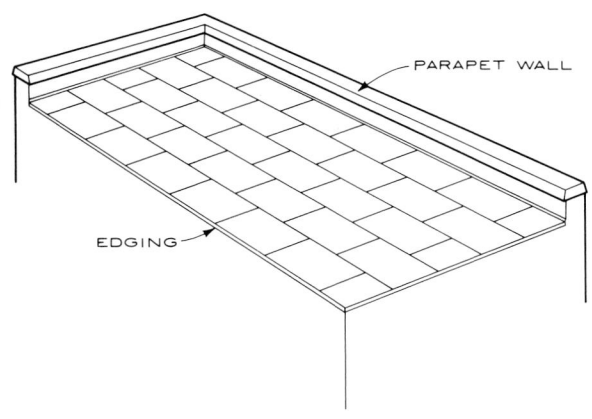

FLAT SEAM ROOF

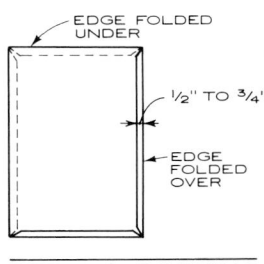

DETAIL 1- ROOFING
SHEET

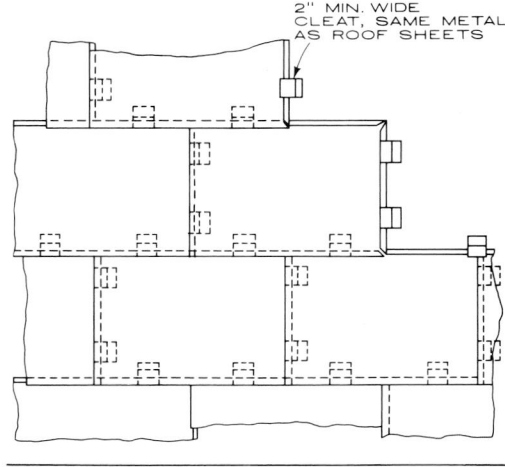

DETAIL 2-FLAT SEAM ROOF

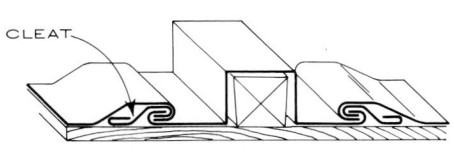

DETAIL 3- EXPANSION BATTEN

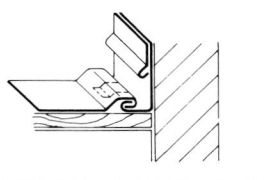

DETAIL 4- JUNCTION AT
PARAPET WALL

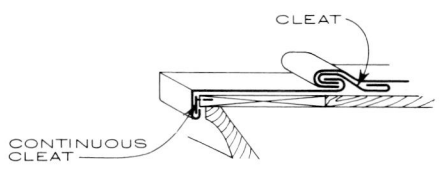

DETAIL 5- ROOF EDGE

NOTES

1. The flat seam method of roofing as illustrated is most commonly used on roofs of slight pitch or for the covering of curved surfaces such as towers or domes.
2. The joints connecting the sheets of roofs having a pitch greater than $1/2$ in./ft may be sealed with caulking compound or white lead. The joints of roofs having a pitch of less than $1/2$ in./ft must be malleted and thoroughly sweated full with solder.
3. Roofs of slight pitch should be divided by expansion batten as shown in detail 3, into sections not exceeding maximum total areas of 30 ft^2.
4. Consult general notes on metal roofs for recommended surface preparation.
5. The metal sheets may be pretinned if required, $1\frac{1}{2}$ in. back from all edges and on both sides of the sheet. Pans are formed by notching and folding the sheets as shown in detail 1.
6. The pans are held in place by cleating as shown. After pans are in place, all seams are malleted and soldered or sealed.
7. Detail 4 shows the junction of a roof and a parapet wall. Metal base flashing is cleated to deck on 2 ft centers and extended up wall; 8 in. pans are locked and soldered to base flashing. Metal counter flashing covers 4 in. of the base flashing. Detail 5 illustrates the installation of flashing at edge of roof. Flashing is formed as shown and attached to the face by a continuous cleat nailed on 1 ft centers and cleated to the roof deck. Pans are locked and soldered or sealed to the flashing. See also general notes below.

GENERAL NOTES

1. Detail drawings for metal roof types are diagrammatic only. The indication of adjoining construction is included merely to establish its relation to the sheet metal work and is not intended as a recommendation of architectural design. Any details that may suggest an architectural period do not limit the application of sheet metal to that or any other architectural style.
2. For weights of metals and roof slopes, see data of the Sheet Metal and Air Conditioning Contractors' National Association and recommendations of manufacturers.
3. Metals used must be of a thickness or gauge heavy enough and in correct proportion to the breadth and scale of the work. Provide expansion joints for freedom of movement.
4. Prevent direct contact of metal roofing with dissimilar metals that cause electrolysis.
5. A wide range of metals, alloys, and finishes are available for metal roofing. The durability as well as the maintenance requirements of each should be taken into consideration when selecting roofing.
6. The surface to receive the metal roofing should be thoroughly dry and covered by a saturated roofing felt in case of leakage due to construction error or wind driven moisture. A rosin paper should be applied over the felt to avoid bonding between felt and metal.
7. Many of the prefabricated batten and standing seam devices are not as watertight as with conventional methods and are therefore more suitable for steeply pitched roofs and mansards.

Straub Associates/Architects; Troy, Michigan
Emory E. Hinkel, Jr.; A. G. Odell, Jr. and Associates; Charlotte, North Carolina

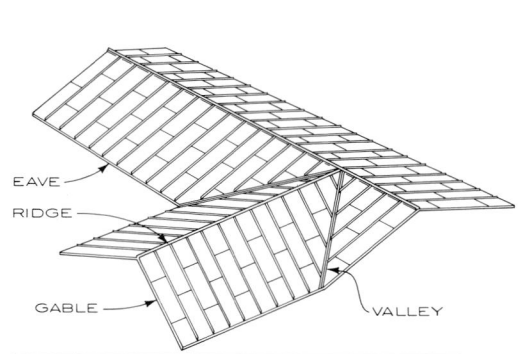

EAVE

RIDGE

GABLE

VALLEY

STANDING SEAM METAL ROOF

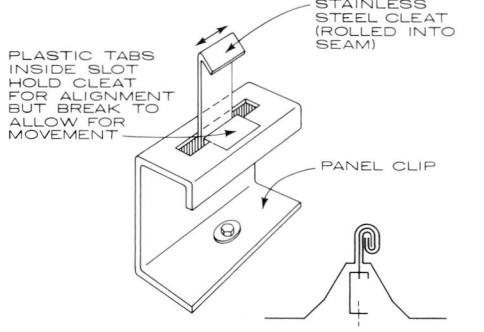

STAINLESS STEEL CLEAT (ROLLED INTO SEAM)

PLASTIC TABS INSIDE SLOT HOLD CLEAT FOR ALIGNMENT BUT BREAK TO ALLOW FOR MOVEMENT

PANEL CLIP

NOTES

To allow for expansion and contraction movement in roof panels, some manufacturers set movable cleats into a stationary panel clip system. The cleat is held in position in the center of a slot in the panel clip by two temporary plastic tabs. This allows for correct alignment of the cleat with the roof panel. Once the cleat has been rolled into the panel seam, it will move with the roof panel by forcing the plastic tabs to break under movement pressure.

MOVABLE CLEAT

NOTES

Roof panels secured at the eave expand up the slope of the roof. Depending on the length of the roof panel, an engineered distance should be left between the end of roof panels on each side of the ridge, thereby allowing for expansion at the ridge. In cases of a very long run of roof panels (usually in excess of 200 ft), expansion joints will be required at other points in addition to the ridge. Any blocking at the ridge should be cut at an angle to provide a space for the panels to bend into when expanding (as in ridge detail A). Ridge coverings can be formed or bowed to move with the expansion of the roof panels (as in ridge details B and C). In addition, the seams can either be flattened or left upright. Upright seams require a closing gasket or panel between seams.

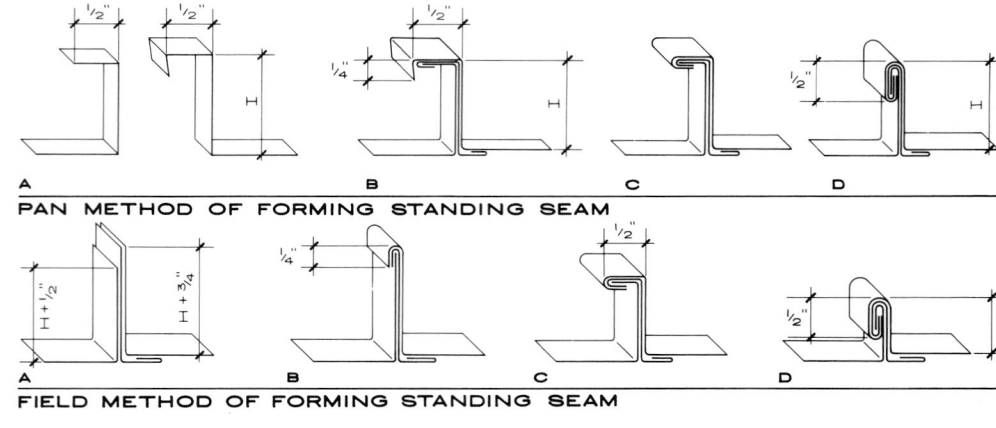

A   B   C   D

PAN METHOD OF FORMING STANDING SEAM

A   B   C   D

FIELD METHOD OF FORMING STANDING SEAM

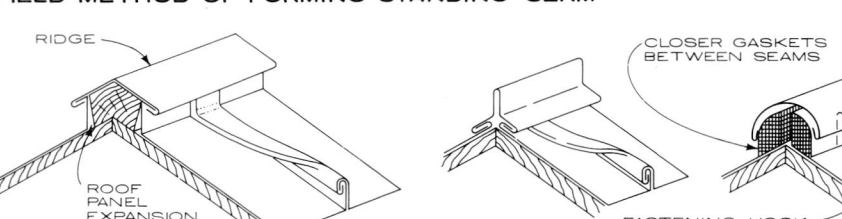

RIDGE

ROOF PANEL EXPANSION SPACE

CLOSER GASKETS BETWEEN SEAMS

FASTENING HOOK FOR RIDGE COVERING

A   B   C

RIDGE CONSTRUCTION

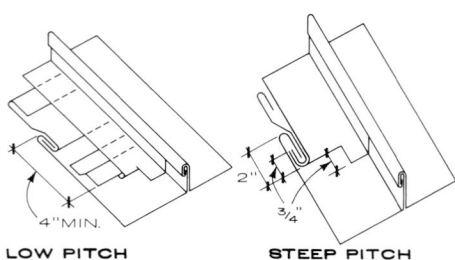

4" MIN.

LOW PITCH   STEEP PITCH

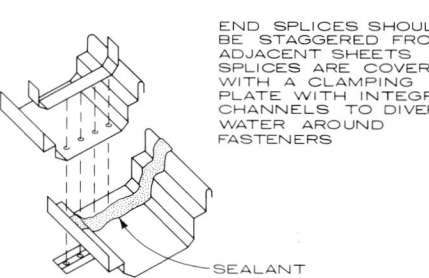

END SPLICES SHOULD BE STAGGERED FROM ADJACENT SHEETS SPLICES ARE COVERED WITH A CLAMPING PLATE WITH INTEGRAL CHANNELS TO DIVERT WATER AROUND FASTENERS

SEALANT

TRANSVERSE SEAM AND PANEL SPLICE

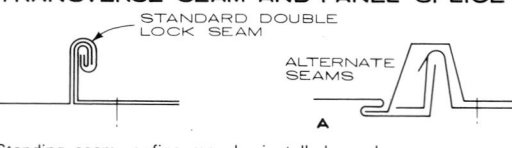

STANDARD DOUBLE LOCK SEAM

ALTERNATE SEAMS

A   B   C   D

Standing seam roofing may be installed on slopes as gentle as ¼ in./ft. Because of the architectural appearance of the roof system, it is more commonly used on steeper roof slopes, allowing the panels to be seen as part of the overall design.

The spacing of seams may vary within reasonable limits to suit the architectural style of a given building. Preformed sheets (as used with preengineered metal buildings) have seam locations set by locations of prepunched holes in the structural framing members.

The two methods of forming a standing seam are the pan method and the roll method. In the pan method, the top, bottom, and sides of the individual sheets are preformed to allow locking together at each edge. Seams at the top and bottom of each sheet are called transverse seams. In the roll method, a series of long sheets are joined together at their ends with double flat lock seams. These field-formed seams can be executed either manually or with a seaming machine (a wheeled electronic device which runs along the sheet joint forming the seam).

In either method, cleats (spaced as recommended by the manufacturer) are formed into the standing seam. Seam terminations are usually soldered.

STANDING SEAM METHODS AND SHAPES

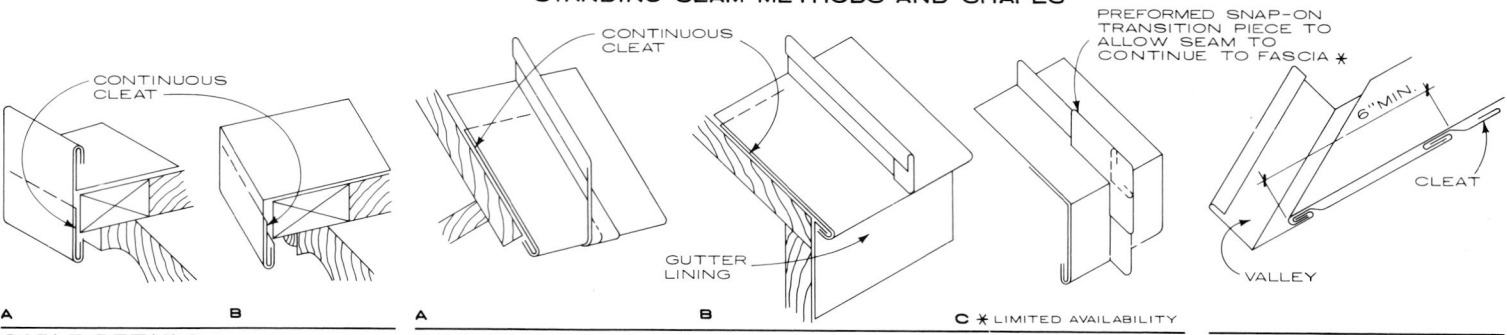

CONTINUOUS CLEAT

A   B

GABLE DETAILS

CONTINUOUS CLEAT

GUTTER LINING

A   B   C * LIMITED AVAILABILITY

EAVE DETAILS

PREFORMED SNAP-ON TRANSITION PIECE TO ALLOW SEAM TO CONTINUE TO FASCIA *

6" MIN.

CLEAT

VALLEY

VALLEY DETAIL

Raso-Greaves, An Architecture Corporation; Waco, Texas
Straub Associates/Architects; Troy, Michigan
Emory E. Hinkel, Jr.; A. G. Odell, Jr. and Associates; Charlotte, North Carolina

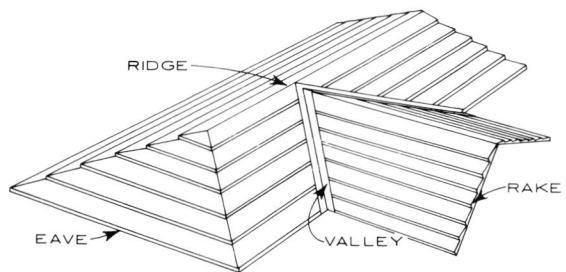

BERMUDA TYPE METAL ROOF

RECOMMENDED GAUGES OR WEIGHTS FOR PAN WIDTHS

WIDTH OF SHEET (IN.)	WIDTH OF PAN "D" (IN.)	COPPER (OZ)	GALVANIZED STEEL (GAUGE)	STAINLESS STEEL (GAUGE)	PAINTED TERNE 40 LB COATING
20	16½	16	26	28	0.015 IN.
22	18½	16	26	28	0.015 IN.
24	20½	16	26	26	0.015 IN.
26	22½	20	24	26	0.0178 IN.
28	24½	20	24	26	0.0178 IN.

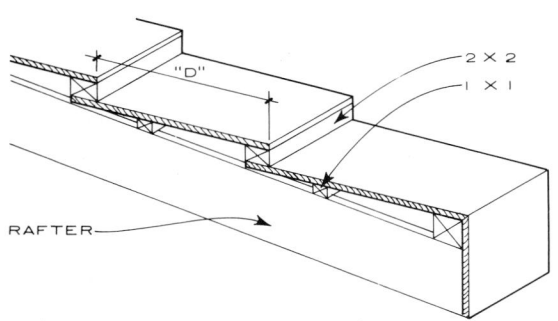

DETAIL 1-WOOD FRAMING

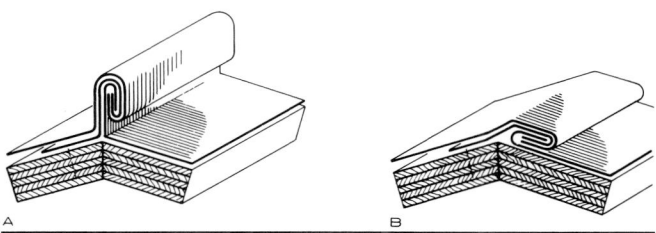

DETAIL 2-SEAM TYPES AT HIP OR RIDGE

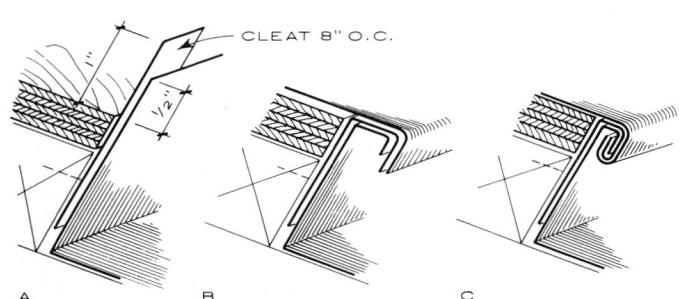

DETAIL 3-CONSTRUCTION AT BATTEN

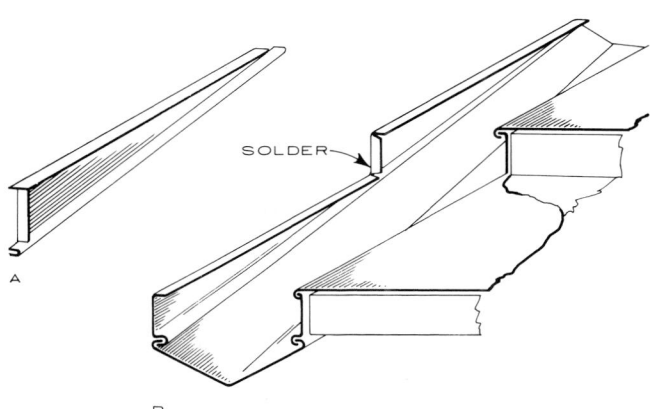

DETAIL 4-CONSTRUCTION AT CLOSURE AND VALLEY

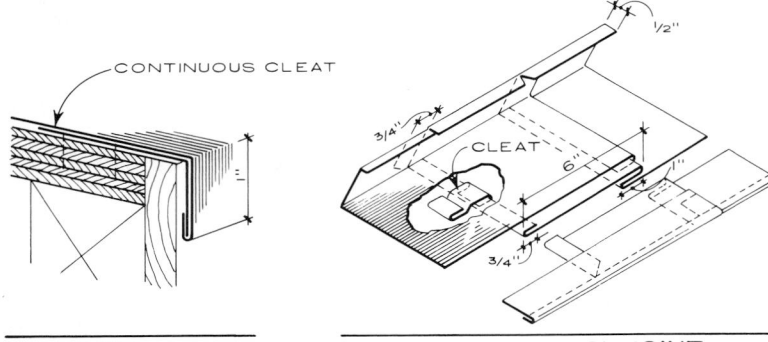

DETAIL 5-EAVE   **DETAIL 6-EXPANSION JOINT**

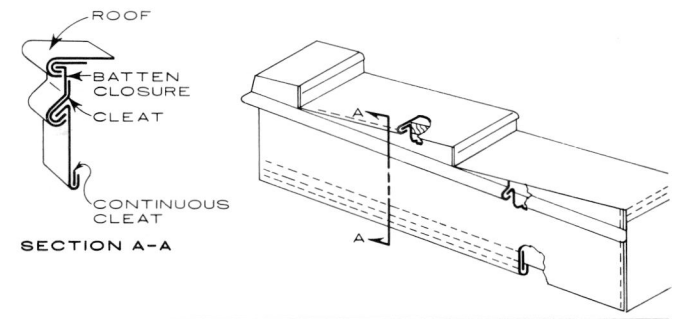

SECTION A-A

DETAIL 7-CONSTRUCTION AT RAKE

NOTES

1. The Bermuda roof may be used for roofs having a slope greater than $2\frac{1}{2}$ in./ft. Wood framing must be provided as shown in detail 1. Dimension "D" and gauge of metal will depend on the size of sheet used. See chart. Consult general notes on metal roofs for recommended surface preparation.

2. Bermuda roof is applied beginning at the eave. The first pan is hooked over a continuous cleat as shown in detail 5. The upper portion of the first and each succeeding pan is attached as shown in detail 3. Cleats spaced on 8 in. centers are nailed to batten as in A of detail 3. Joint is developed as shown in B of detail 3 and malleted against batten as shown in C of detail 3. All cross seams are single locked and soldered except at expansion joints. Cross seams should be staggered. Expansion joints should be used at least every 25 ft and formed as shown in detail 6. Roofing is joined at hip or ridge by use of a standing seam as shown in A of detail 2. Seam may be malleted down as shown in B of detail 2.

3. Detail 4 shows the method of forming valleys. Valley sections are lapped 8 in. in direction of flow.

Individual closures for sides of valley are formed as shown in A of detail 4 and must be soldered as indicated in B of detail 4. A method of terminating the roof at rake is shown in detail 7. The face plate (optional) is held in place by continuous cleats at both top and bottom. The batten closure is formed as a cleat to hold edge of roof pan as shown in section A-A of detail 7.

See also Metal Roofs for general notes.

Straub Associates/Architects; Troy, Michigan
Emory E. Hinkel, Jr.; A. G. Odell, Jr. and Associates; Charlotte, North Carolina

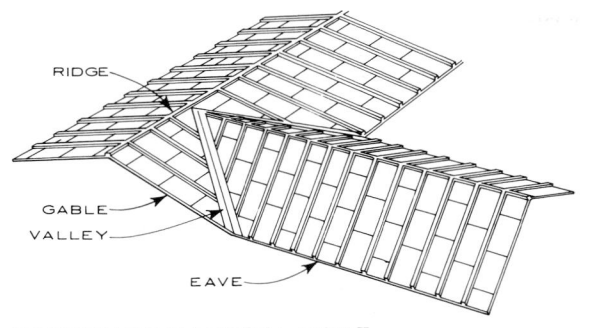

BATTEN SEAM METAL ROOF

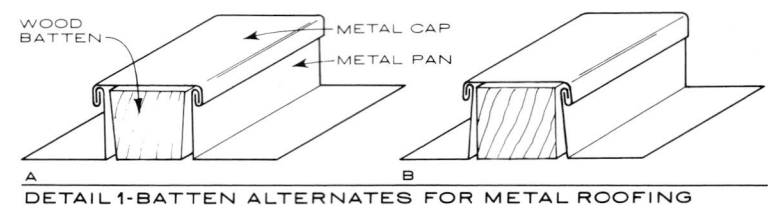

DETAIL 1-BATTEN ALTERNATES FOR METAL ROOFING

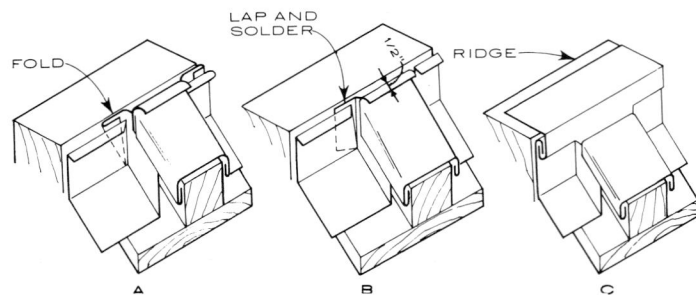

DETAIL 2 - RIDGE CONSTRUCTION

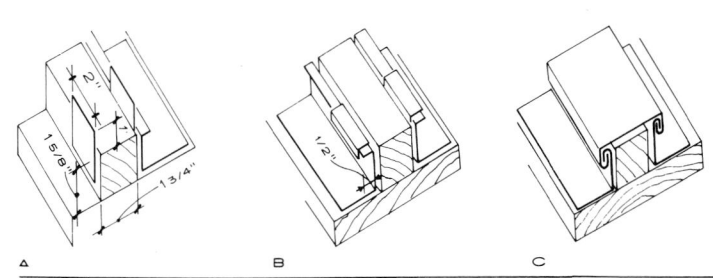

DETAIL 3-BATTEN JOINT CONSTRUCTION

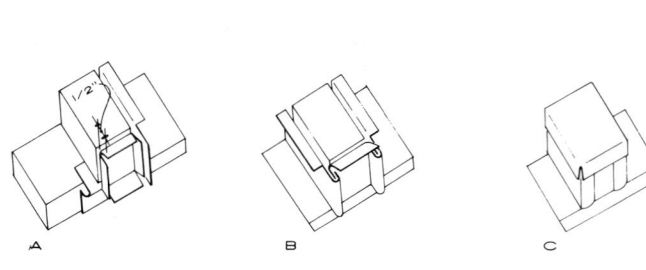

DETAIL 4- BATTEN CAP CONSTRUCTION

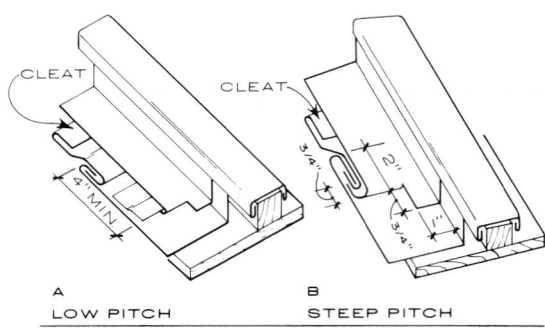

DETAIL 5-TRANSVERSE SEAM

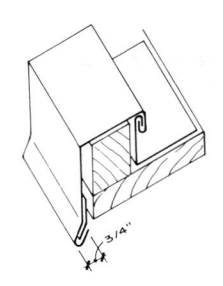

DETAIL 6- GABLE

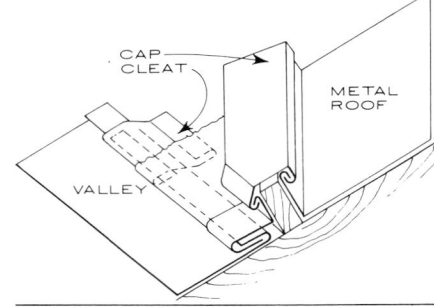

DETAIL 7- VALLEY

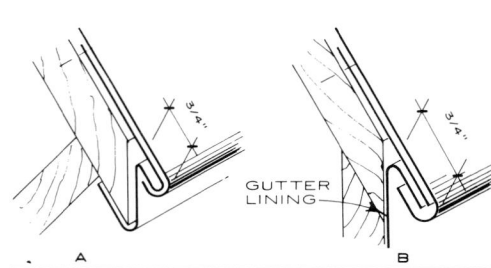

DETAIL 8- EAVES

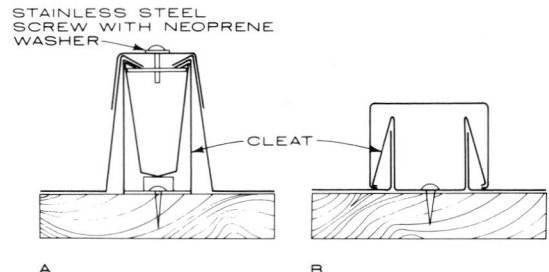

DETAIL 9 - PREFABRICATED BATTENS

NOTES

1. Batten seam roofing may be applied on slopes of 3 in./ft or greater. If the surface to receive the roofing is other than wood, the battens should be bolted into place. All batten fasteners must be countersunk into battens. See general notes on Metal Roofs for recommended surface preparation.

2. The spacing of the wood battens may vary within reasonable limits to suit the architectural style and scale of the building, but the recommended maximum distance is 20 in. between battens. Care should be taken to space the battens in such a manner that waste of metal is held to a minimum. Battens may be shaped as shown in A or B of detail 1.

A is preferred, since it automatically makes allowance for expansion. When battens shown in B are used, care must be taken to provide for expansion by bending the metal where it meets the batten at greater than 90°.

3. Sheets are formed into pans with each side turned up $2^{1}/_{8}$ in. A $^{1}/_{2}$ in. flange is turned toward the center of the pan as shown in B of detail 3. At lower end of the pan, the sheet is notched and a hook edge is formed as in A or B of detail 5. For low pitched roofs the upper end of the sheet is formed as in A of detail 5. On steeper roofs the upper end is formed as shown in B of detail 5. Pans

are installed, starting at the eave, and held in place with cleats spaced not over 12 in. on center as shown in A of detail 3. Each pan is hooked to the one below it and cleated into place. After pans are in place, a cap is installed over the batten as shown in B and C of detail 3.

4. A number of manufacturers have developed metal roofing systems using several prefabricated devices. A and B of detail 9 show two common prefabricated battens in use.

5. See also Standing Seam Metal Roofing for details on combination batten and standing or flat seam roofing. See also Metal Roofs for general notes.

Straub Associates/Architects; Troy, Michigan
Emory E. Hinkel, Jr.; A. G. Odell, Jr. and Associates; Charlotte, North Carolina

MINIMUM THICKNESS (GAUGES OR WEIGHT) FOR COMMON FLASHING CONDITIONS

CONDITIONS / MATERIALS	BASE COURSE	WALL OPENINGS HEAD AND SILL	THROUGH WALL AND SPANDREL	CAP AND BASE FLASHING	VERTICAL AND HORIZONTAL SURFACES	ROOF EDGE RIDGES AND HIPS	CRICKETS VALLEY OR GUTTER	CHIMNEY PAN	LEDGE FLASHING	ROOF PENETRATIONS	COPING WIDTH UP TO 12"	COPING WIDTH ABOVE 12"	EDGE STRIPS	CLEATS	NOTE
Copper	10 oz	10 oz	10 oz	16 oz	16 oz	16 oz	16 oz	16 oz	16 oz	16 oz	16 oz	20 oz	20 oz	16 oz	
Aluminum	0.019″	0.019″	0.019″	0.019″	0.019″	0.019″	0.019″	0.019″	0.019″	0.040″	0.032″	0.040″	0.024″	✕	Note 6
Stainless steel	30 GA	30 GA	30 GA	26 GA	30 GA	26 GA	26 GA	30 GA	26 GA	26 GA	26 GA	24 GA	24 GA	✕	Note 5
Galvanized steel	26 GA	26 GA	26 GA	26 GA	26 GA	24 GA	24 GA	26 GA	24 GA	24 GA	24 GA	22 GA	26 GA	22 GA	Note 2
Zinc alloy	0.027″	0.027″	0.027″	0.027″	0.027″	0.027″	0.027″	0.027″	0.027″	0.027″	0.027″	0.032″	0.040″	0.027″	Note 4
Lead	3#	2½#	2½#	2½#	3#	3#	3#	3#	3#	3#	3#	3#	3#	3#	Note 3
Painted terne	40#	40#	40#	20#	40#	20#	40#	20#	40#	40#			20#	40#	Note 8
elastomeric sheet; fabric-coated metal	See Note 7			✕	✕	✕	✕		See Note 7		✕	✕	✕	✕	Note 7

GENERAL NOTES

1. All sizes and weights of material given in chart are minimum. Actual conditions may require greater strength.
2. All galvanized steel must be painted.
3. With lead flashing use 16 oz copper cleats. If any part is exposed, use 3# lead cleats.
4. Coat zinc with asphaltum paint when in contact with redwood or cedar. High acid content (in these woods only) develops stains.
5. Type 302 stainless steel is an all purpose flashing type.
6. Use only aluminum manufactured for the purpose of flashing.
7. See manufacturer's literature for use and types of flashing.
8. In general, cleats will be of the same material as flashing, but heavier weight or thicker gauge.
9. In selecting metal flashing, precaution must be taken not to place flashing in direct contact with dissimilar metals that cause electrolysis.
10. Spaces marked ✕ in the table are uses not recommended for that material.

GALVANIC CORROSION (ELECTROLYSIS) POTENTIAL BETWEEN COMMON FLASHING MATERIALS AND SELECTED CONSTRUCTION MATERIALS

CONSTRUCTION MATERIALS / FLASHING MATERIALS	COPPER	ALUMINUM	STAINLESS STEEL	GALVANIZED STEEL	ZINC	LEAD	BRASS	BRONZE	MONEL	UNCURED MORTAR OR CEMENT	WOODS WITH ACID (REDWOOD AND RED CEDAR)	IRON/STEEL
Copper		●	●	◐	●	◐	◐	◐	◐			●
Aluminum	○		○	○	○	●	●	●	●	●	●	◐
Stainless steel	◐	●		◐	●	●	●	●	○	○	○	◐
Galvanized steel	●	○	◐		○	◐	◐	●	○	◐	◐	◐
Zinc alloy	●	○	●	○		●	●	●	○	●	●	●
Lead	◐	●	◐	◐	●		◐	●	○	○		○

● Galvanic action will occur, hence direct contact should be avoided.
◐ Galvanic action may occur under certain circumstances and/or over a period of time.
○ Galvanic action is insignificant, metals may come into direct contact under normal circumstances.

GENERAL NOTE: Galvanic corrosion is apt to occur when water runoff from one material comes in contact with a potentially reactive material.

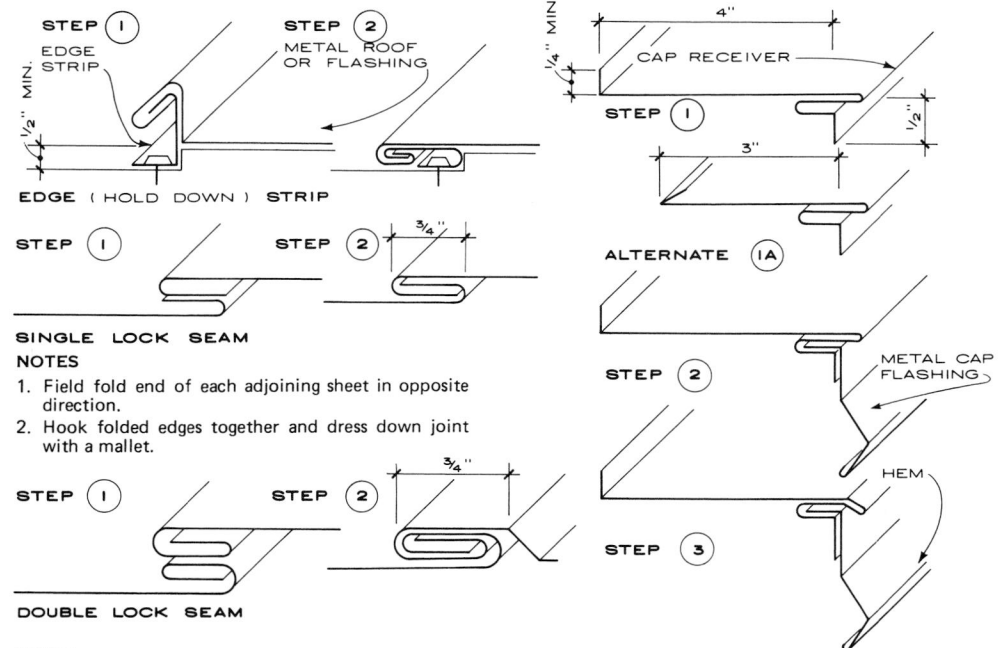

SINGLE LOCK SEAM

NOTES

1. Field fold end of each adjoining sheet in opposite direction.
2. Hook folded edges together and dress down joint with a mallet.

DOUBLE LOCK SEAM

NOTES

1. Double fold end of each adjoining sheet in opposite direction with bar folder.
2. Slide edges together and dress down joint with a mallet.

DEVELOPMENT OF CAP FLASHING
NOTE
Hem in cap flashing recommended for stiffness; but may be omitted if heavier gauge material used.

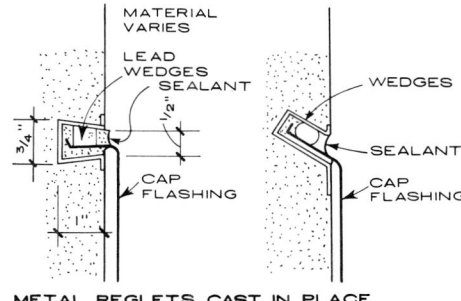

METAL REGLETS CAST IN PLACE

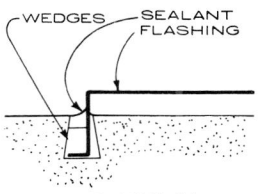

REGLET SAWED IN MATERIAL

TYPICAL REGLETS

NOTE
Various types of metal reglets are available for cast in place and masonry work; see manufacturer's literature. Where material permits, reglets may be sawn. Flashing is secured in reglets with lead wedges at max. 12″ o.c., fill reglet with nonhardening water-resistant compound.

Michael Scott Rudden; The Stephens Associates P.C.—Architects; Albany, New York

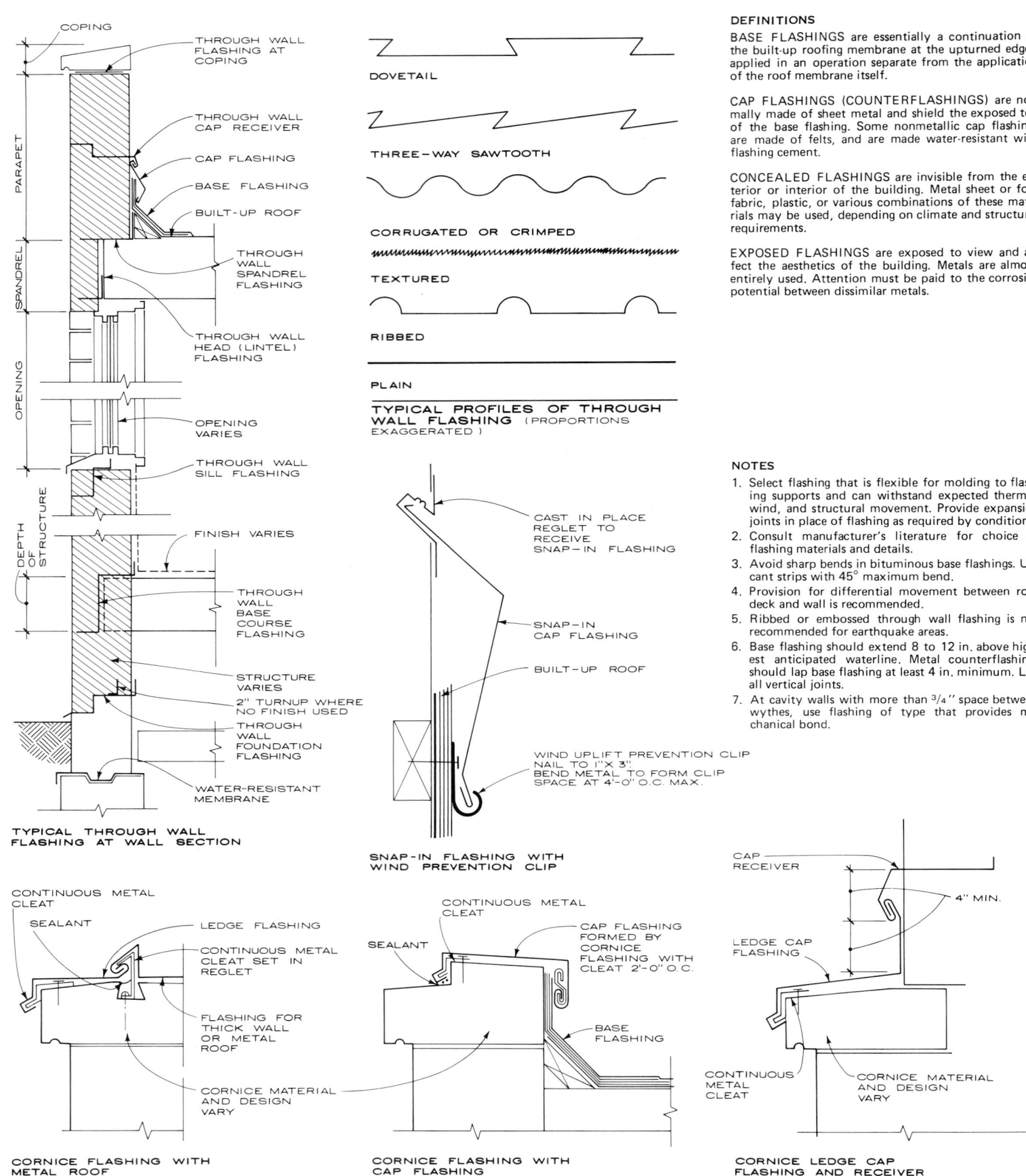

DEFINITIONS

BASE FLASHINGS are essentially a continuation of the built-up roofing membrane at the upturned edges, applied in an operation separate from the application of the roof membrane itself.

CAP FLASHINGS (COUNTERFLASHINGS) are normally made of sheet metal and shield the exposed top of the base flashing. Some nonmetallic cap flashings are made of felts, and are made water-resistant with flashing cement.

CONCEALED FLASHINGS are invisible from the exterior or interior of the building. Metal sheet or foil, fabric, plastic, or various combinations of these materials may be used, depending on climate and structural requirements.

EXPOSED FLASHINGS are exposed to view and affect the aesthetics of the building. Metals are almost entirely used. Attention must be paid to the corrosive potential between dissimilar metals.

DOVETAIL

THREE-WAY SAWTOOTH

CORRUGATED OR CRIMPED

TEXTURED

RIBBED

PLAIN

TYPICAL PROFILES OF THROUGH WALL FLASHING (PROPORTIONS EXAGGERATED)

NOTES

1. Select flashing that is flexible for molding to flashing supports and can withstand expected thermal, wind, and structural movement. Provide expansion joints in place of flashing as required by conditions.
2. Consult manufacturer's literature for choice of flashing materials and details.
3. Avoid sharp bends in bituminous base flashings. Use cant strips with 45° maximum bend.
4. Provision for differential movement between roof deck and wall is recommended.
5. Ribbed or embossed through wall flashing is not recommended for earthquake areas.
6. Base flashing should extend 8 to 12 in. above highest anticipated waterline. Metal counterflashings should lap base flashing at least 4 in. minimum. Lap all vertical joints.
7. At cavity walls with more than 3/4" space between wythes, use flashing of type that provides mechanical bond.

TYPICAL THROUGH WALL FLASHING AT WALL SECTION

SNAP-IN FLASHING WITH WIND PREVENTION CLIP

CORNICE FLASHING WITH METAL ROOF

CORNICE FLASHING WITH CAP FLASHING

CORNICE LEDGE CAP FLASHING AND RECEIVER

CORNICE FLASHING

Michael Scott Rudden; The Stephens Associates P.C.—Architects; Albany, New York

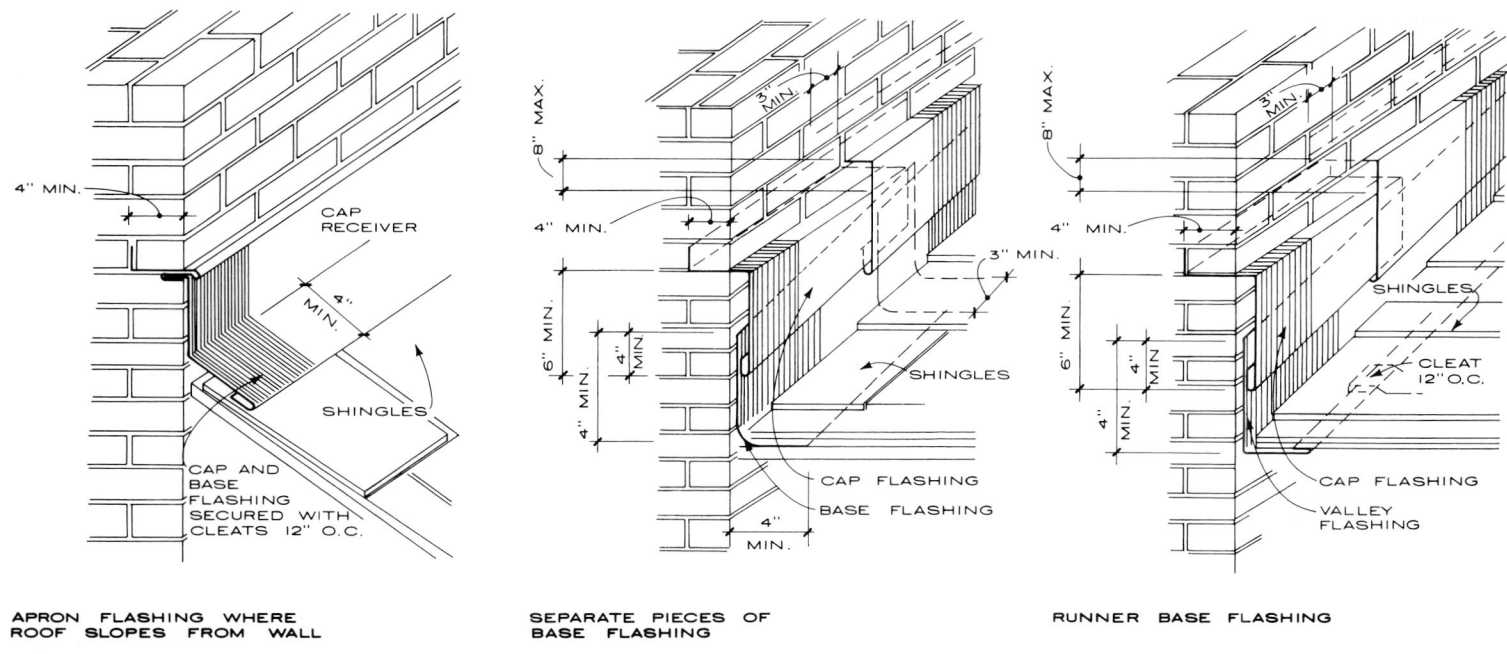

APRON FLASHING WHERE
ROOF SLOPES FROM WALL

SEPARATE PIECES OF
BASE FLASHING

RUNNER BASE FLASHING

PITCHED ROOF WITH WALL FLASHING

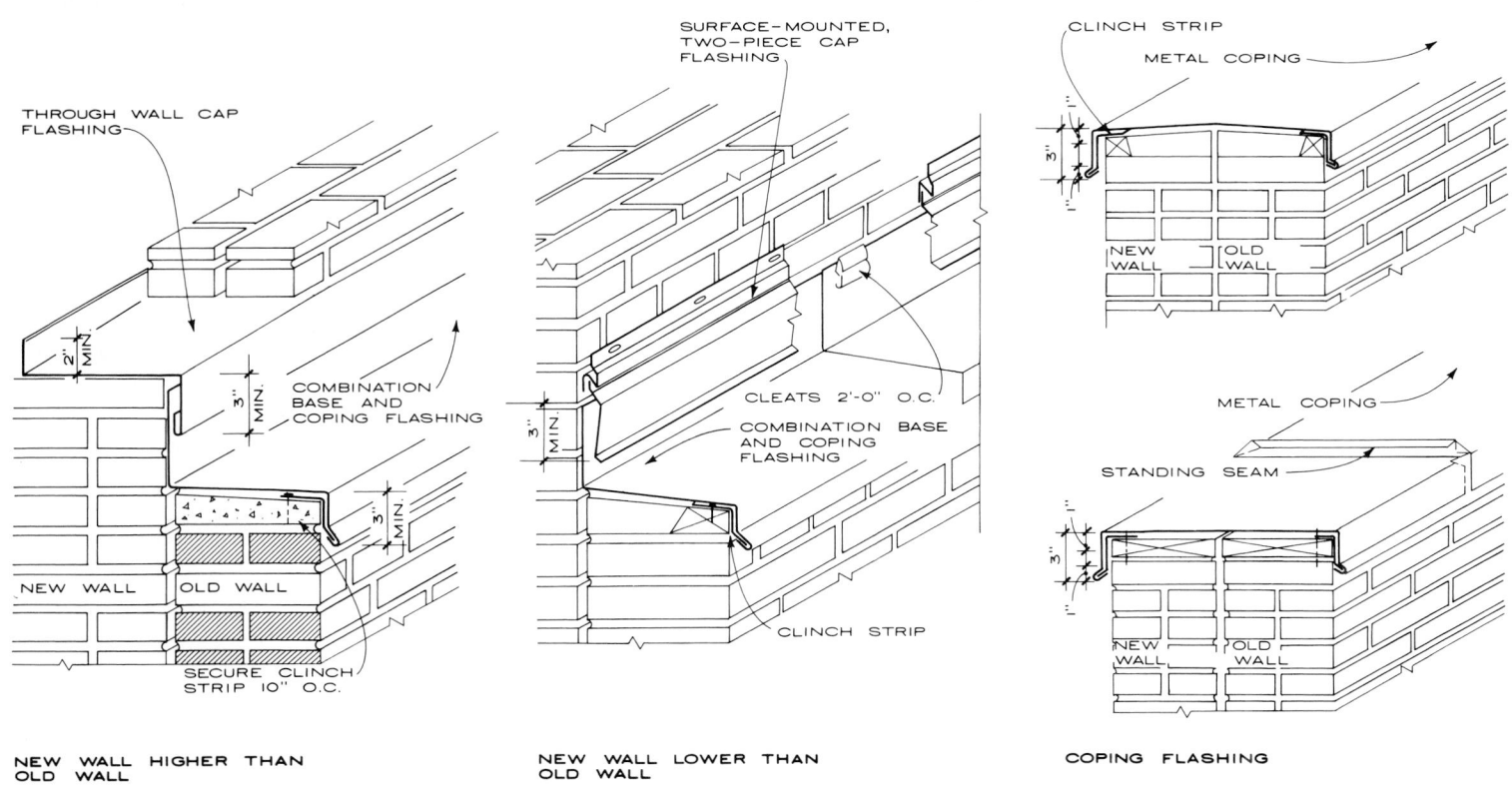

NEW WALL HIGHER THAN
OLD WALL

NEW WALL LOWER THAN
OLD WALL

COPING FLASHING

NEW WALL TO OLD WALL FLASHING

NOTE
Through wall flashing not recommended in earthquake
areas.

Michael Scott Rudden; The Stephens Associates P.C.—Architects; Albany, New York

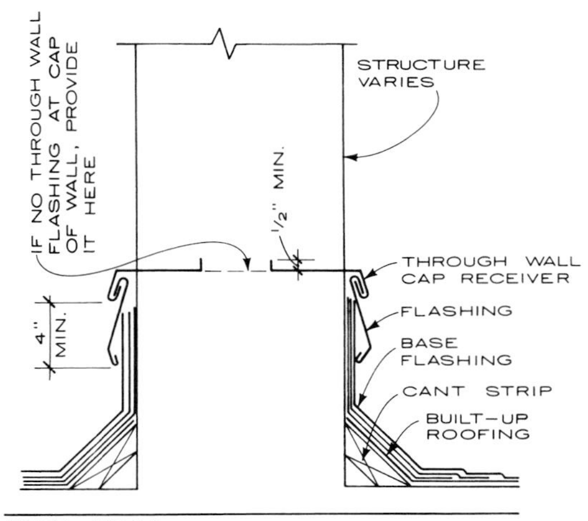

FIRE WALL

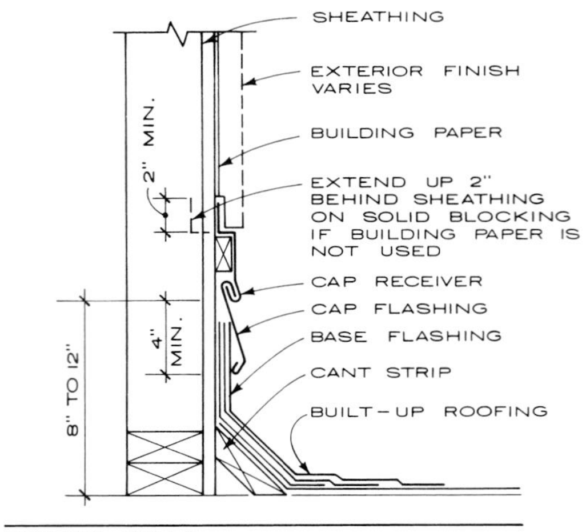

IF NO THROUGH WALL FLASHING AT CAP OF WALL, PROVIDE IT HERE

STRUCTURE VARIES

½" MIN.

4" MIN.

THROUGH WALL CAP RECEIVER

FLASHING

BASE FLASHING

CANT STRIP

BUILT-UP ROOFING

FRAME WALL

SHEATHING

EXTERIOR FINISH VARIES

BUILDING PAPER

EXTEND UP 2" BEHIND SHEATHING ON SOLID BLOCKING IF BUILDING PAPER IS NOT USED

CAP RECEIVER

CAP FLASHING

BASE FLASHING

CANT STRIP

BUILT-UP ROOFING

2" MIN.

8" TO 12"

4" MIN.

MASONRY WALL

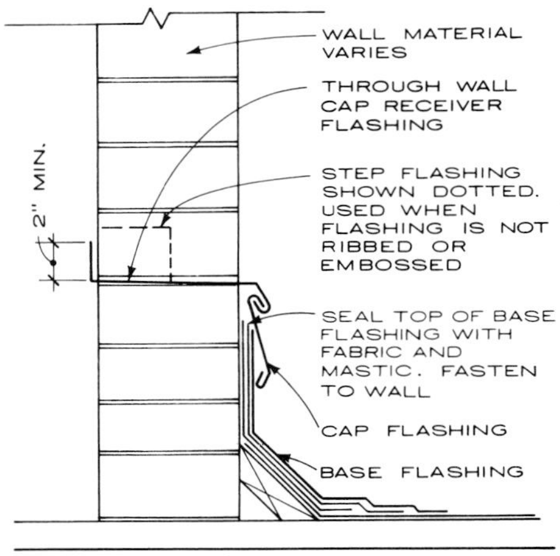

WALL MATERIAL VARIES

THROUGH WALL CAP RECEIVER FLASHING

STEP FLASHING SHOWN DOTTED. USED WHEN FLASHING IS NOT RIBBED OR EMBOSSED

SEAL TOP OF BASE FLASHING WITH FABRIC AND MASTIC. FASTEN TO WALL

CAP FLASHING

BASE FLASHING

2" MIN.

CAST IN PLACE CONC. WALL

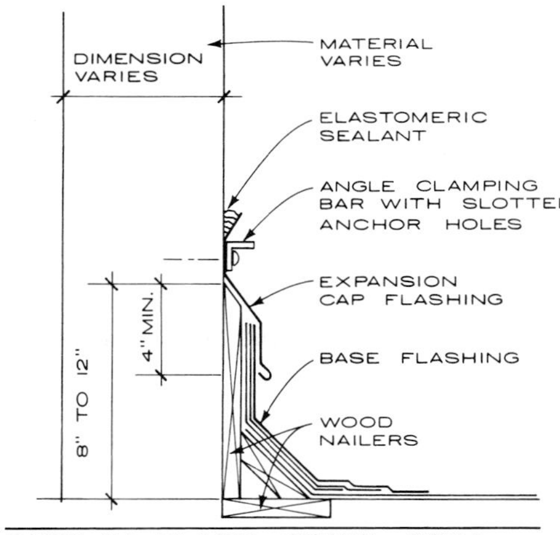

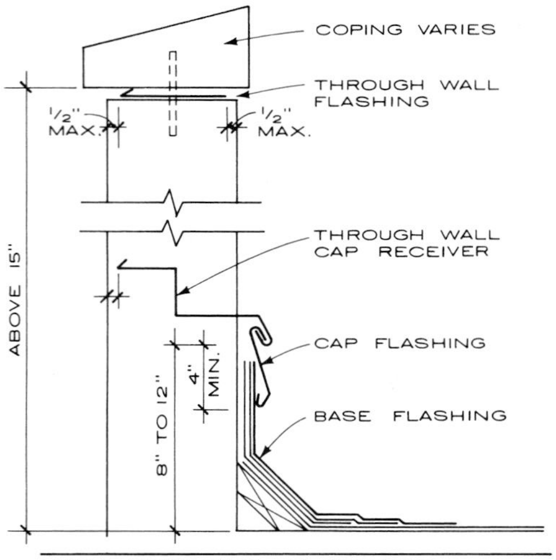

DIMENSION VARIES

MATERIAL VARIES

ELASTOMERIC SEALANT

ANGLE CLAMPING BAR WITH SLOTTED ANCHOR HOLES

EXPANSION CAP FLASHING

BASE FLASHING

WOOD NAILERS

8" TO 12"

4" MIN.

HIGH PARAPET FLASHING

COPING VARIES

THROUGH WALL FLASHING

THROUGH WALL CAP RECEIVER

CAP FLASHING

BASE FLASHING

½" MAX.   ½" MAX.

ABOVE 15"

8" TO 12"   4" MIN.

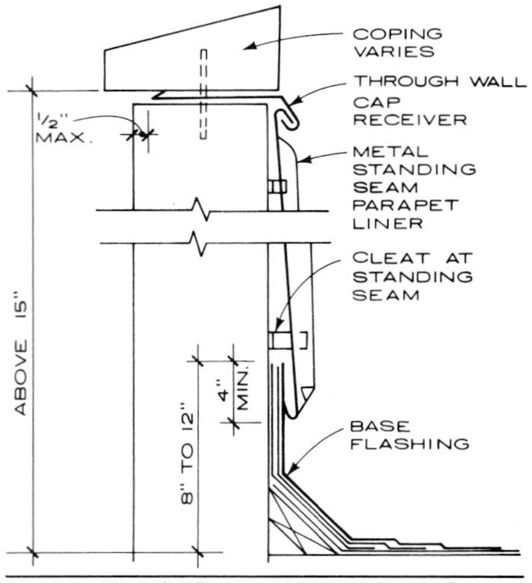

HIGH PARAPET WITH LINING

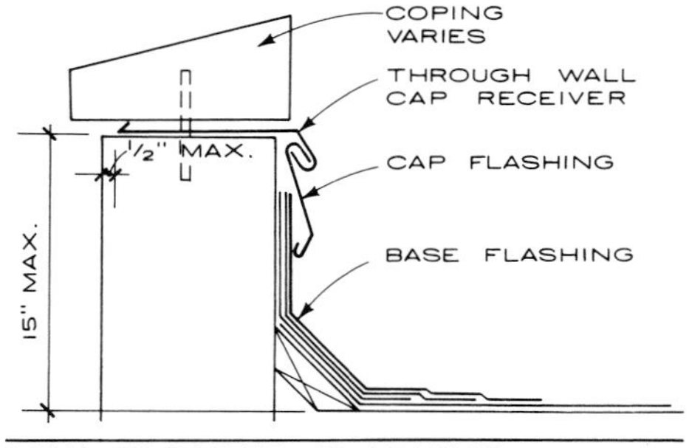

COPING VARIES

THROUGH WALL CAP RECEIVER

METAL STANDING SEAM PARAPET LINER

CLEAT AT STANDING SEAM

BASE FLASHING

½" MAX.

ABOVE 15"

8" TO 12"   4" MIN.

LOW PARAPET FLASHING

COPING VARIES

THROUGH WALL CAP RECEIVER

CAP FLASHING

BASE FLASHING

½" MAX.

15" MAX.

GENERAL NOTES

1. Select flashing that is flexible for molding to flashing supports and that can withstand expected thermal, wind, and structural movement. Provide expansion joints in place of flashing as required by conditions.
2. Consult manufacturer's literature for choice of flashing materials and details.
3. Avoid sharp bends in bituminous base flashings. Use cant strips with 45° maximum bend.
4. Provision for differential movement between roof deck and wall is recommended.
5. A ribbed or embossed pattern should be used for all through wall flashing. Through wall flashing is not recommended for earthquake areas.
6. Base flashing should extend 8 to 12 in. above highest anticipated waterline. Metal counterflashing should lap base flashing by at least 4 in. Lap all vertical joints.

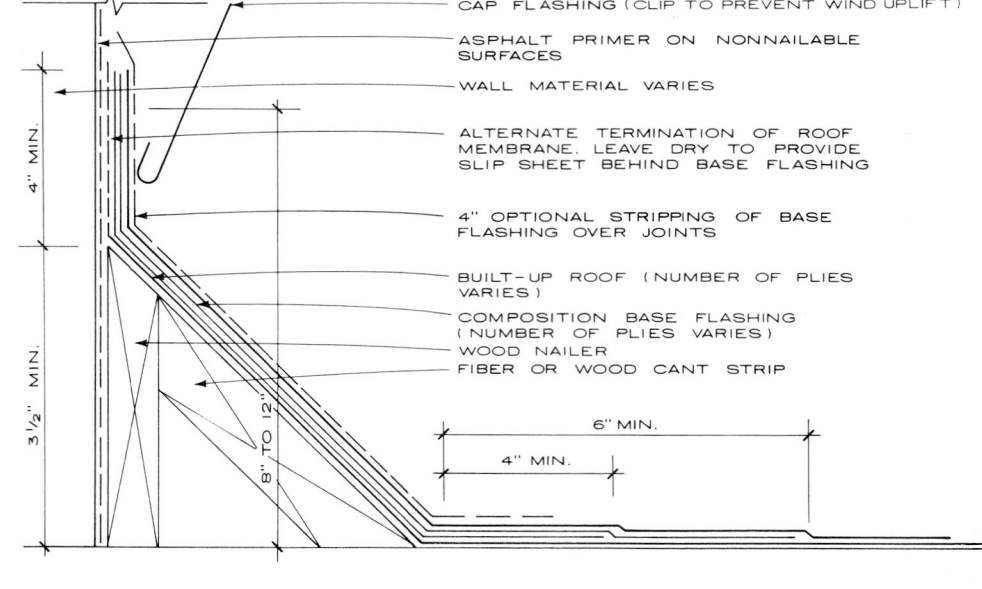

CAP FLASHING (CLIP TO PREVENT WIND UPLIFT)

ASPHALT PRIMER ON NONNAILABLE SURFACES

WALL MATERIAL VARIES

ALTERNATE TERMINATION OF ROOF MEMBRANE. LEAVE DRY TO PROVIDE SLIP SHEET BEHIND BASE FLASHING

4" OPTIONAL STRIPPING OF BASE FLASHING OVER JOINTS

BUILT-UP ROOF (NUMBER OF PLIES VARIES)

COMPOSITION BASE FLASHING (NUMBER OF PLIES VARIES)

WOOD NAILER

FIBER OR WOOD CANT STRIP

4" MIN.

3½" MIN.

8" TO 12"

6" MIN.

4" MIN.

TYPICAL BASE FLASHING

Michael Scott Rudden; The Stephens Associates P.C.—Architects; Albany, New York

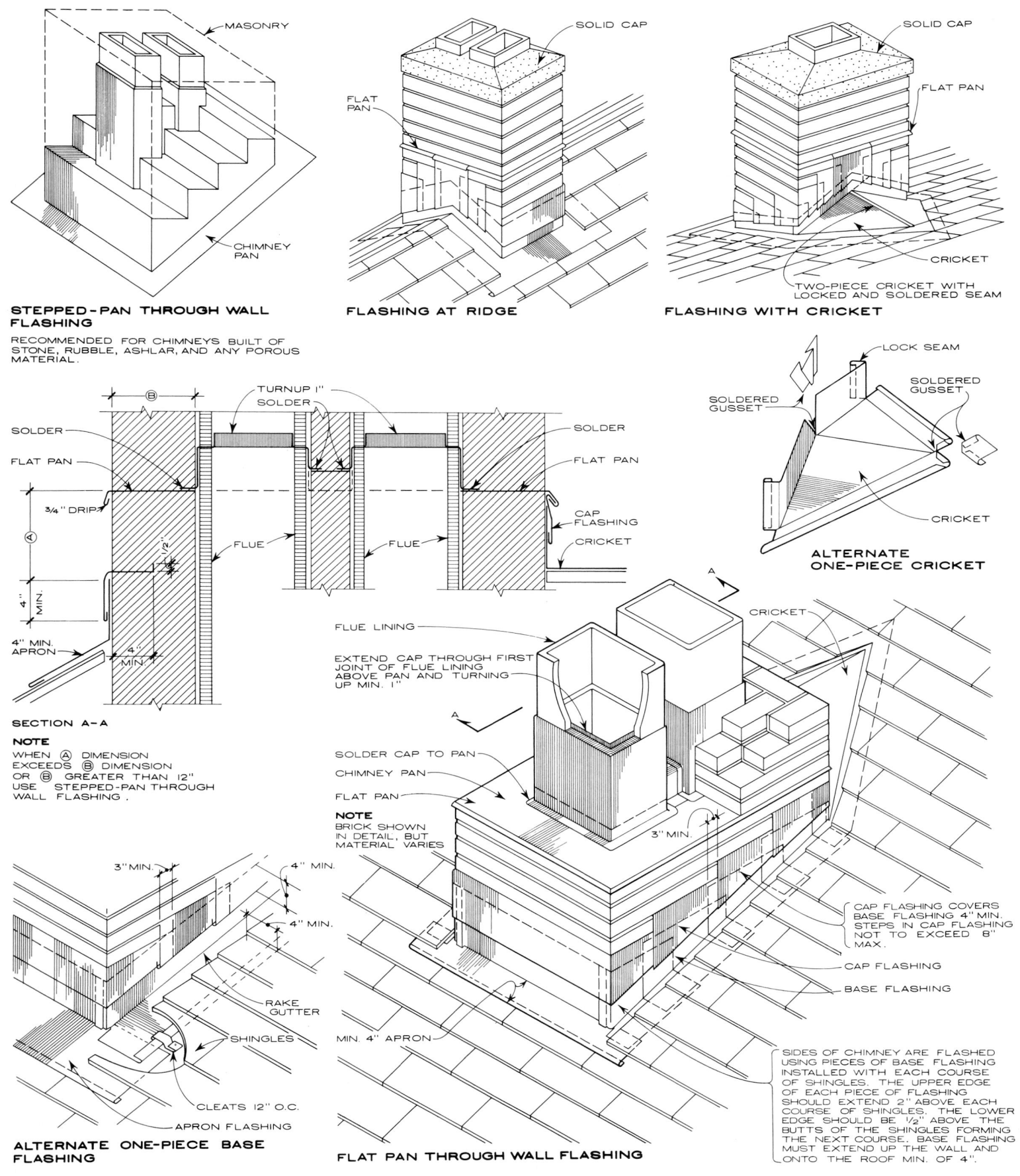

STEPPED-PAN THROUGH WALL FLASHING

RECOMMENDED FOR CHIMNEYS BUILT OF STONE, RUBBLE, ASHLAR, AND ANY POROUS MATERIAL.

MASONRY

CHIMNEY PAN

FLASHING AT RIDGE

SOLID CAP

FLAT PAN

FLASHING WITH CRICKET

SOLID CAP

FLAT PAN

CRICKET

TWO-PIECE CRICKET WITH LOCKED AND SOLDERED SEAM

TURNUP 1"
SOLDER
SOLDER
FLAT PAN
SOLDER
FLAT PAN
3/4" DRIP
CAP FLASHING
FLUE
FLUE
CRICKET
4" MIN. APRON
4" MIN.

SECTION A-A

NOTE
WHEN Ⓐ DIMENSION EXCEEDS Ⓑ DIMENSION OR Ⓑ GREATER THAN 12" USE STEPPED-PAN THROUGH WALL FLASHING.

LOCK SEAM
SOLDERED GUSSET
SOLDERED GUSSET
CRICKET

ALTERNATE ONE-PIECE CRICKET

FLUE LINING
EXTEND CAP THROUGH FIRST JOINT OF FLUE LINING ABOVE PAN AND TURNING UP MIN. 1"
SOLDER CAP TO PAN
CHIMNEY PAN
FLAT PAN

NOTE
BRICK SHOWN IN DETAIL, BUT MATERIAL VARIES

CRICKET
3" MIN.
CAP FLASHING COVERS BASE FLASHING 4" MIN. STEPS IN CAP FLASHING NOT TO EXCEED 8" MAX.
CAP FLASHING
BASE FLASHING

3" MIN.
4" MIN.
4" MIN.
RAKE GUTTER
SHINGLES
CLEATS 12" O.C.
APRON FLASHING

ALTERNATE ONE-PIECE BASE FLASHING

MIN. 4" APRON

FLAT PAN THROUGH WALL FLASHING

SIDES OF CHIMNEY ARE FLASHED USING PIECES OF BASE FLASHING INSTALLED WITH EACH COURSE OF SHINGLES. THE UPPER EDGE OF EACH PIECE OF FLASHING SHOULD EXTEND 2" ABOVE EACH COURSE OF SHINGLES. THE LOWER EDGE SHOULD BE 1/2" ABOVE THE BUTTS OF THE SHINGLES FORMING THE NEXT COURSE. BASE FLASHING MUST EXTEND UP THE WALL AND ONTO THE ROOF MIN. OF 4".

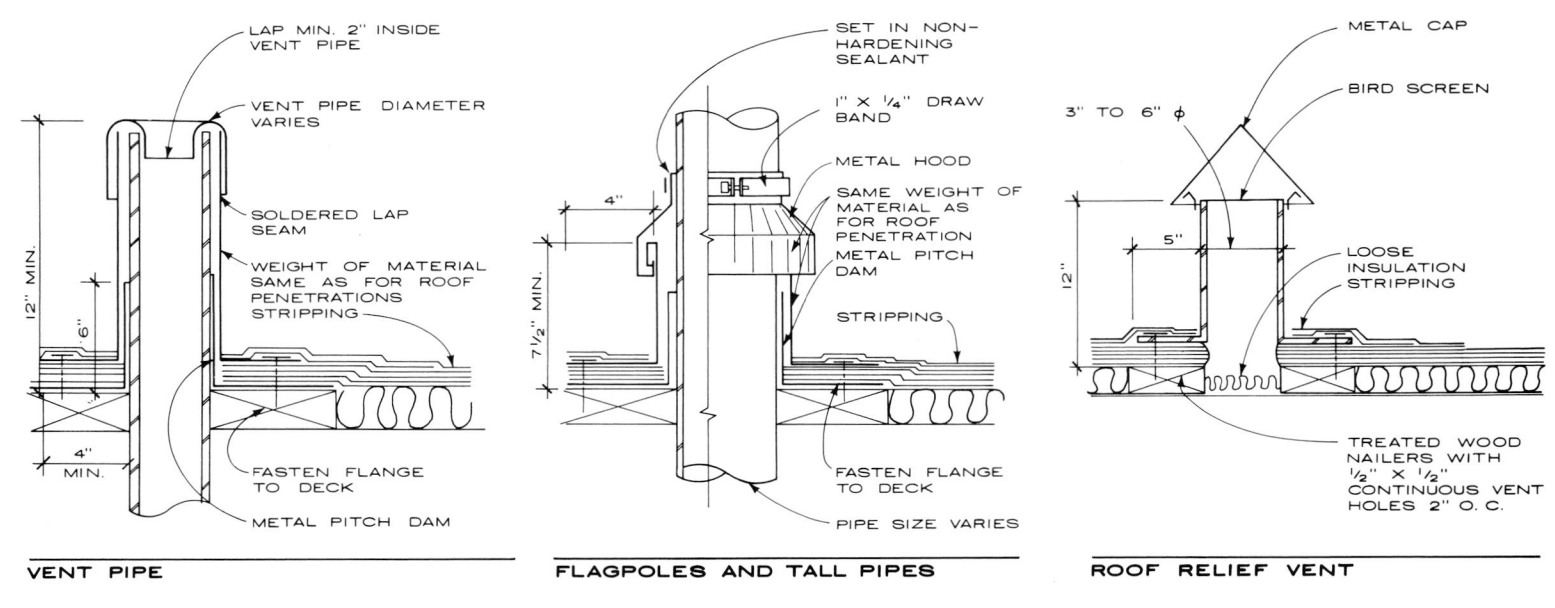

VENT PIPE

FLAGPOLES AND TALL PIPES

ROOF RELIEF VENT

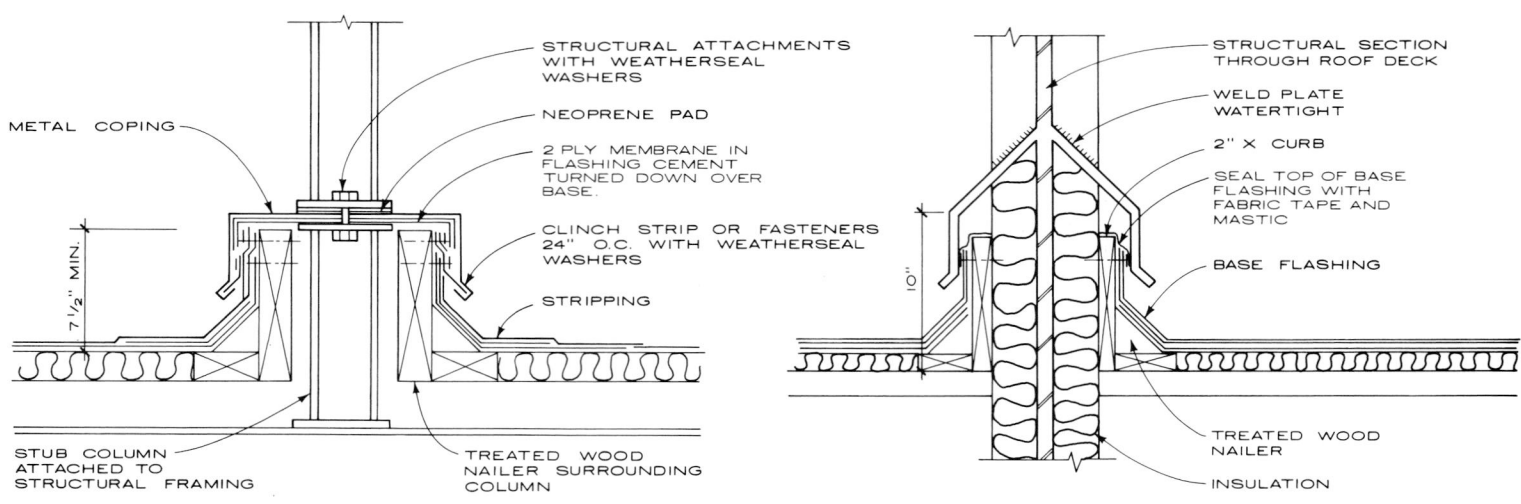

FUTURE COLUMNS, SIGN SUPPORTS, AND STEEL ANGLES

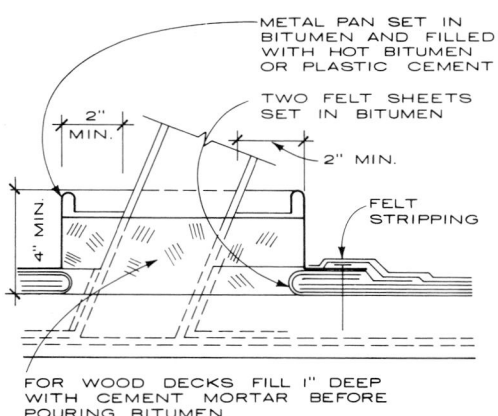

NOTE

Whenever possible avoid the use of pitch pockets in favor of curbs with base and cap flashing around the penetrating member.

PITCH POCKET

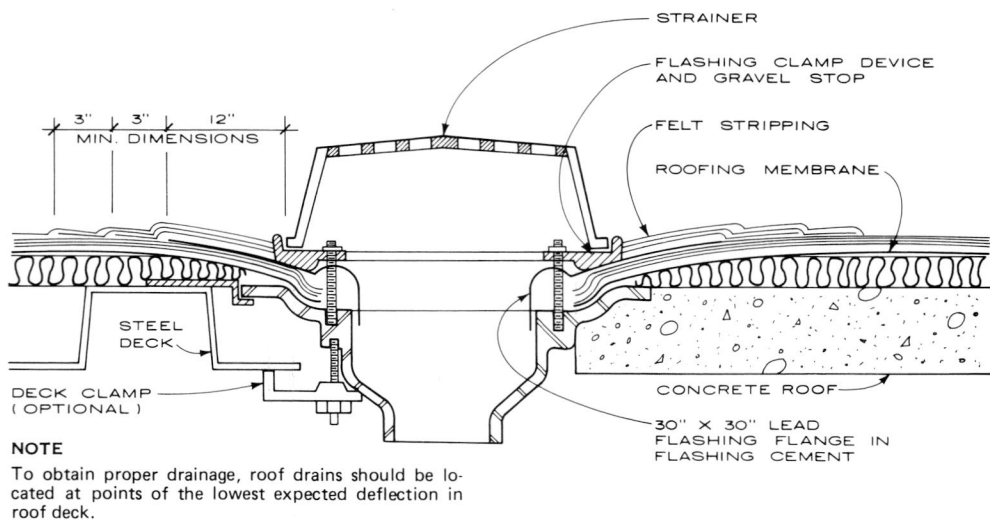

NOTE

To obtain proper drainage, roof drains should be located at points of the lowest expected deflection in roof deck.

ROOF DRAIN

Michael Scott Rudden; The Stephens Associates P.C.—Architects; Albany, New York

7 **FLASHING**

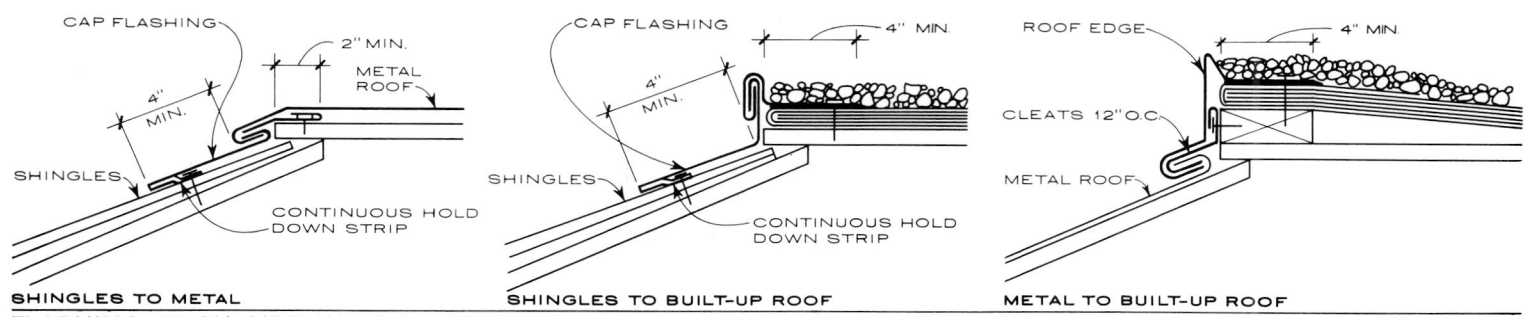

FLASHING AT CHANGE IN ROOF MATERIAL

SHINGLES TO METAL

SHINGLES TO BUILT-UP ROOF

METAL TO BUILT-UP ROOF

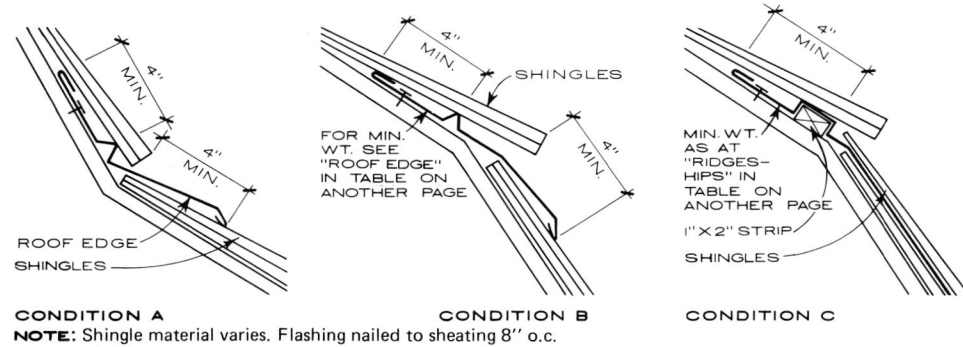

CONDITION A

CONDITION B

CONDITION C

NOTE: Shingle material varies. Flashing nailed to sheating 8" o.c.

FLASHING OF BREAK IN SLOPE OF SHINGLE ROOFS

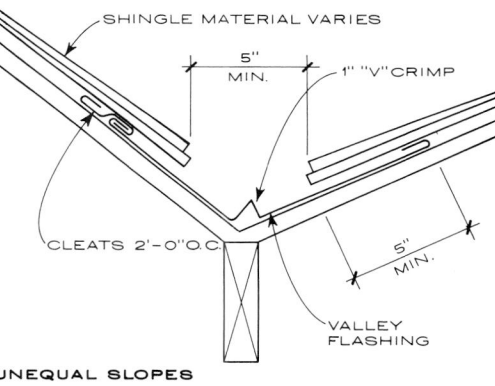

EQUAL SLOPES

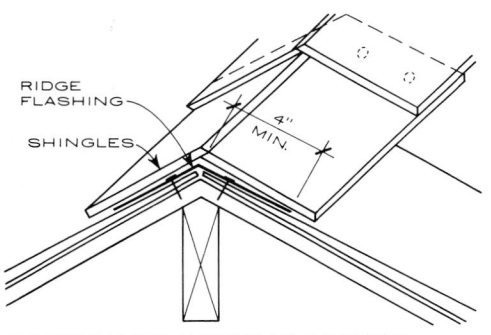

CONCEALED RIDGE FLASHING
NOTE

Ridge flashing formed in 10' lengths and lapped 4". Flashing is nailed to sheathing after shingles are installed, then flashing is covered with ridge shingles.

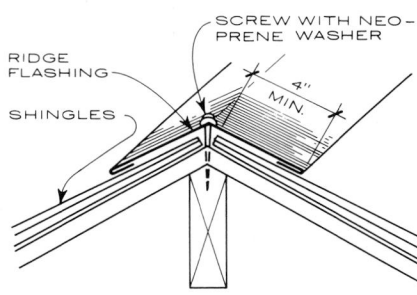

EXPOSED RIDGE FLASHING
NOTE

Ridge flashing formed in 10' lengths and lapped 4".

UNEQUAL SLOPES

OPEN VALLEY FLASHING

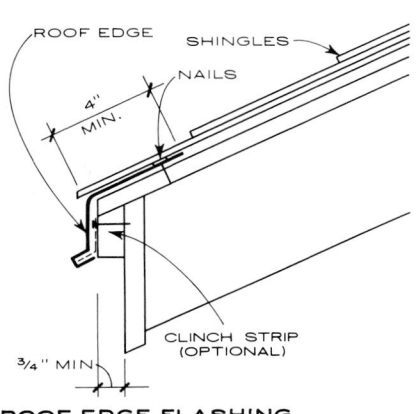

ROOF EDGE FLASHING

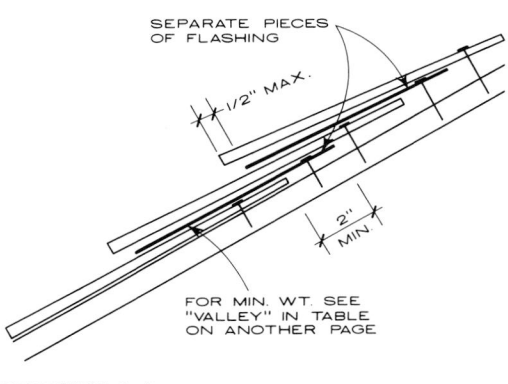

SECTION A-A
CONCEALED VALLEY FLASHING

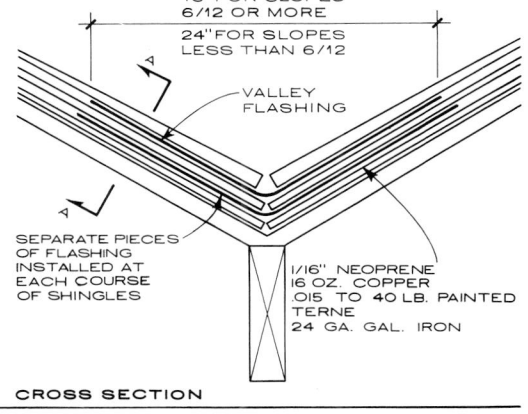

CROSS SECTION

Michael Scott Rudden; The Stephens Associates P.C.—Architects; Albany, New York

GENERAL

A water table is a ledge or slight projection of masonry, wood or other construction on the outside of a foundation wall, or just above. It protects the foundation from rain by throwing the water away from the wall. In the architectural hierarchy of a building form, the water table forms the transitional line between the base and middle sections. A water table is referred to as an offset when the base plane projects out from the upper plane.

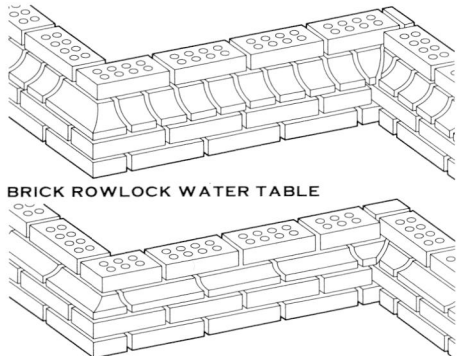

BRICK ROWLOCK WATER TABLE

BRICK STRETCHER WATER TABLE

BRICK VENEER

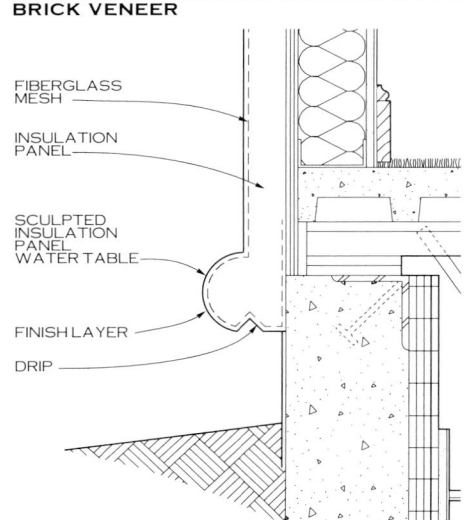

- FIBERGLASS MESH
- INSULATION PANEL
- SCULPTED INSULATION PANEL WATER TABLE
- FINISH LAYER
- DRIP

EXTERIOR INSULATION AND FINISH SYSTEM

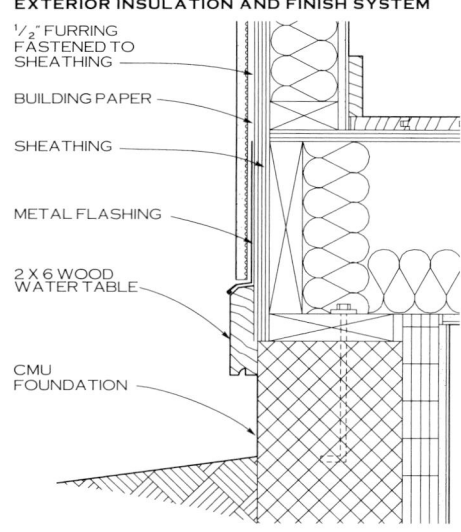

- 1/2" FURRING FASTENED TO SHEATHING
- BUILDING PAPER
- SHEATHING
- METAL FLASHING
- 2 X 6 WOOD WATER TABLE
- CMU FOUNDATION

STUCCO

TROWELED EXTERIOR VENEER

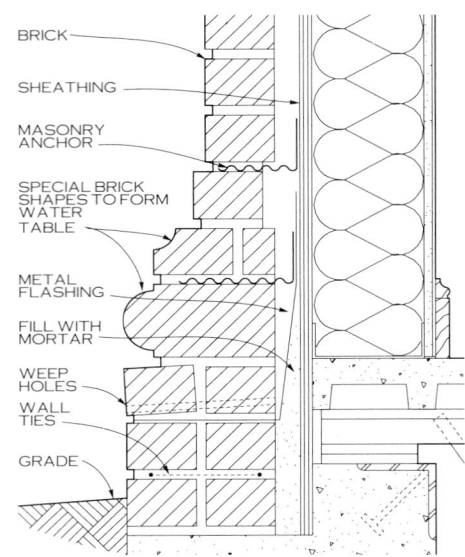

- BRICK
- SHEATHING
- MASONRY ANCHOR
- SPECIAL BRICK SHAPES TO FORM WATER TABLE
- METAL FLASHING
- FILL WITH MORTAR
- WEEP HOLES
- WALL TIES
- GRADE

BRICK WATER TABLE

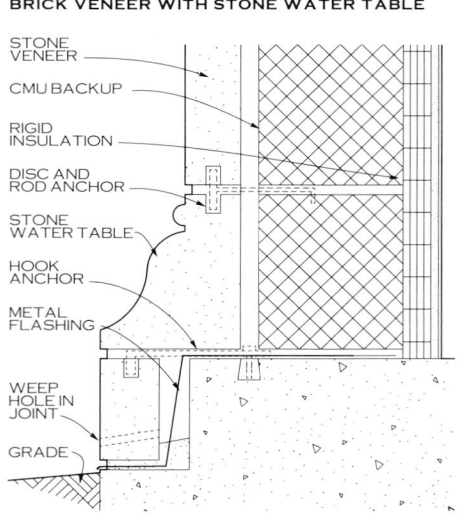

- BRICK
- METAL FLASHING
- STEEL SHELF ANGLE WITH EXPANSION BOLTS 2'- 0" O.C.
- STONE WATER TABLE
- DISC AND ROD ANCHOR
- FLOOR JOIST
- CMU BACKUP
- STONE VENEER
- METAL FLASHING
- WEEP HOLES AT JOINTS

BRICK VENEER WITH STONE WATER TABLE

- STONE VENEER
- CMU BACKUP
- RIGID INSULATION
- DISC AND ROD ANCHOR
- STONE WATER TABLE
- HOOK ANCHOR
- METAL FLASHING
- WEEP HOLE IN JOINT
- GRADE

STONE VENEER WITH STONE WATER TABLE

MASONRY VENEER

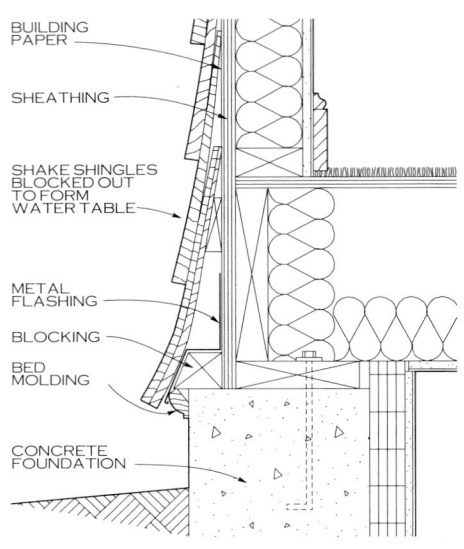

- BUILDING PAPER
- SHEATHING
- SHAKE SHINGLES BLOCKED OUT TO FORM WATER TABLE
- METAL FLASHING
- BLOCKING
- BED MOLDING
- CONCRETE FOUNDATION

BLOCKED-OUT SHAKE SHINGLES WITH PROTRUDED FOUNDATION

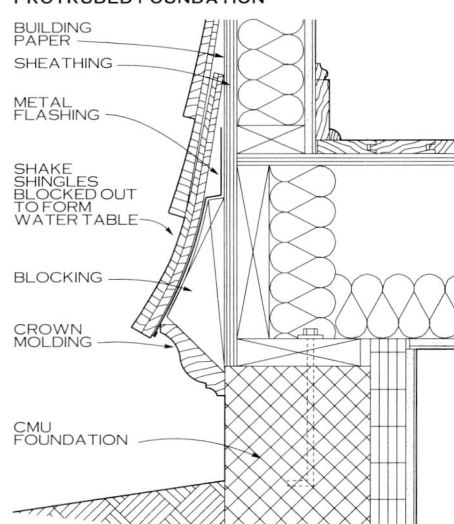

- BUILDING PAPER
- SHEATHING
- METAL FLASHING
- SHAKE SHINGLES BLOCKED OUT TO FORM WATER TABLE
- BLOCKING
- CROWN MOLDING
- CMU FOUNDATION

BLOCKED-OUT SHAKE SHINGLES

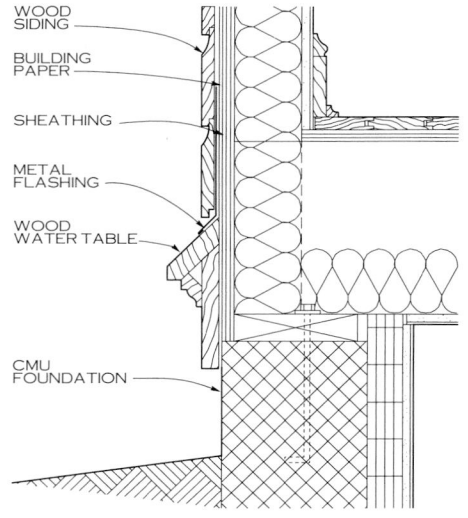

- WOOD SIDING
- BUILDING PAPER
- SHEATHING
- METAL FLASHING
- WOOD WATER TABLE
- CMU FOUNDATION

STRAIGHT SIDING FLUSH WITH FOUNDATION

WOOD SIDING

Richard J. Vitullo, AIA; Oak Leaf Studio; Crownsville, Maryland

7 **FLASHING**

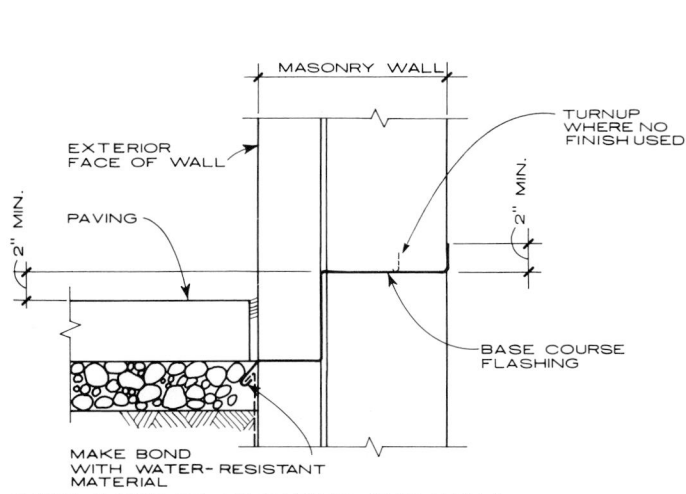

BASE COURSE AT PAVING AND WALL

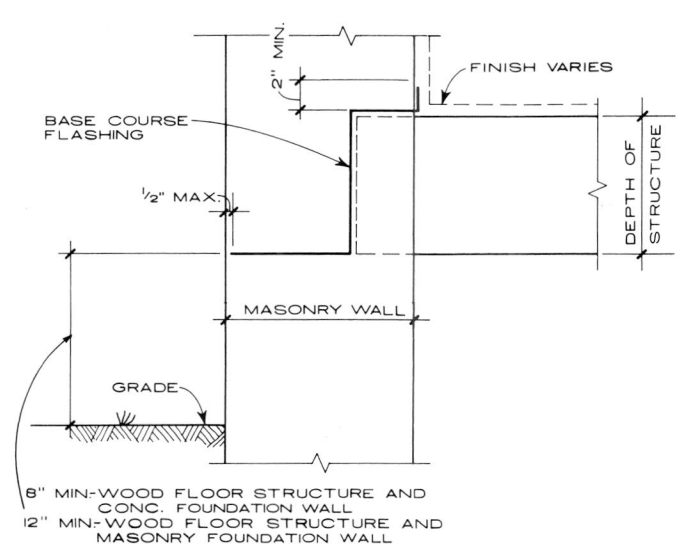

BASE COURSE AT FLOOR CONSTRUCTION

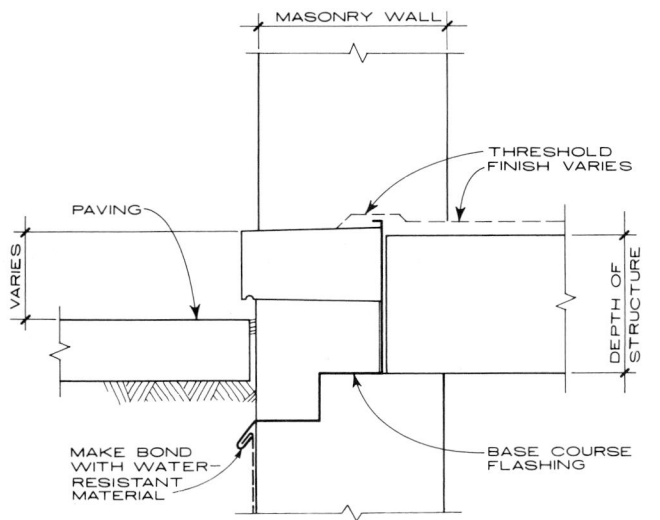

BASE COURSE AT SILL OF MASONRY CONSTRUCTION

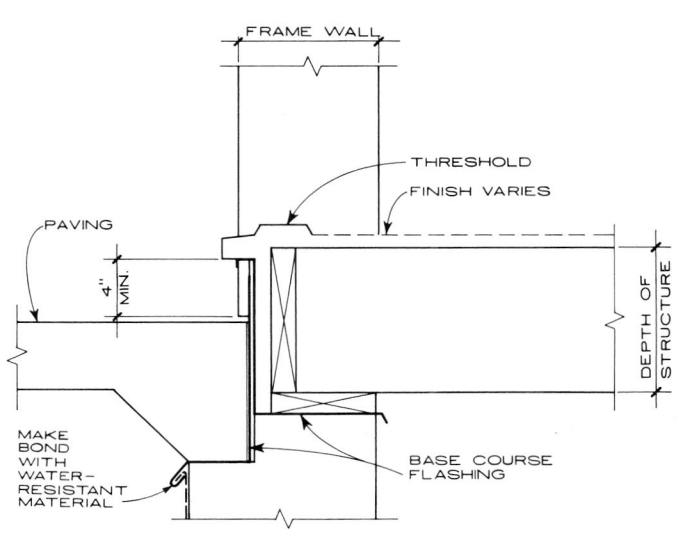

BASE COURSE AT SILL OF FRAME CONSTRUCTION

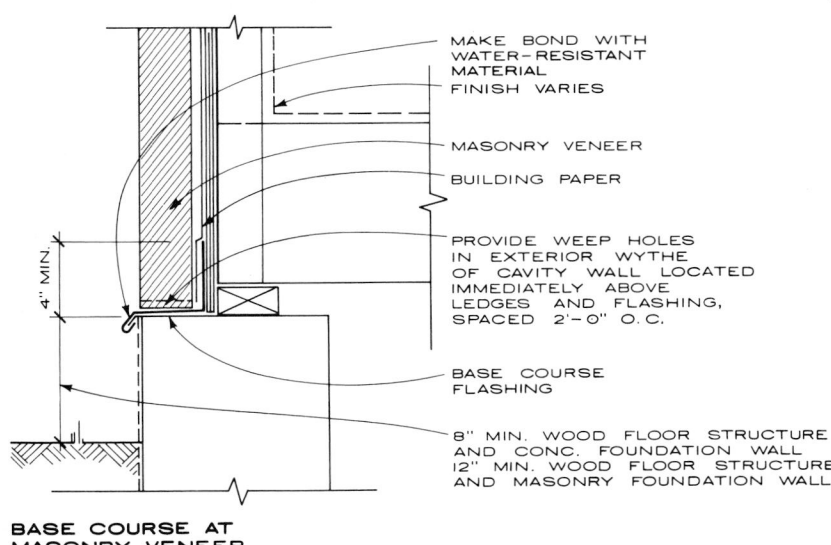

BASE COURSE AT MASONRY VENEER

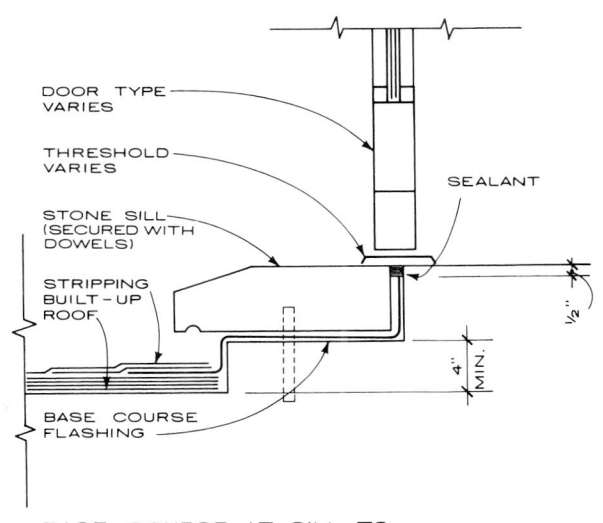

BASE COURSE AT SILL TO BUILT-UP ROOF

Michael Scott Rudden; The Stephens Associates P.C.—Architects; Albany, New York

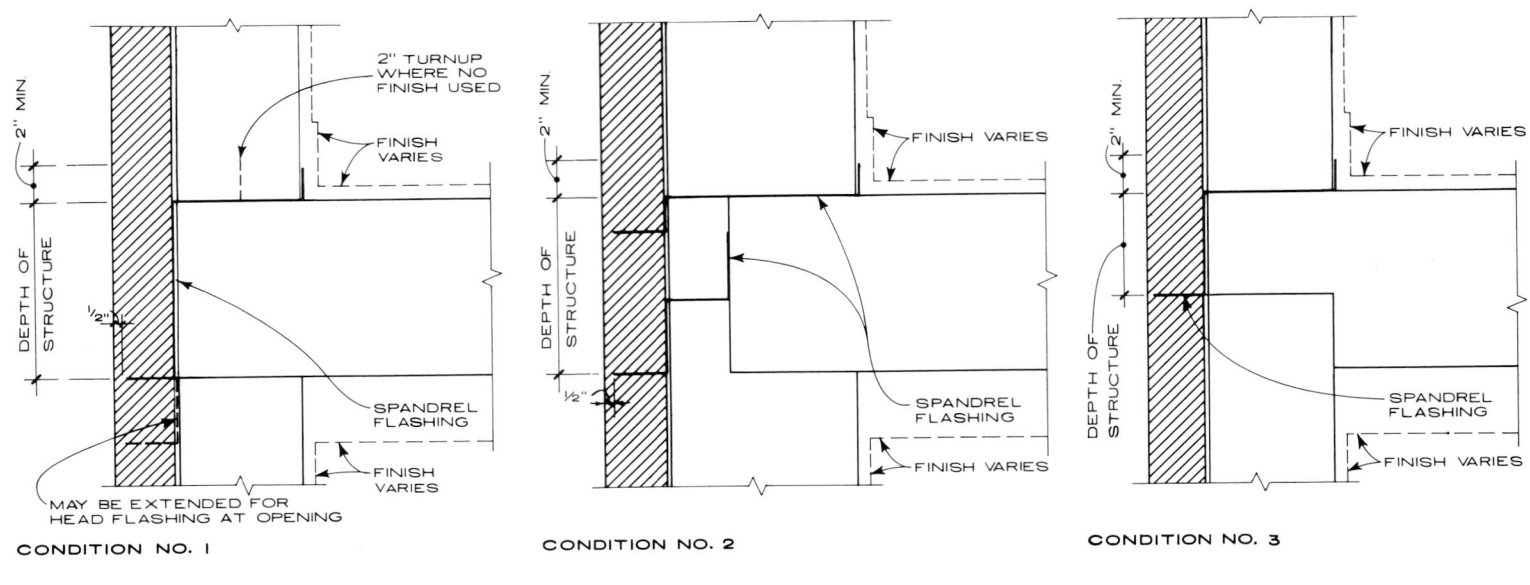

CONDITION NO. 1

2" MIN.

DEPTH OF STRUCTURE

1/2"

2" TURNUP WHERE NO FINISH USED

FINISH VARIES

SPANDREL FLASHING

FINISH VARIES

MAY BE EXTENDED FOR HEAD FLASHING AT OPENING

CONDITION NO. 2

2" MIN.

DEPTH OF STRUCTURE

1/2"

FINISH VARIES

SPANDREL FLASHING

FINISH VARIES

CONDITION NO. 3

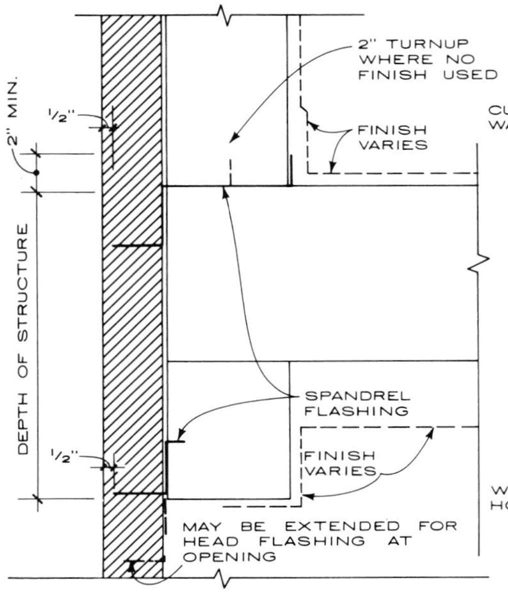

2" MIN.

DEPTH OF STRUCTURE

FINISH VARIES

SPANDREL FLASHING

FINISH VARIES

CONDITION NO. 4

2" MIN.

DEPTH OF STRUCTURE

1/2"

1/2"

2" TURNUP WHERE NO FINISH USED

FINISH VARIES

SPANDREL FLASHING

FINISH VARIES

MAY BE EXTENDED FOR HEAD FLASHING AT OPENING

CONDITION NO. 5

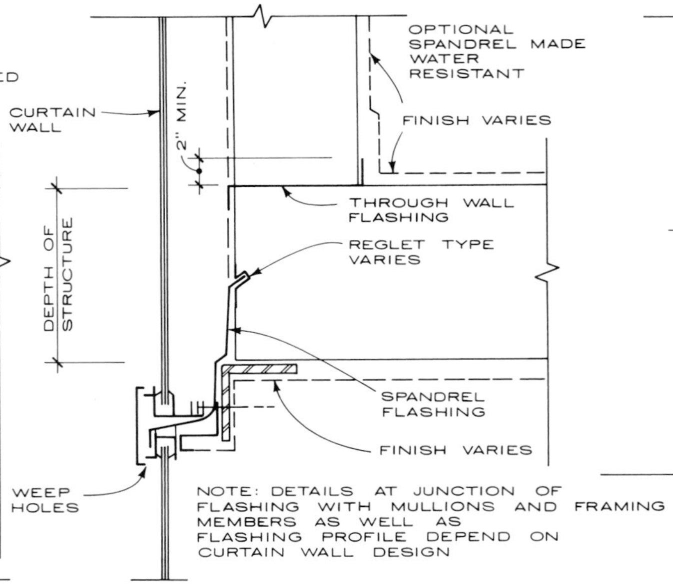

CURTAIN WALL

2" MIN.

DEPTH OF STRUCTURE

OPTIONAL SPANDREL MADE WATER RESISTANT

FINISH VARIES

THROUGH WALL FLASHING

REGLET TYPE VARIES

SPANDREL FLASHING

FINISH VARIES

WEEP HOLES

NOTE: DETAILS AT JUNCTION OF FLASHING WITH MULLIONS AND FRAMING MEMBERS AS WELL AS FLASHING PROFILE DEPEND ON CURTAIN WALL DESIGN

CONDITION NO. 6

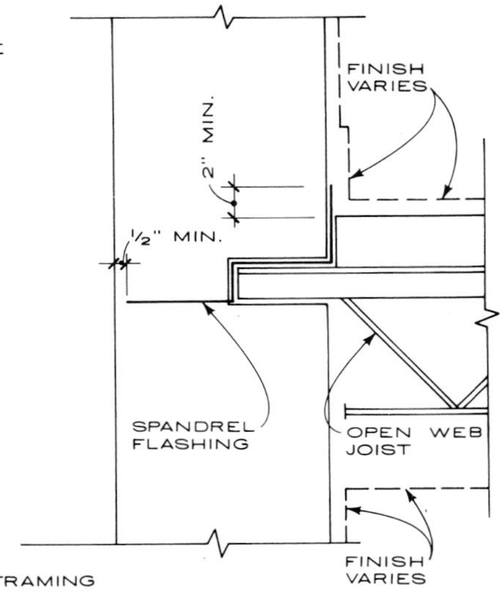

2" MIN.

1/2" MIN.

FINISH VARIES

SPANDREL FLASHING

OPEN WEB JOIST

FINISH VARIES

CONDITION NO. 7

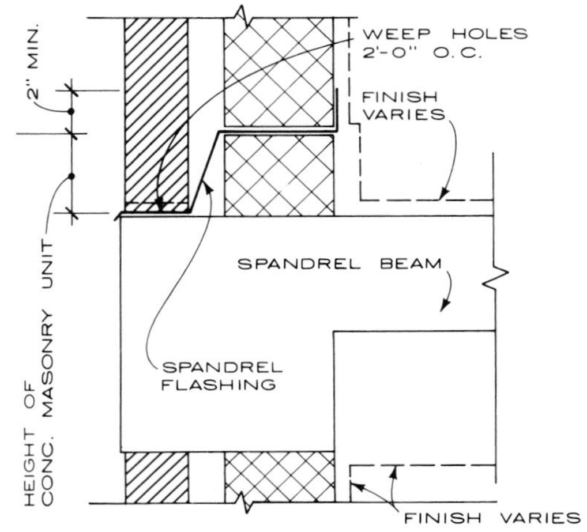

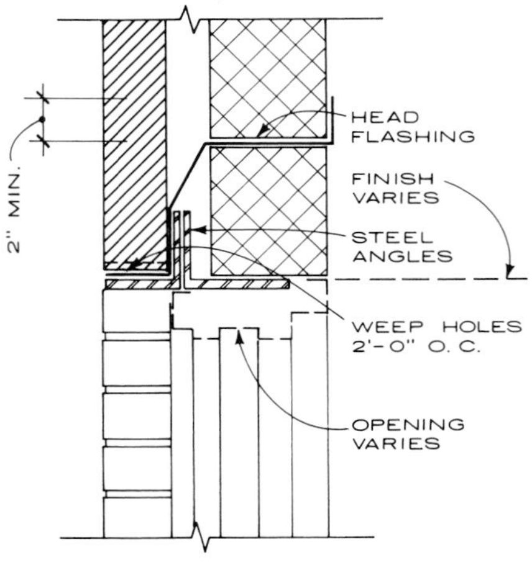

2" MIN.

HEIGHT OF CONC. MASONRY UNIT

WEEP HOLES 2'-0" O.C.

FINISH VARIES

SPANDREL BEAM

SPANDREL FLASHING

FINISH VARIES

HEAD FLASHING

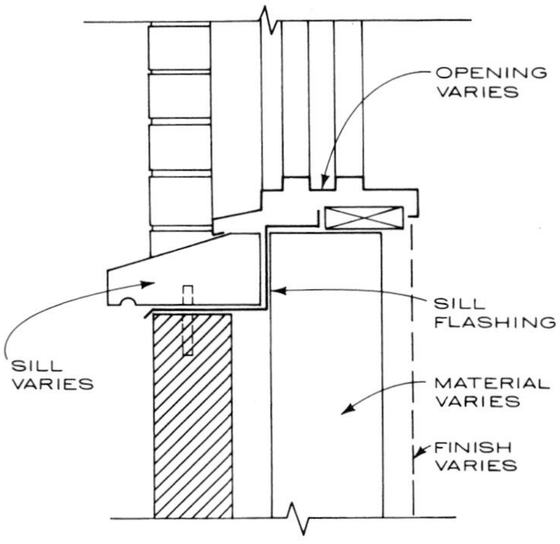

2" MIN.

HEAD FLASHING

FINISH VARIES

STEEL ANGLES

WEEP HOLES 2'-0" O.C.

OPENING VARIES

SILL FLASHING

OPENING VARIES

SILL FLASHING

SILL VARIES

MATERIAL VARIES

FINISH VARIES

Michael Scott Rudden; The Stephens Associates P.C.—Architects; Albany, New York

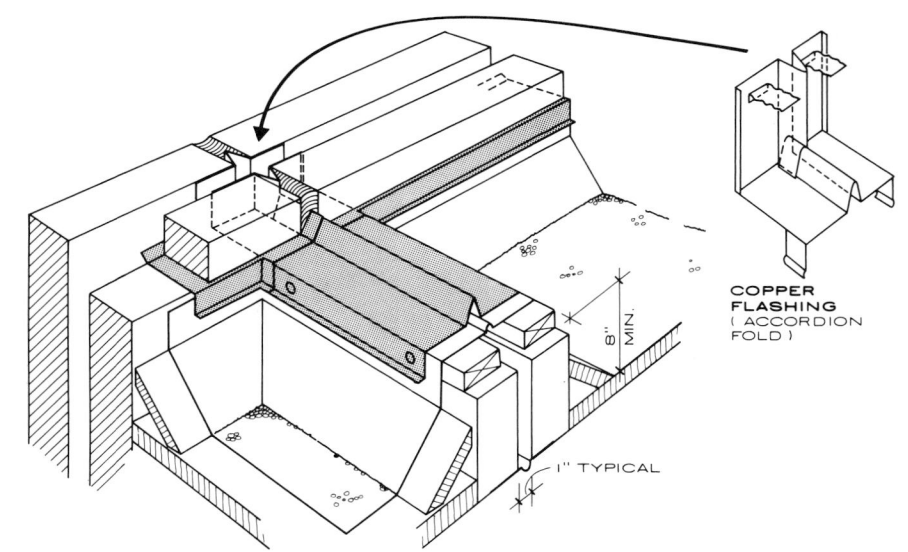
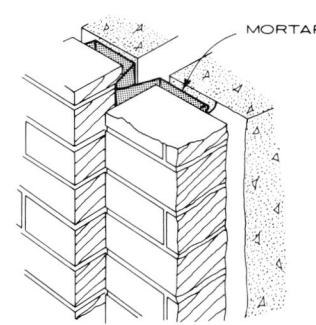

COPPER FLASHING (ACCORDION FOLD)

8" MIN

1" TYPICAL

EXPANSION JOINT AT INTERSECTION OF WALL AND PARAPET

MORTAR

WATERSTOPS SHOULD RUN CONTINUOUS FROM FOOTING TO TOP OF BUILDING. LAP JOINT 4" IN DIRECTION OF FLOW

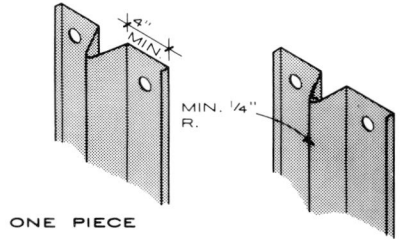

4" MIN

MIN. 1/4" R.

ONE PIECE

TWO PIECE

VERTICAL EXPANSION JOINT AT WALL

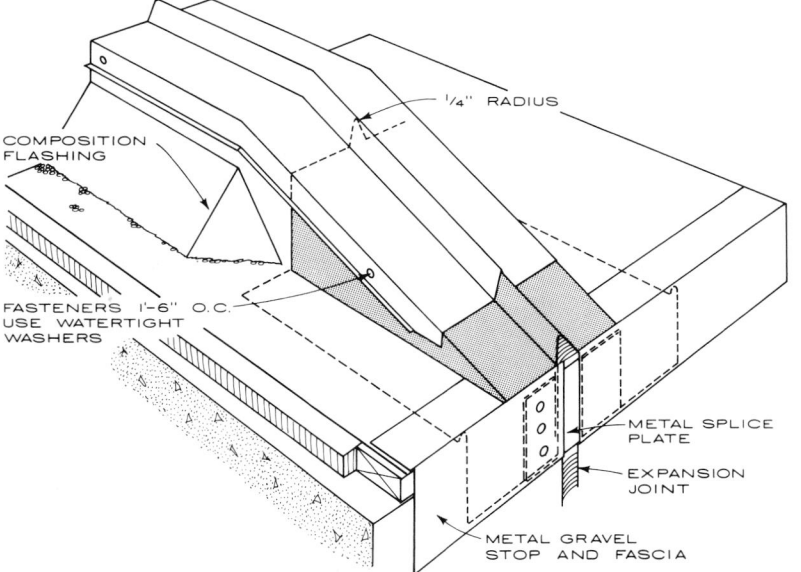

1/4" RADIUS

COMPOSITION FLASHING

FASTENERS 1'-6" O.C. USE WATERTIGHT WASHERS

METAL SPLICE PLATE

EXPANSION JOINT

METAL GRAVEL STOP AND FASCIA

EXPANSION JOINT TRANSITION AT EAVE

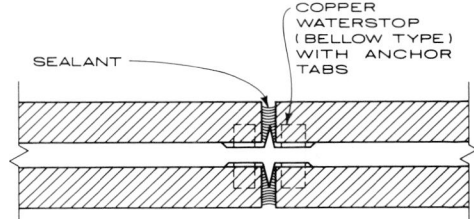

COPPER WATERSTOP (BELLOW TYPE) WITH ANCHOR TABS

SEALANT

PLAN SECTION AT PARAPET WALL

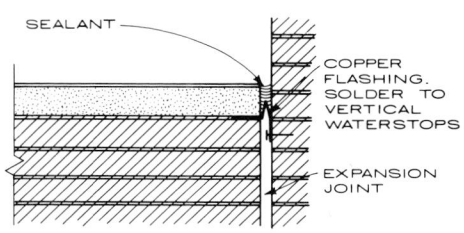

SEALANT

COPPER FLASHING. SOLDER TO VERTICAL WATERSTOPS

EXPANSION JOINT

VERTICAL SECTION AT PARAPET COPING

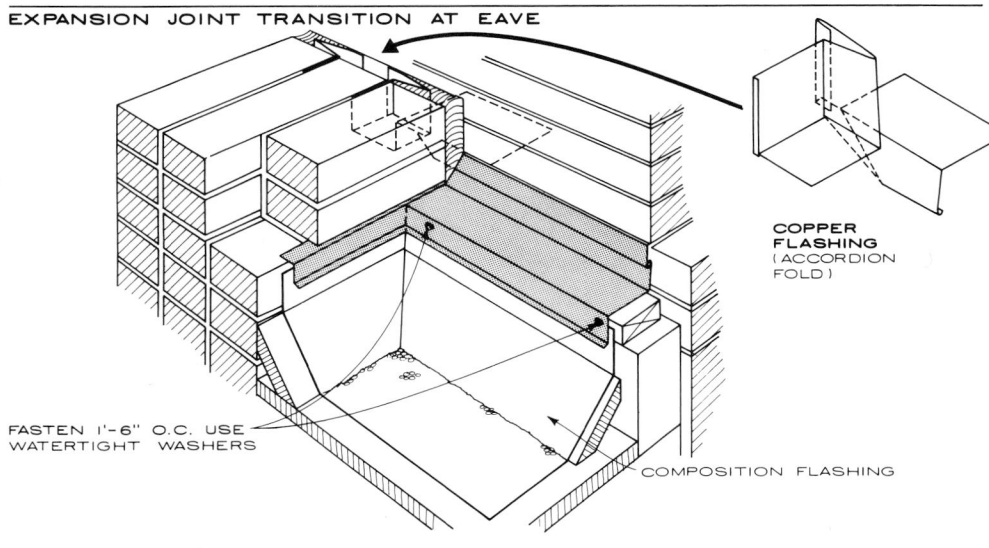

COPPER FLASHING (ACCORDION FOLD)

FASTEN 1'-6" O.C. USE WATERTIGHT WASHERS

COMPOSITION FLASHING

EXPANSION JOINT AT INTERSECTION OF WALL AND PARAPET

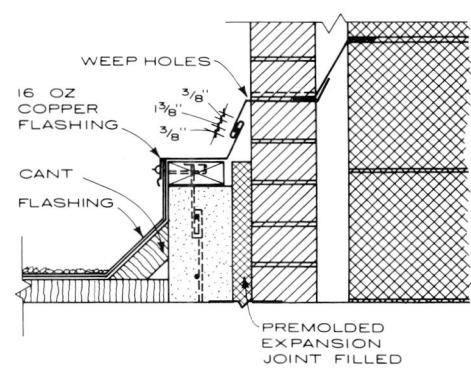

WEEP HOLES

16 OZ COPPER FLASHING

3/8" 1 3/8" 3/8"

CANT FLASHING

PREMOLDED EXPANSION JOINT FILLED

EXPANSION JOINT AT ROOF AND WALL

CTA Architects Engineers; Billings, Montana

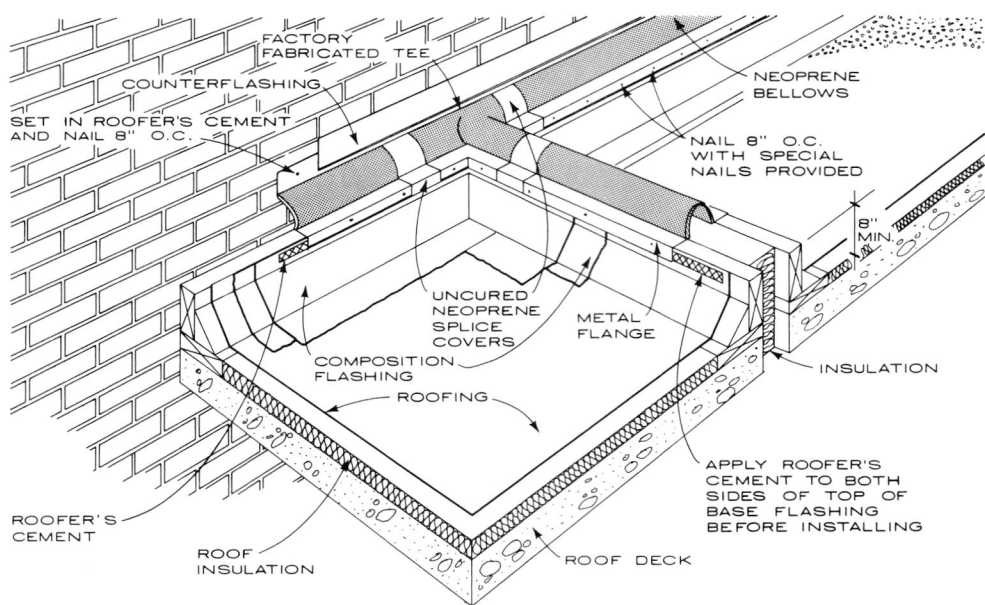

FACTORY FABRICATED TEE

COUNTERFLASHING

SET IN ROOFER'S CEMENT AND NAIL 8" O.C.

NEOPRENE BELLOWS

NAIL 8" O.C. WITH SPECIAL NAILS PROVIDED

8" MIN.

UNCURED NEOPRENE SPLICE COVERS

METAL FLANGE

COMPOSITION FLASHING

INSULATION

ROOFING

ROOFER'S CEMENT

APPLY ROOFER'S CEMENT TO BOTH SIDES OF TOP OF BASE FLASHING BEFORE INSTALLING

ROOF INSULATION

ROOF DECK

CURB FLANGE EXPANSION JOINT COVER AT WALL

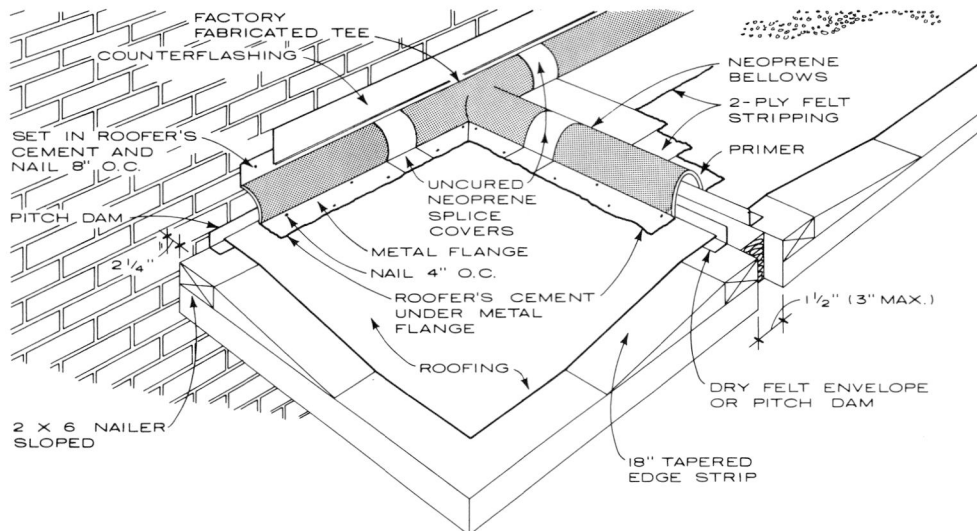

FACTORY FABRICATED TEE

COUNTERFLASHING

SET IN ROOFER'S CEMENT AND NAIL 8" O.C.

PITCH DAM

2 1/4"

NEOPRENE BELLOWS

2-PLY FELT STRIPPING

PRIMER

UNCURED NEOPRENE SPLICE COVERS

METAL FLANGE

NAIL 4" O.C.

ROOFER'S CEMENT UNDER METAL FLANGE

ROOFING

2 X 6 NAILER SLOPED

1 1/2" (3" MAX.)

DRY FELT ENVELOPE OR PITCH DAM

18" TAPERED EDGE STRIP

STRAIGHT FLANGE EXPANSION JOINT COVER AT WALL

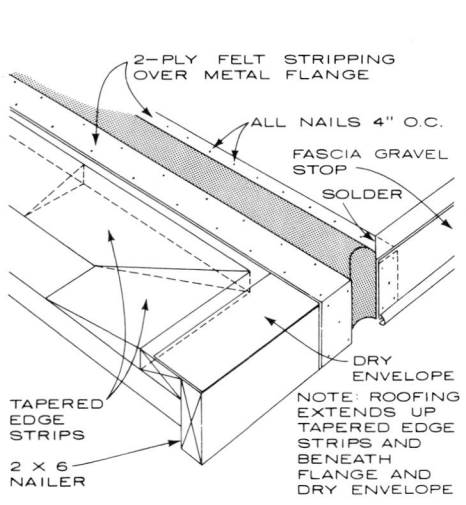

2-PLY FELT STRIPPING OVER METAL FLANGE

ALL NAILS 4" O.C.

FASCIA GRAVEL STOP

SOLDER

DRY ENVELOPE

TAPERED EDGE STRIPS

2 X 6 NAILER

NOTE: ROOFING EXTENDS UP TAPERED EDGE STRIPS AND BENEATH FLANGE AND DRY ENVELOPE

STRAIGHT FLANGE AT GRAVEL STOP

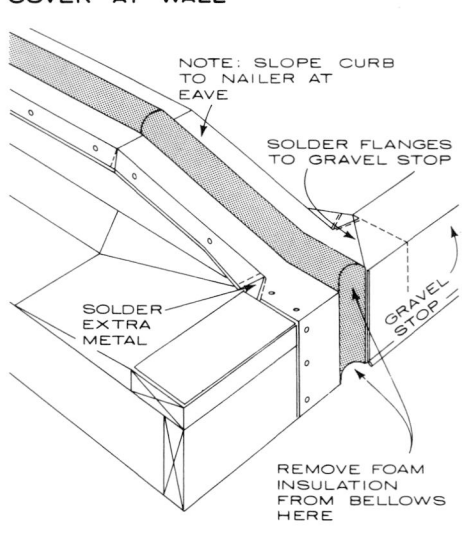

NOTE: SLOPE CURB TO NAILER AT EAVE

SOLDER FLANGES TO GRAVEL STOP

SOLDER EXTRA METAL

GRAVEL STOP

REMOVE FOAM INSULATION FROM BELLOWS HERE

CURB FLANGE AT GRAVEL STOP

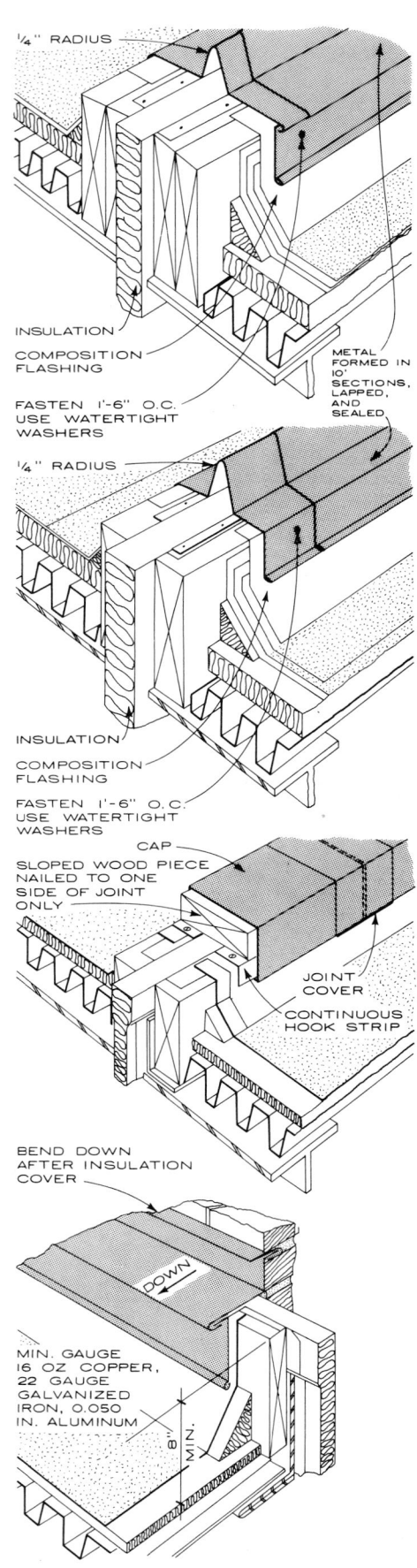

1/4" RADIUS

INSULATION

COMPOSITION FLASHING

FASTEN 1'-6" O.C. USE WATERTIGHT WASHERS

METAL FORMED IN 10' SECTIONS, LAPPED, AND SEALED

1/4" RADIUS

INSULATION

COMPOSITION FLASHING

FASTEN 1'-6" O.C. USE WATERTIGHT WASHERS

CAP

SLOPED WOOD PIECE NAILED TO ONE SIDE OF JOINT ONLY

JOINT COVER

CONTINUOUS HOOK STRIP

BEND DOWN AFTER INSULATION COVER

DOWN

MIN. GAUGE 16 OZ COPPER, 22 GAUGE GALVANIZED IRON, 0.050 IN. ALUMINUM

8" MIN.

BUILDING EXPANSION JOINTS

CTA Architects Engineers; Billings, Montana

WIDTH OF RECTANGULAR GUTTERS FOR GIVEN ROOF AREAS AND RAINFALL INTENSITIES

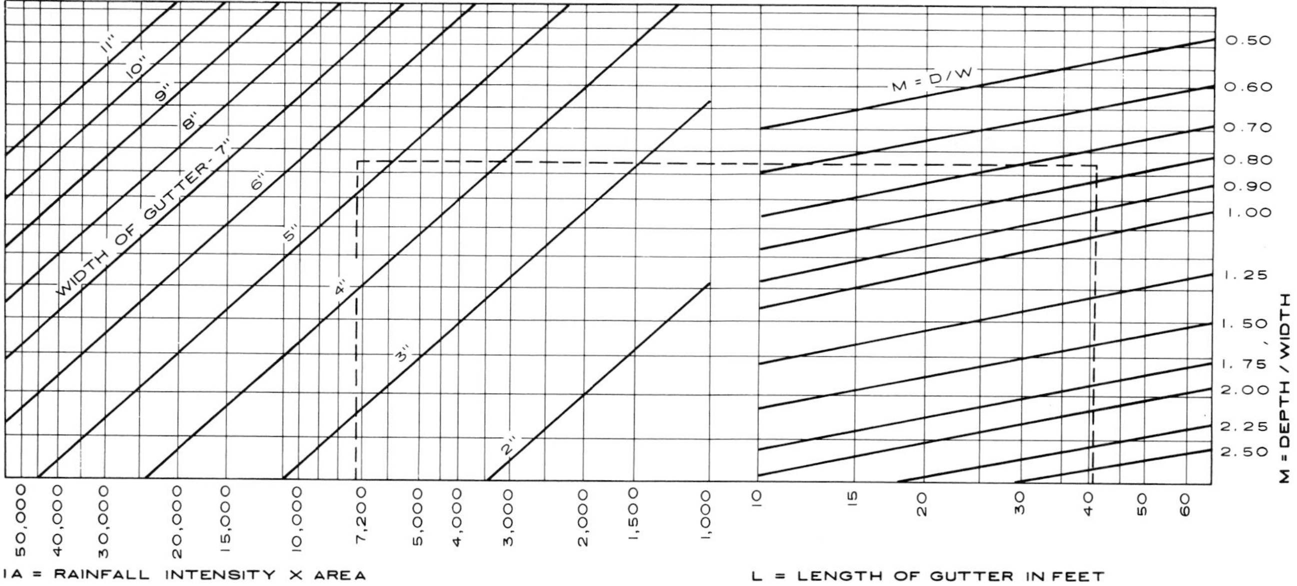

NOTE

The terms "leader," "conductor," and "downspout" all mean the same thing.

SAMPLE PROBLEM

To size rectangular gutter for a building 120 x 30 ft. located in New York City. This building has a flat roof with a raised roof edge on three sides. A gutter is to be located on one of the 120 ft. sides. So that each section of gutter will not exceed 50 ft., three downspouts will be used with 2 gutter expansion joints. The area to be drained by each section of gutter will be 1200 sq. ft., the rainfall intensity from map below is 6 in., the length of each gutter section is 40 ft., and the ratio of gutter depth to width is 0.75. On chart above find the vertical line representing L = 40. Proceed vertically along this line to its intersection with the oblique line representing M = 0.75. Pass horizontally to the left to intersect the vertical line representing IA = 7200. The point of intersection occurs between the oblique line representing gutter widths of 5 and 6 in. The required width of gutter is, therefore, 6 in. and its depth need be only 4 $^{1}/_{2}$ in.

DESIGN AREAS FOR PITCHED ROOFS

PITCH	FACTOR
LEVEL TO 3 IN./FT.	1.00
4 TO 5 IN./FT.	1.05
6 TO 8 IN./FT.	1.10
9 TO 11 IN./FT.	1.20
12 IN./FT.	1.30

NOTE: When a roof is sloped neither the plan nor actual area should be used in sizing drainage. Multiply the plan area by the factor shown above to obtain design area.

INFLUENCE OF GUTTER SHAPE ON DESIGN

1. RECTANGULAR GUTTERS

Use graph at top of page.

2. IRREGULAR SHAPES

Determine equivalent rectangular size and use same method.

3. SEMICIRCULAR GUTTERS

First size downspout from tables below. Then use gutter 1 inch larger in diameter.

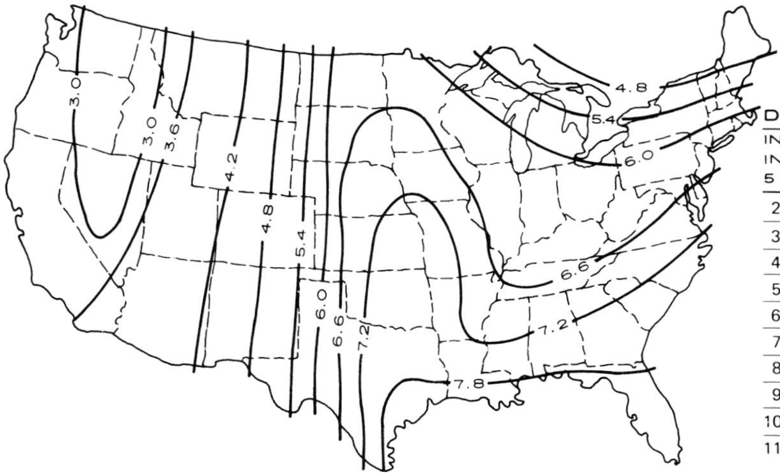

RAINFALL INTENSITY MAP

NOTE

Map shows hourly rainfall intensity in inches per hour for 5 minute periods to be expected once in 10 years. Normally this is adequate for design, but some storms have been twice as intense in some areas. See local records.

DOWNSPOUT CAPACITY

INTENSITY IN IN./HR. LASTING 5 MIN.	SQ.FT. ROOF/ SQ.IN. DOWN-SPOUT
2	600
3	400
4	300
5	240
6	200
7	175
8	150
9	130
10	120
11	110

GENERAL NOTES

Most gutters are run level for appearance. However, a slope of $^{1}/_{16}$ in. per foot is desirable for drainage.

For residential work allow 100 sq. ft. of roof area per 1 sq. in. of downspout.

DOWNSPOUT SIZES

TYPE	AREA SQ. IN.	NOM. SIZE IN.	ACT. SIZE IN.
PLAIN ROUND	7.07	3	3
	12.57	4	4
	19.63	5	5
	28.27	6	6
CORR. ROUND	5.94	3	3
	11.04	4	4
	17.72	5	5
	25.97	6	6
CORR. RECT.	3.80	2	1 $^{3}/_{4}$ x 2 $^{1}/_{4}$
	7.73	3	2 $^{3}/_{8}$ x 3 $^{1}/_{4}$
	11.70	4	2 $^{3}/_{4}$ x 4 $^{1}/_{4}$
	18.75	5	3 $^{3}/_{4}$ x 5
PLAIN RECT.	3.94	2	1 $^{3}/_{4}$ x 2 $^{1}/_{4}$
	6.00	3	2 x 3
	12.00	4	3 x 4
	20.00	5	3 $^{3}/_{4}$ x 4 $^{3}/_{4}$
	24.00	6	4 x 6

Lawrence W. Cobb; Columbia, South Carolina

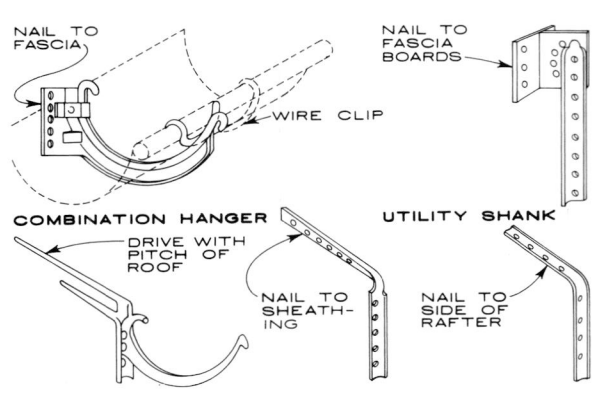

COMBINATION HANGER

DRIVE WITH PITCH OF ROOF

UTILITY SHANK

NAIL TO SHEATH-ING

NAIL TO SIDE OF RAFTER

DRIVE HANGER   VARIOUS SHANKS

SHANK AND CIRCLE HANGERS
Available in malleable and wrought copper, bronze, stainless steel and aluminum. Only a sampling of the wide variety of shapes available is shown. See mfrs. literature.

GUTTER HANGERS

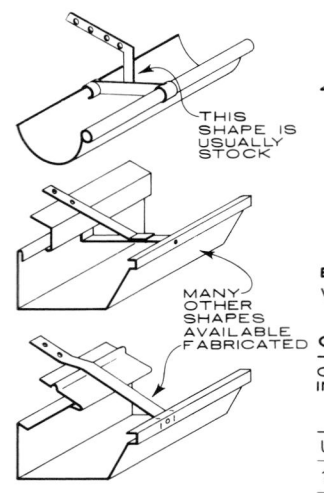

THIS SHAPE IS USUALLY STOCK

MANY OTHER SHAPES AVAILABLE FABRICATED

STRAP HANGERS

BRACKET HANGER
Various shapes are available.

SPIKE AND FERRULE
Not recommended if girth is over 15 in.

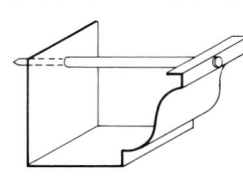

NOTE: Gutter hangers are normally spaced 3'-0" O.C. Reduce to 1'-6" O.C. where ice and snow are long lasting.

GUTTER BRACKET OR STRAP SIZES

GIRTH INCHES	GALV. STEEL INCHES	COPPER INCHES	ALUM. INCHES	STAINLESS INCHES
UP TO 15	1/8 x 1	1/8 x 1	3/16 x 1	1/8 x 1
15 TO 20	3/16 x 1	1/4 x 1	1/4 x 1	1/8 x 1 1/2
20 TO 24	1/4 x 1 1/2	1/4 x 1 1/2	1/4 x 2	1/8 x 2

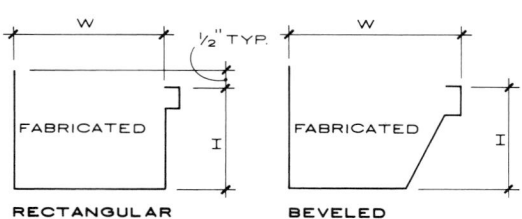

RECTANGULAR   BEVELED   OGEE OR STYLE "K"   SEMICIRCULAR OR HALF-ROUND

METAL GUTTER NOTES
Various sizes and other shapes available.

Always keep front ½ in. lower than back of gutter.

Do not use width less than 4 in. except for canopies and small porches. Minimum ratio of depth to width should be 3 to 4.

OGEE OR STYLE "K"		
2 1/2" H x 3" W		
2 3/4" H x 4" W	G	A
3 3/4" H x 5" W	G	A
4 3/4" H x 6" W	G	
5 1/4" H x 7" W		
6" H x 8" W		

SEMICIRCULAR OR HALF-ROUND	
4" W	G
5" W	G A
6" W	G A
7" W	G
8" W	G

NOTE: Stock sizes—G = galvanized, A = aluminum.

METAL GUTTER SHAPES AND SIZES

NOTES

1. Continuous gutters may be formed at the installation site with cold forming equipment, thus eliminating joints in long runs of gutter.
2. Girth is width of sheet metal from which gutter is fabricated.
3. Sizes listed in table to the left but not marked stock are available on special order.
4. Aluminum and galvanized steel are more commonly used, whereas copper and especially stainless steel are least used.
5. All jointing methods are applicable to most gutter shapes. Lap joints are more commonly used. Seal all joints with mastic or by soldering. Lock, slip, or lap joints do not provide expansion.
6. See SMACNA Architectural Sheet Metal Manual for gutter sizing and details.

EXPANSION JOINTS

Expansion joints should be used on all straight runs over 40 ft. In a 10 ft section of gutter and a 100° temperature change linear expansion will be:

EXPANSION OF METAL GUTTERS IN 40 FT

METAL	COEFFICIENT OF EXPANSION	MOVEMENT
Aluminum	.00128	.15 in.
Copper	.00093	.11 in.
Galvanized steel	.0065	.08 in.

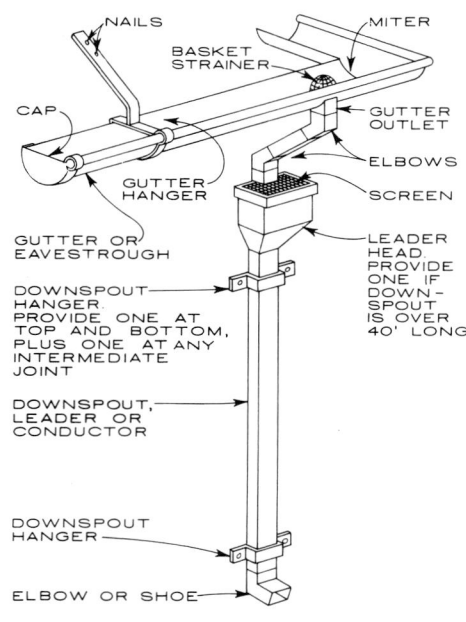

NAILS   MITER   BASKET STRAINER   CAP   GUTTER OUTLET   ELBOWS   GUTTER HANGER   SCREEN   GUTTER OR EAVESTROUGH   LEADER HEAD. PROVIDE ONE IF DOWNSPOUT IS OVER 40' LONG   DOWNSPOUT HANGER PROVIDE ONE AT TOP AND BOTTOM, PLUS ONE AT ANY INTERMEDIATE JOINT   DOWNSPOUT, LEADER OR CONDUCTOR   DOWNSPOUT HANGER   ELBOW OR SHOE

PARTS OF A GUTTER

NOTE
PVC plastic gutter and downspout parts are similar to metal. See manufacturers' data for shapes and sizes.

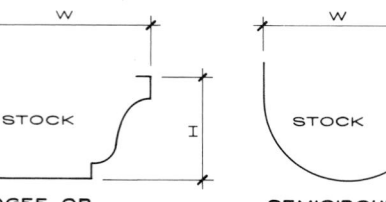

DASH LINE INDICATES ROOF SLOPE

PITCH 12:12   12:7   12:5   12:0

GUTTERS

Gutters should be placed below slope line so that snow and ice can slide clear. Steeper pitch requires less clearance.

PLACING OF GUTTERS

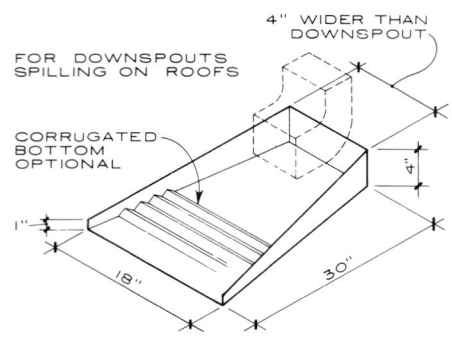

4" WIDER THAN DOWNSPOUT

FOR DOWNSPOUTS SPILLING ON ROOFS

CORRUGATED BOTTOM OPTIONAL

4"

18"   30"   1"

SPLASH PAN

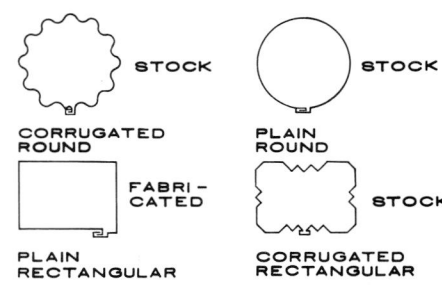

CORRUGATED ROUND   STOCK

PLAIN ROUND   STOCK

PLAIN RECTANGULAR   FABRICATED

CORRUGATED RECTANGULAR   STOCK

NOTES

Space downspouts 20 ft min., 50 ft max., generally. Extreme max. 60 ft.

Do not use size smaller than 7.00 in area except for canopies.

Corrugated shapes resist freezing better than plain shapes.

Elbows available: 45°, 60°, 75°, 90°.

Jones/Richards and Associates; Ogden, Utah
Lawrence W. Cobb; Columbia, South Carolina

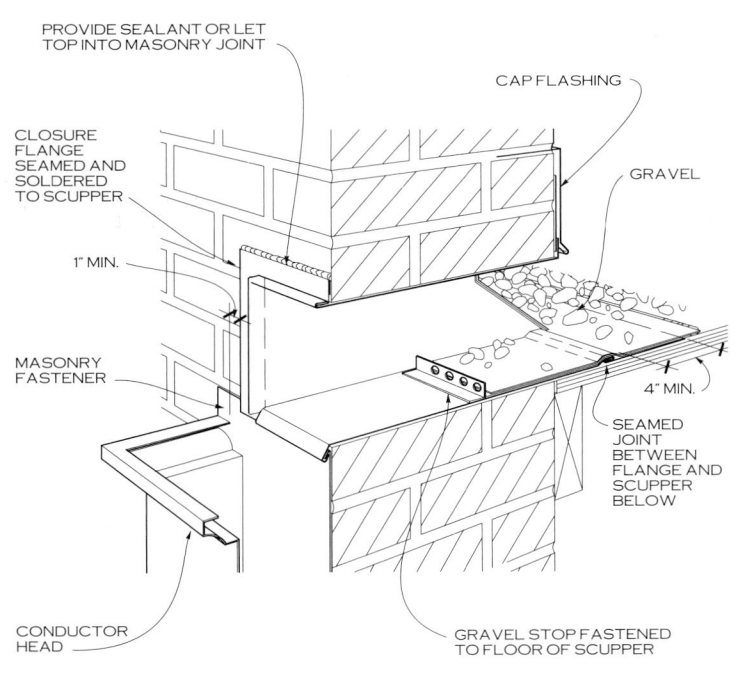

PROVIDE SEALANT OR LET TOP INTO MASONRY JOINT

CAP FLASHING

CLOSURE FLANGE SEAMED AND SOLDERED TO SCUPPER

GRAVEL

1" MIN.

MASONRY FASTENER

4" MIN.

SEAMED JOINT BETWEEN FLANGE AND SCUPPER BELOW

CONDUCTOR HEAD

GRAVEL STOP FASTENED TO FLOOR OF SCUPPER

SCUPPER DETAIL AT PARAPET WALL (CONDUCTOR HEAD SIDE)

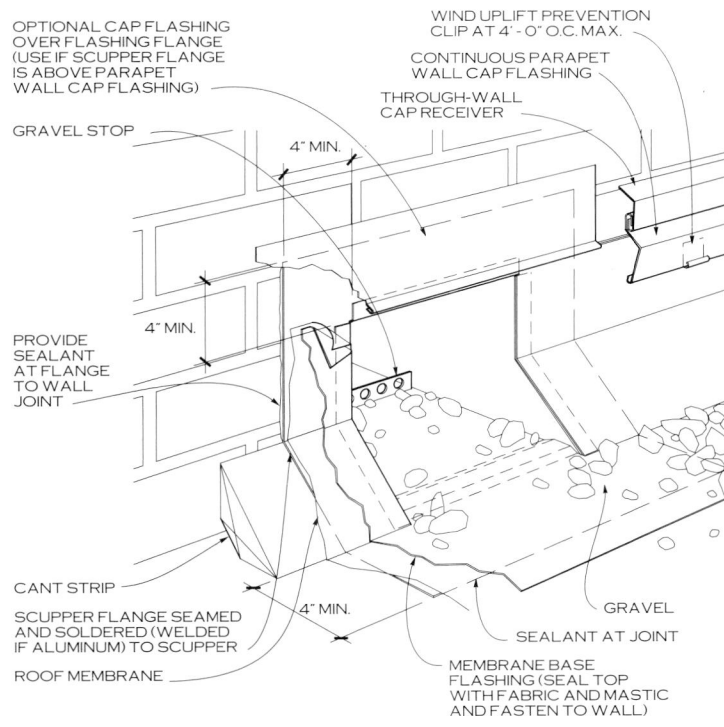

OPTIONAL CAP FLASHING OVER FLASHING FLANGE (USE IF SCUPPER FLANGE IS ABOVE PARAPET WALL CAP FLASHING)

WIND UPLIFT PREVENTION CLIP AT 4'- 0" O.C. MAX.

CONTINUOUS PARAPET WALL CAP FLASHING

THROUGH-WALL CAP RECEIVER

GRAVEL STOP

4" MIN.

4" MIN.

PROVIDE SEALANT AT FLANGE TO WALL JOINT

CANT STRIP

SCUPPER FLANGE SEAMED AND SOLDERED (WELDED IF ALUMINUM) TO SCUPPER

ROOF MEMBRANE

4" MIN.

GRAVEL

SEALANT AT JOINT

MEMBRANE BASE FLASHING (SEAL TOP WITH FABRIC AND MASTIC AND FASTEN TO WALL)

SCUPPER DETAIL AT PARAPET WALL (ROOF SIDE)

NOTES

1. Overflow openings are recommended in heavy icing areas and for drains that may become plugged with leaves or other debris. Check local codes for elevation of overflow opening.

2. Conductor heads and downspouts should be fabricated of the same material. Recommended minimum for construction of conductor heads is 24 gauge galvanized steel, 0.032 in. aluminum, 16 oz. copper, or 26 gauge stainless steel.

3. Edges of conductor head must be suitably stiff, based on dimensional characteristics.

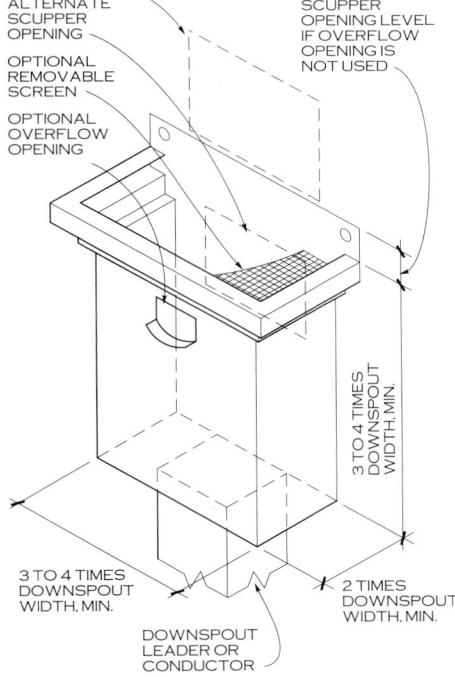

SCUPPER OPENING

ALTERNATE SCUPPER OPENING

OPTIONAL REMOVABLE SCREEN

OPTIONAL OVERFLOW OPENING

SET TOP OF CONDUCTOR HEAD 1" BELOW SCUPPER OPENING LEVEL IF OVERFLOW OPENING IS NOT USED

3 TO 4 TIMES DOWNSPOUT WIDTH, MIN.

3 TO 4 TIMES DOWNSPOUT WIDTH, MIN.

2 TIMES DOWNSPOUT WIDTH, MIN.

DOWNSPOUT LEADER OR CONDUCTOR

TYPICAL CONDUCTOR HEAD

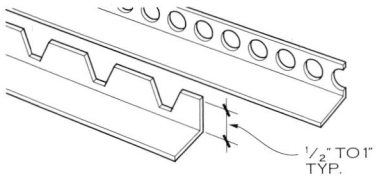

$\frac{1}{2}$" TO 1" TYP.

TYPICAL GRAVEL STOPS

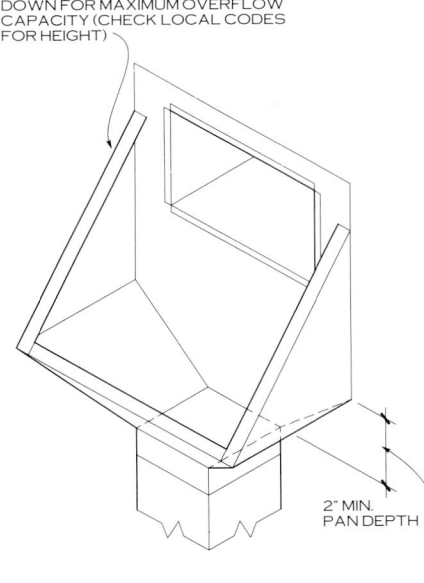

CONDUCTOR HEAD TOP TILTED DOWN FOR MAXIMUM OVERFLOW CAPACITY (CHECK LOCAL CODES FOR HEIGHT)

2" MIN. PAN DEPTH

CONDUCTOR HEAD-MAXIMUM OVERFLOW

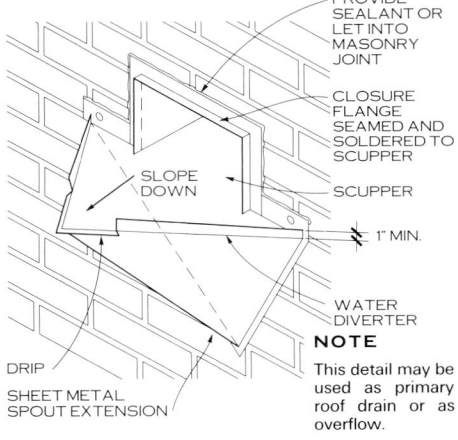

PROVIDE SEALANT OR LET INTO MASONRY JOINT

CLOSURE FLANGE SEAMED AND SOLDERED TO SCUPPER

SCUPPER

SLOPE DOWN

1" MIN.

WATER DIVERTER

DRIP

SHEET METAL SPOUT EXTENSION

NOTE

This detail may be used as primary roof drain or as overflow.

RAINSPOUT DETAIL

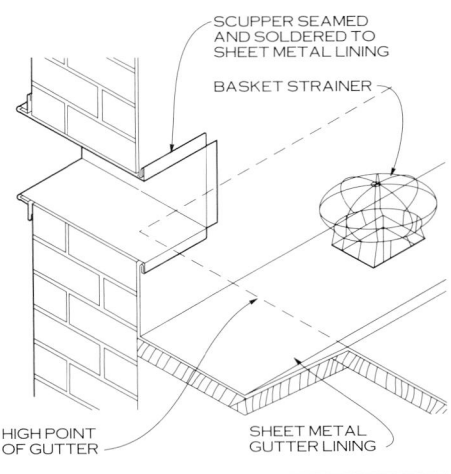

SCUPPER SEAMED AND SOLDERED TO SHEET METAL LINING

BASKET STRAINER

HIGH POINT OF GUTTER

SHEET METAL GUTTER LINING

OVERFLOW SCUPPER AT BUILT-IN GUTTER

Richard J. Vitullo, AIA; Oak Leaf Studio; Crownsville, Maryland

DOWNSPOUTS AND GUTTERS **7**

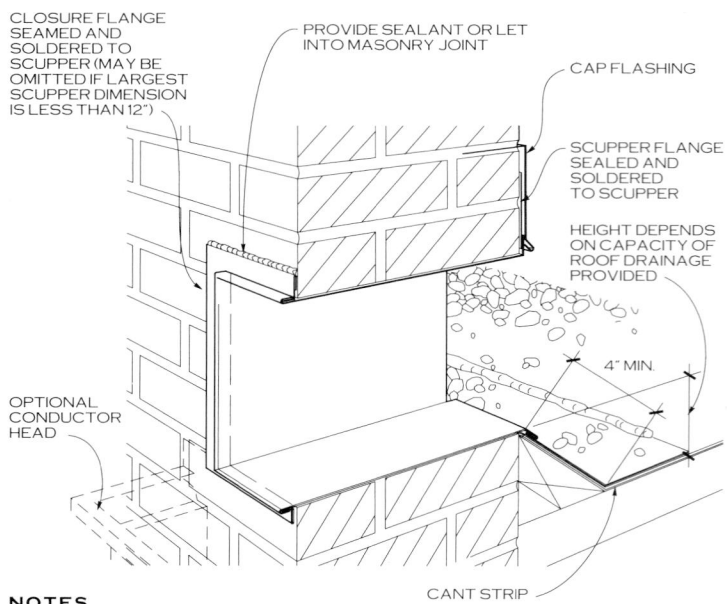

CLOSURE FLANGE SEAMED AND SOLDERED TO SCUPPER (MAY BE OMITTED IF LARGEST SCUPPER DIMENSION IS LESS THAN 12")

PROVIDE SEALANT OR LET INTO MASONRY JOINT

CAP FLASHING

SCUPPER FLANGE SEALED AND SOLDERED TO SCUPPER

HEIGHT DEPENDS ON CAPACITY OF ROOF DRAINAGE PROVIDED

OPTIONAL CONDUCTOR HEAD

4" MIN.

CANT STRIP

NOTES

1. Use overflow scuppers when roof is completely surrounded by parapets and drainage depends on scuppers or internal drainage.
2. Precast concrete panels with scuppers do not need closure flanges on face; all penetrations should be sealed.

OVERFLOW SCUPPER DETAIL AT PARAPET WALL

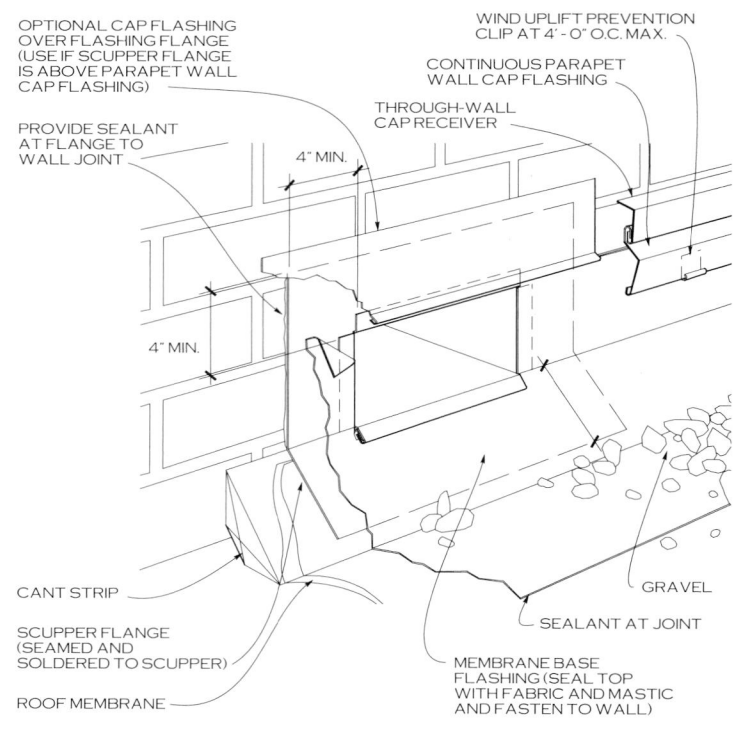

OPTIONAL CAP FLASHING OVER FLASHING FLANGE (USE IF SCUPPER FLANGE IS ABOVE PARAPET WALL CAP FLASHING)

WIND UPLIFT PREVENTION CLIP AT 4'-0" O.C. MAX.

CONTINUOUS PARAPET WALL CAP FLASHING

THROUGH-WALL CAP RECEIVER

PROVIDE SEALANT AT FLANGE TO WALL JOINT

4" MIN.

4" MIN.

CANT STRIP

SCUPPER FLANGE (SEAMED AND SOLDERED TO SCUPPER)

ROOF MEMBRANE

GRAVEL

SEALANT AT JOINT

MEMBRANE BASE FLASHING (SEAL TOP WITH FABRIC AND MASTIC AND FASTEN TO WALL)

OVERFLOW SCUPPER DETAIL AT PARAPET WALL (ROOF SIDE)

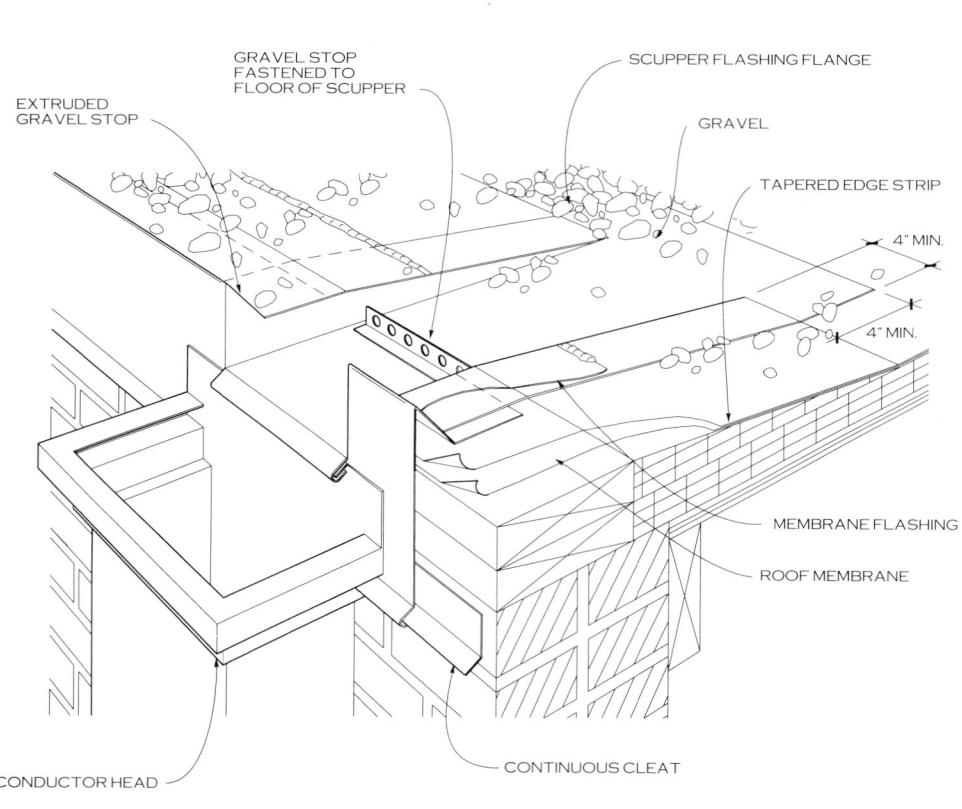

EXTRUDED GRAVEL STOP

GRAVEL STOP FASTENED TO FLOOR OF SCUPPER

SCUPPER FLASHING FLANGE

GRAVEL

TAPERED EDGE STRIP

4" MIN.

4" MIN.

MEMBRANE FLASHING

ROOF MEMBRANE

CONDUCTOR HEAD

CONTINUOUS CLEAT

SCUPPER DETAIL AT GRAVEL STOP (CONDUCTOR HEAD SIDE)

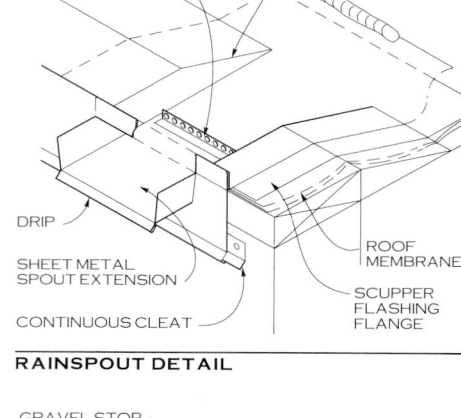

OPTIONAL CAP FASCIA EXTENSION OVER SCUPPER

GRAVEL STOP

DRIP

SHEET METAL SPOUT EXTENSION

CONTINUOUS CLEAT

ROOF MEMBRANE

SCUPPER FLASHING FLANGE

RAINSPOUT DETAIL

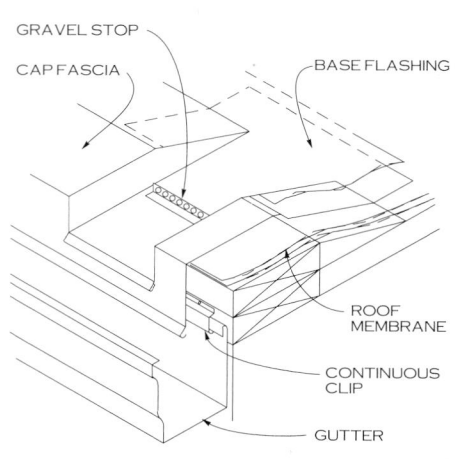

CAP FASCIA

BASE FLASHING

ROOF MEMBRANE

CONTINUOUS CLIP

GUTTER

SCUPPER DETAIL AT RAISED CURB

Richard J. Vitullo, AIA; Oak Leaf Studio; Crownsville, Maryland

7   **DOWNSPOUTS AND GUTTERS**

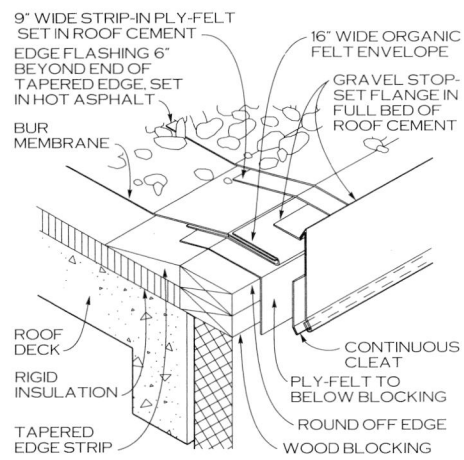

9" WIDE STRIP-IN PLY-FELT SET IN ROOF CEMENT

EDGE FLASHING 6" BEYOND END OF TAPERED EDGE, SET IN HOT ASPHALT

16" WIDE ORGANIC FELT ENVELOPE

GRAVEL STOP-SET FLANGE IN FULL BED OF ROOF CEMENT

BUR MEMBRANE

ROOF DECK

RIGID INSULATION

TAPERED EDGE STRIP

CONTINUOUS CLEAT

PLY-FELT TO BELOW BLOCKING

ROUND OFF EDGE

WOOD BLOCKING

EDGE FLASHING

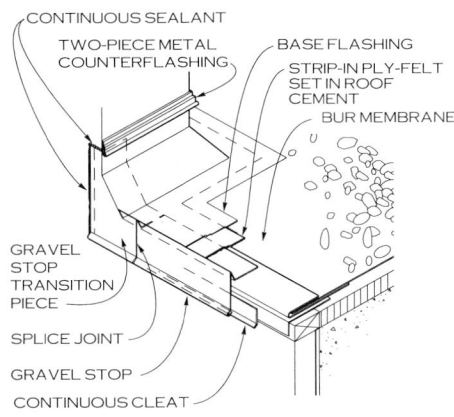

CONTINUOUS SEALANT

TWO-PIECE METAL COUNTERFLASHING

BASE FLASHING

STRIP-IN PLY-FELT SET IN ROOF CEMENT

BUR MEMBRANE

GRAVEL STOP TRANSITION PIECE

SPLICE JOINT

GRAVEL STOP

CONTINUOUS CLEAT

GRAVEL STOP TRANSITION

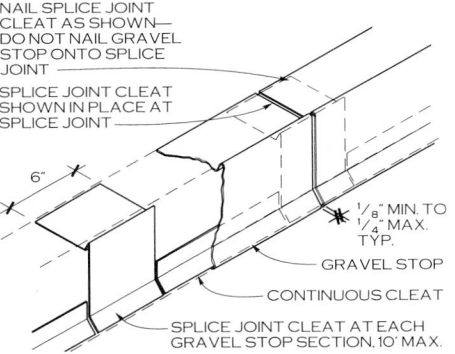

NAIL SPLICE JOINT CLEAT AS SHOWN—DO NOT NAIL GRAVEL STOP ONTO SPLICE JOINT

SPLICE JOINT CLEAT SHOWN IN PLACE AT SPLICE JOINT

6"

1/8" MIN. TO 1/4" MAX. TYP.

GRAVEL STOP

CONTINUOUS CLEAT

SPLICE JOINT CLEAT AT EACH GRAVEL STOP SECTION, 10' MAX.

GRAVEL STOP SPLICE JOINT

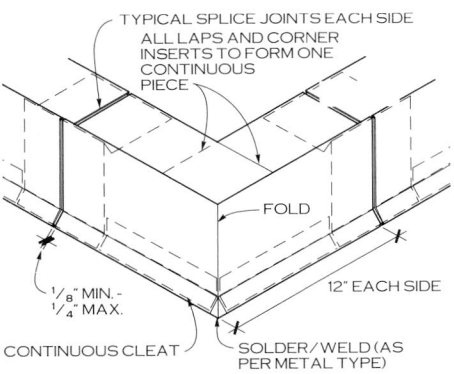

TYPICAL SPLICE JOINTS EACH SIDE

ALL LAPS AND CORNER INSERTS TO FORM ONE CONTINUOUS PIECE

FOLD

1/8" MIN.- 1/4" MAX.

12" EACH SIDE

CONTINUOUS CLEAT

SOLDER/WELD (AS PER METAL TYPE)

GRAVEL STOP OUTSIDE CORNER FABRICATION

RECOMMENDED MINIMUM GAUGES FOR GRAVEL STOP—FASCIA

D (MAX) (IN.)	GALVANIZED STEEL (GAUGE)	COPPER (OZ.)	ALUMINUM (IN.)	ZINC ALLOY (IN.)	STAINLESS STEEL (GAUGE)
4	24	16	0.025	0.020	26
5	24	16	0.032	0.027	26
6	22	20	0.040	0.027	24
7	22	20	0.040	-	22
8	20	20	0.050	-	20

RECOMMENDED MINIMUM GAUGES FOR COPING

WIDTH OF COPING TOP (IN.)	GALVANIZED STEEL (GAUGE)	STAINLESS STEEL (GAUGE)	ALUMINUM (IN.)	COPPER (OZ.)
Through 12	24	26	0.232	16
13 to 18	22	24	0.040	20

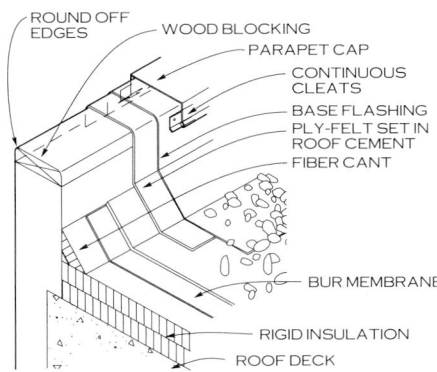

ROUND OFF EDGES

WOOD BLOCKING

PARAPET CAP

CONTINUOUS CLEATS

BASE FLASHING

PLY-FELT SET IN ROOF CEMENT

FIBER CANT

BUR MEMBRANE

RIGID INSULATION

ROOF DECK

PARAPET EDGE DETAIL

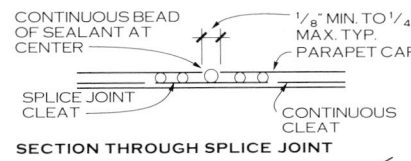

CONTINUOUS BEAD OF SEALANT AT CENTER

1/8" MIN. TO 1/4" MAX. TYP.

PARAPET CAP

SPLICE JOINT CLEAT

CONTINUOUS CLEAT

SECTION THROUGH SPLICE JOINT

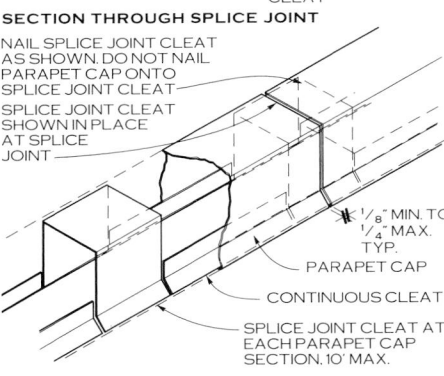

NAIL SPLICE JOINT CLEAT AS SHOWN. DO NOT NAIL PARAPET CAP ONTO SPLICE JOINT CLEAT

SPLICE JOINT CLEAT SHOWN IN PLACE AT SPLICE JOINT

1/8" MIN. TO 1/4" MAX. TYP.

PARAPET CAP

CONTINUOUS CLEAT

SPLICE JOINT CLEAT AT EACH PARAPET CAP SECTION, 10' MAX.

PARAPET CAP SPLICE JOINT

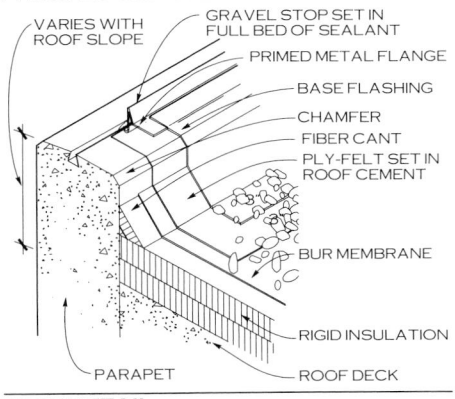

VARIES WITH ROOF SLOPE

GRAVEL STOP SET IN FULL BED OF SEALANT

PRIMED METAL FLANGE

BASE FLASHING

CHAMFER

FIBER CANT

PLY-FELT SET IN ROOF CEMENT

BUR MEMBRANE

RIGID INSULATION

PARAPET

ROOF DECK

EDGE DETAIL

SELECTION OF FLASHING METAL

Each commonly used flashing metal has distinctive characteristics, uses, and limitations. Thickness of materials is a function of material size, aesthetic consideration (prevention of oil-canning), and wind uplift due to metal movement during violent storms.

GALVANIZED STEEL

Galvanized steel flashings should be a minimum of 24 gauge with a G-90 galvanized coating. Of commonly used flashing metals, galvanized steel probably is the most common and least expensive. Although galvanized flashing metal may be left exposed, generally it is painted to further protect the steel from corrosion. Before it is painted, galvanized metal must be prepared. Plain galvanized material chemically etched in the field is preferred for surfaces to be painted. Factory etching, in which the metal is dipped in an acid bath, etches it on all sides. As a result, exposed edges often rust. Field etching is preferred because only the surfaces to be painted are etched. After etching, the surface should be primed and finish painted, preferably with two coats.

Galvanized steel is easy to solder, low in cost, and easy to work. All flashing metal transitions and terminations should be soldered fully for permanent installation; however, this should not be done at metal flashing joints where movement caused by thermal expansion is expected or at building expansion joints.

STAINLESS STEEL

Stainless steel retains many of the advantages of other steel products and yet is generally corrosion resistant. In addition to resisting corrosion, stainless steel can be field soldered so as to accommodate difficult transition and termination conditions. If the mill finish appearance is not acceptable, the stainless steel may be field painted after installation by using a primer followed by finish painting.

COPPER

Copper is also among the lifetime materials that are considered maintenance free. It can be soldered and molds very easily, which makes it adaptable to complicated transitions and changes of plane. Since copper can be soldered in the field, it should be terminated with fully soldered conditions. The designer should be aware, however, that the runoff from the metal can stain adjoining building materials. Copper is generally found to be a softer material than other flashing metals. Copper has a moderate coefficient of expansion in that it is higher than steel and yet less than aluminum.

ALUMINUM

Aluminum is among the permanent materials because it corrodes at a slow rate. Aluminum will, however, oxidize and pit over time, depending on the exposure. Since aluminum can only be connected by welding, field conditions are more difficult to accommodate. Although corner conditions can very often be prefabricated, unusual or difficult changes of plane may be difficult to properly accommodate in aluminum. Aluminum also has a high coefficient of expansion and contraction compared with other flashing metals and field welding is difficult. Due to the limitations of in-field fabrications, aluminum is best used on roofs of simple configurations and few transitions.

Joseph J. Williams, AIA; A/R/C Associates Inc.; Orlando, Florida

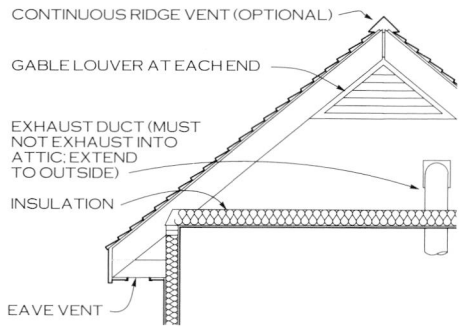

GABLE ROOF WITH UNOCCUPIED ATTIC

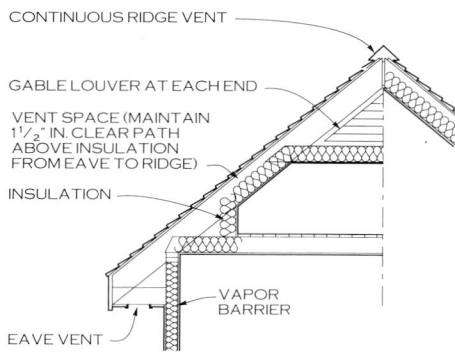

GABLE WITH OCCUPIED SPACE UNDER ROOF

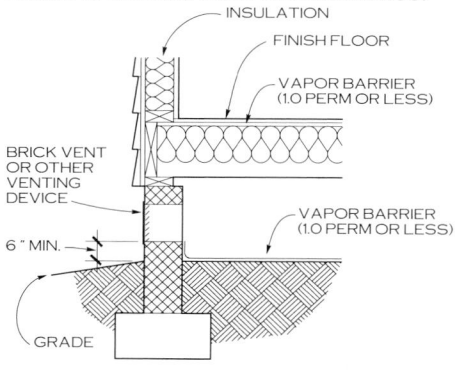

CRAWL SPACE

VENTILATION REQUIREMENTS TO PREVENT CONDENSATION

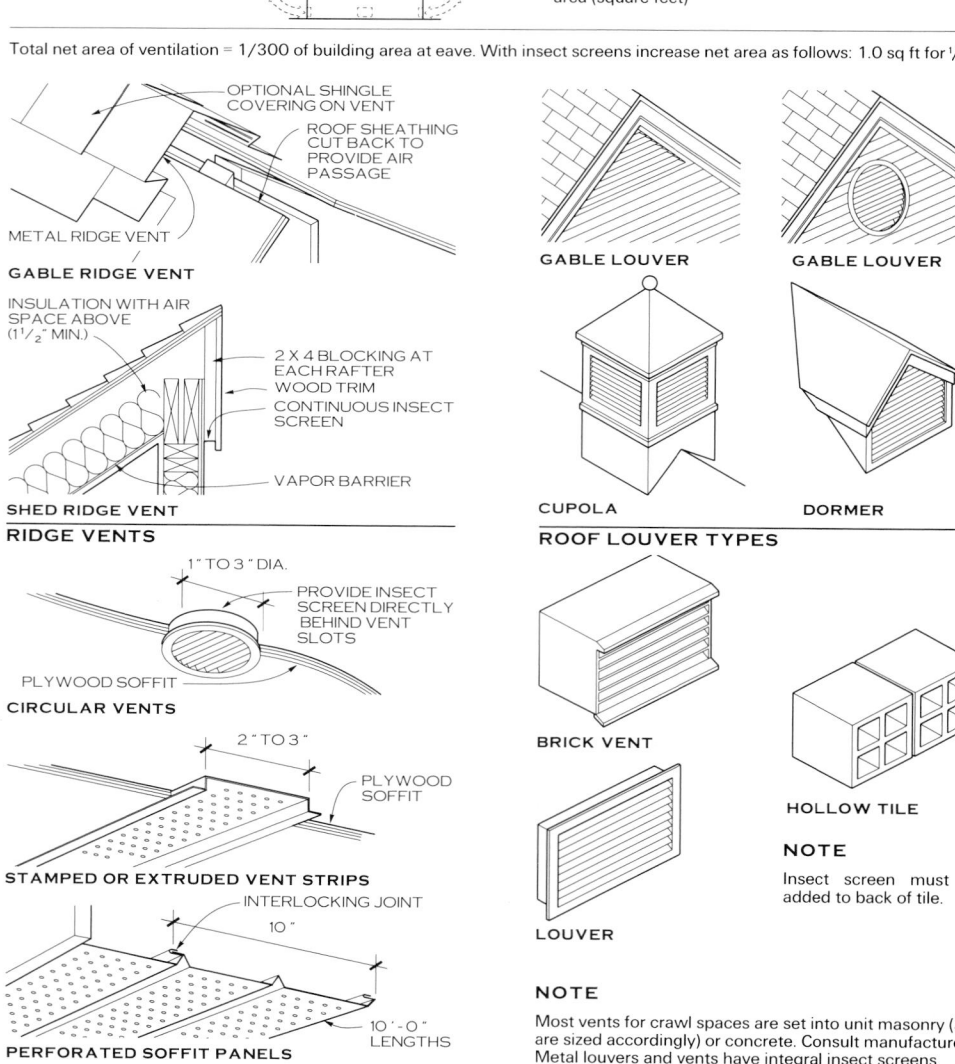

SPACE	DESCRIPTION		TOTAL NET AREA OF VENTILATION (A)	REMARKS
Joist/rafter (finish ceiling attached to underside of joists)	Flat		A = 1/300. Uniformly distributed vents at eaves.	Vent each joist space at both ends. Maintain 1 1/2" min. clear path above insulation for ventilation.
	Sloped		A = 1/300. Uniformly distributed vents at eaves with a continuous ridge vent.	
Attic (unheated)	Gable		A = 1/300. At least two louvers on opposite sides near ridge or one continuous ridge vent. Uniformly distributed vents at eaves.	Any combination of gable/hip louvers and/or ridge vents may be used to achieve required ventilation.
	Hip			
Crawl space/ basement			a = 2L/100 + A/300 Where L = crawl space/basement perimeter (linear feet) A = crawl space/basement area (square feet)	Provide at least one opening per side, as high as possible in wall.

Total net area of ventilation = 1/300 of building area at eave. With insect screens increase net area as follows: 1.0 sq ft for 1/4 in.

GABLE RIDGE VENT

SHED RIDGE VENT

RIDGE VENTS

CIRCULAR VENTS

STAMPED OR EXTRUDED VENT STRIPS

PERFORATED SOFFIT PANELS

EAVE VENTILATION MATERIALS

GABLE LOUVER

GABLE LOUVER

CUPOLA

DORMER

ROOF LOUVER TYPES

BRICK VENT

HOLLOW TILE

NOTE

Insect screen must be added to back of tile.

LOUVER

CRAWL SPACE VENTILATION MATERIALS

NOTE

Most vents for crawl spaces are set into unit masonry (and are sized accordingly) or concrete. Consult manufacturers. Metal louvers and vents have integral insect screens.

VENTILATION APPLICATIONS
GENERAL

Building attics, crawl spaces, and basements must be ventilated to remove moisture and water vapor resulting from human activity within the building. Moisture in basements and crawl spaces can be caused from water in the surrounding soil; these spaces require a high rate of ventilation. The quantity of water vapor depends on building type (e.g., residence, school, hospital), activity (e.g., kitchen, bathroom, laundry), and therefore, air temperature and relative humidity. Proper ventilation and insulation must be combined so that the temperature of the ventilated space does not fall below the dew point; this is especially critical with low outdoor temperatures and high inside humidity. Inadequate ventilation will cause condensation and eventual deterioration of framing, insulation, and interior finishes.

The vent types shown allow natural ventilation of roofs and crawl spaces. Mechanical methods (e.g., power attic ventilators, whole house fans) can combine living space and attic ventilation, but openings for natural roof ventilation must still be provided. Protect all vents against insects and vermin with metal or fiberglass screen cloth. Increase net vent areas as noted in table (above).

Vapor barriers minimize moisture migration to attics and crawl spaces; their use is required for all conditions. Always locate vapor barriers on the warm (room) side of insulation. Provide ventilation on the cold side to permit cold/hot weather ventilation while minimizing heat gain/loss.

Eric K. Beach; Rippeteau Architects, PC; Washington, D.C.

FRAMING

Skylights are available as preassembled units, stock or custom designed, shipped to the site ready to be installed, as assemblies of units, or framed assemblies of stock components, prefabricated off site and then site assembled. Skylight framing systems should provide complete control of both condensation and water infiltration.

Exterior gutter systems should be as simple and functional as possible. Design must take into account compatibility of materials and provision of positive slope for drainage.

The supporting structure, as well as the enclosure itself, must be engineered to carry the total resultant forces of the particular live load, wind load, and dead load in accordance with all building codes.

Framed skylights require somewhat greater mullion widths when glazed with acrylics, due to the expansion and contraction characteristics of plastics that must be taken up at the glazing connection.

Mullion spacing for framed skylights and dimensional limitations on skylight assemblies are governed by building codes responding to the glazing material specified. Maximum widths of glass vary with type:

1. Wire glass—60 in.
2. Laminated glass—48 in.
3. Tempered glass—72 in.

Other factors limiting size are

1. Requirements for positive drainage of rain water
2. Snow and wind loading
3. Condensate gutters in the body of the skylight assembly as well as at its perimeter

Mount on built-up curb with frame and counterflashing. Curb minimum height is 8 in. above roof structure. Prefabricated curbs are available with or without insulation.

Energy efficiency may be increased by use of double and triple glazing and with frames that have thermal breaks. These items will also reduce the probability of condensation.

All skylight units must be securely attached to the roof assembly which may require structural or miscellaneous steel frames at openings in deck.

GLAZING

The thickness, size, and geometric profile of all glass and acrylic glazing material should be carefully selected for compliance with building codes and manufacturer's recommendations.

The following glazing materials are available:

1. Formed acrylic with mar-resistant finish
2. Formed acrylic or flat acrylic
3. Polycarbonates
4. Tempered glass or laminated glass
5. Clear polished wire glass
6. Textured, obscure wire glass

Excessive expansion and contraction of acrylic glazing may cause "rolling" of the sealant between metal framing, causing shifting of glazing material out of the joint.

LOW RISE   MEDIUM RISE   HIGH RISE

The minimum rise to span on curved structures of framed skylights for vaulted and dome shapes is 22%.

Tinted acrylics should be limited to ¼ in. thickness for economy. A combination fiberglass sheet and aluminum frame system which has high insulating and excessive light diffusion may be an economic consideration.

Proper glazing methods have an important influence. Exposed gasketing is subject to material breakdown due to ultraviolet rays of the sun. Small valleys created at the bottom of sloped glazing and horizontal glazing cap will hold water.

Mar-resistant coatings for plastics should be specified if frequent cleaning or heavy pedestrian contact is anticipated.

Glazing with high-performance insulated glass units provides important energy savings and offers the architect numerous functional and aesthetic design choices, but initial cost may be high.

CTA Architects Engineers; Billings, Montana

FINISHES

Finishes for aluminum components are available in the following:

1. Mill finish
2. Clear anodized
3. Duranodic bronze or black
4. Acrylic enamel
5. Fluorocarbons

CONDENSATION

Double glazing and thermal break framing will minimize condensation.

Usually a separation is made where the glazing member is bolted into the framing member by use of a nonheat conductive material.

Insulated assemblies reduce condensation and energy losses.

Thermalized design will help in preventing excessive condensation buildup on the frame of domed skylight units, minimizing corrosion, staining, and general maintenance.

Incorporate a continuous condensation gutter to collect and store moisture until it evaporates.

BUILDING SECURITY

Resistance to forced entry through skylight should include

1. Provision to prevent disassembly of framing from the exterior
2. Elimination of snap-on materials
3. Melting point of glazing: Acrylics can be easily burned through with a torch
4. Use of metal security screens or burglar bars welded to steel angle frame directly below skylight

ENVIRONMENTAL CONTROL

In determining the desired form and size of the skylight unit/assembly, consideration should be given to

1. Environmental conditions, including orientation and the resulting winter and summer solar penetration angles in the given geographic location.
2. Prevailing wind's direction and force
3. Precipitation quantity and patterns
4. Topography and landscaping (trees/shades/leaves)
5. Coordination of the area of skylight with the HVAC system

Views into and out of the building through clear skylights are affected by

1. Overhanging trees and adjacent buildings
2. Nearby street lights
3. Other parts of the same building
4. Views into building from adjacent higher areas (privacy).

The more a formed plastic dome is raised, the greater its ability to refract light of the low early morning and late afternoon sun, which maximizes the use of natural light, but increases the solar heat gain.

AVAILABLE LIGHT ZONES

PERCENTAGE OF ROOF AREA REQUIRED FOR SKYLIGHTING

LIGHT ZONE	LIGHT DESIGN LEVELS		
	30 FT-C	60 FT-C	120 FT-C
1	3.3	5.2	13.3
2	2.8	4.3	10.8
3	1.8	3.2	6.9
4	1.5	2.8	4.0

SKYLIGHTS WITH MOVABLE SECTIONS

Skylights can be designed with movable sections for those locations where a combination indoor–outdoor open-to-the-sky condition is desired. The movable sections are of two basic designs:

1. Complete skylight assemblies of double pitch or barrel vault configurations that roll open horizontally along a track.
2. Individual skylight roof panels of an overall double-pitched enclosure which are normally designed so that the top half slides down over the lower half to open the upper portion of roof.

Consideration should be given to motors, tracks, and other operating parts.

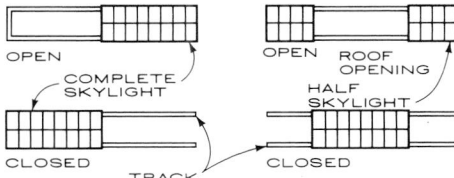

SINGLE UNIT DESIGN 1	DOUBLE UNIT DESIGN 2

MOVABLE SKYLIGHT PLANS

GLASS AND PLASTIC STRUCTURES

Greenhouses, pool enclosures, and covered walkways are applications of skylight assemblies as complete envelopes. Available forms are domes, arches, barrel vaults, and single and double pitch. Lean-to enclosures are available with straight eaves, curved eaves, vertical sides, or slanted sides.

Framing may be of steel, aluminum, or wood, with a variety of glazing options. Secondary component options include doors, operable sash, louvers, shades, blinds, and ventilators. Envelopes are preengineered for specific live and wind loads, which should be checked against requirements of building codes.

FIRE AND SMOKE VENTING

In certain building types and occupancies fire and smoke units that open automatically due to fire-induced temperature increase are required. Their function is to permit the smoke to escape and lower temperatures at floor level.

A sufficient number of vents must be distributed over the entire roof area to assure reasonably early venting of a fire regardless of its location. The size and spacing of the vents must be determined for each building, depending upon

1. Size of building
2. Its particular use or combination of uses
3. The degree of hazard involved

Smoke venting is based upon movement of a specific number of cubic feet of air per minute through the fire vents. Building codes give required capacities, size, and spacing for various types of vents.

Typical roof vent area requirements are:

0.67% of roof area for low heat release occupancies
1% of roof area for moderate heat release occupancies
2% of roof area for high heat release occupancies

Roof vents may be required over stairs, elevator hoistways, atriums, and high hazard occupancies to offer explosion relief, as well as for stages and areas behind the proscenium in theaters.

In determining the number of vents to be used to satisfy the total required venting area, recognize that venting can be better accomplished by several small units than by a few larger ones (NFPA #204). The size of the vent required is based upon its opened area, about equal to its frame size.

Consider also the spacing of vents in relation to interior spaces and their uses, proximity to exits, and their use in providing daylighting. Fire vents may also function as skylights when glazed.

Fire vents may also function as skylights when glazed.

SIZES AND SPANS

2 ft 6 in. to 7 ft 7 in., with dome rise from 10 to 24 in.

GLAZING

1. Generally acrylic, but other glazing available.
2. Single and double glazed normal, triple available.
3. Clear, tinted transparent, and white translucent.
4. Scratches are difficult to remove from acrylic.

FRAMING

1. Self-flashing, with or without integral curb.
2. Insulated curbs available.
3. Areas where excessive snow loading occurs may require additional reinforcement. Consult manufacturer.
4. Skylight—No structural framing within unit.

REMARKS

1. Circular shape may make roofing seal more difficult.
2. Some visual distortion due to curvature of glazing.
3. Side wall installation possible.

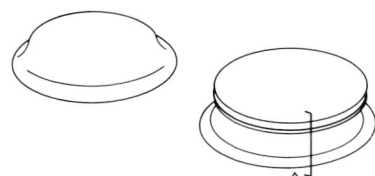

DOME—CIRCULAR

SIZES AND SPANS

Square from 2 ft 0 in. to 10 ft 0 in.; rectangular from 2 ft 0 in. to 5 ft 0 in. wide by 4 ft 0 in. to 8 ft 0 in. long, with dome rise from 8 to 22 in.

GLAZING

1. Acrylic, polycarbonate, glass fiber reinforced.
2. Single and double normal, triple glazing available.
3. Clear, tinted transparent, and white translucent.

FRAMING

1. See framing notes for circular dome skylight.
2. Self-flashing flanged available for pitched roof.

REMARKS

1. Steel security grill inserts available.
2. Explosion relief domes are available.
3. Louvered curbs available to allow skylight to act as ventilator without being opened.

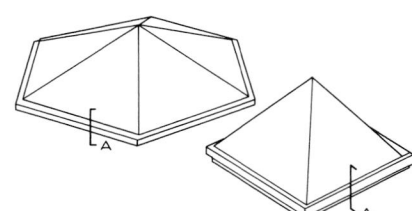

DOME—SQUARE AND RECTANGULAR

SIZES AND SPANS

2 ft 6 in. to 8 ft 0 in., with dome rise from 8 to 22 in.

GLAZING

1. Acrylic and polycarbonate typical.
2. Clear, tinted transparent, and white translucent.
3. Single and double normal.
4. Low visual distortion.

FRAMING

1. See framing notes for circular dome skylight.
2. Triangular base frame available.
3. Octagonal frame with curved dome glazing possible.
4. Normally designed for level roof application.

REMARKS

1. Sealed double domes available from some manufacturers.
2. Secondary dome under pyramid is normally curved.

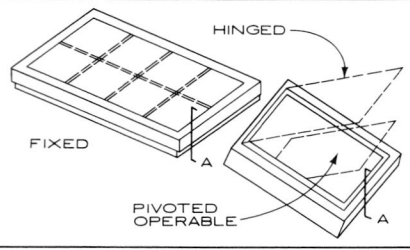

DOME—POLYGON AND PYRAMID

SIZES AND SPANS

Square 1 ft 2 in. to 4 ft 0 in.; rectangular from 2 ft 0 in. to 4 ft 0 in. wide to 4 ft 8 in. long.

GLAZING

1. Double glazed, insulating glass typical.
2. Tempered, laminated, and wire glass available.
3. Clear and tinted transparent normal.
4. Minimum visual distortion.

FRAMING

1. Operable sash: Hinged, pivoted, or sliding types.
2. Lockable frames available.
3. Aluminum and wood frames commonly available.
4. Skylight—No structural framing within unit.

REMARKS

1. Premanufactured screens and shades available.
2. Electric remote control opening operation optional.

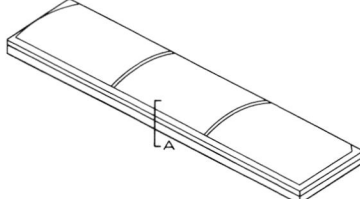

FLAT PANEL—FIXED AND OPERABLE

SIZES AND SPANS

1. 2 ft 0 in. to 10 ft 0 in. wide by any length; rise from 6 to 14 in. or higher as width increases.
2. Larger widths available with vertical ends only.

GLAZING

1. Acrylic and polycarbonate typical.
2. Single or double available.
3. Clear, tinted, and white transluscent.

FRAMING

1. May be installed in series (with structural supports).
2. Expansion and contraction clearances must be considered at frame as size of unit increases.
3. Skylight—No structural framing within unit.

REMARKS

1. Quarter round vault (lean-to) available.
2. May also be used as exterior entry canopy.

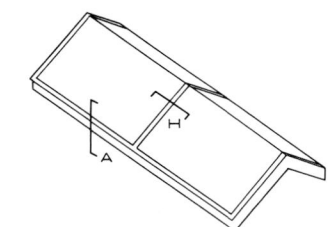

VAULT

SIZES AND SPANS

1. Length and width—almost any design requirement.
2. Variable pitch; up to 4 ft 0 in. along single slope.

GLAZING

1. Generally acrylic, but polycarbonate available.
2. Single or double.
3. Clear, tinted, or white transluscent.
4. Ends may be vertical glazed or hipped.

FRAMING

1. Integral condensation gutters with frame.
2. Expansion and contraction clearances may be needed.
3. Skylight—No structural framing within unit.

REMARKS

Normally used to provide natural light to interior spaces. May be used as exterior entry canopy and walkway protection.

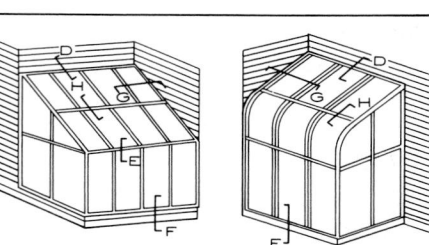

RIDGE

SIZES AND SPANS

Vertical wall and slope to 28 ft 0 in.; rafter spacing of 2, 3, and 4 ft, with glazing lengths of 4, 6, and 8 ft typical.

GLAZING

1. All types of glazing for flat panels; cold formed or thermoplastic for curved shapes.
2. Safety glass or plastic recommended.

FRAMING

1. Tubular or I-beam construction available.
2. May be custom sized to meet retrofit requirements.
3. Glazed structure—Framing within unit is structural to support glazed panels.

REMARKS

1. Shop drawings desirable for these structures.
2. Check local code for requirements of all glazing.

SHED

CTA Architects Engineers; Billings, Montana
Wheeler & Guay Architects P.C.; Alexandria, Virginia

SKYLIGHTS

SIZES AND SPANS

Custom sizes from 3 to 10 ft square, factory assembled. Grid more economical with larger units. Uninterrupted spans of 60 by 90 ft not unusual. Long-span grid networks require a perimeter gutter system to control watersheds.

GLAZING

All types of glazing for flat panels; cold-formed or thermoformed plastic for curved shapes.

FORMS

1. Flat panels used typically for low-pitched roof.
2. Domed units available from most manufacturers.

FRAMING

1. Tubular or I-beam construction available.
2. Glazed structure—framing within unit is structural to support glazed panels.

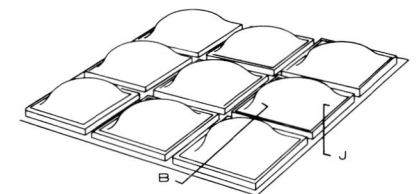

MULTIPLE GRID

SIZES AND SPANS

45 ft across, maximum used. Consult manufacturer before designing custom polygons.

GLAZING

1. All types applicable. Metal panel inserts available.
2. Thickness determined by load and environmental factors.

FORMS

A variety obtainable with varying facets constructed by joining straight framing sections.

FRAMING

1. Tubular and I-beam construction available.
2. Glazed structure—framing within unit is structural to support glazed panels.

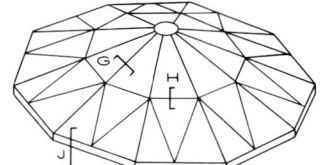

POLYGON

SIZES AND SPANS

10–24 ft usual; available in spans to 300 ft in both static and rollaway structures.

GLAZING

Only plastic glazing materials used. Cold-formed or thermoformed plastic, depending on strength requirements.

FORMS

Can be fabricated to most radii provided rise/span ratio is minimum 22%.

FRAMING

1. Number of curved framing sections can vary within same loading conditions.
2. Glazed structure—framing is structural.

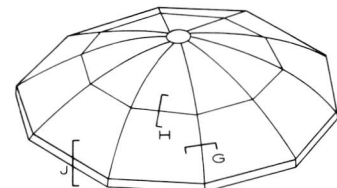

DOME

SIZES AND SPANS

1. Lean-to most economical for up to 20 ft 0 in. common. Slopes vary from 10° to 60°.
2. 40 ft spans possible if rafter depth increased.

GLAZING

1. All types applicable. Insulated glass is tempered.
2. Plastic or safety glass most common.

FORMS

1. Lean-to most commonly used.
2. For double pitch, hip (ridge) detail may vary.
3. Vertical or hip end possible.

FRAMING

1. Tubular or I-beam construction available.
2. Glazed structure—framing within units is structural.

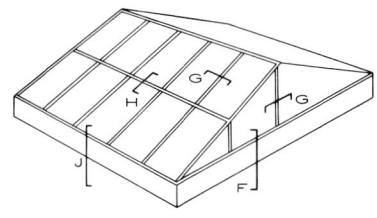

SINGLE OR DOUBLE PITCH

SIZES AND SPANS

1. Common sizes—10–40 ft, standard; one piece thermoformed units up to 10 by 10 ft available.
2. Curb load increases as size increases.

GLAZING

1. All types applicable. Insulated glass is tempered.
2. Plastic or safety glass most common.

FORMS

Three and four sided; standard slopes up to 45°. Maintain minimum rise of 15°.

FRAMING

1. Standard aluminum framing.
2. Many custom framing configurations possible.
3. Glazed structure—framing within unit is structural.

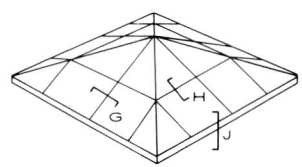

PYRAMID

SIZES AND SPANS

1. 15–25 ft most economical. Up to 40 ft used.
2. Height and width can be customized.

GLAZING

1. All types applicable.
2. Plastic or safety glass most common.
3. Insulated glass usually tempered.

FORMS

Can be used as single or multiple units; hipped gable ends also available.

FRAMING

1. Tubular or I-beam construction available.
2. Use structural gutter network with multiple units.
3. Glazed structure—framing is structural.

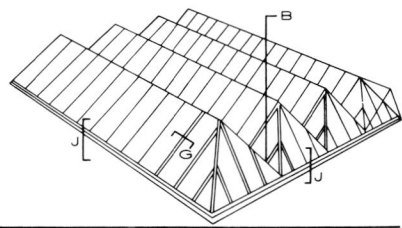

MULTIPLE RIDGE

SIZES AND SPANS

1. 10–40 ft most common. Up to 60 ft available.
2. As width increases, cross purlins become necessary.

GLAZING

1. Plastic glazing materials typical. Glass available in segmented vaults.
2. Glazed panel normally 4 ft wide maximum.

FORMS

Rises from 10 to 50%; 22% most economical.

FRAMING

1. Tubular or I-beam construction available.
2. Glazed structure—framing within unit is structural to support glazed panels.

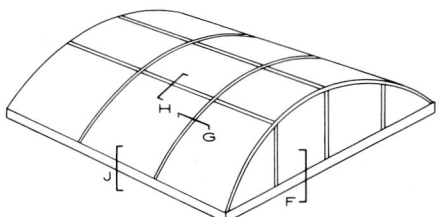

BARREL VAULT

CTA Architects Engineers; Billings, Montana
Wheeler & Guay Architects P.C.; Alexandria, Virginia

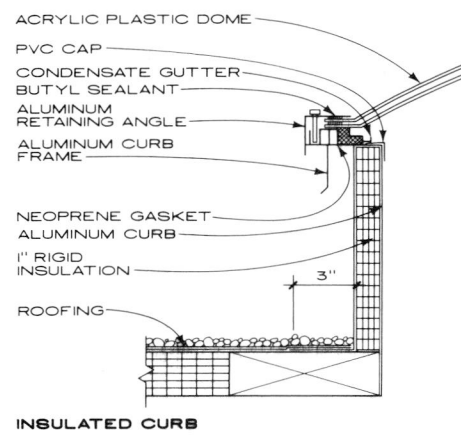

ACRYLIC PLASTIC DOME
PVC CAP
CONDENSATE GUTTER
BUTYL SEALANT
ALUMINUM RETAINING ANGLE
ALUMINUM CURB FRAME
NEOPRENE GASKET
ALUMINUM CURB
1" RIGID INSULATION
ROOFING
3"

INSULATED CURB

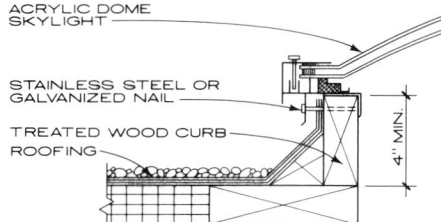

ACRYLIC DOME SKYLIGHT
STAINLESS STEEL OR GALVANIZED NAIL
TREATED WOOD CURB
ROOFING
4" MIN.

WOOD CURB

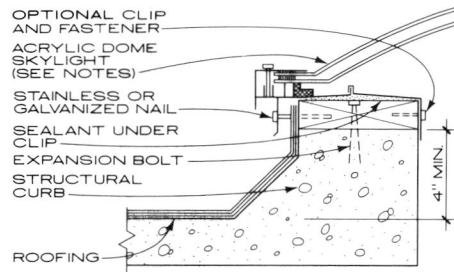

OPTIONAL CLIP AND FASTENER
ACRYLIC DOME SKYLIGHT (SEE NOTES)
STAINLESS OR GALVANIZED NAIL
SEALANT UNDER CLIP
EXPANSION BOLT
STRUCTURAL CURB
ROOFING
4" MIN.

CONCRETE CURB

DETAIL A: CURB TYPES

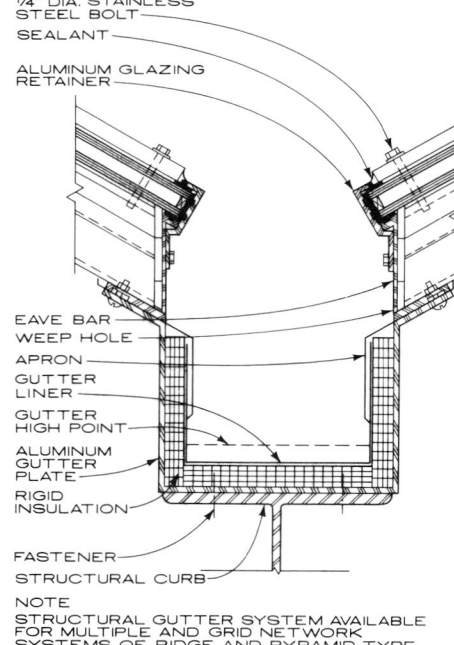

1/4" DIA. STAINLESS STEEL BOLT
SEALANT
ALUMINUM GLAZING RETAINER

EAVE BAR
WEEP HOLE
APRON
GUTTER LINER
GUTTER HIGH POINT
ALUMINUM GUTTER PLATE
RIGID INSULATION
FASTENER
STRUCTURAL CURB

NOTE
STRUCTURAL GUTTER SYSTEM AVAILABLE FOR MULTIPLE AND GRID NETWORK SYSTEMS OF RIDGE AND PYRAMID TYPE ENCLOSURES

DETAIL B: GUTTER

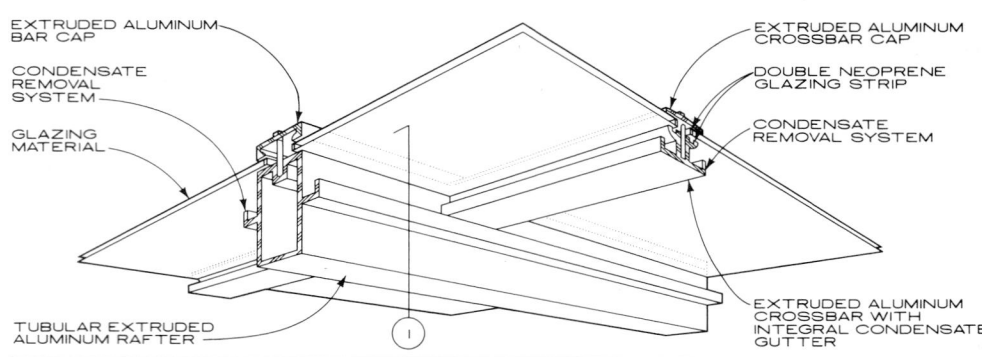

EXTRUDED ALUMINUM BAR CAP
CONDENSATE REMOVAL SYSTEM
GLAZING MATERIAL
TUBULAR EXTRUDED ALUMINUM RAFTER

EXTRUDED ALUMINUM CROSSBAR CAP
DOUBLE NEOPRENE GLAZING STRIP
CONDENSATE REMOVAL SYSTEM
EXTRUDED ALUMINUM CROSSBAR WITH INTEGRAL CONDENSATE GUTTER

1

DETAIL C: TYPICAL TUBULAR ALUMINUM FRAMING

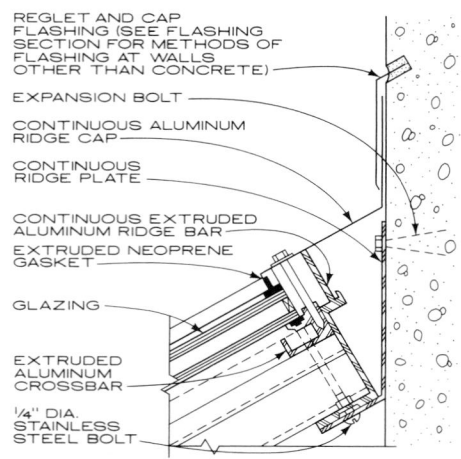

REGLET AND CAP FLASHING (SEE FLASHING SECTION FOR METHODS OF FLASHING AT WALLS OTHER THAN CONCRETE)
EXPANSION BOLT
CONTINUOUS ALUMINUM RIDGE CAP
CONTINUOUS RIDGE PLATE
CONTINUOUS EXTRUDED ALUMINUM RIDGE BAR
EXTRUDED NEOPRENE GASKET
GLAZING
EXTRUDED ALUMINUM CROSSBAR
1/4" DIA. STAINLESS STEEL BOLT

DETAIL D: RIDGE AT SHED

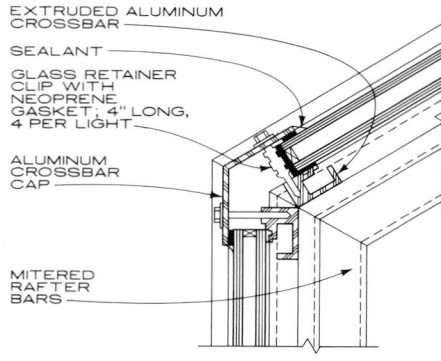

EXTRUDED ALUMINUM CROSSBAR
SEALANT
GLASS RETAINER CLIP WITH NEOPRENE GASKET; 4" LONG, 4 PER LIGHT
ALUMINUM CROSSBAR CAP
1/4" DIA. STAINLESS STEEL BOLT
MITERED RAFTER BARS

DETAIL E: KNEE EDGE

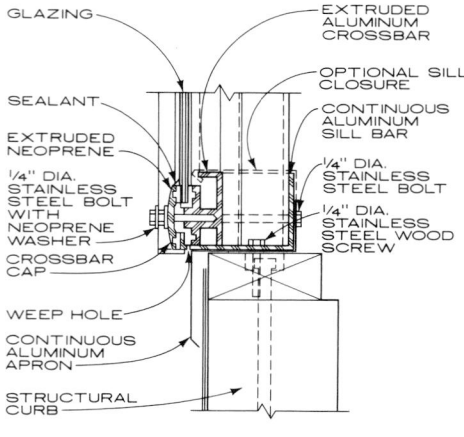

GLAZING
SEALANT
EXTRUDED NEOPRENE
1/4" DIA. STAINLESS STEEL BOLT WITH NEOPRENE WASHER
CROSSBAR CAP
WEEP HOLE
CONTINUOUS ALUMINUM APRON
STRUCTURAL CURB

EXTRUDED ALUMINUM CROSSBAR
OPTIONAL SILL CLOSURE
CONTINUOUS ALUMINUM SILL BAR
1/4" DIA. STAINLESS STEEL BOLT
1/4" DIA. STAINLESS STEEL WOOD SCREW

DETAIL F: VERTICAL SILL

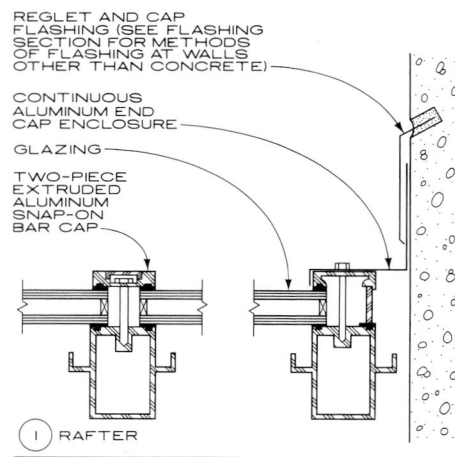

REGLET AND CAP FLASHING (SEE FLASHING SECTION FOR METHODS OF FLASHING AT WALLS OTHER THAN CONCRETE)
CONTINUOUS ALUMINUM END CAP ENCLOSURE
GLAZING
TWO-PIECE EXTRUDED ALUMINUM SNAP-ON BAR CAP

1   RAFTER

DETAIL G: RAFTER AND END WALL

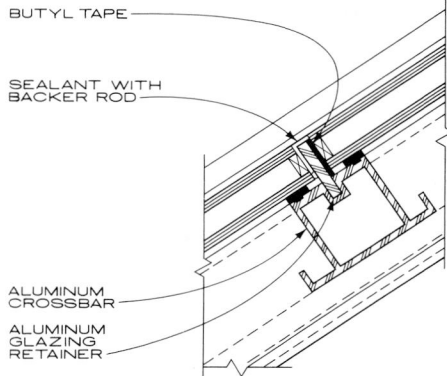

BUTYL TAPE
SEALANT WITH BACKER ROD
ALUMINUM CROSSBAR
ALUMINUM GLAZING RETAINER

DETAIL H: BUTT GLAZING

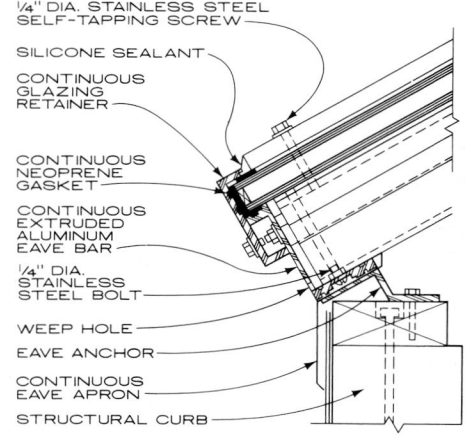

1/4" DIA. STAINLESS STEEL SELF-TAPPING SCREW
SILICONE SEALANT
CONTINUOUS GLAZING RETAINER
CONTINUOUS NEOPRENE GASKET
CONTINUOUS EXTRUDED ALUMINUM EAVE BAR
1/4" DIA. STAINLESS STEEL BOLT
WEEP HOLE
EAVE ANCHOR
CONTINUOUS EAVE APRON
STRUCTURAL CURB

DETAIL J: EAVE OR SILL

CTA Architects Engineers; Billings, Montana
Wheeler & Guay Architects P.C.; Alexandria, Virginia

7   SKYLIGHTS

MAJOR COMPONENTS

The major components of a good joint seal are the substrate, primer, joint filler, bond breaker, and sealant.

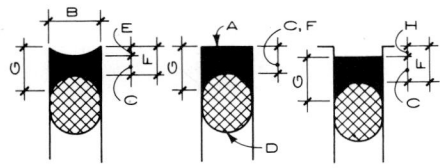

A — sealant
B — sealant width
C — sealant depth
D — joint-filler
E — tooling depth
F — joint-filler depth
G — sealant contact depth
H — sealant recess depth

TYPICAL VERTICAL APPLICATIONS, PROFILES, AND TERMINOLOGY

SUBSTRATE

The more common substrates are masonry concrete, metal, and glass. These are generally classified as porous or nonporous.

Some substrates may not be suitable for achieving a bond unless treated mechanically, chemically, or both.

When the substrate has a coating, the coating must be compatible with the sealant and its bond to the substrate and sealant must be adequate.

Proprietary treatments or protective coatings on metal and waterproofing or water-repellent treatments on concrete may inhibit bonding. Consult both substrate and sealant manufacturers for suitable joint preparation methods and the primers to be used before applying joint materials. Adhesion testing of trial applications in the field is recommended.

Surface laitance and incompatible or bond-inhibiting form release agents on concrete surfaces must be removed.

Substrates must be clean, dry, sound, and free of loose particles, contaminants, foreign matter, water-soluble material, and frost.

Joints in masonry and concrete should be sealed before cleaning exposed surfaces and applying required protective barriers.

PRIMER

The purpose of a primer is to improve the adhesion of a sealant to a substrate. Many sealants require primers on all substrates, some on only certain substrates or on none at all. Most require a primer for maximum adhesion to concrete and masonry surfaces.

JOINT FILLERS

A joint filler is used to control the depth of sealant in the joint and permit full wetting of the intended interface when tooled.

Some joint fillers may be incompatible with the substrate and sealant, causing stains on either one of them or both. Some may be factory coated with a suitable material that provides a barrier to staining. To confirm its suitability, the barrier coating should be acceptable to both the sealant and joint filler manufacturers.

Joint fillers for vertical application may be flexible, compatible, closed cell plastic foam or sponge rubber rod stock and elastomeric tubing of such materials as neoprene, butyl, and EPDM. They should resist permanent deformation before and during sealant application, be nonabsorbent to water or gas, and resist flowing upon mild heating, since this can cause bubbling of the sealant. Open cell sponge type materials such as urethane foam may be satisfactory provided that their water absorption characteristics are recognized. The sealant should be applied immediately after joint filler placement to prevent water absorption from rain. Elastomeric tubing of neoprene, butyl, or EPDM may be applied immediately as a temporary seal until the primary sealant is

put in place, after which they serve to a limited degree as a secondary water barrier. When used as temporary seals, joint fillers should be able to remain resilient at temperatures down to −15°F and have low compression set.

Joint fillers for horizontal application for floors, pavements, sidewalks, patios, and other light-traffic areas may be compatible, extruded, closed cell, high density, flexible foams, corkboard, resin-impregnated fiberboard, or elastomeric tubing or rods. These joint fillers should remain resilient down to −15°F, exhibit good recovery, not cause the sealant to bubble in the joint because of heat, and be capable of supporting the sealant in traffic areas. They should not exude liquids under compression, which could hydraulically cause sealant failure by forcing the sealant from the joint. Combinations of joint filler may be used to form a joint in concrete, and an additional joint filler material may be installed under compression across the width and to the proper depth just before the sealant is applied to provide a clean, dry, compatible backup.

BOND BREAKER

A bond breaker may be necessary to prevent adhesion of the sealant to any surface or material where such adhesion would be detrimental to the performance of the sealant.

The use of a joint filler to which the sealant will not adhere may preclude the need for a bond breaker.

The bond breaker may be a polyethylene tape with pressure-sensitive adhesive on one side or various liquid applied compounds, as recommended by the sealant manufacturer.

SEALANT

Sealants are classified as single component or multicomponent, nonsag or self-leveling, and traffic or nontraffic use, as well as according to movement capability. Characteristics of some generic types are listed in the accompanying table.

CHARACTERISTICS OF COMMON ELASTOMERIC SEALANTS

| | ACRYLIC (SOLVENT) (CURABLE) (ONE-PART) | POLYSULFIDE | | POLYURETHANE | | SILICONE (ONE-PART) |
		TWO-PART	ONE-PART	TWO-PART	ONE-PART	
Chief ingredients	Thermoplastic acrylic, inert pigments, stabilizer, and selected fillers	Polysulfide polymers, activators, pigments, plasticizers, inert fillers, gelling, and curing agents		Polyurethane prepolymer, inert fillers, pigment, plasticizers, accelerators, activators, and extenders	Polyurethane prepolymer, inert fillers, pigment, and plasticizers	Siloxane polymer, pigment, and selected fillers
Percent solids	85–87	95–100	95–100	95–100	95–100	95–100
Curing process	Solvent release	Chemical reaction with curing agent	Chemical reaction with moisture in the air	Chemical reaction with curing agent	Chemical reaction with moisture in air, also oxygen	Chemical reaction with moisture in air
Curing characteristics	Skins on exposed surface; cures progressively inward	Cures uniformly throughout; rate affected by temperature and humidity	Skins over, cures progressively inward; final cure uniform throughout	Cures uniformly throughout; rate affected by temperature and humidity	Skins over, cures progressively inward; final cure uniform throughout	Cures progressively inward; final cure uniform throughout
Primer	Generally not required	Manufacturer's approved primer required for porous surfaces, sometimes for other surfaces		Manufacturer's approved primer required for most surfaces		Required for most surfaces
Application temperature (°F) (substrate)	40–120	40–100	60–100	40–120	40–120	0–120
Tackfree time	24 hr	6–24 hr	6–72 hr	1–24 hr	Slightly tacky until weathered	1 hr or less
Hardness, Shore A Cured 1 to 6 months Aged 5 years	40–70 90	15–45 30–60	25–35 40–50	20–40 35–55	25–45 30–50	20–40 35–55
Joint movement capability (max.)	±12.5%	±25%	±15%	±25%	±15%	±25% high modulus ±50% low modulus
Ultraviolet resistance (direct)	Good	Poor to good	Good	Poor to good	Poor to good	Excellent
Dirt resistance (cured)	Good	Good	Good	Good	Good	Poor
Use characteristics	Excellent adhesion; fair low-temperature flexibility; not usable in traffic areas; unpleasant odor 5–12 days	Wide range of appropriate applications; curing time depends on temperature and humidity	Unpleasant odor; broad range of cured hardnesses available	Sets very fast; broad range of cured hardnesses; excellent for concrete joints and traffic areas	Excellent for concrete joints and traffic areas, but substrate must be absolutely dry; short package stability	Requires contact with air for curing; low abrasion resistance; not tough enough for use in traffic areas

Charles J. Parise, FAIA, FASTM; Smith, Hinchman & Grylls Associates, Inc.; Detroit, Michigan

JOINT DESIGN

The design geometry of a joint seal is related to numerous factors including desired appearance, spacing of joints, anticipated movement in joint, movement capability of sealant to be used, required sealant width to accommodate anticipated movement, and tooling method.

SEALANT WIDTH

The required width of the sealant relative to thermal movement is determined by the application temperature range of the sealant, the temperature extremes anticipated at the site location, the temperature at the time of sealant application, and the movement capability of the sealant to be used. In the absence of specific application temperature knowledge, an ambient application temperature from 4 to 38°C (40 to 100°F) should be assumed in determining the anticipated amount of joint movement in the design of joints. Although affected by ambient temperatures, anticipated joint movement must be determined from anticipated building material temperature extremes rather than ambient temperature extremes.

The accompanying graph provides an average working relationship of recommended joint widths for sealants with various movement capabilities based only on thermal expansion of the more common substrates. These joint widths should be considered as minimal. They do not take into consideration variations in joint dimensions encountered during construction or temperature extremes at the time of sealant application. It is advisable to consider these variables and to also incorporate a safety factor (s.f.) into the joint design by only using a percentage of the stated sealant movement capability, since sealants do not always perform at their stated maximum capabilities.

Many other factors can be involved in building joint movement including, but not limited to, material mass, color, insulation, wind loads, settlement, thermal conductivity, differential thermal stress (bowing), residual growth or shrinkage of materials, building sway, and seismic forces. Of particular importance are material and construction tolerances that can produce joints on the job site smaller than anticipated. The design joint width should be calculated taking all possible movement and tolerance factors into consideration, as shown with the following examples:

$$J = \text{minimum joint width (inches)}$$
$$= \frac{100}{X}(M_t + M_o) + T$$

X = percentage of stated movement capability of the sealant by ASTM Test Method C719

M_t = joint movement due to thermal expansion of substrates (inches)

$\quad = (E_c)(\Delta_t)(L)$

where E_c = coefficient of expansion of substrate from accompanying table (in./in./°F)

$\quad\quad \Delta_t$ = temperature change of substrate (°F)

$\quad\quad L$ = substrate length (inches)

M_o = joint movement due to other factors (inches)

$\quad T$ = tolerances for construction (inches)

A sample calculation for joint width between concrete panels of 10 ft lengths, expecting a temperature change in the concrete of 120°F, construction tolerances of 0.25 in., and sealed with a sealant capable of a maximum ±25% (reduced to 20% for s.f.) movement is

$$J = \frac{100}{X}M_t + T$$
$$= \frac{100}{X}(E_c)(\Delta_t)(L) + T$$
$$= \frac{100}{20}(6 \times 10^{-6} \text{ in./in./°F})(120°F)(120 \text{ in.}) + 0.25 \text{ in.}$$
$$= 0.68 \text{ in.}$$

A more simplified method (but not as accurate) is to use the accompanying graph as follows:

$$J = (\text{joint width scaled}) + T$$
$$= (0.5 \text{ in./in./°F})\left(\frac{120°F}{130°F}\right) + 0.25 \text{ in.}$$
$$= 0.71 \text{ in.}$$

SEALANT DEPTH

The sealant depth, when applied, depends on the sealant width. The following guidelines are normally accepted practice.

1. For a recommended minimum width of ¼ in., the depth should by ¼ in.

2. For joints in concrete, masonry, or stone, the depth of the sealant may be equal to the sealant width in joints up to ½ in. For joints ½ to 1 in. wide, the sealant depth should be one-half the width. For joints 1 to 2 in. wide, the sealant depth should not be greater than ½ in. For widths exceeding 2 in., the depth should be determined by the sealant manufacturer.

3. For sealant widths over ¼ in. and up to ½ in. in metal, glass, and other nonporous surface joints, the minimum of ¼ in. in depth applies, and over ½ in. in width the sealant depth shold be one-half the sealant width and should in no case exceed ½ in.

When determining location of the joint filler in the joint, consideration should be given to the reduction in sealant depth with concave and recessed tooled joints, and the joint should be designed accordingly.

COEFFICIENTS OF EXPANSION

MATERIALS	AVERAGE COEFFICIENT OF LINEAR EXPANSION (MULTIPLY BY 10⁻⁶)	
	CENTIGRADE (MM/MM/°C)	FAHRENHEIT (IN./IN./°F)
Aluminum:		
5005 or 6061 alloy	23.8	13.2
Brass:		
230 alloy	18.7	10.4
Bronze:		
220 alloy	18.4	10.2
385 alloy	20.9	11.6
Clay masonry:		
Clay or shale brick	6.5	3.6
Fire clay brick or tile	4.5	2.5
Concrete masonry:		
Dense aggregate	9.4	5.2
Lightweight aggregate	7.7	4.3
Concrete:		
Calcareous aggregate	9.0	5.0
Siliceous aggregate	10.8	6.0
Quartzite aggregate	12.6	7.0
Copper:		
110 alloy	16.9	9.4
122 alloy	16.9	9.4
Glass	8.8	4.9
Iron:		
Cast, gray	10.6	5.9
Wrought	12.1	6.7
Lead	28.6	15.9
Plastic:		
Acrylic sheet	74.0	41.0
High-impact acrylic sheet	50.0	82.0
Polycarbonate sheet	68.4	38.0
Steel, Carbon	12.1	6.7
Steel, Stainless:		
301 alloy	16.9	9.4
302 alloy	17.3	9.6
304 alloy	17.3	9.6
316 alloy	16.0	8.9
Stone:		
Granite	5.0–11.0	2.8– 6.1
Limestone	4.0–12.0	2.2– 6.7
Marble	6.7–22.1	3.7–12.3
Sandstone	8.0–12.0	4.4– 6.7
Slate	8.0–10.0	4.4– 5.6
Travertine	6.0–10.0	3.3– 5.6
Zinc	32.4	18.0

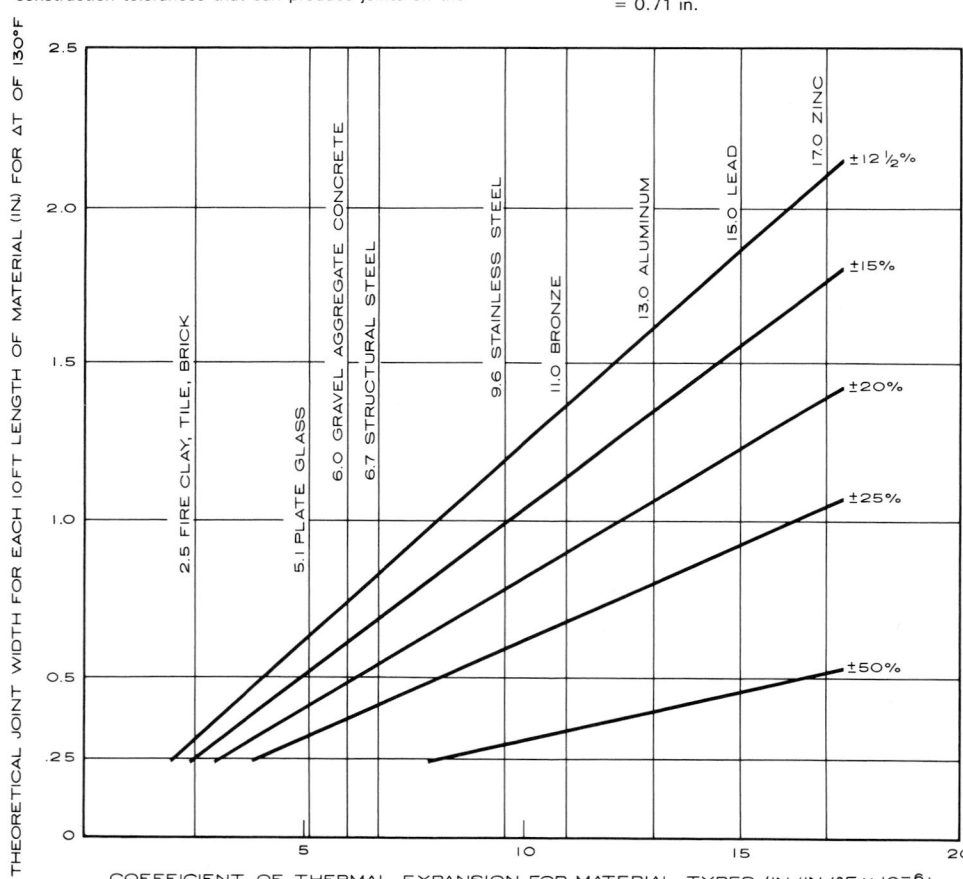

RECOMMENDED JOINT WIDTH FOR SEALANTS WITH VARIOUS MOVEMENT CAPABILITIES

Charles J. Parise, FAIA, FASTM; Smith, Hinchman & Grylls Associates, Inc.; Detroit, Michigan

APPLICATION

To obtain proper adhesion, it is essential that the sealant come in direct contact with the substrate, that the sealant wet the surface of the substrate, and that the substrate be strong enough to provide a firm anchor for the sealant. If any of these conditions is not met, poor adhesion will usually result. The sealant should be installed in such a manner as to completely fill the recess provided in the joint.

Against a porous material, the sealant must enter the pores if good adhesion is to be obtained. Sealants used for this application are thixotropic and will resist flow into the pores unless an external force is applied. Proper filling of the recess accomplishes this, in part, and proper tooling ensures it.

JOINT PREPARATION

Joints to receive sealant should be cleaned out and raked to full width and depth required for installation of joint seal materials. Thoroughly clean all joints, removing all foreign matter such as dust, paint (unless it is a permanent protective coating), oil, grease, waterproofing or water-repellent treatments, water, surface dirt, and frost. Clean porous materials such as concrete, masonry, and unglazed surfaces of ceramic tile by brushing, grinding, blast cleaning, mechanical abrading, acid washing, or a combination of these methods to provide a clean, sound substrate for optimum sealant adhesion. The surface of concrete may be cut back to remove contaminants and expose a clean surface when acceptable to the purchaser.

Remove laitance from concrete by acid washing, grinding, or mechanical abrading and remove form oils from concrete by blast cleaning. Remove loose particles originally present or resulting from grinding, abrading, or blast cleaning by blowing out joints with oil-free compressed air (or vacuuming) prior to application of primer or sealant.

Clean nonporous surfaces, such as metal, glass, porcelain enamel, and glazed surfaces of ceramic tile chemically or by other means that are not harmful to the substrate and are acceptable to the substrate manufacturer.

Remove temporary protective coatings on metallic surfaces by a solvent that leaves no residue. Apply the solvent with clean oil-free cloths or lintless paper towels. Do not dip cleaning cloths into solvent. Always pour the solvent on the cloth to eliminate the possibility of contaminating the solvent. Do not allow the solvent to air-dry without wiping. Wipe dry with a clean dry cloth or lintless paper towels. Permanent coatings that are to remain must not be removed or damaged.

MASKING TAPE

Install masking tape at joint edges when necessary to avoid undesirable sealant smears on exposed visible surfaces. Use a nonstaining, nonabsorbent, compatible type.

PRIMER AND JOINT FILLER

Install primer when and as recommended by the sealant manufacturer for optimum adhesion.

Install compatible joint filler uniformly to proper depth without twisting and braiding.

SEALANT

Install sealant in strict accordance with the manufacturer's recommendations and precautions. Completely fill the recess provided in the joint. Sealants are more safely applied at temperatures above 40°F. Joints must be dry.

TOOLING

Tooling nonsag sealants is essential to force the sealant into the joint and eliminate air pockets and should be done as soon as possible after application and before skinning or curing begins. Tooling also ensures contact of the sealant to the sides of a joint.

Plastic or metal tools may be used. Most applicators use dry tools, but they may be surface-treated to prevent adhesion to the sealant and may be shaped as desired to produce the desired joint profile. Dipping tools in certain liquids decreases adhesion of the sealant to the tool. All liquids should first be tested and accepted for use by the manufacturer. The use of some liquids may result in surface discoloration. In using tooling liquids, care should be taken to ensure that the liquid does not contact joint surfaces prior to the sealant contacting the joint surface. If the sealant overlaps the area contaminated with the liquid, the sealant bond may be adversely affected.

Tool sealant so as to force it into the joint, eliminating air pockets and ensuring contact of the sealant with the sides of the joint. Use appropriate tool to provide a concave, flush, or recessed joint as required.

Immediately after tooling the joint, remove masking tape carefully, if used, without disturbing the sealant.

FIELD TESTING

In cases where the building joints are ready to receive sealant and the question of adhesion of the sealant to novel or untried surfaces arises, it is advisable to install the sealant in a 1.5-m (5 ft) length of joint as a test. It would be good practice to do this as a matter of standard procedure on most projects, even though unusual conditions are not suspected. Following instructions of the sealant manufacturer and using primer as and when recommended, install the sealant in the joint and examine for adhesion after cure to determine whether proper adhesion has been obtained.

Reference: ASTM C-962 "Standard Guide for Use of Elastomeric Joint Sealants." Highlights of text, graph, and figures are reprinted with permission from ASTM Committee C-24 of the American Society for Testing and Materials.

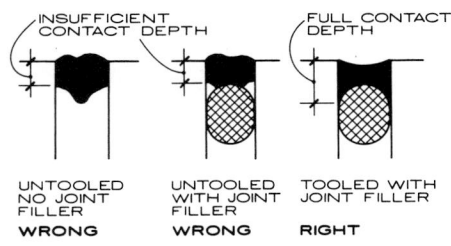

UNTOOLED NO JOINT FILLER **WRONG** — UNTOOLED WITH JOINT FILLER **WRONG** — TOOLED WITH JOINT FILLER **RIGHT**

PURPOSE FOR JOINT FILLER AND TOOLING

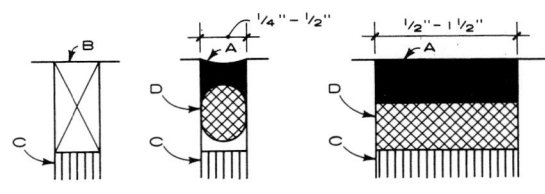

A — sealant
B — removable joint filler
C — premolded joint filler cast in concrete
D — joint filler installed under compression
E — bond breaker (use over sliding metal support in relatively wide joints)
F — concrete shoulder provides vertical support

USE OF MULTIPLE JOINT FILLERS IN HORIZONTAL APPLICATIONS IN CAST-IN-PLACE CONCRETE

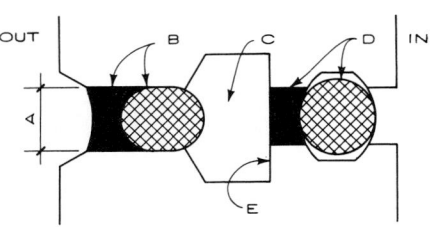

A — 1" minimum for access to interior air seal
B — sealant and joint filler preferred for rain screen; preformed compression seal also used
C — pressure equalization chamber; vent to outside, and chamber baffles at every second floor vertically and same distance horizontally
D — sealant and joint filler installed from outside to facilitate continuity of air seal; building framework hinders application of continuous air seal from interior
E — concrete shoulders required for tooling screed

TWO-STAGE PRESSURE EQUALIZED JOINT SEAL

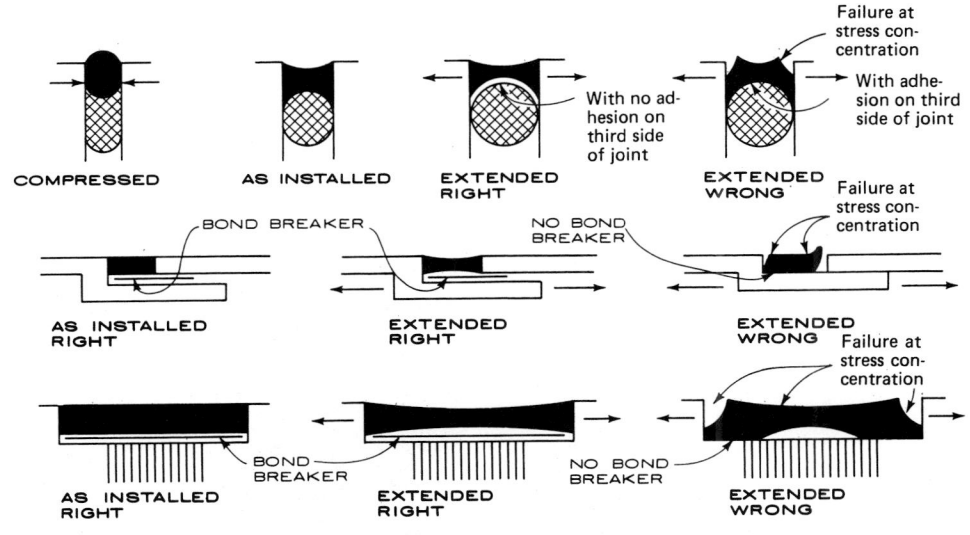

SEALANT CONFIGURATIONS WITH MOVEMENT AND EFFECT OF THREE-SIDED ADHESION

Charles J. Parise, FAIA, FASTM; Smith, Hinchman & Grylls Associates, Inc.; Detroit, Michigan

WATERPROOFING AND DAMPPROOFING
REFERENCES

Building Deck Waterproofing, STP 1084. American Society for Testing and Materials (ASTM), 1990.

Clear Water Repellents Handbook. SWRI, 1991.

Guide for Design of Built-Up Bituminous Membrane Waterproofing Systems of Building Decks, C 981. ASTM.

Guide for Use of High Solids Content, Cold Liquid-Applied Elastomeric Waterproof Membrane with Separate Wearing Course, C 898. ASTM.

Guidelines for Clear Waterproofing Masonry Walls, Masonry Institute of America.

Guide to the Use of Waterproofing, Dampproofing, Protective, and Decorative Barrier Systems for Concrete 515,1R. American Concrete Institute, 1985.

NRCA Waterproofing and Dampproofing Manual. National Roofing Contractors Association, 1989.

Specifying Water Repellents, Monograph 07M181. Construction Specifications Institute, 1990.

VAPOR RETARDERS
REFERENCES

"An Air Barrier for the Building Envelope." *Proceedings of Building Science Insight '86*, NRCC 29943. National Research Center of Canada, 1989.

Air Barriers, TEK-AID Digest 07195. Toronto: Construction Specifications Canada, 1990. [(416) 922-3159]

INSULATION

Cellulose Insulation Manufacturers Association
c/o Dan Lea
136 South Keowee Street
Dayton, OH 45402
Tel: (513) 222-1024
Fax:(513) 222-5794

Center for Insulation Technology
Drexel University
Mechanical Engineering and Mechanics Dept.
Philadelphia, PA 19104
Tel: (215)895-1833
Fax:(215) 895-1478

North American Insulation Manufacturers Association
44 Canal Center Plaza, Suite 310
Alexandria, VA 22314
Tel: (703) 684-0084
Fax:(703) 684-0427

Perlite Institute (PI)
88 New Dorp Plaza
Staten Island, NY 10306-2994
Tel: (718) 351-5723
Fax: (718) 351-5725

Polyisocyanurate Insulation
  Manufacturers Association (PIMA)
1001 Pennsylvania Ave. N.W.
Washington, DC 20004
Tel: (202) 624-2709
Fax:(202) 628-3856

National Insulation and
  Abatement Contractors Association
99 Canal Center Plaza, Suite 222
Alexandria, VA 22314
Tel: (703) 683-6422
Fax:(703) 549-4838

Society of the Plastics Industry, Inc. (SPI)
1275 K Street, N.W., #400
Washington, DC 20005
Tel: (202) 371-5200
Fax:(202) 371-1022

Vermiculite Association (VA)
600 S. Federal Street, Suite 400
Chicago, IL 60605
Tel: (312) 922-6222
Fax:(312) 922-2734

REFERENCES

Watson, Donald, FAIA, ed. *The Energy Design Handbook*. Washington, D.C.: AIA, 1993.

Close, P. *Sound Control and Thermal Insulation of Buildings*. New York: Van Nostrand Reinhold, 1966.

"Thermal Insulation and Vapor Retarder," Ch. 21 and 22. *ASHRAE Handbook*. Fundamentals vol. 1989.

EXTERIOR INSULATION AND FINISH SYSTEMS

Exterior Insulation Manufacturers Association (EIMA)
2759 State Road 580, Suite 112
Clearwater, FL 34621
Tel: (813) 726-6477
Fax:(813) 726-8180

REFERENCES

Gorman, J. R., et al. *Plaster and Drywall Systems Manual* McGraw-Hill,1988.

Guideline Specifications for EIF Systems, Exterior Insulation Manufacturers Association, 1991.

ROOFING

Asphalt Roofing Manufacturers Association (ARMA)
6000 Executive Blvd., Suite 201
Rockville, MD 20852
Tel: (301) 231-9050
Fax:(301) 881-6572

Cedar Shake & Shingle Bureau (CSSB)
515 116th Avenue, NE, #275
Bellevue, WA 98004
Tel: (206) 453-1323
Fax:(206) 455-1314

Institute of Roofing and Waterproofing Consultants
4242 Kirchoff Road
Rolling Meadows, IL 60008
Tel: (708) 991-9292
Fax:(708) 202-8503

National Roofing Contractors Association (NRCA)
O'Hare International Center
10255 W. Higgins Road, Suite 600
Rosemont, IL 60018
Tel: (708) 299-9070
Fax:(708) 2991183

National Roof Deck Contractors Association (NRDCA)
600 South Federal Street, Suite 400
Chicago, IL 60605
Tel: (312) 922-6222
Fax:(312) 922-2734

Roof Coatings Manufacturers Association (RCMA)
6000 Executive Blvd., Suite 201
Rockville, MD 20852-3803
Tel: (301) 881-6572

Roof Consultants Institute (RCI)
7424 Chapel Hill Road
Raleigh, NC 27607
Tel: (919) 859-0742
Fax:(919) 859-1328

Roofing Communications Network (RCN)
3690 Bohicket Road, Suite ID
John's Island, SC 29455
Tel: (800) 522-7663

Roofing Industry Educational Institute (RIEI)
14 Inverness Drive East, Building H, Suite 110
Englewood, CO 80112-5608
Tel: (303) 790-7200
Fax:(303) 790-9006

Roofing Products Division/Rubber
  Manufacturers Association (RPD/RMA)
1400 K Street, N.W., Suite 900
Washington, D.C. 20005
Tel: (202) 682-4800
Fax:(202) 682-4854

Single Ply Roofing Institute (SPRI)
20 Walnut Road, Suite 8
Wellesley Hills, MA 02181
Tel: (617) 237-7879
Fax:(617) 237-1064

REFERENCES

Baker, M. *Roofs: Design, Application, and Maintenance*. Polyscience Publications. National Research Council of Canada, 1980.

Manual for New Roof Construction CSSB.

NRCA Construction Details. NRCA, 1989.

ROOFING TYPES, SHINGLES, AND ROOFING TILES

Cedar Shake & Shingle Bureau (CSSB)
515 116th Avenue, NE #275
Bellevue, WA 98004
Tel: (206) 453-1323
Fax:(206) 455-1314

National Tile Roofing Manufacturers Association, Inc.
P.O. Box 40337
Eugene, OR 97404
Tel: (503) 689-5530

REFERENCES

Design and Application Manual for New Roof Construction. Cedar Shake & Shingle Bureau.

Griffin, C. W. *Manual of Built-Up Roof Systems*. New York: McGraw-Hill.

Installation Manual for Concrete Tile Roofing National Tile Roofing Manufacturers Association.

NRCA Steep Roofing Manual. National Roofing Contractors Association, 1989.

Residential Asphalt Roofing Manual. Asphalt Roofing Manufacturers Association, 1988.

Specification for Clay Roof Tiles, C 1167-90. ASTM, 1991.

MEMBRANE ROOFING
REFERENCES

Building Materials Directory. Underwriters Laboratory. [updated annually]

NRCA Low Slope Roofing Manual National Roofing Contractors Association, 1989.

Reroofing Specifications, Monograph 07M611. Construction Specifications Institute (CSI), 1986.

Single-ply Roofing Systems, Monog. 07M531. CSI, 1987.

Sprayed Polyurethane Foam Roofing Systems, Monograph 07M546. CSI, 1990.

SHEET METAL ROOFING
REFERENCES

Architectural Sheet Metal Manual, 4th ed. Sheet Metal and Air Conditioning Contractors National Association (SMACNA), 1987.

Custom-fabricated Roofing Specifications. SMACNA, 1991.

NRCA Construction Details. National Roofing Contractors Association, 1989.

Sheet Copper Applications. Copper Development Association, 1980.

JOINT SEALERS

Adhesives Manufacturers Association
401 North Michigan Avenue, Suite 2400
Chicago, IL 60611
Tel: (312) 644-6610
Fax:(312) 321-6869

Adhesive and Sealant Council (ASC)
1627 K Street, N.W., Suite 1000
Washington, DC 20006-1707
Tel: (202) 452-1500
Fax:(202) 452-1501

National Paint and Coatings Association (NPCA)
1500 Rhode Island Avenue, N.W.
Washington, DC 20005
Tel: (202) 462-6272
Fax:(202) 462-8549

Sealant, Waterproofing, and Restoration Institute (SWRI)
3101 Broadway, Suite 585
Kansas City, MO 64111
Tel: (816) 561-8230
Fax:(816) 561-7765

REFERENCES

Fenestration Sealants Guide Manual, 850-91. American Architectural Manufacturers Association, 1991.

Guide for Use of Joint Sealants C 1193. ASTM, 1991.

Karpati, K. *Exposure Evaluation of Sealants with Low Movement Capability*, NRCC 29704. National Research Council of Canada, 1988.

Klosowski, J., *Sealants in Construction*. Marcel Dekker, 1989.

O'Conner, T., ed. *Building Sealants: Materials, Properties, and Performance*, STP 1069. ASTM, 1990.

Panek, J., and J. Cook. *Construction Sealants and Adhesives*, 3rd ed. New York: J. Wiley & Sons, 1991.

Sealant Manual. Flat Glass Marketing Association, 1990.

Sealants: The Professional's Guide. Sealant, Waterproofing, and Restoration Institute, 1990.

Selection and Application of Caulks, Sealants, Putties, and Glazing Compounds Structures. National Paint and Coatings Association.

CHAPTER

DOORS
AND WINDOWS

GENERAL

Fire door assemblies, used to protect against the spread of fire and smoke, consist of a fire door, frame, hardware, and accessories such as closers and astragals. Each component is crucial to the overall performance of the assembly as a fire barrier.

NFPA 80, Standard for Fire Doors and Fire Windows, is a consensus standard that establishes minimum criteria for installing and maintaining assemblies and devices used to protect openings in walls, ceilings, and floors from the spread of fire and smoke. The degree of fire protection (in hours) required for a given opening is determined by reference within the model building codes (BOCA, SBCCI, and UBC) and the Life Safety Code (NFPA 101). Classifications of fire doors are given in hourly references determined by testing done in accordance with NFPA 252, Standard Method of Fire Tests of Door Assemblies (also known as UL 10B). Additional information is available in Chapter 6, Section 6 of the NFPA's *Fire Protection Handbook*.

TYPES OF OPENINGS

1. 4-HOUR and 3-HOUR: Openings in fire walls and in walls that divide a single building into fire areas
2. 1 1/2-HOUR and 1-HOUR: Openings in enclosures of vertical communications through buildings and in 2-hr rated partitions providing horizontal fire separations
3. 3/4-HOUR and 20-MINUTE: Openings in walls or partitions between rooms and corridors with a fire resistance rating of 1 hour or less

NOTE

The hourly protection for openings depends on the use of the barrier, as in exit enclosures, vertical openings in buildings, building separation walls, corridor walls, smoke barriers, hazardous locations, and enclosures.

TYPES OF DOORS

Typical construction for swinging fire doors:

1. COMPOSITE fire doors: wood, steel, or plastic sheets bonded to and supported by a solid core material
2. HOLLOW METAL fire doors: flush or panel design with not less than 20-gauge steel face
3. METAL-CLAD fire doors: flush or panel design consisting of metal-covered wood cores or stiles and rails and insulated panels covered with steel of 24 gauge or lighter
4. SHEET METAL fire doors: 22-gauge or lighter steel or corrugated, flush sheet, or panel design
5. TIN-CLAD fire doors: wood core with a terne plate or galvanized steel facing (30 or 24 gauge)
6. WOOD core doors: wood, hardboard, or plastic face sheets bonded to a wood block or wood particleboard core material with untreated wood edges

TYPES OF FRAMES

Fire-rated doorframes can be factory or field assembled. Frames must be adequately anchored at the jambs and floor per manufacturer's specifications. Codes require doors to be installed in accordance with NFPA 80. Section 2-5, Frames, indicates only labeled frames are to be used.

1. LIGHT GAUGE METAL FRAME: Head and jamb members with or without transom panel made from aluminum (45-min. maximum rating) or from light gauge steel (1 1/2-hr maximum rating); installed over finished wall
2. PRESSED STEEL (HOLLOW METAL): Head and jamb members, with or without solid or glazed transoms or sidelights made from 18-gauge or heavier steel (3-hr maximum rating); required for most metal doors

HARDWARE

Door hardware is either provided by the builder independent of the assembly or furnished by the manufacturer with the door assembly. Generally, the manufacturer must prepare the door and frame to receive hardware to ensure the integrity of the fire-rated assembly.

Fire doors are hung on steel ball-bearing hinges and must be self-closing. Labeled automatic latches and door closers can be self-operated or controlled by fail-safe devices that activate in a fire situation. Pairs of doors require coordinators with astragals to ensure that both doors close. Head and jambs should be sealed with gaskets when smoke control is required.

MAXIMUM DOOR SIZES (HOLLOW METAL, ALL CLASSES)

Single door	4 x 10 ft with labeled single-point or 3-point latching device; 4 x 8 ft with fire exit hardware
Pair of doors	8 x 10 ft active leaf, with labeled single-point or 3-point latching device; inactive leaf, with labeled 2-point latching device or top and bottom bolts; 8 x 8 ft with fire exit hardware

Richard J. Vitullo, AIA; Oak Leaf Studio; Crownsville, Maryland
National Fire Protection Association; Quincy, Massachusetts

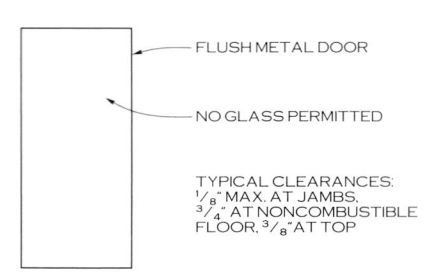

4-HOUR CLASSIFICATION

FLUSH METAL DOOR

NO GLASS PERMITTED

TYPICAL CLEARANCES:
1/8" MAX. AT JAMBS,
3/4" AT NONCOMBUSTIBLE FLOOR, 3/8" AT TOP

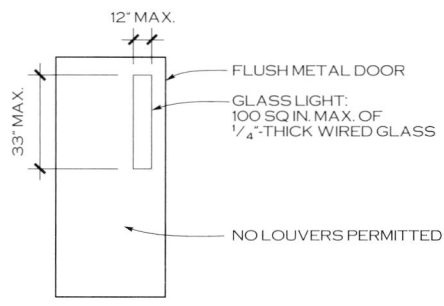

3-HOUR CLASSIFICATION

12" MAX.

33" MAX.

FLUSH METAL DOOR

GLASS LIGHT: 100 SQ IN. MAX. OF 1/4"-THICK WIRED GLASS

NO LOUVERS PERMITTED

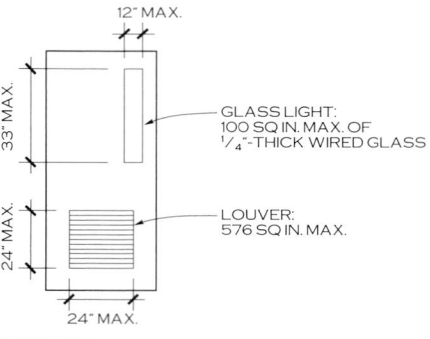

1 1/2-HOUR AND 1-HOUR CLASSIFICATION

12" MAX.

33" MAX.

24" MAX.

24" MAX.

GLASS LIGHT: 100 SQ IN. MAX. OF 1/4"-THICK WIRED GLASS

LOUVER: 576 SQ IN. MAX.

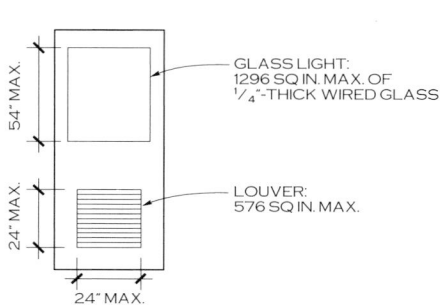

3/4-HOUR AND 20-MIN. CLASSIFICATION

54" MAX.

24" MAX.

24" MAX.

GLASS LIGHT: 1296 SQ IN. MAX. OF 1/4"-THICK WIRED GLASS

LOUVER: 576 SQ IN. MAX.

NOTES FOR ALL CLASSES

1. All hinges or pivots must be steel. Two hinges are required on doors up to 5 ft in height; an additional hinge is required for each additional 2 ft 6 in. of door height or fraction thereof. The same requirement holds for pivots.
2. While wired glass 1/4-in. thick is the most common material used as glass lights, other materials have been listed and approved for installation. Refer to the UL fire protection directory.
3. All authorities having jurisdiction should be consulted before installation of glass lights and louvers.

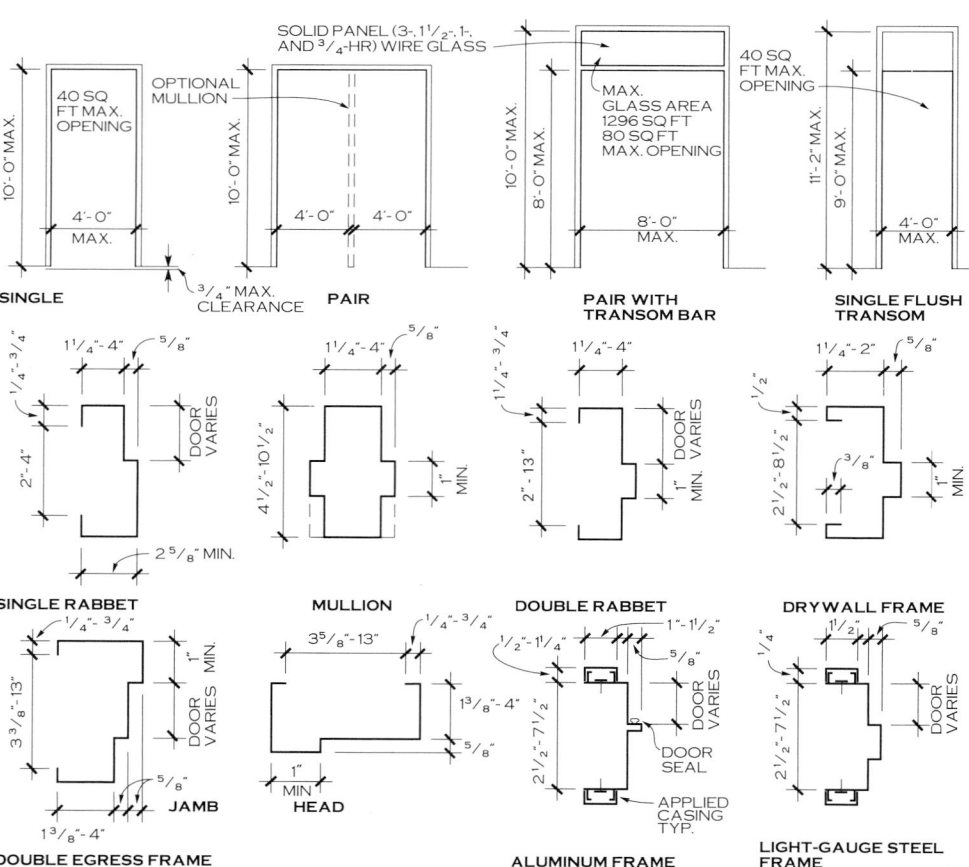

FIRE-RATED STEEL FRAMES—ELEVATIONS AND DETAILS

GENERAL

Door and window security has two functions. In buildings such as prisons, jails, or buildings used for incarceration, security must be focused on detention or keeping people in. In other building types, from residential to commercial to industrial, security is focused on keeping unwanted people out.

Security concerns include hardware, construction details, electronic systems, and building openings such as skylights, roof hatches, and loading areas.

The standards for various degrees of security are based on test methods set up by the National Institute of Law Enforcement and Criminal Justice (NILECJ), now the National Institute of Justice (NIJ), and the American Society for Testing and Materials (ASTM). These standards specify the performance requirements that a door or window must meet in certain testing situations. They do not specify the materials or methods of construction. They do offer a consistent method of evaluation for specified door and window assemblies for each class or grade of security requirement. NILECJ's classes are equivalent to ASTM's grades as defined below.

CLASS I/GRADE 10: Minimum security level; adequate for single family residential buildings located in stable, comparatively low crime areas.

CLASS II/GRADE 20: Low to medium security level; provides security for residential buildings located in average crime rate areas or for apartments in both low and average crime rate areas.

CLASS III/GRADE 30: Medium to high security; provides security for residential buildings located in higher than average crime rate areas or for small commercial buildings in average or low crime rate areas.

CLASS IV/GRADE 40: High security level; provides security for commercial buildings located in medium to high crime rate areas.

SWINGING DOOR ASSEMBLIES

A door, in addition to providing a portal for entry, should resist unwanted intruders. This resistance can be accommodated by requiring that all exterior doors comply with NILECJ 0306.00 Physical Security of Door Assemblies and Components or ANSI/ASTM standard F476-84 Standard Test Methods for Security of Swinging Door Assemblies. The security of a door assembly depends not only on the lock, but also on the strike, buck, hinge, door, and even the surrounding wall.

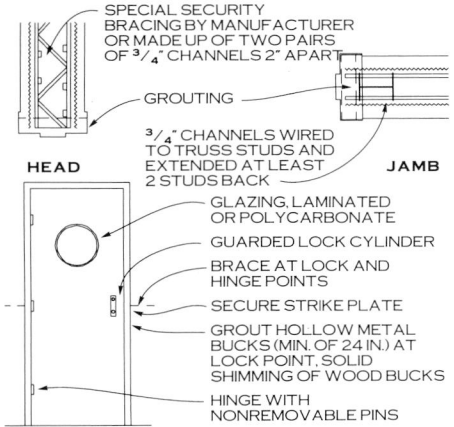

HEAD   JAMB

SPECIAL SECURITY BRACING BY MANUFACTURER OR MADE UP OF TWO PAIRS OF 3/4" CHANNELS 2" APART

GROUTING

3/4" CHANNELS WIRED TO TRUSS STUDS AND EXTENDED AT LEAST 2 STUDS BACK

GLAZING, LAMINATED OR POLYCARBONATE

GUARDED LOCK CYLINDER

BRACE AT LOCK AND HINGE POINTS

SECURE STRIKE PLATE

GROUT HOLLOW METAL BUCKS (MIN. OF 24 IN.) AT LOCK POINT, SOLID SHIMMING OF WOOD BUCKS

HINGE WITH NONREMOVABLE PINS

SECURITY DOOR

FRAME

The stiffness of the bucks is critical; wood bucks should be a minimum of 2 in. thick and have solid, secure shims for 24 in. at the locking point and 12 in. at each hinge point; stops should be milled integral with the buck; wood bucks for Grade 20 should be of premium grade hardwood; Grade 30 bucks should be 16 gauge steel; Grade 40 bucks should be 15 gauge steel; all steel bucks should be grouted full.

WALL

Fire stops or braces should be located at the locking point and each hinge point—for one stud space at grade 10, two stud spaces for Grade 20 and above; if wood studs appear, plywood sheathing should be used on both sides of the studs for two stud spaces to each side of the doorway; if it is a masonry wall, grout all space between frame and wall.

Stuart L. Knoop, AIA; Oudens + Knoop, Architects, P.C.; Washington, D.C.
McCain McMurray, Architect; Washington, D.C.

PERFORMANCE REQUIREMENTS FOR DOOR ASSEMBLIES AND COMPONENTS

DOOR ASSEMBLY TESTS	COMPONENT TEST	MEASURED PARAMETER	REQUIREMENT			
			CLASS I	CLASS II	CLASS III	CLASS IV
Bolt projection strike hole	Lock	Projection Size	9/16 in. (14.3 mm)²	9/16 in. (14.3 mm)²	11/16 in. (17.5 mm)²	11/16 in. (17.5 mm)²
Bolt pressure	Lock	Resistance	150 lbf (670 N)	150 lbf (670 N)	150 lbf (670 N)	150 lbf (670 N)
Jamb/wall stiffness	Jamb/wall	Force to spread	1,350 lbf (6,000 N)	1,800 lbf (8,000 N)	3,600 lbf (16,000 N)	4,950 lbf (22,000 N)
		Increase in lock-front to strike space	3/8 in. (9.5 mm)	3/8 in. (9.5 mm)	1/2 in. (13 mm)	1/2 in. (13 mm)
Knob impact[3]	Lock	Resistance - 74 ft - lbf (100 Joules) impact	One blow	Two blows	Five blows	Ten blows
Cylinder core tension	Lock	Resistance	290 lbf (1,300 N)	1,080 lbf (4,800 N)	2,470 lbf (11,000 N)	2,470 lbf (11,000 N)
Cylinder body tension	Lock	Resistance				3,600 lbf (16,000 N)
Knob torque[3]	Lock	Resistance	18.5 lbf-ft (25 Nm)	37 lbf-ft (50 Nm)	81 lbf-ft (110 Nm)	118 lbf-ft (160 Nm)
Cylinder torque[4]	Lock	Resistance			81 lbf-ft (110 Nm)	118 lbf-ft (160 Nm)
Cylinder impact[4]	Lock	Resistance - 74 ft - lbf (100 Joules) impact			Five blows	Ten blows
Door impact	Door	Impact resistance at center and panel	Two blows of 59 ft-lbf (80 J)	Class I plus two blows of 89 ft-lbf (120 J)	Class II plus two blows of 118 ft-lbf (160 J)	Class III plus two blows of 148 ft-lbf (200 J)
		Impact resistance of glazing - 74 ft - lbf (100 Joules)	One blow	Two blows	Five blows	Ten blows
Hinge pin removal[5]	Hinge	Resistance	50 lbf (225 N)	50 lbf (225 N)	200 lbf (900 N)	200 lbf (900 N)
Hinge impact	Door, hinge, jamb/wall	Impact resistance at hinge	Two blows of 59 ft-lbf (80 J)	Class I plus two blows of 89 ft-lbf (120 J)	Class II plus two blows of 118 ft-lbf (160 J)	Class III plus two blows of 148 ft-lbf (200 J)
Bolt impact	Lock, door, jamb/strike	Impact resistance at bolt	Two blows of 59 ft-lbf (80 J)	Class I plus two blows of 89 ft-lbf (120 J)	Class II plus two blows of 118 ft-lbf (160 J)	Class III plus two blows of 148 ft-lbf (200 J)

NOTES

1. These requirements, promulgated by the National Institute of Law Enforcement and Criminal Justice (NILECJ), Standard 0306.00, were used as the basis for the development of ASTM 476-84 Standard Test Methods for Security of Swinging Door Assemblies.
2. Dead latch plunger must not enter strike hole with latch bolt.
3. Applies to type A locks only. Type A locks use a single dead latch or the combination of a latch or dead latch and a dead bolt which are mechanically interconnected. Type B locks have a latch or dead latch mechanically independent from the dead bolt.
4. Does not apply to key-in-knob locks.
5. Applies to out-swinging doors only.

PERFORMANCE REQUIREMENTS FOR WINDOW UNIT SECURITY

TEST	MEASURED PARAMETER	MINIMUM REQUIREMENT			
		CLASS I	CLASS II	CLASS III	CLASS IV
Loiding force	Force to move locking device	10 lbf (45 N)	10 lbf (45 N)	10 lbf (45 N)	10 lbf (45 N)
Locking device stability, type A	Resistance to unlocking motion	50 cycles by hand	50 cycles by hand	50 cycles by hand	50 cycles by hand
Type B, C, D, and F		50 cycles at 50 lbf (222 N)	50 cycles at 50 lbf (222 N)	50 cycles at 50 lbf (222 N)	50 cycles at 50 lbf (222 N)
Locking device stability, type A	Resistance to static load	50 lbf (222 N)	150 lbf (667 N)	300 lbf (1335 N)	750 lbf (3335 N)
Type B, C, D, and F			150 lbf (667 N)	300 lbf (1335 N)	750 lbf (3335 N)
Window strength, type A	Resistance to static load	Primary 50 lbf (222 N) Secondary 50 lbf (222 N)	Primary 100 lbf (445 N) Secondary 150 lbf (667 N)	Primary 100 lbf (445 N) Secondary 300 lbf (1335 N)	Primary 100 lbf (445 N) Secondary 750 lbf (3335 N)
Type B, C, D, and F			50 lbf (222 N)	150 lbf (667 N)	300 lbf (1335 N)	750 lbf (3335 N)
Impact strength, glazing	Resistance to impact		One impact of 37 ft - lbf (50 J)	One impact of 74 ft - lbf (100 J)	Ten impact of 74 ft - lbf (100 J)
Sash frame			One impact of 37 ft - lbf (50 J)	One impact of 74 ft - lbf (100 J)	Ten impact of 74 ft - lbf (100 J)
Security bars					Ten impact of 74 ft - lbf (100 J)

NOTE

Table from the National Institute of Justice (NIJ) Standard 0316.00, Physical Security of Window Units.

GUIDE SPECIFICATIONS FROM THE HOLLOW METAL MANUFACTURERS ASSOCIATION (HMMA)

	HMMA 860	HMMA 861	HMMA 862	HMMA 863
DOORS				
Face sheets interior	20 ga.	18 ga.	14 ga.	14 or 12 ga.
Face sheets exterior	18 ga.	16 ga.	14 ga.	14 or 12 ga.
Minimum thickness	1 ³/₄"	1 ³/₄"	1 ³/₄"	2"
Stiffeners	22 ga.	22 ga.	18 ga.	18 ga.
Vertical edges	Continuous weld or interlocking seam welded at top and bottom of door	Continuous weld	Continuous weld	Reinforced by 10 ga. continuous steel channel, continuous weld
Top and bottom edges	Closed with 16 ga. continuous recessed steel channel	Closed with 16 ga. continuous recessed steel channel, spot welded to face sheets	Closed with 12 ga. continuous recessed steel channel, spot welded to face sheets	Reinforced with continuous steel channel, 10 ga. spot welded to face sheets 4" on center
Glass molding and stops	Fixed moldings welded to door on security side; loose stops, 20 ga.	Fixed moldings welded to door on security side; loose stops, 20 ga.	Fixed moldings welded to door on security side; all stops, 16 ga.	Fixed moldings, 12 ga. spot welded to face sheets 5" o.c.; removable glass stops, 14 ga. pressed steel channel
FRAMES				
Interior openings	16 ga. (18 ga. for wood doors, 20 ga. for hollow core wood doors)	16 ga.; 14 ga. for openings over 4′-0" in width	12 ga.	12 ga.
Exterior openings	16 ga.	14 ga.	12 ga.	12 ga.
Construction	Welded or knocked-down with integral stop and trim	Welded units with integral stop and trim	Welded units with integral stop and trim	Welded units with integral stop and trim
Floor anchors	16 ga. welded inside jambs	14 ga. welded inside jambs	14 ga. welded inside jambs	Same ga. as frame, welded inside jambs with at least 4 spot welds per anchor
Jamb anchors	In masonry walls 16 ga. steel or 0.156" diameter steel wire. For stud partitions, 18 ga. steel anchors welded inside jambs	In masonry walls 16 ga. steel or 0.156" diameter steel wire. For stud partitions, 18 ga. steel anchors welded inside jambs	In masonry walls 14 ga. steel or 0.156" diameter steel wire. For stud partitions, 16 ga. steel anchors welded inside jambs	Same ga. as frame
Loose glazing stops	20 ga. cold-rolled steel	20 ga. cold-rolled steel	16 ga. cold-rolled steel	10 ga. cold-rolled steel

NOTES

1. HMMA 860: For use in building projects where traffic is relatively light and hard usage is not anticipated.
2. HMMA 861: For use in commercial and industrial applications where rigorous use is anticipated, such as schools, hospitals, industrial buildings, office buildings, hotels, nursing homes, airports, and convention centers.
3. HMMA 862: For use in applications where security is paramount due to high susceptibility to vandalism, break-in, and theft, such as entrances and back doors of businesses, storerooms, warehouses, strip stores, apartments, and condominiums. HMMA 862 incorporates testing procedures and performance requirements promulgated by NILECJ for Class IV doors (ASTM F476-84) including jamb/wall stiffness test, jamb/wall stiffness performance, door impact test, door and glazing panel impact resistance performance.
4. HMMA 863: For applications in jails, prisons, detention centers, and secured areas in hospitals or courthouses. HMMA 863 requires five tests: static load test, rack test, impact load test, removable glazing stop test, and bullet resistance test.
5. Reprinted with permission from the Hollow Metal Manufacturers Association, division of NAAMM.

PERFORMANCE REQUIREMENTS FOR SLIDING GLASS DOOR UNIT SECURITY

	REQUIREMENTS	
PARAMETER	**CLASS I UNIT**	**CLASS II UNIT**
Disassembly	No entry	No entry
Latch operator loiding resistance	10 lbf (45 N)	10 lbf (45 N)
Latch loiding resistance	300 lbf (1335 N) plus weight of panel	600 lbf (2670 N) plus weight of panel
Locking device stability	Horizontal - 50 lbf (222 N) Vertical - 50 lbf (222 N) plus weight of panel (10 cycles)	Horizontal - 50 lbf (222 N) Vertical - 50 lbf (222 N) plus weight of panel (10 cycles)
Door panel removal resistance	Horizontal - 100 lbf (445 N) Vertical - 300 lbf (1335 N) plus weight of panel	Horizontal - 100 lbf (445 N) Vertical - 600 lbf (2670 N) plus weight of panel
Locking device strength	300 lbf (1335 N)	600 lbf (2670 N)
Fixed panel fastening strength	300 lbf (1335 N)	600 lbf (2670 N)
Meeting stile fastening strength	150 lbf (667 N)	Horizontal - 100 lbf (445 N) 300 lbf (1335 N)
Glazing impact strength	None	37 ft-lbf (50 Joules)

NOTES

1. Table from the National Institute of Justice (NIJ) Standard 0318.00, Physical Security of Sliding Glass Door Units.
2. Class I sliding door units provide a minimum level of physical security. Class II sliding door units provide a moderate level of physical security.
3. Loiding is a method of manipulating a locking device from the exterior of a sliding glass door unit by means of a thin, flat object or a thin stiff wire that is inserted between the locking stile and the strike so as to force the locking device toward the unlocked position.

McCain McMurray, Architect; Washington, D.C.

SLIDING DOOR UNITS

Sliding glass doors are a particular concern in securing a building. The locking devices should include vertical rod, or lever bolts, at top and bottom; the frame should be solid or reinforced at the locking points; the stile must also be reinforced at the locking points. The operating panels should be designed so that they cannot be lifted out of their tracks when in the locked position. Glazing and other components should be installed from the inside so that entry cannot be gained by disassembly.

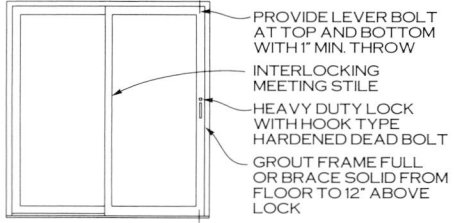

PROVIDE LEVER BOLT AT TOP AND BOTTOM WITH 1" MIN. THROW

INTERLOCKING MEETING STILE

HEAVY DUTY LOCK WITH HOOK TYPE HARDENED DEAD BOLT

GROUT FRAME FULL OR BRACE SOLID FROM FLOOR TO 12" ABOVE LOCK

SLIDING GLASS DOOR

WINDOW SECURITY DESIGN CRITERIA

The following items should be considered when designing and selecting windows:

1. If accessible (residential: 12 ft vertical, 6 ft horizontal; commercial: 18 ft vertical, 10 ft horizontal) and hidden from public view, a higher grade is required.
2. If windows are protected by a detection device (such as shutters, security screens, or bars), the window grade could be irrelevant. If security screens, bars, or shutters are used, requirements for fire exiting must be met.
3. The existence of windbreaks near a building may provide cover for intruders.
4. The use of shades and window coverings may deter intruders, depending on the ease of removal of these devices or the noise from breakage. The use of lockable shutters or rolldown blinds is very effective.
5. Window units should at least comply with ASTM F588-85 Standard Test Methods for Resistance of Window Assemblies to Forced Entry for a minimum grade performance and with NIJ-STD-0316, Physical Security of Window Units, for higher grade performance.

FRAME DESIGN ELEMENTS

1. A rigid frame and sash is important to resist prying and should be removable from the inside only.
2. The quality of the hardware and its placement and anchorage are critical to security. Exposed removable hinges should not be used.
3. Special attention must be given to the use of weather stripping, since this can permit insertion of wires to unlock windows.

GLAZING DESIGN ELEMENTS

1. Multiple glazing systems provide a greater hazard to entry/exit through broken-out windows.
2. Reflective glazing impedes outside daytime surveillance.

MATERIALS AND METHODS FOR WINDOWS

1. Class IV. Very heavy fixed frames with laminated glass over ¹/₄ in. thick security screen, bars, or shutters with special locking device.
2. Class III. Heavy duty sash with laminated glass over ¹/₄ in. thick or polycarbonate glazing ¹/₄ in. thick. Lock should include at least two heavy duty dead locking bolts.
3. Class II. Heavy duty sash with laminated glass or polycarbonate glazing; if wood, sash must be reinforced or heavy; double locks required.
4. Class I. Regular glazing in commercial sash with double locks; can be wood frame.

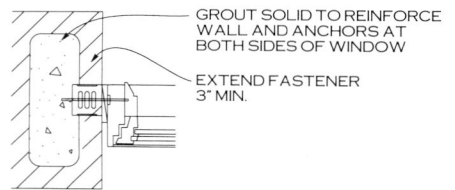

GROUT SOLID TO REINFORCE WALL AND ANCHORS AT BOTH SIDES OF WINDOW

EXTEND FASTENER 3" MIN.

WINDOW JAMB DETAIL

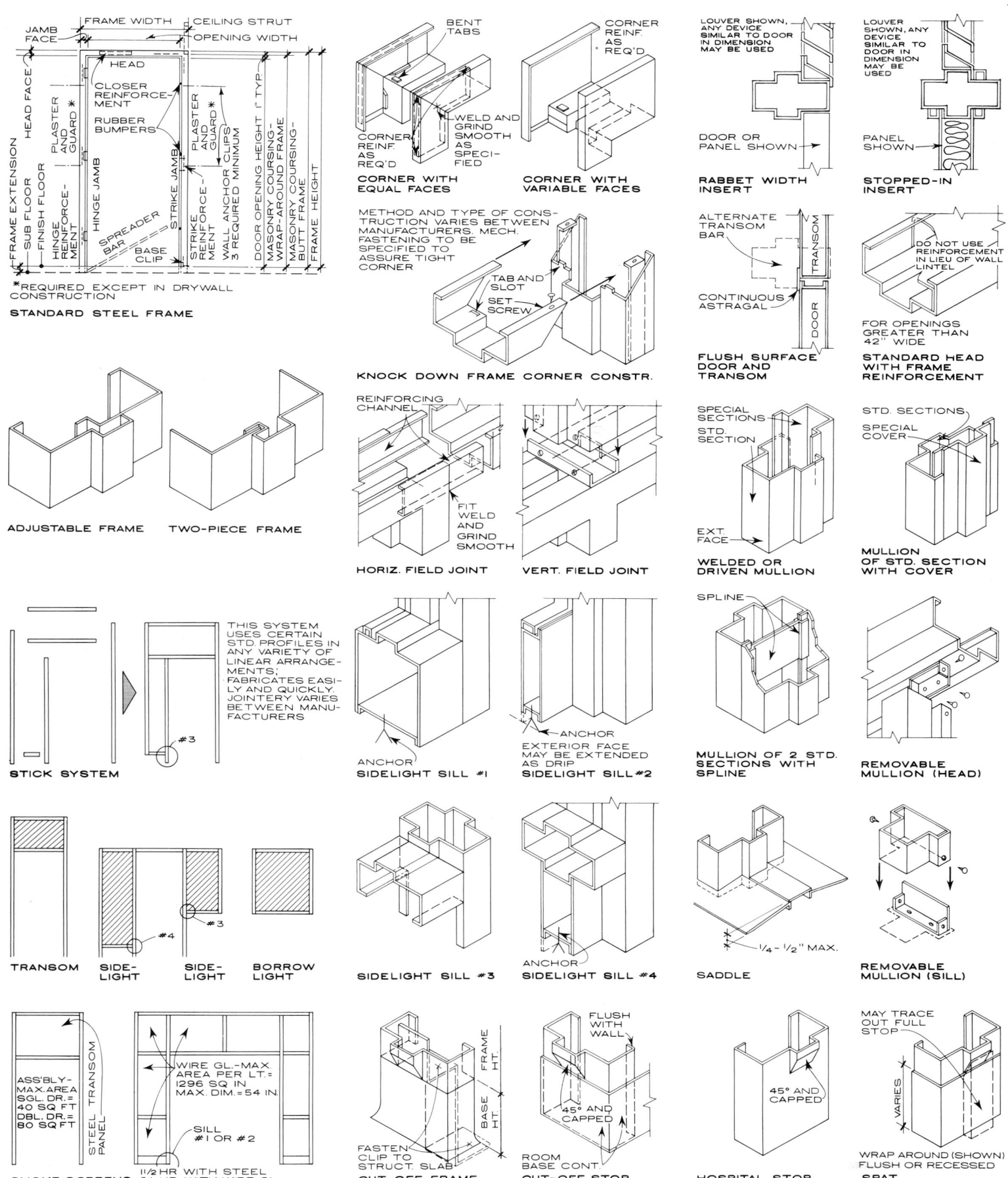

STANDARD STEEL FRAME

*REQUIRED EXCEPT IN DRYWALL CONSTRUCTION

FRAME WIDTH — CEILING STRUT — OPENING WIDTH — JAMB FACE — HEAD FACE — HEAD — CLOSER REINFORCEMENT — RUBBER BUMPERS — PLASTER AND GUARD — HINGE JAMB — STRIKE JAMB — STRIKE REINFORCEMENT — PLASTER AND GUARD — WALL ANCHOR CLIPS 3 REQUIRED MINIMUM — DOOR OPENING HEIGHT 1" TYP. — MASONRY COURSING WRAP-AROUND FRAME — MASONRY COURSING BUTT FRAME — FRAME HEIGHT — FRAME EXTENSION — SUB FLOOR — FINISH FLOOR — HINGE REINFORCEMENT — SPREADER BAR — BASE CLIP

ADJUSTABLE FRAME   **TWO-PIECE FRAME**

STICK SYSTEM

THIS SYSTEM USES CERTAIN STD. PROFILES IN ANY VARIETY OF LINEAR ARRANGEMENTS; FABRICATES EASILY AND QUICKLY. JOINTERY VARIES BETWEEN MANUFACTURERS

#3

TRANSOM   SIDE-LIGHT   SIDE-LIGHT   BORROW LIGHT

#4   #3

SMOKE SCREENS

ASS'BLY-MAX. AREA SGL. DR.= 40 SQ FT DBL. DR.= 80 SQ FT

WIRE GL.-MAX. AREA PER LT.= 1296 SQ IN MAX. DIM.= 54 IN.

SILL #1 OR #2

1 1/2 HR WITH STEEL 3/4 HR WITH WIRE GL.

STEEL TRANSOM PANEL

CORNER WITH EQUAL FACES

BENT TABS — CORNER REINF. AS REQ'D — WELD AND GRIND SMOOTH AS SPECIFIED

CORNER WITH VARIABLE FACES

CORNER REINF. AS REQ'D

KNOCK DOWN FRAME CORNER CONSTR.

METHOD AND TYPE OF CONSTRUCTION VARIES BETWEEN MANUFACTURERS. MECH. FASTENING TO BE SPECIFIED TO ASSURE TIGHT CORNER

TAB AND SLOT — SET SCREW

HORIZ. FIELD JOINT

REINFORCING CHANNEL — FIT WELD AND GRIND SMOOTH

VERT. FIELD JOINT

SIDELIGHT SILL #1

ANCHOR

SIDELIGHT SILL #2

ANCHOR — EXTERIOR FACE MAY BE EXTENDED AS DRIP

SIDELIGHT SILL #3

SIDELIGHT SILL #4

ANCHOR

CUT-OFF FRAME

FRAME HT. — BASE HT. — FASTEN CLIP TO STRUCT. SLAB

CUT-OFF STOP

FLUSH WITH WALL — 45° AND CAPPED — ROOM BASE CONT.

RABBET WIDTH INSERT

LOUVER SHOWN, ANY DEVICE SIMILAR TO DOOR IN DIMENSION MAY BE USED — DOOR OR PANEL SHOWN

STOPPED-IN INSERT

LOUVER SHOWN, ANY DEVICE SIMILAR TO DOOR IN DIMENSION MAY BE USED — PANEL SHOWN

FLUSH SURFACE DOOR AND TRANSOM

ALTERNATE TRANSOM BAR — CONTINUOUS ASTRAGAL — TRANSOM — DOOR

STANDARD HEAD WITH FRAME REINFORCEMENT

DO NOT USE REINFORCEMENT IN LIEU OF WALL LINTEL — FOR OPENINGS GREATER THAN 42" WIDE

WELDED OR DRIVEN MULLION

SPECIAL SECTIONS — STD. SECTION — EXT. FACE

MULLION OF STD. SECTION WITH COVER

STD. SECTIONS — SPECIAL COVER

MULLION OF 2 STD. SECTIONS WITH SPLINE

SPLINE

REMOVABLE MULLION (HEAD)

SADDLE

1/4 - 1/2" MAX.

REMOVABLE MULLION (SILL)

HOSPITAL STOP

45° AND CAPPED

SPAT

MAY TRACE OUT FULL STOP — VARIES — WRAP AROUND (SHOWN) FLUSH OR RECESSED

James W. G. Watson, AIA; Ronald A. Spahn and Associates; Cleveland Heights, Ohio

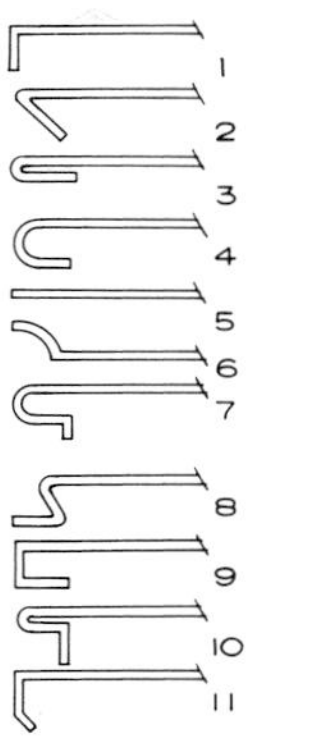
1
2
3
4
5
6
7
8
9
10
11

BACKBENDS

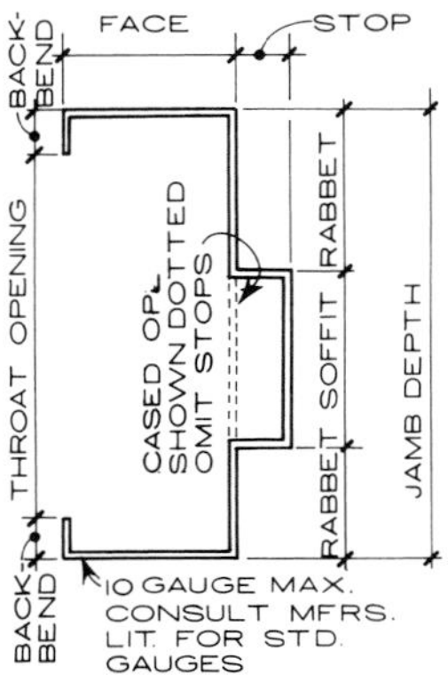
FACE
STOP
BACK-BEND
THROAT OPENING
CASED OPG. SHOWN DOTTED OMIT STOPS
RABBET
SOFFIT
RABBET
JAMB DEPTH
BACK-BEND
10 GAUGE MAX. CONSULT MFRS. LIT. FOR STD. GAUGES

STD. DBL. RABBET

VARIOUS STANDARD PROFILES

JAMB DEPTH	2¾	3	3¾	4¾	5½	5¾	6¾	7¾	8¾	12¾
RABBET 3	SINGLE RABBET ONLY			1 15/16 STD. FOR 1¾" DOOR						
SOFFIT 3										
RABBET 3				1 9/16 STD. FOR 1⅜" DOOR						
BACKBEND	½	7/16	½	½	¾	½	½	½	½	½
THROAT	1¾	2⅛	2	3¾	4	4¾	5¾	6¾	7¾	11¾

NOTES

1. Many others available. Consult mfrs. list for dimensions and options.
2. Depths vary in 1/8" increments to 12 3/4" max.
3. Omit stops for cased opening frames.
4. Std. stop 5/8", 1/2" min. + std. face 2", 1" min.

FRAME GAUGES

GRADE	DUTY	MINIMUM GAUGE
I	Standard	18
II	Heavy duty	16
III	Extra heavy duty	16

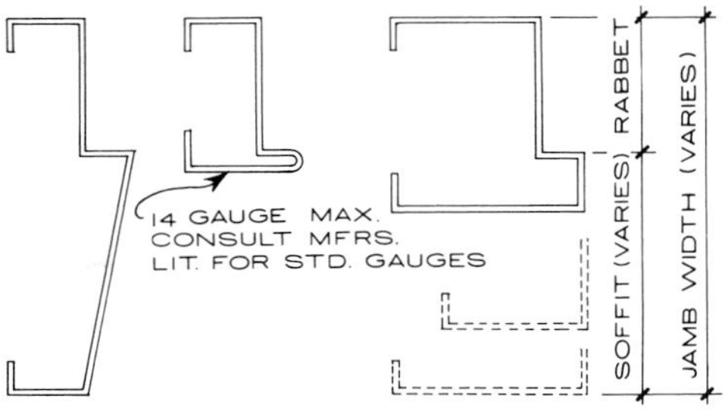
14 GAUGE MAX. CONSULT MFRS. LIT. FOR STD. GAUGES
SOFFIT (VARIES) RABBET
JAMB WIDTH (VARIES)

VARIOUS SINGLE RABBETS

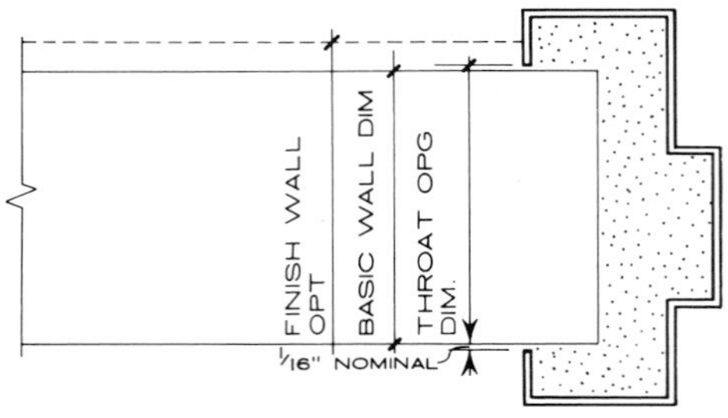
FINISH WALL OPT
BASIC WALL DIM
THROAT OPG DIM.
1/16" NOMINAL

1. Basic wall dim. < throat opening dim. Fin wall mat'l (dotted may encroach on backbend).
2. Anchors appropriate for wall constr. Req'd. min. 3 per jamb.
3. Fill frame w/mortar or plaster as used in wall.
4. Grout frame, backbend at masonry wall.
5. Backbend may vary as selected.

WRAP–AROUND FRAMES

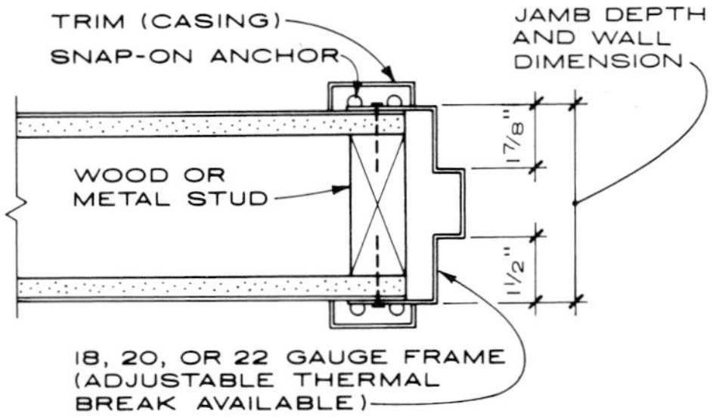
TRIM (CASING)
SNAP-ON ANCHOR
JAMB DEPTH AND WALL DIMENSION
WOOD OR METAL STUD
1 7/8"
1 1/2"
18, 20, OR 22 GAUGE FRAME (ADJUSTABLE THERMAL BREAK AVAILABLE)

LIGHT GAUGE FRAME

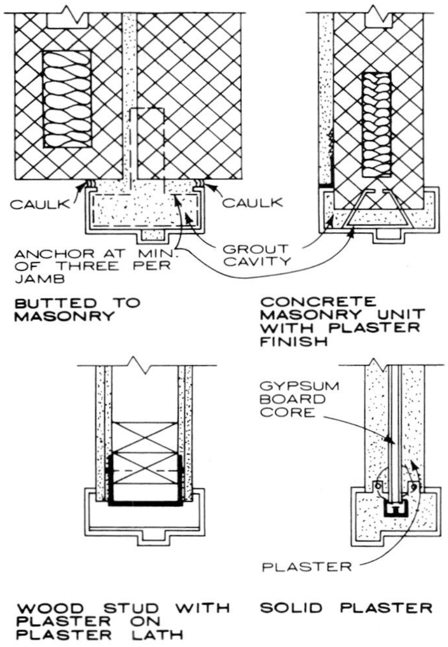
CAULK
CAULK
ANCHOR AT MIN. OF THREE PER JAMB
GROUT CAVITY
BUTTED TO MASONRY
CONCRETE MASONRY UNIT WITH PLASTER FINISH
GYPSUM BOARD CORE
PLASTER
WOOD STUD WITH PLASTER ON PLASTER LATH
SOLID PLASTER

VARIOUS INSTALLATIONS

1. Wall dim. varies from throat opening + 1/2" min. to unlimited max.
2. Anchors appropriate for wall constr. req'd; min. 3 per jamb.
3. Grout frame with mortar or plaster as used in wall.
4. Caulk frame at wall.
5. Dim. 'A'—3" min. in area of pull or knob hardware.
6. Trim may be used to cover joint at wall line #1.
7. Check dim. 'B' on hinge side for door swing >90°.

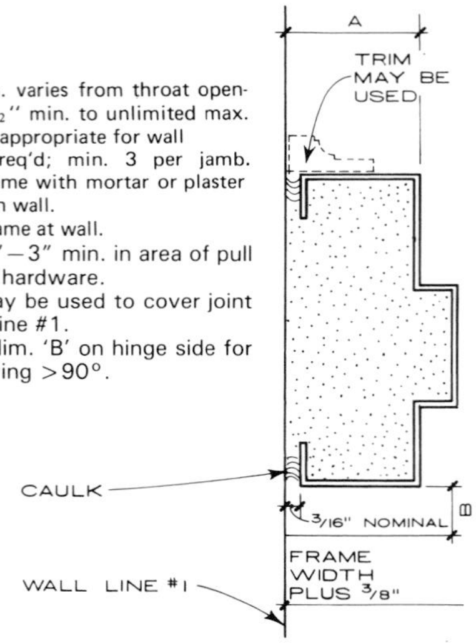
A
TRIM MAY BE USED
CAULK
3/16" NOMINAL
B
WALL LINE #1
FRAME WIDTH PLUS 3/8"

BUTT FRAME

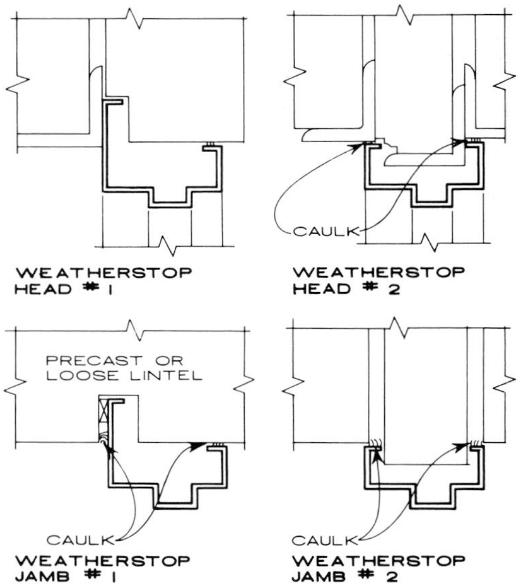
WEATHERSTOP HEAD #1
CAULK
WEATHERSTOP HEAD #2
PRECAST OR LOOSE LINTEL
CAULK
WEATHERSTOP JAMB #1
CAULK
WEATHERSTOP JAMB #2

WEATHERSTOP INSTALLATIONS

NOTES

1. Some details vary between manufacturers.
2. Stock frames stocked in warehouse prior to receipt of order. Certain profiles are warehoused locally.
3. Standard frames manufactured from existing jigs and tooling upon receipt of order. Certain profiles are readily available.
4. Custom frames manufactured in response to specific dimensional requirements of a particular customer. Custom profiles are available with relative delay.
5. Selection should reflect anticipated requirements of construction schedule.
6. Certain detail features will constitute a custom frame, verify with manufacturer.

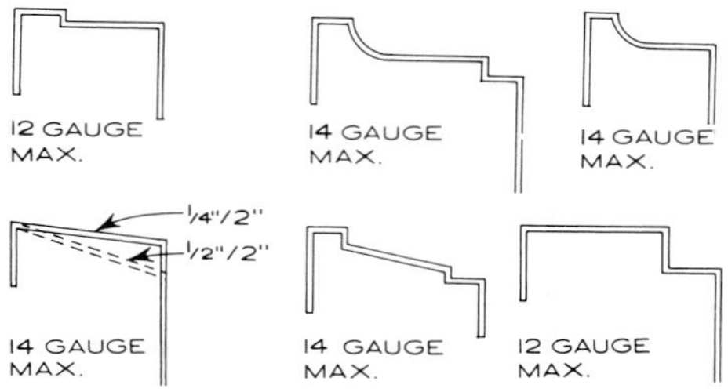
12 GAUGE MAX.
14 GAUGE MAX.
14 GAUGE MAX.
1/4"/2"
1/2"/2"
14 GAUGE MAX.
14 GAUGE MAX.
12 GAUGE MAX.

VARIOUS FACES

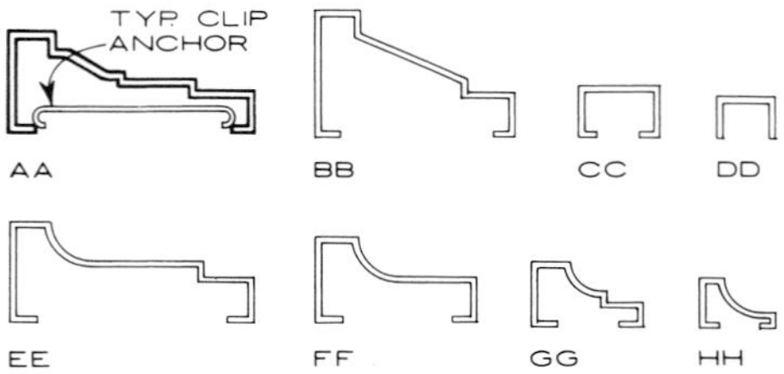
TYP. CLIP ANCHOR
AA
BB
CC
DD
EE
FF
GG
HH

VARIOUS TRIM AND SCRIBE MOLDING

James W. G. Watson, AIA; Ronald A. Spahn and Associates; Cleveland Heights, Ohio

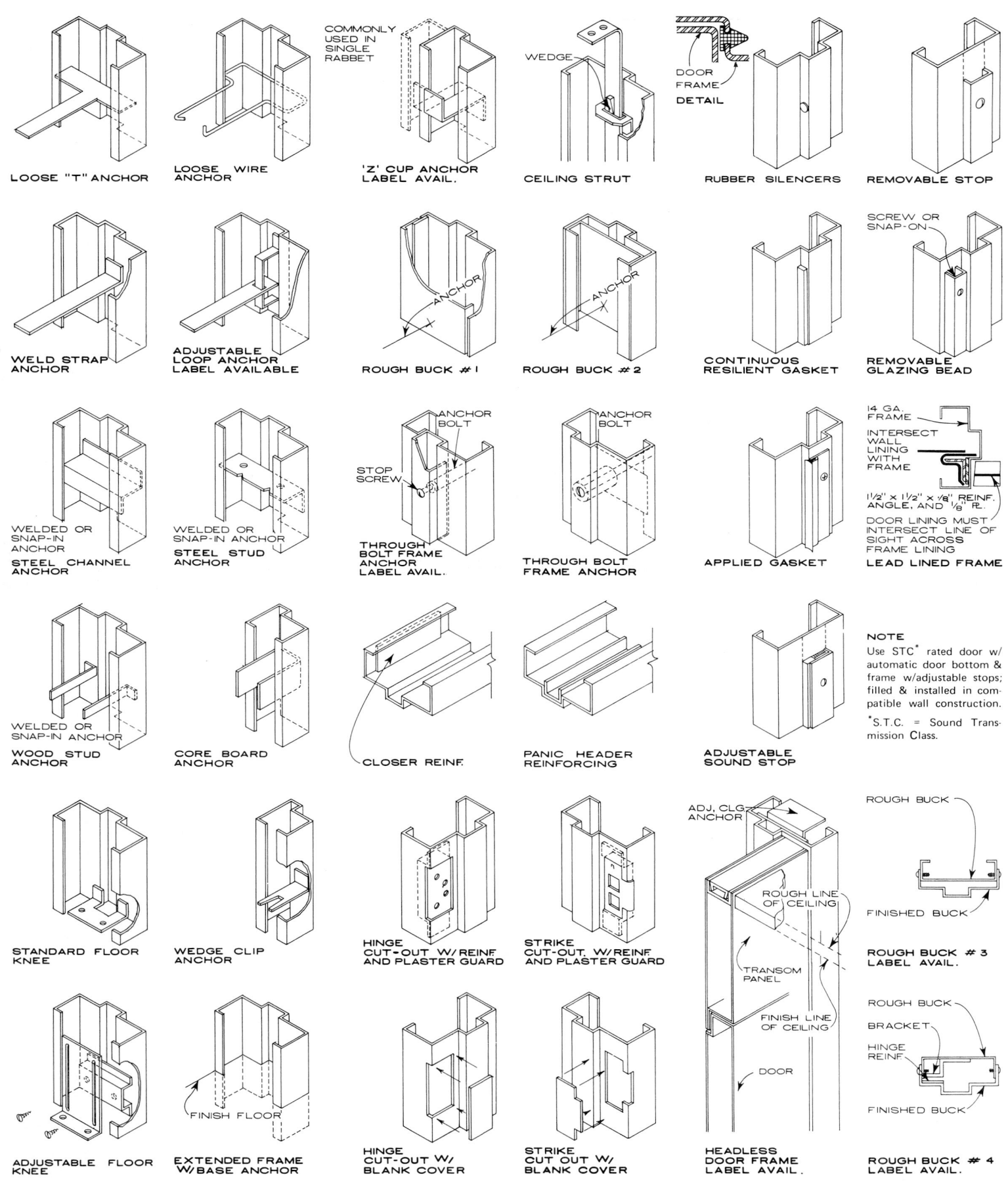

LOOSE "T" ANCHOR

LOOSE WIRE ANCHOR

COMMONLY USED IN SINGLE RABBET

'Z' CUP ANCHOR LABEL AVAIL.

WEDGE

CEILING STRUT

DOOR FRAME DETAIL

RUBBER SILENCERS

REMOVABLE STOP

WELD STRAP ANCHOR

ADJUSTABLE LOOP ANCHOR LABEL AVAILABLE

ANCHOR

ROUGH BUCK #1

ANCHOR

ROUGH BUCK #2

CONTINUOUS RESILIENT GASKET

SCREW OR SNAP-ON

REMOVABLE GLAZING BEAD

WELDED OR SNAP-IN ANCHOR
STEEL CHANNEL ANCHOR

WELDED OR SNAP-IN ANCHOR
STEEL STUD ANCHOR

ANCHOR BOLT
STOP SCREW
THROUGH BOLT FRAME ANCHOR LABEL AVAIL.

ANCHOR BOLT
THROUGH BOLT FRAME ANCHOR

APPLIED GASKET

14 GA. FRAME
INTERSECT WALL LINING WITH FRAME
1 1/2" x 1 1/2" x 1/8" REINF. ANGLE, AND 1/8" PL.
DOOR LINING MUST INTERSECT LINE OF SIGHT ACROSS FRAME LINING

LEAD LINED FRAME

WELDED OR SNAP-IN ANCHOR
WOOD STUD ANCHOR

CORE BOARD ANCHOR

CLOSER REINF.

PANIC HEADER REINFORCING

ADJUSTABLE SOUND STOP

NOTE

Use STC* rated door w/ automatic door bottom & frame w/adjustable stops; filled & installed in compatible wall construction.

*S.T.C. = Sound Transmission Class.

STANDARD FLOOR KNEE

WEDGE CLIP ANCHOR

HINGE CUT-OUT W/REINF. AND PLASTER GUARD

STRIKE CUT-OUT. W/REINF. AND PLASTER GUARD

ADJ. CLG ANCHOR
ROUGH LINE OF CEILING
TRANSOM PANEL
FINISH LINE OF CEILING
DOOR

ROUGH BUCK
FINISHED BUCK
ROUGH BUCK #3 LABEL AVAIL.

ADJUSTABLE FLOOR KNEE

FINISH FLOOR
EXTENDED FRAME W/BASE ANCHOR

HINGE CUT-OUT W/ BLANK COVER

STRIKE CUT OUT W/ BLANK COVER

HEADLESS DOOR FRAME LABEL AVAIL.

ROUGH BUCK
BRACKET
HINGE REINF.
FINISHED BUCK
ROUGH BUCK #4 LABEL AVAIL.

James W. G. Watson, AIA; Ronald A. Spahn and Associates; Cleveland Heights, Ohio

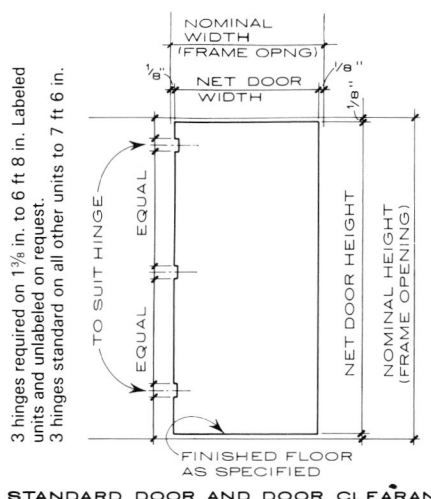

3 hinges required on 1 3/8 in. to 6 ft 8 in. Labeled units and unlabeled units on request. 3 hinges standard on all other units to 7 ft 6 in.

STANDARD DOOR AND DOOR CLEARANCE

Tubular stiles and rails compose structural elements.

A flush or recessed panel is held in place by stiles and rails.

A recessed panel door, generally considered an industrial type door, may be used for decorative purposes.

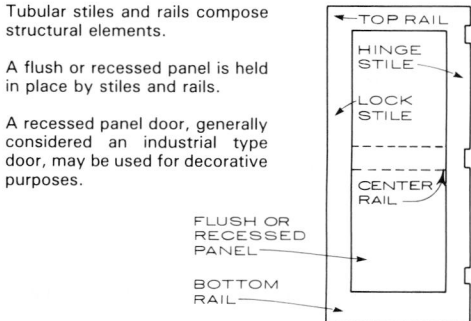

STILE AND RAIL CONSTRUCTION

Relatively wide center panel connected to hinge and lock stile by interlocking and/or welding—forming two exposed vertical seams on door face.

Inverted channel closes top and bottom.

Exterior door is furnished with cap.

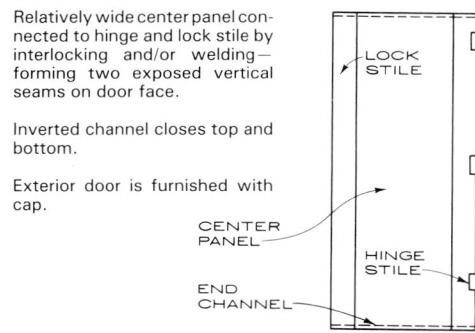

STILE AND PANEL CONSTRUCTION

Pan type or enclosed grid construction.

No seams visible on face.

Exposed seams may be on vertical edges where two pans join.

Top and/or bottom of door may be flush or recessed.

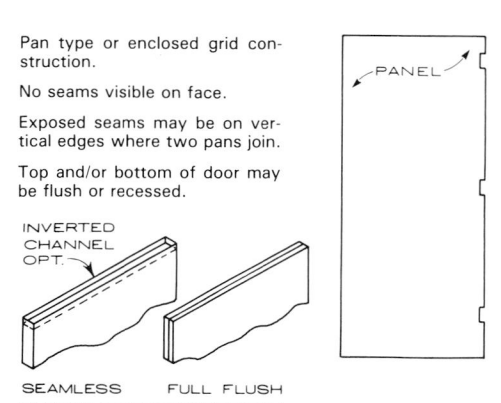

FLUSH CONSTRUCTION

DOOR TYPES

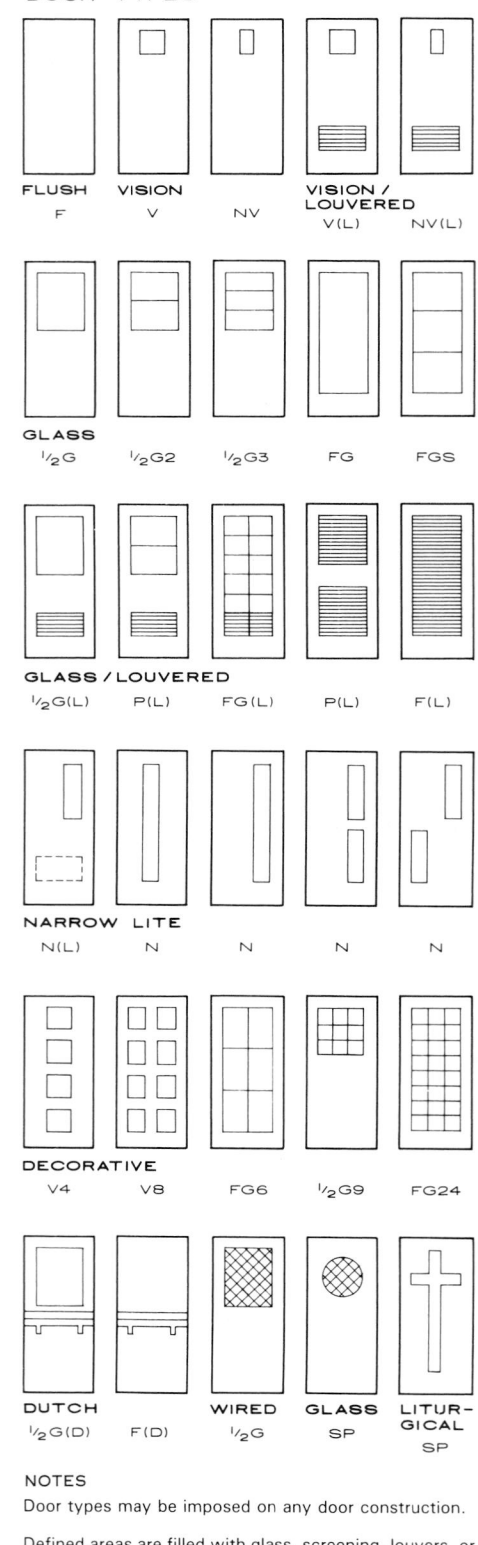

FLUSH F   **VISION** V   NV   **VISION / LOUVERED** V(L)   NV(L)

GLASS 1/2 G   1/2 G2   1/2 G3   FG   FGS

GLASS / LOUVERED 1/2 G(L)   P(L)   FG(L)   P(L)   F(L)

NARROW LITE N(L)   N   N   N   N

DECORATIVE V4   V8   FG6   1/2 G9   FG24

DUTCH 1/2 G(D)   F(D)   **WIRED** 1/2 G   **GLASS** SP   **LITURGICAL** SP

NOTES

Door types may be imposed on any door construction.

Defined areas are filled with glass, screening, louvers, or recessed or flush panels unless otherwise noted.

Stiles and rails or muntins make divisions.

FINISHES

Standard: primed and/or galvanized
Paint: baked enamel
Applied: vinyl clad
Textured, embossed: stainless steel, aluminum
Polished: stainless steel

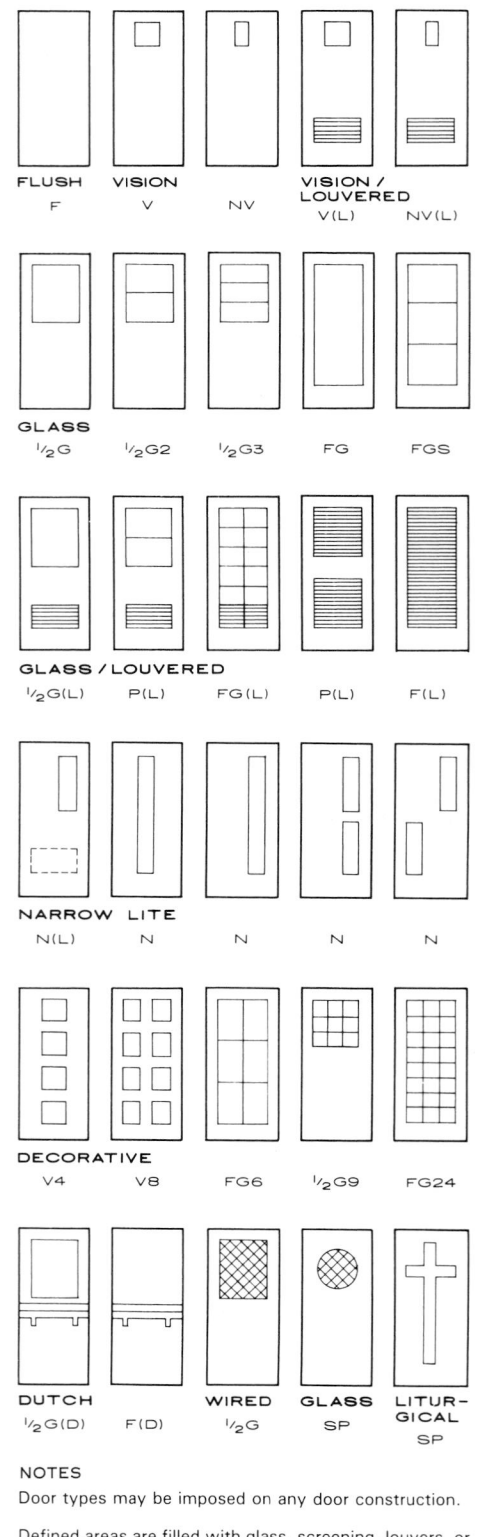

DOOR TOP WITH GLAZED OPENING   **FLUSH DOOR CLOSER REINF.**

STILE AND PANEL DOOR TOP WITH GLAZED OPENING   **STILE AND PANEL JOINT**

HINGE REINFORCEMENT   **STILE AND RAIL DOOR**

STILE AND RAIL CORNER   **FLUSH CONSTR.**

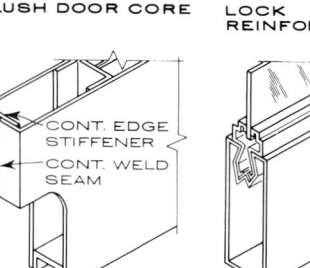

FLUSH DOOR CORE

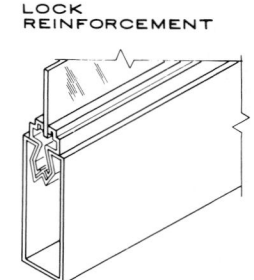

LOCK REINFORCEMENT

FLUSH DOOR BOTTOM AND EDGE CONST.   **STILE AND RAIL DOOR BOTTOM CONST.**

James W. G. Watson, AIA; Ronald A. Spahn and Associates; Cleveland Heights, Ohio

GENERAL NOTES FOR ALL WOOD DOORS
Kiln dried wood, moisture content @ 6-12%.

Type 1 doors: Fully waterproof bond ext. and int.
Type 11 doors: Water resistant bond. Interior only.

Tolerances: Height, width, thickness, squareness and warp per NWMA STANDARDS and vary with solid vs. built-up construction.

Prefit: Doors @ $^3/_{16}$'' less in width and $^1/_8$'' less in height than nominal size, ± $^1/_{32}$'' tolerance, with vertical edges eased.

Premachining: Doors mortised for locks and cut out for hinges when so specified.

Premium: For transparent finish. Good/custom: For paint or transparent finish. Sound: For paint, with 2 coats completely covering defects.

FLUSH WOOD DOORS
CORE MATERIAL
SOLID CORES
Wood block, single specie, @ 2$^1/_2$'' max. width, surfaced two sides, without spaces or defects impairing strength or visible thru hdwd. veneer facing.

HOLLOW CORES
Wood, wood derivative, or class A insulation board.

TYPES OF WOOD FACES
Standard thickness face veneers @ $^1/_{16}$''–$^1/_{32}$'', bonded to hardwood, crossband @ $^1/_{10}$''–$^1/_{16}$''. Most economical and widely used, inhibits checking, difficult to refinish or repair face damage, for use on all cores.

$^1/_8$'' Sawn veneers, bonded to crossband, easily refinished and repaired.

For use on staved block and stile and rail solid cores.
$^1/_4$'' Sawn veneers: same as $^1/_8$'' but without crossband on stile and rail solid cores with horizontal blocks. Decorative grooves can be cut into faces.

LIGHT & LOUVER OPENINGS
Custom made to specifications. Wood beads and slats to match face veneer. 5'' min. between opening and edge of door.

Hollow core: Cut-out area max. $^1/_2$ height of door. Door not guaranteed with openings greater than 40%. Exterior doors: Weatherproofing required to prevent moisture from leaking into core.

FACTORY FINISHING
Partial: Sealing coats applied, final job finish.
Complete: Requires prefit and premachining.

SPECIAL FACING
High or medium-low density overlay faces of phenolic resins and cellulose fibers fused to inner faces of hardwood in lieu of final veneers as base for final opaque finish only.

$^1/_{16}$'' min. laminated plastic bonded to $^1/_{16}$'' min. wood back of two or more piles.

$^1/_8$'' hardboard, smooth one or two sides.

SPECIAL CORES
SOUND INSULATING DOORS
Thicknesses 1$^3/_4$'', 2$^1/_4$''. Transmission loss rating C Stc 36 for 1$^3/_4$'', 42 for 2$^1/_4$''. Barrier faces separated by a void or damping compound to keep faces from vibrating in unison. Special stops, gaskets, and threshold devices required. Mfrs. requirements as to wd. frames and wall specs.

FIRE RATED DOORS
$^3/_4$ hr ''C'' label and 1 hr ''B'' label-maximum size 4'0'' x 10'0''.
1$^1/_2$ hr ''B'' label-maximum size 4'0'' x 9'0''. All doors 1$^3/_4$'' minimum thickness.

LEAD LINED DOORS
See U/L requirements. Optional location within door construction of $^1/_{32}$'' to $^1/_2$'' continuous lead sheet from edge to edge which may be reinforced with lead bolts or glued.

GROUNDED DOORS
Wire mesh located at center of core, grounded with copper wire through hinges to frame.

TYPES OF HOLLOW CORE DOORS

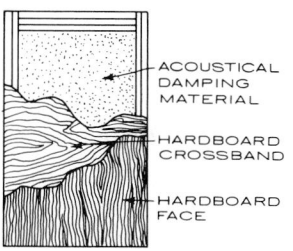

ACOUSTICAL DOOR
Uses gasketed stops and neoprene bottom seals to cut sound transmission.

HONEYCOMB FIBER
INSTITU-
TIONAL:
With cross rail.
INTERIOR:
Without cross rail. Uniform core of honeycomb fiber to form $^1/_2$'' air cells.

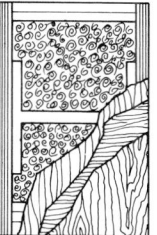

IMPLANTED BLANKS
Spirals or other forms separated or joined, implanted between & supporting outer faces of door.

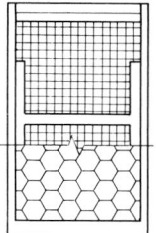

MESH
Interlocked, horizontal & vertical strips, equally spaced, notched into stiles, or expandable cellular or honey-comb core.

TYPES OF SOLID CORES

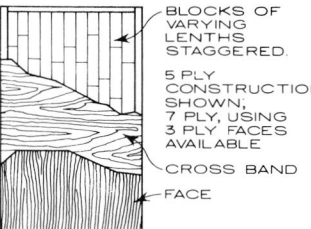

CONTINUOUS BLOCK STAVED CORE
Bonded staggered blocks bonded to face panels. Most widely used & economical solid core.

FRAMED BLOCK STAVED CORE
Non-bonded staggered blocks laid up within stile rail frame, bonded to face panels.

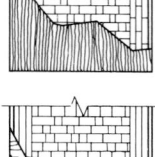

STILE AND RAIL
Horizontal blocks when cross banding is not used. Vertical panel blocks when cross banding is used.

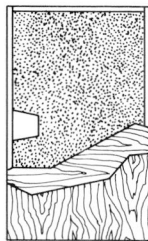

PARTICLE BOARD
Extremely heavy, more soundproof, economical door, available in hardwood face veneer or high pressure laminate face.

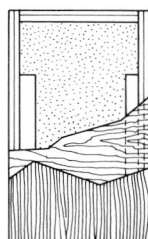

MINERAL COMPOSITION
Lightest weight of all cores. Details, as cut-outs, difficult. Low screw holding strength.

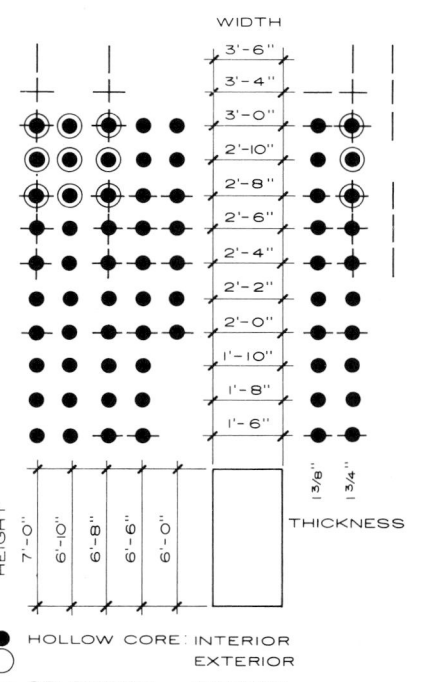

STANDARD SIZES

● HOLLOW CORE: INTERIOR
                EXTERIOR
○ SOLID CORE: INTERIOR
―   INTERIOR
                EXTERIOR

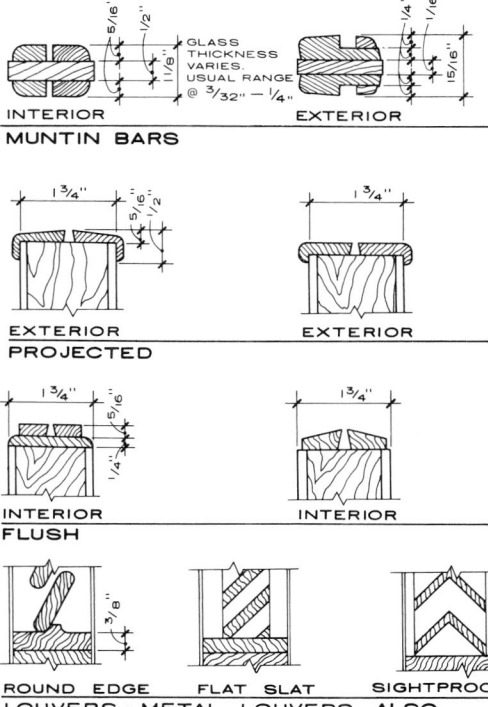

MUNTIN BARS

PROJECTED

FLUSH

ROUND EDGE   FLAT SLAT   SIGHTPROOF
LOUVERS · METAL LOUVERS ALSO AVAILABLE
STOCK OPENING AND LOUVER DETAIL

NOTES

CONSTRUCTION

Solid or built-up stiles, rails, and vertical members or mullions, doweled as in NWWDA standard. Stock material includes ponderosa pine or other Western pine, fir, hemlock, or spruce, and hardwood veneers. Hardboard, metal, and plastic facings available in patterns simulating panel doors.

GRADES

Premium (select) grade: for natural, clear, or stained finish. Exposed wood free of defects that affect appearance.

Standard grade: for opaque finishes. Defects, discoloration, mixed species, and finger joints permitted if undetectable after finishing.

BUILT-UP MEMBERS

Core as in solid core of flush doors. Edge and end strips as in flush doors. Face veneer: hardwood at 1/8 in. minimum.

STICKING, GLASS STOPS, AND MUNTINS

Cove, bead, or ovolo; solid, matching face.

PANELS

Flat: 3-ply hardwood or softwood. Raised—two sides: solid hardwood or softwood built-up of two or more plies. Doors 1 ft 6 in. wide and narrower are one panel wide.

GLAZING

Must be safety glazing. Insulated (dual) glazing is available.

THICKNESS

Interior doors: 1⅜ in.
Exterior doors: 1⅜ in. or 1¾ in.
Storm and screen doors: 1⅛ in.

See index for other door types and door hardware.

ADA ACCESSIBILITY GUIDELINES

For opening width compliance, use doors 3 ft 0 in. wide. Door projections, such as dutch door shelves, may be no more than 4 in. if more than 27 in. above finished floor. Thresholds and saddles must be no higher than ½ in. with beveled edges. Kickplates are recommended outdoors along accessible routes.

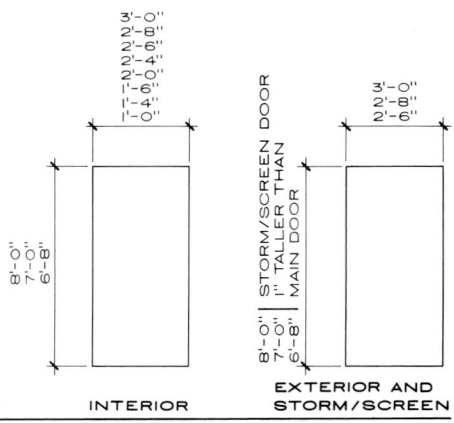

TYPICAL SIZES

SELECTED STANDARD DOOR TYPES (NUMBERS CORRESPOND TO NWWDA STANDARD)

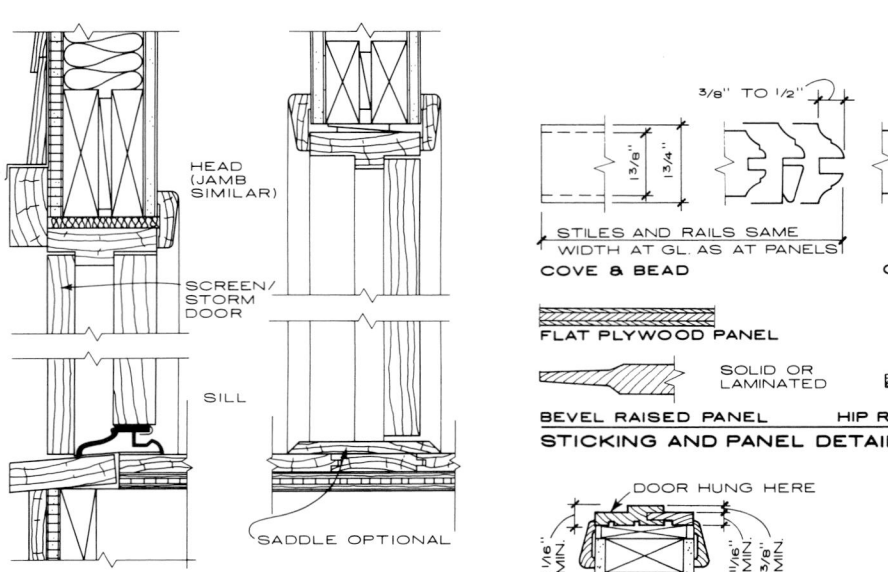

NOTES

Top operable alone or with bottom using joining hardware.

Can swing in or out.

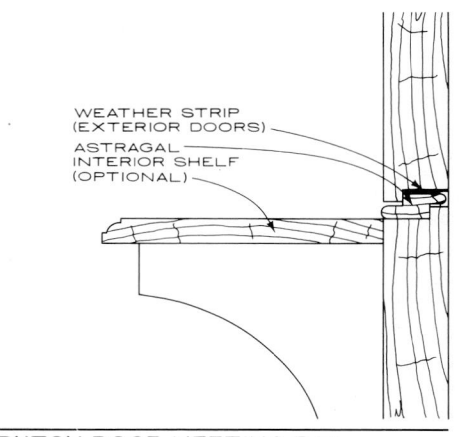

Jeffrey R. Vandevoort; Talbott Wilson Associates, Inc.; Houston, Texas

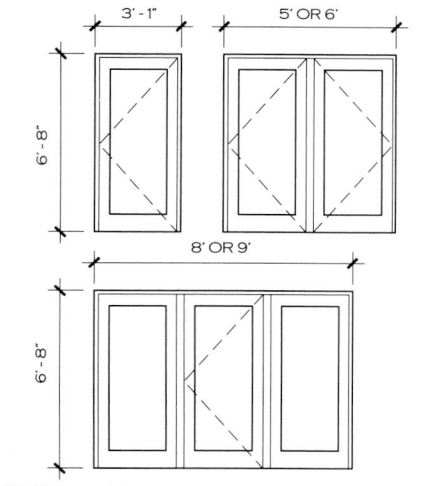

HINGED FRENCH DOOR SIZES

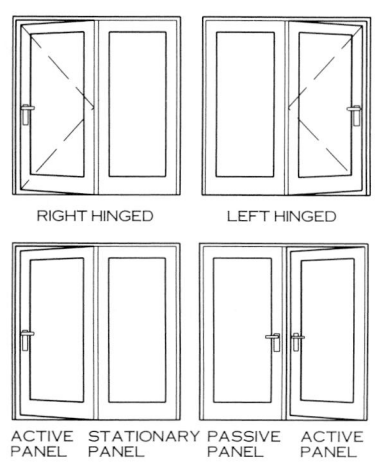

RIGHT HINGED   LEFT HINGED

ACTIVE   STATIONARY   PASSIVE   ACTIVE
PANEL   PANEL   PANEL   PANEL

HINGE AND PANEL CONFIGURATIONS

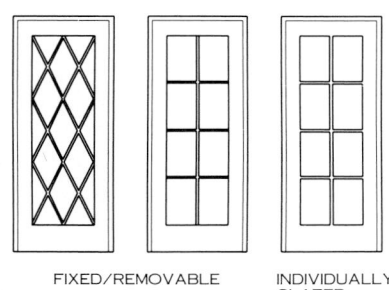

FIXED/REMOVABLE   INDIVIDUALLY
                   GLAZED

OPTIONAL MUNTIN BARS

NOTES

1. Some manufacturers offer doors in 8 ft height.
2. Tempered or laminated safety glass should be used to reduce chance of breakage and dangerous shards if breakage occurs.

DEFINITIONS

ACTIVE—the hinged or operating panel..

PASSIVE PANEL—the panel that can operate only after opening the active panel..

STATIONARY PANEL—a fixed panel..

RIGHT HINGED—hinges mounted on the right stile of the active panel.

LEFT-HINGED—hinges mounted on the left stile of the active panel.

Joseph A. Wilkes, FAIA; Annapolis, Maryland

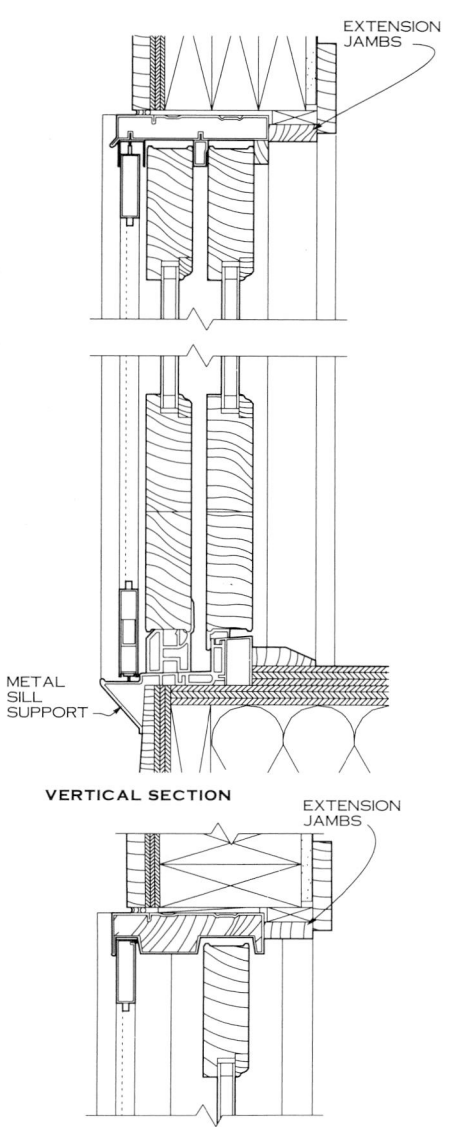

EXTENSION JAMBS

METAL SILL SUPPORT

VERTICAL SECTION

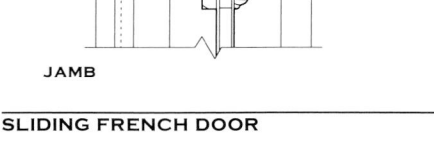

EXTENSION JAMBS

JAMB

SLIDING FRENCH DOOR

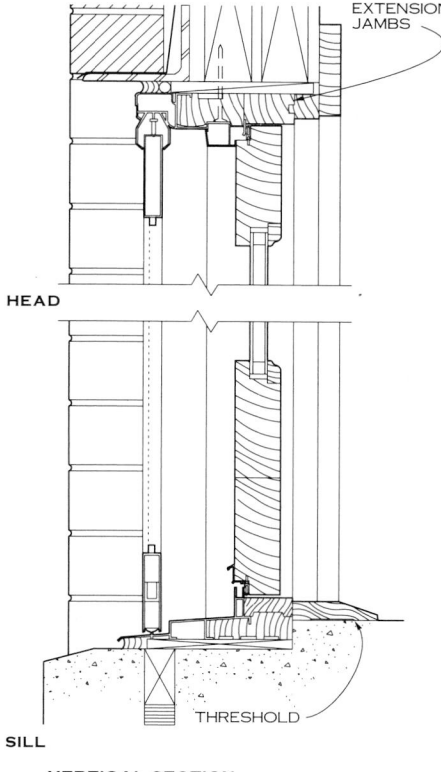

EXTENSION JAMBS

HEAD

THRESHOLD

SILL

VERTICAL SECTION

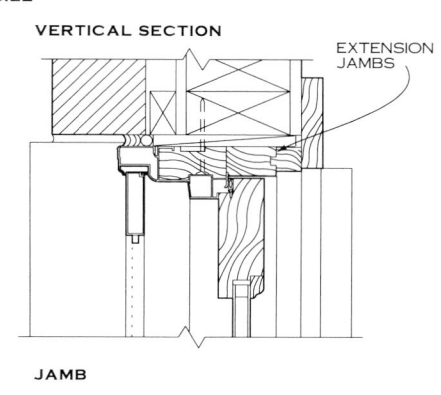

EXTENSION JAMBS

JAMB

HINGED FRENCH DOOR

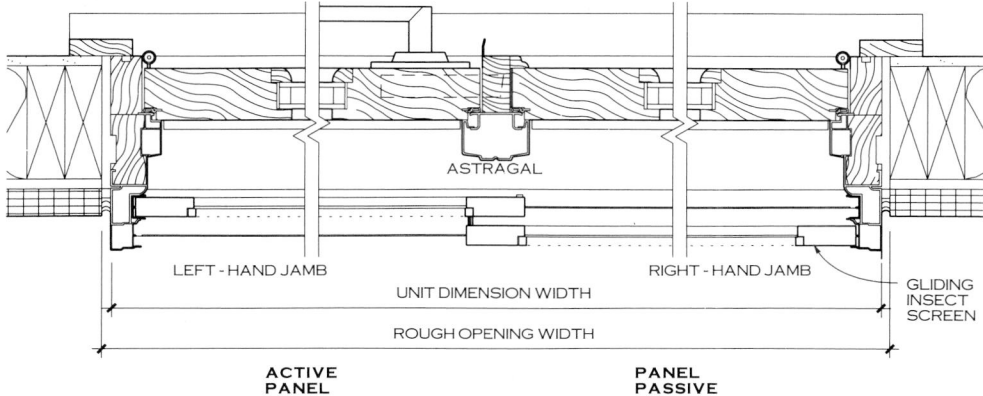

ASTRAGAL

LEFT - HAND JAMB   RIGHT - HAND JAMB

GLIDING INSECT SCREEN

UNIT DIMENSION WIDTH

ROUGH OPENING WIDTH

ACTIVE PANEL   PANEL PASSIVE

SECTION - HINGED FRENCH DOOR

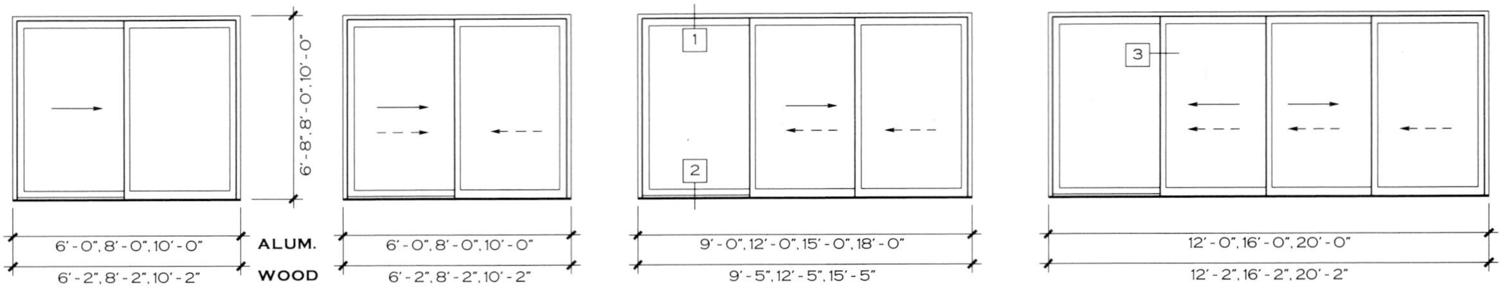

6' - 8", 8' - 0", 10' - 0"

| 6' - 0", 8' - 0", 10' - 0" | ALUM. |
| 6' - 2", 8' - 2", 10' - 2" | WOOD |

| 6' - 0", 8' - 0", 10' - 0" |
| 6' - 2", 8' - 2", 10' - 2" |

1

2

| 9' - 0", 12' - 0", 15' - 0", 18' - 0" |
| 9' - 5", 12' - 5", 15' - 5" |

3

| 12' - 0", 16' - 0", 20' - 0" |
| 12' - 2", 16' - 2", 20' - 2" |

RESIDENTIAL SLIDING DOOR DIMENSIONS AND OPERATION

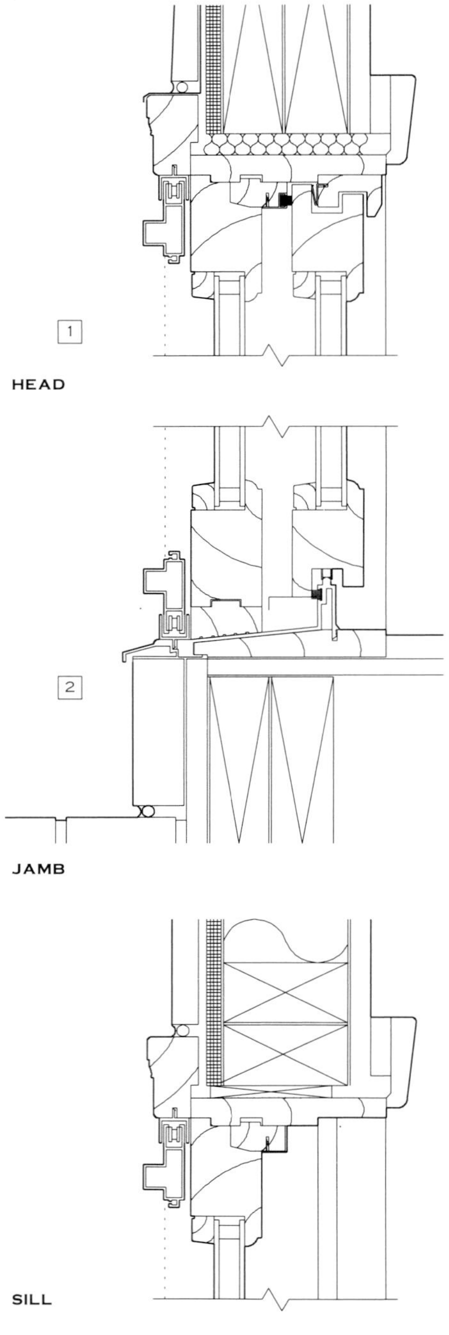

1

HEAD

2

JAMB

SILL

WOOD DETAILS

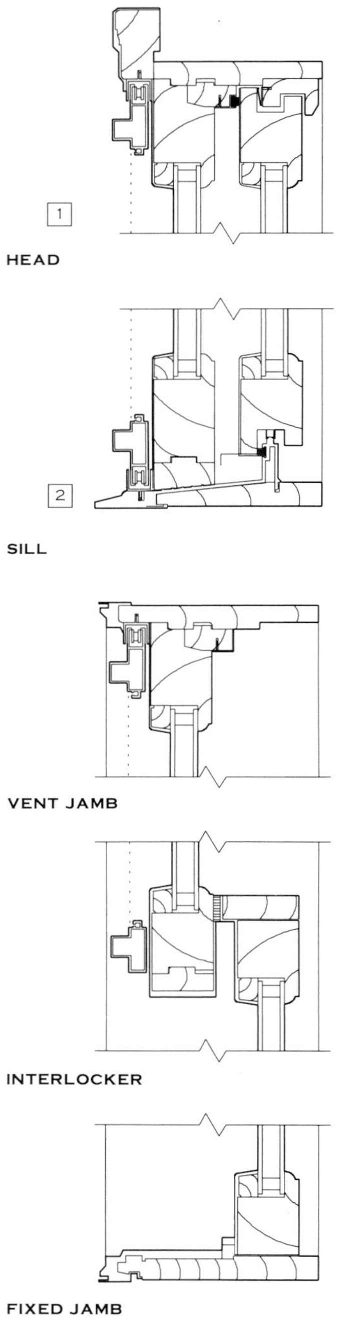

1

HEAD

2

SILL

VENT JAMB

INTERLOCKER

FIXED JAMB

WOOD-CLAD DETAILS

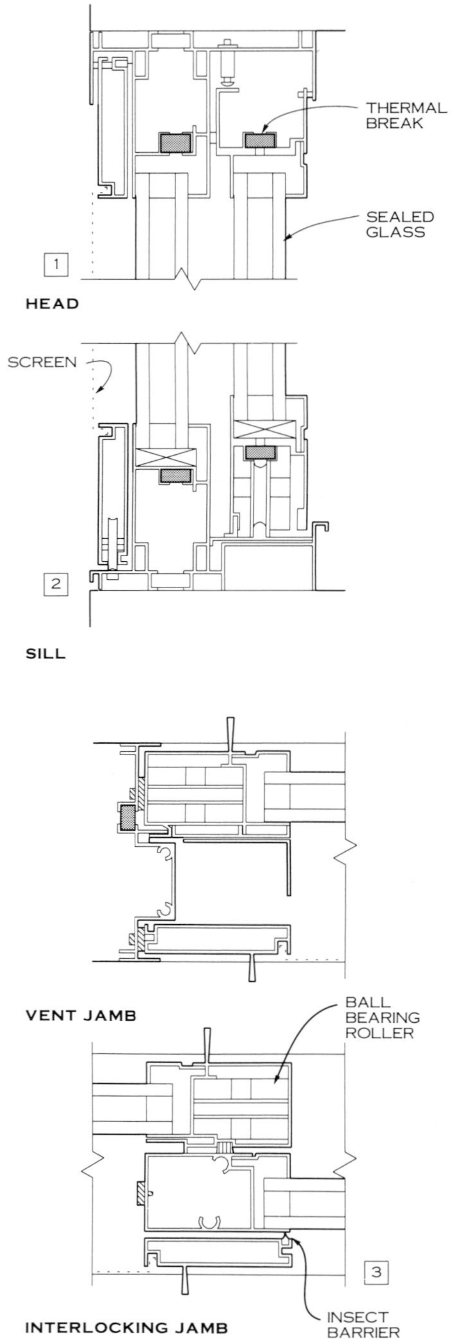

THERMAL BREAK

SEALED GLASS

1

HEAD

SCREEN

2

SILL

VENT JAMB

BALL BEARING ROLLER

3

INTERLOCKING JAMB

INSECT BARRIER

ALUMINUM DETAILS

Joseph A. Wilkes, FAIA; Annapolis, Maryland

WOOD DOORS AND FRAMES

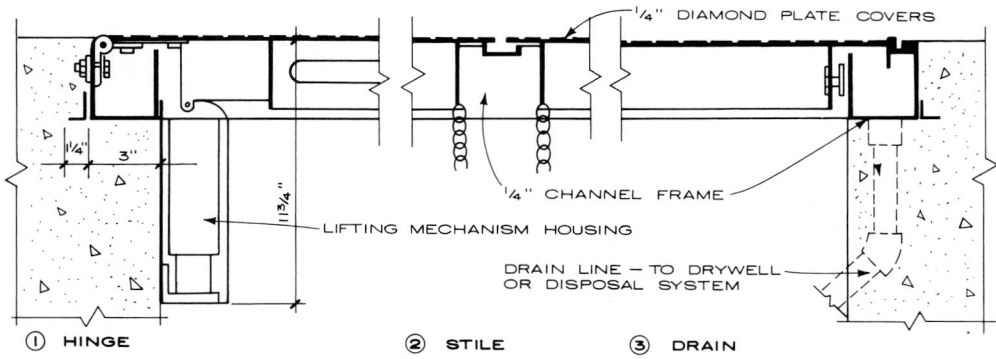

① HINGE ② STILE ③ DRAIN

DETAILS

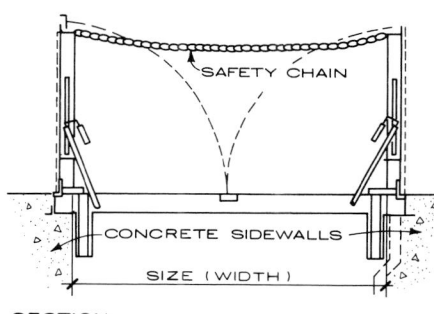

SECTION

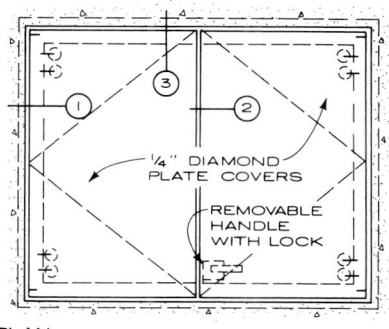

PLAN

SIDEWALK DOORS are available in single and double leaf openings. Single leaf doors range in size from 2 ft to 3 ft 6 in. in 6 in. increments. Double leaf doors range in size from 4 to 6 ft in 1 ft increments. Special sizes are available.

Units are constructed in steel or aluminum. The door leafs are made of ¼ in. diamond plate and are reinforced to withstand 300 psf of live load. Doors can be reinforced for greater loading conditions. The channel frames are made of ¼ in. steel or aluminum with an anchor flange around the perimeter. Each door leaf is equipped with forged brass hinges, stainless steel pins, spring operators, and an automatic hold-open arm with release handle and is locked with a concealed snap lock. A drain coupling is provided to drain the internal gutter system. Safety chains are required to protect the opening.

SIDEWALK DOOR

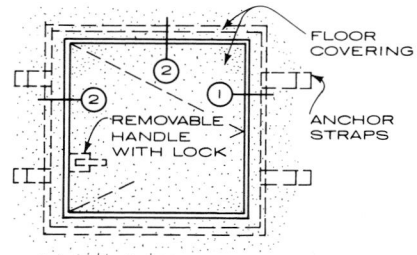

PLAN

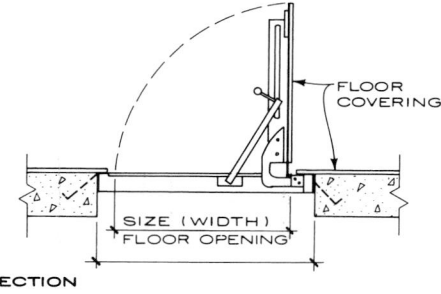

SECTION

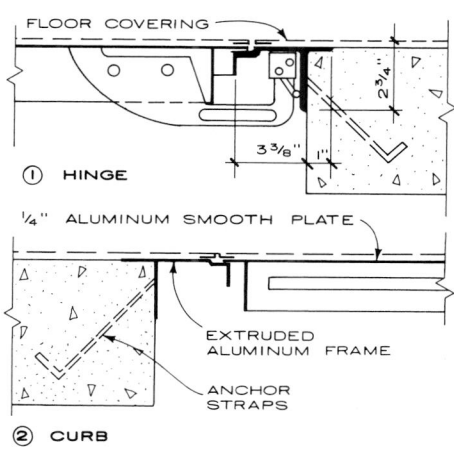

① HINGE

② CURB

FLOOR DOORS are available in single and double leaf openings. Single leaf doors range in size from 2 ft to 3 ft 6 in. in 6 in. increments. Double leaf doors range in size from 4 to 6 ft in 1 ft increments. Special sizes are available. Units are constructed in aluminum.

The door leafs are made of ¼ in. extruded aluminum. Doors are made to accept ⅛ or ³⁄₁₆ in. flooring. Each leaf has cast steel hinges and torsion bars. Doors open by a removable handle and are locked with a concealed snap lock.

FLOOR DOOR

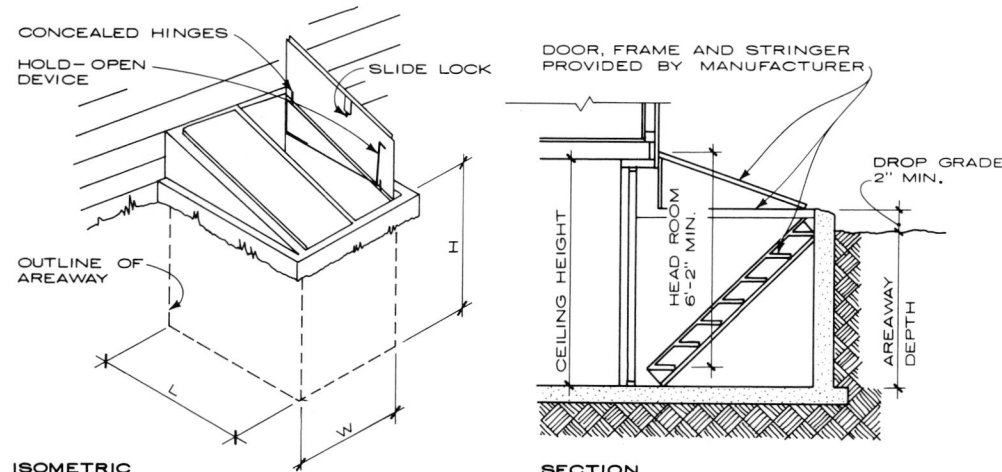

ISOMETRIC

SECTION

CELLAR DOOR

CELLAR DOOR DIMENSIONS

TYPE	LENGTH	WIDTH	HEIGHT
S/L	3'-7¼''	4'-3''	4'-4''
O	4'-10''	3'-11''	2'-6''
B	5'-4''	4'-3''	1'-10''
C	6'-0''	4'-7''	1'-7½''

AREAWAY DIMENSIONS (INSIDE)

TYPE	LENGTH	WIDTH	HEIGHT
S/L	3'-4''	3'-8''	3'-5¼''
O	4'-6''	3'-4''	4'-9¾''
B	5'-0''	3'-8''	5'-6''
C*	5'-8''	4'-0''	6'-2¼''

*Type C door can have a deeper areaway dimension with the use of stringer extensions.

Ronald C. Olech; SRGF, Inc., Architects; Champaign, Illinois

SPECIAL DOORS 8

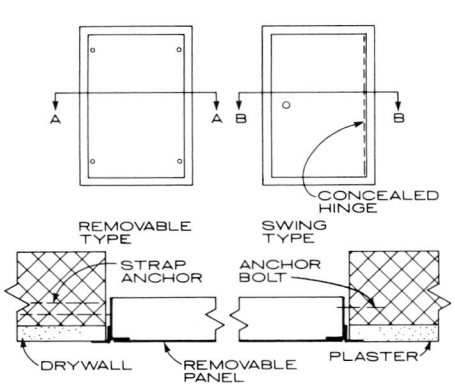

REMOVABLE TYPE   SWING TYPE

CONCEALED HINGE

STRAP ANCHOR   ANCHOR BOLT

DRYWALL   REMOVABLE PANEL   PLASTER

SECTION A-A

NOTES

1. Frames usually are set into building construction; doors are constructed to fit later. Doors may be hinged, set in with clips, or fastened with screws. Hinges may be butt or pivot, separate or continuous, surface or concealed. Assorted stock sizes range from 8 in. x 8 in. to 24 in. x 36 in.
2. Access panels should have a fire rating similar to the wall in which they occur. Access panels of more than 144 sq. ins. require automatic closers.
3. Minimum size for attic and crawl space access often is specified by building code.

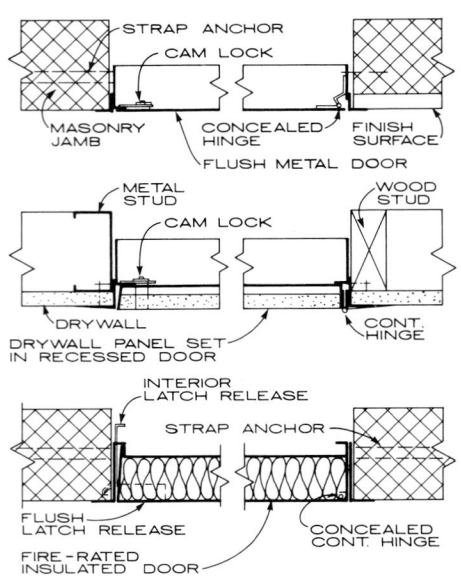

STRAP ANCHOR   CAM LOCK

MASONRY JAMB   CONCEALED HINGE   FINISH SURFACE

FLUSH METAL DOOR

METAL STUD   CAM LOCK   WOOD STUD

DRYWALL   CONT. HINGE

DRYWALL PANEL SET IN RECESSED DOOR

INTERIOR LATCH RELEASE

STRAP ANCHOR

FLUSH LATCH RELEASE

FIRE-RATED INSULATED DOOR   CONCEALED CONT. HINGE

SECTION B-B

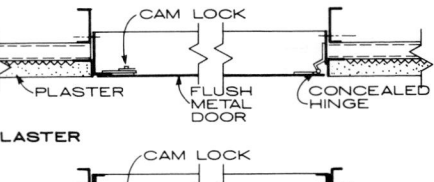

CAM LOCK

PLASTER   FLUSH METAL DOOR   CONCEALED HINGE

PLASTER

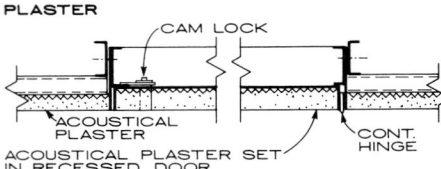

CAM LOCK

ACOUSTICAL PLASTER   CONT. HINGE

ACOUSTICAL PLASTER SET IN RECESSED DOOR

ACOUSTICAL PLASTER

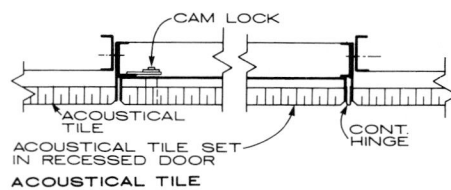

CAM LOCK

ACOUSTICAL TILE   CONT. HINGE

ACOUSTICAL TILE SET IN RECESSED DOOR

ACOUSTICAL TILE

NOTES

1. Spring-operated, swingdown panels and swingup panels frequently are used for ceiling access.
2. Standard sizes range from 12 in. x 12 in. to 24 in. x 36 in.
3. Other finish ceiling panels are detailed similar to acoustical tiles.

ACCESS DOORS

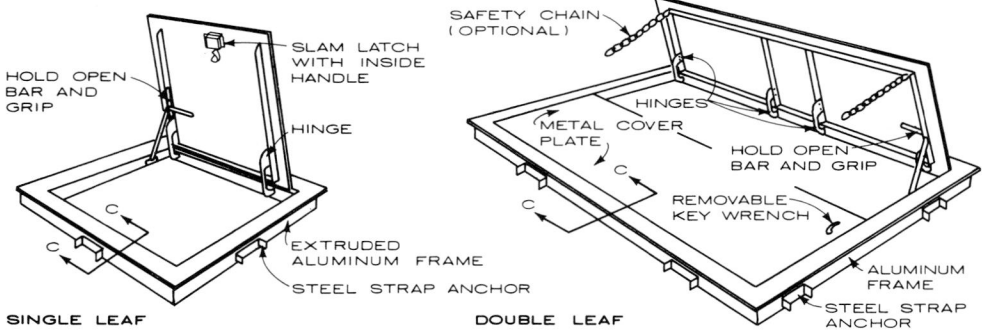

HOLD OPEN BAR AND GRIP   SLAM LATCH WITH INSIDE HANDLE   HINGE

EXTRUDED ALUMINUM FRAME   STEEL STRAP ANCHOR

SINGLE LEAF

SAFETY CHAIN (OPTIONAL)

HINGES   METAL COVER PLATE   HOLD OPEN BAR AND GRIP

REMOVABLE KEY WRENCH   ALUMINUM FRAME   STEEL STRAP ANCHOR

DOUBLE LEAF

1. MATERIAL: Steel or aluminum.
2. SIZES: Single leaf—2 ft. x 2 ft., 2 ft. 6 in. x 2 ft. 6 in., 2 ft. 6 in. x 3 ft., 3 ft. x 3 ft. Double leaf—3 ft. 6 in. x 3 ft. 6 in., 4 ft. x 4 ft., 4 ft. x 6 ft., 5 ft. x 5 ft.

Thickness "T" varies from $\frac{1}{8}$ in. for resilient flooring to $\frac{3}{16}$ in. for carpet; some manufacturers offer $\frac{3}{4}$ in. for terrazzo and tile floor.

Double-leaf floor hatch is recommended for areas where there is danger a person could fall into the opening. Safety codes require that floor openings be protected. Check local codes for special requirements.

CEILING ACCESS PANELS

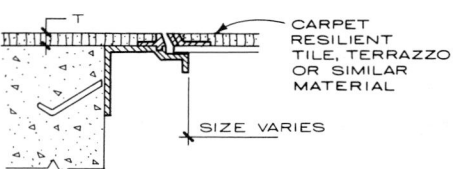

T

CARPET RESILIENT TILE, TERRAZZO OR SIMILAR MATERIAL

SIZE VARIES

FLOOR HATCH – SECTION C-C

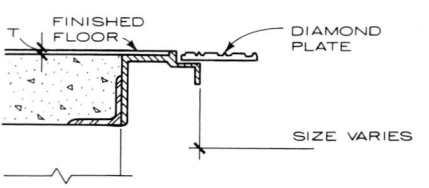

T   FINISHED FLOOR   DIAMOND PLATE

SIZE VARIES

FLOOR HATCH – SECTION C-C

LIGHT-DUTY TRENCH COVERS

1. MATERIAL: Extruded aluminum.
2. SIZE: 2 in. to 36 in. wide. Side frames are available in cut length of 20 ft. stocks that can be spliced to any length. Recessed cover plates are available in 20 ft. stock; other covers are available in 10 ft. and 12 ft. stock.
3. Side frames normally are cast in concrete around trough form.

HEAVY-DUTY TRENCH COVERS

1. MATERIAL: Cast iron or ductile iron.
2. SIZES: Heavy duty cast iron trench covers should be planned carefully to use standard stock length to avoid cutting, or special length casting should be ordered.
3. STOCK COVER SIZE: To 48 in. wide and 24 in. long. Frames are manufactured in standard lengths of 24 in. or 36 in. depending on size and manufacturer. Cast iron troughs are 8 in. deep, 6 in. to 24 in. wide, and 48 in. in stock lengths.
4. Minimum grating size in walkways is specified in ANSI A117.1-1986.

FLOOR HATCHES

2" TO 4"   SIZE VARIES   GASKET   WATER-TIGHT

LIGHT DUTY

3" TO 5" 3/4"   SIZE VARIES   WATERTIGHT   WEEP

HEAVY DUTY

PLAIN PLATE   ABRASIVE COATED   RECESSED PLATE   DIAMOND PLATE

LIGHT DUTY

COVER OR GRATING

CAST-IN-PLACE METAL TROUGH   **HEAVY DUTY**

TRENCH COVERS

Cohen, Karydas & Associates, Chartered; Washington, D.C.
Harold C. Munger, FAIA; Munger Munger + Associates Architects, Inc.; Toledo, Ohio

SPECIAL DOORS

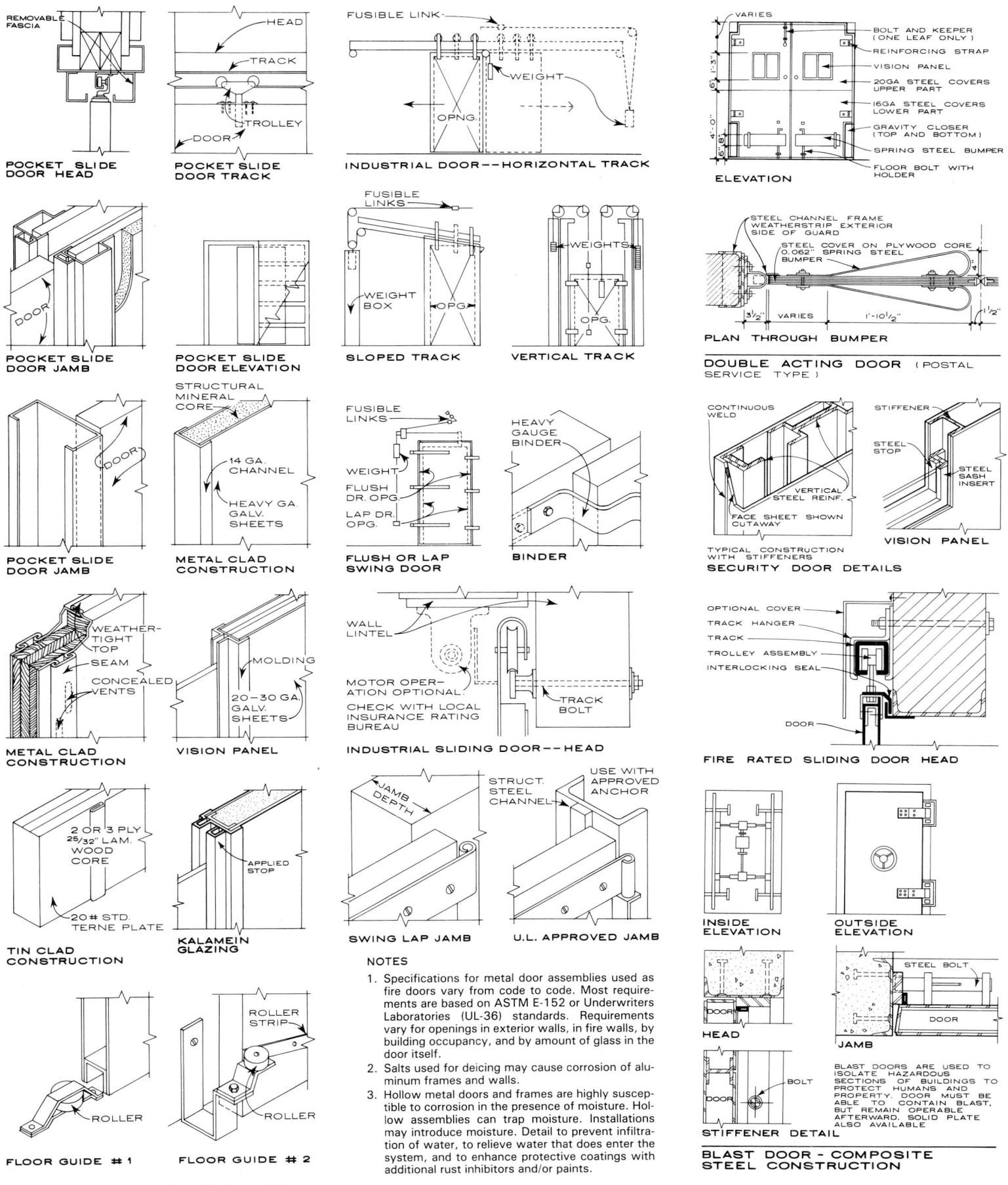

POCKET SLIDE DOOR HEAD

POCKET SLIDE DOOR TRACK

HEAD
TRACK
TROLLEY
DOOR

INDUSTRIAL DOOR--HORIZONTAL TRACK

FUSIBLE LINK
WEIGHT
OPNG.

ELEVATION

BOLT AND KEEPER (ONE LEAF ONLY)
REINFORCING STRAP
VISION PANEL
20GA STEEL COVERS UPPER PART
16GA STEEL COVERS LOWER PART
GRAVITY CLOSER (TOP AND BOTTOM)
SPRING STEEL BUMPER
FLOOR BOLT WITH HOLDER

POCKET SLIDE DOOR JAMB

POCKET SLIDE DOOR ELEVATION

SLOPED TRACK

VERTICAL TRACK

FUSIBLE LINKS
WEIGHTS
OPG.
WEIGHT BOX
OPG.

PLAN THROUGH BUMPER

DOUBLE ACTING DOOR (POSTAL SERVICE TYPE)

STEEL CHANNEL FRAME WEATHERSTRIP EXTERIOR SIDE OF GUARD
STEEL COVER ON PLYWOOD CORE 0.062" SPRING STEEL BUMPER
VARIES
3½" VARIES 1'-10½" 1½"

POCKET SLIDE DOOR JAMB

METAL CLAD CONSTRUCTION

STRUCTURAL MINERAL CORE
14 GA. CHANNEL
HEAVY GA. GALV. SHEETS
DOOR

FLUSH OR LAP SWING DOOR

FUSIBLE LINKS
WEIGHT
FLUSH DR. OPG.
LAP DR. OPG.

BINDER

HEAVY GAUGE BINDER

SECURITY DOOR DETAILS

CONTINUOUS WELD
VERTICAL STEEL REINF.
FACE SHEET SHOWN CUTAWAY
TYPICAL CONSTRUCTION WITH STIFFENERS

VISION PANEL

STIFFENER
STEEL STOP
STEEL SASH INSERT

METAL CLAD CONSTRUCTION

WEATHER-TIGHT TOP SEAM
CONCEALED VENTS

VISION PANEL

MOLDING
20-30 GA. GALV. SHEETS

INDUSTRIAL SLIDING DOOR--HEAD

WALL LINTEL
MOTOR OPER-ATION OPTIONAL: CHECK WITH LOCAL INSURANCE RATING BUREAU
TRACK BOLT

FIRE RATED SLIDING DOOR HEAD

OPTIONAL COVER
TRACK HANGER
TRACK
TROLLEY ASSEMBLY
INTERLOCKING SEAL
DOOR

TIN CLAD CONSTRUCTION

2 OR 3 PLY 25/32" LAM. WOOD CORE
20# STD. TERNE PLATE

KALAMEIN GLAZING

APPLIED STOP

SWING LAP JAMB

JAMB DEPTH
STRUCT. STEEL CHANNEL

U.L. APPROVED JAMB

USE WITH APPROVED ANCHOR

INSIDE ELEVATION

OUTSIDE ELEVATION

HEAD
DOOR

JAMB
STEEL BOLT
DOOR

STIFFENER DETAIL
DOOR
BOLT

FLOOR GUIDE #1
ROLLER

FLOOR GUIDE #2
ROLLER STRIP
ROLLER

BLAST DOORS ARE USED TO ISOLATE HAZARDOUS SECTIONS OF BUILDINGS TO PROTECT HUMANS AND PROPERTY. DOOR MUST BE ABLE TO CONTAIN BLAST, BUT REMAIN OPERABLE AFTERWARD. SOLID PLATE ALSO AVAILABLE

BLAST DOOR - COMPOSITE STEEL CONSTRUCTION

NOTES

1. Specifications for metal door assemblies used as fire doors vary from code to code. Most requirements are based on ASTM E-152 or Underwriters Laboratories (UL-36) standards. Requirements vary for openings in exterior walls, in fire walls, by building occupancy, and by amount of glass in the door itself.
2. Salts used for deicing may cause corrosion of aluminum frames and walls.
3. Hollow metal doors and frames are highly susceptible to corrosion in the presence of moisture. Hollow assemblies can trap moisture. Installations may introduce moisture. Detail to prevent infiltration of water, to relieve water that does enter the system, and to enhance protective coatings with additional rust inhibitors and/or paints.

Darrel Downing Rippeteau, Architect; Washington, D.C.
James W. G. Watson, AIA; Ronald A. Spahn & Associates; Cleveland Heights, Ohio

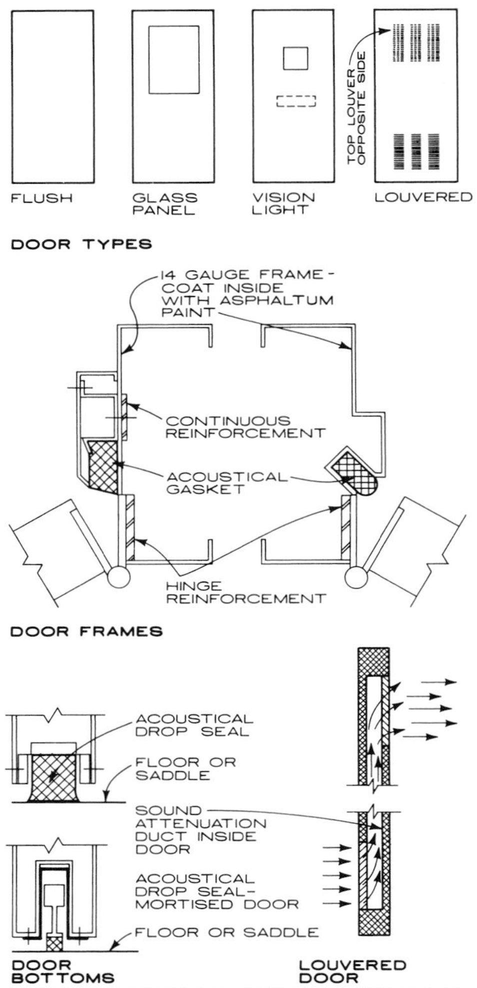

DOOR TYPES

FLUSH · GLASS PANEL · VISION LIGHT · LOUVERED · TOP LOUVER OPPOSITE SIDE

DOOR FRAMES

14 GAUGE FRAME - COAT INSIDE WITH ASPHALTUM PAINT
CONTINUOUS REINFORCEMENT
ACOUSTICAL GASKET
HINGE REINFORCEMENT

ACOUSTIC DOORS AND FRAMES

ACOUSTICAL DROP SEAL
FLOOR OR SADDLE
SOUND ATTENUATION DUCT INSIDE DOOR
ACOUSTICAL DROP SEAL - MORTISED DOOR
FLOOR OR SADDLE

DOOR BOTTOMS · LOUVERED DOOR

NOTE: SURFACE MOUNTED DROP SEALS ARE AVAILABLE

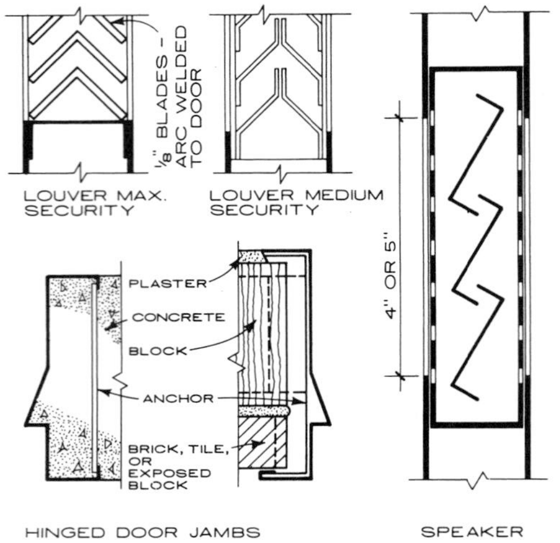

DOOR TYPES

FLUSH · VISION · 2 x 1 VISION WITH BAR · VISION WITH FOOD PASS · VISION WITH OPEN FOOD PASS
OPT. BULLET RESISTANT · SPEAKER OPTIONAL · HINGED COVER SHELF

VISION WITH FOOD PASS AND COVER · VISION WITH SPEAKER · 2 x 2 VISION WITH BARS · PEEPHOLE · LONG VISION
SPEAKER OPTIONAL · AVAILABLE 2 x 3 AND 3 x 3 · PIVOTED COVER · ALT LOCATION

SECURITY LOUVER · DETENTION SCREEN · SOLITARY CONFINEMENT · EXPANDED METAL · LONG VISION

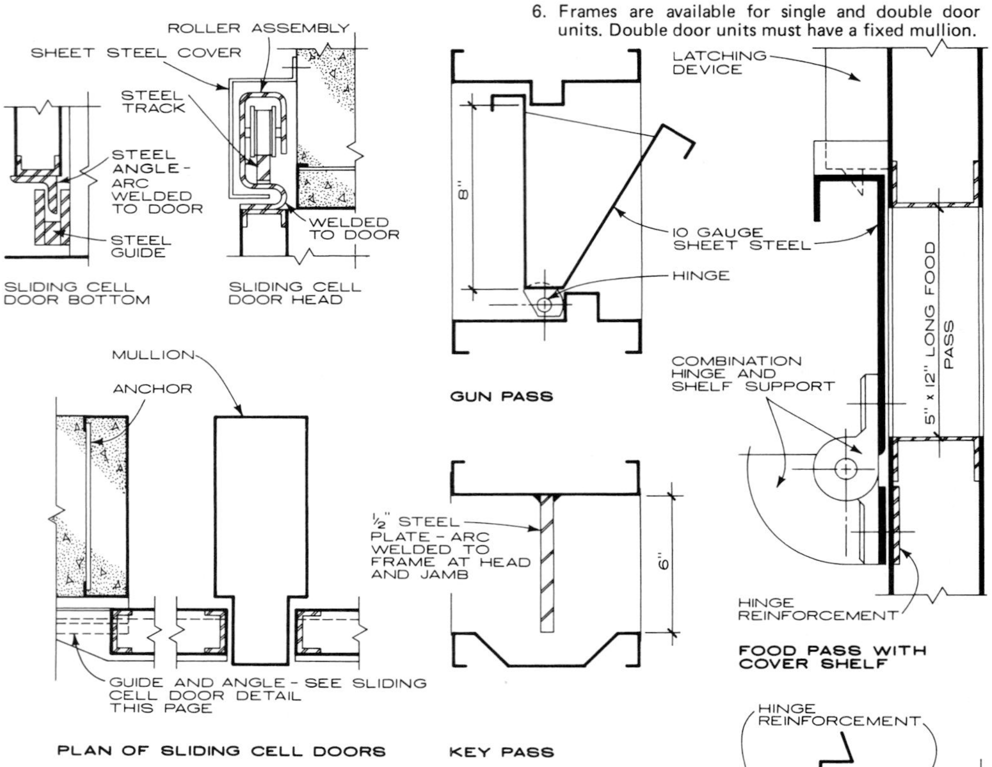

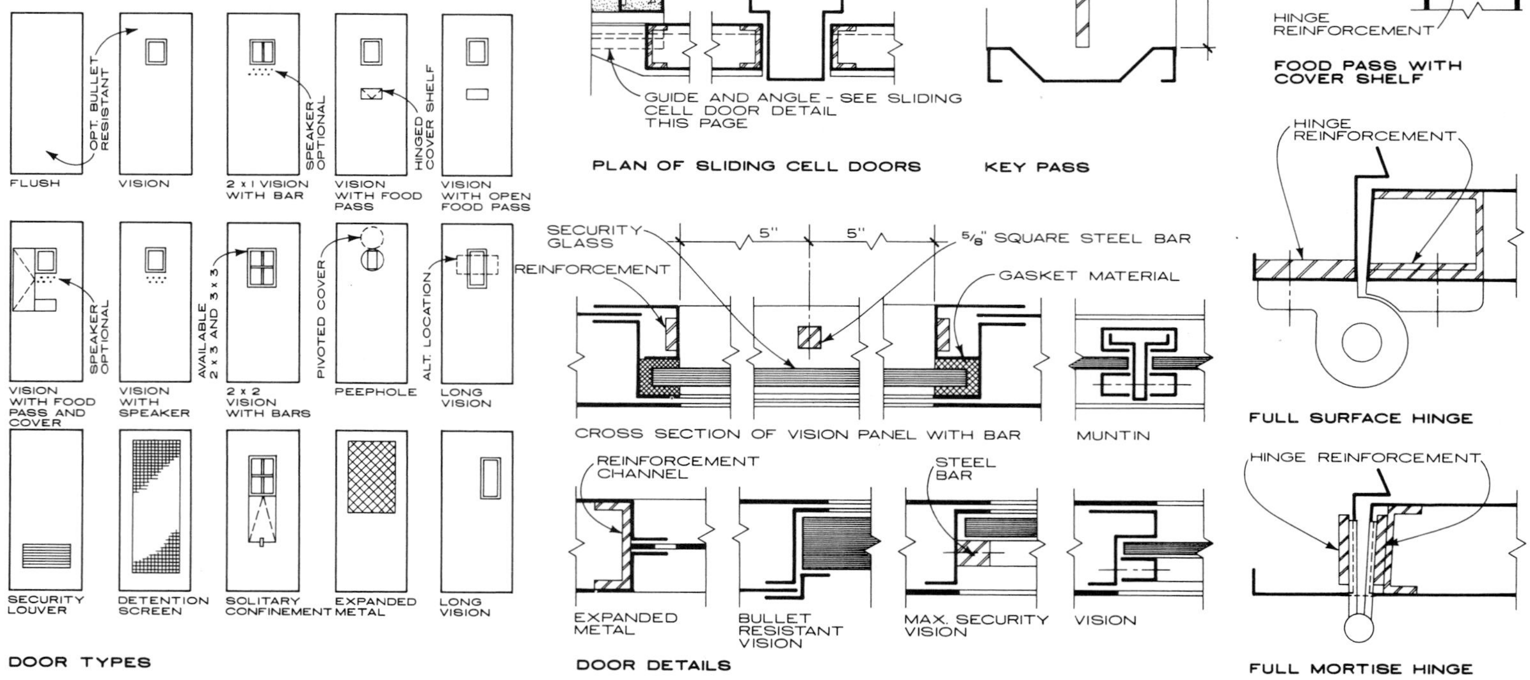

DETENTION DOORS AND DETAILS

Kelly Sacher & Associates; Architects Engineers Planners; N. Babylon, New York

LOUVER MAX. SECURITY · LOUVER MEDIUM SECURITY
⅛" BLADES - ARC WELDED TO DOOR

PLASTER · CONCRETE · BLOCK · ANCHOR · BRICK, TILE, OR EXPOSED BLOCK
HINGED DOOR JAMBS · SPEAKER
4" OR 5"

ROLLER ASSEMBLY · SHEET STEEL COVER · STEEL TRACK · STEEL ANGLE - ARC WELDED TO DOOR · STEEL GUIDE · WELDED TO DOOR
SLIDING CELL DOOR BOTTOM · SLIDING CELL DOOR HEAD

MULLION · ANCHOR
GUIDE AND ANGLE - SEE SLIDING CELL DOOR DETAIL THIS PAGE
PLAN OF SLIDING CELL DOORS

½" STEEL PLATE - ARC WELDED TO FRAME AT HEAD AND JAMB
KEY PASS · 6"

LATCHING DEVICE · 10 GAUGE SHEET STEEL · HINGE
GUN PASS · 8"
COMBINATION HINGE AND SHELF SUPPORT · HINGE REINFORCEMENT
5' x 12" LONG FOOD PASS
FOOD PASS WITH COVER SHELF

SECURITY GLASS · REINFORCEMENT · 5" · 5" · ⅝" SQUARE STEEL BAR · GASKET MATERIAL
CROSS SECTION OF VISION PANEL WITH BAR · MUNTIN

REINFORCEMENT CHANNEL · STEEL BAR
EXPANDED METAL · BULLET RESISTANT VISION · MAX. SECURITY VISION · VISION
DOOR DETAILS

HINGE REINFORCEMENT
FULL SURFACE HINGE
HINGE REINFORCEMENT
FULL MORTISE HINGE

NOTES

1. Security doors must have a minimum nominal thickness of 2 in. so that security locks can be fitted in them. The required door thickness should always be coordinated with the type of security hardware being used.
2. All locking devices should be protected with a ⅛ in. steel plate at the detention side and door edge.
3. Pressed steel security frames should be a minimum of 14 gauge and are made up to 7 gauge. The frame gauge should be selected according to the desired performance. This information is available from the manufacturers.
4. All joints in security frames should be mitered and arc welded.
5. The following hardware reinforcement information should only be used as a guide:

Surface hinges	10 gauge steel channel and a ⅜ in. steel plate
Mortise hinges	10 gauge steel channel and a 3/16 in. steel plate
Surface pull	⅜ x 1 x 12 in. steel plate
Surface closer	12 gauge channel x 2½ x 14 in.

6. Frames are available for single and double door units. Double door units must have a fixed mullion.

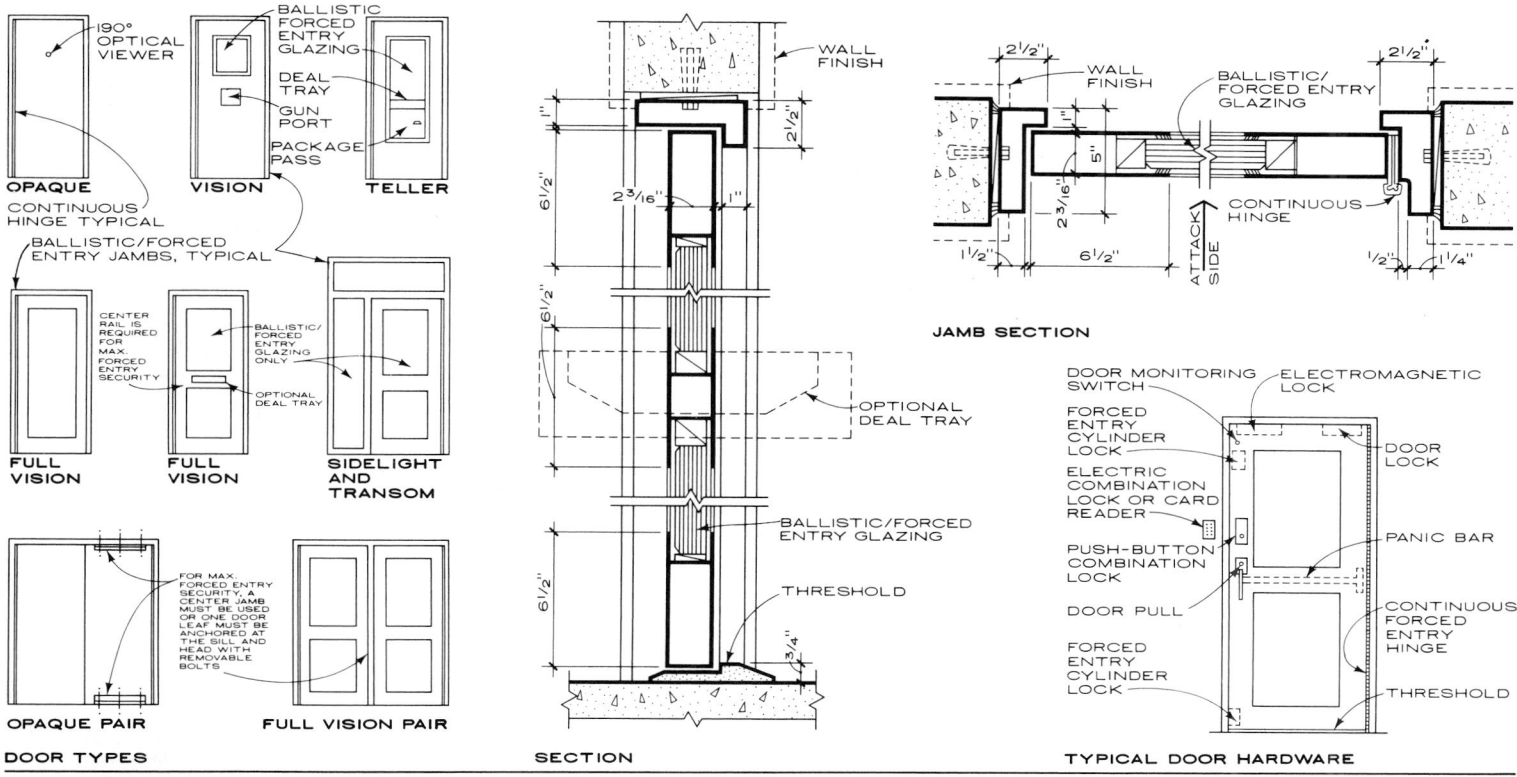

DOOR TYPES **BALLISTIC/FORCED ENTRY DOORS**

SECTION

JAMB SECTION

TYPICAL DOOR HARDWARE

NOTES

1. Ballistic/forced entry modular units from manufacturers can be combined to form a wall or room.

2. Fire-rated opaque security doors are available.

3. Ballistic resistant glazing is manufactured in various thicknesses to attain required levels of resistant standards; e.g., 9 mm, high-powered rifle.

4. To maximize forced entry resistance, security doors must swing toward the attack side.

5. Custom doors can be fabricated when designed within manufacturers' parameters.

6. Walls must be constructed to meet the same level of resistance as the windows and doors installed in them.

7. Doors and windows must be anchored in strict accordance with manufacturers' directions to attain resistant standards.

8. Ballistic/forced entry windows for use in exterior building openings are similar to the teller windows detailed on this page.

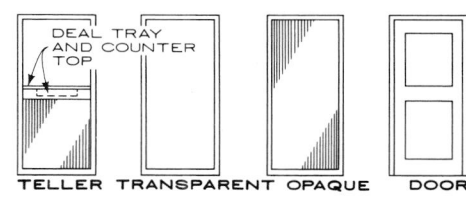

TELLER **TRANSPARENT** **OPAQUE** **DOOR**

MODULAR UNITS

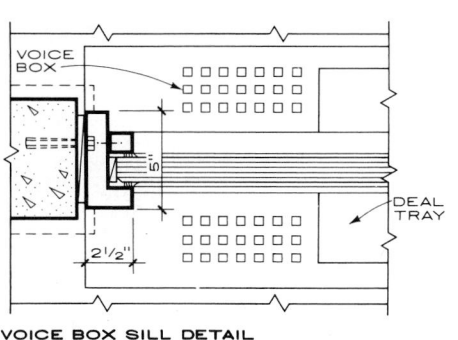

VOICE BOX SILL DETAIL

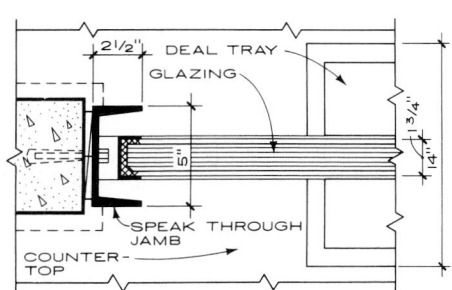

SPEAK THROUGH JAMB DETAIL

BALLISTIC/FORCED ENTRY TELLER WINDOWS

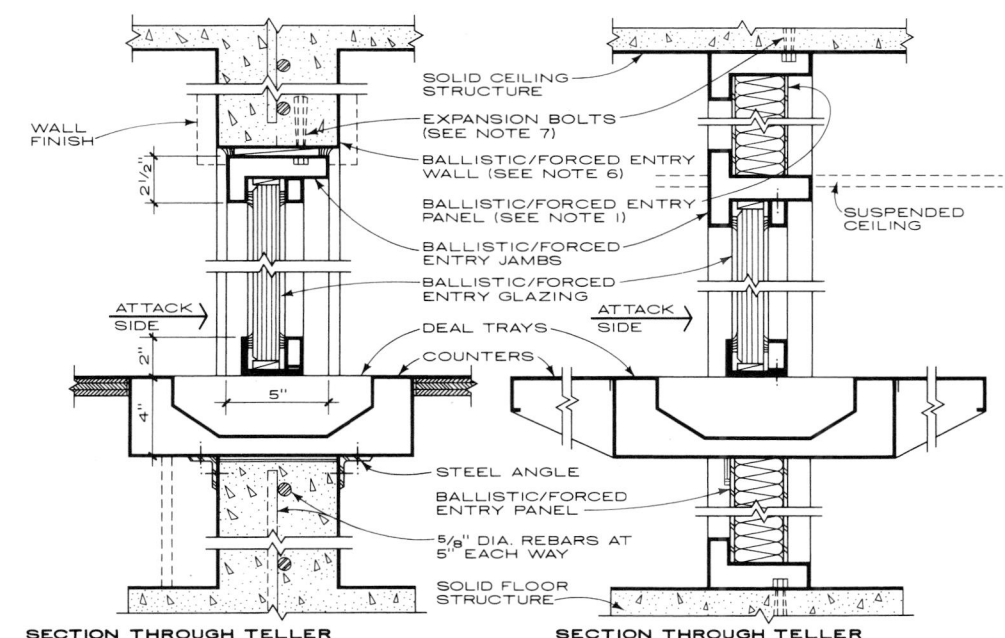

SECTION THROUGH TELLER WINDOW MOUNTED IN BALLISTIC/FORCED ENTRY CONCRETE WALL

SECTION THROUGH TELLER WINDOW MODULAR UNIT

Edwin Daly, AIA; Joseph Handwerger, Architects; Washington, D.C.
William G. Miner, AIA; Washington, D.C.

SPECIAL DOORS   8

BACKGROUND

A successful storefront or retail entrance attracts the casual passerby. In order to attract, a shopfront must:

1. Catch the eye
2. Identify the shop
3. Display the merchandise in the most appealing way
4. Entice the passerby to enter

SHOP CHARACTER

The character of a retail entrance is influenced by the following factors:

1. Neighborhood or retail development character
2. Types of products sold
3. Accessibility—on foot or by car
4. Glazed area in relation to product
5. Fascia—visibility of shop name
6. Lettering—size, color, style, use of logos
7. Illumination—intensity, color, or use of daylight
8. Color—select predominant, coordinate with interior
9. Finishes— cost, design guidelines, and durability

ENVIRONMENTAL FACTORS

The external features of a shop are influenced by the following factors:

1. Solar—shade southern exposures
2. Wind—provide protection with deep lobbies
3. Corrosive—provide protective finishes
4. Street traffic—lobbies or air locks to keep out fumes

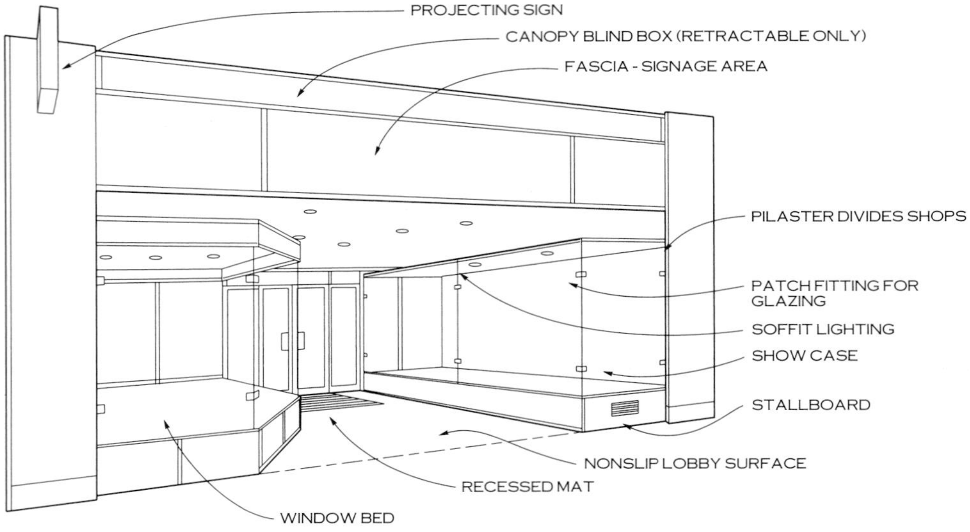
PROJECTING SIGN
CANOPY BLIND BOX (RETRACTABLE ONLY)
FASCIA - SIGNAGE AREA
PILASTER DIVIDES SHOPS
PATCH FITTING FOR GLAZING
SOFFIT LIGHTING
SHOW CASE
STALLBOARD
NONSLIP LOBBY SURFACE
RECESSED MAT
WINDOW BED

STOREFRONT INTERIOR AND EXTERIOR—COMMON ELEMENTS

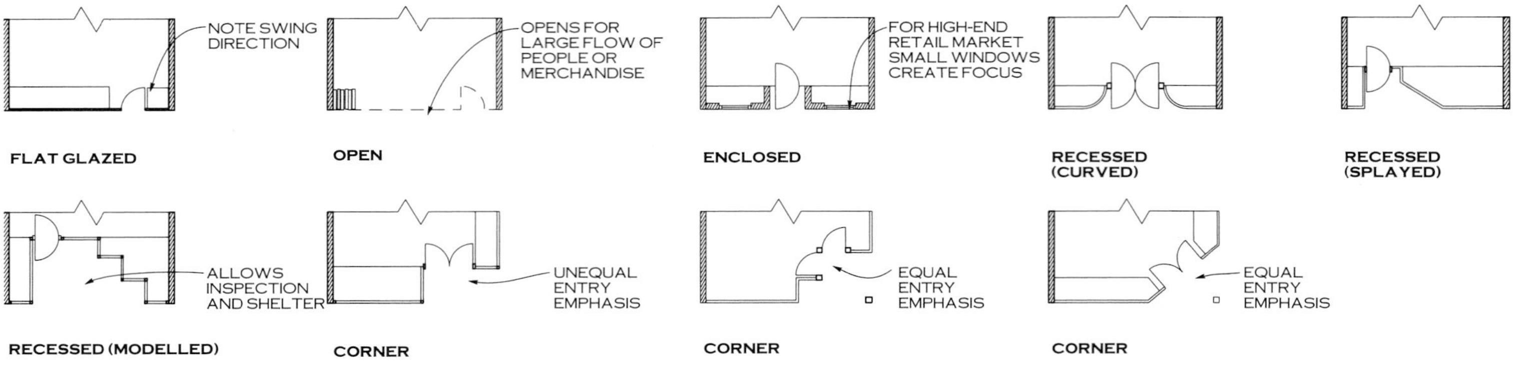
NOTE SWING DIRECTION
OPENS FOR LARGE FLOW OF PEOPLE OR MERCHANDISE
FOR HIGH-END RETAIL MARKET SMALL WINDOWS CREATE FOCUS
FLAT GLAZED
OPEN
ENCLOSED
RECESSED (CURVED)
RECESSED (SPLAYED)
ALLOWS INSPECTION AND SHELTER
UNEQUAL ENTRY EMPHASIS
EQUAL ENTRY EMPHASIS
EQUAL ENTRY EMPHASIS
RECESSED (MODELLED)
CORNER
CORNER
CORNER

STOREFRONT TYPES

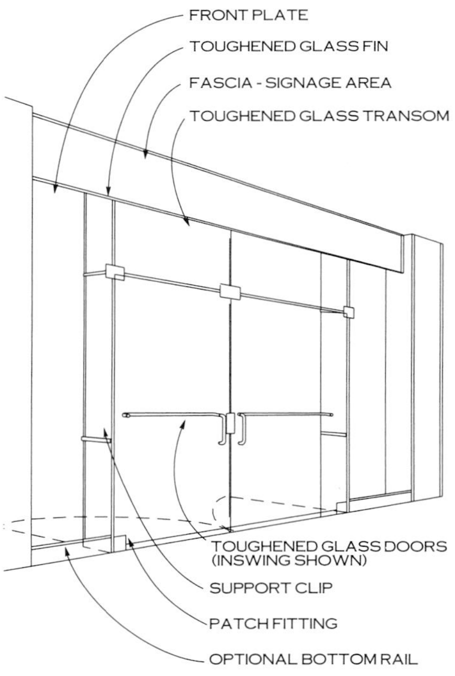
FRONT PLATE
TOUGHENED GLASS FIN
FASCIA - SIGNAGE AREA
TOUGHENED GLASS TRANSOM
TOUGHENED GLASS DOORS (INSWING SHOWN)
SUPPORT CLIP
PATCH FITTING
OPTIONAL BOTTOM RAIL

ALL-GLASS STOREFRONT

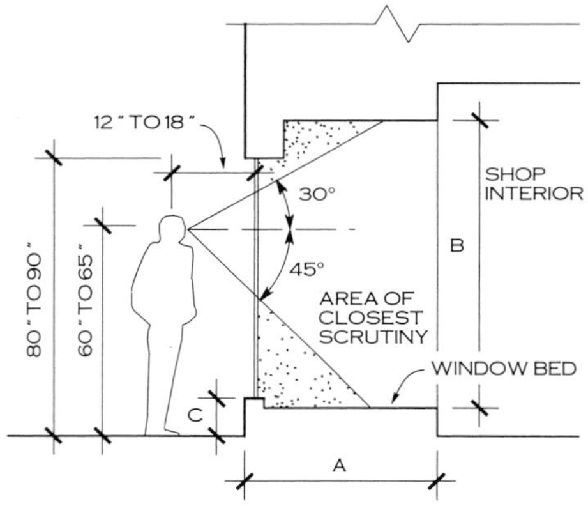
12" TO 18"
30°
45°
SHOP INTERIOR
B
AREA OF CLOSEST SCRUTINY
WINDOW BED
80" TO 90"
60" TO 65"
C
A

REFER TO TABLE BELOW

WINDOW DIMENSIONS

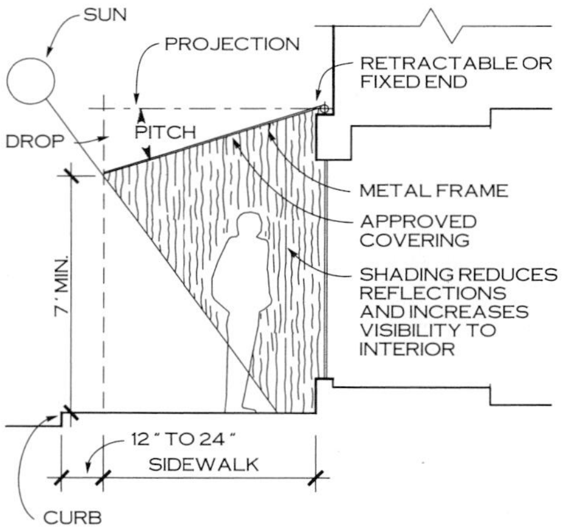
SUN
PROJECTION
RETRACTABLE OR FIXED END
DROP
PITCH
METAL FRAME
APPROVED COVERING
SHADING REDUCES REFLECTIONS AND INCREASES VISIBILITY TO INTERIOR
7' MIN.
12" TO 24"
SIDEWALK
CURB

CHECK LOCAL CODES TO VERIFY REQUIREMENTS

CANOPY DIMENSIONS/SOLAR CONTROL

TYPICAL WINDOW DIMENSIONS

VIEW POINT	TYPE OF SHOP	A WINDOW DEPTH	B WINDOW HEIGHT	C SILL HEIGHT
Very close	Jewelry, eyeglass, picture, and books	18" to 36"	up to 36"	30" to 36"
Close	Toys, shoes, electronic, optical, CD's, and gifts	30" to 60"	up to 80"	18" to 30"
Medium	Clothing, china, glass sporting goods, and appliances	40" to 96"	up to 96"	12" to 18"
Distant	Furniture, floor covering, and automobiles	80" to 120"	Ceiling height	0" to 6"

Eric K. Beach; Rippeteau Architects, PC; Washington, D.C.

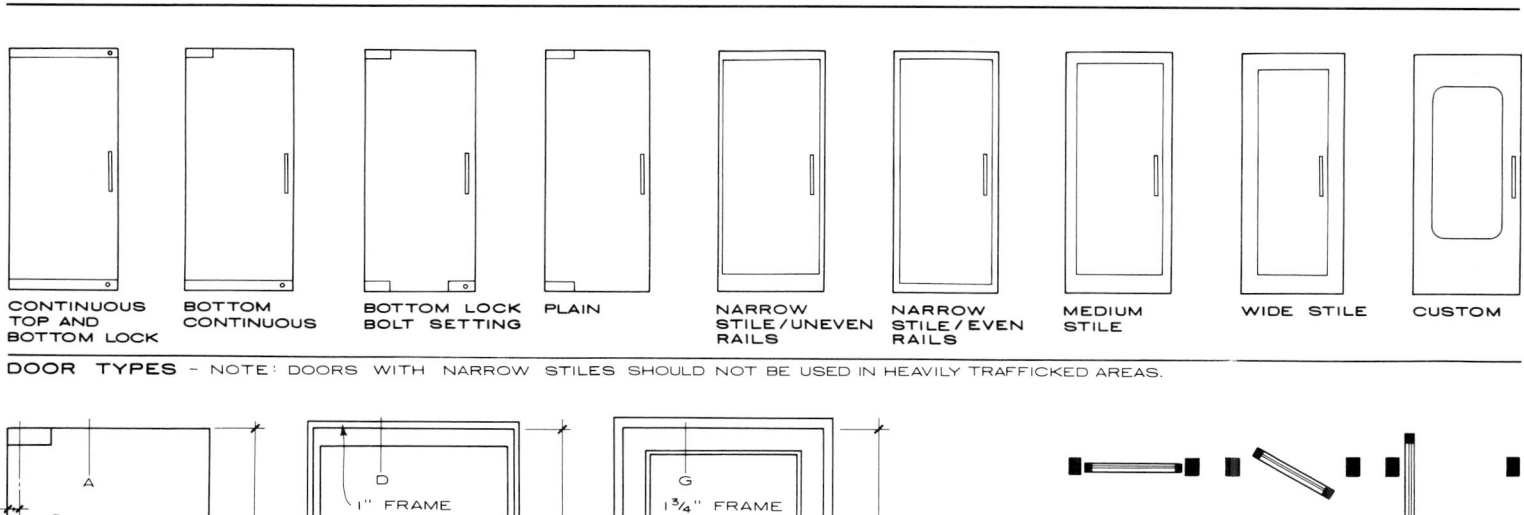

CONTINUOUS TOP AND BOTTOM LOCK | BOTTOM CONTINUOUS | BOTTOM LOCK BOLT SETTING | PLAIN | NARROW STILE/UNEVEN RAILS | NARROW STILE/EVEN RAILS | MEDIUM STILE | WIDE STILE | CUSTOM

DOOR TYPES — NOTE: DOORS WITH NARROW STILES SHOULD NOT BE USED IN HEAVILY TRAFFICKED AREAS.

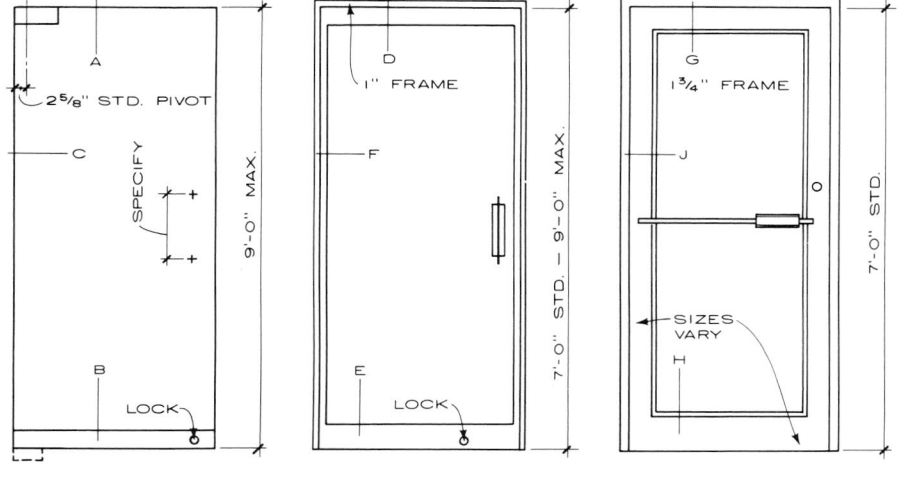

ELEVATION — TYPICAL GLASS DOORS

CLOSED POSITION | PARTLY OPEN | COMPLETELY OPEN

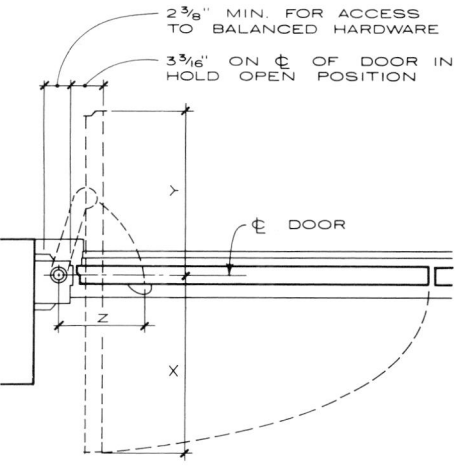

PLAN
BALANCED DOOR

SPACE REQUIREMENTS—VARIOUS DOOR WIDTHS (IN.)

	34	36	38	40	42	44
X	21¼	23¼	25¼	23¼	25¼	27¼
Y	12¾			16¼		
Z	7⅛			8⅞		

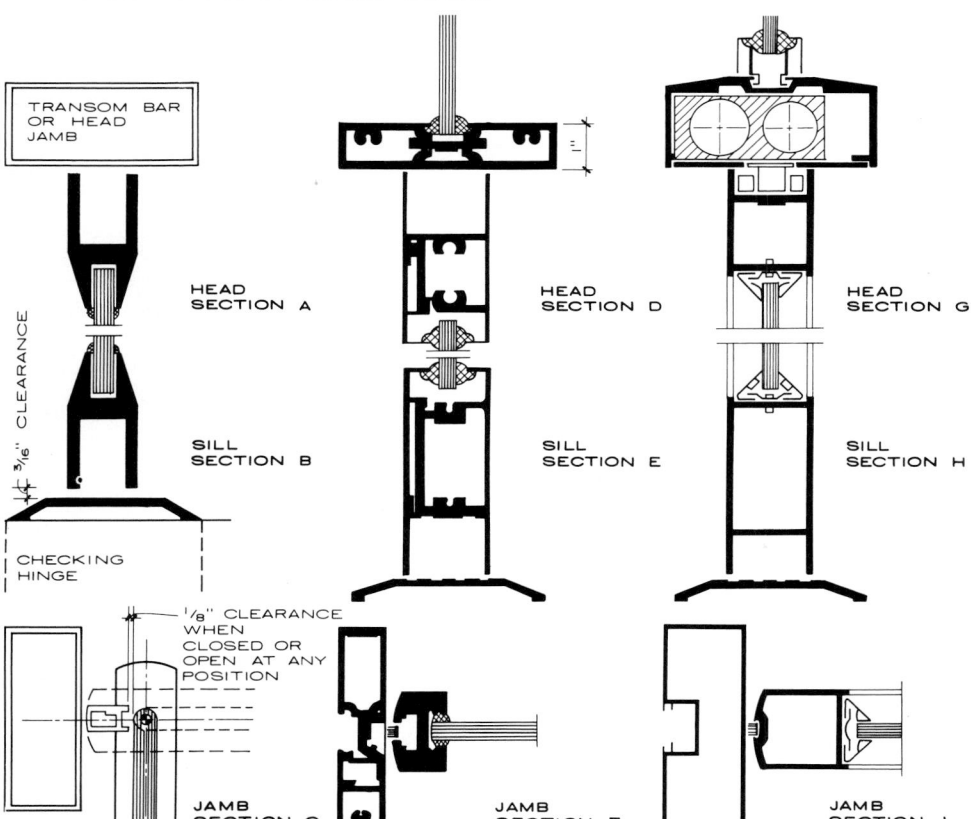

DETAILS—TYPICAL GLASS DOORS

NOTES

1. Consult applicable codes for safety requirements, glass size, thickness, and tempering.
2. Frameless ½ in. glass doors are available in clear, grey, or bronze tints in sizes up to 60 in. x 108 in. Frameless ¾ in. glass doors are available only in clear tint in sizes up to 48 in. x 108 in.
3. Consult manufacturer's data on structural adequacy for required loads and for frames and transom bars reinforcement.
4. Aluminum doors and frames are available in all standard aluminum finishes in sizes up to 6 ft. x 7 ft.
5. Frameless doors may not permit adequate weatherstripping. The use of frameless doors in exterior walls in northern climates should be evaluated for energy efficiency and comfort.
6. Full glass doors should have vision warning marks.
7. ADAAG requires accessible hardware and thresholds.
8. For optimum accessibility, provide automatic door openers.

G. Lawson Drinkard, III, AIA; The Vickery Partnership, Architects; Charlottesville, Virginia

TYPES AND APPLICATIONS

1. Darkroom revolving doors act as a light barrier.
2. Automated revolving doors for large size doors, for persons with disabilities accessibility, etc.
3. Motorized oval doors for small groups, wheelchairs, or grocery carts.
4. Security revolving doors that are noncollapsible until a magnetic shear lock is automatically released in an emergency.
5. Sliding night door of solid metal construction to close off open quadrant at exterior opening.
6. Manually operated.

DESIGN CONSIDERATIONS

1. Mount entirely on one slab.
2. Do not attach to adjacent walls.
3. Floor must be level.

NOTES

1. Circular glass enclosure walls may be annealed $1/4$ in. glass. However, this varies with different government bodies. Some jurisdictions require laminated glass. Tempered glass is not available for this use. Refer to the Consumer Products Safety Commission's standards for glazing.
2. Practical capacity equals 25 to 35 people per minute.
3. Doors fabricated from stainless steel, aluminum, or bronze sections are available. Stainless steel is the most durable; lead times vary with construction techniques. Stainless steel is available in a number of satin and polished finishes. Aluminum is the most common and economical. It is available in anodized or painted finishes. Bronze is most difficult to maintain; satin, polished, or statuary finishes must have a protective lacquer coating. Doors are available with only top and bottom stiles to be used with all-glass storefront doors. Wall enclosures may be all metal, all glass, partial glass, or housed-in construction.
4. Optional heating and cooling source should be placed immediately adjacent to the enclosure.
5. For general planning, use 6 ft 6 in. diameter. For hotels, department stores, airports, or other large traffic areas, use 7 ft or greater diameter.
6. Codes may allow 50% of legal exiting requirements by means of revolving doors. Some do not credit any and require hinged doors adjacent. Verify with local authorities.

REVOLVING DOOR ENCLOSURE DIMENSIONS

DIAMETER	OPENING 4 WING	OPENING 3 WING	WALL LENGTH 4 WING	WALL LENGTH 3 WING	RECOMMENDED MAXIMUM HEIGHT
6'-0"	4'-1"		4'-7 5/8"		10'-0"
6'-2"	4'-2 1/2"		4'-9 1/8"		9'-10"
6'-4"	4'-3 7/8"		4'-10 1/2"		9'-8"
*6'-6"	*4'-5 1/4"	3'-1/4"	*4'-11 7/8"	6'-1/4"	9'-6"
6'-8"	4'-6 5/8"	3'-1 1/4"	5'-1 1/4"	6'-2 1/32"	9'-4"
6'-10"	4'-8 1/8"	3'-2 1/4"	5'-1 1/4"	6'-3 3/4"	9'-2"
*7'-0"	*4'-9 1/2"	*3'-3 1/4"	5'-4 1/8"	*6'-5 1/2"	9'-0"
7'-6"	5'-1 3/4"	3'-6 1/4"	5'-8 3/4"	6'-10 11/16"	8'-6"
8'-0"	5'-6"	3'-9 1/4"	6'-5/8"	7'-3 7/8"	8'-0"
9'-0"		4'-3/4"		8'-2 1/8"	8'-0"
10'-0"		4'-9 1/4"		9'-9/16"	8'-0"
14'-0"	9'-8 7/8"	6'-9 1/4"	10'-3 1/4"	12'-6 1/8"	8'-0"
16'-0"	11'-1 7/8"	7'-9 1/4"	11'-8 1/4"	14'-2 7/8"	8'-0"

* Standard sizes

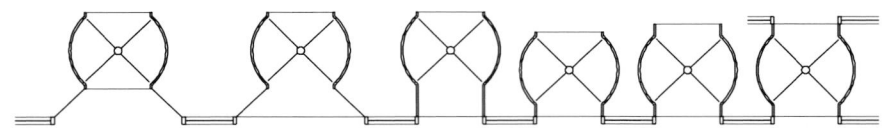

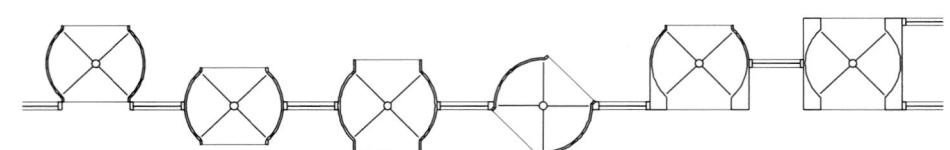

LAYOUT TYPES

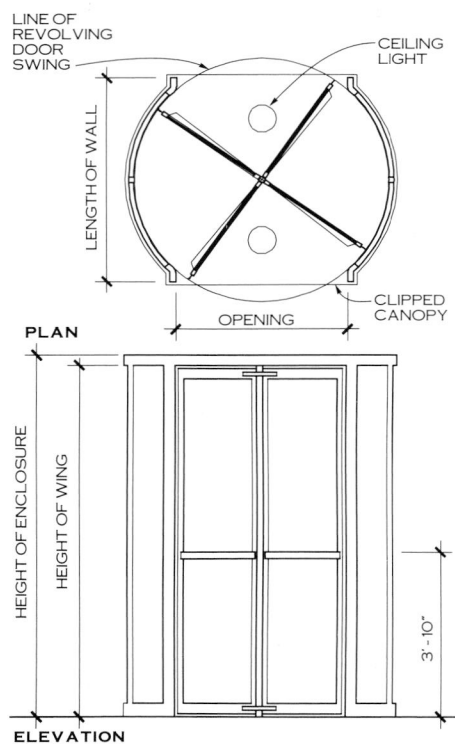

PLAN

ELEVATION

TYPICAL REVOLVING DOOR

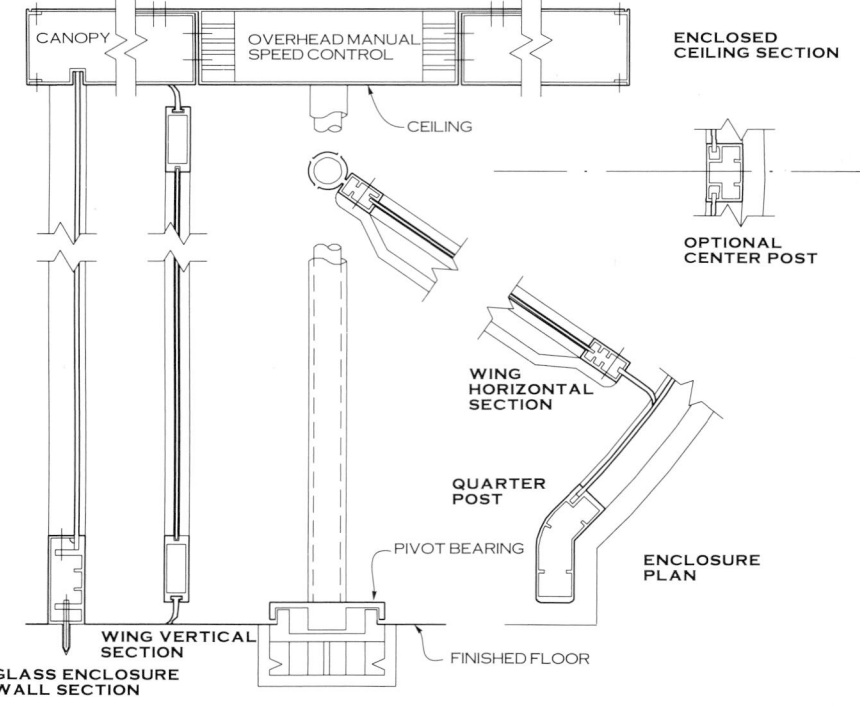

TYPICAL DOOR DETAILS

Jane Hansen, AIA; DeStefano + Partners; Chicago, Illinois

ENTRANCES AND STOREFRONTS

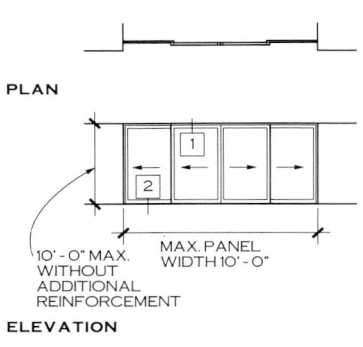

PLAN

ELEVATION

10'-0" MAX. WITHOUT ADDITIONAL REINFORCEMENT

MAX. PANEL WIDTH 10'-0"

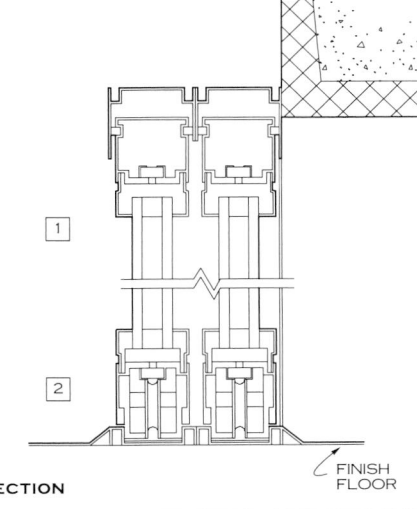

SECTION

FINISH FLOOR

BYPASS DOOR DETAILS

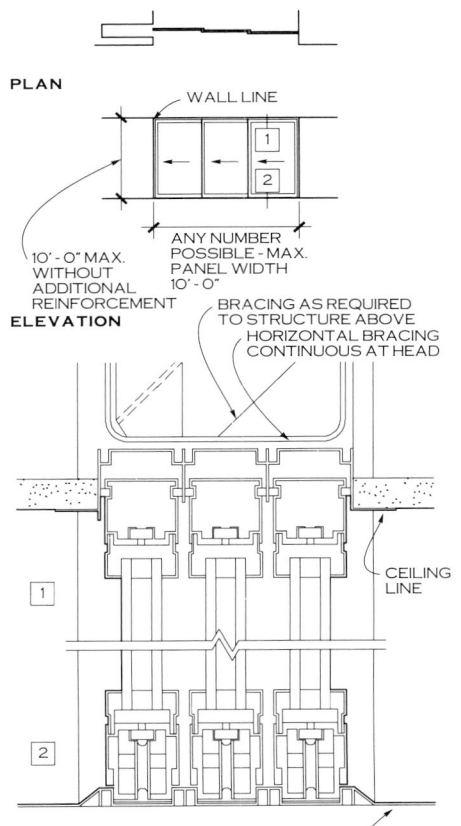

PLAN

WALL LINE

ELEVATION

10'-0" MAX. WITHOUT ADDITIONAL REINFORCEMENT

ANY NUMBER POSSIBLE - MAX. PANEL WIDTH 10'-0"

BRACING AS REQUIRED TO STRUCTURE ABOVE HORIZONTAL BRACING CONTINUOUS AT HEAD

CEILING LINE

SECTION

FINISH FLOOR

POCKET DOOR DETAILS

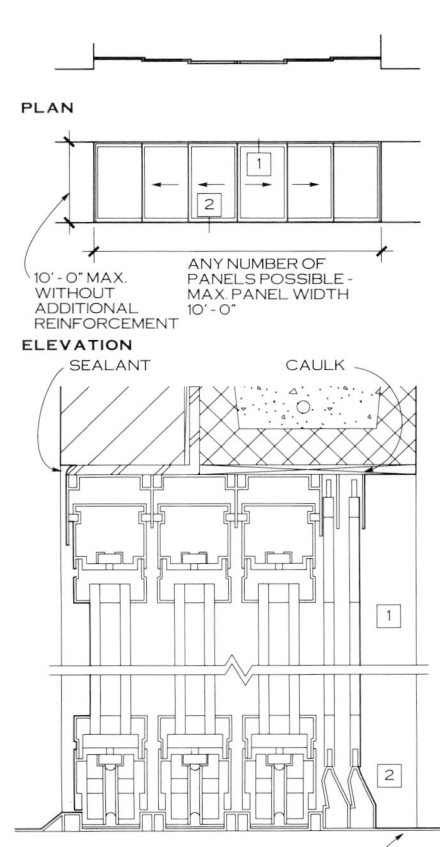

PLAN

ELEVATION

10'-0" MAX. WITHOUT ADDITIONAL REINFORCEMENT

ANY NUMBER OF PANELS POSSIBLE - MAX. PANEL WIDTH 10'-0"

SEALANT

CAULK

SECTION

FINISH FLOOR

MULTIPLE SLIDING DOOR DETAILS

NOTES

1. Sliding glass door wood finishes are available in clear pine with natural varnish, primed, or painted finishes.
2. Cladding for wood doors is available in vinyl or aluminum with electrostatic paint or in anodized aluminum.
3. Aluminum frames are available anodized or with electrostatic paint finishes.
4. Check with manufacturer's literature for material, cladding, and color options.

GLAZING OPTIONS

Standard glazing	Low emissivity insulating glass
	Low emissivity solar insulating glass
Safety glazing	Tempered glass[1]
	Wire glass[1]
	Laminated glass[1]
Nontransparent glass	Obscure glass[1]
	Composite veneer porcelain faced panels
	Glass fiber reinforced plastic
	Spandrel panel
Sound control glazing	Insulated glass

NOTES

1. This glazing can have the same low emissivity coating found on the standard glazings.
2. Most glazing options available with insulating glass with low emissivity films, some also with argon gas.
3. To reduce breakage and avoid injury it is recommended that tempered or safety glass be used.
4. Glazing options vary; check manufacturer's literature for specifics.

PERFORMANCE DATA FOR GLAZING OPTIONS

	ENERGY EFFICIENCY		CENTER OF GLASS U - VALUE	HEAT GAIN (BTU)[1]	INSIDE GLASS SURFACE TEMPERATURES[2]	SHADING COEFFICENTS[3]
	U - VALUE	R - VALUE				
Single pane aluminum frame without thermal breaks	1.31	0.76	1.11	216	17°F	1.00
Ordinary double-pane	0.48	2.10	0.55	190	43°F	0.91
Low emissivity insulating glass	0.30	3.30	0.27	150	56°F	0.73
Low emissivity solar insulating glass	0.30	3.30	0.27	76	56°F	0.36

NOTES

1. Relative heat gain Btu/sq ft/hr: When ASHRAE solar heat gain factor is 200 Btu/hr - sq ft and the outdoor air temperature is 14° warmer than the indoor temperature.
2. Inside glass surface temperatures assume the following: outside temperature, 0°F; inside room temperature, 70°F; outside wind velocity, 15 mph; no air movement inside; and uniform heating conditions.
3. The shading coefficients listed above may vary a few percentage points.
4. R and U values based on Lawrence Berkeley method.

ULTRAVIOLET REDUCTION RATES

Double-pane clear	34%
Low emissivity insulating glass	66%
Low emissivity solar insulating glass	84%

NOTE

Low emissivity insulating glass and low emissivity solar windows help reduce ultraviolet rays.

RELATIVE HEAT GAIN

	HEAT GAIN
Clear	214
Single-pane $^3/_{32}$ or $^1/_8$ in.	208
Single-pane $^3/_{16}$ in.	186
Double-pane insulating	152
Double-pane high-performance insulating	
Tinted grey/bronze	165
Single-pane grey $^3/_{16}$ in.	168
Single-pane bronze $^3/_{16}$ in.	78
Double-pane high-performance sun insulating	
Medium performance reflective	
Single-pane bronze	106

NOTE

Relative heat gain BTU/sq ft/hr: When ASHRAE solar heat gain factor is 200 BTU/hr - sq ft and the outdoor air temperature is 14° warmer than the indoor temperature.

Joseph A. Wilkes, FAIA; Annapolis, Maryland

PROJECTED

This is the workhorse of metal windows, available in many combinations of fixed and operating sash. Usually the lowest light will project in and the upper vents project out for maximum comfort and convenience. However, the flexibility of substituting fixed lights for vents and omitting muntins permits a variety of configurations.

Available in various weights, these windows are frequently used in institutional, commercial, and industrial projects. They will receive single or double glazing, from inside or outside. A wide assortment of hardware has been developed to meet almost every need, including special accessories for manual or mechanical operation of sash above normal reach.

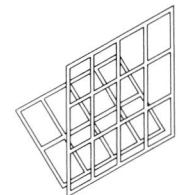

SECURITY

Another variation of the projected sash, this window provides an integral grill permitting ventilation but restricting the size of an object that can pass through the window. Used in institutions requiring detention or tight security against outside entry, this sash minimizes the psychological, installation, and maintenance problems associated with a separate grill.

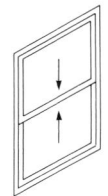

DOUBLE HUNG

The traditional window of the United States wood window industry, metal double hung windows are finding wide application in projects where economy and flush window treatment are paramount. Single hung windows, which provide a fixed light in lieu of the top sash, are employed where economy is particularly critical. Triple hung windows are another variation, providing three operating sash for ease of operation in tall windows.

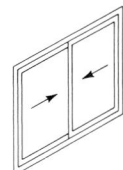

SLIDING

Horizontally sliding or rolling sash provide flush interior and exterior wall surfaces without the need for counterbalancing hardware intrinsic in the double hung window. Initially they were popular as economical sash in residential applications; the sliding window industry has subsequently made substantial product improvements. Their inherent weatherproofing problems have been overcome with careful engineering and workmanship utilizing heavier members. Generally speaking, horizontally or squarely proportioned sash will operate more smoothly than tall, narrow sash. Most manufacturers apply full width insect screens on the exterior.

William A. Klene, AIA, Architect; Herndon, Virginia

COMBINATION

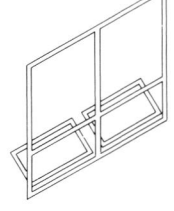

An economical variation of the projected sash that is used where light more than ventilation is desired. Size and height of this type of window will determine its usability as a fire escape in dwelling units and small offices. It may not be used as a fire escape in buildings classified for public assembly such as schools. Operating vents may be designed to project in or out. Insect screens pose different problems in both situations.

CASEMENT

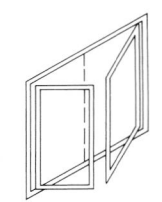

Consisting of vertically proportioned sash that swing outward, somewhat like a door, casement windows offer an aesthetic appeal not furnished by other window types. Insect screens are necessarily placed on the inside. Thus underscreen mechanical operators are usually provided. Otherwise the screen would have to be hinged or equipped with wickets for access to manual pulls.

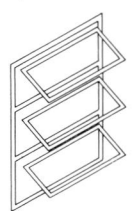

AWNING

A window that has grown in popularity from its Southern residential origins, an awning window offers 100% ventilation combined with a degree of rain protection not attainable with casement sash. Awning sash can be fully weatherstripped and will readily receive double glazing or storm sash. Since their inherent horizontal proportions are not currently in vogue, their use has diminished recently. Insect screens are mounted in the interior, and rotary operators are standard.

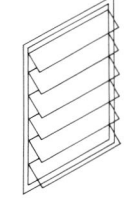

JALOUSIE

When the individual sash depth of the awning window is reduced to the point where it becomes, in effect, an operating louver, horizontal sash members are unnecessary. This has a profound effect on appearance and the ability to provide weatherstripping. Most often found in residences and commercial work, particularly where ventilation is most desirable, jalousie windows are not as widely used as most other sash. Sash widths are limited to the free span capability of the blade materials (usually glass, wood, or metal). Storm sash are readily available and, in some instances, are an integral part of the jalousie. Insect screens are necessarily placed on the interior, with operating hardware usually placed at normal hand height.

PIVOTED

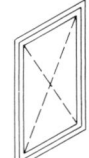

Popular in multistory, air-conditioned commercial buildings, horizontally or vertically pivoting sash are used only for maintenance. Though they usually rotate 90°, some manufacturers produce a sash that rotates 180°. Effective weatherstripping is mandatory in both cases. Wind action on walls of highrise structures must be considered in sash design. Top or side hung sash are also produced by some manufacturers for occasional opening of fixed sash.

GENERAL NOTES

1. Most types are readily available in steel or aluminum. Steel sash tend to be more rigid and have thinner sight lines. They will be galvanized and/or bonderized and primed prior to finishing if so specified. While aluminum sash may be more economical and may offer greater inherent corrosion resistance, they have greater thermal expansion and conductance. Both are available in a variety of finishes.

2. All operating sash are regularly mulled to fixed sash, thus providing for economy, appearance, and a variety of functions.

3. Thoughtful selection of glazing material is as important as window type selection. Plastic glazing materials generally have greater coefficients of thermal expansion than glass, requiring deeper glazing legs and stops.

4. Effective thermal isolation requires double glazing (some manufacturers offer triple glazing or dual sash), continuous weatherstripping, and a "thermal break" in aluminum sash for colder climates.

5. Many manufacturers produce more than one quality window. SWI criteria for various weights of steel sash are useful in making comparisons. Current criteria for aluminum sash are based on performance of a tested specimen, hence require careful consideration unless the manufacturer has a well established reputation.

6. Many manufacturers have ceased using "stock sizes" and produce only custom work. Consequently, special shapes and configurations are easier to obtain, particularly in monumental or commercial grades. Some manufacturers also produce specialized windows that are sound resistant, contain venetian blinds, and so on. Since there is little correlation between the manufacturers' dimensioning systems, individual consultation is imperative where dimensions are critical.

7. Residential grades are somewhat more standardized, generally based on available dimensions of welded edge insulating glass.

8. Muntins, either simulating or forming small glass lights, are usually available for residential sash, if desired.

9. Installation details must take into account internal condensation in most climates. Hardware selection must consider insect screens as well as mounting heights, operating convenience, security, and so on.

10. Most codes have a minimum light and ventilation, minimum wind load resistance, and maximum thermal transmittance requirements, as well as minimum egress provisions from residential sleeping space. All these factors may affect window selection.

11. Prefinished window frames are generally installed after contiguous masonry rather than being built in.

12. Window edges that project more than 4 in. into an accessible route must not be higher than 27 in. above finished floor.

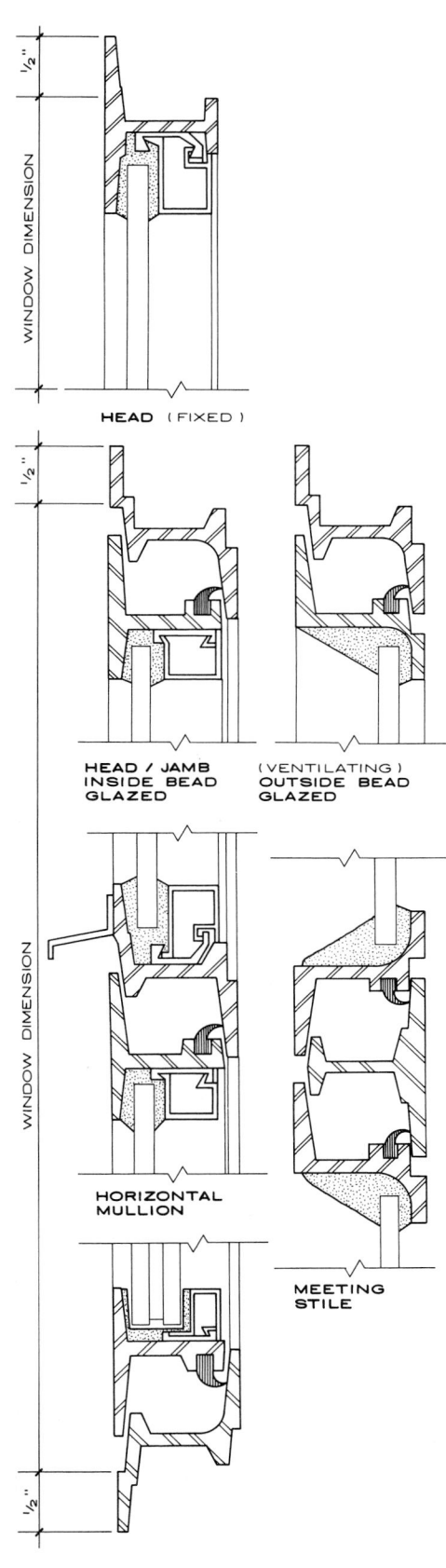

HEAD (FIXED)

HEAD / JAMB
INSIDE BEAD
GLAZED

(VENTILATING)
OUTSIDE BEAD
GLAZED

HORIZONTAL
MULLION

MEETING
STILE

STEEL SASH CONSTRUCTION

William A. Klene, AIA, Architect; Herndon, Virginia

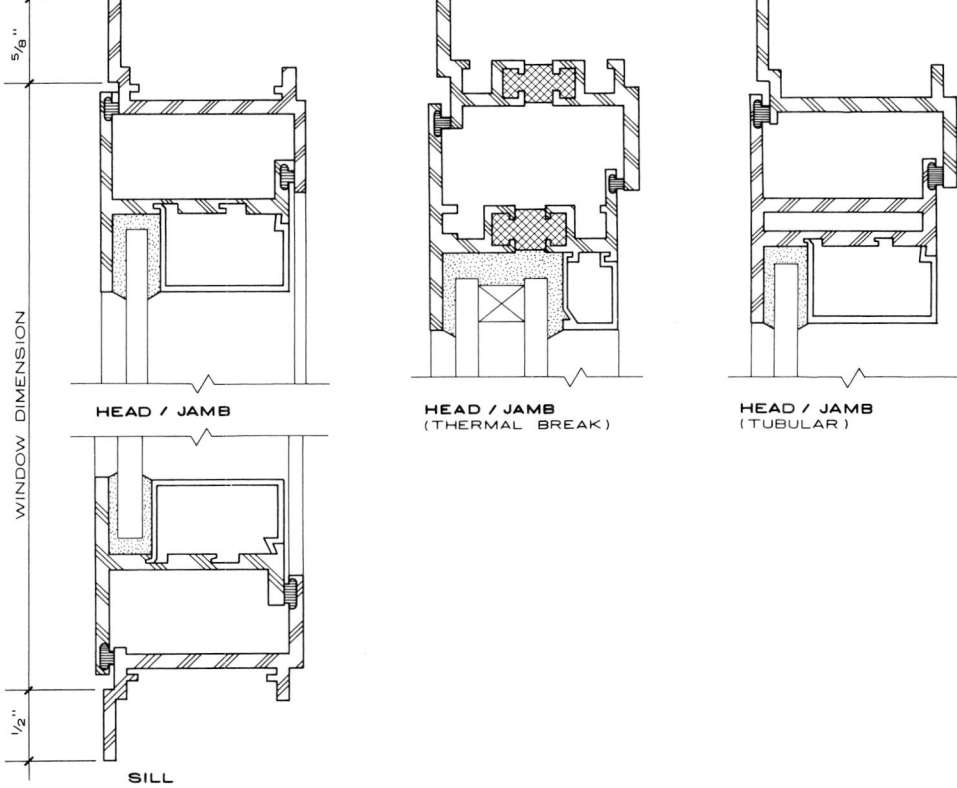

WINDOW NOMENCLATURE

HEAD

MULLION

FIXED
GLASS

HORIZONTAL
MULLION

MEETING
STILE

CASEMENT
VENTILATING
SASH

JAMB

SILL

EXTERIOR

HEAD / JAMB

HEAD / JAMB
(THERMAL BREAK)

HEAD / JAMB
(TUBULAR)

SILL

ALUMINUM SASH CONSTRUCTION

NOTES

1. Window sizes and dimensioning methods, as listed, are not uniform for all manufacturers. Some manufacturers have no stock sizes, producing only custom work. Check with those who supply sash for each geographical area.

2. In general, heavier grades of windows offer greater configuration flexibility. Larger operating sash can be produced with heavier members than with lighter members. Thus the fixed lights shown for taller steel sash can be avoided, if desired.

3. Insect screens are necessarily installed on the interior and must be taken into account when selecting hardware.

4. The raindrip indicated on the horizontal mullion may be required at ventilating heads if sash is placed flush with exterior face of wall.

5. Drawings or specification must contain the following information: window size and location, installation details, sills, stools, flashing, sealing, and anchors; sash material and finish; glazing material; glazing method (tape, putty, or bead, inside or outside); weatherstripping, insect screen material, and hardware.

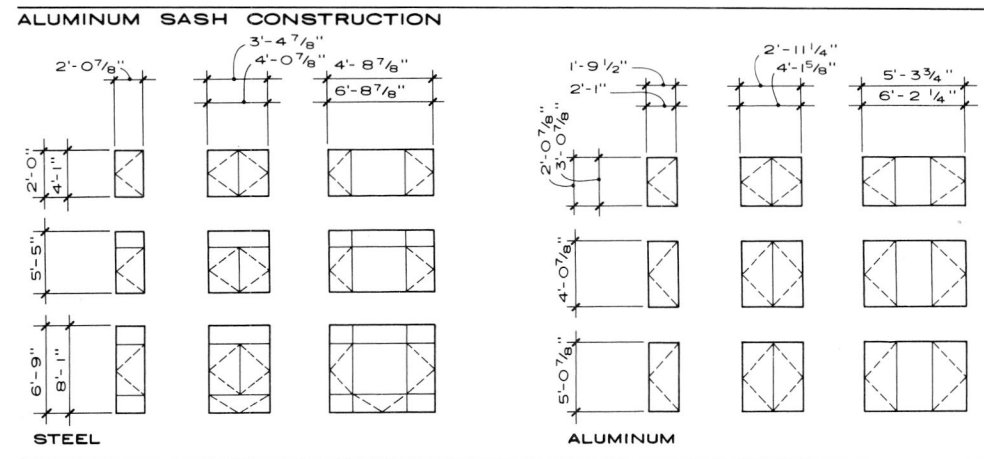

STEEL

ALUMINUM

WINDOW SIZES

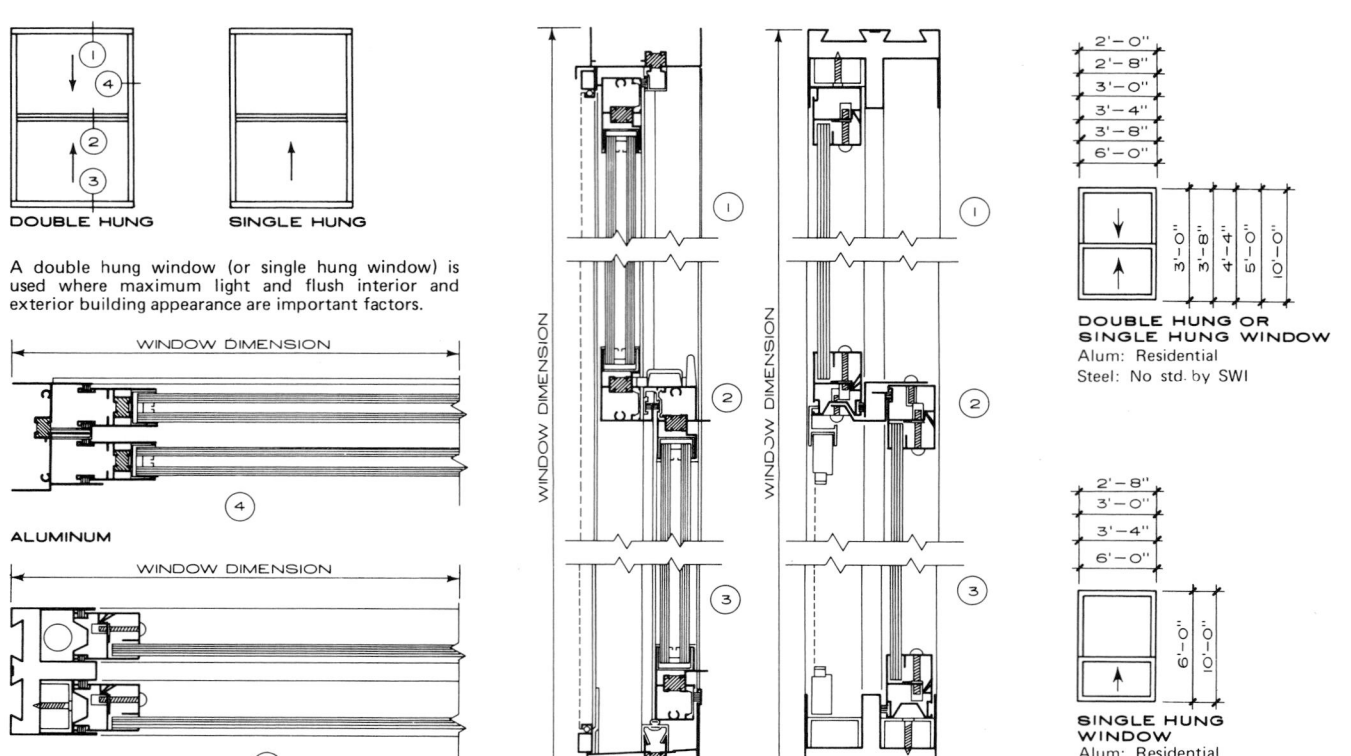

DOUBLE HUNG   **SINGLE HUNG**

A double hung window (or single hung window) is used where maximum light and flush interior and exterior building appearance are important factors.

WINDOW DIMENSION

ALUMINUM

WINDOW DIMENSION

STEEL

JAMB SECTIONS

VERTICAL SECTIONS

ALUMINUM   STEEL

SINGLE AND DOUBLE HUNG WINDOWS

2'-0"
2'-8"
3'-0"
3'-4"
3'-8"
6'-0"

DOUBLE HUNG OR SINGLE HUNG WINDOW
Alum: Residential
Steel: No std. by SWI

2'-8"
3'-0"
3'-4"
6'-0"

SINGLE HUNG WINDOW
Alum: Residential
Steel: No std. by SWI

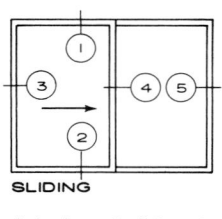

SLIDING

A horizontal sliding glass window (single or double) is used where maximum light, flush interior and exterior building appearance, simple manual operation, and accessibility are important factors.

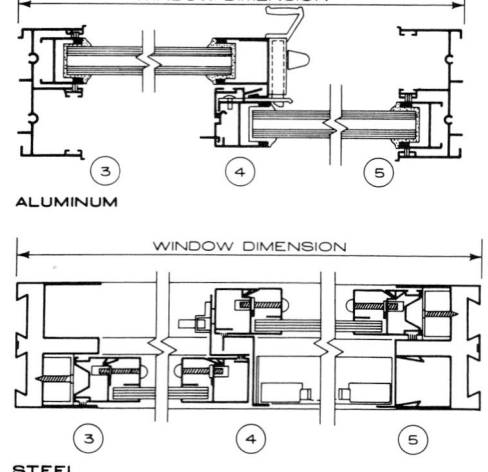

WINDOW DIMENSION

ALUMINUM

WINDOW DIMENSION

STEEL

JAMB SECTIONS

SLIDING WINDOWS

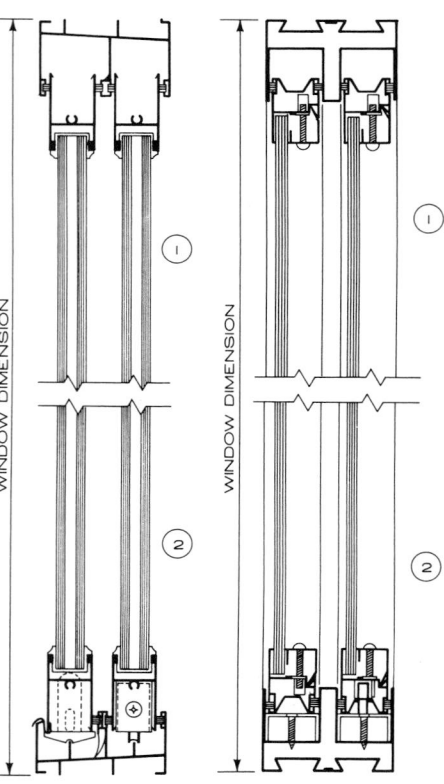

WINDOW DIMENSION   WINDOW DIMENSION

ALUMINUM   STEEL

VERTICAL SECTIONS

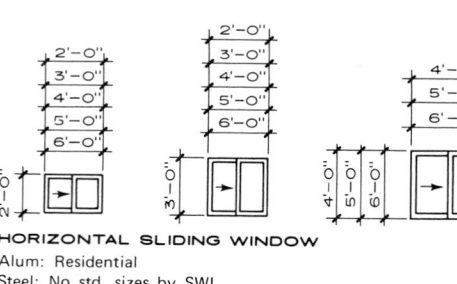

HORIZONTAL SLIDING WINDOW
Alum: Residential
Steel: No std. sizes by SWI

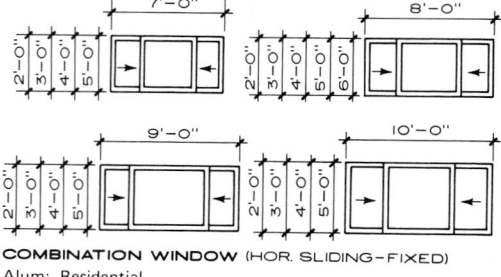

COMBINATION WINDOW (HOR. SLIDING—FIXED)
Alum: Residential
Steel: No std. sizes by SWI

David W. Johnson; Washington, D.C.

  METAL WINDOWS

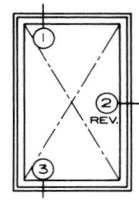

ELEVATION

NOTE

A reversible window is used mostly in multistory, air conditioned buildings where window washing from the interior is desired. It is normally opened for cleaning only; however, it may be combined with a hopper if ventilation is required.

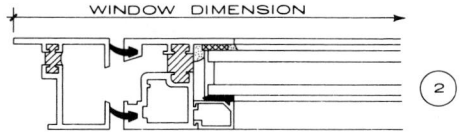

ALUMINUM

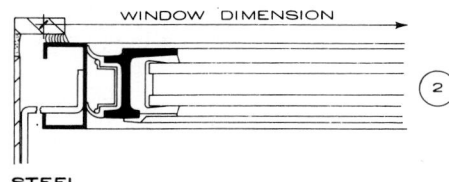

STEEL

JAMB SECTIONS
REVERSIBLE WINDOWS

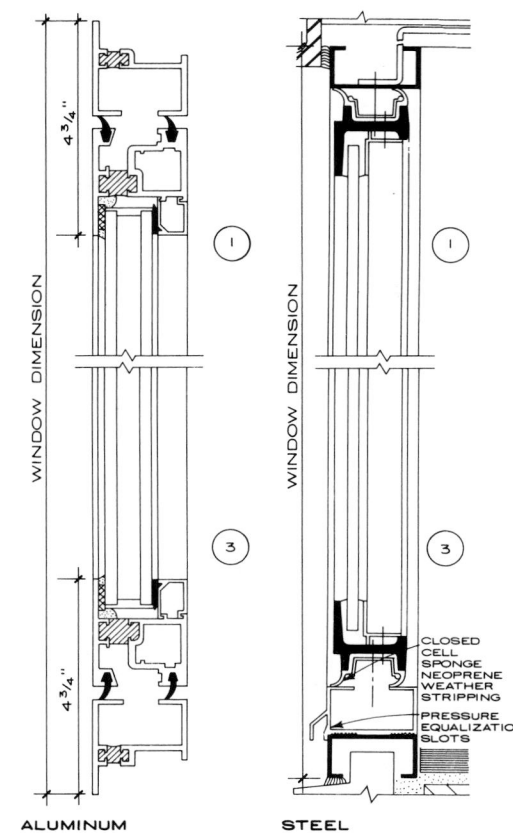

ALUMINUM

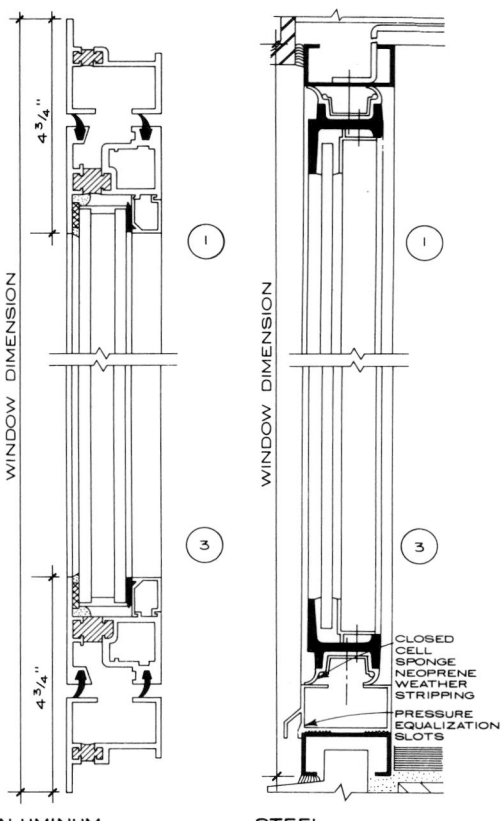

STEEL

VERTICAL SECTIONS

CLOSED CELL SPONGE NEOPRENE WEATHER STRIPPING

PRESSURE EQUALIZATION SLOTS

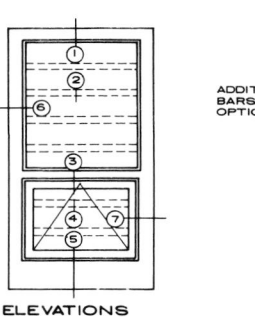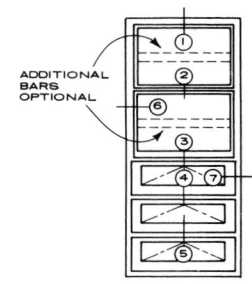

ELEVATIONS

ADDITIONAL BARS OPTIONAL

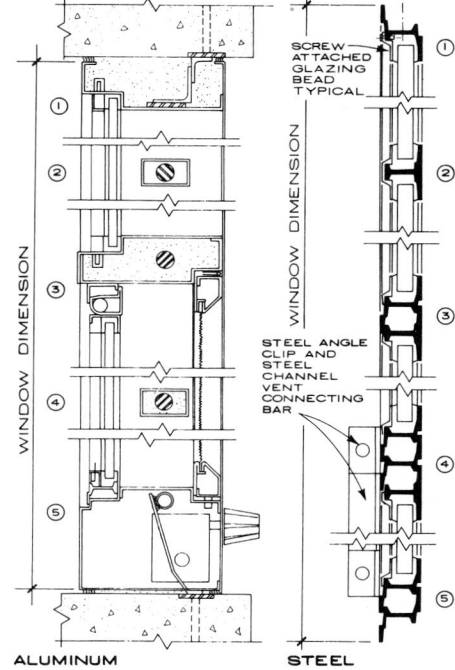

ALUMINUM

STEEL

VERTICAL SECTIONS

SCREW ATTACHED GLAZING BEAD TYPICAL

STEEL ANGLE CLIP AND STEEL CHANNEL VENT CONNECTING BAR

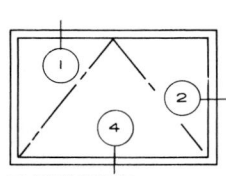

ELEVATIONS
NOTE

A projected (special) window is used mostly in multistory, air conditioned buildings where window washing from the interior is desired. It is normally opened for cleaning only; however, it may be combined with a hopper if ventilation is required. For such use see alternate above.

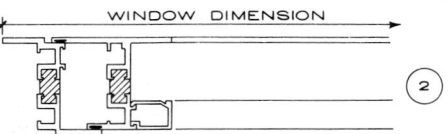

ALUMINUM

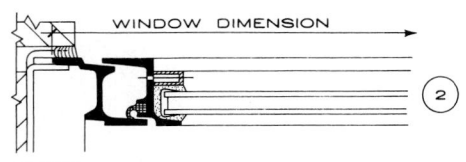

STEEL

JAMB SECTIONS
PROJECTED WINDOWS

David W. Johnson; Washington, D.C.

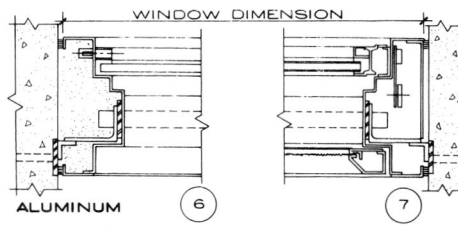

ALUMINUM

STEEL

JAMB SECTIONS

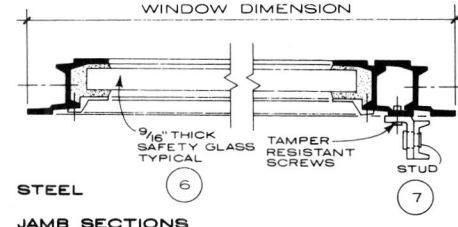

9/16" THICK SAFETY GLASS TYPICAL

TAMPER RESISTANT SCREWS

STUD

STEEL

JAMB SECTIONS

NOTES

1. Housing sill frame size varies with manufacturer of window operator.
2. Muntin and mullion tubes are 12 gauge maximum and 14 gauge medium security, grouted full, and contain a $7/8$ in. diameter tamper resistant bar.
3. Tempered glass is $1/2$ in. on exterior side.
4. Horizontal tube/bars to have maximum spacing of 5 in.

SECURITY WINDOWS

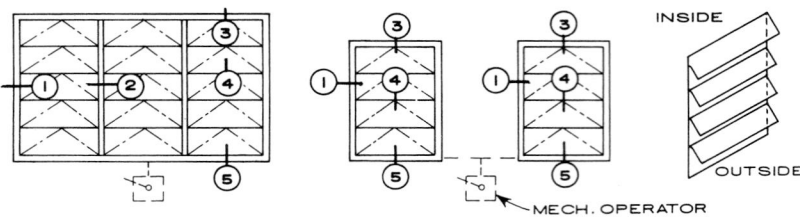

MECH. OPERATOR

INSIDE

OUTSIDE

AWNING

AN AWNING WINDOW is one whose movable units consist of a group of hand operated or gear operated outward projecting ventilators, all of which move in unison. It is used where maximum height and ventilation is required in inaccessible areas such as upper parts of gymnasiums or auditoriums. Hand operation is limited to one window only, while a single gear operator may be connected to two or more awning windows, and may be motorized.

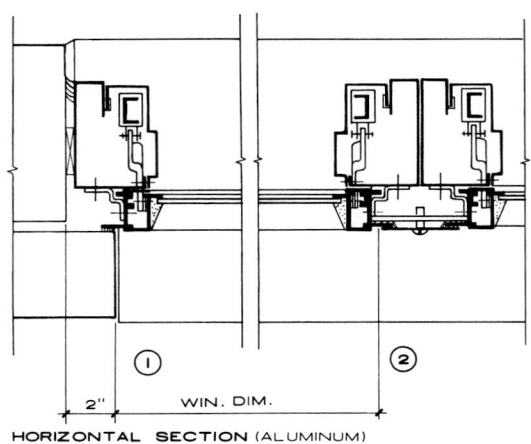

HORIZONTAL SECTION (ALUMINUM)

2" WIN. DIM.

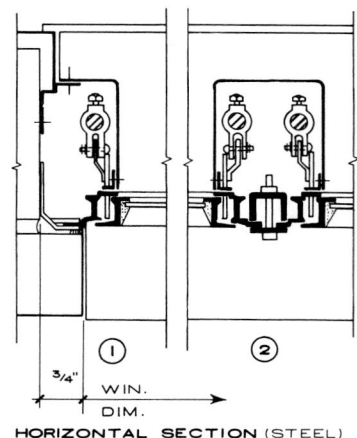

HORIZONTAL SECTION (STEEL)

3/4" WIN. DIM.

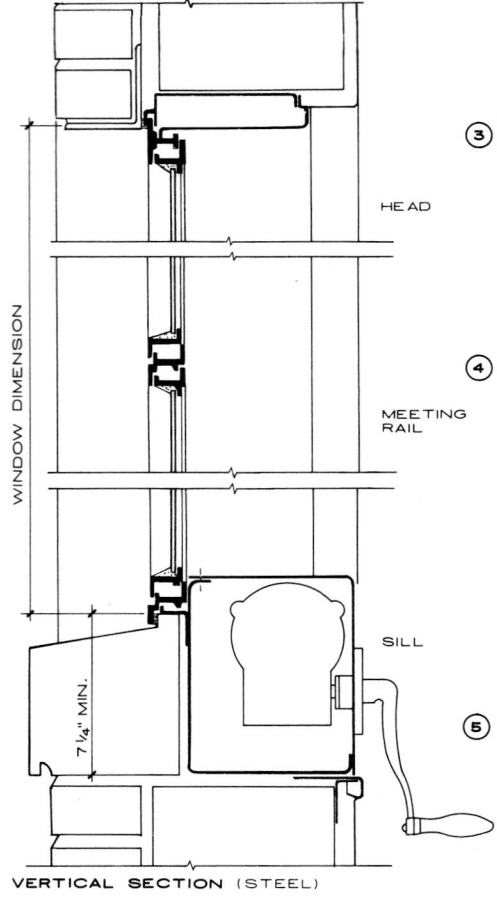

VERTICAL SECTION (STEEL)

HEAD

MEETING RAIL

SILL

WINDOW DIMENSION

7 1/4" MIN.

AWNING WINDOWS

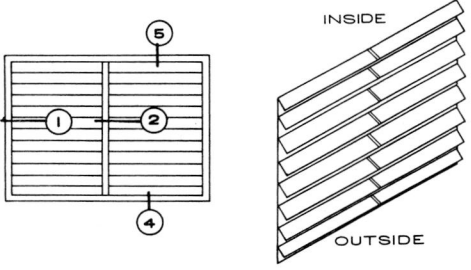

INSIDE

OUTSIDE

JALOUSIE

A JALOUSIE WINDOW (ALUMINUM) consists of a series of operable overlapping glass louvers which pivot in unison. It may be combined in the same frame with a series of operable opaque louvers for climate control. It is used mostly in residential type constructions in southern climates, where maximum ventilation and flush exterior and interior appearance is desired.

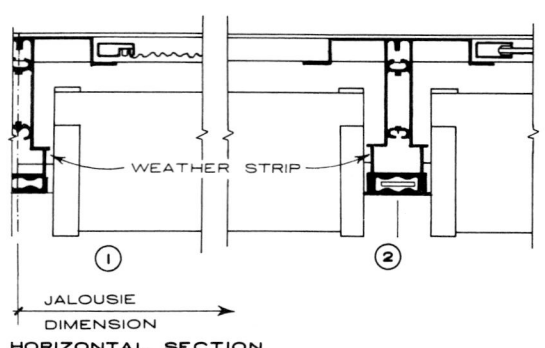

WEATHER STRIP

JALOUSIE DIMENSION

HORIZONTAL SECTION

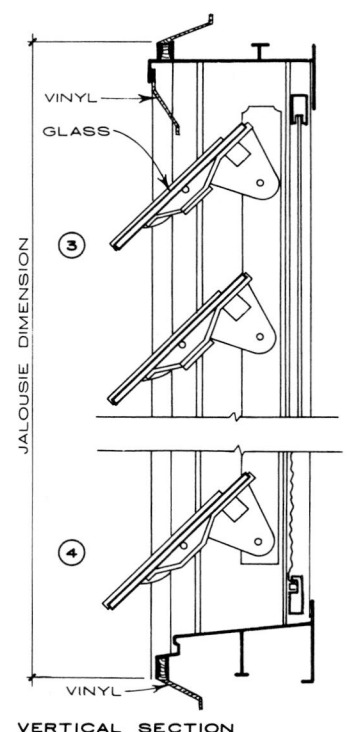

VINYL

GLASS

VINYL

JALOUSIE DIMENSION

VERTICAL SECTION

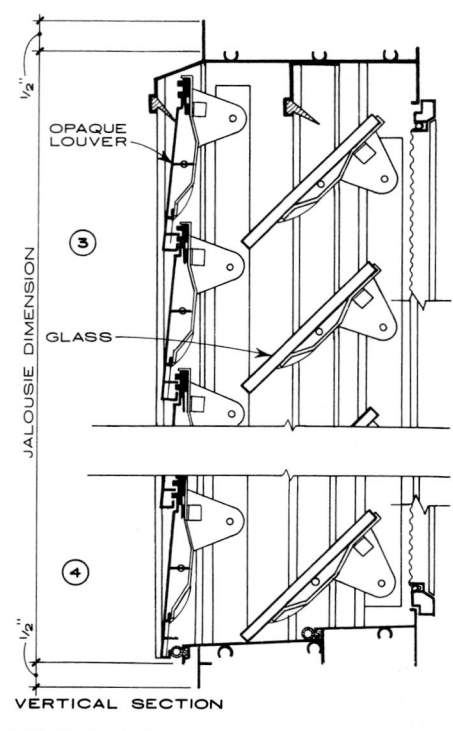

OPAQUE LOUVER

GLASS

1/2"

1/2"

JALOUSIE DIMENSION

VERTICAL SECTION

JALOUSIE WINDOWS

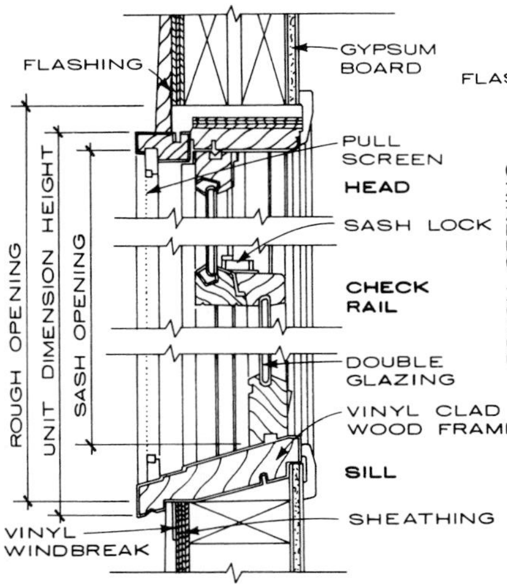

FLASHING
GYPSUM BOARD
PULL SCREEN
HEAD
SASH LOCK
CHECK RAIL
DOUBLE GLAZING
VINYL CLAD WOOD FRAME
SILL
SHEATHING
VINYL WINDBREAK
ROUGH OPENING
UNIT DIMENSION HEIGHT
SASH OPENING

VERTICAL SECTION

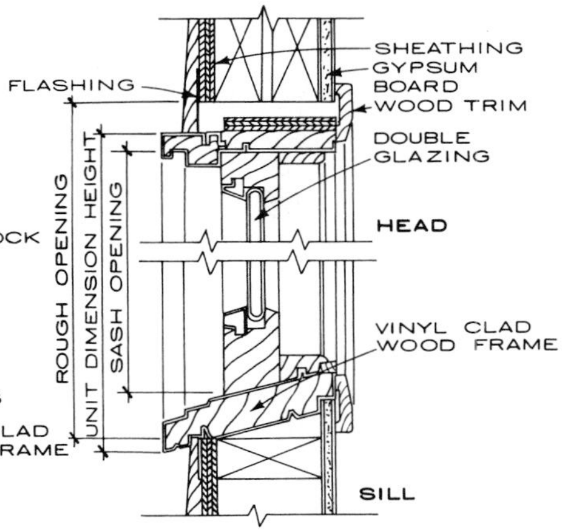

FLASHING
SHEATHING
GYPSUM BOARD
WOOD TRIM
DOUBLE GLAZING
HEAD
VINYL CLAD WOOD FRAME
SILL
ROUGH OPENING
UNIT DIMENSION HEIGHT
SASH OPENING

PICTURE WINDOW DETAIL

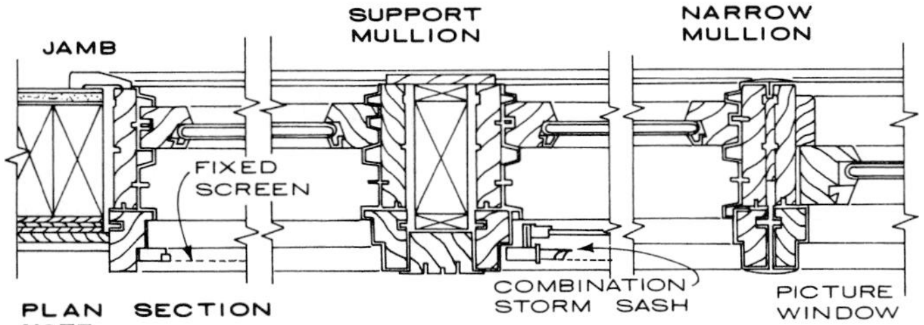

CASING

REPLACEMENT WINDOW

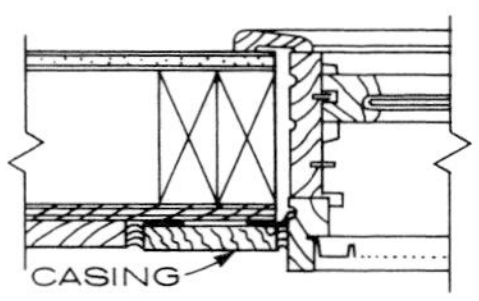

REMODELING AND REPLACEMENT WINDOWS: Stock window sizes of all standard types are available as replacement units with metal or vinyl clad adapter casings added to perimeter to fit existing openings in renovation work.

JAMB
SUPPORT MULLION
NARROW MULLION
FIXED SCREEN
COMBINATION STORM SASH
PICTURE WINDOW

PLAN SECTION
NOTE
Spiral or reel spring balances or pressure weatherstrip operation. Glass size 12 x 12 in. to 44 x 40 in. for 1-light sash.

PLAIN RAIL WINDOW: No parting stop; movable sash slides against fixed sash with hold-open jamb bolts.

DOUBLE HUNG WINDOWS
NOTE
CASEMENT WINDOWS: Stiles and top rail 1 to 2 in., bottom rail 3 in. nominal. Outswinging: screen inside, regular or self-storing flexible type with operation similar to window shade. Sash opening range for 1 sash per frame 1 ft 4 in. x 2 ft 2 in. to 2 x 6 ft. Extension hinges, friction arms, folding push bar or roto worm gear operator.

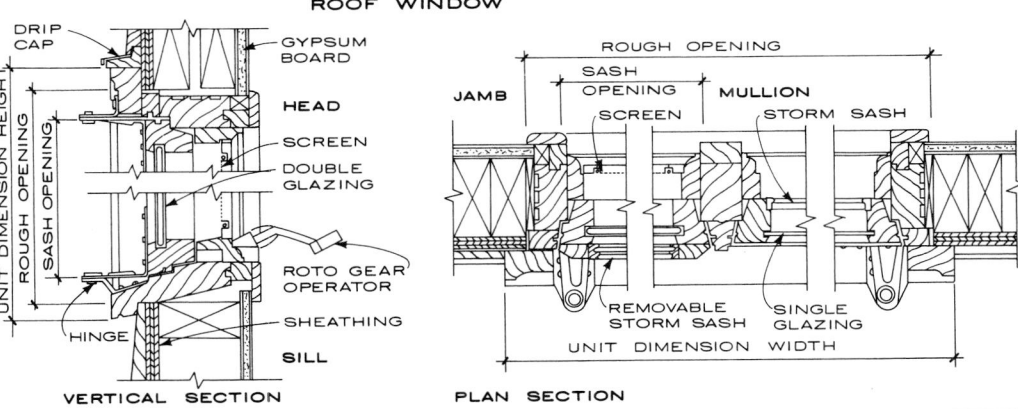

VERTICAL DETAIL
9" FLASHING
OPERATOR
SOFFIT
6" FLASHING
SILL
INSULATING GLASS
6" STEP FLASHING
SCREEN
SASH FRAME
JAMB
HORIZONTAL DETAIL

ROOF WINDOW

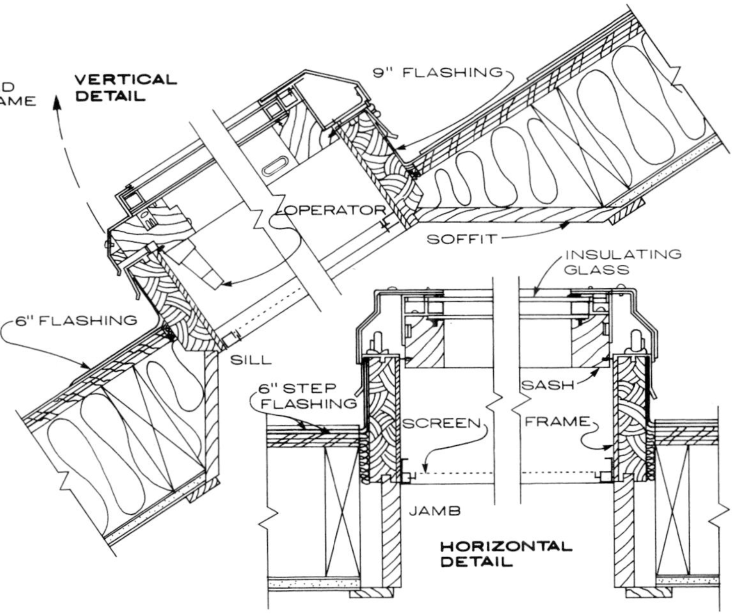

Sash openings approximately 2 to 4 ft wide, 3 to 6 ft high. Awning or pivot. Optional equipment includes shades, blinds, screens, electric operators. May be equipped with automatic closer activated by rain sensor. Weep holes to retard condensation.

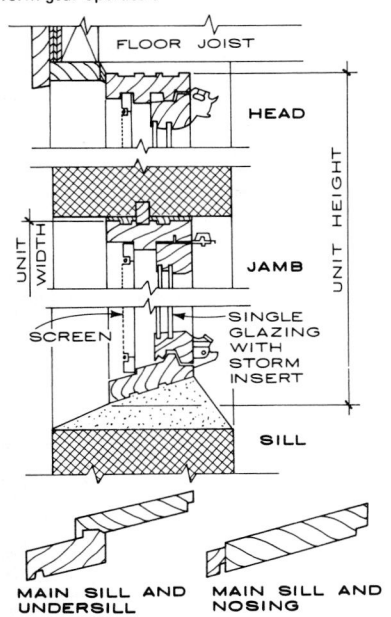

FLOOR JOIST
HEAD
JAMB
SCREEN
SINGLE GLAZING WITH STORM INSERT
SILL
UNIT WIDTH
UNIT HEIGHT

MAIN SILL AND UNDERSILL
MAIN SILL AND NOSING
NOTE
Removable sash and dual purpose hinges for opening from top or bottom.

BASEMENT WINDOWS

DRIP CAP
GYPSUM BOARD
HEAD
SCREEN
DOUBLE GLAZING
ROTO GEAR OPERATOR
HINGE
SHEATHING
SILL
UNIT DIMENSION HEIGHT
ROUGH OPENING
SASH OPENING

VERTICAL SECTION

JAMB
SASH OPENING
SCREEN
MULLION
STORM SASH
REMOVABLE STORM SASH
SINGLE GLAZING
ROUGH OPENING
UNIT DIMENSION WIDTH

PLAN SECTION

CASEMENT WINDOWS

SIDE JAMB
CHECK STILE
SIDE JAMB
TRIPLE GLAZING UNIT

HORIZONTAL SECTION

Sash opening for 2 sash per frame approximately 3 to 6 ft wide by 3 to 5 ft high. Plastic weatherstrip track top and bottom, center lock with handle.

HORIZONTAL SLIDING WINDOWS

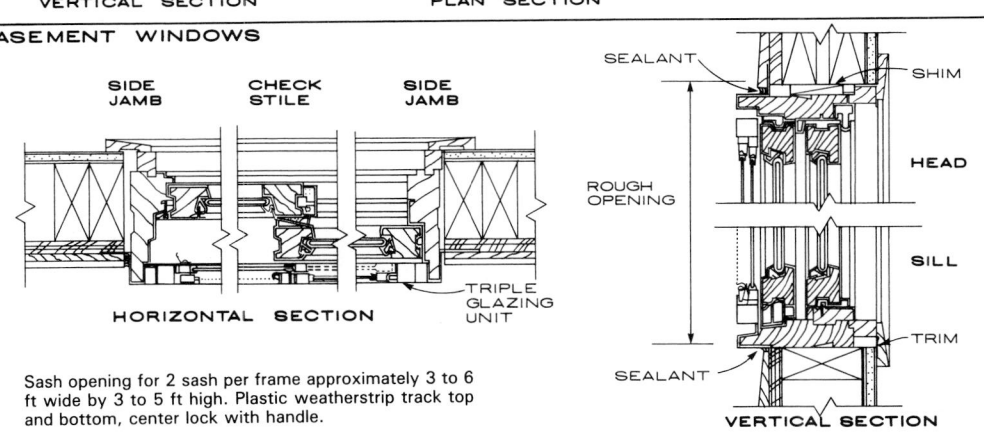

SEALANT
SHIM
HEAD
ROUGH OPENING
SILL
SEALANT
TRIM

VERTICAL SECTION

Carleton Granbery, FAIA; Guilford, Connecticut

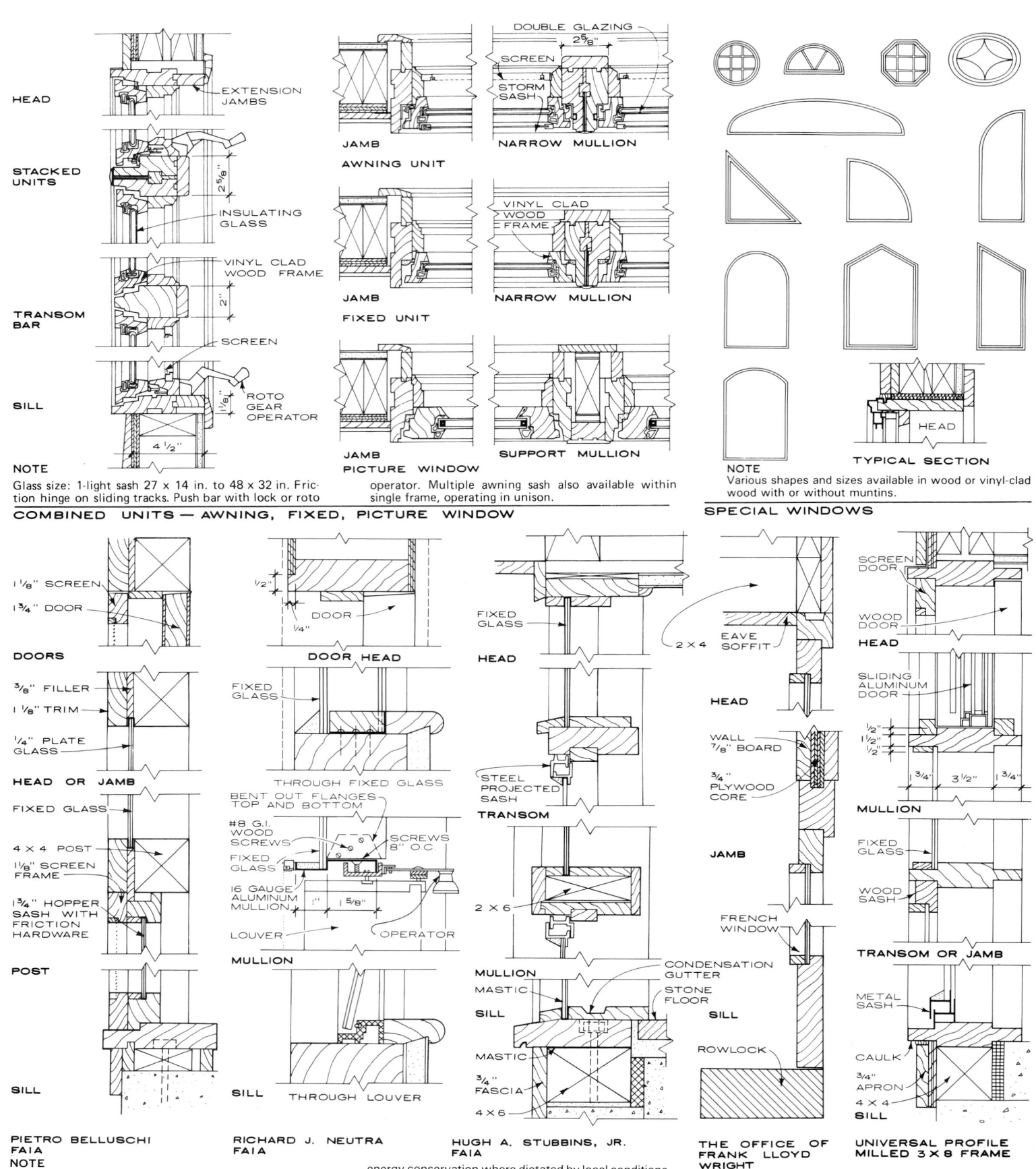

HEAD — EXTENSION JAMBS

STACKED UNITS

INSULATING GLASS

VINYL CLAD WOOD FRAME

TRANSOM BAR

SCREEN

SILL — ROTO GEAR OPERATOR

NOTE
Glass size: 1-light sash 27 x 14 in. to 48 x 32 in. Friction hinge on sliding tracks. Push bar with lock or roto

JAMB — AWNING UNIT

DOUBLE GLAZING — SCREEN — STORM SASH — NARROW MULLION

JAMB — FIXED UNIT

VINYL CLAD WOOD FRAME — NARROW MULLION

JAMB — PICTURE WINDOW

SUPPORT MULLION

operator. Multiple awning sash also available within single frame, operating in unison.

NOTE — TYPICAL SECTION
Various shapes and sizes available in wood or vinyl-clad wood with or without muntins.

COMBINED UNITS — AWNING, FIXED, PICTURE WINDOW

SPECIAL WINDOWS

1 1/8" SCREEN
1 3/4" DOOR

DOORS

3/8" FILLER
1 1/8" TRIM
1/4" PLATE GLASS

HEAD OR JAMB

FIXED GLASS

4 X 4 POST
1 1/8" SCREEN FRAME
1 3/4" HOPPER SASH WITH FRICTION HARDWARE

POST

SILL

PIETRO BELLUSCHI FAIA
NOTE
Selected examples indicating joinery to achieve weathertight narrow profiles. Adaptable to insulating glass for

DOOR
DOOR HEAD

FIXED GLASS

THROUGH FIXED GLASS

BENT OUT FLANGES TOP AND BOTTOM
#8 G.I. WOOD SCREWS
FIXED GLASS
16 GAUGE ALUMINUM MULLION

SCREWS 8" O.C.

LOUVER
OPERATOR

MULLION

SILL

THROUGH LOUVER

RICHARD J. NEUTRA FAIA

energy conservation where dictated by local conditions. See also pages on metal windows. See chapter 19 for historic wood windows.

FIXED GLASS
HEAD

STEEL PROJECTED SASH
TRANSOM

2 X 6

MULLION

MULLION
MASTIC
SILL
MASTIC
3/4" FASCIA
4 X 6

HUGH A. STUBBINS, JR. FAIA

2 X 4
EAVE SOFFIT

HEAD

WALL 7/8" BOARD
3/4" PLYWOOD CORE

JAMB

FRENCH WINDOW

CONDENSATION GUTTER
STONE FLOOR

SILL

ROWLOCK

THE OFFICE OF FRANK LLOYD WRIGHT

SCREEN DOOR
WOOD DOOR
HEAD

SLIDING ALUMINUM DOOR

MULLION

FIXED GLASS

WOOD SASH

TRANSOM OR JAMB

METAL SASH

CAULK
3/4" APRON
4 X 4
SILL

UNIVERSAL PROFILE MILLED 3 X 8 FRAME

CUSTOM DETAILS — FIXED GLASS, HOPPER, CASEMENTS, JALOUSIE, AWNING, AND TRANSOM SASH

Carleton Granbery, FAIA; Guilford, Connecticut

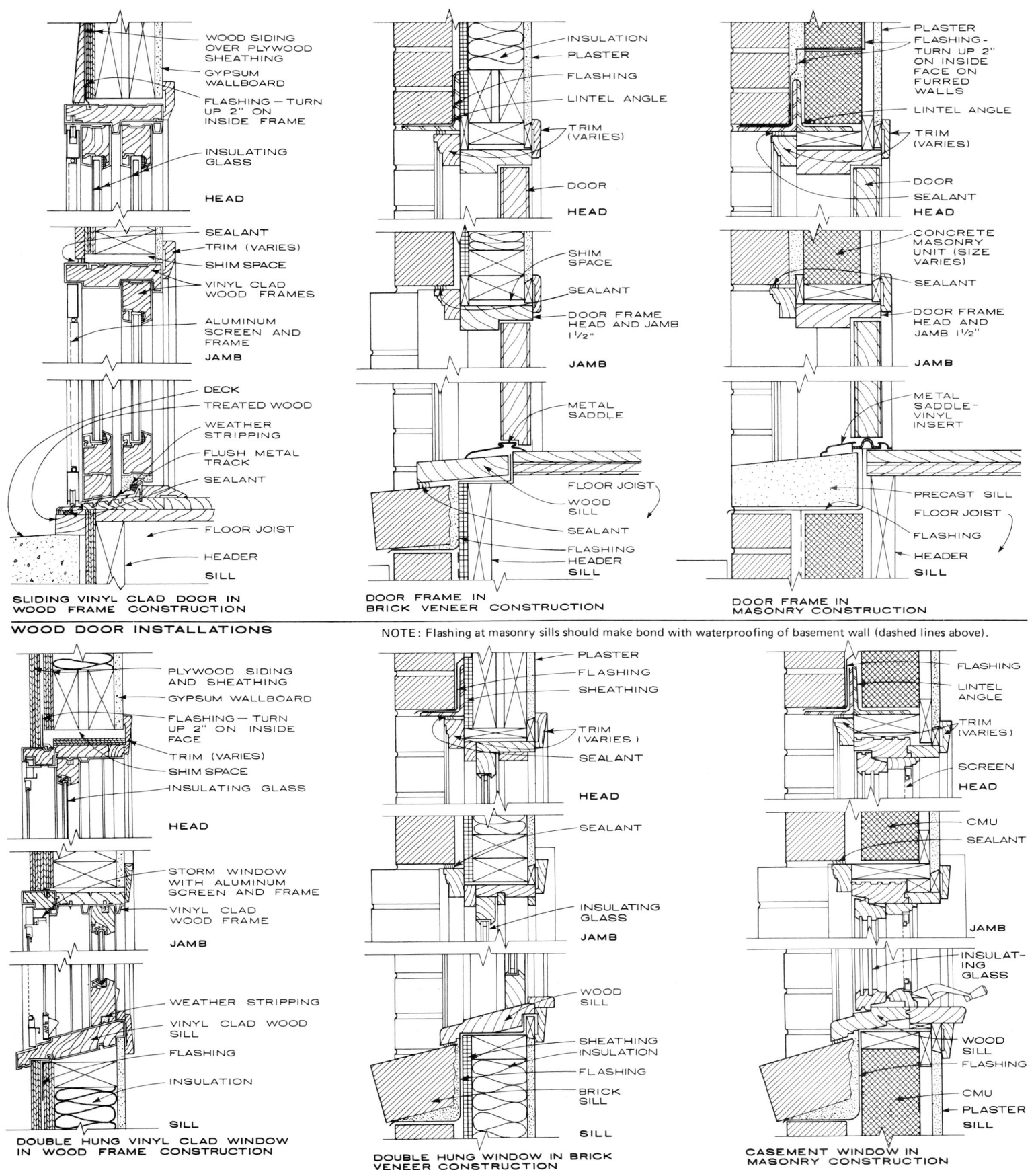

SLIDING VINYL CLAD DOOR IN WOOD FRAME CONSTRUCTION

- WOOD SIDING OVER PLYWOOD SHEATHING
- GYPSUM WALLBOARD
- FLASHING — TURN UP 2" ON INSIDE FRAME
- INSULATING GLASS

HEAD

- SEALANT
- TRIM (VARIES)
- SHIM SPACE
- VINYL CLAD WOOD FRAMES
- ALUMINUM SCREEN AND FRAME

JAMB

- DECK
- TREATED WOOD
- WEATHER STRIPPING
- FLUSH METAL TRACK
- SEALANT
- FLOOR JOIST
- HEADER

SILL

DOOR FRAME IN BRICK VENEER CONSTRUCTION

- INSULATION
- PLASTER
- FLASHING
- LINTEL ANGLE
- TRIM (VARIES)
- DOOR

HEAD

- SHIM SPACE
- SEALANT
- DOOR FRAME HEAD AND JAMB 1½"

JAMB

- METAL SADDLE
- FLOOR JOIST
- WOOD SILL
- SEALANT
- FLASHING
- HEADER

SILL

DOOR FRAME IN MASONRY CONSTRUCTION

- PLASTER
- FLASHING — TURN UP 2" ON INSIDE FACE ON FURRED WALLS
- LINTEL ANGLE
- TRIM (VARIES)
- DOOR
- SEALANT

HEAD

- CONCRETE MASONRY UNIT (SIZE VARIES)
- SEALANT
- DOOR FRAME HEAD AND JAMB 1½"

JAMB

- METAL SADDLE - VINYL INSERT
- PRECAST SILL
- FLOOR JOIST
- FLASHING
- HEADER

SILL

WOOD DOOR INSTALLATIONS

NOTE: Flashing at masonry sills should make bond with waterproofing of basement wall (dashed lines above).

DOUBLE HUNG VINYL CLAD WINDOW IN WOOD FRAME CONSTRUCTION

- PLYWOOD SIDING AND SHEATHING
- GYPSUM WALLBOARD
- FLASHING — TURN UP 2" ON INSIDE FACE
- TRIM (VARIES)
- SHIM SPACE
- INSULATING GLASS

HEAD

- STORM WINDOW WITH ALUMINUM SCREEN AND FRAME
- VINYL CLAD WOOD FRAME

JAMB

- WEATHER STRIPPING
- VINYL CLAD WOOD SILL
- FLASHING
- INSULATION

SILL

DOUBLE HUNG WINDOW IN BRICK VENEER CONSTRUCTION

- PLASTER
- FLASHING
- SHEATHING
- TRIM (VARIES)
- SEALANT

HEAD

- SEALANT
- INSULATING GLASS

JAMB

- WOOD SILL
- SHEATHING
- INSULATION
- FLASHING
- BRICK SILL

SILL

CASEMENT WINDOW IN MASONRY CONSTRUCTION

- FLASHING
- LINTEL ANGLE
- TRIM (VARIES)
- SCREEN

HEAD

- CMU
- SEALANT

JAMB

- INSULATING GLASS
- WOOD SILL
- FLASHING
- CMU
- PLASTER

SILL

WOOD WINDOW INSTALLATIONS

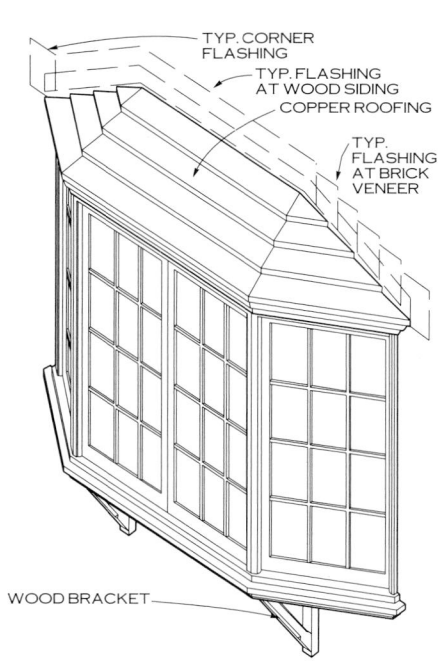

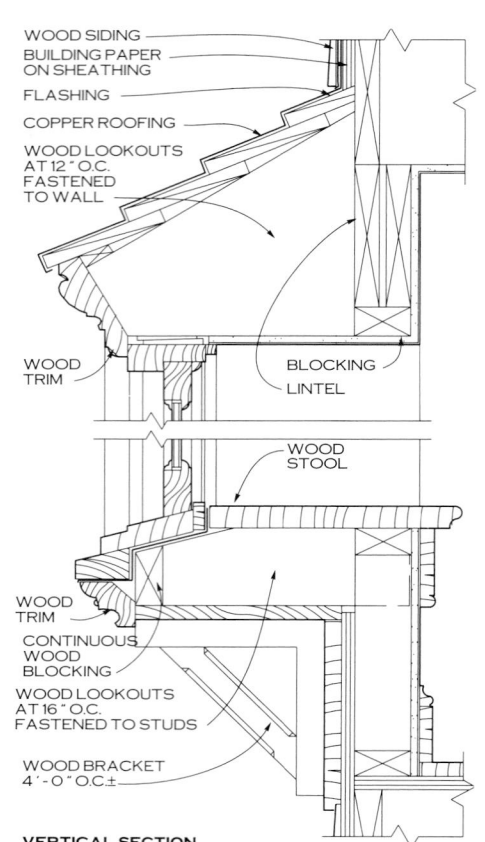

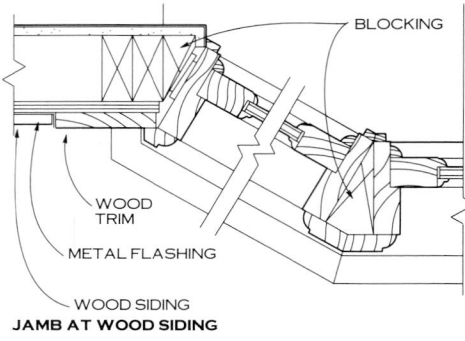

JAMB AT WOOD SIDING

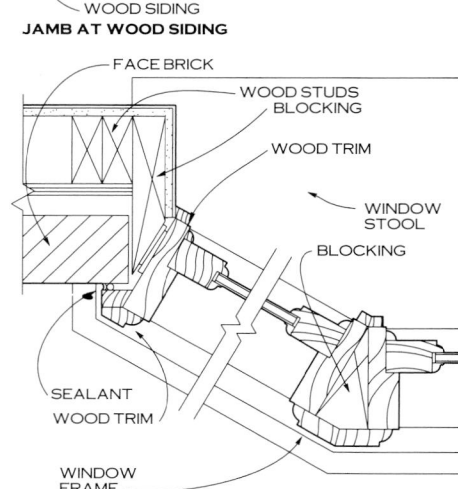

JAMB AT BRICK VENEER

VERTICAL SECTION

GENERAL

An oriel window is a window projecting from the wall face of the upper story of a building and supported on brackets, corbelling, or cantilevered. Oriels were often used in late Gothic and Tudor residential architecture.

ORIEL WINDOW

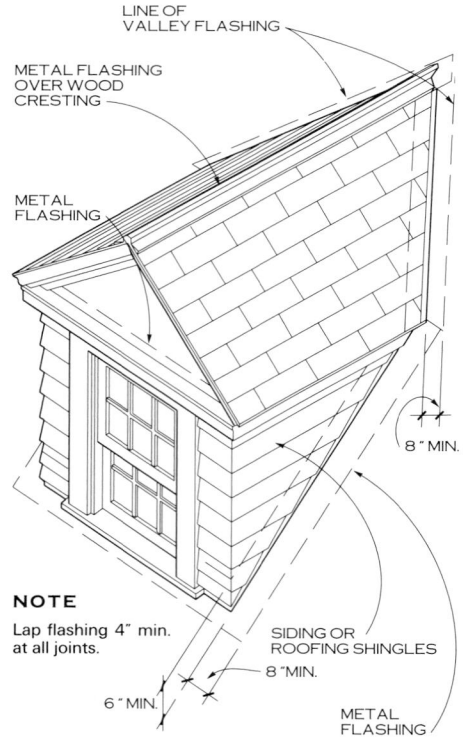

NOTE

Lap flashing 4" min. at all joints.

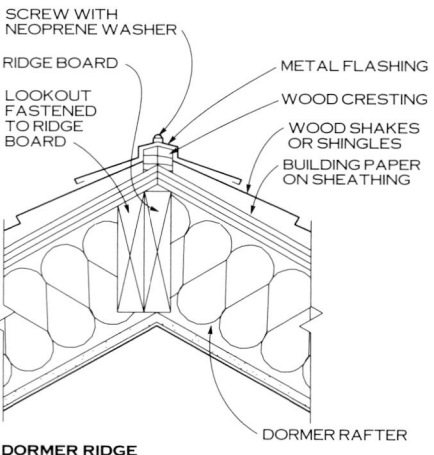

VERTICAL SECTION

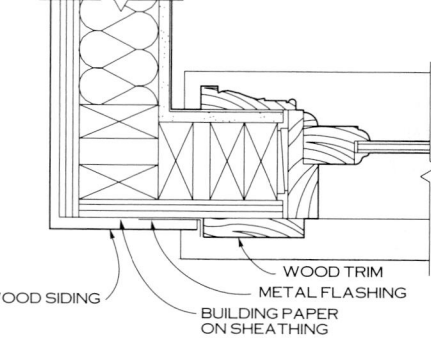

DORMER RIDGE

DORMER CORNER AND JAMB

GENERAL

A dormer is a vertical window projecting from the sloping roof of a building and having vertical sides or cheeks and a gabled or shed roof.

DORMER WINDOW

Richard J. Vitullo, AIA; Oak Leaf Studio; Crownsville, Maryland

WOOD AND PLASTIC WINDOWS

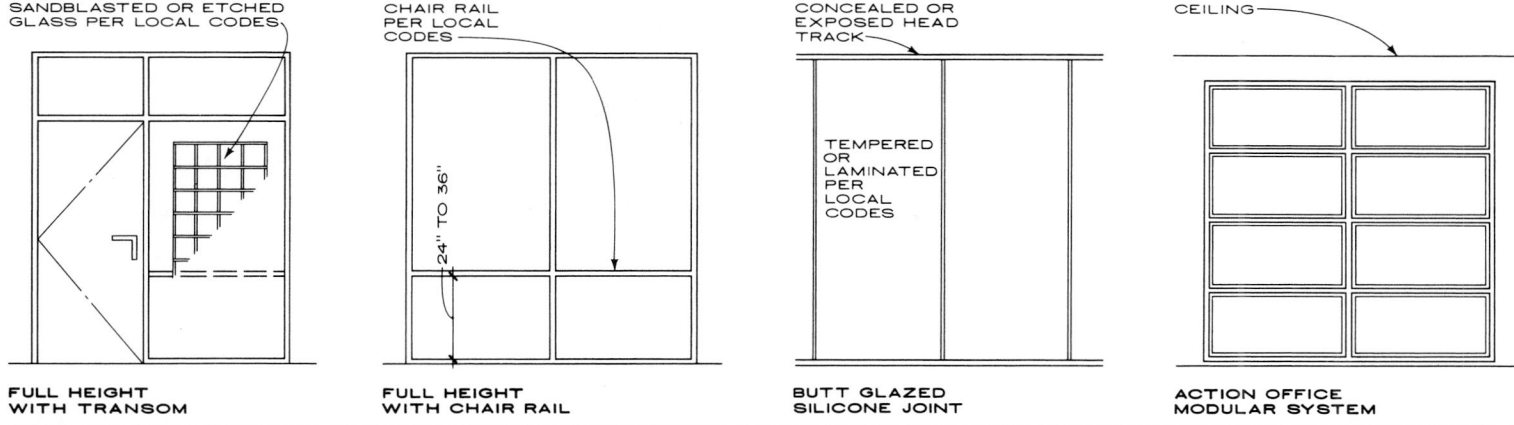

GLASS PARTITION ELEVATIONS

FULL HEIGHT WITH TRANSOM | FULL HEIGHT WITH CHAIR RAIL | BUTT GLAZED SILICONE JOINT | ACTION OFFICE MODULAR SYSTEM

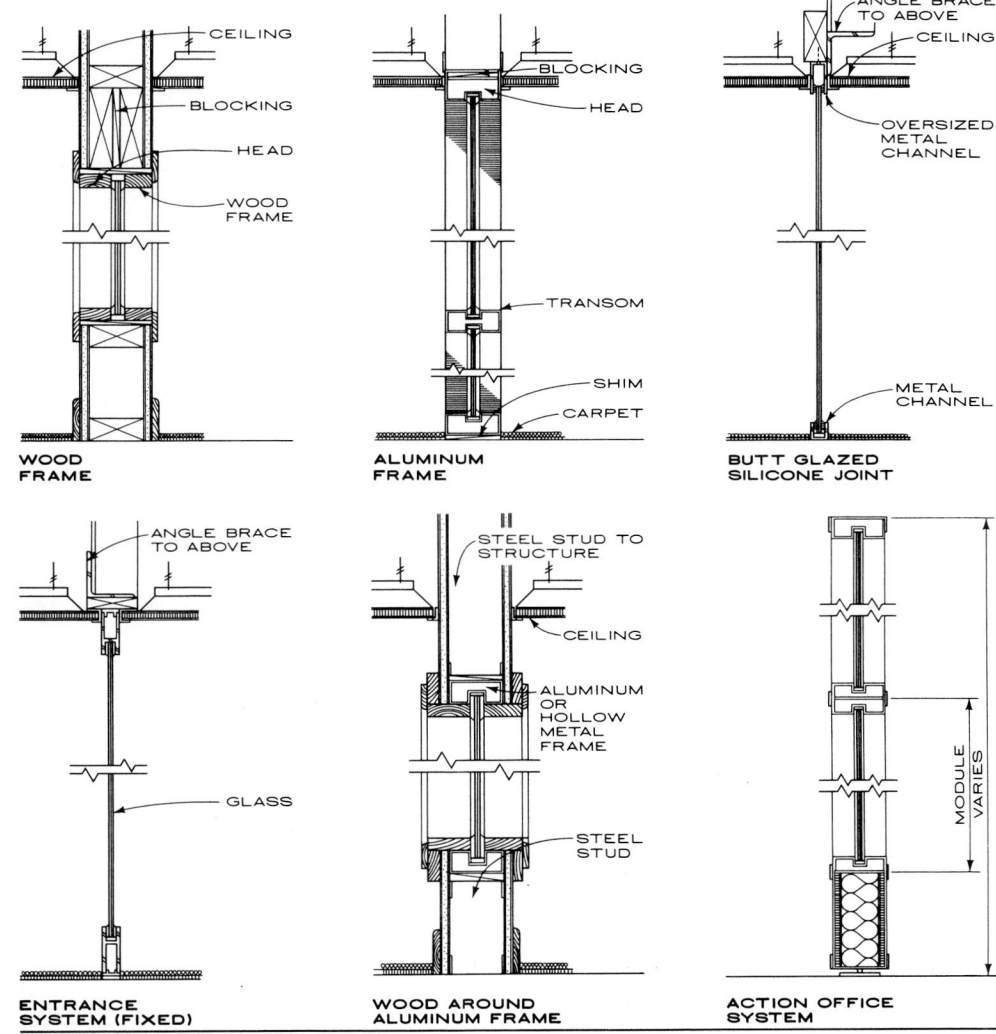

GLASS PARTITION SECTIONS

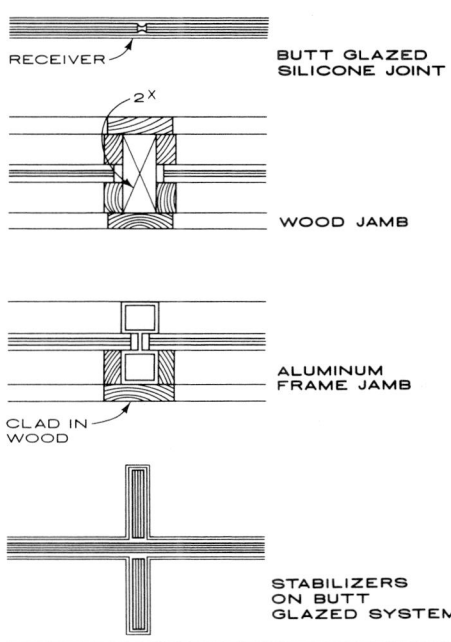

PLAN SECTIONS

GLAZED PARTITION NOTES

1. Interior glazed partitions are available in a variety of standard sizes, materials, and colors. Many manufacturers accommodate special or custom designs.
2. Finishes: Aluminum frames usually come in standard anodized or painted finishes. Many manufacturers now offer rich colors as well. Wood and hollow metal frames can be painted or finished in any tone or color. Action office systems are available in a wide array of colors and finishes, trimmed in wood, metal, or plastic.
3. Silicone glazing (butt glazing) partitions are framed at the top and bottom with either exposed or concealed frames. It is important that the glass thickness be in correct proportion to the unbraced length. If thickness alone cannot handle the span, then glass stabilizers should be used (see diagram).
4. Most manufacturers of action office systems offer a variety of glazed units to be incorporated in their system. Many systems are available with patterned, etched, or tinted glass for safety and privacy.

DRAPERIES

Draperies usually are custom made to specification. Drapery length is unlimited. Fabric width, usually 48 to 118 in. wide, does not limit final drapery width, but affects fabrication only. Considerations in drapery selection include: fabric weight, pleating (fullness), number of seams, track capacity, type of mounting track, type of draw, and control cords location.

SHADES

In addition to the common opaque shade, many shades with excellent shading coefficients that retain a high degree of transparency are available. Single shades usually are limited to 72 in. wide x 198 in. long (manual) or 312 in. long (motorized).

SHUTTERS

Interior shutters are available with fixed or operable vanes in all sizes up to 18 x 78 in. for ¾ in. thick units and 48 x 96 in. for 1¼ in. thick units. Frames usually are painted or stained wood. Some styles use panels of cane, metal, plastic, or solid wood in lieu of vanes.

GLASS COATINGS

A full array of shading films and screens is available for use in new and existing glazing. Films range from totally reflective to slightly tinted. Many also provide excellent shading coefficients.

Sterling Thompson, AIA, and Larry Gawloski, AIA; ARCHIFORMS; Waco, Texas

WOOD AND PLASTIC WINDOWS   (8)

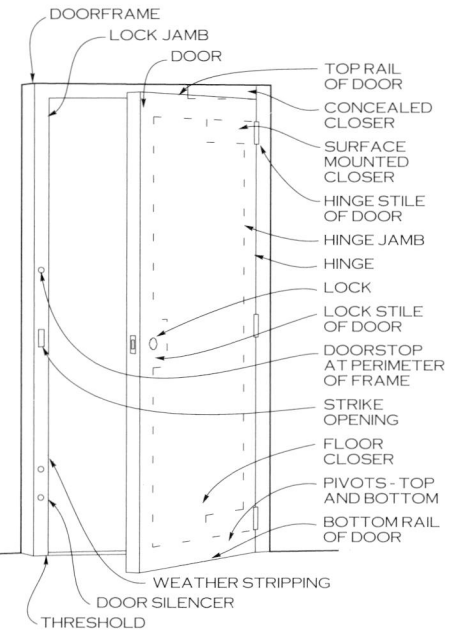

PARTS OF A DOOR

GLOSSARY

Coordinator: A device used on a pair of doors to ensure that the inactive leaf is permitted to close before the active leaf.

Cylinder (of a lock): The cylindrical shaped assembly containing the tumbler mechanism and the keyway, which can be actuated only by the correct keys.

Cylinder lock: A lock in which the locking mechanism is controlled by a cylinder.

Deadbolt (of a lock): A lock bolt having no spring action or bevel, and which is operated by a key or turnpiece.

Door bolt: A manually operated rod or bar attached to a door providing means of locking.

Doorstop: A device to stop the swing or movement of a door at a certain point.

Electric strike: An electrical device that permits releasing of the door from a remote control.

Exit device: A door locking device that grants instant exit when someone presses a crossbar to release the locking bolt or latch.

Flush bolt: A door bolt set flush with the face or edge of the door.

Hand (of a lock, etc.): A term used to indicate the direction of swing or movement, and locking security side of a door.

Lock set: A lock, complete with trim, such as handles, escutcheons, or knobs.

Mortise: A cavity made to receive a lock or other hardware; also the act of making such a cavity.

Mortise lock (or latch): A lock designed to be installed in a mortise rather than applied to the door's surface.

Rabbet: The abutting edges of a pair of doors or windows, shaped to provide a tight fit.

Reversible lock: A lock that, by reversing the latch bolt, may be used by any hand. On certain types of locks, other parts must also be changed.

Rose: A trim plate attached to the door under the handle; sometimes acts as a handle bearing.

Shank (of a handle): The projecting stem of handle into which the spindle is fastened.

Spindle (of a handle): The bar or tube connected with the knob or lever handle that passes through the hub of the lock or otherwise engages the mechanism to transmit the handle action to the bolt(s).

Stop (of a lock): The button, or other small device, that serves to lock the latch bolt against the outside handle or thumb piece or unlock it if locked. Another type holds the bolt retracted.

Strike: A metal plate or box that is pierced or recessed to receive the bolt or latch when projected; sometimes called "keeper."

Richard J. Vitullo, AIA; Oak Leaf Studio; Crownsville, Maryland

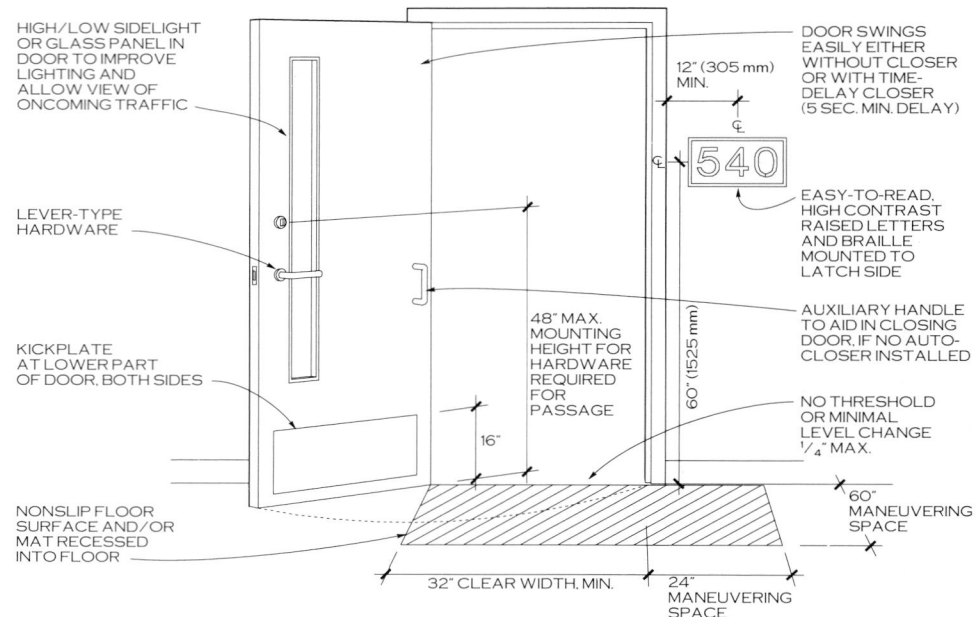

IDEAL ACCESSIBLE DOOR

Three-point lock: A device sometimes required on 3-hour fire doors to lock the active leaf of a pair of doors at three points.

NOTES

1. See also Hollow Metal Frames and Doors.

2. Face the outside of the door to determine its hand. The outside of the door is the "key side," or that side which would be secured should a lock be used. This would usually be the exterior of an entrance door or the corridor side of an office door.

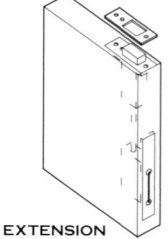

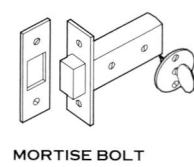

MORTISE BOLT

EXTENSION FLUSH BOLT

NOTE

A miniature deadlock, with bolt projected or retracted by a turn of the small knob.

BOLT MECHANISMS

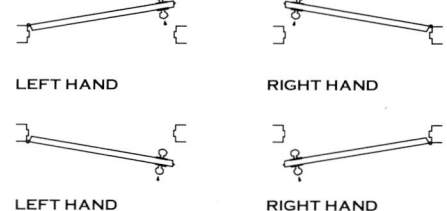

LEFT HAND   **RIGHT HAND**

LEFT HAND REVERSE   **RIGHT HAND REVERSE**

NOTE

In the architectural hardware industry, the position of the hinges on a door — right or left as viewed from outside the entryway — determines the hand.

HANDS OF DOORS

DOOR FINISHES

NEAREST U.S. EQUIVELENT	BHMA CODE	FINISH DESCRIPTION	BASE MATERIAL
USP	600	Primed for painting	Steel
US1B	601	Bright japanned	Steel
US2C	602	Cadmium plated	Steel
US2G	603	Zinc plated	Steel
US3	605	Bright brass, clear coated	Brass*
US4	606	Satin brass, clear coated	Brass*
US9	611	Bright bronze, clear coated	Bronze*
US10	612	Satin bronze, clear coated	Bronze*
US10B	613	Oxidized satin bronze, oil rubbed	Bronze*
US14	618	Bright nickel plated, clear coated	Brass, Bronze*
US15	619	Satin nickel plated, clear coated	Brass, Bronze*
US19	622	Flat black coated	Brass, Bronze*
US20A	624	Dark oxidized, statuary bronze, clear coated	Bronze*
US26	625	Bright chromium plated	Brass, Bronze*
US26D	626	Satin chromium plated	Brass, Bronze*
US27	627	Satin aluminum, clear coated	Aluminum
US28	628	Satin aluminum, clear anodized	Aluminum
US32	629	Bright stainless steel	Stainless steel 300 series
US32D	630	Satin stainless steel	Stainless steel 300 series
-	684	Black chrome, bright	Brass, Bronze*
-	685	Black chrome, satin	Brass, Bronze*

NOTE

* Also applicable to other base metals under a different Builders' Hardware Manufacturers Association code number.

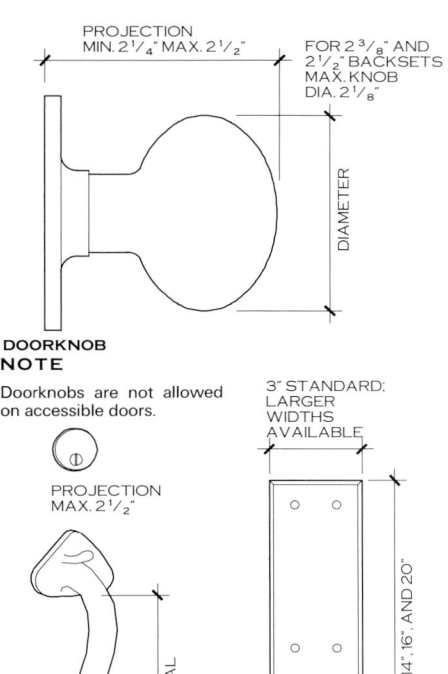

DOORKNOB

NOTE

Doorknobs are not allowed on accessible doors.

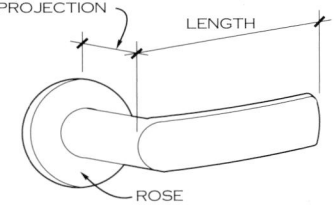

ENTRANCE HANDLE   **PUSH PLATE**

NOTE

Complete lockset for entrance door handle includes mortise lock, handle outside, and knob and rose inside.

LEVER HANDLE

PROJECTION: 1 $^3/_4$ to 2 $^1/_2$ in.
LENGTH: 2 to 4 in.
ROSE: Maximum diameter 1 $^1/_2$ to 3 in.
STILE: Larger stile takes larger rose

NOTE

Local codes may require a return or special clearance on lever handle (e.g., fire codes may require return to prevent fire hose from catching behind lever handle). Also, push-type mechanisms and U-shaped handles are acceptable designs. Consult ANSI and ADAAG and manufacturers' catalogs for other approved designs. Maximum height for accessible hardware is 48 in. above finished floor.

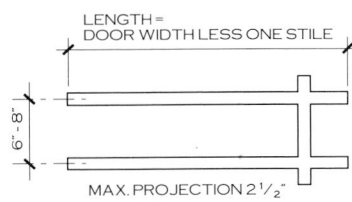

PUSH-PULL BAR

NOTE

Double push-pull bars may be used on the pull side of single-acting doors or on either side of double-acting doors.

KNOB, HANDLES, PLATE, AND BAR

Richard J. Vitullo, AIA; Oak Leaf Studio; Crownsville, Maryland

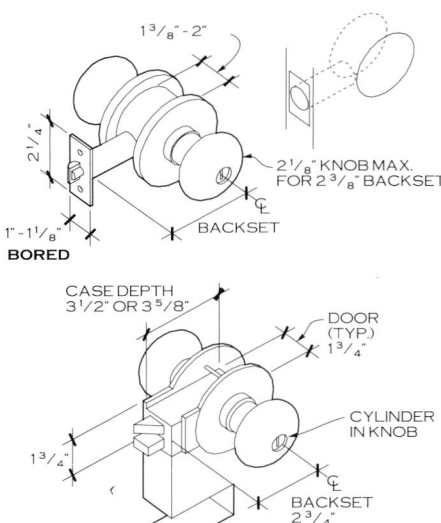

BORED

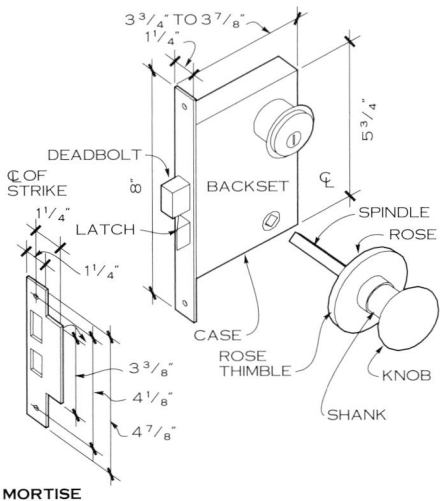

PREASSEMBLED

NOTE

Installation requires notch cut in lock side of door to suit case size. Complete factory assembly eliminates much adjustment on the job.

MORTISE

NOTES

1. Installation requires mortise opening in door.
2. See American Standards Association Lock Strikes A-115V-1959 for metal doorframes. To determine lip length, measure from centerline of strike to edge of jamb and add $^1/_4$ in. Outside strike dimensions standard for all lock types shown.

GENERAL NOTES

Based on use characteristics, there are four main types of latches and locks: passage, privacy, entry, and classroom. (In all cases, latch bolt can be operated by handle from either side.)

1. PASSAGE: Latches can be operated by handle from either side at all times.
2. PRIVACY: Outside handle is locked by push-button inside (or if deadbolt latch, by a turn) and unlocked by emergency key outside.
3. ENTRY: Outside handle is made inoperative by mechanical means, other than a key, on inside; latch bolt is operated by key in outside handle or by manual means at inside handle.
4. CLASSROOM: Outside handle is locked from outside by key; when outside handle is locked, latch bolt may be retracted by key from outside or by rotating inside handle.

LOCK TYPES

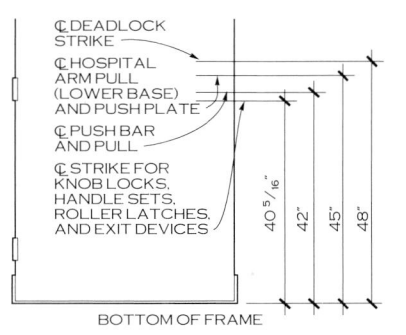

DOOR HARDWARE LOCATIONS

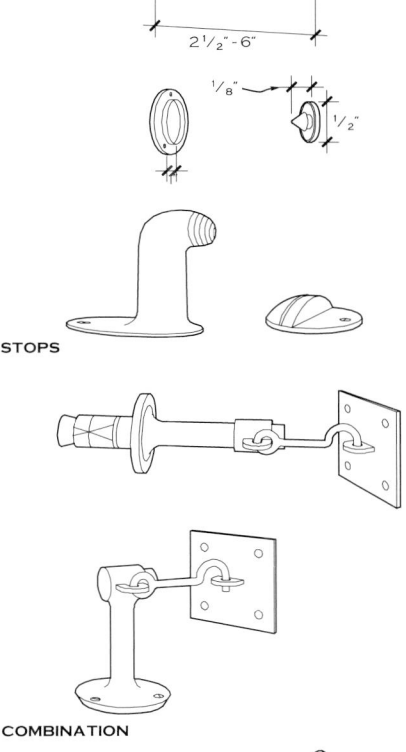

STOPS

COMBINATION

HOLDERS

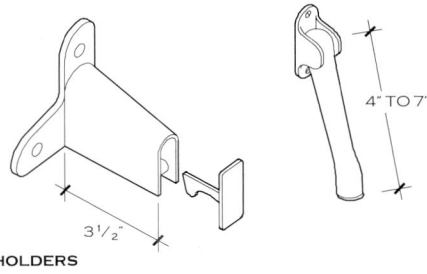

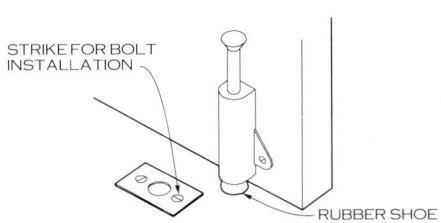

PLUNGER-TYPE HOLDER OR BOLT

STOPS AND HOLDERS

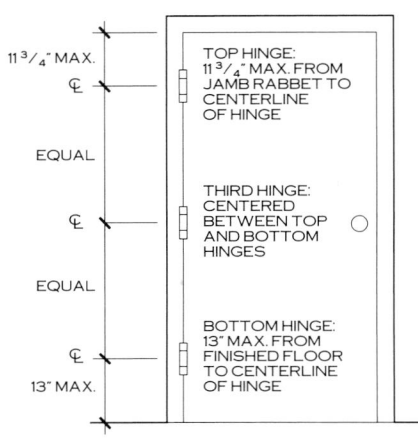

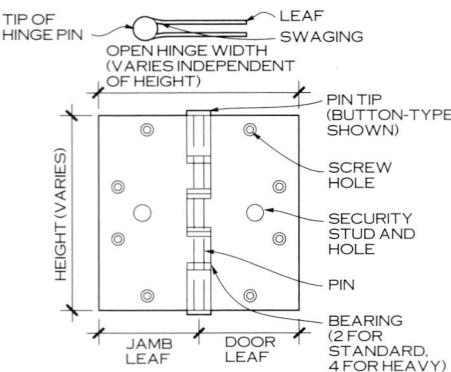

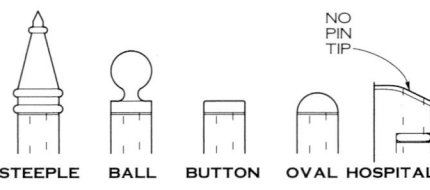

STEEPLE BALL BUTTON OVAL HOSPITAL

TYPES OF HINGE PIN

NOTES

1. Use three hinges for doors as high as 7 ft 6 in. Add one hinge for each additional 30 in. in height.

2. In specifying hinges, the following design criteria are important: door material, weight, and dimensions; hinge weight (standard or heavy), material, finish, and special features (e.g., swing clear, spring hinge, etc.); "clearance," that is, distance between door and frame when door is opened 180°; frequency of use; conditions of use (e.g., exterior, corrosive atmosphere, potential for abuse or vandalism, etc.); type of pin tips; and type of screws.

HINGE LOCATION AND SPECIFICATION

HINGE WIDTH

THICKNESS OF DOOR (IN.)	CLEARANCE REQUIRED* (IN.)	OPEN WIDTH OF HINGES (IN.)
1 3/8	1 1/4 1 3/4	3 1/2 4
1 3/4	1 1 1/2 2 3	4 4 1/2 5 6
2	1 1 1/2 2 1/2	4 1/2 5 6
2 1/4	1 2	5 6
2 1/2	3/4 1 3/4	5 6
3	3/4 2 3/4 4 3/4	6 8 10

NOTE

* Clearance is computed for door flush with doorframe.

HINGE TYPE

TYPE OF BUILDING AND DOOR	DAILY FREQUENCY	HINGE TYPE
HIGH FREQUENCY		Heavy weight
Large department store entrance	5000	
Large office building entrance	4000	
School entrance	1250	
School toilet room	1250	
Store or bank entrance	500	
Office building toilet door	400	
AVERAGE FREQUENCY		Standard weight antifriction bearing (except on heavy doors)
School corridor door	80	
Office building corridor door	75	
Store toilet door	60	
Dwelling entrance	40	
LOW FREQUENCY		Plain bearing hinges may be used on light doors
Dwelling toilet door	25	
Dwelling corridor door	10	
Dwelling closet door	6	

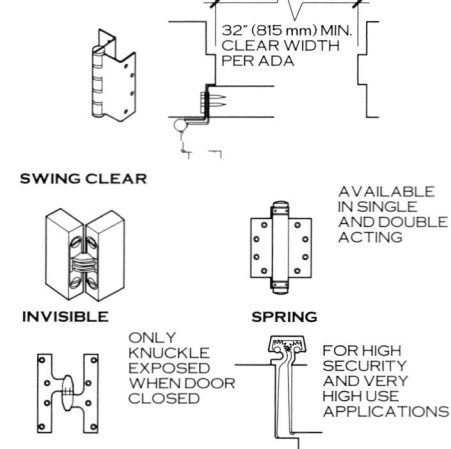

NOTES

1. Swaging is a slight offset of the hinge at the barrel, which permits the leaves to come closer together and improves the operation and appearance of the door.

2. A leaf is one of the two attaching plates that, when fastened together by the hinge pin, form a complete hinge.

3. Bearings (ball, oil-impregnated, or antifriction) offer the best ease of operation and durability.

4. Nonrising pins are a feature of quality hinges. Also available: nonremovable pins (NRP), with set screws; spun pins (FSP), without tips; and floating pins (FTP), with tips driven in both ends.

5. Tolerances: Close tolerances, especially in the pins, prevent excessive wear and are characteristic of high-quality, heavy-duty hinges.

6. A security stud, with matching hole in opposite leaf, is attached to a hinge to prevent door removal even if the pin is removed.

7. Hinges are available in brass, bronze, stainless steel, and carbon steel.

ELEMENTS OF A HINGE

SWING CLEAR

INVISIBLE   SPRING

AVAILABLE IN SINGLE AND DOUBLE ACTING

ONLY KNUCKLE EXPOSED WHEN DOOR CLOSED

FOR HIGH SECURITY AND VERY HIGH USE APPLICATIONS

OLIVE KNUCKLE   CONTINUOUS GEAR

SPECIALTY HINGES

HINGE HEIGHT

THICKNESS (IN.)	WIDTH OF DOORS (IN.)	HEIGHT OF HINGES (IN.)
Doors 3/4 to 1 cabinet	Any	2 1/2
1 1/8 screen or combination	To 36	3
1 3/8	To 36 Over 36	3 1/2 4
1 3/4	To 41 Over 41	4 1/2 4 1/2 heavy
1 3/4 to 2 1/4	Any	5 heavy
Transoms 1 1/4 and 1 3/8 1 3/8 2, 2 1/4, and 2 1/2		3 3 1/2 4

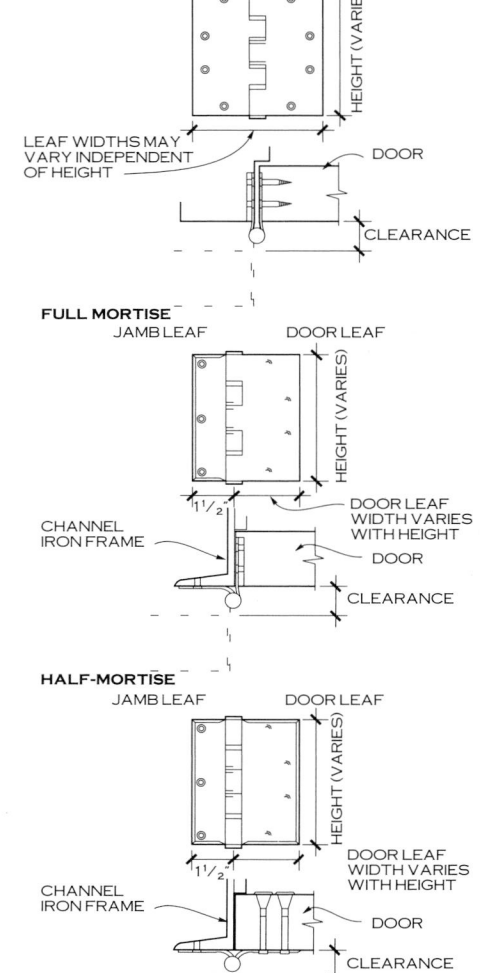

LEAF WIDTHS MAY VARY INDEPENDENT OF HEIGHT

FULL MORTISE

JAMB LEAF   DOOR LEAF

CHANNEL IRON FRAME

DOOR LEAF WIDTH VARIES WITH HEIGHT

DOOR

CLEARANCE

HALF-MORTISE

JAMB LEAF   DOOR LEAF

CHANNEL IRON FRAME

DOOR LEAF WIDTH VARIES WITH HEIGHT

DOOR

CLEARANCE

FULL SURFACE

JAMB LEAF   DOOR LEAF

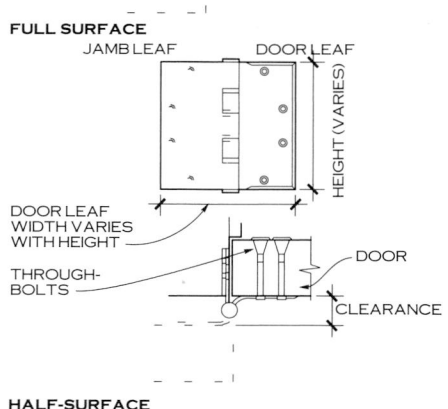

DOOR LEAF WIDTH VARIES WITH HEIGHT

THROUGH-BOLTS

DOOR

CLEARANCE

HALF-SURFACE

TYPES OF HINGES

Richard J. Vitullo, AIA; Oak Leaf Studio; Crownsville, Maryland

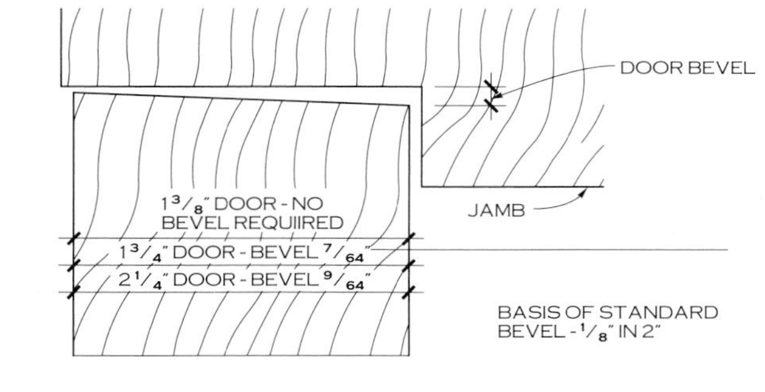

DOOR BEVEL

1 3/8" DOOR - NO BEVEL REQUIRED
1 3/4" DOOR - BEVEL 7/64"
2 1/4" DOOR - BEVEL 9/64"

JAMB

BASIS OF STANDARD BEVEL - 1/8" IN 2"

DOOR BEVELS

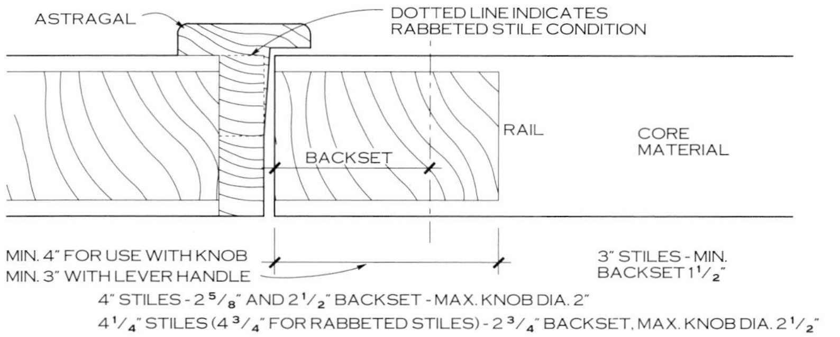

ASTRAGAL

DOTTED LINE INDICATES RABBETED STILE CONDITION

RAIL

BACKSET

CORE MATERIAL

MIN. 4" FOR USE WITH KNOB
MIN. 3" WITH LEVER HANDLE

3" STILES - MIN. BACKSET 1 1/2"

4" STILES - 2 5/8" AND 2 1/2" BACKSET - MAX. KNOB DIA. 2"
4 1/4" STILES (4 3/4" FOR RABBETED STILES) - 2 3/4" BACKSET, MAX. KNOB DIA. 2 1/2"

DOUBLE DOORS WITH FLAT ASTRAGAL (ALSO APPLIES TO DOOR WITH RABBETED MEETING STILES)

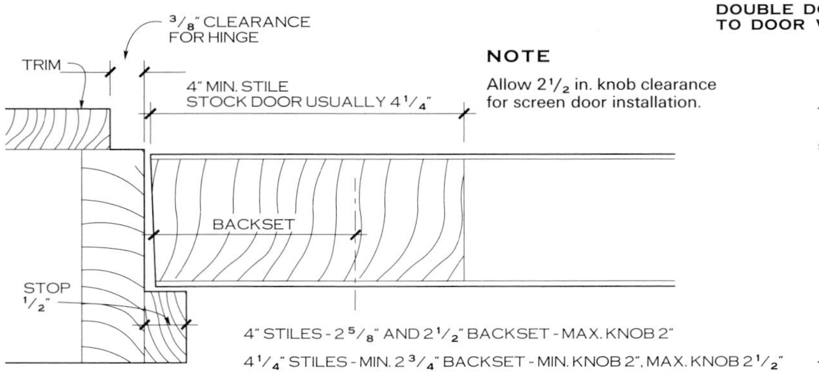

3/8" CLEARANCE FOR HINGE

TRIM

4" MIN. STILE STOCK DOOR USUALLY 4 1/4"

BACKSET

STOP 1/2"

4" STILES - 2 5/8" AND 2 1/2" BACKSET - MAX. KNOB 2"
4 1/4" STILES - MIN. 2 3/4" BACKSET - MIN. KNOB 2", MAX. KNOB 2 1/2"

DOOR WITH LEVER HANDLE OR KNOB USING CYLINDER LOCK

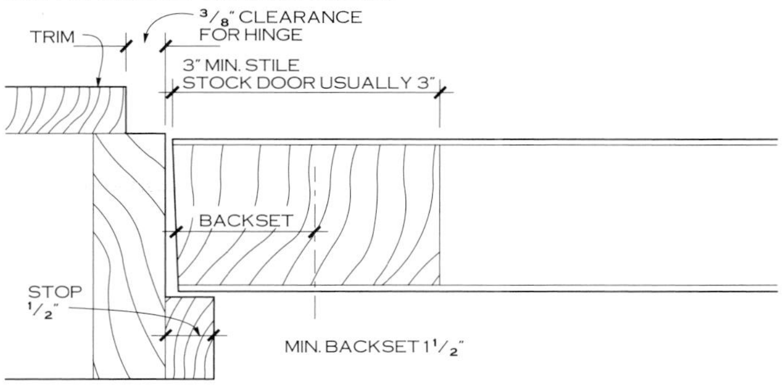

NOTE

Allow 2 1/2 in. knob clearance for screen door installation.

3/8" CLEARANCE FOR HINGE

TRIM

3" MIN. STILE STOCK DOOR USUALLY 3"

BACKSET

STOP 1/2"

MIN. BACKSET 1 1/2"

DOOR WITH LEVER HANDLE USING CYLINDER LOCK

DOOR STILES

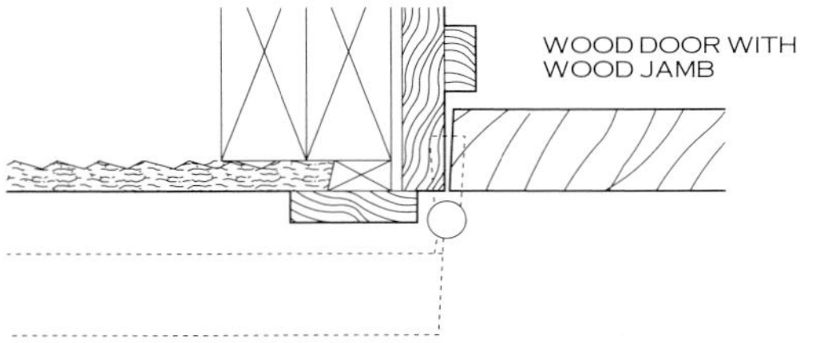

WOOD DOOR WITH WOOD JAMB

FULL MORTISE NONTEMPLATE

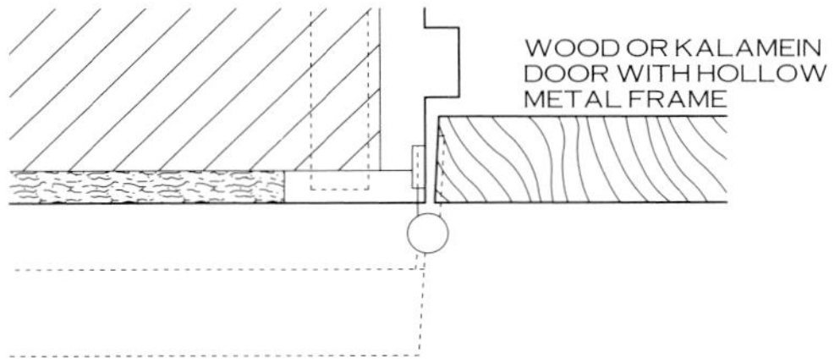

WOOD OR KALAMEIN DOOR WITH HOLLOW METAL FRAME

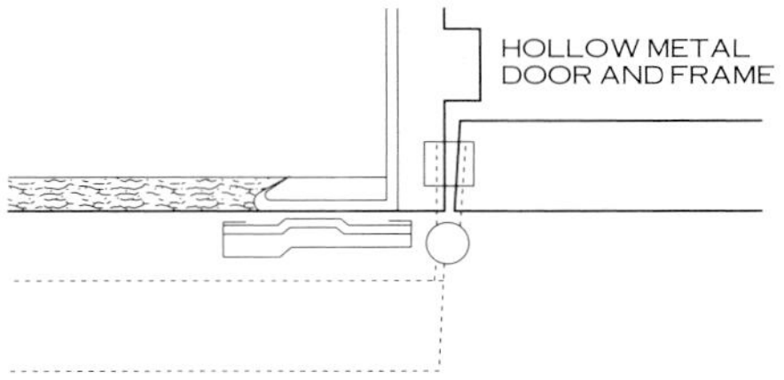

FULL MORTISE TEMPLATE

HOLLOW METAL DOOR AND FRAME

FULL MORTISE TEMPLATE

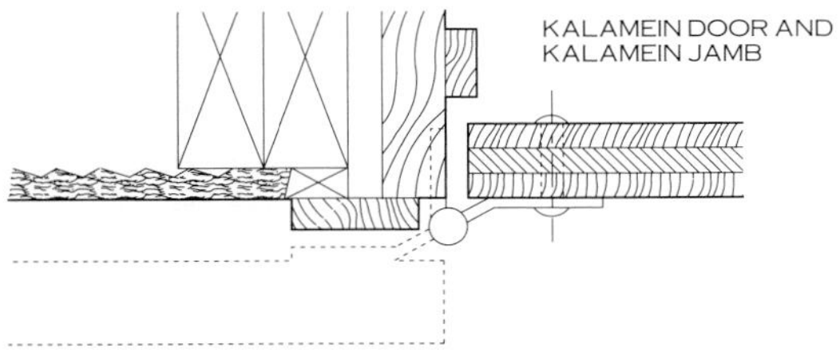

KALAMEIN DOOR AND KALAMEIN JAMB

HALF-SURFACE TEMPLATE

KALAMEIN DOOR WITH HOLLOW METAL FRAME

HALF-SURFACE TEMPLATE

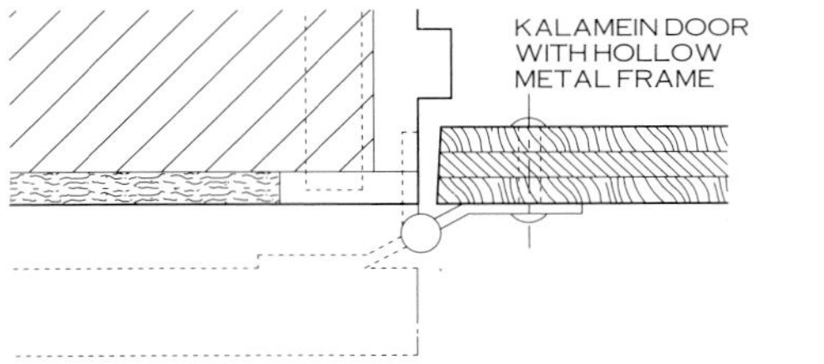

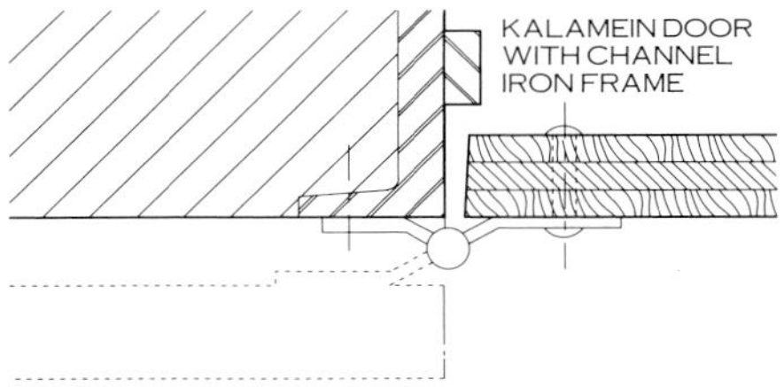

KALAMEIN DOOR WITH CHANNEL IRON FRAME

FULL SURFACE TEMPLATE

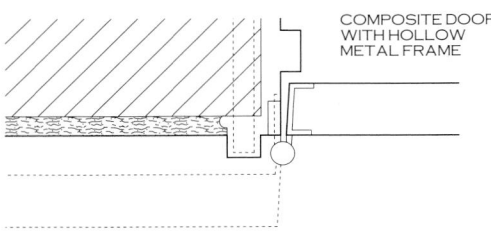

COMPOSITE DOOR WITH HOLLOW METAL FRAME

FULL MORTISE TEMPLATE

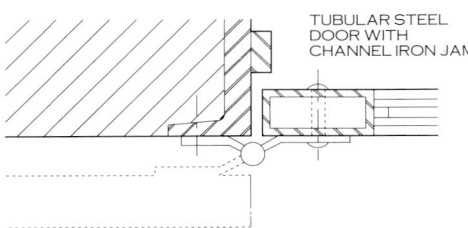
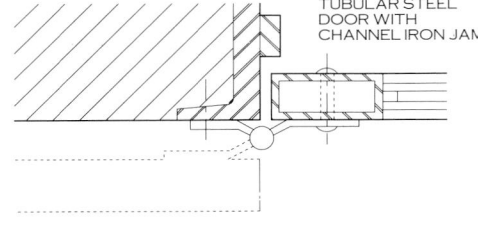

TUBULAR STEEL DOOR WITH CHANNEL IRON JAMB

FULL SURFACE TEMPLATE

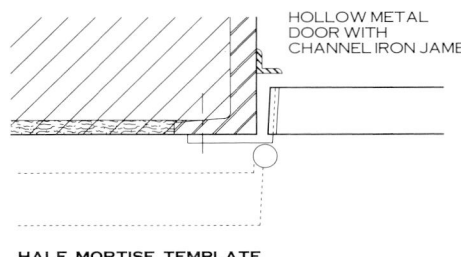

HOLLOW METAL DOOR WITH CHANNEL IRON JAMB

HALF MORTISE TEMPLATE

MORTISE TEMPLATES

Richard J. Vitullo, AIA; Oak Leaf Studio; Crownsville, Maryland

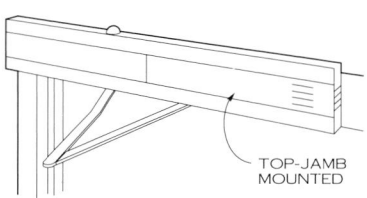

**CLOSER, HOLDER, AND
DETECTOR — STOP SIDE**

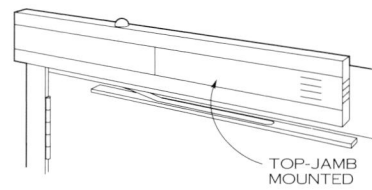

**CLOSER, HOLDER, AND
DETECTOR — HINGE SIDE**

NOTES

1. A combination fire and smoke detector, door holder, and closer is available. Ionization, photoelectric, or heat-sensing devices detect smoke or any combustion products and hold open or close the door.

2. Smoke and fire doors are most commonly held open by electromagnetic or pneumatic devices and are released and closed manually or by means of smoke- or fire-detection devices. Most jurisdictions do not allow the old-fashioned fusible-link door closer in areas of human occupation, except for overhead doors. Consult local codes.

3. Some hold-open devices incorporate an electric switch that allows building maintenance staff to turn off the hold-open feature; however, such a switch should never shut off the detector.

4. A combination device (closer/holder/detector) most often is connected to the fire alarm system but may also be used merely to release and close the fire- or smoke-barrier doors without such a connection.

5. Smoke-sensing devices detect both visible and invisible airborne particles. Various operating principles include ionization, photoelectric, resistance, sampling, and cloud-chamber detection.

6. Ionization detection closers contain a small quantity of radioactive material within the sensing chamber. The resulting ionized air permits an electric current flow between electrodes. When smoke particles reduce the flow of ionized air between electrodes to a certain level, the detection circuit responds. Closing mechanisms usually consist of a detector, electromechanical holding device, and a door closer.

7. Ionization detectors sense ordinary products of combustion from sources such as kitchens, motors, power tools, and automobile exhausts.

8. Photoelectric-detection closers consist of a light source and a photoelectric cell. They activate when smoke becomes dense enough to change the reflectance of light reaching the photoelectric device. Photoelectric detectors may be spot or beam type. Closing mechanisms consist of a detector, electromechanical holding device, and a door closer.

9. Other types of smoke detectors include electrical bridging, sampling, and cloud chambers. Each has operating characteristics similar to ionization and photoelectric detectors.

10. Requirements for closers and detectors vary by code and governing jurisdiction. Refer to local building codes, the life-safety code of the National Fire Protection Association (NFPA), and other applicable regulations.

**COMBINATION CLOSER/HOLDER/
DETECTOR — SURFACE MOUNTED**

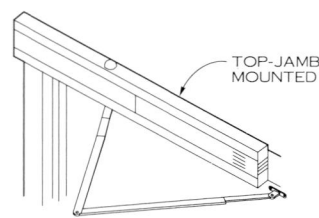

**CLOSER AND HOLDER
ONLY — STOP SIDE**

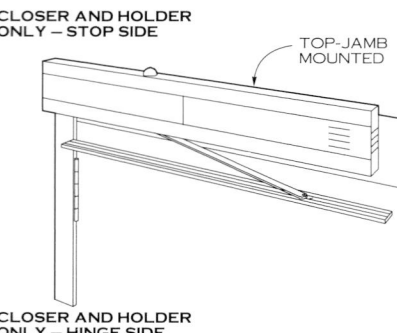

**CLOSER AND HOLDER
ONLY — HINGE SIDE**

NOTES

1. A combination closer and holder (only) will hold door in open position when incorporated with an independent detector or when wired into any type of fire detecting system.

2. All these units have unlimited hold-open from 0° to approximately 170°, or limited hold-open from 85 to 170° for cross-corridor doors.

**COMBINATION CLOSER/HOLDER/
DETECTOR — SURFACE MOUNTED**

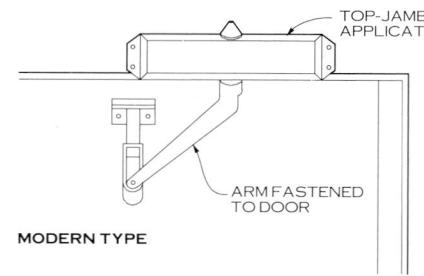

MODERN TYPE

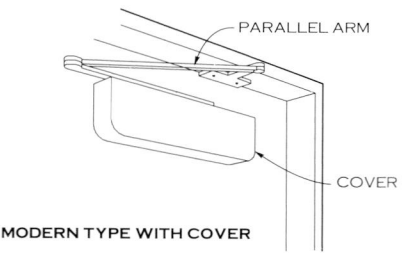

MODERN TYPE WITH COVER

NOTES

1. Door closers may be surface mounted or concealed in the door, frame, or floor. There are three ways to mount surface closers: hinge side, parallel arm, and top jamb. A wide variety of brackets, including corner and soffit types, is available to meet varying door and frame conditions.

2. Surface-mounted and concealed-in-door closers are used exclusively for single-acting doors; floor closers and frame-concealed closers may be used for either single- or double-acting doors.

CLOSER ONLY — SURFACE MOUNTED

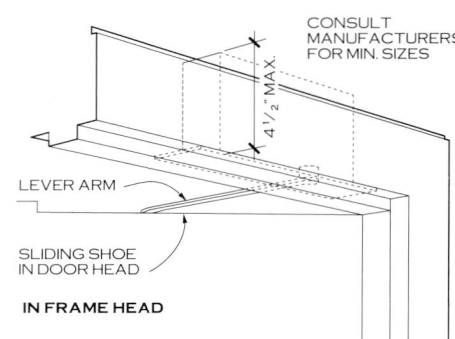

IN FRAME HEAD

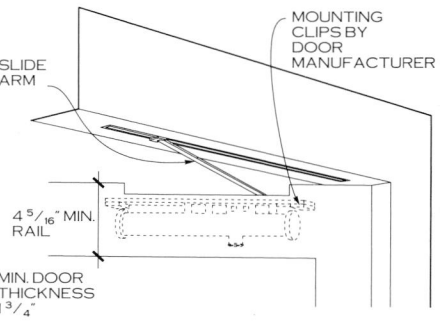

IN DOOR HEAD

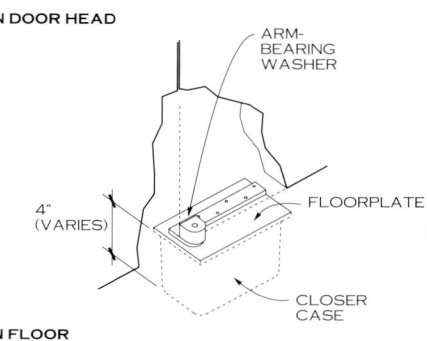

IN FLOOR

CLOSER ONLY — CONCEALED

NOTES

1. A door closer, when properly installed and adjusted, should control the door throughout the opening and closing swings. It combines three basic components: (a) a power source to close a door; (b) a checking source to control the rate at which the door closes; and (c) a connecting component (arm that transmits the closing force from the door to the frame).

   In all modern closers, the power source is a spring and the checking source is a hydraulic mechanism. The spring and checking mechanism are connected to a common shaft, and arms attached to this shaft act as linkage to communicate movement between the door and mechanism. In addition to serving as linkage, the arms, through leverage, can amplify the power of the spring, providing maximum power at the latch point.

2. Additional features for safety and convenience also are available in many types of closers. These include back check, delayed action, adjustable spring power, and a variety of hold-open functions: regular, fusible link, and hospital.

3. A full range of closer sizes is available to suit various door dimensions, locations, and job conditions. The manufacturer's recommendations should be considered carefully.

4. Closers with delayed-action features give a person more time to maneuver through doorways. They are particularly useful on frequently used interior doors such as entrances to toilet rooms. ADAAG requires a closing speed of at least 3 seconds; ANSI requires 5 seconds.

Richard J. Vitullo, AIA; Oak Leaf Studio; Crownsville, Maryland

HARDWARE

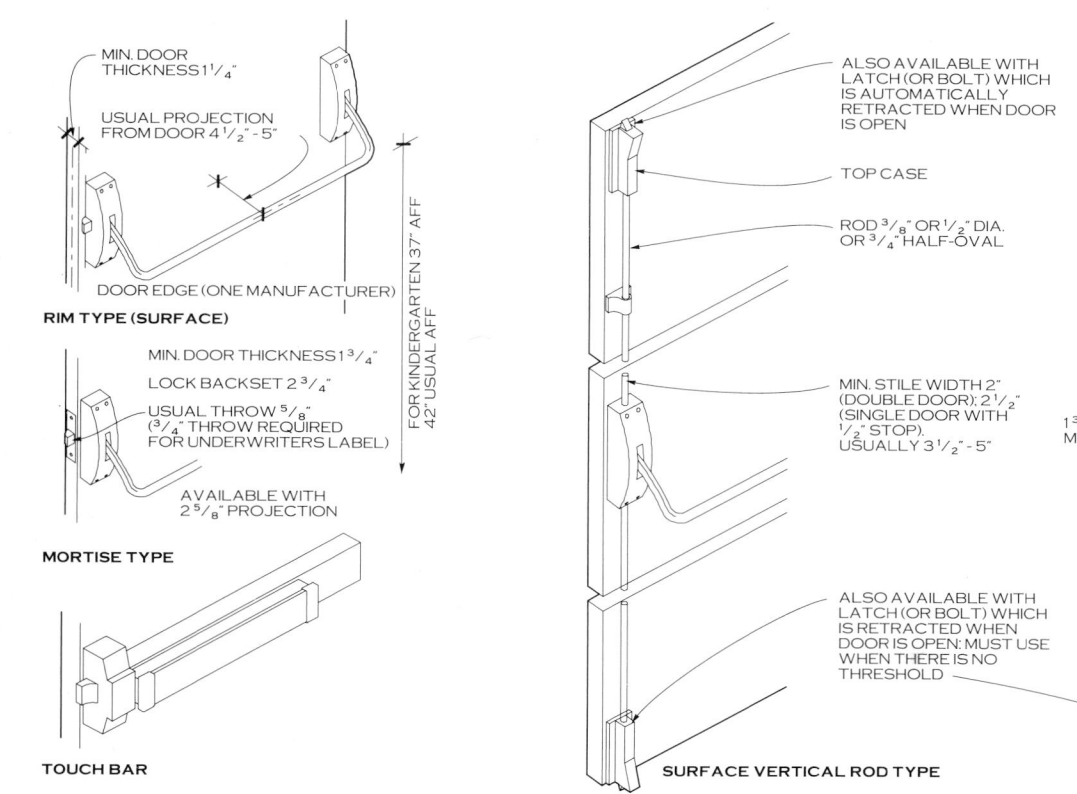

MIN. DOOR THICKNESS 1 1/4"

USUAL PROJECTION FROM DOOR 4 1/2" - 5"

DOOR EDGE (ONE MANUFACTURER)

RIM TYPE (SURFACE)

MIN. DOOR THICKNESS 1 3/4"

LOCK BACKSET 2 3/4"

USUAL THROW 5/8" (3/4" THROW REQUIRED FOR UNDERWRITERS LABEL)

AVAILABLE WITH 2 5/8" PROJECTION

MORTISE TYPE

FOR KINDERGARTEN 37" AFF
42" USUAL AFF

TOUCH BAR

ALSO AVAILABLE WITH LATCH (OR BOLT) WHICH IS AUTOMATICALLY RETRACTED WHEN DOOR IS OPEN

TOP CASE

ROD 3/8" OR 1/2" DIA. OR 3/4" HALF-OVAL

MIN. STILE WIDTH 2" (DOUBLE DOOR); 2 1/2" (SINGLE DOOR WITH 1/2" STOP). USUALLY 3 1/2" - 5"

ALSO AVAILABLE WITH LATCH (OR BOLT) WHICH IS RETRACTED WHEN DOOR IS OPEN: MUST USE WHEN THERE IS NO THRESHOLD

SURFACE VERTICAL ROD TYPE

MIN. STILE 1 3/4" CONSULT MANUFACTURER

2 5/8" - 2 3/4" PROJECTION FROM STILE

1 3/4" MIN.

CONCEALED VERTICAL ROD TYPE (HOLLOW METAL DOORS)

EXIT DEVICES

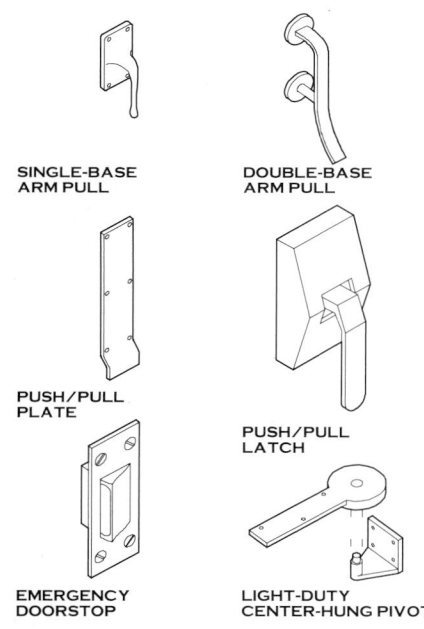

SINGLE-BASE ARM PULL

DOUBLE-BASE ARM PULL

PUSH/PULL PLATE

PUSH/PULL LATCH

EMERGENCY DOORSTOP

LIGHT-DUTY CENTER-HUNG PIVOT

NOTES

1. To permit reverse opening of a door in an emergency, a foldable or collapsible stop, in conjunction with a center-hung pivot, is needed. Such devices typically are used on private or semiprivate toilet doors.

2. If a slowly opening, low-powered automatic door mechanism is used, it shall comply with ANSI 156.19-1984. Such doors shall not open to backcheck faster than 3 seconds and shall require no more than 15 lbf to stop door movement. If a power-assisted door is used, its door opening force shall comply with ANSI 4.13.11 and its closing force shall comply with ANSI A156.19-1984.

HEALTH-RELATED INSTITUTIONAL HARDWARE

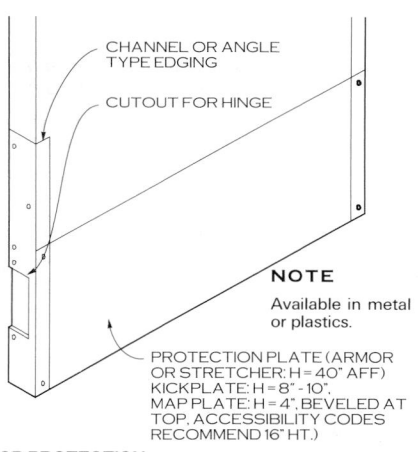

CHANNEL OR ANGLE TYPE EDGING

CUTOUT FOR HINGE

NOTE
Available in metal or plastics.

PROTECTION PLATE (ARMOR OR STRETCHER: H = 40" AFF) KICKPLATE: H = 8" - 10", MAP PLATE: H = 4", BEVELED AT TOP, ACCESSIBILITY CODES RECOMMEND 16" HT.)

DOOR PROTECTION

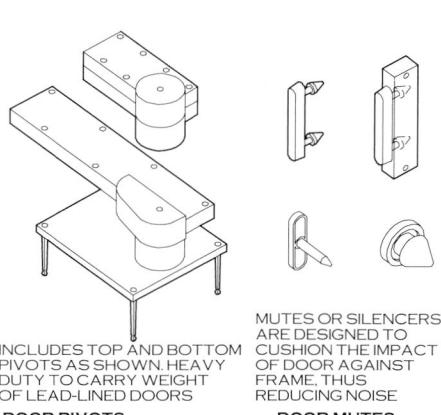

INCLUDES TOP AND BOTTOM PIVOTS AS SHOWN. HEAVY DUTY TO CARRY WEIGHT OF LEAD-LINED DOORS

MUTES OR SILENCERS ARE DESIGNED TO CUSHION THE IMPACT OF DOOR AGAINST FRAME, THUS REDUCING NOISE

DOOR PIVOTS   **DOOR MUTES**

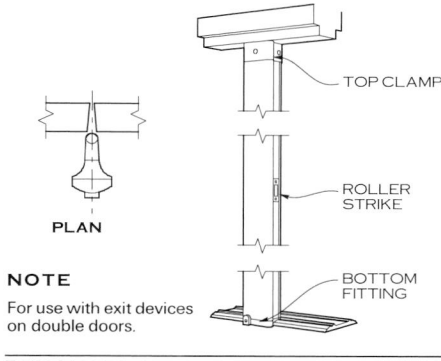

TOP CLAMP

ROLLER STRIKE

BOTTOM FITTING

PLAN

NOTE
For use with exit devices on double doors.

REMOVABLE MULLION

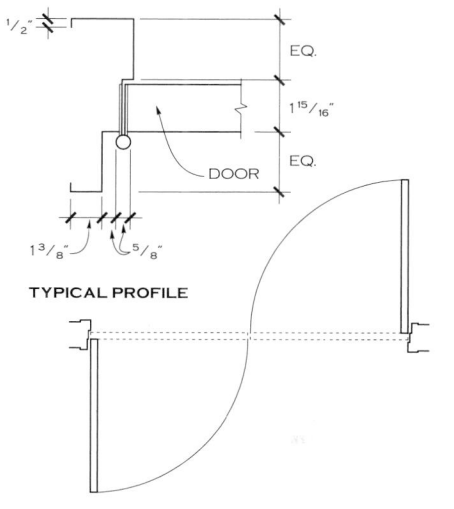

1/2"

EQ.

1 15/16"

EQ.

DOOR

1 3/8"   5/8"

TYPICAL PROFILE

DOUBLE-EGRESS DOORS

Richard J. Vitullo, AIA; Oak Leaf Studio; Crownsville, Maryland

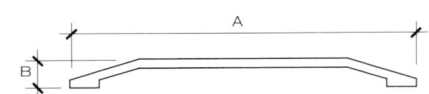

PLAIN, UNFLUTED (IN.)

BRASS		ALUMINUM				BRONZE	
A	B	A	B	A	B	A	B
3	1/4	4 5/64	3/32	4	1/2	2 1/2, 3	1/4
2 1/4	3/16	2 1/4	3/16	4 5/64		4, 5, and 6	1/2
4, 5, and 6	1/2	2 1/2, 3	1/4	5, 6			
		2 1/4	3/16	4	7/16		

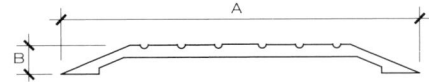

FLUTED (IN.)

BRASS		ALUM.		BRONZE		STEEL	
A	B	A	B	A	B	A	B
3, 3 1/2, 4, 5, and 6	1/2	3, 4, 5, 6, 6 1/2, 7, 7 1/2	1/2	3	5/16	3, 4	1/2
				3	3/8	5 1/2	9/16
				4, 4 1/2, 5, 6, and 7	1/2		

NOTE

Threshold profiles vary among manufacturers. Consult manufacturer's catalog for additional sizes. Standard length is 18 to 20 ft, or thresholds may be cut to size.

ONE-PIECE THRESHOLDS

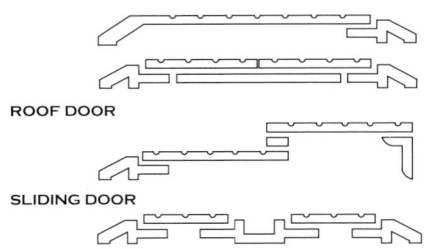

ROOF DOOR

SLIDING DOOR

NOTE

By combining components, saddles may be made to any width; joints will not show as fluting pattern is identical.

TYPICAL ASSEMBLED THRESHOLDS

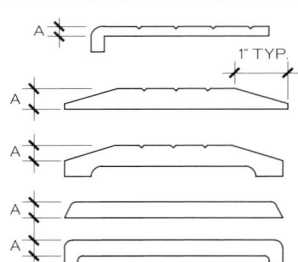

RECOMMENDED PRACTICE

A	IRON	BRONZE	ALUMINUM
1/4"		To 6" wide	To 10" wide
5/16"	To 6" wide	To 10" wide	To 18" wide
3/8"	To 12" wide	To 18" wide	To 24" wide
7/16"	To 24" wide	To 24" wide	To 36" wide
1/2"	To 30" wide	To 30" wide	To 42" wide

NOTE

Length to 9 ft 6 in. When width exceeds 32 in., length should not exceed 7 ft 6 in. Standard widths are 4, 5, and 6 in. Raised threshold shall be beveled with a slope no greater than 1:20.

CAST METAL ABRASIVE-SURFACE THRESHOLD

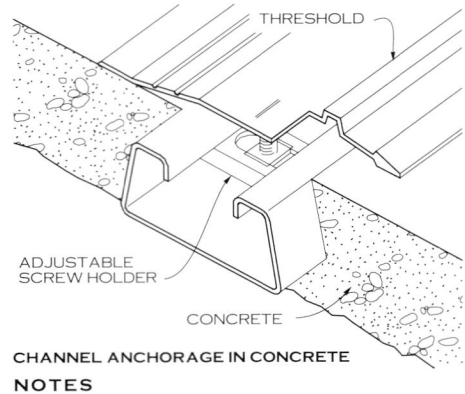

CHANNEL ANCHORAGE IN CONCRETE

NOTES

1. For channel-type threshold anchors, exact location is required at time concrete floor is poured.
2. For installation on wood floors, use wood screws; for masonry floors, use no less than a #10 machine screw and double-cinch anchors for best results. In descending order of holding power, the following may be satisfactory, depending on frequency of use: machine screws with lead anchors, wood screws with lead anchors, wood screws with lead expansion shields, wood screws with plastic anchors.

THRESHOLD ANCHORAGE

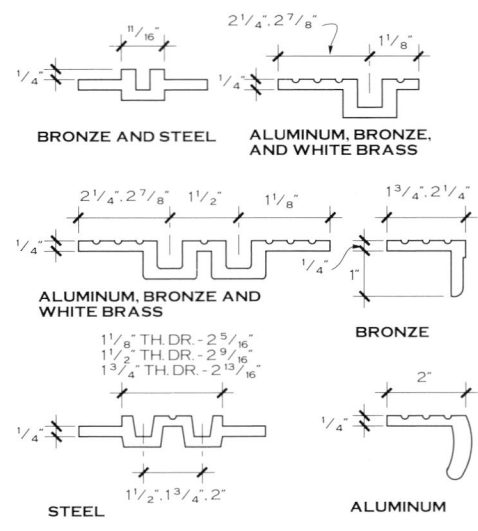

BRONZE AND STEEL

ALUMINUM, BRONZE, AND WHITE BRASS

ALUMINUM, BRONZE AND WHITE BRASS

BRONZE

STEEL

ALUMINUM

COMPONENTS FOR SLIDING DOOR

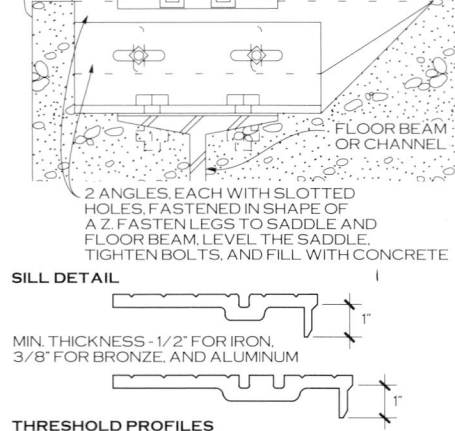

2 ANGLES, EACH WITH SLOTTED HOLES, FASTENED IN SHAPE OF A Z. FASTEN LEGS TO SADDLE AND FLOOR BEAM, LEVEL THE SADDLE, TIGHTEN BOLTS, AND FILL WITH CONCRETE

SILL DETAIL

THRESHOLD PROFILES

MIN. THICKNESS - 1/2 FOR IRON, 3/8 FOR BRONZE, AND ALUMINUM

ELEVATOR THRESHOLDS

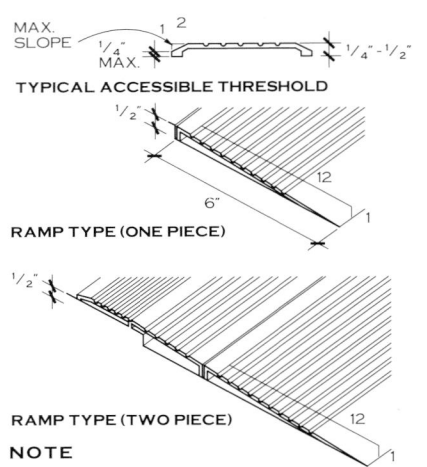

TYPICAL ACCESSIBLE THRESHOLD

RAMP TYPE (ONE PIECE)

RAMP TYPE (TWO PIECE)

NOTE

Level changes at thresholds up to 1/4 in. (6 mm) may be vertical, without edge treatment. Level changes between 1/4 and 1/2 in. shall be beveled with a slope no greater than 1:2. Abrasive finish recommended for threshold surface. Consult manufacturer for other threshold profiles and textures. ADAAG limits new thresholds to 1/2 in. maximum height except at exterior sliding doors (3/4 in. maximum allowed).

ACCESSIBLE THRESHOLD

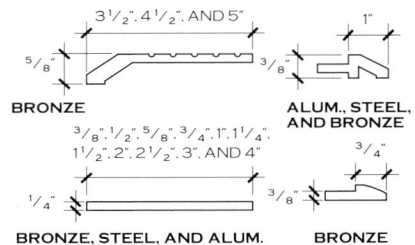

BRONZE

ALUM., STEEL, AND BRONZE

BRONZE, STEEL, AND ALUM.

BRONZE

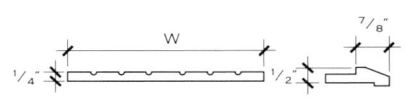

ALUMINUM

ALUMINUM	W = 1 1/2", 2", 3", AND 4"
BRONZE	W = 1", 1 1/2", 2", 2 1/2", 3", 3 1/2", 4", 4 1/2", 5", 5 1/2", AND 6 1/8"
WHITE BRONZE	W = 1 1/2"
STEEL	W = 1 1/2", 2", 3", AND 4"

COMPONENTS FOR REGULAR OPENING

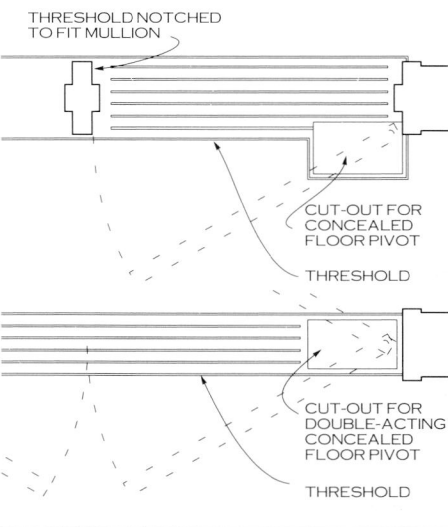

THRESHOLD NOTCHED TO FIT MULLION

CUT-OUT FOR CONCEALED FLOOR PIVOT

THRESHOLD

CUT-OUT FOR DOUBLE-ACTING CONCEALED FLOOR PIVOT

THRESHOLD

FLOOR HINGE CUTOUTS

Richard J. Vitullo, AIA; Oak Leaf Studio; Crownsville, Maryland

HARDWARE

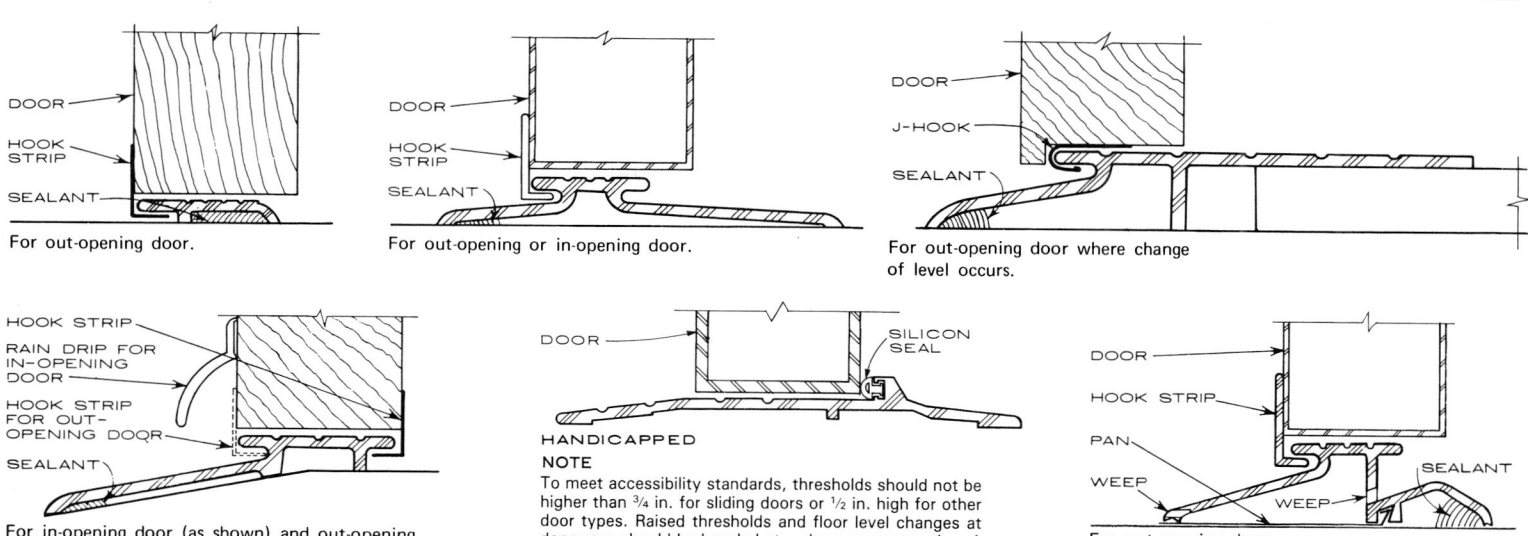

DOOR
HOOK STRIP
SEALANT

For out-opening door.

DOOR
HOOK STRIP
SEALANT

For out-opening or in-opening door.

DOOR
J-HOOK
SEALANT

For out-opening door where change of level occurs.

HOOK STRIP
RAIN DRIP FOR IN-OPENING DOOR
HOOK STRIP FOR OUT-OPENING DOOR
SEALANT

For in-opening door (as shown) and out-opening door where change of level occurs.

DOOR
SILICON SEAL

HANDICAPPED
NOTE
To meet accessibility standards, thresholds should not be higher than ¾ in. for sliding doors or ½ in. high for other door types. Raised thresholds and floor level changes at doorways should be beveled at a slope no greater than 1 in 2.

DOOR
HOOK STRIP
PAN
WEEP
WEEP
SEALANT

For out-opening door.

INTERLOCKING THRESHOLDS

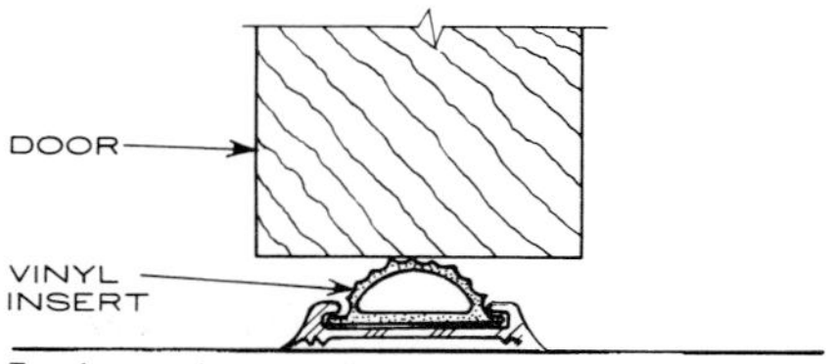

DOOR
VINYL INSERT

For in-opening or out-opening door. For mounting on floor or bottom of door.

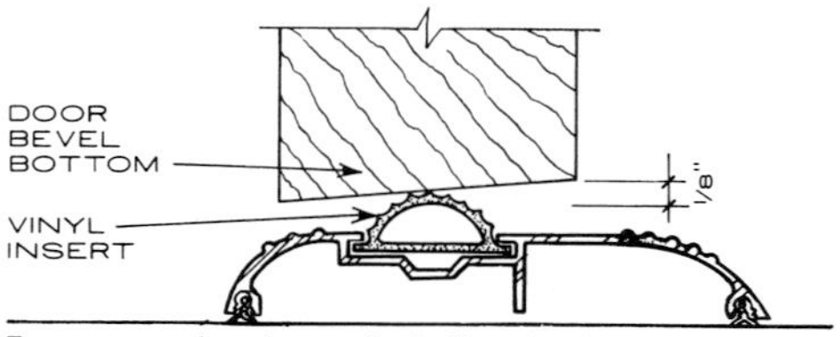

DOOR BEVEL BOTTOM
VINYL INSERT

For out-opening door. A similar threshold is available with weeps and drain pan.

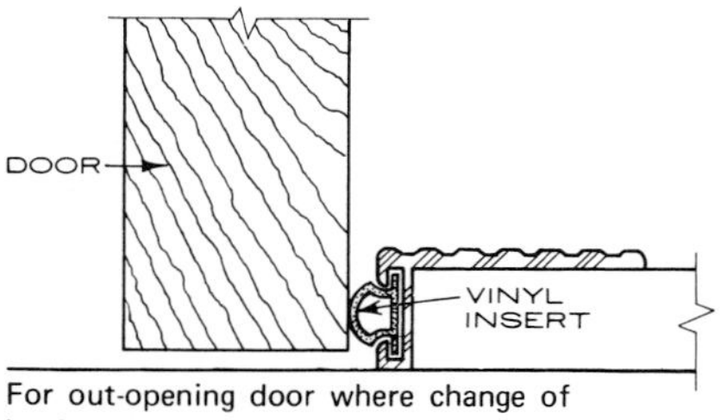

DOOR
VINYL INSERT

For out-opening door where change of level occurs.

DOOR
VINYL INSERT

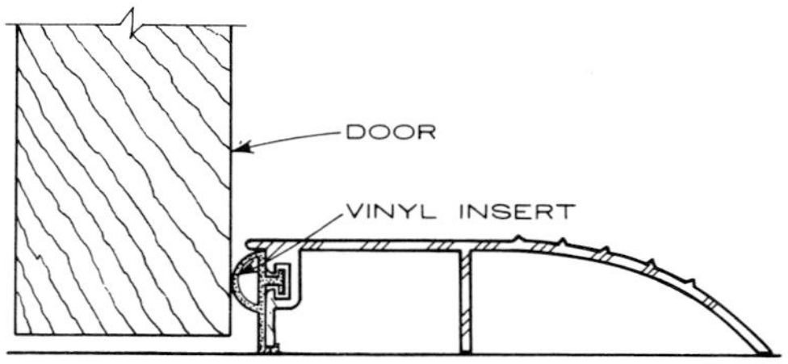

For out-opening doors.

VINYL INSERT THRESHOLDS

DOOR
SEALANT

For out-opening wood door with panic exit hardware.

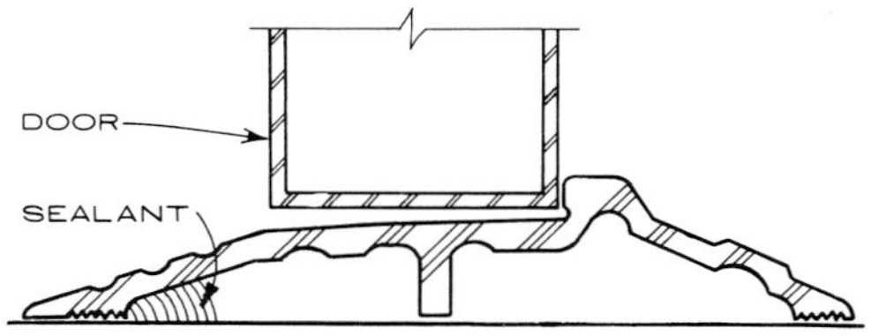

DOOR
SEALANT

For out-opening metal or wood door with panic hardware.

LATCH TRACK THRESHOLDS

DOOR
SEALANT
BUMPER STRIP

For out-opening wood door.

DOOR
SEALANT
BUMPER STRIP

For out-opening metal or wood door.

FLAT SADDLE THRESHOLDS

Dan Cowling & Associates, Inc.; Little Rock, Arkansas

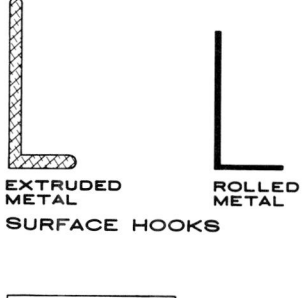

EXTRUDED METAL   ROLLED METAL

SURFACE HOOKS

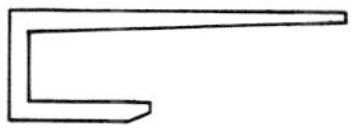

EXTRUDED METAL

ROLLED METAL

CONCEALED HOOKS
INTERLOCKING HOOK STRIPS

NOTE
Hook strips are available in aluminum, brass, bronze, and zinc, and vary in thickness and dimensions. Consult manufacturers' catalogs.

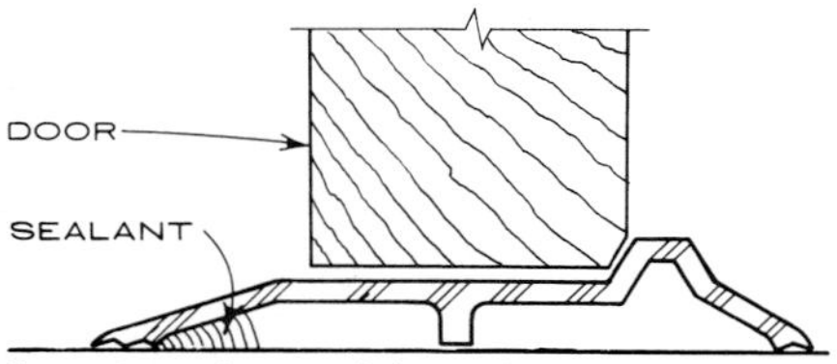

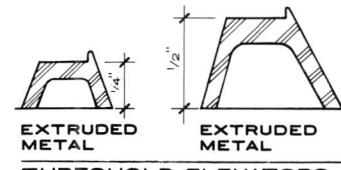

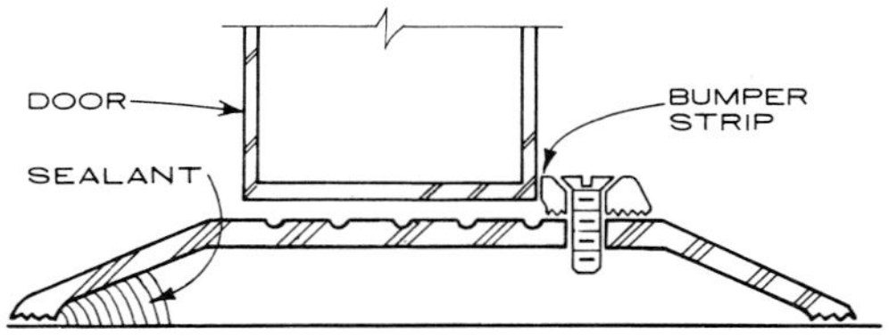

EXTRUDED METAL   EXTRUDED METAL

THRESHOLD ELEVATORS

NOTE
Available in alum. and bronze. Consult manufacturers' catalogs.

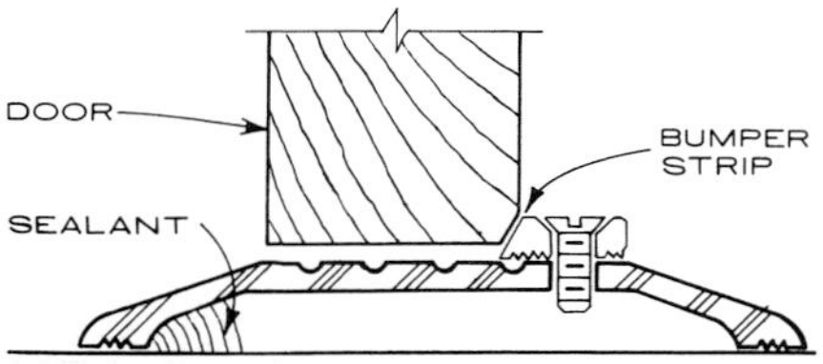

GENERAL NOTE
Thresholds are available in bronze and aluminum with a wide selection of shapes and dimensions.

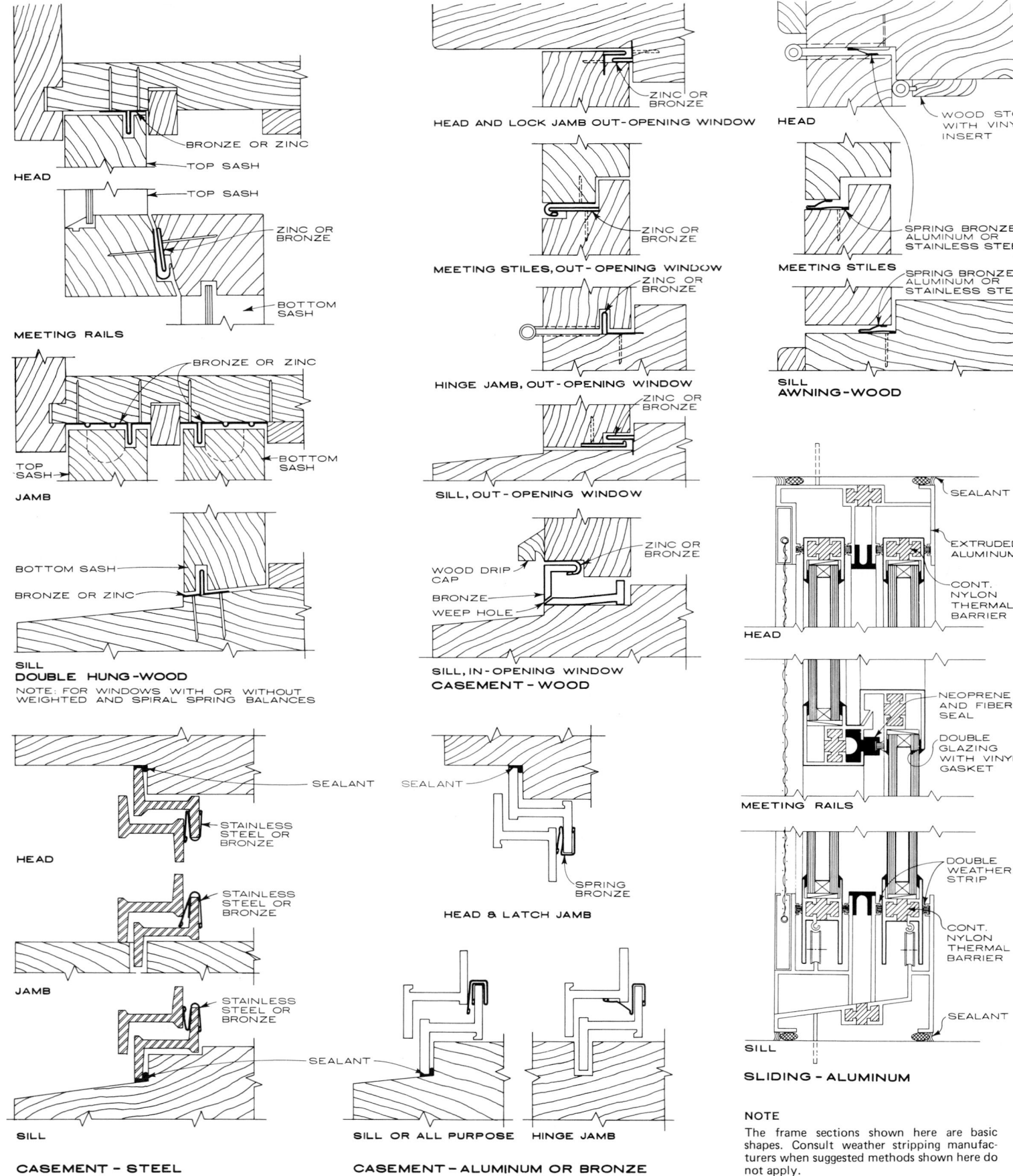

HEAD

BRONZE OR ZINC

TOP SASH

TOP SASH

ZINC OR BRONZE

BOTTOM SASH

MEETING RAILS

BRONZE OR ZINC

TOP SASH

BOTTOM SASH

JAMB

BOTTOM SASH

BRONZE OR ZINC

SILL
DOUBLE HUNG - WOOD
NOTE: FOR WINDOWS WITH OR WITHOUT WEIGHTED AND SPIRAL SPRING BALANCES

HEAD

SEALANT

STAINLESS STEEL OR BRONZE

JAMB

STAINLESS STEEL OR BRONZE

SILL

STAINLESS STEEL OR BRONZE

CASEMENT - STEEL

ZINC OR BRONZE

HEAD AND LOCK JAMB OUT-OPENING WINDOW

ZINC OR BRONZE

MEETING STILES, OUT-OPENING WINDOW

ZINC OR BRONZE

HINGE JAMB, OUT-OPENING WINDOW

ZINC OR BRONZE

SILL, OUT-OPENING WINDOW

WOOD DRIP CAP

ZINC OR BRONZE

BRONZE

WEEP HOLE

SILL, IN-OPENING WINDOW
CASEMENT - WOOD

SEALANT

SEALANT

SPRING BRONZE

HEAD & LATCH JAMB

SEALANT

SILL OR ALL PURPOSE   **HINGE JAMB**

CASEMENT - ALUMINUM OR BRONZE

HEAD

WOOD STOP WITH VINYL INSERT

SPRING BRONZE, ALUMINUM OR STAINLESS STEEL

MEETING STILES

SPRING BRONZE, ALUMINUM OR STAINLESS STEEL

SILL
AWNING - WOOD

SEALANT

EXTRUDED ALUMINUM

CONT. NYLON THERMAL BARRIER

HEAD

NEOPRENE AND FIBER SEAL

DOUBLE GLAZING WITH VINYL GASKET

MEETING RAILS

DOUBLE WEATHER STRIP

CONT. NYLON THERMAL BARRIER

SEALANT

SILL

SLIDING - ALUMINUM

NOTE
The frame sections shown here are basic shapes. Consult weather stripping manufacturers when suggested methods shown here do not apply.

Dan Cowling & Associates, Inc.; Little Rock, Arkansas

GLASS: DEFINITION

A hard, brittle amorphous substance made by fusing silica (sometimes combined with oxides of boron or phosphorus) with certain basic oxides (notably sodium, potassium, calcium, magnesium, and lead) and cooling rapidly to present crystallization or devitrification. Most glasses melt at 800 to 950°C. Heat-resisting glass usually contains a high proportion of boric oxide. The brittleness of glass is such that minute surface scratches in manufacturing greatly reduce its strength.

INDUSTRY QUALITY STANDARDS

ASTM STANDARD C1036: specification for flat glass.

ASTM STANDARD C1048: specification for heat-treated flat glass—Kind HS, Kind FT coated and uncoated glass.

UL STANDARD 752: bullet-resisting material.

UL STANDARD 972: burglary-resisting glazing material.

AAMA STANDARD NO. 12: structural properties of glass, aluminum curtain wall series.

ASTM STANDARD C1300: specification for determining the minimum thickness of annealed glass required to resist a specified load.

CPSC STANDARD 16CFR 1201: standard on architectural glazing materials.

ANSI Z97.1: establishes standards for testing safety glazing material.

INSULATING GLASS CERTIFICATION COUNCIL (IGCC): conducts periodic inspection and independent laboratory tests of insulating glass products.

ASTM STANDARD E546: test method for frost point of sealed insulating glass units in horizontal position.

ASTM STANDARD E576: dew/frost point of sealed insulating glass units in vertical position.

ASTM STANDARD E773: test method for seal durability of sealed insulating glass units.

ASTM STANDARD E774: specification for sealed insulating glass units.

NOTE

Consult glass manufacturers for current information because processes, qualities, finishes, colors, sizes, thicknesses, and limitations are revised continuously. The following information represents one or more manufacturers' guidelines.

BASIC GLASS TYPES (CLEAR GLASS)

WINDOW AND SHEET GLASS

Manufactured by a horizontal flat or vertical draw process, then annealed slowly to produce natural flat fired, high gloss surfaces. Generally has residential and industrial applications. Inherent surface waves are noticeable in sizes larger than 4 sq ft. For minimum distortion, larger sizes are installed with the wave running horizontally. The width is listed first when specifying. Generally, very little glass is produced in the United States by this process. Almost all window and sheet glass is produced by the float process.

FLOAT GLASS

Generally accepted as the successor to polished plate glass, float glass has become the quality standard of the glass industry in architectural, mirror, and specialty applications. It is manufactured by floating molten glass on a surface of molten tin, then annealing slowly to produce a transparent flat glass, thus eliminating grinding and polishing. Float glass is made to the specification requirements of ASTM C1036.

PLATE GLASS

Transparent flat glass is ground and polished after rolling. Within limits, cylindrical and conic shapes can be bent to desired curvature. Only glass for specialty applications is produced by this method.

VARIATIONS OF BASIC GLASS TYPES

PATTERNED GLASS

Known also as rolled or figured glass, patterned glass is made by passing molten glass through rollers that are etched to produce the appropriate design. Most often only one side of the glass is imprinted with a pattern.

WIRE GLASS

Available as clear polished glass or in various patterns, most commonly with embedded welded square or diamond wire. Some distortion, wire discoloration, and misalignment are inherent. Some $1/4$ in. (6 mm) wired glass products are recognized as certified safety glazing materials for use in hazardous locations. For applicable fire and safety codes that govern their use, refer to ANSI Z97.1.

CATHEDRAL GLASS

Known also as art glass, stained glass, or opalescent glass. It is produced in many colors, textures, and patterns; is usually $1/8$ in. thick; and is used primarily in decorating leaded glass windows. Specialty firms usually contract this highly exacting art.

OBSCURE GLASS

To obscure a view or create a design, the entire surface on one or both sides of the glass can be sandblasted, acid etched, or both. When a glass surface is altered by any of these methods, the glass is weakened and may be difficult to clean.

HEAT-ABSORBING OR TINTED GLASS

The glass absorbs a portion of the sun's energy because of admixture contents and thickness. It then dissipates the heat to both the exterior and interior. The exterior glass surface reflects a portion of energy depending on the sun's position. Heat-absorbing glass has a higher temperature when exposed to the sun than clear glass does; thus the central area expands more than the cooler shaded edges, causing edge tensile stress buildup. When designing heat-absorbing or tinted glass windows, consider the following:

1. To minimize shading problems and edge tensile stress buildup, provide conditions so glass edges warm as rapidly as the exposed glass. An example is framing systems with low heat capacity and minimal glass grip or stops. Structural rubber gaskets can be used.
2. The thicker the glass, the greater the solar energy absorption.
3. Indoor shading devices such as blinds and draperies reflect energy back through the glass, thus increasing the glass temperature. Spaces between indoor shading and the glass, including ceiling pockets, should be vented adequately. Heating elements always should be located on the interior side of shading devices, directing warm air away from the glass.
4. The glass can be heat treated to increase its strength and resistance to edge tensile stress buildup.

REFLECTIVE GLASS

Reflective coatings may be applied to float plate, heat strengthened, tempered, laminated, insulated, or spandrel glass, among others. Design considerations for heat-absorbing glass also apply to reflective glass. Reflective glass is available in three basic classifications:

1. Single glazing with a coating on one surface.
2. Laminated glass with the coating between the glass plies or on an exterior surface.
3. Insulating glass units with the coating on an exterior surface or on either of the interior surfaces.

Application of a reflective coating on the exterior surface creates a visually uniform surface on any or all of these glass classifications. Care must be taken in handling, glazing, and cleaning this type of glass to avoid scratching the coating. Some reflective coatings are available only with insulating glass units.

LOW EMISSIVITY GLASS

Low emissivity coatings reflect long-wave room-side infrared energy back to interior spaces, reducing the glazing U-value. Soft coat low emissivity coatings must be used in an insulating glass unit, and hard coat (pyrolitic) low emissivity coatings can be exposed on the glass surface. In general, low emissivity coatings do not provide as good a summer shading coefficient as reflective coated glass; they do provide much better winter U-values. Low emissivity coatings have low reflectivity, in some cases lower than the equivalent uncoated glass product. Design considerations for heat-absorbing glass also apply to low emissivity glass.

HEAT-TREATED GLASS

Heat-strengthened and tempered glass are produced by reheating and rapidly cooling annealed glass. Both have greatly increased mechanical strength and resistance to thermal stresses. Neither type can be altered after fabrication; the manufacturer must furnish the exact size and shape. The inherent warpage may cause glazing problems. Refer to ASTM C1048 for allowable tolerances and other properties.

HEAT STRENGTHENED GLASS: Twice as strong as annealed glass. Unlike tempered glass, it does not pulverize into crystal-like form when broken.

TEMPERED GLASS: Four to five times the strength of annealed glass; it breaks into innumerable small, cubed fragments. It can be much safer than annealed glass. Shallow patterned glass also may be tempered. Tong marks are visible near the edge on the short side when the glass is held vertically during tempering. Most manufacturers temper horizontally to eliminate these marks. Strain patterns are inherent and can be seen under some lighting conditions or through polarizing material.

SPANDREL GLASS

Available as reflective, ceramic frit (patterned and solid colors), direct-to-glass polyvinylidene fluoride (Kynar 500 resin) coatings, and tinted. Can be heat treated or laminated and available as insulating glass units. Insulation and vapor retarders can be added to spandrel glass; however, consult with spandrel glass manufacturer for guidelines.

SOUND CONTROL GLASS

Laminated, insulating, laminated insulating, and double laminated insulating glass products commonly are used for sound control. STC ratings from 31 to 51 are available depending on glass thicknesses, air space size, polyvinyl butyral film thickness, and the number of laminated units used in insulating products.

LAMINATED SAFETY GLASS

A tough, clear plastic polyvinyl butyral sheet (interlayer), ranging in thickness from 0.015 to 0.090 in. (0.381 to 2.3 mm), is sandwiched, under heat and pressure, between plies of sheet, plate, float, wired, heat-absorbing, tinted, reflective, low emissivity, heat-treated glass, or combinations of each. When fractured, particles tend to adhere to the plastic film. Safety glass should be manufactured to comply with ANSI Z97.1 and CPSC 16CFR 1201. (See also Wire Glass, Mirrors.)

SECURITY GLASS

Safety glass with a plastic film of 0.060 in. (1.5 mm) minimum thickness for bullet-resistant (UL 752) and burglar-resistant (UL 972) glass. Bullet-resistant glass consists of three to five plies of glass and, in some cases, high performance plastics, with an overall $3/4$ in. to 3 in. thickness. Avoid sealants with organic solvents or oil, which can react with the plastic film. (See Glazing with Plastic.)

GLAZING ASSEMBLIES

General considerations:

1. Differential thermal movement between frame and glass.
2. Deflection, vertical framing members.
3. Deflection, horizontal framing members.
4. Clearances, shims, drainage, setting blocks.

Thermal movement of the glazing material and stresses the glazing system must withstand are determined by

1. Size of light to be glazed.
2. Minimum and maximum surface temperatures for glazing materials.
3. Sealed insulating units (hotter trapped air). Consult manufacturer and ASTM C1300 and AAMA Standard No. 12 for load capacity information.

Some factors affecting transfer of wind loads to the surrounding structure are

1. Proportion and size of opening, span between supports, and thickness and deflection of glass.
2. Method of support for the glass pane.
3. Movement of the surrounding structure.
4. Setting blocks placed under bottom edge of glass.
5. Spacer shims—to assure proper clearances between face of glazing material and framing channels.
6. Squareness and flatness tolerances of the surrounding glazing channel.

Thomas F. O'Connor, AIA, FASTM; Smith, Hinchman & Grylls; Detroit, Michigan

INSULATING GLASS

Insulating glass, with high performance in thermal resistance and shading coefficient, is used primarily to control heat transfer. Insulating glass units are manufactured from two or more pieces of glass separated by a hermetically sealed air space. Two unit types are available:

1. GLASS EDGE OR GLASS SEAL UNIT: Primarily for residential use. Constructed by fusing edges of two glass lights together with 3/16 in. (5 mm) space filled with a dry gas at atmospheric pressure. Use at high altitudes is not recommended. Do not glaze with lock-strip structural gaskets.

2. ORGANIC SEALED EDGE UNIT: Primarily for commercial and industrial use, as well as for some residential applications. Constructed with two sheets of glass separated by a metal or organic spacer (filled with a moisture absorbing material) around the edges and hermetically sealed. Insulating units should be fabricated to ASTM E546, E576, EE773, and E774 standards.

Available with 1/4 and 1/2 in. airspace in float, patterned, heat absorbing, tinted, reflective coated, annealed, heat-strengthened, tempered, and laminated glass. The thickness of the two glass panes, however, should not differ by more than 1/16 in. The criteria for selecting glass units are appearance, solar-optical properties, thermodynamic properties, and cost.

The heat absorbing glass of a heat absorbing unit should be to the exterior. When sloped insulated glazing is used over occupied areas, heat-strengthened, laminated glass is advisable as the interior light; however, the glass manufacturer and governing codes and authorities on fire and safety should be consulted. Insulated glass units are manufactured in standard maximum sizes up to approximately 84 x 144 in. with a maximum area of 72 sq ft and minimum sizes of approximately 12 x 24 in. Triple glazing units are available for special applications.

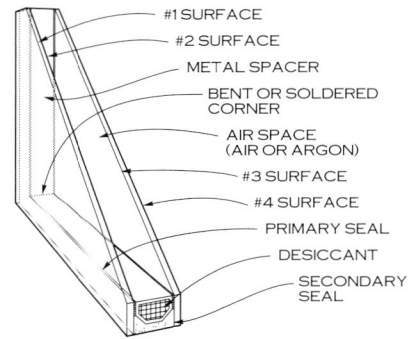

INSULATING GLASS UNIT

REFLECTIVE AND ENERGY EFFICIENT COATINGS

PYROLITIC REFLECTIVE COATING: This coating is applied when the glass is made, allowing the glass to be tempered after the coating is applied. The advantage to this coating is that it is hard and durable and can be applied to surface number 1. The disadvantages are the limited number of coating types available and the poorer thermal, solar, and optical performance.

SPUTTERED REFLECTIVE COATING: This coating is applied after the glass is made. The advantages of this coating are the flexibility of coating types that can be used, a good shading coefficient, and a more universal or more uniform appearance. The disadvantage is that the glass needs to be heat-strengthened before coating. A sputtered coating is affected by the elements and must be used inside the airspace on surface numbers 2 or 3.

LOW EMISSIVE COATING: These coatings are applied to the glass to reflect long-wave room-side infrared energy back in the room. This reduces the U-value while maximizing the amount of natural light allowed in a space. These coatings are generally applied to surface numbers 2 or 3 by either the sputtered or pyrolitic process. The sputtered application gives the best performance with a clearer view and less haze.

Reflective coatings are metallic coatings of stainless steel, titanium, gold, or copper. These coatings can be applied to clear or tinted glass. Tinted glass is generally available in gray, bronze, blue, green, or combinations of these colors.

NOTES

1. Basic industry requirements for insulating glass units are adhesion to required substrates, resistance to ultraviolet attack, unaffected by temperature extremes, resistance to water immersion, resistance to chemical attack of glazing compounds, resistance to cold flow, and resistance to moisture vapor.

2. Insulating glass units fail for the following reasons: edge stress; ultraviolet attack; internal condensation resulting from loss of adhesion of secondary and/or primary seal

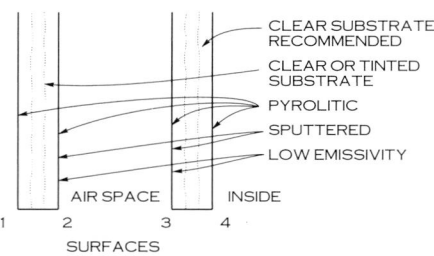

PREFERRED COATING LOCATIONS

to glass, poor corner construction, moisture through seals, or degradation of sealants.

3. Thermodynamic performance considerations for insulating glass units are summer solar heat gain through the glass; winter conducted heat loss through the glass; summer, spring, fall conducted heat gain/loss; infiltration, exfiltration, and ventilation; use of daylight in place of artificial lighting, and building orientation, geometry, and siting.

4. Thermal stresses from solar and interior heat sources can build up in insulating glass units and cause breakage. The following design considerations can help to minimize thermal stresses: building orientation; sizes and shapes of glass units (large lites with large edge areas are more susceptible); indoor shading elements such as blinds or draperies that can trap solar heat between the shading element and the glass; location of heating registers; location of outdoor shading devices such as balconies, awnings, trees, and shrubbery that can cause irregular heating of glass; and heat absorbing capacity of framing systems.

5. Glass units must be designed to withstand certain windloads as determined by building codes. The factors to be considered include geometry of the glass, fabrication techniques, support condition provided by the framing, and type and rate of wind loading.

6. The solar-optical performance of glass units affects the appearance of the building, the comfort of the occupants, and the cost of artificial lighting. Design criteria to be considered are: daylighting requirements; ratio of window to floor areas; interior clutter from random positioning of shading elements or furniture (lower glass transmittances can mask exterior view of clutter); views to the outside (amount of light transmittance of the glass can affect the quality of the outside view); glare/reflectance on computer screens (lower glass transmittances can reduce glare); local climate (fewer sunny days or northern climate may suggest glass with a higher light transmittance); building orientation; and relationship between vision glass and spandrel glass.

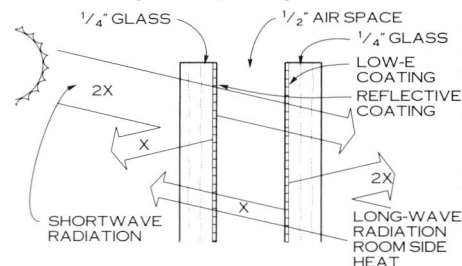

ENERGY DIAGRAM

PERFORMANCE DATA FOR INSULATED GLASS UNITS

		VISIBLE LIGHT		SOLAR RADIATION		U - VALUE		RELATIVE HEAT GAIN SUMMER	SHADING COEFFICIENTS		
		PERCENT TRANSMITTED	PERCENT REFLECTED	PERCENT TRANSMITTED	PERCENT REFLECTED	WINTER	SUMMER		NO SHADING	LIGHT BLINDS	WHITE SHADES
Clear + clear		78 - 82	14 - 15	60 - 76	11 - 15	0.42 - 0.61	169 - 192	0.51 - 0.62	0.79 - 0.92	0.44 - 0.51	0.25
Clear + low-e		49 - 86	12 - 15	17 - 56	17 - 25	0.23 - 0.52	133 - 157	0.28 - 0.54	0.23 - 0.78		
Clear + tinted	green	62 - 78	12 - 14	36 - 62	8 - 12	0.49 - 0.58	116 - 161	0.52 - 0.62	0.54 - 0.76	0.35 - 0.45	0.22
	gray	13 - 56	5 - 13	22 - 56	7 - 9	0.49 - 0.60	74 - 152	0.51 - 0.62	0.33 - 0.71		
	bronze	19 - 62	8 - 13	26 - 57	8 - 9	0.49 - 0.60	76 - 152	0.50 - 0.64	0.25 - 0.73		
	blue	50 - 64	8 - 13	38 - 56	7 - 9	0.49 - 0.58	120 - 154	0.52 - 0.53	0.56 - 0.73		
Clear + coated	silver	7 - 19	22 - 41	5 - 14	18 - 34	0.39 - 0.48	36 - 59	0.43 - 0.52	0.14 - 0.36	0.15 - 0.40	
	blue	12 - 27	16 - 32	12 - 18	15 - 20	0.42 - 0.46	58 - 73	0.44 - 0.54	0.25 - 0.33		
	bronze	7 - 18	14 - 54	5 - 16	13 - 24	0.39 - 0.50	38 - 70	0.40 - 0.54	0.15 - 0.31		
	copper	25	30 - 31	12	45	0.29 - 0.30	44	0.29 - 0.30	0.20		
	gold	7 - 13	42 - 59	3 - 6	42 - 49	0.32 - 0.39	30	0.32 - 0.35	0.13		
Green + coated	silver	6 - 16	17 - 41	3 - 8	13 - 19	0.41 - 0.45	37 - 51	0.43 - 0.53	0.15 - 0.22		
	blue	15 - 24	13 - 32	8 - 12	11 - 13	0.42 - 0.46	50 - 62	0.44 - 0.54	0.21 - 0.27		
Blue + coated	silver	5 - 11	12 - 38	3 - 7	10 - 17	0.41 - 0.45	37 - 51	0.43 - 0.53	0.15 - 0.22		
	blue	5 - 17	9 - 36	3 - 11	6 - 16	0.42 - 0.47	39 - 60	0.46 - 0.55	0.16 - 0.26		
Bronze + coated	silver	5 - 11	11 - 41	3 - 8	11 - 15	0.41 - 0.45	37 - 52	0.43 - 0.53	0.16 - 0.22		
Bronze + low-e		35 - 56	7 - 26	23 - 43	8 - 18	0.31 - 0.43	74 - 101	0.30 - 0.47	0.35 - 0.47		
Grey + coated	silver	4 - 9	9 - 41	3 - 7	10 - 14	0.41 - 0.45	37 - 50	0.43 - 0.53	0.15 - 0.21		

NOTES

1. Winter U-value: Outside = 0°F, 15 mph wind, inside = 70°F. Summer U-value: Outside = 90°F, 7.5 mph wind, inside = 75°F.

2. Relative heat gain = heat gain due to conduction plus heat gain due to solar radiation when outside = 80°F

with a 7.5 mph wind and inside = 75°F with a solar intensity of 200 Btu/hr/sq ft.

3. Shading coefficient is the ratio of the total solar heat gain through the insulating glass to the total solar gain through a standard sheet of clear glass under exactly the same conditions. It is a dimensionless number with a val-

ue from zero to one: the smaller the value of the shading coefficient, the better the glazing is at stopping the entry of solar radiation.

4. Reprinted by permission of McGraw-Hill; New York, NY, from *1991 Sweet's Selection Data*, pp. 5-42, 5-43.

McCain McMurray, Architect; Washington, D.C.
Laurence Saint Germain; DeStefano + Partners; Chicago, Illinois

GLAZING

LEADED STAINED GLASS

Decorative stained glass is characterized by pieces of glass joined together with cames (H-shaped strips) of various widths. Varying the widths adds to the window's decorative effect. Joints are soldered on both sides of the panel. To prevent leakage, a mastic waterproofing material is inserted between the glass and came flange.

Another method of joining the pieces of glass is banding the edges of the glass with a copper foil tape burnished to the glass and then soldered with a continuous bead of solder on both sides.

Bracing bars are fastened to the sash at frequent intervals to strengthen and support the leaded glass. Round bars tied to the leaded glass with twisted copper wires are the most flexible and resilient, allowing for great amounts of thermal movement. Where this system is not suitable, galvanized steel flat bars can be soldered to the surface of the leaded glass.

When the glass requires detail painting, shading, or texturing, it must be done with special mineral pigments and fired at temperatures of 1000 to 1200°F or higher to ensure absolute permanency.

INSTALLATION

It is recommended that decorative glass be installed into specially designed metal frames provided with glazing beads and sealed with a modern flexible glazing material. However, with proper maintenance, high-quality wood frames with suitable division bars are acceptable.

A stained glass studio should be consulted for the location of division bars, mullions, and muntins to best complement the artistic design. Decorative glass weighs approximately 4 lb/ sq ft.

OUTSIDE PROTECTION GLASS

Properly made decorative glass does not necessarily need additional glazing to make it waterproof, but it is valuable for insulating purposes and to afford some protection from external damage. Frames should be designed with a ³/₄ in. ventilated space between glass and should be arranged for the protection glass to be installed from the exterior and the decorative glass from the interior. Clear glass or textured glass ³/₁₆ to ¹/₄ in. thick is most successful.

Depending on geographic location and economics, insulating glass should be considered as the protective outside glazing.

Acrylic and polycarbonate are two types of plastic protection material that can be employed when protection from vandalism is needed. Outside protection glass should be installed by the stained glass studio whenever possible to ensure an integrated system.

GLAZING SEALANTS

Exterior decorative glass must be pressed into a deep back bed of mastic compound or glazing tape. When outside protection glass is used, a watertight seal is not required, and foam tape compressed between the glazing bead and glass may suffice.

SIZE LIMITATIONS

Decorative glass panels should not exceed 12 sq ft, making it necessary to divide larger openings with metal division bars: tee bars for single glazed windows, and special channel bars for windows with outside protection glass.

GLASS COLORS

Machine-made and blown glass from the United States, England, France, and Germany are available in most solid colors; also mixed colors and textures. Uniformity of color will vary from glass of different batches. Special colors are derived by "sumping," or kiln firing.

WORKERS' PROTECTION

Work in decorative glass studios involves handling and storage of many toxic substances and waste such as lead, fluxes, patinas, cleaners, and solvents. The Occupational Safety and Health Administration has established guidelines for use by studios, including blood testing, cleaning, air purification, respirators, work clothing, and toxic waste handling.

Randall S. Lindstrom, AIA; Ware Associates, Inc.; Chicago, Illinois
Joseph A. Wilkes, FAIA; Annapolis, Maryland
Bobbie Burnett Studio; Annapolis, Maryland

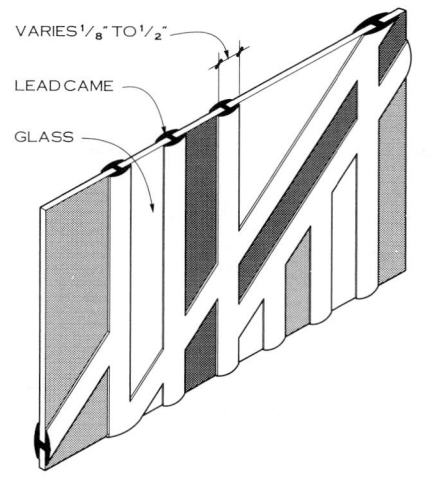

DECORATIVE GLASS PANELS

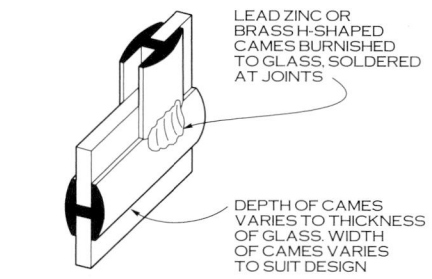

H-SHAPED CAME METHOD

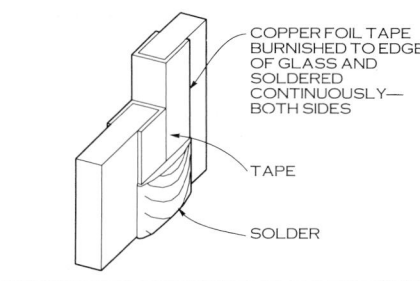

COPPER FOIL METHOD

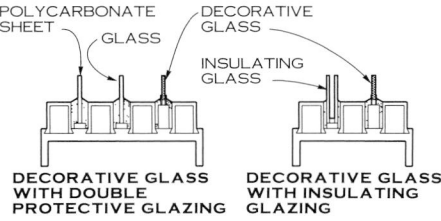

ALUMINUM FRAMES FOR DECORATIVE GLASS

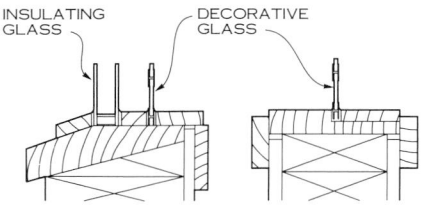

WOOD FRAMES FOR DECORATIVE GLASS

FACETED STAINED GLASS

A 20th century development in the art of stained glass introduced the use of glass dalles 8 x 12 x 1 in., cast in hundreds of different colors that can be cut to any shape and used, in combination with opaque matrix of epoxy resin or reinforced concrete ⁵/₈ to 1 in. in thickness, to create translucent windows and walls of great beauty.

SIZE LIMITATIONS

No single panel of faceted glass should exceed 16 sq ft. The length to width ratio of each panel should not exceed 4:1. Large openings must have horizontal supports to support the weight of stacked panels. When panels are to be stacked vertically, a minimum matrix thickness of ³/₄ in. is recommended. Joints between panels should be sealed with flexible caulking, as described below.

INSTALLATION

Faceted glass can be installed in frames of masonry, metal, or wood. Frames must be detailed to support the weight of the glass and matrix (approximately 10 to 13 lb/sq ft) and the thicker edge of epoxy panels. A stained glass studio should be consulted for the location of division bars and mullions to coordinate with the design.

OUTSIDE PROTECTION GLASS

Because of its high resistance to breakage, waterproof construction, and excellent insulating qualities, faceted glass does not usually need outer glazing. If protection is required, ³/₄ to 1 in. ventilated space between the outer surface of the faceted glass and the inside surface of the protection glass is recommended. Divisions in the protection glass should be designed by the artist to complement the design.

GLAZING SEALANTS

Faceted glass panels should be set into a non-hardening caulking such as butyl, acrylic, silicone, or polysulfide, used both as a bedding and finish bead. For spaces in excess of ¹/₄ in. between faceted glass and frame, fillers such as ethafoam are recommended under the caulking bead. A clearance of ³/₁₆ in. should be allowed between frame and panel edge for proper expansion and contraction. Neoprene spacers are used to ensure proper clearance.

Further information is available from the Stained Glass Association of America.

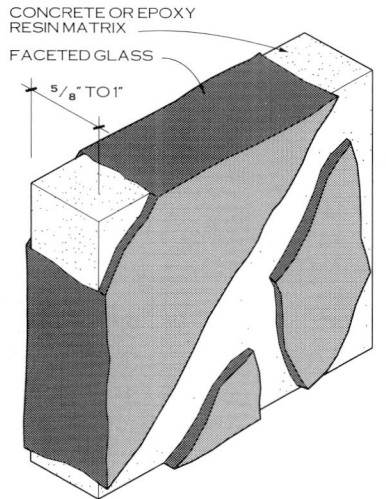

FACETED STAINED GLASS

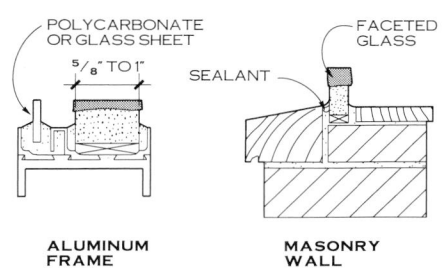

FACETED GLASS WITH PROTECTIVE GLAZING

ACRYLIC PLASTIC AND POLYCARBONATE SHEETS

Both materials are relatively tough, break-, shatter-, or crack-resistant thermoplastics. They are commonly used in the clear transparent form for glazing in schools, factories, skylights, domes, display cases, and protective shields for stained glass assemblies. Certain conditions of varying temperatures and/or humidity on opposing surfaces of a single light may cause it to bow in the direction of the higher temperature and/or humidity. Though this does not affect visibility, it may cause distorted reflections. The surfaces of these materials are susceptible to scratching and abrasions. Abrasive/graffiti-resistant coatings are available, but may cause a distortion in optic quality. As compared with clear glass of equal size and thickness, they maintain greater resistance to impact and breakage and are lighter in weight. Polycarbonates have softer surfaces and are more impact-resistant than acrylics. Acrylics generally weather better than polycarbonates. Because of a somewhat higher coefficient of thermal expansion than in clear glass and other materials with which they are used in construction, acrylics and polycarbonates are subject to a greater degree of dimensional change. In applications that must allow for wide ranges of thermal expansion, avoid inflexible installation methods. Both may be produced with or without light absorbing properties. The allowable continuous service temperature for polycarbonates is slightly higher than that for acrylics. Both may be cold formed to a smooth arc if the resulting radius of curvature is at least 100 times the thickness of the sheet for polycarbonates (180 times for acrylics) and both are supported by curved channel supports following this radius.

Mirrored coatings applied to acrylic sheets are available for interior applications and may be installed with recommended contact cements, double faced tape, clip and channel mounting, and through fastening. Distortion problems indicate that they should not be used for precise image reflectance requirements.

Certain polycarbonate sheets may be used in some bullet resisting and burglar resisting applications.

Consult the manufacturers for current information. Plastics are combustible and cannot be used in fire resistance rated assemblies. Refer to and adhere to all applicable codes and governing authorities on fire and safety.

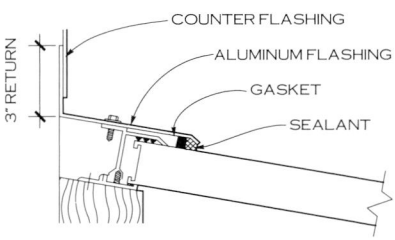

PARAPET/WALL

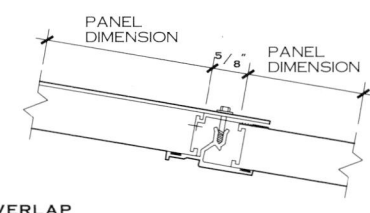

OVERLAP

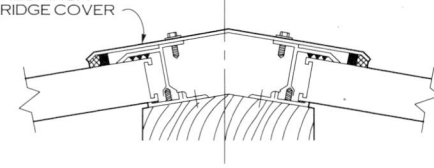

RIDGE

SKYROOF SYSTEM DETAILS

Laurence Saint Germain, AIA; DeStefano + Partners; Chicago, Illinois

POLYCARBONATE GLAZING

	POLY-CAR-BONATE SHEET THICK-NESS	SHORT DIMEN-SION	RABBET DEPTH
Small lights	1/8"	24"	1/2"
Intermediate lights	3/16"	36"	3/4"
	1/4"	48"	3/4"
Large lights	3/8"	60"	1"
	1/2"	72"	1"

NOTES

1. Rabbet width is determined by sheet thickness plus sealant and tape as recommended by sealant tape manufacturers.
2. To select polycarbonate sheet thickness based on wind loads, refer to manufacturers' information.

SMALL ACRYLIC LIGHTS

Maximum dimension to 24 in.
Minimum thickness - 0.100 in.
Minimum rabbet depth 9/32 in.

INTERMEDIATE ACRYLIC LIGHTS

ACRYLIC THICK-NESS	MAXIMUM SASH OPENING		RABBET DIMENSIONS	
	SQUARE	RECTAN-GULAR	DEPTH	WIDTH
0.125"	40" x 40"	30" x 42"	1/2"	3/8"
0.125"	55" x 55"	36" x 68"	3/4"	3/8"
0.187"	42" x 42"	30" x 45"	1/2"	7/16"
0.187"	63" x 63"	36" x 72"	3/4"	7/16"
0.250"	44" x 44"	30" x 46"	1/2"	1/2"
0.250"	69" x 69"	36" x 72"	3/4"	1/2"

LARGE ACRYLIC LIGHTS

ACRYLIC THICKNESS	LONG DIMENSIONS	RABBET DIMENSIONS	
		DEPTH	WIDTH
0.187"	57" to 85"	3/4"	7/16"
0.250"	78" to 96"	1"	5/8"
0.250"	108" to 144"	1 1/8"	3/4"
0.375"	72" to 108"	1"	3/4"
0.375"	108" to 144"	1 1/8"	7/8"
0.500"	114" to 144"	1 1/8"	1"

NOTE

When darker (less than 60% light transmittance) transparent tints of acrylic plastic are used, rabbet depth shown above should be increased by 1/4 in. to allow for greater thermal expansion resulting from solar energy absorption.

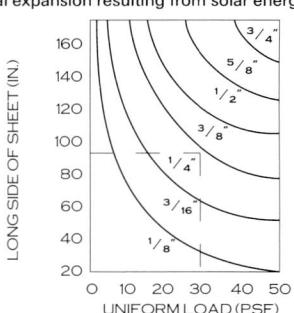

ACRYLIC GLAZING GRAPH

DESIGN LOAD DATA — LARGE AREA ACRYLIC GLAZING

Problem:
Size = 48 x 96 in.
Design load = 30 psf

Solution:
Select 1/4 in. sheet thickness

Data apply to square and rectangular lights of acrylic sheets when the length is no more than three times the width. All edges continuously held.

Sheet thickness section is based on total deflection under uniform load limited to 5% of the short side, or 3 in., whichever is smaller.

COMPARISON OF COEFFICIENTS OF THERMAL EXPANSION

BUILDING MATERIAL	INCHES/INCH/°F
Glass	0.0000050
Aluminum	0.0000129
Polycarbonate	0.0000375
Acrylic	0.0000410[1]
Steel	0.0000063

NOTE

1. Eight times greater than glass.

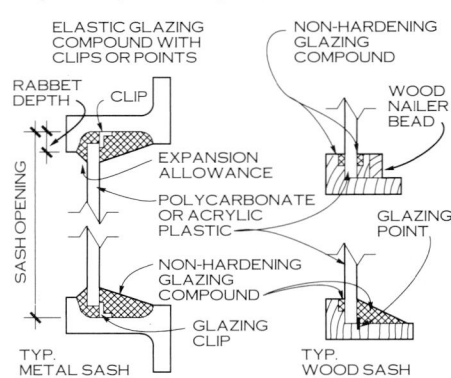

SMALL LIGHTS (WET GLAZING SYSTEM)

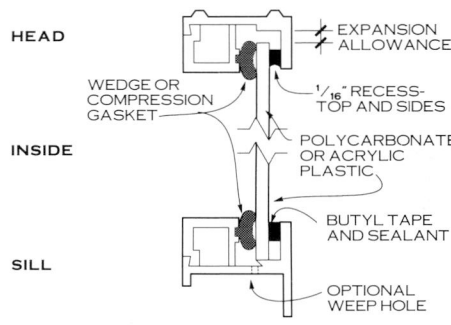

INTERMEDIATE LIGHTS (WET/DRY GLAZING SYSTEM)

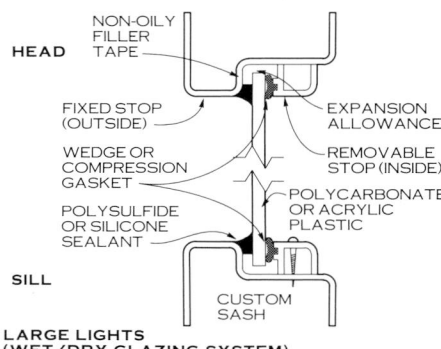

LARGE LIGHTS (WET/DRY GLAZING SYSTEM)

PLASTIC GLAZING DETAILS

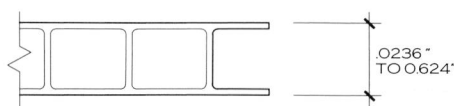

.0236" TO 0.624"

NOTES

1. Double skinned panel available in acrylic and polycarbonate.
2. Less weight than double-pane glass systems.
3. Ribs must run vertically. Curves in direction of ribs possible.

DOUBLE SKINNED PANEL

GENERAL NOTES

1. Information on this page is representative of industry recommendations for vertical glazing applications (within 15° of vertical). Consult with the applicable manufacturers and fabricators for specific applications or for applications at greater than 15° from vertical.
2. It is good practice to glaze at temperatures above 40°F (4°C) to preclude condensation and frost contamination of surfaces that will receive sealants. For sealant glazing below 40°F (4°C), consult the glazing sealant manufacturer.
3. Glazing materials should not be installed more than one day in advance of glass placement to avoid potential damage to the glazing materials by other trades or contamination of the materials.

4. Glazing materials used with high-performance reflective coated glass may require the consideration of additional factors for the glazing materials.
5. Glass should always be cushioned in the glazing opening by resilient glazing materials and should also be free to "float in the opening" so there is no direct contact of the glass with the perimeter framing system.
6. For glazing of polycarbonate and acrylic plastic sheet, particular attention should be given to thermal movement of the sheet and adhesion and compatibility of the sheet with glazing materials, as well as proper preparation of the glazing opening. Consult the manufacturer or fabricator for glazing recommendations.

7. Insulating, wired, and laminated glass must be installed in glazing pockets that are weeped to the exterior to preclude the detrimental effects of moisture.
8. For large glass lites the deflection characteristics of the glass should be investigated to preclude detrimental deflection which can cause glazing seal failure and glass breakage by contact of an edge or corner with the framing.
9. For setting and edge block requirements for casement, vertically pivoted and horizontally pivoted windows refer to the Flat Glass Marketing Association (FGMA) Glazing Manual.

SETTING BLOCK NOTES

1. Blocks should always be wider than the thickness of glass or panel, no more or less than two per glass or panel, and of identical material.
2. For glass using the alternate method, verify acceptability of method with glass manufacturer or fabricator.
3. Setting block length per block
   a. Neoprene, EPDM, or silicone block = 0.1 in./sq ft of glass area; never less than 4 in. long.
   b. Lead block = 0.05 in./sq ft of glass area; never less than 4 in. long.
   c. Lock-strip gasket block = 0.5 in./sq ft of glass area; never less than 6 in. long.
4. For neoprene, EPDM, or silicone blocks, the material should be 85 ± 5 shore A durometer.
5. Lead blocks should never be used with laminated, insulating, or wired glass or in lock-strip gaskets, nor should they be used with glass less than ½ in. thick.

SETTING BLOCK LOCATIONS

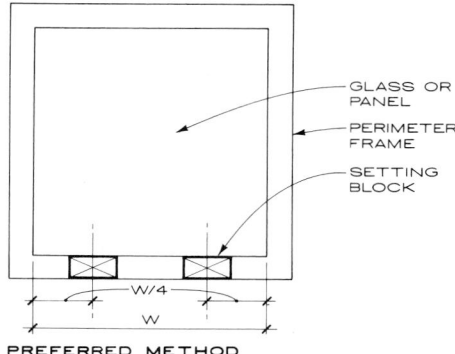

PREFERRED METHOD

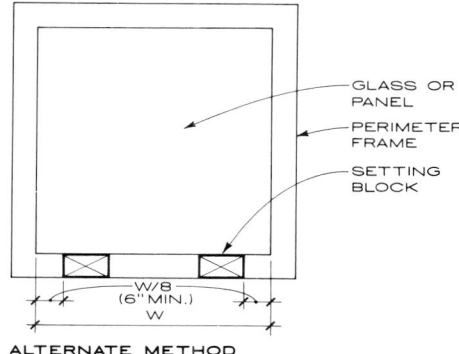

ALTERNATE METHOD

EDGE BLOCK NOTES

1. Edge blocking is used to limit lateral movement of the glass or panel caused by horizontal thermal movement, building vibration, and other causes.
2. Method A is preferred.
3. Material should be neoprene, EPDM, or silicone rubber.
4. Hardness should be 65 ± 5 shore A durometer.
5. Blocks should be a minimum of 4 in. long.
6. Blocks should be placed in vertical frame spaces.
7. Blocks should be sized to permit a nominal ⅛ in. of clearance between the edge of the glass or panel and the block.

EDGE BLOCK LOCATIONS

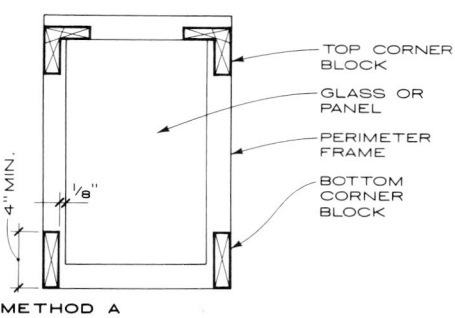

METHOD A

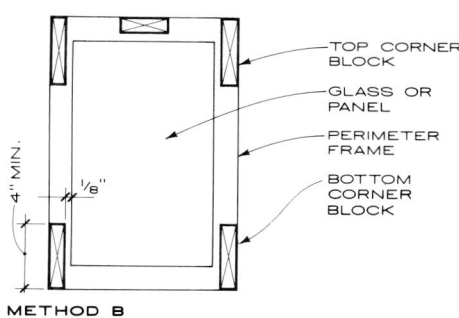

METHOD B

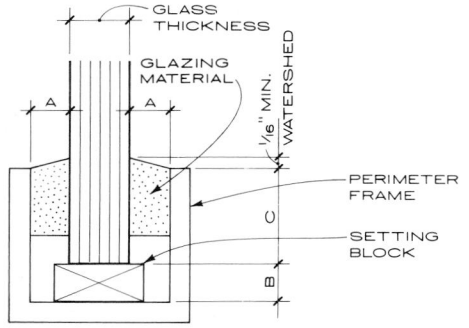

NOTES

1. The typical clearances indicated in the adjacent table may vary by glass manufacturer or fabricator, particularly for special products or applications. Consult the glass manufacturer, fabricator, and sealing material supplier for those conditions.
2. The permissible bow and warp of large lites of heat-strengthened and tempered glass can be substantial, which may require extra face clearance.

TYPICAL FACE AND EDGE CLEARANCE AND BITE

GLASS THICKNESS		MINIMUM CLEARANCES		
IN.	MM	A = FACE	B = EDGE	C = BITE
MONOLITHIC GLASS				
SS*	2.5	1/16	1/8	1/4
1/8 – DS†	3	1/8	1/8	1/4
1/8 – DS‡	3	1/8	1/4	3/8
3/16†	5	1/8	3/16	5/16
3/16‡	5	1/8	1/4	3/8
1/4	6	1/8	1/4	3/8
5/16	8	3/16	5/16	7/16
3/8	10	3/16	5/16	7/16
1/2	12	1/4	3/8	7/16
5/8	15	1/4	3/8	1/2
3/4	19	1/4	1/2	5/8
7/8	22	1/4	1/2	3/4
INSULATING GLASS				
1/2	12	1/8	1/8	1/2
5/8	15	1/8	1/8	1/2
3/4	19	3/16	1/4	1/2
1	25	3/16	1/4	1/2
CERAMIC COATED SPANDREL GLASS				
1/4	6	3/16	1/4	1/2

*SS, Single strength; DS, double strength.
†Annealed glass only.
‡Tempered glass only.

FACE AND EDGE CLEARANCE AND BITE

Thomas F. O'Connor, AIA, FASTM; Smith, Hinchman & Grylls; Detroit, Michigan

GLAZING SYSTEMS NOTES

1. Only rubber materials formulated to recognized standards and of proven durability such as neoprene, EPDM; and silicone should be used for gaskets and blocking.
2. At least two ¼ to ⅜ in. diameter weep holes for the glazing pocket per glass lite or panel are necessary with access to weep holes not prevented by setting blocks or sealants.
3. Glazing compound or putty should not be used to glaze laminated or insulating glass in openings.
4. Sealants in contact or close proximity to gaskets, rubber blocking, insulating glass edge seals, and other sealants must be compatible with those materials to preclude loss of adhesion or lessened durability. Consult with the sealant manufacturer.

5. Sealant must be compatible with the insulating glass edge seal and the polyvinyl butyral laminate of laminated glass to preclude failure of the edge seal or delamination and discoloration of the laminate.
6. The dry glazing method requires careful design and control of tolerances of the frame opening and glazing materials to ensure the development of adequate compression sealing pressure (generally 4–10 lb/lin in. to achieve weathertightness.
7. Closed cell gaskets for dry glazing should have molded or vulcanized corners as the preferred method so as to form a continuous, joint-free glazing material around all sides of the opening.
8. The following table lists sources for specifications and installation practices for glazing materials which should be consulted when designing and specifying.

LOCK-STRIP GASKET NOTES

1. Lock-strip gasket glazing requires careful design and control of framing, gasket, and glazing tolerances to achieve the anticipated weather sealing pressures and structural capacity to resist lateral loads.
2. The best weather sealing performance is achieved with a continuous gasket having factory-formed, injection-molded joints.
3. Concrete gasket lugs require a draft on some surface of the lug to facilitate mold removal. Draft is permissible either on the sides or on top (preferred), not both. Draft on top should slope to the exterior.

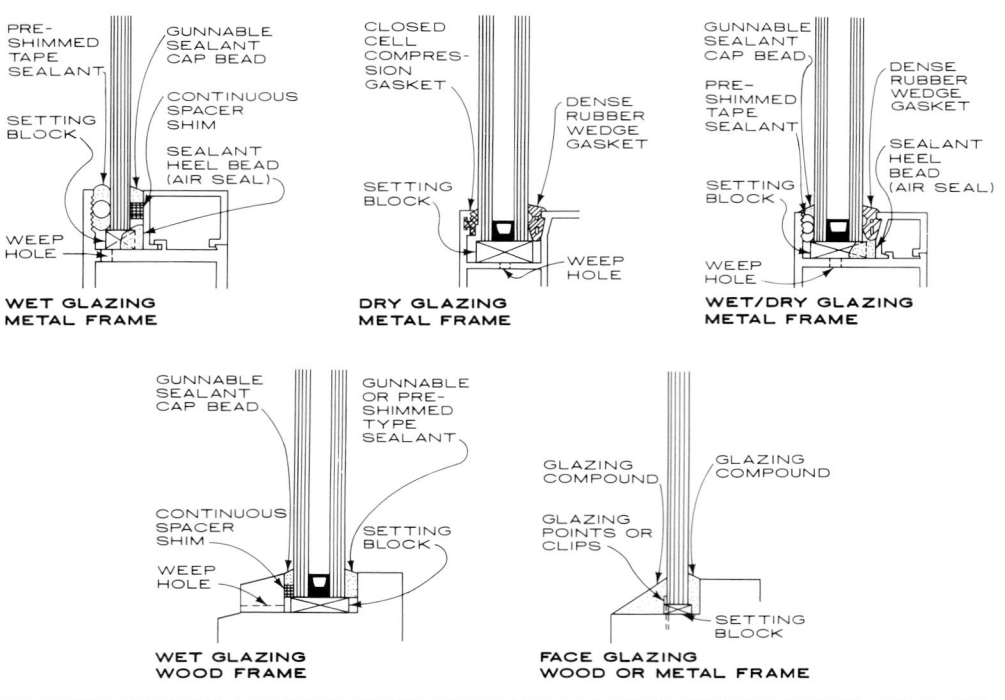

TYPICAL GLAZING SYSTEMS

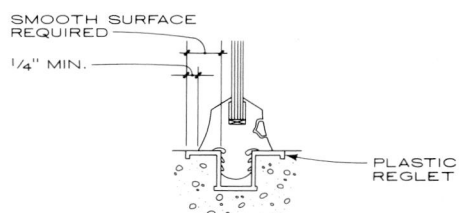

GASKET MOUNTING ON METAL FRAME

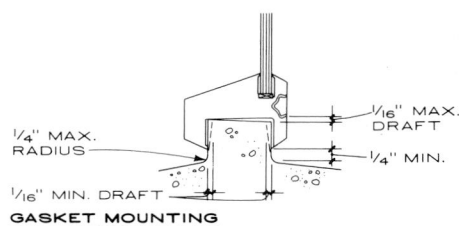

REGLET TYPE GASKET IN CONCRETE

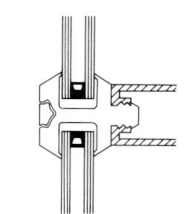

GASKET MOUNTING ON CONCRETE LUG

GLAZING SPECIFICATIONS*

PART	MATERIAL	SPECIFICATION	INSTALLATION PRACTICE
Closed cell rubber gasket	Neoprene Silicone EPDM	ASTM C509	FGMA Glazing Manual
Dense wedge rubber gasket	Neoprene, EPDM Silicone	ASTM C864 ASTM C115	FGMA Glazing Manual
Gunnable sealant	Silicone, polyurethane, and polysulfide Butyl	ASTM C920 ASTM C1085	ASTM C1193
Tape sealant	Butyl Polyisobutylene	AAMA 804.1, 806.1, 807.1	FGMA Glazing Manual
Lock-strip gasket	Neoprene EPDM	ASTM C542	ASTM C716, C963, C964
Setting and edge blocks	Neoprene, EPDM Silicone	ASTM C864 ASTM C115	See setting block and edge block location details and FGMA Glazing Manual
Glazing compound	Oil or resin based	ASTM C570, C669	ASTM C797

*AAMA, Architectural Aluminum Manufacturers Association.
ASTM, American Society for Testing and Materials.
FGMA, Flat Glass Marketing Association.

Thomas F. O'Connor, AIA, FASTM; Smith, Hinchman & Grylls; Detroit, Michigan

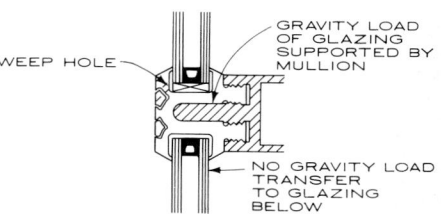

GASKET MOUNTING ON VERTICAL MULLION

HORIZONTAL MULLION AT VERTICALLY STACKED GLAZING

LOCK-STRIP GASKETS

GLAZING

METAL CURTAIN WALLS

Exterior non-load bearing metal and glass enclosure walls require more careful development and skilled erection than traditional wall construction. Because metal and glass react differently to environmental conditions than do other wall materials, the technology for curtain walls is different from all other enclosure systems.

Errors in judgment can be avoided if behavior of the wall is understood. Some of the important considerations for successful curtain wall development are delineated below. Further in-depth material for curtain wall design is available from the Architectural Aluminum Manufacturers Association (AAMA), the Flat Glass Marketing Association (FGMA), and standards developed by American Society for Testing and Materials (ASTM) committees C24 on building seals and sealants and E06 on performance of building constructions. See index under "Structural Sealant Glazing" for additional information that should be considered when developing a structural sealant curtain wall system.

FUNCTION OF THE WALL

The metal and glass curtain wall functions as an "enclosure system" which, when properly developed, can serve multiple functions: (1) withstand the action of the elements; (2) control the passage inward and outward of heat, light, air, and sound; (3) prevent or control access from outside.

NATURAL FORCES

Curtain wall development is determined in part by the impact of natural forces. Natural forces that cause the most concern and failures are (1) water, (2) wind, (3) sunlight, (4) temperature, (5) gravity, and (6) seismic forces. To understand the impact of these forces on curtain wall development, the effects of each should be separately examined.

WATER

The most frequent cause of problems with all enclosures is leakage from rain, snow, vapor, or condensate. Wind driven moisture can enter very small openings and may move within the wall, appearing far from its point of entry. Water vapor can penetrate microscopic pores and will condense on cool surfaces. Such moisture trapped within a wall can result in lessened durability of the wall, which can result in serious damage that is difficult to detect. Leaks are usually limited to joints and openings, which must be designed to provide a weathertight enclosure.

WIND

Structural design development of the wall must take into account both positive and negative pressures caused by wind action, generally increasing in effect depending on the height and shape of the building. Increases in wind loading will occur in corner and roof areas of the building and must be considered accordingly. Framing members, panels, and glass thicknesses should be determined by maximum wind load anticipated and permissible deflection allowable. Winds contribute to the movement of the wall, affecting joint seals and wall anchorage. The effect of positive or negative wind pressure can cause stress reversal on framing members and glass, and will cause water to travel in any direction (including upward) across the face of the wall. The state of the art is to conduct scale model wind studies in a boundary layer wind tunnel to more realistically establish expected prevailing wind patterns and their effects on the building cladding. Wind is a major factor in potential water leakage.

SUNLIGHT

The ultraviolet component of sunlight will cause breakdown of organic materials such as color pigments, various rubber gaskets, plastics, and sealants. Fading and failure of these materials will cause problems with the appearance and weathertightness of the curtain wall. Only quality organic or inorganic materials should be used, and they should be tested for resistance to ultraviolet radiation and ozone attack.

Sunlight passing through glass can cause excessive brightness and glare and will cause fading of interior furnishings and finishes. Shading devices and the use of glare-reducing or high-performance types of glass should be considered in development of the curtain wall.

TEMPERATURE

Temperature change causes thermal movement of materials. Thermal movement is a result of summer solar heating and winter cooling, and is one of the major problems in curtain wall development. Minimum outdoor temperatures vary about 80°F. Throughout the country, the maximum surface temperature of the darker colored surfaces on buildings can range as high as 180°F. This temperature fluctuation, both daily and seasonally, critically affects wall development. Thermal movement is much greater in metals than in wood or masonry. This movement can cause joints to open and close and, over time, if not accounted

for, can cause air infiltration or exfiltration and water infiltration. Affected joints occur at glass to metal interfaces, expansion joints within the system, and transitions to other materials or systems.

Control of the passage of heat through the wall is also required. Heat passage through the wall causes heat gain in hot weather and heat loss in cold weather, the relative importance of the two varying with geographic location. Thermal insulation of opaque wall areas becomes an extremely important consideration, especially whenever these areas constitute a large portion of the total wall area. When vision glass areas predominate, the use of high-performance glasses and the minimizing of through metal or "cold bridges" (usually by inserting continuous nonmetallic breaks in the metal assembly) are more effective in lowering the heat transfer (U-value) through the wall.

GRAVITY

Because gravity is constant and static rather than variable and dynamic, gravity is a less critical force affecting the development of a curtain wall design, but it should be recognized. Gravity causes deflection in horizontal load carrying members, particularly under the weight of glass. However, because the weight of the wall is transferred at frequent intervals to the building frame, the structural effect of gravity is small in comparison with that imposed by wind action. Far greater gravity forces, in the form of floor and roof loads, are acting on the building frame to which the wall is attached. As these loads may cause deflections and displacements of the frame, connections of the wall to this frame must be designed to provide sufficient relative movement to ensure that the displacements do not impose vertical loads on the wall itself.

SEISMIC

Seismic (earthquake) loadings will produce additional static and dynamic loadings to the curtain wall system. Seismic loadings will produce both vertical and horizontal deflections of the wall. This will necessitate special energy absorption considerations in the detail of all wall anchorages and adequate consideration of the joints between curtain wall members.

DESIGN DEVELOPMENT CONSIDERATIONS: STRUCTURAL INTEGRITY

Structural integrity of the curtain wall is a prime concern involving the same design procedures used in any other exterior wall. However, deficiencies of weathertightness and temperature movements are more prevalent than deficiencies in strength, which will be elaborated upon further.

The structural integrity of the curtain wall must be evaluated using two criteria: strength and deflection. Based on numerous curtain wall tests, it has been found that the ultimate performance of the system is usually dependent on the elastic and inelastic deflections of the system rather than on just the strength of component parts.

Curtain wall fabrication and erection tolerances must be carefully reviewed in conjunction with structural frame tolerances. Many curtain wall failures have been caused by inadequate anchorage details, inadequate consideration of tolerances, and differential movement.

WEATHERTIGHTNESS

Weathertightness ensures protection against the penetration of water and an excessive amount of air through the wall. This depends on adequate provision for movement and is closely related to proper joint design. A major share of the problems experienced over the years has been due to lack of weathertightness.

There are three basic methods of curtain wall design that are utilized to achieve weathertightness: barrier design, internal drainage, and pressure equalization. Of the three, pressure equalization is the most sophisticated and difficult to effectively detail, but is claimed to be 100 percent effective if properly performed. Internal drainage systems are the most commonly used and rely on designed mechanisms within the wall system to collect infiltration moisture and direct it harmlessly to the exterior. A barrier design relies on the exterior seals to achieve a 100 percent weathertight barrier. In actual practice this is very difficult to attain and maintain over the life of a curtain wall. If water bypasses the barrier, there is no internal mechanism to control infiltrated water.

PROVISION FOR MOVEMENT

Development of the wall must accommodate relative movements of the wall components as well as differential movements between the wall assembly and the building structure. Relative movements of the wall components will be primarily affected by thermal movements of the wall el-

ements and erection tolerances of the individual wall elements. Erection tolerances may exceed the tolerance for thermal movement. The differential movements between the wall components and the building structure will be a direct function of the dead and live load deflections of the structure and also the creep, elastic frame shortening, shrinkage, thermal, wind, and seismic deformations of the building structure. These differential movements may be of considerable magnitude, and the effects of such differential movements must not be transferred from the structure directly to the curtain wall system. Usually provisions for such differential movement are provided at the head and jamb anchorage locations between the wall jointery and/or joints between wall and adjacent cladding. Behavior of sealants must be considered. Current recommendations from sealant manufacturers are to limit movement of the joint to a percentage of the sealant's rated movement capacity. This will provide a safety factor to help prevent sealant failure. Temperature of metal parts at time of erection, as well as the anticipated design temperature range, will aid in predicting the extent of movement in a joint. Fabrication and erection tolerances must also be considered when establishing the joint opening width.

MOISTURE CONTROL

Control of condensation is essential because metal and glass are not only impermeable to moisture, but have low heat retention capacity. A vapor barrier should be provided on or near the room side wall face. Impervious surfaces within the wall should be insulated to keep them warmer than the dew point of the air contacting them. Provision should be made for the escape of water vapor to the outside. The wall should be detailed so that any condensation occurring within it will be collected and drained away via weeps to the exterior.

THERMAL INSULATION

High thermal and condensation resistance of the wall is a good long-term investment to minimize heat loss in cold weather or heat gain in hot weather. Such devices as minimizing the exposure of the framing members by using thermal breaks and thermally improved framing, employing high performance glass, and insulating opaque surfaces are recommended.

SOUND TRANSMISSION

By careful selection of details and materials, sound transmission characteristics of the metal and glass wall can be made equal to traditional construction.

Use of insulating and laminated glass separately and in combination as well as increasing the mass of the wall will reduce the transmission of sound.

FIRE AND SMOKE STOPS

Prevention of the spread of fire and smoke by continuous firestopping between the curtain wall and the edge of each floor is necessary. Proper detailing and installation of a quality safing material not subject to breakdown by fire will help to avoid what can become an extremely dangerous condition.

CONCLUSION

The following items can be utilized to further refine the techniques of good curtain wall development and construction. It is very beneficial to work with contractors or manufacturers who have specialized for a period of not less than 5 years in the fabrication and installation of curtain walls. Visits to and interviews with owners or managers of buildings will help give an overall view of the performance of curtain wall systems. It is important at the start of design to work with the metal, glass, and sealant manufacturers' technical personnel when developing a metal curtain wall system. Before fabrication and construction starts, wall and component testing should be done under both laboratory and field conditions.

Materials that are to be incorporated into the wall system should be proven durable by industry recognized testing. The curtain wall system design should be tested using a full size mock-up testing for at least the following: air infiltration by ASTM E283; static water infiltration by ASTM E331; dynamic water infiltration by AAMA 501.1; structural adequacy by ASTM E330; and, if necessary, cyclic structural loading by ASTM 1233. Shortly after the start of installation on the building, a completed portion should be water tested by AAMA 501.2 or ASTM E1105 to determine the quality of installation workmanship. This testing can be randomly repeated during installation as a quality control measure.

Thomas F. O'Connor, AIA, FASTM; Smith, Hinchman & Grylls; Detroit, Michigan
Duane Sohl; DeStefano + Partners; Chicago, Illinois

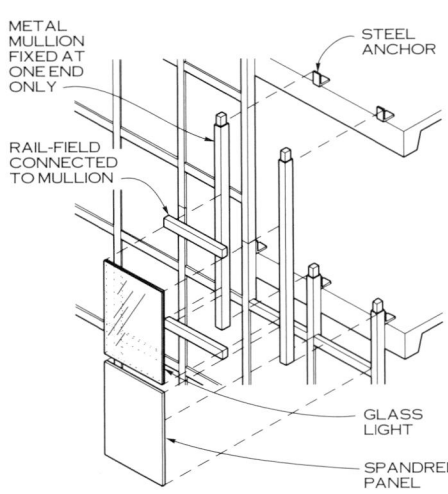

NOTES

1. All components are fabricated and finished off-site and delivered, hoisted, and stored in bundles or packages; they are then assembled and sealed on the building.
2. Mullions may be one or two stories in length, with one end fixed and one end free to move.
3. Infill spandrel panels and glass lights are installed after the framing system is completely installed.
4. Economic considerations: this system is less expensive to assemble (shop-built), ship, handle, and store; however, it is more expensive in terms of on-site labor costs.

STICK SYSTEM

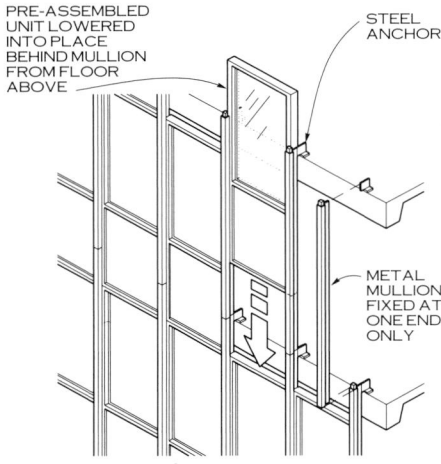

NOTES

1. The unit and mullion system is a combination of the stick and unitized systems where the mullion members are separately installed first, then pre-assembled framed units are placed between them. The system is often employed when the mullion sections are unusually deep or large in cross section, making it impractical to incorporate them as part of a pre-assembled unit.
2. The pre-assembled units used in this system may be one story in height or may be separated into a spandrel unit and a vision glass unit.
3. The advantages and disadvantages of this system are generally comparable to those of the unitized system. The shipping bulk of the units themselves is somewhat less since the mullion sections are shipped separately. However, the on-site labor costs will be greater than those of the unitized system.

UNIT AND MULLION SYSTEM

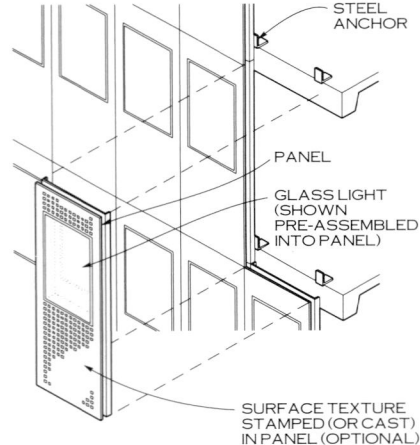

NOTES

1. The panel system is similar to the pre-assembled unitized system except that it consists of homogeneous units formed from sheet metal or castings with few, if any, internal joints except at glass periphery.
2. Panels may be small units, one story or two story in height, with or without openings for glazing.
3. Units may be glazed during shop assembly or glazed after panels are installed on buildings.
4. With present technology in dies and molds, the panel system is economical only when large numbers of identical panels are to be used. Therefore, architectural-type panels, as opposed to more standardized industrial-type panels, are more expensive since they are by nature customized for each job. However, costs for in-shop and on-site labor are both minimized.

PANEL SYSTEM

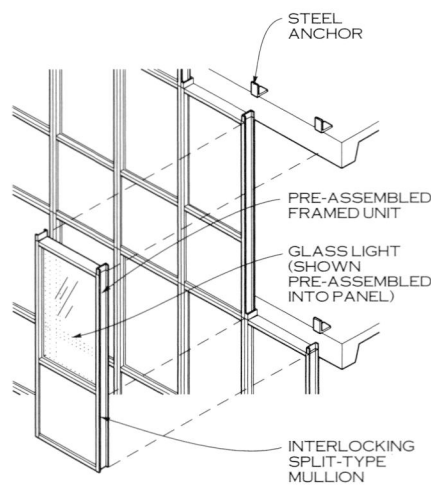

NOTES

1. The unitized system consists of units pre-assembled completely at the factory, except for glazing which is sometimes installed in the field. The vertical edges of adjoining units combine to form mullion members; top and bottom members also join to form horizontal rails.
2. Unit sizes may be one story or two story in height.
3. Advantages of the unit system include assembly under controlled shop conditions which result in a reduction in more costly (and more difficult) on-site labor. However, shipping, handling, and storage may be more difficult due to the bulkiness of the units. Also, when openings need to be left in the wall to facilitate the handling of construction materials ("leave-out" units), special joint details and installation procedures may need to be used to close these openings since the units are designed for sequential interlocking installation.

UNITIZED SYSTEM

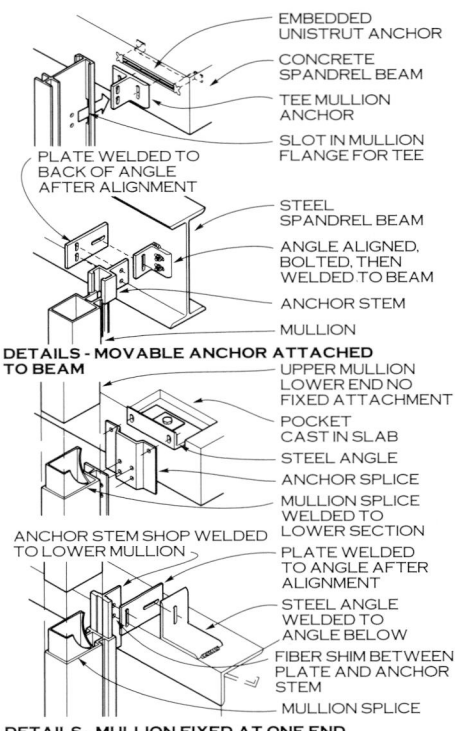

DETAILS - MOVABLE ANCHOR ATTACHED TO BEAM

DETAILS - MULLION FIXED AT ONE END

NOTES

1. Anchorage devices must permit three-dimensional adjustment. Metal-to-metal connections subject to intentional movement should be designed to eliminate noise caused by movement due to temperature change.
2. Anchors must be designed to withstand wind loads acting outward and inward as well as other required loads.
3. Anchors must be permanently secured in position after final assembly and adjustment of wall components.
4. All anchorage members must be corrosion resistant or protected against corrosive forces.
5. Shim plates may be installed between vertical leg of angle anchor and concrete structure, as required, for proper anchor alignment.

ATTACHMENT AND ANCHORAGE DETAILS

PROPERTIES OF COMMON INSULATING PANEL MATERIALS

MATERIALS FOR INFILL PANELS	DENSITY (LB/CU FT)	APPROX. K VALUE
Paper honeycomb	2.5-7.0	0.45-0.55
Paper honeycomb, with foamed plastic fill	4.5-10.0	0.20-0.35
Paper honeycomb, with vermiculite fill	5-14	0.35-0.40
Polystyrene foam, extruded	1.7-3.5	0.20-0.26
Polyurethane foam	1.5-3.0	0.18
Polyisocyanurate	2.0	0.18
Phenolic foam	2.5	0.12
Fiberglass	0.3-2.0	0.23-0.27
Cellular glass	8.5	0.35
Perlite beads in mineral binder	11	0.36

NOTES

1. Consult local codes and ordinances for fire resistance requirements of panel construction. This depends, in part, on conditions of use, degree of fire exposure, and core material type.
2. Choice of core material depends on potential thermal bowing of panel, flatness of facing materials, oil-canning of facing materials, moisture resistance of panel, and thermal resistance aging characteristics of the material.

Thomas F. O'Connor, AIA, FASTM; Smith, Hinchman & Grylls; Detroit, Michigan
Duane Sohl; DeStefano + Partners; Chicago, Illinois

GLAZED CURTAIN WALLS

NOTE

Air chambers surrounding glass panels are open to outside along their lower edges.

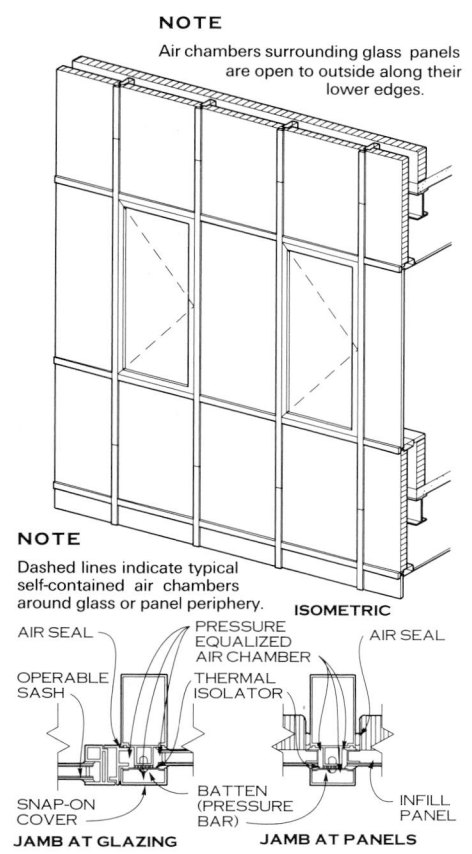

NOTE

Dashed lines indicate typical self-contained air chambers around glass or panel periphery.

ISOMETRIC

AIR SEAL
OPERABLE SASH
PRESSURE EQUALIZED AIR CHAMBER
THERMAL ISOLATOR
AIR SEAL
SNAP-ON COVER
BATTEN (PRESSURE BAR)
INFILL PANEL

JAMB AT GLAZING   JAMB AT PANELS

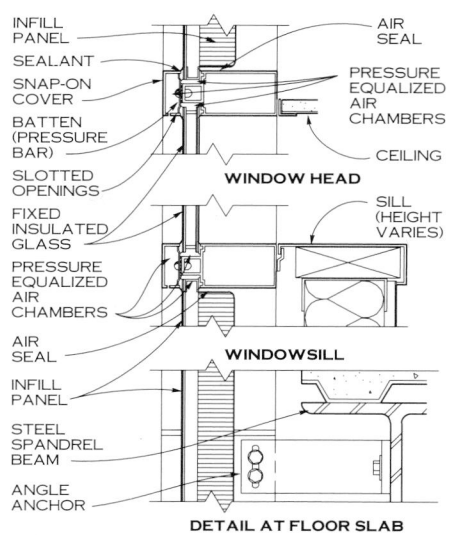

INFILL PANEL
SEALANT
SNAP-ON COVER
BATTEN (PRESSURE BAR)
SLOTTED OPENINGS
FIXED INSULATED GLASS
PRESSURE EQUALIZED AIR CHAMBERS
AIR SEAL
INFILL PANEL
STEEL SPANDREL BEAM
ANGLE ANCHOR
AIR SEAL
PRESSURE EQUALIZED AIR CHAMBERS
CEILING

WINDOW HEAD

SILL (HEIGHT VARIES)

WINDOWSILL

DETAIL AT FLOOR SLAB

GENERAL

The rain screen principle incorporating pressure-equalized design is one of the most reliable systems of eliminating water leakage in metal curtain walls. It does this by neutralizing two of the most difficult forces that cause leakage: wind pressure and kinetic energy. The system itself has three components: the outer layer "rain screen," the pressure-equalized air space, and the inner air seal. The outside wall face (rain screen) keeps a majority of the water out by shedding it. By way of slotted openings in the mullion system which allow an equalization of outdoor and air-space air pressures, the forces that would push any water into the building are stopped at the outside face. Therefore, at the true building seal the inner air seal, water, and the forces that drive it are kept away. Also, the seal is kept away from harmful environmental forces that would otherwise cause deterioration. See AAMA *Aluminum Curtain Wall Design Guide Manual, volume 2* for further information.

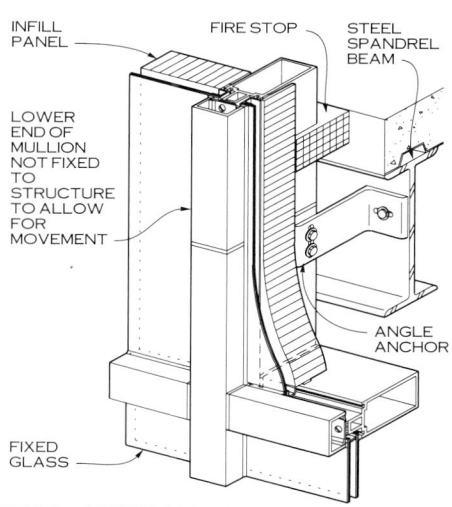

INFILL PANEL
FIRE STOP
STEEL SPANDREL BEAM
LOWER END OF MULLION NOT FIXED TO STRUCTURE TO ALLOW FOR MOVEMENT
ANGLE ANCHOR
FIXED GLASS

DETAIL - ANCHORAGE AND MOVEMENT

NOTES

1. The infill panels and glazing units of the batten pressure-bar system are installed from the exterior of the building and thus are usually considered for low-rise applications only.
2. Adjustability for tolerances and allowances for horizontal and vertical movement must be provided.
3. Slotted openings in snap-on cover plates and battens for pressure equalization are also used as weep holes for the glazing system.
4. The pressure equalization (rain screen) system is an option and is not necessary to the inherent workability of the batten mullion system.
5. For large openings with long perimeters, subdivision of the perimeter pressure equalized air space is advisable.

BATTEN MULLION USING RAIN SCREEN PRINCIPLE AND PRESSURE EQUALIZED WALL DESIGN

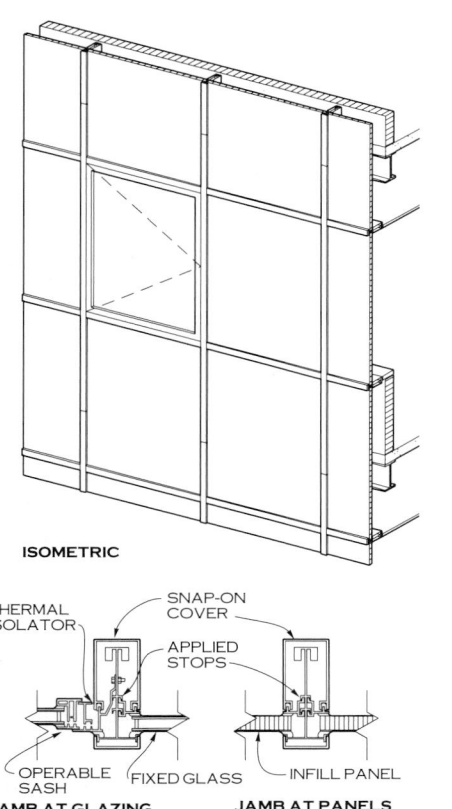

ISOMETRIC

THERMAL ISOLATOR
SNAP-ON COVER
APPLIED STOPS
OPERABLE SASH
FIXED GLASS
INFILL PANEL

JAMB AT GLAZING   JAMB AT PANELS

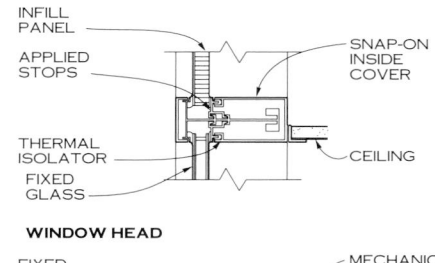

INFILL PANEL
APPLIED STOPS
THERMAL ISOLATOR
FIXED GLASS
SNAP-ON INSIDE COVER
CEILING

WINDOW HEAD

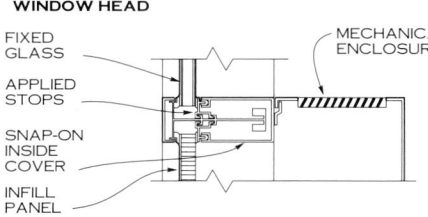

FIXED GLASS
APPLIED STOPS
SNAP-ON INSIDE COVER
INFILL PANEL
MECHANICAL ENCLOSURE

WINDOWSILL

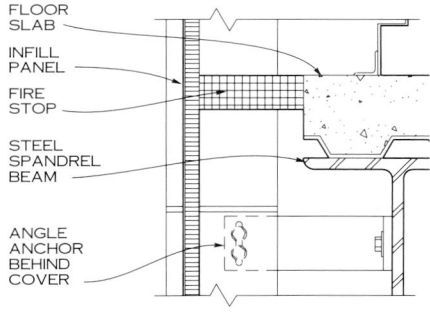

FLOOR SLAB
INFILL PANEL
FIRE STOP
STEEL SPANDREL BEAM
ANGLE ANCHOR BEHIND COVER

DETAIL AT FLOOR SLAB

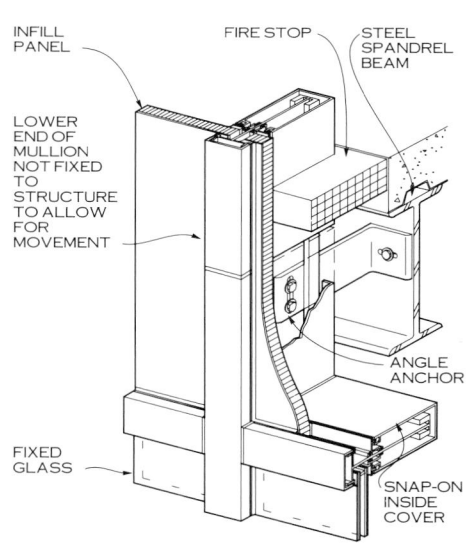

INFILL PANEL
FIRE STOP
STEEL SPANDREL BEAM
LOWER END OF MULLION NOT FIXED TO STRUCTURE TO ALLOW FOR MOVEMENT
ANGLE ANCHOR
FIXED GLASS
SNAP-ON INSIDE COVER

DETAIL - ANCHORAGE AND MOVEMENT

NOTES

1. The infill panels and glazing units of this system are installed from the interior of the building and thus can be considered for low-rise or high-rise applications.
2. Adjustability for tolerances and allowances for horizontal and vertical movement must be provided.
3. Specially designed mullions to carry window washer equipment are frequently used in high-rise designs. Consult manufacturers.
4. All fasteners and anchors in contact with mullion system must be specified and detailed to guard against galvanic action.

INTERIOR APPLIED STOP MULLION

Thomas F. O'Connor, AIA, FASTM; Smith, Hinchman & Grylls; Detroit, Michigan

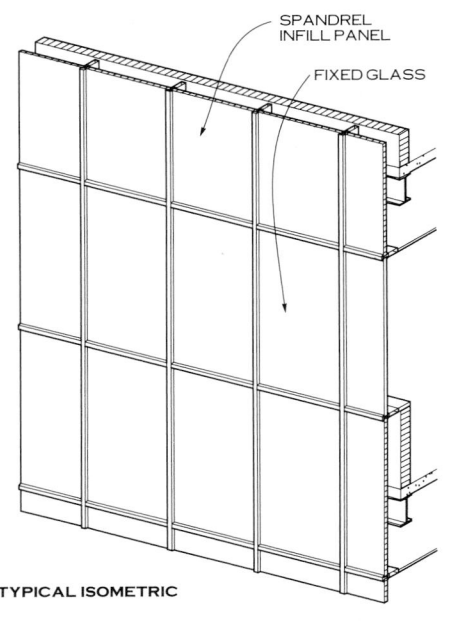

TYPICAL ISOMETRIC

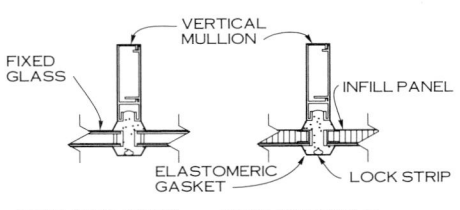

JAMB AT GLAZING   **JAMB AT PANELS**

LOCK-STRIP GASKET MULLION SYSTEM

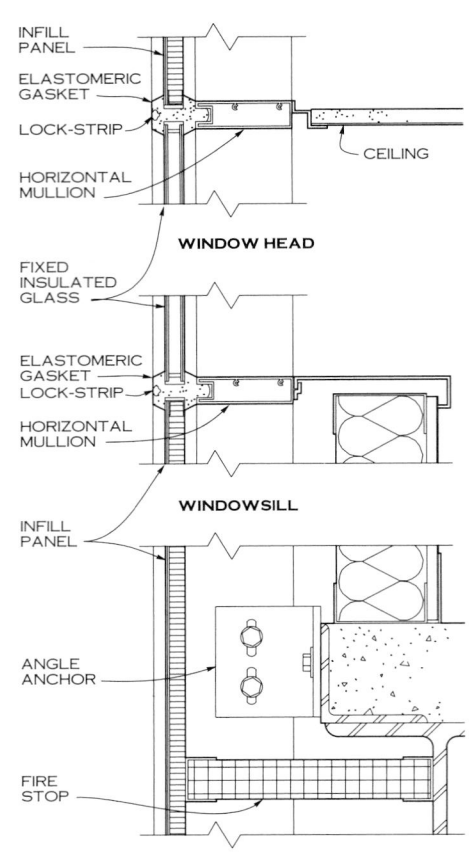

WINDOW HEAD

WINDOW SILL

DETAIL AT FLOOR SLAB

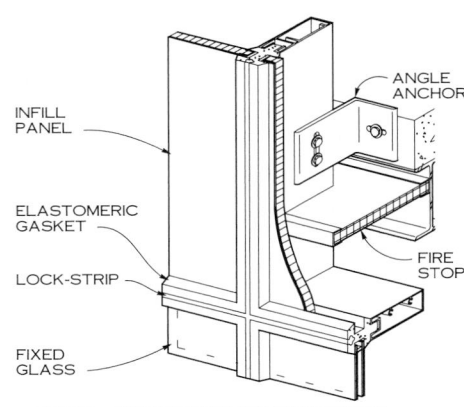

DETAIL—ANCHORAGE AND MOVEMENT

NOTES

1. The inherent high resiliency of the lock-strip gasket system permits wall movement to be accommodated and is one of its most important features. The lock-strip gasket is made in two parts to facilitate installation and provide the pressure required to secure and seal the installed glazing unit or infill panel. Also, since the elastomeric lock-strip gasket is the only part of the mullion exposed to the outside, it acts as a natural thermal break.

2. To facilitate the insertion of the lock-strip and increase the pressure exerted by it, the elastomer used for the lock-strip is harder than that used for the main body of the gasket.

3. Neoprene is the elastomer used for the lock-strip gasket. See ASTM Standard C542 for the physical requirements of the finished gaskets.

4. Ozone resistance and heat aging are important environmental factors that affect the gasket system. During installation, the gasket loses resiliency rapidly below 40° F and must be heated suitably before installation.

5. The lock-strip gasket system is installed directly to the metal mullion in the field and is highly dependent on skilled field labor for its effectiveness.

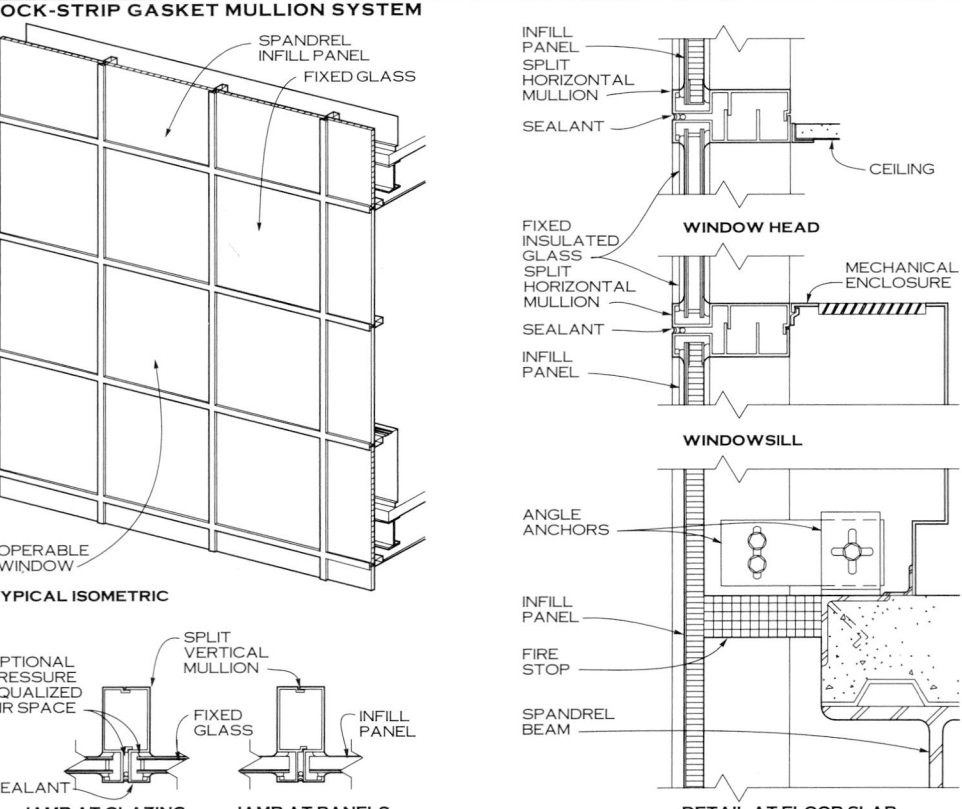

TYPICAL ISOMETRIC

JAMB AT GLAZING   **JAMB AT PANELS**

SPLIT MULLION

WINDOW HEAD

WINDOW SILL

DETAIL AT FLOOR SLAB

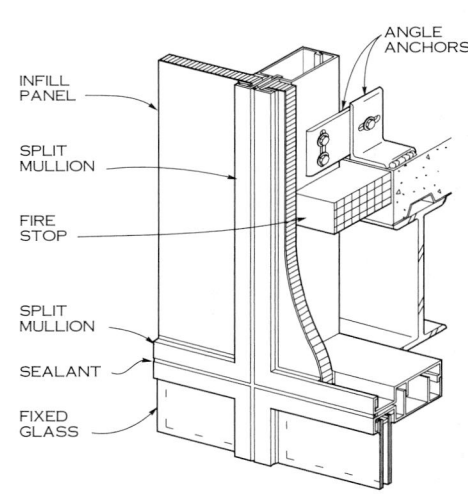

DETAIL—ANCHORAGE AND MOVEMENT

NOTES

1. The split mullion system accommodates movement with slip joints in the mullion construction.

2. Anchorages must have sufficient capacity to permit adjustment in three directions to respond to construction tolerances.

3. Horizontal mullion members are screwed to the split vertical members in the field in a stick-installed system or in the shop unitized system.

Thomas F. O'Connor, AIA, FASTM; Smith, Hinchman & Grylls; Detroit, Michigan

STRUCTURAL SEALANT CURTAIN WALL SYSTEMS

Structural sealant glazing is a system of retaining glass or other materials to the aluminum members of curtain walls using a structural quality sealant specifically designed, tested, and recommended for structural sealant glazing. Consult AAMA Standard No. 13, *Structural Sealant Glazing Systems, A Design Guide*, for additional information. In structural sealant glazing applications, wind-induced and other loadings are transferred by the structural sealant from the glass to the aluminum curtain wall system. There are no mechanical fasteners. Presently only certain silicone sealants are suitable for use in these systems, and references in the balance of the text are to silicone materials.

The design, testing, fabrication, erection, and maintenance of these systems require utmost care and meticulous detailing by the design professional. If the design professional is not fully knowledgeable of structural sealant glazing, then a curtain wall consultant should be retained to be responsible for development and implementation. All parties from the owner to the glazier should be aware of the serious potential liabilities of structural sealant glazing and should be willing to assume their appropriate share of responsibility.

The applicable codes and regulations that apply to the jurisdiction where the structural sealant glazed curtain wall will be erected should be consulted early in the development of the system. Some jurisdictions have regulations that can impact the design as well as the subsequent development and implementation of the system.

Preference should be given to those curtain wall systems, whether 2-side or 4-side structurally glazed, that permit as part of their design the ability to apply the structural silicone sealant in the factory rather than at the construction site. Factory glazing of the structural silicone sealant has fewer variables to control and permits better quality assurance procedures to obtain the high level of sealant workmanship that is necessary for these systems. Construction site glazing is often subject to a multitude of conditions (e.g., rain, dust, storage condition) that can be detrimental to achieving a quality installation of structural silicone sealant. The rain screen (equalized pressure) wall system is not compatible with structural silicone sealant applications.

The following text includes concerns that need to be resolved when developing structurally glazed curtain walls. It is not all inclusive; additional issues may need resolving for each curtain wall system and its particular performance criteria.

QUALITY ASSURANCE
FABRICATION OF COMPONENTS

A quality assurance program should be implemented that adequately monitors and checks the fabrication of the system components, whether in a factory or at the construction site. This type of quality assurance is best performed by an independent inspection agency that has been properly trained to perform this service.

The objectives of the program are to periodically monitor the materials and workmanship to ensure that no undesirable changes occur which would be detrimental to the performance of the system. For example, the quality of materials would be verified (i.e., cleaning solvents for purity, structural sealants for proper mixing or storage life, adhesion of structural sealants to the intended substrates by ASTM test method C794, and lack of adhesion of sealants to joint fillers and backing) as well as workmanship (i.e., substrate cleaning procedures, sealant application, and that the parts of the system are being installed correctly). This monitoring could also include periodic static load testing of assembled components as a statistical check of the fabrication process.

ERECTION OF COMPONENTS

Quality assurance during this part of the process is equally important, particularly if construction site structural sealant glazing is to be performed. A program should be developed that adequately addresses the training of workmen to the system requirements, monitors the initial installation to fine tune procedures, and then periodically monitors the continuing installation.

COMPONENTS

Developing a structurally glazed curtain wall system requires careful, conservative design and consideration of all system components and their interaction, including structural silicone sealant, insulating glass, monolithic glass, aluminum finishes, spacer gaskets, and setting blocks.

STRUCTURAL SILICONE SEALANT

The structural silicone sealant should be chosen by the professional designer, sealant manufacturer, and curtain wall contractor and glazier, all working together to establish the necessary strength, adhesive and cohesive properties, curing characteristics, and fabrication concerns for the intended sealant. The tensile adhesion properties of the structural sealant are established by ASTM test method C1135. An appropriate design factor should be established which includes consideration of the above and also indeterminate variables such as application procedures, whether factory or field assembled, and secondary stresses induced in the structural sealant by thermal movement, wind-induced building movement gravity loads, and other factors. The design stress for the primary forces that the structural sealant will experience should not exceed the industry recommended value of 20 psi (138 k Pa).

INSULATING GLASS

Insulating glass units should be dual seal units, with a secondary seal of structural quality silicone sealant, certified by the Insulating Glass Certification Council (IGCC) to a CBA quality level. Compatibility of the structural silicone sealant with the secondary insulating glass structural sealant should be verified by the sealant manufacturer and the insulating glass manufacturer. If the structural silicone sealant used with the insulating glass units is acetoxy curing (acetic acid liberating), the sealant details must be approved for compatibility by the sealant and insulating glass manufacturers. Caution should be exercised when choosing the structural silicone sealant if it is being used with insulating glass.

Design considerations for the secondary structural silicone seal of insulating glass units include adequate dimensions to resist wind loading and other secondary stresses previously described. The surfaces of insulating glass units should be tested by the sealant and insulating glass manufacturers for compatibility and adhesion of the intended structural silicone sealant. The insulating glass units should be certified by the manufacturer for use in structural silicone sealant glazing.

MONOLITHIC GLASS

Compatibility and adhesion of the structural silicone sealant to the coated or uncoated glass surface should be tested by the sealant manufacturer. Certain silicone sealants may not develop adequate adhesion to some reflective and low emissivity coated glasses. Monolithic glass used for a spandrel area may require an opacifier applied to the interior glass surface. The opacifier should be cut back for the full contact area on all sides where structural adhesion is required. The sealant manufacturer should test for compatibility of the structural silicone sealant with the opacifier and any other adjacent materials that may come in contact with or be in close proximity to the structural silicone sealant.

PANELS

Stone and various metal panels are also structurally glazed in curtain wall systems. The same concerns exist for adhesion and compatibility of the structural sealant with the stone and coated or anodized metal panel surfaces and require adequate testing and verification before use.

ALUMINUM FINISHES

The finish of aluminum panels, framing members, and trim pieces where structural adhesion will occur should be tested for compatibility and adhesion with the intended structural silicone sealant. The sealant manufacturer should verify this by laboratory tests performed before the components are fabricated and also periodically on samples of production run components. If factory applied organic coatings are used, then the adhesion and fatigue resistance of the organic coating to the aluminum is as important as the adhesion and fatigue resistance of the structural sealant to the organic coating and should be laboratory tested to verify the coating's suitability for use in structural sealant glazing. Only high quality factory applied coatings with proven durability, applied by licensed applicators, should be considered.

SPACER GASKETS AND SETTING BLOCKS

Compatibility of spacer gaskets, setting blocks, glazing gaskets, and other accessories with the structural silicone sealant should be established before those components are fabricated and also verified periodically on samples of production run components, with laboratory testing by the sealant manufacturer by ASTM test method C1087. Preference should be given to the use of silicone rubber that meets ASTM specification C1115 or other high quality proven materials for most of these components.

SILICONE WEATHER SEALANTS

Silicone sealants used as a weather seal should be laboratory tested by the sealant manufacturer for adhesion to substrates and for compatibility and stain resistance with adjacent materials before component fabrication and also periodically on samples of production run components.

INTERNAL DRAINAGE

Even though a structural sealant glazing system is essentially a completely sealed system, the curtain wall should be designed to have an interior drainage system to collect any infiltrated or condensed moisture and weep it to the exterior. There are many variables, even in the best designed, fabricated, and installed systems, that affect workmanship so that a 100 percent watertight system should not be expected. Internal undrained moisture can have a detrimental effect on insulating glass edge seals, structural sealant joints, and other system materials.

TESTING OF ASSEMBLED COMPONENTS

Realistic, comprehensive testing criteria for a mock-up of the assembled curtain wall system should be developed by the design professional or curtain wall consultant and the testing laboratory. Performance criteria that should be considered for testing include static air infiltration by ASTM E283; static and dynamic water infiltration by ASTM E330 and AAMA 501.1, respectively; wind loading structural adequacy by ASTM E330 at design loads, at 1.5 times design loads, and perhaps to destruction; deflection characteristics; seismic or racking load resistance; cyclic structural loading by ASTM E1233; steady state thermal performance; verification of reglazing procedures; verification of fabrication and erection techniques; condensation resistance; and aesthetic evaluation.

Mock-up testing helps to verify the curtain wall system design adequacy; it does not predict long-term durability.

The mock-up must be of sufficient size. It also must be representative of the building conditions and should be constructed using the actual production run materials and components, as well as fabrication and erection methods to be used for the building. The mock-up should be erected by the personnel, both supervisory and production, who will fabricate and erect the system. More than one mock-up may be necessary depending on the complexity of the system design.

Any changes or modifications resulting from mock-up testing may require additional laboratory testing of components as well as the mock-up. Any changes or modifications after mock-up testing has been completed should be carefully evaluated. Certain aspects of the mock-up testing and perhaps the curtain wall system design could be invalidated by the changes or modifications.

Production and fabrication of the system for erection on the building should not begin until successful mock-up performance is achieved.

Soon after the start or installation of the system, a field water test, AAMA 501.2 or ASTM E1105, should be performed to verify the adequacy of the installation and then repeated periodically as a continuing check of installation procedures.

MAINTENANCE

The structural sealant curtain wall system design must be capable of being maintained without the need for elaborate or expensive procedures or methods. Glass will break or insulating glass seals will fail, leaks may develop, and the surface will be cleaned periodically. These basic needs should be resolved by the system design. The reglazing of glass is of particular importance, and procedures should be developed in advance of the need. Reglazing may necessitate the use of a different structural sealant from that used for the original work. If this occurs, then this sealant will also have to be tested for compatibility and adhesion during the system design. Factory glazed systems can be designed to greatly ease the field reglazing process.

Consideration should be given to a periodic inspection of the system (particularly a 4-side structurally glazed system) by a qualified professional after installation to verify the continuing performance of the curtain wall system.

Thomas F. O'Connor, AIA, FASTM; Smith, Hinchman & Grylls; Detroit, Michigan

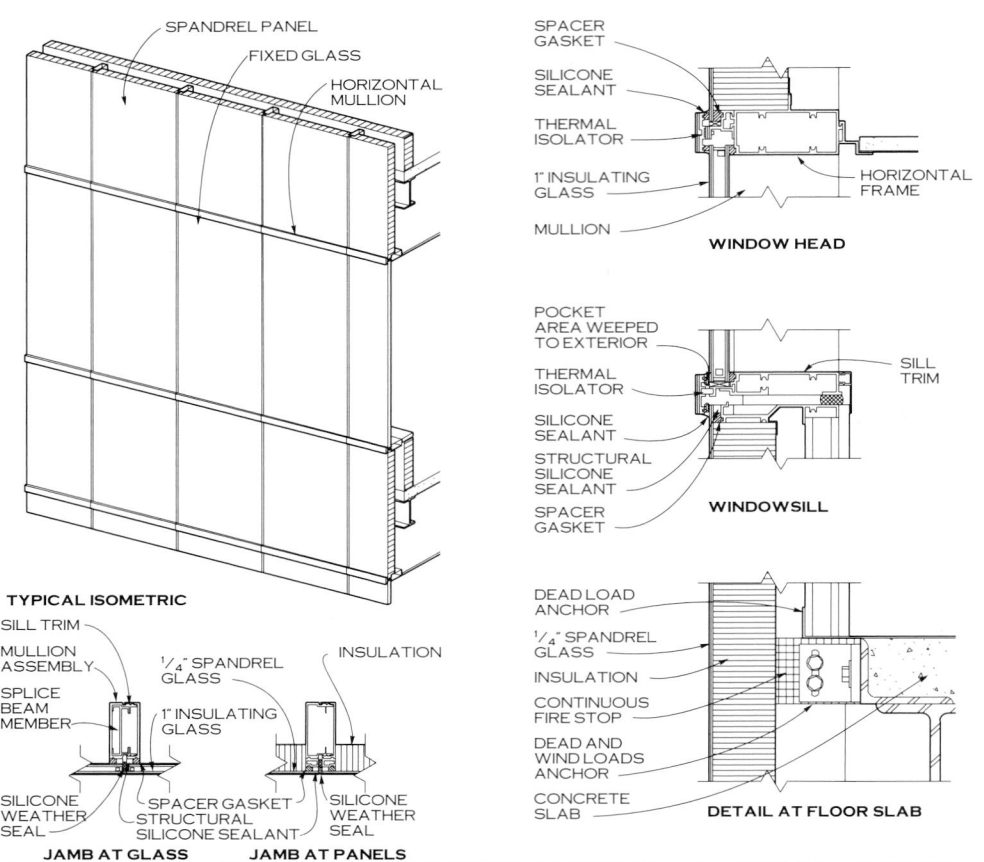

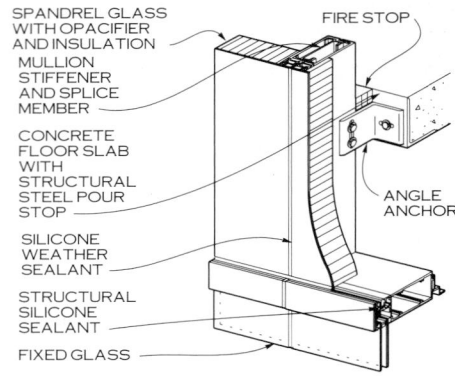

TYPICAL ISOMETRIC

SILL TRIM
MULLION ASSEMBLY
SPLICE BEAM MEMBER
1/4" SPANDREL GLASS
1" INSULATING GLASS
INSULATION
SILICONE WEATHER SEAL
SPACER GASKET STRUCTURAL SILICONE SEALANT
SILICONE WEATHER SEAL

JAMB AT GLASS   **JAMB AT PANELS**

SPACER GASKET
SILICONE SEALANT
THERMAL ISOLATOR
1" INSULATING GLASS
MULLION
HORIZONTAL FRAME

WINDOW HEAD

POCKET AREA WEEPED TO EXTERIOR
THERMAL ISOLATOR
SILICONE SEALANT
STRUCTURAL SILICONE SEALANT
SPACER GASKET
SILL TRIM

WINDOW SILL

DEAD LOAD ANCHOR
1/4" SPANDREL GLASS
INSULATION
CONTINUOUS FIRE STOP
DEAD AND WIND LOADS ANCHOR
CONCRETE SLAB

DETAIL AT FLOOR SLAB

SPANDREL GLASS WITH OPACIFIER AND INSULATION
MULLION STIFFENER AND SPLICE MEMBER
CONCRETE FLOOR SLAB WITH STRUCTURAL STEEL POUR STOP
SILICONE WEATHER SEALANT
STRUCTURAL SILICONE SEALANT
FIXED GLASS
FIRE STOP
ANGLE ANCHOR

DETAIL - ANCHORAGE AND MOVEMENT
NOTES

1. Weather seal joints must be sized to account for, among others, thermal movement, fabrication, and erection tolerances, and adequate access for sealant backup and sealant installation.
2. System weepholes in the bottom of sill or horizontal member snap-on covers must be free to weep to the exterior. Weather seals at these areas must be recessed behind the weepage area.
3. Anchorages must have sufficient capacity to permit adjustment in three directions to respond to construction tolerances.
4. To prevent thermal bridging, a thermal break is needed in the horizontal exposed metal mullion; the structural sealant joint also function as a thermal break.
5. On spandrel glass panels, the opacifier must be cut back at contact width area of the structural sealant; spandrel panel insulation is assembled either directly against glass with an opacifier or 2" away from glass without an opacifier. See AAMA *Structural Sealant Glazing Systems Design Guide* for further information.

STRUCTURAL SEALANT GLAZING ON TWO SIDES

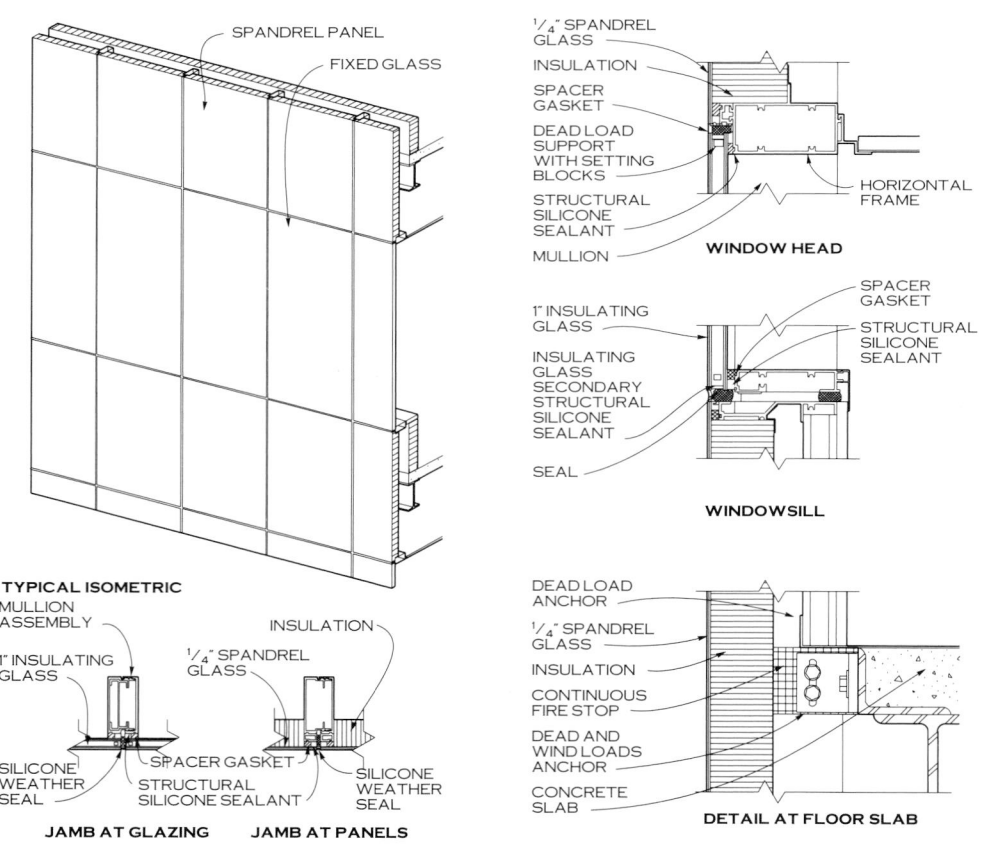

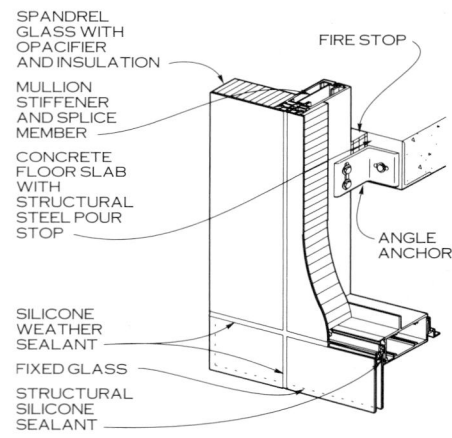

TYPICAL ISOMETRIC

MULLION ASSEMBLY
1" INSULATING GLASS
1/4" SPANDREL GLASS
INSULATION
SILICONE WEATHER SEAL
SPACER GASKET STRUCTURAL SILICONE SEALANT
SILICONE WEATHER SEAL

JAMB AT GLAZING   **JAMB AT PANELS**

1/4" SPANDREL GLASS
INSULATION
SPACER GASKET
DEAD LOAD SUPPORT WITH SETTING BLOCKS
STRUCTURAL SILICONE SEALANT
MULLION
HORIZONTAL FRAME

WINDOW HEAD

1" INSULATING GLASS
INSULATING GLASS SECONDARY STRUCTURAL SILICONE SEALANT
SEAL
SPACER GASKET
STRUCTURAL SILICONE SEALANT

WINDOW SILL

DEAD LOAD ANCHOR
1/4" SPANDREL GLASS
INSULATION
CONTINUOUS FIRE STOP
DEAD AND WIND LOADS ANCHOR
CONCRETE SLAB

DETAIL AT FLOOR SLAB

SPANDREL GLASS WITH OPACIFIER AND INSULATION
MULLION STIFFENER AND SPLICE MEMBER
CONCRETE FLOOR SLAB WITH STRUCTURAL STEEL POUR STOP
SILICONE WEATHER SEALANT
FIXED GLASS
STRUCTURAL SILICONE SEALANT
FIRE STOP
ANGLE ANCHOR

DETAIL - ANCHORAGE AND MOVEMENT
NOTES

1. Weather seal joints must be sized to account for, among others, thermal movement, fabrication, and erection tolerances, and adequate access for sealant backup and sealant installation.
2. Anchorages must have sufficient capacity to permit adjustment in three directions to respond to construction tolerances.
3. Special care in design and detailing is essential for structural silicone systems: the design of the structural silicone "joints"—the adhesive that holds the cladding onto the curtain wall framing members—depends on wind loads, building movement, and related factors.
4. Since quality assurance in the specification and assembly of this system is critical, it is recommended that it be glazed in the shop under controlled conditions. See AAMA *Structural Sealant Glazing Systems Design Guide* for further information.

STRUCTURAL SEALANT GLAZING ON FOUR SIDES

Thomas F. O'Connor, AIA, FASTM; Smith, Hinchman & Grylls; Detroit, Michigan

GLAZED CURTAIN WALLS

GENERAL

The primary element of a translucent wall system is a structural composite sandwich panel formed by permanently bonding specially formulated, reinforced, translucent fiberglass sheets to a grid core constructed of interlocked, extruded structural aluminum I-beams. Panels can be curved or flat. The fiberglass sheets are uniform in thickness and have a weather-resistant, low maintenance composition.

The panel can have an insert of translucent fiberglass insulation. The density of this insulation can be changed to increase the total insulation of the panel to provide a wide range of insulating U factor options of 0.40, 0.24, 0.19, 0.15, 0.10, and even 0.06.

The complete panel is generally only 2 $^3/_4$ in. thick, although it can be 1 $^9/_{16}$ in. thick for economy or 11 in. thick for maximum thermal control.

GRID DESIGNS

Nominal grid size is 12 x 24 in. standard, with 8 x 20 in. optional. Other designs and grid sizes are available; spans will vary with different grid patterns.

TRANSLUCENT COLORS

White and crystal are standard. Other colored faces, including blue, green, and bronze, plus tint option, are available. Colored insulation inserts are also available.

METAL FINISHES

The installation system is available in mill finish or corrosion resistant finish, a coating that meets AAMA 605.2. The finish is resistant to acids, alkalis, salt, and industrial and moisture laden atmospheres.

STANDARD PANEL SIZES

The width is standard in 4 and 5 ft sizes, with width achievable up to 5 ft in any increment. Length is standard from 3 to 20 ft, with other lengths available. Thickness is 2 $^3/_4$ and 1 $^9/_{16}$ in., with $^5/_8$ in. thick glazing panels available; 11 in. is for the 0.006 "U" panel system.

FIRE TESTS

Although some panels contain combustible binder resins (ignition temperature greater than 800° F), they will withstand a 1200°F flame for four hours with no flame penetration. Panels pass the Class A Burning Brand Test (ASTM E-108). A special configuration is a UL listed Class A roof system. All interior faces are 1 in. or less Burn Extent, by ASTM D-635. Several categories of interior flame-spread/smoke developed by ASTM E-84 tunnel tests are available to meet local building codes.

EXPANSION

The coefficient of linear thermal expansion is 1.24 x 10^{-5} in./in./°F (an 8 foot panel will expand approximately $^1/_8$ in. with a temperature differential of 100°F).

CLEAR SPAN AND PRE-ENGINEERED SYSTEMS

Larger skylights, complete with supporting substructures, can span up to 100 ft. Pre-engineered pyramids and domes are larger than the self-supporting skylight. Typical four-sided pyramids from 4 to 20 ft square and roof segmented domes from 8 to 28 ft in diameter are both pre-engineered for a 40 lb/sq ft load.

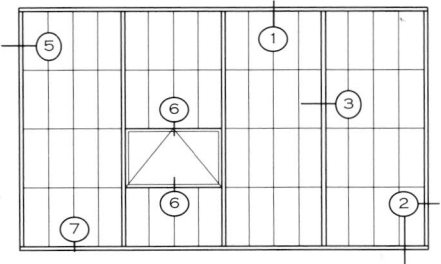

TYPICAL WALL PANEL ELEVATION

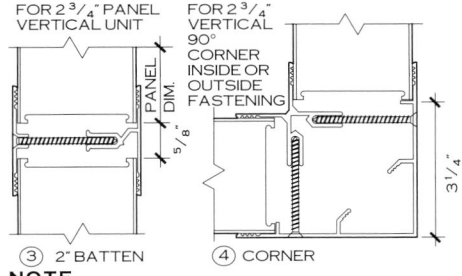

③ 2" BATTEN   ④ CORNER

NOTE

Sealing tapes typical all joints.

EXTERIOR

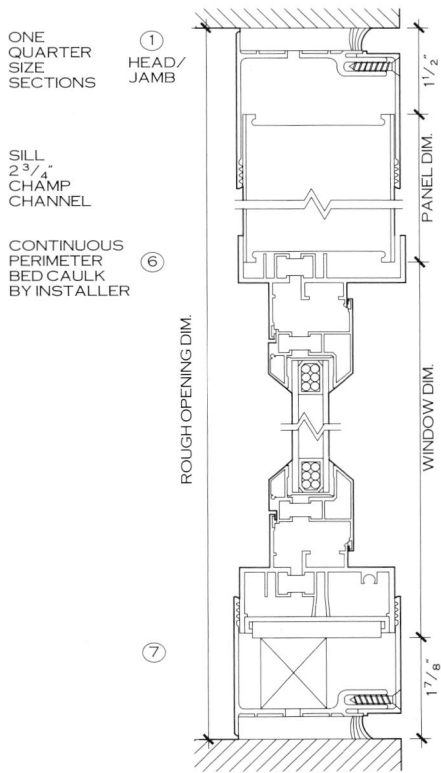

DETAILS OF TRANSLUCENT SKYLIGHT

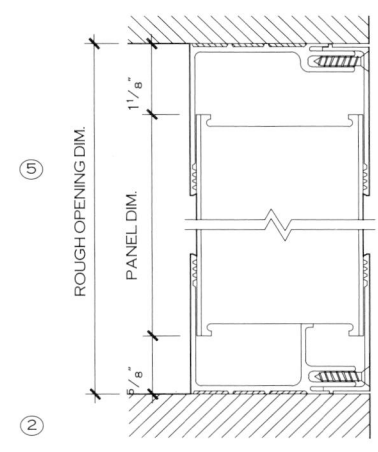

DETAILS OF TRANSLUCENT WALL

HEAT AND LIGHT TRANSMISSION

FACE SHEET COMBINATIONS[2]		PERCENTAGE OF LIGHT TRANSMISSION [3,5]				WALL SHADING COEFFICIENT [5]			
EXTERIOR COLOR	INTERIOR COLOR	0.40 U[4]	0.24 U	0.19 U	0.10 - 0.15 U	0.40 U	0.24 U	0.19 U	0.10 - 0.15 U
Greenish-blue	White	25	14	5	3	0.33	0.26	0.11	0.07
Aqua	White	29	17	6	4	0.40	0.27	0.11	0.07
Rose	White	30	18	6	4	0.41	0.28	0.11	0.07
White[1]	White	30	17	10	6	0.36	0.14	0.09	0.04
Ice blue	White	35	20	7	4	0.46	0.32	0.12	0.07
Greenish-blue	Crystal	37	20	7	4	0.47	0.29	0.12	0.08
Crystal[1]	White	40	20	12	8	0.55	0.20	0.10	0.06
Crystal[1]	Crystal	60	30	15	10	0.76	0.30	0.12	0.09

NOTES

1. Standard: U = 0.41, light transmission 74%, and solar transmission 75%.
2. Many other combinations available.
3. Approximate values by ASTM E-972. Light transmission values over 30% are not recommended for most applications.
4. Wind at 2 mph; 12 x 24 in. grid; 2$^3/_4$ in. panel; perimeter aluminum excluded. Expressed as Btu/hr-sq ft-°F. Mean temperature: + 30°F for 0.24, 0.19, 0.15, 0.10, and + 7°F for 0.40.
5. At 35° incidence angle. Numbers for various panels are calculated based on tests.

Joseph A. Wilkes, FAIA; Annapolis, Maryland

GENERAL
Aluminum Association
900 19th Street, N.W., Suite 300
Washington, DC 20006
Tel: (202) 862-5100
Fax:(202) 862-5164

Aluminum Extruders Council (AEC)
1000 North Rand Road, Suite 214
Wauconda, IL 60084
Tel: (708)526-2010
Fax:(708) 526-3993

American Architectural Manufacturers Association
1540 East Dundee Road, Suite 310
Palatine, IL 60067
Tel: (708) 202-1350
Fax:(708) 202-1480

National Fenestration Rating Council (NFRC)
1300 Spring Street, Suite 120
Silver Spring, MD 20910
Tel: (301) 589-NFRC
Fax:(301) 588-0854

National Sash and Door Jobbers Association (NSDJA)
2400 East Devon Avenue
Des Plaines, IL 60018
Tel: (708) 299-3400
Fax:(708) 299-0489

REFERENCES
ASTM Standards in Building Codes: Specifications, Test Methods, Practices, Classifications, Definitions. Philadelphia: ASTM. [annual]

Beckett, H. E. and J. A. Godfrey. *Windows Performance: Design and Installation.* New York: Van Nostrand Reinhold, 1974.

Environmental Design Research Division. *A Guide for Window Design.* National Bureau of Standards.

"Fenestration," Chapter 27. *ASHRAE Handbook.* Fundamentals vol. 1989.

Hollow Metal Manual. National Association of Architectural Metal Manufacturers (AAMA), 1987. [looseleaf binder]

Simmons, H. L. *Repairing and Extending Doors and Windows.* Van Nostrand Reinhold, 1990.

Stile & Rail Construction. Architectural Woodwork Institute, 1988.

Window Performance and New Technology, NRCC #29348. National Research Council of Canada, 1988.

Window Selection Guide. AAMA, 1988.

FIRE RATING AND SECURITY
National Fire Protection Association (NFPA)
One Batterymarch Park
P.O. Box 9101
Quincy, MA 02269-9101
Tel: (800) 735-0100
Fax:(617) 770-0700

REFERENCES
Fire Doors and Fire Windows, Standard NFPA 80. Quincy, Mass.: National Fire Protection Association, 1990.

Safety Standard for Fire Doors and Frames, UL 63. Underwriters Laboratories.

Smoke Door Assemblies, Standard 105. NFPA, 1989.

Standard NFPA 80-1983. NFPA, 1983.

METAL DOORS AND FRAMES
Insulated Steel Door Institute
30200 Detroit Road
Cleveland, OH 44145-1967
Tel: (216) 899-0010
Fax:(216) 892-1404

WOOD DOORS AND FRAMES
American Hardboard Association
1210 W. Northwest Highway
Palatine, IL 60067
Tel: (708) 934-8800
Fax:(708) 934-8803

National Wood Window and Door Association, Inc.
1400 E. Touhy Avenue
Suite G54
Des Plaines, IL 60018
Tel: (708) 299-5200
Fax:(708) 299-1286

Steel Door Institute (SDI)
30200 Detroit Road
Cleveland, OH 44145-1967
Tel: (216) 899-0010
Fax:(216) 892-1404

REFERENCES
Architectural Flush Doors. Architectural Woodwork Institute, 1988.

Industry Standard for Ponderosa Pine Doors. National Association of Architectural Metal Manufacturers.

Specifiers Guide to Wood Windows and Doors. National Wood Window and Door Assoc. [loose-leaf binder]

ENTRANCES AND STOREFRONTS
REFERENCES
Aluminum Store Front and Entrance Manual, SFM-1. American Architectural Manufacturers Assoc., 1987.

METAL WINDOWS
Steel Window Institute
1300 Sumner Avenue
Cleveland, OH 44115-2851
Tel: (216) 241-7333
Fax:(216) 241-0105

REFERENCES
Specifier's Guide to Steel Windows. Steel Window Inst.

Recommended Specifications for Steel Windows. Steel Window Institute.

Voluntary Guide Specifications for Aluminum Architectural Windows and Sliding Glass Doors, 101V-86. Amer. Architectural Manufacturers Association (AAMA).

Voluntary Specifications for Aluminum Prime Windows and Sliding Glass Doors, ANSI/AAMA 101-88. AAMA.

WOOD AND PLASTIC WINDOWS
National Wood Window and Door Association, Inc.
1400 E. Touhy Avenue, Suite G54
Des Plaines, IL 60018
Tel: (708) 299-5200
Fax:(708) 299-1286

Vinyl Window and Door Institute
355 Lexington Avenue, 11th Floor
New York, NY 10017
Tel: (212) 351-5400
Fax:(212) 697-0156

HARDWARE
American Hardware Manufacturers Association (AHMA)
801 N. Plaza Drive
Schaumberg, IL 60173-4977
Tel: (708) 605-1025
Fax:(708) 605-1093

Builders Hardware Manufacturers Association, Inc.
355 Lexington Avenue, 17th Floor
New York, NY 10017-6603
Tel: (212) 661-4261
Fax:(212) 370-9047

Door and Hardware Institute (DHI)
14170 Newbrook Drive
Chantilly, VA 22021-2223
Tel: (703) 222-2010
Fax:(703) 222-2410

National Retail Hardware Association
5822 West 74th Street
Indianapolis, IN 46278
Tel: (317) 290-0338
Fax:(317) 290-0378

REFERENCES
DHI Handbook. Door and Hardware Institute. [loose-leaf binder]

Finish Hardware, Monograph 08M710. Construction Specifications Institute, 1985.

GLAZING
Art Glass Suppliers Association
1100-H Brandywine Blvd.
P.O. Box 2188
Zanesville, OH 43702-2188
Tel: (614) 452-4541
Fax:(614) 452-2552

Flat Glass Marketing Association (FGMA)
White Lakes Professional Building
3310 S.W. Harrison Street
Topeka, KS 66611-2279
Tel: (913) 266-7013
Fax:(913) 266-0272

Glass Tempering Association (GTA)
White Lakes Professional Building
3310 S.W. Harrison Street
Topeka, KS 66611-2279
Tel: (913) 266-7064

Laminators Safety Glass Association (LSGA)
White Lakes Professional Building
3310 S.W. Harrison Street
Topeka, KS 66611-2279
Tel: (913) 266-7014

National Glass Association (NGA)
8200 Greensboro Drive, Suite 302
McLean, VA 22102
Tel: (703) 442-4890
Fax:(703) 442-0630

Sealed Insulating Glass Manufacturers Association
401 N. Michigan Ave., Suite 2200
Chicago, IL 60611
Tel: (312) 644-6610
Fax:(312) 321-6869

Society of Glass and Ceramic Decorators
888 17th Street, N.W., Suite 600
Brawner Building
Washington, DC 20006-3959
Tel: (202) 728-4132
Fax:(202) 342-0683

Stained Glass Association of America (SGAA)
P.O. Box 22642
Kansas City, MO 64113
Tel: (816) 333-6690

REFERENCES
Johnson, T. E. *Low-E Glazing Design Guide.* Butterworth, 1991.

Peter, John. *Design with Glass.* Van Nostrand Reinhold, 1964.

Plastics in Glazing and Lighting Applications. National Research Council of Canada.

Stained Glass Renaissance. Lead Industries Association.

Voluntary Standard for Thermal Transmittance and Condensation Resistance of Window, Doors, and Glazed Wall Sections, 1503.1-88, AAMA.

GLAZED CURTAIN WALLS
Architectural Translucent
 Skylight and Curtain Wall Association
3421 M Street N.W., Suite 341
Washington, DC 20007
Tel: (715) 842-4616

Flat Glass Marketing Association (FGMA)
White Lakes Professional Building
3310 S.W. Harrison Street
Topeka, KS 66611-2279
Tel: (913) 266-7013
Fax:(913) 266-0272

REFERENCES
Aluminum Curtain Wall Design Guide Manual, CW 1-9. Amer. Architectural Manufacturers Assoc., 1979.

Glazing Manual. Flat Glass Marketing Assoc., 1990.

Guide to Federal Glazing Laws and the Model Safety Glazing Code. National Glass Association, 1990.

Installation of Aluminun Curtain Walls, CWG-1-89. AAMA, 1989.

Laminated Glass Design Guide, I-SGA, 1991.

Recommended Practices for Vertical and Basic Glazing of Organically Seated Insulating Glass Units, TM-3000. Sealed Insulation Glass Manufacturers Association (SIGMA), 1990.

Science and Technology of Glazing Systems, STP 1054. American Society for Testing and Materials, 1990.

Sound Control for Aluminum Curtain Walls and Windows, TIR-AI-1975. AAMA.

Structural Sealant Glazing Systems, CW-13. AAMA, 1985.

Technical Manual for Acoustical Glass, A-6001. SIGMA, 1986.

Voluntary Guidelines for Sloped Glazing, TB-3001. SIGMA, 1990. pp.

CHAPTER

FINISHES

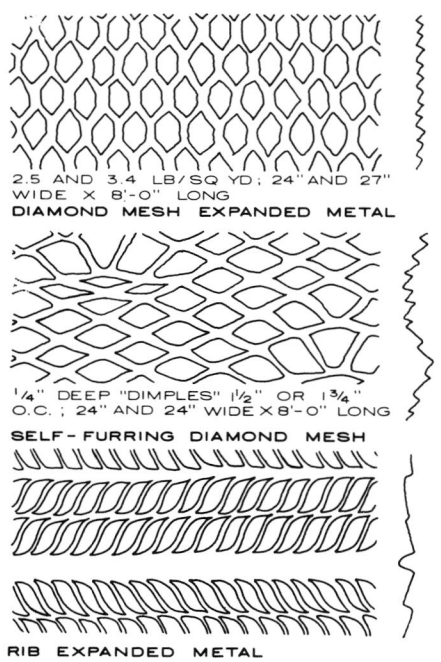

2.5 AND 3.4 LB/SQ YD; 24" AND 27" WIDE X 8'-0" LONG
DIAMOND MESH EXPANDED METAL

1/4" DEEP "DIMPLES" 1 1/2" OR 1 3/4" O.C.; 24" AND 24" WIDE X 8'-0" LONG
SELF-FURRING DIAMOND MESH

RIB EXPANDED METAL

LATHING SYSTEMS

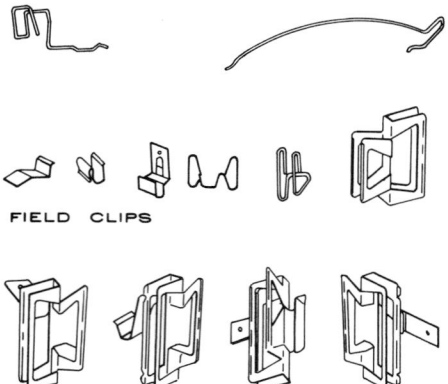

PLASTER COATS LATH SIDE: SCRATCH - BROWN - FINISH
METAL LATH
WIRE TIE
PLASTER COATS CHANNEL SIDE: BACKUP - BROWN - FINISH

SOLID PARTITION SYSTEMS

FIELD CLIPS

CORNER CLIPS

NOTE: OTHER CLIP TYPES ARE AVAILABLE

MISCELLANEOUS

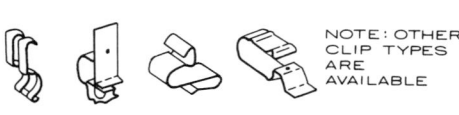

CLIPS FOR GYPSUM LATH SYSTEM

The Marmon Mok Partnership; San Antonio, Texas

LATH AND PLASTER

NOTES

Self-furring paperbacked reinforcing is available in diamond mesh, welded wire, and hexagonal woven wire. Paperbacks are available to conform to Federal Specifications UU-B-790, Type 1, Grade A, Style 2 for highly water-vapor resistant paper.

Metal lath is also manufactured in large diamond mesh 27 x 96 in., 2.5 or 3.4 lb/sq yd, painted steel or galvanized; 1/8 in. flat rib 27 x 96 in., 2.75 or 3.4 lb/sq yd painted or galvanized; 3/8 in. rib expanded 27 x 96 in., 3.4 lb/sq yd painted or galvanized and 3/4 in. rib expanded 24 x 96 in., 5.4 lb/sq yd painted.

Other types of lath are available from some manufacturers.

GYPSUM LATH

Gypsum lath is composed of an air entrained gypsum core sandwiched between two sheets of fibrous absorbent paper and used as a basecoat for gypsum plaster.

1. PLAIN GYPSUM LATH: 3/8 and 1/2 in. thick, 48 in. long, and 16 in. wide (16 1/5 in. in the Western U.S.).
2. PERFORATED GYPSUM LATH: Plain gypsum lath with 3/4 in. diameter holes punched 4 in. o.c. in both directions to provide mechanical key to plaster.
3. INSULATING GYPSUM LATH: Plain gypsum lath with aluminum foil laminated to the backside as insulator or vapor barrier.
4. LONG LENGTH GYPSUM LATH: 16 and 24 in. wide, in lengths up to 12 ft, available insulated or plain with square or vee-jointed Tongue and Groove edges or interlocking as ship-lap edge.

SOLID PLASTER PARTITION CONSTRUCTION

PARTITION CONSTRUCTION	THICKNESS	MAXIMUM HEIGHT
3/4" cold-rolled channels Diamond mesh lath and plaster	2"	12'-0"
3/4" cold-rolled channels Diamond mesh lath and plaster	2 1/2"	16'-0"
1 1/2" cold-rolled channels Diamond mesh lath and plaster	3"	20'-0"
1 1/2" cold-rolled channels Diamond mesh lath and plaster	3 1/2"	22'-0"

NOTE: Maximum partition length is unrestricted if less than 10 ft tall. Twice the height if over 10 ft tall; one and one half the height if over 14 ft tall and equal to the height if over 20 ft tall.

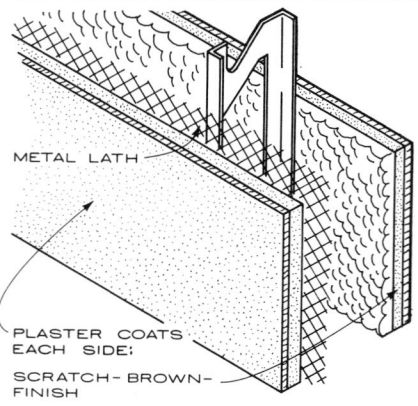

METAL LATH
PLASTER COATS EACH SIDE: SCRATCH - BROWN - FINISH

NOTES

Prefabricated metal studs are used as the supporting elements of lath and plaster hollow partitions. They are available in 1 5/8, 2, 2 1/2, 3 1/4, 4, and 6 in. widths. Lengths are available in various increments up to 24 ft. Prefabricated studs are usually of the nonload bearing type, but load bearing metal studs also are manufactured. Designs vary with the manufacturer, and most manufacturers produce a line of related accessories, such as clips, runners, stud shoes, and similar articles.

HOLLOW PARTITION SYSTEMS

DEFINITIONS

AGGREGATE: Inert material used as filler with a cementitious material and water to produce plaster or concrete. Usually implies sand, perlite, or vermiculite.
BASECOAT: Any plaster coat applied before the finish coat.
BEAD: Light gauge metal strip with one or more expanded or short perforated flanges and variously shaped noses; used at the perimeter of plastered surfaces.
BROWN COAT: In three-coat plaster, the brown coat is the second coat; in two-coat plaster, the base coat.
CALCINED GYPSUM: Gypsum that has been partially dehydrated by heating.
CLIP: A device made of wire or sheet metal for attaching various types of lath and lath sheets to one another.
FIBERED PLASTER: Gypsum plaster containing fibers of hair, glass, nylon, or sisal.
FINISH COAT: The final coat of plaster, which provides the decorative surface.
FURRING: Grillage for the attachment of gypsum or metal lath.
GAUGING: Cementitious material, usually calcined gypsum or portland cement combined with lime putty to control set.
GROUND: A formed metal shape or wood strip that acts as a combined edge and gauge for various thicknesses of plaster to be applied to a plaster base.
GYPSUM: Hydrous calcium sulphate, a natural mineral in crystalline form.
GYPSUM LATH: A base for plaster; a sheet having a gypsum core, faced with paper.
GYPSUM READY MIX PLASTER: Ground gypsum that has been calcined and then mixed with various additives to control its setting and working qualities; used, with the addition of aggregate and water, for basecoat plaster.
HYDRATED LIME: Quicklime mixed with water, on the job, to form a lime putty.
LIME: Obtained by burning various types of limestone, consisting of oxides or hydroxides of calcium and magnesium.
LIME PLASTER: Basecoat plaster of hydrated lime and an aggregate.
NEAT PLASTER: Basecoat plaster, fibered or unfibered, used for job mixing with aggregates.
PERLITE: Siliceous volcanic glass containing silica and alumina expanded by heat for use as a lightweight plaster aggregate.
PLASTER: Cementitious material or combination of cementitious materials and aggregate that, when mixed with water, forms a plastic mass that sets and hardens when applied to a surface.
PORTLAND CEMENT: Manufactured combination of limestone and an argillaceous substance.
SCRATCH COAT: In three-coat plastering, the first coat, which is then scratched to provide a bond for second or brown coat.
SCREED: A device secured to a surface which serves as a guide for subsequent applications of plaster. Thicknesses and widths vary with the thicknesses desired for each operation.
STUCCO PORTLAND CEMENT: Plaster used in exterior application.
VERMICULITE: Micaceous mineral of silica, magnesium, and alumina oxides made up in a series of parallel plates or laminae and expanded by heat for use as a lightweight plaster aggregate.

NOTES

Keene's cement plaster is a specialty finish coat of gypsum plaster primarily used where a smooth, dense, white finish is desired.

Thickness, proportions of mixes of various plastering materials, and finishes vary. Systems and methods of application vary widely depending on local traditions and innovations promoted by the industry.

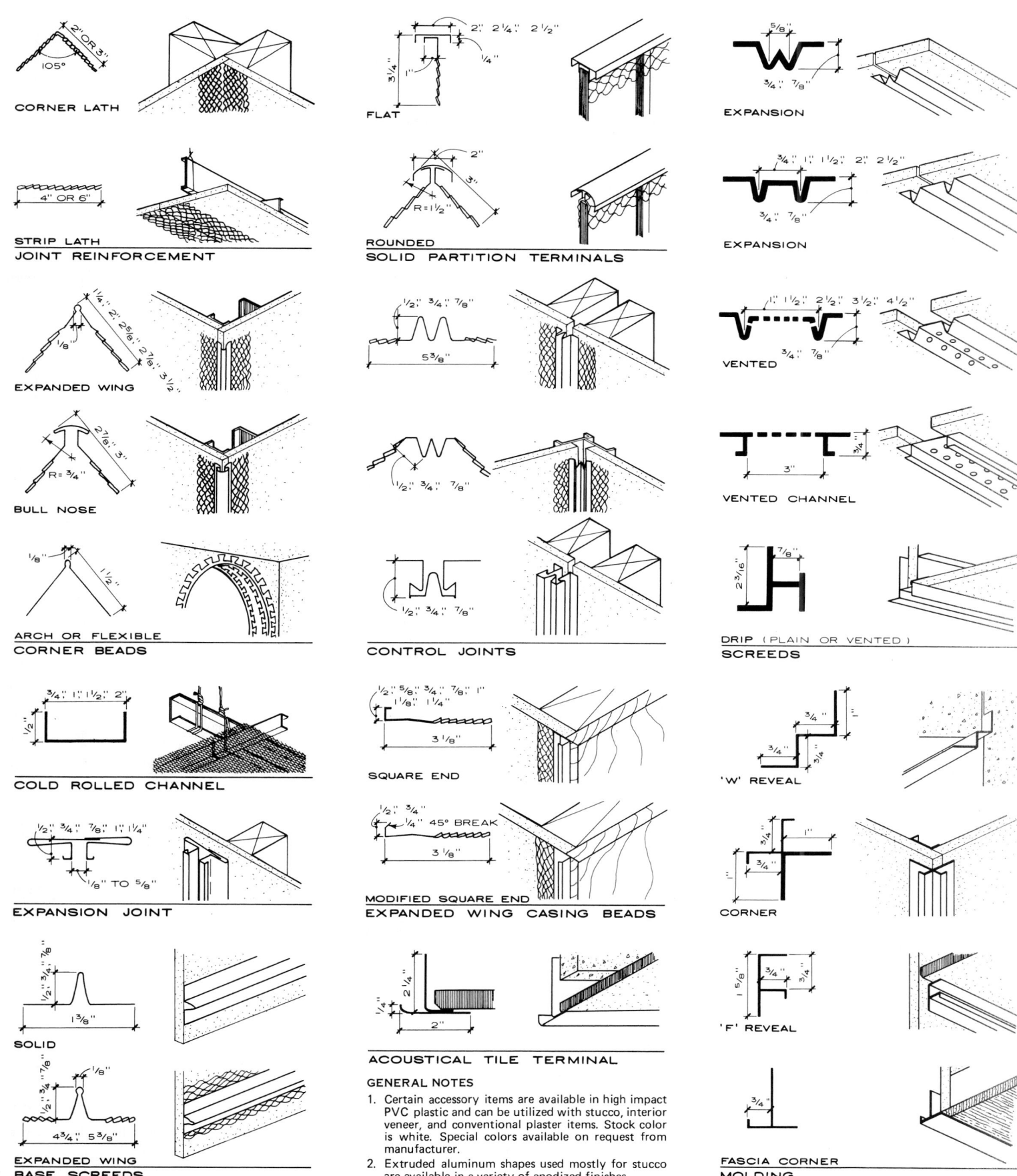

CORNER LATH

STRIP LATH
JOINT REINFORCEMENT

EXPANDED WING

BULL NOSE

ARCH OR FLEXIBLE
CORNER BEADS

COLD ROLLED CHANNEL

EXPANSION JOINT

SOLID

EXPANDED WING
BASE SCREEDS

FLAT

ROUNDED
SOLID PARTITION TERMINALS

CONTROL JOINTS

SQUARE END

MODIFIED SQUARE END
EXPANDED WING CASING BEADS

ACOUSTICAL TILE TERMINAL

GENERAL NOTES
1. Certain accessory items are available in high impact PVC plastic and can be utilized with stucco, interior veneer, and conventional plaster items. Stock color is white. Special colors available on request from manufacturer.
2. Extruded aluminum shapes used mostly for stucco are available in a variety of anodized finishes.

EXPANSION

EXPANSION

VENTED

VENTED CHANNEL

DRIP (PLAIN OR VENTED)
SCREEDS

'W' REVEAL

CORNER

'F' REVEAL

FASCIA CORNER
MOLDING

The Marmon Mok Partnership; San Antonio, Texas

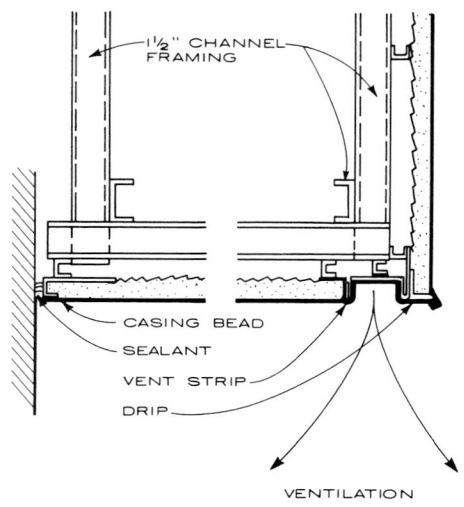

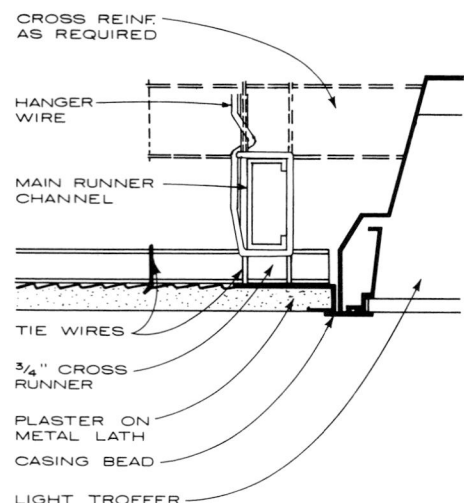

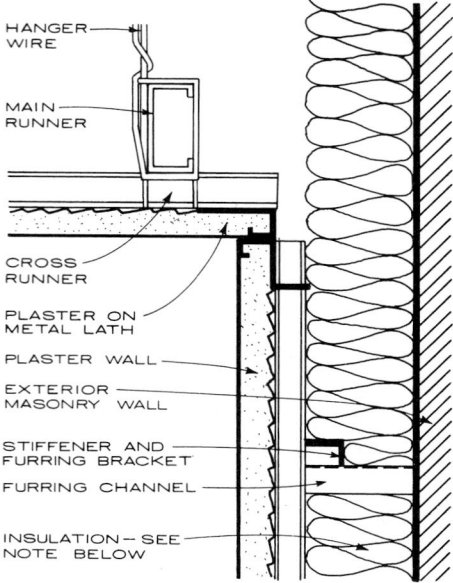

SOFFIT DETAIL

NOTE

Framing details for exterior cement plaster (stucco) are similar to details shown. Wind loads must be considered in designing framing systems for exterior stucco work. Galvanized mesh is available for exterior applications and use in humid areas. Ventilation strips should be used for ventilating all dead airspaces. Where plenum or attic spaces are closed off by ceiling installation, ventilation shall be provided with a minimum of $1/2$ sq. in./sq. ft. of horizontal surface.

SUSPENDED PLASTER CEILING AT RECESSED LIGHT FIXTURE

NOTE

Penetrations of the lath and plaster ceiling—at borrowed light openings, vents, grilles, access panels, and light troffers, for example—require additional reinforcement to distribute concentrated stresses if a control joint is not used. Where a plaster surface is flush with metal, as at metal access panels, grilles, or light troffers, the plaster should be grooved between the two materials.

SUSPENDED PLASTER CEILING AT FURRED MASONRY WALL

NOTE

When interior walls are furred from an exterior masonry wall and insulated, the ceiling should stop short of the furred space. This allows wall insulation to continue above the ceiling line to ceiling or roof insulation, thus forming a complete insulation envelope. In a suspension system that abuts masonry wall, provide 1 in. clearance between ends of main runners or furring channels and wall face.

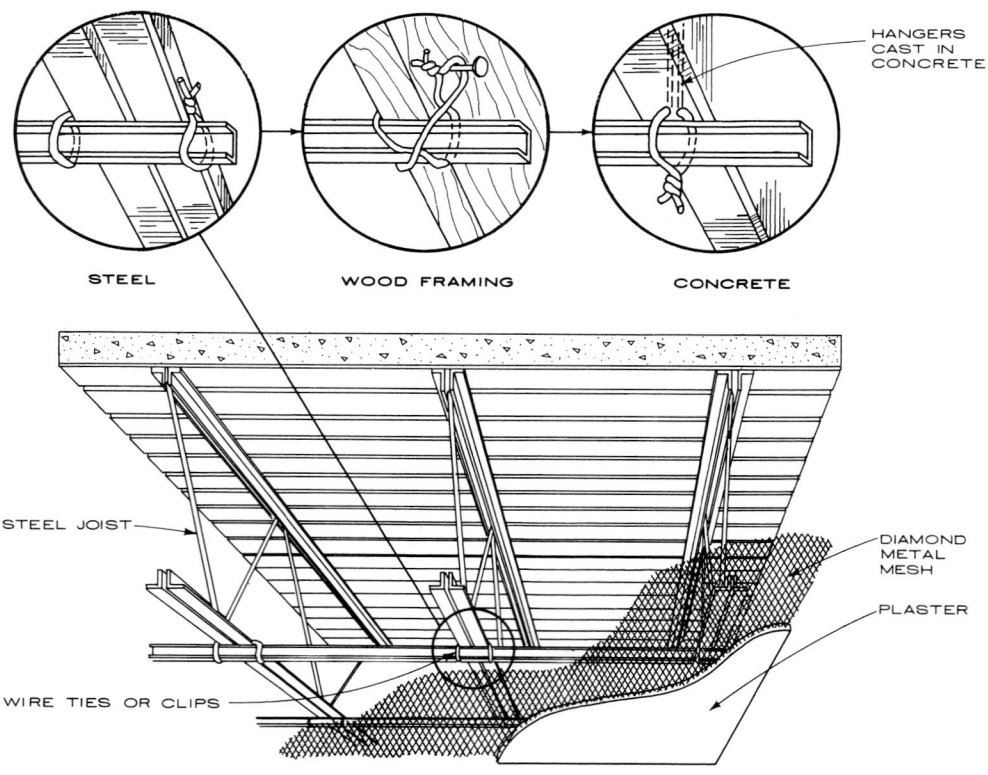

FURRED METAL LATH ON STEEL JOIST

NOTE
RIB METAL LATH MAY BE USED IN LIEU OF DIAMOND MESH LATH AND FURRING CHANNELS IF LATH SPANS DO NOT EXCEED ALLOWABLE MAXIMUM. SEE TABLE 1

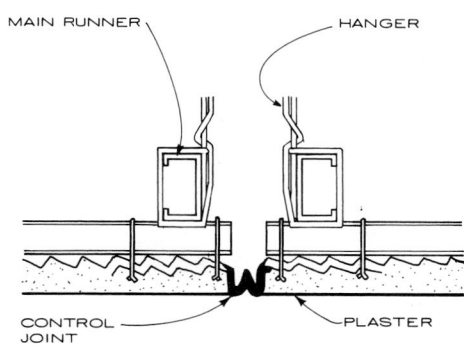

CONTROL JOINT DETAIL

NOTE

Control joints shall be spaced no further than 30 ft on center in each direction for large plastered ceiling areas. Area shall not exceed 900 sq ft without provision for expansion control. Exterior plaster soffits should have control joints spaced no further than 25 ft on center. For portland cement plaster (stucco) areas, interior or exterior, control joints should be placed at 10 ft on center and areas should not exceed 100 sq ft without provisions for expansion/contraction control. Control joints are spaced closer for cement plaster because of its inherent shrinkage during curing.

NOTE

Details shown are for furred (contact) ceilings that are attached directly to the structural members. The architect or ceiling designer should give consideration to the deflection and movement of the structure, since movement and deflection of more than $1/360$ of the span will cause cracking of plaster ceilings. If spacing of structural members exceeds the maximum span of furring members shown in the span charts, the addition of suspended main runners between structural members will be required. Flat rib lath may be attached directly to wood framing members, but is subjected to stresses created by the inherent properties of wood members.

James E. Phillips, AIA; Enwright Associates, Inc.; Greenville, South Carolina

DIRECTIONS FOR USING TABLES

1. Select lath and plaster system.
2. Determine spacing of cross furring channels from Table 1—Lath Span.
3. Determine spacing of main runners from Table 2—Maximum Spacing between Runners.
4. Determine hanger support spacing for main runner from Table 3—Maximum Spacing between Hangers.
5. Calculate area of ceiling supported per hanger.
6. Select hanger type from Table 4—Hanger Selection.
7. Select tie wire size from Table 5—Tie Wire Selection.

TABLE 1. LATH SPAN

	LATH TYPE	WEIGHT/SQ.FT.	SPAN (IN.)
Gypsum lath	3/8" plain	1.5#	16
	1/2" plain	2.0#	16
	1/2" veneer	1.8#	16
	5/8" veneer	2.25#	16
	3/8" perforated	1.4#	16
Metal lath	Diamond mesh	0.27#	12
	Diamond mesh	0.38#	16
	1/8" flat rib	0.31#	12
	1/8" flat rib	0.38#	19
	3/8" flat rib	0.38#	24

TABLE 2. MAXIMUM SPACING BETWEEN RUNNERS

CROSS FURRING TYPE	CROSS FURRING SPACING			
	12"	16"	19"	24"
1/4" diam. pencil rod	2'-0"	—	—	—
3/8" diam. pencil rod	2'-6"	—	2'-0"	—
3/4" CRC, HRC (0.3 lb/ft)	—	4'-6"	3'-6"	3'-0"
1" HRC (0.41 lb/ft)	5'-0"	—	4'-6"	4'-0"

CRC = Cold rolled channel
HRC = Hot rolled channel

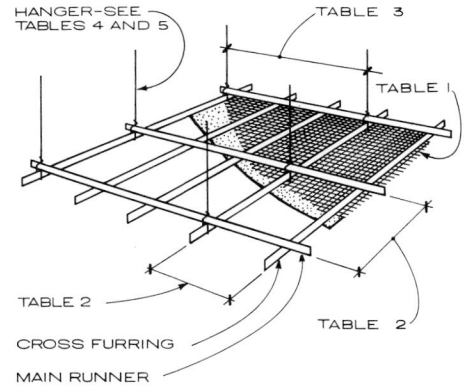

FURRED AND SUSPENSION SYSTEM COMPONENT SELECTION DETAIL

HANGER—SEE TABLES 4 AND 5
TABLE 3
TABLE 1
TABLE 2
TABLE 2
CROSS FURRING
MAIN RUNNER

NOTE

Dimensional requirements for support spacing, runner spacing, hanger spacing, hanger type selection, and tie wire selection are given in tables on this page.

James E. Phillips, AIA; Enwright Associates, Inc.; Greenville, South Carolina

TABLE 3. MAXIMUM SPACING BETWEEN HANGERS

MAIN RUNNER TYPE	MAIN RUNNER SPACING				
	3'-0"	3'-6"	4'-0"	4'-6"	5'-0"
3/4" CRC (0.3 lb/ft)	2'-0"	—	—	—	—
1 1/2" CRC (0.3 lb/ft)	3'-0"*	—	—	—	—
1 1/2" CRC (0.875 lb/ft)	4'-0"	3'-6"	3'-0"	—	—
1 1/2" HRC (1.12 lb/ft)	—	—	—	4'-0"	—
2" CRC (0.59 lb/ft)	—	—	5'-0"	—	—
2" HRC (1.26 lb/ft)	—	—	—	—	5'-0"
1/2" x 1/2" x 3/16" ST1	—	5'-0"	—	—	—

*For concrete construction only—a 10-gauge wire may be inserted in the joint before concrete is poured.

TABLE 4. HANGER SELECTION

MAX. CEILING AREA	MIN. HANGER SIZE
12 sq. ft.	9-gauge galvanized wire
16 sq. ft.	8-gauge galvanized wire
18 sq. ft.	3/16" mild steel rod*
25 sq. ft.	1/4" mild steel rod*
25 sq. ft.	3/16" x 1" steel flat*

*Rods galvanized or painted with rust inhibitive paint and galvanized straps are recommended under severe moisture conditions.

TABLE 5. TIE WIRE SELECTION

	SUPPORT	MAX. CEILING AREA	MIN. HANGER SIZE
Cross furring		8 sq.ft.	14-gauge wire
		8 sq.ft.	16-gauge wire (two loops)
Main runners	Single hangers between beams	8 sq.ft.	12-gauge wire
		12 sq.ft.	10-gauge wire
		16 sq.ft.	8-gauge wire
	Double wire loops at supports	8 sq.ft.	14-gauge wire
		12 sq.ft.	12-gauge wire
		16 sq.ft.	11-gauge wire

ERECTION OF METAL LATH SUSPENSIONS

Metal lath suspensions commonly are made below all types of construction for fire rated plaster ceilings. The lath is supported by framing channels and furring channels suspended with wire hangers from the floor or roof structure above. Framing channels normally are spaced up to 4 ft. o.c. perpendicular to joists and should be erected to conform with the contour of the finished ceiling. Framing channels normally are furred with 3/4 in. channels placed at right angles to the framing. Spacing varies by lath types and weights. The lath should be lapped at both sides and ends and secured to the 3/4 in. channels with wire ties every 6 in. Where plaster on metal lath ceilings abuts masonry walls, partitions, or arch soffits, galvanized casing beads should be installed at the periphery.

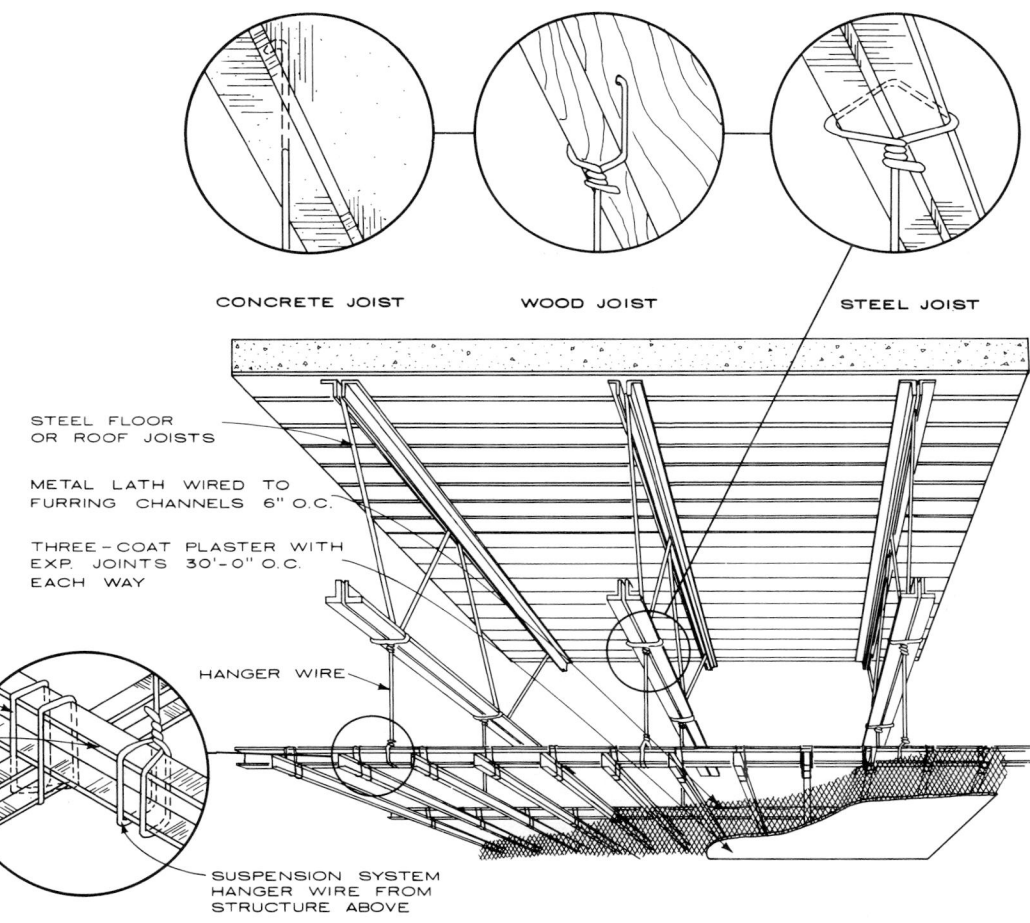

CONCRETE JOIST   WOOD JOIST   STEEL JOIST

STEEL FLOOR OR ROOF JOISTS
METAL LATH WIRED TO FURRING CHANNELS 6" O.C.
THREE-COAT PLASTER WITH EXP. JOINTS 30'-0" O.C. EACH WAY
HANGER WIRE
SUSPENSION SYSTEM TIE WIRES AS REQUIRED
MAIN RUNNER CHANNEL
3/4" CROSS FURRING CHANNEL
SUSPENSION SYSTEM HANGER WIRE FROM STRUCTURE ABOVE

METAL LATH SUSPENDED FROM STEEL JOISTS

LATH AND PLASTER

9

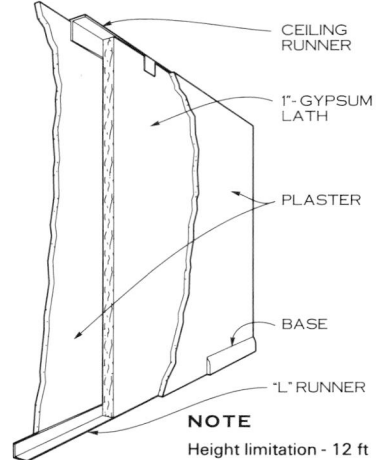

SECTION THROUGH TYPICAL WALL

- CEILING RUNNER
- 1"- GYPSUM LATH
- PLASTER
- BASE
- "L" RUNNER

NOTE
Height limitation - 12 ft

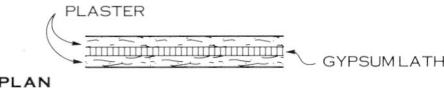

- PLASTER
- GYPSUM LATH

PLAN

2 IN. SOLID GYPSUM LATH

CHANNEL STUD SPACING

TYPE OF LATH	WEIGHT LB/ SQ YD	SPACING OF SUPPORTS
Diamond mesh	2.5	16
	3.4	16
Flat rib	2.75	16
	3.4	24*

*Spacing for solid partitions not to exceed 16'- 0" in height.

CHANNEL STUD SIZE

PARTITION HEIGHT	PARTITION THICKNESS	CHANNEL
12'	2"	
14'	2 1/4"	3/4 in. 300 lb per 1000 ft
16'	2 1/2"	
18'	2 3/4"	1 1/2 in. 475 lb per 1000 ft

METAL STUD WITH METAL LATH STUD SPACING AND HEIGHT LIMITATION*

STUD WIDTH	THICKNESS	MAXIMUM HEIGHT		
		16" O.C.	19"O.C.	24" O.C.
2 1/2"	4"	15'	14'	9'
3 1/4"	4 3/4"	21'	18'	13'
4"	5 1/2"	22'	20'	16'
6"	7 1/2"	26'	24'	20'

*For length not exceeding 1 1/2 times height; for lengths exceeding this, reduce 20%.

METAL STUDS WITH 3/8 IN. GYPSUM LATH HEIGHT LIMITATIONS*

STUD SIZE	LIMIT HEIGHT	I_x MIN.	S_x MIN.
1 5/8"	10'- 6"	0.038	0.044
2 1/2"	13'- 0"	0.103	0.076
3 5/8"	16'- 3"	0.243	0.125
4"	17'- 3"	0.307	0.143
6"	15'- 0"	0.810	0.255

*25 gauge studs (ASTM C-645) spaced at 16 in. o.c..

FRAME AND FASTENER SPACING WITH ROCK LATH PLASTER BASE

FRAMING TYPE	BASE THICKNESS		FASTENER	FRAME SPACING (MAX.)		FASTENER SPACING (MAX.)	
	IN.	MM		IN.	MM	IN.	MM
Unimast Steel stud	3/8"	9.5	1 in. drywall screws	16	406	12	305
	1/2"	12.7		24	610	6	152

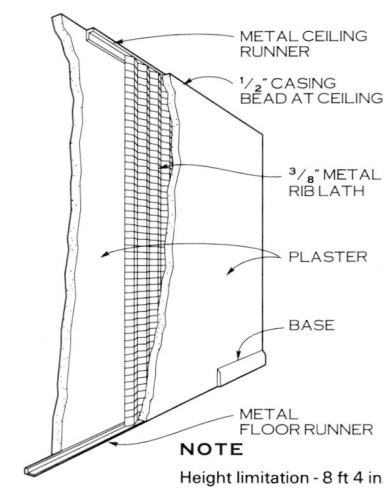

SECTION THROUGH TYPICAL WALL

- METAL CEILING RUNNER
- 1/2" CASING BEAD AT CEILING
- 3/8" METAL RIB LATH
- PLASTER
- BASE
- METAL FLOOR RUNNER

NOTE
Height limitation - 8 ft 4 in

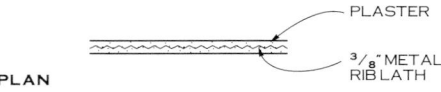

- PLASTER
- 3/8" METAL RIB LATH

PLAN

2 IN. SOLID METAL LATH AND PLASTER

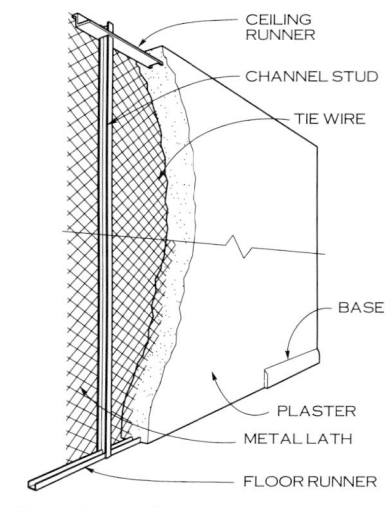

SECTION THROUGH TYPICAL WALL

- CEILING RUNNER
- CHANNEL STUD
- TIE WIRE
- BASE
- PLASTER
- METAL LATH
- FLOOR RUNNER

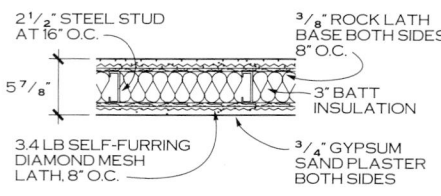

- METAL LATH
- CHANNEL STUD
- PLASTER

PLAN

METAL LATH - CHANNEL STUD - PLASTER- 1 HOUR FIRE RATED

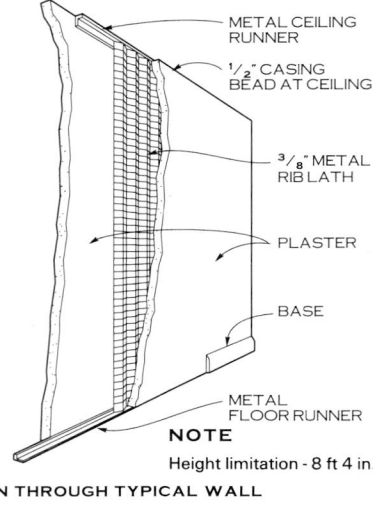

- 2 1/2" STEEL STUD AT 16" O.C.
- 3/8" ROCK LATH BASE BOTH SIDES 8" O.C.
- 5 7/8"
- 3" BATT INSULATION
- 3.4 LB SELF-FURRING DIAMOND MESH LATH, 8" O.C.
- 3/4" GYPSUM SAND PLASTER BOTH SIDES

GYPSUM AND PLASTER LATH - 2 HOUR FIRE RATED PARTITION

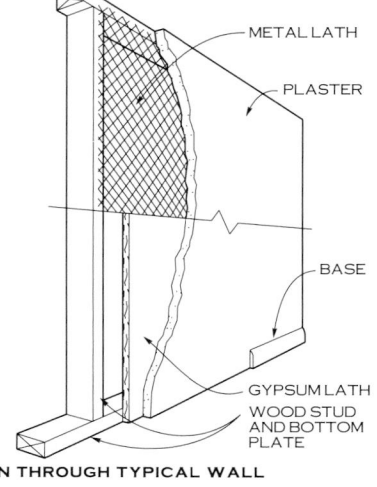

SECTION THROUGH TYPICAL WALL

- METAL LATH
- PLASTER
- BASE
- GYPSUM LATH
- WOOD STUD AND BOTTOM PLATE

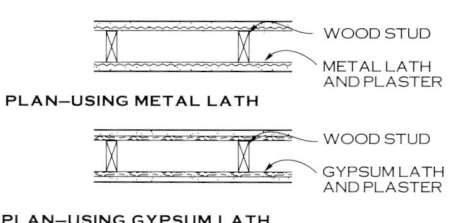

- METAL LATH AND PLASTER
- WOOD STUD

PLAN—USING METAL LATH

- WOOD STUD
- GYPSUM LATH AND PLASTER

PLAN—USING GYPSUM LATH

WOOD STUD AND LATH

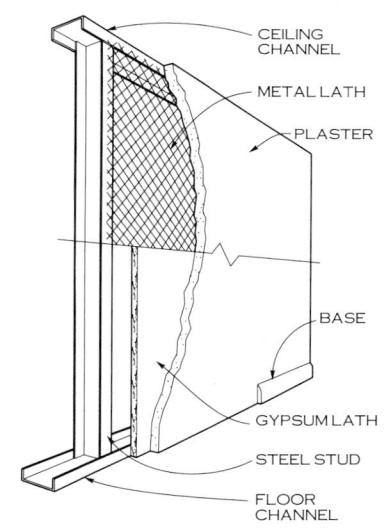

- CEILING CHANNEL
- METAL LATH
- PLASTER
- BASE
- GYPSUM LATH
- STEEL STUD
- FLOOR CHANNEL

SECTION THROUGH TYPICAL WALL

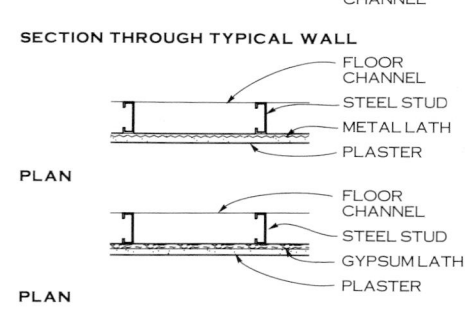

- FLOOR CHANNEL
- STEEL STUD
- METAL LATH
- PLASTER

PLAN

- FLOOR CHANNEL
- STEEL STUD
- GYPSUM LATH
- PLASTER

PLAN

PREFABRICATED METAL STUD

United States Gypsum Company; Chicago, Illinois
Walter H. Sobel, FAIA & Associates; Chicago, Illinois

LATH AND PLASTER

TYPES OF GYPSUM PANEL PRODUCTS

DESCRIPTION	THICKNESS (IN.)	WIDTH/EDGE (FT)	STOCK LENGTH (FT)
Regular gypsum wallboard used as a base layer for improving sound control; repair and remodeling with double layer application	1/4	4, square or tapered	8-10
Regular gypsum wallboard used in a double wall system over wood framing; repair and remodeling	3/8	4, square or tapered	8-14
Regular gypsum wallboard for use in single layer construction	1/2, 5/8	4, square or tapered	8-16
Rounded taper edge system offers maximum joint strength and minimizes joint deformity problems	3/8 1/2, 5/8	4, rounded taper	8-16
Type X gypsum wallboard with core containing special additives to give increased fire resistance ratings. Consult manufacturer for approved assemblies	1/2, 5/8	4, tapered, rounded taper, or rounded	8-16
Aluminum foil backed board effective as a vapor barrier for exterior walls and ceilings and as a thermal insulator when foil faces 3/4'' minimum air space. Not for use as a tile base or in air conditioned buildings in hot, humid climates (Southern Atlantic and Gulf Coasts)	3/8 1/2, 5/8	4, square or tapered	8-16
Water resistant board for use as a base for ceramic and other nonabsorbant wall tiles in bath and shower areas. Type X core is available	1/2, 5/8	4, tapered	8, 10, 12
Prefinished vinyl surface gypsum board in standard and special colors. Type X core is available	1/2, 5/8	2, 2 1/2, 4, square and beveled	8, 9, 10
Prefinished board available in many colors and textures. See manufacturers' literature	5/16	4, square	8
Coreboard for use to enclose vent shafts and laminated gypsum partitions	1	2, tongue and groove or square	8-12
Shaft wall liner core board type X with gypsum core used to enclose elevator shafts and other vertical chases	1, 2	2, square or beveled	6-16
Sound underlayment gypsum wallboard attached to plywood subfloor acts as a base for any durable floor covering. When used with resiliently attached gypsum panel ceiling, the assembly meets HUD requirements for sound control in multifamily dwellings	3/4	4, square	6-8
Exterior ceiling/soffit panel for use on surfaces with indirect exposure to the weather. Type X core is available	1/2, 5/8	4, rounded taper	8, 12
Sheathing used as underlayment on exterior walls with type X or regular core	1/2	2, tongue and groove	8
	1/2, 5/8	4, square	8, 9, 10

NOTE: A large range of adhesives, sealants, joint treatments, and texture products are available from the manufacturers of most gypsum board products. Consult available literature for current recommendations and products.

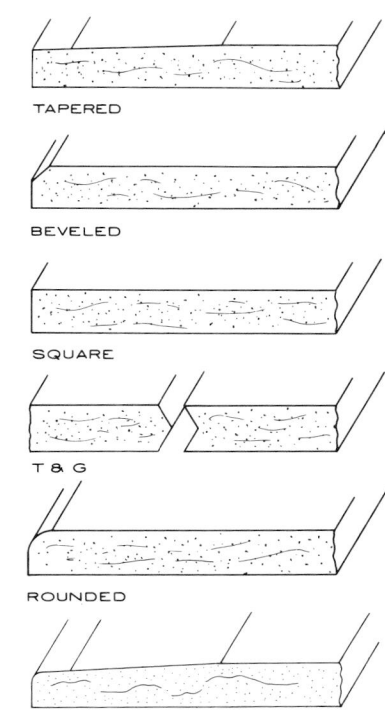

TAPERED

BEVELED

SQUARE

T & G

ROUNDED

ROUNDED TAPER

TYPES OF EDGES

MAX. BENDING FOR DRYWALL

BENDING RADII		
THICKNESS	LENGTHWISE	WIDTH
1/4''	5'-0''	15'-0''
3/8''	7'-6''	25'-0''
1/2''	20'-0''	

Shorter radii may be obtained by moistening face and back so that water will soak well into core of board.

MAXIMUM ALLOWABLE PARTITION HEIGHT (5 PSF LOADING, L240 DEFLECTION, 25 GA STUDS)

STUD SPACING (IN.) (FACING ON EACH SIDE)	STUD DEPTH (IN.)				
	1 5/8 *	2 1/2	3 5/8	4	6
	MAXIMUM ALLOWABLE HEIGHT				
16 (1/2 one-ply)	9'-6''	12'-6''	16'-0''	17'-3''	20'-0''
24 (1/2 one-ply)	8'-3''	10'-9''	13'-6''	14'-3''	15'-0''
24 (1/2 two-ply)	8'-9''	11'-3''	13'-6''	14'-3''	15'-0''

*1 5/8'' stud with single layer of gypsum wallboard recommended for chase walls and closets only.

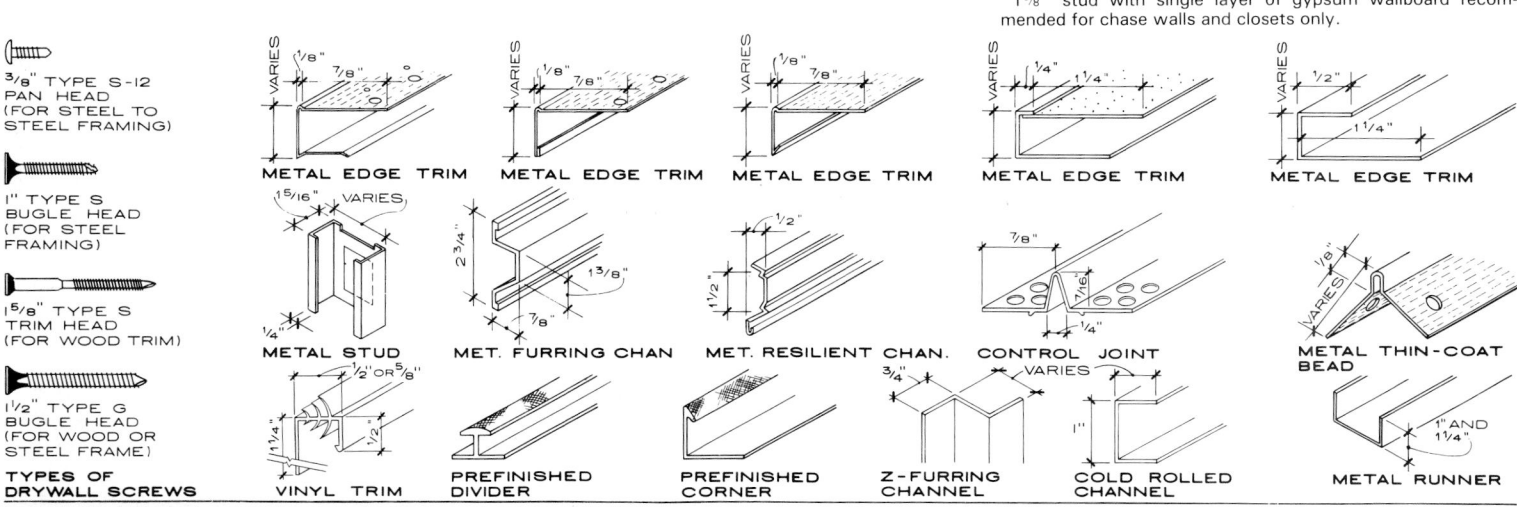

3/8'' TYPE S-12 PAN HEAD (FOR STEEL TO STEEL FRAMING)

1'' TYPE S BUGLE HEAD (FOR STEEL FRAMING)

1 5/8'' TYPE S TRIM HEAD (FOR WOOD TRIM)

1 1/2'' TYPE G BUGLE HEAD (FOR WOOD OR STEEL FRAME)

TYPES OF DRYWALL SCREWS

METAL EDGE TRIM

METAL EDGE TRIM

METAL EDGE TRIM

METAL EDGE TRIM

METAL EDGE TRIM

METAL STUD

MET. FURRING CHAN

MET. RESILIENT CHAN.

CONTROL JOINT

METAL THIN-COAT BEAD

VINYL TRIM

PREFINISHED DIVIDER

PREFINISHED CORNER

Z-FURRING CHANNEL

COLD ROLLED CHANNEL

METAL RUNNER

GYPSUM DRYWALL ACCESSORIES AND COMPONENTS

Ferdinand R. Scheeler, AIA; Skidmore, Owings & Merrill; Chicago, Illinois
James Lloyd; Kennett Square, Pennsylvania

FIRE RATING	STC	WALL THICKNESS	CONSTRUCTION DESCRIPTION	WALL SECTIONS
1 HOUR	30 TO 34	4 7/8"	One layer 1/2 in. type X veneer base nailed to each side of 2 x 4 in. wood studs 16 in. o.c. with 5d coated nails 8 in. o.c. Minimum 3/32 in. gypsum veneer plaster. Joints staggered vertically 16 in. and horizontal joints each side at 12 in.	
		4 7/8"	One layer 5/8 in. type X gypsum wallboard or veneer base nailed to each side of 2 x 4 in. wood studs 16 in. o.c. with 6d coated nails 7 in. o.c. Stagger joints 24 in. on each side.	
	35 TO 39	5 1/8"	Two layers 3/8 in. regular gypsum wallboard or veneer base nailed to each side of 2 x 4 in. wood studs 16 in. o.c. First layer attached with 4d coated nails, second layer applied with laminating compound and nailed with 5d coated nails 8 in. o.c. Stagger joints 16 in. o.c. each side.	
	45 TO 49	5 3/8"	Base layer 3/8 in. regular gypsum wallboard or veneer base nailed to each side of 2 x 4 in. wood studs 16 in. o.c. Face layer 1/2 in. (same as base layer). Use 5d coated nails 24 in. o.c. for base layer and 8d coated nails 12 in. o.c. to edge and 24 in. o.c. to intermediate studs. Stagger joints 16 in. o.c. each layer and side.	
		5 7/8"	Base layer 1/2 in. wood fiberboard to each side of 2 x 4 in. wood studs 16 in. o.c. with 5d coated nails 24 in. o.c. on vertical joints and 16 in. o.c. to top and bottom plates. Face layer 5/8 in. type X gypsum wallboard or veneer base applied to each side with laminating compound and nailed with 8d coated nails 24 in. o.c. on vertical joints and 16 in. o.c. to top and bottom plates. Stagger joints 24 in. o.c. each layer and side.	
		5 7/8"	Both sides resilient channels 24 in. o.c. attached with GWB 54 drywall nails to each side of 2 x 4 in. wood studs 16 in. o.c. One layer 5/8 in. type X gypsum wallboard or veneer base attached with 1 in. type S drywall screws 12 in. o.c. to each side and vertical joints back-blocked. GWB filler strips along floor and ceiling both sides. Stagger joints 24 in. o.c. each side.	
	50 TO 54	5 3/8"	Base layer 1/4 in. proprietary gypsum wallboard applied to each side of 2 x 4 in. wood studs 16 in. o.c. with 4d coated nails 12 in. o.c. Face layer 5/8 in. type X gypsum wallboard or veneer base applied with laminating compound and nailed with 6d coated nails 16 in. o.c. to each side. 1 1/2 in. mineral fiber insulation in cavity. Stagger joints 24 in. o.c. each side.	
		5 3/8"	One side resilient channel 24 in. o.c. with 1 1/4 in. type S drywall screws to 2 x 4 in. wood studs 16 in. o.c. Both sides 5/8 in. gypsum wallboard or veneer base attached to resilient channel with 1 in. type S drywall screws 12 in. o.c. and GWB to stud with 1 1/4 in. type W drywall screws. 1 1/2 in. mineral fiber insulation in cavity. Stagger joints 48 in. o.c. each side.	
	60 TO 64	6 7/8"	One side resilient channels 24 in. o.c. attached with 1 in. type S drywall screws to 2 x 4 in. wood studs 16 in. o.c. Two layers of 5/8 in. type X gypsum wallboard or veneer base. First layer attached with 1 in. type S drywall screws, second layer applied with laminating compound. Other side one layer each of 5/8 in. and 1/2 in. gypsum wallboard or veneer base plus top 3/8 in. gypsum wallboard applied with laminating compound. Use 5d coated nails 32 in. o.c. for base, 8d for 1/2 in. center layer. 2 in. glass fiber insulation in cavity. Stagger all joints 16 in. o.c.	
2 HOUR	40 TO 44	6 1/8"	Two layers 5/8 in. type X gypsum wallboard or veneer base applied to each side of 2 x 4 in. wood studs 24 in. o.c. Use 6d coated nails 24 in. o.c. for base layer and 8d coated nails 8 in. o.c. for face layer. Stagger joints 24 in. o.c. each layer and side.	
	50 TO 54	8"	Two layers 5/8 in. type X gypsum wallboard or veneer base applied to each side of 2 x 4 in. wood studs 16 in. o.c. staggered 8 in. o.c. on 2 x 6 in. wood plates. Use 6d coated nails 24 in. o.c. for base layer and 8d coated nails 8 in. o.c. for face layer. Stagger vertical joints 16 in. o.c. each layer and side.	
	55 TO 59	10 3/4"	Two layers 5/8 in. type X gypsum wallboard or veneer base applied to each side of double row of 2 x 4 in. wood studs 16 in. o.c. on separate plates 1 in. apart. Use 6d coated nails 24 in. o.c. for base layer and 8d coated nails 8 in. o.c. for face layer. 3 1/2 in. glass fiber insulation in cavity. Stagger joints 16 in. o.c. each layer and side. GWB fire stop continuous in space between plates.	

FIRE RATING	STC	WALL THICKNESS	CONSTRUCTION DESCRIPTION	WALL SECTIONS
1 HOUR	35 TO 39	2 7/8"	One layer 5/8 in. type X gypsum wallboard or veneer base applied to each side of 1 5/8 in. metal studs 24 in. o.c. with 1 in. type S drywall screws 8 in. o.c. to edges and 12 in. o.c. to intermediate studs. Stagger joints 24 in. o.c. each side.	
	40 TO 44	3 3/8"	Base layer 3/8 in. regular gypsum wallboard or veneer base applied to each side of 1 5/8 in. metal studs 24 in. o.c. with 1 in. type S drywall screws 27 in. o.c. to edges and 54 in. o.c. to intermediate studs. Face layer 1/2 in. attached on each side to studs with 1 5/8 in. type S drywall screws 12 in. o.c. to perimeter and 24 in. o.c. to intermediate studs. Stagger joints 24 in. o.c. each layer and side.	
		4 7/8"	One layer 5/8 in. type X gypsum wallboard or veneer base applied to each side of 3 5/8 in. metal studs 24 in. o.c. with 1 in. type S drywall screws 8 in. o.c. to vertical edges and 12 in. o.c. to intermediate studs. Stagger joints 24 in. o.c. each side.	
	45 TO 49	3 1/8"	Two layers 1/2 in. regular gypsum wallboard or veneer base applied to each side of 1 5/8 in. metal studs 24 in. o.c. Use 1 in. type S drywall screws 12 in. o.c. for base layer and 1 5/8 in. type S drywall screws 12 in. o.c. for face layer. Stagger joints 24 in. o.c. each layer and side.	
		3 1/8"	Base layer 1/4 in. gypsum wallboard applied to each side of 1 5/8 in. metal studs 24 in. o.c. with 1 in. type S drywall screws 24 in. o.c. to edges and 36 in. o.c. to intermediate studs. Face layer 1/2 in. type X gypsum wallboard or veneer base applied to each side of studs with 1 5/8 in. type S drywall screws 12 in. o.c. Stagger joints 24 in. o.c. each layer and side.	
		5 1/2"	One layer 5/8 in. type X gypsum wallboard or veneer base applied to each side of 3 5/8 in. metal studs 24 in. o.c. with 1 in. type S drywall screws 8 in. o.c. to edge and vertical joints and 12 in. o.c. to intermediate stud. Face layer 5/8 in. (same as other layer) applied on one side to stud with laminating compound and attached with 1 5/8 in. type S drywall screws 8 in. o.c. to edges and sides and 12 in. o.c. to intermediate studs. 3 1/2 in. glass fiber insulation in cavity. Stagger joints 24 in. o.c. each layer and side.	
	50 TO 54	4"	Base layer 1/4 in. regular gypsum wallboard applied to each side of 2 1/2 in. metal studs 24 in. o.c. with 1 in. type S drywall screws 12 in. o.c. Face layer 1/2 in. type X gypsum wallboard or veneer base applied to each side of studs with laminating compound and with 1 5/8 in. type S drywall screws in top and bottom runners 8 in. o.c. 2 in. glass fiber insulation in cavity. Stagger joints 24 in. o.c. each layer and side.	
		4"	Two layers 1/2 in. type X gypsum wallboard or veneer base applied to one side of 2 1/2 in. metal studs 24 in. o.c. Base layer 1 in. and face layer 1 5/8 in. type S drywall screws 8 in. o.c. to edge and adhesive beads to intermediate studs. Opposite side layer 1/2 in. type X gypsum wallboard or veneer base applied with 1 in. type S drywall screws 8 in. o.c. to vertical edges and 12 in. o.c. to intermediate studs. 3 in. glass fiber insulation in cavity. Stagger joints 24 in. o.c. each layer and face.	
	55 TO 59	4 1/4"	Base layer 1/4 in. gypsum wallboard applied to each side of 2 1/2 in. metal studs 24 in. o.c. with 7/8 in. type S drywall screws 12 in. o.c. Face layer 5/8 in. type X gypsum wallboard or veneer base applied on each side of studs with 1 5/16 in. type S drywall screws 12 in. o.c. 1 1/2 in. glass fiber insulation in cavity. Stagger joints 24 in. o.c. each layer and side.	
2 HOUR	40 TO 44	5"	Two layers 5/8 in. type X gypsum wallboard or veneer base applied to each side of 2 1/2 in. metal studs 16 in. o.c. braced laterally. Use 1 in. for base layer and 1 5/8 in. for facelayer type S-12 drywall screws 12 in. o.c. Stagger joints 16 in. o.c. each layer and side.	
	50 TO 54	3 5/8"	Base layer 1/2 in. type X gypsum wallboard or veneer base applied to each side of 1 5/8 in. metal studs 24 in. o.c. Use 1 in. type S drywall screws 12 in. o.c. for base layer and 1 5/8 in. type S drywall screws 12 in. o.c. for face layer. 1 1/2 in. glass fiber insulation in cavity. Stagger joints 24 in. o.c. each layer and side.	
	55 TO 59	6 1/4"	Two layers 5/8 in. type X gypsum wallboard or veneer base applied to each side of 3 5/8 in. metal studs 24 in. o.c. Use 1 in. type S drywall screws 32 in. o.c. for base layer and 1 5/8 in. type S drywall screws 12 in. o.c. to edge and 24 in. o.c. to intermediate studs. One side third layer 1/4 or 3/8 in. gypsum wallboard or veneer base applied with laminating compound. Stagger joints 24 in. o.c. each layer and side.	

FIRE RATING	STC	WALL THICKNESS	CONSTRUCTION DESCRIPTION	WALL SECTIONS
1 HOUR	35 TO 39	3⅛"	1 in. x 24 in. proprietary type X gypsum panels inserted between 2½ in. floor and ceiling J runners with 2½ in. proprietary vented C-H studs between panels. One layer ⅝ in. proprietary type X gypsum wallboard or veneer base applied parallel to studs on side opposite proprietary gypsum panels with 1 in. type S drywall screws spaced 12 in. o.c. in studs and runners. STC estimate based on 1 in. mineral fiber in cavity. (NLB)	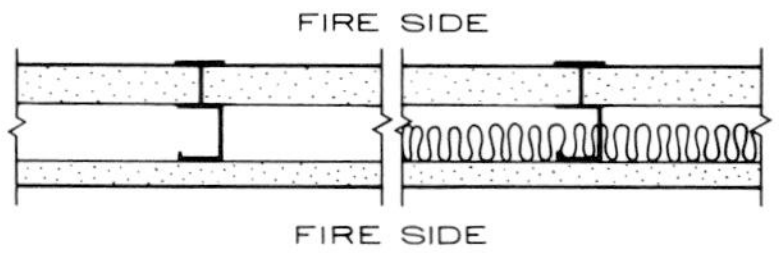 FIRE SIDE / FIRE SIDE
	40 TO 44	2⅞"	¾ in. x 24 in. proprietary type X gypsum panels inserted between 2¼ in. floor and ceiling track and fitted to proprietary 2¼ in. slotted metal I studs with tab-flange. Face layer ⅝ in. type X gypsum board applied at right angles to studs, with 1 in. type S drywall screws, 12 in. o.c. Sound tested with 1 in. glass fiber friction fit in stud space. (NLB)	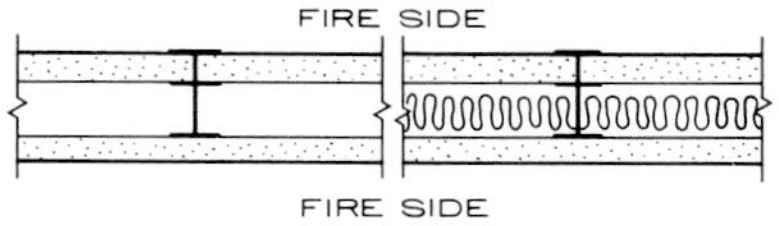 FIRE SIDE / FIRE SIDE
2 HOURS	30 TO 34	2¼"	One layer ⅝ in. type X gypsum wallboard or veneer base applied vertically to each side of 1 in. gypsum board panels (solid or laminated) with laminating compound combed over entire contact surface. Panel supported by metal runners at top and bottom and horizontal bracing angles of No. 22 gauge galvanized steel ¾ in. x 1¼ in. spaced 5 ft. 0 in. o.c. or less on shaft side. (NLB) *Limiting height shown is based on interior partition exposure conditions. Shaft wall exposure conditions may require reduction of limiting height.	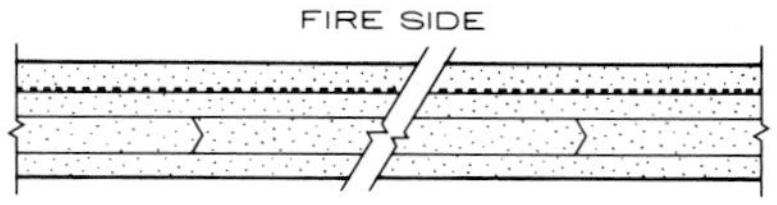 FIRE SIDE
	35 TO 39	4⅛"	Four layers ⅝ in. type X gypsum wallboard or veneer base applied at right angles to one side of 1⅝ in. metal studs 24 in. o.c. Base layer attached to studs with 1 in. type S drywall screws 12 in. o.c. Second layer attached to studs with 1⅝ in. type S drywall screws using only two screws per board. Third layer attached with 2⅝ in. type S drywall screws similar to second layer. Steel strips 1½ in. wide vertically applied over third layer at stud lines and attached 12 in. o.c. to studs with 2⅝ in. type S drywall screws. Third layer also attached to top and bottom track with 2⅝ in. type S drywall screws placed midway between studs. Face layer attached to steel strips with 1 in. type S drywall screws 8 in. o.c. at each stud. Stagger joints of each layer. (NLB)	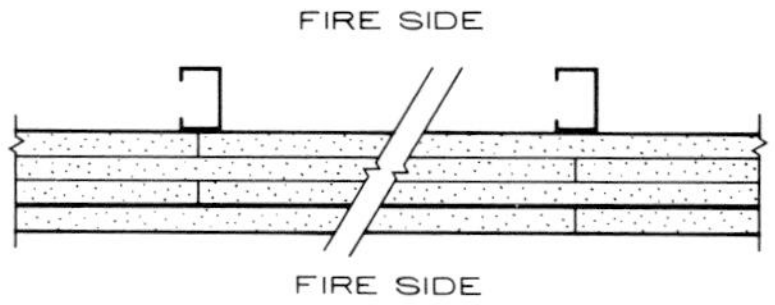 FIRE SIDE / FIRE SIDE
	40 TO 44	3½"	1 in. x 24 in. proprietary type X gypsum panels inserted between 2½ in. floor and ceiling J track with T section of 2½ in. proprietary C-T metal studs between proprietary gypsum panels. Two layers of ½ in. type X gypsum wallboard applied to face of C-T studs. Base layer applied at right angles to studs with 1 in. type S drywall screws 24 in. o.c. and face layer applied at right angles to studs with 1⅝ in. type S drywall screws 8 in. o.c. Stagger joints 24 in. o.c. each layer. (NLB)	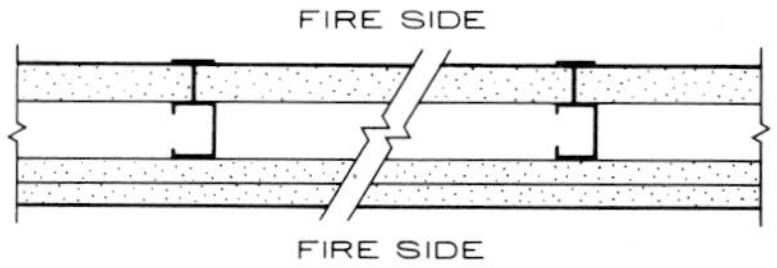 FIRE SIDE / FIRE SIDE
	45 TO 49	3½"	1 in. x 24 in. proprietary type X gypsum panels inserted between 2½ in. floor and ceiling track with tab-flange section of 2½ in. metal I studs between proprietary gypsum panels. One layer of ½ in. proprietary type X gypsum wallboard or veneer base applied at right angles to each side of metal I studs with 1 in. type S drywall screws 12 in. o.c. Sound tested using 1½ in. glass fiber friction fit in stud space. (NLB)	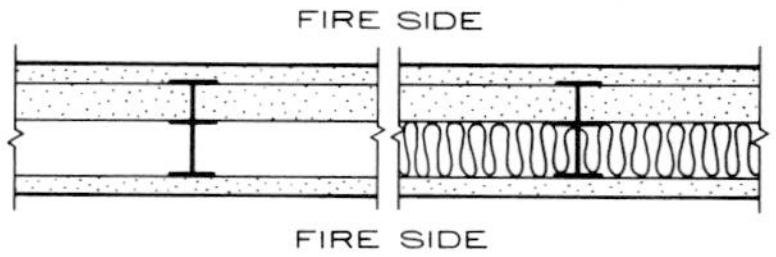 FIRE SIDE / FIRE SIDE
	50 TO 54	4"	1 in. x 24 in. proprietary type X gypsum panels inserted between 2½ in. floor and ceiling track with tab-flange section of 2½ in. metal I studs between proprietary gypsum panels. One layer of ½ in. proprietary type X gypsum wallboard or veneer base applied at right angles to flanges of I studs adjacent to proprietary gypsum panels with 1 in. type S drywall screws 12 in. o.c. Resilient channels spaced 24 in. o.c. horizontally, screw attached to opposite flanges of I studs with ⅜ in. type S screws, one per channel-stud intersection. ½ in. proprietary type X gypsum wallboard or veneer base applied parallel to resilient furring channels with 1 in. type S drywall screws 12 in. o.c. Sound tested using 1 in. glass fiber friction fit in stud space. (NLB)	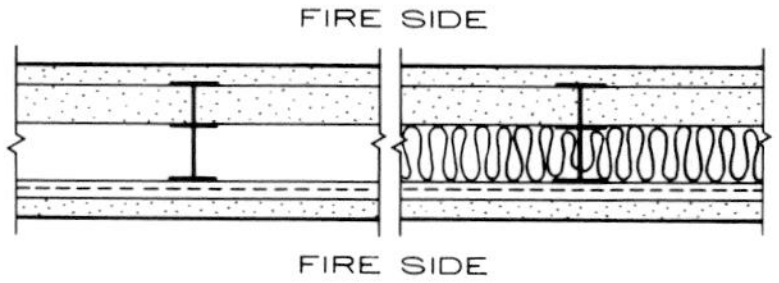 FIRE SIDE / FIRE SIDE
3 HOURS	40 TO 44	4⅛"	2 in. x 24 in. laminated gypsum board panels installed vertically between floor and ceiling 20 gauge J runners with 25 gauge steel H members between panels. Panels attached at midpoint to 2½ in. leg of J runners with 2⅜ in. type S-12 drywall screws. H studs formed from 20 or 25 gauge 2 in. x 1 in. channels placed back to back and spot welded 24 in. o.c. Base layer ⅝ in. gypsum wallboard or veneer base applied parallel to one side of panels, with 1 in. type S drywall screws 12 in. o.c. to H studs. Rigid furring channels horizontally attached 24 in. o.c. to H studs with 1 in. type S drywall screws. Face layer ⅝ in. gypsum wallboard or veneer base attached at right angles to furring channels with 1 in. type S drywall screws 12 in. o.c. Stagger joints 24 in. o.c. each layer and side. (NLB)	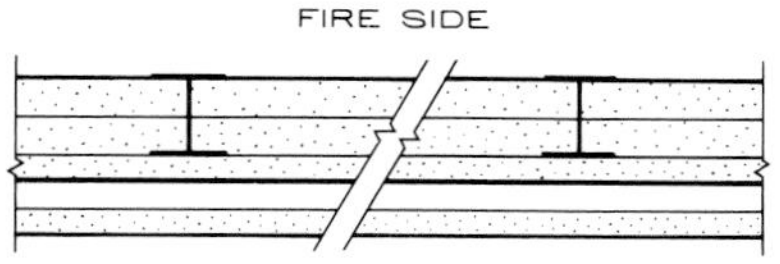 FIRE SIDE
	45 TO 49	5¼"	¾ in. x 24 in. proprietary type X gypsum panels inserted between 2¼ in. floor and ceiling tracks and fitted to 2¼ in. slotted metal I studs with tab-flange. First layer ⅝ in. type X gypsum board applied at right angles to studs with 1 in. type S drywall screws 24 in. o.c. Second layer ⅝ in. type X gypsum board applied parallel to studs with 1⅝ in. type S drywall screws 42 in. o.c. starting 12 in. from bottom. Third layer ⅝ in. type X gypsum board applied parallel to studs with 2¼ in. type S drywall screws 24 in. o.c. Resilient channels applied 24 in. o.c. at right angles to studs with 2¼ in. type S drywall screws. Fourth layer ⅝ in. type X gypsum board applied at right angles to resilient channels with 1 in. type S drywall screws 12 in. o.c. Sound tested with 1 in. glass fiber friction fit in stud space. (NLB)	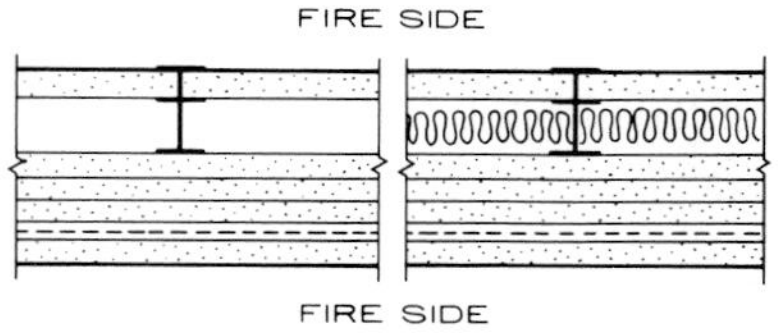 FIRE SIDE / FIRE SIDE

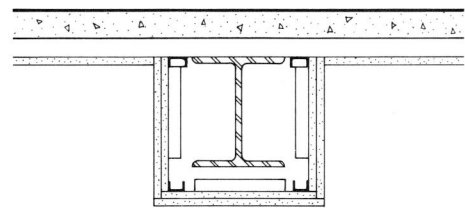

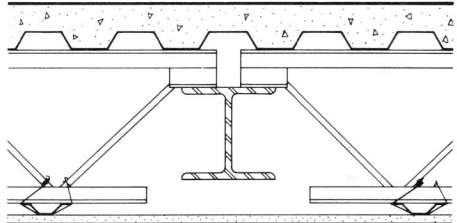

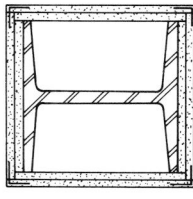

I HOUR FIRE RATING

Base layer ½ in. gypsum wallboard or veneer base tied to column with 18 gauge wire 15 in. o.c. Face layer ½ in. gypsum wallboard or veneer base applied with laminating compound over entire contact surface.

2 HOUR FIRE RATING

Two layers of ⅝ in. type X gypsum wallboard or veneer base around beam. Base layer attached with 1¼ in. type S drywall screws 16 in. o.c., face layer attached with 1¾ in. type S drywall screws 8 in. o.c. to horizontally installed U-shaped steel channels (25 gauge steel 1¹¹⁄₁₆ in. wide and 1 in. legs) located not less than ½ in. from beam flanges. Upper channels secured to steel deck units with ½ in. type S pan head screws spaced 12 in. o.c. U-shaped brackets formed of steel channels spaced 24 in. o.c. suspended from the upper channels with ½ in. type S pan head screws and supported steel channels installed at lower corners of brackets. Outside corners of gypsum board protected by 0.020-in.-thick steel corner beads crimped or nailed. (2 hour restrained or unrestrained beam)

3 HOUR FIRE RATING

One layer ½ in. type X gypsum wallboard or veneer base applied at right angles to rigid furring channels with 1 in. type S drywall screws 12 in. o.c. Wallboard end joints located midway between continuous channels and attached to additional pieces of channel 54 in. long with screws at 12 in. o.c. Furring channels 24 in. o.c. attached with 18 gauge wire ties 48 in. o.c. to open web steel joists 24 in. o.c. supporting ⅜ in. rib metal lath or ⁹⁄₁₆ in. deep, 28 gauge corrugated steel and 2½ in. concrete slab measured from top of flute. Furring channels may be attached to 1½ in. cold-rolled carrying channels 48 in. o.c. suspended from joists by 8 gauge wire hangers not over 48 in. o.c. (3 hour unrestrained beam)

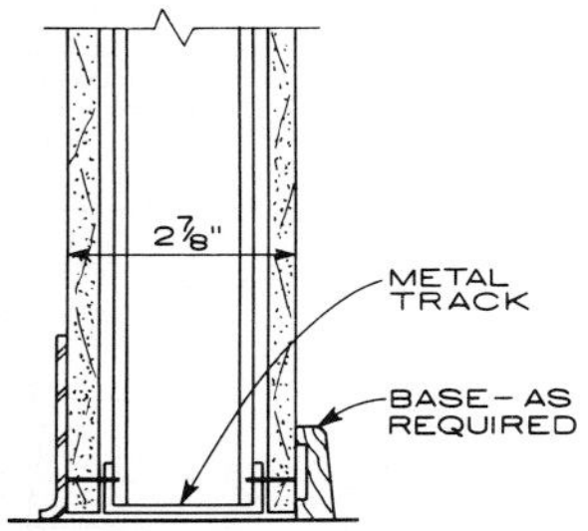

BEAMS, GIRDERS AND TRUSSES

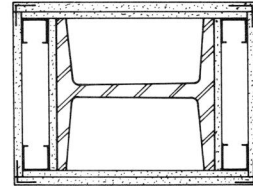

2 HOUR FIRE RATING

Base layer ½ in. type X gypsum wallboard or veneer base against flanges and across web openings fastened to 1⅝ in. metal studs with 1 in. type S drywall screws 24 in. o.c. at corners. Face layers ½ in. type X gypsum wallboard or veneer base screw-attached to studs with 1 in. type S drywall screws 12 in. o.c. to provide a cavity between boards on the flange. Face layers across the web opening laid flat across the base layer and screw attached with 1⅝ in. type S drywall screws 12 in. o.c. Metal corner beads nailed to outer layer with 4d nails 1⅜ in. long, 0.067 in. shank, ¹³⁄₆₄ in. heads, 12 in. o.c.

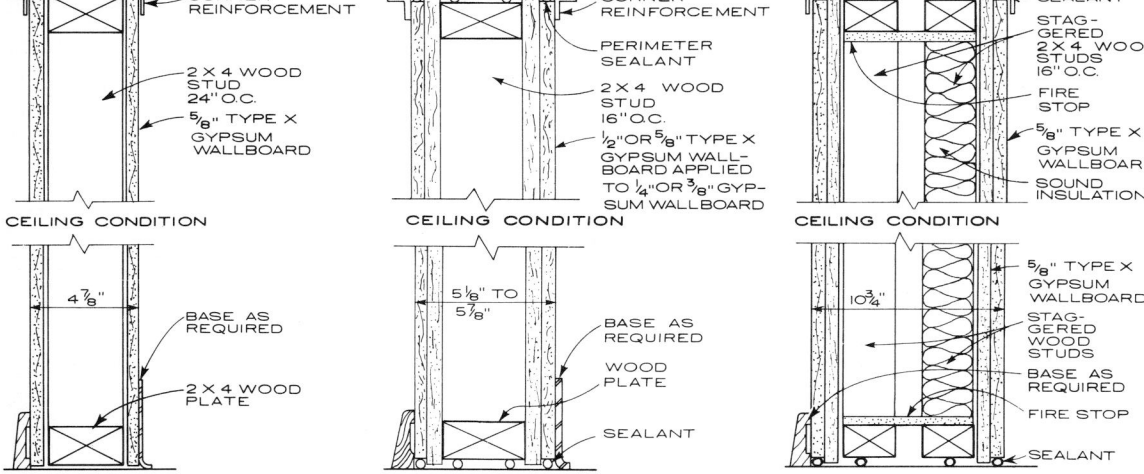

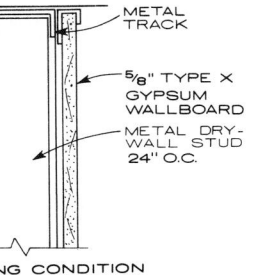

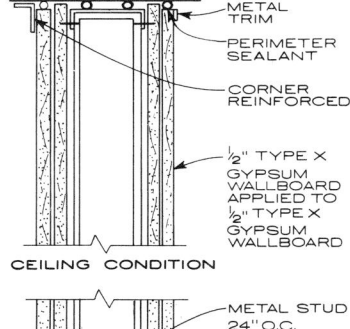

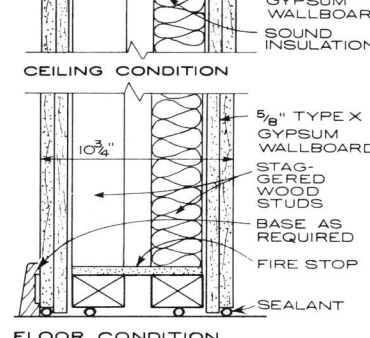

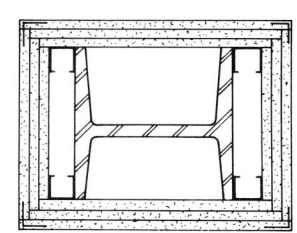

3 HOUR FIRE RATING

Three layers of ⅝ in. type X gypsum wallboard or veneer base screw attached to 1⅝ in. metal studs located at each corner of column. Base layer attached with 1 in. type S drywall screws 24 in. o.c. Second layer with 1⅝ in. type S drywall screws 12 in. o.c. and 18 gauge wire tied 24 in. o.c. Face layer attached with 2¼ in. type S drywall screws 12 in. o.c. and 1¼ in. corner bead at each corner nailed with 6d coated nails, 1⅞ in. long, 0.0915 in. shank, ¼ in. heads, 12 in. o.c.

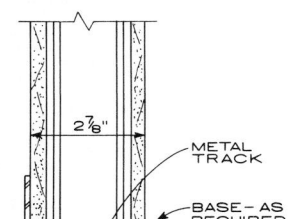

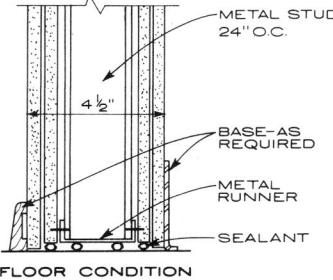

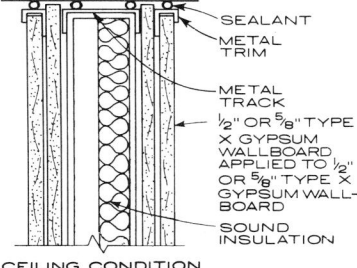

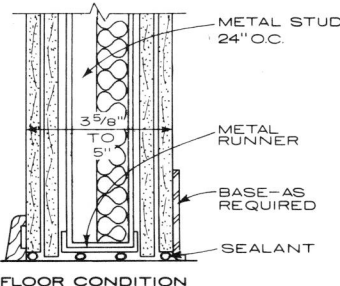

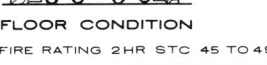

**COLUMNS
FIRE-RESISTIVE
CONSTRUCTION**

GYPSUM WOOD AND METAL FRAMED TYPE PARTITIONS

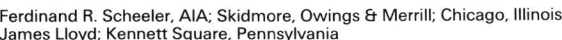

Ferdinand R. Scheeler, AIA; Skidmore, Owings & Merrill; Chicago, Illinois
James Lloyd; Kennett Square, Pennsylvania

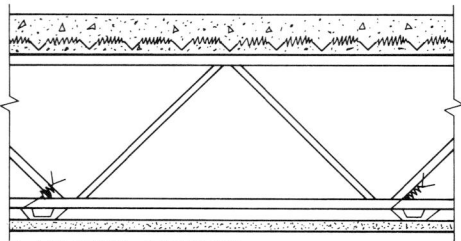

2 HR / STC 50 TO 54

1/2 in. type X gypsum wallboard or veneer base applied to drywall furring channels. Furring channels 24 in. o.c. attached with 18 gauge wire ties 48 in. o.c. to open web steel joists 24 in. o.c. supporting 3/8 in. rib metal lath or 9/16 in. deep, 28 gauge corrugated steel and 2 1/2 in. concrete slab measured from top of flute. Double channel at wallboard end joints.

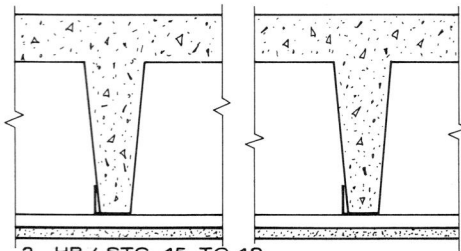

2 HR / STC 45 TO 49

5/8 in. type X gypsum wallboard or veneer base screw attached to drywall furring channels. Furring channels 24 in. o.c. suspended from 2 1/2 in. precast reinforced concrete joists 35 in. o.c. with 21 gauge galvanized steel hanger straps fastened to sides of joists. Joist leg depth, 10 in. Double channel at wallboard end joints.

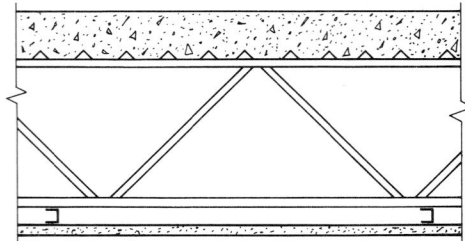

3 HR / STC 45 TO 49

5/8 in. proprietary type X gypsum wallboard or veneer base screw attached to furring channels 24 in. o.c. (double channels at end joints). Furring channel wire tied to open web steel joist 24 in. o.c. supporting 3 in. concrete slab over 3/8 in. rib metal lath. 5/8 x 2 3/4 in. type X gypsum wallboard strips over butt joints.

FLOOR/CEILING ASSEMBLIES, NONCOMBUSTIBLE

1 HR / STC 35 TO 39

5/8 in. type X gypsum wallboard or veneer base applied to wood joists 16 in. o.c. Joists supporting 1 in. nominal wood sub and finish floor, or 5/8 in. plywood finished floor with long edges T & G and 1/2 in. interior plywood with exterior glue subfloor perpendicular to joists with joints staggered.

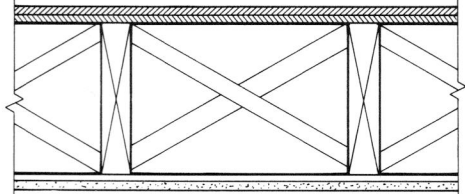

1 HR / STC 40 TO 44

1/2 in. type X gypsum wallboard or veneer base applied to drywall resilient furring channels 24 in. o.c. and nailed to wood joists 16 in. o.c. Wood joists supporting 1 in. nominal T & G wood sub and finish floor, or 5/8 in. plywood finished floor with long edges T & G and 1/2 in. interior plywood with exterior glue subfloor perpendicular to joists with joints staggered.

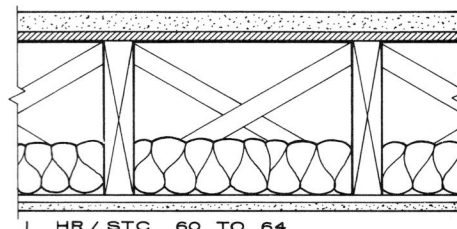

1 HR / STC 60 TO 64

1/2 in. type X gypsum wallboard or veneer base applied to resilient furring channels. Resilient channels applied 24 in. o.c. to wood joists 16 in. o.c. Wood joists support 1/2 in. plywood subfloor and 1 1/2 in. cellular or lightweight concrete over felt. 3 1/2 in. glass fiber batts in joist spaces. Sound tested with carpet and pad over 5/8 in. plywood subfloor.

FLOOR/CEILING ASSEMBLIES, WOOD FRAMED

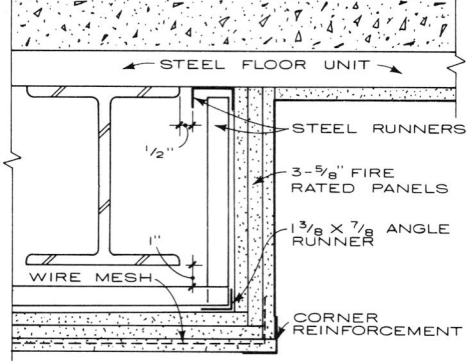

BEAM PROTECTION
3 HR. RESTRAINED   2 HR. UNRESTRAINED

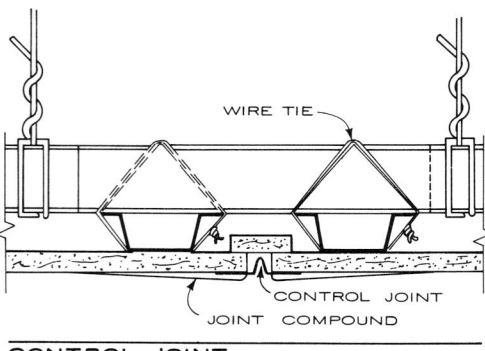

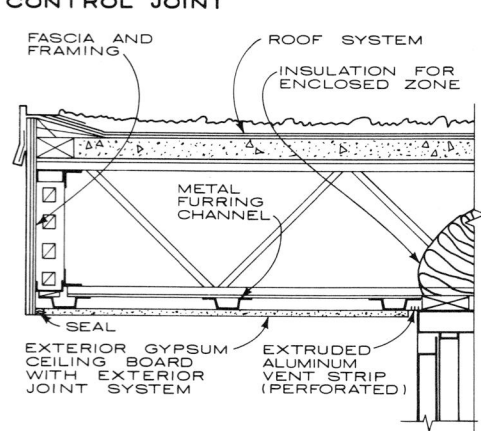

CONTROL JOINT

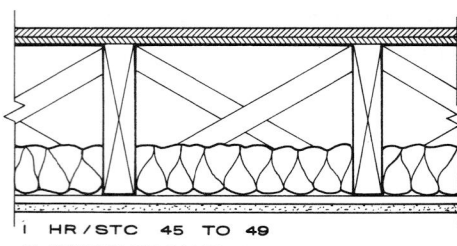

1 HR / STC 45 TO 49
ELECTRIC RADIANT HEAT PANEL

5/8 in. proprietary type X gypsum board electrical radiant heating panels attached to resilient furring channels spaced 24 in. o.c. installed to 2 x 10 in. wood joists 16 in. o.c. 3/12 in. glass fiber insulation friction fit in joist space. Wood floor of nominal 1 in. T & G or 1/2 in. plywood subfloor and nominal 1 in. T & G or 5/8 in. plywood finish floor.

FLOOR/CEILING ASSEMBLIES, WOOD FRAMED

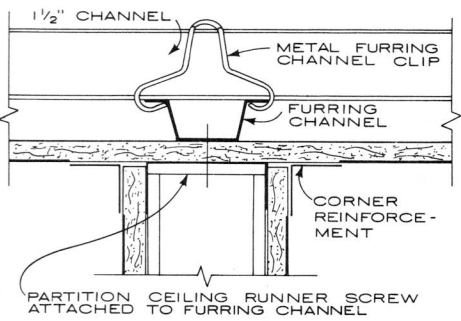

PARTITION ATTACHMENT
(SCREW ATTACHED)

EXTERIOR SOFFIT

CONTINUOUS CEILING

James Lloyd; Kennett Square, Pennsylvania

GYPSUM BOARD

CERAMIC MOSAIC TILE

Ceramic mosaic tile may be either natural clay or porcelain in composition. Special abrasive or slip-resistant surfaces and conductive tile are available only in 1 in. x 1 in. size. Nominal thickness is ¼ in.

GLAZED WALL TILE

Traditional bright and matte glazed wall tile has been supplemented with tile of variegated appearance. Textured, sculptured, embossed, and engraved surface characteristics are coupled with accent designs. Imported tile has increased in availability, and it offers a wide range of variation from the native materials used in the manufacturing process as well as the process itself. Tile from Germany, France, Italy, Mexico, Switzerland, Austria, Brazil, and Spain currently are represented in manufacturer's literature. Nominal thickness is 5/16 in.

QUARRY AND PAVER TILE

Quarry and paver tile may be natural clay, shale, or porcelain in composition. These tile are characterized by their natural earth-tone coloration, high compressive strength, and slip and stain resistance. They are recommended for interior and exterior applications. Nominal thicknesses are ½ in. and ¾ in. for quarry tile and ⅜ in. and ½ in. for paver tile.

NOTES

1. The trim diagram shows typical shapes available for portland cement mortar installations of glazed wall tile. Similar types are available for thin-set installations and for ceramic mosaic tile, quarry tile, and paver tile. See manufacturer's literature for exact shapes, colors, and glazes available.

2. Mounted tile assemblies (sometimes referred to as ready-set systems) are available for glazed tile and ceramic mosaic applications. These assemblies consist of either pregrouted sheets using flexible silicone grout or backmounted sheets that are finished with dry-set grout after installation. Both provide approximately 2 sq ft of coverage per sheet. They are designed to simplify installation and improve uniformity.

3. Ceramic bathroom accessories usually are supplied in sets that include bath and lavatory soap holders, roll-paper holder, towel post, and toothbrush tumbler holder. Designs include surface-mounted and fully recessed models. They may be used with both conventional mortar and thin-set tile installations. Colors and glazes are available to match or harmonize with glazed wall tiles.

Ted B. Richey, AIA; The InterDesign Group; Indianapolis, Indiana

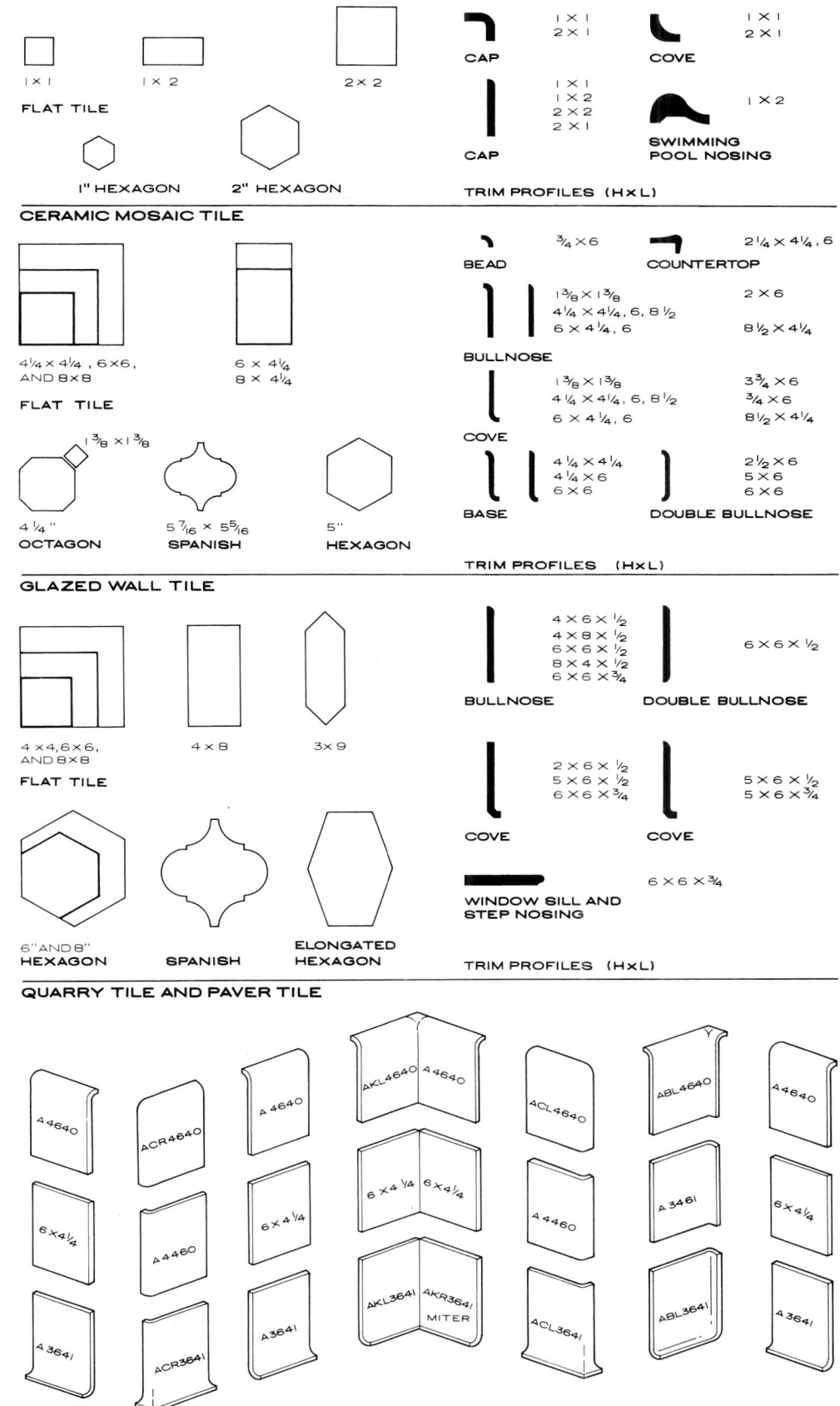

TILE 9

TYPES OF MORTAR

PORTLAND CEMENT MORTAR

A mixture of portland cement and sand (for floors) or lime (for walls) used for thick-bed installation

DRY-SET MORTAR

A mixture of portland cement with sand and additives, imparting water retention that eliminates the need to soak tiles.

LATEX PORTLAND CEMENT MORTAR

A mixture similar to dry-set but with latex (an emulsion of polymer particles in water) added to replace all or part of the water in the mortar. It provides better adhesion, density, and impact strength than dry-set mortar, and it is more flexible and resistant to frost damage.

MODIFIED EPOXY EMULSION MORTAR

As with epoxy mortars, this mixture contains a resin and hardener along with portland cement and sand. Although it is not as chemically resistant as epoxy mortar, it binds well. Compared with straight portland cement, it allows little or no shrinkage.

METHODS OF INSTALLATION

In a thick-bed process tiles may be applied over a portland cement mortar bed $3/4$ to 2 in. thick. The thick-bed allows for accurate slopes or planes in the finished tile work and is not affected by prolonged contact with water. If the backing surface is damaged, cracked, or unstable, use a membrane between the surface and the mortar bed.

In a thin-set process, tiles are set or bonded to the surface with a thin coat of material varying from $1/32$ in. to $1/8$ in. thickness. Bonding materials include dry-set mortar, latex portland cement mortar, organic adhesive, epoxy mortar or adhesive, and modified epoxy emulsion mortar. Thin-set application requires a continuous, stable, and undamaged surface.

THIN-SET MORTAR WITHOUT PORTLAND CEMENT

EPOXY MORTAR

A two-part mixture (resin and hardener with silica filler) used where chemical resistance is important. It has high bond strength and high resistance to impact. This mortar and furan mortar are the only two that can be recommended for use over steel plates.

EPOXY ADHESIVE

Mixture similar to epoxy mortar in bonding capability, but not as chemical or solvent resistant.

ORGANIC ADHESIVE

A one-part mastic mixture that requires no mixing. It remains somewhat flexible (as compared with portland cement mortar), and has good bond strength but should not be used for exterior or wet applications.

FURAN MORTAR

A two-part mixture (furan resin and hardener) excellent for chemical resistant uses and its high temperatures (350°F) tolerance.

GROUT

Grout is used to fill joints between tiles and is selected with a compatible mortar. Types include:

PORTLAND CEMENT BASED GROUTS

Include commercial portland cement grout, sand-portland cement grout, dry-set grout, and latex portland cement grout.

EPOXY GROUT

A two- or three-part mixture (epoxy resin hardener with silica sand filler) highly resistant to chemicals. It has great bond strength. This grout and furan grout are made for different chemical and solvent resistance.

FURAN RESIN GROUT

A two-part furan mixture (similar to furan mortar) that resists high temperatures and solvents.

SILICONE RUBBER GROUT

An elastomeric mixture of silicone rubber. It has high bond strength, is resistant to water and staining, and remains flexible under freezing conditions.

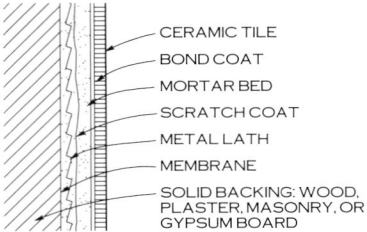

CERAMIC TILE
BOND COAT
MORTAR BED
SCRATCH COAT
METAL LATH
MEMBRANE
SOLID BACKING: WOOD, PLASTER, MASONRY, OR GYPSUM BOARD

Use over solid backing, over wood or metal studs. Preferred method for showers and tub enclosures. Ideal for remodeling.

CEMENT MORTAR

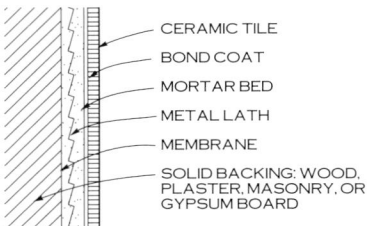

CERAMIC TILE
BOND COAT
MORTAR BED
METAL LATH
MEMBRANE
SOLID BACKING: WOOD, PLASTER, MASONRY, OR GYPSUM BOARD

Use for remodeling or on surfaces that present bonding problems. Preferred method of applying tile over gypsum plaster or gypsum board in showers and tub enclosures.

ONE-COAT METHOD

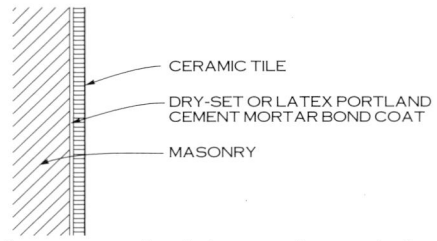

CERAMIC TILE
DRY-SET OR LATEX PORTLAND CEMENT MORTAR BOND COAT
MASONRY

Use over gypsum board, plaster, or other smooth, dimensionally stable surfaces. Use cementitious backer units in wet areas.

DRY-SET MORTAR

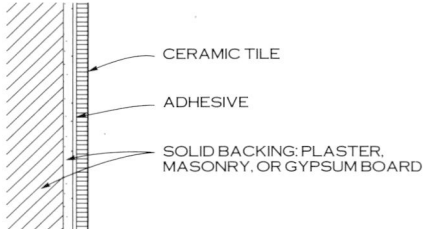

CERAMIC TILE
ADHESIVE
SOLID BACKING: PLASTER, MASONRY, OR GYPSUM BOARD

Use over gypsum board, plaster, or other smooth, dimensionally stable surfaces. Use water-resistant gypsum board in wet areas.

ORGANIC ADHESIVE

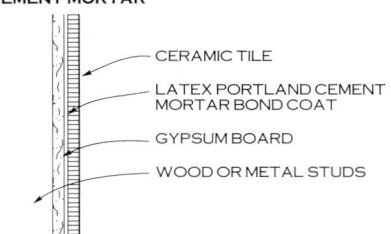

CERAMIC TILE
BOND COAT
MORTAR BED
SCRATCH COAT
METAL LATH
MEMBRANE
WOOD STUDS OR FURRING

Use over dry, well-braced studs or furring. Preferred method of installation in showers and tub enclosures.

CEMENT MORTAR

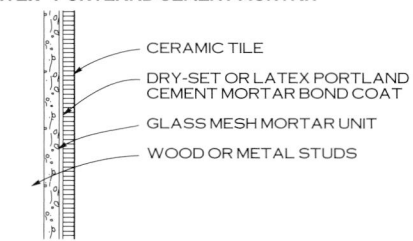

CERAMIC TILE
LATEX PORTLAND CEMENT MORTAR BOND COAT
GYPSUM BOARD
WOOD OR METAL STUDS

Use in dry interior areas in schools, institutions, and commercial buildings. Do not use in areas where temperatures exceed 125°F.

LATEX - PORTLAND CEMENT MORTAR

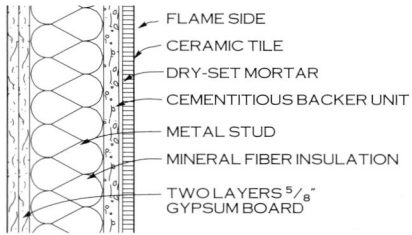

CERAMIC TILE
DRY-SET OR LATEX PORTLAND CEMENT MORTAR BOND COAT
GLASS MESH MORTAR UNIT
WOOD OR METAL STUDS

Use in wet areas over well-braced wood or metal studs. Stud spacing not to exceed 16 in. o.c., and metal studs must be 20 gauge or heavier.

DRY-SET MORTAR (CEMENTITIOUS BACKER)

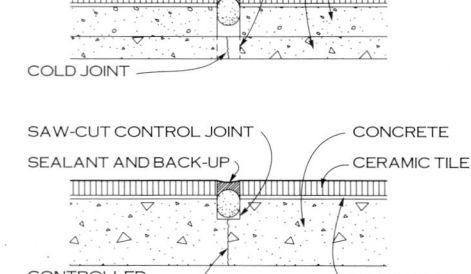

FLAME SIDE
CERAMIC TILE
DRY-SET MORTAR
CEMENTITIOUS BACKER UNIT
METAL STUD
MINERAL FIBER INSULATION
TWO LAYERS $5/8"$ GYPSUM BOARD

Use where a fire resistance rating of 2 hours is required with tile face exposed to flame. Stud spacing not to exceed 16 in. o.c. and mortar dry-set minimum thickness $3/32$ in.

DRY-SET MORTAR (FIRE-RATED WALL)

WALL DETAILS

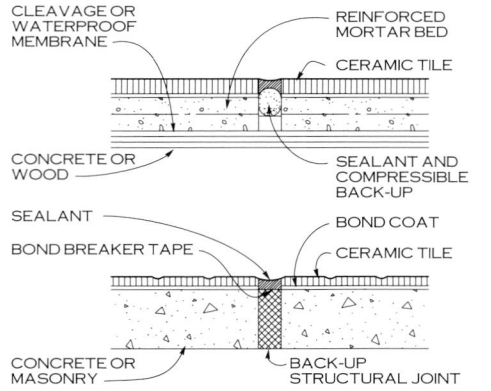

CLEAVAGE OR WATERPROOF MEMBRANE
REINFORCED MORTAR BED
CERAMIC TILE
CONCRETE OR WOOD
SEALANT AND COMPRESSIBLE BACK-UP

SEALANT
BOND BREAKER TAPE
BOND COAT
CERAMIC TILE
CONCRETE OR MASONRY
BACK-UP STRUCTURAL JOINT

SAW-CUT CONTROL JOINT
CONCRETE
SEALANT AND BACK-UP
MORTAR BED
COLD JOINT

SAW-CUT CONTROL JOINT
CONCRETE
SEALANT AND BACK-UP
CERAMIC TILE
CONTROLLED CRACK OR JOINT
BOND COAT

VERTICAL AND HORIZONTAL EXPANSION JOINTS

Tile Council of America, Inc.; Princeton, New Jersey
Jess McIlvain, AIA, CCS, CSI; Jess McIlvain and Associates; Bethesda, Maryland

TILE

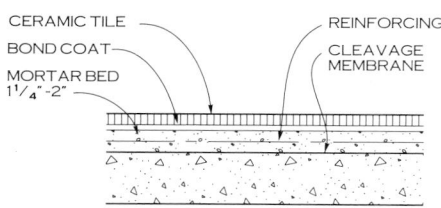

Use over structural floors subject to bending and deflection. Reinforcing mesh mandatory; mortar bed 1¼ to 2 in. thick and uniform.

CEMENT MORTAR

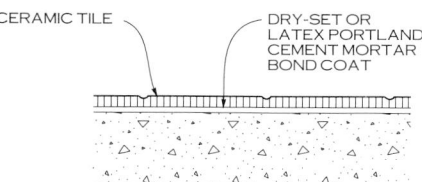

Use on level, clean slab-on-grade construction where no bending stresses occur and expansion joints are installed. Scarify existing concrete floors before installing tile.

DRY-SET OR LATEX PORTLAND CEMENT MORTAR

FLOORING DETAILS—CEMENT

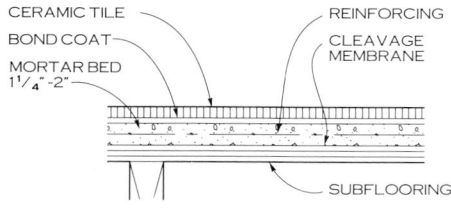

Use over wood floors that are structurally sound and where deflection, including live and dead loads, does not exceed 1/360 of span.

CEMENT MORTAR

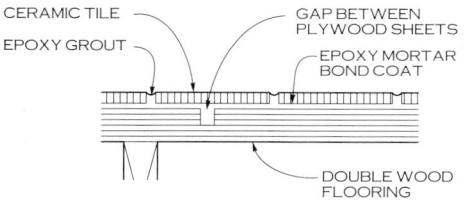

Use in residential, light commercial, and light institutional construction. Recommended where resistance to water, chemicals, or staining is needed.

EPOXY MORTAR AND GROUT

FLOORING DETAILS—WOOD

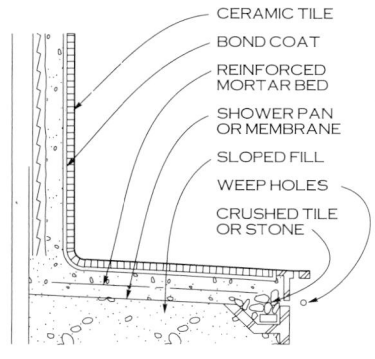

TILE SHOWER RECEPTOR

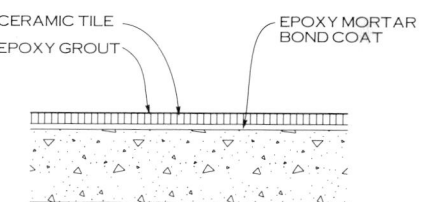

Use where moderate chemical exposure and severe cleaning methods are used, such as in commercial kitchens, dairies, breweries, and food plants.

EPOXY MORTAR AND GROUT

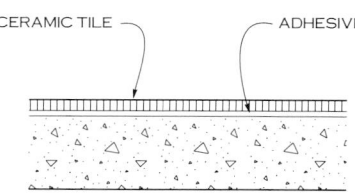

Use over concrete floors in residential construction only. Will not withstand high impact or wheel loads. Not recommended in areas where temperatures exceed 140°F.

ORGANIC OR EPOXY ADHESIVE

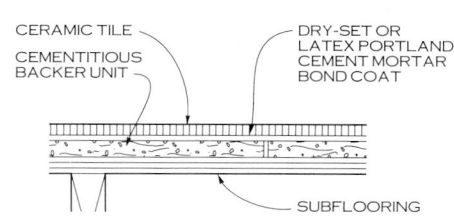

Use in light commercial and residential construction, deflection not to exceed 1/360, including live and dead loads. Waterproof membrane is required in wet areas.

DRY-SET MORTAR

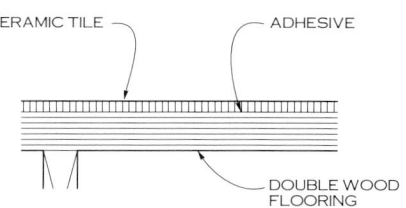

Use over wood or concrete floors in residential construction only. Not recommended for use in wet areas.

ORGANIC ADHESIVE

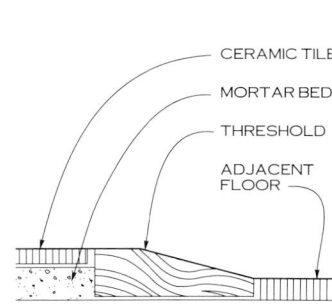

THRESHOLDS AND SADDLES

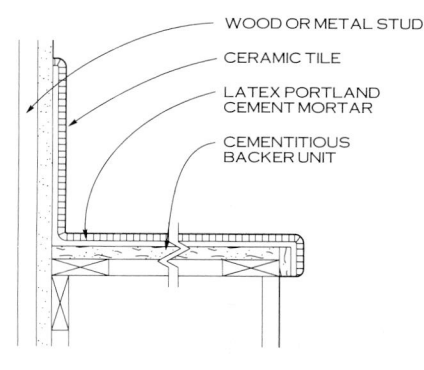

CERAMIC TILE TUB ENCLOSURE

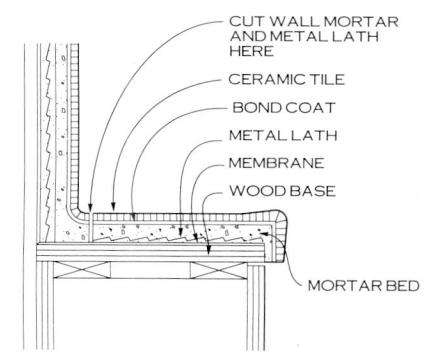

THIN-SET COUNTERTOP

CEMENT MORTAR COUNTERTOP

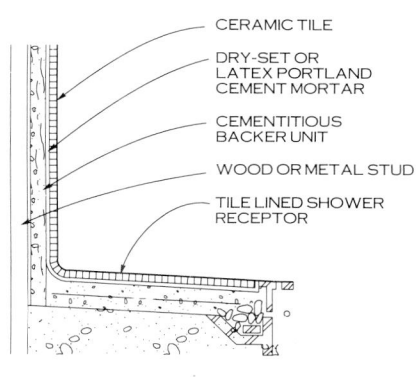

CERAMIC TILE SHOWER RECEPTOR AND WALL

Tile Council of America, Inc.; Princeton, New Jersey
Jess McIlvain, AIA, CCS, CSI; Jess McIlvain and Associates; Bethesda, Maryland

Terrazzo is a material composed of stone chips and cement matrix and is usually polished. There are four generally accepted types, classified by appearance:

1. STANDARD TERRAZZO: The most common type; relatively small chip sizes (#1 and #2 size chips).
2. VENETIAN TERRAZZO: Larger chips (size #3 through #8), with smaller chips filling the spaces between.
3. PALLADIANA: Random fractured slabs of marble up to approximately 15 in. greatest dimension, 3/8 to 1 in. thick, with smaller chips filling spaces between.
4. RUSTIC TERRAZZO: Uniformly textured terrazzo in which matrix is depressed to expose chips, not ground or only slightly ground.

MATRIX DATA

Two basic types exist: portland cement and chemical binders. Color pigments are added to create special effects. Limeproof mineral pigments or synthetic mineral pigments compatible with portland cement are required. Both white and grey portland cement is used depending on final color.

CHEMICAL BINDERS

All five types of chemical binders provide excellent chemical and abrasion resistance, except for latex, which is rated good.

1. EPOXY MATRIX: Two component resinous matrix.
2. POLYESTER MATRIX: Two component resinous matrix.
3. POLYACRYLATE MATRIX: Composite resinous matrix.
4. LATEX MATRIX: Synthetic latex matrix.
5. CONDUCTIVE MATRIX: Special formulated matrix to conduct electricity with regulated resistance, use in surgical areas and where explosive gases are a hazard.

PRECAST TERRAZZO

Several units are routinely available and almost any shape can be produced. Examples include: straight, coved, and splayed bases; window sills; stair treads and risers; shower receptors; floor tiles; and wall facings.

STONE CHIPS

Stone used in terrazzo includes all calcareous serpentine and other rocks capable of taking a good polish. Marble and onyx are the preferred materials. Quartz, granite, quartzite, and silica pebbles are used for rustic terrazzo and textured mosaics not requiring polishing.

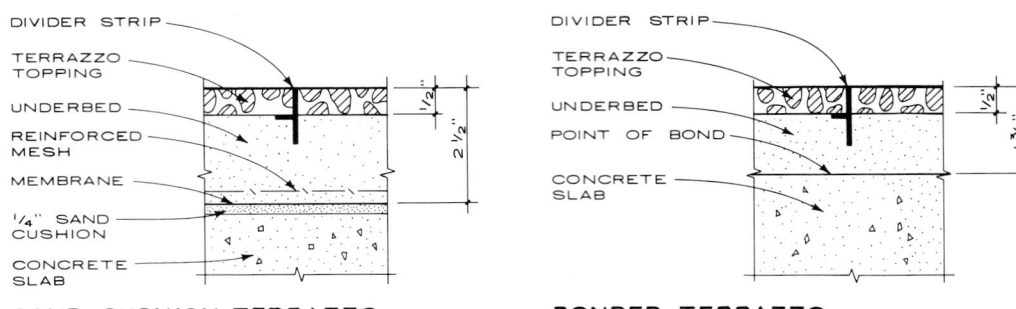

SAND CUSHION TERRAZZO   BONDED TERRAZZO

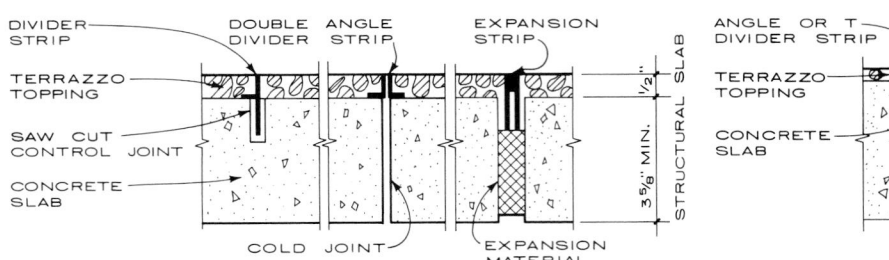

MONOLITHIC TERRAZZO   THIN-SET TERRAZZO

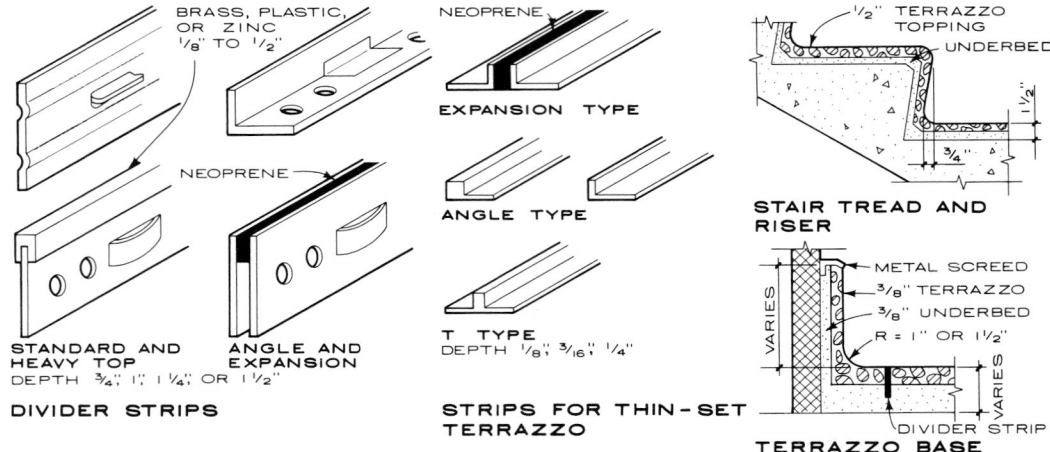

DIVIDER STRIPS   STRIPS FOR THIN-SET TERRAZZO

STAIR TREAD AND RISER

TERRAZZO BASE

TERRAZZO SYSTEMS

TERRAZZO SYSTEM	MINIMUM ALLOWANCE FOR FINISH	MINIMUM WEIGHT/ SQ FT	CONTROL JOINT STRIP LOCATION	SUGGESTED PANEL SIZE AND DIVIDER STRIP LOCATION	COMMENTS
Sand cushion terrazzo	2 1/2"	27 lb	At all control joints in structure	9 to 36 sq ft	Avoid narrow proportions (length no more than twice the width) and acute angles
Bonded underbed or strip terrazzo	1 3/4"	18 lb	At all control joints in structure	16 to 36 sq ft	Avoid narrow proportions as in sand cushion
Monolithic terrazzo	1/2"	7 lb	At all control joints in structure and at column centers or over grade beams where spans are great	At column centers in sawn or recessed slots maximum 24 x 24 ft	T or L strips usually provide decorative feature only
Thin-set terrazzo (chemical binders)	1/4"	3 lb	At all control joints	Only where structural crack can be anticipated	
Modified thin-set terrazzo	3/8"	4 1/2 lb	At all control joints	Only where structural crack can be anticipated	
Terrazzo over permanent metal forms	Varies, 3" minimum	Varies	Directly over beam	Directly over joist centers and at 3 to 5 ft on center in the opposite direction	
Structural terrazzo	Varies, 4" minimum	Varies	At all control joints at columns and at perimeter of floor	Deep strip (1 1/2 in. min.) at all column centers and over grade beams	Use divider strip at any location where structural crack can be anticipated

NOTES
1. Venetian and Palladiana require greater depth due to larger chip size; 2 3/4 in. minimum allowance for finish 28 lb/sq ft.
2. Divider and control joint strips are made of white alloy of zinc, brass, aluminum, or plastic. Aluminum is not satisfactory for portland cement matrix terrazzo; use brass and plastic in chemical binder matrix only with approval of binder manufacturer.
3. In exterior terrazzo, brass will tarnish and white alloy of zinc will deteriorate.

John C. Lunsford, AIA; Varney Sexton Sydnor Architects; Phoenix, Arizona

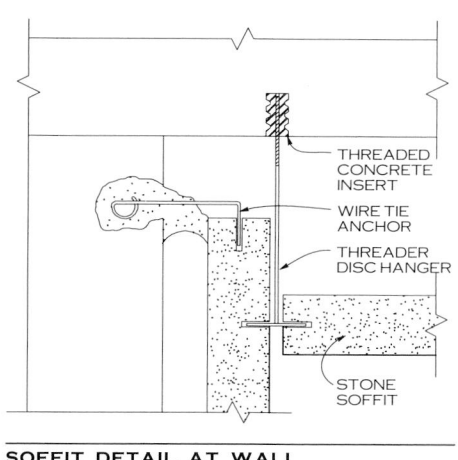

SOFFIT DETAIL AT WALL

Labels: THREADED CONCRETE INSERT, WIRE TIE ANCHOR, THREADER DISC HANGER, STONE SOFFIT

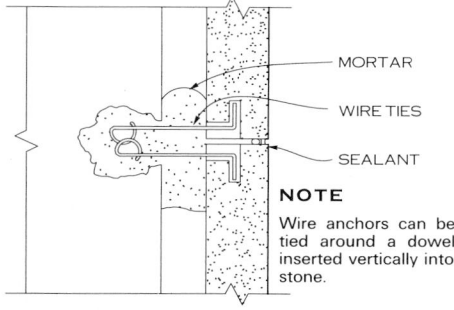

VERTICAL JOINT DETAIL – PLAN

Labels: MORTAR, WIRE TIES, SEALANT

NOTE
Wire anchors can be tied around a dowel inserted vertically into stone.

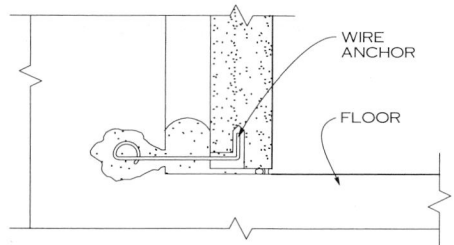

BASE DETAIL

Labels: WIRE ANCHOR, FLOOR

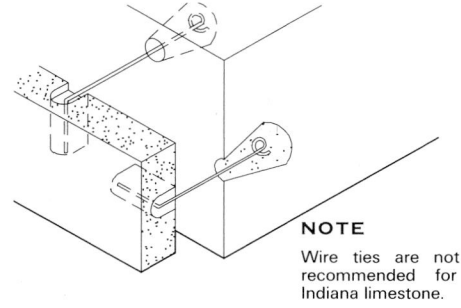

SIMPLE WIRE ANCHOR CONNECTION

NOTE
Wire ties are not recommended for Indiana limestone.

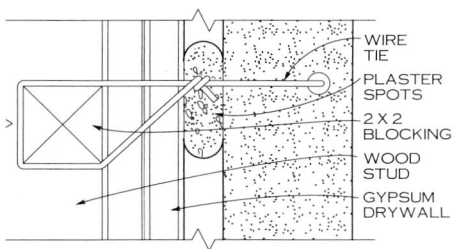

STONE PANEL ON WOOD STUDS

Labels: WIRE TIE, PLASTER SPOTS, 2 X 2 BLOCKING, WOOD STUD, GYPSUM DRYWALL

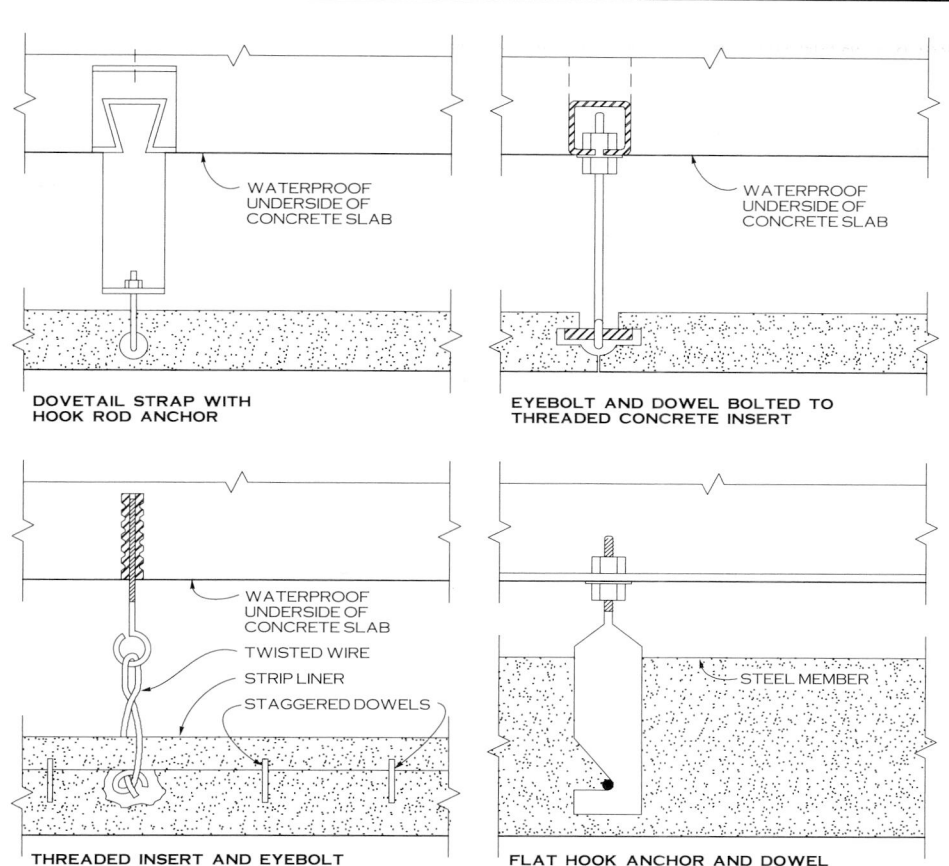

DOVETAIL STRAP WITH HOOK ROD ANCHOR — WATERPROOF UNDERSIDE OF CONCRETE SLAB

EYEBOLT AND DOWEL BOLTED TO THREADED CONCRETE INSERT — WATERPROOF UNDERSIDE OF CONCRETE SLAB

THREADED INSERT AND EYEBOLT — WATERPROOF UNDERSIDE OF CONCRETE SLAB, TWISTED WIRE, STRIP LINER, STAGGERED DOWELS

FLAT HOOK ANCHOR AND DOWEL — STEEL MEMBER

TYPICAL SYSTEMS FOR HANGING INTERIOR VENEER STONE

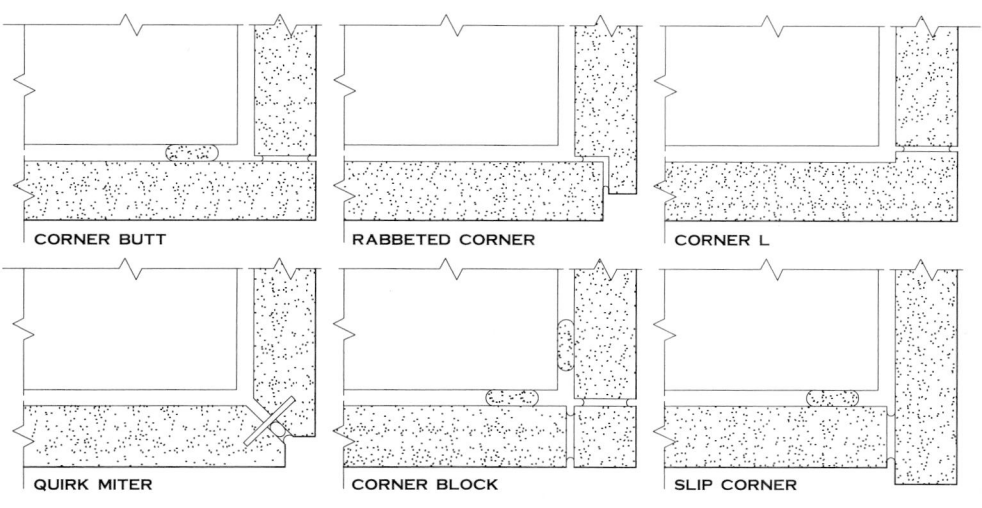

CORNER BUTT, RABBETED CORNER, CORNER L, QUIRK MITER, CORNER BLOCK, SLIP CORNER

TYPICAL CORNER DETAILS

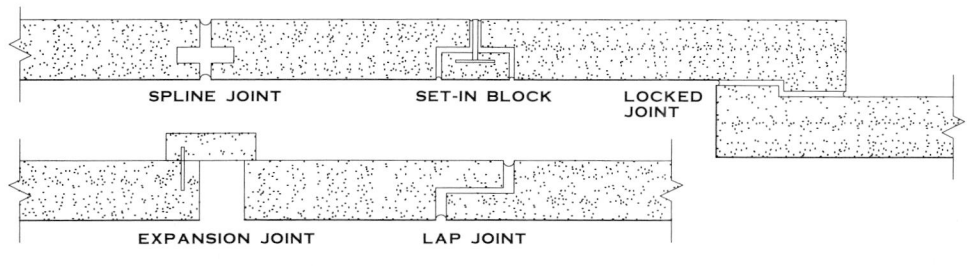

SPLINE JOINT, SET-IN BLOCK, LOCKED JOINT, EXPANSION JOINT, LAP JOINT

TYPICAL HORIZONTAL JOINTS

Building Stone Institute; New York, New York
George M. Whiteside, III, AIA, and James D. Lloyd; Kennett Square, Pennsylvania
Alexander Keyes; Darrel Downing Rippeteau, Architect; Washington, D.C.

STONE FACING 9

ACOUSTICAL CEILING SYSTEMS

CEILING TYPE	Main, Cross T	Access T's	Z channel	H channel	T spline	Flat spline	Spacer	Modular T	Metal pan T	Special	Bent steel	Bent steel alum. cap	Bent aluminum	Extruded aluminum	Galvanized	Painted	Anodized	Embossed pattern	Fire rating available	12 x 12	12 x 24	24 x 24	24 x 48	24 x 60	20 x 60	NOTES
	COMPONENTS										MATERIALS				FINISHES					ACOUSTIC TILE SIZES (IN.)						
Gypsum wallboard																										
Suspended	•										•				•	•			•							
Exposed grid	•										•	•	•	•	•	•	•	•	•			•	•			
Semiconcealed grid	•				•		•				•				•	•			•			•	•			
Concealed H & T				•	•	•					•				•	•			•	•						
Concealed T & G			•								•				•	•			•	•						
Concealed Z			•			•					•				•	•			•	•						
Concealed access	•	•			•	•	•				•				•	•			•	•		•				
Modular	•				•	•		•			•					•			•					•	•	50 or 60" sq main grid
Metal pan									•		•		•		•	•			•	•	•					12" sq pattern
Linear metal										•						•	•									4" o.c. typical
Perforated metal	•						•				•		•			•										1 way grid 4'-8' o.c.
Luminous ceiling										•						•	•									1" to 4" sq grid

ACOUSTICAL CEILING MATERIALS

MATERIALS	12 x 12	12 x 24	24 x 24	24 x 48	24 x 60	20 x 60	30 x 60	60 x 60	48 x 48	Custom sizes	1/2	5/8	3/4	1	1 1/2	3	Square	Tegular	T & G	Kerfed and rabbeted	.45-.60	.60-.70	.70-.80	.80-.90	.90-.95	High humidity	Exterior soffit	High abuse/impact	Scrubbable	Fire rating available
	SIZES (IN.)										THICKNESS (IN.)						EDGES				NRC RANGE					USES				
Mineral fiber:																														
Painted	•	•	•	•	•	•	•			•	•	•	•	•			•	•	•	•	•	•	•	•						•
Plastic face			•	•								•					•					•					•		•	•
Aluminum face	•		•	•								•					•				•	•				•	•		•	•
Ceramic face			•	•								•					•				•					•	•			•
Mineral face	•			•								•	•				•	•			•								•	
Glass fiber:																														
Painted		•	•	•			•					•	•	•			•							•						
Film face		•	•	•		•						•	•	•	•		•							•	•					
Glass cloth face		•	•	•	•	•	•	•					•	•	•		•							•	•			•		
Molded			•	•			•	•	•		Varies						•													
Gypsum		•	•								•						•				•							•		•
Mylar face	•		•	•								•	•				•	•		•	•									
Tectum		•	•		•			•	•		1 - 3						•	•			•									

SPECIAL ACOUSTICAL SYSTEMS
SOUND ISOLATION

When it is necessary to isolate a high noise area from a building or a "quiet room" from a high surrounding noise level, floors, walls, and ceilings should be built free of rigid contact with the building structure to reduce sound and vibration transmission.

CUSTOM WALLS

Auditoriums, concert halls, and other special acoustically conditioned space may require both absorptive and reflective surfaces and, in some cases, surfaces that can be adjusted for varying absorption coefficients to "tune" the space.

SPECIAL PATTERNS AND PROFILES

Screen printed, scored, and face-cut acoustical panels with a variety of edge treatments are available in narrow profile, tegular ceilings. Compatible grid systems, some offering features to facilitate partition and equipment attachment, install in similar fashion to conventional T-bar components.

LOOSE BATTS

USE: Reduce sound transmission through or over partitions; installed over suspended acoustical tile. Also used between gypsum wall partitions.
MATERIALS: Expanded fiberglass or mineral fiber.
STC: Based on total designed system; can range from 40 to 60.

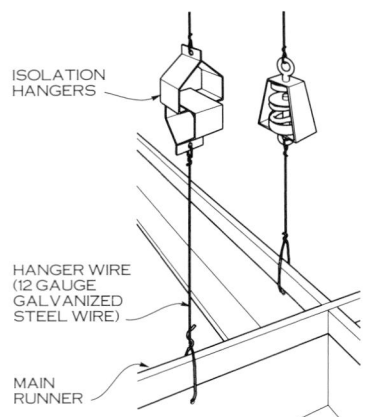

ISOLATION HANGER
CEILING ISOLATION HANGER

Isolates ceilings from noise traveling through the building structure. Hangers are also available for isolating ceiling systems to shield spaces from mechanical equipment and aircraft noise.

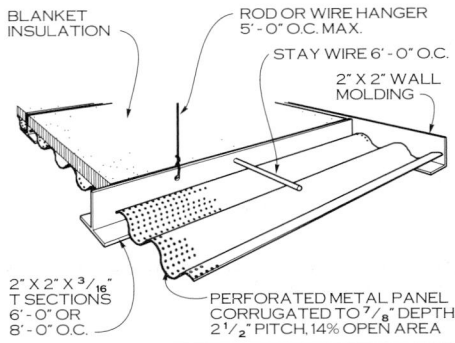

PERFORATED METAL CEILING

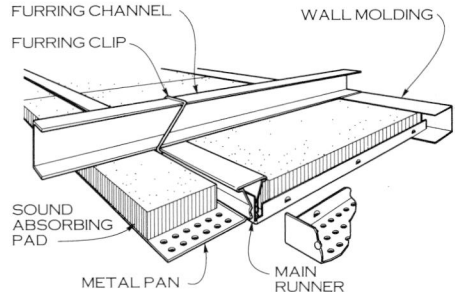

METAL PAN CEILING

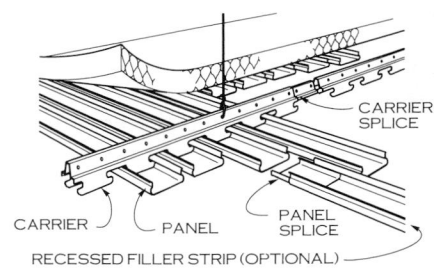

LINEAR METAL CEILING
METAL CEILINGS

USE: Sound absorption depends on batt insulation.
MATERIALS: Bent steel, aluminum, or stainless steel.
NRC: 0.70 to 0.90.
FINISH: Painted, anodized, or stainless steel.

Setter, Leach & Lindstrom, Inc.; Minneapolis, Minnesota

ACOUSTICAL TREATMENT

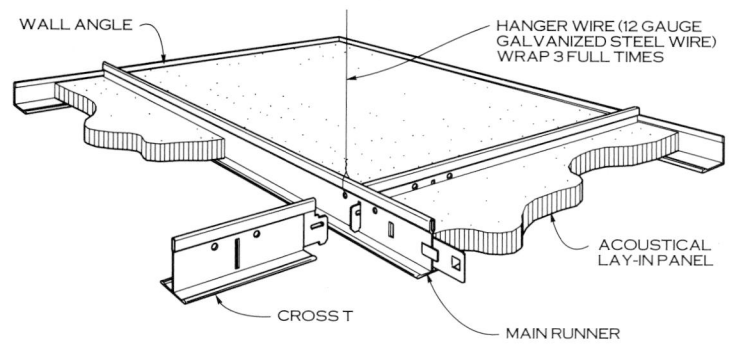

WALL ANGLE

HANGER WIRE (12 GAUGE GALVANIZED STEEL WIRE) WRAP 3 FULL TIMES

ACOUSTICAL LAY-IN PANEL

CROSS T

MAIN RUNNER

EXPOSED GRID

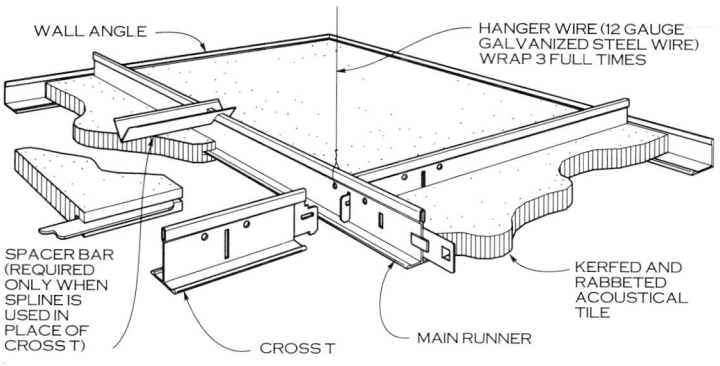

WALL ANGLE

HANGER WIRE (12 GAUGE GALVANIZED STEEL WIRE) WRAP 3 FULL TIMES

SPACER BAR (REQUIRED ONLY WHEN SPLINE IS USED IN PLACE OF CROSS T)

CROSS T

MAIN RUNNER

KERFED AND RABBETED ACOUSTICAL TILE

CONCEALED GRID

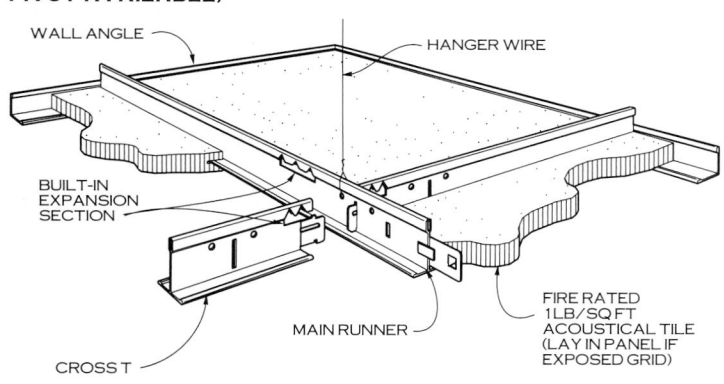

ACCESS T

CROSS T

ACCESS ANGLE

FLAT SPLINE

T SPLINE

MAIN RUNNER

NOTE
Fire rated grid shown.

CONCEALED GRID - UPWARD ACCESS (SIDE PIVOT SHOWN; END PIVOT AVAILABLE)

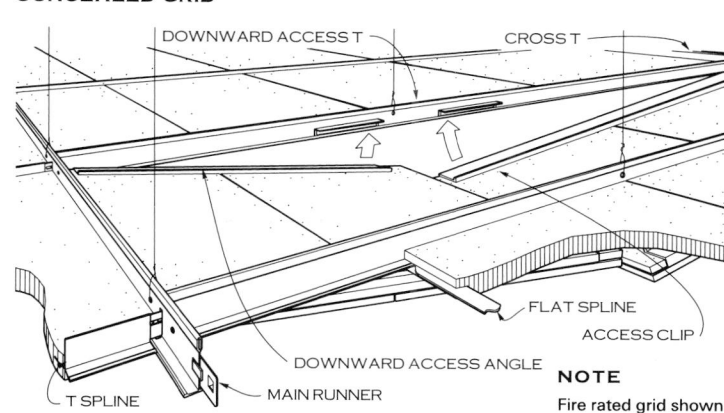

DOWNWARD ACCESS T

CROSS T

FLAT SPLINE

ACCESS CLIP

DOWNWARD ACCESS ANGLE

T SPLINE

MAIN RUNNER

NOTE
Fire rated grid shown.

CONCEALED GRID—DOWNWARD ACCESS (END PIVOT SHOWN; SIDE PIVOT AVAILABLE)

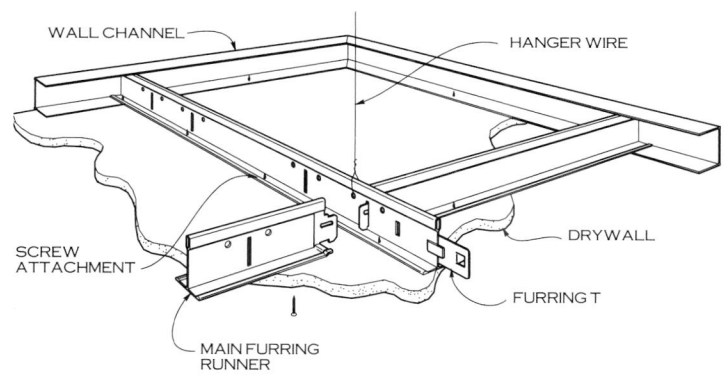

WALL ANGLE

HANGER WIRE

BUILT-IN EXPANSION SECTION

FIRE RATED 1 LB/SQ FT ACOUSTICAL TILE (LAY IN PANEL IF EXPOSED GRID)

MAIN RUNNER

CROSS T

WALL CHANNEL

HANGER WIRE

SCREW ATTACHMENT

DRYWALL

FURRING T

MAIN FURRING RUNNER

FIRE RATED GRID (CONCEALED GRID SHOWN)

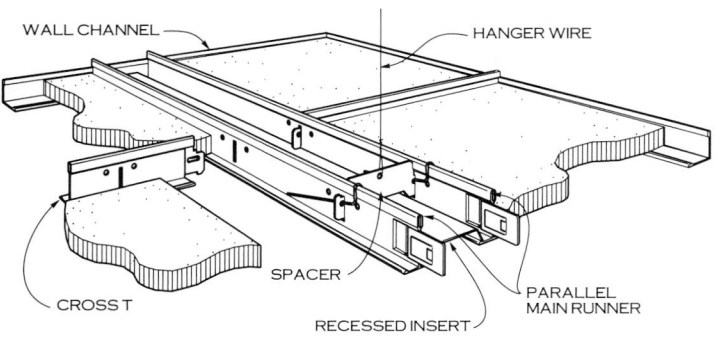

WALL CHANNEL

HANGER WIRE

CROSS T

SPACER

RECESSED INSERT

PARALLEL MAIN RUNNER

DRYWALL FURRING SYSTEM

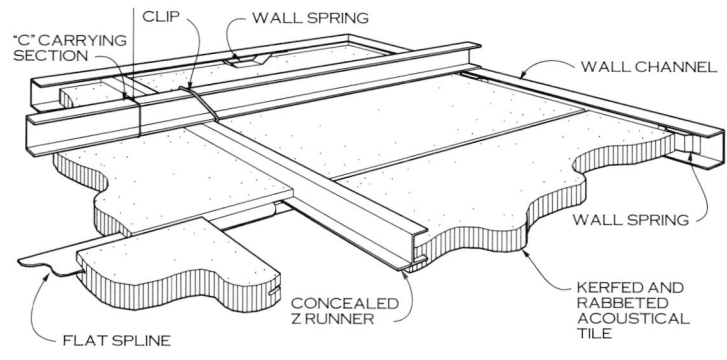

CLIP

WALL SPRING

"C" CARRYING SECTION

WALL CHANNEL

WALL SPRING

FLAT SPLINE

CONCEALED Z RUNNER

KERFED AND RABBETED ACOUSTICAL TILE

LINEAR SYSTEM

CONCEALED Z SYSTEM

Setter, Leach & Lindstrom, Inc.; Minneapolis, Minnesota
Blythe & Nazdin Architects, Ltd.; Bethesda, Maryland

ACOUSTICAL TREATMENT

9

WALL TREATMENT

1. USE: Sound absorption.
2. MATERIALS: Fabric-wrapped glass fiber or mineral wool.
3. N.R.C.: .55–.85
4. NOTES: Wall panels may be used individually or grouped to form an entire wall system. Noise reduction coefficient varies with material thickness and acoustical transparency of fabric facing. Maximum panel sizes vary with manufacturer up to 4 x 12 ft.

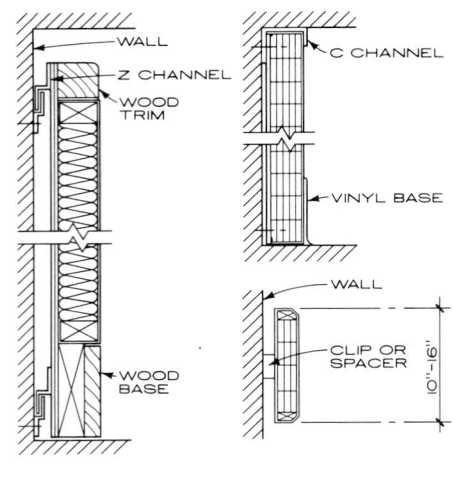

SECTIONS

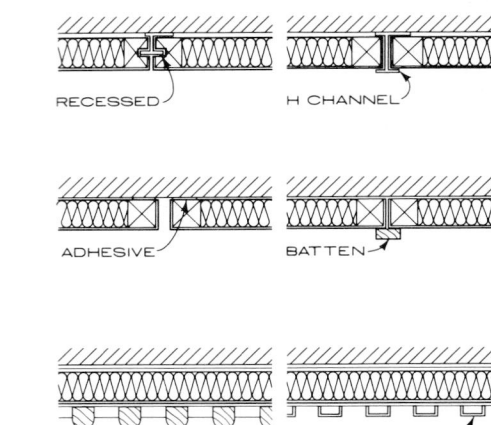

PLAN SECTIONS

WALL TREATMENT

PLENUM BARRIER

1. USE: Reduce sound transmission through plenum above partitions.
2. MATERIALS: 1/64 in. sheet lead, lead-loaded vinyl, perforated aluminum, or foil-wrapped glass fiber.
3. S.T.C.: 18–41 dB improvement.
4. NOTES: All openings through barrier for pipes, ducts, etc., must be sealed airtight for maximum effectiveness.

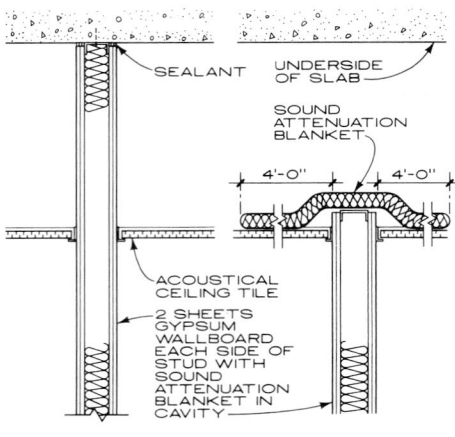

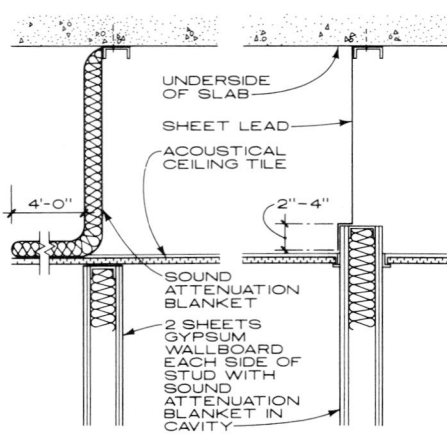

PLENUM BARRIERS

SUSPENDED PANELS

1. USE: Sound absorption.
2. MATERIALS: Vertical suspension–glass fiber blanket wrapped with perforated aluminum foil or fabric stretched over frame. Horizontal suspension–perforated steel or aluminum with glass fiber blanket, or similar to vertical.
3. N.R.C.: .55–.85
4. NOTES: Panels may be suspended from structure or attached directly to ceiling grid. May be arranged in a variety of patterns including linear, square, zigzag vertical, or regular or random spaced horizontal panels.

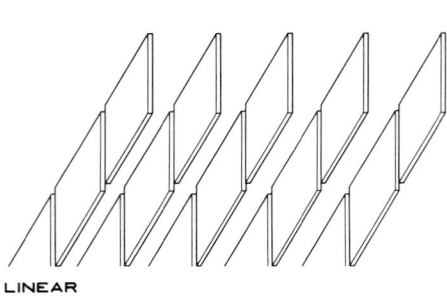

LINEAR

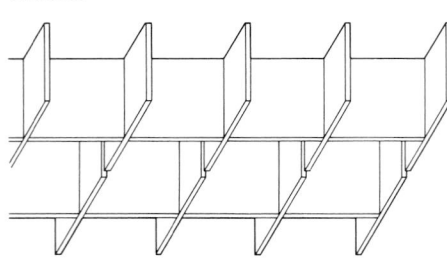

EGGCRATE

CLOUD

SUSPENDED PANELS

ACOUSTICAL MASONRY UNITS

1. USE: Sound absorption
2. MATERIALS: Concrete masonry unit, 4, 6, or 8 in. thick, with metal baffle and/or fibrous filler in slotted areas.
   Structural glazed facing tile, 4, 6, or 8 in. thick; 8 x 8 in. or 8 x 16 in. (nominal) face dimensions, with fibrous filler in cores.
3. N.R.C.: .45–.65

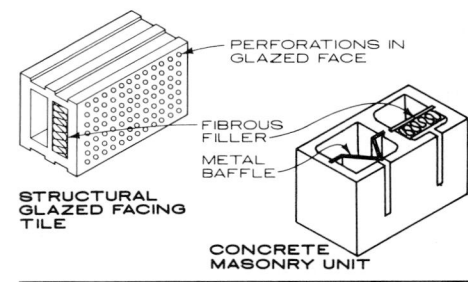

ACOUSTICAL MASONRY UNITS

SPRAY-ON ACOUSTICAL MATERIAL

1. USE: Sound absorption.
2. MATERIALS: Mineral or cellulose fibers spray applied to metal lath or directly to hard surfaces such as concrete, steel, masonry, or gypsum wallboard.
3. N.R.C.: .50–.95.
4. NOTES: Application to metal lath provides slightly better sound absorption and permits irregular shapes. Available with a hard surface for wall applications. Available with fire protection rating.

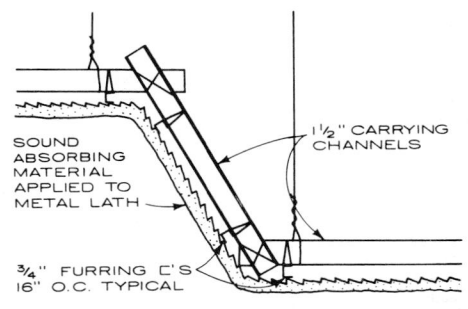

SPRAY-ON ACOUSTICAL MATERIAL

Setter, Leach & Lindstrom, Inc.; Minneapolis, Minnesota
Blythe + Nazdin Architects, Ltd.; Bethesda, Maryland

ACOUSTICAL TREATMENT

NOTES

1. Flooring can be manufactured from practically every commercially available species of wood. In the United States wood flooring is grouped for marketing purposes roughly according to species and region. There are various grading systems used with various species, and often different specifications for different sized boards in a given species. For instance, nail size and spacing varies among the several board sizes typically available in oak.

2. Information given here should be used for preliminary decision making only. Precise specifications must be obtained from the supplier or from the appropriate industry organization named below.

3. Several considerations in wood flooring selection and installation are applicable industrywide. These are shown graphically at right.

4. The table below includes typical grades and sizes of boards for each species or regional group. Grade classifications vary, but in each case one can assume that the first grade listed is the highest quality, and that the quality decreases with each succeeding grade. The best grade will typically minimize or exclude features such as knots, streaks, spots, checks, and torn grain and will contain the highest percentage of longer boards. Grade standards have been reduced in recent years for practically all commercially produced flooring, hence a thorough review of exact grade specifications is in order when selecting wood flooring.

5. End matching gives a complete tongue and grooved joint all around each board. Board length is reduced as required to obtain the matched ends.

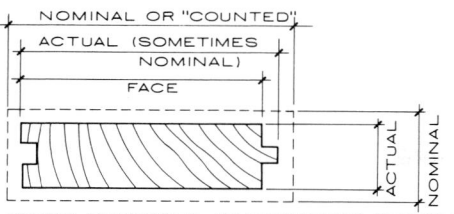

THE UNDERSIDE OF FLOORING BOARDS MAY BE PATTERNED AND OFTEN WILL CONTAIN MORE DEFECTS THAN ARE ALLOWED IN THE TOP FACE. GRAIN IS OFTEN MIXED IN ANY GIVEN RUN OF BOARDS

CROSS SECTIONAL DIMENSIONS

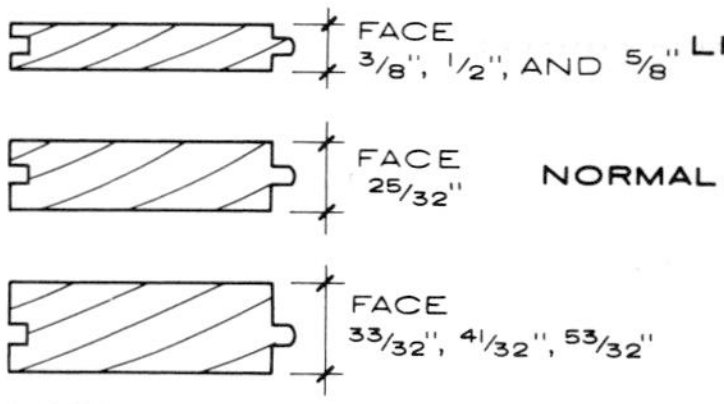

CROSS SECTIONAL DIMENSIONING SYSTEMS VARY AMONG SPECIES, PATTERNS, MANUFACTURERS. TRADE ORGANIZATIONS PROVIDE PERCENTAGE MULTIPLIERS FOR COMPUTING COVERAGE

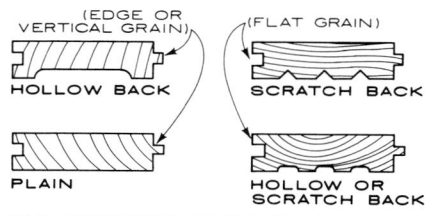

BOARD CHARACTERISTICS

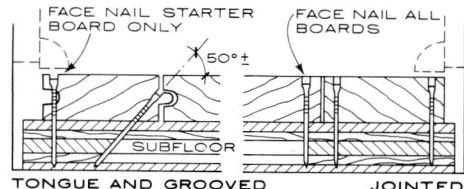

MOST FLOORING MAY BE HAD IN VARYING THICKNESSES TO SUIT WEAR REQUIREMENTS. ACTUAL DIMENSIONS SHOWN ARE AVAILABLE IN MAPLE

VARIOUS THICKNESSES

FACE NAIL STARTER BOARD ONLY   FACE NAIL ALL BOARDS

50°±

SUBFLOOR

TONGUE AND GROOVED   **JOINTED**

JOINTED FLOORING MUST BE FACE NAILED, USUALLY WITH FULLY BARBED FLOORING BRADS

TONGUE AND GROOVED boards are blind nailed with spiral floor screws, cement coated nails, cut nails, machine driven fasteners, use manufacturer's recommendations

FASTENING

  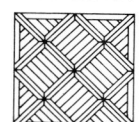

PARQUET FLOORING—SQUARE PANELS

THICKNESS	FACE DIMENSIONS
5/16″ (most common) 9/16″, 11/16″, 3/4″	6″ x 6″, 6¼″ x 6½″, 12″ x 12″, 19″ x 19″ Other sizes are available from certain manufacturers

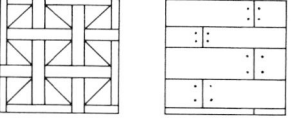

PARQUET FLOORING—INDIVIDUAL STRIPS

THICKNESS	FACE DIMENSIONS
5/16″	2″ x 12″ typical strips can be cut, mitered, etc., to obtain pieces required for special patterns

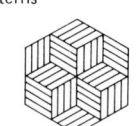

TYPICAL GRADES AND SIZES OF BOARDS BY SPECIES OR REGIONAL GROUP

GROUP	INDUSTRY ORGANIZATION	GRADE	THICKNESS	WIDTH		NOTES
Oak (also beech, birch, pecan, and hard maple)	National Oak Flooring Manufacturers' Assoc.	Quarter Sawn: Clear Select Plain Sawn: Clear Select No. 1 Common No. 2 Common	3/4″, 1/2″ Standard; also 3/8″ 5/16″	Face 1½″ 2″ 2¼″		This association grades birch, beech, and hard maple. First Grade, Second Grade, Third Grade, and "Special Grades." Pecan is graded: First Grade, First Grade Red, Second Grade, Second Grade Red, Third Grade.
Hard maple (also beech and birch) (acer saccharum—not soft maple)	Maple Flooring Manufacturers' Assoc. Inc.	First Grade Second Grade Third Grade Fourth Grade Combinations	3/8″, 12/32″ 41/32″, 1/2″ 33/32″ 53/32″, 5/8″	Face 1½″ 2″ 2¼″ 3¼″		Association states that beech and birch have physical properties that make them fully suitable as substitutes for hard maple. See manufacturer for available width and thickness combinations.
Southern pine	Southern Pine Inspection Bureau	B & B C C & Btr D No. 2	3/8″, 1/2″ 5/8″, 1″ 1¼″, 1½″	Nom. 2″ 3″ 4″ 5″ 6″	Face 1⅛″ 2⅛″ 3⅛″ 4⅛″ 5⅛″	Grain may be specified as edge (rift), near-rift, or flat. If not specified, manufacturer will ship flat or mixed grain boards. See manufacturer for available width and thickness combinations.
Western woods (Douglas fir, hemlock, Englemann spruce, Idaho pine, incense cedar, lodgepole pine, Ponderosa pine, sugar pine, Western larch, Western red cedar)	Western Wood Products Association	Select: 1 & 2 clear- B & Btr C Select D Select Finish: Superior Prime E	2″ and thinner	Nominal 3″ 4″ 6″		Flooring is machined tongue and groove and may be furnished in any grade agreeable to buyer and seller. Grain may be specified as vertical (VG), flat (FG), or mixed (MG). Basic size for flooring is 1″ x 4″ x 12′; standard lengths 4′ and above.
Eastern white pine Norway pine Jack pine Eastern spruce Balsam fir Eastern hemlock Tamarack	Northern Hardwood & Pine Manufacturers' Association	C & Btr Select D Select Stained Select	3/8″, 1/2″ 5/8″, 1″, 1¼″, 1½″	Nom. 2″ 3″ 4″ 5″ 6″	Face 1⅛″ 2⅛″ 3⅛″ 4⅛″ 5⅛″	The various species included in this "Lake States Region" group provide different visual features. Consult manufacturer or local supplier to determine precisely what is available in terms of species and appearance.

Darrel Downing Rippeteau, Architect; Washington, D.C.

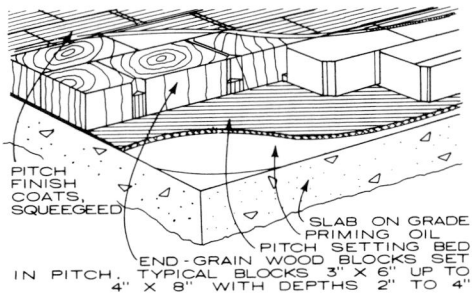

INDUSTRIAL WOOD BLOCK URETHANE FINISH COATS AVAILABLE FOR NONINDUSTRIAL USES

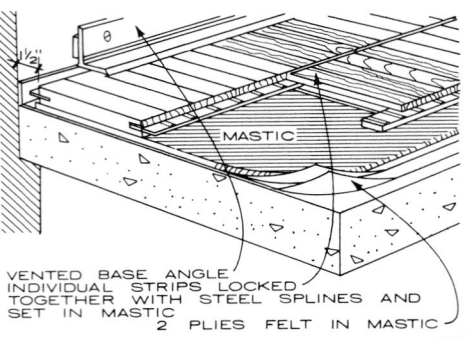

STEEL SPLINED ROWS OF STRIPS CORK UNDERLAYMENT ADDED FOR NON-INDUSTRIAL USE

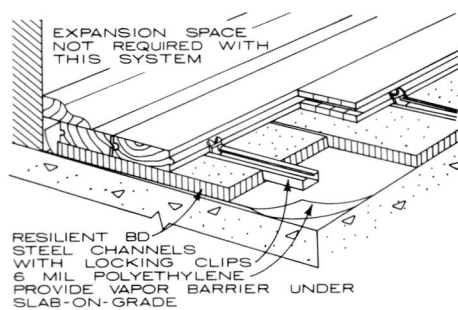

METAL CHANNEL RUNNERS WITH CLIPS

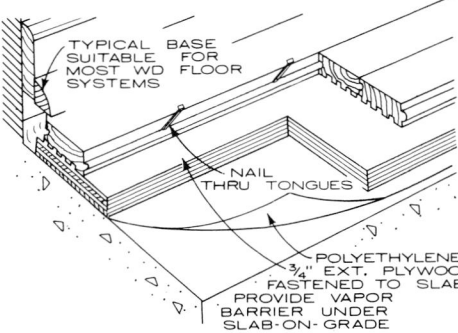

STRIPS OVER PLYWOOD UNDERLAYMENT A NOFMA STANDARD

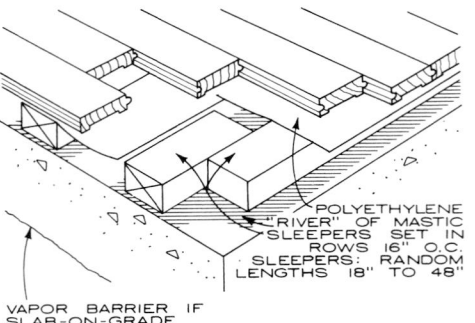

STRIPS OVER STAGGERED 2 X 4 SLEEPERS A NOFMA STANDARD

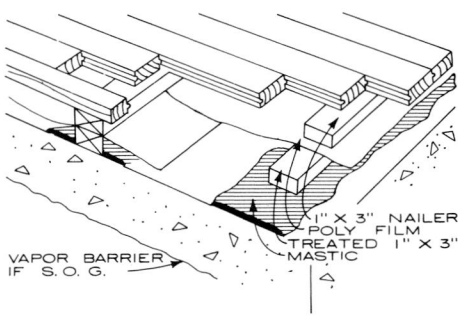

DOUBLE COURSE OF SLEEPER STRIPS A NOFMA STANDARD

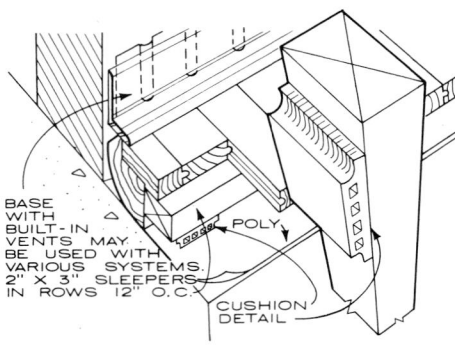

STRIPS OVER CUSHIONED SLEEPERS

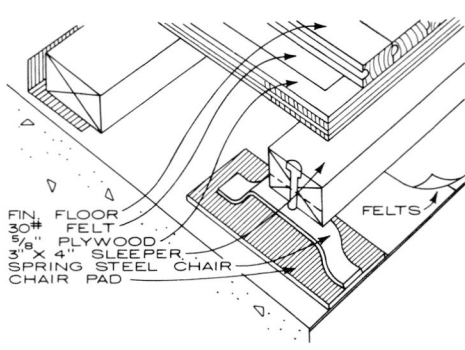

STRIPS OVER SLEEPERS MOUNTED ON SPRING-STEEL CHAIRS

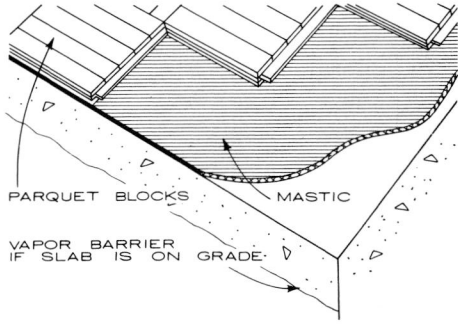

PARQUET BLOCKS SET IN MASTIC

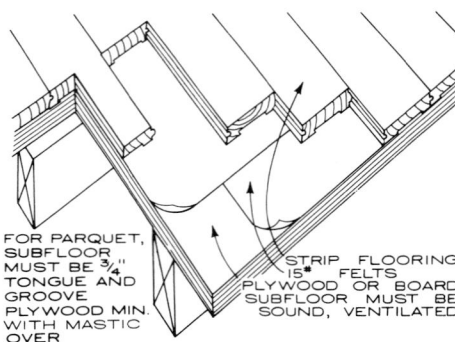

STRIPS OVER SUBFLOOR ON WOOD JOISTS

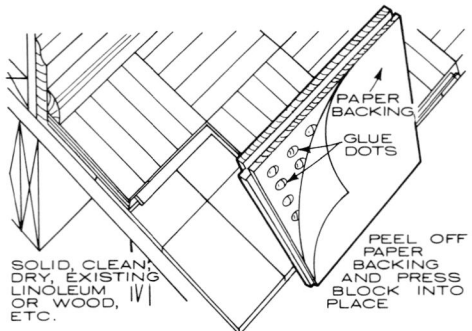

PRESSURE-SENSITIVE "DO-IT-YOURSELF" PANELS (PRE-FINISHED)

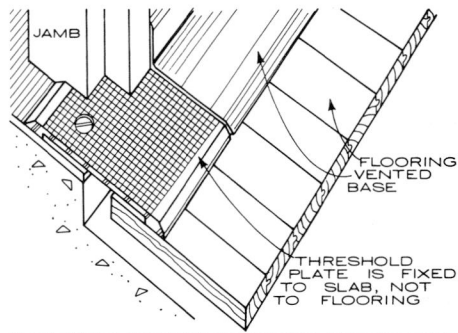

EXPANSION PLATE AT DOORWAY /JOINT WITH DISSIMILAR CONSTRUCTION

Wood flooring is visually attractive and provides an excellent wearing surface. However, wood requires particular care in handling and installation to prevent moisture attack. Minimize moisture attack on wood floors by avoiding proximity to wet areas. Installation should occur after all "wet" jobs are completed. All the permanent lighting and heating plant should be installed to ensure constant temperature and humidity.

Darrel Downing Rippeteau, Architect; Washington, D.C.

Expansion and contraction is a fact of life with most wood flooring. Perimeter base details that allow for movement and ventilation are included in the details above. Moisture control is further enhanced by use of a vapor barrier under a slab on or below grade. This provision should be carefully considered for each installation. Wood structures require adequate ventilation in basement and crawl space.

Wearing properties vary from species to species in wood flooring and should be considered along with appearance. In addition, grain pattern will affect a given species wearability. For instance, industrial wood blocks are typically placed with the end grain exposed because it presents the toughest wearing surface. The thickness of the wood above tongues in T & G flooring may be increased for extra service.

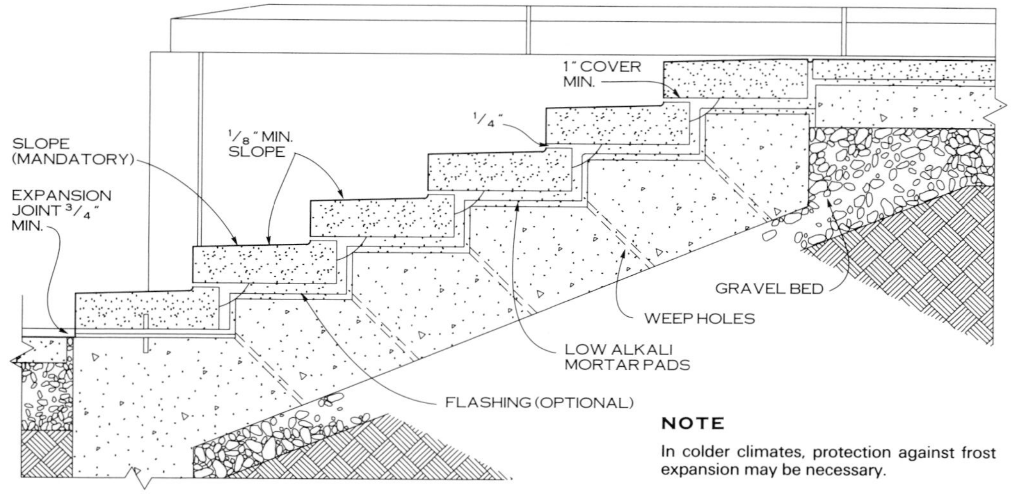

EXTERIOR STAIR SECTION

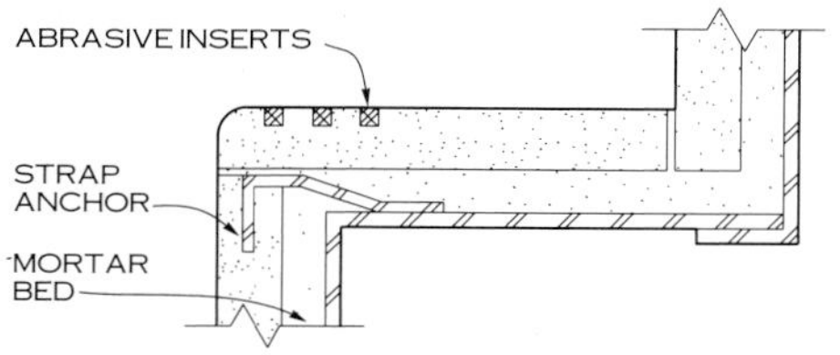

SLOPE (MANDATORY)

EXPANSION JOINT ³/₄" MIN.

1/8" MIN. SLOPE

1" COVER MIN.

1/4"

GRAVEL BED

WEEP HOLES

LOW ALKALI MORTAR PADS

FLASHING (OPTIONAL)

NOTE

In colder climates, protection against frost expansion may be necessary.

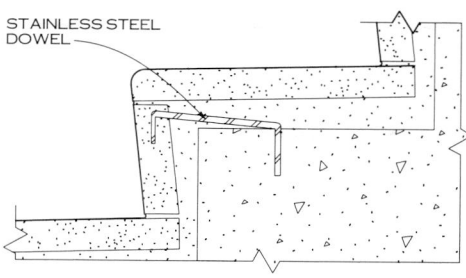

STAINLESS STEEL DOWEL

OPTIONAL FLASHING

SLOPE TREAD 1/8" TO FRONT

WIRE ANCHOR

MORTAR BED

CONCRETE FRAME

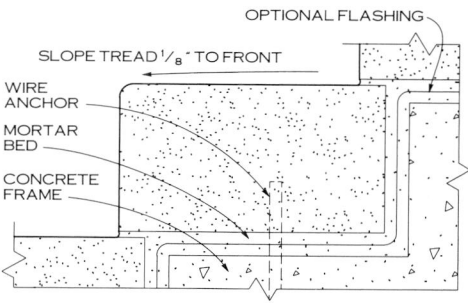

DOWEL

FLASHING (OPTIONAL)

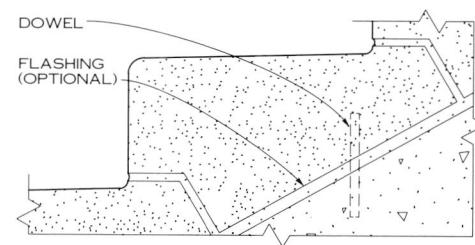

STONE STAIRS WITH CONCRETE FRAME

STONE STAIRS WITH STEEL FRAME

ABRASIVE INSERTS

STRAP ANCHOR

MORTAR BED

METAL PAN WITH STONE SAFETY TREAD

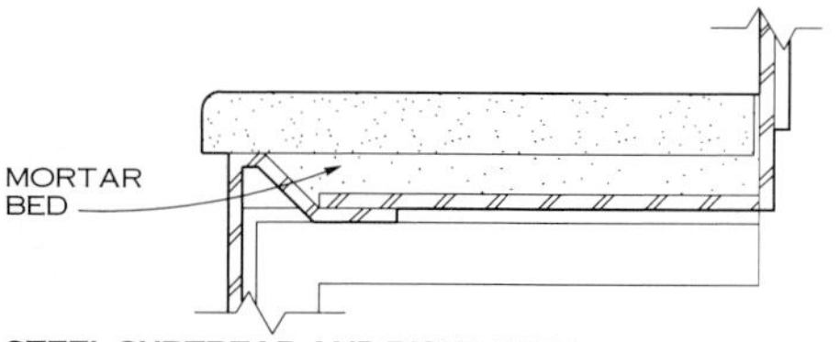

MORTAR BED

STEEL SUBTREAD AND RISER WITH STONE TREAD

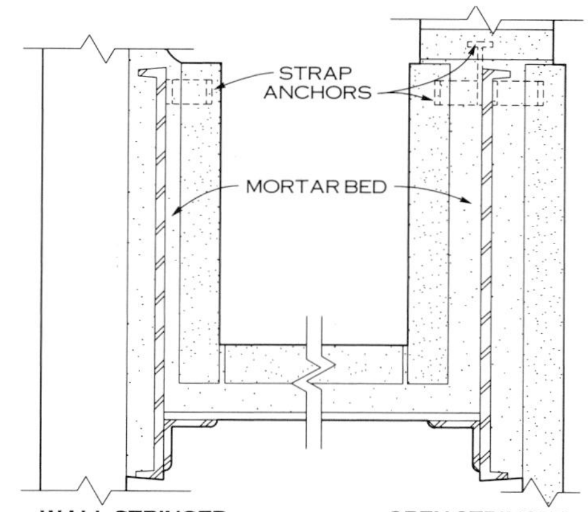

STRAP ANCHORS

MORTAR BED

WALL STRINGER   OPEN STRINGER

DESIGN FACTORS FOR STONE STAIRS

Stone used for steps should have an abrasive resistance of 10 (measured on a scale from a minimum of 6 to a maximum of 17). When different varieties of stone are used, their abrasive hardness should be similar to prevent uneven wear.

Dowels and anchoring devices should be noncorrosive. If a safety tread is used on stairs, a light bush hammered soft finish or nonslip finish is recommended.

To prevent future staining, dampproof the face of all concrete or concrete block, specify low alkali mortar, and provide adequate drainage (slopes and weep holes).

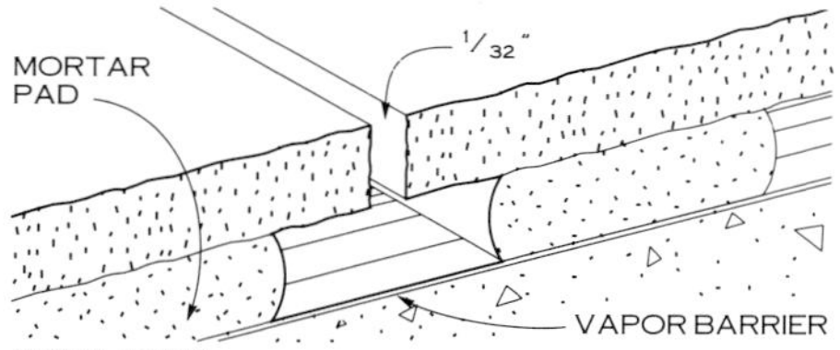

STONE FLOORING

1/32"

MORTAR PAD

VAPOR BARRIER

OPEN JOINT

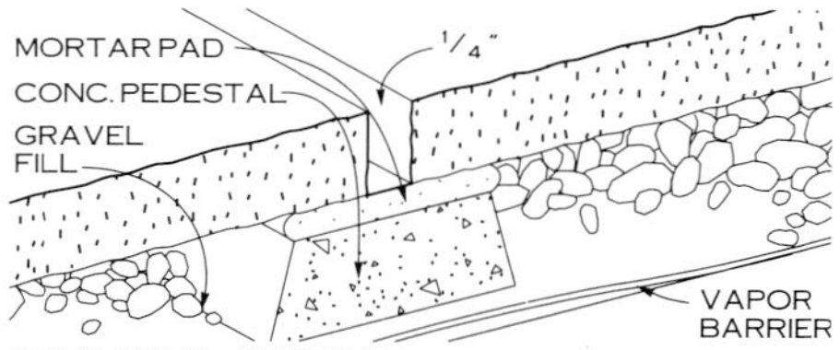

MORTAR PAD
CONC. PEDESTAL
GRAVEL FILL

1/4"

VAPOR BARRIER

OPEN JOINT—PEDESTAL

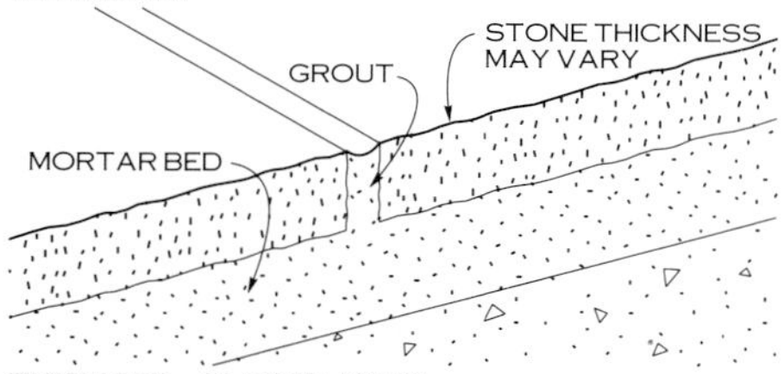

GROUT

STONE THICKNESS MAY VARY

MORTAR BED

THICK SET—CLOSED JOINT

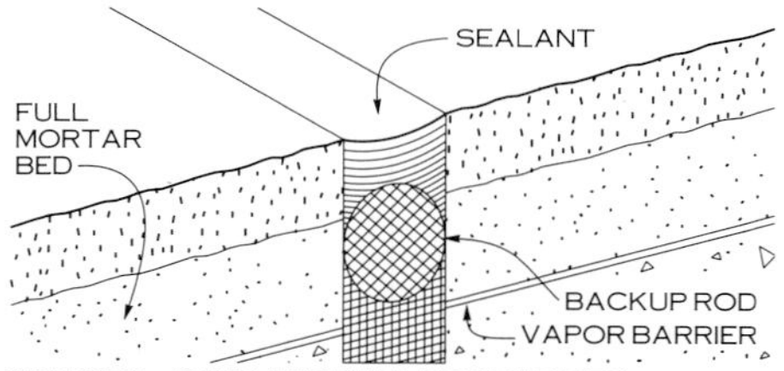

SEALANT

FULL MORTAR BED

BACKUP ROD
VAPOR BARRIER

CONTROL JOINT AND FULL MORTAR BED

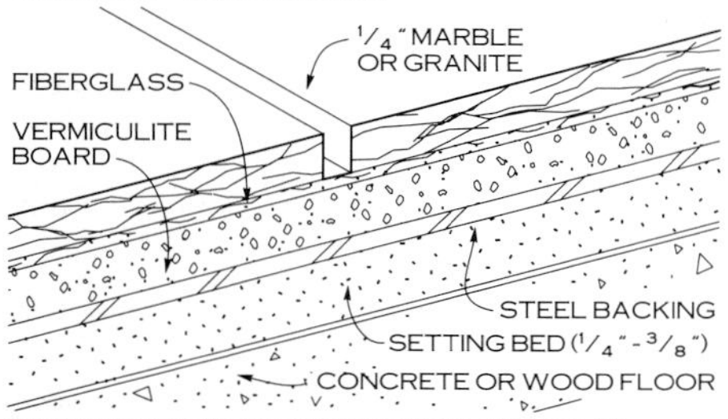

1/4" MARBLE OR GRANITE

FIBERGLASS

VERMICULITE BOARD

STEEL BACKING
SETTING BED (1/4"-3/8")
CONCRETE OR WOOD FLOOR

STONE SANDWICH FLOOR PANEL (PREFAB)

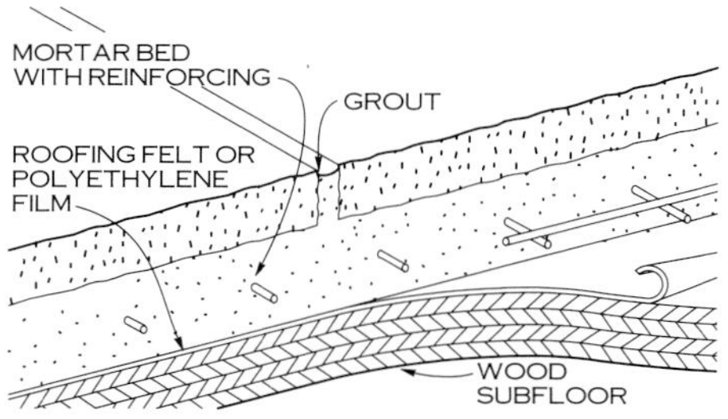

MORTAR BED WITH REINFORCING

GROUT

ROOFING FELT OR POLYETHYLENE FILM

WOOD SUBFLOOR

STONE OVER WOOD FLOOR

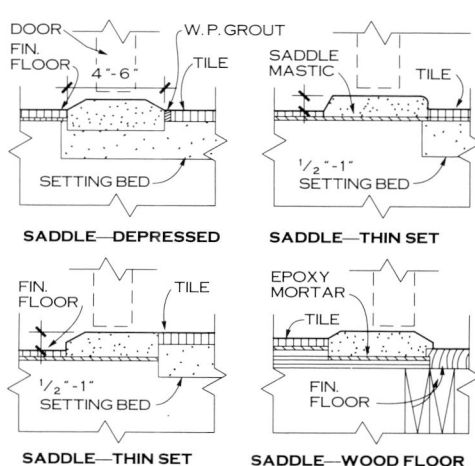

DOOR
FIN. FLOOR
W. P. GROUT
TILE
4"-6"
SETTING BED

SADDLE—DEPRESSED

SADDLE MASTIC
TILE
1/2"-1"
SETTING BED

SADDLE—THIN SET

FIN. FLOOR
TILE
1/2"-1"
SETTING BED

SADDLE—THIN SET

EPOXY MORTAR
TILE
FIN. FLOOR

SADDLE—WOOD FLOOR

STONE THRESHOLDS

Eric K. Beach; Rippeteau Architects, PC; Washington, D.C.
Building Stone Institute; New York, New York; George M. Whiteside, III, AIA, and James D. Lloyd; Kennett Square, Pennsylvania

STONE FLOORING   ⑨

RESILIENT FLOORING CHARACTERISTICS

TYPE OF RESILIENT FLOORING	BASIC COMPONENTS	SUBFLOOR APPLICATION*			RECOMMENDED LOAD LIMIT (PSI)	DURA- BILITY†	RESIS- TANCE TO HEEL DAMAGE	EASE OF MAINTE- NANCE	GREASE RESIS- TANCE	SURFACE ALKALI RESIS- TANCE	RESIS- TANCE TO STAINING	CIGARETTE BURN RESISTANCE	RESIL- IENCE	QUIET- NESS
Vinyl sheet	Vinyl resins with fiber back	B	O	S	75–100	2–3	2–5	1–2	1	1–3	3–4	4	4	4
Homogeneous vinyl tile	Vinyl resins	B	O	S	150–200	1–3	1–4	2–4	1	1–2	1–5	2–5	2–5	2–5
Vinyl composition tile	Vinyl resins and fillers	B	O	S	25–50	2	4–5	2–3	2	4	2	6	6	6
Cork tile with vinyl coating	Raw cork and vinyl resins			S	150	4	3	2	1	1	5	3	3	3
Cork tile	Raw cork and resins			S	75	5	4	4	4	5	4	1	1	1
Rubber tile	Rubber compound	B	O	S	200	2	4	4	3	2	1	2	2	2
Linoleum	Cork, wood, floor, and oleoresins			S	75	3	4–5	4–5	1	4	2	4	4	4

*B: below grade; O: on grade; S: suspended.
†Numerals indicate subjective ratings (relative rank of each floor to others listed above), "1" indicating highest.
  Bruce A. Kenan, AIA, Pederson, Hueber, Hares & Glavin; Syracuse, New York.

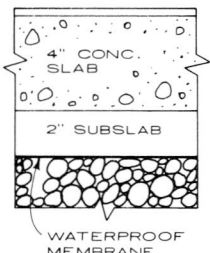
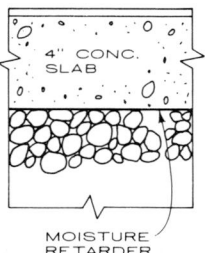
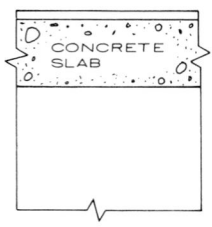
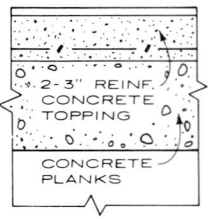
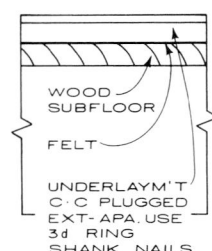
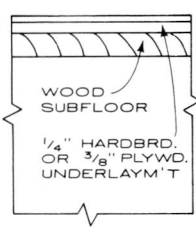

SLAB BELOW GRADE	SLAB ON GRADE	SLAB ABOVE GRADE	SLAB OVER PRECAST	WOOD SUBFLOOR	WOOD SUBFLOOR

RESILIENT FLOORING

PREPARING OLD WOOD FLOORS

TYPE OF SUBFLOOR		COVER WITH
Single wood floor	Tongue and groove not over 3"	Hardboard or plywood, 1/4" or heavier
	Not tongue and groove	Plywood 1/2" or heavier
Double wood floor	Strips 3" or more	Hardboard or plywood 1" or heavier
	Strips less than 3" tongue and groove	Renail or replace loose boards, remove surface irregularities

PREPARING OLD CONCRETE FLOORS

1. Check for dampness.
2. Remove all existing surface coatings.
3. Wirebrush and sweep dusty, porous surfaces. Apply primer.

PREPARING LIFT SLABS

Remove curing compounds prior to resilient flooring installation.

CONCRETE SLABS BY DENSITY

Density			
Light	Medium		Heavy
Pounds per cubic foot			
20/40	60/90	90/120	120/150
Type of concrete			
Expanded perlite, vermiculite, and others	Expanded slag shale, and clay		Standard concrete of sand, gravel, or stone
Recommendations			
Top with 1" thickness of standard concrete mix	Approved for use of resilient flooring if troweled smooth and even		

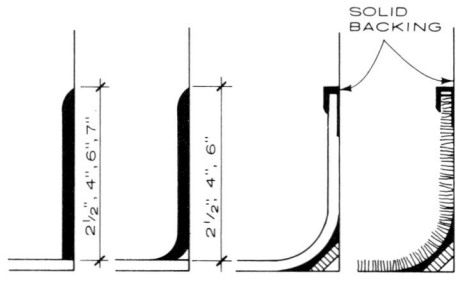
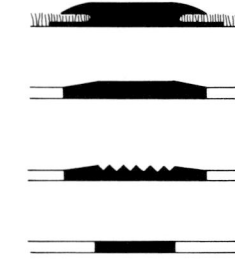
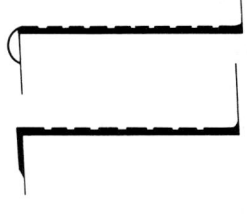

BASES - STRAIGHT OR COVED	COVE STRIP AND CAP STRIP	REDUCERS	STAIR NOSINGS	THRESHOLDS, SADDLES FEATURE STRIP	STAIR TREAD

RESILIENT FLOORING ACCESSORIES, CARPET ACCESSORIES

Broome, Oringdulph, O'Toole, Rudolf & Associates; Portland, Oregon

RESILIENT FLOORING

Carpet 481

BACKGROUND

The word "carpet" comes from the Latin carpere, "to card wool." Carpet production in the U.S. has grown from 100 million square yards in 1910 to over 1 billion square yards in the 1990s. Three events account for the increase.

1. 1930s: man-made fibers developed
2. 1950s: tufting replaced weaving
3. 1960s: tufting machine combined with piece dyeable bulked continuous filament (BCF) nylon. This gave the industry the ability to produce carpet styles with long color lines of up to 50 or more colors without large inventory costs.

CARPET FIBERS

Until the 1930s, nature accounted for 100% of face fiber production for floor coverings. The uncertain supply of desirable wools from about 20 countries, as well as variation in fiber length and increasing costs of scouring and processing, encouraged development of man-made fibers. Man-made fibers are easy to clean, mildew resistant, mothproof, and nonallergenic.

WOOL

Of 1992 U.S. carpet production, 1% was wool. Its qualities have been copied but never quite duplicated. The natural tendency of animal fibers to stretch and return to their original length makes wool carpet resilient, with excellent recovery from crushing. Problems of supply make it the most expensive fiber and the only one requiring antimoth treatment.

COTTON

Negligible current usage. Tufted carpet was an offshoot of the "tufted" bedspread cottage industry in the South and had single-color, loop, or cut-pile fibers made of cotton.

NYLON

Of 1992 carpet production, 80% was nylon, a petrochemical engineered for carpet use, with easy dying characteristics. Successfully introduced into carpet in continuous filament, it was later cut and processed in staple lengths (like wool) to give more natural qualities to the finished product. Recent developments combine topical treatments with modified extrusions to give antisoil properties to the fibers. Adequate maintenance provisions should accompany specifications for these products, since soil will cause fiber damage unless removed by vacuuming and cleaning.

ACRYLIC

Negligible current usage. This hydrocarbon synthetic is considered to be the most wool-like of all man-made fibers.

POLYPROPYLENE (OLEFIN)

Of 1992 production, 12% and growing. This man-made hydrocarbon normally lacks resilience and the ability to be post-dyed. Its simplified extrusion capabilities plus the ability to be solution-dyed prior to extrusion, encouraged many carpet makers to install polypropylene fiber-making facilities.

POLYESTER

Of 1992 production, 7%. A high tensile strength synthetic made by the esterification of ethyl glycol, it has easy care and water-repellent qualities.

CARPET CONSTRUCTION

Woven carpet represents 2% of the total carpet production in the U.S. today. Whether hand-knotted, loomed, or mechanically produced, there are many similarities in production methods. The side-to-side progression in hand-knotted production is accelerated in a loom as the shuttle propels the weft (or woof) yarn back and forth over the 12 or 15 ft width of the finished carpet. This is missing in tufted and later methods. Common to all, however, is a progression of the leading edge of this 12–15 ft finished width in the direction of manufacture. This sets up the direction of lay of the finished face fibers, always in the opposite direction. The exception is in hand-knotted carpet, where the direction of lay of the face fibers falls to one side or the other, depending on the style of knot; the direction of lay changes during cleaning to follow the direction of brushing.

In tufted or woven broadloom, it is imperative that the direction of lay run in the same direction within a continuous installation. Otherwise, adjacent pieces, although perfectly seamed, will appear mismatched in color and texture.

Neil Spencer, AIA; North Canton, Ohio

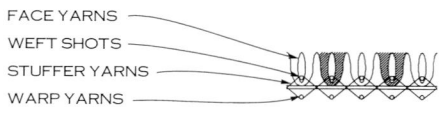

VELVET CONSTRUCTION

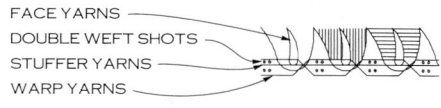

AXMINSTER CONSTRUCTION

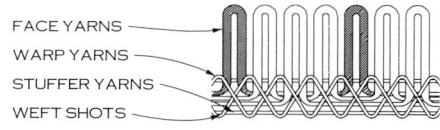

WILTON CONSTRUCTION

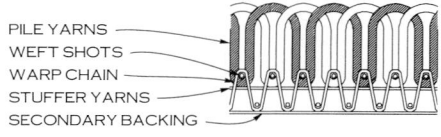

KNITTED CONSTRUCTION

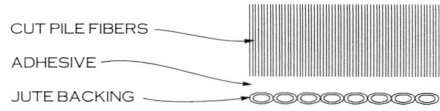

FLOCKED CONSTRUCTION

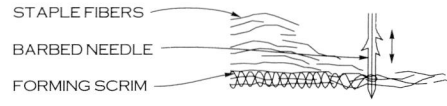

NEEDLEPUNCHED CONSTRUCTION

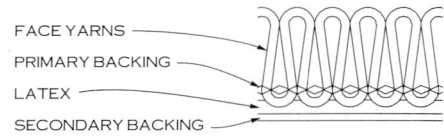

TUFTED CONSTRUCTION

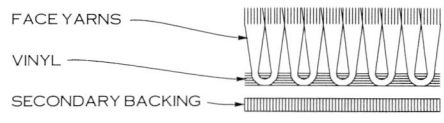

FUSION BONDED CONSTRUCTION

CONSTRUCTION MODES

VELVET: Simplest of all carpet weaves. Although the simplicity of the loom does not permit patterned designs, beautiful yarn color combinations can produce tweed effects. Pile forms as the warp yarns loop over removable "wires" inserted consecutively across the loom (weft-wise). Alternate height wires create high-low loop texture, while wires with a raised knife blade at the trailing end are used to create cut-pile upon retraction.

AXMINSTER: Has a smooth cut-pile surface, with almost all of the yarn appearing on the surface. Colors and patterns are limited only by the number of tufts in the carpet. Identifying feature is the heavy ribbed backing that only allows the carpet to be rolled lengthwise.

WILTON: Basic velvet loom, improved in the early 1800s by a Jacquard mechanism that feeds yarn through as many as six separate punched hole patterns to vary the texture or colored design. Uses only one color at a time on the surface; the other yarns remain buried; thus the reputation that Wiltons have a hidden quality because of the extra "hand" or feel this gives the finished carpet.

KNITTED: Resembles weaving in that knitted carpet is a warp-knitted fabric composed of warp chains, weft-forming yarns, and face yarns and is knitted in single operation. Warp chain stitches run longitudinally and parallel to each other. The backing yarns are laid weft-wise into the warp stitches and pass over three or four rows of warp stitches overlapping in the back of the carpet for strength and stiffness. As in tufted carpet, latex is applied to the back for stability and tuft lock. An additional backing may also be attached. Knitted carpets usually are solid colors or tweeds, with level loop textures.

FLOCKED: Made by propelling short strands of pile fiber (usually nylon) electrostatically against an adhesive-coated, prefabricated backing sheet (usually jute). As many as 18,000 pile fibers per inch become vertically embedded in the adhesive before a secondary backing is laminated to the fabric and the adhesive is cured. The pile fibers can be dyed prior to flocking or the finished surface can be printed after fabrication.

NEEDLEPUNCHED: First made of polypropylene fibers in solid colors for outdoor use (patios and swimming pools), they are now made for indoor and automotive use as well, using wool, nylon, acrylic, and/or olefin fibers in variegated colors and designs. They are made by impinging loose layers of random, staple carpet fibers into a solid sheet of polypropylene, from both sides, by means of thousands of barbed needles until the entire mass is compressed to a solid, bonded fiber mass of indoor/outdoor carpet.

TUFTED: This technique developed from an early method for making tufted bedspreads. Spacing of as many as 2000 needles on a huge sewing machine (12-15 ft wide) determines the carpet gauge. Face yarn is stitched through the primary backing, where it is bonded to a secondary backing with latex before curing in a drying oven. To conserve energy, some mills substitute hot-melt adhesive for latex, though this results in a loss of ability to pass flammability tests. "Single needle" tufting machines have a small stitching head that moves from side to side during carpet construction. They are used mainly for special orders for odd-shaped spaces to eliminate installation waste.

FUSION BONDED: This process produces dense cut-pile or level-loop carpet in solid or moresque colors. For cut-pile, the face yarn, fed simultaneously from the total width of the supply roll, or "beam," is folded back and forth between two vertically emerging primary backings as they are coated with a viscous vinyl paste that hardens, binding the folded face yarns alternately to the vertical backing sheet on each side. Final operation is a mid-line cutting that separates the vertical "sandwich" into two identical cut-pile finished rolls. To make loop-pile fusion-bonded carpet, one primary backing and the cutting operation are omitted. Fusion bonding is especially suited to making carpet tiles.

ORIENTAL RUGS: Defined by Oriental Rug Retailers of America as "a rug of either wool or silk, knotted entirely by hand by native craftsmen in some parts of Asia, from the shores of the Persian Gulf, north to the Caspian Sea, and eastward through Iran, the Soviet Union, Afghanistan, Pakistan, India, China, and Japan." An Oriental rug is classed an antique if it is more than 75 years old, semi-antique if less than 75 years old, and new if made in the past 15 years.

Dhurrie and Kilim rugs are flat woven rugs; they usually cost less than hand-knotted Orientals. They can be either machine- or hand-made and have primitive as well as modern designs. Other types of rugs are ryas from Scandinavia, Native American woven rugs, and Greek flotakis. Braided and rag rugs are also available. Many carpet and rug makers offer custom designs (some computer aided) in a variety of fibers and modes of construction.

CARPET 9

USES FOR CARPET

Carpet may be used in locations other than the floor. Tapestries, traditionally hung on walls, were useful as well as beautiful: they prevented through-wall drafts and were acoustically beneficial. In modern use, edges of full room carpeting may be upturned and used as a wall base. Used with wood trim and glued, carpet may be used in a wainscot, wall, or ceiling panel application. Flame-resistance of carpet should be checked before specifying.

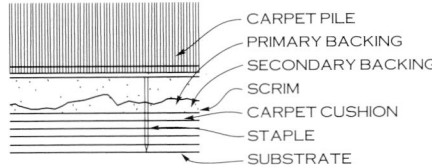

CARPET PILE
PRIMARY BACKING
SECONDARY BACKING
SCRIM
CARPET CUSHION
STAPLE
SUBSTRATE

STRETCH-IN TACKLESS

Over separate cushion. Best condition for maximum carpet wear and most effective cleaning.

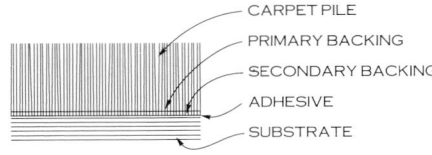

CARPET PILE
PRIMARY BACKING
SECONDARY BACKING
ADHESIVE
SUBSTRATE

DIRECT GLUE DOWN

For large surface areas that make power-stretching and tackless installations prohibitive. Adhesive must be tailored to match carpet backing and substrate, as recommended by carpet manufacturer.

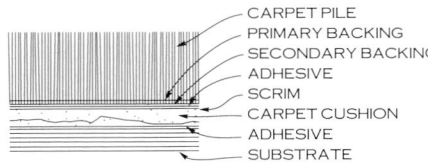

CARPET PILE
PRIMARY BACKING
SECONDARY BACKING
ADHESIVE
SCRIM
CARPET CUSHION
ADHESIVE
SUBSTRATE

DOUBLE GLUE DOWN

Developed to counter early fiber failure, occurring in direct glue-down areas, due to lower than normal resilience level of man-made fibers. Provides ease of large area coverage plus benefits of separate pad.

CARPET CUSHION OR UNDERLAYMENT

Four major categories of carpet cushion are

1. Felt padding
2. Sponge rubber
3. Urethane foam
4. Foam rubber

Four reasons for considering separate carpet cushion in wall-to-wall installations are

1. Adds as much as 50% to the life of the carpet.
2. Absorbs as much as 90% of the traffic noise.
3. Can reduce installation costs by eliminating need for repairs to imperfect substrate.
4. Improves thermal environment by insulation, which varies depending on material.

ACCESSIBILITY FOR PERSONS WITH DISABILITIES

Carpet should be securely attached, have a firm underlayment (if provided), and have a level loop, textured loop, level cut pile, or level cut/uncut pile texture. The maximum pile thickness should be $1/2$ in. (13 mm). Exposed edges should be fastened to floor surfaces and have trim along the entire length of the exposed edge. Carpet edge trim should not exceed $1/2$ in. in height; if more than $1/4$ in., the trim should be beveled 1:20.

TRAFFIC CLASSIFICATION

CARPETED AREAS	TRAFFIC RATING
Educational	
Schools and colleges	
Administration	Medium
Classroom	Heavy
Dormitory	Heavy
Corridor	Heavy
Libraries	Medium
Museums and art galleries	
Display room	Heavy
Lobby	Heavy
Medical	
Health care	
Executive	Light/medium
Patient's room	Heavy
Lounge	Heavy
Nurse's station	Heavy
Corridor	Heavy
Lobby	Heavy
Commercial	
Retail establishments	
Aisles	Heavy
Sales counters	Heavy
Small boutiques, etc.	Heavy
Office buildings	
Executive	Medium
Clerical	Heavy
Corridor	Heavy
Cafeteria	Heavy
Supermarkets	Heavy
Food services	Heavy
Recreational	
Recreation areas	Heavy
Clubhouse	Heavy
Locker room	Heavy
Convention centers	
Auditorium	Heavy
Corridor and lobby	Heavy
Religious	
Churches/temples	
Worship	Light/medium
Meeting rooms	Heavy
Lobby	Heavy

NOTE

If rolling traffic is a factor, carpet may be of maximum density for minimum resistance to rollers. Select only level loop or dense low cut pile for safety.

FIBER CHARACTERISTICS

FEATURES	NYLON	POLYPROPYLENE	POLYESTER	ACRYLIC	WOOL
Durability	EX	EX	VG	G	VG
Soil Resistance	G	F	F	F	G to EX
Resilience	G to EX	P	G	F	EX
Abrasion resistance	EX	EX	EX	G	G
Cleanability	VG	VG	VG	VG	VG

EX - Excellent, VG - Very good, G - Good, F - Fair, and P - Poor.

MAINTENANCE PROGRAMMING

The following maintenance-related factors should be considered in the selection of carpet:

COLOR: Carpets in the mid-value range show less soil than very dark or very light colors. Consider the typical regional soil color. Specify patterned or multicolored carpets for heavy traffic areas in hotels, hospitals, theaters, and restaurants.

TRAFFIC: The heavier the traffic, the heavier the density of carpet construction.

TOPICAL TREATMENT: The soil-hiding qualities of advanced generation fibers do not reduce the need for regular maintenance. Regular cleaning is important to remove hidden dirt that may contribute to early fiber failure.

PLACEMENT: The location of carpeted areas within a building affects the maintenance expense. Walk-off carpet areas can help reduce tracked-in soil near entrances.

DEFINITIONS

CARPET TILES: Square 18 to 36 in. modules, dense cut-pile or loop, heavy backed. Can be made to cover flat, regular wiring; low-voltage lighting systems ("safe-lites"), or underfloor utilities.

CARPET WEAR: As defined by fiber manufacturers, refers to percentage of face fiber lost over the life of a guarantee.

COMMERCIAL: Includes all contract, institutional, transportation; any use where carpet is specified by other than the end user.

RESIDENTIAL: Includes all carpet specified and purchased for residential use by the owner.

LIFE CYCLE COSTING: Permits comparison of diverse flooring methods by totaling initial cost, installation, and detailed predictable maintenance expenses over the expected life of the carpet.

TRAFFIC: Expressed in terms of floor traffics (person) per unit of time or as light, medium, or heavy, to define need for matching carpet construction, which normally increases in density as traffic increases. See table at left.

PILE HEIGHT: Height of loop or tuft from the surface of the backing to the top of the pile, measured in fractions, or decimals, of an inch.

PILE WEIGHT (face weight): Total weight of pile yarns in the carpet (measured in oz/sq yd excluding backing).

PILE DENSITY: D = 36 times the finished pile weight, in oz/yd, divided by the average pile height.

WEIGHT DENSITY (WD) = $\dfrac{(\text{Face weight})^2 \times 36}{\text{Pile height}}$

PITCH (in woven carpet): The number of yarn ends in a 27 in. finished width of carpet.

GAUGE: In tufted carpet, the number of needles per inch across the width of the finished carpet.

STITCHES: Number of rows of yarn ends per inch, finished carpet. Tufts per sq in.: Calculation made by multiplying pitch x wires for woven carpet, or gauge x stitches per inch for tufted.

DERNIER: Weight in grams of 9000 meters (9750 yd) of a single extruded filament of nylon. Based on the standard weight of 450 meters of silk weighing 5 centigrams.

FILAMENT: Continuous strand of extruded synthetic fiber, combined into a "singles" yarn by simply twisting, without the need for spinning.

PLY: Refers to the number of strands of "singles" yarn twisted together (for color or texture) to create a two-ply or three-ply yarn system.

POINT: A single tuft of carpet tile.

BCF: Bulked continuous filament.

CUT-PILE PATTERN: Plush or saxony type carpet with woven, tufted, or printed design or pattern.

LEVEL LOOP: Carpet made from uncut tufts in looped form and having all tufts the same pile height.

CUT-PILE VELVET: Solid color, tweed, or heather blend yarns that give smooth velvety or velour texture.

CUT AND LOOP: Carpet with areas of both cut pile and loop pile, most often with the cut pile being higher than the loop.

FREEZE: Cut pile carpet made from highly twisted yarns that are heat-set to give a curled random configuration to the pile yarns.

PRIMARY BACKING: The matrix used in making tufted carpet, consisting of woven or nonwoven fabric, usually jute or polypropylene, into which pile yarn tufts are stitched.

SECONDARY BACKING: The woven or nonwoven material adhered to the underside of a carpet during construction to provide additional tuft bind for tufted carpet and dimensional stability and body. Usually jute, or polypropylene, latex foam, or vinyl.

Neil Spencer, AIA; North Canton, Ohio

CARPET

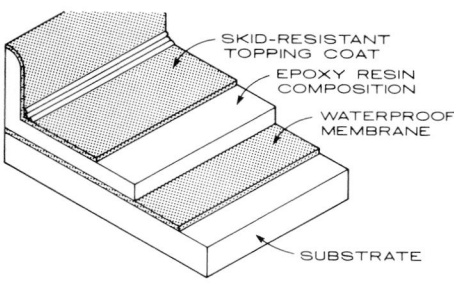

An epoxy resin composition flooring resistant to a large number of corrosive materials, $^3/_{16}$ in. to $^1/_4$ in. thickness, weight 3 psf. Used in manufacturing areas, food processing, hotel and restaurant kitchens, beverage bottling plants and loading docks.

EPOXY RESIN COMPOSITION FLOORING

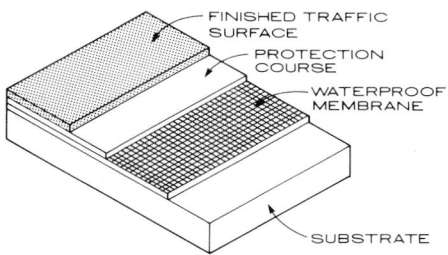

A multicolored installation consisting of a fabric reinforced latex membrane, a neoprene-cement protection course, and a flexible, oil-resistant finish. Thickness $^3/_{16}$ in., weight 1.5 psf. Used on interior or exterior auto parking facilities.

REINFORCED LATEX MEMBRANE

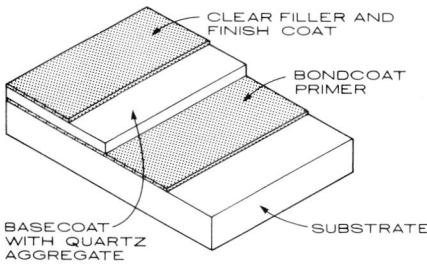

A jointless flooring in which quartz aggregates are embedded either by trowel or broadcast into a wet epoxy binding coat followed by clear filler coat. Used in laboratories, pollution control facilities, locker rooms, light manufacturing.

EPOXY/QUARTZ AGGREGATE

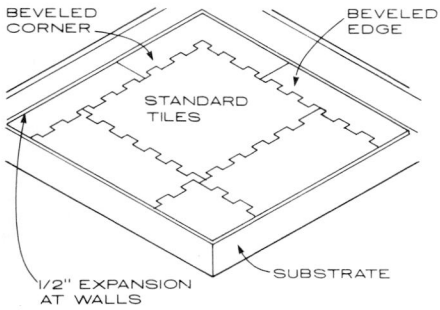

An interlocking rubber tile flooring system made in various thicknesses and types according to user requirements. Can be used in saunas, deck areas, weight, exercise, and locker rooms, on assembly lines, in industrial art rooms.

INTERLOCKING RUBBER FLOORING

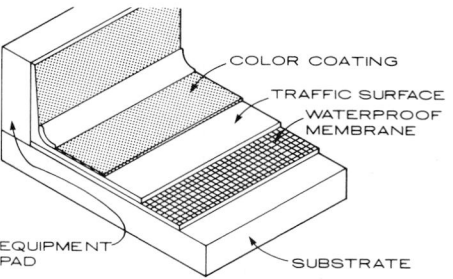

A troweled surface over a fabric reinforced latex-type waterproof membrane. Flooring thickness $^3/_{16}$ in., weight 2$^1/_2$ psf. Used in mechanical equipment rooms and plenum rooms.

WATERPROOF LATEX MEMBRANE FLOORING

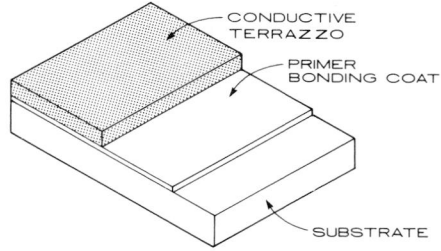

Static-dissipating, nonsparking trowel-applied jointless flooring of elastomeric resin terrazzo, incorporating marble chips. Thickness $^1/_4$ in. to $^1/_2$ in., weighing 3 psf ($^1/_4$ in. thick). Used in hospital operating suites.

CONDUCTIVE FLOORING

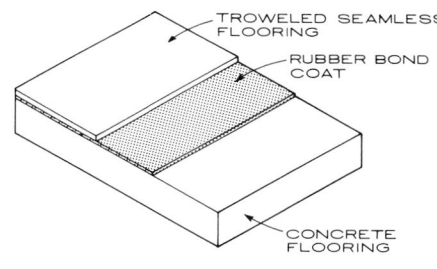

A trowel-applied cupric oxychloride flooring that is nonsparking and solvent resistant, weighing 3.2 psf at $^3/_8$ in. thick. Used in hospitals, arsenals and ammunition plants, light manufacturing areas, warehouses, laboratories.

CUPRIC OXYCHLORIDE FLOORING

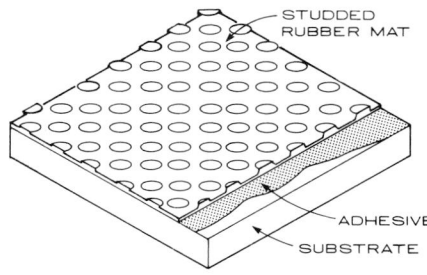

A solid, nonconductive rubber flooring with a raised circular, square, "H" or ribbed pattern. Applied to substrate by use of an adhesive. Used in terminals, malls, recreation facilities, elevators and offices.

STUDDED RUBBER FLOORING

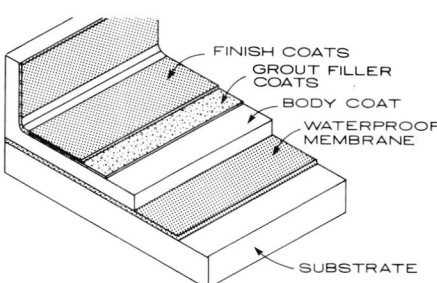

A trowel-applied elastomeric latex resin forming a jointless floor with good chemical resistance, is waterproof in conjunction with membrane. Thickness $^1/_4$ in., weight 3 psf. Used in showers and locker rooms, laboratories, pollution control facilities, TV studios.

ELASTOMERIC LATEX RESIN FLOORING

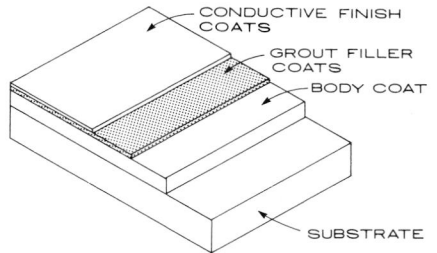

Static-dissipating and nonsparking trowel-applied jointless flooring, $^1/_4$ in. thick, weighing 3 psf. Used in arsenals and ammunition plants, flammable materials storage areas and explosion-hazardous industrial locations.

CONDUCTIVE FLOORING

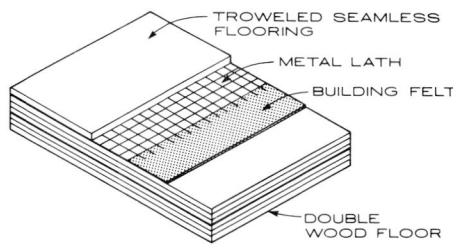

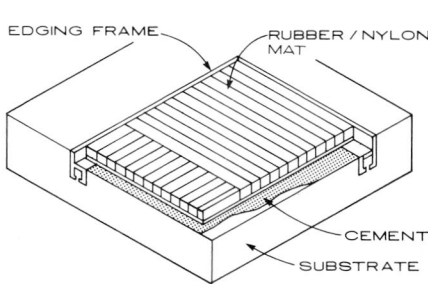

Manufactured from recycled synthetic rubber tires containing nylon fibers for strength and bonded to a glass-cloth backing. Applied to substrate cement adhesive. Used in golf clubs, stores, malls, and air terminals.

RUBBER/NYLON FLOORING

Timothy B. McDonald; Washington, D.C.

SPECIAL FLOORING AND TRIM

GENERAL

Ceilings and Interior
  Systems Construction Association (CISCA)
579 W. North Ave., Suite 301
Elmhurst, IL, 60126
Tel: (708) 833-1919
Fax:(708) 833-1940

National Association of
  Decorative Architectural Finishes
2414 Taylor Avenue
Alexandria, VA 22302-3306
Tel: (703) 836-6504

Wallcovering Manufacturers Association
401 N. Michigan Avenue
Chicago, IL 60611-4267
Tel: (312) 644-6610
Fax:(312) 321-6869

REFERENCES

Exterior Wood in the South: Selection, Applications, and Finishes. Southern Forest Products Assoc., 1991.

Simmons, H. L. *Repairing and Extending Finishes.* Part I: Plaster, Gypsum Board, Ceramic Tile. Van Nostrand Reinhold, 1990.

Simmons, H. L. *Repairing and Extending Finishes.* Part II: Acoustical Treatment, Resilient Flooring, Paint, Transparent Finishes. Van Nostrand Reinhold, 1990.

Reznikoff, S. C. *Specifications for Commercial Interiors.* Whitney Library of Design.

Tolerances, Variation, and Pre-Existing Site Conditions for the Wall and Ceiling Industries. Foundation of the Wall and Ceiling Industry, 1990. [looseleaf binder]

LATH AND PLASTER

Association of Wall and Ceiling International
307 East Annandale Road, Suite 200
Falls Church, VA 22042
Tel: (703) 534-8300
Fax:(703) 534-8307

Foundation of the Wall and Ceiling Industry (FWCI)
307 East Annandale Road, Suite 200
Falls Church, VA 22042
Tel: (703) 534-8300
Fax:(703) 534-8307

International Institute for Lath and Plaster (IILP)
820 Transfer Road
St. Paul, MN 55114-1406
Tel: (612) 645-0208
Fax:(612) 645-0209

REFERENCES

Jointing and Metalwork for Portland Cement Plaster, Monograph 09M221. Construction Specifications Institute,1990.

Gorman, J., et al. *Plaster and Drywall Systems Manual.* McGraw-Hill, 1988.

Van Den Branden, F., and T. Hartsell. *Plastering Skills.* Homewood, Ill.: American Technical Publishers, 1984. [(708) 957-2200]

Portland Cement Plaster, Monograph 09M220. Construction Specifications Institute, 1989.

Portland Cement Plaster (Stucco) Manual, EB049M. Portland Cement Association, 1980.

"The Preservation and Repair of Historic Stucco." Preservation Brief 22, #024-005-01066-1, 1990.

"Preserving Historic Ornamental Plaster," Preservation Brief 23, #024-005-01067-0, 1990.

"Repairing Historic Flat Plaster Walls and Ceilings," Preservation Brief 21, #024-005-01055-6, US GPO, 1989.

"Repairing Historic Stucco," *P/A* (Feb. 1992), pp.119-22.

Specifications for Metal Lathing and Furring, ML/SFA 920. National Association of Architectural Metal Manufacturers, 1991.

Shivers, N. *Walls and Molding: How to Care for Old Historic Wood and Plaster.* Washington, D.C.: Preservation Press, 1990.

GYPSUM BOARD

Gypsum Association
810 First St., NE, Suite 510
Washington, DC 20002
Tel: (202) 289-5440
Fax:(202) 289-3707

REFERENCES

Application and Finishing of Gypsum Board, GA-216. Gypsum Association, 1989.

Gypsum Board, Monograph 09M250. Construction Specifications Institute, 1990.

Using Gypsum Board for Walls and Ceilings. Gypsum Association, 1985.

TILE

Ceramic Tile Institute of America, Inc.
12061 Jefferson Blvd.
Culver City, CA 90230-6219
Tel: (310) 574-7800
Fax:(310) 821-4655

Facing Tile Institute
Box 8880
Canton, OH 44711
Tel: (216) 488-1211
Fax:(216) 488-0333

Italian Tile Association (ITA)
305 Madison Avenue, Suite 3120
New York, NY 10165
Tel: (212) 661-0435
Fax:(212) 949-8192

Materials and Methods Standards Association (MMSA)
c/o Harvey Powell, Noble Co.
P.O. Box 350
Grand Haven, MI 49417
Tel: (616) 842-7844
Fax:(616) 842-1547

Tile Council of America, Inc.
P.O. Box 326
Princeton, NJ 08542-0326
Tel: (609) 921-7050
Fax:(609) 452-7255

REFERENCES

Design Data for Structural Facing Tile. Facing Tile Institute.

Recommended Standard Specifications for Ceramic Tile, ANSI/TCA. Tile Council of America.

American National Standard Specifications for Installation of Ceramic Tile, ANSI A-108 series. Tile Council of America, 1985.

American National Standard Specifications for Ceramic Tile, ANSI A-137.1. Tile Council of America, 1988.

Bulletins 1-16. Materials and Methods Standards Association, 1988.

Ceramic Tile, Monograph 09M310. Construction Specifications Institute, 1984.

Ceramic Tile, SpecGUIDE G09310. Construction Specifications Institute, 1987.

CTI Tile Manual. Ceramic Tile Institute, 1991.

Handbook for Ceramic Tile Installation. Tile Council of America. [updated annually]

TERRAZZO

National Terrazzo and Mosaic Association, Inc.
3166 Des Plaines Avenue, Suite 132
Des Plaines, IL 60018
Tel: (708) 635-7744
Fax:(708) 635-9127

REFERENCES

Terazzo, SpecGUIDE G09400. Construction Specifications Institute, 1987.

Terrazzo Ideas and Design Guide. National Terrazzo and Mosaic Association, 1990.

ACOUSTICAL TREATMENT

Acoustical Society of America (ASA)
500 Sunnyside Blvd.
Woodbury, NY 11797
Tel: (516) 576-2360

REFERENCES

Schultz, T. *Acoustical Uses for Perforated Metals.* Industrial Perforators Association.

"Acoustics for Small Spaces." *P/A* (April 1991), pp.36-40.

Warnock, A. "Reverberant Noise Control in Room Using Sound Absorbing Materials," Building Research Note 163. National Research Council of Canada, 1980.

Egan, M. "Sound Absorption," Ch. 2. *Architectural Acoustics.* McGraw-Hill, 1988.

FLOORING

American Floor Covering Association
13-154 Merchandise Mart
Chicago, IL 60654
Tel: (312) 644-1243
Fax:(312) 644-2787

Fine Hardwood Veneer Association
5603 West Raymond, Suite O
Indianapolis, IN 46241-4356
Tel: (317) 244-3312
Fax:(317) 244-3386

Hardwood Manufacturer's Association (HMA)
400 Penn Center Blvd., Suite 530
Pittsburgh, PA 15235-5605
Tel: (412) 829-0770
Fax:(412) 829-0844

Maple Flooring Manufacturers Association
60 Revere Drive, Suite 500
Northbrook, IL 60062-1563
Tel: (708) 480-9138
Fax:(708) 480-9282

National Oak Flooring Manufacturers Association
P.O. Box 3009
Memphis, TN 38173-0009
Tel: (901) 526-5016
Fax:(901) 526-7022

National Wood Flooring Association
233 Old Meramec Station Road
Manchester, MO 63021
Tel: (800) 422-4556
Fax:(314) 391-6137

Western Wood Products Association (WWPA)
522 S.W. Fifth Avenue, Yeon Building
Portland, OR 97204
Tel: (503) 224-3930
Fax:(503) 224-3934

Wood & Synthetic Flooring Institute
4415 West Harrison Street, Suite 242C
Hillside, IL 60162
Tel: (708) 449-2933
Fax:(708) 449-0837

REFERENCES

Care and Preservation of Your Wood Floors. Wood and Synthetic Flooring Institute.

Hardwood Floors. National Wood Flooring Association. [monthly]

Laminated Hardwood Flooring Standard. Hardwood Plywood Manufacturers' Association.

Resinous Flooring, SpecGUIDE G09680. Construction Specifications Institute (CSI), 1989.

Stone Flooring, SpecGUIDE 09600. CSI, 1991.

Vinyl Composition, Solid Vinyl & Asphalt Tile. Resilient Floor Covering Institute.

Wood Flooring, SpecGUIDE G09550. CSI, 1988.

Recommendations for the Correct Preparation, Finishing and Testing of Concrete Subfloor Surfaces to Receive Wood Finishing. Wood and Synthetic Flooring Institute.

RESILIENT FLOORING

Resilient Floor Covering Institute
966 Hungerford Drive, Suite 12-B
Rockville, MD 20850
Tel: (301) 340-8580
Fax:(301) 340-7283

REFERENCES

Addressing Moisture Related Problems Relevant to Resilient Floor Coverings Installed over Concrete. Resilient Floor Covering Institute (RFCI), 1985.

Recommended Work Procedures for Resilient Floor Coverings. RFCI.

CARPET

Carpet and Rug Institute
P.O. Box 2048
Dalton, GA 30722-2048
Tel: (706) 278-3176
Fax:(706) 278-8835

Jute Carpet Backing Council, Inc. (JCBC)
30 Rockefeller Plaza, 27th Floor
New York, NY 10112
Tel: (212) 408-1040

Chapter

10

SPECIALTIES

NOTES

1. Compartment types: ceiling hung (marble or metal), overhead braced, and wall hung (metal only).

2. Metal finishes: baked-on enamel, porcelain enamel, and stainless steel. Phenolic core, plastic laminate, solid polyethylene, tempered glass, and marble panels also are available.

3. A = standard compartment widths: 32 in., 34 in., and 36 in. (34 in. is used most frequently).

4. B = standard door widths: 20, 22, 24, 26, 28, and 30 in. (24 in. metal doors are standard with marble compartments). Nonstandard sizes that sometimes are used: 23, 27, and 29 in. Doors 34 and 36 in. are used on accessible stalls.

5. C = standard pilaster widths: 3, 4, 5, 6, 8, 10, and 12 in. Nonstandard sizes that sometimes are used: 2, 7, and 14 in.

6. D = standard panel widths: 18–57 in. in 1-in. increments. All panels are 58 in. high.

7. Accessories include such items as paper holders, coat hooks, and purse shelves.

8. In toilet rooms with fewer than 6 stalls, make one compartment accessible. When there are more than 6, design an additional stall 36 in. wide with parallel grab bars and an outswinging door.

9. When possible, design accessible stalls with in-swinging doors. Although this requires more space, the stall doors will be damaged less frequently.

10. Where multiple accessible stalls are provided, design grab bars for left and right side use since people have different arm strengths.

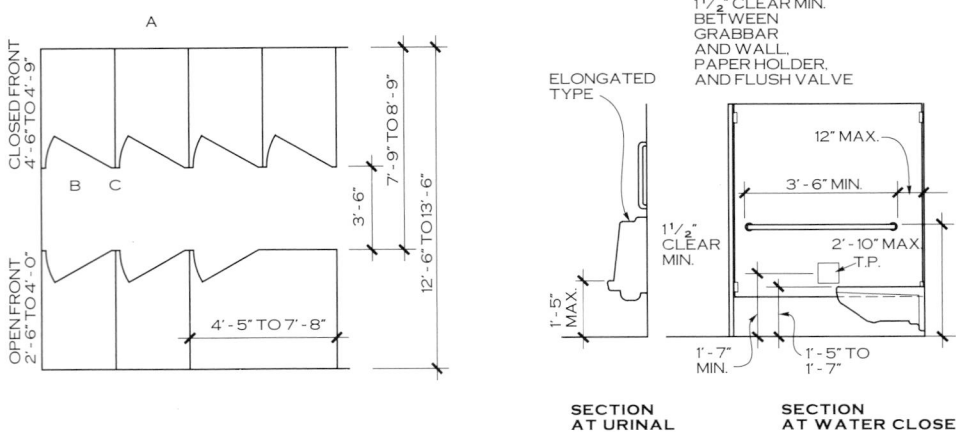

GENERAL STALL PLANNING

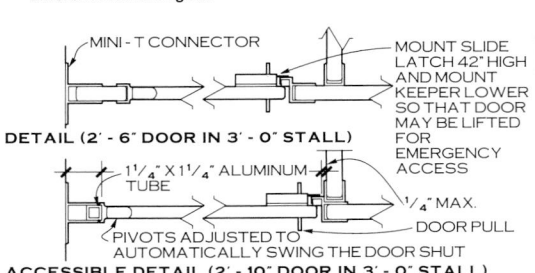

DETAIL (2'- 6" DOOR IN 3'- 0" STALL)

ACCESSIBLE DETAIL (2'- 10" DOOR IN 3'- 0" STALL)

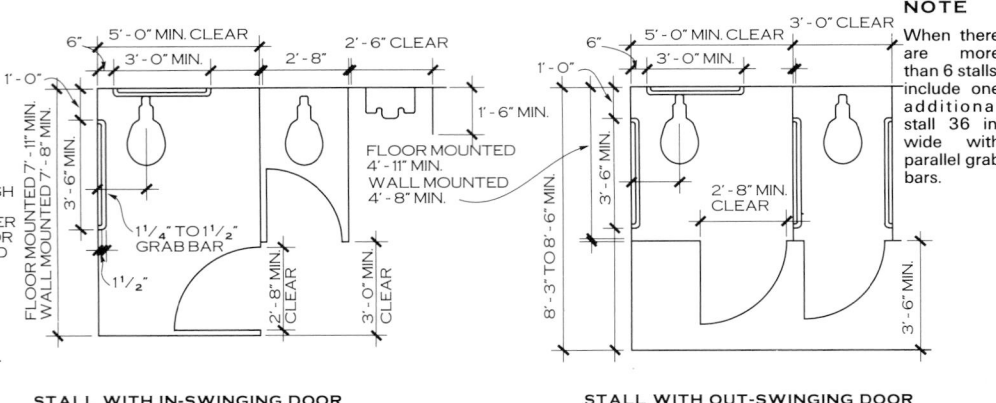

NOTE

When there are more than 6 stalls, include one additional stall 36 in. wide with parallel grab bars.

STALL WITH IN-SWINGING DOOR

STALL WITH OUT-SWINGING DOOR

ACCESSIBLE TOILET PARTITION LAYOUT

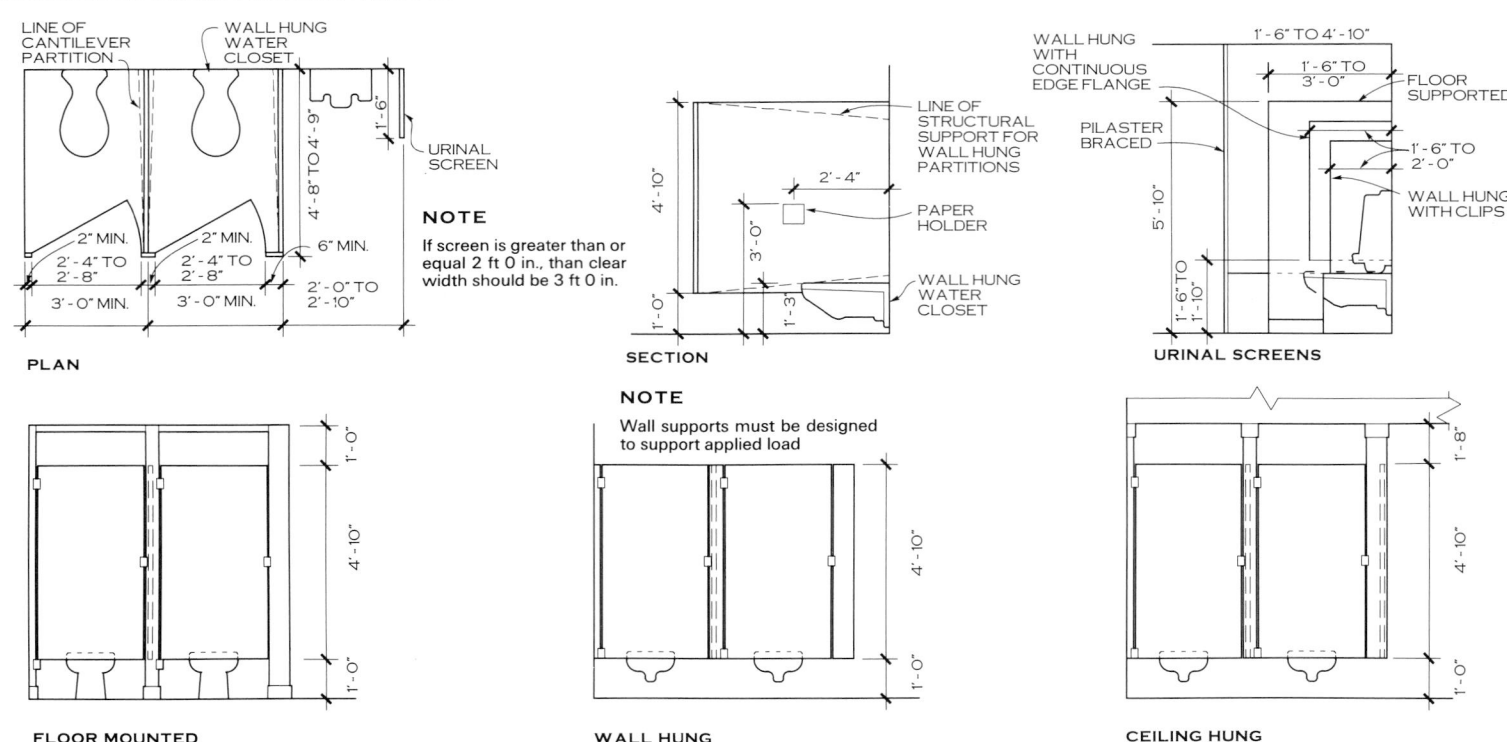

PLAN

NOTE
If screen is greater than or equal 2 ft 0 in., than clear width should be 3 ft 0 in.

SECTION

URINAL SCREENS

NOTE
Wall supports must be designed to support applied load

FLOOR MOUNTED

WALL HUNG

CEILING HUNG

METAL AND PLASTIC LAMINATE TOILET PARTITIONS

Mark J. Mazz, AIA; CEA, Inc.; Hyattsville, Maryland

10   **TOILET AND BATH COMPARTMENTS AND ACCESSORIES**

NOTES

1. SIZE: 1 1/2 in. or 1 1/4 in. O.D. with 1 1/2 in. clearance at wall.
2. MATERIAL: Stainless steel chrome plated brass with knurled finish, optional.
3. INSTALLATION: Concealed or exposed fasteners; return all ends to wall, intermediate supports at 3 ft maximum. Use heavy duty type bars and methods of installation.
4. Other grab bars are available for particular situations.

Consult ANSI and ADAAG requirements, as well as applicable local and federal regulations.

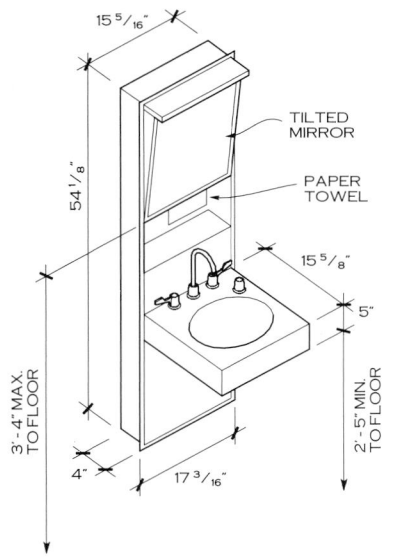

ACCESSIBLE SINK

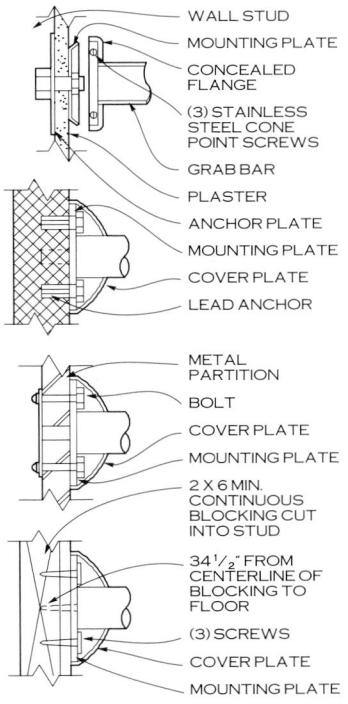

ATTACHMENT DETAILS

Mark J. Mazz, AIA; CEA, Inc.; Hyattsville, Maryland

NOTE

Depending upon configuration of clear floor space, maximum height of controls ranges from 3 ft 8 in. to 4 ft 8 in. and the minimum height ranges from 9 in. to 2 ft 10 in.

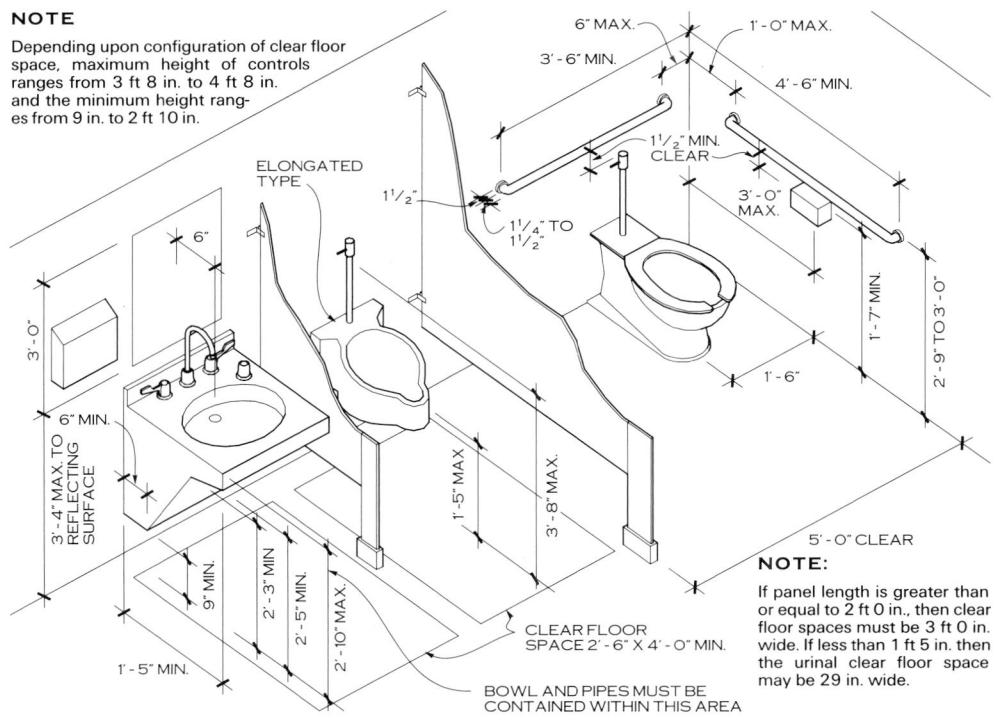

NOTE:
If panel length is greater than or equal to 2 ft 0 in., then clear floor spaces must be 3 ft 0 in. wide. If less than 1 ft 5 in. then the urinal clear floor space may be 29 in. wide.

LOCATION OF ACCESSIBLE FIXTURES AND ACCESSORIES

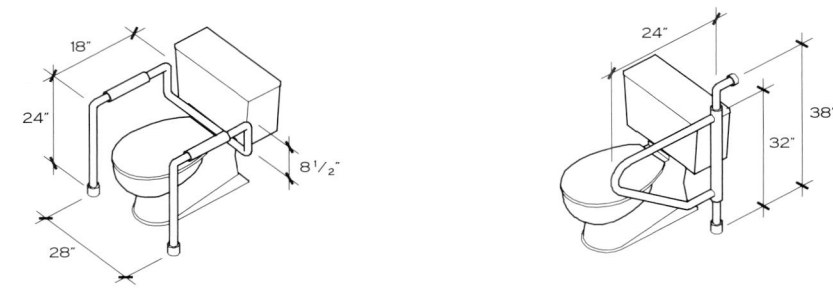

ALTERNATE GRAB BAR CONFIGURATIONS

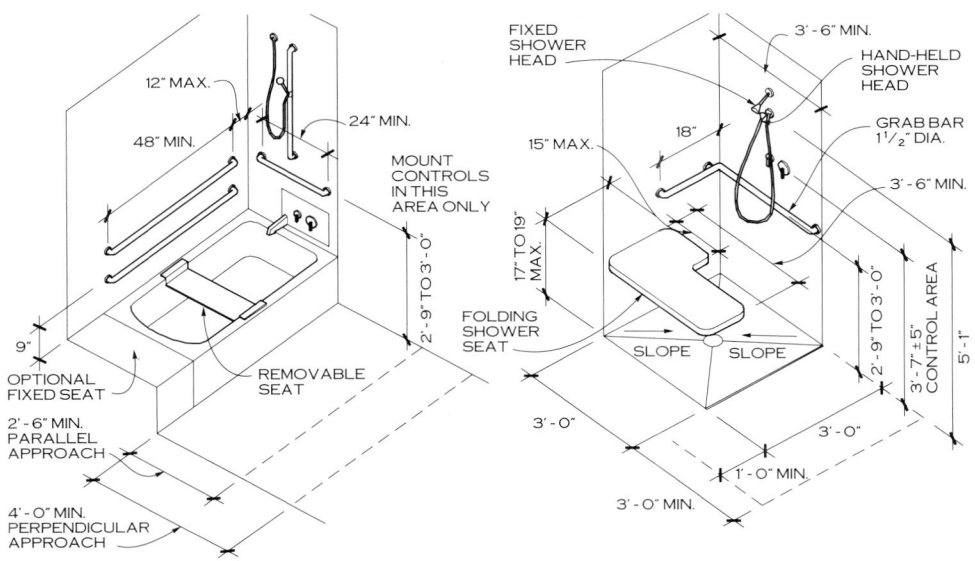

ACCESSIBLE BATHTUB AND SHOWER

GUIDELINES

1. Residential cabinets: enameled steel, stainless steel, aluminum, wood, plastic, etc.
2. Commercial cabinets: stainless steel and enameled steel
3. Accessories: chrome, stainless steel, brass, aluminum, plastic, and vitreous china
4. Cabinet and accessory types: recessed, semi-recessed, or surface mounted.
5. Light fixtures can be part of cabinets.
6. ADA requires reach height not to exceed 48 in. for forward reach or 54 in. for side reach.

NOTE

All dispensers and disposals can be recessed, semirecessed, or surface mounted.

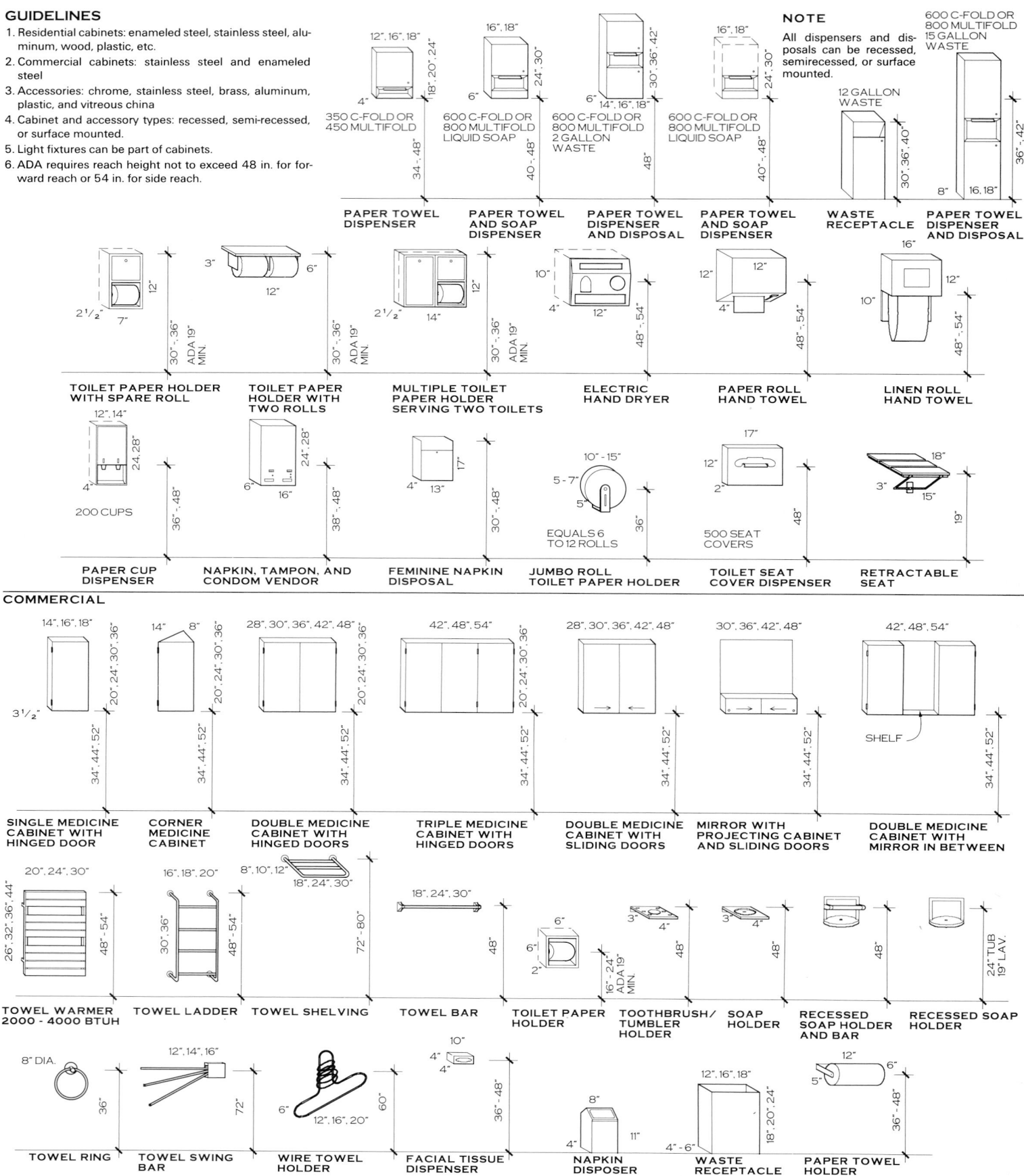

COMMERCIAL

RESIDENTIAL AND HOTEL

Charles A. Szoradi, AIA; Washington, D.C.

10   TOILET AND BATH COMPARTMENTS AND ACCESSORIES

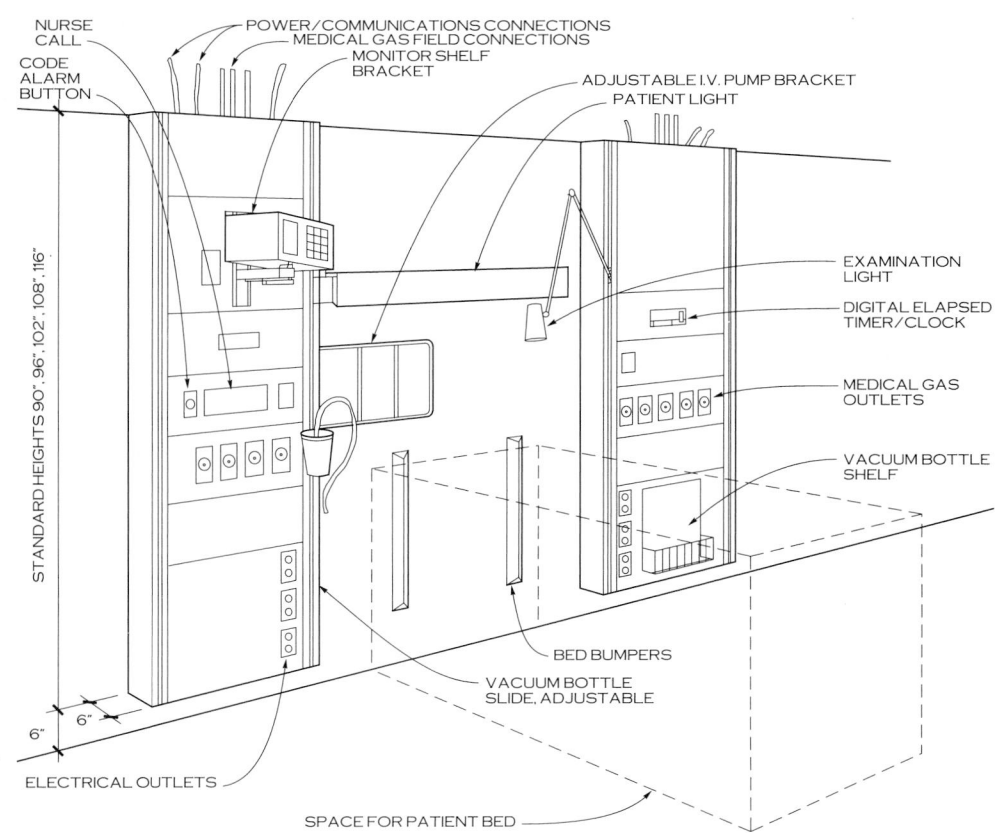

NURSE CALL
CODE ALARM BUTTON
POWER/COMMUNICATIONS CONNECTIONS
MEDICAL GAS FIELD CONNECTIONS
MONITOR SHELF BRACKET
ADJUSTABLE I.V. PUMP BRACKET
PATIENT LIGHT
EXAMINATION LIGHT
DIGITAL ELAPSED TIMER/CLOCK
MEDICAL GAS OUTLETS
VACUUM BOTTLE SHELF
BED BUMPERS
VACUUM BOTTLE SLIDE, ADJUSTABLE
ELECTRICAL OUTLETS
SPACE FOR PATIENT BED
STANDARD HEIGHTS 90", 96", 102", 108", 116"
6" 6"

VERTICAL WALL-MOUNTED MODULES

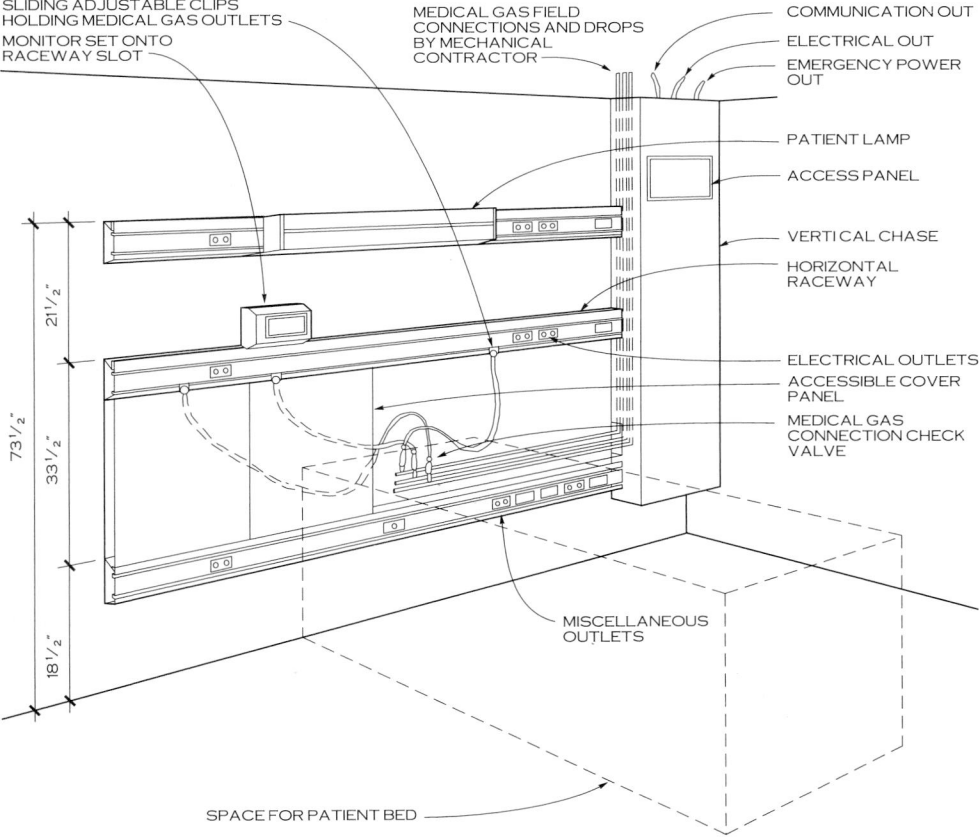

SLIDING ADJUSTABLE CLIPS HOLDING MEDICAL GAS OUTLETS
MONITOR SET ONTO RACEWAY SLOT
MEDICAL GAS FIELD CONNECTIONS AND DROPS BY MECHANICAL CONTRACTOR
COMMUNICATION OUT
ELECTRICAL OUT
EMERGENCY POWER OUT
PATIENT LAMP
ACCESS PANEL
VERTICAL CHASE
HORIZONTAL RACEWAY
ELECTRICAL OUTLETS
ACCESSIBLE COVER PANEL
MEDICAL GAS CONNECTION CHECK VALVE
MISCELLANEOUS OUTLETS
SPACE FOR PATIENT BED
21 1/2"
73 1/2"
33 1/2"
18 1/2"

VERTICAL CHASE WITH HORIZONTAL RACEWAY

Richard J. Vitullo, AIA; Oak Leaf Studio; Crownsville, Maryland
Andrew Sumners; University Park, Maryland

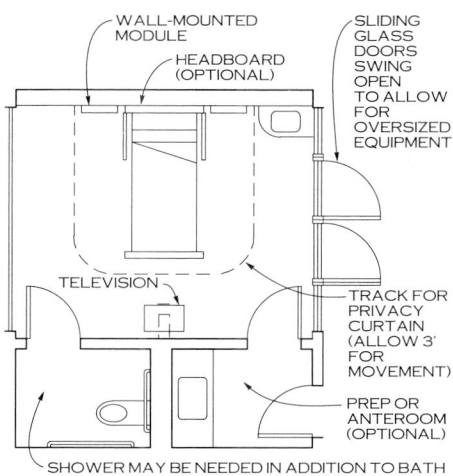

WALL-MOUNTED MODULE
HEADBOARD (OPTIONAL)
SLIDING GLASS DOORS SWING OPEN TO ALLOW FOR OVERSIZED EQUIPMENT
TELEVISION
TRACK FOR PRIVACY CURTAIN (ALLOW 3' FOR MOVEMENT)
PREP OR ANTEROOM (OPTIONAL)
SHOWER MAY BE NEEDED IN ADDITION TO BATH

NOTE

Creating an efficient and unhampered space is important in the design of intensive care units. Several manufacturers offer modular units to help organize the distribution of services to the patient. These services include medical gases such as oxygen and nitrous oxide, air and vacuum service, communications, and power. Wall-mounted systems organize services in vertical or horizontal raceways or modules and are designed for beds that position the patient's head against a wall. Modules can be custom designed to serve the particular needs of each ICU and are flexible and adaptable to meet the needs of individual patients. These modules can be designed to serve one or two patient beds.

TYPICAL LAYOUT/PLAN

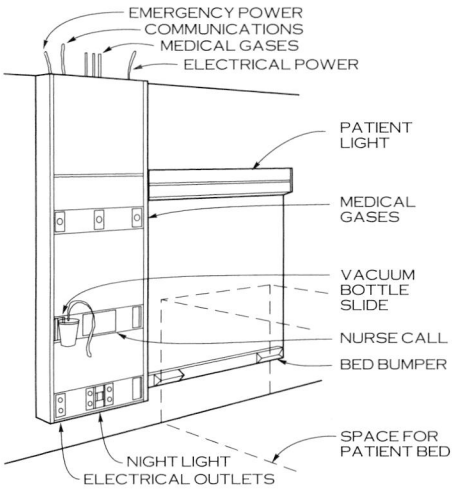

EMERGENCY POWER
COMMUNICATIONS
MEDICAL GASES
ELECTRICAL POWER
PATIENT LIGHT
MEDICAL GASES
VACUUM BOTTLE SLIDE
NURSE CALL
BED BUMPER
SPACE FOR PATIENT BED
NIGHT LIGHT
ELECTRICAL OUTLETS

SINGLE VERTICAL WALL-MOUNTED MODULE

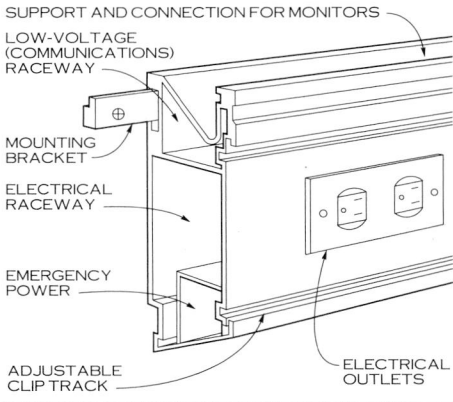

SUPPORT AND CONNECTION FOR MONITORS
LOW-VOLTAGE (COMMUNICATIONS) RACEWAY
MOUNTING BRACKET
ELECTRICAL RACEWAY
EMERGENCY POWER
ADJUSTABLE CLIP TRACK
ELECTRICAL OUTLETS

RACEWAY DETAIL

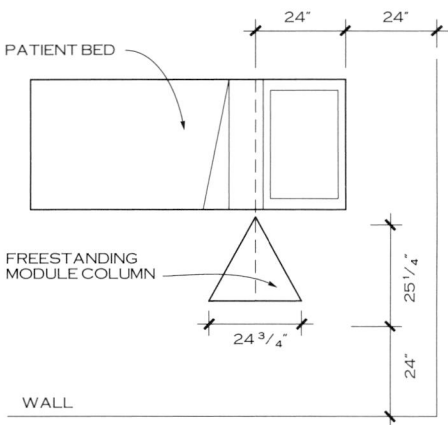

NOTE

Freestanding intensive care unit modules help organize and distribute patient services by accommodating situations in which the patient's bed is not against a wall, thereby allowing hospital staff access to the patient from all sides, particularly near the head. This system also reduces the clutter, inconvenience, and danger of disconnection created by long cords and hoses stretching from a wall-based system to a remote bed. In the rectangular and triangular models, the module is installed permanently, with all wiring and pipes accessed through the top of the unit. The pivoting module column pivots on fixed points in the floor and ceiling, rotating around a zone centered on the patient's chest.

Some of the services provided at the modules are electricity, nurse call, physiological monitor, telephone, emergency power, and medical gas piping (typically, oxygen, air, and vacuum). Each module can accommodate the design and component flexibility required by individual health care facilities.

TYPICAL LAYOUT/PLAN

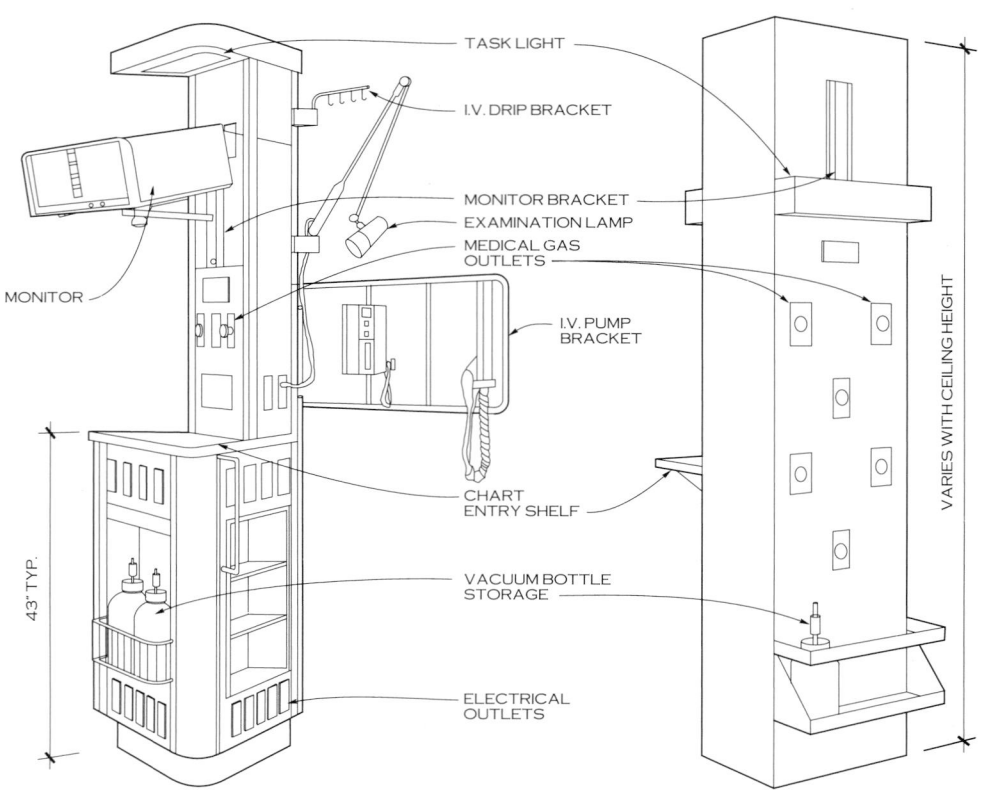

FREESTANDING MODULE

TRIANGULAR MODULE COLUMN   RECTANGULAR MODULE COLUMN

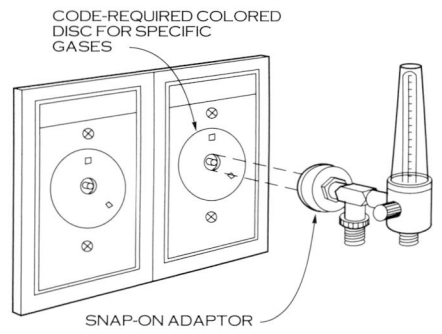

STANDARD GAS OUTLET

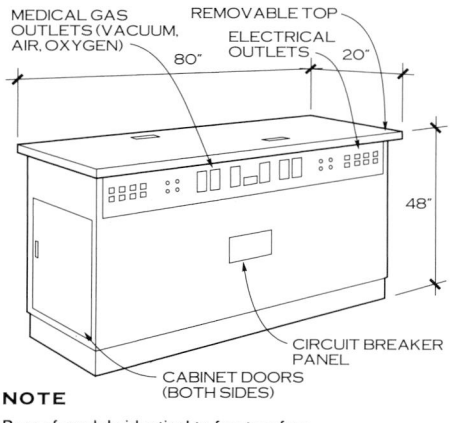

NOTE

Rear of module identical to front surface

NEONATAL MODULE

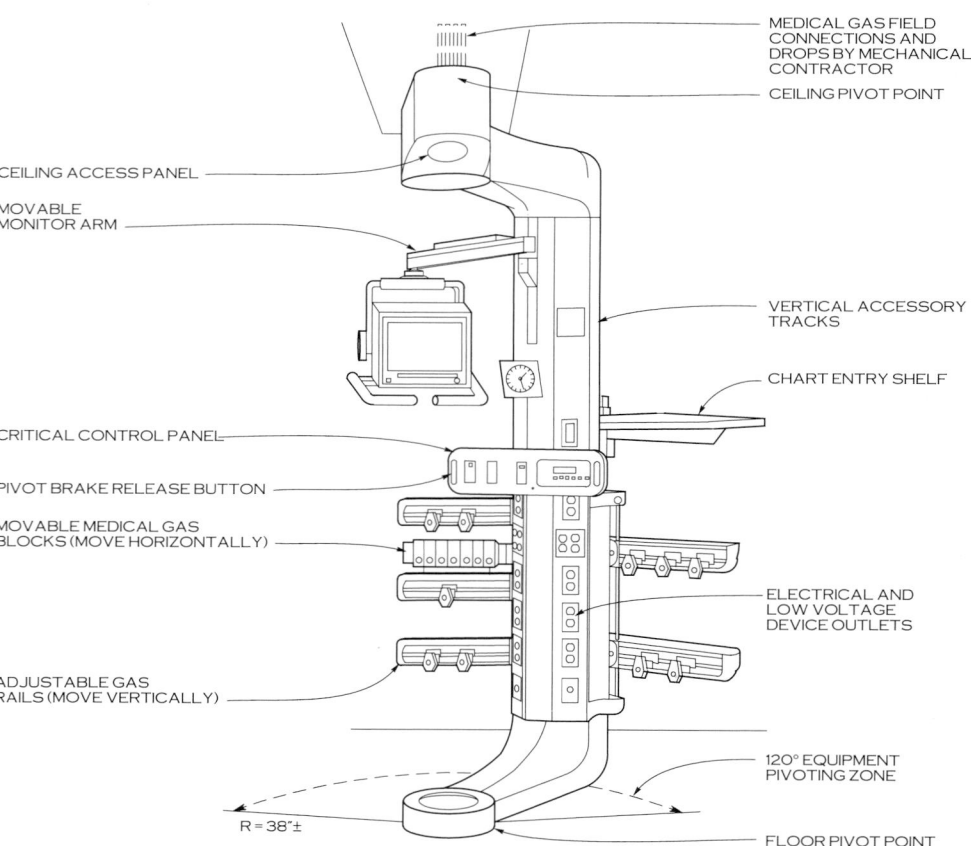

PIVOTING MODULE COLUMN

Richard J. Vitullo, AIA; Oak Leaf Studio; Crownsville, Maryland
Andrew Sumners; University Park, Maryland

10 **SERVICE WALL SYSTEMS**

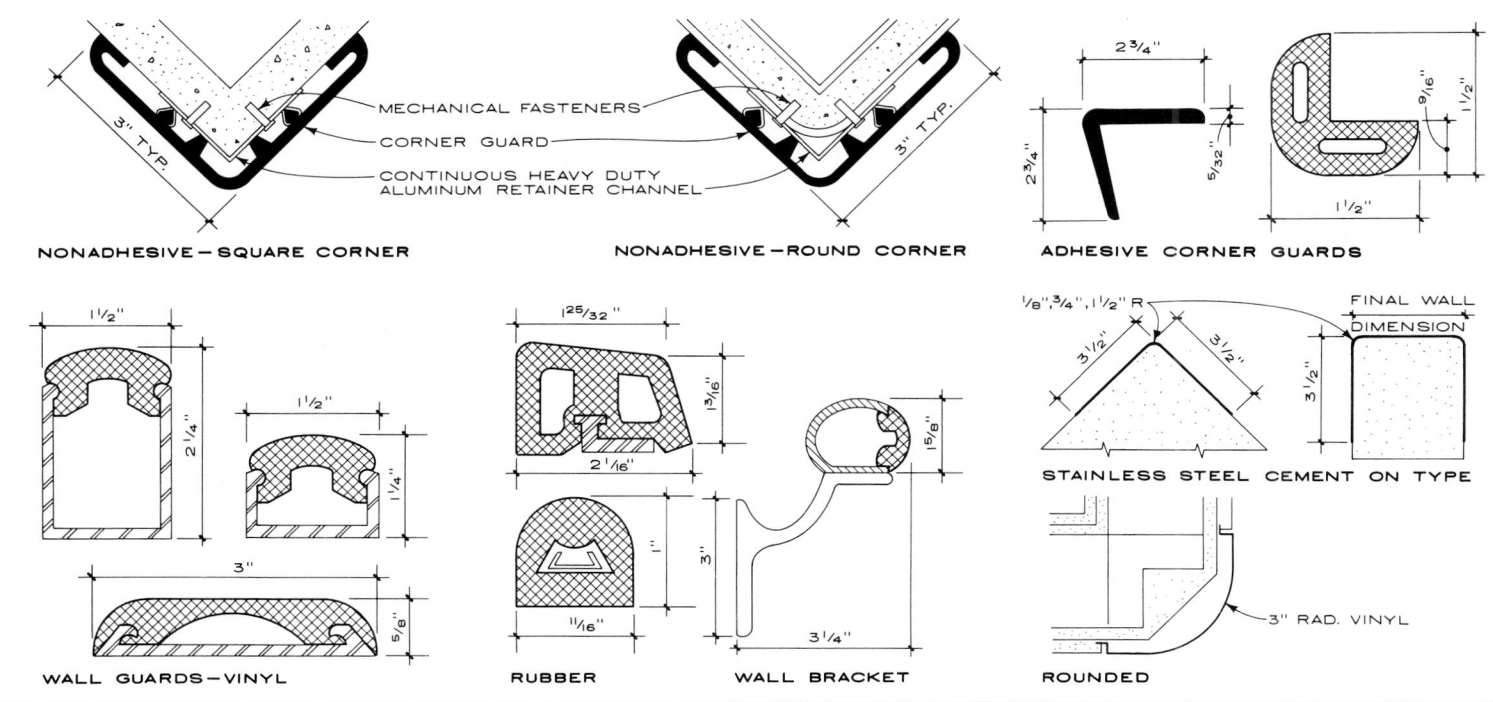

NONADHESIVE—SQUARE CORNER

- MECHANICAL FASTENERS
- CORNER GUARD
- CONTINUOUS HEAVY DUTY ALUMINUM RETAINER CHANNEL

NONADHESIVE—ROUND CORNER

ADHESIVE CORNER GUARDS

WALL GUARDS—VINYL

RUBBER

WALL BRACKET

STAINLESS STEEL CEMENT ON TYPE

FINAL WALL DIMENSION

3" RAD. VINYL

ROUNDED

INTERIOR WALL AND CORNER GUARDS

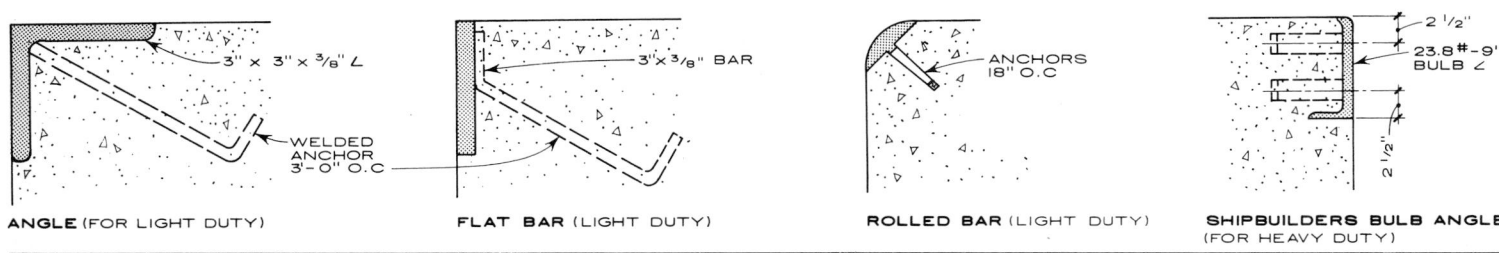

ANGLE (FOR LIGHT DUTY)

- 3" x 3" x 3/8" ∠
- WELDED ANCHOR 3'-0" O.C

FLAT BAR (LIGHT DUTY)

- 3" x 3/8" BAR

ROLLED BAR (LIGHT DUTY)

- ANCHORS 18" O.C

SHIPBUILDERS BULB ANGLE (FOR HEAVY DUTY)

- 23.8# -9" BULB ∠

CURB GUARDS

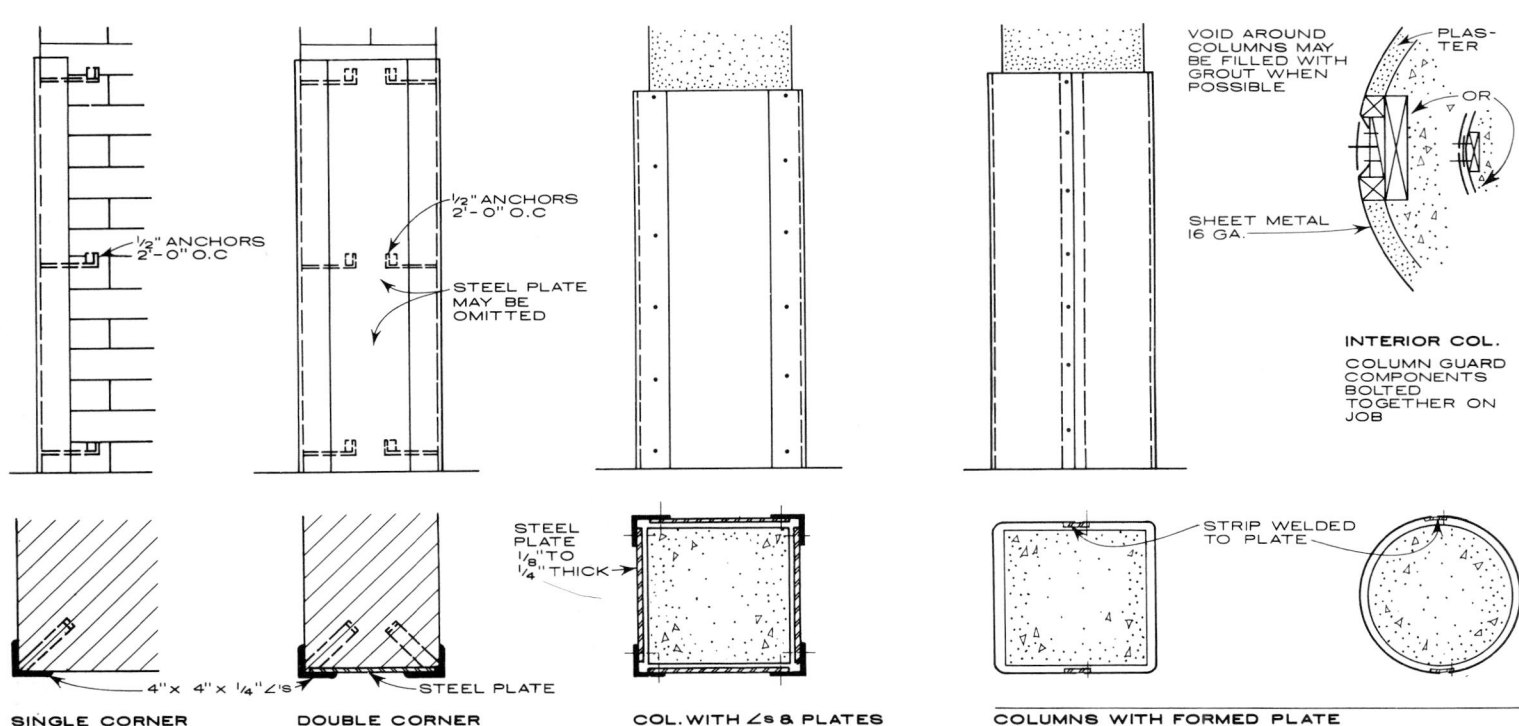

- 1/2" ANCHORS 2'-0" O.C
- 1/2" ANCHORS 2'-0" O.C
- STEEL PLATE MAY BE OMITTED
- VOID AROUND COLUMNS MAY BE FILLED WITH GROUT WHEN POSSIBLE
- PLASTER
- OR
- SHEET METAL 16 GA.

INTERIOR COL.

COLUMN GUARD COMPONENTS BOLTED TOGETHER ON JOB

SINGLE CORNER

- 4" x 4" x 1/4" ∠'s

DOUBLE CORNER

- STEEL PLATE

COL. WITH ∠s & PLATES

- STEEL PLATE 1/8" TO 1/4" THICK

COLUMNS WITH FORMED PLATE

- STRIP WELDED TO PLATE

CORNER AND COLUMN GUARDS

John Sava; The Architects Collaborative, Inc.; Cambridge, Massachusetts
Vincent Cordero, AIA; Arlington, Virginia

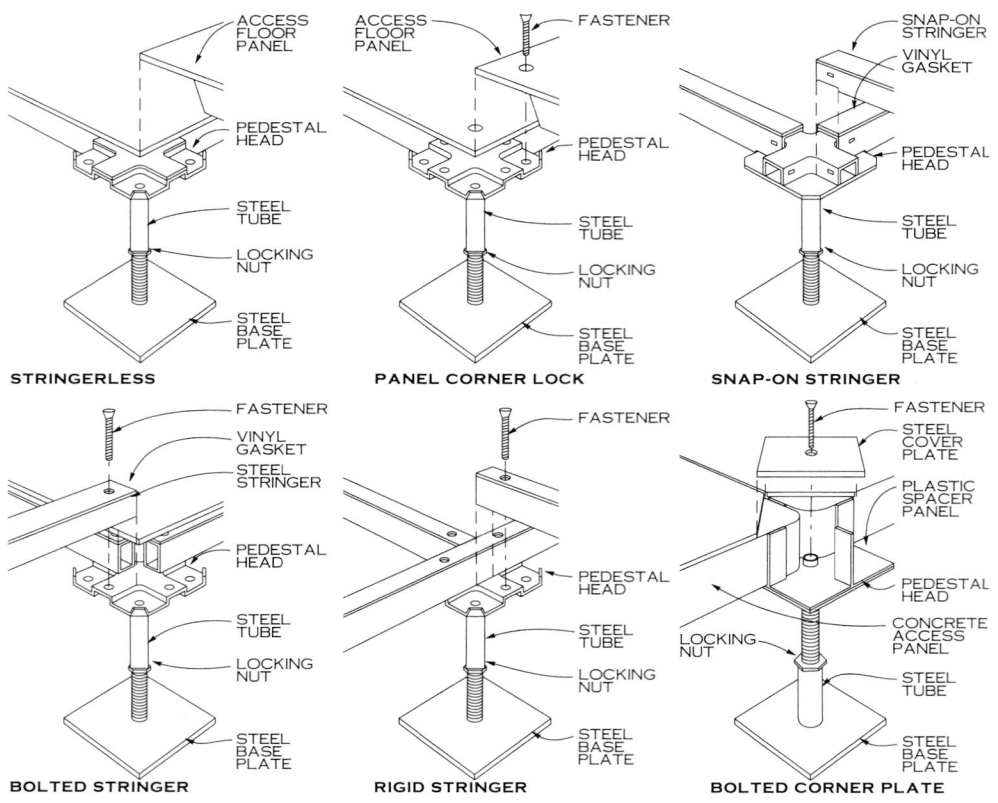

STRINGERLESS

PANEL CORNER LOCK

SNAP-ON STRINGER

BOLTED STRINGER

RIGID STRINGER

BOLTED CORNER PLATE

ACCESS FLOOR SUPPORT SYSTEMS

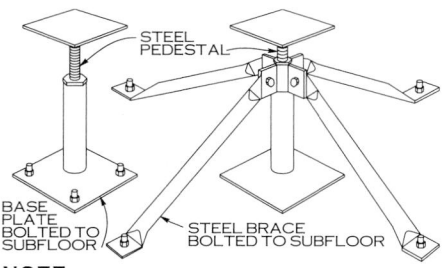

NOTE

Adhesives are commonly used to secure base plate to sub-floor; however, if lateral loads (seismic) are anticipated pedestal should be bolted to floor.

PEDESTAL ATTACHMENT DETAILS

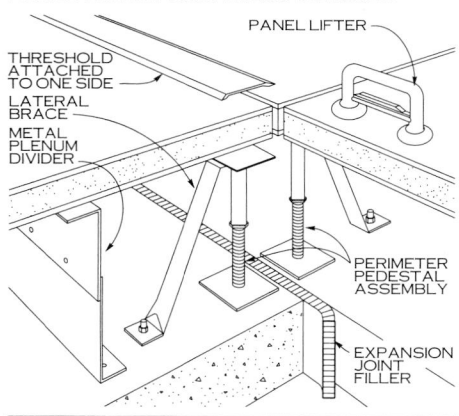

EXPANSION JOINT

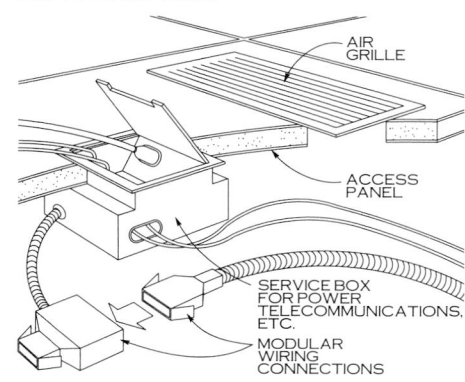

PANEL ACCESSORIES

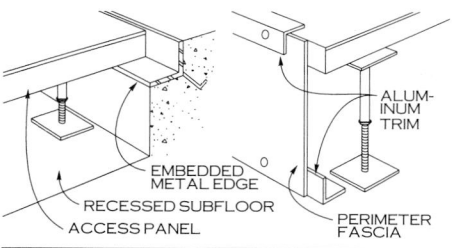

EDGE CONDITION

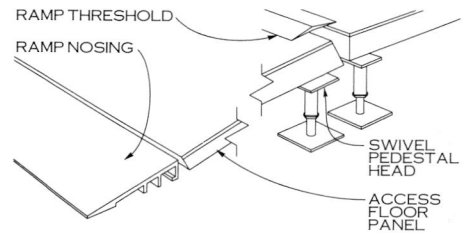

RAMP

COMPARISON TABLE FOR ACCESS FLOOR SUPPORT SYSTEMS

SUPPORT SYSTEM TYPES	RECOMMENDED USES	RECOMMENDED PANEL TYPE	EASE OF PANEL REMOVAL	LATERAL STABILITY	STATIC CONTROL (INHERENT)	PLENUM SEAL (INHERENT)
Stringerless	Computer rooms/ general office	Wood core/ solid steel	Excellent	Fair	Yes	No
Panel corner	General office	Wood core/ solid steel	Fair	Good	Yes	No
Snap-on stringer	Computer rooms/ general office	Wood core/ solid steel	Excellent	Good	Yes	Yes
Bolted stringer	Computer rooms	Wood core/ solid steel	Excellent	Excellent	Yes	Yes
Rigid stringer	Heavy loading in computer rooms	Wood core/ solid steel	Excellent	Excellent	Yes	Yes
Bolted corner plate	General office	Concrete	Fair	Excellent	No	No

GENERAL

Access floor systems are used in offices, hospitals, laboratories, open-area schools, television systems, computer rooms, and telephone-communication centers. They provide mechanical and electrical accessibility and flexibility in placing desks, telephone services, machines, and general office equipment. Equipment can be moved and reconnected quickly using modular wiring. Raised access floors can also be used in a recessed structural floor area. They can create a level floor over an uneven subfloor.

NOTES

1. Panel and pedestal design determine load capacity. Consult manufacturer to determine needs.

2. Floor panel types: reinforced steel, aluminum, steel- or aluminum-encased wood core, steel-encased cementitious fill or lightweight solid reinforced concrete. Basic panels are typically 24 x 24 in.

3. Since the space under the access floor can act as a plenum, special panels can be provided with perforation for maximum air distribution. Also, cable slots and sound and thermal insulation can be provided in the panels.

4. Finishes available: carpet tile (some provided with plastic edging for protection), fire-rated coverings, conductive coverings, vinyl tile, and high-pressure laminate.

COMPUTER ROOMS

Computers place high demands on electrical, mechanical, and floor systems. The floor surface must be conductive and grounded to avoid static electricity and dust accumulation. An automatic fire detection system should be installed in below-floor plenums. Plenums may not exceed 10,000 sq ft and must be divided by noncombustible bulkheads. Computer rooms should be separated from all other occupancies within buildings by walls, floors, and ceilings with a fire-resistant rating of not less than one hour. Structural floors beneath access floors should provide for water drainage to reduce damage to computer systems. All access floor openings should be protected from debris.

Computer rooms require precision temperature and humidity control, even though heat gains are usually concentrated. Package air conditioning units suitable for computer rooms can supply air within a tolerance of ±1.5° and ±5% humidity, using the underfloor plenum with floor registers or special perforated panels. For minimum room temperature gradients, supply air distribution should match closely the load distribution. The distribution system should be flexible enough to accommodate location changes and heat gain with minimum change in the basic distribution system. Supply air systems require about 74 liters per second per kilowatt of cooling to satisfy computer room conditions.

Setter, Leach & Lindstrom, Inc.; Minneapolis, Minnesota
Richard J. Vitullo, AIA; Oak Leaf Studio; Crownsville, Maryland

10   ACCESS FLOORING

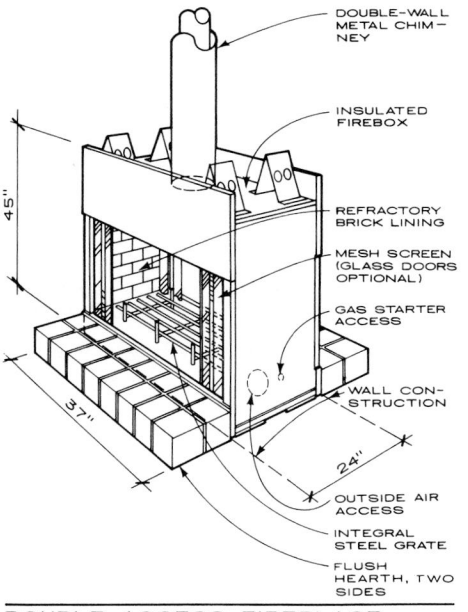

DOUBLE-ACCESS FIREPLACE

Labels: DOUBLE-WALL METAL CHIMNEY; INSULATED FIREBOX; REFRACTORY BRICK LINING; MESH SCREEN (GLASS DOORS OPTIONAL); GAS STARTER ACCESS; WALL CONSTRUCTION; OUTSIDE AIR ACCESS; INTEGRAL STEEL GRATE; FLUSH HEARTH, TWO SIDES; 45"; 37"; 24"

CORNER FIREPLACE

Labels: DOUBLE-WALL METAL CHIMNEY; OUTSIDE AIR ACCESS; GAS STARTER ACCESS; INSULATED FIREBOX; REFRACTORY BRICK LINING; MESH SCREEN (GLASS DOORS OPTIONAL); INTEGRAL STEEL GRATE; FLUSH HEARTH, TWO SIDES; 41 1/2"; 37"; 22"

GENERAL NOTES

1. Verify local/state codes for maximum and minimum chimney height clearances above roof deck.
2. Chimney pipe requires a 2-in. clearance to combustible surfaces. In a multichase installation, chimney pipes should be 20 in. apart, center to center. Chase top must be constructed of noncombustible material.
3. See manufacturer's specifications for chimney joint band and stabilizer locations.
4. Fire-stop spacer must be used whenever a ceiling, floor, or sidewall is penetrated.
5. No special floor support is usually necessary for prefabricated fireplaces; however, local/state codes should be checked to determine exact requirements.
6. Facing material must not obstruct louvered or screened area at sides, top, or bottom of fireplace opening; however, noncombustible finishing material may be used over the black metal on fireplace fronts. See manufacturer's specifications.
7. Inadequate ventilation can occur from air conditioning, heating, or other mechanical systems that generate negative air pressures in the fireplace room. Plan for proper ventilation to ensure smoke-free operation.
8. There is no minimum or maximum horizontal distance for outside air access line.
9. A noncombustible hearth extension must extend at least 8 in. on either side of firebox openings and 16–20 in. in front of firebox.
10. Distances from combustible walls perpendicular to the front of the fireplace—including mantles—vary. Consult manufacturer's specifications.
11. Outlet grilles must be at least 10 in. below ceiling for ducted heat-circulating fireplace.
12. Room furnishings such as drapes, curtains, and chairs must be at least 4 ft 0 in. from firebox opening.

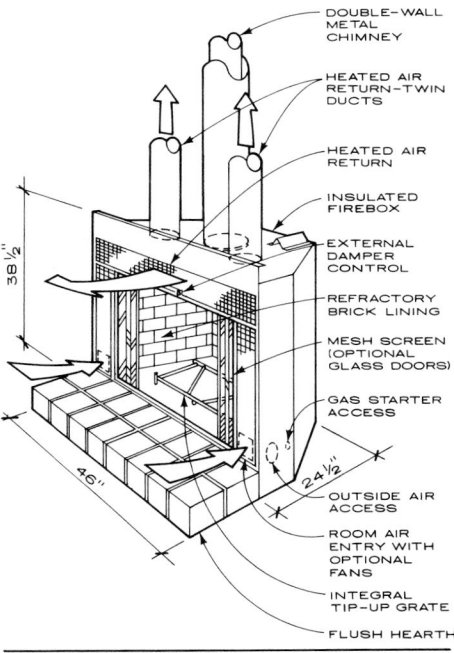

HEAT-CIRCULATING FIREPLACE

Labels: DOUBLE-WALL METAL CHIMNEY; HEATED AIR RETURN; EXTERNAL DAMPER CONTROL; INSULATED FIREBOX; REFRACTORY BRICK LINING; MESH SCREEN (OPTIONAL GLASS DOORS); INTEGRAL TIP-UP GRATE; GAS STARTER ACCESS; OUTSIDE AIR ACCESS; ROOM AIR ENTRY WITH OPTIONAL FANS; HEARTH; 41 1/2"; 48 1/2"; 24"

DUCTED HEAT-CIRCULATING FIREPLACE

Labels: DOUBLE-WALL METAL CHIMNEY; HEATED AIR RETURN—TWIN DUCTS; HEATED AIR RETURN; INSULATED FIREBOX; EXTERNAL DAMPER CONTROL; REFRACTORY BRICK LINING; MESH SCREEN (OPTIONAL GLASS DOORS); GAS STARTER ACCESS; OUTSIDE AIR ACCESS; ROOM AIR ENTRY WITH OPTIONAL FANS; INTEGRAL TIP-UP GRATE; FLUSH HEARTH; 38 1/2"; 46"; 24 1/2"

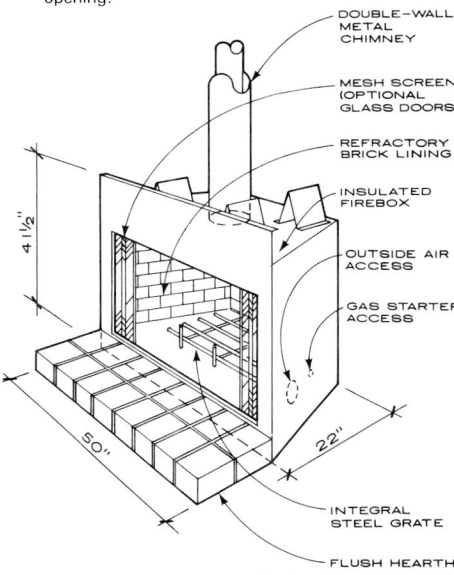

TRADITIONAL FIREPLACE

Labels: DOUBLE-WALL METAL CHIMNEY; MESH SCREEN (OPTIONAL GLASS DOORS); REFRACTORY BRICK LINING; INSULATED FIREBOX; OUTSIDE AIR ACCESS; GAS STARTER ACCESS; INTEGRAL STEEL GRATE; FLUSH HEARTH; 41 1/2"; 50"; 22"

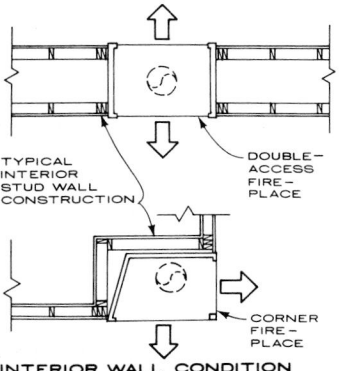

INTERIOR WALL CONDITION CHASE CONSTRUCTED ON ROOF

Labels: TYPICAL INTERIOR STUD WALL CONSTRUCTION; DOUBLE-ACCESS FIREPLACE; CORNER FIREPLACE

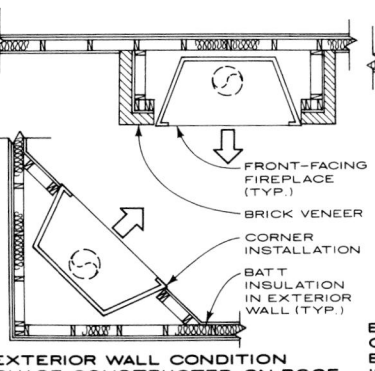

EXTERIOR WALL CONDITION CHASE CONSTRUCTED ON ROOF

Labels: FRONT-FACING FIREPLACE (TYP.); BRICK VENEER; CORNER INSTALLATION; BATT INSULATION IN EXTERIOR WALL (TYP.)

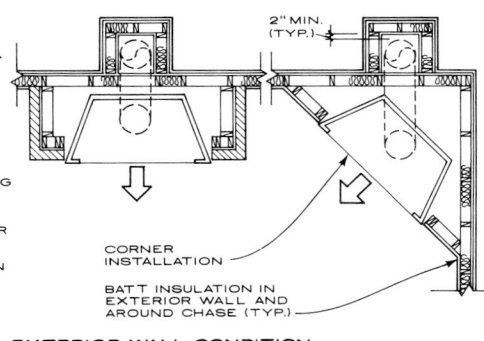

EXTERIOR WALL CONDITION CHIMNEY OFFSET THROUGH EXTERIOR WALL AND ENCLOSED IN CHASE

Labels: CORNER INSTALLATION; BATT INSULATION IN EXTERIOR WALL AND AROUND CHASE (TYP.)

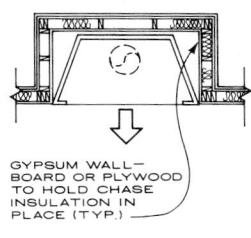

EXTERIOR WALL CONDITION FIREPLACE AND CHIMNEY ENCLOSED IN CHASE

Labels: 2" MIN. (TYP.); GYPSUM WALLBOARD OR PLYWOOD TO HOLD CHASE INSULATION IN PLACE (TYP.)

INSTALLATION CONDITIONS FOR PREFABRICATED FIREPLACES

Richard J. Vitullo, AIA; Oak Leaf Studio; Crownsville, Maryland

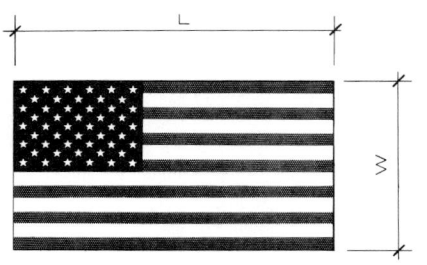

U.S. GOVERNMENT STANDARD L=1.9 W.

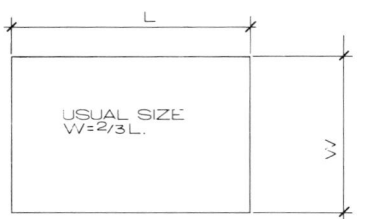

PROPORTIONS OF U.S. FLAG

USUAL SIZE W=2/3L.

U.S. FLAG SIZES AS MANUFACTURED AND USED

WIDTH	LENGTH	WIDTH	LENGTH
3'—0''	5'—0''	10'—0''	18'—0''
4'—0''	6'—0''	10'—0''	19'—0''
4'—4''	5'—6''	12'—0''	20'—0''
5'—0''	8'—0''	15'—0''	25'—0''
5'—0''	9'—6''	20'—0''	30'—0''
6'—0''	10'—0''	20'—0''	38'—0''
8'—0''	12'—0''	26'—0''	45'—0''
10'—0''	15'—0''		

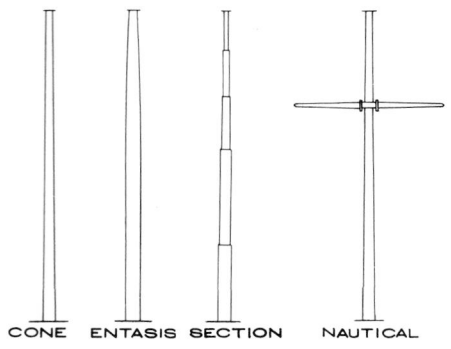

CONE   ENTASIS   SECTION   NAUTICAL

Poles are manufactured in steel, aluminum, bronze, and fiberglass.

Flagpoles must be designed to withstand wind loads while the flag is flying. Design dimensions are dictated by the maximum wind load a pole is exposed to depending on geographical location, whether it is located in a city or open country, whether it is mounted at ground or on top of a building, and size of the flag to be flown. The combination wind load on pole and flag should always be considered. Refer to wind load tests conducted by the National Association of Architectural Metal Manufacturers. (NAAMM)

POLE STYLES

RELATION OF HEIGHT OF POLE TO HEIGHT OF BLDG.

HEIGHT OF POLE	HEIGHT OF BLDG.
20'—0''	1 to 2 stories
25'—0''	3 to 5 stories
33'—0'' to 35'—0''	6 to 10 stories
40'—0'' to 50'—0''	11 to 15 stories
60'—0'' to 75'—0''	over 15 stories

NOTE

This rule serves for preliminary assumptions.

*1/4 LENGTH OF POLE

FROM 5'' DIA. ON 20'-0'' POLE TO 14'' DIA. ON 125'-0'' POLE

BALL

POLE ON GROUND

SIZE OF FLAG IN RELATION TO POLE
RECOMMENDED FLAG SIZES

POLE	FLAG SIZE	POLE	FLAG SIZE
15'—0''	3'—0'' x 5'—0''	50'—0''	8'—0'' x 12'—0''
20'—0''	4'—0'' x 6'—0''	60'—0''	8'—0'' x 12'—0''
25'—0''	4'—0'' x 6'—0''	65'—0''	9'—0'' x 15'—0''
30'—0''	5'—0'' x 8'—0''	70'—0''	9'—0'' x 15'—0''
35'—0''	5'—0'' x 8'—0''	80'—0''	10'—0'' x 15'-.0''
40'—0''	6'—0'' x 10'—0''	90'—0''	10'—0'' x 15'—0''
45'—0''	6'—0'' x 10'—0''	100'—0''	12'—0'' x 18'—0''

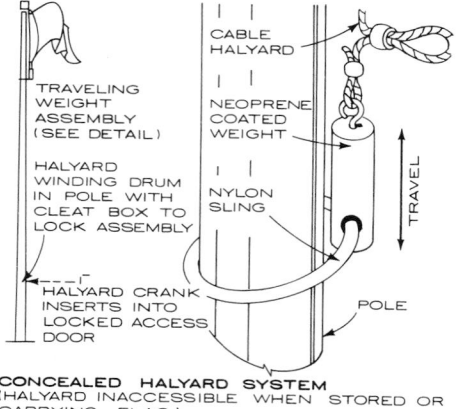

CABLE HALYARD

TRAVELING WEIGHT ASSEMBLY (SEE DETAIL)

NEOPRENE COATED WEIGHT

HALYARD WINDING DRUM IN POLE WITH CLEAT BOX TO LOCK ASSEMBLY

NYLON SLING

TRAVEL

HALYARD CRANK INSERTS INTO LOCKED ACCESS DOOR

POLE

CONCEALED HALYARD SYSTEM
(HALYARD INACCESSIBLE WHEN STORED OR CARRYING FLAG)

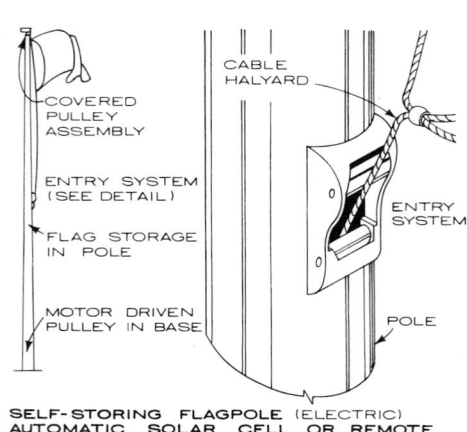

CABLE HALYARD

COVERED PULLEY ASSEMBLY

ENTRY SYSTEM (SEE DETAIL)

FLAG STORAGE IN POLE

ENTRY SYSTEM

MOTOR DRIVEN PULLEY IN BASE

POLE

SELF-STORING FLAGPOLE (ELECTRIC)
AUTOMATIC SOLAR CELL OR REMOTE SWITCH OPERATION

SPECIAL MECHANISMS FOR REMOTE OR VANDAL-PROOF OPERATION

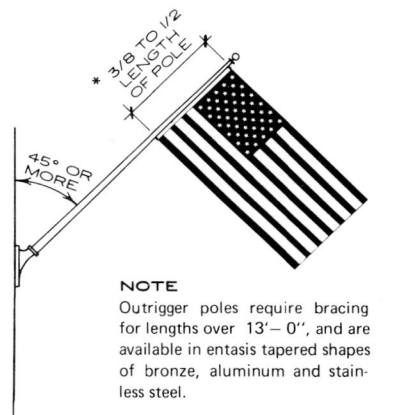

*3/8 TO 1/2 LENGTH OF POLE

45° OR MORE

NOTE

Outrigger poles require bracing for lengths over 13'—0'', and are available in entasis tapered shapes of bronze, aluminum and stainless steel.

OUTRIGGER POLES FOR FLAGS ON BUILDING FRONTS

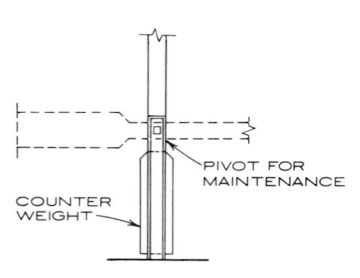

COUNTER WEIGHT

PIVOT FOR MAINTENANCE

TILTING POLE UNIT

METAL COLLAR

POLE

CAULKING

WEDGES

DRY SAND

CONCRETE

METAL TUBE

WEDGES

LIGHTNING PROTECTION

10% OF POLE HGT.

3'-0'' MIN.

8''

CONCRETE ANCHORS

EXPANSION BOLT

FOUNDATION FOR GROUND SET POLES

WALL MOUNTING FLAGPOLES

FOUNDATION AND SURFACE MOUNTING DETAILS

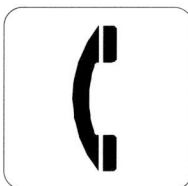
TELEPHONE

MEN'S RESTROOM

GIFT SHOP

SMOKING
PERMITTED

WATERWAY

MAIL

WOMEN'S RESTROOM

LUGGAGE

FIRST AID

EMERGENCY
VEHICLE

DINING

RESTROOMS

LOCKERS

INFORMATION

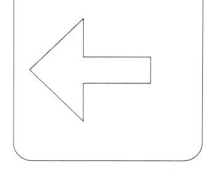
BUS STOP

LOUNGE

ACCOMMODATION
INFORMATION

LOST AND FOUND

PARKING

TRAIN STATION

TEXT TELEPHONE

ACCESSIBLE FOR
HEARING LOSS

PHONE
VOLUME CONTROL
TELEPHONE

INTERNATIONAL
ACCESSIBILITY
SYMBOL

EXIT STAIRS

RAMP

SYMBOLS

NO ENTRY (30 X 30"
RECOMMENDED SIZE)

STOP (24 X 24"
RECOMMENDED SIZE)

NO PARKING (24 X 24"
RECOMMENDED SIZE)

NO SMOKING

emergency
exit
only

USE STAIRWAY

PARKING
FOR
HANDICAPPED
ONLY

VAN
ACCESSIBLE

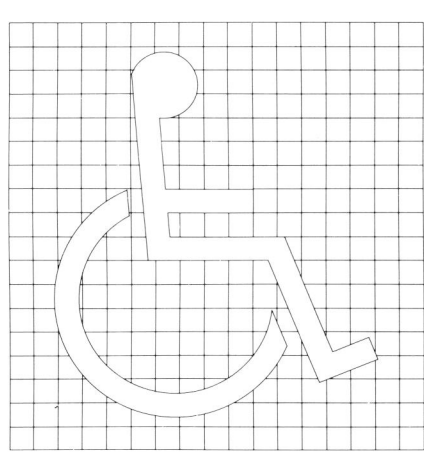
Proportions of the International Symbol of Accessibility

WARNING/PROHIBITORY SIGNS

SYMBOL OF ACCESSIBILITY

Marr Knapp Crawfis Associates, Inc.; Mansfield, Ohio
Richard J. Vitullo, AIA; Oak Leaf Studio; Crownsville, Maryland

IDENTIFYING DEVICES

10

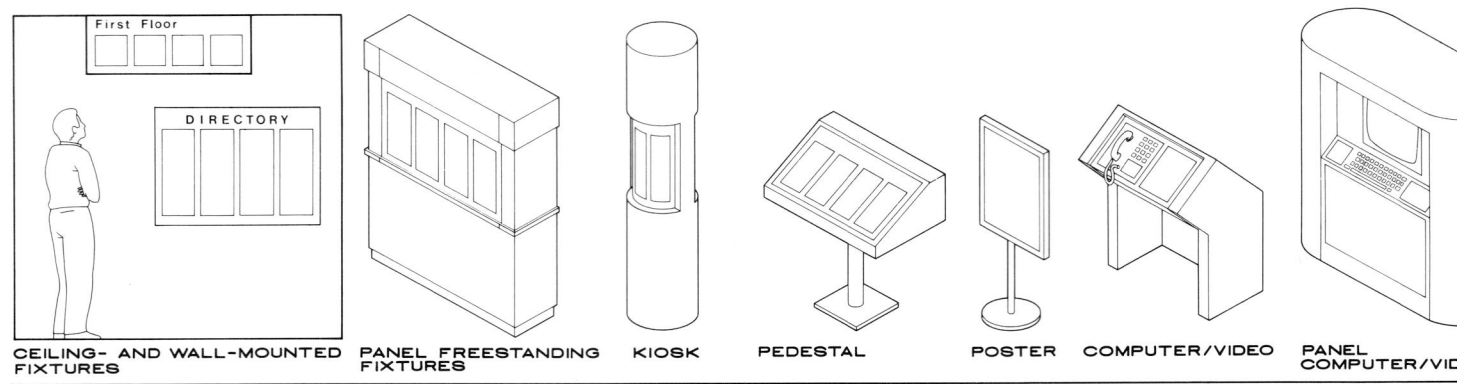

CEILING- AND WALL-MOUNTED FIXTURES | PANEL FREESTANDING FIXTURES | KIOSK | PEDESTAL | POSTER | COMPUTER/VIDEO | PANEL COMPUTER/VIDEO

DIRECTORIES/ORIENTATION MAPS/INFORMATION SYSTEMS

RIGID VINYL INSERTS | MAGNETIC

SLIDING | WINDOW

INTERIOR SIGN TYPES

ACCESSIBLE SIGNAGE FOR PERSONS WITH DISABILITIES

1. Accessible signs should identify permanent rooms and spaces, including room numbers, emergency exits, and toilet facilities. If room numbers are not used, signs such as "Cafeteria" must be accessible.
   a. Letters and numerals: raised $1/32$ in. minimum, uppercase, sans serif, $5/8$ to 2 in. in height, and accompanied by grade 2 Braille.
   b. Pictogram borders should be at least 6 in. high.
   c. Surfaces should have a nonglare finish; level of sheen must be "eggshell" or less.
   d. Provide contrast between the characters and background.
   e. Mounting: 60 in. above finished floor to centerline of sign, preferably on the latch side of door or the closest wall space. Do not mount within the swinging path of a door or where a person cannot approach within 3 in. of the sign.
2. Directional and informational signs for permanent functional spaces (such as signs to auditoriums or elevators) should be accessible.
   a. Character proportions should comply with ADAAG 4.30.2.
   b. Characters should be at least 3 in. high; increase character height as viewing distance increases.
3. Identify such accessible features as assistive listening devices, parking, and text telephones. When not all such features are accessible, identify the accessible ones (e.g., toilet rooms and parking) and provide directional signage from inaccessible ones. Use pictograms at least 6 in. high accompanied by a verbal description.

GENERAL NOTES

EXTERIOR SIGNS

1. Identify entrance and exit of site and building, accessibility information, parking lot location, and facility identification.
2. Signs should be 6 ft 0 in. min. from face of curb, 7 ft 0 in. from grade to bottom of sign, and 100–200 ft from intersections.
3. Building signage materials: fabricated aluminum, illuminated plastic face, back lighted, cast aluminum, applied letter, die raised, engraved, and hot stamped.
4. Plaque and sign materials: cast bronze, cast aluminum, plastic/acrylic, stone (cornerstone), masonry, and wood.
5. For accessibility signage, designate building entrance access, identify parking areas, and direction to facilities. See ADAAG and state regulations for specific requirements.

DIRECTORIES AND MAPS

1. Locate these in main entrances and/or lobbies with appropriate information for persons with disabilities.
2. Place directory information adjacent to "You are here" information.
3. Directories should be placed in stair/elevator lobbies of each floor.
4. Mounting choices: surface mounted, semirecessed, full recessed (flush), cantilevered, chain suspended, rigidly suspended, mechanically fastened, or track mounted.

INTERIOR SIGNS

1. Lightweight freestanding signs should not be used in high-traffic areas. Use when specific location/information maneuverability is required.
2. Electronic, computer, and videotex technologies can provide an innovative and highly flexible directory/sign display system for mapping and/or routing, information (facility and local), advertisement and messages, and management tie-in capabilities.
3. Where changeability and flexibility is a design priority, a modular system is recommended. Rigid vinyl, aluminum, and acrylic inserts as well as magnetic systems may be used.
4. For maximum ease of reading interior signs, any given line in a sign should not exceed 30 characters in width, including upper and lower case letters and spaces between words.
5. Choose the height and "weight" of letter styles and symbols for readability. Consider background materials and contrast when choosing a color scheme.
6. Permanent mounting:
   a. Vinyl tape/adhesive backing, usually factory applied.
   b. Silastic adhesive, usually supplied with vinyl tape strips to hold sign in place until adhesive cures.
   c. Mechanically fastened; specify hole locations.
7. Semipermanent: vinyl tape square can be used on inserts.
8. Changeable: dual-lock mating fasteners, magnets, magnetic tape, or tracks may be used.

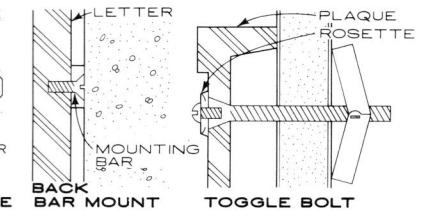

FLUSH MOUNT | PROJECTED MOUNT | INVISIBLE FRAME | BACK BAR MOUNT | TOGGLE BOLT

MOUNTING METHODS/MATERIALS

SYMBOL SIZE (in.)

DISTANCE (FT) FROM VIEWER TO SYMBOL

SYMBOL READABILITY

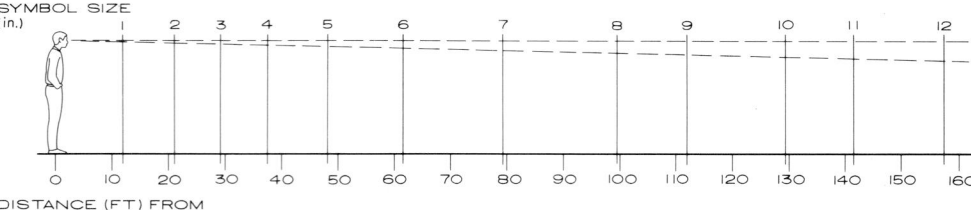

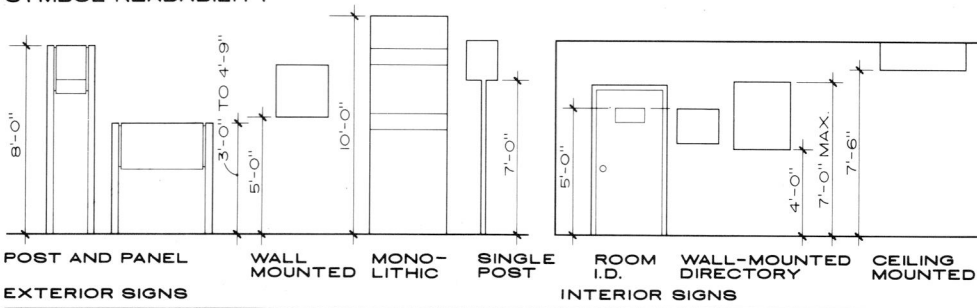

POST AND PANEL | WALL MOUNTED | MONO-LITHIC | SINGLE POST | ROOM I.D. | WALL-MOUNTED DIRECTORY | CEILING MOUNTED

EXTERIOR SIGNS | INTERIOR SIGNS

MOUNTING HEIGHTS

Marr Knapp Crawfis Associates, Inc.; Mansfield, Ohio
Richard J. Vitullo, AIA; Oak Leaf Studio; Crownsville, Maryland

10 IDENTIFYING DEVICES

GENERAL NOTES

1. Construction of locker frame and door typically is of 16 gauge steel for sides and back. Top and bottom are typically 20 to 24 gauge steel. Finishes vary. Number plates, a shelf, and coat hooks on back and side walls are generally included. Other construction such as plastic laminate and wood is also used for club facilities.

2. Door types may be solid, perforated (all or part), or louvered (all or part), and ordered in a variety of steel mesh patterns or in special finishes. Doors and locks may be provided with noise-deadening devices. Locking mechanisms include built-in adjustable combination lock, built-in flat or grooved key, and latching locker handle (for padlock use). All locking mechanisms are available for surface or recessed applications.

3. Optional locker equipment includes sloping top for nonrecessed locations with corner miters available, 6 in. legs for open base installation, interior partitions (some models), multiple shelves, coat rods (for models over 18 in. deep), closed base and closed-end base for legs, and attachable bench elements.

4. Ventilation within locker spaces should provide 15 cu ft/min. air movement for locker.

5. Handicapped user access may suggest use of some multiple tier lockers; shelf and coat hooks on single tier lockers are out of reach of most handicapped.

6. Bench arrangements may be attached to locker front or may be freestanding and require a raised installation. Finishes of lockers may be varied as conditions dictate such as stainless steel bottoms or sides when used in areas where long-term chemical contamination may affect finishes.

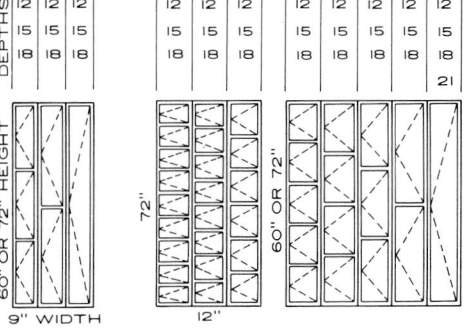
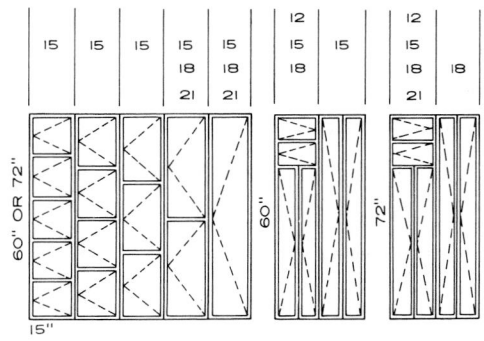
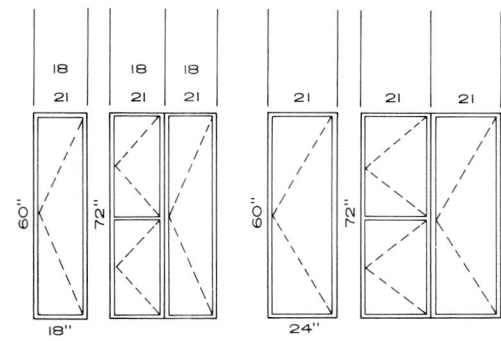

ELEVATIONS
LOCKERS

Checking lockers for heavy duty use are available in enameled steel or stainless steel. Locks are provided with built-in multiple coin selector, which is owner adjustable for coins, tokens, or "free" operation. They may be installed on legs or recessed and may be made movable. Overall height is 6 ft 0 in. on most models, 5 ft 0 in. on some.

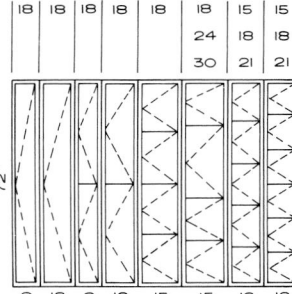

ELEVATION
CHECKING LOCKERS

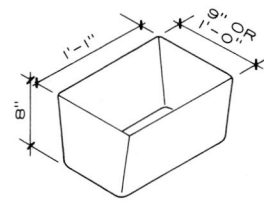

LOCKER SECTION

Basket racks may be arranged in single tier or back to back. Single tier depth is 1 ft 1¼ in. Optional pilfer guards may be installed on sides, top, and bottom, preventing access into adjacent baskets, and should be considered at the back as well. Basket materials include wire mesh (all surfaces), perforated steel ends and mesh sides and bottom, and louvered ends with perforated steel sides and bottom.

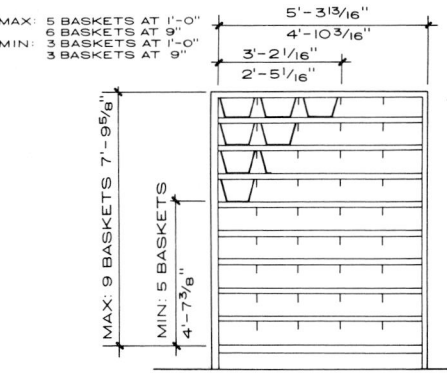

ELEVATION
BASKET RACKS

LOCKER BASKET

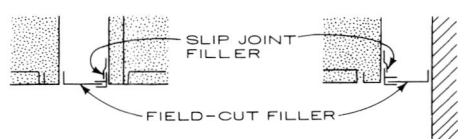

FILLER PIECE   **FLUSH WALL JOINT**

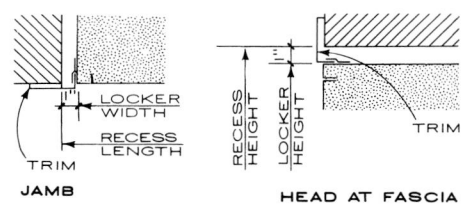

JAMB   **HEAD AT FASCIA**

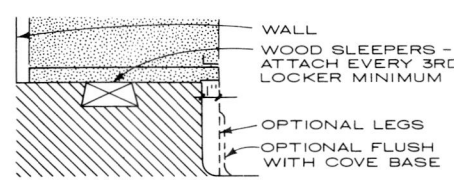

RECESSED/FLUSH BASE AT WALL

RECESSED/FLUSH BASE AT ISLAND

INSTALLATION DETAILS

Frederick C. Krenson, AIA; Rosser Fabrap International; Atlanta, Georgia

FIRE CLASSIFICATION

CLASS Ⓐ
Incipient fires on which quenching or the cooling effect of water is of primary importance. Fires of wood, paper, textile, and rubbish.

CLASS Ⓑ
Incipient fires on which blanketing or smothering effect of extinguishing is of primary importance. Fires of gasoline, oil, grease, and fat.

CLASS Ⓒ
Incipient fires in electrical equipment where a non-conducting extinguishing agent is needed.

OCCUPANCY CLASSIFICATION

Light hazard occupancies (schools, offices, and public buildings) require one unit of extinguishing capacity for every 3000 sq ft of floor area for use on Class A fires.

Ordinary hazard occupancies (dry goods shops and warehouses) require one unit of extinguishing capacity for every 1500 sq ft of floor space for use on Class A fires.

Extra hazard occupancies (paint shops, etc.) require one unit of extinguishing capacity for every 1000 sq ft of floor area for use on Class A fires.

Class A fire extinguishers, regardless of occupancy, shall be located so that maximum travel distance from any point to the nearest extinguisher is less than 75 ft.

The maximum travel distance to a Class B extinguisher is 50 ft (smaller rated extinguishers shall be placed no more than 30 ft from the hazard).

NOTES
1. These classifications are taken from the National Fire Protection Association, Publication #10, Portable Extinguishers, 1978.
2. In all cases check the requirements of local codes.

WATER BASE EXTINGUISHERS

	PRESSURIZED	CARTRIDGE	PUMP TANK	LOADED STREAM
	CLASS A ONLY	CLASS A ONLY	CLASS A ONLY	CLASS A & B
Capacity (gal)	2½	2½	2½ 5	2½
Height	25″	25″	26″ 28″	27″
Diameter	8″	8″	8″ 11″	8″
Weight (lb)	28	26	36 55	42
Class	2A	2A	2A 4A	2A, ½B
Recharge	Weigh cylinder and check annually. In all cases, follow instructions on extinguisher label			
Effective range	45-55 ft		30-40 ft	35-40 ft
Pressure source	Compressed air	Gas cartridge	Hand pump	Pressure
Temperature effect	Will freeze	Will freeze	Will freeze	Will operate at −40°F
Method of extinguishing	Quenches, cools	Quenches, cools	Quenches, cools	Alkametal salt quenches, cools, and fireproofs

NOTE: All water base extinguishing agents are electrical conductors.

Dimensions below are for three makes of extinguisher to show relative sizes

CARBON DIOXIDE
CLASS B & C FIRES

CAPACITY (LB)	2½	5	10	15	20
Height	18″	17″	22″	26″	26″
Diameter	4″	6″	7″	7″	8″
Weight (lb)	10	18	35	44	55
Class	2 B, C	2 B, C	5 B, C	10 B, C	10 B, C
Height	16″	15″	26″	30″	37″
Diameter	7″	10″	13″	12″	11″
Weight (lb)	12	17	34	44	55
Class	2 B, C	5 B, C	10 B, C	10 B, C	10 B, C
Height	18″	17″	26″	33″	33″
Diameter	9″	9″	11″	11″	12″
Weight (lb)	9	17	34	42	55
Class	2 B, C	5 B, C	10 B, C	10 B, C	10 B, C

EFFECTIVE RANGE
3 to 8 ft
DISCHARGE TIME
2½ lb, 12 sec; 5 lb, 22 sec; 10 lb, 23 sec; 15 lb, 26 sec; 20 lb, 25 sec
RECHARGE
after use
PRESSURE SOURCE
compressed gas
TEMPERATURE EFFECT
will operate at minus 40°F
ELECTRICAL CONDUCTIVITY
will not conduct

Dimensions below are for two makes of extinguisher to show relative sizes

PRESSURIZED
HALOGENATED AGENT
CLASS B & C FIRES

CAPACITY (LB)	2½	5
Height	14″	15″
Diameter	3″	3½″
Weight (lb)	7½	9½
Class	5 B, C	10 B, C
Height	15″	15½″
Diameter	3″	4½″
Weight (lb)	5	10
Class	5 B, C	10 B, C

EFFECTIVE RANGE
25 to 30 ft
DISCHARGE TIME
2½ lb, 11 sec; 5 lb, 11 sec
RECHARGE
after use
PRESSURE SOURCE
pump or pressurized
TEMPERATURE EFFECT
will operate at minus 40°F
ELECTRICAL CONDUCTIVITY
will not conduct

DRY CHEMICAL
CLASS A, B, & C

CAPACITY (LB)	5	10	20	30
Height	19″	21″	22″	30″
Diameter	5″	6″	8″	8″
Weight (lb)	15	33	48	70
Class	2A,10B,C	2A,20B,C	2A,80B,C	2A,80B,C
Height	13″	22″	21″	25″
Diameter	5″	7″	9″	9″
Weight (lb)	12	21	35	50
Class	2A,10B,C	2A,20B,C	2A,80B,C	2A,80B,C

EFFECTIVE RANGE
10 to 20 ft
DISCHARGE TIME
5 lb, 10 sec; 10 lb, 11 sec; 20 lb, 15 sec; 30 lb, 34 sec
RECHARGE
after use
PRESSURE SOURCE
compressed gas
TEMPERATURE EFFECT
will operate at minus 40°F
ELECTRICAL CONDUCTIVITY
will not conduct

William G. Miner, AIA, Architect; Washington, D.C.

10 FIRE PROTECTION SPECIALTIES

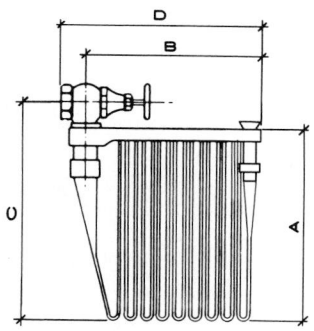

SWING RACK SEMIAUTOMATIC
1½" LINED HOSE

HOSE CAPACITY	25	50	75	100
A	10"	20"	24"	27"
B	15"	16"	19"	20"
C	14"	23"	27"	32"
D	17"	18"	20"	22"
WIDTH	4"	4"	4"	4"

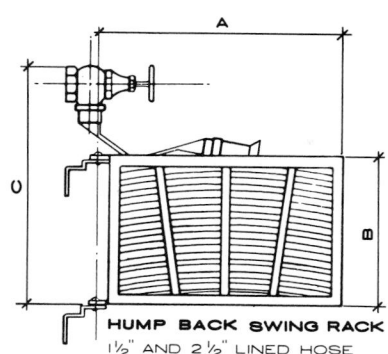

HUMP BACK SWING RACK
1½" AND 2½" LINED HOSE

HOSE CAPACITY	50	100	150	200
A	30"	30"	34"	40"
B	17"	21"	28"	39"
C	30"	33"	40"	50"
WIDTH 1½" HOSE	4"	4"	4"	4"
WIDTH 2½" HOSE	6"	6"	6"	6"

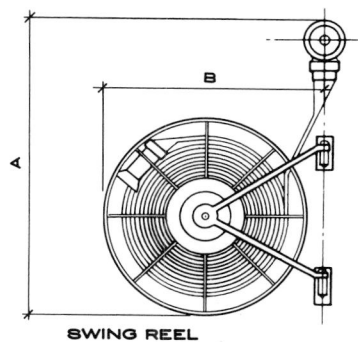

SWING REEL
1½" AND 2½" LINED HOSE

HOSE CAPACITY	50	100	150
A	38"	38"	36"
B	21"	27"	31"
WIDTH 1½" HOSE	4"	4"	4"
WIDTH 2½" HOSE	6"	6"	6"

FIRE HOSE RACK AND REELS

NOTE

Recommended hose size for use with building stand-pipes should not exceed 1½ in. in diameter and 100 ft in length. A larger hose used by amateurs is likely to tangle, cause excessive water damage, and create injuries.

A connection for 2½ in. hose should be available to each station for the use of firemen. Many codes require 2½ in. outlets at all standpipes.

By using a reducing coupling 1½ in. hose can be attached. When a 2½ in. stream is required the coupling may be removed. Industrial installations use 2½ in. hoses and train personnel in the use of the heavier equipment. Valves may be located 5 ft 6 in. above floor (check local code).

Lined synthetic fiber plastic hose is recommended for use on standpipe installations. Cotton rubber lined hose is standard for fire department and heavy equipment hose.

Tables show rack and reels for 1½ and 2½ in. lined hose only. Consult manufacturer's literature for rack and reel dimensions when other types and sizes of hose are used.

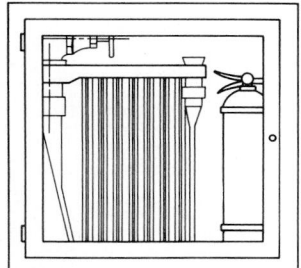

75' 1½" LINED HOSE, RACK, AND ANGLE VALVE; 2½ GAL EXTINGUISHER
2'-9" x 2'-9" x 8½" TO
2'-11" x 2'-11" x 9"

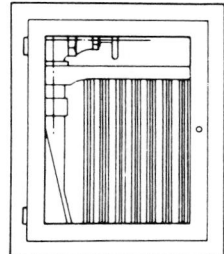

75' 1½" LINED HOSE, RACK, AND ANGLE VALVE
1'-9" x 2'-5" x 8" TO
1'-4" x 2'-7" x 8½"

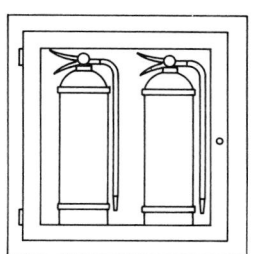

TWO 2½ GAL EXTINGUISHERS
1'-11"X2'-9"X7" TO
2'-2"X2'-11"X8"

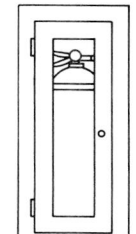

ONE 2½ GAL EXTINGUISHER
1'-0"X2'-6"X8" TO
1'-4"X2'-7"X8½"
NOTE: RESIDENTIAL EXTINGUISHER CABINET
1'-5"X7"X2"

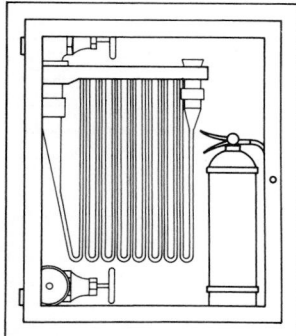

75' 1½" LINED HOSE AND RACK; 1½" AND 2½" ANGLE VALVE; 2½ GAL EXTINGUISHER
2'-9" x 3'-4" x 8½" TO
2'-10" x 3'-7" x 9"

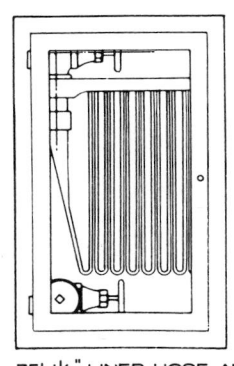

75' 1½" LINED HOSE AND RACK; 1½" AND 2½" ANGLE VALVE
1'-11" x 3'-3" x 8½" TO
2'-4" x 3'-4" x 9"

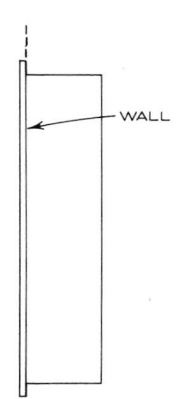

RECESSED

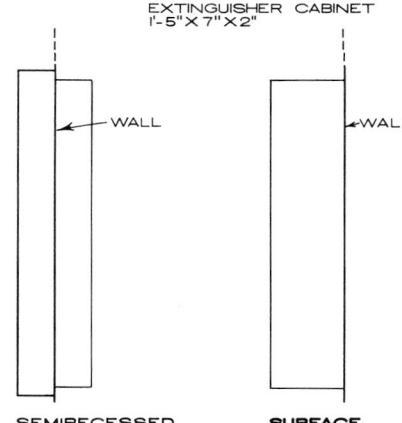

SEMIRECESSED

SURFACE MOUNTED

FIRE HOSE AND EXTINGUISHER CABINETS

NOTE

Cabinets are #18 gauge steel with glass doors as shown or with doors of metal, wood, mirror, and so on.

Consult manufacturer's literature for cabinets with special features such as revolving door, twin doors, pivoting door with attached extinguisher, and curved door.

Cabinets are obtainable for 25, 50, 75, and 100 ft hose racks. Rough dimensions are shown.

William G. Miner, AIA, Architect; Washington, D.C.

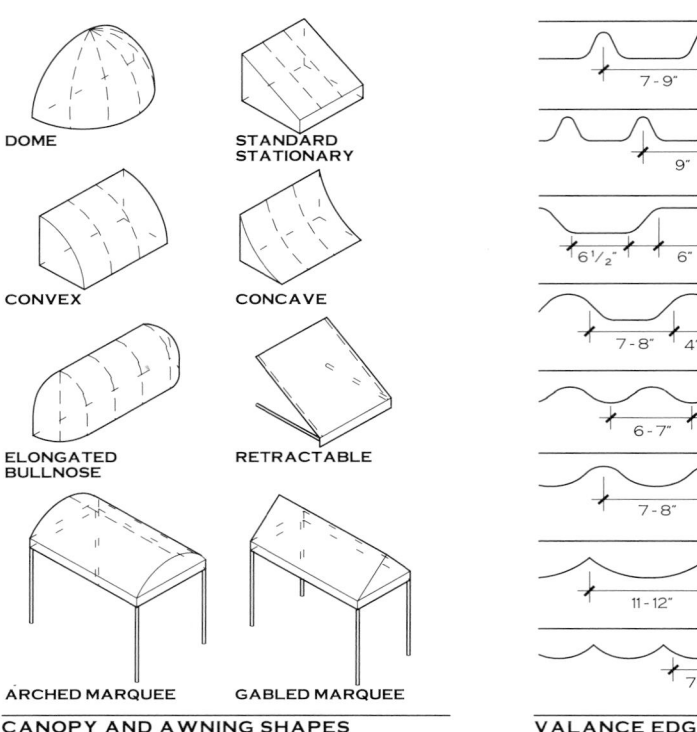

CANOPY AND AWNING SHAPES

DOME

STANDARD STATIONARY

CONVEX

CONCAVE

ELONGATED BULLNOSE

RETRACTABLE

ARCHED MARQUEE

GABLED MARQUEE

VALANCE EDGE TYPES

1 3/4" 7 - 9"

1 3/4" 9"

2" 6 1/2" 6"

2" 7 - 8" 4"

1 1/2" 6 - 7"

1 5/8" 7 - 8"

1 3/4" 11 - 12"

1" 7 - 8"

FABRIC-TO-FABRIC SEAM AND HEM DETAILS

DRESS STITCH SECOND   TOP STITCH FIRST

HALF TURN

REGULAR HEM   DRESS TOP SEAM

TRIPLE HEM   TWO-NEEDLE SEAM (CHAIN STITCH)

FLAT HEM   LAP SEAM

ROPE OR POLYETHYLENE TUBING

BATTLESHIP HEM   GROMMET   BUTT SEAM

POLYETHYLENE TUBING

NOTE
Lap seams and butt seams are "welded" together by means of high radio frequencies at seam overlap joints.

C - RAIL HEM

AWNING FABRIC CHARACTERISTICS

GENERAL CLASSI-FICATION	PAINTED ARMY DUCK	VINYL COATED COTTON	VINYL LAMINATED POLYESTER	SOLUTION DYED ACRYLIC	VINYL COATED POLYESTER	ACRYLIC COATED POLYESTER	VINYL COATED POLY COTTON BLEND	SOLUTION DYED MODACRYLIC
Description	Acrylic painted cotton duck fabric	Vinyl coated on cotton duck fabric	Tri-layer fabric; top and bottom layers are vinyl, middle layer is a woven polyester	Woven fabric, made of 100% acrylic solution dyed fibers with a fluorocarbon finish	Vinyl coated on each side of polyester base fabric	Acrylic coated on each side of a polyester base fabric	Vinyl coated on each side of a 50% polyester base	Woven fabric made of 100% solution dyed modacrylic fiber with fluorocarbon finish
Typical weight	11 oz. per sq yd	15 oz. per sq yd	10 - 16 oz. per sq yd	9.25 oz. per sq yd	11 - 17 oz. per sq yd	9.5 - 12.5 oz. per sq yd	13 oz. per sq yd	9.25 oz. per sq yd
Properties	Resistant to ultraviolet light, mildew, and water	Resistant to ultraviolet light, mildew, and water	Resistant to ultraviolet light, mildew, and water	Resistant to ultraviolet light, color degradation, water, and mildew	Resistant to ultraviolet light, mildew, and water. Cleanable	Resistant to ultraviolet light and mildew; water repellent	Resistant to ultraviolet light and mildew; water repellent	Resistant to ultraviolet light and color degradation; water repellent and resistant
Colors	Stripes or solids, primary colors, pastels, and some earth tones	Stripes or solids; all colors are available	Stripes or solids; primary colors and pastels	Wide variety: stripes and solids, primary colors, and earth tones	Solids; same color on both sides or solid on frost back	Predominantly solids with some stripes. Same color both sides	Solid colors; same color both sides	Solid colors and tweeds. Same color, both sides
Underside	Pearl gray, green, or pearl gray with floral print.	Solid pearl gray	Linen-like pattern, solid coordinating color to match topside or same color as top	Same as top surface	Same as top surface	Same as top surface	Same as top surface	Same as top surface
Surface	Matte finish, with linen-like visible texture.	Smooth, non-glare surface with little or no texture.	Smooth or matte, with slight woven or linen-like texture	Woven texture.	Smooth, somewhat glossy top surface.	Surface is textured with cloth appearance.	Surface is textured.	Woven texture surface
Transparency level	Opaque	Opaque	Translucent, depending on color Certain styles are formulated for backlighting and are highly translucent	Translucent, depending on color	Translucent, depending on color	Translucent, depending on color	Opaque	Translucent, depending on color
Abrasion resistance	Very good	Very good	Good. Base fabric is very strong	Good	Good	Very good	Very good	Good
Dimensional stability (stretch)	Very good	Very good	Very good	Good. Some shrinkage in cold weather, some stretch in hot weather	Stable	Very good	Very good	Good
Mildew resistance	Good. Not recommended for areas of high humidity	Good. Not recommended for areas of high humidity	Very good. Recommended for sustained high humidity.	Very good	Very good	Very good	Very good	Very good
Durability*	5 - 8 years	5 - 8 years	5 - 8 years	5 - 10 years	5 - 8 years	5 - 8 years	5 - 8 years	5 - 10 years
Flame resistance (FR)	Some colors are available with flame retardant treatment	Some colors are available with flame retardant treatment	All colors are flame resistant	Non-flame resistant	All colors are flame resistant	All colors are flame resistant	All colors are flame resistant	All patterns are flame resistant
Width	31 inches	31 inches	31 and 62 inches	46 and 60 inches	37 and 62 inches	31 and 62 inches	60 and 61 inches	46 inches

*Depends on climate and proper care of fabric

Industrial Fabrics Association International; St. Paul, Minnesota
Richard J. Vitullo, AIA; Oak Leaf Studio; Crownsville, Maryland

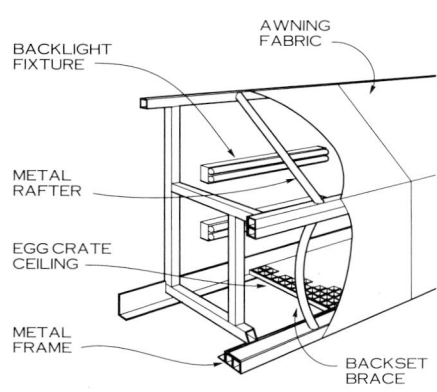

TYPICAL AWNING FRAMEWORK

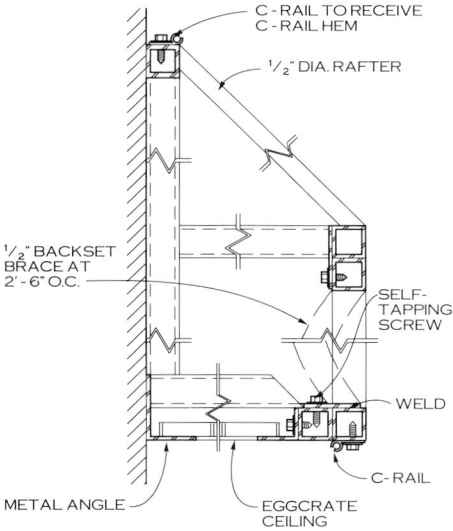

SECTION THROUGH AWNING FRAME

FRAMEWORK DETAILS
FRAME CHARACTERISTICS

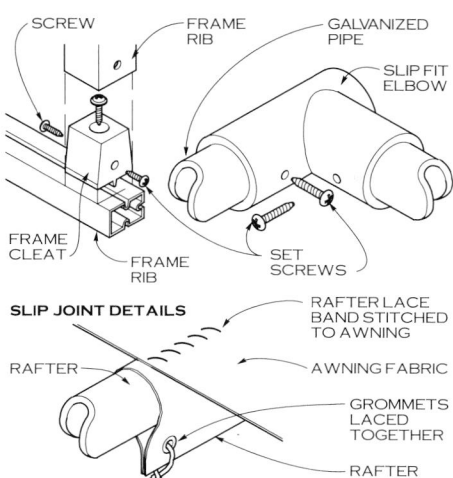

SLIP JOINT DETAILS

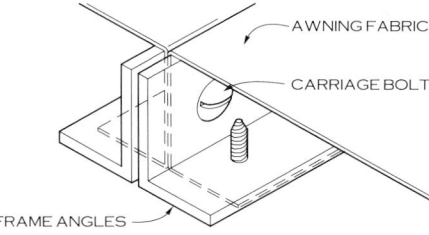

RAFTER LACE DETAIL

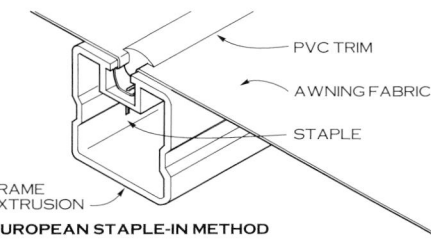

FRAME DETAIL WITH MINIMUM SHADOW LINE

EUROPEAN STAPLE-IN METHOD

FRAMEWORK DETAILS

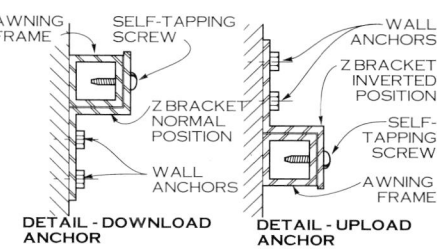

DETAIL - DOWNLOAD ANCHOR **DETAIL - UPLOAD ANCHOR**

NOTE

Consideration should be given to alternating download (snow, wind, and material weight) and upload (wind) anchors on each awning frame. Provide blocking behind anchors as necessary.

FIXED WALL ANCHORS

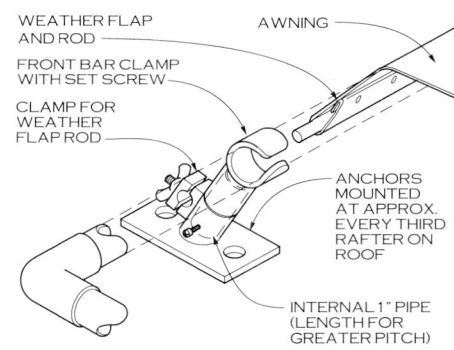

THREADED FRAME DIAMETERS

FRONT BAR SPAN LENGTHS	PIPE DIAMETERS
2' - 0" to 4' - 0"	$3/8$" (or $1/2$" Solid)
4' - 1" to 6' - 0"	$1/2$"
6' - 1" to 9' - 6"	$3/4$"
9' - 7" to 11' - 6"	1"

RETRACTABLE AWNING— HINGE DETAIL

FIXED AWNING—ROOF MOUNT DETAIL

NOTES

1. Awnings and canopies are custom manufactured and engineered to provide sun and rain protection for windows, entrances, and walkways. They can be illuminated with backlighting or graphically embellished and used as signage as well.
2. Code requirements as well as design needs may determine the shape, size, graphics, materials, and lighting chosen. After lighting is installed, the underside of the awning or canopy is finished with a "ceiling," normally a prismatic glass, eggcrating, or an open weave vinyl coated polyester or other translucent fabric in order to hide the hardware and maximize light reflection.
3. Climatic conditions, wind and snow load requirements, and local design customs will affect the construction details of the awning or canopy framework systems.
4. A variety of methods are used to apply graphics to the awning, such as silk screening, hand painting, air brush, cut-out lettering, heat color transfer, pressure-sensitive graphics, and eradicating.
5. Slip fittings with set screws or direct tube-to-tube welding are the most common frame construction practices. Welded joints are more rigid, but shipping, assembly, and disassembly are easier and quicker with slip fitting joints.

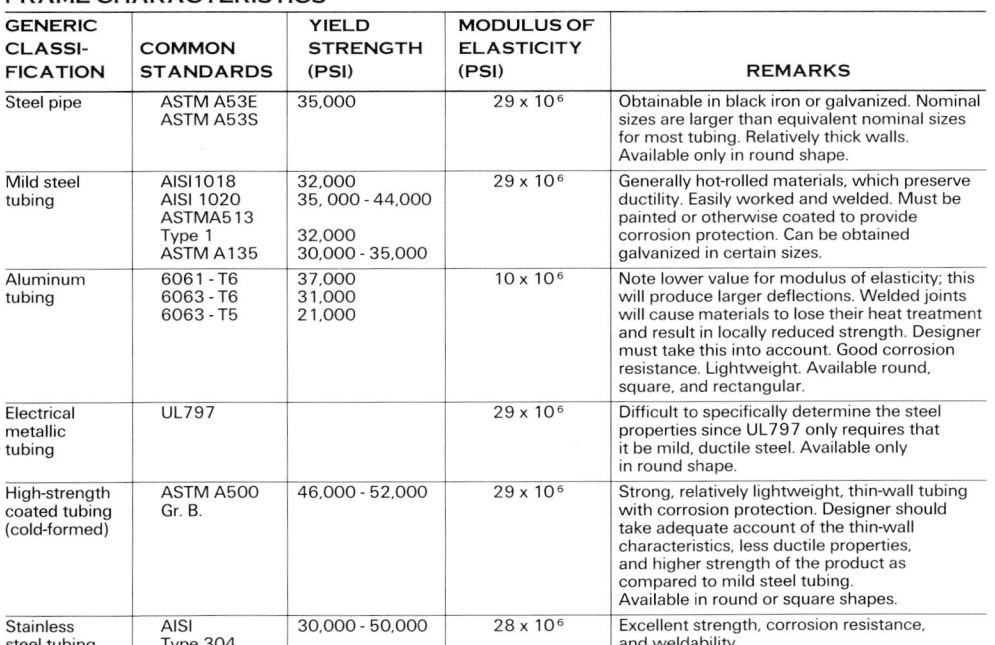

GENERIC CLASSI-FICATION	COMMON STANDARDS	YIELD STRENGTH (PSI)	MODULUS OF ELASTICITY (PSI)	REMARKS
Steel pipe	ASTM A53E ASTM A53S	35,000	29×10^6	Obtainable in black iron or galvanized. Nominal sizes are larger than equivalent nominal sizes for most tubing. Relatively thick walls. Available only in round shape.
Mild steel tubing	AISI 1018 AISI 1020 ASTM A513 Type 1 ASTM A135	32,000 35,000 - 44,000 32,000 30,000 - 35,000	29×10^6	Generally hot-rolled materials, which preserve ductility. Easily worked and welded. Must be painted or otherwise coated to provide corrosion protection. Can be obtained galvanized in certain sizes.
Aluminum tubing	6061 - T6 6063 - T6 6063 - T5	37,000 31,000 21,000	10×10^6	Note lower value for modulus of elasticity; this will produce larger deflections. Welded joints will cause materials to lose their heat treatment and result in locally reduced strength. Designer must take this into account. Good corrosion resistance. Lightweight. Available round, square, and rectangular.
Electrical metallic tubing	UL797		29×10^6	Difficult to specifically determine the steel properties since UL797 only requires that it be mild, ductile steel. Available only in round shape.
High-strength coated tubing (cold-formed)	ASTM A500 Gr. B.	46,000 - 52,000	29×10^6	Strong, relatively lightweight, thin-wall tubing with corrosion protection. Designer should take adequate account of the thin-wall characteristics, less ductile properties, and higher strength of the product as compared to mild steel tubing. Available in round or square shapes.
Stainless steel tubing	AISI Type 304	30,000 - 50,000	28×10^6	Excellent strength, corrosion resistance, and weldability.

Industrial Fabrics Association International; St. Paul, Minnesota
Richard J. Vitullo, AIA; Oak Leaf Studio; Crownsville, Maryland

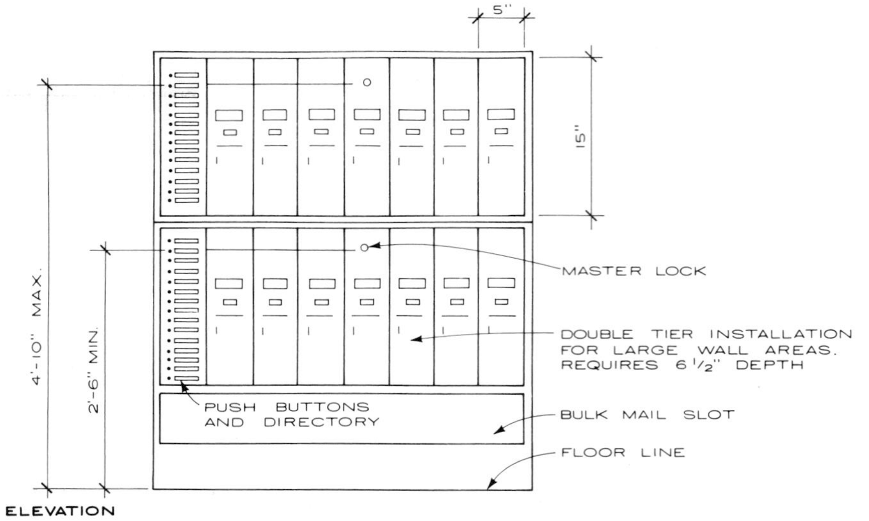

MASTER LOCK

DOUBLE TIER INSTALLATION FOR LARGE WALL AREAS. REQUIRES 6½" DEPTH

PUSH BUTTONS AND DIRECTORY

BULK MAIL SLOT

FLOOR LINE

ELEVATION

VERTICAL COMPARTMENT TYPE
FRONT LOADING

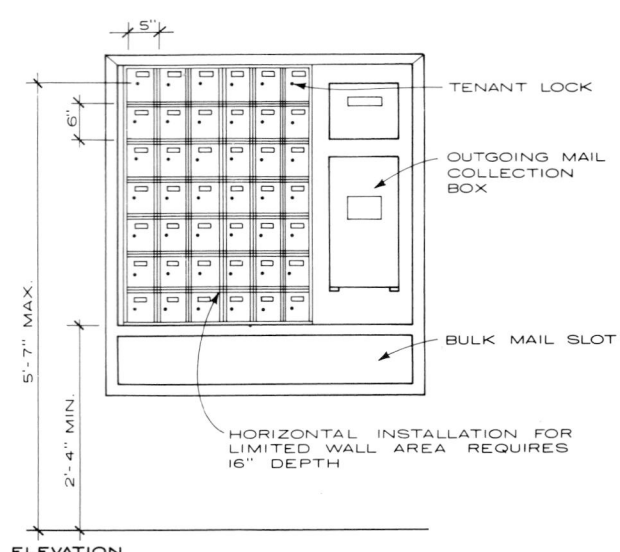

TENANT LOCK

OUTGOING MAIL COLLECTION BOX

BULK MAIL SLOT

HORIZONTAL INSTALLATION FOR LIMITED WALL AREA REQUIRES 16" DEPTH

ELEVATION

HORIZONTAL COMPARTMENT TYPE
FRONT OR REAR LOADING

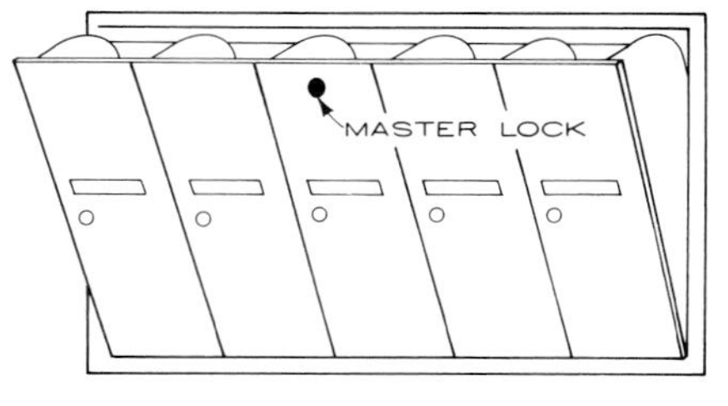

MASTER LOCK

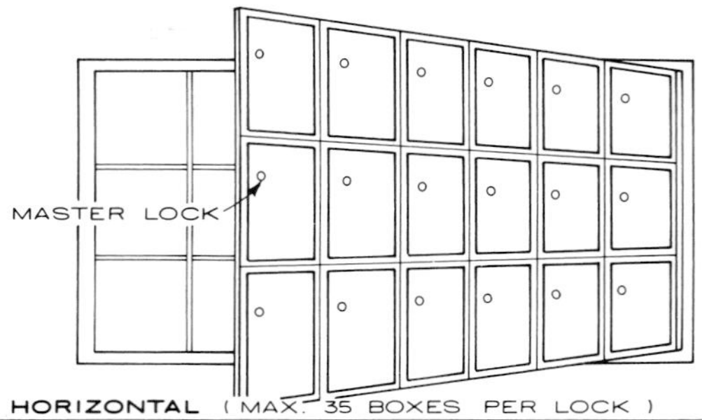

MASTER LOCK

VERTICAL (3 TO 7 BOXES PER LOCK)   **HORIZONTAL (MAX. 35 BOXES PER LOCK)**

FRONT LOADING COMPARTMENTS WITH MASTER LOCK

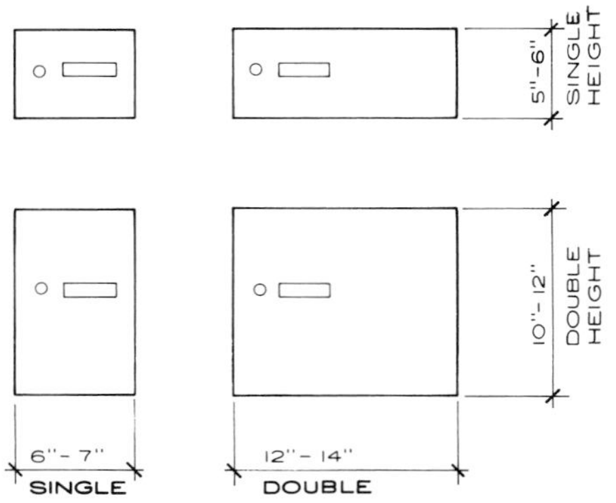

5"-6" SINGLE HEIGHT

10"-12" DOUBLE HEIGHT

6"-7" SINGLE

12"-14" DOUBLE

COMPARTMENT SIZES

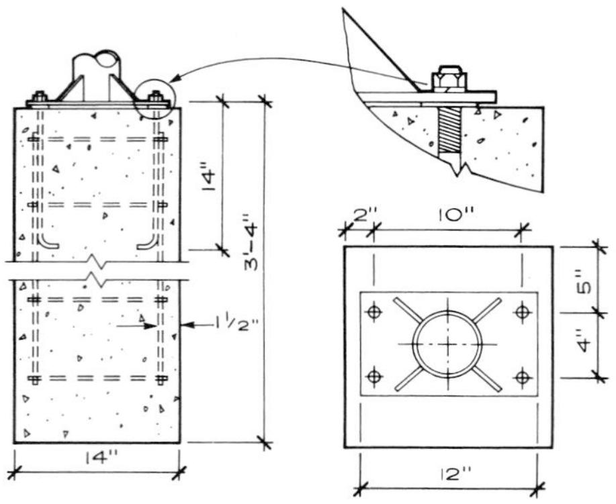

SURFACE

SEMIRECESSED

RECESSED

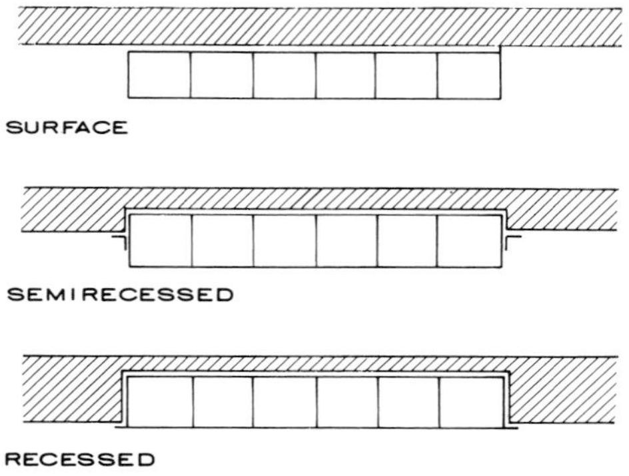

MOUNTING TYPES
FRONT LOADED COMPARTMENTS

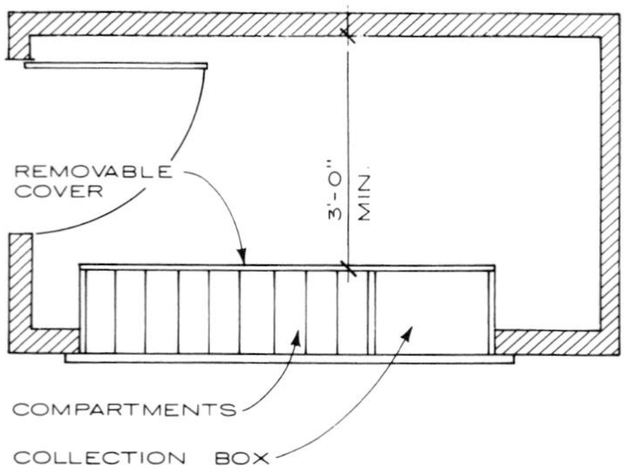

14"

3'-4"

1½"

14"

2" 10"

5"

4"

12"

FOUNDATION DETAILS OF PEDESTAL MOUNTED TYPE

REMOVABLE COVER

3'-0" MIN.

COMPARTMENTS

COLLECTION BOX

MAILROOM PLAN
REAR LOADED COMPARTMENTS

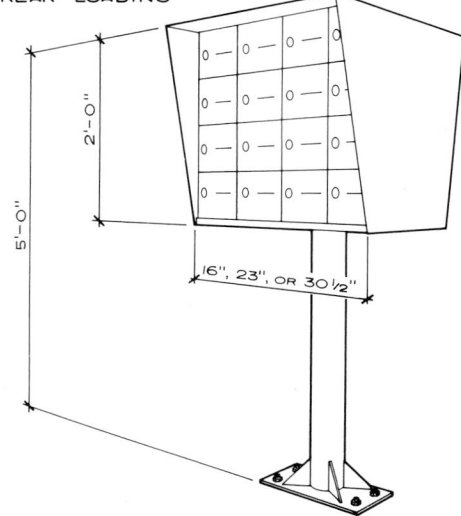

2'-0"

5'-0"

16", 23", OR 30½"

PEDESTAL MOUNTED TYPE

GENERAL NOTES

1. Postal Service approved mail receptacles are required for apartment houses containing three or more apartments with a common building entrance and street number.
2. Individual compartments should be large enough to receive long letter mail 4½ in. wide and bulky magazines 14½ in. long and 3½ in. in diameter.
3. An outdoor installation should preferably be at least 15 ft from a street or public sidewalk, protected from driving rain, and visible from at least one apartment window.
4. All installations must be adequately lighted to afford better protection to the mail and enable carriers to read addresses on mail and names on boxes.
5. A directory, in alphabetical order, is required for installations with more than 15 compartments.
6. Each compartment group is supplied with mounting hardware for master lock.
7. One mailbox door is required for the Postal Service master lock and cannot be used for mail distribution.
8. Call buttons with telephone can be integrated into frame with mailboxes.
9. Depending on occupancy, a certain number of compartments shall be assigned to persons using wheelchairs. Key slots shall be no more than 48 in. from floor. Consult ADAAG and local codes for other requirements.
10. Use of collection boxes is subject to approval by local offices of the United States Postal Service.

Cohen, Karydas & Associates, Chartered; Washington, D.C.

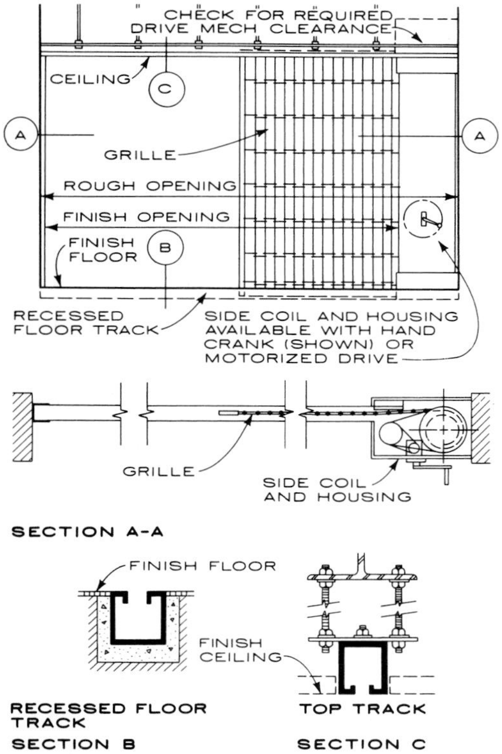

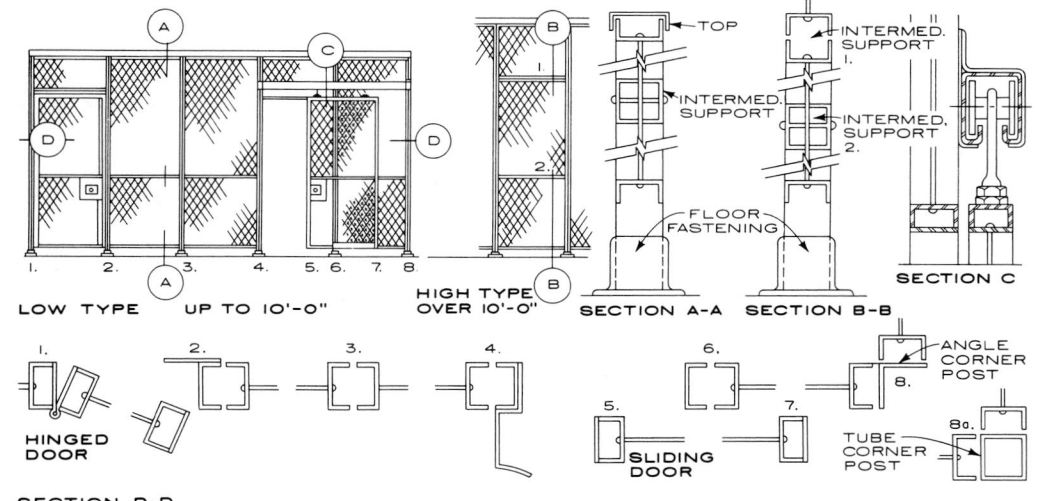

"CHECK FOR REQUIRED DRIVE MECH CLEARANCE"

CEILING
GRILLE
ROUGH OPENING
FINISH OPENING
FINISH FLOOR
RECESSED FLOOR TRACK
SIDE COIL AND HOUSING AVAILABLE WITH HAND CRANK (SHOWN) OR MOTORIZED DRIVE

SECTION A-A

GRILLE
SIDE COIL AND HOUSING

FINISH FLOOR
FINISH CEILING

RECESSED FLOOR TRACK
SECTION B

TOP TRACK
SECTION C

RETRACTABLE GRILLE PARTITIONS

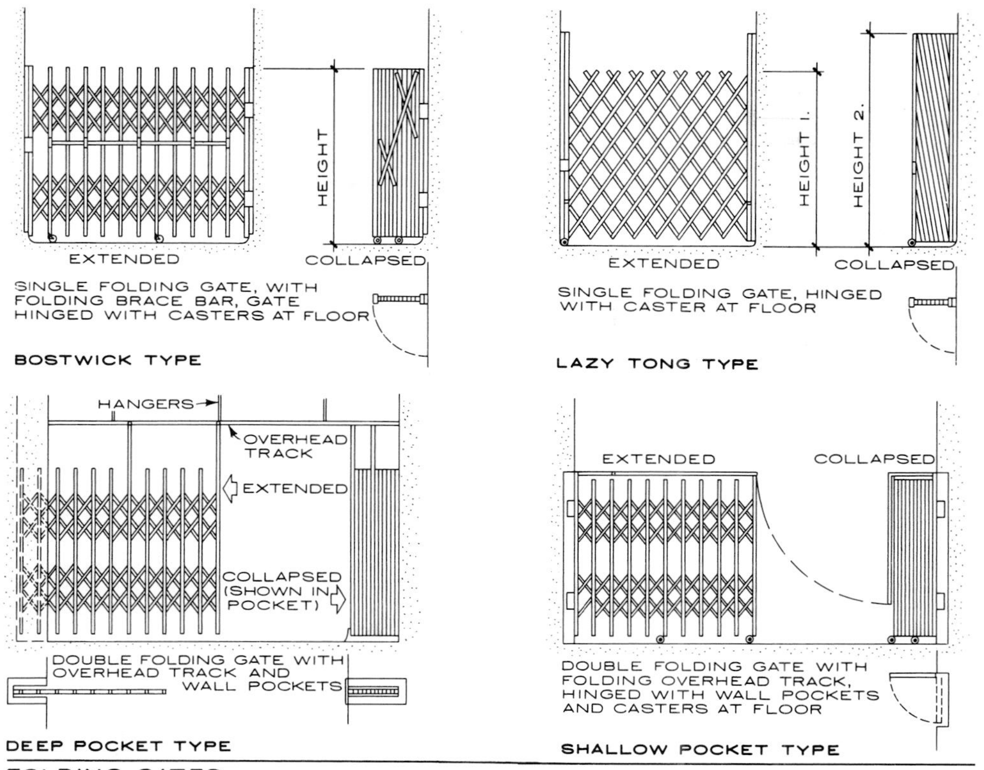

EXTENDED   COLLAPSED
HEIGHT

SINGLE FOLDING GATE, WITH FOLDING BRACE BAR, GATE HINGED WITH CASTERS AT FLOOR

BOSTWICK TYPE

HANGERS
OVERHEAD TRACK
EXTENDED
COLLAPSED (SHOWN IN POCKET)

DOUBLE FOLDING GATE WITH OVERHEAD TRACK AND WALL POCKETS

DEEP POCKET TYPE

FOLDING GATES

EXTENDED   COLLAPSED
HEIGHT 1.   HEIGHT 2.

SINGLE FOLDING GATE, HINGED WITH CASTER AT FLOOR

LAZY TONG TYPE

EXTENDED   COLLAPSED

DOUBLE FOLDING GATE WITH FOLDING OVERHEAD TRACK, HINGED WITH WALL POCKETS AND CASTERS AT FLOOR

SHALLOW POCKET TYPE

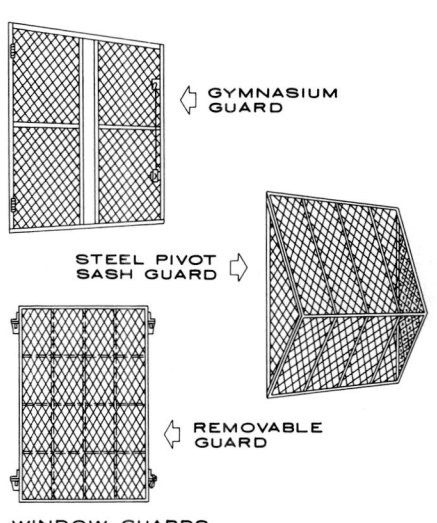

GYMNASIUM GUARD

STEEL PIVOT SASH GUARD

REMOVABLE GUARD

WINDOW GUARDS

LOW TYPE   UP TO 10'-0"
1. 2. 3. 4. 5. 6. 7. 8

HIGH TYPE OVER 10'-0"
TOP
INTERMED. SUPPORT 1.
INTERMED. SUPPORT
INTERMED. SUPPORT 2.
FLOOR FASTENING
SECTION A-A   **SECTION B-B**
SECTION C

HINGED DOOR
SECTION D-D

SLIDING DOOR
ANGLE CORNER POST
TUBE CORNER POST

RECOMMENDED USES FOR WIRE MESH PARTITIONS

MESH	PATTERN		WIRE SIZE	FRAMES	USES
1¼"	◇	☐	11	1" ⊏	Animal cages
1½"	◇		10	1" ⊏	Elevator shafts
1¾"	◇		9	1¼" ⊏	Fire escapes
2"	◇		8	1½" ⊏	Cashier cages
2"	◇		6	1¼" "C"	Runways
				Channel ¾" ⊏	Stair enclosures Locker rooms Departmental divisions Stock rooms Tool rooms

OTHER USES FOR WOVEN WIRE MESH

MESH	PATTERN		WIRE SIZE	FRAMES	USES
¾"	◇	☐	12	5/16" ○ 3/4" ⊏ 1" L	Air intake screens Bird screens
1"	◇	☐	12	3/8" ○ 1" ⊏ 1" L	Basement window guards Shelves and trays Skylight guards
1½"	◇	☐		3/8" ○ 1" ⊏	Door and window guards
2¼"	◇	☐	7	7/16" ○	Wire roof signs
2½"	◇		6	1½" ⊏	Fencing gratings

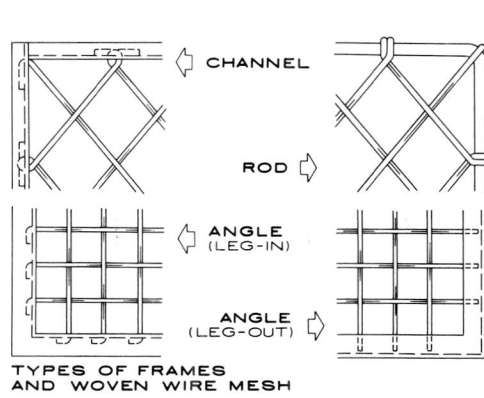

CHANNEL
ROD
ANGLE (LEG-IN)
ANGLE (LEG-OUT)

TYPES OF FRAMES AND WOVEN WIRE MESH

WIRE MESH PARTITIONS

HMC Group; Ontario, California

GENERAL

American National Standards Institute (ANSI)
11 West 42nd Street, 13th Floor
New York, NY 10036-8002
Tel: (212) 642-4900
Fax:(212) 398-0023

Americans with Disabilitites Act Information Office
U.S. Department of Justice
Civil Rights Division
P.O. Box 66378
Washington, DC 20035-998
Tel: (202) 514-0301

American Society for
Testing and Materials (ASTM)
1916 Race St.
Philadelphia, PA 19103-1187
Tel: (215) 299-5400
Fax:(215) 977-9679

Underwriters Laboratories (UL)
333 Pfingsten Road
Northbrook, IL 60062
Tel: (708) 272-8800

Woven Wire Products Association
2515 North Nordica Ave.
Chicago, IL 60635
Tel: (312) 637-1359

TOILET AND BATH COMPARTMENTS AND ACCESSORIES

Cosmetic, Toiletry, and Fragrance Association
1101 17th Street, N.W.
Suite 300
Washington, DC 20036
Tel: (202) 331-1770
Fax:(202) 331-1969

International Sanitary Supply Association
7373 North Lincoln Avenue
Lincolnwood, FL 60646-1799
Tel: (708) 982-0800
Fax:(708) 982-1012

National Association of Mirror Manufacturers
9005 Congressional Court
Potomac, MD 20854
(301) 365-4080

National Association of Service Merchandising (NASM)
118 S. Clinton Street
Suite 300
Chicago, IL 60661-3628
Tel: (312) 876-9494
Fax:(312) 876-5357

Porcelain Enamel Institute
102 Woodmont Blvd., Suite 360
Nashville, TN 37205
Tel: (615) 385-5357
Fax:(615) 385-5463

REFERENCES

Americans with Disabilities Act Accessiblity Guidelines Checklist for Buildings and Facilities (ADAAG). ADA Information Office, 1991.

"Accessibility Guidelines: Design and Constuction Requirements of the Fair Housing Amendments Act of 1988." Center for Accessible Housing, 1992. [80 slides]

Providing Accessibility and Usability for Physically Handicapped People. American National Standards Institute , 1986.

Raeber, John A. "Specification Series: Toilet Compartments." *Architectural Record* (July 1992), p. 36.

Terry, E., Associates. *Americans with Disabilities Act Facilities Compliance Notebook.* New York: J. Wiley & Sons, 1992. [looseleaf] ANSI AI17.1

SERVICE WALL SYSTEMS

Ceilings and Interior Systems
Construction Association (CISCA)
579 West North Avenue, Suite 301
Elmhurst, IL 60126
Tel: (708) 833-1919
Fax:(708) 833-1940

WALL AND CORNER GUARDS

National Association of
Decorative Architectural Finishes
2414 Taylor Avenue
Alexandria, VA 22302-3306
Tel: (703) 836-6504

Wallcovering Manufacturers Association
401 North Michigan Avenue
Chicago, IL 60611
Tel: (212) 661-4261

ACCESS FLOORING
REFERENCES

Access Flooring, CSI Monograph 10M270. Construction Specifications Institute, June 1985.

Shute, Robert W. "Integrating Access Floor Plenums for HVAC Air Distribution." American Society of Heating, Refrigerating, and Air Conditioning Engineers (ASHRAE), October 1992, p. 46.

MANUFACTURED FIREPLACES

Hearth Products Association
1101 Connecticut Avenue, NW, Suite 700
Washington, DC 20036
Tel: (202) 857-1181
Fax:(202)223-4579

FLAGPOLES

National Association of
Architectural Metal Manufacturers (NAAMM)
600 South Federal
Suite 400
Chicago, IL 60605
Tel: (312) 922-6222
Fax:(312) 922-2734

REFERENCES

"Guide Specifications for Design Loads of Metal Flagpoles." ANSI/National Association of Architectural Metal Manufacturers FP 1001-90, 1990.

Metal Flagpole Manual. National Association of Architectural Metal Manufacturers, 1980.

Raeber, John A. "Flagpoles." *Construction Specifier* (August 1992), p. 25.

Wind Load Tests on Poles and Flagpoles. National Association of Architectural Metal Manufacturers.

IDENTIFYING DEVICES

Marking Device Association International
435 N. Michigan Avenue
Suite 1717
Chicago, IL 60611-4067
Tel: (312) 644-0828
Fax:(312)644-8557

National Electric Sign Association
801 North Fairfax Street, Suite 205
Alexandria, VA 22314
Tel: (703) 836-4012
Fax:(703-836-8353

Society for Environmental Graphic Design
1 Story Street
Cambridge, MA 02138
Tel: (617) 868-3381
Fax:(617) 868-3591

World Sign Associates (WSA)
8774 Yates Drive
Westminster, CO 80030
Tel: (303) 427-7252

REFERENCES

"ADA-Compliant Signage Guide." *Facilities Design and Management* (April 1992), p. 9.

International Design (ID), New York. [monthly]

McLendon, Charles B., and Mick Blackistone. *Signage.* New York: McGraw-Hill, 1982.

Follis, John, and David Hammer. *Architectural Signing and Graphics.* New York: Whitney Library of Design, 1988.

Visual Merchandising and Store Design (VM & SD), Cincinnati, OH. [monthly]

FIRE PROTECTION SPECIALTIES

Fire Equipment Manufacturers Association
1300 Sumner Avenue
Cleveland, OH 44115-2180
Tel: (216) 241-7333
Fax:(216) 241-0105

National Association of Fire Equipment Distributors
401 N. Michigan Avenue
Chicago, IL 60611-4267
Tel: (312) 644-6610
Fax:(312) 321-4658

National Fire Protection Association (NFPA)
P.O. Box 9101
1 Batterymarch Park
Quincy, MA 02269
Tel: (800) 735-0100
Fax:(617) 770-0700

REFERENCES

Factory Mutual Approval Guide. 1992.

"Fighting Fire with Fire (Extinguishers)." *Doors and Hardware* (May 1992), p. 54.

NFPA 10—Standard for Portable Fire Extinguishers. National Fire Protection Association, 1990.

Publication #10, Portable Extinguishers. National Fire Protection Association, 1978.

Fire Protection Equipment Directory. Underwriters Laboratories, 1992.

PROTECTIVE COVERS

National Electrical Manufacturers Association (NEMA)
2101 L Street, N.W.
Washington, DC 20037
Tel: (202) 457-8400
Fax:(202) 457-8411

PARTITIONS AND OPERABLE PARTITIONS
REFERENCES

"Light and Power." *Architectural Record* (June 1992), p. 48.

CHAPTER

11

EQUIPMENT

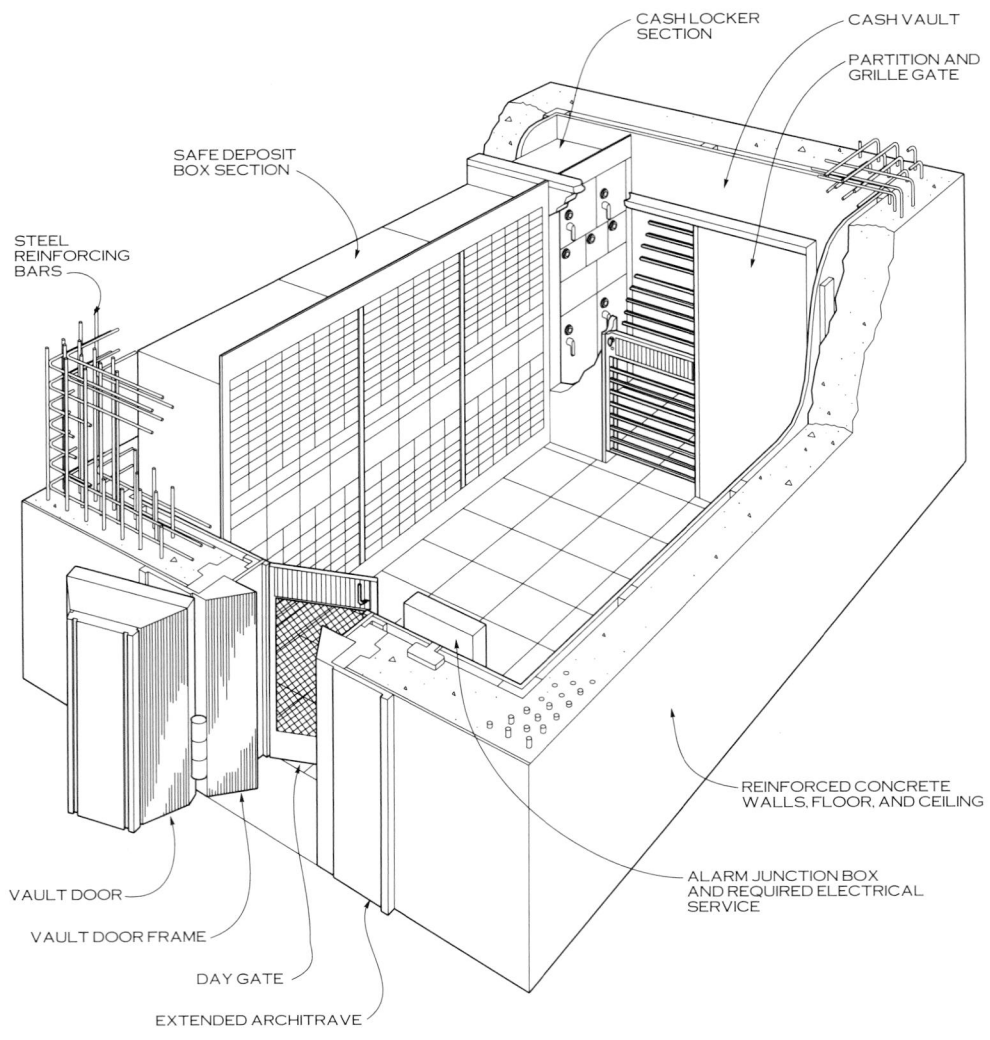

SAFE DEPOSIT BOX SECTION

CASH LOCKER SECTION

CASH VAULT

PARTITION AND GRILLE GATE

STEEL REINFORCING BARS

VAULT DOOR

VAULT DOOR FRAME

DAY GATE

EXTENDED ARCHITRAVE

REINFORCED CONCRETE WALLS, FLOOR, AND CEILING

ALARM JUNCTION BOX AND REQUIRED ELECTRICAL SERVICE

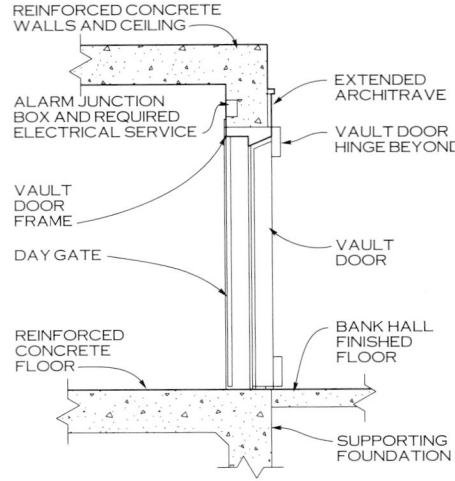

REINFORCED CONCRETE WALLS AND CEILING

ALARM JUNCTION BOX AND REQUIRED ELECTRICAL SERVICE

VAULT DOOR FRAME

DAY GATE

REINFORCED CONCRETE FLOOR

EXTENDED ARCHITRAVE

VAULT DOOR HINGE BEYOND

VAULT DOOR

BANK HALL FINISHED FLOOR

SUPPORTING FOUNDATION

SECTION AT VAULT DOOR

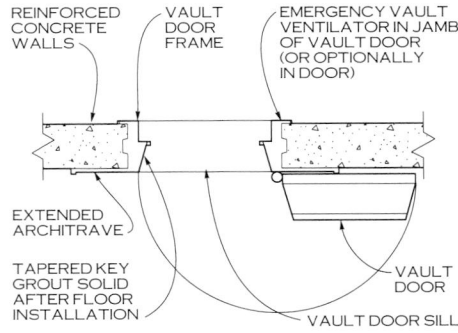

REINFORCED CONCRETE WALLS

VAULT DOOR FRAME

EMERGENCY VAULT VENTILATOR IN JAMB OF VAULT DOOR (OR OPTIONALLY IN DOOR)

EXTENDED ARCHITRAVE

TAPERED KEY GROUT SOLID AFTER FLOOR INSTALLATION

VAULT DOOR

VAULT DOOR SILL

PLAN OF VAULT DOOR

UNDERWRITERS LABORATORIES (UL) PERFORMANCE SPECIFICATIONS FOR VAULTS

Class 1 ½ hr attack resistance time	Not shown — available for application only in existing buildings where structural support (floor load) is critical (does not comply with Bank Protection Act).
Class 2 1 hr attack resistance time	A. 18 in. reinforced concrete B. 8 in. average thickness UL listed modular panel
Class 3 2 hr attack resistance time	A. 27 in. reinforced concrete B. 13 in. average thickness UL listed modular panel.

INSURANCE SERVICES OFFICE NOTES

1. The size, configuration, and specific requirements of all equipment and alarm systems that might be included in a bank vault will vary with different manufacturers and design considerations.

2. Class 2 is the minimum vault panel rating that will meet the requirements of regulation P of the Bank Protection Act.

3. Concrete used in vault construction should develop an ultimate compression strength of at least 3000 lb/sq. in.

4. With fire-resistive materials to meet local building codes, steel lining is not considered acceptable as burglary-resistant material equivalencies for UL vault construction and does not meet the Bank Protection Act requirements. Special approval is required.

5. Class 1 UL listed vault is positioned as equal or superior to the 5R vault classification.

6. Class 2 UL listed vault is positioned as superior to the 9R vault classification.

7. Class 3 UL listed vault is positioned as superior to the 10R vault classification.

8. The above UL listed vaults are superior to traditional ISO and Bank Protection Act construction.

9. The Class 2 UL listed vault is recommended throughout the industry as minimum protection for safe deposit vault operations. A 2-hour, Class 3, is preferable.

SAFE DEPOSIT VAULT—HOMOGENEOUS CONSTRUCTION

GENERAL

Federally insured banks and savings institutions are regulated under the Bank Protection Act of 1968 as revised in 1973, which only recognizes vaults with walls, floor, and ceiling of reinforced concrete at least 12 in. thick. Revisions to the BPA in 1991 should be consulted when planning a new vault. The following comparative classification charts are used to rate security vaults.

MINIMUM NUMBER OF GRIDS FOR DEFORMED BARS

12 in. concrete thickness	3 grids
18 in. concrete thickness	4 grids
27 in. concrete thickness or over	5 grids

MINIMUM NUMBER OF GRIDS FOR #6 EXPANDED STEEL

12 in. concrete thickness	2 grids
18 in. concrete thickness	3 grids
27 in. concrete thickness or over	4 grids

REINFORCING

No. 5 (⅝ in. diameter) deformed steel reinforcing bars located on 4 in. centers in horizontal and vertical rows to form a grid, or expanded steel bank vault mesh weighing 6 lb/sq ft per grid and having a diamond pattern of 3 x 8 in.

Grids are to be located not less than 4 in. apart and shall be staggered in each direction. The number of grids required depends on the thickness of the wall, floor, and ceiling (and specific insurance requirements).

INSURANCE SERVICES OFFICE (ISO)

STEEL DOORS	WALL SPECIFICATIONS EFFECTIVE OCTOBER 30, 1974	ISO CLASSI-FICATION
3½ in.	A. ½ in. steel lining [4] B. 12 in. reinforced concrete	5R
3½ in.	A. 1 in. steel lining [4] B. ½ in. steel lining and 12 in. reinforced concrete C. 18 in. reinforced concrete	6R
7 in.	A. 1 in. steel lining [4] B. ½ in. steel lining and 12 in. reinforced concrete C. 18 in. reinforced concrete	9R
7 in.	A. 1½ in. steel lining [4] B. ½ in. steel lining and 12 in. reinforced concrete B. ½ in. steel lining and 18 in. reinforced concrete C. 27 in. reinforced concrete or 18 in. listed reinforced concrete	10R

Krommenhoek/McKeown and Associates; San Diego, California

BANK EQUIPMENT REQUIREMENTS

1. STANDARDS: Comply with the latest edition of "Comptroller's Manual for National Banks"; see the section on "Minimum Security Devices and Procedures." Higher standards may be specified in the construction documents. The following requirements are based on the Comptroller's Manual.

2. SURVEILLANCE SYSTEM (general) devices should be:
   a. Capable of enlarging images of persons to produce a 1 in. vertical head size.
   b. Reasonably silent in operation.
   c. Taking at least one picture every 2 seconds and operating not less than 3 min.

3. SURVEILLANCE SYSTEM (other than walk-up or drive-in at teller's station or windows):
   a. Placed to reproduce identifiable images of persons either leaving the banking office or in a position to transact business at each station or window.
   b. Capable of actuation by initiating devices located at each teller's station or window.

4. SURVEILLANCE SYSTEM (walk-up or drive-in at teller's station or windows):
   a. Placed to reproduce identifiable images of persons either leaving the banking office or in a position to transact business at each such station or window, and capable of actuation by initiating devices located at each teller's station or window.
   b. Capable of actuation by initiating devices located at each teller's station or window. Such devices may be omitted when the teller is effectively protected by a bullet-resistant barrier. However, if the teller is vulnerable to larceny or robbery, access to actuate a surveillance system should be available.

5. ROBBERY ALARM SYSTEM:
   a. Provide for banking offices at which the police ordinarily can arrive within 5 minutes after an alarm is actuated; all other banking offices should be provided with appropriate devices for promptly notifying the police that a robbery has occurred or is in progress.
   b. Signals the police, through an intermediary, indicating that a crime against the banking office has occurred or is in progress.
   c. Capable of actuation by initiating devices located at each teller's station or window, except those protected by bullet-resistant barrier.
   d. Safeguarded against accidental transmission.

   e. Equipped with a visual and audible signal capable of indicating improper functioning of or tampering with the system.
   f. Equipped with an independent source of power sufficient to assure continuously reliable operation of the system for at least 24 hr.

6. BURGLARY ALARM SYSTEM:
   a. Provide for each banking office.
   b. Capable of detecting promptly an attack on the outer door, walls, floor, or ceiling of each vault and each safe not stored in a vault.
   c. Signals the police, through an intermediary, indicating that a crime against the banking office has occurred or is in progress. Where police cannot arrive within 5 minutes, a loud bell audible inside and 500 ft outside should be provided.
   d. Safeguarded against accidental transmission.
   e. Equipped with a visual and audible signal capable of indicating improper functioning of or tampering with the system.
   f. Equipped with an independent source of power (such as a battery) sufficient to assure continuously reliable operation of the system for at least 80 hr in the event of failure of the usual source of power.

7. WALK-UP AND DRIVE-IN TELLER'S STATIONS OR WINDOWS:
   a. Tellers should be effectively protected by bullet-resistant barriers from robbery or larceny. Such barriers should be of glass at least 1³/₁₆ in. in thickness, or of material of at least equivalent bullet-resistance. Pass-through devices should not afford a person outside a direct line of fire.

8. VAULTS, SAFES, AND SAFE DEPOSIT BOXES: Requirements are described in detail in the manual. See also the Bank Vault page in this chapter.

9. NIGHT DEPOSITORIES:
   a. Should consist of a receptacle chest having cast or welded steel walls, top, and bottom, at least 1 in. thick; a steel door at least 1¹/₂ in. thick, with a combination lock; and a chute, made of steel that is a least 1 in. thick, securely bolted or welded to the receptacle and to a depository entrance of strength similar to the chute. Each depository entrance should be equipped with a burglar alarm and be designed to protect against the "fishing" of a deposit from the deposit receptacle, and "trapping" of a deposit for extraction.

10. AUTOMATED TELLER MACHINES (ATMs):
    a. Should weigh at least 750 lb empty or be securely anchored to the premises. Cash dispensing machines should contain, among other features, a storage chest of cast or welded steel walls, top, and bottom, at least 1 in. thick, with a tensile strength of at least 50,000 psi. Any doors should be constructed of steel at least equivalent in strength to the storage chest and equipped with a combination lock and a relocking device that will effectively lock the door if the combination lock is punched. The housing covering the mechanism for removing the cash from the storage chest should be designed as to provide burglary resistance at least equivalent to the storage chest and should be designed to protect against the "fishing" of cash from the storage chest. The cash dispensing control and delivering mechanism should be protected by steel, at least¹/₂ in. in thickness, securely attached to the storage chest. A cash dispensing machine that also receives deposits should have a receptacle chest having the same burglary resistant characteristics as that of cash dispensing storage chest and should be designed to protect against the fishing and trapping of deposits. Necessary ventilation for the automated machines should be designed so as to avoid significantly reducing the burglary resistance of the machines. The cash dispensing machine should also be designed so as to be protected against actuation by unauthorized persons, should be protected by a burglar alarm, and be located in a well-lighted area.

ATM ACCESSIBILITY

ADA Accessibility Guidelines (ADAAG) Section 4.34 regulate automatic teller machines (ATMs) and require that they be accessible as per 4.1.3, that their controls comply with 4.27 (height of forward reach 48 in., height of side reach 54 in.), that they have clear floor space in compliance with 4.24 (30 x 48 in.), and that they be usable by persons with impaired vision. Each ATM must comply, except where two or more are provided at a location; then only one must comply. Drive-up-only ATMs are not required to comply with clear floor space and reach requirements of 4.27 and 4.34.

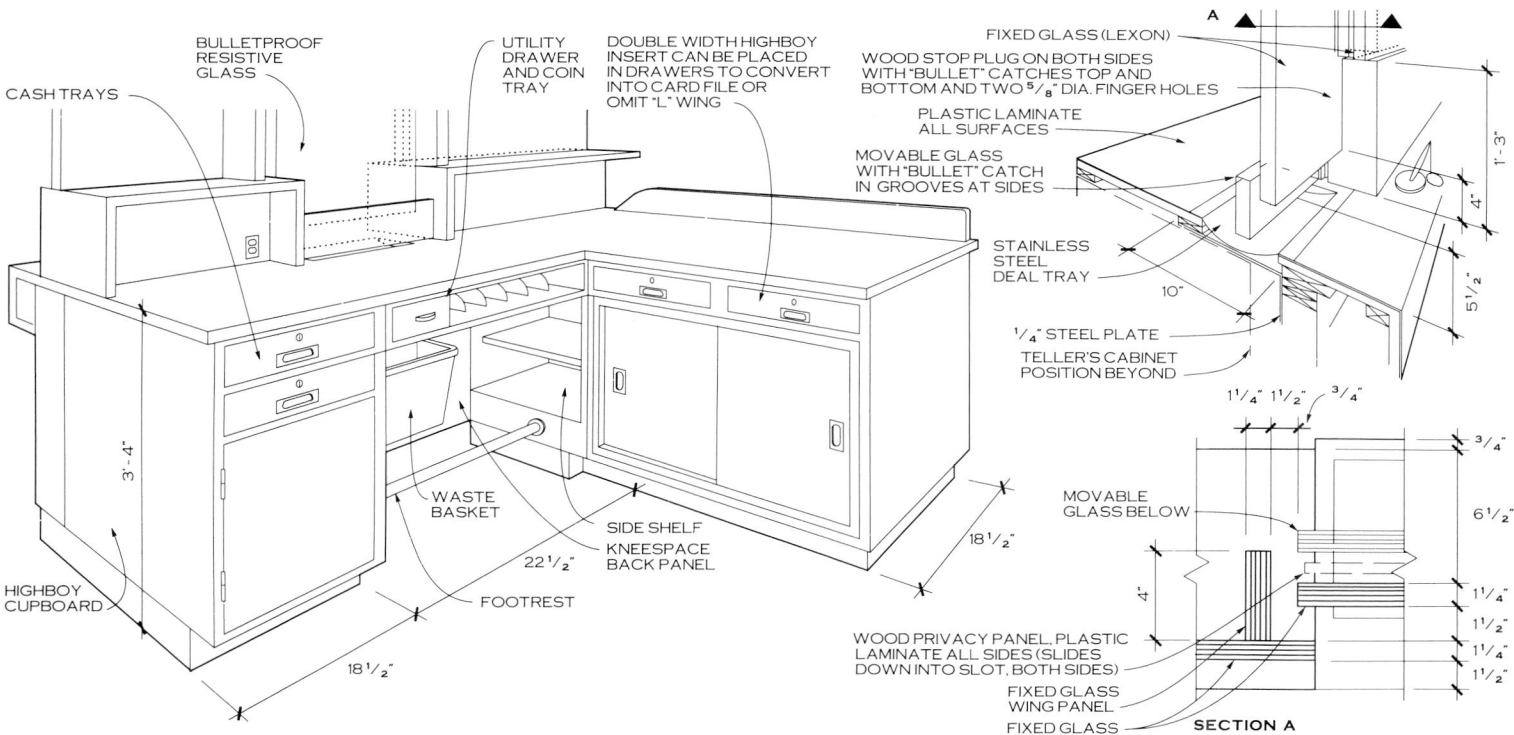

TELLER STATION

Charles Szoradi, AIA; Washington, DC

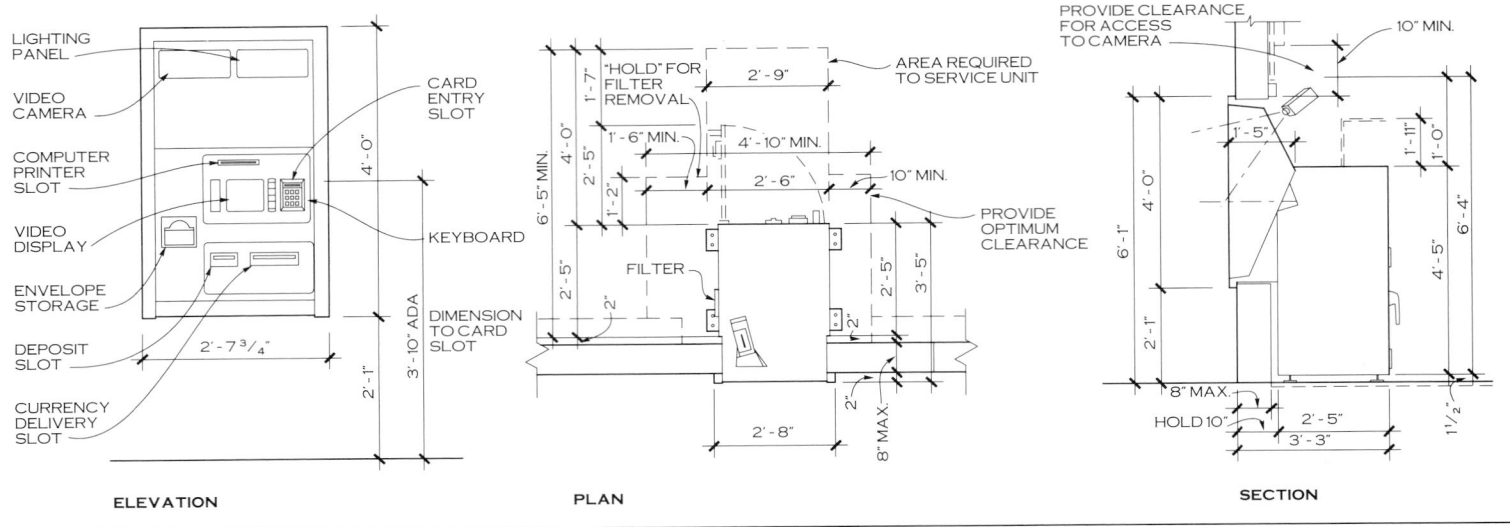

LIGHTING PANEL

VIDEO CAMERA

COMPUTER PRINTER SLOT

VIDEO DISPLAY

ENVELOPE STORAGE

DEPOSIT SLOT

CURRENCY DELIVERY SLOT

CARD ENTRY SLOT

KEYBOARD

DIMENSION TO CARD SLOT

4'-0"

3'-10" ADA

2'-1"

2'-7 3/4"

ELEVATION

"HOLD" FOR FILTER REMOVAL

AREA REQUIRED TO SERVICE UNIT

FILTER

PROVIDE OPTIMUM CLEARANCE

2'-9"

1'-7"

4'-0"

1'-6" MIN.

4'-10" MIN.

2'-5"

10" MIN.

6'-5" MIN.

1'-2"

2'-6"

2'-5"

2'-5"

2"

2"

2'-5"

3'-5"

2'-8"

8" MAX.

PLAN

PROVIDE CLEARANCE FOR ACCESS TO CAMERA

10" MIN.

1'-5"

1'-11"

1'-0"

6'-1"

4'-0"

2'-1"

6'-4"

4'-5"

8" MAX.

HOLD 10"

2'-5"

3'-3"

1 1/2"

SECTION

AUTOMATED TELLER MACHINES (ATM)

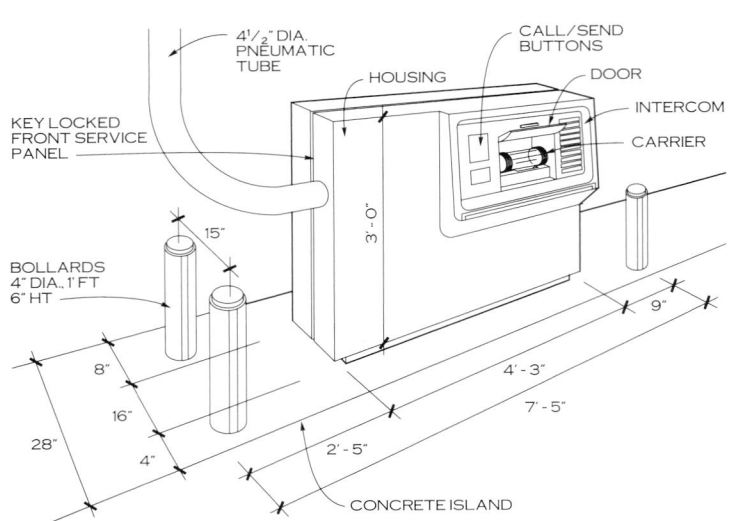

4 1/2" DIA. PNEUMATIC TUBE

HOUSING

CALL/SEND BUTTONS

DOOR

INTERCOM

CARRIER

KEY LOCKED FRONT SERVICE PANEL

BOLLARDS 4" DIA., 1 FT 6" HT

3'-0"

15"

8"

16"

28"

4"

2'-5"

4'-3"

7'-5"

9"

CONCRETE ISLAND

PNEUMATIC AUTO TELLER

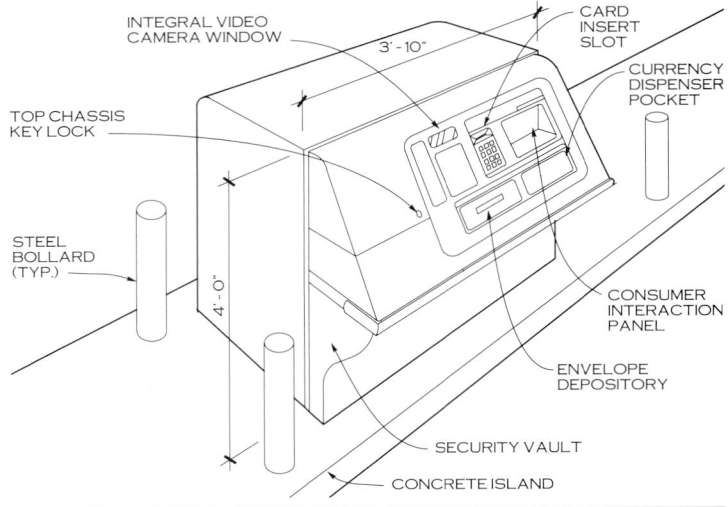

INTEGRAL VIDEO CAMERA WINDOW

CARD INSERT SLOT

CURRENCY DISPENSER POCKET

TOP CHASSIS KEY LOCK

3'-10"

STEEL BOLLARD (TYP.)

4'-0"

CONSUMER INTERACTION PANEL

ENVELOPE DEPOSITORY

SECURITY VAULT

CONCRETE ISLAND

DRIVE-UP AUTOMATIC TELLER MACHINE (ATM)

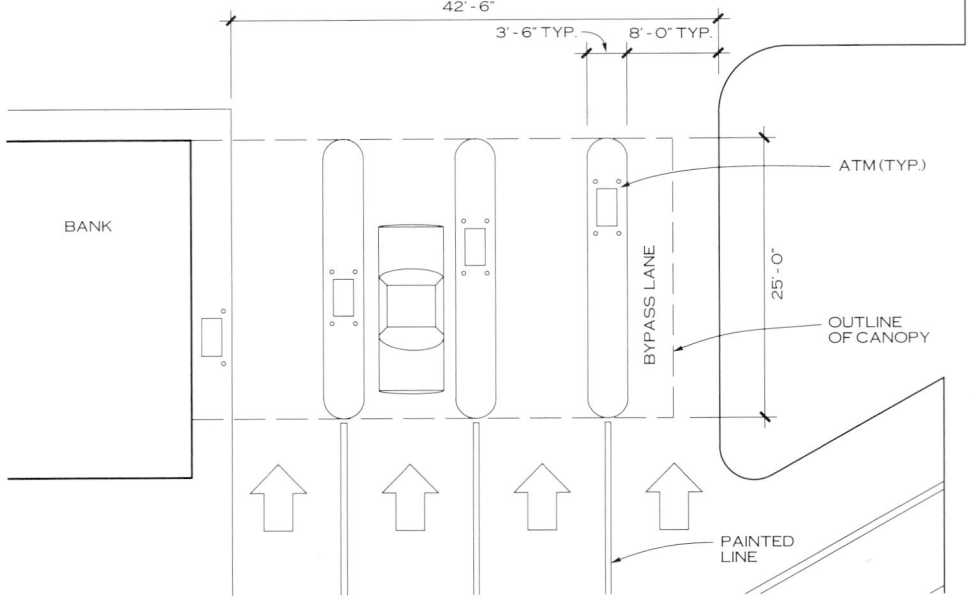

42'-6"

3'-6" TYP.

8'-0" TYP.

BANK

ATM (TYP.)

BYPASS LANE

25'-0"

OUTLINE OF CANOPY

PAINTED LINE

PLAN OF DRIVE-UP TELLERS

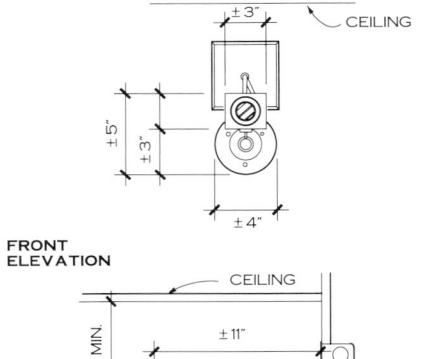

± 3"

CEILING

± 5"

± 3"

± 4"

FRONT ELEVATION

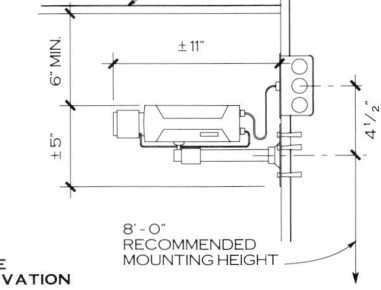

CEILING

± 11"

6" MIN.

± 5"

4 1/2"

8'-0" RECOMMENDED MOUNTING HEIGHT

SIDE ELEVATION

SURVEILLANCE CAMERA

Charles Szoradi, AIA; Washington, D.C.
Equipment information was furnished by Diebold, Inc.; Canton, Ohio

11   TELLER AND BANK SECURITY EQUIPMENT

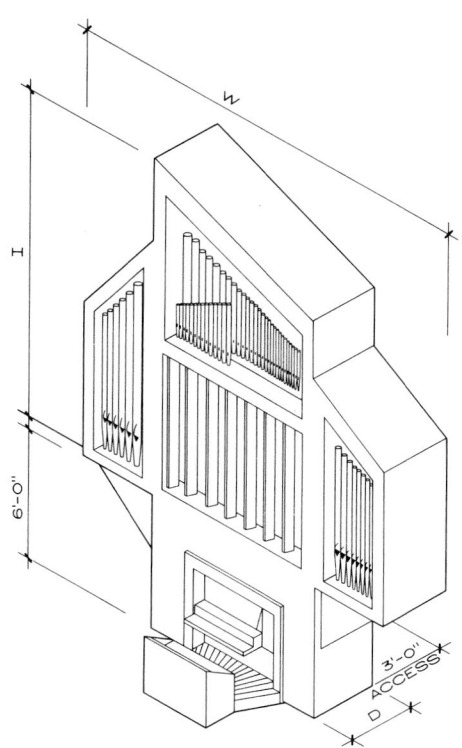

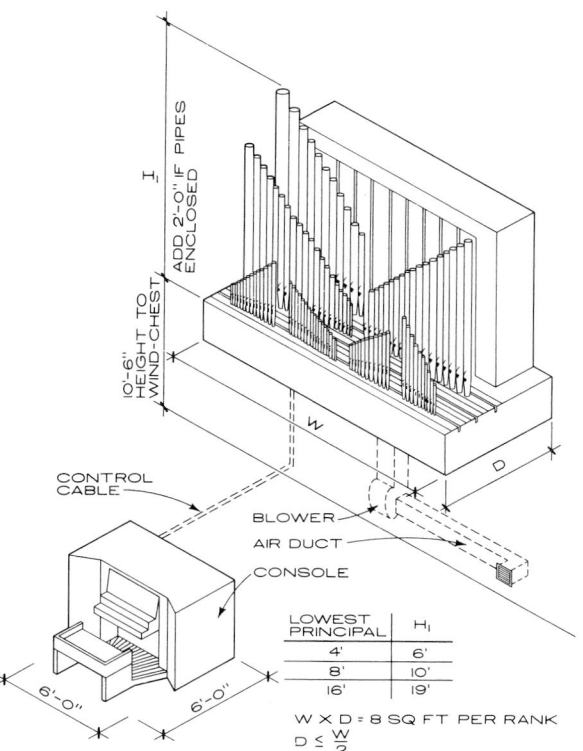

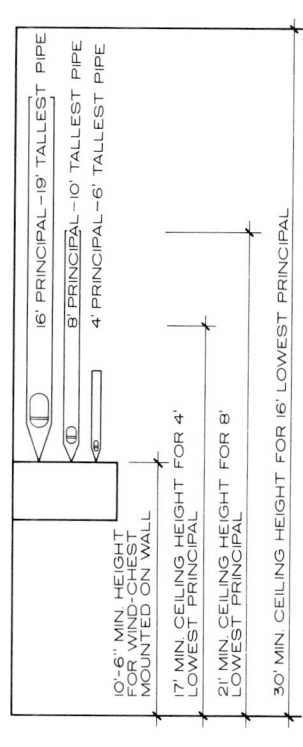

MECHANICAL ACTIONED ORGAN (TRACKER)

ELECTROMECHANICAL OR ELECTROPNEUMATIC ORGAN

PIPE ORGANS

Organ builders recommend that the pipes and casework be located within the space they are to serve, not in an organ chamber. Organ and console, located in proximity to one another, should be placed so that sound can travel freely and directly to the listeners. No furnishings, people, or other barriers should be located in front of the organ pipes. Drafts and sudden temperature changes to the pipes may necessitate more frequent tuning.

While blowers may be built in to the organ casework, quieter operation can be achieved placing the blower in a remote space. However, air for the blower should be drawn from the room in which the organ is located to avoid tuning changes. Sound isolation, power requirements, serviceability, and need for a large duct chase to the organ must be considered when designing the blower room.

The number of stops or ranks required for an organ installation is related to musical flexibility rather than the loudness of an organ. The number of manuals will also vary depending on need for flexibility in the musical program. The table below outlines general guidelines to select the number of ranks for an organ installation.

ELECTROMECHANICAL AND ELECTROPNEUMATIC ORGANS

In these types of instruments, air that passes from the wind-chests into the pipes is controlled by either electromechanical or electropneumatic means. The required size of the organ pipe space will vary depending on the organ builder, but 8 sq ft per rank may be used as a general rule of thumb. If height is available, divisions may be stacked, reducing the floor area required by approximately 25%. All pipes must be accessible for tuning.

Weight of the organ will also vary. A general average is 450 lb per rank. If the organ is enclosed in a case, 50 lb per rank should be added. A stacked arrangement of pipe divisions will increase the floor loading proportionately.

MECHANICAL ACTIONED ORGANS

Commonly know as tracker organs, these instruments introduce air into the pipes through a valve mechanically attached to the keys on the console. The size of tracker organs is measured in terms of stops rather than ranks. Tracker organs are self-contained in wooden cases that house pipes, wind-chests, manuals, and mechanical

components. Such wooden cases may be designed to complement the architecture of the surrounding space. Compared to electromechanical and electropneumatic organs, a tracker organ will usually require more height for pipe cases but consequently less floor area. Often used in chapels because of their compactness, tracker organs are not limited to use in small worship spaces. In larger installations the console may be separated from the pipe chests by a limited distance, but must nonetheless be fixed, due to the mechanical connections between manuals and pipes.

Blowers for this type of instrument are built into the organ casework. Electrical power for the blower must be provided.

Mechanical actioned organs have an average weight of 400–500 lb per stop. A 3 ft 0 in. minimum access space behind the instrument is required for servicing and tuning.

Additional information is available through the Associated Pipe Organ Builders of America.

GENERAL SIZE REQUIREMENTS BASED UPON VARIOUS SEATING CAPACITIES

NO. OF SEATS	NO. OF STOPS	NO. OF RANKS	NO. OF DIVISIONS (1)	LOWEST PRINCIPAL (2)
150	4–9	6–12	2–3	4'
200	9–13	12–16	3	8'
250	12–18	16–23	3	8'
300	15–25	18–34	3	8'
400	20–30	26–44	3	16'
500	25–35	34–50	3–4	16'
750	30–45	44–64	4	16'
1000	35–50	50–78	4	16'

MINIMUM DIMENSIONS FOR A TRACKER ORGAN CASE BASED UPON VARIOUS NUMBERS OF STOPS

NO. OF SEATS	NO. OF STOPS	NO. OF RANKS	NO. OF DIVISIONS	LOWEST PRINCIPAL	W WIDTH	D DEPTH	H HEIGHT
150	4–9	6–12	2–3	4	10'	28''	10'
200	9–13	12–16	3	8	12'	28''	12'
250	12–18	16–23	3	8	15'	36''	14'
300	15–25	18–34	3	8	18'	42''	17'
400	20–30	26–44	3	16	20'	48''	23'
500	25–55	34–50	3–4	16	22'	52''	25'
750	30–45	44–64	4	16	22'	56''	25'
1000	35–50	50–78	4	16	22'	60''	25'

Ware Associates, Inc.; Rockford, Illinois/Chicago/Los Angeles

NOTE
Dimensions given are the maximum length, height, and width found if several models and styles exist.

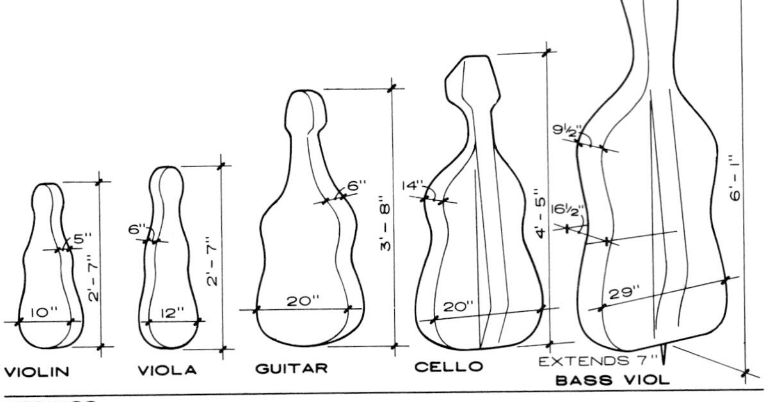

VIOLIN 5" 10" 2'-7"

VIOLA 6" 12" 2'-7"

GUITAR 16" 20" 3'-8"

CELLO 14" 6" 20" 4'-5"

BASS VIOL 9½" 16½" 6'-1" 29" EXTENDS 7"

STRINGS

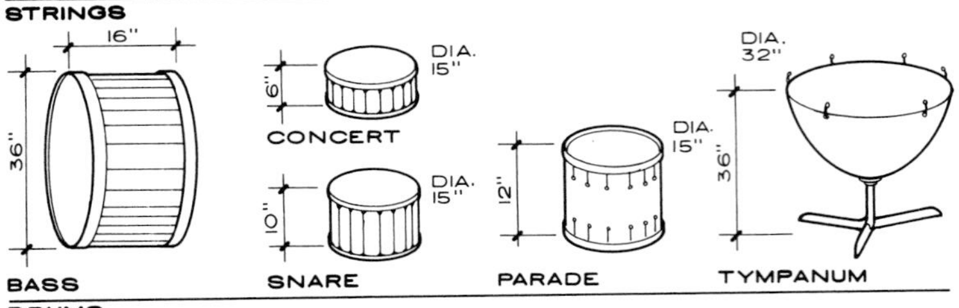

BASS 36" 16"

CONCERT 6" DIA. 15"

SNARE 10" DIA. 15"

PARADE 12" DIA. 15"

TYMPANUM DIA. 32" 36"

DRUMS

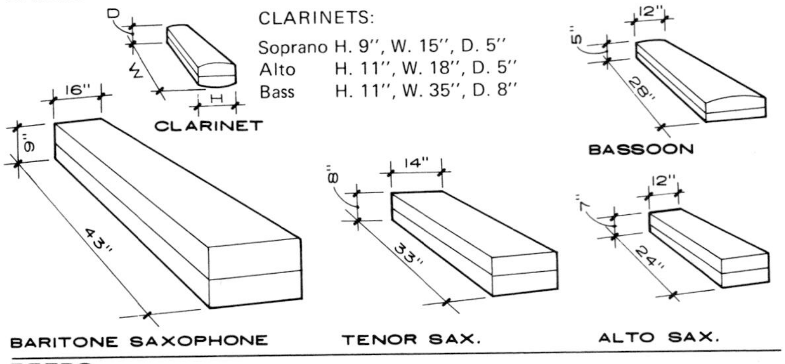

CLARINET 16" 9" D Z H

CLARINETS:
Soprano H. 9", W. 15", D. 5"
Alto   H. 11", W. 18", D. 5"
Bass   H. 11", W. 35", D. 8"

BASSOON 5" 12" 28"

BARITONE SAXOPHONE 16" 9" 43"

TENOR SAX. 8" 14" 33"

ALTO SAX. 7" 12" 24"

REEDS

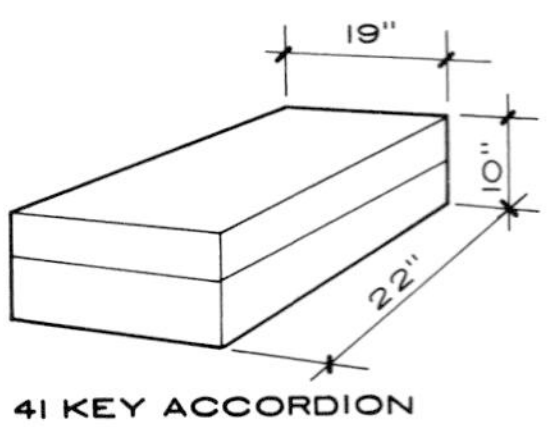

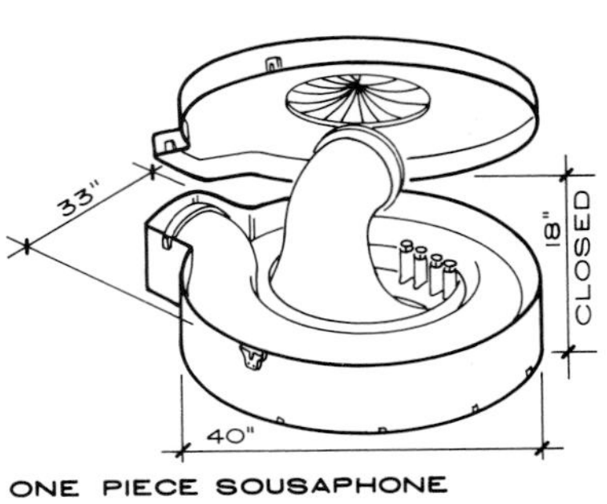

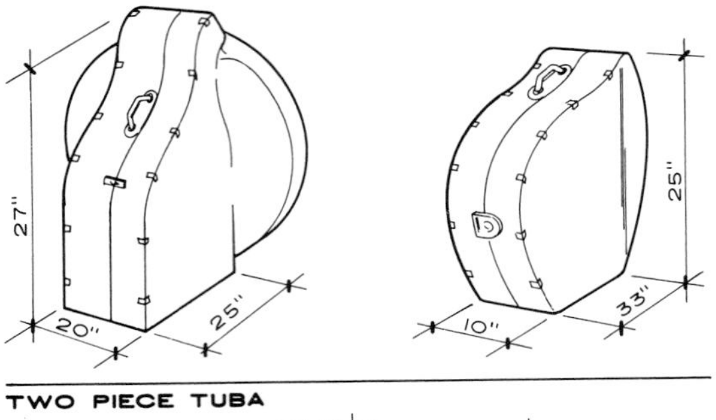

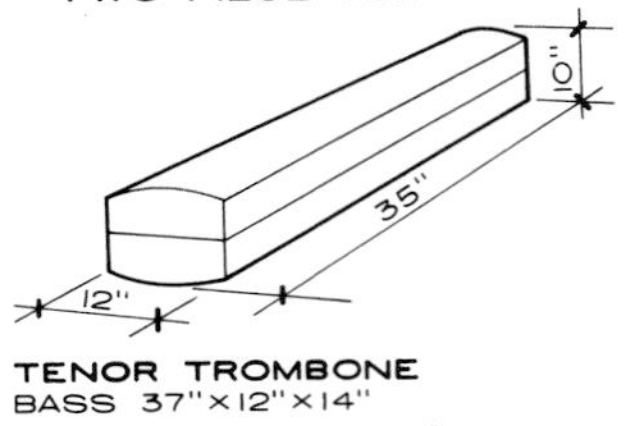

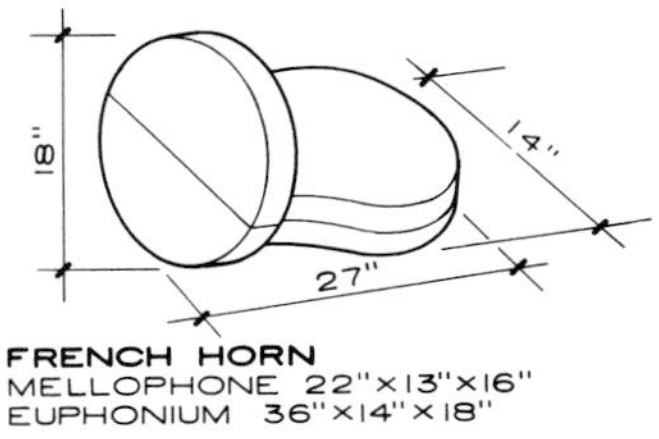

41 KEY ACCORDION 19" 10" 22"

ONE PIECE SOUSAPHONE 33" 40" 18" CLOSED

TWO PIECE TUBA 27" 20" 25" 10" 33" 25"

TENOR TROMBONE 12" 35" 10"
BASS 37"x12"x14"

FRENCH HORN 18" 27" 14"
MELLOPHONE 22"x13"x16"
EUPHONIUM 36"x14"x18"

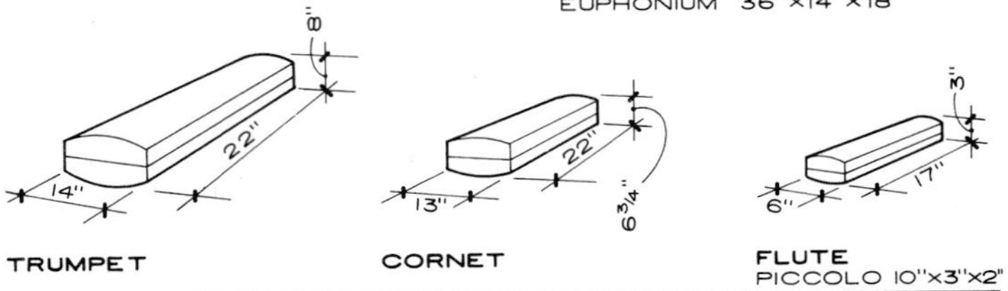

TRUMPET 14" 22" 8"

CORNET 13" 22" 6¾" 6¾"

FLUTE 6" 7" 3"
PICCOLO 10"x3"x2"

BRASS

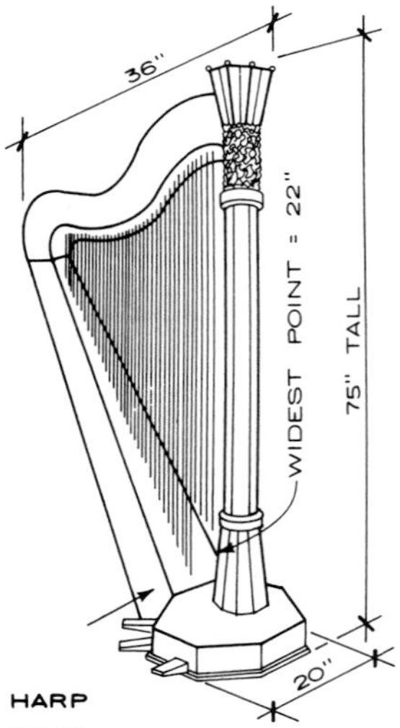

HARP 36" WIDEST POINT = 22" 75" TALL 20"

NOTE
Harps are made in various sizes. A typical larger model is shown. The widest dimension is at the "soundboard" and equals 22 in. A harp case is 25 in. wide x 84 in. deep. Total weight, including harp and case, is approximately 200 lb.

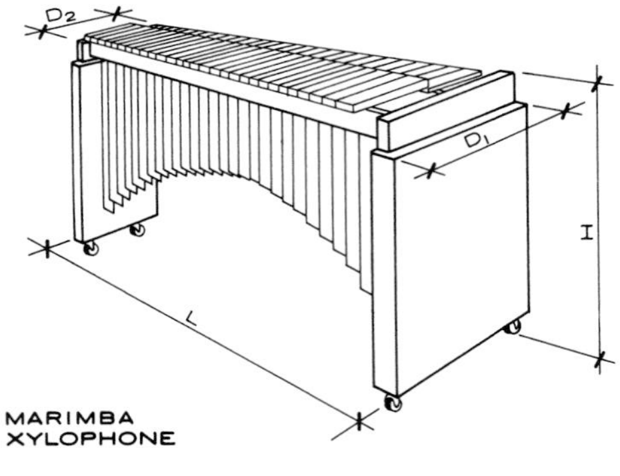

MARIMBA XYLOPHONE D₂ D₁ L H

	L	H	D₁	D₂	WEIGHT
Marimba	87	36	33	16	175 lb
Xylophone	54	34	32	13	70 lb

NOTE: All dimensions are in inches. Many sizes are manufactured. The sizes given above are typical larger size that are available.

MUSIC RACK, WHEN OPEN INCREASES "H" 8" TO 10"

MAX. SIZE SHEET MUSIC ALL INSTRUMENTS

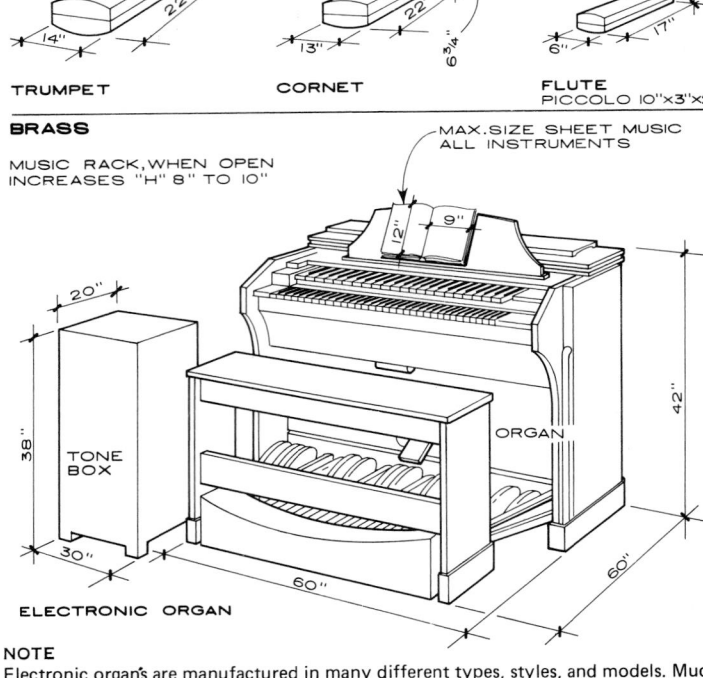

ELECTRONIC ORGAN 9" 12" 20" 38" TONE BOX 30" 60" ORGAN 42" 60"

NOTE
Electronic organs are manufactured in many different types, styles, and models. Much smaller units than that shown are available as well as models weighing several tons. In general, allow space 72 in. wide x 72 in. long x 72 in. high. Also required is a clearance of approximately 50 in. to rear of unit for servicing. Consult organ manufacturers for exact details and models available.

Pipe organs are designed to fit the building in which they are to be used. After factory assembly and testing, they are disassembled and shipped. Pipes may vary from less than 1 in. to more than 30 ft in length. A single organ may have thousands of pipes. Basic components are the pipes, wind chest, blower, valve mechanism, and keyboards.

Leland D. Blackledge, AIA; South St. Paul, Minnesota
John A. Lesire, AIA; Arlington, Virginia

11   **MUSICAL INSTRUMENTS**

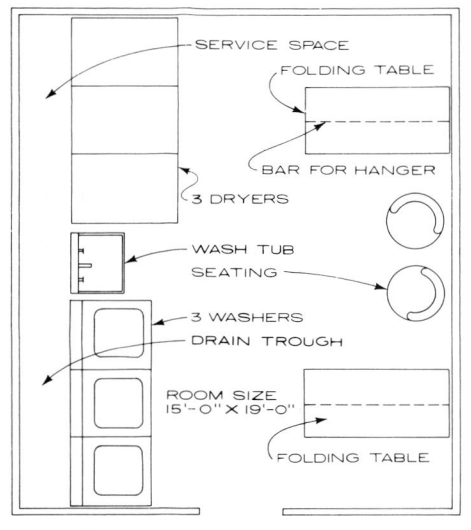

20 UNIT APARTMENT BUILDING

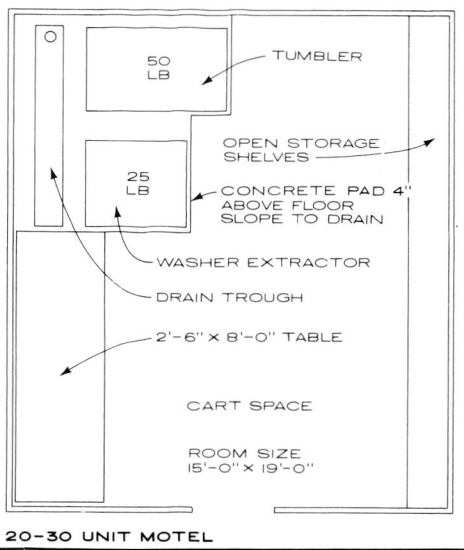

20-30 UNIT MOTEL

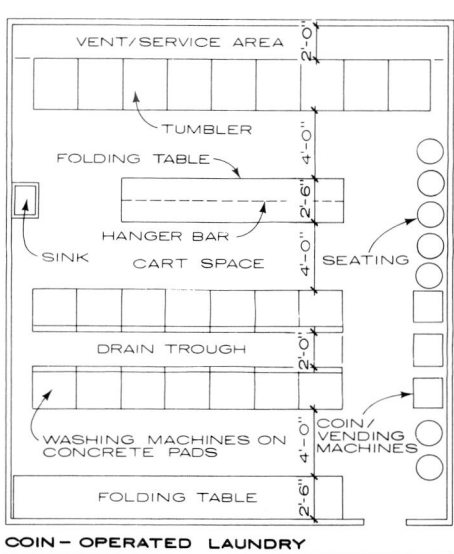

COIN - OPERATED LAUNDRY

TYPICAL PLANS FOR LAUNDRY ROOMS

DRYER SIZES

CAPACITY (LB)	WIDTH	DEPTH
30	31''	44''
50	38''	44''
75	38''	49''
100	46''	62''
200	72''	54''

NOTES

1. Drain trench underneath or behind washers is for washing machine overflow and is sized to contain one complete dump from all machines.
2. Variables that determine size of on-premise laundry machines for hotels include number of rooms and hotel occupancy (at 10 lb of laundry per room).
3. Variables that determine the mix of single, double, and triple load washing machines and size of tumblers in launderettes include the neighborhood and clientele expected.
4. Heavy-duty machines have fewer parts prone to breakage than coin-operated residential machines.
5. Tumbler capacity is twice washer capacity for permanent press fabrics.
6. Venting, electrical, and gas lines should run overhead and drop down to machines.
7. Washing machines in apartment buildings are generally coin-operated residential sizes.
8. Stackable dryers can provide a maximum utilization of space.
9. Commercial laundries must be accessible to persons with disabilities. Front-loading machines with accessible coin boxes are required.

WASHER/EXTRACTOR SIZES

CAPACITY (LB)	WIDTH	DEPTH
20	28''	30''
20-30	30''	32''
30-40	34''	36''
40-50	36''	44''
50-60	46''	40''

Above 60 lb, sizes may vary with manufacturer. Minimum clearances: 18 in. sides, 24 in. behind, and 48 in. front.

TUMBLER SIZES

CAPACITY (LB)	WIDTH	DEPTH
30	32''	45''
50	39''	47''
65	39''	53''
100	47''	64''

Minimum clearances: 24 in. behind, none sides, 48 in. front.

Duane Fisher; Richard Newlon Associates; Washington, D.C.

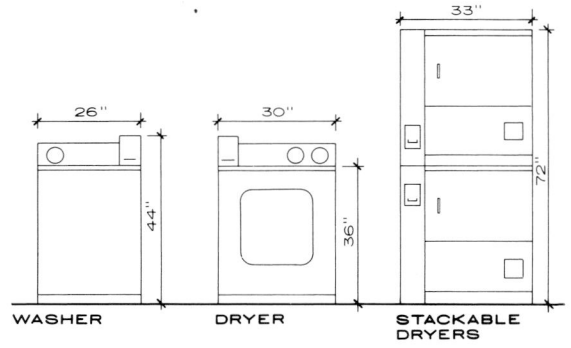

COIN - OPERATED LAUNDRY

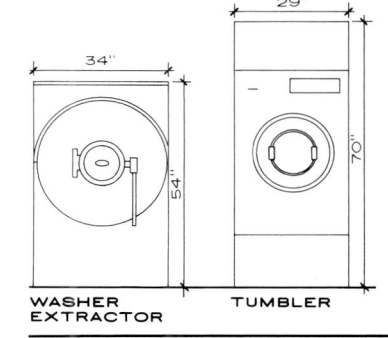

ON-SITE LAUNDRY

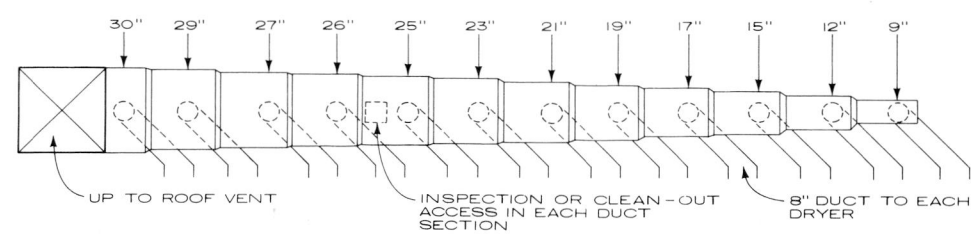

EXHAUST DUCT

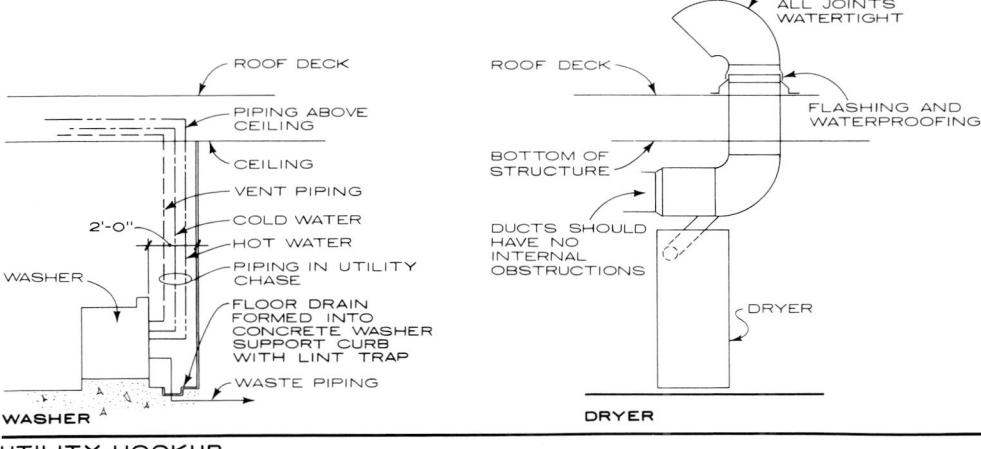

UTILITY HOOKUP

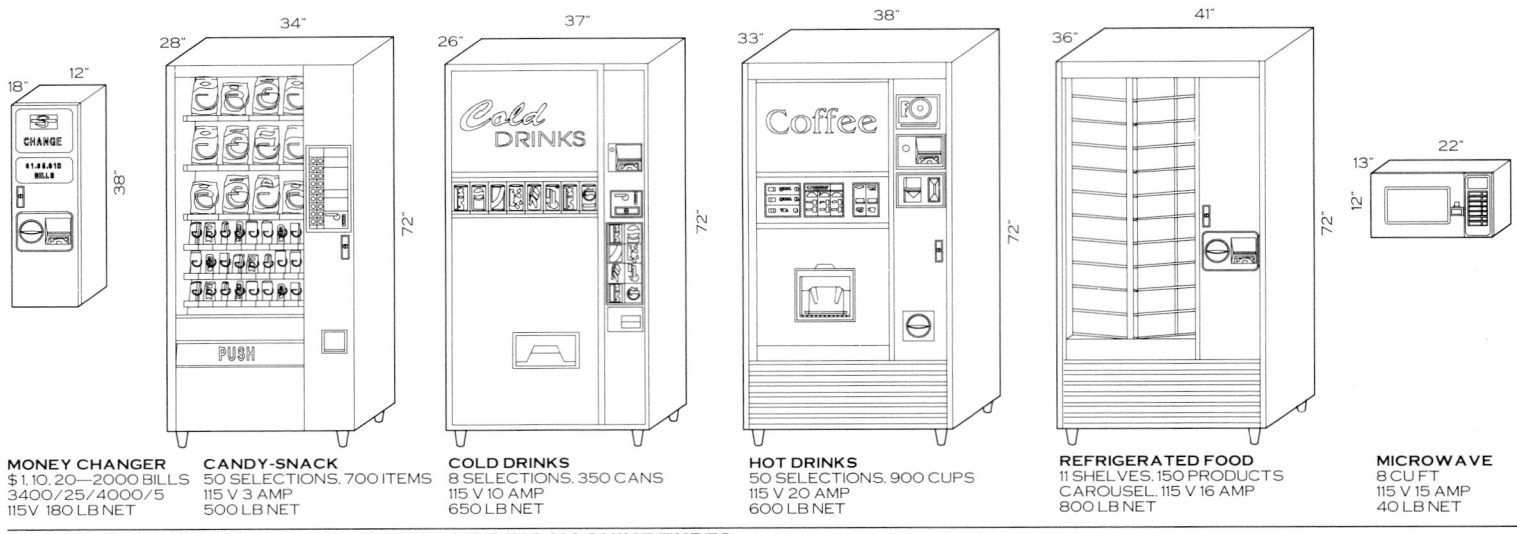

MONEY CHANGER
$1, 10, 20—2000 BILLS
3400/25/4000/5
115V 180 LB NET

CANDY-SNACK
50 SELECTIONS. 700 ITEMS
115 V 3 AMP
500 LB NET

COLD DRINKS
8 SELECTIONS. 350 CANS
115 V 10 AMP
650 LB NET

HOT DRINKS
50 SELECTIONS. 900 CUPS
115 V 20 AMP
600 LB NET

REFRIGERATED FOOD
11 SHELVES. 150 PRODUCTS
CAROUSEL. 115 V 16 AMP
800 LB NET

MICROWAVE
8 CU FT
115 V 15 AMP
40 LB NET

EXAMPLES OF MOST COMMONLY USED VENDING MACHINE TYPES

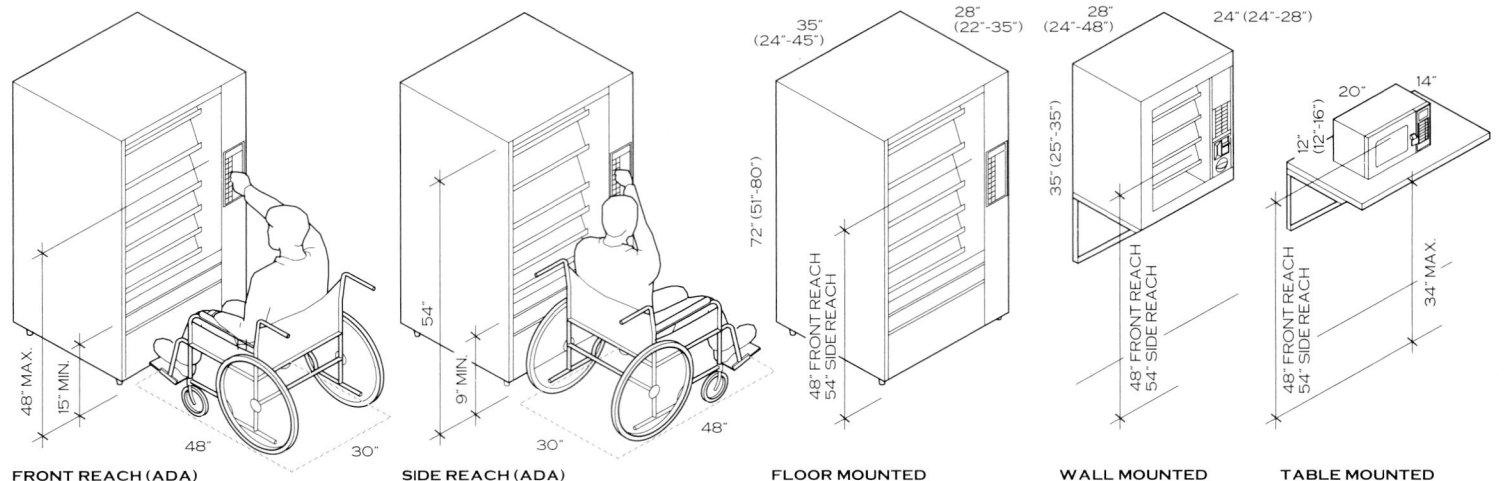

FRONT REACH (ADA) · SIDE REACH (ADA) · FLOOR MOUNTED · WALL MOUNTED · TABLE MOUNTED

NOTE: Equipment dimensions are the most commonly used. Minimum and maximum dimensions are indicated in parentheses.

EQUIPMENT AND CLEARANCE DIMENSIONS

GUIDELINES

1. Front clearance of 5 ft preferred for machines.
2. Double door or larger than 3 ft wide door is preferred for vending machine area.
3. Americans with Disabilities Act (ADA) accessibility guidelines regarding reach heights, floor spaces, and clearance requirements must be followed.
4. Service access of machines is generally from the front. Some cigarette machines require access from the top.
5. Hot water is not required. Some beverage units require cold water supply with shut-off valve. Overflow waste collects into internal tray.
6. Refrigerated vending machines and microwave ovens require a rear wall clearance of up to 8 in. to permit cooling.
7. Electric service is 115 volt. Separate circuit for each machine is preferred. Amperages vary widely from 2 to 20 amp.
8. Merchandising flexibility is important.
9. Electronic controls allow multipricing.

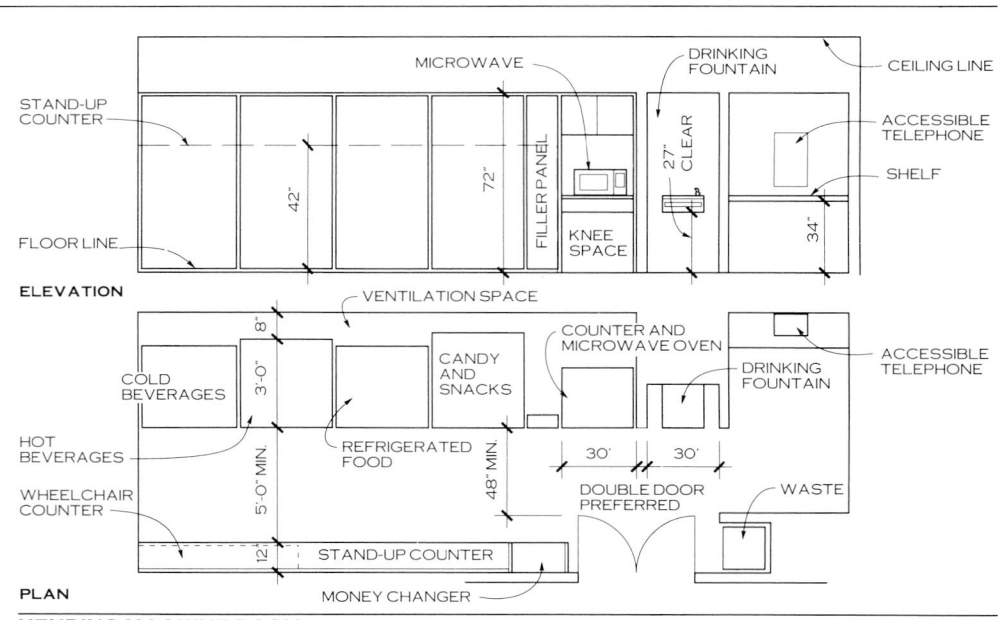

ELEVATION

PLAN

VENDING MACHINE ROOM

Charles A. Szoradi, AIA; Washington, D.C.

11   **VENDING EQUIPMENT**

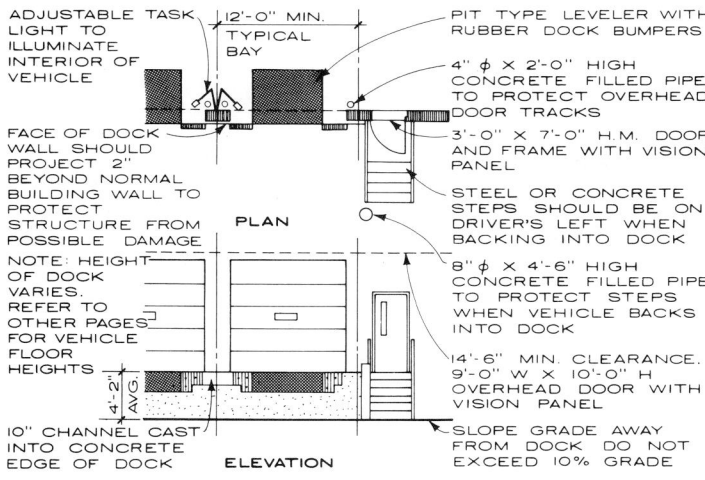

TYPICAL LOADING DOCK BAY

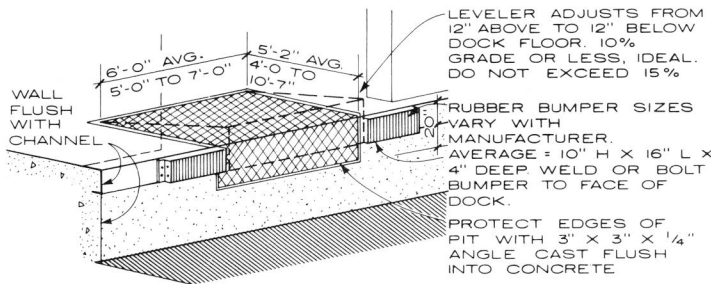

Automatic or manual operation for high volume docks where incoming vehicle heights vary widely; must be installed in a preformed concrete pit. Exact dimensions provided by manufacturer.

PIT TYPE DOCK LEVELER

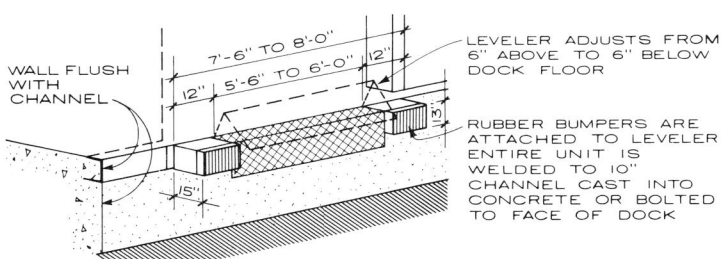

Manual operation for high or medium volume docks where pit type levelers are impractical or leased facilities are being used.

EDGE OF DOCK LEVELER

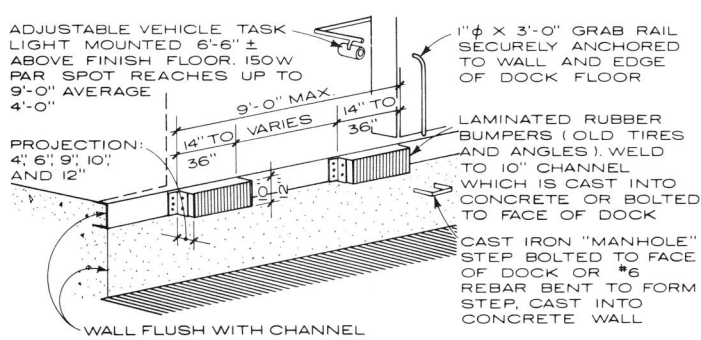

Used for low volume docks where incoming vehicle heights do not vary. Use portable type leveler such as a throw plate.

LOADING DOCK WITHOUT LEVELER

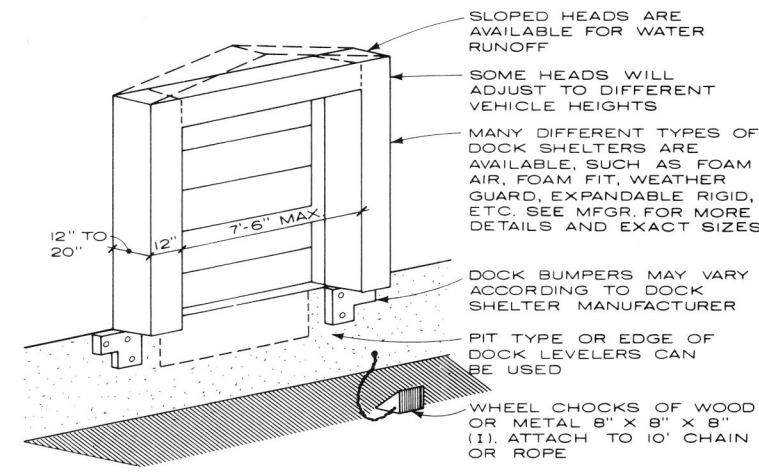

Provides positive weather seal; protects dock from wind, rain, snow, and dirt. Retains constant temperature between dock and vehicle.

CUSHIONED DOCK SHELTER

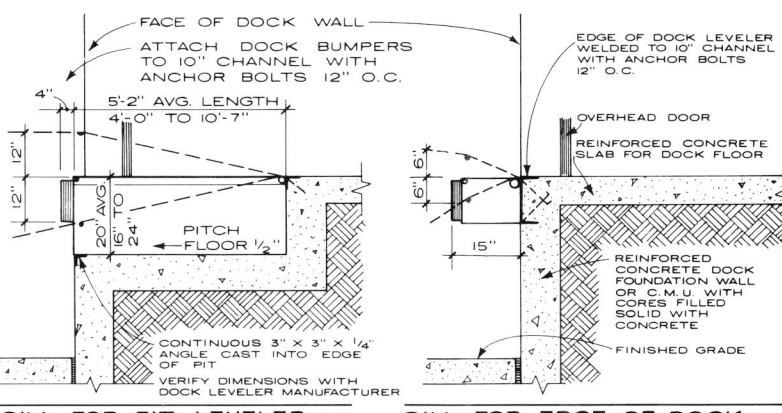

SILL FOR PIT LEVELER   **SILL FOR EDGE OF DOCK LEVELER**

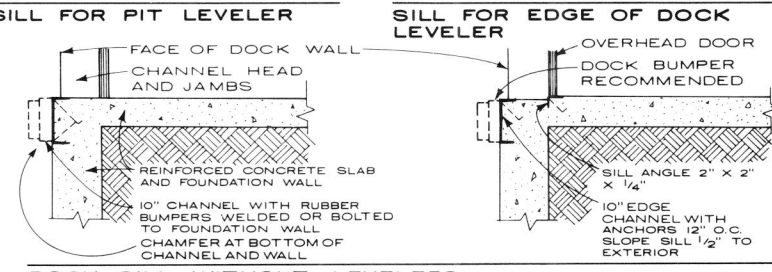

DOCK SILL WITHOUT LEVELERS

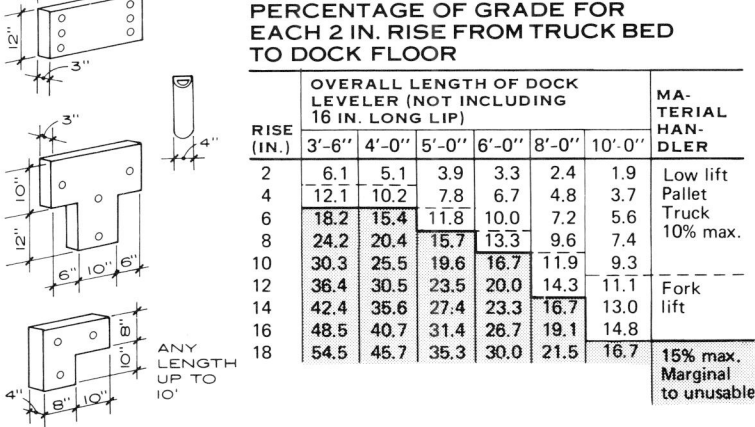

MOLDED HARD RUBBER DOCK BUMPERS

PERCENTAGE OF GRADE FOR EACH 2 IN. RISE FROM TRUCK BED TO DOCK FLOOR

RISE (IN.)	OVERALL LENGTH OF DOCK LEVELER (NOT INCLUDING 16 IN. LONG LIP)						MATERIAL HANDLER
	3'-6"	4'-0"	5'-0"	6'-0"	8'-0"	10'-0"	
2	6.1	5.1	3.9	3.3	2.4	1.9	Low lift
4	12.1	10.2	7.8	6.7	4.8	3.7	Pallet Truck
6	18.2	15.4	11.8	10.0	7.2	5.6	10% max.
8	24.2	20.4	15.7	13.3	9.6	7.4	
10	30.3	25.5	19.6	16.7	11.9	9.3	
12	36.4	30.5	23.5	20.0	14.3	11.1	Fork lift
14	42.4	35.6	27.4	23.3	16.7	13.0	
16	48.5	40.7	31.4	26.7	19.1	14.8	
18	54.5	45.7	35.3	30.0	21.5	16.7	15% max. Marginal to unusable

Robert H. Lorenz, AIA; Preston Trucking Company, Inc.; Preston, Maryland

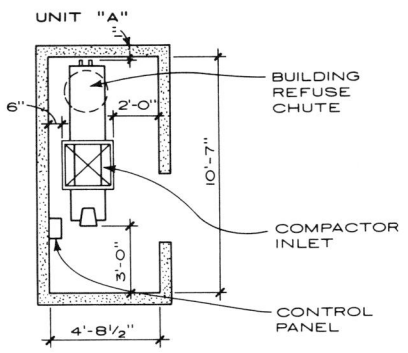

ROOM PLAN

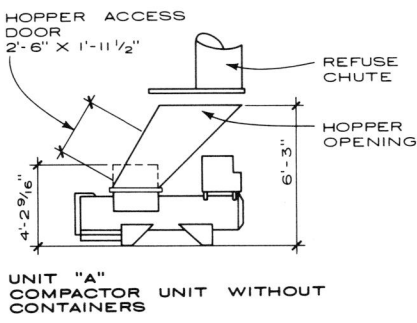

UNIT "A"
COMPACTOR UNIT WITHOUT
CONTAINERS

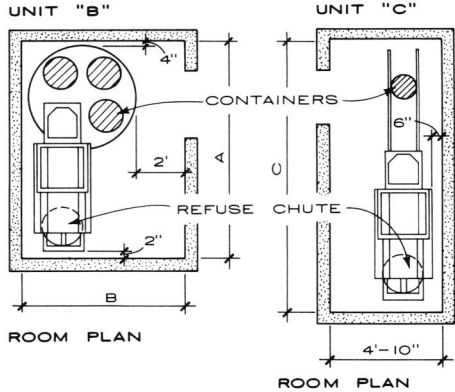

ROOM PLAN

NO. OF CONTAINERS	A	B	C
3			11'-10''
4	9'-8''	7'-0''	13'-5''
5			17'-1''
6	10'-6''	8'-0''	
8	11'-6''	9'-1''	
10	12'-6''	10'-9''	

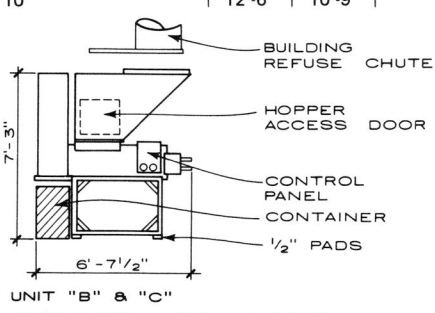

UNIT "B" & "C"
COMPACTOR WITH STORAGE
CONTAINERS

WASTE COMPACTORS AND CONTAINERS

UNIT TYPE	SIZE	CAPACITY OF CONTAINER
Average household compactor	12'' W, 24'' D, 33½''–34½'' H	1.3 cu ft
Small industrial	See units A, B, and C	4 cu ft per bag
Industrial	See unit D	2 cu yd per container
Schools, offices, restaurants	26'' W, 53'' H, 31'' D	6 cu ft
Apartment house stationary compactor with roll away containers	Units vary	2 to 8 cu yd
Industrial waste containers	95'' W, 36'' H, 62'' D to 95'' W, 102'' H, 92'' D	3 to 15 cu yd
Heavy duty industrial waste containers	8' ± W, 8'-10'' H, 23'-2'' L	Up to 43 cu yd
Combination shredder/compactor	45'' W, 29'' D, 78'' H See unit "E"	5.25 cu ft per bag

APARTMENT SELECTION GUIDE

The daily refuse output of 15 to 30 apartments is approximately ½ cu yd (13½ cu ft) weighing about 75 lb. At standard compaction ratios of 4 or 5 to 1, a compactor will reduce the refuse to an approximate volume of 3 cu ft.

If the apartments are large, averaging two or three bedrooms, use the figure of 15 apartments per bag. If apartments average one or two bedrooms, use 20 to 25 apartments per compacted bag, and if the units are small efficiency apartments or one-bedroom apartments occupied by young working people or the elderly, use the figure of 30 apartments per compacted bag per day.

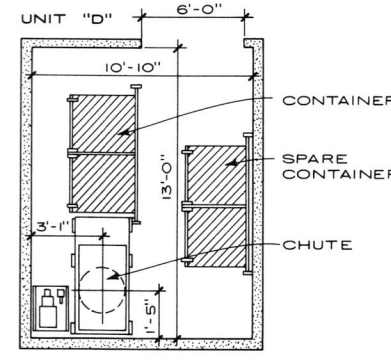

ROOM PLAN

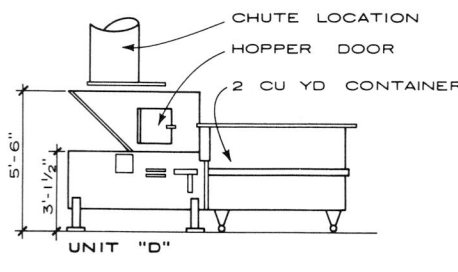

UNIT "D"
INDUSTRIAL COMPACTOR

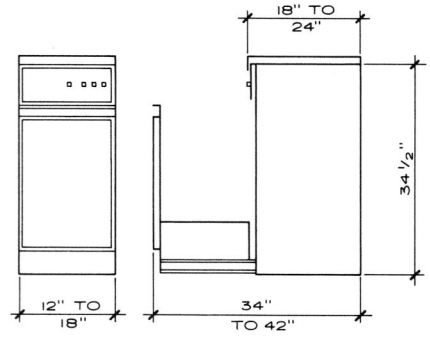

AVERAGE HOUSEHOLD COMPACTOR

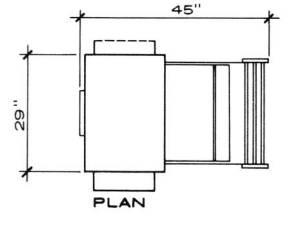

PLAN

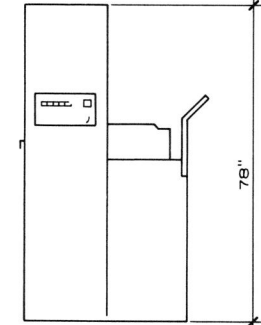

UNIT "E"
COMBINATION SHREDDER
COMPACTOR

Walter H. Sobel, FAIA, & Associates; Chicago, Illinois

BOTTLE AND CASE DIMENSIONS

SIZE	BORDEAUX	BURGUNDY	CHAMPAGNE	WEIGHT
BOTTLE DIMENSIONS (IN.)				
375 ml				
Diameter	2.4	2.6	2.8	
Length	9.5	9.5	10.5	1.5 lb
Incremental height	2.1	2.3	2.5	
750 ml				
Diameter	3.0	3.2	3.5	
Length	12.0	11.8	12.5	2.9 lb
Incremental height	2.6	2.8	3.0	
1.5 L				
Diameter	3.8	4.2	4.4	
Length	14.0	14.0	14.8	5.5 lb
Incremental height	3.3	3.6	3.8	

NOTES

1. Bordeaux bottles represent the majority of wine from Italy, and from parts of France and the United States.
2. Burgundy bottles are from some parts of France and the United States.
3. Champagne bottle sizes are universal.
4. Incremental height of bottles is used where bottles are stacked staggered.

PREMANUFACTURED CELLARS

BOTTLE CAPACITY	HEIGHT (IN.)	WIDTH (IN.)	DEPTH (IN.)
50	34	24	24
465	74	52	27
765	80	73	49
1950	80	73	108

GENERAL NOTES

1. The ideal temperature range is 55-58°F. Temperature consistency is very important. Avoid diurnal swings in temperature, but a yearly variation of 5-10° is acceptable.
2. Relative humidity should stay in the 60-80% range. Lower humidity promotes evaporation loss through bottle corks; higher humidity allows mold, which breaks down the cellulose in labels and storage structures.

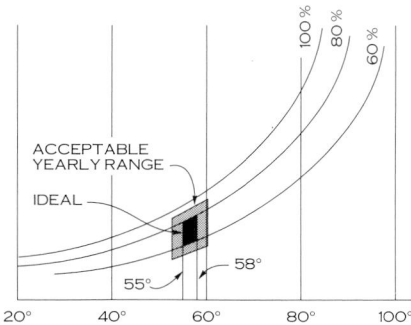

PSYCHROMETRIC CHART

3. Larger cellars should accommodate a range of storage options from individual bottles to full cases.
4. Air conditioning equipment may be single unit or split systems. Use systems designed for wine storage. Standard commercial refrigeration is too cold and lowers humidity. Standard room units are not designed to operate at low enough temperatures and coils tend to ice up.
5. In humid areas, provide a vapor barrier installed on the warm side of walls and ceilings.

SAMPLE ESTIMATION OF AREA REQUIREMENTS

To find the area required for a cellar to hold 2000 bottles of wine:

1. 2000 bottles (divided by) 12 = 166.66 cases
   Total weight = 5800 lbs.
2. One case occupies approximately one square foot of wall area.
3. Assume cases are raised off the floor one foot, and bottles are stacked five feet high. Therefore, 33.33 linear feet of wall area is required (166.66 (divided by) 5).
4. Assuming a minimum 3 ft aisle between storage bins along walls yields a cellar 5 ft wide by 16 ft long.

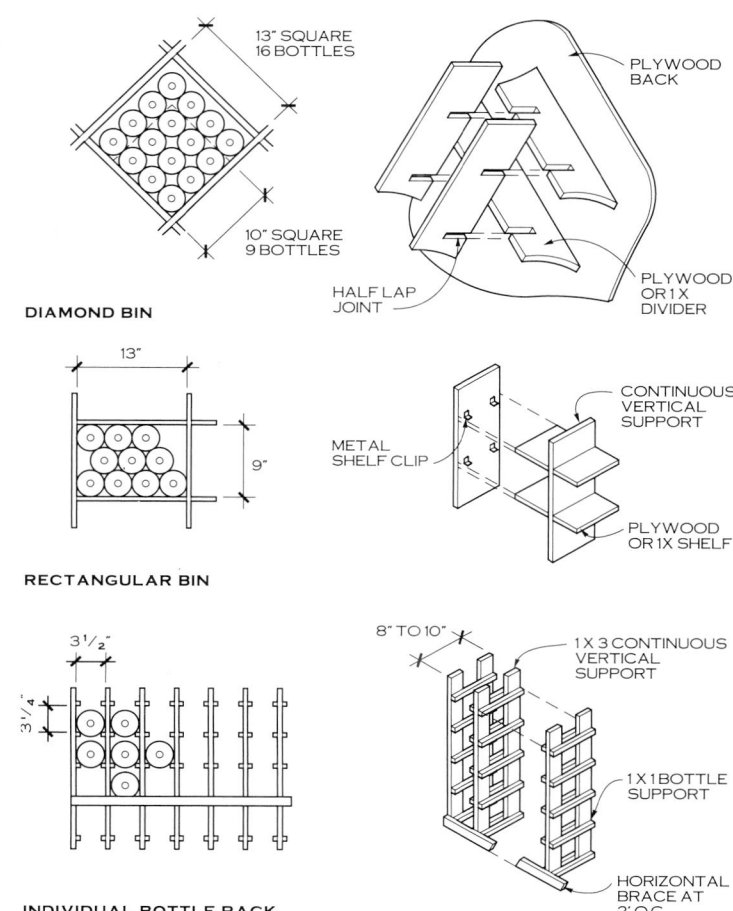

DIAMOND BIN

RECTANGULAR BIN

INDIVIDUAL BOTTLE RACK

BOTTLE STORAGE CONFIGURATIONS

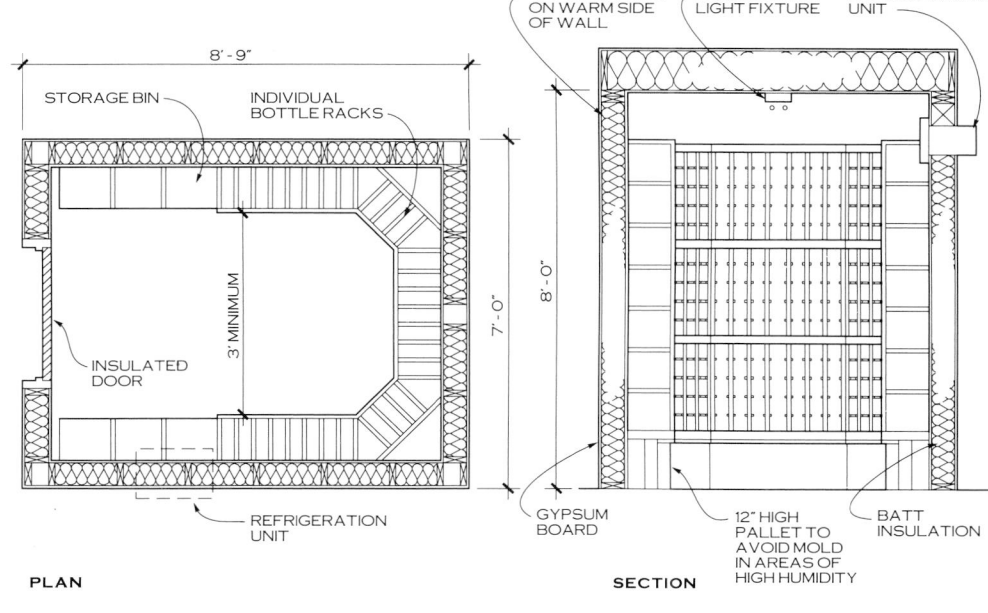

PLAN

SECTION

WOOD FRAME CELLAR FOR 875 BOTTLES

J.T. Devine, AIA, and Robert E. Anderson, AIA; Robert E. Anderson Architect, AIA; Santa Rosa, California

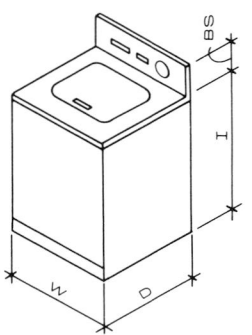

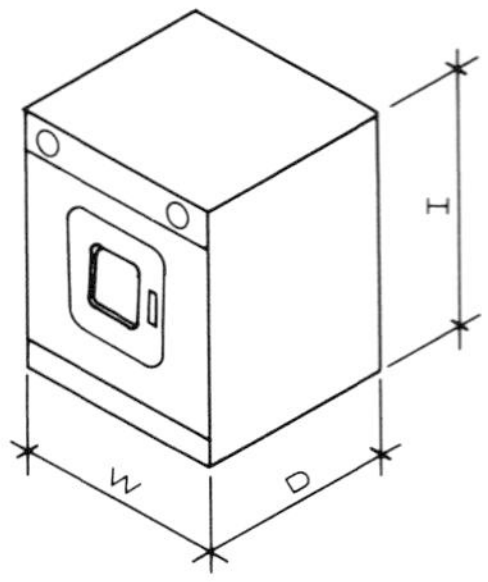

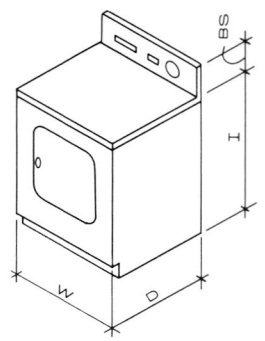

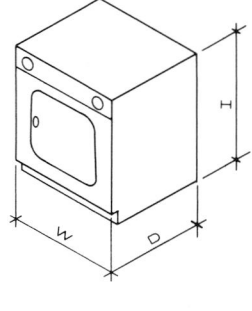

FREESTANDING – TOP OR
FRONT LOADING

UNDER COUNTER

FREESTANDING
FRONT LOADING

UNDER COUNTER

AUTOMATIC WASHERS (SOME HAVE KICK SPACES, SOME NOT)

	MIN.	MAX.	OTHER
W	25½	27	25⅝–26¾
D	24⅞	28²³⁄₃₂	25–28⁵⁄₁₆
H	36	36½	36⅛–36¼
BS	6³⁄₃₂	8¾	6½–8½

	MIN.	MAX.
W	26¾	30¼
D	24⅞	24⅞
H	34½	

AUTOMATIC DRYERS (SOME HAVE KICK SPACES, SOME NOT)

	MIN.	MAX.	OTHER
W	26¾	31½	27–31
D	24⅞	28²³⁄₃₂	25–28⁵⁄₁₆
H	36	36½	36⅛–36¼
BS	6³⁄₃₂	8¾	6½–8½

	MIN.	MAX.
W	26¾	
D	24⅞	
H	34½	

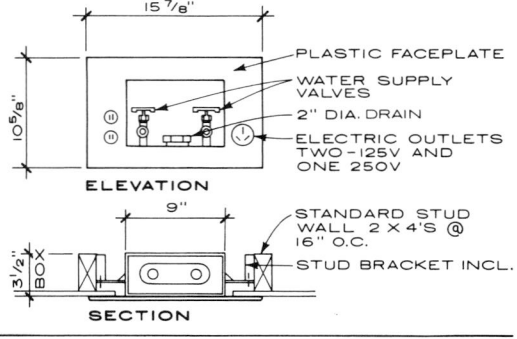

ELEVATION

SECTION

UTILITY CONNECTION BOX (RECESSED)

- PLASTIC FACEPLATE
- WATER SUPPLY VALVES
- 2" DIA. DRAIN
- ELECTRIC OUTLETS TWO – 125V AND ONE 250V
- STANDARD STUD WALL 2 X 4'S @ 16" O.C.
- STUD BRACKET INCL.

GENERAL NOTES

See kitchen & laundry layout pages for locations of washers & dryers and wall chases for pipes & vents and for dishwasher locations.

Where clearances of doors of machines (when open) may be a problem, check manufacturers catalog for "open-door" dimension.

All dimensions given are actual ones but certain variations in body design may affect actual depths of models. Check all units for exact voltage. Some units available with gas.

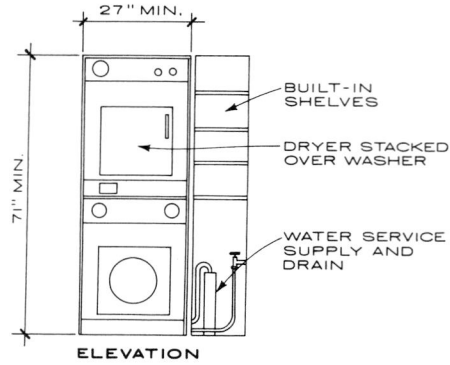

ELEVATION

- BUILT-IN SHELVES
- DRYER STACKED OVER WASHER
- WATER SERVICE SUPPLY AND DRAIN

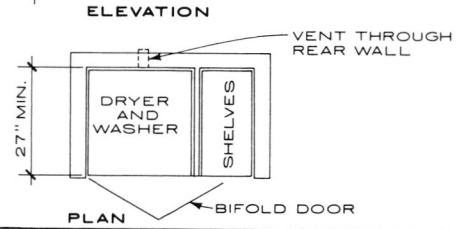

PLAN

- VENT THROUGH REAR WALL
- BIFOLD DOOR

WASHER AND DRYER STACKED
IN CLOSET

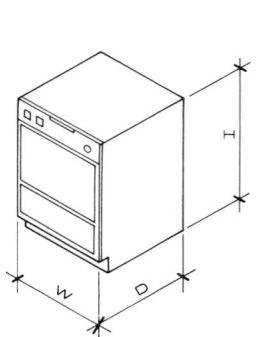

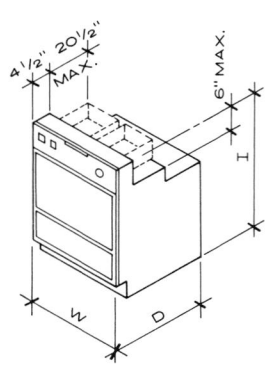

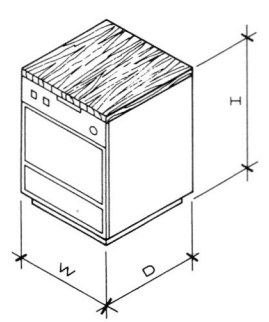

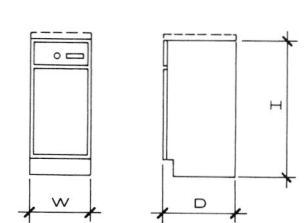

AUTOMATIC DISHWASHERS

UNDER COUNTER				UNDER SINK				MOBILE (WITH COUNTER TOP)			
	MIN.	MAX.	OTHER		MIN.	MAX.	OTHER		MIN.	MAX.	OTHER
W	23	24	23⅞	W	24	24¼	24	W	22½	27	24⅝
D	23¹¹⁄₁₆	26¼	25½	D	24	25½	25	D	23¹¹⁄₁₆	26½	25
H	33½	34½	34⅛	H	34½	34½	34½	H	34⅛	39	36

TRASH COMPACTOR: UNDER COUNTER OR FREESTANDING

	MIN.	MAX.	OTHER
W	11⅞	17¾	14⅞
D	18	24³⁄₁₆	18¼
H	33½	35	34½

William G. Miner, AIA, Architect; Washington, D.C.
R.E. Powe, Jr., AIA; Hugh Newell Jacobsen, FAIA; Washington, D.C.

11   **RESIDENTIAL EQUIPMENT**

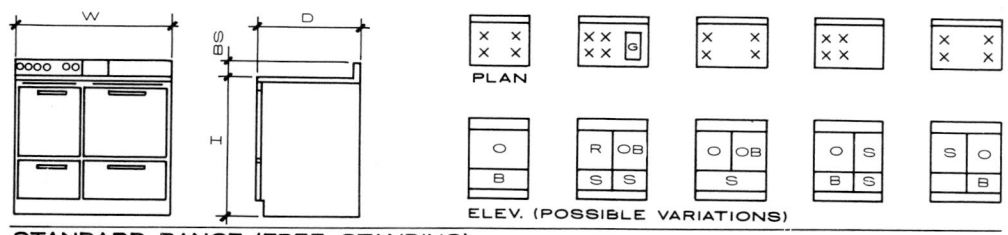

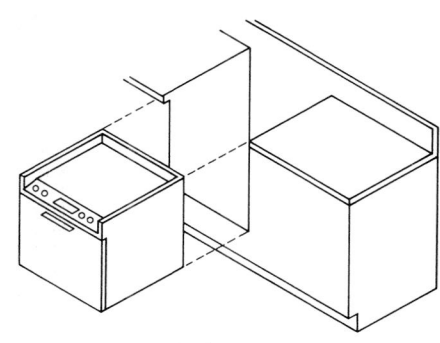

STANDARD RANGE (FREE STANDING)

ELEV. (POSSIBLE VARIATIONS)

ONE OVEN—FOUR UNITS

	MIN.	MAX.	OTHER
W	$19\frac{1}{2}$	40	21–30
D	$24\frac{1}{4}$	$27\frac{1}{2}$	$25–26\frac{1}{4}$
H	$35\frac{1}{8}$	$36\frac{1}{8}$	$35\frac{1}{4}–36$
BS	$4\frac{11}{16}$	$12\frac{1}{2}$	$8\frac{1}{4}–11\frac{1}{2}$

TWO OVENS FOUR UNITS

	MIN.	MAX.	OTHER
W	40		
D	25	$27\frac{1}{2}$	$25\frac{1}{2}–26\frac{1}{4}$
H	$35\frac{1}{8}$	36	$35\frac{1}{4}$
BS	$8\frac{1}{4}$	$11\frac{1}{8}$	$8\frac{1}{8}–10\frac{3}{8}$

SYMBOLS
O–OVEN
B–BROILER
G–REVOLVING GRILL
X–BURNER, GAS OR ELECTRIC
W–WARMING OVEN
S–STORAGE
R–ROTISSERIE

DROP-IN RANGE

	MIN.	MAX.	OTHER
W	$22\frac{7}{8}$	30	$23\frac{7}{8}$
D	$22\frac{1}{8}$	25	$22\frac{1}{2}–24$
H	23	$24\frac{1}{16}$	$23\frac{1}{2}$

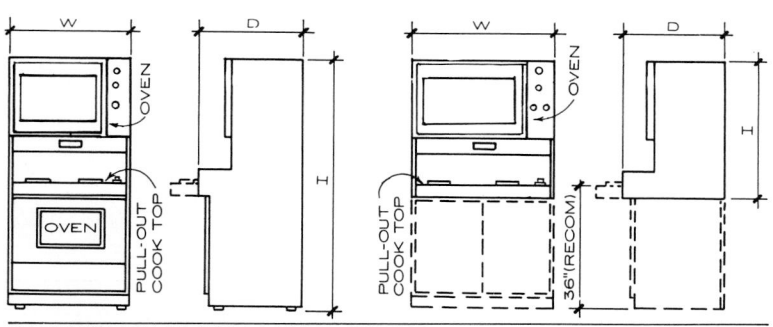

RANGES WITH EYE LEVEL OVENS

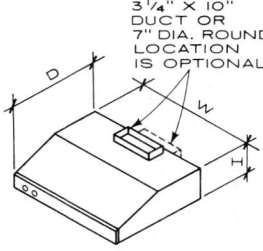

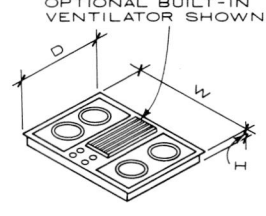

DOUBLE OVEN—4 UNITS

	MIN.	MAX.	OTHER
W	$29\frac{7}{8}$	30	
D	$25\frac{1}{2}$	$27\frac{5}{8}$	$25\frac{5}{8}–27\frac{1}{2}$
H	$61\frac{1}{2}$	$71\frac{1}{4}$	$63\frac{3}{4}–67\frac{7}{16}$

SINGLE OVEN TOP ONLY—4 UNITS

	MIN.	MAX.	OTHER
W	$29\frac{13}{16}$	$38\frac{7}{8}$	$29\frac{7}{8}$
D	$25\frac{1}{2}$	$27\frac{5}{8}$	$27\frac{1}{4}$
H	$33\frac{1}{2}$	$41\frac{1}{16}$	$36\frac{3}{4}$

DOUBLE OVEN TOP ONLY—4 UNITS

	MIN.	MAX.	OTHER
W	39	$40\frac{1}{4}$	40
D	$25\frac{1}{2}$	$27\frac{5}{8}$	$26\frac{3}{4}$
H	$34\frac{7}{8}$	$36\frac{3}{4}$	

Range hoods are available with vents as shown or without vent. Manufacturers provide accessories such as fans, filters, and lights.

RANGE HOOD

	MIN.	MAX.	OTHER
W	24	72	30–66
D	12	$27\frac{1}{2}$	17–26
H	$5\frac{1}{2}$	$8\frac{5}{8}$	$5\frac{5}{8}–7\frac{1}{2}$

Cook tops are available with two to seven heating elements. Griddles, grills, and built-in ventilators are optional.

BUILT-IN COOK TOP ELECTRIC OR GAS

	MIN.	MAX.
W	12	48
D	18	22
H	2	3

NOTE
SELF CLEANING OVENS MUST VENT TO OUTSIDE

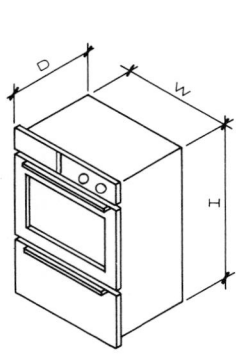

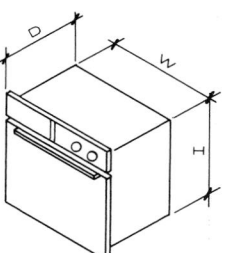

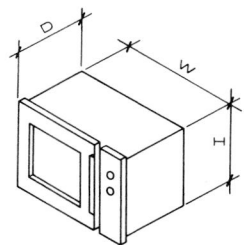

OVEN AND BROILER

	MIN.	MAX.	OTHER
W	21	$24\frac{1}{4}$	$22\frac{1}{2}–24$
D	$21\frac{1}{8}$	24	$22\frac{1}{2}–22\frac{11}{16}$
H	38	$40\frac{7}{16}$	$40\frac{3}{16}$

DOUBLE OVEN

	MIN.	MAX.	OTHER
W	21	$24\frac{1}{4}$	$22\frac{1}{2}–24$
D	$21\frac{1}{8}$	24	$22\frac{1}{2}–22\frac{11}{16}$
H	$39\frac{1}{4}$	$50\frac{3}{8}$	$42–46\frac{13}{16}$

SINGLE OVEN

	MIN.	MAX.	OTHER
W	21	$24\frac{1}{4}$	$22\frac{1}{2}–24$
D	$21\frac{1}{8}$	24	$22\frac{1}{2}–22\frac{11}{16}$
H	$23\frac{1}{2}$	$26\frac{7}{8}$	25

MICROWAVE OVEN

	MIN.	MAX.	OTHER
W	$21\frac{1}{2}$	$24\frac{3}{4}$	$22\frac{1}{2}$
D	$14\frac{1}{2}$	22	$18\frac{3}{4}$
H	$13\frac{5}{8}$	18	17

BUILT-IN WALL OVENS (GAS OR ELECTRIC)

NOTES

1. Check manufacturers requirements for rough clearances.

2. Dimensions shown are in inches.

3. Optional equipment available for ranges or wall ovens are broilers and rotisseries.

William G. Miner, AIA, Architect; Washington, D.C.
R.E. Powe, Jr., AIA; Hugh Newell Jacobsen, FAIA; Washington, D.C.

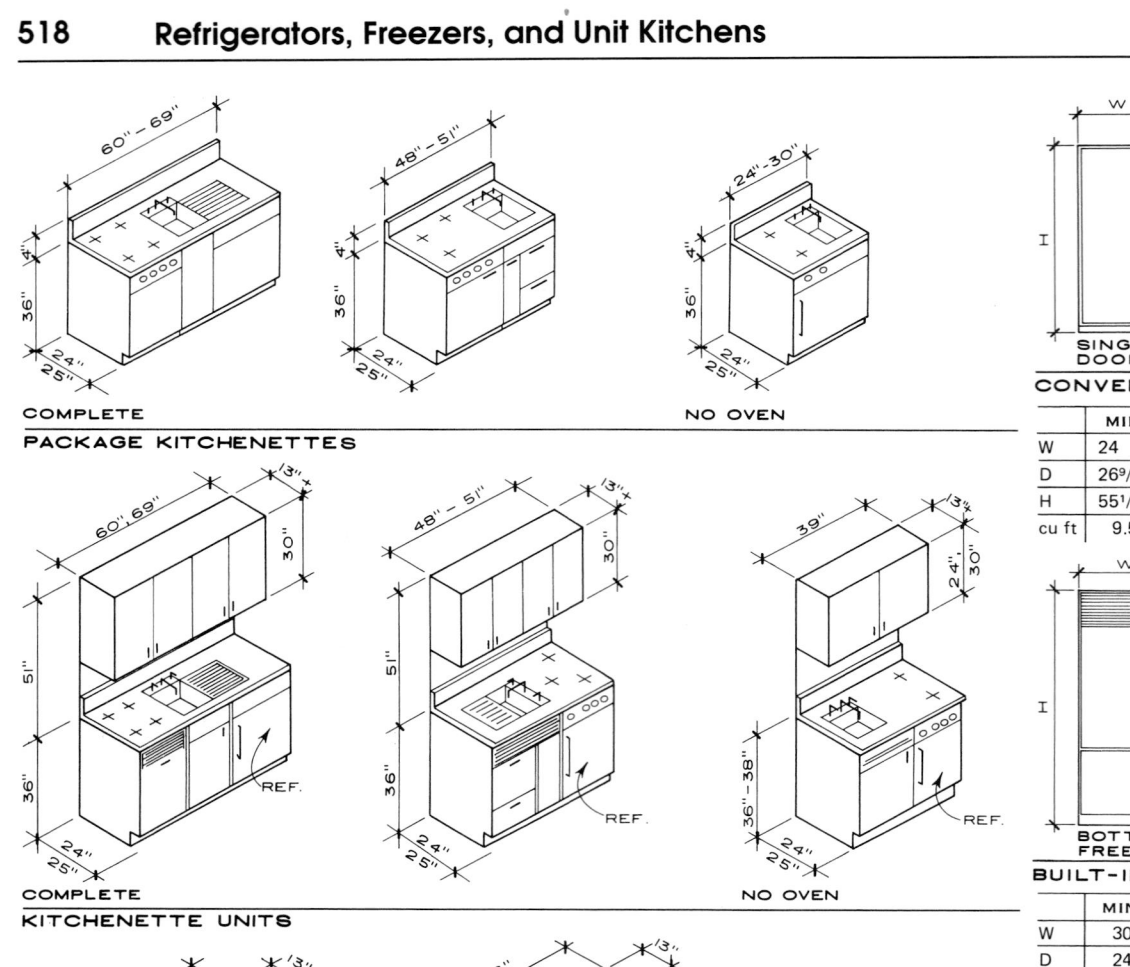

COMPLETE   NO OVEN

PACKAGE KITCHENETTES

COMPLETE   NO OVEN

KITCHENETTE UNITS

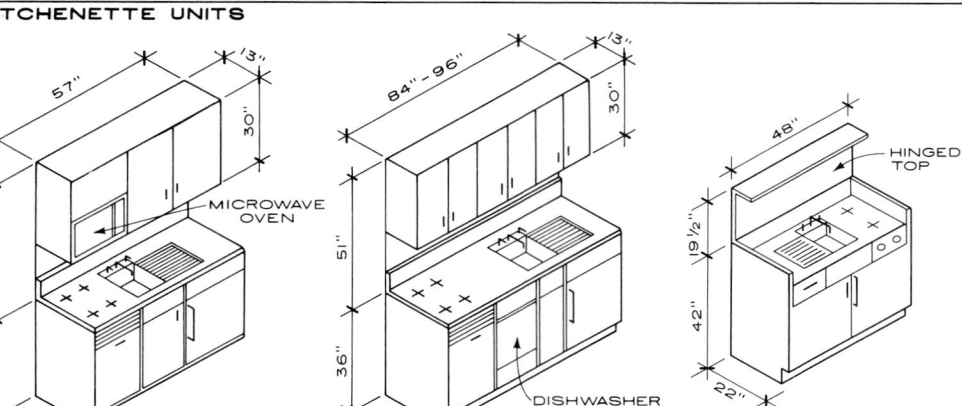

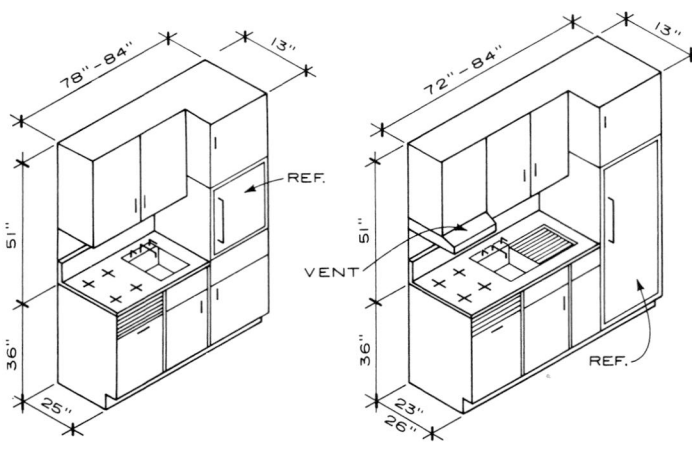

SPECIAL KITCHENETTE UNITS

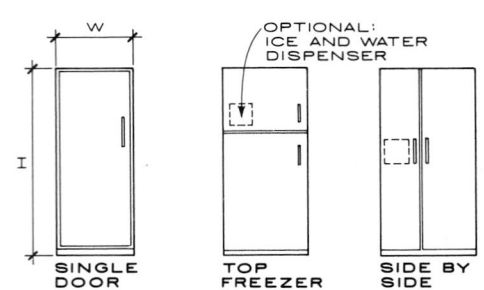

CONVENTIONAL REFRIGERATORS

	MIN.	MAX.	MIN.	MAX.	MIN.	MAX.
W	24	$32^3/_4$	28	$32^3/_4$	$30^1/_2$	$35^3/_4$
D	$26^9/_{16}$	$31^5/_8$	$28^3/_4$	$31^5/_8$	$29^1/_2$	$32^7/_8$
H	$55^1/_2$	$63^1/_2$		66	64	$68^7/_8$
cu ft	9.5	14.0	11.8	22.4	18.5	25.6

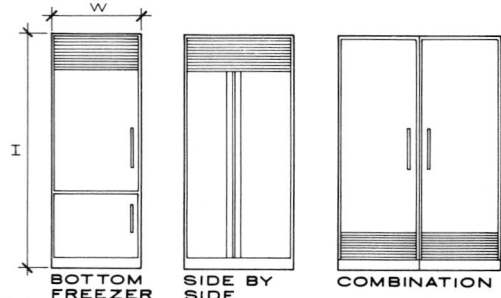

BUILT-IN REFRIGERATORS

	MIN.	MAX.	MIN.	MAX.	OVERALL
W	30	36	36	48	72
D	24	24	24	24	24
H	84	84	84	84	73
cu ft	19	23.6	24	32	42

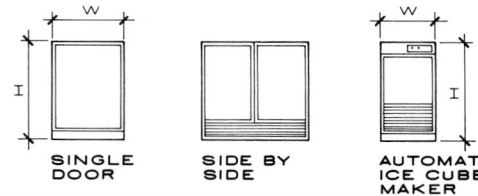

UNDERCOUNTER REFRIGERATORS

	OVERALL	OVERALL	MIN.	MAX.
W	24	36	15	$17^7/_8$
D	$23^3/_4$	$23^3/_4$	$20^3/_8$	$23^{13}/_{16}$
H	$34^1/_2$	$34^1/_2$	$33^1/_8$	$34^{13}/_{32}$
cu ft	5.2	6.0	35 lb of ice	

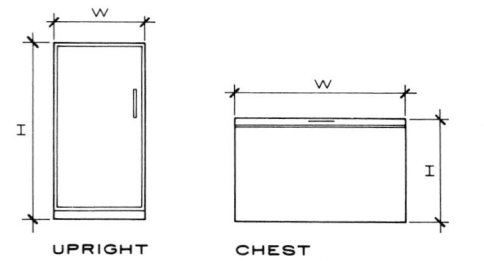

FREEZERS

	MIN.	MAX.	MIN.	MAX.
W	28	32	25	$69^1/_2$
D	$28^7/_8$	$30^{11}/_{16}$	$23^1/_4$	31
H	$59^1/_8$	$70^1/_8$	$34^{11}/_{16}$	35
cu ft	11.6	21.1		25.3

NOTE

See manufacturers' catalogues for actual dimensions of specific units which may include: number of burners, size of refrigerator, size of sink, finish materials, and options such as garbage disposer, range hood, microwave oven, ice maker, dishwasher, or freezer.

William G. Miner, AIA, Architect; Washington, D.C.
R.E. Powe, Jr., AIA; Hugh Newell Jacobsen, FAIA; Washington, D.C.

11   **RESIDENTIAL EQUIPMENT**

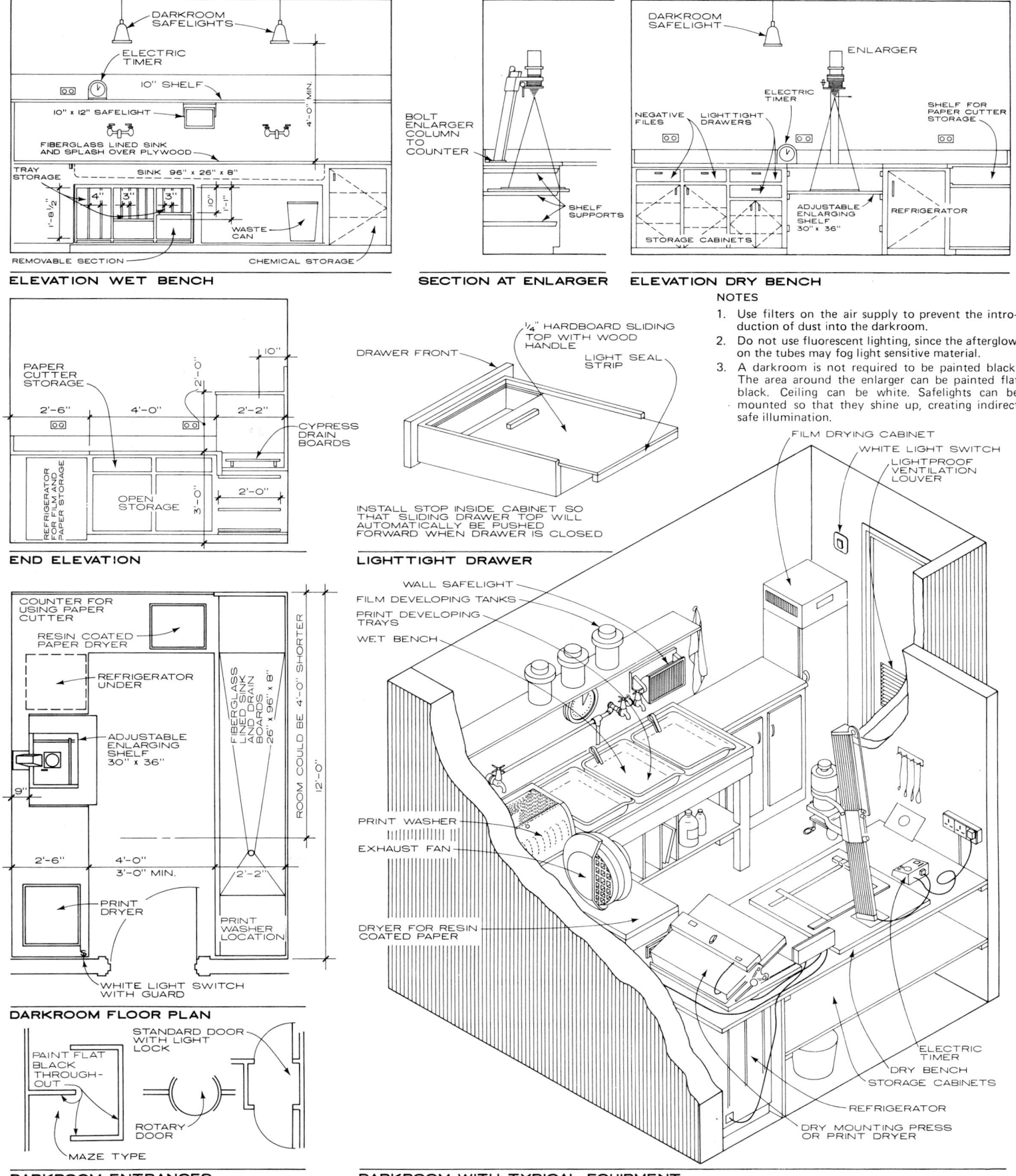

ELEVATION WET BENCH

DARKROOM SAFELIGHTS
ELECTRIC TIMER
10" SHELF
10" x 12" SAFELIGHT
4'-0" MIN.
FIBERGLASS LINED SINK AND SPLASH OVER PLYWOOD
TRAY STORAGE
SINK 96" X 26" X 8"
4" 3" 3"
10" 1'-1"
1'-8½"
REMOVABLE SECTION
WASTE CAN
CHEMICAL STORAGE

SECTION AT ENLARGER

BOLT ENLARGER COLUMN TO COUNTER
SHELF SUPPORTS

ELEVATION DRY BENCH

DARKROOM SAFELIGHT
ENLARGER
ELECTRIC TIMER
NEGATIVE FILES
LIGHTTIGHT DRAWERS
SHELF FOR PAPER CUTTER STORAGE
ADJUSTABLE ENLARGING SHELF 30" x 36"
REFRIGERATOR
STORAGE CABINETS

NOTES

1. Use filters on the air supply to prevent the introduction of dust into the darkroom.
2. Do not use fluorescent lighting, since the afterglow on the tubes may fog light sensitive material.
3. A darkroom is not required to be painted black. The area around the enlarger can be painted flat black. Ceiling can be white. Safelights can be mounted so that they shine up, creating indirect safe illumination.

END ELEVATION

PAPER CUTTER STORAGE
10"
2'-0"
2'-6" 4'-0" 2'-2"
CYPRESS DRAIN BOARDS
REFRIGERATOR FOR FILM AND PAPER STORAGE
OPEN STORAGE
3'-0"
2'-0"

LIGHTTIGHT DRAWER

¼" HARDBOARD SLIDING TOP WITH WOOD HANDLE
DRAWER FRONT
LIGHT SEAL STRIP

INSTALL STOP INSIDE CABINET SO THAT SLIDING DRAWER TOP WILL AUTOMATICALLY BE PUSHED FORWARD WHEN DRAWER IS CLOSED

DARKROOM FLOOR PLAN

COUNTER FOR USING PAPER CUTTER
RESIN COATED PAPER DRYER
REFRIGERATOR UNDER
ADJUSTABLE ENLARGING SHELF 30" x 36"
9"
FIBERGLASS LINED SINK AND DRAIN BOARDS 26" x 96" x 8"
ROOM COULD BE 4'-0" SHORTER
12'-0"
2'-6" 4'-0" 2'-2"
3'-0" MIN.
PRINT DRYER
PRINT WASHER LOCATION
WHITE LIGHT SWITCH WITH GUARD

DARKROOM ENTRANCES

STANDARD DOOR WITH LIGHT LOCK
PAINT FLAT BLACK THROUGHOUT
ROTARY DOOR
MAZE TYPE

DARKROOM WITH TYPICAL EQUIPMENT

FILM DRYING CABINET
WHITE LIGHT SWITCH
LIGHTPROOF VENTILATION LOUVER
WALL SAFELIGHT
FILM DEVELOPING TANKS
PRINT DEVELOPING TRAYS
WET BENCH
PRINT WASHER
EXHAUST FAN
DRYER FOR RESIN COATED PAPER
ELECTRIC TIMER
DRY BENCH
STORAGE CABINETS
REFRIGERATOR
DRY MOUNTING PRESS OR PRINT DRYER

Robert E. Fehlberg, FAIA; CTA Architects Engineers; Billings, Montana

GENERAL

American National Standards Institute (ANSI)
11 West 42nd Street
New York, NY 10036-8002
Tel: (212) 642-4900
Fax:(212) 398-0023

American Society of Mechanical Engineers
1828L Street, NW, Suite 906
Washington, DC 20006
Tel: (202) 785-3756

American Society for
Testing and Materials (ASTM)
1916 Race St.
Philadelphia, PA 19103-1187
Tel: (215) 299-5400
Fax:(215) 977-9679

VAULT EQUIPMENT

National Association of Security and Data Vaults
716 East Washington Street
Syracuse, NY 13210
Tel: (315) 475-7743

Underwriters Laboratories (UL)
333 Pfingsten Road
Northbrook, IL 60062
Tel: (708) 272-8800
Fax:(708) 272-8129

TELLER AND BANK SECURITY EQUIPMENT

National Alarm Association of America
P.O. Box 3409
Dayton, OH 45401
Tel: 1(800) 283-6285

National Burglar and Fire Alarm Association (NBFAA)
7101 Wisconsin Avenue, #1390
Bethesda, MD 20814
Tel: (301) 907-3202

National Independent Bank
Equipment and Systems Association (NIBESA)
1411 Peterson Street
Park Ridge, IL 60068
Tel: (708) 825-8419
Fax:(708) 825-8445

REFERENCES

Americans with Disabilities Act Accessibility Guidelines (ADAAG), Section 4.34, Automatic Teller Machines (ATMs).

Comptrollers Manual for National Banks, Minimum Security Devices and Procedures. [latest edition]

MUSICAL INSTRUMENTS

American Harp Society
6331 Quebec Drive
Hollywood, CA 90068-2831
Tel: (213) 463-0716

Associated Pipe Organ Builders of America
P.O. Box 155
Chicago Ridge, IL 60415
Tel: 1(800) 473-5270

National Association of Band Instrument Manufacturers
38 West 21st Street
5rd Floor
New York, NY 10010-6906
Tel: (212) 924-9175

National Association of Music Merchants
5140 Avenida Encinas
Carlsbad, CA 92008-4391
Tel: (619) 438-8001
Fax:(619) 438-7327

Piano Manufacturers International
4020 McEwen
Suite 105
Dallas, TX 75244-5019
Tel: (214) 233-9107
Fax:(214) 240-4219

COMMERCIAL AND COIN-OPERATED LAUNDRY EQUIPMENT

Coin Laundry Association
1315 Butterfield Road
Suite 212
Downers Grove, IL 60515
Tel: (708) 963-5547
Fax:(708) 963-5864

Laundry and Dry Cleaning International Union
307 Fourth Avenue
Bank Tower, Suite 405
Pittsburgh, PA 15222
Tel: (412) 471-4829
Fax:(412) 471-1840

Multi-Housing Laundry Association
4101 Lake Boone Trail, Suite 201
Raleigh, NC 27607
Tel: (919) 787-5181
Fax:(919) 787-4916

Textile Care Allied Trades Association (TCATA)
1455 Broad Street
Bloomfield, NJ 07003
Tel: (201) 338-7700
Fax:(201) 338-8211

REFERENCES

Herzog, Lee B. "How to Select a Window-Washing System." *Construction Specifier* (Sept. 1992), p. 114.

Turpin, Paul. "My Beautiful Laundry Closet." *JLC* (July 1992), p. 41.

VENDING EQUIPMENT

National Automatic Merchandising Association
20 N. Wacker Drive, Suite 3500
Chicago, IL 60606-3102
Tel: (312) 346-0370
Fax:(312) 704-4140

National Bulk Venders Association
200 N. LaSalle Street
Suite 2100
Chicago, IL 60601-1095
Tel: (312) 621-1400

National Coffee Service Association (NCSA)
4000 Williamsburg Square
Fairfax, VA 22032-1139
Tel: (703) 273-9008
Fax:(703) 273-9011

LOADING-DOCK EQUIPMENT

Association of Professional Material Handling Consultants
8720 Red Oak Blvd.
Suite 224
Charlotte, NC 28217-3957
Tel: (704) 525-4667
Fax:(704) 525-2880

Loading Dock Equipment Manufacturers Association
8720 Red Oak Blvd., Suite 201
Charlotte, NC 28217
Tel: (704) 522-8644

Material Handling Equipment Distributers Association (MHEDA)
201 Route #45
Vernon Hills, IL 60061
Tel: (708) 680-3500
Fax:(708) 362-6989

SOLID-WASTE-HANDLING EQUIPMENT

American Society of Sanitary Engineering (ASSE)
P.O. Box 40362
Bay Village, OH 44140
Tel: (216) 835-3040
Fax:(216) 835-3488

Association of State and Territorial
Solid Waste Management Officials (ASTSWMO)
444 North Capitol Street, N.W.
Suite 388
Washington, DC 20001
Tel: (202) 624-5828

Institute for Solid Wastes
American Public Works Association (ISW/APWA)
106 West 11th Street
Suite 1800
Kansas City, MS 64105-1806
Tel: (816) 472-6100

National Sanitation Foundation
3475 Plymouth Road
P.O. Box130140
Ann Arbor, MI 48113-0140
Tel: (313) 769-8010

National Solid Waste Management Association (NSWMA)
1730 Rhode Island Avenue, N.W.
Suite 1000
Washington, DC 20036
Tel: (202) 659-4613
Fax:(202) 775-5917

Solid Waste Association of North America (SWANA)
1100 Wayne Avenue
Suite 700
Silver Spring, MD 20910
Tel: (301) 585-2898

FOOD SERVICE EQUIPMENT

Wine Institute
425 Market Street
Suite 1000
San Francisco, CA 94105
Tel: (415) 512-0151
Fax:(415) 442-0742

National Association of Food Equipment Manufacturers
401 N. Michigan Avenue
Chicago, IL 60611
Tel: (312) 644-6610
Fax:(312) 321-6869

RESIDENTIAL EQUIPMENT

Association of Home Appliance Manufacturers (AHAM)
20 North Wacker Drive
Suite 1500
Chicago, IL 60606
Tel: (312) 984-5800
Fax:(312) 984-5823

National Association of Retail Dealers of America (NARDA)
10 East 22nd Street
Suite 310
Lombard, IL 60148
Tel: (708) 953-8950
Fax:(708) 953-8957

DARKROOM EQUIPMENT

International Center of Photography
1130 5th Avenue
New York, NY 10128
Tel: (212) 860-1777
Fax:(212) 360-6490

National Associaton of Photographic Manufacturers
550 Mamaroneck Avenue
Harrison, NY 10528
Tel: (914) 698-7603
Fax:(914) 698-7609

Photographic Manufacturers and Distributers Association
866 United Nations Plaza
Suite 436
New York, NY 10017
Tel: (212) 688-3520

CHAPTER

12

FURNISHINGS

INTRODUCTION

Flexibility and adaptability are key factors in the design of accessible furniture. Although dimensional guidelines are given for the pieces shown, furniture that adjusts to unique individual sizes and capabilities will be safer, more comfortable, and more productive for the user whether disabled or not.

To be accessible to wheelchair users, all furniture and controls must meet reach ranges specified by the Americans with Disabilities Act Accessibility Guidelines.

IN THE HOME

1. Furniture should be sturdy and stable even when weight is applied because it is often used for support.
2. Chairs should have armrests to aid rising and may have rollers or wheels (if locking).
3. Cabinets, chests, and desks should have center pulls and be easy to access and operate using one hand. Top drawers should be no higher than 27 in. for wheelchair users to view contents. There should be a 32in. clear space in front of the drawer when fully opened.
4. Hardware should be appropriate for people with poor hand function. Doors should be sliding, rolling, or 180-degree hinged.
5. Bed height should facilitate transfer from a sitting position on the bed to the seat of a wheelchair or to a standing position (18 to 20 in. from floor to the top of the mattress). For access with an assistive device, provide a 36 in. aisle on one side of the bed.
6. Tables and desks should provide kneespace at least 30 in. wide, 19 in. deep, and 27 in. high. The maneuvering room required to access a kneespace depends on its width.

IN THE OFFICE OR PUBLIC PLACE

1. Minimize need for reaching up and behind or bending down.
2. Provide raised work surface to allow for additional kneespace.
3. The most common manufactured office products are seating and work surfaces.

TABLES

1. Conference and worktables should provide kneespace a minimum of 30 in. wide, 19 in. deep, and 27 in. high to be wheelchair accessible. To coordinate with the table height, chairs should have a seat height of approximately 18 in. or should be individually adjustable.
2. See chapter 1 for floor clearance between furniture groupings.

SEATING

1. All chairs, especially task chairs, should have the following adjustable features:
   Back and seat tilt angle and height.
   Armrest width and rotation.
   Swivel base with casters (lockable).
2. A variety of specialty chairs are available.
   Split cushion leg support chair: allows support for a joint that cannot be easily flexed.
   Rising assist cushion or chair: aids rising from chair.
   Rolling chair with brakes: allows safe transfer to and from a wheelchair when breaks are applied; has large (5 in.) wheels to roll over irregular surfaces.
3. Provide approach space for transfer from wheelchair or other mobility aids.

FREESTANDING FURNITURE

1. Common adjustable freestanding furniture includes
   Adjustable worktables or desks:
      Similar to drafting table in appearance
      Adjustable height
      Wide kneespace, wheelchair accessible
      Options: Tilt tops, single or split surfaces, table extensions
   Computer support furniture:
      Split surface tables for monitor and keyboard
      Adjustable height and surface til
   Responsive (stand-up/sit-down) computer tables:
      Wide kneespace, wheelchair accessible
      Fully adjustable height, user responsive

FURNITURE SYSTEMS

1. Furniture systems are especially suited to accessibility because of the modular nature of their components.
   Adjustable height work surfaces:
      Often are made for more than one of a manufacturer's furniture lines and can attach to existing workstations
      Adjusts to various physical needs and various tasks
      Automated, hand-adjustable controls
   Adjustable height storage components:
      Allow for access from workers in wheelchairs or those who have difficulty standing
   Tiered/adjustable computer tables:
      Surface height adjustable
2. For hearing-impaired workers, provide glazed panels in cubicle walls for greater visual access to coworkers and reorient primary work surface to face workstation entrance.

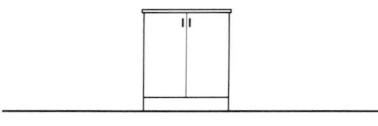

ADJUSTABLE WORKTABLES

Two narrow cabinet doors are easier to access than a single wide door. Pulls on low cabinets should be mounted near the top of the strike-side of doors.

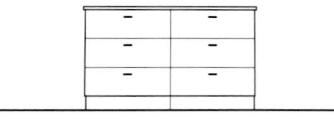

Narrow dresser drawers with a single center-pull can be operated with one hand.

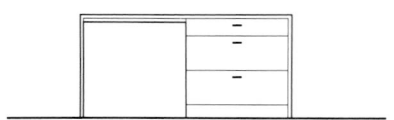

Allow adequate kneespace at desks.

CABINETRY

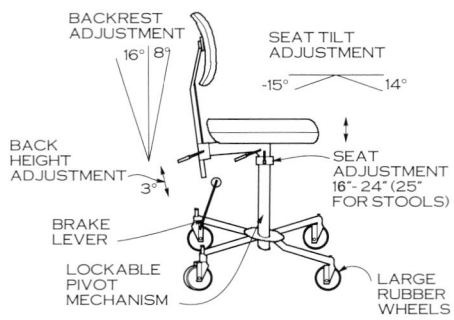

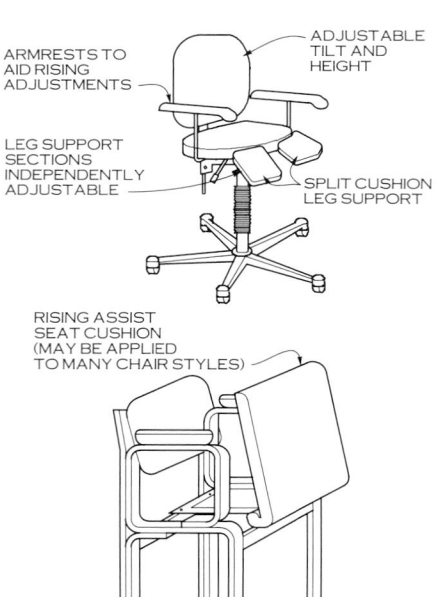

SEATING

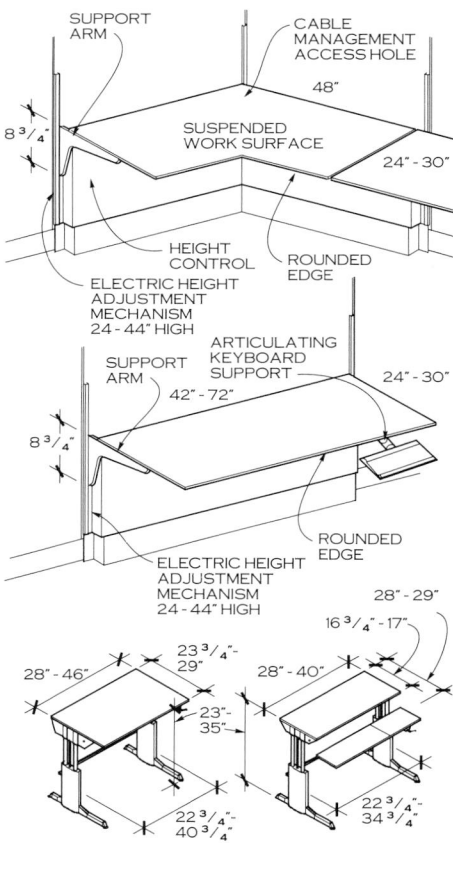

NOTE

Models shown and similar corner models can be used both as freestanding elements or as part of a furniture system. Similar types of work surfaces can also be raised high enough to be used from a standing position.

SYSTEMS FURNITURE

Janet B. Rankin, AIA; Rippeteau Architects; Washington, D.C.

12 **UNIVERSAL ACCESSIBILITY**

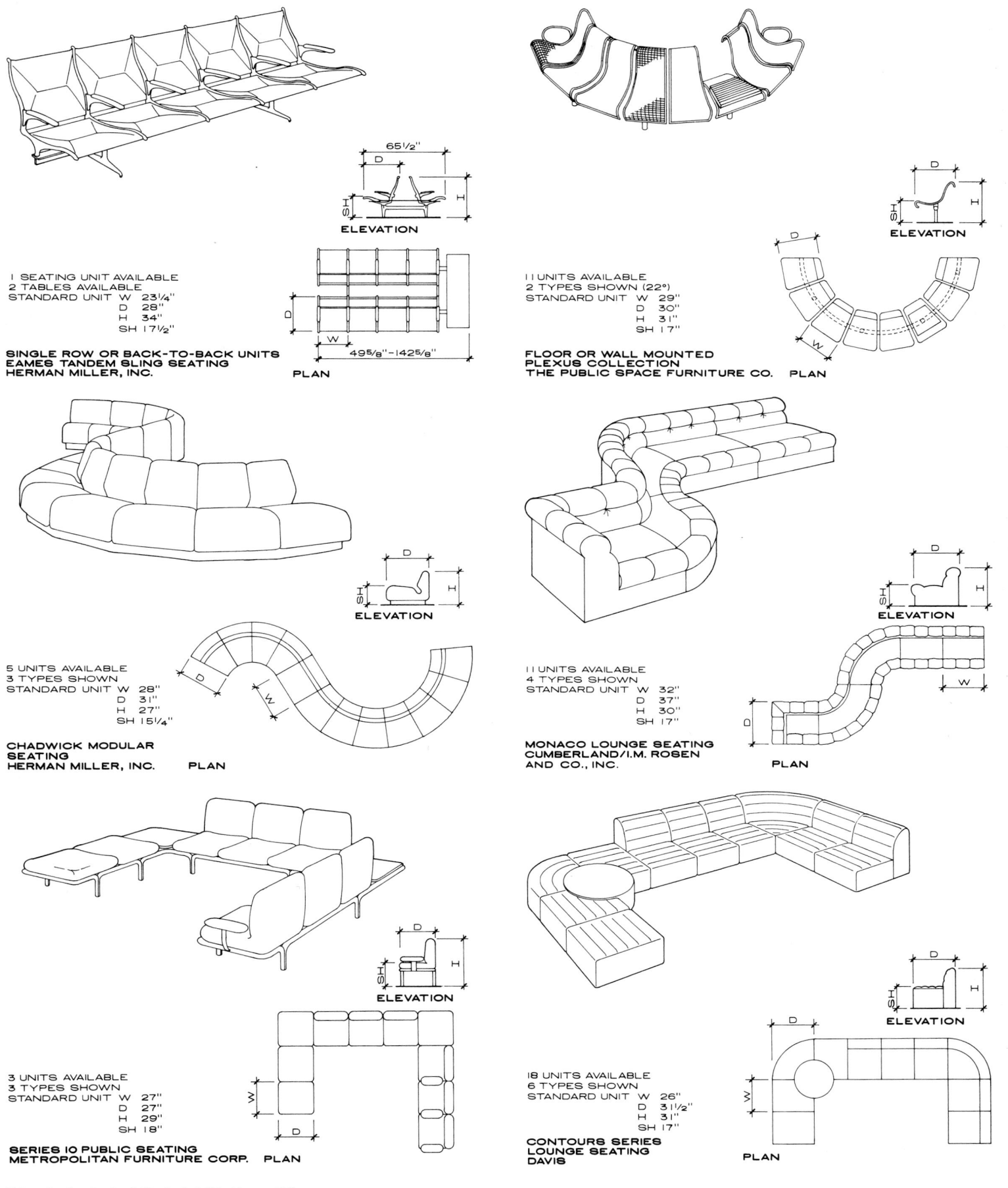

ELEVATION

65½"

I SEATING UNIT AVAILABLE
2 TABLES AVAILABLE
STANDARD UNIT W 23¼"
D 28"
H 34"
SH 17½"

SINGLE ROW OR BACK-TO-BACK UNITS
EAMES TANDEM SLING SEATING
HERMAN MILLER, INC.

PLAN

49⅝"-142⅝"

ELEVATION

II UNITS AVAILABLE
2 TYPES SHOWN (22°)
STANDARD UNIT W 29"
D 30"
H 31"
SH 17"

FLOOR OR WALL MOUNTED
PLEXUS COLLECTION
THE PUBLIC SPACE FURNITURE CO. PLAN

ELEVATION

5 UNITS AVAILABLE
3 TYPES SHOWN
STANDARD UNIT W 28"
D 31"
H 27"
SH 15¼"

CHADWICK MODULAR
SEATING
HERMAN MILLER, INC. PLAN

ELEVATION

II UNITS AVAILABLE
4 TYPES SHOWN
STANDARD UNIT W 32"
D 37"
H 30"
SH 17"

MONACO LOUNGE SEATING
CUMBERLAND/I.M. ROSEN
AND CO., INC. PLAN

ELEVATION

3 UNITS AVAILABLE
3 TYPES SHOWN
STANDARD UNIT W 27"
D 27"
H 29"
SH 18"

SERIES IO PUBLIC SEATING
METROPOLITAN FURNITURE CORP. PLAN

ELEVATION

18 UNITS AVAILABLE
6 TYPES SHOWN
STANDARD UNIT W 26"
D 31½"
H 31"
SH 17"

CONTOURS SERIES
LOUNGE SEATING
DAVIS PLAN

Robert Staples; Staples & Charles Ltd.; Washington, D.C.
Richard J. Vitullo, AIA; Oak Leaf Studio; Crownsville, Maryland

W 19¾"
D 21¼"
H 30"
SH 17¾"

40/4 CHAIR, 1964
DESIGNER: DAVID ROWLAND
GF FURNITURE SYSTEMS

W 21"
D 22"
H 30"
SH 17¼"

MULTI-CHAIR
STACKS 40 ON A DOLLY
SHAW-WALKER

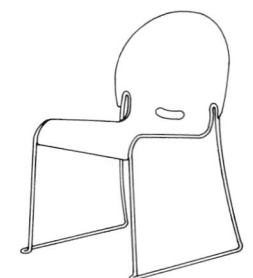

W 20½"
D 24"
H 31½"
SH 18"

STACKING CHAIR
STACKS 20 ON A DOLLY
NIENKAMPER

W 20"
D 22"
H 33¾"
SH 18"

BIBI VADER CHAIR
ACCIAIO, INC.

W 23⅛"
D 25½"
H 31¾"
SH 18"

STACKING CHAIR WITH ARM
DESIGNER: CHARLES EAMES
HERMAN MILLER, INC.

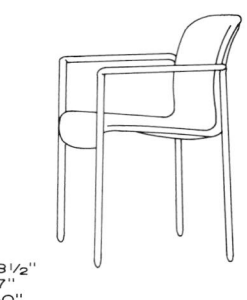

W 18½"
D 17"
H 30"
SH 17½"

PROPER CHAIR
HERMAN MILLER, INC.

W 23"
D 22"
H 30½"
SH 18½"

APTA "SMART" CHAIR
DESIGNER: GIANCARLO PIRETTI
CASTELLI/KRUEGER

W 21½"
D 22½"
H 30½"
SH 18"

STACKING CHAIR
DESIGNERS: THYGESEN/
**   SORENSEN**
RUDD INTERNATIONAL

W 18"
D 20½"
H 29½"
SH 17½"

TABLET ARMCHAIR
TABLET, 23" X 10"
SAMSONITE FURNITURE CO.

W 18½"
D 19½"
H 29½"
SH 17½"

PLIA FOLDING CHAIR
DESIGNER: GIANCARLO PIRETTI
CASTELLI/KRUEGER

W 22"
D 21"
H 32"
SH 18"

STACKING CHAIR
KINETICS

W 22"
D 24"
H 30"
SH 17"

RONDO CHAIR
PERFORATED STEEL
FIXTURES FURNITURE

DIA. 37½"
H 28½"

PLANO FOLDING TABLE
DESIGNER: GIANCARLO PIRETTI
CASTELLI/KRUEGER

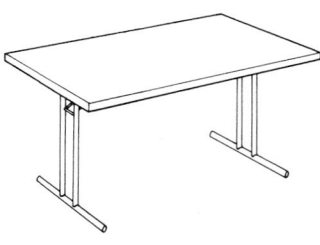

W 24", 30"
D 60", 72"
H 29"

ENCORE FOLDING TABLE
FIXTURES FURNITURE

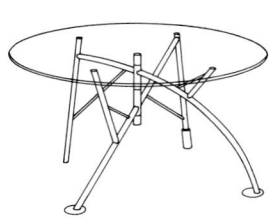

DIA. 48", 54", 60"
H 28¼"

DOLE MELIPONE FOLDING TABLE
DESIGNER: PHILIPPE STARCK
ICF, INC.

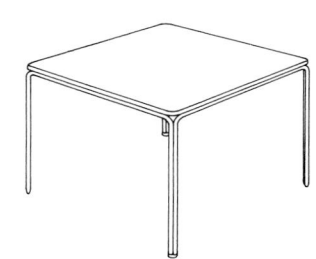

W 24", 30", 34½", 42"
D 24", 30", 34½", 42"
H 29"

SQUARE STACKING TABLE
FIXTURES FURNITURE

Robert Staples; Staples & Charles Ltd.; Washington, D.C.
Richard J. Vitullo, AIA; Oak Leaf Studio; Crownsville, Maryland

12 **GENERAL USE FURNITURE**

TYPICAL END OR SIDE TABLE DIMENSIONS (IN.)

DESCRIPTION	DEPTH		WIDTH		HEIGHT	
	MIN.	MAX.	MIN.	MAX.	MIN.	MAX.
RECTANGULAR	19	28	21	48	17	28
SQUARE	15	32	15	32	17	28
ROUND	16	30	16	30	18	22½

TYPICAL LOW TABLE DIMENSIONS (IN.)

DESCRIPTION	DEPTH		WIDTH		HEIGHT	
	MIN.	MAX.	MIN.	MAX.	MIN.	MAX.
RECTANGULAR	15½	24	21	86	12	18
SQUARE	36	42	32	42	15	17
ROUND	30	42	20	42	15	16½

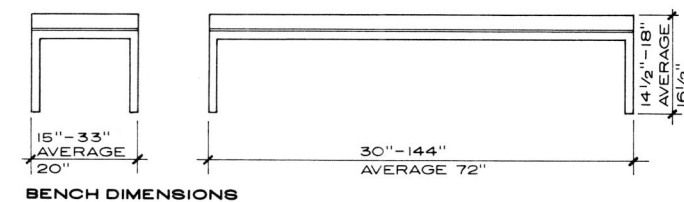

BENCH DIMENSIONS

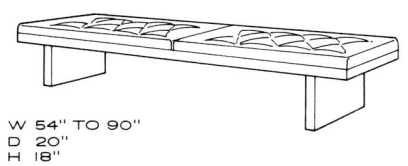

W 54" TO 90"
D 20"
H 18"
BENCH
LEHIGH FURNITURE CORP.

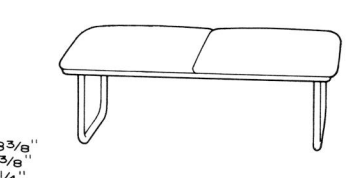

W 48⅜"
D 21⅜"
H 17¼"
BENCH
ALL-STEEL, INC.

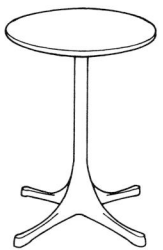

DIA. 17"
H   22"
OCCASIONAL TABLE
DESIGNER: GEORGE NELSON
HERMAN MILLER, INC.

DIA. 13"
H   15"
WOODEN SPOOL TABLE
DESIGNER: RAY EAMES
HERMAN MILLER, INC.

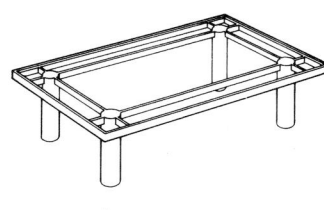

W 45", 60"
D 45", 60"
H 16"
INTERSECT LOW TABLE
BRUETON

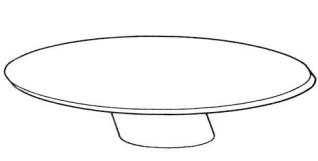

W 63"
D 50"
H 12"
MERCER TABLE
DESIGNER: LUCIA MERCER
KNOLL INTERNATIONAL

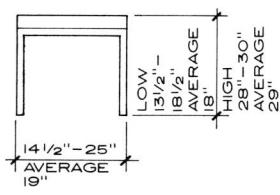
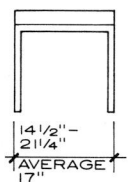

STOOL DIMENSIONS

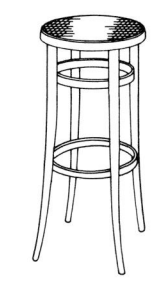

DIA. 17"
H   30"
WOOD STOOL
THONET: DIVISION OF
SHELBY WILLIAMS INDUSTRIES,
INC.

W 22½"
D 18"
H 41½"
SH 30"
FLEDERMAUS BAR CHAIR
THONET: DIVISION OF
SHELBY WILLIAMS INDUSTRIES,
INC.

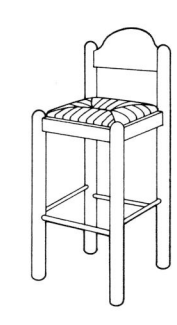

W 16½"
D 19"
H. 43"
SH 30"
PADOVA BAR
STOOL. HANK
LOEWENSTEIN, INC.

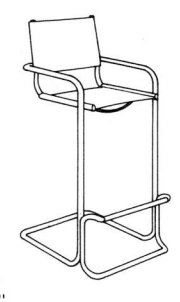

W 18¼"
D 22¼"
H 39½"
SH 27"
BADEN BAR STOOL
LOWENSTEIN/OGGO

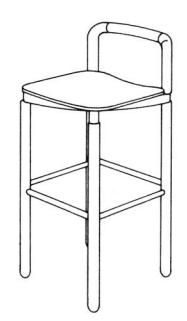

W 18"
D 18"
H 38"
SH 30"
RUBBER BAR STOOL
DESIGNER: BRIAN KANE
METROPOLITAN FURNITURE
CORP.

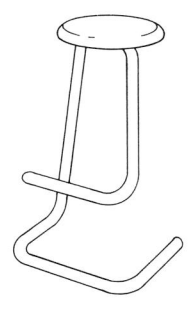

W 16"
D 16"
H 28"
STOOL
KINETICS

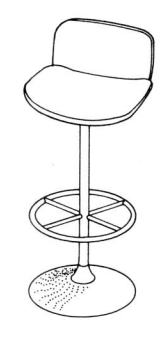

W 19"
D 18"
H 36"
SH 29"
CARIBE BAR STOOL
DESIGNER: ILMARI TAPIOVAARA
ICF, INC.

Robert Staples; Staples & Charles Ltd.; Washington, D.C.
Richard J. Vitullo, AIA; Oak Leaf Studio; Crownsville, Maryland

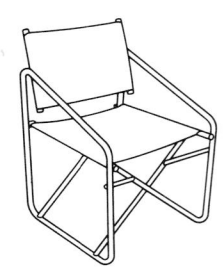

W 22½"
D 22½"
H 34½"
SH 17½"

**NOMAD DINING CHAIR
BROWN JORDAN**

W 24"
D 35"
H 34"
SH 11"

**STEAMER LOUNGE CHAIR
AMBIANT
KNOLL INTERNATIONAL**

W 17½"
D 16"
H 29½"
SH 16"

**STACKING RIO CHAIR
EMU/USA**

DIA. 8'-0", H 9'-0"
UMBRELLA
DIA. 42", H 28"

**TABLE
TRADEWINDS**

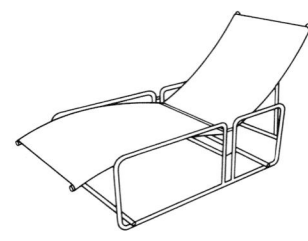

W 25"
D 64"
H 32"
SH 17"

**ADJUSTABLE CHAISE
BROWN JORDAN**

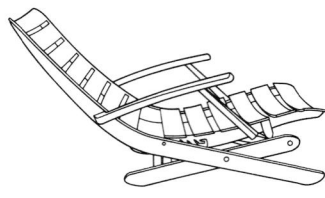

W 25"
D 29"
H 34"
SH 15"

**ADJUSTABLE ARMCHAIR
GROSFILLEX**

W 24½"
D 75½"
H 37½"
SH 10½"

**POOL BED LOUNGE
EMU/USA**

W 28"
D 82"
H 39"
SH 12"

**STACKABLE SUN LOUNGE
TRADEWINDS**

W 26"
D 27½"
H 25½"
SH 13½"

**KANTAN LOUNGE CHAIR
BROWN JORDAN**

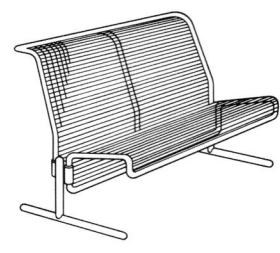

W 48¼"
D 31½"
H 29¾"
SH 17¾"

**TWO-SEAT PARK BENCH
KROIN INC.**

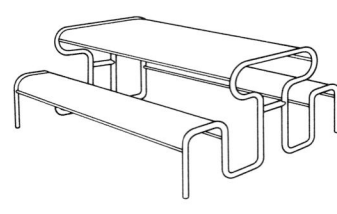

W 72"
D 62"
H 30"
SH 17"

**METAL PICNIC TABLE
FORMS AND SURFACES**

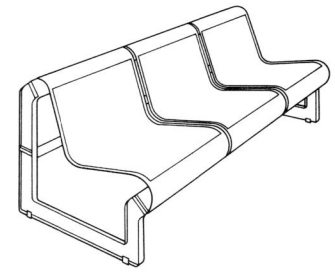

W 70"
D 31½"
H 28"
SH 16"

**LAGOS SEATING
ARTIFORT/KRUEGER**

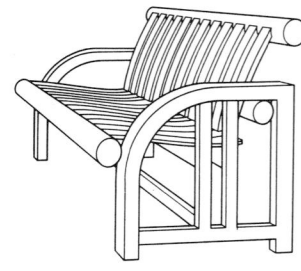

W 55"
D 29"
H 33"
SH 17"

**GARDEN BENCH
SUMMIT FURNITURE INC.**

W 60"
D 23½"
H 43½"
SH 15½"

**LIVERPOOL BENCH
INTERNA DESIGNS, LTD.**

W 72"
D 23"
H 29"
SH 17"

**CHARLESTON BENCH
WOODCRAFTERS OF FLORIDA, INC.**

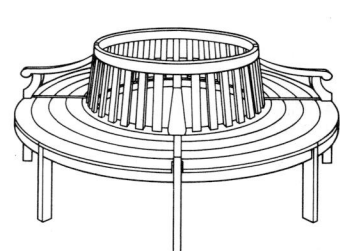

INSIDE DIA.   38"
OUTSIDE DIA. 76"
H   36"
SH   17"

**MONHEGAN TREE BENCH
WEATHEREND/IMAGINEERING, INC.**

Robert Staples; Staples & Charles Ltd.; Washington, D.C.
Richard J. Vitullo, AIA; Oak Leaf Studio; Crownsville, Maryland

GENERAL USE FURNITURE

DESIGN RATIONALE

Systems furniture is designed primarily for utilization in an open office plan which uses few fixed floor-to-ceiling partitions as compared to conventional office layouts. Open office planning receives its impetus from its ability to respond to requirements for increased flexibility and lower long term expenses. Some of the major areas of response are the following:

1. FLEXIBILITY OF PLANNING: Systems furniture in an open plan maximizes the efficient use of net plannable space. This is the result of the use of more vertical space without fixed floor-to-ceiling partitions, thereby freeing floor area and reducing space planning inefficiencies.
2. FLEXIBILITY OF FUNCTION: Systems furniture allows individual workstation modification so that workstation design can reflect functional requirements of the task performed. In this way, changes in function can be accommodated without total furniture replacement.
3. FLEXIBILITY OF PLAN MODIFICATION: Systems furniture in open office planning allows institutions to respond more easily to organizational changes of size, structure, and function. Open planning allows institutions to respond to change at lower cost by reducing expenses related to partition relocation, HVAC modification, lighting relocation, construction, and moving time.

NOTES

1. Any open office plan as commonly applied will utilize some enclosed spaces having fixed, floor-to-ceiling partitions.
2. Systems furniture requires careful planning and engineering consultation to achieve the maximum functional advantage.
3. Systems furniture components are not compatible from one manufacturer to another regardless of generic type.
4. The generic types listed below are broad classifications for descriptive purposes only.

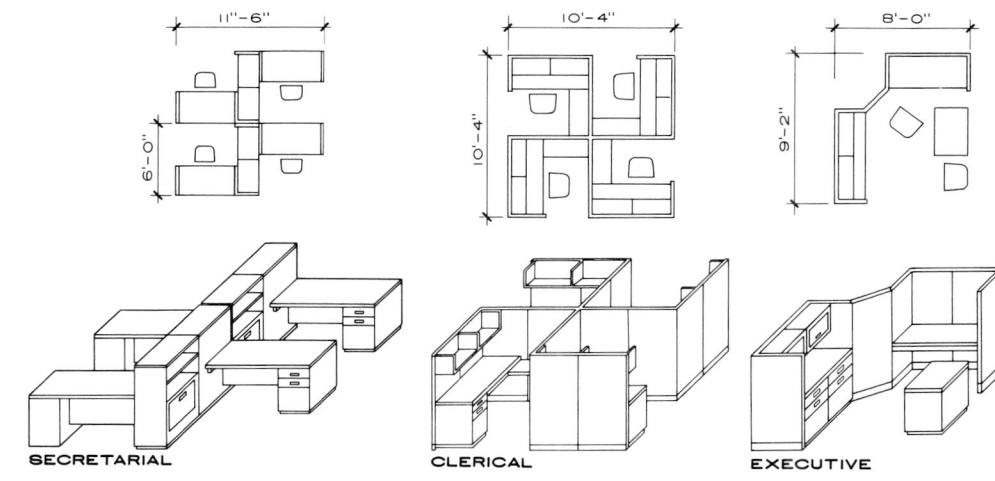

SECRETARIAL   **CLERICAL**   **EXECUTIVE**

CONFIGURATIONS

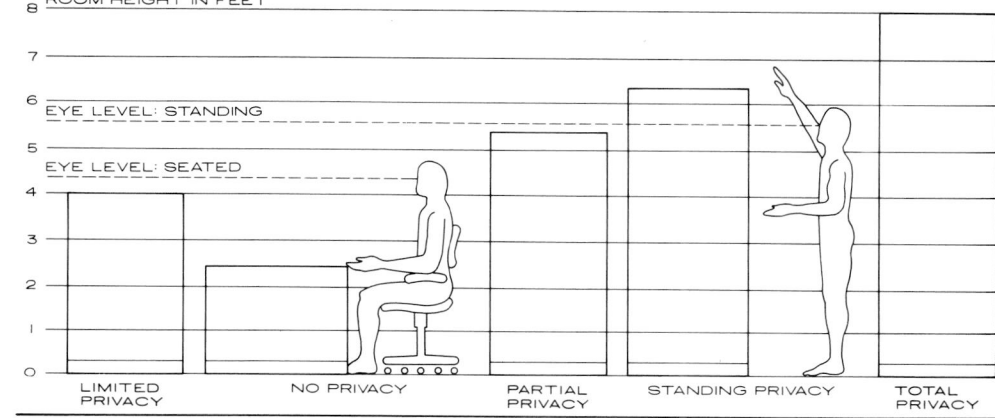

RELATIONSHIP OF PANEL HEIGHT TO PRIVACY

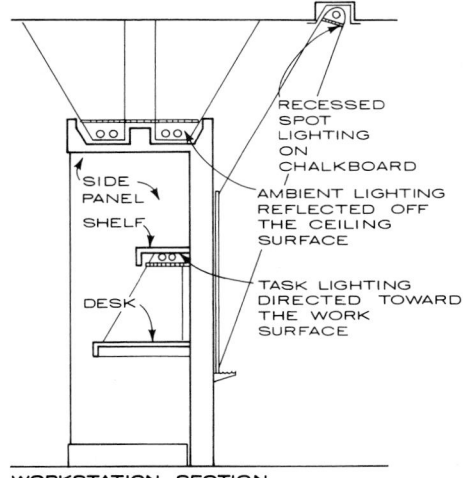

WORKSTATION SECTION

INTEGRATED LIGHTING

Artificial lighting is integrated into most open office furniture systems. The components consist of task oriented downlights located directly over work surfaces, which provide the user with control of intensity and direction of light. Uplights are mounted in the top of workstations to provide indirect light reflected off the ceiling to the ambient surroundings.

Task/ambient lighting provides more flexibility than do standard ceiling mounted fixtures. It can reduce energy consumption by decreasing general light levels and utilizing more efficient light sources. It can also improve acoustics, since fewer fixtures are installed in the acoustical ceiling.

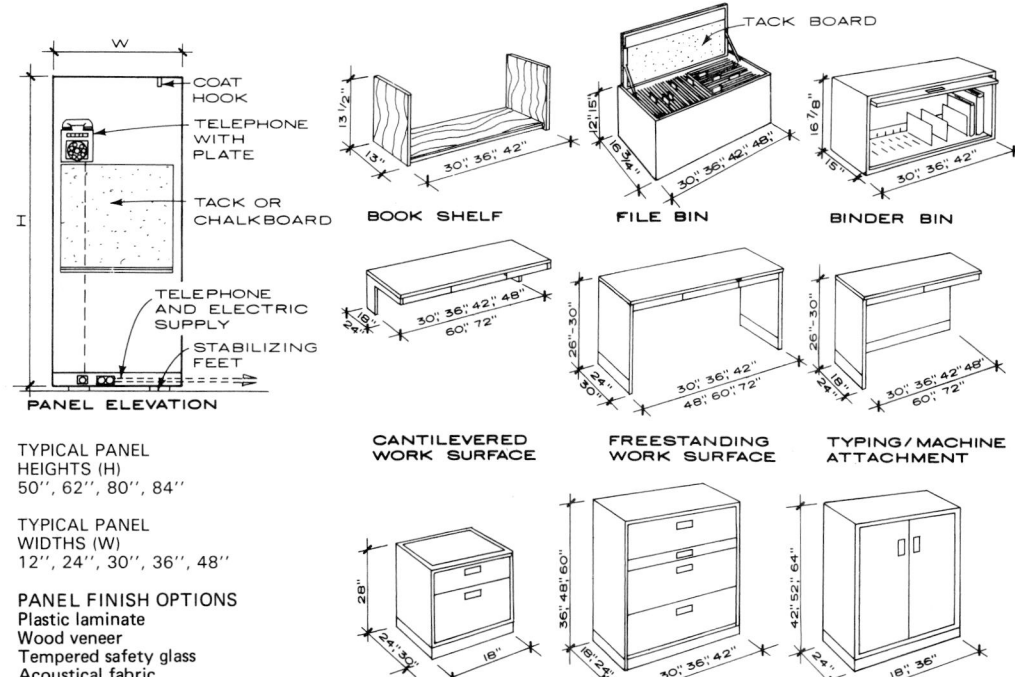

PANEL ELEVATION

TYPICAL PANEL
HEIGHTS (H)
50'', 62'', 80'', 84''

TYPICAL PANEL
WIDTHS (W)
12'', 24'', 30'', 36'', 48''

PANEL FINISH OPTIONS
Plastic laminate
Wood veneer
Tempered safety glass
Acoustical fabric

NOTE: Consult manufacturer for specific sizes and finishes available.

SYSTEMS FURNITURE COMPONENTS

Interspace Incorporated; Washington, D.C.

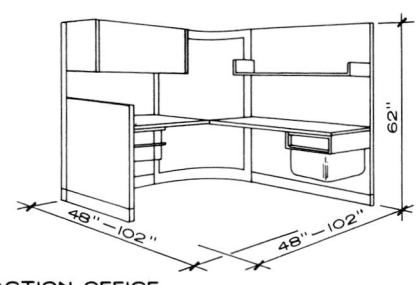

**ACTION OFFICE
HERMAN MILLER, INC.**

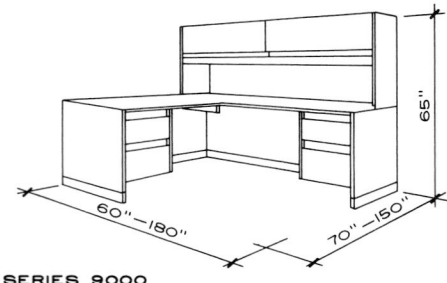

**SERIES 9000
STEELCASE, INC.**

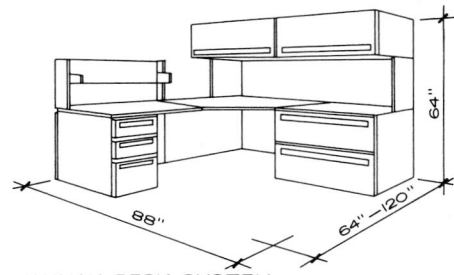

**HANNAH DESK SYSTEM
KNOLL INTERNATIONAL**

PANEL HUNG TYPE

These systems are based on panels that can be connected at various angles (angle options depend on manufacturer). Panels achieve stability through configuration or by attached stabilizing feet. Components are hung on panels at desired heights (usually on 1 in. increments).

SYSTEM ADVANTAGES

Panel hung systems usually have a large variety of components. They offer the highest degree of planning flexibility. These systems are easily modified and are relatively light.

OPTIONS OFFERED (VARY WITH MANUFACTURER)

1. Ability to hang components on fixed, full height partitions.
2. Specialized use components (i.e., hospitals, schools, libraries).
3. Integrated wiring in panels with fast connect or wire manager components for horizontal raceways.
4. Integrated task/ambient lighting components.
5. Multiple standard panel heights (dimensions vary).
6. Fabric covered acoustical panels as structural panel option.
7. Integrated file storage components.

PANEL ENCLOSURE TYPE

These systems are based on building rectilinear enclosures with panel components. Panels achieve stability through right angle panel-to-panel configuration. Components are hung in panel enclosures (usually at several predetermined mounting heights) and are supported by end panels rather than back panels.

SYSTEM ADVANTAGES

Assembled systems have a somewhat unitized appearance. They are stable and, when assembled, are not easily moved. They have a relatively high level of flexibility with a more limited number of components and accessories than in most panel hung systems.

OPTIONS OFFERED (VARY WITH MANUFACTURER)

1. Multiple standard panel heights.
2. Full panel high closed storage units (i.e., wardrobes, shelf).
3. Vertical power poles with lighting outlets, convenience outlets, circuit breakers, telephone raceway.
4. Wire manager components for vertical and horizontal raceways.
5. Integrated task/ambient lighting components and freestanding ambient light units.
6. Fabric covered acoustical panels as structural panel option.
7. Integrated file storage components.

UNITIZED PANEL TYPE

These systems are based on ganging assembled units and panels to form workstations and workstation groupings. Units are individually stable and panels achieve stability by attachment to units and right angle panel-to-panel configuration. Some of these systems are more componentized than others (similar to panel enclosure type) but are marketed as assembled units. Components within assembled units are usually supported by end panels.

SYSTEM ADVANTAGES

Assembled systems have a unitized appearance more closely resembling conventional furniture. They are very stable and, when assembled, are not easily moved. They have a relatively high level of flexibility depending on the degree to which they are unitized. These systems simplify purchase, inventory management, and installation because of their unitized character.

OPTIONS OFFERED (VARY WITH MANUFACTURER)

1. Multiple standard panel heights (dimensions vary).
2. Full panel high closed storage units (i.e., wardrobes, shelf).
3. Wire raceways (horizontal and vertical), convenience outlets, and switches are an integral part of system.
4. Integrated task/ambient light units.
5. Fabric covered acoustical panels usually as hang on or finish panel option.
6. Integrated flexible branch wiring system.
7. Can be used in conventional configurations.

GENERIC TYPES OF SYSTEM FURNITURE

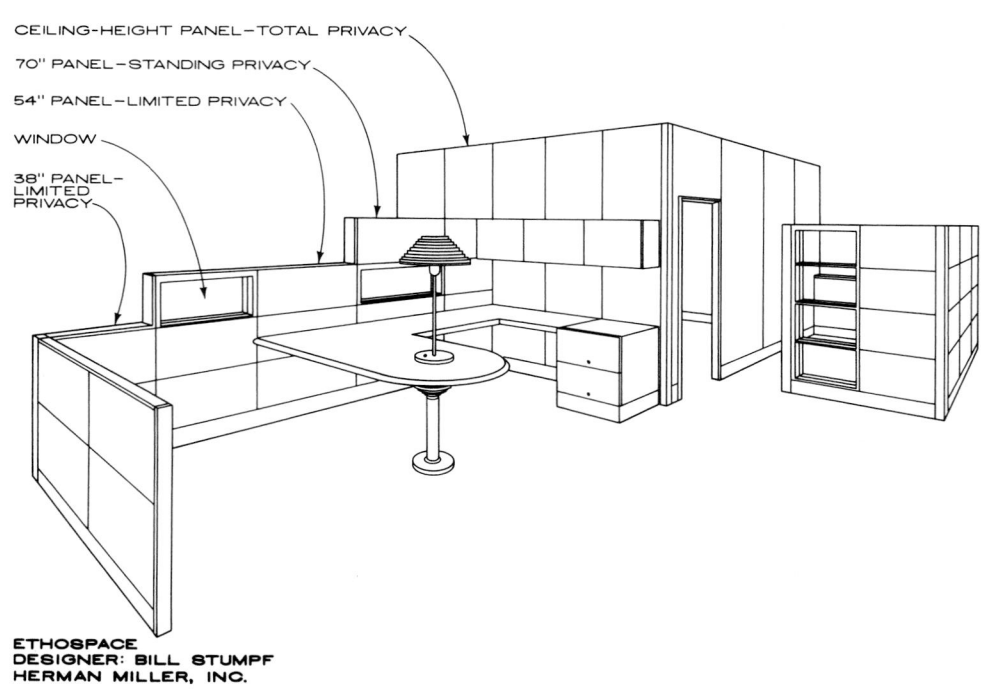

**ETHOSPACE
DESIGNER: BILL STUMPF
HERMAN MILLER, INC.**

COMPONENT WALL AND PARTITION SYSTEM

70" HIGH PANEL—HEIGHT AT TOP OF HEAD

SNAP-IN DETACHABLE TILE (TYPICAL)

FABRIC-COVERED TILE

STEEL FRAME

54" HIGH PANEL—SHOULDER HEIGHT

WINDOW

3 1/2"

THREE-CIRCUIT, SIX-WIRE POWER SYSTEM; CABLES LAY ON EITHER SIDE OF FRAME

HINGED BASE COVER WITH PUNCH-OUT RECEPTACLE COVER

WOOD-COVERED TILE

38" HIGH PANEL—WAIST HIGH

NOTE
PANELS ARE MADE IN 24, 30, OR 48" WIDTH. PANELS ARE BASED ON A 16" VERTICAL MODULE

PANEL COMPONENT

Interspace Incorporated; Washington, D.C.
Richard J. Vitullo, AIA; Oak Leaf Studio; Crownsville, Maryland

12   OFFICE FURNITURE

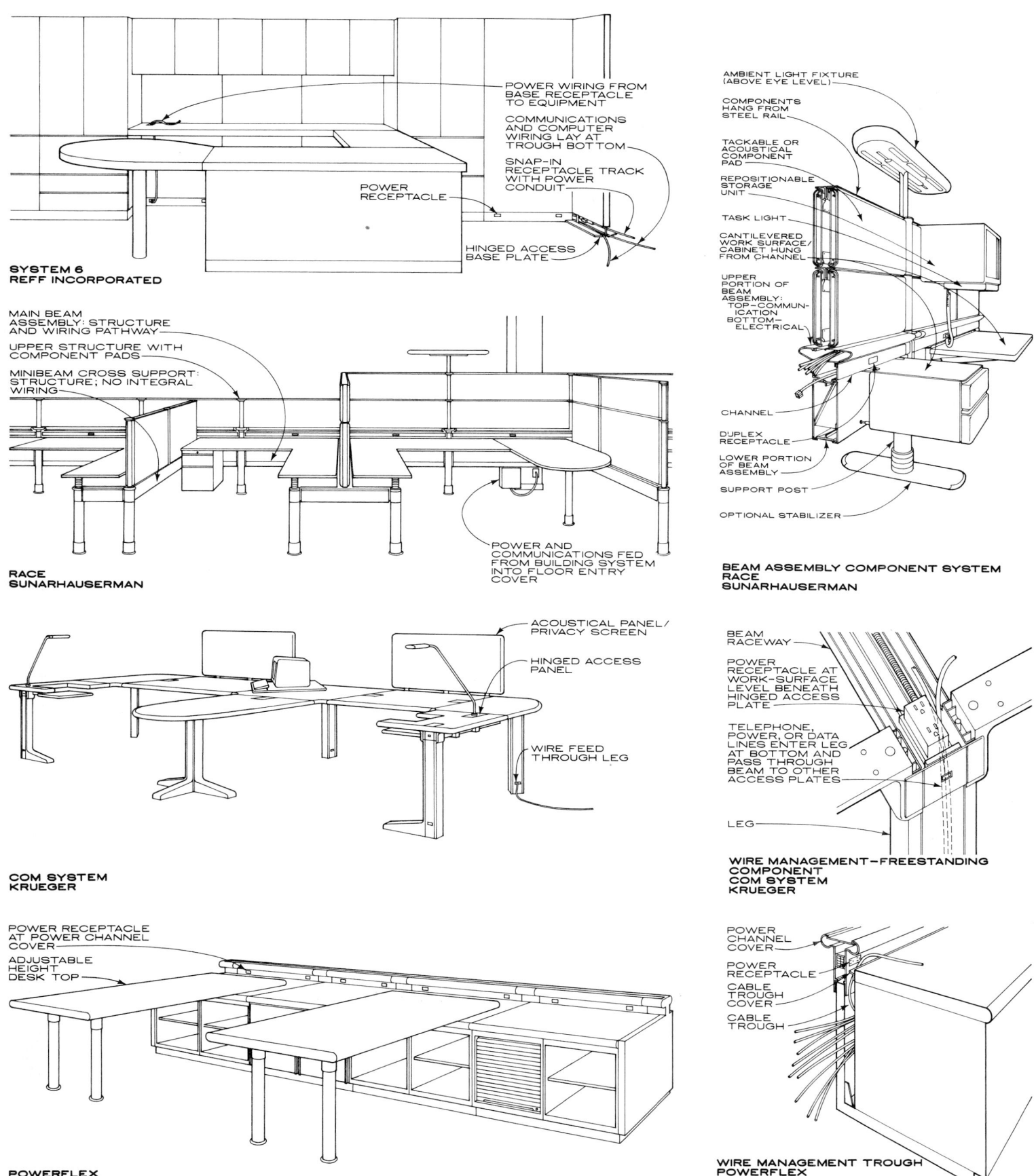

POWER WIRING FROM BASE RECEPTACLE TO EQUIPMENT

COMMUNICATIONS AND COMPUTER WIRING LAY AT TROUGH BOTTOM

SNAP-IN RECEPTACLE TRACK WITH POWER CONDUIT

POWER RECEPTACLE

HINGED ACCESS BASE PLATE

SYSTEM 6
REFF INCORPORATED

MAIN BEAM ASSEMBLY: STRUCTURE AND WIRING PATHWAY

UPPER STRUCTURE WITH COMPONENT PADS

MINIBEAM CROSS SUPPORT: STRUCTURE; NO INTEGRAL WIRING

POWER AND COMMUNICATIONS FED FROM BUILDING SYSTEM INTO FLOOR ENTRY COVER

RACE
SUNARHAUSERMAN

AMBIENT LIGHT FIXTURE (ABOVE EYE LEVEL)

COMPONENTS HANG FROM STEEL RAIL

TACKABLE OR ACOUSTICAL COMPONENT PAD

REPOSITIONABLE STORAGE UNIT

TASK LIGHT

CANTILEVERED WORK SURFACE/ CABINET HUNG FROM CHANNEL

UPPER PORTION OF BEAM ASSEMBLY: TOP—COMMUNICATION BOTTOM— ELECTRICAL

CHANNEL

DUPLEX RECEPTACLE

LOWER PORTION OF BEAM ASSEMBLY

SUPPORT POST

OPTIONAL STABILIZER

BEAM ASSEMBLY COMPONENT SYSTEM
RACE
SUNARHAUSERMAN

ACOUSTICAL PANEL/ PRIVACY SCREEN

HINGED ACCESS PANEL

WIRE FEED THROUGH LEG

COM SYSTEM
KRUEGER

BEAM RACEWAY

POWER RECEPTACLE AT WORK-SURFACE LEVEL BENEATH HINGED ACCESS PLATE

TELEPHONE, POWER, OR DATA LINES ENTER LEG AT BOTTOM AND PASS THROUGH BEAM TO OTHER ACCESS PLATES

LEG

WIRE MANAGEMENT—FREESTANDING COMPONENT
COM SYSTEM
KRUEGER

POWER RECEPTACLE AT POWER CHANNEL COVER

ADJUSTABLE HEIGHT DESK TOP

POWER CHANNEL COVER

POWER RECEPTACLE

CABLE TROUGH COVER

CABLE TROUGH

POWERFLEX
JG FURNITURE SYSTEMS, INC.

WIRE MANAGEMENT TROUGH
POWERFLEX
JG FURNITURE SYSTEMS, INC.

TYPICAL WIRE MANAGEMENT SYSTEMS

Robert Staples; Staples & Charles Ltd.; Washington, D.C.
Richard J. Vitullo, AIA; Oak Leaf Studio; Crownsville, Maryland

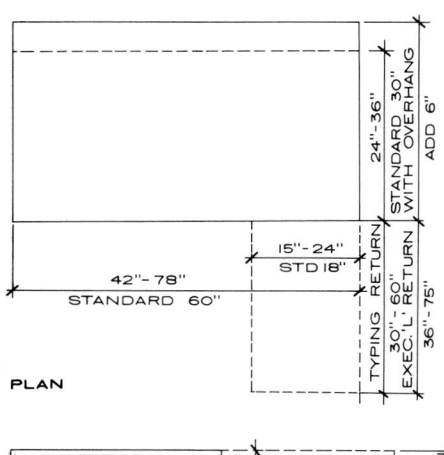

PLAN

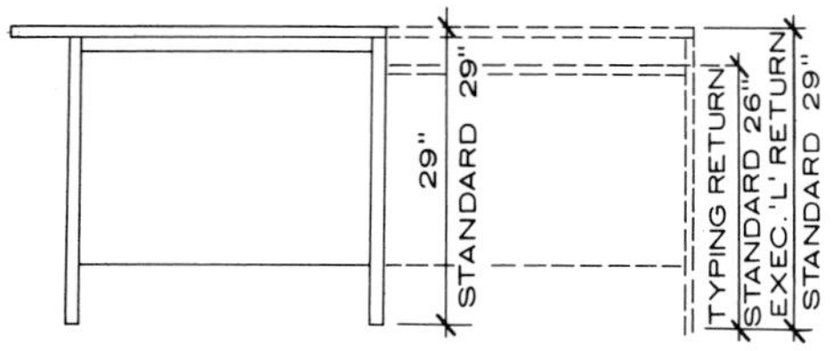

ELEVATION
DESK: SINGLE OR DOUBLE PEDESTAL

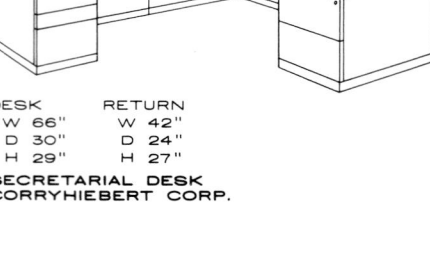

DESK   RETURN
W 66"   W 42"
D 30"   D 24"
H 29"   H 27"

SECRETARIAL DESK
CORRYHIEBERT CORP.

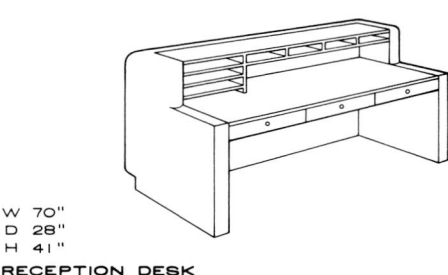

W 70"
D 28"
H 41"

RECEPTION DESK
THE PACE COLLECTION, INC.

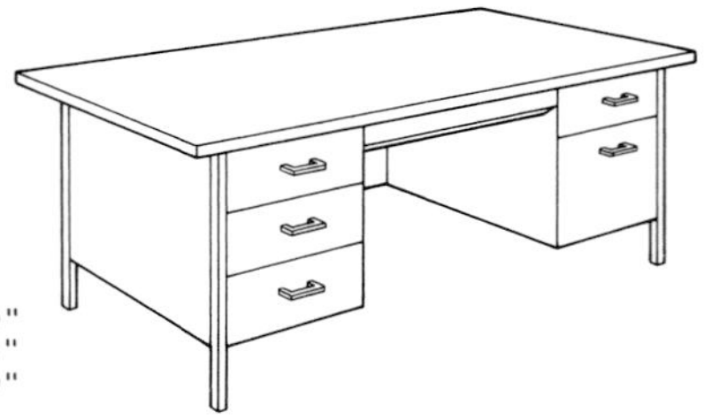

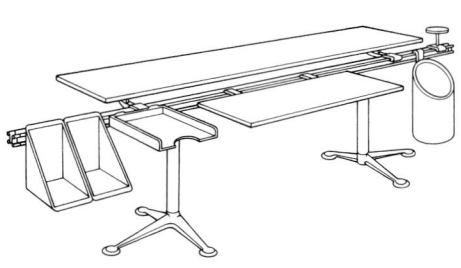

W 70"
D 36"
H 29"

DOUBLE PEDESTAL DESK,
SIDE OVERHANG 4200 SERIES
STEELCASE, INC.

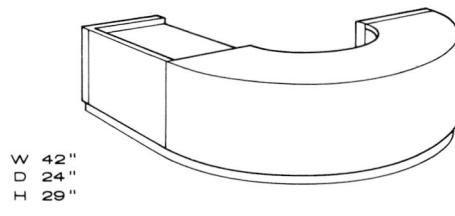

W 42"
D 24"
H 29"

CURVED SEGMENTED DESK
JG FURNITURE SYSTEMS, INC.

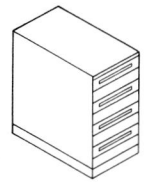 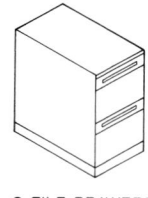 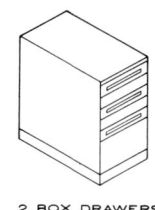 (Burdick / Mueller / Krueger row)

BURDICK GROUP
HERMAN MILLER, INC.

DESK, VARIA CASEGOODS
MUELLER

W 117"
D 66 3/4"
H 29"

MENHIR DESK
KRUEGER INTERNATIONAL DIVISION

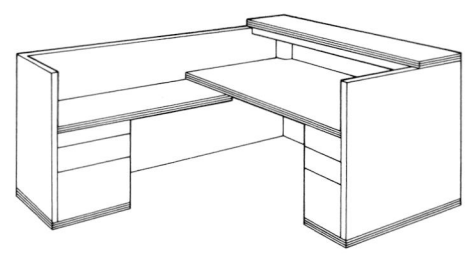 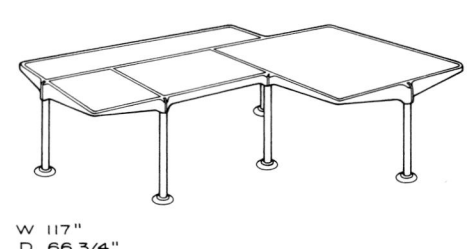

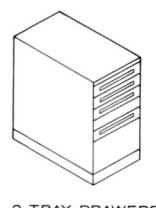 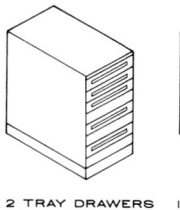 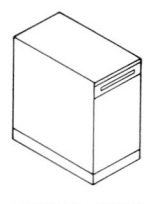 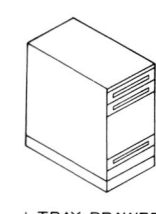

4 BOX DRAWERS   2 FILE DRAWERS   2 BOX DRAWERS
                                      1 FILE DRAWER

2 TRAY DRAWERS   2 TRAY DRAWERS   1 HINGED DOOR   1 TRAY DRAWER
1 BOX DRAWER   3 BOX DRAWERS   1 DATA PROCESSING
1 FILE DRAWER   1 BOX DRAWER

NOTE: ALL PEDESTALS — W 15", D 24", H 29"

4600/8600 CREDENZA PEDESTALS
ALL-STEEL, INC.

TYPICAL CREDENZA DIMENSIONS

	WIDTH (IN.)	DEPTH (IN.)	HEIGHT (IN.)
One component	15–30	17¾–24	25½–29¾
Two component	30–41½	17¾–24	25½–29¾
Three component	45–60½	17¾–24	25½–29¾
Four component	60–79¾	17¾–24	25½–29¾
Five component	75–98½	17¾–24	25½–29¾

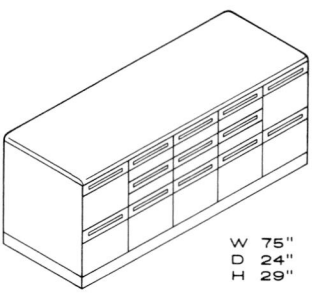

W 75"
D 24"
H 29"

4600/8600 SERIES CREDENZA
ALL-STEEL, INC.

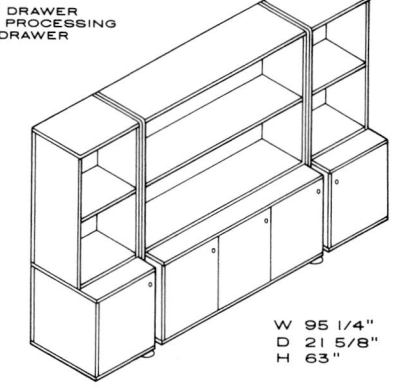

W 95 1/4"
D 21 5/8"
H 63"

MENHIR CABINET
KRUEGER INTERNATIONAL DIV.

Robert Staples; Staples & Charles Ltd.; Washington, D.C.
Richard J. Vitullo, AIA; Oak Leaf Studio; Crownsville, Maryland

RECTANGULAR

WIDTH	LENGTH	APPROXIMATE SEATING
5'-0"	20'-0"	20-22
4'-6"	18'-0"	18-20
4'-6"	16'-0"	16-18
4'-6"	14'-0"	14-16
4'-0"	12'-0"	12-14
4'-0"	11'-0"	10-12
4'-0"	10'-0"	10-12
4'-0"	9'-0"	8-10
4'-0"	8'-0"	8-10
3'-6"	9'-0"	8-10
3'-6"	8'-0"	8-10
3'-6"	7'-6"	6-8
3'-6"	7'-0"	6-8
3'-0"	7'-0"	6-8
3'-0"	6'-6"	6-8
2'-6"	5'-6"	4-6
2'-6"	5'-0"	4-6

SQUARE

WIDTH	LENGTH	APPROXIMATE SEATING
5'-0"	5'-0"	8-12
4'-6"	4'-6"	4-8
4'-0"	4'-0"	4-8
3'-6"	3'-6"	4
3'-0"	3'-0"	4

ROUND

DIAMETER	CIRCUMFERENCE	APPROXIMATE SEATING
8'-0"	25'-1"	10-12
7'-0"	21'-8"	8-10
6'-0"	18'-9"	7-8
5'-0"	15'-7"	6-7
4'-6"	14'-1"	5-6
4'-0"	12'-6"	5-6
3'-6"	11'-0"	4-5

BOAT SHAPED

WIDTH		LENGTH	APPROXIMATE SEATING
CENTER	END		
6'-0"	4'-0"	20'-0"	20-24
5'-6"	4'-0"	18'-0"	18-20
5'-6"	4'-0"	16'-0"	16-18
5'-0"	3'-6"	14'-0"	14-16
4'-6"	3'-6"	12'-0"	12-14
4'-0"	3'-2"	11'-0"	10-12
4'-0"	3'-2"	10'-0"	10-12
3'-6"	3'-0"	9'-0"	8-10
3'-6"	3'-0"	8'-0"	8-10
3'-0"	2'-10"	7'-0"	6-8
3'-0"	2'-10"	6'-0"	6-8

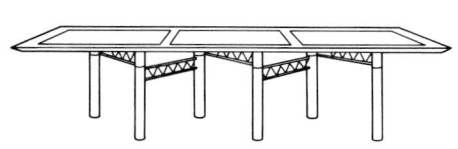

RECTANGLE 48" X 84", 96"
    (EXPANDABLE 48" X 48")
MODULAR UNITS TO 280"
H 29"

ZIPP TABLE
DESIGNER: RODNEY KINSMAN
DAVIS FURNITURE INDUSTRIES, INC.

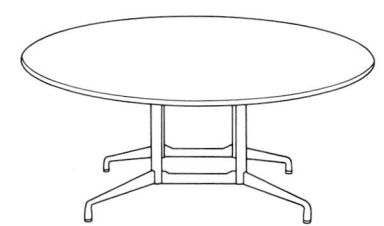

DIA 42"-72"
W 42"-54"
D 72"-144"
H 28½"

SEGMENTED BASE TABLE
DESIGNER: CHARLES EAMES
HERMAN MILLER, INC.

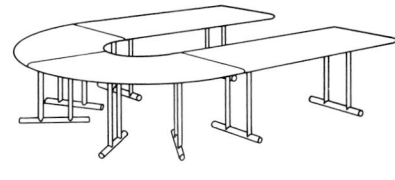

QUARTER CIRCLE: 168" O.D., 48" W
RECTANGULAR: 96" W, 48" D
H 29¼"

OMEGA MODULAR TABLES
STENDIG INTERNATIONAL

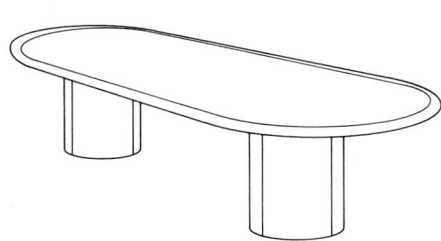

RECTANGULAR OR RADIUS END: 42" X 72" TO
          60" X 240"
ROUND OR SQUARE 42"-72"

CYLINDER BASE TABLES
MUELLER

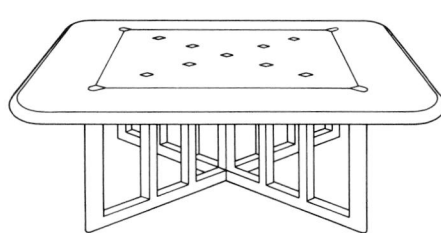

DIA. 36½"-74", SQUARE 31½"-71"
RECTANGULAR 44" X 68", 92", 116"
H 18" OR 28¼"

DE MENIL TABLES
DESIGNER: GWATHMEY SIEGEL
ICF, INC.

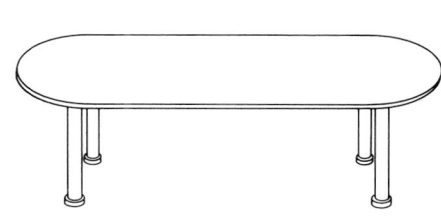

RECTANGULAR OR RADIUS END: 42" X 72" TO
          48" X 192"
ROUND OR SQUARE 42", 48", 54"

THE DONNELLY CONFERENCE TABLE
DESIGNER: PHILIP DONNELLY
JG FURNITURE SYSTEMS, INC.

W 78"
D 48"
H 28"

KNOLL TABLE DESK
DESIGNER: FLORENCE KNOLL
KNOLL INTERNATIONAL

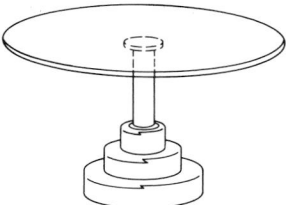

DIA. 24"-57"
SQUARE 39"-57"
RECTANGLE 16" X 51", 59", 71"

MENHIR TABLE CONNECTION
DESIGNERS: L. AKERBIS,
G. STOPPINO
ATELIER INTERNATIONAL

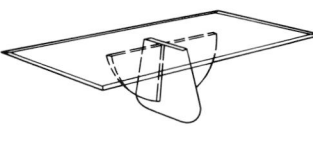

W 42", 48"
D 84", 96"
H 29"

PINNACLE TABLE
DESIGNER: J. WADE BEAM
BRUETON

W 55"-75"
D 39½"
H 28½"

WASHINGTON OVAL
EXTENSION TABLE
DESIGNER: OTTO BLÜMEL
STENDIG INTERNATIONAL, INC.

Robert Staples; Staples & Charles Ltd.; Washington, D.C.

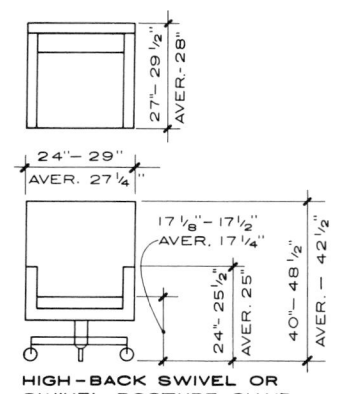

HIGH-BACK SWIVEL OR
SWIVEL POSTURE CHAIR

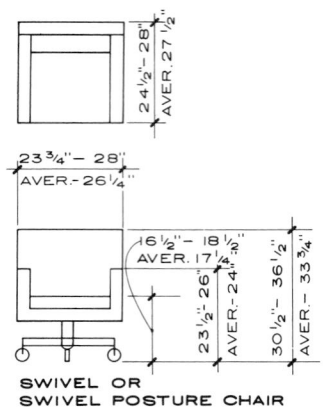

SWIVEL OR
SWIVEL POSTURE CHAIR

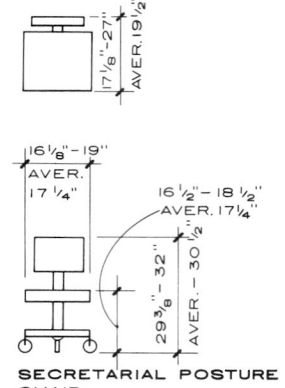

SECRETARIAL POSTURE
CHAIR

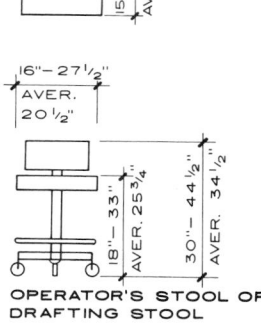

OPERATOR'S STOOL OR
DRAFTING STOOL

W 22 ½"
D 23 ¾"
H 40"–42"
SH 18 ½"–20 ½"

HIGH-BACK ALUMINUM GROUP
DESIGNER: CHARLES EAMES
HERMAN MILLER, INC.

W 26 ½"
D 23 ¼"
H 36 ½"–42"
SH 17"–20"

ERGON EXECUTIVE WITH ARMS
DESIGNER: BILL STUMPF
HERMAN MILLER, INC.

W 25 ½"
D 22 ½"
H 32"–36"
SH 16"–20"

EQUA LOW-BACK WORK CHAIR
DESIGNERS:
BILL STUMPF/DON CHADWICK
HERMAN MILLER, INC.

W 19"
D 18 ½"
H 38 ½"–41 ¾"
SH 25 ¼"–28 ½"

DORSAL OPERATIONAL STOOL
DESIGNERS:
E. AMBASZ/G. PIRETTI
KRUEGER, INC.

W 25 ¾"
D 24 ¼"
H 40"–43 ½"
SH 18"–21 ½"

CONCENTRIX MANAGER CHAIR
STEELCASE, INC.

W 24 ¾"
D 26 ½"
H 32 ¼"–35"
SH 17 ¾"–20 ½"

SAPPER ADVANCED LOW-BACK
DESIGNER: RICHARD SAPPER
KNOLL INTERNATIONAL

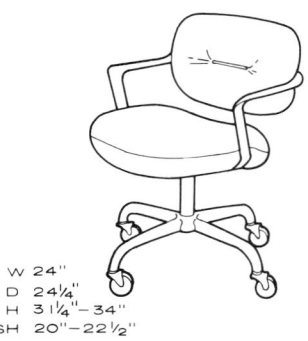

W 24"
D 24 ¼"
H 31 ¼"–34"
SH 20"–22 ½"

MORRISON/HANNAH CHAIR
DESIGNERS:
A.I. MORRISON/B.R. HANNAH
KNOLL INTERNATIONAL

W 25 ½"
D 21"
H 38"–48 ½"
SH 21 ½"–32"

ADVANCED HIGH TASK CHAIR
DESIGNER: NIELS DIFFRIENT
KNOLL INTERNATIONAL

W 27 ¼"
D 27 ½"
H 43"
SH 18 ¾"–21 ½"

BRETON HIGH-BACK CHAIR
STOW AND DAVIS

W 25 ½"
D 25 ½"
H 37"–41"
SH 16 ½"–20 ½"

KELLY PNEUMATIC CHAIR
DESIGNER: WILLIAM RAFTERY
VECTA CONTRACT

W 23"
D 20"
H 31"–39"
SH 17"–22"

SERIES 370 OPERATOR
ARMCHAIR
ELITE/BILRITE

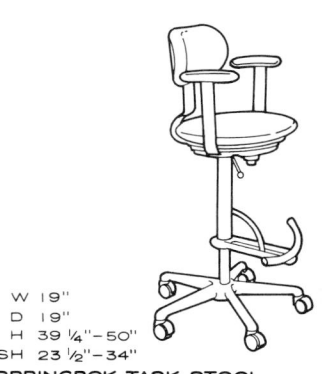

W 19"
D 19"
H 39 ¼"–50"
SH 23 ½"–34"

SPRINGBOK TASK STOOL
DESIGNER: JOHN BEHRINGER
JG FURNITURE SYSTEMS, INC.

Robert Staples; Staples & Charles Ltd.; Washington, D.C.
Richard J. Vitullo, AIA; Oak Leaf Studio; Crownsville, Maryland

OVERFILE STORAGE

TYPE	W	H	D	WEIGHT*
Over 2-drawer letter	30	26 or 37	29	170
Over 2-drawer legal	36		29	308
Over 3-drawer letter	43		29	377
Over 3-drawer legal	54		29	445

VERTICAL FILES

TYPE	W	H	D	WEIGHT*
5-drawer letter	15	60	29	405
5-drawer legal	18	60	29	430
4-drawer letter	15	50	29	324
4-drawer legal	18	50	29	344
3-drawer letter	15	41	29	258
3-drawer legal	18	41	29	162
2-drawer letter	15	30	29	162
2-drawer legal	18	30	29	172

INSIDE DRAWER DIMENSIONS

TYPE	W	H	D
Letter	$12\frac{1}{4}$	$10\frac{1}{2}$	$26\frac{3}{4}$
Legal	$15\frac{1}{4}$	$10\frac{1}{2}$	$26\frac{3}{4}$

*Weights = fully loaded file.

VERTICAL FILE CABINETS

LATERAL FILES

TYPE	W	H	D	WEIGHT*
5-drawer	30, 36, 42	64	18	610–843
4-drawer	30–36–42	52	18	524–720
3-drawer	30, 36, 42	40	18	401–553
2-drawer	30, 36, 42	32	18	285–391

*Weights = fully loaded file.

LATERAL FILE CABINETS

SPECIAL FILES

TYPE	W	H	D
A. Custom stack system	36	52	18
B. Check file	15	52	27
C. Special/double check	22	52	27
D. Card record file	22	52	27
6 drawer (3 × 5, 4 × 6 cards)	22	52	27
5 drawer (3 × 5, 4 × 6, 5 × 8)	22	52	27
E. Pedestal file	15	28	24
Library card file (see index)			

Note: Exact sizes vary with manufacturer.

SPECIAL FILING CABINETS

FIRE INSULATED FILES

TYPE	W	H	D	WEIGHT*
4-drawer letter	17	52	30	600
4-drawer legal	20	52	30	660
3-drawer letter	17	51	30	465
3-drawer legal	20	41	30	515
2-drawer letter	17	28	30	330
2-drawer legal	20	28	30	370
3-drawer lateral	39	56	24	1220
2-drawer lateral	39	39	24	875

*Weight = fully loaded.

FIRE INSULATED FILE CABINETS

Blythe + Nazdin Architects, Ltd.; Bethesda, Maryland
Associated Space Design, Inc.; Atlanta, Georgia

PLANNING

1. Users' filing needs should be tabulated in inches and in turn converted into number of cabinets. Consult manufacturer for inches available in specific cabinets.
2. For open space planning, the following square footage allowances should be used for files and use clearance:

TYPES	SPACE ALLOWANCE (FT^2)
Vertical and 36 in. lateral files	10
Lateral file for computer printout	15

NOTE: All dimensions shown are approximate. Consult manufacturer for actual dimensions.

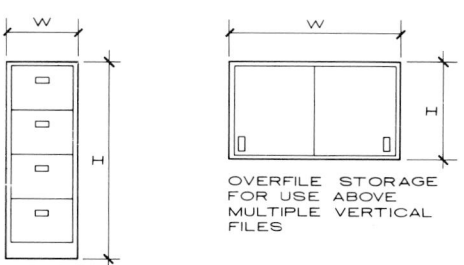

OVERFILE STORAGE FOR USE ABOVE MULTIPLE VERTICAL FILES

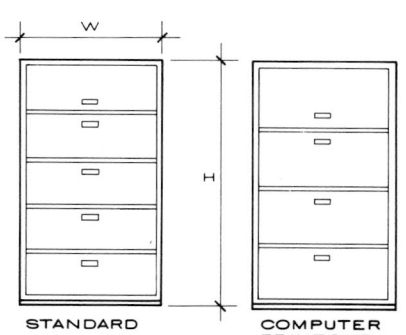

STANDARD   COMPUTER PRINTOUT

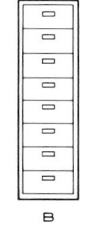 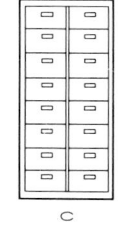 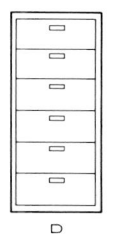 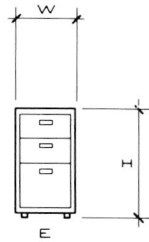

A   B   C   D   E

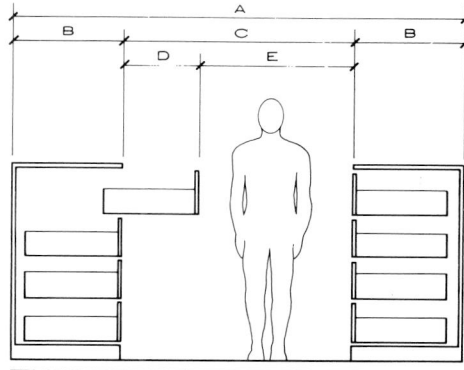

FILE CLEARANCES

	VERTICAL FILES	LATERAL FILES
A	106–120	82–94
B	29	18
C	48–62	46–58
D	18–26	16–22
E	30–36	30–36

DIMENSIONS FOR PLANNING

NOTES

1. Basic types accommodate multiple configurations of drawers, doors, and shelves.
2. 6 in. drawer accommodates cards and vouchers not exceeding 5 in. in one direction.
3. 12 in. drawer accommodates letter and legal files.
4. 15 in. drawer accommodates computer printouts.
5. Files are available to five-drawer height. Files more than five drawers high are not recommended.
6. Typical overfile storage is 26 or 37 in. high.

VERTICAL LETTER   VERTICAL LEGAL   LATERAL

These units are designed to resist forced entry and are fabricated from heavy gauge steel plate. They are available only in legal size vertical format and are essentially the same size as fire insulated cabinets. They are available with or without fire protection.

SECURITY FILES

TYPE	WEIGHT*
5-drawer	1350
5-drawer fire insulated	1650
4-drawer	1050
4-drawer fire insulated	1400
2-drawer	650
2-drawer fire insulated	825

*Weight = fully loaded

SECURITY FILE CABINETS

MOBILE FILE SYSTEM
(2 UNITS DEEP, 12 FT WIDE, FULLY LOADED)

TYPE	WEIGHT (LB)
9 Tier, legal	6200
9 Tier, letter	4850
8 Tier, legal	5550
8 Tier, letter	4350
7 Tier, legal	4900
7 Tier, letter	3850

MOBILE FILE DIMENSIONS

A	36", 42", or 48"
B	$28\frac{1}{2}$" (letter), $34\frac{1}{2}$" (legal), $40\frac{1}{2}$" (x-ray)
Tiers	7, 8, or 9

PAPER WEIGHTS

FILE TYPE	POUNDS PER LINEAR INCH
Letter size	1.5
Legal size	2.0
Computer printout, hanging	1.75

LATERAL CONFIGURATION PLAN

STANDARD CONFIGURATION PLAN

FOOT PEDAL RELEASE ROTATES CARRIAGE 90°
TO NEXT LOCKING POSITION (OPEN OR CLOSED)
ROTATING FILE SYSTEM PLAN

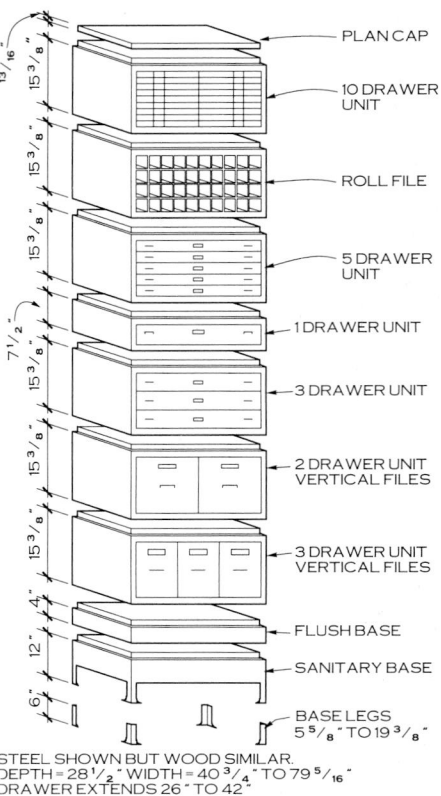

STEEL SHOWN BUT WOOD SIMILAR.
DEPTH = $28\frac{1}{2}$" WIDTH = $40\frac{3}{4}$" TO $79\frac{5}{16}$"
DRAWER EXTENDS 26" TO 42"

PLAN FILE SYSTEMS

HIGH DENSITY MOVING FILE

	MANUAL	MECHANICAL	ELECTRICAL
A	3' to 15'	3' to 45'	6' to 60'
B	24" (letter), 30" (legal), 36" (x-ray), up to 60" (jumbo)		
C	48" standard maximum		
D	36", 42", or 48"		
E	$40\frac{1}{4}$", $64\frac{1}{4}$", $76\frac{1}{4}$", $88\frac{1}{4}$", $97\frac{1}{4}$" or $121\frac{1}{4}$"		
F	48" to 129"		

NOTE
Minimum rated load/carrriage: 30,000 lb or 1000 lb per lineal foot.

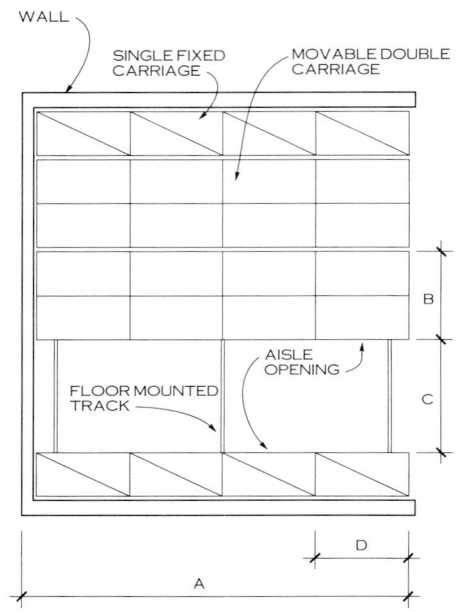

AXONOMETRIC OF CARRIAGE UNIT

HIGH-DENSITY MOVING FILE AND STORAGE SYSTEMS

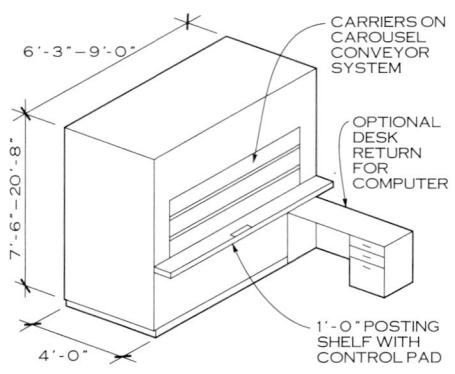

AUTOMATED VERTICAL FILE 8' - 6" WIDE UNIT

Height	8'	9'	10'	12'
Number of carriers	14	16	18	22
Filing inches per carrier	71" (hanging legal) to 88" (lateral letter)			

GENERAL

Filing systems result in significant square footage savings; however, they may produce concentrated loads and require close consultation among engineer, designer, and manufacturer. In areas where the designer must consider seismic shock, check with a manufacturer for equipping file units with special seismic anchors. Records that may be stored in these systems include file folders, binders, plans, books, ledgers, computer tape and print-outs, microfilm, x-ray files, drugs, supplies, parts, checks, cards, or inventory items.

AUTOMATED VERTICAL FILE SYSTEMS

O'Brien - Kilgore, Inc.; Washington, D.C.

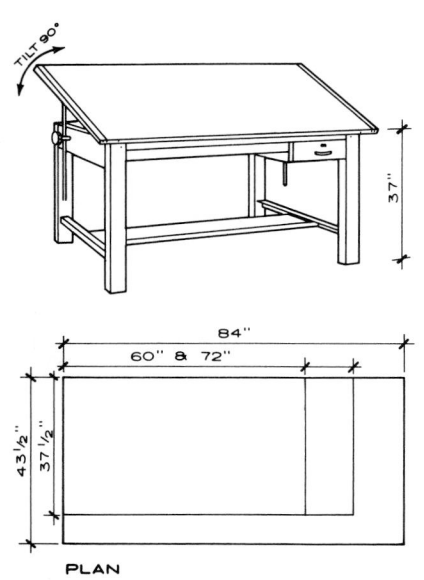

Drafting and/or engineering table is available in wood, in steel, or in combination. Various drawer and pedestal arrangements are available.

DRAFTING TABLE WITH ADJUSTABLE TOP

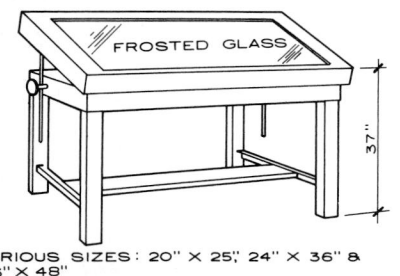

VARIOUS SIZES: 20" X 25"; 24" X 36" & 36" X 48"

FLUORESCENT TRACING TABLE

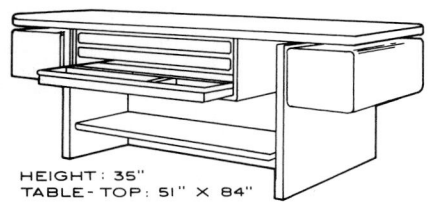

HEIGHT: 35"
TABLE-TOP: 51" X 84"

Service table provides a large worktop and integral storage compartments. Entire offices can be furnished with coordinated units.

SERVICE TABLE

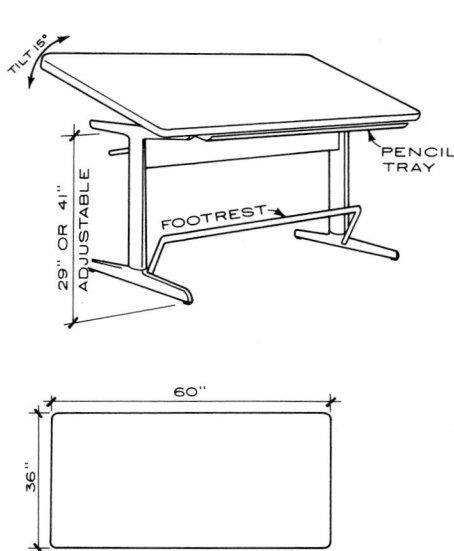

PENCIL TRAY

FOOTREST

29" OR 41" ADJUSTABLE

TILT 15°

ADJUSTABLE WORKING SURFACE

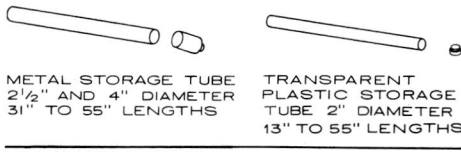

METAL STORAGE TUBE 2½" AND 4" DIAMETER 31" TO 55" LENGTHS

TRANSPARENT PLASTIC STORAGE TUBE 2" DIAMETER 13" TO 55" LENGTHS

STORAGE TUBES

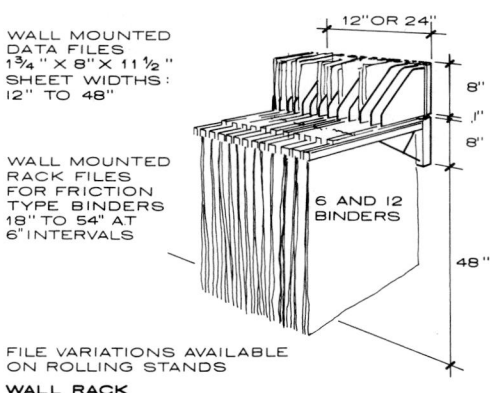

WALL MOUNTED DATA FILES 1¾" X 8" X 11½" SHEET WIDTHS: 12" TO 48"

WALL MOUNTED RACK FILES FOR FRICTION TYPE BINDERS 18" TO 54" AT 6" INTERVALS

12" OR 24"

6 AND 12 BINDERS

FILE VARIATIONS AVAILABLE ON ROLLING STANDS

WALL RACK

PIVOT FILING SYSTEM

ROTATES 360°

BOARD SIZES:
29.5" X 41.3" (75 X 105 CM)
31.5" X 47.3" (80 X 120 CM)
31.5" X 55" (80 X 140 CM)

ADJUSTABLE HEIGHT

ADJUSTABLE TILT TO 90°

Several manufacturers produce an array of drawing tables with adjustable tops, optional footrests, and pencil drawers.

COUNTERBALANCED AUTOMATIC DRAFTING TABLE

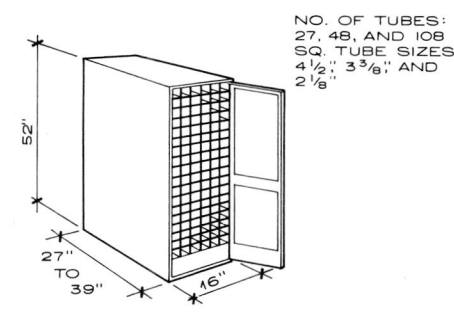

NO. OF TUBES: 27, 48, AND 108
SQ. TUBE SIZES: 4½", 3⅜", AND 2⅛"

52"

27" TO 39"   16"

CABINET ROLL FILE

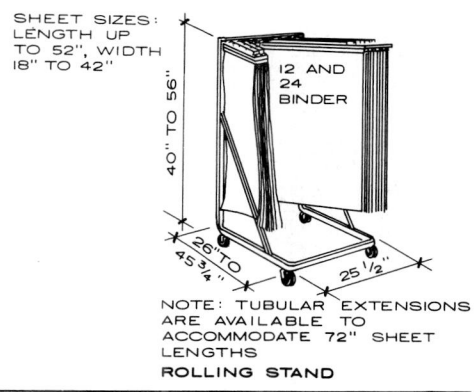

SHEET SIZES: LENGTH UP TO 52", WIDTH 18" TO 42"

12 AND 24 BINDER

40" TO 56"

26" TO 45¾"   25½"

NOTE: TUBULAR EXTENSIONS ARE AVAILABLE TO ACCOMMODATE 72" SHEET LENGTHS

ROLLING STAND

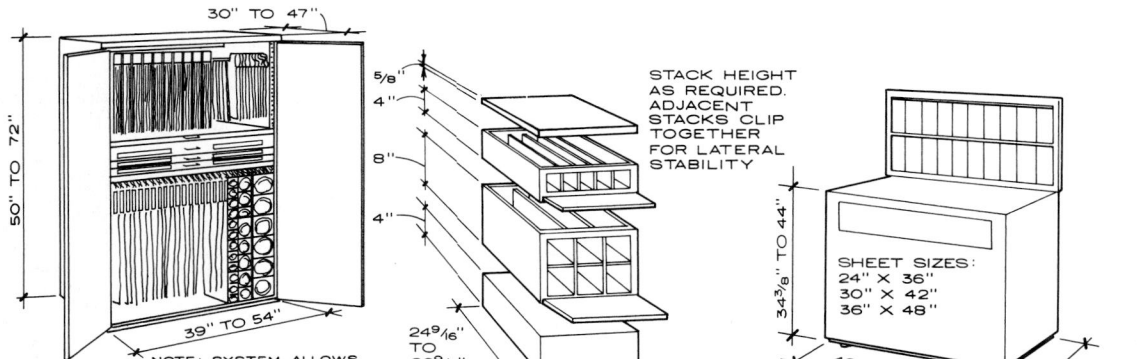

30" TO 47"

50" TO 72"

39" TO 54"

STACK HEIGHT AS REQUIRED. ADJACENT STACKS CLIP TOGETHER FOR LATERAL STABILITY

5/8"
4"
8"
4"

24 9/16" TO 60 9/16"

12 ½"

NOTE: SYSTEM ALLOWS USER TO ADD COMPONENTS AS NEEDED. BINDERS, TUBE PODS, DRAWERS, ENVELOPES, AND BOX FOLDERS ARE ACCESSORIES

MODULAR FILING CABINET

ROLL FILE UNITS

MODULAR FILE SYSTEMS

SHEET SIZES:
24" X 36"
30" X 42"
36" X 48"

34 ⅜" TO 44"

42" TO 54"   15" TO 28"

VERTICAL PLAN FILE

POCKET FILE

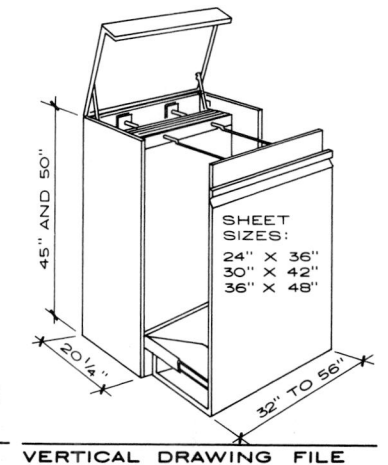

SHEET SIZES:
24" X 36"
30" X 42"
36" X 48"

45" AND 50"

20 ¼"   32" TO 56"

VERTICAL DRAWING FILE

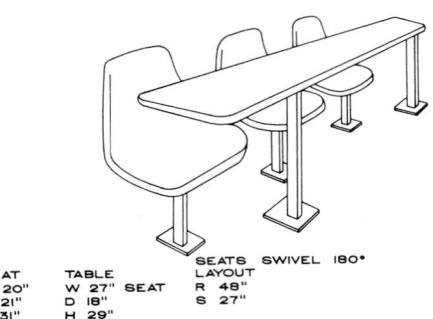

SEAT	TABLE	SEATS SWIVEL 180° LAYOUT
W 20"	W 27" SEAT	R 48"
D 21"	D 18"	S 27"
H 31"	H 29"	

SEMINAR SEATING
KRUEGER

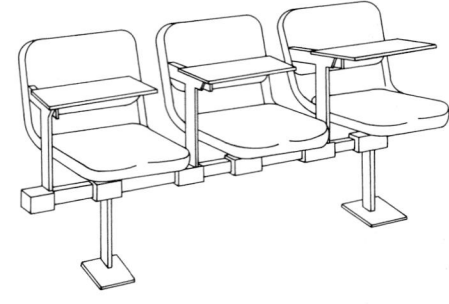

UNIT	LAYOUT
W 22" SEAT	R 36"-39"
D 37"	S 22"
H 31"	

SEQUENCE SEATING
KRUEGER

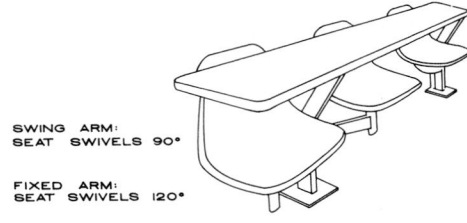

SWING ARM:
SEAT SWIVELS 90°

FIXED ARM:
SEAT SWIVELS 120°

UNIT	LAYOUT
W 27" SEAT	R 41" WITH SWING ARM
D 26" WITH SWING ARM	48" WITH FIXED ARM
34" WITH FIXED ARM	S 27"
H 31"	

UNIVERSITY SEATING
KRUEGER

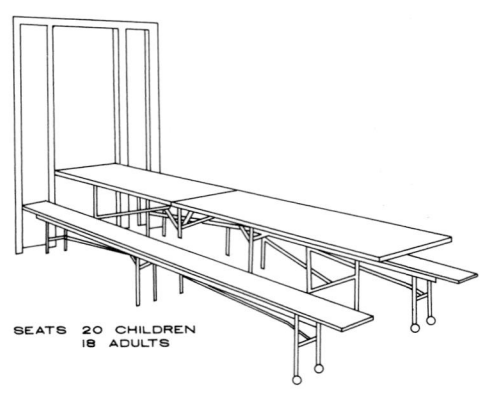

SEATS 20 CHILDREN
18 ADULTS

OPEN	CLOSED
W 168"	H 86"
D 60"	W 60"
H 25-30"	D 6" (SURFACE MOUNT)
	1" (RECESSED)

FOLDING TABLE AND BENCHES
NELSON-ADAMS

NOTES

1. All spacing dimensions are centerline dimensions.
2. Typical seat height is 17 in.
3. Unit dimensions are to farthest extremity.
4. Auditorium seating with tablet arms is used often. See index.
5. Left-handed tablet arms generally are available for fixed arm seating.
6. Ganged seating may be adapted for mounting on level floors, sloped floors and 6 in. to 14 in. risers for tiered seating.

UNIT	LAYOUT
W 24"	R 37"
D 35"	S 39"
H 30"	

COMBINATION STUDY
TOP DESK
SMITH SYSTEM

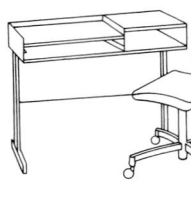

UNIT	LAYOUT
W 24"	R 32"
D 30"	S 39"
H 30"	

COMBINATION STUDY
TOP DESK
SMITH SYSTEM
"SCHOOL FURNITURE"

OPEN	CLOSED
W 60"-96"	L 60"-96"
D 18"-36"	W 18"-36"
H 24"-36"	D 4"

FOLDING TABLE
KRUEGER

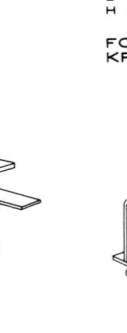

EMPTY	CAPACITY: UP TO 9
W 78"	TABLES DEPENDING
D 27"	ON WIDTH
H 28"	

FOLDING TABLE CADDY
KRUEGER

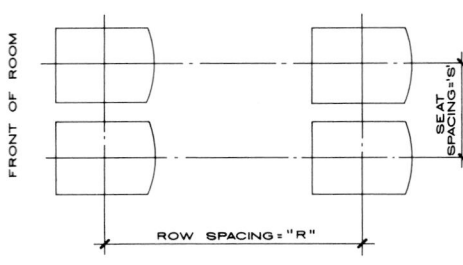

KEY TO LAYOUT DIMENSIONS

UNIT	LAYOUT
W 19"	R 32"
D 30"	S 34"
H 30"	

TABLET ARM CHAIR
SMITH SYSTEM

DESK	CHAIR	LAYOUT
W 34"	W 23"	R 45"
D 18"	D 23"	S 34"
H 29"	H 32"	

TYPING DESK   CHAIR
SMITH SYSTEM   HON

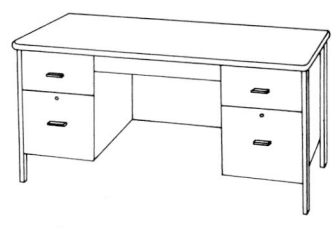

CLOSED
W 60"
D 30"
H 81"-83"

FOLDING TABLE AND CHAIRS
SICO INCORPORATED

SEAT HEIGHT
9½-17½"

DESK	CHAIR	LAYOUT
W 24"	W 18"	R 45"
D 18"	D 20"	S 24"
H 21"-29"	H 24"-30"	

OPEN FRONT DESK
AND CHAIR
SMITH SYSTEM

UNIT	AVAILABLE WITH
W 31" SEAT	26" HIGH DESK
D 30"	TOP FOR USE
H 48"	WITH COMPUTERS

STUDY CARRELL
FLEETWOOD
FURNITURE CO.

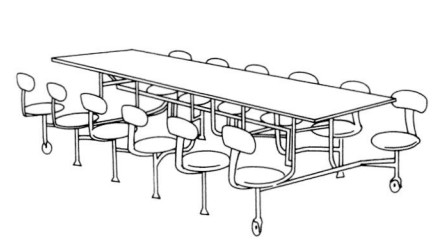

OPEN	BACKRESTS OPTIONAL
W 120"	
D 60"	
H 26"-29"	

W 60"
D 30"
H 29"

DOUBLE PEDESTAL DESK
SMITH SYSTEM

Jeffrey R. Vandevoort; Talbott Wilson Associates, Inc.; Houston, Texas
ISD Incorporated; Chicago, New York, Boston, Houston

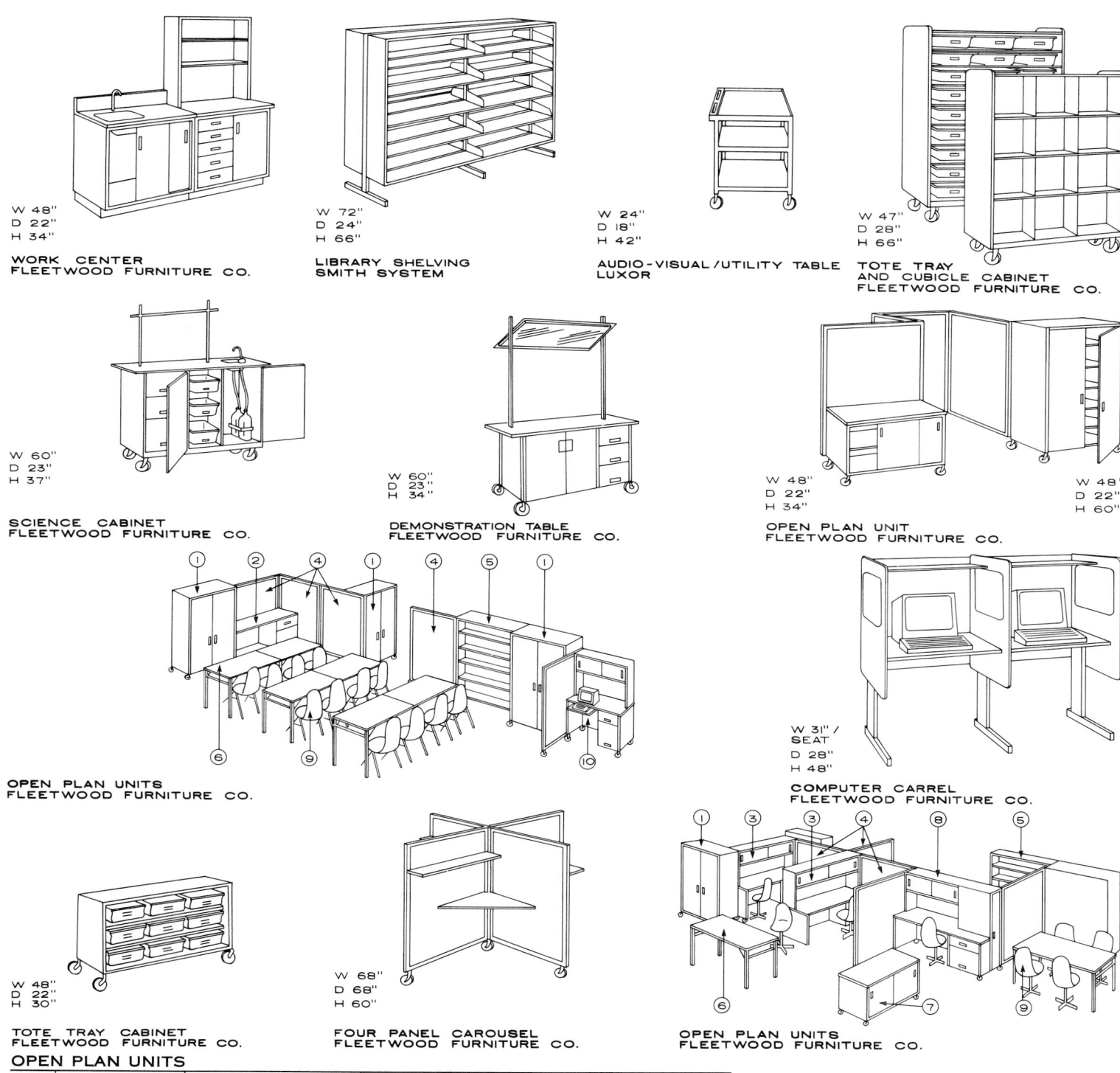

W 48"
D 22"
H 34"

WORK CENTER
FLEETWOOD FURNITURE CO.

W 72"
D 24"
H 66"

LIBRARY SHELVING
SMITH SYSTEM

W 24"
D 18"
H 42"

AUDIO-VISUAL/UTILITY TABLE
LUXOR

W 47"
D 28"
H 66"

TOTE TRAY
AND CUBICLE CABINET
FLEETWOOD FURNITURE CO.

W 60"
D 23"
H 37"

SCIENCE CABINET
FLEETWOOD FURNITURE CO.

W 60"
D 23"
H 34"

DEMONSTRATION TABLE
FLEETWOOD FURNITURE CO.

W 48"
D 22"
H 34"

OPEN PLAN UNIT
FLEETWOOD FURNITURE CO.

W 48"
D 22"
H 60"

OPEN PLAN UNITS
FLEETWOOD FURNITURE CO.

W 31"/
SEAT
D 28"
H 48"

COMPUTER CARREL
FLEETWOOD FURNITURE CO.

W 48"
D 22"
H 30"

TOTE TRAY CABINET
FLEETWOOD FURNITURE CO.

W 68"
D 68"
H 60"

FOUR PANEL CAROUSEL
FLEETWOOD FURNITURE CO.

OPEN PLAN UNITS
FLEETWOOD FURNITURE CO.

OPEN PLAN UNITS

KEY	DESCRIPTION	MANUFACTURER	W (IN.)	D (IN.)	H (IN.)	SHELVES	DRAWER
1	cabinet	Fleetwood Furniture Co.	48	24	72	8	0
2	desk	Fleetwood Furniture Co.	48	28	29	0	2
3	desk	Fleetwood Furniture Co.	48	28	60	1	2
4	partition	Fleetwood Furniture Co.	48		60		
4	partition	Fleetwood Furniture Co.	48		72		
5	bookcase	Fleetwood Furniture Co.	48	22	60	10	
6	table	Krueger	48	24	29		
7	cabinet	Fleetwood Furniture Co.	48	22	34	1	0
8	desk/closet	Fleetwood Furniture Co.	48	28	60	1	2
9	chair	Krueger	21	20	32		
10	comp. desk	Fleetwood Furniture Co.	48	28	60	1	2

NOTES

1. Open classroom layouts are based on modular partition dimensions: 48 in. wide x 60 in. or 72 in. high.
2. Partitions are available with hinges to connect with standard height cabinets, or with casters for freestanding use.
3. Surfaces for partitions are vinyl, porcelain enameled steel, chalkboard, or tackboard.
4. Carrels may be ordered with 31 in. high desktops for use with wheelchairs.
5. Typical seat height is 17 in.
6. Unit dimensions are to farthest extremity.

Jeffrey R. Vandevoort; Talbott Wilson Associates, Inc.; Houston, Texas
ISD Incorporated; Chicago, New York, Boston, Houston

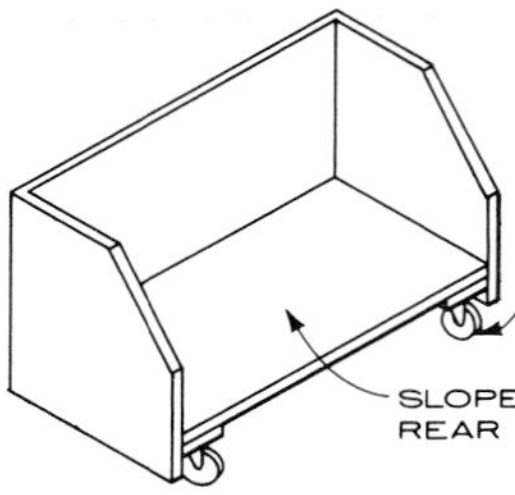

24" W X 12" TO 18" D X 15" TO 18"H
BLOCK CART

CASTERS

SLOPE SHELF TO REAR OF CART

SLOPED SHELVING

3" SHELVING FOR DISPLAY

10" SHELVING

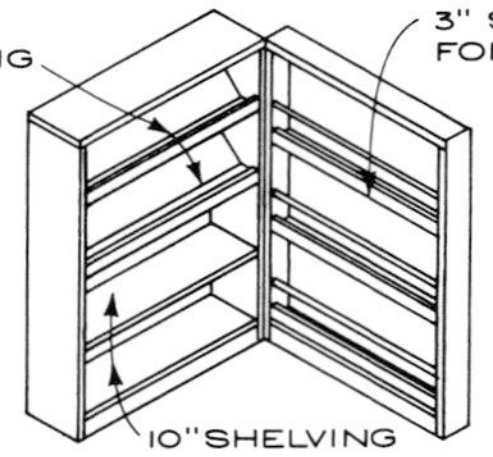

36" W X 52"H
FOLDING BOOKCASE

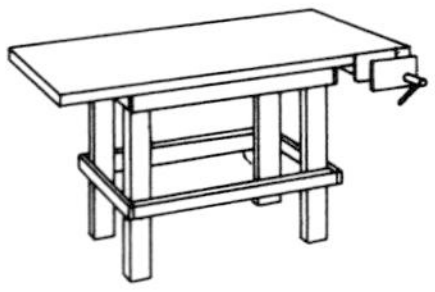

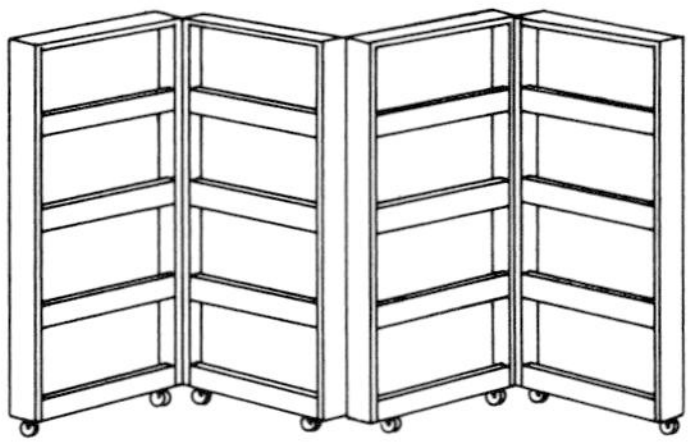

24" W X 3" D X 48"H SECTIONS
FOLDING BOOKSCREEN

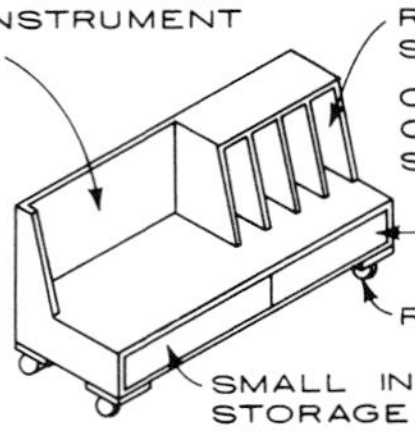

4" PER MAT

CASTERS

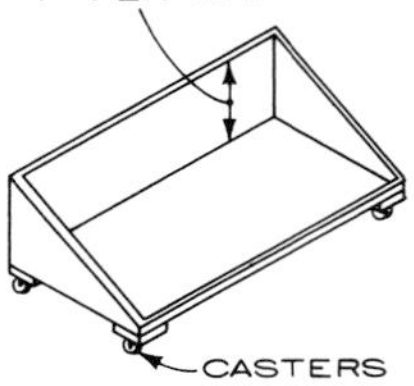

26" W X 14" D
REST MAT CART

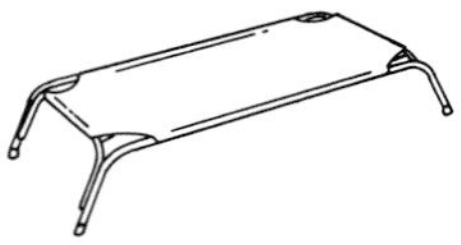

22" TO 27"W X 54" TO 62"D X 12"H
STACKABLE REST COT

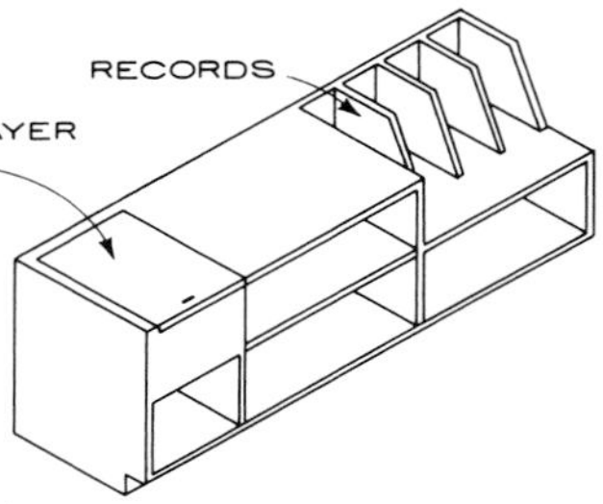

SMALL AND LARGE BLOCKS

TOYS

INDIVIDUAL CUBICLES

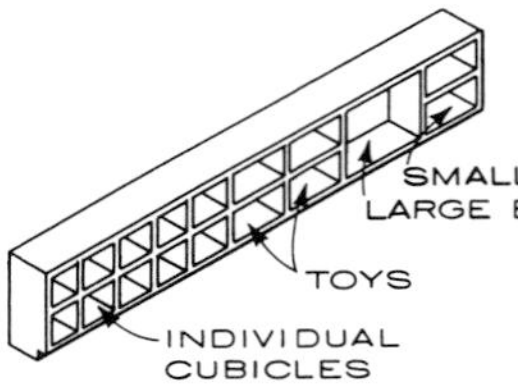

12" TO 18"D X 24"H
BUILT-IN STORAGE CUBICLES

FLOOR EASEL

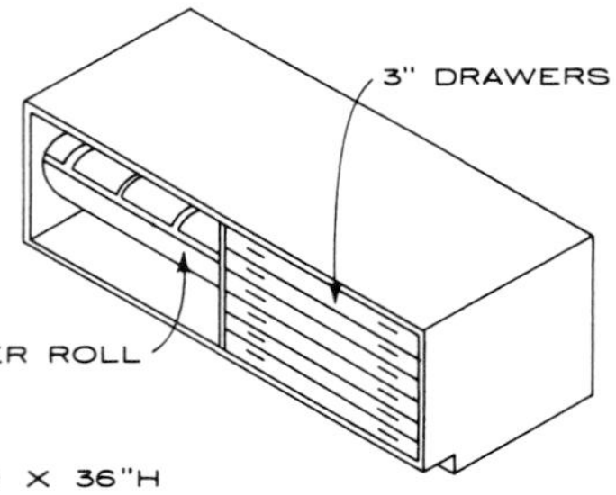

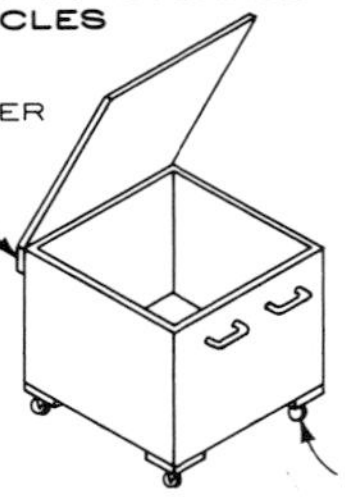

BUMPER

CASTERS

24" SQUARE CARTS TO
CLAY CART

CARRY 50-100 LB
UNDERCOUNTER CLAY CART

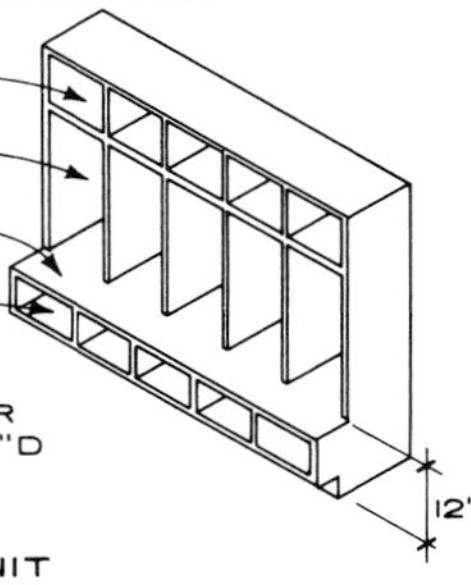

60"L X 41"W X 42"H
EXERCISE LADDER

20"L X 22"W X 19"H SEAT
PLAY HORSE

44"L X 20"W X 26"H
WORKBENCH

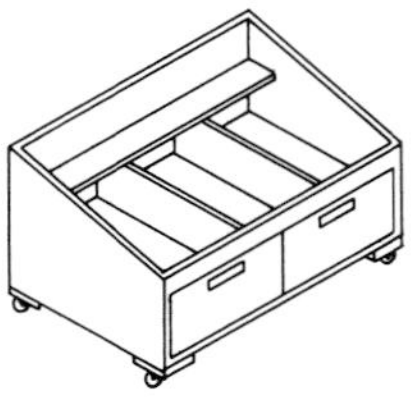

30"W X 24"D X 18" X 24"H
CARPENTRY TOOL CART

LARGE INSTRUMENT STORAGE

RECORD STORAGE

CASSETTE AND CASSETTE PLAYER STORAGE

RUBBER TIRES

SMALL INSTRUMENT STORAGE

54"W X 18"D X 28"H
MUSIC CART

RECORDS

RECORD PLAYER STORAGE

20"D X 24"H
RECORD PLAYER AND STORAGE UNIT

3" DRAWERS

PAPER ROLL

30"D X 36"H
PAPER STORAGE UNIT

HATS

COATS

BENCH

SHOES

12" MODULAR WIDTH X 14"D X 52" H
LOCKER UNIT

12"

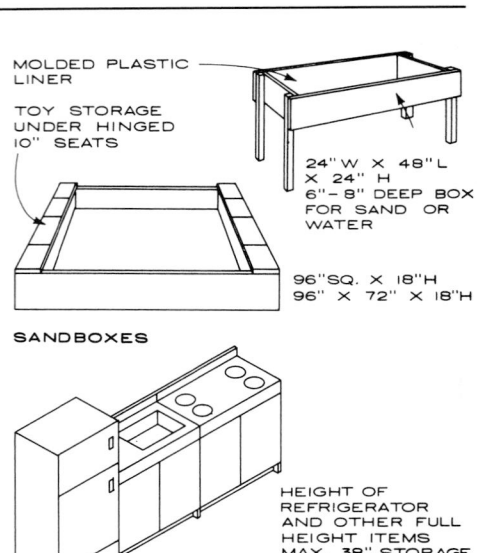

MOLDED PLASTIC LINER

TOY STORAGE UNDER HINGED 10" SEATS

24" W X 48"L X 24" H

6"- 8" DEEP BOX FOR SAND OR WATER

96" SQ. X 18"H
96" X 72" X 18"H
SANDBOXES

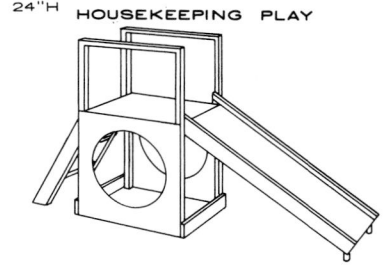

HEIGHT OF REFRIGERATOR AND OTHER FULL HEIGHT ITEMS MAX. 38". STORAGE UNITS FOR POTS, PANS, AND DISHES ARE RECOMMENDED

18" TO 20"W X 12"D X 24"H   **HOUSEKEEPING PLAY**

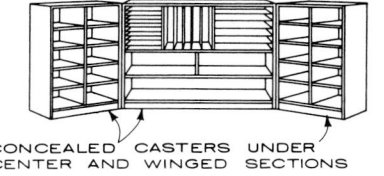

62"L X 24"W X 36"H
INDOOR SLIDE

SHELVES MOVABLE IN 2" INTERVALS

CONCEALED CASTERS UNDER CENTER AND WINGED SECTIONS

46"W (CLOSED) X 14"D X 34"H
FOLDING STORAGE UNIT

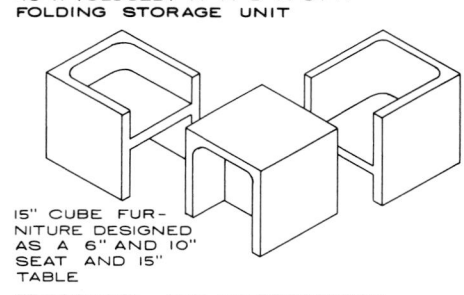

15" CUBE FURNITURE DESIGNED AS A 6" AND 10" SEAT AND 15" TABLE

PRESCHOOL AND KINDERGARTEN SEATING

GENERAL CHAIR AND TABLE REQUIREMENTS

AGE OF CHILD	CHAIR SEAT HEIGHT				TABLE HEIGHT
	8''	10''	12''	14''	
2 years	80%	20%			—
3 years	40%	50%	10%		18''
4 years		25%	75%		20''
5 years			75%	25%	22''

Kent Wong; Hewlett, Jamison, Atkinson & Luey; Portland, Oregon

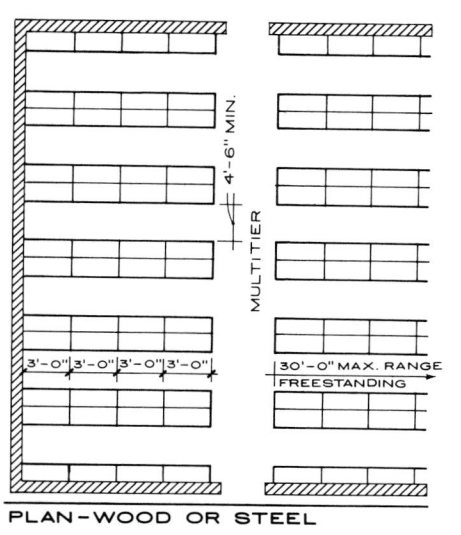

PLAN—WOOD OR STEEL

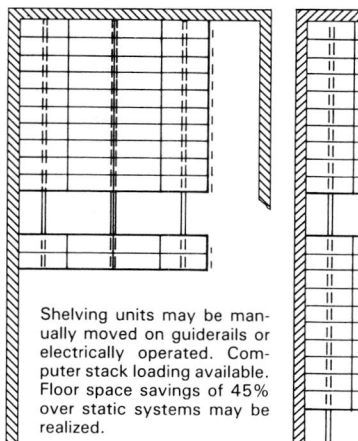
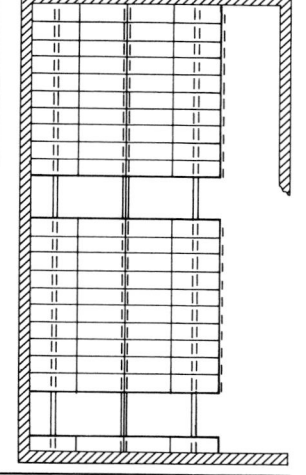

PLAN—TRACK OR STACK SHELVING

Shelving units may be manually moved on guiderails or electrically operated. Computer stack loading available. Floor space savings of 45% over static systems may be realized.

SHELF CAPACITY AND DEPTH

TYPE OF BOOK	VOLUMES PER LINEAR FT	SHELF DEPTH (IN.)
Children's	10-12	8
Fiction and economics	7	8
History and General Literature	7	8
Reference	7	10
Technical and Scientific	6	8
Medical	5	10
Law and public documents	4-5	8
Bound periodicals	5	10-12
U.S. Patent spec.	2	8

BOOK CAPACITY PER GROSS FLOOR AREA

Many variables must be considered: size and kind of books, book lifts, carrels, number and width of aisles, ultimate capacity, and so on. Variances run from 13½ to 19 books/sq ft. For a rule of thumb allow 16 books/sq ft of gross area. The average dead load of books is 25 lb/cu ft.

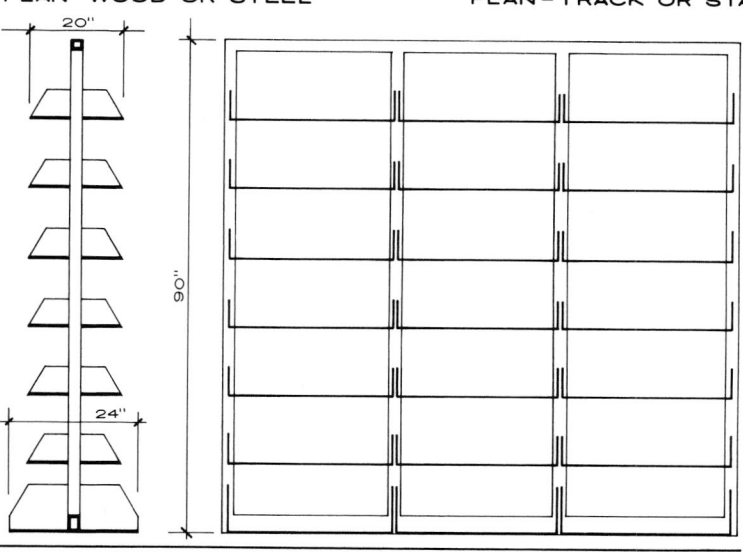

ADJUSTABLE SHELF UNIT, STEEL

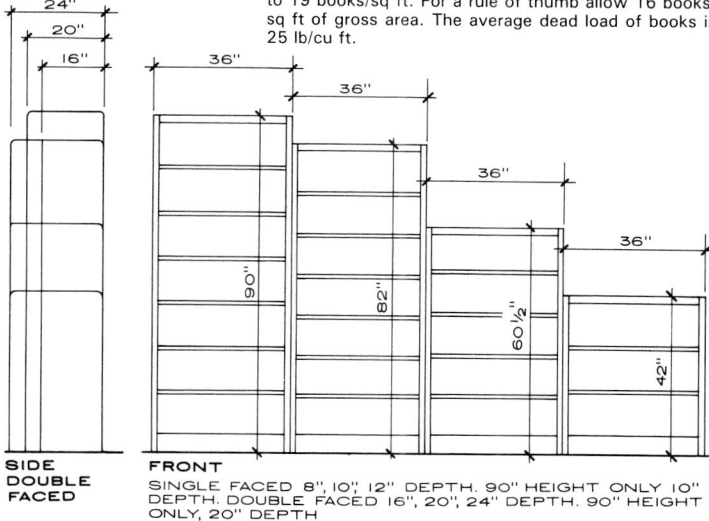

SIDE DOUBLE FACED   **FRONT**

SINGLE FACED 8", 10", 12" DEPTH. 90" HEIGHT ONLY 10" DEPTH. DOUBLE FACED 16", 20", 24" DEPTH. 90" HEIGHT ONLY, 20" DEPTH

ADJUSTABLE SHELF UNIT, WOOD

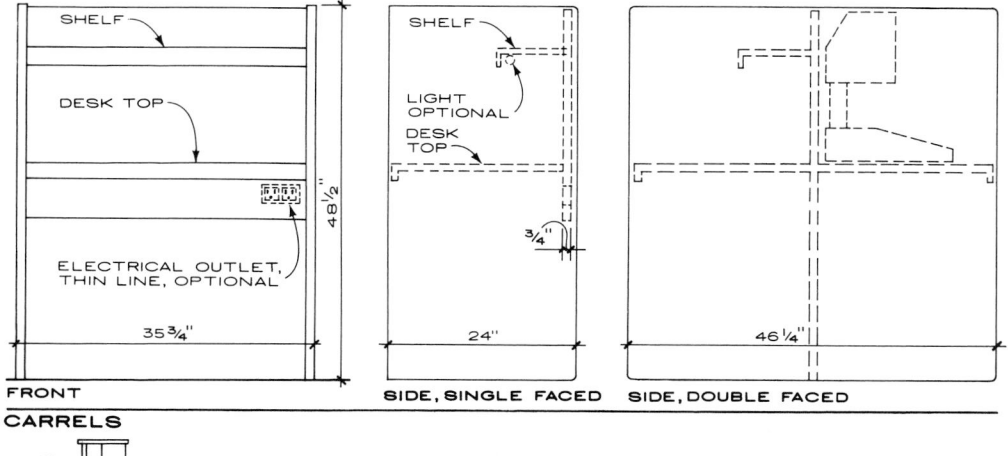

FRONT   **SIDE, SINGLE FACED**   **SIDE, DOUBLE FACED**

CARRELS

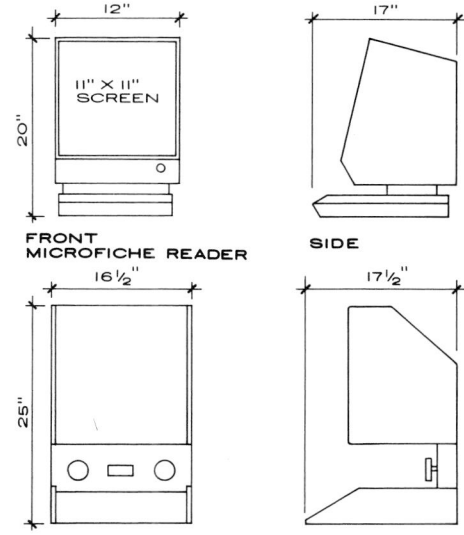

FRONT MICROFICHE READER   **SIDE**

FRONT   **SIDE**
MICROREADER FOR FICHE OR FILM
NOTE

Generally microfilm and microfiche readers and video display terminals (VDT) are positioned on tables.

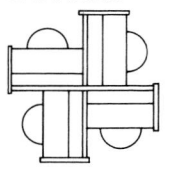

PLAN PINWHEEL   **ELEVATION**

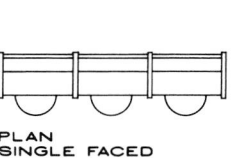

PLAN SINGLE FACED

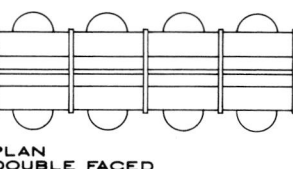

PLAN DOUBLE FACED

CARREL ARRANGEMENTS

LIBRARY EQUIPMENT

Walter Hart Associates, AIA; White Plains, New York

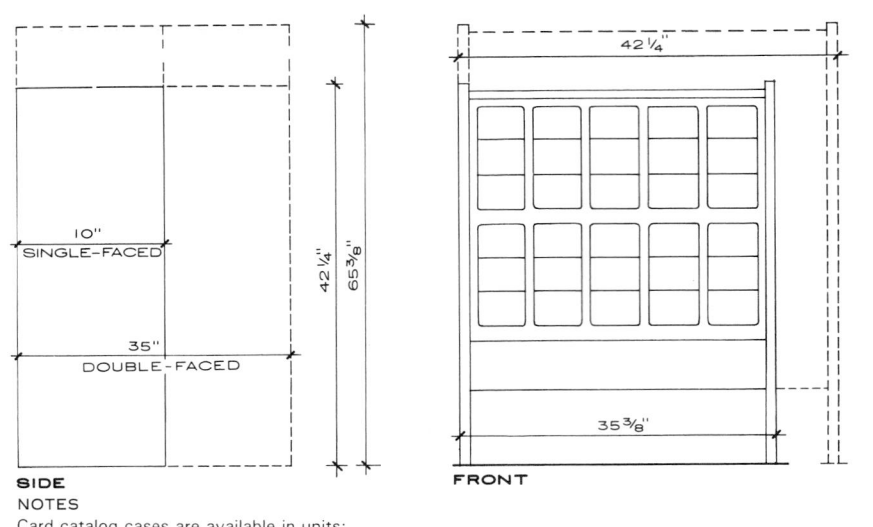

SIDE

FRONT

NOTES

Card catalog cases are available in units:
Single-faced 15–60 trays, 42¼″ H; double-faced 30–120 trays, 42¼″ H; high, single, or double faced with pullout shelves, 72–144 trays, 65⅜″ H. Effective tray card filing depth 14¾″, tray capacity 1250–1300 standard cards of 3″ x 5″.

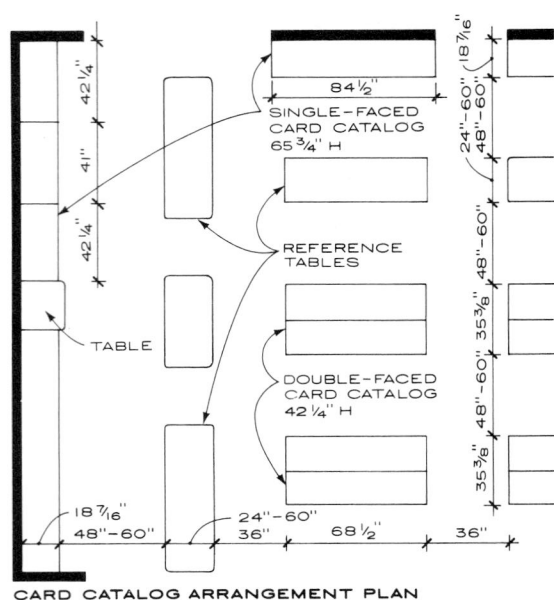

CARD CATALOG ARRANGEMENT PLAN

CARD CATALOG CASES

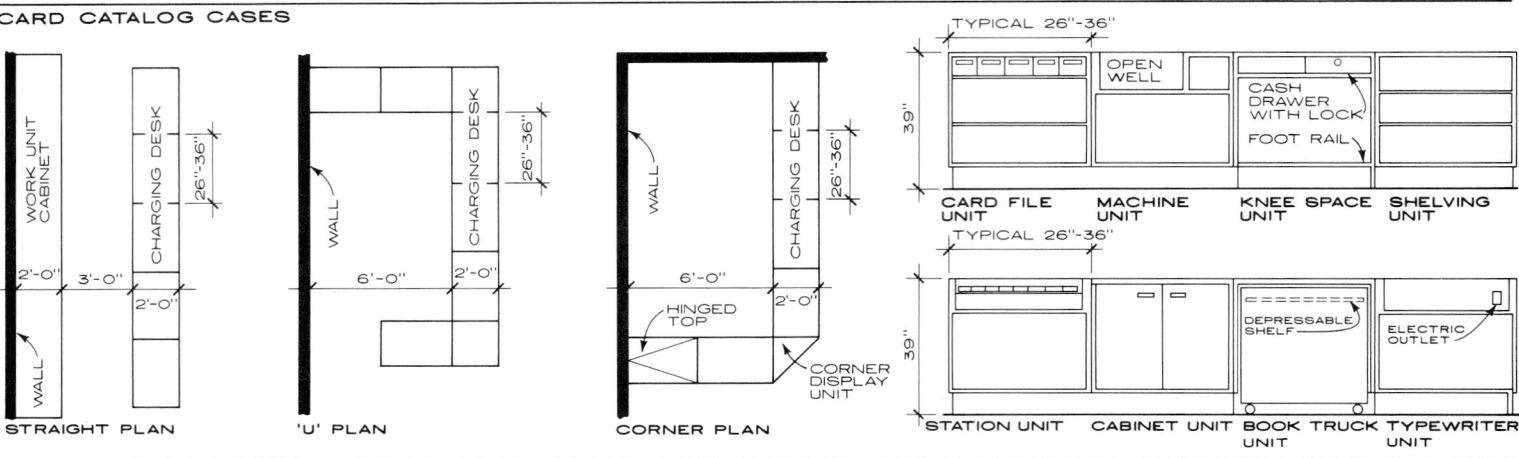

STRAIGHT PLAN

'U' PLAN

CORNER PLAN

CARD FILE UNIT   MACHINE UNIT   KNEE SPACE UNIT   SHELVING UNIT

STATION UNIT   CABINET UNIT   BOOK TRUCK UNIT   TYPEWRITER UNIT

CHARGING DESKS

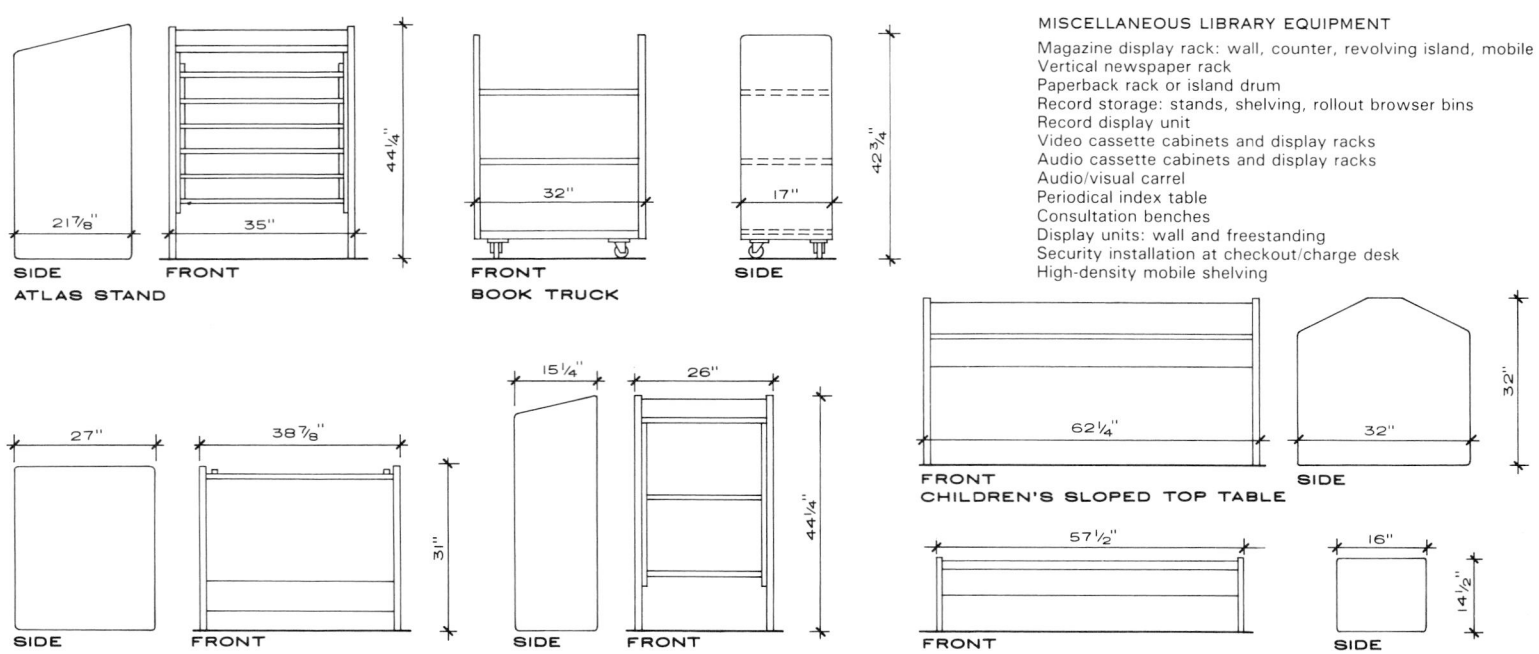

SIDE   FRONT
ATLAS STAND

FRONT
BOOK TRUCK

SIDE

MISCELLANEOUS LIBRARY EQUIPMENT

Magazine display rack: wall, counter, revolving island, mobile
Vertical newspaper rack
Paperback rack or island drum
Record storage: stands, shelving, rollout browser bins
Record display unit
Video cassette cabinets and display racks
Audio cassette cabinets and display racks
Audio/visual carrel
Periodical index table
Consultation benches
Display units: wall and freestanding
Security installation at checkout/charge desk
High-density mobile shelving

SIDE   FRONT
NEWSPAPER STAND

SIDE   FRONT

FRONT   SIDE
CHILDREN'S SLOPED TOP TABLE

FRONT   SIDE
CHILDREN'S BENCH

MISCELLANEOUS LIBRARY EQUIPMENT

Walter Hart Associates, AIA; White Plains, New York

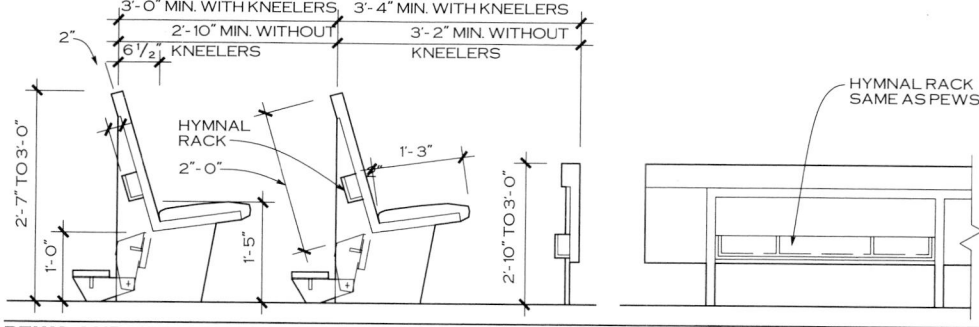

PEWS AND FRONTAL

PEW SPACING

BACK-TO-BACK BETWEEN PEWS			PEW LENGTH*		
NO. OF SPACES	2'-10" SPACING	3'-0" SPACING	NO. OF PERSONS	1'-8" PER PERSON	1'-10" PER PERSON
5	14'-2"	15'-0"	3	5'-0"	5'-6"
10	28'-4"	30'-0"	5	8'-4"	9'-2"
20	56'-8"	60'-0"	7	11'-8"	12'-10"
30	85'-0"	90'-0"	9	15'-0"	16'-6"
			11	18'-4"	20'-0"
			12	20'-0"	

*Minimum space allowed per person is 1 ft 6 in. Based on NFPA 101 Life Safety Code (1985), the maximum number of seats allowed in a row with aisles at both ends of the row is 14; maximum length allowed for a row is 21 ft 0 in.

INTRODUCTION

Ecclesiastical furnishings are as much a part of the ambience, symbolism, and meaning of a worship environment as the structure and architecture itself. Virtually all ecclesiastical furnishings are available from manufacturers in predesigned, prefabricated form. For pews and chairs, in particular, such stock or semicustom items can be quite satisfactory and economical. When special scale, material, or symbolism is desired, custom-designed and custom-built furnishings may be more appropriate, as is often true for chancel/sanctuary furnishings such as the pulpit, communion table, font, and clergy chairs. Illustrations on this and the following page give information about the general size and character of such furnishings. The theological and liturgical attitudes of each church should guide the design and execution of ecclesiastical furnishings.

PEWS

Most pew manufacturers offer a diverse selection of styles, materials, and finishes, and many will custom build special designs prepared by architects. Pew ends contribute most to style and are available in numerous designs, from closed to semiopen to fully open. Kneelers are optional; some are available with hydraulic pistons to govern speed (and noise) when they are lowered and raised. Other options include book, card, pencil, and communion cup holders.

When planning pew locations, leave spaces at the ends of some pews for wheelchair users. Distribute these open areas around the sanctuary, leaving room at some locations for two to three wheelchair users to sit together.

STACKING CHAIRS

A variety of stacking or modular chairs are available and well suited for use in small churches, chapels, and choir areas, where flexibility of arrangement or complete removal is desired. Like pews, these chairs may be upholstered in differing degrees and equipped with kneelers, book holders, and other features. Most manufacturers offer an interlocking device that enables users to join rows of chairs together for temporarily fixed arrangements. In some jurisdictions, interlocking is a code requirement. Stacking capability allows efficient storage of chairs. When worship spaces are large enough to require a sloped floor for proper sight and sound lines, chairs are generally not advisable. (Stacking chairs are illustrated on the following page.)

PULPIT

The pulpit (Protestant) has historically been a fixed chancel/sanctuary furnishing. However, increasing demand for multiple uses of worship space often requires that all furnishings be movable. Among the most important features of a pulpit is an adjustable top, to accommodate the different heights of speakers. A drop-down step may also be desirable. A pulpit should include a concealed reading lamp (especially where A/V darkening is employed), A/V con-

trols, and a built-in clock. Although lavalier or wireless microphones are used extensively, provide a concealed microphone cable raceway and pad the pulpit top to minimize the noise of rustling notes, which sensitive microphones may amplify.

AMBO/READING DESK

The ambo (Roman Catholic), or movable reading desk, is for reading or preaching. It requires an adjustable top to allow for the heights of various users. As shown, the top may be removable to accommodate readers in wheelchairs. A shelf pulled out from behind allows a book to be brought over the lap of a wheelchair-bound person. Size and scale of the desk will vary, depending on the size of the room.

LECTERN/SONG LEADER DESK

Lectors or song leaders use this very flexible, open, and mostly transparent stand. Its top is sloped, with a book stop much like the ambo but of smaller scale.

COMMUNION RAIL

Communion rails should provide for comfortable kneeling and perhaps for the disposition of individual communion cups. In worship spaces also used for concerts or drama, communion rails may need to be easily removable.

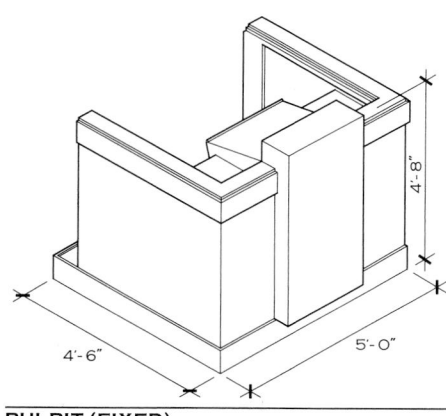

PULPIT (FIXED)

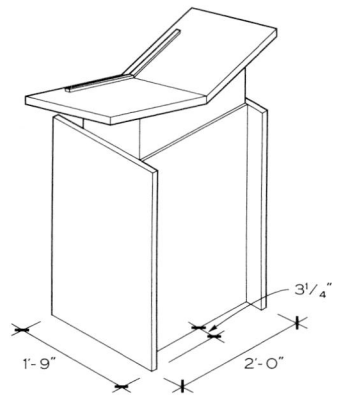

PULPIT (MOVABLE)

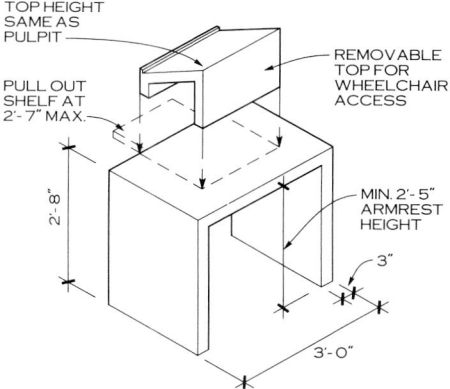

AMBO/READING DESK

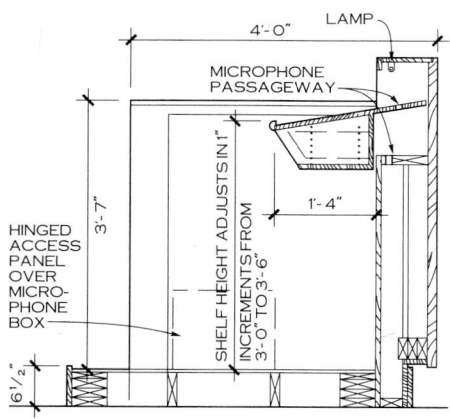

PULPIT (FIXED) SECTION

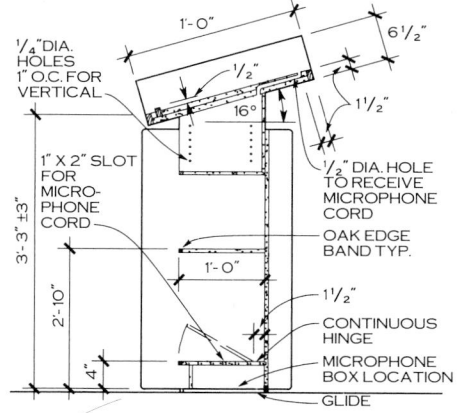

PULPIT (MOVABLE) SECTION

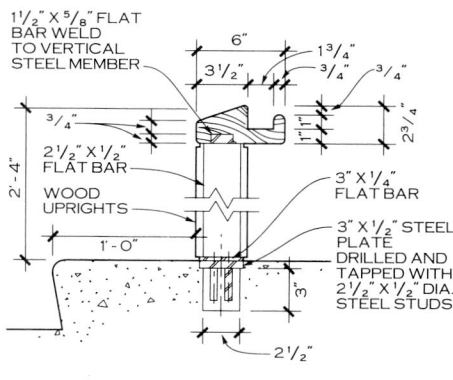

COMMUNION RAIL SECTION

Ware Associates, Inc.; Rockford, Illinois/Chicago/Los Angeles

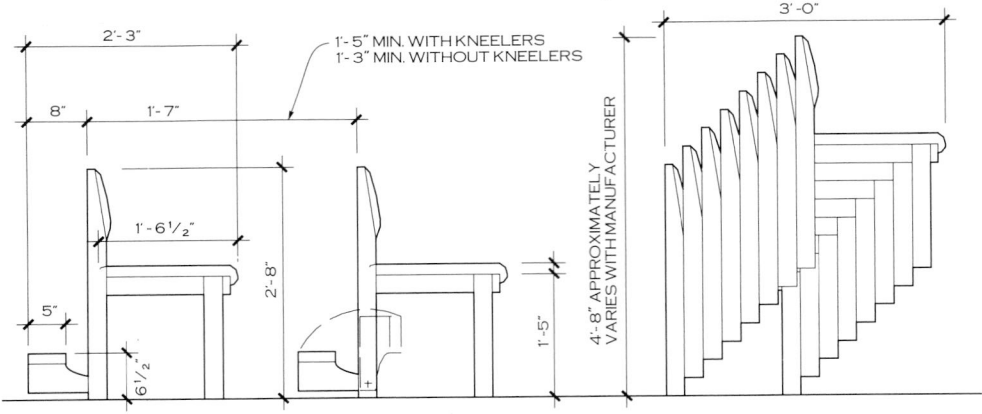

STACKING CHAPEL/CHOIR CHAIRS

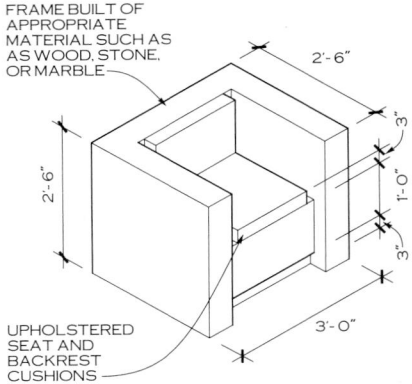

CLERGY/PRESIDER CHAIR

ALTAR/COMMUNION TABLE

In most churches, the altar or communion table is the primary focus and therefore the most visually prominent furnishing. Style and symbolism of the altar/table are deeply rooted in the liturgy of individual churches, and their design usually requires the participation and theological direction of both clergy and laity. Appropriateness of scale and material is particularly important and widely variable. The altar/table is among the furnishings most suited for artist collaboration in design and execution.

BAPTISMAL FONT

A font for baptizing infants and/or adults may be placed in various locations, including at the chancel/sanctuary or at the entrance to the church in the narthex. In some cases, the font may be alternately moved between these locations. Space for family and friends to gather around the

font is usually required. In many churches, the font must be in a position that permits the entire assembly to view the baptism.

BAPTISTRY

Churches practicing baptism by submersion require an altogether different style of baptistry, involving a pool or tank that allows full entry by laity and clergy. Prefabricated baptistry tanks are available and custom installations possible. For churches practicing infant baptism by submersion, allow for a pool 36 x 36 x10 in. deep. For adult immersion, provide a 4 x 4 ft recessed area in the floor with a drain adjacent to the baptistry for water poured over the candidate. Baptistry water is to be heated and continuously circulated by a pump. Significant evaporation may take place and a means for automatic or regular refilling should be accom-

modated. Some areas may require water treatment. Some traditions may require, draining the pool back into the earth. When immersion or submersion is required, locate changing rooms and toilet facilities close to the baptistry.

TABERNACLE

The tabernacle generally associated with Roman Catholic, Orthodox, and Episcopalian (ambry, rather than tabernacle) churches is a very significant element in the worship environment, acting as the place of repose for the consecrated Host—the Body of Christ. It often has a highly artistic and custom furnishing. Pay careful attention to the liturgical attitudes of the individual church, and for Roman Catholic churches review the document *Environment and Art in Catholic Worship* to guide the design and placement of the tabernacle.

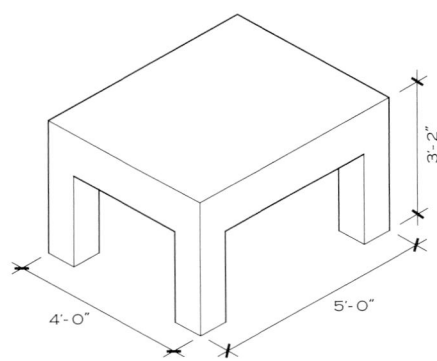

NOTE: May have a solid front

ALTAR

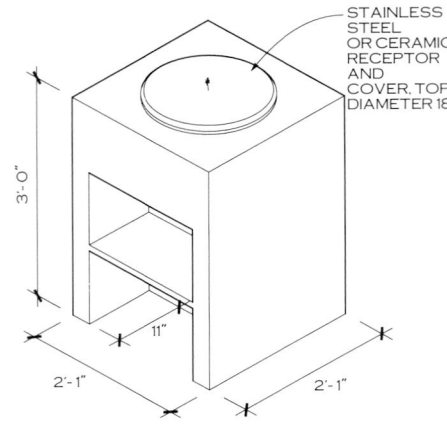

BAPTISMAL FONT

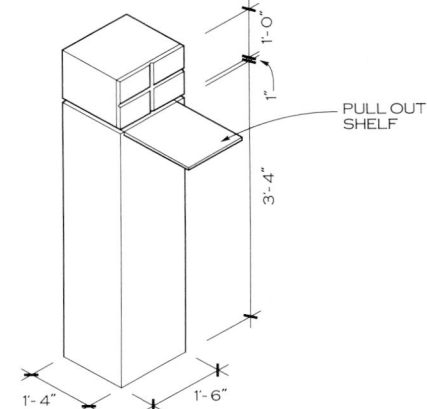

TABERNACLE

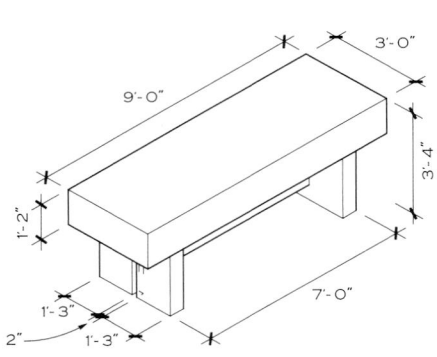

COMMUNION TABLE

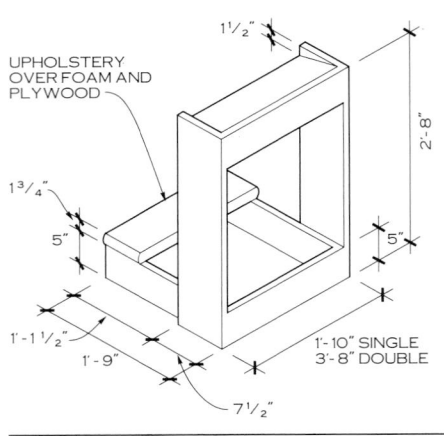

INDIVIDUAL KNEELER

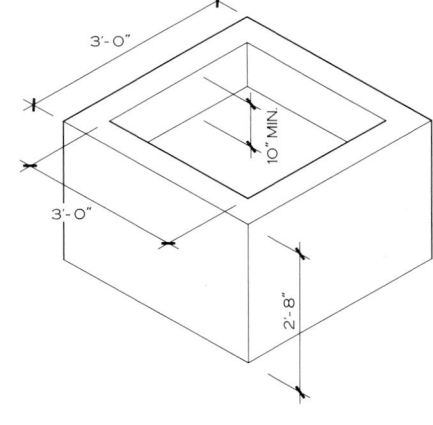

BAPTISTRY

Ware Associates, Inc.; Rockford, Illinois/Chicago/Los Angeles

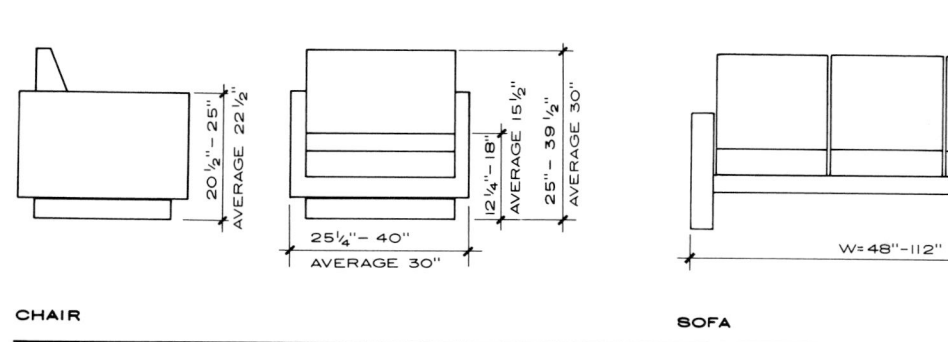

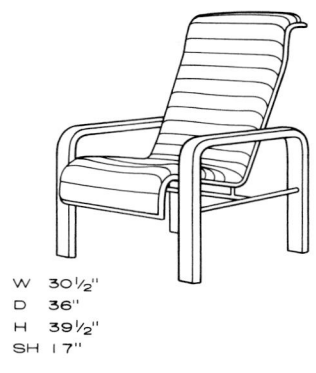

CHAIR

SOFA

TYPICAL LOUNGE SEATING DIMENSIONS

W 30½"
D 36"
H 39½"
SH 17"

**HIGH-BACK CHAIR
MUELLER**

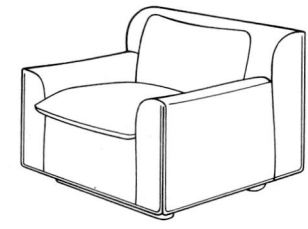

W 36"
D 33"
H 29"

**HELI LOUNGE CHAIR
DESIGNER: OTTO ZAPH
KNOLL INTERNATIONAL**

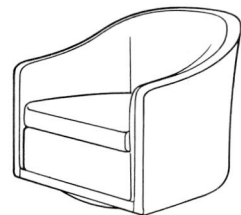

W 32"
D 31"
H 29"
SH 16"

**SWIVEL LOUNGE CHAIR
DESIGNER: BEN BALDWIN
JACK LENOR LARSEN**

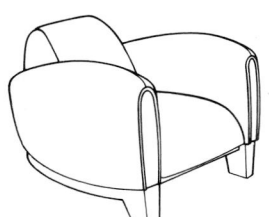

W 35½"
D 39½"
H 26½"
SH 17"

**BUGATTI LOUNGE CHAIR
DESIGNER: FRANZ ROMERO
STENDIG INTERNATIONAL, INC.**

W 36"
D 36"
H 32"
SH 15"

**LOUNGE CHAIR
DESIGNER: GEOFFREY HARCOURT
ARTIFORT / KRUEGER**

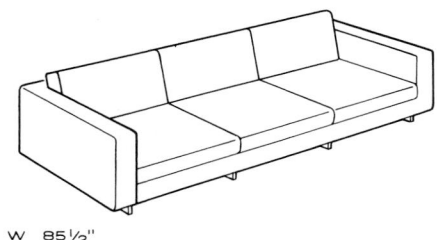

W 85½"
D 36"
H 24¾"
SH 17"

**THREE-PLACE SETTEE
GF**

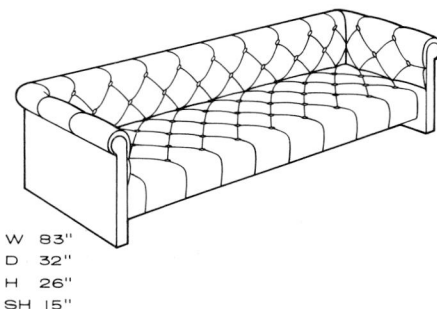

W 83"
D 32"
H 26"
SH 15"

**CLUB SOFA
ZOGRAPHOS DESIGNS, LTD.**

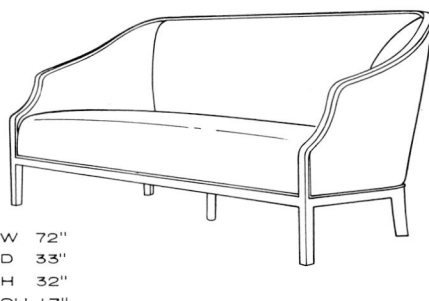

W 72"
D 33"
H 32"
SH 17"

**BANKERS SOFA
DESIGNER: WARD BENNETT
BRICKEL ASSOCIATES, INC.**

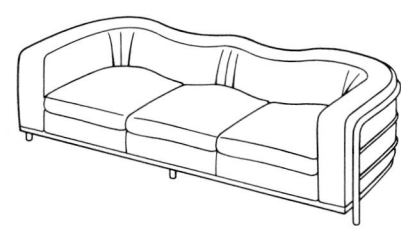

W 76¾"
D 30¾"
H 28½"
SH 17¾"

**ONDA 3-SEAT SOFA
DESIGNERS: DE PAS, D'URBINO, LOMAZZI
ICF, INC.**

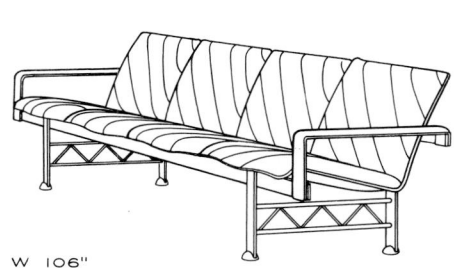

W 106"
D 30"
H 28½"
SH 17"

**SPAN 4-SEAT SOFA
DESIGNER: BURKHARD VOGTHERR
BRAYTON INTERNATIONAL COLLECTION**

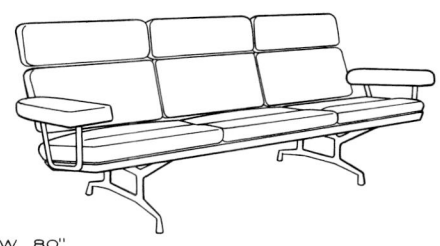

W 80"
D 21"
H 33"
SH 16½"

**3-SEAT SOFA
DESIGNER: CHARLES EAMES
HERMAN MILLER, INC.**

Robert Staples; Staples & Charles Ltd.; Washington, D.C
Richard J. Vitullo, AIA; Oak Leaf Studio; Crownsville, Maryland

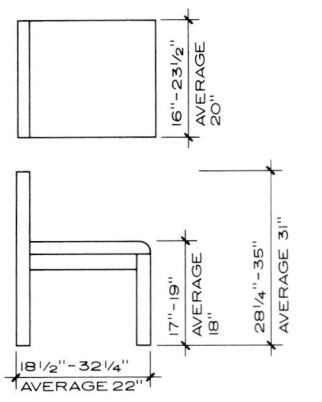

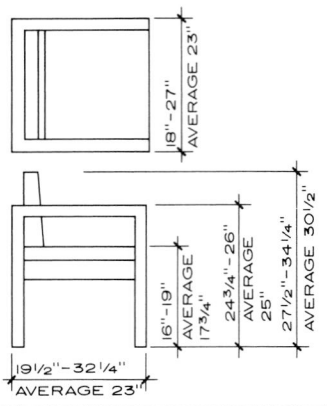

SIDE CHAIR DIMENSIONS

ARMCHAIR DIMENSIONS

W 16"
D 20"
H 35"

VIENNA CHAIR
DESIGNER: MICHAEL THONET
THONET INDUSTRIES, INC.

W 17¼"
D 18¾"
H 34½"
SH 18½"

THALIA SIDE CHAIR
DESIGNER: ANNIG SARIAN
STENDIG INTERNATIONAL, INC.

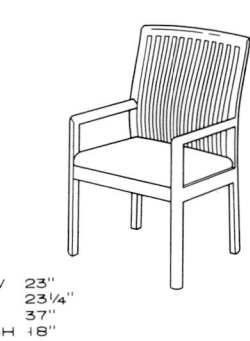

W 19¾"
D 20"
H 32"
SH 18"

PADOVA II SIDE CHAIR
LOWENSTEIN/OGGO

W 21"
D 22½"
H 30"
SH 18"

SIDE CHAIR
DESIGNER: HARRY BERTOIA
KNOLL INTERNATIONAL

W 20"
D 19"
H 34"
SH 17½"

WINDSOR ARMCHAIR
LOWENSTEIN/OGGO

W 23"
D 23¼"
H 37"
SH 18"

CARRINGTON GUEST CHAIR
KIMBALL OFFICE FURNITURE CO.

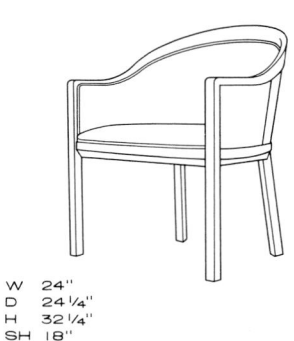

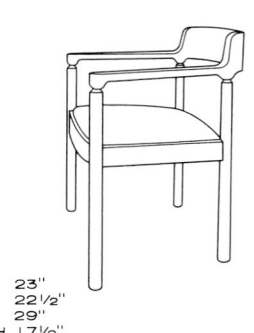

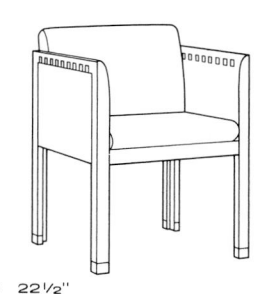

W 22¼"
D 23½"
H 32"
SH 17¾"

COURTHOUSE CHAIR
GUNLOCKE

W 24"
D 24¼"
H 32¼"
SH 18"

WOOD FRAME ARMCHAIR
DESIGNER: WARD BENNETT
BRICKEL ASSOCIATES

W 23"
D 22½"
H 29"
SH 17½"

ARMCHAIR
ZOGRAPHOS DESIGNS LTD.

W 22½"
D 22½"
H 31"
SH 19"

ARMCHAIR
DESIGNER: BRIAN KANE
METROPOLITAN FURNITURE
CORP.

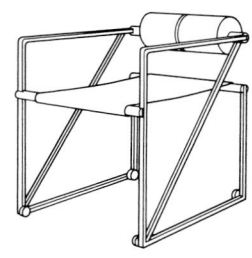

W 22¾"
D 23½"
H 31"
SH 18¼"

SNODGRASS OPEN BACK
ARMCHAIR
STEELCASE

W 23½"
D 22"
H 31"
SH 17½"

VARIX ARMCHAIR
SAMSONITE FURNITURE CO.

W 25"
D 31"
H 29"
SH 16½"

VOLKSCHAIR LOUNGE CHAIR
RUDD INTERNATIONAL CORP.

W 20½"
D 22¾"
H 28¼"
SH 18½"

SECONDA ARMCHAIR
DESIGNER: MARIO BOTTA
ICF, INC.

Robert Staples; Staples & Charles Ltd.; Washington, D.C.
Richard J. Vitullo, AIA; Oak Leaf Studio; Crownsville, Maryland

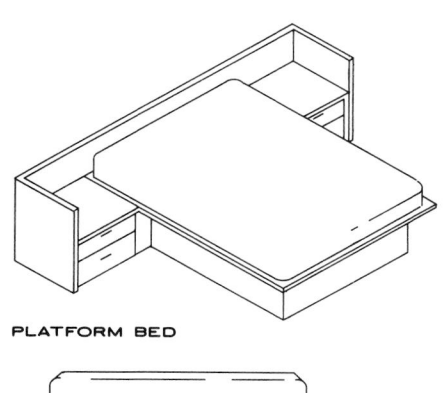

PLATFORM BED

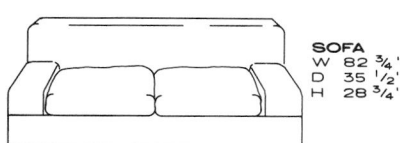

SOFA
W 82¾"
D 35½"
H 28¾"

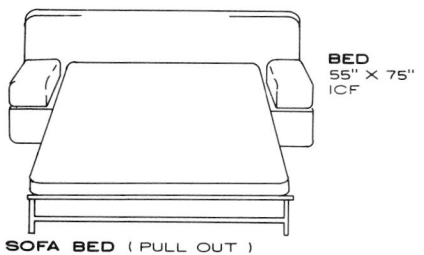

BED
55" X 75"
ICF

SOFA BED (PULL OUT)

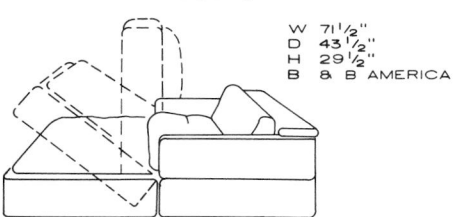

W 71½"
D 43½"
H 29½"
B 8 & B AMERICA

SOFA BED (ROTATING)

MATTRESS
24" X 58"
49" X 58"
74" X 58"

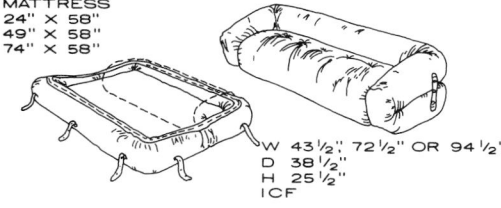

W 43½" 72½" OR 94½"
D 38½"
H 25½"
ICF

SOFA BED (FOLDING)

BEDS

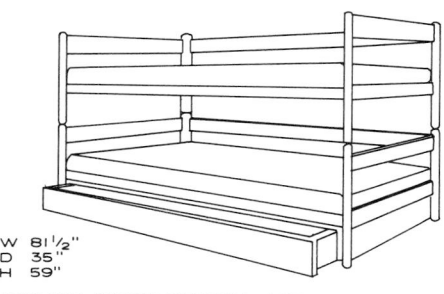

W 81½"
D 35"
H 59"

ATELIER INTERNATIONAL, LTD.
BUNK AND TRUNDLE

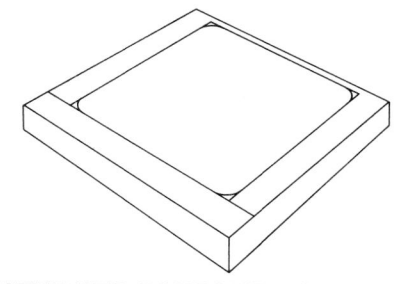

WATER BED COMPONENTS
A. Mattress pad
B. Water mattress
C. Safety liner for mattress
D. Heater
E. Base
F. Headboard
G. Side frame

WATER BED

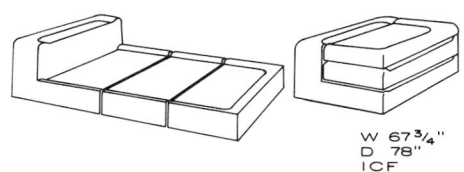

W 67¾"
D 78"
ICF

SECTIONAL DOUBLE BED

BBB BONACINA
FOLDING ARMCHAIR BED

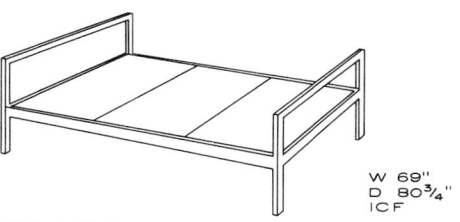

W 69"
D 80¾"
ICF

BED FRAME

STANDARD MATTRESS SIZES
Bunk: 30" x 75", 33" x 75"
Dormitory and hospital: 36" x 75" & 80"
Twin: 39" x 75", 80" & 84"
Double: 54" x 75"
Queen: 60" x 80" & 84"
King: 76" x 80" & 84"
Revolving: 24"D x 41"W
Foldout: 15"D x 41"W
Water bed: Size varies;
  Weight of water 62.4 PCF
Mattress
  Innerspring: 5½"–6½"D
  Foam: 4"–7½"D
Box spring: 5½"–9"D
  (varies with mattress—
  height to equal average)

PILLOW SIZES
Standard: 26"L x 20"W
Queen: 30"L x 20"W
King: 36"L x 20"W

W 25½"
L 51"
H 31½"

THE CHILDREN'S WORKBENCH
JUNIOR CRIB

STANDARD JUVENILE MATTRESS SIZES (IN.)

TYPE	LENGTH	WIDTH
Bassinet	36	18
Bassinet	38¾	22¼
Junior crib	46	23
Junior crib	50¾	25¼
6-year crib	51	27
6-year crib	56¾	31¼
Youth bed	66	33
Youth bed	76	36

FOLDING CHAIR BED

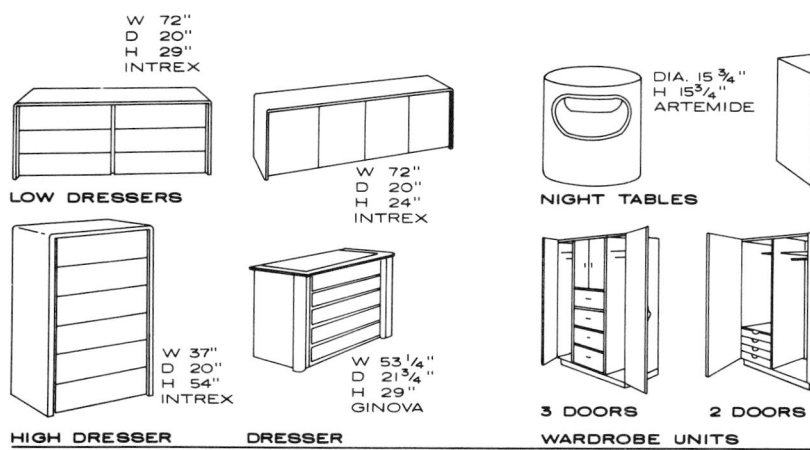

W 72"
D 20"
H 29"
INTREX

LOW DRESSERS

W 72"
D 20"
H 24"
INTREX

W 37"
D 20"
H 54"
INTREX

W 53¼"
D 21¾"
H 29"
GINOVA

HIGH DRESSER   DRESSER

DIA. 15¾"
H 15¾"
ARTEMIDE

W 18"
D 18"
H 24"
INTREX

NIGHT TABLES

3 DOORS   2 DOORS   SLIDING DOORS

WARDROBE UNITS

BEDROOM FURNITURE

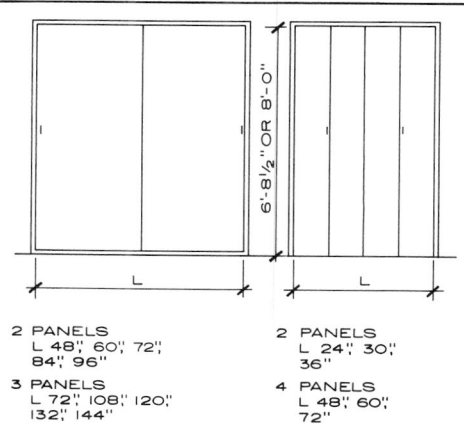

6'-8½" OR 8'-0"

2 PANELS
L 48", 60", 72",
84", 96"

3 PANELS
L 72", 108", 120",
132", 144"

2 PANELS
L 24", 30",
36"

4 PANELS
L 48", 60",
72"

SLIDING   BIFOLD
MIRRORED BED CLOSET DOORS

Associated Space Design, Inc.; Atlanta, Georgia

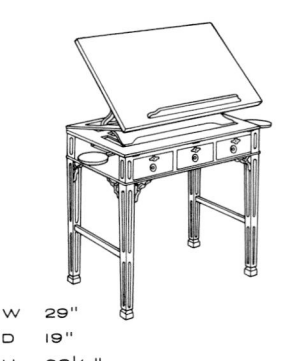

W   29"
D   19"
H   29½"

ARCHITECT'S TABLE
CHIPPENDALE STYLE 1765
BAKER

W   58"
D   28⅜"
H   29"

DOUBLE PEDESTAL DESK
CHIPPENDALE STYLE 1760
BAKER

W   75¾"
D   14½"
H   94½"

BREAKFRONT
CHIPPENDALE STYLE
BAKER

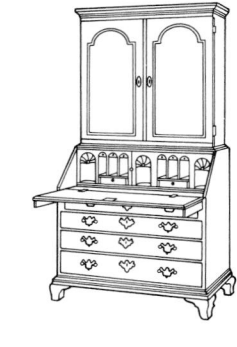

W   40"
D   24½"
H   82½"

DESK BOOKCASE
HISTORIC NEWPORT STYLE
KITTINGER

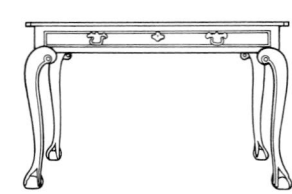

W   46"
D   24"
H   29"

CENTER TABLE
GEORGE I STYLE 1720
BAKER

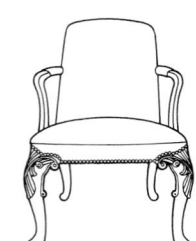

W   25"
D   24"
H   39"
SH 19"

SHEPHERD'S CROOK ARMCHAIR
GEORGE I STYLE 1718
BAKER

W   24"
D   22¾"
H   40½"
SH 19"

OPEN ARMCHAIR
QUEEN ANNE STYLE
KITTINGER

W   26"
D   25¾"
H   39¾"
SH 19"

WENTWORTH ARMCHAIR
GEORGE II STYLE 1750
BAKER

W   23¾"
D   22½"
H   45½"
SH 19"

OPEN ARMCHAIR
CHIPPENDALE STYLE
KITTINGER

W   26"
D   23½"
H   38⅜"
SH 19¼"

OPEN ARMCHAIR
CHIPPENDALE STYLE 1750
BAKER

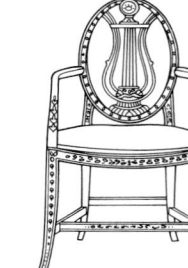
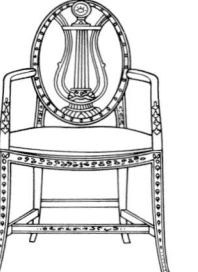

W   22"
D   20⅞"
H   34¼"
SH 19"

OVAL AND LYRE BACK
ARMCHAIR
SHERATON STYLE 1780
BAKER

W   21⅞"
D   22⅝"
H   33"
SH 19"

ARMCHAIR
REGENCY STYLE
KITTINGER

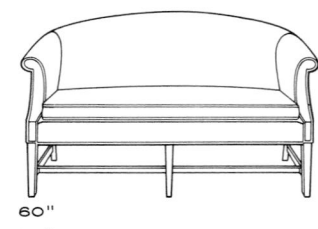

W   60"
D   30"
H   34½"
SH 19"

LOVE SEAT
SHERIDAN / HEPPLEWHITE
STYLE
KITTINGER

W   31"
D   28"
H   45½"
SH 19"

WING CHAIR
CHIPPENDALE STYLE
KITTINGER

W   33"
D   31½"
H   44"
SH 19"

WING CHAIR
CHIPPENDALE STYLE
KITTINGER

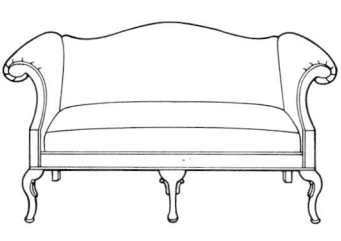

W   66"
D   32"
H   34"   SH 19"

SETTEE
CHIPPENDALE STYLE
HICKORY BUSINESS
FURNITURE

Robert Staples; Staples & Charles Ltd.; Washington, D.C.
Eric J. Gastier; Darrel Downing Rippeteau Architects, PC; Washington, D.C.

CLASSIC AND CONTEMPORARY FURNITURE

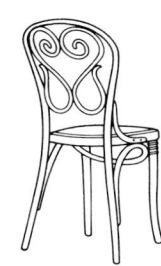
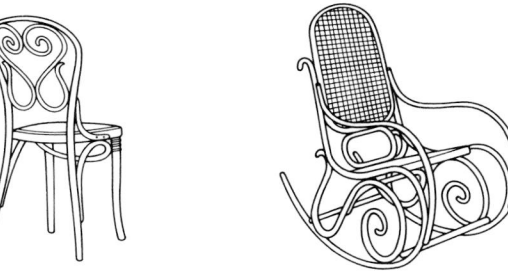
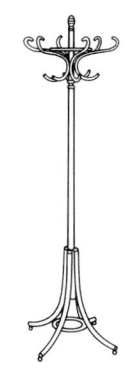

W 18"
D 21"
H 34½"
SH 18"
CAFÉ DAUM CHAIR CIRCA 1849
DESIGNER: MICHAEL THONET
THONET

W 21"
D 40"
H 43"
SH 17"
BENTWOOD ROCKER 1860
DESIGNER: MICHAEL THONET
THONET

DIA. 23½"
H 76"
BENTWOOD COSTUMER
DESIGNER: MICHAEL THONET
THONET

W 21½"
D 22¼"
H 31"
SH 18½"
CORBUSIER CHAIR 1870
DESIGNER: MICHAEL THONET
THONET

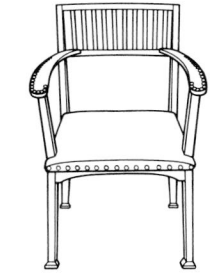
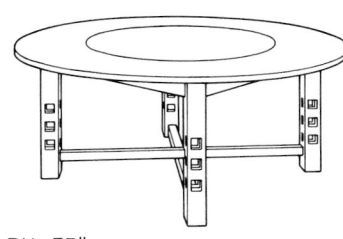
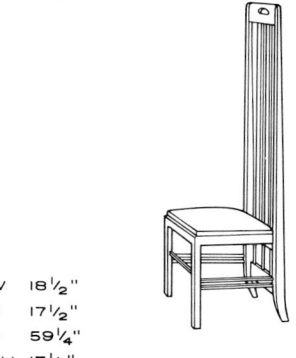
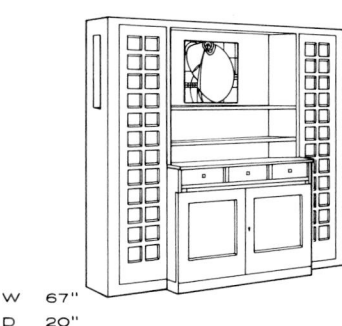

W 27"
D 23"
H 33"
SH 18"
ARMCHAIR CIRCA 1898
DESIGNER: OTTO WAGNER
THONET

DIA. 75"
H 29"
GSA TABLE 1900
DESIGNER:
CHARLES R. MACKINTOSH
ATELIER INTERNATIONAL

W 18½"
D 17½"
H 59¼"
SH 17½"
INGRAM HIGH CHAIR 1900
DESIGNER:
CHARLES R. MACKINTOSH
ATELIER INTERNATIONAL

W 67"
D 20"
H 63"
SIDEBOARD, 2 1918
DESIGNER:
CHARLES R. MACKINTOSH
ATELIER INTERNATIONAL

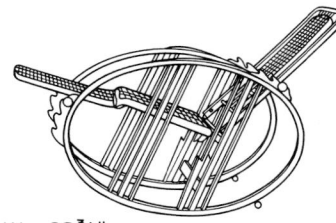
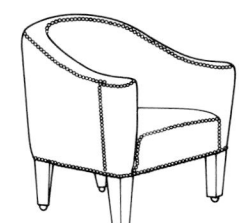

W 19½"
D 18"
H 30½"
FLEDERMAUS CHAIR 1905
DESIGNER: JOSEF HOFFMANN
ICF, INC.

DIA. 25¾"
H 25⅜"
FLEDERMAUS TABLE 1905
DESIGNER: JOSEF HOFFMANN
ICF, INC.

W 28¾"
D 50½"
H 45½"
SH 18"
ROCKING CHAIR 1905
DESIGNER: JOSEF HOFFMANN
ICF, INC.

W 31"
D 28½"
H 30¾"
SH 16½"
VILLA GALLIA ARMCHAIR 1913
DESIGNER: JOSEF HOFFMANN
ICF, INC.

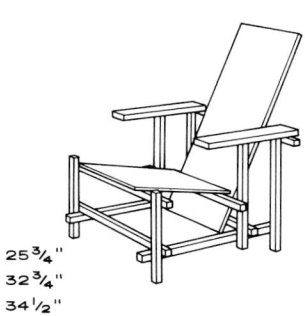
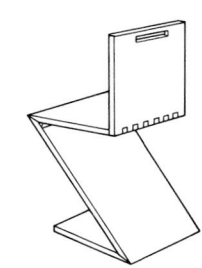
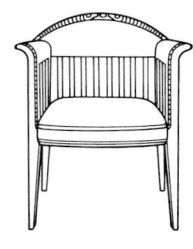
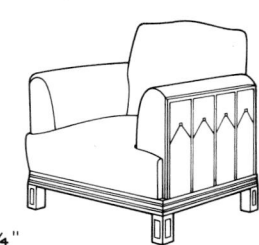

W 25¾"
D 32¾"
H 34½"
SH 13"
RED AND BLUE LOUNGE
CHAIR 1917
DESIGNER: GERRIT RIETVELD
ATELIER INTERNATIONAL

W 14½"
D 17"
H 29"
SH 17"
ZIG ZAG CHAIR 1934
DESIGNER: GERRIT RIETVELD
ATELIER INTERNATIONAL

W 26¾"
D 21¼"
H 33"
SH 17¾"
WHITE CHAIR CIRCA 1910
DESIGNER: ELIEL SAARINEN
ICF, INC.

W 33¾"
D 30½"
H 35½"
SH 17¾"
SAARINEN HOUSE LOUNGE
CHAIR 1929/30
DESIGNER: ELIEL SAARINEN
ARKITEKTURA

Robert Staples; Staples & Charles Ltd.; Washington, D.C.
Eric J. Gastier; Darrel Downing Rippeteau Architects, PC; Washington, D.C.

CLASSIC AND CONTEMPORARY FURNITURE **12**

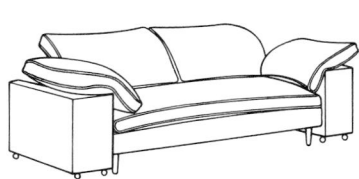

W 94½"
D 35½"
H 34½"
SH 17"
LOTA SOFA 1924
DESIGNER: EILEEN GRAY
PALAZZETTI

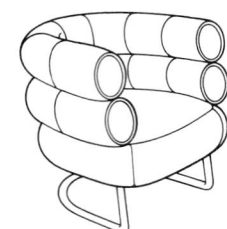

W 35½"
D 32½"
H 29"
SH 16"
POLTRONA ARMCHAIR 1927
DESIGNER: EILEEN GRAY
PALAZZETTI

DIA. 20"
H 21"–36"
ADJUSTABLE HEIGHT TABLE 1927
DESIGNER: EILEEN GRAY
STENDIG INC.

W 21¾"
D 33¾"
H 35¾"
SH 13¼"
LOUNGE CHAIR CIRCA 1920
DESIGNER: RENÉ HERBST
JG FURNITURE SYSTEMS

W 23"
D 22"
H 14½"
BARCELONA STOOL 1929
DESIGNER: MIES VAN DER ROHE
KNOLL INTERNATIONAL

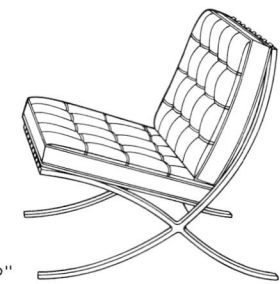

W 30"
D 30"
H 30"
SH 17"
BARCELONA CHAIR 1929
DESIGNER: MIES VAN DER ROHE
KNOLL INTERNATIONAL

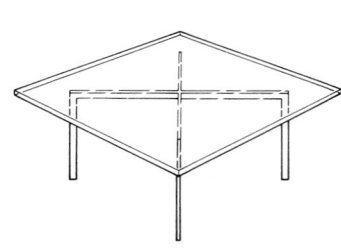

W 40"
D 40"
H 17"
BARCELONA TABLE 1929
DESIGNER: MIES VAN DER ROHE
KNOLL INTERNATIONAL

W 18"
D 23"
H 31½"
SH 17"
BRNO ARMCHAIR 1929
DESIGNER: MIES VAN DER ROHE
PALAZZETTI

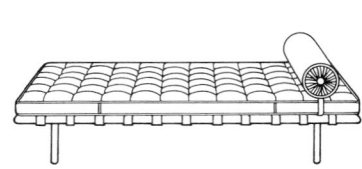

W 78"
D 39"
H 15½"
MIES COUCH
DESIGNER: MIES VAN DER ROHE
KNOLL INTERNATIONAL

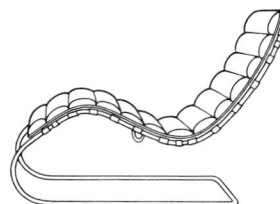

W 23⅝"
D 47¼"
H 37½"
CHAISE LOUNGE 1931
DESIGNER: MIES VAN DER ROHE
KNOLL INTERNATIONAL

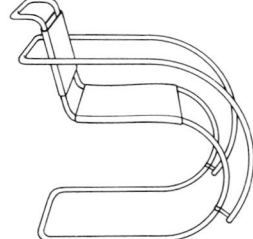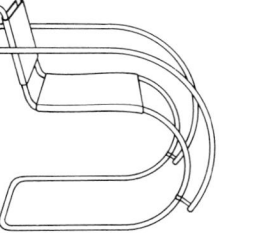

W 21¾"
D 32¼"
H 32¼"
SH 17¼"
MR. CHAIR 1927
DESIGNER: MIES VAN DER ROHE
STENDIG INC.

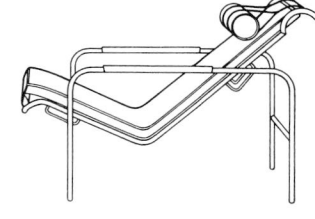

W 21½"
D 43"
H 30"
GENNI LOUNGE CHAIR 1935
DESIGNER: GABRIELE MUCCHI
ICF INC.

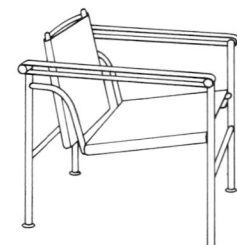

W 23⅝"
D 25⅝"
H 25¼"
SH 15¾"
LC I SLING CHAIR 1928
DESIGNER: LE CORBUSIER
ATELIER INTERNATIONAL

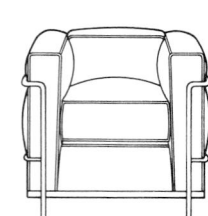

W 30"
D 27½"
H 26½"
SH 17"
LC 2 ARM CHAIR 1929
DESIGNER: LE CORBUSIER
ATELIER INTERNATIONAL

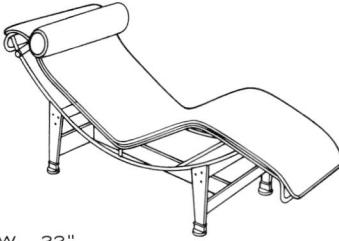

W 22"
D 63"
LC 4 CHAISE LOUNGE 1928
DESIGNER: LE CORBUSIER
ATELIER INTERNATIONAL

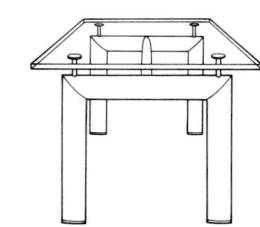

W 90"
D 35½"
H 27"–29"
LC 6 TABLE 1925–28
DESIGNER: LE CORBUSIER
ATELIER INTERNATIONAL

Robert Staples; Staples & Charles Ltd.; Washington, D.C.
Eric J. Gastier; Darrel Downing Rippeteau Architects, PC; Washington, D.C.

12 **CLASSIC AND CONTEMPORARY FURNITURE**

W 22⅝"
D 21⅝"
H 31¾"
SH 18¼"

CESCA ARM CHAIR 1928
DESIGNER: MARCEL BREUER
KNOLL INTERNATIONAL

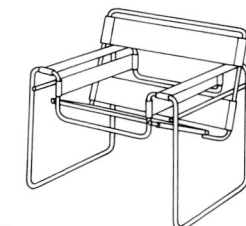

W 30¾"
D 27"
H 28½"
SH 17"

WASSILY CHAIR 1925
DESIGNER: MARCEL BREUER
KNOLL INTERNATIONAL

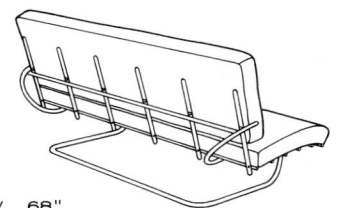

W 68"
D 32"
H 34"
SH 16¾"

SOFA 1931
DESIGNER: MARCEL BREUER
GLOBAL FURNITURE

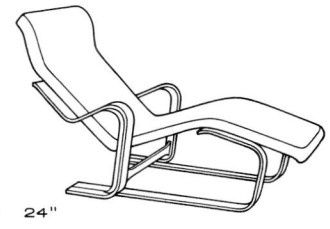

W 24"
D 51"
H 33"

LONG CHAIR 1935/36
DESIGNER: MARCEL BREUER
PALAZZETTI

W 25½"
D 31½"
H 32½"
SH 14½"

BREUER LOUNGE CHAIR 1928
DESIGNER: MARCEL BREUER
ICF, INC.

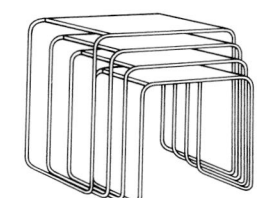

W 26"
D 20"
H 24"

NESTING TABLES 1925
DESIGNER: MARCEL BREUER
THONET

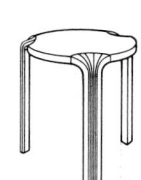

DIA. 15"
H 17¾"

FAN-LEGGED TABLE 1954
DESIGNER: ALVAR AALTO
ICF, INC.

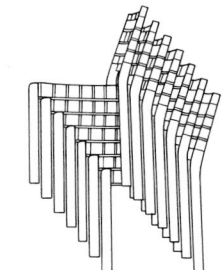

W 19"
D 19¼"
H 31½"
SH 17¾"

STACK CHAIR 1930
DESIGNER: ALVAR AALTO
ICF, INC.

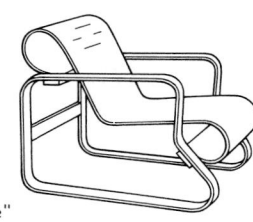

W 23½"
D 31½"
H 25"
SH 13"

"PAIMIO" CHAIR 1930-33
DESIGNER: ALVAR AALTO
PALAZZETTI

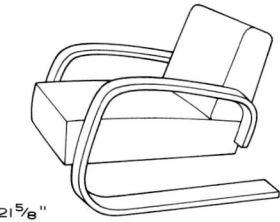

W 21⅝"
D 30¼"
H 25⅝"
SH 14½"

LOUNGE CHAIR 1935
DESIGNER: ALVAR AALTO
ICF, INC.

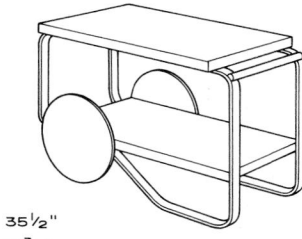

W 35½"
D 19¾"
H 22¼"

TEA TROLLEY 1936/37
DESIGNER: ALVAR AALTO
ICF, INC.

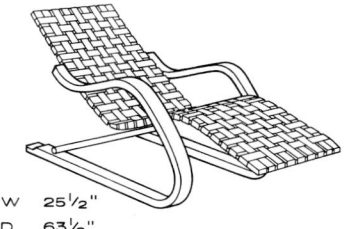

W 25½"
D 63½"
H 26"
SH 10"

CHAISE LOUNGE 1936
DESIGNER: ALVAR AALTO
ICF, INC.

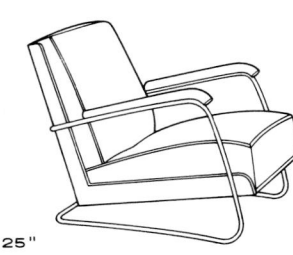

W 25"
D 33¼"
H 31¼"
SH 17¼"

LOUNGE CHAIR 1932-34
DESIGNER: PAULI BLOMSTED
ARKITEKTURA

W 16"
D 18"
H 35"
SH 18"

MIDWAY CHAIR 1914
DESIGNER:
FRANK LLOYD WRIGHT
ATELIER INTERNATIONAL

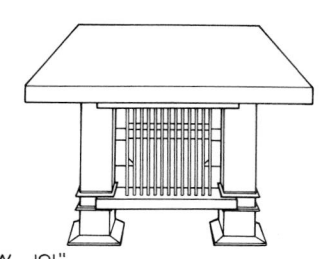

W 101"
D 42"
H 28"

ALLEN TABLE 1917
DESIGNER:
FRANK LLOYD WRIGHT
ATELIER INTERNATIONAL

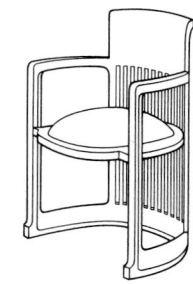

W 21½"
D 22"
H 32"
SH 19½"

BARREL CHAIR 1937
DESIGNER:
FRANK LLOYD WRIGHT
ATELIER INTERNATIONAL

Robert Staples; Staples & Charles Ltd.; Washington, D.C.
Eric J. Gastier; Darrel Downing Rippeteau Architects, PC; Washington, D.C.

W   25½"
D   20"
H   16"

OTTOMAN 1948
DESIGNER: EERO SAARINEN
KNOLL INTERNATIONAL

W   40"
D   34"
H   35½"
SH 16"

WOMB CHAIR 1948
DESIGNER: EERO SAARINEN
KNOLL INTERNATIONAL

W   26"
D   23½"
H   32"
SH 18½"

ARMCHAIR 1956
DESIGNER: EERO SAARINEN
KNOLL INTERNATIONAL

W   78"
D   48"
H   28½"

OVAL TABLE 1956
DESIGNER: EERO SAARINEN
KNOLL INTERNATIONAL

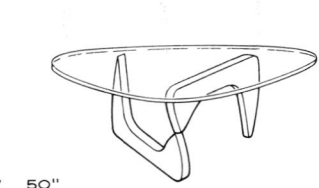

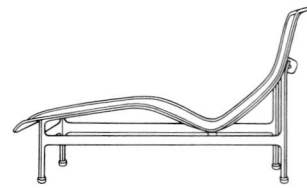

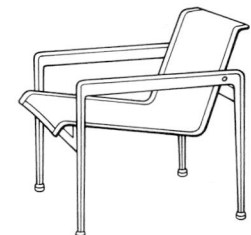

W   50"
D   36"
H   15¾"

NOGUCHI TABLE 1950
DESIGNER: ISAMU NOGUCHI
HERMAN MILLER, INC.

W   33¾"
D   28"
H   30½"
SH 17"

DIAMOND CHAIR 1952
DESIGNER: HARRY BERTOIA
KNOLL INTERNATIONAL

W   24½"
D   58"
H   33¾"
SH 13"

CONTOUR CHAISE LOUNGE
DESIGNER: RICHARD SCHULTZ
ICF, INC.

W   26"
D   28¼"
H   26½"
SH 14"

LOUNGE CHAIR 1966
DESIGNER: RICHARD SCHULTZ
KNOLL INTERNATIONAL

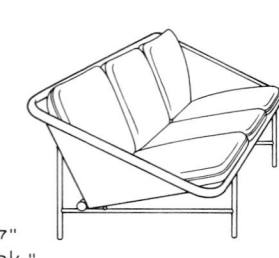

W   87"
D   32¼"
H   29¾"

SLING SOFA 1964
DESIGNER: GEORGE NELSON
HERMAN MILLER, INC.

W   21½"
D   19½"
H   29⅜"
SH 18"

MOLDED PLYWOOD CHAIR 1946
DESIGNER: CHARLES EAMES
HERMAN MILLER, INC.

W   25"
D   25½"
H   31"
SH 17⅝"

MOLDED FIBERGLASS CHAIR 1949
DESIGNER: CHARLES EAMES
HERMAN MILLER, INC.

W   72½"
D   30"
H   35"
SH 16"

COMPACT SOFA 1952
DESIGNER: CHARLES EAMES
HERMAN MILLER, INC.

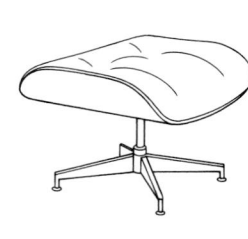

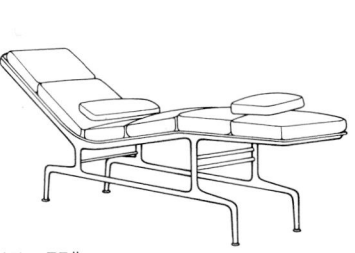

W   32½"
D   32¾"
H   33½"
SH 15"

LOUNGE CHAIR 1956
DESIGNER: CHARLES EAMES
HERMAN MILLER, INC.

W   26"
D   21"
H   15"

OTTOMAN 1956
DESIGNER: CHARLES EAMES
HERMAN MILLER, INC.

W   28½"
D   24¾"
H   33¾"
SH 17½"

ALUMINUM GROUP LOUNGE 1958
DESIGNER: CHARLES EAMES
HERMAN MILLER, INC.

W   75"
D   17½"
H   28¾"
SH 20½"

CHAISE LOUNGE 1968
DESIGNER: CHARLES EAMES
HERMAN MILLER, INC.

Robert Staples; Staples & Charles Ltd.; Washington, D.C.
Eric J. Gastier; Darrel Downing Rippeteau Architects, PC; Washington, D.C.

12   **CLASSIC AND CONTEMPORARY FURNITURE**

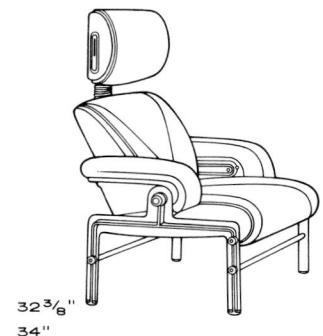

W 32³/₈"
D 34"
H 43½"
SH 16³/₄"

JEFFERSON CHAIR 1986
DESIGNER: NIELS DIFFRIENT
SUNARHAUSERMAN

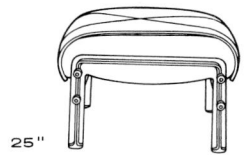

W 25"
D 24"
H 17½"

OTTOMAN 1986
DESIGNER: NIELS DIFFRIENT
SUNARHAUSERMAN

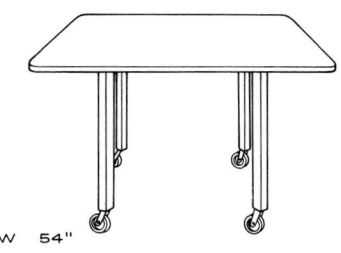

W 54"
D 54"
H 27½"

SQUARE TABLE
DESIGNER: JOSEPH PAUL D'URSO
KNOLL INTERNATIONAL

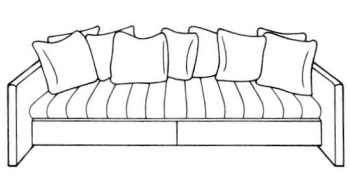

W 96"
D 48"
H 24"
SH 15½"

LARGE SOFA
DESIGNER: JOSEPH PAUL D'URSO
KNOLL INTERNATIONAL

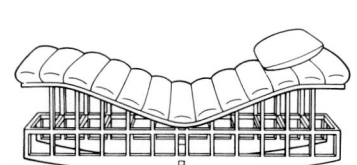

W 72"
D 27½"
H 25⅛"

CHAISE LOUNGE 1982
DESIGNER: RICHARD MEIER
KNOLL INTERNATIONAL

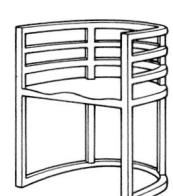

W 21"
D 20"
H 27½"
SH 17½"

CHAIR 1982
DESIGNER: RICHARD MEIER
KNOLL INTERNATIONAL

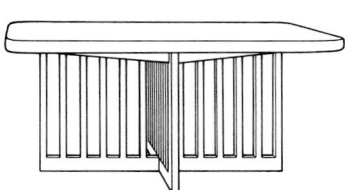

W 60"
D 60"
H 27½"

TABLE 1982
DESIGNER: RICHARD MEIER
KNOLL INTERNATIONAL

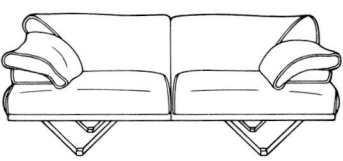

W 72"
D 36"
H 32"

CORNELIUS SOFA 1986
DESIGNER: CARLO SANTI
AXIOM DESIGNS

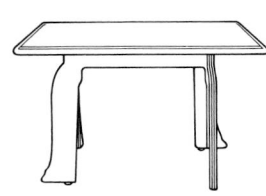

W 48"
D 48"
H 28½"

CABRIOLE LEG TABLE 1984
DESIGNER: ROBERT VENTURI
KNOLL INTERNATIONAL

W 26½"
D 23½"
H 38½"
SH 17½"

QUEEN ANNE CHAIR 1984
DESIGNER: ROBERT VENTURI
KNOLL INTERNATIONAL

DIA. 60"
H 28½"

URN TABLE 1984
DESIGNER: ROBERT VENTURI
KNOLL INTERNATIONAL

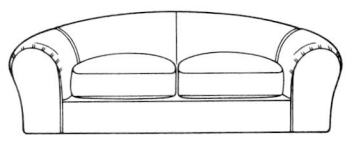

W 87"
D 43½"
H 33³/₄"
SH 20"

SOFA 1984
DESIGNER: ROBERT VENTURI
KNOLL INTERNATIONAL

W 40½"
D 40½"
H 29"

TABLE 1982
DESIGNER: MICHAEL GRAVES
SUNARHAUSERMAN

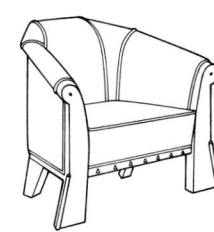

W 32"
D 29"
H 29"

LOUNGE CHAIR 1982
DESIGNER: MICHAEL GRAVES
SUNARHAUSERMAN

DIA. 48"
H 29¼"

TABLE 1986
DESIGNER: MICHAEL MCCOY
ARKITEKTURA

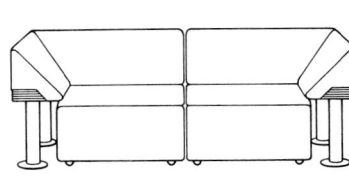

W 74"
D 32"
H 26½"
SH 13½"

QUADRIO SOFA
DESIGNER: MICHAEL MCCOY
KRUEGER INTERNATIONAL DIV.

Robert Staples; Staples & Charles Ltd.; Washington, D.C.
Eric J. Gastier; Darrel Downing Rippeteau Architects, PC; Washington, D.C.

CLASSIC AND CONTEMPORARY FURNITURE **12**

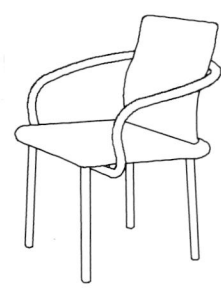

W 26"
D 23 1/2"
H 32 1/2"
SH 16 3/4"

MANDARIN ARMCHAIR 1986
DESIGNER: SOTTSASS ASSOCIATES
KNOLL STUDIO

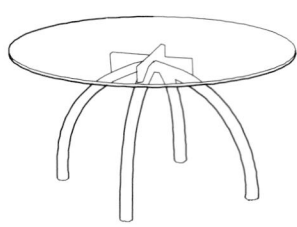

DIA. 53 1/4"
H 28 1/3"

SPYDER TABLE 1987
DESIGNER: SOTTSASS ASSOCIATES
KNOLL STUDIO

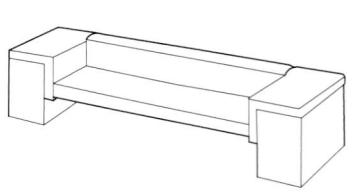

W 70"
D 35 1/2"
H 21 3/4"
SH 15 3/4"

BRIGADIER LOWBACK SEITTEE 1977
DESIGNER: CINI BOERI
KNOLL STUDIO

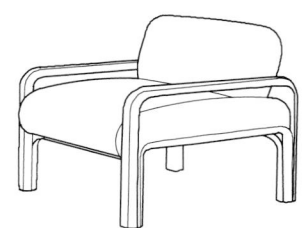

W 31 1/2"
D 33 3/4"
H 30 1/4"
SH 17"

LOUNGE CHAIR 1975
DESIGNER: GAE AULENTI
KNOLL STUDIO

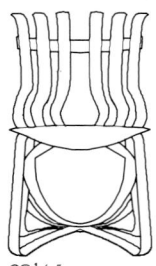

W 28 1/2"
D 24 7/8"
H 33 5/8"
SH 18 1/8"

CROSS CHECK ARMCHAIR 1992
DESIGNER: FRANK GEHRY
KNOLL STUDIO

DIA. 40"
H 28 3/4"

FACE OFF CAFE TABLE 1992
DESIGNER: FRANK GEHRY
KNOLL STUDIO

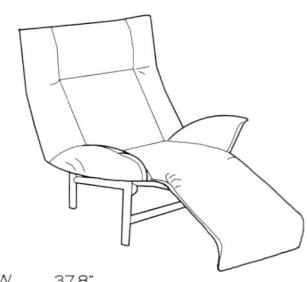

W 37.8"
D 33.5"
H 29.5"-43.3"

VERANDA ARMCHAIR 1983
DESIGNER: VICO MAGISTRETTI
ATELIER INTERNATIONAL

W 41.4"
D 31.5"
H 29.5"
SH 16.2"

685 ARMCHAIR 1973
DESIGNER: MARIO BELLINI
ATELIER INTERNATIONAL

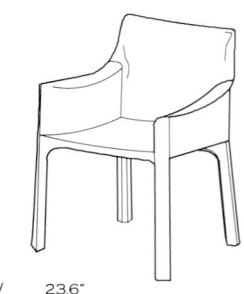

W 23.6"
D 20.5"
H 32.3"
SH 17"

CAB ARMCHAIR 1977,1979
DESIGNER: MARIO BELLINI
ATELIER INTERNATIONAL

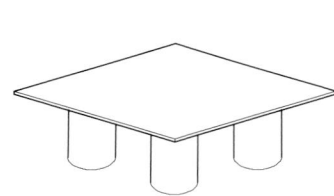

W 49.6"
D 49.6"
H 14.1"

SERENISSIMO 36, LOW TABLE 1985
DESIGNER: LELLA AND MASSIMO
            VIGNELLI AND DAVID LAW
ATELIER INTERNATIONAL

W 23.2"
D 22"
H 34.3"
SH 18.5"

FINESTRA ARMCHAIR 1989
DESIGNER: MICHAEL GRAVES
ATELIER INTERNATIONAL

W 22.8"
D 22.8"
H 34.2"
SH 17.3"

ARCHIZOOM ARMCHAIR 1979
DESIGNER: ARCHIZOOM ASSOCIATES
ATELIER INTERNATIONAL

W 20.3"
D 20"
H 34"
SH 19"

DUO CHAIR 1988
DESIGNER: WERTHER TOFFOLONI
ATELIER INTERNATIONAL

W 57.1"
D 41.7"
H 45.6"
SH 17.7"

TORSO CHAISE LOUNGE 1982
DESIGNER: PAOLO DEGANELLO
ATELIER INTERNATIONAL

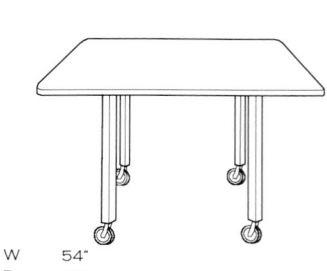

W 54"
D 54"
H 27 1/2"

HIGH ROLLING TABLE 1980
DESIGNER: JOESPH PAUL D'URSO
KNOLL STUDIO

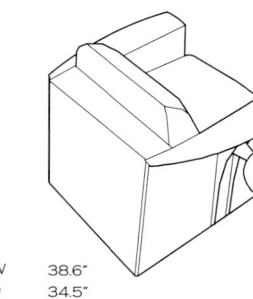

W 38.6"
D 34.5"
H 28.8"
SH 18.2"

LOUNGE CHAIR 1990
DESIGNER: DOUGLAS BALL
ATELIER INTERNATIONAL

McCain McMurray, Architect; Washington, D.C.

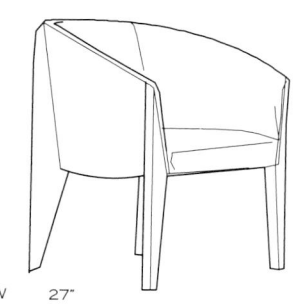

W 27"
D 25 1/2"
H 30"
SH 18"

ARM SESSEL CHAIR 1987
DESIGNER : MARK MACK
BERNHARDT

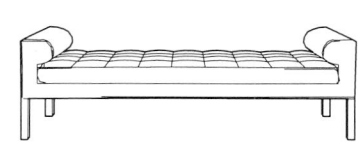

W 66"
D 24"
H 20 3/4"
SH 15 1/2"

MUSEUM BENCH 1982
DESIGNER : CHARLES MCMURRAY
CHARLES MCMURRAY DESIGNS

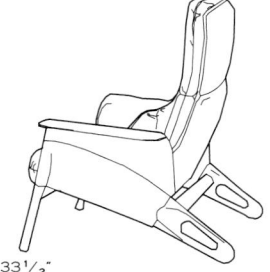

W 33 1/2"
D 34"
H 40"
SH 17"

HOLLINGTON LOUNGE CHAIR
DESIGNER : GEOFF HOLLINGTON
HERMAN MILLER

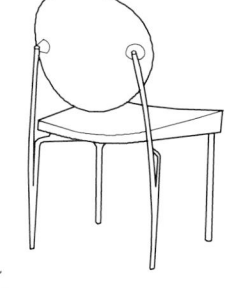

W 19"
D 20"
H 34 3/4"
SH 18"

VIK-TER STACKING CHAIR 1991
DESIGNER : DAKOTA JACKSON
DAKOTA JACKSON, INC

W 32"
D 31"
H 28"
SH 16"

BABY DOLL LOUNGE CHAIR 1989
DESIGNER : BENTLEY LA ROSA SALASKY
BRICKEL ASSOCIATES, INC.

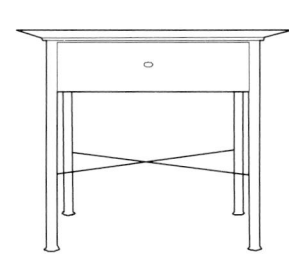

W 23 1/4"
D 23 1/4"
H 20 1/4"

END TABLE 1988
DESIGNER : BENTLEY LA ROSA SALASKY
BRICKEL ASSOCIATES, INC.

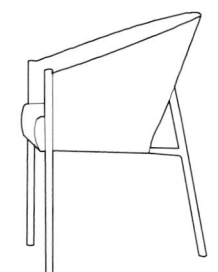

W 18 1/2"
D 21 1/2"
H 31"
SH 18 1/2"

COSTES CHAIR 1984
DESIGNER : PHILIPPE STARCK
DRIADE

W 13"
D 21"
H 19" - 33"
SH 18 1/2"

LOLA MUNDO 1986
DESIGNER : PHILIPPE STARCK
DRIADE

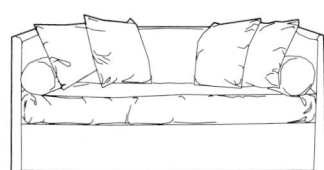

W 72"
D 35"
H 32 1/2"
SH 19"

SHELTER SOFA 1985
DESIGNER : JOHN SALADINO
SALADINO FURNITURE, INC.

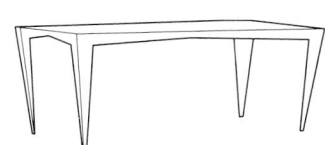

W 72"
D 36"
H 29"

CITIES TABLE
DESIGNER : AL GLASS
BDI

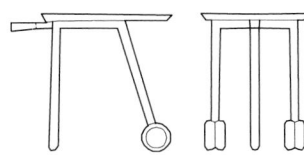

W 24 1/2"
D 15 3/4"
H 21 7/8"

BAISITY SERVOMUTO 1989
DESIGNER : ANTONIO CITTERIO
B & B ITALIA

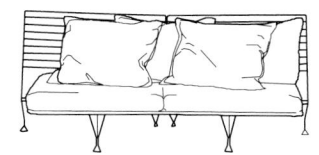

W 85"
D 29 1/2"
H 36 5/8"
SH 16 1/2"

IKMISOU SOFA 1988
DESIGNER : PASCAL MOURGE
VECTA

W 86"
D 41"
H 33 1/2"
SH 15 1/2"

BAISITY SOFA 1989
DESIGNER : ANTONIO CITTERIO
B & B ITALIA

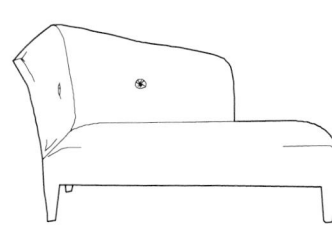

W 70"
D 38"
H 38"
SH 17"

SPIRIT CHAISE
DESIGNER : JOHN HUTTON
DONGHIA FURNITURE

W 36"
D 36"
H 36"
SH 18

LUCIANO CLUB CHAIR
DESIGNER : JOHN HUTTON
DONGHIA FURNITURE

W 20"
D 20"
H 31 1/2"
SH 17 1/2"

ANZIANO CHAIR
DESIGNER : JOHN HUTTON
DONGHIA FURNITURE

McCain McMurray, Architect; Washington, D.C.

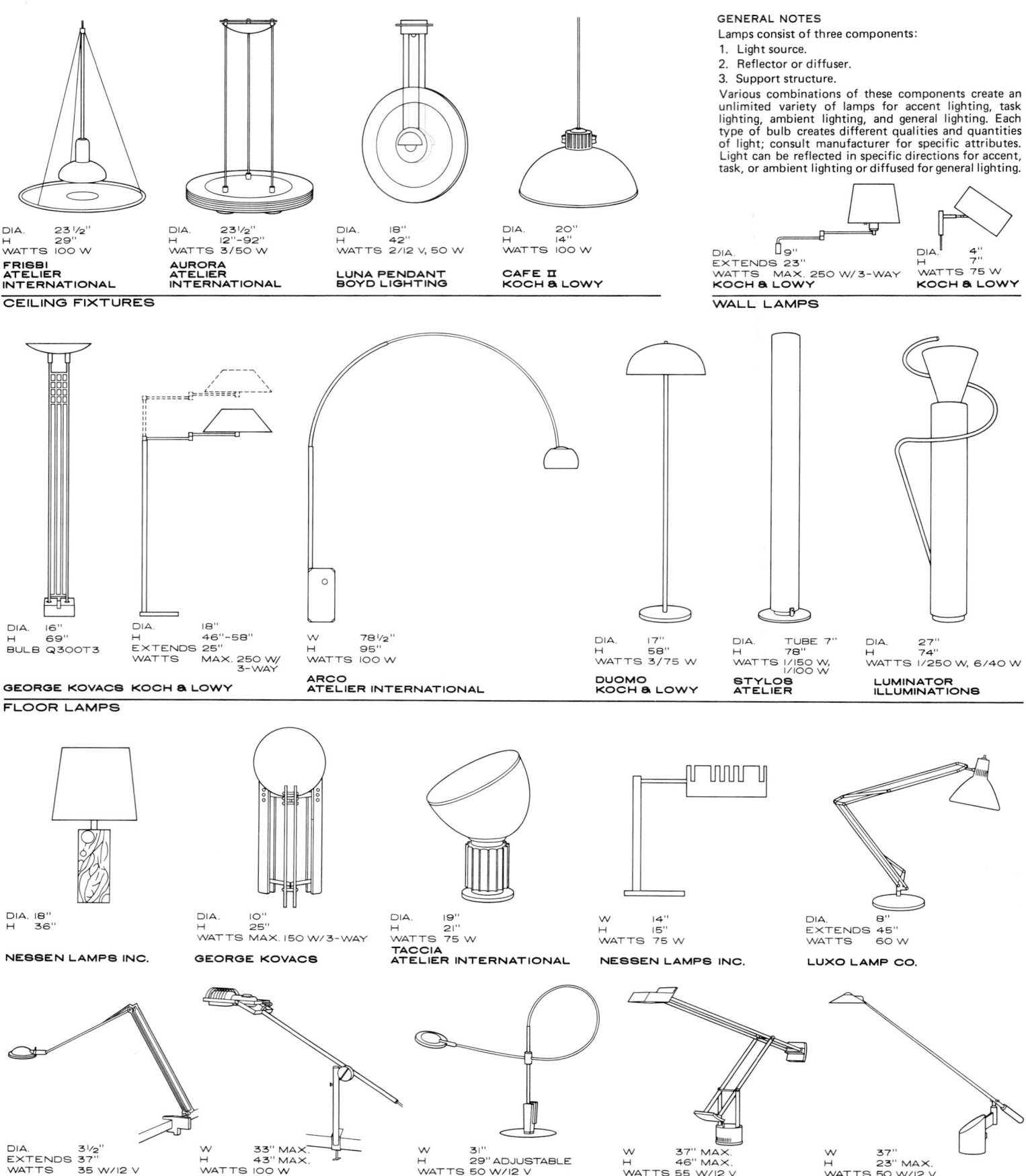

Lamps consist of three components:
1. Light source.
2. Reflector or diffuser.
3. Support structure.

Various combinations of these components create an unlimited variety of lamps for accent lighting, task lighting, ambient lighting, and general lighting. Each type of bulb creates different qualities and quantities of light; consult manufacturer for specific attributes. Light can be reflected in specific directions for accent, task, or ambient lighting or diffused for general lighting.

DIA. 23½"
H 29"
WATTS 100 W
FRISBI
ATELIER
INTERNATIONAL

DIA. 23½"
H 12"-92"
WATTS 3/50 W
AURORA
ATELIER
INTERNATIONAL

DIA. 18"
H 42"
WATTS 2/12 V, 50 W
LUNA PENDANT
BOYD LIGHTING

DIA. 20"
H 14"
WATTS 100 W
CAFE II
KOCH & LOWY

DIA. 9"
EXTENDS 23"
WATTS MAX. 250 W/3-WAY
KOCH & LOWY

DIA. 4"
H 7"
WATTS 75 W
KOCH & LOWY

CEILING FIXTURES

WALL LAMPS

DIA. 16"
H 69"
BULB Q300T3
GEORGE KOVACS

DIA. 18"
H 46"-58"
EXTENDS 25"
WATTS MAX. 250 W/3-WAY
KOCH & LOWY

W 78½"
H 95"
WATTS 100 W
ARCO
ATELIER INTERNATIONAL

DIA. 17"
H 58"
WATTS 3/75 W
DUOMO
KOCH & LOWY

DIA. TUBE 7"
H 78"
WATTS 1/150 W,
1/100 W
STYLOS
ATELIER

DIA. 27"
H 74"
WATTS 1/250 W, 6/40 W
LUMINATOR
ILLUMINATIONS

FLOOR LAMPS

DIA. 18"
H 36"
NESSEN LAMPS INC.

DIA. 10"
H 25"
WATTS MAX. 150 W/3-WAY
GEORGE KOVACS

DIA. 19"
H 21"
WATTS 75 W
TACCIA
ATELIER INTERNATIONAL

W 14"
H 15"
WATTS 75 W
NESSEN LAMPS INC.

DIA. 8"
EXTENDS 45"
WATTS 60 W
LUXO LAMP CO.

DIA. 3½"
EXTENDS 37"
WATTS 35 W/12 V
BERENICE
ARTEMIDE

W 33" MAX.
H 43" MAX.
WATTS 100 W
SINTESI
ARTEMIDE

W 31"
H 29" ADJUSTABLE
WATTS 50 W/12 V
SIGLA T
IPI

W 37" MAX.
H 46" MAX.
WATTS 55 W/12 V
TIZIO
ARTEMIDE

W 37"
H 23" MAX.
WATTS 50 W/12 V
FEATHER
GEORGE KOVACS

TABLE AND DESK LAMPS

Robert Staples; Staples & Charles Ltd.; Washington, D.C.

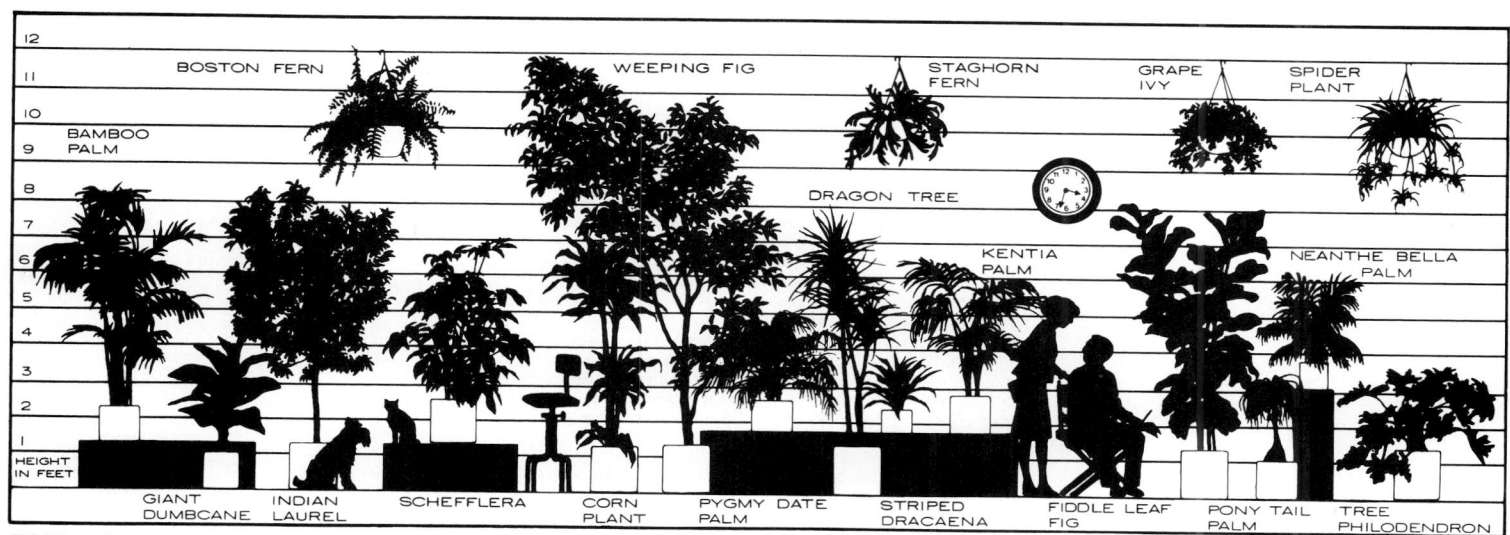

FORM, TEXTURE, AND SIZES OF SOME TYPICALLY USED INTERIOR PLANTS

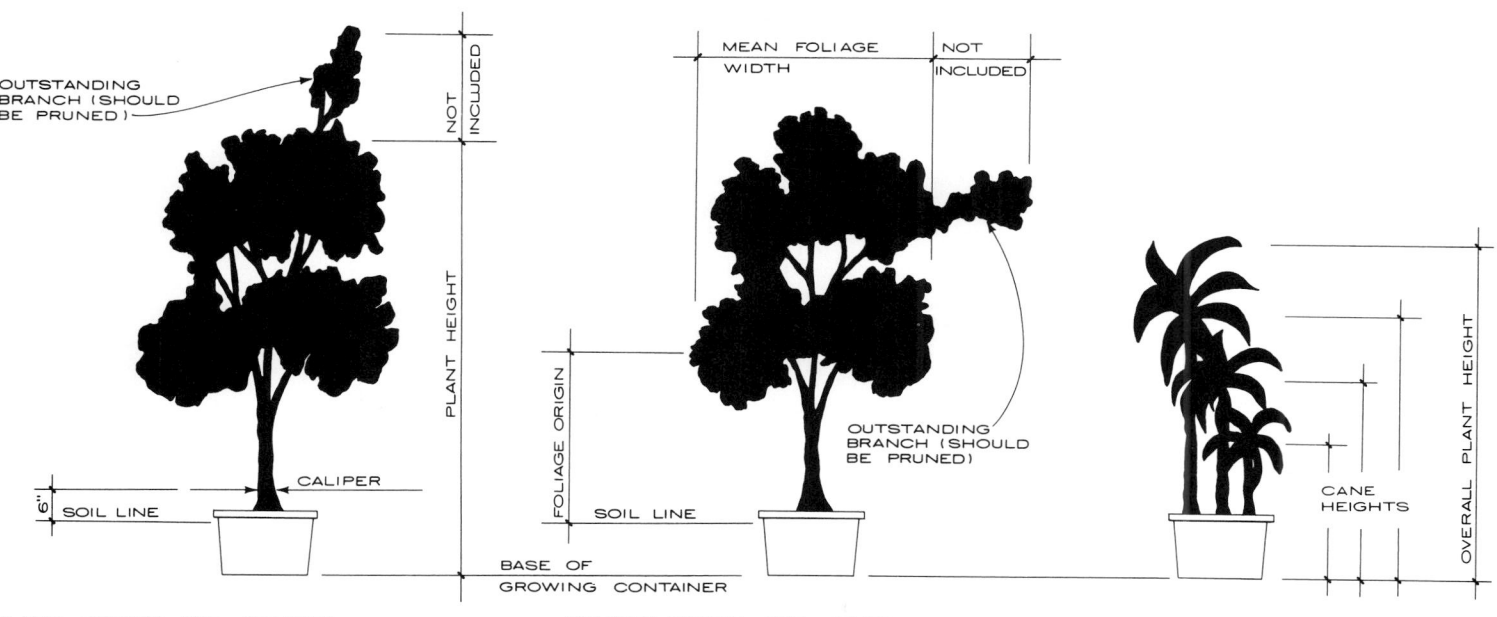

PLANT HEIGHT AND CALIPER   FOLIAGE WIDTH AND ORIGIN   CANE HEIGHTS

INTERIOR PLANT SPECIFICATIONS

NOTE

Plant height should be measured as overall height from the base of the growing container to mean foliage top. Isolated outstanding branches should not be included in height. (Since most plants are installed in movable planters, this overall height measurement should be utilized.)

NOTE

Foliage width should be measured across the nominal mean width dimension. Isolated outstanding branches should not be included in foliage width. Origin or start of foliage should be measured from the soil line.

NOTE

Many plant varieties are grown from rooted canes, with the plant being made up of one or more canes. The number of canes must be specified, if plant form is to be identified. Cane heights should always be measured from the base of the growing container.

OTHER PLANT SPECIFICATION FACTORS

1. Accurately describe plant form (e.g., multistem vs. standard tree form, clump form) and foliage spread desired. Indicate "clear trunk" measurements on trees, if desired. These measurements are from soil line to foliage origin point. Specify caliper, if significant.

2. Indicate lighting intensities designed or calculated for interior space where plants will be installed.

3. Indicate how plants will be used (i.e., in at-grade planter or in movable decorative planter). If movable decorative planters are used, indicate interior diameter and height of planter for each plant specified, since growing container sizes vary considerably.

4. Specify both botanical and common plant names.

5. Indicate any special shipping instructions or limitations.

6. Specify in-plant height column, whether plant height is measured as overall height or above-the-soil line height. Recommended height measurements:

   Interior plants: overall plant height (i.e., from bottom of growing container to mean foliage top).
   Exterior plants: above-the-soil line height.

7. Indicate whether plants are to be container grown or balled and burlapped (B & B) material.

8. Indicate location of all convenient water supply sources on all interior landscaping layouts.

Richard L. Gaines; Plantscape House; Apopka, Florida

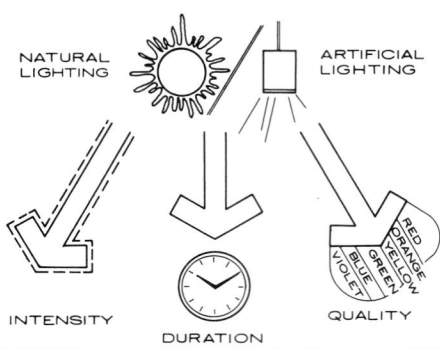

INTERIOR PLANT LIGHTING FACTORS

LIGHTING DURATION NEEDS

1. Adequate lighting is the product of intensity times duration to yield "footcandle-hours"; therefore, compensation between the two exists (e.g., 300 ft-c x 12 hr = 360 ft-c x 10 hr).
2. Recommended rule of thumb: 10–12 hr of continuous lighting on a regular basis, 7 days a week.
3. Generally, it is believed that continuous 24 hr lighting period might be detrimental to plants, but no research bears this out and many projects are under this regime with no apparent bad effects.

LIGHTING INTENSITY NEEDS

1. All plants desire good lighting, but many are tolerant and adaptable to lower light conditions.
2. Because most interior plants are native to areas with intensities of 10–14,000 ft-c, these plants must be "trained" through an acclimatization process of lowered light (2000–4000 ft-c), water and fertilizer levels for survival, and maintained appearance in the interior environment.
3. All plants have varying degrees of interior lighting intensity requirements, best understood as foot-candle (lumens/square foot) requirements.
4. Lighting intensity for plants must be planned and is not simply a footcandle measurement after the building is complete (i.e., footcandle meters are "after the fact" instruments).
5. Intensity must always be above the individual light compensation point for each plant variety, for survival. (LCP is the intensity point at which the plant utilizes as much food as it produces; hence no food storage. Eventually, the plant could die with no food backup.)
6. Recommended rule of thumb: design for a MINIMUM of 50 ft-c on the ground plane for fixed floor type of planters and 75 ft-c at desk height for movable decorative floor planters.
7. Flowering plants and flowers require extremely high intensities (above 2000 ft-c) or direct sunlight to bud, flower, or fruit, as well as lighting high in red and far-red energy.

RECOMMENDED LIGHTING SOURCES FOR PLANTS

Lighting sources are listed in order of priority, based on plant growth efficiency, color rendition preference, and energy efficiency.

CEILING HEIGHT	RECOMMENDED LIGHT SOURCE
10 ft and less	Daylight—sidewall glazing Cool white fluorescent Natural light fluorescent Incandescent Plant growth fluorescent

10–15 ft	Daylight
	  Sidewall glazing
	  Major glazing
	  Skylights
	Metal halide lamp, phosphor coated
	Mercury lamp, deluxe white
	Mercury lamp, warm deluxe white
	High pressure sodium (if color rendition not a design factor)
	Quartz halogen lamp
	Incandescent

15 ft and greater	Daylight
	  Sidewall glazing
	  Major glazing
	  Skylights
	Metal halide lamp, clear
	Metal halide lamp, phosphor coated
	Mercury lamp, deluxe white
	Mercury lamp, warm deluxe white
	High pressure sodium (if color rendition not a design factor)
	Quartz halogen lamp
	Incandescent

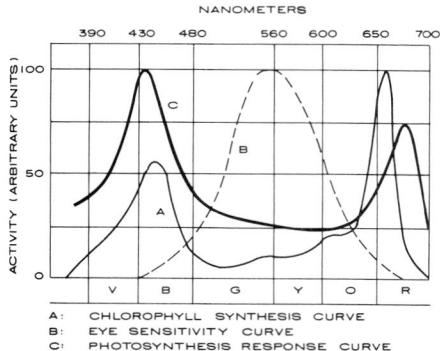

SPECTRAL ENERGY DISTRIBUTION CURVE SHOWING OPPOSING PLANT AND HUMAN EYE RESPONSES

A: CHLOROPHYLL SYNTHESIS CURVE
B: EYE SENSITIVITY CURVE
C: PHOTOSYNTHESIS RESPONSE CURVE

LIGHT QUALITY NEEDS

1. Natural lighting is about twice as efficient as cool white fluorescent lighting for plant growth, because of sunlight's broad range spectrum (i.e., 200 ft-c of CWF = 95 ft-c of natural light).
2. Chlorophyll is most responsive to blue and red wavelength energy in the production of food. The human eye is least responsive to blue and red energy and most responsive to the green-yellow region of the spectrum.
3. High blue energy emitting sources are best for overall plant maintenance (stockier growth, dark green color, little elongation).
4. High red energy emitting sources produce lighter colored foliage, elongated growth, stragglier growth.
5. Designer must be cognizant of color rendition of source, as well as light quality, if lighting is to be used for both plant lighting and illumination. (See Lamp Responses table.)
6. Ultraviolet energy is believed to be somewhat helpful to the photosynthesis process, but is not considered necessary as an integral segment of plant lighting.

LAMP RESPONSES ON INTERIOR PLANTS

BULB	ROOM APPEARANCE	COLORS STRENGTHENED	COLORS GREYED	PLANT RESPONSES
CW	Neutral to cool	Blue, yellow, orange	Red	Green foliage, stem elongates slowly, multiple side shoots, flower life long
WW	Yellow to warm	Yellow, orange	Blue, green, red	
GRO-PL	Purple to pink	Blue, red	Green, yellow	Deep green foliage, stem elongates very slowly, thick stems, multiple side shoots, late flowers on short stems
GRO-WS	Warm	Blue, yellow, red	Green	Light green foliage, stem elongates rapidly, suppressed side shoots, early flowering on long stems, plant matures and dies rapidly
AGRO	Neutral to warm	Blue, yellow, red	Green	
VITA	Neutral to warm	Blue, yellow, red	Green	
HG	Cool	Blue, green, yellow	Red	Green foliage expands, stem elongates slowly, multiple side shoots, flower life long
MH	Cool green	Blue, green, yellow	Red	
HPS	Warm	Green, yellow, orange	Blue, red	Deep green, large foliage, stem elongates very slowly, late flowers, short stems
LPS	Warm	Yellow	All except yellow	Extra deep green foliage, slow, thick stem elongation, multiple side shoots, some flowering, short stems. Some plants require supplemental sun
INC	Warm	Yellow, orange, red	Blue	Pale, thin, long foliage, stems spindly, suppressed side shoots early, short-lived flowers
INC-HG	Warm	Yellow, orange, red	Blue	

KEY

CW: cool white fluorescent.
WW: warm white fluorescent.
GRO-PL: Gro-Lux plant light.
GRO-WS: Gro-Lux wide spectrum.
AGRO: Agro-Lite.
VITA: Vita-Lite.

HG: mercury (all types).
MH: metal halide.
HPS: high pressure sodium.
LPS: low pressure sodium.
INC-HG: incandescent mercury.
INC-PL: incandescent plant light.

Richard L. Gaines; Plantscape House; Apopka, Florida

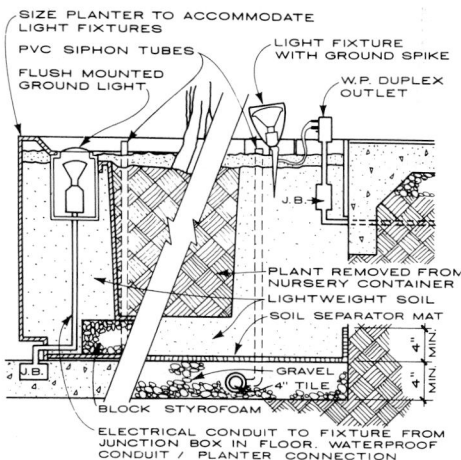

MOVABLE PLANTER/AT-GRADE PLANTER
UPLIGHTING / PLANTING DETAILS

UPLIGHTING AND ELECTRICAL NEEDS

1. May be of some benefit to plants, but inefficient for plant photosynthesis because of plant physiological structure. Chlorophyll is usually in upper part of leaf.
2. Uplighting should never be utilized as sole lighting source for plants.
3. Waterproof duplex outlets above soil line with a waterproof junction box below soil line are usually adequate for "atmosphere" uplighting and water fountain pumps.

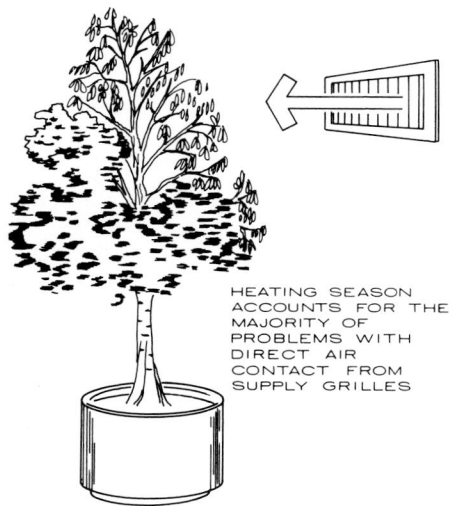

FOLIAGE BURN FROM DIRECT HEAT CONTACT

HVAC EFFECT ON PLANTS

1. Air conditioning (cooled air) generally is not detrimental to plants, even if it is "directed" at plants. The ventilation here is what counts! Good ventilation is a must with plants; otherwise oxygen and temperatures build up. Heat supply, on the other hand, when "directed" at plants, can truly be disastrous. Plan for supplies directed away from plants, but maintain adequate ventilation.
2. Extended heat or power failures of sufficient duration can damage plant health. The lower limit of temperature as a steady state is 65°F for plant survival. Brief drops to 55°F (less than 1 hr) are the lower limit before damage. Temperatures up to 85°F for only 2 days a week can usually be tolerated.
3. The relative humidity should not be allowed to fall below 30%, as plants prefer a relative humidity of 50-60%.

Richard L. Gaines; Plantscape House; Apopka, Florida

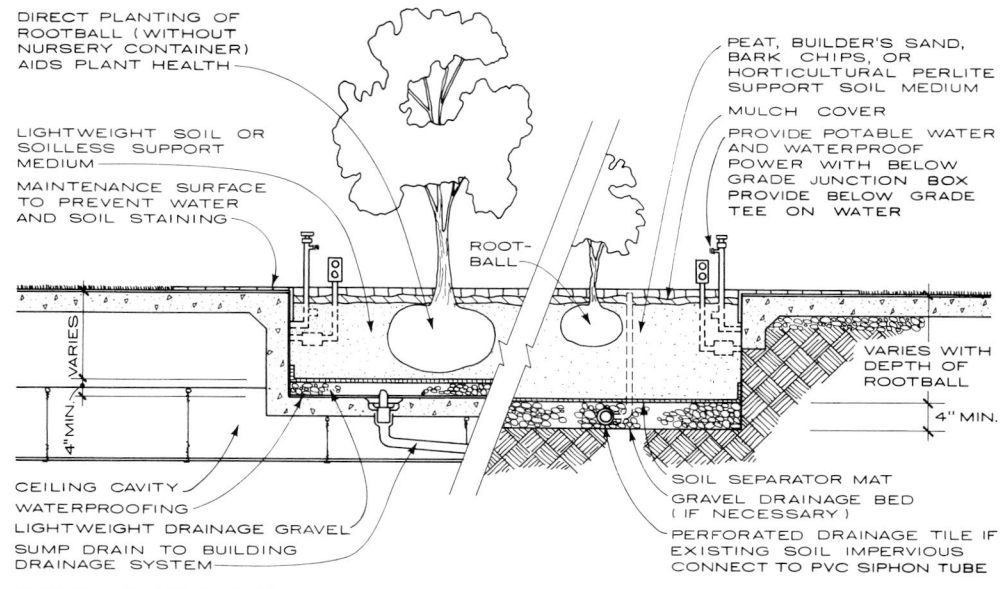

ABOVE-GRADE PLANTER   **AT-GRADE PLANTER**
FLOOR PLANTER DETAILS

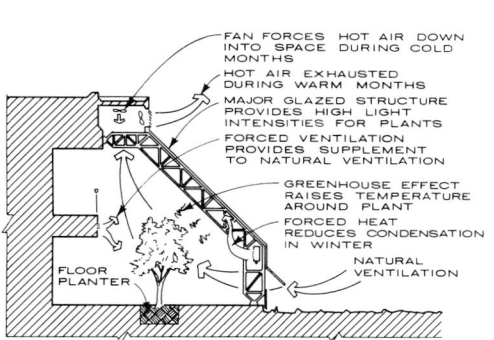

GREENHOUSE EFFECT RAISES NEED FOR ADEQUATE VENTILATION

TEMPERATURE REQUIREMENTS

1. Most plants prefer human comfort range: 70-75°F daytime temperatures and 60-65°F nighttime temperatures.
2. An absolute minimum temperature of 50°F must be observed. Plant damage will result below this figure. Rapid temperature fluctuations of 30-40°F can also be detrimental to plants.
3. "Q-10" phenomenon of respiration: for every 10°C rise in temperature, plants' respiration rate and food consumption doubles.
4. Both photosynthesis and respiration decline and stop with time, as temperatures go beyond 80°F. Beware of the greenhouse effect!

WATER SUPPLY REQUIREMENTS

1. Movable and railing planters are often watered by watering can. Provide convenient access to hot and cold water by hose bibbs and/or service sinks (preferably in janitor's closet) during normal working hours, with long (min. 24 in.) faucet-to-sink or floor distances. Provide for maximum of 200 ft travel on all floors.
2. At-grade floor planters are usually watered by hose and extension wand. Provide hose bibbs above soil line (for maximum travel of 50 ft) with capped "tee" stub-outs beneath soil line. If soil temperature is apt to get abnormally low in winter, provide hot and cold water by mixer-faucet type hose bibbs.
3. High concentrations of fluoride and chlorine in water supply can cause damage to plants. Provide water with low concentrations of these elements and with a pH value of 5.0-6.0. Higher or lower pH levels can result in higher plant maintenance costs.

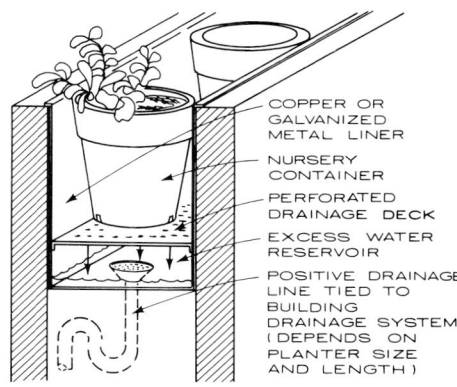

RAILING PLANTER DETAIL

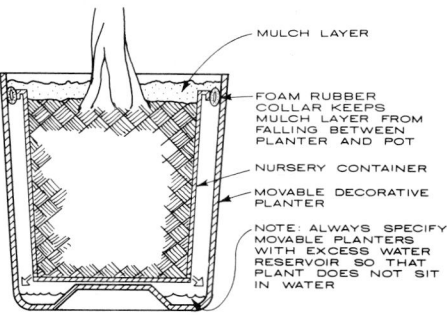

MOVABLE DECORATIVE PLANTER DETAIL

STORAGE REQUIREMENTS

Provide a secured storage space of approximately 30 sq ft for watering equipment and other maintenance materials. It may be desirable to combine water supply and janitor needs in the same storage area.

AIR POLLUTION EFFECTS ON PLANTS

Problems result from inadequate ventilation. Excessive chlorine gas from swimming pool areas can be a damaging problem, as well as excessive fumes from toxic cleaning substances for floor finishes, etc. Ventilation a must here!

GENERAL USE FURNITURE

American Association of
    Textile Chemists and Colorists
P.O. Box 12215
Research Triangle Park, NC 27709-2215
Tel: (919) 549-8141
Fax:(919) 549-8933

American Furniture Manufacturers Association
P.O. Box HP-7
High Point, NC 27261
Tel: (919) 884-5000
Fax:(919) 884-5303

Americans with
    Disabilities Act Information Office
U.S. Department of Justice
Civil Rights Division
P.O. Box 66738
Washington, DC 20035-6738
Tel: (202) 514-0301

American Society of Furniture Designers (ASFD)
1309 Johnson Street
High Point, NC 27262
Tel: (919) 884-4074

American Society of Furniture Designers
mailing address:
P.O. Box 2688
High Point, NC 27261

American Society of Interior Designers (ASID)
608 Massachusetts Avenue, N.E.
Washington, DC 20002
Tel (202) 546-3480

American Textile Manufacturers Institute
1801 K. Street, N.W., Suite 900
Washington, DC 20006
Tel: (202) 862-0500
Fax:(202) 862-0570

Contract Furnishings Council (CFC)
1190 Merchandise Mart
Chicago, IL 60654
Tel: (312) 321-0563

Industrial Fabrics Association International
345 Cedar Building, Suite 800
St. Paul, MN 55101
Tel: (612) 222-2508
Fax:(612) 222-8215

International Furnishings and Design
107 World Trade Center
P.O. Box 580450
Dallas, TX 75258
Tel: (214) 747-2406

REFERENCES

Fiell, Charlotte, and Peter Fiell. *Modern Furniture Classics Since 1945.* Washington, D.C.: AIA Press, 1991.

Habegger, J. *Sourcebook of Modern Furniture.* Van Nostrand Reinhold, 1989.

Pile, J. *Human Factors Design Handbook: Information and Guidelines for the Design of Modern Furniture,* 1979.

Reznikoff, S. C. *Interior Graphics and Design Standards.* Whitney Library, 1986, 622 pp.

OFFICE FURNITURE

Business and Institutional
    Furniture Manufacturers Association (BIFMA)
2680 Horizon Drive, S.E., Suite A1
Grand Rapids, MI 49546
Tel: (616) 285-3963

Computer and Business
    Equipment Manufacturers Association (CBEMA)
1250 I Street, NW, Suite 200
Washington, DC 20005
Tel: (202) 737-8888
Fax:(202) 638-4922

Institute of Business Designers
341 Merchandise Mart
Chicago, IL 60654-1104
Tel: (312) 467-1950
Fax:(312) 467-0779

National Office Products Association (NOPA)
301 North Fairfax Street
Alexandria, VA 22314
Tel: (703) 549-9040
Fax:(703) 683-7552

Office Products Manufacturers Association
P.O. Box 248
Glen Oaks, NY 11004
Tel: (908) 255-1570
Fax:(908) 255-1303

SCHOOL FURNITURE

American Association of School Administrators (AASA)
1801 N. Moore Street
Arlington, VA 22209
Tel: (703) 875-0748

National School Supply and Equipment Associaton
8300 Colesville Road, Suite 250
Silver Spring, MD 20910
Tel: (301) 495-0240
Fax:(301) 495-3330

LIBRARY FURNITURE

American Library Association
50 East Huron Street
Chicago, IL 60611
Tel: (312) 944-6780
Fax:(312) 440-9374

ECCLESIASTICAL FURNITURE

Interfaith Forum on Religion, Art and Architecture (IFRAA)
1777 Church Street, N.W.
Washington, DC 20036
Tel: (202) 387-8333

RESIDENTIAL FURNITURE

Kitchen Cabinet Manufacturers Association (KCMA)
1899 Preston White Drive
Reston, VA 22091-4326
Tel: (703) 264-1690
Fax:(703) 620-6530

National Home Furnishings Association (NHFA)
P.O. Box 2396
High Point, NC 27261
Tel: (919) 883-1650
Fax:(919) 883-1195

National Kitchen and Bath Association
687 Willow Grove Street
Hackettstown, NJ 07840
(908) 852-0033

LAMPS

American Lighting Association
435 North Michigan Avenue, Suite 1717
Chicago, IL 60611-4067
Tel: (312) 644-0828
Fax:(312) 644-8557

International Association of Lighting Designers
18 E. 16th Street, Suite 208
New York, NY 10003-3193
Tel: (212) 206-1281
Fax:(212) 206-1327

INTERIOR PLANTS AND PLANTERS

American Association of Nurserymen (AAN)
1250 I Street, N.W., Suite 500
Washington, DC 20005
Tel: (202) 789-2900
Fax:(202) 789-1893

Associated Landscape Contractors of America
12200 Sunrise Valley Drive
Reston, VA 22091
Tel: (703) 620-6363
Fax:(703) 620-6365

TRADE BUILDINGS AND MARTS

Atlanta Merchandise Mart
240 Peachtree Street, N.W., Suite 2200
Atlanta, GA 30303
Tel: (404) 220-3000

Boston Design Center
One Design Center Place
Boston, MA 02210
Tel: (617) 338-5062

Dallas Design Center
1025 N. Stemmons Freeway, Suite 605
Dallas, TX 75207
Tel: (214) 747-2411

Denver Design Center
595 South Broadway
Denver, CO 80209
Tel: (303) 733-2455

INNOVA
20 Greenway Plaza
Houston, TX 77046
Tel:(713) 963-9955

International Design Center, N.Y. (IDCNY)
29-10 Thomson Avenue, Suite 54
Long Island City, NY 11101
Tel: (718) 937-7474

International Market Square
275 Market Street
Minneapolis, MN 55405
Tel: (612) 338-6250

The L.A. Mart
1933 S. Broadway, Suite 244
Los Angeles, CA 90007
Tel: (213) 749-7911

Marketplace Design Center
2400 Market Street
Philadelphia, PA 19103
Tel: (215) 561-5000

The Merchandise Mart
222 Merchandise Mart Plaza, Suite 470
Chicago, IL 60654
Tel: (800) 677-6278

Miami International Merchandise Mart
777 N.W. 72nd Avenue
Miami, FL 33126
Tel: (305) 261-2900, ext. 169
Fax:(305) 261-3659

Michigan Design Center
1700 Stutz Drive, #25
Troy, MI 48084
Tel: (313) 649-4772

Pacific Design Center
8687 Melrose Avenue, M-60
Los Angeles, CA 90069
Tel: (310) 657-0800

Saint Louis Design Center
917 Locust Street
St. Louis, MO 63101
Tel: (314) 621-6446

San Diego Design Center
6455 Lusk Blvd.
San Diego, CA 92121
Tel: (619) 452-7332

The San Francisco Mart
1355 Market Street
San Francisco, CA 94103
Tel: (415) 552-2311

The Washington Design Center
300 D Street, S.W.
Washington, DC 20024
Tel: (202) 554-5053

RELATED JOURNALS

Architectural Digest
6300 Wilshire Blvd., 11th Floor
Los Angeles, CA 90048
Tel: (213) 965-3700

Architectural Lighting
1515 Broadway, 32nd Floor
New York, NY 10036
Tel: (212) 869-1300

Interior Design
249 West 17th Street
New York, NY 10011
Tel: (212) 645-0067

Interiors
Gralla Publications
1515 Broadway
New York, NY 10036
Tel: (212) 764-7300

Lighting Design and Application (LD+A)
Illuminating Engineering Society of North America
345 East 47th Street
New York, NY 10017
Tel: (212) 705-7926

CHAPTER

13

SPECIAL CONSTRUCTION

GENERAL INFORMATION

Most air structures are primarily designed to resist wind loads. Mechanical blowers must maintain 3 to 5 psf pressure inside the structure at all times. Architectural elements of the building must be detailed to avoid loss of air pressure. Normal entering and exiting should be through revolving doors, while emergency exiting is provided through pressure balanced doors, and vehicles pass through air locks. Avoid using interior furnishings that could possibly puncture the structural membrane. Automatic auxiliary fans should be activated in the event of a pressure drop due to primary power failure.

The structural membrane is usually a nylon, fiberglass, or polyester fabric coated with polyvinyl chloride. Such skins have a life span from 7 to 10 years, and provide fire retardation that passes NFPA 701. A urethane topcoat will reduce dirt adhesion and improve service life. Fluorocarbon top finishes are available that further enhance characteristics and can double service life. Teflon coated fiberglass membranes have a life expectancy of more than 25 years. This material is incombustible, passing ASTM E84, with flame spread rating = 10, smoke developed < 50, and fuel contributed = 10. An acoustical liner (NCR = 0.65) is also available.

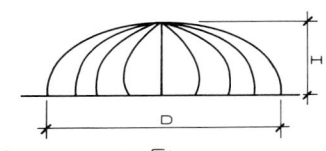

$$D/2 > H > D/(2\sqrt{2})$$

SPAN LIMITATIONS	VAULT	DOME
Without cables	D = 120' – 0''	D = 150' – 0''
With cables	D = 400' – 0''	D = 600' – 0''

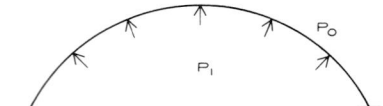

SINGLE MEMBRANE $P_1 > P_0$

This is the most common type of air structure. The internal pressure (P_1) is kept approximately 0.03 psi above the external atmospheric pressure (P_0). It is this pressure difference that keeps the dome inflated.

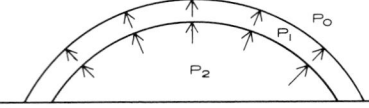

DOUBLE MEMBRANE $P_2 > P_1 > P_0$

The airspace between the two membranes is used for insulation and security. If the outer skin is punctured the inner skin will remain standing. Both single and double membrane air structures require the constant use of blowers to keep them inflated.

AIR SUPPORTED

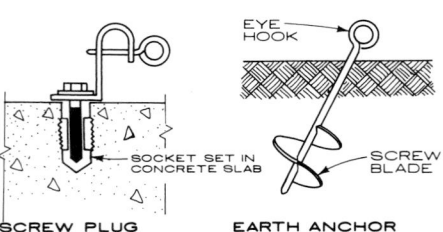

VAULT

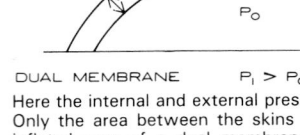

DUAL MEMBRANE $P_1 > P_0$

Here the internal and external pressures are the same. Only the area between the skins is pressurized. The inflated area of a dual membrane structure can be sealed, thus eliminating the need for constant use of blowers, although blowers are recommended to make up losses from leakage.

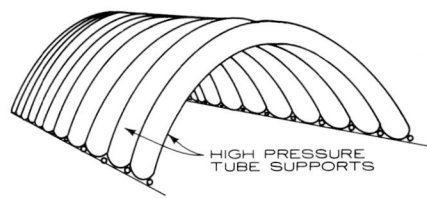

AIR INFLATED

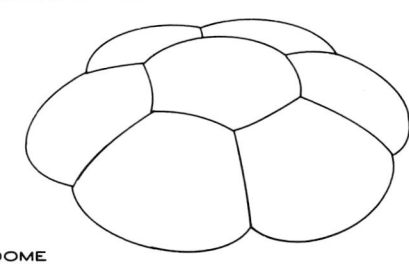

DOME

BASIC CONFIGURATIONS

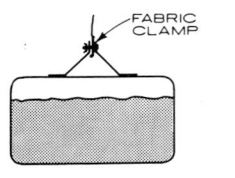

WATER TANK

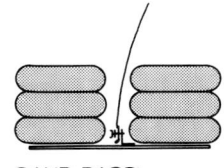

SAND BAGS

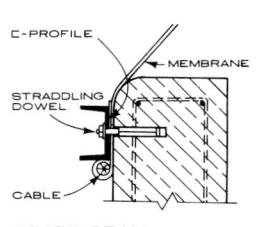

SCREW PLUG   **EARTH ANCHOR**

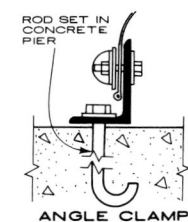

GRADE BEAM   **ANGLE CLAMP**

ANCHORAGE DETAILS

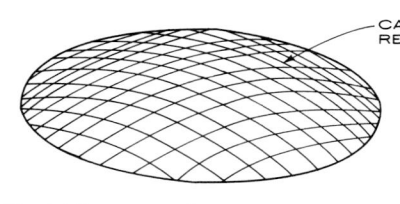

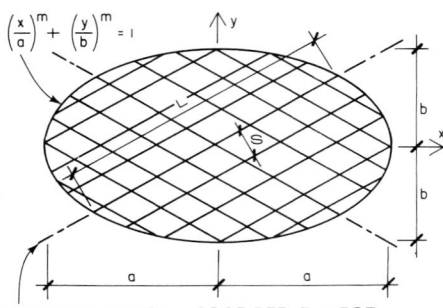

$$\left(\frac{x}{a}\right)^m + \left(\frac{y}{b}\right)^m = 1$$

DIAGONAL OF SUPERSCRIBED ELLIPSE
MAXIMUM CABLE SPACING = 50'-0''

SUPERELLIPSE PLAN

KEY TO NOTATIONS
a/b—One half of major/minor axes of superellipse.
s—Cable spacing.
L—Length of cable along diagonal of superscribed rectangle of proportions 2a and 2b.
e/f—One half of major/minor axes of superscribed

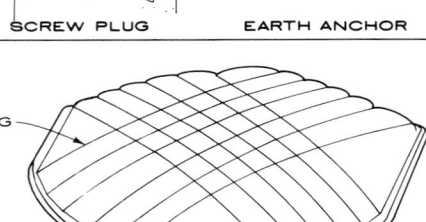

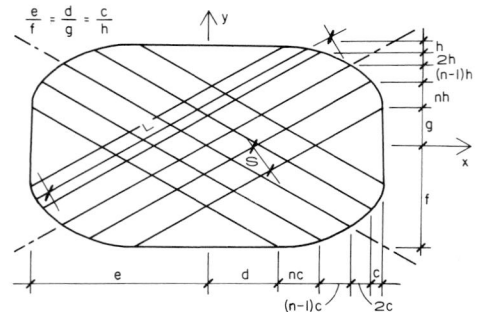

$$\frac{e}{f} = \frac{d}{g} = \frac{c}{h}$$

MAXIMUM STRAIGHT SIDE = 200'-0''
PROGRESSION PLAN

rectangle of plan progression.
d/g—One half of straight sides of and parallel to the major/minor axes of the plan progression.
c, 2c, (n-1)c, nc/h, 2h, (n-1)h, nh—The sequences of curve coordinates parallel to the major/minor axes of the plan progression.

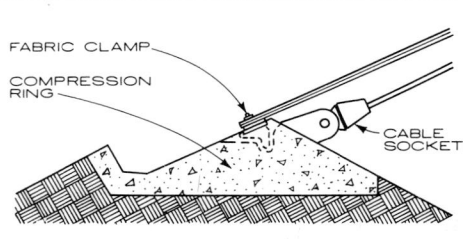

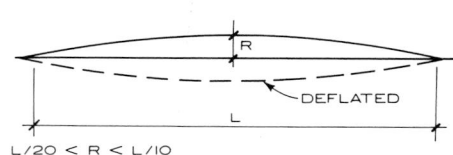

L/20 < R < L/10
200 < L < NO UPPER LIMIT

STRUCTURAL CONSIDERATIONS

Membrane strengths up to 1000 lb/in. are available; a safety factor of 4 for short-term loading and 5 for long-term loading is required. The membrane must be patterned to carry loads without wrinkling. Structural behavior is nonlinear with large displacements. The roof shape shall be established such that the horizontal components of the cable forces result in minimum bending moment in the compression ring under maximum loads. The skewed symmetry indicated permits this condition to be realized. Consult specialist in air structures to integrate structural and architectural requirements.

LONG SPAN STRUCTURES

Geiger Engineers, P.C.; Suffern, New York

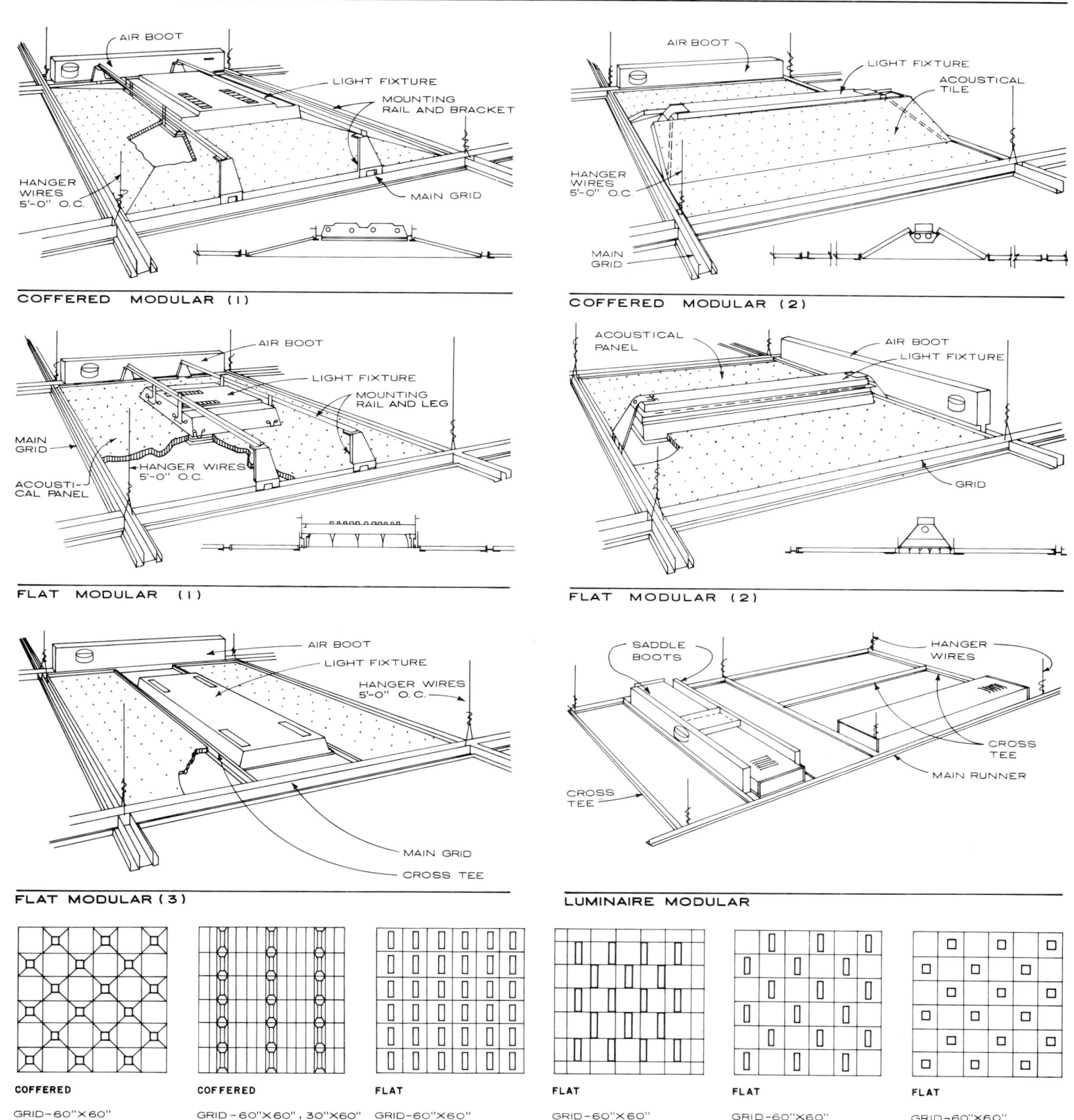

AIR BOOT

LIGHT FIXTURE

MOUNTING
RAIL AND BRACKET

HANGER
WIRES
5'-0" O.C.

MAIN GRID

COFFERED MODULAR (1)

AIR BOOT

LIGHT FIXTURE

ACOUSTICAL
TILE

HANGER
WIRES
5'-0" O.C.

MAIN
GRID

COFFERED MODULAR (2)

AIR BOOT

LIGHT FIXTURE

MOUNTING
RAIL AND LEG

MAIN
GRID

ACOUSTI-
CAL PANEL

HANGER WIRES
5'-0" O.C.

FLAT MODULAR (1)

ACOUSTICAL
PANEL

AIR BOOT
LIGHT FIXTURE

GRID

FLAT MODULAR (2)

AIR BOOT

LIGHT FIXTURE

HANGER WIRES
5'-0" O.C.

MAIN GRID

CROSS TEE

FLAT MODULAR (3)

SADDLE
BOOTS

HANGER
WIRES

CROSS
TEE

MAIN RUNNER

CROSS
TEE

LUMINAIRE MODULAR

COFFERED

GRID-60"X60"
COFFER-60"X60"
LIGHT FIXTURE-1'X4'
2'X2', 2'X4' AND 30"X30"

COFFERED

GRID-60"X60", 30"X60"
COFFER-30"X60"
LIGHT FIXTURE-6½"X48"

FLAT

GRID-60"X60"
LIGHT FIXTURE-10"X48"

FLAT

GRID-60"X60"
LIGHT FIXTURE-20"X60"

FLAT

GRID-60"X60"
LIGHT FIXTURE-10"X48"

FLAT

GRID-60"X60"
LIGHT FIXTURE-24"X24"
OR 30"X30"

REFLECTED   CEILING   PLANS   (INTEGRATED   CEILINGS)

Timothy B. McDonald; Washington, D.C.

INTEGRATED ASSEMBLIES   13

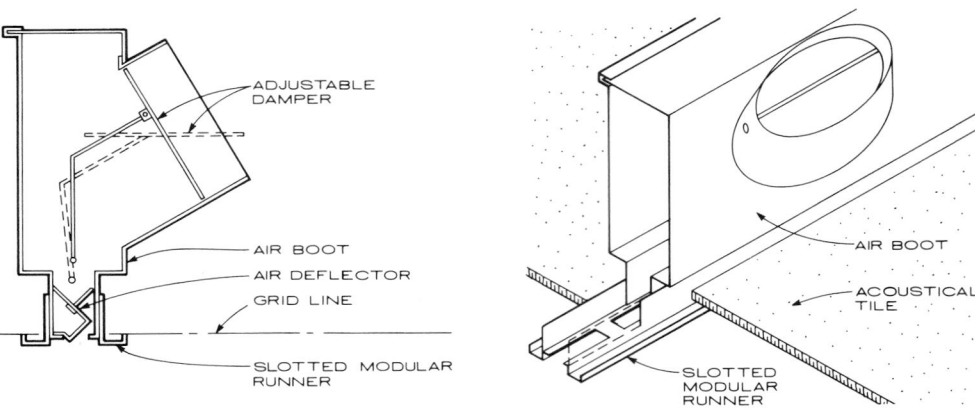

AIR BOOT SECTION AND DETAIL

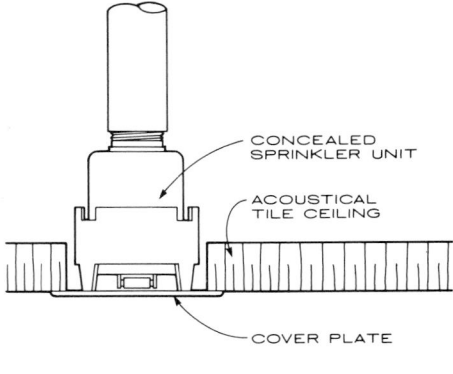

CONCEALED SPRINKLER

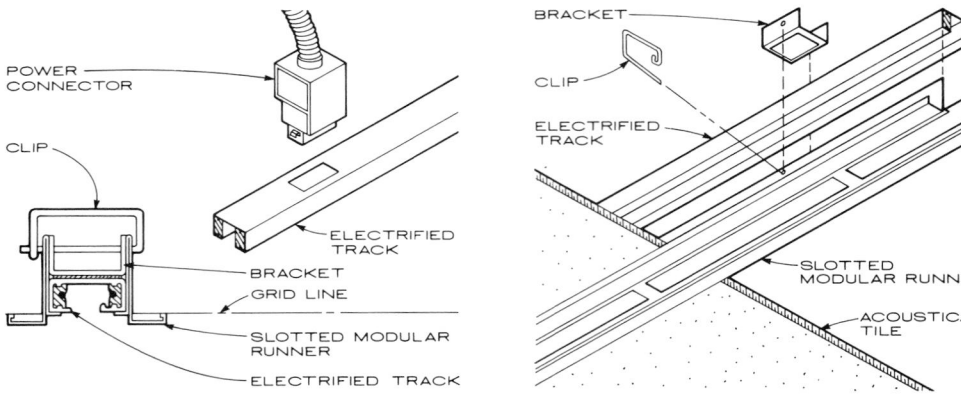

LIGHT TRACK SECTION AND DETAILS

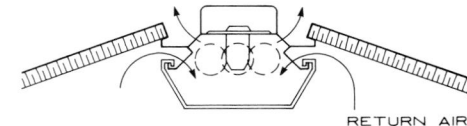

COFFERED FIXTURE

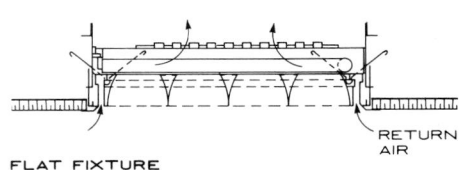

FLAT FIXTURE

LIGHTING FIXTURES

INTEGRATED CEILINGS

Integrated ceilings combine lighting, air diffusion, fire protection, and acoustical control into a single, unified unit. Demountable partitions can be accommodated by the use of an adaptor attached on the modular grid lines. A 60 x 60 in. module is basic to most integrated ceiling systems. Custom sized modules are also available.

LUMINAIRE MODULAR CEILING

The basic configuration is a 60 x 60 in. module divided into four 15 x 60 in. modules.

A recess in the modular defining grid will accommodate demountable partitions, sprinkler heads, and slots for air diffusion.

The basic lighting unit is a $14\frac{1}{2}$ x 48 in. recessed troffer. Air return is by return air light fixtures.

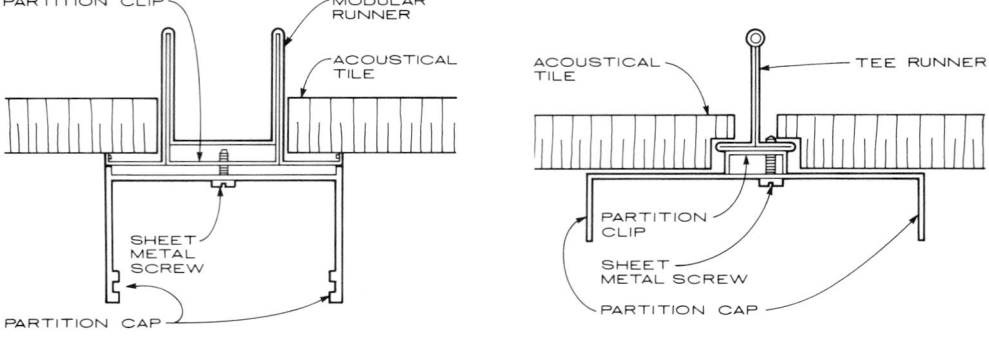

PARTITION ASSEMBLIES

COMPONENTS

CEILING SYSTEMS	HANGER SPACING (o.c.)	WALL MOLDINGS			MAIN RUNNERS			SPACING	CROSS MEMBERS			SPACING (o.c.)	AIR BAR AIR BOOT			ACOUSTIC PANELS			LIGHT FIXTURES		
		L	W	H	L	W	H		L	W	H		L	W	H	L	W	H	L	W	H
Flat modular	2'-6"	10'	$\frac{3}{4}$"	$\frac{3}{4}$"	10'	$\frac{3}{4}$"	$1\frac{1}{2}$"	5'	60"	$\frac{3}{4}$"	$1\frac{1}{2}$"	20"	5'	$3\frac{1}{8}$"	$9\frac{3}{4}$"	5'	20"	$\frac{5}{8}$"	–	1.	–
Coffered lighting	30"	60"	$1\frac{1}{4}$"	$1\frac{1}{4}$"	5'	$2\frac{1}{4}$"	$1\frac{1}{4}$"	5'	60"	$2\frac{1}{4}$"	$1\frac{1}{4}$"	5'	5'	$7\frac{1}{4}$"	8"	5'	15"	$\frac{5}{8}$"	48"	$14\frac{1}{2}$"	5"
Luminair modular	5'	–	–	–	$58\frac{1}{2}$"	3"	$1\frac{1}{2}$"	5'	57"	$\frac{15}{16}$"	$1\frac{1}{2}$"	5'	5'	$7\frac{1}{4}$"	8"	5'	15"	$\frac{5}{8}$"	48"	$14\frac{1}{2}$"	5"
Vertical screen	7' Max.	–	–	–	16'	$1\frac{1}{2}$"	$1\frac{7}{8}$"	7' Max.	16' Max.	$\frac{5}{8}$"	4"	2'-6"	–	2.	–	–	–	–	–	2.	–
Linear screen	5' Max.	–	–	–	16'	$1\frac{27}{32}$"	$1\frac{1}{4}$"	50"	3'-16'	3"	$\frac{5}{8}$"	2"	–	3.	–	–	4.	–	–	5.	–

NOTES

1. Size can vary.
2. No special type necessary.
3. Utilizes slots between panels for delivery and return.
4. Acoustic blanket.
5. Designed to fit panel width.

Timothy B. McDonald; Washington, D.C.

13   **INTEGRATED ASSEMBLIES**

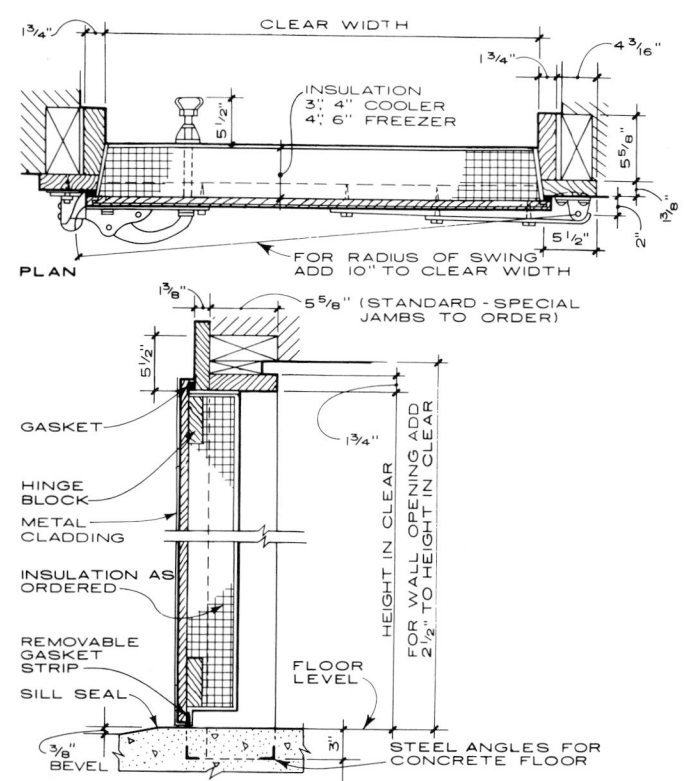

CLEAR WIDTH

INSULATION
3", 4" COOLER
4", 6" FREEZER

FOR RADIUS OF SWING
ADD 10" TO CLEAR WIDTH

PLAN

5⅝" (STANDARD - SPECIAL
JAMBS TO ORDER)

GASKET

HINGE
BLOCK

METAL
CLADDING

INSULATION AS
ORDERED

REMOVABLE
GASKET
STRIP

SILL SEAL

⅜"
BEVEL

FLOOR
LEVEL

STEEL ANGLES FOR
CONCRETE FLOOR

HEIGHT IN CLEAR
FOR WALL OPENING ADD
2½" TO HEIGHT IN CLEAR

SECTION
TYPICAL DOOR DETAILS

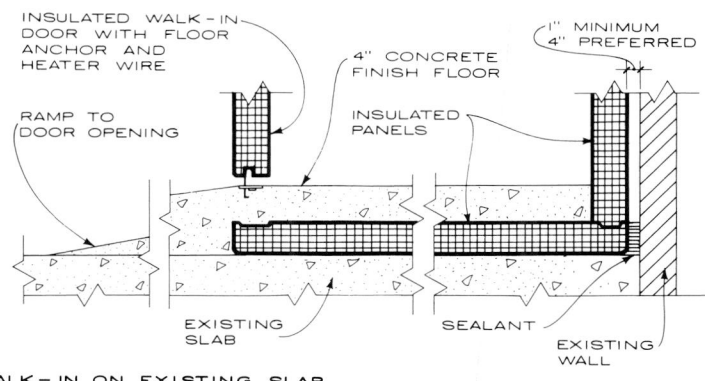

INSULATED WALK-IN
DOOR WITH FLOOR
ANCHOR AND
HEATER WIRE

RAMP TO
DOOR OPENING

4" CONCRETE
FINISH FLOOR

INSULATED
PANELS

1" MINIMUM
4" PREFERRED

EXISTING
SLAB

SEALANT

EXISTING
WALL

WALK-IN ON EXISTING SLAB

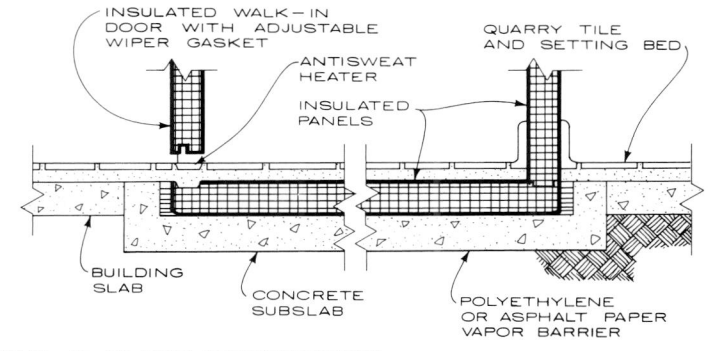

INSULATED WALK-IN
DOOR WITH ADJUSTABLE
WIPER GASKET

ANTISWEAT
HEATER

INSULATED
PANELS

QUARRY TILE
AND SETTING BED

BUILDING
SLAB

CONCRETE
SUBSLAB

POLYETHYLENE
OR ASPHALT PAPER
VAPOR BARRIER

WALK-IN IN NEW CONSTRUCTION
WALK-IN FLOOR DETAILS

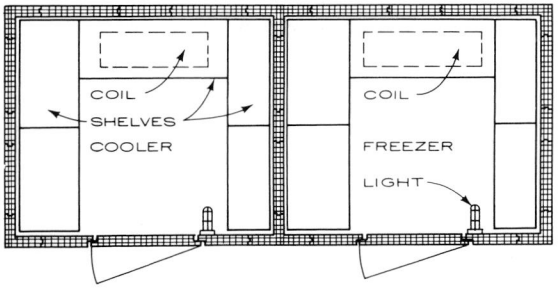

COIL
SHELVES
COOLER

COIL
FREEZER
LIGHT

SIDE-BY-SIDE PLAN
WALK-IN TYPICAL PLANS AND SECTION

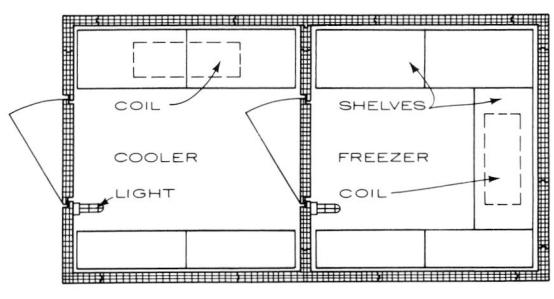

COIL
COOLER
LIGHT

SHELVES
FREEZER
COIL

WALK-THROUGH PLAN

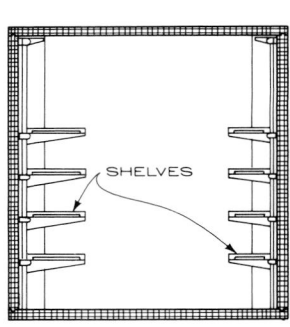

SHELVES

SECTION

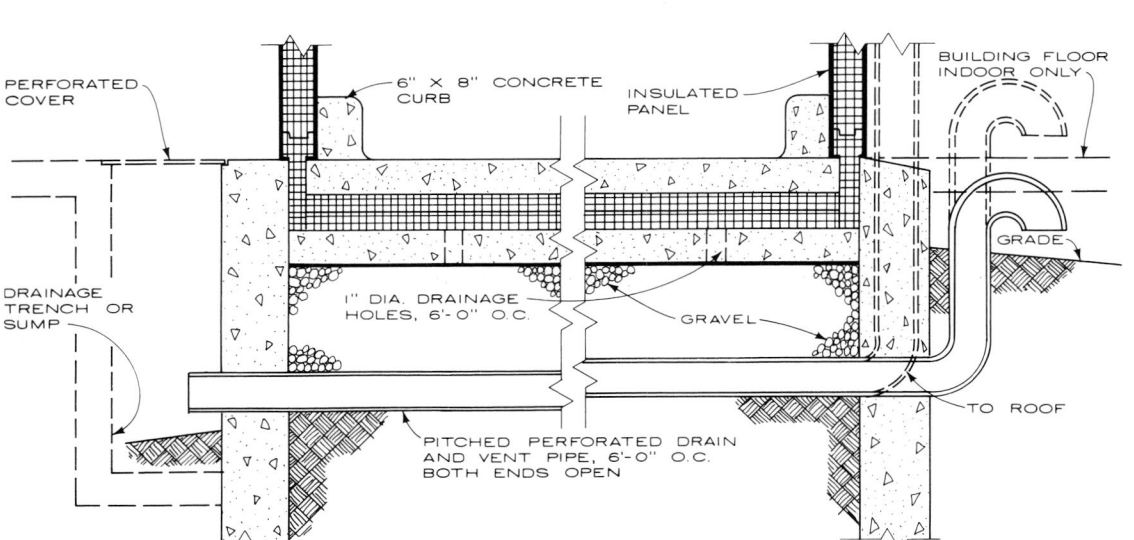

PERFORATED
COVER

DRAINAGE
TRENCH OR
SUMP

6" X 8" CONCRETE
CURB

INSULATED
PANEL

BUILDING FLOOR
INDOOR ONLY

GRADE

GRAVEL

TO ROOF

1" DIA. DRAINAGE
HOLES, 6'-0" O.C.

PITCHED PERFORATED DRAIN
AND VENT PIPE, 6'-0" O.C.
BOTH ENDS OPEN

DRAIN AND VENT DETAIL

Cini-Little International, Inc., Food Service Consultants; Washington, D.C.

GENERAL NOTES

1. DOORS
   Standard sizes: 2'-6", 2'-10", 3'-6", 4'-0", 5'-0" wide x 6'-6" high; 4'-0", 5'-0" wide x 7'-0" high.
   Sliding, double action, and display doors are available.
   Manual or electrically operated.

2. PREFABRICATED INSULATED PANELS
   Standard sizes: 4" thick.
   Width: 11½", 23", and 46".
   Height: 7'-6", 8'-6", 10'-6", and 11'-6".
   Finish material usually aluminum, galvanized steel, or stainless steel.

3. WALK-IN UNIT SIZES
   Widths: 3'-11", 5'-10", 7'-9", 9'-8", and 11'-7".
   Lengths: 5'-10", 7'-9", 11'-7", 13'-6", 15'-5", 17'-4", 19'-3".
   Heights: 7'-6", 8'-6", 9'-6", 10'-6", 11'-6".
   Available accessories: stationary or mobile shelf units and adjustable cantilevered shelves, windows, interior partitions, meat rails, floor racks, ramps, and walk-ins.

4. Check local codes for drainage requirements.

CLEAN ROOM DESIGN

Clean rooms—enclosed areas with carefully controlled environmental conditions for critical operations in electronics, medicine, pharmaceuticals, food processing, bioscience, aerospace, and manufacturing—are classified by the quantity of particulate matter in the air. Temperature, humidity, pressure, noise, vibration, and airflow patterns also are controlled carefully.

Four air cleanliness classes are defined in Federal Standard No. 209: Class 1, Class 10, Class 100, Class 1000, Class 10,000, and Class 100,000. The numbers refer to particles per cubic foot of air. In a Class 100 clean room the particle count cannot exceed 100 particles/cu ft of a size 0.5 μm (meter $\times$ 10^{-6}). For some applications, such as the manufacture of VLSI (very large scale integrated) circuits, an environment cleaner than that defined by Class 100 is required. Class 10 and Class 1 clean rooms have been developed to satisfy this need.

Airborne particles are reduced by HEPA (high efficiency particulate air) filters and controlled airflow. HEPA filters have an efficiency in excess of 99.97% for 0.3 μm particles. For Class 10 and Class 1 clean rooms, HEPA filters are inadequate. ULPA (ultra low penetration air) filters with an efficiency of 99.9995% for 0.12 μm particles are used.

Airflow pattern types for clean rooms are conventional and laminar. In a typical conventional flow, air is supplied through HEPA filters in large ceiling outlets, flows generally downward, and is removed near the floor in wall-mounted return registers. This arrangement is satisfactory for Class 100,000, Class 10,000, or Class 1000 clean rooms, but not for Class 100, Class 10, or Class 1 rooms.

In a laminar flow system, air is supplied through HEPA filters that cover an entire room surface such as the ceiling or a wall. The air travels uniformly across the room and is removed through the entire floor area or opposite wall. The ceiling-to-floor system is a VLF (vertical laminar flow); a wall-to-wall system is a horizontal or crossflow clean room.

In a crossflow room, workstations near the supply air wall are Class 100 or lower; the rest of the room meets Class 10,000 requirements. In downflow clean rooms, the entire work area usually meets Class 100 requirements. Laminar flow workstations can be placed in Class 10,000 rooms for localized Class 100 or lower environments.

Typical airflow quantities to filter dust particles sufficiently via the recirculated air path are:

Class 100,000: 20 air changes/hr—minimum
Class 10,000: 20 air changes/hr—minimum
Class   1000: 50 to 60 air changes/hr—min.
Class   100: 70 to 90 CFM/sq ft

Thus, in a Class 100 vertical laminar flow clean room, air velocity is maintained at 70 to 90 fpm between the ceiling HEPA filters and the perforated tile floor.

To prevent dust infiltration, clean rooms are kept under positive atmospheric air pressure higher than all adjacent areas. Air locks are provided for entry/exit.

Tiles in clean room raised floors have 23 to 60% free area openings, depending on specific applications. Floor equipment loading characteristics and the degree of constant positive pressure affect floor tile selection.

Ambient temperatures normally are between 65° and 75°F, controlled at 72° ± 2°F. Between 40 and 55% relative humidity with ±5% tolerance is usual. Certain critical applications may require a tolerance of ±0.5°F and ±2% relative humidity. Clean rooms requiring 35% or lower relative humidity may use desiccants or low-temperature brine and chilled water cooling coils for depressing the supply air dew point temperature.

Clean room sound control is important. Double wall ductwork and sound attenuators for axial fans are essential if NC levels of 55 dBA or below are desired. In certain applications vibration control warrants special envelope design and mechanical equipment installation. Construction materials and finishes such as floors, walls, ceilings, and lights are crucial in maintaining particulate levels.

Clean rooms must be tested and certified. See the Institute of Environmental Sciences Recommended Practice No. IES-RP-CC-006-84-T, "Testing Clean Rooms."

Joseph R. Loring & Associates, Inc., Consulting Engineers; New York, New York

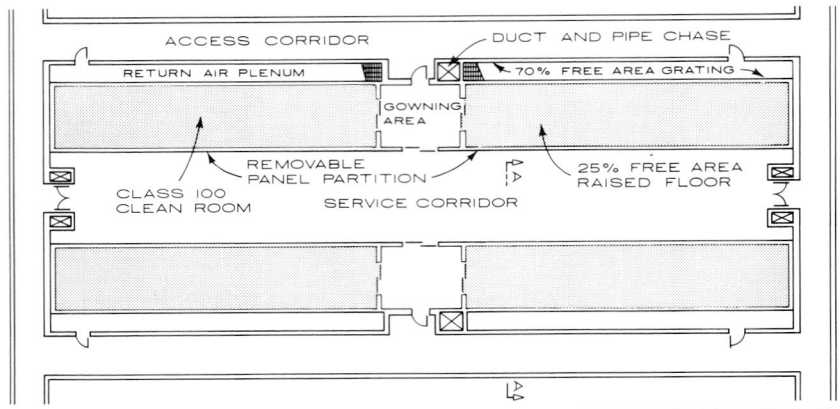

PLAN VIEW OF CLASS 100 CLEAN ROOM

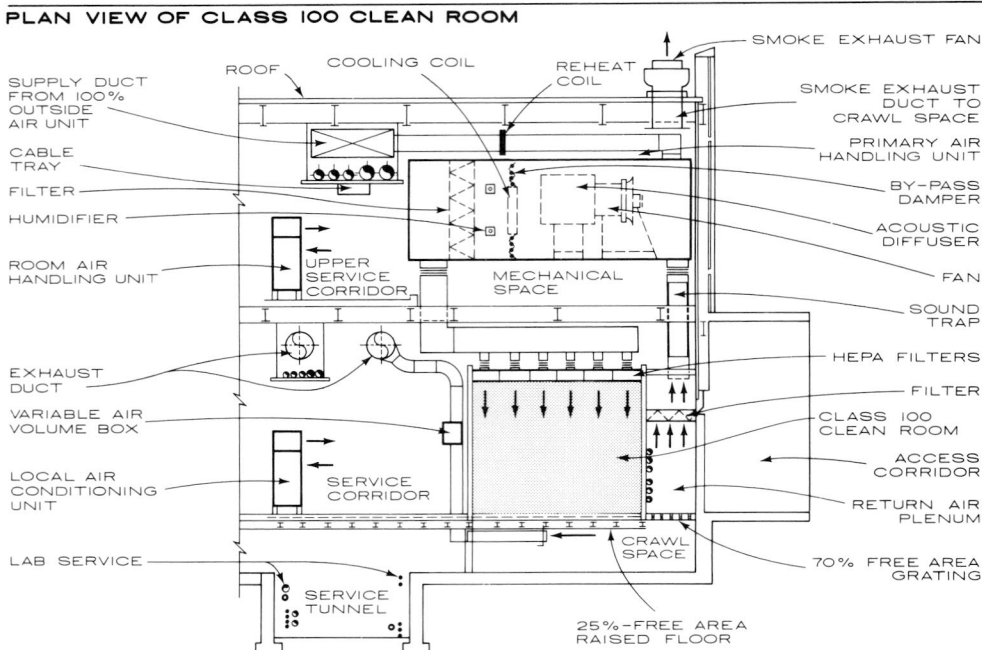

SECTION A-A THROUGH CLASS 100 CLEAN ROOM

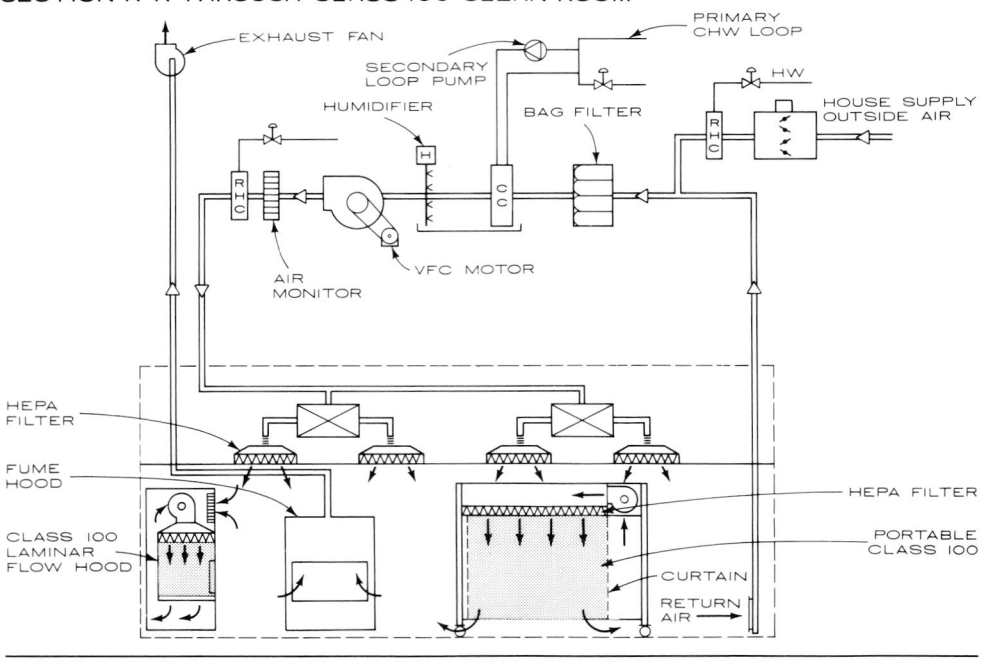

CLASS 10,000 CLEAN ROOM WITH LOCAL CLASS 100 AREAS

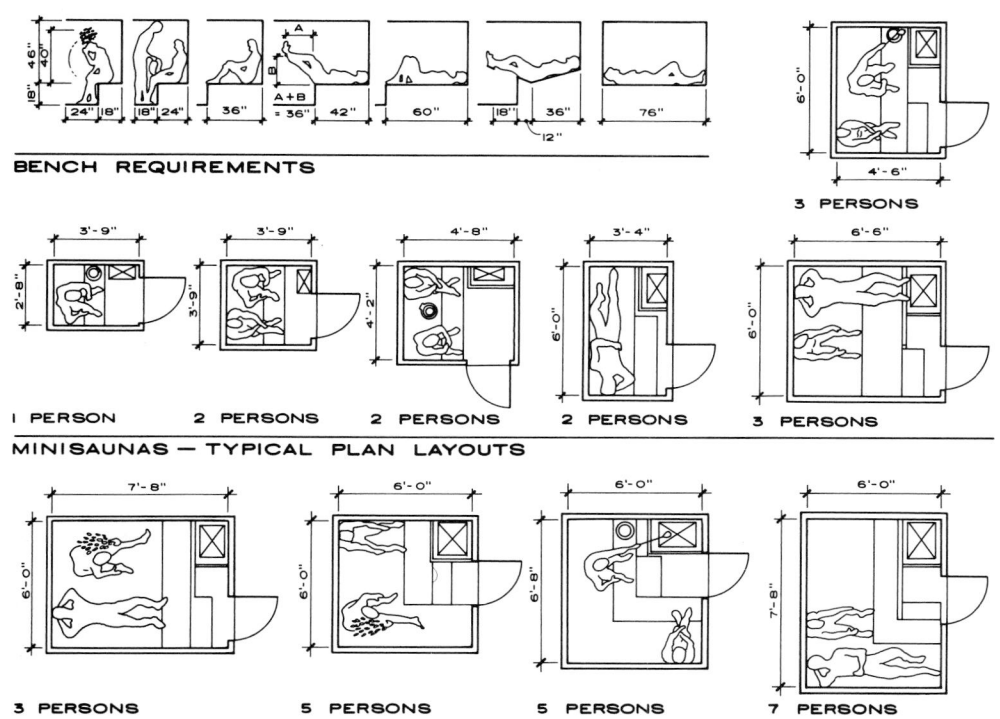

BENCH REQUIREMENTS

MINISAUNAS — TYPICAL PLAN LAYOUTS

1 PERSON   2 PERSONS   2 PERSONS   2 PERSONS   3 PERSONS   3 PERSONS

FAMILY SAUNAS — TYPICAL PLAN LAYOUTS

3 PERSONS   5 PERSONS   5 PERSONS   7 PERSONS

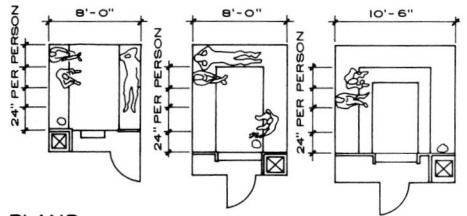

PLANS
PUBLIC SAUNAS

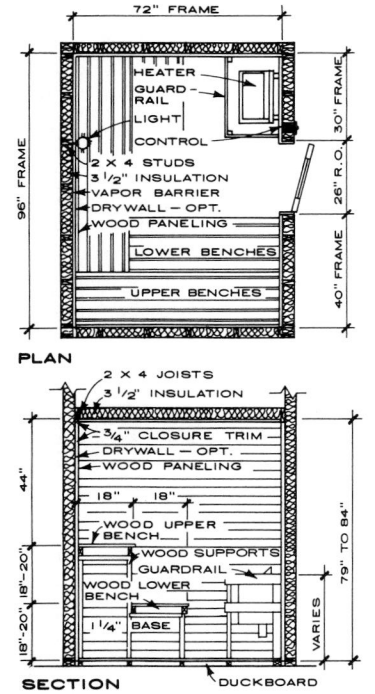

SAUNA ROOM CONSTRUCTION

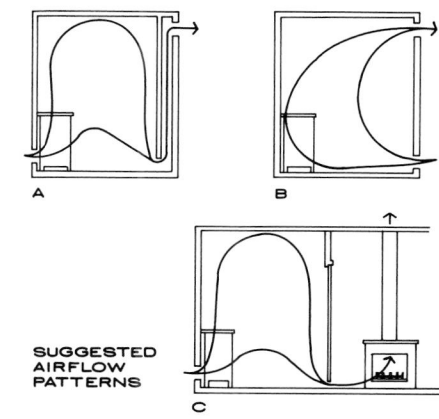

PANEL SAUNA VENTILATION

NATURAL VENTILATION

Air must flow freely into the room—inlet and outlet normally are on opposite walls and at approximately the same level. The inlet situated under the stove creates a strong updraft.

A. A flue or duct provides a chimney action that will pull air off the floor and out.

B. Inlet is low on the wall, with outlet high and directly above it. This ensures ventilation even if wind pressure exists on the wall containing the two ventilators because of the difference in air temperature at the two openings and the effect of normal convection.

C. Suggest fresh air from exterior with outlet through another room, fan, or fireplace.

HEATER: The heater depends on convection for air circulation. It is the preferred method, for the air in a sauna should be as static as possible to heat the sauna in 1 to 1½ hr.

INTERIOR PANELING: Tongue and grooved boards should be at least ⅝ in. thick, or thicker if possible because of the increased ability to absorb vapor and to retain the timber smell. Boards should not be wider than about six times their thickness. Blind nailing with galvanized or aluminum nails is common. Vapor barrier and insulation under the interior paneling must be completely vaporproof and heat resistant. Most conventional insulating materials are effective; mineral base is preferred; avoid using expanded polystyrene.

DOOR: The opening should be kept as small as possible to minimize loss of heat. Maximum height is 6 ft. Door must open outward as a safety measure. A close fitting rebate on all four sides is usually sufficient insurance against heat loss around the edges. The construction should approach the U value of the walls.

HARDWARE: Because of the weight of the door, a pair of 4 in. brass butt hinges with ball bearings are recommended. A heavy ball or roller catch keeps the door closed. Door handles are made of wood.

LIGHTING: The lighting must be indirect and the fitting unobtrusive. The best position for the light is above and slightly behind the bather's normal field of view. The switch is always outside the hot room.

TYPE OF WOOD: White or western red cedar and redwood are the materials suitable for sauna construction. They should be chosen based on their resistance to splitting and decay, color of the wood, and the thermal capacity of the wood. These woods stain badly by metal.

CEILING HEIGHT: The bigger the volume the more heat required; hence, keep the ceiling as low as possible within the limits imposed by the benches.

The main platform or bench will be about 39 in. above floor in a family sauna or at least 60 in. in a large public sauna. The ceiling is about 43 in. above the highest bench. Average family sauna ceiling height is 82 in., public 110 in.

DESIGN CONSIDERATIONS

The fundamental purpose of the sauna is to induce perspiration; the higher the temperature, the more quickly perspiration will begin.

The drier the air, the more heat one can stand. Temperatures on the platform can be as high as 212°F, 230°F, and 240°F. A little warm water thrown over the stove stones just before leaving the sauna produces a slightly humid wave of air that suddenly seems hotter and envelops the bather with an invisible glowing cloud, pleasantly stinging the skin. It is usually better to lie than to sit, for the temperature rises roughly 18°F for every 1 ft above the floor level; if one lies, heat is equally dispensed over the entire body. When lying down one may wish to raise one's feet against the wall or ceiling.

The expanded hot air in the sauna contains proportionately less oxygen than the denser atmosphere outside. Bathers sometimes experience faintness unless the air is changed regularly. An amount of fresh air enters each time the door is opened; this is insufficient, however. Normally two adjustable ventilators are built into the walls. One, the air inlet, is usually placed low near the stove. Fresh air should be drawn from outside and not from adjoining rooms where odors can be present.

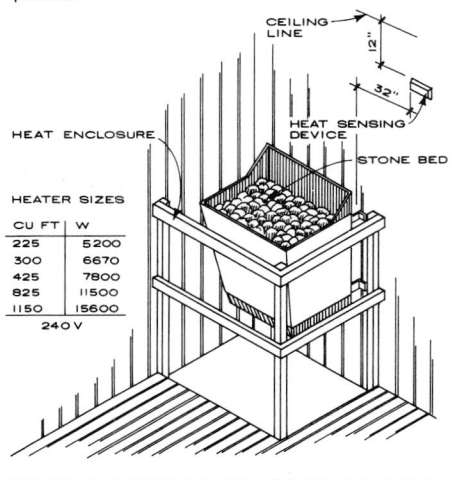

HEATER SIZES	
CU FT	W
225	5200
300	6670
425	7800
825	11500
1150	15600
240 V	

STOVE AND THERMOSTAT LOCATION

Jerry Graham; CTA Architects Engineers; Billings, Montana

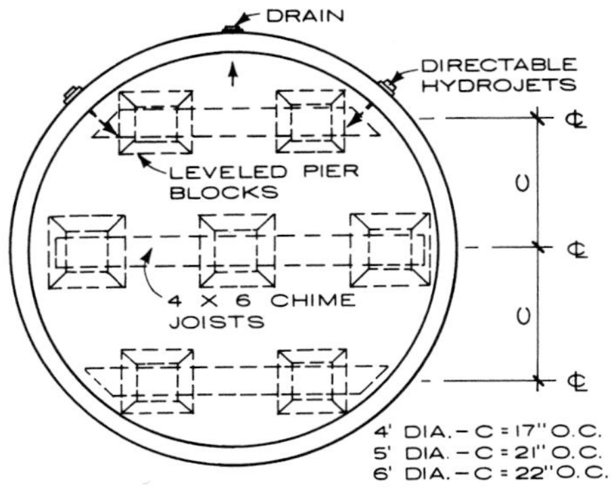

HOT TUB – PLAN

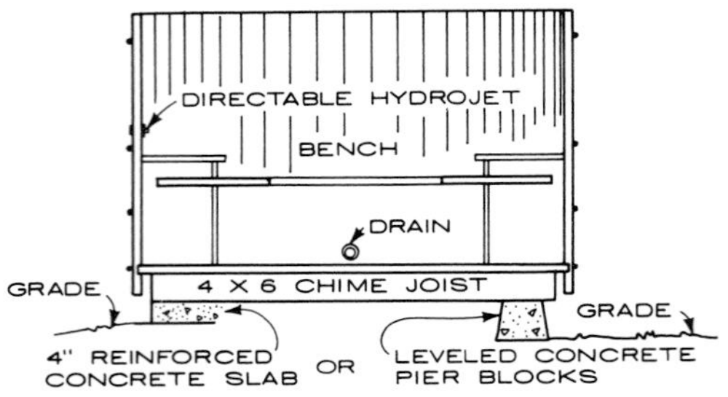

DRAIN

DIRECTABLE HYDROJETS

LEVELED PIER BLOCKS

4 X 6 CHIME JOISTS

4' DIA. – C = 17" O.C.
5' DIA. – C = 21" O.C.
6' DIA. – C = 22" O.C.

HOT TUB – SECTION

DIRECTABLE HYDROJET

BENCH

DRAIN

4 X 6 CHIME JOIST

GRADE

4" REINFORCED CONCRETE SLAB   or   LEVELED CONCRETE PIER BLOCKS

GRADE

MECHANICAL SCHEMATIC

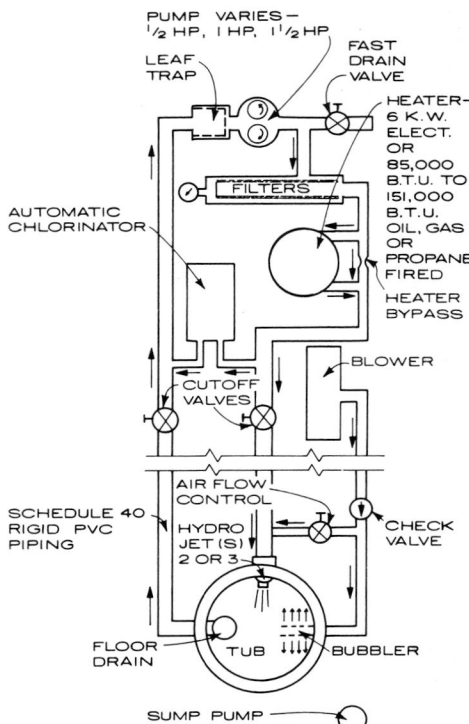

PUMP VARIES –
1/2 HP, I HP, 1 1/2 HP

LEAF TRAP

FAST DRAIN VALVE

HEATER – 6 K.W. ELECT. OR 85,000 B.T.U. TO 151,000 B.T.U. OIL, GAS OR PROPANE FIRED

AUTOMATIC CHLORINATOR

FILTERS

HEATER BYPASS

BLOWER

CUTOFF VALVES

AIR FLOW CONTROL

SCHEDULE 40 RIGID PVC PIPING

HYDRO JET(S) 2 OR 3

CHECK VALVE

FLOOR DRAIN

TUB

BUBBLER

SUMP PUMP SUBGRADE ONLY

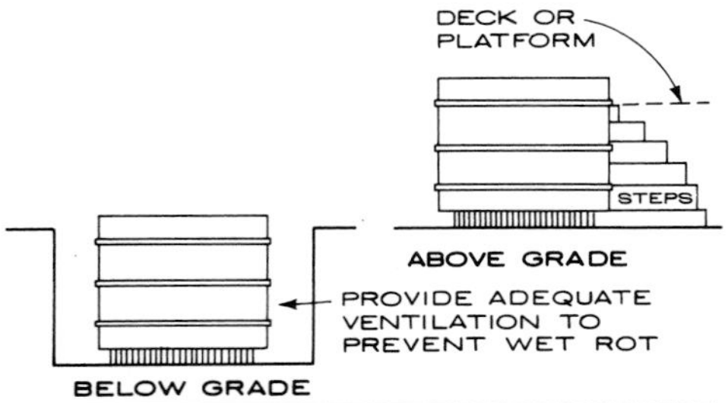

ALTERNATE INSTALLATIONS

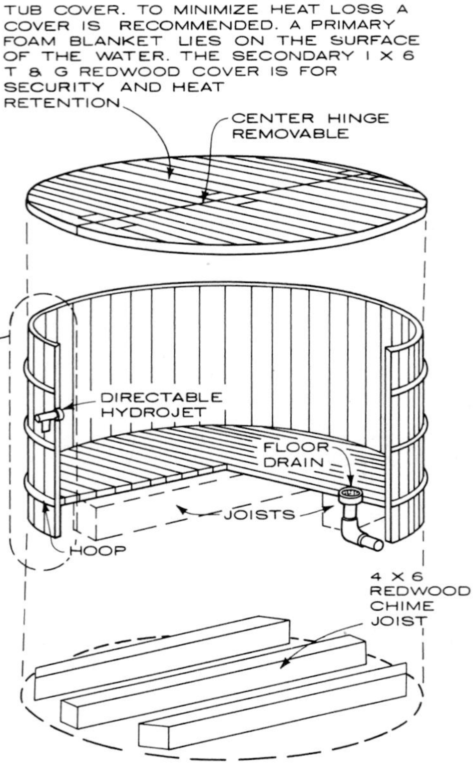

DECK OR PLATFORM

STEPS

ABOVE GRADE

PROVIDE ADEQUATE VENTILATION TO PREVENT WET ROT

BELOW GRADE

TYPICAL TUB

TUB COVER. TO MINIMIZE HEAT LOSS A COVER IS RECOMMENDED. A PRIMARY FOAM BLANKET LIES ON THE SURFACE OF THE WATER. THE SECONDARY 1 X 6 T & G REDWOOD COVER IS FOR SECURITY AND HEAT RETENTION

CENTER HINGE REMOVABLE

DIRECTABLE HYDROJET

FLOOR DRAIN

JOISTS

HOOP

4 X 6 REDWOOD CHIME JOIST

TYPICAL STAVE DETAIL

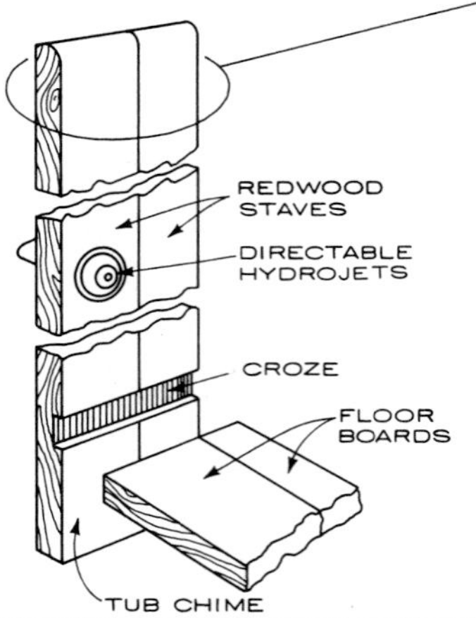

REDWOOD STAVES

DIRECTABLE HYDROJETS

CROZE

FLOOR BOARDS

TUB CHIME

NOTES

Low profile tubs allow the bathers to sit directly on the floor with feet extended. Therapeutically, this style provides direct, close range hydromassage that comes from a floor bubbler. High profile tubs can accommodate more people per diameter foot and allows people to bath standing upright. Tub surfaces are normally left unsealed and will weather naturally to gray. Exterior can be stained or treated with silicone or oil resin to preserve the natural reddish finish. In high altitude, occasional repeated oil treatment is recommended. The size and sophistication of each tub is determined by capacity, budget, and preference for components. The most critical tub support components are the heater, filter system, chlorinator, and automatic cycling and temperature control system. Hydromassage jets are a significant part of every hot tub system. Many types of heaters are available: natural gas, electric, propane, and oil. Their sizes range from 50,000 to 175,000 Btu. All components should be approved and meet local codes and standards. Consult manufacturers for additional information. Tubs made of molded fiberglass with a smooth interior surface are generally referred to as SPAS. Their function and operation is similar to those of the hot tub.

LOW PROFILE TUB

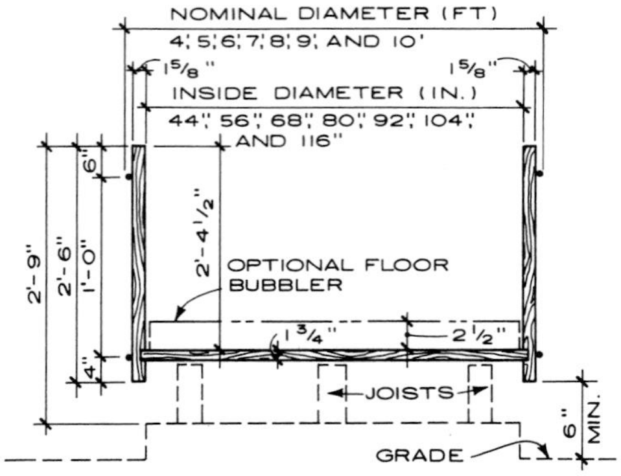

NOMINAL DIAMETER (FT)
4, 5, 6, 7, 8, 9, AND 10'

1 5/8"   1 5/8"

INSIDE DIAMETER (IN.)
44", 56", 68", 80", 92", 104", AND 116"

2'-9" 2'-6" 1'-0" 2'-4 1/2"

OPTIONAL FLOOR BUBBLER

4"

1 3/4"   2 1/2"

JOISTS

6" MIN.

GRADE

STANDARD TUB

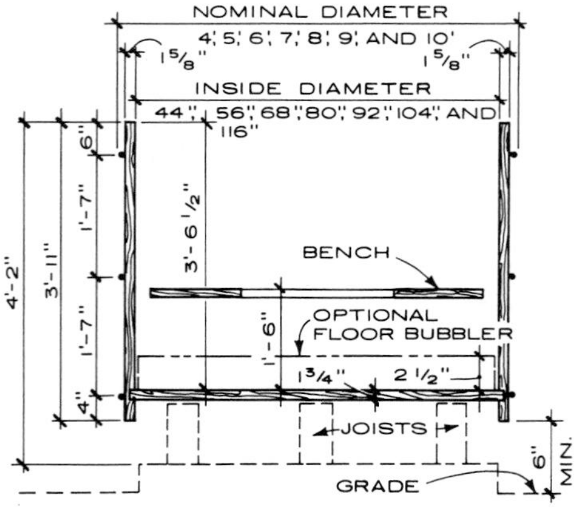

NOMINAL DIAMETER
4, 5, 6, 7, 8, 9, AND 10'

1 5/8"   1 5/8"

INSIDE DIAMETER
44", 56", 68", 80", 92", 104", AND 116"

6" 4'-2" 3'-11" 1'-7" 3'-6 1/2" 1'-7" 1'-6"

BENCH

OPTIONAL FLOOR BUBBLER

4"

1 3/4"   2 1/2"

JOISTS

6" MIN.

GRADE

HOT TUB DIMENSIONS

	STANDARD TUB	LOW PROFILE TUB
NOM. DIA. (FT)	4 5 6 7 8 9 10	4 5 6 7 8 9 10
INSIDE DIA. (IN.)	44 56 68 80 92 104 116	44 56 68 80 92 104 116
NUMBER OF HOOPS	3 3 3 3 4 4	2 2 3 3 3 3
HOOP INTERVAL (IN.)	19 ± 1 IN.	12 ± 1 IN.
SEAT SECTIONS	2 3 4 5	SIT ON FLOOR

SEATING ARRANGEMENTS:

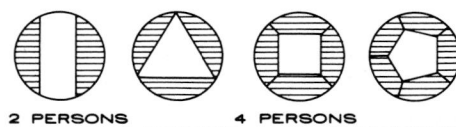

2 PERSONS
3 PERSONS
4 PERSONS
5 PERSONS

Jerry Graham; CTA Architects Engineers; Billings, Montana

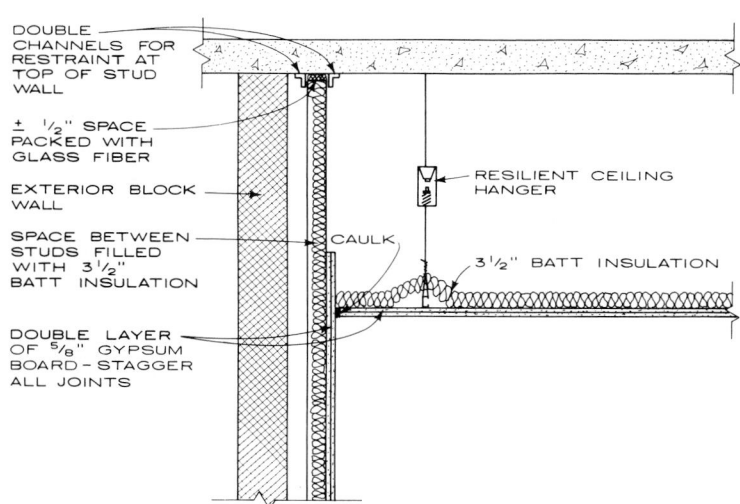

DOUBLE CHANNELS FOR RESTRAINT AT TOP OF STUD WALL

± ½" SPACE PACKED WITH GLASS FIBER

EXTERIOR BLOCK WALL

SPACE BETWEEN STUDS FILLED WITH 3½" BATT INSULATION

DOUBLE LAYER OF ⅝" GYPSUM BOARD - STAGGER ALL JOINTS

CAULK

RESILIENT CEILING HANGER

3½" BATT INSULATION

UPPER EXTERIOR WALL

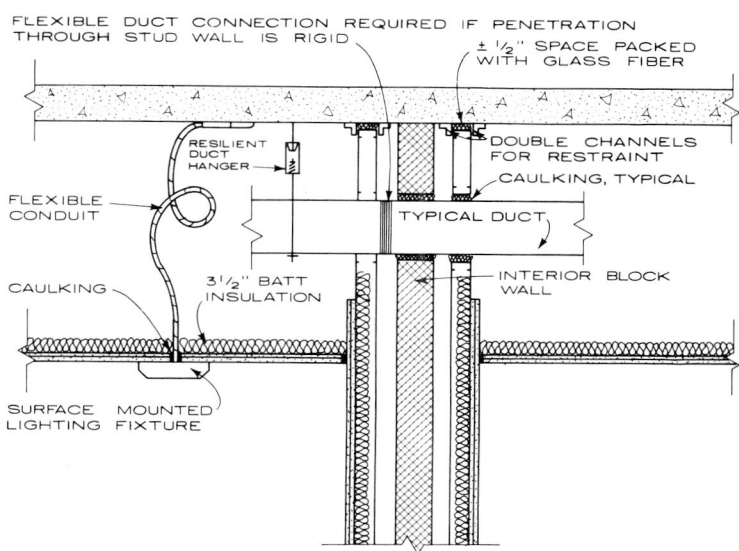

FLEXIBLE DUCT CONNECTION REQUIRED IF PENETRATION THROUGH STUD WALL IS RIGID

± ½" SPACE PACKED WITH GLASS FIBER

RESILIENT DUCT HANGER

FLEXIBLE CONDUIT

DOUBLE CHANNELS FOR RESTRAINT

CAULKING, TYPICAL

CAULKING

TYPICAL DUCT

3½" BATT INSULATION

INTERIOR BLOCK WALL

SURFACE MOUNTED LIGHTING FIXTURE

UPPER INTERIOR WALL WITH HVAC AND ELECTRICAL PENETRATIONS

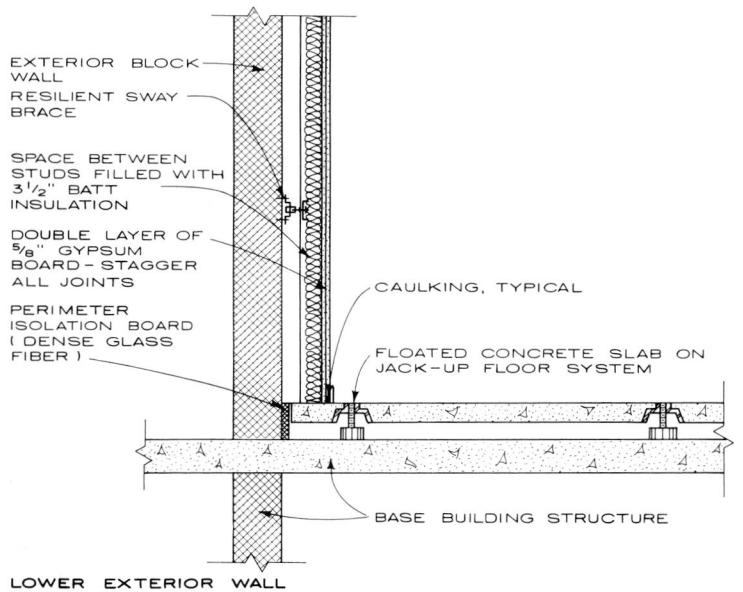

EXTERIOR BLOCK WALL

RESILIENT SWAY BRACE

SPACE BETWEEN STUDS FILLED WITH 3½" BATT INSULATION

DOUBLE LAYER OF ⅝" GYPSUM BOARD - STAGGER ALL JOINTS

PERIMETER ISOLATION BOARD (DENSE GLASS FIBER)

CAULKING, TYPICAL

FLOATED CONCRETE SLAB ON JACK-UP FLOOR SYSTEM

BASE BUILDING STRUCTURE

LOWER EXTERIOR WALL WITH JACK-UP FLOOR

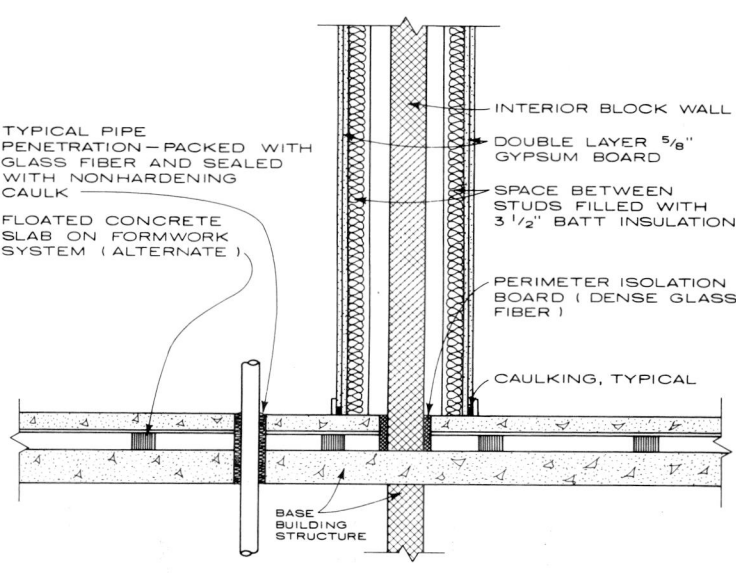

TYPICAL PIPE PENETRATION - PACKED WITH GLASS FIBER AND SEALED WITH NONHARDENING CAULK

FLOATED CONCRETE SLAB ON FORMWORK SYSTEM (ALTERNATE)

INTERIOR BLOCK WALL

DOUBLE LAYER ⅝" GYPSUM BOARD

SPACE BETWEEN STUDS FILLED WITH 3½" BATT INSULATION

PERIMETER ISOLATION BOARD (DENSE GLASS FIBER)

CAULKING, TYPICAL

BASE BUILDING STRUCTURE

LOWER INTERIOR WALL

DETAILS
ISOLATED ROOMS

Isolated rooms incorporate special constructions to reduce intrusive noise and vibration from outside the room or to contain the sound and impact energy that is generated within the room. Typical applications include music practice rooms, sound studios, testing chambers, mechanical equipment rooms near sensitive areas, spaces exposed to nearby aircraft flyovers, and offices under gymnasiums. Isolated room construction can be very expensive; whenever possible, space planning and layout design should isolate high noise sources from acoustically critical uses so that the need for isolated rooms can be minimized.

The correct design of an isolated room is a "box-within-a-box." The inner box, which is the four walls, ceiling and floor of the isolated room, should be an airtight enclosure of dense impervious materials; this box must be isolated by resilient supports from the surrounding structure. It is also important that the base structure that supports the isolated room be as rigid and massive as possible.

The most effective floor construction is a "floated"

Don Klabin, AIA; INCE; Wellesley, Massachusetts

concrete pad, which is separated from the base building structure by steel springs, neoprene, or glass fiber isolation mounts. Inner walls can be supported by this slab. Any necessary structural bracing to the base building structure should be with a resilient nonrigid connection. The ceiling of the box can be suspended from resilient hangers, or it can be supported from the walls of the inner box. The diagram shows typical construction details.

It is necessary to avoid all flanking paths between an isolated room and the base building structure. Any penetrations through the walls or connections to outside services must be as well isolated as the room itself. Therefore, there should be flexible connections in ducts and conduit between the inner and outer box, and all piping must be resiliently supported.

Weatherstripped or sound-rated doors and acoustical double-glazed windows should be part of the continuous air-tight enclosure that defines the inner box.

The degree of noise reduction that can be attained by an isolated room depends on the type of constructions, their resiliency, the elimination of flanking paths, and

the amount of dead airspace that surrounds the inner box. A well-built isolated room can achieve field performance ratings of STC 60 to 70 for airborne sound, and ratings of IIC 80 to 90 for impact noise. However, even minor flanking paths and acoustical short circuits through non-airtight joints can easily degrade these results by 10 points or more. The sound isolation between spaces will be only as great as the weakest sound path.

The advice and assistance of a qualified acoustical consultant should be sought in both the planning and design of isolated rooms and their related special constructions.

In addition to field erected isolated rooms as described above, several manufacturers make prefabricated units. These rooms are sold as self-contained music practice rooms, audiometric booths, and control booths for manufacturing plants. Although the detailing of their constructions is proprietary, one will find the same design approach as outlined here: a separate airtight box kept separate from the building structure. The degree of noise reduction that these prefabricated rooms can attain depends on the parameters used for field erected rooms.

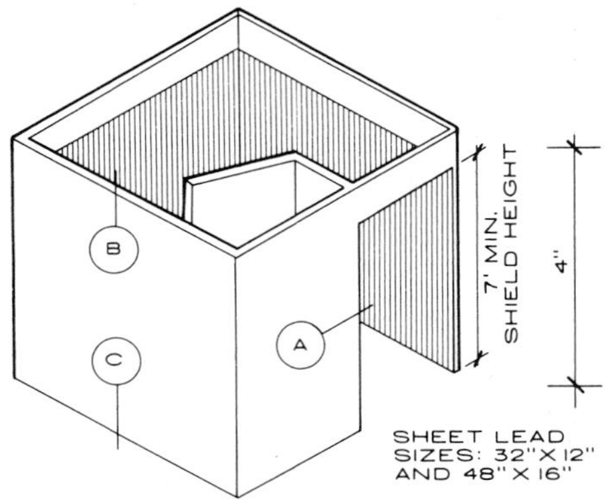

X-RAY ROOM

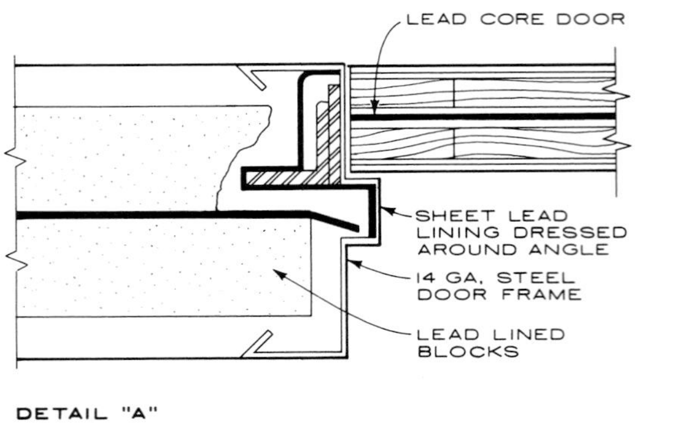

SHEET LEAD SIZES: 32" X 12" AND 48" X 16"

7' MIN. SHIELD HEIGHT

4"

LEAD CORE DOOR

SHEET LEAD LINING DRESSED AROUND ANGLE

14 GA. STEEL DOOR FRAME

LEAD LINED BLOCKS

DETAIL "A"

REINFORCED STEEL DOOR FRAME

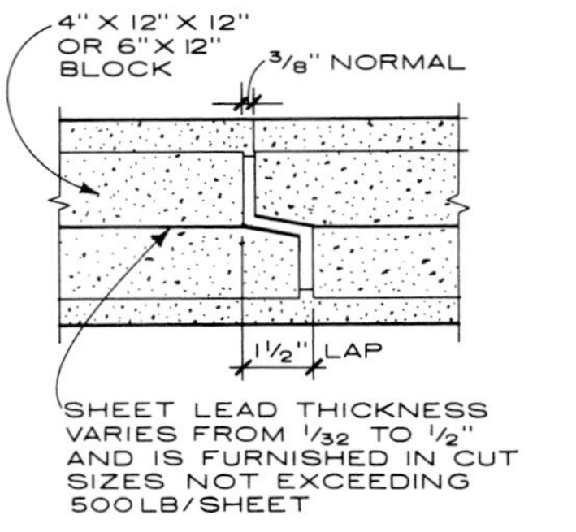

4" X 12" X 12" OR 6" X 12" BLOCK

3/8" NORMAL

1 1/2" LAP

SHEET LEAD THICKNESS VARIES FROM 1/32 TO 1/2" AND IS FURNISHED IN CUT SIZES NOT EXCEEDING 500 LB/SHEET

TYPICAL JOINT

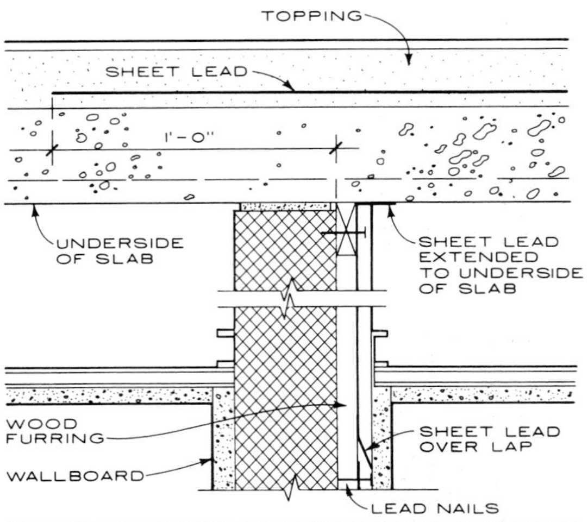

TOPPING

SHEET LEAD

1'-0"

UNDERSIDE OF SLAB

SHEET LEAD EXTENDED TO UNDERSIDE OF SLAB

WOOD FURRING

WALLBOARD

SHEET LEAD OVER LAP

LEAD NAILS

DETAIL WITH SHEET LEAD PLACED ON STRUCTURAL SLAB ABOVE X-RAY ROOM

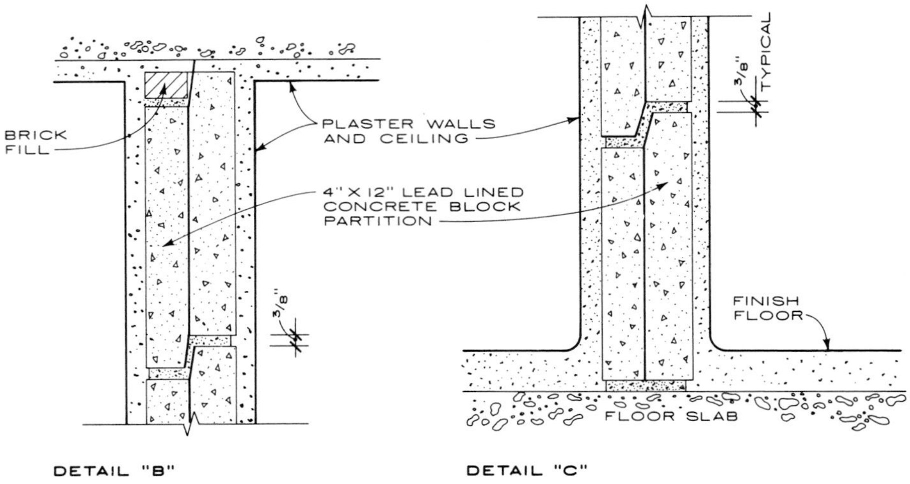

BRICK FILL

PLASTER WALLS AND CEILING

4" X 12" LEAD LINED CONCRETE BLOCK PARTITION

3/8"

DETAIL "B"

3/8" TYPICAL

FINISH FLOOR

FLOOR SLAB

DETAIL "C"

LEAD LINED CONCRETE PARTITIONS

NOTE: WOOD FURRING STRIPS ARE APPLIED VERTICALLY AND HORIZONTALLY IN A GRID PATTERN

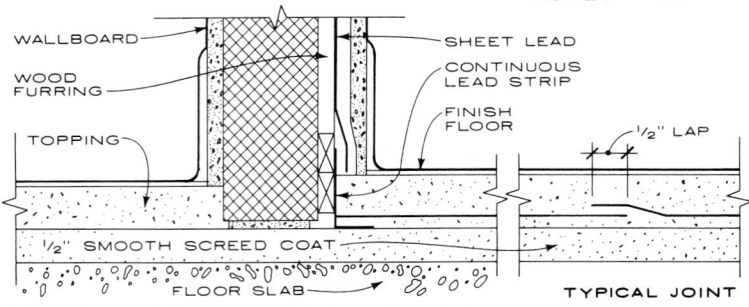

WALLBOARD

WOOD FURRING

TOPPING

SHEET LEAD

CONTINUOUS LEAD STRIP

FINISH FLOOR

1/2" LAP

1/2" SMOOTH SCREED COAT

FLOOR SLAB

TYPICAL JOINT

DETAIL OF SHEET LEAD ON FLOOR UNDER FILL

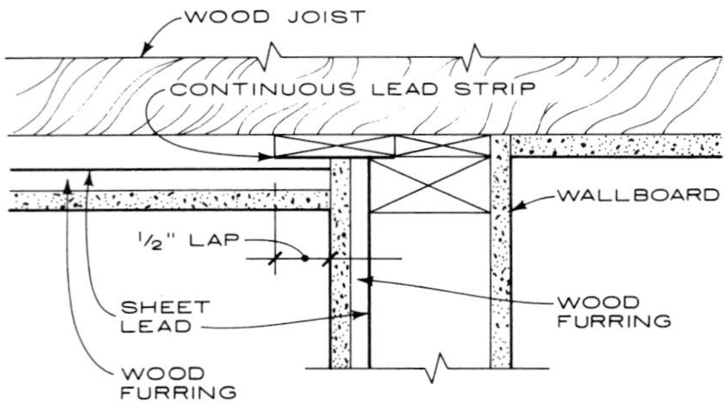

WOOD JOIST

CONTINUOUS LEAD STRIP

1/2" LAP

SHEET LEAD

WOOD FURRING

WALLBOARD

WOOD FURRING

WOOD CONSTRUCTION-CEILING

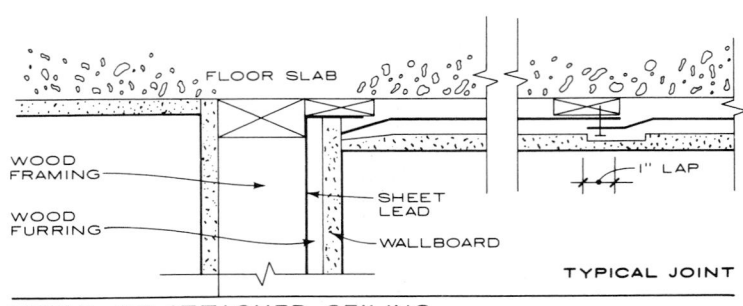

FLOOR SLAB

WOOD FRAMING

WOOD FURRING

SHEET LEAD

WALLBOARD

1" LAP

TYPICAL JOINT

DETAIL OF ATTACHED CEILING

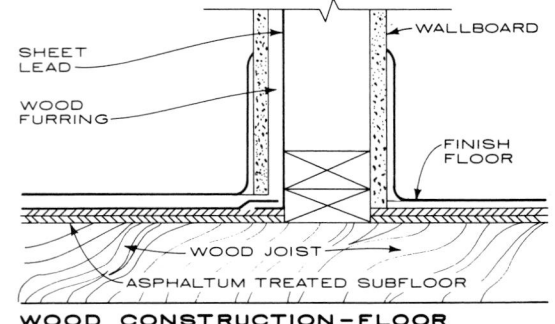

SHEET LEAD

WOOD FURRING

WALLBOARD

FINISH FLOOR

WOOD JOIST

ASPHALTUM TREATED SUBFLOOR

WOOD CONSTRUCTION-FLOOR

John Sava; The Architects Collaborative, Inc.; Cambridge, Massachusetts

BUILDING TYPES AND WIDTHS

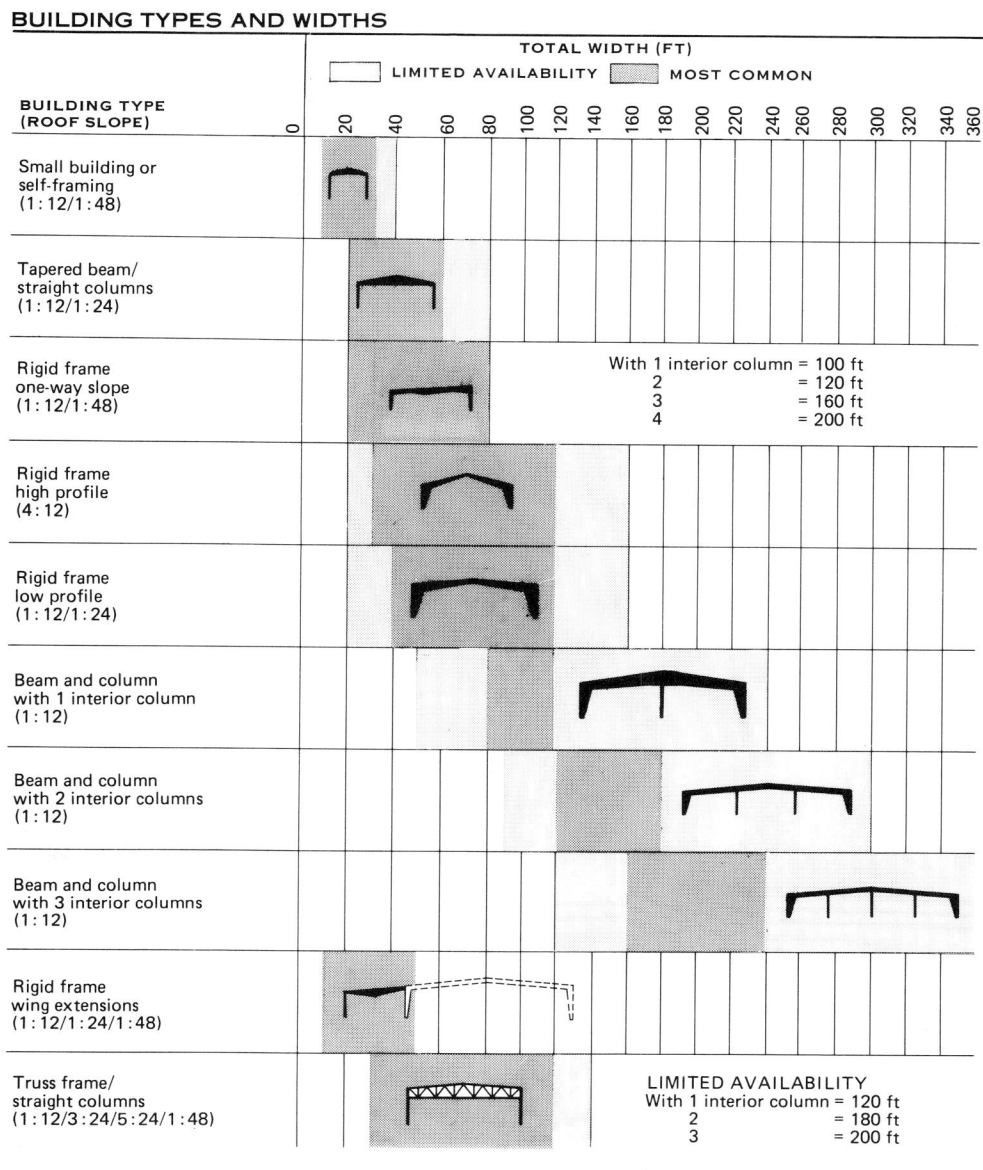

BUILDING TYPE (ROOF SLOPE)	TOTAL WIDTH (FT)
	□ LIMITED AVAILABILITY ▨ MOST COMMON

Small building or self-framing (1:12/1:48)

Tapered beam/ straight columns (1:12/1:24)

Rigid frame one-way slope (1:12/1:48)

With 1 interior column = 100 ft
2 = 120 ft
3 = 160 ft
4 = 200 ft

Rigid frame high profile (4:12)

Rigid frame low profile (1:12/1:24)

Beam and column with 1 interior column (1:12)

Beam and column with 2 interior columns (1:12)

Beam and column with 3 interior columns (1:12)

Rigid frame wing extensions (1:12/1:24/1:48)

Truss frame/ straight columns (1:12/3:24/5:24/1:48)

LIMITED AVAILABILITY
With 1 interior column = 120 ft
2 = 180 ft
3 = 200 ft

DEFINITIONS, NOTES

Preengineered metal buldings are available in standard framing sizes and types from various manufacturers as proprietary products. The table illustrates the most commonly available systems. The following definitions are used commonly by the metal building industry:

1. BAY: refers to the dimension between centerlines of wall columns along a wall, and the dimension from the outside of an end wall corner column and the centerline of the first side wall column. Spacings range from 18 ft. to 30 ft., with 20 ft. to 25 ft. most common.
2. WIDTH: building dimension measured from outside wall girts surface. Inside clearance varies.
3. EAVE HEIGHT: building dimension measured from bottom of wall column to top of eave strut. Nominal 2 ft. increments varying from 10 ft. to 30 ft.
4. LOADS: loading other than those provided by the manufacturer should be specified at the time of building's structural design. Future additional loads also should be considered.
5. ROOF LIVE LOAD: loads, including snow load, exerted on a roof except dead, wind, and lateral loads. Commonly available in 12, 20, or 40 psf.
6. DEAD LOAD: weight of all permanent roof framing and covering materials only. Varies with manufacturer.
7. LATERAL LOADS: additional dead loads other than the metal building framing such as sprinklers, mechanical and electrical systems, and ceilings. Commonly available in 15, 20, or 25 psf.
8. WIND LOAD: additional loading caused by the wind blowing from any horizontal direction. Commonly available in 15, 20, or 25 psf. Site and atmospheric conditions needing special consideration should be specified.
9. SEISMIC LOAD: specify individual design; required for earthquake zones.
10. AUXILIARY LOADS: additional dynamic live loads other than basic design loads, such as cranes, materials handling systems, and impact loads.
11. The user should verify that individual manufacturer's standard practice and any special design considerations meet or exceed established engineering principles, local practice, and applicable building codes.
12. BRACING: diagonal bracing normally is required in the plane of the columns and beams in one or more bays to prevent racking and to resist lateral loading perpendicular to the span of the frames.
13. GIRTS: members span horizontally and transmit lateral loads (pressure and suction) from the exterior walls to the columns. Sag rods supporting the girts about the weak axis may be necessary to achieve design economy.
14. ANCHOR BOLTS: necessary to resist reactions at column bases. Foundations must be designed for reactions transmitted by the column bases and anchor bolts.

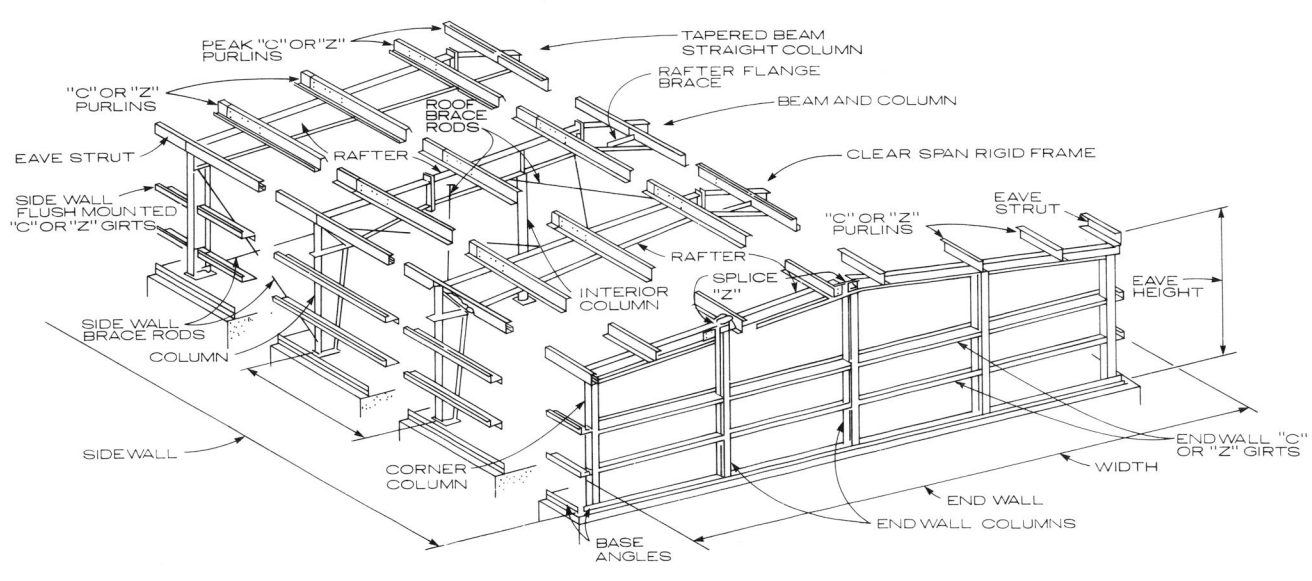

FRAMING SYSTEMS COMPONENTS

Robert P. Burns, AIA, and David Hayes; Robert Burns & Associates; Riverside, Iowa

PRE-ENGINEERED STRUCTURES   **13**

OCCUPANCY SENSORS

There are several types of occupancy sensors for turning lights on and off. They include ultrasonic, infrared, visible light, and audible sound sensors. The first two methods are by far the most prevalent. The infrared is a line-of-sight sensor, but will have some dead spots primarily at long distances from the sensor. The ultrasonic sensor has no dead spots, but is more sensitive to incidental air motion and may respond inappropriately. Either technique can be used in most applications; however, there are applications where the ultrasonic or the infrared occupancy sensor has a slight advantage.

Most occupancy sensor designs have controls that allow selection of a turnoff time and a means to set the sensor's sensitivity to motion. The placement of the sensor is important since it must cover the desired active area. Sensors are generally designed for placement in the ceiling, where there is a clear view of the area to be scanned. Recently simpler occupancy sensors have been designed to be wired directly into the wall switch. Care must be exercised since it is possible there may be many dead spots because the height of the sensor is about four feet off the floor and some active areas could be blocked by furniture.

Sensors are available that can scan an area from 200 sq ft up to about 4000 sq ft. The amount of energy they will save depends upon the amount of power they are controlling and the time of occupancy. Controlling small areas maximizes the time not in the space but controls little power; in controlling large areas, the occupancy time is increased while the controlled power is increased. It is important to have some knowledge of the occupancy time to determine the cost effectiveness of implementing this strategy. The best applications are spaces with limited occupancy such as lavatories, reproduction rooms, filing spaces, and storage spaces. They are also best used in spaces that are separated so that the on-off operation of the lamp does not disturb occupants in other spaces.

PHOTOCELL PLACEMENT

A key element in a successful daylight control system where there are visual tasks is the placement and calibration of the sensing photocell. The ideal position for the placement of the sensing photocell to maintain constant illuminance is on the task being performed. This poses two problems: interference with the task and communication with the lighting control system. Some systems have photocells that sense the illuminance outdoors. This approach is very difficult to calibrate because there is no information about the illuminance on the task. Most systems place the sensing photocell on the ceiling and view the task and the surrounding area. Thus, the information from the photocell can be easily interfaced with the lighting control to properly change the electric light levels. The photocell must also be shielded in such a manner as to block any direct daylight from the window. However, to maintain the specified illuminance on the task, the sensing system must be calibrated at night (no daylighting) and during the day with daylighting available. The reason for this is that the ratio of the electric light and daylight illuminance falling on the task is not the illuminance measured by the sensing photocell. The nighttime calibration (no daylight) is simple and the photocell output sets the light control to provide the specified illuminance. The second calibration is taken during the day, where the daylight on the task is not sufficient and requires an electric lighting contribution in order to provide the specified light level. The photocell output to the control is adjusted so that the electric lights provide sufficient light, supplementing the daylight to maintain the specified task illuminance.

The mechanics of the second calibration could be accomplished electronically with the proper computer software or with a two-cell photocell that independently senses either the electric lights or area surrounding the task. These techniques have been demonstrated and have been shown properly to maintain the specified illuminance on the task.

There are many applications (stores, shopping malls, atria,

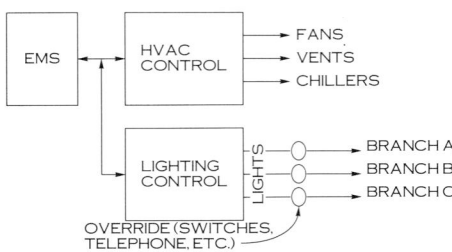

COMPUTERIZED EMS FOR HVAC AND LIGHTING

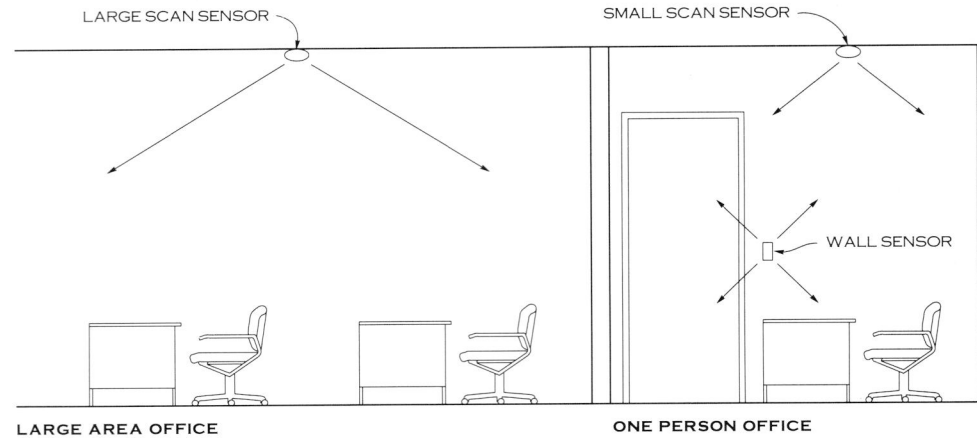

LARGE AREA OFFICE

ONE PERSON OFFICE

OCCUPANCY SENSORS

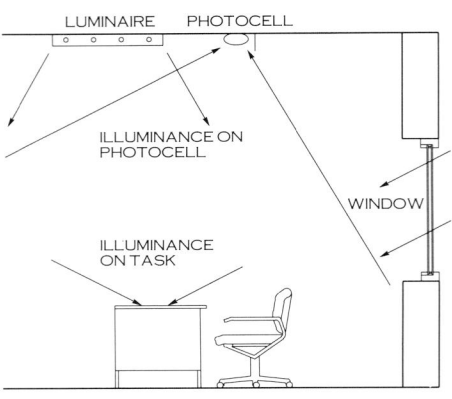

PHOTOCELL PLACEMENT

etc.) where there are no critical visual tasks. With these applications, the location of the photocell has many more options. In such applications the sensing photocell can be placed to view the outside as well as the interior space. The more important aspect is the ease of communication with the electrical lighting controls.

COMPUTERIZED ENERGY MANAGEMENT AND CONTROL SYSTEMS

Today virtually all new buildings incorporate an energy management system (EMS) that controls the HVAC system. Lighting control systems are being designed that will communicate with the EMS and can receive its commands. The simplest, least expensive technique is the use of relays to turn lights on and off at prescribed times based upon the normal working periods. Some states (e.g., California) require automatic lighting control that will at least turn off the lighting for all new construction. For buildings that have an EMS, retrofitting with lighting relay systems is a low cost, effective energy conservation strategy. The relay system can be installed in the electric closet to control branch circuits.

This scheduling technique can be more effective if the occupants must turn on their lights when they arrive at their workspace and the control automatically turns them off at the prescribed times, e.g., at lunch periods and in the evenings. This latter technique is particularly effective if the workforce has scattered starting times. In factories or disciplined offices where all staff is required to start at a particular time, turning on the lights automatically is suitable.

Buildings with automatic control of the lighting must have a suitable override system to accommodate occupants who must work during off hours. The override methods include telephone codes or conveniently located override switches.

The lighting scheduling strategy can also include reducing the light levels during the periods when the space is being maintained or cleaned. Most cleaning crews do not require the full light levels used by the occupants during the normal work periods.

MULTILEVEL SWITCHING

The effectiveness of the simplest low cost method of switching fluorescent lighting systems (relays) can be enhanced by proper wiring of the ballasts in the fixture. By wiring the ballasts to different control points, one can obtain three or four levels of illuminance. For example, in a four-lamp fixture with split wiring, one can obtain full, $1/2$, and 0 light levels. Three-lamp fixtures or six-lamp fixtures can obtain full, $2/3$, $1/3$, and 0 light levels. This flexibility allows these systems to provide lower light levels over some spaces (aisles, storerooms, washrooms, etc.) that do not require full light levels. It enhances the savings for the scheduling strategy as it can reduce the light levels during cleaning periods since the cleaning operation usually does not require full light levels. Other lighting control strategies (lumen depreciation and daylighting) can also be considered. Although the latter two strategies are more energy efficient with continuous dimming controls, they are still cost effective, since the lighting control equipment cost will be less than the dimming control system. The multilevel systems can also address the state lighting codes that require fluorescent lamps to be operated at full and $1/2$ illuminance levels.

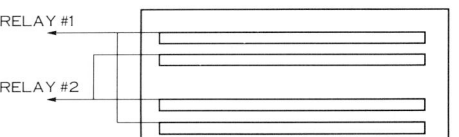

FOUR-LAMP FIXTURE WITH TWO 2-LAMP BALLASTS

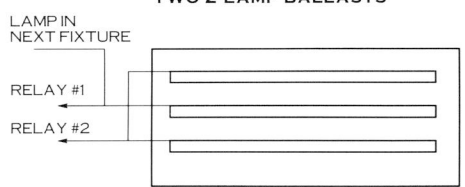

THREE-LAMP FIXTURE WITH ONE 2-LAMP BALLAST AND ONE SHARED 2-LAMP BALLAST

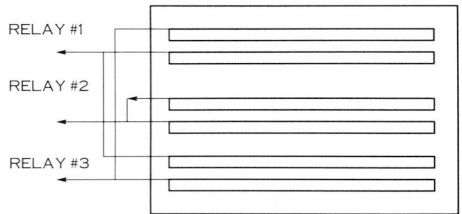

SIX-LAMP FIXTURE WITH THREE 2-LAMP BALLASTS

MULTILEVEL SWITCHING CONNECTIONS

Rudolph R. Verderber; Lawrence Berkeley Laboratory; Berkeley, California

13   BUILDING AUTOMATION SYSTEMS

CONTINUOUS DIMMING LIGHTING CONTROLS

Fluorescent lamps can be continuously dimmed with either standard magnetic ballasts or the new electronic ballasts. Lamps operated with magnetic ballasts are dimmed by conditioning the input power, i.e., the input voltage to the ballast is chopped, reducing the duty cycle. This technique requires switching devices that must control large power levels and is usually cost-effective when switching a large number of lamps. When fluorescent lamps are dimmed much below 50% of full light output, the filament voltage must be maintained at 3 to 4 volts in order to preserve the lamp life. When the duty cycle is reduced, the filament voltage is also reduced, which will accelerate lamp failure at the very low dimming levels, below 50% of full light output. Thus, techniques that condition input power have a practical dimming range. The fact that this technique is only cost-effective when controlling many lamps limits applications to control strategies that demand independent control of small areas, such as tuning and most daylighting strategies.

Electronic dimming ballasts dim fluorescent lamps by limiting the lamp current by a low voltage signal to the ballast's output circuit. The electronic ballasts have feedback circuits that permit the filament voltage to maintain the proper voltage at the very low dimming levels, down to 10% of full light output. Thus, the specified life of fluorescent lamps is still maintained when operated in the dimming mode at very low light levels. The low voltage method of communication allows the control of either large or small areas independent of the electrical power distribution, i.e., the branch circuits. The system efficacy is slightly reduced at the lower light levels since full filament voltage must be maintained; however, the energy use is always reduced. Dimming fluorescent lamps with electronic ballasts permits the effective application of all the lighting control strategies. Since the lamps can be safely dimmed over a wider range, the percentage of energy savings for each lighting control strategy will be maximized. There are additional savings because the electronic lamp-ballast system is more efficacious than the magnetic lamp-ballast systems.

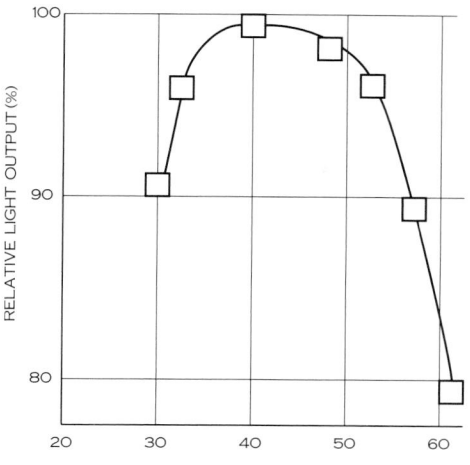

LAMP IN OPEN AIR

RELATIVE LIGHT OUTPUT (%) vs. LAMP WALL TEMPERATURE (°C)

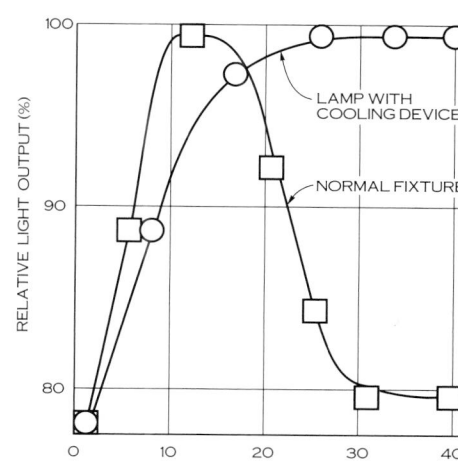

LAMP IN FIXTURE

LAMP WITH COOLING DEVICE

NORMAL FIXTURE

RELATIVE LIGHT OUTPUT (%) vs. TIME OF OPERATION (MINUTES)

LAMP LIGHT OUTPUT VS. TEMPERATURE IN CONTROLLED AND UNCONTROLLED FIXTURES

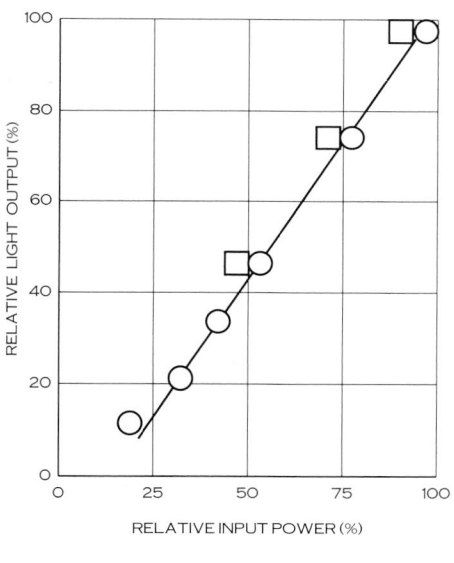

RELATIVE LIGHT OUTPUT (%) vs. RELATIVE INPUT POWER (%)

☐ MAGNETIC BALLAST SYSTEM

◯ ELECTRONIC BALLAST SYSTEM

PRACTICAL CONTINUOUS DIMMING RANGES

ENERGY SAVINGS WITH LIGHTING CONTROLS

Lighting controls are used to provide the proper illumination in accordance with the activity in a space. In addition to improving the quality of the illuminance, considerable energy reduction can be achieved. The amount of energy reduction depends upon the number of control strategies that can be conducted, which depends upon the sophistication of the lighting control equipment. The control strategies include scheduling, tuning, lumen depreciation, and daylighting. Lighting controls also permit load shedding, which is effective in reducing utility demand charges.

Controlling lights with relays limits one to scheduling, turning lights on in the morning and off at night. For some special applications, such as malls and airports, where there is abundant daylighting, relay controls can be effectively employed. Some controls permit the dimming of magnetic ballasts by conditioning the input power. With this method, controlling large banks of luminaires is best considered. Dimming techniques that control large areas limit the strategies to scheduling, lumen depreciation, and simple daylighting applications, that is, where large areas of the space have similar daylighting patterns. The newly introduced dimming electronic ballast systems can perform all of the lighting control strategies. These systems can dim fluorescent lamps over a greater range without any loss in lamp life. It is also economically feasible to dim small areas as well as large areas, i.e., a small number of luminaires. This is because the low voltage control wiring can control lamps independently of the electrical distribution. This allows independent control of daylighted spaces where visual tasks are essential and the daylight distribution is not uniform. These spaces are generally found in offices where there is a great variety of important visual tasks performed during the day.

There have been several lighting control demonstrations that have measured the energy savings for each control strategy. The savings for each technique depends upon the architecture, the operation of space, the type of lamp-ballast system, and the lighting control equipment.

THERMAL CONTROL OF FLUORESCENT LAMPS

The light output from fluorescent lamps is very sensitive to lamp wall temperature and is 10 to 20% below maximum lumen output in most fixtures. There are fixtures available and new techniques being developed that can cool the lamp wall temperature to optimize both the lumen output and the efficiency. There are air handling fixtures in which the return air from the room flows over the lamps, cooling them to near the desired 40°C temperature. New techniques are being developed to employ slots for convective cooling and thermal bridges to obtain reduced lamp wall temperatures.

Of particular interest are many compact fluorescent lamp fixtures in which the internal fixture temperature is sufficiently high that, in addition to the reduction in lumen output and efficiency, there can be premature lamp and/or ballast failures.

By the use of the cooling techniques, full light output can be attained, not only increasing efficiency (reducing operating costs) but also reducing initial and maintenance costs since fewer fixtures (lamps and ballasts) will be required to provide the prescribed light levels.

VENETIAN BLIND CONTROL FOR DAYLIGHTING

Daylighting is most visually effective for a diffuse sky. This condition is generally for the north facing windows. Direct sunlight provides the highest luminance levels, but is usually too high and uncomfortable due to excessive glare. In fact, the discomfort glare may invoke an occupant to perceive the need for higher electric light levels. To effectively take advantage of daylight in the east, west, and south facing spaces, window treatments are needed. Venetian blinds are available that can block or divert the direct sunlight to reduce its glare. Venetian blinds are available that are either manual or automatic. The automatic systems are controlled by responding to a photocell that senses the direction of the sunlight.

The area controlled by either automatic or manual venetian blinds should be coordinated with the electric light control in the same area. This usually requires independent daylight control of relatively small areas. For example, if one designs a system where one photocell controls a large area, occupants may operate the manual blinds in their spaces differently, which will cause the photocell to sense the daylighting from only one area. This could result in one area meeting the specified light levels while other areas are seriously under-illuminated. This illustrates why the daylighting strategy is best applied with lighting control systems that control relatively small areas. There are unique architectural designs that have excellent symmetry with respect to the sun direction that have good results with control systems for relatively large areas. This requires integration of the internal space (usually open floor plans) with the proper positioning of the building with the north, east, south, and west directions.

RANGES OF ENERGY SAVINGS WITH LIGHTING CONTROLS

	SCHEDULING	TUNING	LUMEN DEPRECIATION	DAYLIGHTING[1]
Relays	10 to 30%	NA	NA	15 to 25%
Magnetic ballasts[2]	30 to 40%	NA	6 to 10%	20 to 27%
Electronic ballasts[2]	17 to 50%	25%	8 to 12%	25 to 50%

NOTES

1. Energy savings in the daylight area only.
2. Continuous dimming systems.

Rudolph R. Verderber; Lawrence Berkeley Laboratory; Berkeley, California

GENERAL

The simplest fire alarm system is a self-contained, UL approved residential smoke detector. It senses products of combustion, sounds an alarm, and signals when the battery needs replacement. Most municipalities require the use of smoke detectors in houses, apartments, and motel/hotel rooms. Check local codes for requirements.

More complex systems are needed in buildings where public safety is an issue, such as schools, hospitals, office buildings, and other commercial establishments or institutions. Although there are still applications for small hard-wired and relay-operated alarm signaling systems, the trend is to use microprocessor-based digital multiplex systems that not only signal the presence of a fire but also initiate other measures, including conditioning fans and dampers for smoke control, closing fire doors and shutters, releasing locked doors, capturing elevators, and transmitting voice messages. Voice communication is required in high-rise buildings of specific group occupancies as defined by the BOCA code. It is also recommended for large low-rise buildings to enhance life safety.

Fire alarm systems can either function alone or be integrated with security and building management functions. Processors and their peripheral equipment are generally located in a manned central command center accessible to firemen. Depending on the degree of reliability desired, redundancy can be provided in wiring and processors, along with battery backup.

Alarm system control cabinets can be 36 in. wide x 8 in. deep. They must have battery backup, be UL approved, conform to NFPA no. 72, and may also require local approval. In small systems where only one cabinet may be required, all the functions required at the command center can be incorporated in the same cabinet and located in the main entrance lobby. In larger systems, remote cabinets are generally located in wiring closets throughout the building and can be programmed to function independently of the central processor, should it fail.

SIGNALING SYSTEM TYPES

NONCODED: Evacuation signal sounds continuously.
MASTER CODED: Signal repeats four rounds.
SELECTIVE CODED: Same as "master coded" except individual and assigned number code of up to three groups per round.
PRESIGNAL: Same as "selective coded" except signals sound only at selected areas to prompt investigation. If hazard is determined, evacuation signal is initiated by key.
VOICE: Direct (by microphone) or automatic prerecorded messages are transmitted over speakers, following an "alert" signal.

AUDIBLE ALARMS

Audible alarms must have an intensity and frequency that attract the attention of those with partial hearing loss. Such alarms should produce a sound that exceeds the prevailing sound level in the space by at least 15 dbA or exceeds maximum sound level with a duration of 60 seconds by 5 dbA, whichever is louder. Sound levels should not exceed 120 dbA.

VISUAL ALARMS

Visual alarm signals should be integrated into the building alarm system. Alarm stations should give both audible and visual signals. Visual alarm signals should have the following characteristics:

1. Lamp: xenon strobe type or equivalent.
2. Lamp color: clear or nominal white (i.e., unfiltered or clear filtered white light).
3. Maximum pulse duration: 0.2 sec with a maximum duty cycle of 40%. The pulse duration is defined as the time interval between initial and final points of 10% of maximum signal.
4. Intensity: 75 candela minimum.
5. Flash rate: 1 Hz min., 3 Hz max.
6. Place the alarm 80 in. above the highest floor level within the space or 6 in. below the ceiling, whichever is lower.
7. In any space required to have a visual alarm, generally all areas must be within 50 ft of the signal (measured horizontally). In large spaces, such as auditoriums, exceeding 100 ft across, with no obstructions over 6 ft high, devices may be placed around the perimeter, spaced a maximum of 100 ft apart, in lieu of suspending devices from the ceiling.

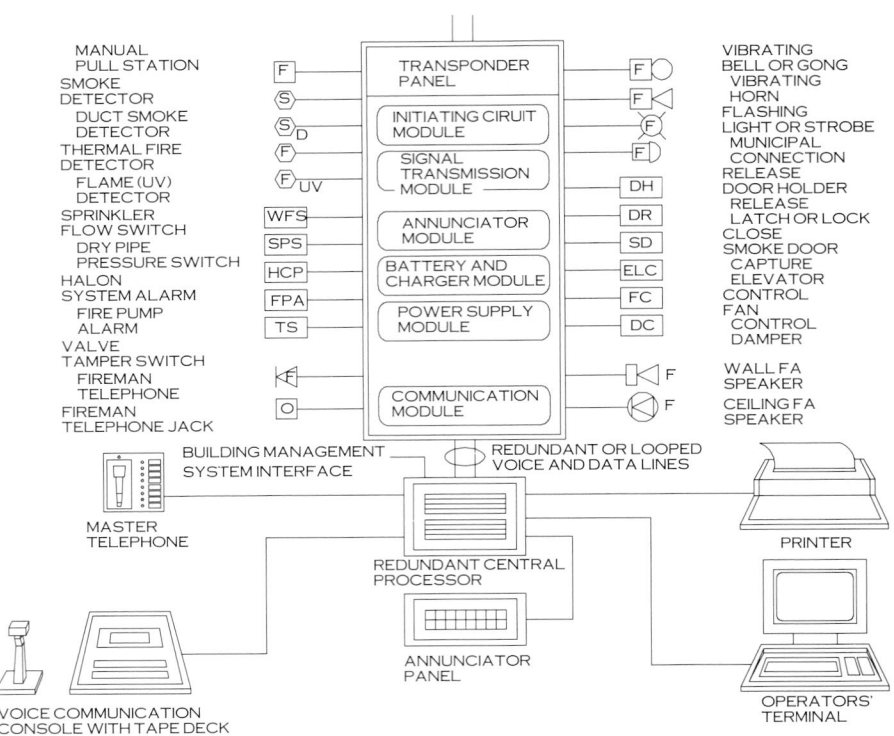

ELECTRONIC FIRE ALARM/COMMUNICATION SYSTEM FUNCTION DIAGRAM

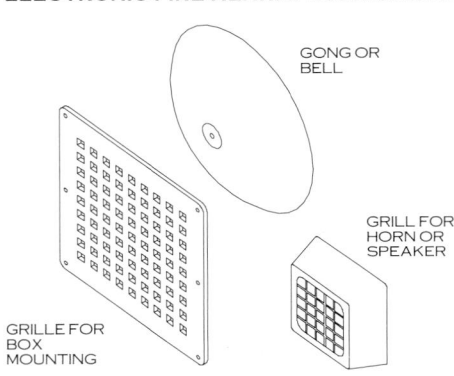

Range in size from 4 to 12 in. diameter. Can be recessed behind a grille. Operation can be single stroke or continuous.

BELL AND COVER

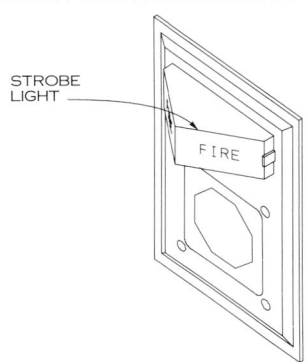

Approximately 10 in. high x 7 in. wide with xenon strobe visual signal. Mounted at 80 in. above finished floor or 6 in. below ceiling, whichever is lower per ADA. Generally located so that no place in any corridor or hallway is more than 50 ft from the signal.

HORN/SPEAKER/VISUAL SIGNAL

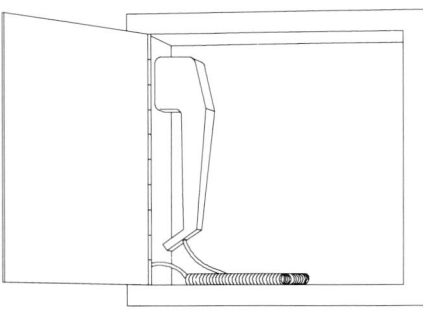

Approximately 12 in. high x 10 in. wide x 3 in. deep, surface or flush. Provided in lieu of jack plates for a total system. Door can be glass or plastic pane.

FIREMAN TELEPHONE CABINET

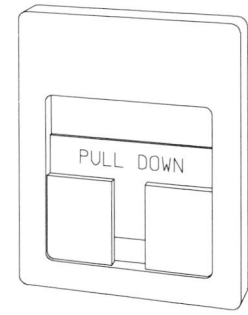

Approximately 7 in. high x 5 in. wide surface or semi-recessed mounted. Mounted 54 in. above finished floor to lever per ADA. Can be provided with break glass rod feature. Operation can be coded or noncoded.

MANUAL PULL STATION

Richard F. Humenn; PE; Joseph R. Loring & Associates, Consulting Engineers; New York, New York
JRS Architect; Mineola, New York

13   **COMMUNICATIONS AND CLOCK SYSTEMS**

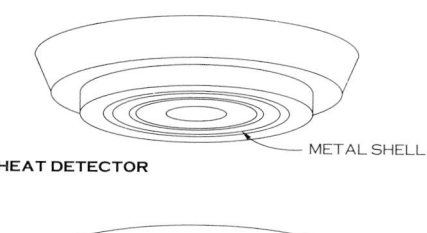

HEAT DETECTOR — METAL SHELL

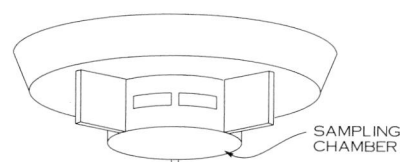

IONIZATION SMOKE DETECTOR — SAMPLING CHAMBER

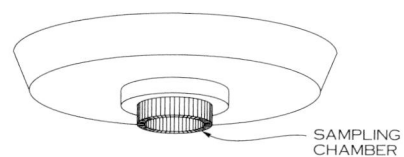

PHOTOELECTRIC SMOKE DETECTOR — SAMPLING CHAMBER

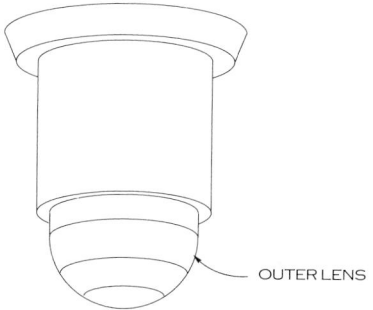

INFRARED AND ULTRAVIOLET FLAME DETECTOR — OUTER LENS

IONIZATION SMOKE DETECTOR

Ionization detectors use the interruption of small current flow between electrodes by smoke in ionized sampling chamber to detect fire. Dual chamber (with reference chamber exposed only to air temperature, pressure, and humidity) and single chamber detectors are available. Ionization detectors can be used in rooms and, when designed for use in air ducts, to detect smoke in air distribution systems.

PHOTOELECTRIC SMOKE DETECTOR

Photoelectric smoke detectors use the scattering of light by smoke into view of photocell. Light source is light emitting diode (LED). Photoelectric detectors can be used in rooms and, when designed for use in air ducts, to detect smoke in air distribution systems.

INFRARED FLAME DETECTOR

Infrared (IR) and ultraviolet (UV) flame detectors respond to the UV and IR radiant energy from flames. Alarm is only triggered when IR (or UV) energy flickers at a rate that is characteristic of flames. Flame detectors can be used in open areas where rapid development of flaming conditions could occur (e.g., flammable liquids, fire hazards).

HEAT DETECTOR

Fixed temperature heat detectors (e.g., those rated at 135 to 197 °F) use low melting point solder or metals that expand when exposed to heat to detect fire. Rate-of-rise heat detectors alarm when rate of temperature change exceeds about 15 °F/min. Expansion of air in chamber with calibrated vent is used to detect rapidly developing fires. Devices are available with both rate-of-rise and fixed temperature detection features.

FIRE AND SMOKE DETECTORS

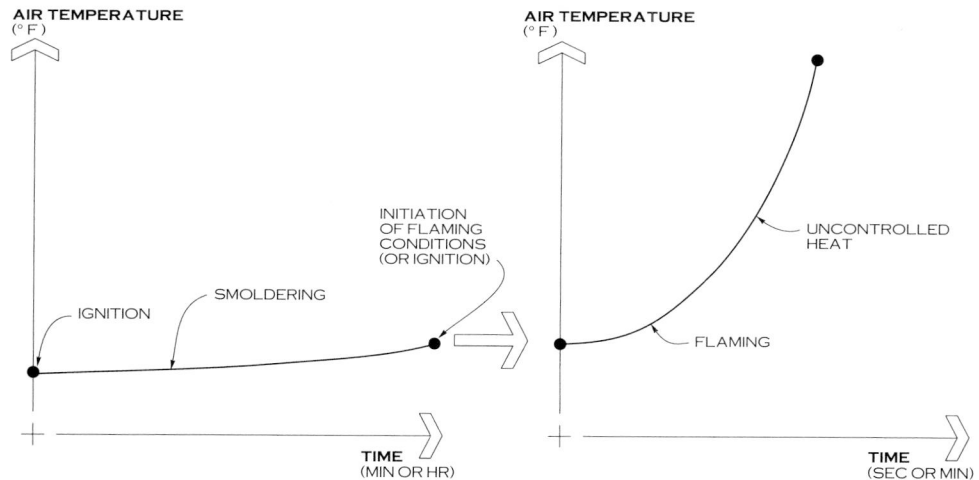

STAGES OF FIRE

Carefully match fire detectors to anticipated fire hazard (e.g., photoelectric smoke detectors for smoldering fires, ionization smoke detectors for flaming fires, flame detectors for flash fires). The time-temperature curves show growth to hazardous conditions for smoldering, flaming, and uncontrolled heat stages of fire.

STAGES OF FIRE

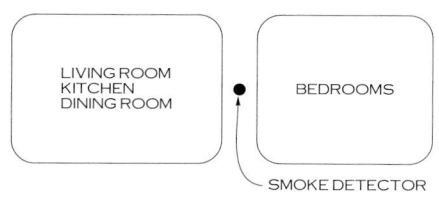

RESIDENTIAL OCCUPANCY (WITH SINGLE SLEEPING AREA)

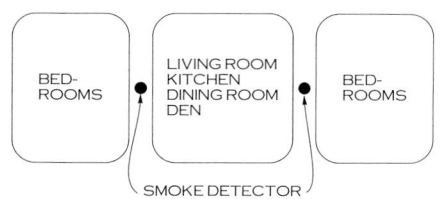

RESIDENTIAL OCCUPANCY (WITH SPLIT SLEEPING AREAS)

CHECKLIST FOR RESIDENTIAL FIRE DETECTION

1. Use smoke detectors to protect the following (in decreasing order of importance.
   a. Every occupied floor and basement.
   b. Sleeping areas and basement near stairs.
   c. Sleeping areas only.
2. Use heat detectors to protect remote areas (e.g., basement shops, attics) where serious fires could develop before smoke would reach smoke detector or in areas such as garages or kitchens where smoke detectors would be exposed to high smoke levels during normal conditions.
3. Locate smoke detectors on ceilings near center of rooms (or on the upper walls 6 to 12 in. from ceiling) where smoke can collect. In long corridors, consider using two or more detectors.
4. Use closer spacing between detectors where ceiling beams, joists, and the like will interrupt flow of smoke to detector.
5. Do not place smoke detectors near supply air registers or diffusers.
6. For guidelines on fire detection for residences, refer to "Household Fire Warning Equipment," NFPA No. 74, available from the National Fire Protection Association.

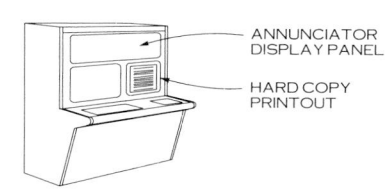

— ANNUNCIATOR DISPLAY PANEL
— HARD COPY PRINTOUT

AUTOMATED CONTROL CONSOLE

NOTE

When fire is detected (e.g., by smoke, heat, flame detectors or water flow indicators in sprinkler system piping), automated control systems immediately summon the fire department. Floor plans of fire area can be projected on annunciator display panel to pinpoint trouble spots. Controls can be designed to automatically shut down fan systems or activate fans and dampers for smoke removal and control. In addition, remote firefighter control panel, with telephone communication to control console and to each floor in building, can be used to control and monitor status of elevators, pumps and emergency generators, fans, dampers, and the like.

M. David Egan, P.E.; College of Architecture, Clemson University; Clemson, South Carolina
John L. Bryan; Fire Protection Engineering, University of Maryland; College Park, Maryland

FIRE SUPPRESSION AND SUPERVISORY SYSTEMS   13

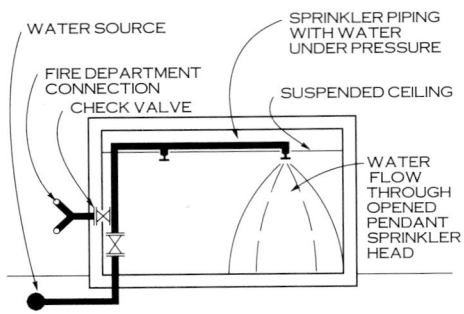

WET PIPE SYSTEM

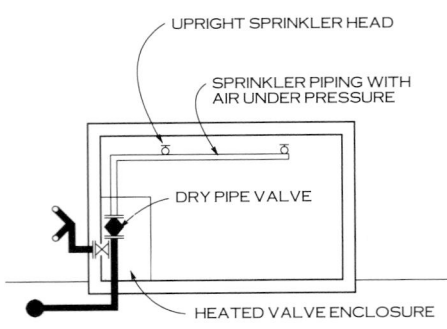

DRY PIPE SYSTEM

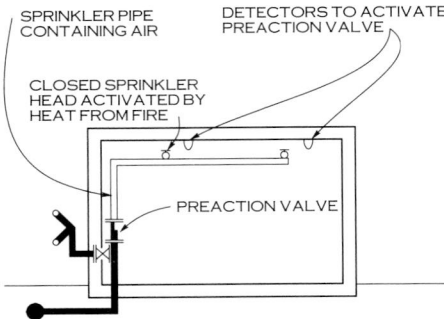

PREACTION SYSTEM

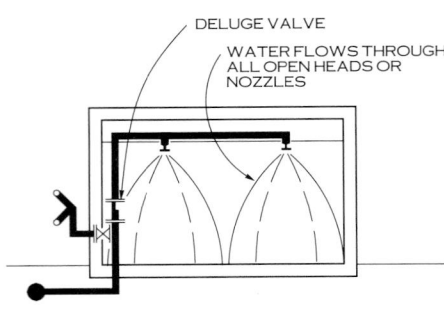

DELUGE SYSTEM

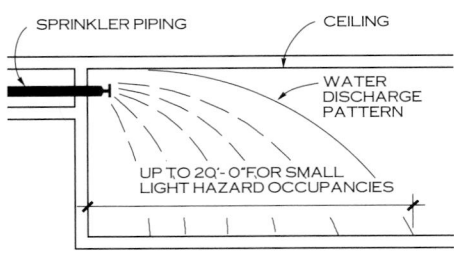

SIDE WALL SPRINKLER HEAD (HORIZONTAL SIDEWALL SHOWN)

Piping can be unobtrusively installed along sides of exposed ceiling beams or joists. In small rooms, sidewall heads provide water discharge coverage without overhead piping.

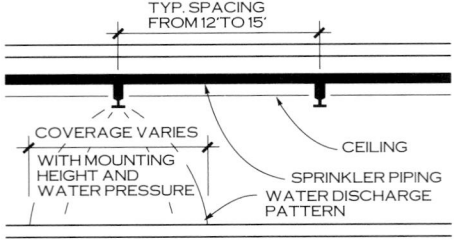

PENDANT SPRINKLER HEAD

Can be recessed in ceiling (e.g., coffered, modeled) or hidden above flat metal cover plate. (Flush sprinkler heads are also available.)

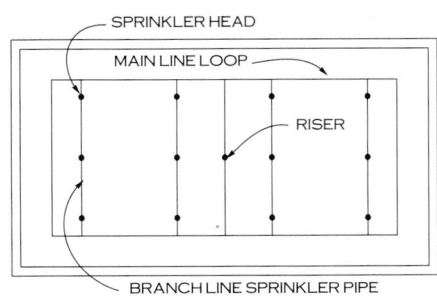

HYDRAULICALLY DESIGNED SPRINKLER SYSTEM LAYOUT

Loop provides water flow from two directions to operating sprinkler heads so pipe sizes will be small. Hydraulic calculations can assure delivery of adequate water flow and pressure throughout piping network to meet design requirements.

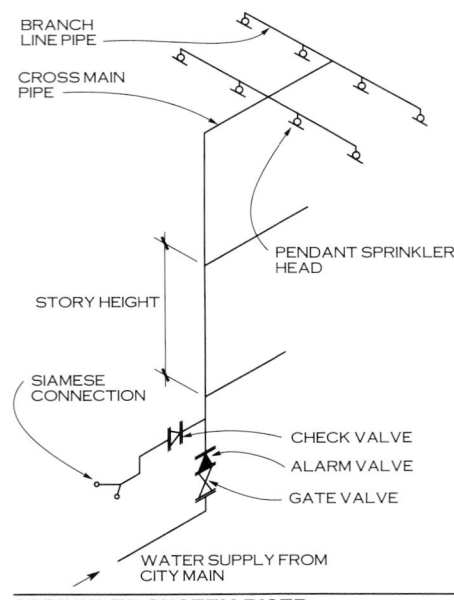

SPRINKLER SYSTEM RISER

TYPES OF SYSTEMS

WET PIPE: Piping network contains water under pressure at all times for immediate release through sprinkler heads as they are activated by heat from fire. Wet pipe system is the most widely used system, since water delivery is faster than with a dry pipe system.

DRY PIPE: Piping network contains air (or nitrogen) under pressure. Following loss of air pressure through opened sprinkler head, dry pipe valve opens, allowing water to enter piping network and to flow through opened sprinkler head (or heads). Used where piping is subject to freezing.

PREACTION: Closed head, dry system containing air in piping network. Preaction valve is activated by heat or smoke detection system more sensitive than sprinkler heads. The opened preaction valve allows water to fill piping network and to flow through sprinkler heads, as they are activated by heat from fire. Used where leakage or accidental discharge would cause water damage.

DELUGE: Sprinkler heads (or spray nozzles) are open at all times and normally there is no water in piping network. Mechanical or hydraulic valves, operated by heat or flame detection systems, are used to control water flow to heads by opening water control deluge valve. Deluge systems are special use systems, as water discharges for all heads (or nozzles) at the same time.

STANDPIPE AND HOSE: Dry standpipes are empty water pipes used by fire fighters to connect hoses in buildings to fire department pumpers. Wet standpipes are water filled pipes permanently connected to public or private water mains for use by industrial fire brigades or by fire fighters.

FOAM: Used to suppress flammable liquid fires. Foam can be distributed by piping network to nozzles or other discharge outlets (e.g., tubes, troughs, monitors) depending on the hazard.

HALON (HALOGINATED HYDROCARBON): Previously used where water damage to building contents would be unacceptable. The use of halon systems is being phased out due to environmental concerns, and new installations are not allowed in many areas. Piping network connects fixed supply of halon to nozzles that discharge uniform, low concentration throughout room. To avoid piping network, discharge cylinders may be installed throughout room or area. Though generally nontoxic, delayed discharge can cause problems by allowing decomposition of halon. Rapid detection is necessary.

CO_2 (CARBON DIOXIDE): Does not conduct electricity and leaves no residue after its use. Piping network connects fixed supply of CO_2 to nozzles that discharge CO_2 directly on burning materials where location of fire hazard is known (called "local application") or discharge CO_2 uniformly throughout room (called "total flooding"). In total flooding systems, safety requirements dictate advance alarm to allow occupants to evacuate area prior to discharge.

DRY CHEMICAL: Can be especially useful on electrical and flammable liquid fires. Powdered extinguishing agent, under pressure of dry air or nitrogen, commonly discharged over cooking surfaces (e.g., frying).

PREPARATION FOR SPRINKLER SYSTEMS

1. Begin planning sprinkler system at the very earliest design stages of project.
2. Determine hazard classification of building and type of system best suited for suppression needs.
3. Refer to national standards (NFPA), state and local codes
4. Check with authority having jurisdiction:
   a. State and local fire marshals
   b. Commercial risk services
   c. Insurance underwriting groups such as IRI or FM (if they have jurisdiction).
5. Use qualified fire protection engineers to design systems. Be sure water supply is adequate (e.g., by water flow tests). Integrate system with structural, mechanical, and other building services.
6. Check space requirements for sprinkler equipment. Sprinkler control room must be heated to prevent freezing of equipment.
7. Consider possible future alterations to building.

M. David Egan, P.E.; College of Architecture, Clemson University; Clemson, South Carolina
John L. Bryan; Fire Protection Engineering, University of Maryland; College Park, Maryland

13   FIRE SUPPRESSION AND SUPERVISORY SYSTEMS

EXPLOSION PREVENTION

Accidental ignition of flammable solids, liquids, and gases can be prevented best by eliminating potential flammable materials and igniters such as sparks or flames. Hard-finish surfaces of inert, spark-resistant, nonflammable materials should be incorporated, as should sloping horizontal surfaces, coved bases, and coved interior corners (see Fig. 1). Continuous cleanup will minimize the accumulation of dust and debris. Hooded dust-collection systems work well in purging dust from localized areas (see Fig. 2).

Provision should be made for containment of spilled liquids and solids. For flammable gases, ventilation for health safety and prevention of concentrated vapors should be provided.

Explosion-proof electrical devices and grounding systems should be provided in accordance with NEC, NFPA, and insurance underwriters.

EXPLOSION SUPPRESSION

Explosion suppression is a specialized application in which an extinguishing agent is discharged to snuff out an explosion in its developing stages. Explosion detection systems detect the pressure rise associated with an explosion and immediately discharge extinguishing or suppression agents before damage can occur.

From start to finish, the entire detection/extinguishing process may take only $^{65}/_{1000}$ of a second. This rapid detection and discharge limits application to only very small confined areas. Ideal applications include the interiors of tanks, hoppers, ductwork, or other equipment containing explosive concentrations of vapors, dust, and powders. Refer to NFPA 69.

SPECIAL EXTINGUISHING SYSTEMS

Automatic fire suppression and extinguishing systems are permanent building installations used to protect the structure, its contents, and its occupants against the hazards of fire and explosion. The nature and magnitude of the hazard will dictate the extinguishing agent and system configuration. Available agents include water (discussed elsewhere), Halon, carbon dioxide, foam, and dry chemicals. Systems may be either total flooding or local application types.

Total flooding systems consist of a fixed supply of extinguishing agent, distribution piping, discharge nozzles, detection devices, alarms, and controls required to achieve a predetermined concentration within an enclosed space or an enclosure around a hazard (see Fig. 3).

Local application systems consist of similar components, as listed above, but are designed to direct extinguishing agents to achieve calculated surface coverages of hazardous areas (see Fig. 4).

HALON SYSTEMS: Halon refers to the family of halogenated hydrocarbon compounds which have very effective fire extinguishing capabilities, but also varying degrees of hazard to human health. Halon 1301 offers the best extinguishing performance with minimum risk to people.

Halon 1301 extinguishes a fire by chemically interrupting the chain reaction of combustion. Halon causes no water damage and leaves no residue, making it ideal for protection of valuable records and electronic equipment. Halon can be discharged in occupied areas, allowing time for orderly shutdown of equipment and evacuation.

The relative high cost of Halon systems mandates that they be used to protect confined areas such as storage vaults, tape libraries or computer rooms, and underfloor spaces.

A typical total-flooding Halon system installation consists of storage cylinders, distribution piping, discharge nozzles, detectors (heat, smoke, UV, etc.), and alarms. Interfaces between the Halon system, HVAC equipment, and electrical equipment are required to ensure adequate shutdown during alarm conditions. Special construction of doors, door closers, partitions, and ceilings is necessary to provide as airtight a space as possible.

Because Halon systems are depleted totally upon discharge, backup or redundant storage cylinders may be required to maintain protection while the system is being serviced and recharged. Local codes or underwriting agencies may require sprinkler backup in areas protected by Halon within sprinklered buildings. Refer to NFPA 12A.

DRY CHEMICAL SYSTEMS: A variety of dry chemical, powderlike products are available for use as extinguishing agents. Although effective against flammable liquid fires and electrical fires, dry chemical systems can result in extensive cleanup problems after discharge and may damage sensitive electronic components or equipment. For these reasons, the most common use of dry chemical systems is for local applications over relatively small areas such as cooking surfaces, dip tanks, and spray booths. Halogenated agents have been found to be ozone depleting. Substitute gases for fire protection use have been developed and are awaiting EPA approval. Refer to NFPA 17.

CARBON DIOXIDE SYSTEMS: Carbon dioxide (CO_2) is a suitable medium for extinguishing flammable liquid fires and fires involving energized electrical equipment. Carbon dioxide systems extinguish fire by reducing the concentrations of oxygen in the air, the vapor phase of the fuel, or both to the point where combustion stops. These systems are generally used in unoccupied areas or where an electrically nonconductive medium is essential. These include electrical equipment rooms, transformers, vaults, or areas containing rotating equipment or flammable liquids. Types of systems include local flooding, local application, hand hose line, and standpipe systems.

Personnel hazards such as suffocation and reduced visibility due to fogging during and after discharge must be considered in the application of total flooding CO_2 systems. Such systems must be designed to allow for total evacuation of the area prior to discharge and must also incorporate audible predischarge alarms. Local application systems usually are installed in confined areas such as restaurant range hoods, open top tanks, and printing presses. Activation of CO_2 systems may be automatic or manual.

In general, large systems requiring sizable quantities of CO_2 use low-pressure storage systems designed for outside installation, while systems requiring small CO_2 quantities can use high-pressure storage cylinders designed for placement inside buildings.

Natural leakage occurring around doors, windows, and dampers generally provides sufficient venting of CO_2 from rooms, ductwork, and equipment enclosures after discharge; therefore, special venting considerations are required only in gas-tight enclosures. Refer to NFPA 12.

FOAM SYSTEMS: Foaming agents used for fire protection fall into one of three major classes: (1) low-, (2) medium-, and (3) high-expansion foams, as determined by their respective foam-to-solution volume ratios. Foam provides a unique agent for total flooding of confined spaces, transporting water to otherwise inaccessible places, and for volumetric displacement of vapor, heat, and smoke.

Foam is used principally to form a floating blanket on flammable or combustible liquids, preventing or extinguishing fire by excluding air and cooling the fuel. It also prevents reignition by suppressing formation of flammable vapors. Film coating characteristics of fire-fighting foams also provide a measure of protection from adjacent fires.

Foam-type fire suppression systems may consist of portable foam-generating equipment with hand-held nozzles or may involve fixed applications for the protection of entire facilities. Liquid fuel storage and unloading facilities and aircraft hangars and fueling areas often employ foam systems. High-expansion foams also have proved effective in high-rack storage areas. Refer to NFPA, Chapters 11 and 11A.

EXPLOSION VENTING

Explosion venting is required in many high-hazard occupancies and is achieved by providing a relief area to the building exterior, thereby controlling the direction of the blast. This requirement depends on the flammability and quantity of the materials within the space and is expressed in square feet of relief area per 100 cubic feet of space.

The relief area may be either brittle material or panels with release fasteners. Brittle relief material such as glass is best placed on the roof and requires a protective screen to limit the size of flying particles. Panel vents normally are placed in walls and require restraining cables. Vents are designed to release at an internal relief pressure, which is a multiple of the design wind load. The remaining walls, roof, and floor are designed to withstand a load that is a multiple of the relief pressure.

Refer to building codes, NFPA, and insurance underwriters for specific requirements and design guidelines.

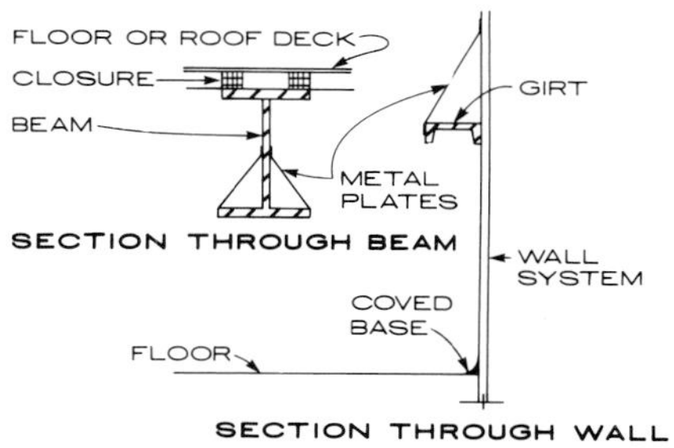

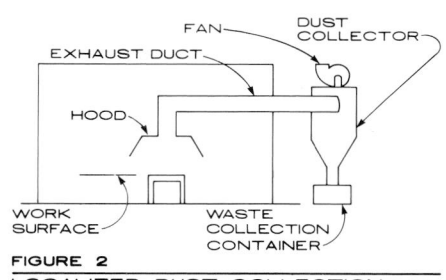

FIGURE 1
MINIMIZING ACCUMULATION OF FLAMMABLE SOLIDS

LOCALIZED DUST COLLECTION
FIGURE 2

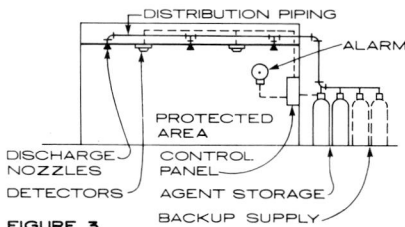

FIGURE 3
TOTAL FLOODING EXTINGUISHING SYSTEM

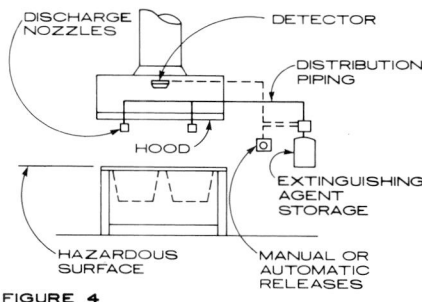

FIGURE 4
LOCAL APPLICATION EXTINGUISHING SYSTEM

GENERAL

American Society for
    Testing and Materials (ASTM)
1916 Race St.
Philadelphia, PA 19103-1187
Tel: (215) 299-5400
Fax:(215) 977-9679

AIR-SUPPORTED STRUCTURES

Industrial Fabrics Association International (IFAI)
345 Cedar Building
Suite 800
St. Paul, MN 55101-1088
Tel: (612) 222-2508
Fax:(612) 222-8215

REFERENCES

Design of Air-Supported Structures, Institution of Structural Engineers. #1351-5. American Society of Civil Engineers, New York, 1984.

SPECIAL PURPOSE ROOMS

Institute of Environmental Sciences (IES)
940 East Northwest Highway
Mount Prospect, IL 60056
Tel: (708) 255-1561
Fax:(708) 255-1699

National Spa and Pool Institute (NSPI)
2111 Eisenhower Avenue
Alexandria, VA 22314
Tel: (703) 838-0083
Fax (703) 549-0493

Sauna Society of America
1001 Connecticut Avenue, N.W.
Washington, DC 20036-5504
Tel: (202) 331-1363

Hivner, Daniel. "Clean Room Technology in the Operating Room." *Consulting-Specifying Engineer* (June 1992), p. 28.

"Hot Stuff "[Saunas]. *Architectural Record* (April 1992), p. 38.

"Testing of Clean Rooms." Institute of Environmental Sciences Recommended Practice No. IES-RP-CC-006-84-T.

SOUND AND VIBRATION CONTROL

Acoustical Society of America
500 Sunnyside Blvd.
Woodbury, NY 11797
Tel: (516) 576-2360
Fax:(516) 349-7669

Audio Engineering Society
60 East 42th Street, Room 2520
New York, NY 10165
Tel: (212) 661-8528
Fax:(212) 682-0417

Concert Hall Research Group
clo Timothy J Foulkes
327 F Boston Post Road
Sudbury, MA 01776
Tel: (508) 443-7871

National Council of Acoustical Consultants (NCAC)
66 Morris Avenue, Suite 1A
Springfield, NJ 07081-1409
Tel: (201) 564-5859
Fax:(201) 564-7480

REFERENCES

Beranek, Leo L. *Noise and Vibration Control*. McGraw-Hill.

Dupree, R. *Catalog of STC and IIC Ratings for Wall and Floor/Ceiling Assemblies*. Office of Noise Control, Calif. Dept. of Health Services, Berkeley, [(415) 540-2604] 1981.

Egan, M.D. "Sound Isolation," Ch. 4, *Architectural Acoustics*. McGraw-Hill, 1988.

Lubman, D. and E. Wetherill. *Acoustics of Worship Spaces*. Acoustical Society of America, 1985.

McCue, E. and R. Talaske. *Acoustical Design of Music Educational Facilities*. Acoustical Society of America, 1990.

MJM Acoustical Consultants. *Research Project on the Noise Isolation Provided by Floor/Ceiling Assemblies in Wood Construction*. CMHC.

MJM Acoustical Consultants. *Research Project on Plumbing Noise in Multi-Dwelling Buildings*. CMHC.

MJM Acoustical Consultants. *Sound Performance of Wood Floor/Ceiling Assemblies*. CMHC.

Noise Control in Buildings, no.27844. National Research Council of Canada, 1987.

Quirt, J. *Controlling Sound Transmission into Buildings*. BPN 56. National Research Council of Canada, 1985.

Rettinger, M. *Handbook of Architectural Acoustics and Noise*. TAB Books, 1988.

"Sound Isolation in Floors." *P/A* (March 1991), pp.121-4.

Talaske, R., et al. *Halls for Music Performance*. Acoustical Society of America, 1982.

Talaske, R. and R. Boner, eds. *Theatres for Drama Performance*. Acoustical Society of America, 1987.

PRE-ENGINEERED STRUCTURES

American Institute of Steel Construction, Inc. (AISC)
1 East Wacker Drive, Suite 3100
Chicago, IL 60601-2001
Tel: (312) 670-2400
Fax:(312) 670-5403

American Iron & Steel Institute
1101 17th Street, N.W.
Suite 1300
Washington, DC 20036
Tel: (202) 452-7100
Fax:(202) 463-6573

American Welding Society
550 N.W. LeJeune Road
P.O. Box 351040
Miami, FL 33135
Tel: (305) 443-9353
Fax:(305) 443-7559

Manufactured Housing Institute
1745 Jefferson Davis Highway, Suite 511
Arlington, VA 22202
Tel: (703) 413-6620
Fax:(703) 413-6621

Metal Building Manufacturers Association (MBMA)
1300 Sumner Avenue
Cleveland, OH 44115
Tel: (216) 241-7333
Fax:(216) 241-0105

National Association of
    Architectural Metal Manufacturers (NAAMM)
600 South Federal, Suite 400
Chicago, IL 60605
Tel: (312) 922-6222
Fax:(312) 922-2734

Steel Window Institute (SWI)
1300 Sumner Avenue
Cleveland, OH 44115
Tel: (216) 241-7333
Fax:(216) 241-0105

REFERENCES

Lee, George C., Robert L. Ketter, and T.L. Hsu. *Design of Single Story Rigid Frames*. Cleveland: Metal Building Manufacturing Association, 1981.

Metal Building Systems Manual. Metal Building Manufacturers Association, 1981.

Metal Building Systems Fact Book. Metal Building Manufacturers Association.

Metal Finishes Manual, 3rd ed. National Association of Architectural Metal Manufacturers.

"Pre-Engineered Systems Expedite Delivery." *Building Design and Construction*, (June 92), p. 76.

Recommended Specifications for Steel Windows, Steel Window Institute.

BUILDING AUTOMATION SYSTEMS

Home Automation Association (HAA)
808 17th Street, NW, Suite 200
Washington, DC 20006-3953
Tel: (202) 333-8579

REFERENCES

Electronic House: Advanced Housing and Home Automation, Home Automation Association. [bimonthly]

"Finding the Competitive Edge Through Intelligent Buildings at Future/Build 2002." *Facilities Design and Management* (Sept. 92), p. 35.

FIRE SUPPRESSION AND SUPERVISORY SYSTEMS

Building and Fire Research Laboratory
National Institute of Standards and Technology
Building 226 Room B216
Gaithersburg, MD 20899
Tel: (301) 975-6850

Factory Mutual Engineering Corp. (FM)
11 51 Boston-Providence Turnpike
Norwalk, MA 02062
Tel: (617) 762-4300
Fax:(617) 762-9375

Fire Research Section (FRS/NRCC)
National Research Council Canada
Ottawa, Canada KIA OR6
Tel: (613) 993-2204

Fire Suppression Systems Association
5024-R Campbell Blvd.
Baltimore, MD 21236
Tel: (410) 931-8100
Fax:(410) 931-8111

National Fire Protection Association (NFPA)
One Batterymarch Park
P.O. Box 9101
Quincy, MA 02269-9101
Tel: (800) 735-0100
Fax:(617) 770-0700

National Fire Sprinkler Association
Route 22 and Robin Hill Corporate Park
Box 1000
Patterson, NY 12563
Tel: (914) 878-4200
Fax:(914) 878-4215

Society of Fire Protection Engineers (SFPE)
One Liberty Square
Boston, MA 02109-4825
Tel: (617) 482-0686

Underwriters Laboratories (UL)
333 Pfingsten Road
Northbrook, IL 60062
Tel: (708) 272-8800
Fax:(708) 272-8129

Underwriters Laboratories of Canada (ULC)
7 Crouse Rd.
Scarborough, Ontario MIR.3A9 Canada
Tel: (416) 757-3611

REFERENCES

Building Manual Directory. Underwriters Laboratories. [updated annually]

Bukowski, R., R. O'Laughlin, and C. Zimmerman. *Fire Alarm Signaling Systems Handbook*, Boston: National Fire Protection Association and Society of Fire Protection Engineers, 1987.

Colburn, Robert E. *Fire Protection and Suppression*. New York: McGraw-Hill, 1975.

Cote, A. and P. Bugbee. *Principles Of Fire Protection*. National Fire Protection Association, 1988.

Factory Mutual. Approval Guide, P7825. [updated annually]

Fire Code Summary. Architectural Woodwork Institute, 1986.

Fire Protection Handbook, 17th ed. Quincy, MA: National Fire Protection Association, c. 1991.

Fire Resistance Design Manual. Gypsum Association, 1992.

Fire Safety in Tall Buildings, Council on Tall Buildings, McGraw-Hill, 1992.

Journal of Fire Protection Engineering, Society of Fire Protection Engineers. [quarterly]

Lathrop, J., ed. *Life Safety Code Handbook*. National Fire Protection Association, 1991.

Loss Prevention Data Books for Architects and Engineers. Factory Mutual. [looseleaf binders, periodic updates]

National Fire Protection Association Codes. Boston: National Fire Protection Association, 1990.

Parking Structures, Standard NFPA 88A. National Fire Protection Association,1985.

The SFPE Handbook of Fire Protection Engineering, DH-HFPE-88. Boston: National Fire Protection Association, 1988.

Sullan, M. "Reducing Fire Hazards in Small Buildings" in *Small Buildings: Technology in Transition*, NRCC 32333. National Research Council of Canada, 1990

Chapter

14

CONVEYING SYSTEMS

GENERAL

An elevator system with its hoistway, machine room, and waiting lobbies is a major element in a building and requires special design consideration. Preengineered or custom-made elevator systems can be constructed to meet virtually all vertical transportation needs for passenger, freight, or service.

In all cases, design of an elevator system must be carefully considered throughout all stages of the building design process. During initial stages, the elevator handling capacity and quality of service desired determines the size, speed, number, type, and location of elevator systems. Proper selection depends on type of tenancy, number of occupants, and the building design (number of floors, floor heights, building circulation, etc.). Elevator ARRANGEMENT locates the elevator within the building plan to provide efficient and accessible service. Each elevator system, once selected, requires OPERATIONAL SPACES, hoistway pit and machine room, and PASSENGER SPACES, lobby, and elevator car.

Proper planning and contact with representatives of the elevator industry and local code officials are essential to each of these design areas.

NOTE: WHERE A HOISTWAY EXTENDS INTO THE TOP FLOOR OF A BUILDING, FIRE RESISTIVE HOISTWAY OR MACHINERY SPACE ENCLOSURES, AS REQUIRED, SHALL BE CARRIED TO THE UNDERSIDE OF THE ROOF IF THE ROOF IS OF FIRE RESISTIVE CONSTRUCTION, AND AT LEAST 3 FT. ABOVE THE TOP SURFACE OF A FIRE NON-RESISTIVE ROOF.

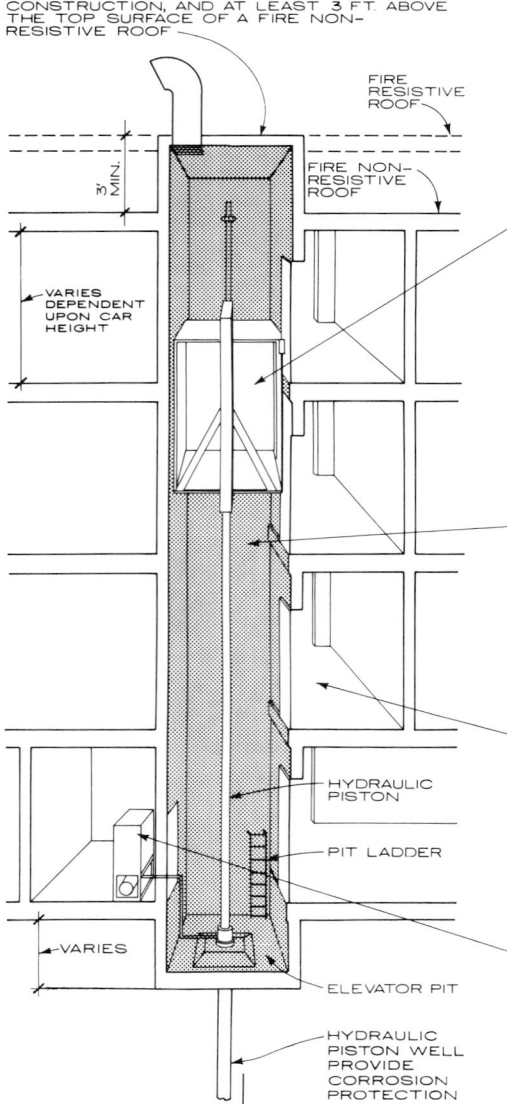

HYDRAULIC ELEVATOR

The two most common systems, the HYDRAULIC ELEVATOR and the ELECTRIC ELEVATOR, are shown in the two diagrams on this page. The systems are distinguished mainly by their hoisting mechanisms.

The HYDRAULIC ELEVATOR uses an oil hydraulic driving machine to raise and lower the elevator car and its load. A hydraulic pump unit is one in which the energy is applied by means of a liquid under pressure in a cylinder equipped with a plunger or piston. The car is supported at the pit floor (hoistway base). Lower speeds and the piston length restrict the use of this system to approximately 55 ft. It generally requires the least initial installation expense, but more power is used during operation because of the greater loads imposed on the driving machine.

An ELECTRIC ELEVATOR is a power elevator where the energy is applied by means of an electric driving machine. In the electric driving machine the energy is applied by an electric motor. It includes the motor, brake, and the driving sheave or drum together with its connecting gearing, if any. Medium to high speeds and virtually limitless rise allow this elevator to serve highrise, medium-rise, and lowrise buildings.

MACHINE ROOM (ELECTRIC ELEVATOR)

Normally located directly over the top of the hoistway—it could also be below at side or rear—the machine room is designed to contain elevator hoisting machine and electronic control equipment. Adequate ventilation, soundproofing, and structural support for the elevator must be considered. Requires self-closing, self-locking access door. Local codes may require that no other electrical or mechanical equipment, not associated with the elevator, be installed in the machine room.

ELEVATOR CAR

Guided by vertical guide rails on each side of the car, the elevator car conveys passenger or freight between floors. It consists of a car constructed within a supporting platform and frame. Design of the car focuses on the finished ceiling, walls, floor, and doors with lighting, ventilation, and elevator signal equipment.

The car and frame of a hydraulic elevator system are supported by a piston or cylinder.

The car and frame of an electric elevator system are supported by the hoist machine. The elevator and its counterweight are connected via steel ropes.

HOISTWAY

The hoistway is a vertical shaft for the travel of one or more elevators. It includes the pit and terminates at the underside of the overhang machinery space floor for electric elevators, or at the underside of the roof over the hoistway of a hydraulic elevator. Access to the elevator car and hoistway is normally through hoistway doors located at each floor serviced by the elevator system. Hoistway design is determined by the characteristics of the elevator system selected and by requirements of the applicable code for fire separation, ventilation, soundproofing, or nonstructural elements.

LOBBY

Elevator waiting areas are designed to allow free circulation of passengers, rapid access to elevator cars, and clear visibility of elevator signals. All elevator lobbies must be enclosed with the exception of the designated main building entry level.

ACCESSIBILITY

Passenger elevators on accessible routes should comply with requirements of ANSI 117.1 and ADAAG.

MACHINE ROOM (HYDRAULIC ELEVATOR)

Normally located near the base of the hoistway, the machine room contains hydraulic pump unit and electronic controls. Provisions of adequate ventilation and soundproofing must be considered. Requires self-closing, self-locking access door. Local codes may require that no other electrical or mechanical equipment, not associated with the elevator, be installed in the machine room.

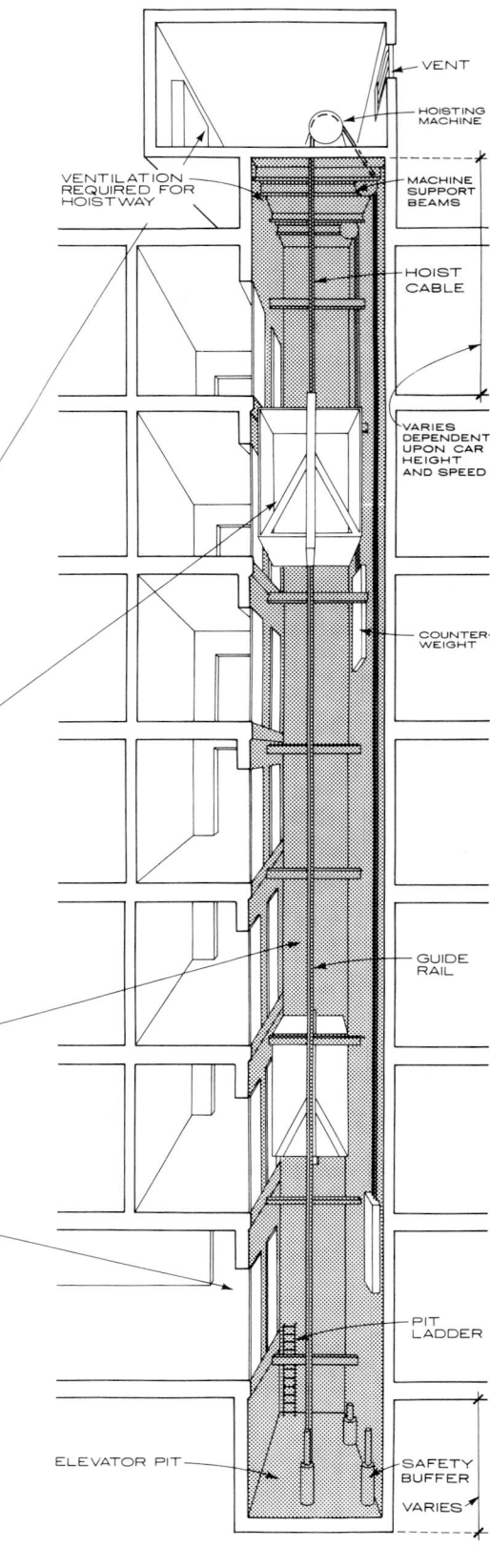

ELECTRIC ELEVATOR

Alexander Keyes; Darrel Downing Rippeteau, Architect; Washington, D.C.

14   INTRODUCTION

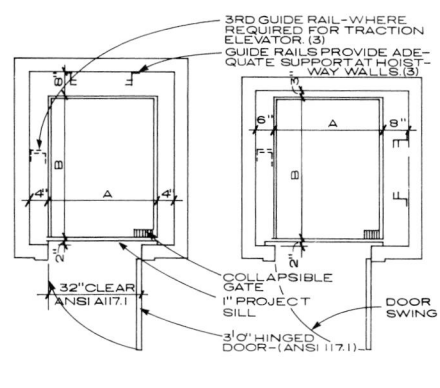

PENTHOUSE

FLOOR

PIT

ELEVATOR SECTION

CAR WITH RAILS AT REAR (4,5)   CAR WITH RAILS AT SIDE (4,5)

RESIDENTIAL ELEVATOR PLANS

RESIDENTIAL ELEVATORS

Typical car sizes, A x B: 36 in. x 36 in., 42 in. x 42 in., 36 in. x 48 in.

12 sq ft platform maximum size allowed by National Elevator Code for residential elevators, ANSI A17.1. This platform size does not meet the National Handicapped Access Code, ANSI A117.1, for use by an unassisted wheelchair-bound person.

Load capacity of drum-type machine is 450 lb. Speed is 30 ft per minute.

Load capacity of traction machine is 700 lb. Speed is 36 ft per minute.

Elevators operate on 220/230 volt, single phase power supply. A disconnect switch must be provided within sight of the machine. A 110V, single phase power supply is required for lighting of machine area of hoistway.

Enclosures are recommended for all hoistways. Fire rating of hoistway enclosure and access doors must be consistent with the fire rating of the building construction. See local codes.

NOTES

1. Dimensions may vary among manufacturers and according to system selected. Elevators carrying greater loads or operating at higher speeds require more clearance overhead and in pit areas.
2. Elevator cars may have higher interior clearances if desired, which increases overhead clearance required in the hoistway.
3. Guide rails usually are provided by the manufacturer in 5 ft sections. Some manufacturers supply rails that can span from floor structure to floor structure. If the existing structure cannot support the guide rails, manufacturers can provide a self-supporting tower that transmits the load to its base. Increased horizontal clearance in the hoistway is required. If a third guide rail is required, it is supplied in 3 ft 4 in. sections.
4. Dimensions given are appropriate for most applications. For exact dimensions required in specific circumstances, consult manufacturers.
5. Elevator cars can be provided with openings on two sides; guide rails must be located accordingly. Consult manufacturers.

DUMBWAITERS

Typical car sizes, A x B: 24 in. x 24 in., 30 in. x 30 in., 36 in. x 36 in., 30 in. x 48 in. Smaller sizes are available.

9 sq ft platform maximum size allowed by National Elevator Code for dumbwaiters, ANSI A17.1.

48 in. high car is maximum allowed by National Elevator Code for dumbwaiters, ANSI A17.1.

Load capacity for drum-type machines is 500 lb. Speed is 50 ft per minute.

Drum-type machines are not recommended for installations with total travel of more than 36 ft–40 ft. Maximum total travel 50 ft.

Load capacity of traction machines is 500 lb. Speeds to 500 ft per minute are available.

Dumbwaiters require 3 phase electrical power. For exact voltage consult manufacturer.

NOTES

1. Dimensions may vary among manufacturers and according to system selected. Dumbwaiters carrying greater loads or operating at higher speeds require more clearance overhead and in pit areas.
2. Guide rails usually are provided by the manufacturer in 5 ft sections. Some manufacturers supply rails that can span from floor structure to floor structure. If existing structure cannot support the guide rails, manufacturers can provide a self-supporting tower that transmits the load to its base. Increased horizontal clearance in the hoistway is required.
3. Vertical dimensions given assume the use of vertical bi-parting doors. The entire door may slide up or down; however, required clearances will vary. Swing hoistway doors also are available. Consult manufacturers.

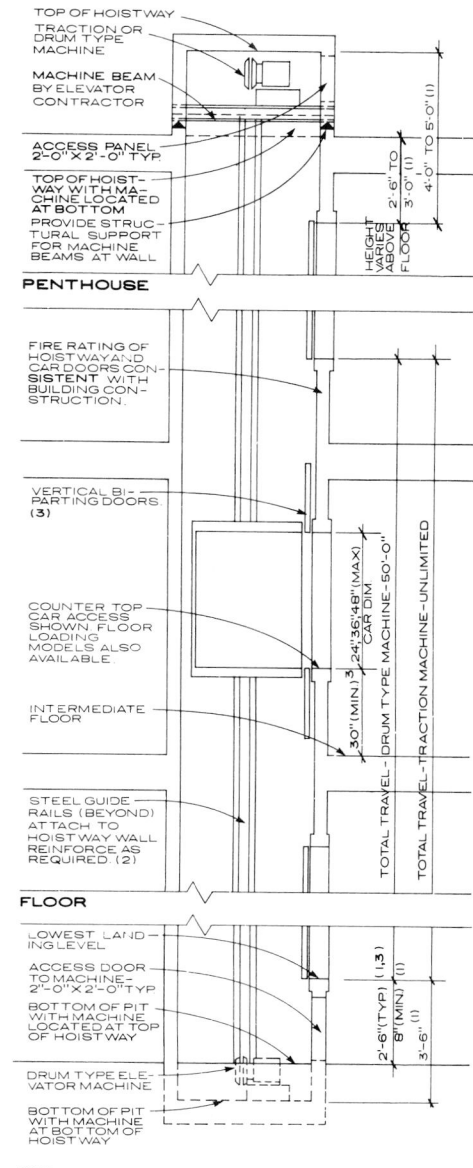

PENTHOUSE

FLOOR

PIT

DUMBWAITER SECTION

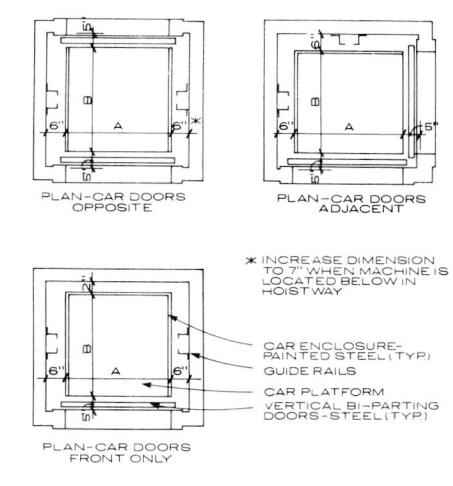

PLAN–CAR DOORS OPPOSITE

PLAN–CAR DOORS ADJACENT

PLAN–CAR DOORS FRONT ONLY

* INCREASE DIMENSION TO 7" WHEN MACHINE IS LOCATED BELOW IN HOISTWAY

CAR ENCLOSURE–PAINTED STEEL (TYP)
GUIDE RAILS
CAR PLATFORM
VERTICAL BI-PARTING DOORS–STEEL (TYP)

PLANS OF TYPICAL DUMBWAITERS

Beth D. Buffington, AIA; Wilkes, Faulkner, Jenkins, and Bass Architects; Washington, D.C.

GENERAL

ELEVATOR SELECTION depends on several factors: the building's physical characteristics, available elevator systems, and code regulations. The functions that relate these selection parameters and indicate the number, size, speed, and type of elevators are, in most cases, complex and are based on the performance of the elevator systems. Representatives of the elevator industry or consulting elevator engineers should be contacted during the selection process to ensure that the most suitable elevator system is chosen.

PRIVATE RESIDENCES

Elevator selection for private residences can be simplified to a few parameters. By code they are limited in size, capacity, rise, and speed and are installed only in a private residence or a multiple dwelling as a means of access to a single private dwelling.

AVAILABLE ELEVATOR SYSTEMS are outlined on another page. The speed, capacity type, aesthetic design, and electronic controls of preengineered systems are generally limited to only a few options.

BUILDING POPULATION analysis involves the identification of the needs of prospective users. Relevant information includes the number of passengers expected to occupy the elevator in one trip and elevator service in a given time period, as well as the type of expected occupancy, i.e., mixed, single occupancy, etc.

BUILDING CHARACTERISTICS affect elevator selection by establishing the building height (distance of elevator travel) and hoistway location. In private residences, the elevator may occupy a tier of closets, an exterior shaft, a room corner, or a stairwell.

ELEVATOR SELECTION—HOSPITAL

The accompanying diagram illustrates elevator selection parameters in the context of a hospital layout. Actual calculations relating these parameters are complex. Consultation with an elevator industry representative or consulting elevator engineer is recommended.

1. BUILDING HEIGHT: Floor-to-floor height and number of floors.
2. BUILDING POPULATION: Total number of building occupants and expected visitors and their expected distribution throughout the building.
3. BUILDING USE ANALYSIS: Location of offices, patients' rooms, service areas, and ancillary spaces conducive to mass assembly. Primary public circulation areas and primary staff circulation areas should be identified.
4. WAITING AREA: Peak loading and waiting time are two important concepts in providing the quality of elevator service expected by hospital visitors and staff. Different standards are applied according to building use. Consult an elevator engineer.
5. LOCATION OF MAJOR ENTRANCES
6. ELEVATOR SYSTEMS: A large selection of elevator capacities, speed, controls, and type are available. In this case, passenger and service elevators are shown. An elevator with a front and rear entrance serves as a passenger elevator during peak visiting hours. The wide variety of elevator alternatives should be discussed with an elevator engineer to select the system most suitable for each individual situation.

SERVICE REQUIREMENTS: Elevators must have sufficient capacity and speed to meet building service requirements. In this case, the elevator must accommodate a 24 x 76 in. ambulance type stretcher with attendants. Check local requirements.

For patient service in hospitals, to accommodate beds with their attachments, use 5000 lb elevators; platforms 6 ft wide x 9 ft 6 in. deep, doors at least 4 ft wide (4 ft 6 in. width is preferred).

CODE AND REGULATIONS: Recommendations and code restrictions regarding accessibility, fire safety, elevator controls, and so on, may affect elevator selection. Consult with an elevator industry representative or consulting elevator engineer. As a minimum, comply with the ANSI A17.1 for Elevators, Dumbwaiters, Escalators and Moving Walks.

NOTE: Elevators should not be considered as emergency exits.

ELEVATOR SYSTEMS IN BUILDINGS OTHER THAN PRIVATE HOMES

Selection of elevator systems increases in complexity with the size and complexity of the project. Even though the vertical transportation needs of low-rise residential and commercial projects may be simply met, all the parameters listed below should be considered and analyzed with a consulting elevator engineer to ensure proper selection.

BUILDING POPULATION

The elevator selection process must begin with a thorough analysis of how people will occupy the building.

1. TOTAL POPULATION AND DENSITY: The total number of occupants and visitors and their distribution by floors within a building.
2. PEAK LOADING: Periods when elevators carry the highest traffic loads. For example, peak loading in office buildings coincides with rush hours and/or lunch periods, while peak loading in hospitals may occur during visiting hours.
3. WAITING TIME: The length of time a passenger is expected to wait for the next elevator to arrive. These demands vary according to building use and building occupant expectations. A person willing to wait 50–70 sec in an apartment building may be willing to wait only 20–35 sec in an office building.
4. DEMAND FOR QUALITY: Sophistication of controls and elevator capacity may be varied to cater to the expected taste of passengers. Large elevator cars and the smooth, long life operation of a gearless elevator may convey an image of luxury even if a smaller elevator having a less sophisticated system would be technically sufficient.

BUILDING CHARACTERISTICS

Physical building characteristics are considered together with population characteristics to determine size, speed, type, and location of elevator systems.

1. HEIGHT: The distance of elevator travel (from lowest terminal to top terminal), number of floors, and floor height.
2. BUILDING USE ANALYSIS: Location of building entrance areas of heavy use such as cafeteria, restaurant, auditorium, and service areas must be identified. Typically, a building should be planned to ensure that no prospective passengers must walk more than 200 ft to reach an elevator.

ELEVATOR SYSTEMS AND REGULATIONS

The parameters previously described outline the environment in which the elevator operates. Local code regulations and ANSI A17.1 requirements provide further elevator guidelines.

Available elevator systems are analyzed to ensure that suitable speed, capacity, controls, and number of cars are selected.

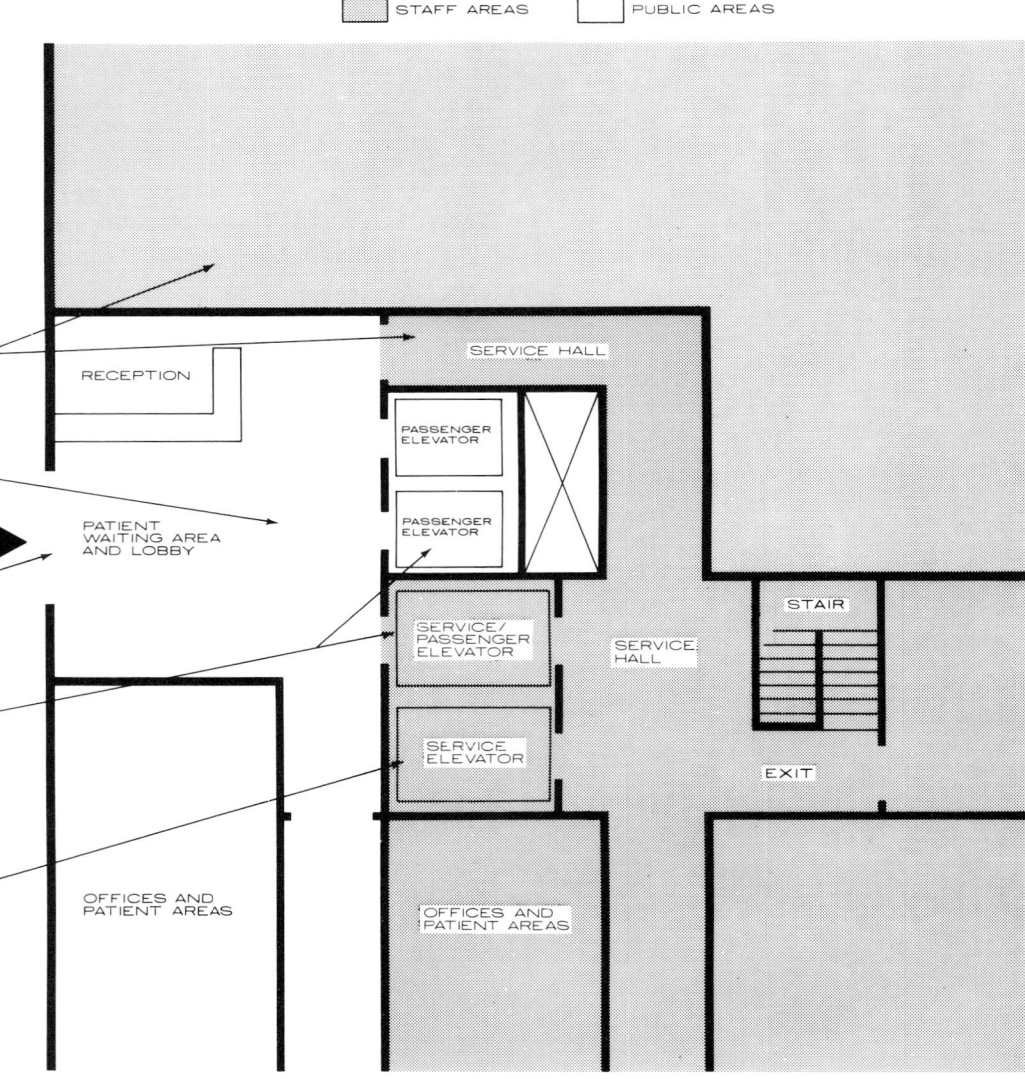

ELEVATOR SELECTION FACTORS – HOSPITAL

Alexander Keyes; Darrel Downing Rippeteau, Architect; Washington, D.C.

 ELEVATORS

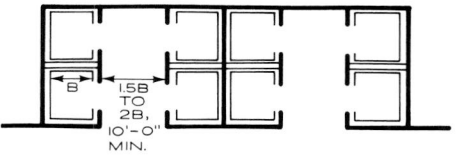

B = DEPTH OF CAR

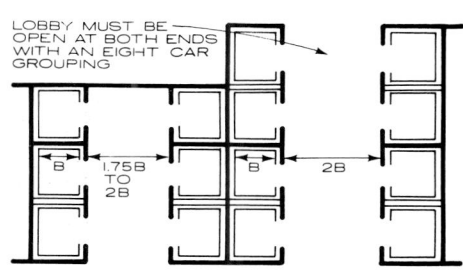

LOBBY MUST BE OPEN AT BOTH ENDS WITH AN EIGHT CAR GROUPING

NOTES

The largest practical grouping of elevators in a building is eight cars. One row of more than four cars is generally unacceptable. With groupings of four or six cars, waiting lobbies may be alcoved (one end closed) or open at both ends. In case of several elevator groupings, one grouping may serve lower floors, while others are express elevators to upper floors.

Where 4 or more elevators serve all or the same portion of a building, they shall be located in not less than 2 hoistways, but in no case shall more than 4 elevators be located in any one hoistway.

ELEVATOR ARRANGEMENTS – FOUR, SIX, AND EIGHT CARS (TYPICAL FOR HIGHRISE APPLICATIONS)

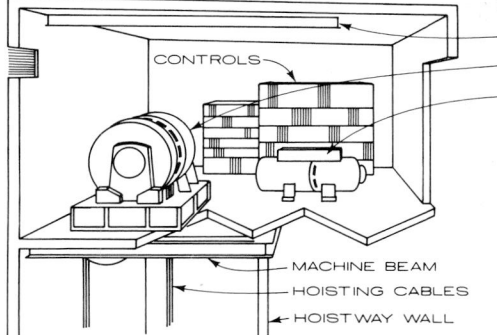

NOTES

The MACHINE ROOM for electric elevators is normally located directly above the hoistway. Space must be provided for the elevator drive, electronic control equipment, and governor with sufficient clearance for equipment installation, repair, or removal. Space requirements vary substantially according to code capacity and speed of the system selected. Adequate lighting and ventilation are required by codes, and sound insulation should be provided. Consult with elevator consultant for requirements.

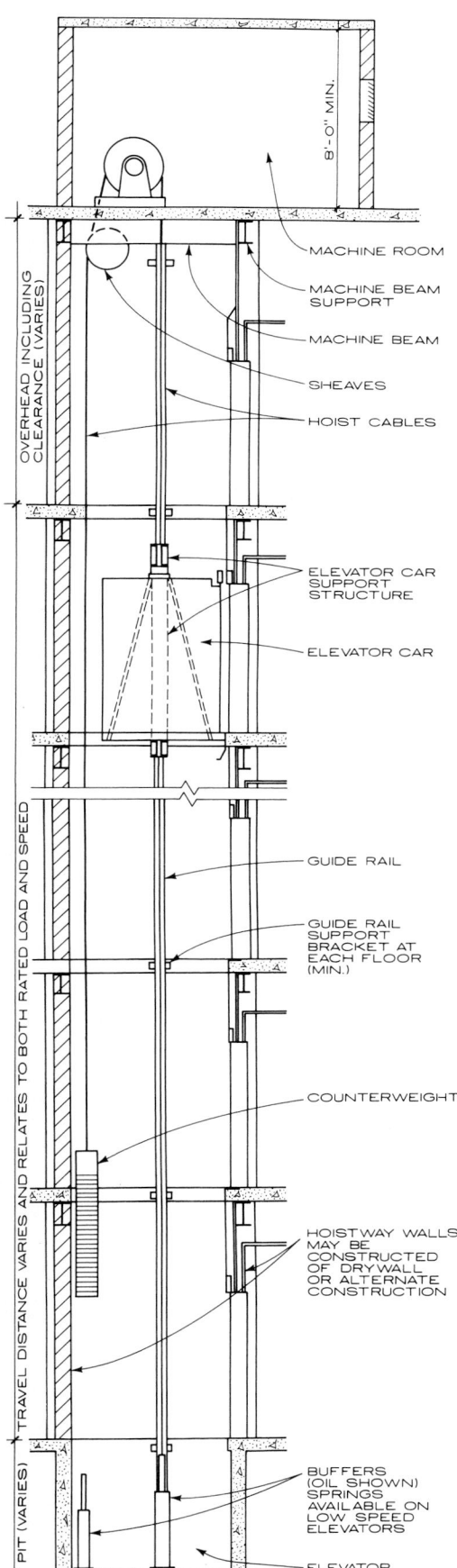

ELECTRIC ELEVATOR – SECTION

MACHINE ROOM (GEARLESS ELEVATOR)

ELECTRIC ELEVATOR DIMENSIONS

RATED LOAD (LB)	DIMENSIONS (FT-IN.)				
	A	B	C	D	E
2000	6-0	5-0	7-4	6-10	3-0
2500	7-0	5-0	8-4	6-7	3-6
3000	7-0	5-6	8-4	7-1	3-6
3500	7-0	6-2	8-4	7-7	3-6
4000	5-8	8-9	7-8	9-8	4-0

NOTES
Dimensions of preengineered units, listed above, are for reference purposes only. Elevator manufacturers or consultants should be consulted for a complete selection.

ELEVATOR HOISTWAY AND CAR – ELECTRIC ELEVATOR

NOTES

Medium and highrise buildings utilize ELECTRIC GEARED TRACTION and ELECTRIC GEARLESS TRACTION elevator systems. The main difference between the two systems lies in the hoisting machinery. General design considerations involving hoistway, machine room, and elevator planning are similar.

ELECTRIC GEARLESS TRACTION ELEVATOR systems are available in preengineered units with speeds of 500 to 1200 fpm. Systems with greater speeds are also available. Gearless elevators, when used in conjunction with appropriate electronic controls, offer the advantages of a long life and smoothness of ride.

ELECTRIC GEARED TRACTION ELEVATOR systems are designed to operate within the range of 100 to 350 fpm, which restricts their use to medium rise buildings.

Both geared and gearless drive units are governed by electronic CONTROLS, which coordinate car leveling, passenger calls, collective operation of elevators, door operation, car acceleration and deceleration, and safety applications. A broad range of control systems are available to meet individual building requirements.

STRUCTURAL REQUIREMENTS call for the total weight of the elevator system to be supported by the MACHINE BEAMS and transmitted to the building (or hoistway) structure. Consult with elevator consultants and structural engineers.

If the elevator machine is to be supported solely by the machine room floor slab, the floor slab shall be designed in accordance with the requirements of ANSI A17.1.

Check local codes for required fire enclosures.

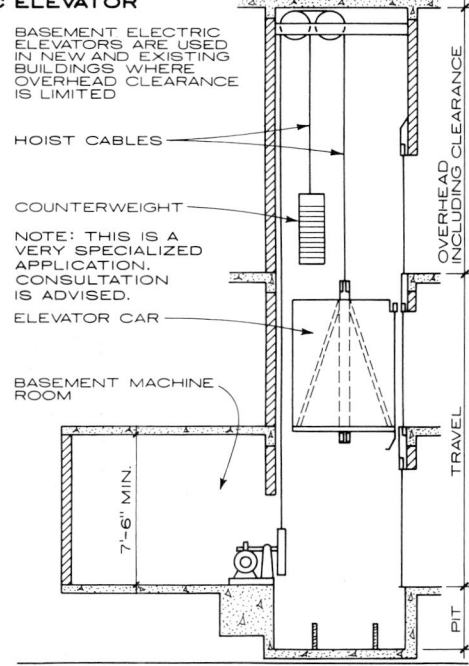

BASEMENT ELECTRIC ELEVATOR – SECTION

BASEMENT ELECTRIC ELEVATORS ARE USED IN NEW AND EXISTING BUILDINGS WHERE OVERHEAD CLEARANCE IS LIMITED

NOTE: THIS IS A VERY SPECIALIZED APPLICATION. CONSULTATION IS ADVISED.

Alexander Keyes; Darrel Downing Rippeteau, Architect; Washington, D.C.

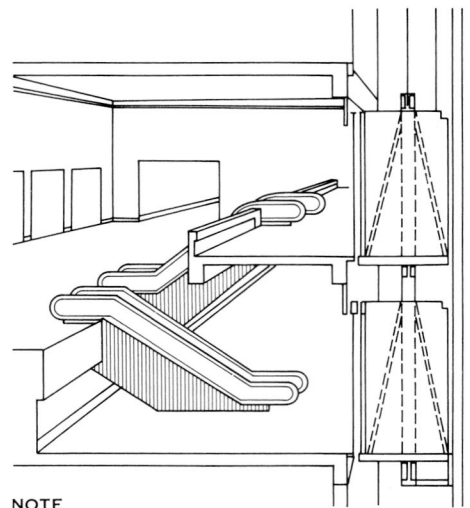

NOTE

In buildings with heavy populations double deck elevators permit an increase in handling capacity without increasing the number of elevators or hoistways. Two cars in tandem operate simultaneously, one serving all floors. Escalators connect the two floors in 2-story lobbies. This is a very specialized application. Consultation is advised.

DOUBLE DECK ELEVATOR

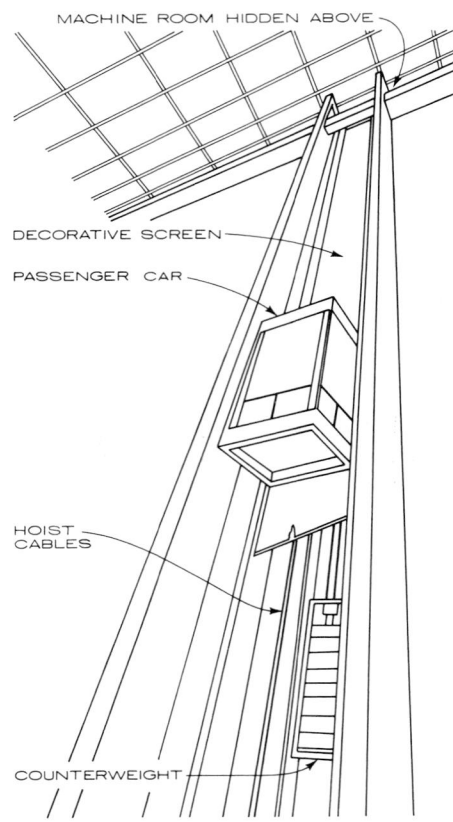

MACHINE ROOM HIDDEN ABOVE

DECORATIVE SCREEN

PASSENGER CAR

HOIST CABLES

COUNTERWEIGHT

NOTE

Observation and glassback elevators travel outside of a hoistway or in a hoistway open on one side. Machinery is concealed or designed to be inconspicuous. Elevators may be engineered for hydraulic, geared, or gearless use. Cabs can be custom designed with over 75% of wall area as glass. Glassback cabs provide glass rear panel only. Safety barriers must be provided at floor penetrations and ground floor, completely surrounding that part of elevator not enclosed by hoistway. This is a very specialized application. Consultation is advised.

OBSERVATION ELEVATOR

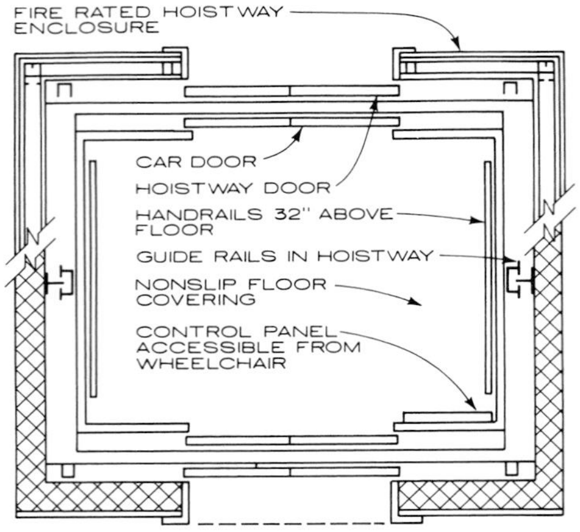

FIRE RATED HOISTWAY ENCLOSURE

CAR DOOR
HOISTWAY DOOR
HANDRAILS 32" ABOVE FLOOR
GUIDE RAILS IN HOISTWAY
NONSLIP FLOOR COVERING
CONTROL PANEL ACCESSIBLE FROM WHEELCHAIR

PLAN OF ELEVATOR CAR WITH REAR DOOR

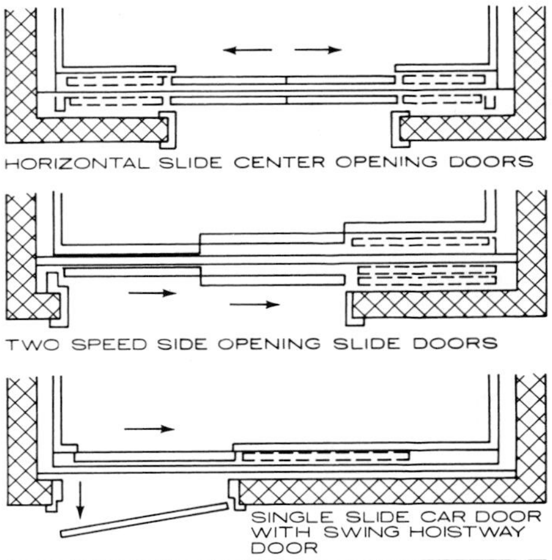

HORIZONTAL SLIDE CENTER OPENING DOORS

TWO SPEED SIDE OPENING SLIDE DOORS

SINGLE SLIDE CAR DOOR WITH SWING HOISTWAY DOOR

ELEVATOR DOOR TYPES

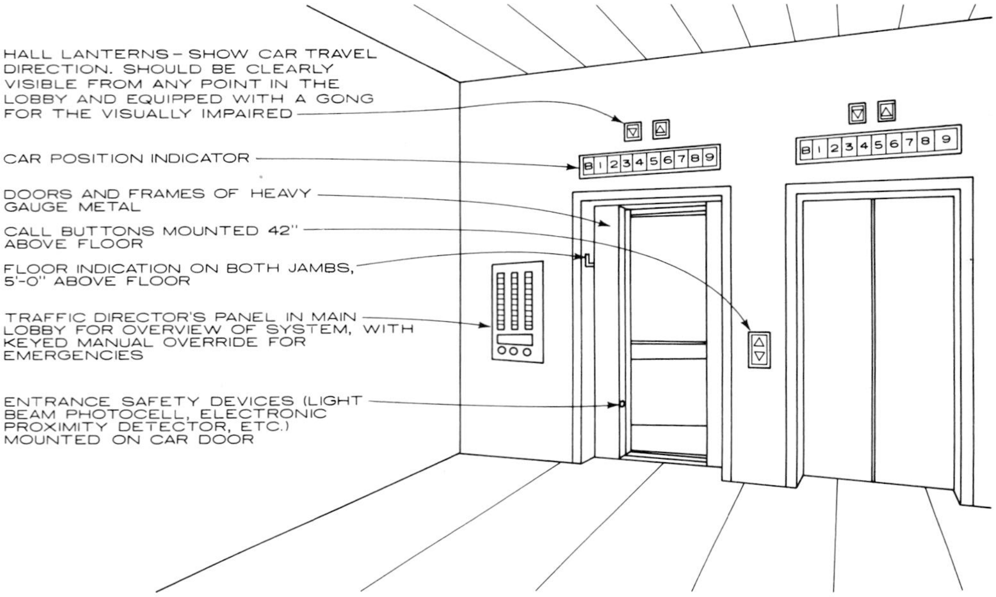

HALL LANTERNS – SHOW CAR TRAVEL DIRECTION. SHOULD BE CLEARLY VISIBLE FROM ANY POINT IN THE LOBBY AND EQUIPPED WITH A GONG FOR THE VISUALLY IMPAIRED

CAR POSITION INDICATOR

DOORS AND FRAMES OF HEAVY GAUGE METAL

CALL BUTTONS MOUNTED 42" ABOVE FLOOR

FLOOR INDICATION ON BOTH JAMBS, 5'-0" ABOVE FLOOR

TRAFFIC DIRECTOR'S PANEL IN MAIN LOBBY FOR OVERVIEW OF SYSTEM, WITH KEYED MANUAL OVERRIDE FOR EMERGENCIES

ENTRANCE SAFETY DEVICES (LIGHT BEAM PHOTOCELL, ELECTRONIC PROXIMITY DETECTOR, ETC.) MOUNTED ON CAR DOOR

ELEVATOR LOBBY

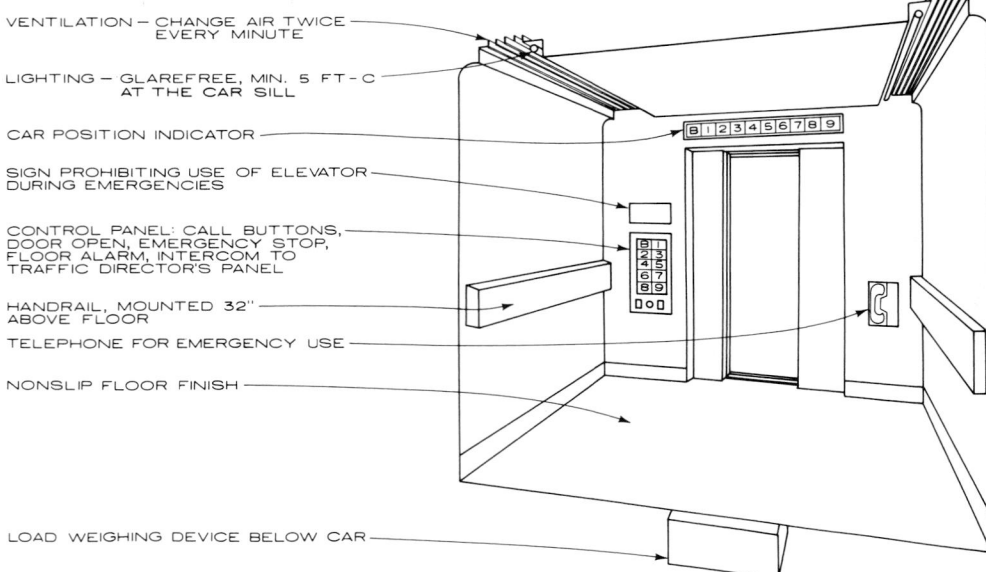

VENTILATION – CHANGE AIR TWICE EVERY MINUTE

LIGHTING – GLAREFREE, MIN. 5 FT-C AT THE CAR SILL

CAR POSITION INDICATOR

SIGN PROHIBITING USE OF ELEVATOR DURING EMERGENCIES

CONTROL PANEL: CALL BUTTONS, DOOR OPEN, EMERGENCY STOP, FLOOR ALARM, INTERCOM TO TRAFFIC DIRECTOR'S PANEL

HANDRAIL, MOUNTED 32" ABOVE FLOOR

TELEPHONE FOR EMERGENCY USE

NONSLIP FLOOR FINISH

LOAD WEIGHING DEVICE BELOW CAR

INTERIOR OF ELEVATOR CAR

Alexander Keyes; Darrel Downing Rippeteau, Architect; Washington, D.C.

GENERAL NOTES

Lowrise buildings may use either oil hydraulic or electric elevator systems. Elevator selection, arrangement, and design of lobby and cars are similar in both cases. The primary differences between the two systems are in their operational requirements. The hydraulic elevator system is described below; the electric elevator system on the next page.

The major architectural considerations of the hydraulic elevator are the machine room, normally located at the base, and the hoistway serving as a fire protected, ventilated passageway for the elevator car. Adequate structure must be provided at the base of the hoistway to bear the load of the elevator car and its supporting piston or cylinder.

Generally speaking, oil hydraulic elevators are used in applications requiring limited vertical travel usage and low speed.

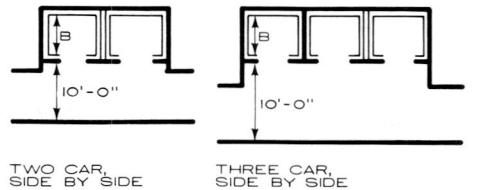

TWO CAR, SIDE BY SIDE

THREE CAR, SIDE BY SIDE

B = DEPTH OF CAR

NOTES

Certain guidelines lead to effective placement, grouping, and arrangement of elevators within a building. Elevators should be: (a) centrally located, (b) near the main entrance, and (c) easily accessible on all floors. If a building requires more than one elevator, they should be grouped, with possible exception of service elevators.

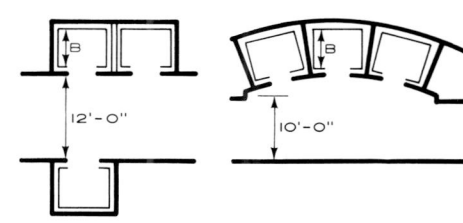

TWO OR THREE CAR, OPPOSITE

THREE CAR, SPECIAL ARRANGEMENT

Within each grouping, elevators should be arranged to minimize walking distance between cars. Sufficient lobby space must be provided to accommodate group movement. Elevators may not open into a corridor.

ELEVATOR ARRANGEMENT, TWO AND THREE CARS (TYPICAL FOR LOWRISE APPLICATIONS)

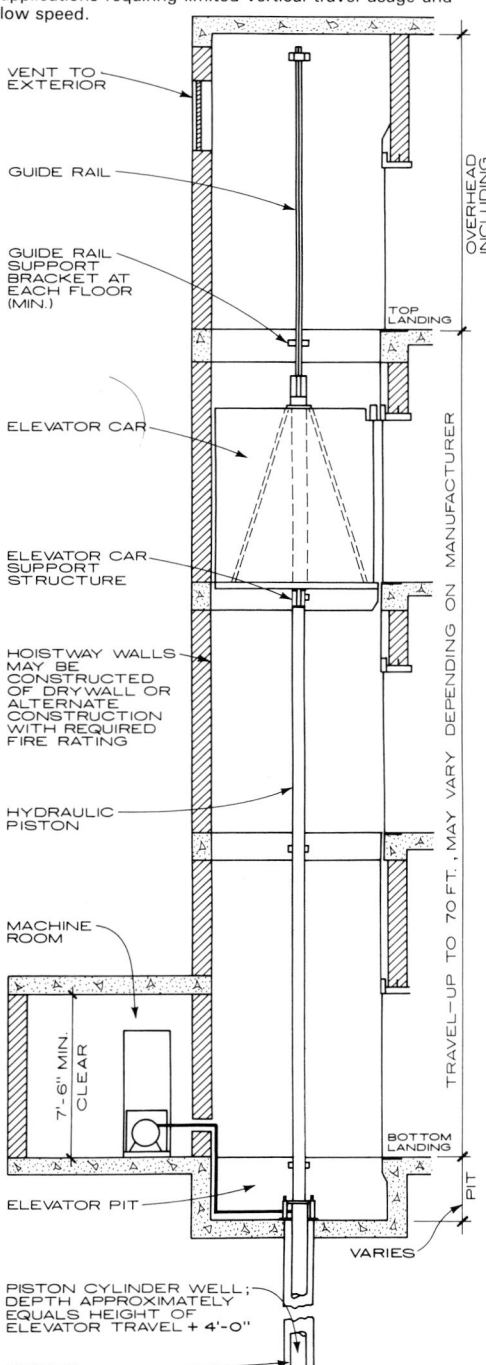

VENT TO EXTERIOR

GUIDE RAIL

GUIDE RAIL SUPPORT BRACKET AT EACH FLOOR (MIN.)

ELEVATOR CAR

ELEVATOR CAR SUPPORT STRUCTURE

HOISTWAY WALLS MAY BE CONSTRUCTED OF DRYWALL OR ALTERNATE CONSTRUCTION WITH REQUIRED FIRE RATING

HYDRAULIC PISTON

MACHINE ROOM

7'-6" MIN. CLEAR

ELEVATOR PIT

PISTON CYLINDER WELL; DEPTH APPROXIMATELY EQUALS HEIGHT OF ELEVATOR TRAVEL + 4'-0"

CASING

OVERHEAD INCLUDING CLEARANCE

TOP LANDING

TRAVEL—UP TO 70 FT., MAY VARY DEPENDING ON MANUFACTURER

BOTTOM LANDING

PIT

VARIES

HYDRAULIC ELEVATOR – SECTION

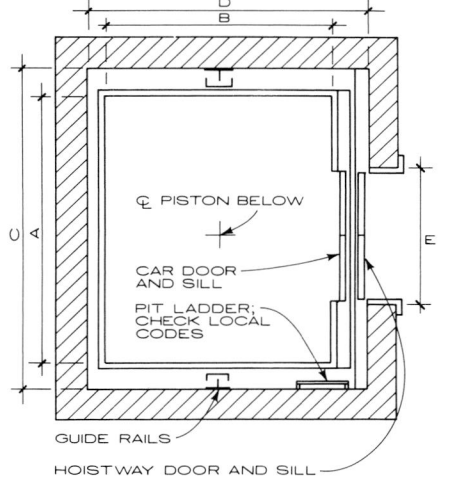

Ċ PISTON BELOW

CAR DOOR AND SILL

PIT LADDER; CHECK LOCAL CODES

GUIDE RAILS

HOISTWAY DOOR AND SILL

ELEVATOR CAR AND HOISTWAY

HYDRAULIC ELEVATOR DIMENSIONS

RATED LOAD (LB)	DIMENSIONS (FT·IN.)				
	A	B	C	D	E
1500	4-10	5-0	6-8	5-9	2-8
2000	6-0	5-0	7-4	5-9	3-0
2500	7-0	5-0	8-4	5-9	3-6
3000	7-0	5-6	8-4	6-3	3-6
3500	7-0	6-2	8-4	6-11	3-6
4000	6-0	6-0	7-4	9-8	4-0

Rated speeds are 75 to 125 fpm.

NOTES

Elevator car and hoistway dimensions of the preengineered units listed above are for reference purposes only. A broad selection of units is available. Representatives of the elevator industry should be contacted for the dimensions of specific systems.

Hoistway walls normally serve primarily as fireproof enclosures. Check local codes for required fire ratings. Guide rails extend from the pit floor to the underside of the overhead. When excessive floor heights are encountered consult the elevator supplier for special requirements.

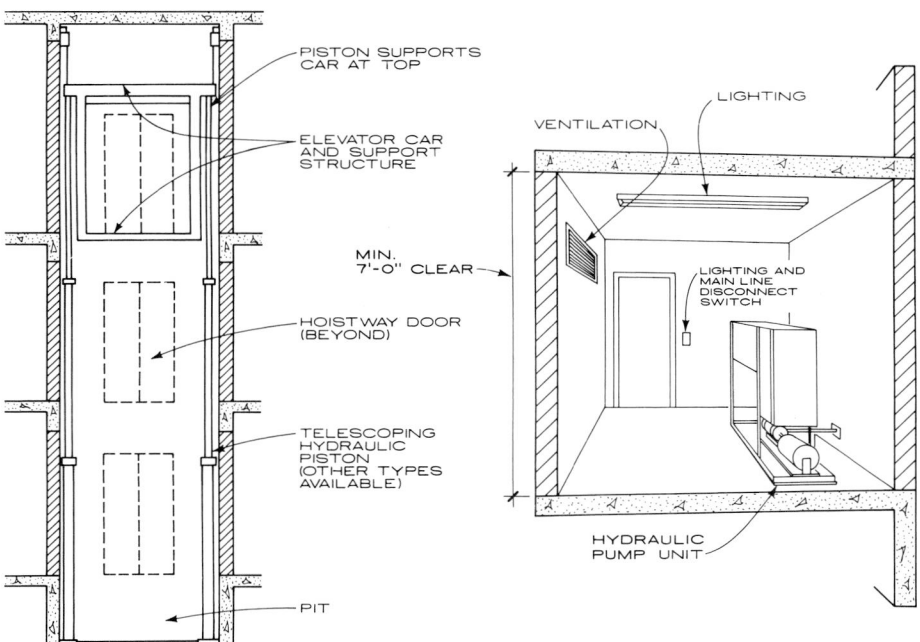

PISTON SUPPORTS CAR AT TOP

ELEVATOR CAR AND SUPPORT STRUCTURE

HOISTWAY DOOR (BEYOND)

TELESCOPING HYDRAULIC PISTON (OTHER TYPES AVAILABLE)

PIT

MIN. 7'-0" CLEAR

VENTILATION

LIGHTING

LIGHTING AND MAIN LINE DISCONNECT SWITCH

HYDRAULIC PUMP UNIT

One type of holeless hydraulic elevator uses a telescoping hydraulic piston as the lifting device, eliminating the need for cylinder well excavation. This system is presently limited to a height of three stories or 21 ft 6 in. Other types of holeless hydraulic elevator units are also available using an inverted cylinder attached to the side of the elevator car.

HOLELESS HYDRAULIC ELEVATOR – SECTION

The MACHINE ROOM of a hydraulic elevator system is usually located next to the hoistway at or near the bottom terminal landing. Consult with elevator manufacturers for required dimensions. Refer to local codes.

Machinery consists of a pump and motor drive unit, hydraulic fluid storage tank, and electronic control panel. Adequate ventilation, lighting, and entrance access (usually 3 ft 6 in. x 7 ft) should be provided.

MACHINE ROOM

Alexander Keyes; Darrel Downing Rippeteau, Architect; Washington, D.C.

GENERAL

Escalators are a very efficient form of vertical transportation for very heavy traffic where the number of floors served is limited, normally a maximum of five to six floors. Escalators are not usually accepted as a required exit.

Dimensions shown are general and will vary somewhat with the manufacturer. Consult manufacturers for structural support, electrical supply, and specific dimensional requirements.

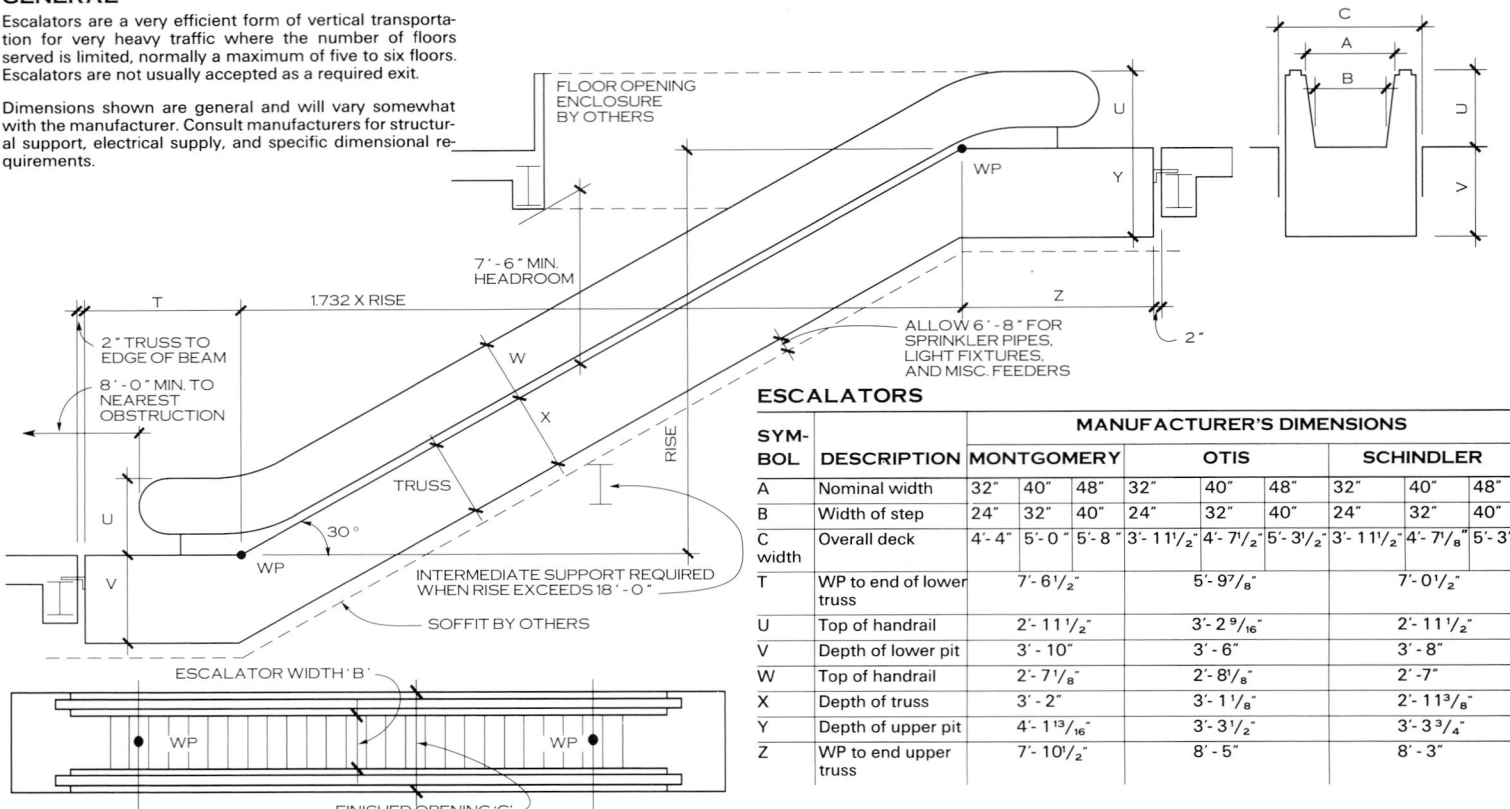

ESCALATORS

SYM-BOL	DESCRIPTION	MANUFACTURER'S DIMENSIONS								
		MONTGOMERY			OTIS			SCHINDLER		
A	Nominal width	32"	40"	48"	32"	40"	48"	32"	40"	48"
B	Width of step	24"	32"	40"	24"	32"	40"	24"	32"	40"
C width	Overall deck	4'-4"	5'-0"	5'-8"	3'-11½"	4'-7½"	5'-3½"	3'-11½"	4'-7⅛"	5'-3"
T	WP to end of lower truss	7'-6½"			5'-9⅞"			7'-0½"		
U	Top of handrail	2'-11½"			3'-2 9/16"			2'-11½"		
V	Depth of lower pit	3'-10"			3'-6"			3'-8"		
W	Top of handrail	2'-7⅛"			2'-8⅛"			2'-7"		
X	Depth of truss	3'-2"			3'-1⅛"			2'-11⅜"		
Y	Depth of upper pit	4'-1 13/16"			3'-3½"			3'-3¾"		
Z	WP to end upper truss	7'-10½"			8'-5"			8'-3"		

ESCALATOR PROFILE

Moving passenger conveyors are particularly useful in transportation terminals, sports arenas, and exposition centers where large numbers of people must move long distances horizontally. The conveyors may be arranged in any combination of horizontal runs and inclines with a practical maximum of 12°.

It is generally not economical to provide moving sidewalks for distances less than 100 ft; for distances greater than 300 ft they invoke passenger frustration by their slow operating speed. Narrower units (26 in.) accommodate one adult; 40 in. widths allow for both walking and standing passengers.

MOVING PASSENGER CONVEYORS

SYM-BOL	DESCRIPTION	MANUFACTURER'S DIMENSIONS						
		MONTGOMERY			OTIS		SCHINDLER	
A	Nominal width	32"	37"	40"	40"	48"	32"	48"
B	Width of walk	24"	32"	40"	32"	40"	26"	40"
C	Overall deck width	4'-4"	5'-0"	5'-8"	4'-7 9/16"	5'-3 9/16"	4'-4½"	5'-8½"
W	Top of handrail		2'-11 7/16"		3'-2⅝"		2'-11 7/16"	
X	Depth of truss		3'-10"		3'-5⅜"		3'-6½"	
Y	Length of pit		18'-10"		18'-0"		18'-10"	
Z	Maximum depth of truss		13"		17¾"		3'-4 7/16"	

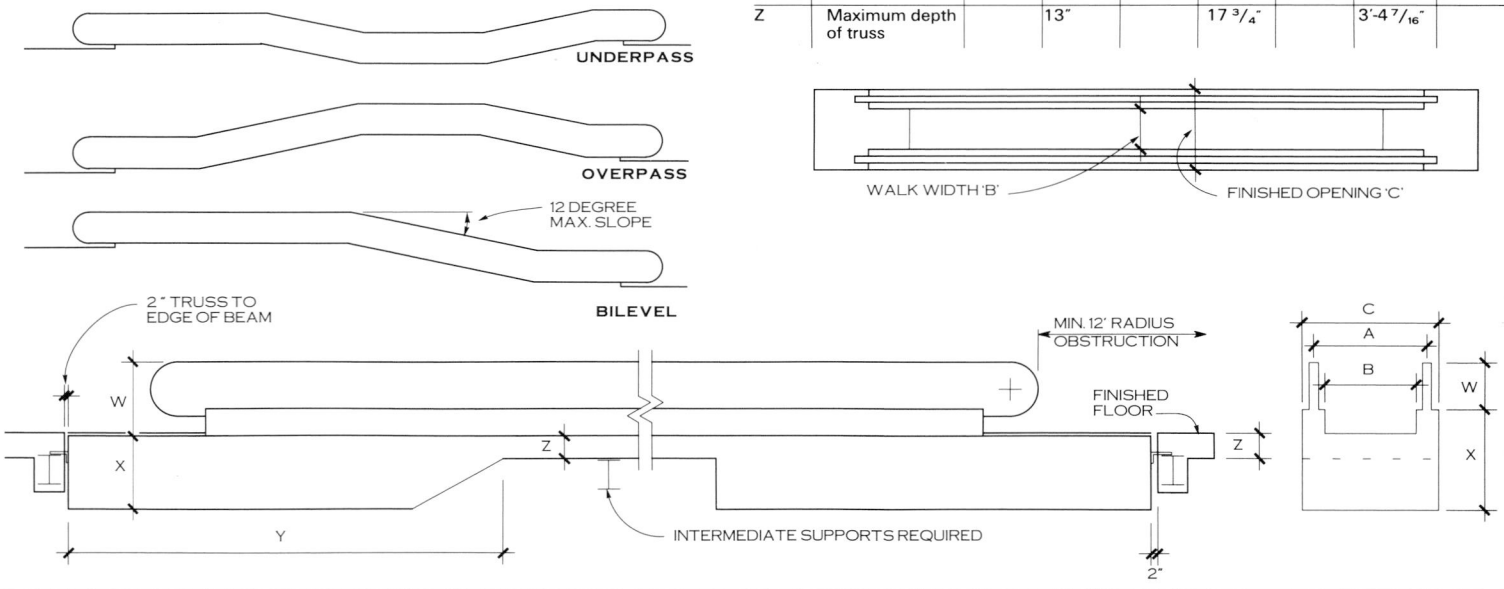

PASSENGER CONVEYOR PROFILE

Alan H. Rider, AIA; Daniel, Mann, Johnson, & Mendenhall; Washington, D.C.

14 **ESCALATORS AND MOVING WALKS**

VERTICAL PALLET LIFT

Used to transport loads from level to level within a conveyor system or for manually loading/unloading at each level. Typically used where basement or second floor serves for storage of reserve or overstock.

Capacity: up to 6000 lb; lift height: up to 20 ft; platform sizes: 13 x 15 to 48 x 72 in.

Lift speed: 20 fpm; installation: floor to floor, with platform either flush with or above floor, depending on loading/unloading technique.

CIRCULAR CONVEYOR LIFT

Used to transport cartons between operating levels and between work stations within a level. Useful where vertical distance is great while horizontal distance is limited.

Lift height: 45 to 144 in. vertical lift per 360° unit. Lift height is relative to radius of unit. Load sizes: width—6 to 48 in.; length—relative to width and radius of conveyor.

Installation: dependent on height of feed and exit conveyors. System requires shaft through floor of O.D. of conveyor plus 12 in.

90° VERTICAL PALLET LIFT

Used to transport unit loads between operating levels in multiple level or multiple floor buildings. Typically used where vertical lift is great and a continuous conveyor system serves in loading/unloading the lift.

Capacity: up to 6000 lb; lift height: up to 80 ft; load sizes: typically 48 x 40 x 72 in.; however, other sizes can be specified; lift speed: 60 fpm; installation: typically installed floor to floor, with shaft through each floor.

NOTE

Lifts presented show various types with data and nomenclature to illustrate systems and equipment available to move loads vertically. Specific sizes and capacity should be obtained from lift manufacturers.

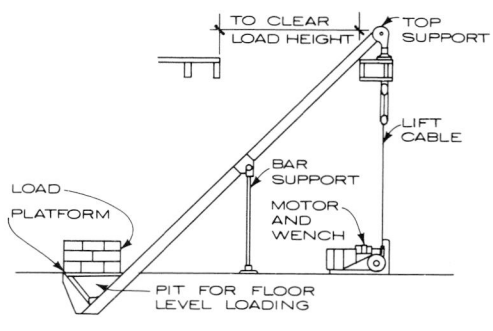

VERTICAL PALLET LIFT

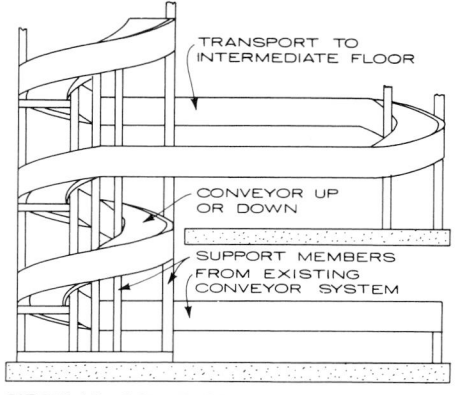

CIRCULAR CONVEYOR LIFT

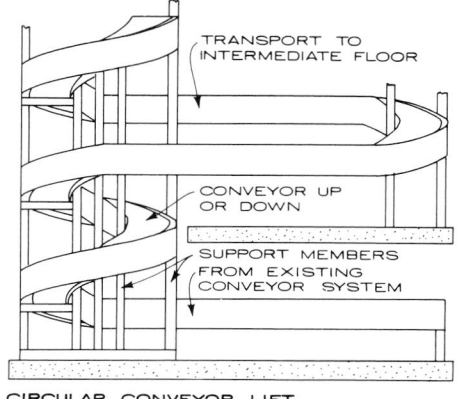

90° VERTICAL PALLET LIFT

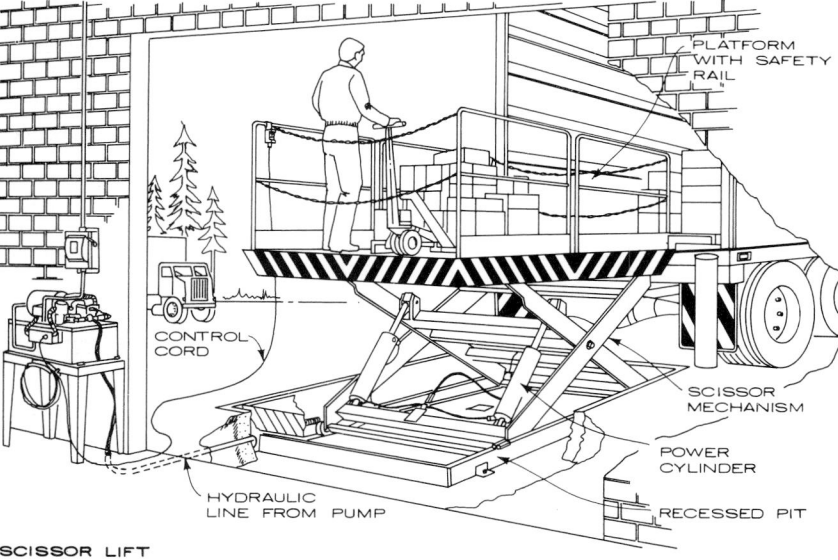

SCISSOR LIFT

MISCELLANEOUS LIFTS

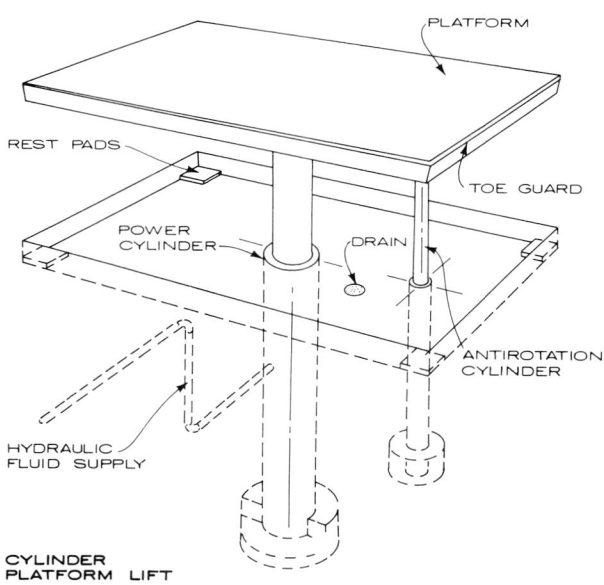

CYLINDER PLATFORM LIFT

SCISSOR LIFT

Used to raise/lower unit loads to delivery vehicles from ground or floor levels that do not align with vehicles.

Load capacity: 2500 to 30,000 lb; lifting height: up to 12 ft; platform sizes: typically 5 x 7 ft to 8 x 12 ft, but other sizes can be specified; lift rate: cycle rate is manually controlled by loading/unloading rate. Up cycle of lift ranges from 40 to 100 sec depending on lift size.

Installation: lifts available in permanent pit installation or portable aboveground units. Limiting factor on installation is electric power source for hydraulic pump and reservoir.

CYLINDER PLATFORM LIFT

Used to move unitized loads from floor or ground to delivery vehicle level to facilitate loading/unloading operations. Used also for machine loading/unloading of heavy/bulky materials.

Load capacity: 2000 to 30,000 lb; lifting height: up to 5 ft; platform sizes: typically 5 x 5 ft to 8 x 15 ft, but other sizes can be specified.

Lift rate: cycle rate is manually controlled by loading/unloading rate. Up cycle of lift ranges up to 12 fpm. Installation: pit used to facilitate platform flush with floor or ground for loading/unloading. Cylinder shaft is centered under platform with antirotational shaft at one end. Both shafts recessed into ground.

St. Onge, Ruff & Associates; York, Pennsylvania

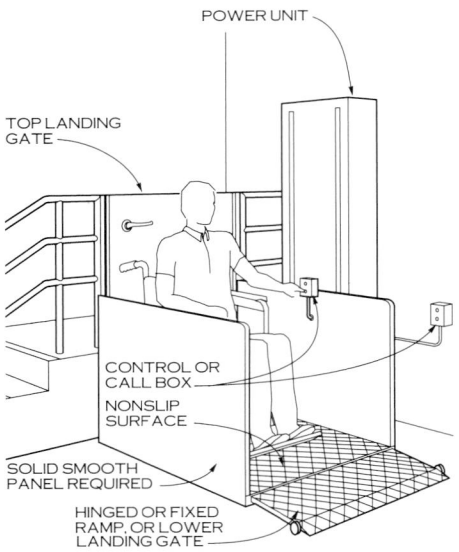

OVERALL VIEW – WHEELCHAIR LIFT

POWER UNIT

TOP LANDING GATE

CONTROL OR CALL BOX

NONSLIP SURFACE

SOLID SMOOTH PANEL REQUIRED

HINGED OR FIXED RAMP, OR LOWER LANDING GATE

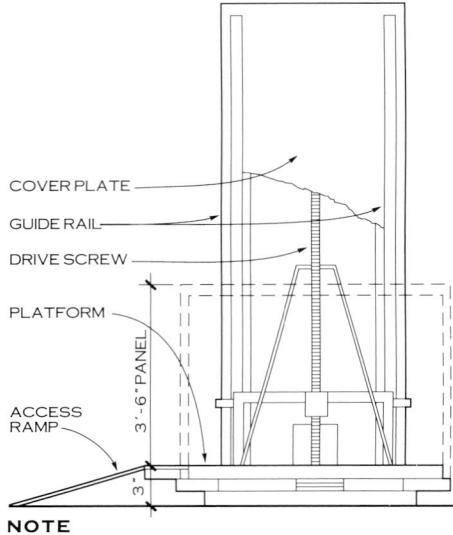

COVER PLATE
GUIDE RAIL
DRIVE SCREW

PLATFORM

3'-6" PANEL

ACCESS RAMP

3'

NOTE

Screw driven lift platform is lifted along a threaded rod, which is rotated by the power unit.

CUT-AWAY SECTION

POWER UNIT
CONTROL BOX
HINGED RAMP

3'-0" (TYP.)

NONSLIP PLATFORM AND RAMP

GATE
18"   4'-0" (TYP.)
RAIL
LANDING

TYPICAL PLAN

WHEELCHAIR LIFT

Eric K. Beach; Rippeteau Architects, PC; Washington, D.C.

GENERAL

Wheelchair lifts are suitable for retrofits of buildings that are not barrier free. Bridges are available from manufacturers for installation over stairs. Recommended speed: 10 to 19 fpm. Capacity: 500 to 750 lb.

Lifts operate on standard household current and are suitable for interior or exterior applications.

WHEELCHAIR LIFT REQUIREMENTS

TYPICAL ANSI A17.1, SEC. 2000.1B	PRIVATE RESIDENCE ANSI A17.1, SEC. 2100.1
42 in. door for top and bottom landings, mechanical/electrical interlock, solid construction	36 in. door for top landing; bottom landing can have guard (other requirements similar to 42 in. door)
Platform sides: 42 in. solid construction	Platform 36 in. solid construction
Grab rails	Same
Enclosure or telescoping toe guard	Obstruction switch on platform
Maximum travel 12 ft	Maximum travel 10 ft
	Automatic guard 6 in. at bottom landing in lieu of door
Key operation	Key operation

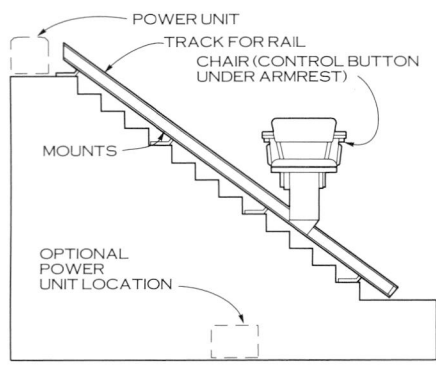

POWER UNIT
TRACK FOR RAIL
CHAIR (CONTROL BUTTON UNDER ARMREST)

MOUNTS

OPTIONAL POWER UNIT LOCATION

NOTE

Chair lift power unit may also be located in chair chassis. Chair lift's compact size may make this lift type more feasible than others for residential use.

CHAIR LIFT – SECTION

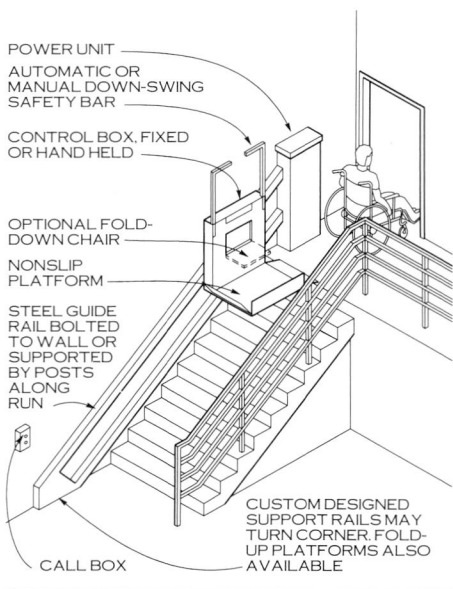

POWER UNIT
AUTOMATIC OR MANUAL DOWN-SWING SAFETY BAR
CONTROL BOX, FIXED OR HAND HELD
OPTIONAL FOLD-DOWN CHAIR
NONSLIP PLATFORM
STEEL GUIDE RAIL BOLTED TO WALL OR SUPPORTED BY POSTS ALONG RUN
CALL BOX
CUSTOM DESIGNED SUPPORT RAILS MAY TURN CORNER. FOLD-UP PLATFORMS ALSO AVAILABLE

STAIR LIFT OR PLATFORM (STRAIGHT RUN)

Inclined stair lifts can be adapted to straight run and spiral stairs. Standard types run along guide rails or tubes fastened to solid wall, stairs, or floor structure. Power units may be placed at the top or bottom of the lift run or in the lift chassis, depending on the manufacturer. Some inclined lift systems fold up out of the way for daily stair use.

Where stair width necessitates a more compact lift, as in residential use, chair lifts are available for straight run or spiral stairs. However, many inclined stair lifts come with standard fold-down seats.

Recommended speed, 20 to 25 fpm on straight runs, 10 fpm on curved sections. Capacity, 500 lb. Typical platform size, 30 x 40 in. Check local code capacities.

INCLINED WHEELCHAIR LIFT REQUIREMENTS

TYPICAL RESIDENCE ANSI A17.1, SEC. 2001	PRIVATE ANSI A17.1, SEC.2100
42 in. self-closing door: solid construction, mechanical/ electrical interlock, lower landing	36 in. self-closing door: solid construction, mechanical/electrical interlock, upper landing
42 in. platform side guard: not used as exit, solid construction	36 in. platform side guard: not used as exit, solid construction
6 in. guard: permitted in lieu of side guard	6 in. guard: permitted in lieu of side guard
6 in. retractable guard: to prevent wheelchair rolling off platform	6 in. retractable guard: to prevent wheelchair rolling off platform
Door required at bottom landing	Underside obstruction switch bottom landing
Travel 3 floors max.	Travel 3 floors max.
Key operation; attendant operation is push button	Key operation: attendant operation is push button and requires door at bottom landing

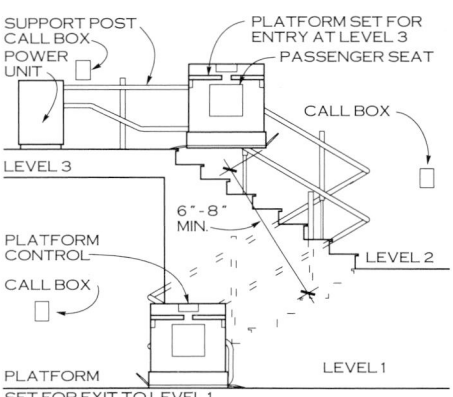

SUPPORT POST
CALL BOX
POWER UNIT

PLATFORM SET FOR ENTRY AT LEVEL 3
PASSENGER SEAT

CALL BOX

LEVEL 3

6"-8" MIN.

PLATFORM CONTROL

CALL BOX

LEVEL 2

LEVEL 1

PLATFORM SET FOR EXIT TO LEVEL 1

STAIR LIFT OR PLATFORM SECTION

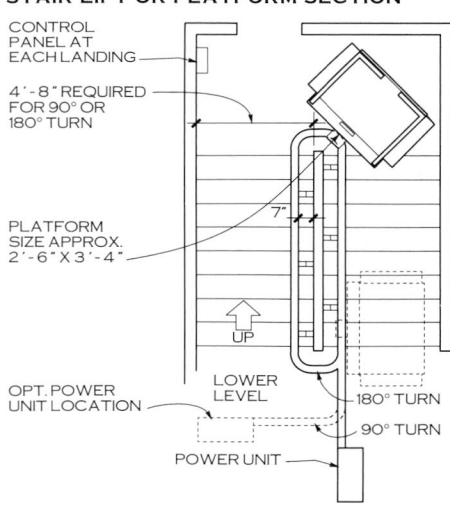

CONTROL PANEL AT EACH LANDING

4'-8" REQUIRED FOR 90° OR 180° TURN

PLATFORM SIZE APPROX. 2'-6" X 3'-4"

7"

UP

PLATFORM

LOWER LEVEL

OPT. POWER UNIT LOCATION

180° TURN
90° TURN

POWER UNIT

STAIR LIFT CHAIR OR PLATFORM PLAN WITH TURNS

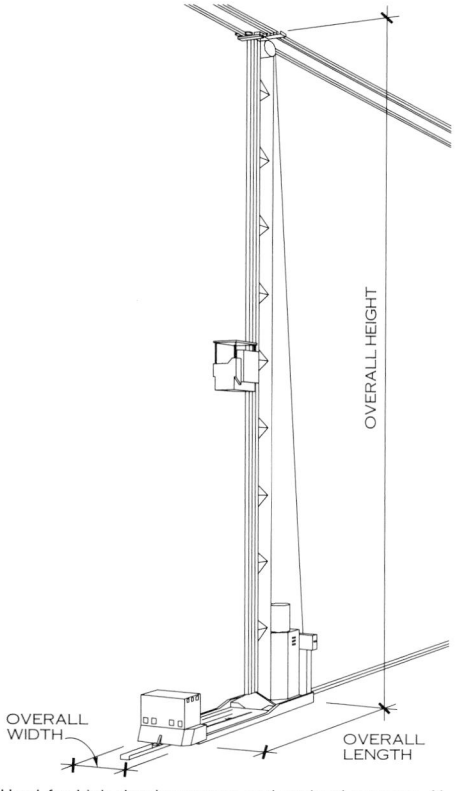

Used for high density storage and retrieval systems. Allows high lift capacity while operating in a narrow aisle. Can be used in numerous aisles unlike dedicated stacker cranes.

HYBRID VEHICLE

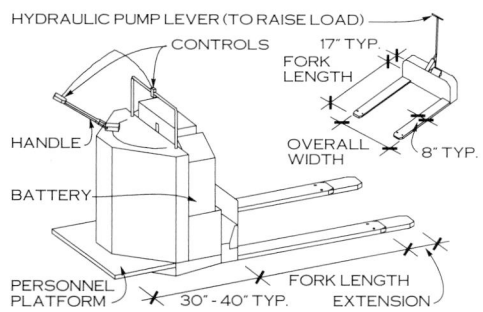

Used to transport unitized loads when stacking of loads is not necessary. Ideal for dock work and production areas.

HAND PALLET TRUCK

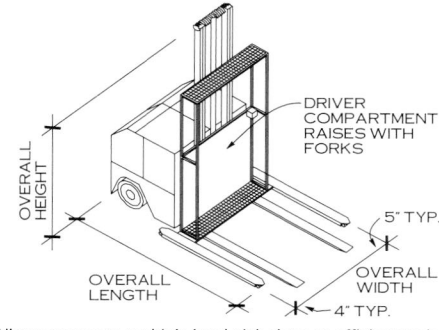

Narrow aisle operations without limiting pallet sizes and rack openings.

REACH TRUCK

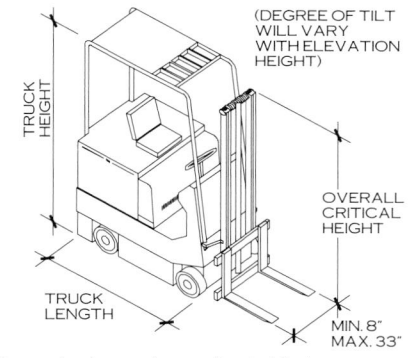

Allows access to multiple level pick slots; an efficient technique with a large item base that has limited space for selection line.

ORDER PICKER TRUCK

Ideal for moving large volumes of material where maneuvering area is not limited.

COUNTERBALANCE TRUCK

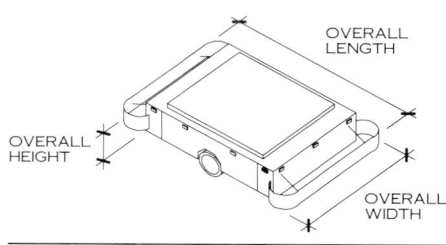

Allows narrow aisle operations. Forks can rotate 180° which allows access to both sides of the aisle without turning the truck around.

TURRET TRUCK

AUTOMATIC GUIDED VEHICLES (AGV)

NOTE

These vehicles are used throughout industry for transporting product from point to point with repeatable accuracy. They are totally automatic and require little or no human interface. The AGV follows a guidepath on the floor or can be radio controlled. The relatively low cost of changing or adding a guidepath makes the AGV a flexible system.

AGV's are controlled by a computer and are powered by industrial batteries.

AGV - DIMENSIONS AND CAPABILITIES

Load capacity	Up to 93,000 lbs
Lift height	Up to 15' - 7"
Turning radius	2' - 0" to 18' - 0"
Weight with battery	2000 to 22,000 lbs
Overall length	6' - 1" to 34' - 4"
Overall width	3' - 6" to 9' - 4"
Overall height	12 1/2" to 7' - 6"
Fork length	Up to 5' - 0"
Travel speeds	Up to 200 FPM

NOTE

Data and figures given are general specifications. AGV's are designed for specific tasks with dimensions and capabilities varying from application to application. Please consult the AGV manufacturer or material handling engineer for specific data.

FORKLIFTS - DIMENSION AND CAPACITIES

	REACH TRUCK	COUNTERBALANCE TRUCK	ORDER PICKER TRUCK	TURRET TRUCK	HYBRID TRUCK	ELECTRIC PALLET TRUCK	HAND JACK
Load capacity (lb)	2000 to 7000	2000 to 15,000	1500 to 3000	3000 to 4000	3900	1500 to 6000	2000 to 6500
Maximum lift height	33' - 3"	22' - 0"	30' - 0"	to 40' - 0"	65' - 6"	6" to 7"	4" to 7 3/4"
Right angle stacking aisle requirement	6' - 0" to 10' - 0"	10' - 4" to 14' - 2"		5' - 7" to 6' - 1"	4' - 6" to 5' - 4"	Truck length plus 3' - 0"	Truck length plus 3' - 0"
Truck weight without load (lb)	4,000 to 8,000	5,400 to 22,000	5,700 to 9,500	7,000 to 15,000		1,000 to 2,000	250 to 300
Overall truck width	3' - 1" to 5' - 4"	2' - 11" to 4' - 10"	3' - 10" to 5' - 10"	4' - 10" to 7' - 1"	4' - 0 5/8"	2' - 7" to 3' - 2"	1' - 6" to 2' - 6"
Overall truck height	6' - 0" to 11' - 8"	5' - 8" to 7' - 6"	7' - 1" to 12' - 4"	7' - 6" to 22' - 6"	70' - 8"	4' - 0" to 5' - 0"	4' - 0"
Overall truck length without load	5' - 2" to 6' - 0"	5' - 6" to 9' - 7"	7' - 4" to 10' - 6"	11' - 3" to 12' - 2"	16' - 9"	5' - 7" to 9' - 7"	3' - 9" to 7' - 5"
Fork length	2' - 6" to 4' - 0"	2' - 6" to 4' - 0"	3' - 0" to 8' - 0"	2' - 6" to 4' - 0"	43"	2' - 6" to 7' - 0"	2' - 0" to 6' - 0"
Ramp slope	15 to 23%	10 to 37%	3 to 16%			Up to 10%	Manually operated

NOTE

Data and figures given here represent the ranges of general specification available on forklift trucks. Aisle width is controlled by type of forklift and pallet size used in a warehouse. Specific data and applications should be obtained from material handling engineers. The trucks presented are electrically powered (excluding the hand jack) using industrial batteries as a source of energy. Industrial batteries typically must be charged after each 8-hr shift. Two batteries per truck are typical to allow back-to-back shift operation. The charging operation should take place in an area segregated from the warehouse or production area and must be designed to meet the various OSHA requirements.

St. Onge, Ruff & Associates; York, Pennsylvania
Richard J. Vitullo, AIA; Oakleaf Studio; Crownsville, Maryland

GENERAL

Pneumatic tube systems can convey materials or information that cannot be sent electronically. These systems, most notably compressed air pneumatic tube systems, were first used in the late 19th century for information and product transportation, particularly by insurance companies who needed and could finance a faster flow of information.

Today most information is transmitted more efficiently by facsimile machines or computer technology. However, some businesses must transport physical materials and need the convenience, speed, and security of tube systems in place of electronic or manual delivery. Banks, for example, use pneumatic tube systems in their drive-through services. Hospitals also use such systems for delivering drugs, blood samples, linen, medical records, and the like. They depend on fast and efficient transport, a prime characteristic of these systems.

Other industries, such as post offices, auto parts handlers, etc., may need to move larger materials or quantities. Conveyance systems, including container carriage and electric track vehicle systems, are effective for horizontal and/or vertical service. Courthouses and jails frequently use these systems to transport personal effects, files, mail, and records securely and quickly.

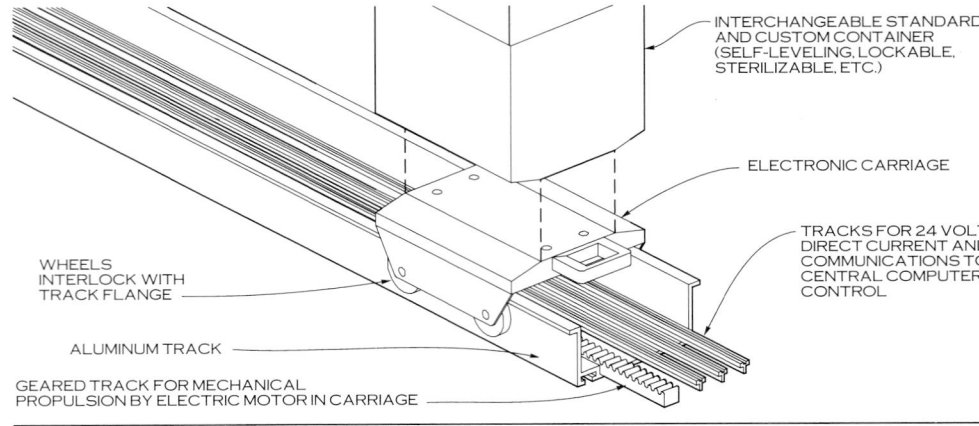

INTERCHANGEABLE STANDARD AND CUSTOM CONTAINER (SELF-LEVELING, LOCKABLE, STERILIZABLE, ETC.)

ELECTRONIC CARRIAGE

TRACKS FOR 24 VOLT DIRECT CURRENT AND COMMUNICATIONS TO CENTRAL COMPUTER CONTROL

WHEELS INTERLOCK WITH TRACK FLANGE

ALUMINUM TRACK

GEARED TRACK FOR MECHANICAL PROPULSION BY ELECTRIC MOTOR IN CARRIAGE

ELECTRIC TRACK VEHICLE SYSTEM

NOTE

The electric track vehicle system is most effective for horizontal movement of payloads up to 50 lb. However, travel may be both horizontal and vertical by employing wheels that lock onto the tracks so that the carriage can ride in an upright, vertical, or inverted position. The system, controlled by a central computer, can be designed to handle point-to-point or loop travel and can stop at many stations.

Fire doors are needed for passage through fire-rated walls. Consult fire codes and manufacturer for specific requirements.

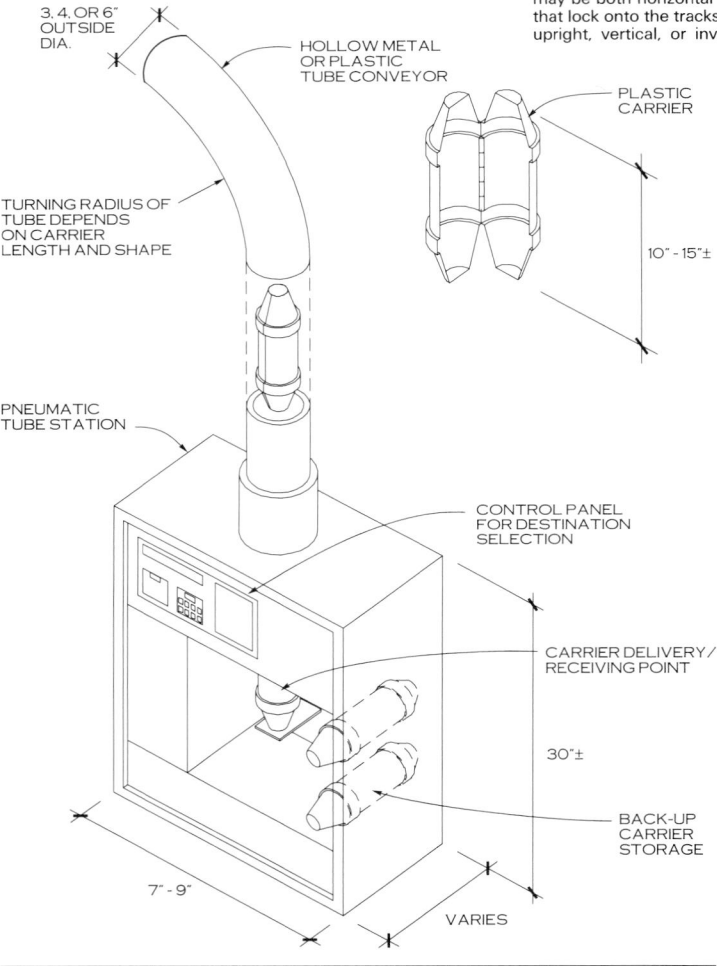

3, 4, OR 6" OUTSIDE DIA.

HOLLOW METAL OR PLASTIC TUBE CONVEYOR

PLASTIC CARRIER

TURNING RADIUS OF TUBE DEPENDS ON CARRIER LENGTH AND SHAPE

10" - 15"±

PNEUMATIC TUBE STATION

CONTROL PANEL FOR DESTINATION SELECTION

CARRIER DELIVERY/ RECEIVING POINT

30"±

BACK-UP CARRIER STORAGE

7" - 9"

VARIES

PNEUMATIC TUBE SYSTEM

NOTE

The pneumatic tube system is effective for both horizontal and/or vertical transport of materials. It allows speeds up to 25 ft per second with payloads up to 15 lb. Materials, placed in a cylindrical carrier, are conveyed by air pressure in hollow tubes. The pressure differential is created by a blower which propels the carrier at a controlled speed. Blowers can be installed at the the tube station or at a remote location. Incoming carriers are slowed upon reaching the destination tube station.

Systems can be designed for two stations or multiple stations grouped into zones. Carriers can be sent and tracked by a computer. In zone systems, carriers are sent by one tube through a long run, then distributed to individual stations at a transfer station. Extra blower units may be required, depending on system length and configuration. Consult manufacturer for specific installation requirements.

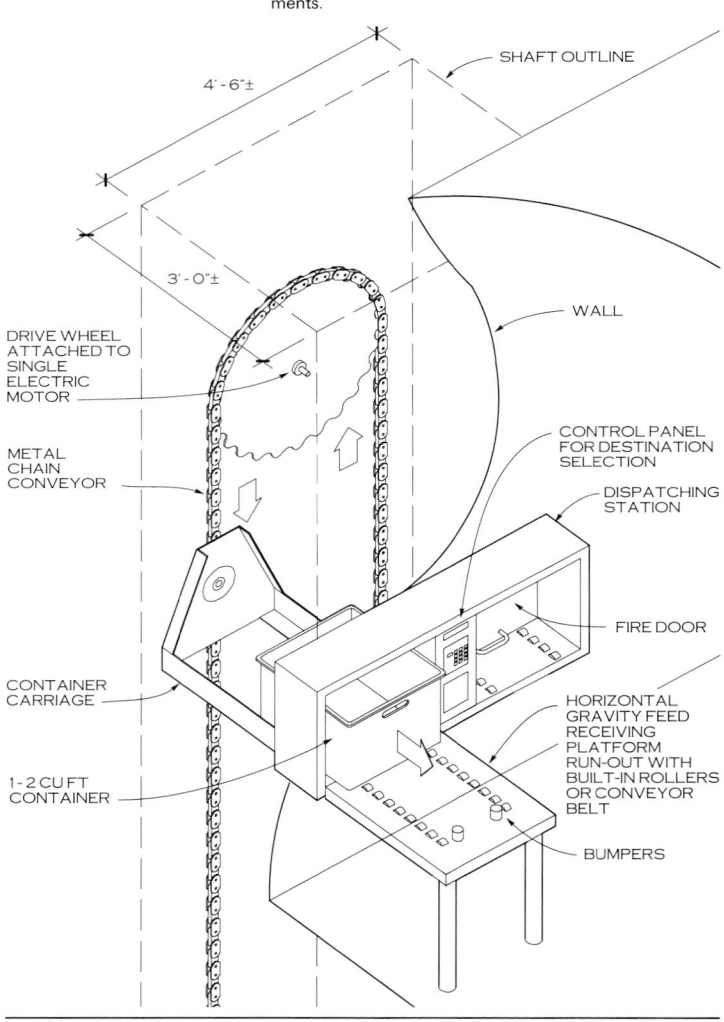

SHAFT OUTLINE

4' - 6"±

3' - 0"±

DRIVE WHEEL ATTACHED TO SINGLE ELECTRIC MOTOR

WALL

METAL CHAIN CONVEYOR

CONTROL PANEL FOR DESTINATION SELECTION

DISPATCHING STATION

FIRE DOOR

CONTAINER CARRIAGE

1 - 2 CU FT CONTAINER

HORIZONTAL GRAVITY FEED RECEIVING PLATFORM RUN-OUT WITH BUILT-IN ROLLERS OR CONVEYOR BELT

BUMPERS

CONTAINER CARRIAGE SYSTEM

NOTE

The container carriage system is effective for the vertical conveyance of materials. Multiple carriages can be attached to the chain to accommodate high-volume movement. The receiving platform runouts can be extended as required. The carriage system can be teamed with conveyor belts for horizontal transport of materials. Consult manufacturer for specific installation requirements.

Translogic Corporation; Denver Colorado
Richard J. Vitullo, AIA; Oakleaf Studio; Crownsville, Maryland

 14 **MATERIAL-HANDLING SYSTEMS**

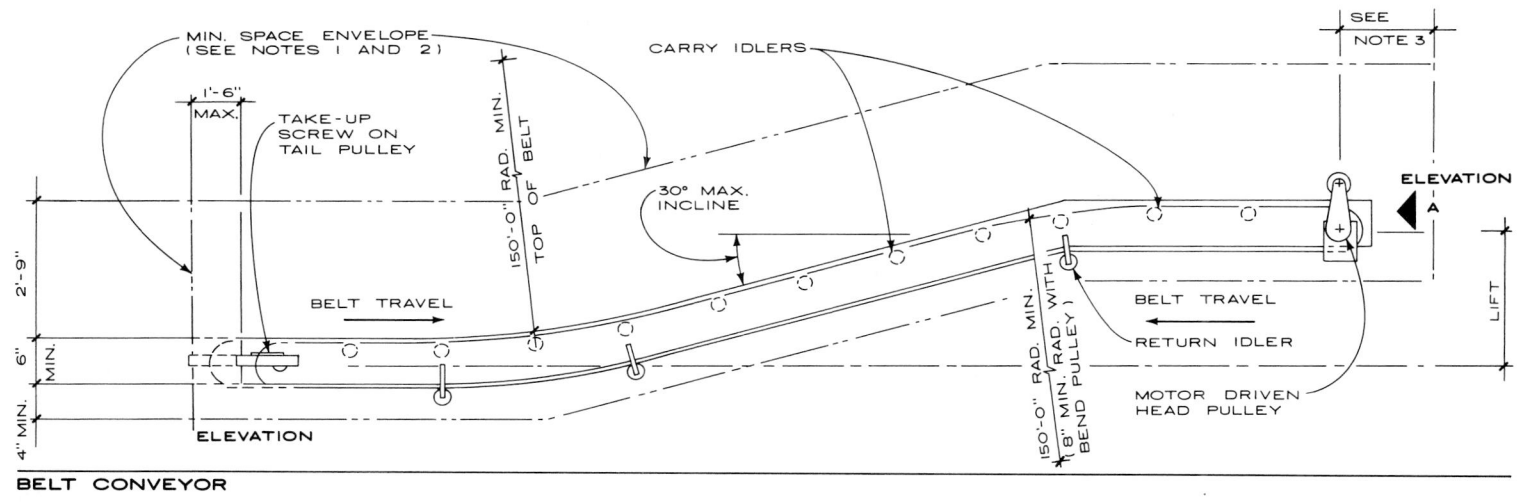

BELT CONVEYOR

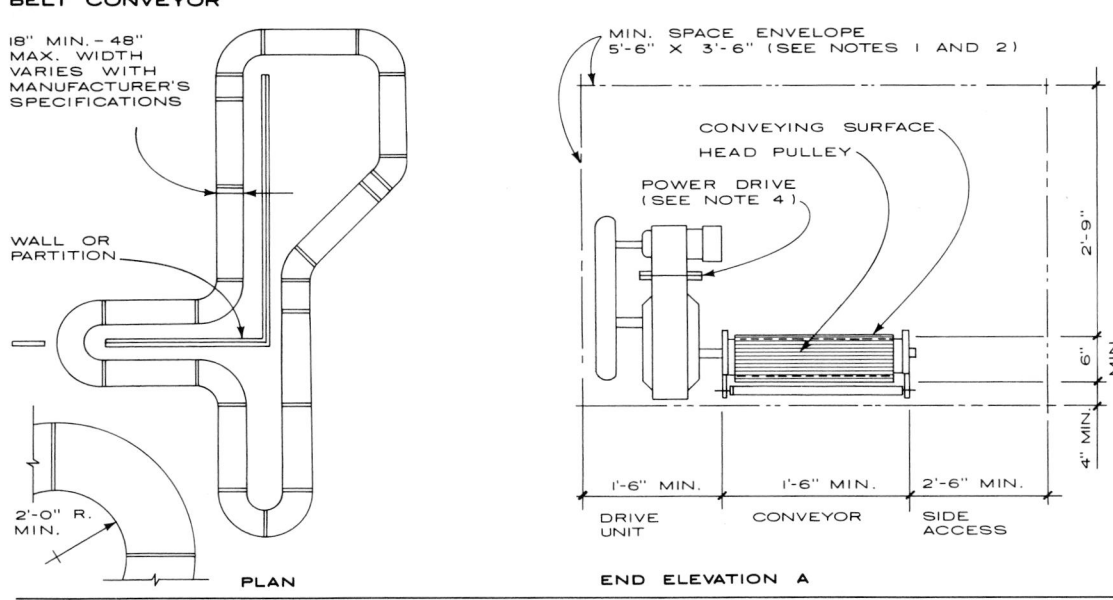

PACKAGE CONVEYOR SYSTEM

PLAN

END ELEVATION A

COMPARISON OF MATERIAL CONVEYORS

CONVEYOR	TYPE	APPLICATION	ADVANTAGES	LIMITATIONS
Belt	Flat (power drive)	Airport baggage Manufacturing, assembly, and inspection Packaged goods	Very common Many vendors Economical High capacity output Extensive speed range	Frequent maintenance required Friction drive pulley slips Belt replacement and realignment required Will not curve horizontally (powered belt curves are available)
	Troughed (power drive)	Bulk handling Dry granular materials Dry solid waste		
Roller	Skate wheel (gravity)	Light duty packages	Mobile units available Can turn in horizontal planes (see typical plan arrangement) Can accumulate loads	Poor for sacked items or resilient outer surfaces Light duty (skate wheel) Limited weight range for rollers Package or unit material Occasional noise problems Regularly inspect wheels or rollers for free rolling
	Gravity roller (unpowered) Live roller (power drive)	Medium to heavy duty handling Pallets or other flat bottom containers or items		
Segmented (articulated) moving surface	Pan Apron Slat (All power driven)	Airport baggage Loose waste handling Solid waste handling	Can handle heavy loads Durable carrying surface Can turn in horizontal planes (see typical plan arrangement) Good for steep inclines Handles hot or wet material	Very costly

NOTES

1. Clearance dimensions shown are nominal. Exact dimensions should be determined after specific equipment has been designed.
2. Service access must be provided at tail pulley, drive area, and along at least one side.
3. Trajectory of material leaving the conveyor depends on the material's characteristics and the speed of its travel.
4. Drive unit does not necessarily protrude above belt surface and can be located below the frame and at locations other than at the head pulley.
5. Access safety rails, guards, etc., should comply with applicable codes and with manufacturers' recommendations.

Alpha Engineers, Inc.; Pocatello, Idaho

GENERAL

Waste and linen chutes should extend full diameter through the roof and be capped with a metal safety vent or glass explosion cap. Sprinklers or flushing spray are recommended at alternate floors. Bottom-hinged hopper doors are commonly used for waste and loose linen. Square side-hinged doors are used for bagged linen. "B" label doors are recommended. To prevent clogging, door size is restricted in proportion to chute diameter. Type "H" hopper discharge doors are installed when discharge is built into wall and the receptacle is a cart or bin. Type "A" direct-open discharge doors (not shown) are commonly used when discharge is into a compactor.

AVERAGE WASTE PRODUCTION/DAY

BUILDING	AMOUNT
Apartment	5 lb/apartment + 1 lb/bedroom
Dormitory	3 lb/person
Hospital	8 lb/bed
Nursing home	6 lb/person
Hotel, motel	3 lb/room
School	10 lb/room +¼ lb/pupil

AVERAGE LINEN PRODUCTION/DAY

BUILDING	AMOUNT
Hospital	15 lb/bed
Hotel, motel	12 lb/bed

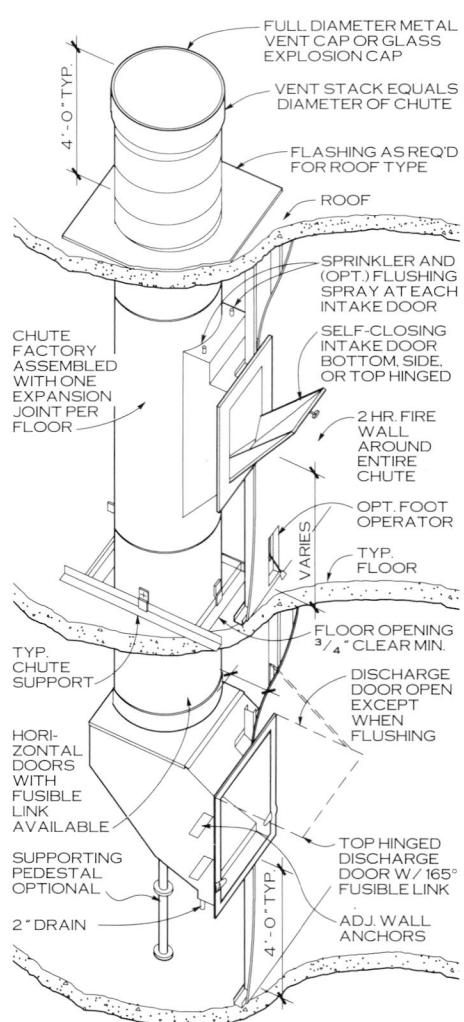

FULL DIAMETER METAL VENT CAP OR GLASS EXPLOSION CAP

VENT STACK EQUALS DIAMETER OF CHUTE

FLASHING AS REQ'D FOR ROOF TYPE

ROOF

SPRINKLER AND (OPT.) FLUSHING SPRAY AT EACH INTAKE DOOR

SELF-CLOSING INTAKE DOOR BOTTOM, SIDE, OR TOP HINGED

2 HR. FIRE WALL AROUND ENTIRE CHUTE

OPT. FOOT OPERATOR

TYP. FLOOR

FLOOR OPENING ¾" CLEAR MIN.

DISCHARGE DOOR OPEN EXCEPT WHEN FLUSHING

TOP HINGED DISCHARGE DOOR W/ 165° FUSIBLE LINK

ADJ. WALL ANCHORS

CHUTE FACTORY ASSEMBLED WITH ONE EXPANSION JOINT PER FLOOR

TYP. CHUTE SUPPORT

HORIZONTAL DOORS WITH FUSIBLE LINK AVAILABLE

SUPPORTING PEDESTAL OPTIONAL

2" DRAIN

WASTE OR LINEN CHUTE
NOTES

1. Fire stops may be required at underside of every slab; check local codes.
2. Chute material: #18 - #16 U.S. gauge aluminized steel or stainless steel.

NOTES

1. Chutes should be used only for first class mail. The chute dimensions should be 2 x 8 in. and extend in a vertical line from beginning point to a receiving box or mailroom. A chute must be accessible its entire length. Chutes in pairs have a divider and dual receiving boxes.
2. Receiving boxes must be placed near the building's main entrance or near the loading area for U.S. Postal Service (USPS) mail collection. Using the shortest line, receiving boxes may not be placed more than 100 ft from the entrance used by the collection person. Locations require local postmaster approval. Receiving boxes must be placed on the same floor the collection person uses to enter the building. Doors must operate freely. Door openings must be at least 12 x 20 in. and not more than 18 x 30 in.
3. Auxiliary boxes should be located near receiving box if receiving box is too small to accommodate the volume of first class mail.
4. A bundle drop must accept a bundle at least 6½ in. wide by 11½ in. long and 4 in. high. To prevent removal of mail, the deposit opening must be fully protected by inside baffle plates. Inlet doors must be inscribed "Letters" and "Letter Mail Tied in Bundles." The bottom of the opening must be at least 61 in. above floor level.

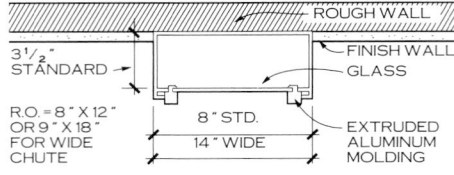

ROUGH WALL

FINISH WALL

GLASS

3½" STANDARD

R.O. = 8" X 12" OR 9" X 18" FOR WIDE CHUTE

8" STD.

14" WIDE

EXTRUDED ALUMINUM MOLDING

MAIL CHUTE PLAN

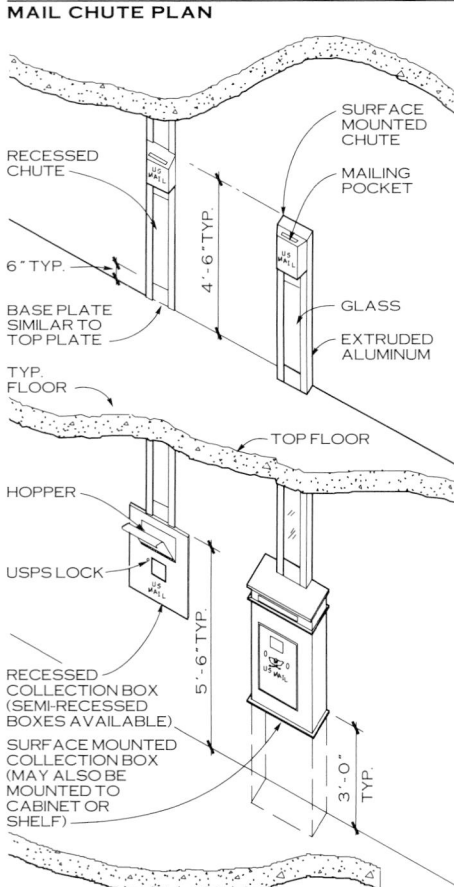

RECESSED CHUTE

6" TYP.

BASE PLATE SIMILAR TO TOP PLATE

TYP. FLOOR

HOPPER

USPS LOCK

RECESSED COLLECTION BOX (SEMI-RECESSED BOXES AVAILABLE)

SURFACE MOUNTED COLLECTION BOX (MAY ALSO BE MOUNTED TO CABINET OR SHELF)

SURFACE MOUNTED CHUTE

MAILING POCKET

GLASS

EXTRUDED ALUMINUM

TOP FLOOR

4'-6" TYP.

5'-6" TYP.

3'-0" TYP.

MAIL CHUTE AND COLLECTION BOXES
NOTES

1. All installations must comply with USPS requirements and are subject to inspection.
2. Floor penetrations may need fire stopping methods.
3. USPS provides listing of approved manufacturers.

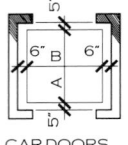 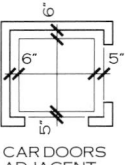 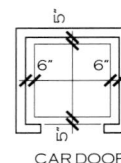

CAR DOORS OPPOSITE   CAR DOORS ADJACENT   CAR DOOR FRONT

PLANS OF TYPICAL DUMBWAITER

ELEVATOR CAPACITY

CAR SIZE			
W	D	H	CAPACITY (LB)
18"	18"	24"	25-75
20"	20"	30"	100
28"	24"	36"	150-250
32"	30"	42"	300-350
36"	36"	48"	400-500

Capacity is determined by the maximum weight of the contents to be transported and the size of the dumbwaiter car. Maximum capacity is 500 lb. Normal speed is 50 ft per minute. The car platform may not exceed 9 sq ft. Car heights cannot exceed 4 ft. Machines may be located above, below, or adjacent to the hatchway. Drum type machines have a maximum rise of 35 to 40 ft; traction type machines have unlimited range of travel.

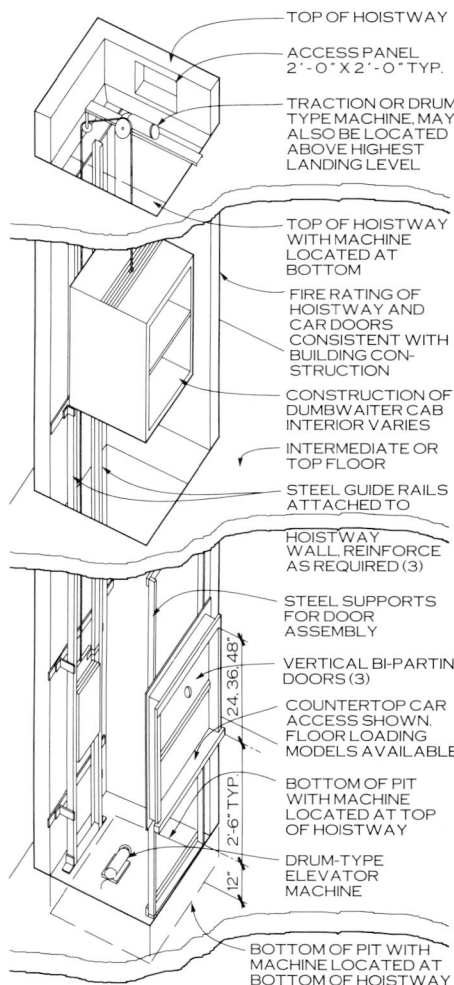

TOP OF HOISTWAY

ACCESS PANEL 2'-0" X 2'-0" TYP.

TRACTION OR DRUM TYPE MACHINE, MAY ALSO BE LOCATED ABOVE HIGHEST LANDING LEVEL

TOP OF HOISTWAY WITH MACHINE LOCATED AT BOTTOM

FIRE RATING OF HOISTWAY AND CAR DOORS CONSISTENT WITH BUILDING CONSTRUCTION

CONSTRUCTION OF DUMBWAITER CAB INTERIOR VARIES

INTERMEDIATE OR TOP FLOOR

STEEL GUIDE RAILS ATTACHED TO

HOISTWAY WALL, REINFORCE AS REQUIRED (3)

STEEL SUPPORTS FOR DOOR ASSEMBLY

VERTICAL BI-PARTING DOORS (3)

COUNTERTOP CAR ACCESS SHOWN. FLOOR LOADING MODELS AVAILABLE

BOTTOM OF PIT WITH MACHINE LOCATED AT TOP OF HOISTWAY

DRUM-TYPE ELEVATOR MACHINE

BOTTOM OF PIT WITH MACHINE LOCATED AT BOTTOM OF HOISTWAY

DUMBWAITERS

NOTE

Consult manufacturer's literature for specific dimensions and load capacity.

Eric K. Beach; Rippeteau Architects, PC; Washington, D.C.
Wilkinson Company, Inc., Cutler Manufacturing Corporation, Atlas Elevator Company, and Sidgwick Lifts, Inc.

 MATERIAL-HANDLING SYSTEMS

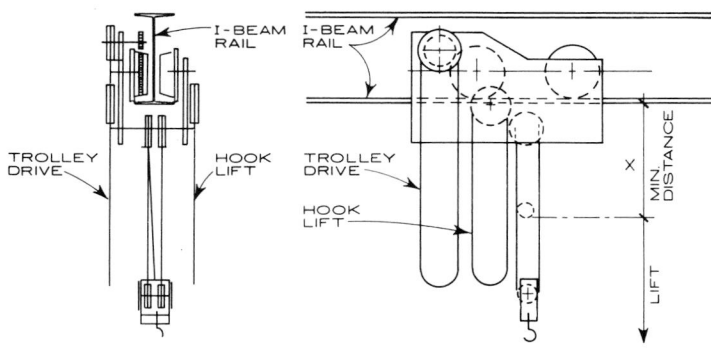

TROLLEY HOIST DATA

CAPACITY (TONS)	STANDARD LIFT (FT)	X	STANDARD I-BEAM	MIN. CURVE RADIUS
1/4	8	8 1/2''	5''	3'-6''
1/2	8	8 1/2''	5''	3'-6''
1	8	11 1/4''	6''	3'-6''
1 1/2	8	13''	7''	3'-6''
2	9	15 1/8''	8''	4'-6''
3	10	18 3/4''	10''	5'-0''
4	10	21 3/4''	10''	7'-6''
5	12	25''	12''	7'-6''
6	12	25''	12''	7'-6''
8	12	31 3/8''	15''	8'-0''
10	12	39''	15''	8'-0''

TROLLEY HOISTS

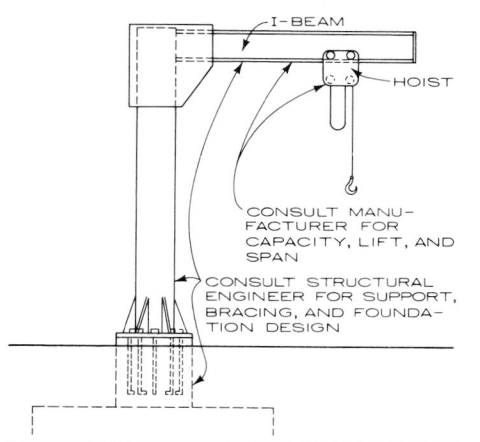

JIB CRANE

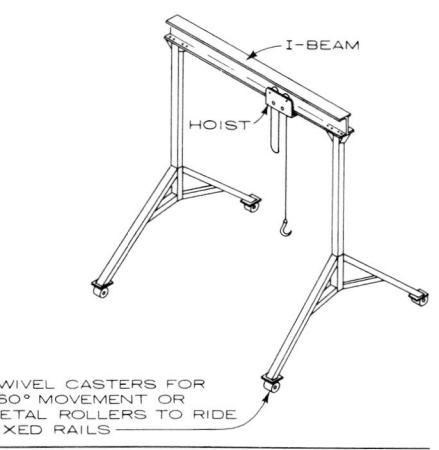

MOVABLE GANTRY

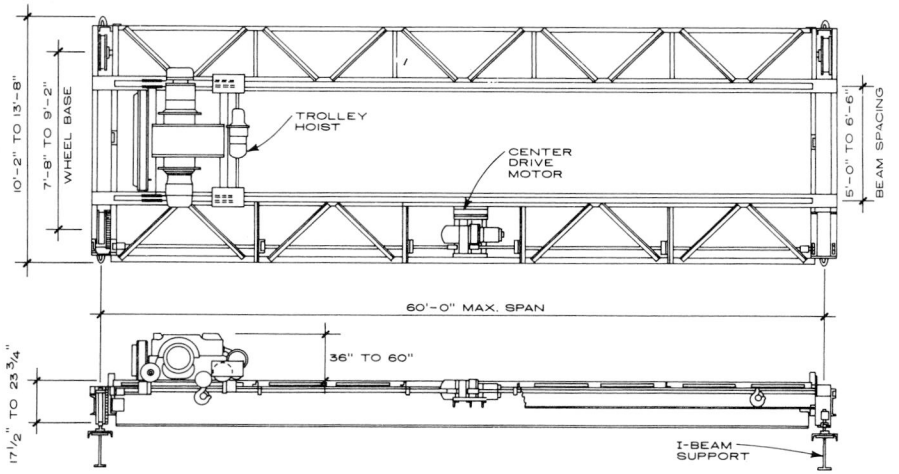

DOUBLE BEAM CRANE (CAPACITY 25 TONS)

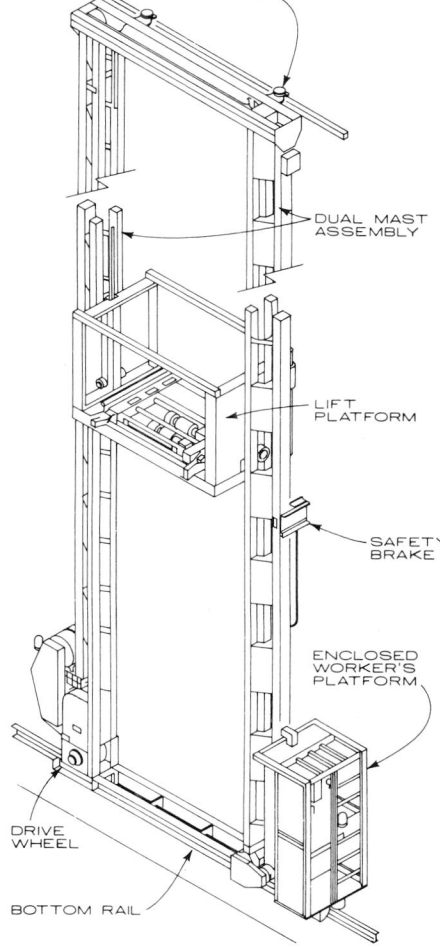

STACKER CRANE (CAPACITY 5 TONS)

CRANES

JIB CRANE

Typically manufactured to lift loads from 1 to 8 tons, with boom located from 10 to 25 ft above ground. Special care must be taken to design foundation to resist large overturning moment. The jib allows 360° movement around the central support, as well as travel of hoist along the I-beam. Larger sizes usually have motorized hoist as well as motorized rotation of boom.

MOVABLE GANTRY

Typically manufactured to lift from 1 to 8 tons, with height of 8 to 35 ft. The gantry allows 360° movement if designed with swivel casters, or it can travel along a fixed steel track mounted on the floor. Larger gantries have motorized hoists as well as motorized travel along

a track. The portable gantry is ideal for retrofit applications since often no structural or foundation modifications are required (as long as slab has capacity to support weight of gantry and load).

DOUBLE BEAM CRANE

Used to handle heavy loads in manufacturing and storage areas where aisle access and load clearances are limited. The beam crane allows two-directional horizontal travel plus vertical lift over the entire area serviced by the crane.

Load capacity: 6000 to 50,000 lb; span: 25 to 60 ft; crane weight: 4500 to 36,000 lb; wheel base: 7 to 13 ft; beam spacing: 5 to 9 ft; working span: 20 to 57 ft; hoist clearance above rail: 37 to 70 in.

STACKER CRANE

Stacker cranes allow storage/retrieval of loads above conventional fork lift truck heights. Also, multiple loads can be handled by manipulating load platform sizes. Cranes can be computer controlled to reduce manpower demands in S/R operations.

Load capacity: up to 10,000 lb; overall height: 40 to 120 ft; working heights: 2 to 112 ft, depending on load heights; aisle width: 4 to 10 ft, depending on load configuration; aisle overrun: 15 to 20 ft, depending on crane structure; crane weight: up to 34,000 lb, depending on load and crane configuration; travel speeds: horizontal—up to 480 fpm; vertical—up to 120 fpm.

NOTE

Stacker cranes are typically built to customer specifications. Specific applications and details should be obtained from crane suppliers.

Rodney D. Burrows, AIA, PE; San Francisco, California
St. Onge, Ruff & Associates; York, Pennsylvania

GENERAL

Accessiblity Equipment Manufacturers Association
4001 East 138th Street
Grandview, MO 64030
Tel: (800) 925-3100
Fax:(816) 763-4467

American Consulting Engineers Council
1015 15th Street, N.W.
Washington, DC 20005
Tel: (202) 347-7474
Fax:(202) 898-0068

American National Standards Institute (ANSI)
11 West 42nd Street, 13th Floor
New York, NY 10036-8002
Tel: (212) 642-4900
Fax:(212) 398-0023

American Society of Mechanical
    Engineers/A17 Committee (ASME)
United Engineering Center
345 East 47th Street
New York, NY 10017
Tel: (212) 605-8793
Fax:(212) 605-8750

REFERENCES

Stein, Benjamin, and John S. Reynolds. *Mechanical and Electrical Equipment for Buildings*, 8th ed. New York: J. Wiley & Sons, 1992.

Strakosh, G. *Vertical Transportation: Elevators and Escalators*, 2nd ed. J. Wiley & Sons, 1983.

ELEVATORS

Elevator Escalator Safety Foundation
P.O. Box 6273
Mobile, AL 36660
Tel: (205) 479-2199

The Elevator Industries Association, Inc. (EIA)
233-43 Bay Street
Douglaston, NY 11363
Tel: (718) 279-3859
Fax:(718) 423-6576

The Elevator World Source
354 Morgan Avenue
P.O. Box 6507
Mobile, AL 36606
Tel: (205) 479-4514
Fax:(205) 479-7043

International Union of Elevator Constructors (IUEC)
Suite 310, Clark Building
5565 Sterrett Place
Columbia, MD 21044
Tel: (410) 997-9000

National Association of Elevator Contractors (NAEC)
1298 Wellbrook Circle N.E.
Conyers, GA, 30207
Tel: (404) 496-1270
Fax:(404) 496-1272

National Association of Elevator Safety Authorities
67 East Weldon, Suite 103
Phoenix, AZ 85012
Tel: (602) 760-9660
Fax: (602) 760-9714

National Association of Elevator Safety Authorities
mailing address:
P.O. Box 15643
Phoenix, AZ 85060

National Association of Vertical
    Transportation Professionals (NAVTP)
1713-19 Ralph Avenue
Brooklyn, NY 11236
Tel: (718) 209-1581
Fax:(718) 531-5059

National Elevator Industry, Inc. (NEI)
185 Bridge Plaza North
Room 310
Fort Lee, NJ 07024
Tel: (201) 944-3211
Fax:(201) 944-5483

National Elevator Industry Educational Program (NEIEP)
11 Larson Way
Attleboro Falls, MA 02763
Tel: (508) 699-2200
Fax:(508) 699-2495

REFERENCES

Beyer, Robert. "Specification Series: Elevators—First things First." *Architectural Record* (Nov. 1992).

"Elevator Modernization: Rising to the Task." *Construction Specifier* (July 1989).

Elevator World [monthly (P.O. Box 6507, Loop Branch, Mobile AL 36606, (205) 479-4514)].

Elevators, Monograph 14M200. Construction Specifications Institute, 1987.

Guide for Emergency Evacuation of Passengers from Elevators, A17.4-91. American Society of Mechanical Engineers, 1991.

Handbook on A17.1 Safety Code for Elevators and Escalators. American Society of Mechanical Engineers, 1990.

Inspector's Manual for Elevators and Escalators, ASME/ ANSI A17.1-88. American Society of Mechanical Engineers/American National Standards Institute, 1988.

Interpretations of A17 Documents—1972-1979. American Society of Mechanical Engineers.

Safety Code for Elevators and Escalators, ASME A17.1-90. American Society of Mechanical Engineers, 1990.

Safety Code for Existing Elevators, ASME A17.3. American Society of Mechanical Engineers, 1990. [includes addenda through 1993]

Safety Standard for Conveyors and Related Equipment, ASME B20.1. ASME, 1990.

Standard for Elevator and Escalator Equipment, CAN/ CSA-B44.1/ASME A17.5-M1991. American Society of Mechanical Engineers, 1991.

Strakosh, G. *Vertical Transportation: Elevators and Escalators*, 2nd ed. J. Wiley & Sons, 1983.

Standard for the Qualification of Elevator Inspectors, ASME QEI-1. American Society of Mechanical Engineers, 1990.

Stein, Benjamin and John S. Reynolds. *Mechanical and Electrical Equipment for Buildings*, 8th ed. New York: J. Wiley & Sons, 1992, 1627 pp.

"The Ups and Downs of Elevator Planning," *Construction Specifier* (April 1989).

ESCALATORS AND MOVING WALKS
REFERENCES

Barney, G. V. *Elevator Abstracts: Including Escalators*. Halstead Press, 1987.

Escalators and Moving Walks, SpecGUIDE G14300, Construction Specifications Institute, 1989.

Standard for Elevator and Escalator Equipment, CAN/ CSA-B44.1/ASME A17.5-M1991, American Society of Mechanical Engineers, 1991.

Strakosh, G. *Vertical Transportation: Elevators and Escalators*, 2nd ed. J. Wiley & Sons, 1983.

LIFTS

Below/Hook Lifters Association
8720 Red Oak Blvd., Suite 201
Charlotte, NC 28217-3957
Tel: (704) 522-8644
Fax:(704) 522-7826

MATERIAL-HANDLING SYSTEMS

Association of Professional Material Handling Consultants
8720 Red Oak Blvd., Suite 224
Charlotte, NC 28217-3957
Tel: (704) 525-4667
Fax:(704) 525-2880

Automatic Guided Vehicle Systems
8720 Red Oak Blvd., Suite 201
Charlotte, NC 28217-3957
Tel: (704) 522-8644
Fax:(704) 522-7826

Conveyor Equipment Manufacturers Association
932 Hungerford Drive, #36
Rockville, MD 20850
Tel: (301) 738-2448
Fax:(301) 738-0076

Loading Dock Equipment Manufacturers
8720 Red Oak Blvd., Suite 201
Charlotte, NC 28217-3957
Tel: (704) 522-8644
Fax:(704) 522-7826

Material Handling Equipment Distributors Association
    (MHEDA)
201 Route #45
Vernon Hills, IL 60061
Tel: (708) 680-3500
Fax:(708) 362-6989

Material Handling Institute
8720 Red Oak Blvd., Suite 201
Charlotte, NC 28217-3957
Tel: (704) 522-8644
Fax:(704) 522-7826

Materials Handling and Management Society
8720 Red Oak Blvd., Suite 224
Charlotte, NC 28217-3957
Tel: (704) 525-4667
Fax:(704) 525-2880

REFERENCES

Material Handling Engineering. Penton Publishing. [monthly]

United States Postal Service (USPS) list of approved manufacturers of mail chutes.

HOISTS AND CRANES

Crane Manufacturers Association of America
8720 Red Oak Blvd., Suite 201
Charlotte, NC 28217-3957
Tel: (704) 522-8644
Fax:(704) 522-7826

Hoist Manufacturers Institute
8720 Red Oak Blvd., Suite 201
Charlotte, NC 28217-3957
Tel: (704) 522-8644
Fax:(704) 522-7826

Power Crane and Shovel Association, a subsidiary of Construction Industry Manufacturers Association
111 East Wisconsin Avenue
Bank One Plaza, Suite 940
Milwaukee, WI 53202-4879
Tel: (414) 272-0943

REFERENCES

Hoists and Cranes, SpecGUIDE G14600. Construction Specifications Institute, 1991.

Safety Standard for Conveyors and Related Equipment, ASME B20.1. American Society of Mechanical Engineers, 1990.

CHAPTER

15

MECHANICAL

SEAMLESS STEEL PIPE

NOMINAL PIPE SIZE	DIMENSION (IN.) O.D.	WALL	CLASS	LB/FT P.E.	LB/FT T&C
2"	2.375	0.154	Std.	3.65	3.68
	2.375	0.218	X.S.	5.02	5.07
	2.375	0.436	XXS.	9.03	-
2 1/2"	2.875	0.203	Std.	5.79	5.82
	2.875	0.276	X.S.	7.66	7.73
	2.875	0.552	XXS.	13.70	-
3"	3.500	0.216	Std.	7.58	7.62
	3.500	0.300	X.S.	10.25	10.33
	3.500	0.600	XXS.	18.58	-
3 1/2"	4.000	0.226	Std.	9.11	9.20
	4.000	0.318	X.S.	12.51	12.63
	4.000	0.634	XXS.	22.85	-
4"	4.500	0.237	Std.	10.79	10.89
	4.500	0.337	X.S.	14.98	15.17
	4.500	0.674	XXS.	27.54	-
5"	5.563	0.258	Std.	14.62	14.81
	5.563	0.375	X.S.	20.78	21.09
	5.563	0.750	XXS.	38.55	-
6"	6.625	0.280	Std.	18.97	19.18
	6.625	0.432	X.S.	28.57	28.89
	6.625	0.864	XXS.	53.16	-
8"	8.625	0.277	-	24.70	25.55
	8.625	0.322	Std.	28.55	29.35
	8.625	0.500	X.S.	43.39	43.90
	8.625	0.875	XXS.	72.42	-
10"	10.750	0.307	-	34.34	35.75
	10.750	0.365	Std.	40.48	41.85
	10.750	0.500	X.S.	54.74	55.82
12"	12.750	0.330	-	43.77	45.45
	12.750	0.375	Std.	49.56	51.15
	12.750	0.406	-	53.53	-
	12.750	0.500	X.S.	65.42	66.71
	12.750	0.687	-	88.50	-
14"	14.000	0.312	-	45.68	-
	14.000	0.375	Std.	54.75	-
	14.000	0.500	X.S.	72.09	-
16"	16.000	0.312	-	52.36	-
	16.000	0.375	Std.	62.58	-
	16.000	0.500	X.S.	82.77	-
18"	18.000	0.312	-	59.03	-
	18.000	0.375	Std.	70.59	-
	18.000	0.500	X.S.	93.45	-
20"	20.000	0.312	-	68.71	-
	20.000	0.375	Std.	78.60	-
	20.000	0.500	X.S.	104.13	-
24"	24.000	0.312	-	79.06	-
	24.000	0.375	Std.	94.62	-
	24.000	0.500	X.S.	125.49	-

SEAMLESS STEEL PRESSURE TUBING

NOMINAL PIPE SIZE	DIMENSION (IN.) O.D.	WALL	CLASS	LB/FT
1/8"	0.405	0.068	Std.	0.240
		0.095	X.S.	0.310
1/4"	0.540	0.088	Std.	0.420
		0.119	X.S.	0.540
3/8"	0.675	0.091	Std.	0.570
		0.126	X.S.	0.740
1/2"	0.840	0.109	Std.	0.850
		0.147	X.S.	1.087
		0.187	-	1.310
		0.294	XXS.	1.714
3/4"	1.050	0.113	Std.	1.130
		0.154	X.S.	1.473
		0.218	-	1.940
		0.308	XXS.	2.440
1"	1.315	0.133	Std.	1.678
		0.179	X.S.	2.171
		0.250	-	2.850
		0.358	XXS.	3.659
1 1/4"	1.660	0.140	Std.	2.272
		0.191	X.S.	2.996
		0.250	-	3.764
		0.382	XXS.	5.214
1 1/2"	1.900	0.145	Std.	2.717
		0.200	X.S.	3.631
		0.281	-	4.862
		0.400	XXS.	6.408

BUTT WELD STEEL PIPE

NOMINAL PIPE SIZE	DIMENSION (IN.) O.D.	STANDARD WEIGHT WALL (IN.)	STANDARD WEIGHT LB/FT P.E.	STANDARD WEIGHT LB/FT T&C	EXTRA STRONG WALL (IN.)	EXTRA STRONG LB/FT P.E.	EXTRA STRONG LB/FT T&C	DOUBLE EXTRA STRONG WALL (IN.)	DOUBLE EXTRA STRONG LB/FT P.E.	DOUBLE EXTRA STRONG LB/FT T&C
1/8"	0.405	0.068	0.24	0.24	0.095	0.31	0.32	-	-	-
1/4"	0.540	0.088	0.42	0.42	0.119	0.54	0.54	-	-	-
3/8"	0.675	0.091	0.57	0.57	0.126	0.74	0.74	-	-	-
1/2"	0.840	0.109	0.85	0.85	0.147	1.09	1.09	-	-	-
3/4"	1.050	0.113	1.13	1.13	0.154	1.47	1.48	0.308	2.441	-
1"	1.315	0.133	1.68	1.68	0.179	2.17	2.18	0.358	2.659	-
1 1/4"	1.660	0.140	2.27	2.28	0.191	3.00	3.02	0.382	5.214	-
1 1/2"	1.900	0.145	2.72	2.73	0.200	3.63	3.66	0.400	6.408	-
2"	2.375	0.154	3.65	3.68	0.218	5.02	5.07	-	-	-
2 1/2"	2.875	0.203	5.79	5.82	0.276	7.66	7.73	-	-	-
3"	3.500	0.216	7.58	7.62	0.300	10.25	10.33	-	-	-
3 1/2"	4.000	0.226	9.11	9.20	0.318	12.51	12.63	-	-	-
4"	4.500	0.237	10.79	10.89	0.337	14.98	15.17	-	-	-

COPPER TUBING

NOMINAL PIPE SIZE	DIMENSION (IN.) O.D.	TYPE K WALL (IN.)	TYPE K LB/FT	TYPE L AND ACR WALL (IN.)	TYPE L AND ACR LB/FT	TYPE M WALL (IN.)	TYPE M LB/FT	REFRIGERATOR TUBE WALL (IN.)	REFRIGERATOR TUBE LB/COIL
	1/8	-	-	-	-	-	-	0.030	1.74
	3/16	-	-	-	-	-	-	0.030	2.88
	1/4	-	-	-	-	-	-	0.030	4.02
	5/16	-	-	-	-	-	-	0.032	5.45
1/4"	3/8	0.035	0.145	0.030	0.126	0.025	0.106	0.032	6.70
3/8"	1/2	0.049	0.269	0.035	0.198	0.025	0.145	0.032	9.10
1/2"	5/8	0.049	0.344	0.040	0.285	0.028	0.204	0.035	12.55
5/8"	3/4	0.049	0.418	0.042	0.362	0.030	0.263	0.035	15.25
3/4"	7/8	0.065	0.641	0.045	0.455	0.032	0.328	0.045	22.75
1"	1 1/8	0.065	0.839	0.050	0.655	0.035	0.465	0.050	32.75
1 1/4"	1 3/8	0.065	1.040	0.055	0.884	0.042	0.682	0.055	44.2
1 1/2"	1 5/8	0.072	1.360	0.060	1.140	0.049	0.940	-	-
2"	2 1/8	0.083	2.060	0.070	1.750	0.058	1.460	-	-
2 1/2"	2 5/8	0.095	2.930	0.080	2.480	0.065	2.030	-	-
3"	3 1/8	0.109	4.000	0.090	3.330	0.072	2.680	-	-
3 1/2"	3 5/8	0.120	5.120	0.100	4.290	0.083	3.580	-	-
4"	4 1/8	0.134	6.510	0.110	5.380	0.095	4.660	-	-
5"	5 1/8	0.160	9.670	0.125	7.610	0.109	6.666	-	-
6"	6 1/8	0.192	13.900	0.140	10.200	0.122	8.920	-	-

RED BRASS PIPE

NOMINAL PIPE SIZE	DIMENSION (IN.) O.D.	STANDARD WEIGHT WALL (IN.)	STANDARD WEIGHT LB/FT	EXTRA STRONG WALL (IN.)	EXTRA STRONG LB/FT
1/8"	0.405	0.062	0.253	0.100	0.363
1/4"	0.540	0.082	0.447	0.123	0.611
3/8"	0.675	0.090	0.627	0.127	0.829
1/2"	0.840	0.107	0.934	0.149	1.230
3/4"	1.050	0.114	1.270	0.157	1.670
1"	1.315	0.126	1.780	0.182	2.460
1 1/4"	1.660	0.146	2.630	0.194	3.390
1 1/2"	1.900	0.150	3.130	0.203	4.100
2"	2.375	0.156	4.120	0.221	5.670
2 1/2"	2.875	0.187	5.990	0.280	8.660
3"	3.500	0.219	8.560	0.304	11.600
3 1/2"	4.000	0.250	11.200	0.321	14.100
4"	4.500	0.250	12.700	0.341	16.900
5"	5.562	0.250	15.800	0.375	23.200
6"	6.525	0.250	19.000	0.437	32.200

PVC (POLYVINYLCHLORIDE) PLASTIC PIPE WATER PRESSURE RATINGS

NOMINAL PIPE SIZE	FOR CEMENTING ONLY - SCH WALL (IN.)	FOR CEMENTING ONLY - SCH PSI AT 73.4°F	FOR CEMENTING OR THREADING - TABLE 80 WALL (IN.)	PSI AT 73.4°F CMNT	PSI AT 73.4°F THRD
1/4"	-	-	0.119	1130	570
3/8"	0.091	620	0.126	920	460
1/2"	0.109	600	0.147	850	420
3/4"	0.113	480	0.154	690	340
1"	0.133	450	0.179	630	320
1 1/4"	0.140	370	0.191	520	260
1 1/2"	0.145	330	0.200	470	235
2"	0.154	280	0.218	400	200
2 1/2"	0.203	300	0.276	420	210
3"	0.216	260	0.300	370	185
4"	0.237	220	0.337	320	160
6"	0.280	180	0.432	280	140

PVC AND CPVC* PIPE DIMENSIONS (IN.)

NOMINAL PIPE SIZE	SCHEDULE 40 OUTSIDE DIA.	SCHEDULE 40 WALL (IN.)	SCHEDULE 80 OUTSIDE DIA.	SCHEDULE 80 WALL (IN.)
1/4"	0.540	0.088	0.540	0.119
3/8"	0.675	0.091	0.675	0.126
1/2"	0.840	0.109	0.840	0.147
3/4"	1.050	0.113	1.050	0.154
1"	1.315	0.133	1.315	0.179
1 1/4"	1.660	0.140	1.660	0.191
1 1/2"	1.900	0.145	1.900	0.200
2"	2.375	0.154	2.375	0.218
2 1/2"	2.875	0.203	2.875	0.276
3"	3.500	0.216	3.500	0.300
3 1/2"	4.000	0.226	4.000	0.318
4"	4.500	0.237	4.500	0.337
5"	5.563	0.258	5.563	0.375
6"	6.625	0.280	6.625	0.432
8"	8.625	0.322	8.625	0.500
10"	10.750	0.365	10.750	0.593
12"	12.750	0.406	12.750	0.687

CPVC* PLASTIC PIPE WATER PRESSURE RATINGS

NOMINAL PIPE SIZE	MAXIMUM OPERATING PRESSURE PSI AT 70°F SCHEDULE 40 SOLVENT CEMENTED	SCHEDULE 80 THREADED	SCHEDULE 80 SOLVENT CEMENTED
1/4"	780	570	1130
3/8"	620	460	920
1/2"	600	420	850
3/4"	480	340	690
1"	450	320	630
1 1/4"	370	260	520
1 1/2"	330	240	470
2"	280	200	400
2 1/2"	300	210	420
3"	260	190	370
4"	220	160	320
6"	180	140	280

* Chlorinated polyvinyl chloride

Piping Systems Council; Chicago, Illinois
P.V.C. Plastic Pipe Institute; New York, New York
Walter H. Sobel, FAIA and Associates; Chicago, Illinois

15 MECHANICAL PIPING AND RELATED EQUIPMENT

STAINLESS STEEL PIPE

NOMINAL PIPE SIZE	DIMENSION O.D. (IN.)	SCHEDULE 5·S		SCHEDULE 10·S		SCHEDULE 40·S	
		WALL (IN.)	LB/FT	WALL (IN.)	LB/FT	WALL (IN.)	LB/FT
1/8	0.405	–	–	0.049	0.186	0.068	0.245
1/4	0.540	–	–	0.065	0.330	0.088	0.425
3/8	0.675	–	–	0.065	0.424	0.091	0.568
1/2	0.840	0.065	0.538	0.083	0.671	0.109	0.851
3/4	1.050	0.065	0.684	0.083	0.857	0.113	1.131
1	1.315	0.065	0.868	0.109	1.404	0.133	1.679
1 1/4	1.660	0.065	1.107	0.109	1.806	0.140	2.278
1 1/2	1.900	0.065	1.274	0.109	2.085	0.145	2.718
2	2.375	0.065	1.604	0.109	2.638	0.154	3.653
2 1/2	2.875	0.083	2.475	0.120	3.531	0.203	5.793
3	3.500	0.083	3.029	0.120	4.332	0.216	7.576
3 1/2	4.000	0.083	3.472	0.120	4.973	0.226	9.109
4	4.500	0.083	3.915	0.120	5.613	0.237	10.790
5	5.563	0.109	6.350	0.134	7.770	0.258	14.620
6	6.625	0.109	7.585	0.134	9.290	0.280	18.970
8	8.625	0.109	9.914	0.148	13.400	0.322	28.550
10	10.750	0.134	15.190	0.165	18.700	0.365	40.480
12	12.750	0.165	22.180	0.180	24.200	0.375	49.550

ALUMINUM PIPE AND SOFT ALUMINUM TUBING

	ALUMINUM PIPE (PLAIN END			SOFT ALUMINUM TUBING		
NOMINAL PIPE SIZE (IN.)	DIMENSION (IN.)		WEIGHT (LB/FT)	DIMENSION (IN.)		LB/50 FT COIL
	O.D.	WALL		O.D.	WALL	
1/2	0.840	0.145	0.294	1/4	0.032	1.30
3/4	1.050	0.113	0.391	3/8	0.035	2.22
1	1.315	0.133	0.581	1/2	0.035	3.03
1 1/4	1.660	0.140	0.786	5/8	0.035	3.84
1 1/2	1.900	0.145	0.940	–	–	–
2	2.375	0.154	1.264	–	–	–
2 1/2	2.875	0.203	2.004	–	–	–
3	3.500	0.216	2.621	–	–	–

COPPER TUBING

1. Type K, L, and M copper tubing is manufactured as a water tube under ASTM standard B88 and is available in both hard drawn lengths and annealed coils.
2. Type K is a water tube for underground and interior service.
3. Type L is a water tube for interior service only.
4. Type K and Type L can be specially cleaned for oxygen service.
5. Type M is a nonpressure water tube for above ground application.
6. Type ACR copper tube is used for air conditioning and refrigeration field service. The ASTM standard for this use is B280. It is available in hard drawn lengths and annealed coils.

STAINLESS STEEL PIPE

Stainless steel is a broad group of alloys. This pipe is available in several different types, each with its own properties regarding strength and corrosion resistance.

ALUMINUM PIPE

This is suitable for water piping and hand railings.

PLASTIC PIPING

When using plastic pipe, it is important to protect the integrity of any fire walls that might be penetrated. Specially approved expanding putty is made for this application, although steel pipe is the safer choice.

Polybutylene and polyethelene tubing is now commonly used for indoor hydronic radiant heating and outdoor snow melting systems.

SEAMLESS STEEL PIPE

1. ASTM Spec. A-53: This is a general service pipe, suitable for bending, coiling, fusion welding, lapping, or flanging. Grade B does not lend itself to close coiling, forge-welding, or cold bends.
2. ASTM Spec. A-106: Manufactured from carbon steel for high temperature, high pressure service. An open hearth steel that comes in Grades A and B. Grade A works well for all forming or welding operations. Grade B has somewhat higher carbon and manganese content, which gives it greater tensile strength but less ductility.

BUTT WELD STEEL PIPE

This pipe is for ordinary use on steam, water, gas, or air. It is not intended for medium or high pressure or close coiling or bending. Specifications require only hydrostatic testing; there are no chemical requirements.

Piping Systems Council; Chicago, Illinois
P.V.C. Plastic Pipe Institute; New York, New York
Walter H. Sobel, FAIA and Associates; Chicago, Illinois

CAST IRON, MALLEABLE, AND DUCTILE IRON PIPE FITTING MATERIALS

The material used in the manufacture of cast iron, malleable, and ductile iron pipe fittings should conform to specifications set by ASTM.

DESIGN: THREADED FITTINGS

Typically, piping 2 in. and below is connected by threaded joints, and piping above 2 in. is joined by welding. Fittings used in welded piping are referred to as "weld els" and "weld tees." Groove joint couplings are often used on fire protection piping systems.

DESIGN: DRAINAGE FITTINGS

Drainage fittings should be designed to give unobstructed flow. Fittings with openings at right angles should have pitched threads with a horizontal line pitch of 1/4 in./ft, assuring positive drainage. Pressure-temperature ratings do not apply to drainage fittings.

DESIGN: PLUGS, BUSHINGS, AND LOCKNUTS

Common plug designs are square head, countersunk, and bar plug. Face bushings and hexagon head bushings are available in a wide range of sizes, and generally are furnished in cast iron or malleable iron. Some small sizes of plugs, bushings, and locknuts are furnished in steel.

Sprinkler lines, heating and air conditioning systems, and plumbing installations utilize cast iron fittings. There is a wide range of types and sizes of fittings available from various manufacturers. Common types of threaded and flanged fittings:

1. ELBOWS: 90°, 90° reducing, 90° side outlet, 45°-90° long radius, 11 1/4°, 22 1/2°, three-way and drop elbows.
2. TEES: Straight run, reducing outlet, reduced run, other end and outlet equal, reduced on run and outlet, side outlet.

Crosses	Laterals
Reducers	Couplings
Double 45° Y's	Increasers
60° Y's	Unions
P traps	Caps
Running traps	Plugs
Return bends	Locknuts

GLASS PIPING

Glass piping is used for acid waste drainlines, and is manufactured to resist fracture from thermal shock between 0° and 100° C.

TEMPER-ATURE (°F)	WORKING PRESSURE NONSHOCK PSIG	
	CLASS 125	CLASS 250
-20 TO 150	175	400
200	165	370
250	150	340
300	140	310
350	125	280
400	–	250

CLASSES 125 AND 250 CAST IRON FLANGED FITTINGS
ANSI STANDARD B16.1

TEMPER-ATURE (°F)	WORKING PRESSURE NONSHOCK PSIG				
	CLASS 125 SIZES			CLASS 250 SIZES	
	1-12	14-24	30-48	1-12	14-24
-20 TO 250	200	150	150	500	300
200	190	135	115	460	280
225	180	130	100	440	270
250	175	125	85	415	260
275	170	120	65	395	250
300	165	110	50	375	240
325	155	105		355	230
350	150	100		335	220
375	145			315	210
400	140			290	200
425	130			270	
450	125			250	

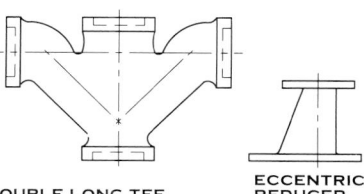

DOUBLE LONG TEE   ECCENTRIC REDUCER

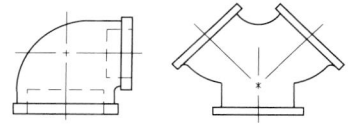

90° REDUCING ELBOW   TRUE Y

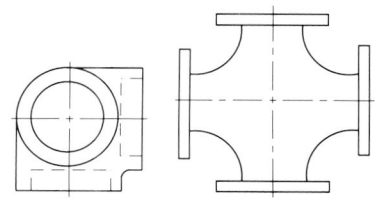

90° SIDE OUTLET ELBOW   CROSS

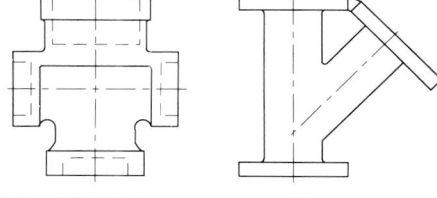

BELL TOP DOUBLE TEE   LATERAL

VARIOUS PIPE FITTINGS

NOTES

The cleanout provides access to horizontal and vertical plumbing lines and stacks and a means to remove obstructions. Generally, cleanouts consist of an iron body and brass plug with neoprene seal. The outlet must be gas tight and watertight and must provide ample space for rodding tools. An adjustable housing will allow for variations in floor fill. Cleanout covers must be designed to support the weight of traffic directed over them. The inside caulk type outlet provides greater ease of installation while the wide flange type assures a waterproof bond between floor covering and cleanout.

Most codes require cleanouts located not more than 50 ft apart in horizontal drainage lines of 4 in. pipe or less and not more than 100 ft apart for larger pipe. Also, install cleanouts at each change of direction greater than 45° and at the base of each vertical waste stack. Access covers should be secured with vandal-proof screws or hinged where these units are likely to be removed.

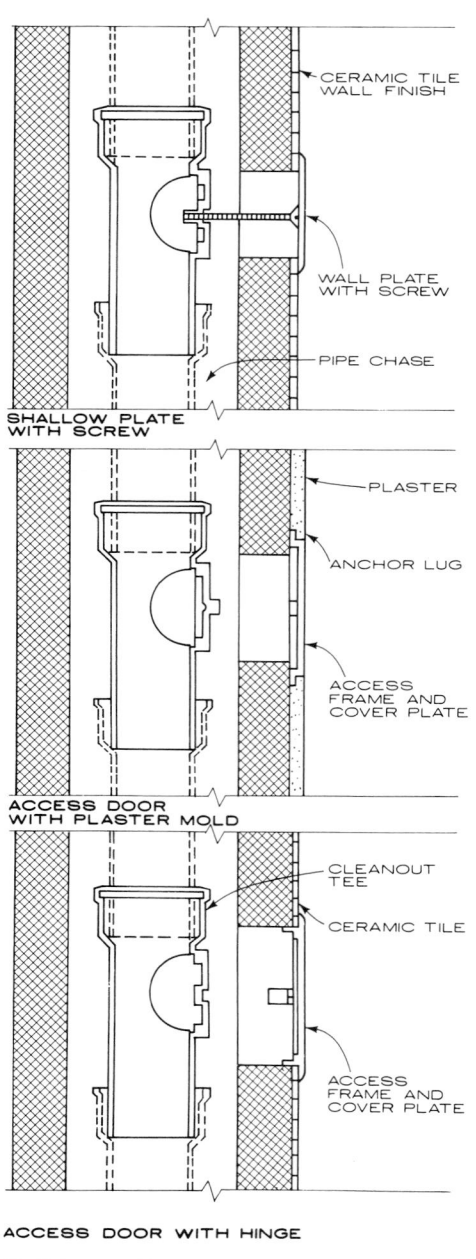

WALL TYPE CLEANOUTS

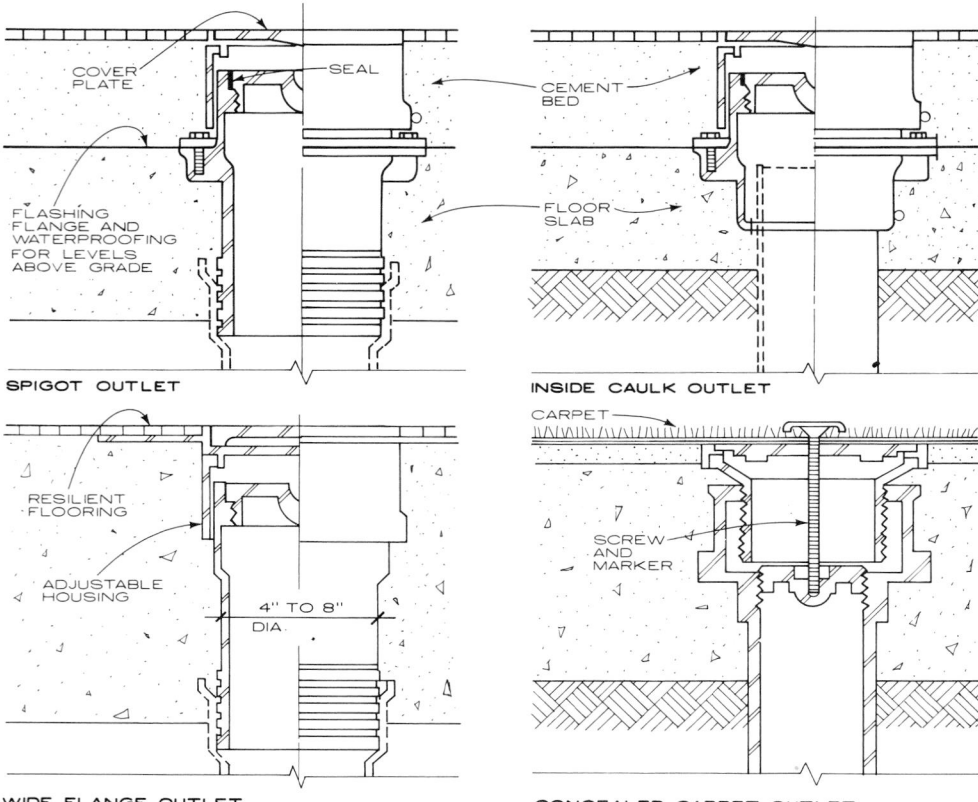

SPIGOT OUTLET

INSIDE CAULK OUTLET

WIDE FLANGE OUTLET

CONCEALED CARPET OUTLET

FLOOR TYPE CLEANOUTS

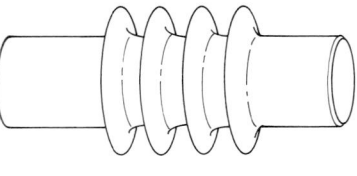

PACKLESS EXPANSION JOINT has stainless steel bellows and carbon steel weld-end nipples (shown) or flanged ends. Sizes 3 in. to 60 in. diameter may have 1 to 10 corrugations. Consult manufacturer for required installation details.

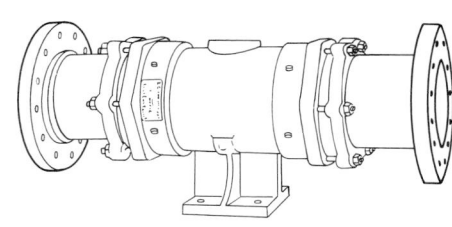

SLIP TYPE EXPANSION JOINT has either internal or external guides. Double joint type is shown with flanged end connections and base. Sizes 1¼ in. to 20 in. are fabricated or cast semi-steel.

EXPANSION JOINT ASSEMBLIES

TOTAL THERMAL EXPANSION OF PIPING MATERIAL (IN.) PER 100 FT ABOVE 32°F

TEMPERATURE (°F)	CARBON AND CARBON MOLY STEEL	CAST IRON	COPPER	BRASS AND BRONZE	WROUGHT IRON	PLASTIC
32	0	0	0	0	0	0
100	0.5	0.5	0.8	0.8	0.5	2.0
150	0.8	0.8	1.4	1.4	0.9	4.25
200	1.2	1.2	2.0	2.0	1.3	6.25
250	1.7	1.5	2.7	2.6	1.7	—
300	2.0	1.9	3.3	3.2	2.2	—
350	2.5	2.3	4.0	3.9	2.6	—
400	2.9	2.7	4.7	4.6	3.1	—
450	3.4	3.1	5.3	5.2	3.6	—
500	3.8	3.5	6.0	5.9	4.1	—
550	4.3	3.9	6.7	6.5	4.6	—
600	4.8	4.0	7.4	7.2	5.2	—
650	5.3	4.7	8.2	7.9	5.6	—
700	5.9	5.3	9.0	8.5	6.1	—
750	6.4	5.8	—	—	6.7	—
800	7.0	6.3	—	—	7.2	—
850	7.4	—	—	—	—	—
900	8.0	—	—	—	—	—
950	8.5	—	—	—	—	—
1000	9.1	—	—	—	—	—

Sargent, Webster, Crenshaw & Folley, Architects Engineers Planners; Syracuse, New York

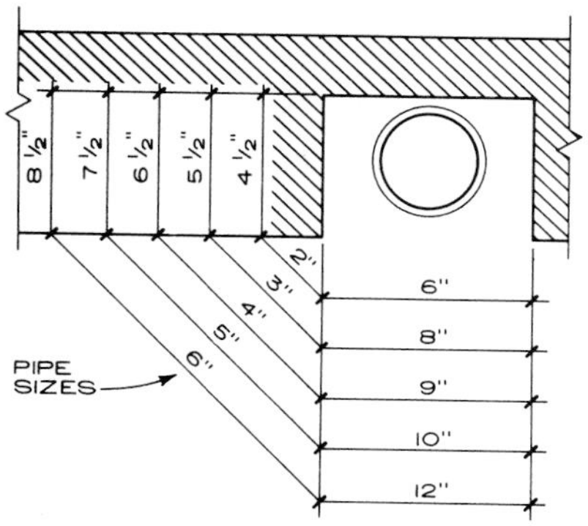

ONE SOIL, WASTE, OR VENT

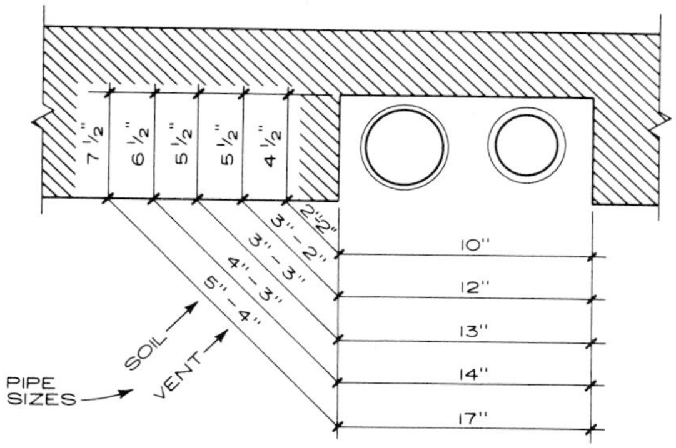

PIPE SIZES →

8½" | 7½" | 6½" | 5½" | 4½"
2"
3"
4"
5"
6"

6"
8"
9"
10"
12"

TWO SOILS, WASTES, OR VENTS

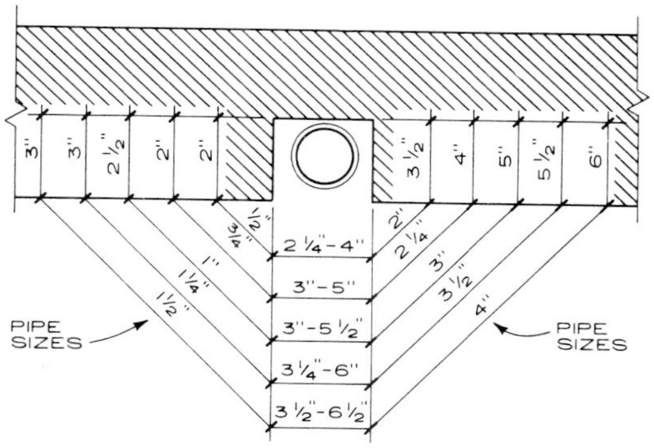

7½" | 6½" | 5½" | 5½" | 4"

PIPE SIZES →

SOIL
VENT

2½"
3"—2"
4"—3"
5"—4"

10"
12"
13"
14"
17"

WATER PIPES

3" | 3" | 2½" | 2" | 2"

PIPE SIZES →

½"
¾"
1"
1¼"
1½"

3½" | 3½" | 3" | 2½" | 2"

2¼"—4"
3"—5"
3"—5½"
3¼"—6"
3½"—6½"

← PIPE SIZES

4"
5"
5½"
6"

RECOMMENDED CHASE SIZES FOR VARIOUS PIPE SIZES WITH HUBS (SEE NOTES 2, 3, AND 4 ON THIS PAGE)

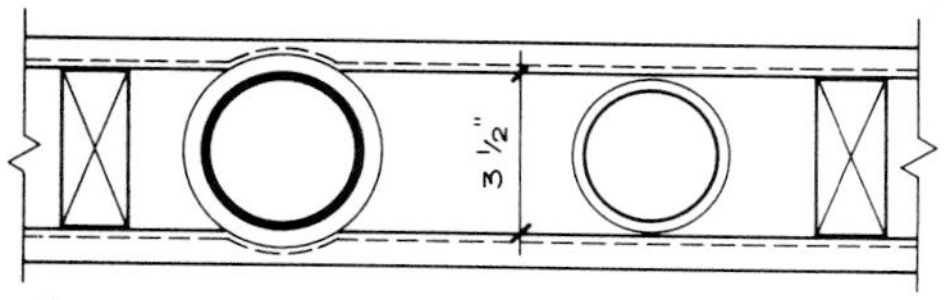

WOOD STUD PARTITIONS WITH 3/4" METAL LATH AND PLASTER

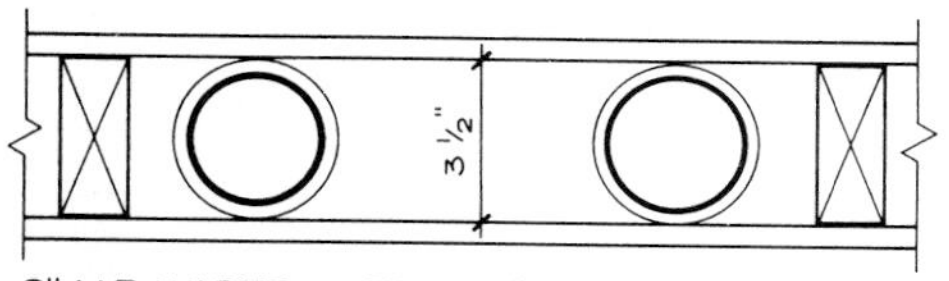

4" STUD — 3½"

2" B & S WASTE PIPE
3" M.P. VENT OR
WATER PIPE

3" C., P., OR N.H. VENT
PIPE
3" C. WATER PIPE
2" M.P. VENT OR WATER
PIPE

6" STUD — 5½"

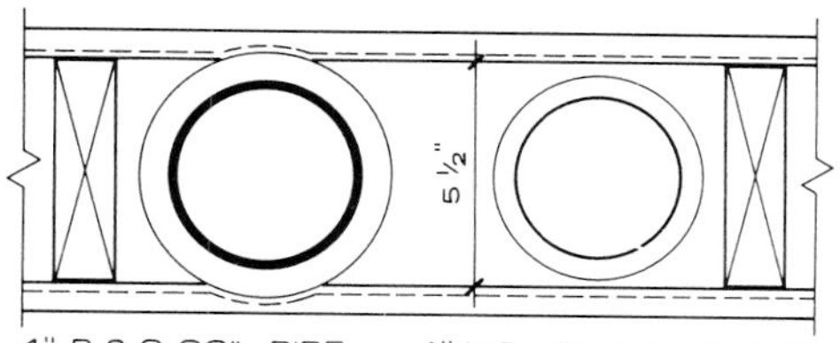

4" B & S. SOIL PIPE
5" M.P. VENT PIPE

4" M.P. VENT OR WATER
PIPE
4" OR 5" N.H. OR P. SOIL
PIPE
4" OR 5" N.H., C., OR P.
VENT PIPE
4" OR 5" C. WATER PIPE

8" STUD — 7½"

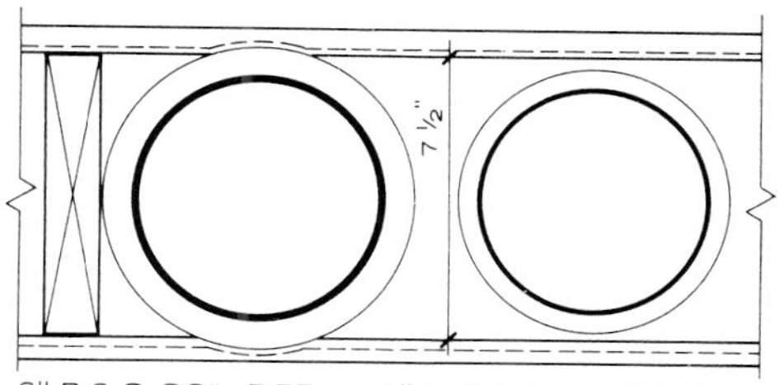

6" B & S SOIL PIPE

6" M.P., N.H., C., OR P.
VENT PIPE
6" N.H. OR P. SOIL PIPE
6" M.P. OR C. WATER PIPE

WOOD STUD PARTITIONS WITH RIGID BOARD OR RIGID LATH

4" STUD — 3½"

2" M.P. WASTE, WATER,
OR VENT PIPE
3" N.H. SOIL PIPE

3" C. WASTE, WATER,
OR VENT PIPE
3" P. WASTE OR VENT
PIPE

6" STUD — 5½"

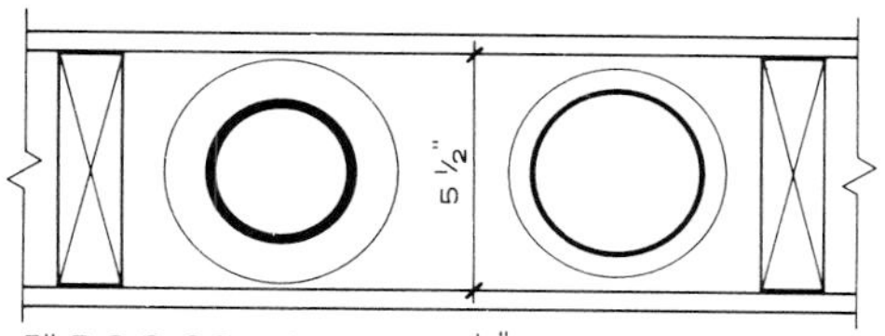

3" B & S SOIL OR
VENT PIPE

3 ½" M.P. WASTE, VENT,
OR WATER PIPE
5" C. WATER OR VENT
PIPE
5" N.H. OR P. SOIL OR
VENT PIPE

8" STUD — 7½"

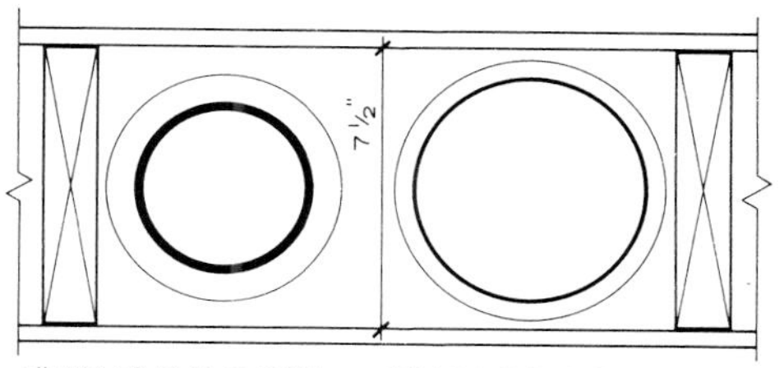

4" OR 5" B & S SOIL
OR VENT PIPE

6" N.H. OR P. SOIL PIPE
6" N.H., M.P., C., OR P.
VENT PIPE
5" M.P. OR 6" C. WATER
PIPE

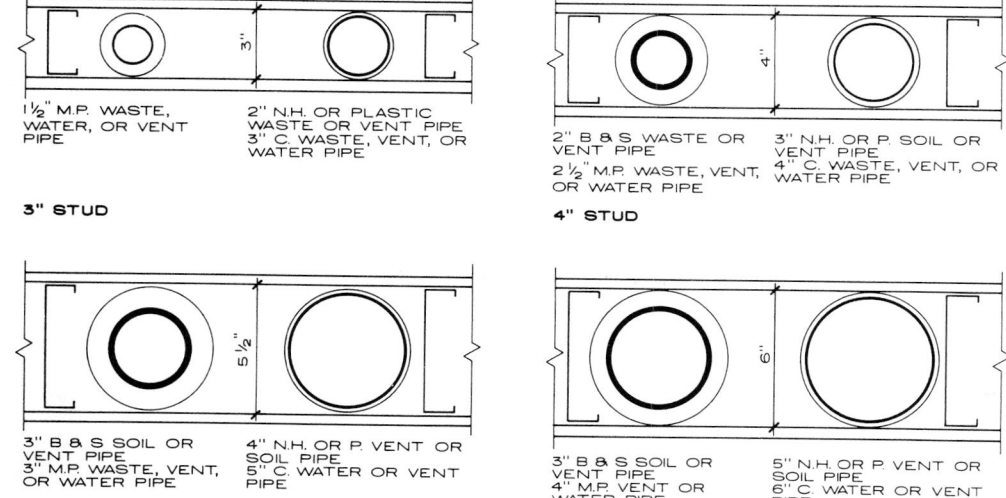

3" STUD — 3"

1½" M.P. WASTE,
WATER, OR VENT
PIPE

2" N.H. OR PLASTIC
WASTE OR VENT PIPE
3" C. WASTE, VENT, OR
WATER PIPE

4" STUD — 4"

2" B & S WASTE OR
VENT PIPE
2 ½" M.P. WASTE, VENT,
OR WATER PIPE

3" N.H. OR P. SOIL OR
VENT PIPE
4" C. WASTE, VENT, OR
WATER PIPE

5½" STUD — 5½"

3" B & S SOIL OR
VENT PIPE
3" M.P. WASTE, VENT,
OR WATER PIPE

4" N.H. OR P. VENT OR
SOIL PIPE
5" C. WATER OR VENT
PIPE

6" STUD — 6"

3" B & S SOIL OR
VENT PIPE
4" M.P. VENT OR
WATER PIPE

5" N.H. OR P. VENT OR
SOIL PIPE
6" C. WATER OR VENT
PIPE

STEEL STUD PARTITIONS WITH RIGID BOARD

Kelly Sacher & Associates; Architects Engineers Planners; N. Babylon, Long Island, New York

NOTES

1. B&S: extra heavy cast iron bell and spigot (push or caulked joints). C: copper tubing. NH: extra heavy cast iron no-hub pipe. MP: malleable pattern (galvanized or nongalvanized). P: plastic pipe.

2. Recommended chase sizes for various pipes include a ¾ in. covering. For additional cover subtract ¾ in. from the amount of cover required; add the result to the desired pipe size dimension.

3. Chases may be provided with or without access. Chases for several pipes, especially those containing main water supply pipes, should be provided with a means of access in case repair is necessary.

4. To size a chase with several pipes, add required widths for each.

5. Partitions with ¾ in. lath and plaster are shown with certain maximum pipe sizes encroaching on the lath and plaster. Encroaching pipe portions should be coated with asphaltic paint to prevent staining the plaster.

6. When rigid board or lath, such as gypsum board, plaster board, or gypsum lath, is used, the extreme diameter of pipe fitting bead or bell should come within the actual clear dimension of the wall core.

7. Pipe spaces can be enlarged by placing piping between two back-to-back partitions with the required clear space between them.

8. Use steel pipe clearances for hubless pipe installation.

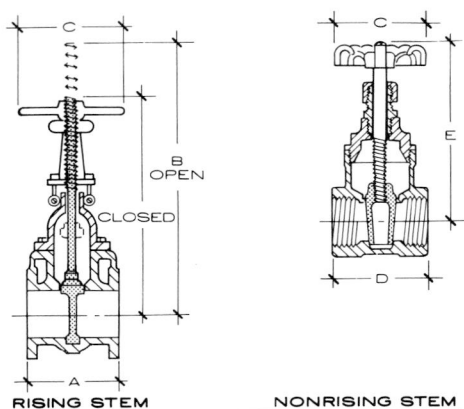

RISING STEM   NONRISING STEM

GATE VALVES

NOTE

Used for on-off service; offers practically no resistance to flow when fully open. Not recommended for throttling or flow modulation. Available in rising and nonrising stems. Suitable for hot and cold water, oil, and gas.

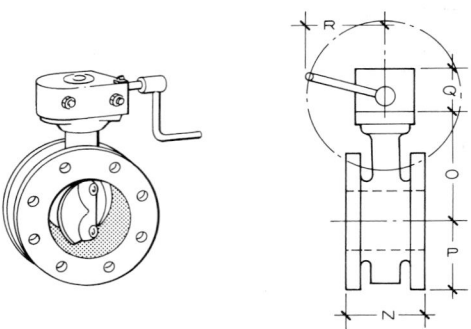

BUTTERFLY VALVE

NOTE

Feature quarter-turn, on-off operation for water, air, gas, or vacuum lines. Recommended for on-off service and some noncritical throttling applications.

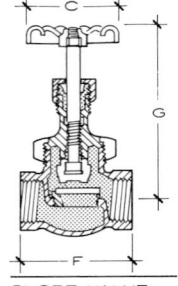

GLOBE VALVE

NOTE

Ideal for throttling service in hot and cold water, oil, and gas piping. Caution must be exercised, however, to avoid extremely close throttling. Vibration may cause valve damage or excessive noise. These valves are seldom used in sizes above 12 in.

NOTES

Effectively utilize the globe valves throttling control while providing for a 90° turn in piping. Conditions regarding excessive throttling and size above 12 in., noted for globe valves, also apply to angle valves.

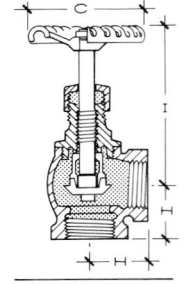

ANGLE VALVE

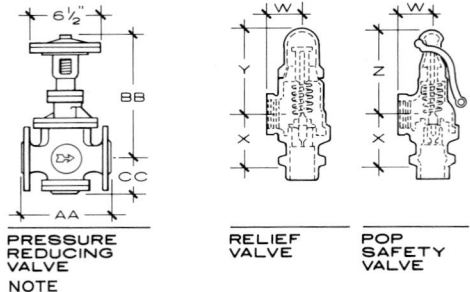

PRESSURE REDUCING VALVE

RELIEF VALVE   POP SAFETY VALVE

NOTE

Used in steam, water, air, or gas lines where it is necessary to reduce incoming pressure to the required service pressure. They also maintain it at the point desired.

NOTE

Usually spring-loaded valves that open automatically when pressure exceeds limit for which the valve is set. Should always be installed with the stem in a vertical position. Relief valves are usually used for liquids. Safety valves are generally used for steam, air, or other gases.

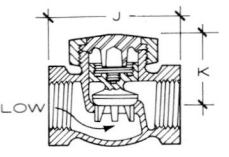

LIFT CHECK VALVE

NOTE

Prevent reversal of flow. For use in horizontal lines only. Generally used in conjunction with globe valves.

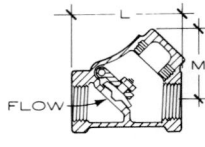

SWING CHECK VALVE

NOTE

Prevent reversal of flow and are particularly suited to low velocity service. Most swing check valves can be installed in horizontal or vertical upward flow piping. Generally used in conjunction with gate valves.

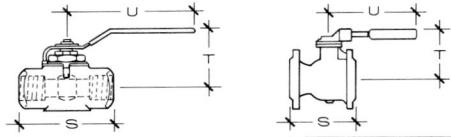

BALL VALVES

NOTE

Feature quarter-turn, on-off operation, straight-through flow, minimum turbulence, low operating torque, tight closure, compact design, and light weight. Available with threaded, solder joint, or flanged ends.

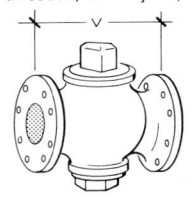

GAS COCK   SPRING—LOADED COCK

NOTE

Available in two-way, three-way, and four-way patterns with threaded or flanged ends. Suitable for cold water, oil, air, or gas.

VALVE DIMENSIONS
THREADED UNLESS OTHERWISE NOTED

SIZE (IN.)	GATE					GLOBE		ANGLE		LIFT CHECK		SWING CHECK		SPRING – LOADED COCK			BALL			COCK	RELIEF AND SAFETY				PRESSURE REDUCING		
	A	B	C	D	E	F	G	H	I	J	K	L	M	O	P	Q	S	T	U	V	W	X	Y	Z	AA	BB	CC
$1/4$	$1^3/4$	$4^1/2$	$1^3/4$	$1^7/8$	$3^3/4$	$1^3/4$	$2^3/4$	$7/8$	3	$1^7/8$	1	$2^1/8$	$1^1/2$				3	$1^1/4$	4	$1^5/8$							
$3/8$	$1^3/4$	$4^1/2$	$1^3/4$	$1^7/8$	$3^3/4$	$1^7/8$	$2^7/8$	1	$3^1/4$	2	$1^1/8$	$2^1/8$	$1^1/2$				3	$1^1/4$	4	$1^3/4$	$1^1/8$	$2^1/4$	$3^1/8$	$3^3/4$	Flanged		
$1/2$	$2^1/8$	$5^1/4$	$2^1/8$	$2^1/8$	$3^3/4$	$2^1/4$	$3^1/2$	$1^1/8$	$3^3/4$	$2^1/2$	$1^3/8$	$2^1/2$	$1^3/4$	$1^1/4$	$2^1/8$	$2^3/8$	$2^1/2$	$1^1/4$	4	$2^1/8$	$1^1/8$	$2^1/4$	$3^1/8$	$3^3/4$	$7^1/2$	$11^3/4$	$3^1/2$
$3/4$	$2^1/4$	$6^1/2$	$2^5/8$	$2^1/4$	$4^1/2$	$2^3/4$	4	$1^3/8$	$4^1/4$	3	$1^7/8$	3	$2^1/8$	$1^5/8$	$2^1/2$	$2^7/8$	$2^3/4$	$1^1/2$	$4^1/2$	$2^1/2$	$1^3/8$	$2^3/4$	$3^1/4$	$3^3/4$	$7^1/2$	$11^3/4$	$3^1/2$
1	$2^3/4$	$7^3/4$	$2^3/4$	$2^7/8$	$5^1/4$	$3^3/8$	$4^1/2$	$1^5/8$	5	$3^1/2$	2	$3^3/4$	$2^1/2$	2	$3^1/8$	$3^1/2$	$3^1/2$	$2^1/8$	6	3	$1^5/8$	$3^1/4$	$3^5/8$	$4^5/8$	$7^1/2$	$11^3/4$	$3^1/2$
$1^1/4$	3	$9^1/4$	$3^1/8$	3	$5^7/8$	$3^7/8$	$4^7/8$	$1^3/4$	$5^1/2$	$4^1/8$	$2^3/8$	$4^1/4$	3				4	$2^5/8$	7	$3^1/2$	$2^1/8$	$3^3/4$	$4^1/4$	$4^3/8$	$7^7/8$	12	$3^3/4$
$1^1/2$	$3^1/4$	$10^1/2$	$3^5/8$	$3^1/4$	$7^1/4$	$4^1/2$	$5^1/2$	$2^1/4$	$6^1/4$	$4^5/8$	$2^5/8$	5	$3^1/2$				$4^1/4$	$2^3/4$	7	$3^3/4$	$2^1/2$	$4^3/8$	$5^3/8$	$5^1/4$	$8^3/8$	$12^1/2$	$4^1/4$
2	$3^3/4$	$12^3/4$	$4^3/4$	$3^3/4$	$8^3/8$	$5^1/4$	6	$2^5/8$	$7^1/2$	$5^3/4$	$3^1/4$	6	$4^1/4$				$4^1/2$	$3^1/8$	8	$4^5/8$	$2^3/4$	$4^1/2$	$6^5/8$	$6^1/8$	$10^1/4$	12	$4^1/2$

VALVE DIMENSIONS
FLANGED UNLESS OTHERWISE NOTED

SIZE (IN.)	GATE					GLOBE		ANGLE		LIFT CHECK		SWING CHECK		BUTTERFLY					RELIEF AND SAFETY				PRESSURE REDUCING		
	A	B	C	D	E	F	G	H	I	J	K	L	M	N	O	P	Q	R	BALL S	T	U	COCK V	AA	BB	CC
2	7.0	18	8	$8^1/2$	11	8	$13^3/4$	4	$12^1/2$	Threaded		8	5	$1^3/4$	$5^1/2$	$2^1/2$	$2^7/8$	5	Threaded						
$2^1/2$	7.5	19	8	$9^1/2$	$13^1/4$	$8^1/2$	$14^1/2$	$4^1/4$	13	$6^7/8$	$3^7/8$	$8^1/2$	$5^1/2$	$1^7/8$	6	$2^3/4$	$2^7/8$	5	$8^5/8$ 3	$4^7/8$	$7^5/8$	$7^3/4$	$11^5/8$	13	6
3	8.0	$19^7/8$	9	$11^1/8$	$14^3/4$	$9^1/2$	$16^1/2$	$4^3/4$	15	8	$4^1/2$	$9^1/2$	6	5	$6^1/4$	$3^1/2$	$2^7/8$	5	8 $3^1/2$	$5^1/4$	$8^1/2$	$9^1/2$	$12^1/2$	$13^3/4$	$6^3/4$
4	9.0	$23^3/4$	10	12	$17^1/2$	$11^1/2$	$19^3/4$	$5^3/4$	$17^3/4$			$11^1/2$	7	5	8.12	$4^1/4$	$2^7/8$	5	9 $7^1/2$	15	$12^1/8$		$14^1/4$	$14^3/4$	$7^5/8$
6	10.5	$32^1/2$	12	$15^7/8$	23	16	$24^1/2$	8	$21^3/4$			14	9	5	9.12	$5^3/4$	$2^7/8$	5	$10^1/2$ $9^1/4$	30			$17^3/4$	$19^1/8$	$10^1/4$
8	11.5	$40^3/4$	14	$16^1/2$	$30^3/4$	$19^1/2$	$26^1/2$	$9^3/4$	24			$19^1/2$	$10^1/4$	6	10.40	$7^1/2$	$2^7/8$	5	$11^1/2$ $10^3/4$	$37^1/2$			$21^1/4$	$43^1/4$	$14^1/4$

NOTES

1. Sizes are nominal; all dimensions are in inches.
2. Refer to manufacturers' literature for other sizes.
3. Operation of 4 in. size and larger located more than 7 ft above the floor requires chains, extensions, etc.

Victor J. Saccaro; Hoyem-Basso Associates; Bloomfield Hills, Michigan

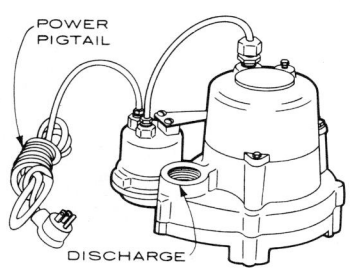

SUBMERSIBLE

Approximate minimum pit size 24 in. x 24 in. Gpm range to 130 gpm; heads to 50 ft.

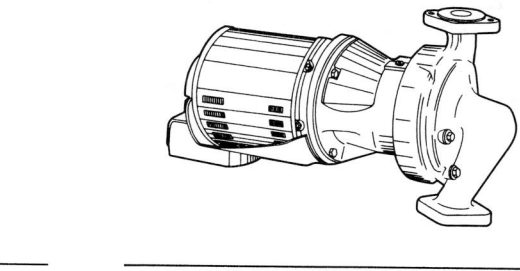

IN-LINE CENTRIFUGAL

Installed directly in pipeline and supported by pipe and structure. Gpm range to 130 gpm; heads to 50 ft.

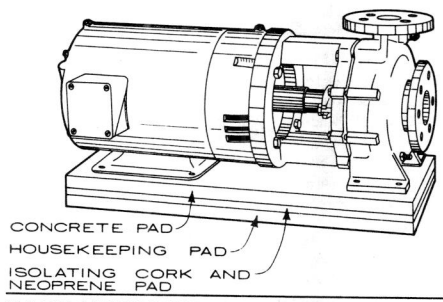

BASE-MOUNTED CENTRIFUGAL CLOSED COUPLED

Gpm range to 3000 gpm; heads to 360 ft. Required floor space approximately 24 in. x 36 in. to 36 in. x 60 in.

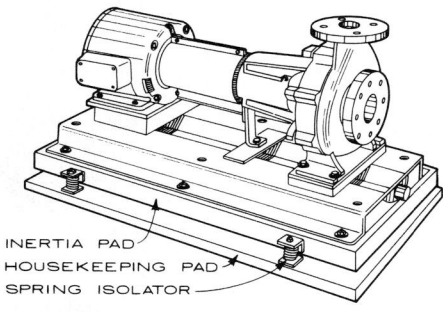

FRAME-MOUNTED CENTRIFUGAL END SUCTION

Gpm range to 25,000 gpm; head range to 600 ft. Required floor space approximately 24 x 48 in. to 72 x 144 in.

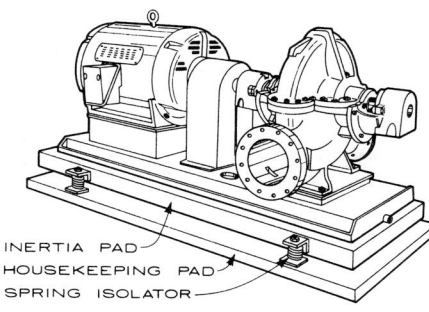

FRAME-MOUNTED CENTRIFUGAL, DOUBLE SUCTION

Gpm range to 14,000 gpm; head range to 1,200 ft. Available with integral suction sump. Ideal for low net positive suction head application. Less floor space required than for centrifugal pumps.

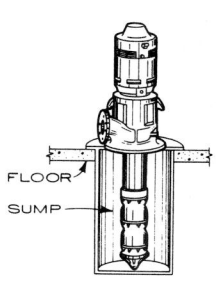

VERTICAL TURBINE

Sewerage or sump pump for small installations up to 150 gpm to 40 ft. total head. Will operate completely submerged in sump. Suitable for negative suction head.

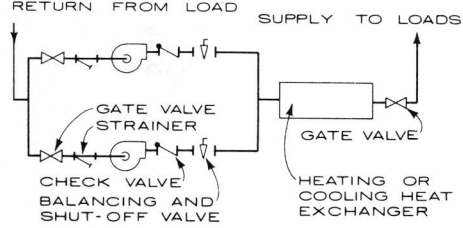

PARALLEL PUMPING

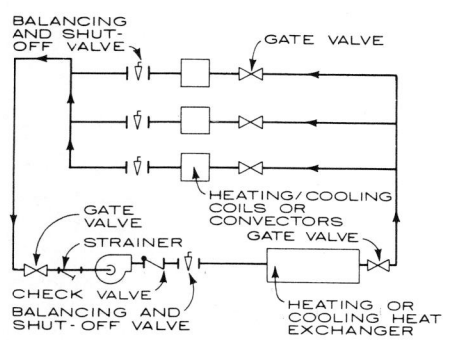

REVERSE RETURN

PARALLEL PUMPING

Provides a degree of standby. If one pump fails, approximately 7 percent of flow can be obtained with one pump. It also can be applied to variable flow rate systems where one pump can be shut down under certain operative conditions; also, if flow required is greater than capacity of a single standard pump, parallel pumps can be installed to achieve desired flow rate.

PRIMARY SECONDARY PUMP

Characteristics of secondary circuit essentially are unaffected by changes in primary circuit or by other secondary circuits. Can be used to provide a different water temperature to each secondary circuit by using mixing valves; also can be used for variable flow primary circuit and constant flow secondary circuits.

REVERSE RETURN

Provides an approximate equal pressure drop to each secondary heat transfer surface, thereby minimizing balancing requirements. Preferred on extensive piping loops for radiation, fan coil units, etc.

CONVENTIONAL PUMPING

Least costly and applicable to systems requiring only basic circulation, such as heat exchangers, chillers, and cooling towers. Also can be used for loops to radiation, fan coil units, etc., where runs are short and balancing can be achieved easily.

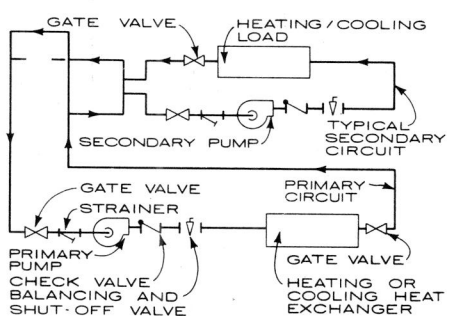

PRIMARY/SECONDARY CIRCUIT

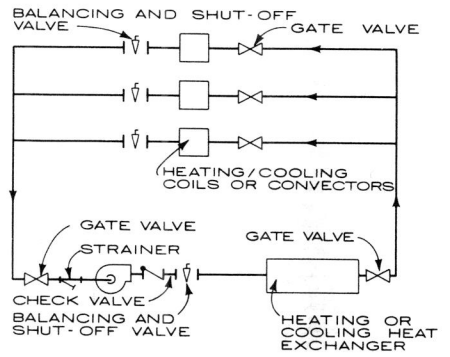

CONVENTIONAL PUMPING

William Tao & Associates, Inc., Consulting Engineers; St. Louis, Missouri

GENERAL

Attention must be given to vibration of mechanical equipment to ensure that there is no transmission of objectionable vibration or structureborne noise to the building and occupied spaces. The following general procedure should be followed to avoid problems of vibration and structureborne noise transmission:

1. Evaluate the inherent quietness of the various types of equipment and try to select the types with the lowest sound and vibration levels, consistent with engineering and cost considerations.
2. Locate equipment rooms so they are not directly adjacent to, above, or below areas that are critical from a noise and vibration standpoint. Equipment with inherently large unbalance or vibratory forces should be installed at grade or remote basement locations whenever possible.
3. Locate pipe and duct shafts in utility or service cores near noncritical areas such as elevator shafts, stairwells, and toilets, rather than adjoining critical areas such as bedrooms or private offices.
4. Design supporting structures to be as stiff as possible. Although most equipment room floors are usually 10 or more times stiffer than equipment isolators, they are capable of deflections resulting in floor natural frequencies in the operating speed range of most HVAC equipment. Primary concern is with low speed equipment on long spans that have low natural frequencies and high speed equipment on short span or rigid floors that have high natural frequencies.
5. Specify maximum allowable equipment vibration levels.
6. Provide appropriate vibration isolation for equipment.

Many types of equipment require some support base to maintain alignment of driving and driven components such as fans or where equipment cannot be supported at individual isolator locations. Support bases may be constructed of structural steel members, concrete, or a combination of concrete and structural members, and should always be designed with ample rigidity to resist all starting and operating forces without supplemental hold-down devices. It is common practice to install many types of equipment on inertia blocks as shown below. Inertia blocks or mass of the system have no effect on the efficiency of isolators; however, they do affect the movement of the equipment itself and, as such, can affect the transmission to the building structure through connected piping and ducts.

Inertia blocks should be used for:

1. Equipment that has large unbalance or vibratory forces such as horizontal air compressors, and some reciprocating compressors and engines. For such equipment, the designer should obtain from the equipment manufacturer the magnitude and frequency of the unbalance forces to permit proper sizing of inertia block.
2. Equipment such as certain large fans, pumps, and compressors, where some type of structural base must be furnished to support driving and driven components and/or maintain alignment.
3. Equipment subject to external forces such as high pressure fans, where use of an inertia block will result in stiffer isolators and thereby limit movement resulting from reaction to pressure thrust.

NOTE

Within earthquake zones, inertia blocks and other support bases must be designed to resist the horizontal and vertical thrusts that can occur during a seismic event. Heavy equipment mounted on a floating base can easily develop enough motion to fly free of its springs. Excessive lateral movement should be prevented through the use of angle iron stops, spring mounts with integral restraints or all-directional snubbers. All of these devices must be carefully installed so that they do not hinder the normal operation of the isolation system.

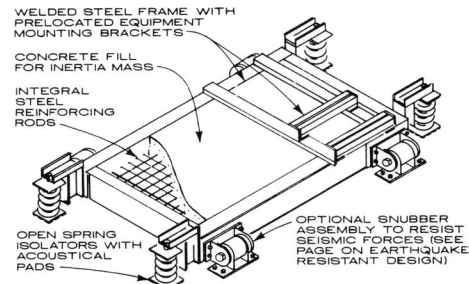

CONCRETE AND STEEL BASE

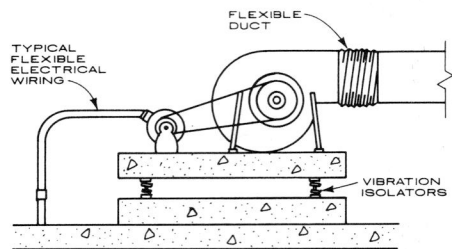

INERTIA BLOCKS

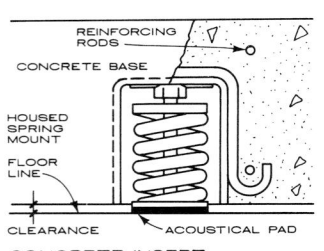

CONCRETE INSERT

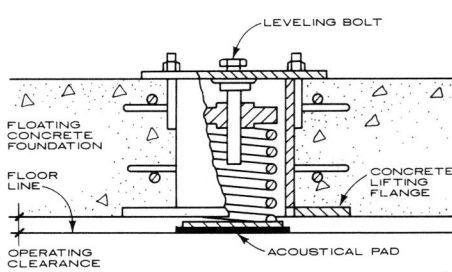

CONCRETE INSERT FOR LARGE BASE

EQUIPMENT SUPPORT BASES

The choice of isolators for any given application primarily depends on required deflection; however, consideration must also be given to life, cost, and suitability for specific application.

STEEL SPRINGS are the most popular and versatile isolators for HVAC application, since they are available for almost any desired deflection and have virtually unlimited lift. Steel springs, when installed outdoors or in corrosive environments, should be properly protected by the electroplating or other protective coatings. The two basic types of spring isolators are open spring mountings and housed spring mountings.

Open spring mountings consist of a steel spring between a bottom and top plate and usually incorporate an adjustment bolt for leveling. Open spring mounts have become popular, since they avoid the binding and "short circuiting" that can occur with housed mountings. However, misalignment (nonparallel condition of floor and base) should generally be avoided.

It is very important that open springs have proper stiffness in the vertical and horizontal directions so that the springs will be stable and equipment will move sideways.

Housed spring mountings consist of a spring element in a housing incorporating an adjustment bolt for leveling that can be internally located to permit installation of the mount under equipment without legs or holes for an adjustment bolt. The springs in housed mountings are not generally designed to meet stability requirements, since housings limit excessive lateral movement.

It should be noted that all spring mounts must incorporate an elastomeric acoustical and friction pad to prevent the transmission of audible high frequency vibration directly through the spring to the structure.

VIBRATION ISOLATORS

OPEN SPRING

HOUSED SPRING

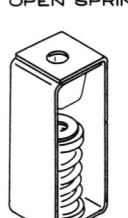

SPRING AND RUBBER

RUBBER HANGER

ISOLATION HANGERS are used for pipe and suspended equipment and usually incorporate rubber, spring, or combination spring and rubber isolator elements. Where spring elements are used, stable springs should be specified. Where isolation hangers are used for suspending piping, provision must be made to accommodate expansion and contraction of pipe due to thermal changes. For pipelines subject to significant thermal movement, this is best accomplished with an eye bolt or swivel arrangement for attachment to structure so that hanger box can swivel to avoid "cocking" of isolation element.

RUBBER MOUNT

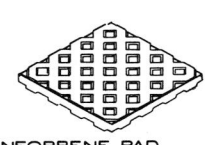

NEOPRENE PAD

RUBBER ISOLATORS are available in mount and pad configuration and are generally molded of rubber or neoprene, although other materials such as fiberglass and cork can be used to meet specific service requirements.

Rubber isolators provide a very high resistance to the transmission of noise (high frequency vibration in the acoustical range). In general, their use should be restricted to minor equipment or basement locations.

COMPARISON TABLE

RANGE	RPM	SPRINGS	ELASTOMERS	CORK
Low	Up to 1200	Required	Unsuitable except for shock	Unsuitable except for shock
Medium	1200–1800	Excellent	Fair	Not recommended
High	Over 1800	Excellent for critical jobs	Good	Fair to good

GENERAL INFORMATION

The insulation and methods described on this page are typical of those used for HVAC work. There are other materials that are equally suitable for use on HVAC and similar systems. The designer should evaluate all available insulating materials and apply what is best suited to the situation with regard to both service and cost. One of the major considerations is the fuel contributed—fire spread—and smoke developed characteristics of various insulating materials. Insulating materials used where air is moved from one area to another such as return and supply air plenums should not exceed a 25/50 fire spread, smoke developed rating.

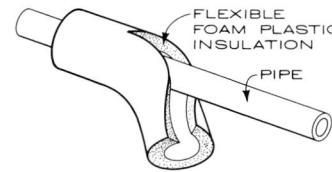

METHOD PD

PA GLASS FIBER: Available in both light and heavy density material and with factory applied jacket. Flame spread 25, smoke developed 50; k value 0.25; thickness 1/2 to 2 in. most commonly used. Use multiple layers for greater thickness. Suitable for −60 to +450°F temperature range.

PB PHENOLIC: Molded rigid insulation from neutral phenolic foam, medium density with factory applied jacket. Flame spread 25, smoke developed 50; k value 0.23; suitable for −40 to +250°F temperature range; available in 1, 1 1/2, and 2 in. thickness.

PC POLYURETHANE: Foamed polyurethane, medium density, available with factory applied jacket. Flame spread 25, smoke developed 50 when covered with jacket of 1 mil thick aluminum foil laminated to Kraft paper; available thickness 1 in.; k value 0.16. Polyurethane without proper jacket exceeds 25/50 flame spread/smoke developed rating. Temperature range −100 to +220°F.

PD FOAMED PLASTIC: Flexible foamed plastic insulation, requires no jacket but may be painted with alkyd paint. Fire retardant type available in 3/8 and 1/2 in. thickness with flame spread of 25, smoke developed 200; standard type available in 3/8, 1/2, 3/4 in. thickness with flame spread and smoke developed exceeding 25/200; k value 0.25; suitable for −40 to +220°F temperature range. Seal joints and seams with adhesive.

PE CALCIUM SILICATE: Rigid pipe insulation, k value 0.40, with factory jacket, for pipe up to 1200°F.

PIPE INSULATION

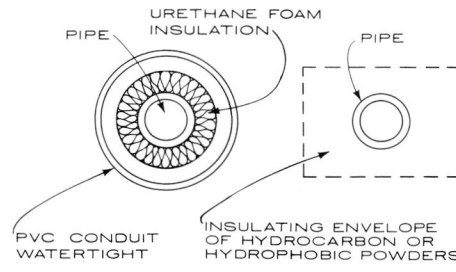

Two of the more common methods of insulating underground piping are shown above. Cathodic protection must be used to prevent corrosion of metallic carrier pipe.

BELOW-GROUND APPLICATIONS

David J. McDade; Tomblinson Harburn Associates; Flint, Michigan
William Tao & Associates, Inc., Consulting Engineers; St. Louis, Missouri

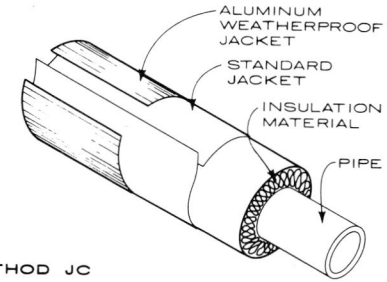

METHOD JC

JA HOT OR COLD PIPE: Glass fiber reinforced vinyl coated paper and aluminum foil laminate.

JB HOT PIPE: Presized glass cloth coated with lagging adhesive.

JC WEATHERPROOF: Same as above with additional aluminum jacket or additional roofing felt jacket.

PIPING JACKETS

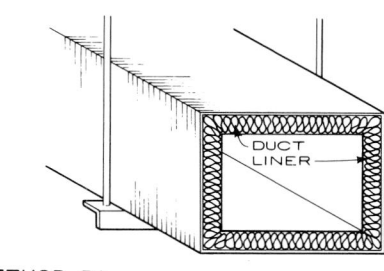

METHOD DA

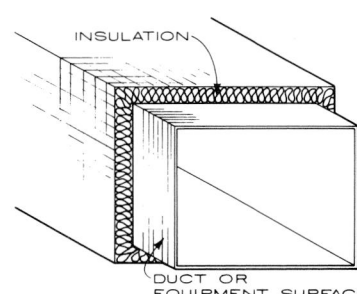

METHOD DB

DA DUCT LINER: Glass fiber duct liner, most used densities 3/4, 1 1/2, and 2 lb/cu ft; thickness 1/2, 3/4, and 1 in. most common; coated with neoprene or similar material to limit erosion and reduce coefficient of friction.

DB EXTERNAL DUCT INSULATION
Blanket type: Blanket type light density glass fiber insulation with reinforced aluminum foil vapor barrier facing. This type of duct covering is especially adaptable to round ducts.
Board type: Glass fiber board type duct insulation with factory applied vapor barrier jacket. This type of duct covering is especially applicable to rectangular ducts and is available in various densities. Heavy density (6 lb/cu ft) should be used where ducts are subject to potential damage.

DUCT INSULATION

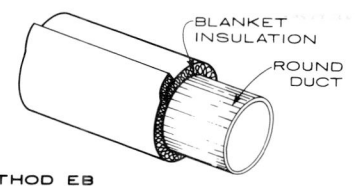

METHOD EB

EA EQUIPMENT TO 220°F: Flexible foamed plastic; k = 0.24; available in sheet form.

EB EQUIPMENT TO 450°F: Glass fiber blanket type low density or rigid board type insulation with factory applied vapor barrier jacket; k = 0.25.

EC EQUIPMENT TO 850°F: Glass fiber board with high temperature binder finished with metal mesh, insulating cement and canvas or glass fabric jacket; k = 0.25.

ED EQUIPMENT AND BREECHING TO 1200°F: Calcium silicate block insulation; k = 0.40; wired in place and troweled with insulating cement and finished with aluminum or glass fabric jacket. Available in scored block to facilitate forming around large cylindrical shapes. Mineral wool insulation with wire mesh cover and aluminum or glass fabric jacket also applicable for high temperature applications.

EQUIPMENT INSULATION

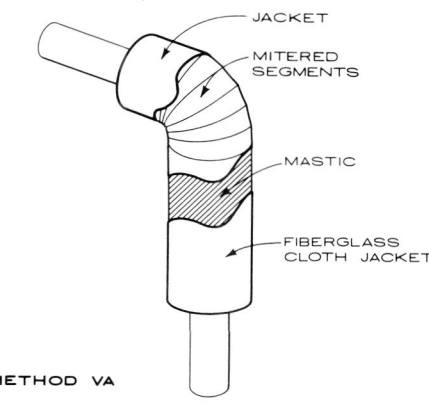

METHOD VA

VA Field mitered glass fiber or calcium silicate of same composition as adjacent pipe insulation with jacket of glass fiber reinforced cloth embedded in mastic. As an alternative fittings may be covered with factory fabricated weatherproof PVC or aluminum fitting covers arranged to fit over blanket type insulation inserts, overmitered pipe insulation or overmolded fitting insulators fabricated from calcium silicate, foam glass, urethane, polystyrene, and so on.

VALVE AND FITTING INSULATION AND JACKETS

APPLICATIONS
EQUIPMENT

1. PUMPS (COLD FLUIDS): Use type EA for pumps handling cold fluids. Insulation can be fabricated into a boxlike enclosure and arranged for easy removal to facilitate servicing.

2. PUMPS (HIGH TEMPERATURE HOT WATER, ETC.): Use type EB for pumps handling hot fluids, fabricated same as indicated above for cold fluid pumps.

3. HEAT EXCHANGERS (TO 850°F SURFACE TEMPERATURE): Use type EB or EC depending on surface temperature of vessel.

4. HEAT EXCHANGERS (TO 1200°F SURFACE TEMPERATURES): Use type ED, either calcium silicate or mineral wool.

5. DOMESTIC WATER AND CHILLED WATER TANKS: Use type EA or EB. EB has 25/50 fire spread/smoke developed rating, whereas type EA exceeds these limits.

6. CHILLERS: Use type EA unless restricted by fire spread/smoke developed ratings, in which case use type EB.

HOT PIPING OPERATING ABOVE AMBIENT DEW POINT

HEAT FLOW

Insulate with enough thickness to satisfy the engineering limits as specified or to maintain the exposed surface temperature below 60°C (140°F) for personnel protection.

VAPOR FLOW

Install with a permeable jacket to allow moisture and gas flow out of the system. Do not establish a vapor dam at the interface of multiple layer installations.

WEATHER PROOFING

Install weather resistant jackets with the laps in a rain shield position, sealing only the areas where rain might enter. Weather resistant mastics may be used in place of a jacket. The mastic should be applied in at least two coats, with an open weave glass fabric embedded in the first coat.

HANGERS

Clevis hangers may be installed directly on pipes operating up to 100°C (212°F). On higher temperature lines the hangers should be external and the pipe should be supported by a saddle and shield.

COLD PIPING OPERATING BELOW AMBIENT DEW POINT

HEAT FLOW

Insulate with enough thickness to satisfy the engineering limits as specified or to maintain the exposed surface at a temperature higher than the ambient dew point temperature, whichever is greater. The condensation of atmospheric moisture on the insulation surface must be avoided.

VAPOR FLOW

Install with a vapor barrier jacket or use insulation of a low permeability, closed cell type. All joints and seams in the vapor barrier must be perfectly sealed and the insulation must be vapor sealed at all terminals, fittings, and valves.

WEATHER PROOFING

Install weather resistant jacket with the laps in a rain shield position, with all seams, joints, and terminals sealed.

HANGERS

Clevis hangers or similar devices may be used, but they should be outside the vapor barrier jacket, with a protective shield having enough area to support the load of the pipe and its contents without crushing or indenting the insulation. Some insulations require a load bearing material insert between the shield and the pipe. The load bearing material should be a high density insulation or a poor conductor of heat such as waterproofed wood. Preinsulated hangers are also available for low temperature pipe support.

INSULATION FOR BOILER BREECHING AND HIGH TEMPERATURE EQUIPMENT

INSULATION CHOICE

First consideration must be given to the operating temperature of the surfaces to be insulated, as each material has a maximum use temperature. A second consideration concerns the size and shape of the surfaces, as these factors will determine whether it is expedient to use blanket, block, or spray-on insulation.

HEAT FLOW

Insulate with a great enough thickness to satisfy the engineering limits or to provide personnel protection by limiting the exposed surface temperature to 60°C (140°F).

VAPOR FLOW

The choice and installation of the insulation and its finish must establish a system that allows free movement of vapor out of the system. Insulation and finishes that contain water or other volatile substances must be exposed to slowly rising temperatures at startup to provide time for vapor escape.

Charles F. Gilbo, Consultant; Lancaster, Pennsylvania

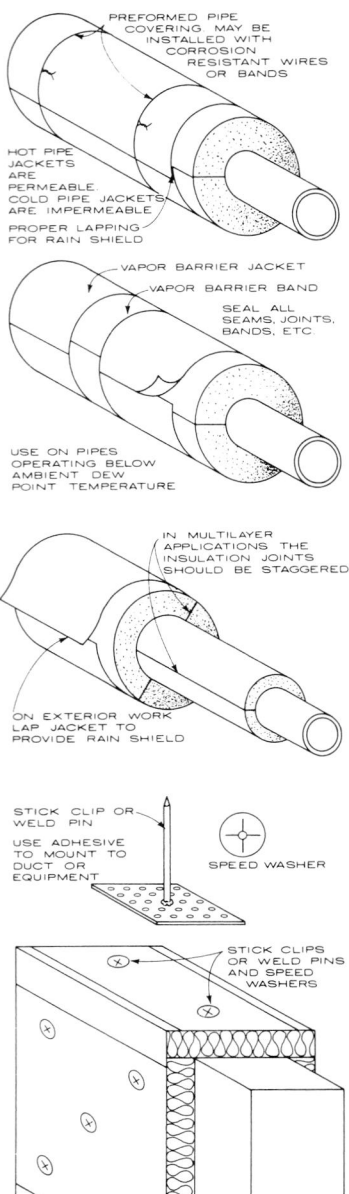

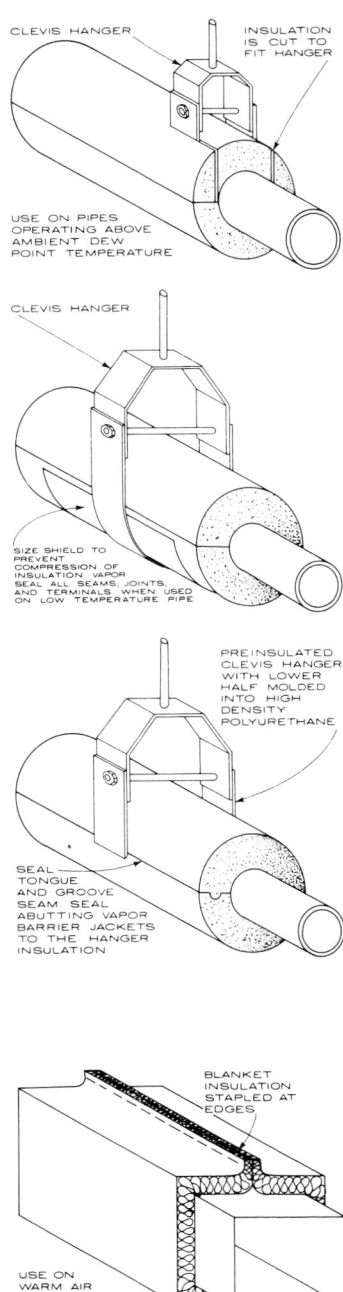

DUCTS FOR LOW TEMPERATURES

VAPOR FLOW

Ducts that operate at temperatures below the ambient dew point temperature must be covered with an insulation system that incorporates a near perfect vapor barrier on the warm side of the insulation. Such ducts may also be successfully insulated with flexible, closed celled, low permeability plastic insulation. If stick clips or weld pins are used to hold board type insulation in place, all penetrations of the vapor barrier must be sealed.

HEAT FLOW

Enough insulation must be used to maintain the temperature of the exposed surface at a level higher than the ambient dew point temperature to prevent the condensation of water. If the engineering specification limits heat flow to the duct, both the limits and condensation control must be considered and the insulation thickness chosen to satisfy the most severe condition.

DUCTS FOR KITCHEN EXHAUST AND HEATING

VAPOR FLOW

Ducts that operate at temperatures above ambient dew point temperature may be insulated without vapor sealing; therefore mechanical anchors and fasteners may be used.

HEAT FLOW

Enough insulation should be used to restrict heat flow to the engineered level. Due consideration must be given to the increased heat flow at the pins, anchors, stick clips, etc.; therefore greater insulation thicknesses are needed when such fasteners are used.

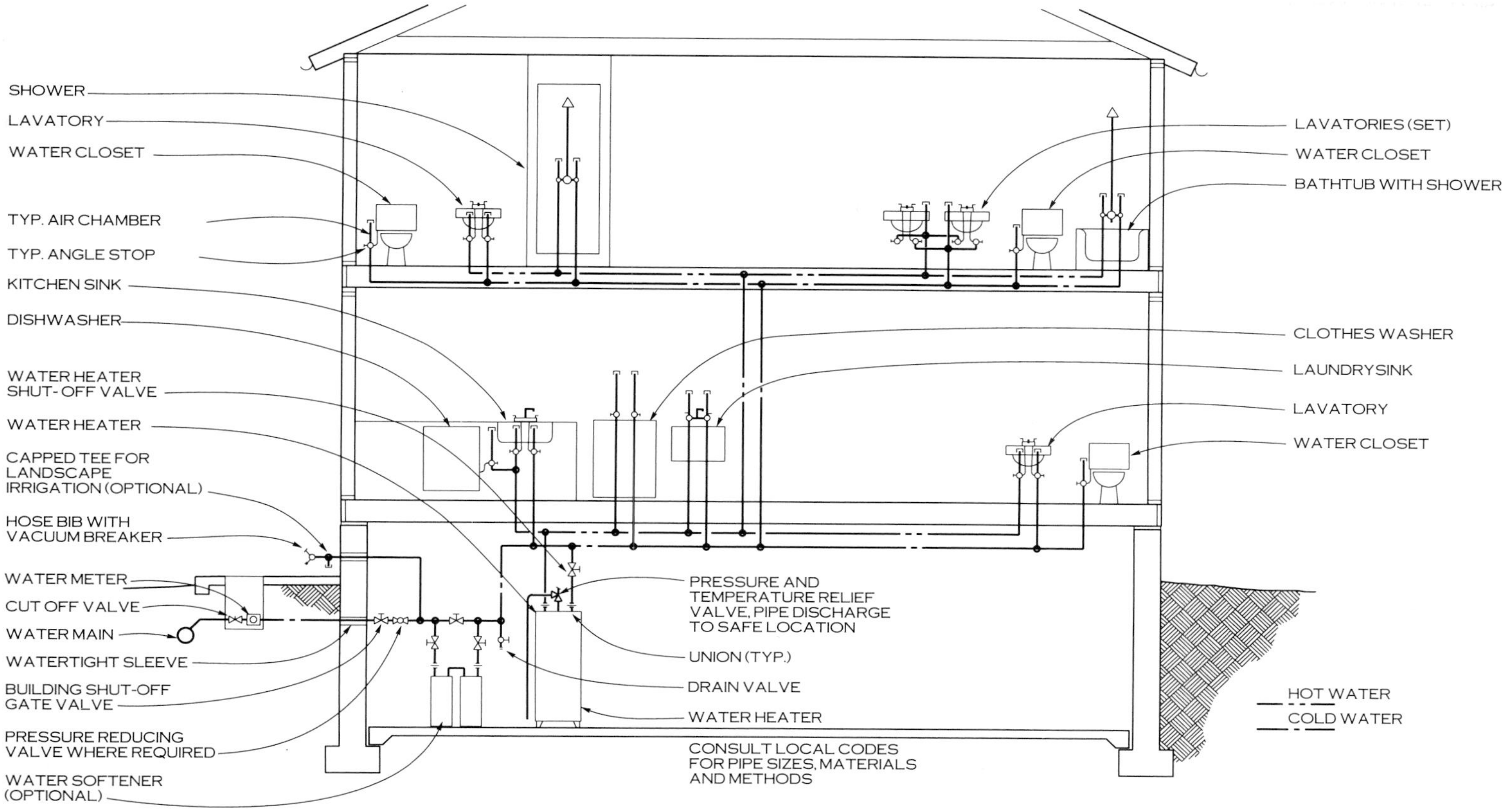

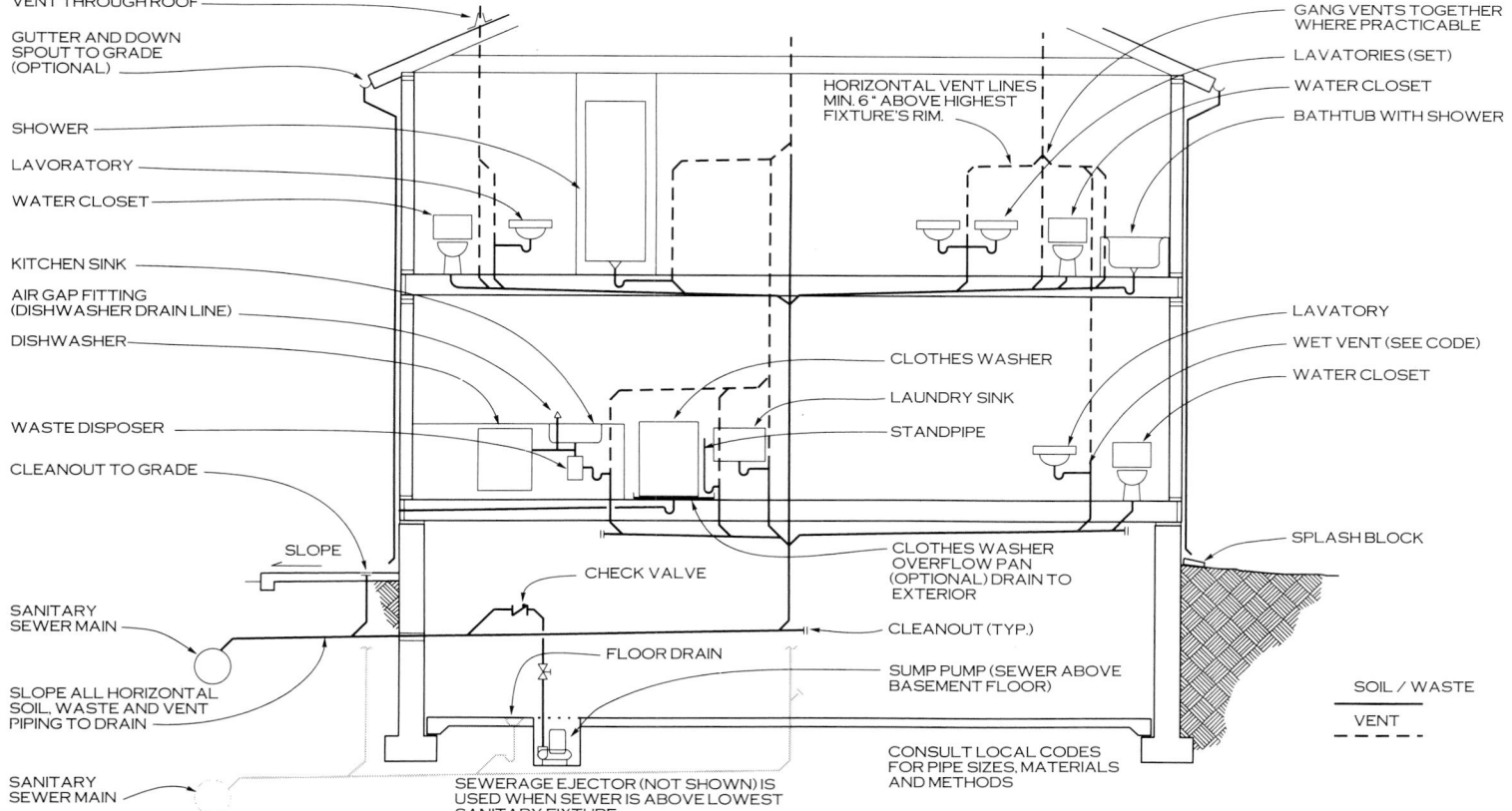

SHOWER
LAVATORY
WATER CLOSET

TYP. AIR CHAMBER
TYP. ANGLE STOP
KITCHEN SINK
DISHWASHER

WATER HEATER
SHUT-OFF VALVE
WATER HEATER
CAPPED TEE FOR
LANDSCAPE
IRRIGATION (OPTIONAL)
HOSE BIB WITH
VACUUM BREAKER

WATER METER
CUT OFF VALVE
WATER MAIN
WATERTIGHT SLEEVE
BUILDING SHUT-OFF
GATE VALVE
PRESSURE REDUCING
VALVE WHERE REQUIRED
WATER SOFTENER
(OPTIONAL)

LAVATORIES (SET)
WATER CLOSET
BATHTUB WITH SHOWER

CLOTHES WASHER
LAUNDRY SINK
LAVATORY
WATER CLOSET

PRESSURE AND
TEMPERATURE RELIEF
VALVE, PIPE DISCHARGE
TO SAFE LOCATION
UNION (TYP.)
DRAIN VALVE
WATER HEATER
CONSULT LOCAL CODES
FOR PIPE SIZES, MATERIALS
AND METHODS

HOT WATER
COLD WATER

WATER SUPPLY PIPING

VENT THROUGH ROOF
GUTTER AND DOWN
SPOUT TO GRADE
(OPTIONAL)

SHOWER
LAVATORY
WATER CLOSET

KITCHEN SINK
AIR GAP FITTING
(DISHWASHER DRAIN LINE)
DISHWASHER

WASTE DISPOSER
CLEANOUT TO GRADE

SLOPE
SANITARY
SEWER MAIN

SLOPE ALL HORIZONTAL
SOIL, WASTE AND VENT
PIPING TO DRAIN

SANITARY
SEWER MAIN

GANG VENTS TOGETHER
WHERE PRACTICABLE
LAVATORIES (SET)
WATER CLOSET
BATHTUB WITH SHOWER

HORIZONTAL VENT LINES
MIN. 6" ABOVE HIGHEST
FIXTURE'S RIM.

LAVATORY
WET VENT (SEE CODE)
WATER CLOSET

CLOTHES WASHER
LAUNDRY SINK
STANDPIPE

CHECK VALVE
FLOOR DRAIN
SUMP PUMP (SEWER ABOVE
BASEMENT FLOOR)

CLOTHES WASHER
OVERFLOW PAN
(OPTIONAL) DRAIN TO
EXTERIOR
CLEANOUT (TYP.)

SPLASH BLOCK

SOIL / WASTE
VENT

CONSULT LOCAL CODES
FOR PIPE SIZES, MATERIALS
AND METHODS

SEWERAGE EJECTOR (NOT SHOWN) IS
USED WHEN SEWER IS ABOVE LOWEST
SANITARY FIXTURE

SOIL, WASTE AND VENT PIPING

Brent Dickens, AIA, Architecture & Planning; San Rafael, California
Drawn by David S. Penney, P.E.

PLUMBING RISER DIAGRAMS   15

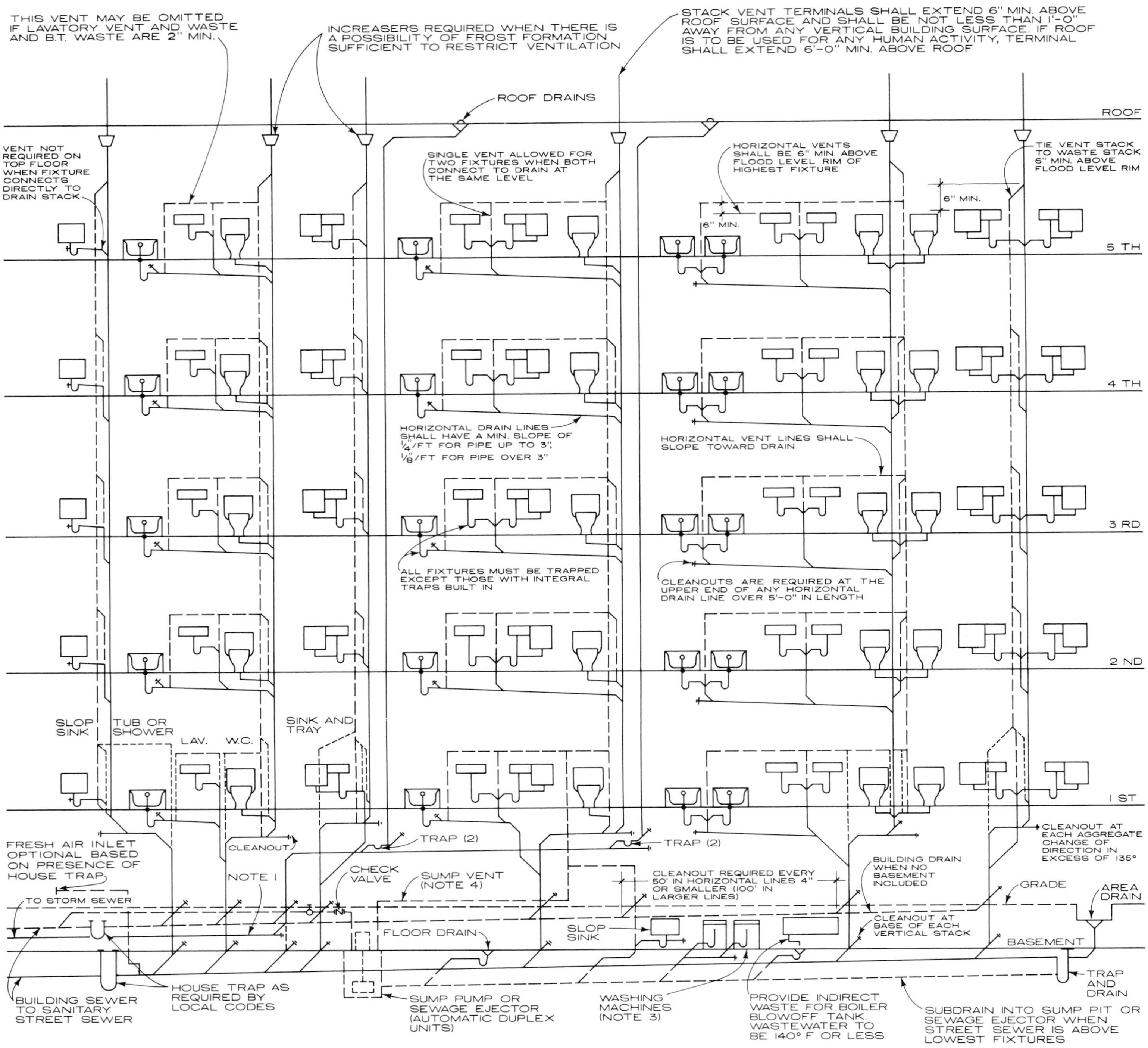

THIS VENT MAY BE OMITTED IF LAVATORY VENT AND WASTE AND B.T. WASTE ARE 2" MIN.

INCREASERS REQUIRED WHEN THERE IS A POSSIBILITY OF FROST FORMATION SUFFICIENT TO RESTRICT VENTILATION

STACK VENT TERMINALS SHALL EXTEND 6" MIN. ABOVE ROOF SURFACE AND SHALL BE NOT LESS THAN 1'-0" AWAY FROM ANY VERTICAL BUILDING SURFACE. IF ROOF IS TO BE USED FOR ANY HUMAN ACTIVITY, TERMINAL SHALL EXTEND 6'-0" MIN. ABOVE ROOF

ROOF DRAINS

ROOF

VENT NOT REQUIRED ON TOP FLOOR WHEN FIXTURE CONNECTS DIRECTLY TO DRAIN STACK

SINGLE VENT ALLOWED FOR TWO FIXTURES WHEN BOTH CONNECT TO DRAIN AT THE SAME LEVEL

HORIZONTAL VENTS SHALL BE 6" MIN. ABOVE FLOOD LEVEL RIM OF HIGHEST FIXTURE

TIE VENT STACK TO WASTE STACK 6" MIN. ABOVE FLOOD LEVEL RIM

6" MIN.

6" MIN.

5 TH

4 TH

HORIZONTAL DRAIN LINES SHALL HAVE A MIN. SLOPE OF $\frac{1}{4}$"/FT FOR PIPE UP TO 3", $\frac{1}{8}$"/FT FOR PIPE OVER 3"

HORIZONTAL VENT LINES SHALL SLOPE TOWARD DRAIN

3 RD

ALL FIXTURES MUST BE TRAPPED EXCEPT THOSE WITH INTEGRAL TRAPS BUILT IN

CLEANOUTS ARE REQUIRED AT THE UPPER END OF ANY HORIZONTAL DRAIN LINE OVER 5'-0" IN LENGTH

2 ND

SLOP SINK

TUB OR SHOWER

LAV. W.C.

SINK AND TRAY

1 ST

FRESH AIR INLET OPTIONAL BASED ON PRESENCE OF HOUSE TRAP

CLEANOUT

NOTE 1

CHECK VALVE

TRAP (2)

SUMP VENT (NOTE 4)

TRAP (2)

CLEANOUT REQUIRED EVERY 50' IN HORIZONTAL LINES 4" OR SMALLER (100' IN LARGER LINES)

BUILDING DRAIN WHEN NO BASEMENT INCLUDED

CLEANOUT AT EACH AGGREGATE CHANGE OF DIRECTION IN EXCESS OF 135°

GRADE

AREA DRAIN

TO STORM SEWER

FLOOR DRAIN

SLOP SINK

CLEANOUT AT BASE OF EACH VERTICAL STACK

BASEMENT

TRAP AND DRAIN

BUILDING SEWER TO SANITARY STREET SEWER

HOUSE TRAP AS REQUIRED BY LOCAL CODES

SUMP PUMP OR SEWAGE EJECTOR (AUTOMATIC DUPLEX UNITS)

WASHING MACHINES (NOTE 3)

PROVIDE INDIRECT WASTE FOR BOILER BLOWOFF TANK WASTEWATER TO BE 140° F OR LESS

SUBDRAIN INTO SUMP PIT OR SEWAGE EJECTOR WHEN STREET SEWER IS ABOVE LOWEST FIXTURES

DIAGRAM NOTES

1. Roof drains and outside area drains must drain into storm drainage sewer where a separate system is available.
2. Traps are required on roof drain and area drain leaders when connected to a combined sanitary and storm sewer system.
3. Provide one washing machine connection for every eight living units (individual connections in each living unit are preferable if space permits). Provide standpipe type indirect waste pipes, 18 in. min. above trap weir. Special consideration must be given to suds pressure zones where washing machines discharge upstream from other fixtures; special venting to nonpressure zones should be provided.
4. Sump vent line shall run independently and unrestricted to the open air when pneumatic type sewage ejectors are used.

NOTE

The diagram generally indicates plumbing drainage solutions that constitute good plumbing practice. Because of variances between different local codes, some of the items shown may be prohibited in some areas, while other items may far exceed the minimum requirements of local codes. Always consult local codes for exact requirements and for such items as fixture unit allotments, pipe sizing, pipe materials, general regulations, and special conditions.

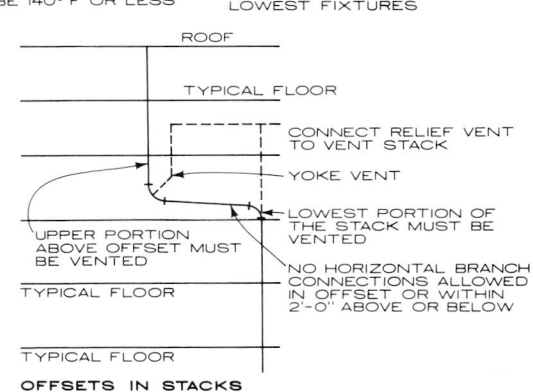

ROOF

TYPICAL FLOOR

CONNECT RELIEF VENT TO VENT STACK

YOKE VENT

LOWEST PORTION OF THE STACK MUST BE VENTED

UPPER PORTION ABOVE OFFSET MUST BE VENTED

NO HORIZONTAL BRANCH CONNECTIONS ALLOWED IN OFFSET OR WITHIN 2'-0" ABOVE OR BELOW

TYPICAL FLOOR

TYPICAL FLOOR

OFFSETS IN STACKS

Killebrew/Rucker/Associates, Inc., Architects/Planners/Engineers; Wichita Falls, Texas

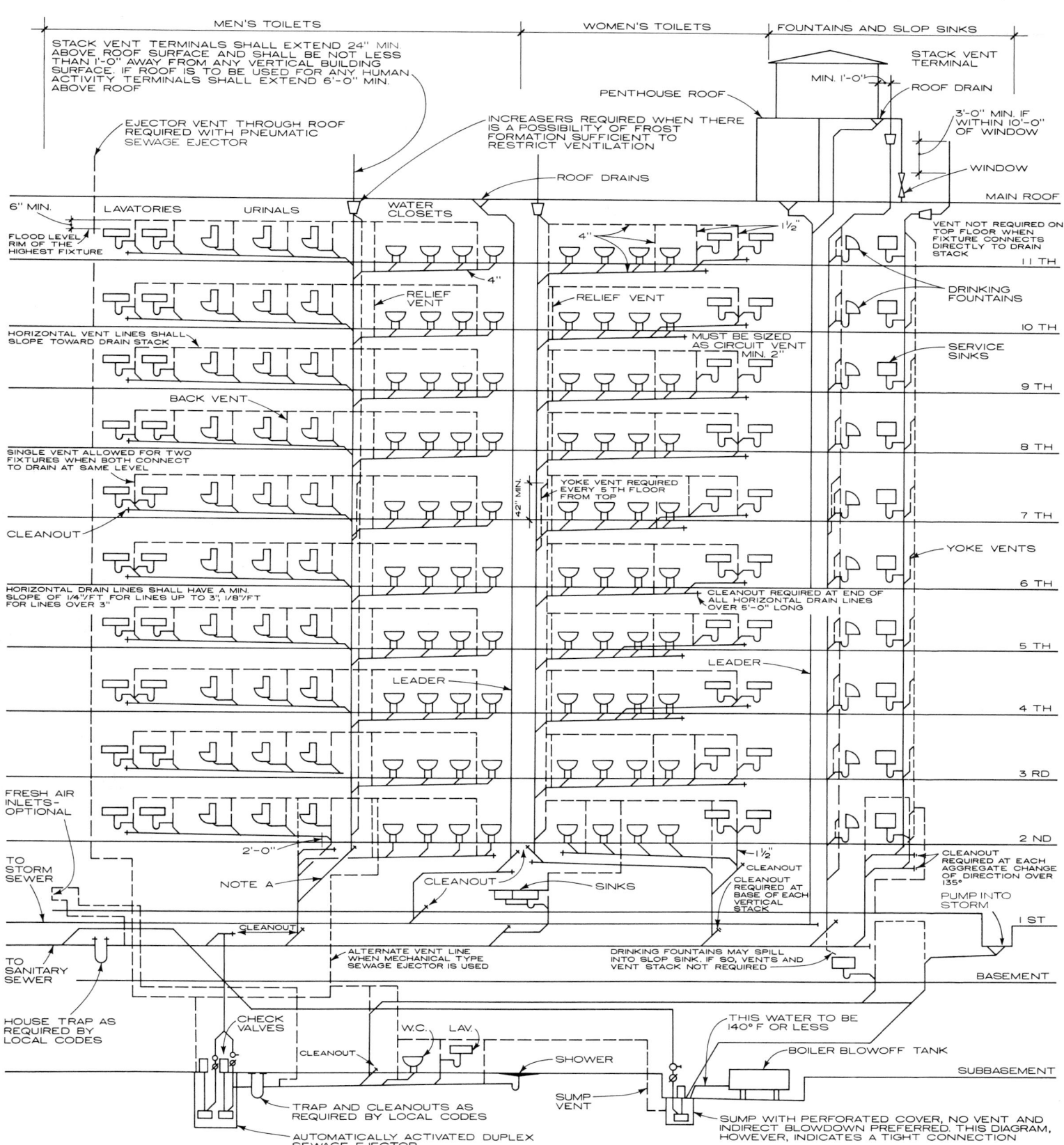

STACK VENT TERMINALS SHALL EXTEND 24" MIN. ABOVE ROOF SURFACE AND SHALL BE NOT LESS THAN 1'-0" AWAY FROM ANY VERTICAL BUILDING SURFACE. IF ROOF IS TO BE USED FOR ANY HUMAN ACTIVITY TERMINALS SHALL EXTEND 6'-0" MIN. ABOVE ROOF

STACK VENT TERMINAL

MIN. 1'-0"

ROOF DRAIN

EJECTOR VENT THROUGH ROOF REQUIRED WITH PNEUMATIC SEWAGE EJECTOR

PENTHOUSE ROOF

INCREASERS REQUIRED WHEN THERE IS A POSSIBILITY OF FROST FORMATION SUFFICIENT TO RESTRICT VENTILATION

3'-0" MIN. IF WITHIN 10'-0" OF WINDOW

WINDOW

MAIN ROOF

ROOF DRAINS

6" MIN.   LAVATORIES   URINALS   WATER CLOSETS

FLOOD LEVEL RIM OF THE HIGHEST FIXTURE

VENT NOT REQUIRED ON TOP FLOOR WHEN FIXTURE CONNECTS DIRECTLY TO DRAIN STACK

1½

4"

11 TH

RELIEF VENT

RELIEF VENT

DRINKING FOUNTAINS

10 TH

HORIZONTAL VENT LINES SHALL SLOPE TOWARD DRAIN STACK

4"

MUST BE SIZED AS CIRCUIT VENT MIN. 2"

SERVICE SINKS

9 TH

BACK VENT

8 TH

SINGLE VENT ALLOWED FOR TWO FIXTURES WHEN BOTH CONNECT TO DRAIN AT SAME LEVEL

42" MIN.

YOKE VENT REQUIRED EVERY 5 TH FLOOR FROM TOP

7 TH

CLEANOUT

YOKE VENTS

6 TH

HORIZONTAL DRAIN LINES SHALL HAVE A MIN. SLOPE OF 1/4"/FT FOR LINES UP TO 3", 1/8"/FT FOR LINES OVER 3"

CLEANOUT REQUIRED AT END OF ALL HORIZONTAL DRAIN LINES OVER 5'-0" LONG

5 TH

LEADER

LEADER

4 TH

3 RD

FRESH AIR INLETS - OPTIONAL

2 ND

TO STORM SEWER

2'-0"

NOTE A

CLEANOUT

SINKS

1½

CLEANOUT

CLEANOUT REQUIRED AT BASE OF EACH VERTICAL STACK

CLEANOUT REQUIRED AT EACH AGGREGATE CHANGE OF DIRECTION OVER 135°

PUMP INTO STORM

1 ST

TO SANITARY SEWER

CLEANOUT

ALTERNATE VENT LINE WHEN MECHANICAL TYPE SEWAGE EJECTOR IS USED

DRINKING FOUNTAINS MAY SPILL INTO SLOP SINK. IF SO, VENTS AND VENT STACK NOT REQUIRED

BASEMENT

HOUSE TRAP AS REQUIRED BY LOCAL CODES

CHECK VALVES

W.C.   LAV.

THIS WATER TO BE 140° F OR LESS

BOILER BLOWOFF TANK

SUBBASEMENT

CLEANOUT

SHOWER

SUMP VENT

TRAP AND CLEANOUTS AS REQUIRED BY LOCAL CODES

AUTOMATICALLY ACTIVATED DUPLEX SEWAGE EJECTOR

SUMP WITH PERFORATED COVER, NO VENT AND INDIRECT BLOWDOWN PREFERRED. THIS DIAGRAM, HOWEVER, INDICATES A TIGHT CONNECTION

GENERAL NOTES

This diagram generally indicates plumbing drainage solutions that constitute good plumbing practice. Because of variances between different local codes, some of the items shown may be prohibited in some areas, while other items may far exceed the minimum requirements of local codes.

Always consult local codes for exact requirements and for such items as fixture unit allotments, pipe sizing, pipe materials, general regulations, and special conditions.

NOTE A

45° or less from vertical may be considered as straight stock in sizing, except that no fixtures or branches may be connected within 2 ft of offset.

Killebrew/Rucker/Associates, Inc., Architects/Planners/Engineers; Wichita Falls, Texas

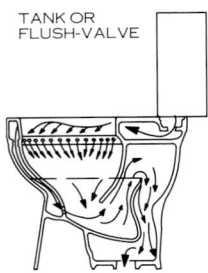

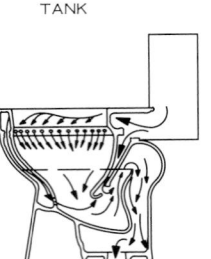

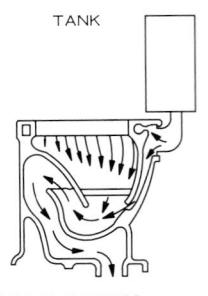

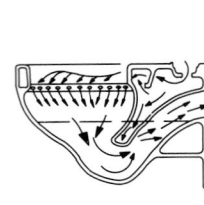

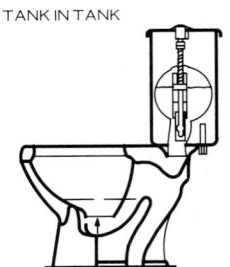

| ONE-PIECE LOW TANK | TANK OR FLUSH-VALVE | TANK | TANK | FLUSH-VALVE | TANK IN TANK |

SIPHON-VORTEX

Water enters through diagonal punching around the rim of the bowl, creating a vortex that draws the water down into the rear trap with a swirling action that scours the walls of the bowl. Water strikes two parallel ridges and folds over forming a jet, producing siphonic action. Large water surface provides a very efficient and clean process, and the flushing is extremely quiet. This model is mostly of one-piece construction with a low profile. Expensive.

SIPHON-JET

Water enters through rim punchings and jets placed in an up-leg of the rear trap, filling the trapway and creating an instant siphon action without rise of water level. The result is quick water withdrawal. Large water surface provides an efficient and clean operation. With quiet flushing and moderate cost, this is the most popular residential model.

REVERSE-TRAP

Water enters through rim punchings and through a jet that fills the rear trapway completely, creating a siphon action and resulting in quick withdrawal of water from the bowl. A water jet is located at the inlet of the trapway. Most of the bowl surface is covered with water. This model is efficient but moderately noisy. Its cost is reasonably low.

WASH-DOWN

Water enters through an open rim, as though a bucket of water were dumped into the bowl, filling the front trapway and creating siphon action. This model provides quick removal of water with minimum water rise. Small water surface makes the model more vulnerable to soiling and clogging. This is the least efficient and most noisy type but lowest in cost.

PRESSURE/ TANKLESS

Strong flushing action is created by a jet of water directed into the rim and jet. The force of the jet draws the bowl contents into the rear trap. It doesn't use siphonic action but relies on the driving force of jet action. At flush valve 25 psi is needed with 1.5-in. inlet spud. Large water surface and large trapway size make this model efficient and suitable for commercial use. Flushing is very noisy. Expensive.

PRESSURE/TANK

A steel tank is located inside the china tank. Uses pressure from the water supply system. A 1.5 in. water supply line provides 25 psi pressure, compressing trapped air in the tank. When flushed the compressed air forces the water out. The bowl is designed to accept the torrent of water. The crest of the surging water empties the bowl through the enlarged trap. Large water surface makes this model efficient. Design features make it suitable for residential use. Flushing is very noisy. Low water usage (1.5 gpf) helps conserve water. Expensive.

TYPES OF FLUSHING SYSTEMS

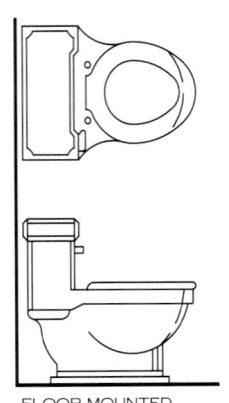

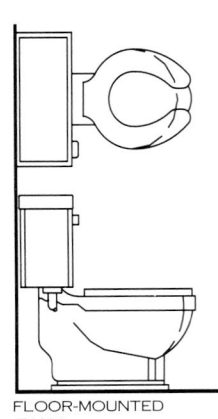

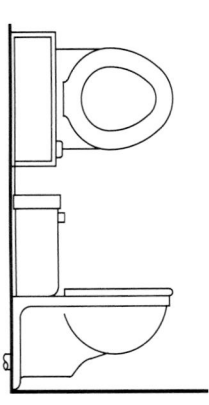

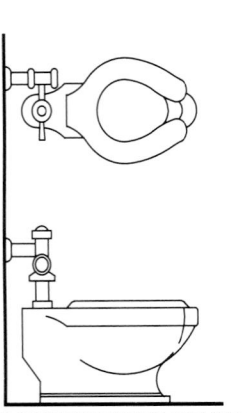

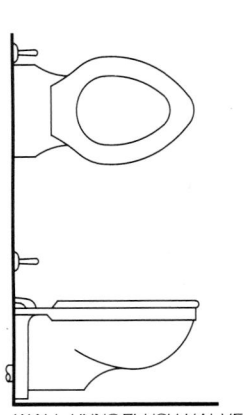

| FLOOR-MOUNTED ONE-PIECE TANK | FLOOR-MOUNTED TANK | WALL-MOUNTED TANK | FLOOR-MOUNTED FLUSH-VALVE | WALL-HUNG FLUSH-VALVE |

WATER CLOSET TYPES

WATER CLOSET NOTES

1. ADA (4.16 Water Closets) describes approach, floor space, and grab bar requirements. (See bathroom planning pages.) Water closet height: 17–19 in. to the top of the toilet seat. Seat shall not spring up. The force required to activate controls shall be max. 5 lbf. Controls shall be mounted on the wide side of the toilet no more than 44 in. above the floor.

2. For rough-in dimensions, refer to manufacturers' manuals.

3. Special toilet types: (1) vacuum-vented toilets, removes odors; (2) composting toilets; (3) chemical toilets.

4. Water usage for most water closets may be regulated between 1.5 and 3.5 gallons per flush.

URINAL NOTES

1. ADA (4.18 Urinals) requirements: Clear floor space: 30 x 48 in. shall be provided in front of urinals to allow forward approach. Urinals shall be stall type or wall-hung with an elongated rim at max. 17 in. above the floor. Shields, if provided, shall not extend beyond the front of the urinal rim and must have a clearance of 29 in. Flush controls shall be accessible, not more than 44 in. above the floor.

2. Urinal tank: 92 to 94 in. above the floor (if provided)

3. Battery stalls: 21 in. to 24 in. on center (except accessible)

4. For styles and rough-in dimensions, refer to manufacturers' manuals.

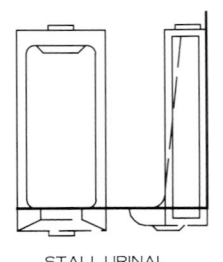

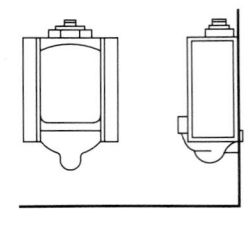

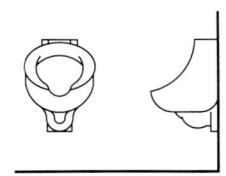

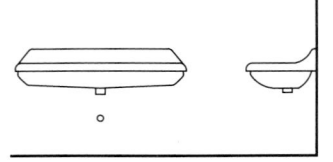

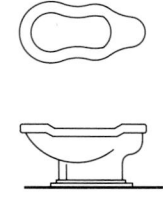

| STALL URINAL | WALL-HUNG WITH WINGS | WALL-HUNG | TROUGH | BIDET |

URINALS AND BIDETS

B.J. Baldwin; Giffels Associates; Detroit, Michigan; Charles Szoradi, AIA; Washington, D.C.
Assistance given by Barbara Munson of American Standard Co. and Leslie Farrel of Kohler Co.

GENERAL NOTES

Lavatories and work sinks are available in vitreous china (V.C.), enameled cast iron (E.C.I.), enameled steel (E.S.), and stainless steel (S.S.). Typically, floor to rim dimension is 2 ft 7 in., unless otherwise noted. The most commonly used means of support is the chair or wall carrier with concealed arms. Other methods are detailed below. Consult manufacturer's data for specific fixture design and support recommendations.

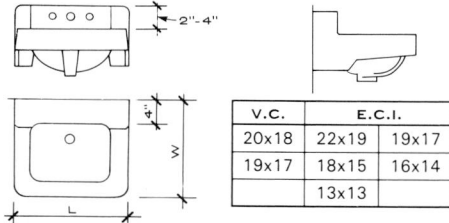

V.C.		E.C.I.
20x18	22x19	19x17
19x17	18x15	16x14
	13x13	

Shelf-back lavatories generally are rectangular with semi-oval basins. Height of the shelf typically is 4 in.; depth is usually 5 in. Support with metal legs and brackets or concealed carrier.

SHELF BACK

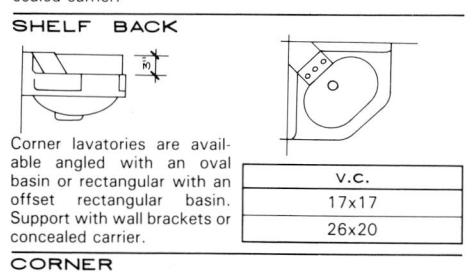

Corner lavatories are available angled with an oval basin or rectangular with an offset rectangular basin. Support with wall brackets or concealed carrier.

V.C.
17x17
26x20

CORNER

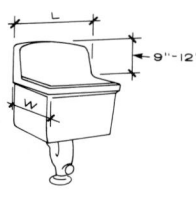

Wash sinks supported with concealed wall brackets for E.C.I. or with angle supports for S.S.

E.C.I.		S.S.		STATIONS
18x36	18x48	20x48		2
18x60	18x72	20x60	20x72	3
		20x96		4

WASH SINKS

Wall-mounted service sinks are designed for janitorial requirements of hospitals, plants, institutions, office buildings, and schools. Floor to rim dimension is 2 ft 3 in. to 2 ft 5 in. Fittings are mounted either on or above the sink back. "H" designates flushing rim design for hospital use specifically.

V.C.		E.C.I.		S.S.	
28x22	26x20 H	24x20	24x18	25x19	23x18
24x22 H	20x20 H	22x18			
22x20					

SERVICE SINKS

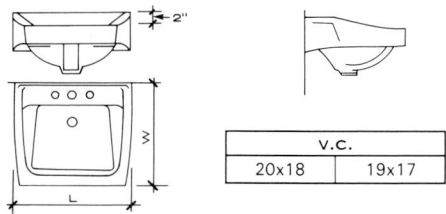

V.C.	
20x18	19x17

Ledge-back lavatories generally are rectangular with rectangular basins. Ledge width usually is 4 in. Typically supported with concealed carrier.

LEDGE BACK

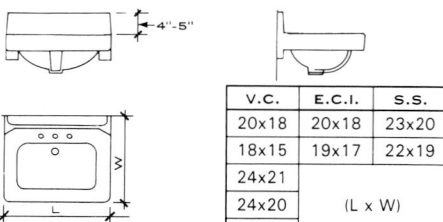

V.C.	E.C.I.	S.S.
20x18	20x18	23x20
18x15	19x17	22x19
24x21		
24x20	(L x W)	
18x16		

Most flat-back lavatories are rectangular with rectangular or semi-oval basins. Typically, floor to rim dimension is 2 ft 7 in. Support using metal legs with brackets or with concealed carrier.

FLAT BACK

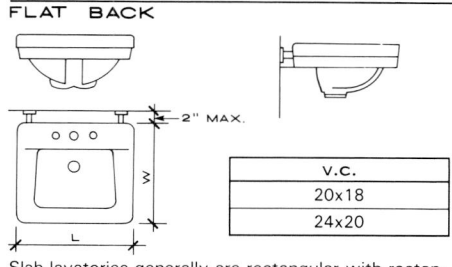

V.C.
20x18
24x20

Slab lavatories generally are rectangular with rectangular basins. A 2 in. escutcheon typically spaces lavatory from finish wall (4 and 6 in. also are available). Vitreous china leg with brackets can be used as alternate means of support.

SLAB

V.C.	S.S.
20x27	23x19

Wheelchair accessible lavatories must be supported using a concealed arm carrier. Height from floor to rim is 2 ft 10 in. Pipes should be covered and should not obstruct. Faucet levers should be accessible or photo-electric.

WHEELCHAIR ACCESSIBLE LAVATORY

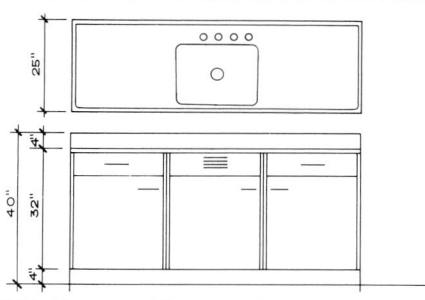

Sink/cabinet assemblies are available in stainless steel with single or double bowls, with or without adjacent drainboards. Lengths of cabinets vary from 42 to 96 in., depending on drawer, door, and bowl options.

CABINET

Built-in lavatories are available oval, rectangular, and circular in a variety of basin shapes. Typically, built-ins are now self-rimming but are available with metal rims, or rimless for undercounter installations.

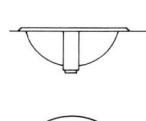

	V.C.			E.S.		E.C.I.		
with Metal Rim								
19x16	19x15	17x14	19x16	18x18		26x18	18x18	
Self-rimming								
28x19	26x20	24x20	20x17	19x19		33x19	28x19	21x19
21x19	21x17	21x13				20x17	19x19	19x16
19x19	19x16							
Rimless								
21x17	19x16	17x14	19x16					

BUILT-IN

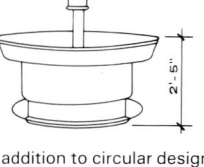

TYPE	DIA. (IN.)	NO. USERS
Circ.	54	8
	36	5
Semi-circ.	54	4
	36	3
Corner	54	3

In addition to circular designs, semicircular and corner types are available, most in precast terrazzo, stainless steel, and some in fiberglass. Most have foot controls, and some have hand controls. Supply from above, below, or through the wall. Vents many rise centrally or come off drain through wall or floor.

WASH SINK

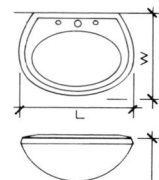
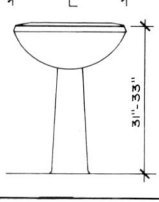

Pedestal lavatories are available in a wide variety of forms, sizes, and basin shapes. See manufacturer for specific designs.

V.C.		
38x22	30x20	28x21
24x19	26x22	25x21
22x21	20x18	

PEDESTAL LAVATORY

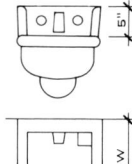

V.C.	E.C.I.
14x13	16x14
14x12	

Institutional lavatories have an integral supply channel to spout and drinking nozzle, strainer, and soap dish. Trap is enclosed in wall. Wall thickness must be specified.

INSTITUTIONAL LAVATORY

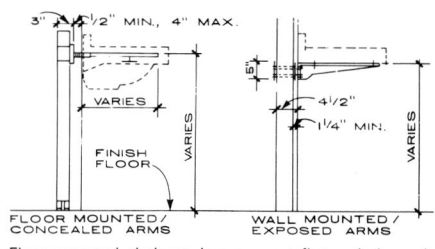

Floor-mounted chair carriers support fixture independent of wall construction. Available with exposed or concealed arms. Wall-mounted carrier with exposed or concealed arms also is available. Additional methods include floor-mounted hanger plate types, floor-mounted bearing plate types, paired metal or single vitreous china leg, in addition to exposed, enameled wall brackets.

METHODS OF LAVATORY SUPPORT

Robert K. Sherrill; Wilkes, Faulkner, Jenkins & Bass; Washington, D.C.

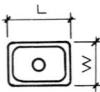

SINGLE BOWL

STAINLESS STEEL

	MIN.	MAX.	OTHER
L	11½	33	12½ ➝ 31
W	13	22⅜	14 ➝ 22¼
D	5½	12	6 ➝ 7½

PORCELAIN ENAMELED STEEL

	MIN.	MAX.	OTHER
L	24	30	
W	21		
D	7⅜	8⅛	

ENAMELED CAST IRON

	MIN.	MAX.	OTHER
L	12	30	
W	12	21	18 ➝ 20
D	6	8	6½ ➝ 7½

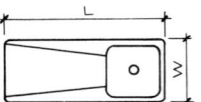

SINGLE BOWL AND DRAINBOARD (RIGHT OR LEFT)

STAINLESS STEEL

	MIN.	MAX.	OTHER
L	33	72	
W	21	25	
D	7	7½	

ENAMELED CAST IRON

	MIN.	MAX.	OTHER
L	42	72	
W	20	25	24
D	6	8	6½ ➝ 7½

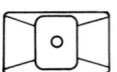

SINGLE BOWL DOUBLE DRAINBOARD

STAINLESS STEEL

	MIN.	MAX.	OTHER
L	54	72	
W	21	25	
D	7	7½	

ENAMELED CAST IRON

	MIN.	MAX.	OTHER
L	54	72	
W	21	25	24
D	6	8	6½ ➝ 7½

DOUBLE BOWL

STAINLESS STEEL

	MIN.	MAX.	OTHER
L	28	46	30 ➝ 42
W	16	22	17 ➝ 21¼
D	5	10	6½ ➝ 7½

PORCELAIN ENAMELED

	MIN.	MAX.	OTHER
L	32		
W	21		
D	7	8⅛	

ENAMELED CAST IRON STEEL

	MIN.	MAX.	OTHER
L	32	42	
W	20	25	
D	6	8	6½ ➝ 7½

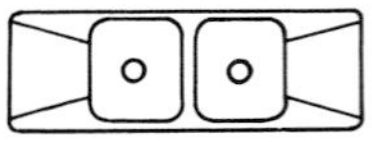

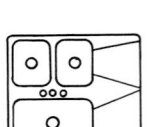

DOUBLE BOWL AND DRAINBOARD

STAINLESS STEEL

	MIN.	MAX.	OTHER
L	60	72	66
W	21	25	
D	7	7½	

ENAMELED CAST IRON

	MIN.	MAX.	OTHER
L	54	72	60
W	24	25	
D	6	8	6½ ➝ 7½

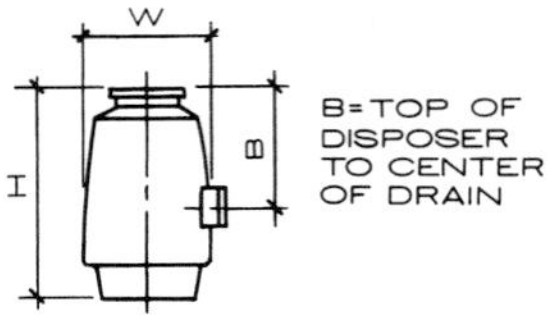

W

B = TOP OF DISPOSER TO CENTER OF DRAIN

GARBAGE DISPOSER

	MIN.	MAX.	OTHER
W	6¼	10⅛	7⅜ ➝ 9½
B	6	9⅜	6⅝ ➝ 8¾
H	12¾	9³⁄₁₆	12⅝ ➝ 16

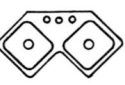

TRIPLE BOWL

STAINLESS STEEL

	MIN.	MAX.	OTHER
L	43	54	45
W	22		
D	5	7½	

TRIPLE BOWL AND DRAINBOARD (ISLAND)

STAINLESS STEEL

	MIN.	MAX.	OTHER
L	54½	57	
W	40½		
D	4	7½	

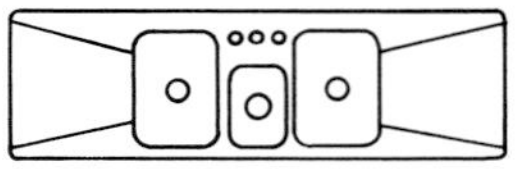

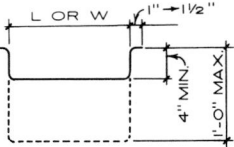

TRIPLE BOWL AND DOUBLE DRAINBOARD

STAINLESS STEEL

	MIN.	MAX.	OTHER
L		84	
W		25	
D		7½	

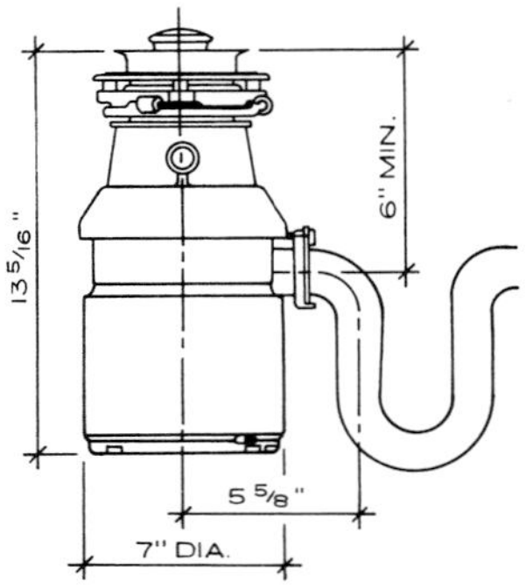

6" MIN.

13⁵⁄₁₆"

5⅝"

7" DIA.

GARBAGE DISPOSER UNITS

CORNER BOWL

STAINLESS STEEL

	MIN.	MAX.	OTHER
L	31⅞	32½	
W	31⅞	32½	
D	7	7½	

BAR SINK

STAINLESS STEEL

	MIN.	MAX.	OTHER
L	14	16¼	15
W	14	20¼	15
D	6	7⅜	6

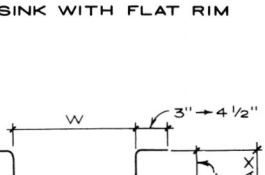

L OR W   1" ➝ 1½"

4" MIN.   1'-0" MAX

SINK WITH FLAT RIM

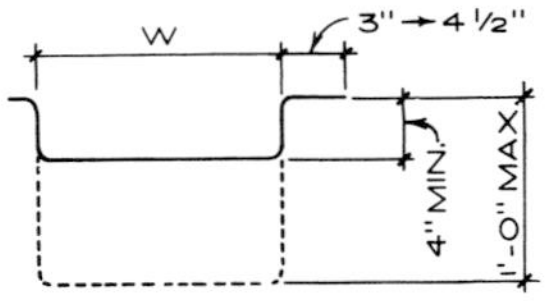

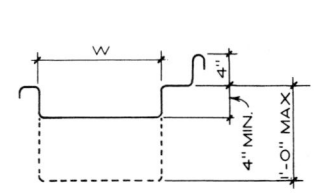

W   3" ➝ 4½"

4" MIN.   1'-0" MAX

SINK WITH BACK LEDGE

W   4"

4" MIN.   1'-0" MAX

SINK WITH BACK LEDGE AND BACKSPLASH

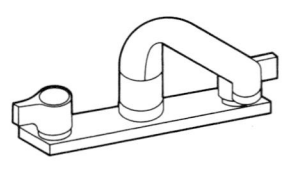

WASHER TYPE

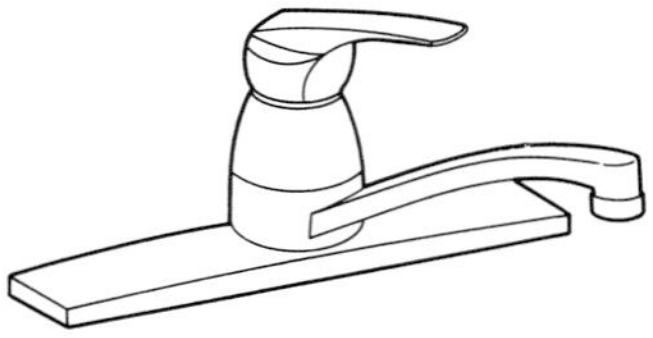

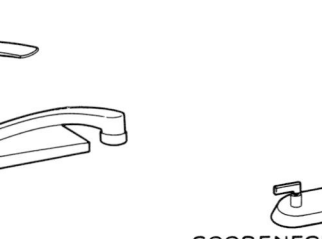

WASHERLESS

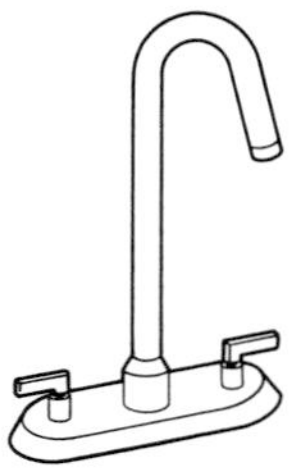

GOOSENECK

KITCHEN FAUCETS

Giffels & Rossetti, Inc.; Detroit, Michigan

NOTES

All dimensions shown on this page are in inches.

Consult manufacturers' literature for variations in bowl finish and available accessories, such as cup strainer, spray head, cutting boards, and trim.

See pages on handicapped accessibility for suggested modifications to mounting height and cabinetry.

15   **PLUMBING FIXTURES**

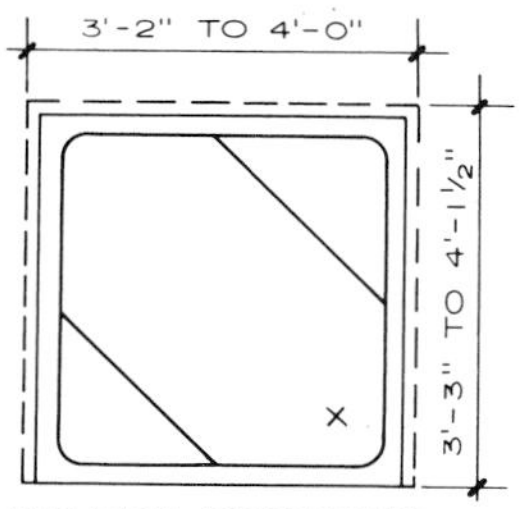

SQUARE AND RECTANGULAR SHOWERS AND BATHTUBS

3'-2" TO 4'-0"

SQUARE RECESSED ENAMELED CAST IRON
HEIGHT: 1'-0" TO 1'-4"

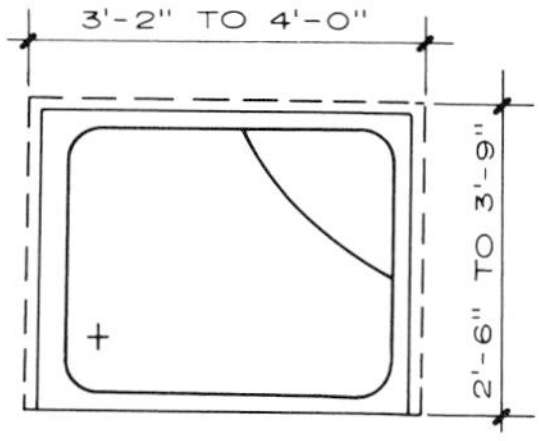

3'-2" TO 4'-0"

SQUARE RECESSED ENAMELED STEEL
HEIGHT: 1'-0" TO 1'-2"

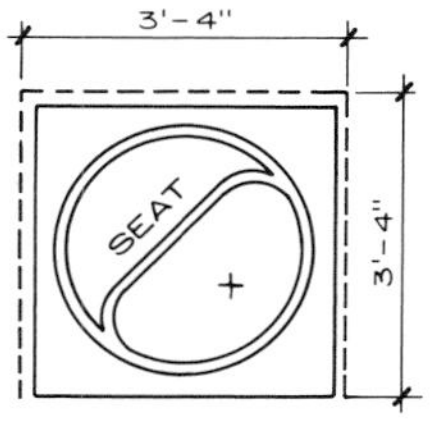

3'-4"

SQUARE RECESSED OR PLATFORM FIBERGLASS
HEIGHT: 2'-9"

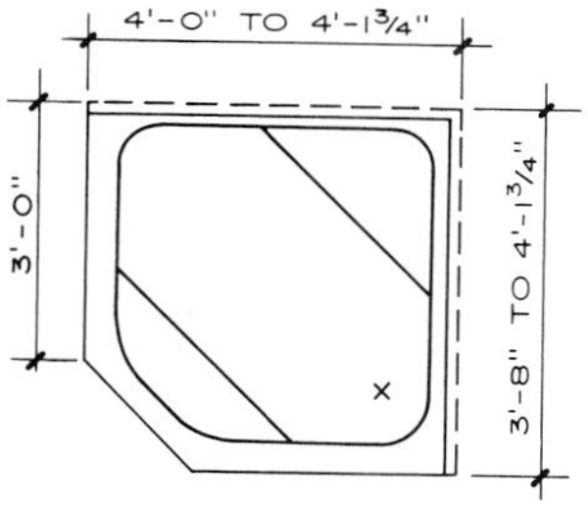

SEAT

4'-0" TO 4'-1¾"

CORNER ENAMELED CAST IRON
HEIGHT: 1'-4"

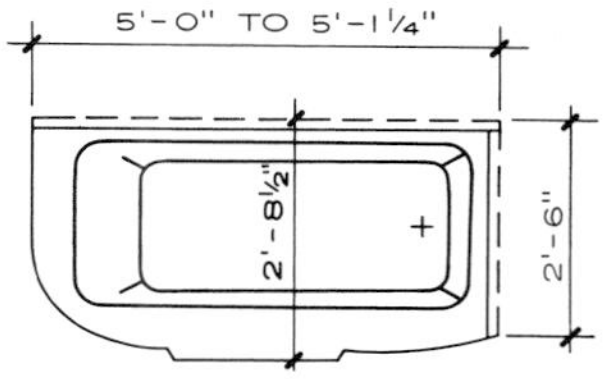

5'-0" TO 5'-1¼"

BUILT-IN-CORNER ENAMELED CAST IRON, VITREOUS CHINA, OR EARTHENWARE
HEIGHT: 1'-4"

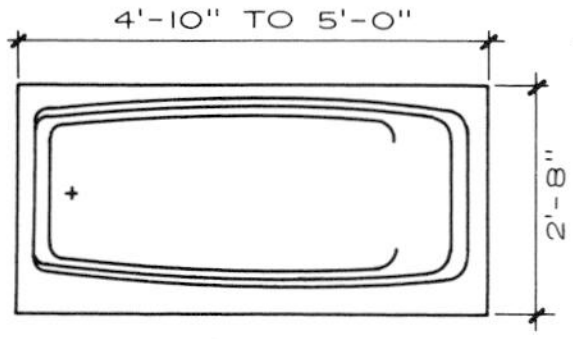

4'-10" TO 5'-0"

BUILT-IN-RECESS FIBERGLASS REINFORCED POLYESTER
HEIGHT: 1'-4"

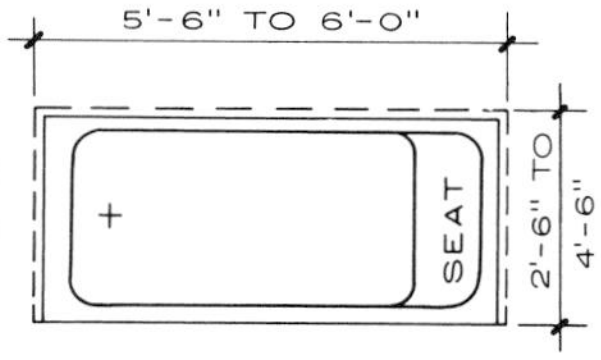

5'-6" TO 6'-0"

SEAT

BUILT-IN-RECESS ENAMELED CAST IRON
HEIGHT: 1'-6" & 1'-8"

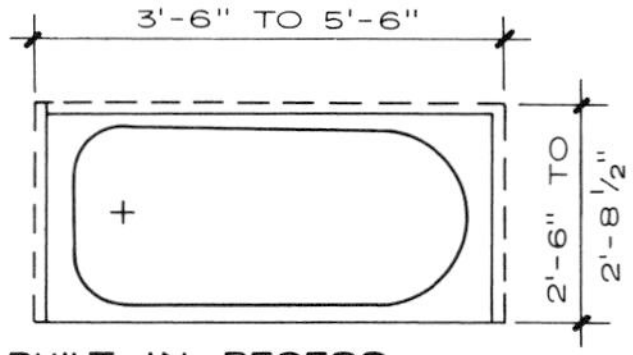

3'-6" TO 5'-6"

BUILT-IN-RECESS ENAMELED CAST IRON, ENAMELED STEEL, OR FIBERGLASS
HEIGHT: 1'-0" & 1'-4"

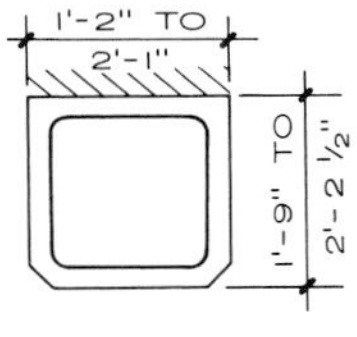

1'-2" TO 2'-1"

FOOT BATH ENAMELED CAST IRON, VITREOUS CHINA, OR EARTHENWARE
HEIGHT: 1'-3"

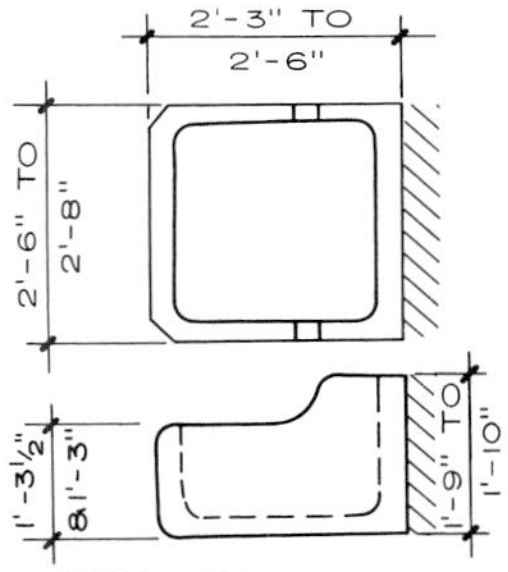

2'-3" TO 2'-6"

SITZ BATH ENAMELED CAST IRON, VITREOUS CHINA, OR EARTHENWARE

FREESTANDING SHOWER CABINETS AND BATHTUBS

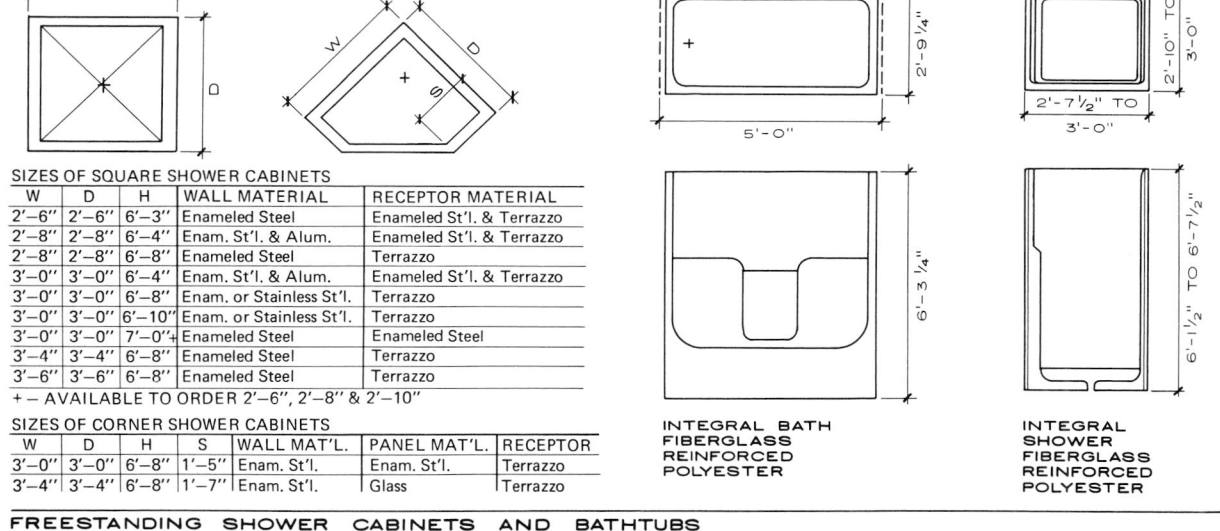

SIZES OF SQUARE SHOWER CABINETS

W	D	H	WALL MATERIAL	RECEPTOR MATERIAL
2'-6"	2'-6"	6'-3"	Enameled Steel	Enameled St'l. & Terrazzo
2'-8"	2'-8"	6'-4"	Enam. St'l. & Alum.	Enameled St'l. & Terrazzo
2'-8"	2'-8"	6'-8"	Enameled Steel	Terrazzo
3'-0"	3'-0"	6'-4"	Enam. St'l. & Alum.	Enameled St'l. & Terrazzo
3'-0"	3'-0"	6'-8"	Enam. or Stainless St'l.	Terrazzo
3'-0"	3'-0"	6'-10"	Enam. or Stainless St'l.	Terrazzo
3'-0"	3'-0"	7'-0"+	Enameled Steel	Enameled Steel
3'-4"	3'-4"	6'-8"	Enameled Steel	Terrazzo
3'-6"	3'-6"	6'-8"	Enameled Steel	Terrazzo

+ – AVAILABLE TO ORDER 2'-6", 2'-8" & 2'-10"

SIZES OF CORNER SHOWER CABINETS

W	D	H	S	WALL MAT'L.	PANEL MAT'L.	RECEPTOR
3'-0"	3'-0"	6'-8"	1'-5"	Enam. St'l.	Enam. St'l.	Terrazzo
3'-4"	3'-4"	6'-8"	1'-7"	Enam. St'l.	Glass	Terrazzo

INTEGRAL BATH FIBERGLASS REINFORCED POLYESTER

INTEGRAL SHOWER FIBERGLASS REINFORCED POLYESTER

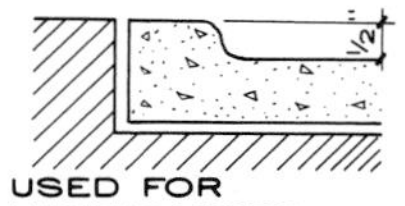

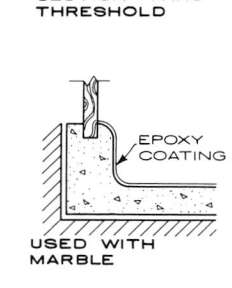

USED FOR HANDICAPPED

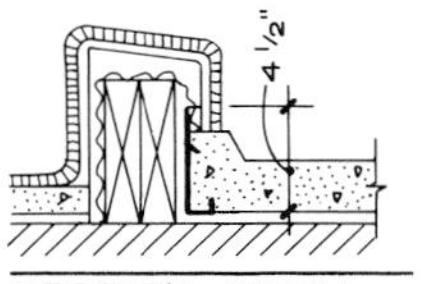

SECTION THRU THRESHOLD

EPOXY COATING

USED WITH MARBLE

SHOWER RECEPTOR TYPES

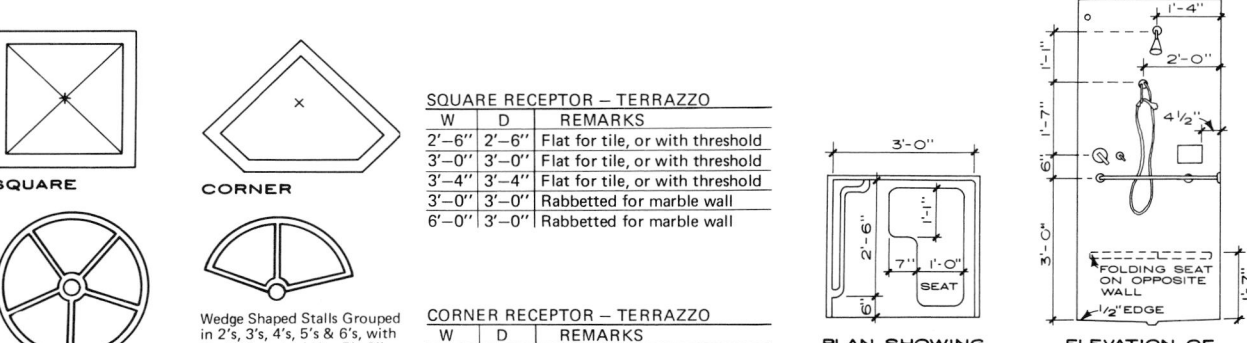

SQUARE

CORNER

SQUARE RECEPTOR – TERRAZZO

W	D	REMARKS
2'-6"	2'-6"	Flat for tile, or with threshold
3'-0"	3'-0"	Flat for tile, or with threshold
3'-4"	3'-4"	Flat for tile, or with threshold
3'-0"	3'-0"	Rabbetted for marble wall
6'-0"	3'-0"	Rabbetted for marble wall

MULTISTALL

Wedge Shaped Stalls Grouped in 2's, 3's, 4's, 5's & 6's, with 6'-0" Standard Ht., 5'-6" Intermediate Ht. & 5'-0" Junior Ht.

CORNER RECEPTOR – TERRAZZO

W	D	REMARKS
3'-0"	3'-0"	Flat for tile, or with threshold
3'-4"	3'-4"	Flat for tile, or with threshold

SHOWER USED BY HANDICAPPED

PLAN SHOWING FOLDING SHOWER SEAT

ELEVATION OF PLUMBING WALL

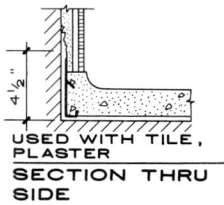

USED WITH TILE, PLASTER

SECTION THRU SIDE

NOTE
Adequate waterproofing should be added to each of the sections.

K. Shahid Rab, AIA; Friesen International; Washington, D.C.

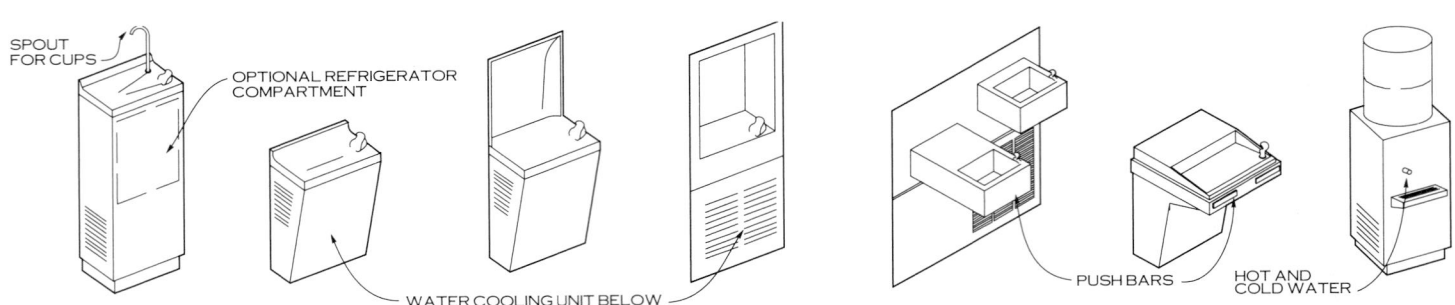

FLOOR MOUNTED				WALL MOUNTED				SEMIRECESSED				FULLY RECESSED				HI-LO ACCESSIBLE				ACCESSIBLE				BOTTLE TYPE			
H	W	D	GPH	H	W	D	GPH	H	W	D	GPH	H	W	D	GPH	H	W	D	GPH	H	W	D	GPH	H	W	D	GPH
30½	15	15	7–12	16	17	13¼	2–5	35¾	17	13½	11–17	50¼	18	12	8–14	38 (6)	38½	12 & 19	8	25	18	19	7.8	36	12	12	1
33½	18	14½	4–20	22	18	14½	4–14	37½	16½	14½	7–15	54¼	19	12¼	7–12	40 (7)	38	11½ & 19	8	23¾	19½	19	4–8	40	14	14	2
40	12	12	3–10	26	17	14	5–15	39¾	18	13½	7–12	55¼	21	13	5–10	39 (7)	38	11¾ & 19	7.8	21¾	18	18½	8	44	17	14	1
41½	18	14½	4–20	29½	18	14½	4–20	44¼	17¼	14	5–13					39 (6½)	32	11 & 19	8	26	17	18	8				

DRINKING FOUNTAINS WITH INTEGRAL COOLERS (DIMENSIONS IN INCHES)

Use air cooled condensers for normal room temperatures; water-cooled units for high room temperature and larger capacities. Many models are available with cold and hot water supply, a cup filling spout, or refrigerated compartments. Fountains are available in a wide selection of colors and finishes.

Floor and wall-mounted fountains are made in lower heights for children's use and can be mounted low on the side of regular height models.

Floor mounted units may be installed flush to a wall or free-standing.

Recommended fountain rim heights above the floor:

1. 40 in.—adults
2. 30 in.—children (often the accessible height will serve)
3. 34 in. max./spout outlet 36 in. max.—accessible

Install half of required fountains at the accessible height.

Design layout such that accessible fountains do not obstruct perambulation of the visually impaired.

Verify clearance dimensions for specific fountains prior to specifying.

Special explosion-proof fountains are recommended for use in hazardous atmospheres. Corrosion resistant fountains are available, as well as a water-cooled type for excessively hot and dusty atmospheres.

Power requirements are 110, 115, 230 V; 50 to 60 cycles, single phase AC; otherwise a transformer is used.

Consult local building codes for minimum number of drinking fountains required.

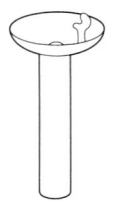 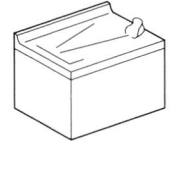 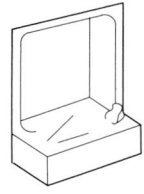 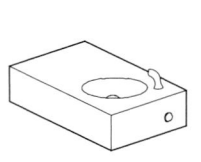 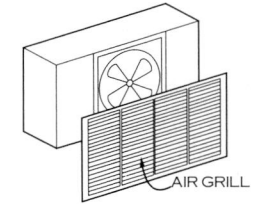

PEDESTAL DISH			WALL MOUNTED				SEMI OR FULLY RECESSED				ACCESSIBLE				REMOTE WATER COOLER			
H	D	SUPPLY & WASTE	H	W	D	SUPPLY & WASTE	H	W	D	SUPPLY & WASTE	H	W	D	SUPPLY & WASTE	H	W	D	GPH
38¼	4	¼ & 1½	7¾	10	10	⅜ & 1¼	27¾	17½	13	⅜ & 1¼	6	12	20	½ & 1¼	16¼	15¾	8	5–6
38¼	14¼	¼ & 1½	16	17	13¼	⅜ & 1¼	29	21	13	⅜ & 1¼	7	15	21	⅜ & 1¼	22¼	30	6½	6–10

DRINKING FOUNTAINS (DIMENSIONS IN INCHES)

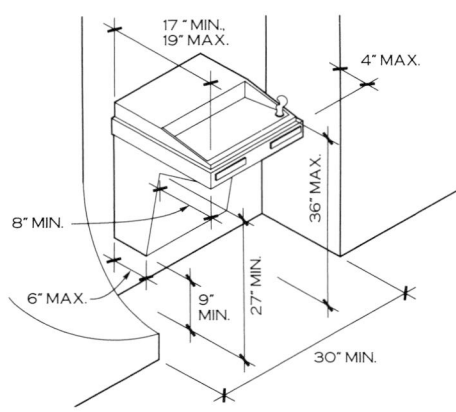

WATER COOLER ALCOVE

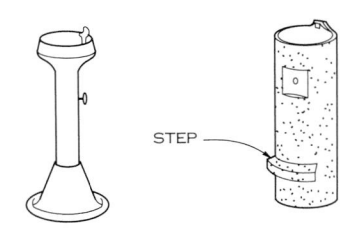 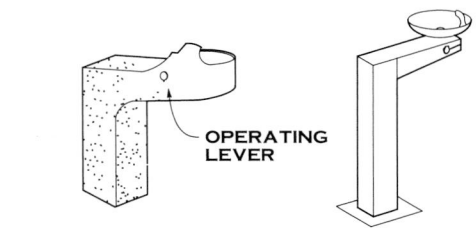

PEDESTAL			CONCRETE CYLINDER			ACCESSIBLE CONC.			ACCESS. PEDESTAL		
H	DIA.	SUPPLY & WASTE	H	DIA.	SUPPLY & WASTE	H	L	SUPPLY & WASTE	H	L	SUPPLY & WASTE
36	12	⅜, 1	36	12	½, 1¼	33	30¾	½, 1¼	33	29¾	½, 1¼

OUTDOOR FOUNTAINS (DIMENSION IN INCHES)

William G. Miner, AIA, Architect; Washington, D.C.
Mark J. Mazz, AIA; CEA, Inc.; Hyattsville, Maryland

PLUMBING FIXTURES

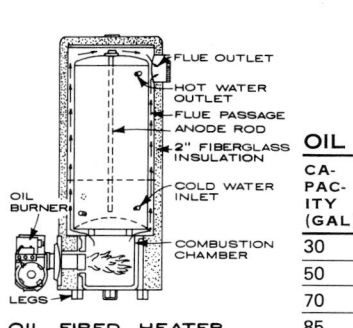

OIL

CAPACITY (GAL)	HEIGHT	DIAMETER
30	57½''	22''
50	69½''	24''
70	74¼''	26''
85	76½''	30''

OIL FIRED HEATER

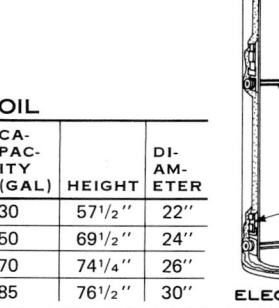

ELECTRIC

CAPACITY (GAL)	HEIGHT	DIAMETER
30	45⅝''	20¼''
52	59⅛''	22¼''
82	60¼''	26¼''
120	62¼''	28¼''

ELECTRIC HEATER

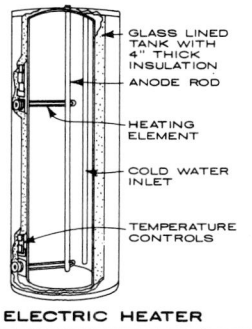

GAS

CAPACITY (GAL)	HEIGHT	DIAMETER
30	55½''	17¾''
50	56⅛''	22¼''
75	60''	24¼''
100	65½''	26¼''

NATURAL GAS HEATER

RESIDENTIAL, STORAGE TYPE WATER HEATERS

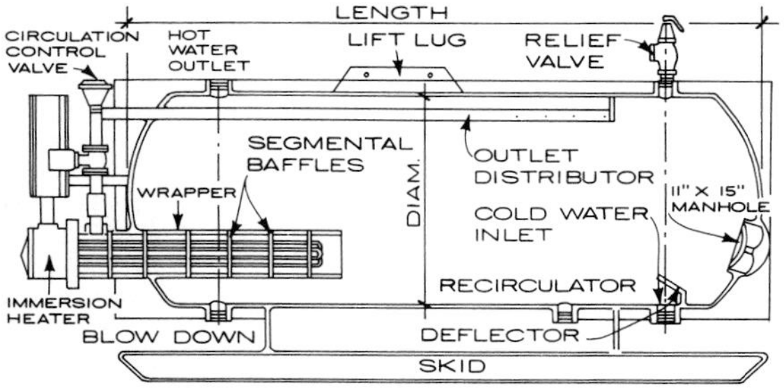

ELECTRIC OR STEAM HEATER

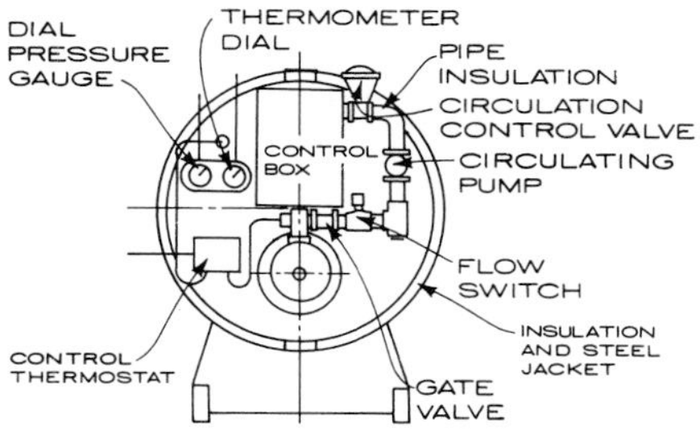

END VIEW

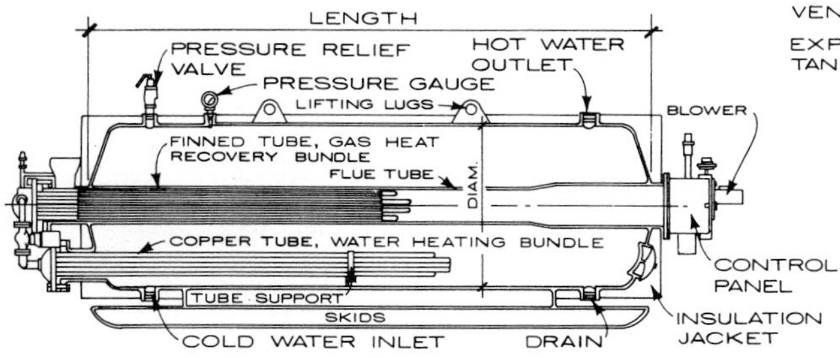

GAS OR OIL FIRED HEATER

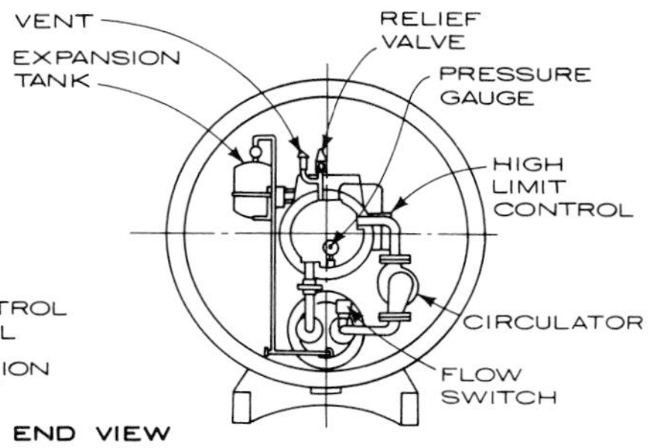

END VIEW

COMMERCIAL, STORAGE TYPE WATER HEATERS

ELECTRIC/STEAM HEATER DIMENSIONS

CAPACITY (GAL)	LENGTH	DIAMETER	SPACE TO REMOVE HEATING SECTION	
			ELECTRIC	STEAM
530	96''	42''	39''	12''
1034	96''	60''	39''	18''
1300	120''	60''	39''	24''
1980	120''	72''	79''	29''
2400	144''	72''	79''	29''
3150	144''	84''	79''	27''
4070	144''	96''	79''	27''

GAS/OIL HEATER DIMENSIONS

CAPACITY (GAL)	LENGTH	DIAMETER	SPACE TO REMOVE HEATING SECTION
560	108''	42''	85''
820	120''	48''	87''
1250	120''	60''	97''
1930	120''	72''	103''
2340	144''	72''	103''
3090	144''	84''	89''
4010	144''	96''	89''

GENERAL NOTE
These dimensions are for horizontal type heaters only. Space saving, vertical type heaters with same capacities are available from most manufacturers.

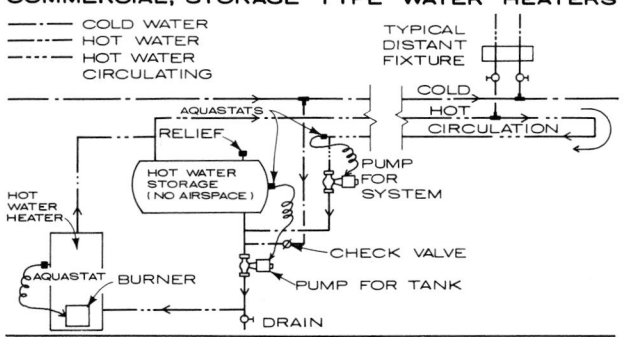

FORCED CIRCULATION SYSTEM

ESTIMATED HOT WATER DEMAND

BUILDING TYPE	HOT WATER[1] PER PERSON DAY'S USE	HOURLY DEMAND	DURATION OF PEAK LOAD	STORAGE CAPACITY DAY'S USE	HEATING CAPACITY DAY'S USE
Residences, apartments, hotels[2]	20-40 gal/day	⅐	4 hr	⅕	⅐
Office buildings	2-3 gal/day	⅕	2 hr	⅕	⅙
Factory buildings	5 gal/day	⅓	1 hr	⅖	⅛

1. At 140°F.
2. Allow additional 15 gal per dishwasher and 40 gal per laundry washer.

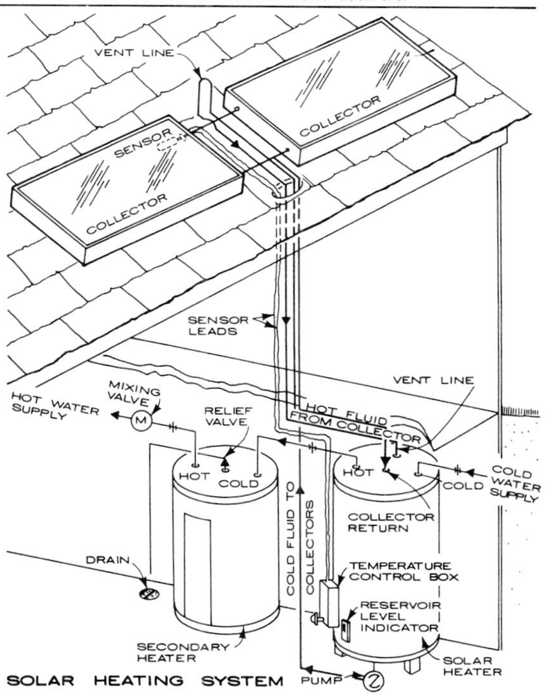

Syska and Hennessy, Consulting Engineers; New York, New York

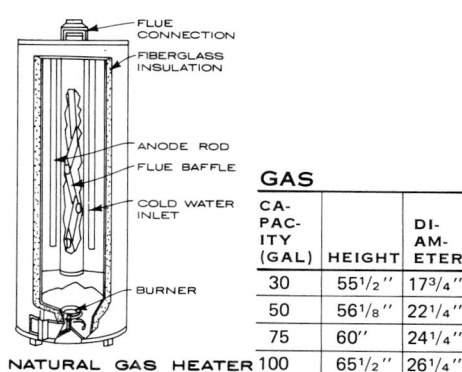

SOLAR HEATING SYSTEM

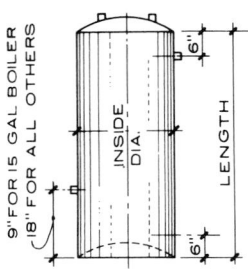

RANGE BOILER

Galvanized Standard
pressure = 85 psi
Extra heavy pressure = 150 psi
Double extra heavy = 150 psi
2'-0'' dia. tank—tapping is
1½'', others 1''

RANGE BOILERS

CAPACITY (GAL)	DIAMETER	LENGTH
15	1'-0''	2'-6''
30	1'-0''	5'-0''
40	1'-2''	5'-0''
66	1'-6''	5'-0''
82	1'-8''	5'-0''
120	2'-0''	5'-0''

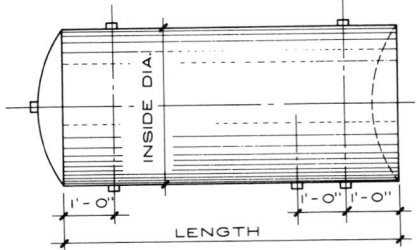

HOT WATER STORAGE TANK

Manhole 11'' x 15'' in shell or head
Standard pressure = 65 psi
Extra heavy pressure = 100 psi
Tanks used vertically or horizontally.
6 tappings in each tank of diameters listed

GENERAL WATER TANK DATA

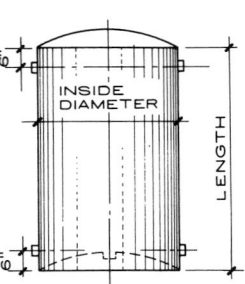

GALVANIZED EXPANSION TANKS

Galvanized, tapping 1'' Φ
Max. pressure = 30 psi
Max. no. of tappings shown

EXPANSION TANKS

CAPACITY (GAL)	DIAMETER	LENGTH
10	1'-0''	1'-8''
15	1'-0''	2'-6''
20	1'-2''	2'-6''
30	1'-0''	5'-0''
40	1'-2''	5'-0''

HOT WATER STORAGE TANKS

CAPACITY (GAL)	DIAMETER	LENGTH
82	1'-8''	5'-0''
118	2'-0''	5'-0''
141	2'-0''	6'-0''
220	2'-6''	6'-0''
294	2'-6''	8'-0''
317	3'-0''	6'-0''
428	3'-0''	8'-0''
504	3'-6''	7'-0''
576	3'-6''	8'-0''
720	3'-6''	10'-0''
904	4'-0''	10'-0''
1008	3'-6''	14'-0''
1504	4'-0''	16'-0''
1880	4'-0''	20'-0''

SOLAR TANK

Galvanized
Double extra heavy = 120 psi
Used vertically only 1'-8''
dia. tank, 1'' tapping, all
others 1½'' tapping

SOLAR TANKS

CAPACITY (GAL)	DIAMETER	LENGTH
66	1'-8''	4'-0''
100	2'-0''	4'-0''
150	2'-6''	4'-0''
210	3'-0''	4'-0''
270	3'-0''	5'-0''

TAP SIZES

TANK DIAMETER	TAP DIAMETER
1'-8''	1½''
2'-0''	1½''
2'-6''	2''
3'-0''	2''
3'-6''	2''
4'-0''	3''

FORMULAS FOR CAPACITY OF CYLINDRICAL TANKS

$Diameter^2$ x 0.7854 x Length = Volume

Cu. Ft. x 7.4805 =

or

$\dfrac{Cu. In.}{1728}$ x 7.4805 =

} Capacity in Gallons

WATER DATA

1 gallon = 231 cu. in. 1 cu. ft. weight 62.5 lbs. Tank sizes may vary. See manufacturer's data.

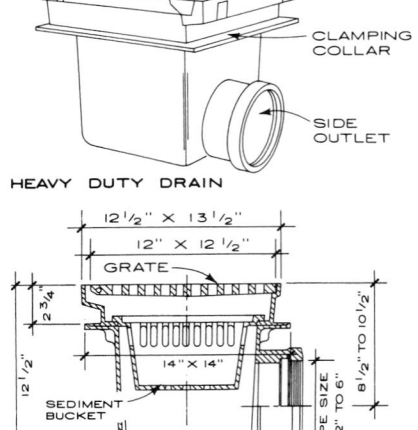

HEAVY DUTY DRAIN

DETAIL

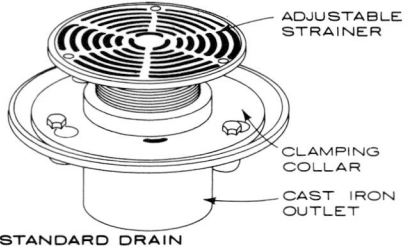

STANDARD DRAIN

SHOWER DRAIN

RECTANGULAR

ANGLE

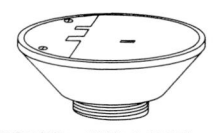

DOME

COVER AND LOCK

NOTE

Heavy duty strainers are constructed of nickel brass or cast iron. Sediment baskets and backwater valves are optional accessories. Vandalproof covers and locks also are available. In water disposal area, spray nozzles are installed for washdown of drains. Consider baskets in shower drains. Consider heel-proof grates where applicable.

FLOOR AND SHOWER DRAINS

William G. Miner, AIA, Architect; Washington, D.C.

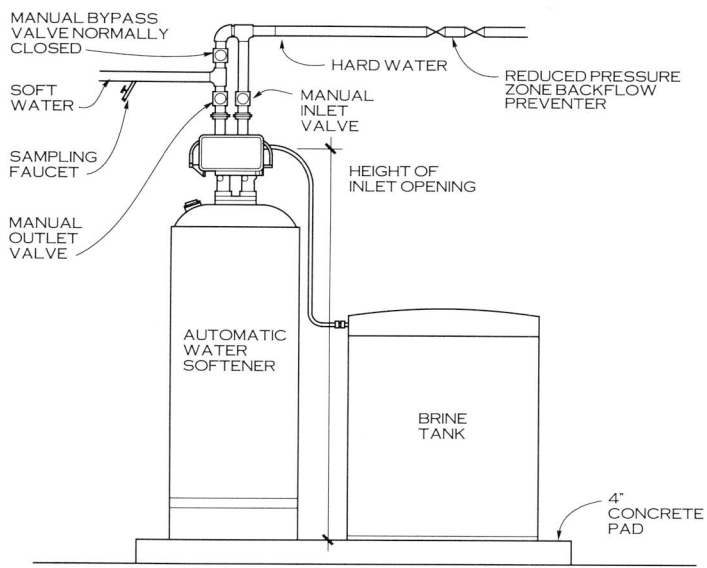

AUTOMATIC WATER SOFTNER PIPING DIAGRAM

AUTOMATIC WATER SOFTENER SCHEDULE—FLOW RATE—17 TO 40 GPM

GRAIN CAPACITY AND SALT DOSAGE PER POUND	SERVICE FLOW RATE (GPM)		PIPE SIZE (IN.)	RESIN QUANTITY (CU FT)	TANK SIZE (IN.)	
	PEAK	CONTINUOUS			SOFTENER	BRINE
14,000 grains/5 lb	25	12	1 1/2	1.5	12 x 40	18 x 38
28,000 grains/10 lb	17	13	1	3.0	16 x 48	24 x 38
43,000 grains/15 lb	17	13	1	4.0	16 x 60	24 x 38
45,000 grains/22 lb	25	12	1 1/2	1.5	12 x 40	18 x 38
90,000 grains/45 lb	40	20	1 1/2	3.0	16 x 48	24 x 38
120,000 grains/60 lb	40	20	1 1/2	4.0	16 x 60	24 x 38

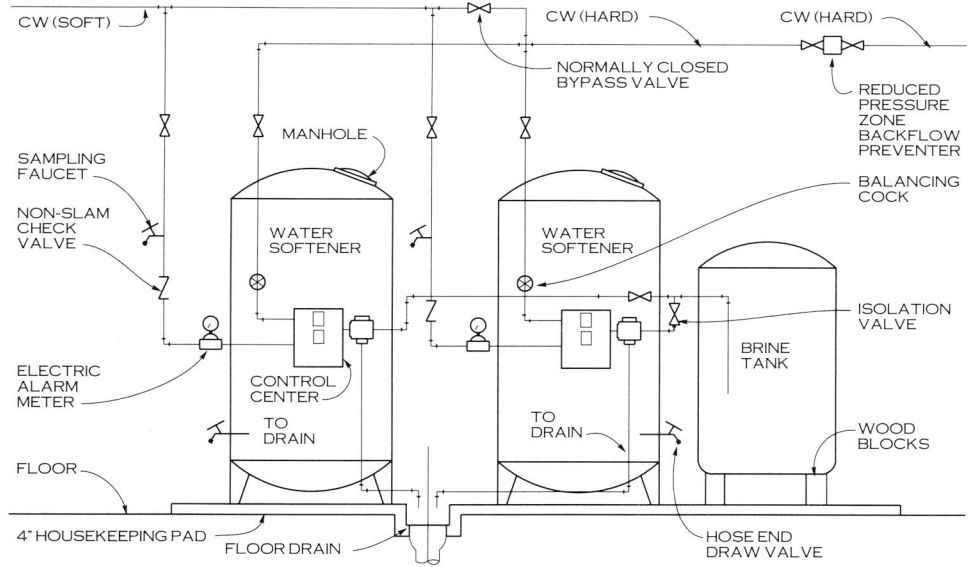

INDUSTRIAL WATER SOFTENER PIPING DIAGRAM

INDUSTRIAL WATER SOFTENER SCHEDULE—FLOW RATE—60 TO 200 GPM

GRAIN CAPACITY AND SALT DOSAGE PER POUND	SERVICE FLOW RATE (GPM)		PIPE SIZE (IN.)	RESIN QUANTITY (CU FT)	TANK SIZE (IN.)	
	PEAK	CONTINUOUS			SOFTENER	BRINE
80,000 grains/20 lb	60	35	1 1/2	5.0	24 x 54	24 x 48
116,000 grains/30 lb	75	50	1 1/2	6.75	24 x 54	24 x 48
250,000 grains/125 lb	75	50	1 1/2	8.5	24 x 54	24 x 48
300,000 grains/150 lb	110	80	2	10.0	30 x 60	30 x 48
450,000 grains/225 lb	110	80	2	15.0	30 x 60	30 x 48
600,000 grains/300 lb	150	110	2 1/2	20.0	36 x 60	36 x 48
800,000 grains/405 lb	200	150	3	27.0	42 x 60	42 x 48

DiClemente - Siegel Engineering, Inc.; Southfield, Michigan

GENERAL

Water hardness is caused by calcium and magnesium salts and is usually expressed in grains per gallon. For example: New York City, 1-5 grains (low); Grand Rapids, Michigan, 9 grains (5-9 moderate); Jacksonville, Florida, 18 grains (over 9 high); well water 0-50 grains.

A water softener is typically one tank for manual operation and two adjacent or concentric tanks with automatic controls. To determine the proper size softener for a residence, use this formula:

No. of people x 50 gal (75 if 3 or more baths) = gal water used /day

Gal water/day x no. of days of service = gal soft water needed

Gal soft water x hardness (grains/gal = capacity of softener needed

If the capacity found necessary by this formula is too large, reduce the number of days of service; the softener will need to be regenerated more often. The table lists data for residential size softeners. If a softener is needed for use in another building type, consult a manufacturer. Rental equipment with service plans is available in some areas, and responsibility for design adequacy should be assumed by the renting company.

When water supplies contain suspended matter, a filter should be placed at the hard water inlet. The softening process often removes any taste the water may have, but filters can also correct bad taste, acidity, or odor problems caused by other salts and minerals.

TYPICAL MANUFACTURERS' DATA

CHARAC-TERISTICS	MODELS		
REGEN-ERATION METHOD	FULLY AUTO-MATIC[1]	SEMI-AUTO-MATIC[2]	MANUAL[3]
Capacity (grains)	18,000	25,000	50,000
Service flow rate (gal)	10	7.5	8
Rinse flow rate (gal)	0.7	0.5	1.0
Ion exchanger (cu ft)	1.0	0.85	1.7
Salt per regeneration (lb)	5.5	10	30
Regeneration time (min)	60	120	90
Service piping (in.)	1	3/4	3/4
Waste piping (in.)	3/8	3/4	1/2
Pressure range (lb)	25-100	25-100	25-100
Electric current (V)	110-60 capacity	110-60 capacity	—
Resin tank diameter (in.)	9 3/16	9	12
Bed area (sq ft)	0.442	0.44	0.78
Shipping weight (lb)	100	116	197
Floor space (in.)	2 x 30	11 x 15	13 x 18
Overall height (in.)	43 3/4	44 3/4	54

NOTES

1. Complete regeneration by time clock.
2. Manually operated switch to start regeneration.
3. Complete manual regeneration by adding dry pellet type salt directly to the softener.

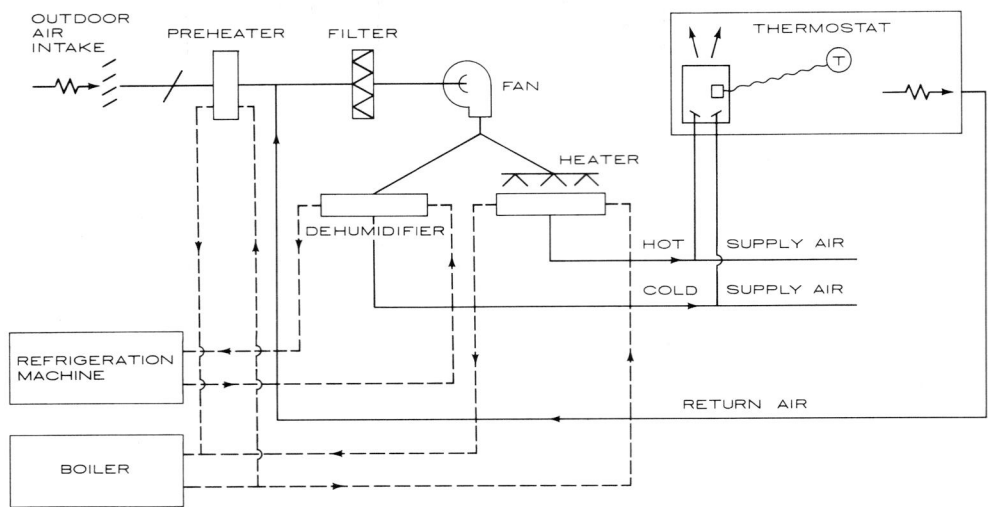

ALL-AIR SYSTEMS

With all-air systems the heating and refrigeration plants may be located in a central mechanical room some distance from the conditioned space. The air handling station not only cleans the air, but also heats or cools it, humidifies or dehumidifies it. Only the final cooled or heated air is brought through ducts into the conditioned space and distributed through outlets or mixing terminals.

Some common all-air systems are: single duct, variable volume; dual conduit; single duct with reheat or fan-powered terminal; multizone; and double duct.

SINGLE DUCT, VARIABLE VOLUME

This central station system supplies a single stream of either hot or cold air at normal velocity. Capacity is adjusted to load by automatic volume control. Exterior room systems are zoned by exposure.

Air terminal diffusers are available with self-contained, self-balancing, system-operated controls, which are factory installed and calibrated.

DOUBLE DUCT, CONSTANT VOLUME
ALL-AIR SYSTEMS

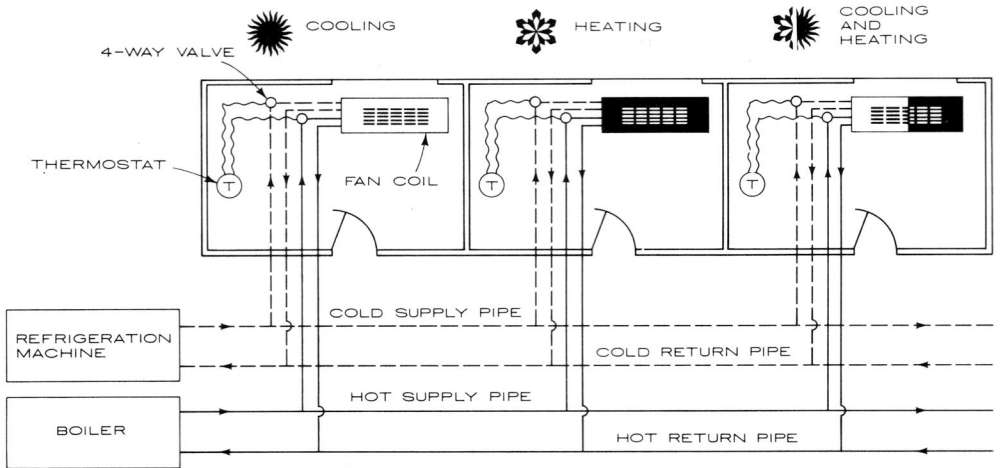

ALL-WATER SYSTEMS

All-water systems have fan coil room terminals with one or two water circuits connected. The cooling medium (such as chilled water or brine) may be supplied from a remote source and circulated through coils in the fan coil terminal located in the conditioned space. These circuits may be either two-pipe or four-pipe distribution. Ventilation comes from a wall opening, from the interior zone system bleed-off, or by infiltration. Another variation uses a separate ventilation unit.

TWO-PIPE SYSTEMS

Either hot or chilled water is piped throughout the building to a number of fan coil units. One pipe supplies water, the other returns it.

FOUR-PIPE SYSTEMS

Two separate piping circuits are used—one for hot and one for chilled medium—to provide simultaneous heating and cooling as needed in various building zones.

FOUR-PIPE DISTRIBUTION
ALL-WATER SYSTEMS

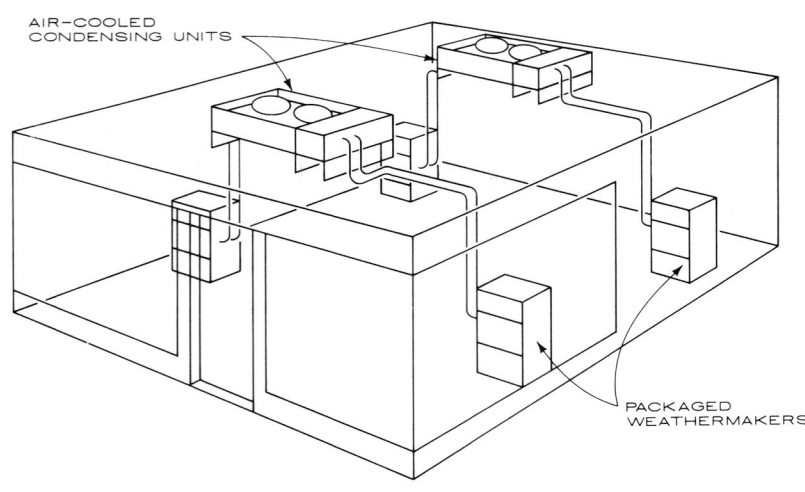

DIRECT EXPANSION SYSTEMS

Expansion systems use self-contained units in windows, cut into the wall, in the roof, or floor-mounted for extracting or adding heat. Units usually are located in or next to the air-conditioned space and consist only of elements essential to producing cool or heat. Heat can be provided either by reverse cycle type, such as a heat pump, or by supplementary heating elements.

ROOFTOP SYSTEMS

Rooftop systems use gas or electricity as energy to supply both heating and cooling. The refrigeration component may be remote or roof-mounted type.

THROUGH-THE-WALL

Cooling normally is achieved in an air-cooled condenser or by centrally circulated water from a cooling tower. Heating is done with gas, electricity, or centrally heated water for year-round air-conditioning.

PACKAGED SYSTEMS

Systems contain roof-mounted, air-cooled condensing units. A reverse cycle heat pump or supplementary heating is required for year-round operation.

DIRECT EXPANSION SYSTEMS

Joseph R. Loring & Associates, Inc., Consulting Engineers; New York, New York
Carrier Corporation; Syracuse, New York

15 HVAC SYSTEMS

GENERAL

The term "sick building syndrome," or "tight building syndrome," applies to any building in which a significant portion of the occupants, usually more than 20%, experience a set of symptoms, including headaches, fatigue, eye, nose, and throat irritation, etc. that ameliorate when the affected persons leave the building. A similar but different condition is "building-related illness," in which the symptoms have recognized medical signs and positive laboratory findings and the causative agent is much more frequently identified. Such illnesses may include Legionnaires' disease, humidifier fever, hypersensitivity pneumonitis, and allergic rhinitis. In theory only one person may be affected with a building-related illness, and these are usually excluded from descriptions of sick building syndrome.

Although most so-called sick buildings have problems with the indoor pollutants in the air, comfort conditions are also important since complaints due to cold, excess heat, or drafts are very common. Humidity can be a problem, as can lighting, noise, vibration, radiation, and odor perception. Other factors include the suitability of furniture, overcrowding, office layout, and personal conflicts, as well as psychological reactions among staff due to anxiety about potential health problems.

Without doubt, however, the single most important factor in dealing with indoor air quality is ventilation. Dilution ventilation is a process whereby fresh or suitable outside air is introduced to an area as stale air is removed. This implies dilution of contaminated air with uncontaminated outside air. The ventilating system has proven to be the best vehicle for optimizing many factors in the indoor environment, including temperature, humidity, electrostatic charges, air movement, and pollution control.

Filtration of outside air and re-circulated air is also vital in ensuring the provision of air of good quality. The importance of removing adequate numbers of the respirable sized particles from indoor air is now accepted, and it is essential, therefore, that filters of satisfactory quality are specified at the design stage.

Cleanliness of the air supply and return systems is also important. The design of air supply equipment must allow easy access to all sections for frequent inspection and cleaning.

AIR QUALITY STANDARDS

The American Society of Heating, Refrigerating, and Air-conditioning Engineers' (ASHRAE) latest standard on indoor air quality (ASHRAE Standard 62-1989, Ventilation for Acceptable Indoor Air Quality) prescribes 20 cubic feet per minute per person (cfm/p) of acceptable outdoor air for office space. This is based on an estimated occupancy rate of about 140 square feet per person. The value of 20 cfm/p was chosen to control carbon dioxide and other contaminants with an adequate margin for safety and to account for health variations among people, varied activity levels, and a moderate amount of smoking.

It is customary for engineers, architects, and designers to be guided by local codes and ordinances for ventilation rates, which are based on ASHRAE recommendations. However, since local codes are updated only every few years, it is inevitable that they will lag behind the most recent thinking on such issues as ventilation rates, and merely meeting the local code requirements may not result in adequate ventilation being provided. It may be wise to seek advice from appropriate experts wherever possible to ensure that the most up-to-date recommendations are being applied to designs.

NEW CONSTRUCTION AND REFURBISHMENT

Many factors affect air quality in buildings, including outdoor air quality, ventilation system, construction materials, people, office equipment, building operations, and maintenance standards. Select system and equipment designs are known to be successful in providing indoor air of acceptable quality. Information is available on selecting environmentally friendly products; on designs and equipment allowing maintainability and durability; on innovative systems offering flexibility; on training of building operating staff; and on recommendations covering the commissioning and subsequent monitoring of air quality throughout a building.

The following checklist outlines suggested steps to follow, extending from design to occupancy and on-going operation of a building.

DESIGN CRITERIA

1. Review of design documentation procedures and compliance of design with indoor air standards, where they exist.
2. Review of ventilation rates and air distribution systems under all projected modes of operation and anticipated outdoor conditions.
3. Review of provision of exhaust from known indoor air pollution sources, including photocopiers, printing operations, and smoking lounges.
4. Review of projected occupant activity, density, and locations on which heating, ventilating, and air conditioning (HVAC) design was based.
5. Identification of major outdoor sources of pollutants in vicinity of building site and prevailing winds to allow correct placement and orientation of air intakes and exhausts.
6. Assessment of room configuration with respect to compatibility of HVAC design.
7. Review of choice of filtration type and design, materials, and locations within the ventilation system for suitability for particular application.

MAINTAINABILITY AND DURABILITY

1. Specification materials that are suited to the job with respect to wind erosion, corrosion, microbial contamination, and the like.
2. Correct use of condensate drains, water baffles, mist eliminators, humidifiers, and cooling towers to control the presence of free water within air handling systems and minimize microbial contamination.
3. Availability of access doors and inspection ports to chambers of air handling systems, plenums, and ductwork systems, including access to re-heat coils, turning vanes, smoke detectors, etc., for inspection, maintenance, and cleaning.
4. Assess integrity, material type, and location of insulating materials associated with HVAC equipment, ducting, and ceiling plenums.
5. Review access to filters, coils, and motors of variable air volume boxes, reheats, perimeter fan coils or induction units.

PRODUCT SELECTION

1. Procure manufacturers' safety data sheets for products that may be suspected contributors to indoor pollutants, including carpets, flooring, linen, adhesives, wall coverings, partitions, and ceilings; insulating and fireproofing materials; sealants on windows, walls, and floors; use of preservatives, paints, varnishes.
2. Request manufacturers of such products to investigate and provide information on curing, drying, and airing procedures to minimize subsequent emission rates after installation.
3. Investigate proposed adhesive materials and work practices of contractors installing sealing compounds, wall and carpet adhesives, paints, varnishes, and the like.

MICROBIAL CONTROL

1. Design precautionary measures to eliminate pests, insects, birds, leaves, and other wind-blown debris from entering the structure, especially the HVAC system and its outdoor air intakes.
2. Minimize standing water in or on a building to decrease levels of bacteria and fungi; take precautions to prevent standing water through the appropriate use of slopes and drains.
3. Design systems to keep the levels of relative humidity within the building below 65% to reduce the chances of water vapor condensing on cooler surfaces and encouraging mold or bacteria growth.

4. Design air filtration systems and their housing in such a way that they are kept dry and operating in as efficient a manner as possible.
5. Design the HVAC system to allow easy access to allow regular maintenance and cleaning of all internal surfaces of the air supply and return systems so that they will be kept in as clean, dry, and dust free a condition as possible.
6. Consider the use of materials and products manufactured with built-in bacteriostats when recommending carpets, floor tiles, ceiling tiles, paints, filters, and insulation materials.
7. Where appropriate, write into the operating specifications the use of high-quality janitorial services that use environmentally friendly products.

COMMISSIONING OVERVIEW

1. Develop and review a formalized transfer of information and hand-over procedures (including on-going operating procedures) from the design team to the building maintenance personnel.
2. Provide specialized, temporary ventilation practices and filtration techniques during and immediately after the commissioning process to ensure protection of the systems before normal operation.
3. Assess the need to use accelerated or extended ventilation capacity during the first few months of occupancy, including the evaluation of "bake-out" procedures for designated spaces to flush out suspected volatile organic compounds.

PROACTIVE MONITORING

An ongoing preventive maintenance or proactive monitoring program may help ensure that the high standards of ventilation, filtration, and hygiene are maintained throughout the building's early life. The initial goal of such a program is to establish a comprehensive air quality data base for the building for use as a reference point for evaluating changes in air quality in the future. The key to a successful program is the use of field-proven techniques for measuring gases, vapors, dusts, bacteria and fungi, etc. that are present within the building. Airborne contamination sensors can be installed into the ventilating system as part of an ongoing monitoring program.

Thereafter, the results of any change in operating practices, substitution of alternative filtration systems, etc. can be evaluated. Improvements can be quantified and then encouraged. Conversely, in the event of any adverse trends in air quality occurring over time, changes can be implemented to rectify the situation.

INDOOR AIR QUALITY AWARENESS

Designers, architects, owners, and builders need to become more aware of the issue known as indoor air quality. Employers nationwide have become increasingly concerned about air quality in their buildings and its potential threats to employees. In several instances, employers have been forced to financially reimburse their employees for illness blamed on the indoor environment of their offices. Part of the issue concerns tenants severing leases and vacating office spaces due to air quality complaints. It is, therefore, very much in the interests of architects, engineers, and HVAC equipment designers to be aware of the importance of the effects on indoor air quality that structures designed by them produce.

Peter Binnie, BA, FIMLS, MIBiol; Healthy Buildings International, Inc.; Fairfax, Virginia

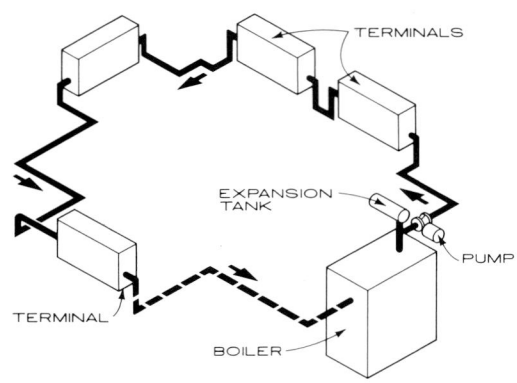

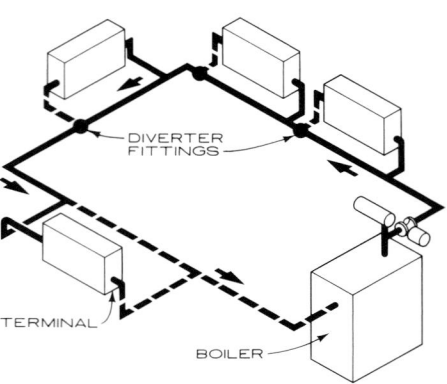

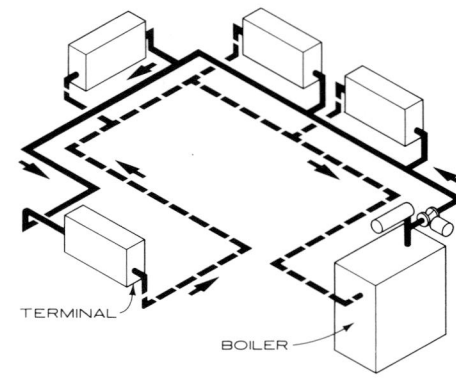

SERIES SYSTEM

(+) MINIMAL PIPING
(−) LIMITED INDIVIDUAL UNIT CONTROL

ONE-PIPE SYSTEM

(+) LESS PIPING THAN TWO-PIPE SYSTEM
(−) REQUIRED DIVERTER FITTINGS
    INCREASE RESISTANCE OF SYSTEM,
    LIMITING SYSTEM SIZE

TWO-PIPE SYSTEM—DIRECT RETURN

(+) CAN USE LESS PIPING THAN REVERSE
    RETURN SYSTEM, ESPECIALLY FOR
    LINEAR SYSTEM CONFIGURATIONS
(−) REQUIRES BALANCING DEVICES TO
    REGULATE FLOW THROUGH EACH
    TERMINAL

HYDRONIC HEATING SYSTEM TYPES

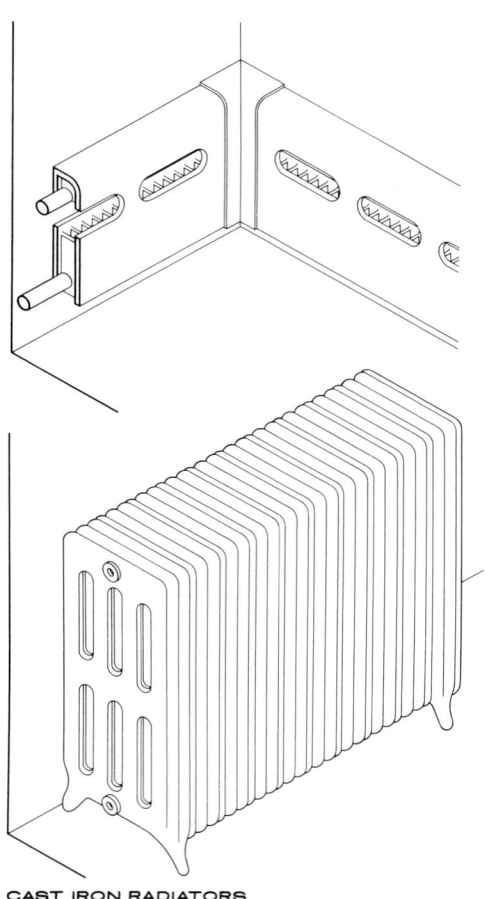

CAST IRON RADIATORS

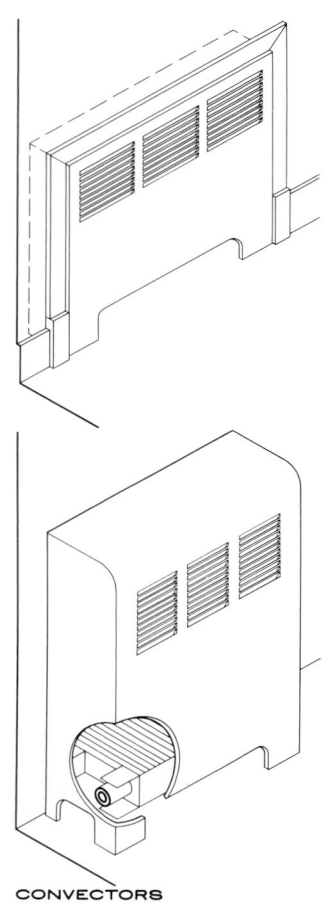

CONVECTORS

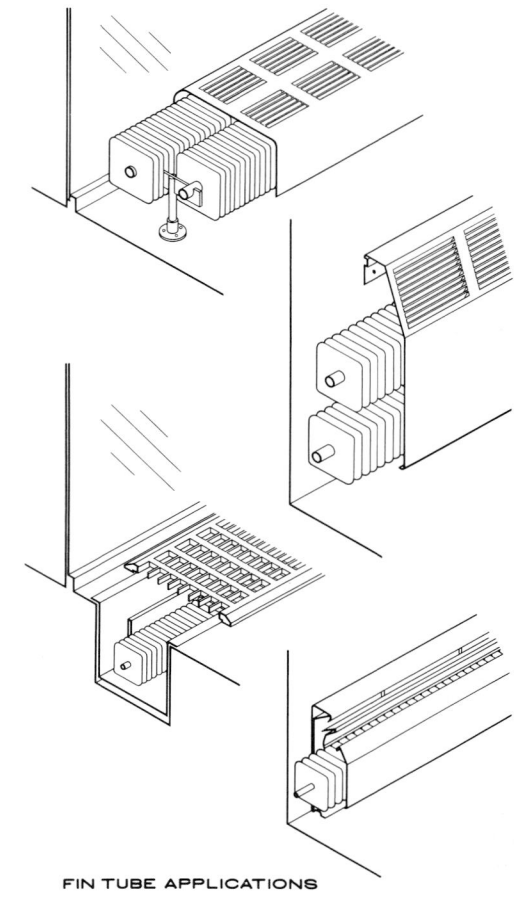

FIN TUBE APPLICATIONS

COMPARATIVE SIZES AND OUTPUT CAPACITIES OF HYDRONIC HEATING TERMINAL UNITS

UNIT TYPE	CAST IRON RADIATOR	STERLING CONVECTOR	VULCAN FIN TUBE RADIATORS		RUNTAL STEEL RADIATORS				
			FLOORLINE (BASEBOARD)	DURA-VANE	"H" PANEL	"V" PANEL	"R" COLUMN	"C" CONVECTOR	"G" GRILLE (GV AND GV-2)
Range of sizes	H 12'' to 3'-9'' L 3'-5'' to 8'-8'' D 4½'' to 1'-1½''	H 1'-8'' to 5'-8'' L 1'-2'' to 3'-0'' D 4¼'' to 8¼''	H 8'' to 1'-2'' L As required D 3½''	H 7'' to 2'-0⁹⁄₁₆'' L As required D 4½'' to 5⁹⁄₁₆''	H 2' to 19'-6'' L 2¾'' to 8'-10⅝'' D 1⅝'' to 3⅜''	H 2¾'' to 2'-5'' L 1'-7¼'' to 19'-6'' D 1⅝'' to 4¾''	H 1'-3⅝'' to 13' L Up to 19'-6'' D 3¾'' to 6¼''	H 2¾'' to 1'-4½'' L 1'-7¼'' to 19'-6'' D 1⅞'' to 1'-3¾''	H 7⅞'' to 3'-11¼'' L 1'-7¾'' to 13'-1½'' D 1¼'' to 2⅜''
Range of output capacities	110 to 250 Btu/sq ft/ hr per unit	Up to 28,000 Btu/hr per unit	Up to 1790 Btu/hr per linear foot	Up to 3180 Btu/ hr per linear foot	Up to 2943 Btu/hr per element	Up to 4715 Btu/hr per linear foot	Up to 5354 Btu/hr per element	Up to 7301 Btu/hr per linear foot	Up to 9473 Btu/hr per linear foot

Eric J. Gastier; Darrel Downing Rippeteau Architects, PC; Washington, D.C.

TERMINAL
BOILER

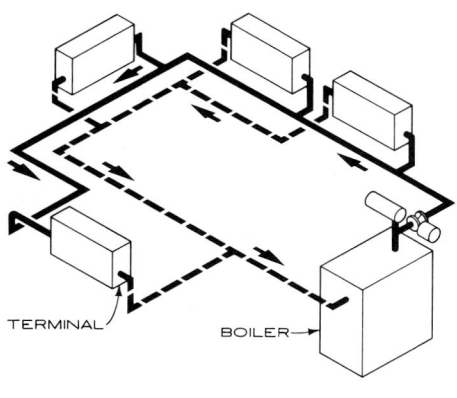

TWO-PIPE SYSTEM—REVERSE RETURN

(+) SIMPLIFIED BALANCING OF TERMINAL UNITS
(−) REQUIRES MAXIMUM PIPING FOOTAGE
(MOST BENEFICIAL WITH LARGE SYSTEMS)

TERMINALS
ZONE "B"
TERMINALS
PUMPS
ZONE "A"
ZONE "C"
TERMINAL
BOILER

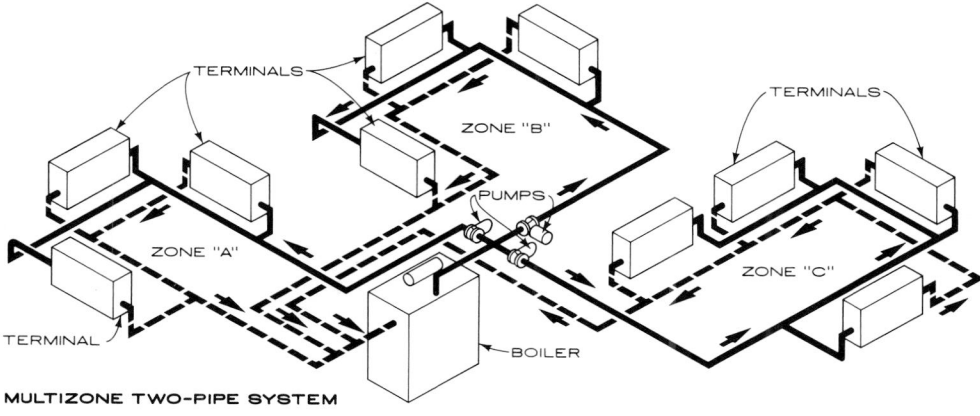

MULTIZONE TWO-PIPE SYSTEM

(+) ALLOWS TEMPERATURES TO VARY BETWEEN ZONES, MAXIMIZING COMFORT AND ENERGY EFFICIENCY
(−) REQUIRES LARGE INITIAL EQUIPMENT COST
(NECESSARY FOR LARGE, MULTIUSE BUILDINGS)

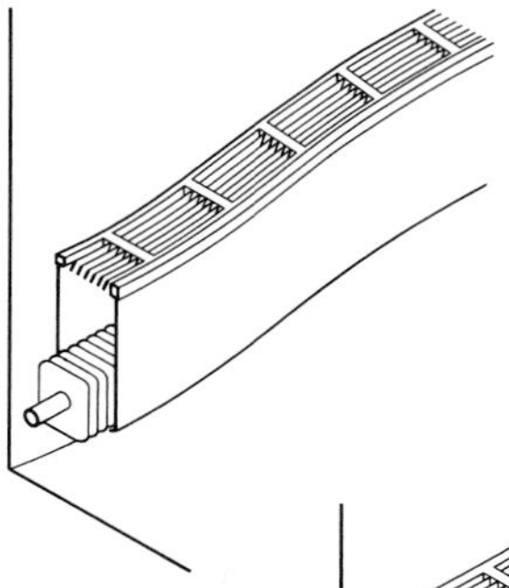

CUSTOM CURVED ENCLOSURE

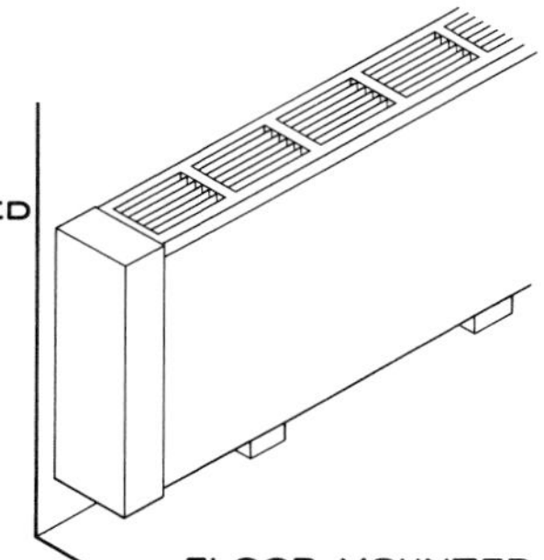

FLOOR-MOUNTED ENCLOSURE ON PEDESTALS

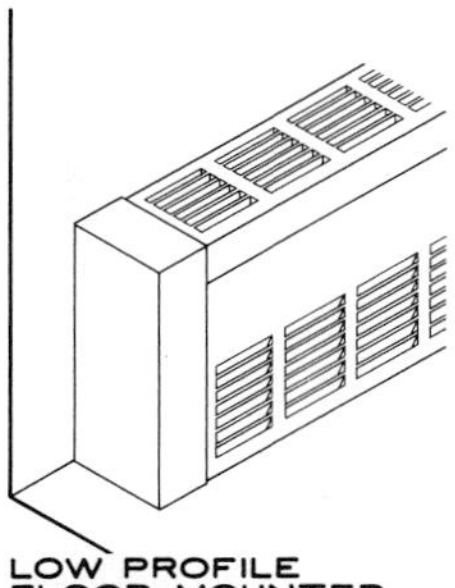

LOW PROFILE FLOOR-MOUNTED ENCLOSURE

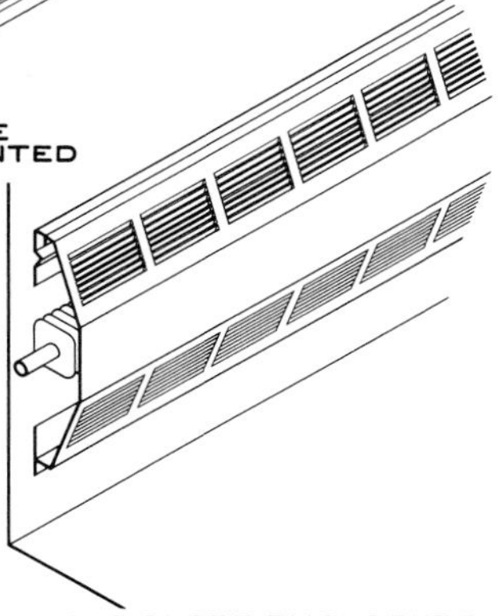

DOUBLE SLOPE ENCLOSURE

VULCAN FIN TUBE RADIATORS

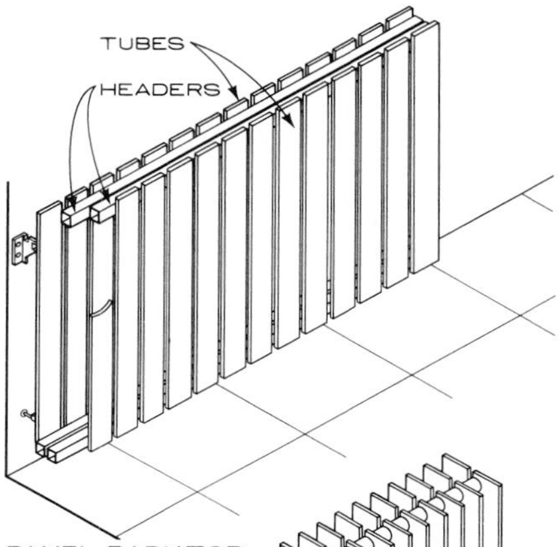

TUBES
HEADERS

"H" PANEL RADIATOR

TUBES
HEADER

"V" PANEL RADIATOR

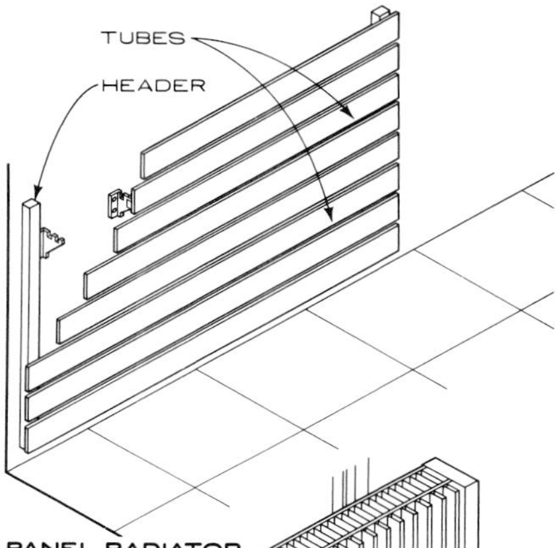

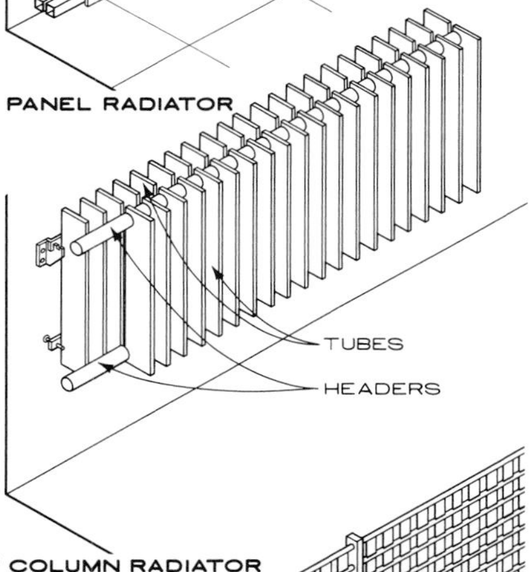

TUBES
HEADERS

"R" COLUMN RADIATOR

HEADER
LAMELLAE (OR FINS)
TUBES

"C" CONVECTOR

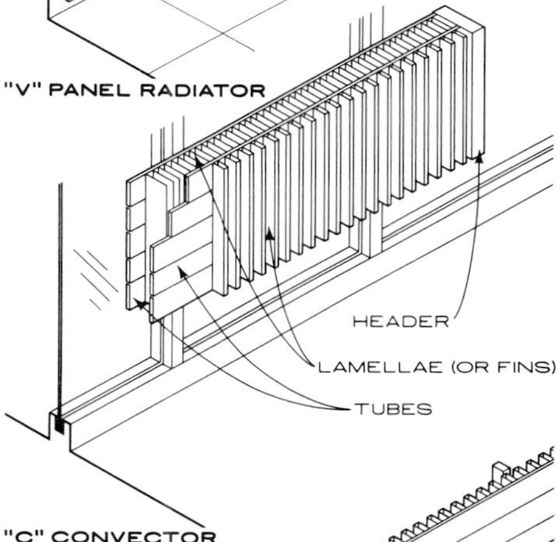

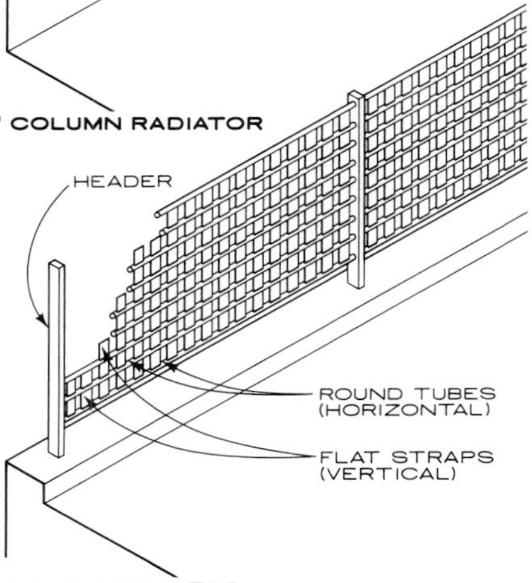

HEADER
ROUND TUBES (HORIZONTAL)
FLAT STRAPS (VERTICAL)

"G" GRILLE RADIATOR

LAMELLAE
TUBES

"C" CONVECTOR

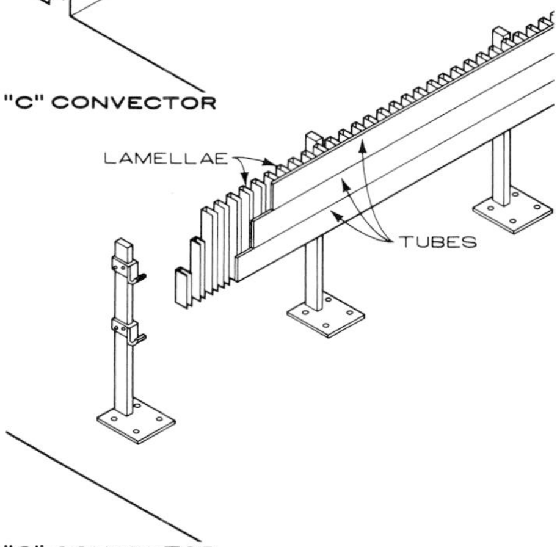

RUNTAL STEEL RADIATORS

Eric J. Gastier; Darrel Downing Rippeteau Architects, PC; Washington, D.C.

GENERAL

The process of removing heat from a refrigerant is called condensing. It is during the condensing process, in a refrigerant cycle, that the refrigerant rejects heat absorbed during the evaporation and compression processes, is reconverted to a liquid state, and becomes ready to repeat the cycle.

To convert the refrigerant from gaseous to liquid state heat exchangers called condensers are used. Air cooled and water cooled condensers are the predominant types used in the building construction industry.

In the less than 50 ton capacity range, water cooled condensers are favored mostly where city water or other water sources such as lake, river, or well are available for once-through use without recirculation of water.

Where water is scarce, as well as in computer rooms and other special air-conditioning applications where year-round temperature and humidity control is required, dry coolers of up to 25 ton capacity are normally used. Where winter ambient is below the water freezing temperature, glycol is added to the condenser water. The heat rejection to the outdoor air is by sensible heat transfer, which is dependent on the dry bulb temperature of the air.

In refrigeration systems larger than 50 ton capacity, water cooled condensers are used to cool the recirculating condenser water. Both the closed circuit evaporative cooler and the cooling tower operate on the principle of evaporative cooling, which is dependent on the wet bulb temperature of the air. The closed circuit evaporative coolers are available in sizes up to 300 tons, and are used when contamination of the condenser water by its direct contact with the outdoor air cannot be tolerated.

Use of a cooling tower is generally acceptable in most installations in the building construction industry. Temperature of the water leaving the cooling tower is approximately 7 to 10°F above the wet bulb temperature of the outside air entering the tower. In cold winter climates, the cooling towers can be used directly to make chilled water and thereby eliminate mechanical refrigeration.

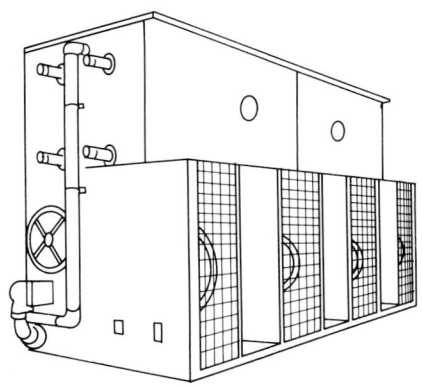

THE EVAPORATIVE CONDENSER combines the functions of a cooling tower and a water cooling condenser. Latent heat transfer is more effective as a means of heat dissipation. This permits a smaller sized unit than an equivalent tonnage air cooled unit, and considerable energy savings in fan horsepower.

Installations can be either indoors in an equipment room with appropriate ducts or outdoors ground mounted or mounted on a roof. When outdoors, adequate protection from freezing must be provided.

For sizing of condensing units, the manufacturers' rating is the only reliable method of determining the unit capacity.

Multiple evaporative condensers may be connected in parallel, or an evaporative condenser may be connected in parallel with a shell and tube condenser. Proper piping and traps must be installed in these cases to prevent unequal loading or overloading.

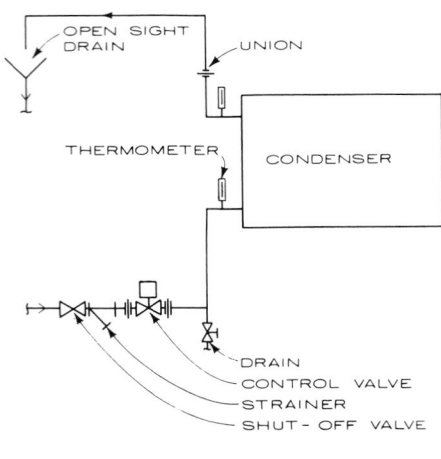

WATER COOLED CONDENSER

For water cooled condenser using city, well, or river water, the return is run higher than the condenser so that the condenser is always full of water. Water flow through the condenser is regulated by a supply line control valve, which is actuated from condenser head pressure control to maintain a constant condensing temperature with variations in load. City water systems usually require check valves and open sight drains, as shown.

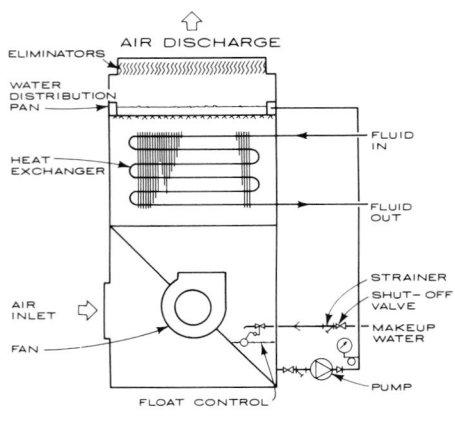

EVAPORATIVE COOLER

The condenser water is circulated inside the tubes of the unit's heat exchanger. Heat flows from the condenser water through the heat exchanger tubes to the spray water outside, which is cascading downward over the tubes. Air is forced upward through the heat exchanger, evaporating a small percentage of the spray water, absorbing the latent heat of vaporization, and discharging the heat to the atmosphere.

The remaining water falls to the sump to be recirculated by the pump. The water consumed is the amount evaporated plus a small amount that is bled off to limit the concentration of impurities in the pan.

The condenser water circulates through the clean, closed loop of the heat exchanger and is never exposed to the airstream or the spray water outside the heat exchanger tubes.

DRY COOLER

The condenser water-glycol solution is circulated inside the finned tubes of the dry cooler's heat exchanger. Heat flows from the condenser water-glycol solution through the heat exchanger tube walls to the fins. Propeller fans draw air over the fins, which transfer its heat to the air passing over it.

An aquastat sensing the temperature of the solution that leaves the dry cooler cycles the fan(s) to maintain the desired temperature.

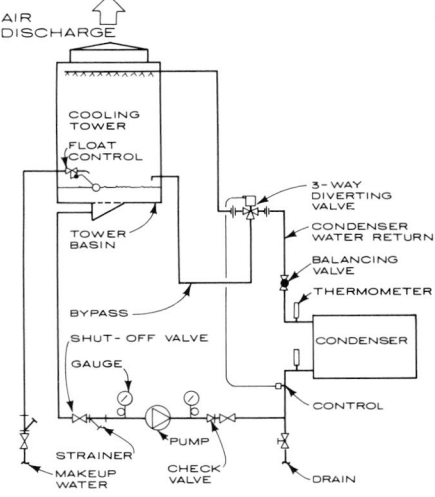

COOLING TOWER

Water flows to the pump from the tower basin and is discharged under pressure to the condenser and back to the tower where it is cooled through the spray deck. Since it is usually desirable to maintain condenser water temperature above a predetermined minimum, return water is partially bypassed around the tower through a control valve to maintain desired supply water temperature.

In this condenser water system, air is continuously in contact with the water. Special consideration for chemical treatment and allowance for impurities, scale, and corrosion in condenser and piping system designs is then required.

Water flow quantity required depends on the refrigeration system employed and the available temperature of the condenser water. Lower condenser water supply temperature results in increased refrigeration machine efficiency.

Anikumar V. Patel; Joseph R. Loring & Associates, Inc., Consulting Engineers; New York, New York

GENERAL NOTES

Chilled water is the most common medium for transferring heat from any type of cooling equipment, such as cooling coils and heat exchangers, to some source of refrigeration.

A chilled water system is a closed circuit system that recirculates water between a mechanical refrigeration water chilling unit and remote cooling equipment, usually operating with water temperatures in the range between 40 and 55°F. There are five types of refrigeration units used in chilled water systems:

1. Centrifugal chiller, with electric motor or steam turbine drive.
2. Reciprocating chiller, with electric motor drive.
3. Rotary screw chiller, with electric drive.
4. Steam absorption chiller.
5. Direct-fired absorption chiller, using fuel oil or gas for firing.

When a chilled water piping system also is used to circulate hot water for winter heating, it is called a dual temperature water system. The design water temperature of chilled water systems usually falls in a rather narrow range because of the necessity for dehumidification and to avoid a possible freeze-up in the chiller. Chilled water supply temperatures usually range from 42° to 60°F for normal comfort applications.

Design flow rates depend on the type of terminal apparatus and the supply temperature. In general, a higher temperature rise (or a greater temperature difference between supply and return temperatures) reduces the initial cost and the operating cost of the distribution system and pumps required and increases the efficiency of the chillers. In a given chilled water system, the selection of the design flow rate and the supply temperature, therefore, are closely related.

Although lower chilled water temperatures permit higher rises (or larger temperature difference), lower chiller efficiencies result. Water treatment may be required in chilled water systems to control corrosion rate, scaling, or algae growth.

Layout of piping systems for chilled water distribution varies greatly depending on system capacity, extent of distribution, type of terminals used, and control scheme to be employed.

Refrigerants that attack the ozone layer above the earth are being phased out and replaced with refrigeration systems that do not degrade the ozone layer, such as R-123, R-134A, and ammonia. This concern has also expanded the use of absorption chillers, both steam and direct-fired types.

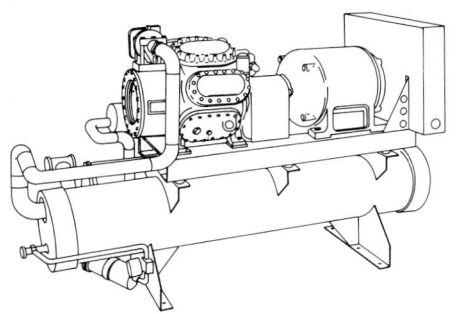

NOTE

A typical reciprocating package chiller, ideally suited to smaller jobs requiring less than 200 tons of cooling. The rotary screw machines are in this range of capacity.

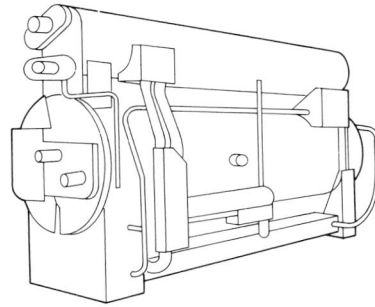

NOTE

A two-stage absorption chiller, steam powered for efficient production of 200 to 800 tons of cooling.

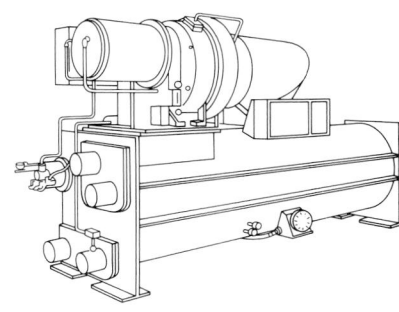

NOTE

A centrifugal chiller with a flooded cooler and condenser. This unit is typically used in ranges of 150 to 1200 tons.

PACKAGE WATER CHILLERS

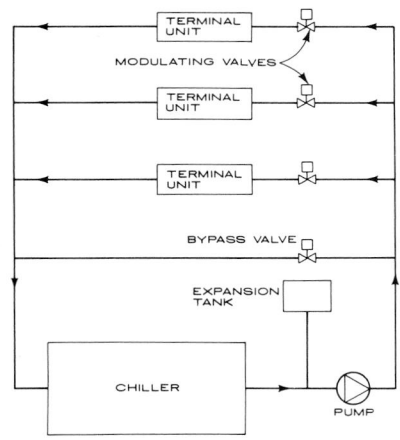

FIGURE 1
ELEMENTARY CHILLED WATER SYSTEM

NOTE

A chilled water system basically consists of a refrigeration water chilling unit, a chilled water recirculating pump, terminal cooling equipment, and an expansion tank. A chilled water bypass valve may be required in systems with two-way modulating valve control at the terminal units. As the cooling load on the terminal equipment decreases, the modulating valve closes and reduces the flow through the terminal. When the water flow through the terminal units is significantly throttled, the bypass valve opens gradually to prevent system pressure buildup and to maintain the water flow required for the proper operation of the chiller.

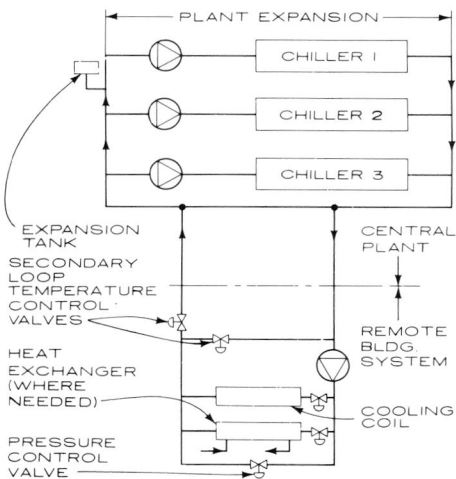

FIGURE 2
PRIMARY/SECONDARY CHILLED WATER PUMPING AND DISTRIBUTION SYSTEM

NOTE

In large campus type applications, the chilled water system consists of multiple chillers and primary and secondary system pumps. The terminal cooling equipment may be chilled water cooling coil of a central air-conditioning unit, closed loop heat exchanger or any other secondary or terminal cooling water system.

The primary loop does not require a pressure control device. The secondary loop pressure control valve operates as described under Elementary Chilled Water System.

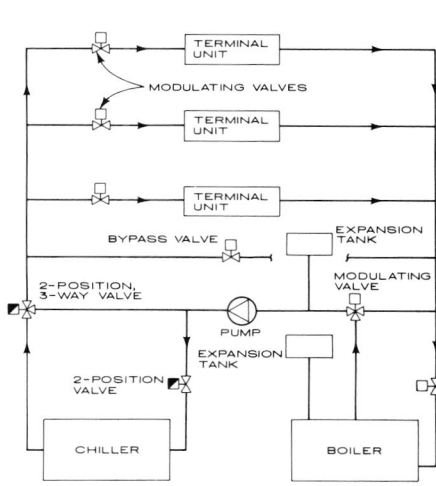

FIGURE 3
TWO-PIPE DUAL TEMPERATURE SYSTEM

NOTE

In a two-pipe dual temperature system hot water is circulated through the terminal units during cold weather and chilled water is circulated during the hot weather. The distribution system may be divided into zones, each of which is capable of changeover from heating to cooling, independent of the other zones.

When the hot and chilled water supply to each terminal unit is in two separate pipes, but the return is in a common pipe, the system is called a three-pipe system. In a four-pipe system, separate supply and return mains for both hot and chilled water are run to each terminal unit.

Joseph R. Loring & Associates, Inc., Consulting Engineers; New York, New York

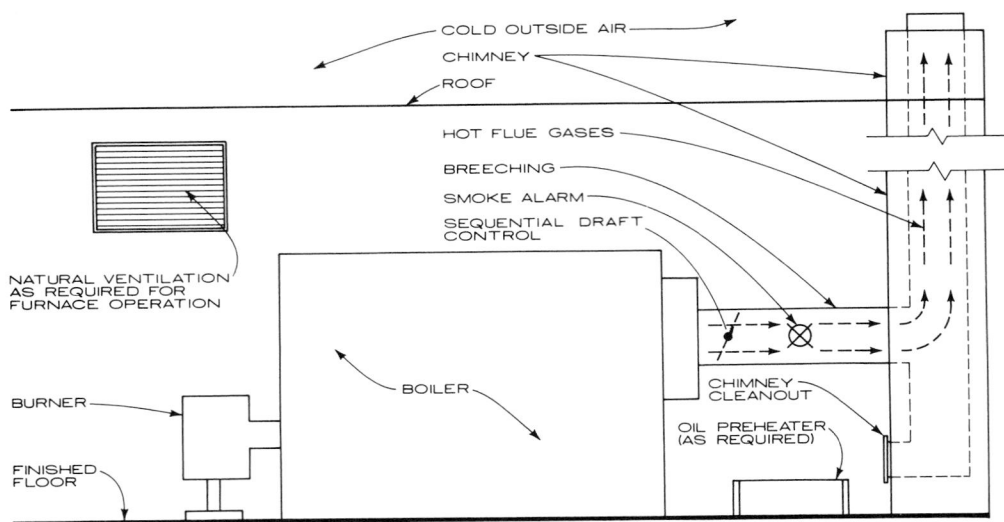

TYPICAL BOILER EQUIPMENT FOR NATURAL DRAFT INSTALLATION

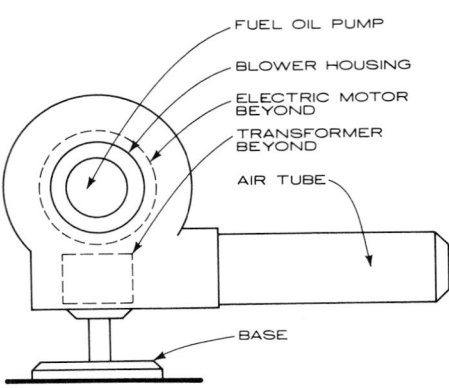

HIGH PRESSURE GUN TYPE BURNER (NO. 2 FUEL OIL)
NOTE: FOR DOMESTIC INSTALLATIONS UP TO 10 FAMILIES AND SINGLE STORY COMMERCIAL INSTALLATIONS UP TO 10,000 SQ FT

BOILERS AND BURNERS

Two main elements determine overall boiler efficiency: (1) heat transfer surface of boiler and its condition—clean or fouled; (2) burner's ability to convert fuel's calorific (heat) value into useful heat.

Burner efficiency depends on the proper combustion of fuel (air-fuel ratio) and the maintenance (annual tune-up) of the burner. To handle a boiler properly and efficiently, the maintenance staff must be trained to operate the unit and to conduct efficiency tests, which include testing for CO_2, stack temperature, smoke, and draft.

NOTE: Air pollution regulations must be obtained from authorities having jurisdiction.

RATINGS

1. Gross rating = input in Btu/hr.
2. Net rating = output in Btu/hr. = gross rating x efficiency.
3. **FUEL RATINGS**

FUEL	HEAT VALUE	EFFICIENCY (%)
Anthracite coal	14,600 Btu/lb	65-75
No. 2 oil	140,000 Btu/gal	70-80
No. 4 oil	145,000 Btu/gal	70-80
No. 6 oil	150,000 Btu/gal	70-80
Natural gas	1052 Btu/cu ft	70-80
Electricity	1 W = 3.4 Btuh	95-100

4. Example: If boiler-burner combination is 80% efficient, No. 2 fuel oil is burned, and the total heat load is 168,000 Btu/hr, what is the required firing rate?

$$\text{Firing rate} = \frac{\text{gross rating}}{\text{fuel rating} \times \text{efficiency}}$$

$$\frac{168,000 \text{ (Btu/hr)}}{140,000 \text{ (Btu/gal)} \times 80\% \text{ (.8)}} = 1.5 \text{ gal/hr}$$

NOTE: Gross and net ratings are found on equipment plates.

CONTROLS

Automatic fuel burning equipment requires a control system that will provide a prescribed sequence of operating events and will take proper corrective action if failure occurs in the equipment or its operation. The basic requirements for oil burners, gas burners, and coal burners (stokers) are the same. The controls can be classified as operating controls, limit controls, and interlocks.

Operating controls initiate the normal starting and stopping of the burner in response to the primary sensor acting through appropriate actuators.

Examples of primary sensors are: a room thermostat for a residential furnace; a pressure actuated switch for a steam boiler; a thermostat for a hot water heater. Since the heat output of a burner may be widely distributed, the location of the primary sensor is important.

An actuator is defined as a device that converts the control system signal into a useful function. Actuators generally consist of valves, dampers, or relays.

Ignition for oil or gas burners is achieved by an electric spark or by a pilot gas flame, all supervised by a flame safeguard system which must meet legal and insurance underwriter's requirements. After ignition is proved, the flame safeguard system then permits the main fuel (gas or oil) to enter the burner for on-line combustion.

Limit controls and interlocks function only when the system exceeds prescribed unsafe operating conditions. They actuate electric switches that will close the fuel valve in the event of an unsafe condition, such as (1) excessive temperature in the combustion chamber or heat exchanger, (2) excessive pressure in a boiler or hot water heater, (3) low water level in a boiler and in larger commercial and industrial burners, (4) high or low gas pressure, (5) low oil pressure, (6) low atomizing media pressure, and (7) low oil temperature when firing residual fuel oil. Separate limit and operating controls are always recommended.

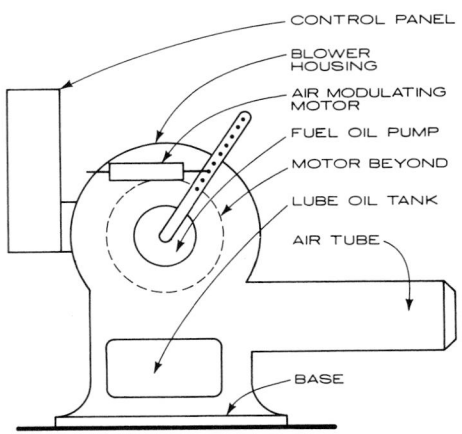

LOW PRESSURE GUN TYPE BURNER (NO. 4 FUEL OIL AND / OR GAS)
NOTE: FOR LARGE DOMESTIC, SEMICOMMERCIAL, AND COMMERCIAL INSTALLATIONS

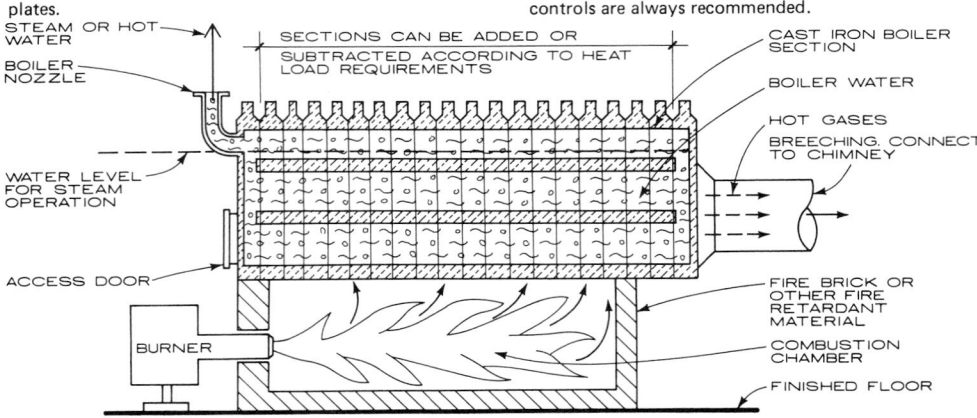

CAST IRON SECTIONAL TYPE BOILER

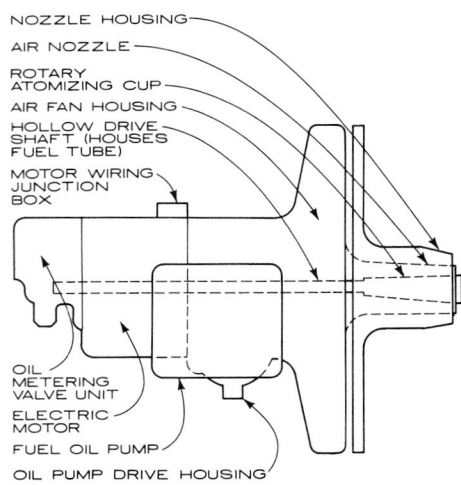

HORIZONTAL ROTARY TYPE BURNER DIRECT DRIVE (NO. 6 FUEL OIL)
NOTE: ALSO AVAILABLE WITH BELT DRIVE, USED IN DOMESTIC, SEMICOMMERCIAL, COMMERCIAL, AND HEAVY INDUSTRIAL

BURNER TYPES

Kelly Sacher & Associates, Architects Engineers Planners; Seaford, New York
Joe H. Shaw; Everett I. Brown Company; Indianapolis, Indiana

15   HEAT GENERATION

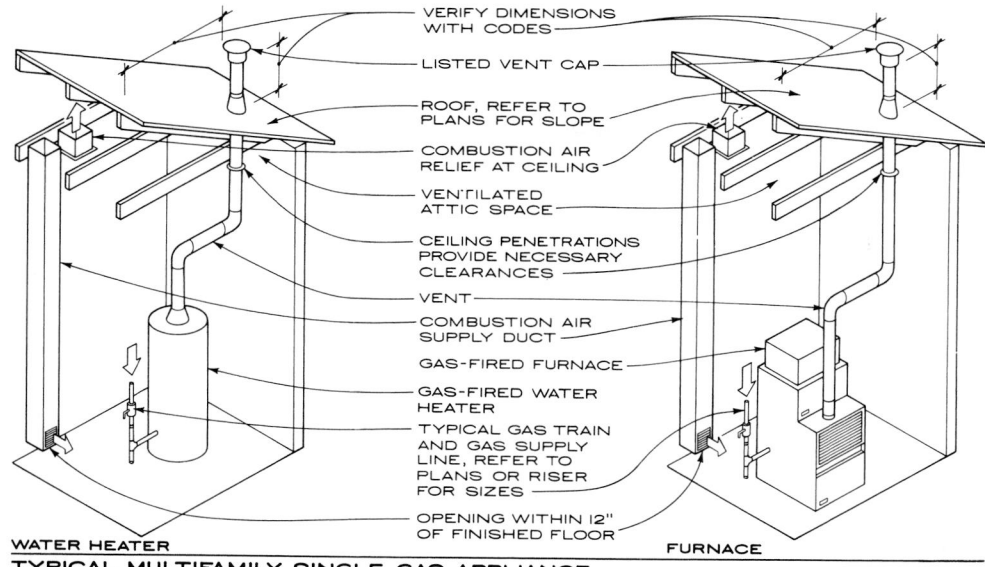

VERIFY DIMENSIONS WITH CODES
LISTED VENT CAP
ROOF, REFER TO PLANS FOR SLOPE
COMBUSTION AIR RELIEF AT CEILING
VENTILATED ATTIC SPACE
CEILING PENETRATIONS PROVIDE NECESSARY CLEARANCES
VENT
COMBUSTION AIR SUPPLY DUCT
GAS-FIRED FURNACE
GAS-FIRED WATER HEATER
TYPICAL GAS TRAIN AND GAS SUPPLY LINE, REFER TO PLANS OR RISER FOR SIZES
OPENING WITHIN 12" OF FINISHED FLOOR

WATER HEATER   FURNACE

TYPICAL MULTIFAMILY SINGLE GAS APPLIANCE

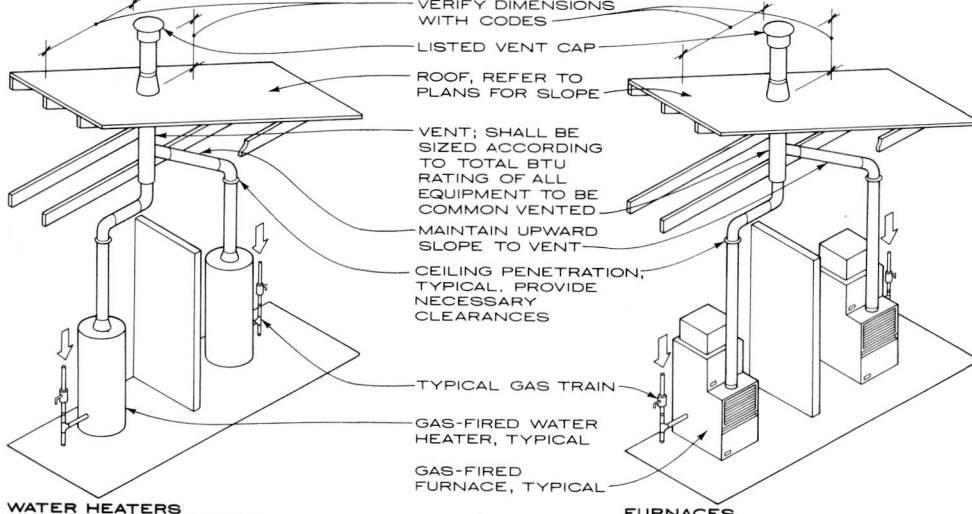

VERIFY DIMENSIONS WITH CODES
LISTED VENT CAP
ROOF, REFER TO PLANS FOR SLOPE
VENT; SHALL BE SIZED ACCORDING TO TOTAL BTU RATING OF ALL EQUIPMENT TO BE COMMON VENTED
MAINTAIN UPWARD SLOPE TO VENT
CEILING PENETRATION, TYPICAL. PROVIDE NECESSARY CLEARANCES
TYPICAL GAS TRAIN
GAS-FIRED WATER HEATER, TYPICAL
GAS-FIRED FURNACE, TYPICAL

WATER HEATERS   FURNACES

TYPICAL MULTIFAMILY COMMON VENTED GAS APPLIANCES

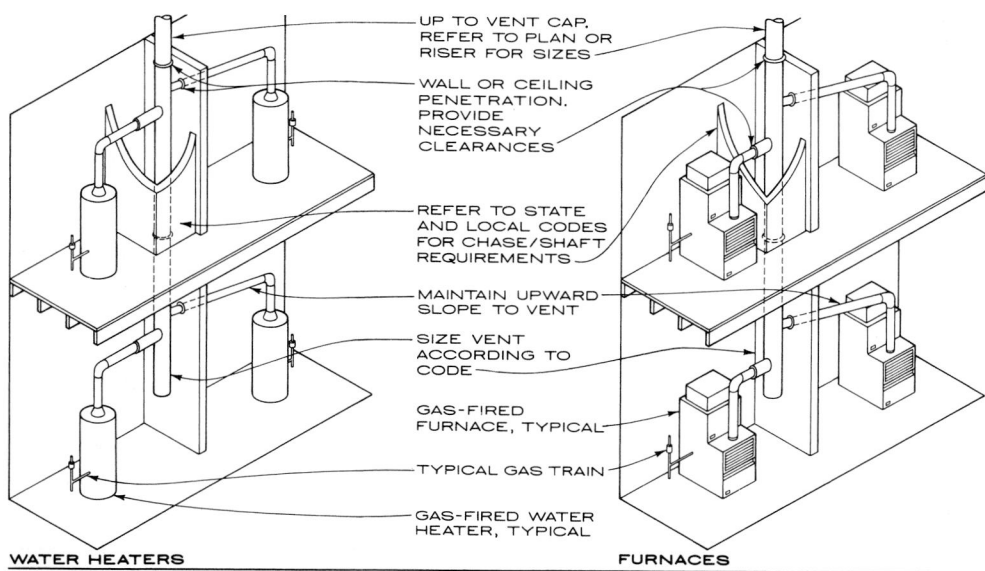

UP TO VENT CAP. REFER TO PLAN OR RISER FOR SIZES
WALL OR CEILING PENETRATION. PROVIDE NECESSARY CLEARANCES
REFER TO STATE AND LOCAL CODES FOR CHASE/SHAFT REQUIREMENTS
MAINTAIN UPWARD SLOPE TO VENT
SIZE VENT ACCORDING TO CODE
GAS-FIRED FURNACE, TYPICAL
TYPICAL GAS TRAIN
GAS-FIRED WATER HEATER, TYPICAL

WATER HEATERS   FURNACES

TYPICAL MULTISTORY/MULTIFAMILY COMMON VENTED GAS APPLIANCES

American Gas Association, Washington, D.C.
Richard J. Vitullo, AIA; Oak Leaf Studio; Crownsville, Maryland

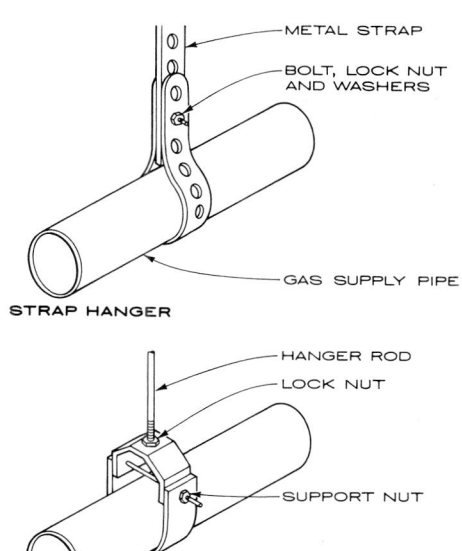

METAL STRAP
BOLT, LOCK NUT AND WASHERS
GAS SUPPLY PIPE

STRAP HANGER

HANGER ROD
LOCK NUT
SUPPORT NUT
GAS SUPPLY PIPE

CLEVIS HANGER

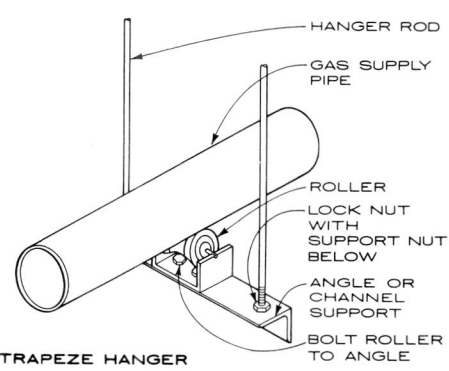

HANGER ROD
GAS SUPPLY PIPE
ROLLER
LOCK NUT WITH SUPPORT NUT BELOW
ANGLE OR CHANNEL SUPPORT
BOLT ROLLER TO ANGLE

TRAPEZE HANGER

NOTE: HANGER SPACING IS DETERMINED BY PIPE SIZES AND AT ALL TURNS AND JUNCTIONS

TYPICAL GAS PIPING HANGERS

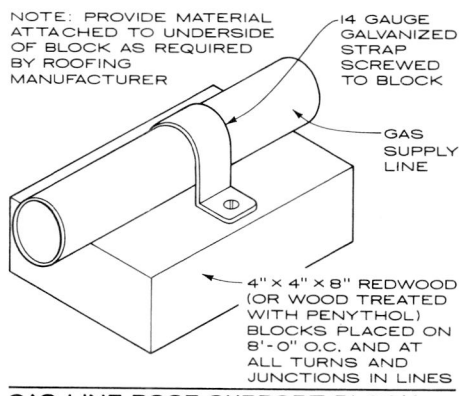

NOTE: PROVIDE MATERIAL ATTACHED TO UNDERSIDE OF BLOCK AS REQUIRED BY ROOFING MANUFACTURER
14 GAUGE GALVANIZED STRAP SCREWED TO BLOCK
GAS SUPPLY LINE
4" × 4" × 8" REDWOOD (OR WOOD TREATED WITH PENYTHOL) BLOCKS PLACED ON 8'-0" O.C. AND AT ALL TURNS AND JUNCTIONS IN LINES

GAS LINE ROOF SUPPORT BLOCK

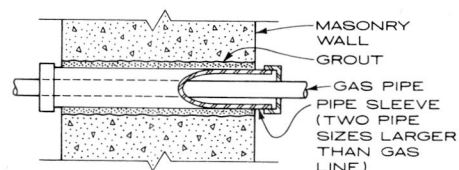

MASONRY WALL
GROUT
GAS PIPE
PIPE SLEEVE (TWO PIPE SIZES LARGER THAN GAS LINE)

NOTE: SLEEVES ENTERING REINFORCED MASONRY WALLS SHALL NOT CONTACT REINFORCING STEEL. SEAL ANNULAR AREA WITH SEALING COMPOUND

TYPICAL WALL PENETRATION

HEAT GENERATION   **15**

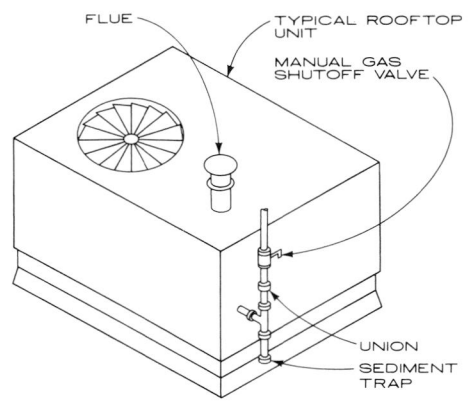

TYPICAL ROOFTOP UNIT
FLUE
MANUAL GAS SHUTOFF VALVE
UNION
SEDIMENT TRAP

TYPICAL GAS-FIRED ROOFTOP UNIT

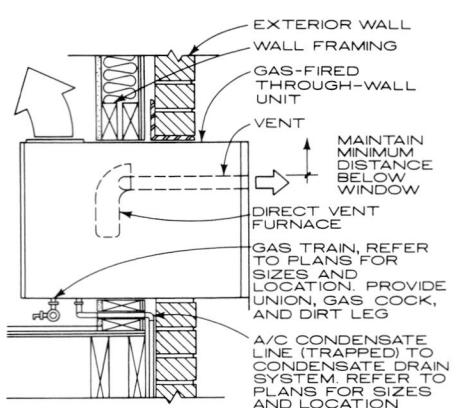

EXTERIOR WALL
WALL FRAMING
GAS-FIRED THROUGH-WALL UNIT
VENT
MAINTAIN MINIMUM DISTANCE BELOW WINDOW
DIRECT VENT FURNACE
GAS TRAIN, REFER TO PLANS FOR SIZES AND LOCATION. PROVIDE UNION, GAS COCK, AND DIRT LEG
A/C CONDENSATE LINE (TRAPPED) TO CONDENSATE DRAIN SYSTEM. REFER TO PLANS FOR SIZES AND LOCATION

TYPICAL GAS HEATING/ELECTRIC COOLING THROUGH-WALL UNIT

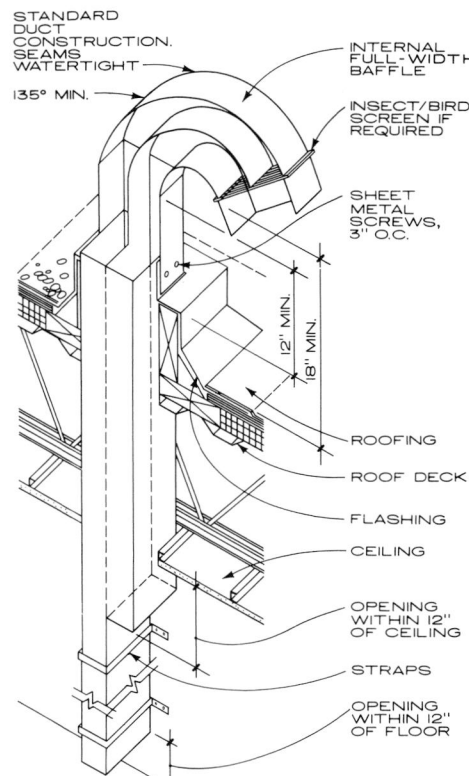

STANDARD DUCT CONSTRUCTION. SEAMS WATERTIGHT
135° MIN.
INTERNAL FULL-WIDTH BAFFLE
INSECT/BIRD SCREEN IF REQUIRED
SHEET METAL SCREWS, 3" O.C.
12' MIN.
18" MIN.
ROOFING
ROOF DECK
FLASHING
CEILING
OPENING WITHIN 12" OF CEILING
STRAPS
OPENING WITHIN 12" OF FLOOR

TYPICAL GOOSENECK COMBUSTION AIR

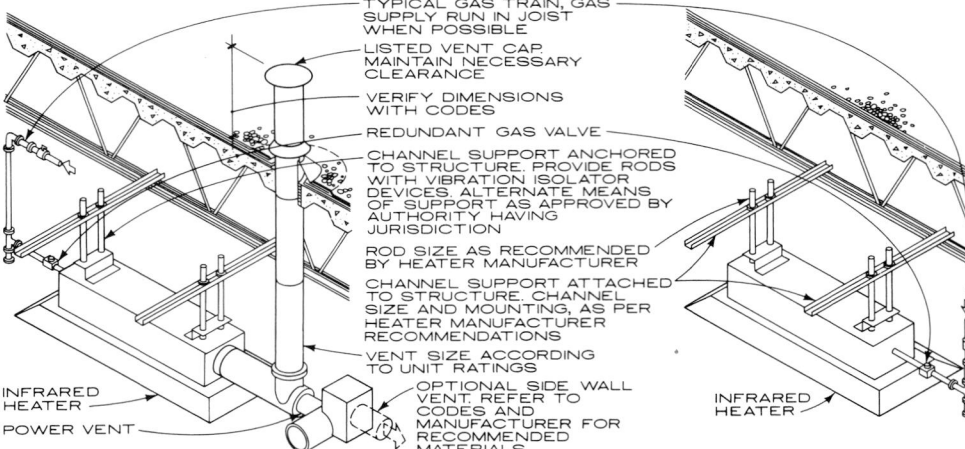

TYPICAL GAS TRAIN, GAS SUPPLY RUN IN JOIST WHEN POSSIBLE
LISTED VENT CAP. MAINTAIN NECESSARY CLEARANCE
VERIFY DIMENSIONS WITH CODES
REDUNDANT GAS VALVE
CHANNEL SUPPORT ANCHORED TO STRUCTURE. PROVIDE RODS WITH VIBRATION ISOLATOR DEVICES. ALTERNATE MEANS OF SUPPORT AS APPROVED BY AUTHORITY HAVING JURISDICTION
ROD SIZE AS RECOMMENDED BY HEATER MANUFACTURER
CHANNEL SUPPORT ATTACHED TO STRUCTURE. CHANNEL SIZE AND MOUNTING, AS PER HEATER MANUFACTURER RECOMMENDATIONS
VENT SIZE ACCORDING TO UNIT RATINGS
OPTIONAL SIDE WALL VENT. REFER TO CODES AND MANUFACTURER FOR RECOMMENDED MATERIALS
INFRARED HEATER
POWER VENT
INFRARED HEATER

LOW-INTENSITY POWER VENTED   HIGH-INTENSITY UNVENTED

TYPICAL GAS-FIRED INFRARED HEATER

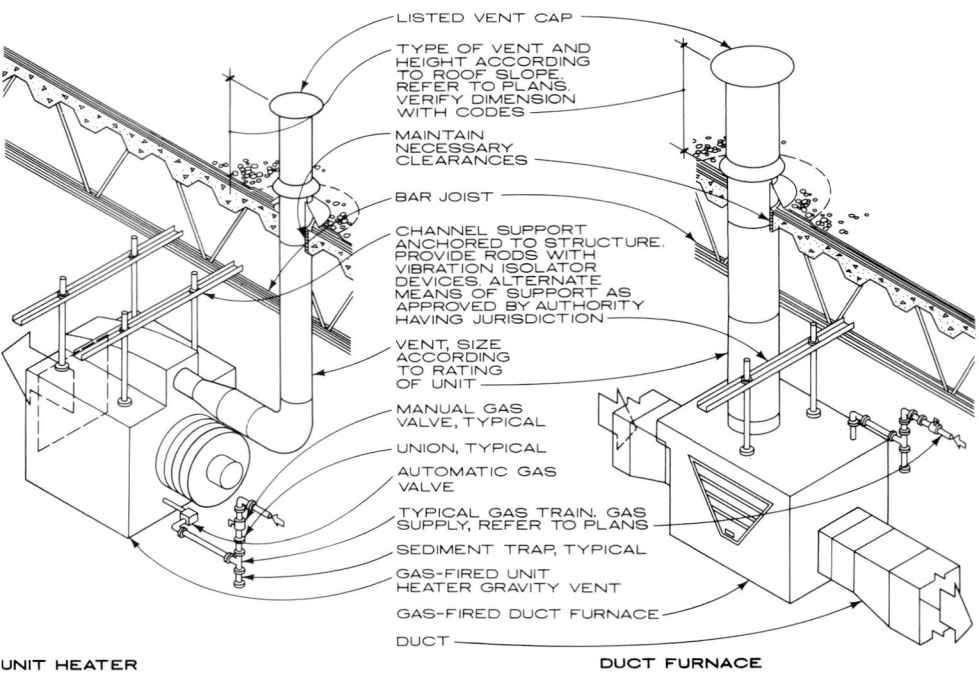

LISTED VENT CAP
TYPE OF VENT AND HEIGHT ACCORDING TO ROOF SLOPE. REFER TO PLANS. VERIFY DIMENSION WITH CODES
MAINTAIN NECESSARY CLEARANCES
BAR JOIST
CHANNEL SUPPORT ANCHORED TO STRUCTURE. PROVIDE RODS WITH VIBRATION ISOLATOR DEVICES. ALTERNATE MEANS OF SUPPORT AS APPROVED BY AUTHORITY HAVING JURISDICTION
VENT, SIZE ACCORDING TO RATING OF UNIT
MANUAL GAS VALVE, TYPICAL
UNION, TYPICAL
AUTOMATIC GAS VALVE
TYPICAL GAS TRAIN. GAS SUPPLY, REFER TO PLANS
SEDIMENT TRAP, TYPICAL
GAS-FIRED UNIT HEATER GRAVITY VENT
GAS-FIRED DUCT FURNACE
DUCT

UNIT HEATER   DUCT FURNACE

TYPICAL GAS-FIRED UNITS

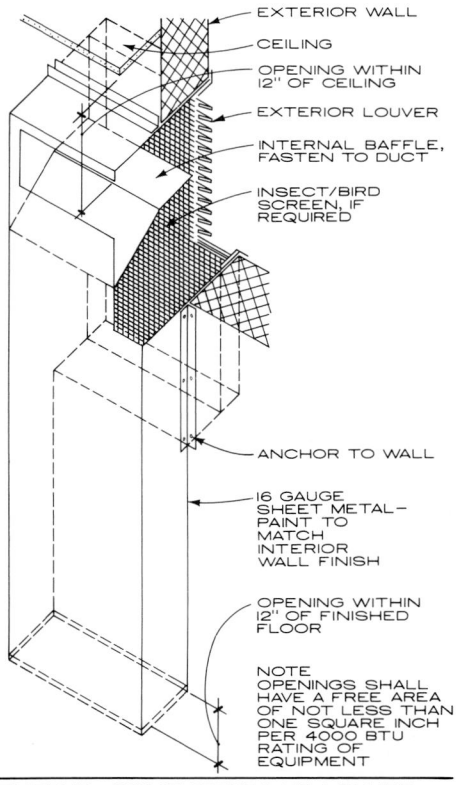

EXTERIOR WALL
CEILING
OPENING WITHIN 12" OF CEILING
EXTERIOR LOUVER
INTERNAL BAFFLE, FASTEN TO DUCT
INSECT/BIRD SCREEN, IF REQUIRED
ANCHOR TO WALL
16 GAUGE SHEET METAL—PAINT TO MATCH INTERIOR WALL FINISH
OPENING WITHIN 12" OF FINISHED FLOOR
NOTE OPENINGS SHALL HAVE A FREE AREA OF NOT LESS THAN ONE SQUARE INCH PER 4000 BTU RATING OF EQUIPMENT

TYPICAL COMBUSTION AIR LOUVER

GENERAL NOTE
THESE DRAWINGS ARE FOR REFERENCE ONLY. REFER TO STATE, LOCAL CODES/ORDINANCES AND MANUFACTURER'S INSTALLATION INSTRUCTIONS FOR PARTICULAR REQUIREMENTS GOVERNING MAINTENANCE CLEARANCES, GAS PIPING, COMBUSTION AIR, VENTING, ETC.

American Gas Association, Washington, D.C.
Richard J. Vitullo, AIA; Oak Leaf Studio; Crownsville, Maryland

15   HEAT GENERATION

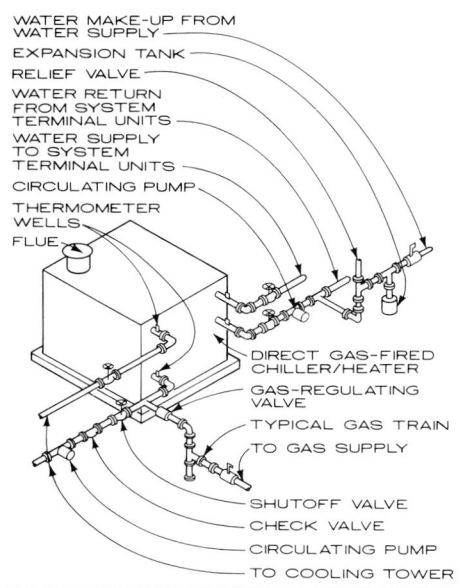

WATER MAKE-UP FROM WATER SUPPLY
EXPANSION TANK
RELIEF VALVE
WATER RETURN FROM SYSTEM TERMINAL UNITS
WATER SUPPLY TO SYSTEM TERMINAL UNITS
CIRCULATING PUMP
THERMOMETER WELLS
FLUE
DIRECT GAS-FIRED CHILLER/HEATER
GAS-REGULATING VALVE
TYPICAL GAS TRAIN
TO GAS SUPPLY
SHUTOFF VALVE
CHECK VALVE
CIRCULATING PUMP
TO COOLING TOWER

DIRECT GAS-FIRED CHILLER/HEATER

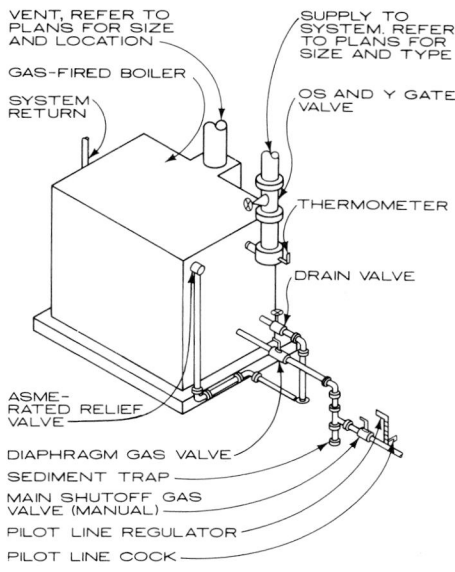

VENT, REFER TO PLANS FOR SIZE AND LOCATION
GAS-FIRED BOILER
SYSTEM RETURN
SUPPLY TO SYSTEM. REFER TO PLANS FOR SIZE AND TYPE
OS AND Y GATE VALVE
THERMOMETER
DRAIN VALVE
ASME-RATED RELIEF VALVE
DIAPHRAGM GAS VALVE
SEDIMENT TRAP
MAIN SHUTOFF GAS VALVE (MANUAL)
PILOT LINE REGULATOR
PILOT LINE COCK

TYPICAL GAS-FIRED BOILER

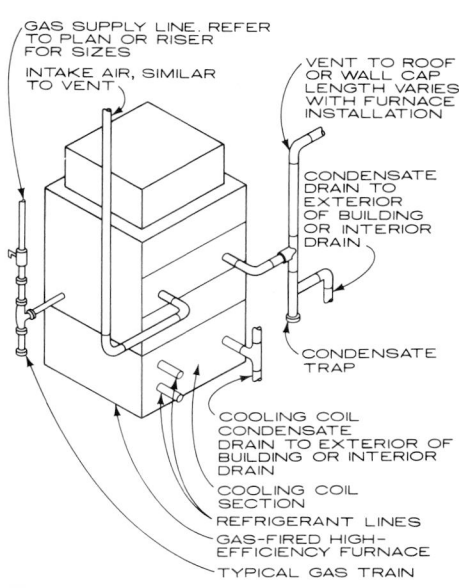

GAS SUPPLY LINE. REFER TO PLAN OR RISER FOR SIZES
INTAKE AIR, SIMILAR TO VENT
VENT TO ROOF OR WALL CAP. LENGTH VARIES WITH FURNACE INSTALLATION
CONDENSATE DRAIN TO EXTERIOR OF BUILDING OR INTERIOR DRAIN
CONDENSATE TRAP
COOLING COIL CONDENSATE DRAIN TO EXTERIOR OF BUILDING OR INTERIOR DRAIN
COOLING COIL SECTION
REFRIGERANT LINES
GAS-FIRED HIGH-EFFICIENCY FURNACE
TYPICAL GAS TRAIN

TYPICAL GAS-FIRED HIGH-EFFICIENCY FURNACE

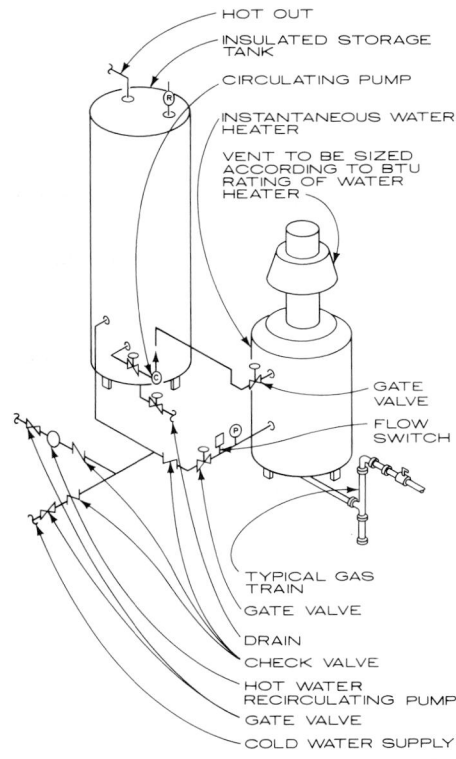

HOT OUT
INSULATED STORAGE TANK
CIRCULATING PUMP
INSTANTANEOUS WATER HEATER
VENT TO BE SIZED ACCORDING TO BTU RATING OF WATER HEATER
GATE VALVE
FLOW SWITCH
TYPICAL GAS TRAIN
GATE VALVE
DRAIN
CHECK VALVE
HOT WATER RECIRCULATING PUMP
GATE VALVE
COLD WATER SUPPLY

TYPICAL INSTANTANEOUS WATER HEATERS WITH STORAGE TANKS

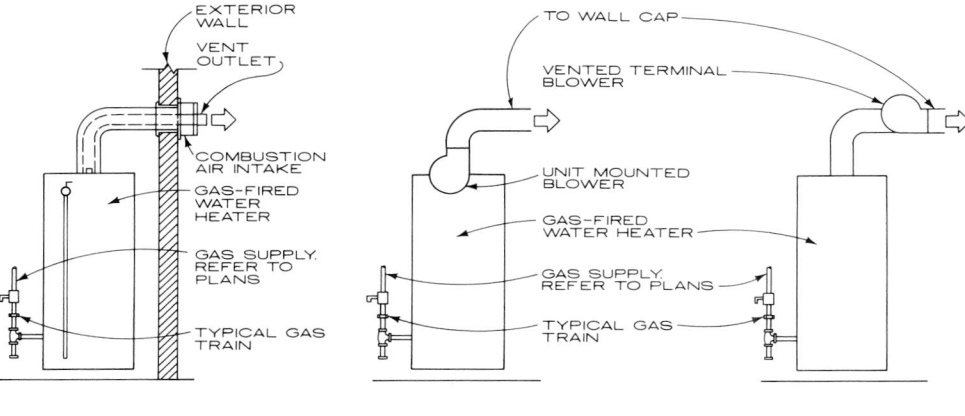

EXTERIOR WALL
VENT OUTLET
COMBUSTION AIR INTAKE
GAS-FIRED WATER HEATER
GAS SUPPLY. REFER TO PLANS
TYPICAL GAS TRAIN
DIRECT VENT

TO WALL CAP
VENTED TERMINAL BLOWER
UNIT MOUNTED BLOWER
GAS-FIRED WATER HEATER
GAS SUPPLY. REFER TO PLANS
TYPICAL GAS TRAIN
POWER VENTED
POWER VENTED

SIDEWALL VENTED GAS-FIRED WATER HEATERS

GENERAL NOTES

1. For high-efficiency furnace, contractor has option of using combination vent/intake air kit (either wall or roof installation) as allowed by code.
2. Combustion air sizing: Free area of inlet and outlet shall be not less than 1 sq in./4000 Btu/hour or equipment rating for system shown. Alternate methods of combustion air ducting and sizing as approved by authority having jurisdiction.
3. These drawings are for reference only. Refer to state and local codes/ordinances and manufacturer's installation instructions for particular requirements governing maintenance, clearances, gas piping, combustion air, and venting.

American Gas Association, Washington, D.C.
Richard J. Vitullo, AIA; Oak Leaf Studio; Crownsville, Maryland

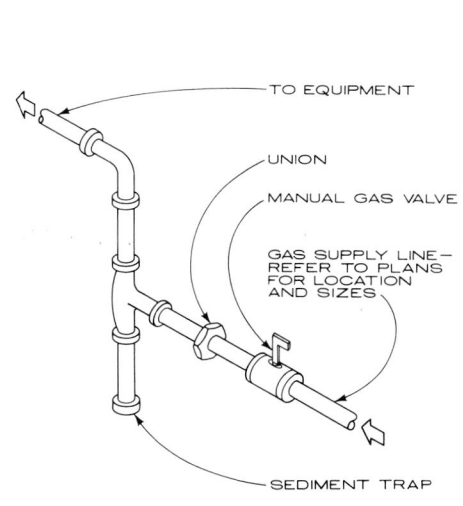

TO EQUIPMENT
UNION
MANUAL GAS VALVE
GAS SUPPLY LINE—REFER TO PLANS FOR LOCATION AND SIZES
SEDIMENT TRAP

TYPICAL GAS TRAIN

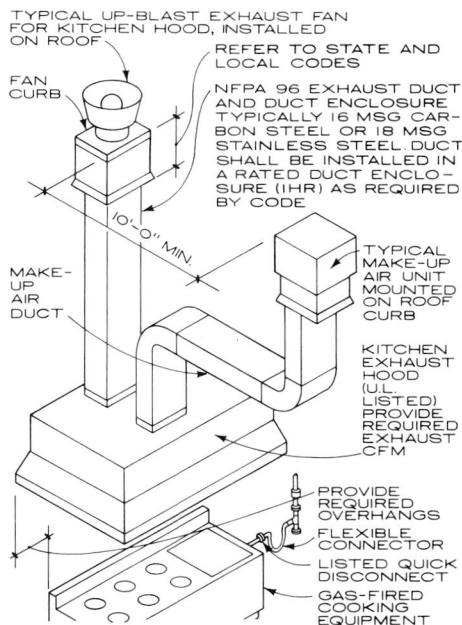

TYPICAL UP-BLAST EXHAUST FAN FOR KITCHEN HOOD, INSTALLED ON ROOF
REFER TO STATE AND LOCAL CODES
FAN CURB
NFPA 96 EXHAUST DUCT AND DUCT ENCLOSURE TYPICALLY 16 MSG CARBON STEEL OR 18 MSG STAINLESS STEEL. DUCT SHALL BE INSTALLED IN A RATED DUCT ENCLOSURE (1HR) AS REQUIRED BY CODE
MAKE-UP AIR DUCT
10'-0" MIN.
TYPICAL MAKE-UP AIR UNIT MOUNTED ON ROOF CURB
KITCHEN EXHAUST HOOD (U.L. LISTED) PROVIDE REQUIRED EXHAUST CFM
PROVIDE REQUIRED OVERHANGS
FLEXIBLE CONNECTOR
LISTED QUICK DISCONNECT
GAS-FIRED COOKING EQUIPMENT

TYPICAL KITCHEN HOOD INSTALLATION

DECENTRALIZED HEATING SYSTEMS

Electric energy is ideally suited to space heating because it is simple to distribute and control. Complete electric heating systems are widely used in residences, schools, and commercial and industrial establishments.

A decentralized electric system applies heating units to individual rooms or spaces. Often the rooms are combined into zones with automatic temperature controls. In terms of heat output, electric in-space heating systems may be classified as natural convection, radiant, or forced air.

NATURAL CONVECTION UNITS

Heating units for wall mounting, recessed placement or surface placement are made with elements of incandescent bare wire or lower temperature bare wire or sheathed elements. An inner liner or reflector is usually placed between elements so that part of the heat is distributed by convection and part by radiation. Electric convectors should be located so that air movement across the elements is not impeded. Small units with ratings up to 1650 W operate at 120 V. Higher wattage units are made for 208 or higher voltages and require heavy duty receptacles.

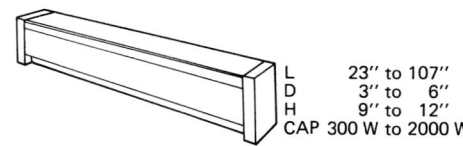

L	24″ to 120″
D	2″ to 8″
H	4″ to 12″
CAP	300 W to 4000 W

BASEBOARD HEATER (Wall Mounted)

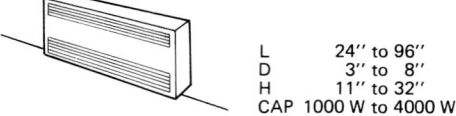

L	24″ to 96″
D	3″ to 8″
H	11″ to 32″
CAP	1000 W to 4000 W

CABINET CONVECTOR (Surface Mounted or Recessed)

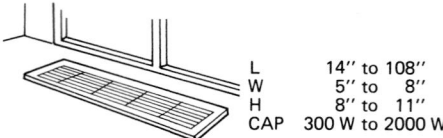

L	14″ to 108″
W	5″ to 8″
H	8″ to 11″
CAP	300 W to 2000 W

FLOOR HEATER (Recessed)

L	23″ to 107″
D	3″ to 6″
H	9″ to 12″
CAP	300 W to 2000 W

HYDRONIC BASEBOARD (Floor Mounted)

NATURAL CONVECTION UNITS

L	14″ to 86″
W	4″ to 12″
H	3″ to 16″
CAP	500 W to 7000 W

INFRARED HEATER (Pendant Mounted) Circular heat lamp is available

L	48″ to 144″
W	24″ to 48″
D	1″
CAP	500 W to 1000 W

RADIANT HEAT PANEL (Surface Mounted or Recessed) Decorative murals are available

Dimensions and capacity vary with coverage

RADIANT CEILING WITH EMBEDDED CONDUCTORS

RADIANT HEATING UNITS

RADIANT HEATING

Heat is produced by a current that flows in a high resistance wire or ribbon and is then transferred by radiation to a heat absorbing body. Manufacturer's recommendations for clearance between a radiant fixture and combustible materials or occupants should be followed.

FORCED AIR UNITS

Unit ventilators and heaters combine common convective heating with controlled natural ventilation.

Unit ventilators are most often mounted on an outside wall for air intake and at windowsills to prevent the down draft of cold air.

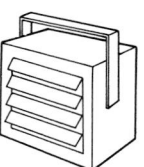

L	10″ to 14″
W	8″ to 14″
D	4″ to 8″
CAP	500 W to 1500 W

CEILING HEATER (Recessed) Circular unit with light is available

W	12″ to 52″
D	6″ to 22″
H	12″ to 26″
CAP	1.5 KW to 50 KW

UNIT HEATER (Bracket Mounted)

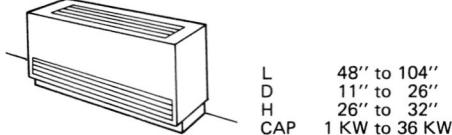

L	48″ to 104″
D	11″ to 26″
H	26″ to 32″
CAP	1 KW to 36 KW

UNIT VENTILATOR (Surface Mounted or Recessed)

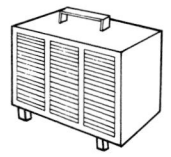

W	10″ to 18″
D	2″ to 6″
H	9″ to 24″
CAP	750 W to 4000 W

WALL HEATER (Recessed)

W	10″ to 72″
D	2″ to 12″
H	7″ to 24″
CAP	500 W to 5000 W

PORTABLE HEATER

FORCED AIR UNITS

CENTRALIZED HEATING SYSTEMS

A central hot water system with terminal radiators can be operated using an electric hot water boiler that contains immersion heating elements.

An electric furnace, consisting of resistance heating coils and a blower, can supply a ducted warm air system. Electric heating units are also installed in supply ducts to provide final temperatures and relative humidities in central air systems.

Integrated recovery systems make use of heat gains from electrical loads such as lights and motors. The excess heat accumulated from these sources can either be transferred or stored for later use.

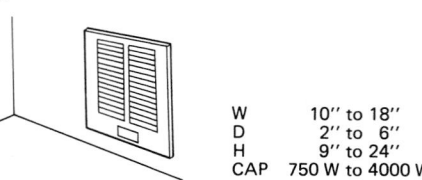

L	25″
W	23″
H	35″
CAP	5 KW to 60 KW

ELECTRIC FURNACE

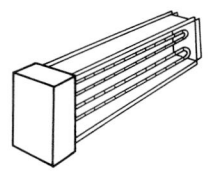

Size varies with duct dimensions
CAP 0.3 KW to 2000 KW

DUCT INSERT HEATER

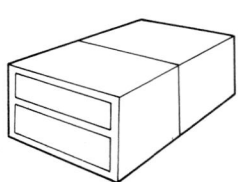

Size varies
CAP 2 KW to 100 KW

HEAT PUMP

Size varies
CAP 6 KW to 40 KW

ELECTRIC BOILER

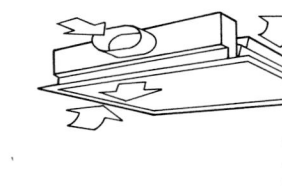

L	24″ to 72″
W	24″ to 72″

Capacity varies with air velocity

INTEGRATED HEAT RECOVERY Heat is gained from light fixtures

CENTRALIZED HEATING SYSTEMS

Tseng-Yao Sun, P.E. and Kyoung S. Park, P.E.; Ayres, Cohen and Hayakawa, Consulting Engineers; Los Angeles/San Francisco, California

15   HEAT GENERATION

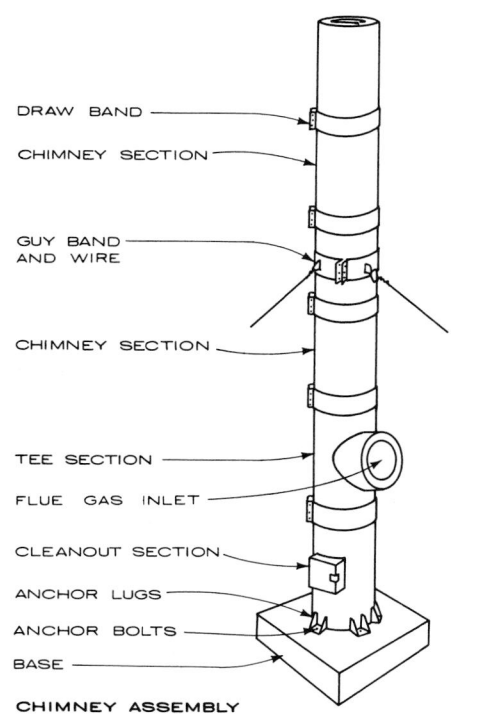

DRAW BAND

CHIMNEY SECTION

GUY BAND AND WIRE

CHIMNEY SECTION

TEE SECTION

FLUE GAS INLET

CLEANOUT SECTION

ANCHOR LUGS

ANCHOR BOLTS

BASE

CHIMNEY ASSEMBLY

MEDIUM HEAT CHIMNEYS

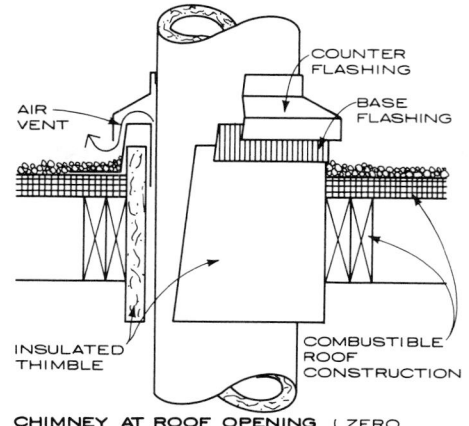

CHIMNEY AT ROOF OPENING (ZERO CLEARANCE)

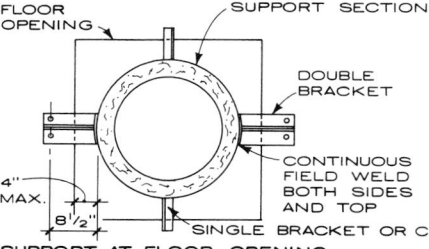

SUPPORT AT FLOOR OPENING

RAIN CAP

ROOF PENETRATION

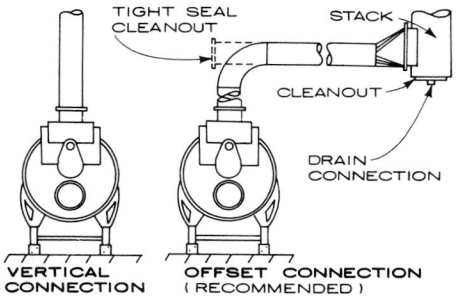

VERTICAL CONNECTION   **OFFSET CONNECTION** (RECOMMENDED)

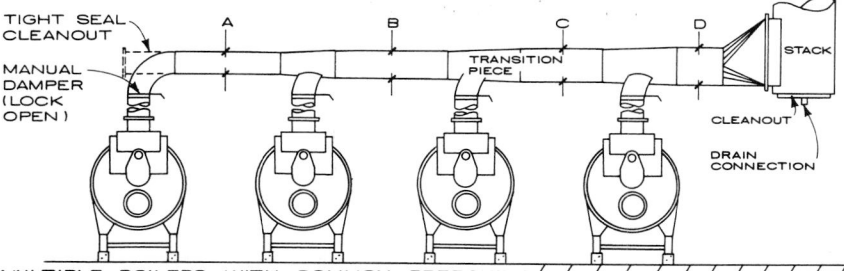

MULTIPLE BOILERS WITH COMMON BREECHING

VENT STACKS

STACK DIAMETER—SINGLE BOILER VENT OR STACK

BOILER HORSE-POWER	STACK DIAMETER (IN.)	A (IN.)	B (IN.)	C (IN.)
15-20	6	15	15	12
25-40	8	20	20	16
50-60	10	25	25	20
70-100	12	30	30	24
125-200	16	40	40	32
250-350	20	50	50	40
400-800	24	60	60	48

STACK DIAMETER— MULTIPLE BOILERS: COMMON BREECHING AND STACK

BOILER HORSE-POWER	MINIMUM STACK DIAMETER (IN.)					
	NUMBER OF BOILERS					
	2		3		4	
	100 FT	200 FT	100 FT	200 FT	100 FT	200 FT
25-40	11	12	13	14	14	16
50-60	13	14	15	16	17	18
70-100	16	17	19	20	21	23
125-200	21	22	24	26	28	30
250-350	26	28	32	34	34	40
400-600	32	34	38	40	42	46

CHIMNEY CONSTRUCTION

The chimney should be supported on a foundation of masonry or reinforced concrete or other noncombustible material having a fire resistance rating of not less than 3 hr. When installed on an appliance, the chimney should be so supported as to not place excessive stress on the appliance. The base of the chimney should be secured to prevent movement of the chimney and anchor lugs should be used for this purpose whenever possible.

A cleanout section may be used in the chimney assembly but must not be used above the chimney inlet.

CLEARANCES

Chimneys of the medium heat appliance or commercial-industrial incinerator type are not intended to be enclosed in walls of combustible materials. These chimneys should be placed in fire resistive or noncombustible shafts where they extend through any story of a building above that in which the connected appliance is located.

An enclosed chimney may be placed adjacent to walls of combustible material with the following minimum clearances:

10 to 15 in. I.D. requires 16 in. clearance
15 to 21 in. I.D. requires 18 in. clearance
21 to 27 in. I.D. requires 20 in. clearance
27 to 36 in. I.D. requires 22 in. clearance

Where the chimney passes through a roof of combustible material it shall be installed with an insulated thimble and flashing. This insulated thimble may be installed at zero inch clearance to combustibles.

The chimney should extend at least 3 ft above the highest point where it passes through the roof and 2 ft higher than any ridge within 10 ft.

VENT STACKS

The purpose of a vent stack is to conduct the products of combustion to a point of safe discharge (atmosphere). Forced draft design eliminates the need for a stack designed to create a draft. An offset type of stack connection to the stub vent on the boiler is preferred. A direct vertical connection can also be made when boiler vent outlets can withstand the direct vertical load of the stack, including the effect of wind and guy wires.

STACK CONSTRUCTION

The stack can be terminated several feet above the top of the roof. (State and local codes may govern the stack height above the roof.) If down drafts are unavoidable, the stack outlet can be provided with a ventilator. Minimum 12 gauge steel is recommended for stack sections. If the stack will be inaccessible, the use of a noncorrosive material (e.g., glass lining) should be considered.

A rain cap or hood should be used at the top of the stack to minimize the entrance of rain or snow.

BREECHING DIAMETER— SINGLE AND MULTIPLE BOILERS

BOILER HORSE-POWER	MINIMUM BREECHING DIAMETER (IN. OD)			
	A (IN.) 1 BOILER	B (IN.) 2 BOILERS	C (IN.) 3 BOILERS	D (IN.) 4 BOILERS
15-20	6	8	9	9
25-40	8	10	11	12
50-60	10	12	14	15
70-100	12	15	17	18
125-200	16	20	22	24
250-350	20	25	28	30
400-600	24	30	33	36
700-800	24	34	38	42

Note: Stack diameter should be larger than breeching diameter.

Syska and Hennessy, Consulting Engineers; New York, New York

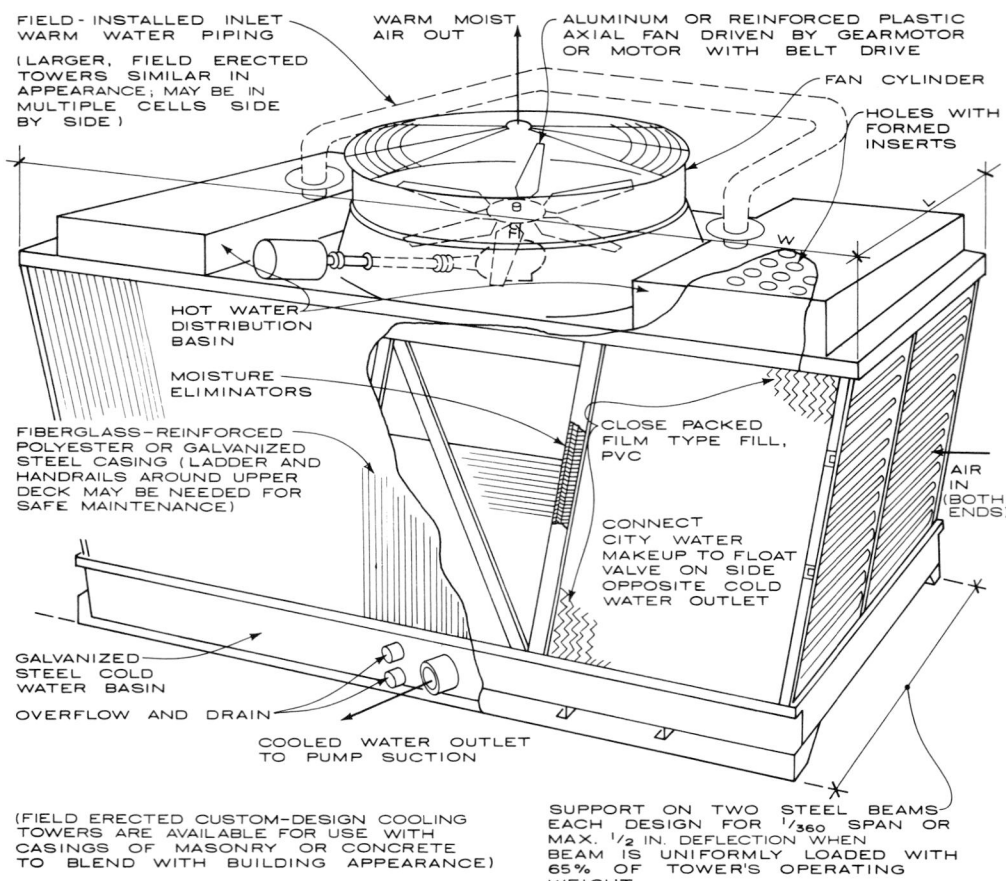

FIELD-INSTALLED INLET WARM WATER PIPING

(LARGER, FIELD ERECTED TOWERS SIMILAR IN APPEARANCE; MAY BE IN MULTIPLE CELLS SIDE BY SIDE)

WARM MOIST AIR OUT

ALUMINUM OR REINFORCED PLASTIC AXIAL FAN DRIVEN BY GEARMOTOR OR MOTOR WITH BELT DRIVE

FAN CYLINDER

HOLES WITH FORMED INSERTS

HOT WATER DISTRIBUTION BASIN

MOISTURE ELIMINATORS

FIBERGLASS-REINFORCED POLYESTER OR GALVANIZED STEEL CASING (LADDER AND HANDRAILS AROUND UPPER DECK MAY BE NEEDED FOR SAFE MAINTENANCE)

CLOSE PACKED FILM TYPE FILL, PVC

CONNECT CITY WATER MAKEUP TO FLOAT VALVE ON SIDE OPPOSITE COLD WATER OUTLET

AIR IN (BOTH ENDS)

GALVANIZED STEEL COLD WATER BASIN

OVERFLOW AND DRAIN

COOLED WATER OUTLET TO PUMP SUCTION

(FIELD ERECTED CUSTOM-DESIGN COOLING TOWERS ARE AVAILABLE FOR USE WITH CASINGS OF MASONRY OR CONCRETE TO BLEND WITH BUILDING APPEARANCE)

SUPPORT ON TWO STEEL BEAMS EACH DESIGN FOR 1/360 SPAN OR MAX. 1/2 IN. DEFLECTION WHEN BEAM IS UNIFORMLY LOADED WITH 65% OF TOWER'S OPERATING WEIGHT

NOTES

1. Cooling towers cool water for reuse in refrigeration condensers or other heat exchangers. Standard ratings are in tons of refrigeration when cooling 3 gal/min per ton from 95 to 85°F with ambient air at 78°F wet bulb. Selection is based on performance at local outdoor design conditions. Frequently the local outdoor ambient wet bulb temperature used for selection is equal to or exceeded by 1% of summer hours.

2. Fans move air horizontally (crossflow) or up (counterflow) against water falling and wetting the fill or packing, to expose maximum water surface to the air. Reduced air flow reduces tower performance. Architectural enclosures should minimize obstruction to air flow.

3. Warm water is distributed at the top of the cooling tower by spray nozzles or basins with multiple orifices, and cooled water is collected in a basin at the bottom and pumped to condensers. Water is cooled by evaporating a very small portion. Water droplets may also be carried out by the air stream. Minerals and impurities present in all water increase concentration as pure water evaporates, so a little water is "bled" and chemicals are added to minimize scaling, corrosion, or biological fouling of condenser tubes. Towers for critical or large systems should be multicell for maintenance without shutdown.

4. Fan, motor, and water splashing noise may be a nuisance. Fan noise is reduced by two speed motors (about 8 dB at half speed, 15% power, and 60% capacity) and by intake and discharge attenuators (about 12 dB) with 10% power increase. Tower noise is louder in line with fan discharge and intake than in other directions. Each doubling of distance decreases noise about 6 dB. Barriers can reflect some noise from critical directions. Locate towers for free air movement. Avoid hot air recirculation, long piping from pumps and condensers, and inadequate substructures. Cooling towers should be located so that noise and water droplet carryover and fog at air discharge in cold weather will not be a nuisance. Consider seismic and wind load in anchoring tower to supports; towers are usually designed to withstand 30 psf wind load. Basins may be heated for winter use.

CROSSFLOW INDUCED-DRAFT PACKAGED COOLING TOWER - 200 TO 700 TON CAPACITY PUMPS AVAILABLE IN DUAL CELLS WITH TWICE THE CAPACITY

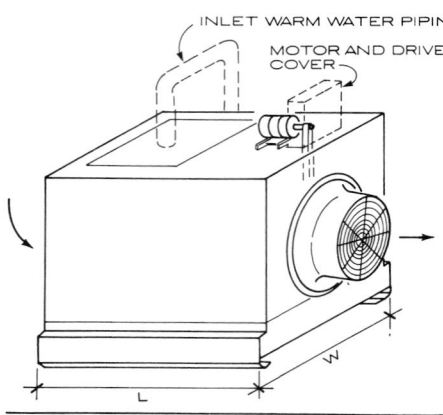

INLET WARM WATER PIPING

MOTOR AND DRIVE COVER

NOTE
AVAILABLE IN SINGLE MODULES AS SKETCHED, OR END-TO-END OR BACK-TO-BACK DOUBLE INLET

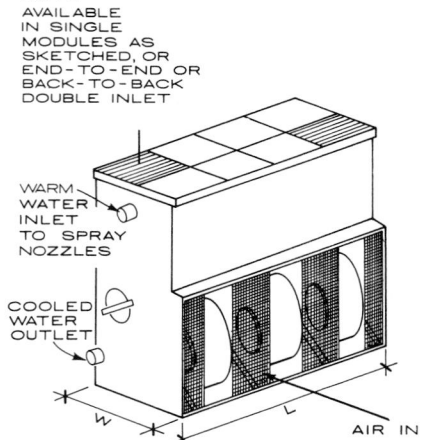

WARM WATER INLET TO SPRAY NOZZLES

COOLED WATER OUTLET

AIR IN

CROSSFLOW INDUCED DRAFT PACKAGE COOLING TOWER

COUNTERFLOW FORCED DRAFT PACKAGE COOLING TOWER

ENCLOSURE CONSIDERATIONS

Provide liberal wall openings on air inlet sides and mount tower so that air outlet is at top of enclosure. Consider effect of wind on nearby structure and enclosure to minimize hot, moist discharge air from being recirculated into inlet.

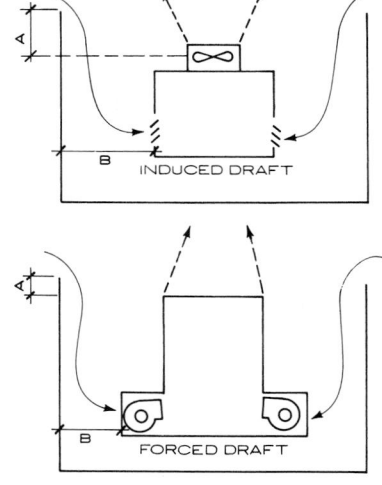

INDUCED DRAFT

FORCED DRAFT

A = Height of enclosure above tower outlet. Minimize or extend shroud up from tower.

B = If enclosure walls have no opening, horizontal distance from tower inlet must increase greatly.

(Power for fan must be increased.)

Consult cooling tower manufacturer for minimum "B" dimension.

TONS 3 GPM/TON 95-85-78	OVERALL DIMENSIONS (IN.)			OPERATING WEIGHT (LB.)	MOTOR (HP)
	L	W	HT.		
5	69	33	60	940	1/4
25	75	46	80	1600	1
50	84	64	92	2500	3
100	93	100	92	4200	5
150	100	144	112	8000	7½

TONS 3 GPM/TON 95-85-78	OVERALL DIMENSIONS (IN.)			OPERATING WEIGHT (LB.)	MOTOR (HP)
	L	W	HT.		
20	36	36	78	950	2
50	72	36	96	1700	7½
150	144	56	122	4800	20
400	140	118	192	14,000	50

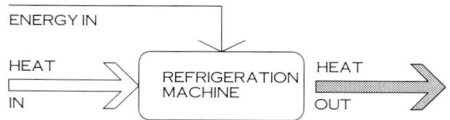

THE REFRIGERATION CYCLE

Refrigeration machines simply move heat from one place to another. Kitchen refrigerators move heat from the storage compartment to the surrounding room. Air conditioners move heat from rooms to the outdoors. Air conditioning equipment's efficiency is indicated by its Seasonal Energy Efficiency Rating (SEER). SEER is an index of the number of Btu's of heat moved per watt of electrical input energy. The higher the SEER for a piece of equipment, the more efficient, and less costly it is to operate.

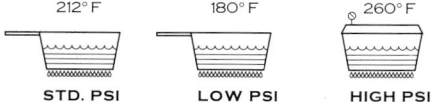

A large quantity of heat is required to boil or evaporate a liquid. This latent or hidden heat is the key to moving large quantities of heat with a small amount of refrigerant. To move heat from an area of low temperature to an area of high temperature (e.g., a building at 75°F to its environment at 95°F) refrigeration equipment needs to change the boiling temperature of the refrigerant. This is accomplished by changing the pressure on the refrigerant.

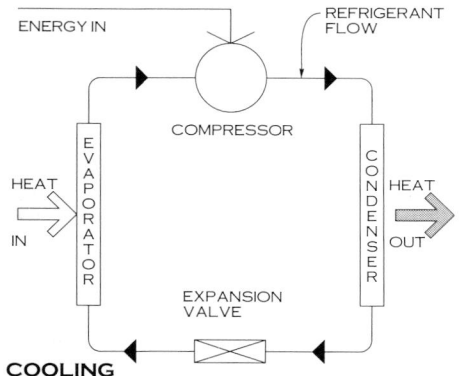

COOLING

During the cooling cycle, an evaporator coil absorbs heat from its surroundings; heated refrigerant within the coil evaporates internally. The refrigerant vapor is drawn into a compressor where pressure and, therefore, boiling (or condensing) temperature are increased. The refrigerant vapor is then discharged into a condenser coil, where it gives up the latent heat absorbed in the evaporator and returns to a liquid state. Finally, liquid refrigerant circulates through an expansion valve, where pressure and evaporation temperature are reduced; the cycle is then repeated.

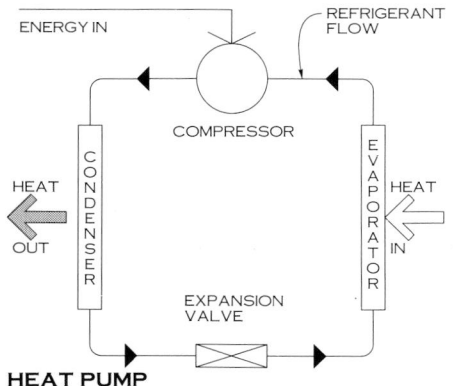

HEAT PUMP

The cooling cycle may be reversed to extract heat from a low temperature source, such as outside air, to heat a building. The basic equipment is unchanged with the exception of a four-way reversing valve and controls that permit the condenser and evaporator to exchange functions. The heat pump is more efficient than electrical resistance heat. Its efficiency, measured as COP (coefficient of performance), is a function of heat source temperature.

J. Trost, AIA; Texas A&M University; College Station, Texas

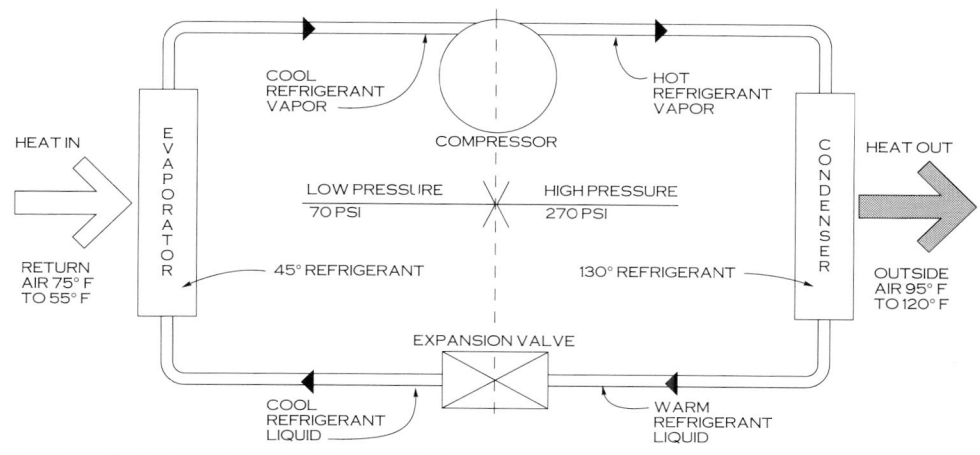

TYPICAL COOLING CYCLE TEMPERATURES AND PRESSURES

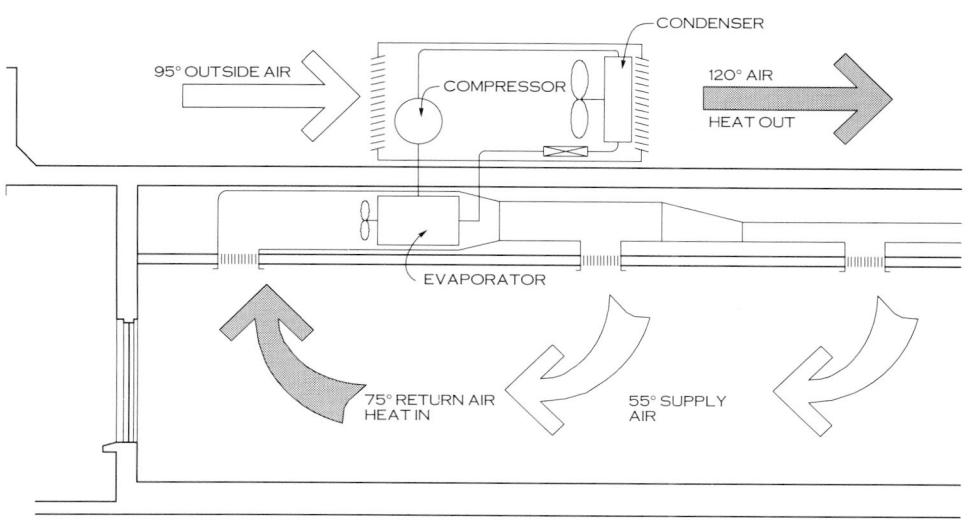

TYPICAL BUILDING APPLICATION

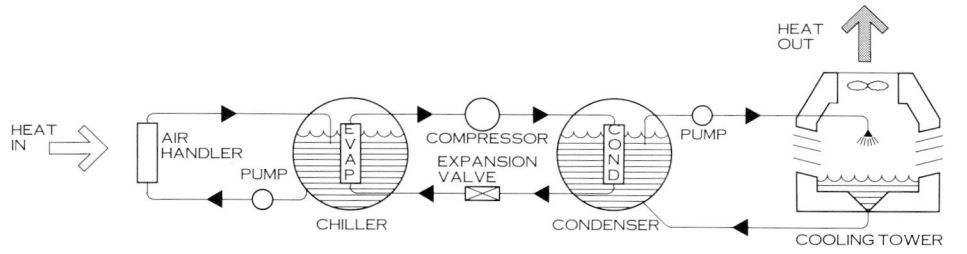

CHILLER AND COOLING TOWER

In large buildings it is impractical to move heat with air only because duct sizes would become excessively large. Therefore, a chiller (water tank) is added to the evaporator, and chilled water is circulated to air-handling units throughout the building. Cooling towers are typically installed in such large systems to increase efficiency. Air conditioning equipment transferring heat to 85°F water in a cooling tower will require less input energy than the same equipment transferring heat to 95°F outside air. A second refrigeration cycle, the absorption cycle, uses a heat source and an absorbent to move heat. This requires electrical energy only for pumps.

The absorber and generator perform the same function as the compressor (see above), and the cycle operates under high vacuum. Generally speaking, absorption systems are less efficient than compressive systems and are a wise choice only when waste heat is available for input energy, such as system operation on emergency power during electrical power outage.

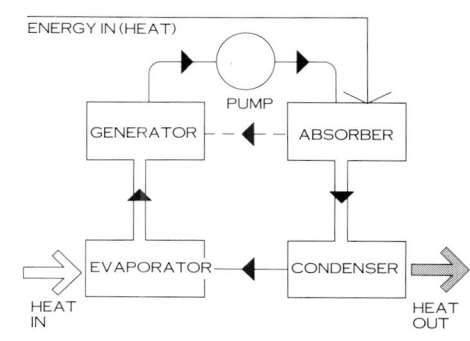

ABSORPTION CYCLE

AIR CONDITIONING IN COMPUTER ROOMS

Computers generate great quantities of heat in concentrated areas. To assure proper operation, a precise temperature and humidity environment is required. The range of control may be as narrow as 72° ± 2°F temperature and 50% humidity ± 5%.

TYPES OF SYSTEMS

Spot Coolers: Direct forced air, located at ceiling in return air plenum or on floor. Short ducting can be used. Capacity: 1 to 3½ tons.

Small System Local Units: Forced air can be used as direct spot units, ducted or for pressurized raised floor. Capacity: 3 to 5 tons.

Large System Local Units: Forced air to be used with pressurized raised floor installation. Capacity 6 to 25 tons.

Mainframe Cooling Systems: Independently generated chilled water circulated to computer's Coolant Distribution Unit (CDU) (an intertwined coiled heat exchanger which distributes special coolant directly to the computer in a closed loop system). Capacity: 2½ to 15 tons.

METHODS OF HEAT REJECTION

Self-Contained Air Cooled: Uses air within building return air plenum, limited to smaller capacity units.

External Air Cooled: Uses outdoor condenser unit and refrigerant lines generally limited to 100 ft above, 30 ft below, or 200 total ft from computer room to outdoor unit.

Water Cooled: Uses closed loop condenser water pumped to external cooling tower to remove heat from condenser within computer room fan coil unit. Cooling tower can be a larger distance from the computer room.

Glycol Cooled: Uses closed loop glycol to carry rejected heat to external dry cooler—allows greater separation of computer room from outside air. With additional coils, the system can provide "free cooling" during colder weather.

Chilled Water: Chilled water pumped from remote chilled water plant to local fan coil unit.

Combination Unit: May use 2 or more means of heat rejection to service the system during different hours of operation or as a backup system in case of primary system failure.

PLANNING PROCEDURE

1. Determine the location of the computer room within the project building.
2. Evaluate the availability of building services and systems, mechanical chases, and electrical power capacities.
3. Determine the overall heat load and plan size of system with client and engineer.
4. Use qualified engineers to design and engineer the systems, supervise all testing and certifications.
5. Detail the construction of walls, ceiling, and floors to provided a complete "vapor seal" and adequate air flow.
6. Evaluate energy efficiency ratios of various kinds of equipment proposed.
7. Select the system most appropriate for the conditions and requirements of the project.

RULES OF THUMB FOR COOLING LOAD ESTIMATES

Room design conditions	
Temperature	72° ± 2°/F
Relative humidity	50% ± 5% RH
Sensible heat ratio	
Sensible heat gain	0.90–0.98
Total heat gain	
Load density (sq ft/ton)	50–100
Air quantity (CFM/ton)	550–650
Ventilation rate (CFM/person)	10–15 max.
Humidification (lb moisture/100 CFM of outside air)	3

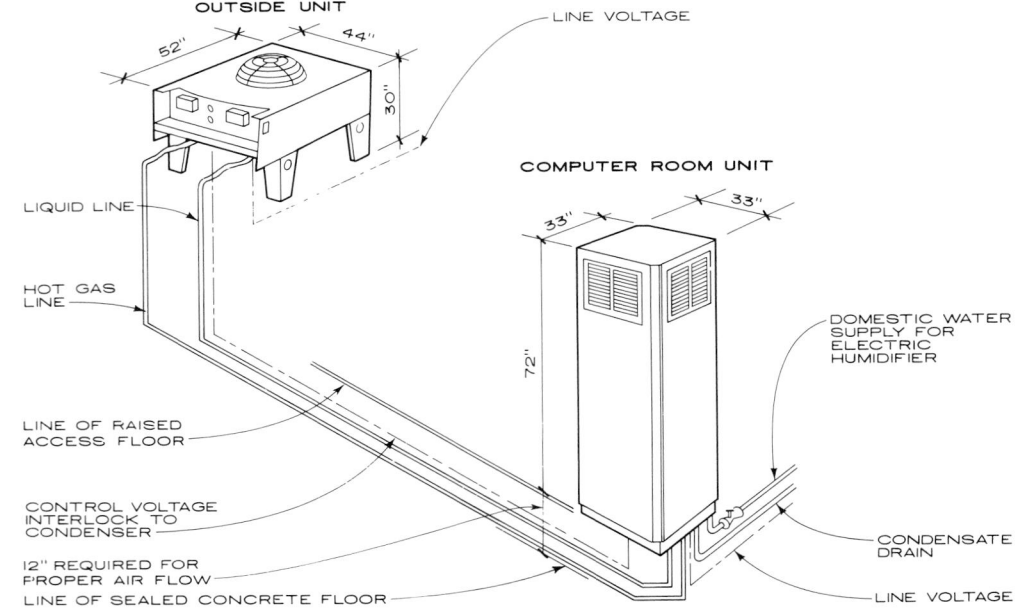

SMALL SYSTEM UNIT WITH OUTSIDE AIR COOLED HEAT REJECTION

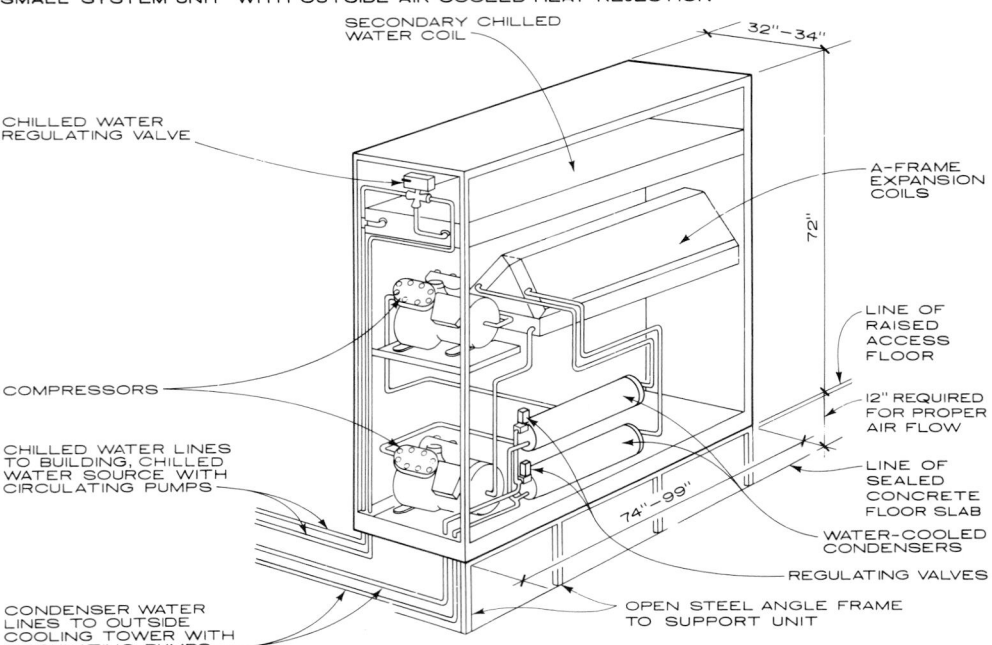

LARGE FORCED AIR SYSTEM WITH COMBINED HEAT REJECTION SYSTEMS

COMPUTER ROOM COOLING UNITS

SELF-CONTAINED AIR COOLED HEAT REJECTION
SPOT COOLER

COMBINED HEAT REJECTION
MAINFRAME COOLING SYSTEM

William R. Arnquist, AIA; Donna Vaughan & Associates, Inc.; Dallas, Texas

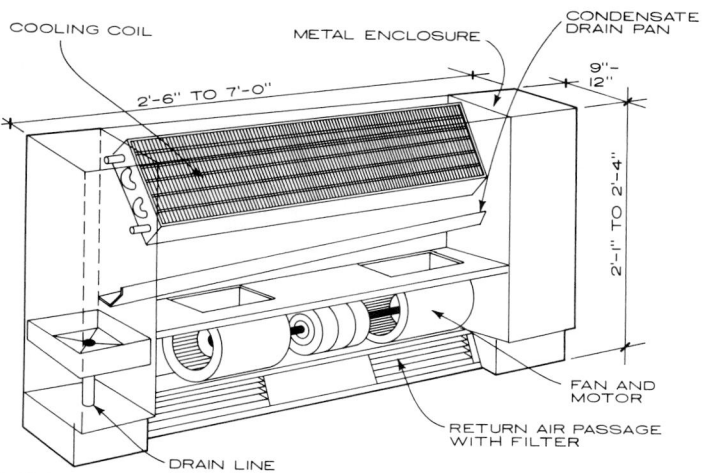

STANDARD FAN COIL UNIT

Labels: COOLING COIL, METAL ENCLOSURE, CONDENSATE DRAIN PAN, 2'-6" TO 7'-0", 9"-12", 2'-1" TO 2'-4", FAN AND MOTOR, RETURN AIR PASSAGE WITH FILTER, DRAIN LINE

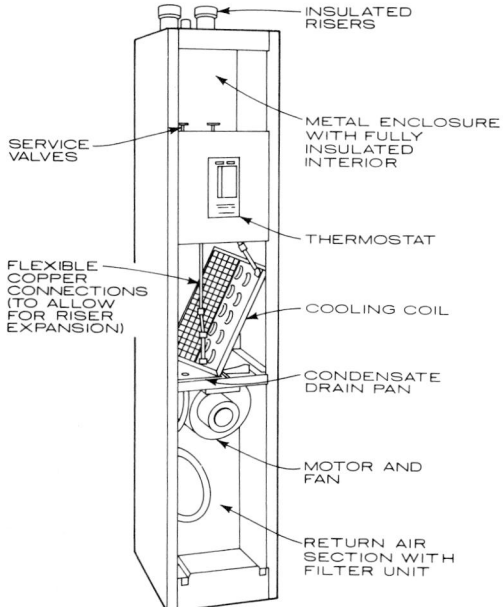

STANDARD HIGHRISE UNIT

Labels: INSULATED RISERS, SERVICE VALVES, METAL ENCLOSURE WITH FULLY INSULATED INTERIOR, THERMOSTAT, FLEXIBLE COPPER CONNECTIONS (TO ALLOW FOR RISER EXPANSION), COOLING COIL, CONDENSATE DRAIN PAN, MOTOR AND FAN, RETURN AIR SECTION WITH FILTER UNIT

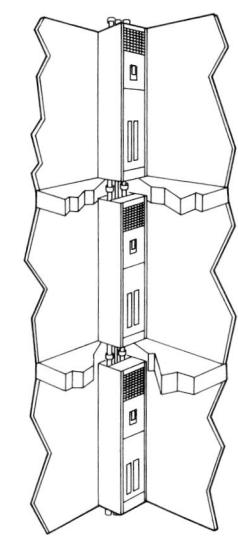

HIGHRISE APPLICATION

NOTE

Highrise corner units can be furred into the walls of the room. They minimize the piping from floor to floor since they are stacked and directly connected to the units above and below for water supply, returns, and drains.

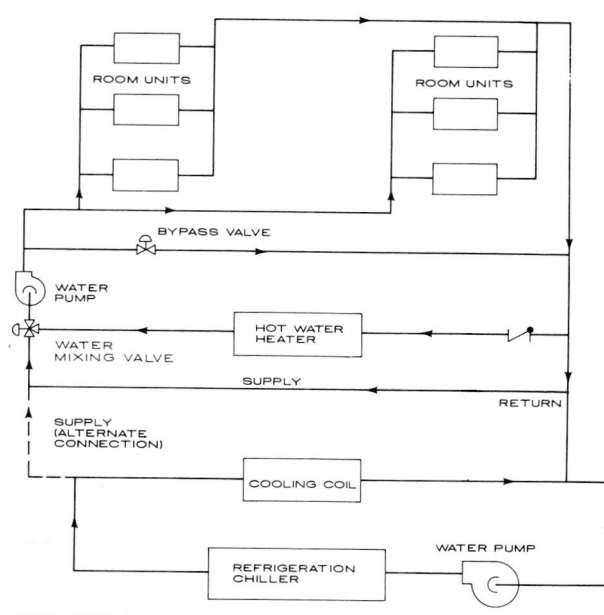

TWO-PIPE (DUAL TEMPERATURE) SYSTEM

Labels: ROOM UNITS, ROOM UNITS, BYPASS VALVE, WATER PUMP, WATER MIXING VALVE, HOT WATER HEATER, SUPPLY, RETURN, SUPPLY (ALTERNATE CONNECTION), COOLING COIL, REFRIGERATION CHILLER, WATER PUMP

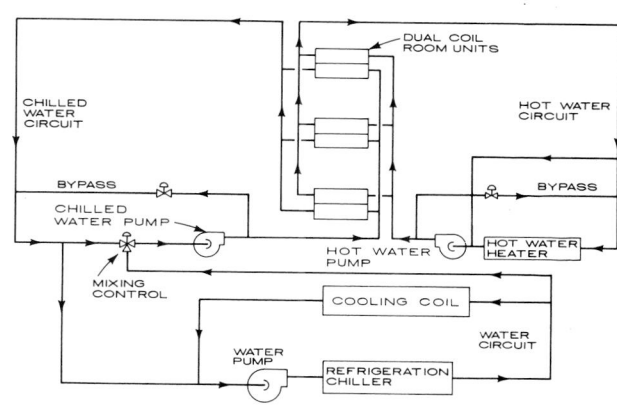

FOUR-PIPE SYSTEM

PIPING SYSTEMS

Labels: DUAL COIL ROOM UNITS, CHILLED WATER CIRCUIT, HOT WATER CIRCUIT, BYPASS, CHILLED WATER PUMP, MIXING CONTROL, HOT WATER PUMP, HOT WATER HEATER, BYPASS, COOLING COIL, WATER PUMP, REFRIGERATION CHILLER, WATER CIRCUIT

NOTES

Chilled water terminals are fan coil units used to dehumidify and cool the airstream injected into the conditioned space.

The typical fan coil unit consists of a finned tube chilled water coil, a fan used to circulate air over the coil and discharge cool air into the conditioned space, a drip pan to collect condensate from the dehumidified air and drain line to transport the condensate away from the fan coil unit.

Fan coil systems are classified into two major groups:

1. A TWO-PIPE SYSTEM uses a single supply pipe (hot or cold depending on the season) and a single return pipe, in a secondary water circuit. Chilled water is introduced into the circuit directly or indirectly from another circuit. If the terminal unit is to provide heat, a hot water, steam, or electric heat exchanger is incorporated into the loop. Direct introduction of hot water from a primary circuit is also employed. The water coil output of each terminal unit is controlled by a local space thermostat.

2. The FOUR-PIPE SYSTEM provides independent sources of heating and cooling to each room unit through separate supply and return chilled water pipes and separate supply and return hot water pipes. The terminal units usually have two separate water coils as well. Local thermostats control the volume of water supplied to each unit.

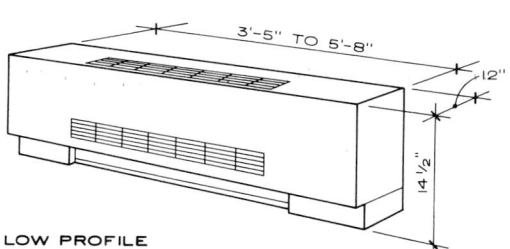

LOW PROFILE

Labels: 3'-5" TO 5'-8", 12", 14 1/2"

NOTE

A low profile fan coil unit is available for installation along window walls, below chalkboards, or in lobbies and hallways where appearance is important. They normally stand free from the wall, with clearance behind the unit for draperies.

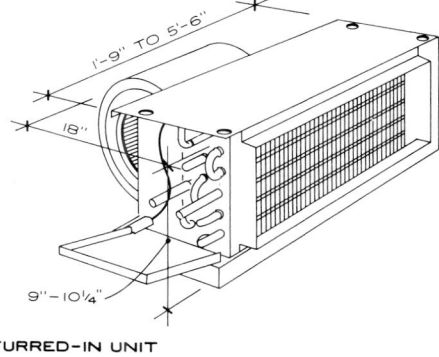

FURRED-IN UNIT

Labels: 1'-9" TO 5'-6", 18", 9"-10 1/4"

NOTE

Furred-in units can be mounted where convenient in the room. They can use ducts to bring in outside air and can be mounted in wall alcoves or ceiling spaces. A removable front panel is needed to conceal the unit and provide complete access to internal components.

WASTE HEAT SOURCES FOR HEAT RECOVERY SYSTEMS

1. Flues of fuel burning heating boilers and furnaces.
2. Refrigeration systems hot gas and condenser water.
3. Exhaust gases from diesel engine and gas turbine driven electric power generating equipment.
4. Cooling water from diesel engine cooling jackets and air compressor aftercoolers.
5. Exhaust steam and condenser water from steam turbine driven electric generators and refrigeration units.
6. Exhaust air from toilet rooms, mechanical equipment rooms, transformer vaults, kitchen range hoods, laundries, laboratory hoods, hospital operating rooms, locker rooms, shower rooms, and swimming pools.
7. Wastewater from washing machines and dishwashers.
8. Internal heat gain from lights, people, and appliances.
9. Heat recovery systems may consist of a direct or indirect heat transfer from airstreams, liquids, refrigerants, water, or gases.

APPLICATIONS FOR WASTE HEAT RECOVERY SYSTEMS

1. Building space heating.
2. Preheating ventilation outdoor air intake.
3. Air conditioning systems supply air reheat.
4. Preheating domestic hot water and boiler feed water.

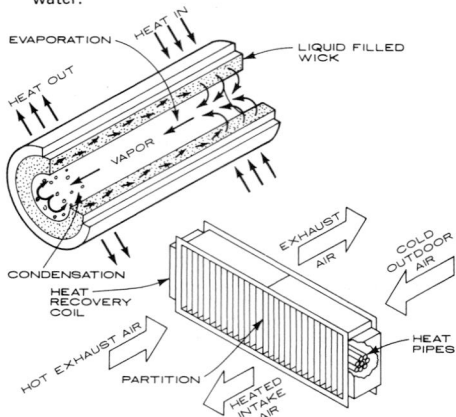

NOTE
Counterflow, indirect air-to-air sensible heat transfer. No leakage between airstreams. Alternate evaporation, condensation, and capillary migration of fluid in porous wick lining of tubes. Coil tilting or fact and bypass damper control. Efficiency 50-70%. Modular sizes to 54 in. x 138 in. x 8 rows deep.

HEAT PIPE

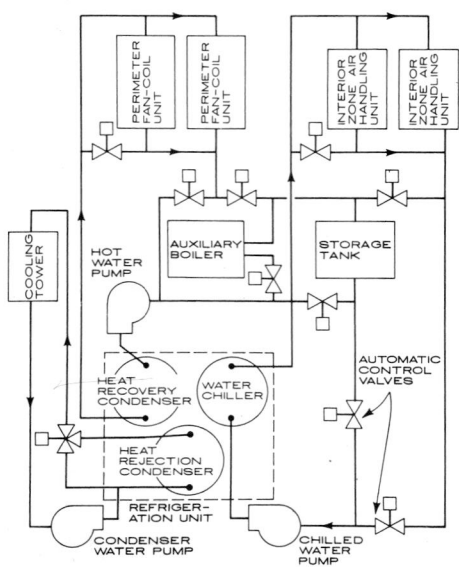

DUAL CONDENSER WATER CHILLER

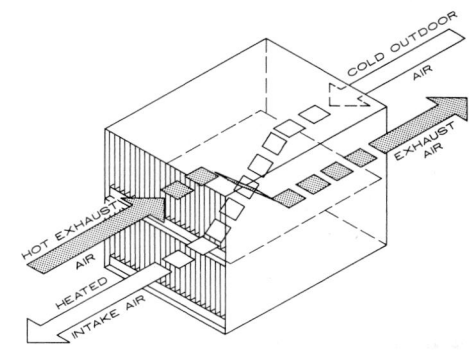

NOTE
Sensible heat absorbing aluminum or stainless steel mesh. Dessicant impregnated for latent heat transfer. Leakage 4-8% between opposing airstreams. Added purging section reduces cross-contamination to less than 1%. Speed variations or face and bypass damper capacity control. Efficiency 70-80%. Sizes to 144 in. diameter.

THERMAL WHEEL

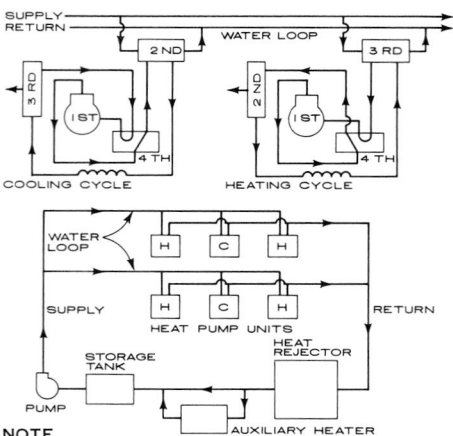

NOTE
Heat transfer from cooled to heated areas. Individually controlled heat pump terminal units with air and water coils. Auxiliary heater operation when heat loss exceeds heat gain. Heat rejector operation when heat gain exceeds heat loss. Tank stores excess capacity. Loop water 60-90°F.

WATER LOOP HEAT PUMPS

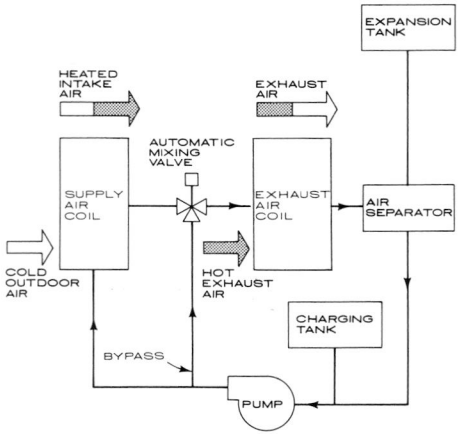

NOTE
Indirect sensible heat transfer between remote air streams with no cross-contamination. Exhaust airstream coil construction to suit application. Antifreeze fluid for low air temperatures. Bypass valve temperature control. Computerized equipment selection. Efficiency 50-70%. Modular coils to 20,000 cfm.

RUNAROUND COILS

NOTE
Counterflow, direct air-to-air type heat exchanger. Sensible heat transfer only. No leakage between airstreams. Corrugated aluminum or stainless steel construction. Washdown spray manifold for dirty exhaust airstreams. Bypass damper temperature control. Modular sizes to 10,000 cfm. Efficiency 60-80%.

PLATE TYPE HEAT EXCHANGER

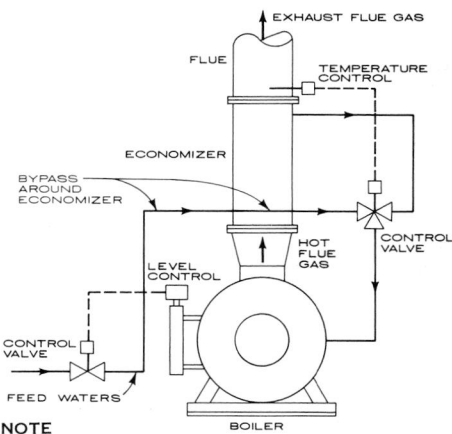

NOTE
Direct flue gas to feed water heat transfer for high pressure steam boilers. Boiler flue gas at 500°F leaving economizer at 325°F, heats feed water from 200 to 248°F. Mixing valve maintains minimum stack temperature leaving economizer to prevent moisture condensation in stack.

BOILER FLUE ECONOMIZER

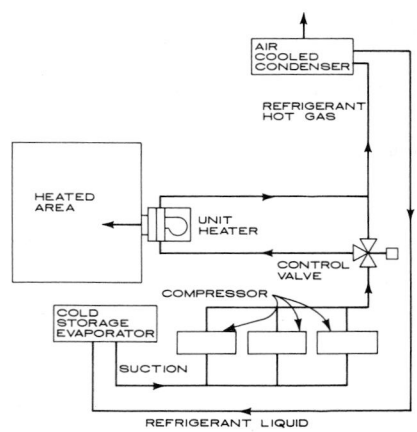

NOTE
Rejected heat from cold storage refrigeration system used to heat occupied areas. For heating, hot gas refrigerant from compressor discharge flows through space heating units to extract heat. When heating is not required, hot gas refrigerant flows directly to air cooled condenser for heat rejection to outdoor air.

REFRIGERANT HOT GAS

Syska and Hennessy, Consulting Engineers; New York, New York

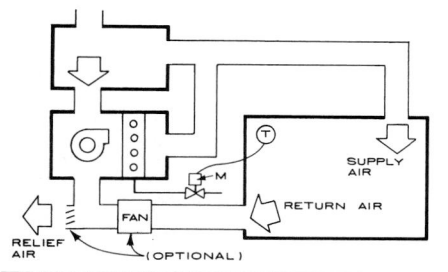
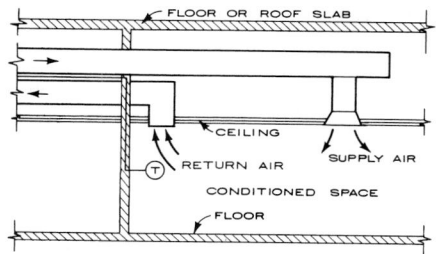

Low pressure system suitable for serving areas requiring only one zone of control. May be used in multiple where more than one zone of control is required. Relatively low first cost. Air handling unit may be blow through or draw through type.

SINGLE ZONE SYSTEM

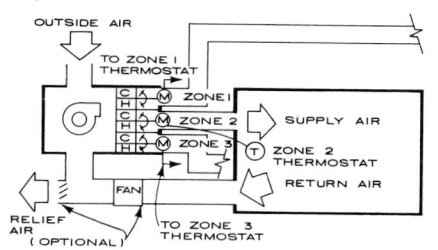
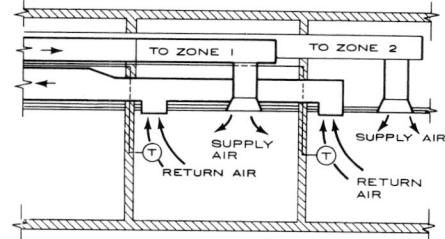

Low pressure system for serving areas requiring more than one zone of control. Practical limit of approximately eight zones per air handling unit. Can be used for simultaneously heating some areas while cooling others; however, control is relatively poor because of leakage at unit dampers and coil wiping. Relatively high first cost and high energy cost. Limited number of manufacturers.

MULTIZONE SYSTEM

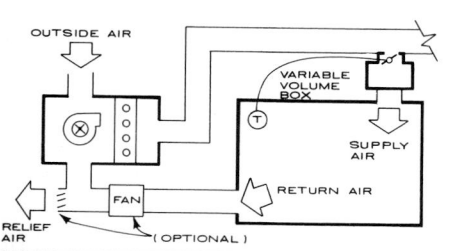
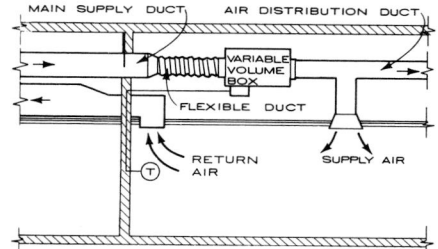

Low, medium, or high pressure system capable of providing a control zone for each box. Can be used for cooling only or for heating and cooling. Changeover from heating to cooling should be zoned by exposure. Provides variable air change rate and not applicable to areas requiring fixed air change rates such as certain hospital and laboratory applications. Relatively low first cost and energy cost. Air handling system may be blow through or draw through type.

SINGLE DUCT VARIABLE VOLUME SYSTEM

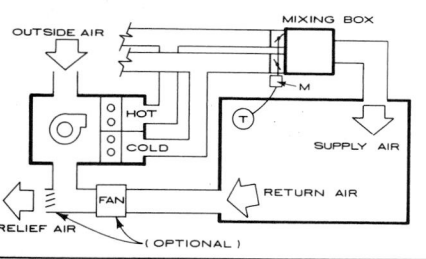
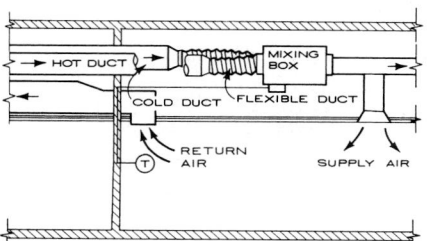

Low, medium, or high pressure system capable of providing a control zone for each box. Provides complete heating and cooling capability with no need for changeover. Available for both constant and variable volume systems (normally does not reduce air flow below 50 percent of maximum). Provides excellent year-round control. Relatively high first cost and energy cost.

DOUBLE DUCT SYSTEM

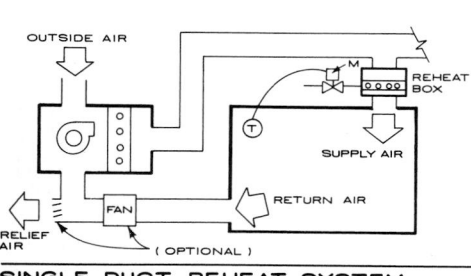
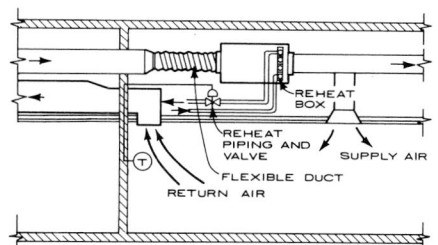

Low, medium, or high pressure system capable of providing a control zone per box. Provides heating and cooling capability (no changeover required). Available for constant and variable volume systems that normally do not reduce airflow below 50% of maximum. Excellent control, high first cost, high energy consumption; use generally limited to laboratory and hospital applications where constant volume and excellent control is required. Air handling system may be blow through or draw through type.

SINGLE DUCT REHEAT SYSTEM

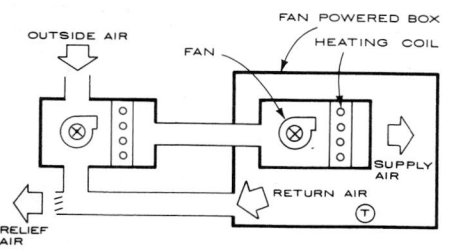
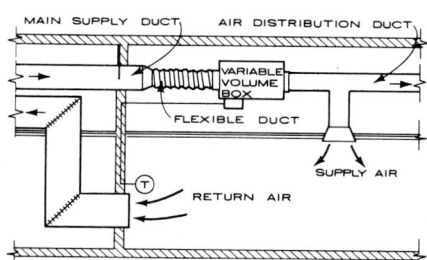

Low, medium, or high pressure system. When heating is required, cooling air damper closes and fan draws air from ceiling void and heats as required. Highly energy efficient control; relatively low first cost. Requires service and maintenance access to fan units at ceiling of occupied areas. Air handling system may be blow through or draw through.

FAN POWERED VARIABLE AIR VOLUME

William Tao & Associates, Inc., Consulting Engineers; St. Louis, Missouri
Krommenhoek/McKeown & Associates Architects & Engineers; San Diego, California

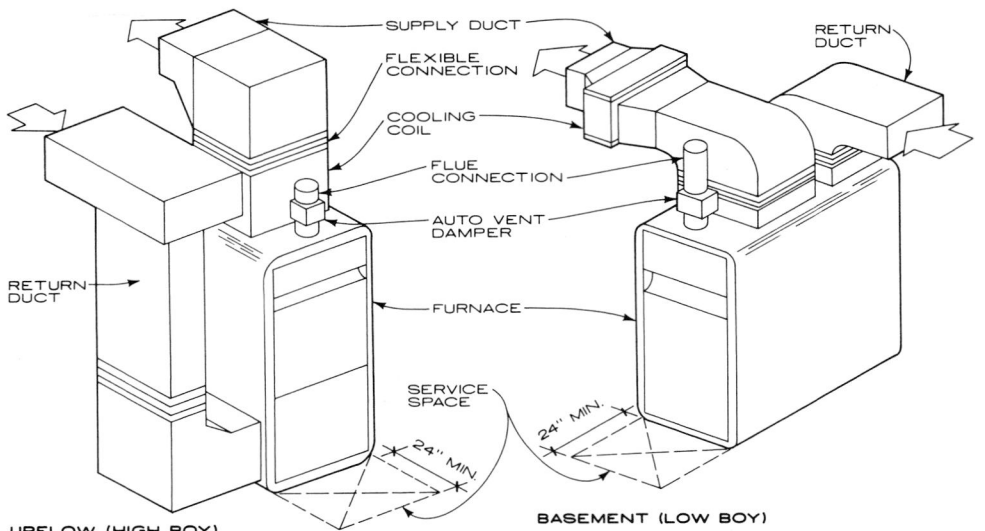

RETURN DUCT / SUPPLY DUCT / FLEXIBLE CONNECTION / COOLING COIL / FLUE CONNECTION / AUTO VENT DAMPER / FURNACE / RETURN DUCT / SERVICE SPACE / 24" MIN.

UPFLOW (HIGH BOY)   BASEMENT (LOW BOY)

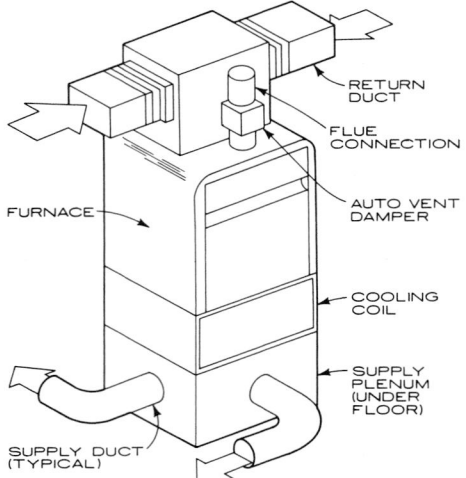

RETURN DUCT / FLUE CONNECTION / FURNACE / AUTO VENT DAMPER / COOLING COIL / SUPPLY PLENUM (UNDER FLOOR) / SUPPLY DUCT (TYPICAL)

DOWNFLOW (COUNTERFLOW)
WARM AIR FURNACES

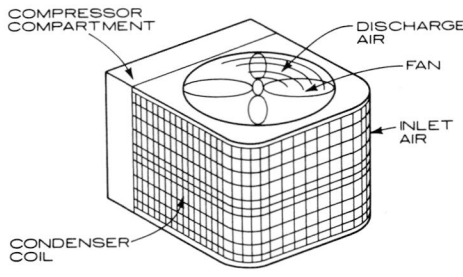

COMPRESSOR COMPARTMENT / DISCHARGE AIR / FAN / INLET AIR / CONDENSER COIL

CONDENSING UNIT

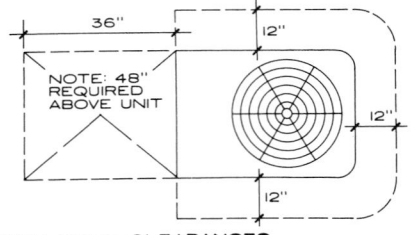

36" / 12" / NOTE: 48" REQUIRED ABOVE UNIT / 12" / 12"

INSTALLATION CLEARANCES
CONDENSING UNIT

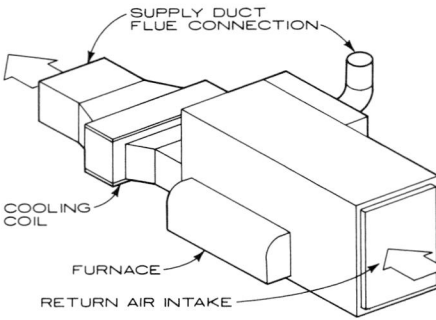

SUPPLY DUCT FLUE CONNECTION / COOLING COIL / FURNACE / RETURN AIR INTAKE

HORIZONTAL

FLOOR AREA REQUIRED BY WARM AIR FURNACE

OUTPUT CAPACITY (BTU/HR)	FURNACE FLOOR AREA (SQ FT)*
Up to 52,000	2.4
52,000–84,000	4.2
84,000–120,000	6.6
120,000–200,000	13.1

*Based on net floor area occupied by the upflow or downflow furnace. Low boy unit requires 50% more floor area. Space for combustion air should be added as required by local codes. Adequate space should be provided for service.

NOTES

1. Warm air furnace units are designed primarily for residential, small commercial, or classroom heating. Cooling can be added to these units by installing a cooling coil downstream from the furnace, with refrigerant compressor and condenser located remotely outside the building.
2. Duct system from the furnace unit can be either above the ceiling or in the floor slab. Above ceiling distribution systems are usually the radial type with high wall registers. Perimeter loop and extended plenum systems in floor slabs provide good air distribution. There are smaller temperature variations across the floor with perimeter loop systems than with radial or extended plenum systems.
3. Duct systems also may be installed below the living spaces, in a crawl space, or in a basement.
4. Two- or three-story buildings using similar warm air furnace and cooling coil combinations are centrally air conditioned via vertical extension of the branch ductwork through walls and partitions. Since all variations of the warm air heating/cooling systems recirculate their air within the building envelope, it is a crucial design requirement to leave return air passage, from each space supplied with air, to the furnace room.

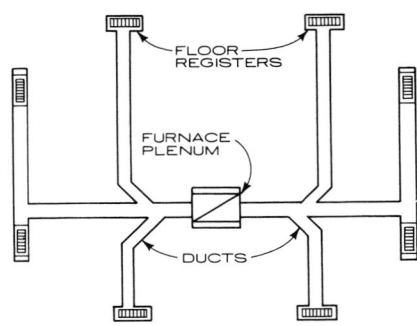

EXTENDED PLENUM SYSTEM

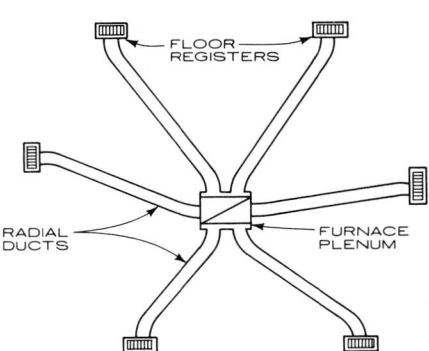

PERIMETER RADIAL SYSTEM

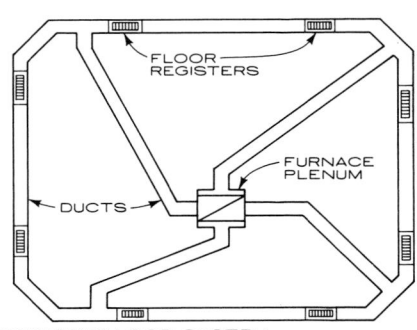

PERIMETER LOOP SYSTEM
DUCT SYSTEMS

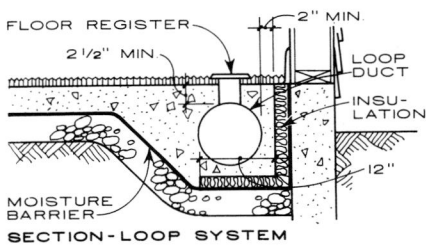

SECTION–LOOP SYSTEM

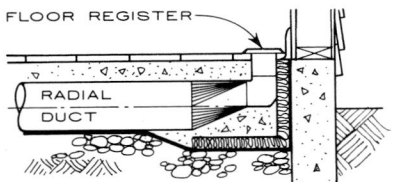

SECTION–RADIAL SYSTEM
AIR OUTLETS

DiClemente-Siegel Engineering, Inc.; Southfield, Michigan

15   AIR DISTRIBUTION

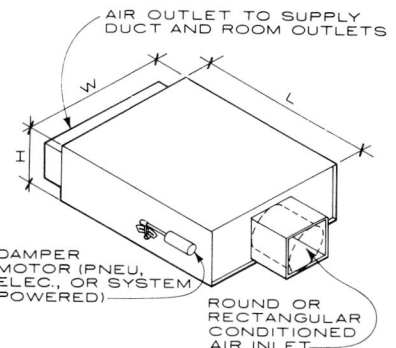

High, medium, or low velocity systems. Inlet pressure required ¼ to 1½ in. W.C. Capacity range 200 to 3200 cfm per box. Box serves as converter from high to low velocity air system, noise attenuator, and control device by modulating air quantity.

RANGE OF DIMENSIONS

CFM	HEIGHT	LENGTH	WIDTH
400	8″– 9″	24″–39″	14″–30″
800	10″–11″	24″–53″	18″–42″
1600	14″	30″–48″	22″–44″
2400	16″	42″–60″	26″–54″
3200	18″	42″–67″	33″–54″

VARIABLE VOLUME PINCH BACK BOX

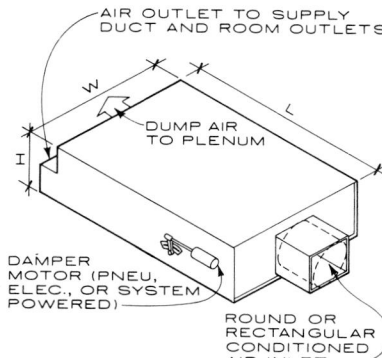

High, medium, or low velocity systems. Inlet pressure required ¼ to 1 in. W.C. Capacity range 200 to 3200 cfm per box. Available with or without reheat coil. Box serves as converter from high to low velocity air system, noise attenuator, and control device by modulating air quantity to space and/or by reheat.

RANGE OF DIMENSIONS

CFM	HEIGHT	LENGTH	WIDTH
200	8″– 9″	24″–39″	12″–19″
400	9″–11″	25″–51″	12″–24″
800	9″–11″	25″–51″	22″–31″
1600	10″–16″	25″–51″	22″–47″
2400	10″–16″	25″–51″	42″–47″
3200	10″–16″	25″–51″	42″–47″

VARIABLE VOLUME DUMP TYPE BOX

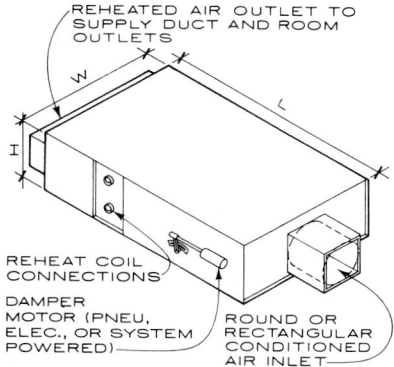

High, medium, or low velocity systems. Inlet pressures ½ to 1½ in. W.C. Capacity range 200 to 5000 cfm. Box serves as converter from high to low velocity air system, noise attenuator, and control device by reheat of conditioned air.

RANGE OF DIMENSIONS

CFM	HEIGHT	LENGTH	WIDTH
200	9″–11″	30″–50″	16″–22″
400	9″–11″	30″–51″	18″–30″
800	9″–11″	30″–51″	22″–42″
1600	14″–16″	48″–51″	40″–44″
2400	16″–18″	60″–55″	40″–54″
3200	16″–18″	60″–55″	16″–66″
5000	20″–18″	60″–55″	20″–80″

REHEAT CONSTANT VOLUME BOX

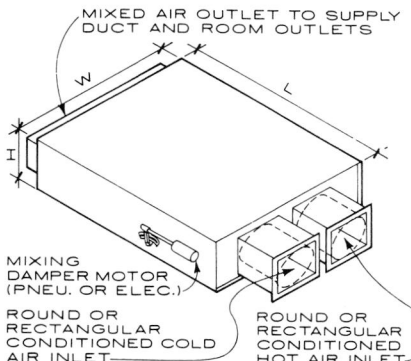

High, medium, or low velocity systems. Inlet pressure ¼ to 1½ in. W.C. Capacity range from 150 to 2000 cfm per box (low velocity) to 5000 cfm (high velocity). Box serves as converter from high to low velocity air system, noise attenuator, and control device by mixing hot and cold air streams.

RANGE OF DIMENSIONS

CFM	HEIGHT	LENGTH	WIDTH
400	6″–10″	40″–51″	30″–19″
800	8″–11″	50″–51″	42″–24″
1600	12″–14″	48″–51″	44″–40″
2400	14″–18″	60″–55″	54″–44″
3200	14″–18″	60″–55″	54″–44″
5000	16″–18″	60″–55″	54″–66″

DUAL DUCT MIXING BOX

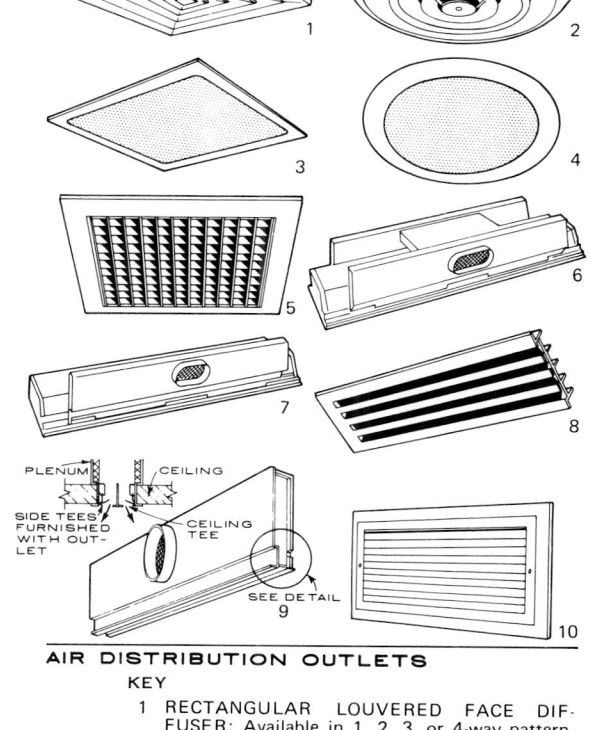

AIR DISTRIBUTION OUTLETS
KEY

1 RECTANGULAR LOUVERED FACE DIFFUSER: Available in 1, 2, 3, or 4-way pattern, steel or aluminum. Flanged overlap frame or inserted in 2 X 2 ft or 2 X 4 ft baked enamel steel panel to fit tile modules of lay-in ceilings. Supply or return.

2 ROUND LOUVERED FACE DIFFUSER: Normal 360° air pattern with blank-off plate for other air patterns. Surface mounting for all type ceilings. Normally of steel with baked enamel finish. Supply or return.

3 RECTANGULAR PERFORATED FACE DIFFUSER: Available in 1, 2, 3, or 4-way pattern, steel or aluminum. Flanged overlap frame or 2 X 2 ft and 2 X 4 ft for replacing tile of lay-in ceiling can be used for supply or return air.

4 ROUND PERFORATED FACE DIFFUSER: Normal 360° air pattern with blank-off plate for other air patterns. Steel or aluminum. Flanged overlap frame for all type ceilings. Can be used for supply or return air.

5 LATTICE TYPE RETURN: All aluminum square grid type return grille for ceiling installation with flanged overlap frame or of correct size to replace tile.

6 SADDLE TYPE LUMINAIRE AIR BOOT: Provides air supply from both sides of standard size luminaires. Maximum air delivery (total both sides) approximately 150 to 170 cfm for 4 ft long luminaire.

7 SINGLE SIDE TYPE LUMINAIRE AIR BOOT: Provides air supply from one side of standard size luminaires. Maximum air delivery approximately 75 cfm for 4 ft long luminaire.

8 LINEAR DIFFUSER: Extruded aluminum, anodized, duranodic, or special finishes, one way or opposite direction or vertical down air pattern. Any length with one to eight slots. Can be used for supply or return and for ceiling, sidewall, or cabinet top application.

9 INTEGRATED PLENUM TYPE OUTLET FOR "T" BAR CEILINGS: Slot type outlet, one way or two way opposite direction air pattern. Available in 24, 36, 48, and 60 in. lengths. Replaces or integrates with "T" bar. Approximately 150 to 175 cfm for 4 ft long, two-slot unit.

10 SIDEWALL OR DUCT MOUNTED REGISTER: Steel or aluminum for supply or return. Adjustable horizontal and vertical deflection. Plaster frame available. Suitable for long throw and high air volume.

William Tao & Associates, Inc., Consulting Engineers; St. Louis, Missouri
Krommenhoek/McKeown & Associates Architects & Engineers; San Diego, California

DUCT CONSTRUCTION

Ductwork must be permanent, rigid, nonbuckling, and nonrattling. Joints in ductwork should be airtight. Galvanized iron or aluminum sheets are usually used in the construction of ducts. The ducts may be either round or rectangular in cross section.

In general, supply ducts should be constructed entirely of noncombustible material. Supply ducts serving a single family dwelling need not meet this requirement, except for the first 3 ft from the unit, provided they are used in conjunction with listed heating units, are properly constructed from a base material of metal or mineral, and are properly applied. Warm air ducts passing through cold spaces or located in exposed walls should have 1 to 2 in. of insulation.

Supply ducts must be securely supported by metal hangers, straps, lugs, or brackets. No nails should be driven through duct walls, and no unnecessary holes should be cut in them.

Supply ducts should be equipped with an adjustable locking type damper for air volume control. The damper should be installed in the branch duct as far from the outlet as possible, where it is accessible.

Automatic smoke dampers are required wherever ductwork passes through a rated smoke barrier partition.

Return systems having more than one return intake may be equipped with balancing dampers.

Attention should be given to the elimination of noise. Metal ducts should be connected to the unit by strips of flexible fire resistant fabric. Electrical conduit and piping, if directly connected to the unit, may increase noise transmission. Return air intakes immediately adjacent to the unit may also increase noise transmission. Installation of a fan directly under a return air grille should be avoided.

DUCT MATERIAL THICKNESS

ROUND DUCT DIA. OR RECTANGULAR DUCT WIDTH (IN.)	GALVANIZED IRON U.S. GAUGE	ALUMINUM B & S GAUGE
	Ducts enclosed in partitions	
14 or less	30	24
Over 14	28	24
	Ducts not enclosed in partitions	
14 or less	28	24
Over 14	26	23

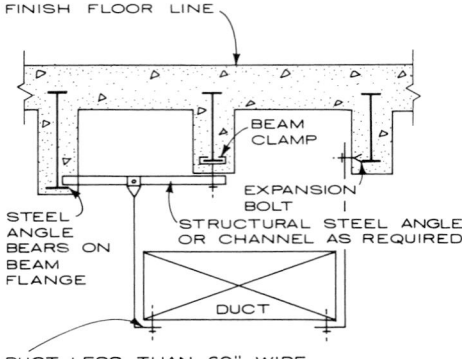

DUCT LESS THAN 60" WIDE USE 1/8" X 1" GALVANIZED IRON HANGER. DUCT OVER 60" WIDE USE 1/8" X 1 3/8" GALVANIZED IRON HANGER

NOTE

On ducts over 48 in. wide hangers shall turn under and fasten to bottom of duct. When cross-sectional area exceeds 8 sq ft duct will be braced by angles on all four sides.

DUCT SUPPORT DETAIL

William G. Miner, AIA, Architect, Washington, D.C.

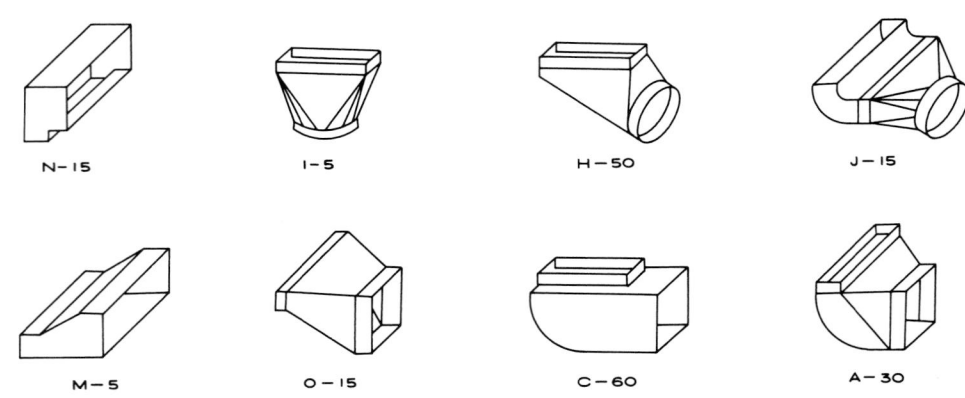

AIR BOOT FITTINGS

NOTE: N-15 ← NUMBER = EQUIVALENT LENGTH (FT)
LETTER = SHAPE DESIGNATION

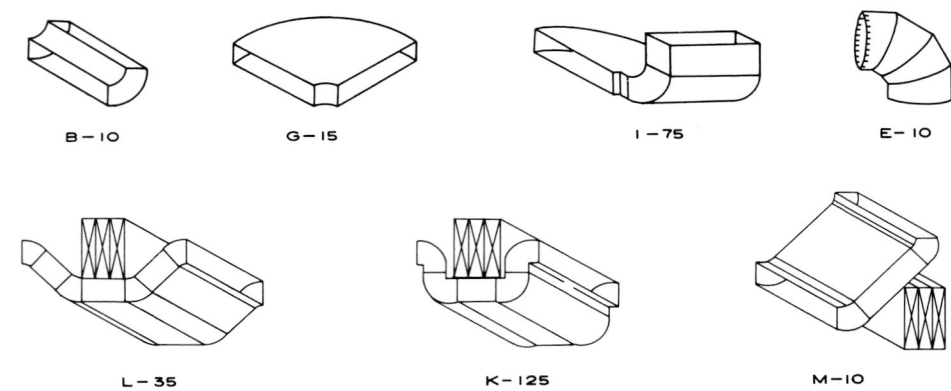

ANGLES AND ELBOWS FOR BRANCH DUCTS

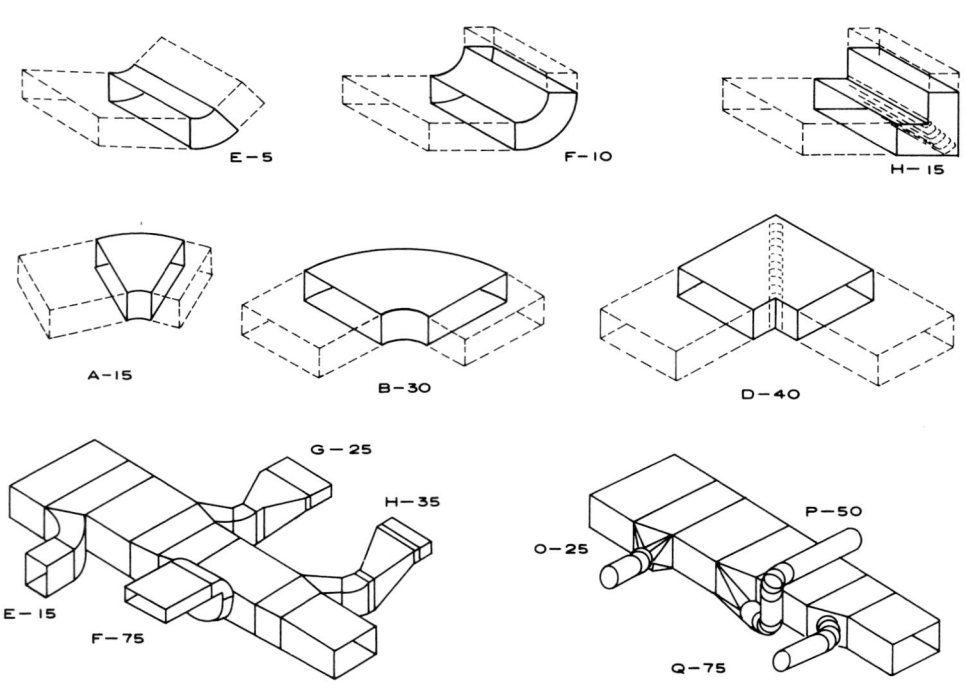

TRUNK DUCTS AND FITTINGS

15   **AIR DISTRIBUTION**

RECOMMENDED AND MAXIMUM AIR VELOCITIES FOR DUCTS

DESIGNATION	RESIDENCES	SCHOOLS, THEATERS, PUBLIC BUILDINGS	INDUSTRIAL BUILDINGS
RECOMMENDED VELOCITIES (FPM)			
Outdoor air intakes (a)	500	500	500
Filters (a)	250	300	350
Heating coils (a), (b)	450	500	600
Cooling coils (a)	450	500	600
Air washers (a)	500	500	500
Fan outlets	1000 - 1600	1300 - 2000	1600 - 2400
Main ducts (b)	700 - 900	1000 - 1300	1200 - 1800
Branch ducts (b)	600	600 - 900	800 - 1000
Branch risers (b)	500	600 - 700	800
MAXIMUM VELOCITIES (FPM)			
Outdoor air intakes (a)	800	900	1200
Filters (a)	300	350	350
Heating coils (a), (b)	500	600	700
Cooling coils (a)	450	500	600
Air washers (a)	500	500	500
Fan outlets	1700	1500 - 2200	1700 - 2800
Main ducts (b)	800 - 1200	1100 - 1600	1300 - 2200
Branch ducts (b)	700 - 1000	800 - 1300	1000 - 1800
Branch risers (b)	650 - 800	800 - 1200	1000 - 1600

(a) These velocities are for total face area, not the net free area; other velocities in table are for net free area.

(b) For low velocity systems only.

DUCT AREA PER SQUARE FOOT OF FLOOR AREA (IN SQ. IN.)

VELOCITY (FT PER MINUTE)
NEARLY SQUARE DUCTS LESS THAN 1000 CFM
FRICTION ALLOWANCE = 1.10

CUBIC FT PER HOUR/ SQ FT	400	600	800	1000	1200	1400	1600
30	0.198	0.132	0.099	0.079	0.069	0.057	0.050
35	0.231	0.154	0.116	0.092	0.077	0.066	0.058
40	0.264	0.176	0.132	0.106	0.088	0.075	0.066
45	0.297	0.198	0.149	0.119	0.099	0.085	0.074
50	0.330	0.220	0.165	0.132	0.110	0.094	0.083
55	0.363	0.242	0.182	0.145	0.121	0.104	0.091
60	0.396	0.264	0.198	0.158	0.132	0.113	0.099
65	0.429	0.286	0.215	0.172	0.143	0.123	0.107
70	0.462	0.308	0.231	0.185	0.154	0.132	0.116
75	0.495	0.330	0.248	0.198	0.165	0.141	0.124
80	0.528	0.352	0.264	0.211	0.176	0.151	0.132
85	0.561	0.374	0.281	0.224	0.187	0.160	0.140
90	0.594	0.396	0.297	0.238	0.198	0.170	0.149
95	0.627	0.418	0.314	0.251	0.209	0.179	0.157
100	0.660	0.440	0.330	0.264	0.220	0.189	0.165
105	0.693	0.462	0.347	0.277	0.231	0.198	0.173
110	0.726	0.484	0.363	0.290	0.242	0.207	0.182
115	0.759	0.506	0.380	0.304	0.253	0.217	0.190
120	0.792	0.528	0.396	0.317	0.264	0.226	0.198
130	0.858	0.572	0.429	0.343	0.286	0.245	0.215
140	0.924	0.616	0.462	0.370	0.308	0.264	0.231
150	0.990	0.660	0.495	0.396	0.330	0.283	0.248

DUCT AREA PER SQUARE FOOT OF FLOOR AREA (IN SQ. IN.)

VELOCITY (FT PER MINUTE)
NEARLY SQUARE DUCTS MORE THAN 1000 CFM
FRICTION ALLOWANCE = 1.05

CUBIC FT PER HOUR/ SQ FT	400	600	800	1000	1200	1400	1600
150	0.945	0.630	0.473	0.378	0.315	0.270	0.236
160	1.008	0.672	0.504	0.403	0.336	0.288	0.252
170	1.071	0.714	0.536	0.428	0.357	0.306	0.268
180	1.134	0.756	0.567	0.454	0.378	0.324	0.284
200	1.260	0.840	0.630	0.504	0.420	0.360	0.315
220	1.386	0.924	0.693	0.554	0.462	0.396	0.347
240	1.512	1.008	0.756	0.605	0.504	0.432	0.378
260	1.638	1.092	0.819	0.655	0.546	0.468	0.410
280	1.764	1.176	0.882	0.706	0.588	0.504	0.441
300	1.890	1.260	0.945	0.756	0.630	0.540	0.473
320	2.016	1.344	1.008	0.806	0.672	0.576	0.504
340	2.142	1.428	1.071	0.857	0.714	0.612	0.536
360	2.268	1.512	1.134	0.907	0.756	0.648	0.567
380	2.394	1.596	1.197	0.958	0.798	0.684	0.599
400	2.520	1.680	1.260	1.008	0.840	0.720	0.630

DUCT AREA PER SQUARE FOOT OF FLOOR AREA

VELOCITY (FT PER MINUTE)
ROUND DUCTS
FRICTION ALLOWANCE = 1.00

CUBIC FT PER HOUR/ SQ FT	400	600	800	1000	1200	1400	1600
30	0.180	0.120	0.090	0.072	0.060	0.051	0.045
35	0.210	0.140	0.105	0.084	0.070	0.060	0.053
40	0.240	0.160	0.120	0.096	0.080	0.069	0.060
45	0.270	0.180	0.135	0.108	0.090	0.077	0.068
50	0.300	0.200	0.150	0.120	0.100	0.086	0.075
55	0.330	0.220	0.165	0.132	0.110	0.094	0.083
60	0.360	0.240	0.180	0.144	0.120	0.103	0.090
65	0.390	0.260	0.195	0.156	0.130	0.111	0.098
70	0.420	0.280	0.210	0.168	0.140	0.120	0.105
75	0.450	0.300	0.225	0.180	0.150	0.129	0.113
80	0.480	0.320	0.240	0.192	0.160	0.137	0.120
85	0.510	0.340	0.255	0.204	0.170	0.146	0.128
90	0.540	0.360	0.270	0.216	0.180	0.154	0.135
95	0.570	0.380	0.285	0.228	0.190	0.163	0.143
100	0.600	0.400	0.300	0.240	0.200	0.171	0.150
105	0.630	0.420	0.315	0.252	0.210	0.180	0.158
110	0.660	0.440	0.330	0.264	0.220	0.189	0.165
115	0.690	0.460	0.345	0.276	0.230	0.197	0.173
120	0.720	0.480	0.360	0.288	0.240	0.206	0.180
130	0.780	0.520	0.390	0.312	0.260	0.223	0.195
140	0.840	0.560	0.420	0.336	0.280	0.240	0.210
150	0.900	0.600	0.450	0.360	0.300	0.257	0.225
160	0.960	0.640	0.480	0.384	0.320	0.274	0.240
170	1.020	0.680	0.510	0.408	0.340	0.291	0.255
180	1.080	0.720	0.540	0.432	0.360	0.309	0.270
190	1.140	0.760	0.570	0.456	0.380	0.326	0.285
200	1.200	0.800	0.600	0.480	0.400	0.343	0.300
220	1.320	0.880	0.660	0.528	0.440	0.377	0.330
240	1.440	0.960	0.720	0.576	0.480	0.411	0.360
260	1.560	1.040	0.780	0.624	0.520	0.446	0.390
280	1.680	1.120	0.840	0.672	0.560	0.480	0.420
300	1.800	1.200	0.900	0.720	0.600	0.514	0.450
320	1.920	1.280	0.960	0.768	0.640	0.549	0.480
340	2.040	1.360	1.020	0.816	0.680	0.583	0.510
360	2.160	1.440	1.080	0.864	0.720	0.617	0.540
380	2.280	1.520	1.140	0.912	0.760	0.651	0.570

DUCT AREA PER SQUARE FOOT OF FLOOR AREA (IN SQ IN.)

VELOCITY (FT PER MINUTE)
THIN RECTANGULAR DUCTS (W TO D 1:5)
FRICTION ALLOWANCE = 1.25

CUBIC FT PER HOUR/ SQ FT	400	600	800	1000	1200	1400	1600
30	0.225	0.150	0.113	0.090	0.075	0.064	0.056
35	0.263	0.175	0.131	0.105	0.088	0.075	0.066
40	0.300	0.200	0.150	0.120	0.100	0.086	0.075
45	0.338	0.225	0.169	0.135	0.113	0.096	0.084
50	0.375	0.250	0.188	0.150	0.125	0.107	0.094
55	0.413	0.275	0.206	0.165	0.138	0.118	0.103
60	0.450	0.300	0.225	0.180	0.150	0.120	0.113
65	0.488	0.325	0.244	0.195	0.163	0.139	0.122
70	0.525	0.350	0.263	0.210	0.175	0.150	0.131
75	0.563	0.375	0.281	0.225	0.188	0.161	0.141
80	0.600	0.400	0.300	0.240	0.200	0.171	0.150
85	0.638	0.425	0.319	0.255	0.213	0.182	0.159
90	0.675	0.450	0.338	0.270	0.225	0.193	0.169
95	0.713	0.475	0.356	0.285	0.238	0.204	0.178
100	0.750	0.500	0.375	0.300	0.250	0.214	0.188
105	0.788	0.525	0.394	0.315	0.263	0.225	0.197
110	0.825	0.550	0.413	0.330	0.275	0.236	0.206
115	0.863	0.575	0.431	0.345	0.288	0.246	0.216
120	0.900	0.600	0.450	0.360	0.300	0.257	0.225
130	0.975	0.650	0.488	0.390	0.325	0.279	0.244
140	1.050	0.700	0.525	0.420	0.350	0.300	0.263
150	1.125	0.750	0.563	0.450	0.375	0.321	0.281
160	1.200	0.800	0.600	0.480	0.400	0.343	0.300
170	1.275	0.850	0.638	0.510	0.425	0.364	0.319
180	1.350	0.900	0.675	0.540	0.450	0.386	0.338
190	1.425	0.950	0.713	0.570	0.475	0.407	0.356
200	1.500	1.000	0.750	0.600	0.500	0.429	0.375
220	1.650	1.100	0.825	0.660	0.550	0.471	0.413
240	1.800	1.200	0.900	0.720	0.600	0.514	0.450
260	1.950	1.300	0.975	0.780	0.650	0.557	0.488
280	2.100	1.400	1.050	0.840	0.700	0.600	0.525
300	2.250	1.500	1.125	0.900	0.750	0.643	0.563
320	2.400	1.600	1.200	0.960	0.800	0.686	0.600
340	2.550	1.700	1.275	1.020	0.850	0.729	0.638
360	2.700	1.800	1.350	1.080	0.900	0.771	0.675
380	2.850	1.900	1.425	1.140	0.950	0.814	0.713

INTRODUCTION

Recent developments in the microprocessor and electronic industries have revolutionized HVAC controls. Today, local temperature control requirements and centralized monitoring and control requirements can be satisfied with a single system as opposed to the two systems historically required. The reason for this is that the lower cost, more powerful microprocessors and electronics available today allow the conventional analog pneumatic and electronic controllers to be cost effectively replaced with digital electronic controllers. As these digital controllers are directly interfaced with the mechanical equipment they control as opposed to interfaced via pneumatic and electric controllers, they are called Direct Digital Controllers (DDCs)

In addition to greatly improving the accuracy of HVAC controls, DDC allows the instrumentation and controls engineer a great deal of flexibility in the development of HVAC sequences of operation and control strategies. Each direct digital control panel (DDCP) is as powerful as the typical personal computer. The DDCP monitors process variables (air temperatures, water temperatures, etc.) with electronic sensors. The DDCP digitizes this information so that it can be analyzed by the microprocessor in accord with the DDCP resident control program. With DDC, these control programs can include proportional, integral, derivative, and even adaptive algorithms. These algorithms allow the elimination of the off-set (error) inherent to conventional analog pneumatic and electric controls. This means that DDC allows controlled variables to be maintained much closer to setpoints than conventional controls, thereby improving comfort and reducing energy costs.

In addition to performing local control functions, DDCPs can be networked together to provide centralized monitoring and control. Today, the communications protocols that dictate how DDCPs communicate with one another tend to be proprietary, and therefore all the DDCPs on a network must be the product of the same manufacturer. Currently, several organizations are developing open protocols (e.g. ASHRAE is developing BACNET). When adopted by manufacturers, these open protocols will allow different manufacturers' DDCPs to communicate with one another. Systems with open protocol capabilities should be considered for projects with facilities at several sites.

OPERATOR INTERFACE

Typically, DDC systems support a variety of operator interfaces. An operator interface is a window through which the system operator can see what is happening to all of the equipment monitored and controlled by the DDC system. The most "user friendly" operator interface is a personal computer with color graphic screen and printer. The personal computer is used to process information and store:

1. Backup copies of the control programs that reside in each DDCP.
2. Graphics depicting how all of the mechanical systems are configured.
3. Graphics of the facility depicting the locations of all monitoring and controlled systems and equipment.
4. Trend logs, alarm logs, and logs of other information to provide a history of the facility's performance.

The color graphic screen is used to display the graphics stored in the personal computer, together with dynamic information (air temperatures, water temperatures, equipment status, etc.) monitored by the DDCPs. Additionally, the operator uses a touch screen, mouse, or keyboard to manipulate the cursor on the screen and command equipment on or off or change setpoints.

The printer is used to provide hard copies of alarm logs and any other information desired.

In addition to personal computers with color graphic screens, most DDC systems support one or more of a variety of less friendly operator interfaces. These operator interfaces include:

1. Portable personal computers with and without color graphic capabilities.
2. Monochromatic screens with and without graphic capabilities.
3. Portable operator terminals with English language capabilities.
4. Portable operator terminals with no English language capabilities.

The operator interface for most systems should be a personal computer with color graphic screen. The other types of operator interfaces should only be used on very small systems and to troubleshoot larger systems.

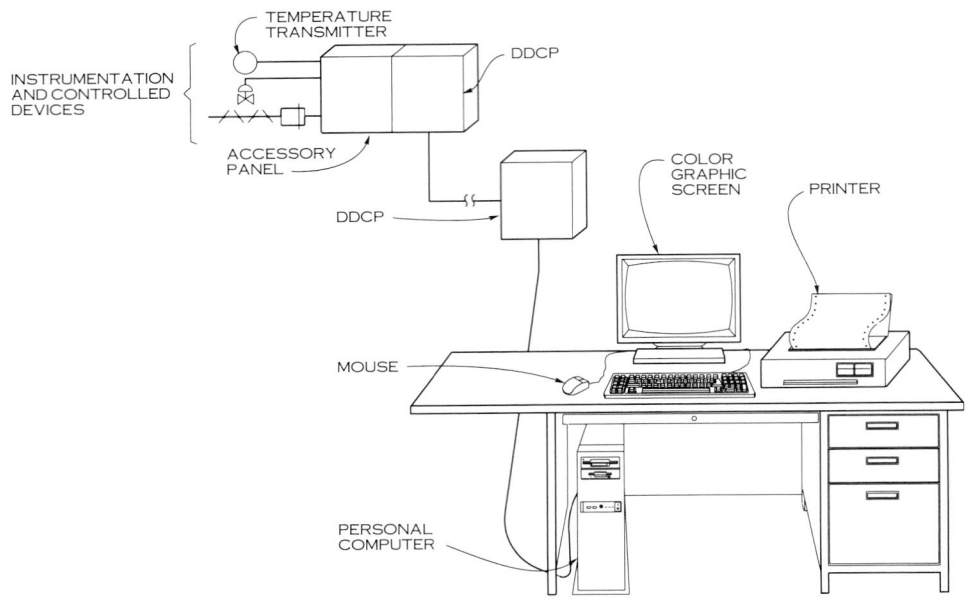

OPERATOR INTERFACE STATION

INSTRUMENTATION AND CONTROLLED DEVICES

DDC systems interface a variety of instrumentation and controlled devices to monitor and control environmental conditions and mechanical equipment. To facilitate start up, commissioning, and maintenance, the transmitters, control wiring, control relays, and transducers required to interface the DDC system with the instrumentation and controlled devices should be housed in accessory panels adjacent to the DDCPs. The quality of this equipment determines the accuracy and capability of the DDC system. If the instrumentation used to monitor controlled variables is not accurate or the controlled devices (valves, dampers, etc.) are improperly sized or are of inferior quality, the DDC system will not function properly.

While advances in the electronic industry have improved the quality (accuracy, repeatability, etc.) of some instruments and controls, they have also resulted in the introduction of several unproven components. Unfortunately, the failure of some of these newly developed and introduced components frequently limits the capabilities of DDC systems. To mitigate the possibility of this occurring, it is imperative that instruments and controls be carefully selected.

Industrial grade instrumentation and controls are more reliable, more accurate, and more expensive than commercial grade instrumentation and controls. Typically, a value engineered combination of industrial and commercial grade instrumentation and controlled devices is most appropriate.

Because the major mechanical systems (refrigeration plants, air handling units, etc.) consume the most energy and have the greatest impact on environmental conditions, the additional cost of industrial grade instrumentation with 4-20mA transmitters is generally justified.

Because smaller mechanical systems and terminal units (VAV boxes, etc.) consume less energy and affect the environmental conditions of fewer occupants, the added cost of industrial grade instrumentation can only be justified for critical applications (laboratories, operating rooms, etc.). Therefore, recently introduced commercial grade sensors (thermistors, semiconductors, etc.) should be considered for small mechanical systems, and terminal units serving noncritical loads.

Generally, commercial grade controlled devices (when properly sized and selected) are adequate for most applications. However, when selecting valves and dampers for large systems, industrial grade controlled devices are frequently required to provide adequate turn down and eliminate leakage.

Electric and electronic valve and damper operators for applications with limited torque requirements can now be purchased for approximately the same cost as convention-

al pneumatic valve and damper operators. They should be considered for terminal units with DDC. Due to the fact that larger mechanical systems generally require controlled devices with much greater torque, pneumatic valve and damper operators are generally appropriate.

CONTROL STRATEGIES

DDC provides the instrumentation and control engineer with power and flexibility to develop and implement control strategies that optimize environmental conditions and minimize energy consumption. The reason for this is that microprocessor-based DDCPs facilitate the sharing of information between control loops and control panels. Examples of how DDC control strategies can reduce energy consumption follow.

VARIABLE AIR VOLUME (VAV) SYSTEMS

When conventional pneumatic and electric/electronic controls are used to control VAV systems, a separate controller is used for each control loop. The wiring and complexity required to share information between conventional controllers generally forces most of the controllers and control loops to be independent.

With DDC, it is easy to share information between control loops. This allows the supply air temperature to be reset based upon supply air volume or VAV box position. Resetting the supply air temperature based on supply air temperature or VAV box position will reduce energy consumption and optimize environmental conditions by:

1. Making the fan operate at an efficient part of the fan curve by reducing supply air temperature when a VAV box approaches its full open position and/or supply air volume approaches system capacity. Reducing the supply air temperature reduces the amount of air required to satisfy the cooling load.
2. Mitigating the possibility of poor air distribution and dumping at the diffusers by increasing supply air temperature. When a VAV box approaches minimum position and/or supply air volume approaches minimum, increasing supply air temperatures increases the amount of air required to satisfy the cooling load. This assures adequate air distribution.
3. Adjusting the position of the outside air and relief air dampers to maintain the volume of outside air at setpoint and adjusting the minimum outside air setpoint as required to maintain indoor air quality. The minimum outside air setpoint can be reset based on the number of people in the area served or by monitoring the quality of the return air.

DDC allows conventional VAV control strategies to be effectively enhanced as described above.

Alfred F. Lyons; Electronic Systems Associates, a subsidiary of Syska & Hennessy, Inc. Engineers; New York, New York

GENERAL NOTES

A computer-based monitoring and control system (MCS) can have many functions: monitoring HVAC and electrical systems, supervisory and intervention control of those systems, energy management (EMCS), direct digital control (DDC), fire/security/telecommunications monitoring and control, maintenance scheduling, data analysis and report generation, and general building management. Continuing improvements in the capacity and capability of DDCs have resulted in systems in which the central console provides very few control functions, while retaining its monitoring and reporting functions.

SYSTEM ELEMENTS

The central console includes the computers, a hard disk for data storage, and the operator–machine interface. The operator–machine interface includes a CRT, a printer, and a keyboard.

The communication link is a coaxial cable or a "twisted pair" of wires. Communication over long distances is usually by telephone lines; modems are used to interface to phone lines. Fiber optics is the newest development in communication; signals are conveyed by light rays rather than electrical impulses.

The field interface device (FID) provides the connection between the MCS and the local loop controls. Intelligent FIDs (IFIDs) can do most of the functions formerly done by the central computer, including intervention control. This cuts down on traffic on the communication link, allowing faster monitoring of error and alarm conditions. If the IFID fails, the local loop devices will continue to function under the "last command" criteria.

A direct digital controller (DDC) takes the place of the controllers in the local loop systems. It can also function as an IFID in interfacing to the MCS. If the DDC fails, the local system will not operate. Local loop controls are those devices contiguous with and used in automatic control of HVAC and electrical systems. This includes DDC, if used. Software includes the programs necessary for correct operation of the computer system.

ENERGY CONSERVATION

A major factor in economic justification of the MCS is energy conservation. The best available data indicate that the MCS, in itself, may be responsible for a 10% energy savings. Additional savings are realized from upgrading existing systems and controls, improvements in control strategies, and improvements in the operator's understanding of the systems.

RETROFITTING

Before installing an MCS in an existing building, it is always necessary to retrofit and upgrade the existing systems and controls.

STAFFING AND TRAINING

A competent, well-trained staff is essential for proper operation of the MCS. Additional skilled personnel or upgrading of existing personnel to a higher skill level will be required to obtain maximum benefit from the MCS. Therefore, personnel costs will be higher, and the owner should be made aware of this.

SPACE REQUIREMENTS

The central console and operator's station requires a 3 by 6 ft desk, a printer stand with paper storage, a four-drawer file cabinet, and a chair. No special environment is needed beyond that normally required for comfort.

SECURITY/FIRE/ TELECOMMUNICATIONS

For reliability and to meet code requirements, it is preferable that security, fire, and telecommunications systems have their own computers and be separate from the MCS serving the HVAC and electrical systems. The several systems should be linked for communication, to trade data, and carry out such coordinated functions as smoke control.

ADAPTIVE AND INTELLIGENT CONTROLS

The use of "adaptive" and "intelligent" software systems should increase the energy conservation capability of computerized systems as well as improve overall control and decision making. Adaptive control programs allow the system to continually readjust parameters, especially controller gains, to match changing load conditions.

Roger W. Haines, PE; Laguna Hills, California

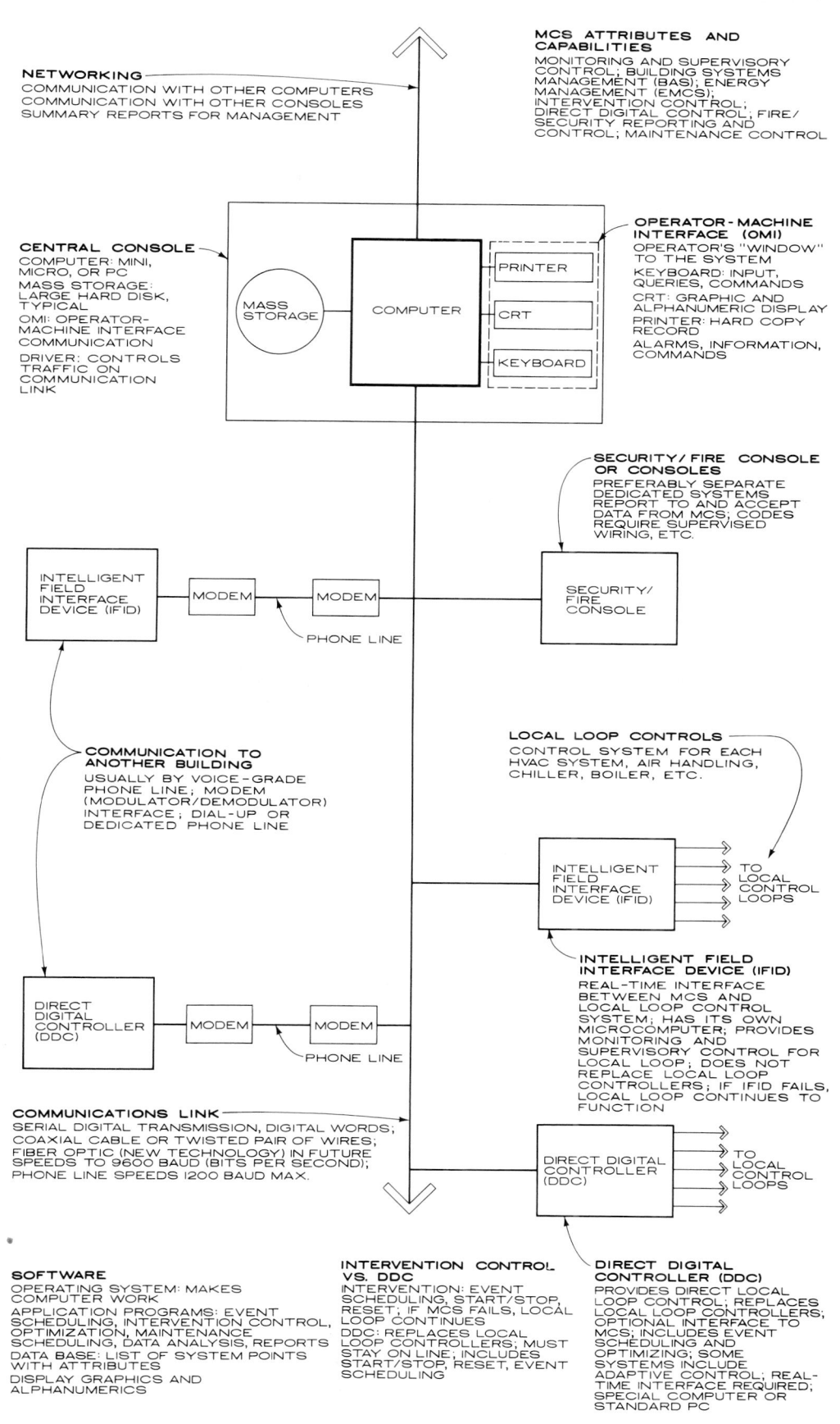

NETWORKING — COMMUNICATION WITH OTHER COMPUTERS COMMUNICATION WITH OTHER CONSOLES SUMMARY REPORTS FOR MANAGEMENT

MCS ATTRIBUTES AND CAPABILITIES — MONITORING AND SUPERVISORY CONTROL; BUILDING SYSTEMS MANAGEMENT (BAS); ENERGY MANAGEMENT (EMCS); INTERVENTION CONTROL; DIRECT DIGITAL CONTROL; FIRE/ SECURITY REPORTING AND CONTROL; MAINTENANCE CONTROL

CENTRAL CONSOLE — COMPUTER: MINI, MICRO, OR PC MASS STORAGE: LARGE HARD DISK, TYPICAL OMI: OPERATOR– MACHINE INTERFACE COMMUNICATION DRIVER: CONTROLS TRAFFIC ON COMMUNICATION LINK

MASS STORAGE — COMPUTER — PRINTER / CRT / KEYBOARD

OPERATOR– MACHINE INTERFACE (OMI) — OPERATOR'S "WINDOW" TO THE SYSTEM KEYBOARD: INPUT, QUERIES, COMMANDS CRT: GRAPHIC AND ALPHANUMERIC DISPLAY PRINTER: HARD COPY RECORD ALARMS, INFORMATION, COMMANDS

SECURITY/FIRE CONSOLE OR CONSOLES — PREFERABLY SEPARATE DEDICATED SYSTEMS REPORT TO AND ACCEPT DATA FROM MCS; CODES REQUIRE SUPERVISED WIRING, ETC.

INTELLIGENT FIELD INTERFACE DEVICE (IFID) — MODEM — MODEM — PHONE LINE — SECURITY/ FIRE CONSOLE

COMMUNICATION TO ANOTHER BUILDING — USUALLY BY VOICE–GRADE PHONE LINE; MODEM (MODULATOR/DEMODULATOR) INTERFACE; DIAL-UP OR DEDICATED PHONE LINE

LOCAL LOOP CONTROLS — CONTROL SYSTEM FOR EACH HVAC SYSTEM, AIR HANDLING, CHILLER, BOILER, ETC.

INTELLIGENT FIELD INTERFACE DEVICE (IFID) — TO LOCAL CONTROL LOOPS

INTELLIGENT FIELD INTERFACE DEVICE (IFID) — REAL-TIME INTERFACE BETWEEN MCS AND LOCAL LOOP CONTROL SYSTEM; HAS ITS OWN MICROCOMPUTER; PROVIDES MONITORING AND SUPERVISORY CONTROL FOR LOCAL LOOP; DOES NOT REPLACE LOCAL LOOP CONTROLLERS; IF IFID FAILS, LOCAL LOOP CONTINUES TO FUNCTION

DIRECT DIGITAL CONTROLLER (DDC) — MODEM — MODEM — PHONE LINE

COMMUNICATIONS LINK — SERIAL DIGITAL TRANSMISSION, DIGITAL WORDS; COAXIAL CABLE OR TWISTED PAIR OF WIRES; FIBER OPTIC (NEW TECHNOLOGY) IN FUTURE SPEEDS TO 9600 BAUD (BITS PER SECOND); PHONE LINE SPEEDS 1200 BAUD MAX.

DIRECT DIGITAL CONTROLLER (DDC) — TO LOCAL CONTROL LOOPS

SOFTWARE — OPERATING SYSTEM: MAKES COMPUTER WORK APPLICATION PROGRAMS: EVENT SCHEDULING, INTERVENTION CONTROL, OPTIMIZATION, MAINTENANCE SCHEDULING, DATA ANALYSIS, REPORTS DATA BASE: LIST OF SYSTEM POINTS WITH ATTRIBUTES DISPLAY GRAPHICS AND ALPHANUMERICS

INTERVENTION CONTROL VS. DDC — INTERVENTION: EVENT SCHEDULING, START/STOP, RESET; IF MCS FAILS, LOCAL LOOP CONTINUES DDC: REPLACES LOCAL LOOP CONTROLLERS; MUST STAY ON LINE; INCLUDES START/STOP, RESET, EVENT SCHEDULING

DIRECT DIGITAL CONTROLLER (DDC) — PROVIDES DIRECT LOCAL LOOP CONTROL; REPLACES LOCAL LOOP CONTROLLERS; OPTIONAL INTERFACE TO MCS; INCLUDES EVENT SCHEDULING AND OPTIMIZING; SOME SYSTEMS INCLUDE ADAPTIVE CONTROL; REAL-TIME INTERFACE REQUIRED; SPECIAL COMPUTER OR STANDARD PC

DIAGRAM OF COMPUTER-BASED MONITORING AND CONTROL SYSTEM

MECHANICAL PIPING AND RELATED EQUIPMENT

American Society of Mechanical Engineers (ASME)
1828L Street, NW, Suite 906
Washington, DC 20006
Tel: (202) 785-3756

International Association of Plumbing
   and Mechanical Officers (IAPMO)
20001 Walnut Drive South
Walnut, California 91789-2825
Tel (909) 595-8449
Fax(909) 594-3690

REFERENCES

ASPE Data Book, Special Plumbing Systems Design Supplement to Vol. 2, Chapter 17, "Compressed Air," and Chapter 19, "Seismic Protection of Plumbing Equipment," 1986.

1989 Boiler and Pressure Vessel Code, Section VIII, "Pressure Vessels," and Section IX, "Welding and Brazing Qualifications," ASME, 1989.

Avallone, Eugene A., and Theodore Baumeister III, eds. *Marks' Standard Handbook for Mechanical Engineers*, 9th ed. New York: McGraw-Hill, 1986.

Building Services Piping, ASME B31.9-88. ASME, 1988.

Karassik, Igor J., William C. Krutzsch, Warren H. Fraser, and Joseph P. Messina, eds. *Pump Handbook*. 2nd Ed. New York: McGraw-Hill, 1986.

Power Piping, ASME B31.1-89, ASME,1989.

Stein, Benjamin and John S. Reynolds. *Mechanical and Electrical Equipment for Buildings*. 8th Ed. New York: Wiley, 1992, 1627 pp.

PLUMBING

American Society of Plumbing Engineers
3617 Thousand Oaks Blvd.
Suite 210
Westlake Village, CA 91362
Tel: (805) 495-7120
Fax:(805) 495-4861

International Association of
   Plumbing and Mechanical Officers (IAPMO)
20001 Walnut Drive South
Walnut, California 91789-2825
Tel: (909) 595-8449
Fax:(909) 594-3690

National Solid Wastes Management Association
1730 Rhode Island Avenue, NW
Suite 1000
Washington, DC 20036
Tel: (202) 659-4613

Plumbing and Drainage Institute (PDI)
1106 West 77th Street, South Drive
Indianapolis, IN 46260
Tel: (317) 251-6970

REFERENCES

Church, J. *Practical Plumbing Design Guide*. New York: McGraw-Hill, 1987.

Crocker, Sabin, P.E. and Reno C. King, P.E., eds. *Piping Handbook*, 5th ed. New York: McGraw-Hill, 1973.

Handbook of Fundamentals. ASHRAE, 1989.

Harris, Cyril M., PhD., editor in Chief. *Handbook of Utilities and Services for Buildings*. New York: McGraw-Hill, 1990.

Hicks, T. *Plumbing Design and Installation Reference Guide*. McGraw-Hill, 1986.

Nayyar, Mohinder L. P.E., ed. *Piping Handbook*, 6th ed. New York: McGraw-Hill, 1992.

Hicks, T. *Plumbing Design and Installation Reference Guide*. McGraw Hill, 1986.

Church, J. *Practical Plumbing Design Guide*. McGraw-Hill, 1987.

Steele, Alfred, P.E. *Advanced Plumbing Technology*. Elmhurst, Ill.: Construction Industry Press, 1984.

PLUMBING FIXTURES AND EQUIPMENT

American Society of Sanitary Engineering (ASSE)
P.O. Box 40362
Bay Village, OH 44140
Tel: (216) 835-3040
Fax:(216) 835-3488

Plumbing Manufacturers Institute (PMI)
800 Roosevelt Road
Building C, Suite 20
Glen Ellyn, IL 60137
Tel: (708) 858-9172

Cast Iron Soil Pipe Institute (CIPSI)
5959 Shallowford Road, Suite 419
Chattanooga, TN 37421
Tel: (615) 892-0137
Fax:(615) 892-0817

REFERENCES

Anderson, Robert. "Energy Efficient Air Compressors" in the 1986 Yearbook, *Edward J. Zimmer Refresher Course*. American Society of Sanitary Engineering, 1986.

Machens, Ronald R., P.E. "Central Vacuum and Compressed Air Systems for Hospitals and Laboratories" in the 1980 Yearbook, *Edward J. Zimmer Refresher Course*, ASSE, 1980.

HVAC SYSTEMS

Air Conditioning Contractors of America
1513 16th Street, N.W.
Washington, DC 20036
Tel: (202) 483-9370
Fax:(202) 234-4721

Air Conditioning and Refrigeration Wholesalers
10251 West Sample Road
Suite B
Coral Springs, FL 33065-3939
Tel: (305) 755-7000
Fax:(305) 755-4103

Air Diffusion Council (ADC)
111 East Wacker Drive
Suite 200
Chicago, IL 60601
Tel: (312) 616-0800
Fax:(312) 616-0233

Cooling Tower Institute
Box 73383
Houston, TX 77273
Tel: (713) 583-4087

Home Ventilating Institute Division of the Air
   Movement and Control Association
30 West University Drive
Arlington Heights, IL 60004
Tel: (708) 394-0150

Hydronics Institute (HI)
P.O. Box 218
Berkeley Heights, NJ 07922
Tel: (908) 464-8200
Fax:(908) 464-7818

Institute of Heating and
   Air Conditioning Industries (IHACI)
606 North Larchment Blvd.
Suite 4A
Los Angeles, CA 90004
Tel: (213) 467-1158

International District
   Heating and Cooling Association
1101 Connecticut Avenue, NW
Suite 700
Washington, DC 20036
Tel: (202) 429-5111

National Association of
   Plumbing-Heating-Cooling Contractors (NAPHCC)
180 South Washington Street
P.O. Box 6808
Falls Church, VA 22046-1148
Tel: (703) 237-8100
Fax:(703) 237-7442

Sheet Metal and Air Conditioning
   Contractor's National Association (SMACNA)
4201 Lafayette Center Drive
Chantilly, VA 22021-1209
Tel: (703) 803-2980
Fax:(703) 803-3732

REFERENCES

Air Conditioning, Heating and Refrigeration News. Business News Publishing. [weekly]

Architectural Sheet Metal Manual. Sheet Metal and Air Conditioning Contractor's National Association, Inc. (SMACNA).

ASHRAE Handbook—HVAC Systems and Equipment. Atlanta: ASHRAE,1992.

CTI News, Cooling Tower Institute. [quarterly]

Engineered Systems. Business News Publishing. [bimonthly]

Heating/Piping/Air Conditioning. Penton Publishing. [monthly]

Intelligent Buildings, 88132. ASHRAE, 1988.

Kitchen Ventilation, 88144. ASHRAE, 1989.

1990 Ventilation Directory, National Conference of States on Building Codes and Standards.

Psychometric Charts, set of five 92200. ASHRAE.

Residential Heating and Cooling, 88108. ASHRAE, 1987.

Rowe, William H. III. *HVAC Design, Criteria, Options, Selections*. Kingston: RS Means, 1988.

Sample Specifications for Hydronic Heating. Hydronics Institute.

Schaffer, A . *Practical Guide to Noise and Vibration Control for HVAC Systems*. ASHRAE, 1991.

Thermal Environmental Conditions for Human Occupancy, Standard 55-1981, 86145. ASHRAE.

Uniform Mechanical Code. International Institute of Plumbing and Mechanical Officials in Plumbing. [annual]

HEAT GENERATION

American Gas Association
1515 Wilson Blvd.
Arlington, VA 22209
Tel: (703) 841-8400
Fax:(703) 841-8406

American Society of Heating, Refrigerating
   and Air Conditioning Engineers, Inc. (ASHRAE)
1791 Tullie Circle, NE
Atlanta, GA 30329
Tel: (404) 636-8400
Fax:(404) 321-5478

Industrial Heating Equipment Association
1901 North Moore Street, Suite 802
Arlington, VA 22209
Tel: (703) 525-2513

Institute of Heating and
   Air Conditioning Industries (IHACI)
606 North Larchment Blvd.
Suite 4A
Los Angeles, CA 90004
Tel: (213) 467-1158

International District
   Heating and Cooling Association
1101 Connecticut Avenue, N..W, Suite 700
Washington, DC 20036
Tel: (202) 429-5111

National Association of
   Plumbing-Heating-Cooling Contractors (NAPHCC)
180 South Washington Street
P.O. Box 6808
Falls Church, VA 22046-1148
Tel: (703) 237-8100
Fax:(703) 237-7442

REFRIGERATION AND HEAT TRANSFER

Air-Conditioning and Refrigeration Institute (ARI)
4301 Northwest Fairfax Drive
Suite 425
Arlington, VA 22203
Tel: (703) 524-8800

Refrigeration Service Engineers Society (RSES)
1666 Rand Road
Des Plaines, IL 60016
Tel: (708) 297-6464
Fax:(708) 297-5038

AIR DISTRIBUTION

Air Distributing Institute
4415 West Harrison Street
Suite 242C
Hillside, IL 60162
Tel: (708) 449-2933

Air Movement and Control Association (AMCA)
30 West University Drive
Arlington Heights, IL 60004
Tel: (708) 394-0150

CHAPTER

16

ELECTRICAL

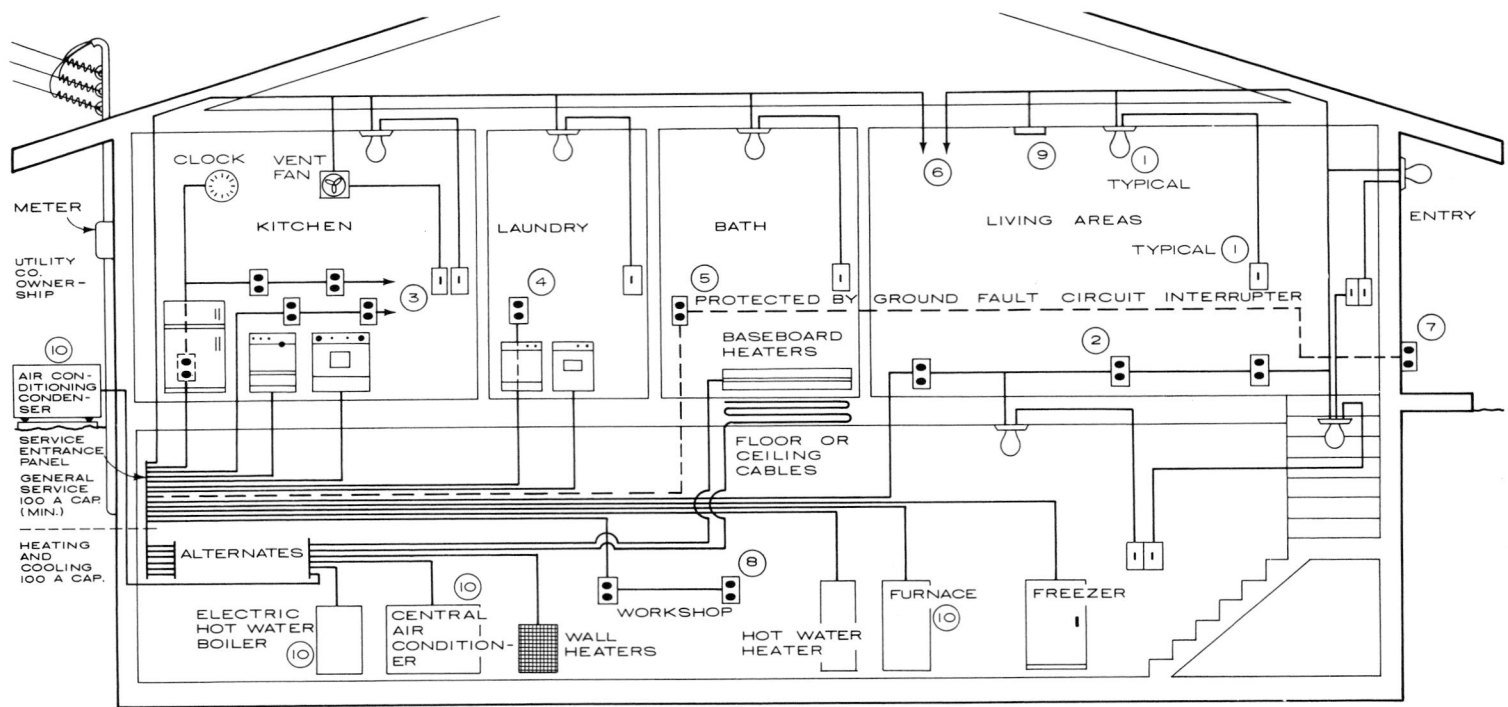

SCHEMATIC DIAGRAM OF TYPICAL RESIDENTIAL ELECTRICAL LAYOUT

GENERAL REQUIREMENTS

1. A minimum of one wall switch controlled lighting outlet is required in every habitable room, in hallways, stairways, and attached garages, and at outdoor entrances. Exception: in habitable rooms other than kitchens and bathrooms one or more receptacles controlled by a wall switch are permitted in lieu of lighting outlets.

2. In every kitchen, family room, dining room, den, breakfast room, living room, parlor, sunroom, bedroom, recreation room, and similar rooms, receptacle outlets are required such that no point along the floor line in any space is greater than 12 ft, measured horizontally, from an outlet in that space, including any wall space 2 ft or more wide and the wall space occupied by sliding panels in exterior walls.

3. A minimum of two #12 wire 20 A small appliance circuits are required to serve only small appliance

outlets, including refrigeration equipment, in kitchen, pantry, dining room, breakfast room, and family room. Both circuits must extend to kitchen; the other rooms may be served by either one or both of them. No other outlets may be connected to these circuits, other than a receptacle installed solely for the supply to and support of an electric clock. In kitchen and dining areas receptacle outlets must be installed at each and every counter space wider than 12 in.

4. A minimum of one #12 wire 20 A circuit must be provided to supply the laundry receptacle(s), and it may have no other outlets.

5. A minimum of one receptacle outlet must be installed in bathroom near the basin and must be provided with ground fault circuit interrupter protection.

6. The code requires sufficient 15 and 20 A circuits to supply 3 W of power for every square foot of floor

space, not including garage and open porch areas. Minimum code suggestion is one circuit per 600 sq ft; one circuit per 500 sq ft is desirable.

7. A minimum of one exterior receptacle outlet is required (two are desirable) and must be provided with ground fault circuit interrupter protection.

8. A minimum of one receptacle outlet is required in basement and garage, in addition to that in the laundry. In attached garages it must be provided with ground fault circuit interrupter protection.

9. Many building codes require a smoke detector in the hallway outside bedrooms or above the stairway leading to upper floor bedrooms.

10. Disconnect switches required.

NOTE

Refer to the National Electrical Code (NEC) for further information on residential requirements.

INDIVIDUAL APPLIANCE CIRCUITS

TYPE	VOLTS	TYPE	VOLTS
Range	240	Dishwasher	120
Separate oven or countertop cooking unit	240	Freezer	120
Water heater	240	Oil furnace motor	120
Automatic washer	240	Furnace blower motor	120
Clothes dryer	240	Water pump	240
Garbage disposal	240	Permanently connected appliances > 1000 W	Varies

BRANCH CIRCUIT PROTECTION

Lighting (general purpose)	#14 wires	15 A
Small appliance	#12 wires	20 A
Individual appliances	#12 wires	20 A
	#10 wires	30 A
	#8 wires	40 A
	#6 wires	50 A

AVERAGE WATTAGES OF COMMON RESIDENTIAL ELECTRICAL DEVICES

TYPE	WATTS	TYPE	WATTS	TYPE	WATTS
Air conditioner, central	2500-6000	Heating pad	50-75	Range oven (separate)	4000-5000
Air conditioner, room type	800-2500	Heat lamp (infrared)	250	Razor	8-12
Blanket, electric	150-200	Iron, hand	600-1200	Refrigerator	150-300
Clock	2-3	Knife, electric	100	Refrigerator, frostless	400-600
Clothes dryer	4000-6000	Lamp, incandescent	10 upward	Roaster	1200-1650
Deep fat fryer	1200-1650	Lamp, fluorescent	15-60	Rotisserie (broiler)	1200-1650
Dishwasher	1000-1500	Lights, Christmas tree	30-150	Sewing machine	60-90
Fan, portable	50-200	Microwave oven	1000-1500	Stereo (solid state)	30-100
Food blender	500-1000	Mixer	120-250	Sunlamp (ultraviolet)	275-400
Freezer	300-500	Percolator	500-1000	Television	50-450
Frying pan, electric	1000-1200	Power tools	Up to 1000	Toaster	500-1200
Furnace blower	380-670	Projector, slide or movie	300-500	Vacuum cleaner	250-1200
Garbage disposal	500-900	Radio	40-150	Waffle iron	600-1000
Hair dryer	350-1200	Range (all burners and oven "on")	8000-14000	Washer, automatic	500-800
Heater, portable	1000-1500	Range top (separate)	4000-8000	Water heater	2000-5000

Ed Hesner; Rasmussen & Hobbs Architects; Tacoma, Washington

 WIRING AND RELATED MATERIALS

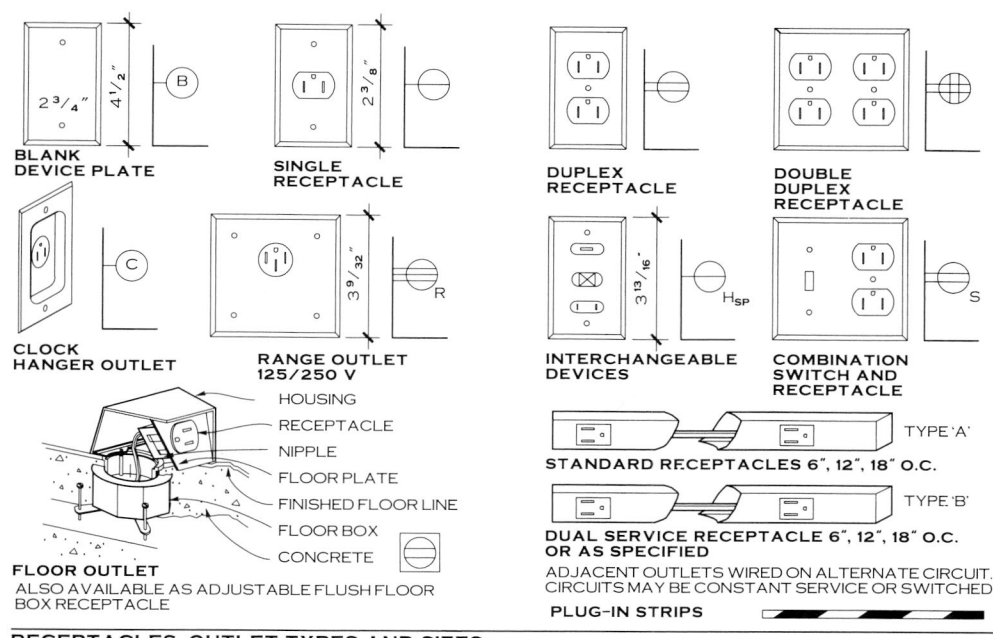

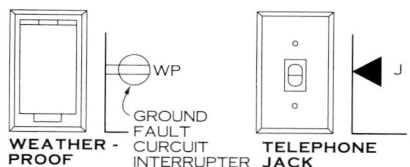

BLANK DEVICE PLATE
SINGLE RECEPTACLE
DUPLEX RECEPTACLE
DOUBLE DUPLEX RECEPTACLE
WEATHER-PROOF
GROUND FAULT CIRCUIT INTERRUPTER
TELEPHONE JACK

CLOCK HANGER OUTLET
RANGE OUTLET 125/250 V
INTERCHANGEABLE DEVICES
COMBINATION SWITCH AND RECEPTACLE

HOUSING
RECEPTACLE
NIPPLE
FLOOR PLATE
FINISHED FLOOR LINE
FLOOR BOX
CONCRETE

FLOOR OUTLET
ALSO AVAILABLE AS ADJUSTABLE FLUSH FLOOR BOX RECEPTACLE

TYPE 'A'
STANDARD RECEPTACLES 6", 12", 18" O.C.

TYPE 'B'
DUAL SERVICE RECEPTACLE 6", 12", 18" O.C. OR AS SPECIFIED
ADJACENT OUTLETS WIRED ON ALTERNATE CIRCUIT. CIRCUITS MAY BE CONSTANT SERVICE OR SWITCHED

PLUG-IN STRIPS

GANG SIZE

GANG	HORIZONTAL	
	HEIGHT	WIDTH
2	4 1/2 "	4 9/16 "
3	4 1/2 "	6 3/8 "
4	4 1/2 "	8 3/16 "
5	4 1/2 "	10 "
6	4 1/2 "	11 13/16 "

NOTES

1. Add 1 13/16 in. for each added gang. Screws are 1 13/16 in. o.c.
2. Plates are made in plastic, brass (.04 to .06 in. thick), stainless steel, and aluminum.
3. All devices to be Underwriters Laboratories approved.
4. All devices to comply with the National Electrical Code.
5. All devices to be of NEMA configuration.
6. Ground fault circuit interrupter or circuits are required in baths, garages, unfinished basements, outdoor at grade level, and within 6 ft of kitchen sinks.

RECEPTACLES, OUTLET TYPES AND SIZES

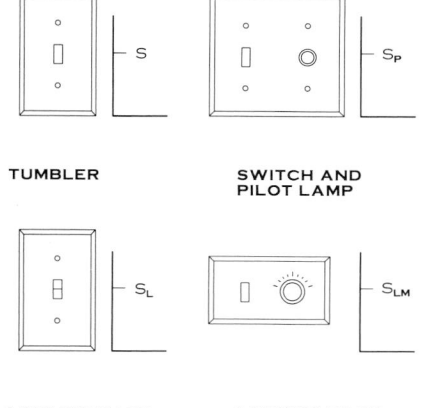

TUMBLER
SWITCH AND PILOT LAMP
LOW VOLTAGE
LOW VOLTAGE MASTER CONTROL

SWITCHES AND OUTLETS
KITCHEN
BATHROOM
BASEMENT, LAUNDRY, UTILITY ROOM

NOTE
1. Outlets and switches shown are most generally used. Number of gangs behind one wall plate depends on the type of devices used.
2. Symbols used are ASA standard. See page on "electric symbols."
3. Interchangeable devices (miniature devices) available in various combinations using any 1, 2, or 3 of the following: switch, convenience outlet, radio outlet, pilot light, bell, button, in one gang. Combined gangs are available.

SWITCHES

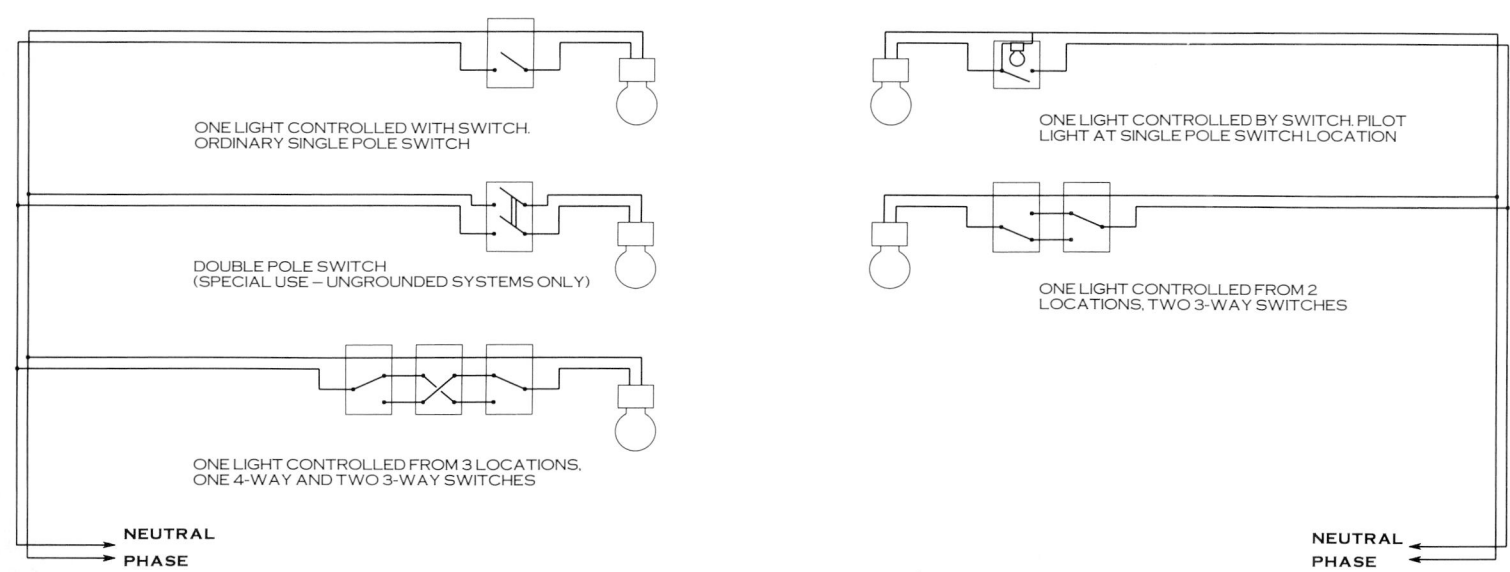

ONE LIGHT CONTROLLED WITH SWITCH. ORDINARY SINGLE POLE SWITCH

ONE LIGHT CONTROLLED BY SWITCH. PILOT LIGHT AT SINGLE POLE SWITCH LOCATION

DOUBLE POLE SWITCH (SPECIAL USE – UNGROUNDED SYSTEMS ONLY)

ONE LIGHT CONTROLLED FROM 2 LOCATIONS, TWO 3-WAY SWITCHES

ONE LIGHT CONTROLLED FROM 3 LOCATIONS, ONE 4-WAY AND TWO 3-WAY SWITCHES

NEUTRAL
PHASE

SWITCH WIRING DIAGRAMS

Michael Dienesch; Giffels Associates, Inc.; Southfield, Michigan

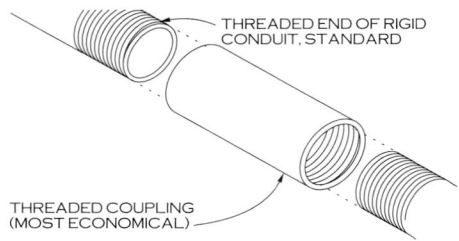

THREADED COUPLING

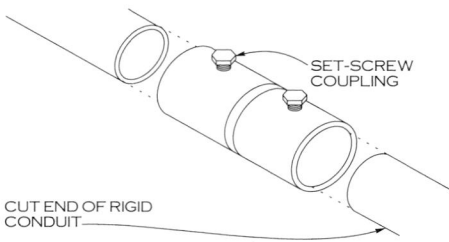

THREADLESS SET-SCREW COUPLING

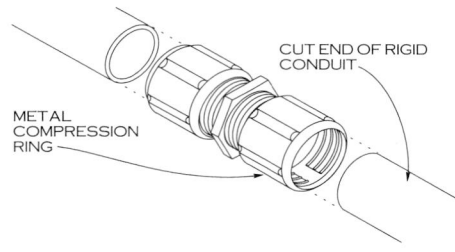

THREADLESS COMPRESSION COUPLING

NOTES

1. Manufactured in 10 ft lengths in diameters from 1/2 to 6 in. Consult manufacturers.
2. Rigid steel conduit provides heavy-duty protection of

RIGID STEEL CONDUIT

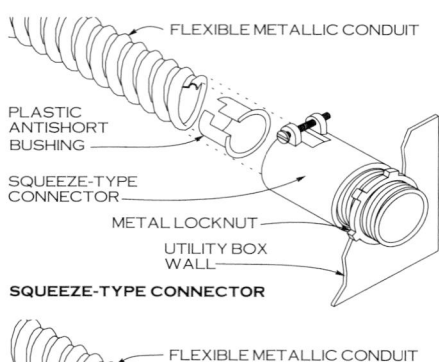

SQUEEZE-TYPE CONNECTOR

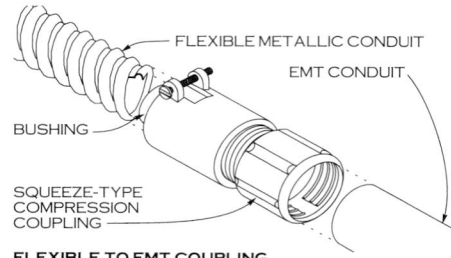

FLEXIBLE TO EMT COUPLING

NOTE

Manufactured in diameters from 5/16 to 4 in.

FLEXIBLE METALLIC CONDUIIT

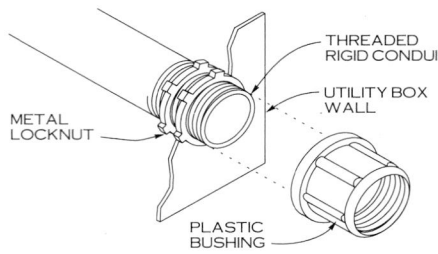

LOCKNUT BUSHING CONNECTION

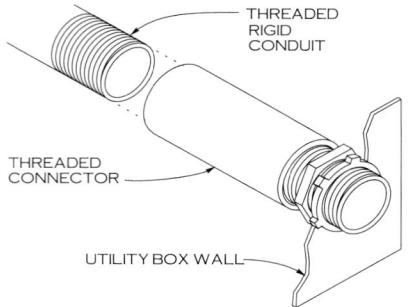

THREADED CONNECTOR

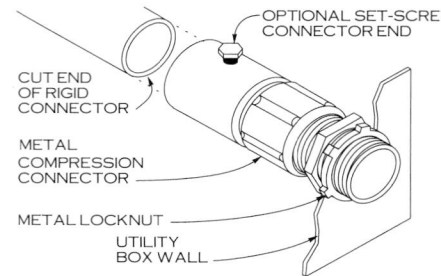

THREADLESS CONNECTORS

wiring from mechanical injury and corrosion and protects surroundings against fire hazard from overheating or arcing of enclosed conductors.

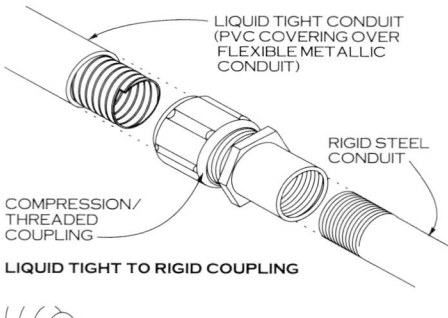

LIQUID TIGHT TO RIGID COUPLING

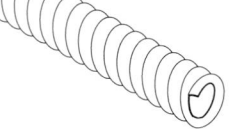

NONMETALLIC LIQUID TIGHT CONDUIT

NOTES

1. Manufactured in various grades according to temperature, range, and resistance factors (moisture, corrosion, and chemicals) in 1/4 to 6 in. diameters.
2. Frequently used for equipment connections in damp or wet locations and outdoors. Consult electrical engineer.

FLEXIBLE LIQUID TIGHT CONDUIT

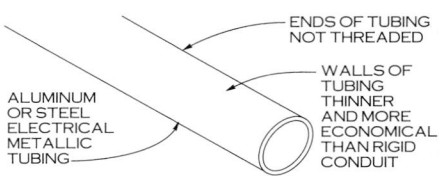

NOTES

1. Manufactured in 10 ft lengths and 1/2 to 4 in. diameters. Consult manufacturers.
2. Uses similar types of threadless couplings and connections as rigid steel conduit.

ELECTRICAL METALLIC TUBING (EMT)

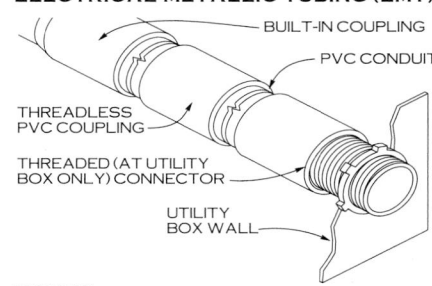

NOTES

1. All threadless connections are joined by means of solvent cement.
2. Commonly used for underground installation or cast into concrete.
3. Manufactured in heavy wall and light wall construction, in 10 ft lengths and 1/2 to 6 in. diameters.
4. Ground wire required for power cables.

RIGID NONMETALLIC CONDUIT

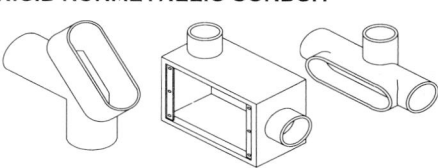

NOTES

1. Conduit outlet bodies are installed as pull outlets for conductors.
2. Fittings are manufactured for rigid steel, EMT, and nonmetallic conduit. Many shapes are available. Consult manufacturers.

CONDUIT OUTLET BODIES

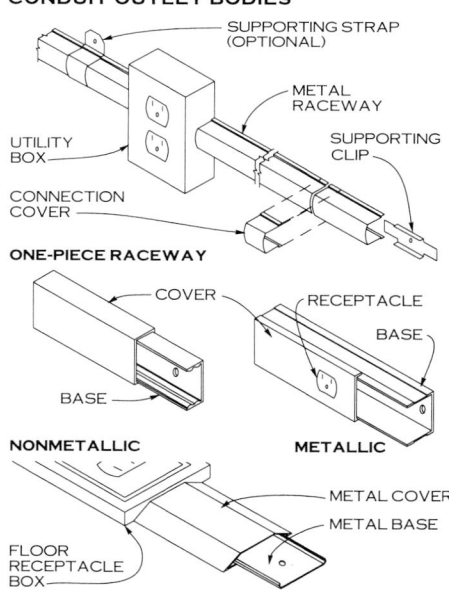

ONE-PIECE RACEWAY

NONMETALLIC   **METALLIC**

METAL FLOOR RACEWAY

SURFACE RACEWAY SYSTEMS

Robert T. Faass, Consulting Engineer; Seabrook, Maryland
Richard J. Vitullo, AIA; Oak Leaf Studio; Crownsville, Maryland

 WIRING AND RELATED MATERIALS

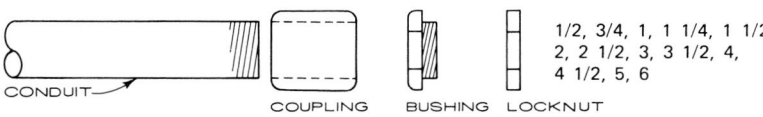

1/2, 3/4, 1, 1 1/4, 1 1/2,
2, 2 1/2, 3, 3 1/2, 4,
4 1/2, 5, 6

CONDUIT   COUPLING   BUSHING   LOCKNUT

RIGID STEEL CONDUIT (RSC) INTERMEDIATE METALLIC CONDUIT (IMC)
For fireproof construction.
See page on "conduits" for graphic size and weights.

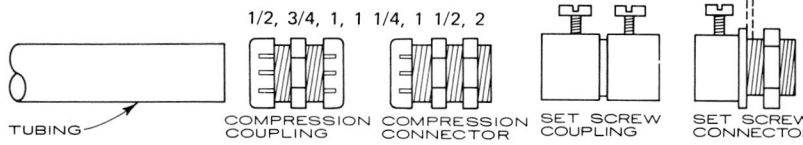

1/2, 3/4, 1, 1 1/4, 1 1/2, 2

TUBING   COMPRESSION COUPLING   COMPRESSION CONNECTOR   SET SCREW COUPLING   SET SCREW CONNECTOR

ELECTRICAL METALLIC TUBING
For fireproof construction. Same use as Rigid Conduit above. Walls are thinner, therefore economical.

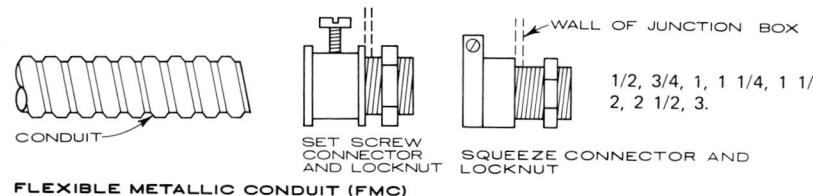

WALL OF JUNCTION BOX

1/2, 3/4, 1, 1 1/4, 1 1/2, 2, 2 1/2, 3.

CONDUIT   SET SCREW CONNECTOR AND LOCKNUT   SQUEEZE CONNECTOR AND LOCKNUT

FLEXIBLE METALLIC CONDUIT (FMC)
For fireproof construction.

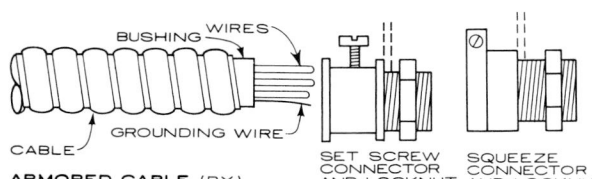

BUSHING   WIRES

GROUNDING WIRE

CABLE

SET SCREW CONNECTOR AND LOCKNUT   SQUEEZE CONNECTOR AND LOCKNUT

2 & 3 Conductor:
#14, 12, 10, 8, 6, 4, 2.
4 Conductor:
#14, 12, 10, 8, 6, 4.
Lead Covered—
2 cond. in #14, 12, 10, 8, & 6; 3 cond. in #14, 12, 10, 8, 6, & 4.

ARMORED CABLE (BX)
For frame construction. Lead covered for wet locations.

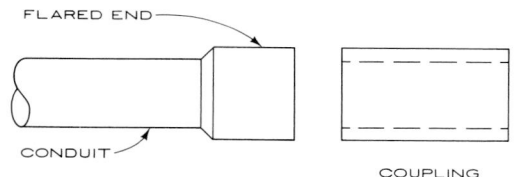

FLARED END

CONDUIT   COUPLING

EPC and EPT same sizes as metallic versions. Available in 3 wall thicknesses (EPT, schedule 40 and 80). Common use underground with or without ·concrete envelope. Ground wire required when used for power cables.

ELECTRIC PLASTIC CONDUIT AND TUBING (EPC AND EPT)

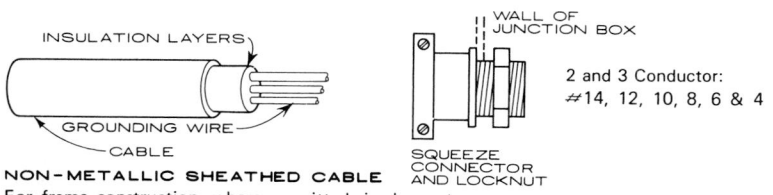

INSULATION LAYERS

WALL OF JUNCTION BOX

GROUNDING WIRE

CABLE

2 and 3 Conductor:
#14, 12, 10, 8, 6 & 4

SQUEEZE CONNECTOR AND LOCKNUT

NON-METALLIC SHEATHED CABLE
For frame construction, where permitted, is cheapest.

CABLES, CONDUITS AND TUBING
STANDARD NOMINAL SIZES IN INCHES

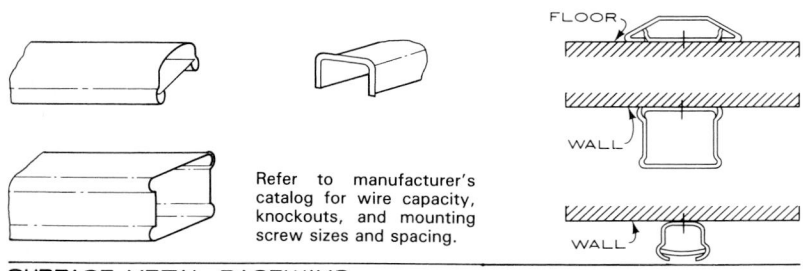

FLOOR

WALL

WALL

Refer to manufacturer's catalog for wire capacity, knockouts, and mounting screw sizes and spacing.

SURFACE METAL RACEWAYS

Syska and Hennessy, Consulting Engineers; New York, New York
Smith, Hinchman & Grylls Associates, Inc.; Detroit Michigan
Achla Bahl Madan, AIA, Architect & Interior Designer; Rochester, New York

---

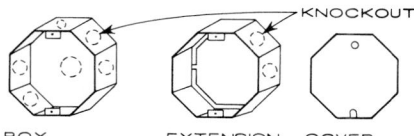
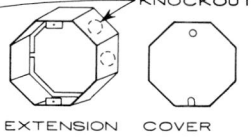

KNOCKOUTS

WIDTH AND DEPTH
3 1/4 x 1 1/2
3 1/2 x 1 1/2
4 x 1 1/2
4 x 2 1/8

BOX   EXTENSION   COVER

OCTAGONAL
Used in ceilings.

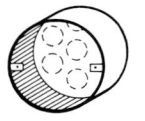
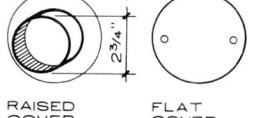

WIDTH AND DEPTH
3 1/4 x 3/4, 1 1/2
3 1/2 x 1/2, 1 1/2
4 x 1/2
*4 x 5/8

* Raised Cover

BOX   RAISED COVER   FLAT COVER

ROUND
Used in ceilings.

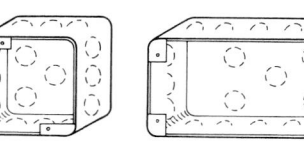

WIDTH AND DEPTH
Square box:
4 x 1 1/2, 2 1/8
4 11/16 x 1 1/2, 2 1/8
2 Gang Box
4 1/2 x 1 3/4 x 6 13/16 long

SQUARE   RECTANGULAR

RECTANGULAR
Used in walls.

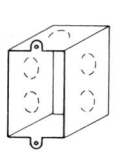
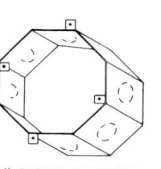
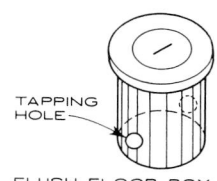

GEM

for switch or receptacle in narrow location
2" wide x 3" long x 2" or 2 1/2" deep
IN MASONRY

4" OCTAGONAL

for concrete 1 1/2, 2, 2 1/2, 3, 3 1/2, 4, 5, 6 deep

TAPPING HOLE

FLUSH FLOOR BOX

for masonry sizes vary

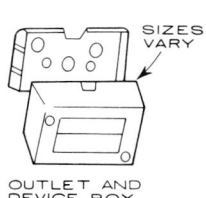

SIZES VARY

ADJUSTABLE JUNCTION BOX   UTILITY BOX   OUTLET AND DEVICE BOX

EXPOSED-FOR SURFACE RACEWAYS
See manufacturers' catalogs for other fittings.

OUTLET AND JUNCTION BOXES
SIZES IN INCHES

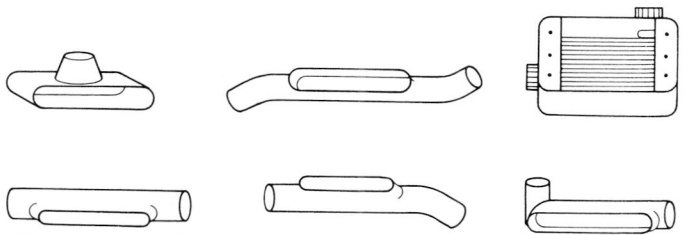

CONDULETS (FOR EXPOSED WORK)
Condulets made in a great many shapes and sizes; consult manufacturers.

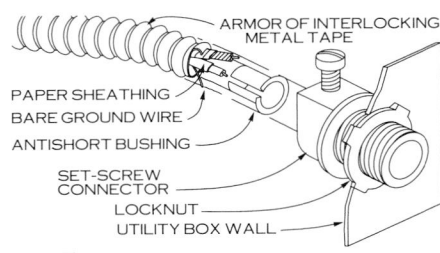

NOTE

Manufactured with 2, 3, and 4 conductor insulated wire in the following sizes: 14, 8, 6, 4, 2, 1. Also contains internal bonds that help the armor itself serve as a bonding conductor for the armor.

ARMORED CABLE (BX)

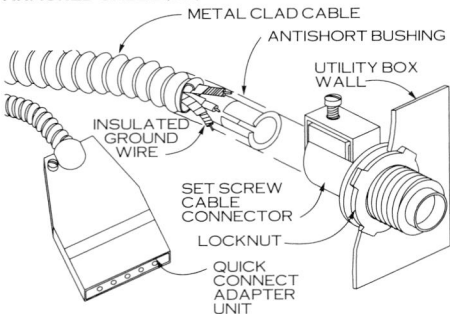

NOTE

Manufactured to similar specifications and sizes as armored cable but with a separate insulated ground conductor. Metal clad cable may be clad in aluminum or steel, corrugated, smooth, or with metal interlocking tape. May be factory assembled with quick connect adapter units for access floor or ceiling wiring systems. Consult with electrical engineer before installation.

METAL CLAD CABLE (MC)

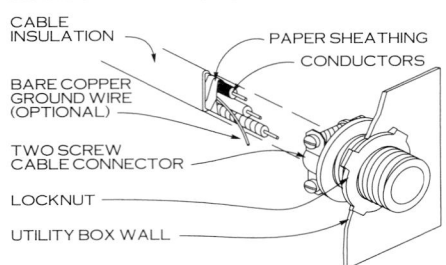

NOTE

Manufactured in 2 and 3 conductor PVC insulated wire in the following sizes: 14, 12, 10, 8, 6, and 4 with or without ground wire.

NONMETALLIC SHEATHED CABLE (NM, ROMEX)

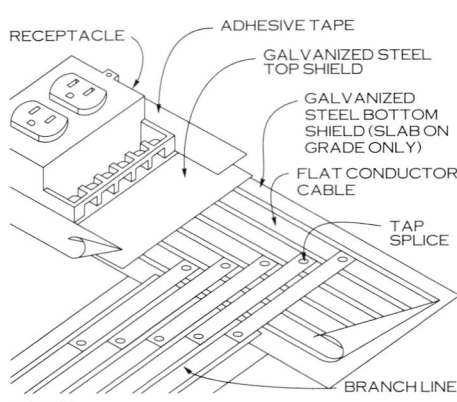

NOTE

Manufactured with combinations of 3, 4, and 5 conductors in cable for easy access under carpet squares. Consult manufacturers before installation.

FLAT CONDUCTOR CABLE

CABLES

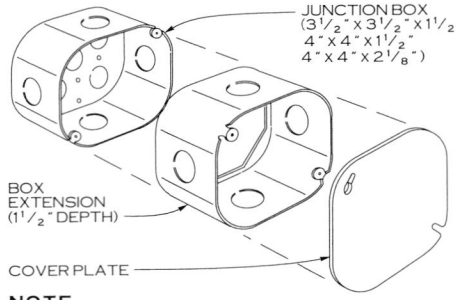

NOTE

Commonly used for flush ceiling outlets.

OCTAGONAL BOX

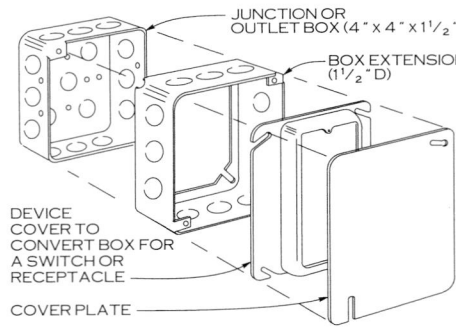

SQUARE BOX

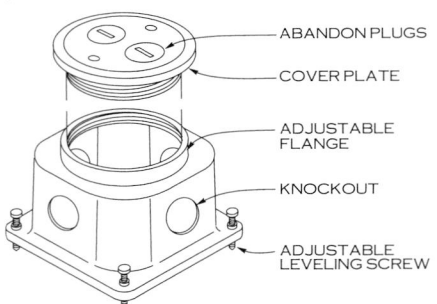

NOTE

Boxes are mounted to wood floor structure (nonadjustable) or for cast-in-place concrete with leveling screws. Concrete box materials include cast iron, stamped steel or nonmetallic.

FLUSH FLOOR BOX

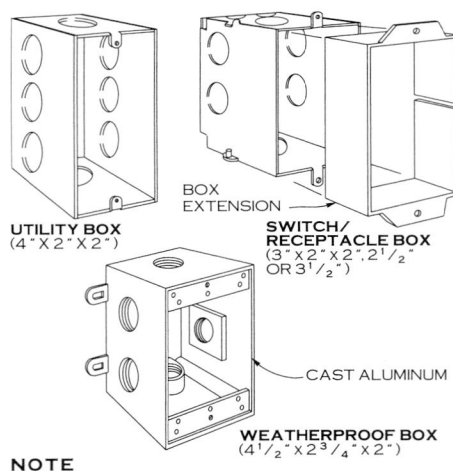

NOTE

These boxes are manufactured in metallic and nonmetallic versions. Knockout locations vary. Utility and exterior boxes are not gangable; switch and masonry boxes may be gangable. Flush mounting in concrete requires a concrete tight box and rigid conduit; in CMU conduit is threaded through the cavities of block.

ELECTRICAL BOXES

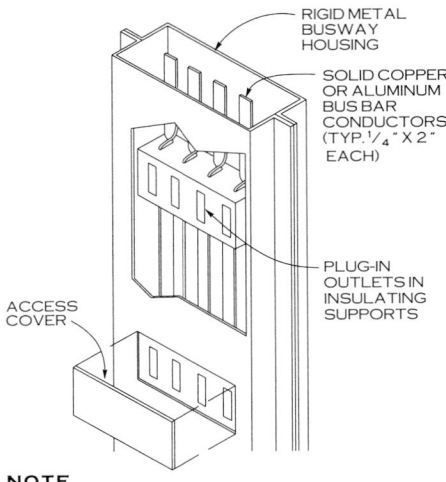

NOTE

Busways carry current from 100 to 4000 amps. They are utilized when large blocks of low voltage power (up to 600V) must be transmitted over long distances or where taps must be made at various points, as in vertical risers in office buildings. Consult electrical engineer before using this system. Busway housing may be hung from overhead support, mounted to wall, or braced to structure in vertical riser installation.

BUSWAY SYSTEM

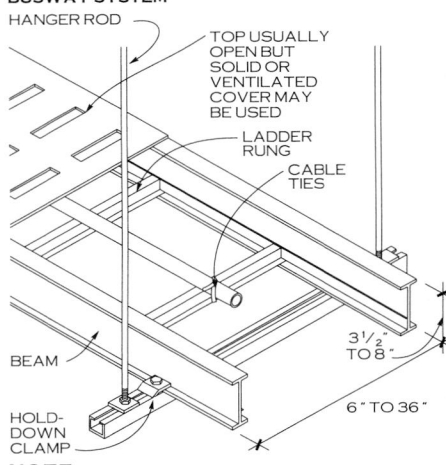

NOTE

Cable trays allow large numbers of insulated cables to be protected and carried in a limited space. For more protection or where heat build-up is not a problem, perforated or solid bottoms and top covers are available. Many fittings, bends, and tees (horizontal and vertical) are available. Consult manufacturers for materials other than aluminum or steel.

CABLE TRAY SYSTEM

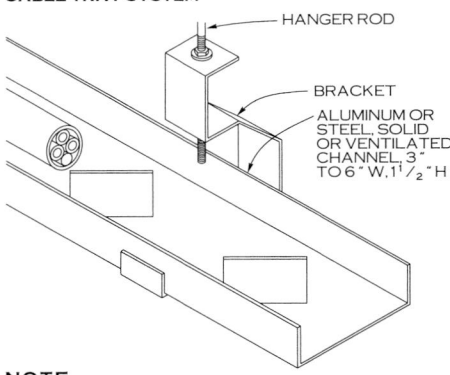

NOTE

Used as branch cable tray to carry single large cable or conduit or several small ones.

CABLE CHANNEL

CONDUIT AND CABLE SUPPORTING DEVICES

Robert T. Faass, Consulting Engineer; Seabrook, Maryland
Richard J. Vitullo, AIA; Oak Leaf Studio; Crownsville, Maryland

16 **WIRING AND RELATED MATERIALS**

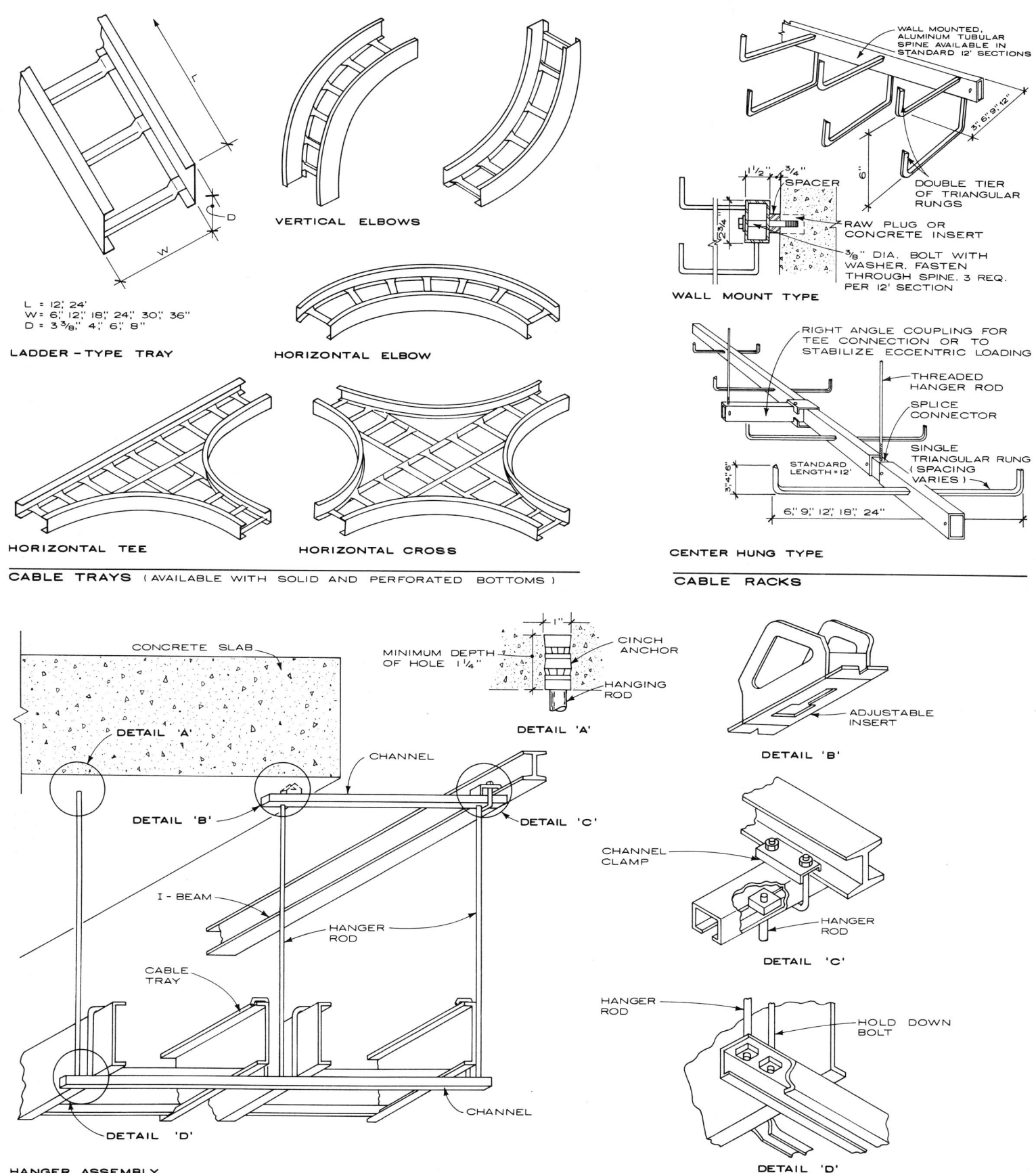

L = 12', 24'
W = 6", 12", 18", 24", 30", 36"
D = 3 3/8", 4", 6", 8"

LADDER-TYPE TRAY

VERTICAL ELBOWS

HORIZONTAL ELBOW

HORIZONTAL TEE

HORIZONTAL CROSS

CABLE TRAYS (AVAILABLE WITH SOLID AND PERFORATED BOTTOMS)

WALL MOUNTED, ALUMINUM TUBULAR SPINE AVAILABLE IN STANDARD 12' SECTIONS

3", 6", 9", 12"

6'

DOUBLE TIER OF TRIANGULAR RUNGS

1 1/2" 3/4" SPACER

2 3/4"

RAW PLUG OR CONCRETE INSERT

3/8" DIA. BOLT WITH WASHER. FASTEN THROUGH SPINE. 3 REQ. PER 12' SECTION

WALL MOUNT TYPE

RIGHT ANGLE COUPLING FOR TEE CONNECTION OR TO STABILIZE ECCENTRIC LOADING

THREADED HANGER ROD

SPLICE CONNECTOR

STANDARD LENGTH = 12'

SINGLE TRIANGULAR RUNG (SPACING VARIES)

3", 4", 6"

6", 9", 12", 18", 24"

CENTER HUNG TYPE

CABLE RACKS

CONCRETE SLAB

DETAIL 'A'

1"

MINIMUM DEPTH OF HOLE 1 1/4"

CINCH ANCHOR

HANGING ROD

DETAIL 'A'

ADJUSTABLE INSERT

DETAIL 'B'

CHANNEL

DETAIL 'B'

DETAIL 'C'

I-BEAM

HANGER ROD

CABLE TRAY

DETAIL 'D'

CHANNEL

HANGER ASSEMBLY

CHANNEL CLAMP

HANGER ROD

DETAIL 'C'

HANGER ROD

HOLD DOWN BOLT

DETAIL 'D'

CABLE TRAY INSTALLATION DETAILS

Ch2M Hill, Inc.; Corvallis, Oregon

WIRING AND RELATED MATERIALS **16**

NOTES

Poke-through systems are used in conjunction with overhead branch distribution systems run in accessible suspended ceiling cavities to serve outlets in full height partitions. When services are required at floor locations where adjacent partitions or columns are not available, as in open office planning, they must either be brought down from a wireway assembly (known as a power pole) or up through a floor penetration containing a fire-rated insert fitting and flush or above-floor outlet assembly. To install a poke-through assembly, the floor slab must either be core drilled or contain preset sleeves arranged in a modular grid. Poke-through assemblies are used in conjunction with cellular deck and underfloor duct systems when precise service location required does not fall directly above its associated system raceway.

With one floor penetration, the single poke-through assembly can serve all the power, communications (telephone), and computer (data) requirements of a workstation. Distribution wiring in the ceiling cavity can be run in raceways. The more cost-effective method is to use armored cable (bx) for power and approved plenum rated cable for communications and data when the ceiling cavity is used for return air. To minimize disturbance to the office space below when a poke-through assembly needs to be relocated or added, a modular system of prewired junction boxes for each service can be provided, although it is more common to elect this option for power only. A different type of wiring system must be selected for a floor slab on grade, above lobby or retail space, above mechanical equipment space, or above space exposed to atmosphere.

Low initial cost of a poke-through system makes it both viable and attractive for investor-owned buildings where tenants are responsible for future changes and for corporate buildings where construction budget is limited. It is effective when office planning includes interconnecting workstation panels containing provisions (base raceways) to extend wiring above the floor, reducing the number of floor penetrations needed for services.

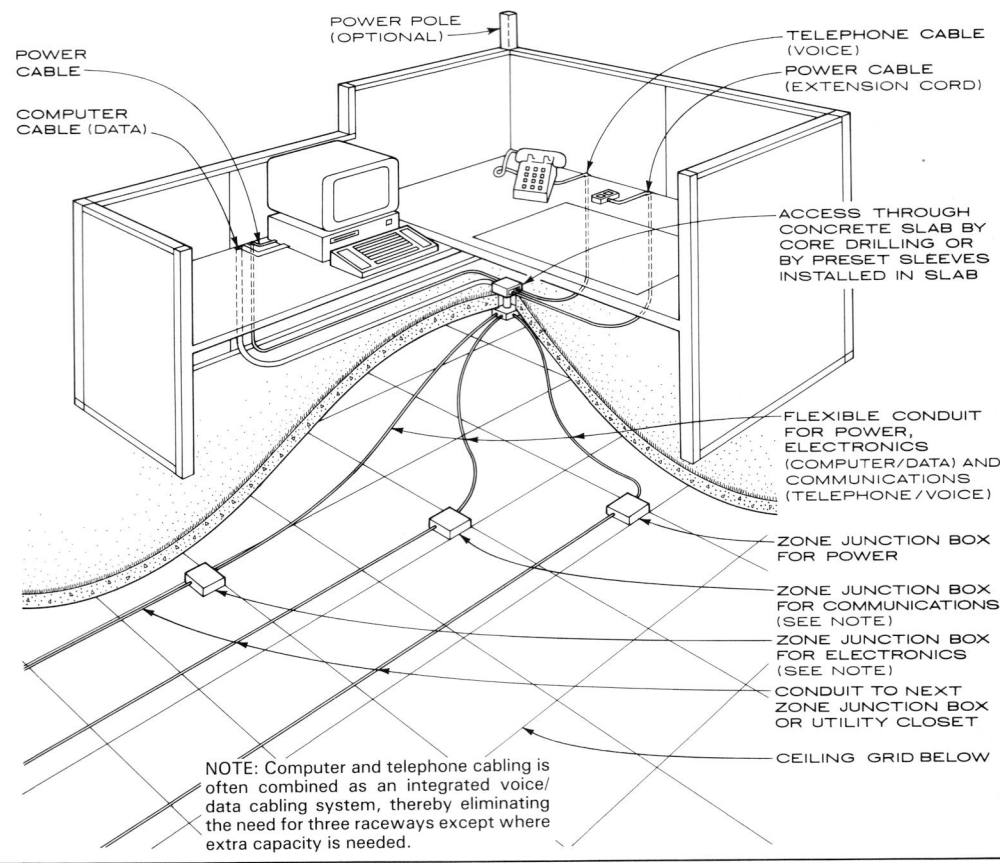

NOTE: Computer and telephone cabling is often combined as an integrated voice/data cabling system, thereby eliminating the need for three raceways except where extra capacity is needed.

POKE-THROUGH HARDWIRE SYSTEM/ZONE JUNCTION BOXES

NOTES

Based on projected frequency of future changes in office furniture layouts, a corporate or government organization may elect to preinvest in a permanent raceway system to minimize cost and disturbance to occupants when changes or additions are made. When structural design dictates the use of metal decking, a cellular floor raceway system utilizing trench header ducts becomes the most likely candidate for selection.

Cellular raceways come in a variety of sizes and configurations ranging from $1\frac{1}{2}$ to 3 in. high with cells 8 or 12 in. o.c. and 2 or 3 cells per section. An overall floor deck can be full cellular, where bottom plates are provided throughout, or blended as shown.

Trench header ducts come in various sizes and configurations. Height is adjustable for slab depths above cells of $2\frac{1}{2}$ to 4 in. and widths vary from 9 to 36 in. Coverplates are $\frac{1}{4}$ in. thick, with lengths from 6 to 36 in., and can either be secured with spring clips or flush, flathead bolts. Two versions of trench design are available, one consisting of a compartmental bottom tray with a grommeted access hole for each cell it crosses and the other a bottomless trench duct consisting of side rails and a separate wireway in the middle, with grommeted access holes only for the power cells.

When service is needed, floor is core drilled above desired cell, the cell top is drilled into, and an afterset insert with above-floor fitting is attached. If data and communication wiring can occupy the same cell, with power wiring in an adjacent cell, two separate service fittings are required for each workstation.

Where it is necessary to eliminate or minimize core drilling, a modular pattern of preset service flush outlets can be provided along the cellular sections before the floor is poured, as shown. Upon activation, one flush outlet can serve all the power, communication, and data requirements of a workstation.

The modular grid and frequency of preset locations will determine the convenience of service provisions for the workstations.

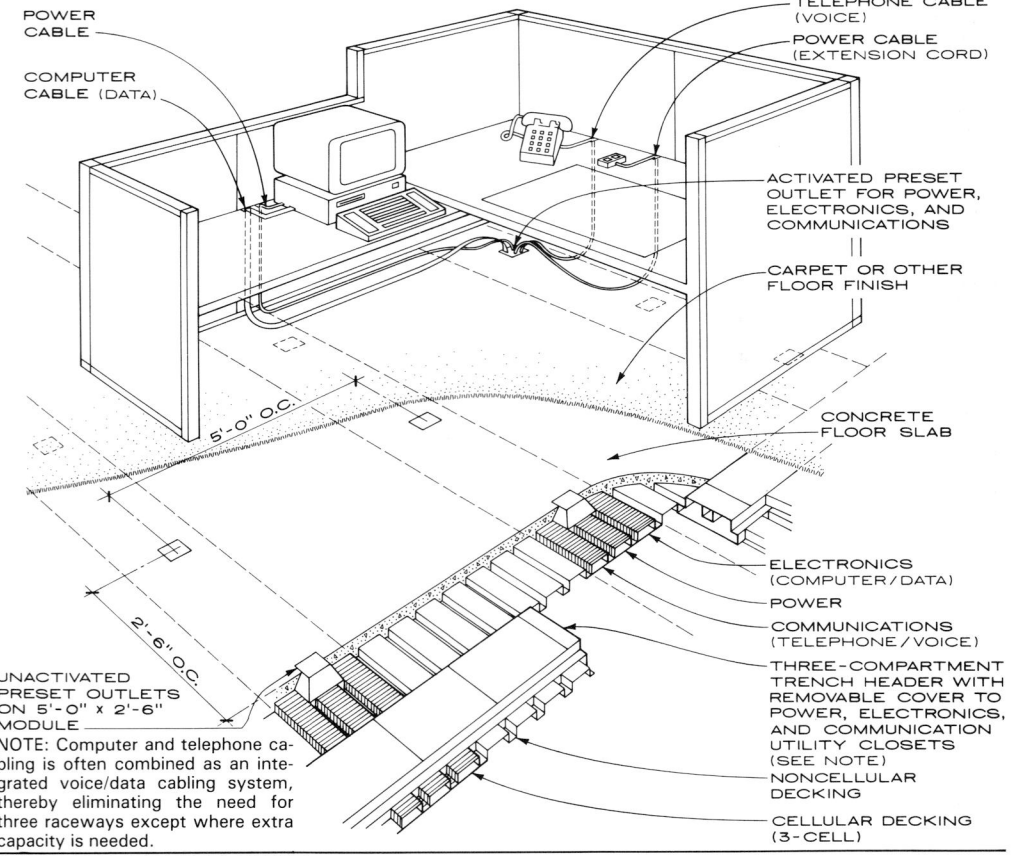

NOTE: Computer and telephone cabling is often combined as an integrated voice/data cabling system, thereby eliminating the need for three raceways except where extra capacity is needed.

ELECTRIFIED CELLULAR DECK SYSTEM/TRENCH HEADER DUCT

Richard F. Humenn, PE; Joseph R. Loring & Associates, Inc., Consulting Engineers; New York, New York
Gary A. Hall; Hammel Green and Abrahamson; Minneapolis, Minnesota

 WIRING AND RELATED MATERIALS

NOTES

Where projected frequency of future changes is relatively high, a raised access floor system will provide the maximum flexibility and lowest cost to relocate or add services for workstations. When used in conjunction with a modular system of power, communication and data wiring plug-in receptacles, and cable connector sets, changes can be made without the need of an electrician or wiring technician. Advantages come at a premium, as access floor systems are the highest in initial cost of all systems described in this section.

A raised access floor is essentially a basic computer floor that is restricted in application to distribute only power, communication, and data services to workstations. The absence of air distribution and high density of cabling associated with computers permit raised floor height to be reduced to nominal 6 in. As the depth of standard 2 ft sq formed steel floor panel is less than 2 in., over 4 in. clear height under the panels provides sufficient clearance to accommodate hardware associated with distributing services. Virtually any variety of above-floor or flush outlets can be mounted on a floor panel and connected to lengths of cable with plug or connector fitting at the other end.

Access floors can be provided with or without stringers, which are used to minimize "creep" effect. Laser beam equipment speeds up accurate leveling of pedestal heights. For a custom installation without ramps or steps, the base floor is structurally designed to be depressed below permanent building elements such as lobbies, stairs, and toilets. Panels can be ordered with factory-installed carpeting or, alternatively, magnetic-backed carpet squares can be added after installation.

The introduction of an access floor does not necessarily require an increase in floor-to-floor height, and if so, the cubage added is at a much lower per unit cost than for the rest of the building. When special attention is given to coordinating lighting with other elements in the suspended ceiling or when lighting is provided below as from the workstations, the cavity can be compressed to compensate for the raised floor.

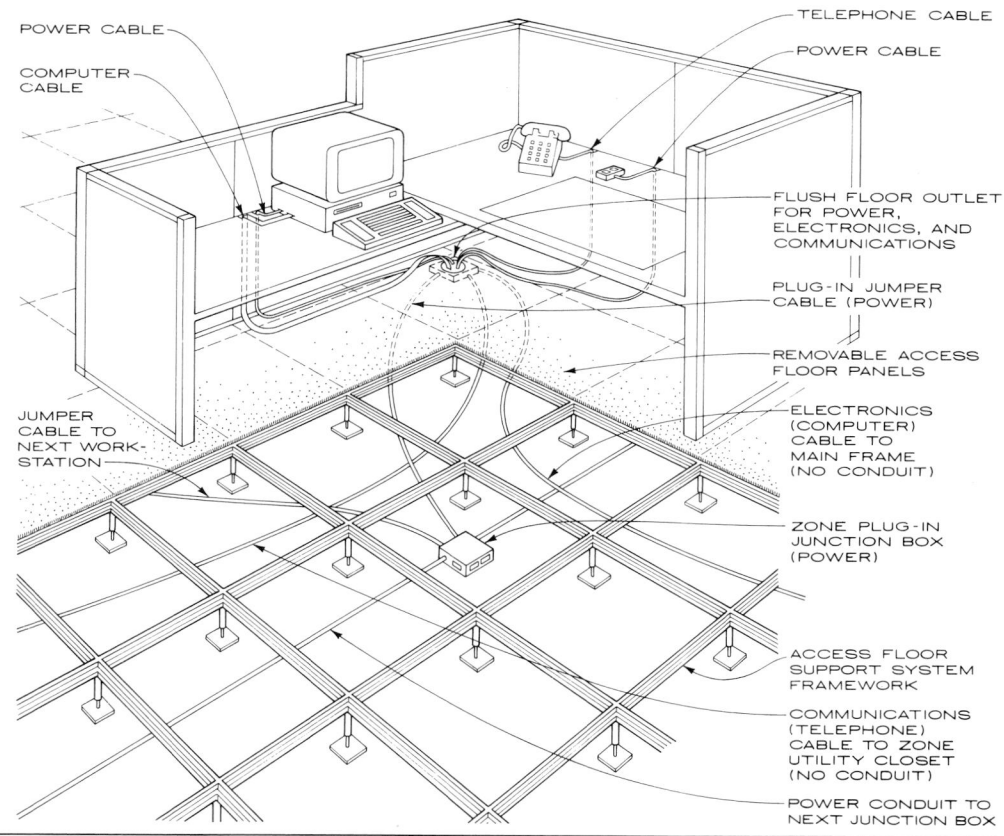

RAISED ACCESS FLOOR SYSTEM / MODULAR PLUG-IN DISTRIBUTION

NOTES

Undercarpet flat cable wiring has developed into a viable system to serve workstations. By code, it can only be used with carpet squares to afford an acceptable degree of access. Although there are some limitations in performance for flat communication (telephone) and computer (data) cables, improvements are continually being made. Flat cables are now available for Local Area Network (LAN) distribution, applicable where communication and data requirements are extensive.

Cables originate at transition boxes located at various intervals along core corridor walls and/or columns that are individually served from distribution centers in utility closets. Boxes can also be cast in the floor or atop a poke-through insert. Cables are not permitted to pass under fixed partitions and must be carefully mapped out to minimize crossovers and clutter.

To install a service fitting, an interface base assembly must first be secured directly to the concrete floor at the flat cable location. The base assembly stabs into conductors of the flat cable and converts them to round wire. When the service fitting is attached, it is activated and ready for use.

Careful consideration must be given to the application of this system based on limitations that may or may not be acceptable under different conditions. For instance, it may be ideal for small areas or renovation of existing buildings where the poke-through or power pole systems are unacceptable or cannot be used. In new buildings where poke-through has been chosen as the base system, the flat cable system is a viable solution in areas where poke-through outlets cannot be installed, such as slab on grade.

Where frequent changes and additions are contemplated, the resulting wear and tear on expensive, glued down carpet tiles may become a distinct disadvantage.

Although this system appears to be simple and inexpensive, it is highly labor intensive and actual installed initial costs and outlet relocation costs are comparable to cellular deck with trench header ducts.

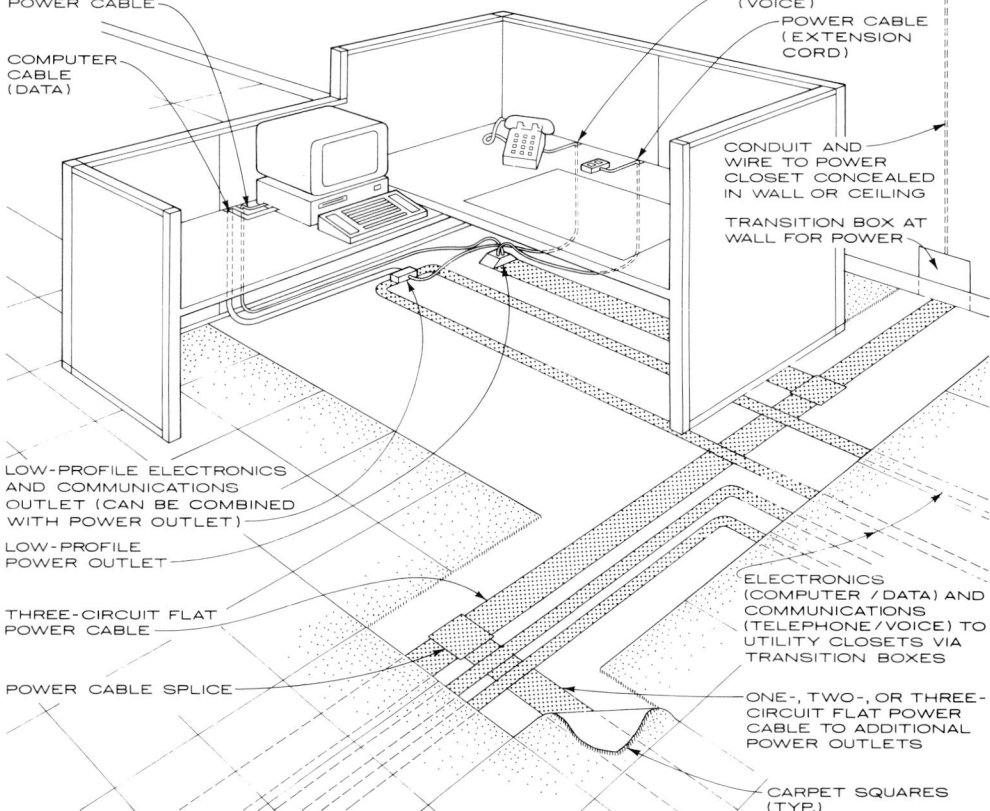

FLAT CABLE WIRING SYSTEM

Richard F. Humenn, PE; Joseph R. Loring & Associates, Inc., Consulting Engineers; New York, New York
Gary A. Hall; Hammel Green and Abrahamson; Minneapolis, Minnesota

UNDERGROUND DISTRIBUTION

Manholes are provided for splicing and pulling of electrical cables for underground distribution. The ductbanks emanating out of the manhole are to be sized according to the latest edition of the National Electrical Code.

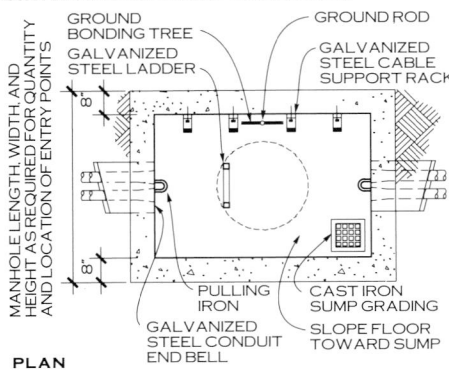

PLAN

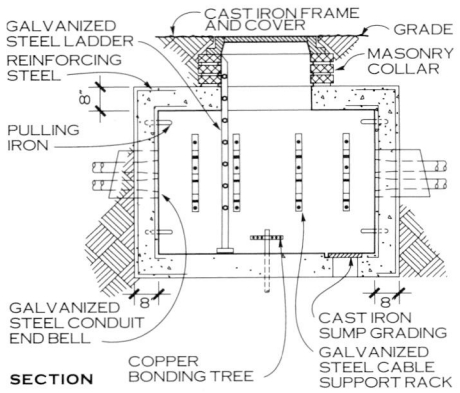

SECTION

MANHOLE DETAILS

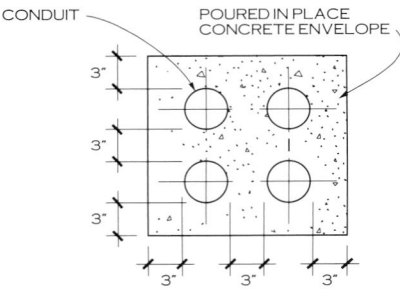

NOTE

Dimensions shown are minimum size overall, dimensions to suit.

CONCRETE ENCASED CONDUIT BANK

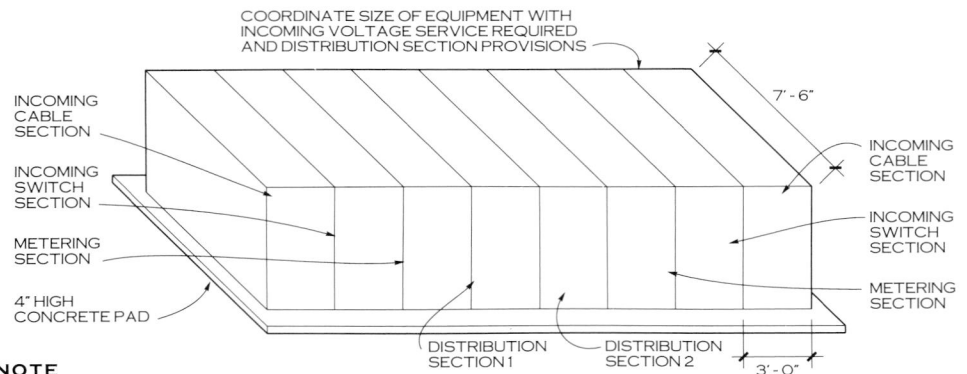

NOTE

Sizes are based on switchgear installed within shelter. If switchgear is to be rated for outdoor use, verify sizes with manufacturer. All clearances shall be coordinated with the National Electrical Code.

PRIMARY SWITCHGEAR WITH PRIMARY POWER FROM TWO SERVICES

OVERHEAD DISTRIBUTION

Overhead distribution lines are supported by poles from the origination of the electric service to the termination point. Poles are fabricated out of various kinds of wood (e.g., pine or cedar) or steel, depending upon the type of equipment to be supported, weather conditions, and cost of material. Transformers mounted directly onto the poles or on platforms provide the required low voltage service to the final point. The spacing between poles, height of poles, and clearances between electric lines and the ground depend upon the type of terrain, weather environment and obstructions (e.g., inhabited area, waterways, railroads, roadways, etc.). Refer to the National Electrical Safety Code for restrictions.

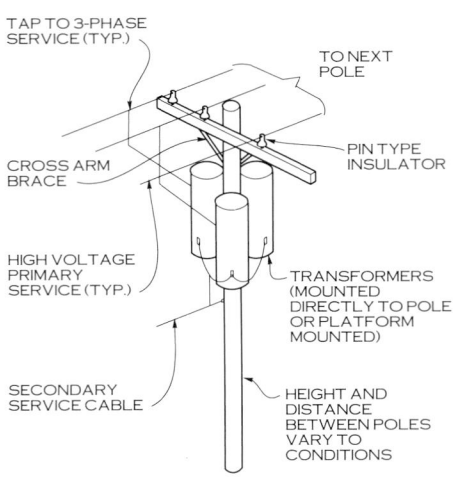

OVERHEAD POLE CONFIGURATION

PRIMARY SERVICE

Primary high voltage electrical service is received at a site via various stages, from the formation of electrical energy (water power, turbines, etc.), to substations that receive the electricity at high voltage and distribute this energy at a lower voltage via switchgear to the point of usage. At each stage, protective devices (switches or circuit breakers) are installed. Transformers are installed to reduce voltage along the lines for the requirements of the end user.

GROUNDING SYSTEMS

All buildings and equipment shall be grounded (or connected to earth) to protect people and equipment from fault currents. A complete interconnected system shall be installed according to the requirements of the National Electrical Code and the National Electrical Safety Code. In the diagram below, the structural steel of the building is connected to a buried "ground grid" to provide this requirement. All electrical equipment is interconnected with this system to provide a direct path to earth or ground.

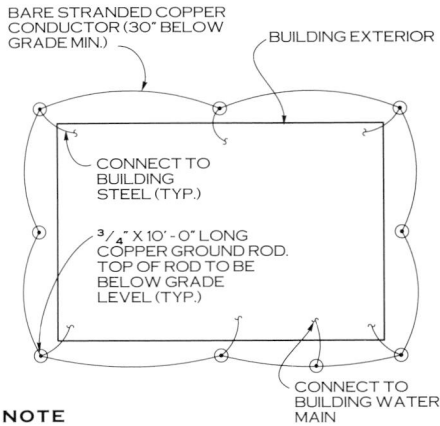

NOTE

Number of ground rods and conductor size according to National Electrical Code requirements.

BUILDING GROUND GRID

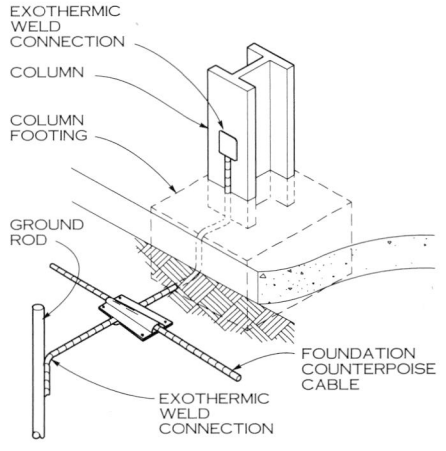

COLUMN BASE GROUNDING

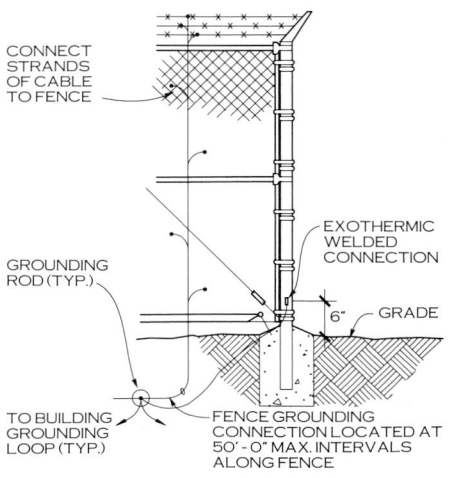

FENCE GROUNDING

F. Holdorf; Flack + Kurtz, Consulting Engineers; New York, New York

16 MEDIUM VOLTAGE DISTRIBUTION

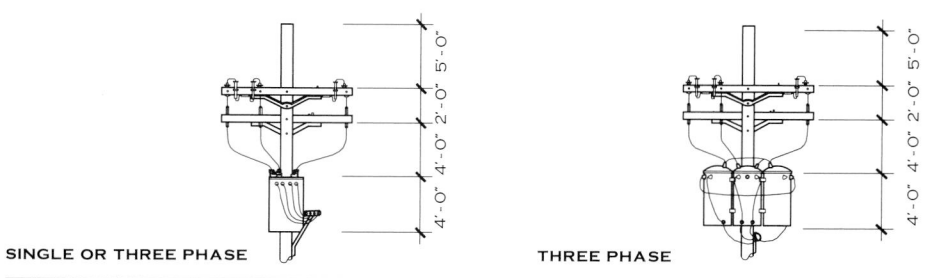

SINGLE OR THREE PHASE   THREE PHASE

OVERHEAD TRANSFORMER

OVERHEAD TRANSFORMER

Three-phase transformers are available up to 500 kVA in a single unit. Three single-phase units can total to 1500 kVA with adequate platform support. Service lateral to building can be either overhead or underground.

Typical dimensions for 15 and 25 kV. See the National Electrical Safety Code (ANSI C2) for required clearances.

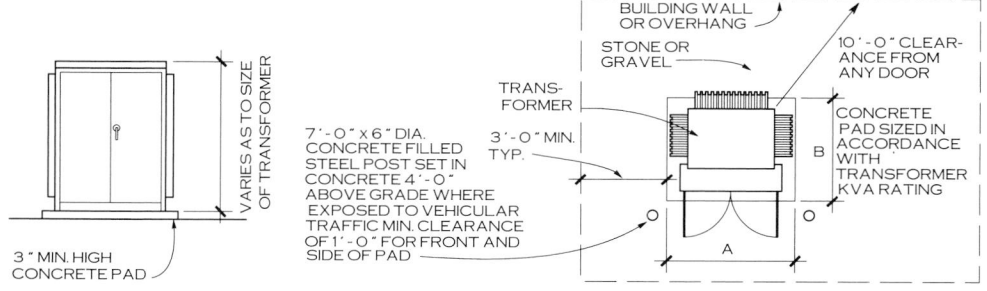

PAD MOUNTED TRANSFORMER

PAD MOUNTED TRANSFORMER

Pad mounted transformers with weatherproof tamper-proof enclosures permit installation at ground level without danger from exposed live parts. Three-phase units up to 1500 kVA are available and are normally used with underground primary and secondary feeders. Customer's grounding grids or grounding electrical conductors should not be connected at pad mounted transformer locations.

TYPICAL PAD SIZES

POWER	A	B
150 - 300 KVA	75 in.	80 in,
500 - 1500 KVA	84 in.	84 in.

High voltage compartment requires 10 ft clearance for on-off operation of the insulated stick located on the transformer (known as "hot stick" operation).

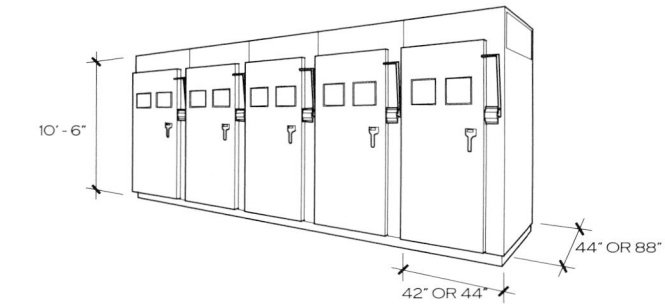

10' - 6"

44" OR 88"

42" OR 44"

PRIMARY SWITCHGEAR

PRIMARY SWITCHGEAR

Where the owner's buildings cover a large area such as a college campus or medical center, the application usually requires the use of medium voltages of 5kV to 34 kV for distribution feeders. Therefore, the utility company will terminate its primary feeders on the owner's metal clad or metal enclosed switchgear. This switchgear may be interior or exterior weatherproof construction. Code clearance in front and back of board must be provided in accordance with the National Electrical Code.

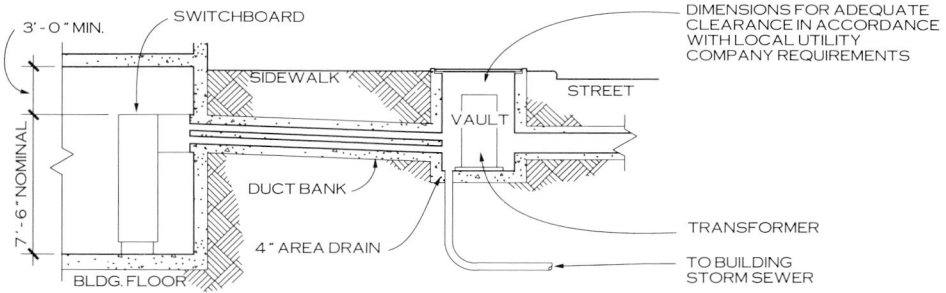

UNDERGROUND VAULT

UNDERGROUND VAULT

Underground vaults are generally used for utility company transformers where all distribution feeders are underground. These systems usually constitute a network or spot network. Vaults often are located below the sidewalks and have grating tops. Transformer is usually liquid filled.

NOTE

If oil-filled transformer is used, oil interceptor is recommended before discharge to building storm sewer.

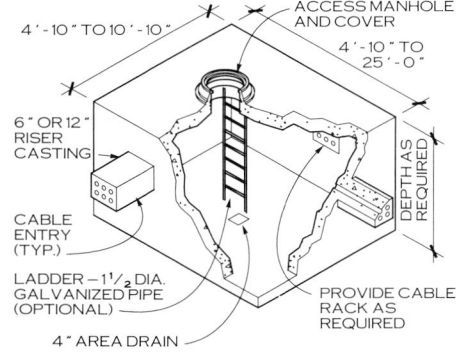

ACCESS BASIN

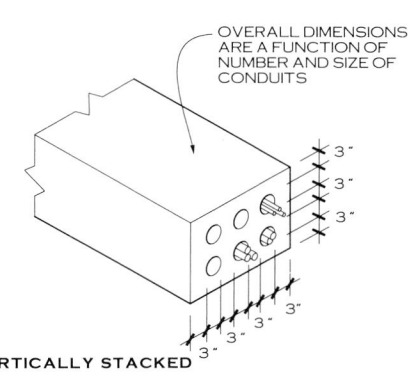

VERTICALLY STACKED

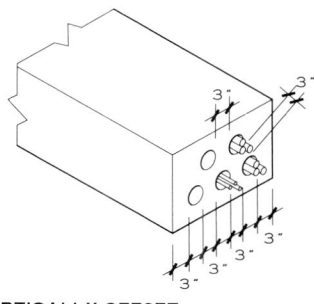

VERTICALLY OFFSET

UNDERGROUND DUCT BANK

William Tao & Associates, Inc., Consulting Engineers; St. Louis, Missouri
Dennis W. Wolbert; Everett I. Brown Company; Indianapolis, Indiana

MEDIUM VOLTAGE DISTRIBUTION   16

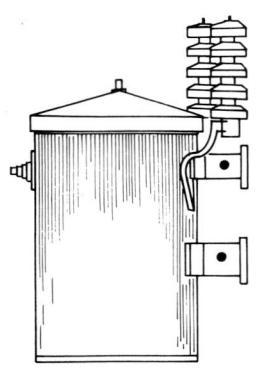
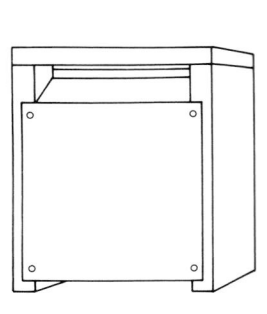
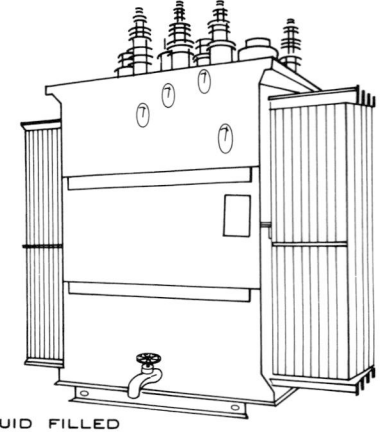
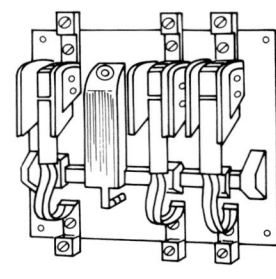

DISTRIBUTION   DRY TYPE   LIQUID FILLED

DISTRIBUTION: Rated secondary voltages: 208, 240, or 480. Immersed in oil. Self-cooled. Primarily mounted on outdoor poles.
DRY: Rated secondary voltages: 120/208 or 240 volts or three phase. Primarily mounted on indoor floors and walls.
LIQUID: Secondary substation transformer with high to low voltage. Primarily a commercial type transformer for the outdoors. Optional external fan cooling.

Rated voltage: 600 VAC. For circuits that are closed and opened repeatedly various design combinations are allowed. Used for all classes of magnetically held loads, open or closed.

TRANSFORMERS

CONTACTOR

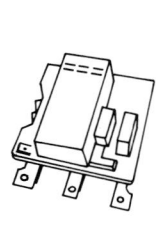
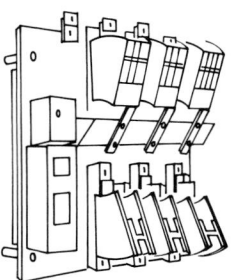
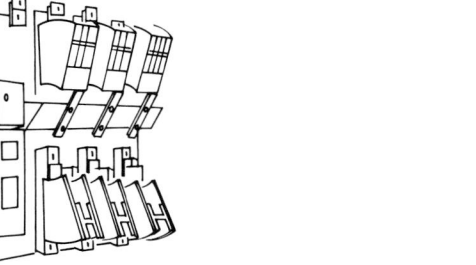
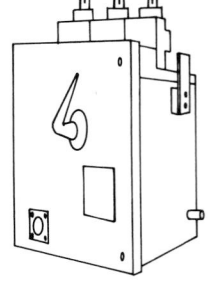

REMOTE CONTROL   AUTOTRANSFER   NETWORK TYPE

REMOTE CONTROL: Provides convenient control of lighting and power circuits from control stations.
AUTOTRANSFER: Automatically transfers loads from a normal source to the emergency source.

Maximum voltage: 125/216 VAC or 277/480 VAC. Interrupting capacity 30,000 and 60,000 A. RMS. SYM. A fault on primary cable or network transformer will open protector to isolate fault from system.

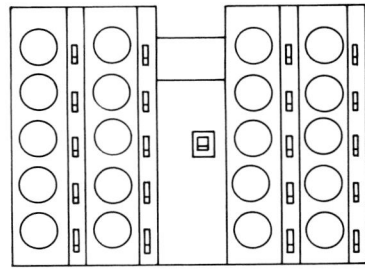

MULTIPLE METER BANK WITH MAIN CIRCUIT BREAKER

Voltage ratings: 120/240, 3 wire, single phase or 208V/120, 4 wire three phase. Either indoor or outdoor construction. Number of sockets as required by application.

SWITCHES

PROTECTOR

METER BANK

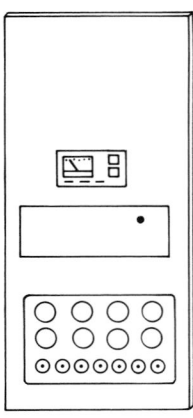
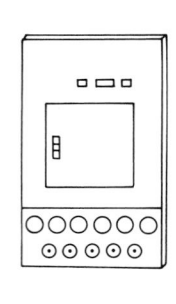
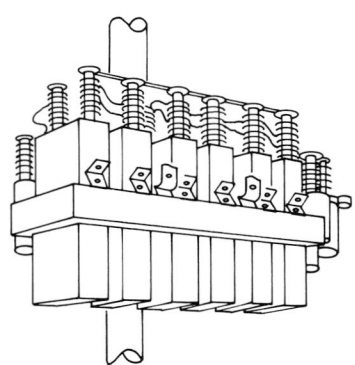
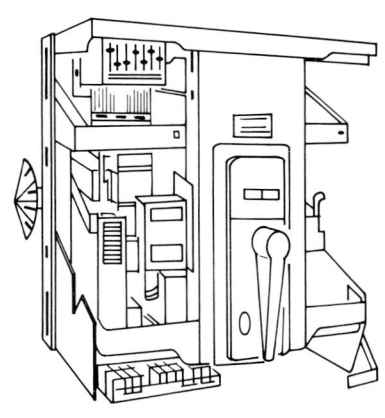

LARGE   SMALL   POLE RACK   LOW VOLTAGE

PRIMARY VOLTAGES: 120, 208, 240, or 277.
SECONDARY VOLTAGE: 120.
APPLICATION: Power and lighting panels, special panels for hospitals (operating, coronary, and X-ray).

Application: Power factor correction on either low or high voltage systems. Types, indoor or outdoor. Size and voltage as required. Switched or floating.

Rated voltages: 240 VAC, 480 VAC, 600 VAC, and 250 VDC. Operation is manual or electric. Breaker trip devices: Electromechanical or solid state. Type: stationary or drawout.

ISOLATED POWER CENTER

CAPACITOR

DISTRIBUTION CIRCUIT BREAKER

A. A. Erdman; Sargent, Webster, Crenshaw & Folley; Architects Engineers Planners; Syracuse, New York

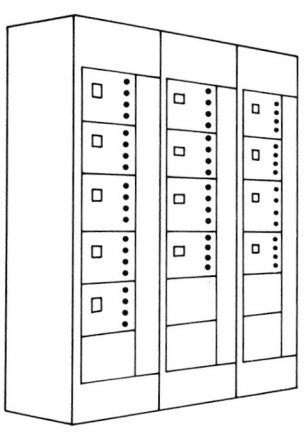

MOTOR CONTROL CENTER

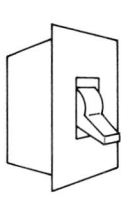
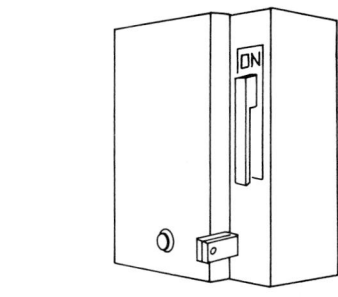

MANUAL   MAGNETIC   COMBINATION

MANUAL: Maximum voltage—240 VAC. Maximum horsepower—1.
MAGNETIC: Maximum voltage—600 VAC. Maximum horsepower—200.

COMBINATION: A magnetic motor starter with a variety of fusible disconnects or circuit breakers.

MOTOR STARTERS

UNIT SUBSTATION: Primary entrance cubicle, air interrupter switch, transformer section, and low voltage distribution sections. See manufacturer's literature for type, size, and arrangements. See National Electric Code for required aisle space, ventilation, servicing area, and special building condition requirements.

UNIT SUBSTATION

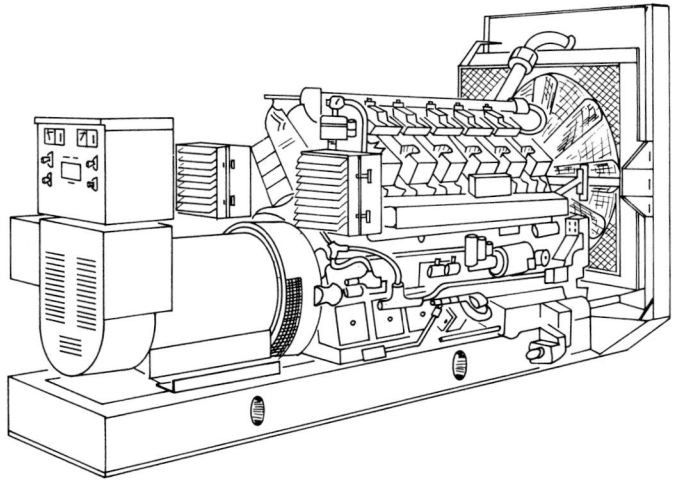

SECONDARY   WITH MAIN

SWITCHBOARD: Metering compartment, main disconnect, check meters, and low voltage distribution section. See manufacturer's literature for type, size, and arrangements. See National Electric Code for required aisle space, servicing area, and room layout.

SWITCHBOARDS

EMERGENCY GENERATOR: Engine driven prime mover, alternator, and controls. Application: to provide emergency power during power outages. See manufacturer's literature for ratings, dimensions, weight, ventilation, and fuel consumption. See National Electric Code for working space requirements and proper application.

EMERGENCY GENERATOR WITH CONTROL PANEL (800 KW)

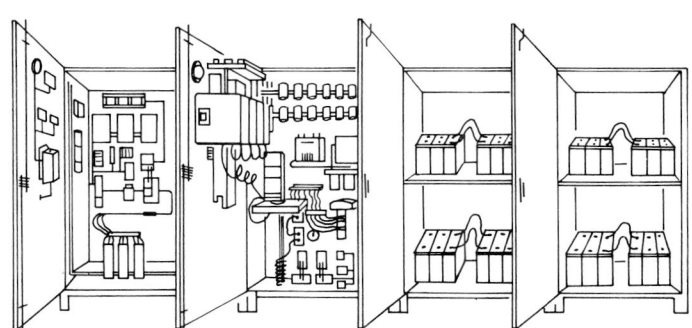

UNINTERRUPTIBLE POWER SUPPLY: D.C. batteries, battery charger, rectifier, and static inverter. Application: to provide continuous power during outage or abnormal transient power conditions. See manufacturer's literature for ratings, dimensions, weight, and ventilation requirements. See National Electric Code for working space requirements.

UNINTERRUPTIBLE POWER SUPPLY

A. A. Erdman; Sargent, Webster, Crenshaw & Folley; Architects Engineers Planners; Syracuse, New York

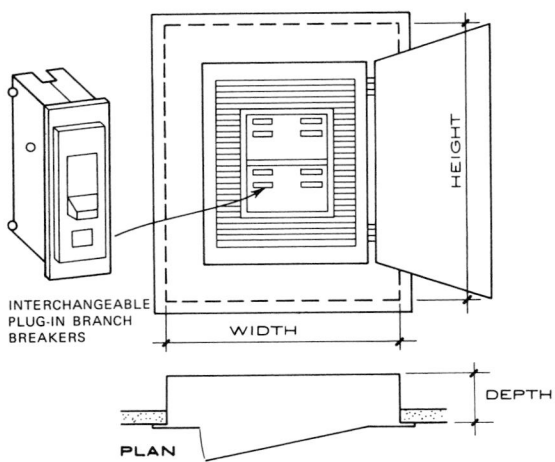

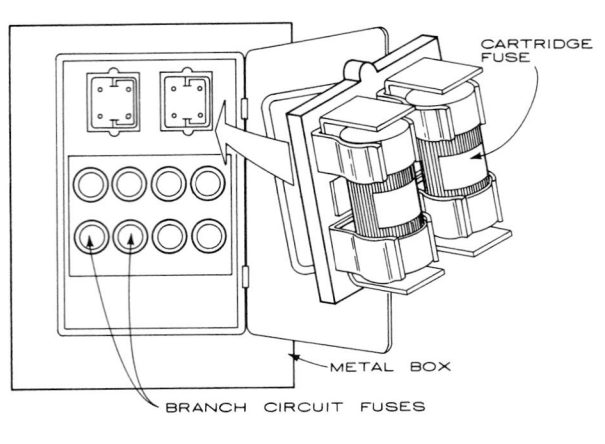

INTERCHANGEABLE PLUG-IN BRANCH BREAKERS

HEIGHT

WIDTH

PLAN

DEPTH

PLUG-IN CIRCUIT BREAKER

CARTRIDGE FUSE

METAL BOX

BRANCH CIRCUIT FUSES

FUSE BOX WITH FUSED MAIN DISCONNECTS

RESIDENTIAL AND SMALL COMMERCIAL PANEL BOARDS

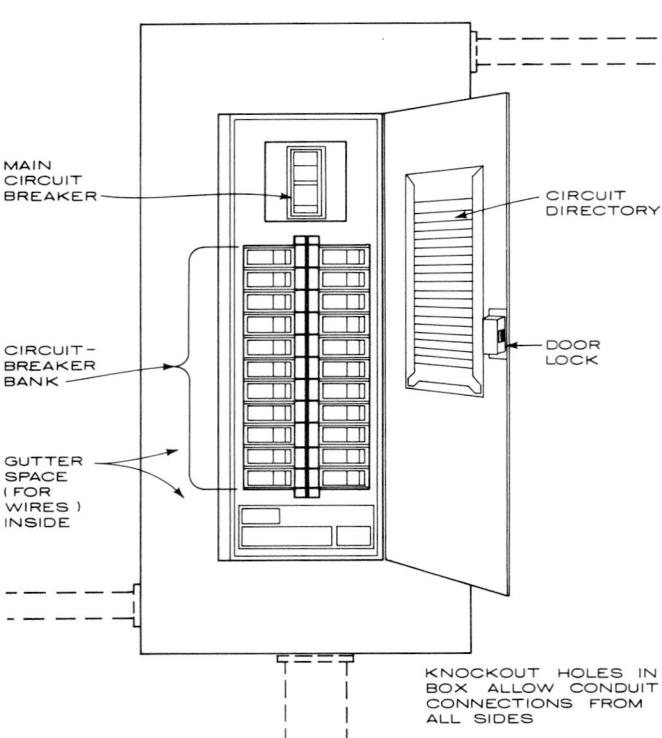

MAIN CIRCUIT BREAKER

CIRCUIT DIRECTORY

CIRCUIT-BREAKER BANK

DOOR LOCK

GUTTER SPACE (FOR WIRES) INSIDE

KNOCKOUT HOLES IN BOX ALLOW CONDUIT CONNECTIONS FROM ALL SIDES

LARGE RESIDENTIAL PANELBOARD

PANELBOARD DIMENSIONS

MAXIMUM NUMBER OF CIRCUITS	BOX DIMENSIONS (IN.)		
	WIDTH	HEIGHT	DEPTH
12	9-15	16-20	$3^3/_4$-$4^5/_8$
20	9-15	$20^1/_4$-24	$3^3/_4$-$4^5/_8$
30	12-15	30-33	$3^3/_4$-$4^5/_8$
40	14-15	34-39	4-$4^5/_8$

Darrel Downing Rippeteau, Architect; Washington, D.C.

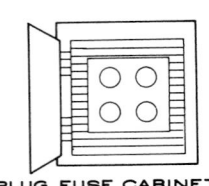

Box dimensions below. For outside dimension add 1 1/4'' to height & width.

PLUG FUSE CABINET

PLUG FUSE

BOX DIMENSIONS (IN.)

BRANCHES	HEIGHT	WIDTH	DEPTH
2	6 5/8	6 5/8	2 3/4
4	6 5/8	6 5/8	2 3/4
6	11 1/8	7 3/8	3 1/8
8	14 1/8	7 3/8	3 1/8

Up to 12 branches same as 8 branches

PLUG FUSE AND PLUG FUSE CABINET
FOR APARTMENTS AND SMALL HOUSES

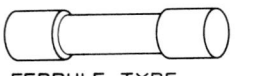

FERRULE TYPE   KNIFE BLADE TYPE

CARTRIDGE FUSES

Ferrule contact 1 to 60 amps.
Knife blade contact 70 to 600 amps and larger.
Ferrule type non-renewable.   Knife blade type non-renewable and renewable link.

STANDARD FUSE SIZES

Plug Fuse: 1, 3, 5, 6, 8, 10, 15, 20, 25 and 30 amperes.
Cartridge: 1, 3, 6, 10, 15, 20, 25, 30, 35, 40, 50, 60, 70, 80, 90, 100, 110, 125, 150, 175, 200, 225, 250, 275, 300, 325, 350, 400, 450, 500, 600 amperes, and larger.

Standard knife switches are rated at 30, 60, 100, 200, 400 & 600 amps, and take cartridge fuses up to and including their rating.

Circuit breakers at 50 (trip at 15, 20, 30, 40, 50); 100 (trip at 15, 20, 30, 40, 50, 70, 100); 225 (70 — 225, increment 25); 600 (125 — 350, increment 25 & 400, 500, 600 amp.)

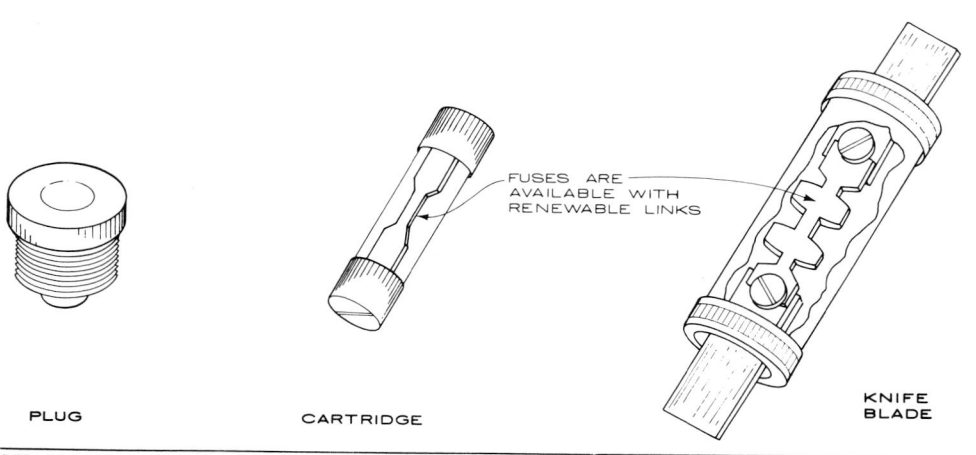

PLUG FUSES
1. RATED VOLTAGE: 125.
2. AMPERE RATING: 1–30 A.
3. FUSE TYPES: S, T

CARTRIDGE FUSES
1. RATED VOLTAGE: 250 AND 600.
2. AMPERE RATINGS: 1/10–60 A.
3. FUSE TYPES: K1, RK1, K5, RK5, J, H, and G.

KNIFE BLADE FUSES
1. RATED VOLTAGE: 250 AND 600.
2. AMPERE RATINGS: 70–6000 A.
3. FUSE TYPES: K1, RK1, K5, RK5, J, H, G, and L.

NOTE: Cartridge and knife blade fuses available for short circuit protection up to 200,000 A (Rms).

FUSES ARE AVAILABLE WITH RENEWABLE LINKS

PLUG   CARTRIDGE   KNIFE BLADE

STANDARD FUSES

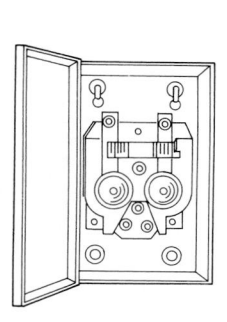
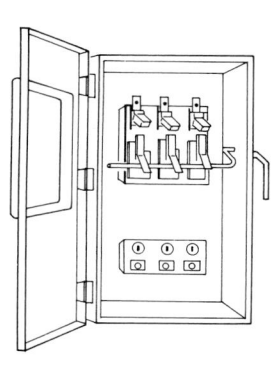
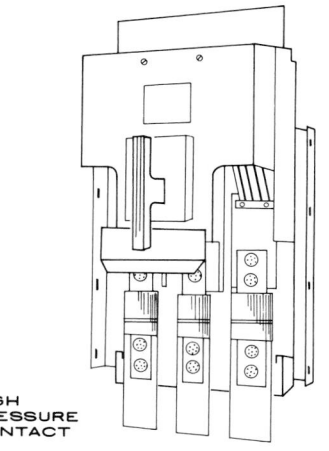

TOGGLE SWITCHES
1. MAXIMUM VOLTAGES: 125 VAC/DC, 125 or 250 VAC/DC, or 240 VAC.
2. RATING: 30 A max.

FUSED SAFETY SWITCHES
1. RATED VOLTAGES: 240 VAC, 125–250 VDC, 600 VAC.
2. POLES: 2, 3, or 4 plus S/N and/or GRD Lug.
3. TYPES: TG, TH, or TC fusible and no fuse.
4. RATING: 30–1200 A.

HIGH PRESSURE CONTACT SWITCHES
1. RATED VOLTAGES: 240 VAC or 480 VAC.
2. POLES: 3.
3. RATINGS: 800–4000 A.

PLUG FUSE BOX   FUSED SAFETY SWITCH   HIGH PRESSURE CONTACT

DISCONNECT SWITCHES

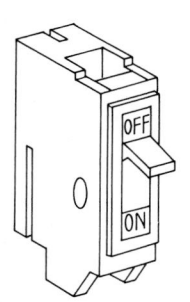

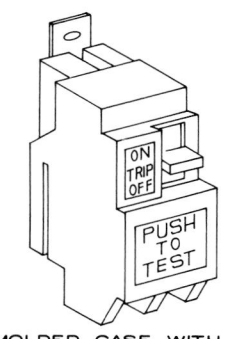

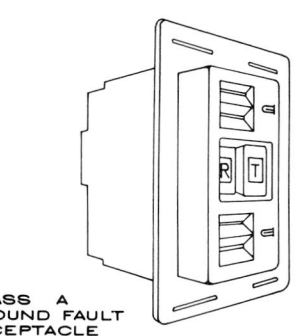

STANDARD MOLDED CASE CIRCUIT BREAKERS
1. RATED VOLTAGES: 120 VAC, 240 VAC, 600 VAC, 125 VDC, and 250 VDC.
2. FRAME SIZES: 100 A, 150 A, 225 A, 400 A, 600 A, 800 A, 1200 A Poles—2 or 3 above 100 A.
3. Current limiting type with fuses.

MOLDED CASE CIRCUIT BREAKERS INCORPORATING GROUND FAULT CIRCUIT INTERRUPTION
1. RATED VOLTAGES: 120 VAC or 120/240 VAC.
2. FRAME SIZE: 100 A ratings, 15–30 A poles—1 or 2.

CLASS A GROUND FAULT CIRCUIT INTERRUPTION RECEPTACLES
1. RATED VOLTAGE: 125 VAC.
2. RATINGS: 15 or 20 A NEMA configuration duplex outlet.

MOLDED CASE   MOLDED CASE WITH GROUND FAULT   CLASS A GROUND FAULT RECEPTACLE

CIRCUIT BREAKERS

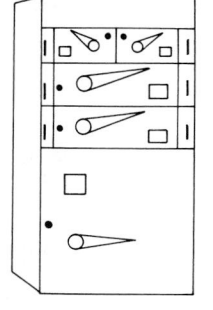

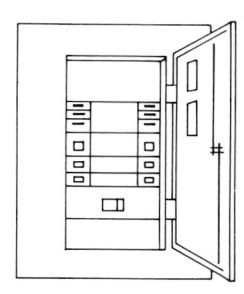

3-PHASE CIRCUIT BREAKER PANELS

MANUFACTURER	MAX. NO. OF POLES	BOX SIZES (IN.)		
		WIDTH	HEIGHT	DEPTH
Square D	12	20	20	5¾
	20	20	23	5¾
	42	20	35	5¾
General Electric Co.	12	20	21½	5¾
	20	20	27½	5¾
	30	20	33½	5¾
	42	20	36½	5¾
Westinghouse	12	20	21	5¾
	18	20	24	5¾
	30	20	30	5¾
	42	20	36	5¾

SWITCH AND FUSE   CIRCUIT BREAKER

DISTRIBUTION PANEL BOARDS

NOTE: Other manufacturers' panels are available in similar sizes.

A. A. Erdman; Sargent, Webster, Crenshaw & Folley; Architects Engineers Planners; Syracuse, New York

A-19

PS-52

PAR-38

R-40

T-6

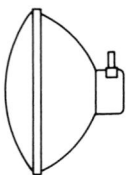

PAR-56

GENERAL SERVICE

BULB	DIA. (IN.)	LENGTH (IN.)	BASE	WATTS
A-15	1 7/8	3 1/2	Med.	15
A-19	2 3/8	4 7/16	Med.	60
A-21	2 5/8	5 5/16	Med.	100
PS-25	3 1/8	6 15/16	Med.	150
PS-30	3 3/4	8 1/16	Med.	300
PS-40	5	9 3/4	Mogul	500
PS-52	6 1/2	13 1/16	Mogul	1000

The efficacy of light production by incandescent filament lamps depends on the temperature of the filament—the higher the temperature, the greater the portion of radiated energy that falls in the visible region. Tungsten filaments have a high melting point (3655°K) and low vapor pressure, which permit higher operating temperatures and, as a result, high efficacies. Past improvements in incandescent lamps have involved changes in filament shape. Recent improvements, however, are primarily a result of changes in the atmosphere inside the glass bulb that encloses the filament. The discovery that inert gases retard evaporation of the filament made it possible to design lamps for higher filament temperatures. Today, most incandescent lamps use a fill mixture of argon and nitrogen.

PARABOLIC REFLECTORS

BULB	DIA. (IN.)	LENGTH (IN.)	BASE	WATTS
R-20	2 1/2	3 15/16	Med.	30
R-30	3 3/4	5 3/16	Med.	75
PAR-38	4 3/4	5 5/16	Med. skt.	150
PAR-38	4 3/4	5 5/16	Med. skt.	150
R-40	5	6 1/2	Med.	150
R-40	5	6 1/2	Med.	300
R-40	5	7 1/4	Mogul	500

The most popular incandescent lamps are general service (GS) ones, which range from the 15-W A-15 to the 1500-W PS-52 types and are designed for 120-, 125-, and 130-V circuits. The letter prefix refers to the lamp shape—for example, PS has a pear straight neck; A is of the standard incandescent shape. Other common designations are G for globe and PAR for parabolic aluminizer reflector. The number following the letter prefix is the bulb diameter in eighths of an inch. For the same wattage, GS lamps (750 to 1000 hr of life) are more efficient than extended service (ES) lamps (2500 hr of life). ES lamps—for use where replacement costs are relatively high, such as hard-to-reach locations—achieve long life by use of a filament that is stronger, but less efficacious.

TUNGSTEN HALOGEN

BULB	DIA. (IN.)	LENGTH (IN.)	BASE	WATTS
T-4	1/2	3 1/8	Minicam	250
T-4	1/2	3 1/8	Rec. S.C.	400
PAR-56	7	5	End prong	500
T-3	3/8	4 11/16	Rec. S.C.	500
T-4	1/2	3 5/8	Minicam	500
T-6	3/4	5 5/8	Rec. S.C.	1000
T-3	3/8	10 1/16	Rec. S.C.	1500

TUNGSTEN HALOGEN lamps are a variation of incandescent filament sources. A halogen additive in the bulb reacts chemically with the tungsten, removing deposited tungsten from the bulb and redepositing it on the filament. This results in a lumen maintenance factor of close to 100%. (Lumen maintenance refers to the ability of a lamp to maintain a constant light output.) However, such a lamp does have a definite life, usually a maximum of 3000 hr. The smaller size, good optical control, and high color temperatures of tungsten-halogen lamps, as well as a continuous spectrum, particularly fit theatrical lighting needs.

INCANDESCENT LAMPS

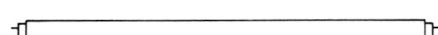

T-12

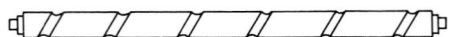

T-12

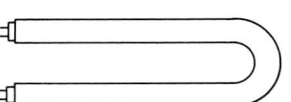

U-BENT

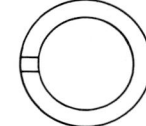

CIRCLINE

STANDARD TUBE

BULB	DIA. (IN.)	LENGTH (IN.)	BASE	WATTS
T-8	1	18	Med. bipin	15
T-12	1 1/2	24	Med. bipin	20
T-12	1 1/2	36	Med. bipin	30
T-12	1 1/2	48	Med. bipin	40
T-12	1 1/2	96	Single pin	75

NOTE: Dimensions are similar for preheat, rapid start, and extended service lamps.

FLUORESCENT lamps offer three to five times the efficacy of incandescent sources and compare favorably with most high intensity discharge sources. Efficacies vary with lamp length, lamp loading, and lamp phosphor coating.

Both geometric design and operating conditions of a fluorescent lamp affect the efficacy with which electrical energy is converted into visible radiation. For example, as lamp diameter increases, efficacy increases, passes through a maximum, then decreases. The length of the lamp also influences its efficacy: the longer it is, the higher the efficacy.

This lamp uses an electric discharge source, in which light is produced predominantly by fluorescent powders activated by ultraviolet energy generated by a mercury arc. The fluorescent lamp cannot be operated directly from the nominal 120-V ac source because the arc discharge would not be established. As a result, it must be operated in series with a ballast that limits the current and provides the starting and operating lamp voltages.

HIGH OUTPUT (800 mA)

BULB	DIA. (IN.)	LENGTH (IN.)	BASE	WATTS
T-12	1 1/2	48	Rec. D.C.	60
T-12	1 1/2	72	Rec. D.C.	85
T-12	1 1/2	96	Rec. D.C.	110
T-12*	1 1/2	72	Rec. D.C.	160
T-12*	1 1/2	96	Rec. D.C.	215

*Requires 1500 milli amps.

The starting process occurs in two stages. Once a sufficient voltage exists between an electrode and ground, ionization of the gas (mercury plus an inert gas) in the lamp occurs. Then a sufficient voltage must exist across the lamp to extend the ionization throughout the lamp and to develop an arc. Three basic types of ballasts—preheat, instant start, and rapid start—provide means of starting.

For the preheat variety, the electrodes are heated before the application of high voltage across the lamp. Arc initiation in instant start lamps depends entirely on the application of a high voltage (400 to 1000 V) across the lamp, which ejects electrons by field emission. These electrons ionize the gas and initiate arc discharge. The rapid start principle makes use of electrodes that are heated continuously by means of low voltage windings built into the ballast. A power saving feature of rapid start circuits is that the lamps show little change in rated life as a result of frequent on/off/ on cycles.

SPECIAL SHAPES

BULB	DIA. (IN.)	LENGTH (IN.)	BASE	WATTS
U-Bent	1 1/2	22 1/2	Med. bipin	40
Circle	1 1/8	8 1/4 dia.	Four pin	22
Circle	1 1/4	12 dia.	Four pin	32
Circle	1 1/4	16 dia.	Four pin	40

NOTE: Fluorescent lamps are available in cool white, warm white, and daylight tints.

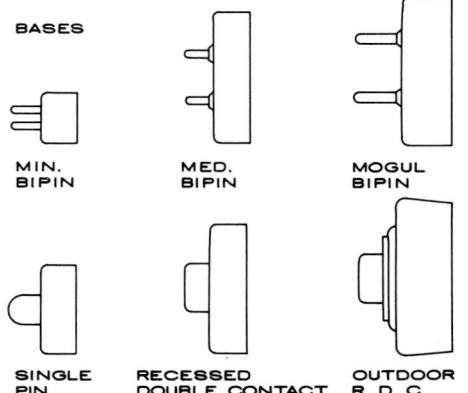

BASES

MIN. BIPIN   MED. BIPIN   MOGUL BIPIN

SINGLE PIN   RECESSED DOUBLE CONTACT   OUTDOOR R. D. C.

FLUORESCENT LAMPS

William G. Miner, AIA, Architect; Washington, D.C.

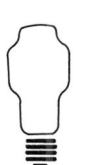

B-21   R-60   BT-28   BT-37   BT-25   E-18

MERCURY VAPOR

BULB	DIA. (IN.)	LENGTH (IN.)	BASE	WATTS
B-17	$2^1/_8$	$5^1/_8$	Med.	40
B-21	$2^5/_8$	$6^1/_2$	Med.	75
BT-25	$3^1/_8$	$7^1/_2$	Mogul	100
BT-28	$3^1/_2$	$8^5/_{16}$	Mogul	250
BT-37	$4^5/_8$	$11^1/_2$	Mogul	400
R-60	$7^1/_2$	$10^7/_8$	Mogul	400
BT-56	7	$15^3/_8$	Mogul	1000

METAL-HALIDE

BULB	DIA. (IN.)	LENGTH (IN.)	BASE	WATTS
BT-28	$3^1/_2$	$8^5/_{16}$	Mogul	175
BT-37	$4^5/_8$	$11^1/_2$	Mogul	400
BT-56	7	$15^3/_8$	Mogul	1000
BT-56	7	$15^3/_8$	Mogul	1500

HIGH PRESSURE SODIUM

BULB	DIA. (IN.)	LENGTH (IN.)	BASE	WATTS
BT-25	$3^1/_8$	$7^5/_8$	Mogul	70
BT-25	$3^1/_8$	$7^5/_8$	Mogul	150
BT-28	$3^1/_2$	$8^5/_{16}$	Mogul	150
E-18	$2^1/_4$	$9^3/_4$	Mogul	250
E-18	$2^1/_4$	$9^3/_4$	Mogul	400
BT-37	$4^5/_8$	$11^1/_2$	Mogul	400
E-25	$3^1/_8$	$15^1/_{16}$	Mogul	1000

MERCURY lamps, which are now popular for lighting commercial interiors, use argon gas to ease starting because mercury has a low vapor pressure at room temperature. When the lighting circuit is energized, the starting voltage is impressed across the gap between the main electrode and the starting electrode, which creates an argon arc that causes the mercury to vaporize. The lamp warmup process takes 5 to 7 min, depending on ambient temperature conditions. Most mercury lamps are constructed with two envelopes—an inner one that contains the arc and an outer one that shields the arc tube from outside drafts and changes in temperature. The outer envelope usually contains an inert gas.

The mercury spectrum results in greenish-blue light at efficacies of 30 to 65 lm/W, which ranks it between incandescent and fluorescent lamps. Economics favor mercury where burning hours are long, service is difficult, and replacement labor is high. Many mercury lamps lose as much as 50% of their initial output during their rated life of 24,000 hr or more.

METAL-HALIDE lamps are similar in construction to the mercury lamp, except that the arc tube contains various metal halides in addition to mercury. When the halide vapor approaches the high temperature, central core of the discharge, it disassociates into the halogen and the metal, with the metal radiating its appropriate spectrum. As the halogen and metal move near the cooler arc tube wall by diffusion and convection, they recombine, and the cycle repeats itself.

These lamps generate light with more than half the efficacy of the mercury arc, offer a small light source size for optical control, and provide good color rendition as compared with clear mercury. They have been applied in nearly every type of interior and exterior lighting application because they offer an efficient "white," light source. The average rated life of this lamp is 15,000 hr.

In both low pressure and high pressure sodium sources, light is produced by electricity passing through sodium vapor. In the LPS lamp, a starting gas of neon produces

a red glow when the lamp is initially ignited. As heat is generated, the sodium metal vaporizes, and the emitted light turns into the characteristic yellow color.

HIGH PRESSURE SODIUM (HPS) lamps are used for roadway and sidewalk illumination and offer more suitable color rendition characteristics. Sodium is a particularly suitable gas because most of its radiation is concentrated in a wavelength interval where the sensitivity of the human eye is high. It also has a relatively low excitation energy.

The HPS lamp is constructed with two envelopes—the inner being polycrystalline alumina, which is resistant to sodium attack. The arc tube contains xenon as a starting gas and a small amount of sodium-mercury amalgam. The outer glass envelope is evacuated and protects against chemical attack of the arc tube and maintains the arc tube temperature.

HPS sources are compact, yet have high efficacies (up to 140 lm/W) and high lumen maintenance characteristics. They radiate energy across the visible spectrum and produce a golden-white color. They are available in sizes from 70 to 1000 W, with the low wattage sources finding application in residential street lighting and shopping mall illumination.

HPS lamps have five times the efficacy of incandescent sources, more than twice that of mercury, and 50% more than metal-halide.

HIGH INTENSITY DISCHARGE LAMPS

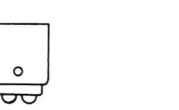

BAYONET SINGLE CONTACT   BAYONET DOUBLE CONTACT   CANDELABRA   CANDELABRA SKIRTED   END PRONG

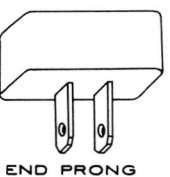
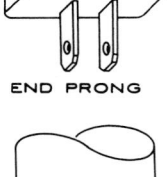
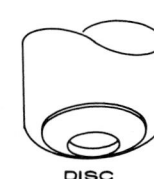

PREFOCUS   MOGUL   MEDIUM   MEDIUM SKIRTED   DISC

LAMP BASES

CHARACTERISTICS OF BASIC LAMP TYPES

CHARACTERISTICS	INCANDESCENT (INCLUDING TUNGSTEN HALOGEN)	FLUORESCENT	HIGH INTENSITY DISCHARGE (HID)		
			MERCURY-VAPOR	METAL-HALIDE	HIGH PRESSURE SODIUM
Wattages (lamp only)	15-1500	40-1000	40-1000	400, 100, 1500	75, 150, 250, 400, 1000
Life (hr)	750-12,000	9000-30,000	16,000-24,000	1500-15,000	10,000-20,000
Efficacy (lm/W, lamp only)	15-25	55-88	20-63	80-100	100-130
Color rendition	Very good to excellent	Good to excellent	Poor to very good	Good to very good	Fair
Light direction control	Very good to excellent	Fair	Very good	Very good	Very good
Source size	Compact	Extended	Compact	Compact	Compact
Relight time	Immediate	Immediate	3-5 min	10-20 min	Less than 1 min

William G. Miner, AIA, Architect; Washington, D.C.

LOW PRESSURE SODIUM LAMPS

BULB	DIA.	LENGTH	LUMENS	WATTS
T-17	2 1/8"	8 1/2"	1,800	18
T-17	2 1/8"	12 3/16"	4,800	35
T-17	2 1/8"	16 3/4"	8,000	55
T-17	2 1/8"	20 3/4"	13,500	90
T-17	2 1/8"	30 1/2"	22,500	135
T-17	2 1/8"	44 1/8"	33,000	180

NOTE: All lamps have DC bayonet bases.

Low pressure sodium lamps are used for security lighting and some roadway lighting. At the higher wattages, they have the highest efficacy of any electric lamps, and so are appealing when operating costs are considered. However, unlike all other electric lamps used for general lighting, they emit light at only two wavelengths: 589 nanometers (about 95% of the output) and 586 nanometers (about 5% of the output). This is light that is of an extremely limited yellow color, and has no color rendering capability.

T-8 LAMPS

LENGTH	NOMINAL WATTS	AVERAGE RATED LIFE	LUMENS
2 ft	17	20,000	±1325
3 ft	25	20,000	±2125
4 ft	32	20,000	±2850
5 ft	40	20,000	±3600

While T-8 (i.e., one-inch diameter) lamps have been available for many years in preheat form (meaning that an external "starter" is required) in short lengths, the newer breed of these narrower lamps is innovative in several ways:

They have an efficacy (lumens per watt) about 10% higher than T-12 lamps.

They are only available in the better color tri-phosphor.

Shorter (2 and 3 ft) and longer (5 ft) lengths are available in a rapid-start design.

When T-8 lamps are used in reflector designs that were developed for the larger T-12 lamps, the overall efficiency of the fixture (lumens out of the fixture relative to input lumens) is somewhat greater.

The increased efficacy of these lamps makes them appealing as an energy-saving strategy. For instance, while a four-foot long T-8 lamp produces about 11% less light (lumens) than a comparable T-12 – a reduction that is often negligible – it does so using about 20% less energy (watts), a significant reduction.

Although a T-8 lamp will physically fit into a fixture designed for a T-12 (since the overall length and the base pin configuration is the same), the ballasts are quite different, and the lamp will not operate. A four-foot T-8 lamp is a 32 watt lamp, whereas a standard four-foot T-12 is a 40 watt lamp. Additionally, there are differences in the ballast designs.

COMPACT FLUORESCENT LAMPS

BULB	±LENGTH (IN.)*	LIGHT OUTPUT EQUIVALENT TO INCANDESCENT (WATTS)	WATTS
Double	4 1/8	25	5
Double	5 1/4	40	7
Double	6 1/2	55	9
Double	7 1/2	60	13
Quad	6	60	13
Quad	6 13/16	75	18
Quad	7 5/8	100	26
Double 4 pin	9 to 10 1/2	75	18
Double 4 pin	12 11/16	100	24–27
Double 4 pin	16 1/2	150	39
Double 4 pin	22 1/2	175	36–39

*Length varies with manufacturer.

Compact fluorescent lamps provide the higher efficacy of fluorescent lamps in envelopes that are approximately the size of incandescent lamps, although of a different shape. Efficacy starts at about 50 lumens per watt for the smallest sizes, and extends to about 80 for the largest.

Compact fluorescent lamps have as good a color range as any fluorescent lamps, using improved phosphors throughout the line. The most commonly used sizes are available in three color temperatures: 2700°K, 3500°K, and 4100°K.

There are three major configurations of compact fluorescent lamps:

1. Two 1/2 in. diameter tubes attached to a base at one end, and joined at the opposite end; these range from about 4 1/4 in. long to about 7 1/2 in.
2. Four 1/2 in. diameter tubes attached to a base at one end, and joined in pairs at the opposite end; these range from just over 4 in. long to just under 8 in. long.
3. Two 5/8 in. diameter tubes attached to a four-pin base at one end, and joined at the opposite end; lengths are from about 9 in. to 22 1/2 in.

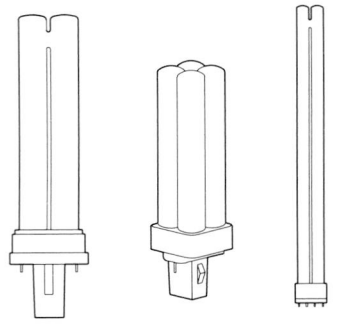

COMPACT FLUORESCENT LAMPS

Some incandescent fixtures, such as wall sconces and other decorative units, are now available with either incandescent sockets or compact fluorescent sockets and ballasts. Downlights and wall-washers, similar to A-lamp incandescent units, are also available with compact fluorescent lamps, in both one- and two-lamp configurations. The table indicates the approximate lumen-output equivalent in an incandescent general service A-lamp; these figures are for bare bulbs only, and do not take into account fixture efficiency, which may be lower, especially with fixtures that rely upon reflectors, for instance, downlights.

At this time the available lamp and ballast combinations are designed to work in a temperature range that limits compact fluorescent lamps to indoor, or warm climate outdoor, use. Dimming is just being developed for some of the quad and 4 pin-based lamps.

ELECTRONIC BALLASTS

COMPARISON OF BALLAST INPUT WATTS[1]

	2 T-12	2 T-8	3 T-12	3 T-8
Magnetic energy-saving	86	71	140	108[2]
Electronic	72	62	108	96

NOTES

1. Figures are averaged from several manufacturers.
2. One 1-lamp ballast + one 2-lamp ballast.

FLUORESCENT LAMP BALLASTS

All fluorescents require a ballast to operate. There are three major circuit designs for fluorescent ballasts: (1) preheat or trigger start, (2) instant start, and (3) rapid start.

1. The preheat is most commonly associated with double-ended fluorescent lamps in lengths of two feet or less, and separates the transformer portion of the ballast from the starting device. These lamps typically flicker a moment before coming onto full intensity, or they require a button to be held down for a moment and then released to start the lamp. Preheat lamps are not commonly used in commercial general lighting situations.

2. Instant start circuits bring the lamp to full intensity immediately by supplying a high voltage surge to the lamp cathodes, with no prior warm-up. This design provides the lowest energy consumption, at the expense of lamp life. For many years only the single-pin lamps known as slimlines used instant start circuits. That has changed with the design of some electronic ballasts.

3. A rapid start ballast applies a small heating voltage to the cathodes for about 750 milliseconds, and then strikes the arc through the lamp. This design provides the most gentle starting conditions, and so results in the longest lamp life, with a slightly higher energy consumption. Lamps designed for rapid start circuits are by far the most common type of fluorescent lamp in commercial and institutional lighting.

ELECTRONIC FLUORESCENT LAMP BALLASTS

Electronic ballasts were developed for several reasons. Among them are:

1. Lower energy use
2. Less weight
3. Reduced flicker
4. Less generation of heat, therefore less air conditioning
5. Quieter

ENERGY USE

Electronic ballasts can be designed that convert power from its line characteristics to the kind of power needed to start and operate a fluorescent lamp in a much more efficient manner than a conventional magnetic ballast. Any ballast draws some power that is not sent on to the lamp. Electronic ballasts draw less power that doesn't result in the production of light than magnetic ballasts. The table included summarizes some average figures on this subject.

The design of magnetic ballasts is such that lumen output is as close to the rated lumen output as possible. Most electronic ballasts are designed to do the same. However, there are electronic ballasts available that are intentionally designed to deliver less than the rated lumens, with a corresponding decrease in the input watts to the ballast, thus saving energy. These may be very useful when tailoring a particular fixture selection to a specific environment, but can be disappointing when they are selected only on the basis of input watts, and on the assumption that the lumen output will be as rated.

WEIGHT

Magnetic ballasts weigh between 3 and 5 lb. Electronic ballasts weigh 1 1/2 to 2 1/2 lb. In some instances, one electronic ballast may replace two magnetic ballasts (three and four lamp operation).

FLICKER

In the United States, power is supplied to buildings in the form of alternating current at 60 hertz (i.e., the current reverses direction 60 times every second). This results in a switching-off of power 120 times per second, and thus a very rapid flicker in all fluorescent lamps.

This flicker should not be confused with the very visible flicker sometimes evident when a lamp or ballast is failing. Although power is similarly switched to incandescent lamps, the heated filament that is producing the light does not extinguish so quickly.

Electronic ballasts provide power to the lamp at around 25,000 hertz, thus raising the flicker to 50,000 times per second, which is considered entirely invisible. Around five to ten percent of the population is consciously sensitive to the 60 cycle flicker in fluorescent lighting systems. Concern has recently been raised about the rest of the population since some studies seem to suggest that fewer symptoms of fatigue develop in offices where the higher frequency electronic ballasts are used. Also there is a potential interaction with the 60 cycle flicker of most computer screens that can be annoying.

AIR CONDITIONING

Since electronic ballasts consume less power that is not passed onto the lamp than magnetic ballasts, they also produce less heat. This means that less heat is generated by the lighting system that the air conditioning system must remove. Estimates suggest that for every three watts less in the lighting system, one or more watts are saved in the air conditioning system.

Robert Prouse, IALD, IES; H.M. Brandston & Partners, Inc.; New York, New York

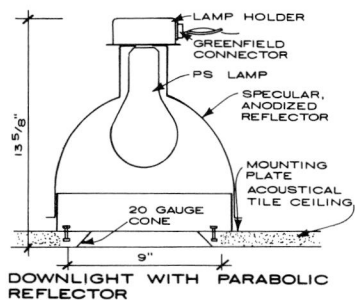

DOWNLIGHT WITH PARABOLIC REFLECTOR

The open reflector downlight uses general service lamps in a polished parabolic reflector to produce controlled light without a lens. The reflector efficiently redirects the upward component of the light source down through the aperture.

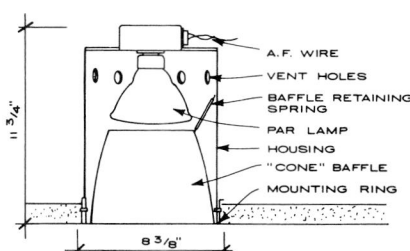

DOWNLIGHT WITH ELLIPTICAL REFLECTOR

A more sophisticated downlight uses a silver bowl lamp to project light up into an elliptical reflector. When the light source is located at one focal point the output light converges and can be redirected through a constricted aperture at the other focal point.

DOWNLIGHT WITH REFLECTOR LAMP

Downlights without reflectors or lenses are commonly called "cans." They have cylindrical housings and rely on a PAR or R lamp for optical control. Cones, annular rings, or lower type baffles will shield an observer from glare in the normal field of view.

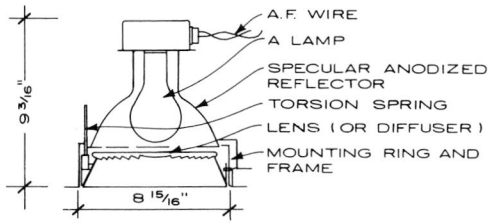

DOWNLIGHT WITH FRESNEL LENS

One downlight type combines a general service lamp with a reflector housing and a diffusing lens. The lens provides directional control of the light as it leaves the luminaire. The lens covers the ceiling aperture, thus keeping dust from the reflector and providing a heat shield.

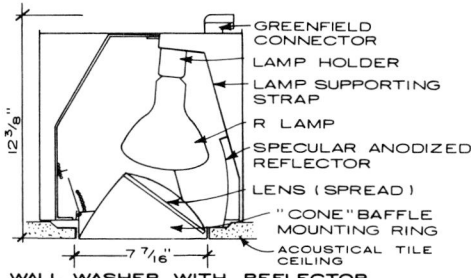

WALL WASHER WITH REFLECTOR LAMP AND LENS

Wall washers provide shadowless coverage of vertical surfaces with an even "wash" of light. They are used to set a mood within a space, to accent surrounding walls, or to obscure undesirable unevenness of the surface.

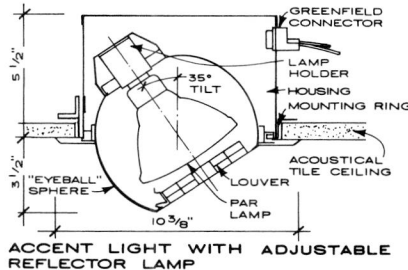

ACCENT LIGHT WITH ADJUSTABLE REFLECTOR LAMP

The accent light produces an asymmetrical distribution of light and normally allows for adjustments in the lamp position. It is used for gallery lighting to emphasize objects or small wall areas.

INCANDESCENT FIXTURES

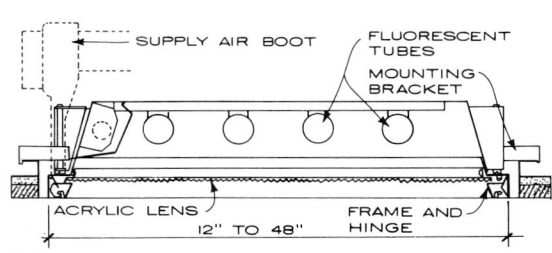

RECESSED UNIT WITH PRISMATIC LENS

The recessed fluorescent luminaire is usually designed to fit into a standard ceiling grid. A transparent, prismatic lens usually encloses the fixture and directs useful light to the work surface.

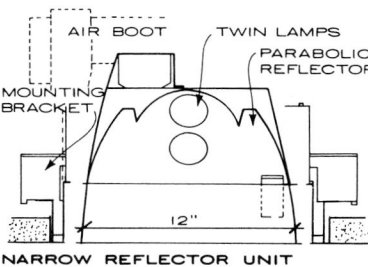

NARROW REFLECTOR UNIT

Parabolic reflectors are used in narrow profile fixtures to redirect the upward component of the light source down to the task area. The fluorescent lamps are stacked so that one may be switched off without sacrificing the even distribution of light.

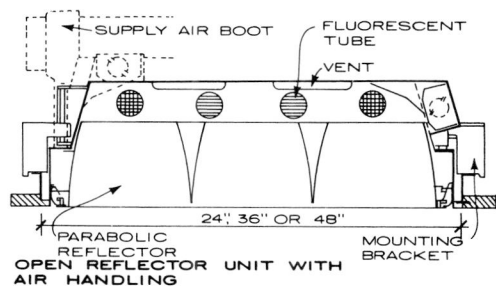

OPEN REFLECTOR UNIT WITH AIR HANDLING

Some open reflector units are fitted with parabola shaped louver blades to better control glare and veiling reflections. Air fittings are also integrated into the lamp housing for ducted air supply or return.

FLUORESCENT FIXTURES

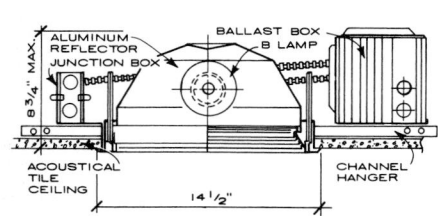

SQUARE LENS AND REFLECTOR UNIT

HID fixtures are usually preassembled and wired for fast installation. A recessed reflector with a fresnel or prismatic lens will maximize the utilization and control of the high lamp output.

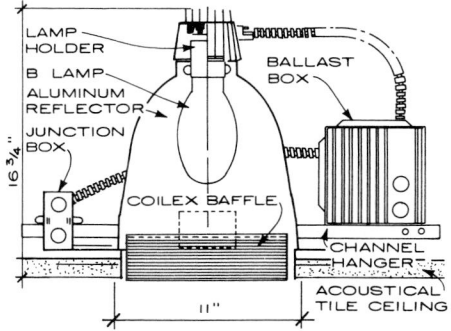

OPEN REFLECTOR DOWNLIGHT

HID luminaires require a deep ceiling space to fully recess the large lamp housing. Open reflector downlights often use elliptical reflectors that focus the lamp light through a small aperture. Coil or cone baffles help reduce fixture surface brightness.

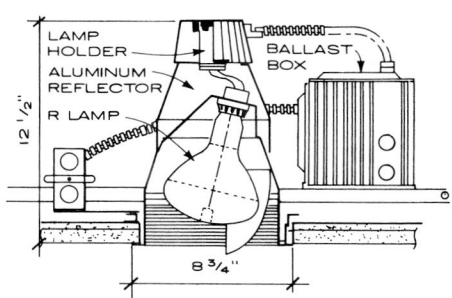

ADJUSTABLE WALL WASHER

A special scoop insert can be added to a standard downlight fixture to create a HID wall washer unit. The reflector and lamp socket can be rotated for desired positioning of light throw.

HIGH INTENSITY DISCHARGE FIXTURES

William G. Miner, AIA, Architect; Washington, D.C.

COEFFICIENTS OF UTILIZATION

TYPICAL LUMINAIRE	TYPICAL DISTRIBUTION AND PERCENT LAMP LUMENS: MAINT. CAT.	MAXIMUM S/MH GUIDE[4]	$\rho cc^{(1)}$ →	80			70			50			30			10			0
			$\rho w^{(2)}$ →	50	30	10	50	30	10	50	30	10	50	30	10	50	30	10	0
			RCR[3] ↓	COEFFICIENTS OF UTILIZATION FOR 20% EFFECTIVE FLOOR CAVITY REFLECTANCE (ρFC = 20)															
 Pendant diffusing sphere with incandescent lamp	V	1.5	0	.87	.87	.87	.81	.81	.81	.69	.69	.69	.59	.59	.59	.49	.49	.49	.44
	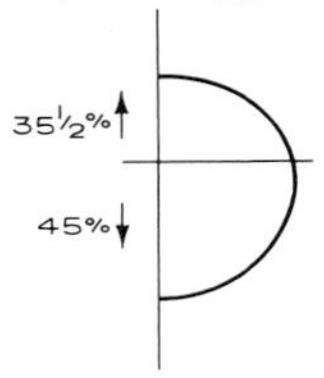35½%↑ 45%↓		1	.71	.67	.63	.66	.62	.59	.56	.53	.50	.47	.45	.43	.39	.37	.35	.31
			2	.61	.54	.49	.56	.50	.46	.47	.43	.39	.39	.36	.33	.32	.29	.27	.23
			3	.52	.45	.39	.48	.42	.37	.41	.36	.31	.34	.30	.26	.27	.24	.22	.18
			4	.46	.38	.33	.42	.36	.30	.36	.30	.26	.30	.26	.22	.24	.21	.18	.15
			5	.40	.33	.27	.37	.30	.25	.32	.26	.22	.26	.22	.19	.21	.18	.15	.12
			6	.36	.28	.23	.33	.26	.21	.28	.23	.19	.23	.19	.16	.19	.15	.13	.10
			7	.32	.25	.20	.29	.23	.18	.25	.20	.16	.21	.16	.13	.17	.13	.11	.09
			8	.29	.22	.17	.27	.20	.16	.23	.17	.14	.19	.15	.12	.15	.12	.09	.07
			9	.26	.19	.15	.24	.18	.14	.20	.15	.12	.17	.13	.10	.14	.11	.08	.06
			10	.23	.17	.13	.22	.16	.12	.19	.14	.10	.16	.12	.09	.13	.09	.07	.05
 Porcelain enameled ventilated standard dome with incandescent lamp	IV	1.3	0	.99	.99	.99	.97	.97	.97	.92	.92	.92	.88	.88	.88	.85	.85	.85	.83
	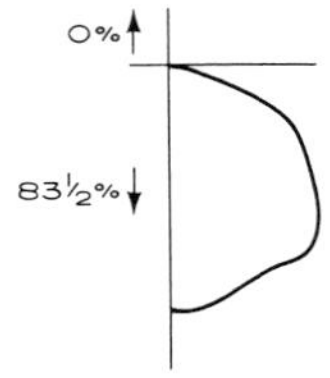0%↑ 83½%↓		1	.88	.85	.82	.86	.83	.81	.83	.80	.78	.79	.78	.76	.77	.75	.73	.72
			2	.78	.73	.68	.76	.72	.67	.73	.69	.66	.71	.67	.64	.68	.65	.63	.61
			3	.69	.62	.57	.67	.61	.57	.65	.60	.56	.63	.58	.55	.61	.57	.54	.52
			4	.61	.54	.49	.60	.53	.48	.58	.52	.48	.56	.51	.47	.54	.50	.46	.45
			5	.54	.47	.41	.53	.46	.41	.51	.45	.41	.50	.44	.40	.48	.43	.40	.38
			6	.48	.41	.35	.47	.40	.35	.46	.39	.35	.44	.39	.34	.43	.38	.34	.32
			7	.43	.35	.30	.42	.35	.30	.41	.34	.30	.39	.34	.30	.38	.33	.29	.28
			8	.38	.31	.26	.38	.31	.26	.37	.30	.26	.36	.30	.26	.35	.30	.26	.24
			9	.35	.28	.23	.34	.27	.23	.33	.27	.23	.32	.27	.23	.31	.26	.22	.21
			10	.31	.25	.20	.31	.24	.20	.30	.24	.20	.29	.24	.20	.29	.23	.20	.18
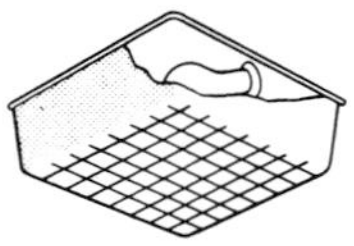 Prismatic square surface drum	V	1.3	0	.89	.89	.89	.85	.85	.85	.77	.77	.77	.70	.70	.70	.63	.63	.63	.60
	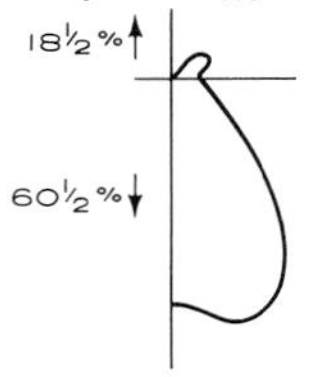18½%↑ 60½%↓		1	.78	.75	.72	.74	.72	.69	.68	.66	.64	.62	.60	.58	.56	.55	.54	.51
			2	.69	.65	.61	.66	.62	.58	.61	.57	.54	.56	.53	.50	.51	.49	.47	.44
			3	.62	.57	.52	.60	.55	.50	.55	.51	.47	.50	.47	.44	.46	.44	.41	.39
			4	.56	.50	.46	.54	.49	.44	.50	.45	.42	.46	.42	.39	.42	.39	.37	.35
			5	.51	.45	.40	.49	.43	.39	.45	.41	.37	.42	.38	.35	.39	.36	.33	.31
			6	.46	.40	.36	.45	.39	.35	.42	.37	.33	.39	.35	.31	.36	.32	.30	.28
			7	.42	.36	.32	.41	.35	.31	.38	.33	.29	.35	.31	.28	.33	.29	.27	.25
			8	.39	.32	.28	.37	.32	.28	.35	.30	.26	.32	.28	.25	.30	.27	.24	.22
			9	.35	.29	.25	.34	.29	.25	.32	.27	.24	.30	.26	.23	.28	.24	.22	.20
			10	.32	.27	.23	.31	.26	.22	.29	.25	.21	.27	.23	.20	.26	.22	.20	.18
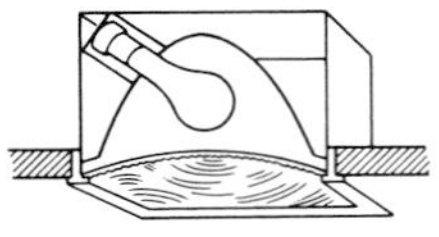 Medium distribution unit with lens plate and inside frost lamp	V	1.0	0	.64	.64	.64	.63	.63	.63	.60	.60	.60	.57	.57	.57	.55	.55	.55	.54
	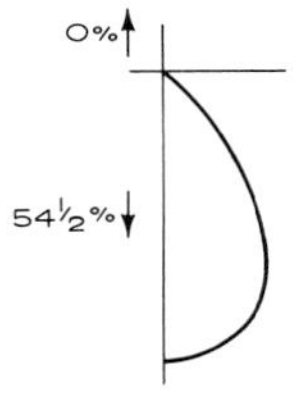0%↑ 54½%↓		1	.60	.58	.57	.58	.57	.56	.56	.55	.54	.54	.53	.52	.52	.52	.51	.50
			2	.55	.53	.51	.54	.52	.50	.52	.50	.49	.51	.49	.48	.49	.48	.47	.46
			3	.51	.48	.46	.50	.47	.45	.49	.46	.44	.47	.45	.44	.46	.44	.43	.42
			4	.47	.44	.41	.47	.44	.41	.45	.43	.41	.44	.42	.40	.43	.41	.40	.39
			5	.44	.40	.38	.43	.40	.38	.42	.39	.37	.41	.39	.37	.40	.38	.37	.36
			6	.41	.37	.35	.40	.37	.35	.39	.36	.34	.39	.36	.34	.38	.36	.34	.33
			7	.38	.34	.32	.37	.34	.32	.37	.34	.31	.36	.33	.31	.35	.33	.31	.30
			8	.35	.32	.29	.35	.31	.29	.34	.31	.29	.34	.31	.29	.33	.30	.29	.28
			9	.33	.29	.27	.32	.29	.27	.32	.29	.26	.31	.28	.26	.31	.28	.26	.25
			10	.30	.27	.25	.30	.27	.24	.30	.27	.24	.29	.26	.24	.29	.26	.24	.23
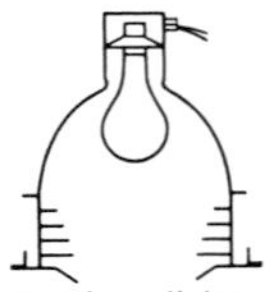 Reflector downlight with baffles and inside frosted lamp	IV	0.7	0	.53	.53	.53	.52	.52	.52	.49	.49	.49	.47	.47	.47	.45	.45	.45	.44
	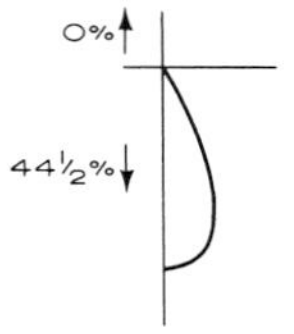0%↑ 44½%↓		1	.51	.50	.49	.50	.49	.48	.48	.47	.47	.46	.46	.45	.45	.44	.44	.43
			2	.48	.47	.46	.48	.46	.45	.46	.45	.44	.45	.44	.44	.44	.43	.43	.42
			3	.47	.45	.44	.46	.45	.43	.45	.44	.43	.44	.43	.42	.43	.42	.41	.41
			4	.45	.43	.42	.44	.43	.42	.43	.42	.41	.43	.41	.41	.42	.41	.40	.40
			5	.43	.41	.40	.43	.41	.40	.42	.40	.39	.41	.40	.39	.41	.40	.39	.38
			6	.42	.40	.39	.41	.40	.38	.41	.39	.38	.40	.39	.38	.40	.39	.38	.37
			7	.40	.38	.37	.40	.38	.37	.39	.38	.37	.39	.38	.37	.38	.37	.36	.36
			8	.39	.37	.36	.38	.37	.36	.38	.37	.35	.38	.36	.35	.37	.36	.35	.35
			9	.37	.36	.34	.37	.35	.34	.37	.35	.34	.36	.35	.34	.36	.35	.34	.33
			10	.36	.34	.33	.36	.34	.33	.36	.34	.33	.35	.34	.33	.35	.34	.33	.32

GENERAL NOTES

Luminaire data in this table are based on a composite of generic luminaire types. The polar intensity sketch (candlepower distribution curve) and the corresponding spacing to mounting height guide are representative of many luminaires of each type shown.

SYMBOLS

1. pcc = percent effective ceiling cavity reflectance.
2. pw = percent wall reflectance.
3. RCR = room cavity ratio.
4. Maximum S/MH guide = ratio of maximum luminaire spacing to mounting or ceiling height above work plane.

Maintenance categories (maint. cat.):

Cat. I	Bare lamps and strips
Cat. II	15% or more uplight, open or louvered Large louvered, 1 in. or more
Cat. III	Less than 15% uplight, open or louvered Small louvered, less than 1 in.
Cat. IV	Recessed with closed top only Lighted ceiling with louvers
Cat. V	Recessed with total enclosure Surface suspended and enclosed
Cat. VI	Totally direct Totally indirect lighting Lighted ceiling with solid diffuser

Illuminating Engineering Society; New York, New York

COEFFICIENTS OF UTILIZATION

TYPICAL LUMINAIRE	MAINT. CAT.	MAXIMUM S/MH GUIDE[4]	RCR[3] ↓	ρCC[1] → 80			70			50			30			10			0
				ρW[2] → 50	30	10	50	30	10	50	30	10	50	30	10	50	30	10	0

COEFFICIENTS OF UTILIZATION FOR 20% EFFECTIVE FLOOR CAVITY REFLECTANCE ($\rho FC = 20$)

R-40 flood without shielding — IV, 0.8, 0%↑, 100%↓

RCR	80/50	80/30	80/10	70/50	70/30	70/10	50/50	50/30	50/10	30/50	30/30	30/10	10/50	10/30	10/10	0
0	1.18	1.18	1.18	1.16	1.16	1.16	1.11	1.11	1.11	1.06	1.06	1.06	1.01	1.01	1.01	.99
1	1.09	1.07	1.04	1.07	1.05	1.02	1.03	1.01	.99	.99	.98	.96	.96	.95	.94	.92
2	1.01	.97	.93	.99	.95	.92	.96	.93	.90	.93	.90	.88	.90	.88	.86	.84
3	.93	.88	.84	.92	.87	.83	.89	.85	.81	.87	.83	.80	.84	.82	.79	.77
4	.87	.81	.76	.85	.80	.75	.83	.78	.75	.81	.77	.74	.79	.76	.73	.71
5	.80	.74	.69	.79	.73	.69	.77	.72	.68	.76	.71	.67	.74	.70	.67	.65
6	.74	.68	.63	.73	.67	.63	.72	.66	.62	.70	.66	.62	.69	.65	.61	.60
7	.69	.62	.57	.68	.62	.57	.67	.61	.57	.65	.60	.56	.64	.60	.56	.55
8	.64	.57	.53	.63	.57	.52	.62	.56	.52	.61	.56	.52	.60	.55	.52	.50
9	.59	.52	.48	.59	.52	.48	.58	.52	.48	.57	.51	.48	.56	.51	.47	.46
10	.55	.49	.44	.55	.48	.44	.54	.48	.44	.53	.48	.44	.52	.47	.44	.42

R-40 flood with specular anodized reflector skirt; 45° cutoff — IV, 0.7, 0%↑, 85%↓

RCR	80/50	80/30	80/10	70/50	70/30	70/10	50/50	50/30	50/10	30/50	30/30	30/10	10/50	10/30	10/10	0
0	1.00	1.00	1.00	.98	.98	.98	.94	.94	.94	.90	.90	.90	.86	.86	.86	.84
1	.96	.94	.92	.94	.92	.91	.90	.89	.88	.87	.86	.85	.84	.84	.83	.82
2	.91	.88	.86	.90	.87	.85	.87	.85	.83	.84	.83	.82	.82	.81	.80	.79
3	.87	.84	.81	.86	.83	.81	.84	.81	.79	.82	.80	.78	.80	.78	.77	.76
4	.83	.80	.77	.82	.79	.77	.81	.78	.76	.79	.77	.75	.78	.76	.74	.73
5	.79	.76	.73	.79	.75	.73	.77	.74	.72	.76	.73	.71	.75	.73	.71	.70
6	.76	.73	.70	.76	.72	.70	.75	.72	.69	.74	.71	.69	.73	.70	.68	.67
7	.73	.69	.66	.73	.69	.66	.72	.68	.66	.71	.68	.66	.70	.67	.65	.64
8	.70	.66	.63	.70	.66	.63	.69	.65	.63	.68	.65	.63	.67	.65	.63	.62
9	.67	.63	.60	.67	.63	.60	.66	.62	.60	.65	.62	.60	.65	.62	.60	.59
10	.64	.60	.58	.64	.60	.58	.63	.60	.58	.63	.60	.57	.62	.59	.57	.56

Intermediate distribution ventilated reflector with clear HID lamp — III, 1.0, 1%↑, 76%↓

RCR	80/50	80/30	80/10	70/50	70/30	70/10	50/50	50/30	50/10	30/50	30/30	30/10	10/50	10/30	10/10	0
0	.91	.91	.91	.89	.89	.89	.84	.84	.84	.81	.81	.81	.77	.77	.77	.75
1	.84	.81	.79	.82	.80	.78	.79	.77	.76	.76	.74	.73	.73	.72	.71	.69
2	.77	.73	.70	.76	.72	.70	.73	.70	.68	.70	.68	.66	.68	.66	.65	.63
3	.71	.66	.63	.69	.65	.62	.67	.64	.61	.65	.62	.60	.63	.61	.59	.57
4	.65	.60	.56	.64	.59	.56	.62	.58	.55	.60	.57	.54	.59	.56	.54	.52
5	.59	.54	.50	.59	.54	.50	.57	.53	.50	.56	.52	.49	.54	.51	.48	.47
6	.54	.49	.45	.54	.49	.45	.52	.48	.45	.51	.47	.44	.50	.47	.44	.42
7	.50	.44	.40	.49	.44	.40	.48	.43	.40	.47	.43	.39	.46	.42	.39	.38
8	.45	.40	.36	.45	.40	.36	.44	.39	.36	.43	.39	.35	.42	.38	.35	.34
9	.41	.36	.32	.41	.36	.32	.40	.35	.32	.39	.35	.32	.38	.35	.32	.30
10	.38	.33	.29	.37	.32	.29	.37	.32	.29	.36	.32	.29	.35	.31	.28	.27

Intermediate distribution ventilated reflector with phosphor coated HID lamp — III, 1.0, 6½%↑, 75½%↓

RCR	80/50	80/30	80/10	70/50	70/30	70/10	50/50	50/30	50/10	30/50	30/30	30/10	10/50	10/30	10/10	0
0	.96	.96	.96	.93	.93	.93	.87	.87	.87	.82	.82	.82	.77	.77	.77	.75
1	.89	.87	.84	.86	.84	.83	.82	.80	.79	.78	.76	.75	.74	.73	.72	.70
2	.82	.79	.76	.80	.77	.74	.76	.74	.72	.73	.71	.69	.70	.68	.67	.65
3	.76	.72	.68	.74	.70	.67	.71	.68	.65	.68	.66	.63	.66	.63	.61	.60
4	.70	.66	.62	.69	.65	.61	.66	.63	.60	.64	.61	.58	.62	.59	.57	.55
5	.65	.60	.56	.64	.59	.56	.62	.58	.54	.60	.56	.53	.58	.55	.52	.51
6	.60	.55	.51	.59	.55	.51	.57	.53	.50	.56	.52	.49	.54	.51	.48	.47
7	.56	.51	.47	.55	.50	.46	.53	.49	.46	.52	.48	.45	.50	.47	.44	.43
8	.52	.47	.43	.51	.46	.43	.50	.45	.42	.48	.44	.41	.47	.43	.41	.40
9	.48	.43	.39	.47	.42	.39	.46	.42	.39	.45	.41	.38	.44	.40	.38	.36
10	.45	.40	.36	.44	.39	.36	.43	.39	.36	.42	.38	.35	.41	.37	.35	.34

Porcelain-enameled reflector with 30°CW x 30°LW shielding — II, 1.0, 23½%↑, 57%↓

RCR	80/50	80/30	80/10	70/50	70/30	70/10	50/50	50/30	50/10	30/50	30/30	30/10	10/50	10/30	10/10	0
0	.90	.90	.90	.85	.85	.85	.76	.76	.76	.68	.68	.68	.60	.60	.60	.57
1	.81	.78	.76	.77	.74	.72	.69	.67	.66	.62	.61	.60	.56	.55	.54	.57
2	.72	.68	.64	.69	.65	.62	.62	.59	.57	.56	.54	.52	.51	.49	.47	.45
3	.65	.59	.55	.62	.57	.53	.56	.52	.49	.51	.48	.46	.46	.44	.42	.39
4	.58	.52	.48	.56	.50	.46	.51	.46	.43	.46	.43	.40	.42	.39	.37	.35
5	.52	.46	.41	.50	.44	.40	.46	.41	.38	.42	.38	.35	.38	.35	.33	.30
6	.47	.41	.36	.45	.39	.35	.41	.37	.33	.38	.34	.31	.35	.31	.29	.27
7	.43	.36	.32	.41	.35	.31	.38	.33	.29	.34	.30	.27	.32	.28	.26	.24
8	.38	.32	.28	.37	.31	.27	.34	.29	.26	.31	.27	.24	.29	.25	.23	.21
9	.35	.29	.24	.33	.28	.24	.31	.26	.22	.28	.24	.21	.26	.22	.20	.18
10	.32	.26	.22	.30	.25	.21	.28	.23	.20	.26	.22	.19	.24	.20	.18	.16

2 lamp prismatic wraparound—multiply by 0.95 for 4 lamps — V, 1.5/1.2, 11½%↑, 58½%↓

RCR	80/50	80/30	80/10	70/50	70/30	70/10	50/50	50/30	50/10	30/50	30/30	30/10	10/50	10/30	10/10	0
0	.80	.80	.80	.77	.77	.77	.71	.71	.71	.66	.66	.66	.60	.60	.60	.58
1	.71	.69	.66	.69	.66	.64	.64	.62	.60	.59	.58	.56	.55	.54	.53	.50
2	.64	.59	.56	.61	.58	.54	.57	.54	.51	.53	.51	.49	.49	.48	.46	.44
3	.57	.52	.48	.55	.50	.47	.51	.48	.45	.48	.45	.42	.45	.42	.40	.38
4	.51	.46	.41	.49	.44	.40	.46	.42	.39	.43	.40	.37	.41	.38	.35	.34
5	.46	.40	.36	.44	.39	.35	.41	.37	.34	.39	.35	.32	.37	.33	.31	.29
6	.41	.35	.31	.40	.35	.31	.38	.33	.30	.35	.31	.28	.33	.30	.27	.26
7	.37	.31	.27	.36	.31	.27	.34	.29	.26	.32	.28	.25	.30	.27	.24	.23
8	.33	.28	.24	.32	.27	.23	.30	.26	.22	.29	.25	.22	.27	.24	.21	.19
9	.30	.24	.20	.29	.24	.20	.27	.23	.19	.26	.22	.19	.24	.21	.18	.17
10	.27	.22	.18	.26	.21	.18	.25	.20	.17	.23	.19	.16	.22	.18	.16	.15

Illuminating Engineering Society; New York, New York

COEFFICIENTS OF UTILIZATION

COEFFICIENTS OF UTILIZATION FOR 20% EFFECTIVE FLOOR CAVITY REFLECTANCE ($\rho FC = 20$)

$\rho cc^{(1)}$ values: 80, 70, 50, 30, 10, 0; with $\rho w^{(2)}$: 50, 30, 10 for each.

2 lamp 1 ft wide troffer with 45° plastic louver—multiply by 0.90 for 3 lamps
MAINT. CAT. IV; MAXIMUM S/MH GUIDE 1.0; 0%↑ 46%↓

RCR	80/50	80/30	80/10	70/50	70/30	70/10	50/50	50/30	50/10	30/50	30/30	30/10	10/50	10/30	10/10	0
0	.54	.54	.54	.53	.53	.53	.51	.51	.51	.48	.48	.48	.46	.46	.46	.45
1	.49	.48	.46	.48	.47	.46	.46	.45	.44	.45	.44	.43	.43	.42	.42	.41
2	.44	.42	.40	.43	.41	.39	.42	.40	.38	.40	.39	.37	.39	.38	.37	.36
3	.40	.37	.34	.39	.36	.34	.38	.36	.34	.37	.35	.33	.36	.34	.33	.32
4	.36	.33	.30	.36	.32	.30	.35	.32	.30	.34	.31	.29	.33	.31	.29	.28
5	.33	.29	.26	.32	.29	.26	.31	.28	.26	.30	.28	.26	.30	.27	.26	.25
6	.30	.26	.24	.29	.26	.24	.29	.26	.23	.28	.25	.23	.27	.25	.23	.22
7	.27	.24	.21	.27	.23	.21	.26	.23	.21	.26	.23	.21	.25	.22	.21	.20
8	.25	.21	.19	.24	.21	.19	.24	.21	.19	.23	.21	.18	.23	.20	.18	.18
9	.22	.19	.17	.22	.19	.17	.22	.19	.17	.21	.18	.16	.21	.18	.16	.16
10	.21	.17	.15	.20	.17	.15	.20	.17	.15	.20	.17	.15	.19	.17	.15	.14

Fluorescent unit with flat prismatic lens, 2 lamp 1 ft wide
MAINT. CAT. V; MAXIMUM S/MH GUIDE 1.4/1.2; 0%↑ 56%↓ 60°

RCR	80/50	80/30	80/10	70/50	70/30	70/10	50/50	50/30	50/10	30/50	30/30	30/10	10/50	10/30	10/10	0
0	.66	.66	.66	.65	.65	.65	.62	.62	.62	.59	.59	.59	.57	.57	.57	.56
1	.61	.59	.57	.59	.58	.56	.57	.56	.54	.55	.54	.53	.53	.52	.51	.50
2	.55	.52	.50	.54	.51	.49	.52	.50	.48	.50	.48	.47	.49	.47	.46	.45
3	.50	.46	.43	.49	.46	.43	.47	.45	.42	.46	.44	.42	.45	.43	.41	.40
4	.45	.41	.38	.45	.41	.38	.43	.40	.38	.42	.39	.37	.41	.39	.37	.36
5	.41	.37	.34	.40	.36	.34	.39	.36	.33	.38	.35	.33	.37	.35	.33	.32
6	.37	.33	.30	.37	.33	.30	.36	.32	.30	.35	.32	.29	.34	.31	.29	.28
7	.34	.30	.27	.34	.29	.27	.33	.29	.26	.32	.29	.26	.31	.28	.26	.25
8	.31	.26	.24	.30	.26	.23	.30	.26	.23	.29	.26	.23	.28	.25	.23	.22
9	.28	.23	.21	.27	.23	.21	.27	.23	.20	.26	.23	.20	.26	.23	.20	.19
10	.25	.21	.18	.25	.21	.18	.24	.21	.18	.24	.21	.18	.23	.20	.18	.17

1 ft wide aluminum troffer with 40°CW x 45°LW shielding and single extrahigh-output lamp
MAINT. CAT. IV; MAXIMUM S/MH GUIDE 1.1/0.8; 0%↑ 42½%↓

RCR	80/50	80/30	80/10	70/50	70/30	70/10	50/50	50/30	50/10	30/50	30/30	30/10	10/50	10/30	10/10	0
0	.50	.50	.50	.49	.49	.49	.47	.47	.47	.45	.45	.45	.43	.43	.43	.42
1	.46	.45	.44	.45	.44	.43	.44	.43	.42	.42	.41	.41	.41	.40	.40	.39
2	.43	.41	.39	.42	.40	.38	.40	.39	.38	.39	.38	.37	.38	.37	.36	.35
3	.39	.37	.35	.39	.36	.34	.37	.35	.34	.36	.35	.33	.35	.34	.33	.32
4	.36	.33	.31	.35	.33	.31	.35	.32	.31	.34	.32	.30	.33	.31	.30	.29
5	.33	.30	.28	.33	.30	.28	.32	.29	.28	.31	.29	.27	.30	.29	.27	.26
6	.31	.28	.26	.30	.28	.26	.30	.27	.25	.29	.27	.25	.28	.26	.25	.24
7	.28	.25	.23	.28	.25	.23	.27	.25	.23	.27	.25	.23	.26	.24	.23	.22
8	.26	.23	.21	.26	.23	.21	.25	.23	.21	.25	.23	.21	.24	.22	.21	.20
9	.24	.21	.19	.24	.21	.19	.23	.21	.19	.23	.20	.19	.22	.20	.19	.18
10	.22	.19	.17	.22	.19	.17	.21	.19	.17	.21	.19	.17	.21	.19	.17	.16

Luminous bottom suspended unit with extrahigh-output lamp
MAINT. CAT. VI; MAXIMUM S/MH GUIDE 1.5; 66%↑ 12%↓

RCR	80/50	80/30	80/10	70/50	70/30	70/10	50/50	50/30	50/10	30/50	30/30	30/10	10/50	10/30	10/10	0
0	.77	.77	.77	.67	.67	.67	.49	.49	.49	.33	.33	.33	.18	.18	.18	.11
1	.67	.64	.62	.59	.57	.54	.44	.42	.41	.30	.29	.28	.17	.16	.16	.10
2	.59	.54	.50	.51	.48	.45	.38	.36	.34	.26	.25	.23	.15	.14	.13	.09
3	.51	.46	.42	.45	.41	.37	.34	.31	.28	.23	.21	.20	.13	.12	.12	.07
4	.45	.40	.35	.40	.35	.31	.30	.27	.24	.20	.18	.17	.12	.11	.10	.06
5	.40	.34	.30	.35	.30	.27	.26	.23	.20	.18	.16	.14	.10	.09	.08	.05
6	.36	.30	.26	.32	.27	.23	.24	.20	.18	.16	.14	.12	.09	.08	.07	.05
7	.32	.26	.22	.28	.23	.20	.21	.18	.15	.15	.12	.11	.08	.07	.06	.04
8	.29	.23	.19	.25	.21	.17	.19	.16	.13	.13	.11	.09	.08	.06	.06	.03
9	.26	.20	.17	.23	.18	.15	.17	.14	.12	.12	.10	.08	.07	.06	.05	.03
10	.24	.18	.15	.21	.16	.13	.16	.12	.10	.11	.09	.07	.06	.05	.04	.03

Diffusing plastic or glass
ρcc from below ~65%

1. Ceiling efficiency ~60%; diffuser transmittance ~50%; diffuser reflectance ~40%. Cavity with minimum obstructions and painted with 80% reflectance paint—use $\rho_c = 70$
2. For lower reflectance paint or obstructions—use $\rho_c = 50$

RCR	70/50	70/30	70/10	50/50	50/30	50/10
1	.60	.58	.56	.58	.56	.54
2	.53	.49	.45	.51	.47	.43
3	.47	.42	.37	.45	.41	.36
4	.41	.36	.32	.39	.35	.31
5	.37	.31	.27	.35	.30	.26
6	.33	.27	.23	.31	.26	.23
7	.29	.24	.20	.28	.23	.20
8	.26	.21	.18	.25	.20	.17
9	.23	.19	.15	.23	.18	.15
10	.21	.17	.13	.21	.16	.13

Louvered ceiling
ρcc from below ~45%

1. Ceiling efficiency ~50%; 45° shielding opaque louvers of 80% reflectance. Cavity with minimum obstructions and painted with 80% reflectance paint—use $\rho_c = 50$

RCR	50/50	50/30	50/10	10/50	10/30	10/10
1	.51	.49	.48	.47	.46	.45
2	.46	.44	.42	.43	.42	.40
3	.42	.39	.37	.39	.38	.36
4	.38	.35	.33	.36	.34	.32
5	.35	.32	.29	.33	.31	.29
6	.32	.29	.26	.30	.28	.26
7	.29	.26	.23	.28	.25	.23
8	.27	.23	.21	.26	.23	.21
9	.24	.21	.19	.24	.21	.19
10	.22	.19	.17	.22	.19	.17

Illuminating Engineering Society; New York, New York

NOTES

UPS (uninterruptible power supply) is designed to provide continuous power with specific electrical characteristics by conditioning utility company power, battery power, or generator-supplied power.

UPS systems are either on-line, routing power through the UPS system continuously, or off-line systems, which route power through the UPS only when the incoming power is interrupted or departs from the design characteristics. The time required for an off-line, solid state UPS to automatically switch on varies with the type of switch selected. Switching equipment generally increases in cost as the time decreases. The time needs to be matched to the tolerances of the critical equipment being supplied by the UPS to prevent loss of data or other problems.

Battery backup time is selected to allow a controlled shutdown of equipment or to allow a backup generator to be started and stabilize at full power.

Redundant UPS systems may be required if UPS power loss cannot be tolerated for system maintenance or equipment breakdown.

Some equipment can produce electrical disturbances that are fed back into the electrical circuit. This must be prevented through filtering in order to maintain clean power to the other equipment being supplied by the UPS.

The UPS unit and battery should be placed together. Some UPS cabinets contain sealed batteries; others require separate batteries.

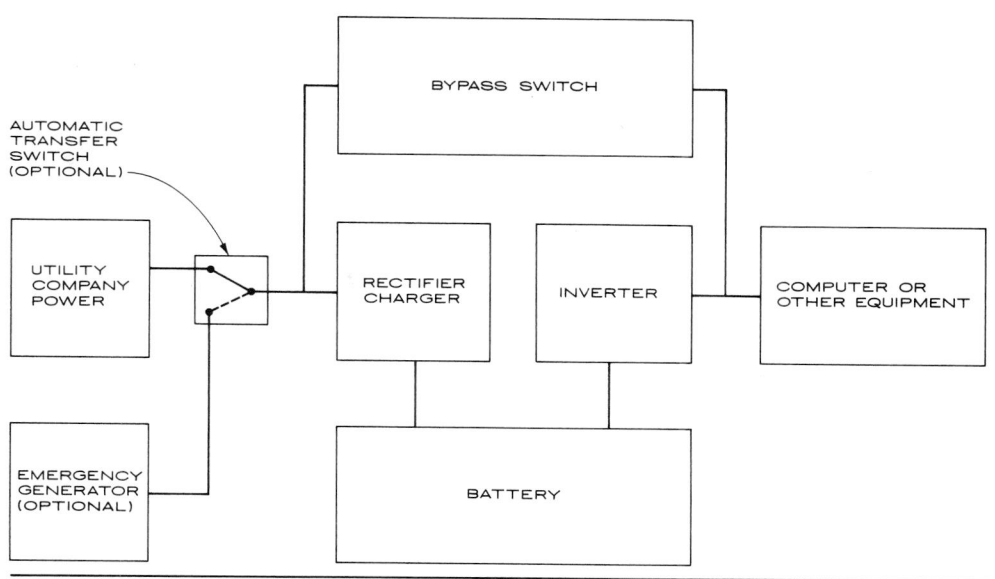

TYPICAL UPS DIAGRAM

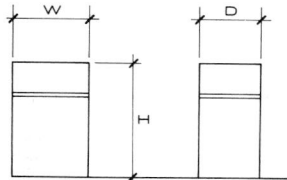

UPS UNDER 10 KVA SIZES

WATTS	W (IN.)	D (IN.)	H (IN.)	TIME (MIN.)
200	8	15	6	15–20
800	22	16	9	15–20
1500	22	16	18	15–20
KVA				
3.0	26	19	52	10
5.0	36	19	52	10
10.0	36	19	52	10

A wide variety of UPS systems is available for smaller applications, ranging from desktop models for single microcomputers to floor models that can supply several computers or other equipment.

UPS UNDER 10 KVA

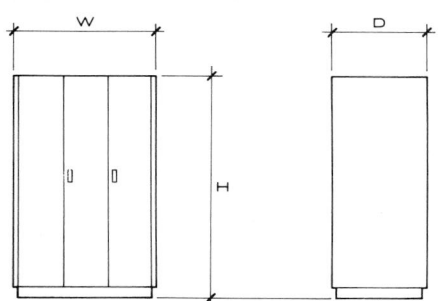

BATTERY CABINET SIZES

KVA	TIME (MIN.)	W (IN.)	D (IN.)	H (IN.)	WEIGHT (LB)	NUMBER REQUIRED
75	15	40	32	76	2300	2
100	15	40	32	76	2300	3
200	15	48	32	76	2300	4
400	10	40	32	76	2300	8
500	7.5	40	32	76	2300	4

BATTERY CABINET

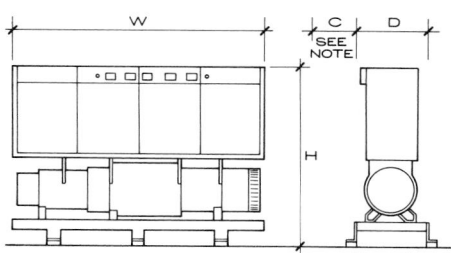

ROTARY UPS SIZES

KVA	W (IN.)	D (IN.)	H (IN.)	WEIGHT (LB)
25	80	24	62	2,600
50	80	24	62	3,400
125	125	32	74	7,000
250	140	32	80	10,000
500	164	60	84	15,000
1000	173	64	98	32,200

Sound level approximately 60 to 80 dB. Heat rejection approximately 400 Btu/hr/KVA at 50 KVA to 250 Btu/hr/KVA at 500 KVA. Maintain room temperature at 70°–80°F. Some units require front and rear clearance for access.

ROTARY UPS

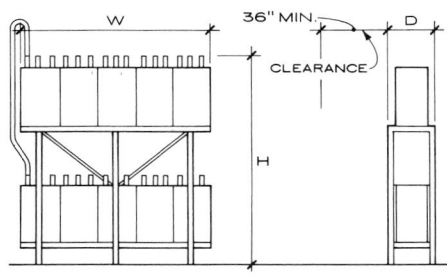

Racks can be placed back to back. Provide shower and eyewash station and ventilation, and maintain approximately 77°F room temperature. Place battery racks close to UPS units. Provide seismic bracing required by code.

BATTERY RACKS

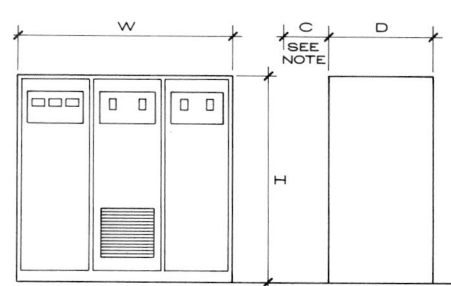

SOLID STATE UPS SIZES

KVA	W (IN.)	D (IN.)	H (IN.)	WEIGHT (LB)
25	28	32	70	1,400
50	72	36	72	4,000
125	72	36	72	5,600
200	72	36	72	6,000
350	168	32	76	12,700
500	168	40	76	14,600

Sound level approximately 65–70 dB. Heat rejection approximately 450–700 Btu/hr/KVA at 50 KVA to 250 Btu/hr/KVA at 500 KVA. Maintain room temperature at 70°–80°F. Some units require clearance (C) for access.

SOLID STATE UPS

BATTERY RACKS
TWO-TIER RACK SIZES

KVA	TIME (MIN.)	W (IN.)	D (IN.)	H (IN.)	WEIGHT (LB)	NUMBER REQUIRED
15	30	96	16	54	3,100	2
100	15	168	18	52	10,000	4
250	15	108	18	52	20,500	6
500	15	156	18	52	34,600	6

THREE-TIER RACK SIZES

KVA	TIME (MIN.)	W (IN.)	D (IN.)	H (IN.)	WEIGHT (LB)	NUMBER REQUIRED
25	15	108	18	79	4,300	1
50	15	108	18	79	5,000	1
100	15	108	18	79	10,000	2
250	15	144	18	79	20,500	3
500	15	108	18	79	34,600	6

Fred W. Hegel, AIA; Denver, Colorado

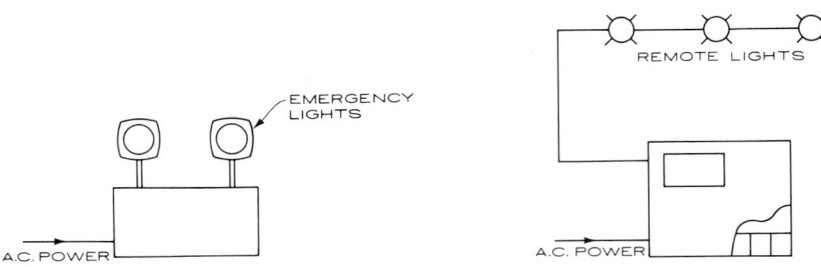

BATTERY PACK

BATTERIES AND INVERTER

BATTERY PACKS AND INVERTERS

Battery powered lighting equipment is utilized to provide minimal emergency illumination required for personnel safety and evacuation purposes in buildings not requiring standby generator power. This equipment is also utilized in buildings requiring standby generator power at central control room, telephone switchboard room, generator room, and electrical switchgear rooms to provide lighting for continuity of critical operations and troubleshooting if the generator fails to start. The batteries require frequent inspection, tests, and maintenance if they are to perform their intended function.

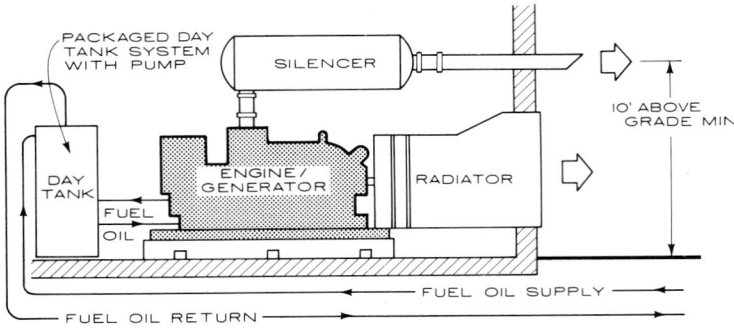

UNIT MOUNTED RADIATOR

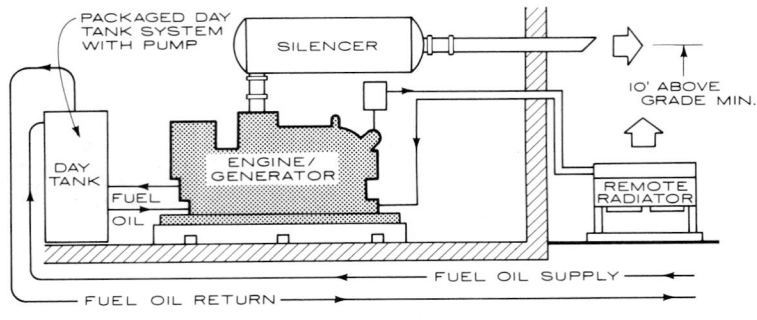

REMOTE RADIATOR

STANDBY GENERATORS

Standby generators are utilized where the life safety lighting requirements and/or the requirements to drive critical equipment are beyond the capacity of battery units, or when required by code (hospitals, high-rise buildings, etc.). Engines are cooled by methods illustrated, and should be located in rooms separate from main electrical switchgear. Engine rooms must have adequate ventilation for engine and generator radiated heat and must be protected against extreme environments under all conditions of airflow. Room size and space at sides of power generating unit(s) must be adequate for service. Access to room must allow for removal of generation unit. Standby generators require frequent inspections, tests under load conditions, and maintenance if they are to perform their intended function. Vibration isolation provisions are required to prevent vibration transmission to surrounding occupied areas. In addition to the cooling methods illustrated, cooling by heat exchanger, submerged pipe, cooling tower, and evaporative cooler should be considered.

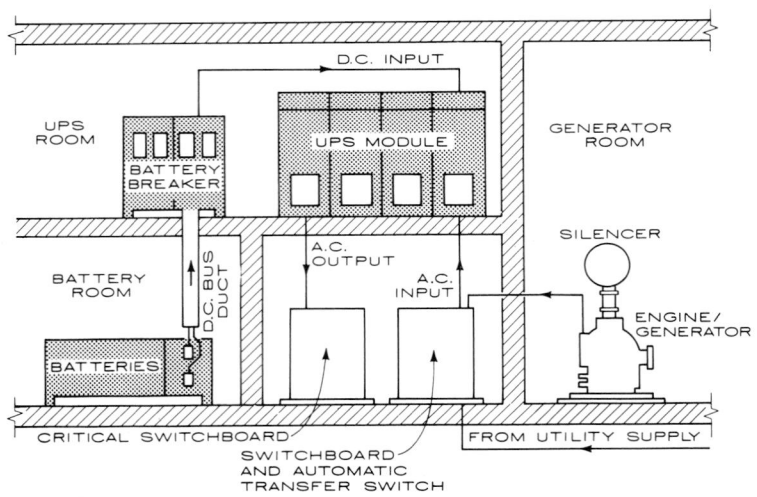

UNINTERRUPTIBLE POWER SUPPLY SYSTEM

UNINTERRUPTIBLE POWER SUPPLY SYSTEM

Uninterruptible power supply (UPS) systems closely control the power supply voltage and frequency to critical equipment such as computers, communications systems, medical instrumentation, and similar sophisticated loads. Such UPS installations often are served from both utility and standby generator sources and provide "buffering" or complete isolation between the service and the critical load. The UPS batteries supply power through the UPS inverter to the critical AC loads until normal or generator power is restored or until the batteries reach end-of-discharge voltage. UPS systems range in size from small self-contained cabinet units to large built-up systems similar to illustration. UPS systems require frequent inspections, tests, and maintenance if they are to perform their intended function.

William Tao & Associates, Inc., Consulting Engineers; St. Louis, Missouri

SPECIAL SYSTEMS

GENERAL

Horizontal telecommunications cabling may be routed between telecommunications closets and workstations via access floors, cellular decks, ceiling plenums, and under-carpet schemes. Access floor distribution facilitates the installation of future cabling as well as the movement of floor boxes and cable feed-throughs to accommodate furniture relocations. Cellular decks provide similar underfloor cable pathways, yet lack the flexibility of relocatable floor boxes. Other distribution approaches include under floor, plenum routing, which requires poke-through fittings for access to workstations, and ceiling routing which is most appropriate for drywall installations. Under-carpet distribution utilizes special cable to provide a relocatable cabling system with minimal modifications to building structures.

Telecommunications closets provide the transition points between riser and horizontal cabling and accommodate associated cable termination hardware and transport electronics. Closets should be designed with respect to service area, environmental, lighting, fire protection, security, and cable pathway requirements. Overhead cable tray, access floors, and D-rings facilitate cable distribution.

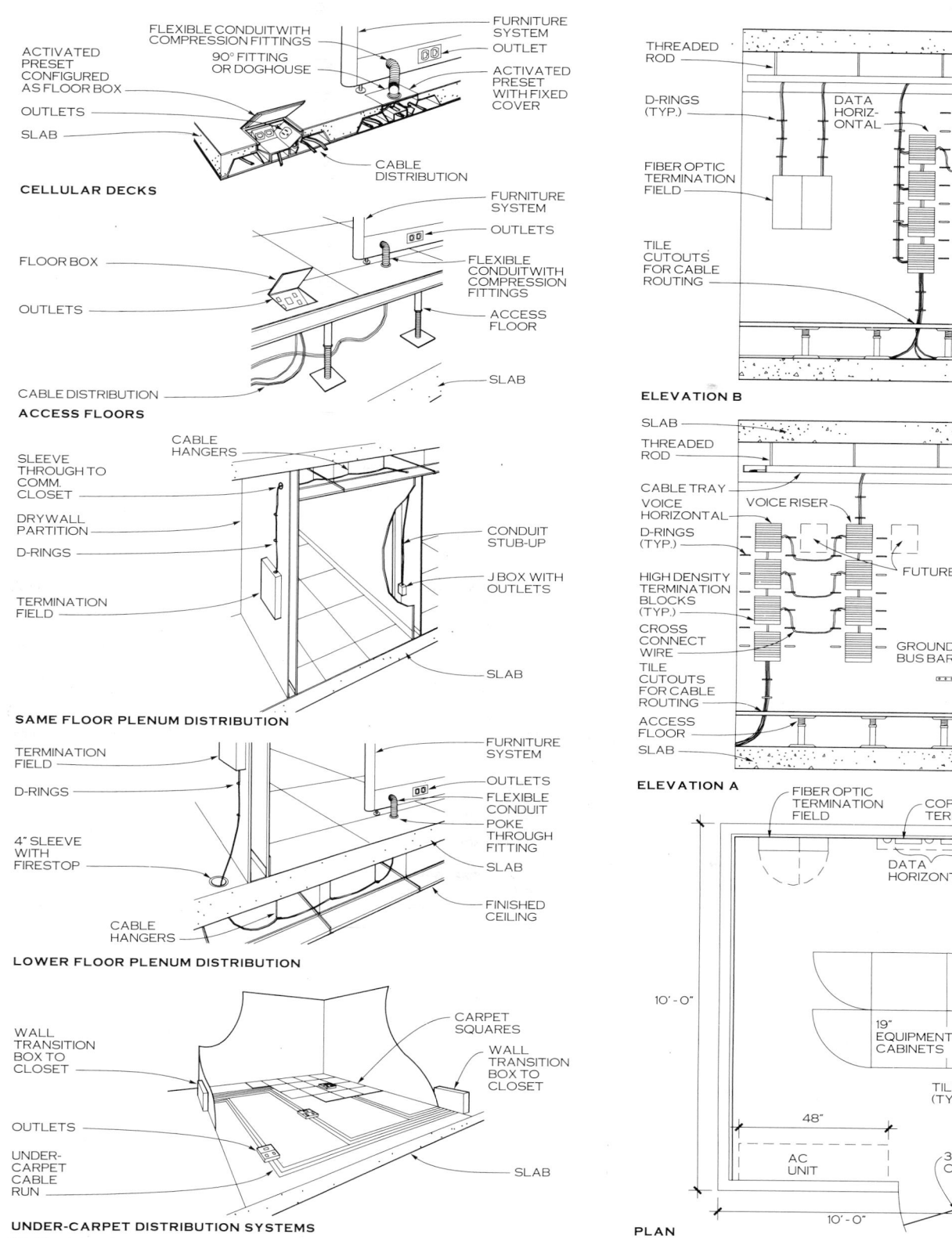

CELLULAR DECKS

ACCESS FLOORS

SAME FLOOR PLENUM DISTRIBUTION

LOWER FLOOR PLENUM DISTRIBUTION

UNDER-CARPET DISTRIBUTION SYSTEMS

HORIZONTAL CABLE DISTRIBUTION

ELEVATION B

ELEVATION A

PLAN

TELECOMMUNICATION CLOSET

Flack + Kurtz, Consulting Engineers; New York, New York

GENERAL

American National Standards Institute (ANSI)
11 West 42nd Street, 13th Floor
New York, NY 10036-8002
Tel: (212) 642-4900
Fax:(212) 398-0023

American Society for
Testing and Materials (ASTM)
1916 Race St.
Philadelphia, PA 19103-1187
Tel: (215) 299-5400
Fax:(215) 977-9679

Association of Edison Illuminating Companies
600 North 18th Street
P.O. Box 2641
Birmingham, AL 35291-0992
Tel: (205) 250-2530

Edison Electric Institute (EEI)
701 Pennsylvania Ave., N.W.
Washington, DC 20004
Tel: (202) 508-5000 or
Tel: (800) EEI-4688
Fax:(202) 508-5794

Illuminating Engineering Society of North America
(IES)
120 Wall St.
New York, NY 10005-4001
Tel: (212) 248-5000
Fax:(212) 248-5017

International Electrical Testing Association
(IETA)
P.O. Box 687
Morrison, CO 80465
Tel: (303) 697-8441

National Electrical Contractors Association (NECA)
3 Bethesda Metro Center, Suite 1100
Bethesda, MD 20814-3299
Tel: (301) 657-3110
Fax:(301) 215-4500

National Electrical
Manufacturers Association (NEMA)
2101 L Street N.W.
Washington, DC 20037
Tel: (202) 457-8400

National Fire Protection Association(NFPA)
P.O. Box 9101
1 Batterymarch Park
Quincy, MA 02269-9101
Tel: (617) 770-3000
Fax:(617) 770-0700

Underwriters Laboratories (UL)
333 Pfingsten Road
Northbrook, IL 60062
Tel: (708) 272-8800
Fax:(708) 272-8129

REFERENCES

Bovay, H.E., Jr., ed. *Handbook Mechanical and Electrical Systems for Buildings.* New York: McGraw-Hill, 1991.

Callogero, J.M., and M. W. Earley and R. H. Murray, eds. *The National Electrical Code Handbook 1993*, 6th ed. Quincy, Mass.: National Fire Protection Association (NFPA), 1992.

Croft, Terrel, and Wilford I. Summers. *American Electricians' Handbook.* 12th ed. New York: McGraw-Hill, 1992.

Electrical Construction Materials Directory, Underwriters Laboratories, 1992.

Fire Protection Handbook, 17th ed. Quincy, Mass.: NFPA, 1991.

Kaufman, John E., ed. Illuminating Engineering Society Handbook—Reference Volume, 1981 and 1984 eds. Illuminating Engineering Society (IES).

International Electrical Testing Association. Standard ATS-1991: Acceptance Testing Specifications for Electrical Power Distribution Systems and Equipment, NETA, 1991.

McPartland, J.F. and B. McPartland, eds. *McGraw-Hill's National Electrical Code Handbook.* 21st ed. New York: McGraw-Hill, 1983.

"NECA Standard of Installation," Washington, DC: National Electrical Contractors Association (NECA), 1988.

Stein, Benjamin and John S. Reynolds. *Mechanical and Electrical Equipment for Buildings.* New York: J. Wiley & Sons, 1992.

Uniform Mechanical Code (see International Institute of Plumbing and Mechanical Officials in Plumbing), annual.

Wilson, A., and J. Morrill, Consumer Guide to Home Energy Savings, ACEEE, 1991, 243 pp.

ELECTRICAL WIRING

American Council for an
Energy-Efficient Economy (ACEEE)
2140 Shattuck Avenue, Suite 202
Berkeley, CA 94704
Tel: (510) 549-9914
Fax:(510) 549-9984

Electric Power Research Institute
Box 10412
Palo Alto, CA 94303-0813
Tel: (415) 855-2000
Fax:(415) 855-2954

Institute of Electrical and
Electronics Engineers (IEEE)
Standards Department
445 Hoes Lane
P.O. Box 1331
Piscataway, NJ 08855-1330
Tel: (908) 562-3800
Fax:(908) 562-1571

National Electrical Manufacturers Association
2101 L Street N.W.
Washington, DC 20037
Tel: (202) 457-8400

Underwriters Laboratories (UL)
333 Pfingsten Road
Northbrook, IL 60062
Tel: (708) 272-8800
Fax:(708) 272-8129

REFERENCES

Fink, Donald G., and H. Wayne Beaty, eds. *Standard Handbook for Electrical Engineers*, 12th ed. New York: McGraw-Hill, 1987.

IEEE Recommended Practice for Electric Power Systems in Commercial Buildings (Gray Book), Standard 241-1990. IEEE, 1990.

IEEE Recommended Practice for Electric Systems in Health Care Facilities (White Book). Institute of Electrical and Electronics Engineers, 1986.

IEEE Recommended Practice for Emergency and Standby Power Systems for Industrial and Commercial Applications (Orange Book), Standard 446. Institute of Electrical and Electronics Engineers, 1987.

LIGHTING

American Lighting Association
435 N. Michigan Ave., Suite 1717
Chicago, IL 60611-4067
Tel: (312) 644-0828
Fax:(312) 644-8557

Certified Ballast Manufacturers
772 Hanna Building
Cleveland, OH 44115
Tel: (216) 241-0711

Commission Internationale de L'Eclairage (CIE)
U.S. National Committee
c/o TLA Consultants
72 Pond Street
Salem, MA 01970
Tel: (508) 745-6870
Fax:(508) 741-4420

Edison Electric Institute (EEI)
701 Pennsylvania Ave., N.W.
Washington, DC 20004
Tel: (202) 508-5000 or (800) EEI-4688
Fax:(202) 508-5794

Illuminating Engineering Society
of North America (IES)
120 Wall St.
New York, NY 10005-4001
Tel: (212) 248-5000
Fax:(212) 248-5017

International Association of Lighting Designers
(IALD)
18 E. 16th Street Suite 208
New York, NY 10003
Tel: (212) 206-1281

Lawrence Berkeley Laboratory (LBL)
Lighting Systems Research Group
Mail Stop 46-125
1 Cyclotron Road
Berkeley, CA 94720
Tel: (510) 486-5388
Fax:(510) 486-6940

Lighting Research Center (LRC)
Rensselaer Polytechnic Institute
Greene Bldg., #115
Troy, NY 12180-3590
Tel: (518) 276-8716
Fax:(518) 276-2999

Lighting Research Institute (LRI)
120 Wall St.
New York, NY 10005-4001
Tel: (212) 248-5014

National Lighting Bureau (NLB)
2101 L St. NW
Washington, DC 20037
Tel: (202) 457-8437
Fax:(202) 457-8437

REFERENCES

Architectural Lighting, Aster Publishing. [monthly]

Choosing Light Sources for General Lighting, CP-32. Illuminating Engineering Society, 1988.

Design Criteria for Lighting Interior Living Spaces, RP-11-80. Illuminating Engineering Society.

Egan, M. D. *Concepts in Architectural Lighting.* New York: McGraw-Hill.

Electronic Ballasts. Specifier Reports, Lighting Research Center, 1992.

Guide on Interior Lighting, CIE 29.2, 1986, 114 pp.

Guide to Performance Evaluation of Efficient Lighting Products, Lighting Research Center, 1991, 56 pp.

Kaufman, John E., ed. *Illuminating Engineering Society Handbook*, Reference vol., 1981 and 1984 eds. Illuminating Engineering Society (IES).

Industrial Lighting, RP-7. Illuminating Engineering Society, 1991.

Journal of the Illuminating Lighting Society. Illuminating Engineering Society.

Library Lighting, RP-4. Illuminating Engineering Society, 1974, 32 pp.

Lighting and Human Performance: A Summary Report. Lighting Research Institute. [monthly]

Lighting Design and Application. Illuminating Engineering Society, monthly.

Lighting Handbook, 1984 Reference vol. Illuminating Engineering Society.

Lighting Handbook, 1987 Application vol. Illuminating Engineering Society.

Lighting Merchandising Areas, RP-2. Illuminating Engineering Society, 1986.

Lighting Ready Reference. IES, 1989.

Minimum Efficiency Standards for Flourescent and Incandescent Lamps, A902. Berkeley: American Council for an Energy-Efficient Economy, 1990.

Nelson, G., et al. *Light Structures Analysis and Design.* Van Nostrand Reinhold, 1987.

Smith, F., and F. Bertolone. *Bringing Interiors to Light: The Principles and Practices of Lighting Design.* Watson-Guptill, 1986.

COMMUNICATIONS

National Communications Association
16 East 34th Street
15th Floor
New York, NY 10016
Tel: (212) 239-4255

North American Telecommunications Association
2000 M. Street, N.W.
Suite 550
Washington, DC 20036
Tel: (202) 296-9800
Fax:(202) 296-4993

Telecommunications Association
701 North Haven Avenue
Suite 200
Ontario, CA 91764-4925
Tel: (909) 945-1122
Fax:(909) 483-3888

Chapter

17

SPORTS AND GAME FACILITIES

SITE ACCESSIBILITY

1. Total accessible parking spaces, dispersed and serving all arena entrances, should be 2% of the total number of stadium parking spaces.
2. Accessible parking spaces should be located as close as possible to all arena entrances, and should be served by pedestrian walkways.
3. Provide curb ramps for access to walks, arena entrances, driveways and parking lots, and at each access aisle connected to a walkway.
4. Accessible parking spaces should serve both cars and vans, and should meet ADAAG specifications for width of access aisle and identifying signage. Higher clearances in parking garages may be required for vans.
5. Identify each accessible space with a post-mounted sign with the bottom edge at least 84 in. high. Signs should bear the international symbol of access and the words "Reserved Parking."
6. Provide signage to direct visitors to accessible parking spaces and to designate routes to accessible building entrances.
7. Provide outdoor lighting at accessible parking and along accessible routes to arena entrances.
8. Mark vehicular and pedestrian entrances to the arena property; routes to the arena entrances should be clearly marked with illuminated outdoor signage.
9. Locate passenger loading zones to permit mobility impaired visitors to be discharged and picked up close to arena entrances.
10. Access aisles adjacent to passenger loading zones should be 4 ft wide and 20 ft long with a slope less than 1:20.

See other *AGS* pages for additional information on accessible parking and curb ramps.

TICKET WINDOWS, RETAIL SHOPS, AND FOOD SERVICE

1. Sales counters should have a minimum height of 27 in. and a maximum height of 34 in., allowing visitors in wheelchairs to use the countertop as an aid to open a purse or to write. At least a portion of the counter should be unobstructed by waiting line railings.
2. Tray slides at food service areas must meet ADAAG height and reach requirements.
3. Condiment stands should be cantilevered for wheelchair access.
4. Wheelchair accessible ticket windows should be provided, and should be located on an accessible route. Windows should be at least 36 in. wide with sills 34 in. high.

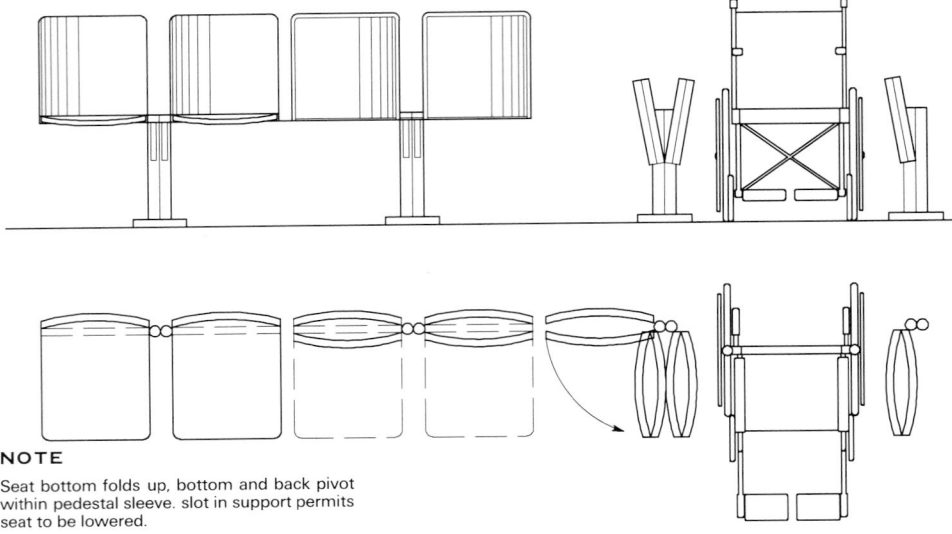

NOTE

Seat bottom folds up, bottom and back pivot within pedestal sleeve. slot in support permits seat to be lowered.

ACCESSIBLE SEATING

Make at least one percent of the total seating accessible. Flexible solutions, such as foldable or removable seating, can accommodate large numbers of people in wheelchairs and can be modified for standard seating when needed.

1. Integrate seating for mobility impaired people with standard seating throughout the stadium; encompass a full range of seat locations and prices.
2. Intersperse accessible seating with standard seating to allow parties with all levels of mobility to sit together.
3. Space for wheelchair seating should be level, 33 in. wide and 54 in. deep if accessible from the front or rear. Spaces accessible only from the side should be 60 in. deep.
4. Provide an accessible route to all wheelchair seating areas. Wheelchair seating is only practical in the front or rear rows of seating sections and on the level platforms separating the standard, stepped seating. Blocks of seating should occur adjacent to vomitory openings. If floors in the vomitory (or elsewhere) exceed a 1:20 slope they must meet the specified ADA criteria for a ramp.

NOTE

The above items primarily address the needs of mobility impaired visitors. Modification to standard arena seating for hearing and visually impaired guests should also be addressed.

VERTICAL CIRCULATION

1. Elevators meeting ADAAG specifications should be available to serve all levels and should be clearly indicated by signage.
2. Ramps used as part of an accessible route must comply with ADA specifications:
   Slope —1:12 maximum
   Maximum rise for any run —30 in.
   Clear width — 36 in.
   Ramps must also follow guidelines for landings and handrails.

ARENA ENTRANCES

1. All arena entrances serving the public should be accessible and served by an accessible route.
2. Provide gates adjacent to turnstiles to permit passage of visitors with mobility impairments.
3. Concourses and public corridors must have 80 in. of clear headroom and be free of protruding objects, as specified by ADAAG.

PUBLIC RESTROOMS

All public restrooms should provide at least one set of accessible toilet room fixtures. Requirements increase as toilet room size increases.

For restroom design, refer to ANSI A117.1 and ADAAG, which establish general requirements for public restrooms. Layouts must allow individuals in wheelchairs to enter, use the fixtures, reopen the door, and exit the room. Provide an unobstructed turning space, a 60 in. diameter clear circular area, in at least one location in the room.

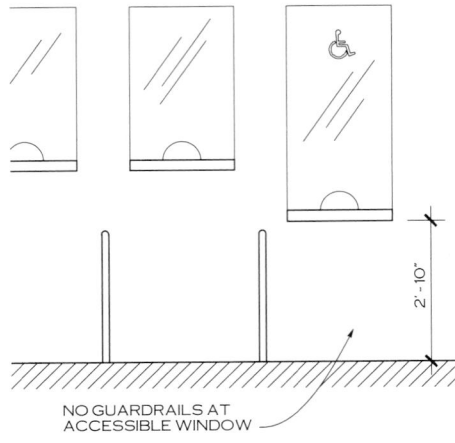

NO GUARDRAILS AT ACCESSIBLE WINDOW

2'-10"

TICKET WINDOW

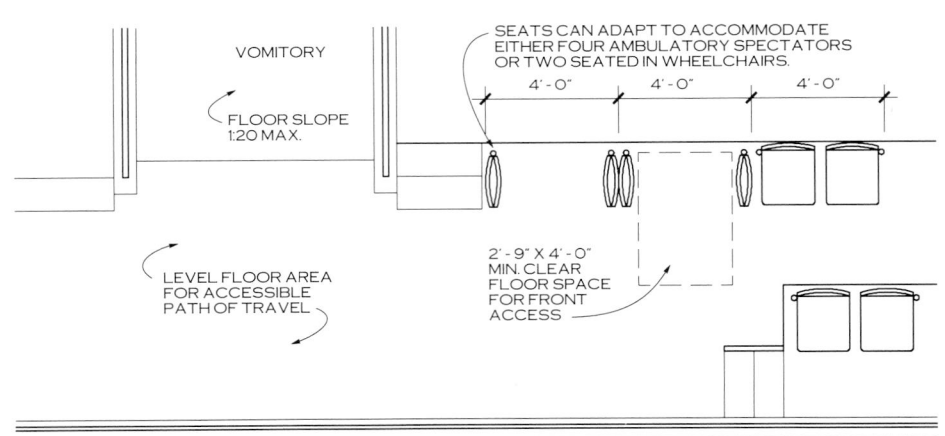

VOMITORY

FLOOR SLOPE 1:20 MAX.

LEVEL FLOOR AREA FOR ACCESSIBLE PATH OF TRAVEL

SEATS CAN ADAPT TO ACCOMMODATE EITHER FOUR AMBULATORY SPECTATORS OR TWO SEATED IN WHEELCHAIRS.

4'-0"   4'-0"   4'-0"

2'-9" X 4'-0" MIN. CLEAR FLOOR SPACE FOR FRONT ACCESS

INTEGRATED ACCESSIBLE SEATING EXAMPLE

Janet B. Rankin, AIA; Rippeteau Architects; Washington, D.C.
Thomas D. Davies, Jr., AIA; Kim A. Beasley, AIA; Paradigm Design Group; Washington, D.C.

17 **UNIVERSAL ACCESSIBILITY**

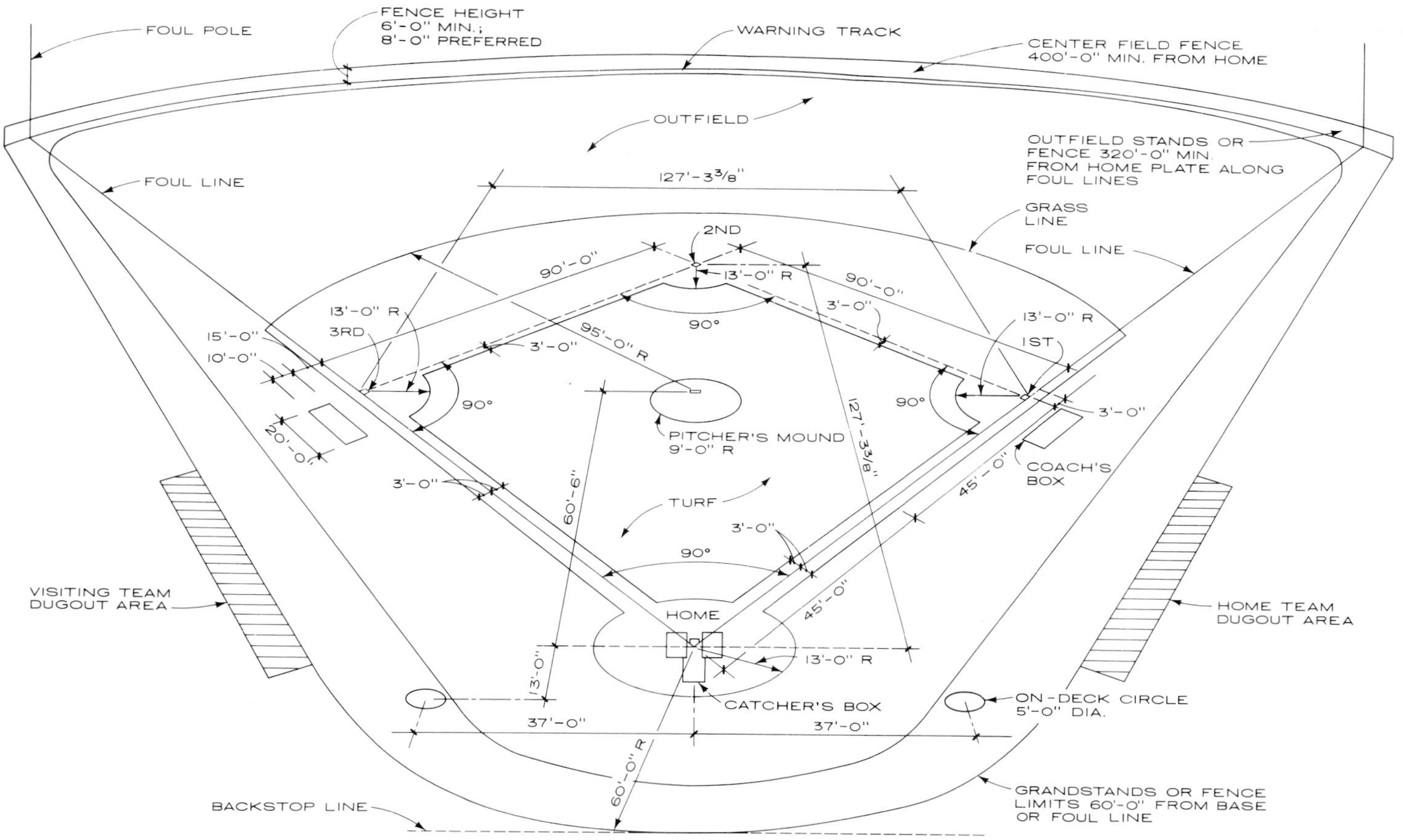

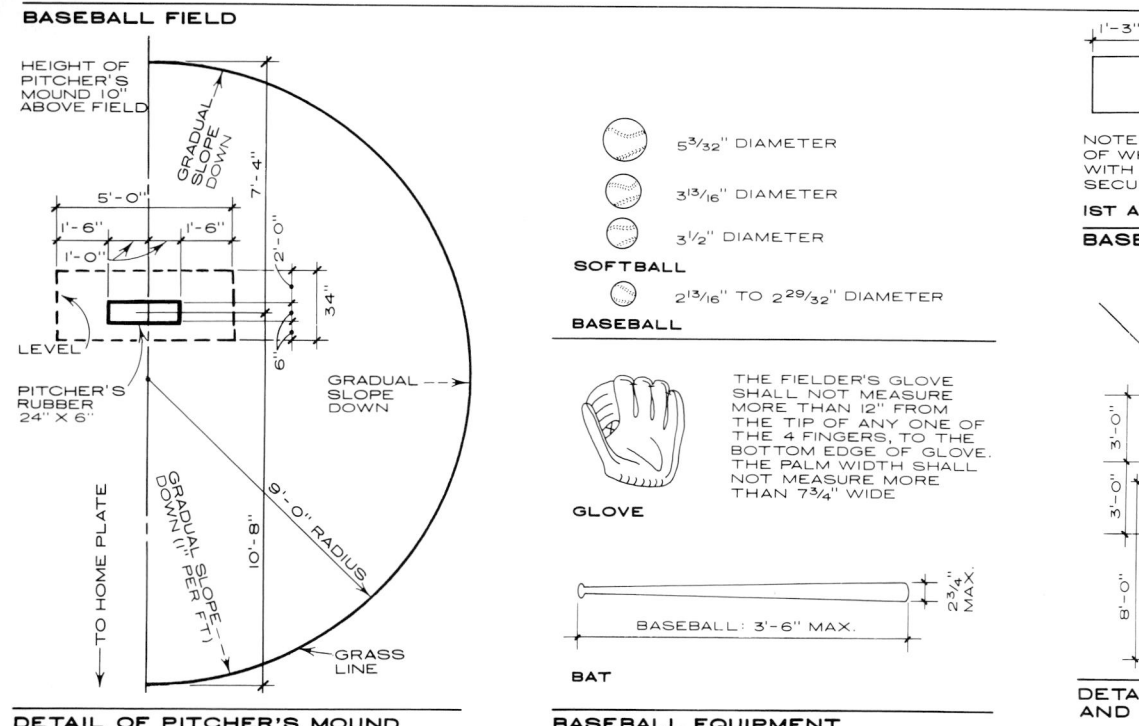

FENCE HEIGHT
6'-0" MIN.;
8'-0" PREFERRED

FOUL POLE

WARNING TRACK

CENTER FIELD FENCE
400'-0" MIN. FROM HOME

FOUL LINE

OUTFIELD

OUTFIELD STANDS OR
FENCE 320'-0" MIN.
FROM HOME PLATE ALONG
FOUL LINES

127'-3³⁄₈"

GRASS
LINE

FOUL LINE

2ND

90'-0"

13'-0" R

90'-0"

13'-0" R

3'-0"

13'-0" R
3RD

90°

1ST

15'-0"

3'-0"

95'-0" R

10'-0"

90°

90°

3'-0"

20'-0"

PITCHER'S MOUND
9'-0" R

127'-3³⁄₈"

45'-0"

COACH'S
BOX

3'-0"

3'-0"

TURF

60'-6"

3'-0"

90°

VISITING TEAM
DUGOUT AREA

HOME TEAM
DUGOUT AREA

45'-0"

HOME

13'-0" R

ON-DECK CIRCLE
5'-0" DIA.

3'-0"

CATCHER'S BOX

37'-0"

37'-0"

60'-0" R

BACKSTOP LINE

GRANDSTANDS OR FENCE
LIMITS 60'-0" FROM BASE
OR FOUL LINE

NOTE

This information is for preliminary
planning and design only. For final
layouts and design, investigate current rules and regulations of the athletic organization or other authority
whose standards will govern.

ORIENTATION

No standard—consider time of day for
games; months when played; location of field, surrounding buildings
and stands. East-northeast recommended by NCAA (home plate to center field).

BASEBALL FIELD

HEIGHT OF
PITCHER'S
MOUND 10"
ABOVE FIELD

GRADUAL
SLOPE
DOWN

7'-4"

5'-0"

1'-6"

1'-6"

2'-0"

1'-0"

3'4"

LEVEL

6"

PITCHER'S
RUBBER
24" X 6"

GRADUAL
SLOPE
DOWN

GRADUAL SLOPE
DOWN (1" PER FT.)

TO HOME PLATE

10'-8"

9'-0" RADIUS

GRASS
LINE

DETAIL OF PITCHER'S MOUND

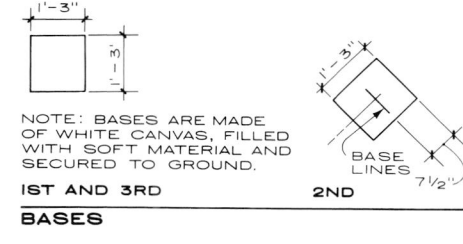

5³⁄₃₂" DIAMETER

3¹³⁄₁₆" DIAMETER

3¹⁄₂" DIAMETER

SOFTBALL

2¹³⁄₁₆" TO 2²⁹⁄₃₂" DIAMETER

BASEBALL

THE FIELDER'S GLOVE
SHALL NOT MEASURE
MORE THAN 12" FROM
THE TIP OF ANY ONE OF
THE 4 FINGERS, TO THE
BOTTOM EDGE OF GLOVE.
THE PALM WIDTH SHALL
NOT MEASURE MORE
THAN 7³⁄₄" WIDE

GLOVE

2³⁄₄"
MAX.

BASEBALL: 3'-6" MAX.

BAT

BASEBALL EQUIPMENT

1'-3"

1'-3"

NOTE: BASES ARE MADE
OF WHITE CANVAS, FILLED
WITH SOFT MATERIAL AND
SECURED TO GROUND.

1'-3"

1'-3"

BASE
LINES

7¹⁄₂"

1ST AND 3RD

2ND

BASES

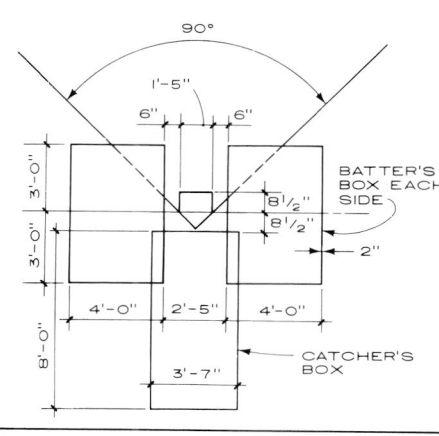

90°

1'-5"

6"

6"

3'-0"

8¹⁄₂"

3'-0"

8¹⁄₂"

BATTER'S
BOX EACH
SIDE

2"

4'-0"

2'-5"

4'-0"

8'-0"

3'-7"

CATCHER'S
BOX

**DETAIL OF HOME BASE BATTER'S
AND CATCHER'S BOX**

Richard J. Vitullo, AIA; Oak Leaf Studio; Crownsville, Maryland

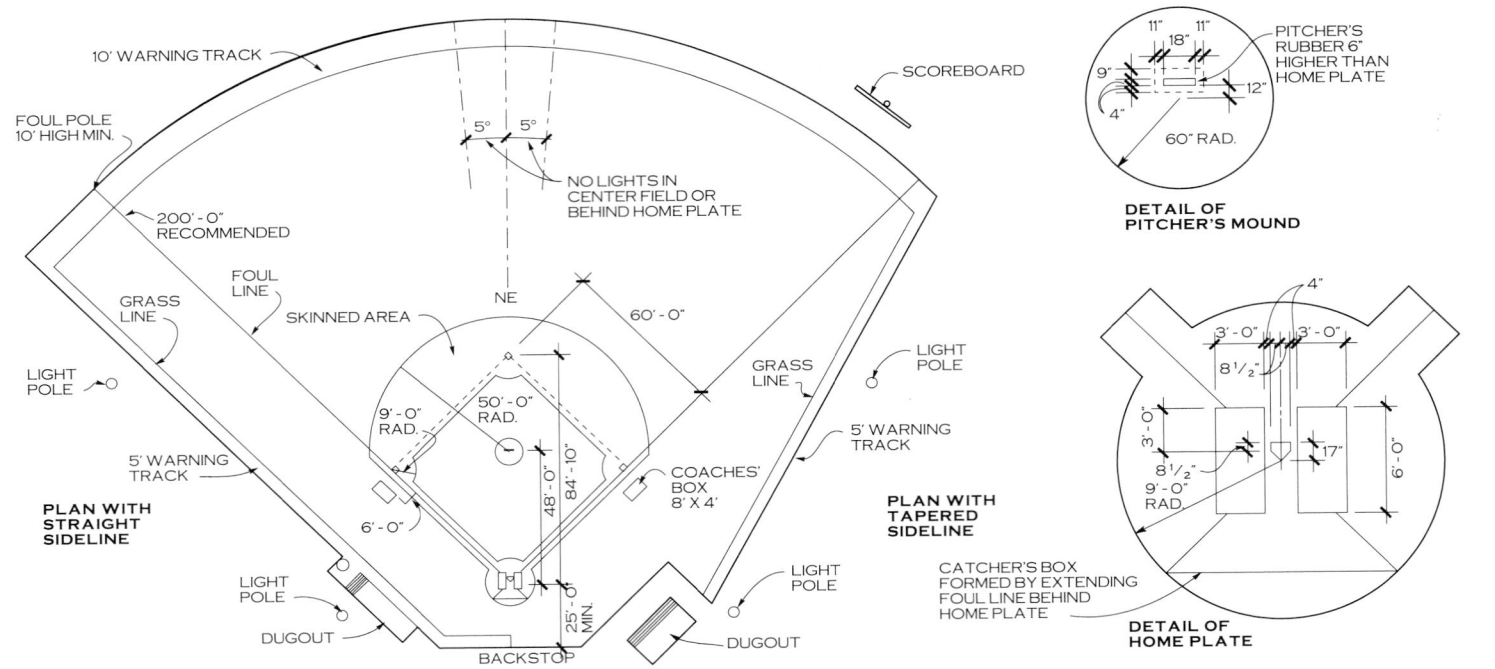

DETAIL OF PITCHER'S MOUND

- 11"
- 18"
- 11"
- 9"
- 12"
- 4"
- 60" RAD.
- PITCHER'S RUBBER 6" HIGHER THAN HOME PLATE

10' WARNING TRACK

SCOREBOARD

FOUL POLE 10' HIGH MIN.

5° 5°

NO LIGHTS IN CENTER FIELD OR BEHIND HOME PLATE

200' - 0" RECOMMENDED

GRASS LINE

FOUL LINE

NE

60' - 0"

LIGHT POLE

SKINNED AREA

GRASS LINE

LIGHT POLE

9' - 0" RAD.

50' - 0" RAD.

5' WARNING TRACK

5' WARNING TRACK

84' - 10"

48' - 0"

COACHES' BOX 8' X 4'

PLAN WITH STRAIGHT SIDELINE

6' - 0"

PLAN WITH TAPERED SIDELINE

LIGHT POLE

DUGOUT

25' - 0" MIN.

LIGHT POLE

DUGOUT

BACKSTOP

CATCHER'S BOX FORMED BY EXTENDING FOUL LINE BEHIND HOME PLATE

DETAIL OF HOME PLATE

- 4"
- 3' - 0"
- 3' - 0"
- 8½"
- 3' - 0"
- 3' - 0"
- 8½"
- 17"
- 9' - 0" RAD.
- 6' - 0"

PLAN OF LITTLE LEAGUE BASEBALL FIELD

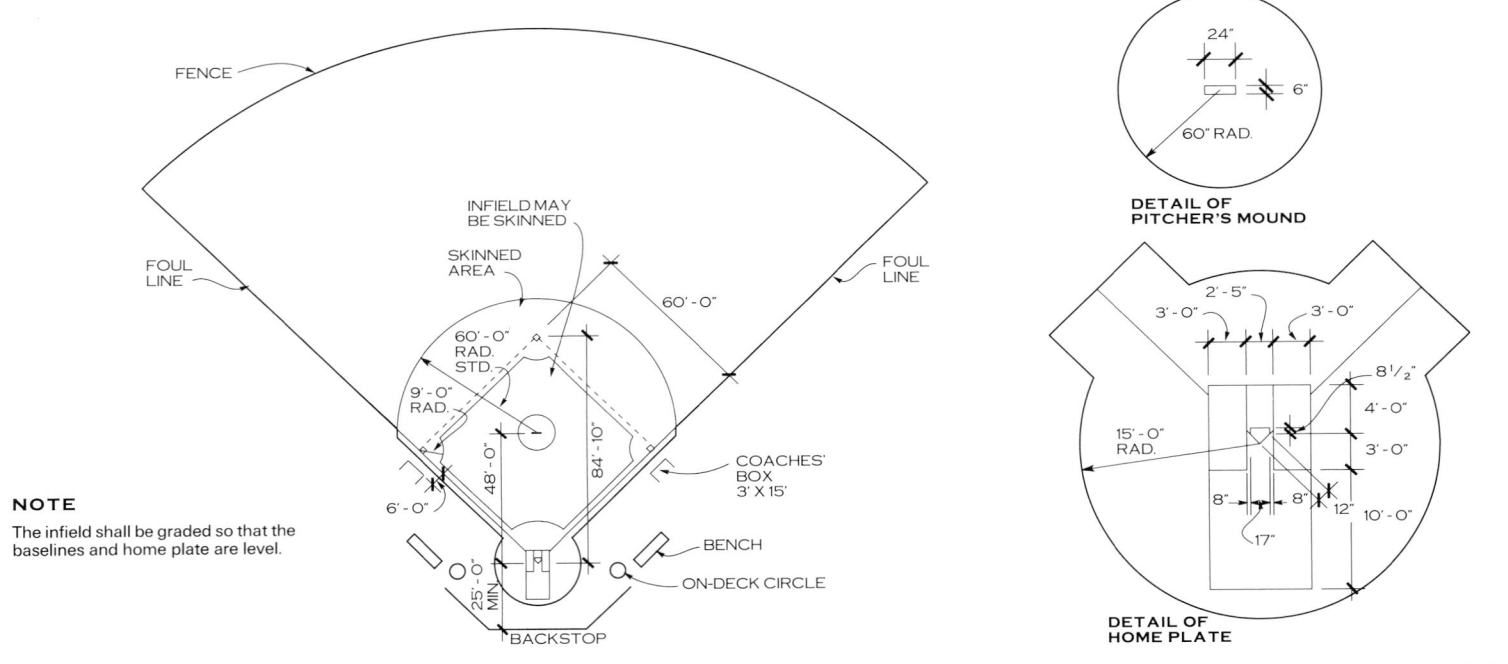

FENCE

DETAIL OF PITCHER'S MOUND

- 24"
- 6"
- 60" RAD.

INFIELD MAY BE SKINNED

SKINNED AREA

FOUL LINE

FOUL LINE

60' - 0"

60' - 0" RAD. STD.

9' - 0" RAD.

84' - 10"

48' - 0"

COACHES' BOX 3' X 15'

NOTE

The infield shall be graded so that the baselines and home plate are level.

6' - 0"

25' - 0" MIN.

BENCH

ON-DECK CIRCLE

BACKSTOP

DETAIL OF HOME PLATE

- 2' - 5"
- 3' - 0"
- 3' - 0"
- 8½"
- 15' - 0" RAD.
- 4' - 0"
- 3' - 0"
- 8"
- 8"
- 12"
- 10' - 0"
- 17"

PLAN OF SOFTBALL FIELD

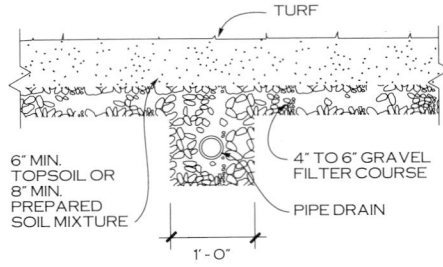

TURF

6" MIN. TOPSOIL OR 8" MIN. PREPARED SOIL MIXTURE

4" TO 6" GRAVEL FILTER COURSE

PIPE DRAIN

1' - 0"

NOTES

1. Baselines should be level; if the diamond must pitch, the slope should not be more than 2% from third to first base, or vice versa. The minimum slope of turf areas outside the skinned area is 1% when there is good subsoil drainage, 2.5% when drainage is poor.
2. The softball backstop is covered in detail on page 674.

SECTION OF TURF AND SUBSOIL DRAIN

17   FIELD SPORTS

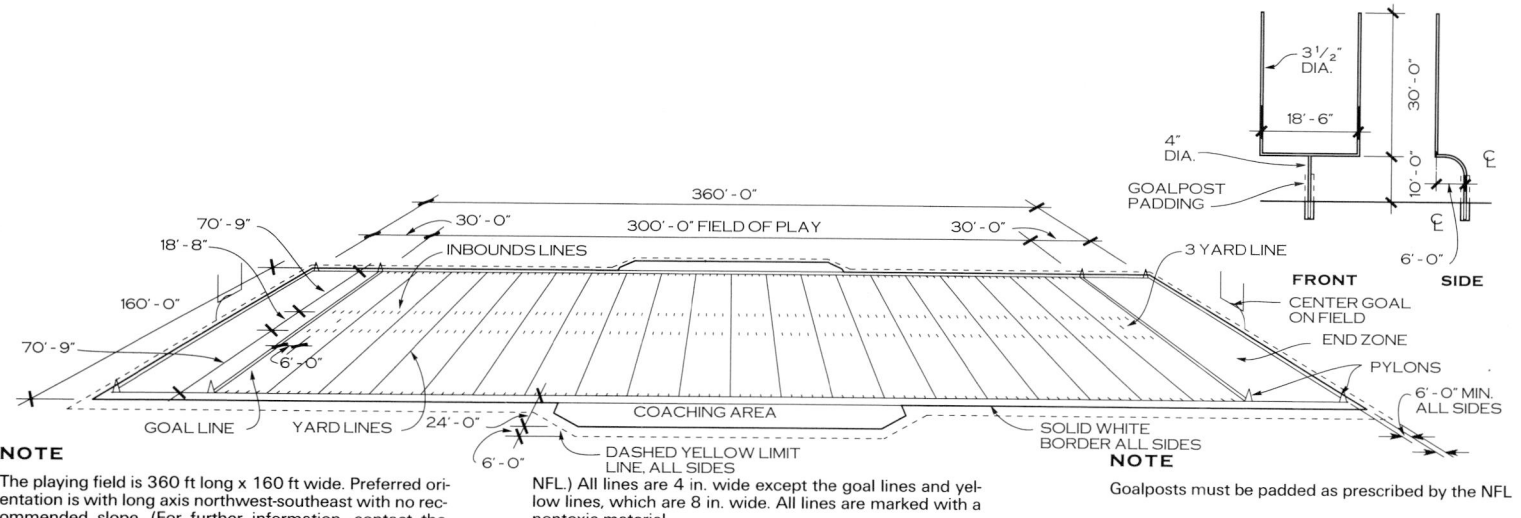

NOTE

The playing field is 360 ft long x 160 ft wide. Preferred orientation is with long axis northwest-southeast with no recommended slope. (For further information, contact the NFL.) All lines are 4 in. wide except the goal lines and yellow lines, which are 8 in. wide. All lines are marked with a nontoxic material.

NOTE

Goalposts must be padded as prescribed by the NFL

PROFESSIONAL FOOTBALL (NFL)

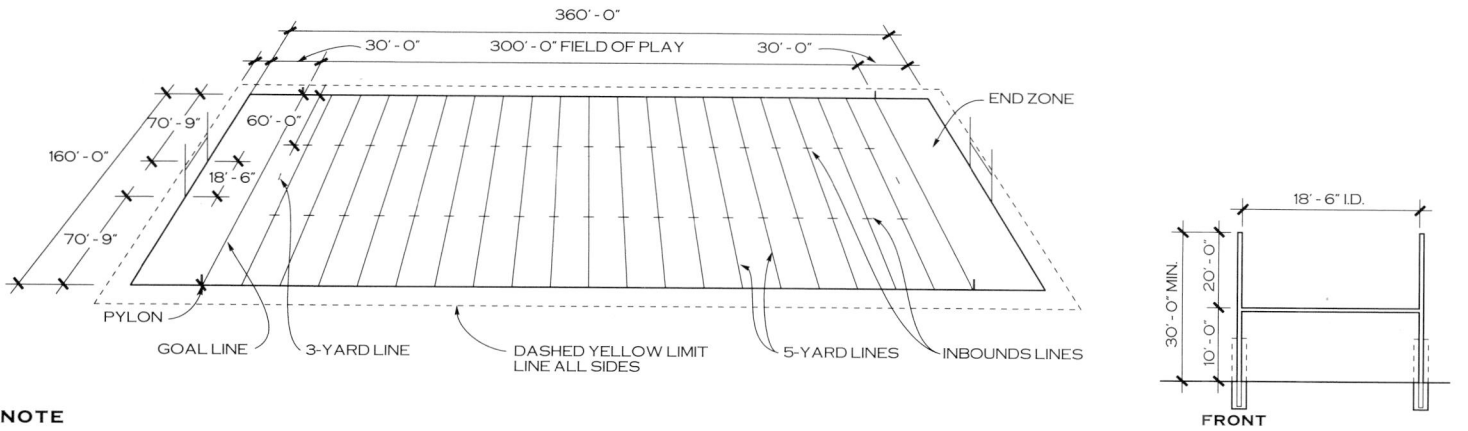

GOALPOSTS

Goalposts should be padded to a height of 6 ft. Color of posts should be yellow or white.

NOTE

The playing field is 360 ft long x 160 ft wide with an additional 12 ft recommended (6 ft minimum) on all sides. Preferred orientation is with the long axis northwest-southeast. Grading of the field should be from the center-line. Subsoil drainage may be necessary. All field dimension lines are 4 in. wide and are marked with a white, nontoxic material. All measurements are from the edge of the line closest to the center of the playing field. End zone marking should not overlap goal lines, side lines, and end lines. Location of inbounds lines is 60 ft (53 ft 4 in. for high school) for college football. Marks should be 4 in. wide x 2 ft long.

COLLEGE FOOTBALL (NATIONAL COLLEGIATE ATHLETIC ASSOCIATION)

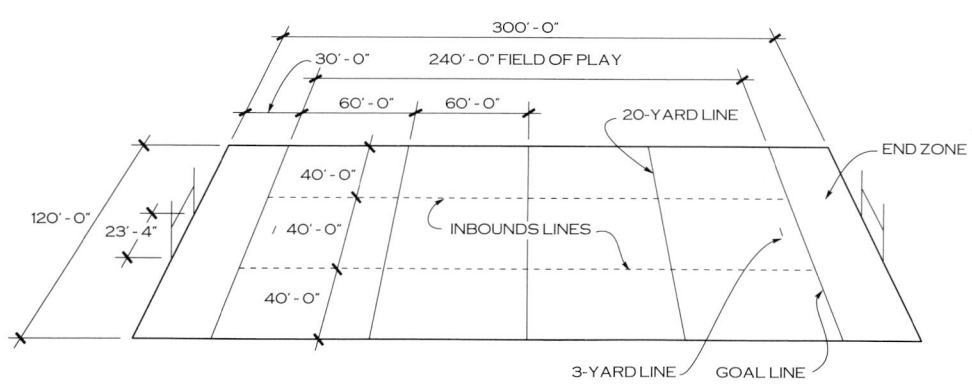

FOOTBALL

NOTE

The playing field is 300 ft long x 120 ft wide with an additional 6 ft allowed on all sides. Preferred orientation is for the long axis to run northwest-southeast. The recommended slope of 1% for proper drainage should run away from each side of the center long axis. All measurements are from the inside edge of the lines, which are 4 in. wide and marked with a white, nontoxic material. Goalposts are similar to those in college football.

NOTE

The football, a prolate spheroid with a long axis of 11 to 11 1/4 in., weighs from 14 to 15 oz.

TOUCH AND FLAG FOOTBALL

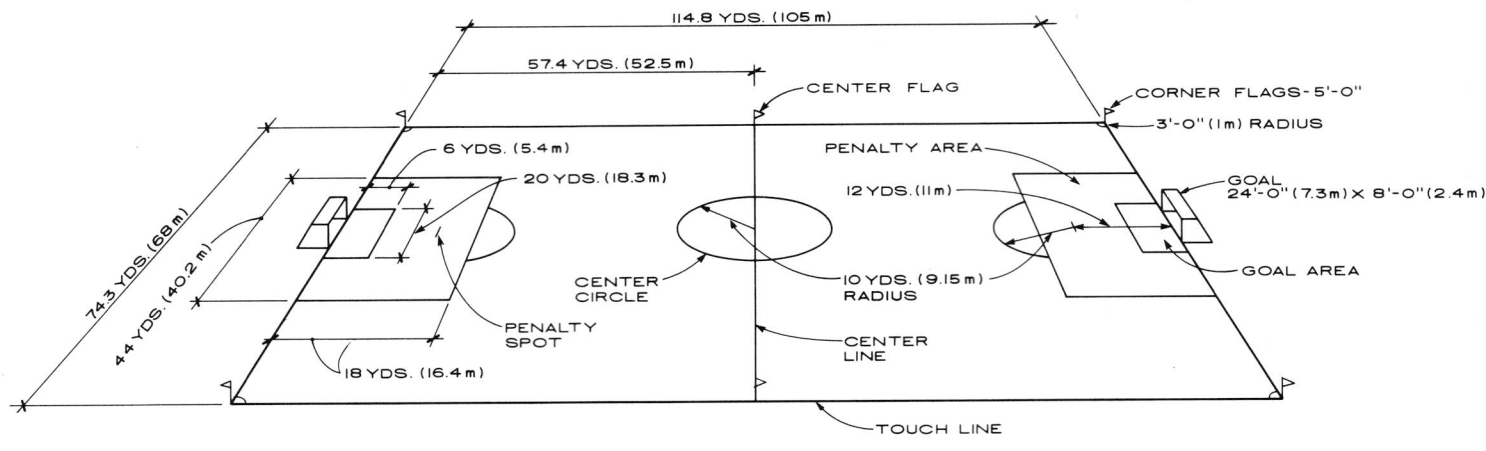

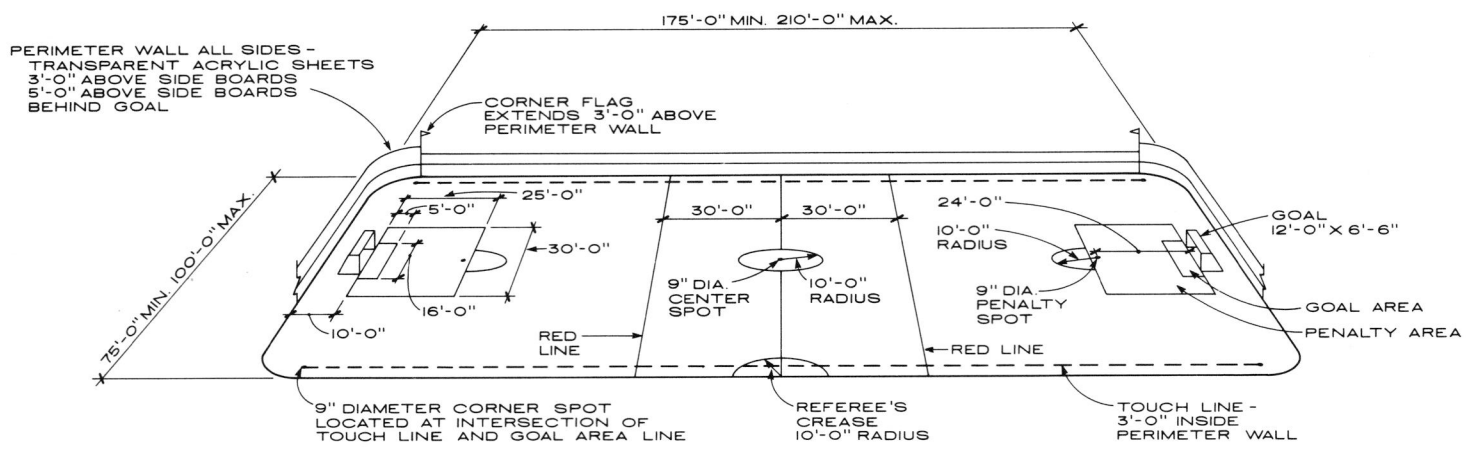

NOTE: OVERALL FIELD DIMENSIONS DEPEND ON AVAILABLE PLAYING SURFACE.

INDOOR SOCCER - MAJOR INDOOR SOCCER LEAGUE

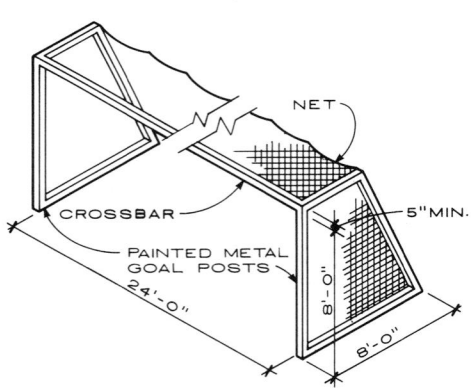

GOAL

The goal posts and crossbar shall not exceed 5 in. nor be less than 4 in. wide and shall present a flat surface to the playing field. The net must be attached to the ground, goal posts, and crossbar. It must extend back and level with the crossbar for 2 ft. 0 in. (.61 M).

SOCCER GOAL

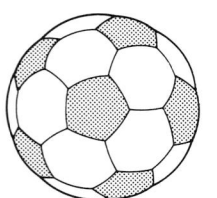

27" (68.58CM) IN CIRCUMFERENCE 14 TO 16 OZ. (453-897 GRAMS)

BALL

The ball's surface has thirty-odd black and white panels that enable the players to estimate its direction and speed of spin.

NOTES AND DEFINITIONS

All dimensions shown are to the inside edge of lines. All lines are to be white and 2 in. wide, except the centerline, which is 5 in. wide.

The long-field orientations in the northern hemisphere should be northwest-southeast for best sun angle during the fall playing season. The preferred drainage is a longitudinal crown with a 1 percent slope from center to each side.

Touchlines are the side boundaries, which are 114 yards (105 M) long.

The centerline is 5 in. (12.7 cm) wide and divides the playing field in half.

The center circle is a 10 yard (9 M) radius from the center of the centerline. At the beginning of each half the ball is kicked off from this circle by one team or the other.

The goal area is the smaller of the two rectangular zones: 20 yards (18.3 M) wide, 6 yards (5.4 M) in front of each goal. Other players can enter the goal area but cannot charge the goalie when he does not have the ball.

The penalty area is the larger of the two rectangular zones: 44 yards (40 M) wide, 18 yards (16.4 M) deep. A major rule infraction in this area allows the other team a penalty kick from the penalty spot.

Refer to rule setting body involved for actual dimensions required. Information shown here is for initial planning only.

Besides all the architectural differences between indoor and outdoor soccer, the natures of the games are deeply contrasted. Refer to the governing bodies, the Major Indoor Soccer League, the U.S. Soccer Federation, the North American Soccer League.

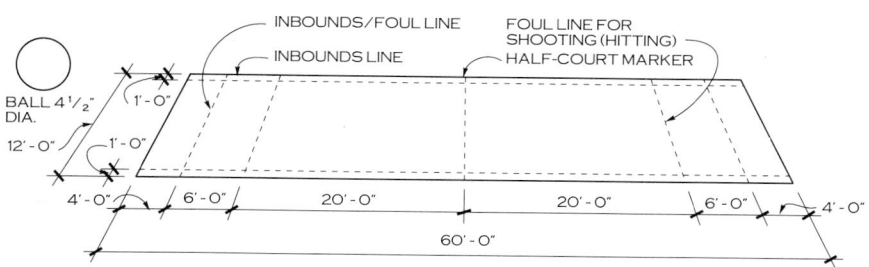

BOCCE BALL (BOCCIE)

BOCCE

The playing field is 60 x 12 ft (18.28 x 3.65 m). Although orientation is of minor importance, it is preferred that the long axis run north-south. The surface should be flat without slope when it is stone, dust, or clay with adequate underdrainage and 1% slope in any direction when turf.

The ball is 4 1/2 in. in diameter and weighs 32 oz.

Further information is available from the International Bocce Association, Inc.

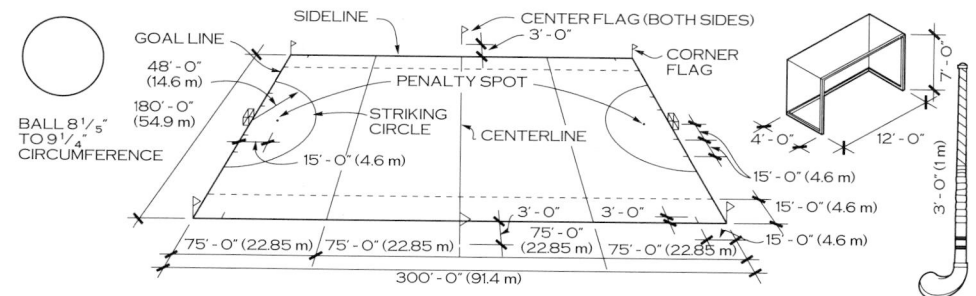

FIELD HOCKEY

FIELD HOCKEY

The playing field is 300 x 180 ft (91.4 x 54.9 m) with an additional 10 ft (3.05 m) safety zone recommended on all sides. The preferred long axis orientation is northwest-southeast. Recommended grading is a 1% slope on each side of the longitudinal axis. All measurements shown are from the inside edge of the lines. Lines are 3 in. wide and marked with a white, nontoxic material.

The field hockey ball is 8 1/5 to 9 1/4 in. (20.8 - 23.5 cm) in circumference and weighs 5 1/2 oz. (155 g). The stick is 3 ft (1 m) long with a wooden head and cane handle with a cork or rubber insert.

Further information is available from the U. S. Field Hockey Association.

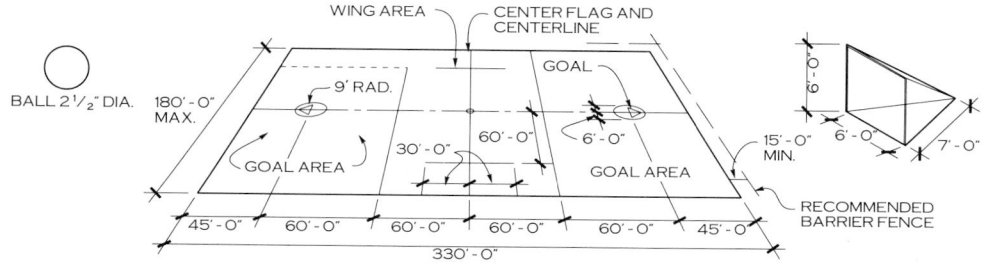

LACROSSE

LACROSSE

The playing field is 300 ft (100.58 m) long and from 160 to 180 ft (48 - 55m) wide, with an additional 15 ft (6.10 m) recommended on all sides. The preferred long axis orientation is northwest-southeast and preferred drainage is a 1% slope away from each side of the longitudinal axis. All dimensions shown are to the inside of the lines except for the centerline. Lines are 2 in. wide and marked with a white, nontoxic material. Flexible flag markers are placed at each corner and on field sidelines at the centerline.

Diameter of lacrosse ball is 2 1/2 in.; the stick is 3 to 6 ft in length.

Further information is available from the National Collegiate Athletic Association.

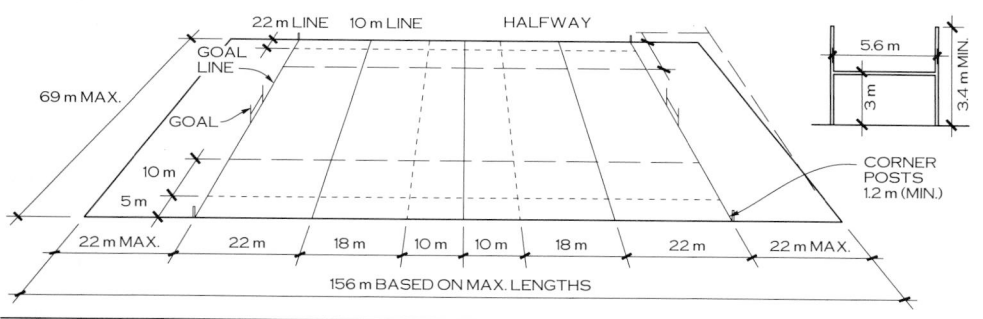

RUGBY

RUGBY

The playing field is 156 x 69 m with an additional 3 m safety zone recommended on all sides. The preferred long axis orientation is northwest-southeast; recommended grading is a 1% slope from each side of the axis. All measurements are from the inside line edges, which are marked with a white, nontoxic material.

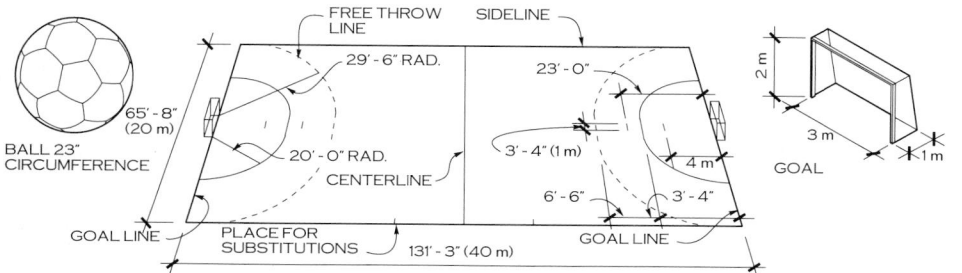

TEAM HANDBALL

TEAM HANDBALL

The playing field is 131 ft 3 in. x 65 ft 8 in. (40 x 20 m), with an additional 6 ft (2 m) unobstructed space on all sides. Preferred orientation is northwest-southeast along the longitudinal axis with a 1% slope away from each side of that axis. All dimensions shown are from the inside line edges except the centerline. All lines are 2 in. wide and marked with a white, nontoxic material.

The men's handball is 23 in. (58.4 cm) in circumference and weighs 16 oz. (453.6 g).

REGULATION COURSES

Among the types of golf courses – regulation, executive, and par-3 courses – the regulation course is the most popular and truest of form, having originated from early Scottish courses. In 18 holes, the course should play to a par of 72 and be at least 6000 yards from middle tees with 6500 yards a good median. A 6500-yard course, complete with clubhouse, parking, practice, and related facilities, will require 160 to 180 acres.

Beginning and ending at the clubhouse, a par-72 course should contain a combination of:

10 par-4 holes   4 par-3 holes   4 par-5 holes = 18 holes
or
5 par-4 holes   2 par-3 holes   2 par-5 holes = 9 holes

A par-70 or 71 is acceptable if the size of the property or nature of terrain prevents the layout of four good par-5 holes. Then replace one or two par-5s with par-4 holes.

GOLF COURSE CONFIGURATIONS

The typical golf course configurations are:

1. Core
2. Core with fingers
3. Double-fairway loop
4. Single-fairway loop
5. Loop with returning nines
6. Loop without returning nines

To gain lot frontage for housing developments, finger or loop configurations should be used. Disadvantages include greater distances between hole and next tee; overall maintenance cost may be higher; and golf balls will be hit off the property.

COURSE LAYOUT

Lay out holes according to their centerline of play, which should run from the center of the tee to the center of the green. On par-4 and par-5 holes the centerline should run on a straight line from the tee to a dogleg point 225 yards down the fairway. On par-5 holes a second dogleg point should be set at 425 yards.

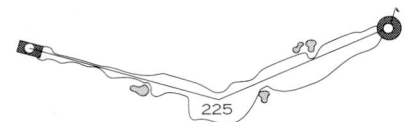

TYPICAL PAR FOUR LAYOUT

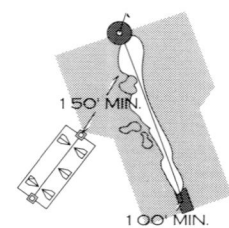

The centerline of a golf hole should be located a minimum of 150 ft from any road, right-of-way, boundary, clubhouse, or maintenance building, except a minimum of 100 ft at the tee. At a distance of 100 to 120 yd from the tee, the width should be 150 ft. On double-fairway loop courses, a minimum width of 500 ft is required.

SAFTETY ZONE

FACILITIES

Clubhouse facilities occupy 6 to 12 acres.

PARKING

Space may be needed for as many as 300 cars:

18 holes x 3 foursomes = 216 cars
25 percent course overlap = 54 cars
Employee/customer parking = 30 cars

PRACTICE FACILITIES

Ideal range is 300 yd long and 100 yd wide. At a 12-to-20 ft per practice station, a 600-ft wide facility should serve 30 to 50 golfers.

PLANNING PROCESS

Ease of utility connections is essential for clubhouse, maintenance area, and the irrigation system. Excessive front-end costs can be avoided by locating near existing infrastructure. Potable water may be from wells or the existing water supply. Irrigation water is usually contained in ponds dug on the golf course.

For an 18-hole golf course, 160 acres is an optimal size. If land is rugged, 175 to 180 acres may be needed. An area less than 150 acres is possible, although this may involve risk of injury to players.

The two most important natural factors in site selection are drainage and soil condition. Many prefer a gently rolling land with positive surface drainage. Fine old trees standing alone in open areas should be noted for use as design features. Developer may want to reserve wooded areas for housing.

VIEWS, NOISE, SUN, AND WIND ORIENTATION

Prevailing wind direction in both summer and winter should be noted. Thin or plant trees according to needs. Study sun orientation to avoid unpleasant views into the setting sun. Generally most favorable location for a clubhouse is at the "high noon" position. Any dramatic views should be noted, although screening or elimination of unpleasant views is more often necessary.

DESIGN DETAILS
GREENS

1. Backdrop of trees or natural slope needed.
2. Should vary in size and shape according to the shot being played.
3. Subdivide greens if desired.
4. Should have six pin-placement areas on each green.
5. Slopes on putting surface should range from 2 to 4 percent.
6. Back usually should be raised two-to-three feet above the front.
7. Blend contours into natural environments.
8. Sides should slope 4:1, 5:1, 6:1, or 7:1, unless contour changes dramatically.

TEES

1. Provide separate tees for different caliber of golfers.
2. Single block tee should be 100 yd to accommodate four sets of tee markers.
3. Need not be rectangular boxes.
4. Tees should be distinct and integrated into the site.
5. For every 1000 rounds per year requires 100 to 200 sq ft.
6. Tees for first and 10th holes and par-3 holes should be larger than others.

HAZARDS

1. Hazards give a golf course its character and flavor and provide challenge to the golfer.
2. Use sand where there are no natural features to provide a desired golfing challenge.
3. Sand can be used to provide depth perception, to define a target area, to frame and accentuate a green, and to divide and buffer parallel fairways.
4. Don't over or under use certain types of sand traps.
5. Use water because of the need to store large amounts for source irrigation, the desire to create strategic and heroic holes, the relative ease to construct ponds and lakes, and to emphasize its esthetic value.
6. Water can be placed across the line of play or parallel to the fairway.
7. There should be water on each classification of hole– par-3, par-4, and par-5.
8. The rough defines the fairways and generally is used as a supplemental hazard.
9. Trees typically line inland courses and serve as hazards but also as physical separators between golf holes. Trees also provide shade and add to esthetics.
10. Planting and clearing of trees should provide a variety of wide and narrow fairways, open and wooded holes, woods, and individual stands.
11. Subtle mounding and contouring of greens and aprons can define fairway limits, separating parallel fairways where there are no existing trees, providing protection for dangerous, tightly spaced areas on a golf course, create a feeling of spatial enclosure, and provide for raised spectator areas at tournaments.
12. Prevailing wind affects the routing of a course.
13. Poor drainage results in weak turf and delays the opening of a course after rain. Therefore, every square foot of a golf course should have positive surface flow to a pond or sewer pipe, either by the natural contour or installed drainage system.

Consultation with a golf course architect is recommended.

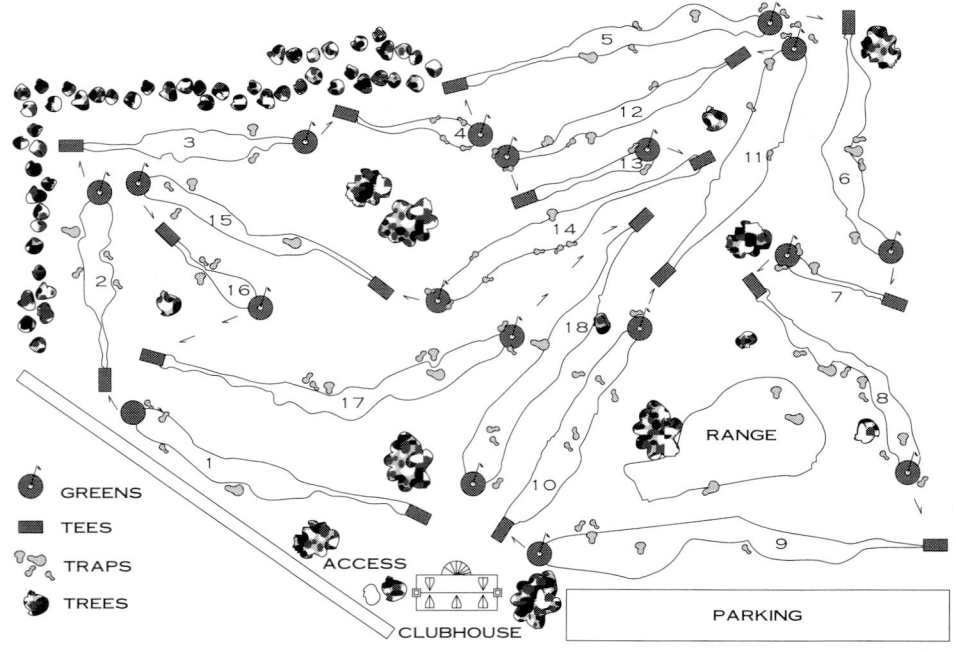

DOUBLE FAIRWAY LOOP

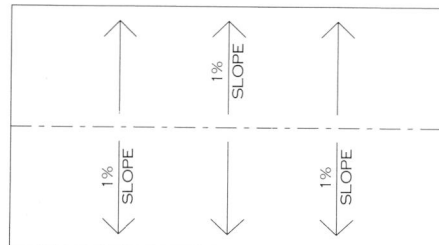

PREFERRED GRADING

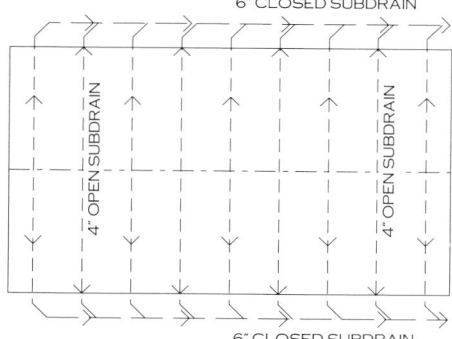

SUBSOIL DRAINAGE

RECTANGULAR SPORTS FIELDS

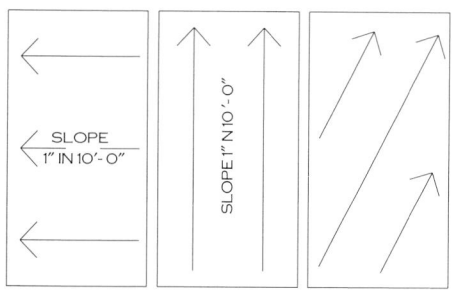

DRAINAGE DIAGRAMS

SPORTS COURTS

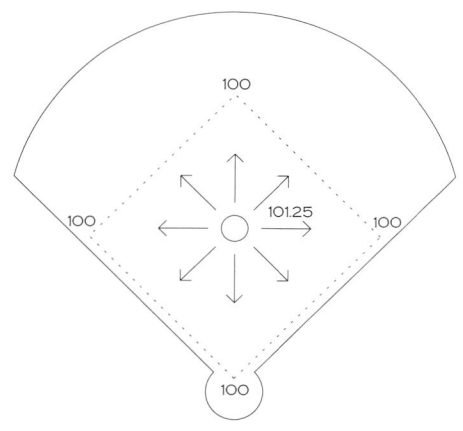

BASEBALL AND SOFTBALL DIAMONDS

NOTES

It is preferable that the baselines be level. If the diamond must pitch, the average slope shall be 2% from first base to third base or vice versa.

The minimum slope for drainage on turf areas outside the skinned area is 1% when adequate subsoil drainage is provided. The maximum is 2.5%.

Sheryl Ananich; Tomblinson Harburn Associates; Flint, Michigan
J. Paul Raeder; Beckett & Raeder, Inc.; Ann Arbor, Michigan
Lawrence Cook Associates P.C., Architects; Falls Church, Virginia

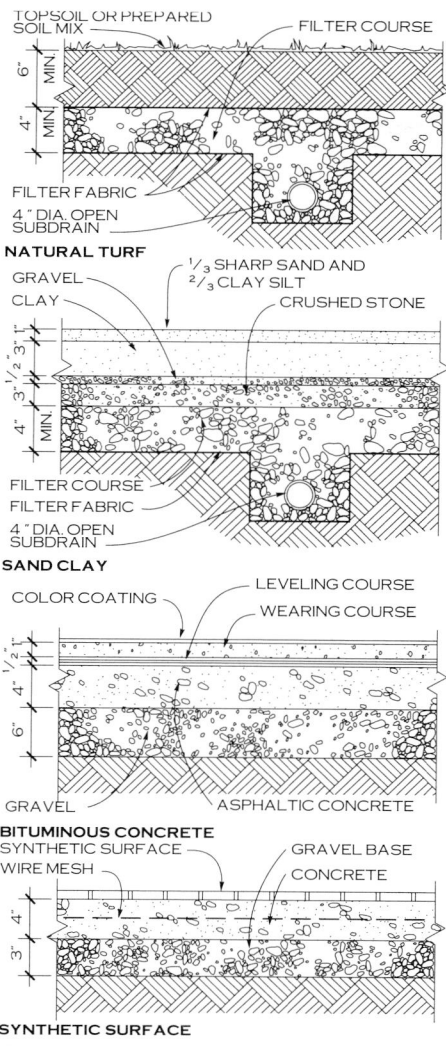

NATURAL TURF

SAND CLAY

BITUMINOUS CONCRETE

SYNTHETIC SURFACE

PLAYING SURFACES

TYPICAL GRADING AND DRAINAGE DETAILS COURT SURFACES

Paved playing surfaces should be in one plane and pitched from side to side, end to end, or corner to corner diagonally, instead of two planes pitched to or from the net. Minimum slope should be 1 in. to every 10 ft. Subgrade should slope in the same direction as the surface. Perimeter drains may be provided for paved areas. Underdrains are not recommended beneath paved areas.

PLAYING FIELDS

Preferred grading for rectangular field is a longitudinal crown with 1% slope from center to each side.

Grading may be from side to side or corner to corner diagonally, if conditions do not permit the preferred grading.

Subsoil drainage should slope in the same direction as the surface. Subdrains and filter course are to be used only when subsoil conditions require. Where subsoil drainage is necessary, the spacing of subdrains is dependent on local soil conditions and rainfall.

Subdrains are to have a minimum gradient of 0.15%.

Baseball and softball fields should be graded so that the bases are level.

LINE PAINTING

All line markings should be acrylic water-base paint only. Oil-base or traffic paints crack, craze, or peel. Spray painting usually is used. High quality courts should be hand painted. Accuracy of track layouts should be verified by registered land surveyor.

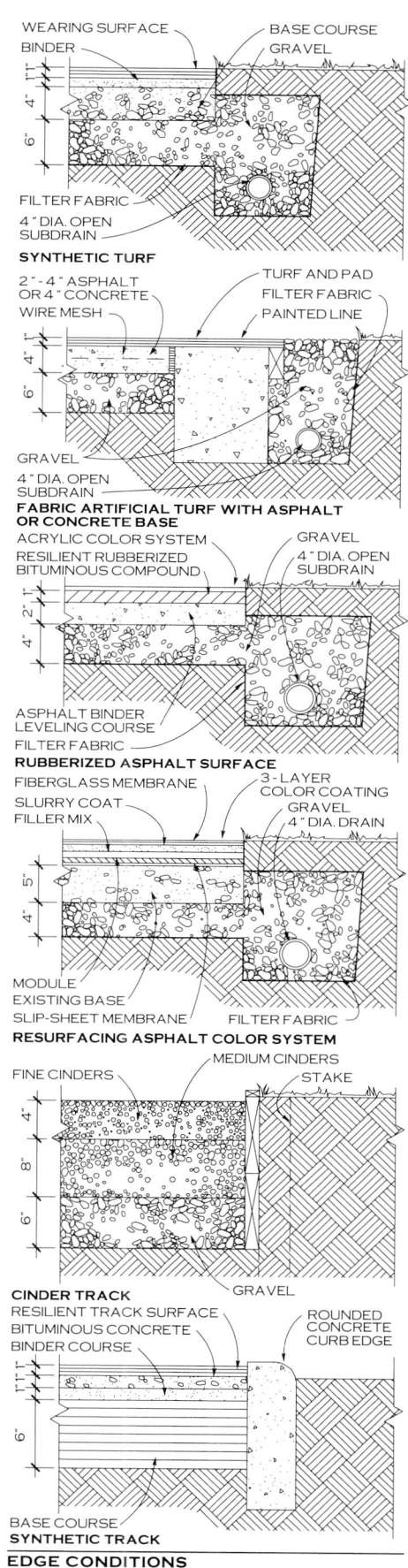

SYNTHETIC TURF

FABRIC ARTIFICIAL TURF WITH ASPHALT OR CONCRETE BASE

RUBBERIZED ASPHALT SURFACE

RESURFACING ASPHALT COLOR SYSTEM

CINDER TRACK

SYNTHETIC TRACK

EDGE CONDITIONS

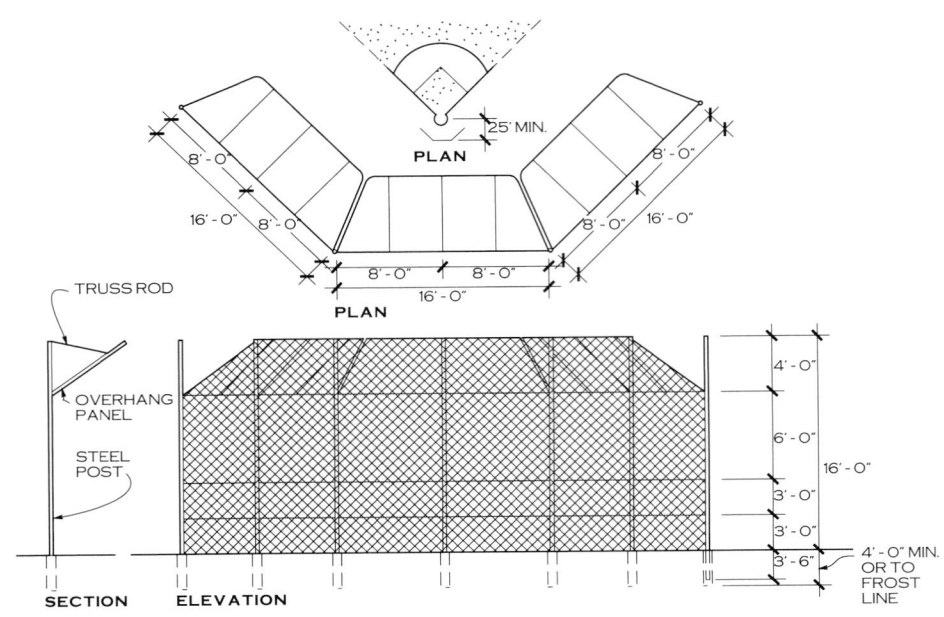

PLAN

PLAN

TRUSS ROD

OVERHANG PANEL

STEEL POST

SECTION   ELEVATION

4' - 0"

6' - 0"

16' - 0"

3' - 0"

3' - 0"

3' - 6"

4' - 0" MIN. OR TO FROST LINE

25' MIN.

8' - 0"   8' - 0"

16' - 0"

8' - 0"   8' - 0"

16' - 0"

8' - 0"   8' - 0"

16' - 0"

TYPICAL SOFTBALL BACKSTOP

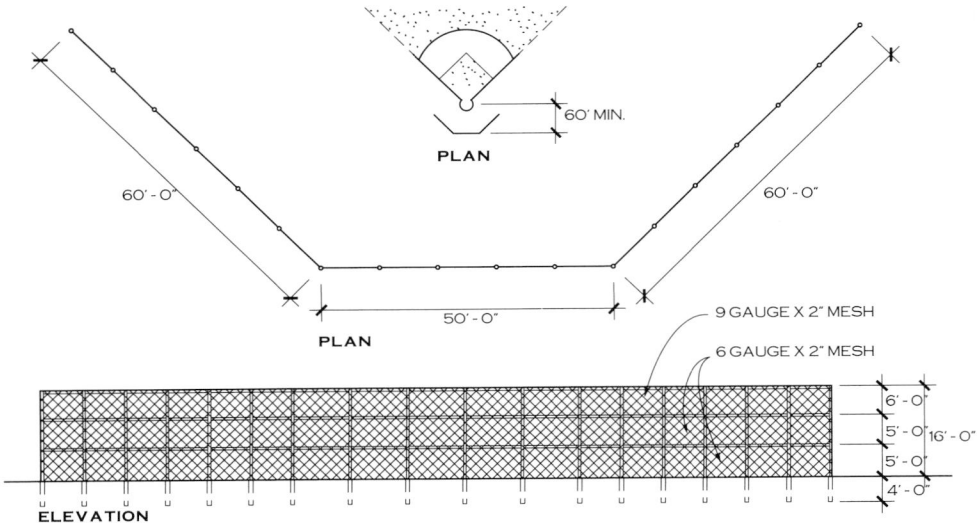

PLAN

60' MIN.

60' - 0"   60' - 0"

50' - 0"

PLAN

ELEVATION

9 GAUGE X 2" MESH

6 GAUGE X 2" MESH

6' - 0"
5' - 0"   16' - 0"
5' - 0"
4' - 0"

REGULATION BASEBALL BACKSTOP

BACKSTOP SIZE AND DIMENSION

Height and width of baseball backstops are to be determined by sports authorities and local requirements.

Posts for backstop heights up to 16 ft: use 3 in. outside diameter; posts for backstop heights 18 to 24 ft: use 4 in outside diameter; top, intermediate, and bottom rails: 1 5/8 in. outside diameter.

WIREO MESH FABRIC

Fabric shall be chain link with galvanized coating or aluminum (optional PVC-coated steel). All ferrous metal parts are to be hot dip galvanized after fabrication.

BASKETBALL STANDARDS

NCAA: Minimum backboard support overhang is 4 ft; minimum outside diameter of post is 3 1/2 in.

AAU: 5 ft 5 in. overhang (and optional NCAA overhang of 4 to 6 ft) requires minimum post outside diameter of 4 1/2 in.

Concrete footing: minimum 2 ft diameter and 4 ft depth. Method of bracing and backboard support varies with manufacturer.

J. Paul Raeder; Beckett Raeder Rankin, Inc.; Ann Arbor, Michigan
Lawrence Cook & Associates; Falls Church, Virginia

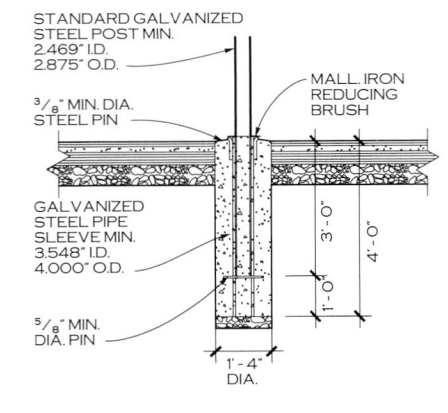

STANDARD GALVANIZED STEEL POST MIN. 2.469" I.D. 2.875" O.D.

MALL. IRON REDUCING BRUSH

3/8" MIN. DIA. STEEL PIN

GALVANIZED STEEL PIPE SLEEVE MIN. 3.548" I.D. 4.000" O.D.

5/8" MIN. DIA. PIN

3' - 0"

4' - 0"

1' - 0"

1' - 4" DIA.

REMOVABLE POST

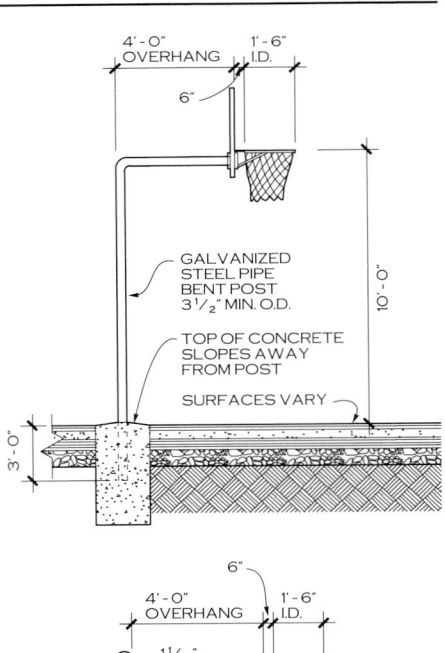

4' - 0" OVERHANG   1' - 6" I.D.

6"

GALVANIZED STEEL PIPE BENT POST 3 1/2" MIN. O.D.

TOP OF CONCRETE SLOPES AWAY FROM POST

SURFACES VARY

10' - 0"

3' - 0"

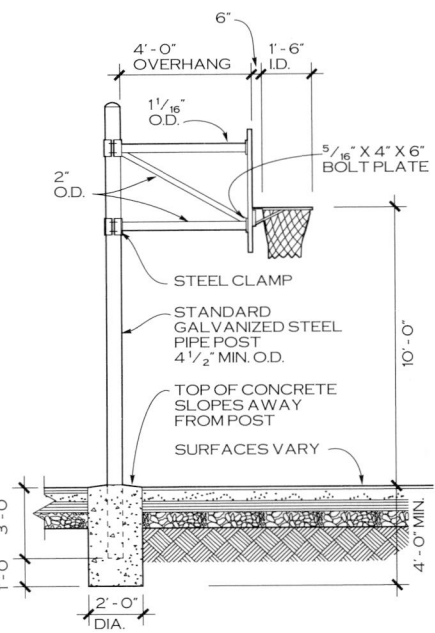

6"

4' - 0" OVERHANG   1' - 6" I.D.

1 1/16" O.D.

2" O.D.

5/16" X 4" X 6" BOLT PLATE

STEEL CLAMP

STANDARD GALVANIZED STEEL PIPE POST 4 1/2" MIN. O.D.

TOP OF CONCRETE SLOPES AWAY FROM POST

SURFACES VARY

10' - 0"

3' - 0"

1' - 0"

4' - 0" MIN.

2' - 0" DIA.

BASKETBALL STANDARDS

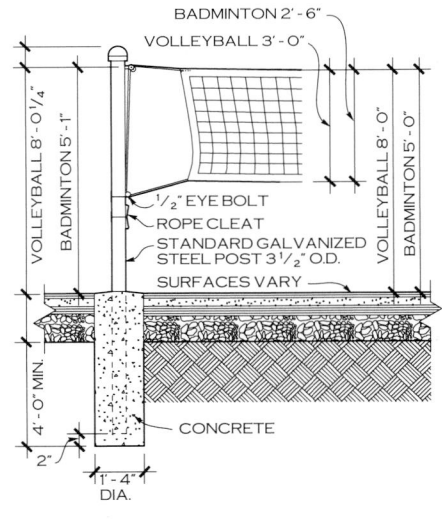

BADMINTON 2' - 6"

VOLLEYBALL 3' - 0"

VOLLEYBALL 8' - 0 1/4"
BADMINTON 5' - 1"

1/2" EYE BOLT

ROPE CLEAT

STANDARD GALVANIZED STEEL POST 3 1/2" O.D.

SURFACES VARY

VOLLEYBALL 8' - 0"
BADMINTON 5' - 0"

4' - 0" MIN.

CONCRETE

2"

1' - 4" DIA.

VOLLEYBALL AND BADMINTON NET AND POST

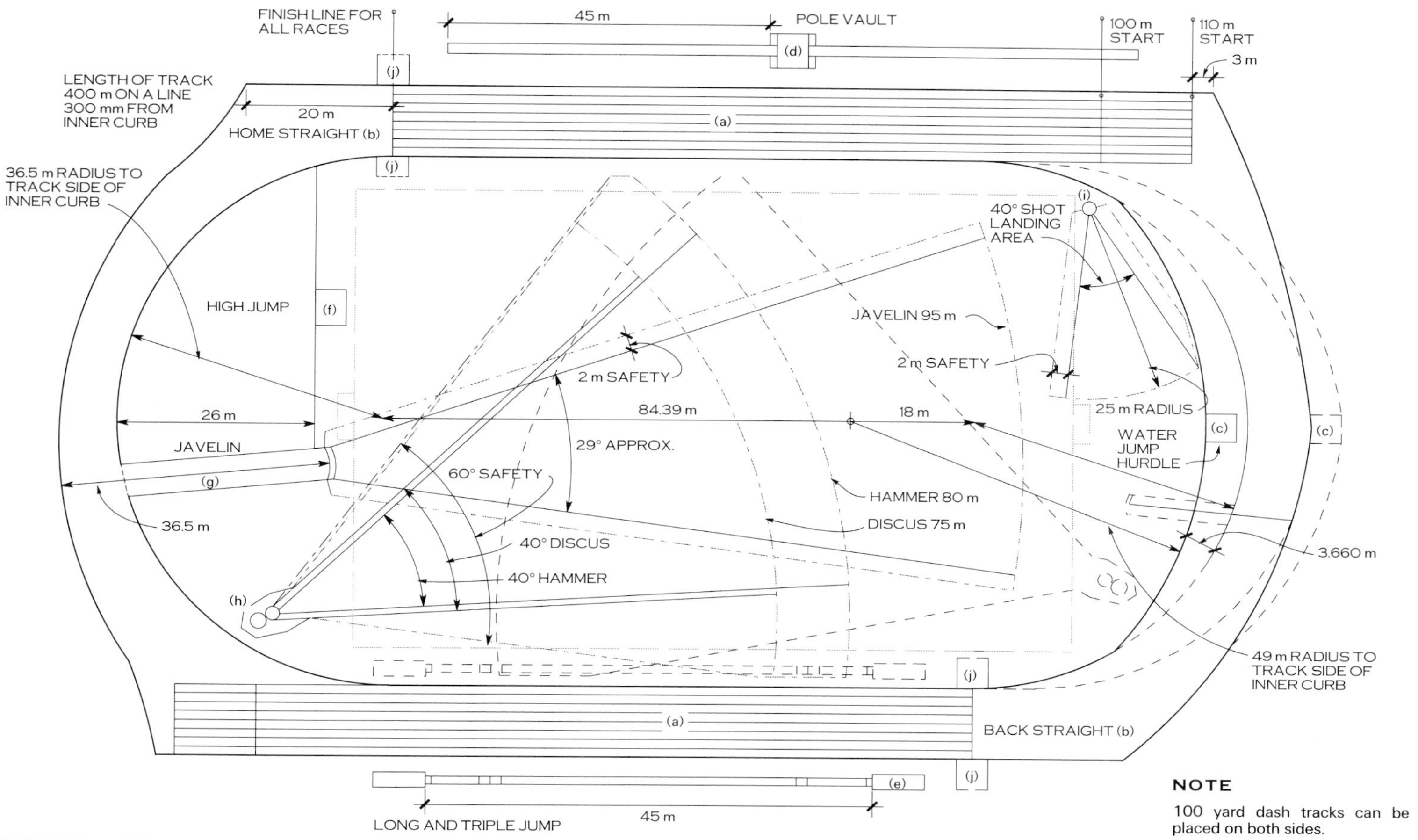

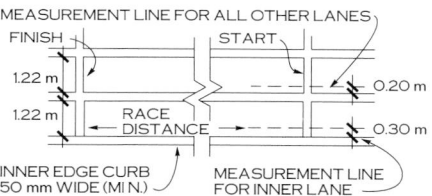

FINISH LINE FOR ALL RACES

45 m

POLE VAULT

(d)

100 m START

110 m START

3 m

LENGTH OF TRACK 400 m ON A LINE 300 mm FROM INNER CURB

20 m

HOME STRAIGHT (b)

(a)

(j)

(j)

36.5 m RADIUS TO TRACK SIDE OF INNER CURB

HIGH JUMP   (f)

40° SHOT LANDING AREA

(i)

JAVELIN 95 m

2 m SAFETY

2 m SAFETY

25 RADIUS

WATER JUMP HURDLE

(c)

(c)

26 m

84.39 m

18 m

JAVELIN

(g)

29° APPROX.

60° SAFETY

HAMMER 80 m

DISCUS 75 m

3.660 m

36.5 m

40° DISCUS

40° HAMMER

(h)

49 m RADIUS TO TRACK SIDE OF INNER CURB

(j)

(a)

BACK STRAIGHT (b)

(j)

(e)

LONG AND TRIPLE JUMP

45 m

NOTE

100 yard dash tracks can be placed on both sides.

LAYOUT GUIDE FOR 400 m RUNNING TRACK AND FIELD EVENT LOCATIONS

LEGEND

(a) Number of lanes
(b) Straights
(c) Steeplechase and water jump
(d) Pole vault
(e) Long and triple jumps
(f) High jump
(g) Javelin
(h) Hammer and discus in cage
(i) Putting and shot
(j) Paved areas

NATIONAL AND INTERNATIONAL COMPETITION

The diagram indicates how a 400 m track with a synthetic surface might be laid out for national and international competition. Different arrangements are possible to suit particular circumstances. For high level competition, however, alternatives for the siting of the throwing circles are of necessity limited if maximum distances are to be safely thrown. For Rules of Competition, refer to the handbook of the International Amateur Athletic Foundation.

TRACK AND LANES

The length of the track should be not less than 400 m. The track should be not less than 7.32 m in width and should, if possible, be bordered on the inside with concrete or other suitable material, approximately 50 mm high, minimum 50 mm wide. The curb may be raised to permit surface water to drain away, in which case a maximum height of 65 mm must not be exceeded.

Where it is not possible for the inner edge of the running track to have a raised border, the inner edge shall be marked with lines 50 mm wide.

The measurement of length shall be taken 0.30 m outward from the inner border of the track or, where no border exists, 0.20 m from the line marking the inside of the track.

In all races up to and including 400 m, each competitor shall have a separate lane, with a minimum width of 1.22 m to be marked by lines 50 mm in width. The inner lane shall be measured as stated in the preceding text, but the remaining lanes shall be measured 0.20 m from the outer edges of the lines.

ALL WHITE LINES 55 mm WIDE

MEASUREMENT LINE FOR ALL OTHER LANES

FINISH

START

1.22 m

1.22 m

RACE DISTANCE

0.20 m

0.30 m

INNER EDGE CURB 50 mm WIDE (MIN.)

MEASUREMENT LINE FOR INNER LANE

METHOD OF MARKING LANES

In international meetings, the track should allow for at least six lanes and, where possible, for eight lanes, particularly for major international events.

The maximum allowance for lateral inclination of tracks shall not exceed 1:100, and the inclination in the running direction shall not exceed 1:1000.

The lateral inclination of the track should, wherever possible, be toward the inside lane.

SURFACE

Synthetic materials provide a consistently good surface capable of continuous and unlimited use in most weather conditions. Maintenance is minimal, consisting of periodic cleaning by hosing down or brushing, the repainting when necessary of the line markings, and an occasional repair.

Cinder surfaces require considerable maintenance by a skilled groundsman every time a track is used. They are not all-weather and seldom provide a consistently good running surface. They are, however, much cheaper to construct and are suitable for club use and training.

On cinder tracks an extra lane is necessary so that sprint and hurdle events can be run on the six outer lanes to avoid the inner lane, which is subject to heavy use during long distance events.

ORIENTATION

It is often difficult to reconcile the requirements of wind direction and the need to avoid an approach into the setting sun. For these reasons, it is now becoming common practice to provide, where possible, alternative directions for running, jumping, and throwing.

THE FINISH

Two white posts shall denote the extremities of the finish line, and shall be placed at least 30 cm from the edge of the track.

The finish posts shall be of rigid construction about 1.4 m high, 80 mm wide, and 20 mm thick.

FORMULA FOR OTHER TRACK PROPORTIONS

Where a track of wider or narrower proportions or of different length is required, the appropriate dimensions can be calculated from the following formula:

$$L = 2P + 2\pi (R + .3 \text{ m})$$

where:

L = length of track (m)
P = length of parallels or distance apart of centers of curves (m)
R = radius to track side of inner curb (m)
$\pi = 3.1416$ (not $^{22}/_7$)

It is recommended that the radius of the semicircles should not normally be less than 32 m or more than 42 m for a 400 m circuit.

NUMBER OF LANES

	SYNTHETIC	CINDER
International competition	8 lanes (9.76 m)	8 lanes (9.76 m) 9 lanes (straights)
Area or regional competition	6 lanes (7.32 m)	7 lanes (8.54 m)

Charles F. D. Egbert, AIA; Egbert, Clarens, and Associates, P.C. Architects; Washington, D.C.

400 M TRACK AND FIELD EVENTS—CONSTRUCTION DETAILS

These details are based on international standards. For additional information, consult the International Amateur Athletic Foundation (IAAF).

These details were provided by the National Playing Fields Association, London, England.

NOTE

To avoid adverse wind conditions during competition, landing areas for the long and triple jumps are desirable at both ends of the runway. A surround of paving slabs (450 x 600 mm) is an advantage. Takeoff board to be of wood or other suitable rigid material, set level with surface and painted white. See detail.

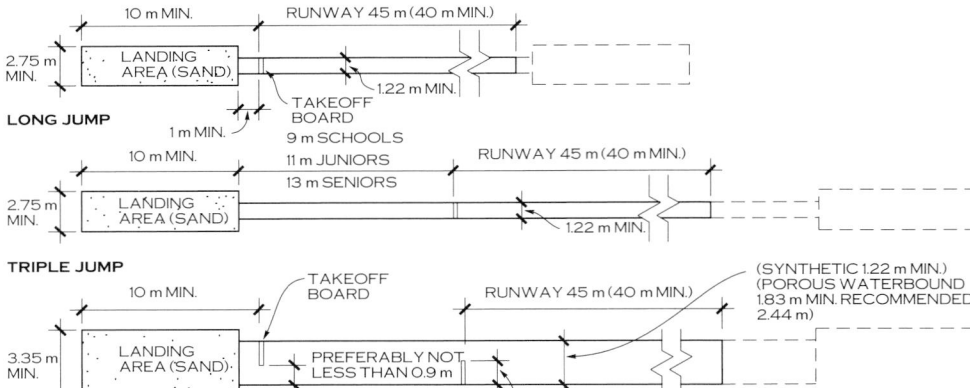

LONG JUMP

TRIPLE JUMP

COMBINED LONG AND TRIPLE JUMP

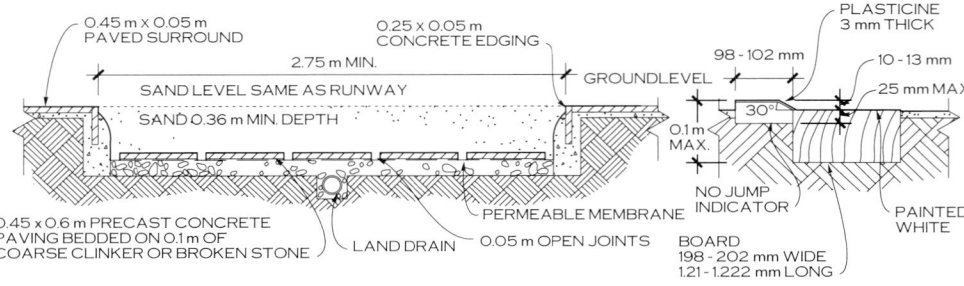

LONG AND TRIPLE JUMP

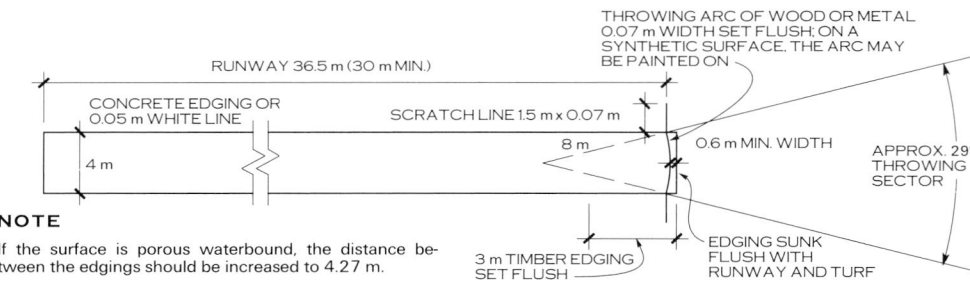

NOTE

If the surface is porous waterbound, the distance between the edgings should be increased to 4.27 m.

JAVELIN THROW

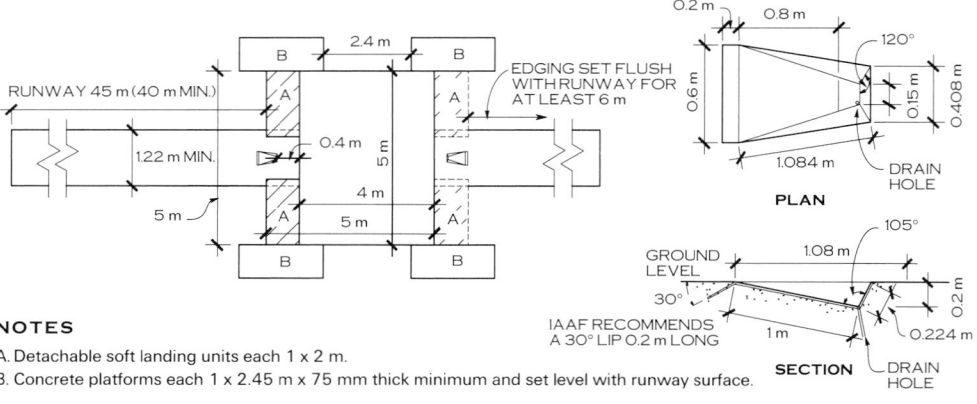

NOTES

A. Detachable soft landing units each 1 x 2 m.

B. Concrete platforms each 1 x 2.45 m x 75 mm thick minimum and set level with runway surface.

POLE VAULT

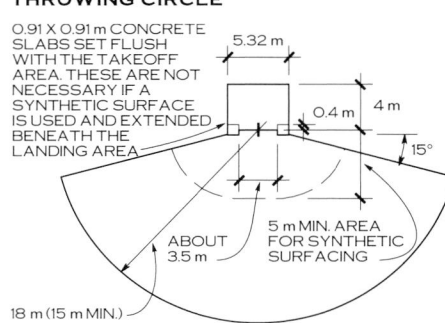

THROWING CIRCLE

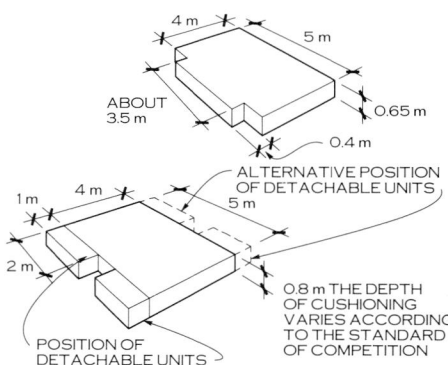

HIGH JUMP

SOFT LANDING AREAS

The soft landing area to be 5 x 5 m minimum. The distance between uprights or extension arms to be 3.660 m minimum/4.370 m maximum. A larger soft landing unit with a 1.300 m extension for the pole vault box cutout giving a total size of 5 x 6.300 m may be provided. The diagram shows a double runway with detachable A units and thus gives a choice of runways according to the wind direction.

For outdoor use, soft landing units should be laid on duckboards on an ash base or other suitable materials (e.g., precast concrete paving on a porous base with 50 mm open joints).

Charles F. D. Egbert, AIA; Egbert, Clarens, and Associates, P.C. Architects; Washington, D.C.

ORIENTATION

For the northern states, a true north-south orientation is recommended. North-northwest by south-southwest at approximately 22 degrees west of true north is recommended for outdoor courts south of the 38th parallel. Particular site characteristics, length of tennis season, and latitude should be taken into consideration when deciding on the most desirable court orientation angle.

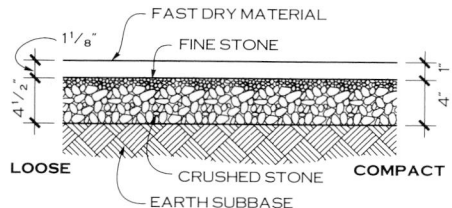

Fast-drying courts are successive layers of crushed green stone or burnt brick and finely ground rock particles mixed with a chemical binder. This surface provides a uniform bounce and allows sliding. A watering system, frequent maintenance, and annual resurfacing are recommended.

FAST-DRYING SURFACE

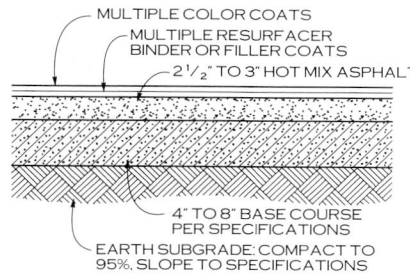

Hot mix asphalt is a mixture of asphalt and aggregate laid in place and compacted before cooling. This surface is laid on a 4 to 8 in. base of stone, gravel, or perforated macadam, depending on soil conditions.

For cushioned surface, place cushion material between resurfacer and color coat.

NON-POROUS/NON-CUSHIONED SURFACE

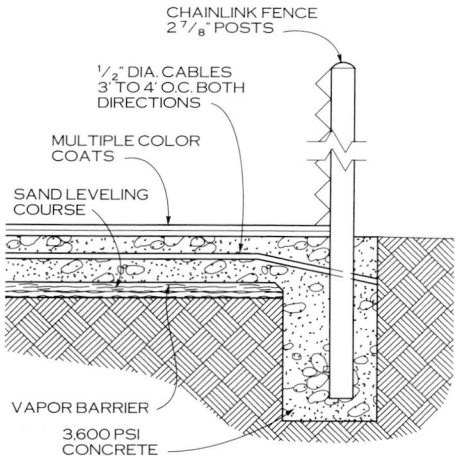

NOTE
No curing compound applied to concrete

Concrete slab 4 to 5 in. thick, placed over a vapor barrier and compacted sand base. Reinforcing cables spaced 3 to 4 ft on center. After concrete has attained sufficient strength, cables are tensioned and maintained in their final tension.

POST-TENSIONED CONCRETE SURFACE

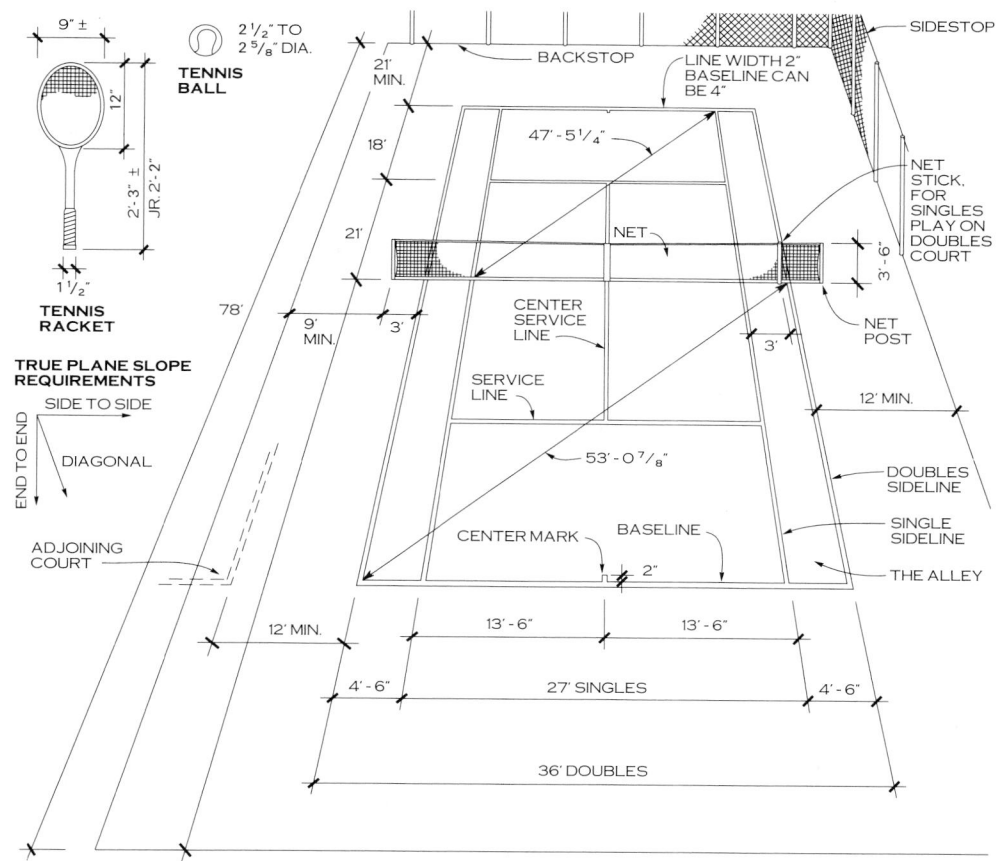

TENNIS BALL

TENNIS RACKET

TRUE PLANE SLOPE REQUIREMENTS

SURFACE DRAINAGE NOTES

1. Hard surface 1 in. over 10 ft
2. Porous courts without underground watering system 1 in. over 20 to 30 ft
3. Porous courts with underground watering system 1 in. over 40 ft
4. Slope should always be in a true plane, side to side, end to end, or corner to corner; never up to middle of court.
5. Subsoil drainage depends on soil conditions.

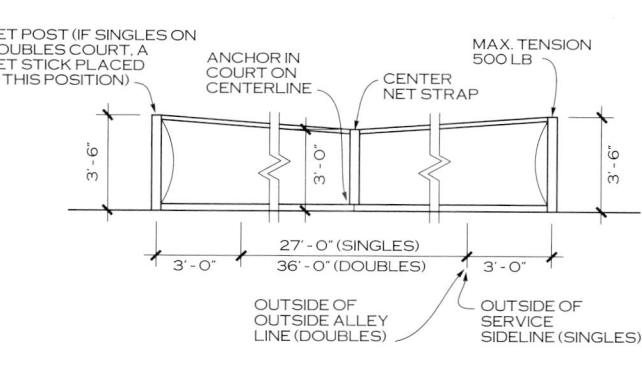

TENNIS COURT AND NET

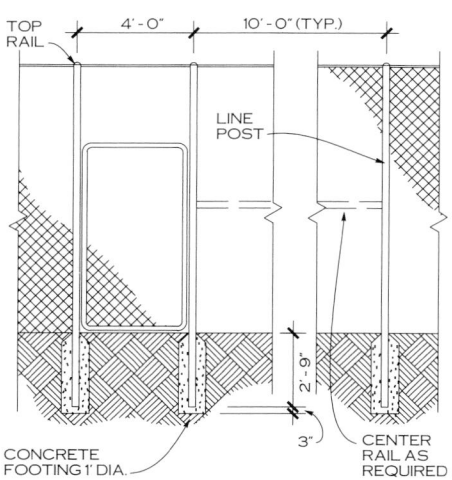

ELEVATION OF ENCLOSURE

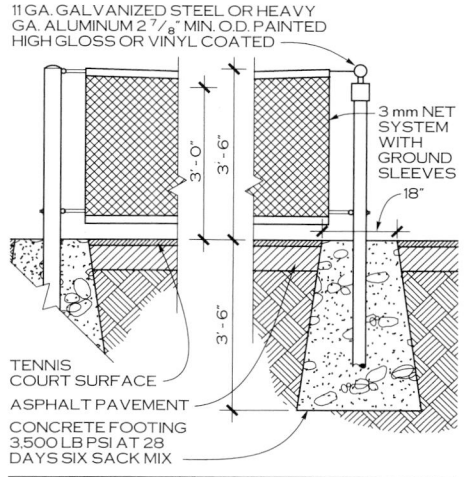

TENNIS POSTS

U.S. Tennis Court and Track Builders Association; Baltimore, Maryland

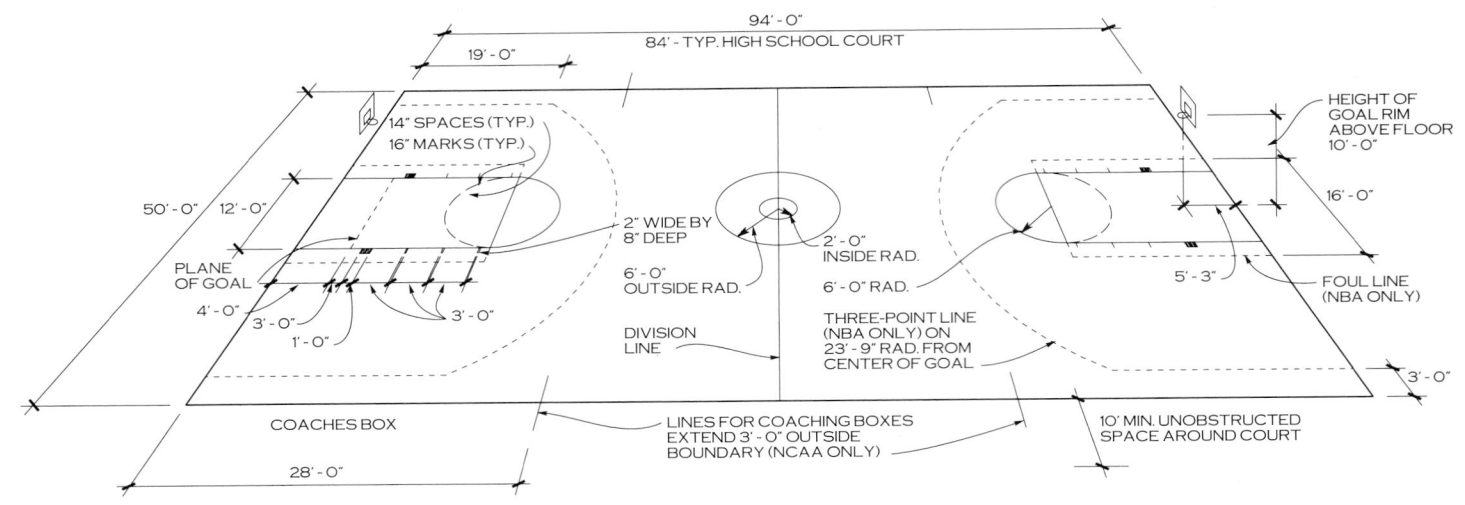

BASKETBALL COURT

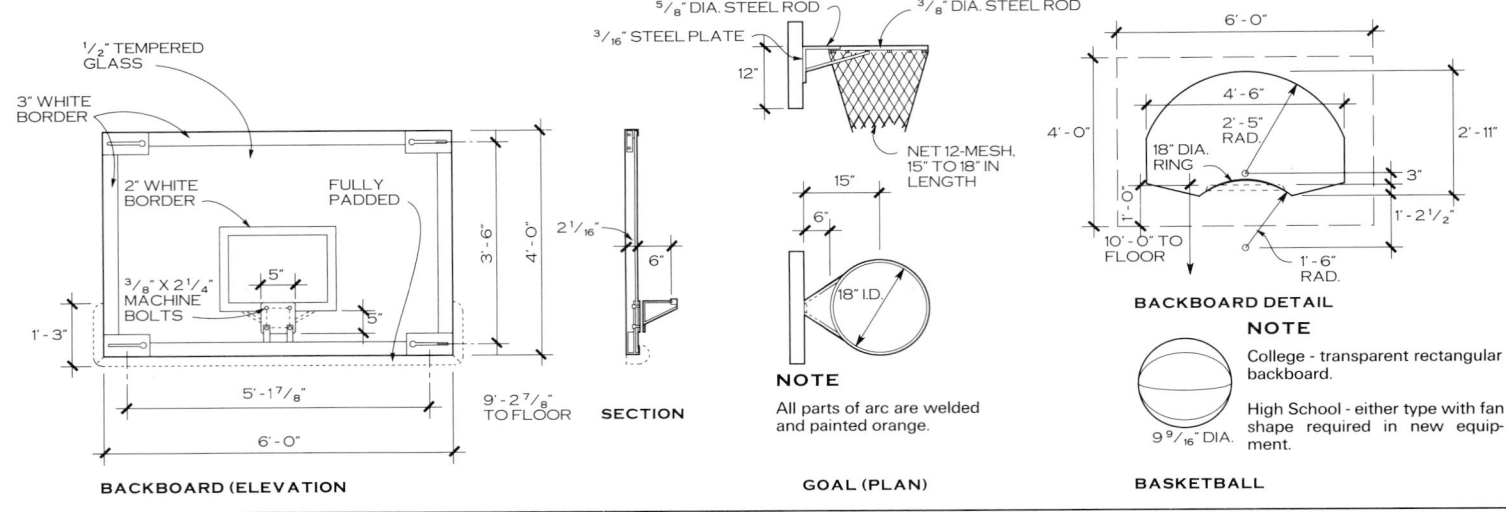

BACKBOARD (ELEVATION

GOAL (PLAN)

BASKETBALL

BACKBOARD AND GOAL (NBA AND NCAA STANDARDS)

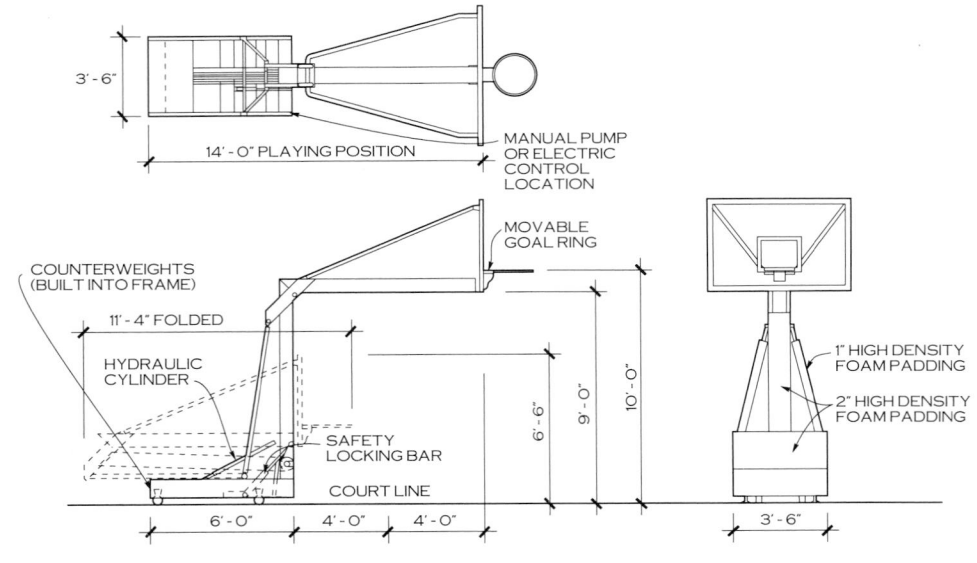

TYPICAL PORTABLE HYDRAULIC GOAL

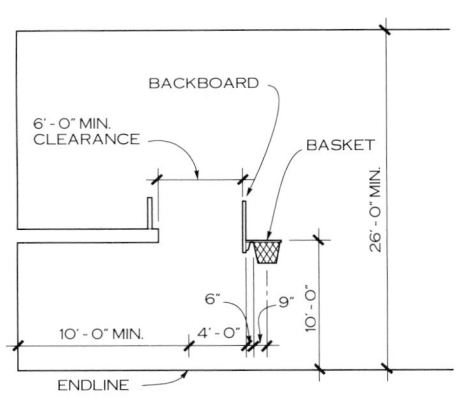

BUILDING SECTION SHOWING ENCROACHMENTS

NOTE

A variety of backboards that swing down from the ceiling structure is available. These require no storage areas on the floor.

GENERAL NOTES

1. Materials and installation of glass wall systems shall comply with the safety and performance standards for walls established by the International Squash Rackets Federation, the American Association of Racquetsports Manufacturers and Suppliers, and local building codes.

2. Temperature and humidity for racquetball courts shall be maintained during storage, installation, and thereafter as follows: temperature range is 65°-78°F and humidity between 40 and 60%.

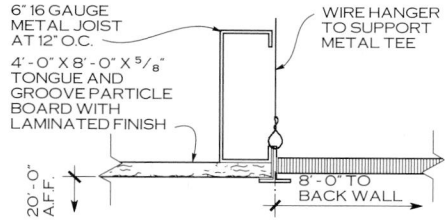

6" 16 GAUGE METAL JOIST AT 12" O.C.

WIRE HANGER TO SUPPORT METAL TEE

4'-0" X 8'-0" X 5/8" TONGUE AND GROOVE PARTICLE BOARD WITH LAMINATED FINISH

20'-0" A.F.F.

8'-0" TO BACK WALL

DETAIL AT CEILING

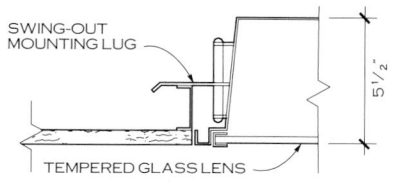

SWING-OUT MOUNTING LUG

5 1/2"

TEMPERED GLASS LENS

DETAIL OF LIGHT

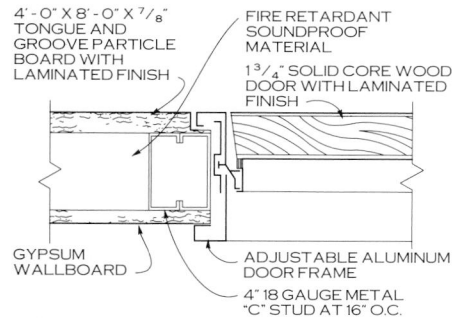

4'-0" X 8'-0" X 7/8" TONGUE AND GROOVE PARTICLE BOARD WITH LAMINATED FINISH

FIRE RETARDANT SOUNDPROOF MATERIAL

1 3/4" SOLID CORE WOOD DOOR WITH LAMINATED FINISH

GYPSUM WALLBOARD

ADJUSTABLE ALUMINUM DOOR FRAME

4" 18 GAUGE METAL "C" STUD AT 16" O.C.

DETAIL OF DOOR AT JAMB

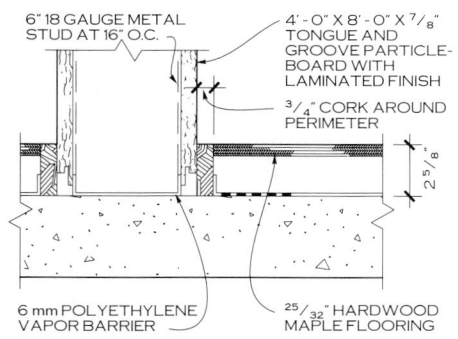

6" 18 GAUGE METAL STUD AT 16" O.C.

4'-0" X 8'-0" X 7/8" TONGUE AND GROOVE PARTICLE-BOARD WITH LAMINATED FINISH

3/4" CORK AROUND PERIMETER

2 5/8"

6 mm POLYETHYLENE VAPOR BARRIER

25/32" HARDWOOD MAPLE FLOORING

SECTION AT COMMON SIDEWALL

NOTES FOR INTERNATIONAL SQUASH COURT—SINGLES

1. All lines on the court are to be 50 mm wide, painted bright red.

2. The back wall may be transparent if it is either exactly 7 ft 0 in. (2130 mm) above the finished floor (in this case, the back wall line may be omitted) or 7 ft 2 in. (2180 mm) or higher above the finished floor. Dimensions are measured to the bottom edge of the line. A transparent wall may not be used if the top of the wall is between 7 ft 0 in. and 7 ft 2 in. above the finished floor.

3. All playing walls of the court shall have a hard, smooth finish and be constructed of the same materials with a strength and deflection characteristic as defined in the International Squash Rackets Federation manual.

Timothy B. McDonald; Washington, D.C.;
Sherry Funston, executive director; Squash Ontario; Willowdale, Ontario
J. Michael Taylor; Playcon Recreational Equipment Limited; Kitchener, Ontario

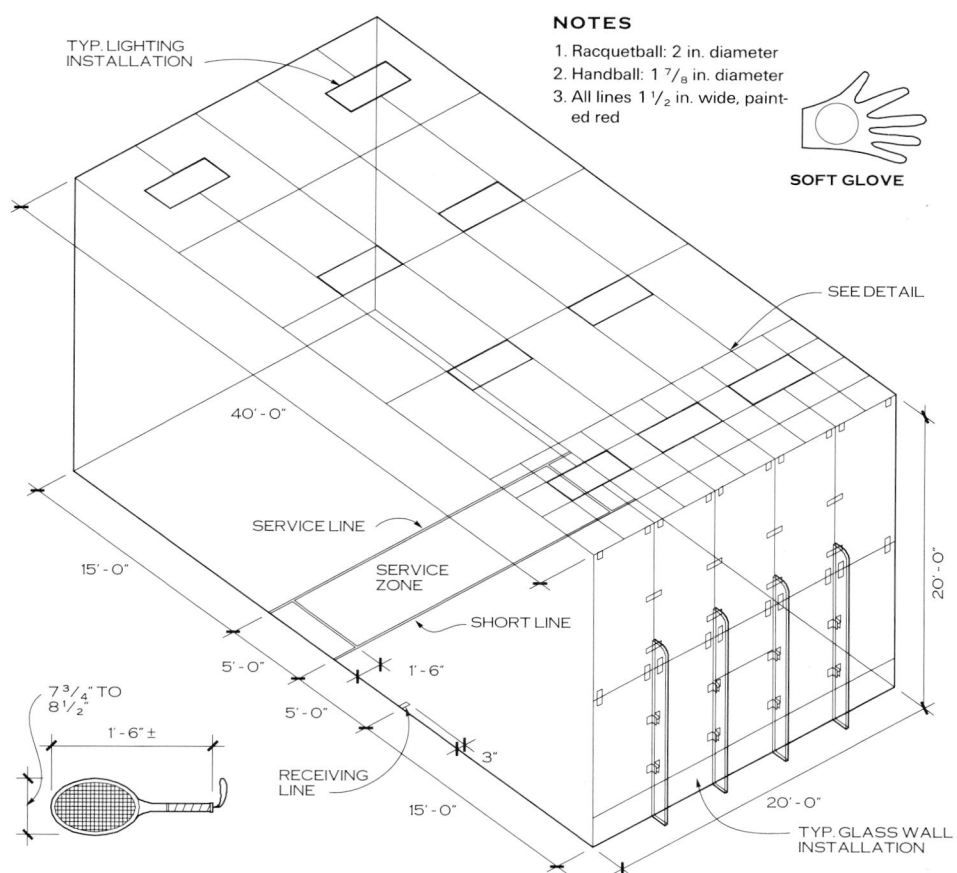

NOTES

1. Racquetball: 2 in. diameter
2. Handball: 1 7/8 in. diameter
3. All lines 1 1/2 in. wide, painted red

SOFT GLOVE

TYP. LIGHTING INSTALLATION

SEE DETAIL

40'-0"

SERVICE LINE

SERVICE ZONE

SHORT LINE

20'-0"

15'-0"

5'-0"

1'-6"

7 3/4" TO 8 1/2"

1'-6" ±

5'-0"

3"

RECEIVING LINE

15'-0"

20'-0"

TYP. GLASS WALL INSTALLATION

HANDBALL/RACQUETBALL/PADDLEBALL COURT

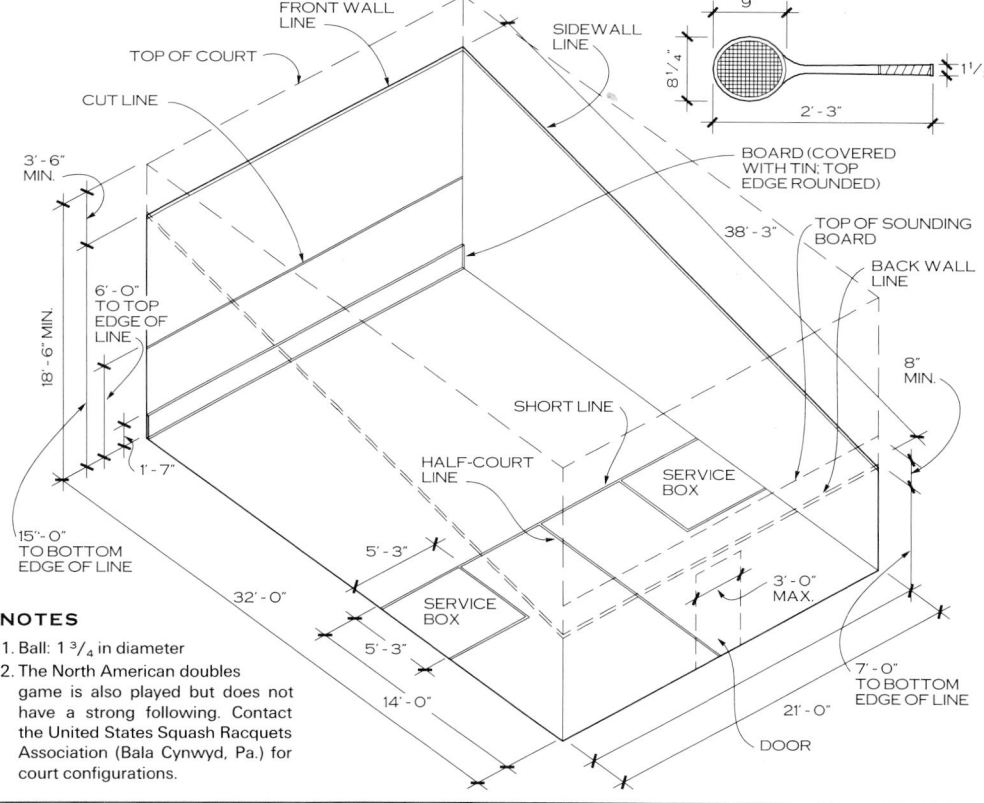

FRONT WALL LINE

SIDEWALL LINE

TOP OF COURT

CUT LINE

9"

8 1/4"

1 1/2"

2'-3"

BOARD (COVERED WITH TIN; TOP EDGE ROUNDED)

TOP OF SOUNDING BOARD

BACK WALL LINE

3'-6" MIN.

6'-0" TO TOP EDGE OF LINE

38'-3"

18'-6" MIN.

SHORT LINE

8" MIN.

1'-7"

HALF-COURT LINE

SERVICE BOX

15"-0" TO BOTTOM EDGE OF LINE

32'-0"

5'-3"

SERVICE BOX

5'-3"

14'-0"

3'-0" MAX.

7'-0" TO BOTTOM EDGE OF LINE

21'-0"

DOOR

NOTES

1. Ball: 1 3/4 in diameter
2. The North American doubles game is also played but does not have a strong following. Contact the United States Squash Racquets Association (Bala Cynwyd, Pa.) for court configurations.

SQUASH COURT (INTERNATIONAL SINGLES)

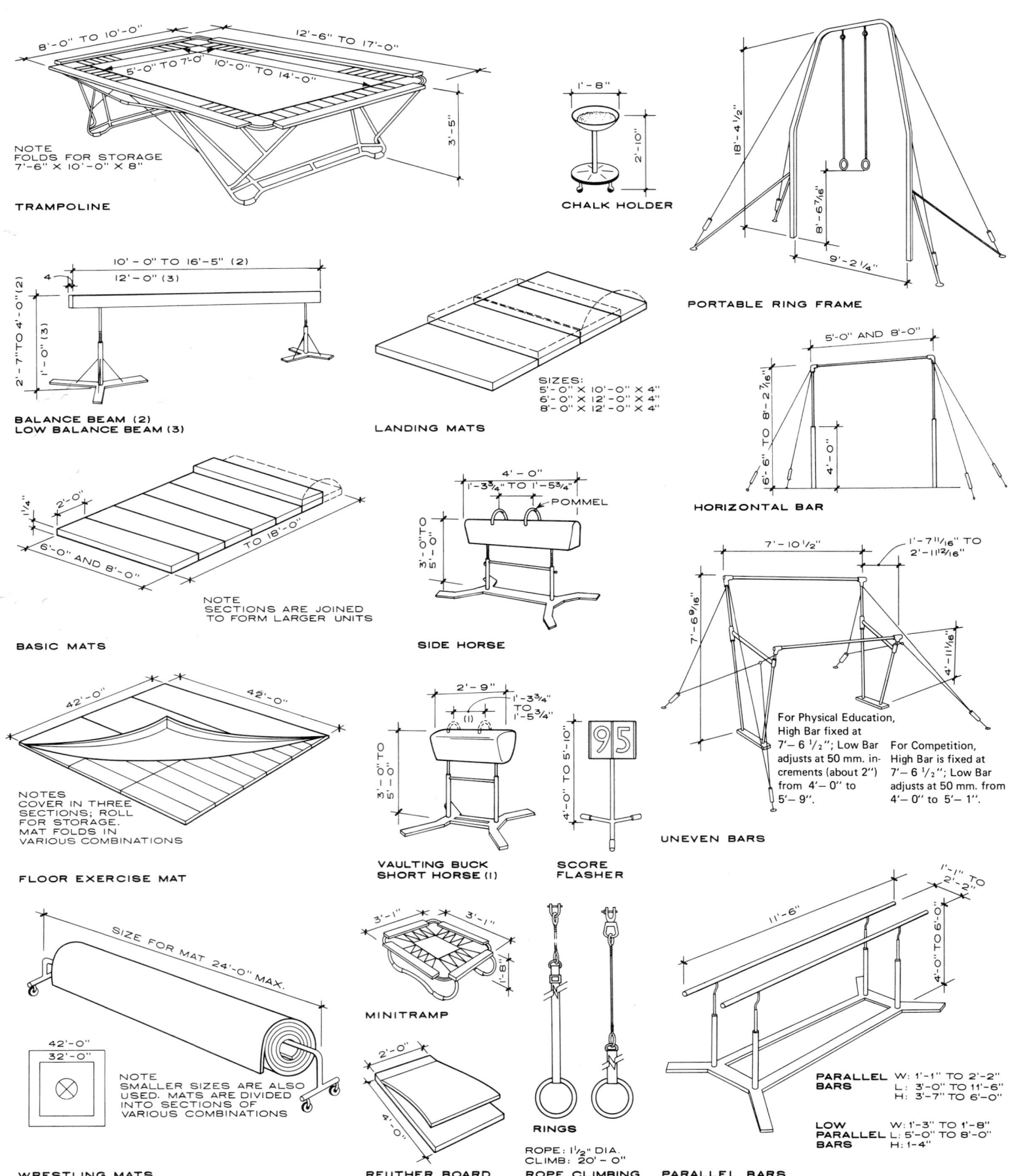

TRAMPOLINE

NOTE
FOLDS FOR STORAGE
7'-6" × 10'-0" × 8"

8'-0" TO 10'-0"
12'-6" TO 17'-0"
5'-0" TO 7'-0"
10'-0" TO 14'-0"
3'-5"

CHALK HOLDER

1'-8"
2'-10"

PORTABLE RING FRAME

18'-4 1/2"
8'-6 7/16"
9'-2 1/4"

BALANCE BEAM (2)
LOW BALANCE BEAM (3)

10'-0" TO 16'-5" (2)
12'-0" (3)
4
2'-7" TO 4'-0" (2)
1'-0" (3)

LANDING MATS

SIZES:
5'-0" × 10'-0" × 4"
6'-0" × 12'-0" × 4"
8'-0" × 12'-0" × 4"

HORIZONTAL BAR

5'-0" AND 8'-0"
6'-6" TO 8'-2 7/16"
4'-0"

BASIC MATS

1'-4"
2'-0"
6'-0" AND 8'-0"
TO 18'-0"

NOTE
SECTIONS ARE JOINED
TO FORM LARGER UNITS

SIDE HORSE

4'-0"
1'-3 3/4" TO 1'-5 3/4"
POMMEL
3'-0" TO 5'-0"

UNEVEN BARS

7'-10 1/2"
1'-7 11/16" TO 2'-11 12/16"
7'-6 9/16"
4'-11/16"

For Physical Education,
High Bar fixed at
7'-6 1/2"; Low Bar
adjusts at 50 mm. in-
crements (about 2")
from 4'-0" to
5'-9".

For Competition,
High Bar is fixed at
7'-6 1/2"; Low Bar
adjusts at 50 mm. from
4'-0" to 5'-1".

FLOOR EXERCISE MAT

42'-0"
42'-0"

NOTES
COVER IN THREE
SECTIONS; ROLL
FOR STORAGE.
MAT FOLDS IN
VARIOUS COMBINATIONS

VAULTING BUCK
SHORT HORSE (1)

2'-9"
1'-3 3/4" TO 1'-5 3/4"
(1)
3'-0" TO 5'-0"

SCORE
FLASHER

95
4'-0" TO 5'-10"

WRESTLING MATS

SIZE FOR MAT 24'-0" MAX.

42'-0"
32'-0"
⊗

NOTE
SMALLER SIZES ARE ALSO
USED. MATS ARE DIVIDED
INTO SECTIONS OF
VARIOUS COMBINATIONS

MINITRAMP

3'-1"
3'-1"
1'-8"

REUTHER BOARD

2'-0"
4'-0"

RINGS

ROPE CLIMBING

ROPE: 1 1/2" DIA.
CLIMB: 20'-0" O

PARALLEL BARS

11'-6"
1'-1" TO 2'-2"
4'-0" TO 6'-0"

PARALLEL   W: 1'-1" TO 2'-2"
BARS   L: 3'-0" TO 11'-6"
           H: 3'-7" TO 6'-0"

LOW   W: 1'-3" TO 1'-8"
PARALLEL   L: 5'-0" TO 8'-0"
BARS   H: 1-4"

John C. Lunsford; AIA, Varney Sexton Sydnor Associates; Phoenix, Arizona

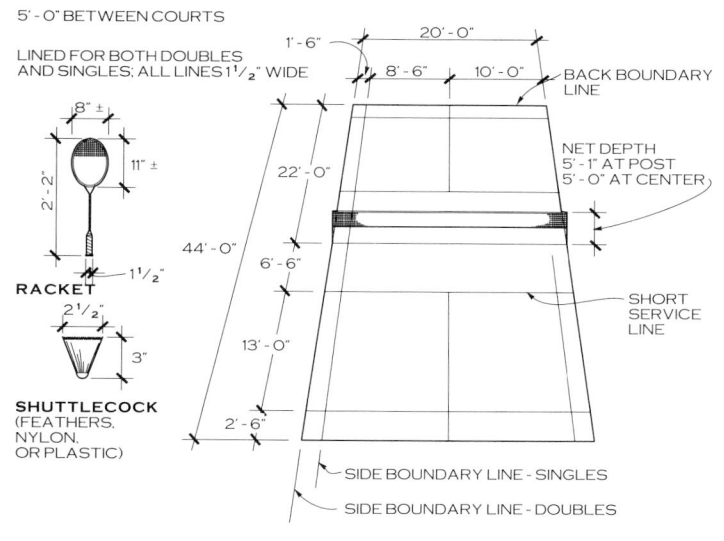

5'- O" BETWEEN COURTS

LINED FOR BOTH DOUBLES
AND SINGLES; ALL LINES 1½" WIDE

RACKET

SHUTTLECOCK
(FEATHERS,
NYLON,
OR PLASTIC)

1'- 6"
20'- O"
8'- 6"
10'- O"
BACK BOUNDARY LINE
NET DEPTH
5'- 1" AT POST
5'- O" AT CENTER
22'- O"
44'- O"
6'- 6"
SHORT SERVICE LINE
13'- O"
2'- 6"
SIDE BOUNDARY LINE - SINGLES
SIDE BOUNDARY LINE - DOUBLES

8" ±
11" ±
2'- 2"
1½"

2½"
3"

BADMINTON

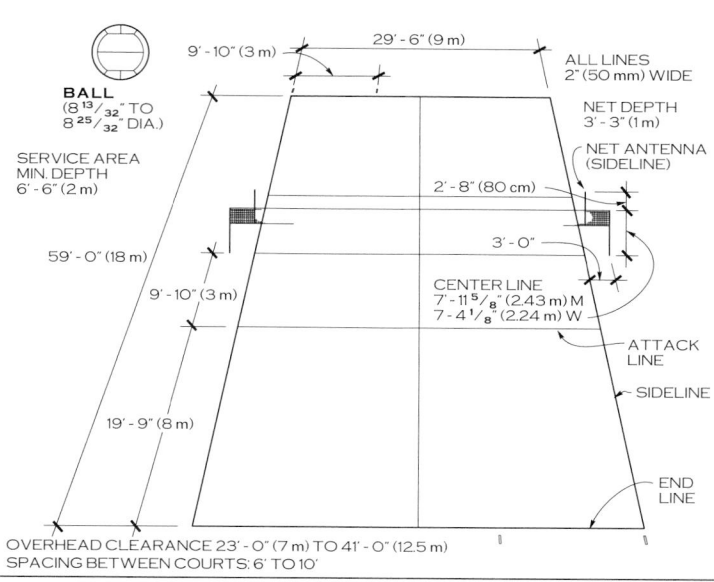

BALL
(8 13/32" TO
8 25/32" DIA.)

SERVICE AREA
MIN. DEPTH
6'- 6" (2 m)

59'- O" (18 m)

9'- 10" (3 m)

19'- 9" (8 m)

9'- 10" (3 m)

29'- 6" (9 m)

ALL LINES
2" (50 mm) WIDE

NET DEPTH
3'- 3" (1 m)

NET ANTENNA
(SIDELINE)

2'- 8" (80 cm)

3'- O"

CENTER LINE
7'- 11 5/8" (2.43 m) M
7'- 4 1/8" (2.24 m) W

ATTACK LINE

SIDELINE

END LINE

OVERHEAD CLEARANCE 23'- O" (7 m) TO 41'- O" (12.5 m)
SPACING BETWEEN COURTS: 6' TO 10'

VOLLEYBALL

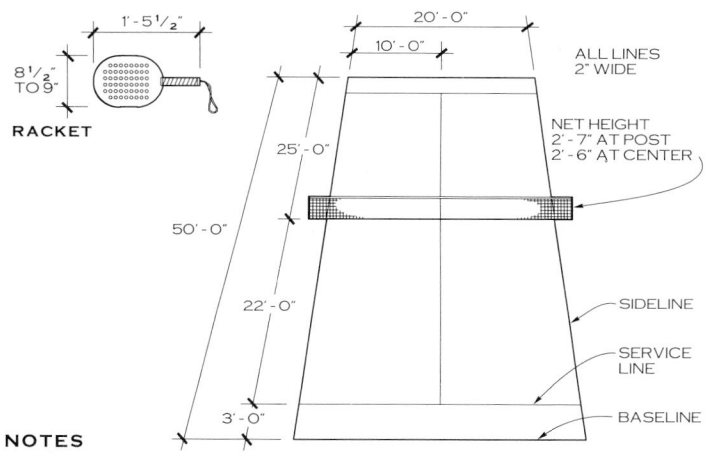

RACKET

1'- 5½"

8½"
TO 9"

20'- O"
10'- O"

ALL LINES
2" WIDE

NET HEIGHT
2'- 7" AT POST
2'- 6" AT CENTER

25'- O"

50'- O"

22'- O"

3'- O"

SIDELINE

SERVICE LINE

BASELINE

NOTES

1. Space behind each baseline to back fence is 15 ft minimum.
2. Space from each sideline to side fence is 10 ft minimum.
3. Fence shall be 8 ft high unless otherwise noted.
4. Ball is a punctured tennis ball.

PADDLE TENNIS

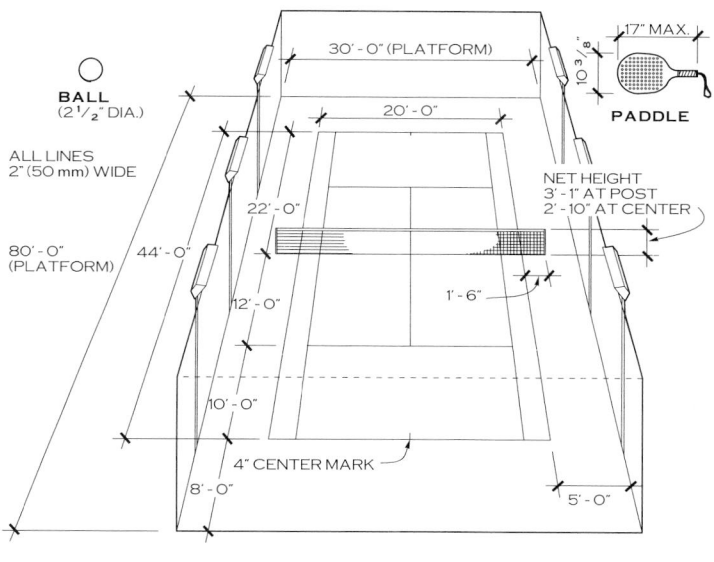

BALL
(2½" DIA.)

ALL LINES
2" (50 mm) WIDE

80'- O"
(PLATFORM)

44'- O"

30'- O" (PLATFORM)

20'- O"

22'- O"

12'- O"

10'- O"

4" CENTER MARK

8'- O"

17" MAX.

10 3/8"

PADDLE

NET HEIGHT
3'- 1" AT POST
2'- 10" AT CENTER

1'- 6"

5'- O"

PLATFORM TENNIS

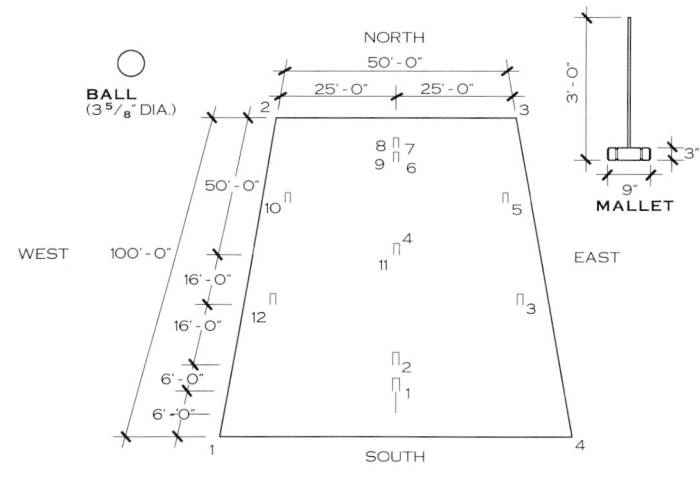

BALL
(3 5/8" DIA.)

NORTH
50'- O"
25'- O"   25'- O"

3'- O"

3"

9"

MALLET

WEST   100'- O"

50'- O"

16'- O"

16'- O"

6'- O"

6'- O"

EAST

SOUTH

8 7
9 6
5
10
4
11
12
3
2
1
1   4

CROQUET

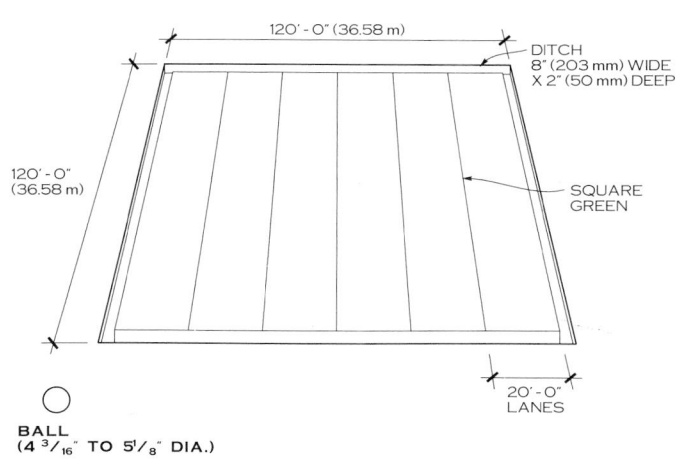

120'- O" (36.58 m)

DITCH
8" (203 mm) WIDE
X 2" (50 mm) DEEP

120'- O"
(36.58 m)

SQUARE GREEN

20'- O"
LANES

BALL
(4 3/16" TO 5 1/8" DIA.)

LAWN BOWLING

COURT SPORTS   17

NOTE

A dart board in a hanging box needs no additional storage. Lighting can be artificial, natural, or both. An adjustable spotlight is advisable. For safety reasons, the playing area should be placed away from doorways and traffic ways. Walls around the board should be surfaced with a material that will not be defaced by the darts. Provide a small chalkboard for scoring.

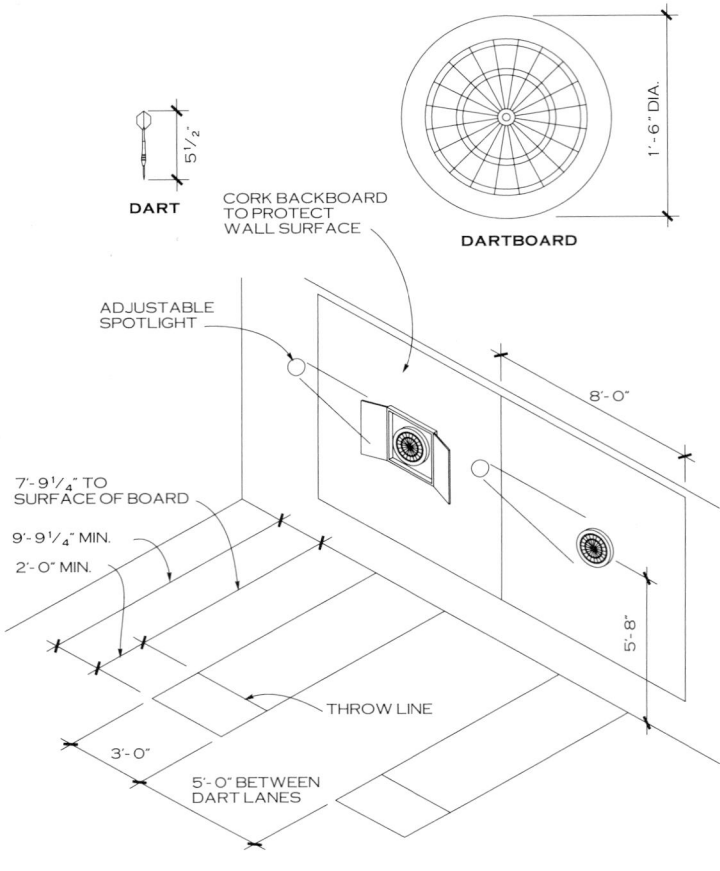

DART

CORK BACKBOARD TO PROTECT WALL SURFACE

DARTBOARD

1'-6" DIA.

5½"

ADJUSTABLE SPOTLIGHT

8'-0"

7'-9¼" TO SURFACE OF BOARD

9'-9¼" MIN.

2'-0" MIN.

5'-8"

THROW LINE

3'-0"

5'-0" BETWEEN DART LANES

DARTS

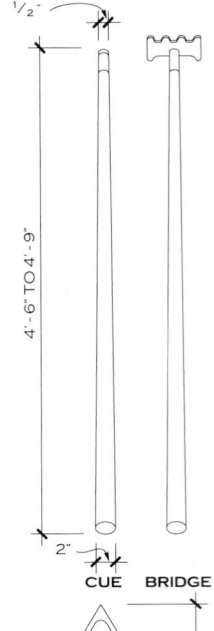

½"

4'-6" TO 4'-9"

2"

CUE   BRIDGE

EIGHT BALL RACK

12¾"

11⅜"

The flooring must be level permanently and be able to withstand point loads. Traditionally designed billiard tables weigh about 1.5 tons spread over eight legs. Lighting must not produce harsh shadows, but some modeling of the ball is desirable. Direct or reflected glare should be avoided, and true color rendering is important in snooker. An overall bright light is needed for each table; natural lighting is not essential. Lighting at the table surface should be approximately 375 lumens, which can be achieved by three 150-watt tungsten filament lamps suspended in a lighting trough. Fluorescent lamps are unacceptable. Some sound insulation is required to prevent distractions from outside the playing area.

TABLE TYPES AND DIMENSIONS

TYPE OF TABLE	PLAYING SURFACE		TABLE SIZE	
	W	L	W	L
English (Snooker)	7'-2"	14'-4"	8'-2"	15'-4"
Standard 9'-0"	4'-2"	8'-4"	5'-2"	9'-4"
Standard 8'-0"	3'-8"	7'-4"	4'-8"	8'-4"
Standard 7'-0"	3'-2"	6'-4"	4'-2"	7'-4"
Oversized 8-0"	3'-10"	7'-8"	4'-10"	8'-8"

NOTES

1. Table height 2'-6"
2. Typical coin operated table is the standard 7'-0".

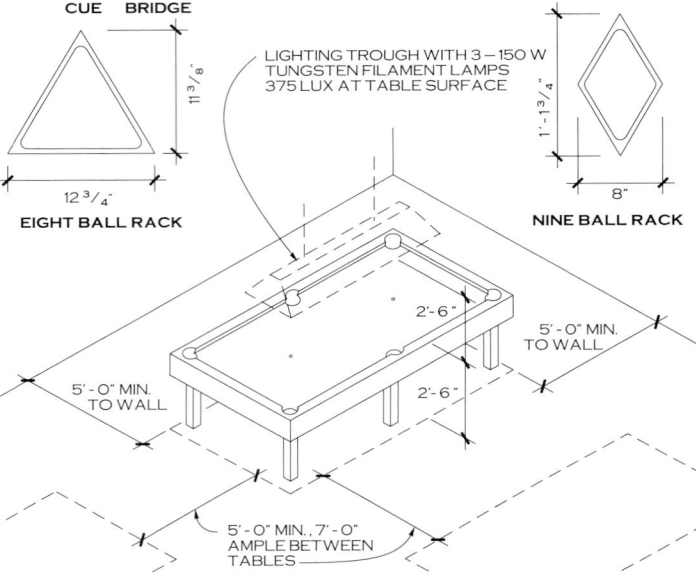

LIGHTING TROUGH WITH 3 – 150 W TUNGSTEN FILAMENT LAMPS 375 LUX AT TABLE SURFACE

NINE BALL RACK

1'-1¾"

8"

2'-6"

5'-0" MIN. TO WALL

5'-0" MIN. TO WALL

2'-6"

5'-0" MIN., 7'-0" AMPLE BETWEEN TABLES

BILLIARDS / POCKET BILLIARDS / SNOOKER

NOTE

Flooring should be level, slightly resilient, and not of non-skid material. Walls should be a uniformly dark nongloss background to provide enough contrast to help players follow the ball. Lighting often varies for different standards of play, but 150 to 500 lumens at table height is the acceptable range. This should not be fluorescent or natural lighting, but preferably tungsten halogen. Sectional tables are stored upright when not in use.

9'-6"

4'-6"

5'-0"

2'-6"

7'-0" MIN. TO WALL

11'-6"

4'-0" MIN. TO WALL

6"

2'-6"

10'-0" MIN. BETWEEN TABLES

6'-0" MIN. BETWEEN TABLES

TABLE TENNIS

NOTES

1. The drawings below illustrate the use of a 7-point dimension grid that expresses the minimum desirable dimensions to be used when either specifying or designing a rectangular shaped pool for residential use.
2. Width, length, and depth dimensions may apply to residential pools of any shape.
3. The minimum length with diving board and wading area is 28 ft. The average length of a residential pool is 28 to 40 ft.
4. Standards for residential swimming pools have been published by the National Spa and Pool Institute (1974).

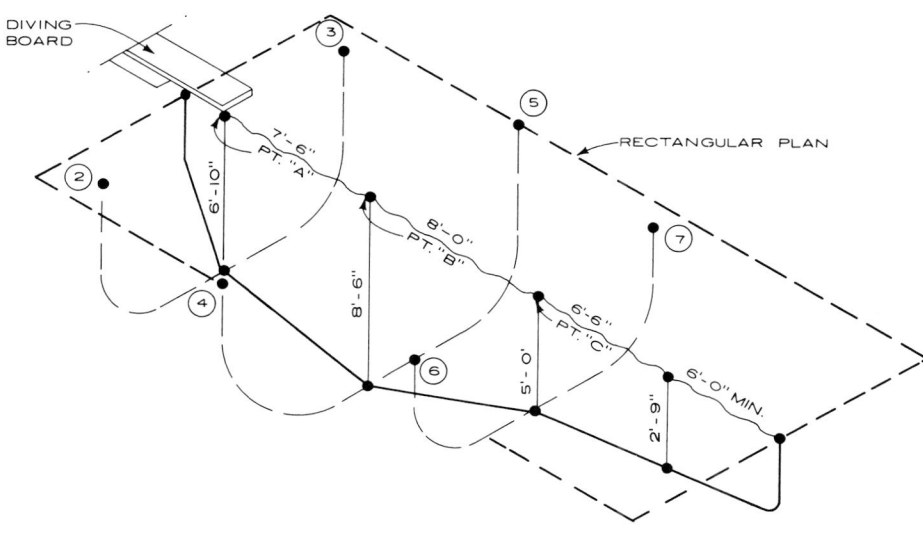

ISOMETRIC OVERLAY VIEW

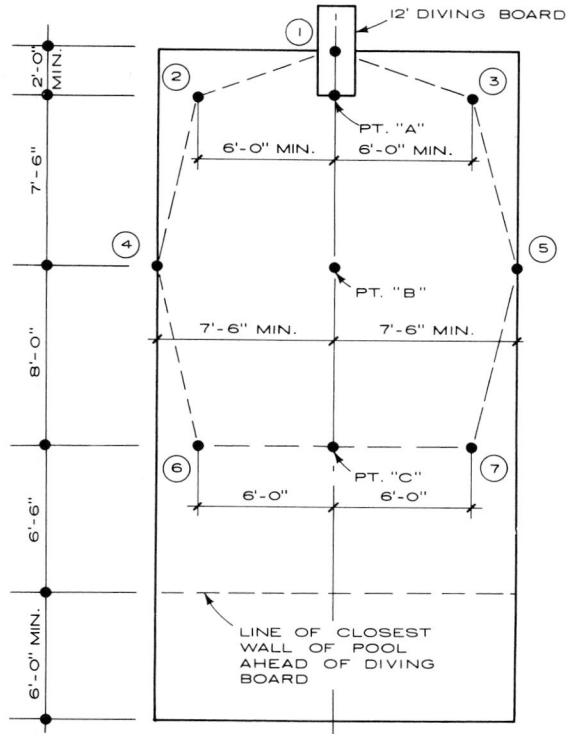

7-POINT GRID DIMENSION PLAN

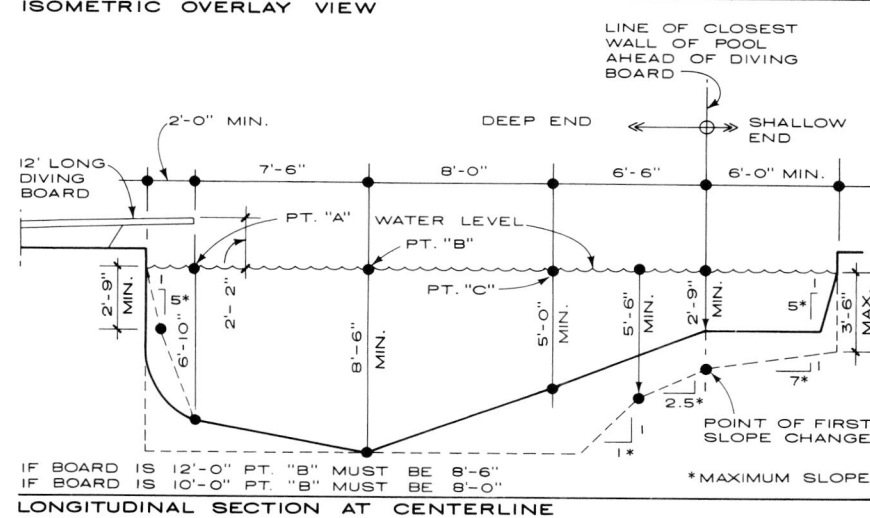

LONGITUDINAL SECTION AT CENTERLINE

IF BOARD IS 12'-0" PT. "B" MUST BE 8'-6"
IF BOARD IS 10'-0" PT. "B" MUST BE 8'-0"

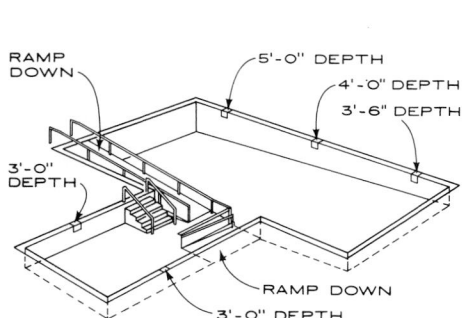

HANDICAPPED POOL ACCESS

Haver, Nunn, and Collamer; Phoenix, Arizona

PERMITS AND RESTRICTIONS

Required in most areas from building, health, plumbing, and electrical departments and zoning boards. Check for setback restrictions and easements covering power and telephone lines, sewers, and storm drains.

SITE CONSIDERATIONS

Check the site for the following conditions, each of which will considerably increase the cost.

1. Fill that is more than 3 ft below pool deck.
2. Hard rock that requires drilling and blasting.
3. Underground water or springs that necessitate pumping or drains.
4. Accessibility of the site for mechanical equipment, minimum entry 8 ft wide by 7 ft 8 in. high, with a grade easy enough for a truck to reach the site.
5. Place the pool where it will get the most sun during swimming season. If possible, place deep end so a diver dives away from, not into, the afternoon sun. Avoid overhanging tree branches near the pool.
6. The slope of the site should be as level as possible; a steep slope requires retaining walls for the pool.
7. The surface deck around the pool should be of a slip-resistant surface.
8. A surrounding fence is recommended to protect pool area from unwanted visitors and to prevent accidents.

CONSTRUCTION AND SHAPES

Pools may be made of reinforced concrete (poured on the job, precast, or gunite sprayed), concrete block, steel, aluminum, or plastic with or without block backup. Concrete, aluminum, fiberglass, and steel pools are available in any shape—rectangular, square, kidney, oval or free form. Complete plastic installations and plastic pool liners with various backups are available only in manufacturers' standard shapes and sizes.

A rectangular pool is the most practical if site permits, since it gives the longest swimming distance.

POOL CAPACITY

Rule of thumb: 36 sq ft for each swimmer, 100 sq ft for each diver. A pool of 20 x 40 ft accommodates 14 persons at a time, but since not everyone is in the pool at once, pool and surroundings are adequate for 30 to 40 people.

FILTER REQUIREMENTS

Filter, motor, and electrical equipment shall be sheltered and waterproofed.

GENERAL

Public pools are generally considered to be those that belong to municipalities, schools, country clubs, hotels, motels, apartments, and resorts. Permits for their construction are required in most areas from local and state boards of health as well as the departments of building, plumbing, and electricity.

Community pools should be integrated with existing and projected recreational facilities, such as picnic areas and parks, for maximum usage. Transportation access should be good, and there should be ample parking space. In a hot climate, enough shade should be provided, particularly in the lounging areas, and be so located that it can be easily converted to spectator space by erecting bleachers.

POOL DESIGN

Formerly most public pools were designed to meet competitive swimming requirements. The trend today is to provide for all-around use. The following should be considered:

1. Ratio of shallow water to deep water. Formerly 60% of pool area 5 ft deep and less was considered to be adequate. Now 80% is considered more realistic.
2. Ratio of loungers to bathers. Generally, no more than one-third of people attending a public pool are in the water at one time. Consequently the 6 to 8 ft walks formerly surrounding pools and used for lounging have been enlarged so that lounging area now approximates pool size.
3. For capacity formula see "Public Swimming Pool Capacity" diagram on another page.

RECOMMENDED DIMENSIONS

MAX. BOARD LENGTH	MAX. HEIGHT OVER WATER	D₁	D₂	R	L₁	L₂	L₃	L₄	L₅	PT.A	PT.B	PT.C
		MINIMUM DIMENSIONS								MINIMUM WIDTH OF POOL AT:		
10'	2/3 m 26''	2.13 m 7'-0''	2.59 m 8'-6''	1.68 m 5'-6''	0.76 m 2'-6''	2.44 m 8'-0''	3.20 m 10'-6''	2.13 m 7'-0''	8.53 m 28'-0''	4.88 m 16'-0''	5.49 m 18'-0''	5.49 m 18'-0''
12'	3/4 m 30''	2.29 m 7'-6''	2.74 m 9'-0''	1.83 m 6'-0''	0.91 m 3'-0''	2.74 m 9'-0''	3.66 m 12'-0''	1.22 m 4'-0''	8.53 m 28'-0''	5.49 m 18'-0''	6.10 m 20'-0''	6.10 m 20'-0''
16'	1 m	2.59 m 8'-6''	3.05 m 10'-0''	2.13 m 7'-0''	1.22 m 4'-0''	3.05 m 10'-0''	4.57 m 15'-0''	0.61 m 2'-0''	9.45 m 31'-0''	6.10 m 20'-0''	6.71 m 22'-0''	6.71 m 22'-0''
16'	3 m	3.35 m 11'-0''	3.66 m 12'-0''	2.59 m 8'-6''	1.83 m 6'-0''	3.20 m 10'-6''	6.40 m 21'-0''	0	11.43 m 37'-6''	6.70 m 22'-0''	7.32 m 24'-0''	7.32 m 24'-0''

Data source: National SPA and Swimming Pool Institute.

L_2, L_3, and L_4 combined represent the minimum distance from the tip of board to pool wall opposite diving equipment.

For board heights exceeding 3 m or for platform diving facilities; comply with dimensional requirements of FINA, USS, NCAA, N.F., etc.

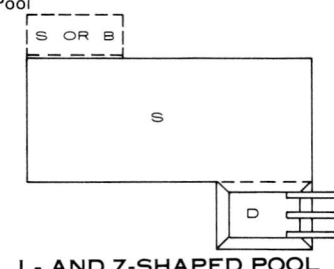

NOTE: Placement of boards shall observe the following minimum dimensions. With multiple board installations minimum pool widths must be increased accordingly.

1 m or deck level board to pool side	9' (2.74 m)
3 m board to pool side	11' (3.35 m)
1 m or deck level board to 3 m board	10' (3.05 m)
1 m or deck level to another 1 m or deck level board	8' (2.44 m)
3 m to another 3 m board	10' (3.05 m)

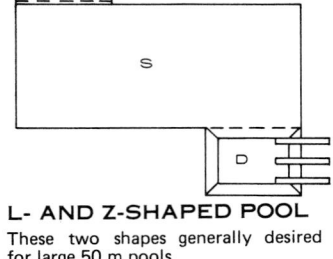

T-SHAPED POOL

Provides large shallow area(s). Diving area off to one side. Water in large part of pool from 3 ft 6 in. to 5 ft deep, adequate for regular competitive events.

L- AND Z-SHAPED POOL

These two shapes generally desired for large 50 m pools.

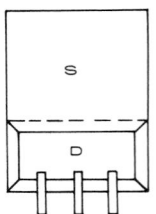

RECTANGULAR POOL

Standard design. Good for competitive swimming and indoor pool design. Shallow area often inadequate.

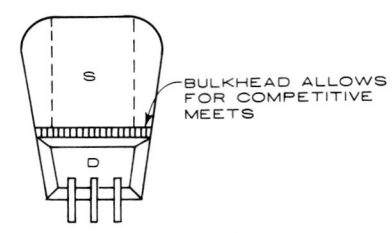

FAN SHAPED POOL

Successful where there is a high percentage of children. Largest area for shallow depth. Deep area can be roped off or separated by bulkhead.

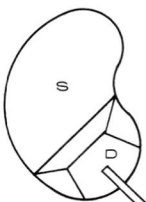

FREE FORM POOL

Kidney and oval shapes are the most common free forms. Use only where competitive meets are not a consideration.

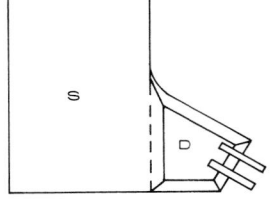

MODIFIED L POOL

Provides for separate diving area. Shallow area with 4 ft min. depth may be roped off for competitive meets.

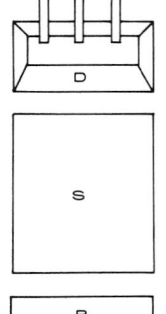
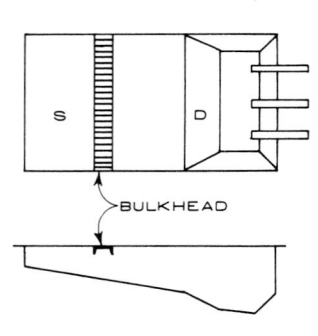

MULTIPLE POOLS

Separate pools for beginners, divers, and swimmers. Ultimate in desirability especially if pool is intended for large numbers of people. Variation at left shows single pool and bulkhead over it with advantage that swimmers are kept out of area reserved for beginners. Both designs may use common filtration system.

WADING POOLS

Generally provided in connection with community and family club pools. Placed away from swimming area to avoid congestion. If near swimming pool, wading area should be fenced off for children's protection. To add play appeal provide spray fittings and small fountains in pool. Also provide seats and benches for adults who accompany children to pool.

PUBLIC POOL SHAPES

NOTE: S = swimming pool, D = diving pool, B = beginners' pool.

R. Jackson Smith, AIA; Designed Environments, Inc.; Stamford, Connecticut
National Swimming Pool Institute; Washington, D.C.

AQUATICS

LENGTH OF POOLS

25 yards is the minimum length for American records, and meets interscholastic and intercollegiate requirements. (Pool should be 75 ft-1½ in. long to allow for electronic timing panels at one end.)

Standards for international competition are shown on 50 meter pool page.

WIDTH OF POOLS

Drawing below shows 7 ft lanes with pool width of 45 ft (6 lanes). Strictly competitive pools should have 8 ft lanes, with pool width of 83 ft (10 lanes). Minimum widths include additional 18 in. width outside lanes on both sides of pool.

NOTES

Gutters at sides of pool are desirable to reduce wave action in swimming meets or water polo. See lighting standards and diving board standards on other pages of this series for additional requirements for competitive pools.

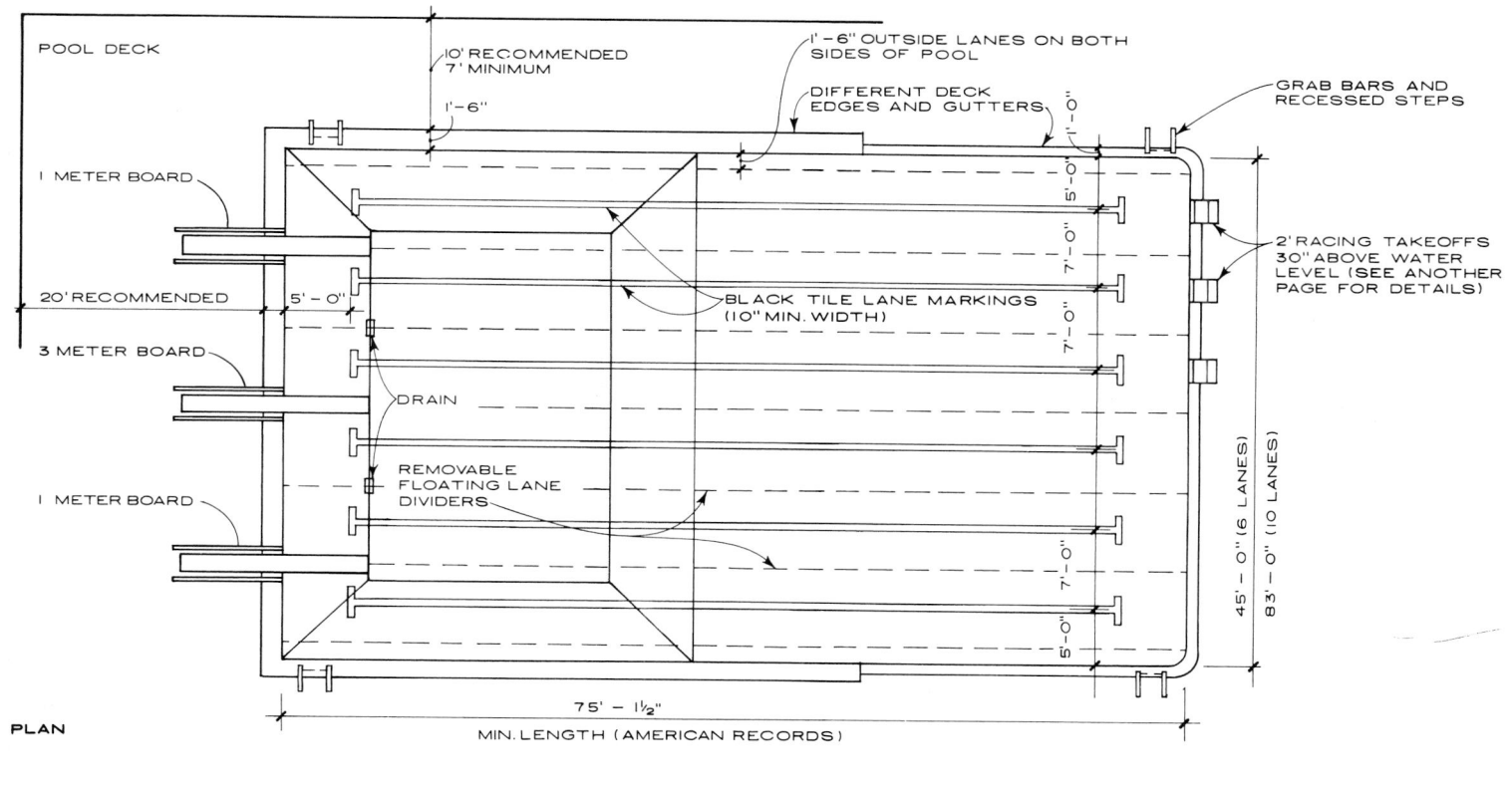

PLAN

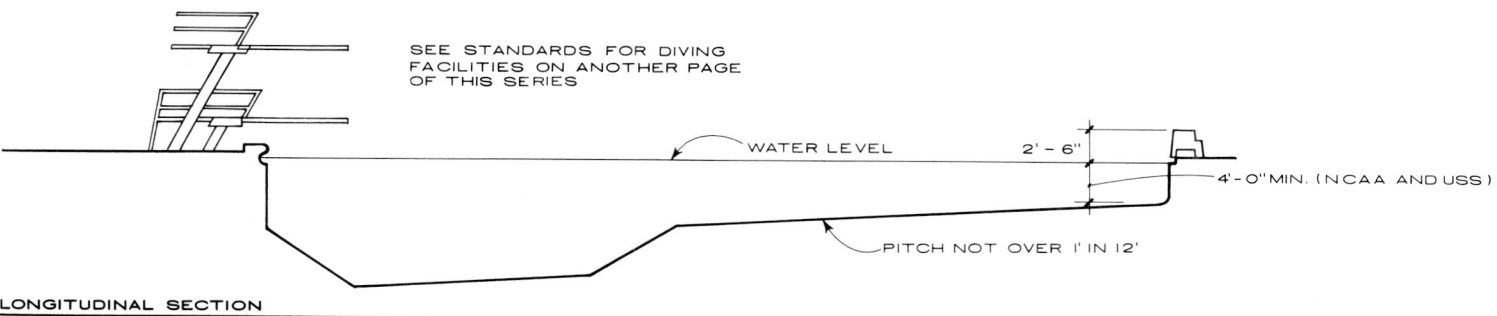

LONGITUDINAL SECTION
25 YARD POOL

Swimming pool capacity requirements vary from one locality to another: check local regulations. The following is suggested by the American Public Health Association.

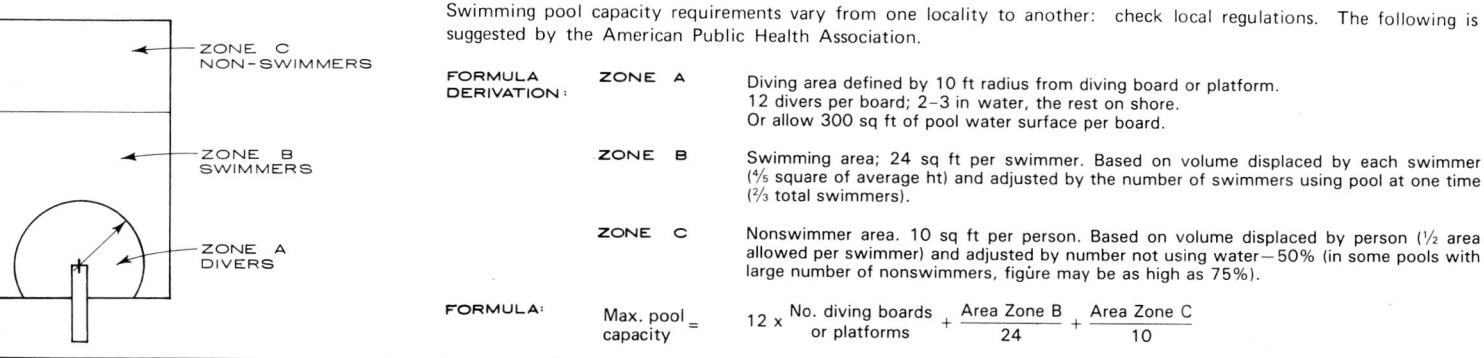

FORMULA DERIVATION:

ZONE A Diving area defined by 10 ft radius from diving board or platform. 12 divers per board; 2–3 in water, the rest on shore. Or allow 300 sq ft of pool water surface per board.

ZONE B Swimming area; 24 sq ft per swimmer. Based on volume displaced by each swimmer (⅘ square of average ht) and adjusted by the number of swimmers using pool at one time (⅔ total swimmers).

ZONE C Nonswimmer area. 10 sq ft per person. Based on volume displaced by person (½ area allowed per swimmer) and adjusted by number not using water—50% (in some pools with large number of nonswimmers, figure may be as high as 75%).

FORMULA:

$$\text{Max. pool capacity} = 12 \times \frac{\text{No. diving boards or platforms}}{} + \frac{\text{Area Zone B}}{24} + \frac{\text{Area Zone C}}{10}$$

PUBLIC SWIMMING POOL CAPACITY

R. Jackson Smith, AIA; Designed Environments, Inc.; Stamford, Connecticut

GENERAL NOTES

For judging competitive meets, FINA officials recommend the springboard and diving platform arrangement indicated below in plan. Diving dimensions meet minimum FINA standards. Fifty meters is minimum length for world records.

NOTE

*Length should be 50.03 m allowing an extra .03 m to compensate for possible future tile facing, structural defects and electrical timing panels.

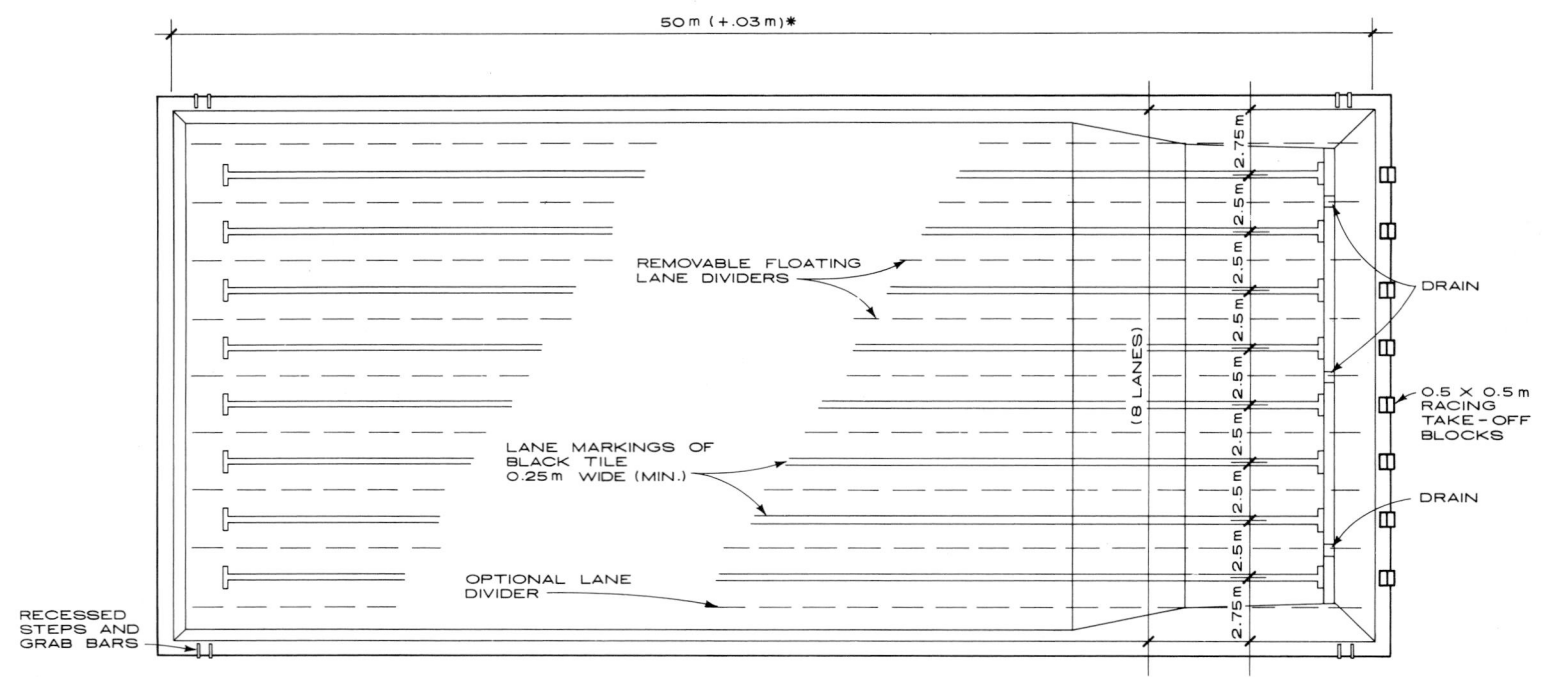

50 m (+.03 m)*

2.75 m
2.5 m
2.5 m
2.5 m
2.5 m
2.5 m
2.5 m
2.5 m
2.75 m

(8 LANES)

REMOVABLE FLOATING LANE DIVIDERS

LANE MARKINGS OF BLACK TILE 0.25 m WIDE (MIN.)

OPTIONAL LANE DIVIDER

RECESSED STEPS AND GRAB BARS

DRAIN

0.5 X 0.5 m RACING TAKE-OFF BLOCKS

DRAIN

PLAN

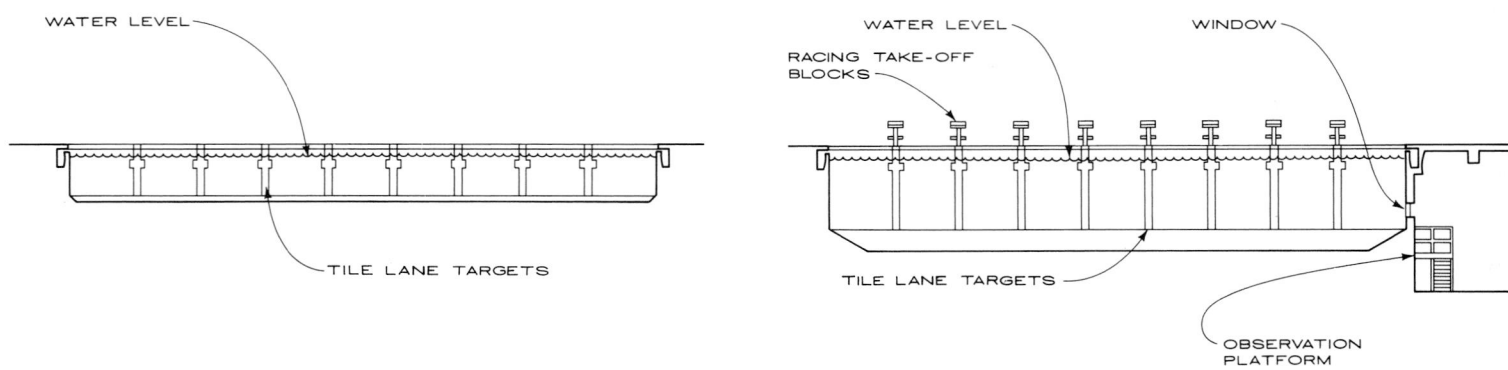

WATER LEVEL

TILE LANE TARGETS

CROSS SECTION

WATER LEVEL

WINDOW

RACING TAKE-OFF BLOCKS

TILE LANE TARGETS

OBSERVATION PLATFORM

CROSS SECTION

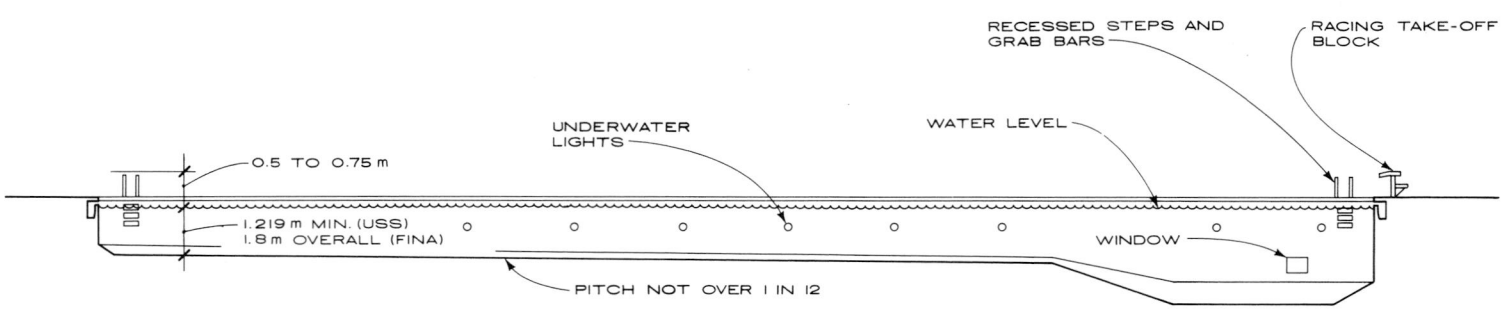

RECESSED STEPS AND GRAB BARS

RACING TAKE-OFF BLOCK

UNDERWATER LIGHTS

WATER LEVEL

0.5 TO 0.75 m

1.219 m MIN. (USS)
1.8 m OVERALL (FINA)

WINDOW

PITCH NOT OVER 1 IN 12

LONGITUDINAL SECTION

Flewelling & Moody; Los Angeles, California
Richard J. Vitullo, AIA; Oak Leaf Studio; Crownsville, Maryland

17 **AQUATICS**

INTRODUCTION

Swimming is excellent recreation and exercise for older people and people with restricted mobility because the body's natural buoyancy in water allows more freedom of movement than other forms of exercise; however, exiting and entering the pool is often a major obstacle. A variety of equipment is available to improve access to pools.

GENERAL REQUIREMENTS

Provide at least one form of accessible entry for every public pool. An accessible route should connect the room entrance to the pool. Surrounding paving should have a slip-resistant, nonabrasive finish. Highlight the edge of the pool with a contrasting color or different paving. Clearly display depth markings.

LIFTS

Lifts to assist people in wheelchairs can be permanently mounted or portable. Manual, hydraulic, pneumatic, or electric lifts are available.

With a manual lift, a wheelchair user slides the sling below his or her body, the pool staff turns the rachet handle to raise the person clear of the wheelchair, the lift is rotated over the pool, and the person is lowered into the water.

Electric or pneumatic lifts can be operated independently.

TRANSFER TIER

Tiered platforms also allow a person to independently enter a swimming pool or whirlpool. The platform is positioned in front of the pool steps; users transfer from a wheelchair to the top step and lower themselves, step-by-step, into the pool. Pool steps should have a second low rail at a height of 6 to 12 in; provide a clear area 5 ft square at the top of the steps for the wheelchair and platform. A second type of platform has two tiers of steps and can be positioned anywhere in the pool.

RAMPS

Use ramps in the shallow end of the pool if space is available. Ramps can be custom built and adapted to a particular situation or be prefabricated, removable units. Provide special wheelchairs that may be fully submerged in water. Ramps and handrails must comply with ADA standards:

Ramp slope—not to exceed 1:12
Handrails—must be provided on both sides
Ramp surface—should be nonslip and nonabrasive
Ramp width—36 in. minimum.

STEPS

Steps may be provided for pool access. Steps must have handrails on both sides. Handrails, handrail extensions, and stair treads and risers must meet ADA standards. Treads should have a nonslip and nonabrasive finish.

MOVABLE POOL FLOORS

Movable pool floors are hydraulically raised and lowered to the level of the surrounding deck so that wheelchair users can enter and exit with ease. The movable area may be a portion of the pool floor or the entire floor. See manufacturer information for design requirements.

RAISED POOL-EDGE COPING

Raised pool-edge copings with grab bars are acceptable means of providing access.

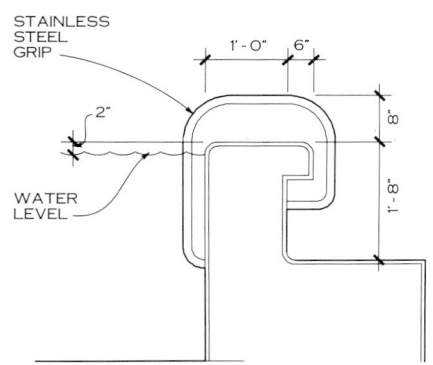

RAISED COPING

Janet B. Rankin; Rippeteau Architects; Washington, D.C.

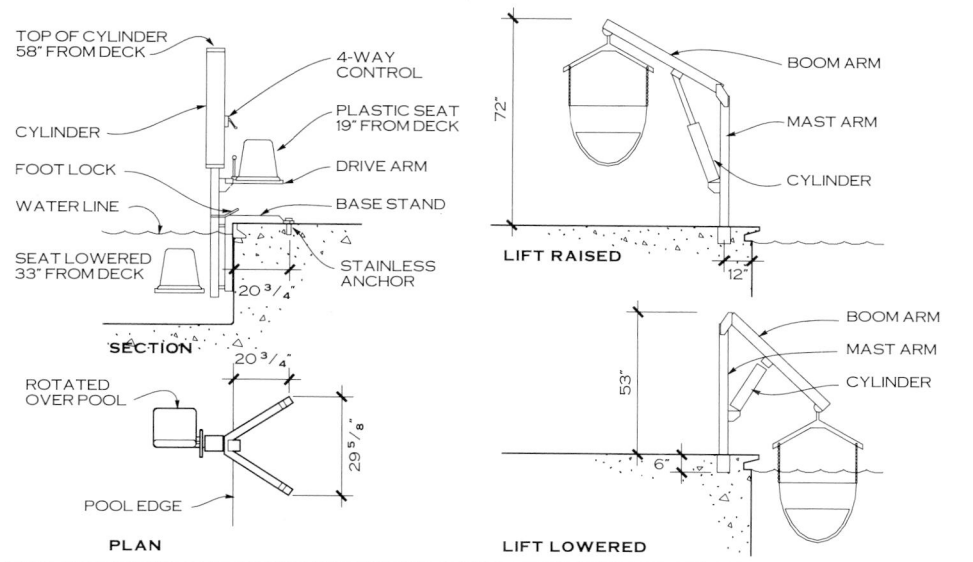

LIFTS

TRANSFER TIER

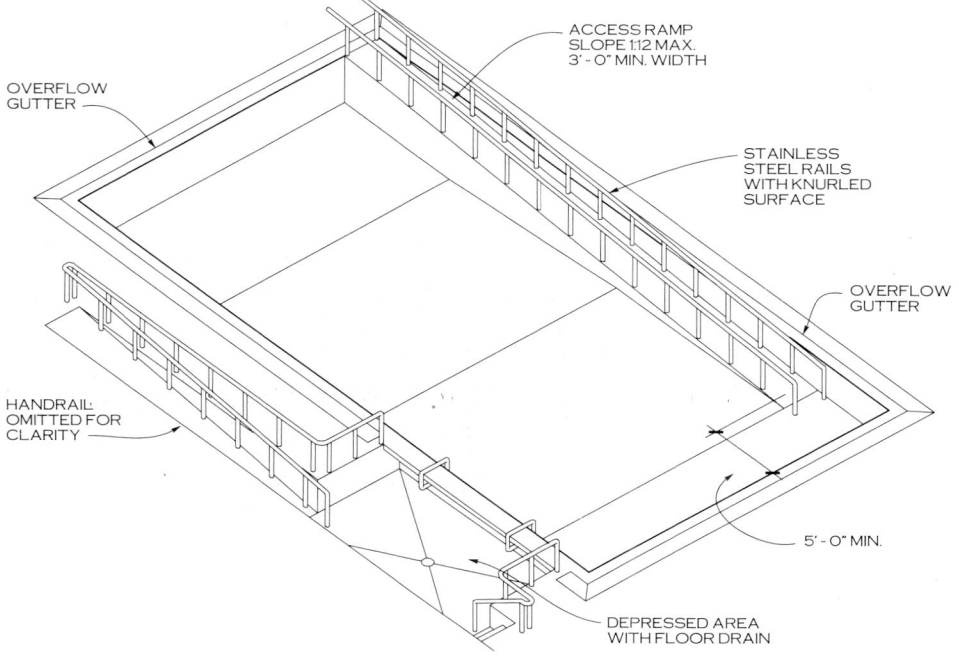

POOL ACCESS RAMP

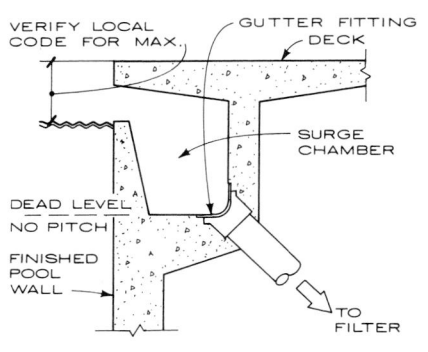

FULLY RECESSED OVERFLOW GUTTER

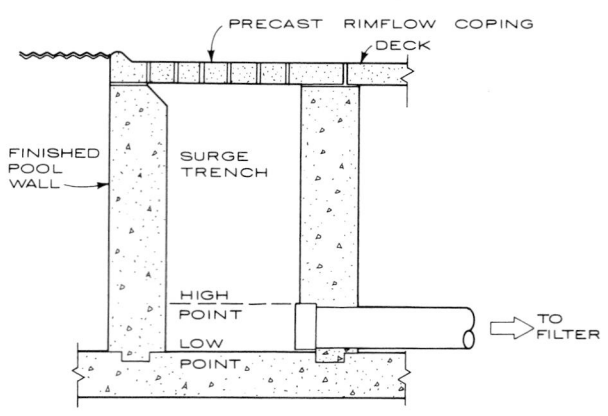

RIMFLOW SYSTEM

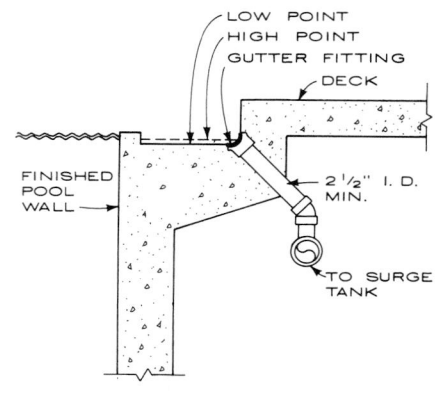

ROLL-OUT OVERFLOW GUTTER

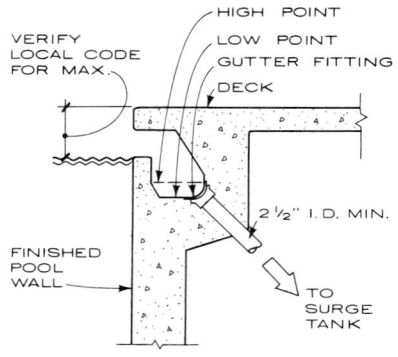

FULLY RECESSED GUTTER

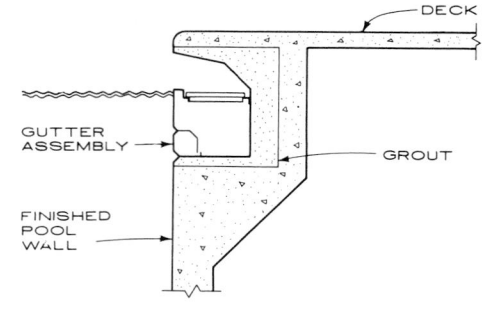

STAINLESS STEEL RECESSED SKIMMER

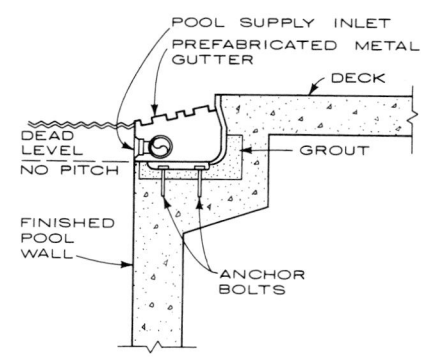

PREFABRICATED OVERFLOW GUTTER

PERIMETER OVERFLOW SYSTEMS

NOTES

1. A perimeter overflow system must be provided on all public swimming pools. It must be designed and constructed so that the water level of the pool is maintained at the operating level of the overflow rim or weir device. Dimension from the deck to the water level is determined by applicable codes.

2. Perimeter type overflow systems, when used as the only overflow system on the pool, must extend around a minimum 50% of the swimming pool perimeter. Perimeter overflow systems must be connected to the circulation system with a system surge capacity of not less than 1 gal/sq ft of pool surface.

3. The perimeter overflow system in combination with the upper rim of the pool must constitute a handhold. It must be designed to prevent the entrapment of swimmer's arms, legs, or feet and to permit inspection and cleaning.

4. The hydraulic capacity of the overflow system must be sufficient to handle 100% of the circulation flow.

5. When roll-out or flush deck type of perimeter overflows are used on competitive pools, the ends of the pool must be provided with a visual barrier that can be seen by swimmers.

6. Perimeter overflows are commonly used on public swimming pools. Some state health departments do not approve skimmers on public swimming pools that exceed a certain surface area. Current state codes or swimming pool regulations must be checked to determine limits of use, minimum dimensions, and other factors dealing with overflow design.

7. Metal swimming pool systems are available that have a built-in perimeter overflow. In addition to the overflow channel, the metal liner may also contain the return waterline from the filtration system. A metal liner that incorporates a cove between wall and floor is desirable to facilitate cleaning.

8. Deck areas adjoining the overflow system are generally required to slope away from it to separate drains. When deck is sloped to pool overflow, provide for diverting pool overflow to waste during deck cleaning.

National Swimming Pool Institute; Washington, D.C.

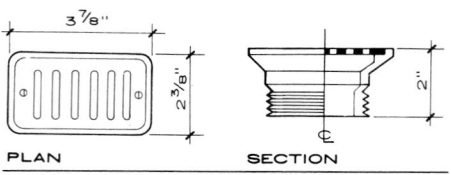

PLAN SECTION
FLAT TYPE GUTTER FITTINGS

ELEVATION SECTION
ANGLE TYPE GUTTER FITTINGS

9. Perimeter type overflows may be custom built to conform to the design selected. Ceramic tile is the preferred material for the top 6 in. of the pool wall, the pool rim, the gutter, and the deck for indoor swimming pools. Gratings for deep overflow gutters may be of precast concrete, plastic, or metal.

10. Proprietary overflow systems are available that have the characteristics of many of the perimeter overflow types shown. Stainless steel is commonly used because of its corrosion resistance. Aluminum overflow systems have a coating or enamel finish. Slotted precast concrete units are also available.

11. Surfaces subject to traffic must be nonslip.

SURFACE SKIMMERS

When surface skimmers are used, one must be provided for each 500 sq ft, or fraction thereof, of the pool surface. When two or more skimmers are used, they must be located so as to maintain effective skimming action over the entire surface of the swimming pool. Skimmers may not be permitted on larger pools. See local health department codes for limitation on public pools. Skimmers are not recommended for competitive pools.

Surface skimmers are available from many swimming pool suppliers. Metal or plastic units are available in various capacities. An access cover in the deck permits removal and cleaning of the strainer. Surface skimmers should comply with the joint National Swimming Pool Institute—National Sanitation Foundation performance standards.

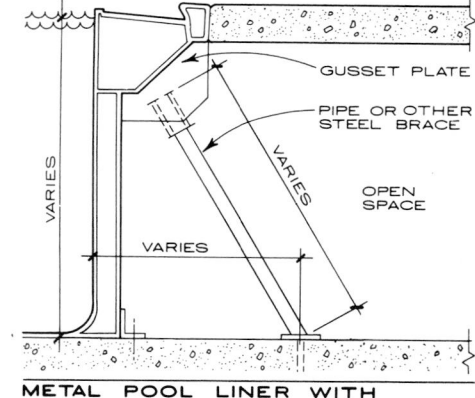

METAL POOL LINER WITH OVERFLOW

Often used in rooftop or other above grade installations where weight is a primary factor in design.

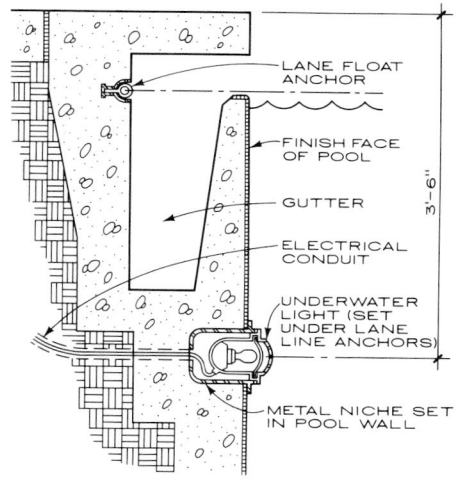

SECTION
GUTTER DETAIL SHOWING UNDERWATER LIGHTING

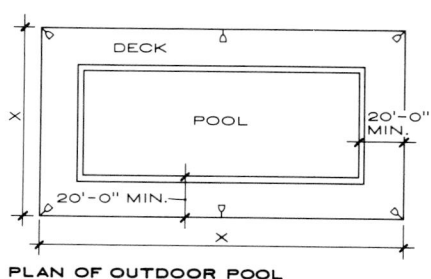

PLAN OF OUTDOOR POOL
OVERHEAD FLOOD LIGHTING

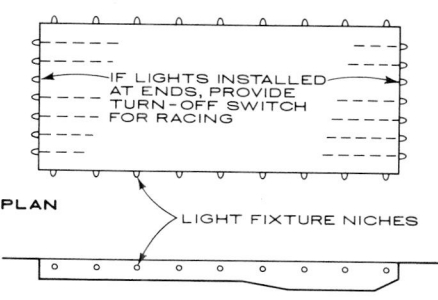

PLAN

SECTION
UNDERWATER POOL LIGHTING

NOTE

Distance ''x'' for spacing of lights not to exceed four times the actual mounting height of lamp in light fixture. For outdoor above-water lighting, flood lights should be mounted at least 20 ft above the water. Select lamps to allow 1.0 W/sq ft minimum for flood lights. Consult USS or NCAA for specific requirements for championship meets. USS rules for championship meets require a minimum of 40 fc 3 ft above the water surface. For interior above-water lighting, concentration of 100 fc is recommended and should be directly over turning end and finish line. (This is a specific requirement for national championship meets.) A power source for additional lighting should be available for use with television, movies, and special events. Buildings housing indoor pools should not have deck-level windows in walls facing pool ends to prevent glare. Deck-level windows at side should be tinted.

NOTES FOR WET AND DRY NICHE UNDERWATER LIGHTS

Underwater lighting type and dimensions should be in accordance with NEC (article 680) regulations.

Underwater lights will require 0.5 to 2.0 W/sq ft of water area and should be sized accordingly.

Box connections for dry or wet niches should be a minimum of 4 ft 0 in. away from the side wall of the pool and 8 in. above the deck. Low voltage wiring should be used for all dry or wet niche lighting fixtures. This requires a transformer located, by code, a specific distance away from pool wall and above deck.

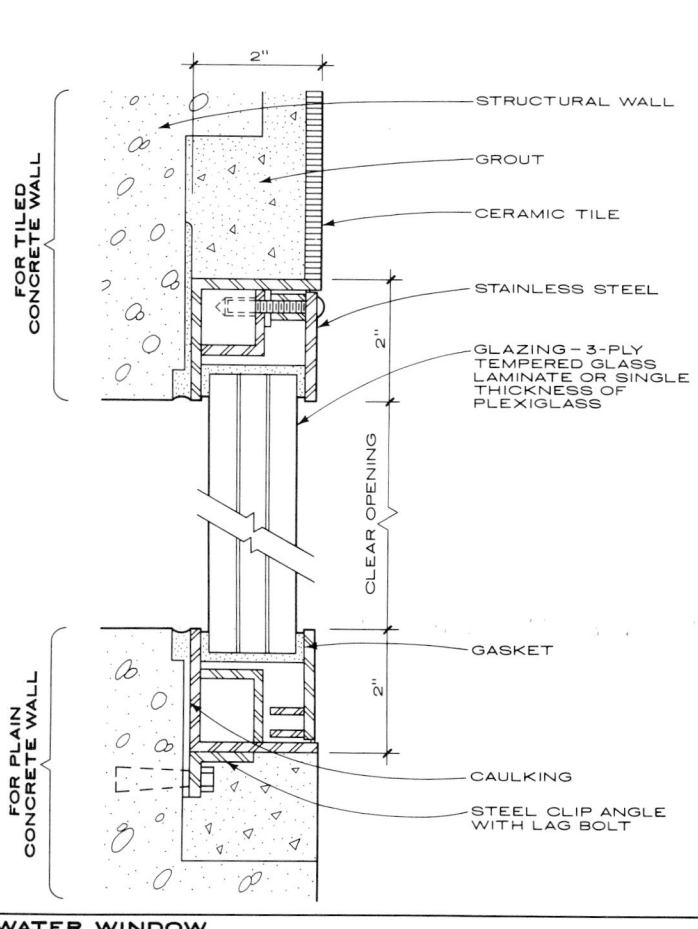

WATER WINDOW

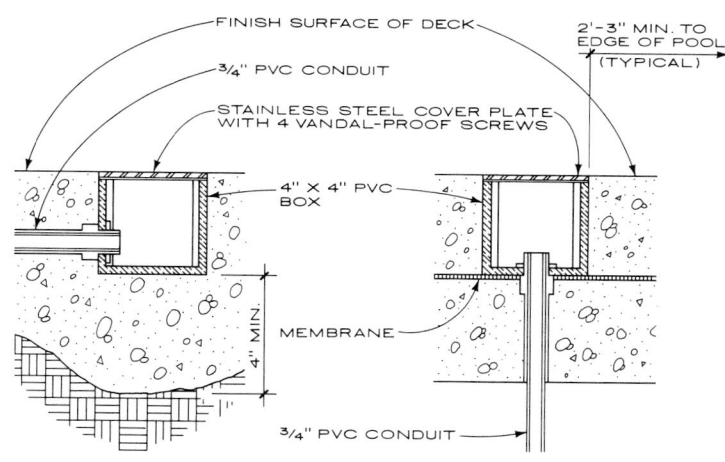

SLAB ON GRADE   **SUSPENDED SLAB**
ELECTRONIC TIMING DECK BOXES

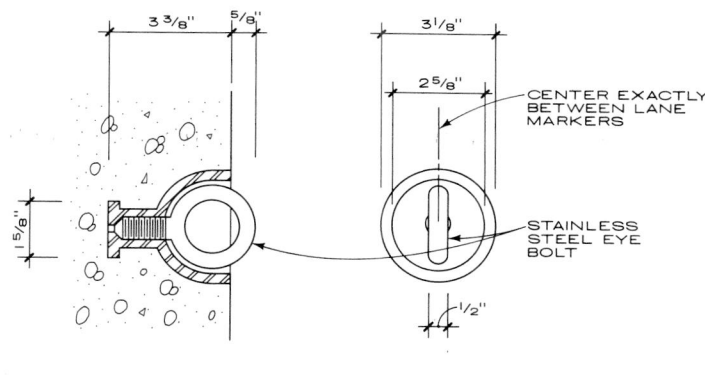

SECTION   **ELEVATION**
LANE FLOAT ANCHOR

Flewelling & Moody; Los Angeles, California
Richard J. Vitullo, AIA; Oak Leaf Studio; Crownsville, Maryland

AQUATICS **17**

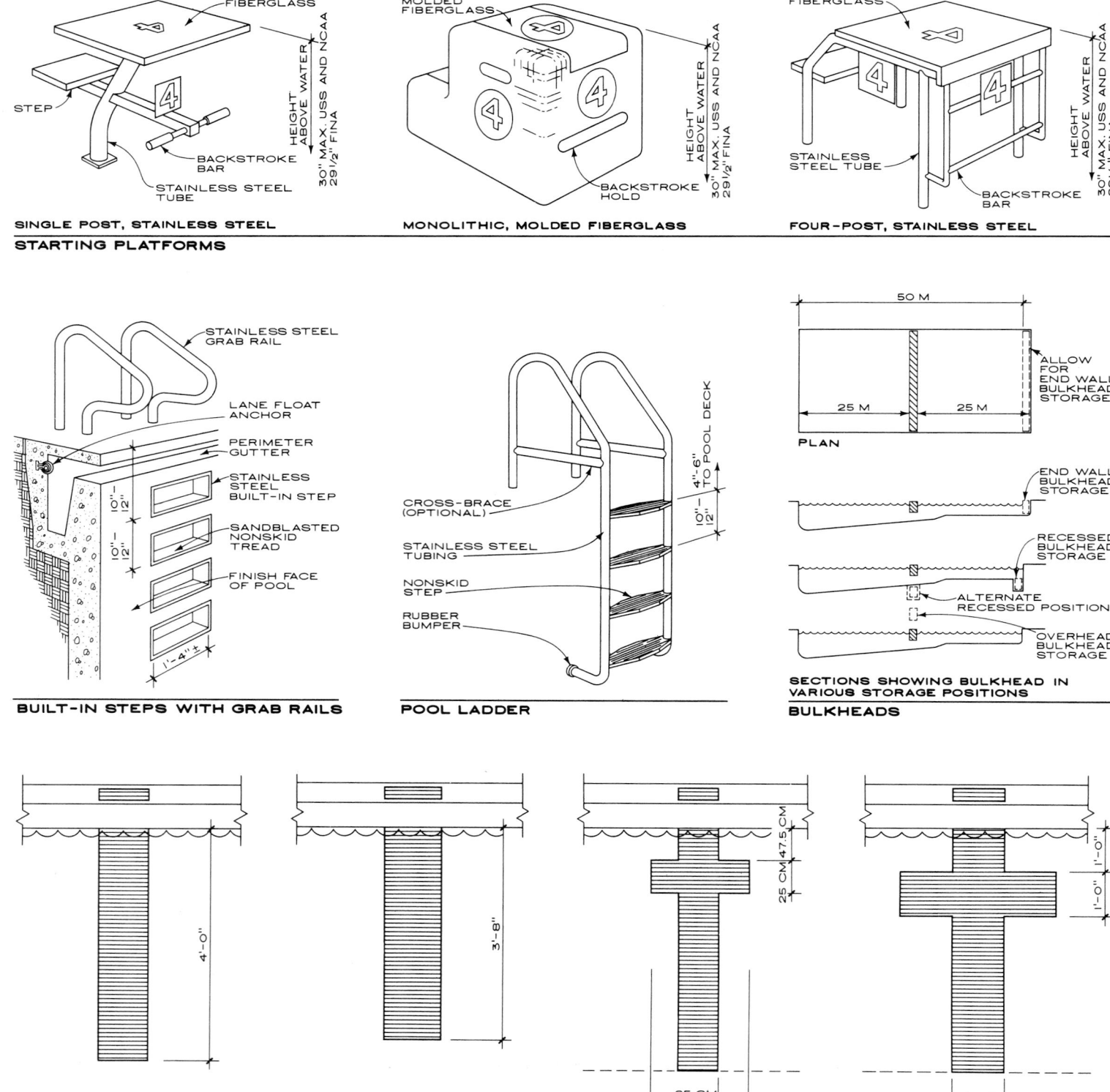

FIBERGLASS

STEP

BACKSTROKE BAR

STAINLESS STEEL TUBE

HEIGHT ABOVE WATER
30" MAX, USS AND NCAA
29 1/2" FINA

SINGLE POST, STAINLESS STEEL

MOLDED FIBERGLASS

BACKSTROKE HOLD

HEIGHT ABOVE WATER
30" MAX, USS AND NCAA
29 1/2" FINA

MONOLITHIC, MOLDED FIBERGLASS

FIBERGLASS

STAINLESS STEEL TUBE

BACKSTROKE BAR

HEIGHT ABOVE WATER
30" MAX, USS AND NCAA
29 1/2" FINA

FOUR-POST, STAINLESS STEEL

STARTING PLATFORMS

STAINLESS STEEL GRAB RAIL

LANE FLOAT ANCHOR

PERIMETER GUTTER

STAINLESS STEEL BUILT-IN STEP

SANDBLASTED NONSKID TREAD

FINISH FACE OF POOL

10"-12" 10"-12"

1'-4"±

BUILT-IN STEPS WITH GRAB RAILS

CROSS-BRACE (OPTIONAL)

STAINLESS STEEL TUBING

NONSKID STEP

RUBBER BUMPER

4"-6" TO POOL DECK

10"-12"

POOL LADDER

50 M

25 M   25 M

ALLOW FOR END WALL BULKHEAD STORAGE

PLAN

END WALL BULKHEAD STORAGE

RECESSED BULKHEAD STORAGE

ALTERNATE RECESSED POSITION

OVERHEAD BULKHEAD STORAGE

SECTIONS SHOWING BULKHEAD IN VARIOUS STORAGE POSITIONS

BULKHEADS

4'-0"

USS

3'-8"

NFHS

25 CM / 47.5 CM

25 CM

50 CM

FINA

1'-0"

1'-0"

1'-0"

NCAA

NOTE: COLOR OF END WALL TARGETS SHOULD BE DARK AND CONTRASTING TO THE GENERAL COLOR OF THE POOL (BLACK PREFERABLE)

END WALL TARGETS

Richard J. Vitullo, AIA; Oak Leaf Studio; Crownsville, Maryland

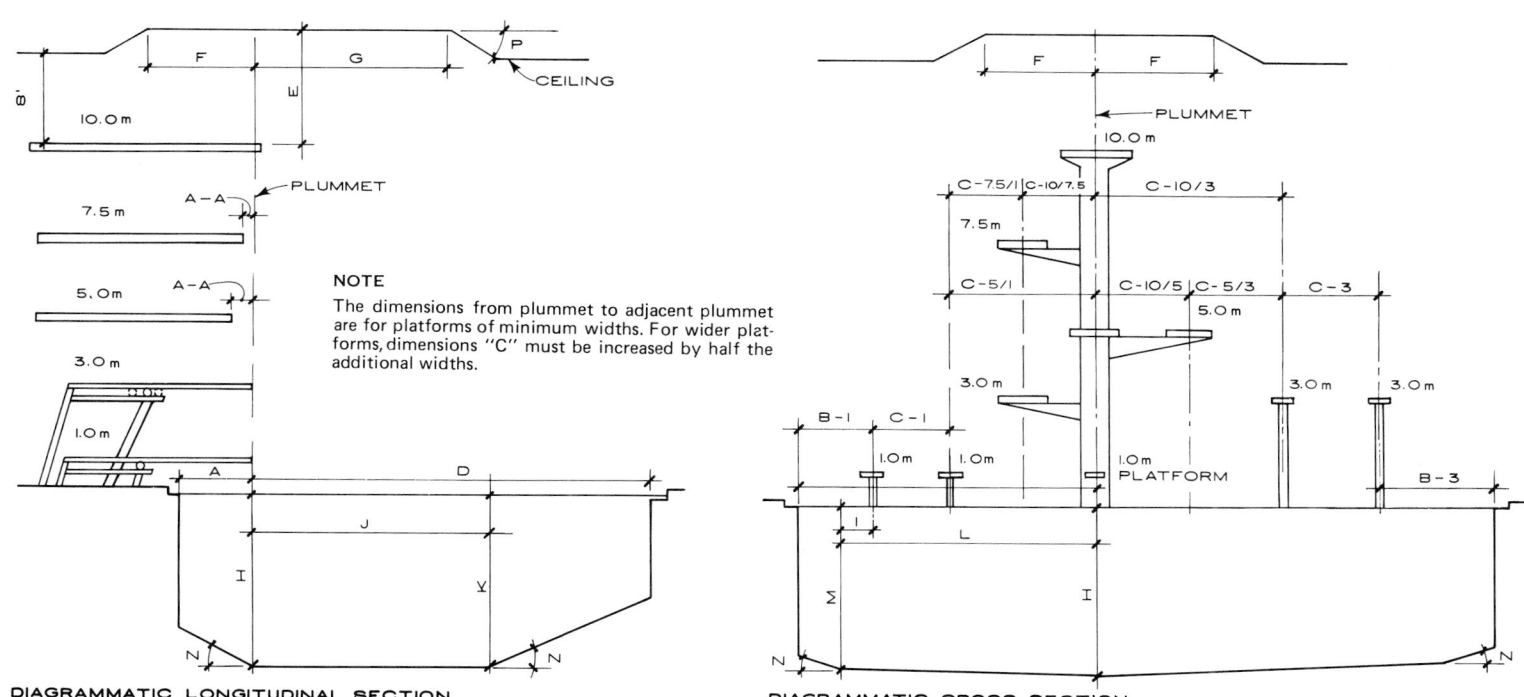

DIAGRAMMATIC LONGITUDINAL SECTION

DIAGRAMMATIC CROSS SECTION

NOTE

The dimensions from plummet to adjacent plummet are for platforms of minimum widths. For wider platforms, dimensions "C" must be increased by half the additional widths.

FINA INTERNATIONAL AMATEUR SWIMMING AND DIVING FEDERATION STANDARDS

DIMENSIONS FOR DIVING FACILITIES			SPRINGBOARDS				PLATFORMS								
			1 METER	3 METER	1 METER	3 METER	5 METER		7.5 METER		10 METER				
		LENGTH	5.0	5.0	4.5	5.0	6.0		6.0		6.0				
		WIDTH	0.5	0.5	0.6	0.8	1.5		1.5		2.0				
		HEIGHT	1.0	3.0	1.0	0.8	5.0		7.5		10.0				
A	FROM PLUMMET: BACK TO POOL WALL	DESIG.	A-1	A-3	A-1 (PL)	A-3 (PL)	A-5		A-7.5		A-10				
		MIN.	1.50	1.50	0.75	1.25	1.25		1.50		1.50				
		PREF.	1.80	1.80			1.50								
A-A	FROM PLUMMET: BACK TO PLATFORM DIRECTLY BELOW	DESIG.					AA-5/1		A-7.5/3		AA-10/5				
		MIN.					0.75		0.75		0.75				
		PREF.							1.50		1.50				
B	FROM PLUMMET: TO POOL WALL AT SIDE	DESIG.	B-1	B-3	B-1 (PL)	B-3 (PL)	B-5		B-7.5		B-10				
		MIN.	2.50	3.50	2.30	2.90	4.25		4.50		5.25				
		PREF.	3.00												
C	FROM PLUMMET TO ADJACENT PLUMMET	DESIG.	C-1	C-3	C-3/1	C-1/1 (PL)	C-3/1 (PL)	C-5/3 (PL)	C-5/1	C-7.5/3/1	C-10/7.5	C-10/7.5/3	C-10/3/1			
		MIN.	2.40	2.60	2.60	1.65	2.10	2.10	2.10	2.10	2.50	2.75	2.75			
		PREF.	2.40	2.40	1.4/3.0											
D	FROM PLUMMET TO POOL WALL AHEAD	DESIG.	D-1	D-3	D-1 (PL)	D-3 (PL)	D-5		D-7.5		D-10				
		MIN.	9.00	10.25	8.00	9.50	10.25		11.00		13.50				
		PREF.													
E	PLUMMET, FROM BOARD TO CEILING OVERHEAD	DESIG.		E-1	E-3	E-1 (PL)	E-3 (PL)		E-5		E-7.5		E-10		
		MIN.		5.00	5.00	3.00	3.00		3.00		3.20		3.40		
		PREF.							3.40		3.40		5 00		
F	CLEAR OVERHEAD, BEHIND AND EACH SIDE OF PLUMMET	DESIG.	F-1	E-1	F-3	E-3	F-1 (PL)	F-3 (PL)	F-5	E-5	F-7.5	E-7.5	F-10	E-10	
		MIN.	2.50	5.00	2.50	5.00	2.75	2.75	2.75	3.00	2.75	3.20	2.75	3.40	
		PREF.								3.40		3.40		5.00	
G	CLEAR OVERHEAD, AHEAD OF PLUMMET	DESIG.	G-1	E-1	G-3	E-3	G-1 (PL)	G-3 (PL)	G-5	E-5	G-7.5	E-7.5	G-10	E-10	
		MIN.	5.00	5.00	5.00	5.00	5.00	5.00	5.00	3.00	5.00	3.20	6.00	3.40	
		PREF.								3.40		3.40		5.00	
H	DEPTH OF WATER AT PLUMMET	DESIG.		H-1		H-3	H-1 (PL)	H-3 (PL)		H-5		H-7.5		H-10	
		MIN.		3.40		3.80	3.40	3.60	3.40	3.80		4.10		4.50	
		PREF.		3.80		4.00		3.80	4.00			4.50		5.00	
J-K	DISTANCE, DEPTH OF WATER, AHEAD OF PLUMMET	DESIG.	J-1	K-1	J-3	K-3	J/K-1 (PL)	J/K-3 (PL)	J-5	K-5	J-7.5	K-7.5	J-10	K-10	
		MIN.	5.00	3.30	6.00	3.70	5.0/3.3	6.0/3.3	6.00	3.70	8.00	4.00	11.00	4.25	
		PREF.		3.70		3.90		3.70	3.90			4.40		4.75	
L-M	DISTANCE, DEPTH OF WATER, EACH SIDE OF PLUMMET	DESIG.	L-1	M-1	L-3	M-3	L/M-1 (PL)	L/M-3 (PL)	L-5	M-5	L-7.5	M-7.5	L-10	M-10	
		MIN.	2.50	3.30	3.25	3.70	2.05/3.3	2.65/3.5	4.25	3.70	4.50	4.00	5.25	4.25	
		PREF.		3.70		3.90		3.70	3.90			4.40		4.75	
N P	MAXIMUM ANGLE OF SLOPE TO REDUCE DIMENSIONS BEYOND FULL REQUIREMENTS	POOL BOTTOM	= 30 Degrees (Approximately 1 ft vertical to 2 ft horizontal)												
		CEILING HEIGHT	= 30 Degrees												

R. Jackson Smith, AIA; Designed Environments, Inc.; Stamford, Connecticut

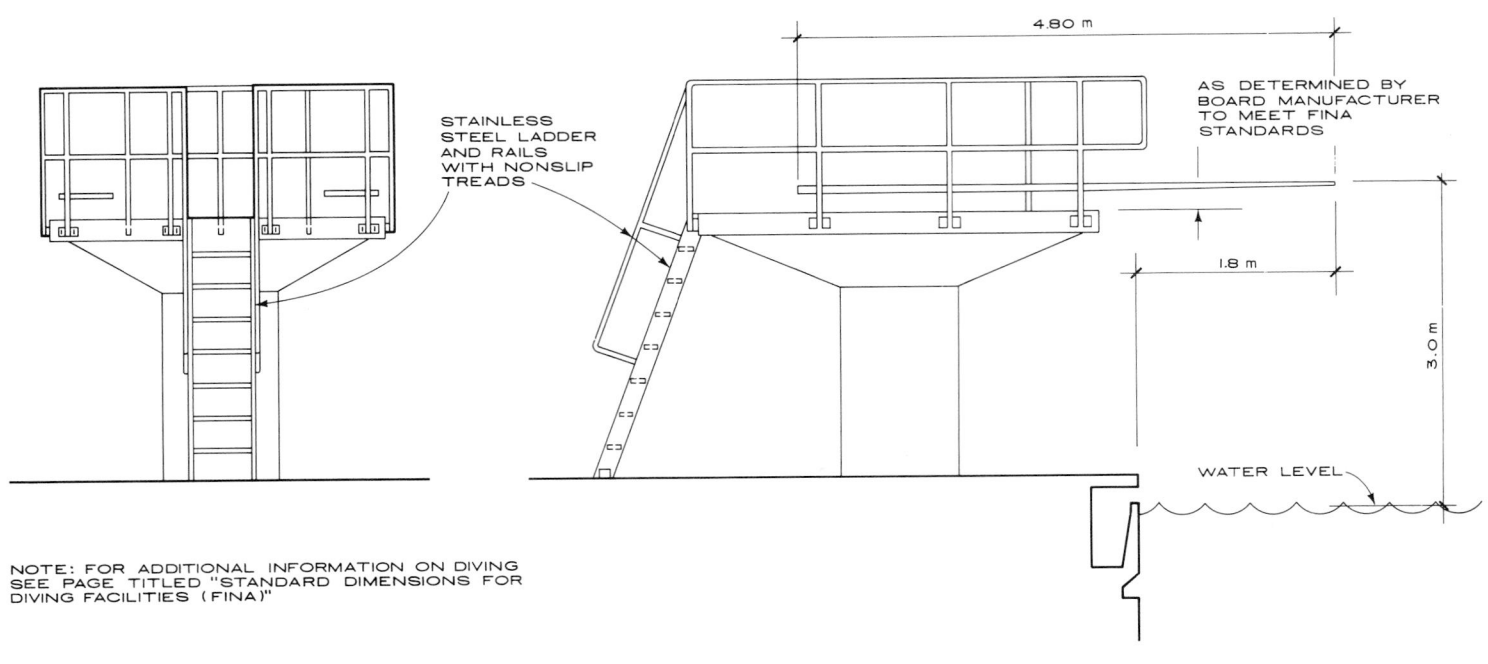

STAINLESS STEEL LADDER AND RAILS WITH NONSLIP TREADS

4.80 m

AS DETERMINED BY BOARD MANUFACTURER TO MEET FINA STANDARDS

1.8 m

3.0 m

WATER LEVEL

NOTE: FOR ADDITIONAL INFORMATION ON DIVING SEE PAGE TITLED "STANDARD DIMENSIONS FOR DIVING FACILITIES (FINA)"

REAR ELEVATION   SIDE ELEVATION

3 METER DIVING BOARD

GENERAL NOTES

Both 1 m and 3 m boards are required for amateur, collegiate, and international meets. All boards shall have a nonslip surface. Consult FINA Handbook. FINA is the Fédération Internationale de Natation Amateur.

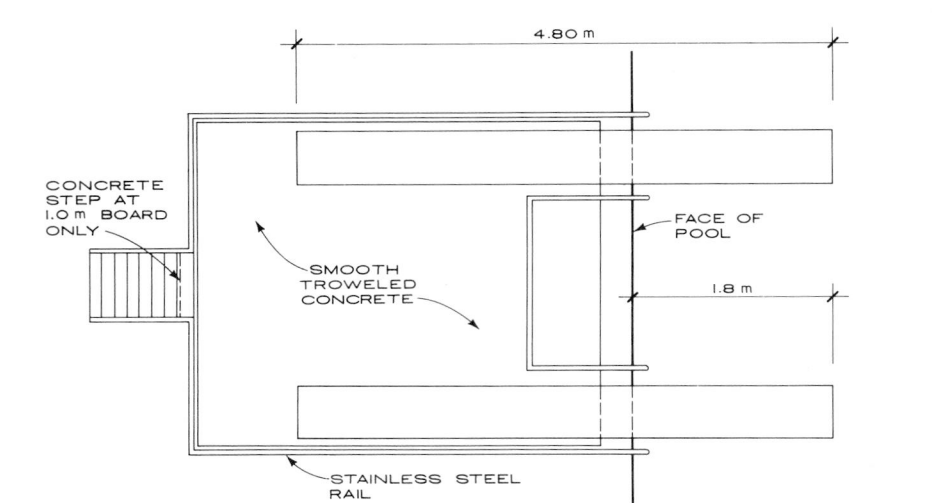

CONCRETE STEP AT 1.0 m BOARD ONLY

4.80 m

SMOOTH TROWELED CONCRETE

FACE OF POOL

1.8 m

STAINLESS STEEL RAIL

PLAN

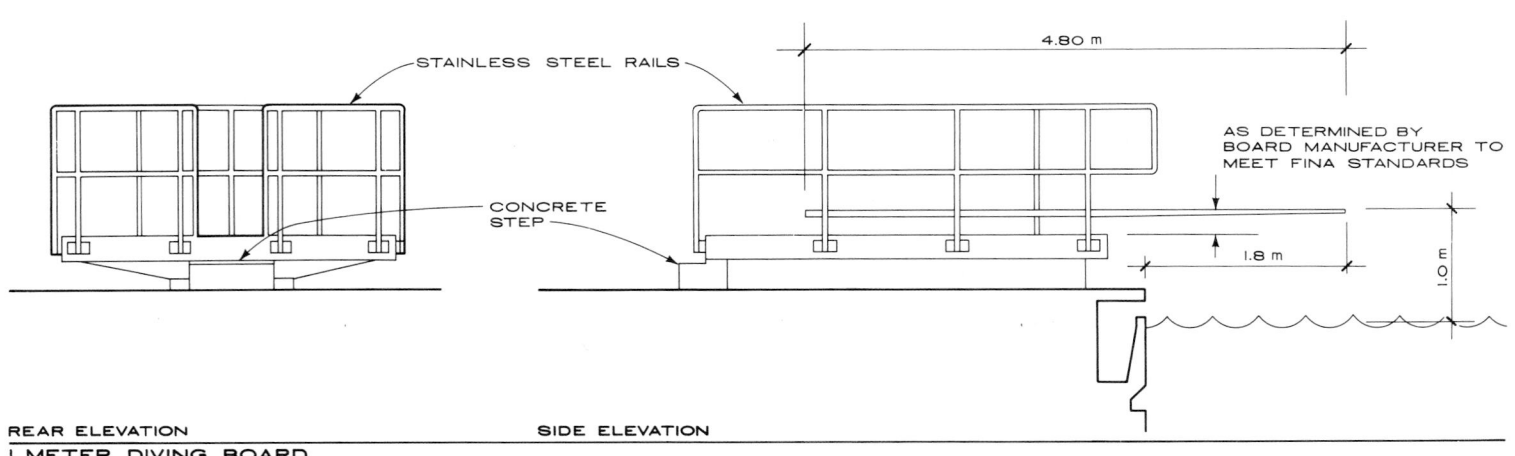

STAINLESS STEEL RAILS

4.80 m

AS DETERMINED BY BOARD MANUFACTURER TO MEET FINA STANDARDS

CONCRETE STEP

1.8 m

1.0 m

REAR ELEVATION   SIDE ELEVATION

1 METER DIVING BOARD

Flewelling & Moody; Los Angeles, California
Richard J. Vitullo, AIA; Oak Leaf Studio; Crownsville, Maryland

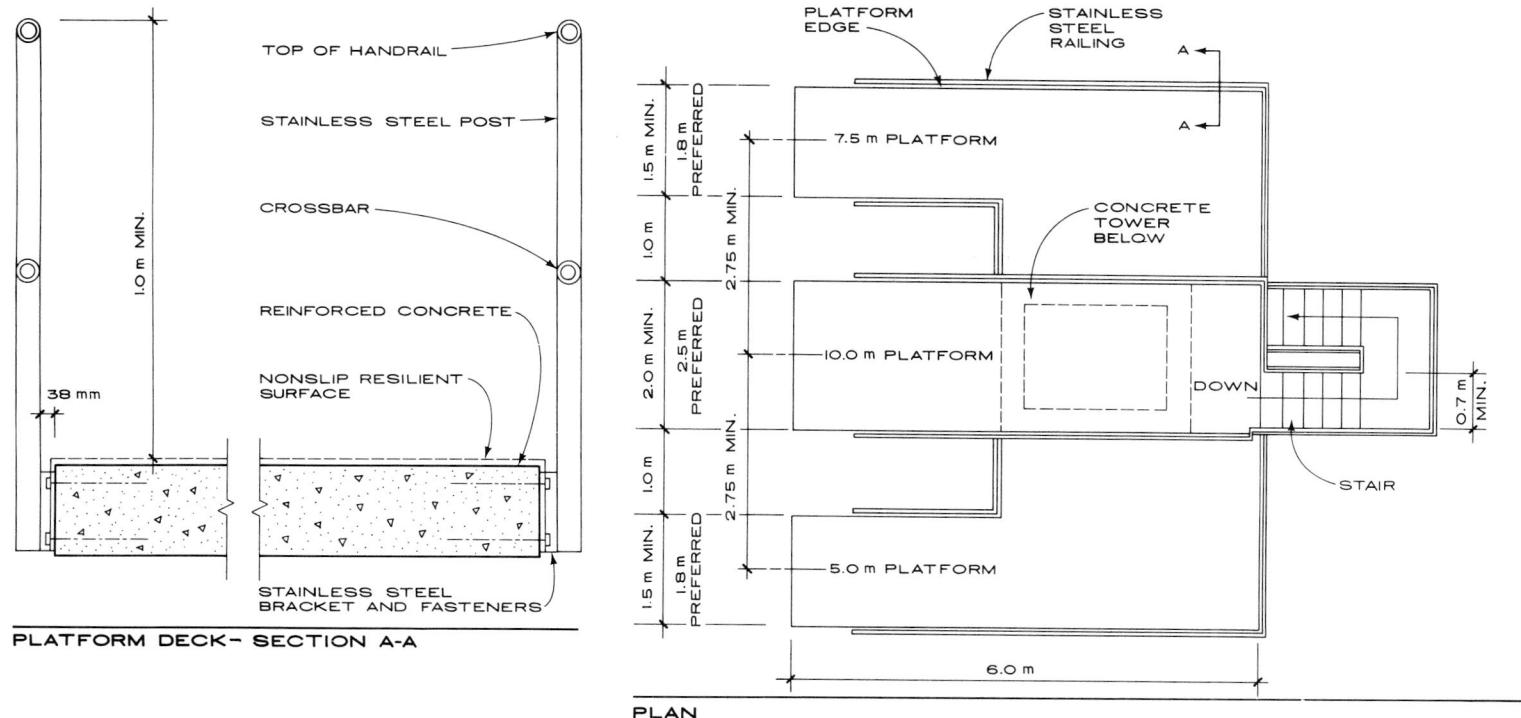

TOP OF HANDRAIL

STAINLESS STEEL POST

CROSSBAR

REINFORCED CONCRETE

NONSLIP RESILIENT SURFACE

1.0 m MIN.

38 mm

STAINLESS STEEL BRACKET AND FASTENERS

PLATFORM DECK- SECTION A-A

PLATFORM EDGE

STAINLESS STEEL RAILING

A

A

1.5 m MIN.
1.8 m PREFERRED

7.5 m PLATFORM

1.0 m

2.75 m MIN.

CONCRETE TOWER BELOW

2.0 m MIN.
2.5 m PREFERRED

10.0 m PLATFORM

DOWN

0.7 m MIN.

1.0 m

2.75 m MIN.

1.5 m MIN.
1.8 m PREFERRED

5.0 m PLATFORM

STAIR

6.0 m

PLAN

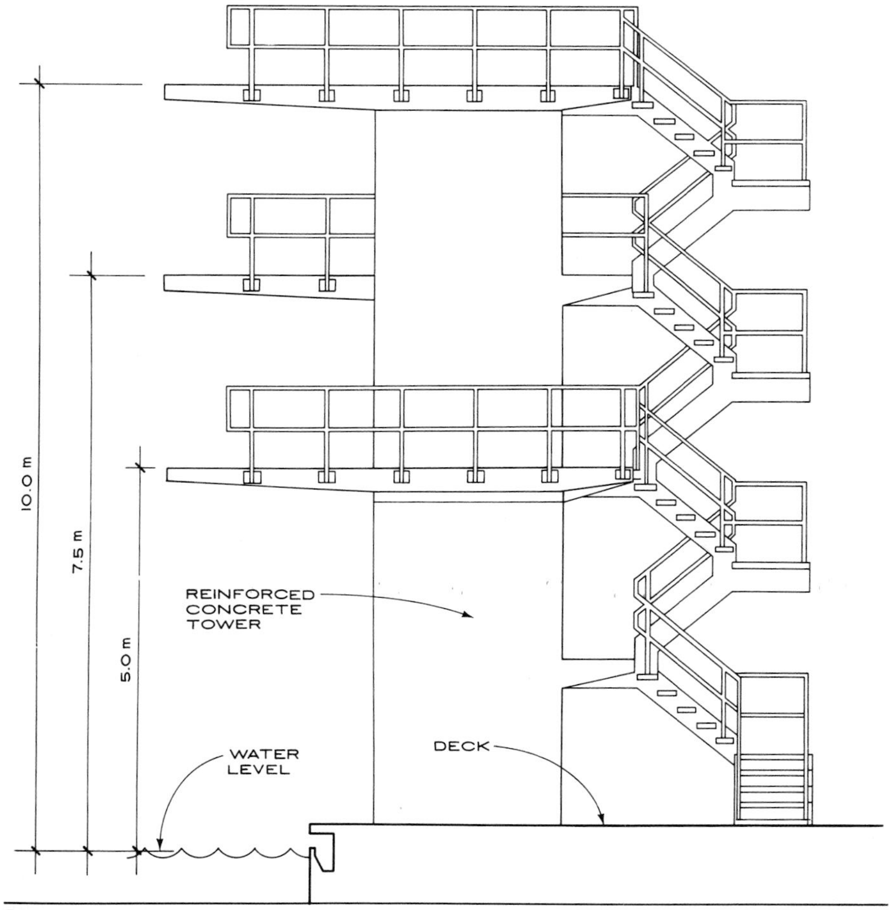

10.0 m

7.5 m

5.0 m

REINFORCED CONCRETE TOWER

WATER LEVEL

DECK

SIDE ELEVATION

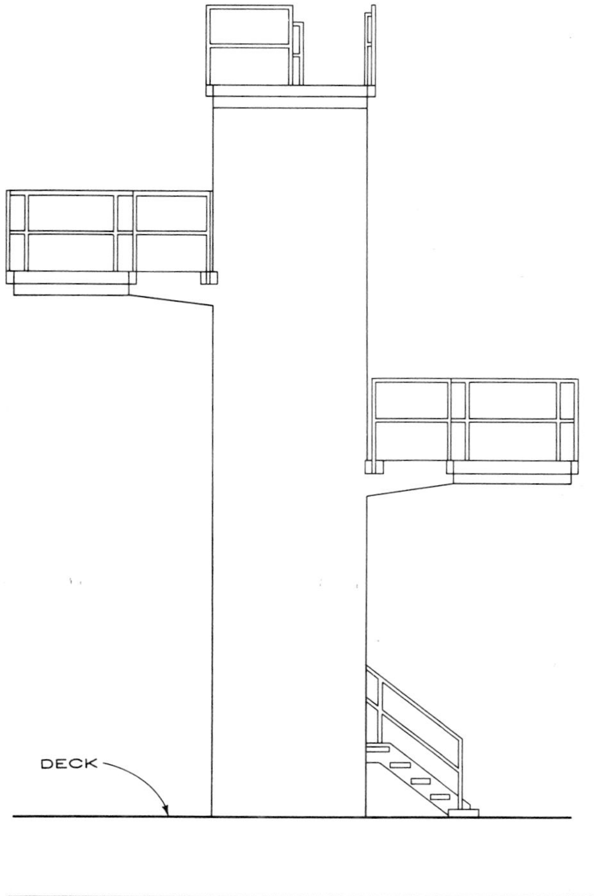

DECK

FRONT ELEVATION

Flewelling & Moody; Los Angeles, California
Richard J. Vitullo, AIA; Oak Leaf Studio; Crownsville, Maryland

AQUATICS   **17**

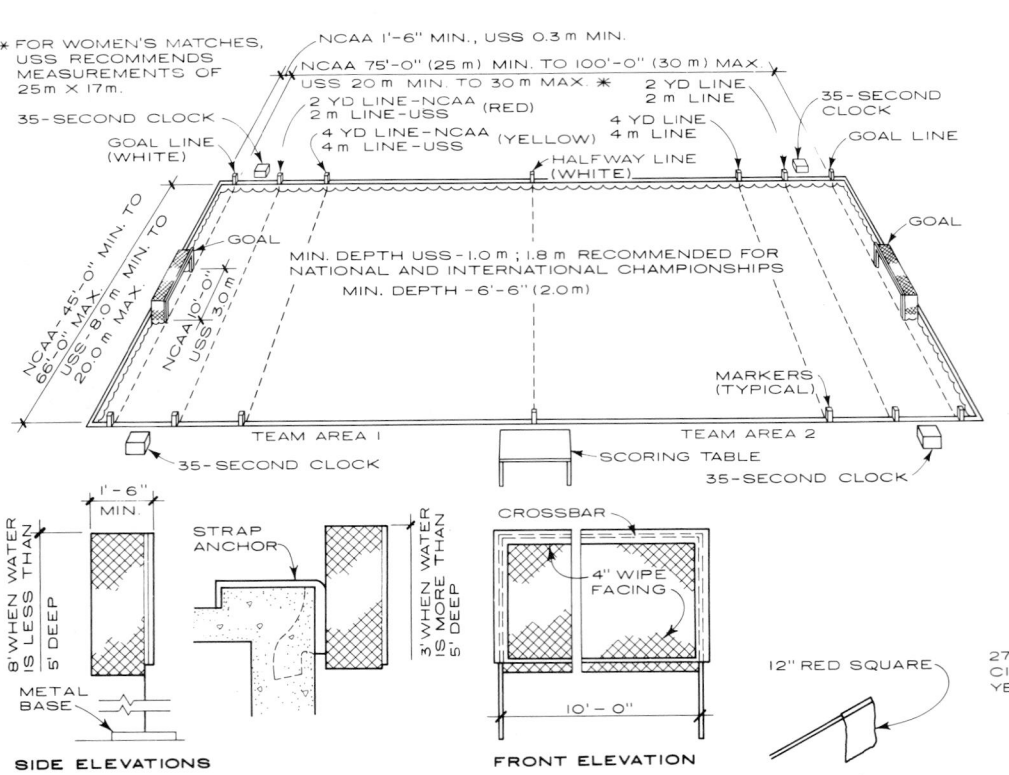

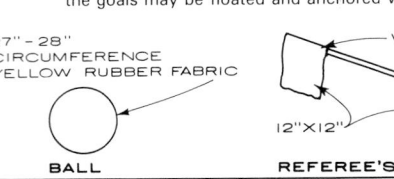

NOTES

1. Distinctive marks must be provided on both sides of field of play indicating goal lines, 2 and 4 yd (or meter) lines, and ½ distance between goal lines. These must be clearly visible from any position within the field of play. Allow sufficient space on walkways so referees may move freely from end to end of field of play. Provide space at goal lines for goal judges.

2. There must be distinctive markers on both ends of the pool to denote the ejection area on the goal line or the ends of the field of play 2 yd (2.0 m) from the corner of the field of play and to the right of the goal at the corner where the goal judge is located.

GOAL REQUIREMENTS

Posts and crossbar, rigid and perpendicular. USS, wood or metal, 3 in. sq, painted white; NCAA, metal 1½ in. diameter, painted yellow or orange. Nets to hang loosely on frame. For USS, the underside of the crossbar must be 0.90 m above water surface when water is 1.50 m or more in depth, and 2.40 m from the bottom of the bath when the depth of the water is less than 1.50 m.

Frames are custom made, with bracing placed where necessary. It is recommended that they be collapsible for easy storage. Anchorage methods depend on pool design, with those above commonly used, or brass couplings may be placed in pool walls to which frame is attached. If pool is longer than required length, one of the goals may be floated and anchored with guy wires.

WATER POLO

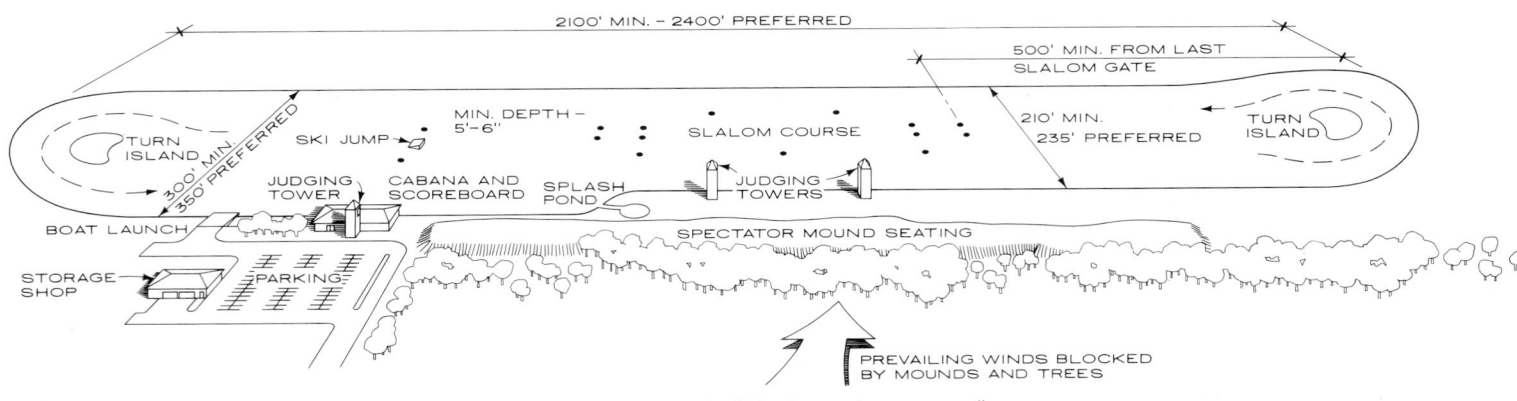

NOTES

1. To decrease turbidity caused by boat wake, an island running down the center of the lake may be built in addition to turn islands. Floating breakwaters may also be used; islands should be riprapped to prevent soil erosion.

2. A gradual (ratio 6:1) sandy slope along shorelines lets wave action die without rolling back.

WATER SKI LAKE

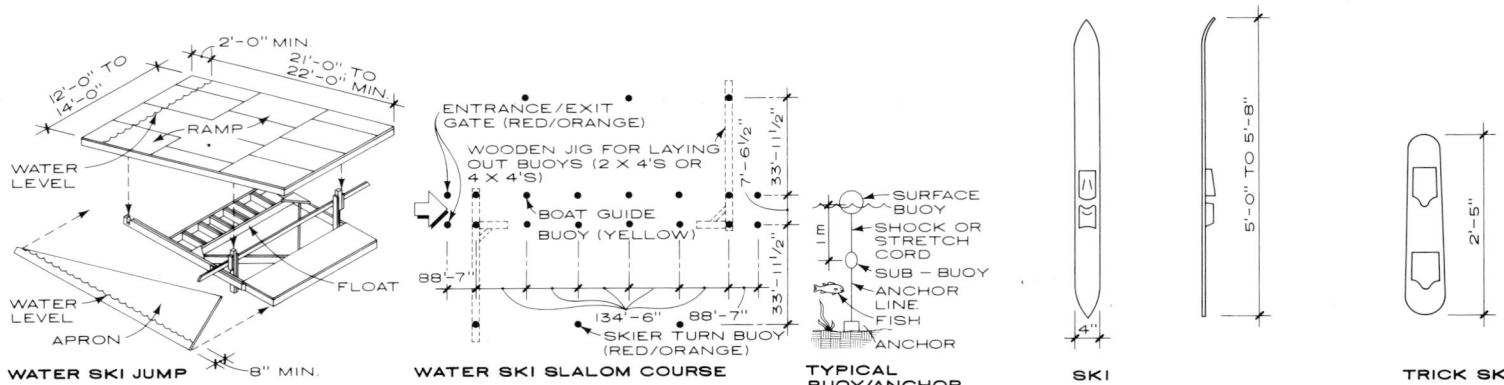

WATER SKIING AND JUMPING

Richard J. Vitullo, AIA; Oak Leaf Studio; Crownsville, Maryland

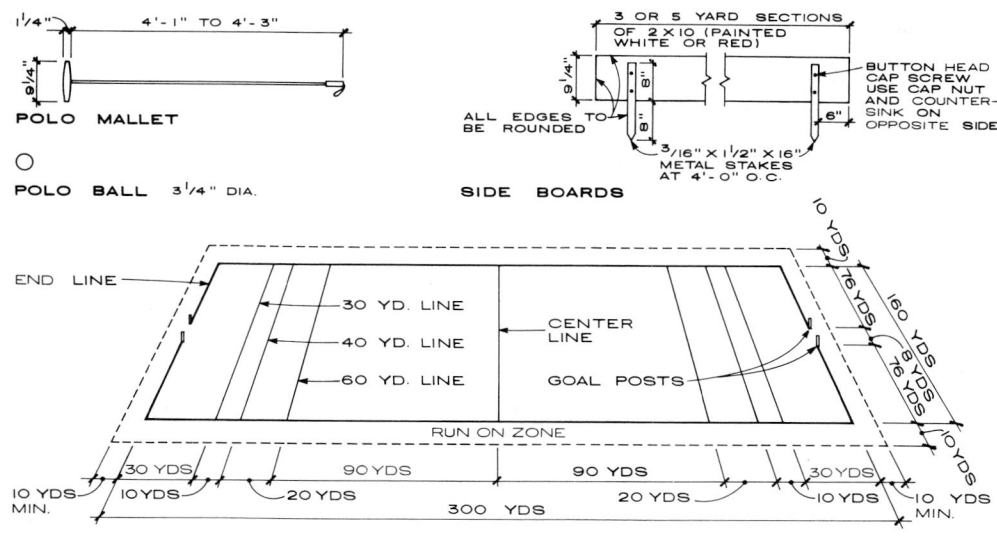

OUTDOOR POLO FIELD

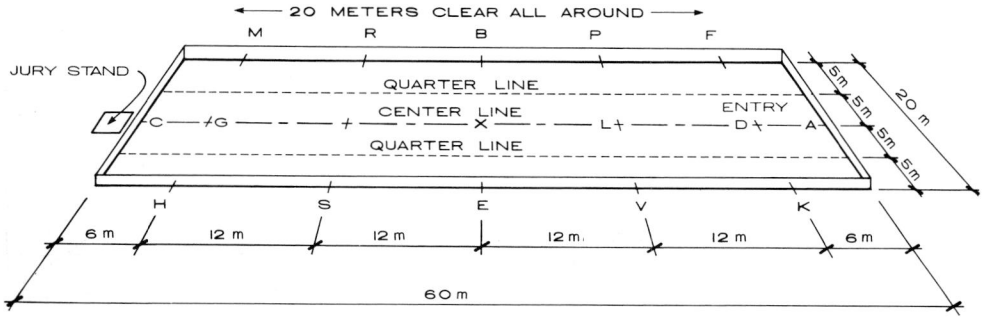

STANDARD DRESSAGE ARENA

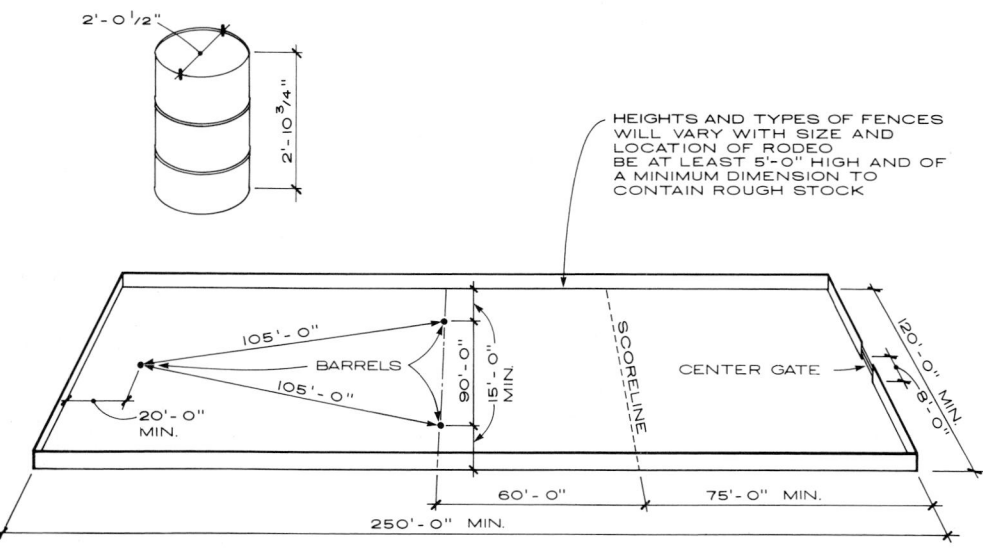

STANDARD BARREL COURSE

Theodore M. Ceraldi & Associates, Architects; Nyack, New York

POLO

Outdoor or high goal polo is played with two teams of four players each. There can be as many as forty horses per team, and stabling and picket areas are needed for the horses. Spectator stands to accommodate three to six thousand people are needed, depending on the level of play.

The field surface should be grass cut smooth and short enough for the ball to roll straight and easily. The field side boundaries are 10 in. high side boards with a minimum of 10 yards run on, known as the safety zone, beyond. Goal posts must be vertical and light enough to break upon collision. Goal posts are 10 ft. high, and 8 yds. apart. About twenty balls are used in a game.

Arena polo is played at smaller clubs or indoors where less space is available. A playing area of 300 ft. by 150 ft. is considered ideal. Goals, at opposite ends of the field, are 10 ft. in width by 12 ft. in height, inside measurement. In smaller arenas the goal size may be reduced, but to not less than 8 ft. in width by 10 ft.in height. The arena shall be clearly marked at the center and at points 15 yds. and 25 yds. perpendicular to each goal. The inflated arena polo ball shall be not less than $4\frac{1}{4}$ in. nor more than $4\frac{1}{2}$ in. in diameter.

Further information: United States Polo Association, Oak Brook, Ill.

DRESSAGE

The arena should be on as level ground as possible. The standard arena is 60 meters x 20 meters. The small arena is 40 meters x 20 meters. The enclosure itself should consist of a low fence about 0.30 meters high. The part of the fence at letter A should be easily removable to let competitors in and out of the arena. Arenas must be separated from the public by a distance of not less than 20 meters.

The letters, clearly marked, should be placed outside the enclosure about 0.50 meters from the fence. A red line painted on the fence 20 cm. high locates the exact point of the letters on the track. The center line, throughout its length, and the three points D, X, and G should be as clearly marked as possible, without frightening the horses. It is recommended, on grass arenas, to mow the grass on the center line shorter than other parts of the arena, and on a sand arena, to roll or rake the center line.

An exercise area must be provided far enough away from the arena so as not to disturb the competitors.

SHOW

Horse show rings vary in size according to type of activity performed. A basic outdoor ring size for hunters and jumpers is 150 ft.x 300 ft. Combined training requires a stadium show ring of 80 meters x 80 meters, as well as a dressage ring. The appropriate breed or show association should be contacted for current and specific regulations.

Flat classes need a level arena with solid footing. There should be one definite opening for an 'in' gate; preferable are separate openings for in and out gates. Rings for flat classes should be large enough to accommodate comfortably the number of horses.

Show management must provide sufficient area for schooling horses. It is recommended that separate schooling areas be provided for hunters and jumpers since different types of jumps are used for each. Jumps may vary from a single jump consisting of a single bar 4 in. in diameter and 6 ft. long, hung in cups from two uprights, to various combinations of two and three fences, water jumps, banks, and ditches—depending on the skill level of the class.

Further information: American Horse Show Association, New York, N.Y.

RODEO

Rodeo consists of several events involving timed contests such as calf roping and barrel riding, and rough stock events such as steer wrestling and bull riding. Arenas may vary in size but must be enclosed with fencing to control the various livestock. Barriers and chutes for timed events should be at the opposite end of arena from chutes for rough stock events. Stables, pens, and corrals for holding stock must be provided, as well as area for contestants to exercise their animals. Grandstand seating is standard; the number of spectators varies with the number and competition level of rodeo participants.

Barrels must be regulation 55 gal. size metal or rubber and enclosed on both ends.

Further information: International Professional Rodeo Association, Pauls Valley, Okla.

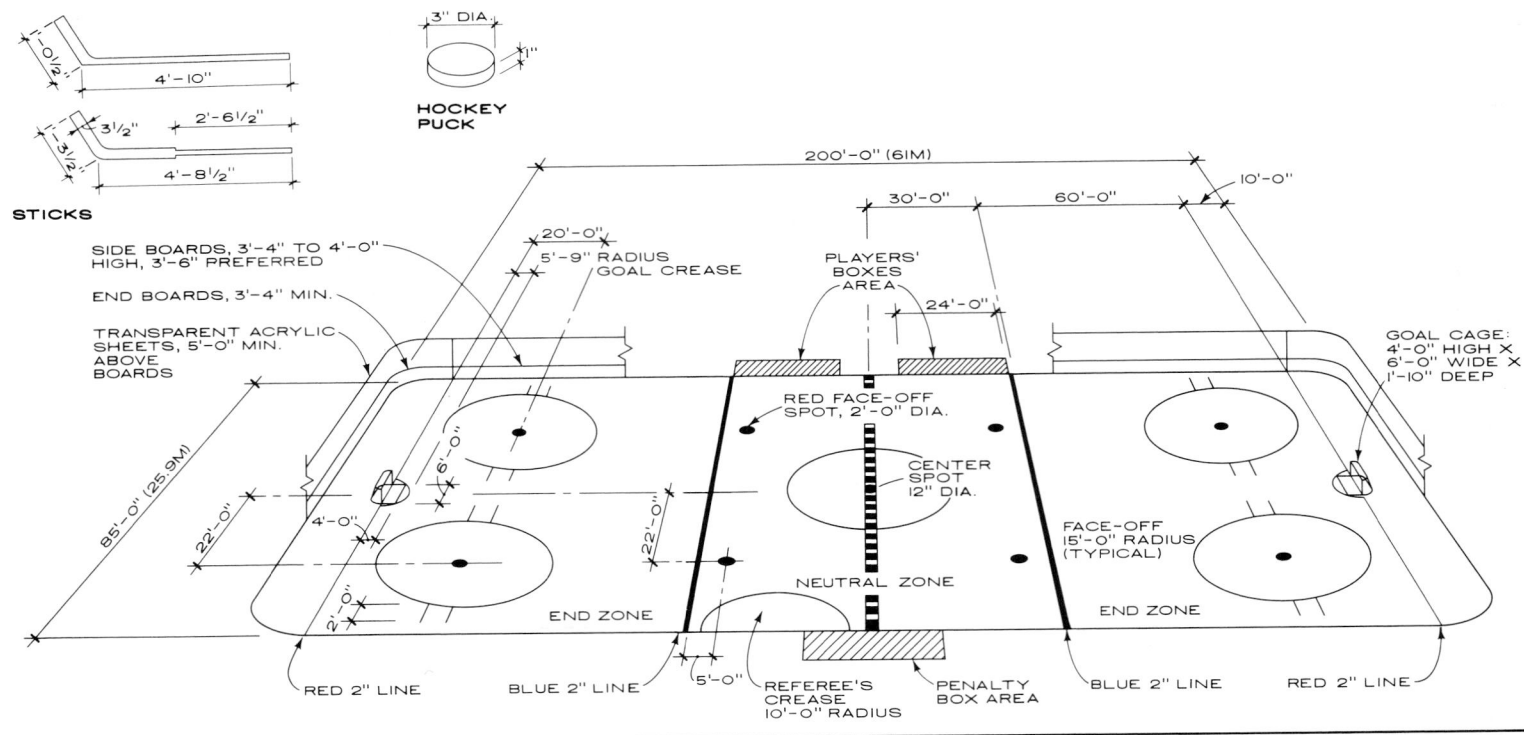

STICKS

HOCKEY PUCK

ICE HOCKEY

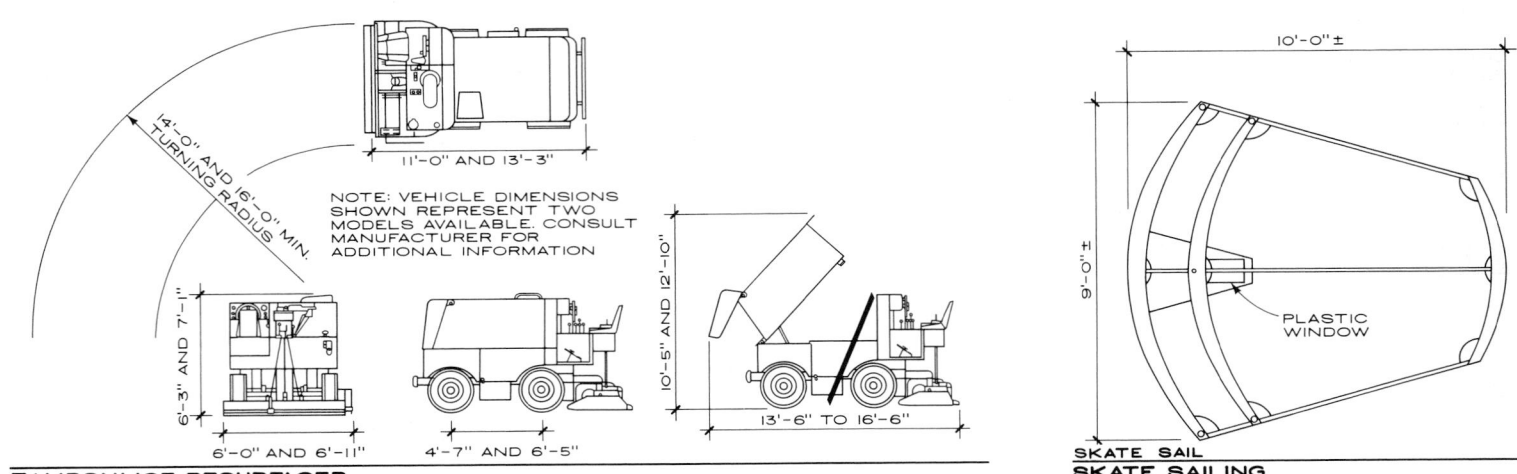

ZAMBONI ICE RESURFACER

NOTE: VEHICLE DIMENSIONS SHOWN REPRESENT TWO MODELS AVAILABLE. CONSULT MANUFACTURER FOR ADDITIONAL INFORMATION

SKATE SAIL
SKATE SAILING

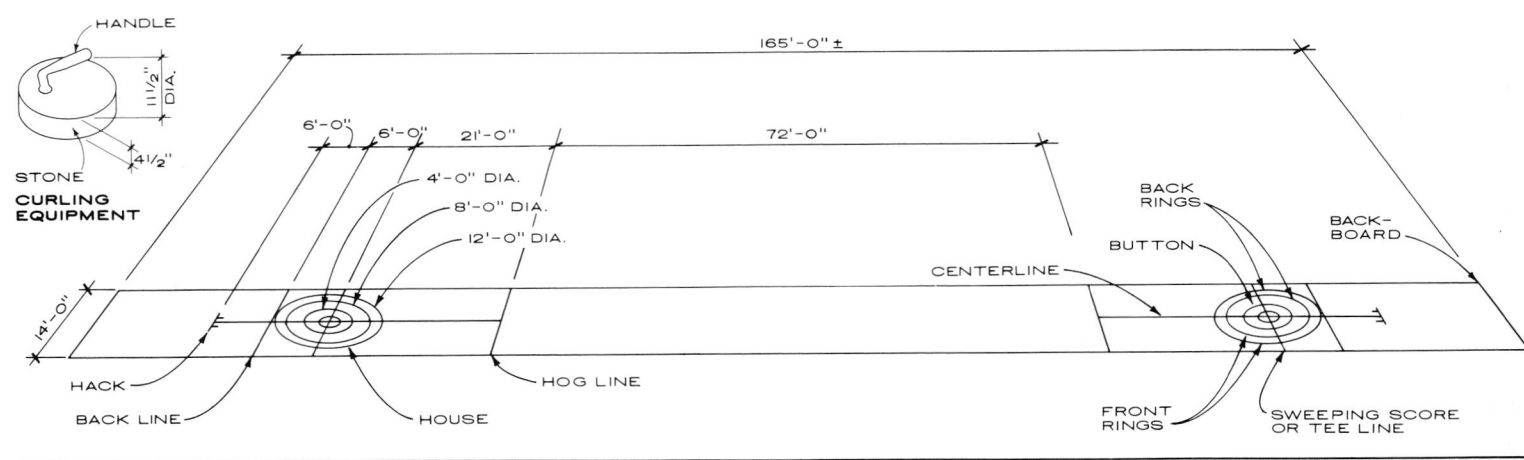

CURLING EQUIPMENT

CURLING

Richard J. Vitullo, AIA; Oak Leaf Studio; Crownsville, Maryland

17 ICE AND SNOW SPORTS

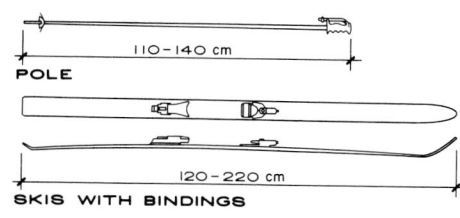

POLE   110-140 cm

120-220 cm

SKIS WITH BINDINGS

BOOT

BASIC EQUIPMENT

VERTICAL DROP AND GATE SPECIFICATIONS FOR FIS AND USSA COURSES

EVENT	FIS DROP (M) MIN.	FIS DROP (M) MAX.	NO. OF GATES MIN.	NO. OF GATES MAX.	USSA DROP (M) MIN.	NO. OF GATES MIN.
DOWNHILL						
One-run:						
men	500	1000			400	
women	500	700			400	
Two-run:						
(each)	450					
SLALOM						
Men	140	220	52	78	120	42
Women	120	180	42	63	120	42
GIANT SLALOM						
Men	250	400	30	60	250	33
Women	250	350	30	53	250	33
SUPER GIANT SLALOM						
Men	500	650	35	65	350	30
Women	350	500	30	50	350	30

FIS = Federation Internationale de Ski

USSA = United States Ski Association

ACCEPTABLE TERRAIN GRADIENTS FOR SLOPES AND TRAILS

SKILL LEVEL	TERRAIN GRADIENTS LOW	HIGH
Beginner/novice	8%	25%
Intermediate	15%	40%
Advanced intermediate/expert	25%	70%
Average Olympic downhill	23%	30%

BASE LODGE

Base lodge size in sq ft = (mountain capacity/seat turnover rate x sq ft/person.

Seat turnover rate—number of persons served per seat per day depends upon weather and temperature.

Typically: 3 (cold/overcast)
5 (warm/clear)

Typical sq ft/person at ski lodge:
30 (local ski area)
35 (destination ski area)

Edge of lodge to be: minimum 100 ft
optimal 150 ft
suitable 100-300 ft
from lift terminals.

Stairs with long treads (14-16 in.) and low risers (6 in.) to accommodate ski boots.

Protect entry/doorways from snowfall/dripping.

Locate windows above snow level.

Ski rental space = 3 sq ft per rental setup (skis, boots, poles).

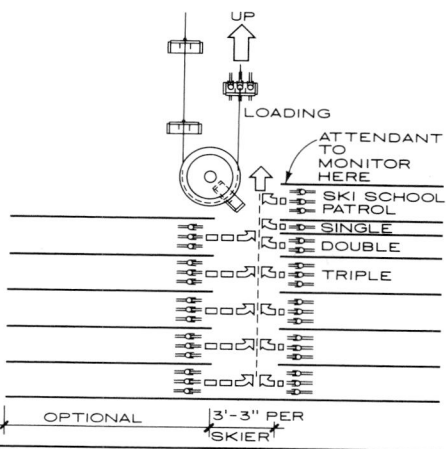

LIFT MAZE

LIFT MAZE AREA REQUIRED FOR 10-MINUTE LIFT LINE

LIFT TYPE	WIDTH (EACH ROW)	AREA (SQ FT)
Double	5 ft 0 in.	2500
Triple	7 ft 6 in.	3750
Quad	10 ft 0 in.	5000

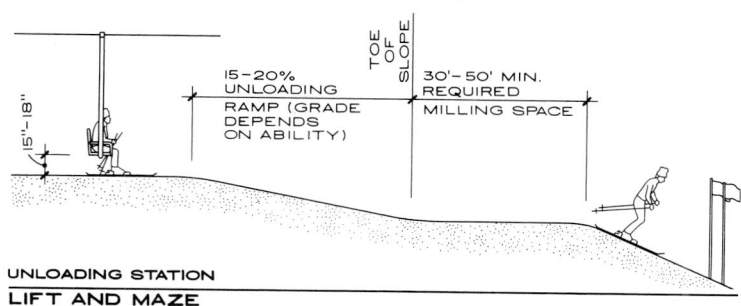

UNLOADING STATION

LIFT AND MAZE

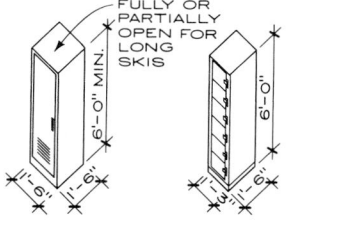

SEASON LOCKER   **COIN-OPERATED LOCKER**   **REGULAR TYPE**   **COIN-OPERATED TYPE**

LOCKERS   **SKI RACKS**

LOCKERS AND SKI RACKS

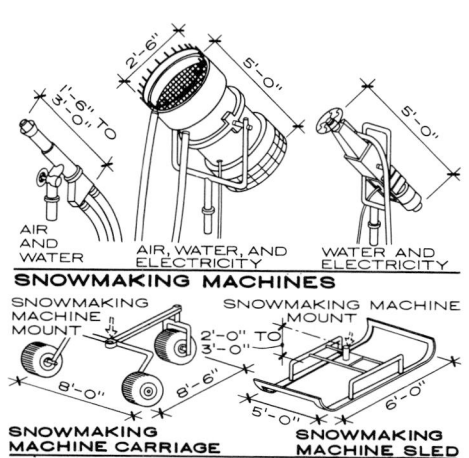

AIR AND WATER   AIR, WATER, AND ELECTRICITY   WATER AND ELECTRICITY

SNOWMAKING MACHINES

SNOWMAKING MACHINE MOUNT   SNOWMAKING MACHINE MOUNT

SNOWMAKING MACHINE CARRIAGE   **SNOWMAKING MACHINE SLED**

MAINTENANCE AND SNOWMAKING EQUIPMENT

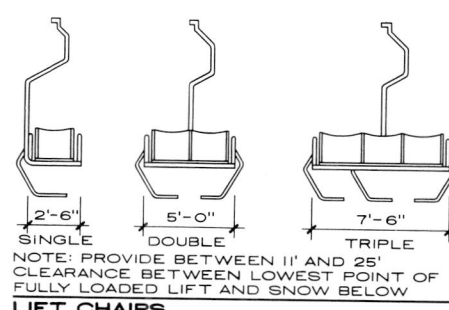

SINGLE   **DOUBLE**   **TRIPLE**

NOTE: PROVIDE BETWEEN 11' AND 25' CLEARANCE BETWEEN LOWEST POINT OF FULLY LOADED LIFT AND SNOW BELOW

LIFT CHAIRS

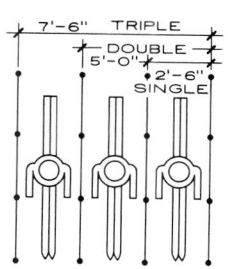

MAZE ROW

NOTE

Lift mazes to be located downhill of or to the side of loading point.

Mazes to be graded as flat as possible.

Approach to loading point to be graded at 3% downhill for distance of 50 ft minimum.

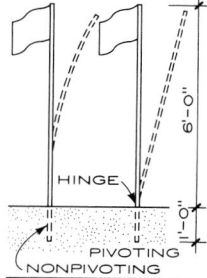

SLALOM POLES

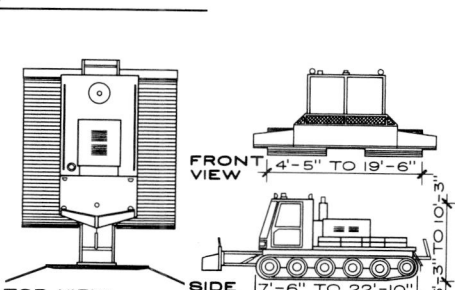

TOP VIEW   **FRONT VIEW**   **SIDE VIEW**

OVERSNOW VEHICLES

MAINTENANCE BUILDING

Area required: 100 sq ft per oversnow vehicle includes vehicle storage, parts and general storage, office, toilets. Does not include snowmaking system.

Doors: 16-20 ft wide, 14-16 ft high for main vehicle entry doors.

Eliot W. Goldstein, AIA, and Chan Li Lin; James Goldstein & Partners; Millburn, New Jersey

ICE AND SNOW SPORTS   17

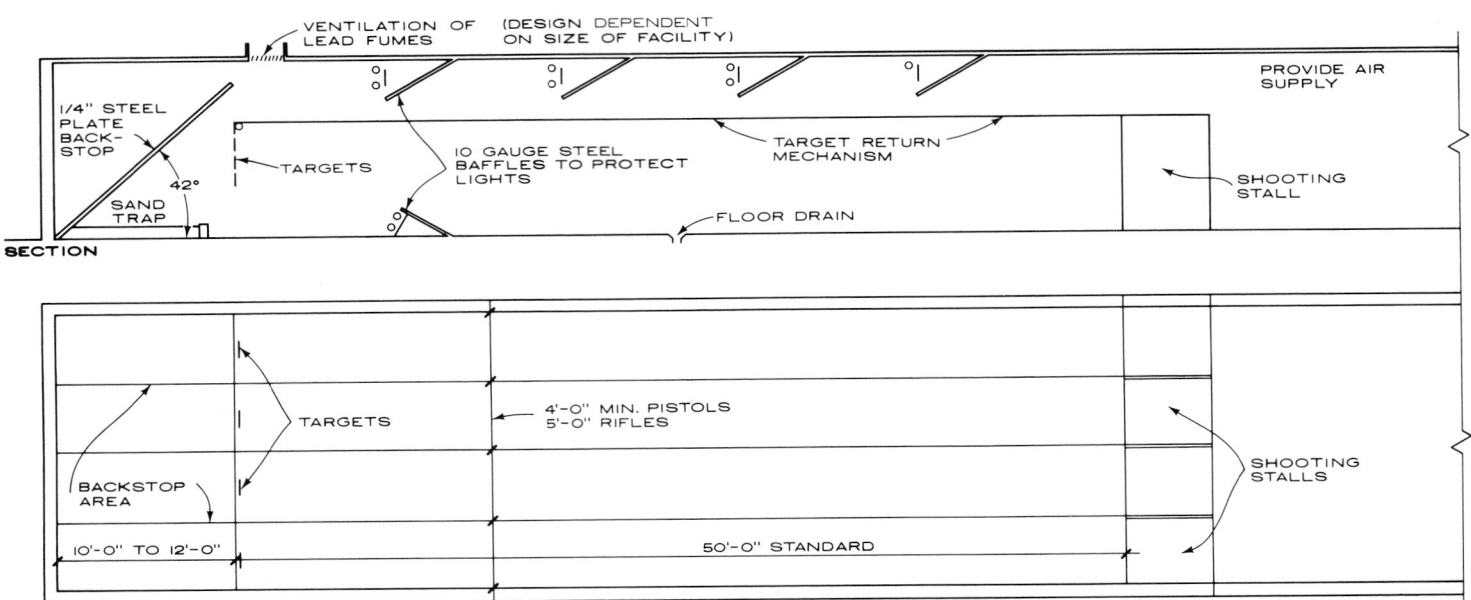

VENTILATION OF LEAD FUMES (DESIGN DEPENDENT ON SIZE OF FACILITY)

PROVIDE AIR SUPPLY

1/4" STEEL PLATE BACK-STOP

42°

SAND TRAP

TARGETS

10 GAUGE STEEL BAFFLES TO PROTECT LIGHTS

TARGET RETURN MECHANISM

FLOOR DRAIN

SHOOTING STALL

SECTION

TARGETS

4'-0" MIN. PISTOLS
5'-0" RIFLES

BACKSTOP AREA

SHOOTING STALLS

10'-0" TO 12'-0"

50'-0" STANDARD

PLAN

DESIGN PROBLEMS

When planning a firearms range, the following safety considerations must be made:

1. Placement of traps; use of stalls and placement of firing line; provision for space for spectators; protection from ricochet; prevention of spilled powder explosions.
2. Ventilation adequate to dissipate lead fumes.
3. Noise abatement.
4. Lighting.

The use of range design consultants is advisable. Contact the National Rifle Association for information.

TARGET SHOOTING

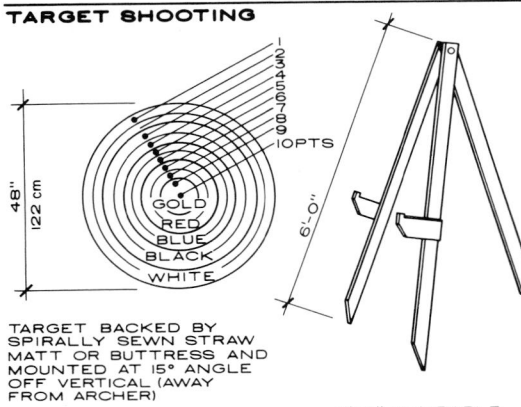

1-2-3-4-5-6-7-8-9
10 PTS

48" 122 cm

6'-0"

GOLD
RED
BLUE
BLACK
WHITE

TARGET BACKED BY SPIRALLY SEWN STRAW MATT OR BUTTRESS AND MOUNTED AT 15° ANGLE OFF VERTICAL (AWAY FROM ARCHER)

Archery ranges should be orientated, in the northern hemisphere, so the archer is facing north ±45°. The range surface is to be turf, and free from obstructions or hard objects; likewise, spaces behind and to either side should be clear.

Target backings are made of stitched compressed straw rope called mat or buttress. Targets are made of thick paper with five concentric color zones. Both the mat and target are slanted at a 15° angle off vertical away from the archer.

Modern bows often are wood composites, fiberglass, and graphite. Lengths vary from 72 in. (1.82 M) to 62 in. (1.57 M). Bows are categorized by their draw weight, the amount of energy needed to pull a 28 in. (71 cm) arrow to full draw. Male archers usually use a 50 lb. to 55 lb. bow; female archers usually use 35 lb. to 40 lb. bow.

Arrow shafts are made of wood, graphite, or aluminum tubing. The flecking is made of plastic or feathers.

LIMBS
SIGHT APPARATUS
HAND GRIP
STABILIZER
STABILIZER WEIGHT

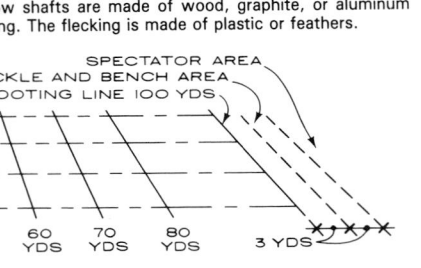

15'-0" DESIRABLE
10'-0" MIN.

SPECTATOR AREA
TACKLE AND BENCH AREA
SHOOTING LINE 100 YDS

90'-0" m

(45'-0" WITH BUNKER BEHIND TARGETS)

TARGETS

SAFETY AREA

30'-0" MIN.

20 YDS 30 YDS 40 YDS 50 YDS 60 YDS 70 YDS 80 YDS   3 YDS

RANGE LAYOUT

ARCHERY

Wooden nonskid flooring is ideal. A rubber piste is used on slippery floors. When a special metallic piste is used, a rubber mat must be placed beneath it to prevent hits on the floor being registered by the electronic scoring device. In competitive fencing, the score is kept by an electronic apparatus, which records each hit, and is linked to the fencers by wires. The wires are kept from trailing the ground by a spring-loaded spool. These spools often are recessed in a pit at each end of the piste.

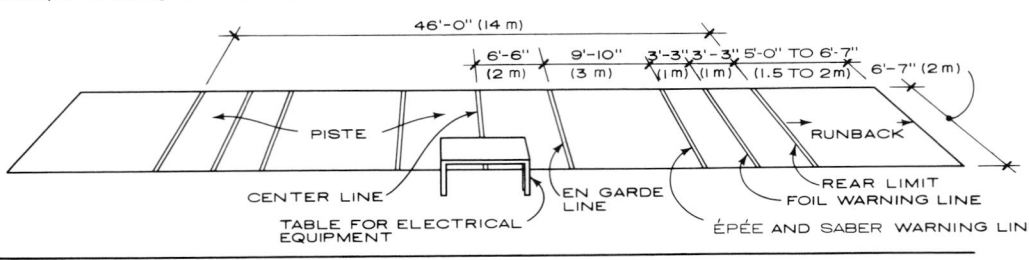

46'-0" (14 m)

6'-6" (2 m) 9'-10" (3 m) 3'-3" (1m) 3'-3" (1m) 5'-0" TO 6'-7" (1.5 TO 2m) 6'-7" (2 m)

PISTE
CENTER LINE
TABLE FOR ELECTRICAL EQUIPMENT
EN GARDE LINE
ÉPÉE AND SABER WARNING LINE
RUNBACK
REAR LIMIT
FOIL WARNING LINE

FENCING

3'-0" (90 cm) 17 5/8 OZ (500 G)
3'-0" (90 cm) 27 1/8 OZ (770 G)
2'-11 1/8" (88 cm) 17 5/8 OZ (500 G)

FOIL
FRENCH HANDLE
ÉPÉE
AMERICAN HANDLE
SABER

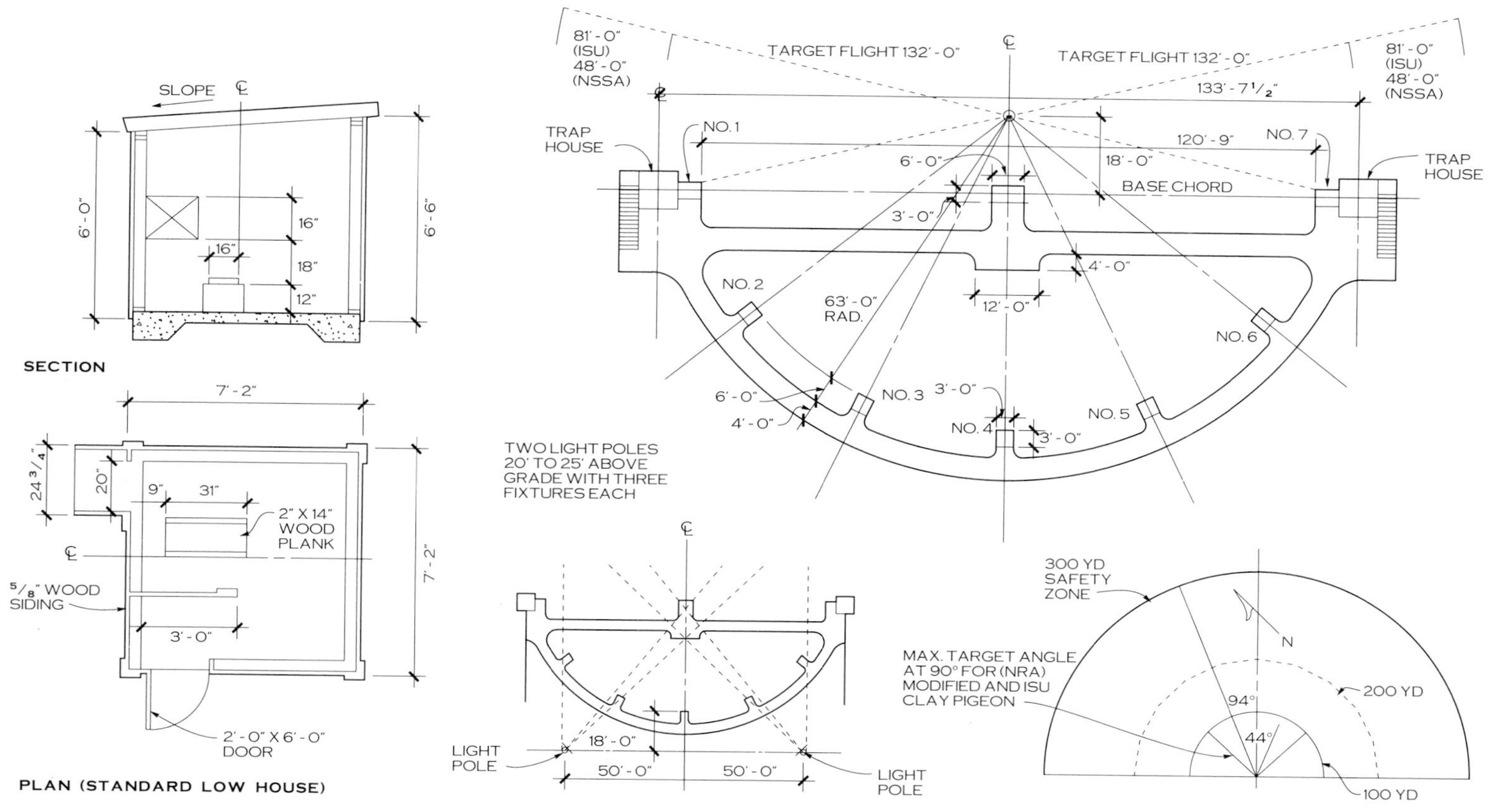

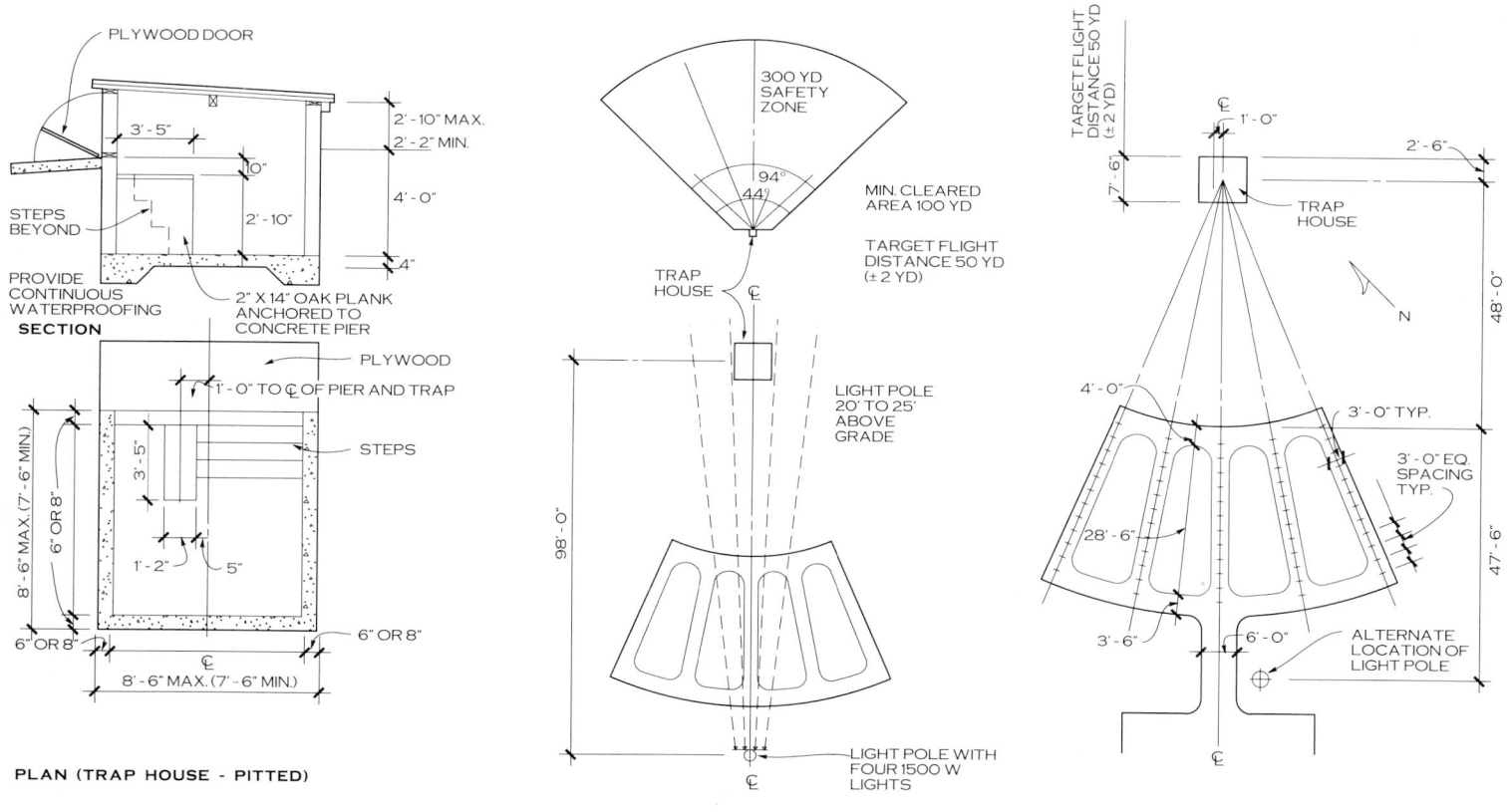

SLOPE ℄

SECTION

PLAN (STANDARD LOW HOUSE)

⅝" WOOD SIDING

2" X 14" WOOD PLANK

2'-0" X 6'-0" DOOR

SKEET SHOOTING

81'-0" (ISU)
48'-0" (NSSA)

TARGET FLIGHT 132'-0"

TARGET FLIGHT 132'-0"

81'-0" (ISU)
48'-0" (NSSA)

133'-7½"

TRAP HOUSE

NO. 1

6'-0"

120'-9"

NO. 7

18'-0"

TRAP HOUSE

BASE CHORD

3'-0"

12'-0"

4'-0"

NO. 2

NO. 6

63'-0" RAD.

NO. 3

3'-0"

6'-0"

4'-0"

NO. 4

3'-0"

NO. 5

TWO LIGHT POLES 20' TO 25' ABOVE GRADE WITH THREE FIXTURES EACH

LIGHT POLE

18'-0"

50'-0"

50'-0"

LIGHT POLE

300 YD SAFETY ZONE

N

MAX. TARGET ANGLE AT 90° FOR (NRA) MODIFIED AND ISU CLAY PIGEON

94°

44°

200 YD

100 YD

PLYWOOD DOOR

3'-5"

2'-10" MAX.
2'-2" MIN.

10"

2'-10"

4'-0"

STEPS BEYOND

4"

PROVIDE CONTINUOUS WATERPROOFING

2" X 14" OAK PLANK ANCHORED TO CONCRETE PIER

SECTION

PLYWOOD

1'-0" TO ℄ OF PIER AND TRAP

3'-5"

STEPS

8'-6" MAX. (7'-6" MIN.)

6" OR 8"

1'-2"

5"

6" OR 8"

℄

8'-6" MAX. (7'-6" MIN.)

6" OR 8"

PLAN (TRAP HOUSE - PITTED)

300 YD SAFETY ZONE

94°

44°

MIN. CLEARED AREA 100 YD

TARGET FLIGHT DISTANCE 50 YD (± 2 YD)

TRAP HOUSE

℄

LIGHT POLE 20' TO 25' ABOVE GRADE

98'-0"

LIGHT POLE WITH FOUR 1500 W LIGHTS

℄

TARGET FLIGHT DISTANCE 50 YD (± 2 YD)

7'-6"

1'-0"

2'-6"

℄

TRAP HOUSE

N

4'-0"

3'-0" TYP.

3'-0" EQ. SPACING TYP.

28'-6"

48'-0"

47'-6"

3'-6"

6'-0"

ALTERNATE LOCATION OF LIGHT POLE

℄

TRAP SHOOTING

GENERAL

Amateur Athletic Union of the United States (AAU)
3400 West 86th Street
P.O Box 68207
Indianapolis, IN 46268
Tel: (317) 872-2900
Fax:(317) 875-0548

National Collegiate Athletic Association
6201 College Blvd.
Overland Park, KS 66211
Tel: (913) 339-1906
Fax:(913) 339-1950

National Council of
Young Men's Christian Association (YMCA-USA)
101 N. Wacker Drive
Chicago, IL 60606
Tel: (312) 977-0031
Fax:(312) 977-9063

National Recreation and Park Association (NRPA)
2775 South Quincy Street
Suite 300
Arlington, VA 22206
Tel: (703) 820-4940
Fax:(703) 671-6772

UNIVERSAL ACCESSIBILITY

Americans with
Disabilities Act Information Office
U.S. Department of Justice
Civil Rights Division
P.O. Box 66738
Washington, DC 20035-6738
Tel: (202) 514-0301

FIELD SPORTS

American Society of Golf Course Architects
221 N. LaSalle Street
35th Floor
Chicago, IL 60601
Tel: (312) 372-7090
Fax:(312) 372-6160

American Professional Soccer League
122 C Street, N.W.
Washington, DC 20001
Tel: (202) 638-0022
Fax:(202) 638-4185

College Football Association
6688 Gunpark Drive
Suite 201
Boulder, CO 80301-3339
Tel: (303) 530-5566
Fax:(303) 530-5371

National Association of Professional Baseball Leagues
P.O. Box A
St. Petersburg, FL 33731
Tel: (813) 822-6937
Fax:(813) 821-5819

National Football League (NFL)
410 Park Avenue
New York, NY 10022
Tel: (212) 758-1500
Fax:(212) 758-1742

National Golf Foundation
1150 South U.S. Highway 1
Jupiter, FL 33477
Tel: (407) 744-6006
Fax:(407) 744-6107

Sports Turf Managers Association
401 N. Michigan Ave.
Chicago, IL 60611-4267
Tel: (312) 644-6610
Fax:(312) 321-6869

United States Soccer Federation
National Headquarters
1801-1811 South Prairie Avenue
Chicago, IL 60616
Tel: (312) 808-1300
Fax:(312) 808-1301

TRACK AND FIELD

U.S. Tennis Court and Track Builders Association
720 Light Street
Baltimore, MD 21230
Tel: (410) 752-3500
Fax:(410) 752-8295

COURT SPORTS

International Racquet Sports Association
253 Summer Street
Boston, MA 02110
Tel: (617) 951-0055
Fax:(617) 951-0056

National Basketball Association (NBA)
645 Fifth Avenue
15th Floor
New York, NY 10022
Tel: (212) 826-7000
Fax:(212) 826-0579

Professional Squash Association
12 Sheppard Street
Suite 419
Toronto, Ontario M5H 3A1
Tel: (416) 777-2542
Fax:(416) 869-3902

Tennis Industry Association
200 Castlewood Drive
North Palm Beach, FL 33408
Tel: (407) 848-1026

U.S. Professional Tennis Association
One USPTA Center
3535 Briarpark Drive
Houston, TX 77042
Tel: (713) 978-7782
Fax:(713) 978-7780

U.S. Tennis Association
70 West Red Oak Lane
White Plains, NY 10604
Tel: (914) 696-7000
Fax:(914) 696-7167

U.S. Tennis Court and Track Builders Association
720 Light Street
Baltimore, MD 21230-3816
Tel: (410) 752-3500
Fax:(410) 752-8295

TABLE AND BAR SPORTS

Billiard and Bowling Institute of America
200 Castlewood Drive
North Palm Beach, FL 33408
Tel: (407) 840-1120

AQUATICS

American Water Ski Association
799 Overlook Drive
Winterhaven, FL 33884
Tel: (813) 324-4341

National Swimming Pool Foundation
10803 Gulfdale
Suite 300
San Antonio, TX 78216
Tel: (210) 525-1227

National Spa and Pool Institute (NSPI)
2111 Eisenhower Avenue
Alexandria, VA 22314
Tel: (703) 838-0083
Fax:(703) 549-0493

Ski Industries America (SIA)
8377-B Greensboro Drive
McLean, VA 22102
Tel: (703) 556-9020
Fax:(703) 821-8276

Water Sports Industry Association
200 Castlewood Drive
North Palm Beach, FL 33408
Tel: (407) 840-1185
Fax:(407) 863-8984

EQUESTRIAN

American Horse Shows Association
220 East 42nd Street, Suite 409
New York, NY 10017-5876
Tel: (212) 972-2472
Fax:(212) 983-7286

Professional Rodeo Cowboys Association
101 Prorodeo Drive
Colorado Springs, CO 80919-9989
Tel: (719) 593-8840
Fax:(719) 593-9315

United States Polo Association
Kentucky Horse Park
4059 Iron Works Pike
Lexington, KY 40511
Tel: (606) 255-0593
Fax:(606) 231-9738

ICE AND SNOW SPORTS

American Hockey League
425 Union Street, #D3
West Springfield, MA 01089-4108
Tel: (413) 781-2030
Fax:(413) 733-4767

American Ski Federation
207 Constitution Ave., N.E.
Washington, DC 20002
Tel: (202) 543-1595

National Hockey League (NHL)
1800 McGill College Avenue
26th Floor
Montreal, Quebec H3A 3J6
Tel: (514) 288-9220
Fax:(514) 284-1663

United States Skiing Association
1500 Kearns Blvd.
Park City, UT 84060
Tel: (801) 649-9090
Fax:(801) 649-3613

TARGET SHOOTING AND FENCING

Archery Manufacturers Association
2622 N.W. 43rd Street, Unit C-4
Gainesville, FL 32606
Tel: (904) 377-8262
Fax:(904) 375-3961

National Rifle Association of America
1600 Rhode Island Ave., N.W.
Washington, DC 20036
Tel: (202) 828-6000
Fax:(202) 861-0306

National Shooting Sports Foundation (NSSF)
11 Mile Hill Road
Newtown, CT 06470
Tel: (203) 426-1320
Fax:(203) 426-1087

Professional Archers Association
26 Lakeview Drive
Stansbury Park, UT 84074
Tel: (801) 882-3817

STRATEGIES OF CLIMATE CONTROL

The bioclimatic chart (Olgyay, *Design with Climate*, updated by Givoni and Arens) is presented here in standard psychrometric format. Plotting temperature and humidity data on the chart identifies cooling strategies for buildings dominated by envelope loads. The heavy lines in Figure 1 delineate limits within which ventilation, massive construction, evaporative space cooling, and clothing can maintain thermal comfort indoors.

VENTILATION

Whole-house (exhaust) fans provide up to 20 air changes per hour and, like continuous cross ventilation, maintain indoor temperatures close to the outdoors. As long as outdoor conditions are within the comfort zone, "air-exchange ventilation" maintains indoor comfort. "Body ventilation" is best provided by ceiling (paddle) fans. They are effective up to 70% relative humidity and 85°F ET° (effective temperature), with a maximum air speed of 3 fps and light clothing (0.4–0.6 clo).

THERMAL MASS

A very massive building envelope can maintain indoor comfort if outdoor air temperature does not exceed the thermal mass limit on the chart (roughly equal to 89°F ET*). This requires that (1) the envelope is shaded or reflective enough that its average daily outside surface temperature is no higher than the daily mean air temperature; (2) the envelope is massive enough to average daily temperature fluctuations; and (3) there is no daytime ventilation of the indoors. Nighttime ventilation extends the upper limit by cooling the envelope from both sides.

EVAPORATIVE SPACE COOLING

Intake ventilation air is evaporatively cooled by drawing it through wetted mats or filters. The technique is suited to arid and semiarid regions and requires a fan-powered ventilation system. The limits are 71.5°F wet-bulb temperature and in excess of 105°F dry bulb, which is a conservative upper bound.

OTHER CLIMATIC ELEMENTS

Wind speeds and direction are important for site analysis and for orienting the building for shelter from winter winds and to capture cooling breezes. Solar radiation data ("irradiation" or "insolation") is necessary for solar heating and daylighting design. Insolation, measured in BTU/sq ft/day or per hour, is a function of latitude, sky conditions, and angle of incidence to the receiving surface (see Kusuda and Ishii, 1977). Ground temperatures at various depths can be estimated from well-water temperatures (see Labs, 1981).

REFERENCES

1. *Local Climatic Summaries*, National Climatic Center, Environmental Data Service, Asheville, NC 28801.
2. T. Kusuda and K. Ishii, *Hourly Solar Radiation Data for Vertical and Horizontal Surfaces on Average Days in the U.S. and Canada*, NBS BSS 96, National Technical Information Service, #PB 265-551, 1977.
3. *Engineering Weather Data*, Air Force Design Manual 88-29 (Army TM 5-785, Navy NAVFAC P-89), 1978.
4. K. Labs, *Regional Analysis of Ground and Above-Ground Climate*, Oak Ridge National Laboratory (NTIS No. ORNL/Sub-81/40451/1), 1981.
5. D. Watson and K. Labs, *Climatic Design*, McGraw-Hill, New York, 1983.
6. E. Arens et al., "Thermal Comfort under an Extended Range of Environmental Conditions," ASHRAE *Transactions*, vol. 92, part 1B, 1986, pp. 18–26.
7. J. Cook, ed., *Passive Cooling*, vol. 8 of Solar Heat Technologies series, MIT Press (Cambridge, Mass.), 1989.

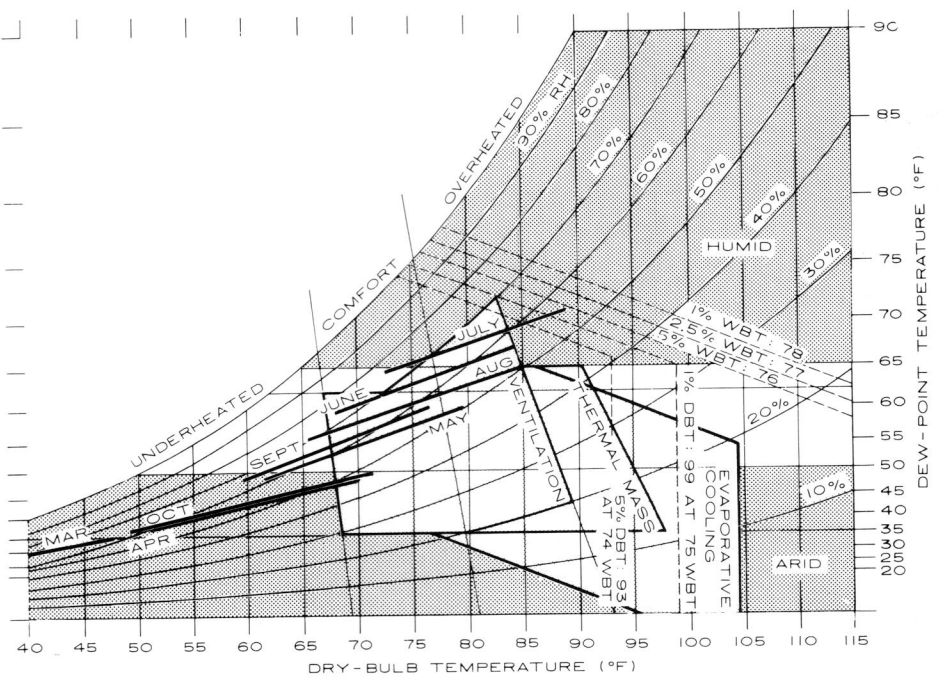

FIGURE 1
BUILDING BIOCLIMATIC CHART (AFTER GIVONI)

FIGURE 2
EXAMPLE ANALYSIS: KANSAS CITY (WATSON AND LABS)

TERMINOLOGY

The effective temperature, ET*, refers to any set of temperature and humidity conditions that gives the same sensation of comfort as the stated temperature at 50% relative humidity (RH). ET* plotted here assumes light office clothing (0.6 clo) and very little air movement. One can feel as comfortable at 80°F with 20% RH as at 76°F at 80% RH; both are 78°F ET*. The ASHRAE comfort zone is bounded by an upper humidity limit of about 62°F dew point; 65°F is a conservative limit. A mean daily dew-point temperature of 50°F produces diurnal air temperature swings in excess of 30°F.

Donald Watson, FAIA; Rensselaer Polytechnic Institute; Troy, New York

PLOTTING DATA ON THE CHART

Combined temperature and humidity conditions at any moment can be plotted as a point on the chart. Graphing hourly data tracks the daily pattern, but daily maximum and minimum temperatures with their coincident humidities are usually adequate. Plotting a single day for each month summarizes the year at a glance (see Watson and Labs, 1983).

Example: Figure 2 plots 7 months of the year in Kansas City and shows ASHRAE summer air-conditioning design temperatures. The daily minimum dry-bulb temperature is coupled with the daily minimum dew point, while the daily maximum dry bulb is coupled with the daily maximum wet bulb. Much of the year falls below the lower comfort limit of 68°F ET* and is "underheated." Conditions exceeding 78°F ET* are "overheated." Ventilation satisfies most cooling needs, but the fact that design temperatures exceed the ventilation limit shows that some air conditioning is necessary.

DESIGN FOR ENERGY CONSERVATION

Regional design for energy conservation aims to minimize use of conventionally powered heating, cooling, and lighting by using natural energy available at the building site. Site planning and building orientation, massing, and envelope design are the principal means for managing climate-driven conduction, convection, radiation, and vapor transfer. Climatic design strategies are selected in response to outdoor microclimatic conditions, defined as "underheated" or "overheated" with respect to indoor human comfort parameters.

CLIMATIC REGIONS (MAP 1)

Map 1 delineates regions according to climatic control strategies. Regions exceeding 8000 annual heating degree days (HDD) are predominantly "underheated," in which cooling is subordinate to solar heating and heat conservation strategies. Regions with fewer than 2000 annual HDD require little heating in comparison to cooling and are predominantly "overheated" for design purposes. The large temperate region between 2000 and 8000 HDD has both heating and cooling requirements that must be balanced so that design features favoring heating do not add to the cooling load, and vice versa.

Suitability of ventilation and evaporative cooling are related to atmospheric humidity during summer months. Regions having a combined July and August average dew point temperature greater than 65°F may be considered "humid," and those averaging less than 50°F dew point may be considered "arid." The entire southeast quadrant of the U.S. has mean daily humidities exceeding comfort limits under still air conditions. The main control problem in this region is to balance ventilation with dehumidification and mechanical cooling.

The 50°F dew point temperature is an arbitrary way of defining atmospheric aridity, but it is convenient since it produces an outdoor daily temperature range of roughly 30°F dry-bulb. Arid and semiarid conditions favor evaporative and radiative cooling and generally disfavor summer daytime ventilation. While massive building envelopes can be advantageous in any region with a significant number of days having average daily temperatures in the upper 70s, mass is especially valuable in arid regions with extremely high daily maxima.

SOLAR HEATING POTENTIAL (MAP 2)

Map 2 depicts solar heating capability in relation to heating load for envelope-dominated buildings. The lines plot the average daily solar gain transmitted through vertical south-facing double glazing, coincident with the need for heat. It is calculated by the relation

$$\text{Average solar gain} = \frac{\text{sum(solar gain} \times \text{HDD)}}{\text{sum(HDD)}}$$

HDD is the base 65°F degree days. The units are Btu/sq ft of glazing. Values assume a ground reflection of 30%. The map indicates that, for instance, useful solar gains are the same in Philadelphia, PA; Huntsville, AL; Oshkosh, WI; and Eugene, OR.

UNDISTURBED GROUND TEMPERATURE (MAP 3)

At "steady state" depth (20–30 ft), ground temperature is the same as well water temperature, as plotted on Map 3. Ground temperatures vary considerably throughout the first 10 ft of earth and are elevated by heat losses from buildings. Heated buildings lose some heat to the deep ground throughout most of the U.S., but the earth is not an effective heat sink in the regions where cooling is most needed. Earth-tempered design requires special analysis of thermal soil–structure interaction.

Donald Watson, FAIA; Rensselaer Polytechnic Institute; Troy, New York
Kenneth Labs; New Haven, Connecticut

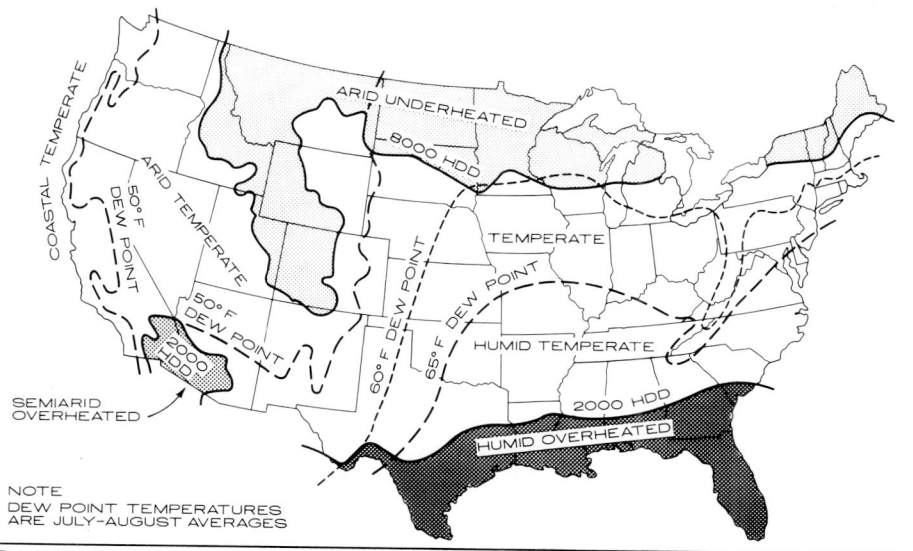

MAP I: U.S. REGIONS BASED UPON CLIMATIC DESIGN CONDITIONS

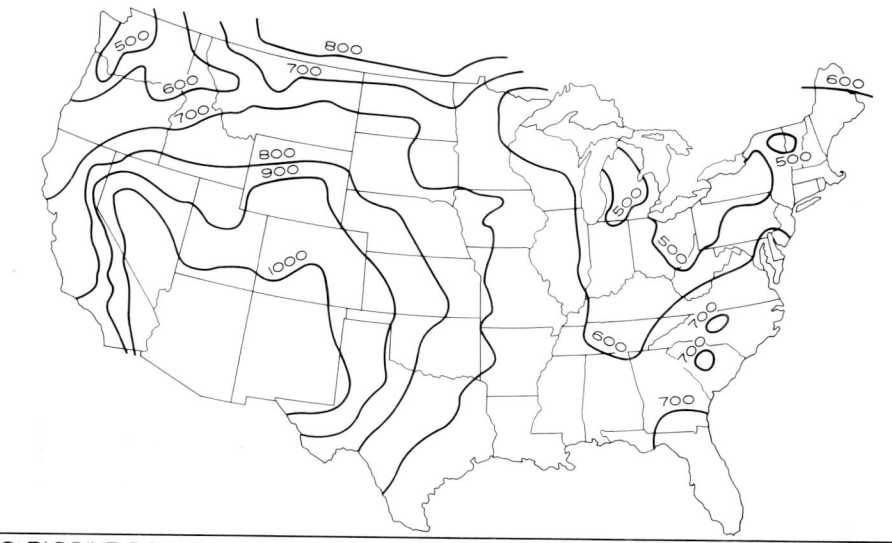

MAP 2: PASSIVE SOLAR HEATING POTENTIAL OF SOUTH WINDOWS (BTU/SQ FT/DAY)
DATA SOURCE: DR. DOUGLAS BALCOMB, SOLAR ENERGY RESEARCH INSTITUTE

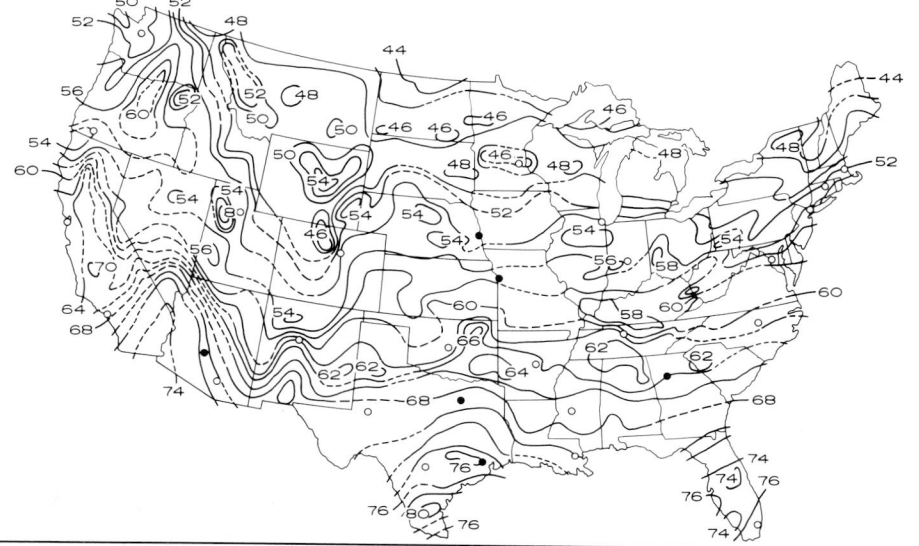

MAP 3: DEEP-GROUND TEMPERATURES (°F)
DATA SOURCE: NATIONAL WELL WATER ASSOCIATION

WINTER WEATHER DATA AND DESIGN CONDITIONS FOR THE UNITED STATES AND CANADA

STATE OR PROVINCE	CITY	LATITUDE (° ')	LONGITUDE (° ')	ELEVATION (FT)	WINTER DESIGN TEMP.*	AVE WINTER TEMP.†	AVERAGE MONTHLY HEATING DEGREE DAYS‡									TOTAL
							SEPT	OCT	NOV	DEC	JAN	FEB	MAR	APR	MAY	
Ala.	Birmingham	33 3	86 5	61	21	54.2	6	93	363	555	592	462	363	108	9	2551
	Mobile	30 4	88 1	119	29	59.9	0	22	213	357	415	300	211	42	0	1560
Alaska	Fairbanks	64 5	147 5	436	-47	6.7	642	1203	1833	2254	2359	1901	1739	1068	555	14,279
	Juneau	58 2	134 4	17	1	32.1	83	725	921	1135	1237	1070	1073	810	601	9075
Ariz.	Flagstaff	35 1	111 4	6973	4	35.6	201	558	867	1073	1169	991	911	651	437	7152
	Tucson	32 1	111 0	2584	32	58.1	0	25	231	406	471	344	242	75	6	1800
Ark.	Little Rock	34 4	92 1	257	20	50.5	9	127	465	716	756	577	434	126	9	3219
Calif.	Bakersfield	35 2	119 0	495	32	55.4	0	37	282	502	546	364	267	105	19	2122
	Sacramento	38 3	121 3	17	32	54.4	0	62	312	533	561	392	310	173	76	2419
	San Diego	32 4	117 1	19	44	59.5	21	43	135	236	298	253	214	135	90	1458
	San Francisco	37 5	122 3	52	40	55.1	102	118	231	388	443	336	319	279	239	3001
Colo.	Alamosa	37 3	105 5	7536	-6	29.7	279	639	1065	1420	1476	1162	1020	696	440	8529
	Denver	39 5	104 5	5283	1	37.6	117	428	819	1035	1132	938	887	558	288	6283
Conn.	Hartford	41 1	73 1	7	9	37.3	117	394	714	1101	1190	1042	908	519	205	6235
Del.	Wilmington	39 4	75 3	78	14	42.5	51	270	588	927	980	874	735	387	112	4930
D.C.	Washington	38 5	77 0	14	17	45.7	33	217	519	834	871	762	626	288	74	4224
Fla.	Miami	25 5	80 2	7	47	71.1	0	0	0	65	74	56	19	0	0	214
	Tallahassee	30 2	84 2	58	30	60.1	0	28	198	360	375	286	202	36	0	1485
Ga.	Atlanta	33 4	84 3	1005	22	51.7	18	124	417	648	636	518	428	147	25	2961
	Savannah	32 1	81 1	52	27	57.8	0	47	246	437	437	353	254	45	0	1819
Hawaii	Honolulu	21 2	158 0	7	63	74.2	0	0	0	0	0	0	0	0	0	0
Idaho	Boise	43 3	116 1	2842	10	39.7	132	415	792	1017	1113	854	722	438	245	5809
Ill.	Chicago	42 0	87 5	658	-4	35.8	117	381	807	1166	1265	1086	939	534	260	6639
	Springfield	39 5	89 4	587	2	40.6	72	291	696	1023	1135	935	769	354	136	5429
Ind.	Indianapolis	39 4	86 2	793	2	39.6	90	316	723	1051	1113	949	809	432	177	5699
Iowa	Des Moines	41 3	93 4	948	-5	35.5	96	363	828	1225	1370	1187	915	438	180	6588
Kan.	Goodland	39 2	101 4	3645	0	37.8	81	381	810	1073	1166	955	884	507	236	6141
	Topeka	39 0	95 4	877	4	41.7	57	270	672	980	1122	893	722	330	124	5182
Ky.	Lexington	38 0	84 4	979	8	43.8	54	239	609	902	946	818	685	326	105	4683
La.	New Orleans	30 0	90 2	3	33	61.8	0	12	165	291	344	241	177	24	0	1254
	Shreveport	32 3	93 5	252	25	56.2	0	47	297	477	552	426	304	81	0	2184
Me.	Portland	43 4	70 2	61	-1	33.0	195	508	807	1215	1339	1182	1042	675	372	7511
Md.	Baltimore	39 1	76 4	146	3	43.7	48	264	585	905	936	820	679	327	90	4654
Mass.	Boston	42 2	71 0	15	9	40.0	60	316	603	983	1088	972	846	513	208	5634
Mich.	Detroit	42 2	83 0	633	6	37.2	87	360	738	1088	1181	1058	936	522	220	6232
	Escanaba	45 4	87 0	594	-7	29.6	243	539	924	1293	1445	1296	1203	777	456	8481
Minn.	Duluth	46 5	92 1	1426	-16	23.4	330	632	1131	1581	1745	1518	1355	840	490	10,000
	Minneapolis	44 5	93 1	822	-12	28.3	189	505	1014	1454	1631	1380	1166	621	288	8322
Miss.	Jackson	32 2	90 1	330	25	55.7	0	65	315	502	546	414	310	87	0	2239
Mo.	Columbia	39 0	92 2	778	4	42.3	54	251	651	967	1076	875	716	324	121	5046
Mont.	Billings	45 5	108 3	3367	-10	34.5	186	487	897	1135	1296	1100	970	570	285	7049
	Missoula	46 5	114 1	3200	-6	31.5	303	651	1035	1287	1420	1120	970	621	391	8125
Neb.	North Platte	41 1	100 4	2779	-4	35.5	123	440	885	1166	1271	1039	930	519	248	6684
	Omaha	41 2	95 5	978	-3	35.6	105	357	828	1175	1355	1126	939	465	208	6612
Nev.	Las Vegas	36 1	115 1	2162	28	53.5	0	78	387	617	688	487	335	111	6	2709
	Reno	39 3	119 5	4404	10	39.3	204	490	801	1026	1073	823	729	510	357	6332
N. H.	Concord	43 1	71 3	339	-3	33.0	177	505	822	1240	1358	1184	1032	636	298	7383
N.J.	Trenton	40 1	74 5	144	14	42.4	57	264	576	924	989	885	753	399	121	4980
N.M.	Albuquerque	35 0	106 4	5310	16	12.0	12	229	642	868	930	703	595	288	81	4348
N.Y.	Buffalo	43 0	78 4	705	6	34.5	141	440	777	1156	1256	1145	1039	645	329	7062
	New York	40 5	74 0	132	15	42.8	30	233	540	902	986	885	760	408	118	4871
N.C.	Charlotte	35 0	81 0	735	22	50.4	6	124	438	691	691	582	481	156	22	3191
	Wilmington	34 2	78 0	30	26	54.6	0	74	291	521	546	462	357	96	0	2347
N.D.	Bismarck	46 5	100 5	1647	-19	26.6	222	577	1088	1463	1708	1442	1203	645	329	8851
Ohio	Cleveland	41 2	81 5	777	5	37.2	105	384	738	1088	1159	1047	918	552	260	6351
	Columbus	40 0	82 5	812	5	39.7	84	347	714	1039	1088	949	809	426	171	5660
Okla.	Oklahoma City	35 2	97 4	1280	13	48.3	15	164	498	766	868	664	527	189	34	3725
	Tulsa	36 1	95 5	650	13	47.7	18	158	522	787	893	683	539	213	47	3860
Ore.	Salem	45 0	123 0	195	23	45.4	111	338	594	729	822	647	611	417	273	4754
Pa.	Pittsburgh	40 3	80 1	1137	5	38.4	105	375	726	1063	1119	1002	874	480	195	5987
	Williamsport	41 1	77 0	527	7	38.5	111	375	717	1073	1122	1002	856	468	177	5934
R.I.	Providence	41 4	71 3	55	9	38.8	96	372	660	1023	1110	988	868	534	286	5954
S.C.	Columbia	34 0	81 1	217	24	54.0	0	84	345	577	570	470	357	81	0	2484
S.D.	Rapid City	44 0	103 0	3165	-7	33.4	165	481	897	1172	1333	1145	1051	615	326	7345
Tenn.	Nashville	36 1	86 4	577	14	48.9	30	158	495	732	778	644	512	189	40	3578
Texas	Brownsville	25 5	97 3	16	39	67.6	0	0	66	149	205	106	74	0	0	600
	Dallas	32 5	96 5	481	22	55.3	0	62	321	524	601	440	319	90	6	2363
	El Paso	31 5	106 2	3918	24	52.9	0	84	414	648	685	445	319	105	0	2700
	Houston	29 4	95 2	50	32	61.0	0	6	183	307	384	288	192	36	0	1396
Utah	Salt Lake City	40 5	112 0	4220	8	38.4	81	419	849	1082	1172	910	763	459	233	6052
Vt.	Burlington	44 3	73 1	331	7	29.4	207	539	891	1349	1513	1333	1187	714	353	8269
Va.	Lynchburg	37 2	79 1	947	16	46.0	51	223	540	822	849	731	605	267	78	4166
Wash.	Seattle	47 4	122 2	14	27	46.9	129	329	543	657	738	599	577	396	242	4424
W. Va.	Charleston	38 2	81 4	939	11	44.8	63	254	591	865	880	770	648	300	96	4476
Wisc.	Green Bay	44 3	88 1	683	-9	30.3	174	484	924	1333	1494	1313	1141	654	305	8029
Wyo.	Casper	42 5	106 3	5319	-5	33.4	192	524	942	1169	1290	1084	1020	651	381	7410
CANADA																
Alta.	Edmonton	53 34	113 31	2219	-25	-	411	738	1215	1603	1810	1520	1330	765	400	10,268
B.C.	Vancouver	49 11	123 10	16	19	-	219	456	657	787	862	723	676	501	310	5515
Man.	Winnipeg	49 54	97 14	786	-27	-	322	683	1251	1757	2008	1719	1465	813	405	10,679
N.S.	Halifax	44 39	63 34	83	5	-	180	457	710	1074	1213	1122	1030	742	487	7361
Ont.	Toronto	43 41	79 38	578	-1	-	151	439	760	1111	1233	1119	1013	616	298	6827
Que.	Montreal	45 28	73 45	98	-10	-	165	521	882	1392	1566	1381	1175	684	316	8203

*Based on 97.5% Design Dry-Bulb values found in ASHRAE Handbook of Fundamentals, 1977.
†October-April, inclusive. ASHRAE Systems Handbook, 1976.
‡Based on the period 1931-1960, inclusive. ASHRAE Systems Handbook, 1976.

NOTES

To visualize the thermal impacts on differently exposed surfaces four locations are shown approximately at the 24°, 32°, 40° and 44° latitudes. The forces are indicated on average clear winter and summer days. The air temperature variation is indicated by the outside concentric circles. Each additional line represents a 2°F difference from the lowest daily temperature. The direction of the impact is indicated according to the sun's direction as temperatures occur. (Note the low temperatures at the east side, and the high ones in westerly directions.)

The total (direct and diffuse) radiation impact on the various sides of the building is indicated with arrows. Each arrow represents 250 Btu/sq ft · day radiation. At the bottom of the page the radiations are expressed in numerical values.

The values show that in the upper latitudes the south side of a building receives nearly twice as much radiation in winter as in summer. This effect is even more pronounced at the lower latitudes, where the ratio is about one to four. Also, in the upper latitudes, the east and west sides receive about 2½ times more radiation in summer than in winter. This ratio is not as large in the lower latitudes; but it is noteworthy that in summer these sides receive two to three times as much radiation as the south elevation. In the summer the west exposure is more disadvantageous than the east exposure, as the afternoon high temperatures combine with the radiation effects. In all latitudes the north side receives only a small amount of radiation, and this comes mainly in the summer. In the low latitudes, in the summer, the north side receives nearly twice the impact of the south side. The amount of radiation received on a horizontal roof surface exceeds all other sides.

Experimental observations were conducted on the thermal behavior of building orientation at Princeton University's Architectural Laboratory. Below are shown the summer results of structures exposed to the cardinal directions. Note the unequal heat distribution and high heat impact of the west exposure compared to the east orientation. The southern direction gives a pleasantly low heat volume, slightly higher, however, than the north exposure.

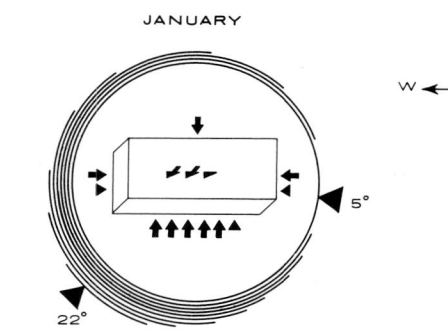

JANUARY

N

W ← → E

MINNEAPOLIS, MINN.

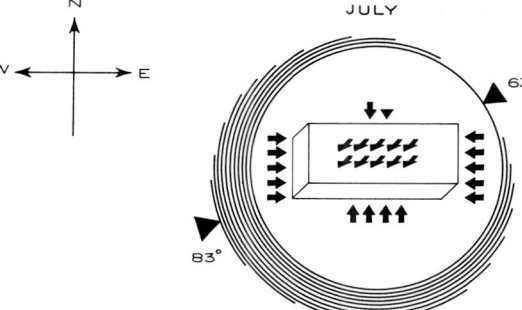

JULY

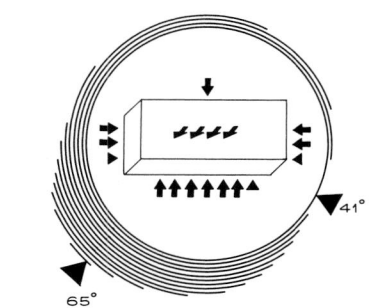

NEW YORK AREA

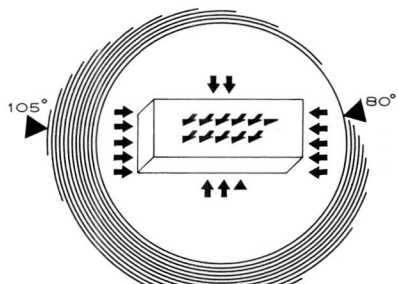

PHOENIX, ARIZ.

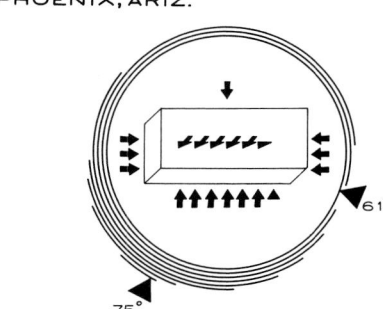

MIAMI, FLA.

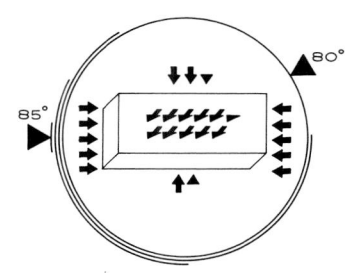

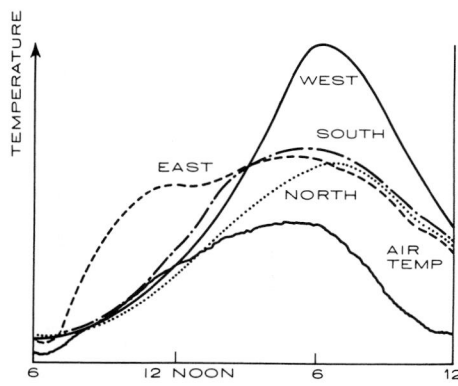

ROOM TEMPERATURE IN
DIFFERENTLY ORIENTED HOUSES

ORIENTATION: CONCLUSIONS

1. The optimum orientation will lie near the south; however, will differ in the various regions, and will depend on the daily temperature distribution.
2. In all regions an orientation eastward from south gives a better yearly performance and a more equal daily heat distribution. Westerly directions perform more poorly with unbalanced heat impacts.
3. The thermal orientation exposure has to be correlated with the local wind directions.

Victor Olgyay, AIA; Princeton University; Princeton, New Jersey

TOTAL DIRECT AND DIFFUSED RADIATION (BTU/SQ FT · DAY)

LATITUDE	SEASON	EAST	SOUTH	WEST	NORTH	HORIZONTAL
44° LATITUDE	WINTER	416	1374	416	83	654
	SUMMER	1314	979	1314	432	2536
40° LATITUDE	WINTER	517	1489	517	119	787
	SUMMER	1277	839	1277	430	2619
32° LATITUDE	WINTER	620	1606	620	140	954
	SUMMER	1207	563	1207	452	2596
24° LATITUDE	WINTER	734	1620	734	152	1414
	SUMMER	1193	344	1193	616	2568

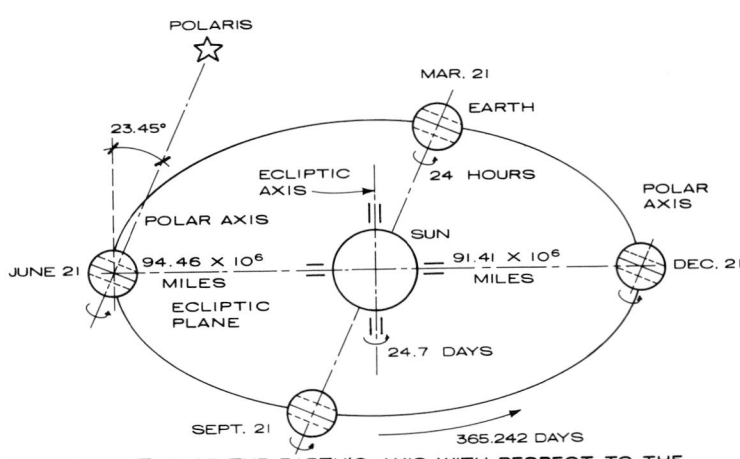

NOTE: THE TILT OF THE EARTH'S AXIS WITH RESPECT TO THE ECLIPTIC AXIS CAUSES THE CHANGING SEASONS AND THE ANNUAL VARIATIONS IN NUMBER OF HOURS OF DAYLIGHT AND DARKNESS

ANNUAL MOTION OF THE EARTH ABOUT THE SUN

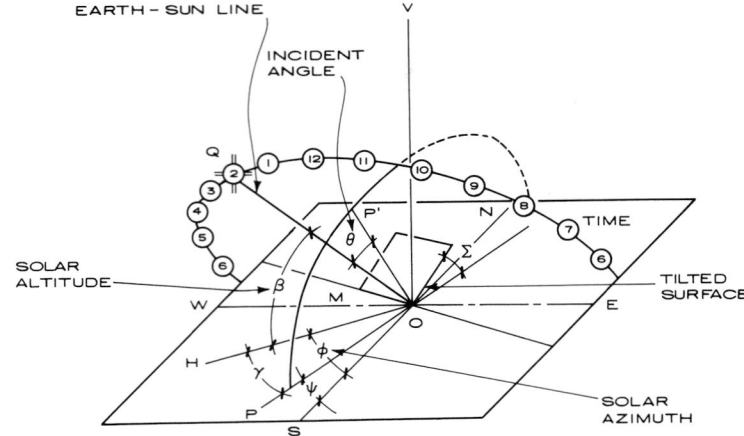

NOTE: Q DESIGNATES THE SUN'S POSITION SO OQ IS THE EARTH – SUN LINE WHILE OP' IS THE NORMAL TO THE TILTED SURFACE AND OP IS PERPENDICULAR TO THE INTERSECTION, OM, BETWEEN THE TILTED SURFACE AND THE HORIZONTAL PLANE

SOLAR ANGLES WITH RESPECT TO A TILTED SURFACE

SOLAR CONSTANT

The sun is located at one focus of the earth's orbit, and we are only 147.2 million km (91.4 million miles) away from the sun in late December and early January, while the earth-sun distance on July 1 is about 152.0 million km (94.4 million miles).

Solar energy approaches the earth as electromagnetic radiation at wavelengths between 0.25 and 5.0 μm. The intensity of the incoming solar irradiance on a surface normal to the sun's rays beyond the earth's atmosphere, at the average earth-sun distance, is designated as the solar constant, I_{sc}. Although the value of I_{sc} has not yet been precisely determined by verified measurements made in outer space, the most widely used value is 429.2 Btu/sq ft · hr (1353 W/sq m) and the current ASHRAE values are based on this estimate. More recent measurements made at extremely high altitudes indicate that I_{sc} is probably close to 433.6 Btu/sq ft · hr (1367 W/sq m). The unit of radiation that is widely used by meteorologists is the langley, equivalent to one kilogram calorie/square centimeter. To convert from langleys/day to Btu/sq ft · day, multiply Ly/day by 3.67. To convert from W/sq m to Btu/sq ft · hr, multiply the electrical unit by 0.3172.

SOLAR ANGLES

At the earth's surface the amount of solar radiation received and the resulting atmospheric temperature vary widely, primarily because of the daily rotation of the earth and the fact that the rotational axis is tilted at an angle of 23.45° with respect to the orbital plane. This tilt causes the changing seasons with their varying lengths of daylight and darkness. The angle between the earth-sun line and the orbital plane, called the solar declination, d, varies throughout the year, as shown in the following table for the 21st day of each month.

JAN -19.9° APR +11.9° JUL +20.5° OCT -10.7°
FEB -10.6° MAY +20.3° AUG +12.1° NOV -19.9°
MAR   0.0°   JUN +23.5° SEP 0.0°   DEC -23.5°

Very minor changes in the declination occur from year to year, and when more precise values are needed the almanac for the year in question should be consulted.

The earth's annual orbit about the sun is slightly elliptical, and so the earth-sun distance is slightly greater in summer than in winter. The time required for each annual orbit is actually 365.242 days rather than the 365 days shown by the calendar, and this is corrected by adding a 29th day to February for each year (except century years) that is evenly divisible by 4.

To an observer standing on a particular spot on the earth's surface, with a specified longitude, LON, and latitude, L, it is the sun that appears to move around the earth in a regular daily pattern. Actually it is the earth's rotation that causes the sun's apparent motion. The position of the sun can be defined in terms of its altitude β above the horizon (angle HOQ) and its azimuth φ, measured as angle HOS in the horizontal plane.

At solar noon, the sun is, by definition, exactly on the meridian that contains the south-north line, and consequently the solar azimuth φ is 0.0°. The noon altitude β is:

$$= 90° - L + \delta$$

Because the earth's daily rotation and its annual orbit around the sun are regular and predictable, the solar altitude and azimuth may be readily calculated for any desired time of day as soon as the latitude, longitude, and date (declination) are specified.

SHADOW CONSTRUCTION WITH TRUE SUN ANGLES

Required information: angle of orientation in relation

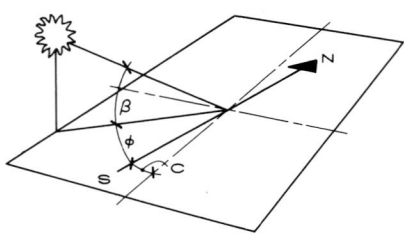

FIGURE 1

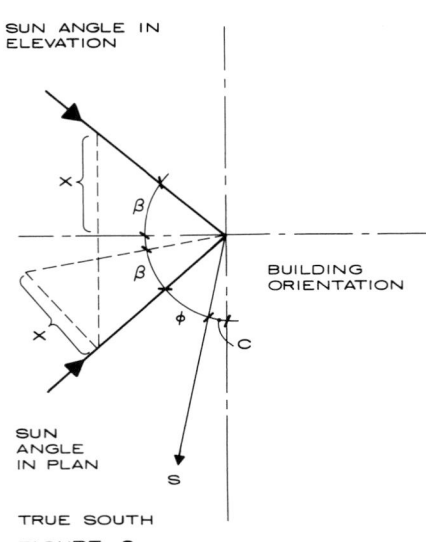

SUN ANGLE IN ELEVATION

SUN ANGLE IN PLAN

TRUE SOUTH

FIGURE 2

to north-south axis (C), azimuth φ, and altitude angle β of the sun at the desired time (Figure 1).

STEP 1. Lay out building axis, true south and azimuth φ of sun in plan (Figure 2).

STEP 2. Lay out altitude β upon azimuth φ. Construct any perpendicular to φ. From the intersection of this perpendicular and φ project a line perpendicular to elevation plane (building orientation). Measure distance x along this line from elevation plane. Connect the point at distance x from elevation plane to center to construct sun elevation β (Figure 2).

STEP 3. Use sun plan φ + C and sun elevation β to construct shadows in plan and elevation in conventional way (Figure 3).

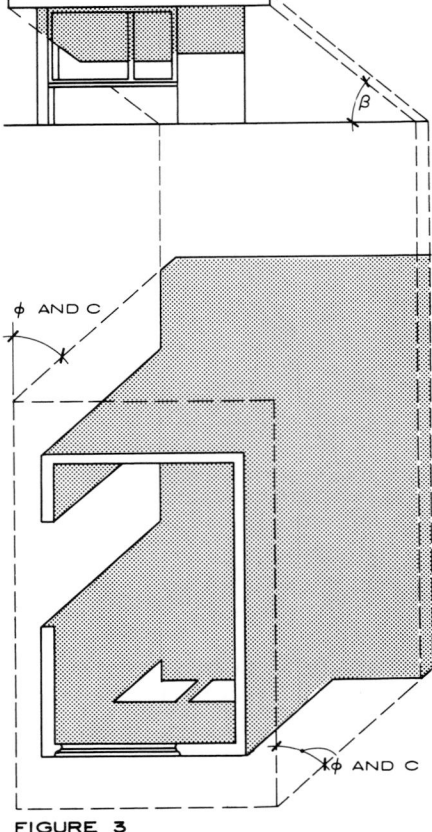

FIGURE 3

John I. Yellott, P.E.; College of Architecture, Arizona State University; Tempe, Arizona

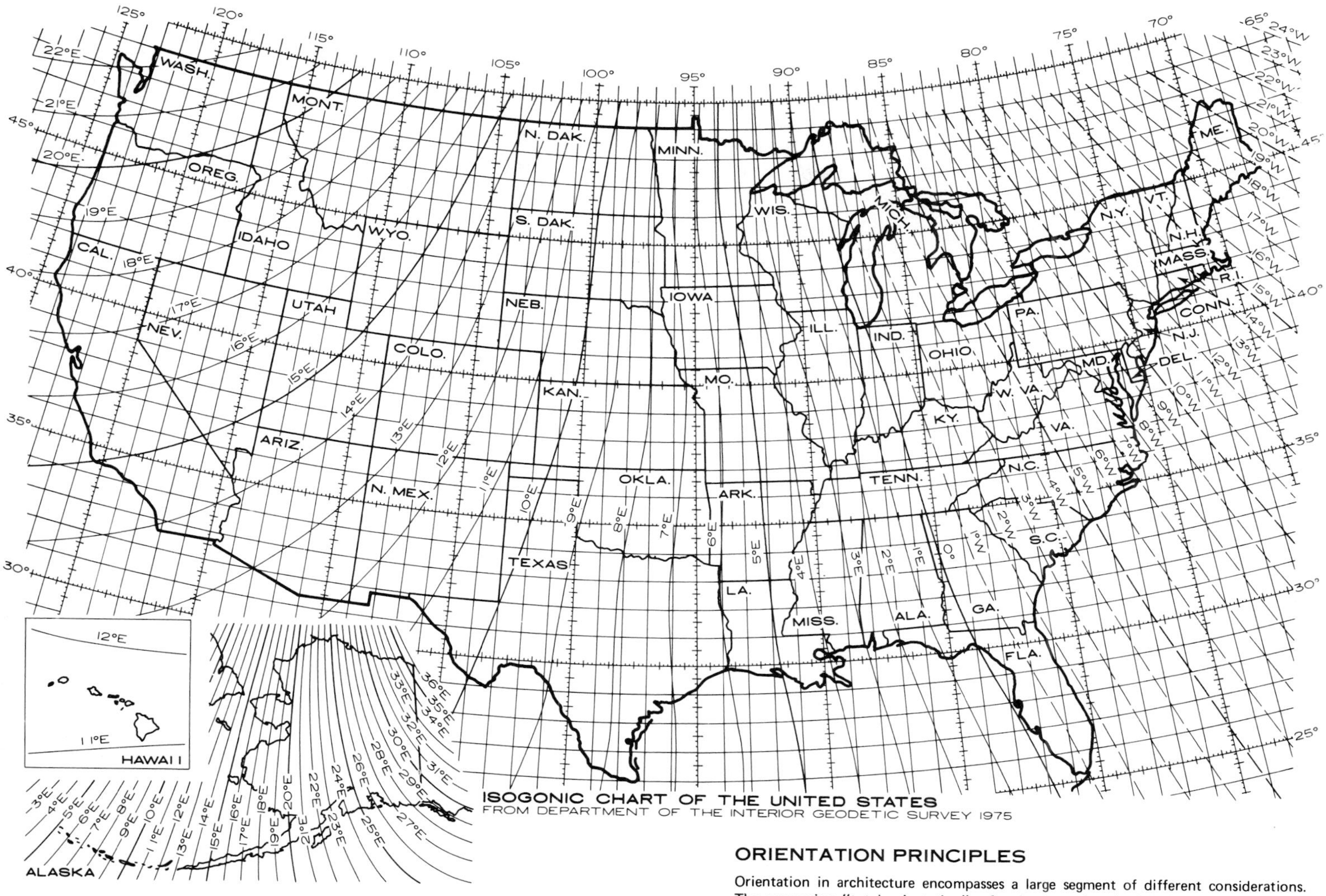

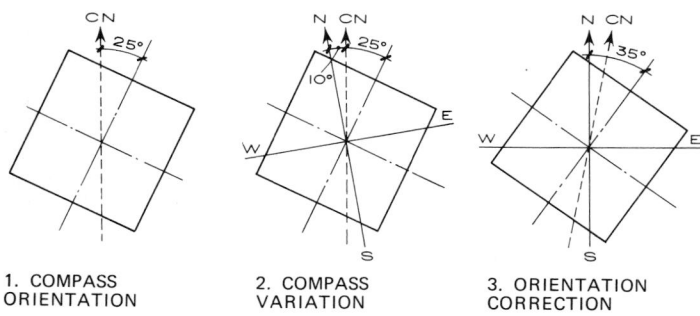

ISOGONIC CHART OF THE UNITED STATES
FROM DEPARTMENT OF THE INTERIOR GEODETIC SURVEY 1975

COMPASS ORIENTATION

The above map is the isogonic chart of the United States. The wavy lines from top to bottom show the compass variations from the true north. At the lines marked E the compass will point east of true north; at those marked W the compass will point west of true north. According to the location, correction should be done from the compass north to find the true north.

EXAMPLE: On a site in Wichita, Kansas, find the true north.

STEP 1.   Find the compass orientation on the site.

STEP 2.   Locate Wichita on the map. The nearest compass variation is the 10°E line.

STEP 3.   Adjust the orientation correction to true north.
The graphical example illustrates a building which lies 25° east with its axis from the compass orientation.

1. COMPASS ORIENTATION

2. COMPASS VARIATION

3. ORIENTATION CORRECTION

Victor Olgyay, AIA; Princeton University; Princeton, New Jersey

ORIENTATION PRINCIPLES

Orientation in architecture encompasses a large segment of different considerations. The expression "total orientation" refers both to the physiological and psychological aspects of the problem.

At the physiological side the factors which affect our senses and have to be taken into consideration are: the thermal impacts—the sun, wind, and temperature effects acting through our skin envelope; the visible impacts—the different illumination and brightness levels affecting our visual senses; the sonic aspects—the noise impacts and noise levels of the surroundings influencing our hearing organs. In addition, our respiratory organs are affected by the smoke, smell, and dust of the environs.

On the psychological side, the view and the privacy are aspects in orientation which quite often override the physical considerations.

Above all, as a building is only a mosaic unit in the pattern of a town organization, the spatial effects, the social intimacy, and its relation to the urban representative directions—aesthetic, political, or social—all play a part in positioning a building.

THERMAL FORCES INFLUENCING ORIENTATION

The climatic factors such as wind, solar radiation, and air temperature play the most eminent role in orientation. The position of a structure in northern latitudes, where the air temperature is generally cool, should be oriented to receive the maximum amount of sunshine without wind exposure. In southerly latitudes, however, the opposite will be desirable; the building should be turned on its axis to avoid the sun's unwanted radiation and to face the cooling breezes instead.

At right the figure shows these regional requirements diagrammatically.

Adaptation for wind orientation is not of great importance in low buildings, where the use of windbreaks and the arrangement of openings in the high and low pressure areas can help to ameliorate the airflow situation. However, for high buildings, where the surrounding terrain has little effect on the upper stories, careful consideration has to be given to wind orientation.

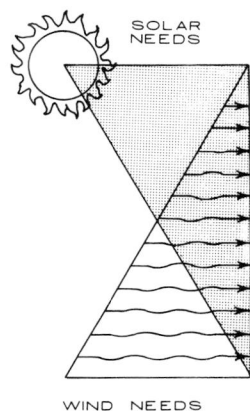

SOLAR NEEDS

WIND NEEDS

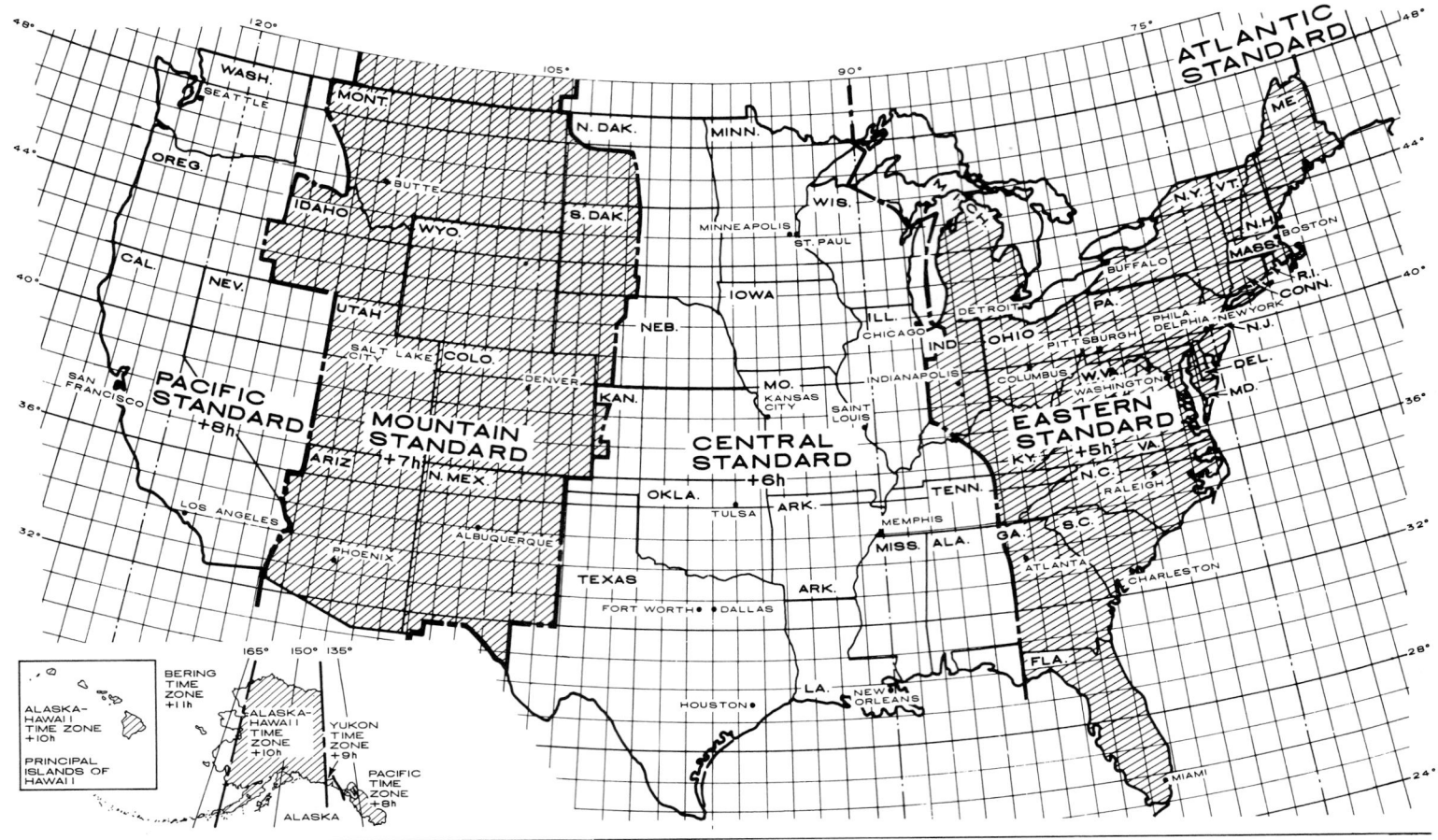

STANDARD TIME ZONES OF THE UNITED STATES
NOTE: Greenwich Standard Time is 0 h.

SOLAR TIME

Solar time generally differs from local standard or daylight saving time, and the difference can be significant, particularly when DST is in effect.

Because the sun appears to move at the rate of 360°/24 hr, its apparent motion is 4 min/1° of longitude. The procedure for finding AST (apparent solar time), explained in detail in the references cited previously, is

$$AST = LST + ET + 4(LSM - LON)$$

where ET = equation of time (min)
  LSM = local standard time meridian (degrees of arc)
  LON = local longitude, degrees of arc
  4 = minutes of time required for 1.0° rotation of earth

The longitudes of the six standard time meridians that affect the United States are: eastern ST, 75°; central ST, 90°; mountain ST, 105°; Pacific ST, 120°; Yukon ST, 135°; Alaska-Hawaii ST, 150°.

The equation of time is the measure, in minutes, of the extent by which solar time, as told by a sundial, runs faster or slower than civil or mean time, as determined by a clock running at a uniform rate. The table below gives values of the declination and the equation of time for the 21st day of each month of a typical year (other than a leap year). This date is chosen because of its significance on four particular days: (a) the winter solstice, December 21, the year's shortest day, $\delta = -23°\ 27$ min; (b) the vernal and autumnal equinoxes, March 21 and September 21, when the declination is zero and the day and night are equal in length; and (c) the summer solstice, June 21, the year's longest day, $\delta = +23°\ 27$ min.

EXAMPLES

Find AST at noon, local summer time, on July 21 for Washington, D.C., longitude = 77°; and for Chicago, longitude = 87.6°.

SOLUTIONS

In summer, both Washington and Chicago use daylight saving time, and noon, local summer time, is actually 11:00 a.m., local standard time. For Washington, in the eastern time zone, the local standard time meridian is 75° east of Greenwich, and for July 21, the equation of time is -6.2 min. Thus noon, Washington summer time, is actually

$$11:00 - 6.2 \text{ min} + 4 \times (75 - 77) = 10:46 \text{ a.m.}$$

For Chicago, in the central time zone, the local standard time meridian is 90°. Chicago lies 2.4° east of that line, and noon, Chicago summer time, is

$$11:00 - 6.2 \text{ min} + 4 \times 2.4 = 11:03 \text{ a.m.}$$

The hour angle, H, for these two examples would be

for Washington: $H = 0.25 \times (12:00 - 10:46)$
  $= 0.25 \times 74 = 18.8°$ east

for Chicago: $H = 0.25 \times (12:00 - 11:03)$
  $= 14.25°$ east

YEAR DATE, DECLINATION, AND EQUATION OF TIME FOR THE 21st DAY OF EACH MONTH; WITH DATA* (A, B, C) USED TO CALCULATE DIRECT NORMAL RADIATION INTENSITY AT THE EARTH'S SURFACE

MONTH	JAN.	FEB.	MAR.	APR.	MAY	JUNE	JULY	AUG.	SEPT.	OCT.	NOV.	DEC.
Day of the year†	21	52	80	111	141	173	202	233	265	294	325	355
Declination, (δ) degrees	-19.9	-10.6	0.0	+11.9	+20.3	+23.45	+20.5	+12.1	0.0	-10.7	-19.9	-23.45
Equation of time (min)	-11.2	-13.9	-7.5	+1.1	+3.3	-1.4	-6.2	-2.4	+7.5	+15.4	+13.8	+1.6
Solar noon	Late			Early			Late			Early		
A: Btuh/sq ft	390	385	376	360	350	345	344	351	365	378	387	391
B: 1/m	0.142	0.144	0.156	0.180	0.196	0.205	0.207	0.201	0.177	0.160	0.149	0.142
C: dimensionless	0.058	0.060	0.071	0.097	0.121	0.134	0.136	0.122	0.092	0.073	0.063	0.057

*A is the apparent solar irradiation at air mass zero for each month; B is the atmospheric extinction coefficient; C is the ratio of the diffuse radiation on a horizontal surface to the direct normal irradiation.
†Declinations are for the year 1964.

John I. Yellott, P.E.; College of Architecture, Arizona State University; Tempe, Arizona

SOLAR ANGLES

The position of the sun in relation to specific geographic locations, seasons, and times of day can be determined by several methods. Model measurements, by means of solar machines or shade dials, have the advantage of direct visual observations. Tabulative and calculative methods have the advantage of exactness. However, graphic projection methods are usually preferred by architects, as they are easily understood and can be correlated to both radiant energy and shading calculations.

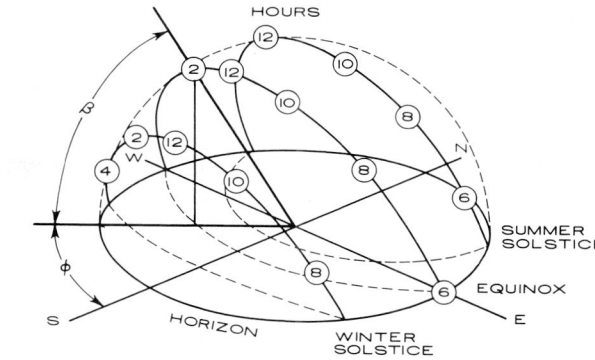

SOLAR PATH DIAGRAMS

A practical graphic projection is the solar path diagram method. Such diagrams depict the path of the sun within the sky vault as projected onto a horizontal plane. The horizon is represented as a circle with the observation point in the center. The sun's position at any date and hour can be determined from the diagram in terms of its altitude (β) and azimuth (ϕ). (See figure on right.) The graphs are constructed in equidistant projection. The altitude angles are represented at 10° intervals by equally spaced concentric circles; they range from 0° at the outer circle (horizon) to 90° at the center point. These intervals are graduated along the south meridian. Azimuth is represented at 10° intervals by equally spaced radii; they range from 0° at the south meridian to 180° at the north meridian. These intervals are graduated along the periphery. The solar bearing will be to the east during morning hours, and to the west during afternoon hours.

(CONTINUED NEXT PAGE)

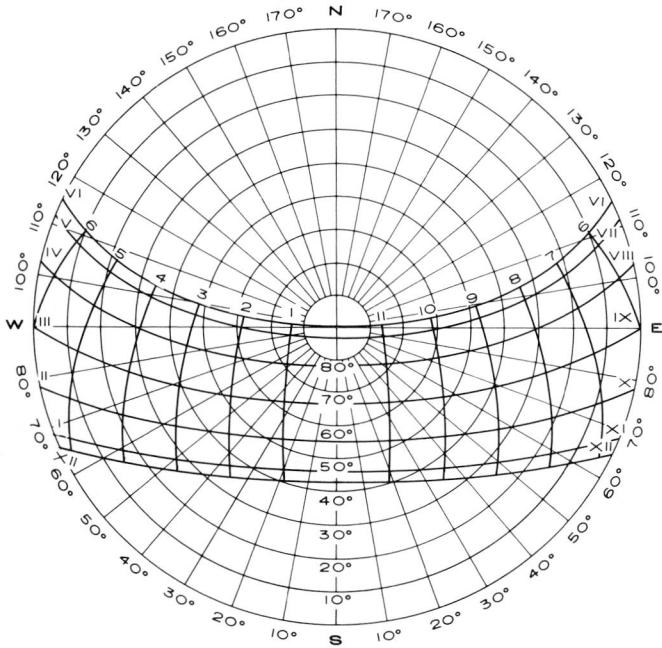

24°N LATITUDE

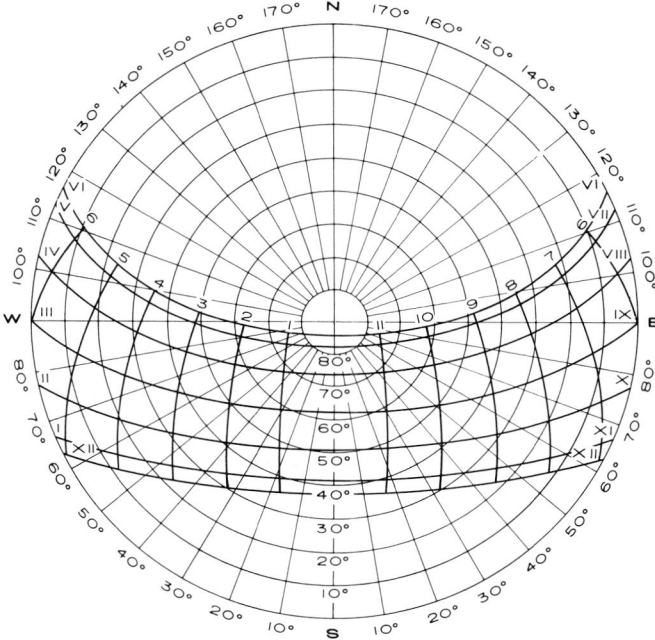

28° N LATITUDE

32°N LATITUDE

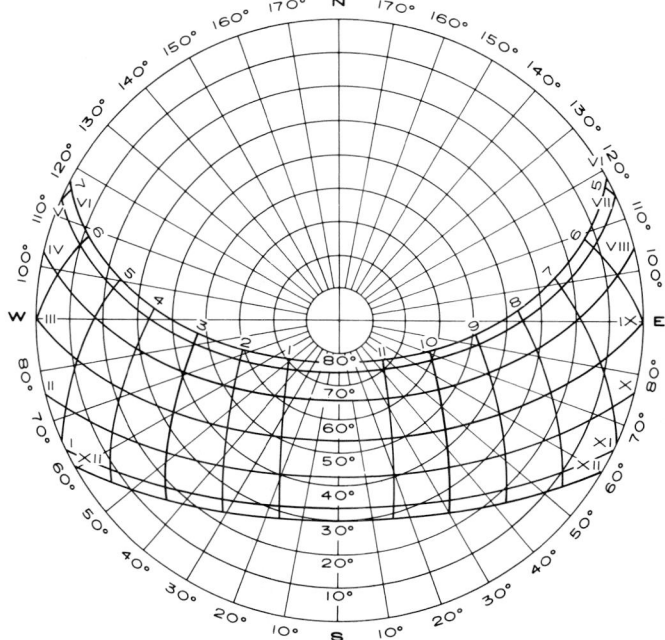

36°N LATITUDE

Victor Olgyay, AIA; Princeton University; Princeton, New Jersey

SOLAR RADIATION AND BUILDING ORIENTATION   18

SOLAR PATH DIAGRAMS (CONTINUED)

The earth's axis is inclined 23°27' to its orbit around the sun and rotates 15° hourly. Thus, from all points on the earth, the sun appears to move across the sky vault on various parallel circular paths with maximum declinations of ±23°27'. The declination of the sun's path changes in a cycle between the extremes of the summer solstice and winter solstice. Thus the sun follows the same path on two corresponding dates each year. Due to irregularities between the calendar year and the astronomical data, here a unified calibration is adapted. The differences, as they do not exceed 41', are negligible for architectural purposes.

DECLINATION OF THE SUN

DATE	DECLINATION	CORRESP. DATE	DECLINATION	UNIFIED CALIBR.
June 21	+23°27'			+23°27'
May 21	+20°09'	July 21	+20°31'	+20°20'
Apr. 21	+11°48'	Aug. 21	+12°12'	+12°00'
Mar. 21	+0°10'	Sep. 21	+0°47'	+0°28'
Feb. 21	−10°37'	Oct. 21	−10°38'	−10°38'
Jan. 21	−19°57'	Nov. 21	−19°53'	−19°55'
Dec. 21	−23°27'			−23°27'

The elliptical curves in the diagrams represent the horizontal projections of the sun's path. They are given on the 21st day of each month. Roman numerals designate the months. A cross grid of curves graduate the hours indicated in arabic numerals. Eight solar path diagrams are shown at 4° intervals from 24°N to 52°N latitude.

EXAMPLE

Find the sun's position in Columbus, Ohio, on February 21, 2 P.M.:

STEP 1. Locate Columbus on the map. The latitude is 40°N.

STEP 2. In the 40° sun path diagram select the February path (marked with II), and locate the 2 hr line. Where the two lines cross is the position of the sun.

STEP 3. Read the altitude on the concentric circles (32°) and the azimuth along the outer circle (35°30'W).

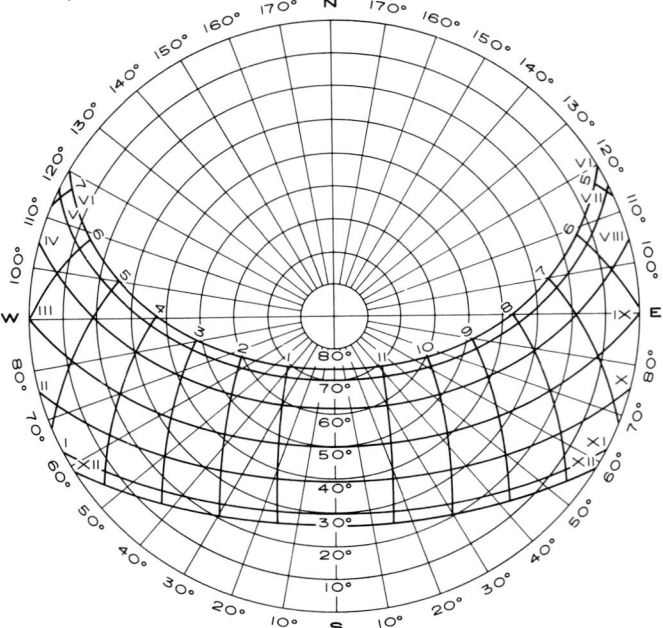

40°N LATITUDE

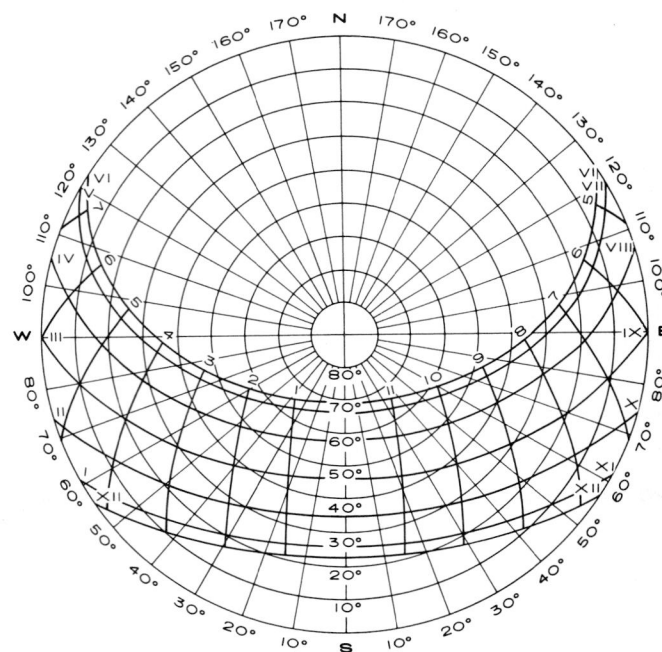

44°N LATITUDE

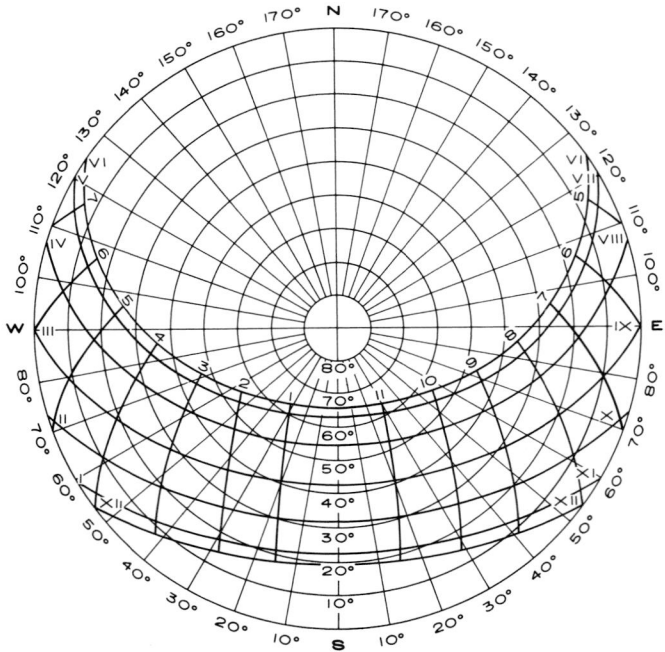

48°N LATITUDE

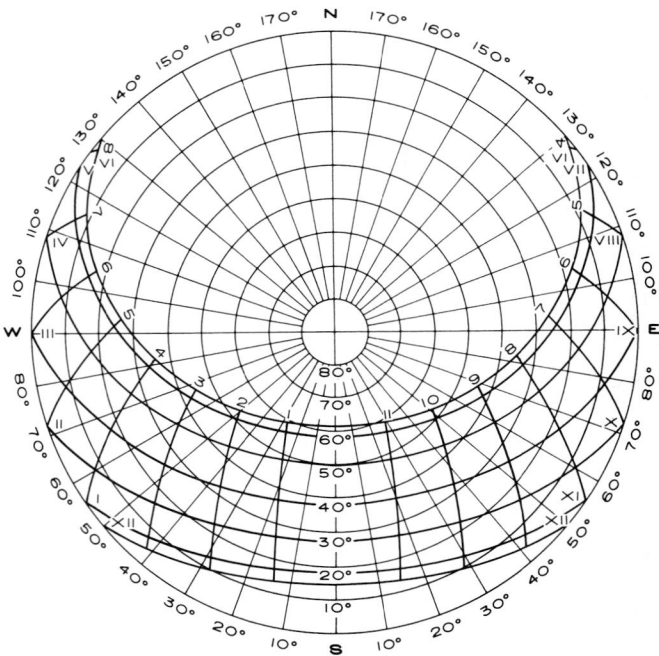

52°N LATITUDE

Victor Olgyay, AIA; Princeton University; Princeton, New Jersey

CALCULATION OF SOLAR POSITION

The solar position to any location and time can be accurately calculated by relating the spherical triangle formed by the observer's celestial meridian, the meridian of the sun, and the great circle passing through zenith and the sun. The following formulas can be used to find the solar altitude and azimuth angles:

$$\sin \beta = \cos L \cos \delta \cos H + \sin L \sin \delta$$
$$\cos \phi = (\sin \beta \sin L - \sin \delta)/(\cos \beta \cos L)$$

where:

- β = solar altitude above the horizon
- L = latitude of the location; conventionally negative for southern hemisphere latitudes
- δ = declination of the sun at the desired date, which is the angle between the earth-sun line and the equatorial plane (north declinations are conventionally positive; south declinations negative)
- H = hour angle of the sun = 0.25 x (number of minutes from local solar noon); H is zero at solar noon and changes 15 degrees per hour
- ϕ = solar azimuth, which is the angular distance measured from the south between the south-north line and the projection of the earth-sun line in the horizontal plane

SOLAR-SURFACE ANGLES

The direction of the earth-sun line OQ is defined by the solar altitude A (angle HOQ) and the solar azimuth B (angle HOS). These can be calculated when the location (latitude), date (declination), and time of day (hour angle) are known. The surface azimuth S is the angle SOP between the south-north line SON and the normal to the surface OP. The surface-solar azimuth G is the angle HOP.

The angle of incidence θ depends on the orientation and tilt of the irradiated surface. For a horizontal surface, θ_H is the angle QOV between the earth-sun line OQ and the vertical line OV. For the vertical surface shown above as facing SSE, the angle of incidence θ_V is the angle QOP between the earth-sun line OQ and the normal to the surface, OP. For surfaces such as solar collectors, which are generally tilted at some angle T upward from the horizontal, the incident angle θ_T may be found from the equation:

$$\cos \theta_T = \cos A \cos S \sin T + \sin A \cos T$$

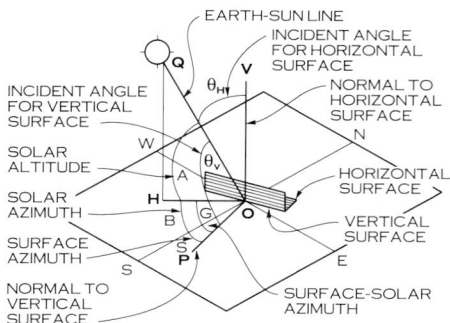

CALCULATION OF SOLAR IRRADIATION

It is necessary to know the amount of solar energy falling on exposed surfaces in order to evaluate the importance of solar shading. Because shading devices primarily protect surfaces from direct solar irradiation, only these energy calculations are described here.

The magnitude of direct solar irradiation is, first of all, a function of the sun's altitude and the apparent solar constant and atmospheric extinction coefficient. The latter two parameters take into account the annual variation of the earth-sun distance and the atmospheric water vapor content. The intensity of direct solar irradiation under clear atmospheric conditions at normal incidence can be calculated by:

$$I_{DN} = A \exp(-B/\sin \beta)$$

where:

- I_{DN} = direct normal solar intensity at the earth's surface on clear days
- exp = base of natural logarithms
- A = apparent solar constant or apparent normal incidence intensity at air mass zero
- B = atmospheric extinction coefficient

The following tables indicate direct normal solar irradiation on clear days as a function of solar altitude on the solstices and the equinoxes.

I_{DN} AS A FUNCTION OF SOLAR ALTITUDE (BTU/SQ FT/HOUR)

β	JUNE 21	MAR. 21/ SEPT. 21	DEC. 21
5	33	55	77
10	106	142	173
15	156	195	226
20	189	228	258
25	212	250	279
30	229	266	294
40	251	286	314
50	264	298	325
60	272	306	332
70	277	310	336
80	280	313	339
90	281	314	339

SOLAR IRRADIATION

The direct irradiation received by any given surface is also a function of the angle of incidence of the solar beam relative to that surface. The angle of incidence is the angle between the direct solar rays and a line normal to the irradiated surface.

For horizontal surfaces, the cosine of the angle of incidence is equal to the sine of the solar altitude. The direct irradiation on horizontal surfaces is thus calculated by:

$$I_{DH} = I_{DN} \times \sin \beta$$

For vertical surfaces, the incident angle depends on the solar altitude and the surface-solar azimuth. The surface-solar azimuth (γ) is the angular distance between the solar azimuth and the azimuth of the surface. The surface azimuth is the angle between south and the normal to the surface, measured counterclockwise from south. The direct irradiation on vertical surfaces can thus be calculated by:

$$I_{DV} = I_{DN} \times \cos \beta \cos \gamma$$

In the following tables, calculated values of solar position in degrees, and direct irradiation in BTU/sq ft/hour are given for horizontal surfaces and various vertical orientations. The tables indicate values for 26°N to 46°N latitude at 4° intervals on the solstices and the equinoxes.

26°N LATITUDE   INCIDENT DIRECT SOLAR RADIATION

JUNE 21

AM		ALT	AZM	S	SE	E	NE	N	SW	HOR
6	6	10.05	111.30		42	98	96	38		19
7	5	22.82	105.97		91	180	164	52		79
8	4	35.93	101.15		110	193	164	38		143
9	3	49.24	96.45		107	171	134	19		199
10	2	62.69	91.17		87	126	91	3		243
11	1	76.15	82.61	9	53	66	41			271
12		87.45	0.00	13	9				9	281
	PM	β	ϕ	S	SW	W	NW	N	SE	HOR

MARCH/SEPTEMBER 21

AM		ALT	AZM	S	SE	E	NE	N	SW	HOR
6	6	0.00	90.00							
7	5	13.45	83.30	21	138	175	109			42
8	4	26.71	75.80	56	196	222	117			115
9	3	39.46	66.33	88	205	202	80			181
10	2	51.11	52.79	114	186	150	25			233
11	1	60.25	31.43	130	148	79			36	266
12		64.00	0.00	135	95				95	277
	PM	β	ϕ	S	SW	W	NW	N	SE	HOR

DECEMBER 21

AM		ALT	AZM	S	SE	E	NE	N	SW	HOR
6	6									
7	5	2.23	62.48	5	10	9	3			
8	4	13.76	54.88	120	206	171	36			51
9	3	24.12	45.30	177	252	179	1			113
10	2	32.66	33.01	212	248	138			53	162
11	1	38.46	17.65	232	216	74			112	194
12		40.55	0.00	239	169				169	204
	PM	β	ϕ	S	SW	W	NW	N	SE	HOR

30°N LATITUDE   INCIDENT DIRECT SOLAR RADIATION

JUNE 21

AM		ALT	AZM	S	SE	E	NE	N	SW	HOR
6	6	11.48	110.59		50	113	110	42		25
7	5	23.87	104.30		97	184	163	47		84
8	4	36.60	98.26		117	194	157	28		146
9	3	49.53	91.79		117	171	125	5		200
10	2	62.50	83.46	14	99	126	79			243
11	1	75.11	67.48	27	66	66	27			270
12		83.45	0.00	32	23				23	279
	PM	β	ϕ	S	SW	W	NW	N	SE	HOR

MARCH/SEPTEMBER 21

AM		ALT	AZM	S	SE	E	NE	N	SW	HOR
6	6	0.00	90.00							
7	5	12.95	82.37	23	137	170	104			40
8	4	25.66	73.90	63	199	218	110			109
9	3	37.76	63.43	100	212	200	71			173
10	2	48.59	49.11	128	196	148	14			223
11	1	56.77	28.19	147	159	79			48	254
12		60.00	0.00	153	108				108	265
	PM	β	ϕ	S	SW	W	NW	N	SE	HOR

DECEMBER 21

AM		ALT	AZM	S	SE	E	NE	N	SW	HOR
6	6									
7	5	0.38	62.40							
8	4	11.44	54.15	110	185	152	30			38
9	3	21.27	44.12	177	246	171			4	96
10	2	29.28	31.73	217	248	134			59	143
11	1	34.64	16.77	240	221	72			119	173
12		36.55	0.00	247	175				175	183
	PM	β	ϕ	S	SW	W	NW	N	SE	HOR

Gary L. Powell, Ph.D.; Salt River Project; Phoenix, Arizona

34°N LATITUDE — INCIDENT DIRECT SOLAR RADIATION

JUNE 21

AM		ALT	AZM	S	SE	E	NE	N	SW	HOR
					BTU/SQ FT/HR					
6	6	12.86	109.78		57	126	121	45		
7	5	24.80	102.54		103	188	162	42		34
8	4	37.07	95.28		125	195	151	18		99
9	3	49.49	87.10	9	127	171	115			158
10	2	61.79	76.00	31	111	125	67			205
11	1	73.17	55.10	46	79	66	14			234
12		79.45	0.00	51	36				36	244
PM	β	φ		S	SW	W		NW	N	SE	HOR

MARCH/SEPTEMBER 21

AM		ALT	AZM	S	SE	E	NE	N	SW	HOR
					BTU/SQ FT/HR					
6	6	0.00	90.00							
7	5	12.39	81.48	25	134	165	99			37
8	4	24.49	72.11	69	201	215	103			103
9	3	35.89	60.79	110	217	197	61			163
10	2	45.89	45.92	142	204	147	3			211
11	1	53.21	25.60	163	170	78			60	241
12		56.00	0.00	169	120				120	251
PM	β	φ		S	SW	W	NW	N	SE	HOR

DECEMBER 21

AM		ALT	AZM	S	SE	E	NE	N	SW	HOR
					BTU/SQ FT/HR					
6	6									
7	5									
8	4	9.08	53.57	93	155	126	23			25
9	3	18.38	43.12	173	236	162			8	79
10	2	25.86	30.65	219	246	130			63	123
11	1	30.81	16.05	245	223	70			123	152
12		32.55	0.00	253	179				179	162
PM	β	φ		S	SW	W	NW	N	SE	HOR

38°N LATITUDE — INCIDENT DIRECT SOLAR RADIATION

JUNE 21

AM		ALT	AZM	S	SE	E	NE	N	SW	HOR
					BTU/SQ FT/HR					
6	6	14.18	108.87		64	137	130	47		37
7	5	25.60	100.70		109	190	160	36		93
8	4	37.33	92.25		133	195	144	8		149
9	3	49.13	82.47	23	137	171	105			199
10	2	60.58	69.06	48	122	125	55			238
11	1	70.61	45.67	64	92	66	1			262
12		75.45	0.00	70	50				50	270
PM	β	φ		S	SW	W	NW	N	SE	HOR

MARCH/SEPTEMBER 21

AM		ALT	AZM	S	SE	E	NE	N	SW	HOR
					BTU/SQ FT/HR					
6	6	0.00	90.00							
7	5	11.77	80.63	26	130	158	93			33
8	4	23.20	70.43	75	202	210	96			96
9	3	33.86	58.38	120	222	194	53			153
10	2	43.03	43.16	155	212	145			7	198
11	1	49.57	23.52	177	180	77			71	227
12		52.00	0.00	185	131				131	236
PM	β	φ		S	SW	W	NW	N	SE	HOR

DECEMBER 21

AM		ALT	AZM	S	SE	E	NE	N	SW	HOR
					BTU/SQ FT/HR					
6	6									
7	5									
8	4	6.69	53.12	69	114	92	16			13
9	3	15.44	42.30	164	221	149			10	61
10	2	22.40	29.74	216	240	124			66	103
11	1	26.96	15.45	246	222	68			126	130
12		28.55	0.00	255	180				180	139
PM	β	φ		S	SW	W	NW	N	SE	HOR

42°N LATITUDE — INCIDENT DIRECT SOLAR RADIATION

JUNE 21

AM		ALT	AZM	S	SE	E	NE	N	SW	HOR
					BTU/SQ FT/HR					
6	6	15.44	107.87		70	147	137	47		43
7	5	26.28	98.78		115	192	157	30		96
8	4	37.38	89.19	3	140	196	136			150
9	3	48.45	77.96	36	146	170	95			196
10	2	58.95	62.79	64	133	125	43			233
11	1	67.64	38.62	82	105	66			12	256
12		71.45	0.00	88	63				63	263
PM	β	φ		S	SW	W	NW	N	SE	HOR

MARCH/SEPTEMBER 21

AM		ALT	AZM	S	SE	E	NE	N	SW	HOR
					BTU/SQ FT/HR					
6	6	0.00	90.00							
7	5	11.09	79.84	27	126	151	87			30
8	4	21.81	68.88	79	201	205	89			88
9	3	31.70	56.21	128	225	191	45			142
10	2	40.06	40.79	166	218	143			16	184
11	1	45.88	21.82	190	188	76			81	211
12		48.00	0.00	198	140				140	220
PM	β	φ		S	SW	W	NW	N	SE	HOR

DECEMBER 21

AM		ALT	AZM	S	SE	E	NE	N	SW	HOR
					BTU/SQ FT/HR					
6	6									
7	5									
8	4	4.28	52.82	35	58	46	8			4
9	3	12.46	41.63	148	197	131			12	44
10	2	18.91	29.00	209	229	116			66	82
11	1	23.09	14.96	242	217	65			125	107
12		24.55	0.00	253	179				179	115
PM	β	φ		S	SW	W	NW	N	SE	HOR

46°N LATITUDE — INCIDENT DIRECT SOLAR RADIATION

JUNE 21

AM		ALT	AZM	S	SE	E	NE	N	SW	HOR
					BTU/SQ FT/HR					
6	6	16.63	106.77		76	155	142	47		48
7	5	26.82	96.80		121	194	154	23		99
8	4	37.22	86.15	13	147	195	129			149
9	3	47.47	73.66	50	155	169	85			192
10	2	56.95	57.25	80	144	124	31			226
11	1	64.40	33.33	99	116	65			24	248
12		67.45	0.00	106	75				75	255
PM	β	φ		S	SW	W	NW	N	SE	HOR

MARCH/SEPTEMBER 21

AM		ALT	AZM	S	SE	E	NE	N	SW	HOR
					BTU/SQ FT/HR					
6	6	0.00	90.00							
7	5	10.36	79.09	27	120	142	81			26
8	4	20.32	67.45	83	199	199	82			80
9	3	29.42	54.27	134	227	187	37			130
10	2	36.98	38.75	175	223	140			24	169
11	1	42.14	20.43	201	195	75			89	194
12		44.00	0.00	210	148				148	203
PM	β	φ		S	SW	W	NW	N	SE	HOR

DECEMBER 21

AM		ALT	AZM	S	SE	E	NE	N	SW	HOR
					BTU/SQ FT/HR					
6	6									
7	5									
8	4	1.86	52.65	3	5	4	1			
9	3	9.46	41.12	122	162	107			11	27
10	2	15.41	28.41	194	212	105			63	61
11	1	19.23	14.56	232	207	60			122	84
12		20.55	0.00	244	173				173	92
PM	β	φ		S	SW	W	NW	N	SE	HOR

Gary L. Powell, Ph.D.; Salt River Project; Phoenix, Arizona

18   SOLAR RADIATION AND BUILDING ORIENTATION

BASIC PRINCIPLES

The diagrams presented in this discussion are based on an isolated building. Neighboring buildings and landscaping can substantially affect airflow and should be taken into account when evaluating ventilation strategies.

As wind approaches the face of a building the airflow is slowed, creating positive pressure and a cushion of air on the building's windward face. This cushion of air, in turn, diverts the wind toward the building sides. Airflow as it passes along the sidewalls separates from building wall surfaces and, coupled with high-speed airflow, creates suction (negative pressure) along these wall surfaces. On the building leeward side a big slow-moving eddy is created. Suction on the leeward side of the building is less than on the sidewalls (see Figure 1).

If windows are placed in both windward and leeward faces, the building would be cross ventilated and eddies will develop against the main airflow direction (see Figure 2). Ventilation can be enhanced by placing windows in sidewalls due to the increased suction at this location; also, greater air recirculation within the building will occur due to air inertia (see Figure 3). Winds often shift direction, and for oblique winds, ventilation is best for rooms with windows on three adjacent walls (see Figure 4) than on two opposite walls (see Figure 5). However, if wind is from the one windowless side, then ventilation is poor, since all openings are in suction (see Figure 6).

If the building configuration only allows for windows in one wall, then negligible ventilation will occur with the use of a single window, because there is not a distinct inlet and outlet. Ventilation can be improved slightly with two widely spaced windows. Airflow can be enhanced in these situations by creating positive and negative pressure zones by use of architectural features such as wing walls (see Figure 7). Care must be exercised in developing these features to avoid counteracting the natural airflow, thereby weakening ventilation (see Figure 8).

AIR JETS

As airflow passes through a well-ventilated room, it forms an "air jet." If the windows are centered in a room, it forms a free jet (see Figure 9). If, however, the openings are near the room walls, ceiling, or floor, the airstream attaches itself to the surface, forming a wall jet (see Figure 10). Since heat removal from building surfaces is enhanced with increased airflow, the formation of wall jets is important in effecting rapid structure cooling. To improve the overall airflow within a room, offsetting the inlet and outlet will promote greater mixing of room air (see Figure 11).

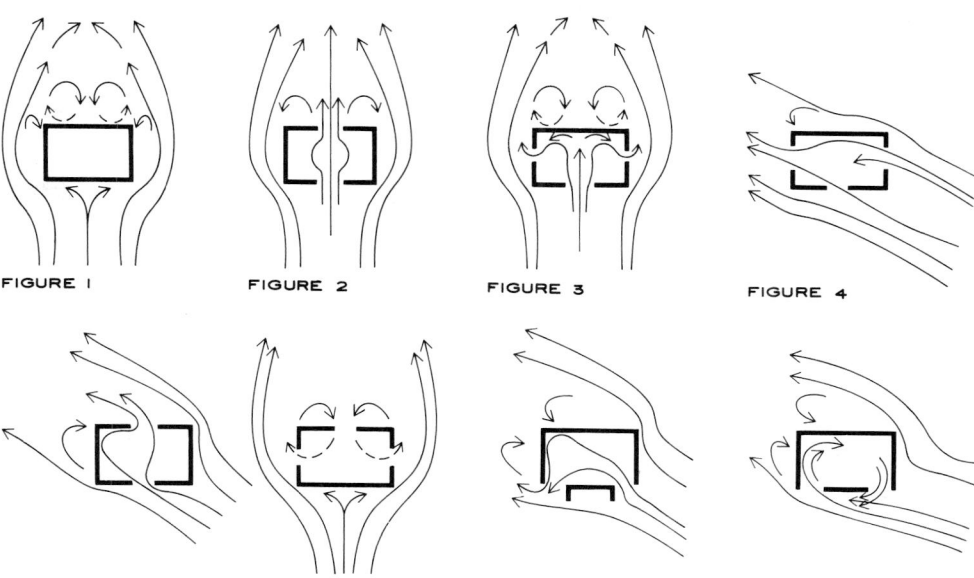

FIGURE 1   FIGURE 2   FIGURE 3   FIGURE 4

FIGURE 5   FIGURE 6   FIGURE 7   FIGURE 8

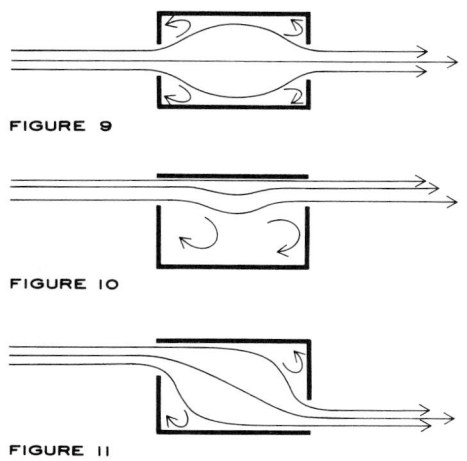

FIGURE 9

FIGURE 10

FIGURE 11

WINDOW SIZE

Airflow within a given room increases as window size increases, and to maximize airflow, the inlet and outlet opening should be the same size. Reducing the inlet size relative to the outlet increases inlet velocities. Making the outlet smaller than the inlet creates low but more uniform airspeed.

W. Fred Roberts Jr., AIA; Roberts & Kirchner Architects; Lexington, Virginia

VENTILATION AIR CHANGE RATE

The natural air change rate within a building depends on several factors: speed and direction of winds at building site; the external geometry of building and adjacent surroundings; window type, size, location, and geometry; and the building's internal partition layout. Each of these factors may have an overriding influence on the air change rate of a given building.

Natural ventilation can be accomplished by wind-driven methods or by solar chimneys (stack effect). However, the stack effect is weak and works best during hours when air temperatures are highest and ventilation may not be desirable. In many areas ventilation is best accomplished during the night hours when temperatures are lowest. The night average wind speed is generally about 75% of the 24-hr average wind speed reported by weather bureaus. Often wind speeds are insufficient to accomplish effective people cooling; therefore, ventilating for structure cooling rather than people cooling should be the first design goal. As a rule of thumb, an average of 30 air changes per hour should provide adequate structure cooling, maintaining air temperatures most of the time within 1.5°F of outdoor temperatures.

EXTERNAL EFFECTS

The leeward wake of typical residential buildings extends roughly four and one-half times the ground-to-eave height. For buildings spaced greater than this distance, the general wind direction will remain unchanged. For design purposes, vegetation should be considered for its effect on wind speed, which can be as great as 30–40% in the vegetation's immediate vicinity. Its effect on wind direction is not well established and should not be relied upon in establishing ventilation strategies.

RULE OF THUMB EXAMPLE

Determine inlet window opening area to achieve 30 air changes per hour in a house of 1200 sq ft with a ceiling height of 8 ft and awning windows with insect screens.

Required airflow (CFM)
= House volume x air changes per hr/60

Required airflow = (1200 x 8) x 30/60 = 4800 CFM

From local National Oceanic and Atmospheric Administration (NOAA) weather data, determine site wind conditions for design month. For the example above, average wind speed at 10 m above ground level = 7 mph or 616 ft/min at 30° incidence angle to the house face. Note that site wind speeds are generally less than NOAA data, usually collected at airports.

To determine the required inlet area, divide the house airflow by the wind speed passing through openings in the windward building face. To establish this wind speed, the site wind speed must be modified by the effects of building angle relative to wind direction and porosity of the window opening.

Figure 12 charts the effect of wind incidence angle on airflow rates (based on wind tunnel tests on model buildings with equal inlet and outlet areas equaling 12% of inlet wall areas). Table 1 establishes porosity factors for typical window arrangements. By multiplying the site wind speed by the window air speed factor (WAF) and window porosity factor (WPF), the effective wind speed can be determined. Therefore:

$$\text{Inlet window area} = \frac{\text{Airflow}}{\text{Wind speed x WAF x WPF}}$$

$$\text{Inlet window area} = \frac{4800}{616 \times 0.35 \times 0.75} = 29.7 \text{ sq ft}$$

In the example above, therefore, providing a total of 60 sq ft of insect screened awning windows will provide the required ventilation of 30 air changes per hour.

For best results, the 60 sq ft of windows should be split equally between inlets and outlets. However, adequate airflows can be maintained for anywhere from 40/60 to 60/40 split between inlets and outlets.

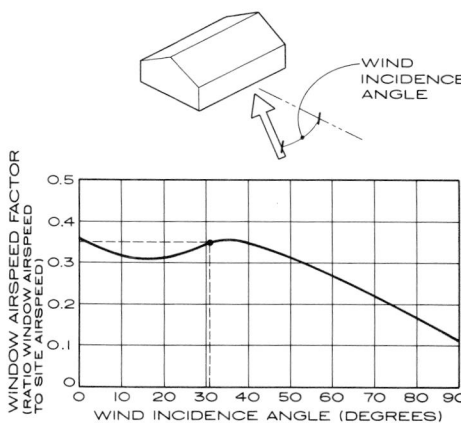

FIGURE 12

TABLE 1 POROSITY FACTORS

WINDOW TYPE	FACTOR
Fully open awning or projecting window	0.75
Awning window with 60% porosity insect screen	0.65
60% porosity insect screen only	0.85

CLIMATE

Cold climates in North America are generally north of the 40th parallel. Very cold is identified by the southern boundary of the 32°F mean annual temperature and includes most of Canada and Alaska except along the Pacific coast. Permafrost extends from below Hudson Bay and just north of the southern coast of Alaska to the Arctic Ocean. The Arctic Circle designates the southernmost point where continuous daylight in summer and continuous darkness in winter exist.

PLANNING DETERMINANTS

Cold climates generally require multidisciplined considerations for extremes of physical, economic, sociological, and environmental conditions. These include very cold temperatures, high winds, drifting snow, continuous darkness and low sun angles, permafrost, minimal and costly transportation and communication, and subsequent isolation.

DESIGN

Responses to planning determinants suggest aerodynamic design, isolation from permafrost, maximum insulation, self-sufficient utilities, backup systems for emergency, privacy without isolation, variety, and color. Labor is costly, suggesting maximum prefabrication. (Modular components can be used where barges can navigate.)

THERMOPILES AND PROBES

Both self-contained convection (passive) and mechanically refrigerated (active) systems are used for new construction and stabilization of existing foundations, either directly as pipe piles or in smaller pipes (probes) that can be placed beside a pile or under slab or foundation. Passive systems rely on natural convection of a liquid or gas medium to remove heat from the ground to keep it frozen; active systems use pumps and refrigeration technology. Recent concerns regarding global warming have caused renewed interest in the design parameters for passive systems.

UTILITIES

Utilidors or utiliducts are the most common way to provide protection, easy access, and insulation of utility lines to avoid disturbance to the permafrost. Human waste at isolated facilities may be handled by compost privies (waterless toilets) and chemical toilets or self-contained treatment systems. Disposal systems include incineration and sewage lagoons.

PERMAFROST, ICE WEDGES AND LENSES, AND FROST HEAVE

DEFINITION OF PERMAFROST: Ground of any kind that stays colder than the freezing temperature of water throughout several years. Depth can extend to 2,000 ft below active layer.

TERMS

ACTIVE LAYER: Top layer of ground subject to annual freezing and thawing. Up to 10 ft or only 18 in. over some permafrost.

FROST HEAVING: Lifting or heaving of soil surface created by the freezing of subsurface frost-susceptible material.

FROST-SUSCEPTIBLE SOIL: Soil that has enough permeability and capillary action (wickability) to expand upon freezing.

ICE LENSE (TABER ICE): Subsurface pocket of ice in soil.

ICE WEDGE: Wedge-shaped mass of ice within thaw zone. Wedges range up to 3 or 4 ft wide and 10 ft deep.

PERELETOK: Frozen layer at the base of the active layer that remains unthawed during some cold summers.

RESIDUAL THAW ZONE: Layer of unfrozen ground between the permafrost and active layer. This layer does not exist when annual frost extends to the permafrost, but is present during some warm winters.

SITE PLANNING

Blowing snow with high winds, low sun angles, and long periods of darkness are the dominant design factors. Minimizing obstructions that cause snow drifting and

Edwin B. Crittenden, FAIA, and John N. Crittenden, AIA; Anchorage, Alaska

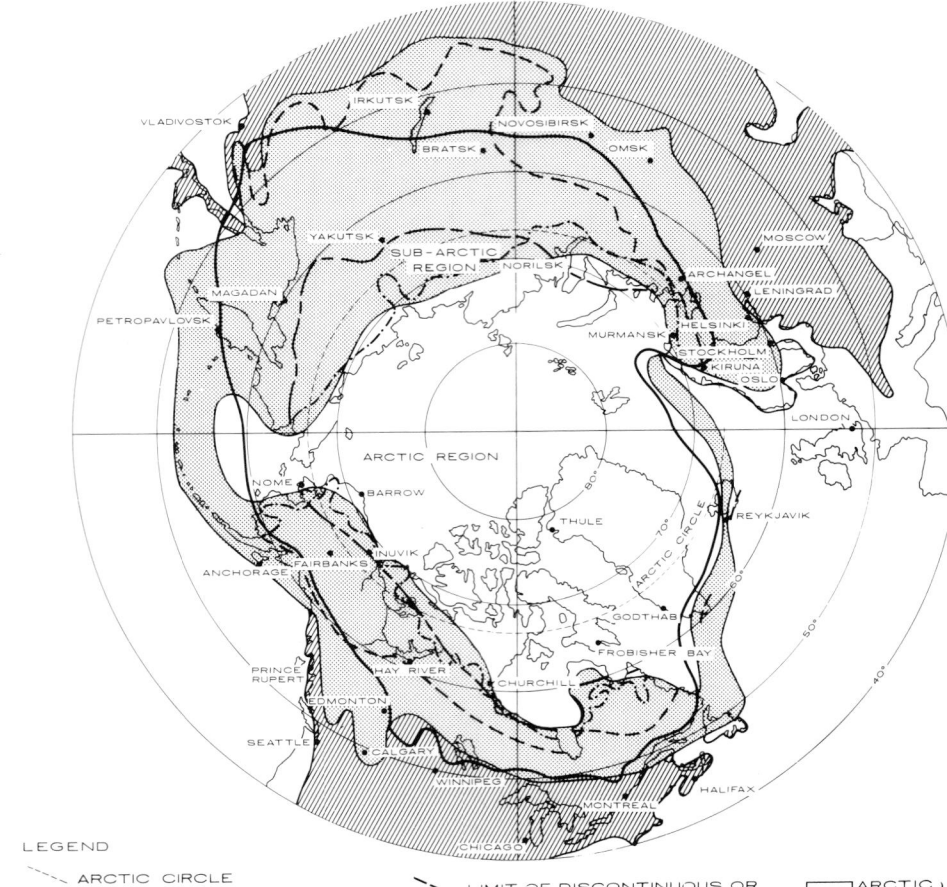

LEGEND

- – – – – ARCTIC CIRCLE
- ───── 32°F MEAN ANNUAL TEMPERATURE
- – – – – LIMIT OF CONTINUOUS PERMAFROST
- – ·· – ·· – LIMIT OF DISCONTINUOUS OR SPORADIC PERMAFROST
- – · – · – NORTHERN BOUNDARY OF TREES

	ARCTIC	COLD DRY
	SUB-ARCTIC	
	COLD WET	

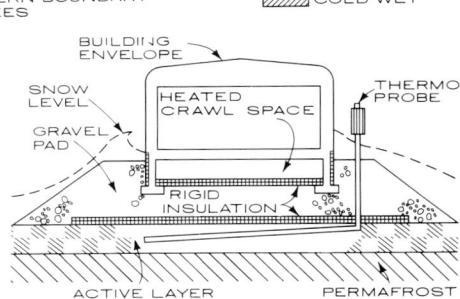

CONDITION 1: ELEVATED BUILDING ON PILES

CONDITION 2: BUILDING ON GRAVEL PAD

placing the long axis of a structure parallel to the prevailing wind help. Buildings can be spaced to avoid the long shadows cast by low winter sun angles. Darkness is a physical and psychological problem that suggests adequate lighting and signage.

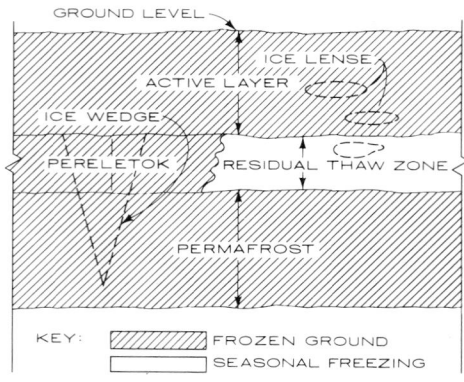

KEY: ▨ FROZEN GROUND
▢ SEASONAL FREEZING

CONDITION OF BUILDINGS ON PERMAFROST

CONDITION 1: Building elevated on piles allows the dispersion of building heat to prevent ground thaw and allow the wind to remove snow. Wooden piles, with low thermal conductivity, induce minimal heat into frozen ground while thermopiles can remove heat to retain frozen state.

CONDITION 2: Building elevated on non-frost-susceptible gravel pad to provide insulation in addition to existing ground cover. Rigid insulation adds to the protection from thaw of the permafrost. Thermoprobes are used to refreeze fill and keep permafrost frozen.

REFERENCES

Johnston, G. H., Permafrost Engineering, Design and Construction, National Research Council of Canada, John Wiley & Sons, New York, 1981.

Phukan, Arvind, Frozen Ground Engineering, Prentice Hall, Englewood, NJ, 1985.

Rice, Eb, Building in the North, Geophysical Institute, University of Alaska, Fairbanks, AK, 1975.

Zrudlo, Leo R., Psychological Problems and Environmental Design in the North, Collection Nordicana, Université Laval, Montreal, Canada, 1972.

GENERAL

Successful design of building envelopes for cold regions requires that all air-vapor retarders, wind barriers, and insulation be continuous. Air-vapor retarders prevent warm, moist indoor air from entering and condensing in portions of the envelope. Wind barriers prevent cold outdoor air from entering the insulation. Seal the wind barrier and air-vapor retarder at all joints and penetrations in the envelope to prevent air leakage and moisture problems. Metal or concrete bridging across the insulated layer can cause thermal short circuits. Minimize thermal short circuits with continuous insulation; this saves energy and reduces condensation and mold. Adequate slopes and continuity at flashing prevent problems due to snow and ice on roofs.

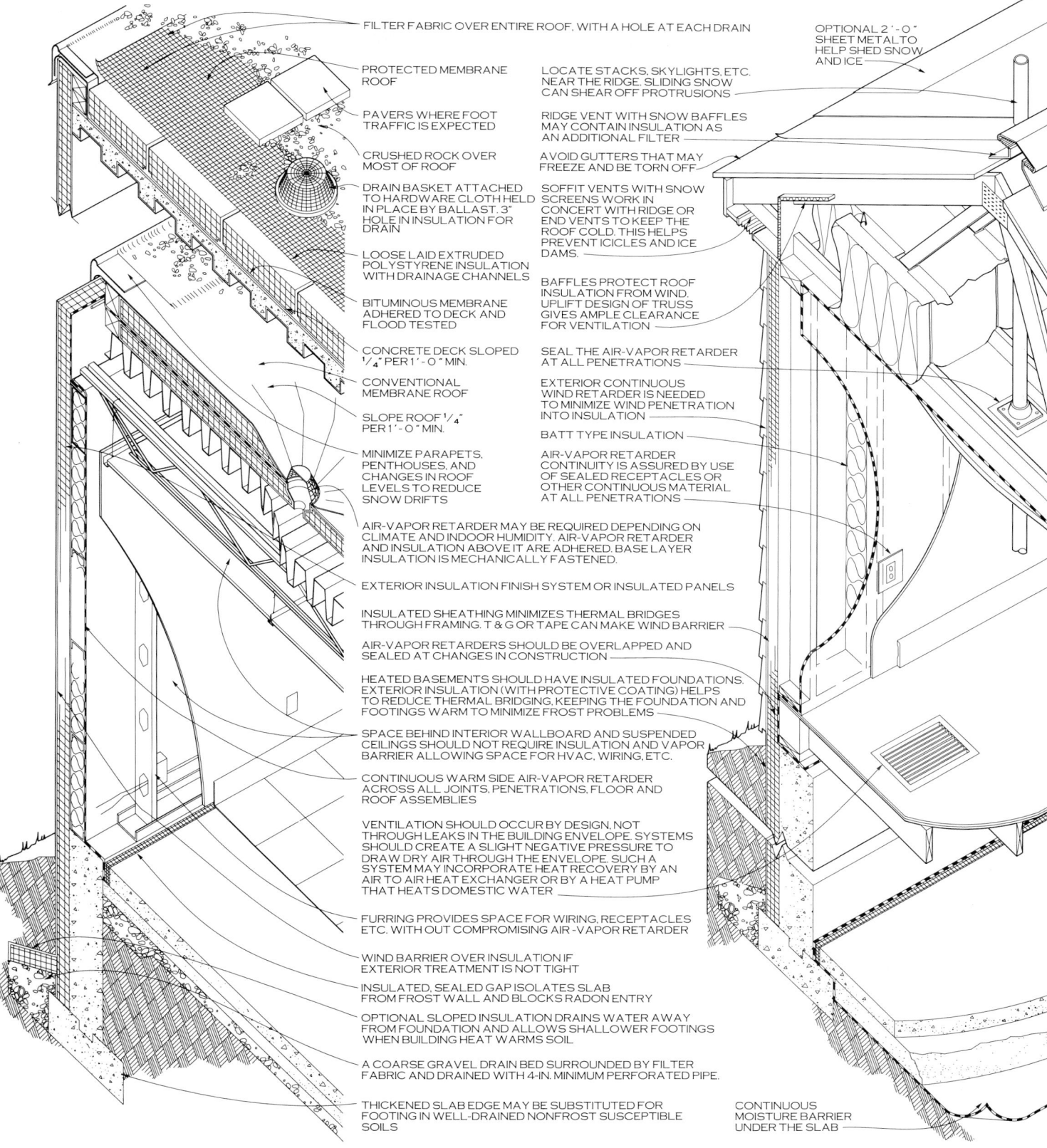

FILTER FABRIC OVER ENTIRE ROOF, WITH A HOLE AT EACH DRAIN

PROTECTED MEMBRANE ROOF

PAVERS WHERE FOOT TRAFFIC IS EXPECTED

CRUSHED ROCK OVER MOST OF ROOF

DRAIN BASKET ATTACHED TO HARDWARE CLOTH HELD IN PLACE BY BALLAST. 3" HOLE IN INSULATION FOR DRAIN

LOOSE LAID EXTRUDED POLYSTYRENE INSULATION WITH DRAINAGE CHANNELS

BITUMINOUS MEMBRANE ADHERED TO DECK AND FLOOD TESTED

CONCRETE DECK SLOPED 1/4" PER 1'-0" MIN.

CONVENTIONAL MEMBRANE ROOF

SLOPE ROOF 1/4" PER 1'-0" MIN.

MINIMIZE PARAPETS, PENTHOUSES, AND CHANGES IN ROOF LEVELS TO REDUCE SNOW DRIFTS

AIR-VAPOR RETARDER MAY BE REQUIRED DEPENDING ON CLIMATE AND INDOOR HUMIDITY. AIR-VAPOR RETARDER AND INSULATION ABOVE IT ARE ADHERED. BASE LAYER INSULATION IS MECHANICALLY FASTENED.

EXTERIOR INSULATION FINISH SYSTEM OR INSULATED PANELS

INSULATED SHEATHING MINIMIZES THERMAL BRIDGES THROUGH FRAMING. T & G OR TAPE CAN MAKE WIND BARRIER

AIR-VAPOR RETARDERS SHOULD BE OVERLAPPED AND SEALED AT CHANGES IN CONSTRUCTION

HEATED BASEMENTS SHOULD HAVE INSULATED FOUNDATIONS. EXTERIOR INSULATION (WITH PROTECTIVE COATING) HELPS TO REDUCE THERMAL BRIDGING, KEEPING THE FOUNDATION AND FOOTINGS WARM TO MINIMIZE FROST PROBLEMS

SPACE BEHIND INTERIOR WALLBOARD AND SUSPENDED CEILINGS SHOULD NOT REQUIRE INSULATION AND VAPOR BARRIER ALLOWING SPACE FOR HVAC, WIRING, ETC.

CONTINUOUS WARM SIDE AIR-VAPOR RETARDER ACROSS ALL JOINTS, PENETRATIONS, FLOOR AND ROOF ASSEMBLIES

VENTILATION SHOULD OCCUR BY DESIGN, NOT THROUGH LEAKS IN THE BUILDING ENVELOPE. SYSTEMS SHOULD CREATE A SLIGHT NEGATIVE PRESSURE TO DRAW DRY AIR THROUGH THE ENVELOPE. SUCH A SYSTEM MAY INCORPORATE HEAT RECOVERY BY AN AIR TO AIR HEAT EXCHANGER OR BY A HEAT PUMP THAT HEATS DOMESTIC WATER

FURRING PROVIDES SPACE FOR WIRING, RECEPTACLES ETC. WITH OUT COMPROMISING AIR-VAPOR RETARDER

WIND BARRIER OVER INSULATION IF EXTERIOR TREATMENT IS NOT TIGHT

INSULATED, SEALED GAP ISOLATES SLAB FROM FROST WALL AND BLOCKS RADON ENTRY

OPTIONAL SLOPED INSULATION DRAINS WATER AWAY FROM FOUNDATION AND ALLOWS SHALLOWER FOOTINGS WHEN BUILDING HEAT WARMS SOIL

A COARSE GRAVEL DRAIN BED SURROUNDED BY FILTER FABRIC AND DRAINED WITH 4-IN. MINIMUM PERFORATED PIPE.

THICKENED SLAB EDGE MAY BE SUBSTITUTED FOR FOOTING IN WELL-DRAINED NONFROST SUSCEPTIBLE SOILS

LOCATE STACKS, SKYLIGHTS, ETC. NEAR THE RIDGE. SLIDING SNOW CAN SHEAR OFF PROTRUSIONS

RIDGE VENT WITH SNOW BAFFLES MAY CONTAIN INSULATION AS AN ADDITIONAL FILTER

AVOID GUTTERS THAT MAY FREEZE AND BE TORN OFF

SOFFIT VENTS WITH SNOW SCREENS WORK IN CONCERT WITH RIDGE OR END VENTS TO KEEP THE ROOF COLD. THIS HELPS PREVENT ICICLES AND ICE DAMS.

BAFFLES PROTECT ROOF INSULATION FROM WIND. UPLIFT DESIGN OF TRUSS GIVES AMPLE CLEARANCE FOR VENTILATION

SEAL THE AIR-VAPOR RETARDER AT ALL PENETRATIONS

EXTERIOR CONTINUOUS WIND RETARDER IS NEEDED TO MINIMIZE WIND PENETRATION INTO INSULATION

BATT TYPE INSULATION

AIR-VAPOR RETARDER CONTINUITY IS ASSURED BY USE OF SEALED RECEPTACLES OR OTHER CONTINUOUS MATERIAL AT ALL PENETRATIONS

OPTIONAL 2'-0" SHEET METAL TO HELP SHED SNOW AND ICE

CONTINUOUS MOISTURE BARRIER UNDER THE SLAB

CONCRETE OR STEEL CONSTRUCTION WITH MEMBRANE ROOF

FRAME CONSTRUCTION WITH A COLD ROOF

Eric K. Beach; Rippeteau Architects, PC; Washington, D.C.
Stephen N. Flanders and Wayne Tobiasson; Cold Regions Research and Engineering Laboratory, U.S. Army Corps of Engineers; Hanover, New Hampshire

CLIMATE RESPONSE AND BUILDING DESIGN

18

STRATEGIES OF CLIMATE CONTROL

Underheated conditions occur in both humid and arid regions and dominate much of the U.S. The strategies are to minimize conduction and infiltration losses and to take advantage of winter solar gain. Humidity affects sky clearness and availability of solar radiation, making optimization of solar glazing area one of the main opportunities of regional design. Moisture movement through the building shell must be controlled. It is driven by air leakage (exfiltration) and by vapor diffusion, which is related to temperature differences.

MINIMIZE CONDUCTION LOSSES

Minimize ratio of envelope to heated floor area. Minimize foundation perimeter length. Insulate envelope components in proportion to indoor–outdoor temperature difference. Minimize areas of windows, doors, and other envelope components of inherently low R value. Detail to avoid thermal bridging. Provide movable insulation for glazed areas.

MINIMIZE INFILTRATION LOSSES

Plant vegetation to create wind-sheltered building sites. Shape building to minimize exposure to winter wind. Orient doors and windows away from winter wind. Specify weatherstripping and infiltration barrier.

CAPTURE SOLAR GAIN

Provide high-transmittance south-facing glazing. Provide thermal mass indoors to store solar gains.

INSULATION

Insulation requirements are proportional to heating loads. The foundation is often underinsulated and can be a major source of heat loss. The desirable insulation level depends on basement temperature and insulation levels in the rest of the building. An approximate thermal optimum is:

$$R_{ins} = \frac{T_{bsmt} - T_0}{T_1 - T_0} R_{ref} - R_{wall}$$

R_{ins} = R value to be added to basement wall above grade

R_{ref} = R value of superstructure wall

R_{wall} = R value of uninsulated basement foundation wall

T_{bsmt} = average seasonal temperature of basement

T_1 = average seasonal temperature of living space

T_0 = average seasonal outdoor temperature

The added foundation insulation above grade is R_{ins}. It should decrease with depth by R − 2 per foot in ordinary soils and R − 1.5 in wet soils. A horizontal skirt can be used to reduce floor perimeter losses. Exterior insulation keeps the wall warm and eliminates condensation and thermal bridges. As seasonal basement temperature decreases, losses to it from the superstructure increase, and basement ceiling R value should increase. As a very rough rule, the basement ceiling R value should be greater than $(R_{ref} - R_{ins})$.

SOLAR DESIGN AND DAYLIGHTING

The most advantageous south glazing area depends on thermal and climatic factors. Rules of thumb have been prepared (Los Alamos National Laboratory) and more sophisticated methods are available for desktop computers.

The advantage of glazing for daylighting has to be weighed against the penalty of winter heat loss. In predominantly cloudy climates, skylighting can be designed without significant shading, but not without concern for glare. In clear, sunny climates and in warmer regions, daylight glazing may require shading to reduce undesired heat gain. South glazing has the combined advantages of daylighting, winter heat gain, and economical summer shading.

REFERENCES

1. Los Alamos National Laboratory, *Passive Solar Heating Analysis*, ASHRAE, Atlanta, 1984.
2. National Research Council, Canada, Ottawa, Ontario, K1A OR6: *Construction Details for Air Tightness* (nonresidential), NRCC 18291, 1980; *Exterior Walls: Understanding the Problems*, NRCC 21203, 1983; *Humidity, Condensation and Ventilation in Houses*, NRCC 23293, 1984; J. Latta, *The Principles and Dilemmas of Designing Durable House Envelopes for the North*, Building Practice Note 52, 1985.

Donald Watson, FAIA; Rensselaer Polytechnic Institute; Troy, New York
Kenneth Labs, New Haven, Connecticut

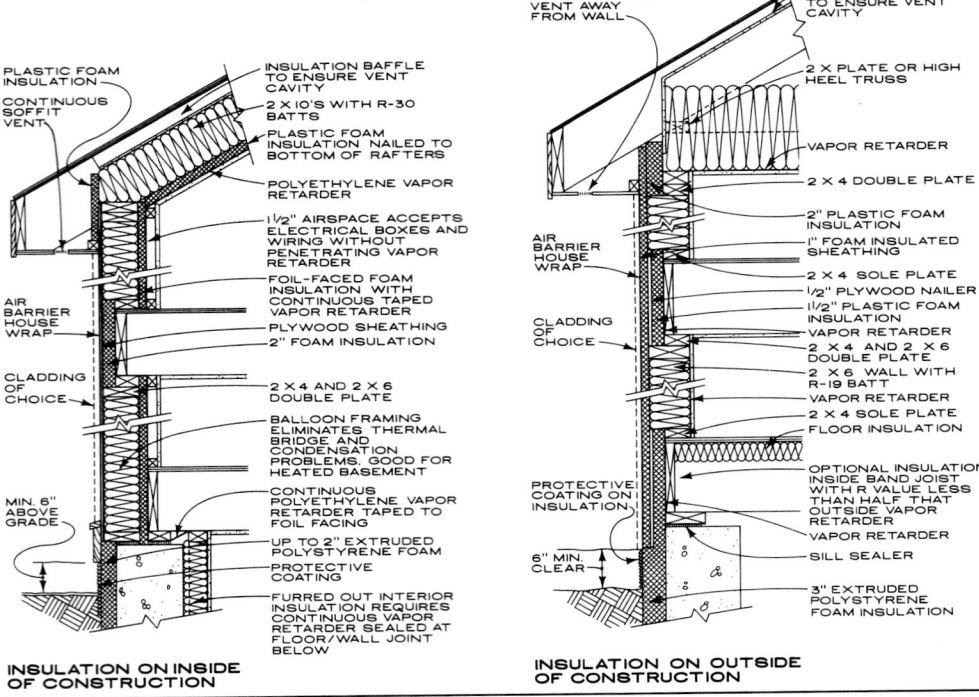

ENERGY-EFFICIENT WALL SECTIONS

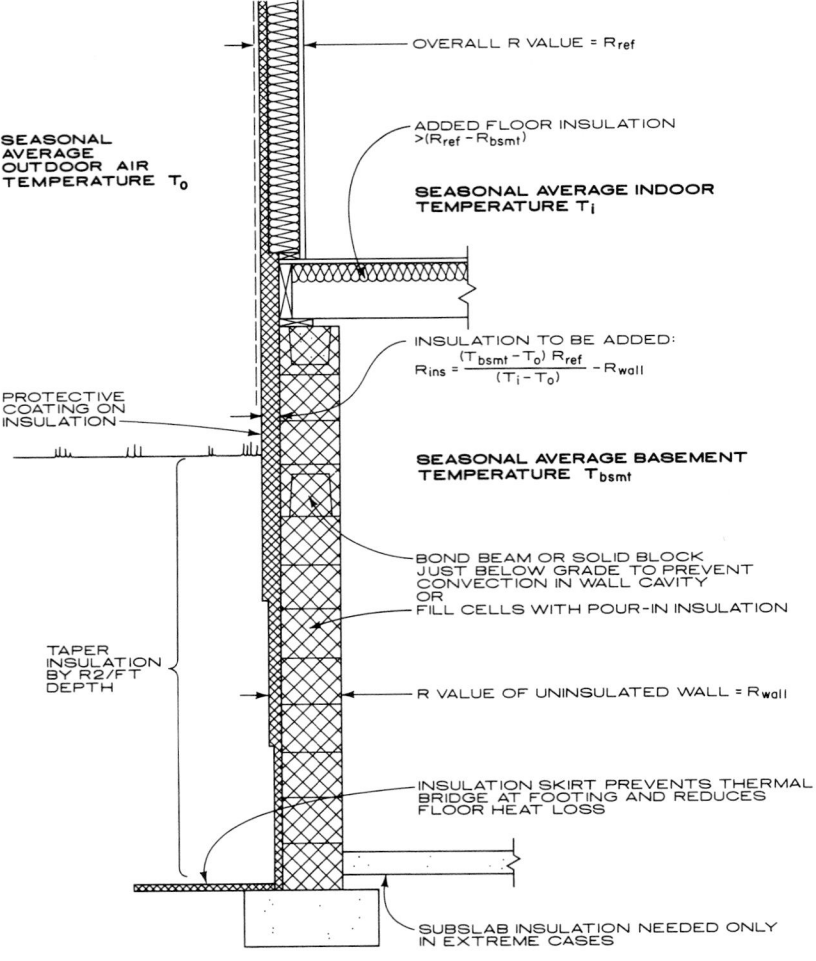

BASEMENT FOUNDATION AND FLOOR INSULATION

CLIMATE: IMPLICATIONS

Although classified as arid and overheated, severe desert climates in the United States typically have four distinct periods for determining comfort strategies. The hot dry season, occurring in late spring, early summer, and early fall, has dry, clear atmospheres that provide high insolation levels, high daytime air temperatures, very high sol-air temperatures, and large thermal radiation losses at night producing a 30 to 40°F daily range. Nighttime temperatures may fall below the comfort limits and are useful for cooling. Low humidity allows effective evaporative cooling. The hot humid season occurs in July and August. In addition to high insolation, it is characterized by high dew point temperatures (above 55°F), reducing the usefulness of evaporative cooling for comfort conditioning. Cloudiness and haze prevent nighttime thermal reradiation, resulting in only a 20°F or less daily range. Lowest nighttime temperatures are frequently higher than the comfort limits. Thus refrigeration or dehumidification may be needed to meet comfort standards. The winter season typically has clear skies, cold nights, very low dew point temperatures, a daily range of nearly 40°F, and the opportunity for passively meeting all heating requirements from isolation. The transitional or thermal sailing season occurs before and after the winter season and requires no intervention by environmental control systems. This season can be extended by the passive features of the building. Other desert climates have similar seasons but in different proportions and at cooler scales.

MINIMIZE SOLAR AND CONDUCTIVE GAINS

Solar radiation is the greatest liability to comfort conditions in this region. Summer solar intensity is highest on horizontal surfaces. A vented attic above an insulated ceiling is very effective. Ideally the entire building, both transparent and opaque surfaces, should be shaded, as well as outdoor pedestrian and living areas (ramadas and pergolas). Plant trees to shade roof and east and west walls, and to develop a modified microclimate around the building. Shape massing to minimize solar load on envelope; thus multistory schemes with narrow east-west exposures are efficient. Cluster buildings to shade one another; position carport or garage as a buffer on the west side. Use light-colored surfacing on walls and roof.

Insulate envelope components in proportion to the difference between sol-air and indoor temperatures. In addition, use radiant barriers in attic, cathedral ceilings, and walls. Perimeter insulation of slab-on-grade floors is desirable but not critical. In this region, deep-ground temperatures are too high and soil conductivity is too low for the earth to be a useful cooling sink. But low conductivity makes the soil a good buffer against surface conditions. Earth berms work.

SELECTIVE FENESTRATION

Shading of glass during the full overheated period also has the highest priority. Minimize glass on the west. Balance fenestration between north and south, although both orientations require solar control. For all uses, residential and light commercial, direct solar gain is not desired except in the coldest months. For small area windows that will be shaded, single pane glazing is acceptable. With larger areas (over 20 sq ft), in addition to the conductive heat gain, the higher inside surface temperature of single glazing raises the mean radiant temperature and adversely affects comfort. Generally fenestration should be double pane with a low "e" coating on the inside surface of the outside pane. If fenestration is unshaded, replace low "e" coating with "heat mirror," which also reduces visible transmission. Multiple glazing should have low conductance frames, using either thermal breaks, if metal, or thermally resistant materials such as wood or plastic. Clear, sunny skies make daylighting dependable and predictable for design. Although glazings with low shading coefficients block considerable insolation, they also prevent daylighting the space, thus requiring higher wattages for electric lighting. Small windows and skylight areas are effective but apertures need exterior shade to avoid solar gain and high contrast. Reflected light from the ground and from light shelves is useful, but glare from uncontrolled reflecting surfaces must be kept from view.

VENTILATION

Although nighttime breezes are slight, design for ventilation. Arrange floor plans for internal air movement, especially to cool thermal mass. Wholehouse fans, powered ventilation and economizer cycle systems are strongly recommended for accelerated night cooling.

THERMAL MASS AND INSULATION

Uninsulated Mass Construction: Vernacular house designs in hot, arid regions use low mass construction for sleeping areas, and high mass for daytime activity areas. These strategies also apply to other building types. The low mass zone is ventilated or is mechanically cooled off quickly at night, while the high massive zone has little window area and cools off slowly.

Uninsulated exterior mass delays the transfer of heat to the interior. Its usefulness depends on occupancy and space-conditioning schedules. For example, a masonry west wall can relieve an office building by delaying peak loads during business hours, but would be inappropriate for a west-facing bedroom. The delay rate of most mass materials is approximately 40 to 50 minutes per inch thickness. A completely shaded, uninsulated massive wall can do no better than maintain an average daily temperature near the outdoor average, unless the space is well ventilated at night. Uninsulated mass walls have low R values and generally are not economically suitable for heated and air-conditioned buildings. Insulating a mass wall in a composite construction is beneficial in most climates.

Adobe or rammed earth walls for thermal mass can be more expensive than poured concrete or concrete masonry units. Most economical may be full weight concrete block (not lightweight aggregate) with open cells filled by a weak sand or gravel grout to add mass and conductivity. Freestanding interior walls or partitions of mass materials allow thermal access to both sides, and they are protected from the elements (important if earthen materials).

Insulated Mass Construction: Insulation outside the mass has the greatest benefit: It reduces heat gain while allowing the wall to discharge heat during nighttime ventilation. In winter it doubles usefulness with thermal storage for passive solar heat. Insulation also allows less mass to be used to reduce interior temperature swings. Calculation of the thermal dampening, delay rate and storage dynamics of composite walls is complex and benefits from computer modeling. A minimum of 2 in. thickness and a maximum of surface area can stabilize the interior environment, whether mechanically or passively conditioned.

Insulating inside the mass or adding mass outside an insulated frame wall (brick veneer) improves performance over either case alone. Both are inferior to outside insulation and slightly less effective than walls with integral insulation (masonry with core insulation). An ideal wall would have thermal mass on both surfaces with resistance insulation between. The optimal insulation and mass combinations vary with climate and conditioning hours of the building. Carpeting on the floor slab and the use of paper faced drywall reduces the immediate thermal effect of their mass. Lightweight wall construction, if used, should have minimum R-19.

MECHANICAL EQUIPMENT

Zone cooling for two or more units of mechanical equipment to provide comfort control, minimize duct lengths, and allow partial cooling when one unit is inoperative. Thermostat setbacks can be used to discharge the thermal mass at night when costs are lower. Place outdoor equipment away from doors and windows. Because of lower efficiencies, and defrost requirements below 45°F, heat pumps are not preferred. Multiple fuel heating and cooling units are recommended. Refrigeration units should have SEER above 10. (Supply ducts sized for silence have velocities below 600 fpm, for efficiency below 1000 fpm and never more than 1500 fmp.) Ducts should be inside the insulated building envelope.

Evaporative space coolers can provide comfort more than 90% of the cooling season at elevations above 1500 ft and more than 50% of the cooling season at elevations below 1500 ft throughout the Southwest. Operating costs for electricity and water are between 25 to 30% of refrigeration. Two stage evaporative units perform well in the most demanding locations at operating costs of 30 to 35% of refrigeration but cannot provide 100% comfort during peak humid times. Evaporative cooling requires exhaust, and security is a risk if open windows are used. Exhaust through chimneys or provide secondary cooling through barometric dampers to a vented attic or ducted to attached garages or sunspaces.

Multiple speed ceiling fans over seating and beds can add to comfort choices and extend the capacities of cooling systems by providing comfort at higher temperatures.

CONSTRUCTION DETAILS

1. Coolant and refrigerant pipes from remote evaporative towers and condensers should be insulated for their entire length.
2. Roof construction similar to the cold climate roof detail is also appropriate in hot locations.
3. Exposed wood (especially in small cross sections) and many plastics deteriorate from excessive heat and high ultraviolet exposure.
4. Although vapor barriers may not be critical to control condensation, they are important as a building wrap or wind shield, both to control dust penetration and to avoid convective leaks from high temperature differentials.
5. Avoid thermal bridges such as extensive cantilevered slabs.
6. Radiant barriers and details appropriate to humid overheated climates are at least as effective, but assembly must avoid holes where convection would leak their thermal advantage.
7. Ventilate building skin (attic or roof, walls) to relieve sol-air heat transfer.

REFERENCES

K. Clark and P. Paylore, *Desert Housing: Balancing Experience and Technology for Dwelling in Hot Arid Zones*, Office of Arid Land Studies, University of Arizona, Tucson.

J. Cook, *Cool Houses for Desert Suburbs*, Arizona Solar Energy Commission, Phoenix, 1984.

A. Olgyay and V. Olgyay, *Solar Control and Shading Devices*, Princeton, 1957.

S. Byrme and R. Ritschard, "A Parametric Analysis of Thermal Mass in Residential Buildings," LBL-20288, Lawrence Berkeley Laboratory, Berkeley, CA, 1985.

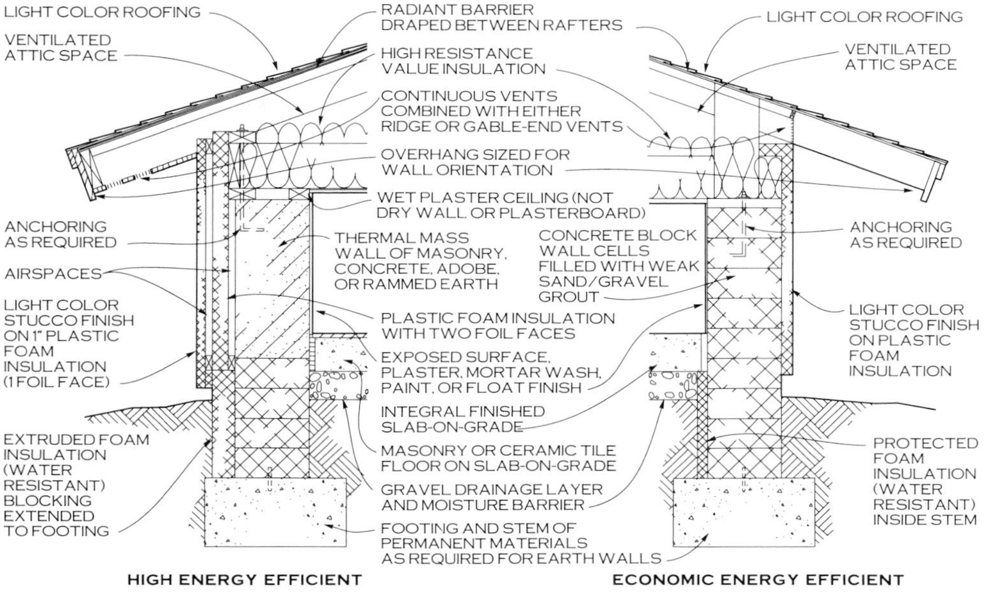

LIGHT COLOR ROOFING
VENTILATED ATTIC SPACE
RADIANT BARRIER DRAPED BETWEEN RAFTERS
HIGH RESISTANCE VALUE INSULATION
CONTINUOUS VENTS COMBINED WITH EITHER RIDGE OR GABLE-END VENTS
OVERHANG SIZED FOR WALL ORIENTATION
WET PLASTER CEILING (NOT DRY WALL OR PLASTERBOARD)
ANCHORING AS REQUIRED
AIRSPACES
THERMAL MASS WALL OF MASONRY, CONCRETE, ADOBE, OR RAMMED EARTH
CONCRETE BLOCK WALL CELLS FILLED WITH WEAK SAND/GRAVEL GROUT
LIGHT COLOR STUCCO FINISH ON 1" PLASTIC FOAM INSULATION (1 FOIL FACE)
PLASTIC FOAM INSULATION WITH TWO FOIL FACES
EXPOSED SURFACE, PLASTER, MORTAR WASH, PAINT, OR FLOAT FINISH
INTEGRAL FINISHED SLAB-ON-GRADE
EXTRUDED FOAM INSULATION (WATER RESISTANT) BLOCKING EXTENDED TO FOOTING
MASONRY OR CERAMIC TILE FLOOR ON SLAB-ON-GRADE
GRAVEL DRAINAGE LAYER AND MOISTURE BARRIER
FOOTING AND STEM OF PERMANENT MATERIALS AS REQUIRED FOR EARTH WALLS
LIGHT COLOR ROOFING
VENTILATED ATTIC SPACE
ANCHORING AS REQUIRED
LIGHT COLOR STUCCO FINISH ON PLASTIC FOAM INSULATION
PROTECTED FOAM INSULATION (WATER RESISTANT) INSIDE STEM
HIGH ENERGY EFFICIENT
ECONOMIC ENERGY EFFICIENT

TYPICAL WALL SECTIONS

Donald Watson, FAIA; Rensselaer Polytechnic Institute; Troy, New York
Jeffrey Cook; Arizona State University; Tempe, Arizona
Kenneth Labs; New Haven, Connecticut

STRATEGIES OF CLIMATE CONTROL

Humid overheated conditions are most severe along the Gulf Coast, but occur across the entire southeastern U.S. Atmospheric moisture limits radiation exchange, resulting in daily temperature ranges less than 20°F. High insolation gives first priority to shading. Much of the overheated period is only a few degrees above comfort limits, so air movement can cool the body. Ground temperatures are generally too high for the earth to be useful as a heat sink, although slab-on-grade floor mass is useful. The strategies are to resist solar and conductive heat gains and to take best advantage of ventilation.

MINIMIZE SOLAR GAINS

1. Plant trees to shade roof and east and west walls.
2. Shape building to minimize solar load on envelope.
3. Shade all glazing during overheated period.
4. Shade north elevation in subtropical latitudes.
5. Use light-colored surfacing on walls and roof.

MINIMIZE CONDUCTIVE GAINS

1. Insulate envelope components in proportion to sol-air–indoor temperature difference.
2. Use radiant barrier in attic space.
3. Consider thermally massive envelope materials to reduce peak air-conditioning loads.
4. Use slab-on-grade instead of crawl space and insulate only at perimeter.

PROMOTE VENTILATION LOSSES

1. Orient building to benefit from breezes.
2. Use plantings to funnel breezes into building, but be careful not to obstruct vent openings.
3. Use wing walls and overhangs to direct breezes into building.
4. Locate openings and arrange floor plan to promote cross ventilation.
5. Plan interior for effective use of whole-house fan.
6. Ventilate building envelope (attic or roof, walls).

SPACE VENTILATION

"Air-change ventiliation" brings outdoor temperatures indoors by breezes or whole-house exhaust fans. Whole-house fans yield about 20 air changes per hour (ACH) and are useful only as long as outdoor conditions are within comfort limits (72°–82°F). They may offer 30–50% savings in electricity costs over air conditioning. Whole-house fans do not provide high enough airflow rates for body ventilation. Ceiling (paddle) fans are recommended for air movement and can maintain comfort with indoor temperatures up to 85°F ET*. Air conditioning is necessary above 85°F ET*. The issue of when to ventilate and when to air condition is a function of building type, occupancy hours, heat and moisture capacity of the structure, and climatic subregion. Humidity is a factor, as night air may be cool but excessively humid.

ROOFS AND ATTICS

The attic should be designed to ventilate naturally. Most of the heat gain to the attic floor is by radiation from the underside of the roof. While ventilation is unable to interrupt this transfer, most of it can be stopped by an aluminum foil radiant barrier. Foil facings on rigid insulation and sheathing can be used as radiant barriers when installed facing an airspace.

Roof spray systems can dissipate most of the solar load, leaving the roof temperature near the ambient dry-bulb instead of the sol-air temperature. The theoretical lowest temperature that the roof can be cooled to by evaporation is the wet-bulb, but is not attainable under real daytime conditions. The cost-effectiveness of spray systems depends on the roof section, R value, building type, climatic region, and other factors. Spray systems are most advantageous for poorly insulated flat roofs.

WALLS

Radiant barriers enhance the performance of walls by reducing solar gain. They are most effective on east and west walls and are recommended for predominantly overheated regions [< 2000 heating degree days (HDD), >2500 cooling degree days (CDD)]. They are not recommended on south walls except where CDD exceed 3500. Radiant barriers must face an airspace and can be located on either side of the wall structure. Outside placement allows the cavity to be vented. This enhances summer wall performance, but admitting cold air degrades it during winter. Venting is recommended for regions having more than 3500 CDD. Discharging the cavity into the attic ensures best vent action. Thermal mass in walls reduces peak air-conditioning loads and delays peak heat gain. By damping off some of the peak load, massive walls help keep indoor temperatures in the range where ceiling (paddle) fans and airflow from cross ventilation provide comfort.

DAYLIGHTING

Windows and skylights should be shaded to prevent undesired heat gain. North- and south-facing glazing is shaded most easily for predictable daylighting. Light-colored reflective sunshades and ground surfaces will bounce the light and minimize direct gain. Cloudy or hazy sky conditions are a source of brightness and glare.

REFERENCES

1. S. Chandra et al. Cooling with Ventilation, Solar Energy Research Institute, Golden, CO, 1982.
2. K. E. Wilkes, Radiant Barrier Fact Sheet, CAREIRS, Silver Spring, MD.
3. P. Fairey, S. Chandra, A. Kerestecioglu, "Ventilative Cooling in Southern Residences: A Parametric Analysis," PF-108-86, Florida Solar Energy Center, Cape Canaveral, 1986.

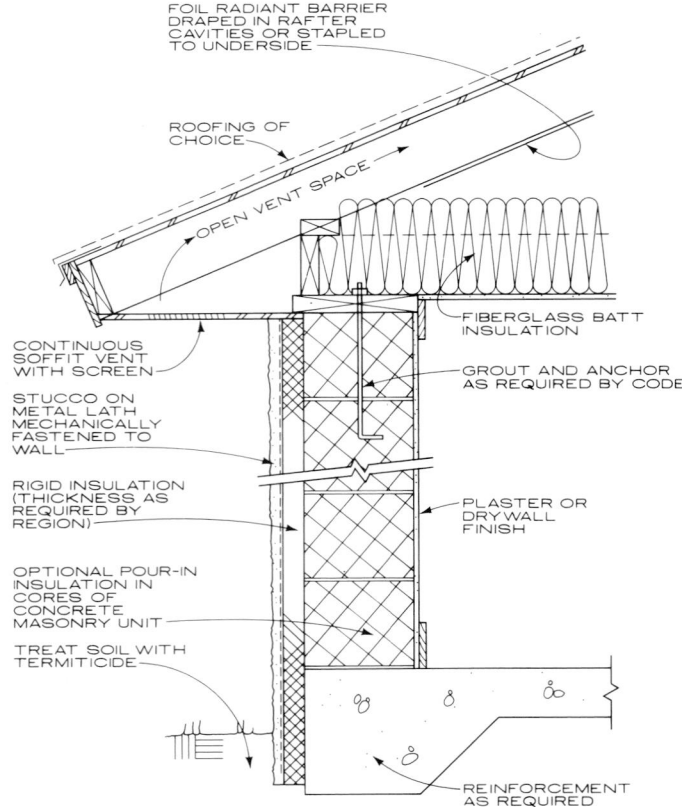

ENERGY-EFFICIENT WALL SECTION: VENTED SKIN MASONRY WALL WITH INSIDE INSULATION

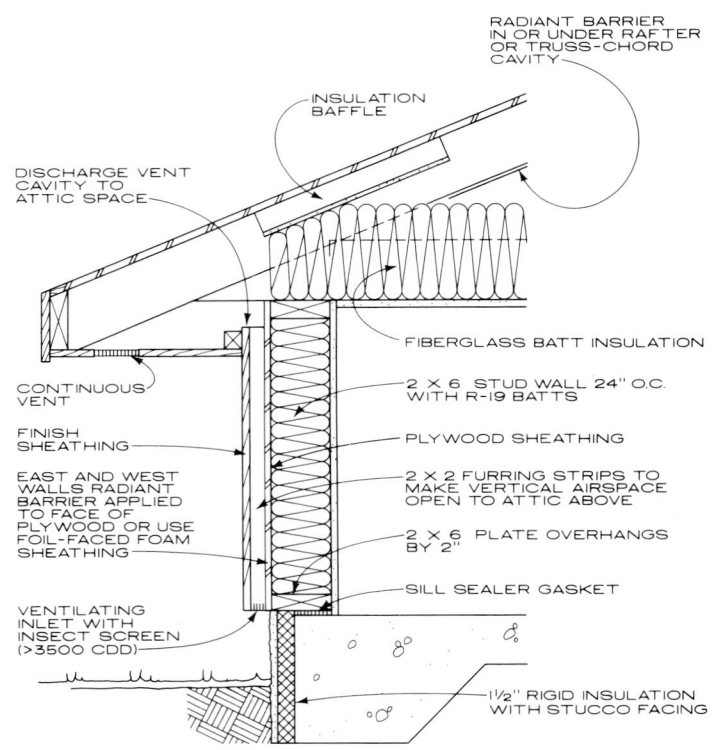

ENERGY-EFFICIENT WALL SECTION: VENTED SKIN WALL WITH RADIANT BARRIER

Donald Watson, FAIA; Rensselaer Polytechnic Institute; Troy, New York
Kenneth Labs; New Haven, Connecticut

18 CLIMATE RESPONSE AND BUILDING DESIGN

The term "alternate energy systems" describes uses of climatic resources—sun, wind, precipitation/humidity, and temperature—to provide all or part of the energy requirements of a building. Their development has paralleled the uncertain cost and availability of conventional energy supplies. New design concepts—passive solar and cooling and daylighting designs—have become part of recommended building practice. More advanced technologies have been developed, but their widespread use awaits either more experience with them or more penalizing energy prices. Some can be easily incorporated into a building design, requiring only careful design integration of architectural and heating, cooling, and lighting systems. A number of factors can change the economic constraints upon what is and is not cost-justified: the need for emergency preparedness, the prospect of interruptible or increasingly costly conventional fuel supplies, environmental pollution from fossil fuel combustion, and limited capacity of existing power plants. These concerns suggest that they be given full consideration together with energy conservation/load reduction techniques so that our long-term reliance upon conventional and nonrenewable energy sources can be minimized.

The practical approach to alternate energy system design begins with analysis of the energy requirement of the building "end use": the temperature, humidity, air flow, and lighting levels required for human comfort, and the related power demands for productive activity. The various sources for supplying heating, cooling, lighting, and electric power can then be matched to the end use in terms of "thermodynamic" efficiency, comfort, operational cost, and reliability. High levels of energy conservation and renewable energy use can make life-cycle economic gains possible, such as by downsizing mechanical system sizes or through "off-peak" loading of the building's energy requirement to reduce or eliminate "demand charges," as is possible when a building has a large energy storage system.

The figure diagrams the various alternate energy system components. The building itself is shown as an energy collection, storage, and distribution system. Choices include system components that are separate from the building (though presumably nearby) and those that must be integrated with it.

REMOTE ENERGY COLLECTORS
(ELECTRICAL)

Three contenders for alternate electric power are windmills, microhydro dams, and photovoltaic panels. Photovoltaic systems use the photons of sunlight to generate electricity across a grid of cells in a solar collector. These can be mounted on the roof of a building or can be "remote," since electricity is easily distributed from its point of collection. Site engineering concerns are major, but building design criteria are minor, limited only to storage battery location and the electric distribution system within the building. The economic viability of these choices is greatly improved by reduction of the electric load requirement achievable by energy-efficient lighting and equipment.

REMOTE ENERGY STORAGE
(THERMAL)

Energy storage near a building site has proved to be viable when the site is large enough, made part of seasonal (6-month) storage, and serves groups of buildings (district heating/cooling). These include:

Underground thermal storage: Heat generated by solar collectors (either air type or liquid type) can be stored within a large mass of earth, in existing caverns, or in newly dug clay or soil beds. In Kerava Solar Village near Helsinki, Finland, solar collectors mounted on the south-facing roofs of 44 apartments supply solar-heated water to a 400,000 gal water tank which in turn heats 338,500 cu ft of rock surrounding the tank embedded 66 ft in the earth.

Acquifier systems: A variation of thermal storage that is "charged" by solar collectors are systems using natural or man-made acquifiers for seasonal storage, thus utilizing groundwater temperature for heating and cooling, generally relying upon a water-to-water heat pump to change the groundwater temperature to the end-use requirement for heating and cooling.

Ice storage systems: Ice storage systems use ice-making, either "seasonal" for 6-month storage or "diurnal," at night for next-day use, to provide building cooling. The advantage of making ice in winter is obvious, imposing

Donald Watson, FAIA; Rensselaer Polytechnic Institute; Troy, New York

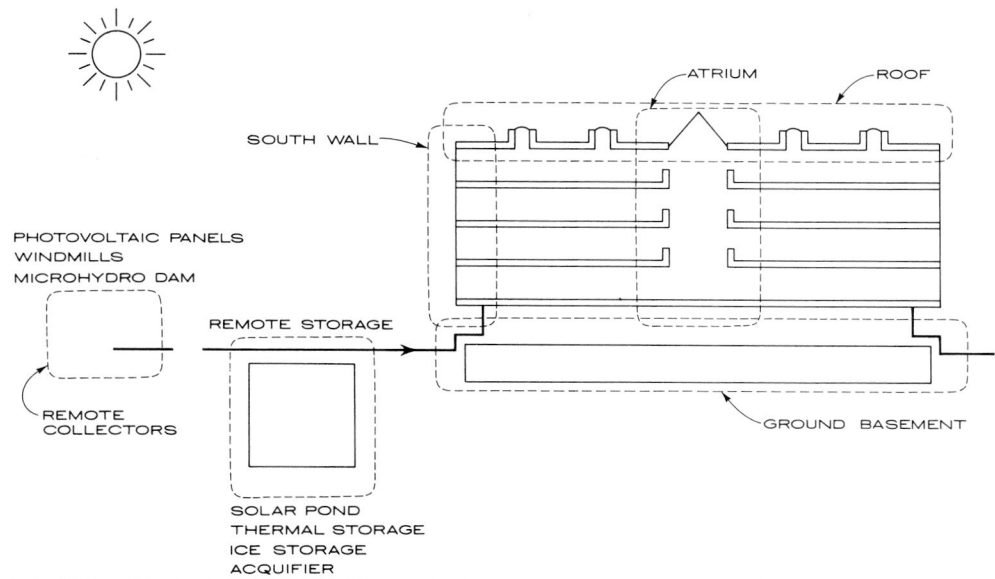

SOUTH WALL — ATRIUM — ROOF

PHOTOVOLTAIC PANELS
WINDMILLS
MICROHYDRO DAM

REMOTE STORAGE

REMOTE COLLECTORS

GROUND BASEMENT

SOLAR POND
THERMAL STORAGE
ICE STORAGE
ACQUIFIER

SITE AND BUILDING AS ENERGY COLLECTION, STORAGE, AND DISTRIBUTION SYSTEM

only the cost of a large storage area logically located within the subgrade basement of a building, but which can also be separate. Diurnal systems are cost-effective when there are advantages of "off-peak" utility rates and/or significantly cooler nighttime temperatures.

Solar ponds: Solar ponds are salt ponds that exploit the temperature gradient effect of salt water. First documented by Russian scientist von Kaleczinsky in 1902, water a few feet below a confined body of salt water reaches temperatures up to 185°F due to the varying salinity of the water: The bottom of the pond is a bed of salt in which heat is efficiently stored because heated salt-rich water does not rise, while the surface of relatively fresh water above is clear, allowing solar heat to be transmitted through it and at the same time insulating the denser layers below. In Israel and Australia, such solar ponds have been used as a source of thermal energy and to drive engines for electric generation. While only half as efficient as a solar collector, the relatively low cost of solar ponds (reportedly ten times less costly per unit of collector surface) indicates their potential.

INTEGRATED BUILDING SYSTEMS

A building designed to efficiently use climatic resources for heating, cooling, lighting, and electric power generation is properly considered an alternate energy system. Means for doing so are tabulated in the table and summarized below as a checklist for designers.

South wall: The south-facing wall of a building (in the Northern hemisphere) is an efficient energy resource. The low-angled winter sun can bring into a building interior the benefits of winter heat and light. Shading the south facade in summer can be efficiently accomplished with relatively short overhangs. Because of this, passive solar heating, summer shading, and year-round daylighting can

and ought to be made part of south-wall design. Solar heat can be stored in thermal storage placed in the sun behind glass or ducted/piped to the building interior.

Roof: The roof of a building can be used for mounting "active" solar collectors for heating, photovoltaic collectors for generating electricity, or skylights for daylighting. In hot climates, the roof is also an alternate energy resource if used for evaporative or radiant cooling.

Atrium: Atria design can be integrated into a "whole building" daylighting system and combined with the mechanical air movement system wherein it can economically replace ducting in ventilative cooling and heat recovery systems. Skylights, enhanced with light and heat reflectors, can be designed to reflect sunlight deep within a building.

Below-ground/basement: The below-ground construction of a building can be used for thermal storage, as described above. In single-storied or low-rise buildings, "ground coupling" utilizes the relatively stable temperatures of the surrounding earth to provide an economical heating/cooling flywheel effect.

OTHER ENERGY FLOWS WITHIN A BUILDING

Alternate energy design addresses all energy and resource requirements involved in building construction and use, including plant growth in interior and exterior gardens; water collection, purification, and reuse; and resource recycling and organic waste treatment/nutrient recovery. These energy flows, together with the ecological role of the surrounding landscape, are properly considered as biological system requirements of living efficiently within the limits of climate and environment.

EXAMPLES OF ENERGY-EFFICIENT ARCHITECTURAL ELEMENTS

ELEMENTS	HEATING	COOLING	LIGHTING
South wall	South-facing glass Trombe wall Sunspace	Reflective glass Sunshades	Venetian blinds Light shelf
Roof	Active solar collectors South-facing clerestories	Evaporative cooling Skytherm (radiant cooling)	Skylighting Photovoltaic collectors
Atrium	South-oriented glazing Storage mass in sun	Shaded courtyard Ventilating chimney	Light shaft Light reflectors
Ground/basement	Thermal storage	"Coolth" storage	

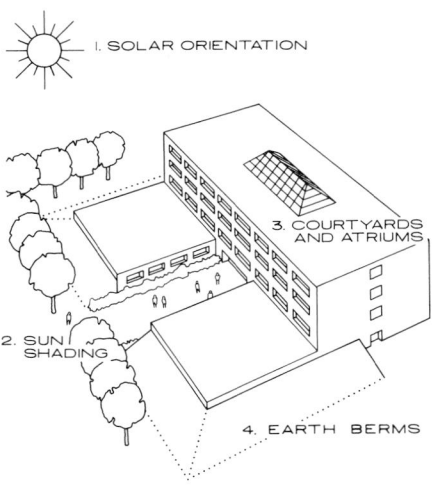

SITE PLANNING AND ORIENTATION

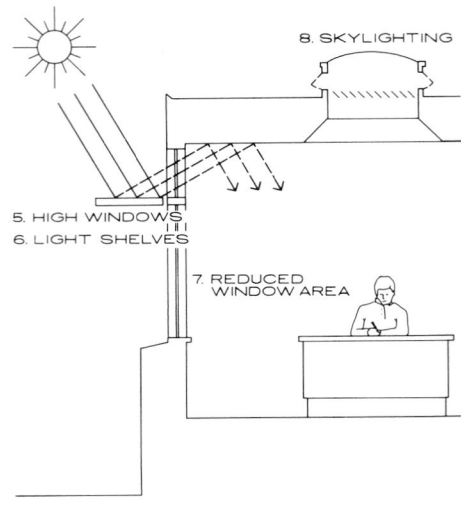

DAYLIGHTING

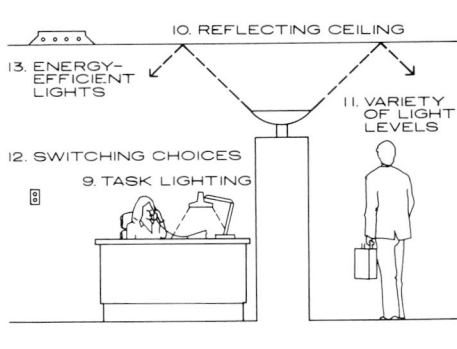

ENERGY-EFFICIENT LIGHTING

ENERGY-CONSERVING DESIGN: NONRESIDENTIAL BUILDINGS

Energy-conserving design for nonresidential buildings is justified by savings in operating costs which result in a lower "life-cycle" investment. For large buildings of all types, the best opportunities are most likely to be found in electricity costs; depending upon the demand charges of the local utility, "peak load" reduction and/or "shifting" (diurnal or seasonal) measures may prove to be cost-effective. Concurrently, lower electric use by effective daylighting and by cooling load reduction (window orientation and solar controls) will be cost-effective, since these loads are typically interrelated and use expensive forms of energy. When these loads and costs are reduced, heating cost reduction by solar and energy-conserving techniques also applies to larger buildings. Energy-conserving opportunities are best addressed by a whole-systems team approach of architecture, HVAC, lighting, and controls engineering. For example, high levels of insulation or of thermal mass may be cost justified when these also result in substantially reduced mechanical system sizes and power requirements.

The architect should consider the following items in designing an energy-efficient nonresidential building, regardless of size and building type.

SITE PLANNING AND ORIENTATION

1. ORIENT THE LONGER WALLS OF A BUILDING TO FACE NORTH–SOUTH

Walls that face the equator (e.g., the noonday sun) are ideal for windows oriented to admit daylighting with minimum cost for shading or sun control (i.e., relatively small horizontal overhangs create effective shading). Walls and windows facing east and west, on the other hand, are sources of undesirable overheating and are difficult to shade effectively. In a cool climate, windows facing the equator can gain useful wintertime heating from the sun. (See also "Daylighting" criteria.)

2. PROVIDE SUN SHADING TO SUIT CLIMATE AND USE VARIATIONS

Buildings can be located in groups to shade one another. Landscaping and sun shading can be used to shade building surfaces, especially windows, during overheated hours. Functions can be located within a building to coincide with solar gain benefit or liability. For example, cafeterias are ideally exposed to noontime winter sun in cool and temperate climates or placed in the midday shade in warm climates; low-use areas (storage areas) can be used as climatic buffers placed on the east or west in hot climates or on the north in cool climates.

3. CREATE COURTYARDS AND ENCLOSED ATRIUMS

Semienclosed courtyards (in warm climates) and enclosed atriums (in temperate and cool climates) can be formed by groups of buildings to provide areas for planting, shading, water fountains, and other microclimatic benefits. Atriums can also be used as light courts and

ventilating shafts. Indoor or outdoor planted areas provide evaporative cooling for local breezes when located near buildings.

4. USE EARTH BERMS FOR CLIMATIC BUFFERING

Earth berms (sloped or terraced, formed simply by grading earth against the wall of a building) help to buffer the building against temperature extremes of both heat and cold. The planting on earth berms also provides evaporative cooling near the building. Earth berms can be construction cost savers because the foundation does not have to be as deep (in single-storied construction); the earth and ground cover is often less costly than other wall finishing materials. Its long-term maintenance can also be lower than conventional materials.

DAYLIGHTING

5. PLACE WINDOWS HIGH IN THE WALL OF EACH FLOOR

Windows placed high in the wall near the ceiling provide the most daylight for any given window area, permitting daylight to penetrate more deeply into the interior.

6. USE LIGHT SHELVES

Light shelves are horizontal projections placed on the outside and below a window to reflect sunlight into the interior. Typically placed just above eye level, the light shelf reflects daylight onto the interior ceiling, making it a light-reflecting surface (instead of a dark, shaded surface typical of a conventional interior ceiling). At the same time, the light shelf shades the lower portion of the window, reducing the amount of light near the window, which is typically overlit. The result is more balanced daylighting with less glare and contrast between light levels in the interior.

7. SIZE WINDOWS ACCORDING TO USE AND ORIENTATION

Because window glass has little or no resistance to heat flow, it is one of the primary sources of energy waste and discomfort. Window areas should be shaded against direct solar gain during overheated hours. Even when shaded, windows gain undesired heat when the outdoor temperature exceeds the human comfort limit. Window areas should therefore be kept to a reasonable minimum, justified by clearly defined needs for view, visual relief, ventilation, and/or daylighting. Double glazing should be considered for all windows for energy efficiency and comfort in cool and temperate climates. In warm climates, double, tinted, or reflective glass should be considered, depending upon building size and use.

8. USE SKYLIGHTING FOR DAYLIGHTING, WITH PROPER SOLAR CONTROLS

Skylighting that is properly sized and oriented is an efficient and cost-effective source of lighting. Consider that for most office buildings, sunlight is available for nearly the entire period of occupancy and that the lighting re-

quirement for interior lighting is only about 1% of the amount of light available outside. Electric lighting costs, peak demand charges, and work interruptions during power brownouts can be greatly reduced by using daylight. Cost-effective, energy-efficient skylights can be small, spaced widely, with "splayed" interior light wells that help reflect and diffuse the light. White-painted ceilings and walls further improve the efficiency of daylighting (by as much as 300% if compared with dark interior finishes). Skylights should include some means to control undesired solar gain by one or more of the following means: (a) Face the skylight to the polar orientation; (b) provide exterior light-reflecting shading; (c) provide movable sunshades on the inside, with a means to vent the heat above the shade.

ENERGY-EFFICIENT LIGHTING

9. USE TASK LIGHTING, WITH INDIVIDUAL CONTROLS

Lamps for task lighting are ideally located near the work surface and are adjustable to eliminate reflective glare. The energy-efficient advantages are that less light output is required (reduced geometrically as a function of its closer distance to the task) and the lamp can be switched off when not needed.

Note: General light levels should be reduced below conventional standards and sources of reflective glare from ceiling lights and windows eliminated in areas where cathode ray tubes (CRTs) are used.

10. USE THE CEILING AS A LIGHT-REFLECTIVE SURFACE

By using "uplights," either ceiling pendants or lamps mounted on partitions and/or cabinets, the ceiling surface can be used as a light reflector. This has several advantages: (a) fewer fixtures are required for general area ("ambient") lighting; (b) the light is indirect, eliminating the sources of visual discomfort due to glare and reflection, (c) if light shelves are used, the ceiling is the light reflector for both natural and artificial light, an advantage for the occupant's sense of visual order.

11. EMPLOY A VARIETY OF LIGHT LEVELS

In any given interior, a variety of light levels improves visual comfort. Light levels can be reduced in low-use areas, storage, circulation, and lounge areas. Daylighting can also be used to provide variety of lighting, thereby reducing monotone interiors.

12. PROVIDE SWITCHING CHOICES, TO ACCOMMODATE SCHEDULE AND DAYLIGHT AVAILABILITY

Areas near windows that can be naturally lit should have continuous dimming controls to dim lights that are not needed. Other areas should have separate switching to coincide with different schedules and uses. Consider occupant-sensing light switches in areas of occasional use, such as washrooms, storage, and warehouse areas.

Donald Watson, FAIA; Rensselaer Polytechnic Institute; Troy, New York

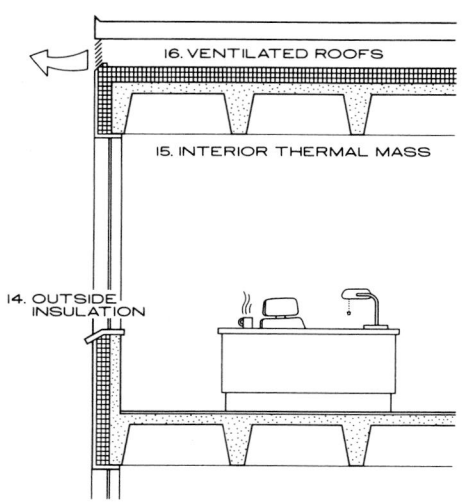

THERMAL CONSTRUCTION

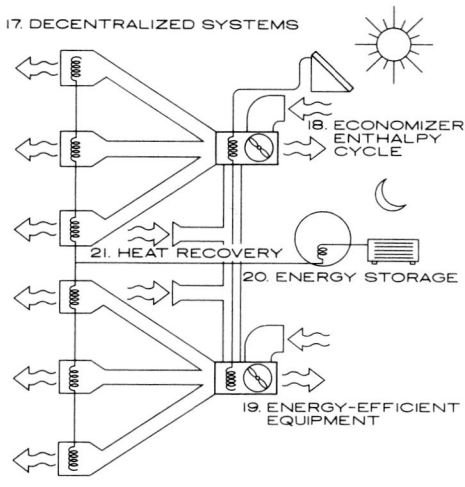

ENERGY-EFFICIENT MECHANICAL SYSTEMS

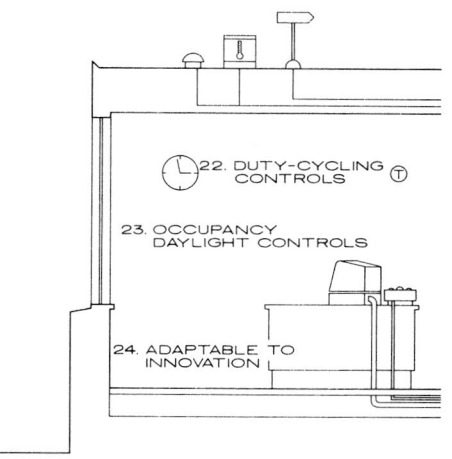

SMART BUILDING CONTROLS

13. USE ENERGY-EFFICIENT LIGHTS AND LUMINAIRES

Use the most efficient light source for the requirement: these might be fluorescent bulbs, high-intensity discharge lamps, or high-voltage/high-frequency lights. Compact fluorescent lights with high-efficiency ballasts have advantages of low wattage, low waste heat, long life, and good color rendering. Incandescent lights use less energy when switched on, so these are appropriate for occasional use and short-term lighting. Luminaires should also be evaluated for how efficiently they diffuse, direct, or reflect the available light.

THERMAL CONSTRUCTION

14. PLACE INSULATION ON THE OUTSIDE OF THE STRUCTURE

Insulation is one of the most cost-effective means of energy conservation. Insulation placed on the outer face of a wall or roof protects the structure from the extremes of the outside temperature (with the added benefit of lengthening the life of the roof waterproofing membrane) and adds the massiveness of the structure to the thermal response of the interior (see Criteria 15). In localities where "resistance insulation" is not available, the combination of airspaces and high capacitance materials (such as masonry and/or earth berms) should be designed for effective thermal dampening or time lag (the delay and diffusion of outside temperature extremes that are transmitted to the interior). As an alternative to insulating roof structures in hot climates, a "radiant barrier" consisting of a continuous sheet of reflective foil with a low emissivity coating and an airspace around it serves as an effective shield against undesired heat gain.

15. UTILIZE THERMAL MASS ON BUILDING INTERIOR

In office buildings, thermally massive construction (such as masonry and concrete which have good heat storage capacity) benefits the energy-efficient operation of heating and cooling equipment as follows:

(a) Cooling benefits: Thermal mass absorbs the "overheating" that is inevitable in an office space due to the buildup of heat from people, equipment, lighting, rising afternoon temperature, and solar gain. The more thermal mass that is effectively exposed to an interior space (ceiling and walls), the greater is the saving on air conditioning in the afternoon, with the potential to delay the overheating until early evening when electric rates may be lower and/or outdoor air may be low enough to cool the mass by night ventilation. (The "night cooling" option is especially favorable in warm, dry climates due to predictably cooler nighttime temperatures.)

(b) Heating benefits: In temperate and cool climates, thermal mass helps absorb and store wintertime passive solar heat. This is especially effective if the thermal mass is on the building interior and directly heated by the sun (made possible by design of various corridor, stairway, and half-height partition arrangements).

16. USE LIGHT-CONSTRUCTED VENTILATED ROOFS IN HOT CLIMATES

In hot climates, the roof is the primary source of undesired heat gain. Energy-efficient roof designs should be considered. One of the best for hot climates is a ventilated double roof wherein the outside layer is a light-colored and lightweight material which shades the solar heat from the inner roof, which should be well insulated. As described in Strategy 14, a "radiant barrier" can be considered as an alternative to resistance insulation to serve as a shield against thermal transfer through the ceiling portion of the roof structure.

ENERGY-EFFICIENT MECHANICAL SYSTEMS

17. USE DECENTRALIZED AND MODULAR SYSTEMS

Heating and cooling equipment is most efficient when sized to the average load condition, not the "peak" or extreme condition. Use modular unit boilers, chillers, pumps, and fans in series so that the average operating load can be met by a few modules operating at peak efficiency rather than a single unit that is oversized for normal conditions. Zone the distribution systems to meet different loads due to orientation, use, and schedule. Use variable-air-volume (VAV) systems to reduce fan energy requirements and to lower duct sizes and costs (the system can be designed for the predominant load, not the sum of the peak loads). Decentralized air-handling systems have smaller trunk lines and duct losses. Dispersed air handlers, located close to their end use, can be reduced in size from conventional system sizes if hot and chilled water is piped to them (a decentralized air-handling system with a centralized plant).

18. USE ECONOMIZER/ENTHALPY CYCLE COOLING

Economizer/enthalpy cycle cooling uses outdoor air when it is cool enough for direct ventilation and/or when the outdoor air has a lower heat content than indoor air (so that it can be cooled evaporatively without raising indoor humidity). Although useful in all climates, direct or indirect evaporative cooling systems are especially effective in hot, dry climates.

19. USE ENERGY-EFFICIENT EQUIPMENT

The energy efficiency of mechanical equipment varies greatly. Consider heat pumps for cooling and for heating to replace separate chiller and boiler units. Heat pumps can also use local water sources or water storage (see Criteria 20 below). Newly developed mechanical heating equipment, such as gas-fired pulse combustion boilers, is achieving very high (up to 85%) annual operating efficiencies.

20. USE ENERGY STORAGE FOR COOLING

Chilled water storage has several advantages: It permits water chilling or ice-making at night under more favorable ambient conditions and possible lower electric rates;

perhaps more important, it reduces or eliminates peak-hour energy consumption, thereby reducing demand charges.

21. USE HEAT RECOVERY FOR HEATING

In cool and temperate climates, heat can be recovered from warm zones of a building and recirculated to underheated areas. Recoverable heat sources include equipment, process heat, and passive solar gain. Heat recovery wheels or coils can be used where indoor air needs to be ventilated, transferring heat into the incoming fresh airstream. In all climates, process heat or active solar heat (e.g., from solar collectors) can be used for domestic hot water or for tempering incoming fresh air.

"SMART BUILDING" CONTROLS

22. USE SMART THERMOSTATS

"Duty-cycling" temperature controls can be programmed for different time schedules and thermal conditions, the simplest being the day–night setback. Newer controls are "predictive," sensing outdoor temperature trends and then selecting the system operation most appropriate to the condition.

23. USE OCCUPANCY- AND DAYLIGHT-SENSING LIGHTING CONTROLS

Automatic switching of lights according to the building occupant schedule and the daylight condition is recommended, with manual override for nighttime occupancy. Photosensors should be placed in areas that can be predictably lit by natural light.

24. BE PREPARED FOR RAPID INNOVATION IN BUILDING CONTROL SYSTEMS

Newly developing "smart" building systems include microprocessing for thermal and light control, fire and air-quality precautions, equipment failure, and operations/maintenance requirements (along with new communication and office management systems). These innovations require that electric wiring be easily changed, such as through "double-floor" construction.

REFERENCES

Burt Hill Kosar Rittelmann Associates: *Small Office Building Handbook*, New York: Van Nostrand Reinhold, 1985.

Burt Hill Kosar Rittelmann Associates: *Commercial Building Design*, New York: Van Nostrand Reinhold, 1987.

McGuiness, Stein, and Reynolds: *Mechanical and Electric Equipment for Buildings*, New York: John Wiley & Sons, 7th Edition, 1986.

Solar Energy Research Institute: *Design of Energy-Responsive Commercial Buildings*, New York: John Wiley Interscience, 1985.

Watson, Donald, editor: *Energy Conservation through Building Design*, New York: McGraw-Hill Book Company, 1979.

Donald Watson, FAIA; Rensselaer Polytechnic Institute; Troy, New York

ENERGY-EFFICIENT ATRIUM DESIGN

In its original meaning, an atrium was the open courtyard of a Roman house. Today an atrium is a glazed courtyard on the side of or within a building. If issues of heating, cooling, and lighting are ignored, atrium designs can add significantly to the energy cost of the building as well as require above-average energy to maintain comfort within them. On the other hand, energy-efficient atrium spaces can contribute savings through natural lighting, passive heating, and natural cooling strategies. (Any multistoried space raises concerns for fire safety and requires special attention.)

Atrium spaces are more responsive to the influence of the outside climate than conventional buildings, and their design therefore will follow local climate requirements. Design also will depend on the specific function and goals of the atrium: to supply daylighting for itself or to adjacent spaces; to provide comfort for sedentary human occupancy or plants; or to serve only as a semiconditioned space for circulation. The challenge of energy-efficient atrium design is to combine various and perhaps conflicting requirements for passive heating, natural cooling, and daylighting using the geometry of the atrium, its orientation, and solar and insulation controls at the glazing surfaces. These architectural choices need to be integrated with the mechanical engineering to assure that the passive energy opportunities will in fact effectively reduce building energy use.

PASSIVE SOLAR HEATING OPPORTUNITIES

Atriums designed with large glass areas overheat during the day, providing potentially recoverable heat to parts of the adjacent building, such as its outer perimeter, which can be transferred by air or by an air-to-water heat pump. In cool climates and in buildings with a predominant heat load (such as a residential or hotel structure), using this solar heat gain can be cost-effective. In such a case, vertical glass facing the south captures winter sun while incurring minimum summer heat gain liability. If the atrium space requires sedentary occupant comfort, heat storage within the space and energy-efficient glazing also are beneficial.

NATURAL COOLING OPPORTUNITIES

To reduce required cooling in an atrium, protection from the summer sun is essential. Natural cooling can be accomplished by glass orientation, protective coatings as part of the glazing, and shading devices, which may or may not be movable. In hot, sunny climates, relatively small amounts of glass can meet daylighting objectives while reducing the solar gain liability. In warm, humid climates with predominantly cloudy skies (the sky is nonetheless a source of undesirable heat gain), the north-facing orientation should be favored for large glazed areas. Mechanical ventilation should facilitate the upward flow of natural ventilation. Spot cooling by air conditioning lower atrium areas is a relatively efficient means of keeping some areas comfortable for occupancy without fully conditioning the entire volume of air.

DAYLIGHTING OPPORTUNITIES

An atrium with the predominant function to provide natural lighting takes its shape from the predominant sky condition. In cool, cloudy climates, the atrium cross-section ideally would be stepped outward as it gets higher in order to increase overhead lighting. In hot, sunny locations with clear sunny skies, the cross-section is like a large lighting fixture designed to reflect, diffuse, and make usable the light from above. Daylighting design is complicated by the movement of the sun as it changes position with respect to the building throughout the day and the year.

WINTERGARDEN ATRIUM DESIGN

Healthy greenery can be incorporated in atrium design. The designer needs to know the unique horticultural requirements for the plant species for lighting, heating, and cooling, which could be quite different from those for human occupancy. Generally, plants need higher light levels and cooler temperatures than might be comfortable for humans. The most efficient manner to keep plants heated is with plant bed or root heating, as with water tubes or air tubes in gravel or earth. Plants also benefit from gentle air movement, which reduces excessive moisture that might rot the plants and circulates CO_2 needed for growth.

RELATIVE IMPORTANCE OF DESIGN PRINCIPLES IN VARIOUS CLIMATES

ATRIUM ENERGY-DESIGN PRINCIPLE	COLD/CLOUDY SEATTLE CHICAGO MINNEAPOLIS	COOL/SUNNY DENVER ST. LOUIS BOSTON	WARM/DRY LOS ANGELES PHOENIX MIDLAND, TX	HOT/WET HOUSTON NEW ORLEANS MIAMI
HEATING				
H1 To maximize winter solar heat gain, orient the atrium aperture to the south.	●	■	△	
H2 For radiant heat storage and distribution, place interior masonry directly in the path of the winter sun.		■	●	
H3 To prevent excessive nighttime heat loss, consider an insulating system for the glazing.	●	■		
H4 To recover heat, place a return air duct high in the space, directly in the sun.	■	●	△	
COOLING				
C1 To minimize solar gain, provide shade from the summer sun.		■	■	●
C2 Use the atrium as an air plenum in the mechanical system of the building.	■	■	■	■
C3 To facilitate natural ventilation, create a vertical "chimney" effect with high outlets and low inlets.	■	■	■	●
LIGHTING				
L1 To maximize daylight, use a stepped section (in predominantly cloudy areas)	■	△		
L2 To maximize daylight, select skylight glazing for predominant sky condition (clear and horizontal in predominantly cloudy areas)	■	■	■	■
L3 Provide sun and glare control	■	■	●	■

KEY

● = Very important
■ = Positive benefit
△ = Discretionary use

REFERENCES

William M. C. Lam's *Sunlighting as Formgiver for Architecture* (Van Nostrand Reinhold, 1986) discusses accurate scale modeling to calculate the daylighting contribution of a particular atrium or lightwell design.

"Sizing Atria for Daylighting" (unpublished ms., 1986), by Virginia Cartwright, describes nomographs to estimate the daylight contribution from lightwells of various length, width, and height ratios.

Michael J. Bednar's *The New Atrium* (McGraw-Hill, 1986) discusses and provides examples of atrium design criteria, including energy, fire safety, circulation, and amenity.

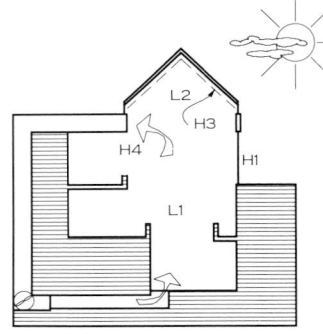

COLD/CLOUDY

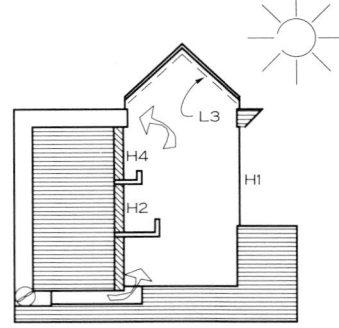

COOL/SUNNY

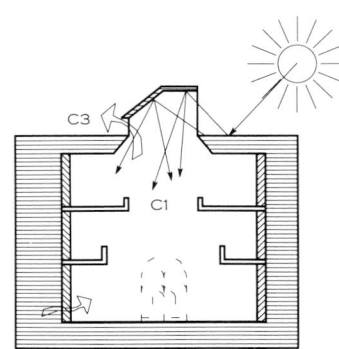

WARM/DRY

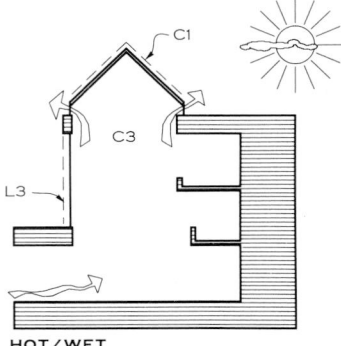

HOT/WET

Donald Watson, FAIA; Rensselear Polytechnic Institute; Troy, New York

INTRODUCTION

This page concerns thermal storage applications for heating and cooling buildings and heating domestic or service water. Nearly 80% of the energy used in buildings is for these purposes. The discussion here focuses on thermal storage in materials that are not an integral part of the building structure.

LIMITED CAPACITY HEATING/COOLING DEVICE

This includes applications where the momentary demand for heating/cooling exceeds the capacity of the heating/cooling device. In such cases thermal storage is used in conjunction with limited capacity heating/cooling equipment to meet peak demand.

LOW-COST ENERGY

The availability of low-cost energy often does not coincide with the need. Thermal storage can be charged with low-cost energy when it is available and discharged when the stored energy is needed later. A conventional heating or cooling appliance may be used to augment stored energy. Waste heat from refrigeration equipment may be useful for heating service water. Because the demand for hot water may not coincide with the availability of waste heat, waste heat storage is required.

APPLICATIONS

Limited capacity appliance: The most widespread application of thermal storage is probably that of storage-type electric resistance water heaters. A tank of water is heated by an electric resistance element that is not of sufficient capacity to heat the water during peak demand for hot water. However, enough hot water is stored so that when the peak demand occurs, there is sufficient hot water stored to satisfy demand.

By using thermal storage in conjunction with a smaller air-conditioning unit than would normally be used to handle a given cooling load, a substantial savings in operating costs can often be realized. The savings comes primarily from operating the unit at night. The lower heat rejection temperature at night means that the compressor does less work even though it accomplishes the same amount of cooling. Since the need for cooling is usually greatest during the day, the coolness generated at night must be stored for use during the day. Chilled water storage, ice reservoirs, and phase change materials are being used increasingly in buildings for coolness storage.

Off-peak power: Storage of warmth generated by off-peak power can effectively reduce operating costs. Off-peak power is often available from electric utility companies at a significantly lower cost than normal electric power. Energy storage is essential for the customer to satisfy their needs throughout the day when off-peak power is not available and yet realize the savings resulting from use of off-peak power. Off-peak rates are widely available for domestic water heating and to a lesser degree for space heating and air conditioning.

Waste heat: Without thermal storage, use of waste heat may not be feasible because waste heat is often not available when heating is needed. Heat that is normally dumped to the atmosphere from refrigeration condensers can be used to heat buildings and service water. A rapidly growing approach to waste heat recovery is the use of a heat exchanger in the refrigerant line leaving the compressor of an air conditioner.

The envelope and structure of many buildings are of sufficiently low mass that the amount of heat that can be stored in those components is so small as to be not worth the trouble. A wood-frame building is an example of a low-mass structure. A thermal storage chamber could be installed in the building to store coolness during the summer and to store heat during the winter. The chamber could be cooled during the summer by nighttime ventilation, by evaporative cooling, or by the nighttime operation of mechanical cooling equipment. During the winter the storage chamber could be heated by passive gain to the building.

Active solar heat storage: Thermal storage is usually an essential part of solar water and space heating systems. Solar heat is collected and stored during the day and released at night as needed. Commercial applications are similar.

Everett M. Barber Jr.; Guilford, Connecticut

PRINCIPAL DESIGN CONCERNS

Quality of thermal energy to be stored: Energy to be stored must be available at a temperature level sufficient for it to be useful when needed.

Suitability of storage media: Certain thermal storage materials are more appropriate than others for a given thermal storage task. For example, a phase change material (PCM) with a phase change temperature of 150°F would be inappropriate for passive solar heating/cooling because the temperatures available for storage are not that high.

Encouraging thermal gradients in the storage media: A heat source that has a much higher temperature than the heat storage media will give up its heat to that storage much more readily than will a heat source that is close to the temperature of the storage media. A similar effect occurs with storage of coolness. The greater the temperature difference between the stored energy and that needed to satisfy the load, the less energy must be expended to satisfy the load.

Interface with auxiliary heating/cooling system: It is usually not cost-effective to size a thermal storage system to handle the entire load under all conditions. Some type of auxiliary system is therefore necessary to supplement the storage system. The two systems should be configured so that the thermal storage can be drawn upon first to satisfy the entire load. Once the quality of energy in the thermal storage has been depleted to the point that it is no longer practical to use alone, then the auxiliary system can be used to augment the flow of heat from the storage media. If the thermal storage is entirely depleted, then the auxiliary system can assume the entire load.

When both thermal energy generated at off-peak rates and heat such as solar energy are to be stored, the solar heat storage should be separated from heat produced by off-peak power. If they are not separated, the electric heaters, commonly used for off-peak storage, can heat the stored energy to a temperature level above which the solar collectors would collect little useful heat.

In instances where the cost of conventional energy does not vary with the time of day, the storage and auxiliary systems should be controlled so that the relatively inexpensive stored energy is consumed before the more expensive conventional fuel. This may not be the best practice where the cost of the conventional fuel varies with the time of day.

Duration of thermal storage: The duration over which warmth or coolness is stored is an important factor. At present, thermal storage is most often used in applications of several hours' to several days' duration.

Choice of heat transfer fluid: All other factors being equal, less energy is needed to transport the same amount of heat in a system using a liquid such as water than in a system using air; that is, the pumping energy used to move water is a fraction of the fan energy needed to move the same amount of heat with air. Often factors other than pumping costs will determine the fluid to be used.

CHARACTERISTICS OF HEAT STORAGE MATERIALS

Thermal storage materials may be separated into sensible heat storage materials and phase change materials. Sensible heat storage materials such as water and rock change temperature as heat is added or removed, but they do not change in physical state. Phase change materials also change in temperature as heat is added or removed over a portion of their heating/cooling cycle, but at the temperature at which they change phase, heat can be added or removed without a change in temperature.

SENSIBLE HEAT STORAGE MATERIALS

Both water and rock are commonly used sensible heat storage materials. Water may be contained by a tank, an aquifer, a cavern or mine, or a pond. Rock is most frequently used in pebble form. Heat is added to or removed from the water while it is in liquid form and added to or removed from rock in solid form. In some types of systems the same water used to store heat can also be used as the heat transfer fluid. This precludes the cost and inefficiency inherent with heat exchangers. Where water is used for thermal storage, thermal gradients can be encouraged by the choice and location of supply and return openings to the tank, by use of a diffuser to minimize mixing of fluid entering the tank, and by use of diaphragms, baffles, segmented tanks, or multiple tanks. Containers having a high ratio of height to diameter are also useful for encouraging stratification.

Water has a higher heat capacity than pebbles; thus the volume of water needed to store a given quantity of heat is about one-third of the volume of pebbles needed.

When air is the heat transfer fluid used to charge and discharge a pebble bed, no heat exchanger is required.

Where pebbles are used for thermal storage, temperature gradients can be developed easily and preserved by charging the bed with air moving through in one direction and discharging it with air moving through in the opposite direction. An alternative approach involves charging and discharging the bed with flow in one direction only. One-way flow significantly lessens the quality of heat available from the pebble bed and results in a considerable lag before recently added heat is available from the bed.

PHASE CHANGE MATERIALS

Water is often used as a thermal storage medium for cooling buildings. If water is cooled to the freezing point, it changes phase and becomes ice. Once the water reaches its freezing point, then heat must be removed from the water until it has solidified before it can drop further in temperature.

Materials other than water exist which change phase at temperatures suitable for a variety of thermal storage applications. A given PCM can be selected because it has a phase change temperature that is suited for the temperature of the heat available to be stored and for the load.

As a PCM passes through its phase change point, it can absorb a great deal of heat. A PCM continues to absorb heat at a constant temperature until it has completely changed phase. Primarily due to their high heat capacity at the phase change temperature, PCMs store much more heat than can water or pebbles in the same volume. Thus, a phase change system takes up far less space in a building than does a sensible heat storage container to store the same quantity of useful heat.

The efficiency of a solar collector depends on the temperature difference between the collector and the surrounding air. The lower the temperature at which the collector must operate, the higher its efficiency. If a sensible heat storage medium is uniform in temperature because efforts were not made to encourage stratification, then the collectors will not operate as efficiently as they would if they were connected to a stratified storage. Since a PCM can absorb heat for a long time at the phase change point, a solar collector delivering heat to a PCM can often operate more efficiently than it would if it were delivering heat to a sensible heat storage container at a uniform temperature.

SYSTEM SIZING

The variation of the load over time must be known or estimated. The temperature level of the energy needed to satisfy the load must be known. An estimate must be made of the amount of heat available for storage and of the temperature level of that heat.

A number of computer programs exist that can be used to estimate the heating and cooling load of residential and small commercial buildings. Several such programs are EEDO, CALPASS, SLR, and FLOAD. For large buildings the most well-documented, verified, and maintained computer program for building energy requirement estimating is DOE2.1c. The program has a separate thermal storage module that can be used for thermal storage studies.

REFERENCE

For detailed information on thermal storage design, see R. L. Cole et al.: "Design and Installation Manual for Thermal Energy Storage," Argonne National Laboratory Report No. ANL-79-15, second edition, 1980.

ENERGY ANALYSIS

An energy analysis can be accomplished by a variety of techniques: manual, graphic, calculator, microcomputer, and mainframe computer. The purpose of energy analysis is to evaluate mathematically the energy required to maintain the interior environment of proposed or existing buildings and their support systems. When estimating energy needs of a proposed or existing building, it is necessary to account for the energy use in each of the following categories:

1. Offsetting heat losses through the building envelope (heating).
2. Offsetting heat gains through the building envelope (cooling).
3. Heating or cooling ventilation air.
4. Offsetting or using heat gain from occupants, lights, and process loads.
5. Offsetting or using solar gain.
6. Energy required for lights and miscellaneous use.
7. Motor loads for air movement and energy transfer.
8. Heating domestic hot water.
9. Energy used to reheat and recool.
10. Energy for humidification and dehumidification.
11. Energy for vertical, horizontal movement of people.
12. Miscellaneous—convenience outlets, etc.
13. Food service.

With the wide range of energy analysis tools available, it is important to select the appropriate tool for each design stage. Less sophistication is needed in the early design stages than in the final stages. To obtain maximum benefit from energy analysis, the process should start in the early schematic design stages. Following is a possible energy analysis sequence.

SCHEMATIC DESIGN PHASE

Calculated manually, graphically, or with simple computer programs, analysis in the schematic design phase should take into consideration building orientation and solar and daylighting impact on the energy required for heating, cooling, and lighting. The ideal analysis tool is a microcomputer program that permits the designer to incorporate more and more data about the building as the design progresses, without reentering previous data. Results of the schematic analysis should guide the designer in deciding on orientation, massing, and building configuration. The decision made in these early studies will have a major impact on optimum energy use in the final design.

DESIGN DEVELOPMENT PHASE

As design decisions become final and construction materials are selected, the energy analysis should be upgraded. The analysis procedure should allow adjustments for daylighting and building mass. Operating, occupancy, lighting, and motor profiles should be accommodated. Also to be considered are mechanical equipment responses and ventilation loads. As a minimum, the analysis procedure should include a variable base degree hour or bin factor for weather data.

CONSTRUCTION DOCUMENT PHASE

As the construction documents near completion, a more sophisticated analysis can be made. An hour-by-hour analysis can be made by a mainframe computer. The mechanical equipment can be modeled as it would respond to the hourly heating and cooling loads. Thus, energy wasted by mechanical systems is accounted for. Profiles of building operation, occupancy, lighting, etc. are adjusted to the final design, and the energy needs projection is close to that of the final building.

Energy analysis for existing buildings being modified or recycled can be done by any of the above procedures that track building operation, occupancy, lighting, ventilation, and motor profiles. This can be done by mainframe computers on an hour-by-hour analysis or by microcomputers using programs with a variable base degree hour or bin method of processing weather data. Existing buildings are easier to analyze than new buildings because operational profiles are known.

For an energy analysis to provide maximum benefit to the designer, the building's annual energy use should be broken down as in the example at right. As modifications are made, projected increase or decrease percentages should be shown.

EXAMPLE OF TOTAL ANNUAL ENERGY USE BY FUEL TYPE	ENERGY USE PER YEAR	PERCENT OF TOTAL	REDUCTION IN ENERGY USE	PERCENT OF REDUCTION
ELECTRICITY (In kilowatt hours)				
Cooling	42,424 KWH	(16.3%)	−16,753 KWH	(28.3%)
Lighting	150,573 KWH	(58.0%)		
Motor operation	58,829 KWH	(22.7%)	−21,598 KWH	(26.9%)
Miscellaneous power	7,781 KWH	(3.0%)		
TOTAL ELECTRICAL USE	259,607 KWH		−38,351 KWH	(12.9%)
NATURAL GAS (In thousands of square feet)				
Heating	1,397 MCF	(84.8%)	−1,863 MCF	(57.1%)
Domestic water heating	58 MCF	(3.5%)		
Food service	193 MCF	(11.7%)		
TOTAL NATURAL GAS USE	1,648 MCF		−1,863 MCF	(53.1%)
BREAKDOWN OF TOTAL ANNUAL ENERGY USE				
HEATING (In millions of BTU)				
Roof loss	877.8 MMBTU	(34.0%)	−719.0 MMBTU	(45.0%)
Wall loss	127.1 MMBTU	(4.9%)	−104.1 MMBTU	(45.0%)
Window loss	26.2 MMBTU	(1.0%)	−21.5 MMBTU	(45.0%)
Door loss	115.2 MMBTU	(4.5%)	−94.3 MMBTU	(45.0%)
Slab Edge loss	77.3 MMBTU	(3.0%)	−63.3 MMBTU	(45.0%)
Infiltration loss—doors	166.2 MMBTU	(6.4%)	−136.2 MMBTU	(45.0%)
Ventilation loss	0.1 MMBTU	(0.0%)	−812.9 MMBTU	(100.0%)
Morning warm-up	49.1 MMBTU	(1.9%)	+32.7 MMBTU	(200.0%)
TOTAL	1,439.1 MMBTU	(55.7%)	−1,918.4 MMBTU	(57.1%)
COOLING (In millions of BTU)				
Conduction solid surfaces	13.9 MMBTU	(0.5%)	−1.4 MMBTU	(9.0%)
Conduction glazed surfaces	2.9 MMBTU	(0.1%)	−0.3 MMBTU	(9.0%)
Solar gain	27.8 MMBTU	(1.1%)	+0.3 MMBTU	(1.1%)
Ventilation gain	0.1 MMBTU	(0.0%)	−55.8 MMBTU	(99.9%)
Lighting gain	39.0 MMBTU	(1.5%)	+1.3 MMBTU	(3.4%)
Equipment gain	4.1 MMBTU	(0.2%)		
Occupant gain	35.7 MMBTU	(1.4%)	+1.6 MMBTU	(4.7%)
Air handler gain	21.4 MMBTU	(0.8%)	−2.8 MMBTU	(11.5%)
TOTAL	144.8 MMBTU	(5.6%)	−57.2 MMBTU	(28.3%)
LIGHTING (In millions of BTU)	513.9 MMBTU	(19.9%)		
MOTOR OPERATION (In millions of BTU)	200.8 MMBTU	(7.8%)	−73.7 MMBTU	(26.9%)
DOMESTIC WATER HEATING (In millions of BTU)	60.0 MMBTU	(2.3%)		
MISCELLANEOUS USE (In millions of BTU)				
Convenience electric power	26.6 MMBTU	(1.0%)		
Food Service	198.3 MMBTU	(7.7%)		
TOTAL	224.8 MMBTU	(8.7%)		
TOTAL ANNUAL ENERGY USE (In millions of BTU)				
70,147 BTU/per sq. ft.	2,583.4 MMBTU	TOTAL	−2,049.3 MMBTU	(44.2%)

ANALYSIS PROCEDURE CAPABILITY AT VARIOUS DESIGN STAGES

CONCEPT	ANALYSIS MODE	DESIGN STAGE		
		SCHEMATIC	DESIGN	CONSTRUCTION
Orientation	M,G,MC	X	X	X
Solar	M,G,MC	X	X	X
Daylighting	M,G,MC	X	X	X
Configuration	G	X	X	X
Mass	MC		X	X
Oper. profiles	M,MC		X	X
Occup. profiles	M,MC		X	X
Light. profiles	M,MC		X	X
Motor profiles	M,MC		X	X
Mech. response	MC,MF			X
Hourly analysis	MF			

M = Manual   MC = Microcomputer
G = Graph   MF = Mainframe

COMPONENTS OF ENERGY USE IN BUILDING

COMPONENT	ENERGY LOADS			IMPACT TOTAL
	HEATING ENERGY	COOLING ENERGY	OTHER ENERGY	
Building envelope	+	+		+
Solar gain	−	+		+ or −
Ventilation	+	+		+
Occupants	−	+		+ or −
Lights	−	+	+	+
Motors	−	+	+	
Domestic hot water	0	0	+	+
Reheat	+	0		+
Recool	0	+		+
Humidification	+	0		+
Dehumidification		+		+
Vertical and horizontal movement of people	0	0	+	+

+   Add to load
−   Reduces load
0   Has no impact

Huber H. Buehrer, AIA, PE; Buehrer Group; Maumee, Ohio

18   **ENERGY CONSERVATION**

PASSIVE SOLAR DESIGN

Passive solar heating and cooling systems, which rely on natural energy flow through and around a building, are divided into three generic categories, including:

1. DIRECT SYSTEMS: Heat is collected directly within the space or, for cooling, lost or dissipated directly from the space.
2. INDIRECT SYSTEMS: Heat gain or loss occurs at the weatherskin.
3. ISOLATED SYSTEMS: Heat gain or loss occurs away from the weatherskin. Cooling, for example, can include induced air precooled from the earth's mass using air to earth heat exchangers ("coolth" tubes) or cooling ponds.

Systems can be combined depending on thermal needs.

SPACE HEATING CONCEPTS

As part of any passive system's development, energy conservation elements should be considered. With passive solar heating, minimizing and preventing heat loss is fundamental to ensure that the heating system is most effective. These elements include adequate insulation, building orientation, surface-to-volume ratios, and appropriate materials, texture, and finish choices. The space heating success depends on adequate solar energy collection, storage, distribution, and control, all of which occur by natural, nonchemical means using the three basic heat transfer processes: conduction, convection, and radiation. Efficient passive system operation often involves some user control to alter or override energy flows within a building or at its weatherskin.

1. Solar collection surfaces generally are transparent or translucent plastics, fiberglass, or glass oriented in a southerly direction. Material degradation can be caused by solar exposure and other weather elements. Insulating these collection areas to control nighttime loss is especially important in extreme climates.
2. Thermal storage materials include concrete, brick, sand, tile, stone, and water or other liquids. Phase change materials such as eutectic salts and paraffins also are feasible. Storage should be placed to receive maximum solar exposure, either directly or indirectly. Adequate thermal storage capacity allows the sun's heat to be absorbed and retained until it is needed, and it helps to reduce internal temperature fluctuations.
3. Heat distribution occurs naturally by conduction, convection, and radiation. Generally, fans and other mechanical energy distribution equipment are avoided; however, sometimes they are required for fine-tuned operations.
4. Control mechanisms such as vents, dampers, movable insulation, and shading devices can assist in balanced heat distribution.

SPACE COOLING CONCEPTS

Passive solar cooling, like passive heating, tempers interior space temperatures using natural thermal phenomena. A structure designed for natural cooling should incorporate features that reduce external heat gains and dissipate internal heat gains, including adequate insulation, overhangs, shading, orientation, surface color and texture, proper ventilation, and similar factors. When possible, external heat gain should be controlled before it reaches or penetrates the weatherskin.

When cooling is necessary, heat dissipation is accomplished by cooling interior thermal mass, air, or both with conduction, convection, and radiation. Evaporation in hot arid regions and dehumidification in hot humid regions are primary cooling design concerns. Many passive cooling concepts and methods exist:

1. Site cooling: through vegetative control, water bodies, and adjacent land forms and materials.
2. Earth cooling: by using groundwater or the earth's mass with earth sheltering or "coolth" tubes.
3. Radiative cooling: heat loss to the sky or cooler objects.
4. Ventilative cooling: cross ventilation through spaces, double roofs, attics, or walls, induced or forced ventilation by pressure or temperature differences.
5. Vapor cooling: evaporative cooling to remove sensible heat, dehumidification to remove latent heat.
6. Flywheel cooling: cooling by internal thermal mass or rockbeds.

PASSIVE SOLAR TYPES

		HEATING	COOLING
DIRECT SYSTEMS	**DIRECT GAIN/LOSS** Direct gain is the most common passive solar building approach; most structures use it to some degree. Collection and storage are integral with the space. Southerly oriented glazing (collector) admits winter solar radiation to the space beyond. Thermal storage, incorporated within the building structure, absorbs solar energy. During the cooling season, windows, walls, and roofs can be operable or openable for natural or induced ventilation, cooling both the mass and space.		
INDIRECT SYSTEMS	**THERMAL STORAGE WALL — MASS WALL** Thermal storage walls are based on a "sun to mass to space" concept. Collection and storage are separated from the space, but linked thermally. Energy is transferred by conduction through the wall, then by radiation to the space. A mass wall can be vented during the day, if warranted, to the interior by a convective heat flow. (If vents are used, then the mass wall is often referred to as a Trombe wall.) In the mass wall system, storage usually is in masonry or concrete directly behind the south glazing. Mass walls should be vented to the exterior and shaded during summer months.		
	THERMAL STORAGE WALL — WATER WALL Water wall systems use a liquid, often held in barrels or tubes directly behind south-facing glass acting as the thermal storage medium. Solar radiation is absorbed by the contained water. This energy is released gradually as needed to the interior. Potential water problems are corrosion and bacteria and algae growth. A water wall should be shaded or vented to the exterior during cooling periods. Provide freeze protection where required.		
	ROOF POND In a roof pond system the liquid storage mass is in the ceiling or roof. During heating seasons, insulation panels are moved to expose the storage mass to the sun in the day. Energy is absorbed by the roof pond. At night the panels are replaced over the storage, allowing stored heat to radiate to the building's interior. The process is reversed in summer. The roof pond, insulated from the high summer sun during the day, absorbs the building's internal heat. At night the insulation is opened to allow stored heat to radiate to the sky.		
ISOLATED SYSTEMS	**SUNSPACE** In sunspace designs, solar collection and primary thermal storage often are isolated from living spaces, although variations are possible. The solar system functions independently of the building interior, although heat can be drawn from the sunspace as needed. (Thermal storage in the living area is classed as an indirect system.) Even on clear winter days sunspaces may overheat sometimes because of large glazed areas. For cooling, the sunspace can be used to induce a convective flow from the exterior, and should be shaded, preferably on the exterior.		
	THERMOSIPHON Thermosiphon, natural convection systems, rely on the rise and fall of heated and cooled elements such as air. As temperatures change, air moves without mechanical assistance. When the sun warms a collector surface, warm air rises. Simultaneously cooler air is pulled from the storage bottom, causing a natural convection loop. Heat is convected into the space or stored in the thermal mass until needed. In cooling seasons, collectors may be used as a thermal chimney. Warm air rises, inducing precooled air from the ground or other source up through the storage mass to cool it.		

Dennis A. Andrejko, AIA; Andrejko & Associates; Williamsville, New York

PASSIVE SOLAR HEATING—DESIGN PROCEDURE

The focus of this section is on winter heating between U.S. latitudes 32°N and 48°N. The following design and calculation procedure is applicable to

1. Building types that have space heating requirements dominated by heat loss through the exterior skin of the building.

2. Buildings with a small internal heat contribution from lights, people, and equipment such as residences, small commercial, industrial, and institutional buildings, and large daylit buildings whose internal heat gain is only a small portion of their total heating requirement.

Passive solar heating systems are integral to building design. The concepts relating to system operation must be applied at the earliest stages of design decision making.

Passive systems demand a skillful integration of all the architectural elements within each space—glazing, walls, floor, roof, and in some cases even interior surface colors. The way in which the glazing and thermal mass (heat storage materials, i.e., masonry, water) are designed generally determines the efficiency and level of thermal comfort provided by the system. Two concepts are critical to understanding the thermal performance of passively heated space. They are

1. That the quantity of south glazing, insulating properties of the space, and the outdoor climatic conditions will determine the number of degrees the average indoor temperature in a space is above the average outdoor temperature on any given day (ΔT).

2. That the size, distribution, material, and in some cases (direct gain systems) surface color of thermal mass in the space will determine the daily fluctuation above and below the average indoor temperature (see Figure 1).

Calculating heat gain and loss is a relatively straightforward procedure. The storage and control of heat in a passively heated space, however, is the major problem confronting most designers. In the process of storing and releasing heat, thermal mass in a space will fluctuate in temperature, yet the object of the heating system is to maintain a relatively constant interior temperature. For each system, the integration of thermal mass in a space will determine the fluctuation of indoor temperature over the day.

EXAMPLE

In a direct gain system, with masonry thermal mass, the major determinant of fluctuations of indoor air temperature is the amount of exposed surface area of masonry in the space; in a thermal storage wall system, it is the thickness of the material used to construct the wall. The following is a procedure for sizing both direct gain and thermal storage wall systems.

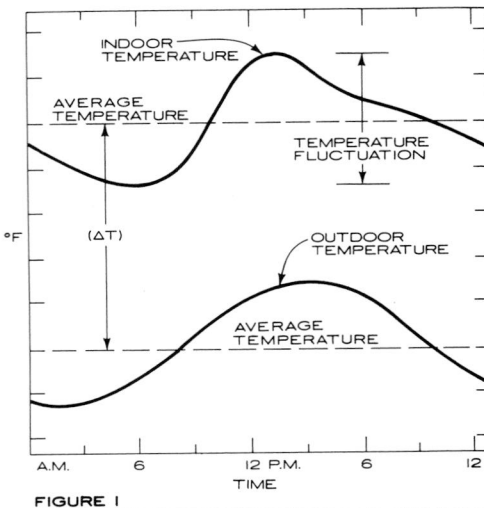

FIGURE I
DAILY TEMPERATURE FLUCTUATION

DIRECT GAIN

Direct gain systems are characterized by daily fluctuations of indoor temperatures, which range from only 10°F to as much as 30°F. The heating system cannot be turned on or off, since there is little control of natural heat flows in the space. To prevent overheating, shading devices are used to reduce solar gain, or excess heat is vented by opening windows or activating an exhaust fan.

The major glass areas (collector) of each space must be oriented to the south (±30°) for maximum solar heat gain in winter. These windows can serve other functions as well, such as openings for light and for views.

Each space must also contain enough mass for the storage of solar heat gain. This implies masonry in the building, but the masonry can be as thin as 4 in. in cold climates and 1½–2 in. in very mild climates.

SOUTH GLAZING: One criterion for a well-designed space is that it gains enough solar energy, on an average sunny day in winter, to maintain an average space temperature of ±68°F over the 24-hr period. By establishing this criterion, it is possible to develop ratios for the preliminary sizing of south glazing. Table 1 (see next page) lists ratios for various climates and locations.

In a direct gain system, sunlight can also be admitted into a space through clerestories and skylights as well as vertical south-facing windows. This approach may be taken (1) for privacy, (2) because of shading on the south

facades, (3) because spaces are located along facades other than south, and (4) to avoid direct sunlight on people and furniture. Use the following guidelines when designing clerestories and skylights:

1. CLERESTORY: Locate the clerestory at a distance in front of interior mass wall of roughly 1 to 1.5 times the height of the clerestory above the finished floor. Make the ceiling of the clerestory a light color to reflect and diffuse sunlight down into the space. In regions with heavy snowfall, locate the sill of the clerestory glazing 18 in. or more above the roof surface (see Figure 2, next page).

2. SAWTOOTH CLERESTORIES: Make the angle (as measured from horizontal) equal to or smaller than the altitude of the sun at noon on December 21, the winter solstice. Make the underside of the clerestories a light color (see Figure 3, next page).

3. SKYLIGHT: Use a south-facing or horizontal skylight with a reflector to increase solar gain in winter, and shade both horizontal and south-facing skylights in summer to prevent excessive solar gain (see Figure 4, next page).

THERMAL STORAGE MASS: The two most common materials used for storing heat are masonry and water. Masonry materials transfer heat from their surface to the interior at a slow rate. If direct sunlight is applied to the surface of a dark masonry material for an extended period of time, it will become uncomfortably hot, thereby

giving much of its heat to the air in the space rather than heat conducting it away from the surface for storage. This results in daytime overheating and large daily temperature fluctuations in the space. To reduce fluctuations, direct sunlight should be spread over a large surface area of masonry. To accomplish this:

1. Construct interior walls and floors of masonry at least 4 in. in thickness.

2. Diffuse direct sunlight over the surface area of the masonry either by using a translucent glazing material—placing a number of small windows so that they admit sunlight in patches—or by reflecting direct sunlight off a light-colored interior surface first (see Figure 5, next page).

3. Use the following guidelines for selecting interior surface color and finishes:
   a. Masonry floors of a medium to dark color.
   b. Masonry walls of any color.
   c. Lightweight construction (little thermal mass) of a light color to reflect sunlight onto masonry surfaces.
   d. No wall-to-wall carpeting over masonry floors.

By following these recommendations, one can control temperature fluctuations in the space on clear winter days to approximately 10°–15°F. These temperature fluctuations are for clear winter days and for at least 6 sq ft of exposed masonry surface area for each square foot of south glazing.

THERMAL STORAGE WALLS

The predominant architectural expression of a thermal storage wall building is south-facing glass. The glass functions as a collecting surface only and admits no natural light into the space. However, windows can be included in the wall to admit natural light and direct heat and to permit a view.

Either water or masonry can be used for a thermal storage wall (a masonry thermal storage wall with thermocirculation vents is often referred to as a Trombe wall). Since the mass is concentrated along the south face of the building, there is no limit to the choice of construction materials and interior finishes in the remainder of the building.

SOUTH GLAZING: The criterion for a double-glazed thermal storage wall is the same as for a direct gain system—that it transmit enough heat on an average sunny winter day to supply a space with all its heating needs for that day. Tables 1 and 2 (see next page) list guidelines for sizing the glazing of masonry or water walls, respectively.

WALL DETAILS: While the procedure above gives guidelines for the overall size (surface area) of a thermal storage wall, the efficiency of the wall as a heating system depends mainly on its thickness, material, and surface color. (See Table 3, next page.) If the wall is too thin, the space will overheat during the day and be too cool in the evening; if it is too thick, it becomes inefficient as a heating source, since little energy is transmitted through it.

The choice of wall thickness, within the range given for each material in Table 3 (see next page), will determine the air temperature fluctuation in the space over the day. As a general rule, the greater the wall thickness, the smaller the indoor fluctuation. Table 4 (see next page) can be used to select a wall thickness.

The greater the absorption of solar energy at the exterior face of a thermal wall, the greater the quantity of incident energy transferred through the wall in the building. Therefore, make the outside face of the wall dark (preferably black) with a solar absorption of at least 85%.

Edward Mazria, AIA, Architect; Edward Mazria & Associates; Albuquerque, New Mexico

PASSIVE SOLAR

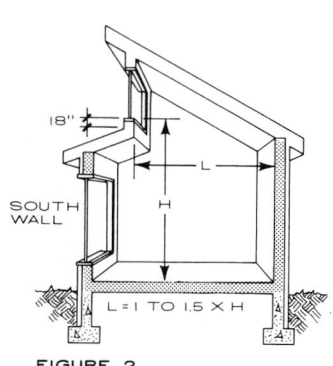

FIGURE 2.
CLERESTORY

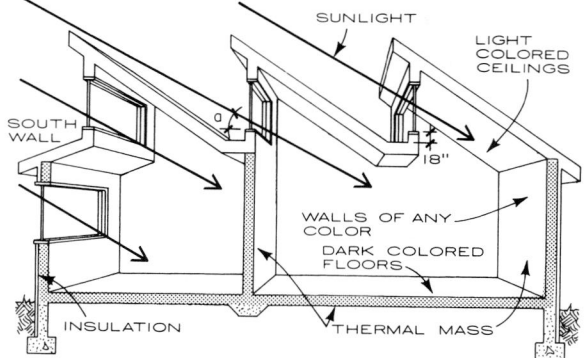

FIGURE 3. SAWTOOTH CLERESTORIES

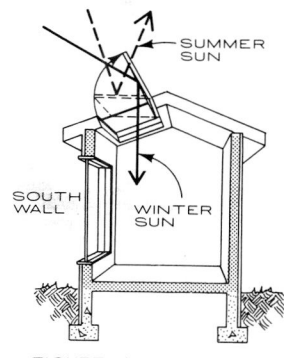

FIGURE 4.
SKYLIGHT

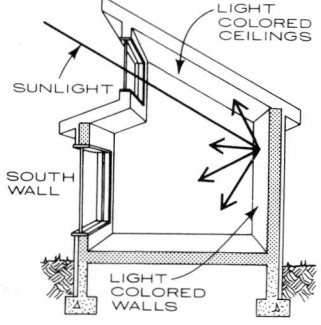

FIGURE 5.
REFLECTING DIRECT
SUNLIGHT

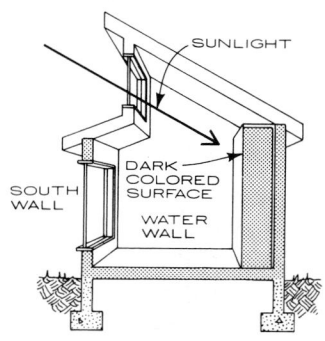

FIGURE 6.
WATER WALL

DIRECT GAIN SYSTEMS

TABLE 1. SIZING SOLAR GLAZING FOR DIRECT GAIN, VENTED TROMBE WALL, AND WATER WALL SYSTEMS

| | SQUARE FEET OF GLAZING NEEDED FOR EACH SQUARE FOOT OF FLOOR AREA | | | |
| | 36°F NL | | 44°F NL | |
AVERAGE WINTER TEMPERATURE (CLEAR DAY)	LOW HEAT LOSS	HIGH HEAT LOSS	LOW HEAT LOSS	HIGH HEAT LOSS
Cold climates				
20°F	0.23	0.46	0.30	0.60
25°F	0.18	0.37	0.23	0.46
30°F	0.15	0.30	0.17	0.34
Temperate climates				
35°F	0.12	0.23	0.13	0.26
40°F	0.09	0.18	0.10	0.20
45°F	0.06	0.13	0.08	0.15

NOTES

1. Convective connections to building.
2. Temperatures listed are for December and January (usually the coldest months) and are monthly averages.
3. Low heat loss: Space with a net load coefficient (NLC) = 3 Btu/day/sq ft/°F. A space with little exposed external surface area.
4. High heat loss: Space with an NLC = 6 Btu/day/sq ft/°F. A space with a large amount of exposed external surface area.
5. The NLC is the total building heat loss less the loss through the solar aperture.

TABLE 2. SIZING SOLAR GLAZING FOR UNVENTED MASONRY THERMAL STORAGE WALL SYSTEMS

| | SQUARE FEET OF GLAZING NEEDED FOR EACH SQUARE FOOT OF FLOOR AREA | | | |
| | 36°F NL | | 44°F NL | |
AVERAGE WINTER TEMPERATURE (CLEAR DAY)	LOW HEAT LOSS	HIGH HEAT LOSS	LOW HEAT LOSS	HIGH HEAT LOSS
Cold climates				
20°F	0.33	0.66	0.43	0.85
25°F	0.30	0.60	0.35	0.70
30°F	0.26	0.52	0.30	0.60
Temperate climates				
35°F	0.20	0.40	0.23	0.46
40°F	0.15	0.30	0.17	0.34
45°F	0.12	0.23	0.13	0.26

NOTES

1. No convective connections to building.
2. Temperatures listed are for December and January (usually the coldest months) and are monthly averages.
3. Low heat loss: Space with a net load coefficient (NLC) = 3 Btu/day/sq ft/°F. A space with little exposed external surface area.
4. High heat loss: Space with an NLC = 6 Btu/day/sq ft/°F. A space with a large amount of exposed external surface area.
5. The NLC is the total building heat loss less the loss through the solar aperture.

TABLE 3. SUGGESTED MATERIAL THICKNESS FOR INDIRECT GAIN THERMAL STORAGE WALLS

MATERIAL	RECOMMENDED THICKNESS
Brick (common)	10 to 14 in.
Concrete (dense)	12 to 18 in.
Water	6 in. or more

NOTE: When using water in tubes, cylinders, or other types of circular containers, have a container of at least a 9½ in. diameter or holding ½ cu ft (31 lb, 3.7 gal) of water for each one square foot of glazing.

TABLE 4. APPROXIMATE SPACE TEMPERATURE FLUCTUATIONS AS A FUNCTION OF INDIRECT GAIN THERMAL STORAGE WALL MATERIAL AND THICKNESS

| | THICKNESS (IN.) | | | | | |
MATERIALS	4	8	12	16	20	24
Brick (common)	—	24°	11°	7°	—	—
Concrete (dense)	—	28°	16°	10°	6°	5°
Water (31°F)	—	18°	13°	11°	10°	9°

NOTE: Assumes a double glazed thermal wall. If additional mass is located in the space, such as masonry walls and/or floors, then temperature fluctuations will be less than those listed. Values are given for clear winter days.

Edward Mazria, AIA, Architect; Edward Mazria & Associates; Albuquerque, New Mexico

PRINCIPLES

Thermal storage wall systems are solar space heating devices that can also be used for space cooling in some climates. They consist generally of south-facing massive walls, an airspace, and are then sealed to the exterior by a glass or plastic glazing system. As solar radiation is transmitted through the glazing material, the wall is heated during sunlit hours; in turn the heated wall then radiates warmth to the interior space during the night. Additional components can be added to enhance cold climate performance, such as selective surface foils, night insulation systems, reflectors, and exterior vents to control overheating in mild climates.

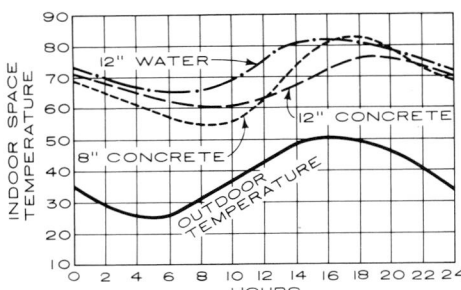

FIGURE 1

WALL PERFORMANCE

Figure 1 illustrates the characteristic performance of three thermal storage walls during one clear January day 24-hr cycle in a well-insulated house with ½ sq ft of wall for each square foot of room area, located in the U.S. Pacific Northwest. The two thicknesses of concrete wall shown in the graph demonstrate that by adding wall depth the resulting fluctuation in interior space temperature is reduced, and wall peak temperature is shifted toward the night hours when heat is most needed. Also it can be seen that by using a water wall with the same volume as the 12 in. concrete wall, the response of the wall to solar heating is enhanced; however, maximum heat transmission to the building interior occurs earlier in the evening when less heat is needed.

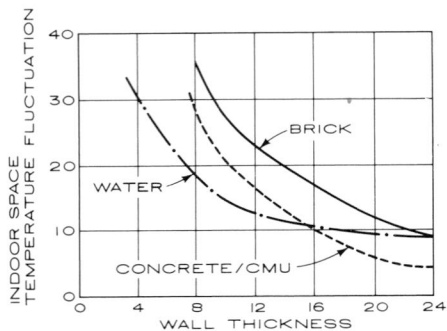

FIGURE 2

TEMPERATURE FLUCTUATION

Figure 2 illustrates space temperature fluctuations that can be expected for a one-day cycle using three different wall materials of varying thicknesses and the same design conditions as depicted in Figure 1. The wall types shown are solid brick, concrete or concrete masonry units grouted solid, and water.

WALL AREA VS. FLOOR AREA

Figure 3 gives rule of thumb guidelines for surface area of storage wall, using a wall thickness of between 8 and 18 in., compared to square feet of floor area to be heated for four latitudes. Example: Find the required wall area for a 250 sq ft room located at 40° north latitude with an average outdoor temperature of 34°F during the coldest winter month. On the "Y" axis find 34°, move right on the graph to the 40° latitude line, and then down the graph to the "X" axis, finding the wall vs. floor ratio of 0.45. Multiply 0.45 times the floor area of 250 sq ft, for a suggested wall area of 112.5 sq ft.

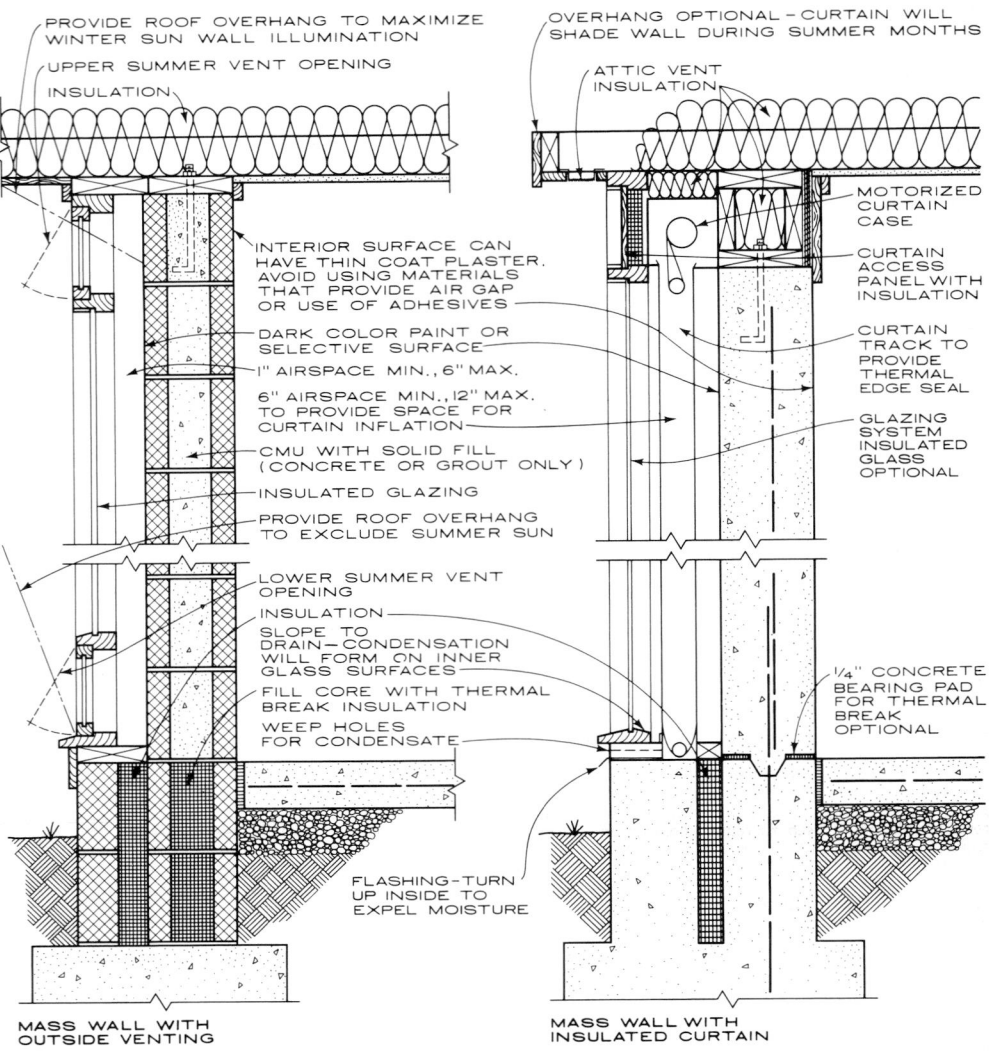

MASS WALL WITH OUTSIDE VENTING

MASS WALL WITH INSULATED CURTAIN

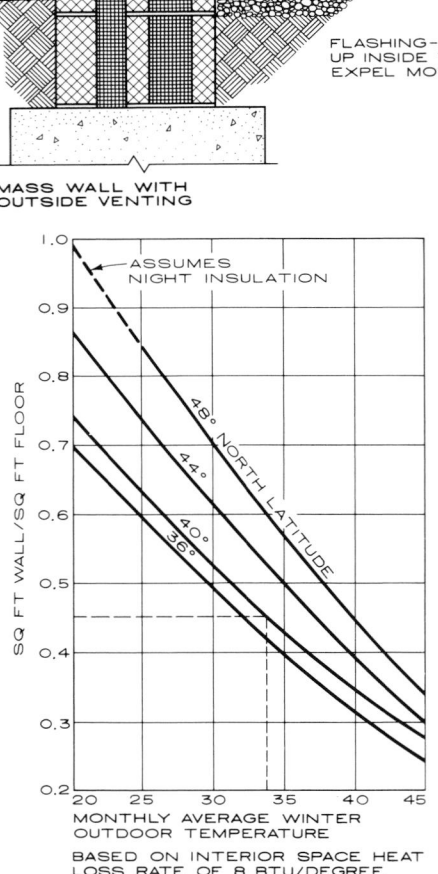

FIGURE 3

BASED ON INTERIOR SPACE HEAT LOSS RATE OF 8 BTU/DEGREE DAY/SQ FT FLOOR AREA /°F 8"–18" WALL THICKNESS

WATER WALLS

Thermal storage walls of the water container type are generally designed as an integral part of the heated space. Fiberglass, plastic, glass, or metal containers can be used; however, if steel is used, a rust inhibitor should be added to the water, and in all cases algicide should be added to prevent algae growth. Water containers are also manufactured that fit within wood-framed walls and appear as translucent windows from the interior or that can be covered with dry wall.

INTERNAL MASS

Mass thermal walls can also be used within rooms that are directly heated by solar radiation entering through windows (direct gain system), but where the wall is not directly illuminated by the sun. In this application the wall acts as a heat sink, absorbing excess spacial heat during sunlit hours and giving back heat during the night, reducing spacial temperature swings. As a rule of thumb, provide internal mass wall area at the rate of six times the direct gain window area.

COOLING

The use of thermal storage walls for cooling involves the isolation of the wall from the exterior and, in particular, solar radiation during the sunlit hours, then exposing the wall surfaces to air jets of cool night air either by forced or natural ventilation to reduce the wall's internal temperature. The wall then functions as a heat sink during the warm hours the following day, to absorb internal spacial heat, thereby maintaining comfortable indoor temperatures.

W. Fred Roberts Jr., AIA; Roberts & Kirchner Architects; Lexington, Virginia

SOLAR RADIANT ENERGY

Solar energy reaches the earth's surface in the form of electromagnetic radiation in the wavelength band between 0.3 and 3.0 micrometers (μm). Beyond the earth's atmosphere, at the average earth-sun distance (about 93 million miles) the radiant flux density on a surface normal to the solar rays is now thought to be 1377 W/sq m or 437 Btu/hr · sq ft. This quantity, known as the solar constant, is apparently subject to minor fluctuations caused by small changes in the sun's output of shortwave (ultraviolet) radiation. An earlier value, 1353 W/sq m or 429.2 Btu/hr · sq ft continues to be widely used pending further measurements from outer space.

At the surface of the earth, solar irradiance falling on horizontal surfaces varies from zero at sunrise to a maximum that, at sea level, may be as high as 325 Btu/hr · sq ft (945 W/sq m) at noon on a clear day. The intensity falls to zero again at sunset. Clear day irradiance values for horizontal and tilted surfaces with varying orientations are given in ASHRAE Publication GRP 170. Values for average day conditions can be found in "Hourly Solar Radiation Data for Vertical and Horizontal Surfaces on Average Days in the United States and Canada" published by the National Bureau of Standards in their Building Science Series 96. A wealth of data on horizontal irradiance is to be found in the "Climatic Atlas of the U.S." and in the publications of the National Weather Service, Asheville, NC. Methods of estimating direct, diffuse, and reflected radiation are given in Chapter 26, 1977 ASHRAE Handbook of Fundamentals.

SOLAR COLLECTION AND UTILIZATION

Solar radiant energy can be put to use at low and moderate temperatures by flat plate collectors, Figure 1, in which a blackened sheet of metal is used to absorb the incoming radiation and covert it to heat. This heat is then conducted to a fluid that passes through tubes or passages integral with or attached to the plate. To minimize loss of heat from the absorber plate, glazing (single or double, with glass or a heat resistant plastic) is used to reduce convection and to suppress longwave radiation exchange with the sky. The rear surface of the collector plate is insulated carefully, preferably with glass fiber that can withstand the relatively high temperatures (300 to 400°F) that can exist under "stagnation" conditions. This occurs when the collector is exposed to full sunshine with no heat transfer fluid flowing through it. The entire unit is contained within a weatherproof box, and connecting pipes or ducts are provided to bring the fluid to the collector and to carry it away after it has been heated. Details of many types of flat plate collectors are given in Chapter 58, 1978 ASHRAE Handbook of Applications. Performance calculations and test data are given in ASHRAE Publication GRP 170.

When high temperatures are required for industrial or power generation applications, concentrating collectors must be used. These reflect or refract a large amount of solar energy onto a relatively small absorber area, thus reducing the surface available for heat loss and enabling the fluid to attain temperatures that can exceed 1000°F. Such collectors must "track the sun" because they can use only the direct beam radiation from the solar disk. Some concentrating collectors remain essentially fixed, but these are limited to concentration ratios of less than 3 : 1.

SOLAR ENERGY UTILIZATION SYSTEMS

A system for using solar energy consists of an array of collectors, a storage subsystem, and another subsystem, which is generally quite conventional, for distributing the heated fluid and returning it to storage. Pumps or fans are used to circulate the heat transfer fluid, and control devices are used to start and stop the circulators. Auxiliary or standby heat sources are generally needed to carry part of the load when demand is exceptionally heavy and the thermal storage is depleted due to long periods of unfavorable weather.

Figure 2 shows a simple system for providing space heating and domestic hot water, using a drain-down procedure in which the collectors are emptied whenever the pump P1 stops. A differential controller senses the temperatures of the collector plate and the water and starts the circulating pump P1 when the sun has heated the plate above the water temperature. The pump is stopped when the plate temperature drops to

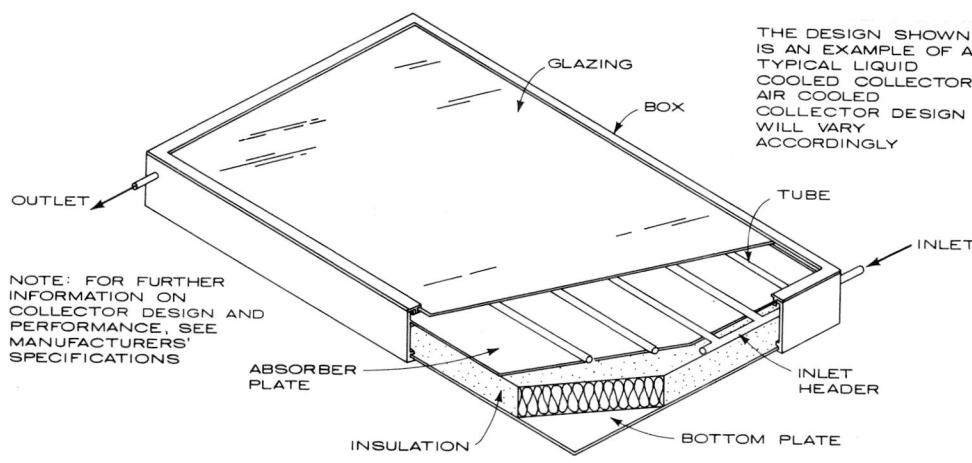

FIGURE I. TYPICAL FLAT PLATE COLLECTOR

NOTE: FOR FURTHER INFORMATION ON COLLECTOR DESIGN AND PERFORMANCE, SEE MANUFACTURERS' SPECIFICATIONS

THE DESIGN SHOWN IS AN EXAMPLE OF A TYPICAL LIQUID COOLED COLLECTOR. AIR COOLED COLLECTOR DESIGN WILL VARY ACCORDINGLY

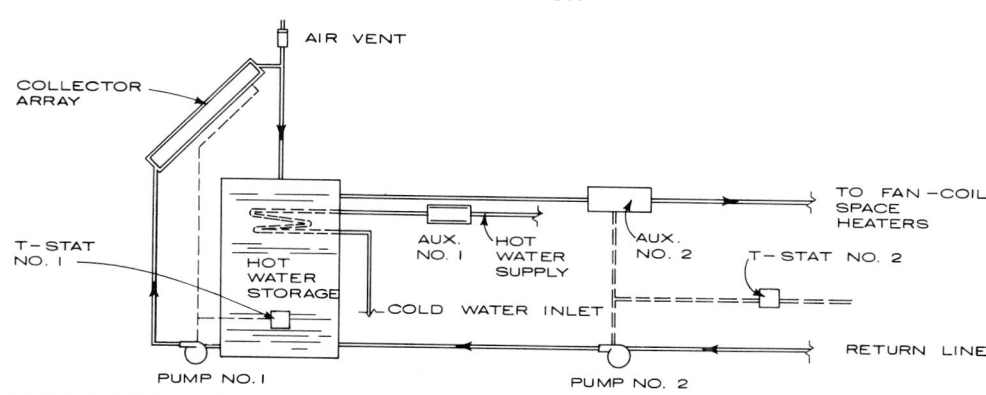

FIGURE 2. DRAIN – BACK SOLAR WATER SYSTEM

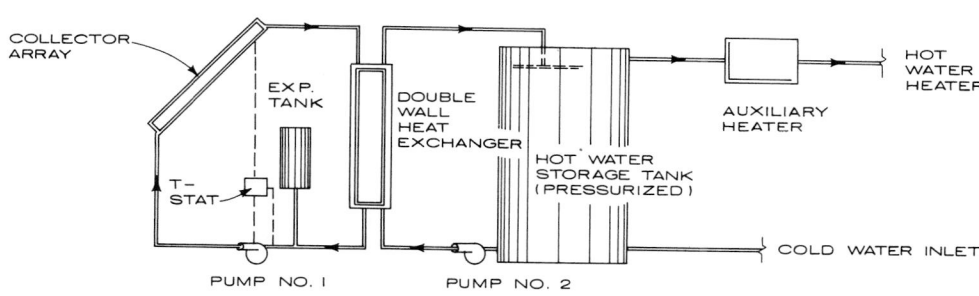

FIGURE 3. SOLAR WATER HEATING SYSTEM

the point where collection of heat is no longer possible.

Domestic hot water is provided by a pipe coil or a small tank located near the top of the main storage tank. The domestic hot water system operates under full line pressure whereas the main tank is at essentially atmospheric pressure, so any leakage would normally be into the main tank. Because of the very remote possibility of a back flow from the main tank into the city water supply, some plumbing codes require a double wall heat exchanger for this service. An auxiliary heater is provided to ensure an adequate supply of hot water at all times.

Since solar heat collection systems work more efficiently when the temperature difference between the collector and the ambient air is relatively low, fancoil units with large areas of finned tube heat transfer surface are generally selected for the space heating assignment. These can be used with water temperatures as low as 100°F. The auxiliary heat source in many solar installations will be electricity, and the heater may use simple direct resistance elements. When cooling is required as well as heating, a heat pump may

prove to be a wise choice, particularly when large amounts of auxiliary energy are likely to be needed.

FREEZE PROTECTION FOR LIQUID SYSTEMS

When water is used as the heat transfer fluid, freeze protection must always be provided, since there is no location within the continental United States where freezing has never been known to occur. The drain-down system shown in Figure 2 is a fail-safe method to provide such protection but it has certain disadvantages that, in many applications, make the use of a freezing point depressant advisable. Figure 3 shows a widely used system in which water plus ethylene glycol or propylene glycol, or some similar antifreeze fluid, is circulated through the collector array by pump P1. A double wall heat exchanger is used to transfer the collected heat to the service hot water which is under full line pressure, and a standby heater is provided to raise the temperature of the sun heated water to the conventional 140°F. Since domestic hot water is rarely actually used at 140°F, it is beneficial to use a lower thermostat setting for the hot water and to use less cold water for dilution.

John I. Yellott, P.E., and Gary Yabumoto; College of Architecture, Arizona State University; Tempe, Arizona

AIR SYSTEMS

Air collectors carry serious limitations, primarily because the temperatures that they deliver are low and the space requirements for air ducts are high. Air collectors can be appropriate, however, for applications requiring low process heat or involving the regeneration of desiccant material for dehumidification.

The key issue in air system design is to minimize air leakage in areas where cold outside air is present—between collectors, for example, or in uninsulated chases. One effective installation approach entails mounting the collectors integrally with the roof and keeping all duct connections below the roof. Air collectors have also been mounted on flat roofs, at an angle, with housings erected to protect the back of the collector enclosures and their ductwork. Steps should always be taken to prevent exposure of collector connections and ductwork to the weather.

An air system's heat storage container should allow air moving to and from the container to circulate through the entire storage mass, without "short-circuiting." The container should be adequately insulated, and all joints—especially around the top—should be tightly sealed. Do not install a drain at the bottom of the container; it might provide access for animals, insects, or odors.

The system's fan and duct configuration must allow for the delivery of heated air directly from collectors to load, from collectors to storage, and, indirectly, from storage to load. This requires two pairs of interconnected dampers. Solar fan components that provide integral fan dampers and controllers are available. If a coil is to be used to heat water, it should be located beyond the fan to minimize any chance of its freezing.

These issues, reviewed here as a checklist for architects, have been thoroughly documented. Correction measures can be incorporated into the specification, manufacture, and installation of active solar collection systems.

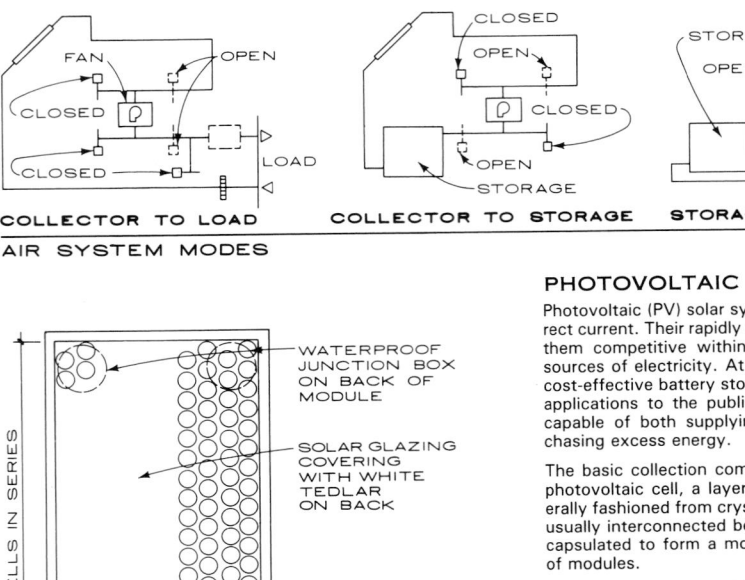

AIR SYSTEM

AIR SYSTEM MODES

COLLECTOR TO LOAD　　COLLECTOR TO STORAGE　　STORAGE TO LOAD

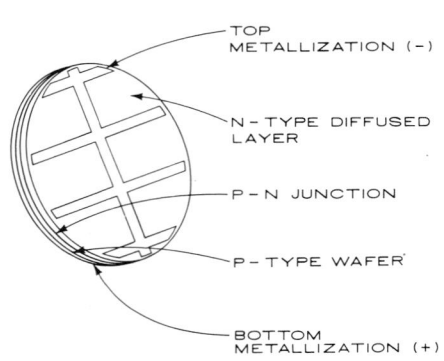

PHOTOVOLTAIC CELL

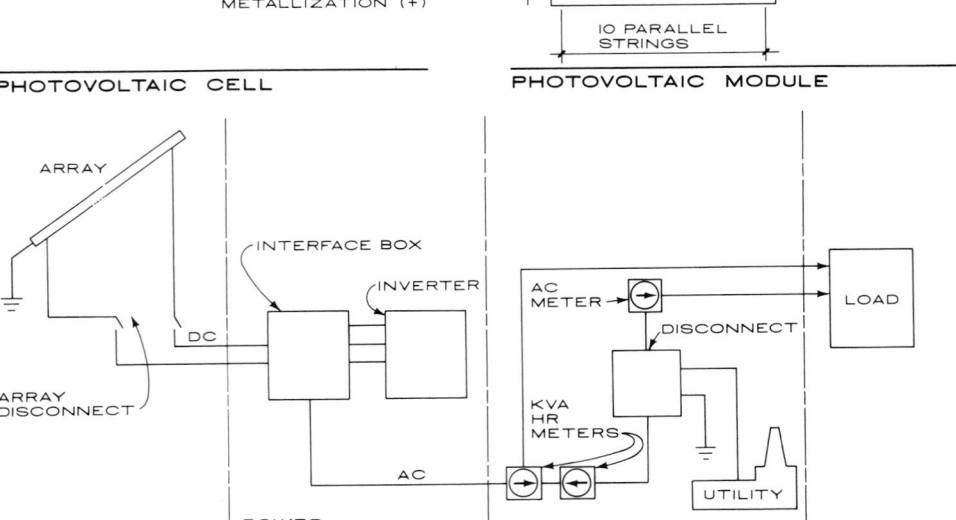

PHOTOVOLTAIC MODULE

PHOTOVOLTAIC SYSTEMS

Photovoltaic (PV) solar systems convert sunlight into direct current. Their rapidly decreasing cost may well make them competitive within the next decade with some sources of electricity. At present, however, the lack of cost-effective battery storage limits common PV system applications to the public utilities, which are uniquely capable of both supplying additional energy and purchasing excess energy.

The basic collection component of a PV system is the photovoltaic cell, a layered semiconductor that is generally fashioned from crystalline silicon. A group of cells, usually interconnected both in series and parallel, is encapsulated to form a module. An array is an assembly of modules.

The major factors considered in the sizing of a PV array are its anticipated loads and its power conditioning system (PCS) capacities. The design of an array depends on the module to be installed. Since no single module provides the commonly required voltage, several modules must be installed in series to achieve the proper voltage; groups of similar modules are then connected in parallel to provide the required amperage. The design of an array must facilitate this grouping of modules in series and parallel.

Modules can be installed in three ways: integrally (replacing the sheathing and roofing); applied (set directly on the sheathing, as roofing, or directly on the roofing itself); and standoff, or rack mounted (above the roof and either parallel or at an angle to it). The primary installation considerations are the tilt and orientation of the roof and the vent requirements of the module. The latter consideration can seriously affect system efficiency. Modules are adversely affected by heat, losing approximately ±0.003% efficiency for each degree Farenheit rise in temperature. Applied installations, therefore, are less efficient, because the modules are unable to discharge heat. Rack mounting, which allows air to circulate freely behind the modules, is often the most efficient installation technique. Some PV systems capture the heat discharged by the modules and supply it directly to interior spaces as heated air or exhaust it directly to the exterior; in these installations, the collectors are attached and ducted as they would be in an air collector system.

The major component of the PCS is the inverter, which converts the DC power generated by the array into AC power used by the load. The PCS also synchronizes the PV array's power output to make it compatible with the local utility company's output. The number of available PCS capacities is limited and is thus a controlling factor in the sizing of PV systems.

PHOTOVOLTAIC SYSTEM

COLLECTOR　　POWER CONDITIONING　　UTILITY INTERFACE　　LOAD

Stephen Weinstein, AIA; The Ehrenkrantz Group; New York, New York

The design of a solar collector array and its support structure can have an important influence on overall building appearance and be a key determinant of the total cost of the solar heating system. It is also the aspect of the system that the architect can most easily control.

Because there are no industry standards for collector size, piping, or mounting hardware, it is essential that the architect know which collector system will be installed before he or she begins final detailing and design. If the collector array is to be selected as part of a total bid package, for example, sizing and coordination problems may result, and the architect may lose control of the array's structural underpinnings and the building's overall appearance.

ANCHORING THE SUPPORT STRUCTURE

Rooftop collector supports should be anchored directly to structural members, not to wood or metal decking; otherwise, wind-induced uplift forces and point loading may cause roofing—and possibly structural—failure. In steel buildings, vertical supports must be secured directly to joists or beams. In wood buildings, securing the collector supports directly to structural members will normally require the installation of some form of blocking, under the decking and between rafters, to transfer the load.

DESIGNING THE ARRAY

When a collector array is to be placed on a light steel-framed roof, the direction of the joints in the array's support structure becomes a critical design issue. It is often necessary to stagger the array's vertical supports to ensure an even distribution of the load. Some roofs cannot support such a load and thus must be clear-spanned. The array support structure in such cases is likely to be particularly expensive; intricate long-span space-frame structures are invariably costly and cost-ineffective.

AVOIDING ROOFING PROBLEMS

Leaky roofs are a persistent problem in solar installations. Problems can be anticipated and minimized by following these guidelines:

- Minimize roof penetrations. Collector supports constructed of pipe, if used in a large array as shown, require one roof penetration for every 60 sq ft of roof area, approximately; long-span design, by comparison, calls for one roof penetration roughly every 225 sq ft. Roof penetrations can also be avoided by using solar piping supports that rest directly on the roof, as shown; these prevent undue roof stress caused by pipe movement.
- Properly detail the flashing of vertical supports at the roofline. Except on pitched roofs (and often even then), wood-blocking bolted directly through the roof will ultimately generate leaks, regardless of the amount of roofing cement applied. The best approach is to use a neoprene roofing sleeve. The next best is base flashing and canopy detail. Less preferable is a pitch pocket, properly constructed. Other approaches—those using site-fabricated curbs and other techniques—tend to fail. If blocking is to be secured directly to a sloped roof, then roofing cement should be applied between each layer of shingles, between shingles and deck, and between shingles and blocking.

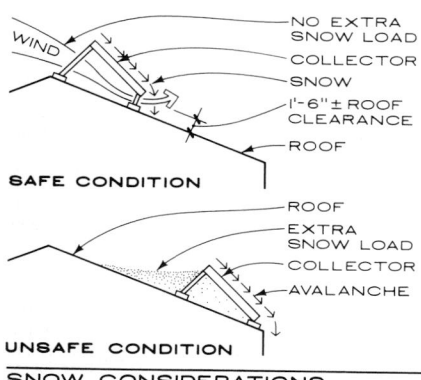

SAFE CONDITION

NO EXTRA SNOW LOAD
COLLECTOR
SNOW
1'-6"± ROOF CLEARANCE
ROOF
WIND

UNSAFE CONDITION

ROOF
EXTRA SNOW LOAD
COLLECTOR
AVALANCHE

SNOW CONSIDERATIONS

Stephen Weinstein, AIA; The Ehrenkrantz Group; New York, New York

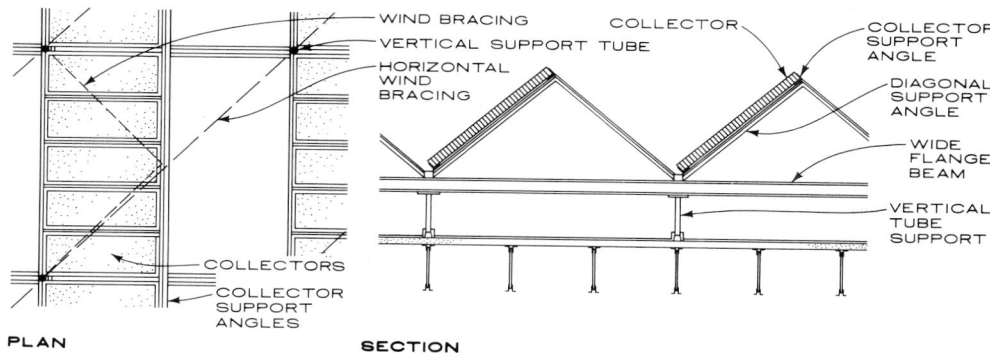

WIND BRACING
VERTICAL SUPPORT TUBE
HORIZONTAL WIND BRACING
COLLECTOR
COLLECTOR SUPPORT ANGLE
DIAGONAL SUPPORT ANGLE
WIDE FLANGE BEAM
VERTICAL TUBE SUPPORT
COLLECTORS
COLLECTOR SUPPORT ANGLES

PLAN   **SECTION**

COLLECTOR SUPPORT

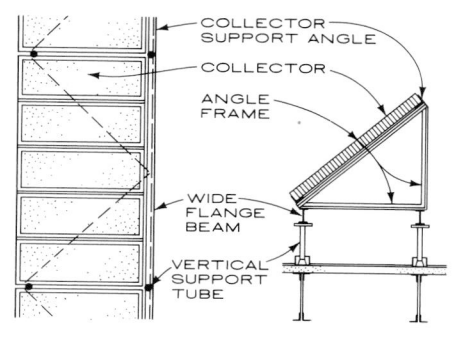

COLLECTOR SUPPORT ANGLE
COLLECTOR
ANGLE FRAME
WIDE FLANGE BEAM
VERTICAL SUPPORT TUBE

PLAN   **SECTION**

COLLECTOR SUPPORT

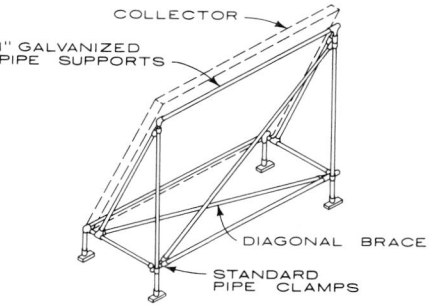

COLLECTOR
1" GALVANIZED PIPE SUPPORTS
DIAGONAL BRACE
STANDARD PIPE CLAMPS

PIPE RACK MOUNTING

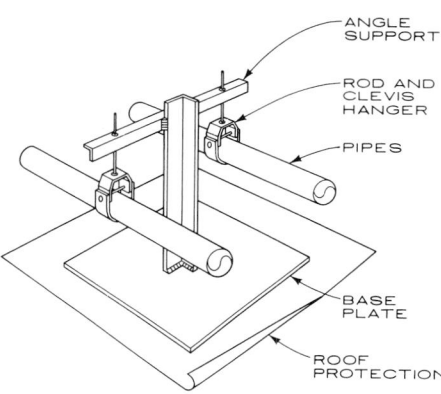

ANGLE SUPPORT
ROD AND CLEVIS HANGER
PIPES
BASE PLATE
ROOF PROTECTION

PIPE SUPPORT

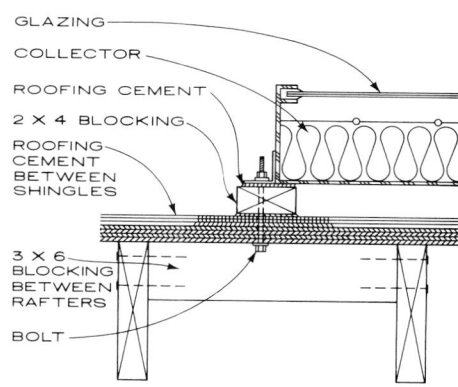

GLAZING
COLLECTOR
ROOFING CEMENT
2 X 4 BLOCKING
ROOFING CEMENT BETWEEN SHINGLES
3 X 6 BLOCKING BETWEEN RAFTERS
BOLT

SLOPED ROOF

- Do not create dams. Any form of continuous blocking or curb will—unless installed at a right angle to the slope of a pitched roof—invariably dam a portion of the roof and ultimately cause built-up roofing to fail.
- Specify that all work be performed by the appropriate trade. Support flashing, for instance, is often installed by the steel erector or the plumbing contractor rather than by the roofing contractor.
- Protect the roof. Specify that the roof in general be protected during construction and that permanent walkways be installed to provide access to the system once it is in use.
- Mount collectors on a sloped roof unless the pitch is so flat that the loss of year-round efficiency in performance will be too great. When collectors and

sloped roof are parallel, allow a 1½ in. airspace between them to prevent deterioration of the roofing material and the collector enclosures. Do not mount collectors integrally with the roofing unless the collectors are specifically designed for integral mounting; as a rule, only air collectors are so designed. In cold regions, mount collectors as near the roof peak as possible to minimize damming and snow buildup and to lessen the chance of a dangerous snow slide—a particular threat when an array is located above an entry.

- On a flat roof, mount collectors between 2 ft 6 in. and 3 ft above the roof rather than directly on the roof. This prevents snow buildup, permits adequately sloped pipe runs, and—most important—allows for the installation of proper roof penetrations and for future roof repair and replacement.

SHADING DEVICES

The effect of shading devices can be plotted in the same manner as the solar path was projected. The diagrams show which part of the sky vault will be obstructed by the devices and are projections of the surface covered on the sky vault as seen from an observation point at the center of the diagram. These projections also represent those parts of the sky vault from which no sunlight will reach the observation point; if the sun passes through such an area the observation point will be shaded.

SHADING MASKS

Any building element will define a characteristic form in these projection diagrams, known as "shading masks." Masks of horizontal devices (overhangs) will create a segmental pattern; vertical intercepting elements (fins) produce a radial pattern; shading devices with horizontal and vertical members (eggcrate type) will make a combinative pattern. A shading mask can be drawn for any shading device, even for very complex ones, by geometric plotting. As the shading masks are geometric projections they are independent of latitude and exposed directions, therefore they can be used in any location and at any orientation. By overlaying a shading mask in the proper orientation on the sun-path diagram, one can read off the times when the sun rays will be intercepted. Masks can be drawn for full shade (100% mask) when the observation point is at the lowest point of the surface needing shading; or for 50% shading when the observation point is placed at the halfway mark on the surface. It is customary to design a shading device in such a way that as soon as shading is needed on a surface the masking angle should exceed 50%. Solar calculations should be used to check the specific loads. Basic shading devices are shown below, with their obstruction effect on the sky vault and with their projected shading masks.

SHADING MASK PROTRACTOR

The half of the protractor showing segmental lines is used to plot lines parallel and normal to the observed vertical surface. The half showing bearing and altitude lines is used to plot shading masks of vertical fins or any other obstruction objects. The protractor is in the same projection and scale as the sun-path diagrams (see pages on solar angles); therefore it is useful to transfer the protractor to a transparent overlay to read the obstruction effect.

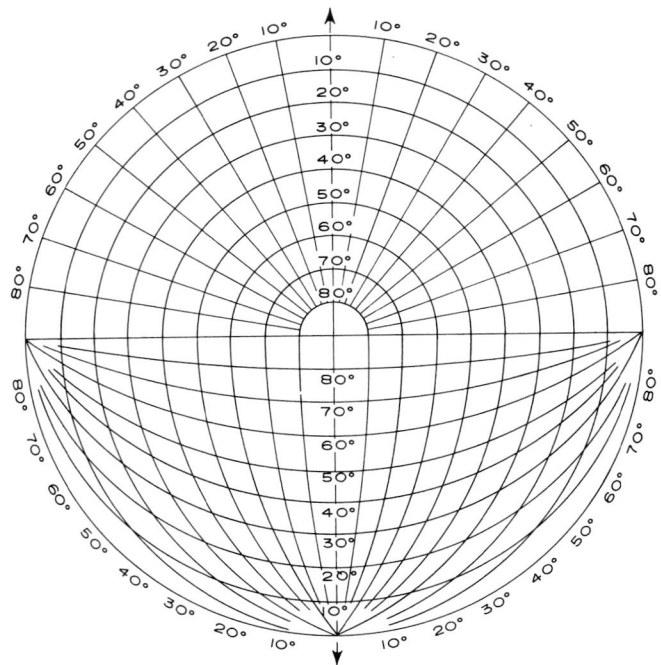

SHADING MASK PROTRACTOR

HORIZONTAL

VERTICAL

EGGCRATE

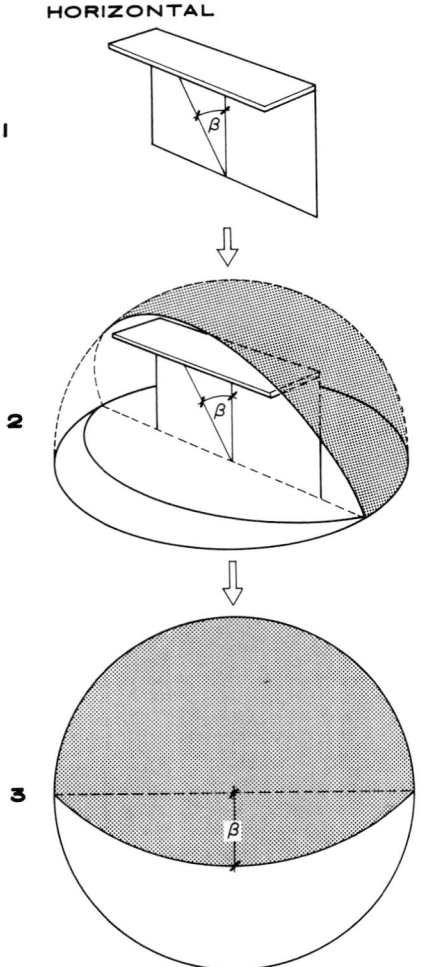

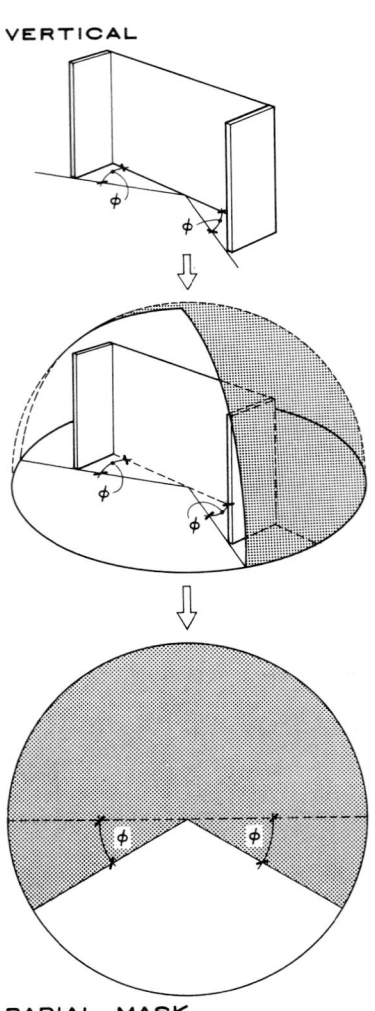

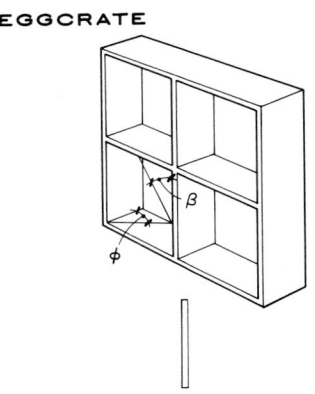

Horizontal devices produce segmental obstruction patterns, vertical fins produce radial patterns, and eggcrate devices produce combination patterns.

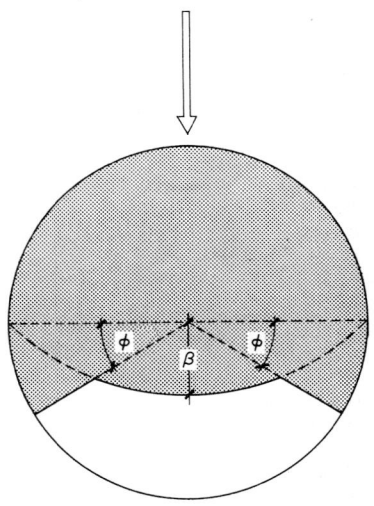

SEGMENTAL MASK

RADIAL MASK

COMBINATION MASK

Victor Olgyay, AIA; Princeton University; Princeton, New Jersey

18   SHADING

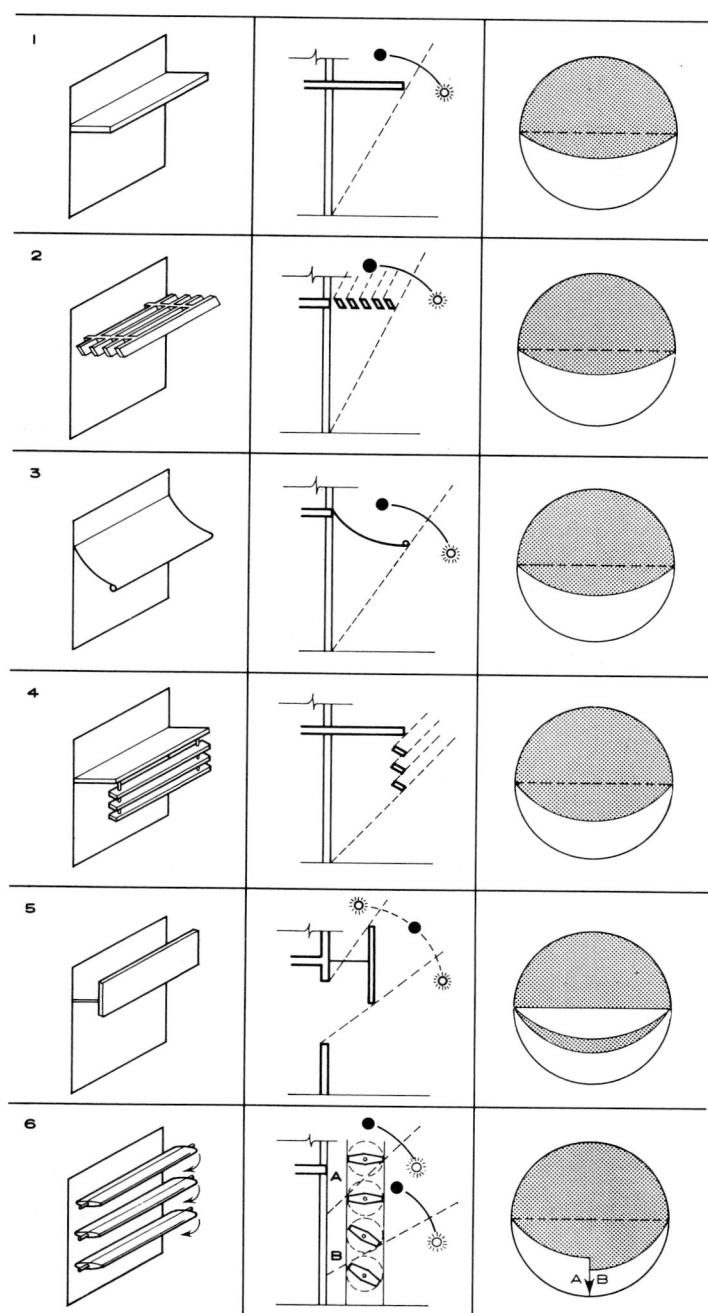

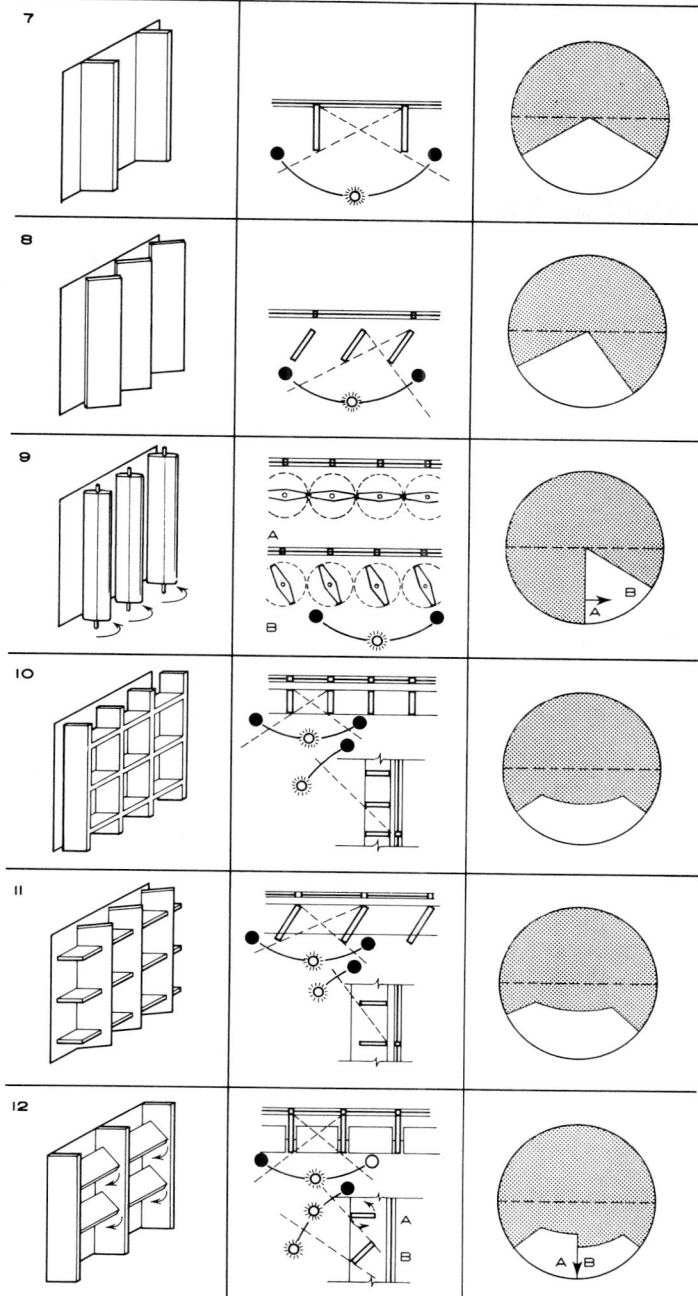

EXAMPLES OF VARIOUS TYPES OF SHADING DEVICES

The illustrations show a number of basic types of devices, classified as horizontal, vertical, and eggcrate types. The dash lines shown in the section diagram in each case indicate the sun angle at the time of 100% shading. The shading mask for each device is also shown, the extent of 100% shading being indicated by the gray area.

General rules can be deduced for the types of shading devices to be used for different orientations. Southerly orientations call for shading devices with segmental mask characteristics, and horizontal devices work in these directions efficiently. For easterly and westerly orientations vertical devices serve well, having radial shading masks. If slanted, they should incline toward the north, to give more protection from the southern positions of the sun. The eggcrate type of shading device works well on walls facing southeast, and is particularly effective for southwest orientations. Because of this type's high shading ratio and low winter head admission; its best use is in hot climate regions. For north walls, fixed vertical devices are recommended; however, their use is needed only for large glass surfaces, or in hot regions. At low latitudes on both south and north exposures eggcrate devices work efficiently.

Whether the shading devices be fixed or movable, the same recommendations apply in respect to the different orientations. The movable types can be most efficiently utilized where the sun's altitude and bearing angles change rapidly: on the east, southeast, and especially, because of the afternoon heat, on the southwest and west.

Victor Olgyay, AIA; Princeton University; Princeton, New Jersey

HORIZONTAL TYPES 1. Horizontal overhangs are most efficient toward south, or around southern orientations. Their mask characteristics are segmental. 2. Louvers parallel to wall have the advantage of permitting air circulation near the elevation. Slanted louvers will have the same characteristics as solid overhangs, and can be made retractable. 4. When protection is needed for low sun angles, louvers hung from solid horizontal overhangs are efficient. 5. A solid, or perforated screen strip parallel to wall cuts out the lower rays of the sun. 6. Movable horizontal louvers change their segmental mask characteristics according to their positioning.

VERTICAL TYPES 7. Vertical fins serve well toward the near east and near west orientations. Their mask characteristics are radial. 8. Vertical fins oblique to wall will result in asymmetrical mask. Separation from wall will prevent heat transmission. 9. Movable fins can shade the whole wall, or open up in different directions according to the sun's position.

EGGCRATE TYPES 10. Eggcrate types are combinations of horizontal and vertical types, and their masks are superimposed diagrams of the two masks. 11. Solid eggcrate with slanting vertical fins results in asymmetrical mask. 12. Eggcrate device with movable horizontal elements shows flexible mask characteristics. Because of their high shading ratio, eggcrates are efficient in hot climates.

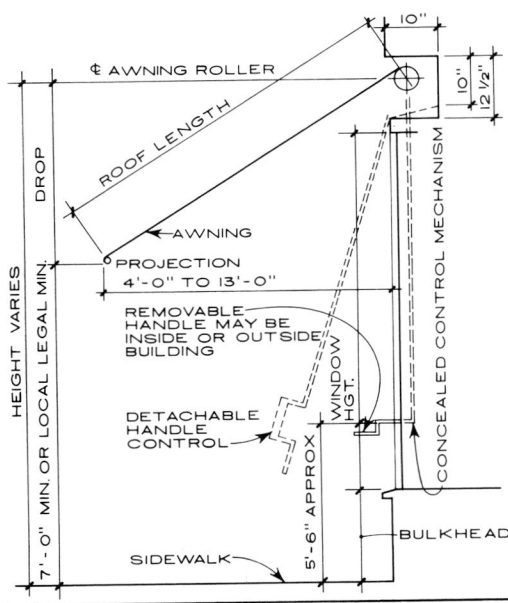

DIAGRAMMATIC SECTION RECESSED BOX INSTALLATION

AWNING MATERIALS:
1. Painted cotton duck
2. Vinyl-coated cotton duck
3. Vinyl-laminated polyester
4. Solution-dyed acrylic
5. Vinyl-coated polyester
6. Acrylic-coated polyester
7. Vinyl-coated polycotton
8. Solution-dyed modacrylic

AWNING OPERATORS:
1. Detachable handle control
2. Gear box & shaft (concealed or exposed) with removable handle inside or outside of building
3. Electric control

RETRACTABLE WINDOW AWNINGS: Retractable awnings are manufactured in widths from 10 to 50 ft. Pitch can vary from horizontal to 45 degrees.

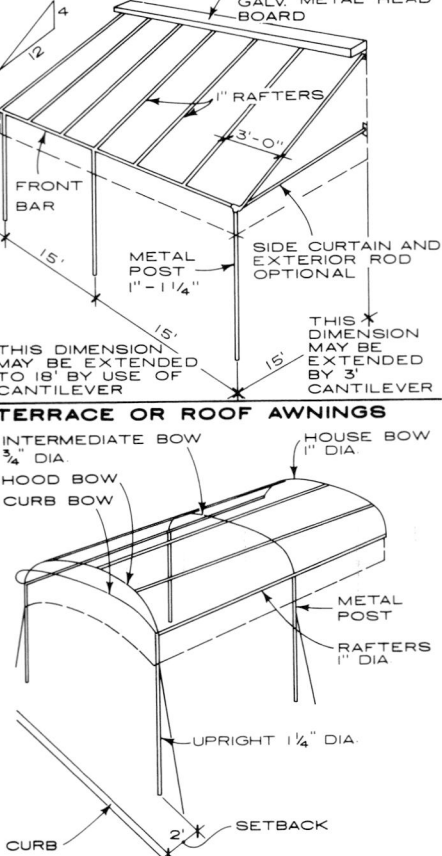

TERRACE OR ROOF AWNINGS

CANOPIES - LOW CURVED BOW SHOWN

TERRACE OR ROOF AWNINGS

To provide complete sun protection and shade, the overall length of the awning bar should extend 3 in. past the glass line on both sides. For proper sunshade protection, awnings should project at least as far forward from the face of the window as the bottom of the window is below the front bar of the awning.

The wall measurement of an awning is the distance down the face of the building from the point where the awning attaches to the face of the building (or from the center of the roller in the case of the roller type awning).

The projection of an awning is the distance from the face of the building to the front bar of the awning in its correct projected position.

Right and left of an awning are your right and left as you are facing the awning looking into the building.

Framework consists of galvanized steel pipe, with non-rattling fittings. Awning is lace-on type canvas with rope reinforced eave. Protector hood is galvanized sheet metal or either bronze, copper, or aluminum.

Sizes of members should be checked by calculation for conditions not similar to those shown on this page.

Consult local building code for limitations on height and setback.

COVERED WALKWAYS

Covered walkways are available with aluminum fascia and soffit panels in a number of profiles. The fascia panels are supported with pipe columns and steel or aluminum structural members if necessary. Panels can cantilever up to 30% of span. Canopy designs can be supported from above.

Another method of providing covered exterior space is with stressed membrane structures. Using highly tensile synthetic fabric and cable in collaboration with compression members, usually metal, dynamic and versatile tentlike coverings can be created. Membrane structures are especially suited to temporary installations.

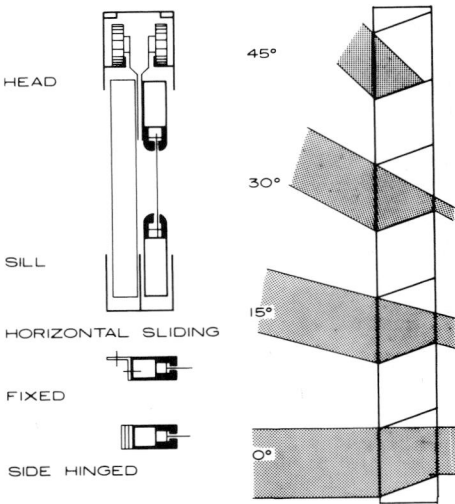

NOTE

These miniature external louvers shade windows from direct sunlight and glare while allowing a high degree of visibility, light, ventilation, insect protection, and day-time privacy. Much like a woven metal fabric, they are not strong architectural elements but present a uniform appearance in the areas covered. The solar screen is installed in aluminum frames and can be adapted to suit most applications.

SOLAR SCREEN SIZES

MATE-RIAL	LOUVERS	TILT	VERTICAL SPACING	SIZE (WIDTHS)
Aluminum	17"	17°	1" o.c.	18"–48"
Bronze	17", 23"	20°	1/2" o.c.	Up to 72 1/2"

Aluminum screens are available in black or light green. Bronze screens come in black only.

SOLAR SCREENS

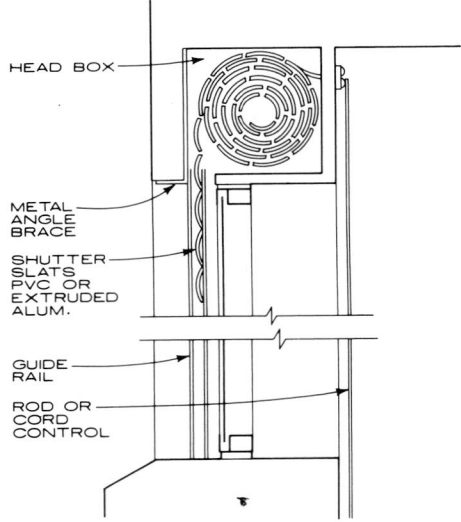

NOTE

Rolling shutters provide sun control not only by shading windows from direct sun rays but also by way of two dead airspaces—one between shutter and window, the other within the shutter extrusions to serve as insulation. The dead airspaces work as well in winter to prevent the escape of heat from the interior. In addition, shutters are useful as privacy and security measures. They can be installed in new or existing construction and are manufactured in standard window sizes.

ROLLING SHUTTERS

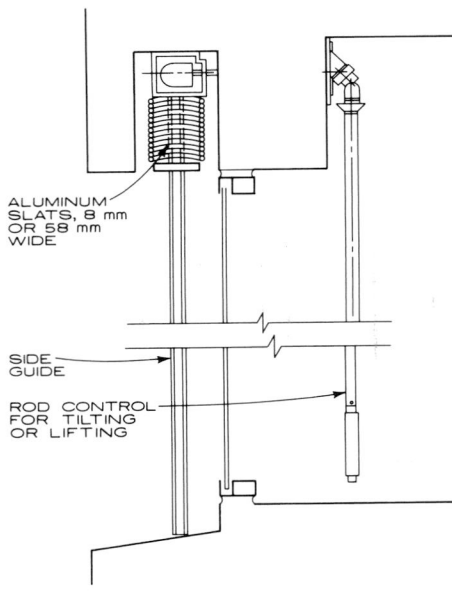

NOTE

External blinds protect the building interior from solar gain and glare, but can be raised partially or fully to the head when not needed. Manual or electric control is from inside the building.

EXTERNAL VENETIAN BLINDS

Graham Davidson, Architect; Washington, D.C.

TYPES OF UNDERGROUND SPACE

Commercial underground buildings can be classified in a number of ways:

1. Cut-and-cover buildings: Buildings relatively near the surface. The structure supports earth loads from above and on the sides. The term "earth-sheltered" usually refers to cut-and-cover buildings. Also, distinctions can be made between buildings that are fully beneath existing grade and those that are bermed.
2. Mined space: Building area is created by excavating in self-supporting soil or rock.

Underground building type is determined primarily by the site, topography, and program requirements. The ability to create mined space is determined by local soils and geology. Further classification of underground buildings often is based on the surface opening. Categories include windowless chambers, atrium designs, and elevational designs (windows along a single wall).

GENERAL ADVANTAGES

Some of the many advantages associated with underground buildings are:

1. Limited visual impact of the building in natural or historical settings.
2. Preservation of surface open space above the building in dense urban or campus settings.
3. Efficient land use by extending buildings beyond normal setbacks or by building into otherwise unbuildable slopes.
4. Environmental benefits such as reducing water runoff and preserving or increasing plant and animal habitat.
5. Protection from tornadoes, storms, and fire.
6. Provision of civil defense shelters.
7. Increased security against vandalism and theft.
8. Insulation from noise and vibration, permitting some incompatible uses to be located in closer proximity.
9. Reduced exterior maintenance.
10. Reduced construction costs for exterior finishing materials and mechanical equipment.
11. Reduced life-cycle costs of the building based on reduced heating, cooling, maintenance, and insurance costs.

ENERGY-RELATED ADVANTAGES AND LIMITATIONS

In most climates underground buildings have characteristics that reduce heating and cooling loads when compared with above-ground structures. Advantages from improved energy efficiency include:

1. Reduced winter heat loss because of moderate below-grade temperatures and reduced cold air infiltration.
2. Reduced summer heat gain especially when earth-bermed walls are planted with grass or ground cover. Peak cooling loads are reduced.
3. Direct cooling from earth in summer.
4. Daily and seasonal temperature fluctuations are reduced, resulting in smaller HVAC equipment sizes.
5. Large mass below-grade concrete buildings can store solar heat and off-peak electric power.

The U.S. deep-ground temperature map illustrates variations in the below-grade environment. At about 25 ft and deeper, temperatures of undisturbed ground remain approximately constant. Ground temperatures around an in-ground building rise. Buildings nearer to the surface initially experience some temperature variations that stabilize in time.

Energy-conserving benefits are affected by climate, ground temperatures, degree of exposure, building depth, mechanical system design, and building use. Buildings requiring high levels of mechanical ventilation are less likely to benefit from below-grade placement than buildings with low to moderate ventilation requirements. Maximum energy benefits are derived from building uses such as cold storage, or spaces where precision temperature and humidity conditions must be controlled (e.g., laboratories, libraries, and special materials storage).

DISADVANTAGES

Underground building limitations present a number of disadvantages over conventional construction. Most of these can be overcome by design. Among the limitations are:

1. Limited opportunities for natural light and exterior views;
2. Limited entrance and service access;
3. Limited view of the building and its entrance;
4. Increased costs on sites that have water tables, bedrock near the surface, or adjacent buildings with shallow foundations;
5. Increased construction costs for heavier structures (especially if earth is placed on the roof) and high-quality waterproofing systems.

SPECIAL DESIGN CONCERNS

Entrance design: Entrances should be visible and clear from the exterior. Descending may occur inside or outside the building. If possible, large spaces and natural light should be provided in the entrance area. Various underground building entrance approaches are shown in drawings at the right.

Natural light and view: A primary concern in designing underground buildings is offsetting the possible negative psychological and physiological effects of windowless environments. In addition to admitting sunlight, windows provide orientation, variety, and a similarity to above-ground space. As shown in drawings at the right conventional windows, skylights, and courtyards are effective means of providing light and view in near-surface underground buildings. Where these techniques are inadequate, beamed or reflected daylighting systems may be explored.

Interior design: In underground spaces with limited opportunities for natural light and view, building interior should be organized to provide maximum exposure to light and view for the greatest number of users at each opportunity. Design techniques include large interior courtyards, high ceilings, glass walls, plants, warm colors, variety in design and lighting, and full spectrum artificial lights.

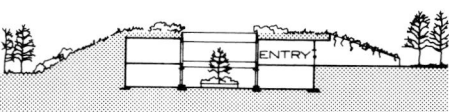
ENTRANCE INTO A BERMED STRUCTURE

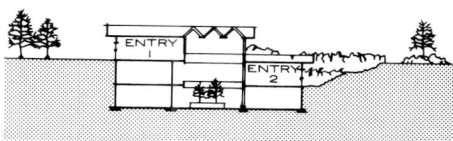
ENTRANCES AT GRADE AND SUBGRADE LEVELS

BUILDING ENTRANCE DESIGN

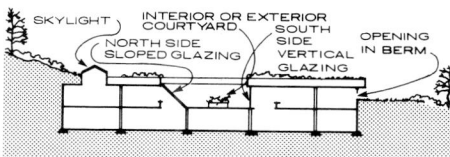
BUILDING SET INTO A SLOPING SITE

NATURAL LIGHT AND VIEW

INSULATION AND WATERPROOFING

Generally, waterproofing should be applied to all below-grade roofs and walls. When a building floor is below the water table level, waterproofing must be placed beneath the floor as well. On below-grade roofs and walls, waterproofing applied directly on the substrate (concrete, wood) is recommended. Insulation and drainage layers then can be placed over the waterproofing (see roof detail below).

When insulation is used in a below-grade application outside of the waterproofing, two characteristics are crucial:

1. Ability to resist structural loads from the earth (this limits selection to rigid board products).
2. Ability to maintain R-value and to resist degradation during constant and severe exposure to water and moisture.

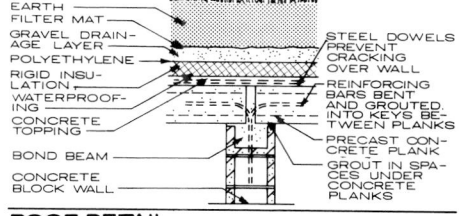
ROOF DETAIL

U.S. DEEP-GROUND TEMPERATURE MAP

SUGGESTED AMOUNTS OF BELOW-GRADE INSULATION

HEATING/COOLING DEGREE DAYS (BASE: 65°F)	SUGGESTED RANGE OF BELOW-GRADE INSULATION[1]		
	ROOFS AND[2] UPPER WALL	LOWER WALL[3]	REMOTE FLOOR[4] AREAS
8,000–11,000/0–500	R-20–R-40	R-10–R-20	0–R-5
5,000–8,000/500–1,500	R-15–R-30	R-5–R-15	0–R-5
2,000–5,000/1,500–2,500	R-5–R-20	5–R-10	0
under 2,000/over 2,000	R-5–R-20	0	0

NOTES

1. This table is a general guide only and assumes an earth cover thickness in the range of 12 to 30 in. for the earth-covered roof.
2. Earth-covered roof with 12 to 30 in. of cover and walls within 4 ft of the ground surface.
3. Earth-covered wall surfaces farther than 4 ft from the ground surface.
4. Remote floor areas (i.e., more than 10 ft from the ground surface) not used as a solar storage area or for heat distribution.

John Carmody; Underground Space Center, University of Minnesota; Minneapolis, Minnesota
Kyle Williams, AIA; BRW Architects, Inc.; and David Eijadi, AIA; The Weidt Group; Minneapolis, Minnesota

STRUCTURAL CONSIDERATIONS

Earth sheltered structures are usually deeper and the loads greater than for basements. Hydrostatic and compaction loads add to the triangular soil loading on walls (Figure 1). Floors below water level are subjected to uplift of 62.4 psf per foot depth below water level and may require special design (Figure 2) to resist the load and to provide a uniform support plane for the waterproof membrane. Roof live loads in urban areas may include public assembly at 100 psf, in addition to soil, plants, and furnishings. Saturated soils and gravel are usually taken at 120 pcf. Tree loads are related to species and size. Tree weights can be estimated for preliminary design by the logarithmic relation

$$\log(wt) = x + 2.223 \log(dia.) + 0.339 \log(ht)$$

where (wt) is in pounds, (dia.) is trunk diameter in inches at breast height, and (ht) is in feet. Forest trees range in x from 0.6 for fir to 0.8 for birch, with spruce and maple at about 0.7. The equation has not been tested for lawn trees, so it must be used with caution. Site investigation is important to determine soil bearing and drainage capacity, shearing strength, and water level. Hillside designs produce unbalanced lateral loads that may recommend interior wall buttressing.

LANDSCAPE CONSIDERATIONS

Rooftop plantings require adequate soil depth (Figure 3), underdrainage, and irrigation. Lightweight soil mixes reduce roof loads, but are not suitable under foot. Highly trafficked roofs may require special sandy soil mixes used for golf greens and athletic fields to resist compaction and root damage. Plant materials should be drought-resistant and hardier than normal, since roof soil may be colder than lawn soil.

DRAINAGE AND MOISTURE CONSIDERATIONS

Footing drains draw down the water table and prevent ponding in the backfill. Exterior location is more effective, but is subject to abuse during backfilling and to subsequent settlement. Underslab drains are easier to install correctly and are less likely to fail. Unless both are used, weep holes should be installed through the footing to connect underfloor and perimeter systems. A polyethylene sheet keeps water vapor from entering the slab, and through-joint flashing prevents capillary transfer of soil moisture through the footing to the wall. The waterproofing system must be suited to the structural system and the surface condition of the substrate. Plastic waterstops complicate joint forming and may conceal the source of leaks, disadvantages that usually outweigh whatever benefit they may provide. Chemical (e.g., bentonite base) waterstops do not have these disadvantages.

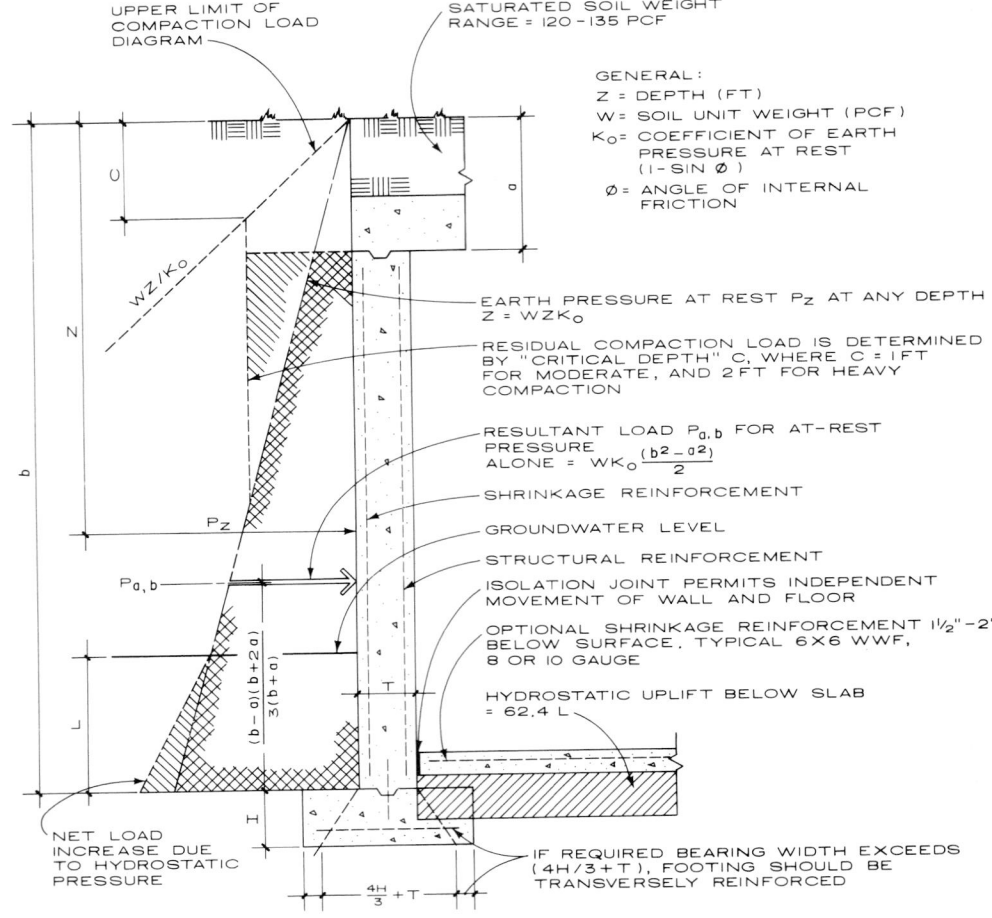

General:
Z = DEPTH (FT)
W = SOIL UNIT WEIGHT (PCF)
K_0 = COEFFICIENT OF EARTH PRESSURE AT REST $(1 - \sin \emptyset)$
$\emptyset$ = ANGLE OF INTERNAL FRICTION

SATURATED SOIL WEIGHT RANGE = 120 - 135 PCF

UPPER LIMIT OF COMPACTION LOAD DIAGRAM

EARTH PRESSURE AT REST P_z AT ANY DEPTH Z = WZK_0

RESIDUAL COMPACTION LOAD IS DETERMINED BY "CRITICAL DEPTH" C, WHERE C = 1FT FOR MODERATE, AND 2FT FOR HEAVY COMPACTION

RESULTANT LOAD $P_{a,b}$ FOR AT-REST PRESSURE ALONE = $WK_0 \dfrac{(b^2 - a^2)}{2}$

SHRINKAGE REINFORCEMENT

GROUNDWATER LEVEL

STRUCTURAL REINFORCEMENT

ISOLATION JOINT PERMITS INDEPENDENT MOVEMENT OF WALL AND FLOOR

OPTIONAL SHRINKAGE REINFORCEMENT 1½"-2" BELOW SURFACE, TYPICAL 6X6 WWF, 8 OR 10 GAUGE

HYDROSTATIC UPLIFT BELOW SLAB = 62.4 L

IF REQUIRED BEARING WIDTH EXCEEDS (4H/3+T), FOOTING SHOULD BE TRANSVERSELY REINFORCED

NET LOAD INCREASE DUE TO HYDROSTATIC PRESSURE

FIGURE 1 COMPOSITE LOAD DIAGRAM

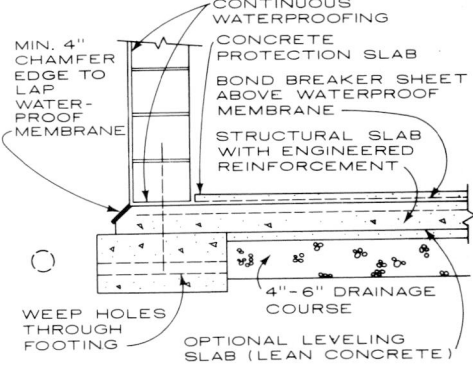

CONTINUOUS WATERPROOFING

CONCRETE PROTECTION SLAB

BOND BREAKER SHEET ABOVE WATERPROOF MEMBRANE

STRUCTURAL SLAB WITH ENGINEERED REINFORCEMENT

MIN. 4" CHAMFER EDGE TO LAP WATERPROOF MEMBRANE

WEEP HOLES THROUGH FOOTING

4"-6" DRAINAGE COURSE

OPTIONAL LEVELING SLAB (LEAN CONCRETE)

FIGURE 2 REINFORCED SLAB (GERMAN APPROACH)

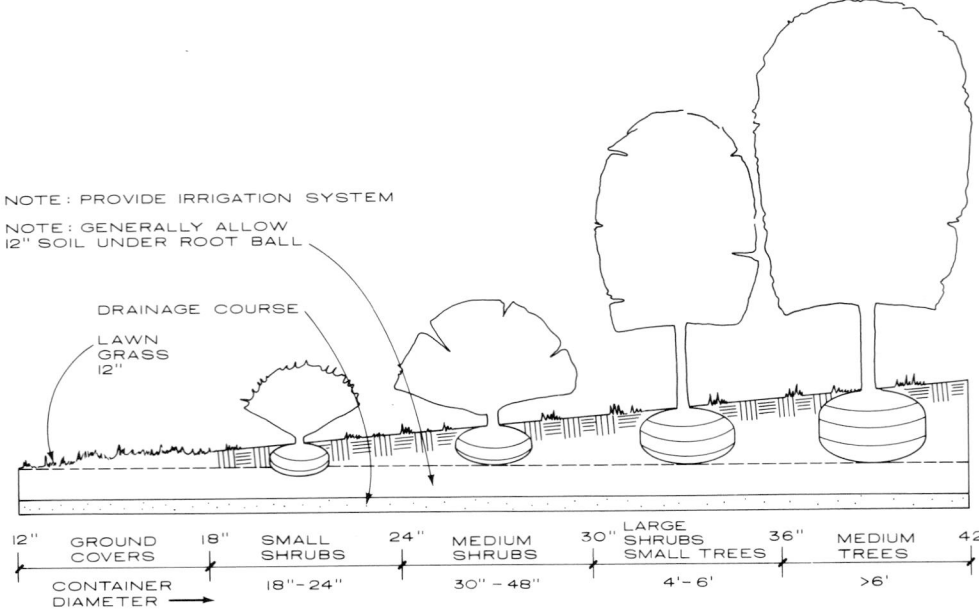

NOTE: PROVIDE IRRIGATION SYSTEM

NOTE: GENERALLY ALLOW 12" SOIL UNDER ROOT BALL

DRAINAGE COURSE

LAWN GRASS 12"

12"	GROUND COVERS	18"	SMALL SHRUBS	24"	MEDIUM SHRUBS	30"	LARGE SHRUBS SMALL TREES	36"	MEDIUM TREES	42"
	CONTAINER DIAMETER →		18"-24"		30"-48"		4'-6'		>6'	

FIGURE 3 PLANT SOIL COVER REQUIREMENTS

Kenneth Labs; New Haven, Connecticut

RECOMMENDED REFERENCES

1. J. Carmody and R. Sterling, *Earth Sheltered Housing Design*, 2d ed. (New York: Van Nostrand Reinhold, 1985).
2. L. Gish, *Building Deck Waterproofing*, STP 1084 (Philadelphia: ASTM, 1990).
3. K. Labs, "Roofs for Use," *Progressive Architecture* (July 1990): 36–42.
4. K. Labs and J. Carmody et al., *Building Foundation Design Handbook* (Minneapolis: University of Minnesota Underground Space Center, 1988).
5. U.S. Navy, *Earth Sheltered Buildings*, NAVFAC DM 1.4, no. 008-050-00230-1 (Washington: Government Printing Office, 1983).

18   **EARTH SHELTERS**

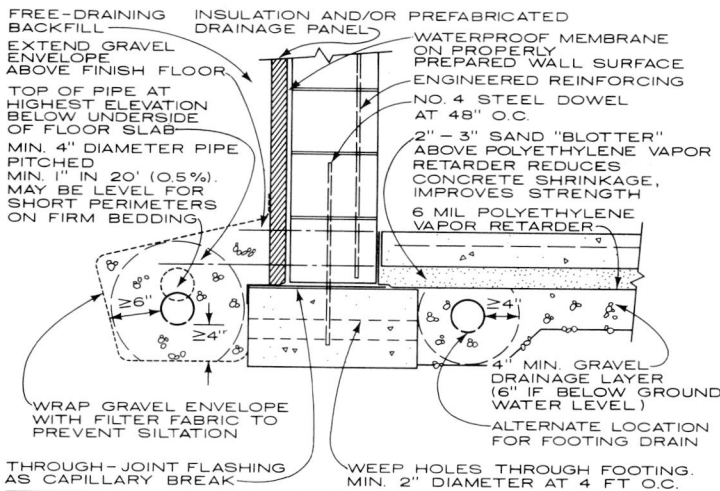

FREE-DRAINING BACKFILL
EXTEND GRAVEL ENVELOPE ABOVE FINISH FLOOR

TOP OF PIPE AT HIGHEST ELEVATION BELOW UNDERSIDE OF FLOOR SLAB

MIN. 4" DIAMETER PIPE PITCHED MIN. 1" IN 20' (0.5%). MAY BE LEVEL FOR SHORT PERIMETERS ON FIRM BEDDING

INSULATION AND/OR PREFABRICATED DRAINAGE PANEL

WATERPROOF MEMBRANE ON PROPERLY PREPARED WALL SURFACE

ENGINEERED REINFORCING

NO. 4 STEEL DOWEL AT 48" O.C.

2" – 3" SAND "BLOTTER" ABOVE POLYETHYLENE VAPOR RETARDER REDUCES CONCRETE SHRINKAGE, IMPROVES STRENGTH

6 MIL POLYETHYLENE VAPOR RETARDER

WRAP GRAVEL ENVELOPE WITH FILTER FABRIC TO PREVENT SILTATION

THROUGH-JOINT FLASHING AS CAPILLARY BREAK

WEEP HOLES THROUGH FOOTING. MIN. 2" DIAMETER AT 4 FT O.C.

4" MIN. GRAVEL DRAINAGE LAYER (6" IF BELOW GROUND WATER LEVEL)

ALTERNATE LOCATION FOR FOOTING DRAIN

TYPICAL FOOTING CONDITION

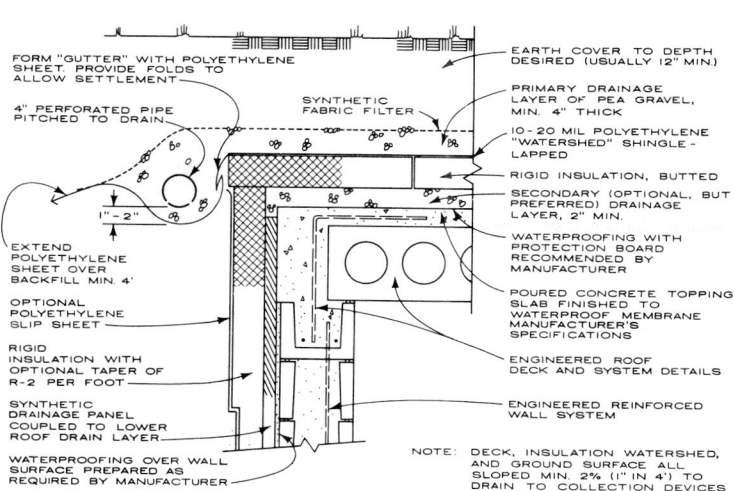

FORM "GUTTER" WITH POLYETHYLENE SHEET. PROVIDE FOLDS TO ALLOW SETTLEMENT

4" PERFORATED PIPE PITCHED TO DRAIN

SYNTHETIC FABRIC FILTER

EXTEND POLYETHYLENE SHEET OVER BACKFILL MIN. 4'

OPTIONAL POLYETHYLENE SLIP SHEET

RIGID INSULATION WITH OPTIONAL TAPER OF R-2 PER FOOT

SYNTHETIC DRAINAGE PANEL COUPLED TO LOWER ROOF DRAIN LAYER

WATERPROOFING OVER WALL SURFACE PREPARED AS REQUIRED BY MANUFACTURER

EARTH COVER TO DEPTH DESIRED (USUALLY 12" MIN.)

PRIMARY DRAINAGE LAYER OF PEA GRAVEL, MIN. 4" THICK

10-20 MIL POLYETHYLENE "WATERSHED" SHINGLE-LAPPED

RIGID INSULATION, BUTTED

SECONDARY (OPTIONAL, BUT PREFERRED) DRAINAGE LAYER, 2" MIN.

WATERPROOFING WITH PROTECTION BOARD RECOMMENDED BY MANUFACTURER

POURED CONCRETE TOPPING SLAB FINISHED TO WATERPROOF MEMBRANE MANUFACTURER'S SPECIFICATIONS

ENGINEERED ROOF DECK AND SYSTEM DETAILS

ENGINEERED REINFORCED WALL SYSTEM

NOTE: DECK, INSULATION WATERSHED, AND GROUND SURFACE ALL SLOPED MIN. 2% (1" IN 4') TO DRAIN TO COLLECTION DEVICES

ROOF EDGE DETAIL

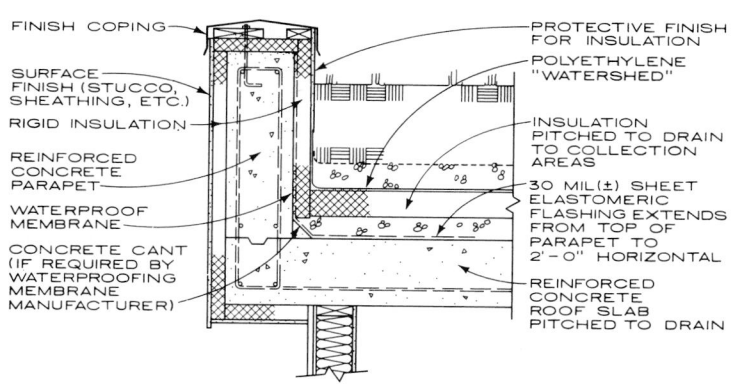

FINISH COPING

SURFACE FINISH (STUCCO, SHEATHING, ETC.)

RIGID INSULATION

REINFORCED CONCRETE PARAPET

WATERPROOF MEMBRANE

CONCRETE CANT (IF REQUIRED BY WATERPROOFING MEMBRANE MANUFACTURER)

PROTECTIVE FINISH FOR INSULATION

POLYETHYLENE "WATERSHED"

INSULATION PITCHED TO DRAIN TO COLLECTION AREAS

30 MIL(±) SHEET ELASTOMERIC FLASHING EXTENDS FROM TOP OF PARAPET TO 2'-0" HORIZONTAL

REINFORCED CONCRETE ROOF SLAB PITCHED TO DRAIN

CONCRETE PERIMETER PARAPET

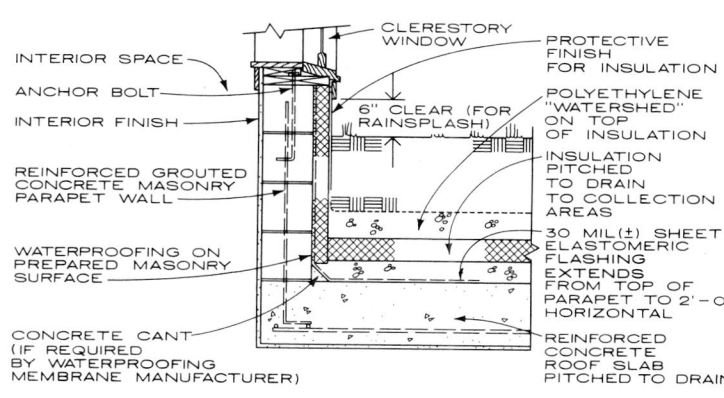

INTERIOR SPACE

ANCHOR BOLT

INTERIOR FINISH

REINFORCED GROUTED CONCRETE MASONRY PARAPET WALL

WATERPROOFING ON PREPARED MASONRY SURFACE

CONCRETE CANT (IF REQUIRED BY WATERPROOFING MEMBRANE MANUFACTURER)

CLERESTORY WINDOW

6" CLEAR (FOR RAINSPLASH)

PROTECTIVE FINISH FOR INSULATION

POLYETHYLENE "WATERSHED" ON TOP OF INSULATION

INSULATION PITCHED TO DRAIN TO COLLECTION AREAS

30 MIL(±) SHEET ELASTOMERIC FLASHING EXTENDS FROM TOP OF PARAPET TO 2'-0" HORIZONTAL

REINFORCED CONCRETE ROOF SLAB PITCHED TO DRAIN

MASONRY INTERIOR PARAPET

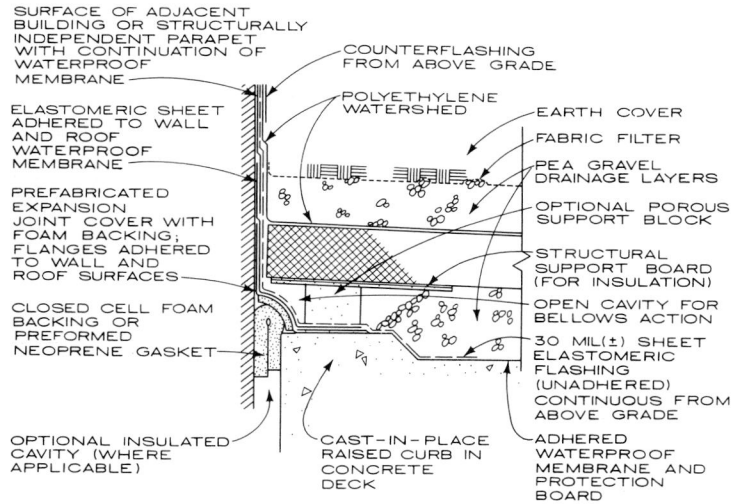

SURFACE OF ADJACENT BUILDING OR STRUCTURALLY INDEPENDENT PARAPET WITH CONTINUATION OF WATERPROOF MEMBRANE

ELASTOMERIC SHEET ADHERED TO WALL AND ROOF WATERPROOF MEMBRANE

PREFABRICATED EXPANSION JOINT COVER WITH FOAM BACKING; FLANGES ADHERED TO WALL AND ROOF SURFACES

CLOSED CELL FOAM BACKING OR PREFORMED NEOPRENE GASKET

OPTIONAL INSULATED CAVITY (WHERE APPLICABLE)

COUNTERFLASHING FROM ABOVE GRADE

POLYETHYLENE WATERSHED

EARTH COVER

FABRIC FILTER

PEA GRAVEL DRAINAGE LAYERS

OPTIONAL POROUS SUPPORT BLOCK

STRUCTURAL SUPPORT BOARD (FOR INSULATION)

OPEN CAVITY FOR BELLOWS ACTION

30 MIL(±) SHEET ELASTOMERIC FLASHING (UNADHERED) CONTINUOUS FROM ABOVE GRADE

CAST-IN-PLACE RAISED CURB IN CONCRETE DECK

ADHERED WATERPROOF MEMBRANE AND PROTECTION BOARD

FLEXIBLE JOINT AT ROOF EDGE

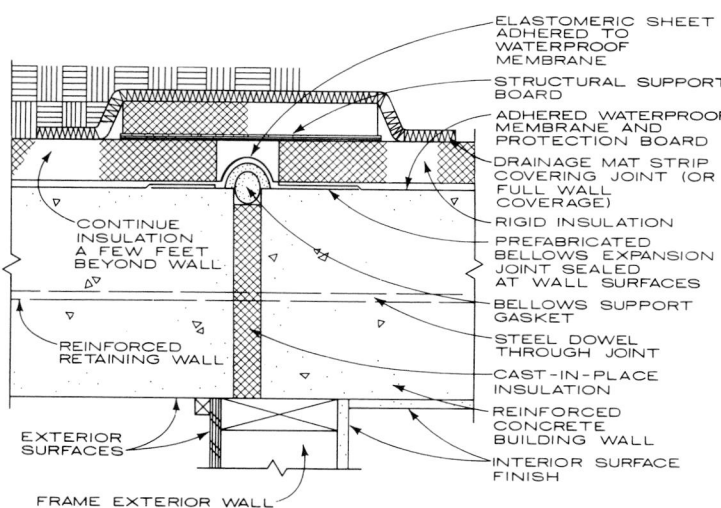

CONTINUE INSULATION A FEW FEET BEYOND WALL

REINFORCED RETAINING WALL

EXTERIOR SURFACES

FRAME EXTERIOR WALL

ELASTOMERIC SHEET ADHERED TO WATERPROOF MEMBRANE

STRUCTURAL SUPPORT BOARD

ADHERED WATERPROOF MEMBRANE AND PROTECTION BOARD

DRAINAGE MAT STRIP COVERING JOINT (OR FULL WALL COVERAGE)

RIGID INSULATION

PREFABRICATED BELLOWS EXPANSION JOINT SEALED AT WALL SURFACES

BELLOWS SUPPORT GASKET

STEEL DOWEL THROUGH JOINT

CAST-IN-PLACE INSULATION

REINFORCED CONCRETE BUILDING WALL

INTERIOR SURFACE FINISH

THERMAL BREAK AT RETAINING WING WALL (PLAN)

THERMAL CONSIDERATIONS

Exterior insulation keeps walls and roofs warm and at a stable temperature. This minimizes dimensional change and indoor surface condensation and keeps elastomeric waterproofing pliable. Exterior insulation consumes no indoor space, but it is sometimes attacked by rodents and insects. Extruded polystyrene is usually preferred for its resistance to water absorption. Roof insulation should be placed within the drainage layer so that it does not

sit in water or impede drainage. Gravel is not always needed under the insulation, especially if the insulation is pitched to drain and is covered with polyethylene sheets. All seepage planes should be sloped a minimum of 1 in. in 4 ft.

Soil has little thermal resistance, so roof winter thermal performance depends largely on added insulation. Heat

loss from earth-covered roofs is nearly constant at

$$Q = (T_1 - T_0)/R$$

where Q is heat loss in Btu/ft²[hr]°F, T_1 and T_0 are indoor and outdoor air temperatures (°F) averaged over the preceding few days, and R is the thermal resistance of the overall roof assembly. Wet soil has an R value of slightly less than 1.0 per foot thickness.

Kenneth Labs; New Haven, Connecticut

DEFINITIONS AND SYMBOLS

BRITISH THERMAL UNIT (Btu): The quantity of heat required to raise the temperature of one pound of water one degree Fahrenheit (specifically, from 59°F to 60°F).

DEGREE DAYS (DD): A temperature-time unit used in estimating building heating requirements. For any given day, the number of DD equals the difference between the reference temperature, usually 65°F, and the mean temperature of the outdoor air for that day. DD per month or per year are the sum of the daily DD for that period. (Check locality for reference temperatures.)

DEWPOINT TEMPERATURE: The temperature corresponding to 100% relative humidity for an air-vapor mixture at constant pressure.

EMITTANCE (e): The ratio of the radiant energy emitted by a surface to that emitted by a perfect radiator (a black body) at the same temperature.

HUMIDITY, ABSOLUTE: The weight of water vapor contained in a unit volume of an air-vapor mixture.

HUMIDITY RATIO: The ratio of the mass of water vapor to the mass of dry air in a given air-vapor mixture.

HUMIDITY, RELATIVE (RH): The ratio of the partial pressure of the water vapor in a given air-vapor mixture to the saturation pressure of water at the existing temperature.

ISOTHERM: A line on a graph or map joining points of equal temperature.

OVERALL HEAT TRANSFER COEFFICIENT (U or $1/R_T$): The rate of heat transfer under steady state conditions through a unit area of a building component caused by a difference of one degree between the air temperatures on the two sides of the component. In U.S. practice, the units are Btu/sq ft · hr · °F.

PERM: Unit of water vapor transmission through a material, expressed in grains of vapor per hour per inch of mercury pressure difference (7000 grains = 1 lb).

REFLECTANCE: The ratio of the radiant energy reflected by a surface to the energy incident upon the surface.

SURFACE HEAT TRANSFER COEFFICIENT (h): The rate of heat transfer from a unit area of a surface to the adjacent air and environment caused by a temperature difference of one degree between the surface and the air. In U.S. practice, the units are Btu/sq ft · hr · °F.

THERM: A unit of thermal energy equal to 100,000 Btu.

THERMAL CONDUCTANCE (C or 1/R): Time rate of heat flow through unit area of a material when a temperature difference of one degree is maintained across a specified thickness of the material. In U.S. practice, the units are Btu/hr · sq ft · °F.

THERMAL CONDUCTIVITY (k): Time rate of heat flow through unit area and unit thickness of a homogeneous material when a temperature of gradient of one degree is maintained in the direction of heat flow. In U.S. practice, the units are: Btu/hr · sq ft · (F/in.) or, when thickness is measured in feet, Btu/hr · ft · °F.

THERMAL RESISTANCE (R): Unit of resistance to heat flow, expressed as temperature difference required to cause heat to flow through a unit area of a building component or material at the rate of one heat unit per hour. In U.S. practice, the units are F/Btu/hr · ft^2).

TOTAL THERMAL RESISTANCE (R_t): The total resistance to heat flow through a complete building section or construction assembly, generally expressed as the temperature difference in °F needed to cause heat to flow at the rate of 1 Btu per hour per sq ft of area.

VAPOR RETARDANT LOW PERMEABILITY: A layer applied to surfaces enclosing a humid space to prevent moisture migration to a point where it may condense because of reduced temperature.

VAPOR PERMEABILITY: The property of a material that permits migration of water vapor under the influence of a difference in vapor pressure across the material.

VAPOR PERMEANCE: The ratio of the water vapor flow rate, in grains per hour, through a material of any specified thickness to the vapor pressure difference between the two surfaces of the material, expressed in inches of mercury. The unit is the perm.

VAPOR PRESSURE (P_v): The partial pressure of the water vapor in an air-vapor mixture. It is determined by the dewpoint temperature or by the drybulb temperature and the relative humidity of the mixture. The units are psi or inches of mercury.

THERMAL TRANSMISSION

Problems in the performance of building construction materials and assemblies are frequently associated with undesirable flow of heat, moisture, or both. The heat transfer characteristics of most building materials are published in standard references such as the ASHRAE Handbook of Fundamentals. While the published data are subject to manufacturing and testing tolerances and judgment must be used in applying them, they may generally be used with confidence for design purposes.

Heat transmission coefficients are generally expressed as conductivities, k, for which the thickness unit is 1 in., or in conductances, C, for a specified thickness. The resistance to heat flow through a material, R, is the reciprocal of the conductance. For a homogeneous material of thickness L in., the thermal resistance R = L/k.

For a surface or an airspace, where the heat flows by both radiation and convection, combined coefficients are used, symbolized by h with a subscript to designate which particular surface or airspace is being considered. Thermal resistances at surfaces and across airspaces are again designated by R with an appropriate subscript, where R = 1/h. Such R values are strongly influenced by the nature and orientation of the surfaces.

To estimate the rate of heat flow through a building section, the total resistance (R_t) of that section is found by reference to published standard value or by adding the resistances of the individual components of the section. The overall coefficient U is then found as the reciprocal of the total resistance: $U = 1/R_t$. The rate of heat flow Q (Btu/hr) through a wall section of exposed area A sq ft is the product of the overall coefficient U, the area A and the temperature difference $(t_i - t_o)$: $Q = U \times A \times (t_i - t_o)$. This heat flow may be inward or outward, depending on t_i and t_o. The general procedure for finding the total thermal resistance and the U value for a given building section on which the sun is not shining is as follows:

1. Select the design outdoor conditions of air temperature (dry bulb), wind speed, and wind direction from local Weather Service records or ASHRAE recommendations. From this information select an outer surface coefficient h_o which will generally be 4.0 Btu/sq ft · hr · °F for summer and 6.0 for winter. Determine the indoor surface coefficient h_i which will be 1.46 Btu/sq ft · hr · °F under most conditions unless forced airflow exists along the wall of the window. Convert these to resistances with $R_o = 1/h_o$ and $R_i = 1/h_i$.
2. List all of the component elements of the section and determine the thermal resistance of each element by dividing the actual (not the nominal) thickness by its thermal conductivity k, except for airspaces. For airspaces, the thickness is taken into account in the conductance h_{as} and the thermal resistance R_{as} is the reciprocal of the conductance.
3. The total resistance of the building section is simply the sum of the individual resistances (make sure that every component is included properly). The U value of the section is then found from: $U = 1/R_t$. The U x A product is often needed to simplify the calculation of the total heat flow into or out of the building's envelope, as well as for the computations used to determine compliance with building energy performance standards.
4. For such building components as windows, skylights, and doors, U values may be found in standard references, for example, the ASHRAE Handbook of Fundamentals. Thermal resistances for a wide variety of common building materials are given in the table presented later in this section.

GENERAL NOTES

The foregoing does not include consideration of heat losses or gains due to ventilation air in large buildings or to infiltration of outdoor air through openings, cracks around windows and doors, construction imperfections, and so on. The energy required to heat this air in winter or to cool and dehumidify it in summer must be carefully estimated by methods given in the ASHRAE Handbook of Fundamentals. During both summer and winter, effects of the sun on both walls and windows must be taken into account.

The solution to the basic problem of attaining acceptable heat flow rates involves the selection of materials that are appropriate for the intended service and the incorporation of enough insulation within the building section to reduce the inward or outward heat flow to the desired rate. Since the indoor-outdoor temperature difference is one of the essential factors in the heat flow equation, the indoor temperature must be selected to comply with the pertinent code or other restriction. Temperatures from 65 to 72°F are generally used in winter while 75 to 78°F are typical summer values.

Selection of the outdoor design values involves careful consideration of the number of hours per year during which exceptionally low or high temperatures are encountered. National Weather Service temperature data are available for most locations in the United States and similar data exist for principal cities throughout the world. For winter design purposes, dry bulb temperatures are usually listed, which are exceeded by 99 and 97.5% of the total hours (2160) in December, January, and February. The 97.5% value is generally used for designing. Since the 54 hr (approximately) during which the outdoor air temperature will be lower than the stated value are experienced at intervals throughout the winter months. These temperatures are usually encountered in the early morning hours before sunrise, so that winter design heating loads tend to ignore solar effects. In summer, solar loads tend to dominate the air-conditioning picture.

Thermal conductances for walls, roofs, doors, and windows are combined in many of the energy conservation building standards to give a weighted average U value, designated as U_o. Allowable values for U_o depend on the building type and size and the number of heating degree days experienced at the building's location.

$$U_o = \frac{U_{xw} \times A_w + U_f \times A_f + U_d \times A_d}{A_w + A_f + A_d}$$

where the subscripts w, f, and d designate walls, fenestration, and door, respectively.

In many locations, allowable U_0 values may be specified in the applicable building code directly or by reference to an accepted standard, such as ASHRAE Standard 90. Estimation of summer cooling loads is also accomplished by using the U x A products as determined above, to which solar loads from fenestration must be added. Thermal resistances may be slightly higher in summer than in winter for the same building section. By far the largest factor in most building heat gain is the load imposed by solar radiation entering through fenestration. Cooling load is also increased by internal heat sources within the structure, including lighting, miscellaneous electrical loads, and the people in the building. Latent heat loads from moisture removal must also be considered. Properly qualified consultants should be called in to give advice in this field even before the orientation and fenestration of a proposed new building are fixed.

The energy conservation standards mentioned above also include provisions dealing with summer cooling requirements, which are set primarily by the latitude of the city in which the structure will be erected. The mass of the proposed building in terms of weight per square foot of wall area is also introduced to compensate in part for time lags caused by the thermal capacity of building components. It should be noted that cooling, a year-round requirement in many large buildings with high internal loads, is more costly in terms of energy consumption and cost than is heating. The internal heat gains that are helpful in winter are harmful in summer, since they can add greatly to the building's cooling load.

John I. Yellott, P.E.; College of Architecture, Arizona State University; Tempe, Arizona

THERMAL VALUES OF MATERIALS

MATERIAL & DESCRIPTION	DENSITY (lb per cu ft)	RESISTANCE (R)[a] Per inch thickness (1/k)	For thickness listed (1/C)
BUILDING BOARDS, PANELS, FLOORING, ETC.			
Gypsum or plaster board ⅜ in.	50	—	0.32
Gypsum or plaster board ½ in.	50	—	0.45
Plywood	34	0.04	—
Sheathing, fiberboard ½ in.	18	—	1.32
²⁵⁄₃₂ in.	18	—	2.06
	22	2.44	—
	25	2.28	—
Wood fiberboard, lam. or homogeneous	30	2.00	—
	50	1.37	—
Particleboard ⅝ in.	40	—	0.82
Wood subfloor ¾ in.	—	—	0.44
BUILDING PAPER			
Vapor-permeable felt	—	—	0.06
Vapor-seal, 2 layers of mopped 15 lb felt	—	—	0.12
Vapor-seal, plastic film	—	—	Negl.
FINISH FLOORING MATERIALS			
Carpet and fibrous pad	—	—	2.08
Carpet and rubber pad	—	—	1.23
Hardwood ²⁵⁄₃₂ in.	—	—	0.71
Terrazzo 1 in.	—	—	0.08
Tile-asphalt, linoleum, vinyl, rubber	—	—	0.05
INSULATING MATERIALS			
Blanket and Batt[b]			
Mineral wool, fibrous form			
processed from rock, slag, or glass			
1–3 in.		4.16	—
3–4 in.	0.3–2.0	—	11.0
5½–6½ in.		—	19.0
9–10 in.		—	30.0
Wood fiber			
Boards and slabs			
Cellular glass	8.5	2.86	—
Glass fiber	4–9	4.00	—
Expanded rubber (rigid)	4.5	4.55	—
Expanded polyurethane (R-11 blown)	1.5	6.25	—
(Thickness 1 in. & greater)			
Expanded polystyrene, extruded			
Cut cell surface	1.8	4.00	—
Smooth skin surface	1.8–3.5	5.00	—
Expanded polystyrene, molded beads	1.0	3.85	—
		—	
Mineral fiber with resin binder	15	3.45	—
Mineral fiberboard, wet felted			
Core or roof insulation	16–17	2.94	—
Acoustical tile	18	2.86	—
Acoustical tile	21	2.70	—
Mineral fiberboard, wet molded			
Acoustical tile[c]	23	2.38	—
Wood or cane fiberboard			
Acoustical tile[c] ½ in.	—	—	1.19
Acoustical tile[c] ¾ in.	—	—	1.78
Interior finish (plank, tile)	15	2.86	—
Cement fiber slabs (shredded with portland cement boards)	25.0–27.0	2.00	—
Loose Fill			
Mineral fiber			
(glass, slag, or rock)			
5 in.	0.6–2.0	—	11.00
6½–8¾ in.	0.6–2.0	—	19.00
10¼–13¾ in.	0.6–2.0	—	30.00
Vermiculite (exfoliated)	4.0–6.0	2.27	—
	7.0–8.2	2.13	—
Perlite (expanded)	2.0–4.1	3.50	—
	4.1–7.4	3.00	—
	7.4–11.0	2.60	—
Wood fiber, softwoods	2.0–3.5	3.33	—
MASONRY MATERIALS—CONCRETES			
Cement mortar	116	0.20	—
Gypsum-fiber concrete, 87½% gypsum, 12½% wood chips	51	0.60	—
Lightweight aggregates including	120	0.19	—
expanded shale, clay or slate;	100	0.28	—
expanded slags; cinders; pumice;	80	0.40	—
perlite; vermiculite; also	60	0.59	—
cellular concretes	40	0.86	—
	30	1.11	—
	20	1.43	—
Sand & gravel or stone aggregate (oven dried)	140	0.11	—
Sand & gravel or stone aggregate (not dried)	140	0.08	—
Stucco	116	0.20	—

THERMAL VALUES OF MATERIALS

MATERIAL & DESCRIPTION	DENSITY (lb per cu ft)	RESISTANCE (R)[a] Per inch thickness (1/k)	For thickness listed (1/C)
MASONRY UNITS			
Brick, common[d]	120	0.20	—
Brick, face[e]	130	0.11	—
Clay tile, hollow:	—	—	
1 cell deep 3 in.	—	—	0.80
1 cell deep 4 in.	—	—	1.11
2 cells deep 6 in.	—	—	1.52
2 cells deep 8 in.	—	—	1.85
Concrete blocks, three oval core:			
Sand & gravel aggregate 4 in.	—	—	0.71
8 in.	—	—	1.11
12 in.	—	—	1.28
Cinder aggregate 3 in.	—	—	0.86
4 in.	—	—	1.11
8 in.	—	—	1.72
12 in.	—	—	1.89
Lightweight aggregate 3 in.	—	—	1.27
(expanded shale, clay, slate 4 in.	—	—	1.50
or slag; pumice) 8 in.	—	—	2.00
12 in.	—	—	2.27
Concrete blocks, rectangular core:			
Sand & gravel aggregate			
2 core, 8 in. 36 lb.	—	—	1.04
Lightweight aggregate (expanded shale, clay, slate or slag; pumice)			
3 core, 6 in. 19 lb.	—	—	1.65
2 core, 8 in. 24 lb.	—	—	2.18
3 core, 12 in. 38 lb.	—	—	2.48
Granite, marble	150–175	0.05	—
Stone, lime or sand	—	0.08	—
METALS			
Aluminum	171	0.0007	—
Brass, red	524–542	0.0010	—
Brass, yellow	524–542	0.0012	—
Copper, cast rolled	550–555	0.0004	—
Iron, gray cast	438–445	0.0030	—
Iron, pure	474–493	0.0023	—
Lead	704	0.0041	—
Steel, cold drawn	490	0.0032	—
Steel, stainless, type 304		0.0055	—
Zinc, cast		0.0013	—
PLASTERING MATERIALS			
Cement plaster, sand aggregate	116	0.20	—
Sand aggregate ½ in.	—	—	0.10
Sand aggregate ¾ in.	—	—	0.15
Gypsum plaster:			
Lightweight aggregate ½ in.	45	—	0.32
Lightweight aggregate ⅝ in.	45	—	0.39
Lightweight aggregate, on metal lath ¾ in.	—	—	0.47
Perlite aggregate	45	0.67	—
Sand aggregate	105	0.18	—
Sand aggregate ½ in.	105	—	0.09
Sand aggregate ⅝ in.	105	—	0.11
Sand aggregate, on metal lath ¾ in.	—	—	0.13
Vermiculite aggregate	45	0.59	—
ROOFING			
1-ply membrane 0.048 in.	83	—	0.50
Asphalt roll roofing	70	—	0.15
Asphalt shingles	70	—	0.44
Built-up roofing ⅜ in.	70	—	0.33
Slate ½ in.	—	—	0.05
SIDING MATERIALS			
(On Flat Surface)			
Shingles:			
Wood, 16 in., 7½ in. exposure	—	—	0.87
Wood, double, 16 in., 12 in. exposure	—	—	1.19
Wood, plus insul. backer board, ⁵⁄₁₆ in.	—	—	1.40
Siding:			
Aluminum (hollow backed over sheathing)	—	—	0.61
Vinyl (hollow backed over sheathing) 0.04 in.	—	—	1.00
Cedar shakes ½ in.	—	—	0.94
¾ in.	—	—	1.69
Wood, drop, 1 x 8 in.	—	—	0.79
Wood, bevel, ½ x 8 in., lapped	—	—	0.81
Wood, bevel, ¾ x 10 in., lapped	—	—	1.05
Architectural glass	—	—	0.10

D. Richard Stroup, AIA; Craig, Gaulden & Davis, Architects; Greenville, South Carolina

THERMAL TRANSMISSION   **18**

THERMAL VALUES OF MATERIALS

MATERIAL & DESCRIPTION		DENSITY (lb per cu ft)	RESISTANCE (R)[a] Per inch thickness (1/k)	For thickness listed (1/C)
WOODS				
Maple, oak, and similar hardwoods		45	0.91	—
Fir, pine, and similar softwoods		32	1.25	—
Fir, pine, and similar softwoods	25/32 in.	32	—	0.98
	1½ in.	32	—	1.89
	2½ in.	32	—	3.12
	3½ in.	32	—	4.35
Door, 1-¾ in. thick solid wood core				3.13
1⅜ in. hollow core				2.22

STEEL DOORS (NOMINAL THICKNESS 1¾ IN.)

Mineral fiber core	—	—	1.69
Solid urethane foam core*	—	—	5.56
Solid polystyrene core*	—	—	2.13

*With thermal break.

AIR SURFACES

Position of Surface	Direction of Heat Flow	Type of Surface: Non-Reflective Materials Resistance (R)	Reflective Aluminum Coated Paper Resistance (R)	Highly Reflective Foil Resistance (R)
STILL AIR				
Horizontal	Upward	0.61	1.10	1.32
45° slope	Upward	0.62	1.14	1.37
Vertical	Horizontal	0.68	1.35	1.70
45° slope	Down	0.76	1.67	2.22
Horizontal	Down	0.92	2.70	4.55
MOVING AIR (any position)				
15 mph wind	Any	0.17 (winter)	—	—
7½ mph wind	Any	0.25 (summer)	—	—

AIR SPACES

Position of Air Space and Thickness (inches)		Heat Flow Dir.	Season	Types of Surfaces on Opposite Sides: Both Surfaces Non-Reflective Materials Resistance (R)	Aluminum Coated Paper/ Non-Reflective Materials Resistance (R)	Foil/ Non-Reflective Materials Resistance (R)
Horizontal	¾	Up	W	0.87	1.71	2.23
	¾		S	0.76	1.63	2.26
	4		W	0.94	1.99	2.73
	4		S	0.80	1.87	2.75
45° slope	¾	Up	W	0.94	2.02	2.78
	¾		S	0.81	1.90	2.81
	4		W	0.96	2.13	3.00
	4		S	0.82	1.98	3.00
Vertical	¾	Down	W	1.01	2.36	3.48
	¾		S	0.84	2.10	3.28
	4		W	1.01	2.34	3.45
	4		S	0.91	2.16	3.44
45° slope	¾	Down	W	1.02	2.40	3.57
	¾		S	0.84	2.09	3.24
	4		W	1.08	2.75	4.41
	4		S	0.90	2.50	4.36
Horizontal	¾	Down	W	1.02	2.39	3.55
	1½		W	1.14	3.21	5.74
	4		W	1.23	4.02	8.94
	¾		S	0.84	2.08	3.25
	1½		S	0.93	2.76	5.24
	4		S	0.99	3.38	8.08

D. Richard Stroup, AIA; Craig, Gaulden & Davis, Architects; Greenville, South Carolina

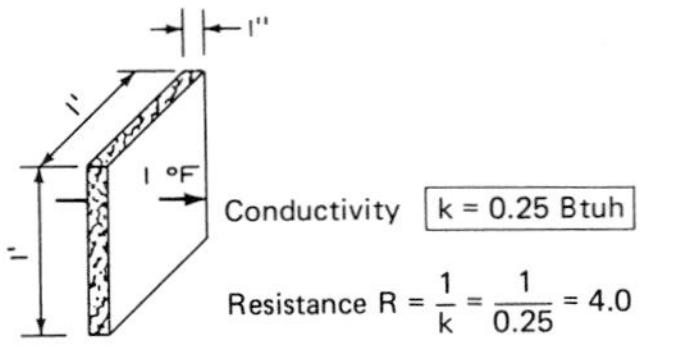
1"
1 °F
1'
1'
Conductivity k = 0.25 Btuh
Resistance R = 1/k = 1/0.25 = 4.0

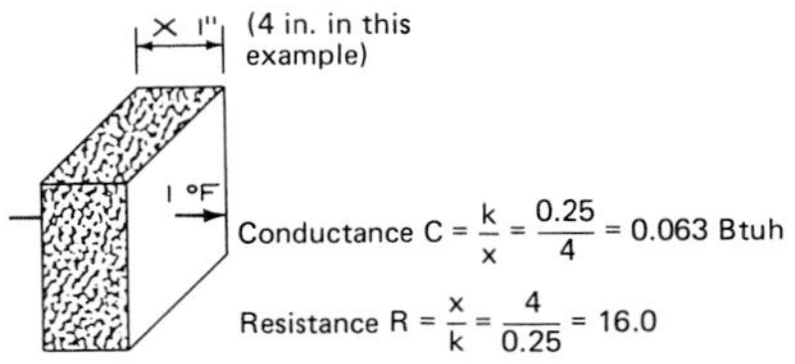
X 1" (4 in. in this example)
1 °F
Conductance C = k/x = 0.25/4 = 0.063 Btuh
Resistance R = x/k = 4/0.25 = 16.0

GLASS FIBER INSULATION BOARD

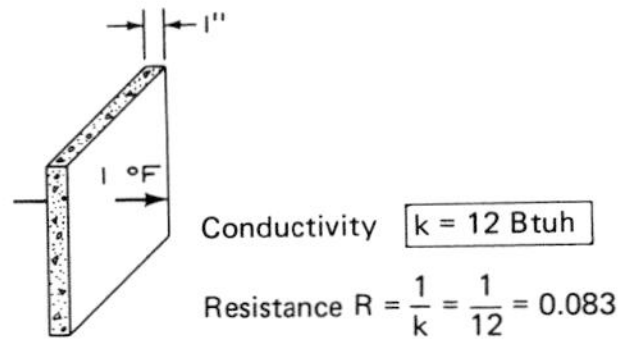
1"
1 °F
Conductivity k = 12 Btuh
Resistance R = 1/k = 1/12 = 0.083

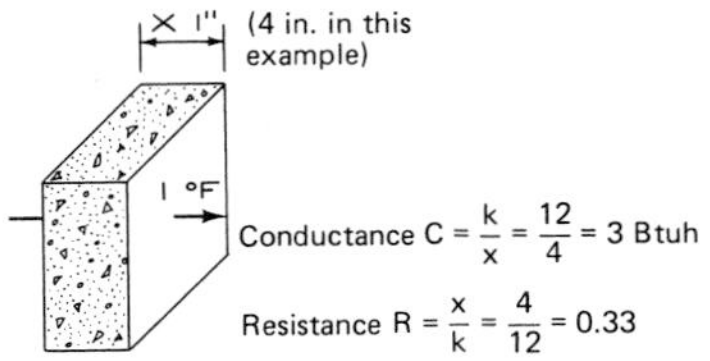
X 1" (4 in. in this example)
1 °F
Conductance C = k/x = 12/4 = 3 Btuh
Resistance R = x/k = 4/12 = 0.33

SAND AND GRAVEL CONCRETE

NOTES: Standard unit of area 1 sq ft.
Standard unit temperature differential 1 °F.

HEAT FLOW RATE

FOOTNOTES

a. Resistances are representative values for dry materials and are intended as design (not specification) values for materials in normal use. Unless shown otherwise in descriptions of materials, all values are for 75°C mean temperature.

b. Includes paper backing and facing if any. In cases where insulation forms a boundary (highly reflective or otherwise) of an airspace, refer to appropriate table for the insulating value of the airspace. Some manufacturers of batt and blanket insulation mark their products with R value, but they can ensure only the quality of the material as shipped.

c. Average values only are given, since variations depend on density of the board and on the type, size, and depth of perforations.

d. Thicknesses supplied by different manufacturers may vary depending on the particular material.

e. Values will vary if density varies from that listed.

f. Data on rectangular core concrete blocks differ from the data for oval core blocks because of core configuration, different mean temperature, and different unit weight. Weight data on oval core blocks not available.

g. Weight of units approx. 7⅝ high by 15⅝ long are given to describe blocks tested. Values are for 1 sq ft area.

h. Thermal resistance of metals is so low that in building constructions it is usually ignored. Values shown emphasize relatively easy flow of heat along or through metals so that they are usually heat leaks, inward or outward.

i. Spaces of uniform thickness bounded by moderately smooth surfaces.

j. Values shown not applicable to interior installations of materials listed.

k. Winter is heat flow up; summer is heat flow down.

l. Based on area of opening, not on total surface area.

Based on data from ASHRAE Handbook of Fundamentals, 1977, Chapter 22.

GLASS, GLASS BLOCK AND PLASTIC SHEET

MATERIAL AND DESCRIPTION	OVERALL HEAT TRANSMISSION COEFFICIENT (U)	SEASONS	RESISTANCE (R)
VERTICAL PANELS—EXTERIOR			
Flat Glass			
Single glass	1.10	Winter	0.91
	1.04	Summer	0.96
Insulating glass, two lights of glass			
3/16 in. airspace	0.62	Winter	1.61
	0.65	Summer	1.54
1/4 in. airspace	0.58	Winter	1.72
	0.61	Summer	1.64
1/2 in. airspace	0.49	Winter	2.04
	0.56	Summer	1.79
Insulating glass, three lights of glass			
1/4 in. airspaces	0.39	Winter	2.56
	0.44	Summer	2.22
1/2 in. airspaces	0.31	Winter	3.23
	0.39	Summer	2.56
1/2 in. airspaces, low emittance coating			
e = 0.20	0.32	Winter	3.13
	0.38	Summer	2.63
e = 0.40	0.38	Winter	2.63
	0.45	Summer	2.22
e = 0.60	0.43	Winter	2.33
	0.51	Summer	1.96
Storm windows			
1–4 in. airspace	0.50	Winter	2.00
	0.50	Summer	2.00
Glass Block			
6 x 6 x 4 in. thick (nom.)	0.60	Winter	1.67
	0.57	Summer	1.76
8 x 8 x 4 in. thick (nom.)	0.56	Winter	1.79
	0.54	Summer	1.85
With cavity divider	0.48	Winter	2.08
	0.46	Summer	2.17
12 x 12 x 4 in. thick (nom.)	0.52	Winter	1.92
	0.50	Summer	2.00
With cavity divider	0.44	Winter	2.27
	0.42	Summer	2.38
12 x 12 x 2 in. thick (nom.)	0.60	Winter	1.67
	0.57	Summer	1.76
Single Plastic Sheet			
1/8 in. thick (nom.)	1.06	Winter	0.94
	0.98	Summer	1.02
1/4 in. thick (nom.)	0.96	Winter	1.04
	0.89	Summer	1.12
HORIZONTAL PANELS—EXTERIOR			
Flat Glass			
Single glass	1.23	Winter	0.81
	0.83	Summer	1.20
Insulating glass, two lights of glass			
3/16 in. airspace	0.70	Winter	1.43
	0.57	Summer	1.75
1/4 in. airspace	0.65	Winter	1.54
	0.54	Summer	1.85
1/2 in. airspace	0.59	Winter	1.69
	0.49	Summer	2.04
Glass Block			
11 x 11 x 3 in. thick with cavity divider	0.53	Winter	1.89
	0.35	Summer	2.86
12 x 12 x 4 in. thick with cavity divider	0.51	Winter	1.96
	0.34	Summer	2.94
Plastic Bubbles[k]			
Single walled	1.15	Winter	0.87
	0.80	Summer	1.25
Double walled	0.70	Winter	1.43
	0.46	Summer	2.17

NOTES

The thermal conductivity of glass is relatively high (k = 7.5), and, for single glazing, most of the thermal resistance is imposed at the indoor and outdoor surfaces. Indoors, approximately two-thirds of the heat flows by radiation to the room surfaces and only one-third flows by convection. This can be materially affected by the use of forced airflow from induction units, for example. The inner surface coefficient of heat transfer, h_i, can be substantially reduced by applying a low emittance metallic film to the glass.

For glazing with airspaces, the U value can be reduced to a marked degree by the use of low emittance films. This process imparts a variable degree of reflectance to the glass, thereby reducing its Shading Coefficient. Manufacturers' literature should be consulted for more details on this important subject. Also consult Chapter 27 of the 1981 ASHRAE Handbook of Fundamentals.

FOOTNOTES

a. Resistances are representative values for dry materials and are intended as design (not specification) values for materials in normal use. Unless shown otherwise in descriptions of materials, all values are for 75°C mean temperature.

b. Includes paper backing and facing if any. In cases where insulation forms a boundary (highly reflective or otherwise) of an airspace, refer to appropriate table for the insulating value of the airspace. Some manufacturers of batt and blanket insulation mark their products with R value, but they can ensure only the quality of the material as shipped.

c. Average values only are given, since variations depend on density of the board and on the type, size, and depth of perforations.

d. Thicknesses supplied by different manufacturers may vary depending on the particular material.

e. Values will vary if density varies from that listed.

f. Data on rectangular core concrete blocks differ from the data for oval core blocks because of core configuration, different mean temperature, and different unit weight. Weight data on oval core blocks not available.

g. Weight of units approx. 7$^5/_8$ high by 15$^5/_8$ long are given to describe blocks tested. Values are for 1 sq ft area.

h. Thermal resistance of metals is so low that in building constructions it is usually ignored. Values shown emphasize relatively easy flow of heat along or through metals so that they are usually heat leaks, inward or outward.

i. Spaces of uniform thickness bounded by moderately smooth surfaces.

j. Values shown not applicable to interior installations of materials listed.

k. Winter is heat flow up; summer is heat flow down.

l. Based on area of opening, not on total surface area.

Based on data from ASHRAE Handbook of Fundamentals, 1977, Chapter 22.

John I. Yellott, P.E.; College of Architecture, Arizona State University; Tempe, Arizona

SOLAR GAINS THROUGH SUNLIT FENESTRATION

Heat gains through sunlit fenestration constitute major sources of cooling load in summer. In winter, discomfort is often caused by excessive amounts of solar radiation entering through south facing windows. By contrast, passive solar design depends largely on admission and storage of the radiant energy falling on south facing and horizontal surfaces. Admission takes place both by transmission through glazing and by inward flow of absorbed energy. With or without the sun, heat flows through glazing, either inwardly or outwardly, whenever there is a temperature difference between the indoor and outdoor air. These heat flows may be calculated in the following manner.

The solar heat gain is estimated by a two-step process. The first step is to find, either from tabulated data or by calculation, the rate at which solar heat would be admitted under the designated conditions through a single square foot of double strength ($1/8$ in.) clear sheet glass. This quantity, called the solar heat gain factor (SHGF), is set by (a) the local latitude; (b) the date, hence the declination; (c) the time of day (solar time should be used); (d) the orientation of the window.

Tabulated values of SHGF are given in the 1981 ASHRAE Handbook of Fundamentals, Chapter 27, for latitudes from $0°$ (the equator) to $64°$ N by $8°$ increments and for orientations around the compass from N to NNW, by $22.5°$ increments. Selected values from the $40°$ table are given in an adjacent column.

Each individual fenestration system, consisting of glazing and shading devices, has a unique ability to admit solar heat. This property is evaluated in terms of its shading coefficient (SC), which is the ratio of the amount of solar heat admitted by the system under consideration to the solar heat gain factor for the same conditions. In equation form, this becomes:

solar heat gain (Btu/sq ft · hr) = SC x SHGF

Values of the shading coefficient are given in Chapter 27 of the 1981 ASHRAE Handbook of Fundamentals for the most widely used glazing materials alone and in combination with internal and external shading devices. Selected values for single and double glazing are given below:

SHADING COEFFICIENT FOR SELECTED GLAZING SYSTEMS

TYPE OF GLASS	SOLAR TRANS- MISSION	SHADING COEFFICIENT, SC
Clear		
$1/8$ in.	0.86	1.00
$1/4$ in.	0.78	0.94
Heat absorbing		
$1/8$ in.	0.64	0.83
$1/4$ in.	0.46	0.69
Insulating glass, clear both lights		
$1/8$ + $1/8$ in.	0.71	0.88
$1/4$ + $1/4$ in.	0.61	0.81
Heat absorbing out		
Clear in, $1/4$ in.	0.36	0.55

For combinations of glazing and shading devices, see the ASHRAE chapter cited above.

The heat flow due to temperature difference is found by multiplying the U-value for the specified fenestration system by the area involved and by the applicable temperature difference:

$$Q = A \times [SC \times SHGF + U \times (t_o - t_i)]$$

The same equation is used for both summer and winter, with appropriate U-values, but in winter the conduction heat flow is usually outward because the outdoor air is colder than the indoor air.

Example: find the total heat gain, in Btu/sq ft · hr, for 1000 sq ft of unshaded $1/4$ in. heat absorbing single glass, facing west, in Denver ($40°$N latitude) at 4:00 P.M. solar time on October 21. Indoor air temperature is $70°$F; outdoor air temperature is $40°$F.

Solution: from the accompanying table, for 4:00 P.M. on October 21 find the SHGF for west facing fenestration on October 21 to be 173 Btu/sq ft · hr. For $1/4$ in. heat absorbing glass, SC = 0.69 and U for winter conditions is 1.10 Btu/sq ft · hr · °F.

$$Q = 1000 \times [0.69 \times 173 + 1.10 \times (40 - 70)]$$
$$= 1000 \times (119.4 - 33.0) = 86,400 \text{ Btu/hr}$$

Even though the outdoor air is $30°$ cooler than the indoor air, the net heat gain through the window in question would be equivalent to 7.2 tons of refrigeration.

For the same window area in summer, on August 21 at 4:00 P.M. solar time, SHGF = 216, and the air temperatures may be taken as $95°$F outdoors and $78°$F indoors. The total heat gain will be:

$$Q = 1000 \times [0.69 \times 216 + 1.04 \times (95 - 78)]$$
$$= 1000 \times (149.0 + 17.7) = 166,700 \text{ Btu/hr}$$
$$= 13.9 \text{ tons of refrigeration}$$

The cooling load can be reduced by selecting a fenestration system with lower shading coefficient and U-value. Under the same conditions, a double glazed window with two lights of $1/4$ in. clear glass and a highly reflective translucent inner shading device would have U = 0.52 and SC = 0.37. The cooling load would then be reduced to 88,760 Btu/hr or 7.4 tons of refrigeration.

SOL-AIR TEMPERATURE

When the opaque surfaces of a structure are struck by solar radiation, much of the energy is absorbed by the irradiated surface, raising its temperature and increasing the rate of heat flow into the roof or wall. The time lag between the onset of irradiation and the resulting rise in the indoor surface temperature depends on the thickness and mass per unit area of the building element and on the thermal conductivity, specific heat, and density of the materials. The time lag is negligible for an uninsulated metal roof, but it can be a matter of hours for a massive concrete or masonry wall.

Heat flow through sunlit opaque building elements is estimated by using the sol-air temperature, t_{sa}, defined as an imaginary outdoor temperature that, in the absence of sunshine, would give the same rate of heat flow as actually exists at the specified time under the combined influence of the incident solar radiation and the ambient air temperature.

$$t_{sa} = I \times Abs./h_o$$

where I = solar irradiance (Btu/sq ft · hr)

Abs. = surface absorptance, dimensionless

h_o = outer surface coefficient (Btu/sq ft · hr · °F)

Surface absorptances range from as low as 0.30 for a white surface to 0.95 for a black built-up roof. Values of h_o range from the conventional 4.0 for summer with an assumed wind speed of 7.5 mph to a still air value of 3.0.

Example: find the rate of heat flow through a 1000 sq ft uninsulated black built-up roof, U = 0.3, under strong summer sunshine, I = 300 Btu/sq ft · hr, still air with $100°$F outdoors, $78°$F indoors.

Solution: the sol-air temperature is found from

$$t_{sa} = 300 \times \frac{0.95}{3.0} + 100 = 195°F$$

The rate of heat flow, neglecting the time lag, is

$$Q = 1000 \times 0.3 \times (195 - 78) = 35,100 \text{ Btu/hr}$$

With no sunshine on the roof, the heat flow is

heat flow = $1000 \times 0.3 \times (100 - 78) = 6600$ Btu/hr

The effect of the solar radiation is thus to increase the heat flow rate by 88%. A more massive roof with a lower U-value would show considerably less effect of the incoming solar radiation.

SOLAR INTENSITY AND SOLAR HEAT GAIN FACTORS FOR 40°N LATITUDE

DATE	SOLAR TIME (A.M.)	DIRECT NORMAL (BTUH/SQ FT)	SOLAR HEAT GAIN FACTORS (BTUH/SQ FT) N	E	S	W	HOR	SOLAR TIME (P.M.)
Jan 21	8	142	5	111	75	5	14	4
	10	274	16	124	213	16	96	2
	12	294	20	21	254	21	133	12
Feb 21	8	219	10	183	94	10	43	4
	10	294	21	143	203	21	143	2
	12	307	24	25	241	25	180	12
Mar 21	8	250	16	218	74	16	85	4
	10	297	25	153	171	25	186	2
	12	307	29	31	206	31	223	12
Apr 21	6	89	11	88	5	5	11	6
	8	252	22	224	41	21	123	4
	10	286	31	152	121	31	217	2
	12	293	34	36	154	36	252	12
May 21	6	144	36	141	10	10	31	6
	8	250	27	220	29	25	146	4
	10	277	34	148	83	34	234	2
	12	284	37	40	113	40	265	12
June 21	6	155	48	151	13	13	40	6
	8	246	30	216	29	27	153	4
	10	272	35	145	69	35	238	2
	12	279	38	41	95	41	267	12
Jul 21	6	138	37	137	11	11	32	6
	8	241	28	216	30	26	145	4
	10	269	35	146	81	35	231	2
	12	276	38	41	109	41	262	12
Aug 21	6	81	12	82	6	5	12	6
	8	237	24	216	41	23	122	4
	10	272	32	150	116	32	214	2
	12	280	35	38	149	38	247	12
Sep 21	8	230	17	205	71	17	82	4
	10	280	27	148	165	27	180	2
	12	290	30	32	200	32	215	12
Oct 21	8	204	11	173	89	11	43	4
	10	280	21	139	196	21	140	2
	12	294	25	27	234	27	177	12
Nov 21	8	136	5	108	72	5	14	4
	10	268	16	122	209	16	96	2
	12	288	20	21	250	21	132	12
Dec 21	8	89	3	67	50	3	6	4
	10	261	14	113	146	14	77	2
	12	285	18	19	253	19	113	12
			N	W	S	E	HOR	PM

John I. Yellott, P.E.; College of Architecture, Arizona State University; Tempe, Arizona

18   **THERMAL TRANSMISSION**

GENERAL

For years the building industry in the United States has depended upon a seemingly endless supply of high quality materials, supplies, and energy resources. Manufacturers have been producing building materials abundantly, and architects generally have been specifying them for reasons of aesthetics, budget, performance, code compliance, and availability. Consideration is rarely given to the environmental impact of using these materials, i.e., what environmental "costs" go into extracting, producing, shipping, and installing them. These costs include depletion of nonrenewable raw materials and resources; production of waste by-products; and exposure of toxicity to the air, water, soils, and inhabitants of nearby areas.

For the building industry of the future, it will be good business to use materials that are environmentally friendly, sustainable, and renewable and that contain recycled materials. A building industry that depends upon depletable resources to manufacture its materials will become more and more costly as the resources are depleted. More important, the world in which we build will become more and more uninhabitable because of the toxins and waste left by our present materials and methods of construction. To do its part in keeping the world safe to live in, the architecture profession must incorporate procedures and standards of resource conservation into our design philosophies.

BUILDING MATERIALS ANALYSIS
LIFE CYCLE OF BUILDING MATERIALS

To analyze a building material from an environmental standpoint, an understanding of the life cycle of that material must be reached. Examine the environmental burdens that accrue through extraction or acquisition of the raw materials and their processing/manufacture and the packaging, distribution, use, and ultimate recovery (reuse/recycling) or disposal of the finished product.

Three aspects of the life of a building material are most significant in considering environmental impact: Is the raw material renewable or nonrenewable? How much total waste or how many toxic by-products are produced in its production and during the life of the product? How much energy is consumed in its life cycle? A building material that is both environmentally "pure" and readily available–that is, one made from a 100% renewable raw material that uses only renewable energy in its extraction, production, and transport and can be infinitely reclaimed and recycled (as well as healthy to the occupants of a building)–will be hard to find. Even to have that "perfect" material as a goal, we need a frame of reference from which to choose materials based on environmental concerns, something like ingredient and nutrition labeling on food products. If this information was available on materials for the building industry, we would be able to specify materials that are healthy and "nutritious" for a sustainable planet.

EMBODIED ENERGY OF BUILDING MATERIALS

The embodied energy of a building material comprises all the energy consumed in acquiring and transforming the raw materials into finished products and transporting them to the building site. The life-cycle chart below details where energy is consumed in producing building materials. The embodied energy or energy "content" of a building material will act as a rough guide to its environmental friendliness. The energy content reflects the material's "closeness" to the earth; the more it is refined or processed, the more energy it "contains" and hence the more "expensive" it is environmentally.

If we must produce and use high-energy materials, it is important that we not waste that energy by burying them in a landfill but rather reuse or recycle them.

To compare one material to another, we must take into account the following characteristics:

1. Regional availability–local extraction/manufacture
2. Recyclability (how many times the material can be recycled and retain viability)
3. Reusability
4. Durability and life span
5. Toxicity of the product or of the materials used to maintain the product during its life
6. Efficiency of product's performance as an architectural component
7. Savings on other materials not used because this product is used
8. Savings in energy not consumed over the life span of the building because this product is used
9. Any combination of these factors

Some construction methods and systems bind materials together to render them difficult or costly to recycle or reuse. One example of this is reinforced concrete, which efficiently uses steel in its role of spanning distances but also makes it impractical to recycle after a building has outlived its usefulness. A structural steel frame, although it uses a great deal more steel than a similar reinforced concrete frame, can be unbolted, disassembled, and reused or melted down and reformed infinitely.

NOTE

Evaluating whether a certain material is used in construction is a complicated process involving many factors. Certain regions or markets may be more familiar with or more suitable for certain types of construction or materials, and this may be an unavoidable factor that nullifies all others in determining which structural or other material is used.

LIFE-CYCLE CHECKLIST FOR BUILDING MATERIALS

This checklist can be used to analyze the environmental impact of building materials:

1. Raw material acquisition (mining, harvesting, drilling, extraction)
   a. Is the resource renewable or sustainable (reproducible indefinitely)?
   b. How much nonrenewable waste is produced?
   c. What is the amount and type of energy consumed? (Is it sustainable?)
   d. How does acquisition affect the environment? (Does it destroy forests or other habitats, produce silt or toxic runoff or air pollution?)
2. Raw material processing and manufacturing
   a. How much nonrecyclable waste is produced?
   b. What is the type and amount of energy consumed to manufacture the product?
   c. What toxicity to air, water, or soils is produced by processing?

APPROXIMATE VALUE OF EMBODIED ENERGY IN BUILDING MATERIALS

MATERIALS		ENERGY CONTENT (BTU/LB)
Low energy materials	Sand/gravel	18
	Wood	185
	Sand-lime brickwork	730
	Lightweight concrete	940
Medium energy materials	Gypsum board	1,830
	Brickwork	2,200
	Lime	2,800
	Cement	4,100
	Mineral fiber insulation	7,200
	Glass	11,100
	Porcelain	11,300
High energy materials	Plastic	18,500
	Steel	19,200
	Lead	25,900
	Zinc	27,800
	Copper	29,600
	Aluminum	103,500

3. Product packaging and final packaging (for shipping)
   a. Is packaging recyclable or made of recycled material?
   b. Is packaging excessive?
   c. Does packaging use nonrenewable resources (e.g., petroleum or materials harmful to the environment, such as CFC insulation packing material)?
4. Product distribution
   a. Would the product travel an excessive distance from the manufacturing site to the building site when more local products could be used?
   b. What is the type and amount of energy consumed to transport the material?
5. Product installation, use, maintenance
   a. Does installation produce excessive and/or nonrenewable site waste?
   b. What energy is consumed to install and maintain the product?
   c. Does installation, use, or maintenance of the product pollute the outdoor or indoor environment for installers or occupants?
   d. How durable is the product and what is its rate of degradation?
   e. Does the product add to the energy efficiency of the building?
6. Disposal, recycling, reuse
   a. Does the product use virgin materials wisely?
   b. Is it recyclable after use and, if so, to what degree?
   c. Can the product be reused?
   d. What energy is consumed to recycle the product?
   e. What energy is consumed to dispose of its nonrecyclable elements?
   f. What is the toxicity to the environment when the product is thrown away?

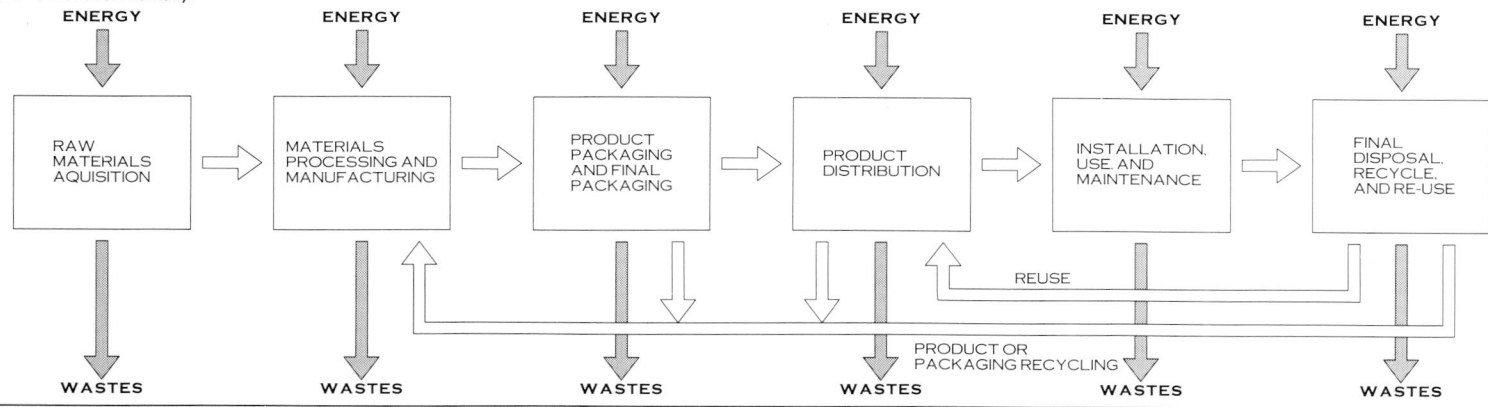

LIFE-CYCLE CHART

Energy consumption considerations of building materials should not override basic respect for the earth. Degradation of the landscape in materials extraction, transport, and manufacturing, as well as in construction, should be minimized.

Richard J. Vitullo, AIA; Oak Leaf Studio; Crownsville, Maryland
AIA Environmental Resource Guide

ENVIRONMENTAL CONSTRUCTION   18

LIFE CYCLE OF COMMON BUILDING MATERIALS

	ALUMINUM	STEEL	PARTICLEBOARD
Raw materials acquisition and preparation	• Manufacturing depletes the mineral bauxite, a finite resource (only 125 years remain at the current rate of consumption). • Bauxite strip mining causes loss of large tracts of land, including some loss of tropical forests and habitats. • Reclamation of strip mines reduces long-term effects but some species may be lost. • Other raw materials consumed during acquisition include lime, caustic, soda, crude oil, and coal. • Degradation of ground and surface water and air may occur from mining.	• Manufacturing depletes supplies of iron ore, limestone, and coal, all finite resources. • Processing of coal into coke produces toxic air pollutants. • Deep pit mining causes loss of virgin forests and lands; land reclamation may reduce long term effects • Degradation of ground and surface water and air may occur from mining	• Approximately 90% of the wood component of this product comes from sawmill waste; if managed, sustainable and renewable wood cellulose sources are used, natural resource depletion is eliminated; if sawmill waste from old growth trees is used, those forests and habitats will be lost. • Size of wood chips varies from 25mm to particles as fine as flour. • 98% of the resin binder in particleboard is urea formaldehyde (urea is derived from petroleum and formaldehyde from natural gas); 1.6% of the resin used is phenol formaldehyde (phenol is derived from coal tar and petroleum).
Raw materials processing and manufacturing	• Smelting and ingot casting is energy intensive. • Different finishes vary in their environmental burdens: anodizing and powdered paint coatings have few negative environmental effects, while electroplating and related finishes are highly polluting.	• Raw materials and resources used in processing include nickel, manganese, chromium, lubricating oils, solvents, acids, and alkalies. • Iron is produced from iron ore, coke, and lime, which is heated in blast furnaces. • Steel is made from iron by either the basic oxygen furnace method, using 30% scrap, or the electric furnace method, using all scrap steel and iron.	• Gaseous formaldehyde emissions occur in drying and mat pressing stages of processing.
Product packaging and final packaging	• Packaging of materials varies; choose products that use minimal packaging or packaging made of recycled materials and/or that is itself recyclable.		
Product distribution	• Distribution varies; choose products made and/or distributed from a place as close to the building site as possible.		
Product installation, use, and maintenance	• Generally a low maintenance material, depending on finish. Painted aluminum surfaces require periodic repainting; anodized finishes and powdered paint coatings require occasional cleaning.	• Maintenance depends on which alloy is used (e.g., stainless steel), whether electrolytic treatment has been done (e.g., galvanized steel), and whether a coating has been applied. • Preparation of the surface for repainting or other maintenance may require use of solvents or acids. • Weathering steel, which forms a protective oxidized coating, is also available.	• Most uses are for applications such as cabinet and furniture core stock (MDF), nonstructural floor underlayment, and manufactured home decking. Since the uses are located in protected and confined areas beneath finishes, degradation and air pollution are minimized. Nonetheless, some interior air pollution from offgassing may occur.
Final disposal, reuse, or recycle	• Scrap can be recovered, recycled, and reused endlessly; use of recycled aluminum reduces total energy requirements by 90–95%, however, only 15–20% of aluminum in construction is recovered and recycled since it is "bound up" with other materials and difficult to separate. • Final disposal causes no ill environmental effects, except ground water contamination from coatings and landfill overcrowding.	• By way of magnetic separating processes, scrap is easily recovered and recycled. Recycled steel saves energy and raw materials and reduces contamination of the environment. • Final disposal causes no ill environmental effects except groundwater contamination from coatings and landfill overcrowding; steel eventually oxidizes back into a natural state. Limited sorting of steel alloys required in recycling.	• Since particleboard is usually bound tightly into assemblies with other materials and finishes such as laminates, recycling is difficult, although possible.
Energy consumption totals	• The aluminum industry accounts for 1.4% of annual world energy consumption. • Embodied energy at point-of-use for one pound of aluminum is estimated at 102,500 BTUs. Aluminum produced from recovered scrap and recycled aluminum rather than bauxite ore saves 80% of total energy consumption.	• Embodied energy at point-of-use for one pound of steel is estimated at 19,200 BTUs. Processes using scrap steel and iron save energy by skipping blast furnace energy consumption.	• Embodied energy at point-of-use for one pound of underlayment particleboard is estimated at 7,000 BTUs, 30-40% of which is derived from the resin adhesive. • Energy consumed in production is mostly used for heat to dry particles, heat resins, and create steam for hot presses. Depending on the manufacturing plant, wood, gas, and oil are used for energy; however, 78% of the total energy bound up in wood products comes from the burning of wood waste.
Waste generation total	• Bauxite refining yields large volumes of mud containing trace amounts of hazardous waste. • Although most airborne emissions are contained by wet scrubbing, small amounts of carcinogenic hydrocarbons escape during smelting and forming. • Fabrication and finishing may produce heavy metal sludges and large amounts of waste waters that require treatment with toxic chemicals. • Solid wastes include used potliners of carbon, insulation material, fluoride, and cyanide.	• Both deep pit and strip mining of iron ore, coal, and limestone yield large amounts of discarded rock and soil, resulting in erosion and contamination of water by dissolved toxic minerals. The production of one ton of steel creates 1.5 tons of waste materials. • Mine spoils from coal mining may acidify nearby soils and water. • Coke ovens may emit toxic sulphur dioxide fumes, carbon monoxide, and other particulate emissions; processing limestone into lime releases carbon dioxide emissions into the air. • Liquid wastes produced by processing include lubricants, electrolytic coatings, pickling solutions, paints, and contaminated water. • Solid wastes include by-products from the processing of iron ore, limestone, and coal.	• Most solid waste from particleboard manufacturing is recovered in the mill or used as fuel; panel trim pieces and defective panels are ground up and put back into raw material stock. • Production of resins results in waste waters that may contain toxic monomers.
Conclusion for designers	• Although its embodied energy is very high, when compared pound for pound to alternative materials aluminum may be preferable as it is very strong and durable, lightweight, and readily recyclable. • Specify aluminum products that are made fully or partially from recycled scrap. • Consider designs that will facilitate recycling; avoid, if possible, mixed-material assemblies. • Anodized finishes and powdered paint coatings may be the most environmentally friendly finishes. • In applications where the uniquely advantageous characteristics of aluminum are not needed, consider low energy-consuming alternative materials that are recyclable.	• Since many steel products are made totally or partially from recycled steel, steel is considered less environmentally harmful than other alternatives. • Steel can be used very efficiently in reinforced concrete as a structural material. However, this practice usually binds the steel permanently with concrete, making it nonrecyclable. • Steel, regardless of coating, treatments, and alloys, can be recovered and recycled easily.	• Urea formaldehyde (UF) particleboard offgasses formaldehyde into indoor air. Levels of emission are higher in spaces with high temperature and humidity levels; all emission levels decrease over time. • Specify low-emitting, UF-bonded particleboard where practical, or consider sealing UF particleboard or using phenol formaldehyde-bonded particleboard (exterior grade plywood, etc.).

Richard J. Vitullo, AIA; Oak Leaf Studio; Crownsville, Maryland
AIA Environmental Resource Guide

18 ENVIRONMENTAL CONSTRUCTION

RESOURCE CONSERVATION METHODS AND SYSTEMS

Choosing building materials containing recycled materials is but one step in the process of environmentally conscious design. Sensitive environmental design takes the holistic view, regarding every aspect of how a building works in its context. Consideration must be given to how a building performs and relates to its surroundings throughout its life, before (design and specification), during (construction), and after (lifetime maintenance and energy costs) it is built. The following guidelines can be used for designing with resource conservation goals:

1. Design with nature's patterns in mind so the building works with them and the resources of its site rather than overpowering and controlling them. The following methods will help you achieve this goal:

   a. Building and site planning. To achieve the goal of overall environmental design, it is critical to orient the building to the landscape at the site. Working with site features will allow you to take advantage of natural systems, such as ventilation by means of windows and chimneys or full-spectrum light sources.

   b. Earth-sheltered design. Solar heat and light can be used to reduce the nonrenewable energy requirements of a building. The temperature- moderating feature of the earth is an aspect of the surrounding environment often ignored. Through earth berms, earth-covered roofs, and underground design, a building can make use of the consistent 55° F± of the earth

below the local frost line or at least the inherent R-value of earth material. A well-designed earth-sheltered structure also reduces the need for exterior maintenance of building materials.

2. Preserving existing site features may benefit the local habitat and make the building harmonize with the site.

   a. Tree, plant, and soil preservation. Establish environmental priorities for the building site. Inventory natural features such as viable trees and shrubs and wetland areas. Trees provide an enormous environmental benefit to the health of buildings (shading, etc.), sites (soil enrichment from leaves, etc.), and birds and other wildlife. Locate buildings, driveways, and land to be disturbed during construction far enough from existing trees to avoid root compaction. A good rule of thumb is to stay out of the drip line of a tree during construction. Have a landscape architect, arborist, forester, or environmental consultant assist in the survey.

   b. Construction and demolition site waste recycling or reuse. The construction of a single-family home in the U.S. generates 2.5 tons of waste. Since landfill overcrowding has caused dumping fees to increase significantly, it is becoming economically feasible to recycle construction and demolition wastes. Identify materials that could be used more efficiently, salvaged, reused on site, or recycled. Common materials that generally can be recycled from construction sites are (with percentages based on total site waste volume): wood

(27%), cardboard/paper (18%), gypsum board (15%), insulation (9%), roofing (8%), metals (7%), concrete/asphalt rubble (6%), landscaping debris (5%), and miscellaneous (5%). These are national averages, and each site will be different. Identify positions for recycling bins on site so materials can be separated as they are recovered. Prevent storm sewer and ground water pollution and reduce soil erosion with sensitive design and site construction methods.

3. Energy-efficient design should reduce or eliminate nonrenewable fossil fuel consumption for heating, cooling, and lighting. Although it is good to create a building with resource conservative materials, it is critical to ensure that once the building is built it either continues to conserve energy resources or uses renewable energy resources throughout its life. Consider using durable, low-maintenance materials. Where practical, design full-cycle systems such as solar water heating that will capture renewable energy on site. The following equipment can help achieve this goal:

   a. Heat recovery ventilators. This system extracts the heat from the air as it is exhausted and transfers that it to incoming air (or the reverse in the summer). This system allows a tight, energy-efficient building to be ventilated but still retain the heat-energy used to maintain the indoor environment. Depending on the climate, this system can be up to 80% efficient in recovering energy and is recommended for either very cold or very hot, humid climates. Consult with a mechanical engineer or equipment manufacturer.

   b. Ground source heat pump. Like earth-sheltered building design, this system takes advantage of the stability of underground temperatures. Long lengths of copper tubing are buried either horizontally or vertically in the earth and circulated with a heat-exchanging medium.

NONTOXIC BUILDING MATERIALS

Some building materials contain substances or release particles that can be an irritant and cause the medical problem called "sick building syndrome." Some of these airborne substances can also cause long-term problems such as chronic allergies and even cancer. Chemically sensitive people are at risk, as well as otherwise healthy installers or building occupants. The origins of these toxic substances–including by-products of manufacture and installation (e.g., chemicals released as adhesives and mastics cure), by-products of decay and age (e.g., offgassing of particleboard or plywood), and by–products of burning (e.g., toxic fumes from plastics)–are varied.

The U.S. Environmental Protection Agency (EPA) has identified five major causes of indoor air pollution:

1. Biogenic particles–mold, bacteria, etc.
2. Combustion by-products–tobacco products, gas ranges, furnaces, and fireplaces
3. Organic chemicals–benzene, formaldehyde
4. Natural substances–radon, lead
5. Fibrous materials and airborne particles–fiberglass, asbestos, pollen, dust, etc.

Ideally, materials and systems selected for a building should be durable, easily maintained, safe for the installer and user, and produced without excess energy use. Good maintenance features allow a material to be cleaned of other hazards and irritants, such as mold, moisture, and dust, with nontoxic cleaners and treatments. However, building materials should not be chosen for good maintenance features alone, as hazardous materials like vinyl, synthetics, and plastics can be very easy to clean.

As in any design process, designing a healthy building requires establishing priorities. However, this may not be an easy task, as it can be difficult to define "healthy" and difficult to implement "healthy" practices. Alternative products are not as well known or marketed as standard products, making them harder to find. In addition, these products can be more expensive and occasionally more difficult to install or apply if contractors are unfamiliar with them. Nonetheless, carefully selecting appropriate alternatives where possible and minimizing the most toxic materials and methods make constructing a "healthier" building an achievable goal.

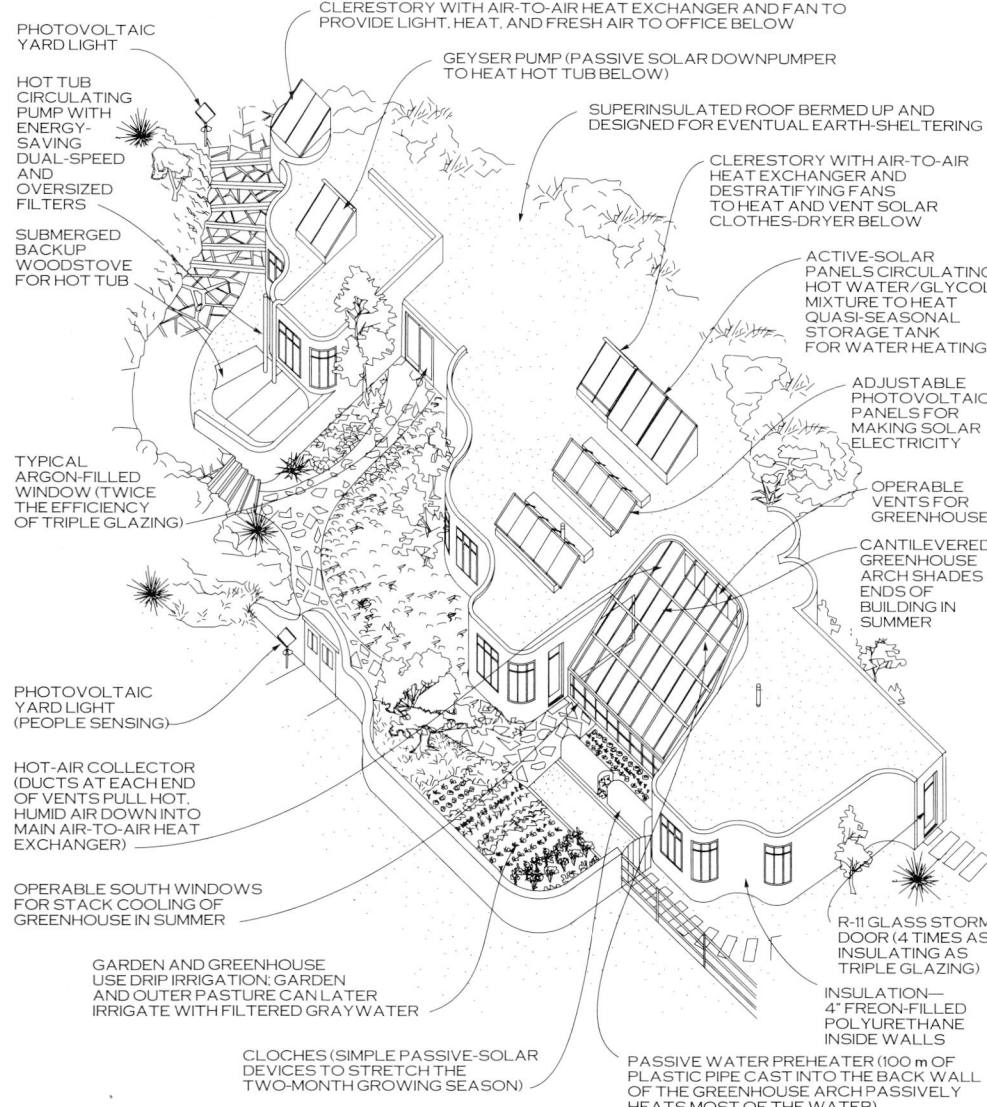

PHOTOVOLTAIC YARD LIGHT

HOT TUB CIRCULATING PUMP WITH ENERGY-SAVING DUAL-SPEED AND OVERSIZED FILTERS

SUBMERGED BACKUP WOODSTOVE FOR HOT TUB

TYPICAL ARGON-FILLED WINDOW (TWICE THE EFFICIENCY OF TRIPLE GLAZING)

PHOTOVOLTAIC YARD LIGHT (PEOPLE SENSING)

HOT-AIR COLLECTOR (DUCTS AT EACH END OF VENTS PULL HOT, HUMID AIR DOWN INTO MAIN AIR-TO-AIR HEAT EXCHANGER)

OPERABLE SOUTH WINDOWS FOR STACK COOLING OF GREENHOUSE IN SUMMER

GARDEN AND GREENHOUSE USE DRIP IRRIGATION; GARDEN AND OUTER PASTURE CAN LATER IRRIGATE WITH FILTERED GRAYWATER

CLOCHES (SIMPLE PASSIVE-SOLAR DEVICES TO STRETCH THE TWO-MONTH GROWING SEASON)

CLERESTORY WITH AIR-TO-AIR HEAT EXCHANGER AND FAN TO PROVIDE LIGHT, HEAT, AND FRESH AIR TO OFFICE BELOW

GEYSER PUMP (PASSIVE SOLAR DOWNPUMPER TO HEAT HOT TUB BELOW)

SUPERINSULATED ROOF BERMED UP AND DESIGNED FOR EVENTUAL EARTH-SHELTERING

CLERESTORY WITH AIR-TO-AIR HEAT EXCHANGER AND DESTRATIFYING FANS TO HEAT AND VENT SOLAR CLOTHES-DRYER BELOW

ACTIVE-SOLAR PANELS CIRCULATING HOT WATER/GLYCOL MIXTURE TO HEAT QUASI-SEASONAL STORAGE TANK FOR WATER HEATING

ADJUSTABLE PHOTOVOLTAIC PANELS FOR MAKING SOLAR ELECTRICITY

OPERABLE VENTS FOR GREENHOUSE

CANTILEVERED GREENHOUSE ARCH SHADES ENDS OF BUILDING IN SUMMER

R-11 GLASS STORM DOOR (4 TIMES AS INSULATING AS TRIPLE GLAZING)

INSULATION— 4" FREON-FILLED POLYURETHANE INSIDE WALLS

PASSIVE WATER PREHEATER (100 m OF PLASTIC PIPE CAST INTO THE BACK WALL OF THE GREENHOUSE ARCH PASSIVELY HEATS MOST OF THE WATER)

ENERGY SAVING SYSTEMS (THE ROCKY MOUNTAIN INSTITUTE; SNOWMASS, COLORADO)

Richard J. Vitullo, AIA; Oak Leaf Studio; Crownsville, Maryland
AIA Environmental Resource Guide

BUILDING MATERIALS COMPARISON CHART

CSI DIVISIONS	STANDARD PRODUCTS	ENVIRONMENTAL IMPACT	TOXICITY TO INDOOR ENVIRONMENT	ENVIRONMENTALLY SOUND ALTERNATIVE PRODUCTS OR SUGGESTIONS	ENVIRONMENTAL IMPACT	TOXICITY TO INDOOR ENVIRONMENT
Concrete	Concrete material	• Concrete has high embodied energy content		• Autoclaved cellular concrete (ACC)	• Uses fly-ash, a by-product of coal combustion • Aluminum powder additive reacts with lime to create hydrogen bubbles and a lightweight, cellular cementitious material (provides high strength to weight ratio); also self-insulating (R-10 for 8 in. wall)	• No harmful by-products
Metals	Steel studs/ framing members	• Reduces depletion of old and new growth timber • Can be made from recycled scrap into identical product • Consumes more energy to produce (high embodied energy content) • Steel production pollutes air, water, and soil	• Inert; produces no harmful by-products	• Use materials with less embodied energy content if recycled steel not available	• See alternative product chosen	• See alternative product chosen
Wood	Standard wood framing	• Depletes old and new growth timber • Can be recycled into particleboard and other wood products • Pressure-treated woods contain toxic inorganic arsenates (site waste needs to be contained)	• Produces no significant harmful by-products	• Interior: Engineered lumber Finger-jointed structural lumber Plastic framing members • Exterior: Decking - pav lope Mudsills - douglas fir treated with resin oil, beechwood distillates, etc.	• Engineered lumber made from recycled wood fiber and small diameter trees • Finger-jointed wood made from small wood pieces • Plastic members made from recycled soda bottles • Pav lope, a plantation grown, rot-resistant hardwood • Natural wood treatments not toxic	• Engineered lumber may offgas formaldehyde • Plastic members may offgas chemical fumes and give off toxic fumes when burned
	Plywood	• Made from large diameter, old growth peeler logs	• Interior grade offgases high-emitting levels of urea formaldehyde • Exterior grade offgases low-emitting phenol formaldehyde • Formaldehyde a possible carcinogen and is irritating to respiration • Offgassing half-life is ± 6 months	• Lumber-core plywood • Cellulose fiberboard underlayment • Exterior - grade plywood with sealing finishes • Tongue and groove pine sheathing	• All plywood still made from old growth peeler logs • Cellulose fiberboard made from recycled newspapers • Tongue and groove pine usually locally grown and can be from smaller diameter trees	• Lumber core and exterior grade plywoods have reduced levels of formaldehyde offgassing • Cellulose fiberboard and tongue and groove pine have no harmful offgassing
	Particleboard: Oriented - strand board (OSB) Medium density fiberboard (MDF)	• Can be made from recycled wood scrap, sustainable woods, and cellulose fibers	• Same characteristics as plywood	• Laminated or sealed MDF		• Covering finishes or sealers reduce offgassing
	Finish woods	• Use of exotic tropical woods depletes rain forests	• Produces no harmful by-products	• Domestic temperate hardwoods (plum, cherry, alder, black locust, and persimmon) • Veneer woods with recycled backup • Reclaimed and re-used woods	• Domestic woods can be managed as sustainable tree farms • Use of veneers instead of solid woods saves tree resources • Use of re-used woods saves tree resources	• Some finishes may be harmful to indoor air
Thermal and moisture protection	Fiberglass batt insulation	• Can be made from recycled glass	• Airborne fibers can be irritating to skin, lungs, and nasal passages • Offgases formaldehyde	• Cellulose insulation • Cotton insulation • Cementitious foam insulation • Mineral fiber insulation	• Cellulose insulation made from recycled newsprint • Cotton batt insulation made from recycled cotton denim fibers • Cementitious foam made from silicate-based magnesium (CFC-free) • Mineral fiber made from mineral slag, a waste by-product of steel production	• Cotton and cellulose insulation may be treated with chemical fire treatment
	Rigid insulation	• Many types made from nonrenewable petrochemicals • Many types also made with CFCs, which are harmful to ozone layer	• Gives off toxic fumes when burned • Those made with isocyanurate, polyurethane, and phenolic foam offgas chemical fumes	• Recycled extruded polystyrene insulation • CFC-free insulation • Expanded polystyrene	• Re-use of recycled plastic does not deplete oil resources • HCFC foaming agent $1/20$ as damaging to ozone as CFC • Expanded polystyrene only R-3.6 per inch (extruded polystyrene R-4.4 per inch)	• Some recycled plastic materials may offgas chemical fumes • Plastics give off toxic fumes when burned
	Exterior siding/ trim	• Vinyl siding made from nonrenewable petrochemical source • Wood siding and shakes deplete mature slow growth cedar and redwood trees		• Hardboard siding • Fiber-cement composite siding • Composite trim	• Hardboard siding made from recycled wood fiber • Fiber cement siding made from wood sawmill chips and portland cement • Composite trim made from recycled plastic and recycled wood fiber	
	Wood and asphalt roof shingles	• Asphalt is derived from nonrenewable petrochemicals • Wood shingles, either cedar or redwood, from old growth, slow growth tree stands	• Many contain fiberglass fibers (mostly harmful to installers), an irritant • Chemical treatment of wood shingles harmful to installers	• Fiber-cement composite shingles • Natural slate and terra-cotta • Recycled aluminum shingles • Recycled plastic shingles • Metal roofing of recycled steel or copper	• Fiber-cement shingles made from recycled wood sawmill chips or paper and portland cement (also recyclable) • Recycled aluminum from soda cans and scrap • Recycled plastic from computer housings	• Plastic offgases harmful fumes (negligible to indoor air) and gives off toxic fumes when burned

Richard J. Vitullo, AIA; Oak Leaf Studio; Crownsville, Maryland
AIA Environmental Resource Guide

18 **ENVIRONMENTAL CONSTRUCTION**

BUILDING MATERIALS COMPARISON CHART

CSI DIVISIONS	STANDARD PRODUCTS	ENVIRONMENTAL IMPACT	TOXICITY TO INDOOR ENVIRONMENT	ENVIRONMENTALLY SOUND ALTERNATIVE PRODUCTS OR SUGGESTIONS	ENVIRONMENTAL IMPACT	TOXICITY TO INDOOR ENVIRONMENT
Doors and windows	Doors	• Some doors made with endangered old growth woods such as teak or mahogany (lauan) veneers and solids	• Few harmful by-products in wood; finishes may contain offgassing materials	• Recycled-content doors • Fiberglass doors	• Some doors made from recycled plastic and wood waste; also recycled steel • Fiberglass uses a few petrochemicals in production	• Recycled wood may be bound by urea formaldehyde resin • Recycled plastic offgases and gives off toxic fumes when burned
	Windows	• Many windows in older structures not energy efficient	• Vinyl windows offgas harmful fumes and give off toxic fumes when burned	• Recycled-content windows • High efficient, low E glass windows • Argon-filled insulated glass windows	• Fiberglass same coefficient of expansion as glass • See doors above	• See doors above
Finishes	Gypsum board wall and ceiling systems	• Many types use predominantly virgin gypsum mineral, depleting resources	• Many carcinogens in standard joint compounds	• Wallboard made with recycled or reclaimed materials • Nontoxic powdered joint compound	• Some alternative "gypsum" board cores contain recycled scrap wallboard, by-product gypsum (from emissions of fossil-fueled factories), recycled cellulose fiber, perlite, ryegrass straw (an agricultural by-product), mixed waste papers. Some wallboard facings made with recycled paper	• Nontoxic joint compounds contain no harmful agents (must be site-mixed and may be difficult to use)
	Flooring	• PVC and vinyl tiles made from nonrenewable petrochemicals	• PVC and vinyls offgas harmful fumes	• Natural linoleum tile • Recycled-content tile • Natural grouts • Reclaimed and re-used wood floors	• Linoleum made from linseed oil, pine resins, softwood flour, cork, and jute • Tile made from recycled light bulbs and auto glass • Tile made from recycled auto tires • Grouts made from silica, calcium rock, and iron-oxide pigments	
	Carpet	• Many made from petrochemicals, a nonrenewable resource	• Plastic fibers, backing, mastics, and treatments offgas many gasses harmful to respiratory systems (major component of "sick building syndrome") • All carpets may harbor dust and mites, both respiratory irritants • Plastic gives off toxic fumes when burned	• Natural fiber carpets • Recycled-content carpets	• Choose untreated carpets made with natural fibers and backing such as wool or cotton • Some carpets made from recycled plastic (soft drink bottles) • Choose natural jute padding	• Use tackable edging instead of adhesives or just edge and seam application of adhesives • Use low-voc adhesives • Recycled plastic offgases harmful fumes and gives off toxic fumes when burned
	Paint, finishes, and wood treatments	• Unused paint etc. can cause groundwater and soil pollution if disposed of improperly • Volatile organic compounds (VOCs) can cause smog and ground level ozone pollution	• Many enamels, varnishes, and polyurethanes contain VOCs and offgas these causing harmful respiratory reactions	• Citrus-based paints • Acrylic-based stains • Natural wood treatments and finishes	• Citrus-based paints have low-biocide content but contain some petrochemicals • More organic type finishes present less disposal problems	• Citrus-based paints have low-biocide, nonirritating content (must be thinned and color-mixed by installer) • Acrylic-based stains are low-VOC • Natural wood treatments of tung oil, ointment of beeswax, etc. contain no harmful irritants (more maintenance required)
	Adhesives and mastics	• Unused containers can cause groundwater and soil pollution if disposed of improperly	• Some adhesives and mastics offgas hazardous fumes to installers and occupants • Many types of adhesives are flammable and give off toxic fumes when burned	• Low-voc, environmentally safer adhesives and mastics	• Some adhesives and mastics are nontoxic, nonflammable, and safer for disposal (water-soluble)	• Low-voc content emits less toxic fumes
Electrical	Electrical wiring		• Electromagnetic fields are created around any electrical source and may cause cancer	• Electromagnetic shielding		• Install shielding for wiring at spaces that will have prolonged exposure to occupants (e.g., bedrooms)

NOTES

1. This chart is intended as a guide to selecting environmentally friendly materials. As a rule of thumb, use locally produced environmentally friendly materials to save transportation-related energy.

2. In comparing building materials, the choice that promotes resource conservation may not always be as straightforward as it appears. For example, wood may seem a better choice than plastic for a park bench, as it is a natural, renewable material rather than a petroleum-based one. However, in an outdoor usage, where durability and good maintenance characteristics are preferred, offgassing from plastic is not an issue. When the aesthetics of wood are not important, plastic made from recycled soda bottles may be an appropriate solution. Choosing recycled plastic would conserve wood materials–old-growth cedar, redwood, or chemically treated pine–and reuse something made from a nonrenewable resource, making it an acceptable solution sympathetic with resource conservation principles. At issue is the definition of a "resource" that must be conserved. A great deal of material and embodied energy are tied up in existing plastic. The reuse of these materials not only allows those resources to continue a useful life but also saves the embodied energy that would have been used to create a new product in its place. Plastic, particularly, is very durable and very slow to degrade.

Richard J. Vitullo, AIA; Oak Leaf Studio; Crownsville, Maryland
AIA Environmental Resource Guide

GENERAL

Association of Energy Engineers
4025 Pleasantdale Road, Suite 420
Atlanta, GA 30340
Tel: (404) 447-5083
Fax:(404) 446-3969

Department of Energy
1000 Independence Avenue, S.W.
Washington, DC 20585
Tel: (202) 586-5000

Environmental Protection Agency
401 M Street, S.W.
Washington, DC 20460
Tel: (202) 382-2090

Renewable Natural Resources Foundation
5430 Grosvenor Lane
Bethesda, MD 20814
Tel: (301) 493-9101

REFERENCES

Brown, Lester R. *State of the World*. Worldwatch Institute.
Environmental Resource Guide (ERG). [quarterly]
Lam, William M. C. *Sunlighting as Formgiver for Architecture*. New York: Van Nostrand Reinhold, 1986.
Lawrence Berkeley Laboratory and Eley Associates. *Skylight Handbook Design Guidelines*. Palatine, Ill.: American Architectural Manufacturers Association. (AAMA), 1988.
McHarg, Ian L. *Design with Nature*.
Moore, Fuller. *Concepts and Practice of Architectural Daylighting*. New York: Van Nostrand Reinhold, 1985.
Oak Ridge National Laboratory. *Builder's Foundation Handbook*. Springfield, Va.: National Technical Information Service, 1991.
Pearson, David. *The Natural House Book*.
Van der Ryn, Sim and Peter Calthorpe. *Sustainable Communities: A New Design Synthesis for Cities, Suburbs, and Towns*.
Wann, David. *Biologic: Environmental Protection by Design*.
Watson, Donald, and Kenneth Labs. *Climatic Design: Energy-Efficient Building Principles and Practices*. New York: McGraw-Hill, 1983 (revised 1993).
Watson, Donald, FAIA, ed. *The Energy Design Handbook*. Washington, D.C.: AIA Press, 1993.

CLIMATE

International Society of
  Indoor Air Quality and Climate (ISIAQ)
Box 22038, Sub 32
Ottawa, Canada KIV 0W2
Tel: (613) 731-2559
Fax:(613) 737-2005

REFERENCES

Burt Hill Kosar Rittelmann Associates/Min Kantrowitz Associates. *Commercial Building Design: Integrating Climate, Comfort, and Cost*. New York: Van Nostrand Reinhold, 1987.
Givoni, B. *Man, Climate, and Architecture*. New York: American Elsevier Publishing.
Lowry, W. P. *Atmospheric Ecology for Designers and Planners*. Van Nostrand Reinhold, 1991.
Olgyay, V. *Bioclimatic Approach to Architecture*. Princeton, N.J.: Princeton University Press.

SOLAR RADIATION AND BUILDING ORIENTATION
REFERENCES

AWNSHADE 1.0 (Sun Shading Calculations), MS DOS program, FSEC, 1990.
Evans, Benjamin E. *Daylight in Architecture*. New York: McGraw-Hill, 1981.

NATURAL VENTILATION
REFERENCES

Boutet, T. *Controlling Air Movement: A Manual for Architects and Builders*. McGraw-Hill, 1987.
Building Air Quality: A Guide for Building Owners and Facility Managers, Environmental Protection Agency,

1991. [S/N 055-000-00390-4, Superintendent of Documents, Box 371954, Pittsburgh, PA 15250-7954]
Cooling with Ventilation. SERI/SP-273-2966. Florida Solar Energy Center.
Cone, J. and M. Hodgson, eds. *Problem Buildings: Building-Associated Illness and the Sick Building Syndrome*. Occupational Medicine, State of the Art Reviews, Hanley and Belfus, 1989.
Dupont, P. and J. Morrill. *Residential Air Quality and Energy Efficiency*. Berkeley: American Council for an Energy-Efficient Economy, 1989. [(510) 549-9914]
Guide for Radon Control Options for the Design and Construction of New Low-Rise Residential Buildings, ASTM E 14655. ASTM, 1992.
Indoor Air Bulletin. Indoor Air Information Service. [monthly (Santa Cruz, CA 95060, (408) 426-6624)]
Indoor Air: International Journal of Indoor Air Quality and Climate, ISIAQ. [quarterly]
Radon Handbook for the Building Industry. NAHB, 1989.
Radon Reduction in Schools: Technical Guidance, EPA/520/1-89-020. Environmental Protection Agency, 1989.
Radon Resistant Construction Techniques for New Residential Construction. EPA/6252/2-91/032, EPA, 1991.
Ventilation Acceptability, Indoor Air Quality, Standard 62-1989. ASHRAE.

ENERGY CONSERVATION

Conservation and Renewable
Energy Inquiry and Referral Service (CAREIRS)
P. O. Box 8900
Silver Spring, MD 20907
Tel: (800) 523-2929

Energy Efficient Building Association (EEBA)
Northcentral Technical College
1000 Campus Drive
Wausau, WI 54401-1899
Tel: (715) 675-6331
Fax:(715) 675-9776

National Renewable Energy Laboratory (NREL)
(formerly the Solar Energy Research Institute)
1617 Cole Blvd.
Golden, CO 80401-3393
Tel: (303) 231-7000
Fax:(303) 231-1199

REFERENCES

McPherson, E. G., ed. *Energy-Conserving Site Design*. ASLA Bookstore, 1984.
Shaw, A. *Energy Design for Architects*. Fairmont Press, 1989.
Pacific Northwest Laboratories. *Architect's and Engineer's Guide to Energy Conservation in Existing Buildings*. 2 vols. Springfield, Va.: National Technical Information Service, 1990.
U. S. Congressional Office of Technology Assessment. *Fueling Development: Energy Technologies for Developing Countries*. Washington, D.C.: U.S. Government Printing Office (GPO), 1991.
U.S. Department of Energy. *National Energy Strategy: Powerful Ideas for America*. Washington, D.C.: GPO, 1991.
Vale, Brenda, and Robert Vale. *Green Architecture: Design for an Energy-Conscious Future*. Boston: Bulfinch Press, Little Brown, 1991.
Watson, Donald, and Kenneth Labs. *Climatic Design: Energy-Efficient Building Principles and Practices*. New York: McGraw-Hill, 1983 (revised 1993).

SOLAR COLLECTION

American Solar Energy Society
2400 Central Avenue G-1
Boulder, CO 80301
Tel: (303) 443-3130
Fax:(303) 443-3212

Interstate Solar Coordination Council
P.O. Box 65874
St. Paul, MN 55165
Tel: (612) 296-4737
Fax:(612) 297-1959

Passive Solar Industries Council
1090 Vermont Ave., N.W., Suite 1200
Washington, DC 20005
Tel: (202) 393-5043

Solar Energy Industries Association
777 N. Capitol Street, N.E., Suite 805
Arlington, VA 20002
Tel: (202) 408-0660
Fax:(202) 408-8536

REFERENCES

Allen, Patricia A., ed. *A Bibliography of Reports by Sandia Photovoltaic Projects*. Albuquerque: Sandia National Laboratories, 1981. [Available from NTIS, Springfield, VA 21161, order #SAND 81-0135]
Anderson, B. ed. *Solar Building Architecture*. MIT Press, 1990.
Balcomb, J.D. *Passive Solar Buildings*. MIT Press, 1992.
Brown, G.Z., et al. *Inside Out: Design Procedures for Passive Environmental Technologies*. New York: J. Wiley & Sons, 1992.
Burgess, E. L. *Summary of Photovoltaic Application Experiments Designs*. Springfield, Va.: National Technical Information Service (NTIS), 1981.
Gupta, Yudi, and Stephen K. Young. *Design Handbook for Photovoltaic Power Systems*. Albuquerque: Sandia National Laboratories, 1981.
Krieder, Jan F., and Frank Krieth. *Solar Energy Handbook*. New York: McGraw-Hill, 1981.
Los Alamos National Laboratory and Solar Energy Research Institute. *Engineering Principles and Concepts for Active Solar Systems*. New York: Hemisphere Publishing Corporation, 1988.
Los Alamos National Laboratory. *Passive Solar Heating Analysis*. #90110. ASHRAE, 1984.
Los Alamos National Laboratory. *Passive Solar Heating Analysis-Supplement*, #90112. ASHRAE, 1987.
Mazria, Edward. *The Passive Solar Energy Book*, expanded professional edition. Emmaus, Penn.: Rodale Press, 1979.
Solar Energy Research Institute (SERI). *Energy Conservation Technical Information Guide*, 3 vols. NTIS, 1987-89.

SHADING
REFERENCES

Boyer, Lester, and Walter Groudzik. *Earth Shelter Technology*. Texas A&M Univ. Press, 1987.
Brown, G.Z., et al. *Inside Out: Design Procedures for Passive Environmental Technologies*. New York: J. Wiley & Sons, 1992.
Cook, J., ed. *Passive Cooling*. MIT Press, 1989.

EARTH SHELTERS
REFERENCES

Carmody, J. and R. Sterling. *Earth Sheltered Housing Design*, 2nd ed. New York: Van Nostrand Reinhold, 1982.
Earth Sheltered Buildings, NAVFAC Design Manual 1.4, SN 008-050-00230-1. US GPO, 1984.
Moreland Associates. *Earth Covered Buildings: An Exploratory Analysis for Hazard and Energy Performance*, Federal Emergency Management Agency, 1981.

THERMAL TRANSMISSION
REFERENCES

Egan, M. David. *Concepts in Thermal Comfort*. Englewood Cliffs, NJ: Prentice-Hall, Inc.,1975.
Moore, Fuller. *Environmental Control Systems: Heating, Cooling, Lighting*. New York: McGraw-Hill, 1993.
Portland Cement Association. *Simplified Thermal Design of Building Envelopes*.

ENVIRONMENTAL CONSTRUCTION

Environmental Design Research Association (EDRA)
PO Box 24083
Oklahoma City, OK 73124
Tel: (405) 843-4863

CHAPTER
19
HISTORIC PRESERVATION

INTRODUCTION

Historic buildings are tangible evidence of the nation's history and culture. They add interest, identity, and variety to our streets and neighborhoods. At the same time, because of their age, methods of construction, materials, and finishes, they present special challenges to architects. Historic buildings frequently involve materials and systems that are difficult to evaluate in terms of their physical behavior, especially when applying modern standards and codes. Because historic buildings are essentially different from new buildings in these respects, it is important to remember that the approaches that would be taken in designing a new building generally do not apply to the preservation, rehabilitation, or restoration of a historic building.

UNDERSTANDING HISTORIC PRESERVATION OBJECTIVES

Almost any historic preservation project will involve a variety of work, which may include stabilization, repair, and partial or total replacement of deteriorated historic materials. Overall "preservation objectives" must be balanced against the client's needs for building alterations and additions, life safety, seismic code requirements, and a host of other real-life demands on the building program. When undertaking rehabilitation work on a historic building, there are two basic objectives: to preserve historic materials and to preserve the historic character. If these objectives are met, then the building will continue to convey its sense of history.

Historic materials are those materials used in construction (e.g., the wooden siding, the slate roof, or the terra-cotta cornice) of a building. Although every building has undergone repair, replacement, and alteration over the years, the purpose of any preservation project should be to retain as much as possible of the surviving historic materials in the course of treatment. By historic character we mean those tangible features of the building that help to distinguish it from other buildings. Aspects that give a historic building its individuality may include its overall form or shape, materials, craftsmanship details, interior spaces, and applied detailing. The historic character can be seriously affected by small changes; for example, applying a layer of paint to a historically unpainted building, replacing windows with new ones of different size and shape, or introducing a suspended ceiling within a tall room.

Each historic building is unique in its evolution, use, performance, and maintenance. Part of this uniqueness involves the changes to the building in its past, to its finishes, form, or floor plan. The architect should remember that changes that may have occurred in the past frequently have acquired historic value or possess architectural significance in their own right, just as the new work on historic buildings may acquire some historic significance in the future. A building is not fixed in time at the date of its construction but represents a continuity of history.

Many historic buildings are rehabilitated for new uses. If the primary objective is to preserve the historic building while accommodating new needs, the architect must first understand the building and the character of its materials, features, and spaces. The challenge is to make both the historic building and new uses work together. The federal government's Standards for Rehabilitation, from the Secretary of the Interior's Standards for the Treatment of Historic Properties, rev. 1992, provides a framework to guide work on historic buildings when repairs, alterations, and additions are planned for a continued or new use. (It should be noted that there are separate Standards for Preservation, Restoration, and Reconstruction.) The ten rehabilitation standards are general principles that present a balance between preserving the historic character and making respectful changes in order to accommodate continuing or new uses; the guidelines present recommended treatments and approaches that help meet the Standards and also explain the consequences of undertaking irresponsible work. The Guidelines are organized in broad categories such as materials (masonry, wood and architectural metals); roofs; windows; storefronts; structural systems; interior spaces, features, and finishes; and mechanical systems.

The Standards and Guidelines form the basis for the following historic preservation section in Architectural Graphic Standards. The guidance recommends the identification of character-defining spaces, features, materials, and finishes as a first step in the rehabilitation process and suggests a hierarchy in selecting appropriate work, from minor actions such as maintenance and repair of historic materials to major actions such as the replacement of deteriorated and missing features and design for new addi-

tions. Considering the unknown conditions that will be encountered during the progress of any work on historic buildings, frequent reference to the Standards and Guidelines is recommended when planning and executing a project.

UNDERSTANDING THE HISTORIC BUILDING AS A SYSTEM

The architect should remember that building materials are not inert and that they have many other properties than their compressive or tensile strength. The architect should never look at the materials in isolation, but as part of the historic building system. Such systems will react to changes in the environment, and the materials are frequently chemically active. Both the systems and the materials will react to almost any human intervention. For example, applying a chemical coating to the exterior walls of a building is a treatment that could affect the transmission of moisture and vapor through the walls.

COMMON REHABILITATION PROJECT PROBLEMS

The following is a list of problem areas that frequently arise in rehabilitation projects which should be investigated and considered in advance. A historic preservation specialist may be required to address some of these problem areas.

1. Moisture problems: Perhaps the single most pervasive problem of existing buildings is the penetration of moisture both from within and without. Without understanding the cause (rather than the symptoms) of this problem, it is difficult to select a remedial solution. Many high-tech products (coatings, water repellents) may cause more harm than good. To reduce moisture problems, buildings should be made weathertight (e.g., install proper gutters and downspouts, repair roof, repoint cracks, provide proper surface grading).

2. Hard-to-find crafts: Stonecutters, wood-carvers, slaters, stencilers, wood turners, parquet floor layers, ornamental plasterers, gilders, grainers, and marblers provide custom art and craft services, generally for large-scale restoration and rehabilitation projects. The architect should provide a sample or prototype of the specific effect desired to the craftsperson in order to establish preservation objectives and work quality. The sample may be an isolated artifact, may be in place on the historic building, or may even be on another building.

3. Hard-to-find replacement materials: Careful, long-range planning may be required to obtain special materials such as decorative terra cotta or certain brownstones, sandstones, and marbles. Some metal components may be difficult to repair or fabricate, especially deteriorated ornamental sheet metal cornices, window hoods, roof cresting, and certain ornamental metal shingles.

4. Energy conservation: Improving the energy performance of historic buildings is a generally desirable goal, but some energy-conserving features, such as tinted glazing, can alter the historic appearance of the building. Any energy conservation treatments that will visually or physically alter the building's historic features should be carefully evaluated. Furring out the inside surface of exterior walls for insulation will require that paneling and trim be carefully removed and reapplied, otherwise the extra thickness of the insulation and wall finish will change the architectural relationships between openings, wall surfaces, and trim.

5. The unintended impact of new technology: Problems can result from the indiscriminate application of modern architectural practices to historic buildings. The introduction of high-strength portland cements, elastomeric compounds, water repellents, or epoxy coatings may create a host of secondary problems not anticipated by the architect; these problems may result from using standardized specifications.

FOR THE RECORD

Working on a historic building is both a challenge and an opportunity. If the building is significant, the architect has a responsibility not only to preserve it but to leave a record for the future. Such a record should include a summary of the research; measured drawings of the building before rehabilitation; information discovered during work on the building; and documentation of the work as planned and as carried out. Measured drawings should follow the Standards for Architectural and Engineering Documentation, 1983, developed by the Historic American Buildings Survey/Historic American Engineering Record of the National Park Service.

THE SECRETARY OF THE INTERIOR'S STANDARDS FOR THE TREATMENT OF HISTORIC PROPERTIES (REV. 1992)

STANDARDS FOR REHABILITATION

1. A property shall be used as it was historically or be given a new use that requires minimal change to its distinctive materials, features, spaces, and spatial relationships.

2. The historic character of a property shall be retained and preserved. The removal of distinctive materials or alteration of features, spaces, and spatial relationships that characterize a property shall be avoided.

3. Each property shall be recognized as a physical record of its time, place, and use. Changes that create a false sense of historical development, such as adding conjectural features or elements from other historic properties, shall not be undertaken.

4. Changes to a property that have acquired historic significance in their own right shall be retained and preserved.

5. Distinctive materials, features, finishes, and construction techniques or examples of craftsmanship that characterize a property shall be preserved.

6. Deteriorated historic features shall be repaired rather than replaced. Where the severity of deterioration requires replacement of a distinctive feature, the new feature shall match the old design, color, texture, and, where possible, materials. Replacement of missing features shall be substantiated by documentary and physical evidence.

7. Chemical or physical treatments, if appropriate, shall be undertaken using the gentlest means possible. Treatments that cause damage to historic materials shall not be used.

8. Archeological resources shall be protected and preserved in place. If such resources must be disturbed, mitigation measures shall be undertaken.

9. New additions, exterior alterations, or related new construction shall not destroy historic materials, features, and spatial relationships that characterize the property. The new work shall be differentiated from the old and shall be compatible with the historic materials, features, size, scale and proportion, and massing to protect the integrity of the property and its environment.

10. New additions and adjacent or related new construction shall be undertaken in such a manner that, if removed in the future, the essential form and integrity of the historic property and its environment would be unimpaired.

Lee H. Nelson, FAIA, and Kay D. Weeks; Preservation Assistance Division, National Park Service; Washington, D.C.
Eric J. Gastier; Darrell Downing Rippeteau Architects; Washington, D.C.

INTRODUCTION

INTRODUCTION

This checklist indicates the range of preservation factors that should be considered when rehabilitating historic buildings. It is not exhaustive, and some factors will not apply to all structures or preservation projects.

CHECK HISTORIC PRESERVATION DESIGNATION AND AVAILABLE DOCUMENTATION

Is your building a local landmark or located in a locally designated historic district? Is it in a historic district listed in the National Register of Historic Places? Does it contribute to the historic significance of the district?

What historical or architectural documentation is available about the building(s) or site? For example:

- National Register nominations
- recorded by Historic American Buildings Survey/Historic American Engineering Record
- state or local historical survey or inventory
- local documents, views, photographs in libraries, archives, historical societies

CHECK LEGAL REQUIREMENTS

Are there easements or local ordinances governing alterations to the property (deed records, zoning offices)?

Depending on the current or anticipated use, how does the 1990 Americans with Disabilities Act, a federal civil rights law, apply to your historic building?

How do state and local building codes apply to your historic building? What effect will they have upon its character and integrity? Are code variances available? Are there code equivalency possibilities for your particular building?

Will there be federal funds involved in the project, which will require review by the State Historic Preservation Office and consultation with the Advisory Council on Historic Preservation? Will federal investment tax credits be used? If so, are you familiar with the Secretary of the Interior's Standards for Rehabilitation and Guidelines for Rehabilitating Historic Buildings as well as the National Park Service certification procedures in Chapter 1, Title 36 of the Code of Federal Regulations, Part 67? Have you obtained a copy of the Historic Preservation Certification Application form from the State Historic Preservation Office?

Note that for federal investment tax credits, the Secretary's Standards (36 CFR 67) take precedence over local requirements.

EVALUATE HISTORIC CHARACTER AND SIGNIFICANCE OF STRUCTURE

Have you identified, listed, and prioritized the character defining aspects of the building? These may include its form, materials, workmanship, features, color, and spatial relationships, that is, those tangible aspects of the building that define its historic character.

Usually, original materials and features are central to the building's historical significance; sometimes, however, an original feature may not be as important as the changes that have been made to it over time. For example, if a brick building was painted at an early date, its painted appearance may be an important aspect of its historic character.

What is the original configuration of the building? What architectural changes have been made over time? Changes may include

- additions such as a porch, wing, or upper story.
- changes to surfaces and finishes (unpainted to painted, slates to asphalt, polychrome to monochrome).
- blocking of windows, removal of shutters.
- changes to grade.
- change to a cornice; loss of stairs or steps.
- false fronts.
- changes to basic plan (single family to multiple family).

Most buildings change over time with different occupancies and uses. These changes are an integral part of the building's historic character and should be evaluated very carefully prior to work.

Has the architectural integrity of the building been assessed? Architectural integrity means the intactness of the building as an architectural system (its plan, features, materials, finishes, structural system, and the presence of architectural features).

ASSESS PHYSICAL CONDITION

Are there gross physical problems that threaten the building's architectural and structural integrity?

Has a structural survey been performed to determine deficiencies due to settlement, deflection of beams, seismic inadequacy, and cuts through structural members for mechanical pipes and ducts?

Is there inherent materials damage, such as materials failure due to poor original design, poor original materials, severe environmental or moisture problems, neglect, improper maintenance, etc.?

Is there man-inflicted damage, such as ornamentation removed, inappropriate coatings, bad repointing or cleaning, insensitive additions, or partitioning of significant interior spaces? Are historic features hidden behind later alterations? These may include ornamental ceilings or cornices hidden above dropped ceilings.

What aspects of the Americans with Disabilities Act apply to your rehabilitation project? Are there accessible public entrances? Is there proper signage?

DEVELOP PRESERVATION PROJECT PLANS

Will it be necessary to write unique specifications rather than use standard specifications for work performed on a historic building?

Will testing be needed to determine the performance of the materials or the systems? Note that it may be necessary to review test results with consultants or laboratories.

Will the project involve hard-to-find replacement materials such as terra-cotta or ornamental metals that may require critical path logistical planning?

Will the project require hard-to-find crafts such as stone carving or ornamental plastering? If so, can the necessary expertise be found?

Can samples or models be made available to establish the standard of craftsmanship for the project?

Will the project involve energy conservation measures? Have measures been chosen that retain historic materials and finishes to the maximum extent possible?

Will new uses require upgrading the live loading capacity of wooden floor joists? How do the preservation objectives affect the decision-making? For instance, it is better to double up existing joists with a parallel member than to remove historic materials, and if an ornamental ceiling would be damaged by this approach, a structural engineer should investigate other alternatives.

Are new additions and adjacent new construction sympathetic to the historic building, site, or district? Minimize adverse effects by maintaining the scale, shape, materials, and detailing of the adjacent historic structures.

What protective measures will be taken to preserve important character-defining features and finishes during the construction work?

Will the project involve making bathrooms and amenities accessible to persons with disabilities? Have options been studied to achieve access without threatening or destroying significant interior spaces, features, and finishes?

Will rehabilitation work on the building result in the loss of distinctive historic fabric or seriously damage the historic character? Loss of historic fabric or change of historic character can occur on the exterior when

- storefronts are altered.
- visible skylights are added on top of an existing building.
- new dormers are added on prominent roofs.
- whole new floors are added on top of an existing building.
- porches are enclosed.
- new window openings are created.
- tinted films or reflective coatings are added to windows.
- new window sash are historically inappropriate in configuration and detailing.

Loss of fabric or change of character often occurs on the interior when

- interiors are partitioned and significant sequences of spaces are lost.
- plaster is removed to expose brickwork.
- interiors are gutted to reconfigure spaces, insert new floor levels, or create new atria.
- significant stairs are removed or altered.

Will there be a professional on site during construction to ensure work is carried out according to established preservation principles?

Have construction personnel received adequate training in undertaking historic preservation work?

SOURCES OF TECHNICAL PRESERVATION INFORMATION

PRESERVATION ASSISTANCE DIVISION

National Park Service
P.O. Box 37127
Washington, DC 20013-7127

The Preservation Assistance Division has developed numerous technical publications on preserving and rehabilitating historic buildings. These publications are available from the Superintendent of Documents, Government Printing Office, Washington, DC 20402. Write to the Preservation Assistance Division at the above address for a free copy of the current Catalog of Historic Preservation Publications, which includes stock numbers and prices. Free leaflets are also available on the preservation of historic landscapes and accessibility to historic buildings. "America's Landscape Legacy" defines designed and vernacular landscapes, and includes a selected bibliography and listing of professional contacts. "Preserving the Past and Making it Accessible for People with Disabilities" explains accessibility and preservation requirements, describes the administrative process in meeting both, and suggests organizations and officials to contact for further information.

NATIONAL PARK SERVICE REGIONAL OFFICES WITH NATIONAL REGISTER PROGRAMS

Cultural Resources Division
Alaska Regional Office, National Park Service
2525 Gambell Street, Room 107
Anchorage, AK 99503

Preservation Assistance Division
Mid-Atlantic Regional Office, National Park Service
Second and Chestnut Street, Second Floor
Philadelphia, PA 19106

Division of Cultural Resources
Rocky Mountain Regional Office, National Park Service
12795 West Alameda Parkway
P.O. Box 25287
Denver, CO 80225

Preservation Services Division
Southeast Regional Office, National Park Service
75 Spring Street, SW, Room 1140
Atlanta, GA 30303

National Register Programs
Western Regional Office, National Park Service
600 Harrison Street, Suite 600
San Francisco, CA 94107-1372

ORGANIZATIONS/CONTACTS

AIA State Preservation Coordinators
Call the Historic Resources Committee staff director at the AIA Headquarters (Tel: 202.626.7589) to make contact with the AIA state preservation coordinator.

The Association for Preservation Technology International
P.O. Box 8178
Fredericksburg, VA 22404

National Trust for Historic Preservation
1785 Massachusetts Avenue, NW
Washington, DC 20036

National Alliance of Preservation Commissions
Hall of States
444 North Capitol Street, NW, Suite 342
Washington, DC 20001-1512

The Old-House Journal Corporation
2 Main Street
Gloucester, MA 09130

STATE HISTORIC PRESERVATION OFFICERS

For the name and address of the state historic preservation officer in your state, contact:

The National Conference of State Historic Preservation Officers (NCSHPO)
Hall of the States
444 North Capitol Street, NW, Suite 332
Washington, DC 20001-1512

Lee H. Nelson, FAIA, and Kay D. Weeks; Preservation Assistance Division, National Park Service; Washington, D.C.
Eric J. Gastier; Darrel Downing Rippeteau Architects; Washington, D.C.

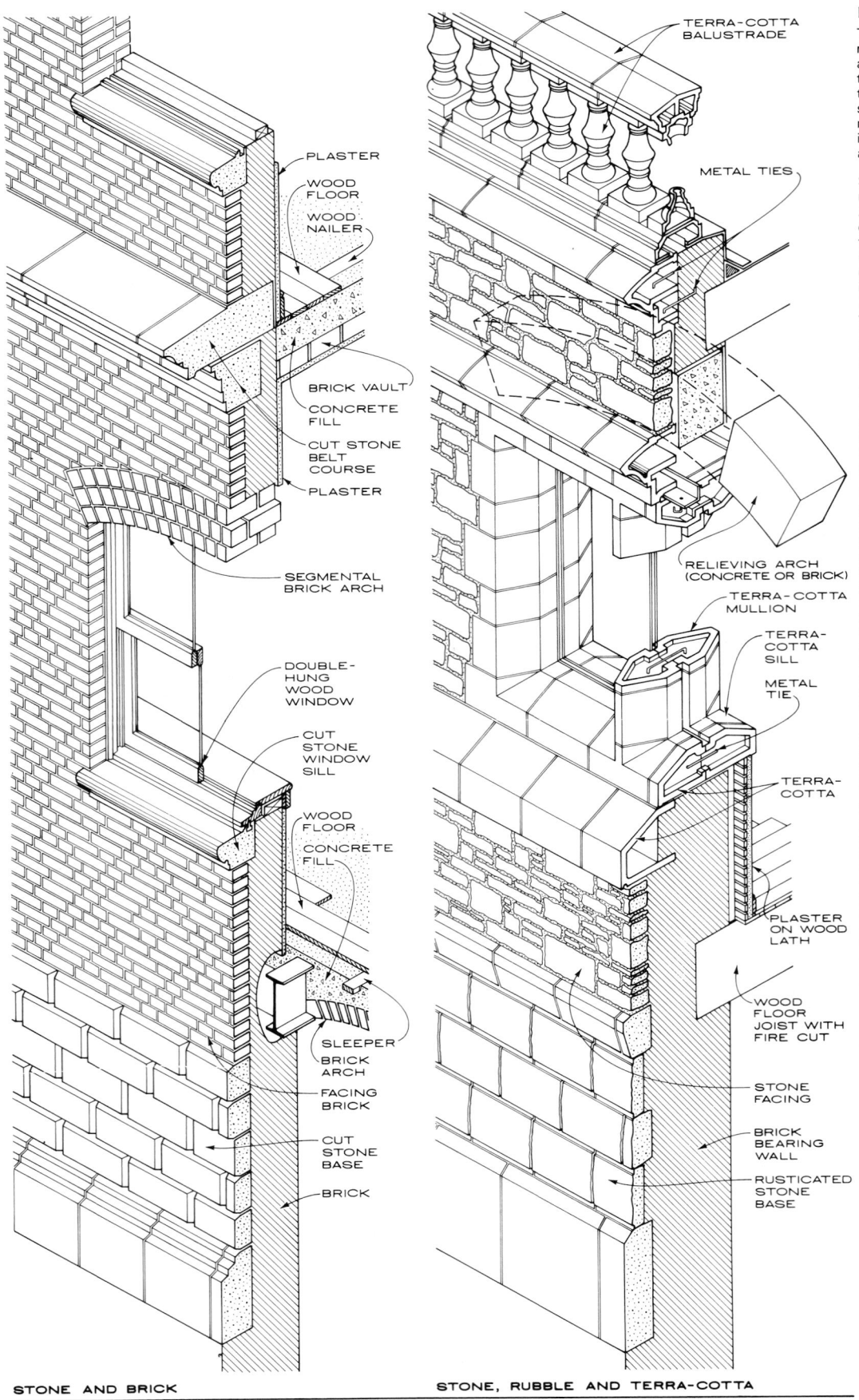

STONE AND BRICK

Labels (left drawing):
PLASTER
WOOD FLOOR
WOOD NAILER
BRICK VAULT
CONCRETE FILL
CUT STONE BELT COURSE
PLASTER
SEGMENTAL BRICK ARCH
DOUBLE-HUNG WOOD WINDOW
CUT STONE WINDOW SILL
WOOD FLOOR
CONCRETE FILL
SLEEPER
BRICK ARCH
FACING BRICK
CUT STONE BASE
BRICK

STONE, RUBBLE AND TERRA-COTTA

Labels (right drawing):
TERRA-COTTA BALUSTRADE
METAL TIES
RELIEVING ARCH (CONCRETE OR BRICK)
TERRA-COTTA MULLION
TERRA-COTTA SILL
METAL TIE
TERRA-COTTA
PLASTER ON WOOD LATH
WOOD FLOOR JOIST WITH FIRE CUT
STONE FACING
BRICK BEARING WALL
RUSTICATED STONE BASE

MASONRY — TYPICAL LOAD-BEARING WALL SECTIONS

INTRODUCTION

The function of masonry units such as brick or stone is related to the thickness of a wall, the mortar, the bond, and the quality of workmanship. The relationship of all these materials determines the historic building's structural soundness as well as its appearance. While masonry is among the most durable of historic building materials, it is also the most susceptible to damage by improper maintenance or repair techniques and harsh or abrasive cleaning methods.

Stone is one of the more lasting of masonry building materials and has been used throughout the history of American building construction. In the 17th and 18th centuries, stone was often used only for decorative details, trimwork, foundations, and chimneys on brick buildings. Where stone was plentiful, however, it was used to construct even simple houses and outbuildings. Stonework on most buildings was roughly finished, but more elaborate stone structures often featured finely tooled or carved decorative surfaces. The kinds of stone most commonly encountered on historic buildings in the U.S. include various types of sandstone, limestone, marble, granite, slate, and fieldstone.

Brick varied considerably in size and quality. Before 1870, brick clays were pressed into molds and were often unevenly fired. The quality of brick depended on the type of clay available and the brick-making techniques; by the 1870s—with the perfection of an extrusion process—bricks became more uniform and durable.

Terra-cotta is also a kiln-dried clay product popular from the late 19th century until the 1930s. Brownstone terra-cotta was the earliest type used throughout the last half of the 19th century. It was hollow cast, glazed or unglazed, and was generally used in conjunction with brick to imitate brownstone. Fireproof terra-cotta was developed for use in high-rise buildings. Inexpensive, lightweight, and fireproof, these rough-finished hollow building blocks were well suited to span I-beams in floor, wall, and ceiling construction. Glazed architectural terra-cotta consists of hollow units hand cast in molds or carved in clay and heavily glazed and fired. The development of the steel-frame office building in the early 20th century and the eclectic taste of the time contributed to the widespread use of architectural terra-cotta.

Adobe, which consists of sun-dried earthen bricks, was one of the earliest permanent building materials used in the U.S., primarily in the Southwest where it is still a popular building material.

Mortar is used to bond together masonry units. Historic mortar was generally quite soft and consisted primarily of lime, sand, and other additives such as crushed oyster shells, partially burned lime, animal hair, particles of clay, or pigments to color the mortar to match or contrast with the masonry units. While natural cement was included in some mortars beginning in the early 19th century, most historic mortar did not contain portland cement until after 1880 when it was used in combination with the newly available, harder extruded bricks, which required a more rigid and nonabsorbing mortar.

Traditional stucco, sometimes referred to as plaster, was also heavily lime based and had much the same composition as historic mortar, with regional variations that reflected the availability of certain materials. Like mortar, the composition of stucco increased in hardness with the addition of portland cement toward the end of the 19th century. In the 18th and 19th centuries, stucco was often scored to resemble cut stone and was used as a finish coat directly over stone, brick, or log construction. In the early 20th century, stucco took on significance as a building material in its own right and was applied (often with a decorative textured finish) directly over wood or metal lath attached to the building's structural framework.

Concrete has a long history, being variously made of tabby, volcanic ash, and later of natural hydraulic cements; the latter was first given limited use in the early 19th century in some mortars before the introduction of portland cement in the 1870s. From that time on, concrete has been used in its precast form for structural blocks or "cast stone" to simulate entire stone facades or smaller architectural details. In the 20th century, this has further evolved into precast structural elements.

Lee H. Nelson, FAIA, H. Ward Jandl, Anne Grimmer, Kay D. Weeks; Preservation Assistance Division, National Park Service; Washington, D.C.
Eric J. Gastier; Darrel Downing Rippeteau Architects, PC; Washington, D.C.

PRESERVATION APPROACHES

Masonry features that are important in defining the over-all historic character of the building include walls, brackets, railings, cornices, window architraves, door pediments, steps, and columns, with tooling and bonding patterns, coatings, color, and joint details.

Making inappropriate visual changes to historic masonry surfaces in the process of rehabilitation, such as applying paint or other coatings to masonry that has been historically unpainted, can easily change the entire character of the building. Similarly, paint should not be removed from historically painted masonry.

The various causes of mortar joint deterioration (such as leaking roofs or gutters, differential settlement of the building, capillary action, or extreme weather exposure) should be identified before selecting an appropriate remedial treatment.

Masonry should only be cleaned in order to halt deterioration or to remove heavy soiling. Cleaning masonry surfaces when they are not heavily soiled in order to create a new appearance can needlessly introduce chemicals or moisture into historic materials. If it is determined that cleaning is appropriate, tests should be conducted prior to cleaning and observed over a sufficient period of time so that both the immediate effects and the long-range effects are known.

Brick or stone surfaces should be cleaned with the gentlest method possible, such as water and detergents, using natural bristle brushes. They should never be sandblasted using dry or wet grit or other abrasives. These methods of cleaning permanently erode the surface of the material. Cleaning methods involving water or liquid chemical solutions should not be used when there is any possibility of freezing temperatures, and chemical products should never be used that will damage masonry, such as using acid on limestone or marble.

If repainting of historically painted masonry is necessary, the damaged paint should be removed to the next sound layer using the gentlest method possible prior to repainting. Colors should be used that are historically appropriate to the building and district.

Masonry walls and other masonry features should be repaired whenever there is evidence of deterioration. This may include disintegrating mortar, loose bricks, damp walls, or damaged plasterwork.

In preparation for repointing, deteriorated mortar should be removed by carefully hand-raking the joints to avoid damaging the masonry. Never use electric saws.

Old mortar should be duplicated in strength, composition, color, and texture. Repointing with mortar of high portland cement content can create a bond that is stronger than the historic material, damaging historic masonry as a result of the differing coefficient of expansion and the differing porosity of the material and the mortar.

When repointing, the use of traditional materials and methods is strongly recommended rather than synthetic caulking compounds and "scrub" coating techniques. Old mortar joints should be duplicated in width and in joint profile.

Stucco should be repaired by removing only the damaged material and patching with new stucco that duplicates the old in strength, composition, color, and texture. Mud plaster should be used as a surface coating over unfired, unstabilized adobe, in order to bond to the adobe. Cement stucco, on the other hand, will not bond properly, enabling moisture to become entrapped between materials. Concrete may be repaired by cutting the deteriorated portion back to a sound surface, then removing the source of deterioration—often corrosion of metal reinforcement bars—by sandblasting or chemical cleaning of the re-bars. The new concrete patch must be applied carefully so it will bond satisfactorily with, and match, the historic concrete.

Masonry features may be repaired by patching, piecing in, or consolidating the masonry using recognized preservation methods. Repair may also include the limited replacement in kind of those extensively deteriorated or missing parts of masonry features such as terra-cotta brackets or stone balusters when there are surviving prototypes.

A masonry feature that is too deteriorated or damaged to repair should be replaced in kind whenever possible. If the historic form and detailing are still evident, they should be used as a model to reproduce the feature.

If a masonry feature is completely missing and there is sufficient historical, pictorial, and physical documentation, the missing feature should be accurately reproduced. In the absence of documentation, the replacement masonry feature may be a new design that is compatible with the size, scale, and color of the historic building.

Finally, for both repair and replacement treatments, using the same kind of material is always preferred; however, if this is not technically or economically feasible, a compatible substitute material with the same visual and physical qualities may be considered.

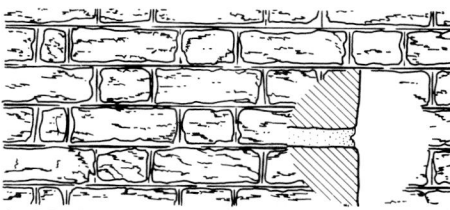

A. COLONIAL GRAPEVINE JOINT, FLEMISH BOND CIRCA 1720

B. BEADED JOINT, FLEMISH BOND CIRCA 1809

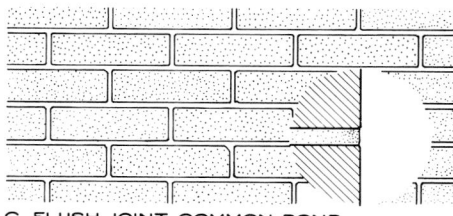

C. FLUSH JOINT, COMMON BOND MID-19TH CENTURY

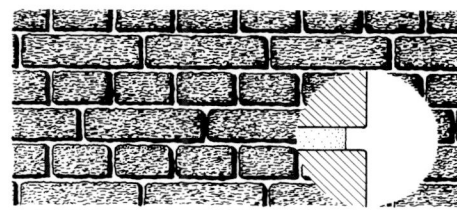

D. RAKED JOINT, ENGLISH BOND EARLY 20TH CENTURY

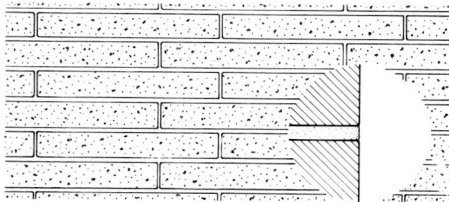

E. FLUSH JOINT, ONE-THIRD RUNNING BOND EARLY 20TH CENTURY

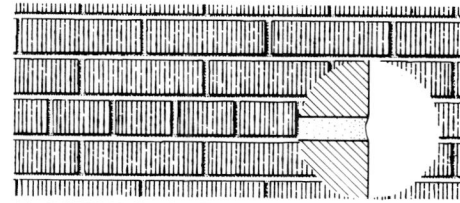

F. CONCAVE JOINT, COMMON BOND EARLY 20TH CENTURY

NOTE THE DIFFERENCE IN UNIFORMITY OF HANDMADE (A AND B) AND MACHINE-MADE (C-F) BRICKS. IN A, B AND F, THE VERTICAL JOINTS WERE STRUCK BEFORE THE HORIZONTALS. IN B AND E, THE VERTICAL JOINTS ARE NARROWER THAN THE HORIZONTALS

JOINT TYPES AND BRICK BONDING PATTERNS

A. FLEXIBLE MORTAR (LIME)	B. INFLEXIBLE MORTAR (CEMENT)
NORMAL	
HOT (BRICKS EXPAND) — MORTAR COMPRESSES	SPALLING
COLD (BRICKS CONTRACT) — MORTAR FLEXES	CRACKS OPEN UP

FLEXIBLE MORTAR (A) EXPANDS AND CONTRACTS WITH TEMPERATURE CHANGES. BRICKS BONDED BY INFLEXIBLE MORTAR (B) TEND TO SPALL AT THE EDGES (THE AREA OF GREATEST STRESS) IN HOT WEATHER AND SEPARATE FROM THE MORTAR IN COLD WEATHER

EFFECTS OF TEMPERATURE CHANGE ON MASONRY

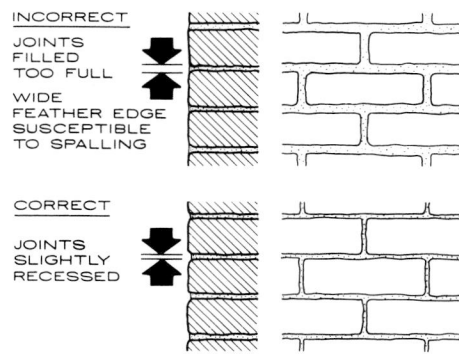

INCORRECT
MORTAR NOT CLEANED OUT TO A SUFFICIENT UNIFORM DEPTH

EDGES OF BRICKS DAMAGED BY TOOL OR GRINDER, CREATES WIDER JOINT

CORRECT
MORTAR CLEANED OUT TO A UNIFORM DEPTH OF ABOUT 1"

UNDAMAGED EDGES OF BRICK

PREPARATION OF MORTAR JOINTS FOR REPOINTING

INCORRECT
JOINTS FILLED TOO FULL

WIDE FEATHER EDGE SUSCEPTIBLE TO SPALLING

CORRECT
JOINTS SLIGHTLY RECESSED

PROPER REPOINTING OF MASONRY JOINTS

Lee H. Nelson, FAIA, H. Ward Jandl, Anne Grimmer, Kay D. Weeks; Preservation Assistance Division, National Park Service; Washington, D.C.
Eric J. Gastier; Darrel Downing Rippeteau Architects, PC; Washington, D.C.

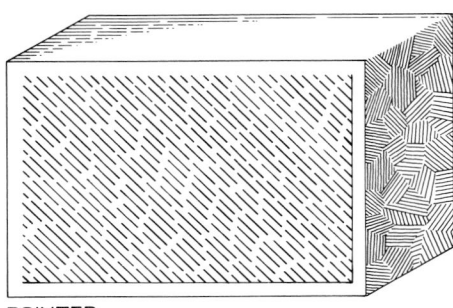

POINTED

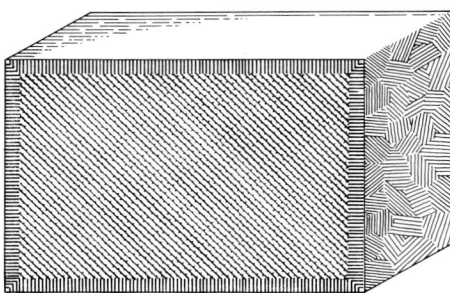

BROACHED

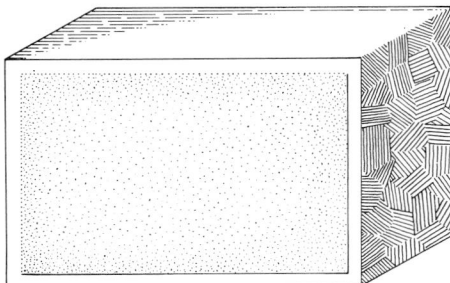

BUSH-HAMMERED

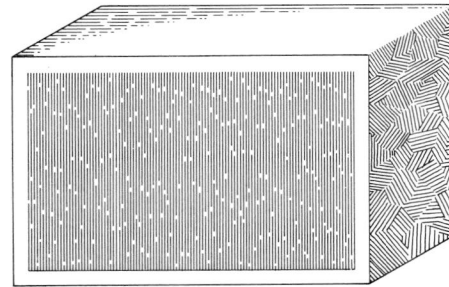

PATENT-HAMMERED

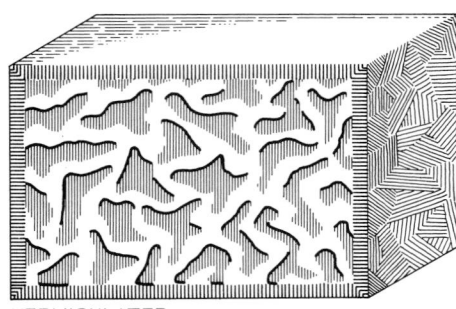

VERMICULATED

STONEWORK FINISHES

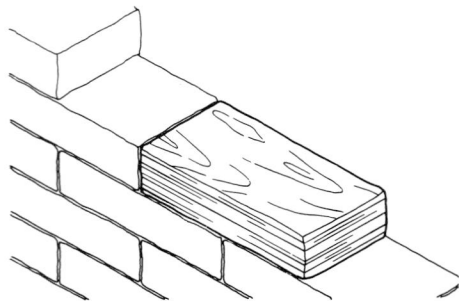

THE CORRECT CONSTRUCTION METHOD IS TO PLACE STONE ON ITS NATURAL BED AS IT ORIGINALLY LAY IN THE QUARRY

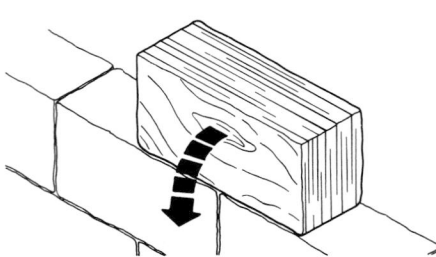

A FACE-BEDDED STONE SCALES IN LAYERS BECAUSE IT WAS PLACED ON END WITH ITS BEDDING PLANES PARALLEL TO THE FACE OF THE WALL. FACE BEDDING ACCOUNTS FOR THE POOR CONDITION OF MANY MID-19TH CENTURY BROWNSTONE BUILDINGS (ARROW INDICATES SCALING)

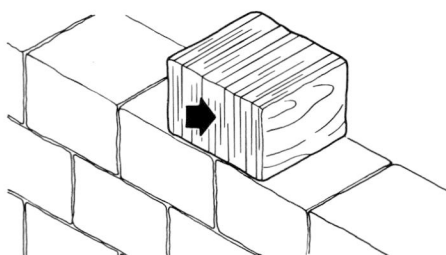

AN EDGE-BEDDED STONE HAS ITS BEDDING PLANES PERPENDICULAR TO THE FACE OF THE WALL. SEAMS ON THE EXPOSED SURFACE (INDICATED BY THE ARROW) WILL WASH OUT IN TIME

STONE BEDDING METHODS

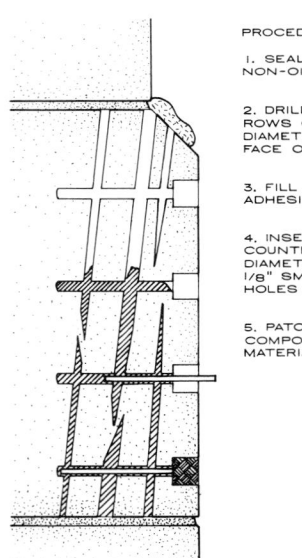

PROCEDURE

1. SEAL CRACKS WITH NON-OILY CLAY

2. DRILL STAGGERED ROWS OF HOLES (MAX. DIAMETER 1/4") THROUGH FACE OF STONE

3. FILL HOLES WITH ADHESIVE GROUT

4. INSERT AND COUNTERSINK PINS. DIAMETER SHOULD BE 1/8" SMALLER THAN HOLES

5. PATCH HOLES WITH COMPOSITE PATCHING MATERIAL

THROUGH-SURFACE STONE REPAIR

PROCEDURE

1. CLEAN SURFACES TO BE JOINED

2. PROTECT ADJACENT SURFACES WITH RUBBER CEMENT

3. DRILL STAGGERED ROWS OF HOLES: DEPTH = 4 X PIN DIAMETER DIAMETER = PIN DIAMETER + 1/8"

4. FILL HOLES WITH RIGID (HIGH MODULUS) EPOXY ADHESIVE

5. SET PINS

6. COAT STONE SURFACES TO BE JOINED WITH FLEXIBLE (LOW MODULUS) EPOXY ADHESIVE

7. SET DETACHED PIECE IN PLACE. GENTLY TAP WITH RUBBER MALLET TO SEAT STONE

8. CLEAN OFF RUBBER CEMENT

CONCEALED REPAIR FOR STONE

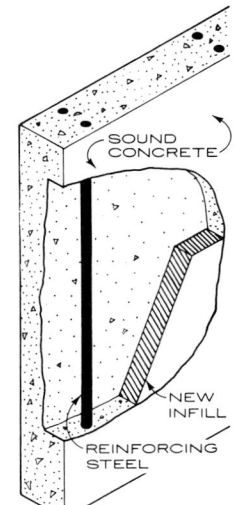

PROCEDURE

1. REMOVE LOOSE DETERIORATED CONCRETE TO SOUND CONCRETE. CUT SQUARE SHOULDERS AT EDGE OF REPAIR AREA. EXPOSE ALL SIDES OF REINFORCING STEEL

2. SANDBLAST CONCRETE AND REINFORCING STEEL CLEAN

3. IMMEDIATELY APPLY PROTECTIVE COATING SYSTEM TO REINFORCEMENT

4. MOISTEN CONCRETE SURFACE AND ALLOW TO DRY UNTIL DAMP

5. INSTALL MORTAR, EPOXY-MODIFIED BOND COAT AND CONCRETE, OR EPOXY-MODIFIED BOND COAT AND PORTLAND CEMENT CONCRETE, DEPENDING ON REPAIR DEPTH

6. CURE AS NECESSARY

SOUND CONCRETE

NEW INFILL

REINFORCING STEEL

SPALLED CONCRETE REPAIR (EXTERIOR WALLS)

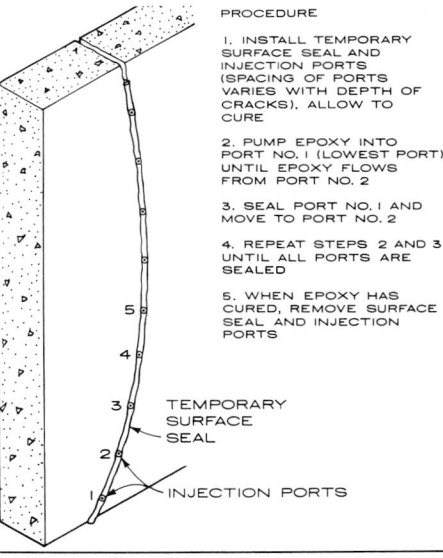

PROCEDURE

1. INSTALL TEMPORARY SURFACE SEAL AND INJECTION PORTS (SPACING OF PORTS VARIES WITH DEPTH OF CRACKS). ALLOW TO CURE

2. PUMP EPOXY INTO PORT NO. 1 (LOWEST PORT) UNTIL EPOXY FLOWS FROM PORT NO. 2

3. SEAL PORT NO. 1 AND MOVE TO PORT NO. 2

4. REPEAT STEPS 2 AND 3 UNTIL ALL PORTS ARE SEALED

5. WHEN EPOXY HAS CURED, REMOVE SURFACE SEAL AND INJECTION PORTS

TEMPORARY SURFACE SEAL

INJECTION PORTS

FRACTURED CONCRETE REPAIR (WALLS AND SLABS)

Lee H. Nelson, FAIA, H. Ward Jandl, Anne Grimmer, Kay D. Weeks; Preservation Assistance Division, National Park Service; Washington, D.C.
Eric J. Gastier; Darrel Downing Rippeteau Architects, PC; Washington, D.C.

19 **HISTORIC MASONRY**

INTRODUCTION

Wood has played a central role in American building during every period and in every style. Because it can be easily shaped by sawing, planing, carving, and gouging, wood is used for architectural features such as clapboards, cornices, brackets, entablatures, shutters, columns, and balustrades. These features may be important in defining the building's historic character and thus their retention, protection, and repair are important in rehabilitation projects.

PRESERVATION APPROACHES

While loss of some exterior wood to weathering is inevitable, taking steps to maximize its retention should be an integral part of any work on a historic building. Radical changes to the historic appearance of wood surfaces should be avoided, such as changing the type of finish or its color, or stripping historically painted surfaces to bare wood, then applying clear finishes or stains in order to create a ''natural'' look. Special finishes, such as marbling or graining, are evidence of individual craftsmanship and should be preserved. The causes of wood deterioration should be identified and corrected, such as faulty flashing, leaking gutters, cracks and holes in siding, deteriorated caulking, or insect or fungus infestation.

Painted wood surfaces should be inspected to determine whether repainting is necessary or if cleaning is all that is required. Paint should not be removed that is firmly adhering to and, thus, protecting wood surfaces. If surfaces need painting, deteriorated paint should only be removed to the next sound layer, using the gentlest method possible (hand scraping/sanding).

Precautions need to be taken when removing lead-based paint. Personal protective gear should be worn, and the environment should be protected from lead-laden dust and debris. All toxic residue should be disposed of in compliance with applicable laws.

It is never appropriate to use destructive paint removal methods such as propane or butane torches, sandblasting, or waterblasting. These methods can irreversibly damage woodwork and could penetrate through to damage interior fabric. Electric hot-air guns may be used effectively on decorative wood features and electric heat plates on flat wood surfaces when paint is so deteriorated that total removal is necessary.

Wood features can be repaired by patching, consolidating, or otherwise reinforcing the wood using recognized preservation methods. A wood feature too deteriorated to repair should be replaced in kind whenever possible. If the historic form and detailing are still evident, they should be used to restore the feature. If a wood feature is missing and there is sufficient historical, pictorial, and physical documentation, the missing feature should be restored. Replacing a deteriorated or missing wood feature based on insufficient documentation can create a false historic appearance and can have a more significant negative impact on the historic character than not replacing the feature at all. For both repair and replacement, using the same kind of material is always preferred. If this is not feasible, a compatible substitute material may be used if it conveys the same historic appearance as wood and is physically and chemically compatible.

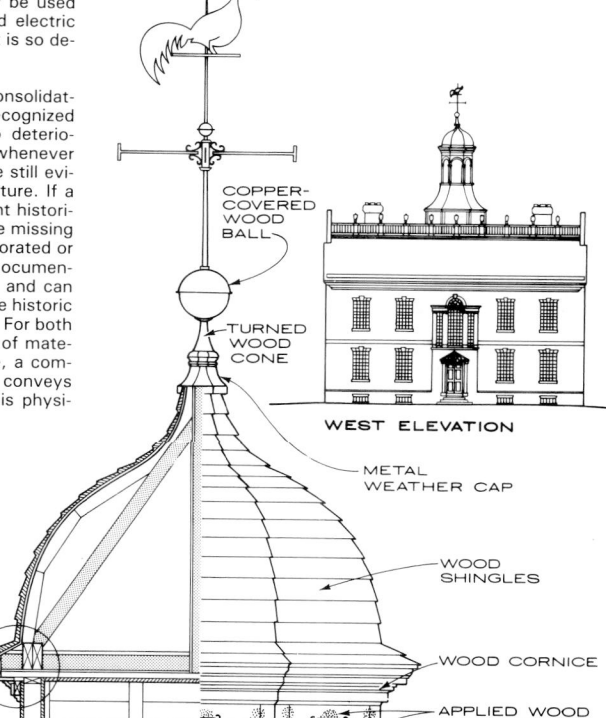

COPPER-COVERED WOOD BALL

TURNED WOOD CONE

WEST ELEVATION

METAL WEATHER CAP

WOOD SHINGLES

WOOD CORNICE

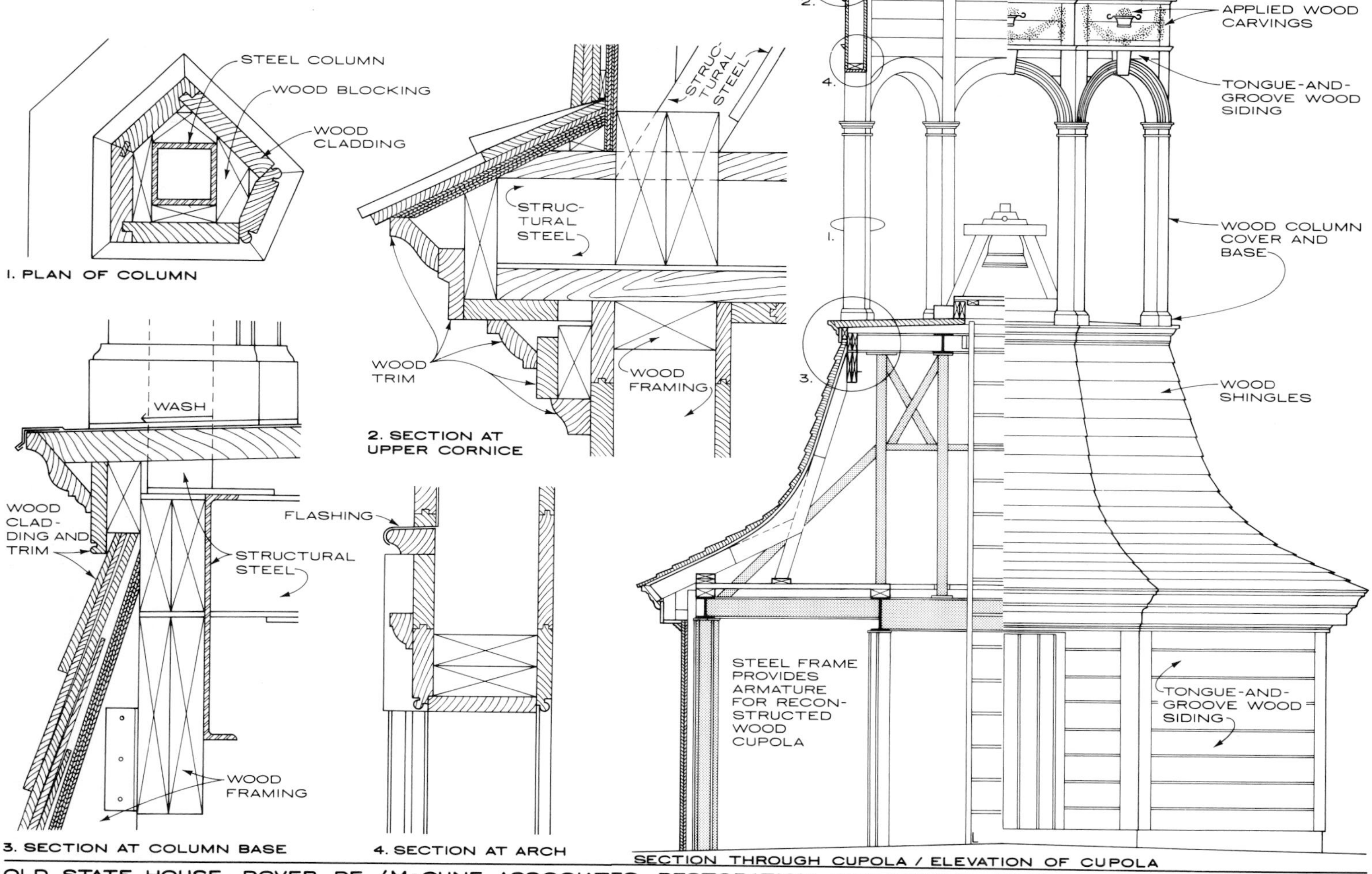

APPLIED WOOD CARVINGS

TONGUE-AND-GROOVE WOOD SIDING

WOOD COLUMN COVER AND BASE

WOOD SHINGLES

STEEL FRAME PROVIDES ARMATURE FOR RECONSTRUCTED WOOD CUPOLA

TONGUE-AND-GROOVE WOOD SIDING

SECTION THROUGH CUPOLA / ELEVATION OF CUPOLA

STEEL COLUMN

WOOD BLOCKING

WOOD CLADDING

1. PLAN OF COLUMN

STRUCTURAL STEEL

STRUCTURAL STEEL

WOOD TRIM

WOOD FRAMING

2. SECTION AT UPPER CORNICE

WASH

WOOD CLADDING AND TRIM

STRUCTURAL STEEL

WOOD FRAMING

3. SECTION AT COLUMN BASE

FLASHING

4. SECTION AT ARCH

OLD STATE HOUSE, DOVER, DE (McCUNE ASSOCIATES, RESTORATION ARCHITECTS, 1977)

Lee H. Nelson, FAIA, H. Ward Jandl, Sharon C. Park, AIA, Michael J. Auer; Preservation Assistance Division, National Park Service; Washington, D.C.

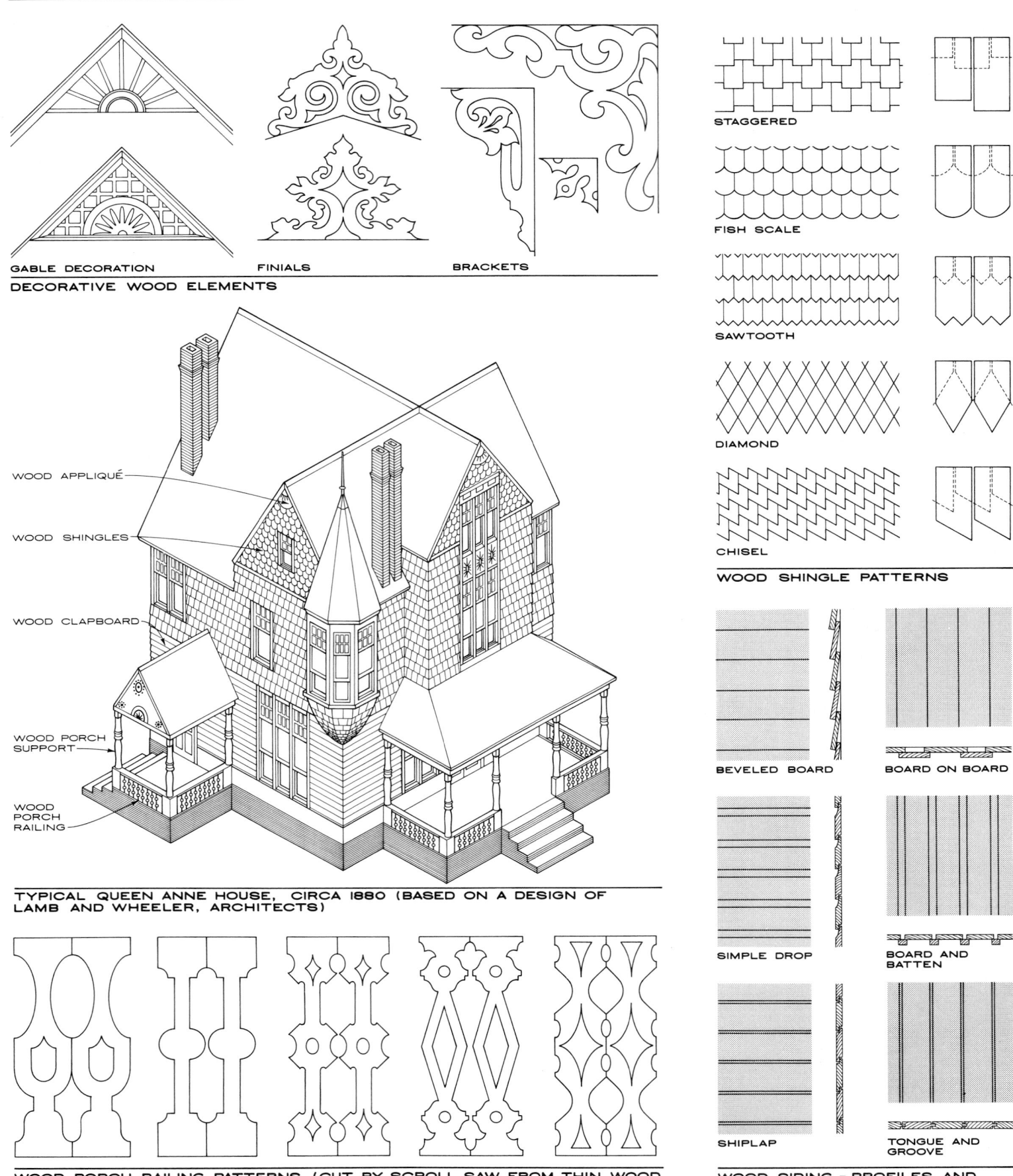

GABLE DECORATION   FINIALS   BRACKETS

DECORATIVE WOOD ELEMENTS

STAGGERED

FISH SCALE

SAWTOOTH

DIAMOND

CHISEL

WOOD SHINGLE PATTERNS

WOOD APPLIQUÉ

WOOD SHINGLES

WOOD CLAPBOARD

WOOD PORCH SUPPORT

WOOD PORCH RAILING

TYPICAL QUEEN ANNE HOUSE, CIRCA 1880 (BASED ON A DESIGN OF LAMB AND WHEELER, ARCHITECTS)

BEVELED BOARD   BOARD ON BOARD

SIMPLE DROP   BOARD AND BATTEN

SHIPLAP   TONGUE AND GROOVE

WOOD PORCH RAILING PATTERNS (CUT BY SCROLL SAW FROM THIN WOOD STOCK)

WOOD SIDING - PROFILES AND PATTERNS

Lee H. Nelson, FAIA, H. Ward Jandl, Sharon C. Park, AIA, Michael J. Auer; Preservation Assistance Division, National Park Service; Washington, D.C.
Eric J. Gastier; Darrel Downing Rippeteau Architects, PC; Washington, D.C.

INTRODUCTION

Architectural metal features—such as cast-iron facades, porches, and steps; sheet metal cornices, siding, roofs, roof cresting, and storefronts; and cast or rolled metal doors, window sash, entablatures, and hardware—are often highly decorative and may be important in defining the overall historic character of the building.

Metals commonly used in historic American building construction include lead, tin, zinc, copper, bronze, brass, iron, steel, and, to a lesser extent, nickel alloys, stainless steel, and aluminum. A high degree of craftsmanship went into fabrication of the metals in older American buildings. Often it was local artisans who designed and built fine staircases, exterior light standards, railings, or metal sculptures.

PRESERVATION APPROACHES

Before beginning any preservation work on metal features, it is critical that the metal be correctly identified; different metals have unique properties and thus require distinct preservation treatments. Inappropriate treatments to metal features can inadvertently result in their damage or loss.

Changes to architectural metal finishes can result in changing the historic character of a building.

Protecting architectural metals from corrosion should be the focus of a cyclical maintenance program. Proper drainage should be provided so that water does not stand on flat, horizontal surfaces or accumulate in curved, decorative features.

Incompatible metals should never be placed together without a reliable separation material or galvanic corrosion of the less noble metal will occur; e.g., copper corrodes cast iron, steel, tin, and aluminum.

Architectural metals should be carefully cleaned with the gentlest method possible to remove corrosion prior to repainting or applying other appropriate protective coatings. Local codes should also be checked to ensure compliance with environmental safety requirements. For some metals, such as bronze or copper, the surface coating or patina may serve as a protective coating and should not be removed. Soft metals such as lead, tin, copper, terneplate, and zinc should be cleaned with appropriate chemical methods because their finishes can be abraded by blasting methods, such as grit blasting.

The paint used to protect historic metal surfaces often contains lead. Care should be taken if lead-based paints are removed. Workers should wear protective gear, and lead-laden dust and other debris should not be introduced into the air. Any toxic residue that has been removed should be disposed of in compliance with local, state, and federal laws.

Harder metals, such as cast iron, wrought iron, and steel, may be hand scraped and wire-brushed to remove paint buildup and corrosion. If these methods prove ineffective, low-pressure grit blasting may be appropriate if the surface is not damaged or abraded. Adjacent wood or masonry should be protected from all cleaning efforts.

Applying appropriate paint or other coating systems immediately after cleaning decreases the corrosion rate of metals or alloys. If an architectural metal is being repainted, the colors should be appropriate to the historic building or district.

Architectural metal features can often be repaired by patching, splicing, or otherwise reinforcing the metal following recognized preservation methods. Repairs also involve the limited replacement in kind of those extensively deteriorated or missing parts of features when there are surviving prototypes. Examples are porch railings or roof cresting. An architectural metal feature that is too deteriorated to repair should be replaced in kind whenever possible. If the historic form and detailing are still evident, they can be used to guide the new work.

If an architectural metal feature is completely missing and there is sufficient historical, pictorial, and physical documentation, the missing features should be accurately restored. In the absence of sufficient documentation, the replacement metal feature may be a new design that is compatible with the size, scale, material, and color of the historic building.

Finally, for both repair and replacement treatments, using the same kind of metal is always preferred. If this is not feasible, a compatible substitute material may be used if it conveys the same visual appearance as the historic material and is chemically and physically compatible.

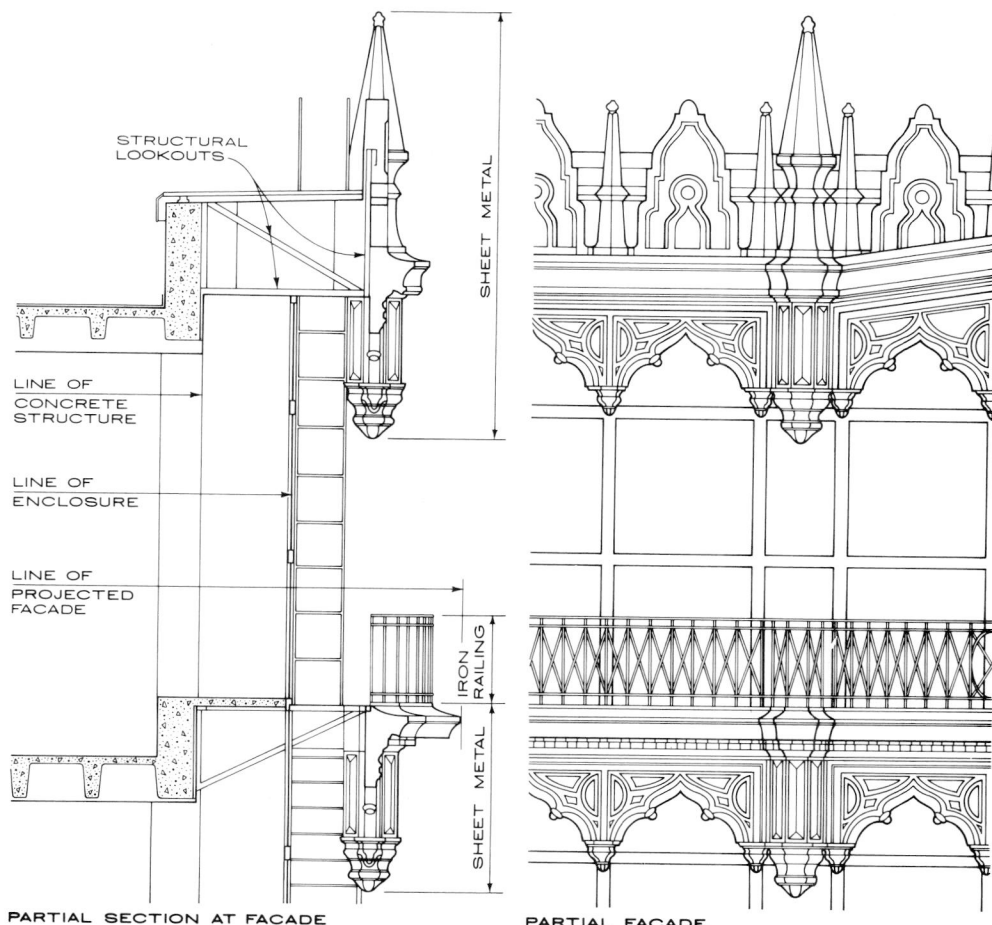

PARTIAL SECTION AT FACADE

PARTIAL FACADE

HALLIDIE BUILDING, SAN FRANCISCO, CA, 1918 (WILLIS POLK – ARCHITECT)

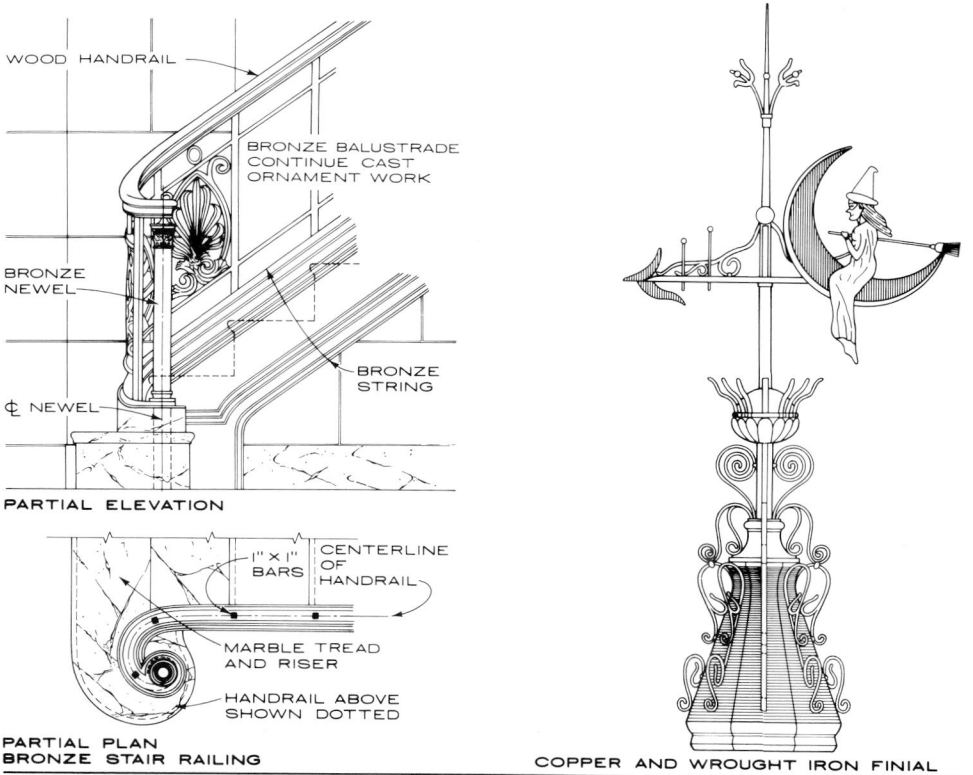

PARTIAL ELEVATION

PARTIAL PLAN
BRONZE STAIR RAILING

METAL ORNAMENT

COPPER AND WROUGHT IRON FINIAL

Lee H. Nelson, FAIA, H. Ward Jandl, Camille Martone, Kay D. Weeks; Preservation Assistance Division, National Park Service; Washington, D.C.
Eric J. Gastier; Darrel Downing Rippeteau Architects, PC; Washington, D.C.

HISTORIC ARCHITECTURAL METALS

758   **Preservation of Historic Roofs**

INTRODUCTION

The roof—with its shape; features such as cresting, dormers, cupolas, and chimneys; and the size, color, and patterning of the roofing material—is an important design element of many historic buildings. In addition a weathertight roof is essential to the long-term preservation of the entire structure.

Historic roofing is in large measure a reflection of available materials, levels of construction technology, the weather, and cost. For example, throughout the country in all periods of history, wood shingles have been used—their size, shape, and detailing differing according to regional craft practices. European settlers used clay tile for roofing as early as the mid-17th century. In some cities, such as New York and Boston, clay was popularly used as a precaution against fire. The Spanish influence in the use of clay tiles is found in the southern, southwestern, and western states. In the mid-19th century, tile roofs were often replaced by sheet-metal roofs, which were lighter and easier to install and maintain. Another practice settlers brought to the New World was slate roofing, and evidence of its use dates from the mid-17th century. Slate has been popular for its durability, fireproof qualities, and its decorative applications. The use of metals for roofing and roof features dates from the 18th century and includes the use of sheet iron, corrugated iron, galvanized metal, tinplate, and zinc. Awareness of these and other traditions of roofing materials and their detailing will contribute to more sensitive treatments.

PRESERVATION APPROACHES

The configuration of a historic building can be radically changed by adding new features to the roof, such as dormer windows, vents, skylights, or mechanical and service equipment. Adding an additional floor or floors at the roofline is possibly the most difficult rehabilitation change to accomplish without dramatically changing the historic character of the building. For this reason, the roof's shape, size, color, and patterning should be retained in any preservation project.

Routine maintenance of the building includes cleaning of gutters and downspouts and replacing deteriorated flashing. Roof sheathing should also be checked for proper venting to prevent moisture condensation and water penetration and to ensure that materials are free from insect infestation. When water and debris are permitted to collect, damage may occur to roof fasteners, sheathing, and the underlying structure.

In certain cases, such as storm or fire damage, only portions of a roof or a damaged roofing feature will need repair. The repaired area should match the visual qualities of the historic roof. Some repairs involve less difficulty than others. Normally, individual slates can be replaced without major disruption to the rest of the roof; replacing flashing, on the other hand, can require substantial removal of surrounding materials. If it is the substrate or a support material that has deteriorated, many of the more durable surface materials such as slate or tile can be reused if handled carefully during the repair.

A roof feature that is too deteriorated to repair should be replaced in kind, whenever possible. With some exceptions, most historic roofing materials are available today. Manufacturers of more common roofing materials can usually fill orders for less frequently requested items, such as unusual tile or embossed metal shingles.

For both repair and replacement of historic roofing, compatible substitute materials may be considered if the same kind of material is technically or economically infeasible; however, the substitute material needs to convey the same visual appearance and be physically and chemically compatible with the surrounding materials.

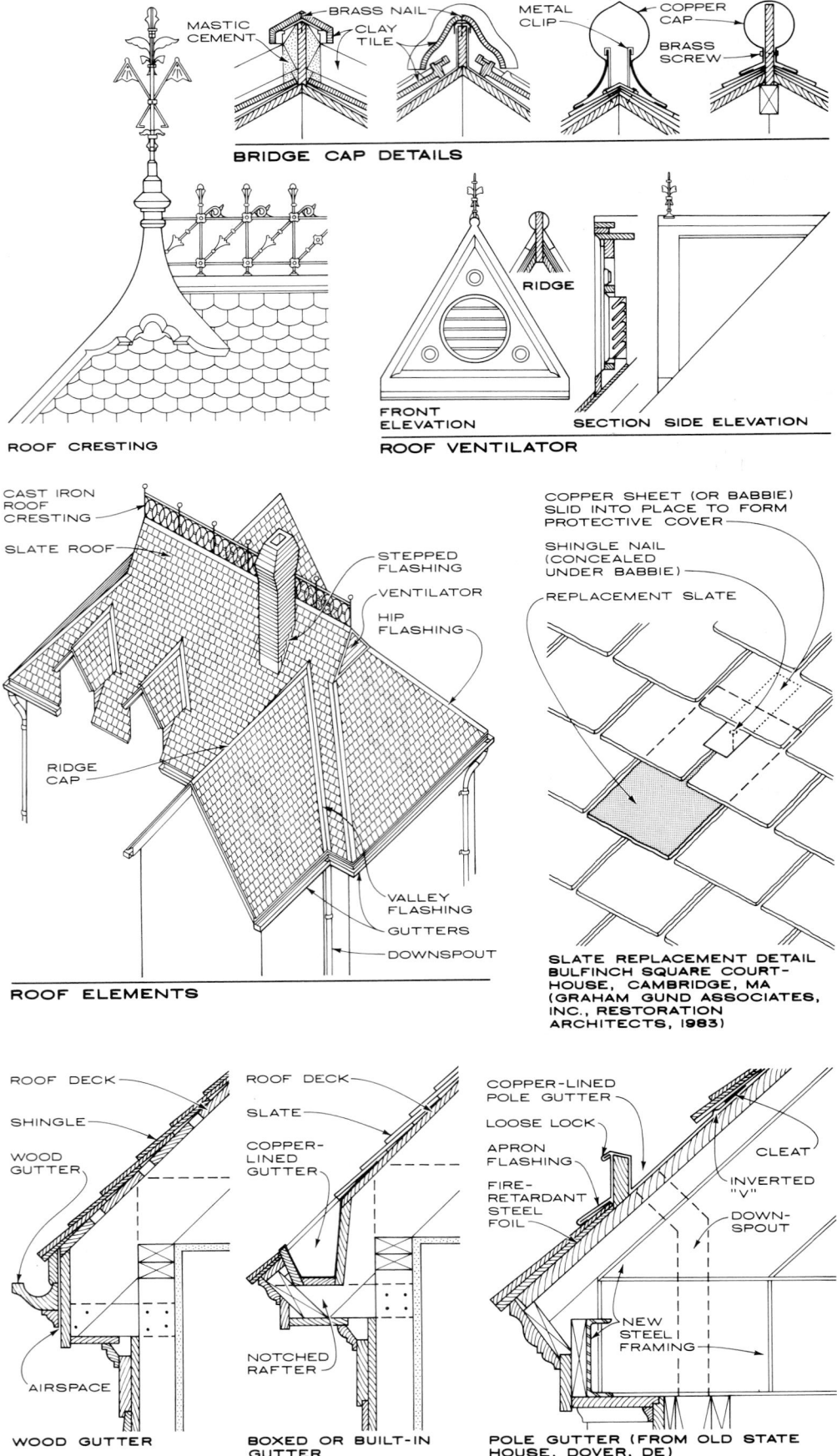

BRIDGE CAP DETAILS

MASTIC CEMENT — BRASS NAIL — CLAY TILE — METAL CLIP — COPPER CAP — BRASS SCREW

ROOF CRESTING

ROOF VENTILATOR

RIDGE

FRONT ELEVATION

SECTION SIDE ELEVATION

ROOF ELEMENTS

CAST IRON ROOF CRESTING
SLATE ROOF
STEPPED FLASHING
VENTILATOR
HIP FLASHING
RIDGE CAP
VALLEY FLASHING
GUTTERS
DOWNSPOUT

COPPER SHEET (OR BABBIE) SLID INTO PLACE TO FORM PROTECTIVE COVER
SHINGLE NAIL (CONCEALED UNDER BABBIE)
REPLACEMENT SLATE

SLATE REPLACEMENT DETAIL BULFINCH SQUARE COURTHOUSE, CAMBRIDGE, MA (GRAHAM GUND ASSOCIATES, INC., RESTORATION ARCHITECTS, 1983)

GUTTER DETAILS

ROOF DECK
SHINGLE
WOOD GUTTER
AIRSPACE

WOOD GUTTER

ROOF DECK
SLATE
COPPER-LINED GUTTER
NOTCHED RAFTER

BOXED OR BUILT-IN GUTTER

COPPER-LINED POLE GUTTER
LOOSE LOCK
APRON FLASHING
FIRE-RETARDANT STEEL FOIL
NEW STEEL FRAMING
CLEAT
INVERTED "V"
DOWNSPOUT

POLE GUTTER (FROM OLD STATE HOUSE, DOVER, DE)

Lee H. Nelson, FAIA, H. Ward Jandl, Sharon C. Park, AIA; Preservation Assistance Division, National Park Service; Washington, D.C.
Eric J. Gastier; Darrel Downing Rippeteau Architects, PC; Washington, D.C.

19   **HISTORIC ROOFS**

INTRODUCTION

As one of the few parts of a building serving both as an interior and exterior feature, windows are nearly always an important part of the historic character of a building. In most buildings, windows also comprise a considerable amount of the historic fabric of the wall plane and thus are deserving of special consideration. It is essential that the historic character of the windows be assessed together with their physical condition before specific repair or replacement work is undertaken. Emphasis should be placed on repairing existing windows, where possible, and improving their performance, such as with retrofitting weatherstripping to reduce air infiltration. Replacement windows should closely match the historic ones.

PRESERVATION APPROACHES

Technology and prevailing architectural styles have shaped the history of windows in the United States, starting in the 17th century with wooden casement windows with tiny glass panes seated in lead cames. From the transitional single-hung sash in the early 1700s to the true double-hung sash later in the same century,

VENETIAN WINDOW FROM THE OLD STATE HOUSE DOVER, DE (McCUNE ASSOCIATES, RESTORATION ARCHITECTS)

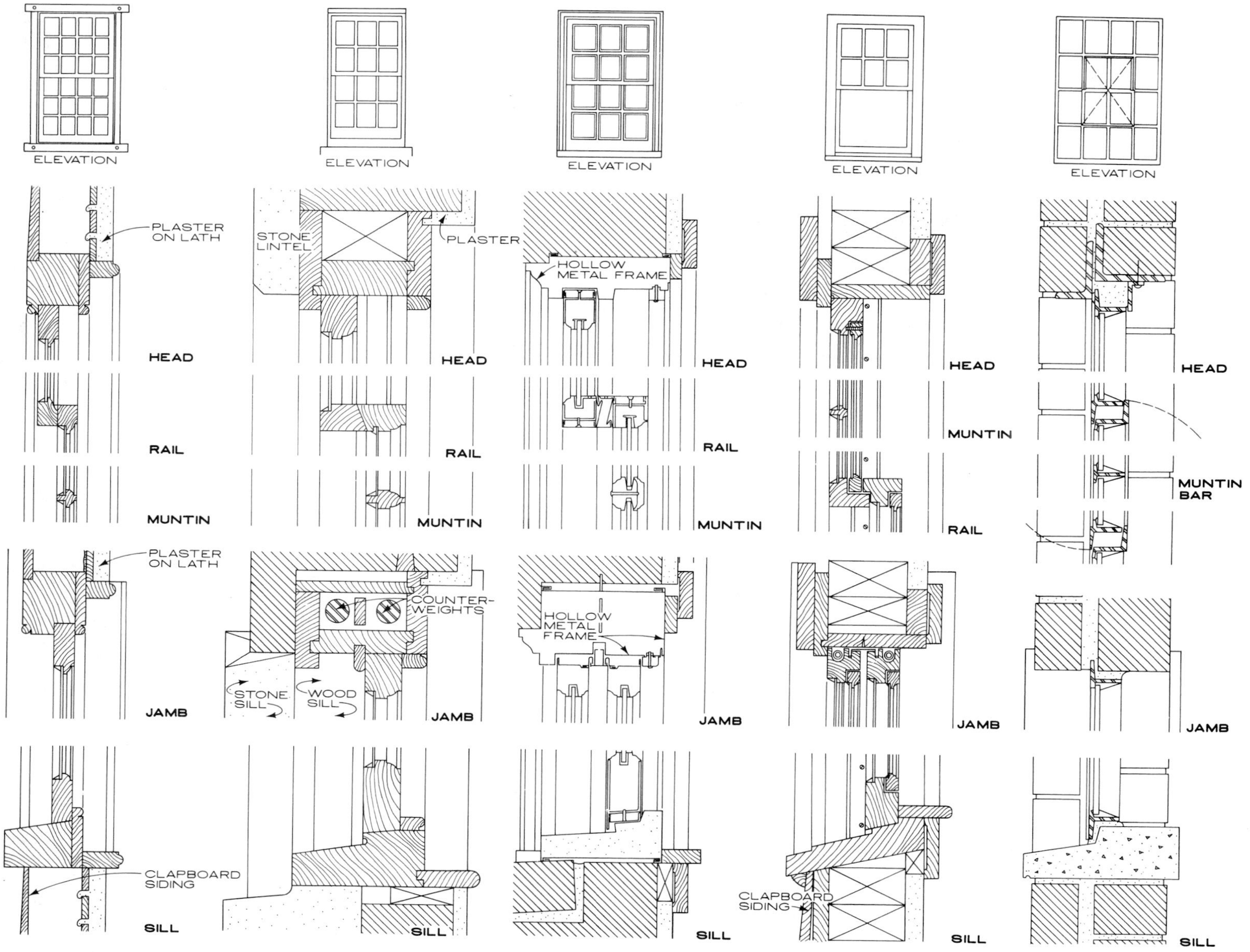

these early wooden windows were characterized by small panes, wide muntins, and the way in which decorative trim was used on both the exterior and interior of the window. As the sash thickness increased by the turn of the 19th century, muntins narrowed in width but increased in thickness according to the size of the window and design practices. Regional traditions continued to have an impact on window design, such as with the long-term use of ''French windows'' in the deep South. By the mid-19th century, two-over-two lights were common; the manufacturing of plate glass in the United States by the late 19th century allowed for dramatic use of large sheets of glass in commercial and office buildings. With mass-produced windows, mail order distribution, and changing architectural styles, it was possible to obtain a wide range of window designs and light patterns in sash. Popular versions of Arts and Crafts houses constructed in the early 20th century frequently utilized smaller lights in the upper sash set in groups or pairs and saw the reemergence of casement windows. In the early 20th century, the desire for fireproof building construction in dense urban areas contributed to the growth of a thriving steel window industry along with a market for hollow metal and metal clad wooden windows.

| ELEVATION | ELEVATION | ELEVATION | ELEVATION | ELEVATION |

| HEAD | HEAD | HEAD | HEAD | HEAD |

PLASTER ON LATH — STONE LINTEL — PLASTER — HOLLOW METAL FRAME

| RAIL | RAIL | RAIL | | |

| MUNTIN | MUNTIN | MUNTIN | MUNTIN | MUNTIN |

| | | | RAIL | MUNTIN BAR |

PLASTER ON LATH — COUNTER-WEIGHTS — HOLLOW METAL FRAME

| JAMB | JAMB | JAMB | JAMB | JAMB |

STONE SILL — WOOD SILL

| SILL | SILL | SILL | SILL | SILL |

CLAPBOARD SIDING

SINGLE-HUNG WOODEN WINDOW SOLID MORTISE AND TENON FRAME EARLY 18TH CENTURY

DOUBLE-HUNG WOODEN WINDOW MID-19TH CENTURY

STANDARD HOLLOW GALVANIZED IRON DOUBLE-HUNG WINDOW CIRCA 1910

DOUBLE-GLAZED DOUBLE-HUNG WOODEN WINDOW 1930S

HORIZONTAL PIVOTED STEEL WINDOW EARLY 20TH CENTURY

Lee H. Nelson, FAIA, H. Ward Jandl, Charles Fisher; Preservation Assistance Division, National Park Service; Washington, D.C.
Eric J. Gastier; Darrel Downing Rippeteau Architects, PC; Washington, D.C.

PRESERVATION APPROACHES

An in-depth survey of the condition of existing windows should be undertaken early in the planning of a rehabilitation to allow time to fully explore repair and upgrading methods and possible replacement options, if merited. Peeling paint, broken glass, stuck sash, and high air infiltration are no indication that existing windows are beyond repair and that their performance cannot be enhanced.

The wood and architectural metal which comprise the window frame, sash, muntins, and surrounds should be maintained through appropriate surface treatments such as cleaning, rust removal, limited paint removal, reapplication of protective coating systems, and reglazing where necessary.

Windows should be made weathertight by recaulking and replacing or installing weatherstripping. These actions also improve thermal efficiency. Retrofitting or replacing windows should never be a substitute for proper maintenance of the sash, frame, and glazing.

Window frames and sash can be repaired by patching, splicing, consolidating, or otherwise reinforcing historic materials.

Window repair can include replacement of deteriorated components such as sash cords, muntins, and sills.

Serviceable window hardware such as brass lifts and sash locks can be reused in the course of repairs and should not be discarded in favor of new hardware.

Thermal efficiency can be improved with weatherstripping, storm windows, caulking, interior shades, and, if historically appropriate, blinds and awnings. Replacing historic multipaned sash with new thermal sash is inappropriate when the historic sash are in repairable condition.

Interior storm windows should have airtight gaskets, ventilating holes, and/or removable clips or operability features to ensure proper maintenance and to avoid potential condensation damage to historic windows.

Exterior storm windows should be selected that do not damage or obscure the windows and frames. It is not appropriate to install new exterior storm windows that are inappropriate in size and are not painted the same color as the sash trim.

Tinted or reflective glazing should never be used on character-defining or other conspicuous elevations. Lightly tinted glazing could be used on non-character-defining elevations if other energy retrofitting alternatives are not possible and after conclusively establishing a need for such a treatment.

A historic window that is too deteriorated to repair should in most cases be replaced in kind, that is, using the same kind of material (wood for wood; steel for steel) and using the same sash and pane configuration and other design details.

In some cases, the historic windows (frame, sash, and glazing) may be completely missing. The preferred option for replacement is always an accurate restoration using historical, pictorial, and physical documentation.

Where fixed windows are being installed, the glass and frames should be set in the same planes as the historic sash, with all detailing duplicated.

When replacing historic multipaned sash with new sash, true integral muntins should be utilized, particularly on smaller buildings, windows on large buildings close to the pedestrianway, on ornate windows, where windows are part of a significant interior space, and where a building has high historic merit.

On certain types of large buildings, particularly high-rises, aluminum windows may be a suitable replacement for historic wooden sash provided wooden replacements are not practical and the design detail of the historic windows can be matched. Historic color duplication, custom contour panning, incorporation of 5/8 in. deep trapezoidal exterior muntin grids where applicable, retention of the same glass-to-frame ratio, matching of the historic reveal, and duplication of the frame width, depth, and such existing decorative details as arched tops should all be components in aluminum replacement windows selected for use on historic buildings.

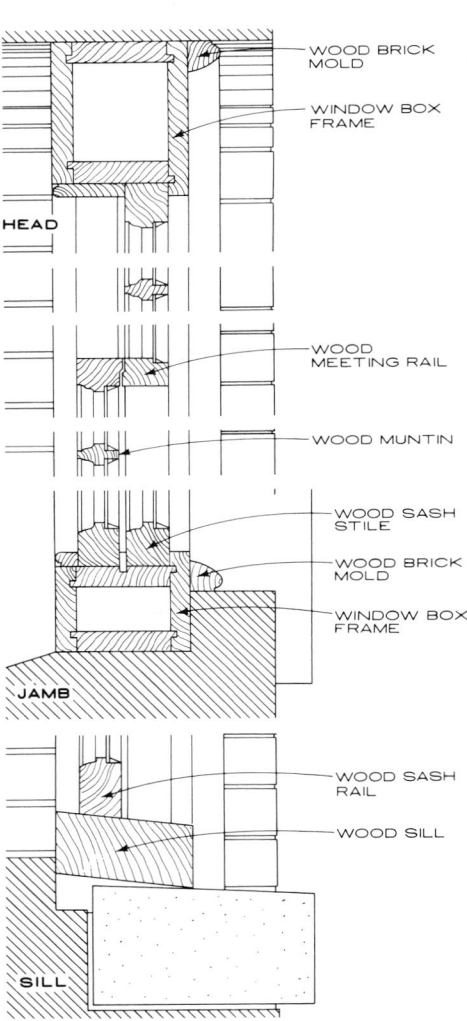

LATE 19TH CENTURY MILL WINDOW

REPAIR WHENEVER POSSIBLE.
IN SOME CASES, REPLACEMENT OF SASH
AND REUSE OF FRAMES AND HARDWARE
MAY BE POSSIBLE

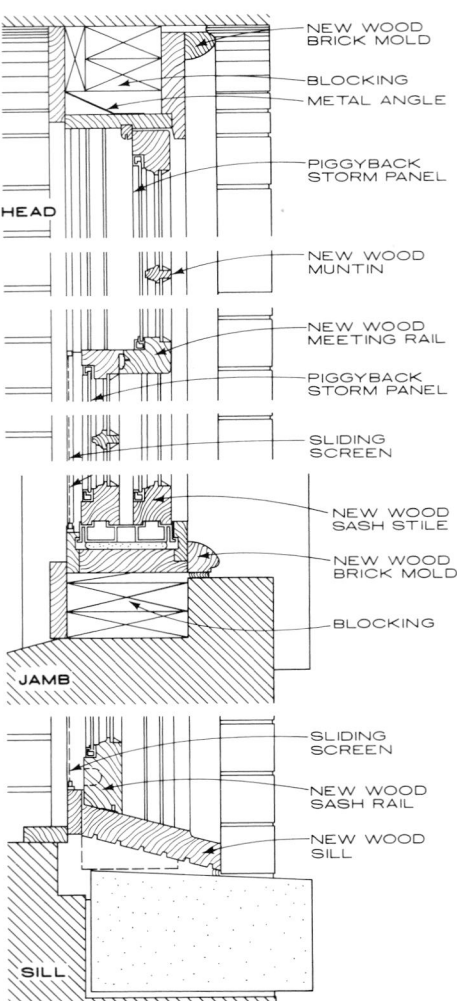

WOOD REPLACEMENT WINDOW

APPROPRIATE WHEN HISTORIC WINDOW IS
BEYOND REPAIR. IN MANY CASES, PIGGYBACK
INTERIOR STORM PANELS ATTACHED TO NEW
SASH AND/OR INTERIOR MOUNTED INSECT
SCREENS ARE SUITABLE UPGRADED
FEATURES. EXTERIOR APPEARANCE OF
HISTORIC WINDOW SHOULD BE RETAINED

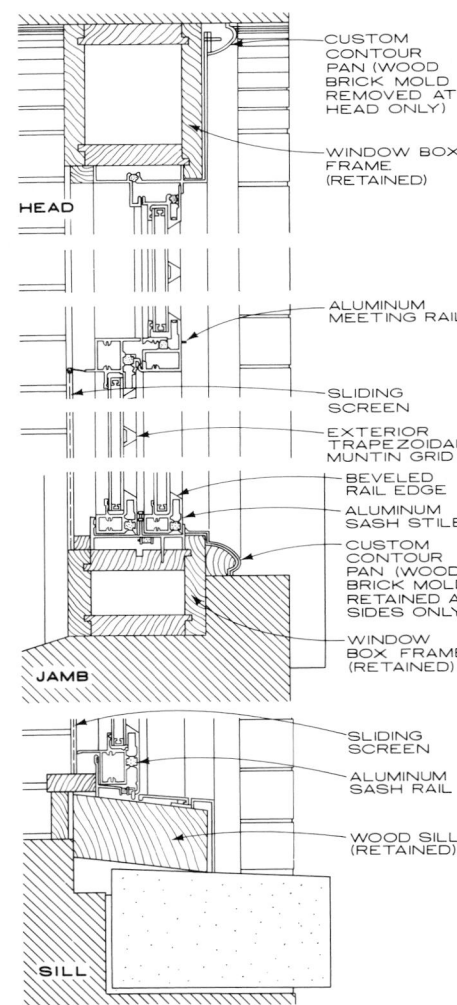

**ALUMINUM REPLACEMENT
WINDOW (CUSTOM)**

APPROPRIATE IN SOME CASES, PARTICULARLY
IN EARLY 20TH CENTURY HIGH-RISES.
SPECIAL FEATURES TO BE SPECIFIED:
BEVELED RAIL AND STILE EDGES, CUSTOM
CONTOUR PANNING, CUSTOM COLOR,
TRAPEZOIDAL EXTERIOR MUNTIN GRID, AND
CLOSELY MATCHED SIGHT LINES

REPAIR/REPLACEMENT STRATEGIES FOR HISTORIC WOOD WINDOWS

Lee H. Nelson, FAIA, H. Ward Jandl, Charles Fisher; Preservation Assistance Division, National Park Service; Washington, D.C.
Eric J. Gastier; Darrel Downing Rippeteau Architects, PC; Washington, D.C.

ACCESSIBLE ENTRANCE DESIGN

Providing entrances that are accessible to everyone requires a balance between historic preservation goals and the special needs of disabled people. Careful planning is required to achieve solutions that provide the highest level of access with the lowest level of impact to character-defining materials and features. Each building should thus be evaluated to determine the best design and best placement of accessibility features. Solutions on a primary facade may range from a minimal threshold wedge to a small ramp to much longer ramps, inclines, and grade changes. Designing a ramp that does not exceed 1 in. of rise for every 12 in. of run and is as unobtrusive as possible are dual preservation goals. (It should be noted that regrading to 1 in. of rise for 20 in. of run eliminates the need for handrails.) Retaining existing doors and hardware and using an automatic door opener are also recommended, whenever possible. If a significant primary facade would be threatened or destroyed in the process of providing access, a secondary facade may be used to provide an alternative public entrance. In general, nonmechanical means of overcoming physical barriers are preferable because mechanical devices require more maintenance and can easily break down.

If there is inadequate space for an accessible ramp, an incline or vertical lift may be considered. Each type of lift requires adequate maneuvering space at the head and foot of steps. Mechanical motors and electrical activators must have proper covers to reduce breakdowns. Lifts are often allowed for retrofit work but are generally not allowed in new construction. If new construction is to be part of an overall rehabilitation project, it may be possible to locate accessible entrances in a new addition with service to the historic building.

New additions, built to achieve accessibility requirements, should be

1. properly scaled (not too large in comparison to adjacent features).

2. of compatible materials (similar in quality, type, color values).

3. of compatible design (differentiated from the historic elements).

4. "reversible" (basic integrity of building left intact if a new accessibility feature were to be removed).

If the historical significance of a major facade would be threatened or destroyed if a new ramp or lift were added, every effort should be made to find a convenient alternative public entrance. Alternative public entrances located close to parking areas may provide a more direct path of travel for persons with disabilities. With careful planning, successful solutions can usually be found to balance accessibility and historic preservation requirements.

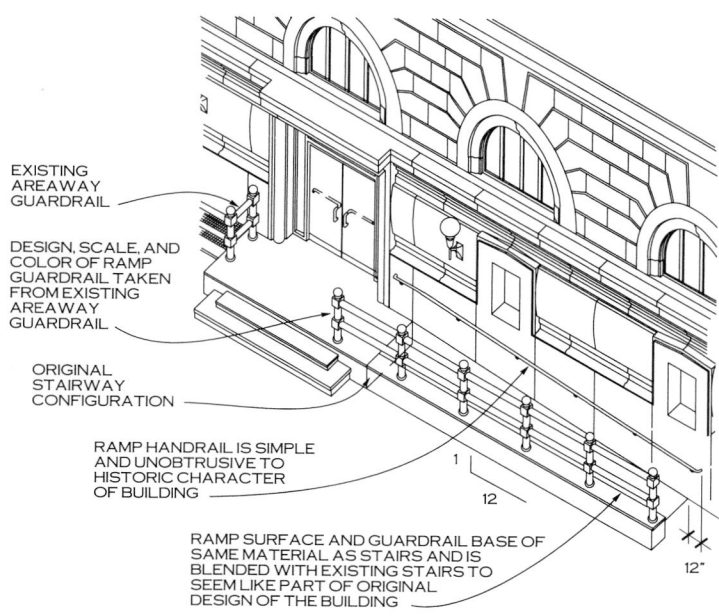

EXISTING AREAWAY GUARDRAIL

DESIGN, SCALE, AND COLOR OF RAMP GUARDRAIL TAKEN FROM EXISTING AREAWAY GUARDRAIL

ORIGINAL STAIRWAY CONFIGURATION

RAMP HANDRAIL IS SIMPLE AND UNOBTRUSIVE TO HISTORIC CHARACTER OF BUILDING

RAMP SURFACE AND GUARDRAIL BASE OF SAME MATERIAL AS STAIRS AND IS BLENDED WITH EXISTING STAIRS TO SEEM LIKE PART OF ORIGINAL DESIGN OF THE BUILDING

1 / 12

12"

ACCESSIBLE RAMP INTEGRATED WITH ENTRY

NOTE

Platform lifts are allowed in retrofit situations, but are generally not in new construction.

TERRACE

PORTION OF BALUSTRADE REMOVED TO ACCOMMODATE PLATFORM LIFT

SIDEWALK

WHEELCHAIR PLATFORM LIFT: COLOR TO BE COMPATIBLE WITH SURROUNDING MATERIALS

FOR ELEVATIONAL DIFFERENCES THIS GREAT, A RAMP COULD BE PROHIBITIVELY EXPENSIVE AND LONG

PLATFORM LIFT INTEGRATED INTO STAIR ENTRY

NOTES

1. Temporary ramp solution complies with ADA, and the design is durable and refined enough to be in place until a permanent solution is constructed.
2. Both designs retain the symmetry of the entry portal, allow maximum circulation, and are compatible with building color and historic character.
3. Temporary ramp should be easily "reversible" to original design.

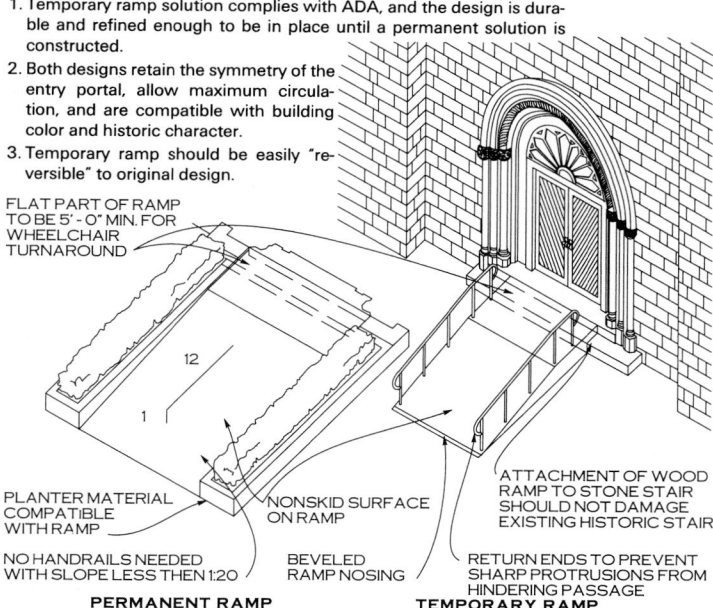

FLAT PART OF RAMP TO BE 5' - 0" MIN. FOR WHEELCHAIR TURNAROUND

12

1

PLANTER MATERIAL COMPATIBLE WITH RAMP

NONSKID SURFACE ON RAMP

ATTACHMENT OF WOOD RAMP TO STONE STAIR SHOULD NOT DAMAGE EXISTING HISTORIC STAIR

NO HANDRAILS NEEDED WITH SLOPE LESS THEN 1:20

BEVELED RAMP NOSING

RETURN ENDS TO PREVENT SHARP PROTRUSIONS FROM HINDERING PASSAGE

PERMANENT RAMP   **TEMPORARY RAMP**

ACCESSIBLE RAMP REPLACING ENTRY

ACCESSIBLE SIDE DOORS ARE SALVAGED FROM SECOND REVOLVING DOOR

ONE OF ORIGINAL TWO REVOLVING DOORS REALIGNED TO CENTER OF OPENING

EXISTING ENTRY AT SAME GRADE AS SIDEWALK

ACCESSIBLE SIDE DOORS ARE SALVAGED FROM SECOND REVOLVING DOOR

PUSH PLATE ACTIVATES AUTOMATIC DOOR OPENER

ACCESSIBLE DOORS INTEGRATED INTO EXISTING ENTRY

Ward Jandl, Kay D. Weeks, Sharon C. Park, AIA, Timothy A. Buehner; Preservation Assistance Division, National Park Service; Washington, D.C.
Richard J. Vitullo, AIA; Oak Leak Studio, Crownsville, Maryland

INTRODUCTION

Entrances and porches are quite often the focus of historic buildings, particularly when they occur on primary elevations. Together with their functional and decorative features such as doors, steps, balustrades, pilasters, and entablatures, they can be extremely important in defining the overall character of a building.

Usually entrances and porches were integral components of a historic building's design; for example, porches on Greek Revival houses, with Doric or Ionic columns and pediments, echoed the architectural elements and features of the larger building. Central one-bay porches or arcaded porches are evident in Italianate style buildings of the 1860s. Doors of Renaissance Revival style buildings frequently supported entablatures or pediments. Porches were particularly prominent features of Eastlake and Stick Style houses; porch posts, railings, and balusters were characterized by a massive and robust quality, with members turned on a lathe. Porches of bungalows of the early 20th century were characterized by tapered porch posts, exposed post and beams, and low-pitched roofs with wide overhangs. Art Deco commercial buildings were entered through stylized glass and stainless steel doors.

PRESERVATION APPROACHES

The materials that comprise entrances and porches—masonry, wood, and architectural metal—should be protected and maintained through appropriate surface treatments such as cleaning, rust removal, limited paint removal, and reapplication of protective coating systems. The overall condition of materials should be evaluated to determine whether more than protection and maintenance are required.

Removing or radically changing primary entrances will in most cases change the overall appearance of the building. Entrances and porches should never be removed because the building has been reoriented to accommodate a new use.

If barrier-free access is required to a historic building, it should be introduced in a way that does not destroy significant material or interfere with the historic design.

Entrances and porches can be repaired by reinforcing deteriorated historic materials—patching, splicing, and reinforcing with epoxies are examples. Limited replacement in kind of extensively deteriorated or missing parts of repeated features may be undertaken where there are surviving prototypes. Examples include balustrades, cornices, entablatures, columns, sidelights, and stairs.

Only when an entire entrance or porch is too deteriorated to repair—or is missing—should total replacement be considered. If the historic form and detailing are still evident, this evidence should be used to restore the entrance or porch.

If the entrance or porch is missing, restoration should be based on historical, pictorial, and physical evidence rather than on conjectural designs or the availability of elements from neighboring buildings.

When insufficient documentation exists for an accurate restoration, the replacement entrance or porch may be a new design that is consistent with the size, scale, material, and color of the historic building. Care must be taken not to create a false historic appearance in the new work.

Compatible substitute material may be considered if replicating with the historic material is technically or economically infeasible; the substitute material needs to convey the same visual appearance and be physically and chemically compatible. It is important to note that historic exterior wood elements were typically of rot-resistant species.

PORCH AND ENTRY

655 HUGHES STREET, CAPE MAY, NJ

PORCH AND ENTRY

FENDALL HALL, EUFAULA, AL (NICHOLAS H. HOLMES, RESTORATION ARCHITECT, 1975)

PORCH AND ENTRY

GUNSTON HALL, FAIRFAX COUNTY, VA

WOOD BALUSTRADE

TAPERED WOOD COLUMN AND BASE

SLOPED WOOD FLOOR

MASONRY STOOP

CROWNS

LONGITUDINAL FLOOR JOISTS TO ACCOMMODATE SLOPING FLOOR

TYPICAL BUNGALOW PORCH AND ENTRY, EARLY 20TH CENTURY

Lee H. Nelson, FAIA, H. Ward Jandl, Camille Martone, Kay D. Weeks; Preservation Assistance Division, National Park Service; Washington, D.C.
Eric J. Gastier; Darrel Downing Rippeteau Architects, PC; Washington, D.C.

HISTORIC ENTRANCES AND PORCHES

INTRODUCTION

The storefront is usually the most prominent feature of a historic commercial building, playing a crucial role in a store's advertising and merchandising strategy. Although a storefront usually does not extend beyond the first story, the rest of the building is often related to it visually in form and detail. Planning should always consider the entire building; window patterns on the upper floors, cornice elements, and other decorative features should be carefully retained, in addition to the storefront itself.

The earliest extant storefronts in the United States, dating from the late 18th and early 19th centuries, had bay or oriel windows and provided limited display space. The 19th century witnessed the progressive enlargement of display windows as plate glass became available in increasingly larger sizes. The use of cast-iron columns and lintels at ground floor level permitted structural members to be reduced in size. Recessed entrances provided shelter for sidewalk patrons and further enlarged display areas. In the 1920s and 1930s, aluminum, colored structural glass, stainless steel, glass block, neon, and other new materials were introduced to create Art Deco storefronts. The growing appreciation of historic buildings in recent years has prompted many owners to remove inappropriate changes and restore the historic appearance of their storefronts.

PRESERVATION APPROACHES

Functional and decorative features that make up the historic storefront include display windows, lower window panels, transoms, business signs, entrance doors, and entablatures. Materials that make up a storefront—cast iron, bronze, wood, pressed metal, structural glass—should be identified before undertaking any preservation work.

Removal of inappropriate, nonhistoric cladding and later alterations such as oversized awnings and signs can enhance a historic storefront.

The historic storefront should be secured by boarding up windows and installing alarm systems prior to and during rehabilitation. Unsecured doors and broken windows permit interior features and finishes to be damaged by weather or vandalism.

Damaged historic features such as cracked display windows, deteriorated wooden panels below windows, and rusted metal structural members should be repaired wherever possible rather than replaced.

Repairs are best made using historic materials; however, substitute materials may be appropriate if they convey the same visual appearance as the surviving components of the storefront.

Only if an entire storefront is missing or is too deteriorated to repair should total replacement be considered. The form and detailing should replicate the historic storefront.

Restoration should be based on historical and pictorial evidence rather than on conjectural designs or the availability of elements from neighboring buildings. When insufficient documentation exists for an accurate restoration, the replacement storefront may be a new design that is consistent with the size, scale, material, and color of the historic building.

Alterations to storefronts for the purpose of providing access to persons with disabilities should not result in the destruction of significant historic materials. For example, if paired door panels are each less than 32 in. wide or if historic decorative hardware is not the "lever-action type," doors and hardware should be retained and automatic door openers considered as a preservation solution.

Whenever possible, high thresholds or one step up should be modified with a ramp. Full sets of steps on a primary facade are often architectural features that cannot be altered without threatening or destroying the building's historical significance; secondary entrances should be considered in such situations.

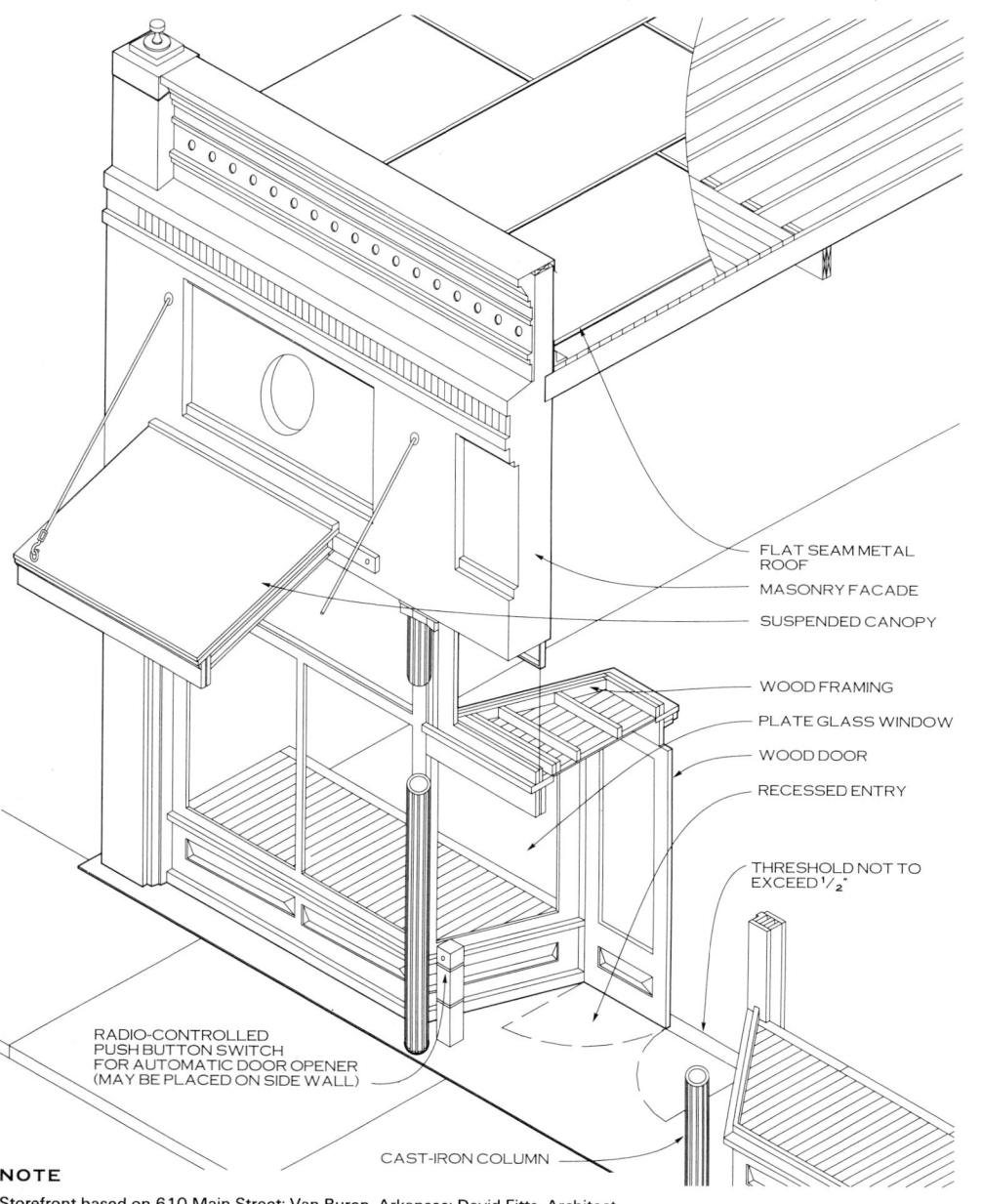

FLAT SEAM METAL ROOF
MASONRY FACADE
SUSPENDED CANOPY
WOOD FRAMING
PLATE GLASS WINDOW
WOOD DOOR
RECESSED ENTRY
THRESHOLD NOT TO EXCEED ¹/₂"
RADIO-CONTROLLED PUSH BUTTON SWITCH FOR AUTOMATIC DOOR OPENER (MAY BE PLACED ON SIDE WALL)
CAST-IRON COLUMN

NOTE
Storefront based on 610 Main Street; Van Buren, Arkansas; David Fitts, Architect

TYPICAL STOREFRONT, LATE 19TH CENTURY, WITH ACCESSIBILITY MODIFICATIONS

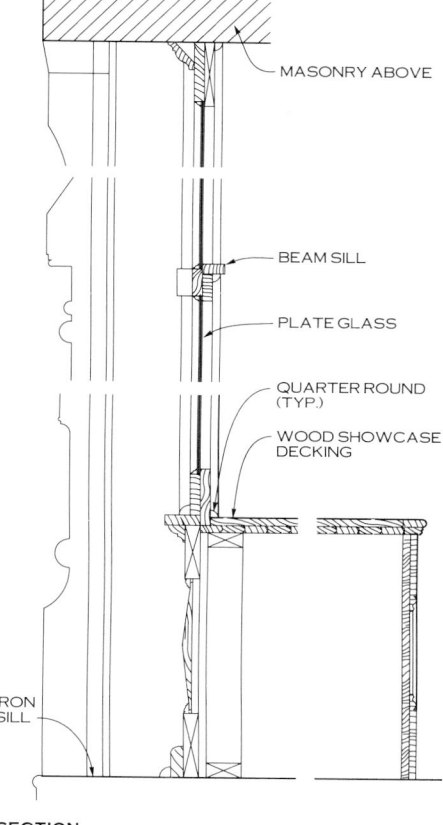

MASONRY ABOVE
BEAM SILL
PLATE GLASS
QUARTER ROUND (TYP.)
WOOD SHOWCASE DECKING
IRON SILL

SECTION

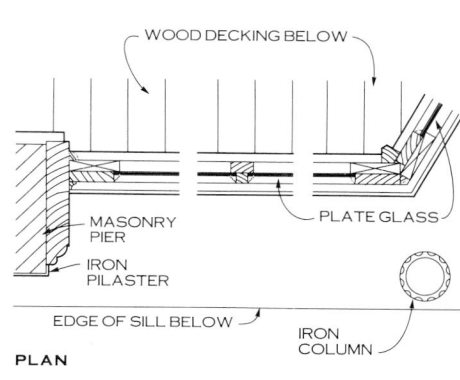

WOOD DECKING BELOW
MASONRY PIER
IRON PILASTER
PLATE GLASS
EDGE OF SILL BELOW
IRON COLUMN

PLAN

STOREFRONT DETAILS

Lee H. Nelson, FAIA, H. Ward Jandl, Michael J. Auer, Kay D. Weeks, Sharon C. Park, AIA, Timothy A. Buehner; Preservation Assistance Division, National Park Service; Washington, D.C.

INTRODUCTION

Structural systems in architecture are composed of structural elements (such as beams, piers, and trusses) and building materials (wood, steel, and masonry) that together form the walls, floors, and roofing of buildings.

If features of the structural system are exposed, such as load-bearing brick walls, cast iron columns, roof trusses, posts and beams, vigas, or stone foundation walls, they may be important in defining the building's overall historic character.

The types of structural systems found in America include, but certainly are not limited to, the following: wooden frame construction (17th century), balloon frame construction (19th century), load-bearing masonry construction (18th century), brick cavity wall construction (19th century), heavy timber post and beam industrial construction (19th century), fireproof iron construction (19th century), heavy masonry and steel construction (19th century), skeletal steel construction (19th century), and concrete slab and post construction (20th century).

PRESERVATION APPROACHES

A significant structural system or distinctive structural features should be identified prior to any work. To accommodate new uses within a historic building, structural upgrading should be done in a sensitive manner. Installing equipment or mechanical systems that result in numerous cuts, splices, or alterations to historic structural members should always be avoided.

If excavations or regrading—either adjacent to or within a historic building—are being planned, studies should be

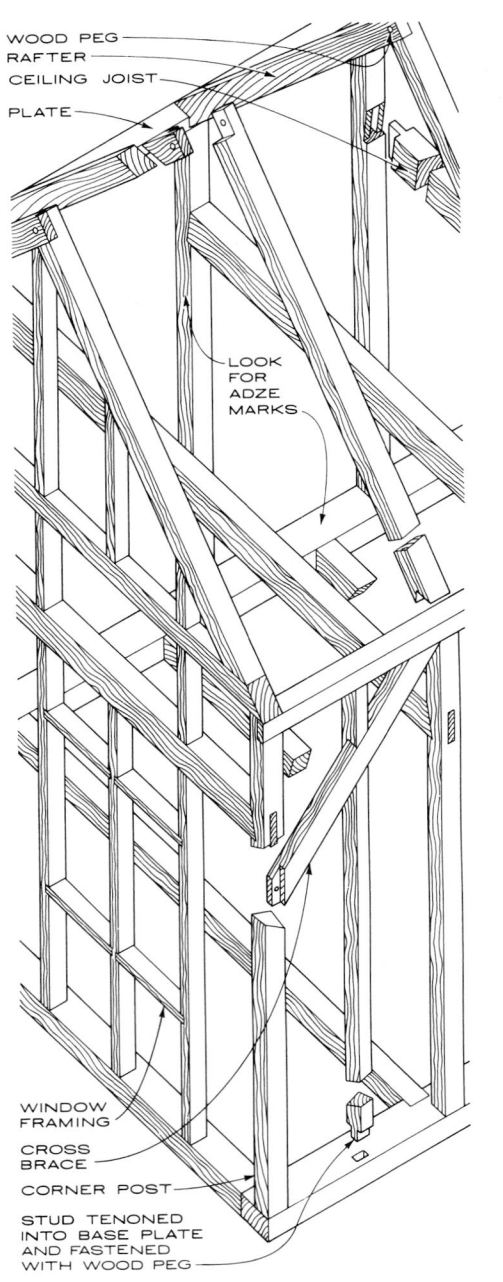

WOOD PEG
RAFTER
CEILING JOIST
PLATE

LOOK FOR ADZE MARKS

WINDOW FRAMING
CROSS BRACE
CORNER POST
STUD TENONED INTO BASE PLATE AND FASTENED WITH WOOD PEG

TYPICAL 18TH CENTURY MORTISE AND TENON WOOD FRAMING

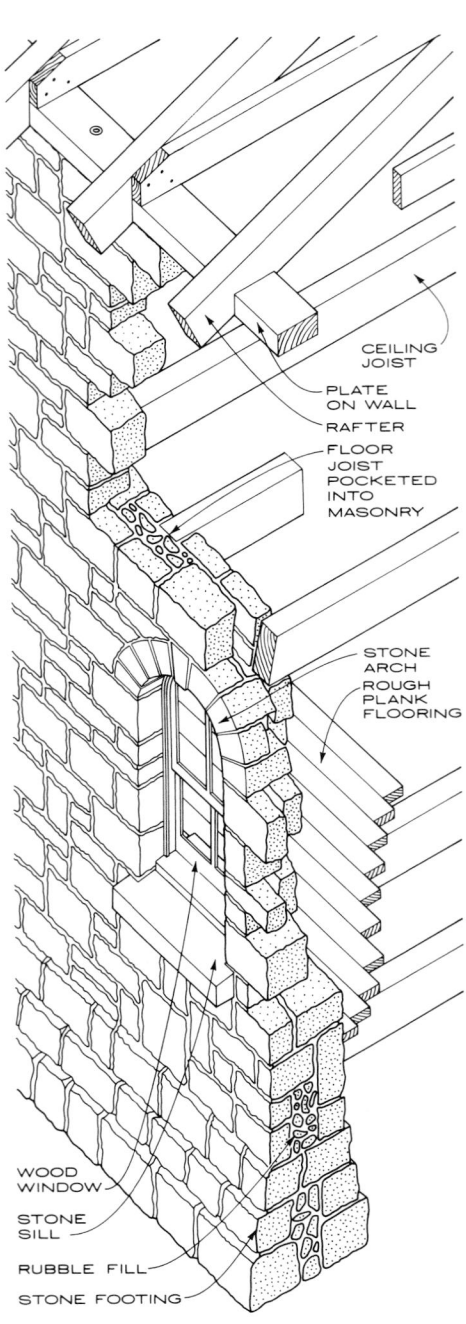

CEILING JOIST
PLATE ON WALL
RAFTER
FLOOR JOIST POCKETED INTO MASONRY

STONE ARCH
ROUGH PLANK FLOORING

WOOD WINDOW
STONE SILL
RUBBLE FILL
STONE FOOTING

18TH AND 19TH CENTURIES LOAD-BEARING MASONRY

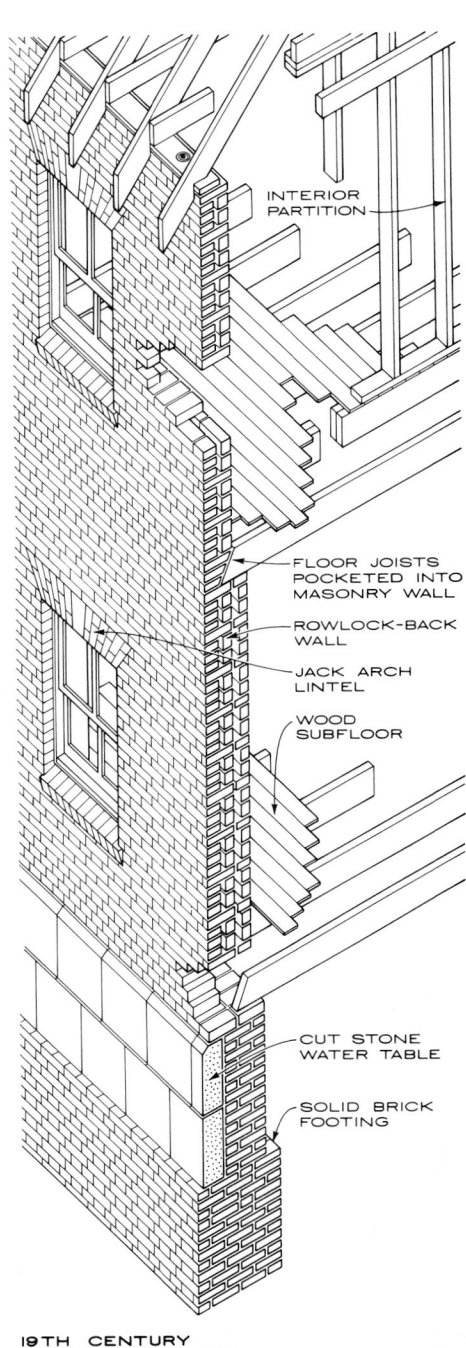

INTERIOR PARTITION

FLOOR JOISTS POCKETED INTO MASONRY WALL
ROWLOCK-BACK WALL
JACK ARCH LINTEL
WOOD SUBFLOOR

CUT STONE WATER TABLE
SOLID BRICK FOOTING

19TH CENTURY BRICK CAVITY WALL

STRUCTURAL SYSTEMS

Lee H. Nelson, FAIA, H. Ward Jandl, Sharon C. Park, AIA, Kay D. Weeks; Preservation Assistance Division, National Park Service; Washington, D.C.
Eric J. Gastier; Darrel Downing Rippeteau Architects, PC; Washington, D.C.

HISTORIC STRUCTURAL SYSTEMS

done first to ascertain potential damage to archeological resources and to the historic building itself. If significant archeological resources will be disturbed, appropriate mitigation measures need to be incorporated into the project. Inappropriate excavations can cause the historic foundation to settle, shift, or fail.

Structural problems, such as deflection of beams, racking of structural members, or cracking and bowing of walls, should be treated—not cosmetically covered over. A deteriorated load-bearing masonry wall should be reinforced and retained wherever possible, not replaced with a new wall that is veneered using old brick.

Structural deterioration can be the result of subsurface ground movement, vegetation growing too close to

foundation walls, improper grading, uncontrolled moisture, poor maintenance of exterior materials, leaking roofs, insect infestation, fungal rot, poor interior ventilation that results in condensation, inadequate attention to the effects of moisture in original structural detailing, and general deterioration of materials over time. Cyclical maintenance and annual inspections should be routine for historic buildings.

The structural system should be repaired by augmenting or upgrading individual parts or features. For example, weakened structural members such as floor framing can be paired with a new member sistered, braced, or otherwise supplemented and reinforced.

Permanent structural upgrading should never be undertaken in a manner that diminishes the historic character of the building, such as installing exterior strapping channels.

In instances where seismic upgrading is necessary, it is best to use grouted bolts as opposed to exposed plates and to locate diaphragms on unornamented surfaces or to consider other options that reduce the visual and physical impact of the code-required change.

If exposed elements of the structural system are beyond repair, the replacements need to convey the same form, design, and overall visual appearance as the historic feature, to equal the load-bearing capabilities of the historic material, and to be physically and chemically compatible.

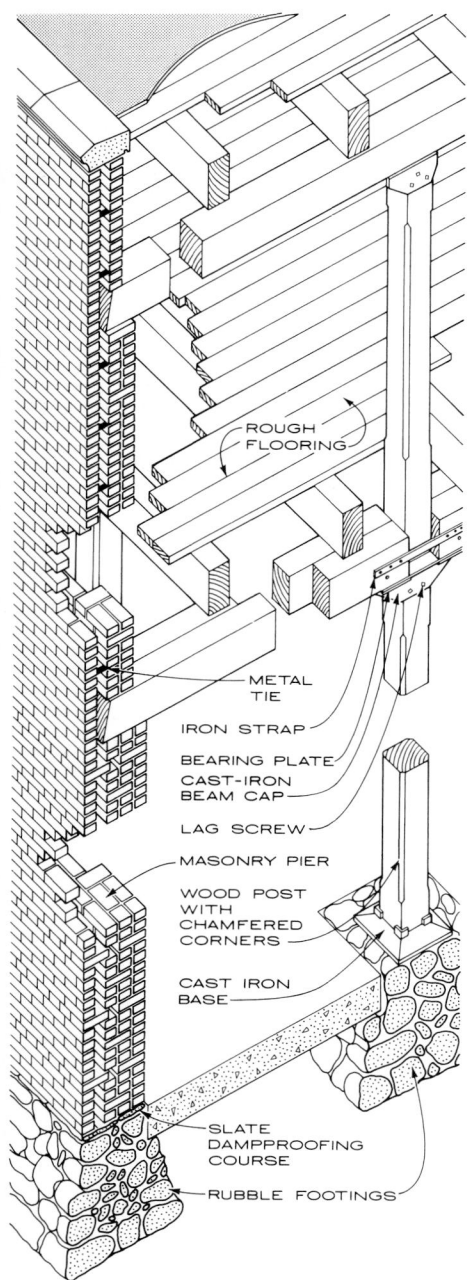

ROUGH FLOORING

METAL TIE
IRON STRAP
BEARING PLATE
CAST-IRON BEAM CAP
LAG SCREW
MASONRY PIER
WOOD POST WITH CHAMFERED CORNERS
CAST IRON BASE
SLATE DAMPPROOFING COURSE
RUBBLE FOOTINGS

19TH AND EARLY 20TH CENTURIES HEAVY TIMBER POST AND BEAM

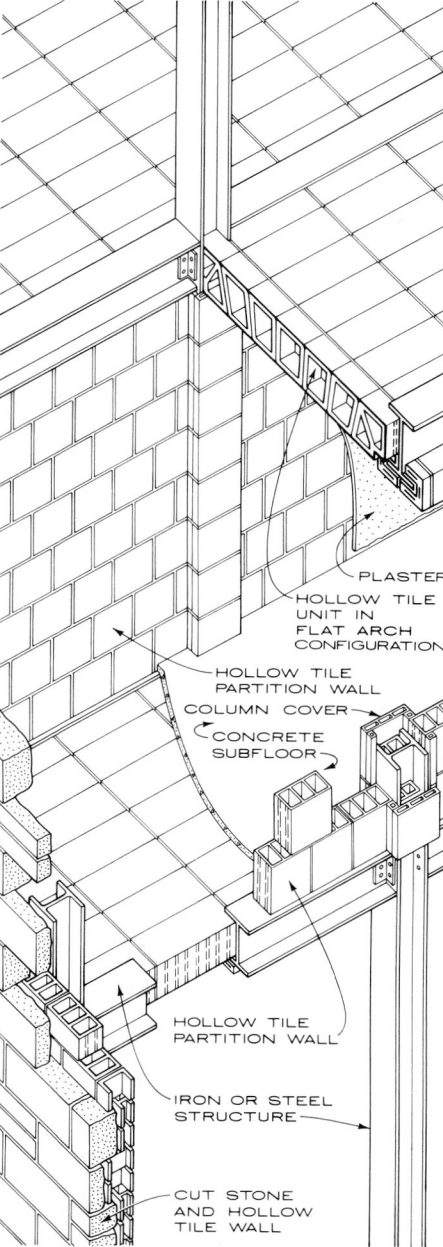

PLASTER
HOLLOW TILE UNIT IN FLAT ARCH CONFIGURATION
HOLLOW TILE PARTITION WALL
COLUMN COVER
CONCRETE SUBFLOOR
HOLLOW TILE PARTITION WALL
IRON OR STEEL STRUCTURE
CUT STONE AND HOLLOW TILE WALL

LATE 19TH AND EARLY 20TH CENTURIES FIREPROOF CONSTRUCTION

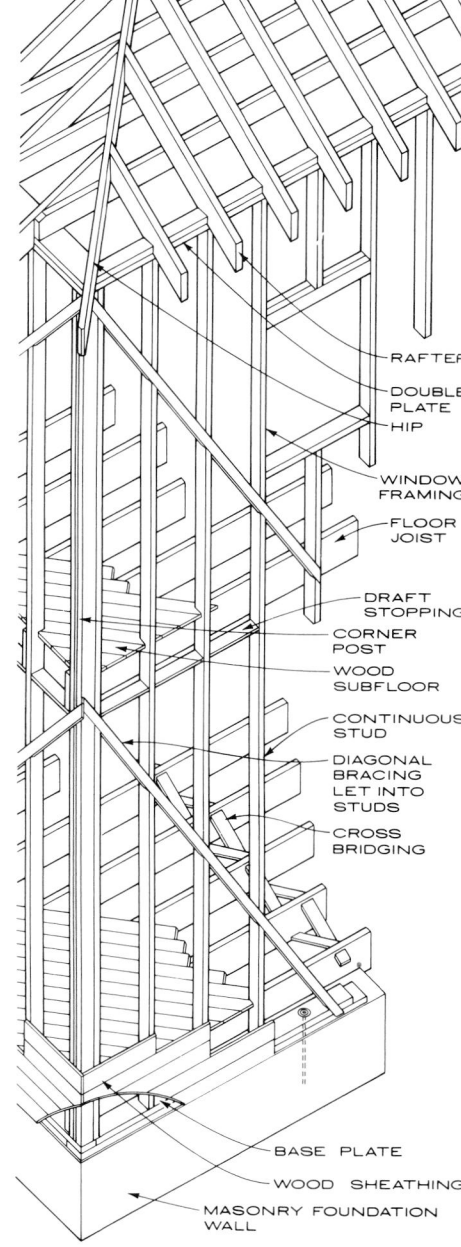

RAFTER
DOUBLE PLATE
HIP
WINDOW FRAMING
FLOOR JOIST
DRAFT STOPPING
CORNER POST
WOOD SUBFLOOR
CONTINUOUS STUD
DIAGONAL BRACING LET INTO STUDS
CROSS BRIDGING
BASE PLATE
WOOD SHEATHING
MASONRY FOUNDATION WALL

20TH CENTURY BALLOON FRAMING

STRUCTURAL SYSTEMS

Lee H. Nelson, FAIA, H. Ward Jandl, Sharon C. Park, AIA, Kay D. Weeks; Preservation Assistance Division, National Park Service; Washington, D.C.
Eric J. Gastier; Darrel Downing Rippeteau Architects, PC; Washington, D.C.

HISTORIC STRUCTURAL SYSTEMS 19

MAKING INTERIORS ACCESSIBLE

Making historic interiors accessible to persons with disabilities requires careful planning to ensure that significant historic spaces, features, and finishes are not threatened or destroyed. Because historic buildings are in a special category for code compliance, several design options may need to be developed and reviewed prior to implementing a solution.

Spaces that are of secondary importance often provide excellent locations for improved services to comply with the accessibility requirements. Interior alterations may involve developing an accessible path along corridors or through spaces to reach areas of principal activities (dining, banking, shopping), public restrooms and amenities (telephone, water fountains, etc.), elevator lobbies, or fire egress. This path should have corridors and doors of adequate width

and hardware designed for use by persons with disabilities. Properly designed accessible bathrooms, telephones, counters, and water fountains need to be provided. Existing historic elevators may be successfully altered to accommodate the needs of disabled people by adding a lowered control panel, or a new elevator may be added. With careful planning, a high level of access can be achieved with a minimum amount of alteration to significant historic features.

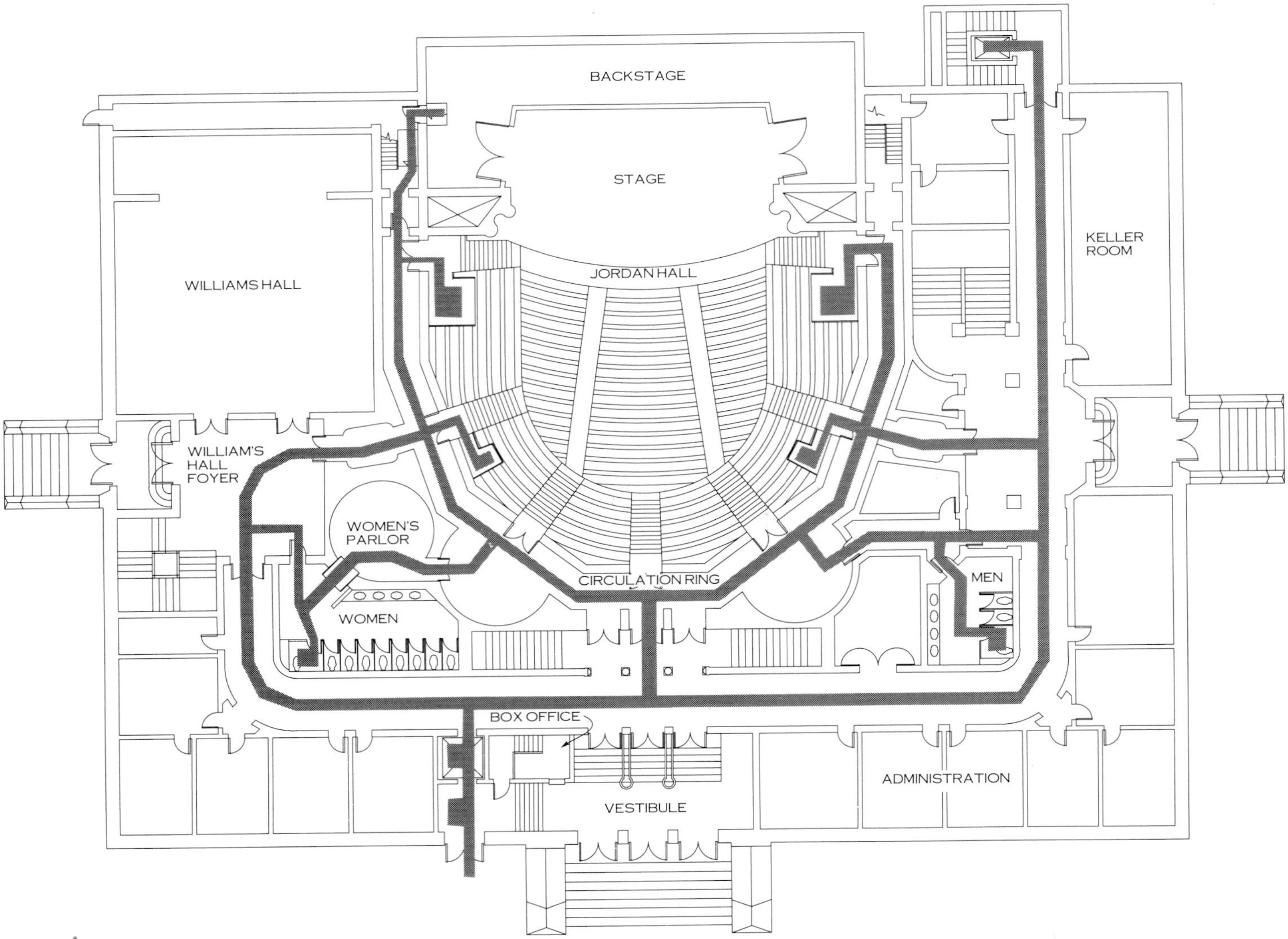

BACKSTAGE

STAGE

KELLER ROOM

WILLIAMS HALL

JORDAN HALL

WILLIAM'S HALL FOYER

WOMEN'S PARLOR

CIRCULATION RING

MEN

WOMEN

BOX OFFICE

ADMINISTRATION

VESTIBULE

NOTES

When making interior changes for accessibility, it is important to preserve character-defining spaces, features, and finishes. The historic entrance vestibule to this concert hall has been expanded to provide room for a grade-level entry and elevator. The restrooms have been enlarged, platform areas for wheelchair seating provided, and plush carpet removed from the path of travel.

- Avoid alterations to primary, significant spaces.
- Develop an accessible path to principal areas of activity with a minimum of alterations.
- Investigate the possibility of offset hinges to widen door openings.

- Avoid plush carpets; consider refinishing or repairing original floor surfaces.
- Install custom-designed lever hardware if compatible with historic hardware.

NEW ENGLAND CONSERVATORY OF MUSIC - DESIGN DEVELOPMENT DRAWING (ANN BAHA ASSOCIATES)

H. Ward Jandl, Kay D. Weeks, Sharon C. Park, AIA, Timothy Buehner; Preservation Assistance Division, National Park Service; Washington, D.C.

19   HISTORIC INTERIORS

INTRODUCTION

An interior floor plan, the arrangement and sequence of spaces, and built-in features and applied finishes are individually and collectively important in defining the historic character of the building. Their identification, retention, protection, and repair should be given prime consideration in every rehabilitation project.

In evaluating historic interiors prior to rehabilitation, it should be kept in mind that interiors are comprised of a series of primary and secondary spaces. This is applicable to all buildings, from courthouses to cathedrals to cottages and office buildings. Primary spaces, including entrance halls, parlors, living rooms, assembly rooms, and lobbies, are defined not only by their features and finishes, but by the size and proportion of the rooms themselves—purposely created to be the visual attraction or functioning "core" of the building. Care should be taken to retain the essential proportions of primary interior spaces and not to damage, obscure, or destroy distinctive features and finishes.

Secondary spaces include areas and rooms that "service" the primary spaces and may include kitchens, bathrooms, mail rooms, utility spaces, secondary hallways, firestairs, and office cubicles in a commercial or office space. Extensive changes can often be made in these less important areas without having a detrimental effect on the overall historic character.

PRESERVATION APPROACHES

Distinctive interior spaces, features, and finishes should be identified, then carefully retained and preserved in any work project. Examples include columns, cornices, baseboards, fireplaces and mantels, paneling, light fixtures, hardware, flooring, and wallpaper, plaster, paint, and finishes such as stenciling, marbling, and graining.

Distinctive interior spaces should not be altered by inserting a floor, cutting through the floor, lowering ceilings, or adding or removing walls.

Historically finished surfaces such as paint, plaster, or other finishes should not be stripped (e.g., removing plaster to expose masonry surfaces such as brick walls or a chimney piece). It is also inappropriate to strip painted wood to a bare wood surface, then apply a clear finish or stain to create a "natural, new look." Distinctive finishes such as marbling or graining on doors or paneling should be repaired, not covered over or removed. Conversely, paint, plaster, or other finishes should not be applied to surfaces that have been historically unfinished to create a new appearance.

Code-required fire suppression systems (such as a sprinkler system for a wood-frame mill building) should be sensitively designed so that character-defining features are not covered.

Interior features should be protected against gouging, scratching, and denting during project work by covering them with heavy canvas or plastic sheets. Destructive methods of paint removal such as propane or butane torches or sandblasting should never be used because they can irreversibly damage the historic materials that comprise interior features.

Interior features and finishes can often be repaired and preserved by reinforcing the historic materials. Repair may involve the limited replacement in kind of those extensively deteriorated or missing parts of repeated features when there are surviving prototypes such as stairs. Examples include balustrades, wood paneling, columns, or decorative wall coverings or ornamental tin or plaster ceilings. If an interior feature or finish is too deteriorated to repair or is missing, its replacement should be based on historical and pictorial evidence rather than on conjectural designs or the availability of elements from neighboring buildings.

In cases where insufficient documentation exists for an accurate restoration of an interior feature or finish, the replacement should be compatible in scale, design, materials, color, and texture with the surviving interior features and finishes. A new design element should be distinguishable from the old and not create a false historic appearance.

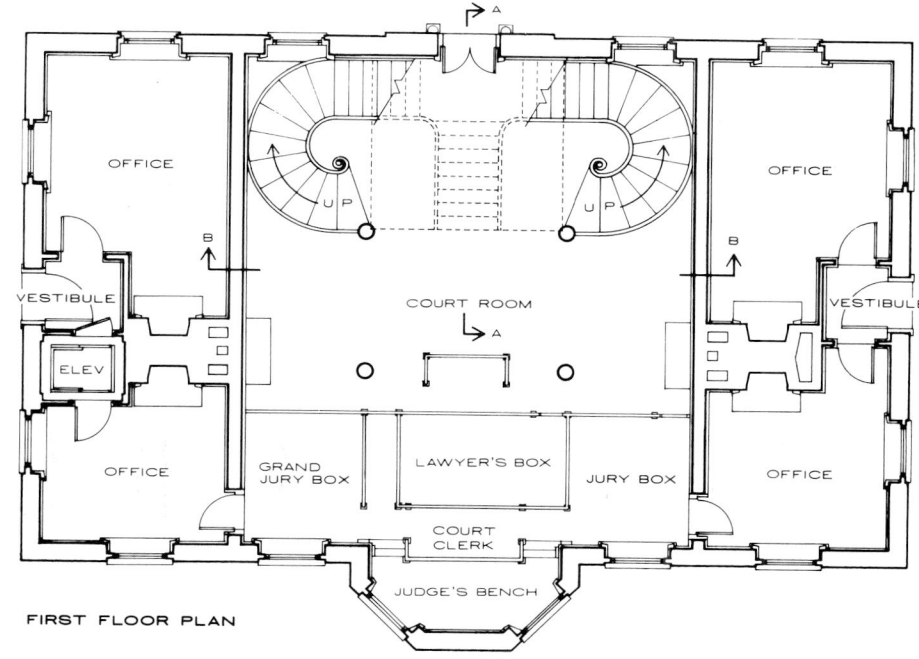

FIRST FLOOR PLAN

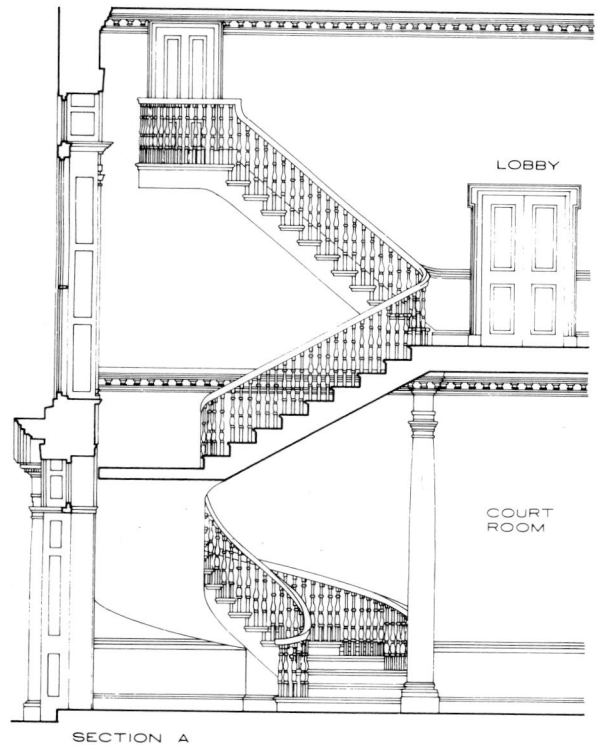

SECTION A

PARTIAL TRANSVERSE SECTION

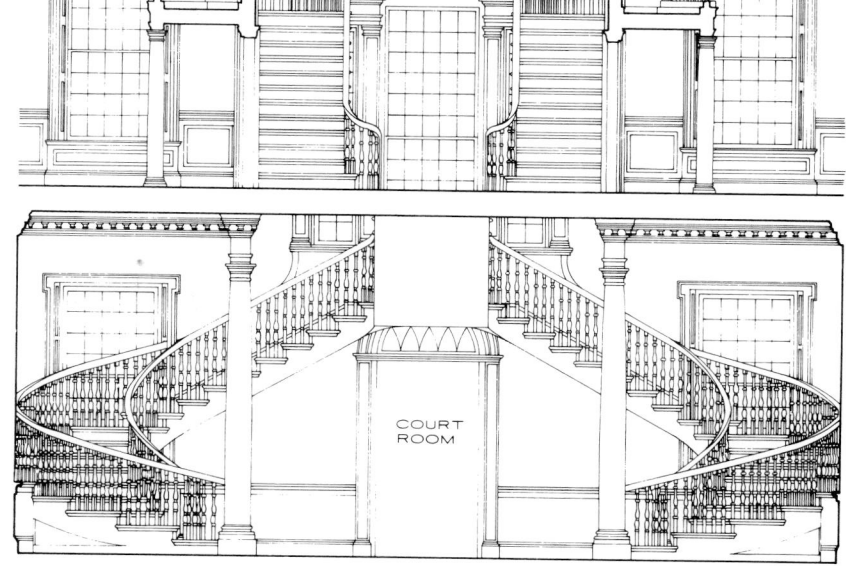

SECTION B

PARTIAL LONGITUDINAL SECTION

OLD STATE HOUSE, DOVER, DE (McCUNE ASSOCIATES, RESTORATION ARCHITECTS, 1977)

Lee H. Nelson, FAIA, H. Ward Jandl, Camille Martone, Kay D. Weeks; Preservation Assistance Division, National Park Service; Washington, D.C.
Eric J. Gastier; Darrel Downing Rippeteau Architects, PC; Washington, D.C.

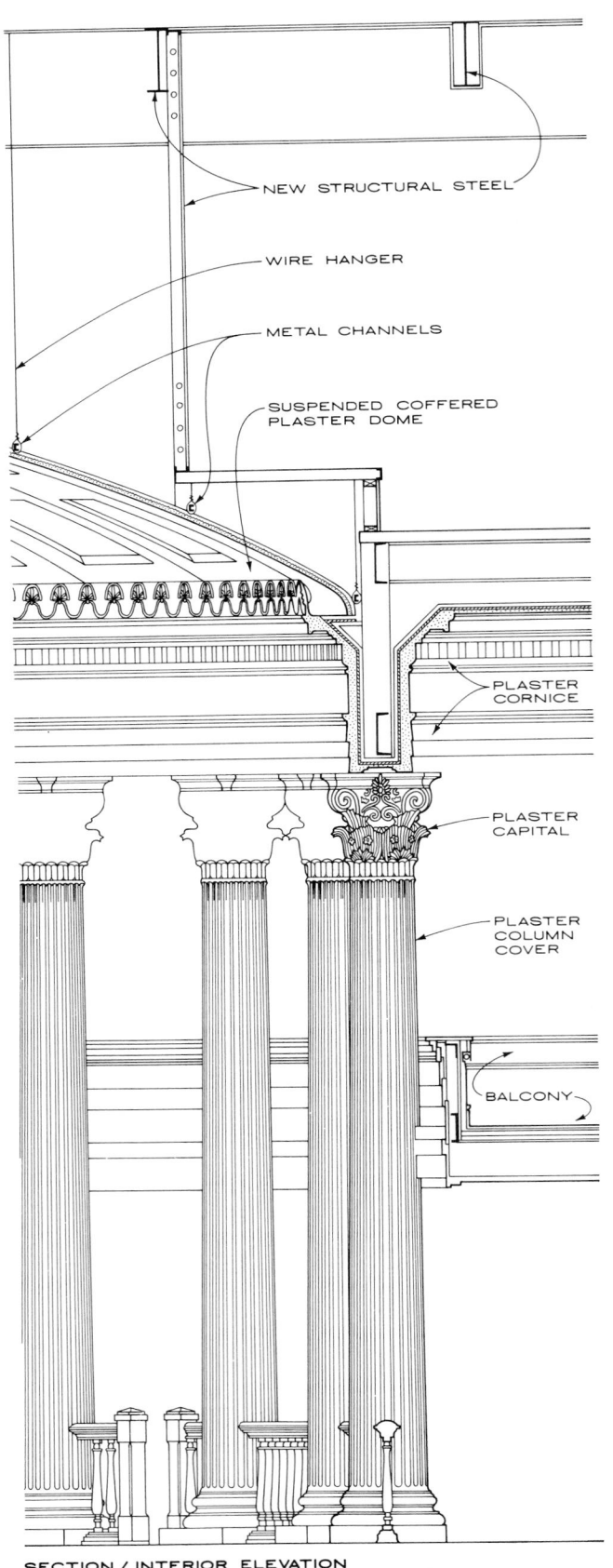

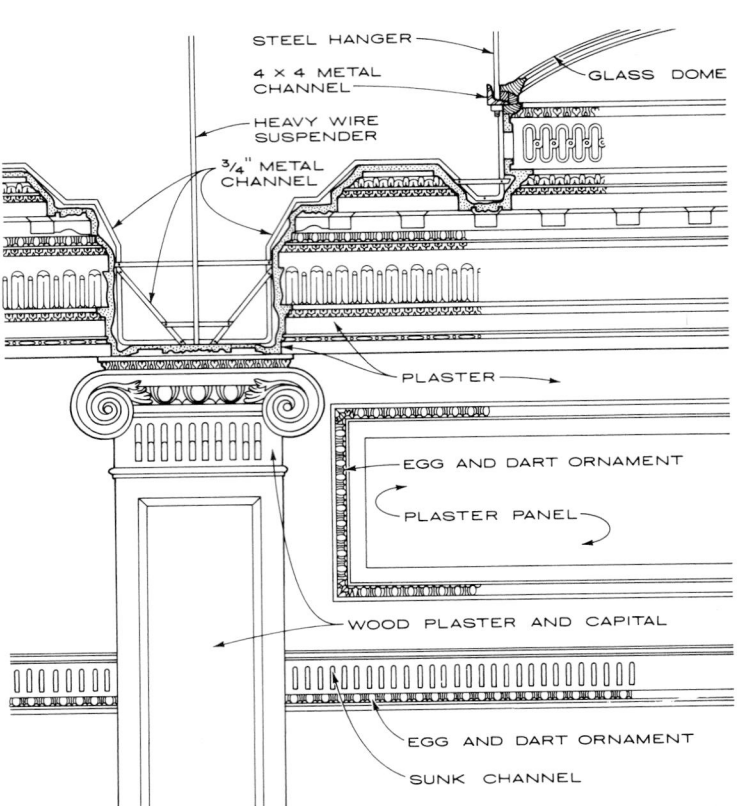

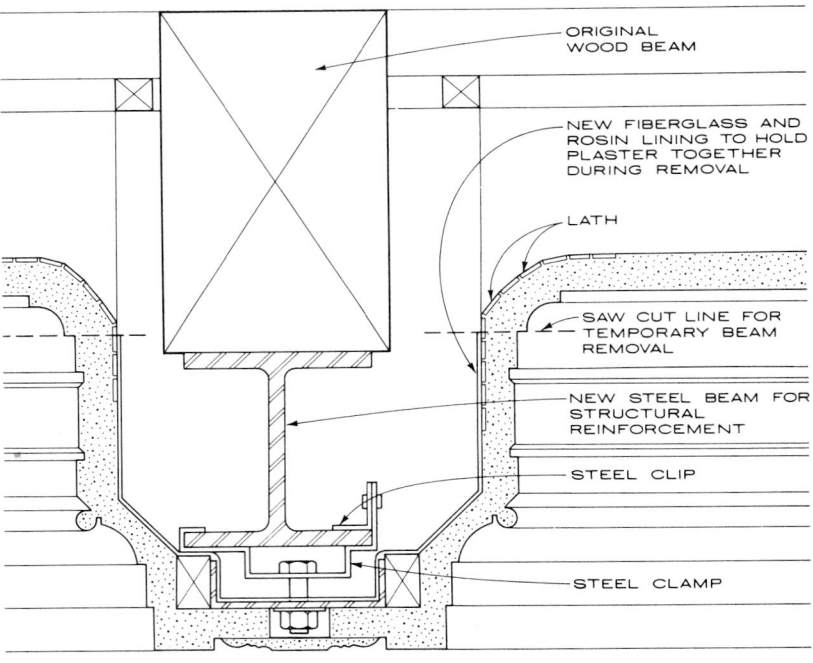

NEW STRUCTURAL STEEL

WIRE HANGER

METAL CHANNELS

SUSPENDED COFFERED PLASTER DOME

PLASTER CORNICE

PLASTER CAPITAL

PLASTER COLUMN COVER

BALCONY

SECTION / INTERIOR ELEVATION
OLD CAPITOL BUILDING, SPRINGFIELD, IL
(FERRY AND HENDERSON – ARCHITECTS FOR
RESTORATION, 1967)

STEEL HANGER

4 X 4 METAL CHANNEL

GLASS DOME

HEAVY WIRE SUSPENDER

3/4" METAL CHANNEL

PLASTER

EGG AND DART ORNAMENT

PLASTER PANEL

WOOD PLASTER AND CAPITAL

EGG AND DART ORNAMENT

SUNK CHANNEL

SECTION / INTERIOR ELEVATION
VENTURA COUNTY COURTHOUSE, SAN BUENA, VENTURA, CA,
1911 (ALBERT C. MARTIN – ARCHITECT)

ORIGINAL WOOD BEAM

NEW FIBERGLASS AND ROSIN LINING TO HOLD PLASTER TOGETHER DURING REMOVAL

LATH

SAW CUT LINE FOR TEMPORARY BEAM REMOVAL

NEW STEEL BEAM FOR STRUCTURAL REINFORCEMENT

STEEL CLIP

STEEL CLAMP

ORNAMENTAL PLASTER BEAM REMOVAL AND REPLACEMENT DETAIL
CROCKER ART GALLERY, SACRAMENTO, CA
(ROSEKRANS AND BRODER, INC. – ARCHITECTS FOR RESTORATION,
1978)

ORNAMENTAL PLASTER

Lee H. Nelson, FAIA, H. Ward Jandl, Camille Martone, Kay D. Weeks; Preservation Assistance Division, National Park Service; Washington, D.C.
Eric J. Gastier; Darrel Downing Rippeteau Architects, PC; Washington, D.C.

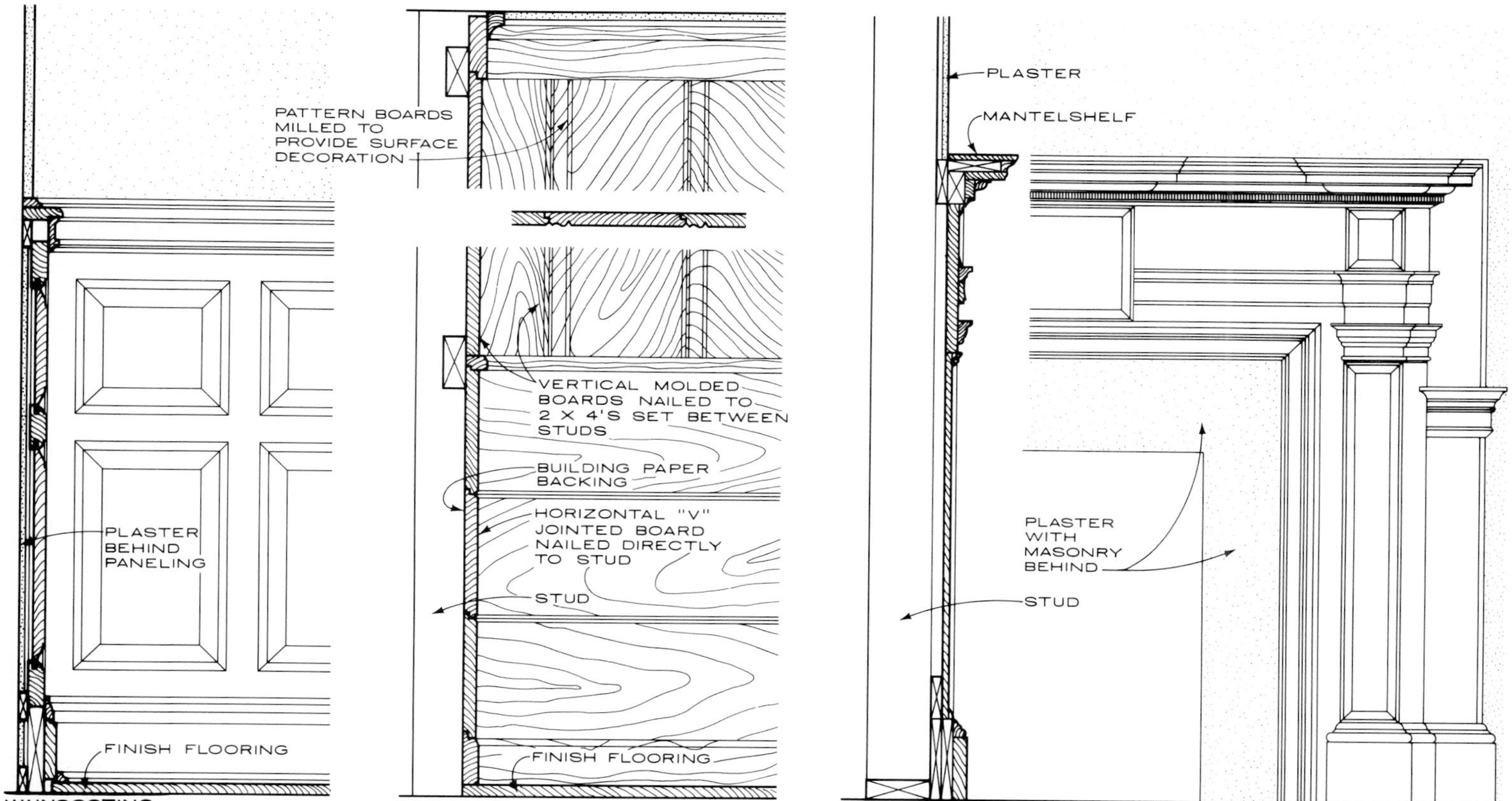

PATTERN BOARDS
MILLED TO
PROVIDE SURFACE
DECORATION

PLASTER

MANTELSHELF

PLASTER
BEHIND
PANELING

VERTICAL MOLDED
BOARDS NAILED TO
2 X 4'S SET BETWEEN
STUDS

BUILDING PAPER
BACKING

HORIZONTAL "V"
JOINTED BOARD
NAILED DIRECTLY
TO STUD

STUD

PLASTER
WITH
MASONRY
BEHIND

STUD

FINISH FLOORING

FINISH FLOORING

WAINSCOTING

BOARDING

FIREPLACE (FROM OLD STATE HOUSE, DOVER, DE)

WOOD PANELING AND CABINETRY WORK

CORNER
FIREPLACE

WOOD PANELING FROM THE LIVING ROOM OF THE TAYLOE HOUSE, WILLIAMSBURG, VA (PERRY, SHAW AND HEPBURN, CONSULTING ARCHITECTS FOR RESTORATION, 1949)

Lee H. Nelson, FAIA, H. Ward Jandl, Camille Martone, Kay D. Weeks; Preservation Assistance Division, National Park Service; Washington, D.C.
Eric J. Gastier; Darrel Downing Rippeteau Architects, PC; Washington, D.C.

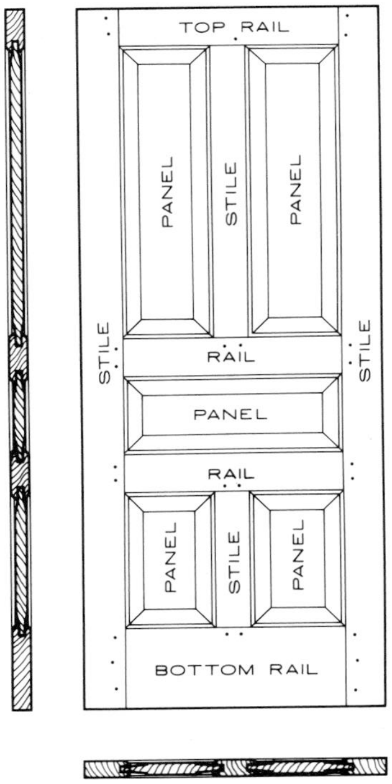

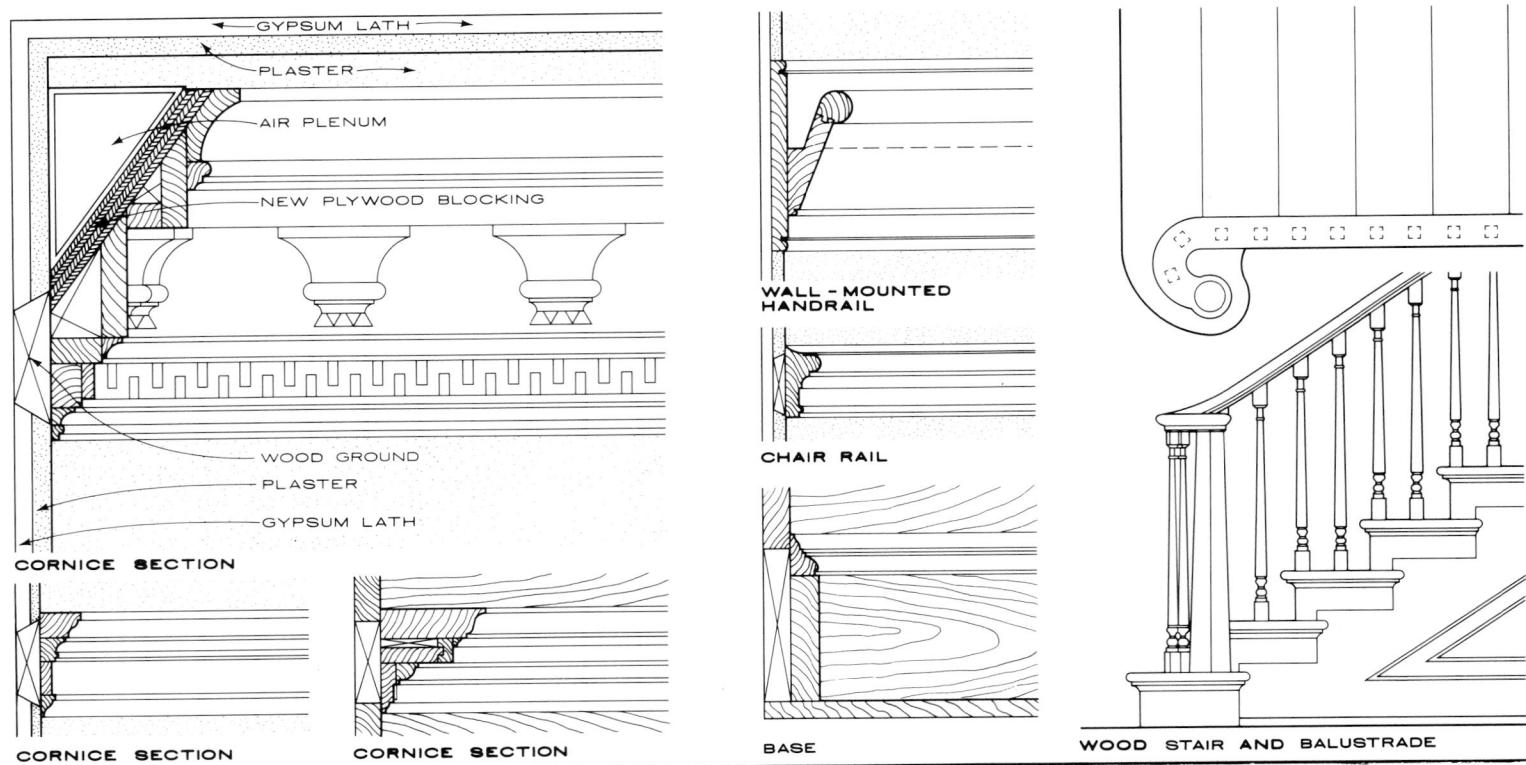

SOLID MOLDED STILE
WOOD DOOR

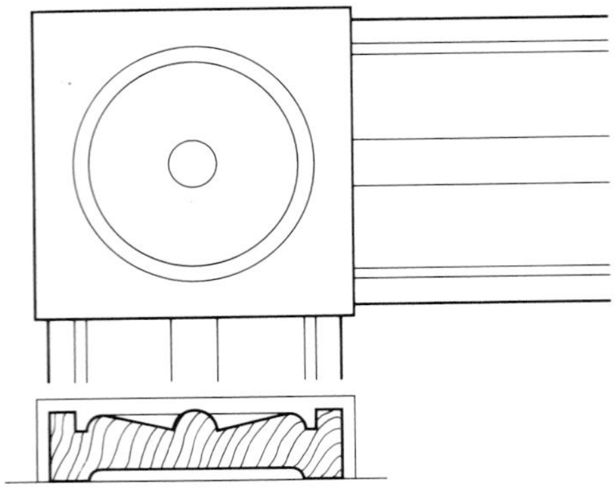

BLOCK AND PILASTER ARCHITRAVE

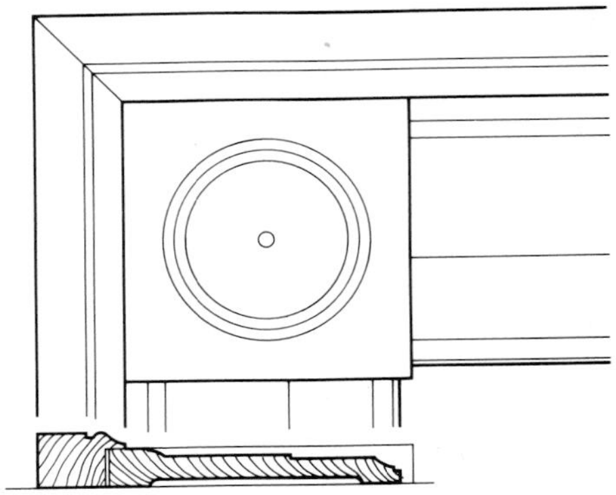

CORNER BLOCK AND MITERED
BACKBAND MOLDING

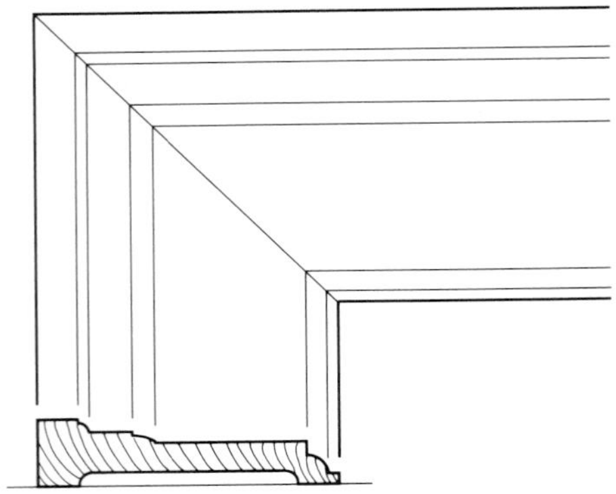

MITERED ARCHITRAVE

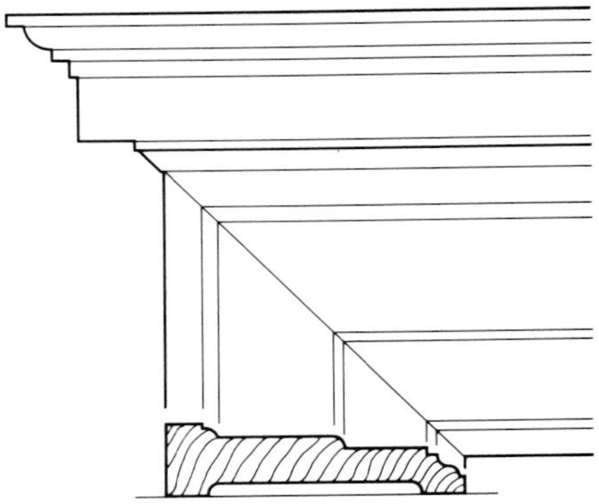

DOOR TRIM

MITERED ARCHITRAVE WITH CORNICE

CORNICE SECTION

CORNICE SECTION

CORNICE SECTION

WALL-MOUNTED
HANDRAIL

CHAIR RAIL

BASE

WOOD STAIR AND BALUSTRADE

INTERIOR WOOD DETAILS FROM THE OLD STATE HOUSE, DOVER, DE (McCUNE ASSOCIATES, RESTORATION
ARCHITECTS, 1977)

Lee H. Nelson, FAIA, H. Ward Jandl, Camille Martone, Kay D. Weeks; Preservation Assistance Division, National Park Service; Washington, D.C.
Eric J. Gastier; Darrel Downing Rippeteau Architects, PC; Washington, D.C.

19   HISTORIC INTERIORS

INTRODUCTION

The visible features of historic heating, lighting, ventilating, and plumbing systems may sometimes help define the overall historic character of the building and should thus be retained and repaired whenever possible. Realistically, the systems themselves (the compressors, boilers, generators, and their ductwork, wiring, and pipes) will generally need to be upgraded or entirely replaced in order to accommodate the new use and to meet code requirements. However, the visible portions of a system, the grilles, registers, lighting fixtures, and ornamental switchplates may be important in helping to define the interior historic character of a building. Therefore, the identification of such character-defining features should take place together with an evaluation of their physical condition early in project planning. The distinctive visual features of a building's mechanical, plumbing, and electrical system should be retained in the rehabilitation.

Mechanical, lighting, and plumbing systems were largely a product of the industrial age. The 19th century interest in hygiene, personal comfort, and the reduction of the spread of disease were met with the development of central heating, piped water, piped gas, and a network of underground cast iron sewers. Vitreous tiles in kitchens, baths, and hospitals could be easily and regularly cleaned. The mass production of cast iron radiators made central heating affordable to many; some radiators were elaborate and included special warming chambers for plates or linens. Ornamental grilles and brass registers created decorative covers for functional heaters in public spaces. By the turn of the 20th century, it was common to have all these modern amenities in a building.

The greatest impact of the 20th century was the use of electricity for the interior lighting, forced air ventilation, elevators for tall buildings, exterior lighting, and electric heat. The new age of technology brought an increasingly high level of design and decorative art to the functional elements of mechanical, electrical, and plumbing systems.

PRESERVATION APPROACHES

Mechanical, plumbing, and electrical systems and their features should be maintained through cyclical cleaning and other appropriate measures. Adequate ventilation of attics, crawl spaces, and cellars should be provided to prevent accelerated deterioration of mechanical systems due to moisture problems.

New systems should be installed in a manner that does not destroy or damage significant architectural material and that makes use of decorative elements of older systems—switchplates, ventilator grilles, lighting fixtures, etc.

Before total replacement of historic mechanical systems is considered, efforts should be made to evaluate the upgrading of the present system. Any ornamental features, such as significant lighting fixtures, should be retained after rewiring.

Often, to accommodate a continuing or new use, the historic mechanical system needs to be totally replaced with a new system. This new system needs to be installed in a manner that minimizes alterations to the building's floor plan and exterior elevations and causes the least damage to the historic building materials.

If a new mechanical system needs to be installed in a historic building, the vertical runs of ducts, pipes, and cables should be placed in closets, service rooms, and wall cavities rather than in architecturally significant spaces. Mechanical equipment should not be concealed in walls or ceilings in a manner that requires the removal of significant historic building materials.

New "dropped" acoustical ceilings that hide mechanical equipment should not be installed when this destroys the proportions of character-defining interior spaces, obscures window openings, or covers over decorative ceilings.

Cutting through features such as masonry walls to install heating/air-conditioning units should always be avoided. If new air-conditioning units are installed in window frames, the sash and frames should be protected from moisture condensation. Window installations should be considered only when all other viable heating/cooling systems would result in significant damage to historic materials.

ADDING NEW MECHANICAL SYSTEMS TO HISTORIC BUILDINGS

The need for modern mechanical systems is one of the most common reasons to undertake work on historic buildings. For historic properties, it is critical to understand what spaces, features, and finishes are historic in the building, what should be retained, and what the realistic heating, ventilating, and cooling needs are for the building, its occupants, and its contents. In too many cases, applying modern standards of interior climate comfort to historic buildings has proven detrimental to historic materials and decorative finishes. A systematic approach, involving preservation planning, preservation design, and a follow-up program of monitoring and maintenance, can ensure that new systems are successfully added—while preserving the historic integrity of the building.

In planning a new mechanical system for a historic building, it should be noted that climate control systems are generally classified according to the medium used to condition the temperature: air, water, or a combination of both. The complexity of choices means that a systematic approach is critical in determining the most suitable system for a building, its contents, and its occupants. No matter which system is installed, a change in the interior climate will result. The physical change will, in turn, affect how the building materials perform. Installing new climate control systems along with thermal upgrades to the building envelope, such as wall insulation, can dramatically change interior moisture levels, potentially damaging interior finishes and furnishings. For example, insulating historic walls without providing for ventilation channels may create condensation within the wall and cause deterioration of historic materials. Whenever the building's interior climate will be changed, a mechanical engineer specializing in historic buildings should be consulted.

MINIMIZING THE VISUAL EFFECT OF NEW HEAT/AIR DELIVERY SYSTEMS

Conditioned air or radiant heat is delivered through a system of grilles, registers, diffusers, cabinets, or radiators. In the case of new registers and grillework, decorative elements should be retained and ideally reused in the new or upgraded mechanical system. If new registers are needed, custom-designed diffusers may be incorporated into historic designs with a minimum of visual intrusion. For example, painted or grained baseboards can minimize the visual impact of a low register; and long-slot diffusers in the ceiling, soffits, or fascias of balconies can be almost invisible.

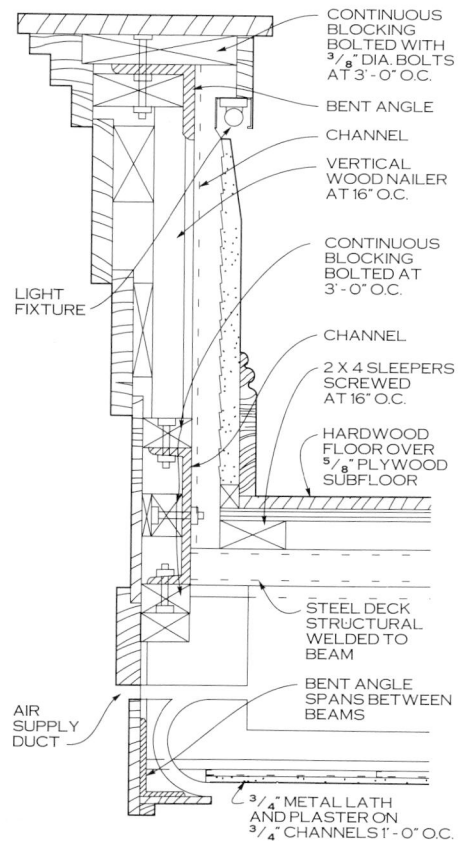

BALCONY SECTION

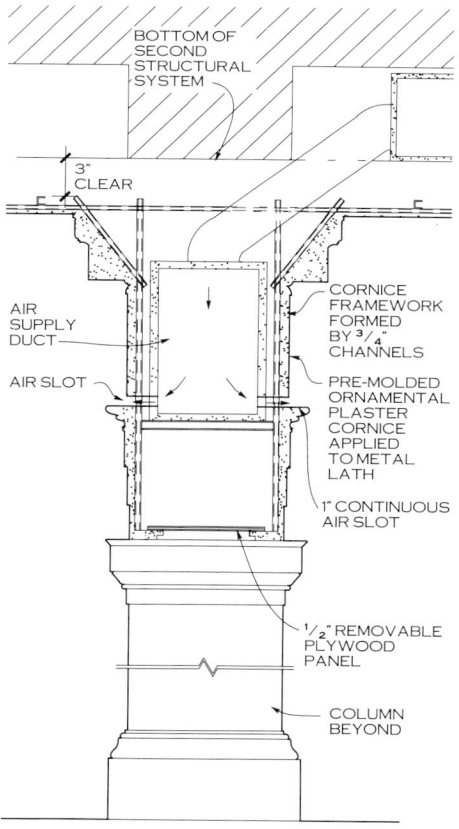

BEAM/ENTABLATURE DETAIL

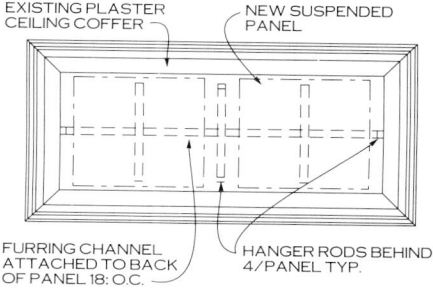

DIFFUSER IN COFFER

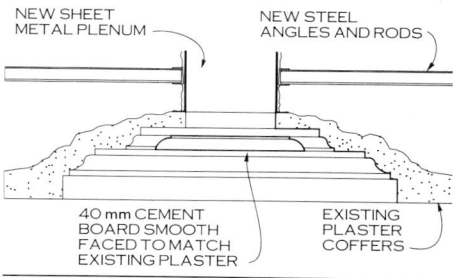

DIFFUSER SECTION

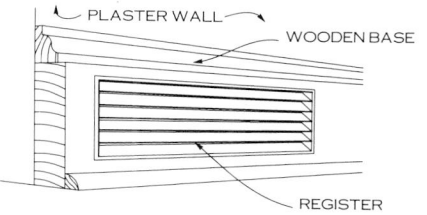

BASEBOARD REGISTER

H. Ward Jandl, Kay D. Weeks, Sharon C. Park, AIA, Timothy A. Buehner; Preservation Assistance Division, National Park Service; Washington, D.C.

INTRODUCTION

Historic landscapes are cultural resources that are part of our national heritage. Like historic buildings and districts, these special places reveal aspects of our country's origins and development through their form and features and the ways they were used. They also reveal much about our evolving relationship with the natural world. Historic landscapes are more than gardens and parks; they include scenic highways, rural communities, cemeteries, battlefields, and zoological gardens. In addition to vegetation and topography (the configuration of natural and cultural features), historic landscapes may include other features such as water, roads, paths, steps, walls, buildings, or furnishings such as fences or benches. Historic landscapes are generally termed designed or vernacular in nature.

A historic designed landscape is one that was consciously designed or laid out by a landscape architect, master gardener, architect, or horticulturist according to design principles or by an amateur gardener working in a recognized style or tradition. The landscape may be associated with a significant person(s), trend, or event in landscape architecture or illustrate an important development in its theory and practice. Designed landscapes evolved to fulfill aesthetic objectives. Examples may include parks, campuses, and estates.

A vernacular historic landscape is one shaped by the everyday life of an individual, family, or community. It evolved because of functional requirements and can be a single property or collection of single properties. Examples include rural villages, industrial complexes, and agricultural landscapes.

UNDERSTANDING HISTORIC PRESERVATION OBJECTIVES

Historic landscapes can be composed of a number of features and their components that, individually or collectively, contribute to its historic character. They include small-scale elements such as fountains or statuary, as well as patterns of fields and forests that define the spatial character of the landscape. Professional techniques for identifying, documenting, and preserving historic landscapes have evolved in the public and private sectors over the past 25 years. It is now recognized that historic landscapes are constantly evolving and cannot be frozen in time. Historic landscapes are just as complex and fragile as historic structures. Their documentation, treatment, and management require a careful, comprehensive approach. Today we view historic landscapes as living organisms that are important not merely as settings associated with historic structures, but as significant places in their own right.

PRESERVATION APPROACHES

The process for making treatment decisions is the same for landscapes as it is for other historic resources.; it requires a keen understanding of the property's history, significance, and existing condition. Though the exact process of preserving a historic landscape may vary from site to site, it generally involves four major steps:

1. Historical research is essential before work is begun on a landscape. The landscape's historic period(s) and their relative significance are revealed through information gathered from a variety of sources, such as historical photos, plans, nursery records, household records, personal correspondence, and oral histories. Articles in journals and magazines as well as other published sources may also provide information about the landscape's history (see PLAN 1).

2. Inventory and documentation of the landscape provides a detailed record of the existing materials and features and their condition. This survey should include drawings to scale, photographs, and narrative text; it may also include videotaping (see PLAN 2).

3. Analysis of the site provides a basis for understanding the landscape's change over time. Compare the landscape's current features, materials, spaces, and overall organization to those that existed during its historic period(s). Based on an understanding of their evolution, these features may be attributed to specific time frames. Treatment options for the overall landscape may now be weighed (see PLAN 3).

4. The selection of a treatment for the landscape determines the type and scope of work for each project, i.e., the extent of repair and replacement of historic features and materials. The type and scope of work, in turn, determines how the property will relate to the viewer. Decisions made at this step will determine how the history of the property will be perceived (see PLAN 4).

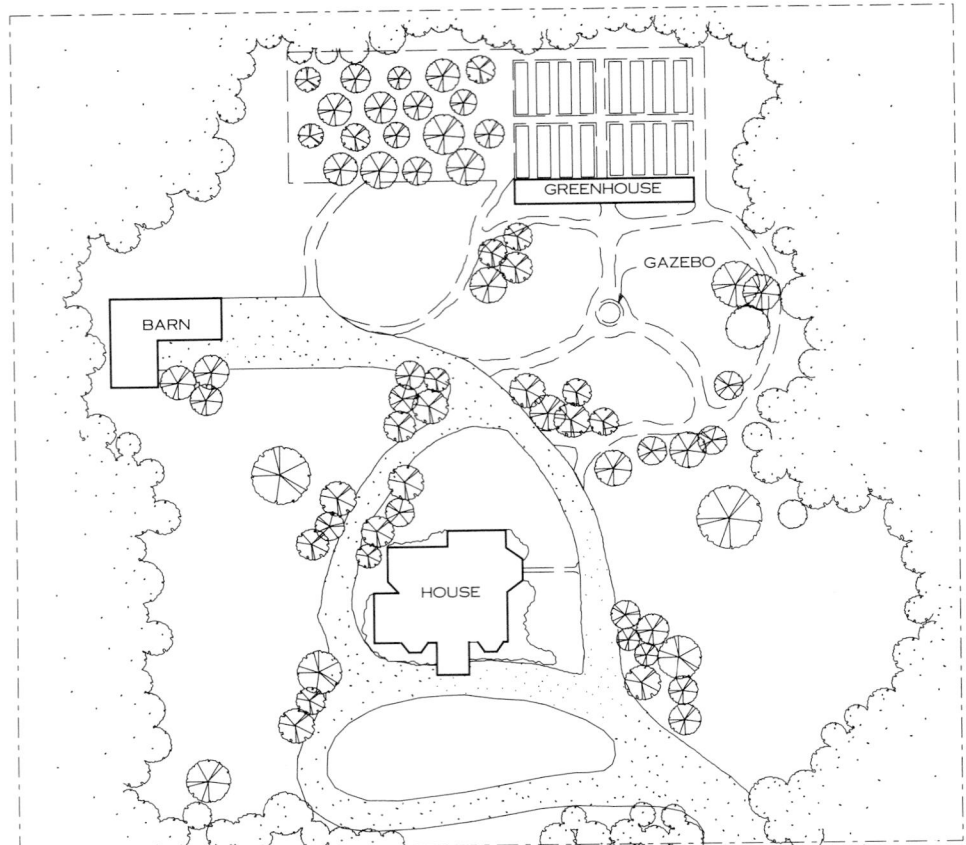

PLAN 1. HISTORIC SURVEY (AS BUILT)

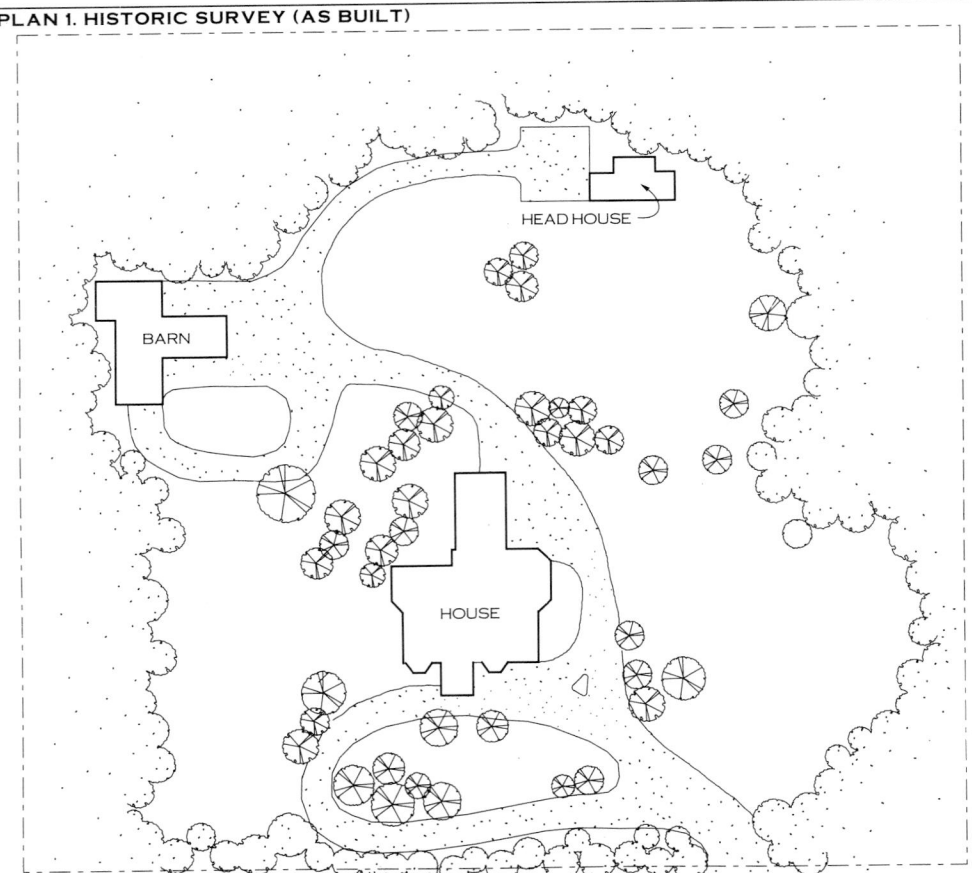

PLAN 2. INVENTORY AND DOCUMENTATION OF EXISTING CONDITIONS

H. Ward Jandl, Charles A. Birnbaum, Kay D. Weeks; Preservation Assistance Division, National Park Service; Washington, D.C.

HISTORIC LANDSCAPES

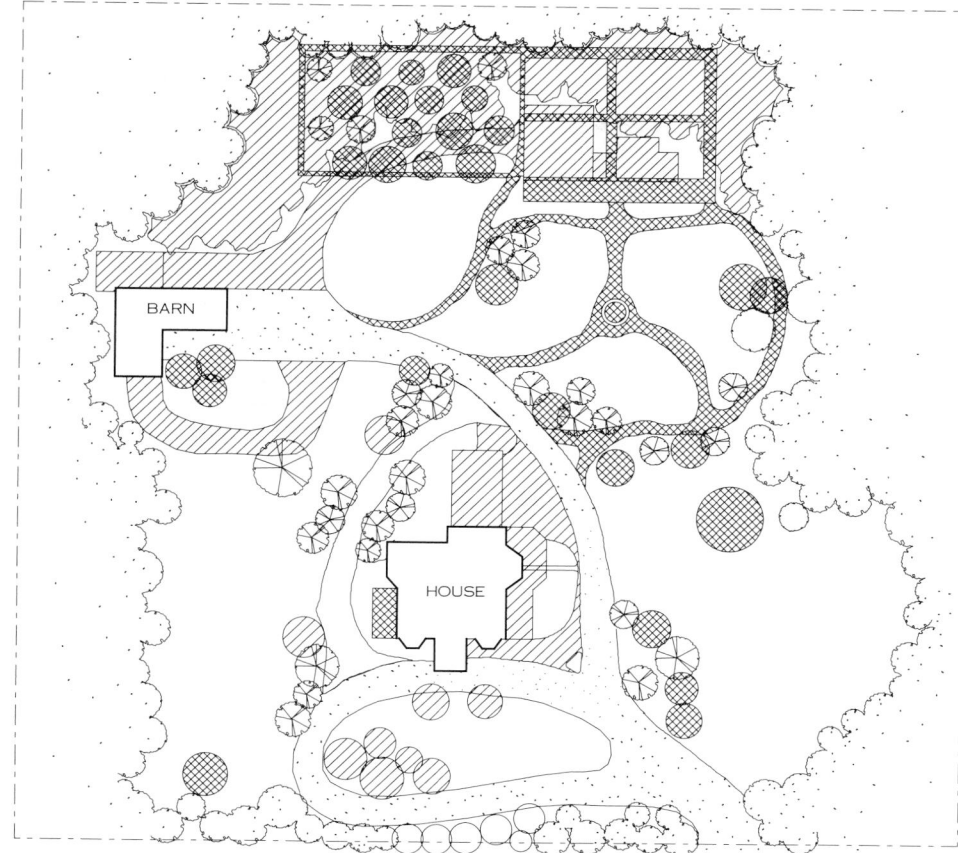

PLAN 3. ANALYSIS

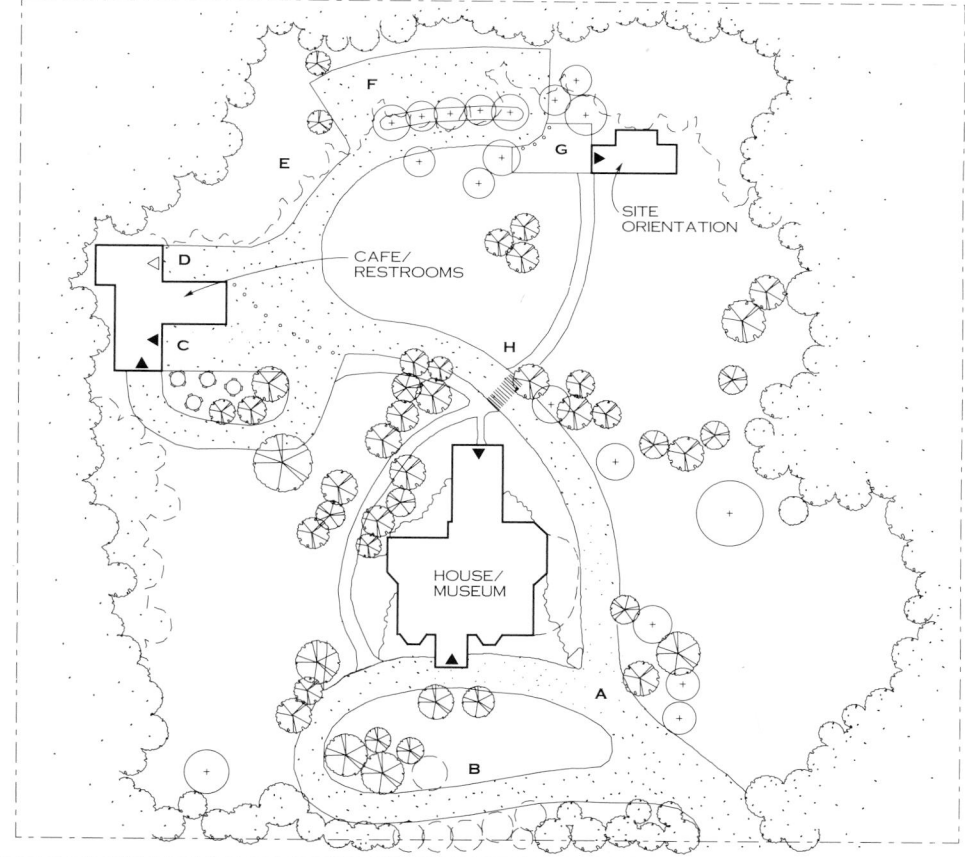

PLAN 4. TREATMENT

H. Ward Jandl, Charles A. Birnbaum, Kay D. Weeks; Preservation Assistance Division, National Park Service; Washington, D.C.

REHABILITATION

When repair and replacement of deteriorated features are necessary; when alterations or additions to the property are planned for a new or continued use; and when its depiction at a particular period of time is not appropriate, rehabilitation of the landscape may be considered as a treatment. Before work begins, a documentation plan for rehabilitation should be developed.

Initial, or temporary, measures of protection or stabilization may be applied to existing features before more substantial rehabilitation work can be implemented. These measures guard the existing condition of a property or its features by preventing further deterioration, loss, or attack and shield the public from danger or injury. Protection may include putting up fencing, closing an area of the landscape, or other actions that will prevent damage from human or natural causes such as vandalism, weather, and fire. Stabilization reestablishes the strength of a structurally unsafe, damaged, or deteriorated property, while retaining its essential form. Stabilization may involve reinforcing earth, water features, or vegetation after natural disasters such as earthquakes, hurricanes, or floods.

The goal of rehabilitation is to retain the historic character of a property while allowing alterations and additions necessary for contemporary uses. In landscapes, rehabilitation is a common treatment, since it allows changes to satisfy present-day demands. For example, when a formerly private property is adapted for public use, it may require the addition of features such as parking and visitor centers, and other public facilities. Additions must be carefully designed and located so the historic character of the property is retained, and the new design must be compatible without distinguishable from the property's historic features.

NOTES
PLAN 1—HISTORIC SURVEY (AS BUILT)

This plan reflects information derived from historical research. Note buildings, structures, furnishings, drives, walks, areas of woodland, trees, and shrubs.

PLAN 2—INVENTORY AND DOCUMENTATION OF EXISTING CONDITIONS

This plan is an inventory of the property as currently configured. It includes every aspect of the property as originally constructed and all extant additions.

PLAN 3—ANALYSIS

This plan shows in detail the changes that have taken place in the landscape over time.

⊠ = Lost features
⧄ = Later additions

PLAN 4—TREATMENT

This plan illustrates rehabilitation of the historic landscape shown in plans 1, 2, and 3. Alterations and changes reflect continuing and new uses. Distinctive materials, features, spaces, and spatial relationships that characterize the historic landscape have been preserved and convey the property's historic significance.

--- = Features to be removed
  + = New trees
  △ = Universal building access
A-H= Project work sectors

A. Removal of later circulation that compromises the integrity of the house/museum and landscape. This allows for rehabilitation of the house's setting.
B. Reopening of the historic vista between the front terrace and neighboring community. Trees that block the vista are removed, while later tree plantings not in the viewshed are retained.
C. Reuse of barn as a cafe/restroom. Semicircular road to south is adapted as an outdoor cafe terrace. New paved area meets barn and historic circulation; new materials demarcate this new use. Area is secured with four bollards.
D. Delivery access.
E. Restoration of open area. Invasive woodland removed.
F. Visitor and staff parking.
G. Visitor orientation/interpretation station. New trees screen parking from the historic house and its setting.
H. New pedestrian circulation connects visitor facilities. Layout is sympathetic to the original design but meets today's safety and accessibility standards.

MEASURED DRAWINGS OF HISTORIC STRUCTURES

Measured drawings are similar to as-built architectural drawings except that they are generally produced years after a structure is built, not immediately after construction. They are used as base drawings for projects involving existing structures, but also record the architect's careful examination and study of both older and newer building components. Measured drawings portray conditions at the time of documentation, including the accretions, alterations, and deletions that have occurred from the original. Their content will vary depending upon the nature of the project.

A preliminary step in producing measured drawings should be to make an on-site reconnaissance of the site. Take notes on a systematic basis, recording the overall dimensions, design, materials, structural and decorative details, and present condition. Making sketched floor plans will help to organize the information. From the gathered observations, determine the number, type, and scale of the required measured drawings.

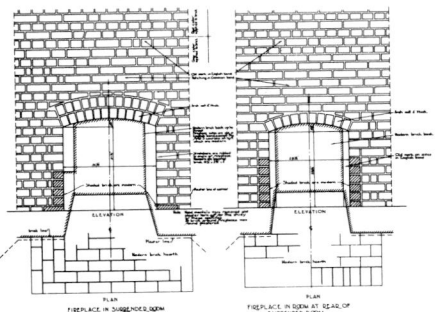

Moore House, Yorktown, VA (by F. Nichols)

Measured drawings of existing conditions at the site of the British surrender at Yorktown were part of the first historic structures report prepared by the National Park Service in 1935. The architect has annotated conditions and apparent periods of various elements. Plaster was removed from the chimney, revealing its brick construction, which was recorded before being replastered.

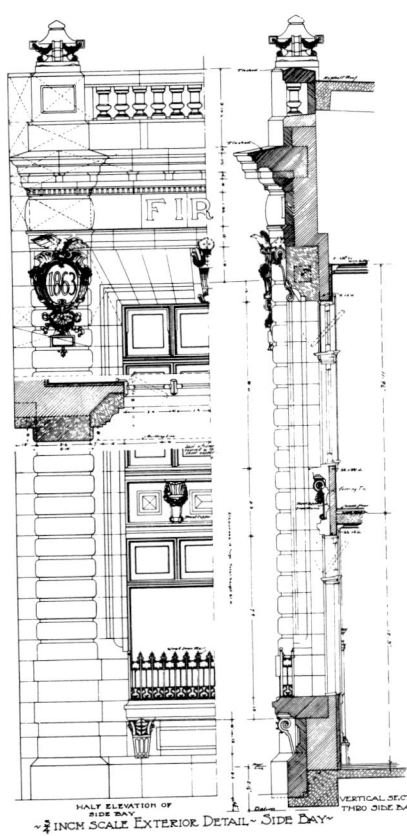

~½ INCH SCALE EXTERIOR DETAIL~ SIDE BAY~

First National Bank, Toledo, OH (George S. Mills, Architect)

John A. Burns, AIA; HABS/HAER, National Park Service; Washington, D.C.

When existing condition measured drawings are needed:

1. Do any drawings or measurements exist or must they be produced?
2. If drawings or measurements exist, are they accurate and useful to the current need?
3. If measurements must be taken, what tools and expertise are required and available to produce them?
4. Does the structure itself, its size, condition, use, and accessibility dictate the manner in which it can be measured?

Structural members were located and sized in this axonometric drawing that both explains and interprets historic building techniques.

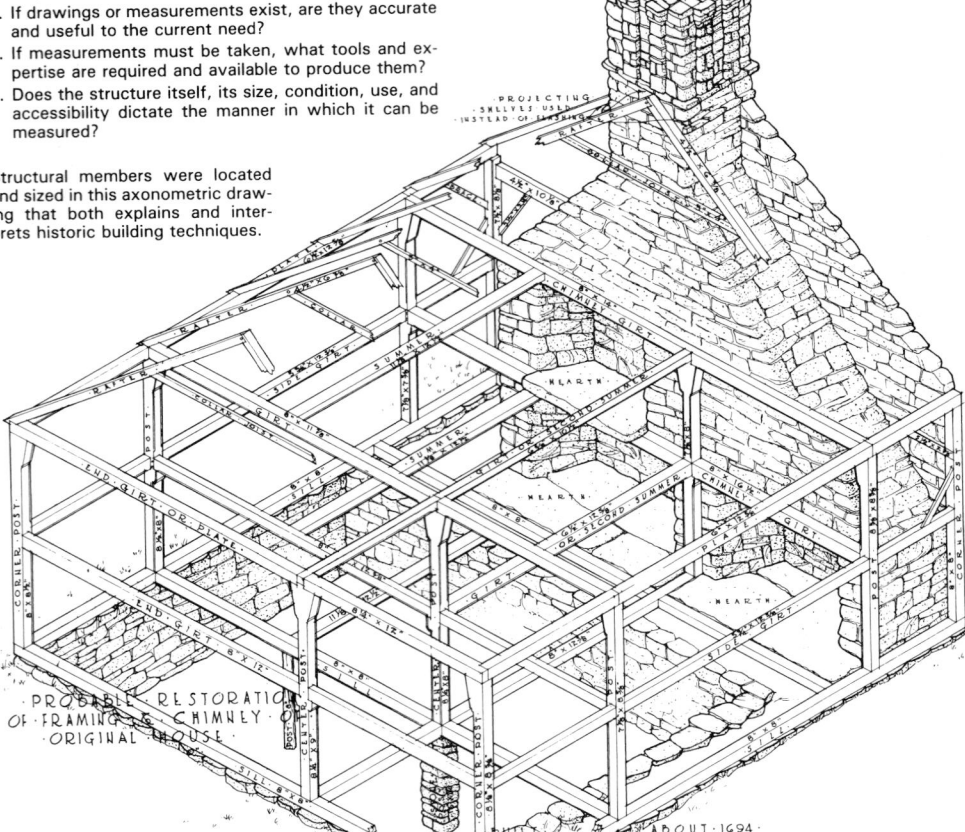

Valentine Whitman, Jr., House, Limerock, RI (by W.R. Colvin)

HISTORICAL RESEARCH

A basic assumption in producing measured drawings is that other sources for drawings do not meet the needs of the project being undertaken. Measured drawings are based primarily on physical evidence, but may rely on other sources for information. Documentary sources can provide evidence of former conditions and help to interpret physical fabric. Historic views, whether drawn or photographed, can be invaluable. A key factor in any measured drawing is understanding the accuracy and limitations of the sources for the measurements.

Original architectural drawings are most likely found in the possession of the original architectural firm or its successor firm. They may also be found in the building, in the company archives, or in the owner's papers. The National Union Index to Architectural Records, which tracks the location of architectural records throughout the United States, can be searched by contacting the Prints and Photographs Division, Library of Congress, Washington, DC 20540. Regional and local repositories of historical records may have architectural records. Another source for locating graphic records are finding aids such as the *Avery Index to Architectural Periodicals* (Boston: G.K. Hall & Co., 1973). Because of the expense of producing measured drawings, it is worth the effort to attempt to locate original drawings, specifications, and photographs.

The original 1904 drawings for this bank (left) were located in the files of another firm and photographically copied. They provide both dimensional information and construction details that would have required destructive investigation to determine.

The historic evolution of a house (right) explained in graphics and words. The drawings alone would not give historical data; description alone would not convey how the various alterations appeared.

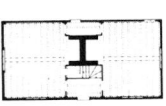

FIRST PERIOD 1680

The structure's original center chimney plan contained two principal rooms on each floor. The interior was lit by groups of three casement windows with transom lights above. Two large facade gables were arranged symmetrically on the south slope of the roof.

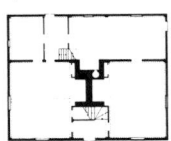

SECOND PERIOD 1720

For an unknown reason the east end of the house was taken down about 1720 and replaced by a one-story lean-to. A lean-to against the north wall was also added at this time. In addition to these changes in plan, the remaining facade gable was removed.

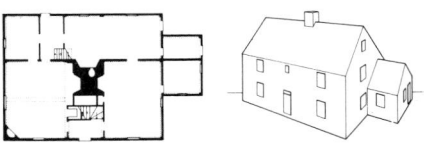

THIRD PERIOD 1750

The major alterations of the house about 1750 were the rebuilding of the east end to two full stories and the addition of a small one-story structure to the east wall. The west end was left substantially unaltered.

Mulford House, East Hampton, NY (by Anne E. Weber)

DEGREE OF COMPLETENESS

The significance of the building and its individual features and the type of information essential in the finished drawings determine the degree of completeness of the drawings. A large and elaborate historic building will require more drawings than a more modest structure.

1. Decide what drawings will best explain and illustrate the various features of the structure. Then determine what measurements are needed to produce the drawings.
2. Decide on the level of detail required in the finished drawings. This will determine both the scales of the drawings and the precision of the measurements needed to make the drawings. For instance, at the common scale of 1/4'' = 1'-0'', the smallest distance that can be accurately drawn is approximately 1 in.
3. Determine what level of accuracy is needed in the measurements. Dimensions to the nearest inch may be adequate for plans but inadequate for details, where measurements to the nearest 1/16 in. or 1/8 in. would be required.

Measured drawings will require differing levels of detail and annotation depending on the ultimate use of the drawings. Measured drawings intended to provide the basis for restoration will require extensive dimensions and annotations to record all the historical and conditional information. Measured drawings intended for maintenance purposes may need little more than material indications and basic dimensions in order to be able to calculate gross areas needing treatment. Measured drawings produced as mitigation are the ''last rites'' for a structure planned to be demolished, recording for future generations all its salient features. Measured drawings intended to serve as protection from catastrophic loss must be detailed enough to allow the exact replication of a highly significant building should it be destroyed.

MEASUREMENT TECHNIQUES

1. DOCUMENTARY. Locating and duplicating copies of original drawings is the simplest way to produce measured drawings. The copies must be checked against the actual structure to determine their accuracy, whether the building was constructed as drawn, and how closely the drawings portray current conditions.
2. HAND MEASURING. When hand measuring, all dimensions are assumed to be either horizontal or vertical. Inclined dimensions can be converted by using trigonometry. The most accurate way to hand measure a string of dimensions is by measuring from a common point so that the dimensions are cumulative. Consecutive measurements made individually are less accurate because any errors are compounded when strings of dimensions are added.

Time can be saved if certain assumptions can be made, such as using the floor as a level datum plane and assuming the rooms are square and the walls are plumb. Whatever assumptions are made when taking the measurements will govern the accuracy of the measured drawings. Inaccessible features can be measured by counting repetitive materials of known dimension such as brick courses in a chimney.

There are two basic hand measuring techniques. One system is to directly measure the architectural features to locate them in relation to each other. Control points can be established by measuring a network of triangles that can be drawn as rigid figures. Room shapes can be determined by measuring the diagonals of a room. This technique works well on structures that are reasonably regular.

The second method establishes a grid from which the structure is measured. Features are located in relation to the grid rather than to each other. This technique is especially useful for irregular or distorted buildings.

3. SURVEYING. It may be necessary to survey a traverse to establish accurate control points from which to measure a structure or to locate site features that cannot be measured directly.
4. PHOTOGRAPHIC. The science of measuring from photographs is photogrammetry. The simplest form of photogrammetry of interest to architects is rectified photography. Rectified photography manipulates and enlarges a photograph so that an architectural feature with a few known dimensions is reproduced at a given scale. It is best used to record features in a single plane, such as room elevations or flat facades. It is not accurate for measuring objects either in front of or behind the plane of the subject that has been enlarged to scale. Positioning targets at known locations on the subject and placing a measuring stick in the field of view can increase accuracy.

Stereophotogrammetry uses two photographs taken from known positions in relation to the building. After taking some dimensions in the field of view and determining the specifications of the camera, accurate plottings can be made at any desired scale. Because this technique uses photographs, conditional information is recorded. Also, photographs record in a generalized way all that the camera ''sees,'' so that many different measurements can be made. Hand measuring, by contrast, only records measurements that are consciously taken and written down.

Analytical photogrammetry can produce measurements of missing or deteriorated features from historic photographs if some dimensions can be determined in the photographs. Accuracy is dependent on the quantity and quality of the historic photographs. The technique is more accurate if the historic photographs can be combined with contemporary photogrammetry.

Photogrammetry records large structures without scaffolding and in much less time than by hand measuring or surveying. Other benefits are that photogrammetric images record conditional information and that the plates can be stored and plotted when necessary.

John A. Burns, AIA; HABS/HAER, National Park Service; Washington, D.C.

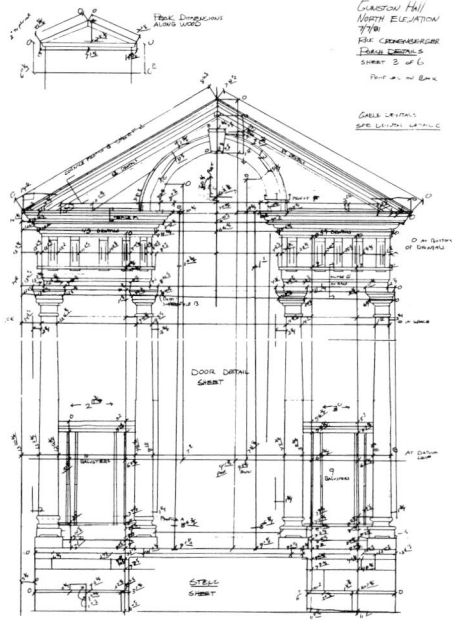

Gunston Hall, Lorton vic., VA (by Richard J. Cronenberger)

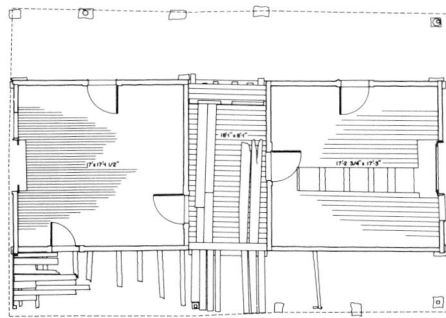

Butler Dogtrot, Tishomingo vic., MS (by Peter Darlow)

Buildings too irregular to measure directly are measured from a grid established in and around the structure. The dimension strings give only the overall measurements necessary to describe the basic configuration. More precise information on the shape and distortions of the house is accessible in the field records.

Comparison of direct field measurements of a porch and the finished detail drawing. Field notes are the primary source; the drawings cannot be more accurate than the field measurements. Many more dimensions are recorded in the field notes than are actually written on the final drawing, so it is important to save and organize the field notes for future reference.

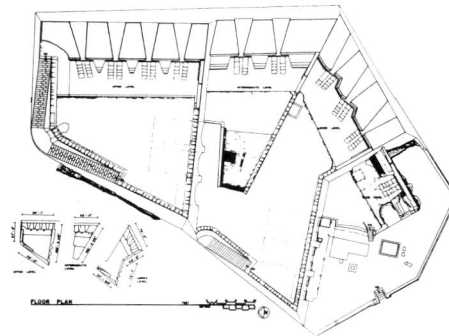

La Trinidad Counterguard, San Juan, PR (by Todd Wambach)

A large and irregular structure such as a fort can be measured accurately using an electronic distance measuring theodolite to produce angle and distance measurements.

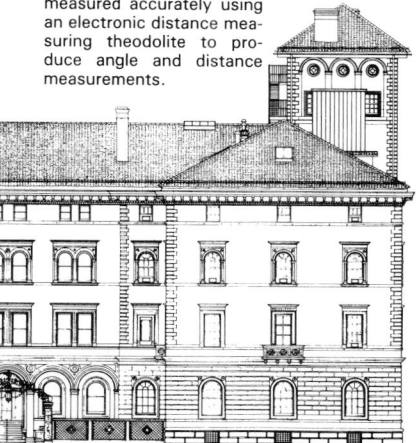

Villard Houses, New York, NY (by Perry Borchers, Soottipong Winyoopradist, and Varathorn Bookman)

Independence Hall (north elevation), Philadelphia, PA (by Dennett, Muessig, Ryan & Associates)

THE HISTORIC AMERICAN BUILDINGS SURVEY

The Historic American Buildings Survey (HABS) is a collection of graphic and written documentation on more than 20,000 historic buildings throughout the United States. The graphic records consist of 44,000 architectural measured drawings and 120,000 large format photographs, supported by 48,000 pages of written data. Administered by the National Park Service, with technical assistance from the American Institute of Architects, the completed records are reproducible and are accessible through the Prints and Photographs Division of the Library of Congress.

HABS measured drawings show conditions at the time a structure was recorded, including alterations and additions to the original since it was built. While measured drawings are utilitarian, HABS measured drawings must additionally meet all HABS standards for content, accuracy, verifiability, archival stability, and reproducibility. HABS measured drawings are prepared for historic structures:

1. When restoration or rehabilitation work is planned, to establish existing conditions prior to beginning treatment.
2. As part of normal conservation and maintenance of a structure.
3. As insurance against catastrophic loss, should something happen to the structure.
4. As easement documentation.
5. When demolition is planned, to keep a permanent record for future generations.
6. For public information or interpretation.
7. As scholarship.

HABS measured drawings are produced for any or several of the above reasons. HABS drawings include site plans, landscape plans, floor plans, elevations, sections, details, and interpretive drawings. Field records and measurements are retained for future use and reference.

TALL CASE CLOCK

Glass plate photogrammetric stereopairs of Independence Hall were produced so that the entire exterior and significant portions of the interior could be plotted. Objects as small as ⅛ in. are discernible in the plates. The original of the HABS drawing of the north elevation was produced for public information and maintenance purposes at 3/16″ = 1′-0″ and thus cannot portray all the detail recorded in the plates. Even so, the differences between the basement window arches on either side of the door and the fact that the tower is off-center are easily visible. The larger scale drawing of the clock was plotted from plates made at the same distance from the building.

PRODUCING HABS MEASURED DRAWINGS

Architects interested in producing HABS measured drawings as part of a rehabilitation or restoration project, as mitigation, or as part of their professional practice should consult *Recording Historic Structures* (Washington, DC: AIA Press, 1988). Additional information and mylar drawing sheets preprinted with the HABS title blocks are available from the HABS office (Historic American Buildings Survey, National Park Service, P.O. Box 37127, Washington, DC 20013-7127).

The standards for documentation to be included in the HABS collection are as follows:

1. Content. Documentation shall adequately explicate and illustrate what is significant or valuable about the historic building, site, structure, or object being documented.

2. Quality. Documentation shall be prepared accurately from reliable sources with limitations clearly stated to permit independent verification of the information.
3. Materials. Documentation shall be prepared on materials that are readily reproducible, durable, and in standard sizes.
4. Presentation. Documentation shall be clearly and concisely produced.

Completed HABS measured drawings are a secure, permanent record of a historic structure prepared on archival materials and stored under controlled archival conditions. They make information on historic buildings available to the public and serve as a form of insurance against catastrophic loss.

HABS relies on the generosity of architects and organizations as a major source for architectural documentation. Donated records have been and continue to be a significant part of the HABS collection.

John A. Burns, AIA; HABS/HAER, National Park Service; Washington, D.C.

A longitudinal section of Adler and Sullivan's Auditorium Building reveals the overall configuration of the structure and the major interior spaces. The hotel portion is on the left with a dining hall on the top floor, stage house and theater in the center, banquet hall above the sloping roof of the theater, rehearsal hall above the rear of the theater, and office space on the right. HABS recorded the structural and mechanical systems of the building as part of a master plan for renovation and restoration work. This drawing was produced from historic drawings, photographs and specifications, and contemporary field measurements, and illustrates the building as it was completed in 1890. Large structures such as this must be composed on several HABS sheets to be drawn at a reasonable scale.

Auditorium Building, Chicago, Il (by August Ventura)

Villard Houses Dining Room, New York, NY (by Perry Borchers, Soottipong Winyoopradist, and Kun-Hyuck Ahn)

Decorative and sculptural details are difficult to measure and delineate because there are few hard edges. Photogrammetry offers the capability of making precise contour maps of sculptural surfaces.

REPRODUCTIONS OF HABS DOCUMENTATION

All Historic American Buildings Survey documentation is in the public domain and may be reproduced for the cost of the reproductions. For each measured drawing there is a reproducible copy; for each photograph there is a large format negative; data pages can be photocopied. The HABS collection is accessible to the public in the Prints and Photographs Division of the Library of Congress in Washington, DC, either in person or by mail inquiry. Questions concerning documentation in the HABS collection should be sent to the Prints and Photographs Division, Library of Congress, Washington, DC 20540. Reproductions can be ordered through the Library of Congress Photoduplication Service at the same address. If used in a publication, HABS requests that the program and the individual responsible (delineator, photographer, historian) be appropriately credited.

John A. Burns, AIA; HABS/HAER, National Park Service; Washington, D.C.

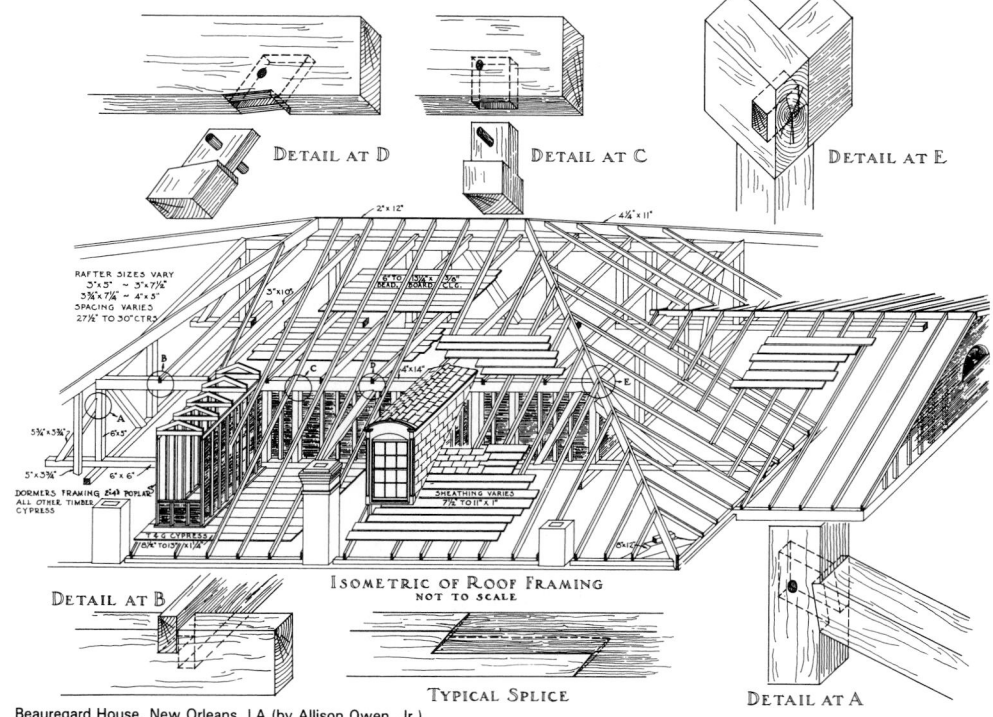

Beauregard House, New Orleans, LA (by Allison Owen, Jr.)

Cutaway isometric drawings depict complex shapes such as roof framing in an effective manner. HABS records structural and mechanical systems when they are accessible. Buildings undergoing restoration offer the opportunity to record historic structural and mechanical systems while they are exposed.

GENERAL

Advisory Council on Historic Preservation
1100 Pennsylvania Avenue, N.W., Suite 809
Washington, DC 20004
Tel:(202) 786-0503

AIA Committee on Historic Resources (AIA/CHR)
1735 New York Ave., N.W.
Washington, DC 20006
Tel: (202) 626-7789

American Historical Association
400 A Street, S.E.
Washington, DC 20003
Tel: (202) 544-2422

American Institute for Conservation (AIC)
1717 K Street N.W., Suite 301
Washington, DC 20006
Tel: (202) 452-9545
Fax:(202) 452-9328

Association for Preservation Technology
904 Princess Anne Street
P.O. Box 8178
Fredericksburg, VA 22404
Tel: (703) 373-1621
Fax:(703) 373-6050

Campbell Center for Historic Preservation Studies
203 E. Seminary, Box 66
Mt. Carroll, IL 61053
Tel: (815) 244-1173
Fax:(815) 244-1619

Center for Architectural Conservation
Georgia Institute of Technology
245 4th Street, Room 225
Atlanta, GA 30332-0155
Tel: (404) 894-3390
Fax:(404) 894-8738

Heritage Canada Foundation (HCF)
412 Mclaren Street
Ottawa, Ontario K2P OM8
Tel: (613) 237-1066

National Alliance of Preservation Commissions
c/o University of Georgia
609 Caldwell Hall
Athens, GA 30602
Tel: (706) 542-4731
Fax:(706) 542-4485

National Alliance of Statewide Preservation Commissions
c/o Historic Massachusetts
45 School Street
Boston, MA 02108
Tel: (617) 723-3383

National Conference of State Historic Preservation Officers
444 North Capitol Street, N.W., Suite 342
Washington, DC 20001-1512
Tel: (202) 624-5465

National Endowment for the Arts
1100 Pennsylvania Ave., N.W., Rm. 624
Washington, DC 20506
Tel:(202) 682-5442

National Preservation Institute (NPI)
National Building Museum
401 F St., N.W., Suite 301
Washington, DC 20001
Tel: (202) 393-0038

National Trust for Historic Preservation
1785 Massachusetts Avenue, N.W.
Washington, DC 20036
Tel: (202) 673-4000

National Trust for Historic Preservation Library
McKeldin Library/University of Maryland
College Park, MD 20742
Tel: (301) 405-6320

Office of Park Historic Architecture/National Park Service
(OPHA/NPS)
800 North Capitol St., N.W., Room 360
Washington, DC 20002
Tel: (202) 343-8146

Preservation Action
1350 Connecticut Ave., N.W., Suite 401
Washington, DC 20036
Tel: (202) 659-0915

Preservation Assistance Division
National Park Service
P.O. Box 37127
Washington, DC 20013-7127
Tel: (202) 343-9573

Society of Architectural Historians
1232 Pine Street
Philadelphia, PA 19107
Tel: (215) 735-0224
Fax:(215) 735-2590

REFERENCES

Delahanty, Randolph, and E. Andrew McKinney. *Preserving the West.* New York: Pantheon, 1985.

Fitch, James Marston. *Historic Preservation: Curatorial Management of the Built World.* New York: McGraw-Hill, 1982.

Glass, James A. *The Beginnings of a New National Historic Preservation Program, 1957-69.* Nashville: American Association for State and Local History, 1989.

Kay, Jane Holtz, with Pauline Chase-Harrell. *Preserving New England.* New York: Pantheon, 1986.

Maddex, Diane, ed. *All About Old Buildings: The Whole Preservation Catalog.* Washington, D.C.: Preservation Press, 1983.

Murtagh, William J. *Keeping Time: The History and Theory of Preservation in America.* Pittstown, N.J.: Main Street Press, 1987.

RECORDING HISTORIC STRUCTURES

Historic American Buildings Survey
800 North Avenue Street, N.W.
Suite 300
Washington, DC 20001
Tel: (202) 343-9604

National Register of Historic Places
National Park Service
P.O. Box 37127 (413)
Washington, DC 20013-7127
Tel: (202) 343-9536

National Trust for Historic Preservation
1785 Massachusetts Avenue, N.W.
Washington, DC 20036
Tel: (202) 673-4000

REFERENCES

Burns, John A., and the Historic American Buildings Survey/Historic American Engineering Record. *Recording Historic Structures.* HABS/HAER, 1989.

Guidelines for Completing National Register of Historic Places Forms. Washington, D.C.: U.S. Department of the Interior, National Park Service.

National Register of Historic Places: Cumulative List 1966-88. Nashville: American Association for State and Local History, 1989.

National Register of Historic Places Index on CD-ROM. Mineral, VA: Buckmaster Publishing, 1989.

National Register of Historic Places Subscription. Nashville: American Association for State and Local History, 1988-90.

ADAPTIVE REUSE
REFERENCES

Austin, Richard L., ed. *Adaptive Reuse: Issues and Case Studies in Building Preservation.* New York: Van Nostrand Reinhold, 1987.

Diamondstein, Barbaralee. *Remaking America: New Uses, Old Places.* New York: Crown, 1986.

Schmertz, Mildred F., and the editors of Architectural Record. *New Life for Old Buildings.* New York: McGraw-Hill, 1982.

Shopsin, William C. *Restoring Old Buildings for Contemporary Uses.* New York: Whitney Library of Design, 1986.

ENERGY CONSERVATION
REFERENCES

Advisory Council on Historic Preservation. *Assessing the Energy Conservation Benefits of Historic Preservation: Methods and Examples.* Washington, D.C.: U.S. Government Printing Office, 1979.

National Trust for Historic Preservation. *New Energy from Old Buildings.* Washington, D.C.: Preservation Press, 1981.

HISTORIC PRESERVATION LAW

National Center for Preservation Law
1015 31st Street, N.W.
Suite 400
Washington, DC 20007
Tel: (202) 828-9611

REFERENCES

Duerkson, Christopher, ed. *A Handbook on Historic Preservation Law.* Washington, D.C.: Conservation Foundation, 1983.

Robinson, Nicholas A., ed. *Historic Preservation Law.* New York: Practicing Law Institute. [annual]

NEIGHBORHOODS
REFERENCES

Palen, John, and Bruce London, eds. *Gentrification, Displacement and Revitalization.* Albany: State University of New York Press, 1985.

Robin, Peggy. *Saving the Neighborhood.* Kensington, Md.: Woodbine House, 1990.

PLANNING AND URBAN DESIGN

Alliance for Historic Landscape Preservation
82 Wall Street
Suite 1105
New York, NY 10005
Tel: (617) 491-3727

Urban Design and Preservation Division of the
American Planning Association (UDPD/APA)
7320 26th Avenue, NW
Seattle, WA 98117
Tel: (206) 462-4072

Urban Land Institute (ULI)
625 Indiana Ave, N.W.
Suite 400
Washington, DC 20004
Tel: (800) 321-5011
Fax:(202) 624-7140

REFERENCES

Gratz, Roberta Brandes. *The Living City.* New York: Simon and Schuster, 1989.

Jackson, Kenneth T. *Crabgrass Frontier: The Suburbanization of America.* New York: Oxford University Press, 1987. 406 pp.

Stokes, Samuel N., et al. *Saving America's Countryside: A Guide to Rural Conservation.* Baltimore: John's Hopkins University Press, 1989.

REHABILITATION

Association of Specialists in Cleaning & Restoration
10830 Annapolis Junction Road, Suite 312
Annapolis Junction, MD 20701
Tel: (301) 604-4411

Center for Preservation
and Rehabilitation Technology
Virginia Polytechnic and State University
1001 Prince Street Alexandria, VA 22314
Tel: (703) 739-6089

REFERENCES

Gayle, Margot, et al. *Metals in America's Historic Buildings: Uses and Preservation Treatments.* U.S. Dept. of the Interior. Washington, D.C.: U.S. Government Printing Office, 1980.

London, Mark. *Masonry: How to care for Old and Historic Brick and Stone.* Washington, D.C.: Preservation Press, 1988.

Moss, Roger W. *Lighting for Historic Buildings.* Washington, DC: Preservation Press, 1988.

Seale, William. *Recreating the Historic House Interior.* Nashville: American Association for State and Local History, 1985.

Stahl, Frederick A. *A Guide to the Maintenance, Repair, and Alteration of Historic Buildings.* New York: Van Nostrand Reinhold, 1984.

Stephen, George. *New Life for Old Houses.* rev. ed. Washington, DC: Preservation Press, 1989.

Von Rosenstiel, Helene, and Gail Caskey Winkler. *Floor Coverings for Historic Buildings.* Washington, DC: Preservation Press, 1988.

BED SIZES (IN.)

TYPES	W	L
King	72	84
Queen	60	82
Double	54	82
Single	39	82
Daybed	30	75
Crib	30	53

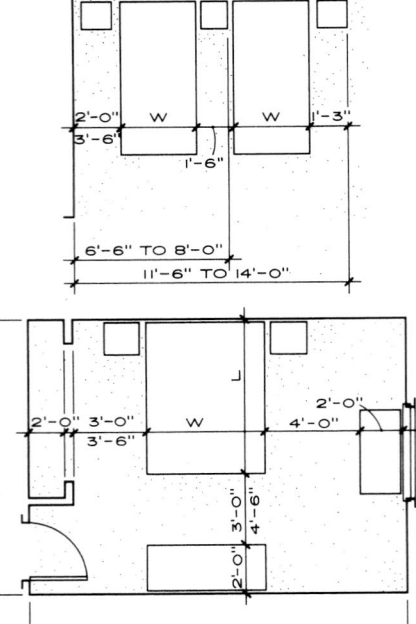

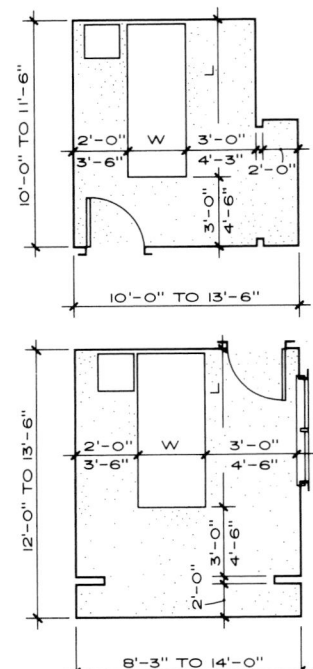

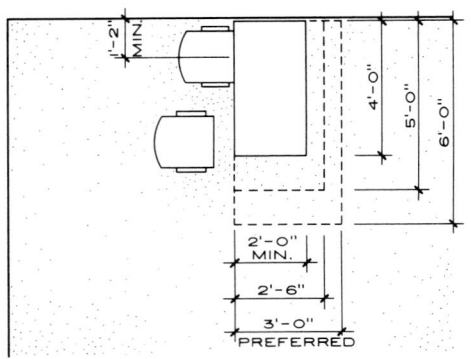

BED CLEARANCES

BEDROOM FURNITURE

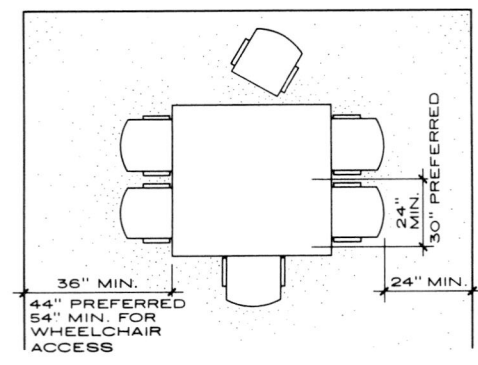

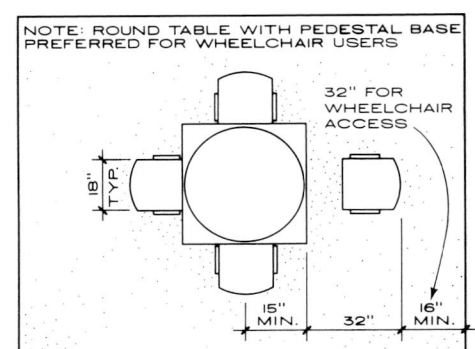

RECTANGULAR TABLES (IN.)

SIZE	SEAT	WHEELCHAIR
24 x 48	4	
30 x 48	4	2
30 x 60	4-6	2-4
36 x 72	4-6	4-6
36 x 84	6-8	6

SQUARE TABLES (IN.)

SIZE	SEAT	WHEELCHAIR
30 x 30	2	
36 x 36	2-4	
42 x 42	4	2 (TIGHT)
48 x 48	4-8	2
54 x 54	4-8	4

ROUND TABLES (IN.)

SIZE	SEAT	WHEELCHAIR
30	2	
36	2-4	
42	4-5	
48	5-6	2
54	5-6	4

DINING ROOM FURNITURE

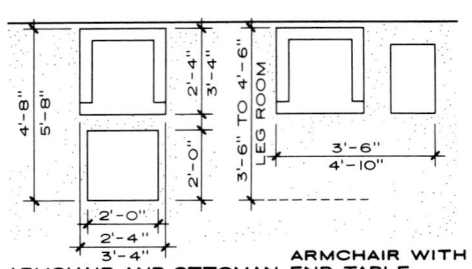

ARMCHAIR AND OTTOMAN   **ARMCHAIR WITH END TABLE**

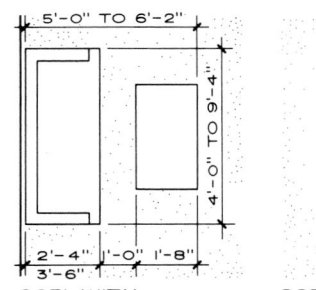

ARMCHAIRS WITH COFFEE TABLE

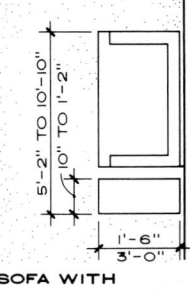

SOFA WITH COFFEE TABLE   **SOFA WITH END TABLE**

LIVING ROOM FURNITURE

Robin Andrew Roberts, AIA; Washington, D.C.
Arthur J. Pettorino, AIA; Hicksville, New York

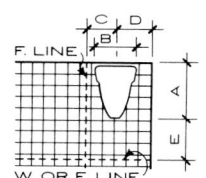
WATER CLOSET

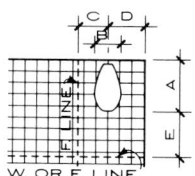
BIDET

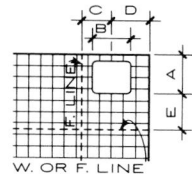
LAVATORY

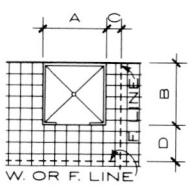
SHOWER

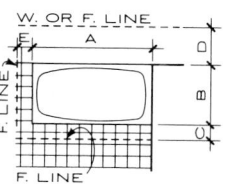
TUB (RECTANGULAR)

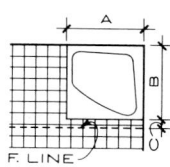
TUB (SQUARE)

FIXTURE SIZES AND CLEARANCES (IN.) W = WALL F = FIXTURE

FIXTURE	A		B		C		D		E	
	MINIMUM	LIBERAL	MINIMUM	LIBERAL	MINIMUM	LIBERAL	MINIMUM	LIBERAL	MINIMUM	LIBERAL
Water closet	27	31	19	21	12	18	15	22	W = 18 F = 18	W = 36 F = 34
Bidet	25	27	14	14	12	18	15	22	W = 18 F = 18	W = 36 F = 34
Lavatory	16	21	18	30	2	6	14	22	18	30
Shower	32	36	34	36	2	8	18	34		
Tub (rectangular)	60 STD.	72	30 STD.	42	2	8	W = 20 F = 18	W = 34 F = 30	2	8
Tub (square)	38		39		2	4				

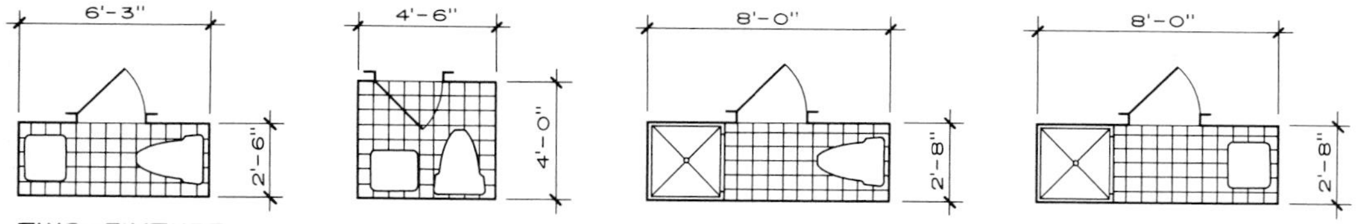

NOTES

1. Typical bathroom accessories include medicine cabinet, mirror, soap dish, towel rack, and toilet paper holder.
2. Convenience outlets for electric toothbrushes, razors, and hair dryers should be provided. They should be electrically grounded for user safety.
3. Bathroom ventilations may be achieved by natural means (window or operable skylight) or with mechanical exhaust fan.

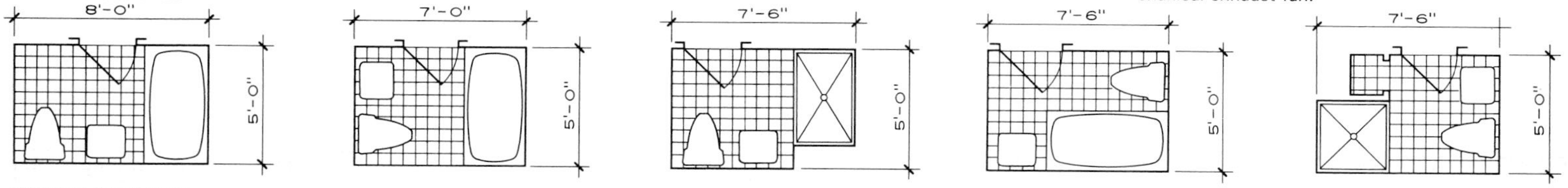

TWO-FIXTURE

THREE-FIXTURE

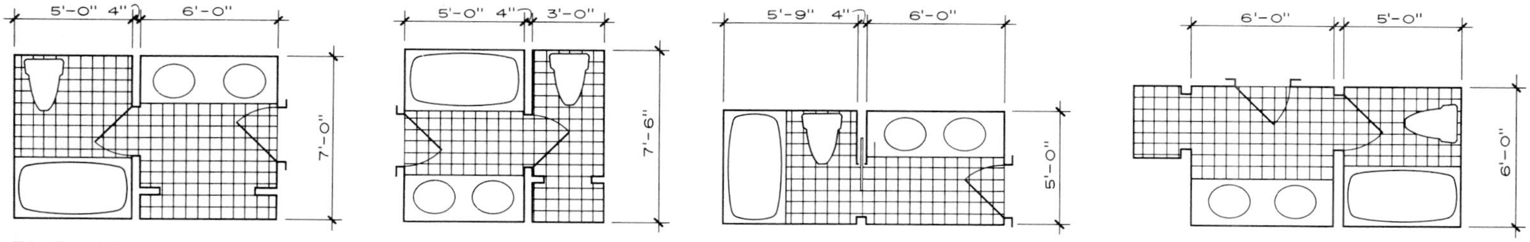

FOUR-FIXTURE

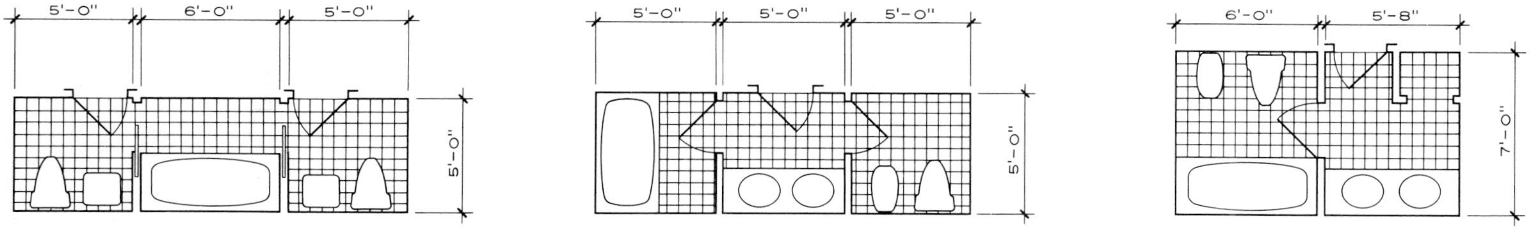

FIVE-FIXTURE

TYPICAL ARRANGEMENTS

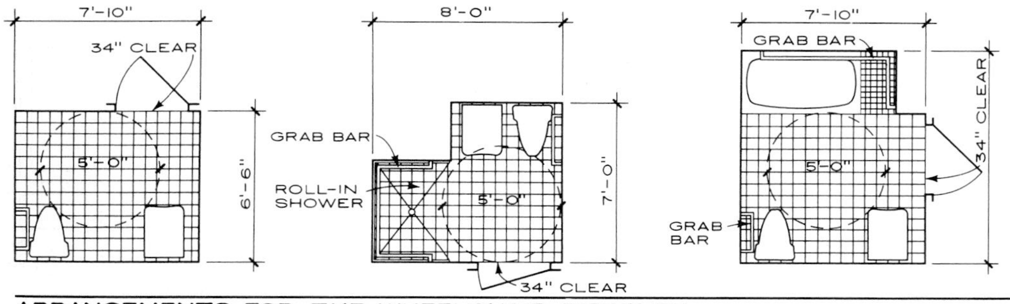

NOTES

1. Provide space for wheelchair maneuverability; observe 5 ft minimum radius.
2. Additional space next to water closet will allow for side transfer from wheelchair.
3. Provide knee space under sink. Insulate pipes to avoid scalding.
4. Use grab bars around water closet and tub.
5. Roll-in shower may replace tub and is more convenient for many wheelchair disabled.
6. Bathroom door to be minimum 32 in. clear opening and to swing outward. Use lever hardware on both sides.

ARRANGEMENTS FOR THE WHEELCHAIR DISABLED

Robin Andrew Roberts, AIA; Washington, D.C.
Arthur J. Pettorino, AIA; Hicksville, New York

KITCHEN SPACE PLANNING

The layouts shown here, together with their general area requirements, are based on studies of furniture, appliances, storage, and clearances for the average residential kitchen. They have been developed to accommodate work, storage, and floor areas required for various food preparation functions. The location and order of both appliances and associated work surfaces should be de-

termined by physical limitations, traffic flow, individual preferences, and appliance type in determining kitchen size during the early planning stages. To simplify comparison of the various room types, basic sizes of furniture, appliances, and clearances have been standardized.

Storage: Minimum 18 sq ft of space for basic storage with an additional 6 sq ft/person served.

Work Flow: Work flow should move from refrigerator work center (A) to sink work center (B) to cooking work center (C), then to the serving spot. The total length of the work triangle (ABC) should average less than 23 lineal feet and never exceed 26 lineal feet.

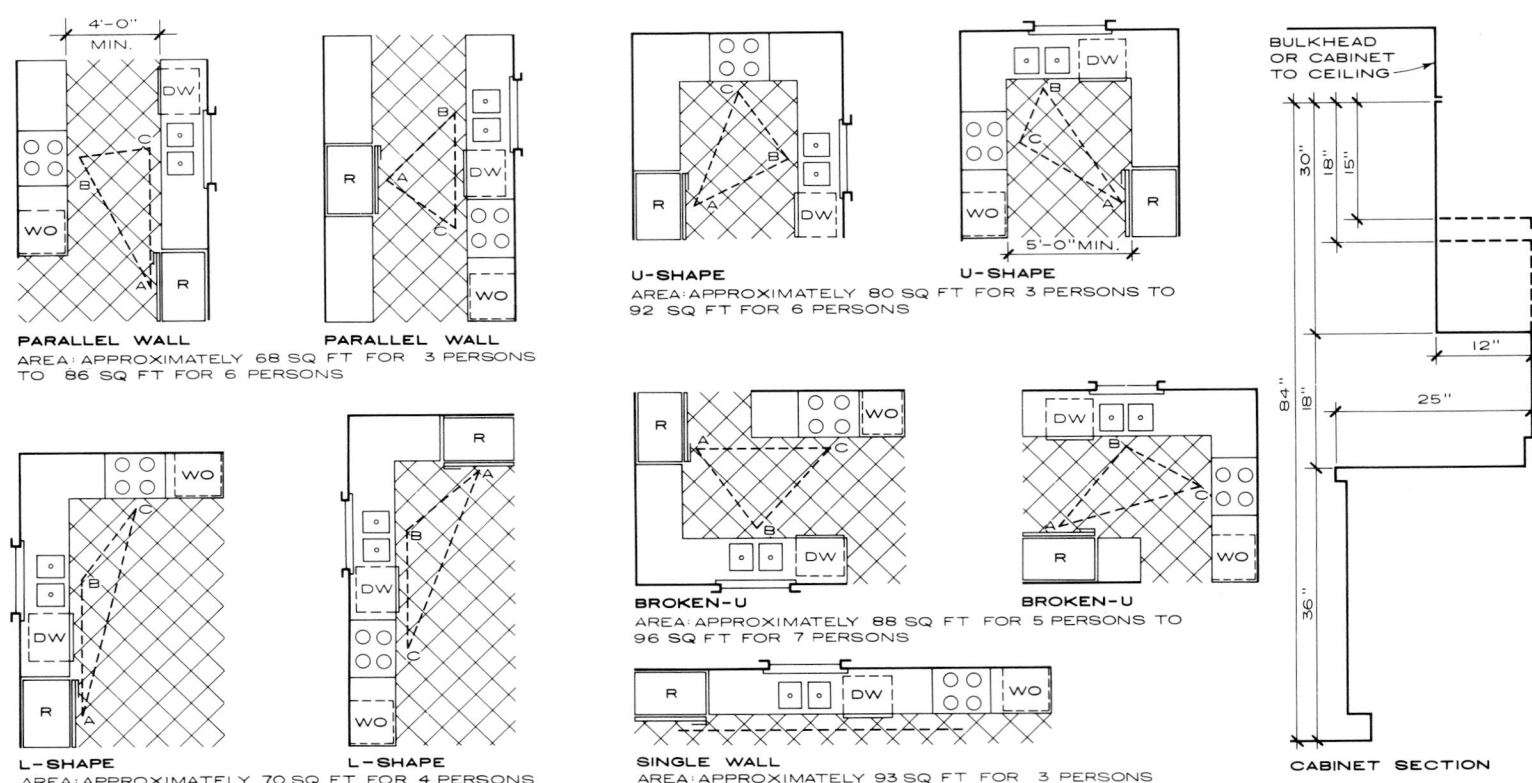

PARALLEL WALL
AREA: APPROXIMATELY 68 SQ FT FOR 3 PERSONS TO 86 SQ FT FOR 6 PERSONS

U-SHAPE
AREA: APPROXIMATELY 80 SQ FT FOR 3 PERSONS TO 92 SQ FT FOR 6 PERSONS

L-SHAPE
AREA: APPROXIMATELY 70 SQ FT FOR 4 PERSONS TO 86 SQ FT FOR 6 PERSONS

BROKEN-U
AREA: APPROXIMATELY 88 SQ FT FOR 5 PERSONS TO 96 SQ FT FOR 7 PERSONS

SINGLE WALL
AREA: APPROXIMATELY 93 SQ FT FOR 3 PERSONS TO 111 SQ FT FOR 6 PERSONS

CABINET SECTION

RESIDENTIAL KITCHEN ARRANGEMENTS

NOTE: SMALL KITCHENS USUALLY HAVE UP TO 10 RUNNING FEET OF COUNTER AND EQUIPMENT. AVERAGE KITCHENS HAVE UP TO 20 RUNNING FEET OF THE SAME. USUAL EQUIPMENT INCLUDES UNDERCOUNTER REFRIGERATOR.

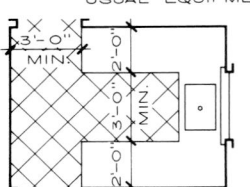
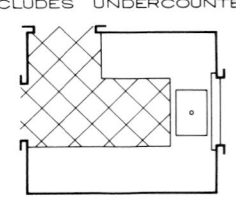
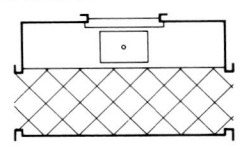
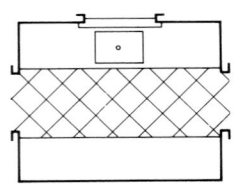
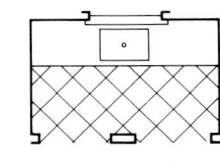

PANTRY TYPES

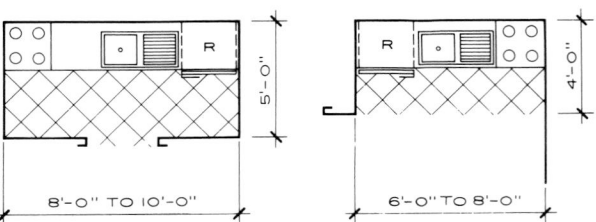
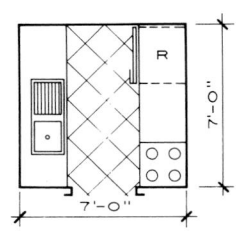

ABBREVIATIONS
DW = DISHWASHER
WO = WALL OVEN
R = REFRIGERATOR

KITCHENETTES

Robin Andrew Roberts, AIA; Washington, D.C.
R. E. Powe, Jr., AIA; Hugh N. Jacobsen, FAIA; Washington, D.C.

RESIDENTIAL ROOM PLANNING

KITCHEN WORK CENTERS

A residential kitchen may be considered in terms of three interconnected work centers: A, B, and C, as shown below. Each encompasses a distinct phase of kitchen activity, and storage should be provided for the items that are most used in connection with each center.

The functions of the sink center are most common to the other two centers. It is recommended, therefore, that the sink center's location be convenient to each of the others (usually between them). The refrigerator center is best located near the entry and the range center near the dining area.

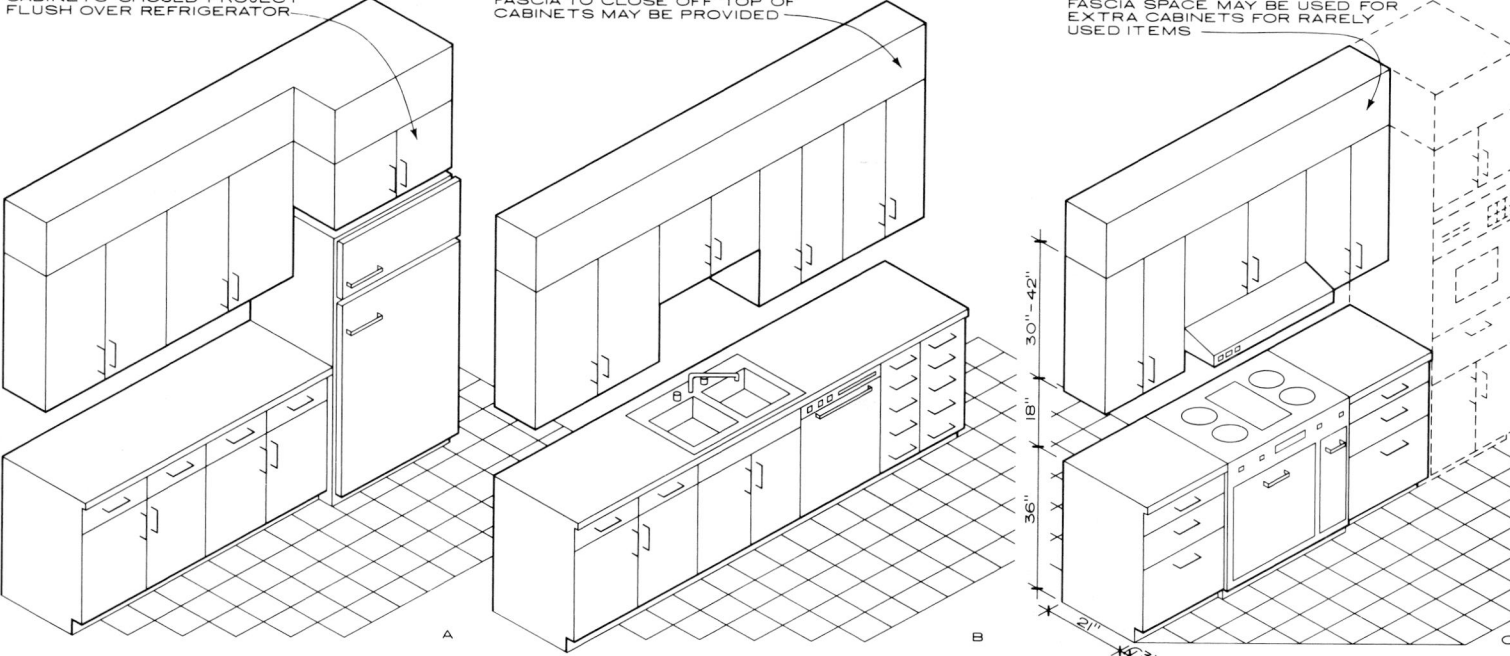

REFRIGERATOR CENTER
(Receiving and Food Preparation)

Provide storage for mixer and mixing bowls; other utensils: sifter, grater, salad molds, cake and pie tins, occasional dishes, condiments, staples, canned goods, brooms, and miscellaneous items.

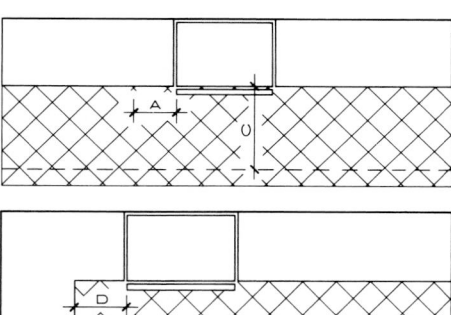

A = 15 in. minimum counter space at latch side of refrigerator for loading and unloading.
B = 18 in. minimum clearance between latch side of refrigerator and turn of counter.
C = 40 to 42 in. clearance from face of refrigerator to wall or facing counter.

SINK CENTER
(Food Preparation, Cleaning, and Cleanup)

Provide storage for everyday dishes, glassware, pots and pans, cutlery, silver, pitchers and shakers, vegetable bins, linen, towel rack, wastebasket, cleaning materials and utensils, garbage can or disposal, and dishdrain. Some codes require louvers or other venting provisions in the doors under enclosed sinks.

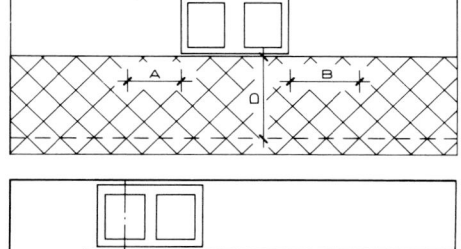

A = 18 to 36 in. counter space on side of sink.
B = 24 to 36 in. counter space on side of sink.
Provide 24 in. counter space at either right or left if dishwasher is used.
C = 14 in. minimum clearance between center of bowl and the turn of counter.
D = 40 to 42 in. minimum clearance from face of sink to wall or facing counter.

RANGE CENTER
(Cooking and Serving)

Provide storage for pots, potholders, frying pans, roaster, cooking utensils, grease container, seasoning, canned goods, breadbin, breadboard, toaster, plate warmer, platters, serving dishes, and trays.

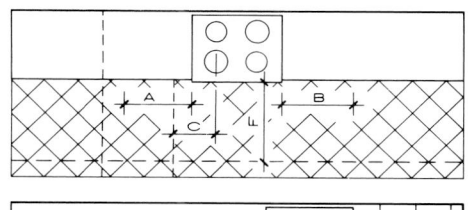
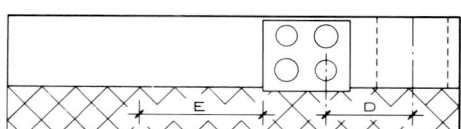

A, B = 18 to 24 in. counter space on either side of cooking facility.
C = 14 in. minimum clearance between center of front unit and the turn of counter.
D = 16 in. minimum clearance between center of front unit and nearest piece of high equipment or wall, or between center of wall oven and adjoining wall.
E = 36 to 42 in. counter space between range and nearest piece of equipment.
F = 40 to 42 in. clearance from face of range or oven to face of wall or facing counter.

CLEARANCES

WHEELCHAIR ACCESSIBLE KITCHENS

The preferred cooktop and counter height is 30 to 33 in., but may be standard 36 in. Open floor space is necessary for wheelchair maneuverability; observe a 5 ft minimum turning radius. Smooth, nonskid flooring is required. Indoor–outdoor carpet is preferred, but difficult to maintain in a kitchen. Linoleum or vinyl tile is acceptable. Knee space is necessary under sink counter. Insulate pipes to avoid scalding. Provide cooktop controls at front to avoid reaching across hot surfaces. Wall ovens should preferably be set so that top of open oven door is 2 ft 7 in. above floor. Side-by-side refrigerator-freezer is preferred, although units with freezer on bottom are acceptable. Dishwashers should be front-loading.

Round tables with pedestal bases are preferred. A 4 ft diameter will accommodate two wheelchair users; a 4 ft 5 in. diameter will accommodate four wheelchair users.

Storage considerations for wheelchair users include use of pegboard for pots, pans, and utensils. Vertical drawers in base cabinets allow for storage of food that would otherwise be out of reach of wheelchair users. Narrow shelving mounted to the backs of doors in cabinets or closets provides accessible storage for food and utensils.

Robin Andrew Roberts, AIA; Washington, D.C.
Arthur J. Pettorino, AIA; Hicksville, New York
R. E. Powe, Jr., AIA; Hugh N. Jacobsen, FAIA; Washington, D.C.

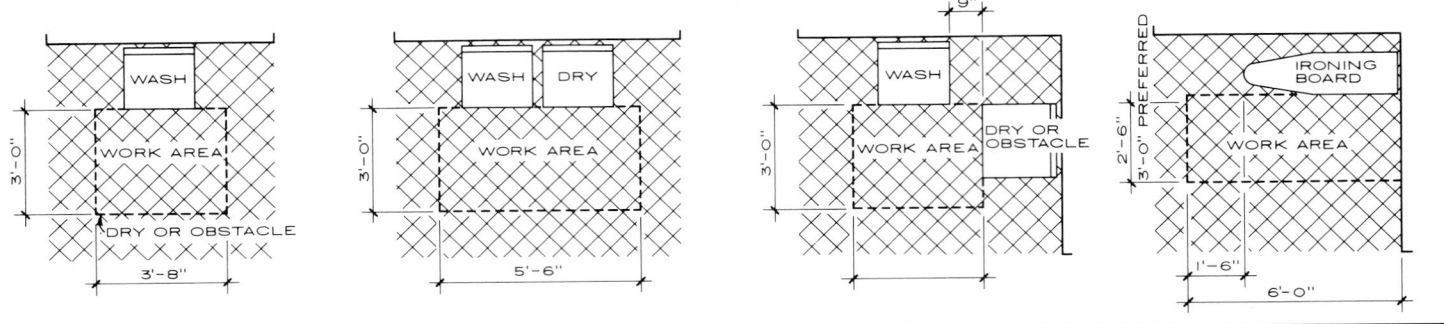

LAUNDRY EQUIPMENT CLEARANCES

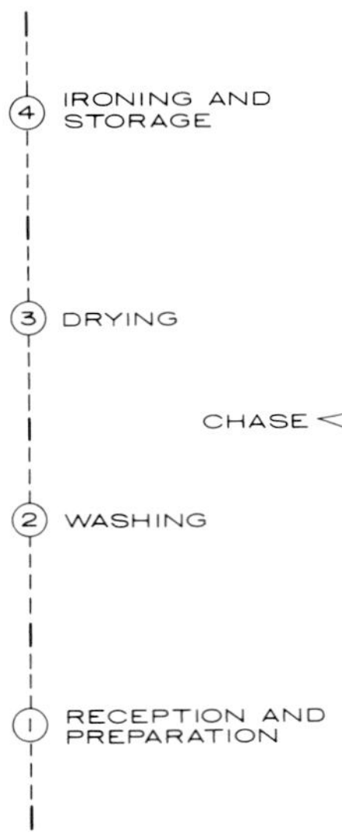

SEQUENCE:
- (4) IRONING AND STORAGE
- (3) DRYING
- (2) WASHING
- (1) RECEPTION AND PREPARATION

SEQUENCE

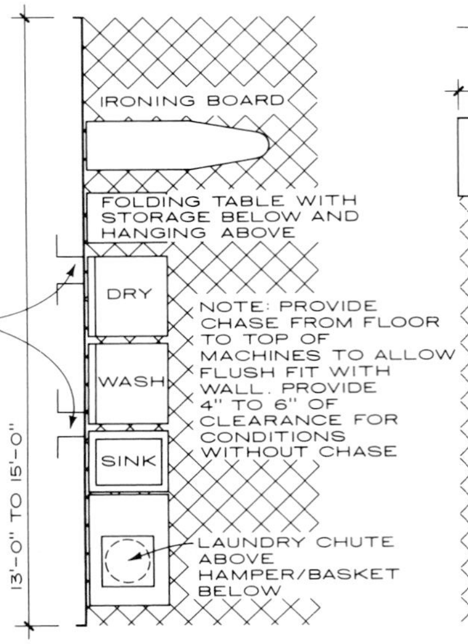

ONE-WALL LAUNDRY:
IRONING BOARD, FOLDING TABLE WITH STORAGE BELOW AND HANGING ABOVE, CHASE, DRY, WASH, SINK, LAUNDRY CHUTE ABOVE HAMPER/BASKET BELOW

NOTE: PROVIDE CHASE FROM FLOOR TO TOP OF MACHINES TO ALLOW FLUSH FIT WITH WALL. PROVIDE 4" TO 6" OF CLEARANCE FOR CONDITIONS WITHOUT CHASE

13'-0" TO 15'-0"

ONE-WALL LAUNDRY

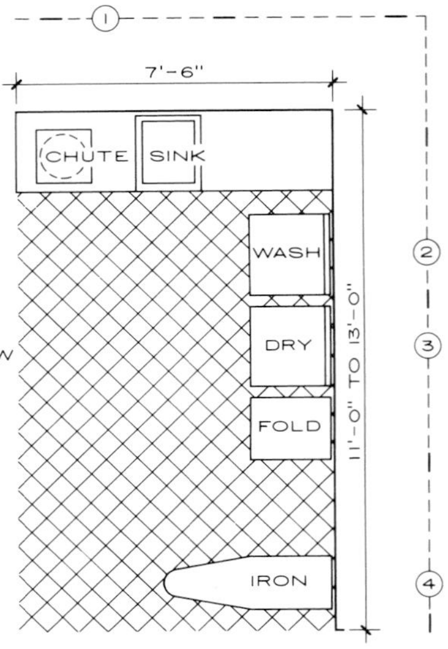

"L" LAUNDRY:
7'-6", CHUTE, SINK, WASH, DRY, FOLD, IRON, 11'-0" TO 13'-0"

"L" LAUNDRY

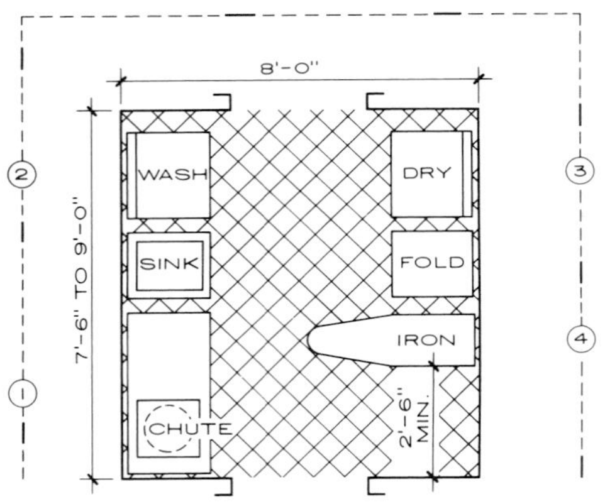

PARALLEL LAUNDRIES:
8'-0", WASH, DRY, SINK, FOLD, IRON, CHUTE, 7'-6" TO 9'-0", 2'-6" MIN.

PARALLEL LAUNDRIES

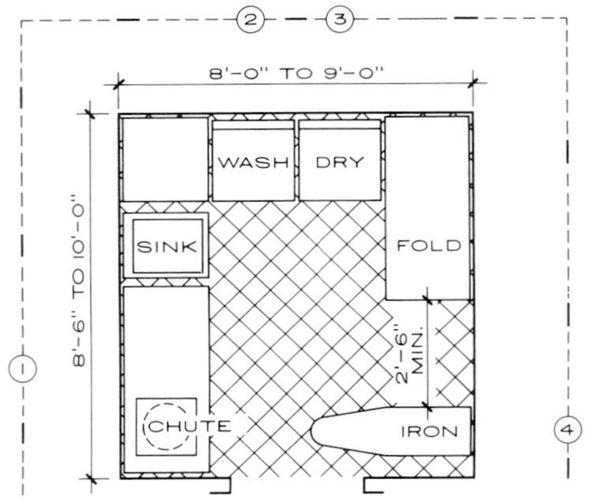

"U" LAUNDRY:
8'-0" TO 9'-0", WASH, DRY, SINK, FOLD, CHUTE, IRON, 8'-6" TO 10'-0", 2'-6" MIN.

"U" LAUNDRY

TYPICAL LAUNDRIES

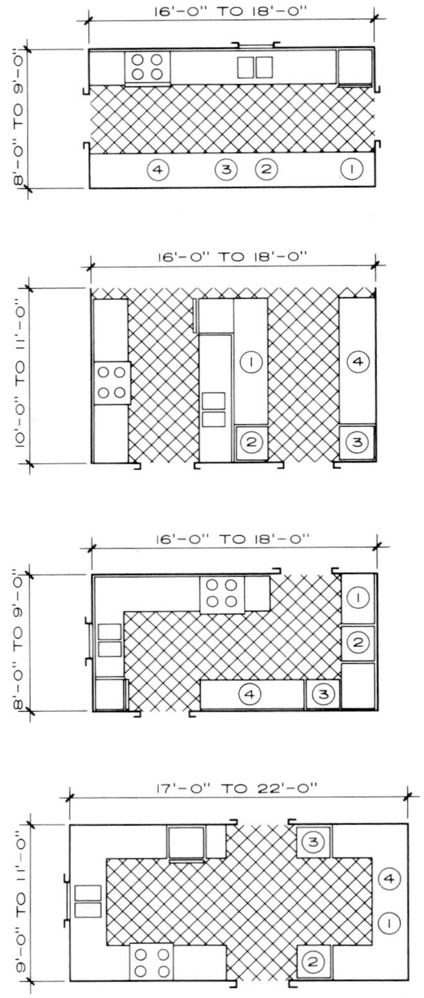

LAUNDRIES WITH KITCHEN:
- 16'-0" TO 18'-0" / 8'-0" TO 9'-0"
- 16'-0" TO 18'-0" / 10'-0" TO 11'-0"
- 16'-0" TO 18'-0" / 8'-0" TO 9'-0"
- 17'-0" TO 22'-0" / 9'-0" TO 11'-0"

LAUNDRIES WITH KITCHEN

LAUNDRIES FOR WHEELCHAIR USERS

For wheelchair users, having laundry facilities close to the kitchen combines several time-consuming activities with a minimum of movement from place to place.

The basic necessities for an accessible laundry facility are the following: front-loading automatic washer, dryer, storage shelving for supplies, lightweight steam iron, ironing board, and a surface for folding.

Laundry equipment controls are to be within high forward or side reach ranges. Controls shall be operable with one hand and not require tight grasping, pinching, or twisting of the wrist.

For an accessible laundry area, provide storage for supplies within high forward or side reach ranges and all working surfaces at a comfortable seated work height of 29 in. with knee clearance below.

APARTMENT HOUSE LAUNDRIES

In apartment houses, locate laundry rooms in the basement or on the ground floor of the building near necessary mechanical equipment, piping, and ventilation.

Locate laundry rooms on grade, to provide surfaces to absorb vibrations from operation and to not disturb the apartment dwellers.

Provide convenient access from dwelling units to laundry room. Incorporate into the laundry room design folding tables and vending machines for soap, bleach, and other laundry powders.

Provide the ability for visual inspection of the laundry room for the security of the users. Also, laundry rooms in large apartment buildings are public areas where apartment dwellers socialize and meet each other, so provide area to accommodate this necessary function.

Robin Andrew Roberts, AIA; Washington, D.C.
Arthur J. Pettorino, AIA; Hicksville, New York
R. E. Powe, Jr., AIA; Hugh N. Jacobsen, FAIA; Washington, D.C.

RESIDENTIAL ROOM PLANNING

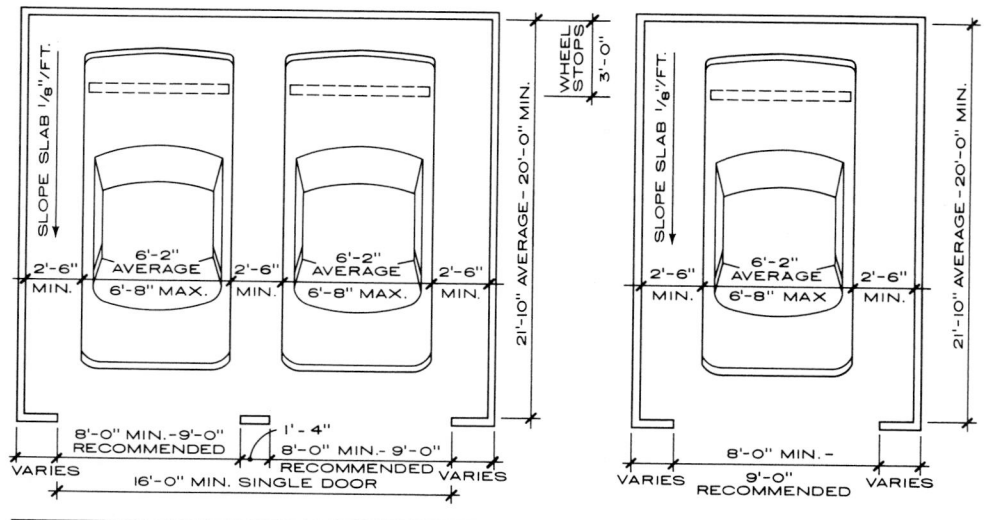

TWO-CAR GARAGE   **ONE-CAR GARAGE**

NOTES

1. Site location varies because of site constraints and design concept. Design considerations include circulation, visual safety for backing out, and visual consideration if garage is exposed to public view.
2. Garages may be enlarged to provide circulation ease by allowing spaces of 2 ft 6 in. minimum between all walls and other vehicles, and to provide space for work areas, photography laboratories, laundry room, and storage.
3. Garages may be attached directly to the house or be connected by a covered passage. Connection is preferable at or near the kitchen or utility area off the kitchen. If attached, refer to local code requirements.

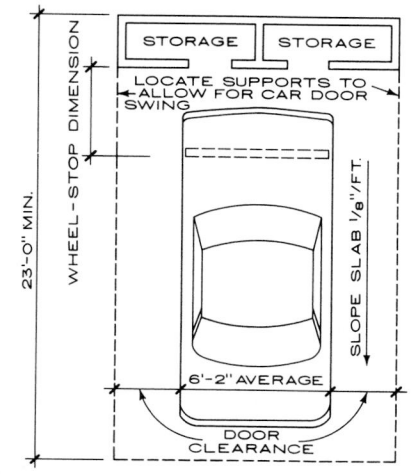

BACKOUT TYPE CARPORT

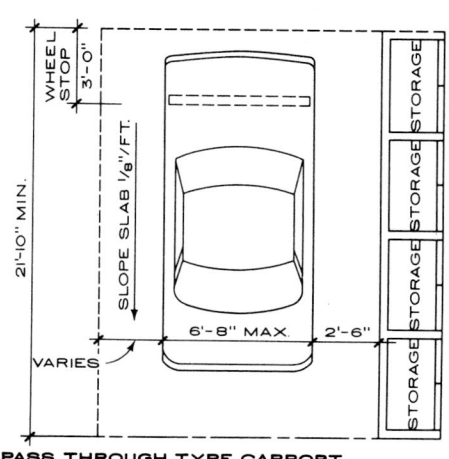

PASS THROUGH TYPE CARPORT

CARPORTS

SECTIONAL DOOR SIZES

DOOR WIDTH	NUMBER OF PANELS ACROSS
To 8'-11''	2
9'-0''–11'-11''	3
12'-0''–14'-11''	4
15'-0''–17'-11''	5

NOTE: Doors up to 8'-6'' high require 4 sections.

HINGED GARAGE DOOR WIDTHS

OPENING	TWO-DOOR	THREE-DOOR	FOUR-DOOR
8'-0''	4'-0''	2'-8''	2'-0''
8'-6''	4'-3''	2'-10''	2'-1½''
9'-0''	4'-6''	3'-0''	2'-3''

OFFSET HINGE–MULTI-LEAVE

MULTIPLE HINGED DOOR TWO OR MORE CARS

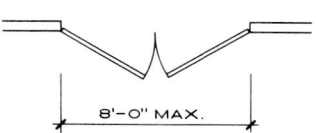

DOUBLE OR TRIPLE HINGED

NOTE

For multiple and offset hinged doors, swinging to one or both sides, hinged in or out, and used for two or more cars: 6½ to 11 in. necessary from top of opening to ceiling.

HINGED DOORS

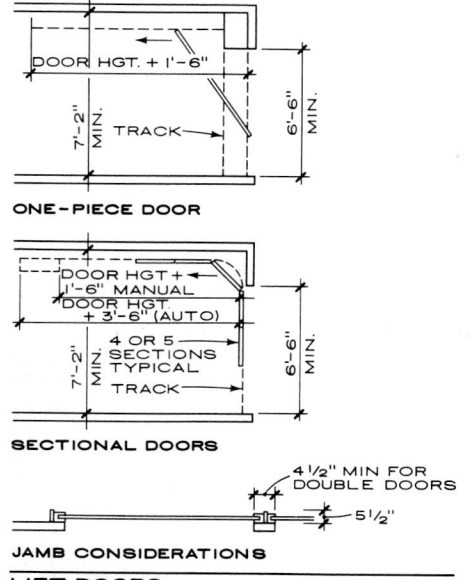

ONE-PIECE DOOR

SECTIONAL DOORS

JAMB CONSIDERATIONS

**LIFT DOORS –
MOST WIDELY USED –
AUTOMATIC OPTIONAL**

NOTE: HEIGHTS 6'-6'', 6'-10'', 7'-0'', 7'-6'' AND 8'-0''

William T. Cannady, FAIA; Houston, Texas

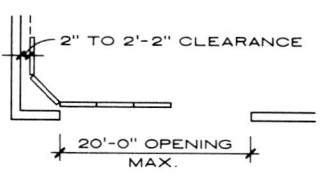

HINGED SECTION

**MULTIPLE DOORS –
TWO OR MORE CARS**

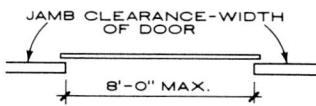

SINGLE DOOR

NOTE

6½ to 9 in. necessary from top of opening to ceiling (all sliding doors).

SLIDING DOORS

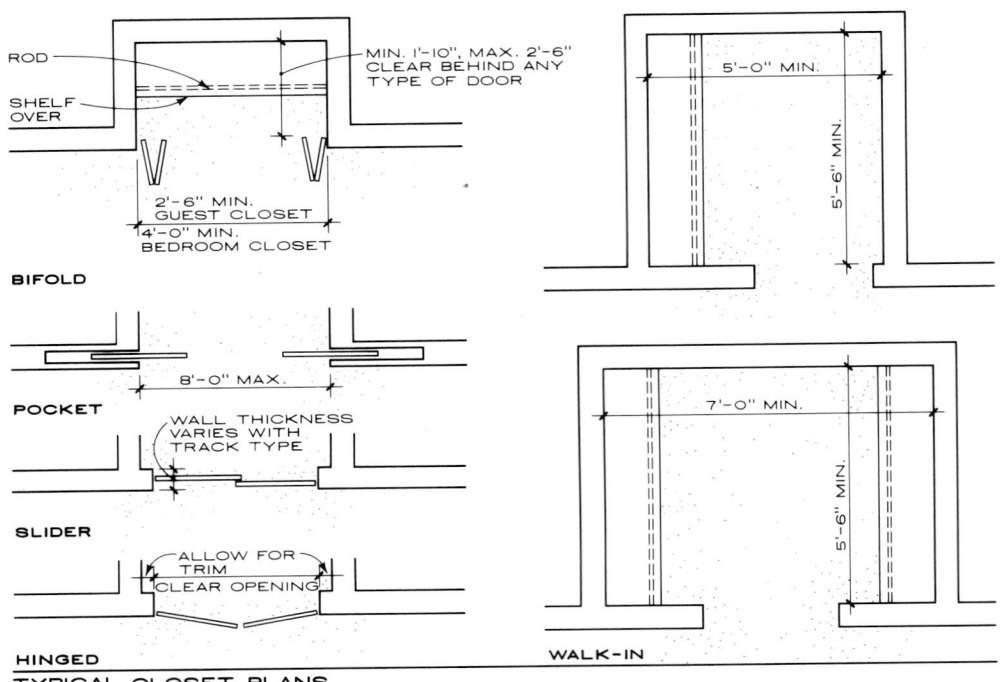

TYPICAL CLOSET PLANS

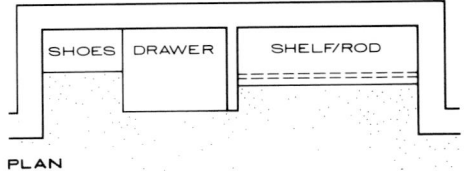

PLAN

NOTES

1. No closet bifold door should exceed a 2 ft panel. Largest door stock in pocket and sliding door is 4 ft.
2. All closet doors should allow easy access to top shelves.
3. Doors for children's closets can be used as tackboards, chalkboards, or mirrors.
4. Consider use of hinged doors for storage fittings and mirrors.
5. Walk-in closets should be properly ventilated and lit.
6. Provide clear floor space at least 30 by 48 in. for wheelchair approach. Pole and shelf height is 54 in. maximum for wheelchair access. Doors to shallow closets, where wheelchair passage is not required, may have a clear opening width of 20 in. minimum.
7. Percentage of accessibility of closets varies with door types used: Bifold at $66^{2}/_{3}$% minimum; pocket at 100%; sliding at 50% or more; and hinged at 90% depending on hardware and door thickness.

TYPICAL CLOSET SECTIONS

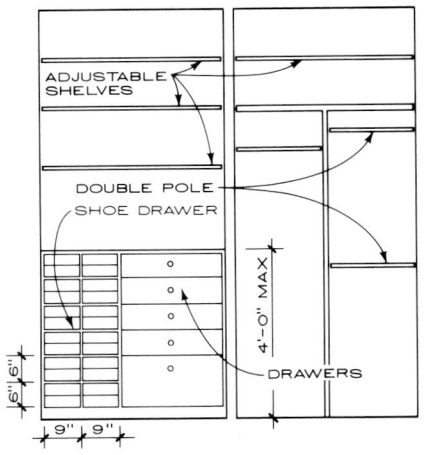

ELEVATION
DIVIDED CLOSET

RESIDENTIAL STORAGE

SHELVING. Standard shelving sizes are 6, 8, 10, and 12 in., although shelving up to 18 in. deep is desirable for closet shelving. Shelving may be either fixed or adjustable.

DRAWERS. Typical drawers are from 16 to 24 in. deep, 12 to 36 in. wide, and 2 to 8 in. deep or deeper. Often built into casework, drawers may be of wood, metal, or molded plastic.

CLOSETS. Standard closet depth is 24 to 30 in. for clothing and 16 to 20 in. for linens.

BOXES. Closet storage fittings such as boxes and garment bags can be used for supplemental or seasonal storage.

STORAGE REQUIREMENTS

BEDROOM. Allow a minimum of 4 to 6 ft of hanging space per person. Allow 8 linear ft of hanging space for closets shared by 2 people. Allow 12 in. of hanging space for 6 suits, 12 shirts, 8 dresses, or 6 pairs of pants.

LINEN STORAGE. Place near bedrooms and bathrooms in a closet with 12 to 18 in. deep shelves. Supplemental storage in bins or baskets may be needed. Provide minimum 9 sq ft for 1–2 bedroom house; 12 sq ft for 3–4 bedroom house.

BATHROOMS. A mirrored wall cabinet 4 to 6 in. deep is typical bathroom storage, supplemented by space for supplies of soap, toothpaste, and other toiletries.

COATS. A closet near an entry door for coats and rainwear is desirable in most areas of the country. Provide

extra 2 to 3 in. in depth for air circulation and added bulkiness of overcoats.

CLEANING EQUIPMENT. A closet at least 24 in. wide for storage of vacuum cleaners and household cleaning supplies is helpful. Locate closet near center of house and provide electrical outlet so vacuum can be left connected.

KITCHEN/DINING. See pages on kitchen planning for recommendations.

OTHER STORAGE. Most families have additional storage needs. For custom design work, these needs must be analyzed and storage planned. Storage rooms and attic and basement areas are possible supplemental storage locations.

Robin Andrew Roberts, AIA; Washington, D.C.
R. L. Speas, Jr.; Hugh N. Jacobsen, FAIA; Washington, D.C.

RESIDENTIAL ROOM PLANNING

GENERAL

Closet systems can be assembled from prefabricated materials cut in the field to custom fit an existing closet. Closet systems are typically constructed of either solid particleboard covered in plastic laminate or steel wire coated with vinyl, polyvinyl chloride, or epoxy.

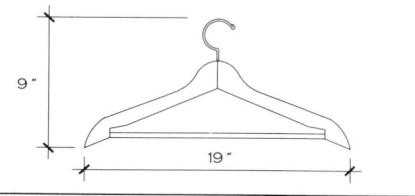

HANGER

TYPICAL LAYOUT DIMENSIONS

REFERENCE	DIMENSION	DESCRIPTION
A	96"	Minimum ceiling height (typical)
B	42"	Hanging storage for shirts, jackets, pants, and skirts for men and women
C	24"	Standard width for drawers and baskets; height for children's hanging clothes
D	36"	Storage for 3 pairs of men's shoes and 4 pairs of women's shoes
E	68"	Hanging storage for dresses and full length robes, evening gowns
F	14"	Standard shelf depth
G	12"	Distance rod is to be mounted from back of closet
H	04"	Distance from top of shelf above to centerline of rod
J	06"	Distance between shelves to allow for shoe storage
K	24"	Minimum required inside clear depth for closet (typical)
L	12"	Shelf width for 1 stack of clothes
M	06"	Clearance from floor to allow for vacuuming
N	30"	Standard height for children's hanging clothes

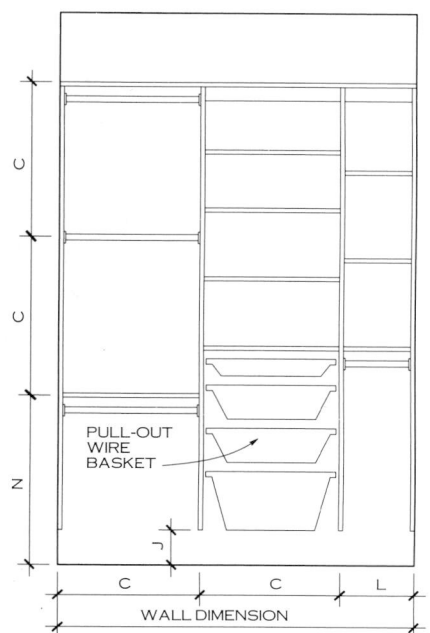

CHILD'S CLOSET

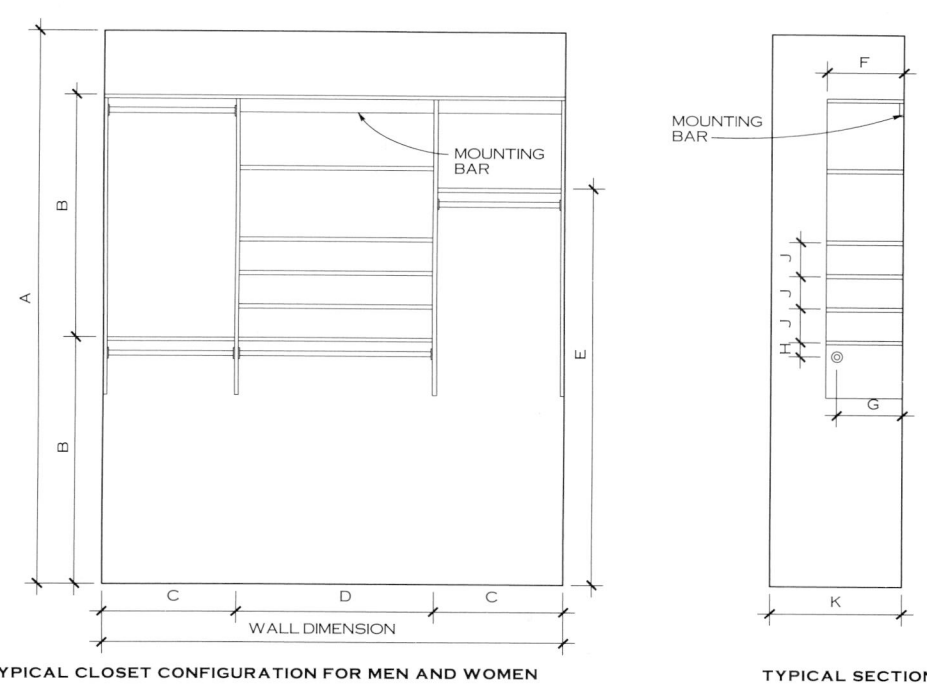

TYPICAL CLOSET CONFIGURATION FOR MEN AND WOMEN **TYPICAL SECTION**

SOLID SHELVING SYSTEMS

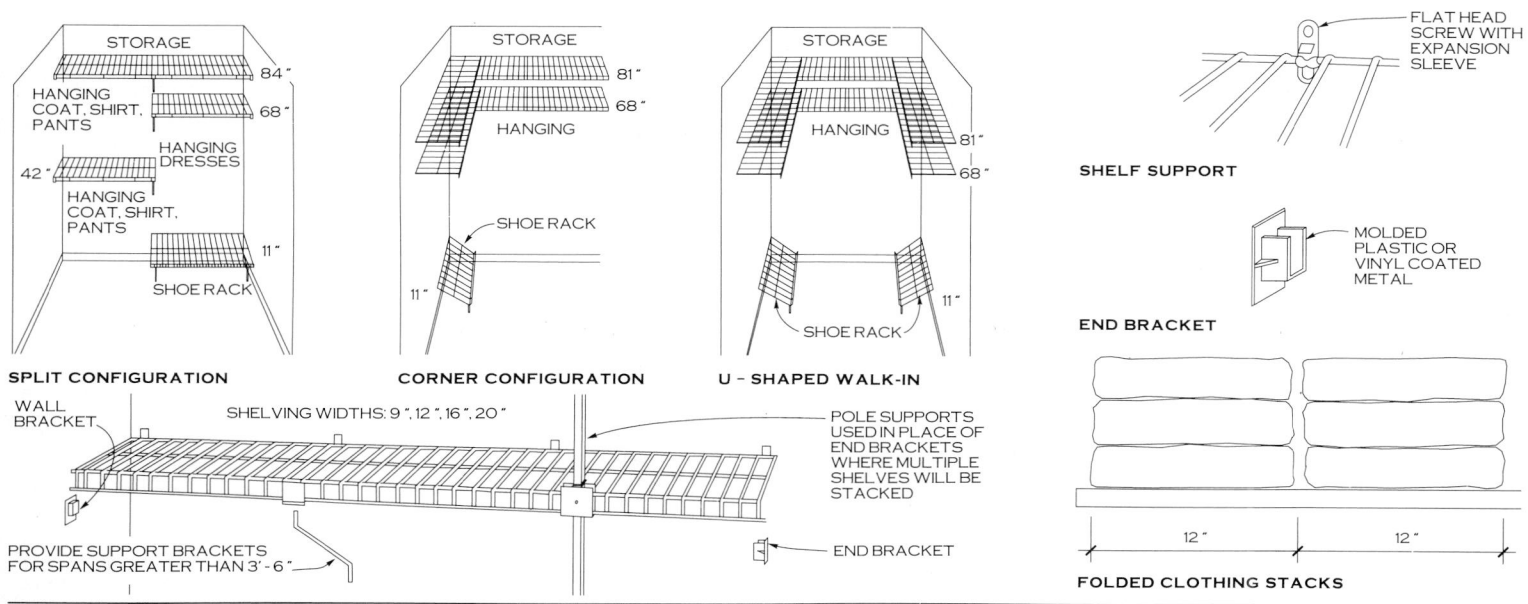

SPLIT CONFIGURATION   **CORNER CONFIGURATION**   **U – SHAPED WALK-IN**   **SHELF SUPPORT**   **END BRACKET**   **FOLDED CLOTHING STACKS**

COATED STEEL WIRE SHELVING SYSTEMS

O'Brien - Kilgore, Inc.; Washington, D.C.

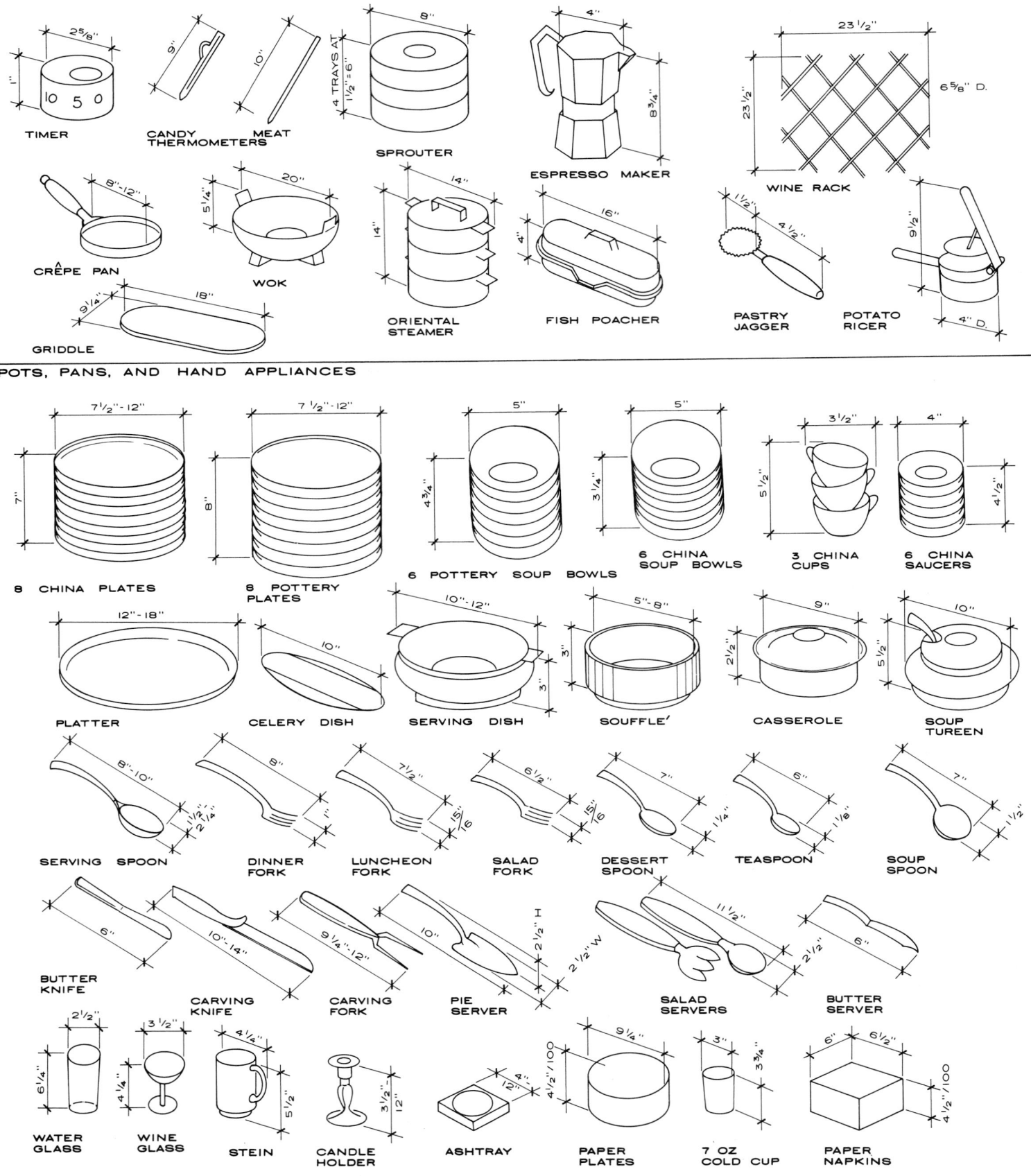

TIMER   CANDY THERMOMETERS   MEAT   SPROUTER   ESPRESSO MAKER   WINE RACK

CRÊPE PAN   WOK   ORIENTAL STEAMER   FISH POACHER   PASTRY JAGGER   POTATO RICER

GRIDDLE

POTS, PANS, AND HAND APPLIANCES

8 CHINA PLATES   8 POTTERY PLATES   6 POTTERY SOUP BOWLS   6 CHINA SOUP BOWLS   3 CHINA CUPS   6 CHINA SAUCERS

PLATTER   CELERY DISH   SERVING DISH   SOUFFLE'   CASSEROLE   SOUP TUREEN

SERVING SPOON   DINNER FORK   LUNCHEON FORK   SALAD FORK   DESSERT SPOON   TEASPOON   SOUP SPOON

BUTTER KNIFE   CARVING KNIFE   CARVING FORK   PIE SERVER   SALAD SERVERS   BUTTER SERVER

WATER GLASS   WINE GLASS   STEIN   CANDLE HOLDER   ASHTRAY   PAPER PLATES   7 OZ COLD CUP   PAPER NAPKINS

DINING ROOM TABLEWARE

E. H. & M. K. Hunter, Architects; Raleigh, North Carolina

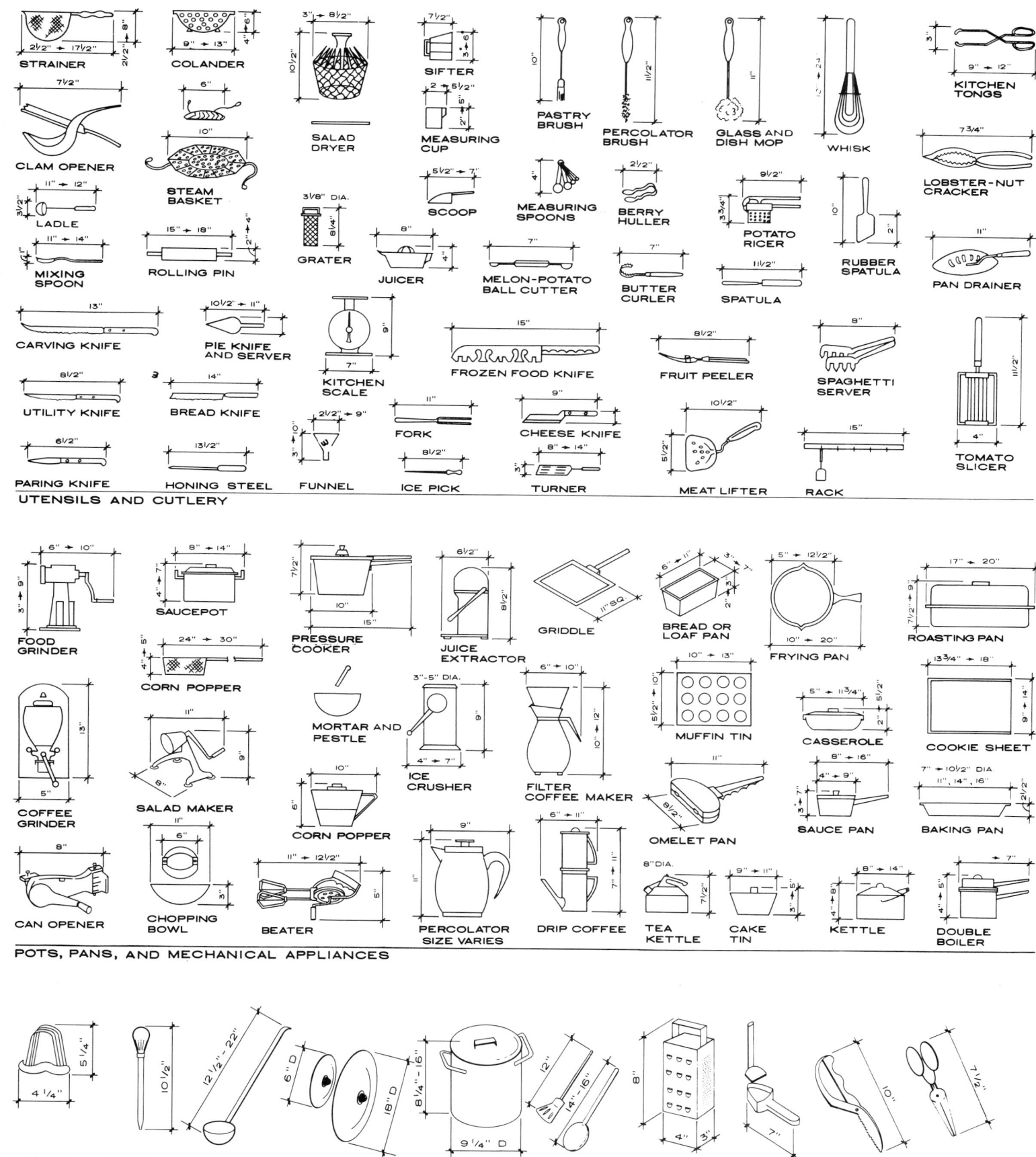

UTENSILS AND CUTLERY

STRAINER · COLANDER · SIFTER · SALAD DRYER · MEASURING CUP · PASTRY BRUSH · PERCOLATOR BRUSH · GLASS AND DISH MOP · WHISK · KITCHEN TONGS

CLAM OPENER · STEAM BASKET · SCOOP · MEASURING SPOONS · BERRY HULLER · POTATO RICER · RUBBER SPATULA · LOBSTER-NUT CRACKER

LADLE · MIXING SPOON · ROLLING PIN · GRATER · JUICER · MELON-POTATO BALL CUTTER · BUTTER CURLER · SPATULA · PAN DRAINER

CARVING KNIFE · PIE KNIFE AND SERVER · KITCHEN SCALE · FROZEN FOOD KNIFE · FRUIT PEELER · SPAGHETTI SERVER · TOMATO SLICER

UTILITY KNIFE · BREAD KNIFE · FORK · CHEESE KNIFE · MEAT LIFTER

PARING KNIFE · HONING STEEL · FUNNEL · ICE PICK · TURNER · RACK

POTS, PANS, AND MECHANICAL APPLIANCES

FOOD GRINDER · SAUCEPOT · PRESSURE COOKER · JUICE EXTRACTOR · GRIDDLE · BREAD OR LOAF PAN · FRYING PAN · ROASTING PAN

CORN POPPER · MORTAR AND PESTLE · MUFFIN TIN · CASSEROLE · COOKIE SHEET

COFFEE GRINDER · SALAD MAKER · ICE CRUSHER · FILTER COFFEE MAKER · OMELET PAN · SAUCE PAN · BAKING PAN

CAN OPENER · CHOPPING BOWL · BEATER · PERCOLATOR SIZE VARIES · DRIP COFFEE · TEA KETTLE · CAKE TIN · KETTLE · DOUBLE BOILER

POTS, PANS, AND HAND APPLIANCES

PASTRY BLENDER · BULB BASTER · LADLE · PAN LIDS · STOCKPOT · SPATULA SPOON · GRATER SHREDDER · GARLIC PRESS · POULTRY SHEARS · KITCHEN SHEARS

E. H. & M. K. Hunter, Architects; Raleigh, North Carolina

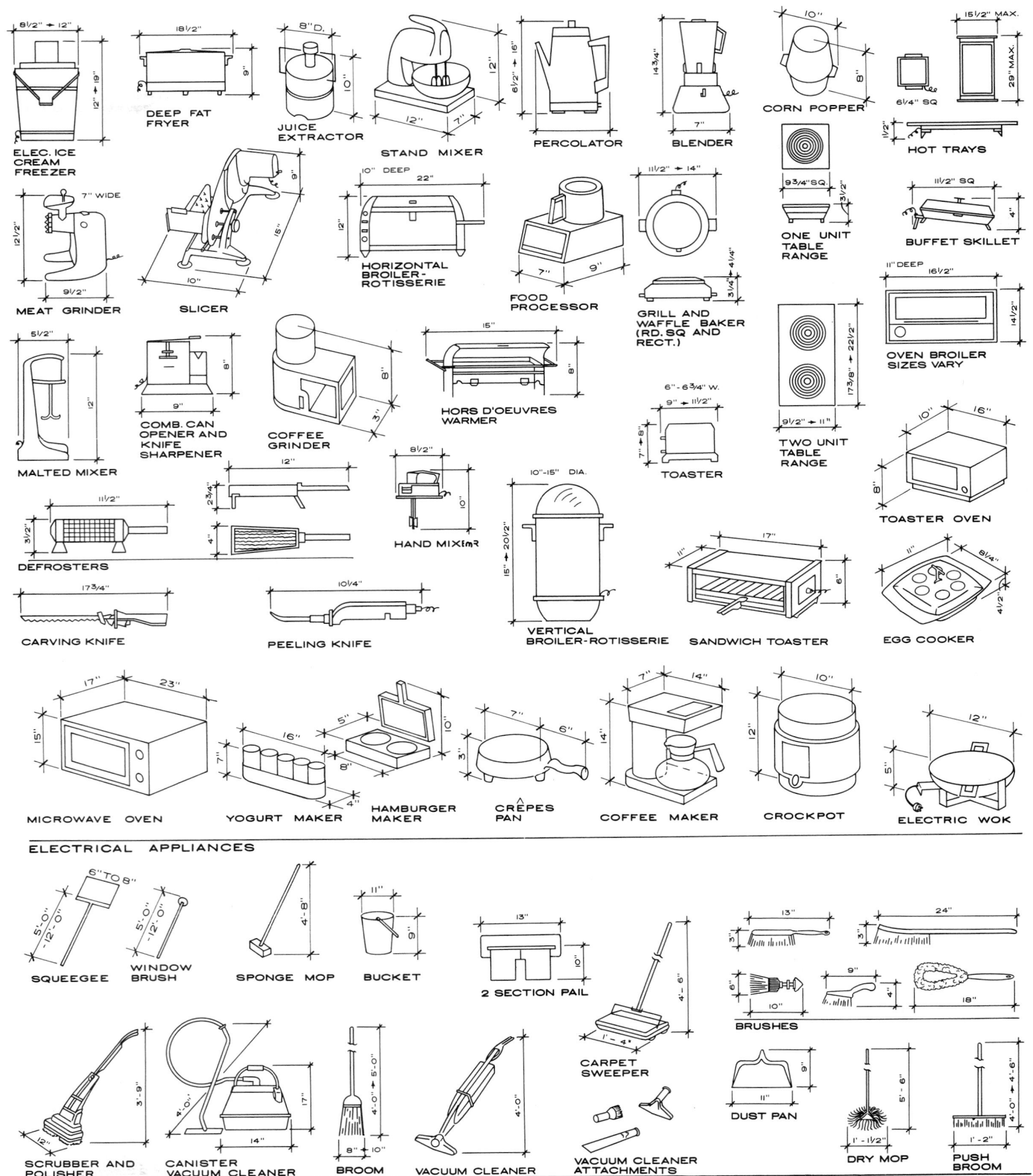

ELEC. ICE CREAM FREEZER

DEEP FAT FRYER

JUICE EXTRACTOR

STAND MIXER

PERCOLATOR

BLENDER

CORN POPPER

HOT TRAYS

MEAT GRINDER

SLICER

HORIZONTAL BROILER-ROTISSERIE

FOOD PROCESSOR

GRILL AND WAFFLE BAKER (RD. SQ AND RECT.)

ONE UNIT TABLE RANGE

BUFFET SKILLET

OVEN BROILER SIZES VARY

MALTED MIXER

COMB. CAN OPENER AND KNIFE SHARPENER

COFFEE GRINDER

HORS D'OEUVRES WARMER

TWO UNIT TABLE RANGE

TOASTER

TOASTER OVEN

DEFROSTERS

HAND MIXER

CARVING KNIFE

PEELING KNIFE

VERTICAL BROILER-ROTISSERIE

SANDWICH TOASTER

EGG COOKER

MICROWAVE OVEN

YOGURT MAKER

HAMBURGER MAKER

CREPES PAN

COFFEE MAKER

CROCKPOT

ELECTRIC WOK

ELECTRICAL APPLIANCES

SQUEEGEE

WINDOW BRUSH

SPONGE MOP

BUCKET

2 SECTION PAIL

CARPET SWEEPER

BRUSHES

DUST PAN

SCRUBBER AND POLISHER

CANISTER VACUUM CLEANER

BROOM

VACUUM CLEANER

VACUUM CLEANER ATTACHMENTS

DRY MOP

PUSH BROOM

CLEANING EQUIPMENT

E. H. & M. K. Hunter, Architects; Raleigh, North Carolina

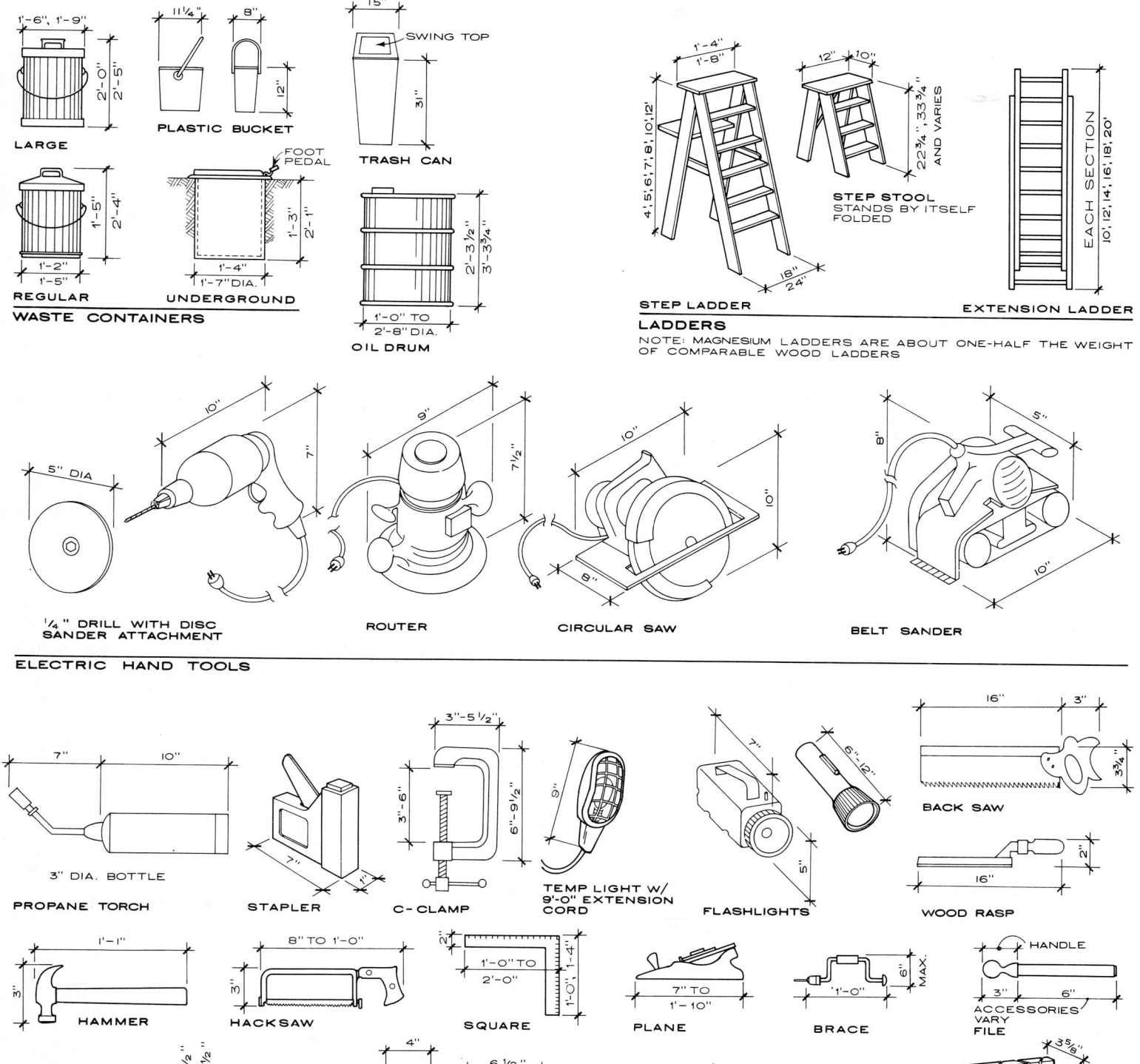

WASTE CONTAINERS

LARGE

REGULAR

UNDERGROUND

PLASTIC BUCKET

TRASH CAN

OIL DRUM

LADDERS

STEP LADDER

STEP STOOL
STANDS BY ITSELF
FOLDED

EXTENSION LADDER

NOTE: MAGNESIUM LADDERS ARE ABOUT ONE-HALF THE WEIGHT
OF COMPARABLE WOOD LADDERS

ELECTRIC HAND TOOLS

1/4" DRILL WITH DISC
SANDER ATTACHMENT

ROUTER

CIRCULAR SAW

BELT SANDER

PROPANE TORCH

STAPLER

C-CLAMP

TEMP LIGHT W/
9'-0" EXTENSION
CORD

FLASHLIGHTS

BACK SAW

WOOD RASP

HAMMER

HACKSAW

SQUARE

PLANE

BRACE

FILE

MONKEY WRENCH

HANDSAW

COPING SAW

CHISEL

PLIERS

MITER BOX

WOOD LEVEL

HATCHET OR AXE

CROW BAR

TOOL BOX

SCREWDRIVER

TYPICAL HOUSEHOLD HAND TOOLS

E. H. & M. K. Hunter, Architects; Raleigh, North Carolina

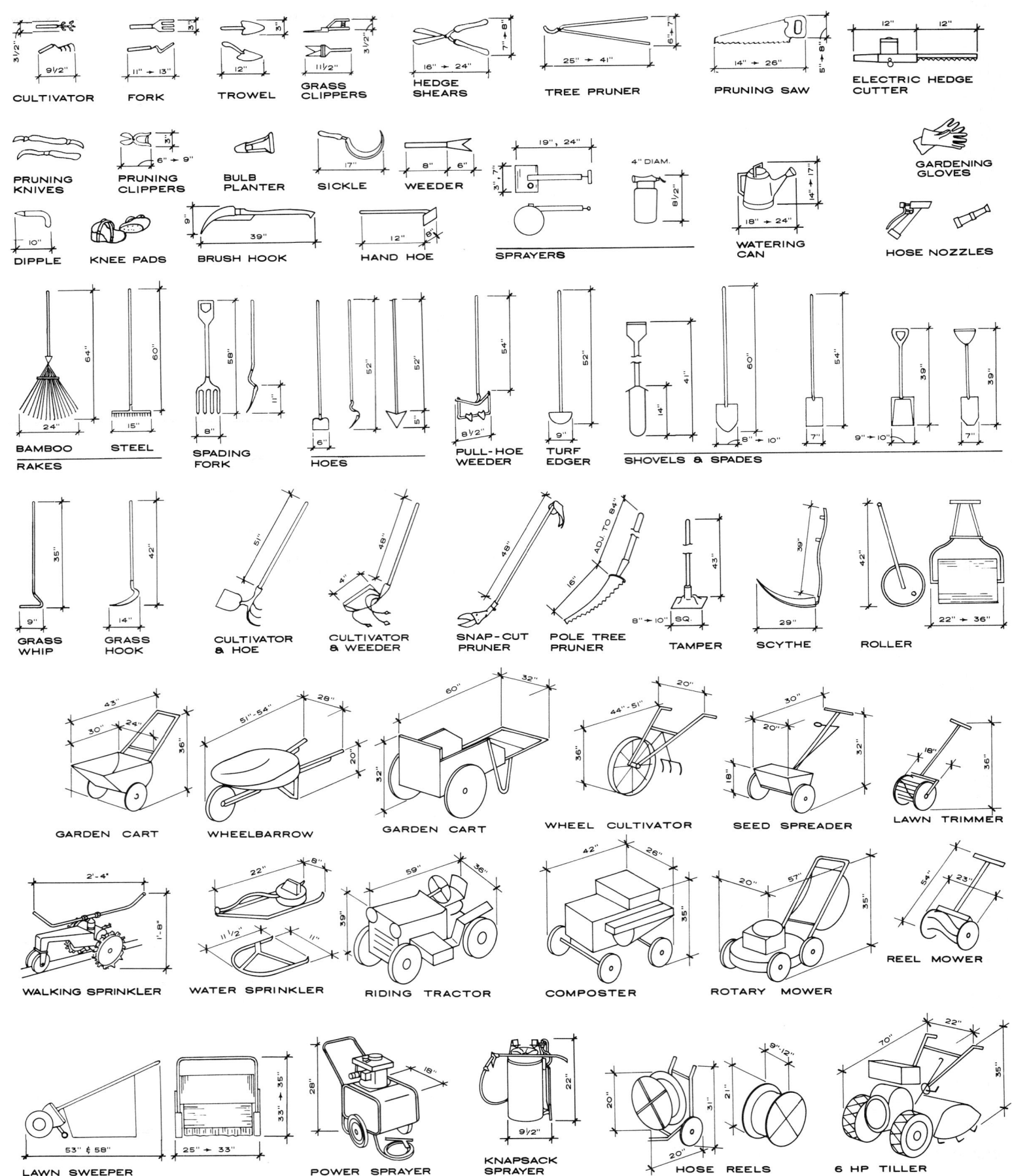

E. H. & M. K. Hunter, Architects; Raleigh, North Carolina

GENERAL

1. Typical height for work surface, desk, and credenza is 29 in. Return height is typically 27 in.
2. Universal work surface height is 28 in.
3. Minimum dimension between face of credenza and face of desk is 42 in.
4. Typical transaction counter is 12 to 15 in. deep and 42 to 48 in. high.
5. Freestanding credenzas may be used as computer work surfaces by increasing depth from 20 to 24 in. and by adding a kneehole.
6. Chairman's office may also include an executive storage unit or bookcase.

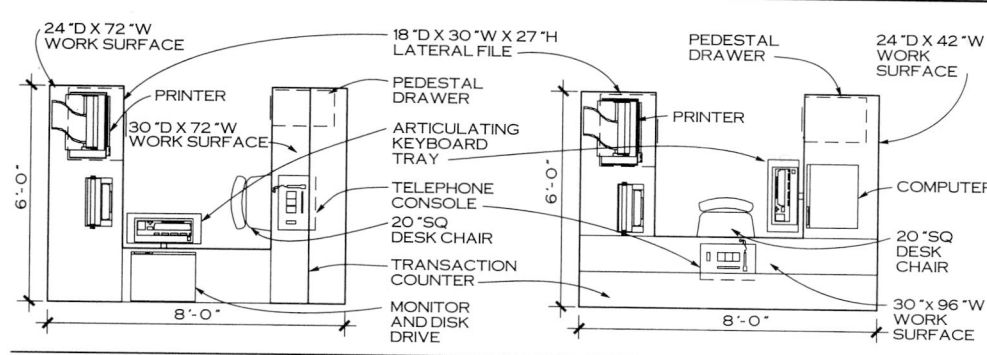

RECEPTIONIST – OPEN AREA

24"D X 72"W WORK SURFACE
18"D X 30"W X 27"H LATERAL FILE
PEDESTAL DRAWER
24"D X 42"W WORK SURFACE
PRINTER
PEDESTAL DRAWER
30"D X 72"W WORK SURFACE
ARTICULATING KEYBOARD TRAY
PRINTER
COMPUTER
TELEPHONE CONSOLE
20"SQ DESK CHAIR
20"SQ DESK CHAIR
TRANSACTION COUNTER
30"x 96"W WORK SURFACE
MONITOR AND DISK DRIVE
8'-0"

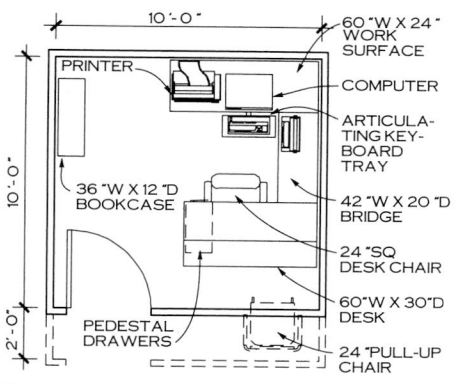

SUPERVISOR – INTERIOR OFFICE

10'-0"
60"W X 24" WORK SURFACE
PRINTER
COMPUTER
ARTICULATING KEYBOARD TRAY
36"W X 12"D BOOKCASE
42"W X 20"D BRIDGE
24"SQ DESK CHAIR
60"W X 30"D DESK
PEDESTAL DRAWERS
24"PULL-UP CHAIR

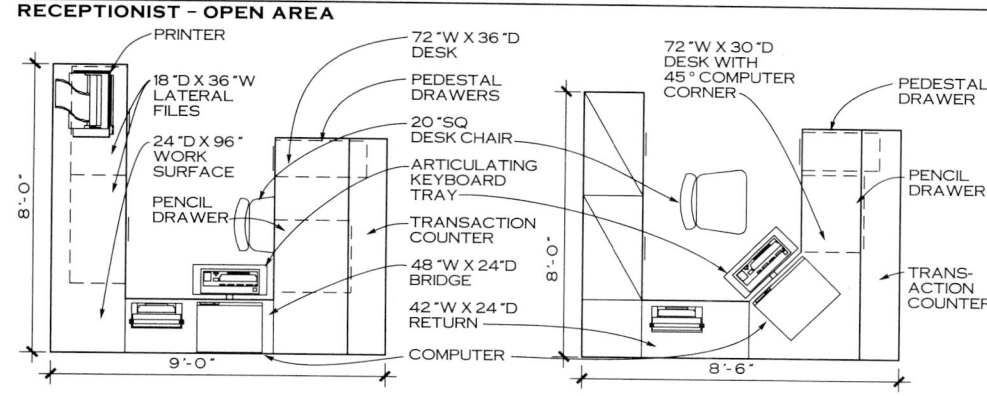

SECRETARY / CLERICAL

PRINTER
72"W X 36"D DESK
72"W X 30"D DESK WITH 45° COMPUTER CORNER
PEDESTAL DRAWERS
PEDESTAL DRAWER
18"D X 36"W LATERAL FILES
20"SQ DESK CHAIR
24"D X 96" WORK SURFACE
ARTICULATING KEYBOARD TRAY
PENCIL DRAWER
PENCIL DRAWER
TRANSACTION COUNTER
48"W X 24"D BRIDGE
TRANSACTION COUNTER
42"W X 24"D RETURN
COMPUTER
9'-0"
8'-6"

MANAGER – PERIMETER WINDOWED OFFICE

10'-0"
15'-0"
72"W X 20"D CREDENZA
36"W X 18"D BOOKCASE OR LATERAL FILE
27"W X 30"D HIGH BACK SWIVEL CHAIR
72"W X 36"D DESK
27"SQ PULL-UP ARMCHAIR

PRESIDENT – PERIMETER WINDOWED CORNER OFFICE

20'-0"
15'-0"
24"SQ END TABLE
30"SQ LOUNGE CHAIR
PLANTER
27"SQ PULL-UP ARMCHAIR
72"W X 36"D DESK
30"SQ HIGH BACK SWIVEL CHAIR
72"W X 20"D CREDENZA
48"W X 24"D COFFEE TABLE
84"W X 30"D SOFA
72"W X 18"D EXECUTIVE STORAGE UNIT

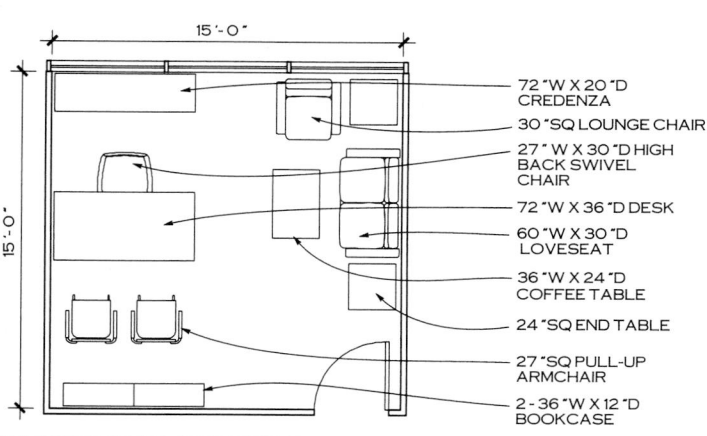

VICE-PRESIDENT – PERIMETER WINDOWED OFFICE

15'-0"
15'-0"
72"W X 20"D CREDENZA
30"SQ LOUNGE CHAIR
27"W X 30"D HIGH BACK SWIVEL CHAIR
72"W X 36"D DESK
60"W X 30"D LOVESEAT
36"W X 24"D COFFEE TABLE
24"SQ END TABLE
27"SQ PULL-UP ARMCHAIR
2-36"W X 12"D BOOKCASE

CHAIRMAN – PERIMETER WINDOWED CORNER OFFICE

20'-0"
20'-0"
78"W X 20"D CREDENZA
PLANTER
30"SQ HIGH BACK SWIVEL CHAIR
78"W X 36"D DESK
48"W X 36"D COFFEE TABLE
27"SQ PULL-UP ARMCHAIR
30"SQ LOUNGE CHAIR
24"SQ END TABLE
48"DIAMETER CONFERENCE TABLE
96"W X 30"D SOFA

O'Brien - Kilgore, Inc.; Washington, D.C.

GENERAL

Conference rooms should be located for proximity to user groups within a building and for accessibility to outside guests. Since a conference room typically serves to communicate a firm's "image" to others, finishes are usually selected from higher quality materials to suggest a prominent and visible location. When a conference room functions as a multiuser or multigroup space, the position of access doors is altered and acoustical folding partitions or movable walls may be used. The designer should note the additional requirements imposed by building codes for assembly occupancy for larger rooms.

FINISHES

Carpeted floors, acoustical wall panels, or fabric wall coverings and acoustic ceilings should be used. Avoid using "attention-getting" patterns and colors on walls which may decrease focal emphasis of tables, seating,

and speaker or projection area. All finishes should be carefully examined for flame spread and smoke-generated ratings.

LIGHTING

Parabolic lens fluorescent fixtures provide good general lighting with less glare. Directional fixtures such as track lighting may be used for presentation areas. Use dimming switches.

MECHANICAL

Provide a minimum of eight air changes per hour plus a minimum of 10 cu ft/min of outside air per person for odor-free air and good ventilation. Provide an exhaust system to be manually controlled from the room. Careful attention should be given to sound attenuation of diffusers.

TELECONFERENCING

The space and furniture requirements for teleconferencing are different from the typical conference room. All aspects are geared toward video camera requirements. Typically, the conference is held between groups in separate locations linked by video satellite. The standard layout includes two ceiling-mounted video cameras to cover the participants and an optional direct downward-aimed document camera, a projection television monitor (front or rear projecting) for the remote participants, and a control console which interfaces the video cameras, telephone, and satellite linkage. The room arrangement is such that all participants may view and be viewed simultaneously. Mixing presentation media (projection, boards, flip charts, etc.) becomes more difficult in teleconferencing, while the requirements for acoustics and ventilation remain unchanged from the typical conference room. Lighting must be in accordance with the requirements of the video system used.

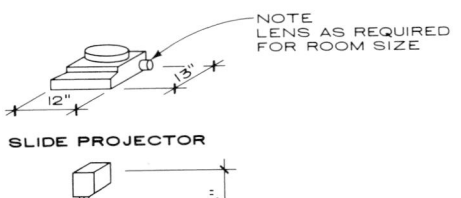

SLIDE PROJECTOR

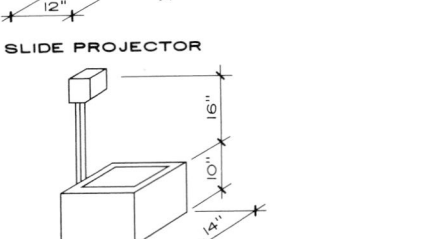

OVERHEAD PROJECTOR

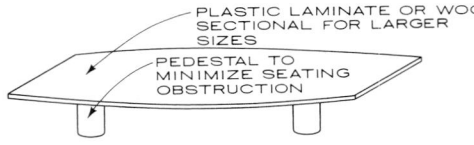

CONFERENCE TABLE
REFER TO FURNITURE SECTION
FOR SIZE BASED ON SEATING

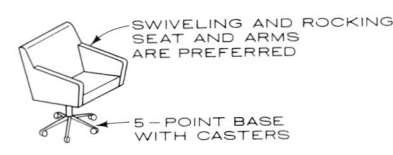

CHAIR

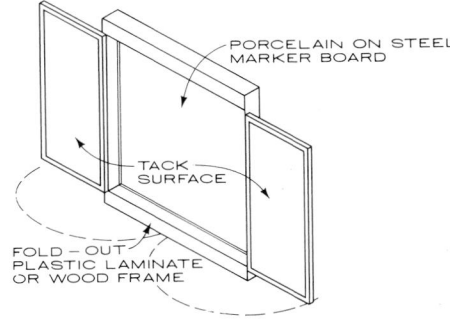

WALL-MOUNTED VISUAL CENTER

CONFERENCE ROOM FURNITURE AND EQUIPMENT

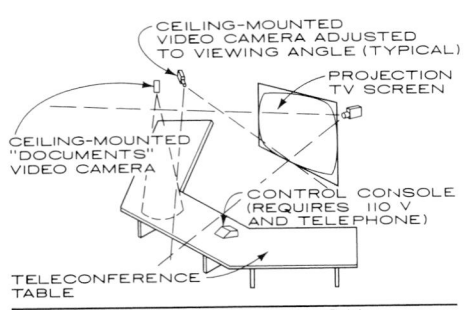

COMPONENTS OF A TYPICAL TELECONFERENCE ROOM

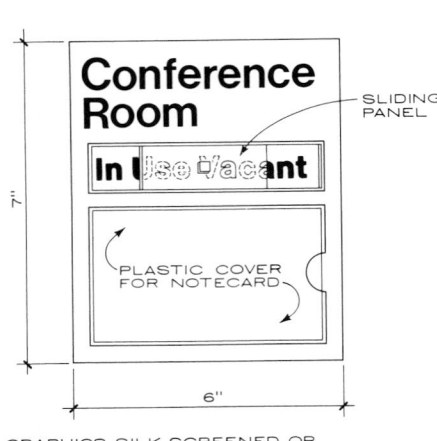

CONFERENCE ROOM SIGN

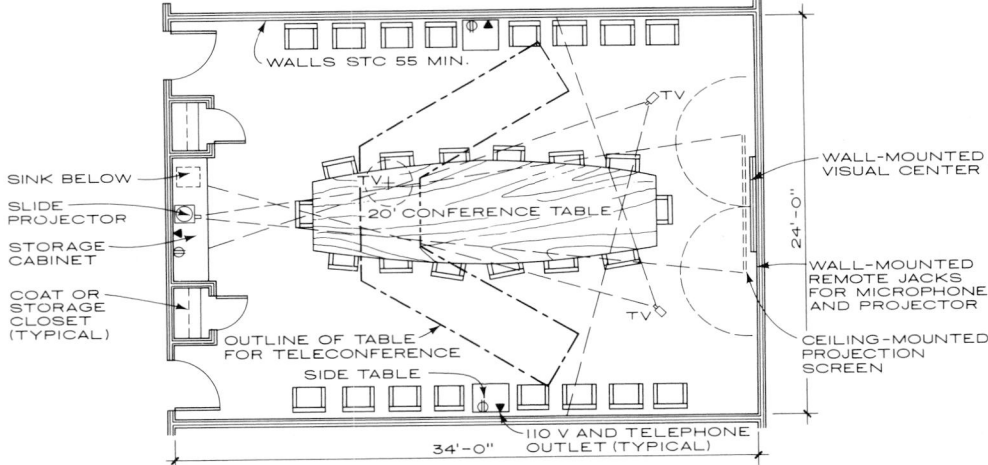

PLAN

NOTE

Components of both traditional and teleconferencing conference rooms are shown. The "board room" layout rendered here is not recommended for teleconferencing. See dashed layout, components at left, and general notes above.

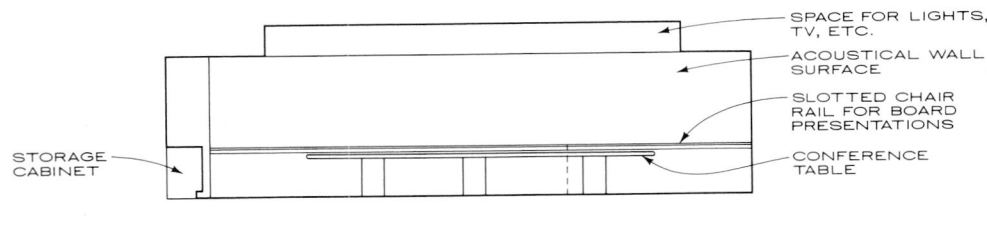

SECTION

TYPICAL CONFERENCE ROOM (25 – 30 PERSONS)

J. Kevin Lloyd, AIA; Barge, Waggoner, Sumner & Cannon; Nashville, Tennessee

 NONRESIDENTIAL ROOM PLANNING

GENERAL PLANNING NOTES

During the early stages of planning, consult with regional Postmaster General for regulations concerning postal facilities in office buildings.

PLATFORM

A dock area that provides off-the-street loading and unloading of mail.

MAILROOM

A security type room located at platform level, which has its own access door to the platform for off-hour service. Platform door should be 48 in. wide, security type. If window or lockbox service is provided, the mailroom should be located at the principal building entrance level. Standard interior treatment should apply in this space. Provide heavy-duty wall and corner guards.

SERVICES

The size of mailroom and services provided by the post office vary with size and occupancy of the building. The U.S. Postal Service recognizes for its staffing and servicing two types of mailrooms for small, medium, and large office buildings.

1. LOCKBOX SERVICE: Buildings up to 200,000 sq ft of leasable space or with a maximum of 75 tenants. Provide one receptacle for each tenant and rear loading for 11 or more tenants. A building directory must be maintained.

   The vertical distance from floor to tenant locks on top tier of receptacles is 66 in. maximum; to bottom lowest tier 10 in. minimum, preferably 30 in. Install only at one entrance. Allow a minimum of 3 ft of clear working space behind units. Provide

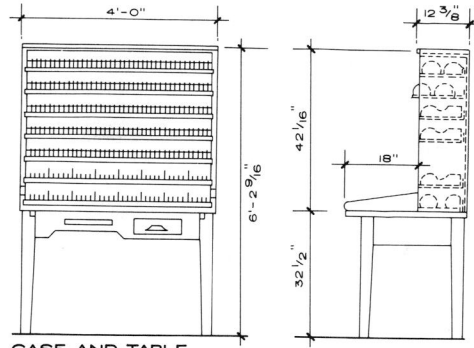

CASE AND TABLE

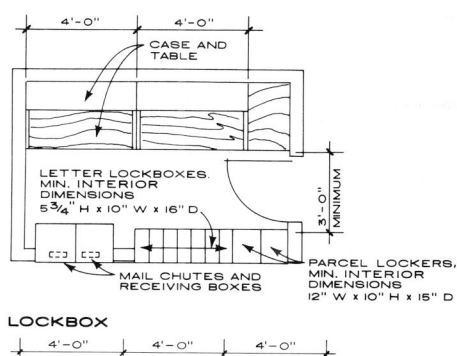

LOCKBOX

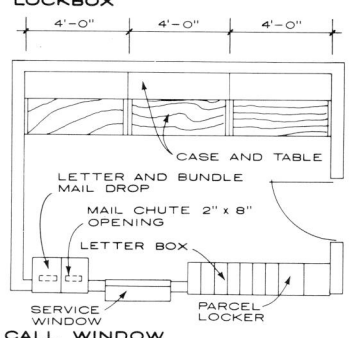

CALL WINDOW

80 sq ft of working space for each additional carrier. Allow 1 sq ft of working space for every 1000 sq ft of leasable office space. Specifications for construction of mail receptacles shall be identical to those for Type II, horizontal apartment house receptacles as prescribed in USPS Publication 17, except that the minimum inside dimensions shall be 5¾ in. high, 10½ in. wide, and 16 in. deep.

2. CALL WINDOW SERVICE: Buildings with 75 or more tenants, one carrier for each 100,000 sq ft of leasable office space up to 500,000 sq ft, plus one carrier for each additional 200,000 sq ft of office building. Allow 1.5 sq ft for every 1000 sq ft of leasable space; the minimum call window service space is 100 sq ft.

POSTAL SERVICES

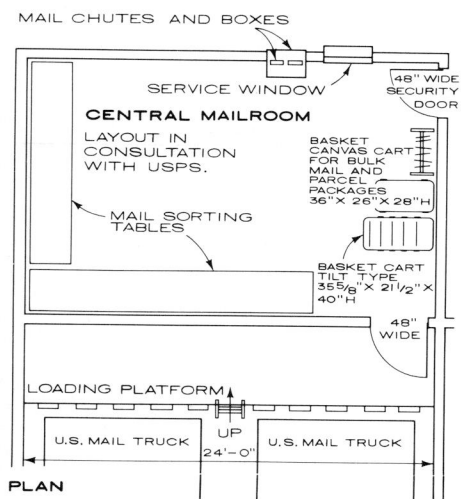

PLAN

CENTRAL MAILROOM

CENTRAL MAILROOM

Buildings larger than 200,000 sq ft and up to 2,000,000 sq ft of leasable space can be served on each floor from a central mailroom using a containerized mechanical system. Allow a minimum of 400 sq ft for first 50 tenants plus 135 sq ft for each additional 50 tenants, or 2 sq ft for each 1000 sq ft of leasable space.

Service mailrooms shall be provided on each multitenant floor, unless containers are conveyed mechanically to tenant offices. Allow 5 x 7 ft minimum floor area for service mailroom. Mechanical systems accommodating 8 to 19 containers may require a minimum area of 7 x 8 ft. Minimum inside container dimensions are 12 x 16 x 6 in.

Existing mechanical systems often are disbanded. U.S. Postal Service recommends a central mailroom with rear-loading lock boxes and parcel lockers. For high mail and parcel volumes, nutting trucks and BMC containers as shown may be used for transport to mailroom floor (48 in. wide security doors required).

NOTES

1. Centralized mail delivery: Neighborhood Delivery & Collection Box Units (NDCBU) are popular in home and office complex developments. USPS can help plan centralized mail delivery (Pub. 265, August 1983).

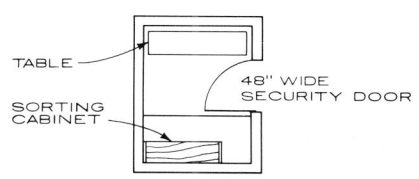

SERVICE MAILROOM PLAN

2. USPS lobby layouts in postal buildings designate specific vending machine areas, customer service lobby, and box lobby with parcel lockers having a lock system similar to public lockers, and customer leased box lockers. See USPS guidelines, "New Directions in Lobby Design Practices." Some equipment and features are applicable to office buildings.

3. Rehabilitating existing buildings: the form of mail handling should not change, i.e., an original central mailroom installation may not be changed to mail delivery on each floor. Same applies to mail chute installations. Relocation may be necessary, but discontinuation or introduction of a new installation needs approval. In all cases, early consultation with the local Postmaster should be initiated.

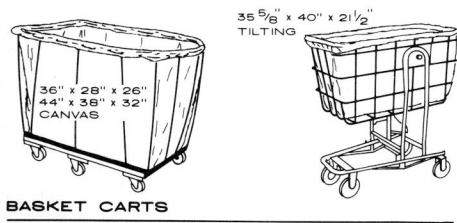

BASKET CARTS

EQUIPMENT

MAIL CHUTES AND RECEIVING BOXES

1. Chutes: Used in buildings of at least four stories for first class mail only. The chute cross section must be approximately 2 x 8 in. and extend in a continuously vertical line from beginning point to receiving box or mailroom. Chute interior must be accessible its entire length. Chutes in pairs have a divider and dual receiving boxes.

MAIL CHUTES AND RECEIVING BOXES

2. Receiving boxes: Must be placed near the building's main entrance or near the loading, unloading area for USPS mail collection. Using the shortest line, receiving boxes may not be placed more than 100 ft from the entrance used by the collection person. Locations require local Postmaster approval. Receiving boxes must be placed on the same floor the collection person uses to enter the building. Doors must operate freely. Door openings must be at least 12 x 20 in. and not more than 18 x 30 in.

3. Auxiliary boxes: Located near receiving box when receiving box is too small to accommodate first class mail volume. Openings must be large enough to receive tied bundles of first class mail.

4. Bundle drops: Receiving boxes must have bundle drops with an opening for a bundle at least 6½ in. wide by 11½ in. long and 4 in. high. To prevent removal of mail through it, the deposit opening must be fully protected by inside baffle plates. Inlet doors must be inscribed "Letters" and "Letter Mail Tied in Bundles." Bottom of the opening must be at least 61 in. above floor level.

Reference: USPS Publication 16, August 1989

NOTES

1. All installations must comply with USPS requirements and are subject to inspection.
2. Floor penetrations may need firestopping methods.
3. USPS provides listing of approved manufacturers.

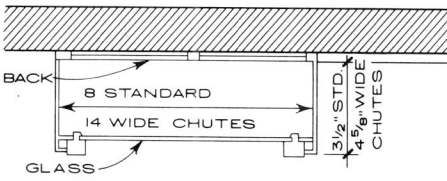

MAIL CHUTE—PLAN

NOTES

1. May be recessed.
2. Use wide chutes for 8 x 10 in. envelopes.
3. Tempered glass at least 3/16 in. thick, or heavy, shatterproof plate glass at least ¾ in. thick, or transparent, fire-resistant plastic material of equal or greater strength than 3/16 in. tempered glass.

Walter Hart Associates, AIA; White Plains, New York

GENERAL NOTES

Coatrooms should be adjacent to and have line-of-sight connections with lobby or with circulation path between building entry and destination (auditorium, gallery, etc). Care should be taken to provide ample space for orderly queuing out of the mainstream of circulation. This is of particular importance in theaters, concert halls, and similar facilities where check in and out of massive numbers of people occurs in a very brief period of time. In galleries, museums, and restaurants, the flow of people is more even, resulting in a diminished need for queuing space and a smaller staffing requirement for the checkroom itself.

For general planning purposes, allow between 1.1 and 1.5 in. of rack space per garment, depending on climate. Hats, umbrellas, and packages should be stored with the garment rather than segregating items by type. Most racks contain from one to three overhead shelves for this purpose. For ease of access, these shelves should not extend above 6 ft 8 in.

For small to medium size facilities, conventional coatrooms are adequate. In large facilities where hundreds of garments will be accommodated, the designer should consider using automated conveyors. These systems save a great deal of time by eliminating the need to access aisles searching for a garment. In addition, the aisles are eliminated, resulting in a more efficient use of space. These systems function as follows:

The coatroom attendant hangs incoming garments on a conveyor in prenumbered slots that correspond to the claim check number. Hats and other items are placed in bins over the patron's garments. When departing patrons present their claim check, the attendant keys in the number on a control panel, and the conveyor revolves until it automatically stops at the correct number.

COATROOM AREA REQUIREMENTS

CAPACITY	AREA, CONVENTIONAL	AREA, AUTOMATED
100	75	N.A.
200	140	100
300	200	130
400	240	150
500	310	180
1000	575	320
1500	760	460
2000	1025	600

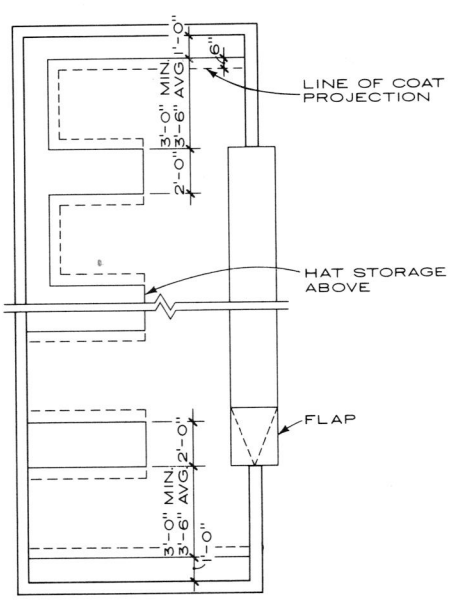

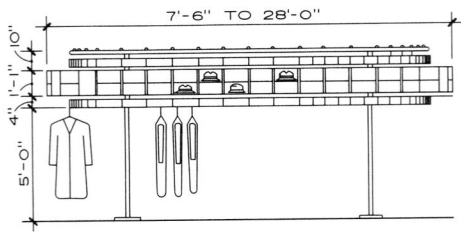

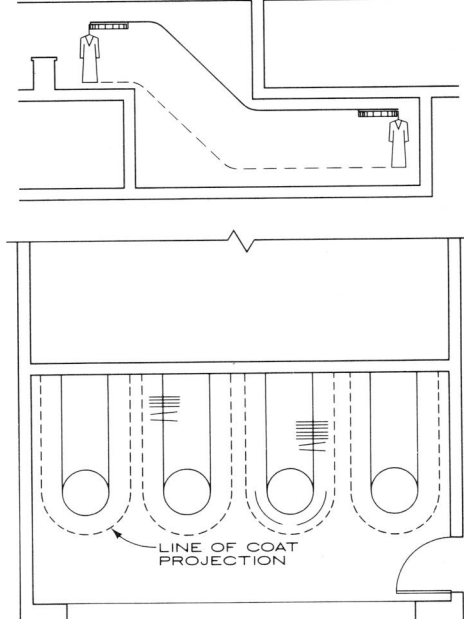

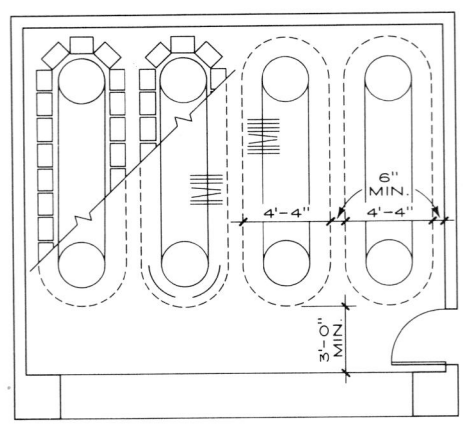

CONVENTIONAL COATROOM

AUTOMATED COATROOMS

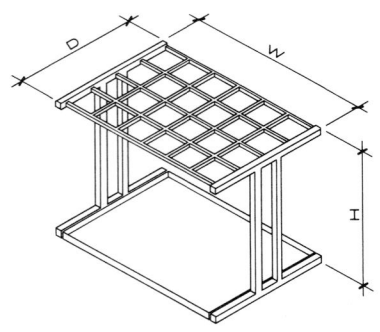

UMBRELLAS	HEIGHT	DEPTH	WIDTH
12	18″	12″	10″
18	18″	9″	18″
24	18″	12″	18″

UMBRELLA RACK

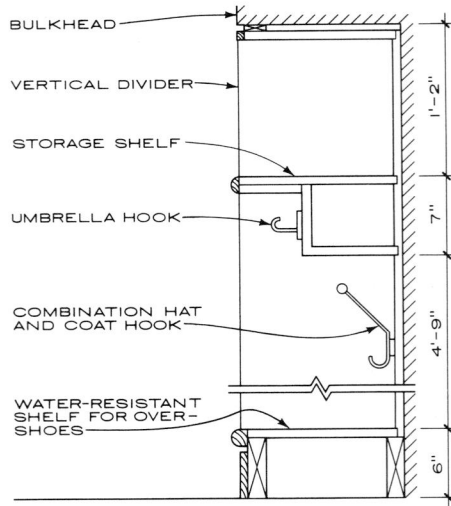

"CUSTOM" COATROOM RACK

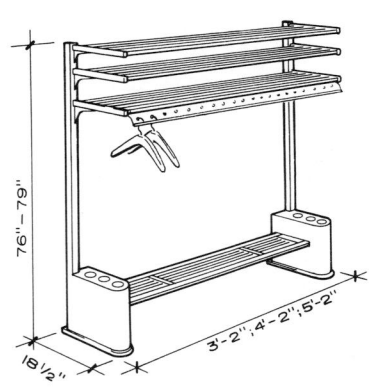

COMBINATION COAT, HAT, UMBRELLA, OVERSHOE RACK

Above model may be mounted back-to-back. Portable models are mounted on casters. Models available with or without umbrella and overshoe racks, and some are collapsible.

COATROOM EQUIPMENT

Blythe + Nazdin Architects, Ltd.; Bethesda, Maryland

GENERAL

Round tables are usually recommended for seating four or more persons.

Dimension "A" depends on the perimeter length necessary per seat (1 ft 10 in. to 2 ft 0 in. per person). For cocktails, 1 ft 6 in. is sufficient.

Tables 3 ft 0 in. and wider will seat at least one person at each end.

Smaller sizes are satisfactory for drink service; larger sizes for food. Tables with center bases accommodate coupled table arrangements better than four-legged tables.

The type and style of service affect tables and arrangements. Consider the use of service carts, high chairs, as well as accessibility for the disabled. See the Americans with Disabilities Act (ADA) requirements below.

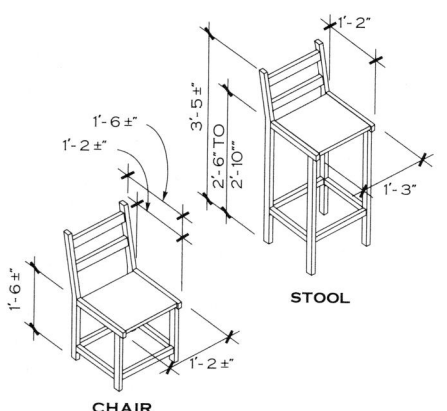

STOOL

CHAIR

TYPICAL DIMENSIONS

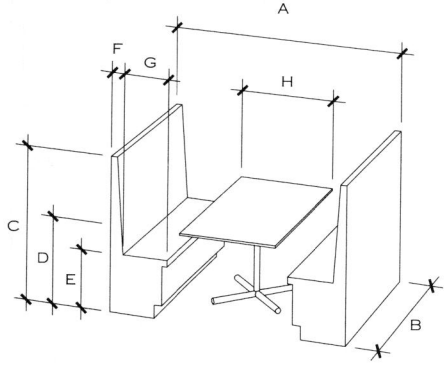

BOOTH DIMENSIONS

A = Seat back to seat back: 5′ - 6″ to 6′ - 2″
B = One person per side: 2′ - 0″ to 2′ - 6″
    Two persons per side: 3′ - 6″ to 4′ - 6″
    Three persons per side: 5′ - 0″ to 6′ - 2″
C = 3′ - 0″ to 4′ - 0″
D = 2′ - 6″
E = 1′ - 6″
F = 2″ to 4″
G = 1′ - 6″±
H = 2′ - 0″ to 2′ - 6″

NOTES

1. Local building codes may determine actual booth sizes. Tables are often 2 in. shorter in length than seats and may have rounded ends. Circular booths have overall diameter of approximately 6 ft 4 in.

2. Eliminate one booth and replace with table to provide access for wheelchair.

BOOTHS

BAR DIMENSIONS

A = 8′ - 4″ to 11′ - 7″
B = 1′ - 6″ to 2′ - 0″
C = 2′ - 4″ to 3′ - 2″
D = 2′ - 6″ to 3′ - 0″
E = 2′ - 0″ to 2′ - 6″
F = 6″ to 7″
G = 1′ - 10″ to 2′ - 2″
H = 2′ - 6″ to 2′ - 10″
I = 11″ to 1′ - 10″
J = 7″ to 9″
K = 6″ to 9″
L = 2′ - 6″
M = 3′ - 6″ to 3′ - 9″
N = 3′ - 0″ to 3′ - 6″
O = 5′ - 0″ to 5′ - 9″

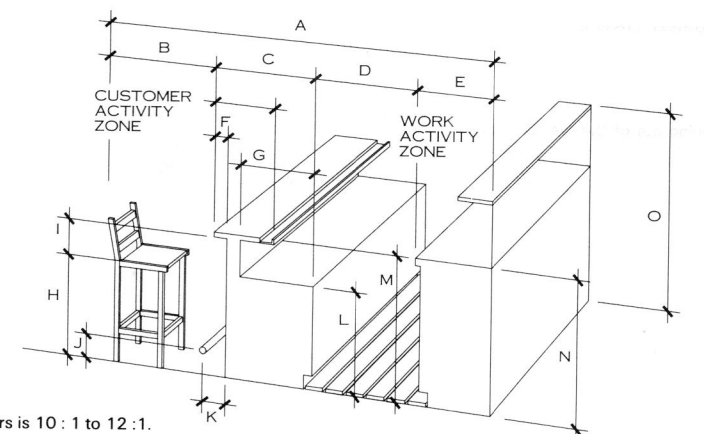

NOTE

Ratio of counter seating to servers is 10 : 1 to 12 :1.

LOW COUNTER DIMENSIONS

A = 4′ - 11″ to 5′ - 6″
B = 3′ - 1″ to 3′ - 3″
C = 1′ - 10″ to 2′ - 0″
D = 1′ - 7″ minimum
E = 1′ - 6″ to 2′ - 0″
F = 2′ - 4″ to 2′ - 8″
G = 2′ - 3″ minimum
H = 4″ to 8″
I = 5′ - 0″ minimum

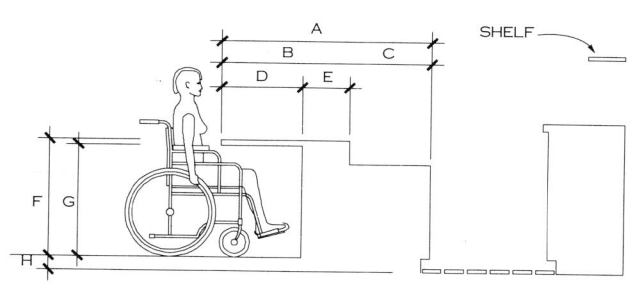

NOTE

A continental bar with low seating is one means of achieving accessibility. The bartender's area can be lowered or the seating area can be on a raised platform accessed by ramp.

BARS AND COUNTERS

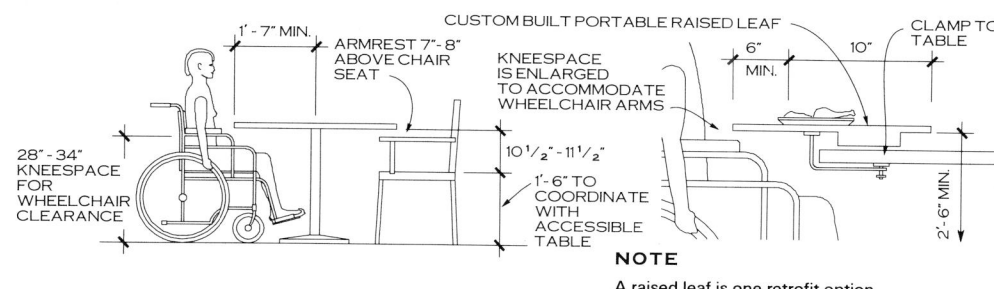

NOTE

A raised leaf is one retrofit option.

ACCESSIBLE FURNITURE

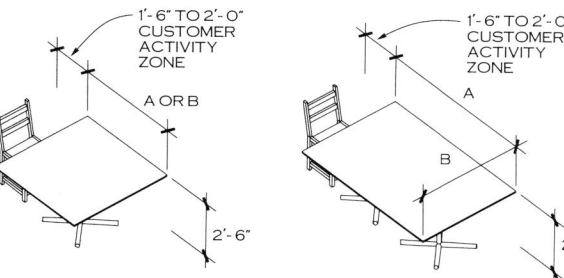

SQUARE TABLES

PERSONS	A OR B
2	2′ - 0″ to 2′ - 6″
4	3′ - 0″ to 3′ - 6″

RECTANGULAR TABLES

PERSONS	A	B
2 (on one side)	3′ - 6″ to 4′ - 0″	
6 (3 on each side)	5′ - 10″ to 7′ - 0″	2′ - 6″ to 3′ - 0″
8 (4 on each side)	7′ - 6″ to 9′ - 0″	

ROUND TABLES

PERSONS	A
4 - 5	3′ - 0″ to 3′ - 6″
6 - 7	3′ - 6″ to 4′ - 6″
7 - 8	4′ - 6″ to 5′ - 0″
8 - 10	5′ - 0″ to 6′ - 0″

TABLES

Janet B. Rankin, AIA; Rippeteau Architects; Washington, D.C.
Cini-Little International, Inc., Food Service Consultants; Washington, D.C.

CLEARANCES:

A =6" minimum (no passage)
B =1'-6" (limited passage)
C =1'-7"
D =2'-6"
E =3'-0"
F =3'-6"
G =4'-0"
H =4'-6"
I =6'-0"

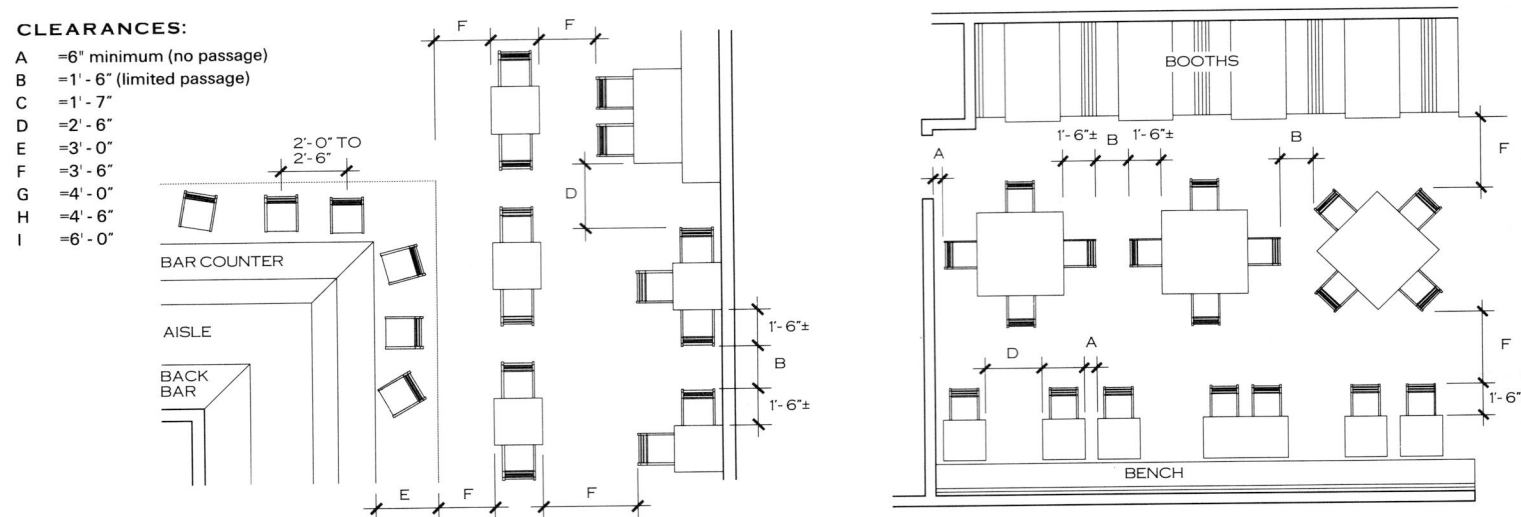

NOTE

All dimensions are minimum clearances. Seating layouts show general configurations and are not intended to depict any specific type of operation. Tables may be converted from square to round to generally enlarge seating capacity. Booth seating makes effective use of corner space.

A wheelchair accessible route, at least 36 in. wide, is required to connect the entrance, accessible fixed seating, and restrooms.

TYPICAL SEATING ARRANGEMENTS

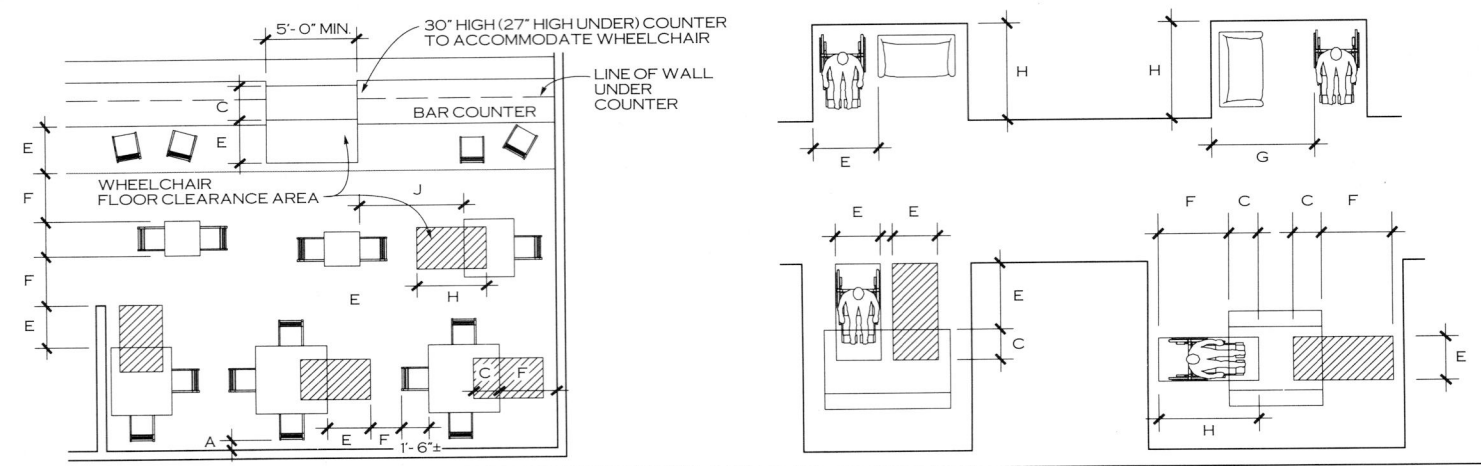

SEATING ARRANGEMENTS FOR PERSONS USING WHEELCHAIRS

GENERAL DESIGN CRITERIA
SERVICE AISLES

1. For square seating, allow 72 in. minimum between tables (30 in. aisle plus two chairs back to back).
2. For diagonal seating, allow 36 in. minimum between corners of tables.
3. For wall seating, allow 30 in. minimum between wall and seat back.
4. Allow a minimum of 30 in. for bus carts and service carts.

CUSTOMER AISLES

1. Refer to local codes for restrictions on requirements.
2. For wheelchair access, allow 36-44 in. aisle.
3. For wall seating, allow 30 in. minimum between walls and table.
4. Clear floor space must be provided for table access. Such clear floor space shall not overlap kneespace by more than 19 in.

TABLE PLACEMENT

1. Allow circulation space adjacent to doors and food service areas.
2. Restaurants should offer a variety of seating options.

ACCESSIBLE SEATING

1. If fixed or built-in seating areas are provided, make at least 5%, or a minimum of one fixed/built-in seating area, accessible. Review ADA requirements.
2. Accessible seating should be integrated within the dining area, and should accommodate both large and small groups.
3. Raised and sunken areas must be accessible. Mezzanines must also be accessible unless certain conditions are met (see ADAAG 5.4).

TABLE AND COUNTER CRITERIA

1. Tables average 29 in. high.
2. The tops of accessible tables and counters should be 28 in. to 34 in. high. A portable raised leaf may be provided to adapt lower tables.
3. If seating for people in wheelchairs is provided at tables or counters, kneespace at least 27 in. high, 30 in. wide, and 19 in. deep shall be provided.
4. Where food and drink are served at counters exceeding 34 in. in height, a portion of the main counter, 60 in. in length, should be made accessible, or accessible tables shall be located in the same area.
5. Corners and edges of table and countertops should be rounded for safety.

SEATING CRITERIA

1. Chair seat height is usually 18 in. Seat heights should be slightly higher at wheelchair accessible tables.
2. Seats should be a minimum of 16 in. deep and 16 in. wide.
3. Padding and cushions should be firm.
4. Seat backs should be slightly inclined.
5. Armrests should be provided to aid in rising.
6. Table or counter supports should not interfere with seat kneespace so the feet can be positioned for rising.

DINING SPACE AVERAGES

TYPE OF ROOM	SQUARE FEET PER PERSON
Banquet	10 - 12
Cafeteria	12 - 18
Tearoom	10 -16
Lunchroom/coffee shop	12 - 16
Dining room/restaurant	13 - 16
Specialty/formal dining	17 - 22

NOTE

Area figures represent the average minimum. Seating requirements may vary widely to suit individual operations.

Janet B. Rankin, AIA; Rippeteau Architects; Washington, D.C.
Cini-Little International, Inc., Food Service Consultants; Washington, D.C.

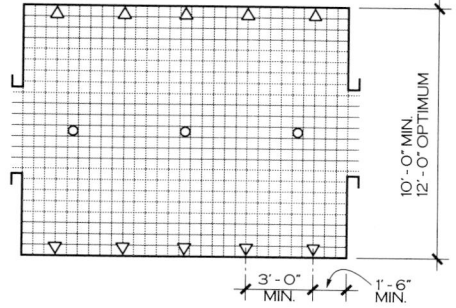

NOTE

Educational facilities with time constraints should have 10 shower heads for the first 30 persons and one shower head for every four additional persons. In recreational facilities one shower head for each 10 dressing lockers is a minimum. Temperature controls are necessary to keep water from exceeding 110° F. Both individual and master controls are needed for group showers.

GROUP SHOWERS

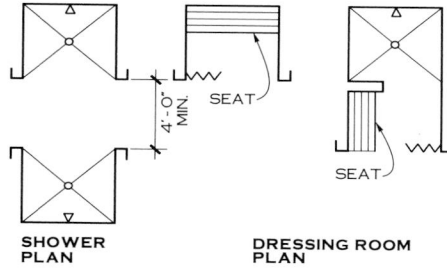

SHOWER PLAN   DRESSING ROOM PLAN

TYPICAL DIMENSIONS

	MINIMUM	OPTIMUM
Showers	3' - 0" x 3' - 6"	3' - 6" x 3' - 6"
Dressing Rooms	3' - 0" x 3' - 6"	3' - 6" x 4' - 0"

NOTE

Individual dressing rooms and showers can be combined in a variety of configurations to obtain 1:1, 2:1, 3:1, and 4:1 ratios.

INDIVIDUAL SHOWERS AND DRESSING ROOMS

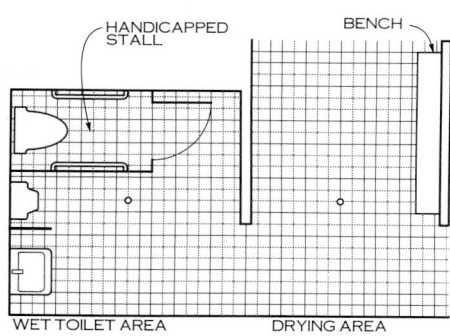

WET TOILET AREA   DRYING AREA

NOTE

The drying room should have about the same area as the shower room. Provision for drainage should be made. Heavy duty towel rails, approximately 4 ft from the floor, are recommended. A foot drying ledge, 18 in. high and 8 in. wide as shown in the drawing, is desirable. An adjacent wet toilet is suggested. Avoid curbs between drying room and adjacent space. Size of towel service area (which can be used for distributing uniforms) varies. Size of area varies with material to be stored; 200 sq ft is usually sufficient.

DRYING ROOM AND WET TOILET

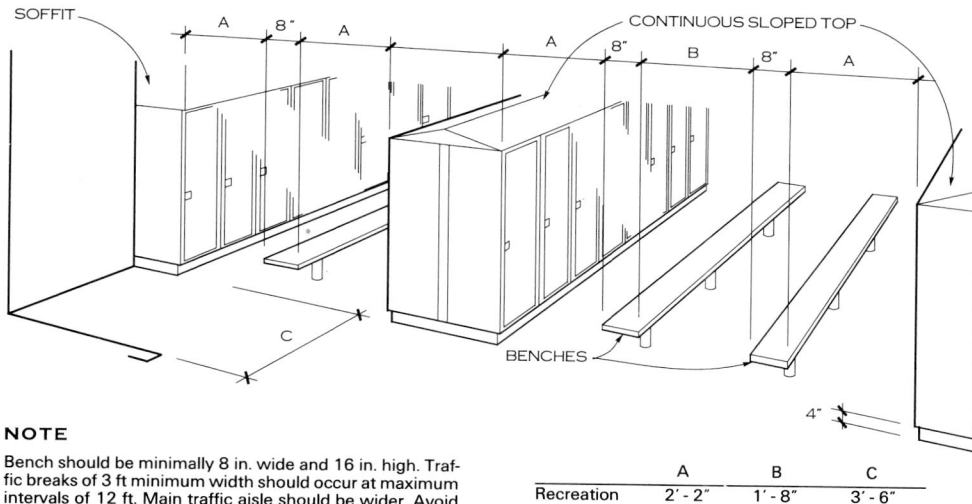

BENCHES

NOTE

Bench should be minimally 8 in. wide and 16 in. high. Traffic breaks of 3 ft minimum width should occur at maximum intervals of 12 ft. Main traffic aisle should be wider. Avoid lockers that meet at 90° corner.

	A	B	C
Recreation	2' - 2"	1' - 8"	3' - 6"
School	2' - 6"	2' - 6"	4' - 0"

LOCKER ROOM

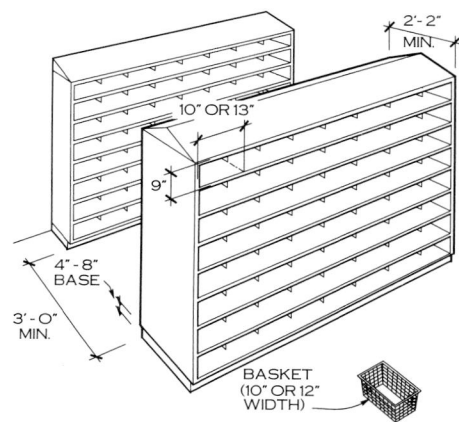

BASKET (10" OR 12" WIDTH)

Basket racks vary from 7 to 10 tiers in height. Wide baskets require 1 ft shelf space, small baskets 10 in. shelf space; both fit 1 ft to 1½ ft deep shelf. Back-to-back shelving is 2 ft 3 in. wide. Height is 9¼ in.

BASKET ROOM AND BASKET RACK

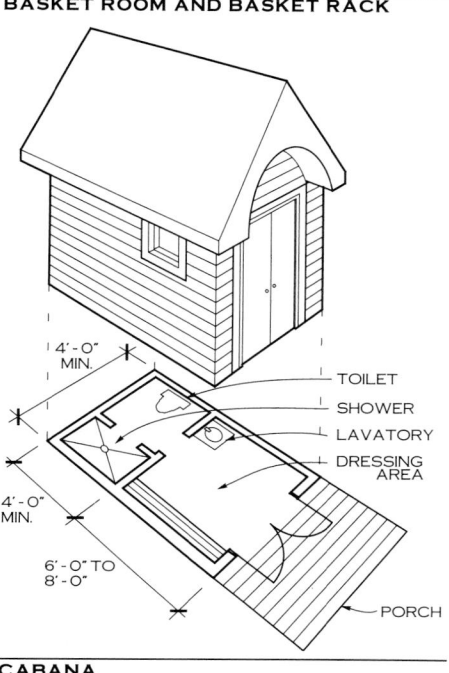

CABANA

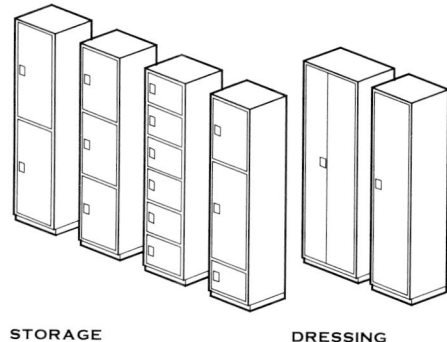

STORAGE   DRESSING

STANDARD SIZES (IN.)

Width	9	12	15	18
Depth	12	15	18	
Height	60	72 (overall)		

NOTE

For schools, standard storage locker is 9 in. or 12 in. x 12 in. x 12 in. to 24 in. Standard dressing lockers are 12 in. x 12 in. x 60 in. or 72 in. Number of dressing lockers should be equal to the peak period load plus 10 to 15% for expansion.

LOCKER TYPES

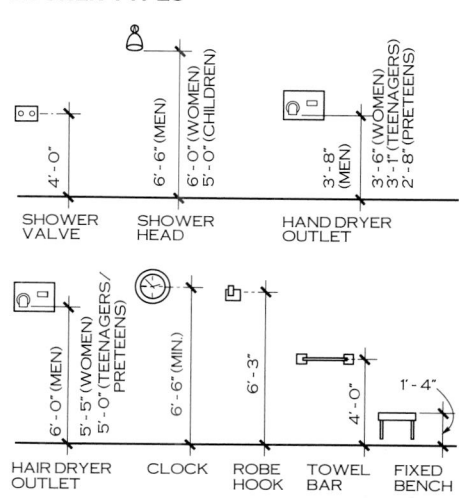

RECOMMENDED MOUNTING HEIGHTS

Richard J. Vitullo, AIA;Oak Leaf Studio; Crownsville, Maryland
BFS Architectural Consulting and Interior Design, YMCA of the USA; Chicago, Illinois

LOCKER ROOM FACILITIES CHECKLIST

1. Fixed benches 16 in. high.
2. Lockers on raised base.
3. Locker numbering system.
4. Hair dryers—one per 20 lockers.
5. Mirrors at lavatory.
6. Makeup mirror and shelf.
7. Drinking fountain (height as required).
8. Bulletin board.
9. Dressing booths, if required.
10. Full - length mirror.
11. Clock.
12. Door signs.
13. Sound system speaker, if required.
14. Lighting at mirrors for grooming.
15. Lighting located over aisles and passages.
16. Adequate ventilation for storage lockers.
17. Windows located with regard to height and arrangement of lockers.
18. Visual supervision from adjacent office.

GENERAL NOTES

1. The most widely used arrangement of lockers is the bay system, with a minimum 4 ft circulation aisle at each end of the bays. Ordinarily, the maximum number of lockers in a bay is 16. Locate dry (shoe) traffic at one end of the bays and wet (barefoot) traffic at the other end. For long bays with a single bench, make 3 ft breaks at 15 ft intervals.

2. Supervision of school lockers is the easiest if they are located in single banks along the two walls, providing one or more bays that run the length of the room.

3. The number of lockers in a locker room depends on the anticipated number of members and/or size of classes. For large numbers separate locker areas should be encouraged. In small buildings interconnecting doors provide flexibility and allow for the handling of peak loads.

4. Individual dressing and shower compartments and a shower stall for the handicapped may be required.

5. Basket storage, if included, generally is self-service. Maximum height is 8 tiers. A dehumidifying system should be provided to dry out basket contents overnight. Separate auxiliary locker rooms for teams, part-time instructors, faculty, or volunteer leaders may be required. A small room for the coach's use may be desirable.

6. The shower room should be directly accessible to the drying room and locker room that it serves. When a shower room is designed to serve a swimming pool, the room should be located so that all must pass through showers before reaching the pool deck.

7. Separate wet and dry toilet areas are recommended. Wet toilets should be easily accessible from the shower room. When designed for use with a swimming pool, wet toilets should be located so that users must pass through the shower room after use of toilets.

8. Locker room entrance and exit doors should have vision barriers.

9. All facilities should be barrier-free.

10. Floors should be of impervious material, such as ceramic or quarry tile, with a Carborundum impregnated surface, and should slope toward the drains. Concrete floors (nonslip surface), if used, should be treated with a hardener to avoid the penetration of odors and moisture.

11. Walls should be of materials resistant to moisture and should have surfaces that are easily cleaned. All exterior corners in the locker rooms should be rounded.

12. Heavy duty, moisture resistant doors at locker room entrances and exits should be of sufficient size to handle the traffic flow and form natural vision barriers. Entrance/exit doors for the lockers should be equipped with corrosion resistant hardware.

13. Ceilings in shower areas should be of ceramic tile or other material impervious to moisture. Locker room ceilings should be acoustically treated with a material impervious to moisture and breakage. Floor drains should be kept out of the line of traffic, where possible.

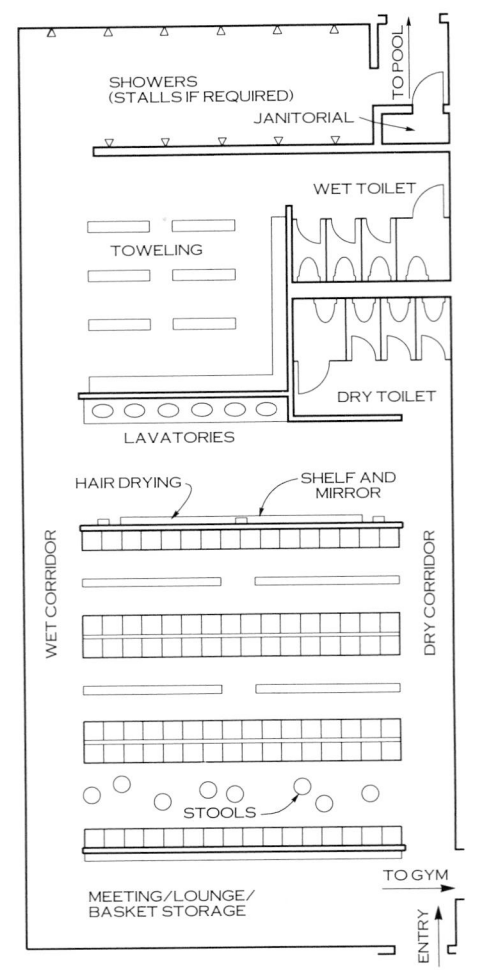

GYMNASIUM AND POOL LOCKER ROOM

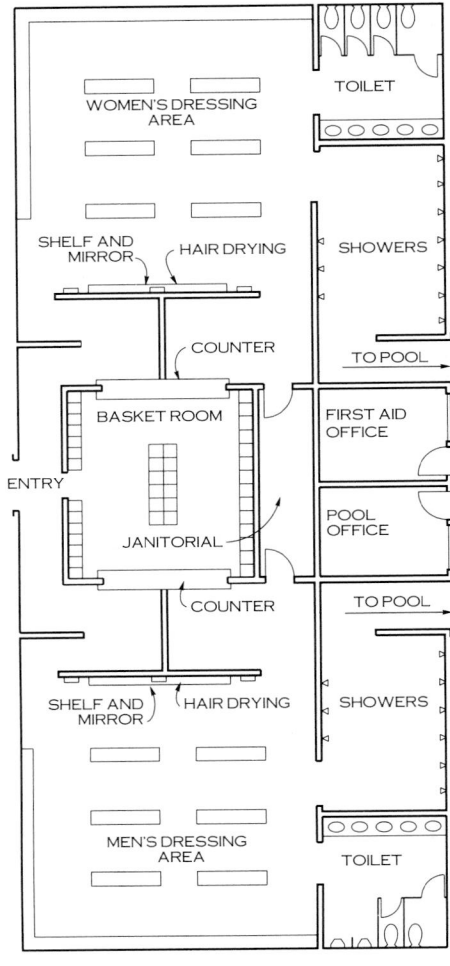

POOL LOCKER ROOM

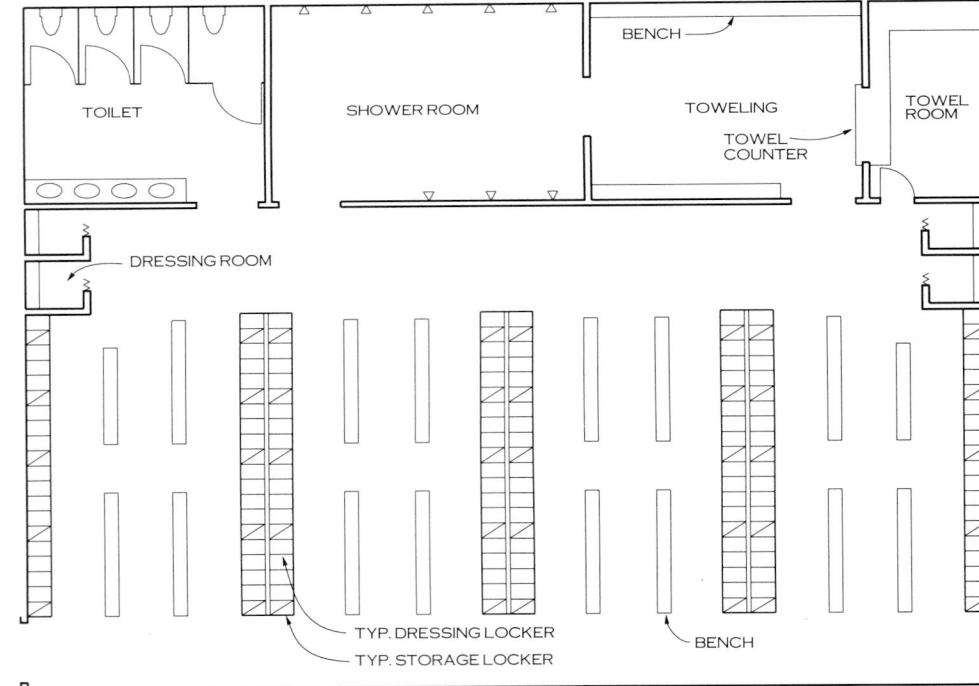

GYMNASIUM LOCKER ROOM

BFS Architectural Consulting and Interior Design, YMCA of the USA; Chicago, Illinois

LOCATION WITHIN THE BUILDING

The courtroom is often the major space in the building and should be centrally located, with primary access to its support spaces (e.g., judge's chamber, jury rooms, witness rooms, court officer's spaces), the public lobby, and toilet facilities.

REQUIRED SPACES

Courtrooms require 3 main areas or zones

1. The public space
2. The courtroom, including the jury box
3. The judge's bench and witness stand

The public space is open to the public for observation of the trial proceedings. Defendants and attorneys also use this space as a waiting area before their trial. The public space should have access to the public corridor and good access to public toilet facilities. It is usually divided from the courtroom space by a low divider rail with swinging gates.

The courtroom space is a restricted access space. Access to this space should be from private corridors, jury rooms, court officer offices, or the gates to the public space. This space contains the majority of courtroom activity. The jury, attorneys, defendants, and sometimes the press occupy this space. The jury box, part of the courtroom space, usually has a raised floor to provide better visibility of the trial proceedings. The jury box should have direct access to the jury room(s) or to a private corridor leading to the jury room(s). The courtroom space should not be accessible from any public corridor.

The judge's bench and witness stand have the most restricted access. They are usually divided from the courtroom space by a divider rail. The floor of the judge's bench is usually raised above the raised floor level of the jury box and witness stand to provide the judge(s) the most prominent position in the courtroom space. The judge's bench has direct access to the judge's chamber or to a private corridor leading to the judge's chamber. The witness stand is located adjacent to the judge's bench and is accessible only from the courtroom space. The witness stand has a raised floor, usually at the same level as the jury box.

SPACE RELATIONSHIPS

The jury should have direct access to the jury room without crossing the courtroom or any public space. A separate entrance to the jury room should be provided from the building corridor. Private toilet facilities should be provided, with direct access to the jury room. The judge should have direct access to the courtroom from his office. The size of the courtroom and its support spaces varies considerably, depending on the volume of court proceedings. For example, in a small municipal or magistrate's courtroom, 50 seats in the public space and 6 seats for jury members are adequate, whereas in a federal district court or state circuit court, 80–100 seats should be provided for the public, 12–14 for jury members (includes 2 alternates), 3 for judges, 1 for clerk of court, and 1 for court reporter. Seating for the press reporters should be provided in or near the courtroom space. All areas must be accessible to persons with disabilities.

CONSTRUCTION

The courtroom does not require natural lighting. A lighting level of 50 fc at the attorneys' table and judge's bench and a lighting level of approximately 30 fc in the public space should be adequate. All perimeter walls should be insulated to reduce sound transmission (STC 47 minimum). Resilient floor covering should be used in the public space and carpet may be used in the courtroom itself.

AREA REQUIREMENTS FOR SUPPORT SPACES

The jury room should be approximately 200 sq ft for municipal court and 350 sq ft for federal district court. Multiple jury rooms are often required for busy court facilities. A judge's chamber should be 150–350 sq ft. If pretrial hearings are held in the judge's chamber, the area should be increased to approximately 750 sq ft. A clerk of court's office should be 150–350 sq ft.

T. John Gilmore, AIA; O'Cain Forrester Gilmore Architects; Spartanburg, South Carolina

TYPES OF COURTS

Municipal or magistrate's courtrooms are usually small courtrooms located in City Hall or other municipal buildings. Municipal courts handle traffic and minor criminal cases. Magistrate's courts handle small civil and minor criminal cases.

State circuit courtrooms are usually large courtrooms located in the county courthouse of each county. State circuit courts handle all state trial proceedings, both civil and criminal.

Federal district courtrooms are usually large courtrooms located in federal governmental buildings serving each federal judicial district. Federal district courts handle all federal trial proceedings, both civil and criminal.

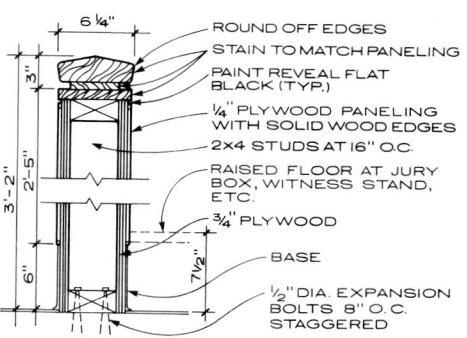

RAIL DIVIDER

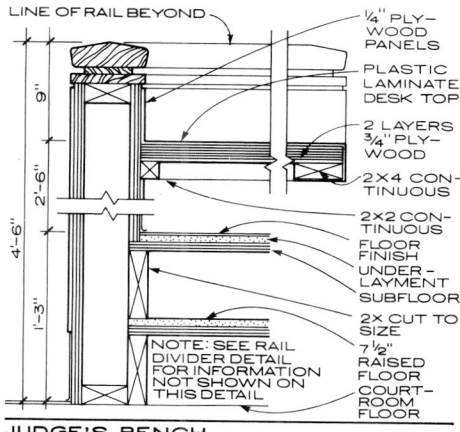

JUDGE'S BENCH

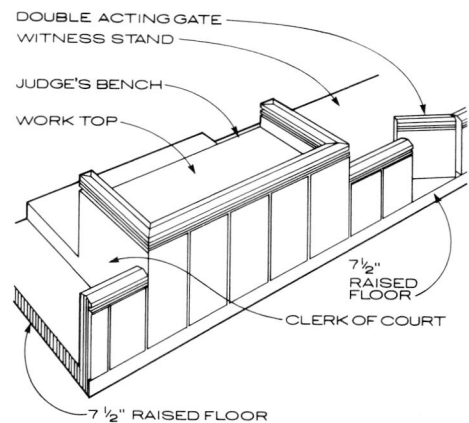

VIEW OF JUDGE'S BENCH

FLOOR PLAN—MUNICIPAL COURTROOM

GENERAL ACUTE CARE

Patient rooms must be accessible, easily maintained, and spacious enough to contain high-tech life support and monitoring equipment. Entry doors should be a minimum of 48 in. wide. Wider openings are sometimes required to accommodate large equipment and surgical teams during emergency situations. A clear area of 48 in. should be maintained at the foot of patient beds. Equip patient rooms with basic amenities such as a patient chair, visitor chair, television set (VCR optional), wardrobe for full-length garments and luggage, drawers for clothing and personal items, and a countertop for flowers and cards. Patient rooms include toilet facilities, though central bathing areas may be provided in lieu of individual showers. Doors to accessible toilet rooms must provide a clear opening of 32 in. minimum. If doors swing in, equip them with hardware that permits emergency access. Universal precautions require a lavatory in, or near the entrance to, each patient room and a place to store gloves, masks, and gowns. Space for electronic equipment, such as a patient data terminal and printer, may be required. Semiprivate patient rooms should contain cubicle curtains for visual privacy.

INTENSIVE CARE

Patients in an intensive care unit are under continuous observation. Each room should be visible from the nurse station or a staffed corridor workstation. Each unit must contain equipment for continuous monitoring. Provide a nurse call at each bed for summoning assistance. Beds should be within view of an exterior window, preferably an operable window. Provide bedside space for visitors and a curtain for visual privacy. Doors should be a minimum of 48 in. wide. Sliding doors may be used for access to rooms or cubicles within a suite. Provide at least one private room or cubicle in each ICU for patients requiring isolation and/ or separation. Toilet units can be provided in each bed area, along with a sink, countertop for preparing medications, and universal precautions storage. IV tracks and exam lights are typically placed above each bed. Because of the acuity of illness of these patients, rolling life-support equipment often occupies space at the side and foot of the bed. Maintain a minimum of 48 in. on three sides of each bed. Utility columns allow 360 degree access around the patient.

FINISHES AND HEADWALLS

Finishes in patient rooms should be durable and easy to maintain: vinyl flooring, vinyl wall coverings, or painted gypsum board partitions, etc. are typically used. Epoxy paint is sometimes used at wet or medication preparation areas. Some hospitals contain less "institutional" patient rooms with carpeted floors and other homelike finishes. Consult local codes for restrictions on finishes in patient rooms.

Depending on the room type, bed headwalls may include a nurse call button, reading light, room light switches, television controls, electrical outlets, central monitoring capabilities, suction, vacuum, and various medical gas outlets. Headwalls are available as prefabricated units or can be built into the partition. Wall thicknesses may vary depending on the type of equipment used.

Consult the Americans with Disabilities Act (ADA) for specific accessibility guidelines.

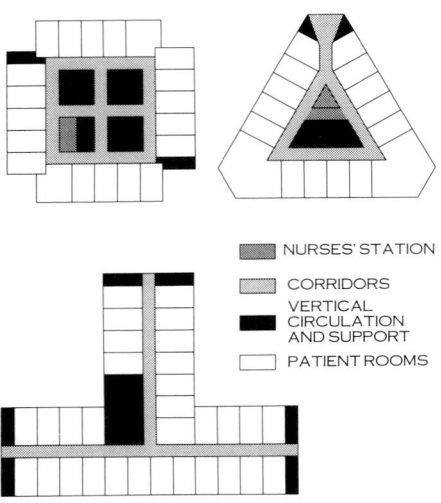

▨	NURSES' STATION
▩	CORRIDORS
■	VERTICAL CIRCULATION AND SUPPORT
☐	PATIENT ROOMS

TYPICAL UNIT CONFIGURATION

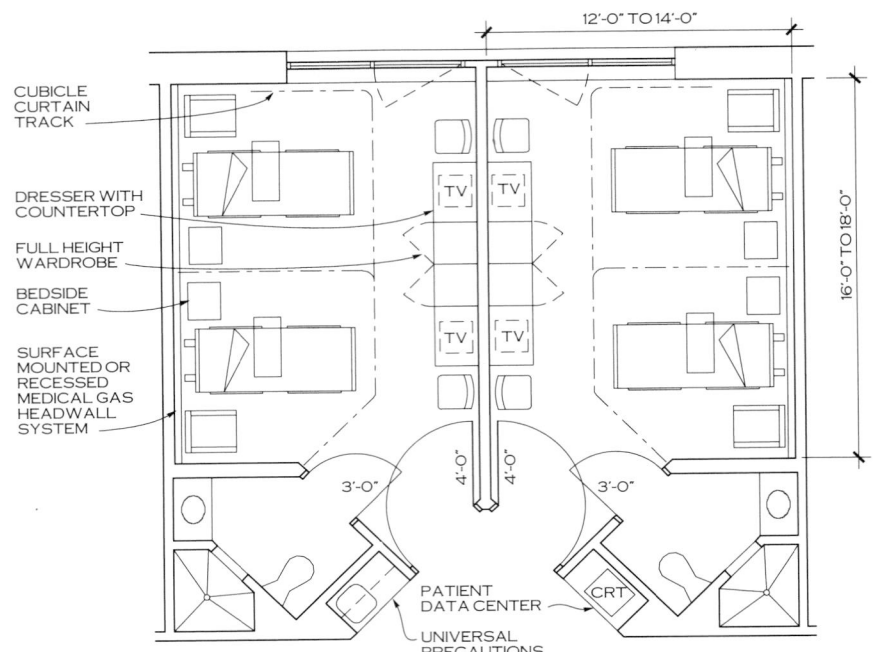

SEMIPRIVATE PATIENT ROOM

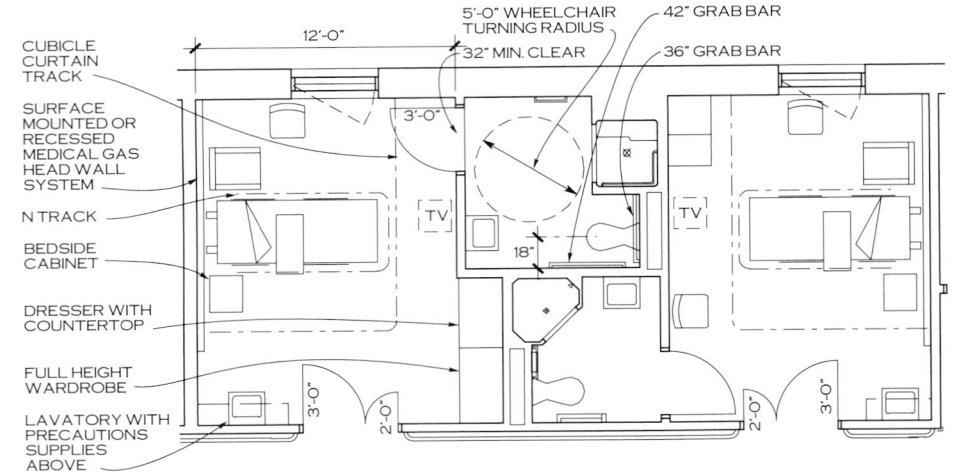

PRIVATE PATIENT ROOM

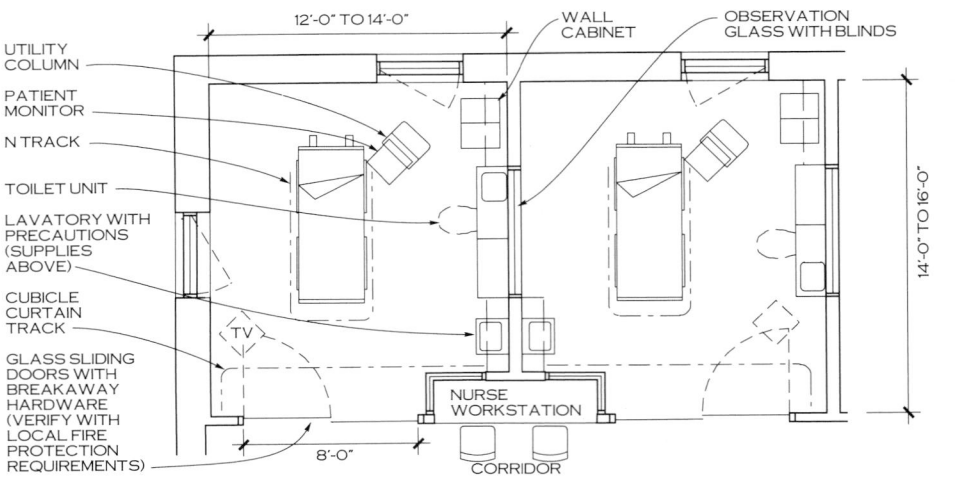

INTENSIVE CARE UNIT PATIENT ROOM

Timothy J. Cowan; Burt Hill Kosar Rittelmann Associates; Pittsburgh, Pennsylvania

NONRESIDENTIAL ROOM PLANNING

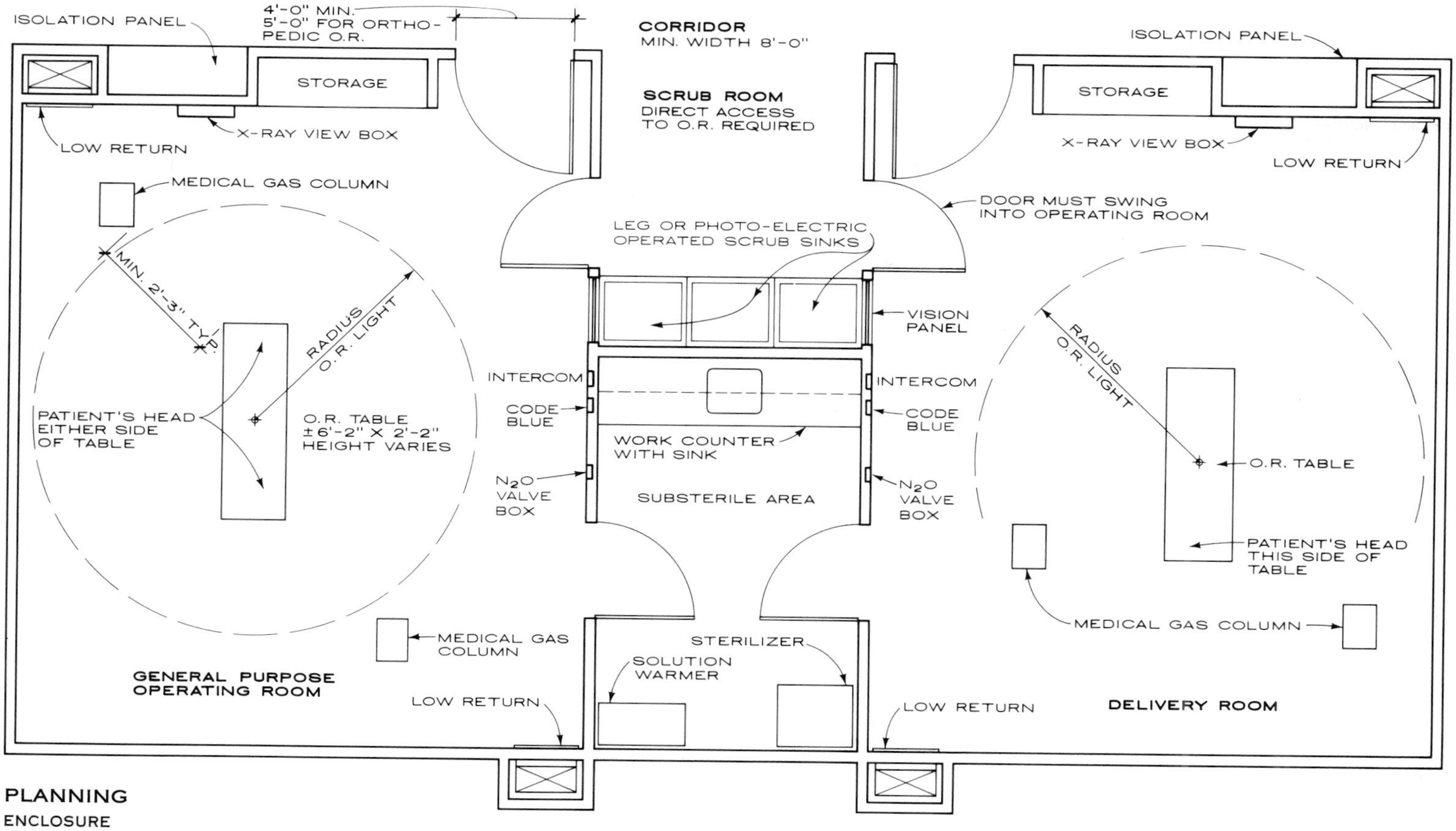

ISOLATION PANEL

4'-0" MIN.
5'-0" FOR ORTHO-
PEDIC O.R.

STORAGE

LOW RETURN

X-RAY VIEW BOX

MEDICAL GAS COLUMN

MIN. 2'-3" TYP.

RADIUS O.R. LIGHT

PATIENT'S HEAD
EITHER SIDE
OF TABLE

O.R. TABLE
±6'-2" X 2'-2"
HEIGHT VARIES

GENERAL PURPOSE
OPERATING ROOM

MEDICAL GAS
COLUMN

LOW RETURN

CORRIDOR
MIN. WIDTH 8'-0"

SCRUB ROOM
DIRECT ACCESS
TO O.R. REQUIRED

LEG OR PHOTO-ELECTRIC
OPERATED SCRUB SINKS

VISION
PANEL

INTERCOM

CODE
BLUE

WORK COUNTER
WITH SINK

N₂O
VALVE
BOX

SUBSTERILE AREA

STERILIZER
SOLUTION
WARMER

LOW RETURN

ISOLATION PANEL

STORAGE

X-RAY VIEW BOX

LOW RETURN

DOOR MUST SWING
INTO OPERATING ROOM

INTERCOM

CODE
BLUE

N₂O
VALVE
BOX

RADIUS O.R. LIGHT

O.R. TABLE

PATIENT'S HEAD
THIS SIDE OF
TABLE

MEDICAL GAS COLUMN

LOW RETURN

DELIVERY ROOM

PLANNING

ENCLOSURE

General purpose operating rooms must be extremely flexible due to widely varying spatial requirements of surgical procedures and personal preferences of the surgical staff. Public health codes limit the minimum size of these operating rooms to 360 sq ft, exclusive of casework. Certain procedures can require significantly more space. Operating rooms should be roughly square in plan and free of columns, with the operating room table located in the approximate center of the room to allow for maximum flexibility in positioning of equipment and personnel. Delivery rooms may be a minimum of 300 sq ft, exclusive of casework, for noncesarian births and 360 sq ft for cesarian. In delivery rooms, the operating room table is typically shifted from the center of the room to provide more space at the foot end. Endoscopy operatories may be as small as 250 sq ft, while orthopedic rooms should be at least 450 sq ft. Operating room finished ceiling height should be no lower than 9 ft 0 in., with an ample ceiling cavity for service space above.

FINISHES

The primary concern in surgical room finishes is cleanliness. Flooring materials should be seamless and have an integral base for ease of maintenance. Walls should be finished with a scrubbable epoxy base paint or with vitreous ceramic tile and bacteria-resistant grout. Ceiling finishes should be either plaster or gypsum board. Built-in casework, countertops, sinks, and similar items should be stainless steel.

In operating rooms where flammable gases will be used an antistatic flooring surface must be specified to avoid sparks that could cause an explosion. Finishes throughout the operating room should be of light, neutral colors to avoid any distortion in skin color.

ENVIRONMENTAL CONTROLS

Temperature and humidity in operating rooms must be strictly regulated to maintain a suitable environment for surgery. Positive air pressure must be maintained with respect to other areas to avoid infiltration of contaminants from outside the operating room. Air should be supplied at low velocities, with diffusers positioned to avoid formation of air eddies. Return registers should be near floor level, adjacent to medical gas columns, and at furthest points from each other for evacuation of an-

esthetic gases, dust, and microbes. In areas where flammable gases will be used, electrical outlets must be explosion-proof or be placed 5 ft 0 in. above finished floor; high-hazard fire protection systems should be installed.

EQUIPMENT

Medical gas columns typically contain a variety of gases, vacuum lines, and power used by the anesthesiologist during surgical procedures. They should be located adjacent to the anesthesiologist, who is positioned near the head of the patient. These columns are ceiling mounted and typically extend down to approximately 5 ft 6 in. above the floor. Retractable columns are also available. Depending on the anticipated use of the facility, a great variety of additional, highly specialized equipment will also be required.

Because of the extreme complexity of these areas, extensive participation by doctors, technicians, equipment manufacturers, and engineers is required throughout the design process.

TYPICAL SURGICAL SUITE

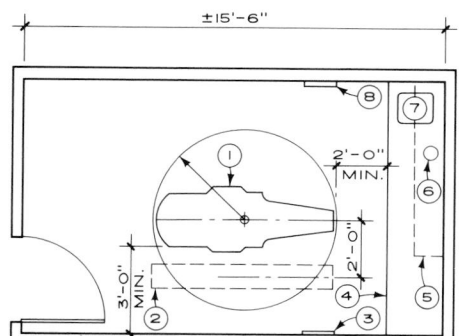

±15'-6"

2'-0" MIN.

3'-0" MIN.

DENTAL EQUIPMENT KEY

1. Dental chair
2. Dual operating room light track
3. Medical gas console
4. Counter (cabinets below)
5. Overhead storage
6. Cutout in counter for waste
7. Stainless steel sink with foot control
8. Film illuminators (2)

PLANNING

The dental chair base is equipped with hot and cold water, wet suction, compressed air, drainage if required for cuspidor, and power. In addition, a chair-mounted operating light may be used in lieu of a ceiling-mounted fixture.

The wall-mounted medical gas console typically includes nitrogen, oxygen, and nitrous oxide. If nitrous oxide gas is included, a scavenging system should be provided. Medical gases can be supplied by tanks on movable carts.

While room finishes are not as critical in dental operatories as in operating rooms, all surfaces should be washable.

DENTAL OPERATORIES

Deborah Hershowitz and Frank Giese; Rogers, Burgun, Shahine and Deschler Architects; New York, New York
Blythe + Nazdin Architects, Ltd.; Bethesda, Maryland

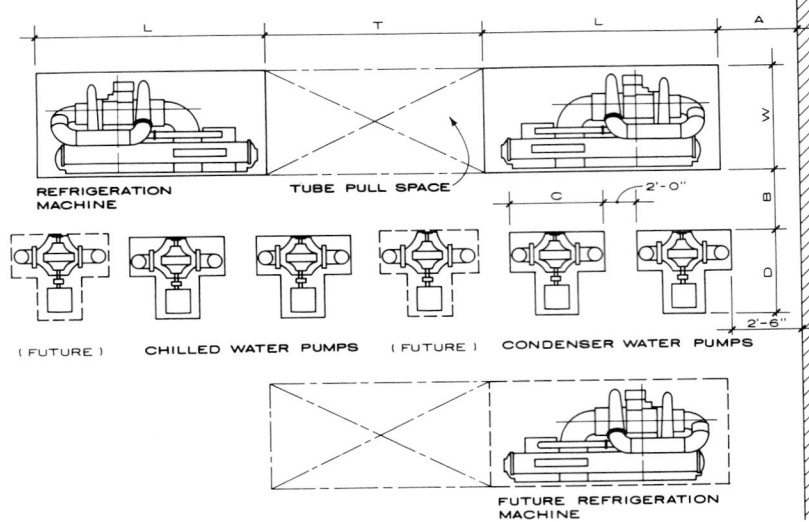

REFRIGERATION MACHINE — TUBE PULL SPACE

(FUTURE)   CHILLED WATER PUMPS   (FUTURE)   CONDENSER WATER PUMPS

FUTURE REFRIGERATION MACHINE

GENERAL

The capacity of each refrigeration machine is equal to 50% of the peak cooling load. Each water pump provides the flow requirement of one refrigeration machine. Therefore, one pair of condenser and chilled water pumps is needed for each machine.

The cooling tower may be located on the roof of the refrigeration equipment room or on the ground adjacent to the equipment room. When located on ground, the condenser water outlet(s) on the cooling tower must be not less than 5 ft above the equipment room floor elevation for proper functioning of condenser water pumps.

See ASHRAE Standard 15-1992, ''Safety Code for Mechanical Regrigeration,'' for required ventilation of chiller plant and monitoring of toxic refrigerants.

EXPANSION OF EQUIPMENT

For operational flexibility of a refrigeration plant, the size of the future refrigeration machine is generally planned to be the same as of the present machines. It may be economically advantageous to oversize some portions of the chilled and condenser waterpipes to handle the future flow rates.

Provision must also be made for expansion of the cooling tower capacity when the future refrigeration machine is installed.

REFRIGERATION EQUIPMENT ROOM SPACE REQUIREMENTS

EQUIPMENT (TONS)	L	W	HEIGHT	T	A	B	C	D	MINIMUM ROOM HEIGHT
RECIPROCATING MACHINES									
Up to 50	10'-0''	3'-0''	6'-0''	8'-6''	3'-6''	3'-6''	4'-0''	3'-0''	11'-0''
50 to 100	12'-0''	3'-0''	6'-0''	9'-0''	3'-6''	3'-6''	4'-0''	3'-6''	11'-0''
CENTRIFUGAL MACHINES									
120 to 225	17'-0''	6'-0''	7'-0''	16'-6''	3'-6''	3'-6''	4'-6''	4'-0''	11'-6''
225 to 350	17'-0''	6'-6''	7'-6''	17'-6''	3'-6''	3'-6''	5'-0''	5'-0''	11'-6''
350 to 550	17'-0''	8'-0''	8'-0''	16'-6''	3'-6''	3'-6''	6'-0''	5'-6''	12'-0''
550 to 750	17'-6''	9'-0''	10'-6''	17'-0''	3'-6''	3'-6''	6'-0''	5'-6''	14'-0''
750 to 1500	21'-0''	15'-0''	11'-0''	20'-0''	3'-6''	3'-6''	7'-6''	6'-0''	15'-0''
STEAM ABSORPTION MACHINES									
Up to 200	18'-6''	9'-6''	12'-0''	18'-0''	3'-6''	3'-6''	4'-6''	4'-0''	15'-0''
200 to 450	21'-6''	9'-6''	12'-0''	21'-0''	3'-6''	3'-6''	5'-0''	5'-0''	15'-0''
450 to 550	23'-6''	9'-6''	12'-0''	23'-0''	3'-6''	3'-6''	6'-0''	5'-6''	16'-0''
550 to 750	26'-0''	10'-6''	13'-0''	25'-6''	3'-6''	3'-6''	6'-0''	5'-6''	17'-6''
750 to 1000	30'-0''	11'-0''	14'-0''	29'-6''	3'-6''	3'-6''	7'-0''	6'-0''	17'-6''

Note: Direct-fired absorption machines are roughly the same size as steam absorption machines.

REFRIGERATION ROOM LAYOUT

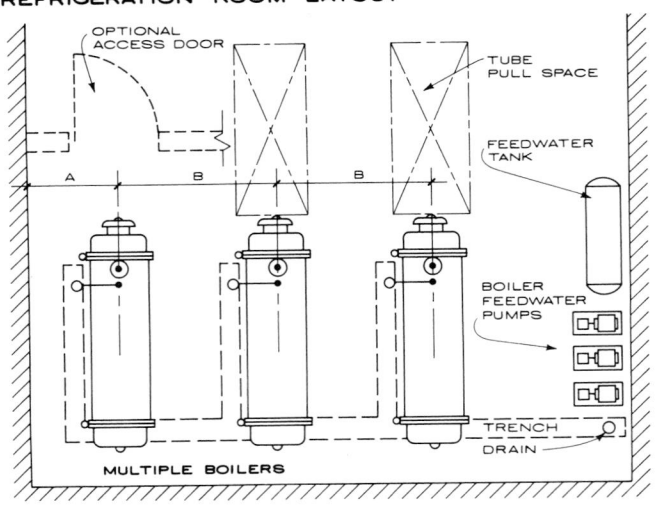

OPTIONAL ACCESS DOOR — TUBE PULL SPACE — FEEDWATER TANK — BOILER FEEDWATER PUMPS — TRENCH DRAIN — MULTIPLE BOILERS

ROOM DIMENSIONS

Dimension A allows for a minimum 3 ft 6 in. aisle between the water column on the boiler and the wall. Dimension B between boilers allows for a clear aisle of:

    3'-6''— 15–200 hp
    4'-0''—250–350 hp
    5'-0''—400–800 hp

The shortest boiler room length is obtained by allowing for possible future tube replacement (from front or rear of boiler) through a window or doorway. Allowance is only made for minimum door swing at each end of the boiler.

AIR SUPPLY

Two permanent air supply openings on opposite walls of the boiler room are recommended. These openings should be located below a height of 7 ft with a total clear area of at least 1 sq ft. Air supply openings can be louvered for weather protection. Check applicable codes for minimum supply air requirements.

Size the openings by using the following formula:

$$\text{area (sq ft)} = \frac{CFM}{FPM}$$

Amount of air required (CFM):

    Combustion air—max. boiler HP x 2 CMF/BHP
    Ventilation air—max. boiler HP x 2 CFM/BHP

NOTE: a total of 10 CFM/BHP applies up to 1000 ft elevation. Add 3% more per 1000 ft of added elevation.

Air velocity required (FPM):

    Up to 7 ft height— 250 FPM
    Above 7 ft height— 500 FPM
    Supply air duct to boiler—1000 FPM

If chillers and boilers are located in the same room, combustion air supply must be ducted to boilers (see ASHRAE 15-1992).

BOILER ROOM SPACE REQUIREMENTS

BOILER HP	15–40	50–100	125–200	250–350	400–800
Dimension A	5'-9''	6'-6''	6'-10''	7'-9''	8'-6''
Dimension B	7'-5''	8'-9''	9'-7''	11'-9''	14'-3''

NOTE: Above requirements apply to both steam and hot water boilers.

BOILER ROOM LAYOUT FOR STEAM BOILERS

Joseph R. Loring & Associates, Inc., Consulting Engineers; New York, New York

 20   NONRESIDENTIAL ROOM PLANNING

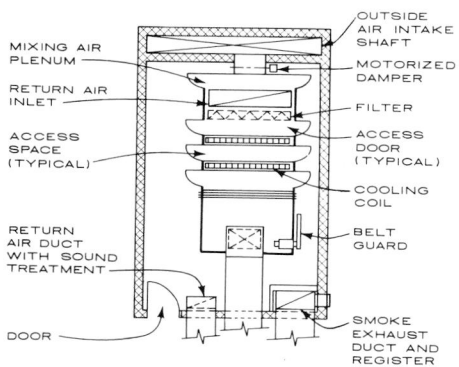

**FIGURE 2
EQUIPMENT ROOM PLAN**

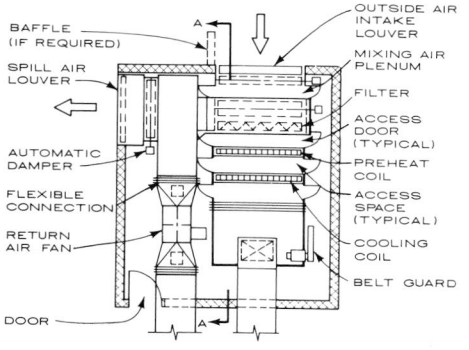

**FIGURE I
EQUIPMENT ROOM PLAN**

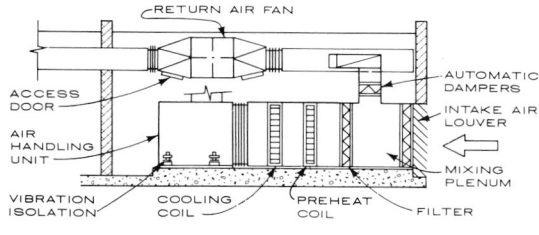

EQUIPMENT ROOM SECTION A—A

NOTES

1. The air-handling equipment room should be located centrally to reduce distances conditioned air must travel from the equipment room to the farthest air-conditioned space. Fan noise transmission to adjacent spaces also must be considered. If the equipment room is located near conference rooms, sleeping quarters, broadcasting studios, or other sound sensitive areas, special treatment of the equipment room area will be required to provide adequate sound and vibration isolation from surrounding areas.

2. Adequate access space must be provided to maintain and replace heating coils, cooling coils, filters, damper motors and linkage, control valves, bearings, fan motors, fans, belts, pulleys, and other parts.

3. Figure 1 shows a typical equipment room plan with one floor-mounted air-conditioning unit and one suspended return air fan. The air-conditioning unit shown is a horizontal draw-through type consisting of fan, cooling coil, preheat coil, filters, return air plenum, outdoor air intake plenum, and access sections on either side of the coils.

4. The outdoor air intake louver and exhaust air louver are located on different walls. Where both intake and exhaust louver must be located on the same wall, they must be as far apart as possible, but not less than 10 ft. in order to reduce the short circuiting between the exhaust and intake air.

5. Figure 2 shows the same system without a return fan, but with exhaust capability via a remote fan.

6. When a horizontal blow-through unit is used, the length of the unit essentially is the same as shown for the draw-through unit.

7. Where higher headroom is available, a vertical unit, which can be only the draw-through type, may be used to reduce the unit's length. Depending on the size of the unit, this reduction in length will range from 2 ft. to 3 ft. 6 in.

8. Figure 1 shows an axial fan for returning air from the conditioned space. The return air fan may not be required where the air-conditioning system is not designed to operate under economizer cycle (cooling by cold outdoor air) mode.

9. A floor-mounted centrifugal single width, single inlet type fan or double width, double inlet type fan, may be used instead of the suspended axial fan shown; however, this generally increases equipment room width.

10. Outside air intake louvers are weatherproof with 50 percent to 60 percent free area. Louver size for conventional intake and exhaust air systems can be determined by allowing 800 ft. to 1,000 ft. per minute velocity through the free area.

11. The quantity of outside air drawn into a system depends on the ventilation criteria of the space being served and the amount of make-up air needed to balance any exhaust air drawn from the same space. The ratio of outside air to the total amount being supplied to a space may be very small. An office may need 10 percent to 20 percent outside air; a laboratory may require 100 percent outside air because of its non-recirculating aspect.

12. The total air quantity supplied to any individual space may vary from 0.5 CFM per sq. ft. for light occupancy (public circulation type office space) to 2 to 3 CFM per sq. ft. for laboratories, restaurants, ballrooms, and similar areas with large internal or external cooling loads.

EQUIPMENT ROOM SPACE REQUIREMENTS

CFM RANGE	APPROXIMATE OVERALL DIMENSION OF SUPPLY AIR UNITS			RECOMMENDED ROOM DIMENSIONS		
	W	H	L	W	H	L
1,000– 1,800	4'-9''	2'-9''	14'-9''	12'-6''	9'-0''	18'-9''
1,801– 3,000	5'-0''	3'-6''	16'-0''	13'-9''	9'-0''	20'-0''
3,001– 4,000	6'-9''	4'-6''	16'-0''	17'-6''	9'-0''	20'-0''
4,001– 6,000	7'-6''	4'-6''	16'-9''	18'-0''	9'-0''	20'-9''
6,001– 7,000	7'-6''	4'-9''	18'-3''	18'-6''	9'-6''	22'-3''
7,001– 9,000	8'-0''	5'-0''	18'-9''	19'-0''	10'-0''	22'-9''
9,001–12,000	10'-0''	5'-6''	21'-0''	23'-0''	11'-0''	25'-0''
12,001–16,000	10'-3''	6'-0''	22'-0''	23'-6''	12'-6''	26'-0''
16,001–19,000	10'-6''	6'-6''	23'-9''	24'-0''	13'-0''	27'-9''
19,001–22,000	11'-9''	7'-3''	25'-0''	26'-9''	15'-0''	29'-0''
22,001–27,000	11'-9''	8'-6''	26'-0''	27'-0''	16'-0''	30'-0''
27,001–32,000	13'-0''	9'-9''	27'-9''	29'-0''	18'-0''	31'-9''

AIR HANDLING EQUIPMENT ROOM REQUIREMENTS

AIR FILTRATION AND ODOR REMOVAL

Air filter selection is determined by the degree of cleanliness required. The initial cost, ease of maintenance, improvement of housekeeping, health benefits, and product quality are considerations. Size and quantity of dust and contaminants are also factors.

Filters most often are located at the air inlet of the heating, ventilating, and air-conditioning equipment, providing protection to the equipment and the area served. Filters are located at the equipment discharge and at entry of air into clean rooms, operating rooms, critical health care rooms, and various industrial process areas. Filters located in return air and exhaust air limit the contamination of other areas and the atmosphere.

AIR FILTER types are dry media, viscous (sticky) media, renewable media, and electronic. Filter performance tests and ratings have been established by ASHRAE, NBS, and AFI. The three operating characteristics that distinguish the various types of air cleaners are efficiency, air flow resistance, and dust holding capacity. Efficiency measures the ability of the air cleaner to remove particulate matter from an air stream. Average efficiency over the life of the filter is the most important consideration. Airflow resistance is the static pressure drop across the filter at a given airflow rate. Dust holding capacity defines the amount of a particular type of dust that an air cleaner can hold when operated at a specified airflow rate to some

maximum resistance value, or before its efficiency is seriously reduced as a result of the collected dust. Filter efficiency comparisons should always be based on the same test conditions.

PREFILTERS are required to extend the life of costlier high efficiency filters. High efficiency particulate filters (HEPA), and their integral frames, should be tested and certified in place. Filter pressure

drop gauges are recommended as an aid to economical replacement scheduling for all types of filters.

ODOR REMOVAL is best controlled by limiting the source. Dilution of odors by direct exhaust ventilation is the most common control method. Air washer and carbon filters are usually used for reclaiming odorous air. Ozone treatment and aerosol masking of odors are sometimes used.

AIR FILTER CHARACTERISTICS

MEDIA AND TYPE	PERCENT EFFICIENCY RANGE		DUST HOLDING CAPACITY	AIRFLOW RESISTANCE (IN. WATER)
	ATMOSPHERIC DUST	SMALL PARTICLES		
Dry panel throwaway	15–30	NA	Excellent	0.1–0.5
Viscous panel throwaway	20–35	NA	Good	0.1–0.5
Dry panel cleanable	15–20	NA	Superior	0.08–0.5
Viscous panel cleanable	15–25	NA	Superior	0.08–0.5
Mat panel renewable	10–90	0–60	Good to superior	0.15–1.0
Roll mat renewable	10–90	0–55	Good to superior	0.15–0.65
Roll oil bath	15–25	NA	Superior	0.3–0.5
Close pleat mat panel	NA	85–95	Varies	0.4–1.0
High efficiency particulate	NA	95–99.9	Varies	1.0–3.0
Membrane	NA	to 100	NA	NA
Electrostatic with mat	80–98	NA	Varies	0.15–1.25

John O. Samuel; Joseph R. Loring & Associates, Inc., Consulting Engineers; New York, New York

NOTES

1. Some of the toilet room layouts shown are similar. Variations are in the direction of the door swing and whether the width or depth is the more constraining dimension. Dimensions show "comfortable" minimums and preferred dimensions.

2. Overall room dimensions include a 2 in. construction tolerance.

3. Each layout shows the required clear floor space for the fixtures and the doors. Frequently the clear floor space at the fixture is more stringent than the 60 in. diameter or the T-shaped maneuvering space required. Both must be considered.

4. References to ADAAG are to the Americans with Disabilities Act Accessibility Guidelines for Buildings and Facilities.

5. Clearances for wheelchair turning space require either a 60 in. diameter circle or a T-shape with each leg 36 in. wide and overall length and width of 60 x 60 in.

6. Typical clear floor space at plumbing fixtures:
   a. Water closet with adjacent lavatory: 48 in. wide x 66 in. deep (front approach); 48 in. wide x 56 in. deep (side approach)
   b. Water closet without adjacent lavatory: 60 in. wide x 56 in. deep
   c. Lavatory: 30 in. wide x 48 in. deep

7. Door maneuvering clearances: see ADAAG (section 4.13.6 and fig. 25) for various requirements and conditions. Variables include direction of swing, direction of approach, size of door, door hardware.

8. Doors to bathrooms are assumed to be 36 in. wide, with a closer and latch for privacy. Where noted, the overall dimension may decrease if there is no closer.

9. Mount accessible coat hooks between 48 and 54 in. maximum above finished floor, depending on the direction of approach (48 in. preferred).

10. Maneuvering clearances at base of water closets are based on American Standard model #2108 (floor mounted tanktype) and #2257 (wall-mounted flush-valve type), mounted per manufacturer recommendations. Confirm actual water closet dimensions for other makes and models.

11. Maneuvering clearances below lavatories are based on American Standard model #0355 (wall hung) and #0475 (mounted in countertop). Confirm actual lavatory dimensions for other makes and models.

12. Some states and local jurisdictions have adopted more strigent accessibility requirements.

DRAWING NOTES

1. See the ADAAG for the following figures:
   Wheelchair turning space - Figure 3
   Maneuvering clearance at doors - Figure 25
   Clear floor space required at plumbing fixtures - Figures 28, 31, and 32

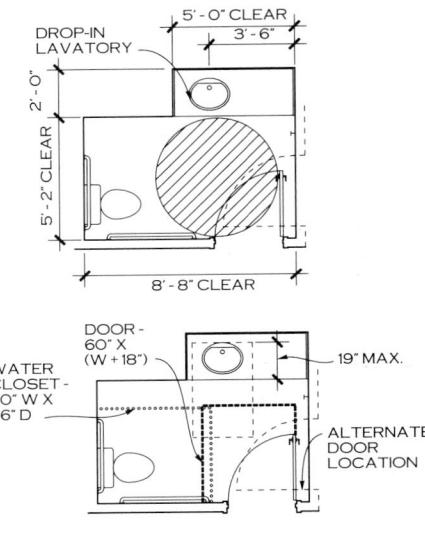

LAVATORY ON SIDE WALL

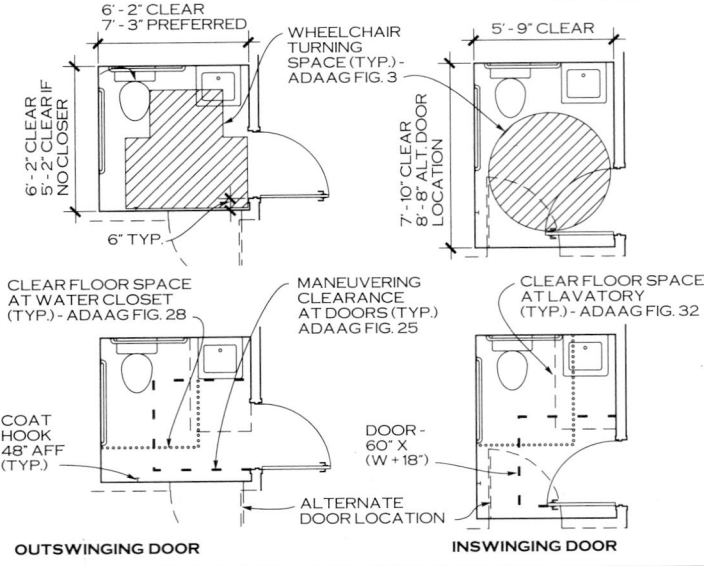

SHORT AND COMPACT

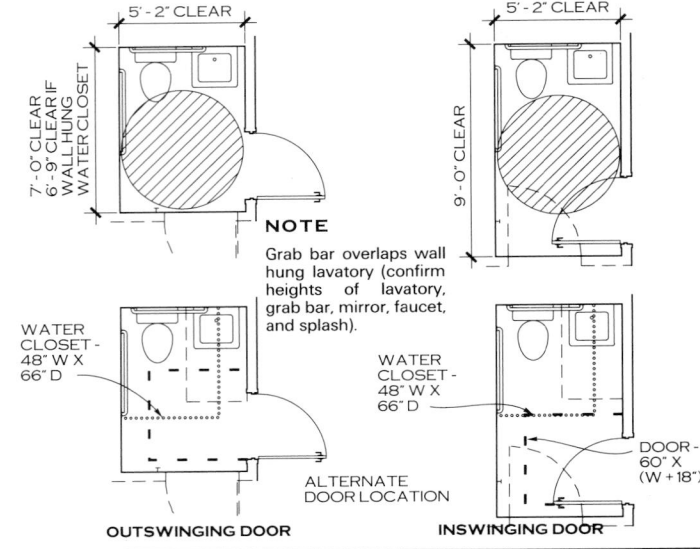

NOTE

Grab bar overlaps wall hung lavatory (confirm heights of lavatory, grab bar, mirror, faucet, and splash).

LONG AND NARROW

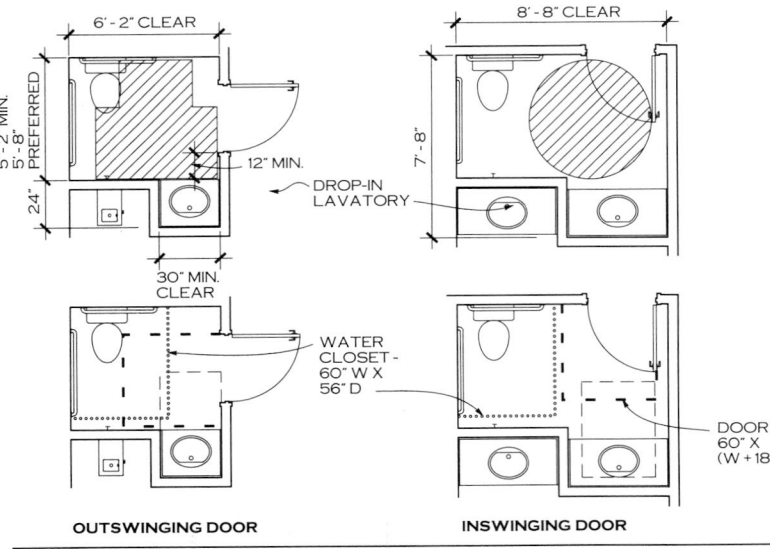

LAVATORY ON OPPOSITE WALL

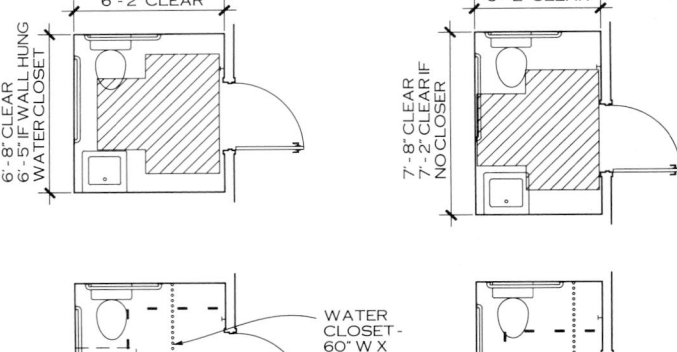

Dan E. Woosley, AIA, and James L. Terry, AIA; Evan Terry Associates, P.C.; Birmingham, Alabama

GENERAL

When laying out multiple fixture toilet rooms, consider the following:

1. Number of fixtures required by code or needed for use.
2. Protection of sight lines into the toilet rooms.
3. Appropriate wall space for toilet accessories: towel dispensers, waste and ash receptacles, feminine napkin dispensers, electric hand dryers, coat hooks, mirrors (especially full-length, recommended in women's rooms).
4. Minimize plumbing walls; keep it simple.
5. Plumbing chases appropriate to fixture support (wall-hung versus floor mounted) and piping (sanitary and supply).
6. Accessibility for those with varying disabilities.
7. Flow of people during peak use in very large toilet rooms; increase aisle and vestibule widths accordingly.

LARGE TOILET ROOMS

When laying out large commercial toilet rooms, always consult current plumbing codes for minimum requirements. Generally, the number of fixtures required for men's rest rooms is usually sufficient. However, for places of assembly, building codes have a history of seriously undersizing the number of stalls for women's rest rooms. Consider the maximum number of people the rest rooms will serve, typical gender ratio, type of event, and whether they are subject to surges (e.g., intermissions, half-times) during which women's toilet rooms become especially crowded.

The chart and rule-of-thumb guidelines on this page are useful in finding a more reasonable balance of fixtures between genders. Compare them with local code minimums. A general ratio of 3:2 total fixtures (water closets/urinals) for women-to-men is a good guideline, assuming an equal number of each gender.

WOMEN'S WATER CLOSETS IN LARGE FACILITIES

	RECOMMENDED RATIO (WC/WOMEN)	PREFERRED
Theaters, convention halls, auditoriums, etc.	1:50	1:40
Stadiums, arenas	1:100	1:75
Places of worship	1:75	1:75

GUIDELINES FOR MULTIPLE FIXTURE REST ROOMS

TYPE OF BUILDING OR OCCUPANCY	OCCUPANT CONTENT	WATER CLOSETS (FIXTURE/PERSON)		URINALS (FIXTURE/MALE)
Assembly places: theaters, auditoriums, convention halls, etc., for public use	Number of persons equals number of seating spaces	Male 1: 1 - 100 1: 101 - 200 3: 201 - 400	Females One for each 25 females up to 200 11: 201 - 400	1: 1 - 100 2: 101 - 200 3: 201 - 400 4: 401 - 600
		Over 400, add 1 fixture for each additional 500 males and 1 for each additional 50 females		Over 600, add 1 fixture for each additional 300 males
Assembly places: stadiums, arenas, and sporting facilities for public use	Number of persons equals number of seating spaces	Male 1: 1 - 100 1: 101 - 200 3: 201 - 400	Females One for each 25 females up to 200 11: 201 - 400	1: 1 - 100 2: 101 - 200 3: 201 - 400 4: 401 - 600
		Over 400, add 1 fixture for each additional 500 males and 1 for each additional 100 females		Over 600, add 1 fixture for each additional 300 males
Places of worship: principal assembly places	Number of persons equals number of seating spaces	Male 1: 150	Females 1: 75	1: 150

* Based on Appendix C of the 1991 Uniform Plumbing Code, with permission of IAPMO.

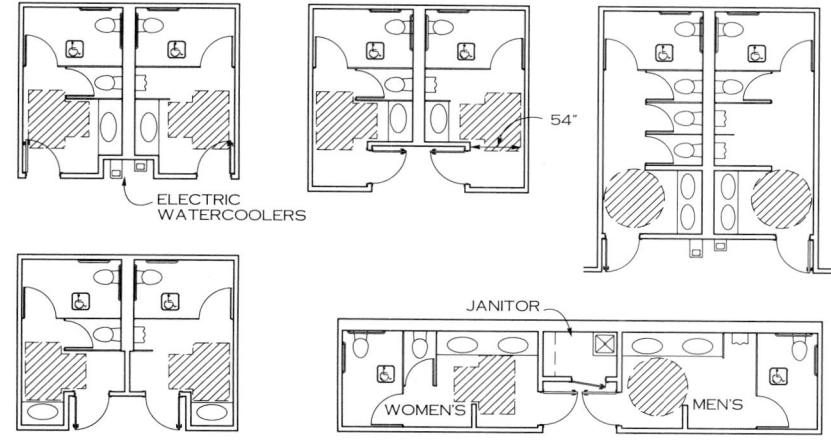

ELECTRIC WATERCOOLERS

54"

JANITOR

WOMEN'S   MEN'S

EXAMPLES OF MID-SIZED TOILET ROOMS

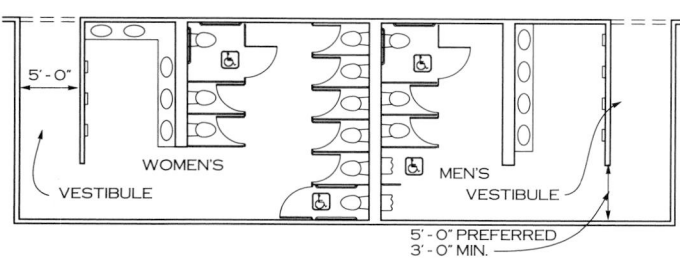

5' - 0"

WOMEN'S

VESTIBULE

MEN'S

VESTIBULE

5' - 0" PREFERRED
3' - 0" MIN.

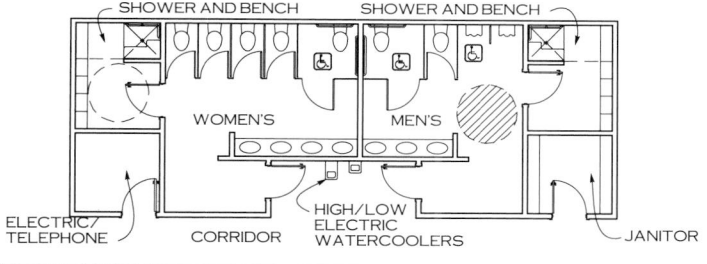

SHOWER AND BENCH   SHOWER AND BENCH

WOMEN'S   MEN'S

ELECTRIC/ TELEPHONE   CORRIDOR   HIGH/LOW ELECTRIC WATERCOOLERS   JANITOR

TOILET ROOMS WITH SHOWER AND LOCKERS

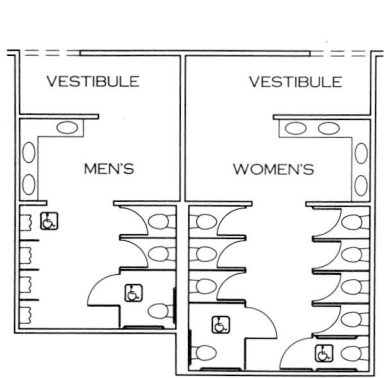

VESTIBULE   VESTIBULE

MEN'S   WOMEN'S

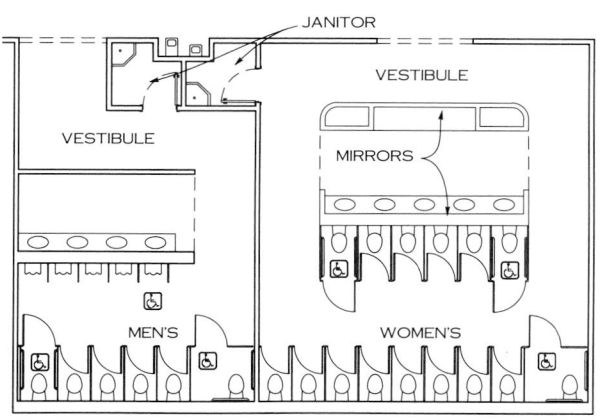

JANITOR

VESTIBULE

VESTIBULE

MIRRORS

MEN'S   WOMEN'S

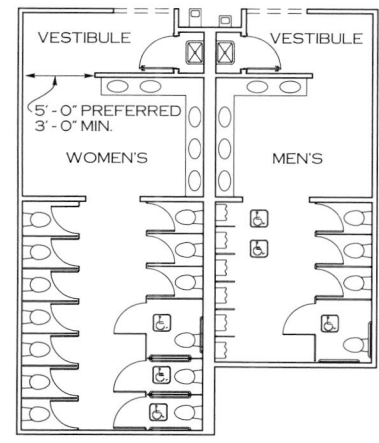

VESTIBULE   VESTIBULE

5' - 0" PREFERRED
3' - 0" MIN.

WOMEN'S   MEN'S

EXAMPLES OF MEGA TOILET ROOMS (AIRPORTS, ARENAS, AUDITORIUMS, STADIUMS, THEATERS, ETC.)

Dan E. Woosley, AIA, Neil King, AIA, and James L. Terry, AIA; Evan Terry Associates, P.C.; Birmingham, Alabama
Charles Easterberg; University of Washington; Seattle, Washington

PROJECT PROGRAM

A powerful tool in office design is the project program. Speculative offices by definition have a far simpler program than client occupied offices, which must locate and support every individual and piece of equipment that will occupy the finished building.

There are many approaches to programming, but all successful programs are highly interactive and require the involvement and commitment of all key participants. All programs involve the following:

1. Data collection
2. Data analysis
3. Data organization
4. Data development
5. Conceptual communication
6. Evaluation of concepts.

Design programs have become very complex and may take longer to develop than the design of the building. The program seeks to measure the influence of every element affecting the proposed project. These range from the effects of the sun and wind to the interrelationships of various organizational groupings to the most beneficial levels of light, temperature, and sound for individuals and equipment. Not all program communication is verbal. Many graphic techniques exist to aid in the analysis and communication of data and concept. The most important, but not only, product of the program is the facilities plan. Other important products are a clearly defined chain of communications, a command structure for decision making in a timely manner, a project schedule with milestones clearly defined, and a project budget. Other less objective goals are an energy conservation policy and image projection.

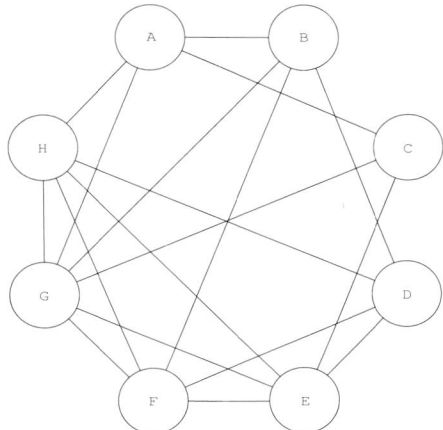

INTERACTION NET

An interaction net illustrates the number of interactions each function or space has with its peers. The items being analyzed are shown as nodes on the perimeter of a net. Each interaction is shown as a line between the relating item.

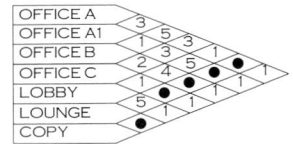

MATRIX

A matrix of relationships shows a variety of relationships within a large group. It does this by dividing the large group into several obvious classifications. A series of yes/no questions are then asked of each group and subsequent subgroup. The elements with a positive response form a subgroup, and the negative responses form a companion subgroup.

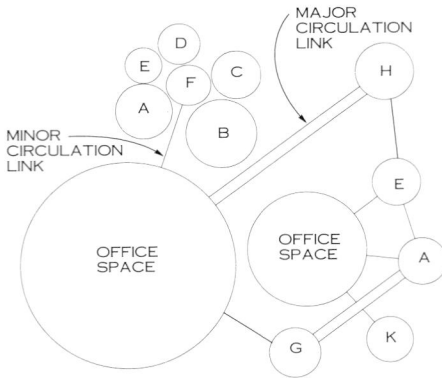

BUBBLE DIAGRAM

The bubble diagram is one of the first attempts to place spaces in their proper relationship. Bubble diagrams approximate space sizes and show strong and weak relationships by proximity of represented spaces. A loose circulation or "flow" path between spaces is generated.

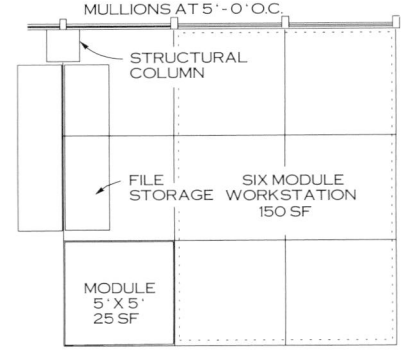

5 FT MODULE

Large modules do not necessarily create larger workstations as illustrated here. The module is a device for coordinating different building systems. Large modules reduce spacing options

MODULE

One of the first tasks of the design process is the selection of a building module. The module affects all future design decisions from furniture systems to mullion spacing and structural system. The module must successfully integrate all these systems. Once selected, the module aids in dimensionally locating the structural frame, the core, the utility risers and distribution closets and has an impact on almost every component of the building.

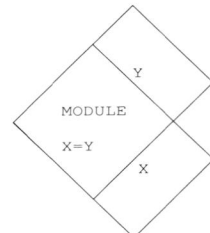

Modules range from 4 ft x 4 ft (16 sq ft) to 6 ft x 6 ft (24 sq ft) and are adjustable in 4 or 6 in. increments. Structural bay sizes are established as multiples of module dimensions.

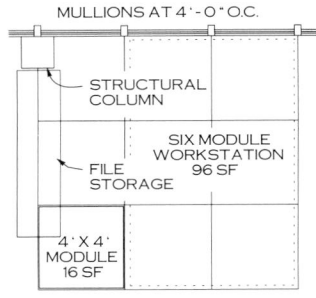

4 FT MODULE

Small modules promote flexibility and complexity.

MODULES

Offices can be broadly grouped into two categories: speculative and client occupied. Nearly all speculative office projects are designed using the open plan concept. The flexibility in defining tenant spaces and the reduced cost of this system are overwhelming advantages to the developer. Client occupied office designs have increasingly moved from conventional plan to the open plan concept by utilizing more developed concepts like office landscaping and cellular plans.

CONVENTIONAL PLAN

The conventional office plan is used primarily today in corporate executive offices. Conventional office plans are characterized by shallow bays and long narrow footprints with central cores that maximize window space. Conventional plans define space by creating offices with floor-to-ceiling partitions opening onto enclosed corridors. Bearing walls and interior columns are easier to accommodate in conventional plans than other types.

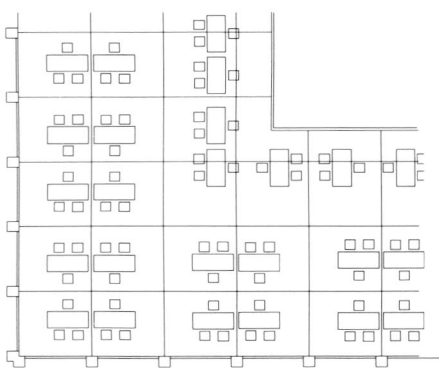

OPEN PLAN

Open plans are characterized by deep open bays with few internal columns. Privacy, acoustics, and territoriality issues are handled with integrated furniture systems incorporating privacy/acoustical panels. Delivery of power and communication to point of use has inspired the creation of several new delivery technologies: raised flooring, flatwire, and furniture systems with integrated cable raceways are examples.

MODULES

Laird Ueberroth, Architect, and Associates; McLean, Virginia

GENERAL

Most elements of a building are composed of many identical components assembled in a pattern or grid to form the "whole." Examples include the structural frames, glazing panels, distribution closets for Power and communication, lighting, etc. Modularity is the attempt to bring all these patterns or grids into harmony. The advantage in this is a more efficient use of space and systems by eliminating "gaps" of unusable or unserviceable space. Harmony is established by defining a lowest common denominator or module and using it as a basis for all elemental grids. The most basic relationship from a planning standpoint is between the depth of bays (established by the structural frame) and the work station. The goal, which is more important in shallow bays, is to maximize the flexibility of workstation, corridor, and file space, within the bay without creating any "gaps" of unused space.

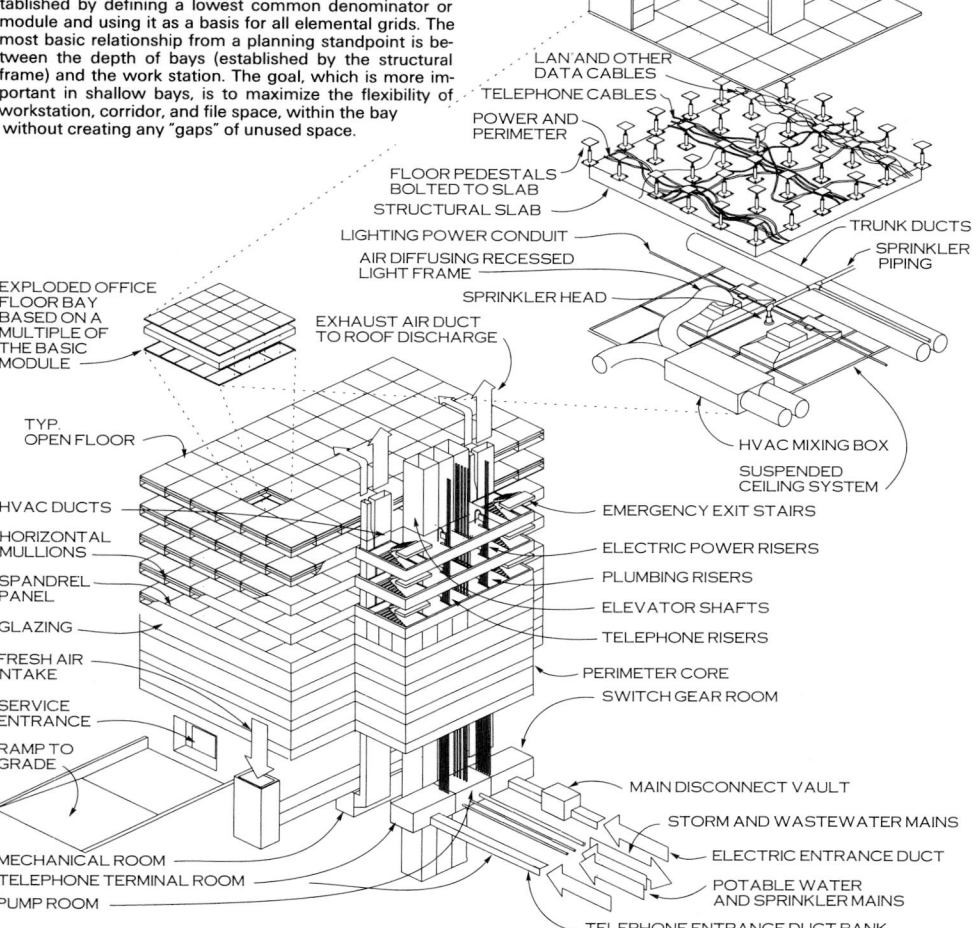

SYSTEM FURNITURE WORKSTATION FIT TO THE MODULE
RAISED ACCESS FLOOR COVERED WITH FLOOR TILES
LAN AND OTHER DATA CABLES
TELEPHONE CABLES
POWER AND PERIMETER
FLOOR PEDESTALS BOLTED TO SLAB
STRUCTURAL SLAB
LIGHTING POWER CONDUIT
AIR DIFFUSING RECESSED LIGHT FRAME
SPRINKLER HEAD
EXPLODED OFFICE FLOOR BAY BASED ON A MULTIPLE OF THE BASIC MODULE
EXHAUST AIR DUCT TO ROOF DISCHARGE
TRUNK DUCTS
SPRINKLER PIPING
HVAC MIXING BOX
SUSPENDED CEILING SYSTEM
TYP. OPEN FLOOR
HVAC DUCTS
HORIZONTAL MULLIONS
SPANDREL PANEL
GLAZING
FRESH AIR INTAKE
SERVICE ENTRANCE
RAMP TO GRADE
EMERGENCY EXIT STAIRS
ELECTRIC POWER RISERS
PLUMBING RISERS
ELEVATOR SHAFTS
TELEPHONE RISERS
PERIMETER CORE
SWITCH GEAR ROOM
MAIN DISCONNECT VAULT
STORM AND WASTEWATER MAINS
ELECTRIC ENTRANCE DUCT
POTABLE WATER AND SPRINKLER MAINS
TELEPHONE ENTRANCE DUCT BANK
MECHANICAL ROOM
TELEPHONE TERMINAL ROOM
PUMP ROOM

AVERAGE ILLUMINATION LEVEL FOR TYPICAL AREAS (IN FOOTCANDLES)

General offices	50
Drafting rooms	75
Conference rooms	50
Computer rooms	50
Corridors/stairs	20
Lobbies	20
Reception desks	50
Cafeterias	30

AVERAGE ELECTRICAL LOAD FOR TYPICAL SPACES (WATTS/SQ FT)

General offices	3
Copier rooms	15
Conference rooms	1
Word processing	4
Computer room	40

MINIMUM LIVE LOAD FOR TYPICAL OFFICE AREAS (LB/SQ FT)

General office	50
Equipment rooms	100
Corridors	80
Telephone exchange	150
Transformer rooms	200
File storage rooms	80

ARCHITECTURAL GRAPHIC STANDARDS REFERENCE CHART FOR NINTH EDITION

Critical work station dimensions	page 5
Vending rooms	pages 512
Conference rooms	page 794
Acoustics	pages 59-64
Lighting	pages 51-54
Fire suppression	pages 572-574
Structural assemblies	page 37-42
Loading dock	page 513
Area & volume calculations	page 118
Concrete floor system	page 173
Stone veneer	page 235
Curtain wall	pages 446-449
Ceiling systems	page 474
Office furnishings	page 533
Seismic design	page 47
Elevators	page 578
Plumbing	pages 604-605
HVAC	pages 620-630
Floor wiring systems	page 646
Uninterruptible power	page 661

OFFICE SPACE ALLOWANCE GUIDE (SF)

Top executive	400 –600
Managers	150 –200
Assistant managers	100 –125
Supervisors	80 –100
Operator (60 inch desk)	50 – 60
Operator (55 inch desk)	50 – 55
Operator (50 Inch Desk)	45
Standard letter file	6
Standard legal file	7
Letter lateral file	6.5
Legal lateral file	7.5
Video studio	900
Meeting room (over 200 people)	2000

OFFICE BUILDING AUXILIARY SPACES

Office buildings serve a wide variety of users, with a diverse set of requirements. No single office building type or configuration could satisfy all of the potential requirements. As new buildings are constructed to meet the needs of individual users, new services are continuously being incorporated into their designs. Listed below are many of the auxiliary spaces found in office buildings today. Some are almost universal and some are quite rare.

1. Fire control room
2. Facilities maintenance and storage
3. Building control center
4. Video conference room
5. Shipping / receiving dock
6. Cafeteria
7. Secure storage/vault room
8. Copy / graphics room
9. UPS battery room and generator room
10. PBX frame room
11. Telephone terminal room
12. Electric power switch room
13. Record storage
14. Library

Laird Ueberroth, Architect, and Associates; McLean, Virginia

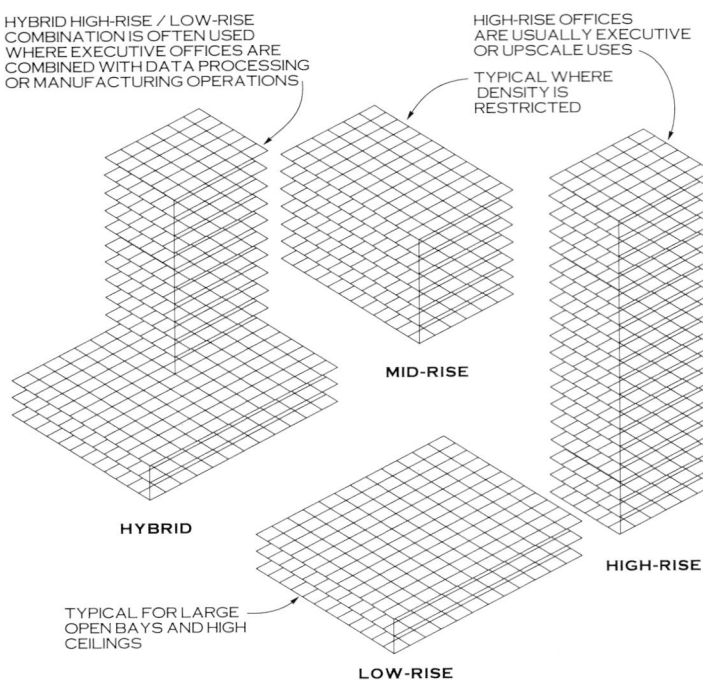

HYBRID HIGH-RISE / LOW-RISE COMBINATION IS OFTEN USED WHERE EXECUTIVE OFFICES ARE COMBINED WITH DATA PROCESSING OR MANUFACTURING OPERATIONS

HIGH-RISE OFFICES ARE USUALLY EXECUTIVE OR UPSCALE USES

TYPICAL WHERE DENSITY IS RESTRICTED

MID-RISE

HYBRID

HIGH-RISE

TYPICAL FOR LARGE OPEN BAYS AND HIGH CEILINGS

LOW-RISE

OFFICE ENVELOPE CONFIGURATIONS

FACILITIES PLAN

The program statement sets down in detail the relationships and space allocations of the components of the project. The Facilities Plan takes the information presented in the Program Statement and applies it to the Proposed building envelope as determined by Zoning, Code, and site restrictions to establish building form and orientation. All rooms/areas are laid out with spaces provided for all employees and functions.

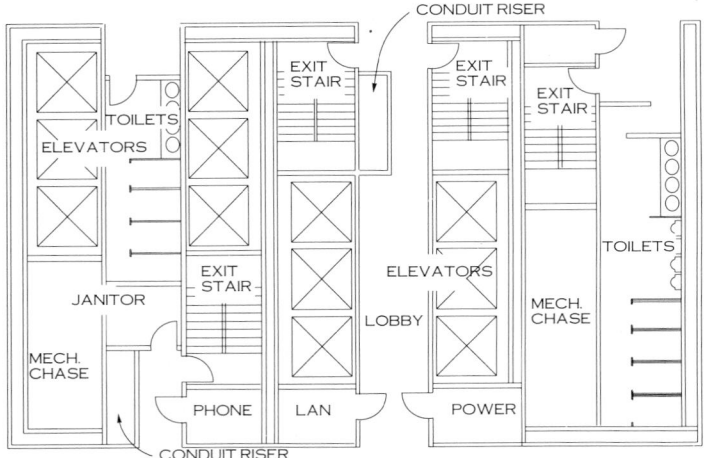

CONDUIT RISER
EXIT STAIR
EXIT STAIR
EXIT STAIR
TOILETS
ELEVATORS
TOILETS
EXIT STAIR
ELEVATORS
JANITOR
LOBBY
MECH. CHASE
MECH. CHASE
PHONE
LAN
POWER
CONDUIT RISER

TYPICAL HIGH-RISE OFFICE BUILDING CORE CONFIGURATION

CONCEPTUAL CORE COMPONENT GUIDELINES

Power, communication, and signal cables	2% net area
Toilet rooms	1 sq ft of toilet room per 150 sq ft net area
Maximum travel distance to elevator	200 ft
Maximum wait for elevator	30 seconds
Stair towers	2 minimum, 300 sq ft each

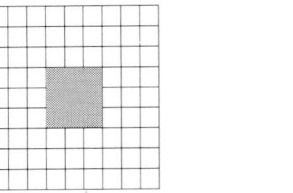

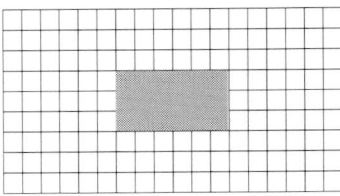

SYMMETRICAL CENTRAL CORE

ELONGATED CENTRAL CORE

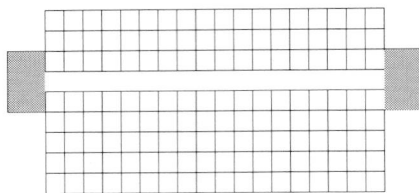

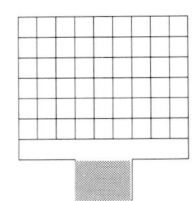

SPLIT PERIMETER CORE

PERIMETER CORE

CORE CONFIGURATIONS

The core is the consolidated placement of the major service and support structures. Because the core links the entire building together, its components are enclosed within fireproof cells. The integrity of these enclosures is critical, because once a fire or smoke enters the core it can quickly spread to all other floors. Typical cores include stair towers (2), elevators, toilets, HVAC risers, power and communication distribution closets, modularity.

Many broad core placement categories exist with many more variations. Factors that influence the placement of the core are:
1. the planning concept selected
2. site characteristics which affect the building footprint
3. structural/seismic considerations
4. the type and number of end users
5. the degree of flexibility required.

Split cores and cores located on the building perimeter increase flexibility and open planning options. Central and elongated cores lend themselves to more conventional rigid plans, although the depth of the bay can have a great influence on flexibility.

Once the core has been established, protected and unprotected circulation corridors are mapped onto individual floors in conjunction with the facilities plan. The location of the core and circulation plan must work in relation with the module developed. Careful consideration must be given to the present and possible future uses of the proposed spaces, because the distances established by the building shape and the core/circulation locations will determine what type of planning concepts can be accommodated efficiently.

OFFICE SUPPORT SYSTEMS

The trend for the foreseeable future is toward increasing the power and flexibility available in the modern office building. To accomplish this, greater demands are being made to deliver worker support—like voice and data integration, video services, security, energy, and environmental management—to more points in the building and to do so in a way that does not restrict redesign of workstation layouts or hinder free travel between stations. Thought must be given to how these systems will be accommodated within the building structure. In areas where raised floors are not provided, the structural system should be designed to place minimal restriction on poke-through accessibility of power and communication cables and easy access for rewiring large areas. In addition to flexible distribution, these systems require more support space. Computer supported voice/data switching services will require increased dedicated space in new office buildings. Local Area Networks (LAN) with distributed processing features will require increased cabling areas. Uninterrupted power supply (UPS) is another new requirement of many office buildings. UPS systems require an electric power generator, fuel storage, a monitor room, and a large battery storage room. The increased power requirements of automated workstations and computers in office buildings require increased power distribution. The increased power requirement and the need to dedicate larger amounts of power for specific uses mean an increase in the amount of space set aside for electric power panel closets and conduit risers.

ACCESS FLOOR: High first cost, but relocation is inexpensive. Floor plenum can accommodate HVAC as well as cable. Outlets are flush with floor, and relocations are easy.

POKE-THROUGH: Least expensive first cost, uses traditional distribution methods in ceiling plenum. One outlet per 65 sq ft maximum is drilled through floor above and fitted with a fireproof assembly. Outlets sit 4 in. above floor. Relocations require interference with floor below.

PLUG-IN DUCT: Power poles bring cables from ceiling space to floor or prewired furniture systems. Very flexible system but aesthetically questionable.

FLAT WIRE: Flat copper conductors are taped to the floor under carpet. Wires cannot be crossed and the system does not handle lighting, but it is flexible and accessible. Transitions from flat to round cables make the system expensive.

CELLULAR FLOOR: A metal tray is poured integral with a composite concrete floor slab. Trays are laid out on a modular grid with outlets set on the module. Inexpensive, but does not handle lighting, and difficult to adjust out of the module.

Laird Ueberroth, Architect, and Associates; McLean, Virginia

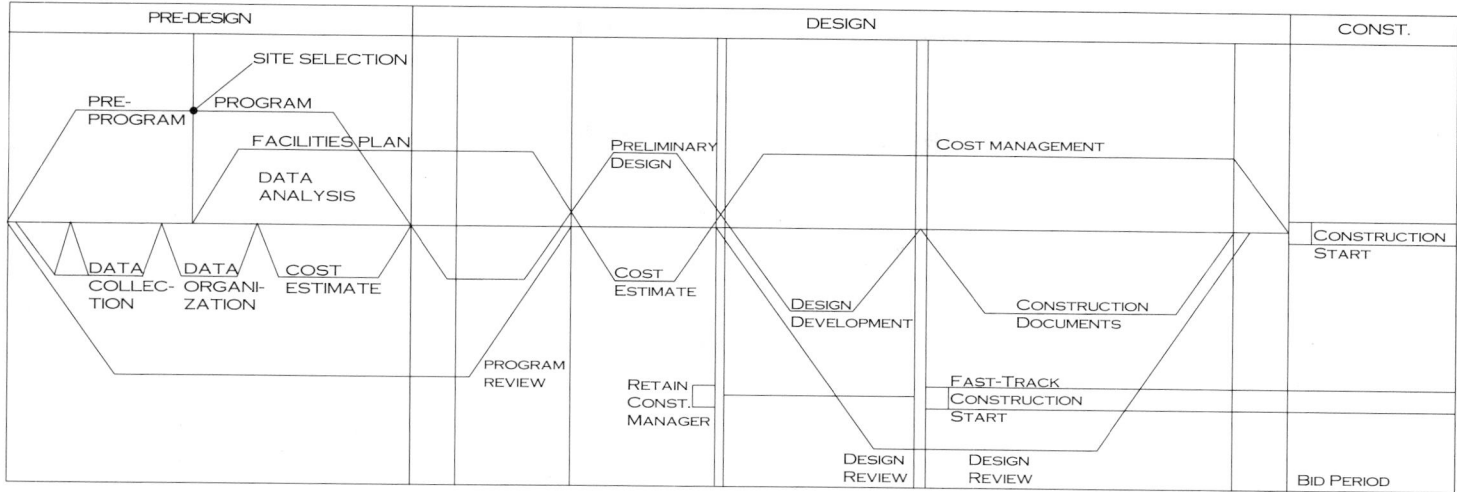

DESIGN SCHEDULE

Time and cost control has become an important part of office building design. A well thought-out schedule has become an essential management tool for tracking and controlling project progress. Many different scheduling techniques exist; CPM, Gantt Chart, and PERT are a few common examples. Most project scheduling today is automated and managed by popular computer software packages.

Office building schedules can be broken down into several broad categories; preprogram, program, design, construction, and postconstruction. The preprogram involves all work related to preparing for the project. Site selection and raw data collection are examples of this phase. In the program phase project specific information is collected, organized, and analyzed, and concepts are developed and presented for review. The program culminates in the facilities plan. The design phase selects all building components and systems and dimensionally locates and sizes them. This phase is further broken down into design development and construction documents. Construction may start in the construction documents stage of the design, depending on the type of delivery approach selected.

DELIVERY APPROACHES

Design and construction have evolved as separate disciplines. The separation of these two essential components of a building project has many logical and time tested advantages. Increased competition and the importance of time have generated several new delivery approaches which are gaining popularity in office building. Delivery approaches differ in two fundamental ways: whether the design and construction are seen as integrated or separated responsibilities, and whether construction begins before or after construction documents are fully developed.

CONSTRUCTION

The importance of time in the creation of office buildings has generated many new construction approaches. Design/build and fast track are increasingly popular new construction options. Their acceptance has spurred the wider use of construction managers and overlapped design and construction techniques. These techniques tend to limit the fluidity of the design and places greater emphasis on locking in decisions during the predesign and early design phases.

FAST TRACK

As its name implies, the primary advantage of this approach is speed. It saves time by overlapping design and construction. Architects and contractors are in their traditional roles in fast track projects. With added demands of construction coordination and cost and time control, fast tracking has stimulated the emergence of the construction manager (CM). With the advantage of reduced delivery time comes the disadvantage of reduced cost control. There are two approaches to this problem. One is to proceed with construction without a fixed overall price. This requires a cost-management strategy to establish contingencies and alternates for all subcontracts. The other approach is to contract the work based on partially developed documents. Guaranteed maximum price contracts are popular with owners. It is impossible to avoid risk when an overall price is set on the basis of partially completed documents.

DESIGN BUILD

Design/build unifies the design and construction responsibilities under one contract. The advantages of this approach are: the owner has only one point of responsibility for the project, the unproductive adversarial relationship between architect and contractor is eliminated, the builder becomes a member of the decision team lending his expertise in cost control and constructability to the process, thereby fixing costs at an early stage. The primary disadvantage of this approach is that the owner loses the professional advice of an agent working for his interests. Since the owner is purchasing a complete package he gives up many opportunities to choose the best products for his purposes. Often an administrative architect is used to try and reestablish the role of an agent for the owner's interest in this process.

DESIGN-AWARD-BUILD

In this traditional approach to building, the owner writes at least two prime contracts: one with the architect and one with the contractor. The architect provides a professional service to the owner and acts as his agent, lending his expertise to the design and selection of a contractor. Traditionally a contractor is selected when the design is complete; construction is started only when the total construction cost is known. Variations of this approach allow for the writing of several prime contracts and overlapping design and construction. The construction manager is often hired by the owner when these options are used.

FAST TRACK

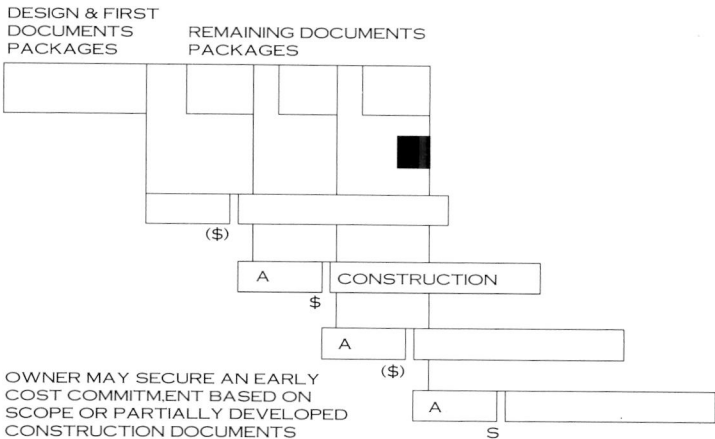

DESIGN & FIRST DOCUMENTS PACKAGES

REMAINING DOCUMENTS PACKAGES

OWNER MAY SECURE AN EARLY COST COMMITMENT BASED ON SCOPE OR PARTIALLY DEVELOPED CONSTRUCTION DOCUMENTS

DESIGN /BUILD

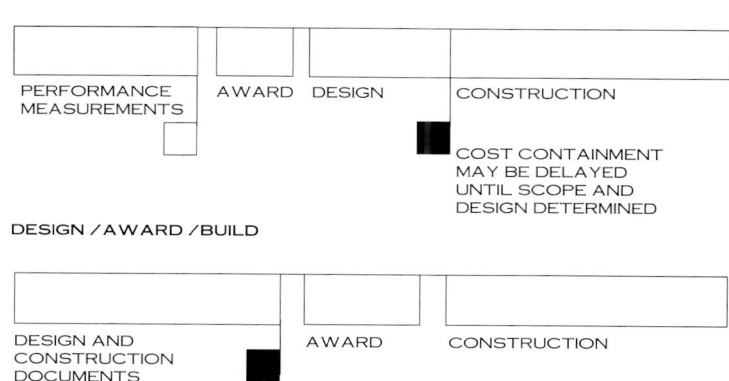

PERFORMANCE MEASUREMENTS — AWARD — DESIGN — CONSTRUCTION

COST CONTAINMENT MAY BE DELAYED UNTIL SCOPE AND DESIGN DETERMINED

DESIGN /AWARD /BUILD

DESIGN AND CONSTRUCTION DOCUMENTS — AWARD — CONSTRUCTION

Laird Ueberroth, Architect, and Associates; McLean, Virginia

PURPOSE OF CHILD CARE CENTERS

Child care centers designed specifically to meet the needs of working parents with pre-school age children are a relatively new institution in the United States. Centers can serve as few as 20 children; however, they are usually sized to accommodate 60 to 150 children. Larger centers are overwhelming to young children and should be subdivided into smaller groupings. Centers provide care for children as young as 6 weeks old, to children of kindergarten age. Some centers also provide before- and after-school care for older children. Centers are expected to provide a rich variety of learning experiences, provide a secure environment, and meet the children's physical needs.

For children, all activities are learning experiences, and the key to good design is providing design elements that enhance the child's self-esteem and relate to the children through scale. Developmentally appropriate environments should be stressed. Materials, interiors, and equipment should be selected to create a non-institutional setting, and include such humanizing elements as soft textures, non-poisonous plants, and animals.

CRITICAL DESIGN DETERMINANTS

Major issues that will influence the ultimate design include: the number of classrooms required, and the total number and age of the children in each classroom. State and possibly local regulations pertaining to the requirements for the licensing of child care centers (in addition to building and life safety codes) will be the defining factor in many of these issues. The operator and staff of the center will also provide valuable input.

Many children enrolled in child care centers are too young to walk, talk, or follow directions; therefore, evacuation of the children during an emergency is critical. Cribs are generally used to evacuate infants. Centers, especially those serving infants, should be located only on the ground floor level, and each classroom and napping area should have an exit leading directly to the exterior at grade. Centers should also be designed to meet the requirements of the American National Standards Institute for Accessibility and Usability for Physically Handicapped People.

MULTI-PURPOSE AREA

This area should accommodate a wide variety of activities: group games, play in inclement weather, holiday activities, parent meetings, etc. The area should be a minimum of 400 square feet, and provided with adjacent storage space to accommodate the furniture and equipment that will be used at various times in the space. Toilets should be located adjacent to this area. If a before/after school program is provided, it may be located in this space.

SITE REQUIREMENTS

In addition to the building, there are numerous special site features that should be considered.

Centers should be located in friendly environments, away from natural and constructed hazards. The best location is a residential neighborhood; also utilized but less desirable locations are employment areas and major commuter routes.

A parking area for the parents to drop off and pick up the children should be located close to the building entrance; parents and children should be able to enter the center without crossing vehicular circulation areas. The main entrance to the center should be controlled to prevent unauthorized visitors. On-site parking for staff and visitors should be provided; however, parking should be divided into several small areas, and screened to support an inviting appearance. Deliveries and trash pickup should occur at a screened service entrance.

Outdoor play should be divided into a minimum of two separate spaces, one for older children and one for younger children. Each area should include developmentally appropriate equipment and activities and be provided with specifically selected landscaping materials.

SIZES FOR PLANNING PURPOSES

Child care regulations generally require classrooms of 20-40 net square feet (NSF) per child, with 35 NSF being the average minimum. Support functions will increase the total square footage required. Small classrooms, designed to accommodate two teachers and the related number of children as required by the licensing regulations, are recommended.

TYPICAL SIZES

No. of children	60-150
Building size	80-100 sq ft/child
Total building	6000-12,000 sq ft
Outdoor play	75-100 sq ft/child
Overall lot size	$1/2$-2 acres

MAJOR FUNCTIONS

Classrooms are the focal point of a child care center; however, there are many other functions necessary to ensure the smooth operation of the center.

Administrative areas, including reception areas, offices, and a staff lounge are essential to center operations. The staff lounge provides a refuge for teachers from the hectic activities and the demands of the children and provides a space to accomplish paperwork. Conference rooms may also be desirable. Staff and visitors should be provided with toilet facilities separate from the children's toilet rooms.

An isolation area should be provided for children who become sick during the day and need to be separated from the other children. This area must be provided with adult supervision, whether located in a separate, but nearby space or in a space shared with an office function. This area should be near a toilet, and have adequate space for a cot/crib.

The size of the kitchen and related storage area will vary depending on the kinds of food to be prepared and whether food is prepared at the center, supplied by the parents, or catered. Most centers will provide, at a minimum, snacks, milk, and juice. Many centers rely on paper products, so that dishwashing is not a major concern. However, trash accumulation from these products, as well as from disposable diapers, can be significant; a separate trash area should be provided.

A central storage area is required to store extra furniture, seasonal decorations, toys, educational materials, paper products, and office supplies.

MULTI-PURPOSE AREA, LIBRARY, ART, AND MEDIA CENTERS

Depending on the operational needs of the center, and the budget, additional activity areas for the children outside of the classroom may be desired.

A multi-purpose area should accommodate a wide variety of activities: group games, play in inclement weather, holiday activities, and parent meetings. If a before and after school program is provided, it may be located here. The area should be a minimum of 400 square feet, and provided with adjacent storage space and toilets. Art, media, and library functions are usually found within the classrooms. However, they could be located in separate spaces, providing specialized instruction and an opportunity for the children to be in a different space.

CLASSROOM ACTIVITIES

Classrooms should be divided into clearly defined activity areas, using child-scaled furniture and equipment pertinent to each activity. Activity areas should be separated from traffic patterns and segregated by noise level. Classrooms should be designed for easy rearrangement of furniture and equipment to provide flexibility. Most daily activities including napping, eating, and learning should occur within the classroom to promote continuity and develop feelings of security in the children.

Older children, over two, require individual, small group and large group activity spaces. Cubbies should be provided for storage of children's clothing and belongings. Storage areas for cots, paints, and other supplies should be located within each classroom; however, they should be accessible only to the teachers.

Toilet rooms, art and handwashing sinks should be provided within the classroom to improve sanitation and develop healthy habits, independence, and self-reliance. Fixtures should be child-scaled. One toilet and lavatory fixture should be provided for each 10-15 children, depending on regulations and available budget.

INFANT AREAS

Most regulatory agencies define infants as children under the age of two. Their physical and developmental needs are very different from those of older children, and the infants should be physically separated from the older children. Infant classrooms should be the smallest groups of children at the center, accommodating 6-12 children, depending on the child/teacher ratios.

Physical needs include frequent and irregular feeding and sleeping patterns. Diapering areas designed to ensure that diapering is a safe, sanitary procedure should be provided in each infant area. All the items that the teacher requires in changing the child including wipes, diapers, water, paper towels, a trash receptacle, etc. should be within easy reach of the changing table. Some jurisdictions require that toilets be provided near the diapering area.

Infant areas require more space because of the need for cribs; one crib should be provided for each infant. Cribs should be permanently located in separate areas adjacent to the classroom so that the infants can sleep on their own schedule and in a quiet area. The amount of physical separation from other activities will be determined by applicable child care regulations, and by the staffing patterns. Napping areas will generally require an additional 20-30 square feet/child, depending on the crib size and the child care regulations for separation between cribs.

Because eating in the infant area occurs frequently and at irregular intervals, a small kitchen area should be provided in each infant classroom. The area requires storage, a sink, refrigerator, and either a microwave or a stove for warming food and milk.

A small laundry area should be provided to wash soiled linens and clothes. Close proximity to the infant area is recommended.

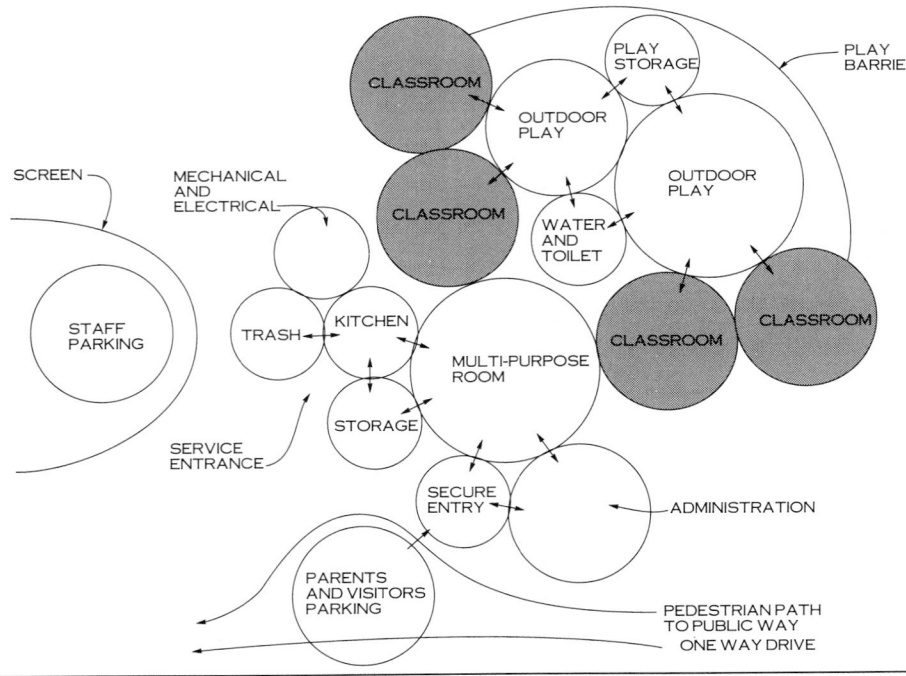

SITE RELATIONSHIPS

Linda Clark, AIA; Archi-tots, Inc.; Silver Spring, Maryland

 CHILD CARE

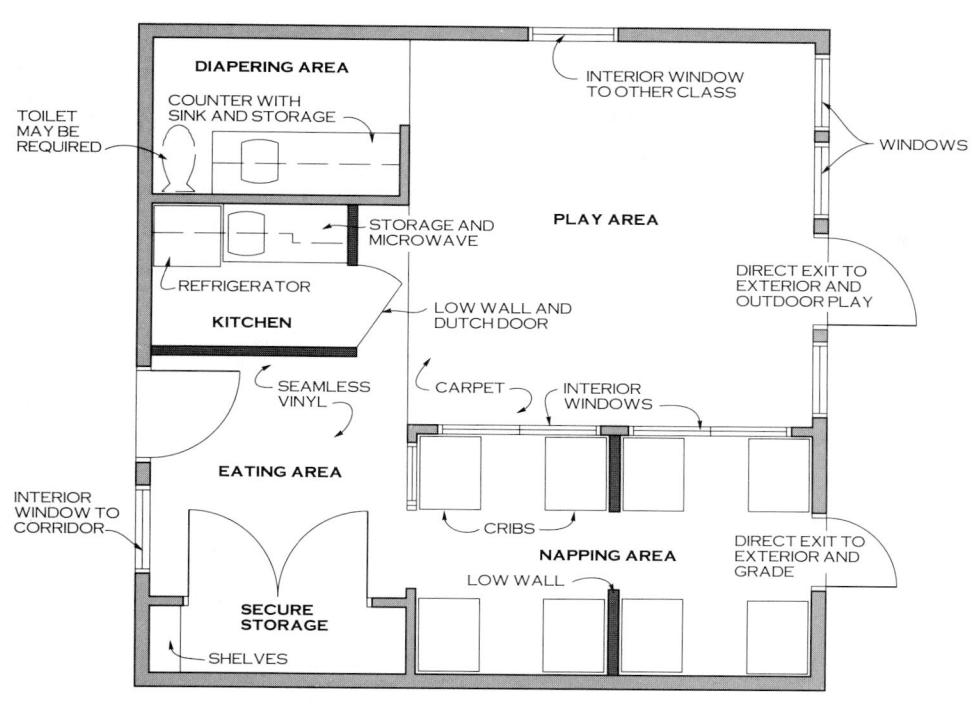

CLASSROOM FOR EIGHT INFANTS

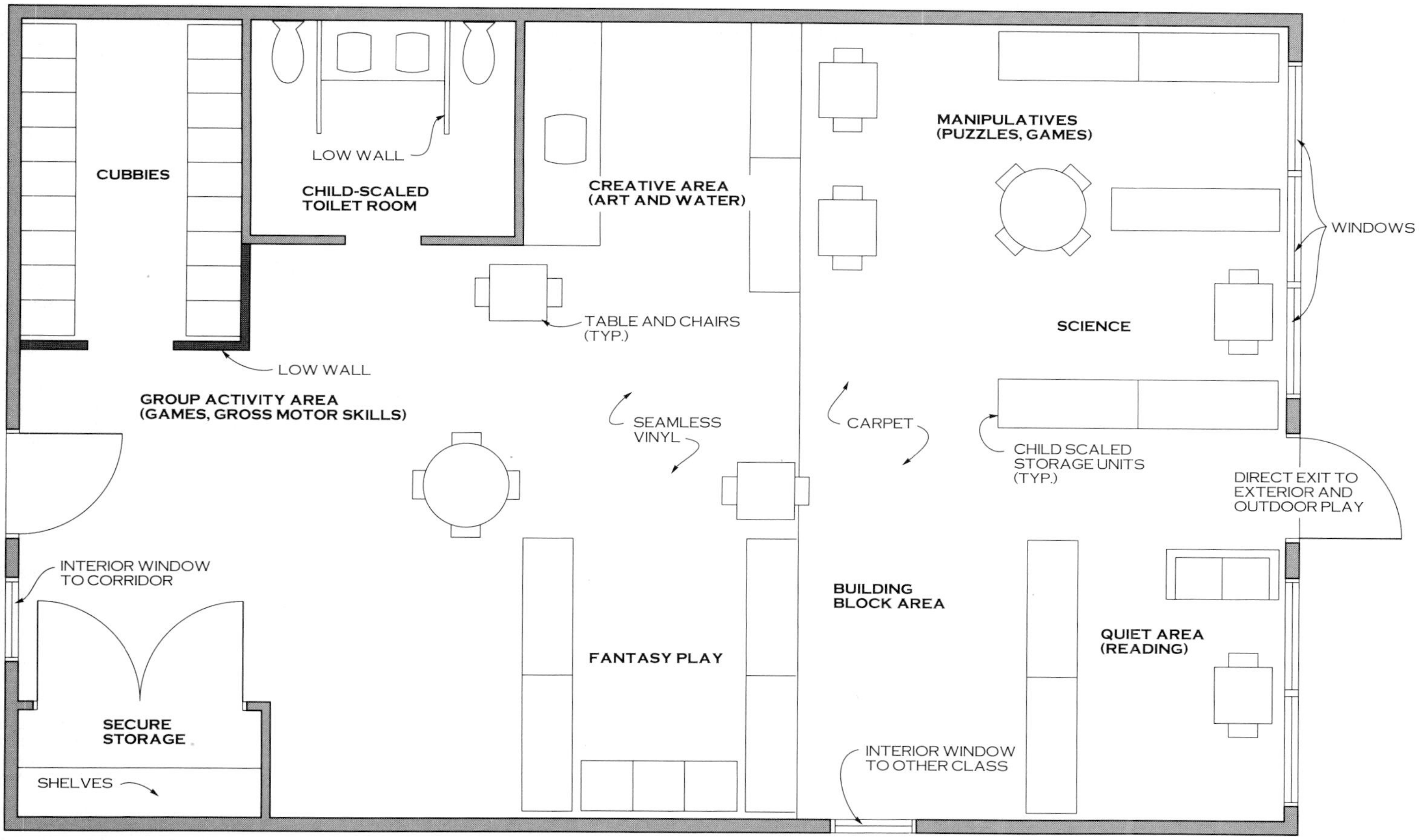

Labels within diagram:
- DIAPERING AREA
- COUNTER WITH SINK AND STORAGE
- TOILET MAY BE REQUIRED
- INTERIOR WINDOW TO OTHER CLASS
- WINDOWS
- STORAGE AND MICROWAVE
- PLAY AREA
- REFRIGERATOR
- KITCHEN
- LOW WALL AND DUTCH DOOR
- DIRECT EXIT TO EXTERIOR AND OUTDOOR PLAY
- SEAMLESS VINYL
- CARPET
- INTERIOR WINDOWS
- EATING AREA
- CRIBS
- INTERIOR WINDOW TO CORRIDOR
- NAPPING AREA
- DIRECT EXIT TO EXTERIOR AND GRADE
- LOW WALL
- SECURE STORAGE
- SHELVES

HVAC, PLUMBING, ACOUSTICAL AND ELECTRICAL REQUIREMENTS

Design temperatures should range between 68-78 °F, measured at the children's level, 1 to 3 ft. above the floor. Additional humidification should be provided. Buildings that are too hot or cold can create problems at an otherwise smoothly running center. An adequate ventilation system, with provisions for fresh and exhaust air, is critical to the health of the children. Stagnant air filled with bacteria can contribute to the spread of illness, which is one of the major problems associated with child care centers.

Hot and cold water should be provided in each classroom; however, hot water to child accessible fixtures should not exceed 110°F. Drinking water should also be provided in each classroom.

Noise is a major concern. Classrooms, infant napping areas, and offices should be sound insulated from one another. Finishes that absorb sound should be selected.

Lighting should be a combination of natural, fluorescent and incandescent to provide developing eyes with a full spectrum of light. Windows, both to the exterior and to other classroom are necessary to help the children learn about the world. Receptacles should be either installed above the children's reach, or be of a type which can only be activated when turned or twisted.

SCALE AND FINISHES

All furniture, fixtures, and equipment should be sized to accommodate the children and to promote self-esteem, learning, and independence. Building materials should be selected to relate to the children's scale, i.e., small panes of glass instead of picture windows.

Finishes are important and variety in their selection encourages interest and promotes learning. Basic colors should be neutral to offset the intense and often hectic activities of the children, their equipment, and their artwork. However, accent colors could be provided. Finishes should also be selected for their acoustical properties and ease of maintenance. Both carpeting and seamless vinyl flooring should be provided in the classrooms to support different activities.

CLASSROOM FOR TWENTY, THREE- TO FIVE-YEAR-OLDS

Labels within diagram:
- CUBBIES
- LOW WALL
- CHILD-SCALED TOILET ROOM
- CREATIVE AREA (ART AND WATER)
- MANIPULATIVES (PUZZLES, GAMES)
- WINDOWS
- TABLE AND CHAIRS (TYP.)
- SCIENCE
- LOW WALL
- GROUP ACTIVITY AREA (GAMES, GROSS MOTOR SKILLS)
- SEAMLESS VINYL
- CARPET
- CHILD SCALED STORAGE UNITS (TYP.)
- DIRECT EXIT TO EXTERIOR AND OUTDOOR PLAY
- INTERIOR WINDOW TO CORRIDOR
- BUILDING BLOCK AREA
- QUIET AREA (READING)
- SECURE STORAGE
- FANTASY PLAY
- INTERIOR WINDOW TO OTHER CLASS
- SHELVES

Linda Clark, AIA, Archi-tots, Inc.; Silver Spring, Maryland

CHILD CARE

20

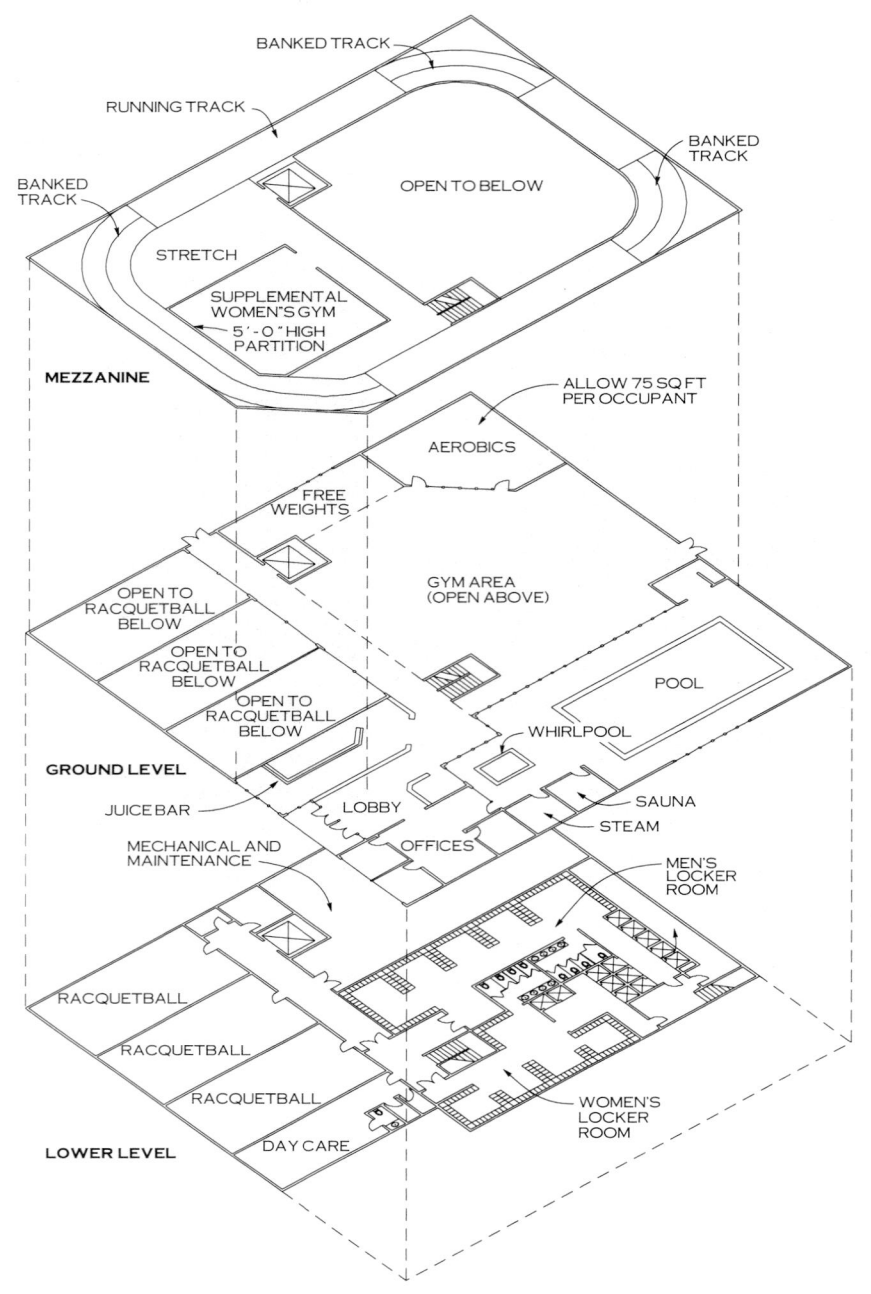

BANKED TRACK

RUNNING TRACK

BANKED TRACK

BANKED TRACK

OPEN TO BELOW

STRETCH

SUPPLEMENTAL WOMEN'S GYM 5'-0" HIGH PARTITION

MEZZANINE

ALLOW 75 SQ FT PER OCCUPANT

AEROBICS

FREE WEIGHTS

OPEN TO RACQUETBALL BELOW

OPEN TO RACQUETBALL BELOW

OPEN TO RACQUETBALL BELOW

GYM AREA (OPEN ABOVE)

POOL

WHIRLPOOL

GROUND LEVEL

JUICE BAR

LOBBY

SAUNA

STEAM

MECHANICAL AND MAINTENANCE

OFFICES

MEN'S LOCKER ROOM

RACQUETBALL

RACQUETBALL

RACQUETBALL

WOMEN'S LOCKER ROOM

LOWER LEVEL

DAY CARE

TYPICAL HEALTH CLUB LAYOUT

GENERAL

Health clubs combine many activities, services, and equipment types under one roof. The areas for each activity are usually open to each other. This promotes interaction and incentive for individuals to continue their participation. This layout visually exposes each member to other activities in which they may want to participate. The visual center of the plan is where the fitness and aerobic machines are located. Some uses are separated for privacy (e.g. locker rooms, supplemental women's gym, etc.) and for particularly high noise activities like aerobics and racquetball. Restaurants, juice bars, and lounges are also incorporated and are usually connected to the common areas.

Planning criteria for health clubs can be broken down into the following four main categories:

1. Aerobic/Cardiovascular
   a. Running track
   b. Treadmill/stair climbing machines
   c. Stationary bicycle
   d. Rowing machine
   e. Swimming pool
   f. Racquetball/squash
   g. Aerobic exercises
2. Anaerobic/Muscular Development
   a. Resistance and repetition fitness machines (includes weight, electronic, or air compression resistance)
   b. Free weights
3. Muscle and Blood Circulation Stimulation
   a. Whirlpool (hydrotherapy)
   b. Steam room (heat therapy)
   c. Sauna (heat therapy)
   d. Massage (direct muscle therapy)
4. Services and Support
   a. Fitness profile (check of weight, blood pressure, percentage of body fat, flexibility, grip strength, and cardiovascular endurance)
   b. Locker and shower rooms
   c. Restaurant and lounge
   d. Administration
   e. Day care
   f. Mechanical and maintenance

NOTES

1. Wet areas such as pools and saunas should be segregated from dry areas such as weight rooms.
2. Heavy traffic and wet areas should be finished with impervious floor materials such as ceramic tile. Wet areas should have a nonslip surface and slope to drains.
3. Open gym areas should be finished in a durable carpet with shock resistant padding.
4. Sound isolation systems should be used in all walls, ceilings, and floors that border occupied spaces. Of particular concern is impact noise from aerobic exercise, running, and free-weight training. Resiliency and mass should be built into the structure to reduce sound transmission.
5. Intense human activity, shower facilities, and the pool and sauna areas all contribute major concentrations of moisture that must be vented to the outside.
6. Lighting quality is an important issue for each activity. A diffuse or indirect system is preferred. However, moods can be created through the use of spot lighting, which can highlight activities. Use water resistant lighting in such areas as pools and steam rooms.

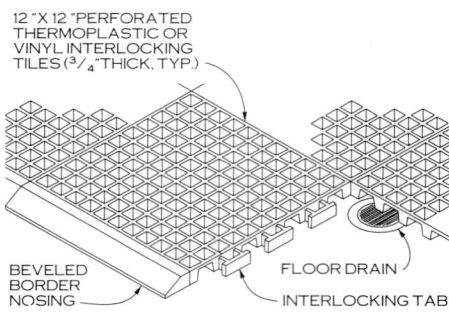

12"X 12 "PERFORATED THERMOPLASTIC OR VINYL INTERLOCKING TILES (3/4"THICK, TYP.)

BEVELED BORDER NOSING

FLOOR DRAIN

INTERLOCKING TAB

NOTE

Used in pool areas, locker rooms, etc.

FLOORING FOR WET AREAS

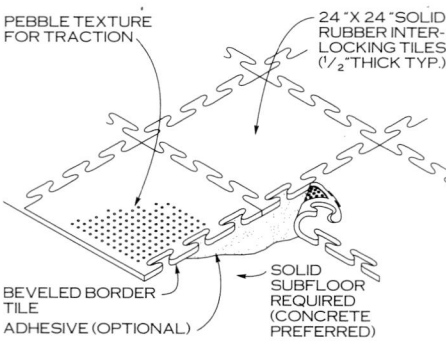

PEBBLE TEXTURE FOR TRACTION

24"X 24 "SOLID RUBBER INTERLOCKING TILES (1/2"THICK TYP.)

BEVELED BORDER TILE

ADHESIVE (OPTIONAL)

SOLID SUBFLOOR REQUIRED (CONCRETE PREFERRED)

NOTE

Used in weight rooms and for aerobic classes.

FLOORING FOR HIGH-IMPACT AREAS

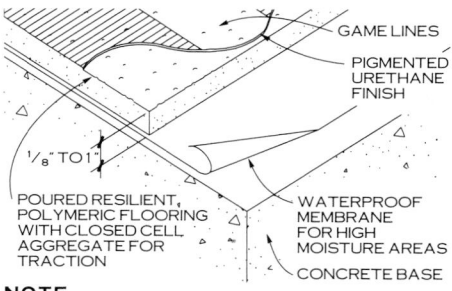

GAME LINES

PIGMENTED URETHANE FINISH

1/8" TO 1"

POURED RESILIENT, POLYMERIC FLOORING WITH CLOSED CELL AGGREGATE FOR TRACTION

WATERPROOF MEMBRANE FOR HIGH MOISTURE AREAS

CONCRETE BASE

NOTE

Used on running tracks.

POURED RESILIENT FLOORING DETAIL

Brosso, Wilhelm, & McWilliams; Baltimore, Maryland
Richard J. Vitullo, AIA; Oak Leaf Studio; Crownsville, Maryland

DIFFERENT TYPES OF MUSEUMS

The defining characteristic of any museum is its collection. Without a collection, an institution should not ordinarily be called a museum. For instance, a scientific public institution that has interpretive and interactive galleries demonstrating scientific principles and perhaps an Imax theater, but no collections, would be referred to as a science center, not a museum. Similarly, an institution that has an art school and an active art exhibition and lecture program, but no collections, would be called an art center, not an art museum.

Museums are as varied as their collections and their exhibitions. Each has its own special character and special requirements. Nevertheless, all museums do have certain things in common, which is the basis for this section of Graphic Standards.

Listed here are a few of the more common kinds of museums:

1. Art museums: paintings and sculpture, decorative arts, folk art, and textiles
2. Children's museums
3. College and university museums
4. History museums: historic houses, historical society museums, archives, military museums, maritime and naval museums and historic ships
5. Nature centers
6. Park museums and visitor centers
7. Science museums: anthropology; ethnology; aquariums and oceanariums; archaeology; entomology; geology, mineralogy and paleontology; herpetology; medical; natural history and natural science; physical science
8. Specialized museums: aeronautics and space, agriculture, architecture, circus, costume, firefighting, forestry, guns, horology, and military

Following are some of the most basic museum design considerations.

SITE CONSIDERATIONS

PUBLIC PARKING. Urban museum sites generally rely on nearby public parking, while suburban and rural sites require off-street parking convenient to the main public entrance. Typically, daily parking requirements are relatively modest. Maximum requirements will be for special opening events and "blockbuster" exhibitions. Consider sharing parking with nearby churches or businesses that have different peak hours. Valet and remote, bussed parking may be possible for a few events.

STAFF PARKING. This should be convenient to the staff entrance, which will be near shipping and receiving and will have special security measures.

SCULPTURE GARDENS. Such gardens must be either inside or outside the museum security envelope. If inside, they must be enclosed and secure (e.g., MOMA in N.Y.). If they are outside, they must be inaccessible from within the galleries (e.g., the Hirschorn in Washington, D.C.).

SHIPPING AND SERVICE FACILITIES. It is critically impor-

tant for any museum to be able to receive and send large crated and uncrated museum objects safely and efficiently, receive construction and other kinds of materials, and to dispose of trash in a sightly and efficient manner. Requirements vary according to the kinds of objects the museum will house and exhibit, but for most museums the service drive, service yard, and shipping dock must be built to accommodate full-sized over-the-road semi-trailer trucks. Provision also must be made for trash dumpsters and temporary parking for other smaller delivery and service vehicles. A 4 ft high dock will accommodate high-bed trucks but will be very awkward for low-bed trucks and vans. A 2 ft dock will be best for low trucks, but a portable ramp will be required for use with high bed trucks. Two separate docks, one at 2 ft and the other at 4 ft, is ideal. A dock leveler is an alternative. Convenient and attractive accommodation for transformers, emergency generators, chilled water machines, and similar pieces of mechanical equipment should be considered at the beginning of the design process.

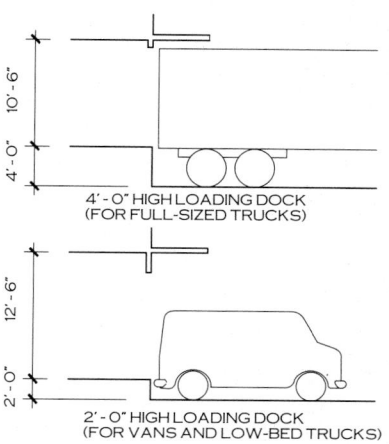

4'-0" HIGH LOADING DOCK
(FOR FULL-SIZED TRUCKS)

2'-0" HIGH LOADING DOCK
(FOR VANS AND LOW-BED TRUCKS)

LOADING DOCKS

PLANNING RELATIONSHIPS AND TYPICAL MUSEUM SPACES

Museums consist of several discrete blocks of space that must be kept separate for secure and efficient operations. Museums consist of several discrete blocks of space that must be kept separate for secure and efficient operations. Usually the main departments include: public services, educational facilities, galleries, temporary exhibitions support facilities, general staff services, collections management, collections storage, and curatorial and administrative offices. The following diagram illustrates how these relate to each other.

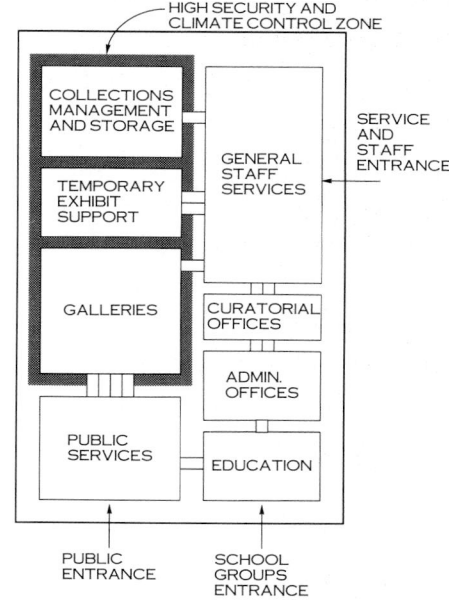

OVERALL SPACE RELATIONSHIPS

PROGRAMMING

The importance of developing a thorough program for museum planning cannot be overemphasized. Museums are composed of many different spaces, each accommodating a particular function. Different kinds of museums require very different spaces, so each anticipated function must be analyzed and accommodated individually. The two most common program mistakes are

1. Emphasizing public spaces and slighting staff support spaces (which often comprise half the museum).
2. Failing to design for future growth.

The following are the main elements that could be found in most museums, although they vary widely, depending on size, type, location, collecting goals, educational mission, etc.

PUBLIC SERVICES

These public non-gallery spaces should be located together near the public entrance. They include vestibule, public lobby, information desk, coat and parcel checkroom, museum shop, auditorium, meeting rooms, A/V presentation/orientation room, public toilets, drinking fountains, and phones.

PUBLIC LOBBY

Generally thought of as a monumental space, this lobby has many practical functions: orientation and access to all public service functions (not just the galleries) and a setting for social functions. This is the one space where windows and skylights can be effective. Size is often governed by the capacity needed for banquet dinners (at 10-12 sq ft per person plus entry and circulation space) and/or receptions (at 8-10 sq ft per person plus entry and circulation space). During receptions visitors may be dispersed throughout the galleries as well, depending on the kinds of events being held.

MEETING ROOMS AND AUDITORIUMS

These will vary widely according to the expected events program. Smaller museums usually have either a sloped floor auditorium or a multi-purpose room. Larger museums may have both. Rooms may be used for museum events, or rented to other public and private groups. The museum board should develop a policy about the use of these rooms before they are designed. For security and operating economy, auditoriums and meeting rooms must be accessible when the galleries are closed.

MUSEUM SHOP AND BOOKSTORE

This sales function is increasingly important both as an educational program and as a source of income. The retail shop should open to the lobby where it will be especially visible and attractive as visitors leave the museum. An adjacent office and inventory space are essential. Size will be determined by the intended marketing and sales program.

PUBLIC TOILETS

Toilets should be sized to accommodate the largest anticipated exhibition openings or auditorium audiences. Plumbing codes often overstate fixture requirements for gallery spaces. Galleries are never crowded all of the time. Interpretations should be clarified with appropriate building code officials.

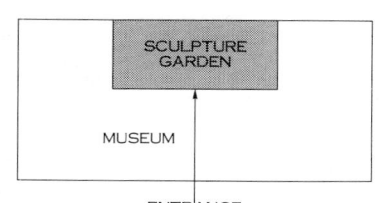

ENCLOSED SCULPTURE GARDEN (SECURE)

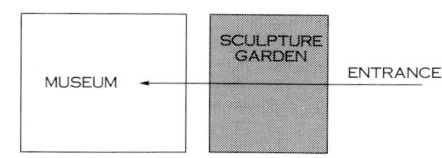

OUTDOOR SCULPTURE GARDEN (NOT SECURE)

SCULPTURE GARDENS

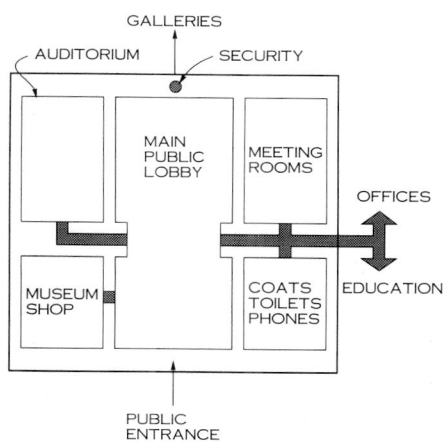

PUBLIC SERVICE RELATIONSHIPS

John D. Hilberry, AIA; John Hilberry & Associates Inc., Architects and Museum Planners; Detroit, Michigan

GALLERIES

Galleries vary widely according to the objects being exhibited. Gallery sizes and proportions as well as floor, wall, and ceiling materials and lighting must be appropriate for the specific kinds of objects exhibited. Discussed here are some of the most common gallery types:

ART GALLERIES generally are well-finished rooms where objects are displayed to aesthetic advantage but with relatively little interpretive material. Art collections include paintings, sculpture, furniture, decorative arts, murals, architectural fragments and reconstructions, prints, drawings, and photographs.

INTERPRETIVE GALLERIES are simpler architecturally, but the environment is dominated by interpretive material (historical reconstructions, photomurals, graphics, explanatory text, etc.). Interpretive exhibits cover subjects such as history and natural history and use techniques such as dioramas, period rooms, and dark rides.

SCIENCE CENTER GALLERIES may have no museum objects at all, but may feature educational interactive devices that illustrate scientific principles. These rooms may resemble classrooms or even play areas rather than traditional gallery spaces.

VISIBLE STORAGE GALLERIES contain dense presentations of large numbers of museum objects from the collection with little interpretation but with reference materials available for study.

CHANGING EXHIBITION GALLERIES are flexible galleries used for a wide variety of exhibitions, each installed for a limited period.

COMBINATION GALLERIES integrate several gallery types. Most galleries should be capable of being deinstalled and used for special exhibitions from time to time.

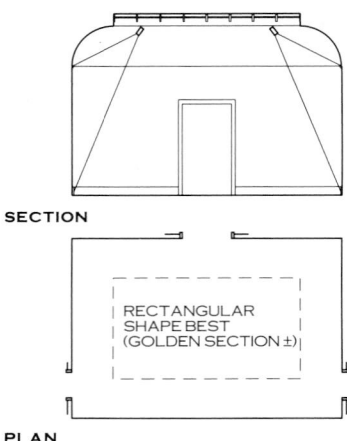

SECTION

PLAN

TRADITIONAL ART GALLERY

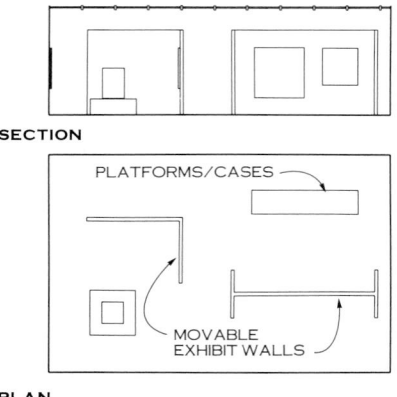

SECTION

PLAN

FLEXIBLE OPEN-PLAN GALLERY

GALLERY CHARACTERISTICS

DISCRETE ROOMS: Galleries should be isolated spaces conducive to concentrating on the objects exhibited. The museum-viewing experience is a private one and should not be interrupted by other people moving on balconies, peeking in windows, etc. When the museum is closed, the galleries should become secure dark vaults.

GALLERY FLEXIBILITY. Even "permanent" exhibitions change over time, and all galleries must provide an appropriate amount of flexibility. Traditional art museums achieve this by providing a variety of well designed, proportioned, and organized gallery rooms of different sizes and characters. This arrangement provides the ability to locate different exhibitions in different rooms at different times. A more modernist approach has been to provide open floor space, a modular ceiling system, and movable exhibition walls, so the space can be reconfigured at will. This solution offers the ultimate in plan flexibility, but sacrifices spatial variety and richness in favor of anonymous continuity. The former may be better for permanent galleries and the latter for contemporary art and changing exhibition galleries. A middle ground is to provide some level of physical changeability within the context of fixed gallery rooms.

GALLERY PROPORTIONS. Galleries with pleasing proportions provide the best exhibit spaces. Generally a rectangular floor plan is best. Ceiling heights should be proportional to the plan size of the room and to the objects to be exhibited. Generally 11 to 14 ft is appropriate. Lower ceilings may be acceptable in certain intimate galleries such as those exhibiting old master prints, photographs, or other especially small objects. Ceilings higher than 16 ft are useful occasionally, but generally they are difficult to work with and tend to dwarf the objects being exhibited.

GALLERY FINISH MATERIALS: Galleries must be finished as attractive working exhibit spaces. Floors, wall, and (ideally) ceilings all should be capable of having fasteners secured to them that can support considerable weight. Floors and walls should have securely attached $^3/_4$ in. tongue and groove plywood substrate. Suitable flooring materials are tongue and groove hardwood strip flooring or carpet. Suitable wall materials are thin ($^1/_4$ or $^3/_8$ in.) drywall or stretched fabric. Wall carpet sometimes is appropriate. Ceilings can be plain painted drywall or an acoustical grid. If the floor is hard, an acoustical ceiling is especially useful. Ceiling grids should be simple, orderly, and unobtrusive. Recessed lighting tracks are less obtrusive than surface-mounted tracks.

GALLERY SUPPORT SPACES: Storage space for track lighting fixtures and bulbs, pedestals, vitrines, cases, movable exhibition partitions and panels, and other items should be immediately accessible to the galleries. If necessary, this space can be provided in a remote location, but nearby is much more convenient.

INDIVIDUAL GALLERY SIZES AND CEILING HEIGHTS

GALLERY TYPE	FLOOR AREA (SQ FT)	CEILING HEIGHT (FT)
Intimate Galleries Old Master prints & drawings Archival documents Jewelry Small decorative arts Small artifacts Miniature dioramas Gems & minerals Insects, small animals	300 - 900	9 - 11
Medium Galleries 14-19 C. paintings Traditional sculpture Furniture Decorative arts Small historical exhibits Medium-sized artifacts Most scientific exhibits Interactive galleries Most temporary exhibits	1,000 - 2,000	11 - 14

Large Galleries
Central gallery among
  smaller galleries
Large Baroque paintings
20th C. paintings & sculpture
Temporary exhibitions
Industrial history
Architectural reconstructions
Historical reconstructions
Large dioramas
Large natural history
  exhibits (dinosaurs,
  whales, etc.)
	2,000 - 5,000	14 - 20

TEMPORARY EXHIBITION STORAGE AND STAGING

Adequate spaces must be provided for receiving and handling exhibition materials, which usually arrive by truck in crates. These materials consist of museum objects borrowed from other institutions and/or individuals, which means that conservation-standard climate control and security must be provided in order to avoid liability for damage and to meet the strict requirements sophisticated modern lenders often impose on borrowing institutions. The main temporary exhibition support facilities are discussed here:

SHIPPING AND RECEIVING FACILITIES. Receiving and sending major traveling exhibitions require first-rate facilities. A good shipping and receiving room has an appropriate loading dock with a large shipping door and immediate access to the crating/uncrating room and to the freight elevator. Very close monitoring of this space by security personnel is essential.

CRATING/UNCRATING ROOM. A large room must be provided as a work space for crating and uncrating borrowed museum objects, for temporarily storing both the objects and their crates, and for examining, photographing, and organizing the objects in preparation for gallery installation. Space may be required to handle several exhibitions simultaneously. The space must be secure and climate controlled to museum conservation standards. This must be a clean room, not a carpentry or paint shop. Appropriate work surfaces, supplies storage, and collection storage equipment must be provided.

TEMPORARY COLLECTIONS STORAGE. After objects are removed from their crates, they must be examined, organized, and safely stored prior to installation. After the exhibition closes, they must be stored and prepared for crating.

TEMPORARY CRATE STORAGE. While the objects are in the museum, the crates must be stored and maintained under proper humidity conditions.

COLLECTIONS MANAGEMENT

These are the facilities that accommodate the handling, care, storage, and conservation of the museum's own collections. Clear unobstructed passageways are essential between the shipping dock to the carpentry shop, crating/uncrating room, galleries, and collections storerooms. Door openings, freight elevators, and passageway heights, widths, and corner configurations must be uniformly large. Placement of ducts and piping must be carefully coordinated to avoid bottlenecks.

The extent of the facilities for collections management will vary widely depending on the extent and nature of the collections and the level of registration, research, and conservation activity that is appropriate or that the institution can afford. Following are discussions of the most important of these facilities.

REGISTRATION. This is one of the most basic museum functions. The registrar generally is responsible for handling all museum objects, keeping track of their location within the museum, and maintaining records about each object, whether owned by the museum or loaned as part of a temporary exhibition. Whenever an object enters or leaves the museum, or even if it is moved around within the museum, the registrar must record that event, make a condition report if necessary, and make sure the movement or removal of the object is appropriate and authorized. These activities require office and work space, facilities for extensive paper files and computer operations, and sometimes space for temporary object storage.

COLLECTIONS STORAGE. The collection storerooms are extremely important and should be located with the other collections management facilities (see Museum Storage).

MATTING AND FRAMING. Any museum that exhibits works of art on paper, photographs, documents, or other two-dimensional paper objects will have an active matting and framing operation. Since paper objects cannot be exhibited for long periods of time without damaging them, they must be constantly taken in and out of frames, and all framed objects must first be matted. This must be a clean room (not a carpentry shop) with work tables and storage for materials. Minor conservation procedures also may take place here if the museum does not have a conservation laboratory.

CONSERVATION LABORATORIES. Most smaller museums do not have conservation labs. Larger museums, however, may have extensive facilities, including separate laboratories for specialized conservation procedures such as those required for paintings, sculpture, 3-D decorative arts, textiles, cars, industrial machinery, fossils, taxidermy, or anthropological artifacts. Each kind of conservation requires special facilities and equipment.

John D. Hilberry, AIA; John Hilberry & Associates Inc., Architects and Museum Planners; Detroit, Michigan

MUSEUM STORAGE

Collections storage and general storage are very different and should not be confused. General storage space can be inexpensive and its location is not critical. Collections storage, however, must meet the most exacting security and climate control requirements and must be correctly located.

GENERAL STORAGE

Museums require large amounts of miscellaneous material that must be stored, either on the premises or in some remote location. On-premises storage is much more convenient. Provision of adequate general storage space is cost-effective, since this space is relatively inexpensive and, if sufficient space is not allowed, general storage items inevitably pre-empt space in more expensive parts of the museum. Storage may be required for grounds and building maintenance equipment and supplies, lifts, ladders, materials-handling equipment, mechanical and electrical equipment and supplies, central office supplies, museum shop inventory, exhibition light fixtures and bulbs, general lighting fluorescent tubes and bulbs, seasonal paraphernalia, volunteer committee supplies, general furniture (tables, desks, chairs, lecterns, etc.), exhibition furniture (pedestals, vitrines, cases, exhibition walls, platforms, etc.), laboratory equipment, audio/visual equipment, and crates (other than those associated with traveling exhibitions). Storage requirements for each of these items should be identified and quantified separately, even if they are to be stored together.

COLLECTIONS STORAGE

Proper care of its collections is one of the main responsibilities of any museum. Location and design of the collections storerooms, therefore, should be a primary planning and design consideration. Since the mission of most museums is to collect continuously, provision for growth is fundamental. Collections storerooms must be clean, dry, secure, well lighted, free of overhead pipes containing liquids, and properly air conditioned to conservation climate control standards. They must be located conveniently near shipping and receiving, curatorial offices, and registration and other collections management facilities. An interior location is ideal. Minimizing the possibility of flooding or other water damage is essential. Whether collections storage is separated into distinct rooms or kept together in large open vaults depends on the nature of the collections and on administrative policies about staff responsibilities.

COLLECTIONS STORAGE EQUIPMENT

Different objects require different kinds of storage equipment. Types and numbers of storage units and the floor area that will be required must be determined by analysis of the collections in close cooperation with the collections management staff. Space must be provided for storage of fork lifts, dollies, and other materials-handling equipment. Some of the more common types of storage equipment are painting screens, painting bins, open steel shelving, closed steel cabinets, wet specimen cabinets, drawer units, flat files, wardrobe units, rolled textile storage racks, hand racks, pallet racks, floor pallets, and oversized objects storage areas. In addition to the storage units, many museum objects are kept in containers, such as acid-free boxes, solander boxes, textile screens, and rolled textile tubes, which are placed in or on the storage units.

COMPACTOR SYSTEMS

A number of companies manufacture systems that permit aisles of shelving units to roll, permitting substantially higher density of objects in storerooms. These systems, though efficient, are costly, less convenient, and may inhibit the ability of fire suppression systems to extinguish flames inside the collections storage units when in the closed position. They require either depressed floor construction for built-in recessed floor tracks or ramps for the surface installation of tracks. Since storage is always at a premium, prudent programming often suggests that adequate storage space be built without compactors, but that provisions be made so they can be added in case of unanticipated collections growth.

SCIENTIFIC RESEARCH LABORATORIES

Science museums often involve significant research programs, which require laboratories of various kinds, including clean, dirty, and wet laboratories, and special storage and equipment rooms. The requirements for each of these rooms must be programmed in close cooperation with the scientists involved.

EDUCATION SPACES

Many museums have active educational programs, ongoing A/V presentations, and orientation talks for groups of both children and adults. The following list includes some important education spaces:

1. Holding areas for children's coats, etc.
2. Orientation rooms
3. Studio classrooms
4. Lecture classrooms
5. Staff and docent offices

ADMINISTRATIVE AND CURATORIAL OFFICES AND WORK SPACES

The offices themselves will not be much different from business or academic offices. The appropriate number and size of spaces must be based on projected staff and activities. Generally, museum staffs grow faster than anticipated after new facilities are completed, and ample allowance should be made for "future office" space. These offices can be located with the collections management and general staff areas, or they can be separated. Practical planning considerations often dictate that they be separated. Curators may need larger than usual offices if they will have museum objects in their offices for examination and research. Security and HVAC implications of this possibility must be considered.

GENERAL STAFF SERVICES

Back-of-house facilities required for museums to operate efficiently may include shipping and receiving room(s), shipping clerk's office, sallyport, central security station, maintenance shop, carpentry shop, paint shop, graphics studio, typesetting room, exhibition preparation room, taxidermy shop, isolation room, trash room, compactor room, recycling center, dermistid room, greenhouse, X-ray laboratory, photography studio, darkroom, refrigerated specimen room, flammable liquids storeroom, instrument room, A/V storage and work room, and guards' toilets, showers, and dressing rooms. Not all museums will have all of these spaces, and in smaller museums some spaces will be combined. In larger ones, several spaces may be dedicated to one function.

MUSEUM SECURITY

Good museum security results from a combination of good museum planning, good lock and alarm systems, and good professional and security staff practices. A specialized museum security consultant can assist the museum staff and the architect with all of these issues. Planning for security involves understanding the zones that must be kept separate and how public, staff, and objects will move through the facility under different circumstances. When entering and leaving the galleries, the public should be required to pass one easily monitored checkpoint. Non-gallery public functions (such as auditorium, museum shop, or toilets) should not be accessed through the galleries. When closed, galleries should function as secure vaults. Emergency fire exits from galleries should be minimal, alarmed, and located and designed for easy observation of anyone using them.

Staff areas should be clearly separated from galleries and public services. Shipping and receiving and staff entrances must be tightly monitored and easily controlled by the security staff. Collections storerooms should be treated as vaults and should contain no mechanical or electrical equipment that might require access for maintenance or in emergencies. Mechanical ductwork and grilles must be designed to prevent access by burglars to locked galleries and collection storerooms.

Electronic alarm systems should be designed by professionals specializing in museum security systems. Such specialized professionals also should be consulted with regard to locking systems. Often alarm system work is not part of the general A&E contract for reasons of confidentiality. Sometimes alarm company sales personnel design these systems, but this can produce less than ideal results. Because of the liabilities involved, this issue should be discussed carefully with appropriate museum authorities.

Public and staff movement through the museum must be carefully separated. There should be only one public and one staff/shipping entrance to the museum. Public and staff areas will be open at different times, and each should be securable when not open. Public service areas should be easily accessible during open hours. Ideally, there should be only one point of access to the galleries from the public services area. Access from public to staff areas should be strictly limited and easily monitored. Staff should not need to move through galleries when they are closed. The staff entrance and shipping and receiving dock should be together and both easily monitored and controlled by security personnel.

Auditoriums, theaters, and food service facilities present special service access problems because they operate on different schedules from other museum functions and these operations may conflict with the museum's needs for security and cleanliness. Separate service access for these facilities may be appropriate.

In most small and medium sized museums, the central security station should be located at the service entrance with secure windows opening to the outdoors, to the shipping and receiving room, and to a staff entrance sallyport. In large museums, the central station may be in a more secure location away from all entrances, with a shipping clerk's station at the service entrance. The following is a typical security station layout.

```
                    GENERAL STORAGE

COLLECTIONS STORAGE

                                    BUILDING
                                    MAINT.

            OTHER
            GENERAL
            STAFF
            SERVICES
TEMPORARY, EXHIBIT SUPPORT          CARPENTRY
                                    GENERAL
                                    SHOPS

                                    SHIPPING
                                    AND          SHIPPING DOCK
                                    RECEIVING

            STAFF
            TOILETS
                                    SECURITY

GALLERIES                           SALLYPORT    STAFF ENTRANCE

                ADMINISTRATIVE
                AND CURATORIAL
                OFFICES
```

GENERAL STAFF RELATIONSHIPS

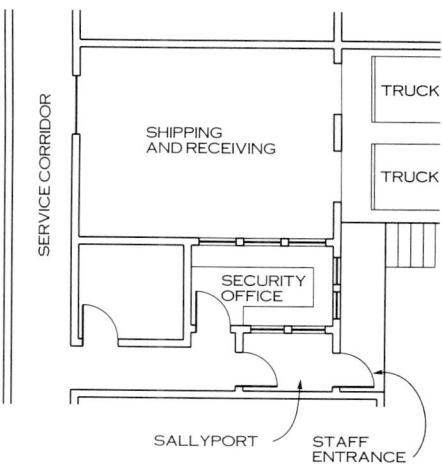

TYPICAL SECURITY ARRANGEMENT AT SHIPPING AND STAFF ENTRANCE

John D. Hilberry, AIA; John Hilberry & Associates Inc., Architects and Museum Planners; Detroit, Michigan

MUSEUM LIGHTING

Museum lighting presents a fundamental paradox, since the very light that is essential to appreciation of the exhibited objects also may be an agent for their destruction. Lighting requirements vary widely from museum to museum and from one part to another of a single museum.

PUBLIC SERVICES. Lighting for public functions should be treated in the most aesthetically pleasing way, since these spaces set the tone for the entire institution and introduce the gallery exhibitions. Public service spaces generally do not contain museum objects, so the use of natural light is acceptable if the galleries are distinctly separate from these spaces. If this separation is less distinct, however, natural lighting in the lobby will have to be strictly limited. In any case, lighting levels in the lobby must not be so high that the galleries seem dark by comparison.

GALLERY LIGHTING. Basic gallery lighting consists of a good track lighting system properly placed in relation to the exhibition walls (see drawing). Line voltage (120V) track offers more flexibility in selection of fixtures (a key consideration), and the fixtures generally produce a softer effect with less glare. Low voltage fixtures can produce more highly focused beams for special effects. Small low voltage fixtures (MR-16) are less intrusive but more expensive and, since the sources are more concentrated, the light quality is harsher. Concealed or shielded lighting sources are desirable (see drawing). General lighting ordinarily is neither required nor desirable. Track lighting can be exposed, shielded, or concealed.

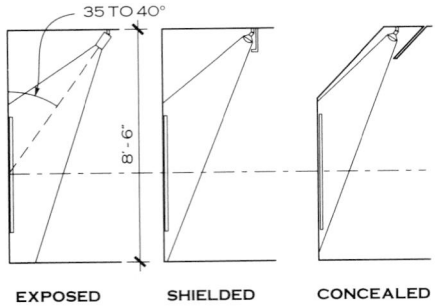

TRACK LIGHTING CONFIGURATIONS

WINDOWS generally are undesirable in galleries because of glare, photochemical degradation, visual competition with the objects exhibited, and security issues. Sculpture galleries are a possible exception, since stone and bronze are essentially unaffected by light.

SKYLIGHTING can be effective, but must be fully understood and very skillfully designed. Many expensive gallery daylighting schemes fail to perform well. Special lighting design consultation is recommended. Risks include photochemical degradation and fading of museum objects due to too high light levels, too much ultraviolet light, too much heat gain, lack of light control for special exhibitions where natural light may be undesirable, inability to eliminate all light when the galleries are closed, and possible security exposure.

If used, skylighting should be placed in the center of fixed galleries so that the light generally comes from behind viewers as they look at the exhibition walls. Overall top lighting in flexible gallery spaces can result in lighting that is too flat and can produce glare. Some of the most successful uses of skylighting have limited the natural light to general diffused reflected light on ceiling surfaces, leaving the actual exhibition lighting to track lighting fixtures. Clerestories are safer and more easily controlled than horizontal or pitched skylights and can result in satisfactory background light levels. Accent and nighttime lighting still will be required in any case.

The ultraviolet component of gallery lighting is especially dangerous. UV rays can be avoided almost entirely by using incandescent light sources. If natural or other light sources are involved, careful UV filtration is essential. Light reflected from surfaces covered with white (titanium dioxide) paint contains much less UV than direct light.

The intensity of all forms of light must be carefully controlled. Lighting intensities should be discussed with a qualified conservator, but the following are commonly recommended maximum lighting levels for various kinds of common museum objects.

MAXIMUM LIGHT LEVELS FOR VARIOUS MUSEUM OBJECTS

TYPE OF OBJECT	MAXIMUM LIGHT LEVEL
Oil paintings	200 lux
Prints and drawings	50 lux
Photographs	50 lux
Textiles	50 lux
Organic materials (painted leather, wood, etc.)	50 lux
Bronze and stone	no limit

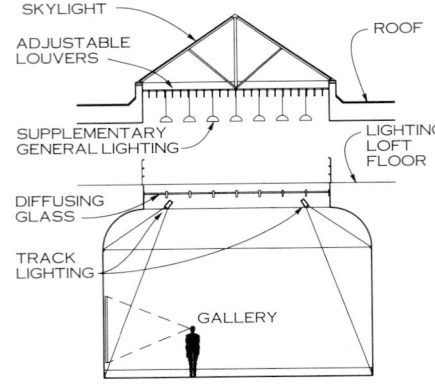

TRADITIONAL SKYLIT GALLERY

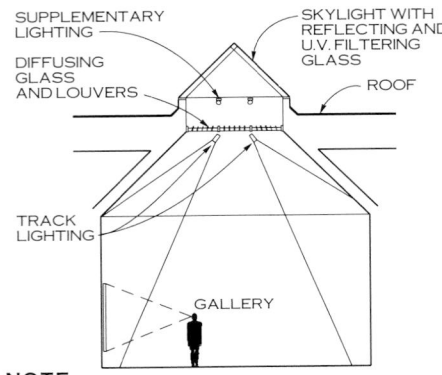

NOTE

All light above and behind observer

MODERN SKYLIT GALLERY

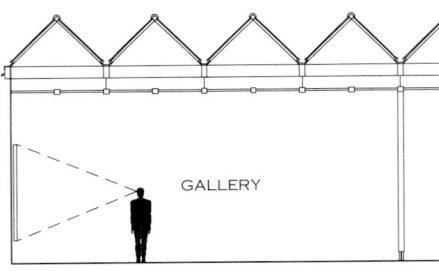

NOTE

Light above but also in front of observer (glare)

CONTINUOUS SKYLIT GALLERY

LIGHTING IN COLLECTIONS STOREROOMS. Lighting in collections storerooms should provide adequate light for safe handling and examination of objects while protecting them from unnecessary exposure, especially to ultraviolet light. In large storerooms, lighting should be switched so that general light is provided for safe passage in main aisles, and additional light can be switched on when needed in particular areas. This will make for an economical operation and will prevent unnecessary exposure of the objects.

Fluorescent lighting is most common because it is inexpensive, but it must be provided with UV shielding, usually through use of sleeves for individual tubes. Indirect systems that reflect light from a white ceiling painted with titanium dioxide paint will greatly reduce the UV component and result in even light distribution. Light from high pressure sodium bulbs contains almost no ultraviolet light and is excellent from the point of view of conservation. Color discrimination is difficult in this light, however, necessitating separate examining areas with continuous spectrum lighting. Portable lighting also may be used for examination of objects in place.

CLIMATE CONTROL

ZONING. At the outset of any museum project, it must be decided whether the entire building will be maintained at conservation standards or only those areas containing collections items (galleries and collections storerooms). If the conservation-standard areas are limited, the rest of the building can be treated like any other public building. Adequate physical separations, including vapor barriers, must be provided, however, between conservation and human comfort zones. In particular, this may mean the galleries will have to be separated from the main public lobby with glass doors (which are also desirable for security reasons). If galleries and collections storerooms are located in interior zones only, many problems and expenses can be avoided.

HUMIDITY CONTROL. Control of relative humidity is the single most critical factor in museum environments. Although ideal conditions vary for different kinds of collections, desirable R.H. for most museum objects is approximately 50%. This level must be held constant, day and night, summer and winter. Fluctuations in R.H. are very destructive, repeatedly stressing the materials of which museum objects are made.

Maintenance of 50% relative humidity throughout the winter months in cold climates tends to produce severe condensation on windows and within the exterior wall construction. Prevention of condensation requires installation of exceptionally good vapor barriers and insulation systems. A completely continuous "zero perm" vapor barrier system is essential in these circumstances. In this context, "zero perm" means a permeability rating of less than .01 grains of water per square foot per hour per inch of mercury vapor pressure in accordance with ASTM E 96 test procedure A, B, or BW. The design of wall and roof systems to accommodate such vapor barriers is difficult and should not be undertaken casually.

If, in a cold climate situation, it is determined that installation of zero perm vapor barriers and required mechanical equipment is impossible or impractical, the fall-back position should be to design the wall and roof systems to permit one slow controlled cycle per year, varying from about 25% R.H. in winter to about 50% in summer. Climate control for museums housed in historic buildings reviewed on a case-by-case basis to weigh the importance of protecting the building against the importance of protecting the collection. Hourly, daily, or weekly fluctuations must be avoided under any circumstances.

AIR FILTRATION. Requirements for air filtration vary depending on the quality of the outside air and the conservation demands of the museum objects to be housed. Generally, a good choice would be bag filters with throwaway pre-filters, UL Rating Class 1: particulates removed to 95% efficiency on ASHRAE 52/76. Electrostatic filters must not be used because they produce destructive ozone. Activate carbon filters are effective in removing gaseous pollutants, but they are expensive and require active maintenance.

OPERATING CYCLES. Heating and cooling loads vary greatly between occupied galleries (with lights and people) and unoccupied ones (closed and dark). When unoccupied, systems should be designed to operate at a low maintenance level. Since air volumes are large and pollutant sources nearly non-existent, when a gallery is closed it should be possible to reduce or eliminate outside air in order to improve environmental stability and operating economy.

LOCATION OF PIPING. All piping containing liquids should be kept out of areas containing museum objects. In particular, plumbing should not be located above galleries and collections storerooms.

LOCATION OF OUTLETS, SWITCHES, AND CONTROLS. All convenience outlets, switches, HVAC thermostats, humidistats, and other control devices must be kept off gallery walls. Outlets should be in the base and in the floor. Switches should be remote. Thermostats and humidistats can be located in return air ducts. Gallery walls must be for exhibition purposes only.

John D. Hilberry, AIA; John Hilberry & Associates Inc., Architects and Museum Planners; Detroit, Michigan

AIRFIELD

The principal component of an airport site is the airfield, which includes the runways, taxiways, and areas for navigational aids. The airfield configuration is the primary factor in determining the layout of the airport site. Basic types of runway configurations are illustrated below. Runways are oriented to take advantage of prevailing winds and to minimize crosswind conditions. Runway length varies for climate conditions (elevation and maximum air temperature) and type of aircraft. The number of runways is a function of the volume of aircraft activity.

SITE LAYOUT

The layout plan illustrates a large airport with a diverse assembly of facilities that are typically required to support the principal aviation function of transporting passengers and cargo. The facilities of the terminal area include the aircraft gates, which should be located to optimize aircraft movement to and from the runways, the terminal itself, and the interface with the ground transportation system, which includes access roadways and parking, and may also include a rail or rapid transit station. Facilities with restrictive location requirements include the air traffic control tower (ATCT), which requires clear sightlines to runways, taxiways, and other areas of aircraft operations, and the aircraft rescue and fire fighting (ARFF) facility, whose site is determined by mandatory response time criteria. Another element of the site layout is the security perimeter, which must encompass all aircraft operating areas. Typically, passenger terminals and cargo buildings are incorporated into the security perimeter. Among the recent trends in airport facilities are the use of automated transit systems (people movers) and the incorporation of large commercial developments (hotels, retail, offices, and conference centers) on the landside of the terminal.

REGULATIONS AND STANDARDS

In the United States, the Federal Aviation Administration (FAA) is principally responsible for the regulations and standards applicable to the design of airports. On a worldwide basis, the International Civil Aviation Organization (ICAO) defines uniform standards and recommended procedures. Enforcement and practice, however, remain within the jurisdiction of individual countries. The reference section lists FAA and ICAO documents that contain useful planning information.

RUNWAY AND TAXIWAY CLEARANCES

The location and height of buildings and other obstacles on or near the airport are regulated by a defined set of imaginary surfaces. The transitional surfaces begin at a prescribed distance from either side of the runway centerline and extend upward at a 7:1 slope. The section illustrates the transitional surface for a precision instrument runway. The approach surfaces extend from beyond the ends of the runway beginning at a 50:1 slope. The runway protection zone, which corresponds to the first part of the approach surface, is usually depicted on site plans. The separation criteria for runway centerlines and taxiway centerlines is based on aircraft wingspan clearances. Clearances illustrated will accommodate a Boeing 747-400.

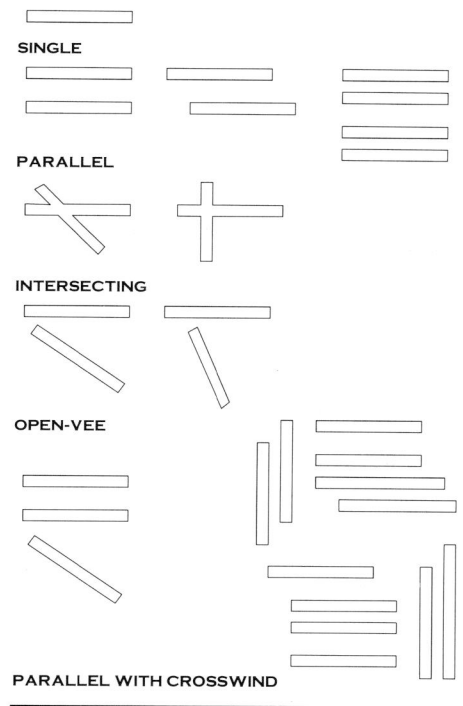

SINGLE

PARALLEL

INTERSECTING

OPEN-VEE

PARALLEL WITH CROSSWIND

RUNWAY CONFIGURATIONS

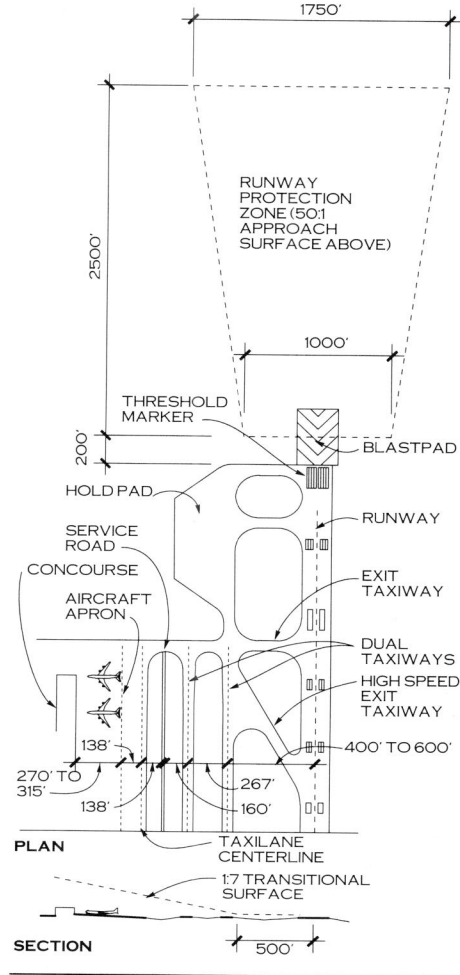

RUNWAY AND TAXIWAY CLEARANCES

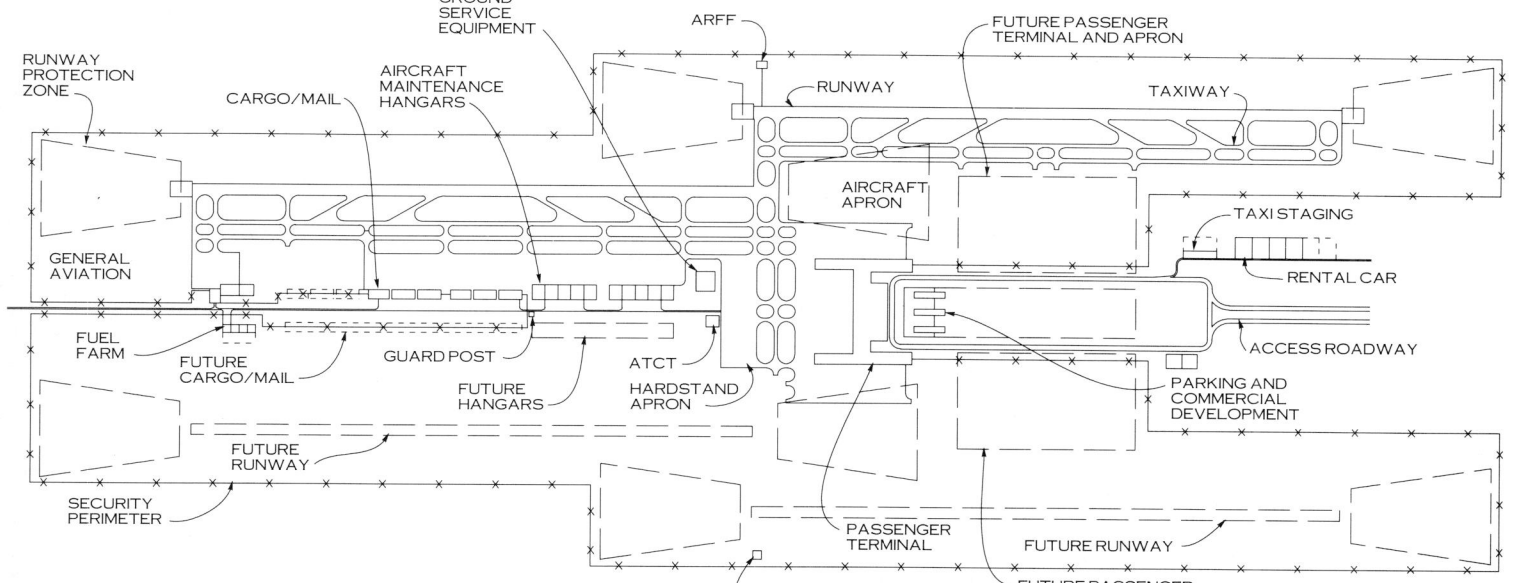

SITE LAYOUT

Mark Romack, Perkins & Will; Chicago, Illinois

AIRCRAFT DESIGN GROUPS

The FAA groups aircraft into six (6) categories based on wingspan. Representative airplanes of groups II, III, IV, and V are illustrated.

GROUP I (WINGSPAN UP TO 49')
NOT DEPICTED

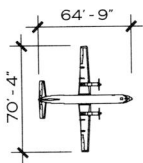

SAAB SF-340

GROUP II (WINGSPAN 49' TO 79')

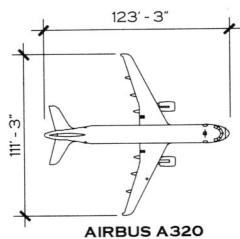

AIRBUS A320

GROUP III (WINGSPAN 79' TO 118')

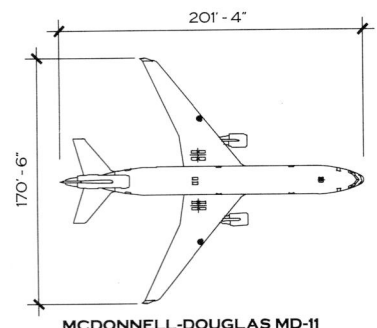

MCDONNELL-DOUGLAS MD-11

GROUP IV (WINGSPAN 118' TO 171')

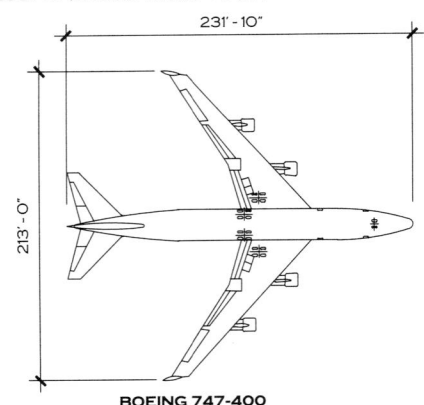

BOEING 747-400

GROUP V (WINGSPAN 171' TO 214')

GROUP VI (WINGSPAN 214' TO 262')
NOT DEPICTED

AIRPLANE CLASSIFICATIONS

TERMINAL CONFIGURATIONS

The most important determinant in the configuration of the terminal is the arrangement of aircraft gates. The four basic types—pier, linear, satellite, and transporter—are illustrated. The pier arrangement results in a compact aircraft apron but creates cul-de-sacs that can restrict aircraft movement. Linear arrangements offer unrestricted aircraft movement but are problematic for hub locations where an airline with many gates will find its operations spread over considerable distances. Satellite configurations use under-apron pedestrian corridors or automated transit systems to connect terminal processing areas with remote concourse gates. Transporter schemes use buses or mobile lounges to convey passengers between the terminal and noncontact (hardstand) gates. Many airports have some noncontact gates, but few rely on this concept as the principal terminal configuration. Combinations of the four types are often used.

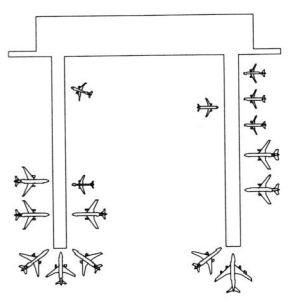
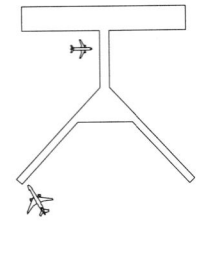
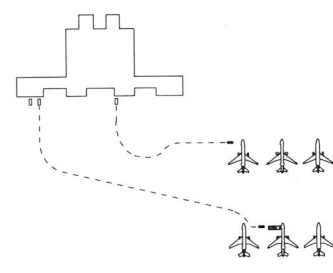

PIER

TRANSPORTER

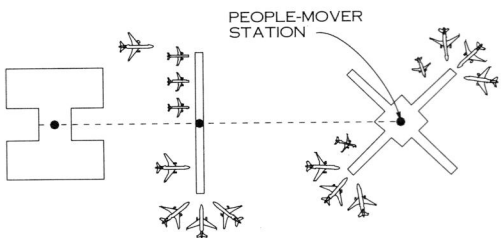
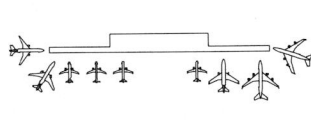

SATELLITE

LINEAR

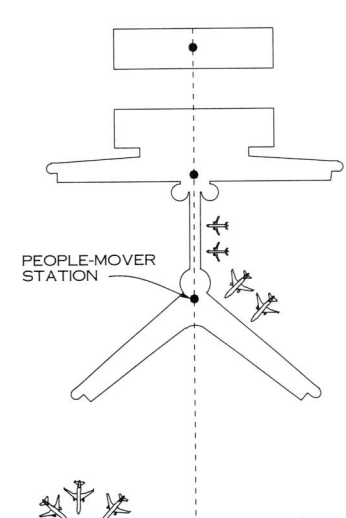
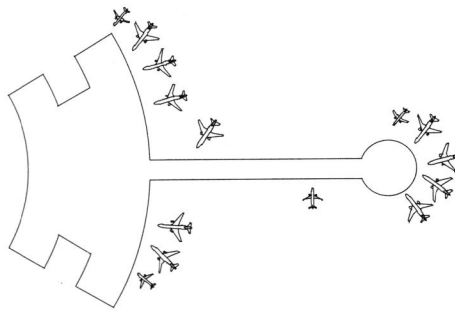

LINEAR AND PIER (TEE)

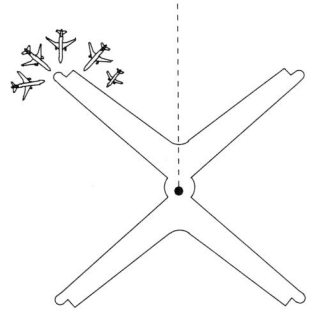
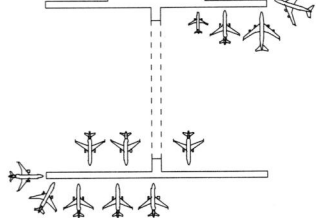

PIER AND SATELLITE

LINEAR AND SATELLITE

TERMINAL CONFIGURATIONS

Mark Romack, Perkins & Will; Chicago, Illinois

 AIRPORTS

TERMINAL PLANNING

The organization of the interior spaces of a terminal chiefly depends on the flow of passengers and their baggage through a series of processing steps between aircraft and ground transportation, or from aircraft to aircraft in the case of connecting passengers. Typical flows for arrivals and departures at U.S. airports are diagrammed. Floor plans illustrate the general layout and adjacencies for a small airport serving commuter aircraft and narrow-body jets.

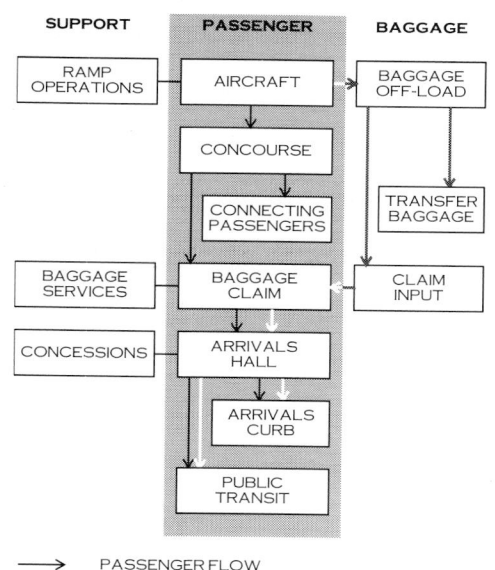

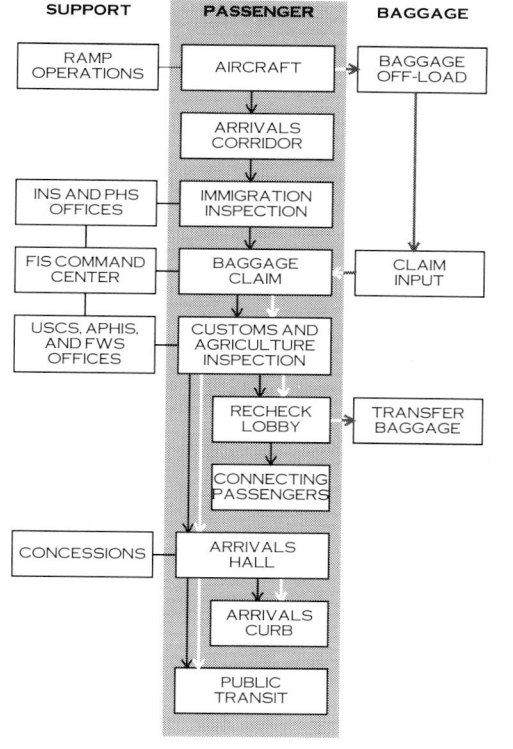

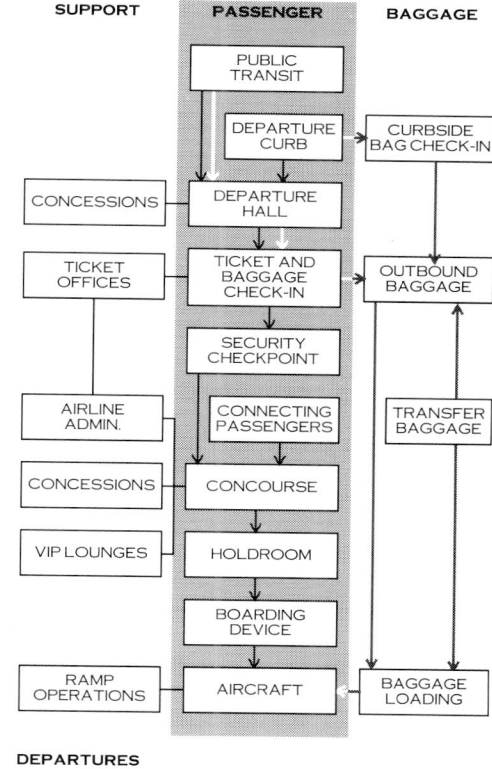

ARRIVALS (DOMESTIC)

ARRIVALS (INTERNATIONAL)

DEPARTURES

PASSENGER FLOW

CHECKED BAGGAGE FLOW

NOTE

Federal Inspection Services (FIS) consist of Immigration and Naturalization Services (INS), Public Health Services (PHS), United States Customs Service (USCS), Animal and Plant Health Inspection Service (APHIS), and Fish and Wildlife Service (FWS).

FLOW DIAGRAMS

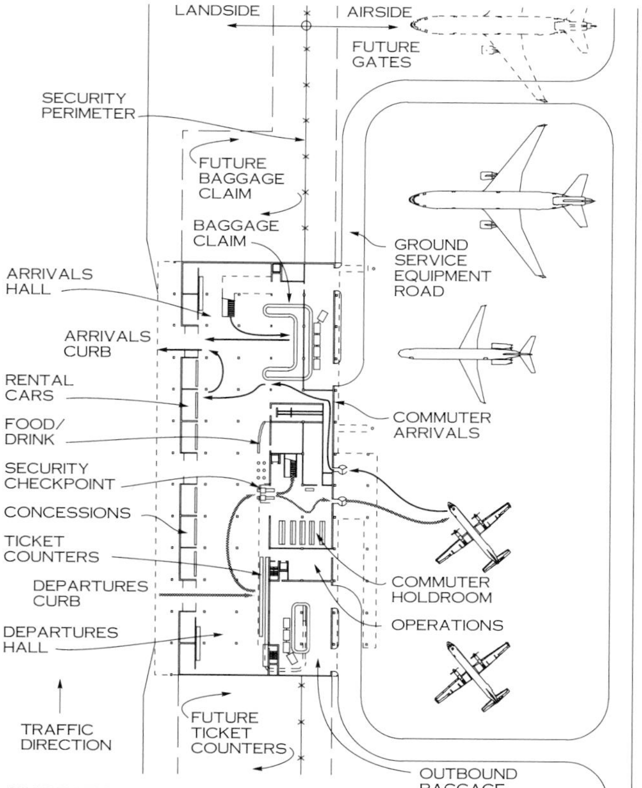

GRADE LEVEL PASSENGER FLOW

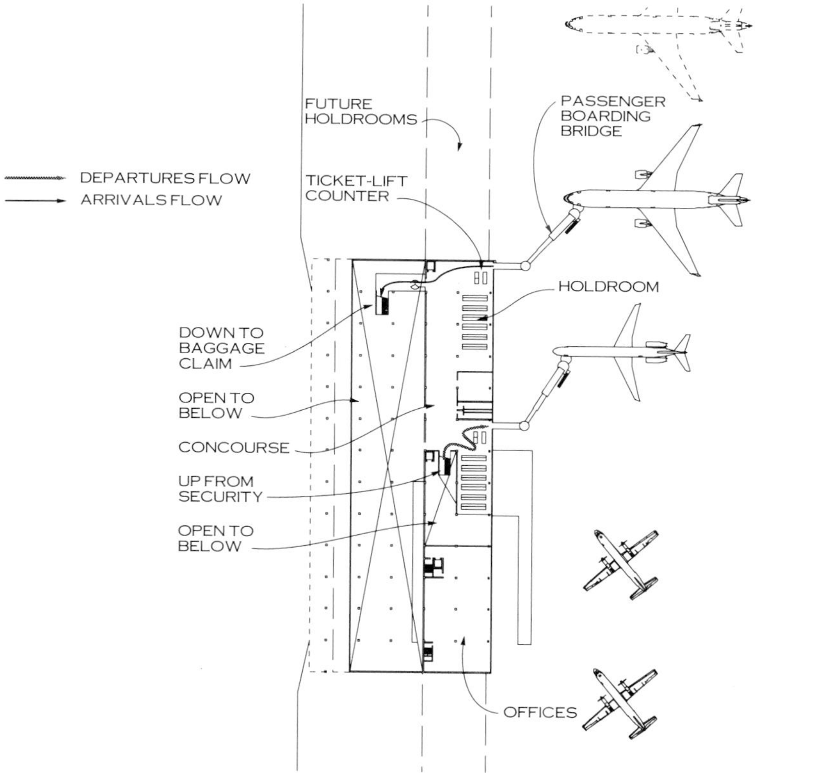

UPPER LEVEL PASSENGER FLOW

DEPARTURES FLOW
ARRIVALS FLOW

PASSENGER TERMINAL

Mark Romack, Perkins & Will; Chicago, Illinois

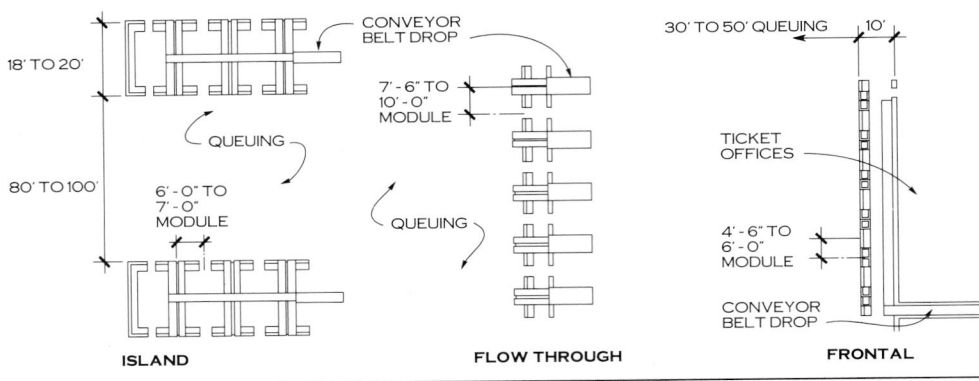

ISLAND   **FLOW THROUGH**   **FRONTAL**

TICKET COUNTER CONFIGURATIONS

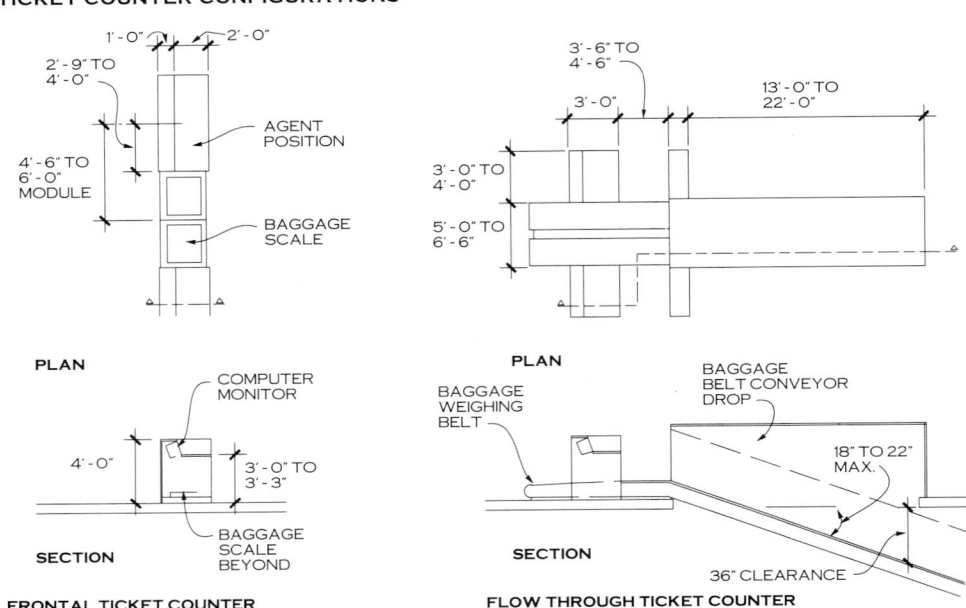

FRONTAL TICKET COUNTER   **FLOW THROUGH TICKET COUNTER**

TICKET COUNTERS

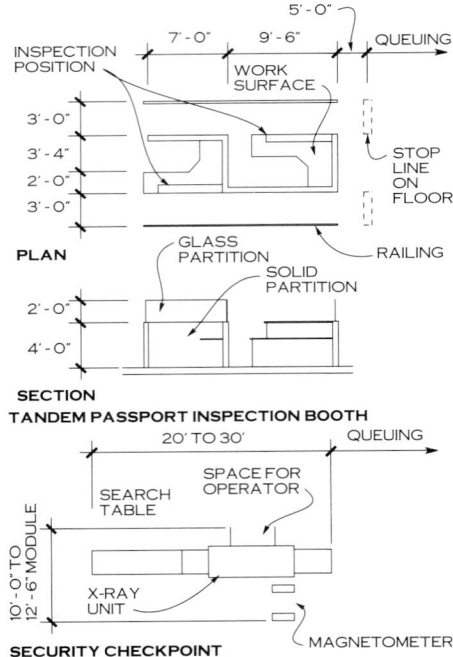

TANDEM PASSPORT INSPECTION BOOTH

SECURITY CHECKPOINT

INSPECTION AREAS

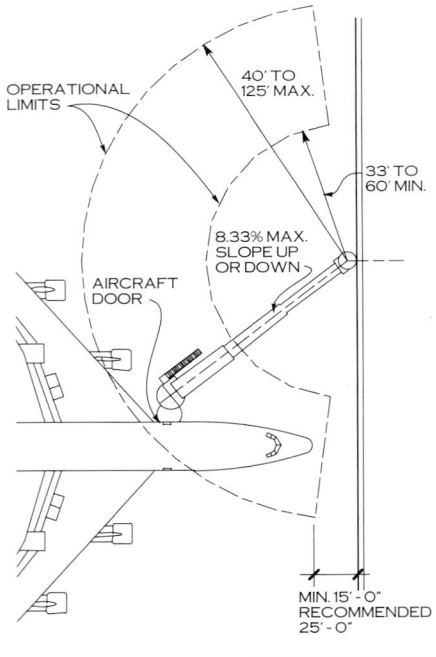

PASSENGER BOARDING BRIDGE

SYSTEMS

In addition to conventional mechanical and electrical systems, a large amount of space in an airport terminal will be devoted to systems unique to this building type. The baggage handling system requires space for baggage conveyor routes and floor areas for outbound and inbound systems. The types of handling systems vary widely but all include some means of sorting outbound baggage by flight (either manually or with automated devices) and a method of conveying baggage from check-in to gate (typically by a combination of belt conveyors and tug-and-cart trains). Inbound baggage requires a device for displaying baggage for claim by arriving passengers. Several systems are required to support aircraft at the gates: pre-conditioned (PC) air, ground power (400 Hz), and hydrant fueling, among others. These systems can be supplied from mobile ground service equipment but often are incorporated within the terminal building (or apron, in the case of aviation fuel lines) for reasons of economy and efficiency. Space is required for equipment and distribution runs. Communication requirements tend to be extensive due to the multiple number of systems: public address, flight information and display (FIDS), dynamic signage, ground radio, CCTV and security monitoring, as well as individual or shared information systems for airlines, government agencies, and other tenants.

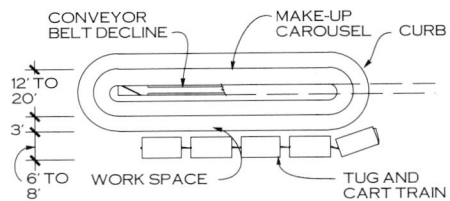

OUTBOUND BAGGAGE MAKE-UP CAROUSEL PLAN

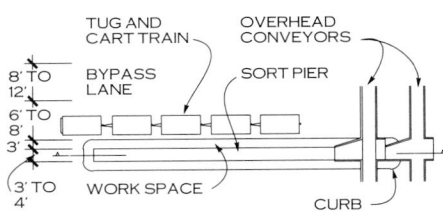

SORT PIER PLAN

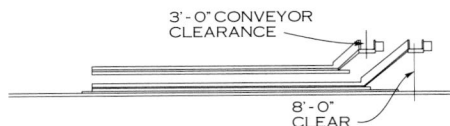

SORT PIER SECTION

OUTBOUND BAGGAGE

REFERENCES

1. Airport Capacity and Delay, FAA Advisory Circular 150/5060-5, September 23, 1983.
2. Airport Design, FAA Advisory Circular 150/5300-13, September 29, 1989.
3. Planning and Design of Airport Terminal Facilities at Nonhub Locations, FAA Advisory Circular 150/5360-9, April 4, 1980.
4. Federal Aviation Regulations Part 77, Objects Affecting Navigable Airspace, FAA, January 1975.
5. Aerodromes, Annex 14 to the Convention on International Civil Aviation, volume 1, ICAO, July 1990.
6. Airport Terminals Reference Manual, International Air Transport Association (IATA), January 1989.

Mark Romack, Perkins & Will; Chicago, Illinois

PRINCIPLES OF SCHOOL PLANNING AND DESIGN

The environment of a school should actively stimulate human development—socially, intellectually, physically, and emotionally. Creating an environment, not just a space, is essential.

Flexibility and design are inherently important in school design. The school facility must be able to adapt to the continuing evolution of education, in methods and approach. The school building must meet the needs of civic scale and of its users. It should provide a focal point for the community, a center of education and enlightenment. On a more intimate level, the design of the school building should create an environment in scale to its inhabitants. The facility should offer a comfortable work environment and maximize interaction between students, teachers, and staff. The resolution of human and civic scale will give students a sense of confidence within their environment, while providing a connection with the world outside.

NEW TRENDS

School planning has evolved in response to changing teaching methods and school organization. The educational process has become more active and interrelated.

Educational programming is often formulated and facilities planned in response to the educational, recreational, cultural, and social needs of both the students and the adult community. This coordination makes the school an integral part of the wider community.

Over the years, the trends in curricula have grown toward individualized instruction, with more specialized and diverse course offerings, and greater reliance on mechanical, electronic, and audiovisual aids to the learning process.

Extracurricular activities such as foreign language and science clubs, school publications, special music groups, and drama organizations are carried over into after school hours and evening. Also, in many communities summer school sessions are becoming conventional both for make-up work and for acceleration programs.

SITE LAYOUT

Requirements for site layout differ according to the local climate, the nature and character of the community setting and its people, the size of the school, the age groups to be taught, and the projected rate of growth.

Flexibility should allow for a building layout solution that can adapt to specific site constraints and, more important, become an integrated part of the community. The scale must allow the building to take on a site specific form sensitive to its context.

Urban sites generally call for higher densities and multistory buildings, possibly sharing amenities with the community or utilizing rooftops for open spaces and athletics. Rural sites, on the other hand, are more self-sufficient and sometimes have extensive athletic fields and open areas.

The relationship of site elements is very important to the successful and safe function of the school:

1. Differentiate and provide for three types of automobile traffic—faculty, student, and visitor.
2. Separate drop-off facilities from buses.
3. Separate service areas and access from other circulation systems.
4. Provide protection from the weather via enclosed hallways, canopies, and sheltered courtyards.
5. Site design flexibility should allow for public areas to be accessible after school hours, while the academic wings are secured.

The accompanying site plans show designs for schools that have successfully addressed many of the factors above.

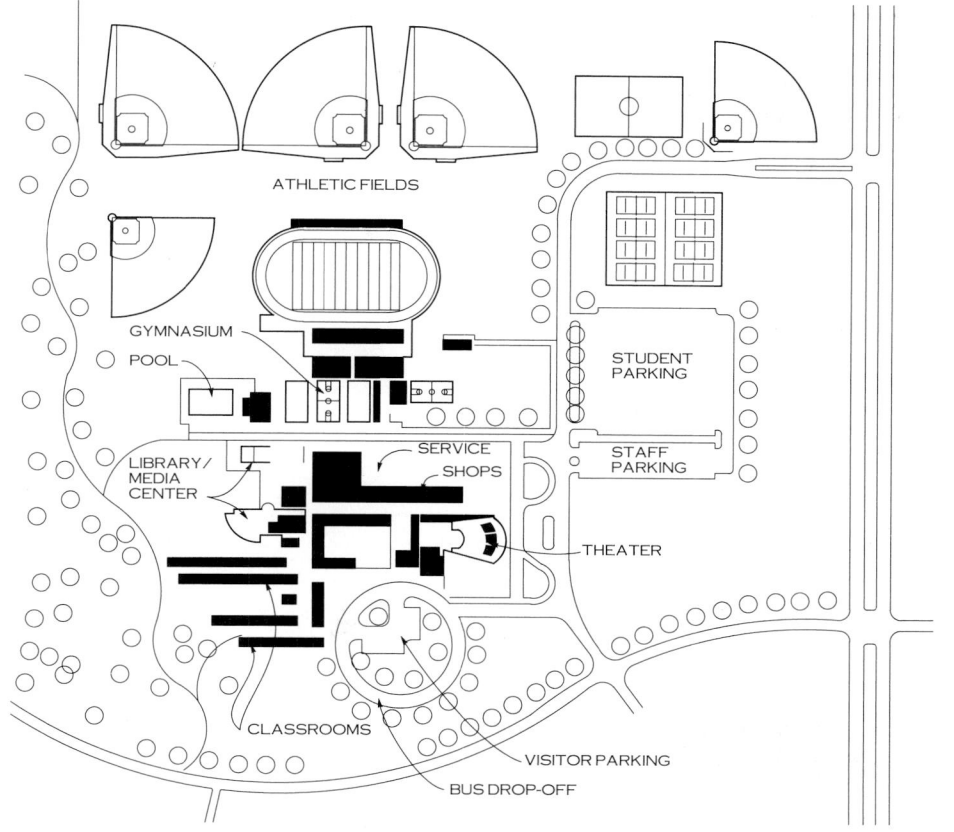

FIGURE 1 — SITE PLAN

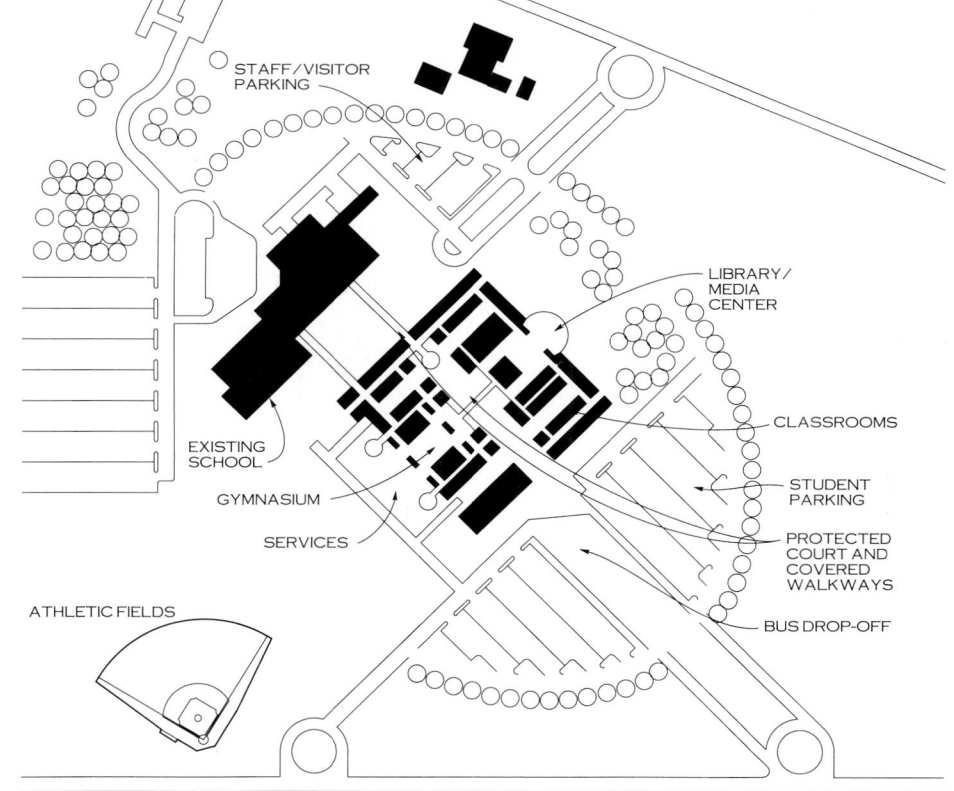

FIGURE 2 — SITE PLAN

Perkins & Will; Chicago, Illinois

BUILDING TYPES

There are many ways of organizing space that will allow a school to respond better to ways of teaching certain age groups, site and climate conditions, construction and funding phasing, and code restraints.

Circulation within the school, along with the physical needs of the spaces, establishes the plan. There are four basic plan concepts or building types: linear, modular, courtyard/campus, and high-rise. Often a combination of the above can be found in the same school building complex.

The plan examples shown represent the basic four types:

LINEAR

Building elements are organized along a linear circulation spine or "corridor" that separates activity zones and con-trols access. Corridors can vary over their length, corresponding with outdoor spaces, and identify classroom entrances.

CLUSTER (OPEN PLAN)

Instructional areas and other functions are arranged in groups or clusters around a common area with no specially designated bands of space for circulation. Instructional areas are divided through partitions in various size spaces, accommodating groups working together and separately.

COURTYARD/CAMPUS

Building elements are closely related and linked around one central outdoor space or a series of courts and entrances.

In the campus plan, the relationship of building functions to outdoor spaces is similar to the courtyard type but on a much larger scale. A campus-type plan resolves a large school into smaller elements (components), with the library as the academic focus. Gyms and auditoriums are in separate structures appropriate to their function, as are the academic elements. The illustrations show a compact campus plan for a high school and a 700,000-sq ft K-12 school complex for 4300 students in a rural area, the latter combined with a physical education/community fitness center.

HIGH-RISE

This city building type developed out of a demand for high density with emphasis on vertical arrangement of building functions. Typically, specialized and public-oriented facilities are on the ground floor, with classrooms on upper floors. The illustration of this type shows two stories of a five-story K-5 school.

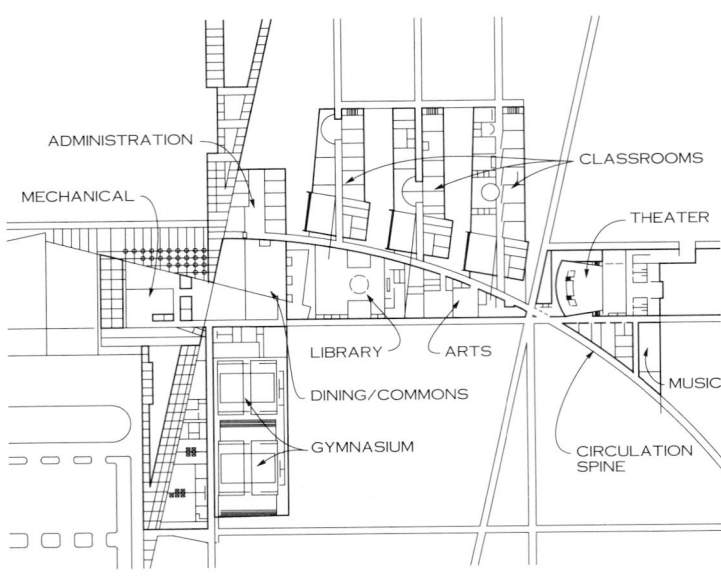

LINEAR EXAMPLE

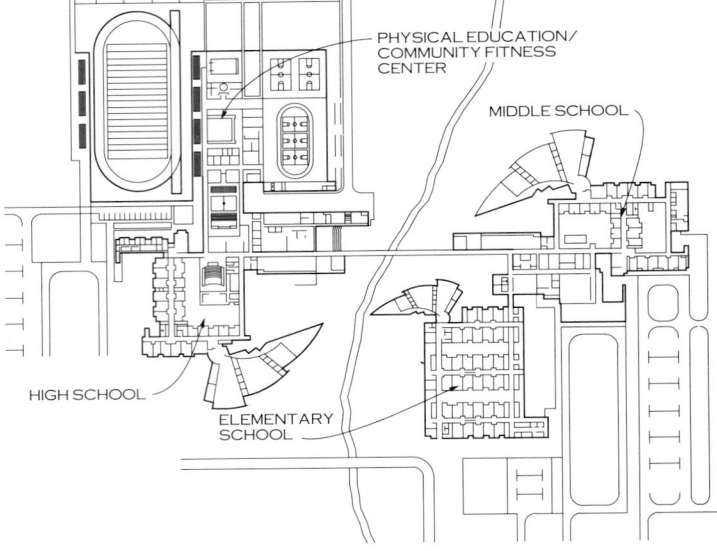

RURAL CAMPUS EXAMPLE

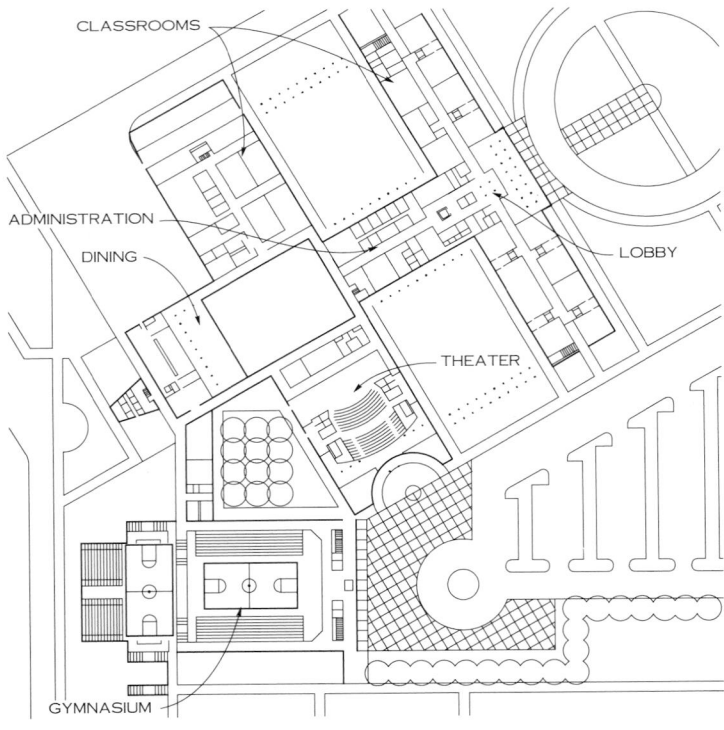

COURTYARD EXAMPLE

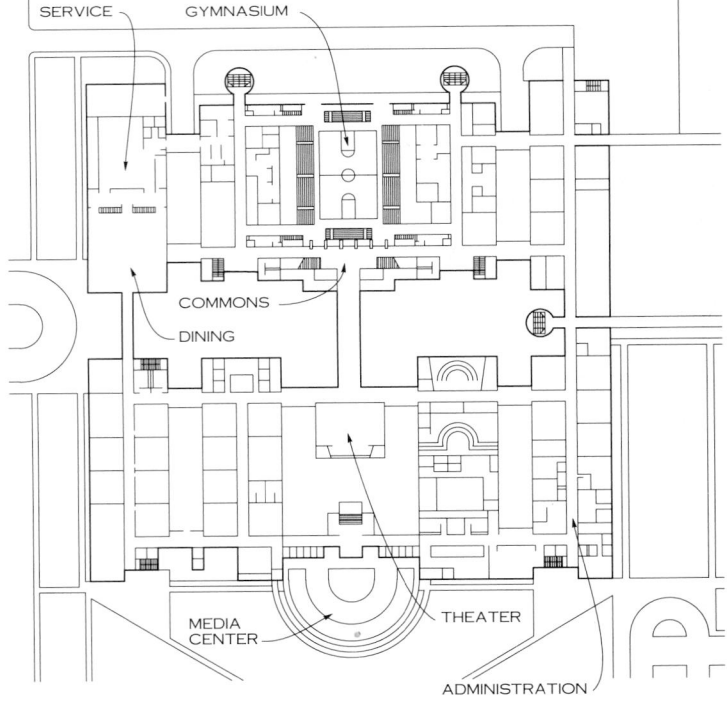

COMPACT CAMPUS EXAMPLE

Perkins & Will; Chicago, Illinois

SCHOOLS

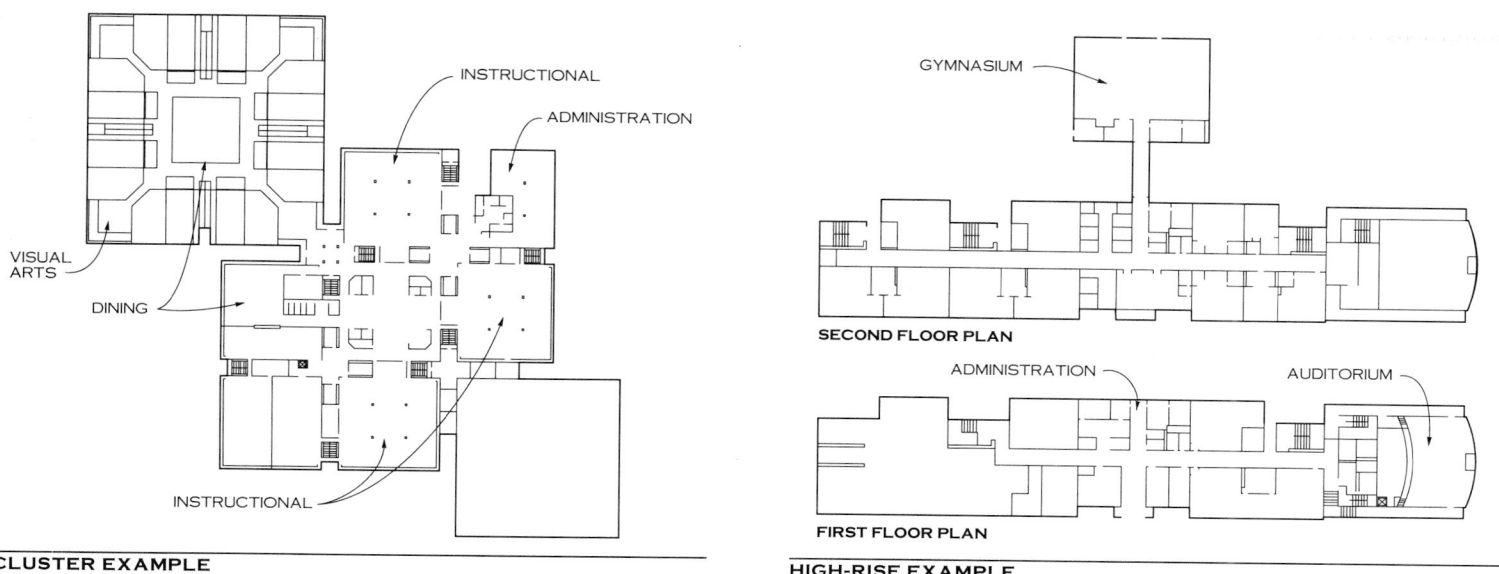

CLUSTER EXAMPLE

SECOND FLOOR PLAN

FIRST FLOOR PLAN

HIGH-RISE EXAMPLE

BUILDING ELEMENTS

Based on the philosophy that mind, soul, and body must all be part of education, five basic elements must be accommodated in a school building. Activities addressing the children's mind, soul, and body and administrative and support functions are each divided into subelements directly relating to them. These elements are more complex, more distinct, and larger in secondary education than they are in elementary education. Building elements are connected by circulation via entrances, corridors, arcades, and open or enclosed courts.

LIBRARY/MEDIA CENTER

The library/media center is the central information resource area for all students, faculty, and staff. In addition to books and periodicals, it houses records, tapes and cassettes, facilities for closed-circuit TV programming and production, film, cameras, and projection equipment.

The library/medica center should be physically and educationally at the heart of the school, equally accessible to classrooms, administration offices, and possibly the community. It may be open after school hours and located to allow direct access to it.

CLASSROOMS

The classroom is a repetitive element in a school building. Its area has increased in recent years to accommodate the extension of classroom activities, the use of audiovisual equipment in teaching, and group instruction techniques. Typical classroom layouts are the standard-size classroom, the large group and demonstration classroom, and the double classroom composed of two large classrooms separated by a movable partition. In the latter example, when the folding door is open, these rooms become an area for large group instruction or team teaching.

It is very important that all classroom equipment/furniture relate to the size of its occupants. Consider, for example, the mounting height for chalkboards and drinking fountains, as well as desk size, etc.

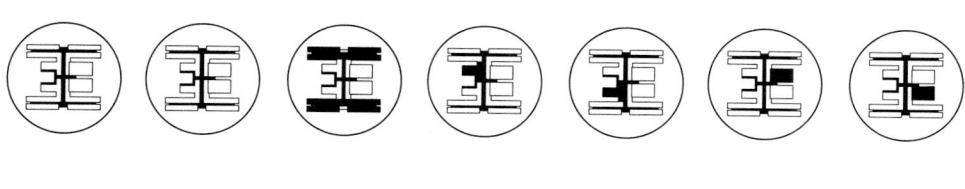

ENTRANCE · CIRCULATION · CLASSROOM · ADMINISTRATION · LIBRARY/MEDIA · DINING · GYMNASIUM/MULTIPURPOSE

ELEMENTARY SCHOOL SPACES

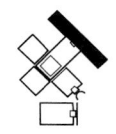 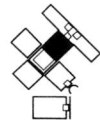 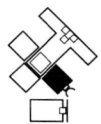 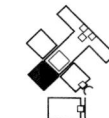 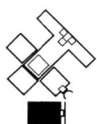 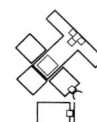 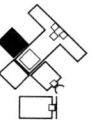

CLASSROOMS · LIBRARY/ADMINISTRATION · THEATER · BAND/CHORUS · GYMNASIUM · DINING HALL · ARTS

HIGH SCHOOL SPACES

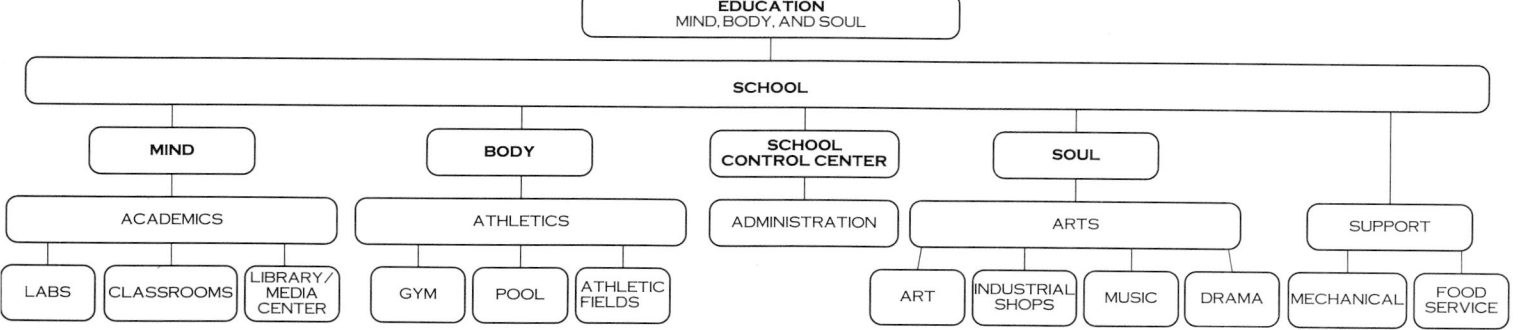

BUILDING ELEMENTS

Perkins & Will; Chicago, Illinois

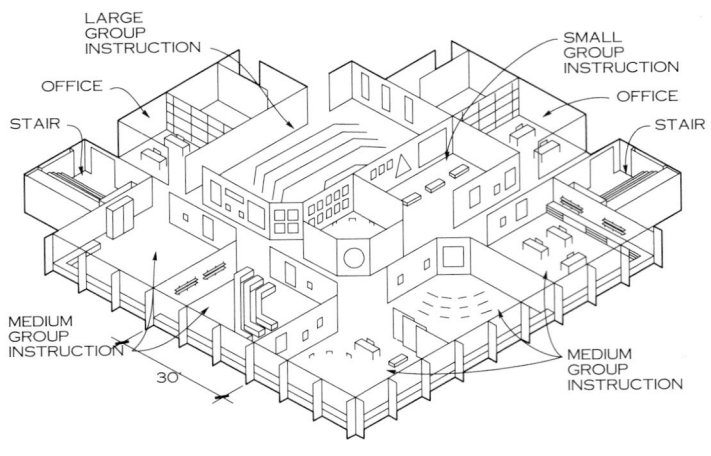

ISOMETRIC SHOWING CLASSROOM TYPES

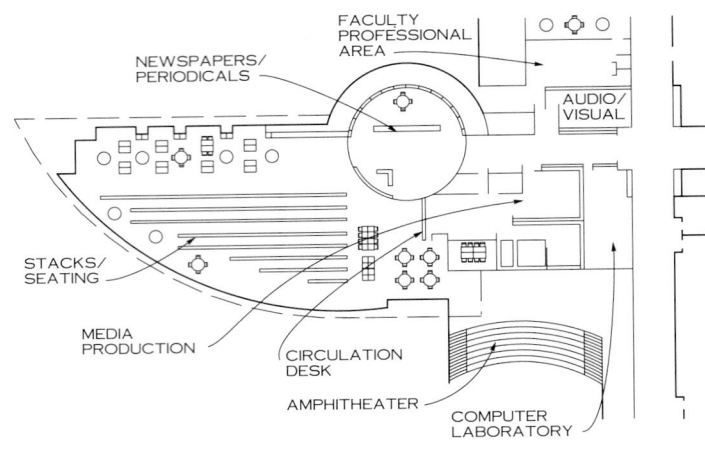

LIBRARY/MEDIA CENTER

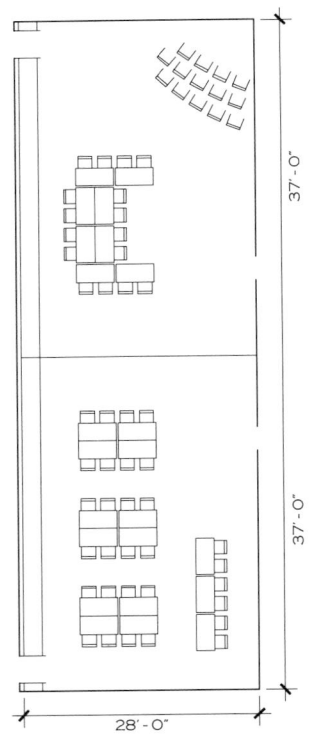

DOUBLE CLASSROOM

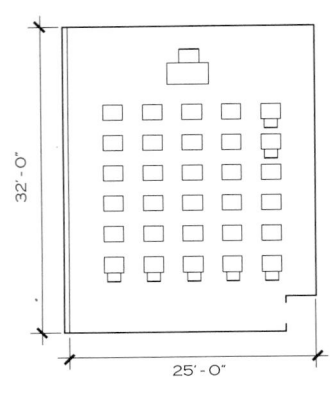

STANDARD CLASSROOM

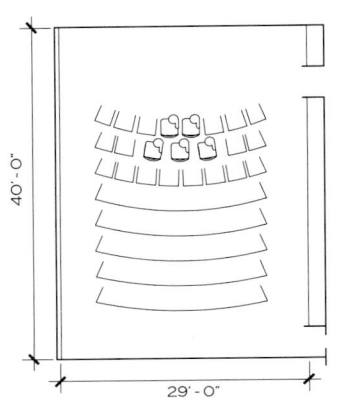

LARGE GROUP AND DEMONSTRATION CLASSROOM

SYSTEMS OUTLINE

Many factors are essential to make a school building function as a total environment conducive to better learning and teaching. The most basic factors are diagrammed in the chart at the bottom of the page.

LIGHTING

Wherever possible, indirect illumination-type fixtures with fluorescent light sources should be used to restrict room surface glare. Both natural and artificial light must be controllable.

HVAC

The system must be capable of maintaining a controlled, comfortable environment throughout, with appropriate zoning flexibility. Good ventilation is very important. Air systems are almost always used in schools for spaces where there are large concentrations of people, such as gymnasiums, auditoriums, cafeterias, and library/media centers.

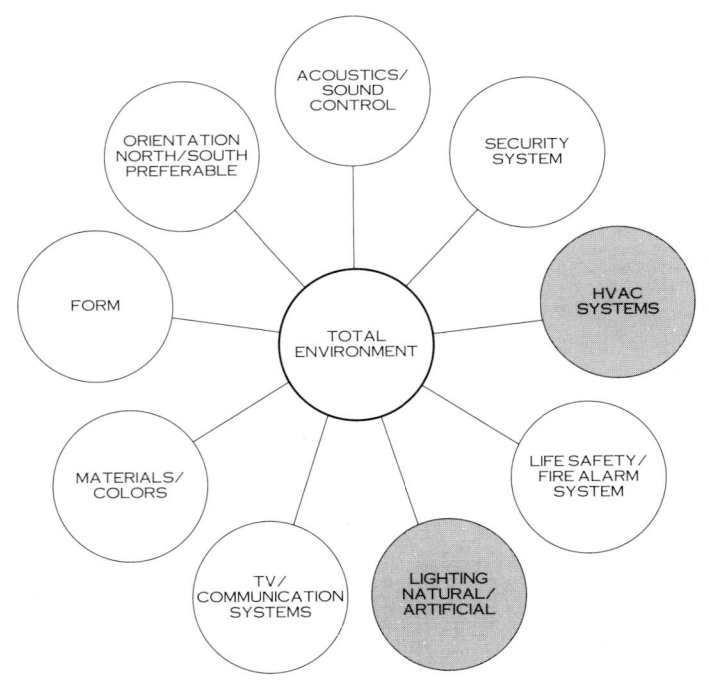

SYSTEMS OUTLINE

Perkins & Will; Chicago, Illinois

INTRODUCTION

The U.S. health care delivery system has changed enormously since the early 1980s. The federal government now attempts to control health care costs for patients receiving Medicare and Medicaid benefits by assigning fixed costs to hundreds of standard diagnoses (called Diagnostic Related Groups, or DRGs) and reimbursing health care facilities only this amount for each patient stay. The result has been a substantial shift to outpatient treatment for many diagnoses, including surgery. Consequently, hospitals now face a surplus of inpatient beds and great pressures to revise physical plants to accommodate many more outpatients. At the same time, health insurance companies have cut benefits for inpatient care. All of this has changed the way hospitals are planned and has stimulated new conceptual responses to the new functional challenges. In addition, hospitals are no longer the only building types responding to health care needs. The following sections describe typical U.S. health care facilities in the 1990s.

HOSPITAL BUILDING TYPES
PRIMARY CARE/COMMUNITY

Like the family doctor, the community hospital is the first contact with the health care system for many people. Hospital primary care provides general treatment and diagnostic services within a limited, well-defined geographic area. Such services usually include general surgery, standard radiography and fluoroscopic imaging, routine laboratory tests, and emergency care, as well as general medicine, maternity, and pediatrics. A small unit usually serves as a combined intensive care unit (ICU) and cardiac care unit (CCU). The number of inpatient beds can range from 25-50 for small rural hospitals to 100-150 for facilities in developed areas.

REGIONAL REFERRAL

Compared to primary care hospitals, referral hospitals serve larger, less well defined areas and provide not only basic care but also more specialized care, including orthopedics; eye, ear, nose, and throat (EENT); urology, cardiology; oncology; or neurology. Computerized tomography (CT) scanning, magnetic resonance imaging (MRI), ultrasonography, and nuclear medicine imaging are also present to support these specialties. Cardiac catheterization, open-heart surgery, and cancer treatment programs are sometimes available. The emergency department has a heavier workload because of the specialty capabilities available. The number of inpatient beds can range from 150-200 to 300-350 or more.

TERTIARY CARE/TEACHING

Because many tertiary care/teaching hospitals have world-class reputations and provide extremely special services, they may attract patients from all over the world. Such facilities seek to provide not just health care but also a setting (and patients) for medical research and education. Balancing these objectives is an important consideration in the design of such hospitals. All the specialties are represented, as well as some state-of-the-art diagnostic and treatment modalities frequently still in development. Imaging devices such as positron emission tomography (PET) scan, procedures such as "gamma knife" treatment for cancer, and "clean rooms" for patients recovering from bone marrow transplants must all be housed in specially designed facilities. Tertiary care hospitals may be physically linked to a medical school's basic science and clinical research laboratories, academic offices, classrooms, and very large outpatient facilities. The number of inpatient beds can vary from 400-450 to 800-900 or more.

SPECIALTY (REHABILITATION, PSYCHIATRIC, PEDIATRIC)

Specialty hospitals treat only one kind of patient. Rehabilitation hospitals treat and provide therapy for patients suffering from illnesses or injuries that have restricted their physical and/or cognitive abilities. Because of such patients' disabilities, fully accessible functional areas with generous clearances and circulation space must be planned. Rehabilitation hospitals may include facilities for cardiac rehabilitation and sports medicine.

Psychiatric hospitals treat patients with mental illness. Since most of these patients are fully mobile physically, patient rooms can be designed like dormitory rooms. Security, access, and unit-to-unit separation must also be considered when planning such facilities.

Other specialty hospitals include those devoted to women's and children's health. While they contain most of the treatment and diagnostic areas of a standard hospital, they also have special design needs: patient privacy, appropriate scale, and nonthreatening environments.

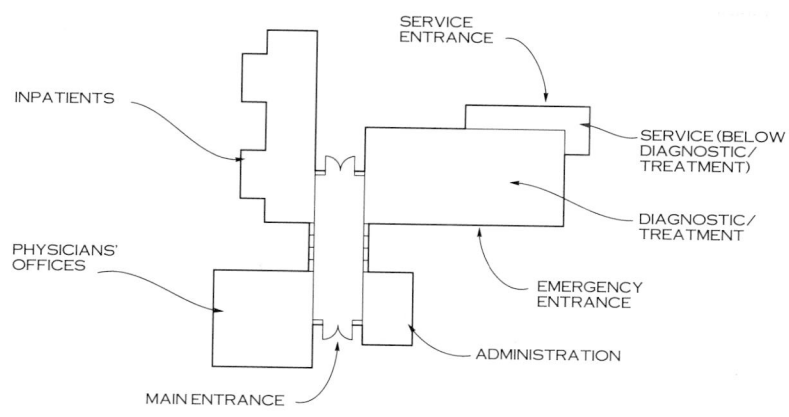

PRIMARY CARE/COMMUNITY HOSPITAL

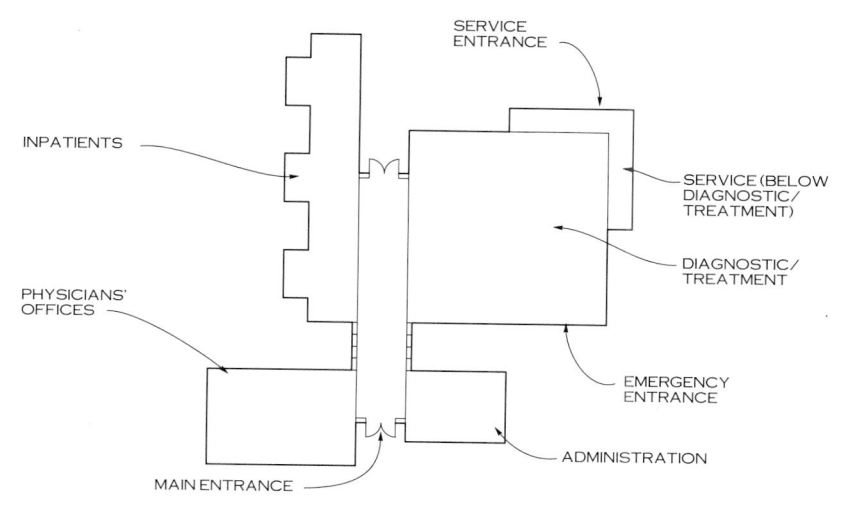

REGIONAL REFERRAL HOSPITAL

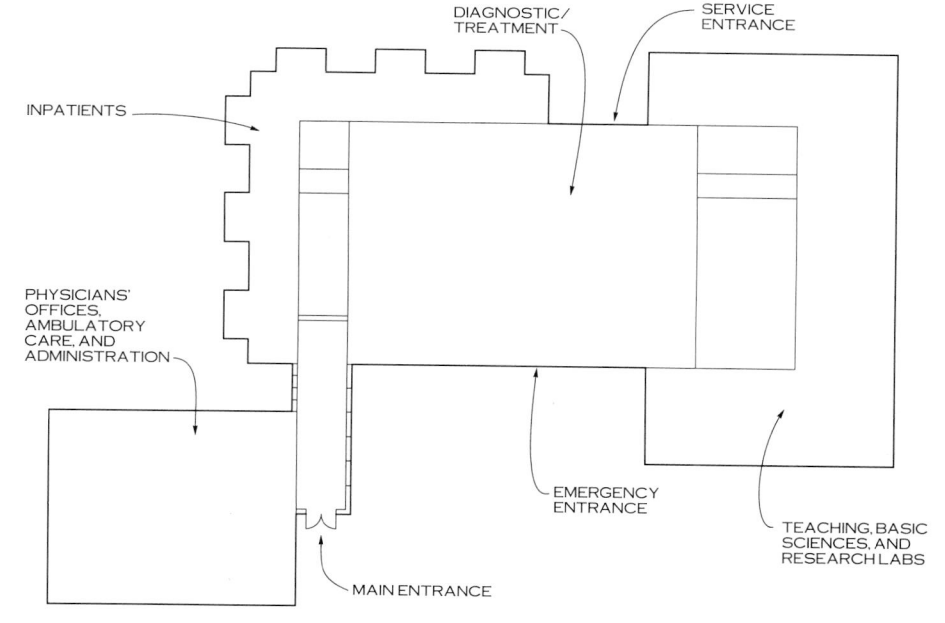

TERTIARY CARE/TEACHING HOSPITAL

Donald W. Velsey, AIA; Ellerbe Becket; Washington, D.C.
Charles F. D. Egbert, AIA; Egbert, Clarens, and Associates, PC Architects; Washington, D.C.

URGICENTERS

The movement toward outpatient care has stimulated the development of freestanding facilities, not necessarily associated with a hospital, for patients to use as they might a family doctor—frequently on a walk-in basis without an appointment. Urgicenters can relieve overburdened hospital emergency rooms of nonemergency work. To compete with freestanding urgicenters, hospitals are starting urgicenters contiguous to their own emergency department; a triage nurse can direct walk-in patients to appropriate treatment in the hospital, but in a less-intensive, nonemergency setting.

SURGICENTERS

The increase in outpatient surgery has also prompted the development of freestanding surgical facilities, where doctors perform surgery that might otherwise be done in a hospital. State regulations limit patient stays to 24 hours, so the surgery performed must not require the potential support of hospital services. To compete with surgicenters, hospitals are providing outpatient surgery as well: up to 80% of all surgery in some hospitals is outpatient.

POSTSURGERY RECOVERY CENTERS

The recent development of postsurgery recovery centers brings the freestanding facility idea full circle, back to the "hospital" model. Surgicenters have recognized some patients' need to stay longer than 24 hours and have created a kind of surgical hotel. Because the costs and amenities are similar to those of a very good hotel, such facilities cater to an affluent clientele.

BIRTHING CENTERS

The movement to limit hospital stays combined with women's increasing desire to deliver babies in a less institutional setting, has resulted in the development of freestanding birthing centers. Such centers provide for normal deliveries, which accounted for 75 to 80% of births in the United States in 1990. Complicated and cesarean-section (C-section) deliveries, which require special support, may remain in the hospital setting. Whether in a hospital or freestanding birthing center, the trend is to reduce the average maternity stay to 24 hours, if possible. Consequently, a new planning theory simplifies and accelerates the functional flow of the maternity patient. Labor, delivery, and postpartum stays are now routinely combined in one room (called the LDRP). The design of the LDRP room must balance the needs for special air conditioning, medical gas outlets, and monitoring capability with the desire to create a homelike atmosphere. To compete with birthing centers, hospitals are providing LDRP suites contiguous to C-section operating rooms.

AMBULATORY CARE FACILITIES

Increased demand for outpatient care has stimulated the development of freestanding ambulatory care facilities — large outpatient clinics operated by groups of physicians or health maintenance organizations (HMOs). These facilities can combine versions of the urgicenter, surgicenter, and birthing center with full diagnostic support; the resulting functional grouping has been called a "hospital without beds." Ambulatory care planning modules must be flexible. Scheduling each clinic module by hours of use is the most important programming and planning factor in designing functional outpatient clinics. To compete with such centers, hospitals are providing on-site ambulatory care facilities, ranging from contiguous office buildings for physicians to large outpatient clinics.

LONG-TERM CARE FACILITIES

Long-term care facilities manage patients who need supervision of or assistance with long-term, chronic conditions but do not need the treatment and diagnostic support of a hospital. Whereas the number of beds in a typical acute care unit in a hospital is ideally about 25 to 30 per nursing station, as many as 60 beds per station are permitted in long-term care units in some jurisdictions. There are various levels of care within the long-term definition: The skilled nursing facility cares for patients whose chronic conditions require constant nursing support, such as ventilators (assisted breathing). Some hospitals are converting empty bed space to these units, which require a less intense level of staffing. The nursing home traditionally provides care for patients, usually elderly, who need some assistance and supervision. Other levels of care are available in congregate care facilities, eldercare, or assisted living complexes, which offer a variety of living accommodations, ranging from apartments to dormitory-style units to supervised units with nurses on duty.

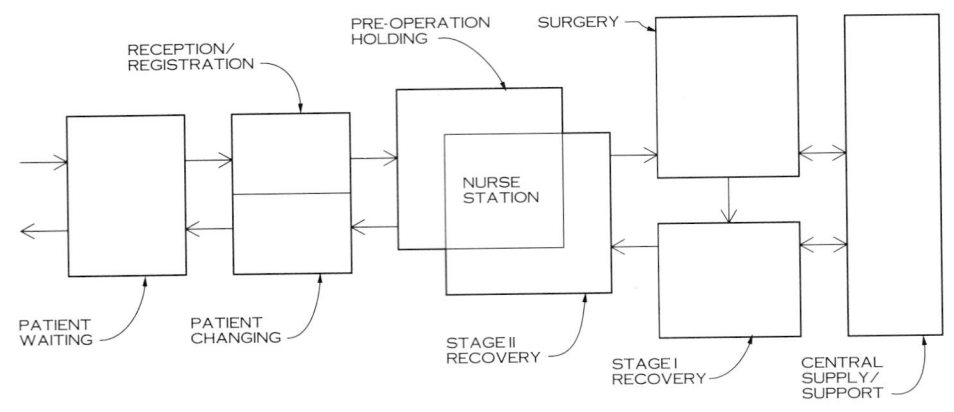

SURGICENTER FLOW DIAGRAM

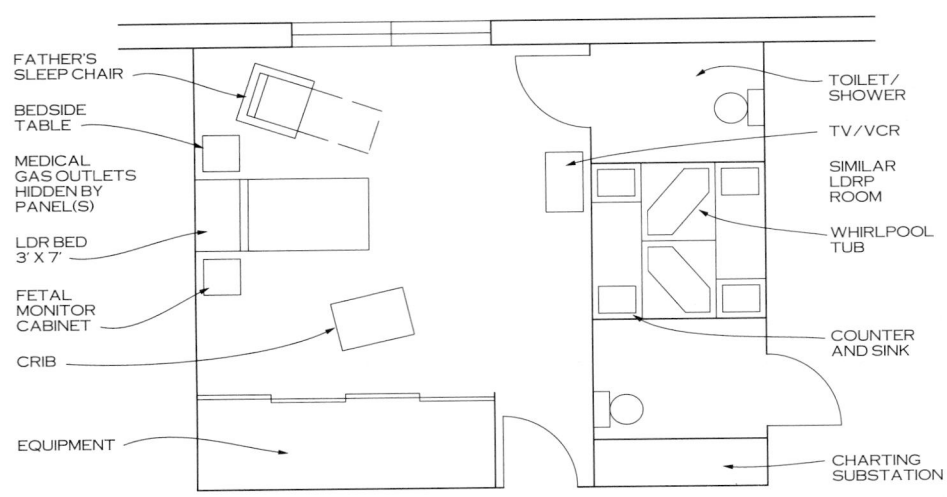

BIRTHING CENTER - TYPICAL LDRP ROOM

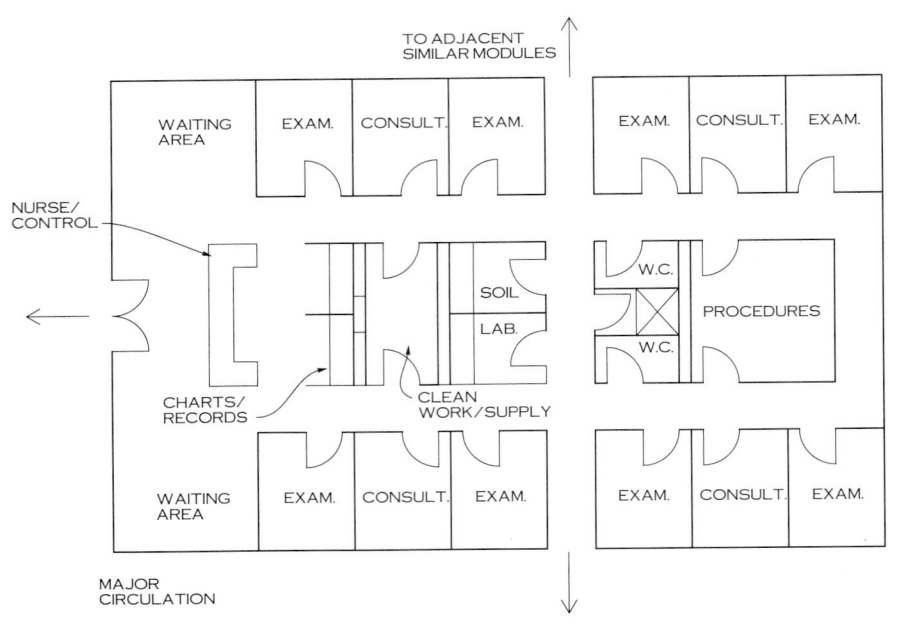

TYPICAL AMBULATORY CARE/OUTPATIENT CLINIC MODULE

Donald W. Velsey, AIA; Ellerbe Becket; Washington, D.C.
Charles F. D. Egbert, AIA; Egbert, Clarens, and Associates, PC Architects; Washington, D.C.

HEALTH CARE

PROGRAMMING
STRATEGIC PLANS

Health care facilities periodically attempt to identify strategies for satisfying probable future needs. Such strategies may involve adding a new treatment or diagnostic service or expanding to capture a larger market share of a particular service and to encourage physicians to use the facilities. A long-range strategic plan documents such goals.

MASTER FACILITY PLANS

Master facility plans are derived from the strategic plan and consist of (1) a projection of future space needs, (2) a comparison of those needs to available existing space, (3) an analysis of existing functional deficiencies, (4) an analysis of existing mechanical and electrical systems and their capacity, (5) block plan diagrams proposing directions for growth and areas of renovation, (6) prioritization and phasing of proposed construction projects, and (7) preliminary construction and project cost estimates based on the proposed phasing.

Note: A reasonable rule of thumb for converting construction cost estimates to project costs is to add 40%. This percentage includes major movable equipment and furnishings, design fees, and design and construction contingencies.

FUNCTIONAL SPACE PROGRAMMING

Functional space programming is often developed in two consecutive levels of detail. The first level is conceptual and is expressed in departmental gross square feet (DGSF). This level of programming is used to develop master facility plans. It consists of a department-by-department calculation of the areas within the overall boundaries of each department, including internal departmental circulation and partitions. DGSF is directly derived from projected departmental workloads or personnel numbers. Earlier popular programming methods, which link the size of a department to the numbers of beds in a hospital, are no longer valid because of the large shift to outpatient workloads.

The conceptual program must be completed by adding estimated mechanical/electrical spaces as DGSF, plus an overall factor (in the range of 1.10 to 1.15) to convert all DGSF to total building gross square feet (BGSF), which adds all general circulation, both vertical and horizontal, and exterior walls.

The second level of detail is a space-by-space program listing, in usable net square feet (NSF), all the functions in the facility. Major mechanical and electrical spaces should also be treated as NSF. These areas can then be factored variously at approximately 1.20 to 1.65 (depending on circulation and partitioning needs) to get DGSF; that result factored by 1.10 to 1.15 yields BGSF. If the assumptions used in the conceptual program are still valid, the DGSF of both conceptual and detailed programs should be approximately the same.

EXAMPLE: A SURGICAL SUITE TO SUPPORT 10,000 PROCEDURES/YR
ASSUMPTIONS

1. 260 days/yr of scheduled operation. (A small percentage of emergency surgery will not affect the results.)
2. 8 hr/day of scheduled operation.
3. 25% of the workload is inpatient procedures requiring general anesthesia in a "major" operating room. Each procedure, including cleanup time, ties up a room for an average of 2.5 hr. Therefore, one room can handle 8 hr divided by 2.5, or 3.2 procedures/day.
4. 50% of the workload is outpatient procedures requiring general anesthesia in a "major" operating room. Each procedure, including cleanup time, ties up a room for an average of 1.5 hr. One room can therefore handle 5.3 procedures/day.
5. 25% of the workload is outpatient procedures requiring local anesthesia in a "minor" procedures room. Each procedure ties up a room for an average of 0.5 hr. One room can therefore handle 16 procedures/day.

CALCULATIONS

1. 10,000 procedures/yr divided by 260 = 38 procedures/day (say 40 procedures/day).
2. Inpatients: 10/day at 3.2/room/day requires 3.1 major operating rooms.
3. Outpatients with general anesthesia: 20/day at 5.3/room/day requires 3.7 major operating rooms.
4. Outpatients with local anesthesia: 10/day at 16/room/day requires 0.6 minor procedures rooms.

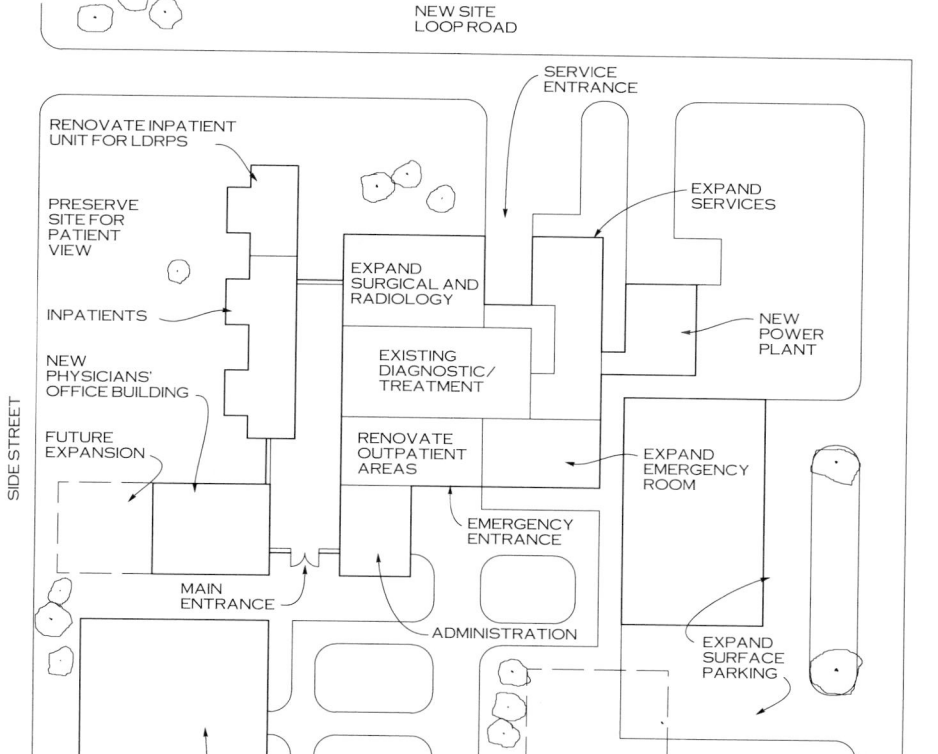

DIAGRAMMATIC MASTER FACILITY PLAN

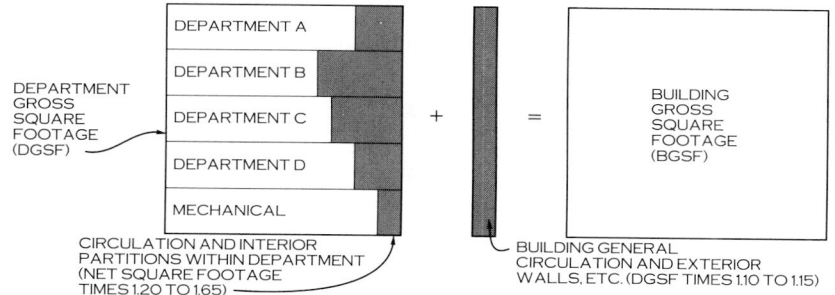

FUNCTIONAL SPACE PROGRAM

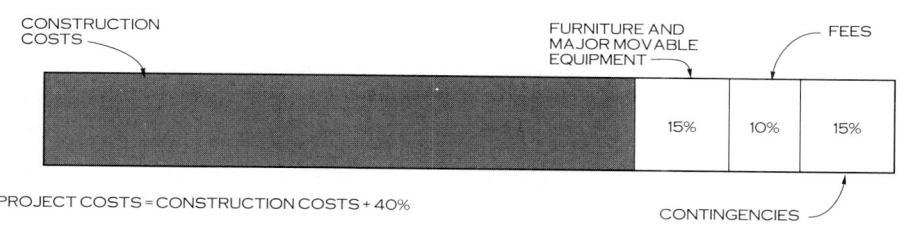

PROJECT COSTS = CONSTRUCTION COSTS + 40%

PROJECT COSTS

RESULTS

A total of 6.8 or 7 major operating rooms is required and only 1 minor procedures room is required.

Rule of thumb for programming: The total area (including all appropriate support spaces) of a surgical suite will be approximately 2200 DGSF/operating room or minor procedures room. Therefore this surgical suite would be 8 rooms x 2200 DGSF, or approximately 17,600 DGSF.

NOTE

There are recognized rules of thumb for sizing every department, using workload methodology like this example. See bibliography for more information.

Donald W. Velsey, AIA; Ellerbe Becket; Washington, D.C.
Charles F. D. Egbert, AIA; Egbert, Clarens, and Associates, PC Architects; Washington, D.C.

PLANNING THE HEALTH CARE FACILITY

Certain attributes of health care facilities clearly distinguish them from other building types. They resemble small towns or cities in the way city planning and zoning criteria can be applied to planning these facilities. Some representative concerns follow along with specific examples.

1. Functional traffic patterns must be kept separate.
   a. At loading docks, incoming clean supplies should have no contact with soiled linens, trash, recyclables, and hazardous waste.
   b. In surgery, restricted areas where scrub suits are worn should be separated from areas where street clothes can be worn.
   c. In all treatment and diagnostic areas, inpatient stretcher traffic should not mix with ambulatory outpatient or waiting area traffic.
   d. In elevators, hospital staff and supply traffic should be separated from public and visitor traffic.
   e. In patient units, those with communicable disease should be separated from others.
2. It is important to respect linear, step-by-step functional flows in certain areas.
   a. Used surgical instruments move, in order, through decontamination, sterile preparation, terminal sterilization, sterile pack storage, and transportation through a restricted zone back to the operating rooms.
   b. Outpatient surgery patients move from reception/registration, to undressing, to pre-op holding, to the operating room, to stage 1 recovery, to stage 2 recovery, to dressing, to checkout.
   c. Radiology film goes from film dispenser, to cassette, to exposure at radiographic table, to film processing and developing, then to quality review, radiologist viewing, and files.
3. The proportion of mechanical and electrical costs to architectural costs is very high, due in part to the following:
   a. Special, filtered air conditioning systems in surgery, with high volumes of air exchange.
   b. Extensive medical gas systems: oxygen, medical compressed air, vacuum, nitrous oxide, nitrogen.
   c. Special exhausts for clinical laboratory fume hoods, nuclear medicine xenon gases, and patient isolation rooms.
   d. Heavy electrical loads in imaging areas, and isolated power and emergency power requirements in many treatment and diagnostic areas.
   e. Special transportation devices such as pneumatic tubes, and automated tote-box systems.
   f. Extensive electronic communications: local computer networks, including provisions for medical information systems; nurse call; intercom; pocket paging; radio communication to emergency services; digital imaging transmission; and television systems for security and for educational and hospital programming.
4. Planning must recognize the need for future flexibility and growth
   a. Structural modules are derived from the various functional planning units. The ideal grid for inpatient units may be different from that for treatment and diagnostic areas.
   b. It is important to locate potential high-growth departments where they can expand into new construction or into adjacent renovated soft space.
   c. When planning large areas with a mix of space sizes, find a common modular dimension to facilitate future changes within a department. For example, program a clinic's exam rooms and utility rooms at 120 NSF. Most partition systems that purport to be easily movable are in fact rarely, if ever, moved; it may be better to plan permanent spaces whose uses can be altered as space demands change.
5. Functional "zoning" determines massing relationships:
   a. Inpatient units have many of the attributes of hotels and dormitories.
   b. Treatment and diagnostic areas resemble areas in high-tech buildings, where "process" is important for performing delicate procedures.
   c. Support and service areas where materials are handled are the health care facility's light industry zones.
   d. Administrative areas are for business functions and thus are suitable to an office building environment.
   e. Outpatient processing, registration, and clinic areas—

along with the necessary public access, shops, services, and lobbies—can be thought of as retail space. In fact as competition for patients steps up, the phrase "medical mall" has been coined to describe the desired atmosphere of such spaces.

A SELECTED BIBLIOGRAPHY

The American Institute of Architects and the U.S. Department of Health and Human Services. *Guidelines for Construction and Equipment of Hospital and Medical Facilities, 1992-93*. Washington, D.C.: AIA Press, 1993.

American Society for Hospital Engineering Technical Document Series. Chicago: American Hospital Association Publishing, Inc.

Association for the Care of Children's Health. *Child Health Care Facilities Design Guidelines*. Washington, D.C.: Association for the Care of Children's Health, 1987.

Bush-Brown, Albert, and Dianne Davis. *Hospitable Design for Healthcare and Senior Communities*. New York: Van Nostrand Reinhold, 1992.

Carpman, Janet R., and Myron A. Grant. *Planning Health Facilities for Patients and Visitors*. Chicago: American Hospital Association Publishing, Inc., 1993.

Evaluation and Space Planning Methodology Series. Ottawa (Canada): Health and Welfare Canada, 1978.

Hardy, Owen B. and Lawrence P. Lammers. *Hospitals: The Planning and Design Process*. Rockville, Md: Aspen Systems Corporation, 1986.

Health Facilities Review. Washington, D.C.: AIA Press, various years.

Laufman, Harold, ed. *Hospital Special Care Facilities*. New York: Academic Press, 1981.

Malkin, Jain. *Hospital Interior Architecture*. New York: Van Nostrand Reinhold, 1992.

Malkin, Jain. *Medical and Dental Space Planning for the 1990s*. New York: Van Nostrand Reinhold, 1990.

Rostenburg, Bill. *Design Planning for Free Standing Ambulatory Care Facilities*. Chicago: American Hospital Association Publishing, Inc., 1986.

Snook, I. Donald, Jr. *Hospitals: What They Are and How They Work*. Rockville, Md.: Aspen Systems Corporation, 1981.

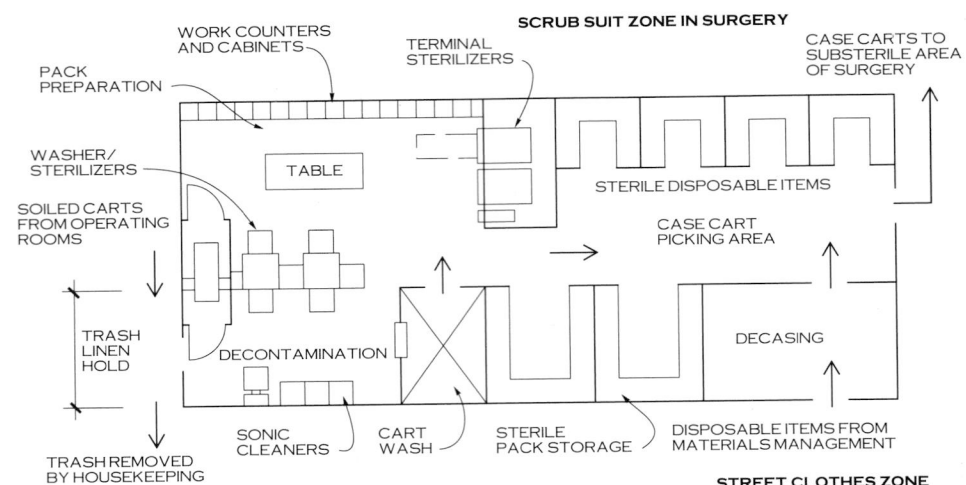

TYPICAL FLOW DIAGRAM: MATERIALS – CENTRAL SUPPLY

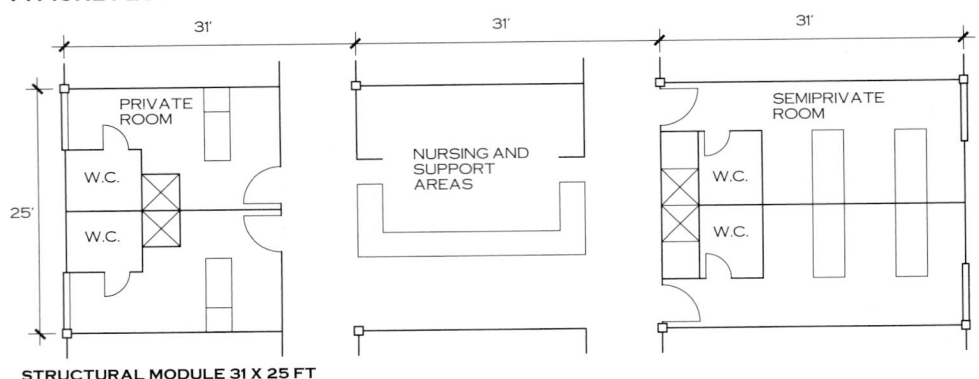

STRUCTURAL MODULE 31 X 25 FT

INPATIENT UNIT

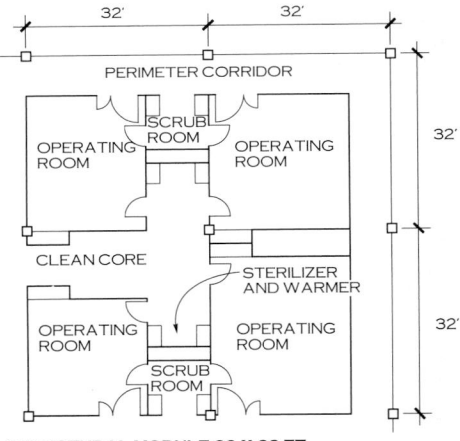

STRUCTURAL MODULE 32 X 32 FT

SURGICAL SUITE

Donald W. Velsey, AIA; Ellerbe Becket; Washington, D.C.
Charles F. D. Egbert, AIA; Egbert, Clarens, and Associates, PC Architects; Washington, D.C.

INTRODUCTION

The word "church" simply denotes a space, or group of spaces, that provides a place for devotion, education, and fellowship. Certain images may come to mind when thinking about a church, yet each built form should be a direct response to its particular faith. Belief systems, traditions, and styles of worship may vary widely, even within groups of similar denominations. The architectural vernacular within the region and the neighborhood may impact design decisions. The inclusion and arrangement of liturgical furnishings and symbols should be carefully discussed so that the result reflects the traditions of the group and provides an environment that evokes the appropriate spiritual response.

SITE PLANNING ISSUES

Land capacity: Actual layouts may vary, but typically a site will accommodate 150 to 200 persons per acre at peak usage. Shared parking on adjacent properties increases this number. Allow for more land for outdoor athletic, worship, or cemetery needs. For long-term growth, plan the possibility of acquiring adjacent land.

Parking: Provide one parking space for every 1.6 to 2.2 seats in the main worship area. Consider shared parking on adjacent or nearby properties to reduce the amount of hard surface needed for limited weekly use. Typical parking arrangements accommodate 100 cars per acre.

Site access: Parking should be visible upon approach to the site, and the main entrance to the building needs to be easily identifiable. More than one entrance to the site is advisable. Include service drives for delivery and removing trash from the kitchen and other facilities. Provide adequate sidewalks to the facility.

Building access: Multiple access points to the building will accommodate the rapid influx of people arriving for services. Where possible, include a covered area to protect people being dropped off or picked up. This is especially important for special services, such as weddings and funerals.

ELEMENTS TO CONSIDER

Worship center (nave, sanctuary, or auditorium): Allow 8 to 10 sq ft per person in the seating area. Several basic arrangements for seating are shown here. Consider style of worship, site constraints, seating capacity, and sight lines. Many variations are possible.

Raised platform (sanctuary, chancel, or platform): Allow room for table or altar, pulpit, reading desk, and usually some seating. Observe rules for sight lines.

Music, choir, instruments: Size of choir is typically 10% of the worship center's capacity. Choir seating should be close to the musical instruments and arranged in no more than three rows. Allow room for special performers, handbells, strings, and piano. Consider fixed instruments, such as the organ, in planning the room.

Special considerations: Sacred or liturgical items that have specific functions, such as the tabernacle, baptismal font or baptistery, devotional areas, and statuary will vary among churches. Think of symbols, artwork, seasonal decorations, and furnishings as part of the room. Discuss room acoustics and sound reinforcement systems, which are a critical component. Consider both natural and artificial lighting. Include preparation rooms (sacristies or communion preparation) and, for floral arrangements, spaces with access to a sink, storage, and perhaps refrigeration. Special sinks for consecrated wine or water may be needed. Dressing rooms with toilets may be required for immersion/submersion baptisms.

Gathering space (narthex or commons): Allow 2 to 3 sq ft for each person in the worship center. This is the circulation hub of the church. Include coat hanging and information areas, as well as other storage space.

Administrative offices: Include reception area (25 to 30 sq ft per waiting person), main office (50 to 75 sq ft per clerical staff member), and individual offices (150 to 300 sq ft, depending on function). Provide counseling space where appropriate. Also provide work/storage space for photocopying, filing, and the like. Staff/meeting rooms may be shared as a classroom or library.

Multipurpose rooms (fellowship rooms or parish hall): These are used for dining, meetings, sports, and education. Configurations should be flexible and easy to alter.

Kitchen/serving facilities: Square footage should be 25% of the multipurpose room square footage. Consider whether the kitchen is full service or only for warming or catering. May house commercial or residential equipment. Check local health department rules. Determine whether to design for staff or volunteer help. If the kitchen is adjacent to the multipurpose room, allow secondary access to serve the rest of the facility.

Music support spaces: Provide a seating layout identical to that of the worship center. Design acoustics to match that of the worship center when full. Provide a music storage and retrieval system. Robing rooms, warm-up rooms, music director's office, and practice spaces may need to be included.

Education spaces: These may be designed for licensed day care; check with appropriate authorities. The following age groups need to be considered:

1. Nursery (0 to 6 months): 30 to 35 sq ft per person. Provide a drop-off area with security, storage for infant paraphernalia, changing area with sink, staff toilets, and toy storage.
2. Small children (6 months to 3 years): 30 sq ft per person. Provide changing area with sink, child-sized toilet facilities, storage, and proper lighting and ventilation.
3. Children (ages 4 to 11): 25 sq ft per person. Classrooms are much like an elementary school's. Provide display space, storage, access to toilets, and appropriate surface finishes for crafts.
4. Youth (junior high through college): 18 to 20 sq ft per person. This group typically enjoys a more casual style of space, which can be modified to match its particular image. Incorporate soft furniture, storage, and appropriate finishes for hard use.
5. Adults: 12 to 15 sq ft per person. Depending on style of classes, the furnishings may vary widely, from tables and chairs to lounge-type furniture. May be shared space with parlor, lounge, or library.

PLANNING ISSUES

Including all programmed spaces described above and support facilities such as toilets and mechanical rooms, the complex will be from 55 to 60 sq ft per seat in the worship center. The center of the complex is the gathering space, which acts as a lobby to orient visitors and users alike. Placing the administrative offices near the main entry provides a measure of security. The worship center, the focus of the complex, is easily accessible to the gathering space. Music support spaces are near the performing location in the worship center.

The gathering space may also serve as a lobby for the multipurpose room. The kitchen should serve the multipurpose room as well as other activity spaces. Food delivery and refuse removal need to be accommodated without using public spaces. Nurseries and young children's rooms should be close to the gathering space. Youth classrooms often have a separate entry, removed from the main entry. Clear, wide, and open circulation paths throughout the entire complex will augment its use, as large numbers of people move through the corridors over very short periods of time.

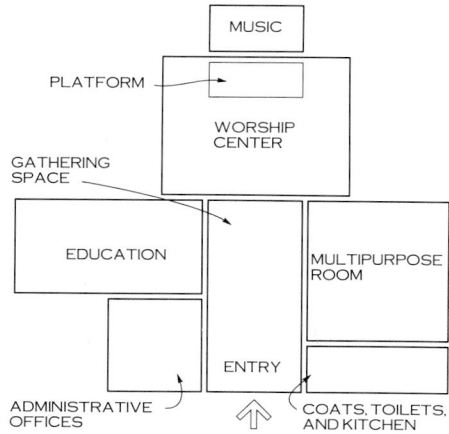

OVERALL SPACE RELATIONSHIPS

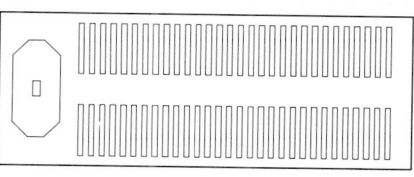
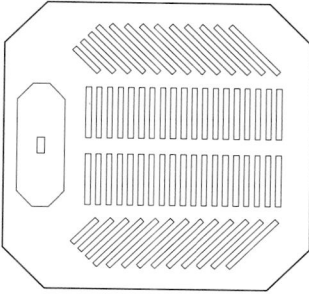
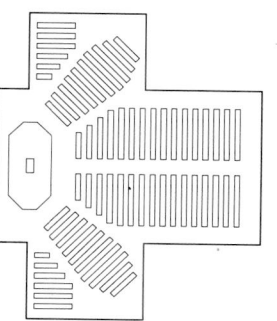
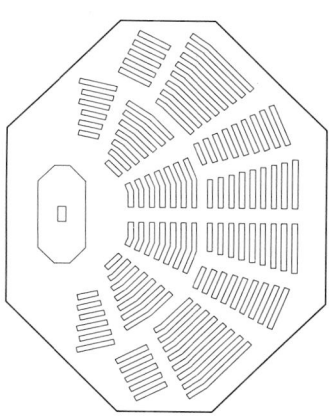
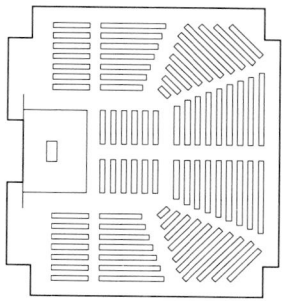

SEATING CONFIGURATIONS

David Cooper, AIA; Ware Associates, Inc.; Rockford, Illinois/Chicago/Los Angeles

GENERAL

The following are activity and space requirements for synagogues:

ACTIVITIES

1. Worship for large and small groups
2. Cantorial (all groups), Music (reform)
3. Bar mitzvah and Bas mitzvah
4. Hospitality/reception
5. Study area
6. Child care
7. School
8. Assembly (non-worship)
9. Food services - Oleg Shabbat
10. Maintenance

SPACES

1. Sanctuary (including expansion of 200% for high holidays)
2. Bemah
3. Ark
4. Lectern, reform or conservative
5. Chairs - four for officers
6. Eternal light

AREAS

1. Social hall - 12 sq ft per person dining
2. Administration - 30% of sanctuary space
3. Kitchen - 10% of sanctuary space
4. Education
   a. 30 sq ft per child in nursery/kindergarten
   b. 30 sq ft per child in grade 1 to 6
   c. 20 sq ft per child in grades 7 to 12
   d. 15 to 20 sq ft per adult
5. Seating - 15 sq ft per person net
6. Aisle dimensions
   a. Main aisle - 5 ft wide
   b. Side aisle - 3 ft 6 in.

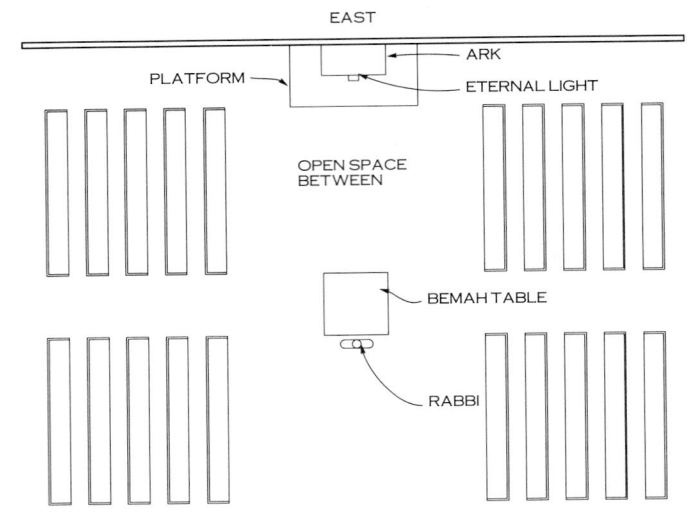

ORTHODOX LAYOUT

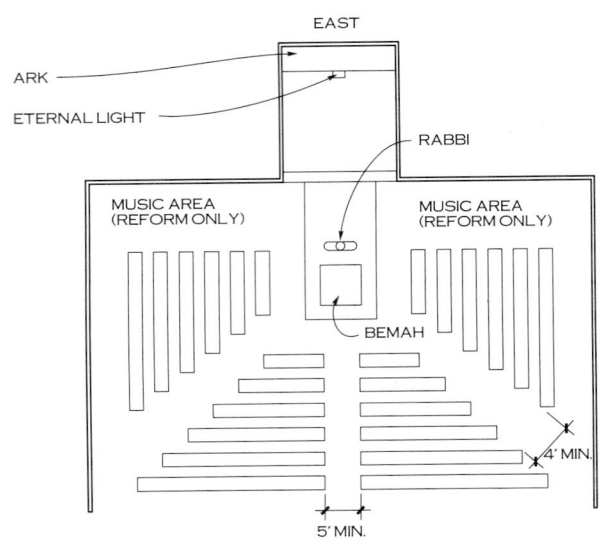

REFORM AND CONSERVATIVE LAYOUT

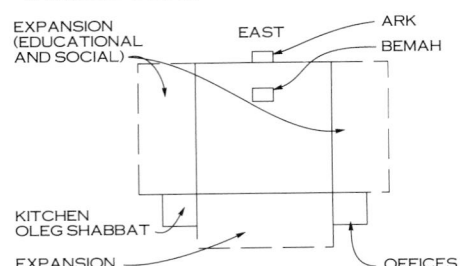

INTERRELATIONSHIP DIAGRAM

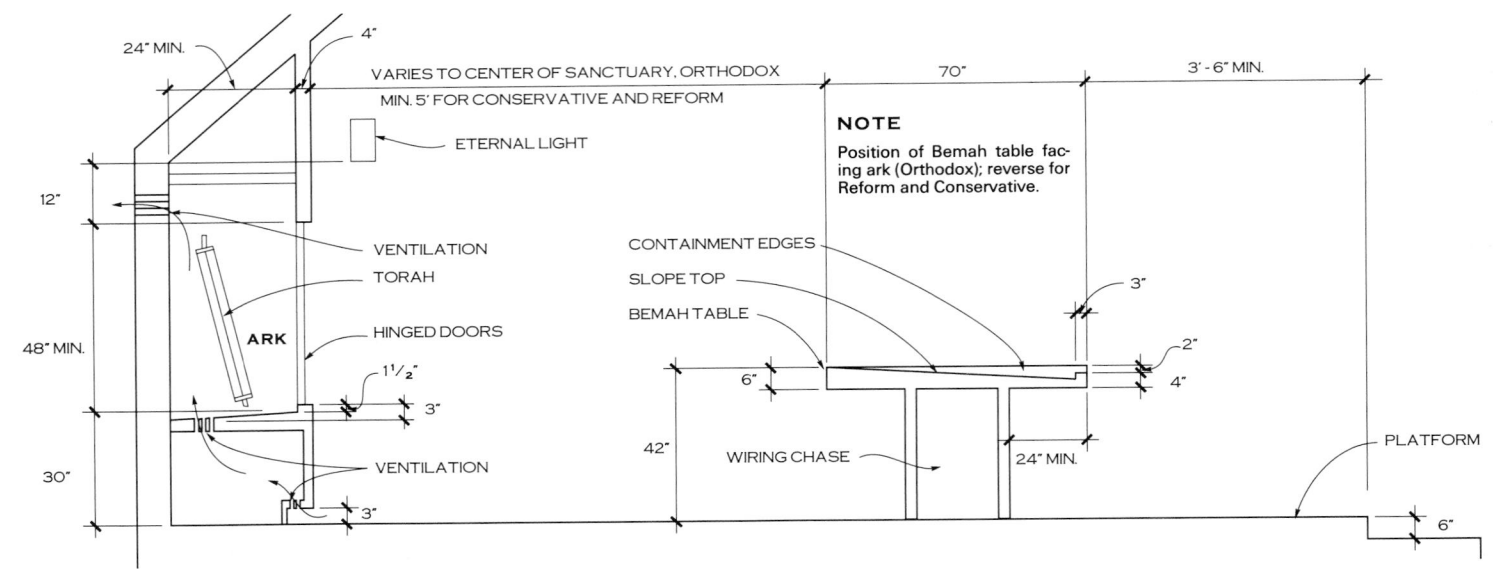

NOTE

Position of Bemah table facing ark (Orthodox); reverse for Reform and Conservative.

SECTION

Norman Jaffe, FAIA; Bridgehampton, New York

SPECIAL DESIGN CONSIDERATIONS

SYMBOLIC ELEMENTS: Most Muslim communities, especially those who consider the pluralistic, freedom, and rights-based Western world as their home, want to express their presence through a structure is easily recognizable as a mosque. The common architectural features that give the mosque a unique silhouette are the dome(s) and minaret(s) that culminate with a clearly visible crescent. A formal entrance, an expressed turn of the prayer hall toward the Qibla, a Mihrab that bulges out on the exterior of the Qibla wall, and some carefully placed arched windows can further enhance the recognizability of the mosque.

LOBBY: Some communities require that male and female members of a family separate before entering the mosque, thus requiring two separate entrances. This has important implications for the planning and formal expression of the mosque.

SHOES AND COAT AREA: For men and boys; separate facilities for women, young girls, and children.

WASHROOMS: Provide regular washrooms, possibly including a European bidet or similar arrangement for washing. One washroom should be planned for fifty prayer spaces. Consideration should be given to providing adequate washrooms for women with children.

ABLUTION AREA: Ablution stations are needed for the ritual cleansing of hands, forearms, mouth, sinuses, face, and feet in a prescribed sequence. At least one enclosed shower stall is needed for the ritual shower of Ghusul. Provide a nonskid surface in this area. Some provision should be made for drying feet before entering the prayer area.

PRAYER HALL: Rectangular or square floor area with simple linear arrangement for prayer spaces. The prayer rows are parallel to the Qibla wall and directed toward Qibla as indicated by Mihrab. No shoes are wore in the designated prayer areas. A separate area for women, young girls, and children must be provided. Special acoustically separated but visually connected area for nursing mothers and mothers with very young children is recommended.

AREA FOR NON-MUSLIM VISITORS: Requests to observe the Islamic payers are common and should be accommodated.

MOSQUE CAPACITY: The mosque should be planned on sound population data and projections. In North America and Europe, construction of a "visible and permanently consecrated" mosque often draws extra people to the congregation.

WOMEN'S ATTENDANCE: Women generally comprise 25 to 33 percent of the total congregation. This will probably increase considerably in the West as women assume a more active role in community affairs.

PARKING: One parking space should be provided for five adult prayer spaces with contingency arrangements for extra parking on high religious holidays.

MOVEMENT THROUGH SPACES: A clear sequence of alternative movement choices from the entrance to the prayer hall should be developed. Areas in which shoes should be removed and stored versus shoeless areas is a planning difficulty. Consult with the client on acceptable situations.

PRAYER AREA: The conventional geometry of a prayer area has been a broadside rectangle with its longer side parallel to the Qibla wall. Religious tradition has established a precedent for longer rows to be closer to the Qibla wall. Floor finishes of the prayer hall should clearly indicate the arrangement of prayer rows at every 48 inches parallel to the Qibla wall. The floor should also be soft enough for the knees, which carry a considerable weight as the body is changes postures. Each prayer module should be 24 x 48 in.

BURIAL PREPARATION: If facilities for the washing and shrouding of the dead are required, follow relevant health regulations.

PROGRAMMING ELEMENTS

1. A marked entrance, gateway
2. A lobby or forecourt with attached facilities
3. Prayer hall and its various sections with clearly marked thresholds of entrances
4. Qibla wall
5. Mihrab
6. Mimbar

Norman Jaffe, FAIA; Bridgehampton, New York
Gulzar Haider, Carleton University; Ottawa, Canada

TYPES OF MOSQUES IN THE CONTEMPORARY WEST

NEIGHBORHOOD MOSQUE: Serve those in a community for which the main or the Friday mosque might be beyond convenient transportation.

FRIDAY MOSQUE (often called the main or the central mosque or given a special name like Al-Farooq Mosque): Large enough for Salat al-Juma', capacity usually above 200. Imam's residence and a caretaker's apartment may be attached to the mosque.

ISLAMIC CENTER: Mosque plus facilities for socioreligious gatherings that cannot be performed in the mosque prayer hall, e.g., weddings, anniversaries, lectures, and light sports. Some centers also have facilities for the ritual washing and shrouding of dead bodies in preparation for burials.

CAMPUS CENTER: Caters to the unique setting and requirements of the Muslim population of a university campus.

HEADQUARTERS MOSQUE: Built as a marker of an Islamic diplomatic or organizational presence (e.g., Washington Islamic Center, United Nations Mosque). Mosques that belong to special spiritual orders of Islam may also fall under this category.

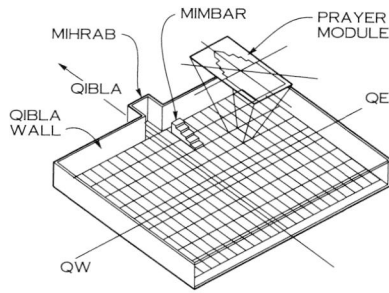

NOTES

1. Number of levels for the Mimbar equals 3, 5, or 7 depending on the size of the congregation.
2. Portability of Mimbar is recommended.
3. Coordination of Mimbar and Mihrab design is recommended.
4. When women attendance exceeds 33 percent to total congregation, a separate floor and/or space is recommended.
5. Mihrab design is achieved by relative manipulation of outside and inside surfaces without violating spatial prayer module for Imam.

PLAN

DEFINITIONS

Salat: Obligatory Islamic ritual prayer to be offered five times a day, preferably in congregation, in the mosque

Imam: Religious leader of Muslim community

Salat al-Juma': Obligatory Friday congregational prayer with khutba by the Imam

Sijdah: Prostration before God in the body position when the forehead, two palms, two knees, and two sets of toes simultaneously touch the earth plane

Masjid/Mosque: Literally the place where Sijdah is enacted. Place for collective Salat whose crescendo is Sijdah in unison by the whole congregation.

Jami Masjid: Mosque large enough hold Salat al-Juma'

Kaa'ba: The cube shaped, black cloth-draped sanctuary erected by Abraham and Ishma'il as "Bait-Allah," the "house of God." Located at the center of the holy precinct in Makkah. The sacred node to which all mosques of the earth are oriented.

Qibla: Orientation toward Kaa'ba

Mihrab: Niche identifying the Qibla wall and the place of the Imam who leads the congregational prayer.

Mimbar: Mosque pulpit, a simple ladder chair for the Imam to rise to a place of higher visibility among a large congregation. Traditionally the symbolic seat of the prophet.

QIBLA ORIENTATION

The following figure and procedure is for cities in the Northern hemisphere west of Makkah. The method can easily be extended to cities over the rest of the globe.

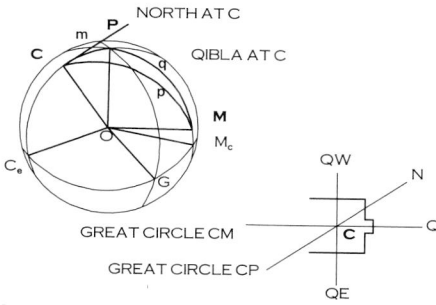

SPHERICAL GEOMETRY

The Qibla orientation for a mosque is calculated by the following equations, using equation 1 to solve for unknown angle p, then substitute the value of angle p into equations 2 to solve angle Q, Qibla orientation:

Equation 1: $\cos p = \cos q \cos m + \sin q \sin m \cos P$

Equation 2: $\sin Q = \dfrac{\sin q \sin P}{\sin p}$

where:

C = City Whose Qibla is to be calculated
C_e = Geometric location of city meridian on equator
M = Makkah, location of Kaa'ba
M_e = Geometric location of Makkah meridian on equator
P = Geometric north pole of earth sphere
O = Geometric center of earth sphere
G = 0° meridian at equator

m = Angle COP (known as 90° - latitude of city C)
q = Angle POM (known as 90° - latitude of Makkah)
p = Angle COM
P = Angle C_eOM_e
Q = Qibla orientation at C, angle between diametric planes CPO and CMO

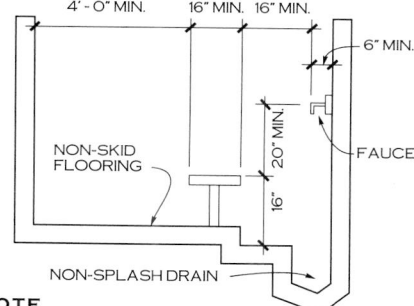

NOTE

Ablution stall should be separated a minimum of 24 in. with the recommended distance of 30 in.

ABLUTION STALL

SUMMARY

It is recommended that before the architect embark on interpretation and invention of a mosque, they acquaint themselves with the many regional traditions and some recent precedents in the design. The following references are recommended:

Burckhardt, T. Art of Islam: Language and Meaning (London, 1976).

Hoag, J.D. Islamic Architecture (New York, 1977).

Michell, G. (ed). Architecture of the Islamic World (London, 1978).

Papadopoul, A. Islam and Muslim Art (Abrams, 1976).

Sevcenko, M.B. (ed). Theories and Principles of Design in the Architecture of Islamic Societies, AKPIA (Cambridge, Mass., 1988).

PLANNING ISSUES

Correctional facility design has experienced a dramatic shift away from the classic cellblock system to a centralized living unit concept. This system provides for greater control of a given number of inmates and economizes on staffing requirements by allowing control of several living units from a centralized location. Living units are sized to provide manageable groups of inmates, maximum flexibility in segregating different groups, and a high degree of fire protection without sacrificing security.

The living unit concept typically groups between 24 and 48 single cells around a communal dayroom, which provides areas for television, reading, conversation, and light activities. Each unit contains its own shower facility, with approximately one shower for every 8 inmates. Units are usually two tiers high, with a two-story dayroom. The inclusion of natural light in both cells and dayrooms is strongly encouraged.

There is a growing trend away from indirect inmate supervision (in which guards are placed in a secure control booth) to direct supervision where guards are in direct contact with the inmates, encouraging an environment of greater interaction.

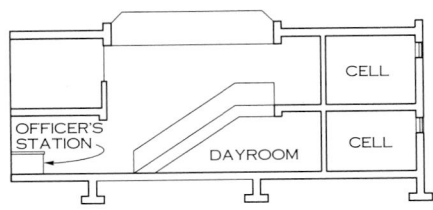

TYPICAL UNIT SECTION

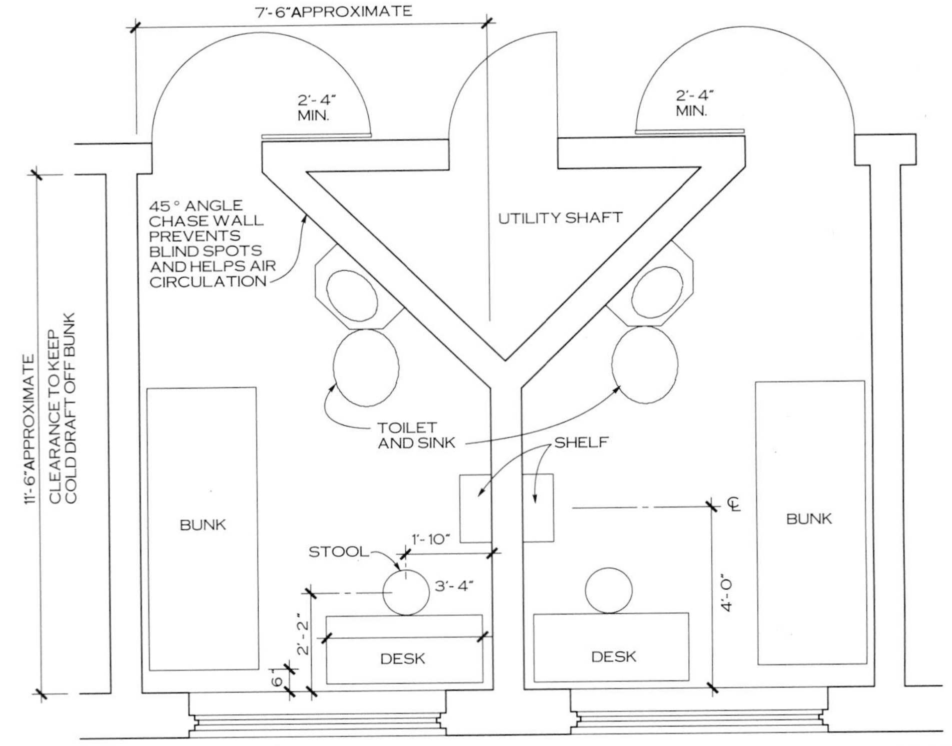

TYPICAL CELL LAYOUT

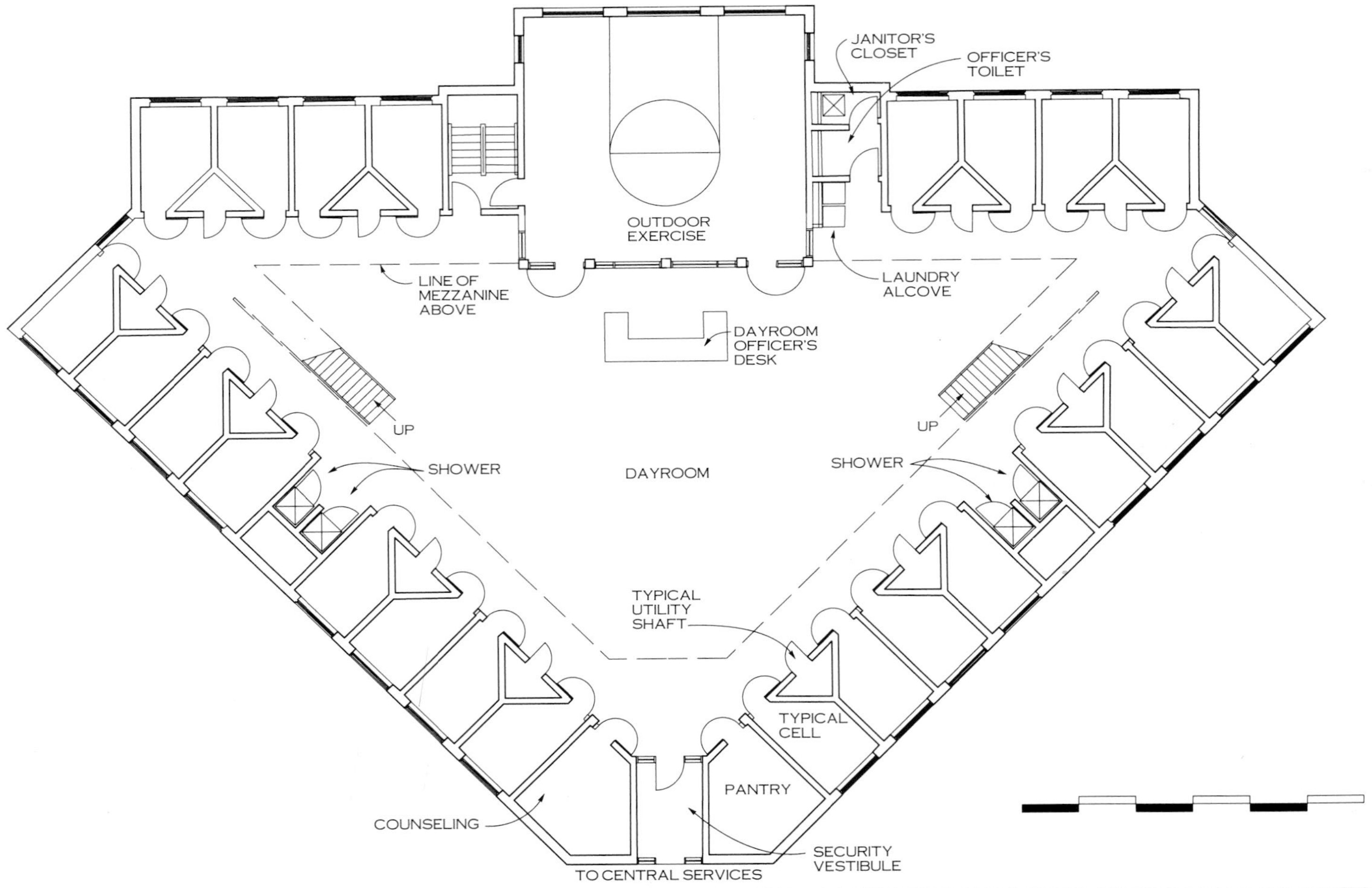

TYPICAL HOUSING UNIT PLAN

Glenn J. Ware, AIA; Hansen Lind Meyer; Orlando, Florida

 DETENTION

GENERAL

A stadium is a pitch or track for individual athletics or team competition in an arena surrounded by stepped tiers for standing or seated spectators. Some stadiums are covered, but these coverings do not necessarily enclose the structure.

The design of a stadium is largely dictated by the type of activity it will house and by the number of spectators to be accommodated. The specific sports and number of spectators are usually outlined in the program.

POSSIBLE ACTIVITIES FOR STADIUMS

soccer
rugby
football (American)
baseball
athletic competition/track and field
equestrian events: polo, jumping, rodeo
entertainment concerts
multi-purpose events

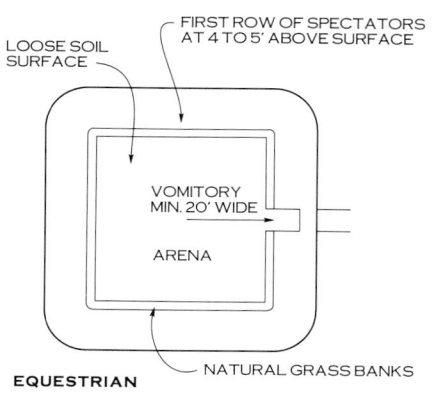

EQUESTRIAN

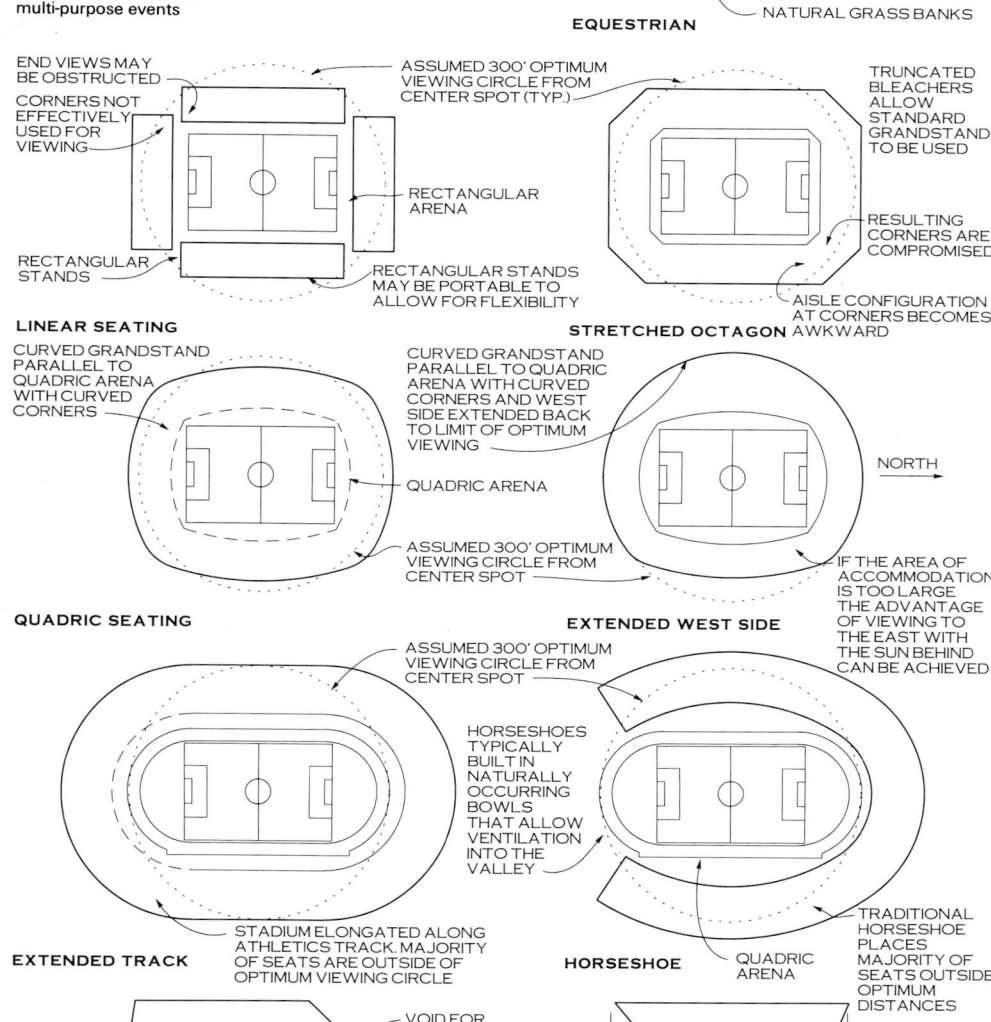

LINEAR SEATING

STRETCHED OCTAGON

QUADRIC SEATING

EXTENDED WEST SIDE

EXTENDED TRACK

HORSESHOE

BASEBALL

MULTI-USE

TYPICAL STADIUM CONFIGURATIONS

NBBJ; Research Triangle Park, North Carolina

PRIORITY PLANNING FOR STADIUMS

1. SAFE for all spectators and participants: Usually dictated by local codes and regulations, safety issues relate to crowd control, fire safety, evacuation, circulation, etc.
2. COMPACT enough to accommodate all spectators within maximum viewing distances to ensure minimum views of all areas of the field of activity.
3. CONVENIENT for spectators and participants: Access to amenities within the complex should be available within minimum time standards.
4. COMFORTABLE: To ensure feasibility, the comfort of spectators and participants should be accommodated as much as the budget will allow.
5. FLEXIBLE: Ensure flexibility in terms of different venues and future growth potential.
6. ECONOMICAL: Evaluate initial capital expenditure and recurring maintenance costs.

GENERAL STADIUM PLANNING GUIDELINES

The plan of all stadia is determined first by the regulation size of the activity and auxiliary areas, i.e., the pitch or track on which the activity takes place, the necessary surrounding areas for linesmen, and the need to move back the first row of spectators for improved viewing.

If possible, orient the stadium with the long axis running north and south so most spectators face east and west. Attempt to give both teams, as nearly as possible, identical lighting conditions.

STADIUM TERMINOLOGY

ARENA: the activity area plus the ancillary area of the stadium.

ATHLETICS: track and field events.

CONTINENTAL SEATING: a seating arrangement not interrupted by a center aisle.

CROWN: the average distance from the eye of the spectator to the top of the head, which is approximately 120mm or 4 3/4 in.

FOCUS: the middle of the innermost athletics track or the near touchline in football or soccer.

HOUSE SEATS: seats normally reserved for house management or special guests. These are not sold but held out for special use.

PITCH: the competition athletic field.

RAKE: the angle of rise of seating stands.

SIGHT LINES: the lines of vision of the spectators in normal and extreme positions in the facility. Sight lines include upper as well as side views.

TIER: one of a series of rows rising one behind and above another.

VOMITORY: areaway for circulation within stadium.

LIMIT OF VIEWING

The limit of viewing distance is determined by the ability of the spectator farthest from the activity to distinguish the smallest moving object.

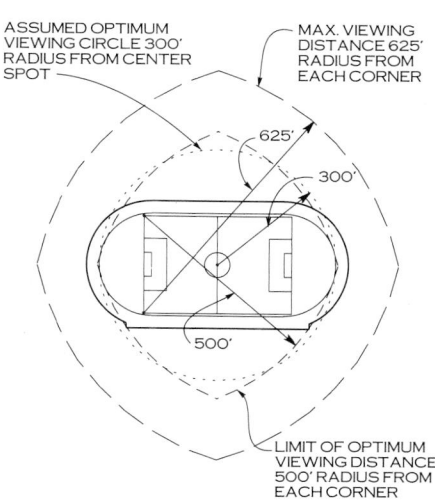

SEATING GUIDELINES

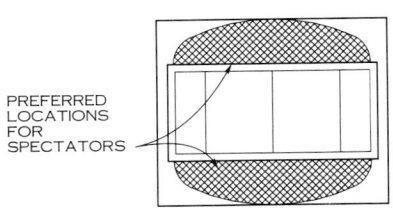

PREFERRED
LOCATIONS
FOR
SPECTATORS

RUGBY

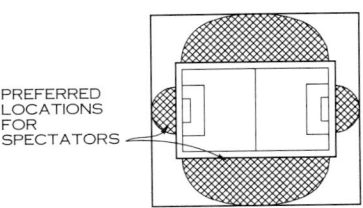

PREFERRED
LOCATIONS
FOR
SPECTATORS

SOCCER

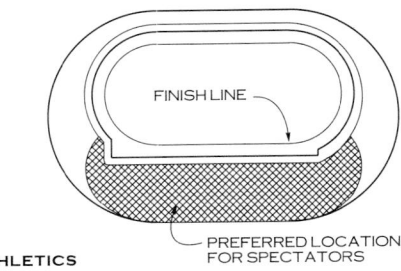

FINISH LINE

PREFERRED LOCATION
FOR SPECTATORS

ATHLETICS

OPTIMUM SEATING

STRAIGHT VS. QUADRIC SEATING

Spectator accommodation in rows parallel to the side lines or touch lines and close to the pitch is self-obscuring. A spectator near a corner of the pitch has difficulty seeing the other corner on the same side, since the view is obscured by other spectators. Quadric, or curved, seating can offer unobscured views (see Tiers Comparison).

TIERS

The rake of the tiering is determined either mathematically or graphically in section, where the principal factors are the assumed constant of the crown and these variables: the horizontal distance between consecutive rows, the focus, and the height of the spectator's eye in the first row.

In determining the rake, the lines of sight from the eyes of spectators in each row to the focus should be clear of, or at worst tangential to, the top of the head of the spectator in the row in front. This will give a profile that is parabolic, the rake increasing with the viewing distance. Tiers in this profile are not economical to construct and are not safe for crowd movement. The stairs in gangways become unequal and therefore unacceptable.

OVERLAPPING TIERS

Overlapping the seating tiers is an obvious method of substantially reducing the maximum viewing distance—the horizontal (plan) distance—by increasing the vertical distance.

CONCESSIONS

Stands for food, beverages, and souvenirs should be designed to handle peak impact loads. Events with half-times or periods will induce the largest crowds. Patrons should be able to reach concessions within 40 to 60 seconds.

The general recommendation for concessions is 20 to 25 linear feet of counter space for every 1,000 seats if there are no vending machines. If vending is provided, use 13 to 18 linear feet.

DRESSING ROOMS

Dressing rooms should include changing areas with stalls or hangers for clothing, showers, drying rooms, tables for taping, and toilets. Equip stalls with a bench or stool, hangers, a shelf, and possibly a lock box for valuables. There should be a trainer's room for athletes' therapy. Dressing rooms for officials should be separate from those for athletes.

ACCESS CONTROL

There should be one turnstile per 1,000 spectators. Viewers, athletes, and staff should be able to empty a stadium in under eight minutes.

If the field is used for concerts, spectators must have access to toilets and concessions. Admissions control should prevent mixing between those who have purchased floor tickets and those with tickets in less expensive seats.

Other items that should be addressed as part of the program include:

Broadcasting studios/press boxes
Emergency medicine/first aid/life safety
Night lighting
Public address system
Restrooms
Scoreboards/sign boards
VIP seating/hospitality provisions

CROSS REFERENCE (AGS 9TH ED.)

Grandstand and bleacher details: p. 837
Playing field construction: p. 673
Individual sports: polo, soccer, football, baseball, for specific size requirements of playing field and ancillary spaces.

CONSULTANTS

Confer with consultants who specialize in athletic surfaces and equipment, long-span structures, lighting, etc.

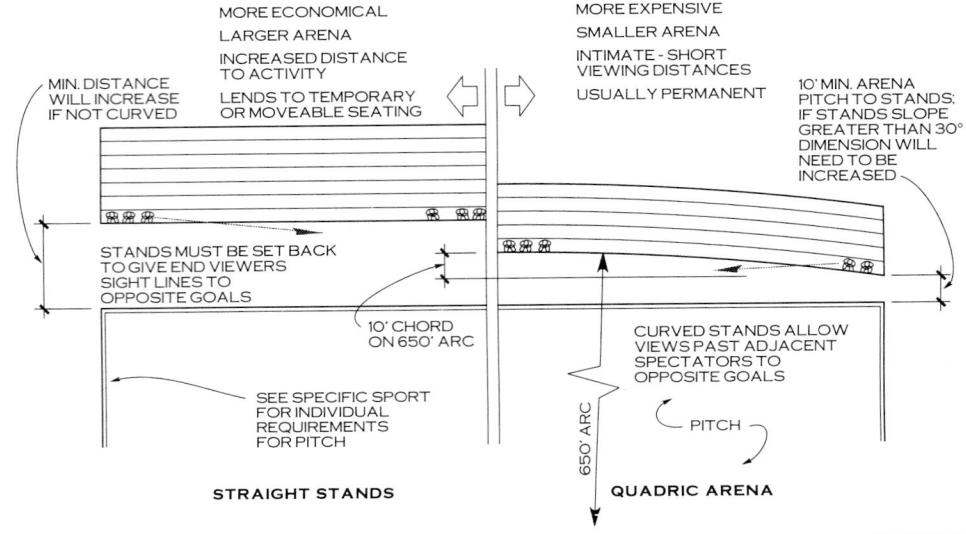

MORE ECONOMICAL
LARGER ARENA
INCREASED DISTANCE TO ACTIVITY
LENDS TO TEMPORARY OR MOVEABLE SEATING

MORE EXPENSIVE
SMALLER ARENA
INTIMATE - SHORT VIEWING DISTANCES
USUALLY PERMANENT

MIN. DISTANCE WILL INCREASE IF NOT CURVED

10' MIN. ARENA PITCH TO STANDS; IF STANDS SLOPE GREATER THAN 30° DIMENSION WILL NEED TO BE INCREASED

STANDS MUST BE SET BACK TO GIVE END VIEWERS SIGHT LINES TO OPPOSITE GOALS

10' CHORD ON 650' ARC

CURVED STANDS ALLOW VIEWS PAST ADJACENT SPECTATORS TO OPPOSITE GOALS

SEE SPECIFIC SPORT FOR INDIVIDUAL REQUIREMENTS FOR PITCH

650' ARC

PITCH

STRAIGHT STANDS

QUADRIC ARENA

STRAIGHT VS. QUADRIC SEATING

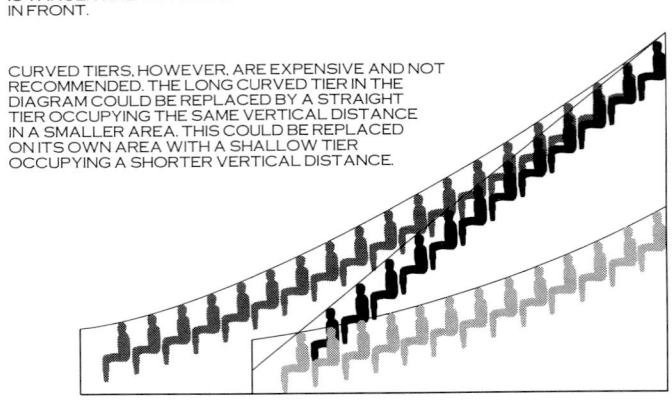

A STEPPED TIER SET OUT FROM A TOUCH LINE PRODUCES A PARABOLIC CURVE IN SECTION, WHEN THE LINE OF VISION IS TANGENTIAL TO THE TOP OF THE HEAD OF THE VIEWERS IN FRONT.

CURVED TIERS, HOWEVER, ARE EXPENSIVE AND NOT RECOMMENDED. THE LONG CURVED TIER IN THE DIAGRAM COULD BE REPLACED BY A STRAIGHT TIER OCCUPYING THE SAME VERTICAL DISTANCE IN A SMALLER AREA. THIS COULD BE REPLACED ON ITS OWN AREA WITH A SHALLOW TIER OCCUPYING A SHORTER VERTICAL DISTANCE.

THREE STRAIGHT TIERS APPROXIMATELY TANGENTIAL TO THE THEORETICAL CURVE IN A SINGLE TIER IS ECONOMICAL IN COST BUT NOT IN SPACE. SEPARATING AND OVERLAPPING THE TIERS REDUCES PLAN AREA. THE ANGLE OF RAKE MAY NEED TO BE INCREASED BUT SHOULD NOT BE STEEPER THAN 35°.

CURVED VS. STRAIGHT

STACKED VS. STRAIGHT RUN

TIERS COMPARISON

NBBJ; Research Triangle Park, North Carolina

ASSEMBLY

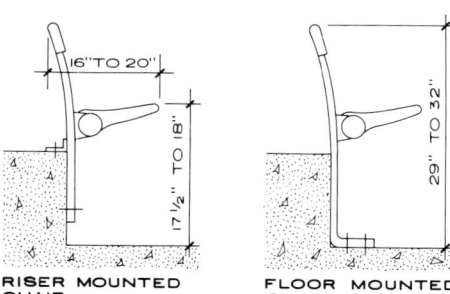

RISER MOUNTED CHAIR

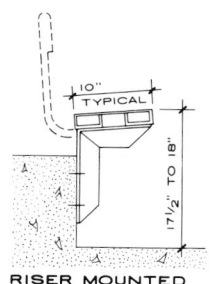

FLOOR MOUNTED CHAIR

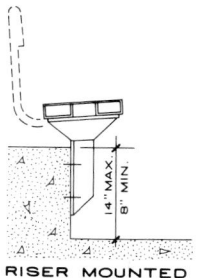

RISER MOUNTED BENCH L

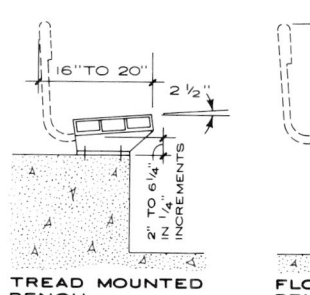

RISER MOUNTED BENCH T

TREAD MOUNTED BENCH

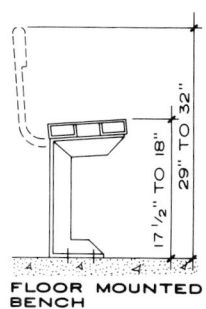

FLOOR MOUNTED BENCH

STANDARD SEATS AND SEAT SUPPORTS

SEATING CAPACITY

Allow 18 in. of bleacher length per person per row. Normal aisle width of 36 in. reduces seating capacity by two seats per row x number of rows x number of aisles. See table below.

SAFETY AREAS

1. BASEBALL FIELDS: Minimum 60 ft from seating to foul line or baseline at each side of home plate.
2. SOFTBALL FIELDS: Minimum 25 ft from seating to foul line or baseline at each side of home plate.
3. BASKETBALL COURTS: Minimum 6 ft from seating to court sides, 4 ft minimum to court ends.
4. SWIMMING POOLS: Minimum 5 ft from seating to pool decks. Spectator area must be separate from pool area to avoid mixing dry and wet traffic.

STADIUM SEATING

Concrete risers and treads with seating attached. See typical seats and seat supports above.

FIXED GRANDSTAND

8 in. rise with 24 in. row spacing typical. Available options include front, end, and back rails, crosswalks, ramps, stairs, aisles, vomitories, closed risers, double foot plates, folding seat backs, and waterproof covers of metal or fiberglass for resurfacing existing wooden bleachers.

PORTABLE BLEACHERS

3, 4, or 5 row sections typical. Transportable options include wheels and trailer attachments. Bleachers of up to 25 rows may be assembled of portable sections.

TELESCOPIC BLEACHERS

1. LOWRISE: $9^5/_8$ in. normal rise for most uses. 22 in. minimum row spacing gives maximum seating capacity. 24 in. spacing gives greater leg room. 30 or 32 in. spacing provides extra passage and leg room space and space for optional folding back rests.
2. HIGHRISE: Models with $11^5/_8$ or 16 in. risers are suggested for pools, balconies, hockey rinks, or similarly difficult viewing situations where seating must be banked more steeply than is normal.

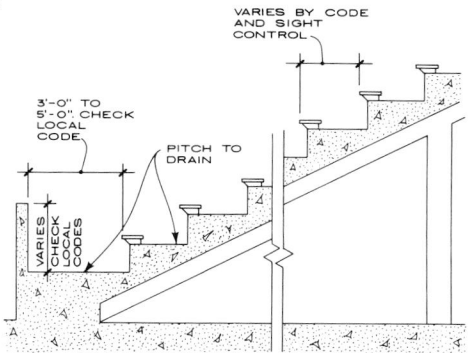

STADIUM SEATING

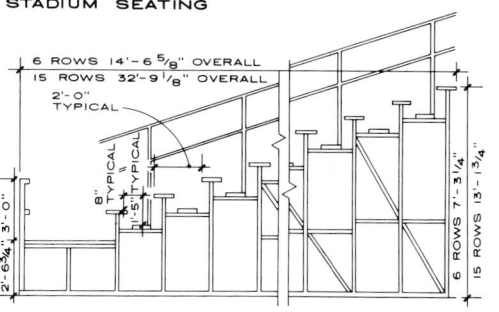

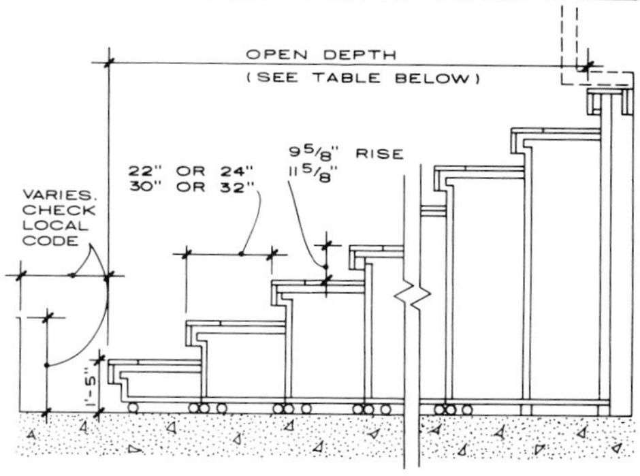

FIXED GRANDSTAND (ELEVATED)

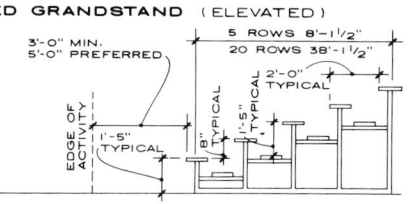

PORTABLE BLEACHERS

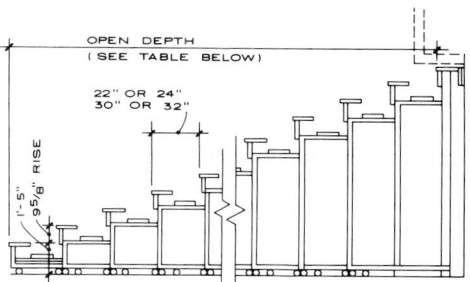

TELESCOPIC BLEACHERS (HIGHRISE)

TELESCOPIC BLEACHERS (LOWRISE)

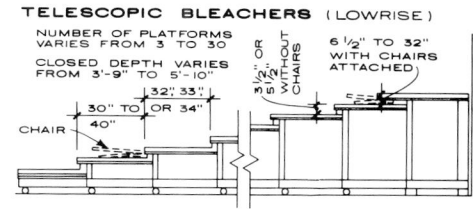

TELESCOPIC PLATFORM

SEATING CAPACITY

LENGTH (FT)

ROW	8	12	16	20	24	28	32	36	40
3	16	24	32	40	48	56	64	72	80
4	21	32	42	53	64	74	85	96	106
5	26	40	53	66	80	93	106	120	133
6	32	48	64	80	96	112	128	144	160
7	37	56	74	93	112	130	149	168	186
8	42	64	85	106	128	149	170	192	213
9	48	72	96	120	144	168	192	216	240
10	53	80	106	133	160	186	213	240	266
12	64	96	128	160	192	224	256	288	320
14	74	112	149	186	224	261	298	336	373
16	85	128	170	213	256	298	341	384	426
18	96	144	192	240	288	336	384	432	480
20	106	160	213	266	320	373	426	480	533

NOTE: Consult manufacturers for additional information.

GRANDSTANDS AND BLEACHERS DIMENSIONS

ROW	OPEN DEPTH				$9^5/_8''$ RISE CLOSED DEPTH		$11^5/_8''$ AND 16'' RISE CLOSED DEPTH	
	22''	24''	30''	32''	22'' OR 24''	30'' OR 32''	22'' OR 24''	30'' OR 32''
3	4'-11½''	5'-1½''	6'-3½''	6'-5½''	3'-1¹³/₁₆''	3'-9¹³/₁₆''	3'-1¹³/₁₆''	3'-9¹³/₁₆''
4	6'-9½''	7'-1½''	8'-9½''	9'-1½''	3'-2⅛''	3'-10⅛''	3'-2⅛''	3'-10⅛''
5	8'-7½''	9'-1½''	11'-3½''	11'-9½''	3'-2⁷/₁₆''	3'-10⁷/₁₆''	3'-2⁷/₁₆''	3'-10⁷/₁₆''
6	10'-5½''	11'-1½''	13'-9½''	14'-5½''	3'-2¾''	3'-10¾''	3'-2¾''	3'-10¾''
7	12'-3½''	13'-1½''	16'-3½''	17'-1½''	3'-3¹/₁₆''	3'-11¹/₁₆''	3'-3¹/₁₆''	3'-11¹/₁₆''
8	14'-1½''	15'-1½''	18'-9½''	19'-9½''	3'-3⅜''	3'-11⅜''	3'-3⅜''	3'-11⅜''
9	15'-11½''	17'-1½''	21'-3½''	22'-5½''	3'-3¹¹/₁₆''	3'-11¹¹/₁₆''	3'-3¹¹/₁₆''	3'-11¹¹/₁₆''
10	17'-9½''	19'-1½''	23'-9½''	25'-1½''	3'-4''	4'-0''	3'-4''	4'-0''
12	21'-5½''	23'-1½''	28'-9½''	30'-5½''	3'-4⅝''	4'-0⅝''	3'-4⅝''	4'-0⅝''
14	25'-1½''	27'-1½''	33'-9½''	35'-9½''	3'-5¼''	4'-1¼''	NOTE: For $11^5/_8''$ rise of 18 or more rows and 16'' rise of 13 or more rows check with manufacturer for modified closed depth dimensions.	
16	28'-9½''	31'-1½''	38'-9½''	41'-1½''	3'-5⅞''	4'-1⅞''		
18	32'-5½''	35'-1½''	43'-9½''	46'-5½''	3'-6½''	4'-2½''		
20	36'-1½''	39'-1½''	48'-9½''	51'-9½''	3'-7⅛''	4'-3⅛''		

Eric Johnson; Lawrence Cook Associates P.C., Architects; Falls Church, Virginia
David W. Johnson; Washington, D.C.

THEATER DESIGN CRITERIA

The planning of seating areas in places of assembly should involve the following considerations:

1. EFFICIENCY: The floor area efficiency in square feet per seat is a function of the row spacing, the average chair width, and the space allocation per seat for aisles. See following pages for further discussion of these factors.

Efficiency (F) = seat factor + aisle factor

$$F \text{ (sq ft/seat)} = \frac{W_s T}{144} + \frac{IT}{144} \times \frac{1}{S_{avg}}$$

where W_s = average seat width (in.)
T = row to row spacing (tread) (in.)
I = average aisle width (in.) (42 in. width is typical)
S_{avg} = average number of seats in a row per single aisle: 8 or fewer—inefficient layout; 14 to 16—maximum efficiency (multiple aisle seating); 18 to 50 and more—continental seating.

2. CAPACITY AND AUDIENCE AREA: Audience area = capacity x efficiency.

35–75	Classroom
75–150	Lecture room, experimental theater
150–300	Large lecture room, small theater
300–750	Average drama theater in educational setting
750–1500	Small commercial theater, repertory theater, recital hall
1500–2000	Medium large theater, large commercial theater
2000–3000	Average civic theater, concert hall, multiple use hall
3000–6000	Very large auditorium
Over 6000	Special assembly facilities

3. PERFORMING AREA (not including adjacent support area) (sq ft):

	MINIMUM	AVERAGE	MAXIMUM
Lectures (single speaker)	150	240	500
Revue, nightclub	350	450	700
Legitimate drama	250	550	1000
Dance	700	950	1200
Musicals, folk opera	800	1200	1800
Symphonic concerts	1500	2000	2500
Opera	1000	2500	4000
Pageant	2000	3500	5000

4. ORIENTATION OF SEATED SPECTATOR: Head strain is minimized by orienting chairs or rows of chairs so that spectators face the center of action of the performing area.

5. ANGLE OF VISION OF SPECTATOR: The human eye has a peripheral spread of vision of about 130°. This angle of view from chairs in the front rows will define the outer limits of the maximum sized performing area.

6. ANGLE OF ENCOUNTER: The angle of encounter is defined by the 130° peripheral spread of vision of a single performer standing at the "point of command." Patrons seated outside the spread of this angle will not have simultaneous eye contact with performer. Natural sound communication will also deteriorate for these patrons.

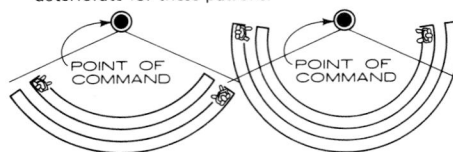

7. DISTANCE BETWEEN PERFORMANCE AND LAST ROW OF SPECTATORS: Achievement of visual and sound communication is enhanced by minimizing this distance while satisfying the preceding parameters.

Peter H. Frink; Frink and Beuchat: Architects; Philadelphia, Pennsylvania

SCREEN PROJECTION

- The minimum distance between the first row and the screen (D_F) is determined by the maximum allowable angle between the sightline from the first row to the top of the screen and the perpendicular to the screen at that point. A maximum angle of 30 to 35° is recommended.
- The maximum distance between the screen and the most distant viewer (MDV) should not exceed eight times the height of the screen image. An MDV two to three times the screen width is preferred.
- Screen width (W) is determined by the use of the appropriate aspect ratio between the screen image width and height.
- Curvature of screens may reduce the amount of apparent distortion for a larger audience area. Curvature of larger screens may help to keep the whole of the image in focus and may provide a more uniform distribution of luminance.

ZERO ENCIRCLEMENT (PROSCENIUM STAGE, PICTURE FRAME STAGE, END STAGE)

- The angle of audience spread in front of a masking frame is determined by the maximum size of the corner cutoff from a rectangularly shaped performing area that can be tolerated by seats at the side.
- Audience may not fill angle of encounter from point of command.
- Audience farthest from performing area.
- Large range in choice of size of performing area.
- Provisions for a large amount of scenic wall surfaces without masking sightlines.
- Horizontal movement of scenery typically made in both perpendicularly and parallel to centerline.
- Possibility of short differences in arrival time between direct and reflected sound at the spectator. This may be beneficial to music performances.

90° TO 130° ENCIRCLEMENT (PICTORIAL OPEN STAGE, WIDE FAN, HYBRID, THRUST STAGE)

- Audience spread defined and limited by angle of encounter from point of command.
- Performing area shape trapezoidal, rhombic, or circular.
- Audience closer to performing area than with zero encirclement.
- Picture frame less dominant.
- Range in choice of size of performing area.
- Provision for an amount of scenic wall surfaces possible without obscuring the performing area.
- Horizontal movement of scenery is possible in directions at 45° to and parallel to centerline.
- Shape of seating area places maximum number of seats within the directional limits of the sound of the unaided voice, beneficial for speech performance.

180° TO 270° ENCIRCLEMENT (GREEK THEATER, PENINSULAR, THREE-SIDED, THRUST STAGE, 3/4 ARENA STAGE, ELIZABETHAN STAGE)

- Audience spread well beyond angle of encounter from point of command in order to bring audience closer to performing area.
- Simultaneous eye contact between performer and all spectators not possible.
- Minimum range of choice in size of performing area.
- Provision of a small amount of scenic wall surfaces possible without masking sightlines.
- Horizontal movement of scenery is possible only parallel to centerline.
- Large encirclement by audience usually demands actor vomitory entrance through or under audience.

360° ENCIRCLEMENT (ARENA STAGE, THEATER IN THE ROUND, ISLAND STAGE, CENTER STAGE)

- Performer always seen from rear by some spectators.
- Simultaneous eye contact between performer and all spectators not possible.
- Audience closest to performance.
- No range of choice in size of performing area.
- No scenic wall surfaces possible without obscuring the view of the performing area.
- Horizontal movement of scenery not readily possible.
- Encirclement by audience demands actor vomitory entrance through audience area.

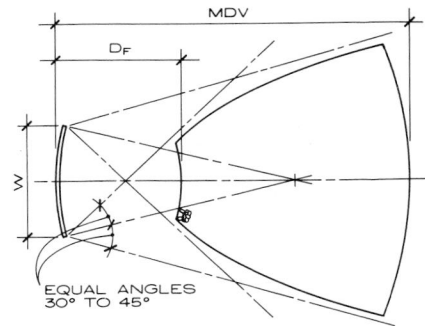

SCREEN PROJECTION

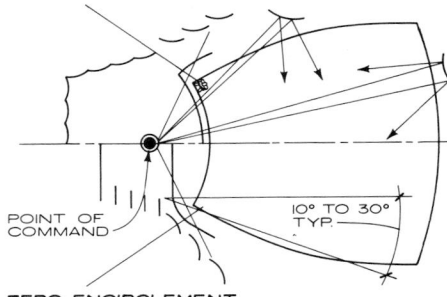

ZERO ENCIRCLEMENT

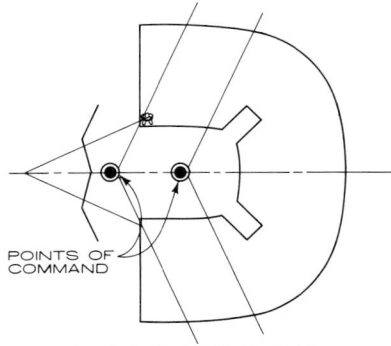

90° TO 130° ENCIRCLEMENT

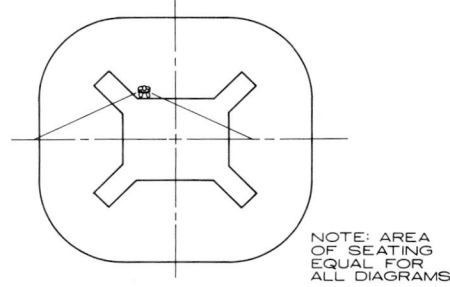

180° TO 270° ENCIRCLEMENT

360° ENCIRCLEMENT

NOTE: AREA OF SEATING EQUAL FOR ALL DIAGRAMS

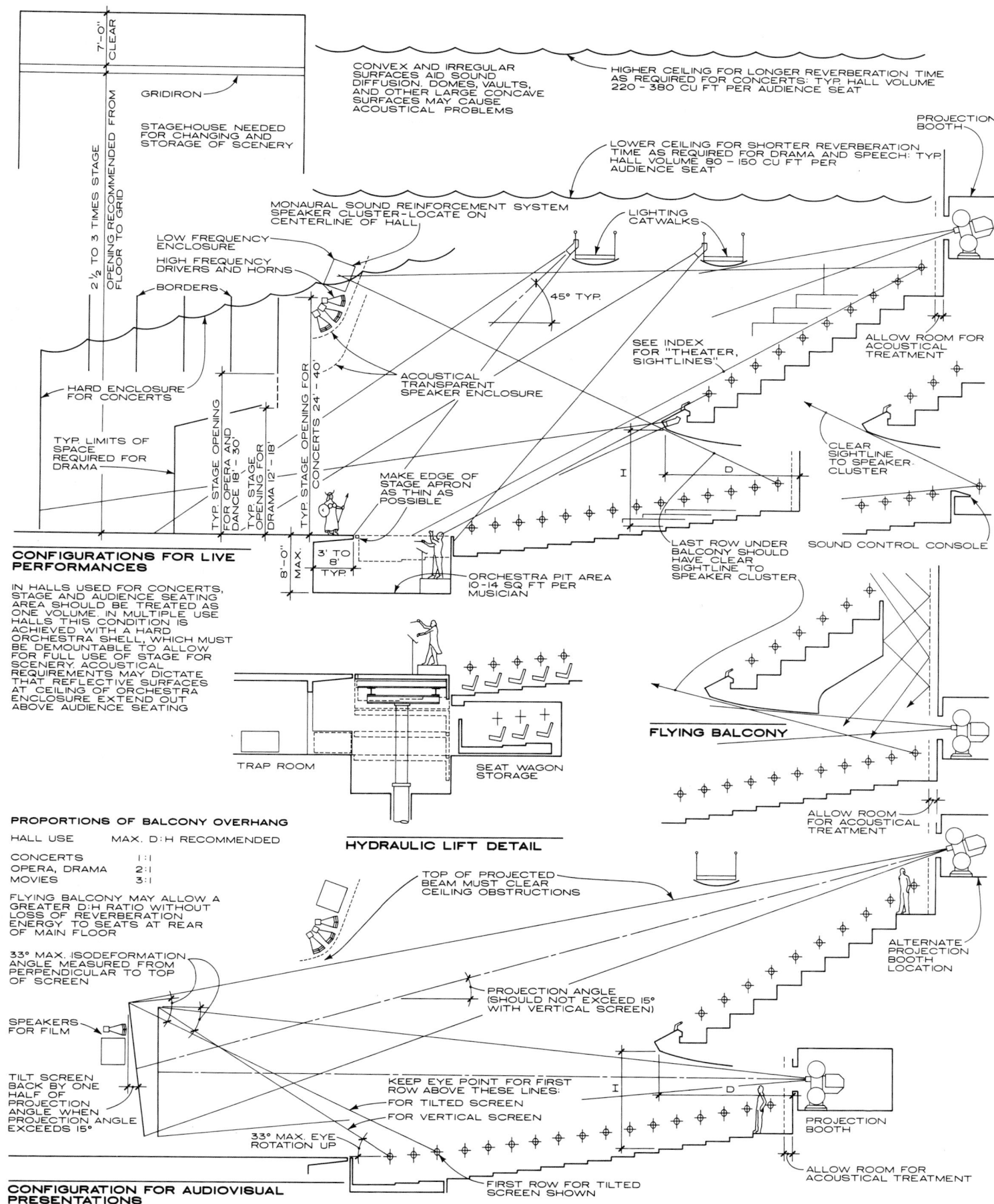

7'-0" CLEAR

GRIDIRON

STAGEHOUSE NEEDED FOR CHANGING AND STORAGE OF SCENERY

2 ½ TO 3 TIMES STAGE OPENING RECOMMENDED FROM FLOOR TO GRID

CONVEX AND IRREGULAR SURFACES AID SOUND DIFFUSION. DOMES, VAULTS, AND OTHER LARGE CONCAVE SURFACES MAY CAUSE ACOUSTICAL PROBLEMS

HIGHER CEILING FOR LONGER REVERBERATION TIME AS REQUIRED FOR CONCERTS: TYP. HALL VOLUME 220 - 380 CU FT PER AUDIENCE SEAT

LOWER CEILING FOR SHORTER REVERBERATION TIME AS REQUIRED FOR DRAMA AND SPEECH: TYP. HALL VOLUME 80 - 150 CU FT PER AUDIENCE SEAT

PROJECTION BOOTH

MONAURAL SOUND REINFORCEMENT SYSTEM SPEAKER CLUSTER-LOCATE ON CENTERLINE OF HALL

LIGHTING CATWALKS

LOW FREQUENCY ENCLOSURE

HIGH FREQUENCY DRIVERS AND HORNS

BORDERS

45° TYP.

ALLOW ROOM FOR ACOUSTICAL TREATMENT

HARD ENCLOSURE FOR CONCERTS

ACOUSTICAL TRANSPARENT SPEAKER ENCLOSURE

SEE INDEX FOR "THEATER, SIGHTLINES"

TYP. LIMITS OF SPACE REQUIRED FOR DRAMA

TYP. STAGE OPENING FOR OPERA AND DANCE 18 - 30'

TYP. STAGE OPENING FOR DRAMA 12'-18'

TYP. STAGE OPENING FOR CONCERTS 24'-40'

CLEAR SIGHTLINE TO SPEAKER CLUSTER

MAKE EDGE OF STAGE APRON AS THIN AS POSSIBLE

I D

LAST ROW UNDER BALCONY SHOULD HAVE CLEAR SIGHTLINE TO SPEAKER CLUSTER

SOUND CONTROL CONSOLE

8'-0" MAX.

3' TO 8' TYP.

ORCHESTRA PIT AREA 10-14 SQ FT PER MUSICIAN

CONFIGURATIONS FOR LIVE PERFORMANCES

IN HALLS USED FOR CONCERTS, STAGE AND AUDIENCE SEATING AREA SHOULD BE TREATED AS ONE VOLUME. IN MULTIPLE USE HALLS THIS CONDITION IS ACHIEVED WITH A HARD ORCHESTRA SHELL, WHICH MUST BE DEMOUNTABLE TO ALLOW FOR FULL USE OF STAGE FOR SCENERY. ACOUSTICAL REQUIREMENTS MAY DICTATE THAT REFLECTIVE SURFACES AT CEILING OF ORCHESTRA ENCLOSURE EXTEND OUT ABOVE AUDIENCE SEATING

FLYING BALCONY

TRAP ROOM

SEAT WAGON STORAGE

PROPORTIONS OF BALCONY OVERHANG

HALL USE	MAX. D:H RECOMMENDED
CONCERTS	1:1
OPERA, DRAMA	2:1
MOVIES	3:1

FLYING BALCONY MAY ALLOW A GREATER D:H RATIO WITHOUT LOSS OF REVERBERATION ENERGY TO SEATS AT REAR OF MAIN FLOOR

HYDRAULIC LIFT DETAIL

ALLOW ROOM FOR ACOUSTICAL TREATMENT

33° MAX. ISODEFORMATION ANGLE MEASURED FROM PERPENDICULAR TO TOP OF SCREEN

TOP OF PROJECTED BEAM MUST CLEAR CEILING OBSTRUCTIONS

PROJECTION ANGLE (SHOULD NOT EXCEED 15° WITH VERTICAL SCREEN)

ALTERNATE PROJECTION BOOTH LOCATION

SPEAKERS FOR FILM

TILT SCREEN BACK BY ONE HALF OF PROJECTION ANGLE WHEN PROJECTION ANGLE EXCEEDS 15°

KEEP EYE POINT FOR FIRST ROW ABOVE THESE LINES: FOR TILTED SCREEN FOR VERTICAL SCREEN

I D

33° MAX. EYE ROTATION UP

FIRST ROW FOR TILTED SCREEN SHOWN

PROJECTION BOOTH

ALLOW ROOM FOR ACOUSTICAL TREATMENT

CONFIGURATION FOR AUDIOVISUAL PRESENTATIONS

Peter H. Frink; Frink and Beuchat: Architects; Philadelphia, Pennsylvania

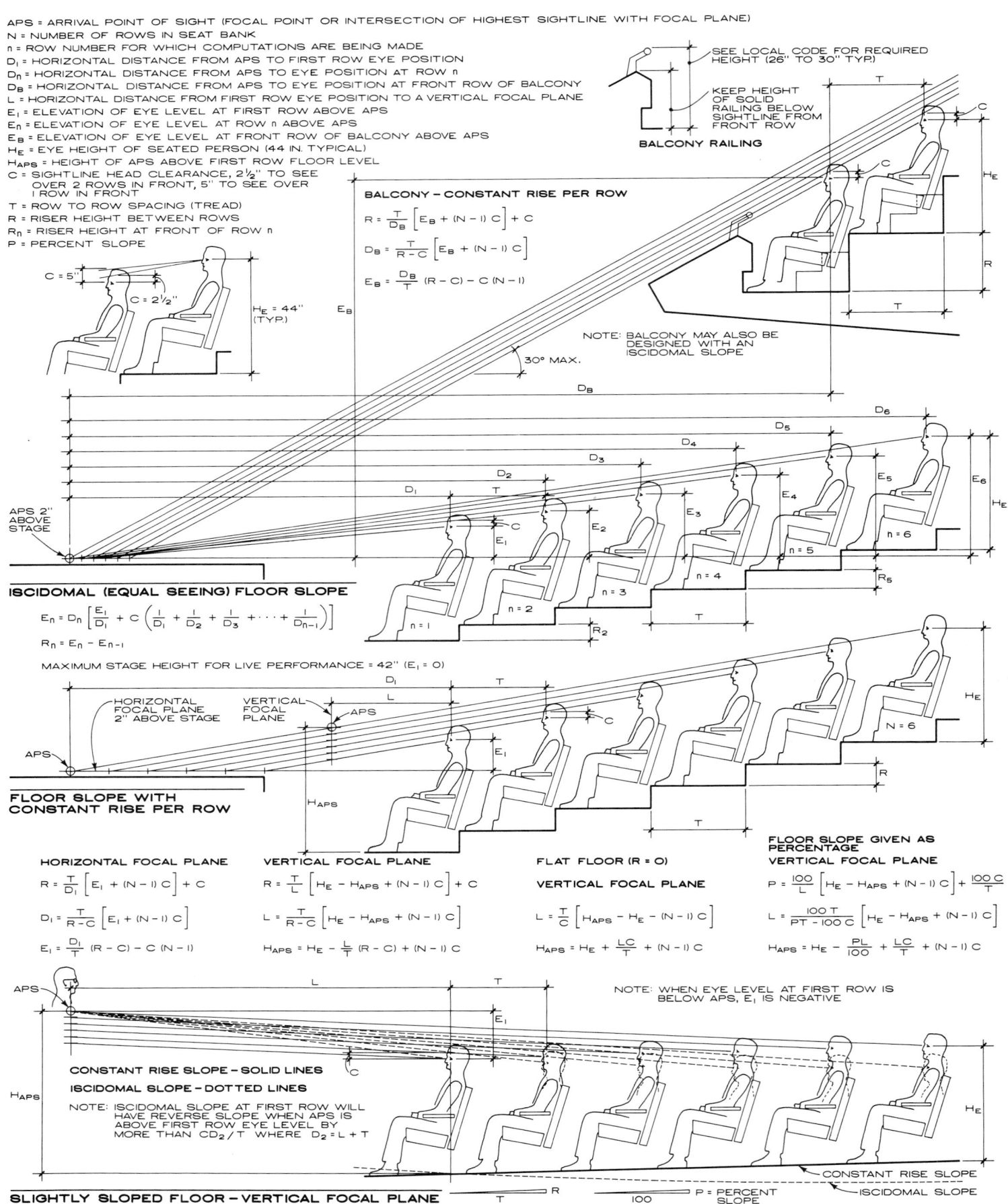

APS = ARRIVAL POINT OF SIGHT (FOCAL POINT OR INTERSECTION OF HIGHEST SIGHTLINE WITH FOCAL PLANE)
N = NUMBER OF ROWS IN SEAT BANK
n = ROW NUMBER FOR WHICH COMPUTATIONS ARE BEING MADE
D_1 = HORIZONTAL DISTANCE FROM APS TO FIRST ROW EYE POSITION
D_n = HORIZONTAL DISTANCE FROM APS TO EYE POSITION AT ROW n
D_B = HORIZONTAL DISTANCE FROM APS TO EYE POSITION AT FRONT ROW OF BALCONY
L = HORIZONTAL DISTANCE FROM FIRST ROW EYE POSITION TO A VERTICAL FOCAL PLANE
E_1 = ELEVATION OF EYE LEVEL AT FIRST ROW ABOVE APS
E_n = ELEVATION OF EYE LEVEL AT ROW n ABOVE APS
E_B = ELEVATION OF EYE LEVEL AT FRONT ROW OF BALCONY ABOVE APS
H_E = EYE HEIGHT OF SEATED PERSON (44 IN. TYPICAL)
H_{APS} = HEIGHT OF APS ABOVE FIRST ROW FLOOR LEVEL
C = SIGHTLINE HEAD CLEARANCE, 2½" TO SEE OVER 2 ROWS IN FRONT, 5" TO SEE OVER I ROW IN FRONT
T = ROW TO ROW SPACING (TREAD)
R = RISER HEIGHT BETWEEN ROWS
R_n = RISER HEIGHT AT FRONT OF ROW n
P = PERCENT SLOPE

C = 5"
C = 2½"
H_E = 44" (TYP.)

SEE LOCAL CODE FOR REQUIRED HEIGHT (26" TO 30" TYP.)
KEEP HEIGHT OF SOLID RAILING BELOW SIGHTLINE FROM FRONT ROW
BALCONY RAILING

BALCONY – CONSTANT RISE PER ROW

$$R = \frac{T}{D_B}\left[E_B + (N-1)C\right] + C$$

$$D_B = \frac{T}{R-C}\left[E_B + (N-1)C\right]$$

$$E_B = \frac{D_B}{T}(R-C) - C(N-1)$$

NOTE: BALCONY MAY ALSO BE DESIGNED WITH AN ISCIDOMAL SLOPE

30° MAX.

ISCIDOMAL (EQUAL SEEING) FLOOR SLOPE

$$E_n = D_n\left[\frac{E_1}{D_1} + C\left(\frac{1}{D_1} + \frac{1}{D_2} + \frac{1}{D_3} + \cdots + \frac{1}{D_{n-1}}\right)\right]$$

$$R_n = E_n - E_{n-1}$$

MAXIMUM STAGE HEIGHT FOR LIVE PERFORMANCE = 42" (E_1 = O)

APS 2" ABOVE STAGE

FLOOR SLOPE WITH CONSTANT RISE PER ROW

HORIZONTAL FOCAL PLANE 2" ABOVE STAGE
VERTICAL FOCAL PLANE
APS

HORIZONTAL FOCAL PLANE

$$R = \frac{T}{D_1}\left[E_1 + (N-1)C\right] + C$$

$$D_1 = \frac{T}{R-C}\left[E_1 + (N-1)C\right]$$

$$E_1 = \frac{D_1}{T}(R-C) - C(N-1)$$

VERTICAL FOCAL PLANE

$$R = \frac{T}{L}\left[H_E - H_{APS} + (N-1)C\right] + C$$

$$L = \frac{T}{R-C}\left[H_E - H_{APS} + (N-1)C\right]$$

$$H_{APS} = H_E - \frac{L}{T}(R-C) + (N-1)C$$

FLAT FLOOR (R = O)

VERTICAL FOCAL PLANE

$$L = \frac{T}{C}\left[H_{APS} - H_E - (N-1)C\right]$$

$$H_{APS} = H_E + \frac{LC}{T} + (N-1)C$$

FLOOR SLOPE GIVEN AS PERCENTAGE
VERTICAL FOCAL PLANE

$$P = \frac{100}{L}\left[H_E - H_{APS} + (N-1)C\right] + \frac{100C}{T}$$

$$L = \frac{100T}{PT - 100C}\left[H_E - H_{APS} + (N-1)C\right]$$

$$H_{APS} = H_E - \frac{PL}{100} + \frac{LC}{T} + (N-1)C$$

APS

NOTE: WHEN EYE LEVEL AT FIRST ROW IS BELOW APS, E_1 IS NEGATIVE

CONSTANT RISE SLOPE – SOLID LINES

ISCIDOMAL SLOPE – DOTTED LINES

NOTE: ISCIDOMAL SLOPE AT FIRST ROW WILL HAVE REVERSE SLOPE WHEN APS IS ABOVE FIRST ROW EYE LEVEL BY MORE THAN CD_2/T WHERE $D_2 = L + T$

CONSTANT RISE SLOPE
ISCIDOMAL SLOPE

$$\frac{R}{T} \qquad \frac{P}{100} = \text{PERCENT SLOPE}$$

SLIGHTLY SLOPED FLOOR – VERTICAL FOCAL PLANE

Peter H. Frink; Frink and Beuchat: Architects; Philadelphia, Pennsylvania

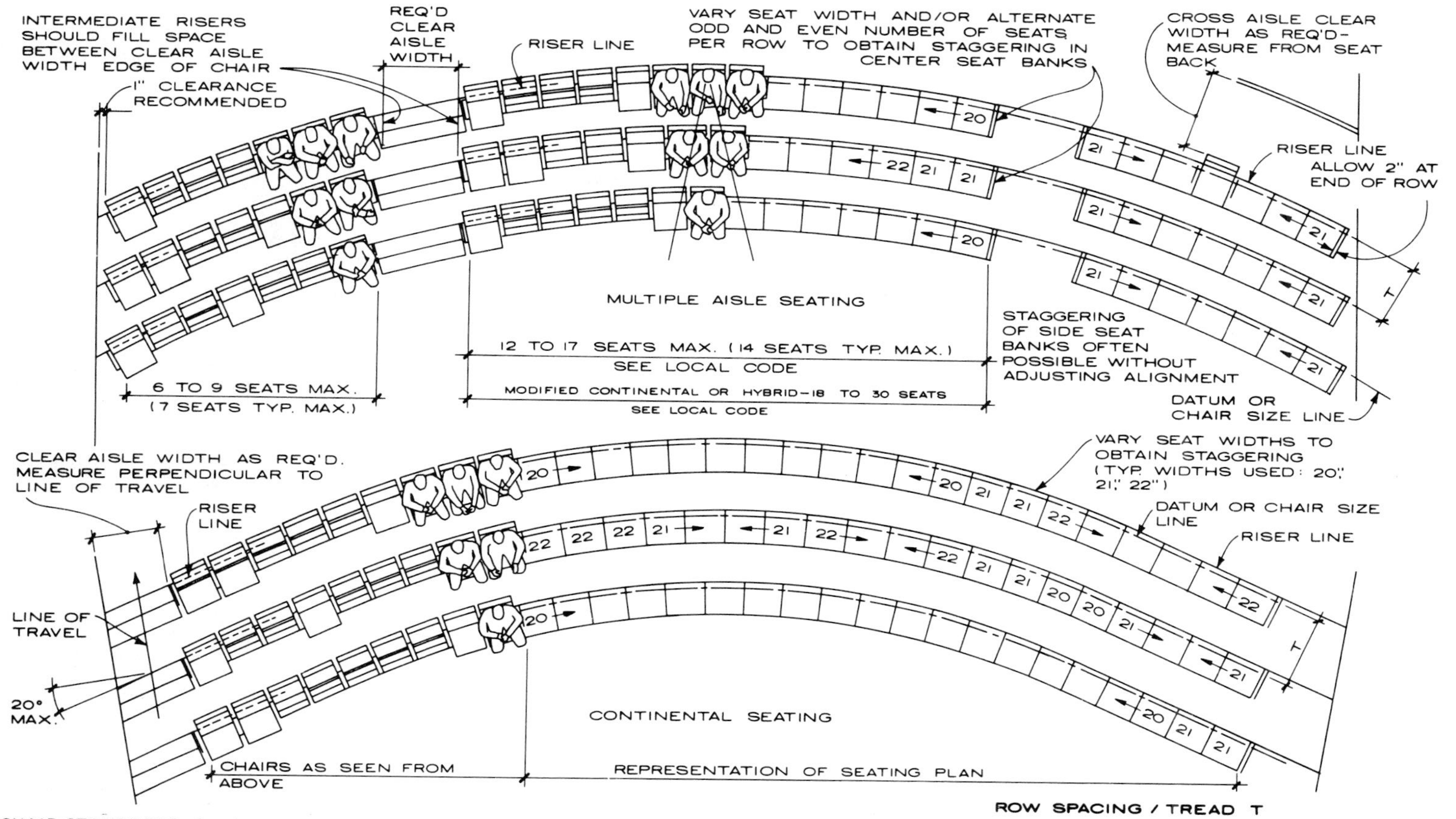

INTERMEDIATE RISERS SHOULD FILL SPACE BETWEEN CLEAR AISLE WIDTH EDGE OF CHAIR
1" CLEARANCE RECOMMENDED
REQ'D CLEAR AISLE WIDTH
RISER LINE
VARY SEAT WIDTH AND/OR ALTERNATE ODD AND EVEN NUMBER OF SEATS PER ROW TO OBTAIN STAGGERING IN CENTER SEAT BANKS
CROSS AISLE CLEAR WIDTH AS REQ'D– MEASURE FROM SEAT BACK
RISER LINE
ALLOW 2" AT END OF ROW
20
22 21 21
21
20
21
21
21
21
MULTIPLE AISLE SEATING
STAGGERING OF SIDE SEAT BANKS OFTEN POSSIBLE WITHOUT ADJUSTING ALIGNMENT
12 TO 17 SEATS MAX. (14 SEATS TYP. MAX.)
SEE LOCAL CODE
6 TO 9 SEATS MAX.
(7 SEATS TYP. MAX.)
MODIFIED CONTINENTAL OR HYBRID–18 TO 30 SEATS
SEE LOCAL CODE
DATUM OR CHAIR SIZE LINE
CLEAR AISLE WIDTH AS REQ'D. MEASURE PERPENDICULAR TO LINE OF TRAVEL
RISER LINE
VARY SEAT WIDTHS TO OBTAIN STAGGERING (TYP. WIDTHS USED: 20", 21", 22")
DATUM OR CHAIR SIZE LINE
RISER LINE
20
20 21 21 22
22 22 22 21 21 22
22 21 21 20 20 21
22
20
21
20 21 21
LINE OF TRAVEL
20° MAX.
CONTINENTAL SEATING
CHAIRS AS SEEN FROM ABOVE
REPRESENTATION OF SEATING PLAN
T

CHAIR STANDARDS: Cast iron, steel, riser mounted and floor mounted. Also pedestal mounting using continuous beam support or cantilevered standards. Folding tablet arms usually available.

CHAIR ARMS: Upholstered fabric, wood, plastic, metal.

CHAIR BACKS: Plastic, molded plywood, rolled stamped metal, upholstered front, rear. Higher backs and bottom extension for scuff protection also available.

CHAIR SEATS: Upholstered, plywood, plastic, metal pan, coil or serpentine springs, polyurethane foam.

20" MAX.
10"–12"
2" ±
VARIES
15 1/2" ±
NOMINAL DEPTH
RISER LINE
VARIES WITH RISER HEIGHT
DATUM OR CHAIR SIZE LINE
WIDTH VARIES
18"–24" AVAILABLE
20"–22" TYP.
21" IDEAL

ROW SPACING / TREAD T

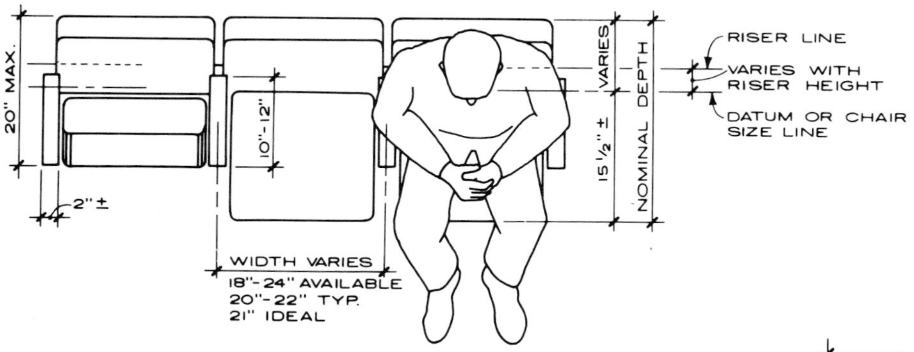

LEGAL CRITERIA: See local code for required minimum spacing. Codes typically stipulate a minimum clear plumbline distance measured between the unoccupied chair and the rear of the back of the chair in front.

- 32"–33": typical minimum for multiple aisle seating
- 34"–37": typical minimum for modified continental seating
- 38"–42": typical minimum for continental seating

COMFORT FOR THE SEATED PERSON:

- 32": knees will touch chair back; uncomfortable
- 34": minimum spacing for comfort
- 36": ideal spacing for maximum comfort
- 38" and up: audience cohesiveness may suffer

EASE OF PASSAGE IN FRONT OF SEATED PERSONS:

- 32"–34": seated person must rise to allow passage
- 36"–38": some seated persons will rise
- 40" and up: passage in front of seated persons possible

SAFETY: Excessive plumbline distance may entice exiting persons to squeeze ahead and cause jam.

EFFICIENCY: Choice of minimum spacing satisfying criteria above reduces maximum distance to stage.

CHAIR WIDTH
3'-8" EYE LEVEL
T
T
DATUM OR CHAIR SIZE LINE
20" MAX.
PLUMBLINE CLEARANCE (SEE NOTE)
ANGLE VARIES
PITCH VARIES 8 1/4" TYP. MAX. 5 1/4" TYP. MIN. 6 3/4", 7 1/2" STANDARD
VARIES
RISER MOUNTED CHAIR
FLOOR MOUNTED CHAIR
T
8 1/2" ±
6" ±
17" ±
15 1/2" ±
VARIES
END PANEL AVAILABLE FOR MOST CHAIRS
1" RECOMMENDED FROM BACK WALL OR RAIL FOR STANDEE

Peter H. Frink; Frink and Beuchat: Architects; Philadelphia, Pennsylvania

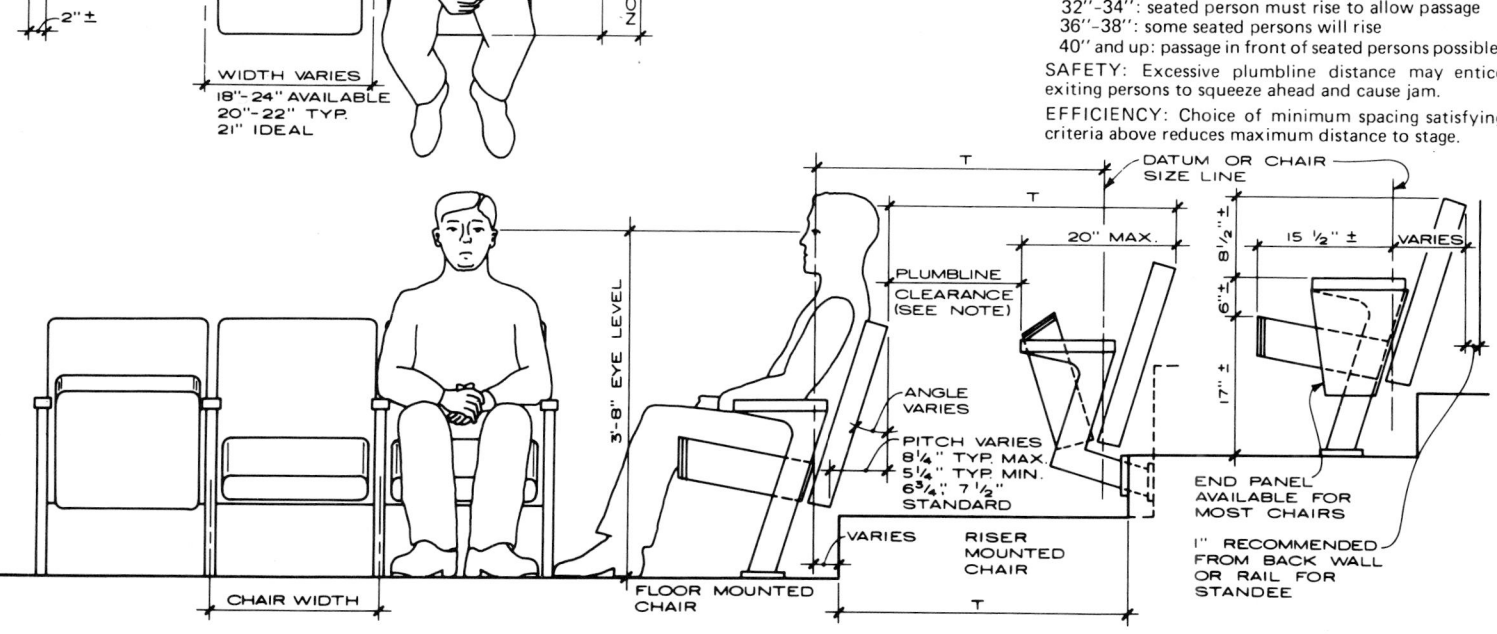

STAGE LIGHTING SYSTEM DESIGN GENERAL COMMENTS

The purpose of a stage lighting system is to provide a flexible arrangement of dimmers, lighting positions, and outlet devices such that stage lighting fixtures may be placed where needed and controlled individually or in groups according to the differing requirements of each production. While it is impossible to develop rules of thumb which will be adequate or appropriate in all cases, several guidelines have been listed below as an aid to determining the proper scope of system required. Several generic cases have been listed. Common terms and equipment components are defined.

CONSIDERATIONS

The planning of a stage lighting system should involve the following considerations:

1. Type of use
2. Size of performing area
3. Size of theater, location of stage lighting positions
4. Budget

Determinations will have to be made about the following subjects:

1. Dimmer-per-circuit or patched circuit system
2. Quantity of dimmers
3. Quantity and distribution of stage lighting circuits
4. Electrical feed size
5. Type of stage lighting outlet devices
6. Type of control console
7. Type and quantity of stage lighting fixtures and accessories

STAGE LIGHTING SYSTEM TERMS AND COMPONENTS DEFINED

DIMMER

A device which controls the intensity of stage lighting fixtures; a remotely controlled electronic device in current practice. Standard sizes are 1.2 kW, 2.4 kW, 6.0 kW, 12.0 kW, at 120 V. Dimmers may be purchased in rack cabinets in large quantities (96 or more) or in small portable packages which can be wall mounted (6, 12, or 18 dimmers).

CIRCUIT

A grounded stage lighting circuit; usually no common neutrals are permitted. Load sizes depend in part on local codes—20 A is average, 15 A is maximum in some areas; some 50 A are often also provided. Circuits are distributed throughout the theater for fixture plug-in and terminate either at a dimmer rack, patch panel, or transfer panel.

DIMMER-PER-CIRCUIT

A configuration whereby every stage lighting circuit home runs to an independent dimmer. This is more economical than a patch panel scheme in most cases.

PATCH PANEL

A custom-made device for interconnecting a large number of stage lighting circuits to a small number of dimmers. This is more expensive than a dimmer-per-circuit configuration in most cases.

TRANSFER PANEL

A custom-made device enabling permanent circuits to be disconnected from the theater's dimming system and connected to a show's touring dimming system. Front-of-house circuits are generally made "transferable" in this way in large multipurpose theaters that must accommodate tours.

FRONT-OF-HOUSE

In a proscenium theater, the audience side of the proscenium. Abbreviated "FOH."

FOLLOWSPOT

A very bright manually operated spotlight used to "follow" a performer around the stage. Light source can be incandescent, carbon arc, xenon, or HMI.

LEKO, FRESNEL, ELLIPSOIDAL, PARCAN, SCOOP, FLOODLIGHT

Theatrical lighting fixtures.

STRIPLIGHT

A continuous fixture containing a number of lamps, used for downlight, backlight, footlight, and cyclorama lighting—usually 6 or 8 ft long with 12 lamps in three or four circuits.

CONTROL CONSOLE

Often called the "light board." A computerized, manual, or hybrid control device for stage lighting dimmers. Generic types include 2, 5, or 10 scene "preset consoles" (manual) and "memory consoles" (computerized). Older installations may have mechanically operated resistance or autotransformer dimmers in which the control console and the dimmer rack are essentially one device.

CONNECTOR STRIP

A type of outlet device for stage lighting circuits; essentially a continuous wireway with outlets or pigtails.

OUTLET BOX

An outlet device for stage lighting circuits. Box size and circuit quantities vary. Surface-mounted or recessed styles available. Circuit numbers must appear on the faceplate (with adhesive labels or engraved).

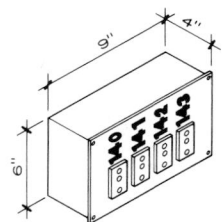

OUTLET BOX

BOX BOOM

An important front-of-house side wall lighting position in a proscenium theater. See diagram below.

COVE, BEAM, SLOT, TRUSS

A front-of-house lighting position located at the auditorium ceiling. See diagram below.

FOLLOWSPOT BOOTH

Houses the followspots. Enclosed, if possible, and ventilated as per code. Usually at or near the rear of the house, and quite high; 30°–45° to the edge of the stage preferred. Four spots require a booth nominally 24 ft wide x 10 ft deep; two spots require one 12 ft wide x 10 ft deep.

CONTROL BOOTH

Primary location for control console. Good view of stage preferred. Often located on the main level at the rear of the house. Houselighting controls should be duplicated here as well as backstage.

DIMMER ROOM

Location for dimmer racks. Can be remote from the stage. Locate for efficiency of load and feed wire conduit runs. Ventilate to accommodate heat load (approximately 5% connected load). Control humidity to protect equipment.

BOOMS, LADDERS, TORMS, TORMENTORS

On-stage side lighting positions. Nonarchitectural; located temporarily for each production as required.

PIPES, BATTENS, ELECTRICS

On-stage overhead lighting positions. Usually rigging pipes or pipe grid members. In a proscenium theater often one or more rigging pipes will be permanently designated as "electrics" and served with connector strips attached directly to the pipe.

CYCLORAMA, CYC

A large seamless white or pale blue backdrop, used scenically to represent the sky or provide a surface on which abstract colors and patterns can be projected with stage lighting fixtures. Usually cloth; some plaster cycs exist, but are difficult (some say impossible) to repair adequately once cracked or marred. Plaster is not recommended.

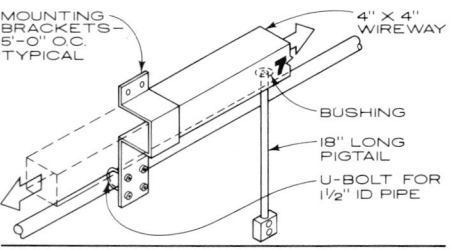

CONNECTOR STRIP

MOUNTING BRACKETS—5'-0" O.C. TYPICAL
4" X 4" WIREWAY
BUSHING
18" LONG PIGTAIL
U-BOLT FOR 1½" ID PIPE

RECOMMENDED PARAMETERS FOR STAGE LIGHTING SYSTEMS

THEATER TYPE	NUMBER OF SEATS	FEED SIZE*	CIRCUIT QUANTITY	DIMMER QUANTITY
Elementary school	Varies	100	24–36	18–36†
Junior high, or middle school	Varies	300	75–100	75–100
High school	Varies	400	100–150	100–150
Studio theater	75–300	400	150–200	36–200†
Educational drama theater	300–750	800	200–400	200–400
Small professional theater	750–1500	1200	300–500	300–500
Medium size theater	1500–2000	1600	400–600	400–600
Large multipurpose theater, civic theater, road house	Over 2000	2400	600–800	600–800

*Feed size shown in amps, 3 phase, 120/208 V Y.
†A simple patch system where the circuits terminate in male pigtails which can be plugged directly into a small quantity of portable dimmer packs is generally more economical for small installations with limited budgets than a dimmer-per-circuit scheme.

Joshua Dachs; Jules Fisher Associates Inc., Theater Consultants; New York, New York

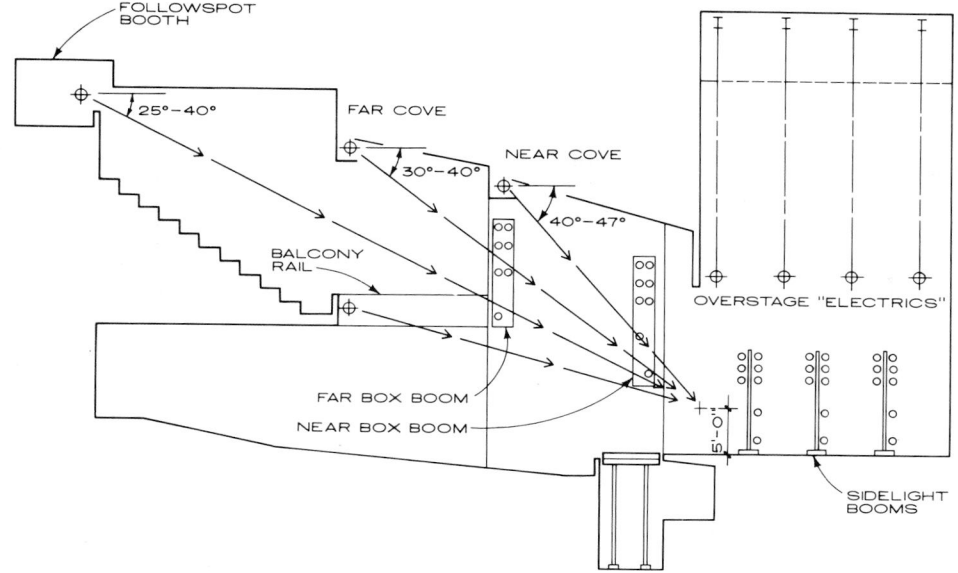

SECTION

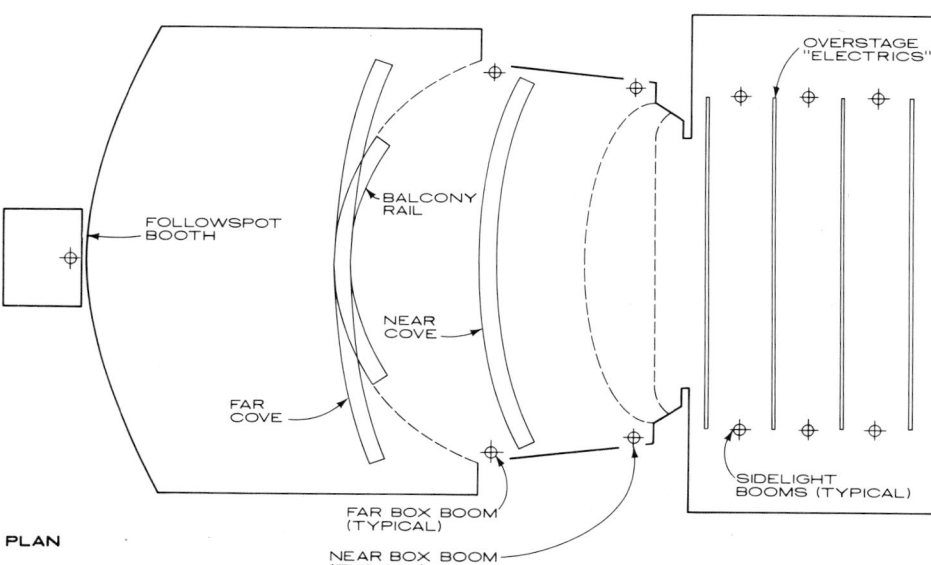

PLAN

PROSCENIUM THEATER

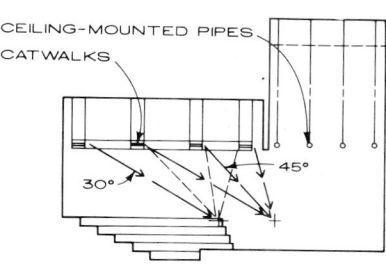

SECTION

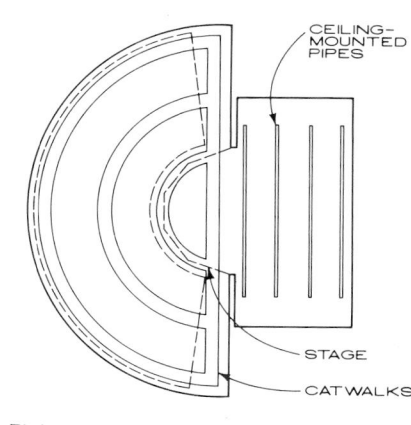

PLAN

THRUST THEATER

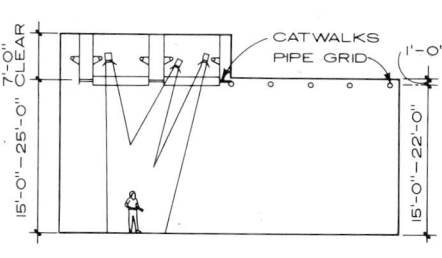

SECTION

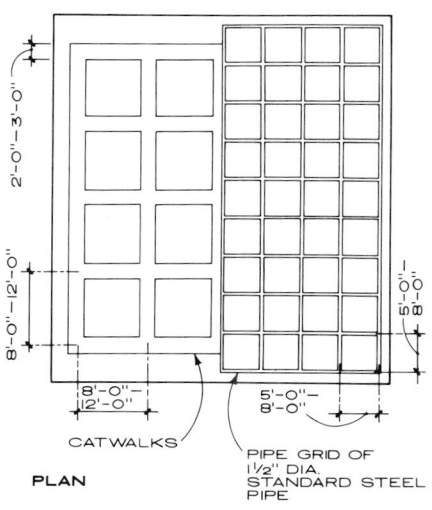

PLAN

STUDIO THEATER ("BLACK BOX")

STAGE LIGHTING POSITIONS

It is crucial that a theater be provided with adequate, easily accessible stage lighting positions, served with an adequate quantity of circuits. Accessibility is a key issue. Lighting positions in an active theater need to be accessed daily to maintain, focus, and color the fixtures. Safety and ease must be kept in mind, as well as crew size, which is crucial to theater economics. Using a ladder is both time-consuming and dangerous and requires more than one stagehand. A catwalk is much safer, less time-consuming, and only requires one stagehand.

In a proscenium theater lighting is done from a variety of positions and angles. Frontlighting is provided by side wall positions called box booms, the balcony railing, and ceiling positions which can be recessed within the ceiling or exposed as catwalks. Followspots are generally located in a booth at the top rear of the theater (see definitions). On stage, rigging sets with dedicated stage lighting outlet devices (connector strips or drop boxes) and portable vertical floor-mounted pipes called booms provide positions for downlighting, sidelighting, and backlighting. These positions are *all* important, and every attempt should be made to provide them.

In flexible studio or black-box theaters a pipe grid or a system of catwalks should be provided over the entire floor area of the theater to which lighting equipment (and scenery) can be attached. This grid should be well served by stage lighting circuits in boxes or connector strips. A two-way grid of 1½ in. diameter pipe, nominally 4–6 ft o.c. should be adequate in most cases, accessed by ladder from the floor. The catwalk system is preferable, but requires a taller room.

In a thrust or arena theater, a grid or a series of catwalks should be provided over the main stage area to accommodate downlighting, sidelighting, and backlighting. Catwalks, ceiling slots, or ceiling-mounted pipes should be provided for frontlight and low washes, similar to the balcony rail or second cove in a proscenium theater. If there is a conventional stagehouse behind the thrust, it should be served in the same way as a proscenium theater's stagehouse, with overhead pipes and side booms.

RECOMMENDED REFERENCE MATERIAL

Stage Lighting—A guide to the planning of theatres and public building auditoriums. Illuminating Engineering Society Report #CP-45, 1983.

In most cases it is recommended that the services of a qualified theater consultant be retained.

Joshua Dachs; Jules Fisher Associates Inc., Theater Consultants; New York, New York

GENERAL

Veterinary clinics are typically divided into three zones—public, procedural and patient—based on use, interior finish, and mechanical zones. The current trend is toward providing full service facilities, including boarding, grooming, and retail areas.

PUBLIC ZONE

It is desirable to have the traffic flow "one way" within the public areas; in one door to reception and waiting and then out another door to the cashier and exit door.

RECEPTION DESK. Allow room for two or three receptionists to work; include space for computer, typewriter, small copier, and files. Files can be accommodated in lateral medical files or an open eggcrate system.

WAITING AREA. Ideally, divide this space into separate dog and cat alcoves with approximately 2 to 3 chairs per exam room. Three-foot clearance in front of each chair, apart from the circulation pattern for pets, is required.

EXAM ROOMS. 1.5 exam rooms per full-time equivalent veterinarian is typical. Exam rooms can be held to a minimum size (rooms exclusively for cats can be as small as 6 ft x 7 ft 6 in.). Two-way traffic flow—a front door for clients and a back door for the veterinarian and for taking animals to treatment—is desirable. One oversized exam room for consultation or for treating large dogs is recommended. Acoustical batt insulation in the walls surrounding exam rooms is suggested. Based on input from the veterinarian, exam rooms should be equipped with undercounter refrigerators and small sinks.

PROCEDURAL ZONE

Includes lab, pharmacy, treatment, X-ray, surgery, and surgery/prep.

LAB/PHARMACY. This facility should be immediately accessible to the exam rooms. Often it forms an acoustical and visual barrier between these rooms and the treatment area.

LAB. In addition to a sink with exhaust fan (a residential range hood is adequate), the lab should include an area for diagnostic equipment (assume 2 ft per piece of equipment minimum), microscope (with kneespace), centrifuge, and workspace.

PHARMACY. This can be a combination of base cabinets with drawers and shelving above (enclosed or open) with risers to make bottles in the back visible. A residential size refrigerator is also necessary.

TREATMENT. Provide one workstation per two exam rooms, with a minimum of two workstations, one dry and one wet, with adjacent layout space for equipment. Workstations can be either peninsular or island. Islands should include a utility column for electrical feed and plumbing vent. Many clinics now include a separate wet workstation for dental procedures. Provide a bank of cages in treatment for intensive care and recovery.

X-RAY. Either an enclosed or open room opening from the treatment area is suitable, depending on local health regulations and the amount of protection desired. Radiation protection needs vary based on the equipment being used, ranging from two layers of gypsum board to lead shielding. A darkroom should be adjacent to the X-ray equipment. Most veterinarians use automatic processors so the old development tanks are no longer necessary. Storage for X-ray films, approximately 14 x 18 in. each, is also required. Wall-mounted X-ray viewers should be provided in exams, treatment, X-ray, and surgery areas.

SURGERY/PREP. This should be a small alcove off the treatment area for preparing packs and scrubbing for surgery. A "hands-free" scrub sink, place for an autoclave, and a work area for preparing packs is required. A cabinet-top pass-through to surgery for prepared packs is often requested.

SURGERY. Provide one or two tables and space for parking equipment and carts. High-efficiency particulate airflow filters should be specified on ducts feeding the surgery, which should be a positive pressure room at minimum.

DOCTORS' OFFICE. In addition to a doctor's station adjacent to the treatment area for filling out charts, a small doctor's office is usually required.

TYPICAL ROOM SIZES

ROOM SIZES	MINIMUM	AVERAGE
Reception	8 x 12	12 x 14
Waiting	8 x 16	10 x 20
Retail		12 x 15
Exam	6 x 8	8 x 10
Oversize exam		10 x 12
Laboratory	6 x 12	8 x 12
Pharmacy	6 x 8	7 x 12
Treatment	14 x 20	18 x 24
X-ray	8 x 10	8 x 12
Darkroom	4 x 6	6 x 6
Surgery		
One table	9 x 10	10 x 12
Two table		12 x 16
Wards	minimum 4' aisle	
Runs	4' aisle, 3 x 5 runs	
Office	8 x 10	12 x 16
Handicap bath	5 x 9	
Grooming	8 x 10	12 x 16
Bathing	8 x 10	10 x 12
Food preparation	6 x 6	8 x 10

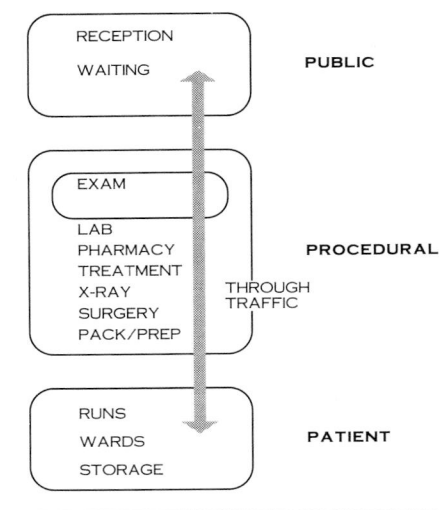

CONVENTIONAL VETERINARY HOSPITAL BUBBLE DIAGRAM

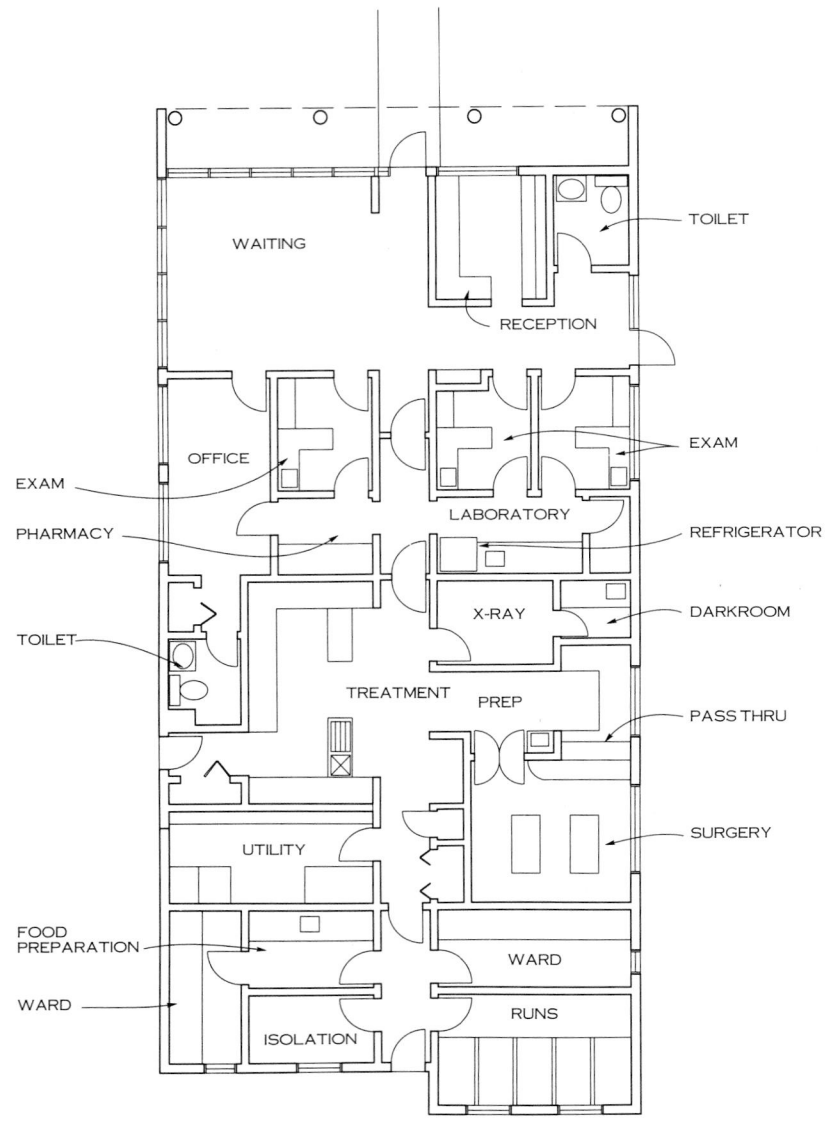

TYPICAL FLOOR PLAN

Mark R. Hafen, AIA; Gates Hafen, P.C.; Boulder, Colorado

ANIMAL CARE

PATIENT ZONE

The patient areas should be acoustically separated from the rest of the facility. The high degree of abuse and constant cleaning requirements of this area make it practical to have painted epoxy concrete block walls, concrete floors, and mylar-faced lay-in acoustical tile ceilings. Ward rooms used for holding small dogs or cats in cages can have walls of drywall.

WARDS. These should have space for no more than 25 animals. Assume approximately 1 to 1.25 cages per linear foot of three-tier caging. Where possible runs or cages should not face each other. Cages are typically placed on 4 in. high built-in curbs. Wards should be provided with natural light when possible and exhaust fans.

RUNS. The number of runs needed depends on the number of larger dogs treated; minimum size is typically 3 x 5 ft each. Drains should be provided in each run. Slope floors a minimum of $1/4$ in. per foot. Caging can be either fabricated aluminum, stainless steel, or chain-link available through veterinary or kennel equipment suppliers. Partitions between runs should be a minimum of 6 ft high with the bottom 4 ft solid to avoid cross-contamination. The solid portion can be of galvanized metal, plastic-laminated exterior plywood, or concrete block. Where possible, noise-reducing baffles and panels should be utilized. Hose bibs with hot and cold water should be provided for hosing down the runs.

UTILITY/GROOMING. Room is needed for dry food storage, food preparation, incidental grooming, and washer/dryer. These functions can be separated in larger facilities. The food preparation area should include a double sink, dry food storage bins, work counter, and undercounter refrigerator. A grooming/bathing area should include a raised grooming tub, place for a cage for dog drying, and a small 2 x 4 ft freestanding grooming table. The washer/dryer is used for both washing soiled blankets from the wards and surgery linens. Space is required for a chest-type necropsy freezer. The service entry should be into this room.

MISCELLANEOUS

A small isolation ward, including a small bank of cages and one run, is often required for isolating highly contagious animals. Usually it is located immediately adjacent to the service entry, where it will be accessible without going through other wards or the treatment area.

HEATING, COOLING, AND VENTILATION

Ideally there should be three mechanical zones: public, procedural, and patient. Three truly separate zones help control acoustical and odor problems. These zones should be pressurized so that air is fed to the public areas and exhausted from the patient areas. Additional exhaust fans should be provided in lab and treatment rooms. A large capacity exhaust fan is necessary in the ward and run areas. Where economically feasible, air should be exhausted to the outside in the run areas to avoid spread of diseases and minimize odors. The acceptable temperature and humidity range in the wards and runs can vary beyond the typical comfort zone, but should not be below 50 or above 85 degrees. Air changes in the wards and runs should be 12 to 14 an hour. The surgery should be a positive pressure room with high-efficiency particulate airflow filters.

ELECTRICAL

In addition to the obvious requirements of the X-ray equipment (typically 100 amp), most veterinary clinics utilize a lot of electrical equipment, including autoclaves, dog dryers, and exam and surgery lights. Be careful not to locate too many pieces of equipment on any one circuit.

MATERIALS

Cleanable and durable materials are a high priority. In the public areas flooring can be welded sheet vinyl or quarry tile (with latex epoxy grout). Walls can be covered with flat latex or vinyl. Ceilings can be of gypsum board or lay-in acoustical tile.

In the procedural areas a higher degree of cleanability/durability is required. Floors should be of welded seam homogeneous PVC sheet vinyl, and walls can be washable latex. The surgery should have water-based epoxy walls and a painted gypsum board ceiling. Other ceilings can be lay-in acoustical tile.

In the patient areas durability is most important. All areas exposed to water should have concrete block walls painted with water-based epoxy (other walls should be of epoxy painted gypsum board). Ceilings exposed to water hoses should have mylar-faced acoustical tile. Floors in wards should be of sealed and colored concrete. In the runs it is possible to paint or tile the floors, but the most foolproof solution is sealed and colored concrete.

Mark R. Hafen; AIA, Gates Hafen, P.C.; Boulder, Colorado

TYPICAL VETERINARY EQUIPMENT AND SIZES[1]

EQUIPMENT	HEIGHT	WIDTH	DEPTH
X-ray control center	53"	21"	$12 1/2$"
X-ray table	22"	57"	39"
X-ray illuminator	$19 3/4$"	29"	$3 1/8$"
X-ray film processor	$18 1/2$"	23"	38"
Surgical equipment sterilizer	14"	$19 1/2$"	$23 1/2$"
Walk-on platform scale	$34 1/2$"	$44 1/2$"	20"
Electric lift exam and weight table	10 to 40"	$44 1/2$"	20"
Pedestal base surgery table	37"	58"	19"
Combination tub/exam table with cabinet[2]	38"	$60 1/2$"	$24 5/8$"
Combination tub/exam table with legs[2]	35"	$60 1/2$"	$24 5/8$"
Kennel assemblies[3]	48 to 84"	48 to 168"	$28 1/4$"

NOTES

1. All dimensions are typical and may vary with manufacturer.
2. Combination tub/exam tables can have tub depth of either 6 or 16 in.
3. Kennel assemblies are modular with cage sizes of 24 x 24 in. , 24 x 30in. , 30 x 30 in. , 36 x 30 in. , and 48 x 30 in.

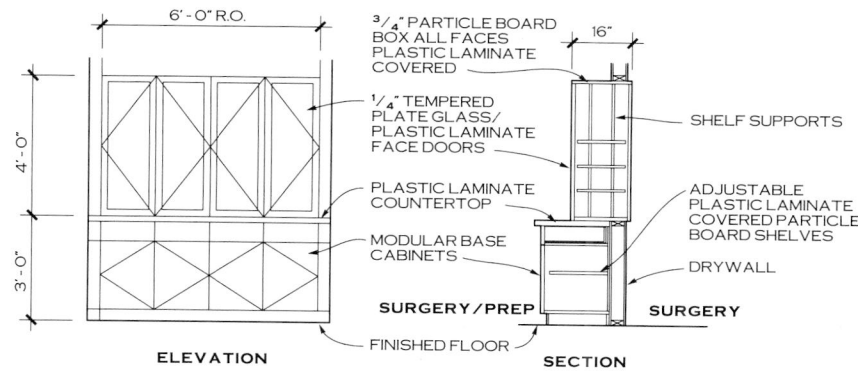

SURGERY/PREP PASS-THROUGH UNIT

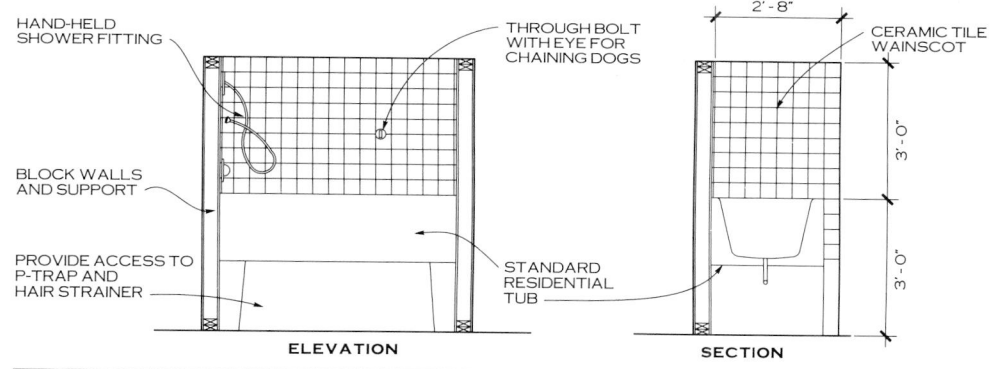

GROOMING TUB

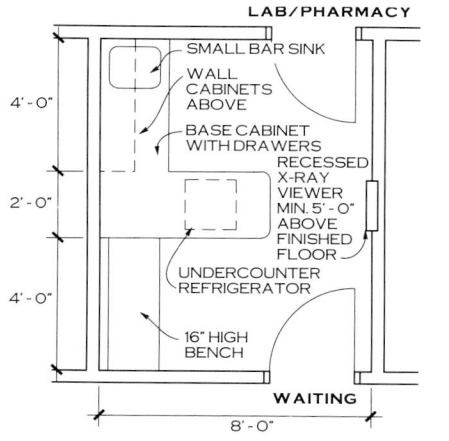

TYPICAL EXAM ROOM

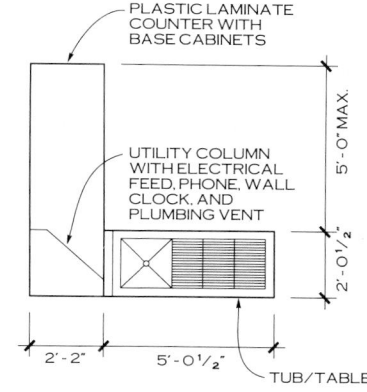

TYPICAL TREATMENT STATION

GENERAL

All kennels for boarding dogs must provide for each animal a primary enclosure (usually indoors) for privacy, eating, and resting and a secondary enclosure (usually outdoors) for exercise.

The primary enclosure should consist of solid dividers to separate adjacent runs and provide privacy with a sloped floor to provide for drainage during cleaning. Enclosures should be large enough to allow for normal movements with minimum sizes of 3 x 4 x 4 ft for small breeds and 3 x 6 x 6 ft for larger breeds.

The secondary enclosure is for exercise and should be large enough for the dog to break into a trot with minimum sizes of 3 x 7 x 4 ft for small breeds and 3 x 11 x 6 ft for larger breeds. Separate each run with a barrier to prevent waste from flowing from one to another. Provide hose bibbs to wash down this area.

Cats are boarded in stacked cages of 2 x 3 x 3/2 ft with a perch at the rear. The materials can be less durable than those for dogs, since cats are not as destructive and cleaning does not require hose down. Each enclosure should contain a litter box and enough floor space for food and water and lying down. A climbing tree and removable den for hiding can be provided. Cat enclosures are usually vented individually to prevent the spread of diseases.

Cats enjoy interesting views and distractions so good lighting, cheerful colors, music, plants, outside views, caged birds, and fish tanks are recommended. Cats, however, will adapt to boarding faster if they are separated visually from one another. Community play areas are not recommended because of the possible spread of diseases.

VENTILATION

Proper ventilation is important to prevent the spread of diseases. Air should be vented to the outside, unless air cleaners are used. Recommended ventilation standards should be 10 to 15 room air changes per hour.

HEATING AND COOLING

Temperatures should be designed and maintained between 60-80°F, with humidity maintained between 30-70%. Radiant heat in the floor is highly recommended as it provides heat at the level of the animal.

DRAINAGE

The flooring of all runs should be sloped 1/4 in. per foot from the rear to the front. Drainage should be quick and complete, with the floor finish being not so smooth that it becomes slippery when wet or so rough that it is hard to clean and harms the animal. Waste materials should be collected outside the runs or cages and run to minimum 3 in. diameter floor drains.

LIGHTING

All areas should be bright and cheerful with abundant natural light for the health of the animals. Skylights and ample windows located a minimum of 6 ft off the floor are desirable. Windows should be operable and hinged at the sill to tilt inward to prevent escapes.

NOISE CONTROL

Noise control is important to decrease boarding stress and employee health problems such as hearing loss and to meet local noise ordinances. Noise reducing materials should be considered including ceiling and wall baffles.

MATERIALS

All materials used should be durable and easy to clean and maintain. Concrete block sealed or painted is the usual choice. Prefabricated and modular runs are available or chain link fencing can be used. Carpeting is not recommended as a flooring material.

NOTES

Kennels for the care and boarding of animals are typically defined as breeding, commercial, private, research, and veterinary/medical. The size, type, quantity, and layout of the equipment is related to the function of the kennel and amount and type of patronage.

The schematic drawing (right) is not meant to dictate a design standard but rather to familiarize the reader with typical characteristics of commercial kennels.

TYPICAL ROOMS

ROOM NAME	MINIMUM SIZES
Reception / retail sales	15 x 20
Private office	10 x 10
Customer service office	8 x 10
Pre-entry exam room	6 x 8
Grooming room	10 x 10
Bathing and drying room	8 x 8
Storage	3 x 6
Utilities	8 x 8
Exotics boarding area	8 x 10
Isolation room	6 x 6

ROOM NAME	MINIMUM SIZES
Service corridor	4 wide
Customer toilet	6 x 7
Storage	8 x 10
Kennel kitchen	10 x 15
Employee locker / lounge	8 x 10
Employee toilet / shower	6 x 8
Storage	3 x 6
Cattery	Related to number of cages
Dog kennel	Related to number of runs
Security fence	6-ft-high

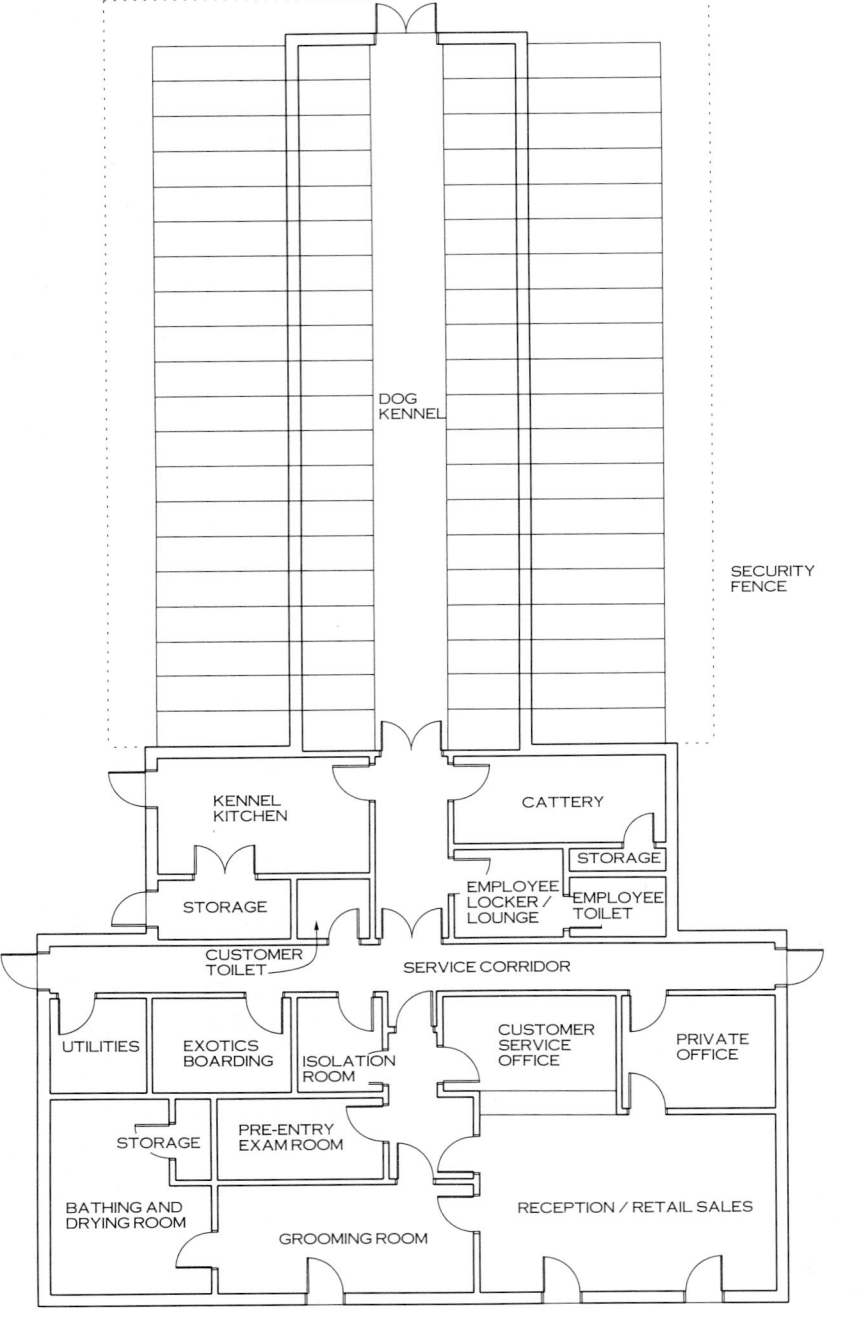

PLAN OF TYPICAL COMMERCIAL KENNEL

Jesse Oak; Anderson Cooper Georgelas; McLean, Virginia
American Boarding Kennels Association; Colorado Springs, Colorado

ANIMAL CARE

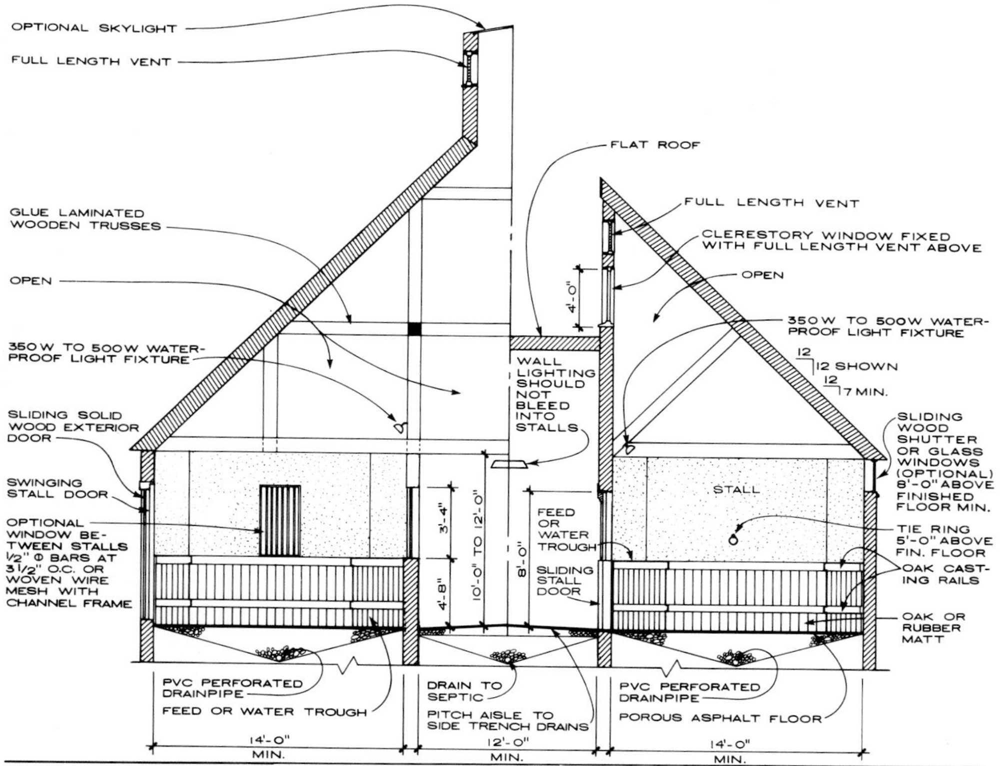

TYPES OF BROODMARE STABLES

OPTIONAL SKYLIGHT

FULL LENGTH VENT

GLUE LAMINATED WOODEN TRUSSES

OPEN

350 W TO 500 W WATER-PROOF LIGHT FIXTURE

SLIDING SOLID WOOD EXTERIOR DOOR

SWINGING STALL DOOR

OPTIONAL WINDOW BETWEEN STALLS 1/2" Φ BARS AT 3 1/2" O.C. OR WOVEN WIRE MESH WITH CHANNEL FRAME

PVC PERFORATED DRAINPIPE — FEED OR WATER TROUGH

FLAT ROOF

FULL LENGTH VENT

CLERESTORY WINDOW FIXED WITH FULL LENGTH VENT ABOVE

OPEN

350 W TO 500 W WATER-PROOF LIGHT FIXTURE

12/12 SHOWN
12/7 MIN.

WALL LIGHTING SHOULD NOT BLEED INTO STALLS

SLIDING WOOD SHUTTER OR GLASS WINDOWS (OPTIONAL) 8'-0" ABOVE FINISHED FLOOR MIN.

STALL

FEED OR WATER TROUGH

SLIDING STALL DOOR

TIE RING 5'-0" ABOVE FIN. FLOOR

OAK CASTING RAILS

OAK OR RUBBER MATT

DRAIN TO SEPTIC

PITCH AISLE TO SIDE TRENCH DRAINS

PVC PERFORATED DRAINPIPE

POROUS ASPHALT FLOOR

14'-0" MIN. / 12'-0" MIN. / 14'-0" MIN.

3'-4" / 4'-8" / 10'-0" TO 12'-0" / 8'-0"

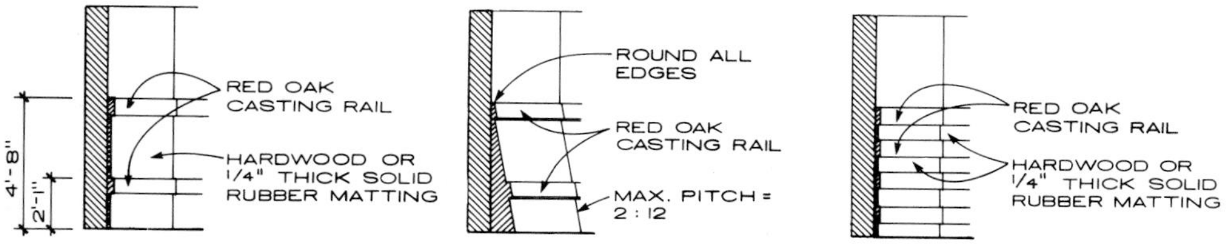

TYPICAL STALL TREATMENT FOR CASTING PREVENTION

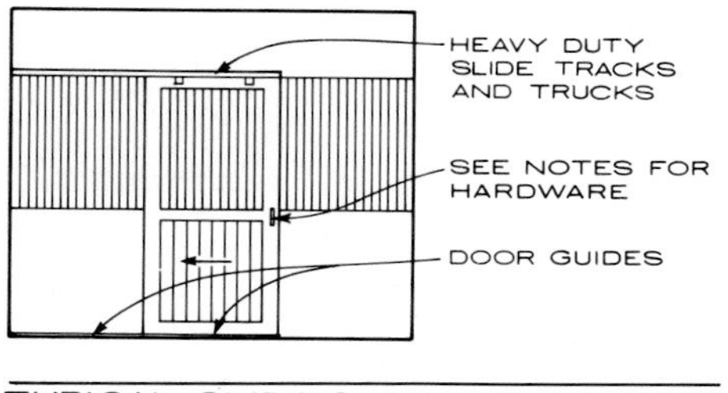

RED OAK CASTING RAIL

HARDWOOD OR 1/4" THICK SOLID RUBBER MATTING

4'-8" / 2'-1"

ROUND ALL EDGES

RED OAK CASTING RAIL

MAX. PITCH = 2:12

RED OAK CASTING RAIL

HARDWOOD OR 1/4" THICK SOLID RUBBER MATTING

TYPICAL SLIDING AISLE DOOR

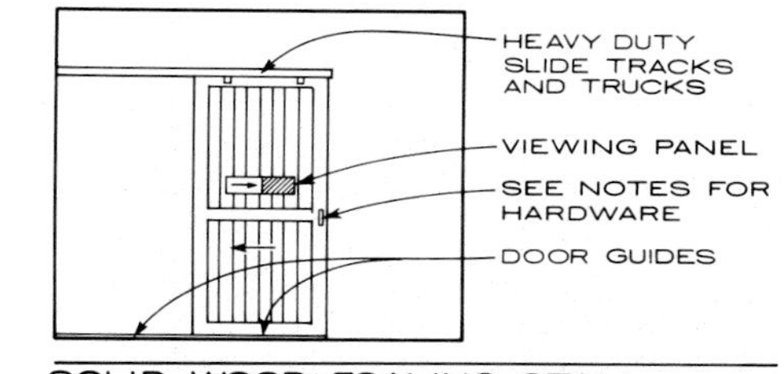

HEAVY DUTY SLIDE TRACKS AND TRUCKS

SEE NOTES FOR HARDWARE

DOOR GUIDES

SOLID WOOD FOALING STALL WITH VIEW THROUGH

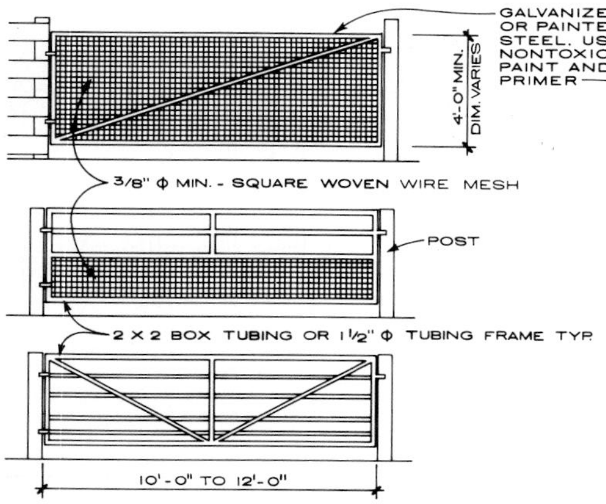

HEAVY DUTY SLIDE TRACKS AND TRUCKS

VIEWING PANEL

SEE NOTES FOR HARDWARE

DOOR GUIDES

STANDARD GATES

GALVANIZED OR PAINTED STEEL. USE NONTOXIC PAINT AND PRIMER

4'-0" MIN. DIM. VARIES

3/8" Φ MIN. - SQUARE WOVEN WIRE MESH

POST

2 X 2 BOX TUBING OR 1 1/2" Φ TUBING FRAME TYP

10'-0" TO 12'-0"

BROODMARE STALL SCREEN

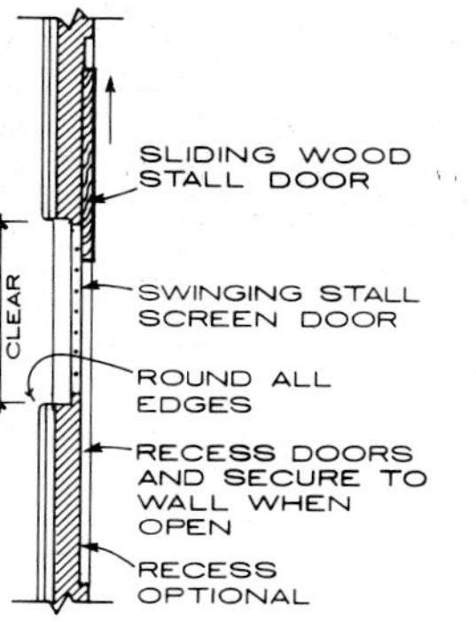

8'-0" / 3'-10" / 4'-0" / 4'-0" CLEAR / 2"

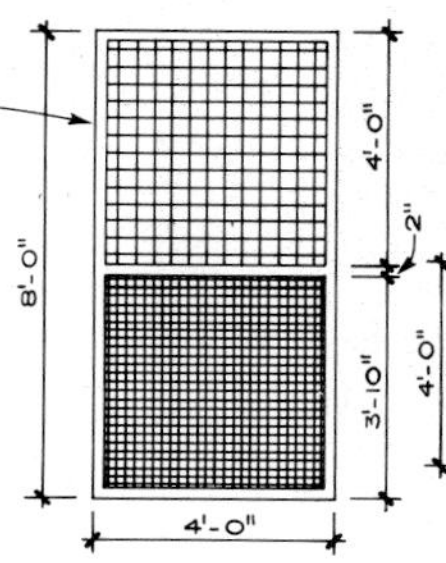

SCREEN DOOR FRAMED W/ 12 GA. BOX TUBING. UPPER HALF 5/8" Φ MIN. WOVEN WIRE AT 3 1/2" O.C. MAX. LOWER HALF 3/8" Φ AT 1 1/2" O.C. MAX. SPACING.

4'-0"

BROODMARE EXTERIOR STALL DOOR PLAN

SLIDING WOOD STALL DOOR

SWINGING STALL SCREEN DOOR

ROUND ALL EDGES

RECESS DOORS AND SECURE TO WALL WHEN OPEN

RECESS OPTIONAL

Theodore M. Ceraldi & Associates, Architects; Nyack, New York

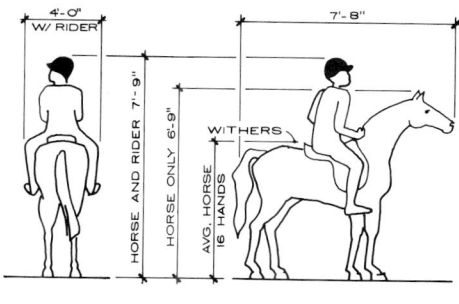

4'-0" W/ RIDER

7'-8"

HORSE AND RIDER 7'-9"

HORSE ONLY 6'-9"

AVG. HORSE 16 HANDS

WITHERS

ONE HAND EQUALS 4"

CLEARANCES FOR HORSE AND RIDER

NOTES

Barns: masonry and glue-laminated construction for fire-resistance. Stalls: furred out, finished with red oak, hardwood, or 1/4 in. rubber matting. Casting rails: 2 in. x 6 in. red oak, edges rounded, sealed with boiled linseed oil. Countersink fastener heads, plug. Stall corners: rounded or 45° walls to casting rail. Ventilation: high open slots with optional sliding wood shutter. Windows: safety glass only, minimum of 8 ft above floor. Floor: 3 in. porous asphalt (percolation of one gallon in ten seconds) over 18 in. crushed stone with a porous drainpipe pitched to take effluent away from barn areas. Check local codes on septic requirements. Floors: rough concrete or skid-resistant brick pavers with a central floor drain to catch basin. Grates: cast iron or precast concrete centered in stall with perforations no larger than 1 in. diameter or 1 in. sq. Floor: sloped to center drain. Provide optional infrared heaters in all horse wash areas at maximum 10 ft above floor. Aisle floors: porous asphalt, paving bricks set in 2 in. sand, or diamond scored concrete with trench drains to each side.

Tack room area varies with the type of stable. Riding stables have at least one bridle and saddle per horse or pony. Saddle and bridle racks can be fastened in rows, one over another. Additional space is needed for groom equipment, sometimes stored in tack trunks. In broodmare stables, tack is mainly halters and grooming supplies. Tack room and foaling stall must be heated. Foaling stall heat: controllable to raise it as quickly as possible to 75° minimum and to maintain it. Foaling stall floor: seamless, rubberized material, minimum 1 in. thick, texturized, and pitched to a separate drain and catch basin (not connected to main barn drainage). Rubberized flooring turned up the walls, minimum of 24 in. Foaling stall adjoined by the situp room (also heated) with a one-way unbreakable glass panel and/or slide shutter for the groom to observe.

All feed and grain storage bins are lined with galvanized steel for vermin control. Feed amounts vary widely. As a guideline, a horse under medium to heavy workload is fed 15 lb of grain plus hay per day. All hay and bedding must be stored in a separate dry barn due to fire risk. As horses are grazing animals, hay managers are not recommended; place hay in a corner on the stall floor. All roofs should have a minimum 7/12 pitch and continuous full length vents under the eaves and at ridges. Sliding doors are preferable. All swinging dutch doors or full doors should have a 180° swing to wall and fasten. Stalls should have heavy duty slide bolts, kick over bolts, and/or locking pins. All hardware should be smooth with no sharp protrusions and inaccessible to horses at the stalls. All light fixtures should be guarded and/or waterproofed. Light switches: located in a central panel away from wet areas. Lighting levels vary. Depending on the program, stalls are lighted with a single floodlight over the inside stall door at the ceiling or 10 to 12 ft. above finished floor. Aisles can be lighted by incandescent or fluorescent lamps. Broodmares and stallions require brighter light and lighting programs to keep fertility levels maximized (approximately 100 footcandles should be achieved at 5 ft 0 in. above finished floor per stall). Aisles may have lower light levels of 40 footcandles, except examination or display areas, which must have additional light available on demand.

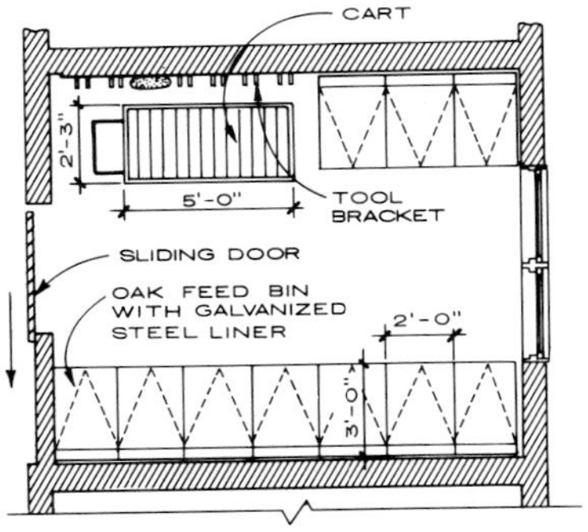

FEED AND EQUIPMENT ROOM PLAN

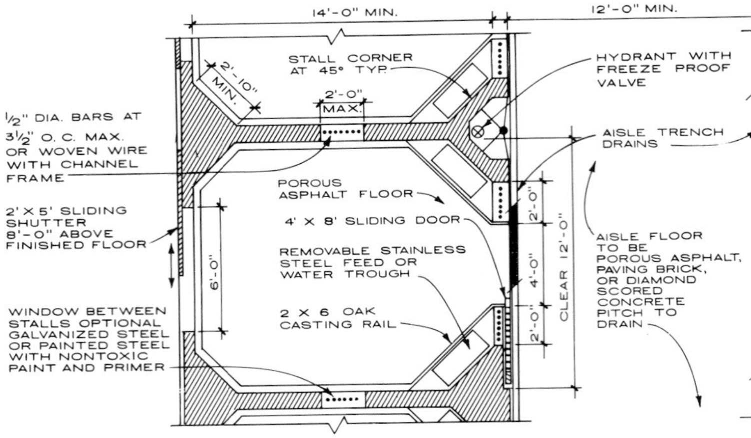

CART

TOOL BRACKET

SLIDING DOOR

OAK FEED BIN WITH GALVANIZED STEEL LINER

5'-0"

2'-0"

TYPICAL STALL PLAN

14'-0" MIN.

2'-10" MIN.

2'-0" MAX.

STALL CORNER AT 45° TYP.

1/2" DIA. BARS AT 3 1/2" O.C. MAX. OR WOVEN WIRE WITH CHANNEL FRAME

2' X 5' SLIDING SHUTTER 8'-0" ABOVE FINISHED FLOOR

WINDOW BETWEEN STALLS OPTIONAL GALVANIZED STEEL OR PAINTED STEEL WITH NONTOXIC PAINT AND PRIMER

POROUS ASPHALT FLOOR

4' X 8' SLIDING DOOR

REMOVABLE STAINLESS STEEL FEED OR WATER TROUGH

2 X 6 OAK CASTING RAIL

6'-0"

AISLE

12'-0" MIN.

HYDRANT WITH FREEZE PROOF VALVE

AISLE TRENCH DRAINS

AISLE FLOOR TO BE POROUS ASPHALT, PAVING BRICK, OR DIAMOND SCORED CONCRETE PITCH TO DRAIN

CLEAR 12'-0"

TACK ROOM PLAN

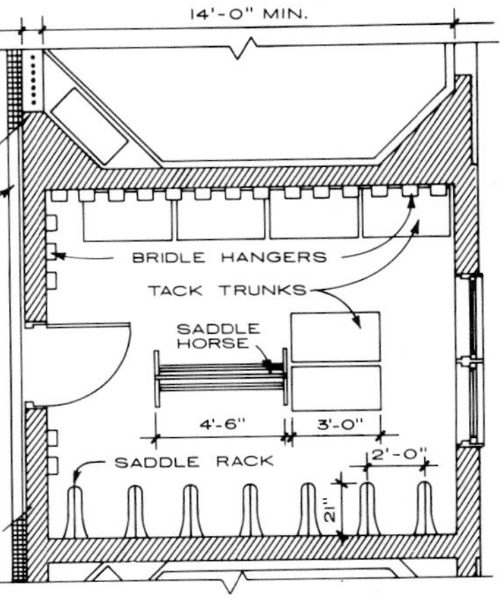

14'-0" MIN.

BRIDLE HANGERS

TACK TRUNKS

SADDLE HORSE

4'-6"   3'-0"

SADDLE RACK

2'-0"

2"

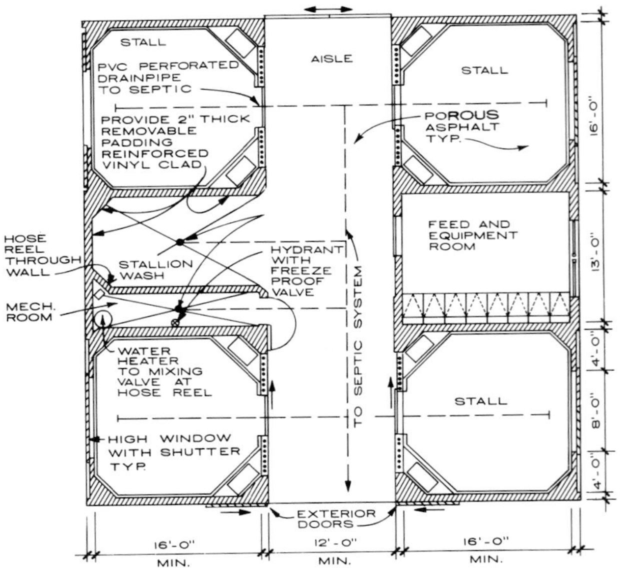

STALLION BARN-4 STALLS — REFER TO NOTES

STALL

AISLE

STALL

PVC PERFORATED DRAINPIPE TO SEPTIC

PROVIDE 2" THICK REMOVABLE PADDING REINFORCED VINYL CLAD

POROUS ASPHALT TYP.

FEED AND EQUIPMENT ROOM

HOSE REEL THROUGH WALL

STALLION WASH

HYDRANT WITH FREEZE PROOF VALVE

MECH. ROOM

WATER HEATER TO MIXING VALVE AT HOSE REEL

TO SEPTIC SYSTEM

STALL

HIGH WINDOW WITH SHUTTER TYP.

EXTERIOR DOORS

16'-0" MIN.   12'-0" MIN.   16'-0" MIN.

16'-0"   13'-0"   4'-0"   8'-0"   4'-0"

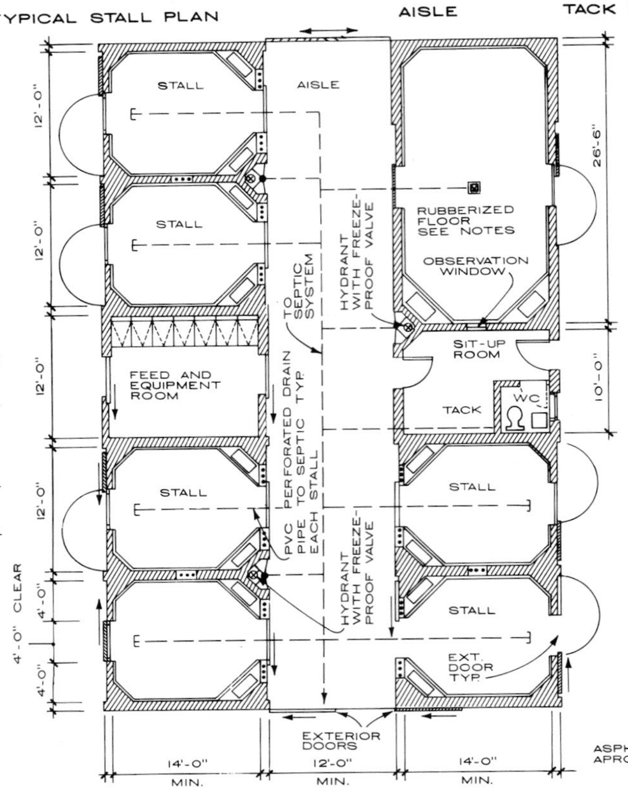

BROODMARE BARN - 7 STALLS — REFER TO NOTES

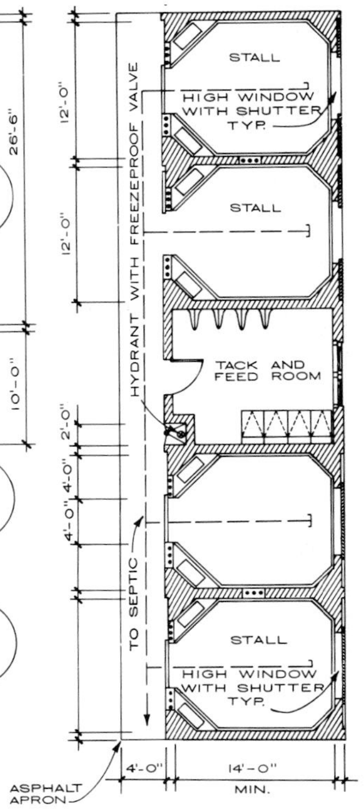

STALL   AISLE

STALL

FEED AND EQUIPMENT ROOM

STALL

STALL

RUBBERIZED FLOOR SEE NOTES

OBSERVATION WINDOW

SIT-UP ROOM

TACK   WC

STALL

STALL

HYDRANT WITH FREEZE-PROOF VALVE

TO SEPTIC SYSTEM

PVC PERFORATED DRAIN PIPE TO SEPTIC EACH STALL

HYDRANT WITH FREEZE-PROOF VALVE

EXT. DOOR TYP.

EXTERIOR DOORS

14'-0" MIN.   12'-0" MIN.   14'-0" MIN.

12'-0"   12'-0"   12'-0"   12'-0"   26'-6"   10'-0"

4'-0" CLEAR   4'-0"   4'-0"

RIDING HORSE BARN 4 STALLS REFER TO NOTES

STALL

HIGH WINDOW WITH SHUTTER TYP.

STALL

HYDRANT WITH FREEZEPROOF VALVE

TACK AND FEED ROOM

TO SEPTIC

STALL

STALL

HIGH WINDOW WITH SHUTTER TYP.

ASPHALT APRON

12'-0"   12'-0"   4'-0"   2'-0"   4'-0"

4'-0"   14'-0" MIN.

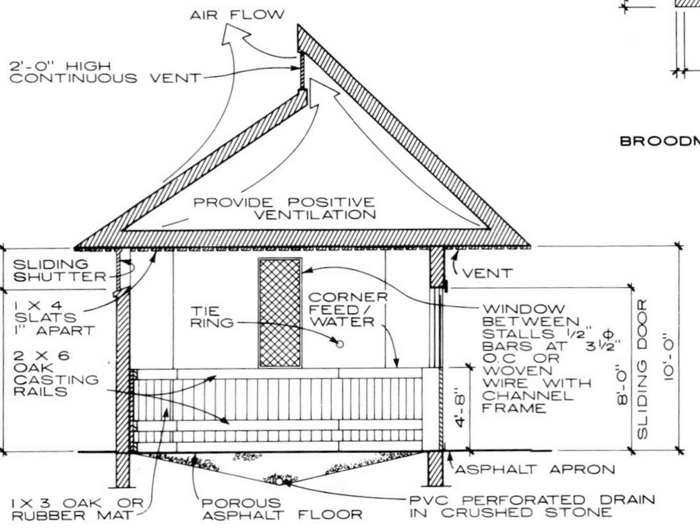

STALL SECTION THROUGH RIDING HORSE BARN

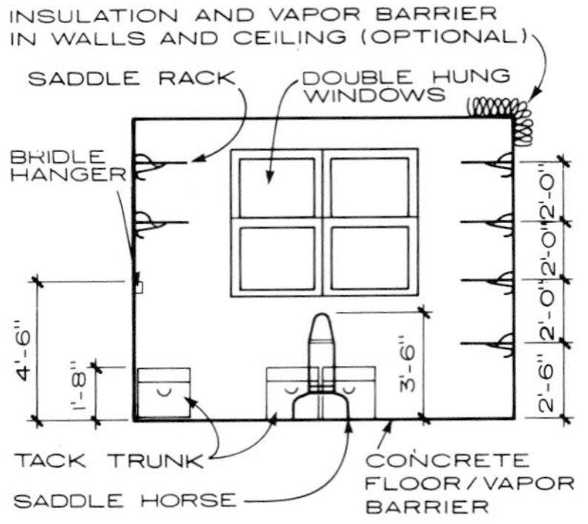

AIR FLOW

2'-0" HIGH CONTINUOUS VENT

PROVIDE POSITIVE VENTILATION

SLIDING SHUTTER

1 X 4 SLATS 1" APART

2 X 6 OAK CASTING RAILS

TIE RING

CORNER FEED/ WATER

VENT

WINDOW BETWEEN STALLS. 1/2" BARS AT 3 1/2" O.C. OR WOVEN WIRE WITH CHANNEL FRAME

SLIDING DOOR

1 X 3 OAK OR RUBBER MAT

POROUS ASPHALT FLOOR

PVC PERFORATED DRAIN IN CRUSHED STONE

ASPHALT APRON

2'-0"   8'-0"   4'-8"   8'-0"   10'-0"

TACK ROOM ELEVATION

SERVES 40 STALLS- HEAT AND HUMIDITY CONTROL REQUIRED

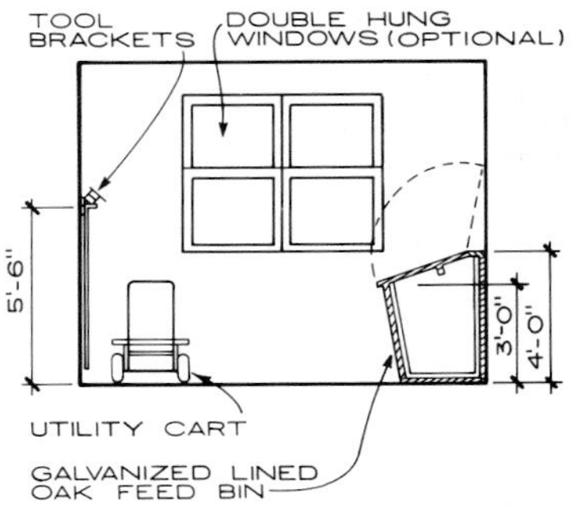

INSULATION AND VAPOR BARRIER IN WALLS AND CEILING (OPTIONAL)

SADDLE RACK

DOUBLE HUNG WINDOWS

BRIDLE HANGER

TACK TRUNK

SADDLE HORSE

CONCRETE FLOOR / VAPOR BARRIER

4'-6"   1'-8"   3'-6"   2'-6"   2'-0"   2'-0"

FEED AND EQUIPMENT ROOM ELEVATION

CAPACITY OF ONE BIN = 100 LB VENTILATION REQUIRED

TOOL BRACKETS

DOUBLE HUNG WINDOWS (OPTIONAL)

UTILITY CART

GALVANIZED LINED OAK FEED BIN

5'-6"   3'-0"   4'-0"

Theodore M. Ceraldi & Associates, Architects; Nyack, New York

ANIMAL CARE

INTRODUCTION

Developments in ventilation, glazing, and horticulture have helped achieve satisfactory plant growth in greenhouses to make the practice economical. Site selection considerations include: topography (flat is advisable), drainage, quantity and quality of water supply, air quality, direction and average wind speed, and, most important, the amount of available light. Orientation for optimal solar gain is east-west except in conditions where shadow casting obstructions outweigh the orientation rule. Once a site has been selected, development of a plan for growth (even if only one greenhouse is built at first) is essential, factoring in access, mechanical room locations, and circulation of materials and labor. Heating and cooling needs will vary with latitude, plant type, skin or glazing, and growth period.

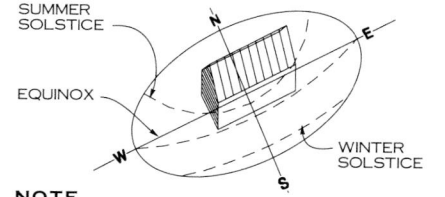

NOTE

Use of an uneven span greenhouse allows for optimal solar orientation. Slope of glass is determined by latitude.

OPTIMAL SOLAR ORIENTATION

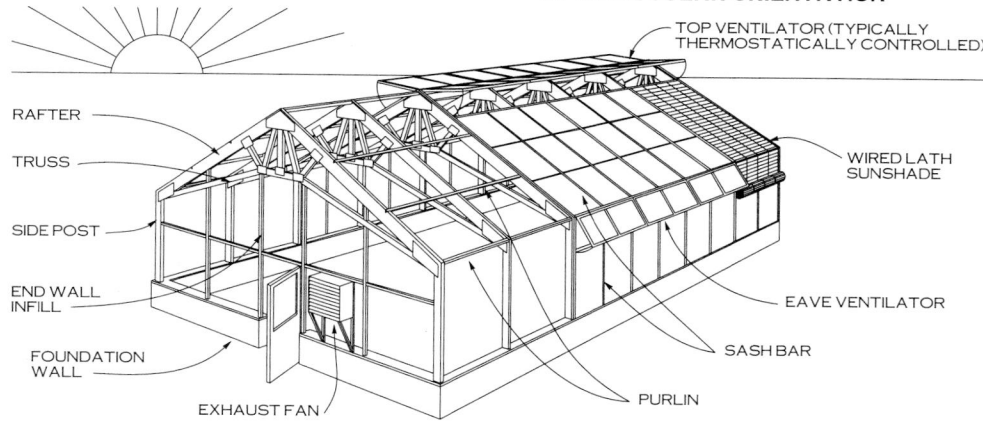

GENERIC GREENHOUSE

When properly maintained, a glass greenhouse will last 40 to 50 years. Structural design of a greenhouse is similar to curtain wall design with live loads of wind, snow, piping, and hanging basket plants.

| EVEN SPAN | UNEVEN SPAN | RIDGE AND FURROW | LEAN-TO |

GLASS-SHEATHED GREENHOUSE

Rigid or flexible plastic greenhouses feature economy, ease of fabrication, and flexibility of form making. Plastic's liabilities are its poor durability, reduced light transmission over time, and discoloration or brittleness.

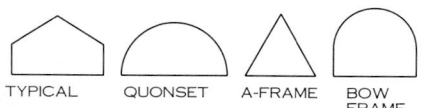

| TYPICAL | QUONSET | A-FRAME | BOW FRAME |

PLASTIC-SHEATHED GREENHOUSE

HEATING SYSTEMS

Heat distribution is achieved through use of solar, hot air, or radiant pipe systems. Solar heating will usually need the augmentation of the two latter systems at the coolest or windiest part of the year.

RADIANT/HOT WATER PIPE

Systems use a boiler to heat and distribute water. Pipes located at the greenhouse perimeter are the most convenient and efficient method of achieving uniform temperature.

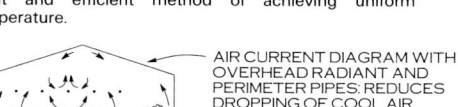

AIR CURRENT DIAGRAM WITH OVERHEAD RADIANT AND PERIMETER PIPES: REDUCES DROPPING OF COOL AIR

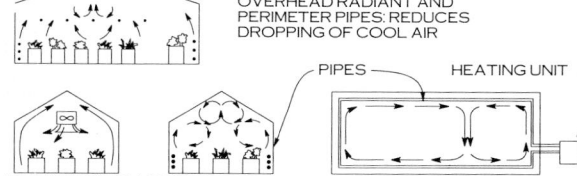

AIR CURRENT DIAGRAMS PIPES HEATING UNIT

HEATING SYSTEMS

FRAME TYPES

MATERIAL	FEATURES
Pipe frame	Economy/simple connections
Steel frame	50' span (installation by professionals)
Aluminum frame	No rust, deeper sections than steel
Wood frame	Pressure treated lifespan: 10-15 yrs.

PLASTIC TYPE	MATERIAL
Flexible	Polyethylene, mylar
Rigid	PVC, acrylic, fiberglass

NOTE

The size of a plastic greenhouse is limited only by the width of a single sheet of plastic.

INSULATION

Insulation augments heating systems and helps reduce heat loss from convection and radiation. Three basic systems are most widely used: movable night curtains, plastic covering over glass, and permanent reflective insulation of north wall and roof.

HOT AIR

Systems burn various fossil fuels and distribute the warmed air with fans.

HORIZONTAL DISCHARGE PLASTIC DUCT

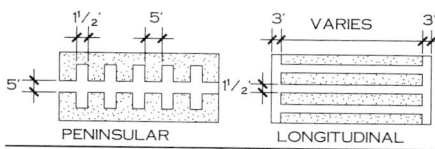

WHERE
A = MIN. ANGLE OF SPAN
H = HEIGHT
Y = CENTERLINE OF HIGHEST POINT TO PROPOSED GREENHOUSE

SOLVE FOR Y
TAN A° = H/Y

SPACING OF STRUCTURES

PENINSULAR LONGITUDINAL

BENCHING

GENERAL

Reduction of summer heat gain is achieved through shading systems, and natural and fan ventilation systems. Shading is most often achieved with the use of paint on the interior glass, lath rolled on the structure's exterior, or cloth of varying density on the structure's interior.

EVAPORATIVE COOLING

Mechanical refrigeration is generally cost prohibitive cooling with the exception of pad systems, or "swamp coolers," involving pulling air through a wet pad the length of the greenhouse wall with a fan mounted high on the opposite wall.

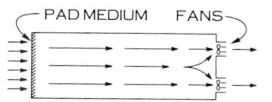

NOTE

Fan and pad water pump are hooked up to the same thermostat.

SWAMP COOLER

EXHAUST FANS

Fan placement depends on greenhouse orientation; optimal placement is the side opposite the normal wind direction. Fans from adjacent greenhouses should be placed opposite each other, spaced at not more than 25 ft. Stratification is desired in summer cooling, where only 15 to 60% of total air volume is moved mechanically.

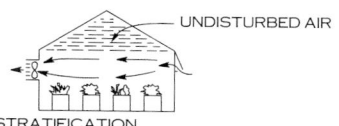

COOLING SYSTEMS

Air exchange is necessary to moderate interior temperature and humidity. High humidity promotes plant disease and inhibits soil drying. The most common means of ventilation are natural venting, tube ventilation, and fan-jet ventilation.

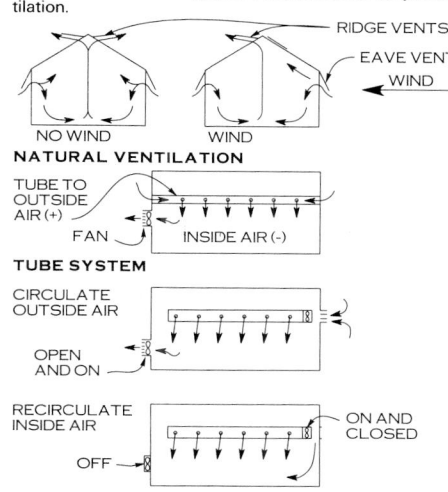

NO WIND WIND

NATURAL VENTILATION

TUBE TO OUTSIDE AIR (+) FAN INSIDE AIR (-)

TUBE SYSTEM

CIRCULATE OUTSIDE AIR OPEN AND ON

RECIRCULATE INSIDE AIR OFF ON AND CLOSED

FAN JET SYSTEM

VENTILATION SYSTEMS

Eric K. Beach; Rippeteau Architects, PC; Washington, D.C.

GENERAL

Solid waste handling, disposal, and recycling are basic building services that require careful planning. Environmental concerns for waste generation, collection, storage, and disposal are essential design considerations. In order to establish the appropriate size and arrangement of waste storage and recycling areas and to determine the need for waste handling equipment, it is necessary to estimate the quantity and types of solid waste to be generated at the project site. Considerations must be given to the type of project, building mass and height, the number of occupants, duration of occupancy, and possible special wastes (such as flammable materials, toxic materials, liquids, and bulk items).

DESIGN REQUIREMENTS

The project design should address the need for special rooms and/or containers within individual building spaces; the means of solid waste and recycling collection within the various parts of a building, frequency of collection, and method for transporting the material; possible use of chutes in multistory buildings; and the frequency and means for removing refuse from the project site. Design consideration should be given to the types of collection containers, holding bins, possible use of compactors, and size, location, and access requirements for equipment.

SOLID WASTE ESTIMATING

The following tables provide some basic data and trends regarding municipal solid waste generation to assist in determining approximate quantities and types of solid waste materials generated in various building types. Make adjustments for special project types, use of compactors, and other conditions resulting in deviations from the normal conditions. Use of disinfectants, insecticides, and deodorizing agents should be considered.

RECYCLING

Recycling occurs when material is diverted from the waste stream and used in lieu of virgin materials. Between 1960 and 1988, the percentage of waste material collected for recycling increased from 6.7% to 13.1%. At least 32 states now have comprehensive recycling laws that require detailed plans and/or separation mandates. With estimates of 25% recycling by the year 2000, the architect should plan for a recycling system.

SOLID WASTE GENERATION RATES

BUILDING TYPE	POUNDS/ DAY	EQUIVALENT IN LOOSE CUBIC YARDS
Apartment	2.5/person	0.025
	4/bedroom	0.040
	8/unit	0.080
Cafeteria	1/meal served	0.005
Department store	75 corrugated[1]	1.500
	15 other waste[1]	0.060
Discount store	60 other waste[1]	1.200
	10 other waste[1]	0.040
Fast food	200[1]	2.500
Hospital	16/occupied bed	0.100
Hotel		
First class	3.2/room	0.030
	2/meal served	0.010
Medium class	1.7/room	0.020
	1.2/meal served	0.006
Manufacturing		
100 - 400 people	3/person	0.020
400 - 3,000 people	7/person	0.047
Motel	2/room	0.020
Nursing and retirement home	5/person	0.030
Office	1/100 sq ft	0.009
Restaurant	1.5/meal served	0.008
School	0.5/person	0.050
Shopping mall	2.5/100 sq ft	0.018
Supermarket	100 corrugated[1]	2.000
	65 other waste[1]	0.260
Warehouse	1/100 sq ft	0.020
Community wide		
Residential[2]	2.5 - 3.5/person	
Commercial[3]	0.9 - 1.6/person	

NOTES

1. Per $1,000 of sales.
2. Solid waste collected by residential collection system only. Usually includes building with 1 - 4 dwelling units.
3. Generally includes apartments and condominiums of more than 4 units collected under a commercial system.

VOLUME OF PRODUCTS DISCARDED IN MUNICIPAL SOLID WASTE - 1988

	1988 DISCARDS[1] (MILLIONS OF TONS)	WEIGHT (% OF TOTAL)	LANDFILL DENSITY (LB/CU YD)	LANDFILL VOLUME[2] (MIL CU YD)	VOLUME (% OF TOTAL)
DURABLE GOODS	23.0	14.7	520	88.5	22.2
NONDURABLE GOODS					
Newspapers	8.9	5.7	800	22.1	5.5
Books and magazines	4.6	2.9	800	11.5	2.9
Office papers	5.7	3.6	800	14.2	3.5
Commercial printing	3.5	2.2	800	8.8	2.2
Tissue paper and towels	3.0	1.9	800	7.6	1.9
Paper plates and cups	0.7	0.4	800	1.6	0.4
Plastic plates and cups	0.4	0.2	355	2.1	0.5
Disposable diapers	2.7	1.7	400	13.3	3.3
Other nonpackaging paper	5.2	3.3	800	12.9	3.2
Clothing and footwear	3.9	2.5	435	18.1	4.5
Other miscellaneous nondurables	4.6	2.9	390	23.4	5.9
Total nondurable goods	43.0	27.6	634	135.6	34.0
CONTAINERS AND PACKAGING					
Glass packaging					
Beer and soft drink	4.3	2.8	2,800	3.1	0.8
Wine and liquor	1.9	1.2	2,800	1.4	0.3
Food and other bottles and jars	3.6	2.3	2,800	2.6	0.6
Total glass packaging	9.8	6.3	2,800	7.0	1.8
Steel packaging					
Beer and soft drink cans	0.1	0.1	560	0.3	0.1
Food and other cans	2.1	1.4	560	7.6	1.9
Other steel packaging	0.2	0.1	560	0.8	0.2
Total steel packaging	2.4	1.6	560	8.7	2.2
Aluminum packaging					
Beer and soft drink cans	0.6	0.4	250	4.8	1.2
Other cans	0.1	0.1	250	0.8	0.2
Foil and closures	0.3	0.2	550	1.1	0.3
Total aluminum packaging	1.0	0.7	299	6.7	1.7
Paper and paperboard packaging					
Corrugated boxes	12.6	8.1	750	33.6	8.4
Milk cartons	0.5	0.3	820	1.2	0.3
Folding cartons	4.1	2.6	820	10.0	2.5
Other paperboard packaging	0.3	0.2	820	0.8	0.2
Bags and sacks	2.7	1.7	740	7.3	1.8
Wrapping paper	0.1	0.1	800	0.3	0.1
Other paper packaging	1.6	1.0	740	4.3	1.1
Total paper and paperboard packaging	21.9	14.0	763	57.5	14.4
Plastics packaging					
Soft drink bottles	0.3	0.2	355	1.7	0.4
Milk bottles	0.4	0.3	355	2.3	0.6
Other containers	1.7	1.1	355	9.7	2.4
Bags and sacks	0.8	0.5	670	2.4	0.6
Wraps	1.1	0.7	670	3.3	0.8
Other plastics packaging	1.2	0.8	185	13.2	3.3
Total plastics packaging	5.5	3.5	341	32.4	8.1
Wood packaging	2.1	1.3	800	5.3	1.3
Other miscellaneous packaging	0.2	0.1	1,015	0.4	0.1
Total containers and packaging	43.0	27.6	729	118.0	29.6
TOTAL NONFOOD PRODUCT WASTE	109.0	69.9	637	342.0	85.8
OTHER WASTES					
Food	13.2	8.5	2,000	13.2	3.3
Yard	31.1	20.0	1,500	41.3	10.4
Miscellaneous inorganics	2.7	1.7	2,500	2.2	0.5
Total other wastes	47.0	30.1	1,659	56.7	14.2
Total Municipal solid waste discarded	156.0	100.0	783	399.0	100.0

NOTES

1. Discards after materials recovery and composting, before combustion and landfilling.
2. This assumes that all waste is landfilled, but some is combusted and otherwise disposed.

THE CHANGING SHAPE OF INTEGRATED WASTE MANAGEMENT

	1960		1970		1980		1988		2000	
	TONS[1]	%	TONS[1]	%	TONS[1]	%	TONS[1]	%	TONS[1]	%
Landfills	54.9	62.5	88.2	72.4	121.4	81.1	130.5	72.7	106.5	49
Recycling	5.9	6.7	8.6	7.1	14.5	9.7	23.5	13.1	54.4	25.0
Incineration[2]	27.0	30.8	24.7	20.3	11.0	7.4	1.0	0.6	0.1	0.1
Waste-to-energy	0.0	0.0	0.4	0.3	2.7	1.8	24.5	13.6	55.0	25.5
Total	87.8	100.0	121.9	100.0	149.6	100.0	179.6	100.0	216.0	100.0

NOTES

1. In millions of tons per year.
2. Without energy recovery.

National Solid Wastes Management Association; Washington, D.C.

INTRODUCTION

Solid waste disposal has become a critical issue for society. Landfills and other waste disposal facilities are reaching capacity and siting new facilities is difficult due to environmental and health concerns, including water pollution, loss of wetlands, poisoning of the soil, and the breeding of vermin. As a result, traditional methods of handling solid waste are becoming more costly. Reducing landfill waste extends the life of existing facilities and lessens the need to build new facilities.

Much of what we have called "waste" is not waste, but marketable materials that can be reused to make new products. Reusing materials already extracted from the earth enables sustainable use as raw resources are depleted. Products require great amounts of energy to be produced from raw natural materials. By recycling we are recapturing energy embodied in a material during initial manufacturing processes. Sorting and recycling waste often reduces operating and disposal costs while conserving natural resources and energy.

Most states and municipalities have laws and programs to encourage waste reduction and recycling, including mandatory quotas, deposit/return arrangements, and disposal bans. Buildings should include the spaces necessary to carry out recycling and waste management programs. Once the waste and recyclable materials generation of a building's users are determined, spaces can be designed for sorting, storage, and removal.

RECYCLABLE MATERIALS

Separating materials by category or product is the first step in recycling (see table at right). Materials are sorted into like kinds to prevent contamination. Contaminated materials are less readily recyclable and therefore less marketable. Sorting is particularly important for paper and glass. Cleaning food packaging of organic material is usually necessary. Some recyclers will accept "commingled" or mixed waste and will sort and clean materials by hand or by mechanical means. (Paper is easily contaminated and can never be recycled this way; it must always be separated from other waste materials.) Communities that pick up commingled recyclable materials have enjoyed a greater participation rate since it requires little, if any, change in waste disposing habits. However, sorting of recyclable materials at their generation point is less labor intensive and produces higher quality, less contaminated reprocessed materials.

SYMBOLS

The recycling symbol signifies the three steps of the recycling loop: collecting materials, manufacturing new products, and selling and using recycled products.

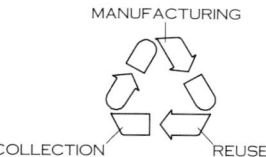

MANUFACTURING

COLLECTION   REUSE

In the marketplace, the recycling symbol is marked on products in the following way:

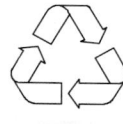

This conformation of the symbol is used to identify items made from materials that can be recycled.

This conformation of the symbol is used to identify products made entirely or primarily from recycled materials.

PLANNING AND DESIGN

When planning a project, make a waste analysis based on the building type or building users and address the following issues:

1. Source generation: identify types and quantities of waste material likely to be generated.
2. Collection and sorting: determine space and equipment needed for the collection and/or separation of waste materials.
3. Disposal: determine the frequency and means of the remover or recycler to collect the waste.

Richard J. Vitullo, AIA; Oak Leaf Studio; Crownsville, Maryland
Tom Lokey; Northeast Maryland Waste Disposal Authority; Baltimore, Maryland

RECYCLABLE MATERIALS

CATEGORY	PRODUCT	MATERIAL DESCRIPTION (RECYCLING LABEL)	CONVERSION OF VOLUME TO WEIGHT
Paper	Ledger paper, white letterhead	SWL – sorted white ledger (high-grade white paper)	Uncompacted – 1 cu yd = 500 lb Compacted – 1 cu yd = 750 lb
	Computer paper	CPO – computer printout	Uncompacted – 1 cu yd = 500 - 600 lb Compacted – 1 cu yd = 1000 - 1200 lb
	Colored paper	SCL – sorted color paper	Uncompacted – 1 cu yd = 500 lb Compacted – 1 cu yd = 750 lb
	Newspaper	Mix – newsprint	Uncompacted – 1 cu yd = 350 - 500 lb Compacted – 1 cu yd = 750 - 1000 lb
	Magazines	Mix – clay-coated paper	Not available
	Telephone books	Mix – mixed papers/adhesives	1 book = 1 - 3 lb
	Cereal boxes	Mix – coated paperboard	Not available
	Shipping boxes	OCC – old corrugated cardboard	Uncompacted – 1 cu yd = 285 lb Compacted – 1 cu yd = 500 lb
Glass	Food jars, beverage bottles	1. Amber glass 2. Green glass 3. Clear glass	Loose, whole – 1 cu yd = 600 lb Manually crushed –1 cu yd = 1000 lb Mechanically crushed – 1 cu yd = 1800 lb
Plastic	Beverage containers	PET – polyethylene terephthalate	Whole – 1 cu yd = 30 lb
	Milk containers	HDPE – high-density polyethylene	Whole – 1 cu yd = 25 lb Crushed –1 cu yd = 50 lb Compacted – 1 cu yd = 600 lb
	"Clamshell" containers	Polystyrene plastic foam	Not available
	Film plastic	LDPE – low-density polyethylene	Not available
Metals	Beverage cans	Aluminum/bi-metal	Whole – 1 cu yd = 50 - 70 lb Crushed – 1 cu yd = 300 - 450 lb
	Food and beverage cans	Steel with tin finish	Whole – 1 cu yd = 125 - 150 lb Crushed – 1 cu yd = 500 - 850 lb
Miscellaneous	Pallets	Wood	Not available
	Food waste	Organic solids and liquids	55 gallon drum – 415 lb
	Yard waste	Organic solids	Leaves, uncompacted – 1 cu yd = 250 lb Leaves, compacted – 1 cu yd = 450 lb Wood chips – 1 cu yd = 500 lb Grass clippings – 1 cu yd= 400 lb
	Used motor oil	Petroleum product	1 gallon = 71 lb
	Tires	Rubber	1 passenger car = 20 lb 1 truck = 90 lb

NOTE

No building or facility will need space for sorting and storing all or even most of the recyclable materials on this list. Generally paper products should be separated from other wastes. The number of products to be sorted within a category should be limited for most users; sorting more than two products may result in contamination.

An effective recycling system in the home, school, or workplace integrates materials sorting with the regular collection of waste. Convenience of use is essential. Recycling systems should be as easy to use as a conventional waste basket (and be usable by the elderly and persons with disabilities). Provide extra space alongside regular waste containers for separating and storing recyclable materials. Conveying systems like waste chutes may also be provided. Collection bins should be clearly distinguished by using different-sized containers and effective graphics; differentiation will encourage proper use and reduce contamination, a serious recycling problem.

NONRESIDENTIAL BUILDINGS

In most commercial and educational buildings, paper is the predominant recyclable waste product (70%+). Paper is readily recyclable into consumable form. High-grade paper, like bond, is used in great volumes and is a generally marketable recycling commodity. Since paper can be easily contaminated, its separation from other waste is critical.

In health care facilities, biomedical waste must be separated from all other wastes and is generally collected and incinerated by waste disposal specialists. Biomedical waste collection spaces should be provided apart from general waste and recycling spaces.

The design of recyclable waste collection rooms used by individual employees, visitors, students, etc. should adequately accommodate the volume of waste generated. Larger waste collection rooms require less frequent removal resulting in lower labor costs. Collection bin sizes should be based on the material weight-to-volume ratio. For example, office paper has a high weight-to-volume ratio; a 96-gallon container, or equivalent, may be the largest one practicable. Collection containers should be placed adjacent to areas where waste materials are generated. Place bins for recycling paper in copy and computer rooms; place bins for glass, metal, and plastic in kitchens, vending rooms, lounges, etc. If waste chutes are used, they should be similarly placed. Manual crushers should be mounted near bins for low weight-to-volume materials (such as aluminum cans and plastic bottles) to help reduce space requirements. Most collection areas should be neat and ordered in appearance as befits most office environments.

In some high-rise office buildings, the service core near the maintenance closet and freight elevator can house a secondary waste storage or chute area. Tenants or service personnel deposit waste and recyclable materials there regularly. Since this is a holding area accessible only to a few building occupants, the space can be utilitarian in appearance.

Consult local building codes regarding fire separation or sprinkler requirements for storage rooms, especially for combustibles like paper.

Once you determine the quantities, number of separations, etc. of a building's waste, design the central storage/disposal space. See illustrations for a typical layout of a large office building space and loading dock area. These layouts can be used for other building types that handle a similar volume of waste. Waste chutes and compactor/balers are used where the building configuration, removal service, and/or waste volume warrant it.

MINIMUM EXTERIOR TRASH AND RECYCLING AREAS FOR NON-RESIDENTIAL BUILDINGS

BUILDING SIZE (SQ FT)	TRASH (SQ FT)	RECYCLABLE MATERIALS (SQ FT)
0 - 5000	12	12
5001 - 10,000	24	24
10,001 - 25,000	48	48
25,000 +	Each additional 25,000 sq ft requires 48 sq ft each for trash and recyclable materials	

SOURCE GENERATION[4]

CLASSIFICATION	BUILDING TYPES	QUANTITIES OF WASTE GENERATED	TYPES OF WASTE GENERATED
Residential	Studio or one bedroom apartment	1 - 1 1/2 cu yd per unit per month (200 - 250 lb)	Newspaper (38/43)[1] Plastic (18/7)[1] Miscellaneous (13/18)[1] Metals (14/9)[1] Yard waste/compost (10/15)[1] Glass (2/8)[1]
	Two or three bedroom apartment or single family house	1 1/2 - 2 cu yd per unit per month (250 - 400 lb)	
Commercial	Office, general	1 1/2 lb per employee per day or 1 cu yd per 10,000 sq ft per day (includes 1/2 lb of high-grade paper per person per day)	Plastics, compost, used oil, metals, and glass (30%)[2] High grade paper (29%)[2] Mixed papers (23%)[2] Newspapers (10%)[2] Corrugated cardboard (8%)[2]
	Department store	1 cu yd per 2500 sq ft per day	Corrugated cardboard, compost, wood pallets, high grade paper, and plastic film[3]
	Wholesale/retail store	Varies with type of tenant	
	Shopping center	Varies with type of tenant	
	Supermarket	1 cu yd per 1250 sq ft per day	Corrugated cardboard, compost, and wood pallets[3]
	Restaurants/ entertainment	Varies with number of meals served and type of food	Compost (38%)[2] Corrugated cardboard (11%)[2] Newsprint (5%)[2] High-grade paper (4%)[2]
	Drugstore	1 cu yd per 2000 sq ft per day	Corrugated cardboard and high grade paper[3]
	Bank/insurance company	Survey required (3/4 lb high-grade paper per person per day)	High-grade paper, mixed paper, and corrugated cardboard[3]
Hotel and motel	High occupancy	1/2 cu yd per room per week (plus restaurants)	Glass, aluminum, plastic, high-grade paper, newspaper, and corrugated cardboard[3]
	Average occupancy	1/6 cu yd per room per week (plus restaurants)	
Institutional	Hospital	1 cu yd per 5 occupied beds per day	Compost, high-grade paper, biomedical waste, corrugated cardboard, glass, and plastics[3]
	Nursing home	1 cu yd per 15 persons per day	
	Retirement home	1 cu yd per 20 persons per day	
Educational	Grade school	1 cu yd per 8 rooms per day	High-grade paper, mixed paper, newspaper, corrugated cardboard, compost, plastic, glass, and metals[3]
	High school	1 cu yd per 10 rooms per day	
	University	Survey required	

NOTES

1. Percentage by volume/percentage by weight.
2. Percentage by volume.
3. Percentages not available.
4. This table approximates by building type the quantity and type of waste generated; the information should be used as a guideline only. Volume (using varying weights per cubic yard) is derived from nationwide U.S. averages of noncompacted waste.

MINIMUM INTERIOR OR EXTERIOR TRASH AND RECYCLING AREAS FOR MULTIFAMILY HOUSING

NUMBER OF UNITS	TRASH (SQ FT)	RECYCLABLE MATERIALS (SQ FT)
2 - 6	12	12
7 - 15	24	24
16 - 25	48	48
25 +	Each additional 25 dwelling units require an additional 48 sq ft for both trash and recyclable materials	

SINGLE-FAMILY HOUSING

Generally, issues regarding collection of recyclable and waste materials in the single-family home are similar to those within an apartment. Sorting of recyclable materials is often accommodated in kitchen base cabinets, especially under the sink, in a trash cabinet "island," or in a nearby utility closet. Most cabinet manufacturers offer a specially designed base cabinet to handle recyclable and waste materials. If organic materials are collected for composting, odors and vermin must be addressed as well as the ability to clean the collection bins. Garages may include recycling storage areas or closets; if adjacent to kitchens, a pass-through system with closable doors can be built.

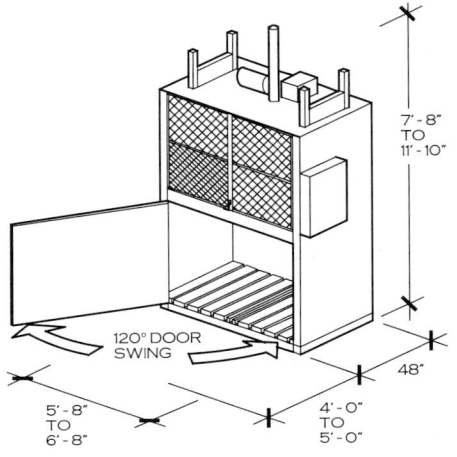

BALER/COMPACTOR

NOTES

1. All baler dimensions are approximate and vary depending upon the manufacturer. Typical bale sizes (in inches) are: 18 x 18 x 18, 20 x 24 x 18, 30 x 24 x 20, 48 x 30 x 42, 60 x 30 x 48, and 72 x 30 x 48

2. To determine whether a baler is needed, consult a recycler to analyze probable waste quantities. Balers can make recycling more efficient by saving space. For example, if the volume of cardboard boxes is high in a certain building, balers can greatly reduce the amount of storage space needed. The bailing of such waste as metal cans, plastic bottles, paper, or cardboard may make the recyclable materials more marketable by increasing trailer payloads.

3. Some balers expand by linking bins together to accommodate a variable recycling program. A sliding ram mechanism will service each bin.

MULTIFAMILY HOUSING

Diverse types of waste are generated in the home; this waste is compounded in multifamily apartment buildings. Waste and recyclable materials often contain organic materials that can attract rodents and insects and produce odors that must be controlled or segregated from the surrounding area. Resident's glass, metal, and plastic materials need to be washed or sealed in containers before placing in collection bins. Consult local health, fire, and building codes regarding these storage areas; sprinklers may be required.

A two-part system is recommended for an effective recycling program in high-rise residential projects. First, provide space in the home kitchen area to collect recyclable and waste products. For multifamily housing, each dwelling unit should have a total of 5 cu ft minimum set aside for waste storage (2.5 cu ft for trash and 2.5 cu ft for recyclable materials). Second, provide convenient space on each floor for sorting and/or deposit of materials. Freight elevator bays or maintenance rooms are usually good locations. In low-rise multifamily buildings or complexes, a central interior space may be desirable. The closer it is to the regular waste drop-off point the better.

In some situations, waste chutes provided on each floor can be effective, especially if deposit space is limited. Two waste chute systems are available. One consists of multiple, separate chutes for trash, metal, plastic, and newspapers. The other is a single waste chute that handles all of the waste, which is "sorted" by a computerized revolving bin in a central storage room. Corrugated cardboard and glass usually cannot be accommodated by the chute system because of jamming and breakage, respectively. Glass also requires color separation and is best handled by other collection methods.

Central storage spaces for recyclable and waste materials may be placed in a variety of locations depending on the layout of the building or complex. When no secondary spaces are possible or practicable for waste drop-off, residents must drop off recyclable and waste materials at a central site. The options for this central site are as follows:

SINGLE EXTERIOR SITE

Place compartmentalized recycling dumpsters or 90-gallon carts in one central location. This system, easiest for the maintenance staff and the remover, is the least expensive method. However, this is the least convenient arrangement for residents, and a large area on the site may be required.

MULTIPLE EXTERIOR SITES

For larger building complexes, place recycling bins or compartmentalized dumpsters adjacent to a conventional waste disposal site. Keep bins separate and clearly marked. Minimum maintenance is required for this layout, designed to be convenient to residents by providing multiple locations. Removal costs may be somewhat higher than a single collection site.

Exterior storage areas are generally prohibited in required front yards, street sideyards, or required parking and landscaped areas. Check local zoning, fire, and building codes.

SINGLE INTERIOR SITE

A recycling area can be set up at an interior location using separate containers on wheels – 32-gallon containers, 55- or 90-gallon drums – to collect and store waste and recyclable materials. This central collection area should be convenient to residents, near elevator lobbies, mailrooms, chuterooms, ends of hallways, or in other common areas like laundry rooms, lounges, or lobbies. If no space is available in any of these locations, use a single storage room that meets code requirements.

Richard J. Vitullo, AIA; Oak Leaf Studio; Crownsville, Maryland
Tom Lokey; Northeast Maryland Waste Disposal Authority; Baltimore, Maryland

WASTE MANAGEMENT

DISPOSAL

To determine waste and recyclable material removal arrangements for a project, contact the municipal or county environmental office for local regulations or guidelines for collection programs. If private arrangements must be made, contact local removal and recycling companies that could service the building. The container type and size compatible with collection vehicles should be noted and provided for in the design. Since recycling is an industry in its infancy, provide extra storage space in or near the building to accommodate future needs.

Some building types, such as grocery stores, generate a large amount of bulky corrugated cardboard, requiring compacting and/or baling. Materials of large volume to weight ratios, such as metal cans and plastic bottles, if not crushed manually at their generation point, may be compacted at a central storage room. The volume of material collected and the number of trips the remover needs to make will generally indicate the cost-effectiveness of a crusher or baler.

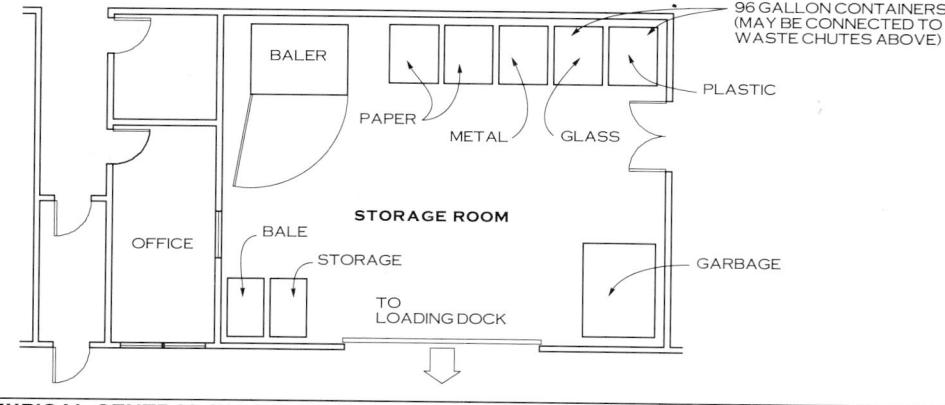

TYPICAL CENTRAL WASTE ROOM PLAN

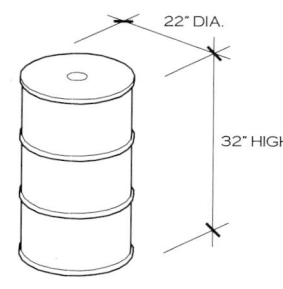

55 GALLON DRUM (.3 CU YD)

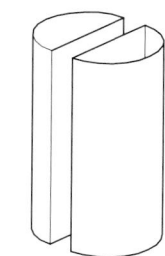

DIVIDERS FOR 55 GALLON DRUM FOR SEPARATION

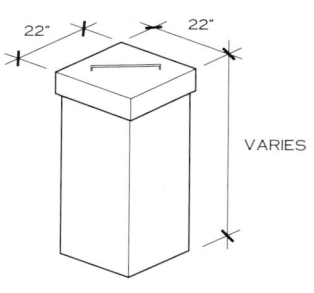

CARDBOARD CONTAINER (CAPACITY VARIES)

TYPICAL CONTAINERS

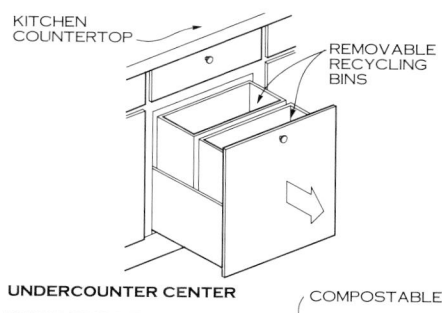

UNDERCOUNTER CENTER

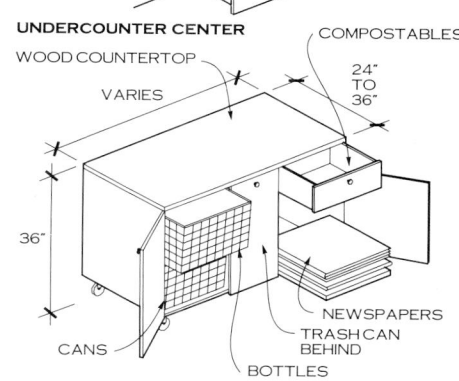

MULTIPURPOSE ISLAND

RESIDENTIAL RECYCLING UNITS

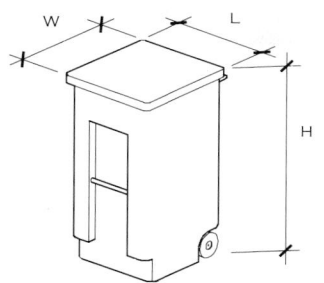

PLASTIC CONTAINER

COMMON SIZES

	LENGTH	WIDTH	HEIGHT
32 gal	21"	19"	36"
64 gal	29"	21"	42"
96 gal	35"	24"	43"

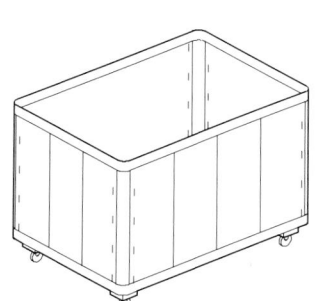

CANVAS BINS

COMMON SIZES

	LENGTH	WIDTH	HEIGHT
8 bushel	35"	26"	21"
16 bushel	42"	30"	30"
18 bushel	44"	31"	29"

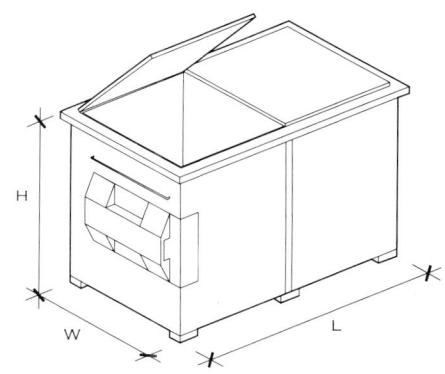

FRONT LOADING STEEL CONTAINER

COMMON SIZES

	LENGTH	WIDTH	HEIGHT	EMPTY WEIGHT
2 cu yd	72"	36"	36"	600 lb
4 cu yd	72"	54"	48"	900 lb
6 cu yd	72"	66"	60"	1200 lb
8 cu yd	72"	66"	80"	1500 lb

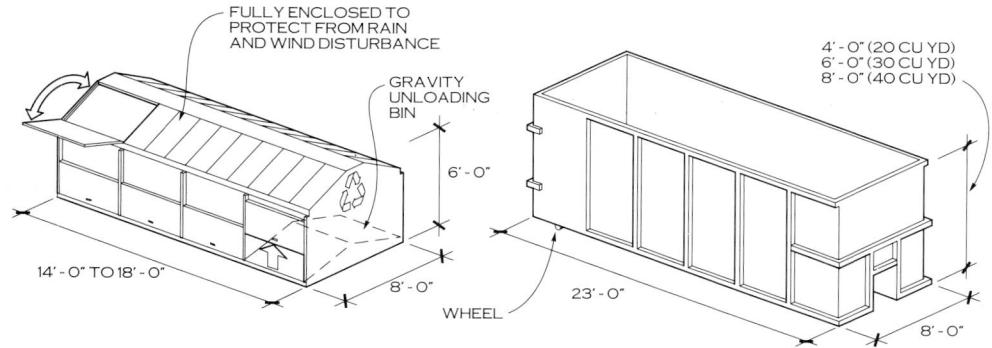

RECYCLING MATERIALS CONTAINER   **CONVENTIONAL "ROLL OFF" WASTE CONTAINER**

STORAGE CONTAINERS

Richard J. Vitullo, AIA; Oak Leaf Studio; Crownsville, Maryland
Tom Lokey; Northeast Maryland Waste Disposal Authority; Baltimore, Maryland

WASTE MANAGEMENT   20

RESIDENTIAL ROOM PLANNING

National Kitchen and Bath Association
687 Willow Grove Street
Hackettstown, NJ 07840
Tel: (908) 852-0033

Society of Certified Kitchen Designers
687 Willow Grove St.
Hackettstown, NJ 07840
Tel: (908) 852–0033

REFERENCES

Design Criteria for Lighting Interior Living Spaces, RP-11, Illuminating Engineering Society, 1980.

NONRESIDENTIAL ROOM PLANNING
REFERENCES

Ching, Frank. *Building Construction Illustrated*, 2nd ed. New York: Van Nostrand Reinhold, 1991.
DeChiara, Joseph. *Time-Saver Standards for Building Types*, 3rd ed. McGraw-Hill, 1991.
DeChiara, Joseph. *Time-Saver Standards for Interior Design and Space Planning*. McGraw-Hill, 1991.
Preiser, Wolfgang F. E. *Professional Practice in Facility Programming*. Van Nostrand Reinhold, 1993.
Spence, William P. *Architectural Working Drawings: Residential and Commercial Buildings*. New York: J. Wiley & Sons, 1993.

OFFICES

Institute of Business Designers (IBD)
341 Merchandise Mart
Chicago, IL 60654
Tel: (312) 467-1950

Office Planners and Users Group (OPUP)
Box 11182
Philadelphia, PA 19136
Tel: (215) 335-9400

REFERENCES

IES Recommended Practice for Lighting Offices Containing Visual Display Terminals, RP-24, Illuminating Engineering Society (IES), 1990.
Industrial Lighting, RP-7. IES, 1991.
NLB Guide to Office Lighting and Productivity, National Lighting Bureau, 1988.
"Office Acoustics." *P/A*, (Sept. 1992).
Office Lighting, RP-1. IES, 1982.
Steffy, G. *Lighting the Workplace*. PBC International, 1991.

CHILD CARE

National Child Care Association
1029 Railroad Street, N.W.
Conyers, GA 30207-5275
Tel: (800) 543-7161
Fax:(404) 388-7772

MUSEUMS

American Association of Museums (AAM)
1225 Eye Street N.W., Suite 200
Washington, DC 20005
Tel: (202) 289-1818

AIRPORTS

Aviation Safety Institute
6797 North High Street
Worthington, OH 43085-0304
Tel: (614) 885-4242
Fax:(614) 885-5891

REFERENCES

Aerodomes, Annex 14 to the Convention on International Civil Aviation, vol. 1. ICAO, July 1990.
Airport Capacity and Delay, FAA Advisory Circular 150/5060-5, September 23, 1983.
Airport Design, FAA Advisory Circular 150/5300-13, September 29, 1989.
Airport Terminals Reference Manual. International Air Transport Association (IATA), January 1989.

Federal Aviation Regulations Part 77, Objects Affecting Navigable Airspace. FAA, January, 1975.
Planning and Design of Airport Terminal Facilities at Non-hub Locations, FAA Advisory Circular 150/5360-9, April 4, 1980.

SCHOOLS

Association of University Architects (AUA)
c/o Austus G. Kellogg, AIA
Yale University School of Medicine
333 Cedar St.
New Haven, CT 06510
Tel: (203) 785-4667

Council of Educational Facility Planners (CEFP)
641 Chatham Lane, Suite 217
Columbus, OH 43221
Tel: (614) 792-8103

REFERENCES

Educational Facilities Lighting, RP-3, IES, 1988.
Graves, Ben E. *School Ways: Design of Public Schools*. McGraw-Hill, 1992.

HEALTH CARE

American Association
of Homes for the Aging (AAHA)
901 E St. NW, Suite 500
Washington, DC 20004-2037
Tel: (202) 783-2242

American Hospital Association (AHA)
840 North Lake Shore Drive
Chicago, IL 60611
Tel: (312) 280-6000

American Society for Hospital Engineering
840 N. Lakeshore Drive
Chicago, IL 60611
Tel: (312) 280-5223

Forum for Health Care Planning
2111 Wilson Blvd, Suite 8500
Arlington, VA 22201
Tel: (203) 516-6192

U.S. Department of Health and Human Services
Division of Health Facilities Planning
5600 Fishers Lane, Room 17A10
Parklawn Building
Rockville, MD 20857
Tel: (301) 443-2265

U.S. Veterans Administration Architectural Service
(USVA/AS)
810 Vermont Avenue
Washington, DC 20420
Tel: (202) 233-3738

REFERENCES

AIA Committee on Architecture for Health with the U.S. Department of Health and Human Services. *Guidelines for Construction and Equipment of Hospital and Medical Facilities: 1992-93 ed*. Washington, D.C.: AIA Press, 1993.
Health Care Facilities, CP-29, IES, 1985.
Health Facilities Review, 1992-93. Washington, D.C.: AIA Press, 1993.

ECCLESIASTICAL

Interfaith Forum on
Religion, Art and Architecture (IFRAA)
1777 Church Street, N.W.
Washington, DC 20036
Tel: (202) 387-8333

REFERENCES

Burckhhardt, T. *Art of Islam: Language and Meaning*. London: 1976.
Hoag, J. D. *Islamic Architecture*. New York, 1977.
Lighting for Houses of Worship, CP-21, IES, 1992.
Mitchell, G., ed. *Architecture of the Islamic World*. London, 1978.
Papadopoul, A. *Islam and Muslim Art*, Abrams, 1976.
Sevcenko, M. B., ed. *Theories and Principles of Design in the Architecture of Islamic Societies*. AKPIA, Cambridge, Mass.: 1988.

DETENTION

American Correctional Association (ACA)
8025 Laurel Lake Court
Laurel, MD 20707
Tel: (301) 206-5100

American Jail Association (AJA)
2053 Day Road, Suite 100
Hagerstown, MD 21740
Tel: (301) 790-3930

Community Research Association
41 East University Blvd., Suite 302
Champaign, IL 61820
Tel: (217) 398-3120

Federal Bureau of Prisons
Facilities Development Division (FBP/FDD)
320 First Street, N.W., Room 5008
Washington, DC 20534
Tel: (202) 514-6460

National Criminal Justice Reference Service
PO Box 6000
Rockville, MD 20850
Tel: (800) 851-3420

National Institute of Corrections, US Department of Justice
(NIC/USDJ)
1860 Industrial Circle, Suite A
Longmont, CO 80501
Tel: (303) 682-0213

REFERENCES

AIA Committee on Architecture for Justice. *Justice Facilities Review, 1992-93*. Washington, D.C.: AIA Press, 1993.

ASSEMBLY

League of Historic American Theaters (LHAT)
1511 K St., N.W., Suite 923
Washington, DC 20005
Tel: (202) 783-6966

National Endowment for the Arts
1100 Pennsylvania Ave., N.W.
Washington, DC 20506
Tel: (202) 682-5400

US Institute for Theater Technology (USITT)
10 West 19th St., Suite 5A
New York, NY 10011-4206
Tel: (212) 924-9088

REFERENCES

Lighting for Theatrical Presentations on Educational and Community Proscenium-Type Stages, IES, 1983.
Lubman, D. and E. Wetherill. *Acoustics of Worship Spaces*. Acoustical Society of America (ASA), 1985.
McCue, E. and R. Talaske. *Acoustical Design of Music Educational Facilities*. ASA, 1990.
Stage Lighting—A Guide to the Planning of Theatre and Public Building Auditoriums, CP-45. IES, 1983.
Talaske, R., et al. *Halls for Music Performance*. ASA, 1982.
Talaske, R. and R Boner, eds. *Theatres for Drama Performance*. ASA, 1987.

GREENHOUSES

American Association of Nurserymen
1250 I. Street, N.W., Suite 500
Washington, DC 20005
Tel: (202) 789-2900
Fax:(202) 789-1893

National Greenhouse Manufacturers Association
6 Honeybee Lane
P.O. Box 1350
Taylors, SC 29687
Tel: (803) 244-3854

WASTE MANAGEMENT

National Solid Waste Management Association
1730 Rhode Island Avenue, N.W., Suite 1000
Washington, DC 20036
Tel: (202) 659-4613
Fax:(202) 775-5917

APPENDIX

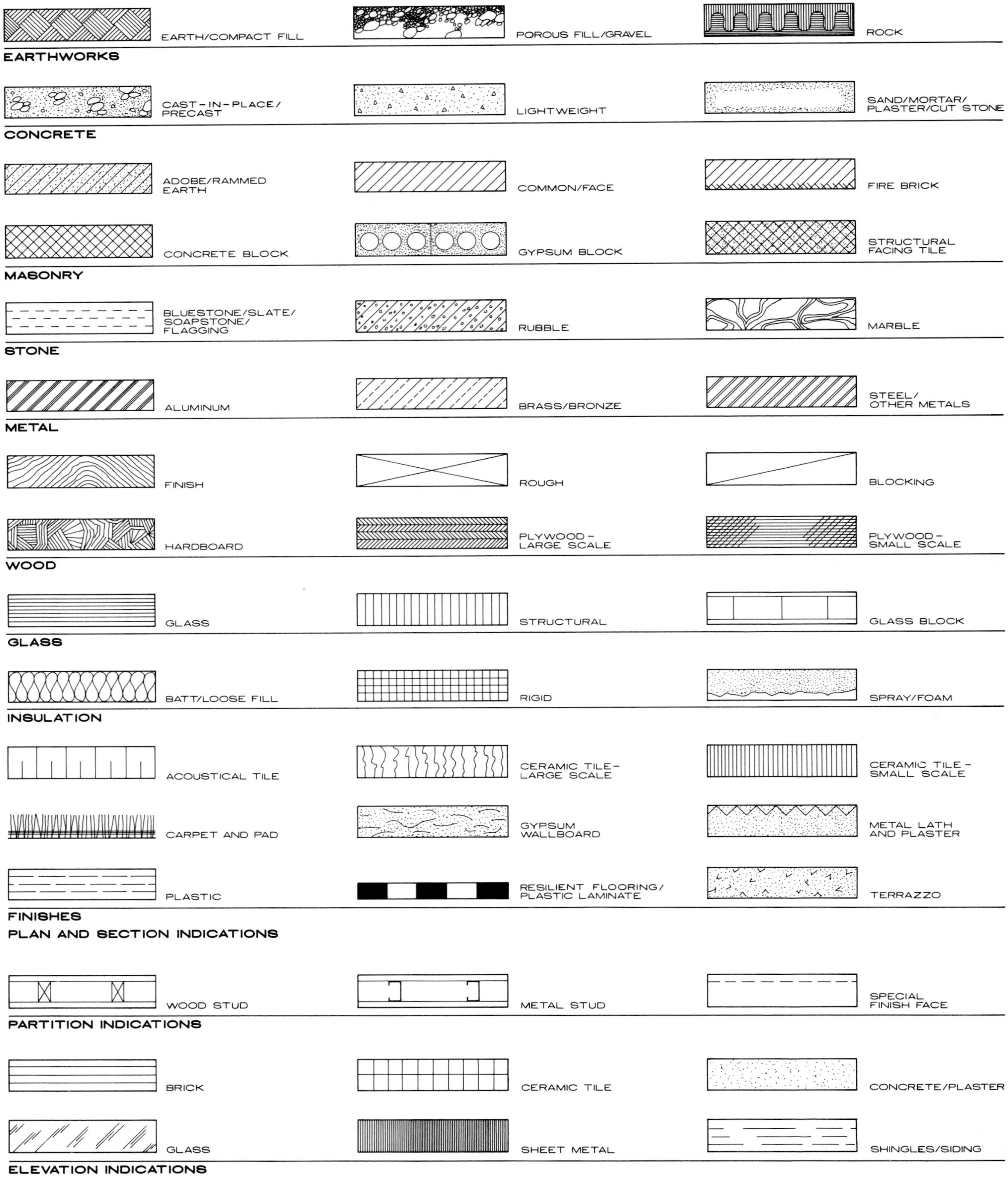

EARTH/COMPACT FILL   POROUS FILL/GRAVEL   ROCK

EARTHWORKS

CAST-IN-PLACE/PRECAST   LIGHTWEIGHT   SAND/MORTAR/PLASTER/CUT STONE

CONCRETE

ADOBE/RAMMED EARTH   COMMON/FACE   FIRE BRICK

CONCRETE BLOCK   GYPSUM BLOCK   STRUCTURAL FACING TILE

MASONRY

BLUESTONE/SLATE/SOAPSTONE/FLAGGING   RUBBLE   MARBLE

STONE

ALUMINUM   BRASS/BRONZE   STEEL/OTHER METALS

METAL

FINISH   ROUGH   BLOCKING

HARDBOARD   PLYWOOD-LARGE SCALE   PLYWOOD-SMALL SCALE

WOOD

GLASS   STRUCTURAL   GLASS BLOCK

GLASS

BATT/LOOSE FILL   RIGID   SPRAY/FOAM

INSULATION

ACOUSTICAL TILE   CERAMIC TILE-LARGE SCALE   CERAMIC TILE-SMALL SCALE

CARPET AND PAD   GYPSUM WALLBOARD   METAL LATH AND PLASTER

PLASTIC   RESILIENT FLOORING/PLASTIC LAMINATE   TERRAZZO

FINISHES

PLAN AND SECTION INDICATIONS

WOOD STUD   METAL STUD   SPECIAL FINISH FACE

PARTITION INDICATIONS

BRICK   CERAMIC TILE   CONCRETE/PLASTER

GLASS   SHEET METAL   SHINGLES/SIDING

ELEVATION INDICATIONS

John Ray Hoke, Jr., FAIA; Washington D.C.

 GRAPHIC SYMBOLS

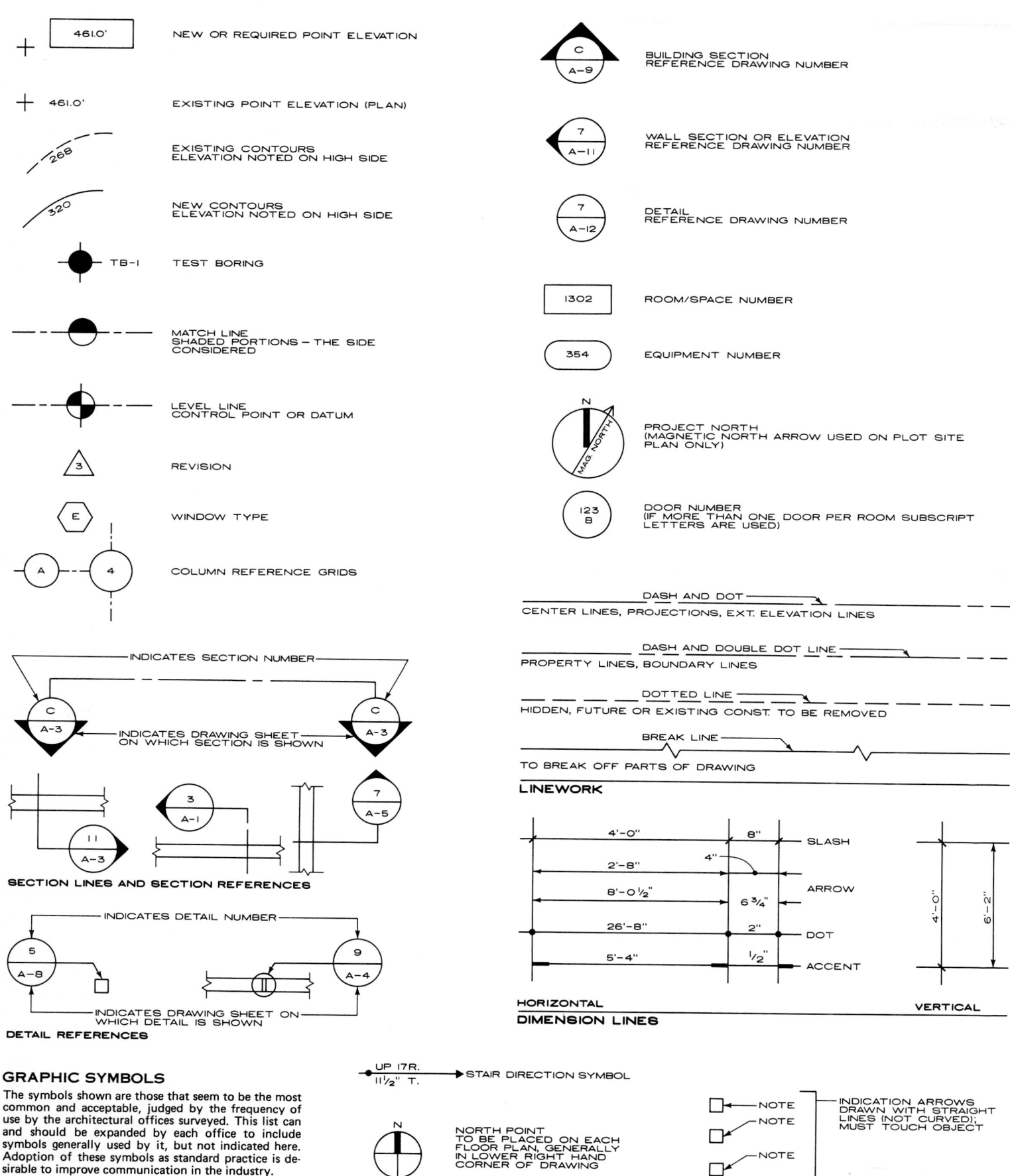

461.0'   NEW OR REQUIRED POINT ELEVATION

461.0'   EXISTING POINT ELEVATION (PLAN)

268   EXISTING CONTOURS
ELEVATION NOTED ON HIGH SIDE

320   NEW CONTOURS
ELEVATION NOTED ON HIGH SIDE

TB-1   TEST BORING

MATCH LINE
SHADED PORTIONS – THE SIDE
CONSIDERED

LEVEL LINE
CONTROL POINT OR DATUM

3   REVISION

E   WINDOW TYPE

A   4   COLUMN REFERENCE GRIDS

INDICATES SECTION NUMBER

C
A-3

C
A-3

INDICATES DRAWING SHEET
ON WHICH SECTION IS SHOWN

11
A-3

3
A-1

7
A-5

SECTION LINES AND SECTION REFERENCES

INDICATES DETAIL NUMBER

5
A-8

9
A-4

INDICATES DRAWING SHEET ON
WHICH DETAIL IS SHOWN

DETAIL REFERENCES

C
A-9   BUILDING SECTION
REFERENCE DRAWING NUMBER

7
A-11   WALL SECTION OR ELEVATION
REFERENCE DRAWING NUMBER

7
A-12   DETAIL
REFERENCE DRAWING NUMBER

1302   ROOM/SPACE NUMBER

354   EQUIPMENT NUMBER

N   PROJECT NORTH
(MAGNETIC NORTH ARROW USED ON PLOT SITE
PLAN ONLY)

123
B   DOOR NUMBER
(IF MORE THAN ONE DOOR PER ROOM SUBSCRIPT
LETTERS ARE USED)

DASH AND DOT
CENTER LINES, PROJECTIONS, EXT. ELEVATION LINES

DASH AND DOUBLE DOT LINE
PROPERTY LINES, BOUNDARY LINES

DOTTED LINE
HIDDEN, FUTURE OR EXISTING CONST. TO BE REMOVED

BREAK LINE
TO BREAK OFF PARTS OF DRAWING

LINEWORK

4'-0"	8"	SLASH
2'-8"	4"	
8'-0 1/2"	6 3/4"	ARROW
26'-8"	2"	DOT
5'-4"	1/2"	ACCENT

4'-0"   6'-2"

HORIZONTAL   **VERTICAL**
DIMENSION LINES

GRAPHIC SYMBOLS

The symbols shown are those that seem to be the most common and acceptable, judged by the frequency of use by the architectural offices surveyed. This list can and should be expanded by each office to include symbols generally used by it, but not indicated here. Adoption of these symbols as standard practice is desirable to improve communication in the industry.

John Ray Hoke, Jr., FAIA; Washington D.C.

UP 17R.
11 1/2" T.   STAIR DIRECTION SYMBOL

N
NORTH POINT
TO BE PLACED ON EACH
FLOOR PLAN, GENERALLY
IN LOWER RIGHT HAND
CORNER OF DRAWING

NOTE
NOTE
NOTE

INDICATION ARROWS
DRAWN WITH STRAIGHT
LINES (NOT CURVED);
MUST TOUCH OBJECT

GRAPHIC SYMBOLS   A

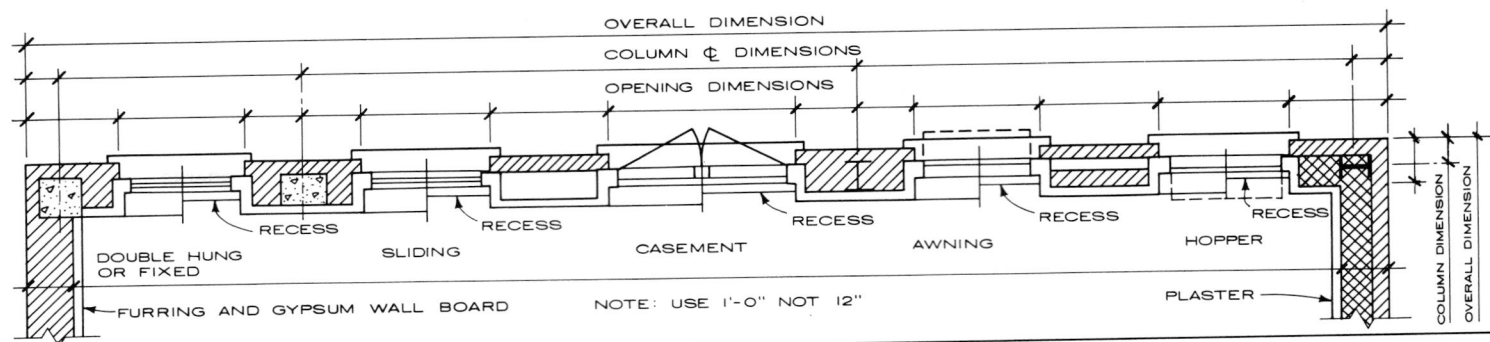

METHOD FOR DIMENSIONING EXTERIOR WINDOW OPENINGS IN MASONRY WALLS (DOORS SIMILAR)

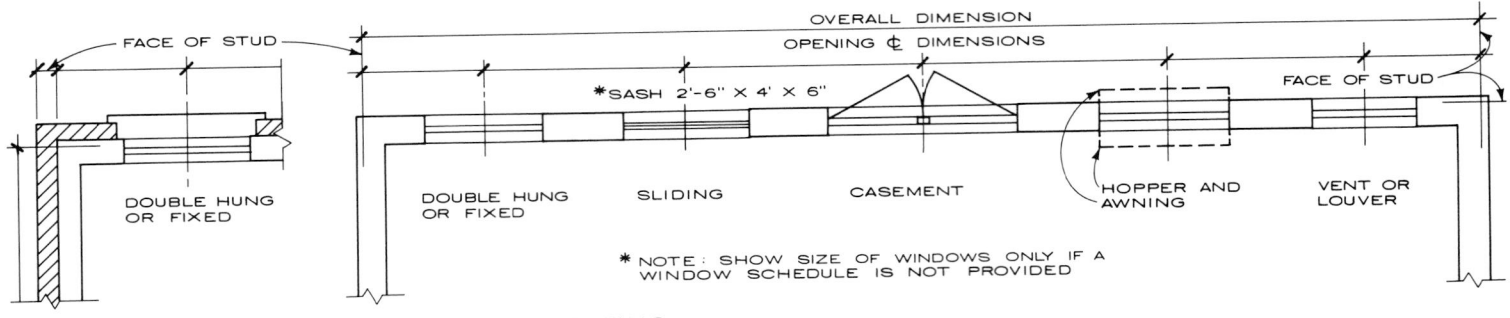

METHOD FOR DIMENSIONING EXTERIOR WINDOW OPENINGS IN FRAME WALLS (DOORS SIMILAR)

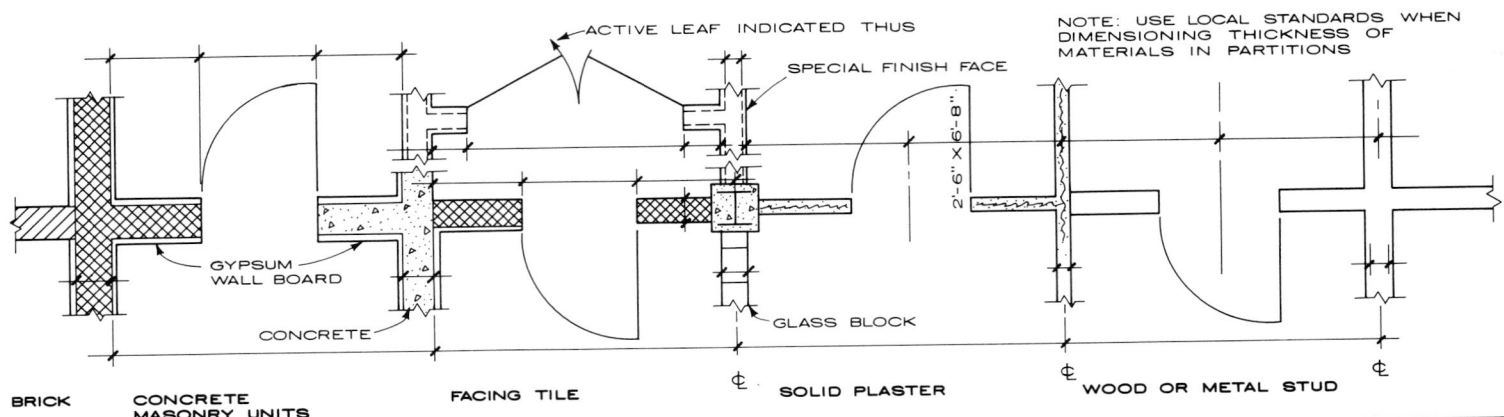

METHOD FOR DIMENSIONING AND INDICATIONS OF INTERIOR PARTITIONS AND DOORS

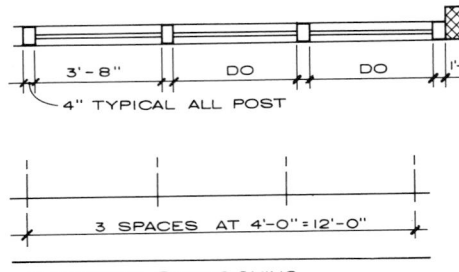

REPETITIVE DIMENSIONING

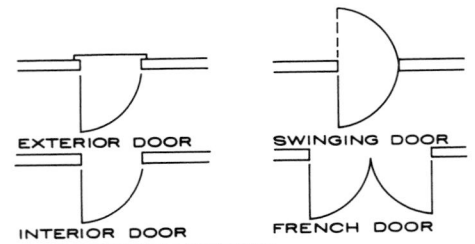

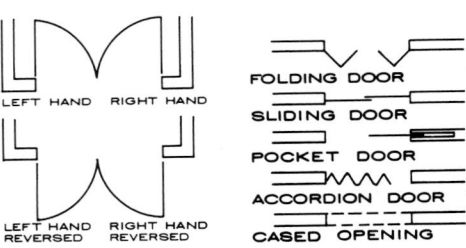

GENERAL NOTES

Dimensioning should start with critical dimensions and should be kept to a minimum. Consideration must be given to the trades using them and the sequencing adjusted to their respective work. It is also necessary to bear in mind that tolerances in actual construction will be varied. This means that as-built dimensions do not always coincide with design dimensions. Dimensioning from established grids or structural elements, such as columns and structural walls, assists the trades that must locate their work prior to that of others.

John Ray Hoke, Jr., FAIA; Washington D.C.

RECOMMENDATIONS

1. Dimensions under 1 ft shall be noted in inches. Dimensions 1 ft and over shall be expressed in feet.
2. Fractions under 1 in. shall NOT be preceded by a zero. Fractions must have a diagonal dividing line between numerator and denominator.
3. Dimension points to be noted with a short blunt 45° line. Dash to be oriented differently for vertical (✳) and horizontal (✳) runs of dimensions. Modular dimension points may be designated with an arrow or a dot.
4. Dimension all items from an established grid or reference point and do not close the string of dimensions to the next grid or reference point.
5. Dimension: to face of concrete or masonry work; to centerlines of columns or other grid points; to centerlines of partitions. In nonmodular wood construction dimension to critical face of studs. When a clear dimension is required, dimension to the finish faces and note as such. Do not use the word "clear."
6. Dimension as much as possible from structural elements.
7. Overall readability, conciseness, completeness, and accuracy must be foremost in any dimensional system. It takes experience to determine how to use dimensions to the best advantage.

GRAPHIC SYMBOLS

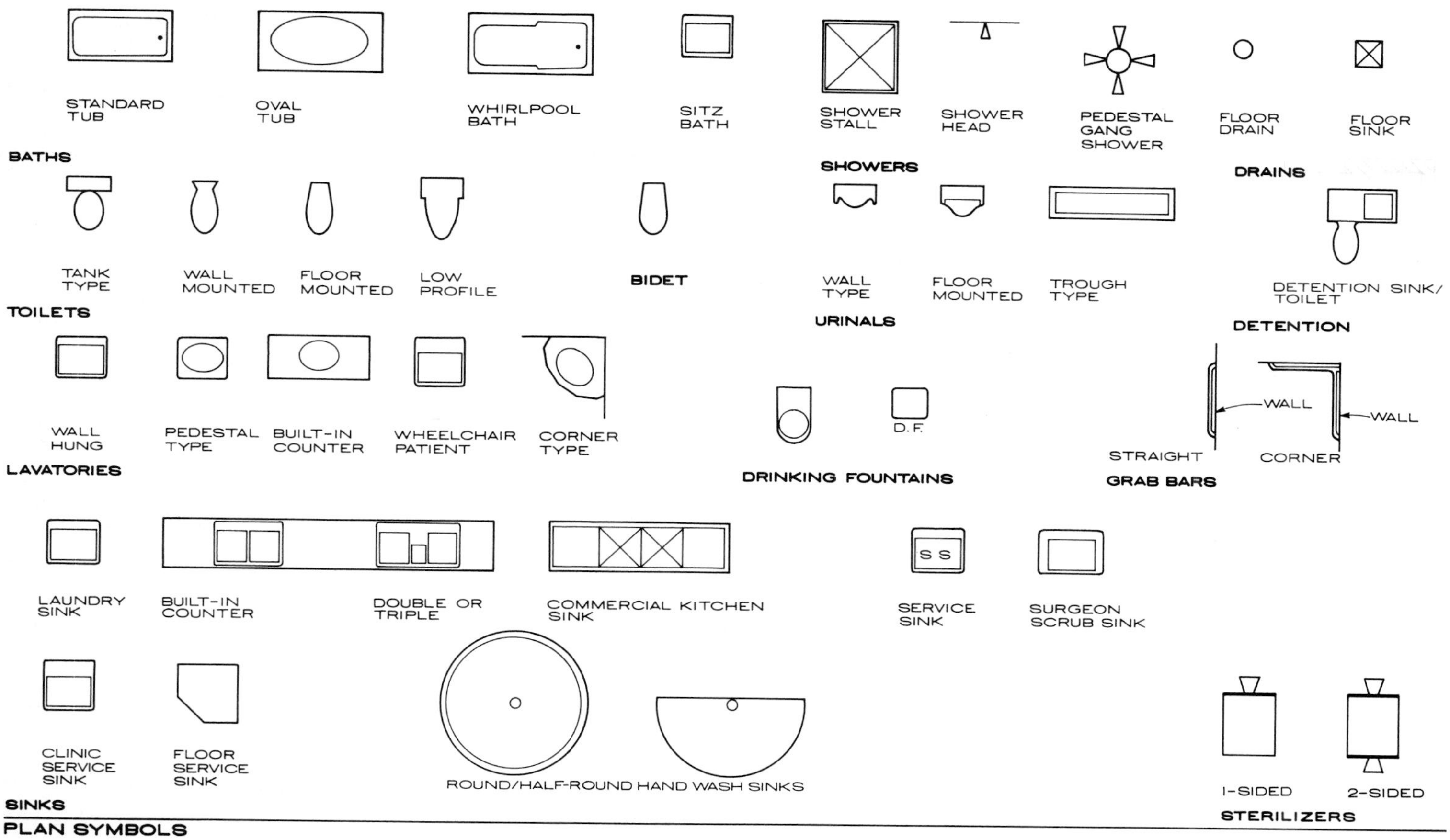

BATHS

STANDARD TUB | OVAL TUB | WHIRLPOOL BATH | SITZ BATH

SHOWERS

SHOWER STALL | SHOWER HEAD | PEDESTAL GANG SHOWER | FLOOR DRAIN | FLOOR SINK

DRAINS

TOILETS

TANK TYPE | WALL MOUNTED | FLOOR MOUNTED | LOW PROFILE | BIDET

URINALS

WALL TYPE | FLOOR MOUNTED | TROUGH TYPE | DETENTION SINK/ TOILET

DETENTION

LAVATORIES

WALL HUNG | PEDESTAL TYPE | BUILT-IN COUNTER | WHEELCHAIR PATIENT | CORNER TYPE

DRINKING FOUNTAINS

D.F.

GRAB BARS

STRAIGHT | CORNER | WALL | WALL

SINKS

LAUNDRY SINK | BUILT-IN COUNTER | DOUBLE OR TRIPLE | COMMERCIAL KITCHEN SINK | SERVICE SINK | SURGEON SCRUB SINK

CLINIC SERVICE SINK | FLOOR SERVICE SINK | ROUND/HALF-ROUND HAND WASH SINKS

STERILIZERS

1-SIDED | 2-SIDED

PLAN SYMBOLS

LEVEL OF COIN SLOT

FLOOR LINE

SANITARY NAPKIN— TAMPON DISPENSER | 3'-4" | SANITARY NAPKIN DISPOSAL UNIT | 2'-4" | GRAB BAR | 2'-9" | PARTITION AT TOILET | 4'-10" | 1'-0" | PARTITION AT URINAL | 3'-6" | 1'-6" | FRAMED MIRROR WITH SHELF | VARIES | 3'-4" HANDICAPPED

MOP HOLDER | 5'-6" | PAPER TOWEL DISPENSER | 3'-4" | MOP RECEPTOR FAUCET | 2'-6" | ROBE HOOK | 5'-8" | 4'-0" HANDICAPPED | SHOWER ROD | 6'-6" | SHOWER HEAD | 4'-0" HANDICAPPED | 6'-7" | SOAP DISPENSER SOAP DISH SOAP DISH/GRAB BAR | 3'-4"

FLOOR LINE

TOILET SEAT COVER DISPENSER | 3'-4" | TOWEL DISPENSER/ WASTE RECEPTACLE | 3'-4" | TOILET PAPER HOLDER | 2'-0" | URINAL (ADULT) | 2'-0" | 1'-5" HANDICAPPED | CHALKBOARD TACKBOARD | VARIES ± 4'-0" | ELECTRIC WATER COOLER | 2'-3" | 2'-9" TO BUBBLER | LAVATORY | 2'-5"

FLOOR LINE

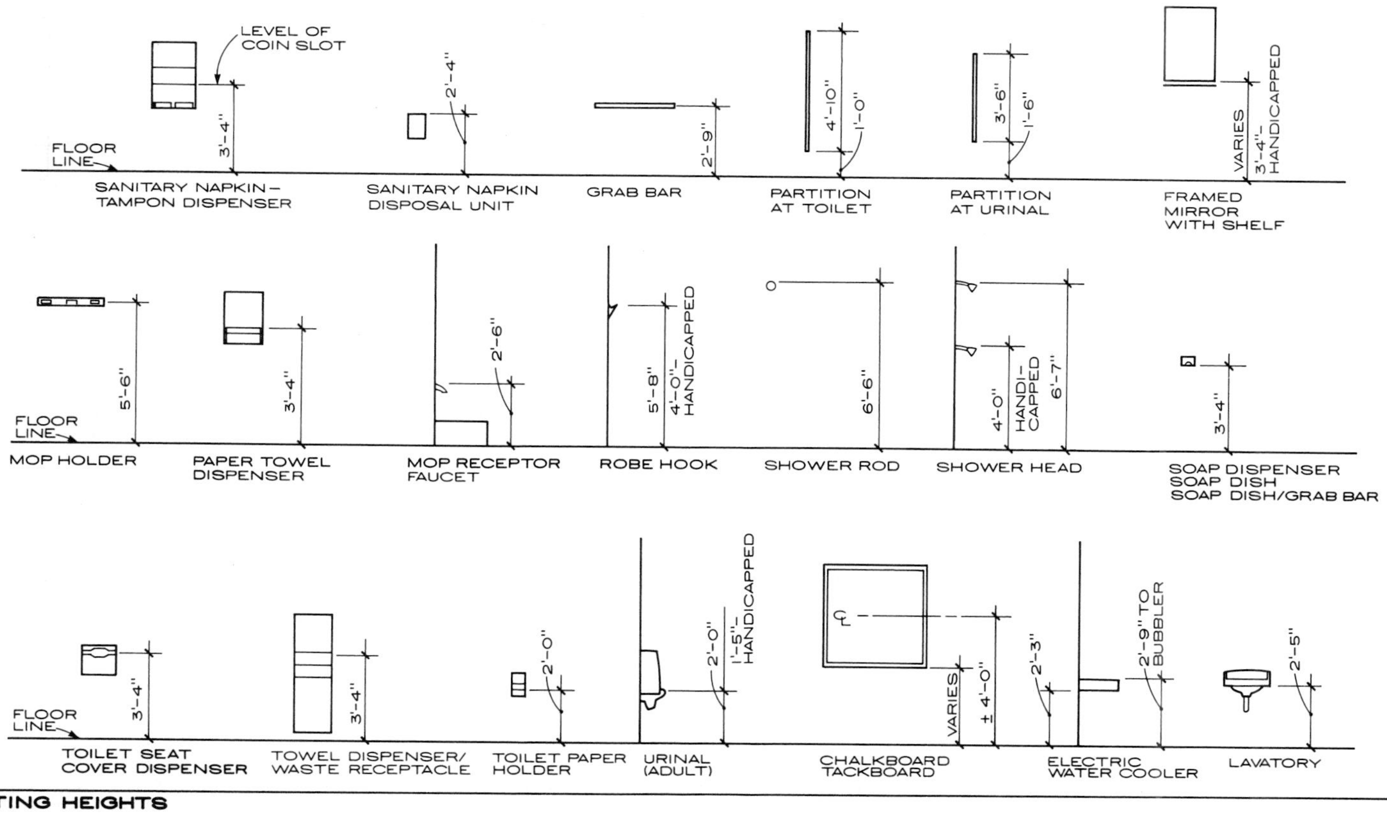

MOUNTING HEIGHTS

Dale Switzer, AIA; Hope Architects & Engineers; San Diego, California

GRAPHIC SYMBOLS

INSTITUTIONAL COMMERCIAL AND INDUSTRIAL OCCUPANCIES

NURSES CALL SYSTEM DEVICES. (ANY TYPE)

PAGING SYSTEM DEVICES (ANY TYPE)

FIRE ALARM SYSTEM DEVICES (ANY TYPE)

STAFF REGISTER SYSTEM (ANY TYPE)

ELECTRICAL CLOCK SYSTEM DEVICES (ANY TYPE)

COMPUTER DATA SYSTEM DEVICES

PRIVATE TELEPHONE SYSTEM DEVICES

WATCHMAN SYSTEM DEVICES

SOUND SYSTEM

FACP — FIRE ALARM CONTROL PANEL

SC — SIGNAL CENTRAL STATION

CR — CARD READER

AUXILIARY SYSTEM CIRCUITS
Any line without further designation indicates two-wire system. For a greater number of wires, designate with numerals in manner similar to: 12- no. 18W - ¾" C. Designate by numbers corresponding to listing in schedule.

A,B,C, ETC. — SPECIAL AUXILIARY OUTLETS
Subscript lettering refers to notes on drawings or detailed description in specifications.

PANELBOARDS

FLUSH MOUNTED PANELBOARD AND CABINET

SURFACE – MOUNTED PANELBOARD AND CABINET

BUSDUCTS AND WIREWAYS

T T T — TROLLEY DUCT

B B B — BUSWAY (SERVICE, FEEDER OR PLUG-IN)

C C C — CABLE THROUGH LADDER OR CHANNEL

W W W — WIREWAY

SIGNALING SYSTEM OUTLETS RESIDENTIAL OCCUPANCIES

• PUSH BUTTON

BUZZER

BELL

BELL AND BUZZER COMBINATION

ANNUNCIATOR

COMPUTER DATA OUTLET

INTERCONNECTING TELEPHONE

TELEPHONE SWITCHBOARD

BT — BELL RINGING TRANSFORMER

D — ELECTRIC DOOR OPENER

CH — CHIME

TV — TELEVISION OUTLET

T — THERMOSTAT

UNDERGROUND ELECTRICAL DISTRIBUTION OR LIGHTING SYSTEM

M — MANHOLE

H — HANDHOLE

TM — TRANSFORMER- MANHOLE OR VAULT

TP — TRANSFORMER PAD

UNDERGROUND DIRECT BURIAL CABLE

UNDERGROUND DUCT LINE

STREET LIGHT STANDARD FED FROM UNDERGROUND CIRCUIT

ELECTRICAL DISTRIBUTION OR LIGHTING SYSTEM, AERIAL

POLE

STREET LIGHT AND BRACKET

TRANSFORMER

PRIMARY CIRCUIT

SECONDARY CIRCUIT

DOWN GUY

HEAD GUY

SIDEWALK GUY

SERVICE WEATHER

PANELS CIRCUITS AND MISCELLANEOUS

LIGHTING PANEL

POWER PANEL

WIRING, CONCEALED IN CEILING OR WALL

WIRING, CONCEALED IN FLOOR

WIRING EXPOSED

HOME RUN TO PANEL BOARD.
Indicate number of circuits by number of arrows. Any circuit without such designation indicates a two-wire circuit. For a greater number of wires indicate as follows: /// (3 wires) //// (4 wires), etc.

FEEDERS
Use heavy lines and designate by number corresponding to listing in feeder schedule.

WIRING TURNED UP

WIRING TURNED DOWN

G — GENERATOR

M — MOTOR

I — INSTRUMENT (SPECIFY)

T — TRANSFORMER (OR DRAW TO SCALE)

CONTROLLER

EXTERNALLY OPERATED DISCONNECT SWITCH

PULL BOX

Frederick R. Brown, PE; Ayres, Cohen and Hayakawa, Consulting Engineers; Los Angeles/San Francisco, California
Richard F. Humenn, PE; Joseph R. Loring & Associates, Inc., Consulting Engineers; New York, New York

 GRAPHIC SYMBOLS

LIGHTING OUTLETS

CEILING, WALL

○ —○ OUTLET BOX AND INCANDESCENT LIGHTING FIXTURE. SLASH INDICATES FIXTURE ON EMERGENCY SERVICE

▭ ▭ INCANDESCENT LIGHTING TRACK

Ⓑ —Ⓑ BLANKED OUTLET

Ⓓ DROP CORD

⊗ —⊗ EXIT LIGHT AND OUTLET BOX, DIRECTIONAL ARROWS AS INDICATED. SHADED AREAS DENOTE FACES

○—•—○ OUTDOOR POLE ARM MOUNTED FIXTURES

Ⓙ —Ⓙ JUNCTION BOX

Ⓛ —Ⓛ LAMP HOLDER WITH PULL SWITCH

ⵉⵉⵉ MULTIPLE FLOODLIGHT ASSEMBLY

EMERGENCY BATTERY PACK WITH CHARGER AND SEALED BEAM HEADS

REMOTE EMERGENCY SEALED BEAM HEAD WITH OUTLET BOX

Ⓛ —Ⓛ OUTLET CONTROLLED BY LOW VOLTAGE SWITCHING WHEN RELAY IS INSTALLED IN OUTLET BOX

INDIVIDUAL FLUORESCENT FIXTURE. SLASH INDICATES FIXTURE ON EMERGENCY SERVICE

⊢—⊣ OUTLET BOX AND FLUORESCENT LIGHTING STRIP FIXTURE

▭▭▭ CONTINUOUS ROW FLUORESCENT FIXTURE

SURFACE-MOUNTED FLUORESCENT

RECEPTACLE OUTLETS

—⊝ SINGLE RECEPTACLE OUTLET

⊜ DUPLEX RECEPTACLE OUTLET

⊕ TRIPLEX RECEPTACLE OUTLET

⊕ QUADRUPLEX RECEPTACLE OUTLET

⊜ DUPLEX RECEPTACLE OUTLET-SPLIT WIRED

⊜ TRIPLEX RECEPTACLE OUTLET-SPLIT WIRED

—△ SINGLE SPECIAL PURPOSE RECEPTACLE OUTLET

—△ DUPLEX SPECIAL PURPOSE RECEPTACLE OUTLET

⊜ R RANGE OUTLET

—▲ DW SPECIAL PURPOSE CONNECTION

CLOSED CIRCUIT TELEVISION CAMERA

—Ⓒ CLOCK HANGER RECEPTACLE

Ⓕ FAN HANGER RECEPTACLE

⊡ FLOOR SINGLE RECEPTACLE OUTLET

⊡ FLOOR DUPLEX RECEPTACLE OUTLET

△ FLOOR SPECIAL PURPOSE OUTLET

▣ DATA OUTLET IN FLOOR

▣ FLOOR TELEPHONE OUTLET-PRIVATE

UNDERFLOOR DUCT AND JUNCTION BOX FOR TRIPLE, DOUBLE, OR SINGLE DUCT SYSTEM AS INDICATED BY NUMBER OF PARALLEL LINES

CELLULAR FLOOR HEADER DUCT

SWITCH OUTLETS

S SINGLE POLE SWITCH

S_2 DOUBLE POLE SWITCH

S_3 THREE-WAY SWITCH

S_4 FOUR-WAY SWITCH

S_D AUTOMATIC DOOR SWITCH

S_K KEY OPERATED SWITCH

S_P SWITCH AND PILOT LAMP

S_{CB} CIRCUIT BREAKER

S_{WCB} WEATHERPROOF CIRCUIT BREAKER

S_{DM} DIMMER

S_{RC} REMOTE CONTROL SWITCH

S_{WP} WEATHERPROOF SWITCH

S_F FUSED SWITCH

S_{WF} WEATHERPROOF FUSED SWITCH

S_L SWITCH FOR LOW VOLTAGE SWITCHING SYSTEM

S_{LM} MASTER SWITCH FOR LOW VOLTAGE SWITCHING SYSTEM

S_T TIME SWITCH

Ⓢ CEILING PULL SWITCH

⊝$_S$ SWITCH AND SINGLE RECEPTACLE

⊜$_S$ SWITCH AND DOUBLE RECEPTACLE

○ A,B,C ETC.

⊜ A,B,C ETC. } SPECIAL OUTLETS

S A,B,C ETC.

Any standard symbol given above with the addition of lowercase subscript lettering may be used to designate some special variation of standard equipment of particular interest in a specific set of architectural plans.

When used they must be listed in the schedule of symbols on each drawing and if necessary further described in the specifications.

Frederick R. Brown, PE; Ayres, Cohen and Hayakawa, Consulting Engineers; Los Angeles/San Francisco, California
Richard F. Humenn, PE; Joseph R. Loring & Associates, Inc., Consulting Engineers; New York, New York

GRAPHIC SYMBOLS

HEATING AND VENTILATING SYMBOLS

HEAT TRANSFER SURFACE, PLAN	
EXPOSED RADIATOR	
RECESSED RADIATOR	
ENCLOSED RADIATOR FLUSH	
ENCLOSED RADIATOR PROJECTING	
UNIT HEATER (PROPELLER), PLAN	
UNIT HEATER (CENTRIFUGAL) PLAN	
UNIT VENTILATOR, PLAN	
STEAM (INDICATE TYPE)	F & T
BLAST THERMOSTATIC TRAP	
FLOW METER, VENTURI	VFM
STRAINER, DUPLEX	
REDUCING PRESSURE VALVE	
AIR LINE VALVE	
LOCK SHIELD VALVE	
DIAPHRAGM VALVE	OR
AIR ELIMINATOR VALVE	
STRAINER	
THERMOMETER	
PRESSURE GAUGE AND COCK	
RELIEF VALVE	

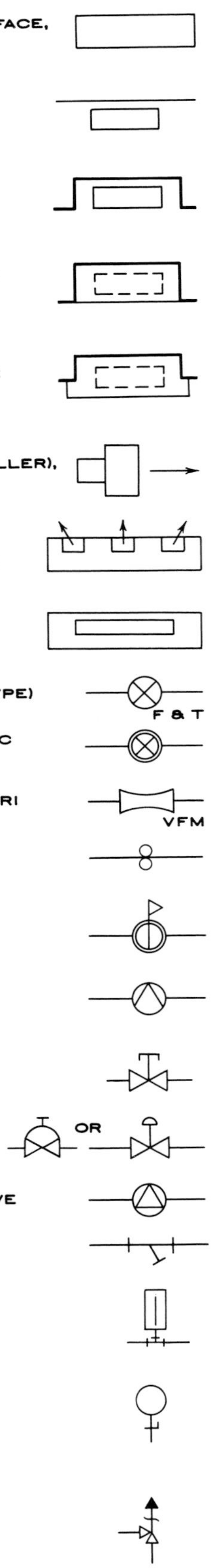

HEATING AND VENTILATING (CONT.)

AUTOMATIC AIR VENT	AV
AUTOMATIC 3-WAY VALVE	
AUTOMATIC 2-WAY VALVE	
SOLENOID VALVE	S
FLEXIBLE CONNECTOR	
THERMOSTAT, ELECTRIC	T
THERMOSTAT, PNEUMATIC	T

DUCTWORK SYMBOLS

DUCT (1ST FIGURE, WIDTH; 2ND, DEPTH)	12 × 20
DIRECTION OF FLOW	
INCLINED DROP IN RESPECT TO AIR FLOW	D
INCLINED RISE IN RESPECT TO AIR FLOW	R
FLEXIBLE CONNECTION	
DUCTWORK WITH ACOUSTICAL LINING	
FIRE DAMPER WITH ACCESS DOOR	FD AD
MANUAL VOLUME DAMPER	VD
AUTOMATIC VOLUME DAMPER	
EXHAUST, RETURN OR OUTSIDE AIR DUCT SECTION	20 × 12
SUPPLY DUCT SECTION	20 × 12
SUPPLY OUTLET, CEILING DIFFUSER	20" DIA. CD 1000 CFM
SUPPLY OUTLET, CEILING DIFFUSER	20 × 12 CD 700 CFM
LINEAR DIFFUSER	96 × 6 -LD 400 CFM

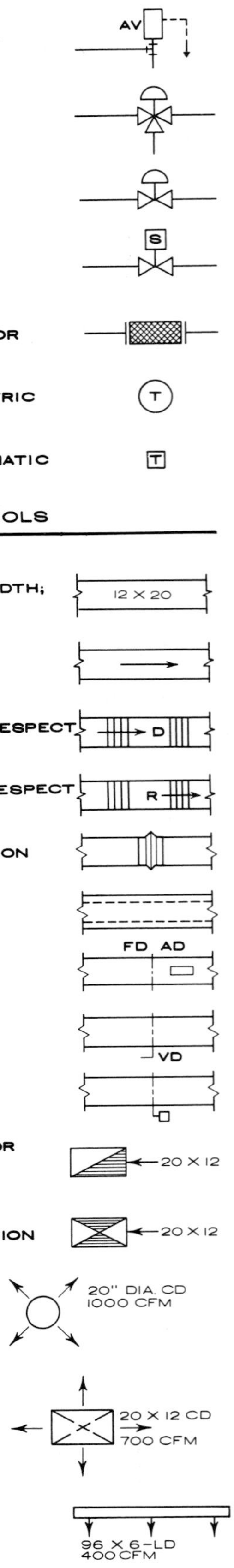

DUCTWORK (CONT.)

TOP REGISTER OR GRILLE	20 × 12 -TR 700 CFM / 20 × 12 -TG 700 CFM
CENTER REGISTER OR GRILLE	20 × 12 -CR 700 CFM / 20 × 12 -CG 700 CFM
BOTTOM REGISTER OR GRILLE	20 × 12 -BR 700 CFM / 20 × 12 -BG 700 CFM
TOP AND BOTTOM REGISTER OR GRILLE	20 × 12 -T AND BR 700 CFM EA. / 20 × 12 -T AND BG 700 CFM EA.
FLOOR REGISTER	20 × 12 FR 700 CFM
MIXING BOX	
ADJUSTABLE PLAQUE	20 × 12 - P 700 CFM / 20" φ P 700 CFM
SPLITTER DAMPER	
SPLITTER DAMPER, UP	
SPLITTER DAMPER, DOWN	
ADJUSTABLE BLANK OFF	20 × 12 TR
TURNING VANES	
FAN AND MOTOR WITH BELT GUARD	
LOUVER OPENING	20 × 12 -L 700 CFM
INTAKE LOUVERS ON SCREEN	

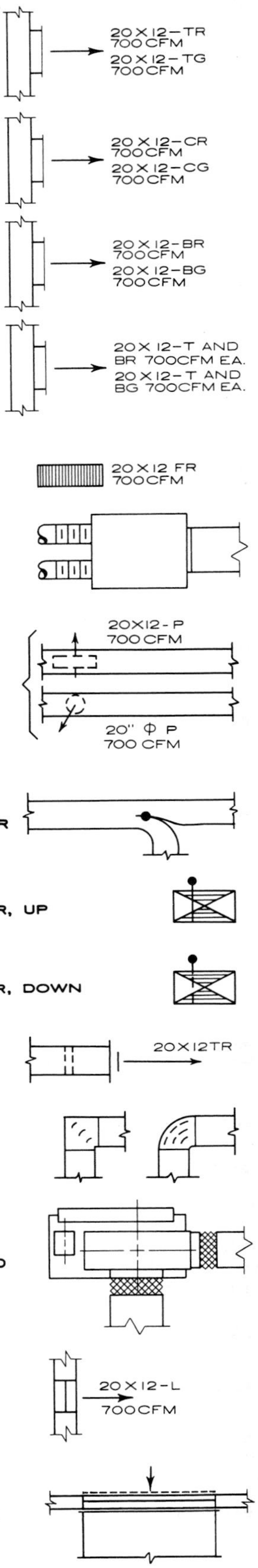

Amor Halperin, PE; Ayres, Cohen and Hayakawa, Consulting Engineers; Los Angeles/San Francisco, California
Joseph R. Loring & Associates, Inc., Consulting Engineers; New York, New York

GRAPHIC SYMBOLS

HEAT-POWER APPARATUS

STEAM GENERATOR (BOILER) .....

FLUE GAS REHEATER
(INTERMEDIATE SUPERHEATER) ..

LIVE STEAM SUPERHEATER ......
OR REHEATER

FEED HEATER WITH
AIR OUTLET ....

CONDENSER, SURFACE ....

STEAM TURBINE ....

CONDENSING TURBINE ....

OPEN TANK ....

CLOSED TANK ....

AUTOMATIC REDUCING VALVE ....

AUTOMATIC BYPASS VALVE .....

AUTOMATIC VALVE
OPERATED BY GOVERNOR ......

BOILER FEED PUMP ....

SERVICE PUMP ....

CONDENSATE PUMP ....

CIRCULATING WATER PUMP ......

AIR PUMP ....

OIL PUMP ....

RECIPROCATING PUMP ....

AIR EJECTOR
(DYNAMIC PUMP)

VACUUM TRAP ....

REFRIGERATION

THERMOSTAT, SELF-CONTAINED

THERMOSTAT, REMOTE BULB ...

PRESSURE SWITCH ....

EXPANSION VALVE, HAND.......

EXPANSION VALVE, AUTOMATIC .

EXPANSION VALVE,
THERMOSTATIC ....

EVAPORATOR PRESSURE
REGULATING VALVE,
THROTTLING TYPE
(EVAPORATOR SIDE)

EVAPORATOR PRESSURE
REGULATING VALVE,
THERMOSTATIC, THROTTLING
TYPE

EVAPORATOR PRESSURE
REGULATING VALVE
SNAP-ACTION

COMPRESSOR SUCTION VALVE,
PRESSURE LIMITING,
THROTTLING TYPE
(COMPRESSOR SIDE)

CONSTANT PRESSURE VALVE,
SUCTION

THERMAL BULB ....

SCALE TRAP ....

DRYER ....

FILTER AND STRAINER   ....

COMBINATION STRAINER
AND DRYER

SIGHT GLASS ....

FLOAT VALVE
HIGH SIDE

FLOAT VALVE
LOW SIDE

GAUGE ....

COOLING TOWER ....

EVAPORATOR,
FINNED TYPE, NATURAL
CONVECTION

EVAPORATOR,
FORCED CONVECTION ....

IMMERSION COOLING UNIT ....

CONDENSER,
AIR-COOLED,
FINNED, FORCED AIR

CONDENSER,
WATER-COOLED,
SHELL AND TUBE

CONDENSER
EVAPORATIVE

HEAT EXCHANGER

CONDENSING UNIT
AIR COOLED

CONDENSING UNIT
WATER COOLED

PRESSURE SWITCH WITH
HIGH PRESSURE CUT-OUT

COMPRESSOR

COMPRESSOR
OPEN CRANKCASE
RECIPROCATING, DIRECT
DRIVE

COMPRESSOR
OPEN CRANKCASE
RECIPROCATING BELTED

COMPRESSOR
ENCLOSED CRANKCASE,
ROTARY, BELTED

Amor Halperin, PE; Ayres, Cohen and Hayakawa, Consulting Engineers; Los Angeles/San Francisco, California

GRAPHIC SYMBOLS

PLUMBING PIPING

SOIL, WASTE OR LEADER (ABOVE GRADE)	————————
SOIL, WASTE OR LEADER (BELOW GRADE)	— — — — -
VENT	- - - - - -
COMBINATION WASTE AND VENT	——SV——
ACID WASTE	——AW——
ACID VENT	— — —AV— — —
INDIRECT DRAIN	——IW——
STORM DRAIN	——S——
COLD WATER	— - — - — -
SOFT COLD WATER	—— SW——
INDUSTRIALIZED COLD WATER	——ICW——
CHILLED DRINKING WATER SUPPLY	——DWS——
CHILLED DRINKING WATER RETURN	——DWR——
HOT WATER	— - - — - - —
HOT WATER RETURN	— - - - — - - - —
SANITIZING HOT WATER SUPPLY (180° F.)	—⧸- -⧸- -⧸
SANITIZING HOT WATER RETURN (180° F.)	—⧸- - -⧸- -
INDUSTRIALIZED HOT WATER SUPPLY	——IHW——
INDUSTRIALIZED HOT WATER RETURN	——IHR——
TEMPERED WATER SUPPLY	——TWS——
TEMPERED WATER RETURN	——TWR——
FIRE LINE	— F — F —
WET STANDPIPE	——WSP——

DRY STANDPIPE	——DSP——
COMBINATION STANDPIPE	——CSP——
MAIN SUPPLIES SPRINKLER	——S——
BRANCH AND HEAD SPRINKLER	—o——o—
GAS - LOW PRESSURE	—G——G—
GAS - MEDIUM PRESSURE	——MG——
GAS - HIGH PRESSURE	——HG——
COMPRESSED AIR	——A——
VACUUM	——V——
VACUUM CLEANING	——VC——
OXYGEN	——O——
LIQUID OXYGEN	——LOX——
NITROGEN	——N——
LIQUID NITROGEN	——LN——
NITROUS OXIDE	——NO——
HYDROGEN	——H——
HELIUM	——HE——
ARGON	——AR——
LIQUID PETROLEUM GAS	——LPG——
INDUSTRIAL WASTE	——INW——
PNEUMATIC TUBES TUBE RUNS	——PN——
CAST IRON	——CI——
CULVERT PIPE	——CP——
CLAY TILE	——CT——
DUCTILE IRON	——DI——
REINFORCED CONCRETE	——RCP——
DRAIN - OPEN TILE OR AGRICULTURAL TILE	= = = =

HEATING PIPING

HIGH PRESSURE STEAM	——HPS——
MEDIUM PRESSURE STEAM	——MPS——
LOW PRESSURE STEAM	——LPS——
HIGH PRESSURE RETURN	——HPR——
MEDIUM PRESSURE RETURN	——MPR——
LOW PRESSURE RETURN	——LPR——
BOILER BLOW OFF	——BD——
CONDENSATE OR VACUUM PUMP DISCHARGE	——VPD——
FEEDWATER PUMP DISCHARGE	——PPD——
MAKE UP WATER	——MU——
AIR RELIEF LINE	——V——
FUEL OIL SUCTION	——FOS——
FUEL OIL RETURN	——FOR——
FUEL OIL VENT	——FOV——
COMPRESSED AIR	——A——
HOT WATER HEATING SUPPLY	——HW——
HOT WATER HEATING RETURN	——HWR——

AIR CONDITIONING PIPING

REFRIGERANT LIQUID	——RL——
REFRIGERANT DISCHARGE	——RD——
REFRIGERANT SUCTION	——RS——
CONDENSER WATER SUPPLY	——CWS——
CONDENSER WATER RETURN	——CWR——
CHILLED WATER SUPPLY	——CHWS——
CHILLED WATER RETURN	——CHWR——
MAKE UP WATER	——MU——
HUMIDIFICATION LINE	——H——
DRAIN	——D——
BRINE SUPPLY	——B——
BRINE RETURN	——BR——

Amor Halperin, PE; Ayres, Cohen and Hayakawa, Consulting Engineers; Los Angeles/San Francisco, California
Joseph R. Loring & Associates, Inc., Consulting Engineers; New York, New York

 GRAPHIC SYMBOLS

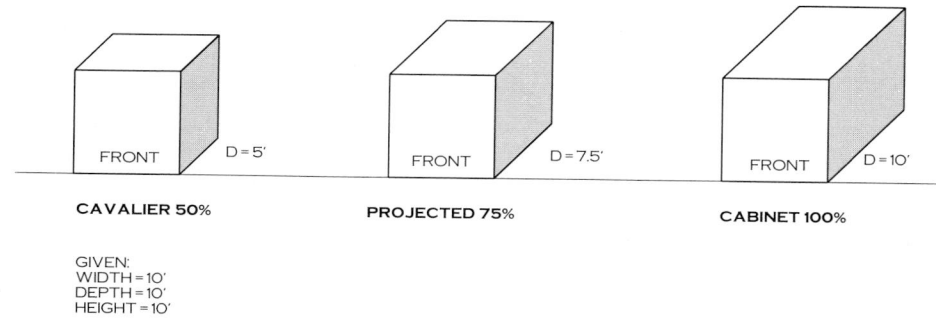

CAVALIER 50%   PROJECTED 75%   CABINET 100%

GIVEN:
WIDTH = 10'
DEPTH = 10'
HEIGHT = 10'

NOTE

If front elevation is drawn at scale, $1/4" = 1' - 0"$
Depth is $3/4 \times 1/4 = 3/16"$
Use scale: $3/16" = 1' - 0"$

OBLIQUE ELEVATION

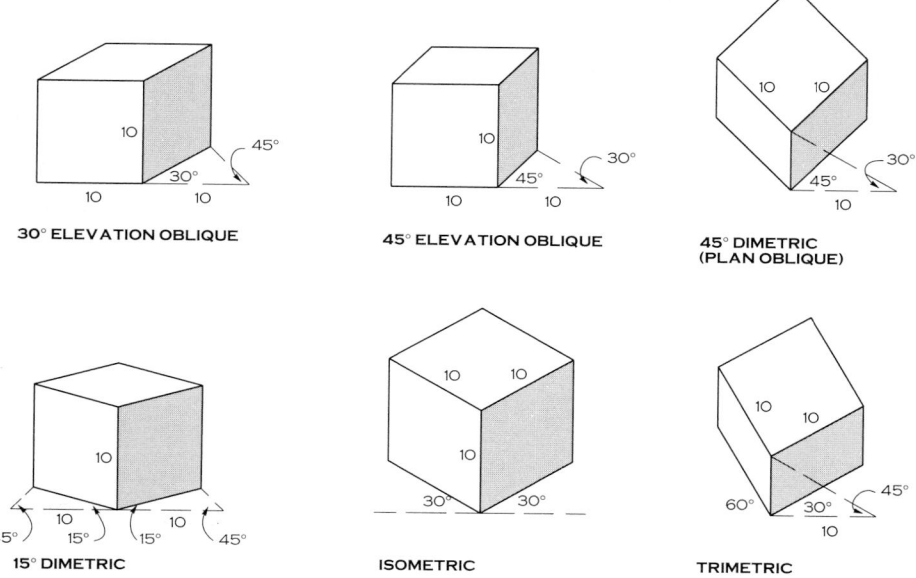

30° ELEVATION OBLIQUE   45° ELEVATION OBLIQUE   45° DIMETRIC (PLAN OBLIQUE)

15° DIMETRIC   ISOMETRIC   TRIMETRIC

AXONOMETRIC – MEASURED METHOD

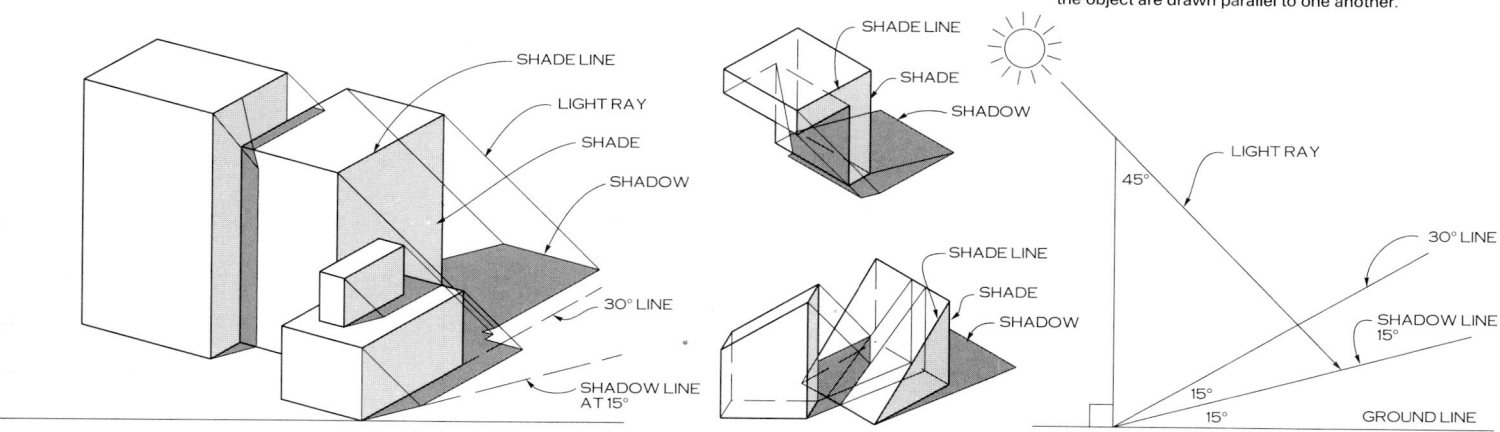

SHADE LINE
LIGHT RAY
SHADE
SHADOW
30° LINE
SHADOW LINE AT 15°

SHADE LINE
SHADE
SHADOW

SHADE LINE
SHADE
SHADOW

LIGHT RAY
30° LINE
SHADOW LINE 15°
GROUND LINE

AXONOMETRIC SHADES AND SHADOWS

PARALINE DRAWINGS

Paraline drawings are sometimes referred to as AXONO-METRIC (Greek) or AXIOMETRIC (English) drawings. These drawings are projected pictorial representations of an object which give a three-dimensional quality. They can be classified as orthographic projections in as much as the plan view is rotated and the side view is tilted. The resulting "front" view is projected at a 90° angle to the picture plane (as illustrated in the projected method). These drawings differ from perspective drawings, since the projection lines remain parallel instead of converging to a point on the horizon.

Drawings prepared using the projection method require three views of the object, which tends to be more time-consuming and complex than drawing by the direct measuring method. The following drawings utilize this method; they are simple to draw and represent reasonably accurate proportions.

OBLIQUE

In an oblique drawing one face (either plan or elevation) of the object is drawn directly on the picture plane. Projected lines are drawn at a 30 or 45° angle to the picture plane. The length of the projecting lines is determined as illustrated and varies according to the angle chosen.

DIMETRIC

A dimetric drawing is similar to oblique, with one exception: the object is rotated so that only one of its corners touches the picture plane. The most frequently used angle for the projecting lines is an equal division of 45° on either side of the leading edge. A 15° angle is sometimes used when it is less important to show the "roof view" of the object.

ISOMETRIC

The isometric, a special type of dimetric drawing, is the easiest and most popular paraline drawing. All axes of the object are simultaneously rotated away from the picture plane and kept at the same angle of projection (30° from the picture plane). All legs are equally distorted in length at a given scale and therefore maintain an exact proportion of 1:1.

TRIMETRIC

The trimetric drawing is similar to the dimetric, except that the plan of the object is rotated so that the two exposed sides of the object are not at equal angles to the picture plane. The plan is usually positioned at 30/60° angle to the ground plane. The height of the object is reduced proportionately as illustrated (similar to the 45° dimetric).

SHADES AND SHADOWS

Shades and shadows are easily constructed and can be very effective in paraline drawings. The location of the light source will determine the direction of the shadows cast by the object. The shade line is the line (or the edge) that separates the light area from the shaded areas of the object. Shadows are constructed by drawing a line, representing a light ray, from a corner of the lighted surface at a 45° angle to the ground plane. Shadows cast by a vertical edge of the object will be drawn midway in the angle created by the intersection of the projected line of the object and the ground, or baseline (the baseline represents the intersection of the picture plane). The 45° light ray is extended until it meets the shadow line (as illustrated), and this point determines the length of the shadow for any given vertical height of the object. Shadow lines of all vertical edges of the object are drawn parallel to one another.

Samuel J. De Santo and Associates; New York, New York
Alvarado Thrun Maeda and Associates; New York, New York; Eric A. Borch; Newburgh, New York

DRAWING METHODS

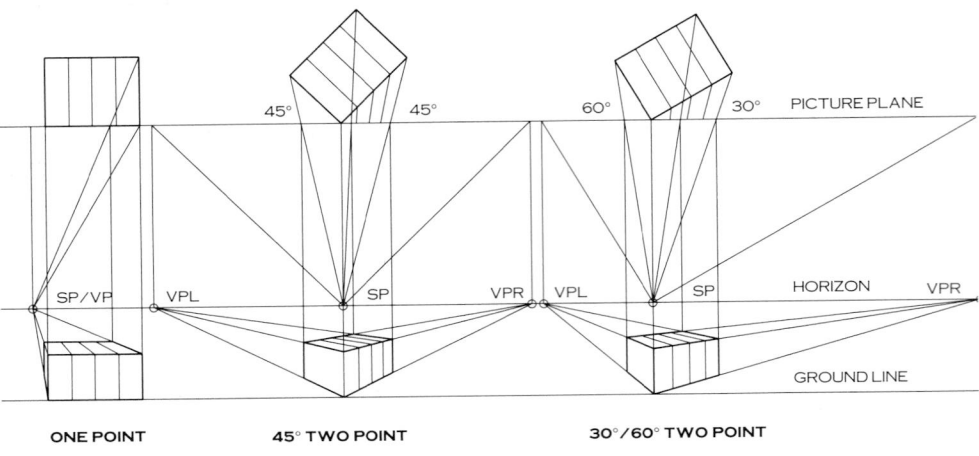

ONE POINT   45° TWO POINT   30°/60° TWO POINT

PERSPECTIVE - PROJECTION METHOD
NOTES

Before the drawing can be laid out, the following information must be obtained:

1. An approximation of the overall dimensions of the building.
2. The location of the building in relation to the picture plane.
3. The orientation of the building, either in front of or behind the picture plane.

While the building can be located anywhere in the drawing—in front of, behind, or at any angle to the picture plane - the simplest approach is to place the building at the picture plane. The horizontal lines of the building would be parallel to the picture plane in a one-point perspective or placed at an angle to the picture plane. Usually this will be a 30/60 or 45° angle in a two-point perspective.

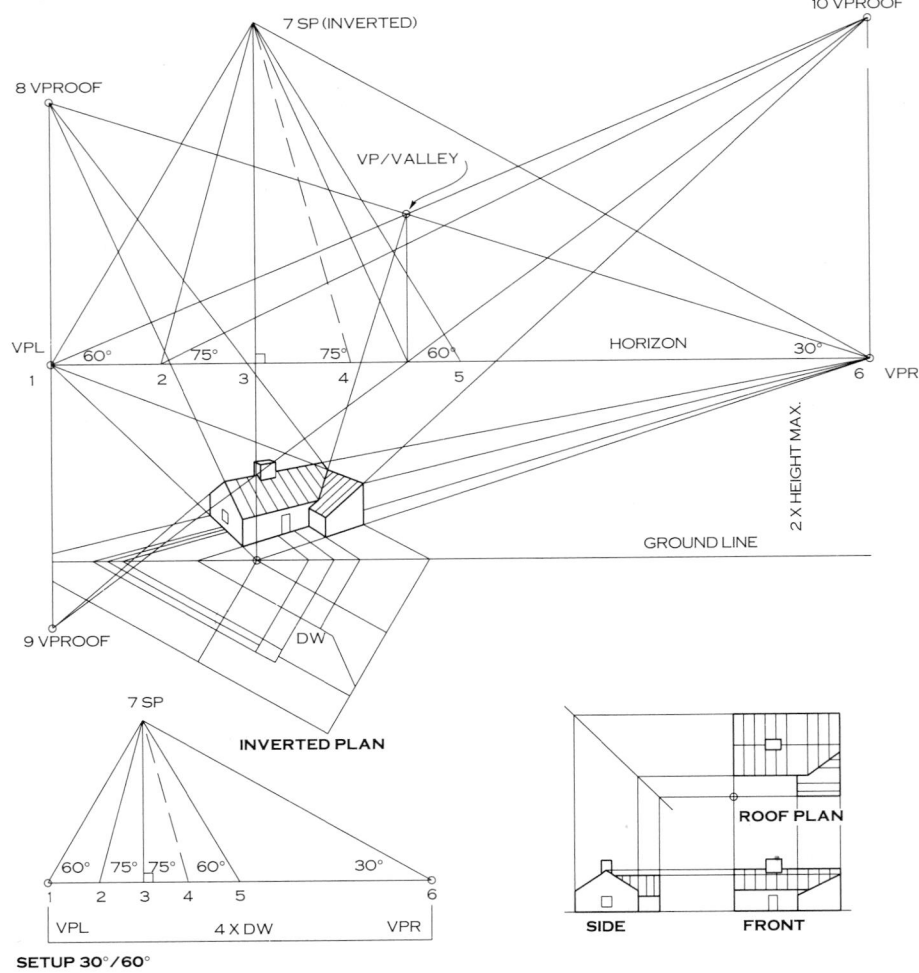

INVERTED PLAN

SETUP 30°/60°

PERSPECTIVE – TWO-POINT CONVENTIONAL METHOD

TERMS AND CONCEPTS

1. THE OBJECT: Called a building in this example.
2. THE PICTURE PLANE: An imaginary, transparent plane, onto or through which the object is perceived in a perspective rendering. It is:
   a. Parallel to one face of the drawing paper, if it is a one-point perspective.
   b. Perpendicular to the ground line and at any angle to the building if it is a two-point perspective.
   c. Tilted and placed at any angle to the building if it is a three-point perspective.
   d. A curved plane if it is a wide angle perspective view.
3. HORIZON LINE: A line drawn on the picture plane to represent the horizon. It is usually located at the point where all parallel lines recede away from the viewer and finally converge. This point is aptly designated as the vanishing point. Note that although the horizon is generally thought of as a horizontal line, in certain applications it could be vertical, or even at an angle, to the picture plane. For example, in drawing shades and shadows it appears to be at a 90°, angle and in a three-point perspective it appears to be slanted.
4. STATION POINT: The point from which the object is being viewed or, in other words, the point from which the viewer is seeing the building. The location of this point will be the factor that determines the width of the drawing. A 30° cone of vision is drawn from the station point; as the viewer moves away from the object, the cone widens, the object becomes smaller, and more material is included in the area surrounding the object. A common way of determining the distance between the station point and the picture plane is by referring to the following parameters:
   a. Minimum - 1.73 times the width of the drawing.
   b. Average - 2.00 times the width of the drawing.
   c. Maximum - 2.5 times the width of the drawing.
5. VANISHING POINT(S): A specific point or points located on the horizon line, where all parallel lines, drawn in perspective, converge or terminate. The location of the vanishing point varies with the type of perspective drawing. In the two-point perspective, the distance between the vanishing point left and the vanishing point right is estimated as being approximately four times the overall size of the building.
6. VISUAL RAY: An imaginary line drawn from the station point to any specific point lying within the designated scope of the plan layout of the object. The point at which this projected line passes through the picture plane will determine the location of that point in the perspective drawing.
7. GROUND PLANE: The ground on which the viewer is standing. In plan, this is determined at the station point. In perspective, it is the primary plane on which the building is sited. When the lines of this plane are extended to infinity, they become the horizon line. The intersection formed when the picture plane and the ground plane come together is called the ground line. In this way the horizontal dimension of the drawing is determined. The vertical dimension is determined by the vertical distance from the ground line to the horizon line. This should be approximately twice the height of object, in perspective, or a 30° cone in elevation.
8. ONE-POINT INTERIOR PERSPECTIVE: The most frequently used application of a one-point perspective. This is the same method as that used in setting up a one-point exterior perspective, except for the limitations that the confinement of space places on the location of the vanishing point. The vanishing point is usually located at the sitting or standing height of an average person within the space (eye level can be considered to be at 5 ft 4 in. from the floor). In most cases, the vanishing point is located within the confines of the enclosed space being represented in the drawing.
9. TWO-POINT PERSPECTIVE USING THE MEASURING POINT METHOD: This is a simplified alternative to the conventional method of laying out the plan picture plane and projecting the vanishing lines. The measuring point method of drawing a two-point perspective eliminates the necessity of the preliminary layout of the plan. One of the obvious advantages of this method is the ease with which the size of the drawing can be adjusted. A perspective can be made larger by simply increasing the scale of the drawing.

Samuel J. De Santo and Associates; New York, New York
Alvarado Thrun Maeda and Associates; New York, New York; Eric A. Borch; Newburgh, New York

 DRAWING METHODS

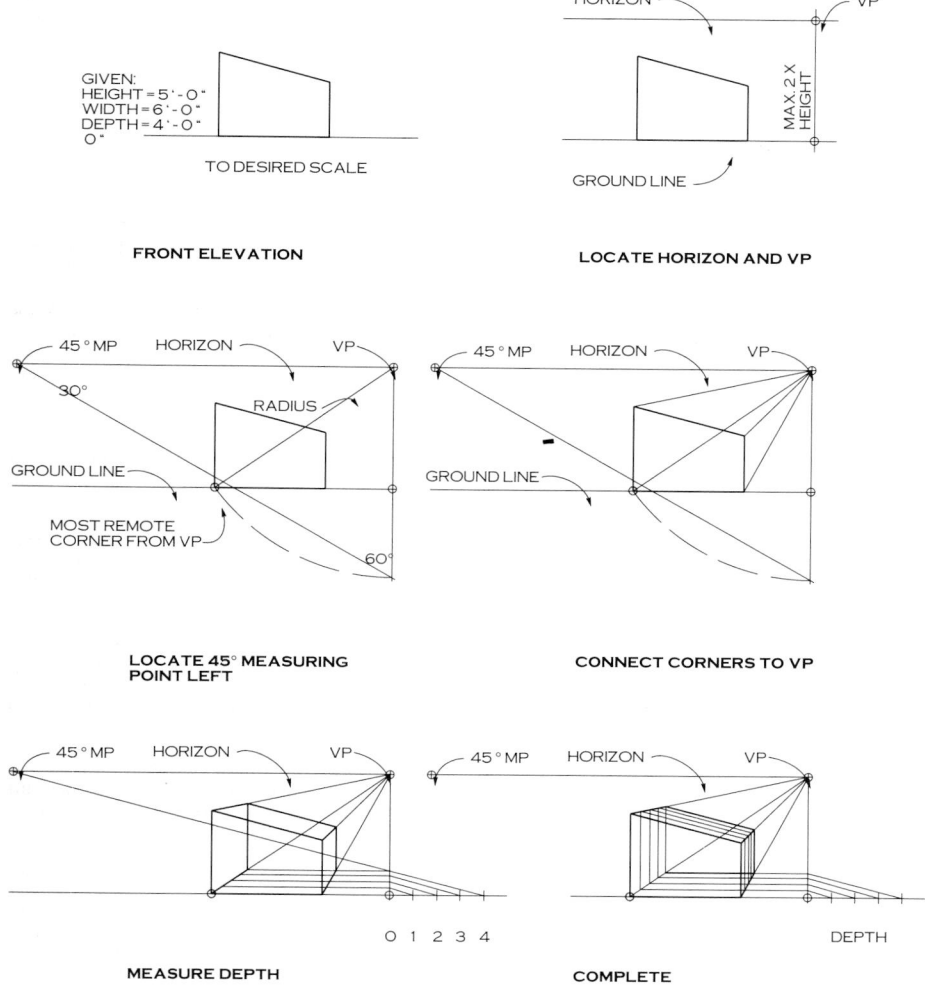

GIVEN:
HEIGHT = 5'-0"
WIDTH = 6'-0"
DEPTH = 4'-0"
0"

TO DESIRED SCALE

FRONT ELEVATION

HORIZON · VP

MAX. 2 X HEIGHT

GROUND LINE

LOCATE HORIZON AND VP

45° MP   HORIZON   VP
30°
RADIUS
GROUND LINE
MOST REMOTE CORNER FROM VP
60°

LOCATE 45° MEASURING POINT LEFT

45° MP   HORIZON   VP

GROUND LINE

CONNECT CORNERS TO VP

45° MP   HORIZON   VP

0 1 2 3 4

MEASURE DEPTH

45° MP   HORIZON   VP

DEPTH

COMPLETE

ONE-POINT PERSPECTIVE BY 45° MEASURING POINT

LOCATE HORIZON
1/3 UP FROM
GROUND LINE
AND VP 1/3 OVER
FROM ONE WALL

HORIZON
VP
2/3
1/3
2/3   1/3

DRAW FRONT ELEVATION
TO DESIRED SCALE
FRONT ELEVATION

45° MP   VP   HORIZON
30°   RADIUS
MOST REMOTE
CORNER FROM VP   60°
GROUND LINE

LOCATE 45° POINT

CONNECT ALL
CORNERS TO VP
HORIZON
45° MP   VP
GROUND LINE
0 1 2 3 4

LOCATE BACK WALL

HORIZON
45° MP   VP   HORIZON

COMPLETE

ONE-POINT DIRECT MEASURED INTERIOR PERSPECTIVE

Samuel J. De Santo and Associates; New York, New York
Alvarado Thrun Maeda and Associates; New York, New York; Eric A. Borch; Newburgh, New York

ONE-POINT PERSPECTIVE

The one-point perspective is probably the least complicated of the projected perspective methods. The primary face of the building or object is placed directly on the picture plane. The adjacent planes, generally connected to the primary plane at right angles, converge to the vanishing point - which can be either in front of or behind the picture plane. The vanishing point, located on the horizon line, also determines the height from which the building is viewed.

The conventional method of laying out a one-point exterior perspective is illustrated on the preceding page. A plan view, roof view, and elevation are required for the layout. The size of the object, and therefore the drawing, can be increased or decreased by moving the plan further in front of or behind the picture plane. This method is more flexible but much more complicated and time consuming than the method that follows.

EXTERIOR ONE-POINT PERSPECTIVE

1. Draw the primary elevation of the building to scale.
2. Locate the horizon above the ground line at the desired level (eye level is approximately 5 ft 4 in.). To ensure that the final perspective will fall within the 60° cone of vision, the height should not exceed 2 times the height of the building. The vanishing point is located left or right arbitrarily depending on the view desired.
3. Locate the 45° measuring point (45° MP) on the horizon by drawing a line from the vanishing point to the most remote corner from the vanishing point to the most remote corner from the vanishing point (as illustrated). Using this line as the radius, strike an arc from the most remote corner, to a vertical line drawn down from the VP. From this intersection draw a line upward, at a 60° angle to meet the horizon. This point (45° MP) will be the vanishing point for all lines that are positioned at a 45° angle and parallel to the picture plane.
4. From each corner of the primary elevation, draw a line to the vanishing point.
5. The room depth is determined by starting at point 0 on the ground line and measuring to the right. Connect this point to the 45° MP on the horizon. The back wall is located where this line intersects the vertical base line drawn from the VP to the ground line.
6. The perspective is completed by constructing the back wall at the location established in step 5 and connecting it to the front wall. Note that the lines that are drawn at 45° angle in the drawing remain parallel to each other as they are extended in perspective.

ONE-POINT INTERIOR AND SECTIONAL PERSPECTIVE

1. Draw the primary elevation, or section, to scale. Locate the horizon line and vanishing point within the confines of the interior space.
2. The 45° measuring point (45° MP), which is also the SP in section, is located similar to the exterior one-point perspective. Strike an arc from the most remote corner of the room to a vertical line drawn from the VP. From this intersection draw a line upward at 60° (to the vertical) to meet the horizon. This intersection shall be the 45° MP.
3. The room depth is determined by starting at point 0 on the ground line and measuring to the right. Connect this point to the 45° MP on the horizon. The back wall is located where the line intersects the vertical base line drawn from the VP to the ground line.
4. Complete the back wall as illustrated. Note that all lines occurring at a 45° angle in the elevation remain parallel in perspective. All surfaces that are parallel to the picture plane will remain parallel in perspective.

DRAWING METHODS

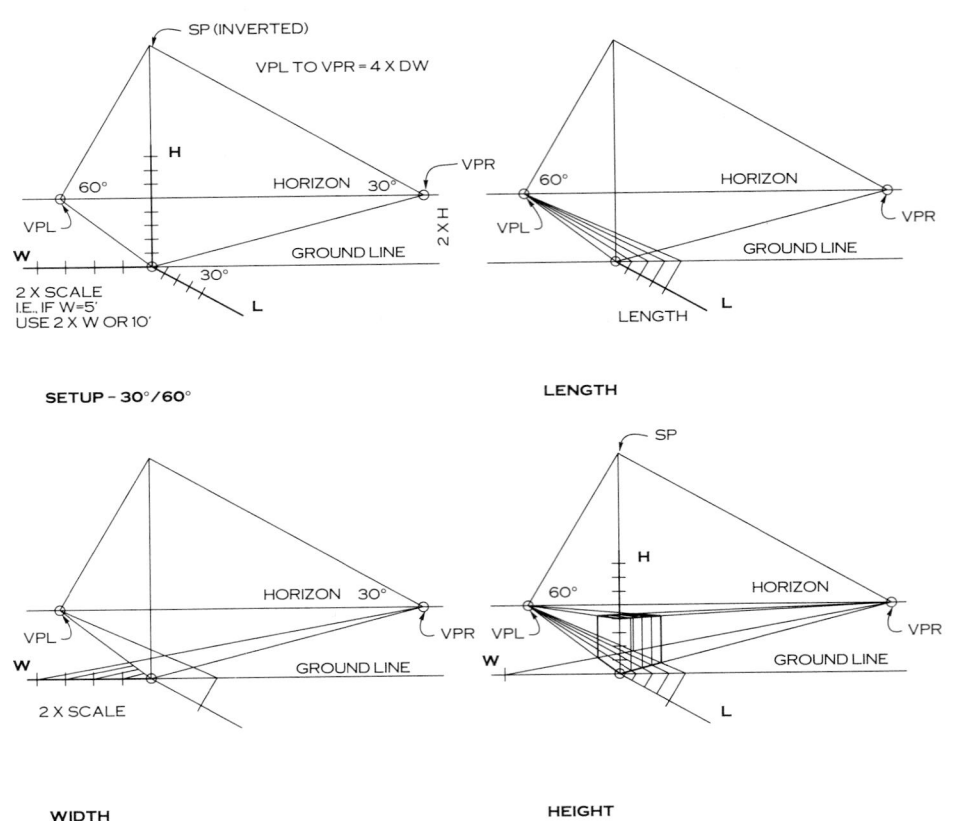

SETUP – 30°/60°   **LENGTH**

WIDTH   **HEIGHT**

TWO-POINT PERSPECTIVE – 30°/60° DIRECT MEASURED SYSTEM

TWO-POINT PERSPECTIVE

The projection method of constructing a two-point perspective is illustrated on page 197. This is the most widely used and most flexible method of drawing a two-point perspective. It can be taken from any viewpoint by simply turning the plan to the desired position in the preliminary layout. The size of the perspective can also be adjusted by moving the plan in front of the picture plane for a larger drawing and behind the picture plane for a smaller drawing. As in all projected methods, an inordinate amount of time and energy is devoted to the layout. The measured method is equally accurate, less time-consuming, and much easier to construct, since it eliminates the need to lay out the drawing in plan. The desired size of the drawing is determined by drawing the primary elevation at the desired scale.

30°/60° DIRECT MEASURED SYSTEM

1. SETUP: Draw a horizon line and locate vanishing point right (VPR) and vanishing point left (VPL) separated at a distance that is approximately 4 to 4.5 times the maximum width of the building. Follow the illustration to locate the station point and leading corner of the building.
2. LENGTH: Measure, to scale, the length of the building along length line L. A perpendicular line is drawn from these designated points to the ground line. The vanishing perspective lines are then drawn directly from these points to the appropriate vanishing point (VPL). In this way the correct length of the line can be determined. Note what happens when equally spaced points are projected from the ground line to the vanishing point. The visual distance (length) between them, as they get closer to the vanishing point, is progressively foreshortened.
3. WIDTH: The width is measured along the width line (see illustration) at double scale. That is, if the perspective is drawn at a scale of $\frac{1}{8}$ in. = 1 ft and a particular line is to be drawn at 5 ft, measure 5 ft at $\frac{1}{4}$ in. scale starting at the corner and measure to the left of the corner horizontally. A line is drawn from each point on the width line to the appropriate vanishing point (VPR). The intersections of the length and width vanishing lines will define the "plan" in perspective.
4. HEIGHT: Since the leading corner of the building is placed directly on the picture plane, the height is measured, to scale, directly on the H line. It is then carried to VPL and VPR as illustrated.

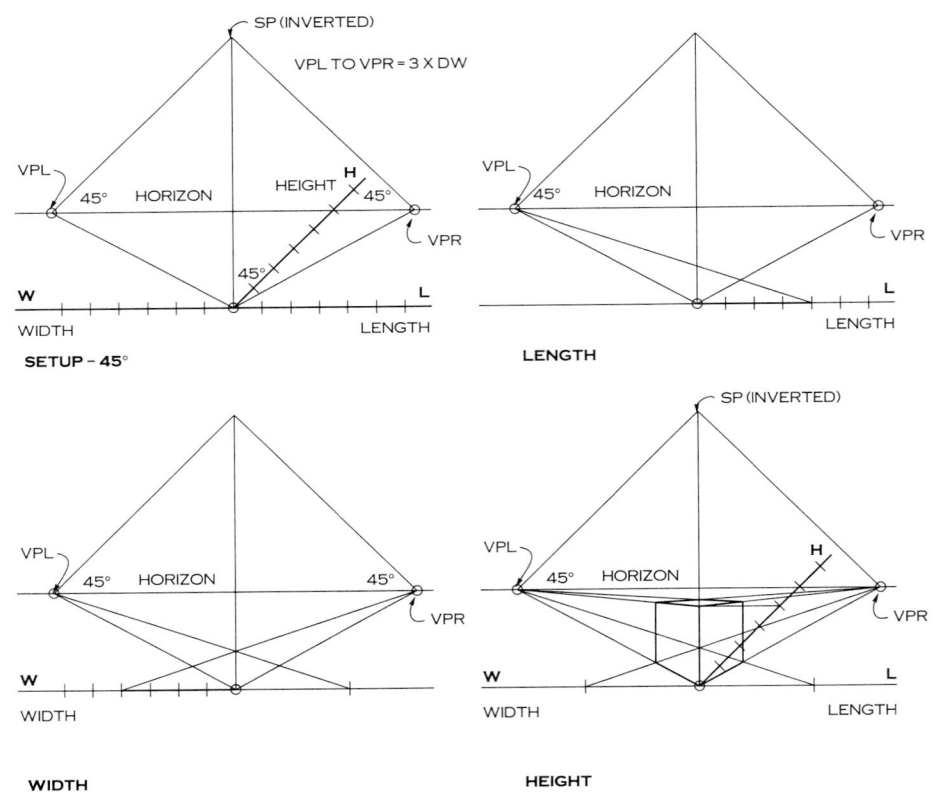

SETUP – 45°   **LENGTH**

WIDTH   **HEIGHT**

TWO-POINT PERSPECTIVE – 45° DIRECT MEASURED SYSTEM

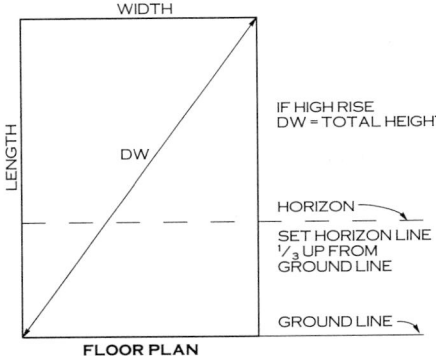

FLOOR PLAN

45° DIRECT MEASURED SYSTEM

1. SETUP: Similar to the method used in the 30°/60° setup, the vanishing points are placed on the horizon line and separated by 3 times the diagonal width. Complete the setup as illustrated.
2. LENGTH: Measure, to scale, the length of the building along the length line L. Connect the points directly to VPL.
3. WIDTH: In this setup, the width is the same as the length scale. Measure the width of the building along the width line W. The length and width lines will form an outline of the "plan" in perspective.
4. HEIGHT: The height line is positioned at a 45° angle and marked off to scale. A line representing the leading corner of the building is drawn perpendicular to the ground line. Connect or draw a line from the measurement points along the height line horizontally to the vertical corner line. As in the 30°/60° setup, these points are then carried to VPR and VPL.

Samuel J. De Santo and Associates; New York, New York
Alvarado Thrun Maeda and Associates; New York, New York; Eric A. Borch; Newburgh, New York

 DRAWING METHODS

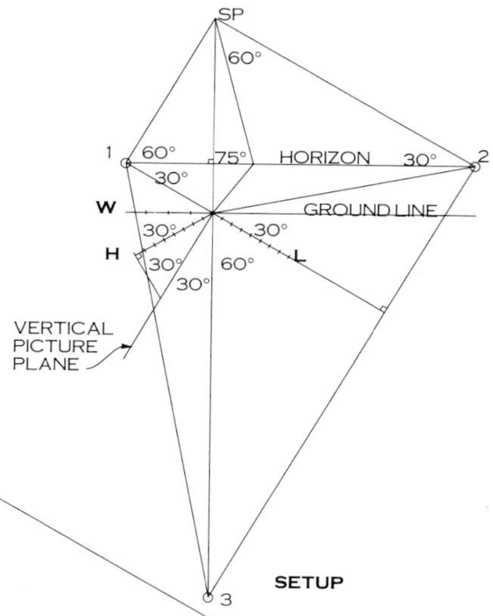

THREE-POINT PERSPECTIVE

In a one- or two-point perspective, the vertical lines of the object are usually parallel to each other and perpendicular to the ground plane. In reality, however, the vertical lines also converge, depending on the height of the observer (or the station point). If the station point is higher than the roof plane, the vertical lines will converge as they get closer to the ground plane; if the station point is lower than the roof plane, the vertical lines will converge as they move farther away from the ground plane.

The three-point perspective is very similar in method to the two-point one. The plan is rotated at any angle to the picture plane, and the location of the station point (in plan) is determined in the same way. The right and left vanishing points will likewise be located on the horizon line. The side view, however, differs from the two-point perspective in that the picture plane is now tilted forward when viewing the building (or object) from a point lower than the roof plane or backward when viewing the building from a point higher than the roof plane. When the lines of vision are drawn to the station point in plan and a side elevation, the combined projections result in a three-point perspective as viewed from the "front." As in the other projected perspective methods, a plan view, side view, and picture plan are required before the perspective can be constructed.

Vanishing point left and vanishing point right (indicated as points 1 and 2 in the illustration) are located on the horizon line. The distance between these two points is approximately four times the maximum length of the object. Once these two points are determined, the entire framework of the construction can be drawn using the 30/60 and 45° triangles (75° = 30 = 45).

LENGTH

The length line is drawn at the same scale as the line connecting points 1 and 2 (which is four times the maximum length of the object). Measured points are projected perpendicularly from the length line L to the ground line (see illustration). From the ground line, the measured points are connected to vanishing point left (or point 1).

WIDTH

At double the original scale, that is, if length (L) is at a $1/4$ in. scale, use $1/2$ in. scale for width (W). Locate the distances along the width line, and connect these points directly to the vanishing point right (or point 2).

HEIGHT

Using the original scale, mark off the measuring points along the height line (H). These points are projected perpendicularly to the line labeled "vertical plane." From these points a line is drawn to vanishing point right (point 2), thereby cutting the vertical lines vanishing to point 2.

45° POINT

This point on the horizon is determined by projecting a line from the upside down station point so that it will meet the horizon line at a 75° angle. All lines occurring at a 45° angle to the picture plane (in viewing) will converge to this point; it is, therefore, often convenient to use this as a reference point when converting exact width to length, or vice versa, in plan.

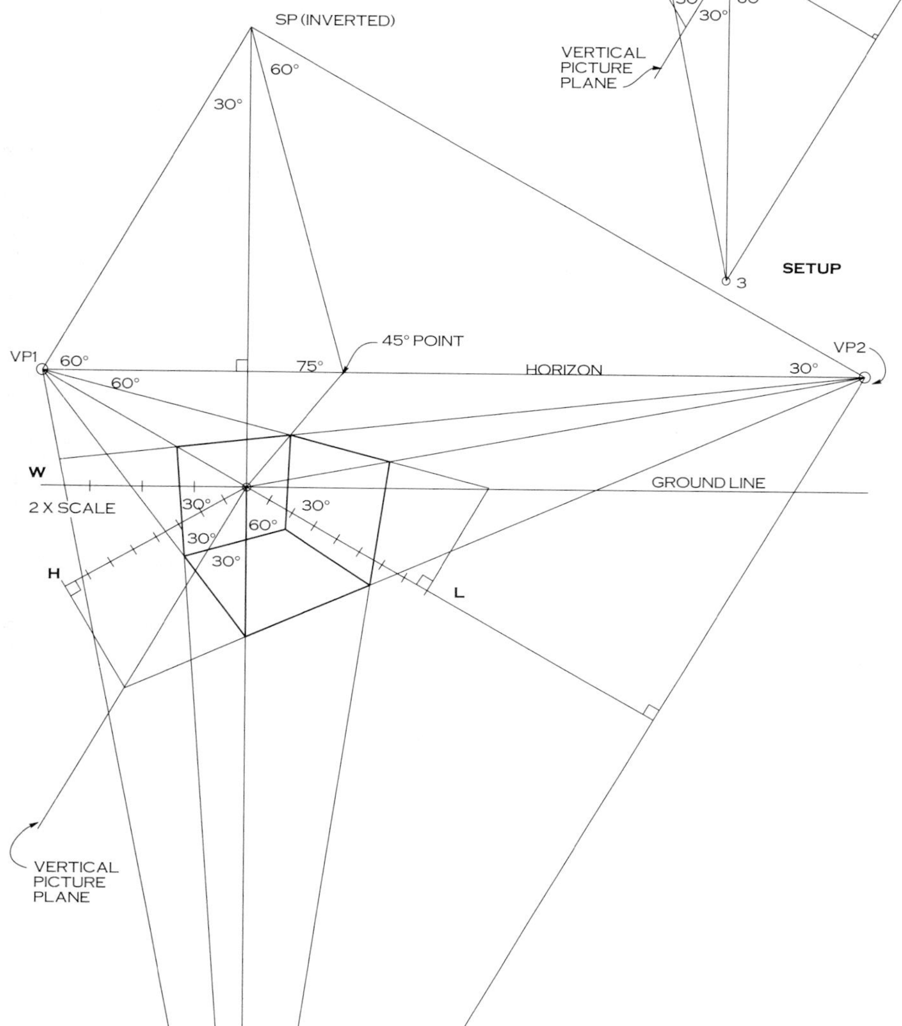

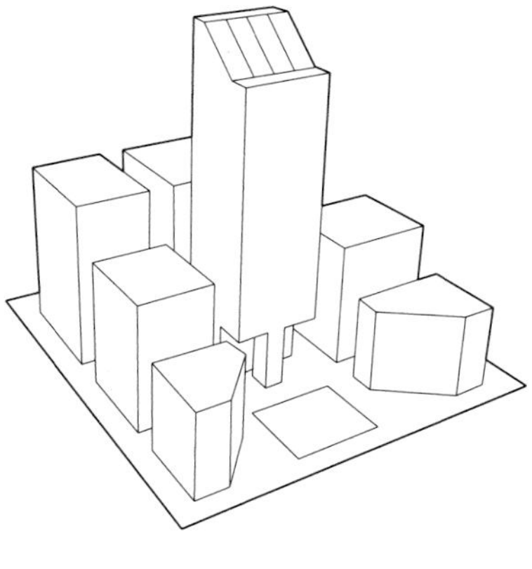

SETUP

VERTICAL PICTURE PLANE

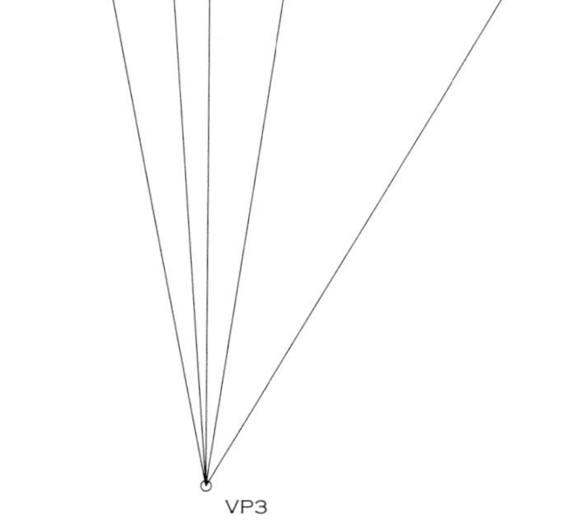

VP1 · VP2 · VP3 · HORIZON · GROUND LINE · 45° POINT · 2 X SCALE · SP (INVERTED)

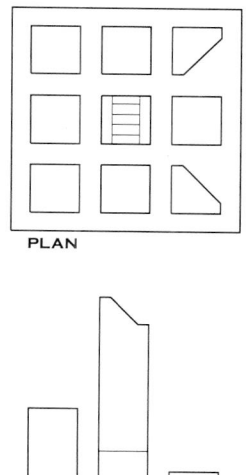

THREE-POINT PERSPECTIVE

PLAN

ELEVATION

PROJECTING THE PERSPECTIVE

Samuel J. De Santo and Associates; New York, New York
Alvarado Thrun Maeda and Associates; New York, New York; Eric A. Borch; Newburgh, New York

DRAWING METHODS

OVERVIEW OF CONDOC

ConDoc is a production methodology developed to improve the quality and usefulness of construction documents while greatly simplifying the process of creating them. ConDoc provides a means to organize and format drawings and to directly link information shown on drawings to that contained in the specifications.

A major feature of ConDoc is the use of a unique keynote system that links drawings and specifications while reducing substantially the text needed on drawings without any loss of information shown on the drawings.

BASIC PRECEPTS OF THE CONDOC METHODOLOGY

1. Will not restrict the creativity or individuality of the user.
2. Works with projects of any size or type.
3. Does not restrict the extent of information to be placed in the documents.
4. Works for all disciplines, but it is not necessary that it be used by all disciplines on a project.
5. Provides conventions for formatting the composition of individual drawings, based upon a modular sheet arrangement.
6. Uses a keynote system which directly interfaces with the specification numbering system.
7. Provides a means for standardizing procedures in the preparation of construction documents.
8. Enhances quality control, coordination, and review of documents.

THE DRAWING FORMAT

Consistency of drawing arrangement is achieved through the use of a modular subdivision of spaces with provisions for a keynote system and legend. The ConDoc modular drawing format relates to standard sheet sizes, although special sizes may be accommodated.

The use of ConDoc organizes and standardizes the arrangement of graphic information within modules (or group of modules). It establishes a standard size and location on for titles and symbols, a standard for placement of information including dimensioning, and simplifies the means to incorporate standard details and schedules.

LINKING DRAWING AND SPECIFICATIONS VIA KEYNOTES

Great advances and benefits have been realized in the preparation of specifications as a result of the development and evolution of the 16-division format and 5-digit code that identifies each of the sections used in the specifications. This same 5-digit code is used throughout the construction industry to categorize technical data and, when used as a keynote, provides immediate recognition as to which specification sections relate to information shown on the drawing.

The use of keynotes and materials legend dramatically reduces the extent of lettering on drawings, without sacrifice in the amount of information shown. The ConDoc methodology removes extraneous information, simplifies and expedites the placement of information, minimizes the time needed to compose drawings, and avoids unnecessary duplication of information.

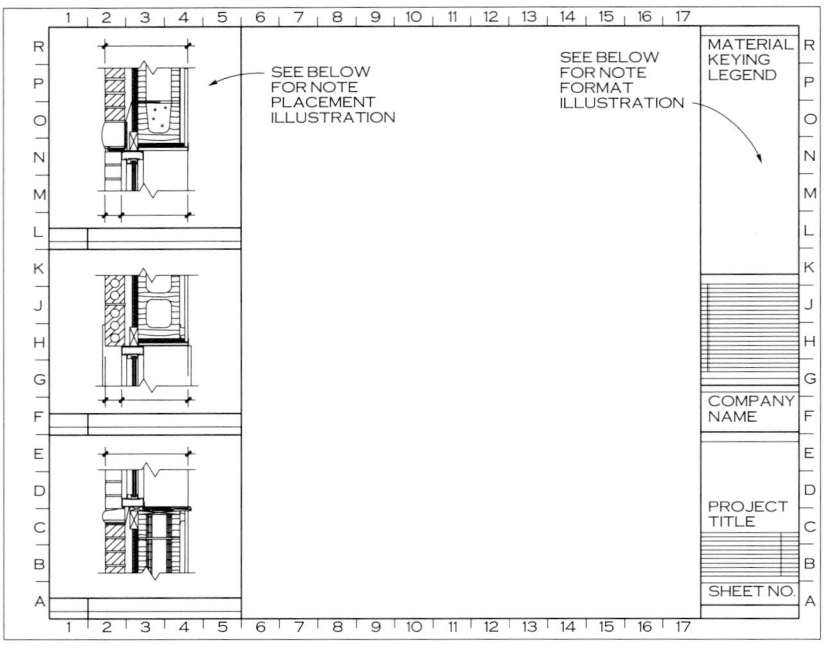

MODULAR TITLE SHEET FOR GRID IDENTIFICATION SYSTEM

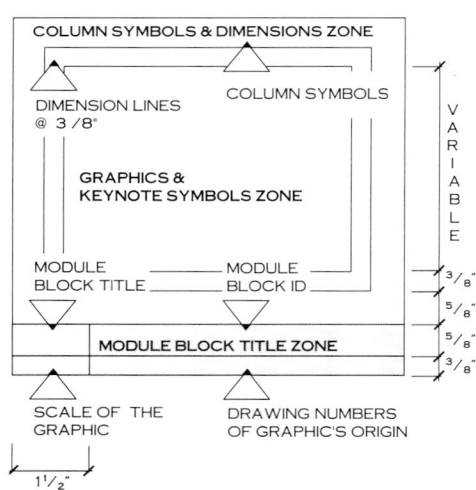

STANDARD CONDOC MODULE BLOCK

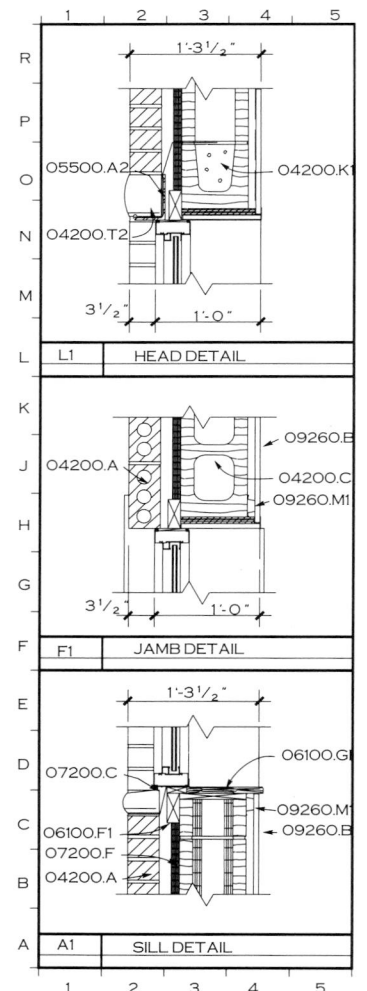

TYPICAL CONDOC DETAIL AND KEYING LEGEND

MATERIAL KEYING LEGEND

DIV. 4 MASONRY

04200.A	FACE BRICK
04200.B	SOLDIER COURSE
04200.C	8" CONCRETE BLOCK
04200.K1	CMU LINTEL - SEE STRUCTURAL
04200.N	WEEP HOLES
04200.Q	MEMBRANE FLASHING
04200.R	BLOCK INSULATION
04200.T2	CAST STONE LINTEL
04200.T3	CAST STONE SILL

DIV. 5 METALS

05500.A2	$3\frac{1}{2}$"X 5 ""X$\frac{5}{16}$ ""AGLE

DIV. 6 WOOD AND PLASTICS

06100.A4	2 X 4 STUDS AT 16 "O.C.
06100.F1	WOOD BLOCKING AS REQUIRED
06100.F6	TREATED 1 X 8
06100.F7	TREATED BLOCKING
06100.G6	$\frac{3}{4}$ "EXTERIOR GRADE PLYWOOD
06100.GI	CULTURED MARBLE SILL

DIV. 7 THERMAL AND MOISTURE PROTECTION

07200.F	1 "BOARD INSULATION
07200.A	SILICONE SEALANT
07200.C	CAULK
07200.D	BACKER ROD

DIV. 8 DOORS AND WINDOWS

08110.A	HOLLOW METAL FRAME
08110.B	HOLLOW METAL DOOR
08110.C	"B" LABEL HOLLOW METAL FRAME
08110.D	JAMB ANCHOR
08110.E	GROUT - FILL HOLLOW METAL FRAME
08211.A	SOLID CORE WOOD DOOR
08360.B	DOOR TRACK
08410.A	ALUMINUM FRAMING - SEE SCHEDULE

DIV. 9 FINISHES

09260.B	$\frac{5}{8}$ "GYP. BD.
09260.F1	$\frac{5}{8}$ "TYPE "X" GYP. BD.
09260.G2	METAL CORNER BEAD (TYP.)
09260.M1	$\frac{7}{8}$ "FURRING CHANNEL

James M. Duda; Herndon, Virginia; Onkal K. Guzey and James N. Freehof; Washington, D.C. Terry Graves; McCarty Architects; Tupelo, Mississippi

 DRAWING METHODS

GUIDELINES FOR COMPUTER-AIDED DESIGN (CAD) LAYERS

Most computer-aided design systems support the concept of grouping information for display, editing, and plotting. The CAD layer feature facilitates using one set of graphic information to produce multiple drawings. For example, a single CAD file could be used to produce a floor plan, reflected ceiling plan, lighting plan, power plan, and furniture plan.

Other applications of CAD layers include

1. Sharing information common to several floor plans in a multistory building
2. Accommodating alternative design schemes or project phases within individual drawings
3. Helping architects, design consultants, and consulting engineers coordinate drawings and share graphic information

CAD Layer Guidelines, prepared by the AIA Task Force on CAD Layer Guidelines, provides a structure for consistent organization of CAD drawings by architects, engineers, facility managers, and design consultants.

CONVENTIONS FOR NAMING LAYERS

Guidelines are organized using a three-level hierarchy for naming layers that provides for flexibility and expandability. The first level designates the major group of information and corresponds to traditional sheet-numbering conventions. Major groups are

A Architecture, interiors, facilities
S Structural
M Mechanical
P Plumbing
F Fire protection
E Electrical
C Civil engineering
L Landscape architecture

This level is followed by a code designating the construction system. For example, a drawing might contain the following layers:

A-WALL   Walls

A-DOOR	Doors
A-GLAZ	Glazing
A-EQPM	Equipment
A-CLNG	Ceiling information
A-ROOF	Roof
E-POWR	Electrical power
S-COLS	Structural columns

Where additional differentiation is needed, an optional modifier can be added:

A-WALL-FULL
A-WALL-PRHT
A-WALL-MOVE
A-WALL-HEAD

USER-DEFINABLE FIELDS

It is possible to add user-defined fields to accommodate special requirements. For example, A-DOOR-METL and A-DOOR-WOOD could designate metal and wood doors, respectively.

BUILDING INFORMATION/DRAWING INFORMATION

CAD layer guidelines define two types of layers: building information layers and drawing information layers. Building information layers relate to the physical form of a building. Examples include walls, doors, columns, and light fixtures. Information on these layers is often shared between drawings. Drawing information layers contain annotation, dimensions, reference symbols, and other information specific to a single drawing. Drawing information layers are organized by drawing and type of information, rather than by construction system.

REMODELING PROJECTS

Renovation and remodeling projects require differentiation between new work, existing items to remain, and existing items to be demolished. This can be accomplished by the use of the following modifiers:

EXST   Existing to remain
DEMO   Existing to demolish

Layers without a modifier designate new work.

ARCHITECTURE, INTERIORS, AND FACILITIES

BUILDING INFORMATION LAYERS

A-WALL	Walls
A-DOOR	Doors
A-GLAZ	Glazed openings, windows, glazed walls and partitions
A-FLOR	Floor information
A-EQPM	Equipment
A-FURN	Furniture
A-CLNG	Ceiling information
A-ROOF	Roof
A-AREA	Area calculations and occupancy information
A-ELEV	Interior and exterior elevations
A-SECT	Sections
A-DETL	Details

DRAWING INFORMATION LAYERS

A-SHBD	Sheet border and title block line work
A-PFLR	Floor plan
A-PLGS	Large-scale floor plan
A-PCLG	Reflected ceiling plan
A-PROF	Roof plan
A-PXFU	Fixtures and furniture plan
A-PEQM	Equipment plan
A-PMFN	Materials and finish plan
A-PDEM	Demolition plan
A-PARE	Area calculations
A-POCC	Occupancy plan
A-P***	Other plan drawings
A-ELEV	Interior and exterior elevations
A-SECT	Building and wall sections
A-DETL	Details
A-SCHD	Schedules and title block sheets

CAD Layer Guidelines is published by AIA Press. For more information call (800) 365-ARCH.

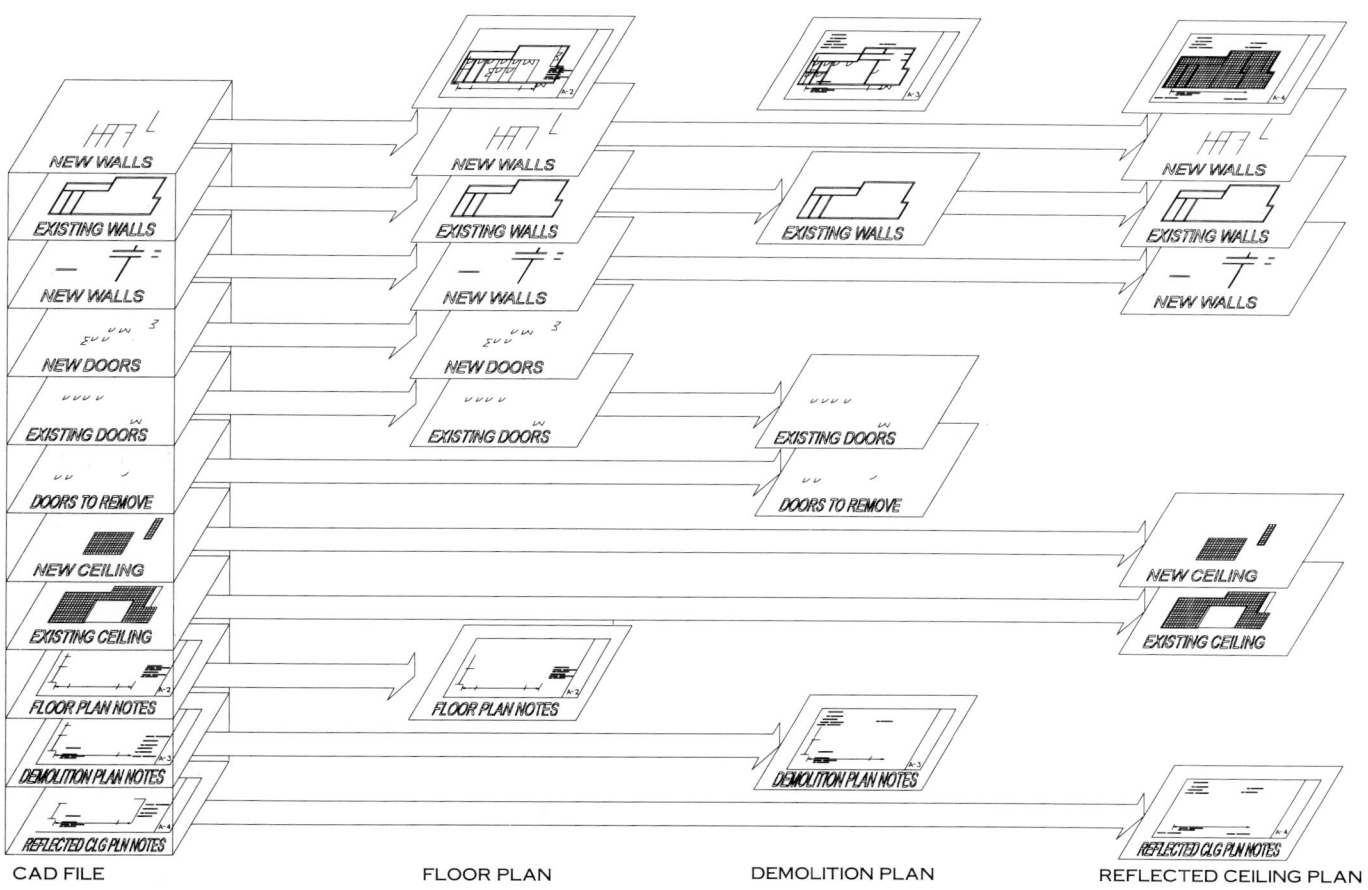

SAMPLE DRAWING STRATEGY FOR A REMODELING PROJECT

Michael K. Schley, AIA; Raleigh, North Carolina
Terry Graves; McCarty Architects; Tupelo, Mississippi

DRAWING METHODS

GENERATIVE GEOMETRY

The archetypal circle and square can geometrically generate many forms. Ancient cultures recognized these forms and relationships as essential and sacred, a metaphor of universal order. The circle and square in the act of self-division give us three generative roots: the square roots of 2, 3, and 5 (figs. 1a and 1b). These root relationships are all that are necessary to form the five regular (Platonic) solids that are the basis for all volumetric forms (fig. 1c). Also, 2, 3, and 5 are the only numbers required to divide the octave into musical scales.

THE $\sqrt{2}$

In seeming paradox, the half of a square produces its double; this is analogous to biological growth from cell division and the generation of musical tone. In fig. 2a, the diagonal of square ABCD (square 1, fig. 2a) is exactly equal to the side of square ACFG (square 2). The area of square 2 is exactly twice that of square 1. The side of a square is called its root. The side of square 1 = 1; the side of square 2 = the square root of 2. The diagonal of square 2 = 2, exactly twice the side of the primary square. The division of the square by the diagonal yields three seemingly contradictory, yet geometrically true, relationships:

$$\frac{\text{root}}{\text{diag}} : \frac{\text{root}}{\text{diag}} :: \frac{1}{\sqrt{2}} : \frac{\sqrt{2}}{2} \qquad \frac{\text{root}}{\text{diag}} : \frac{\text{diag}}{\text{root}} :: \frac{1}{\sqrt{2}} : \frac{\sqrt{2}}{2}$$

$$\frac{\text{root}}{\text{root}} : \frac{\text{diag}}{\text{diag}} :: \frac{1}{\sqrt{2}} : \frac{\sqrt{2}}{2}$$

The square root of 2 represents the power of multiplicity through the geometric progression a:b::b:c (fig. 2b). The relationship of the side to the diagonal may be written

$$\frac{1}{\sqrt{2}} : \frac{\sqrt{2}}{2} : \frac{2}{2\sqrt{2}} : \frac{2\sqrt{2}}{4} : \frac{4}{4\sqrt{2}} \qquad \text{etc}$$

THE VESICA PISCIS AND THE $\sqrt{3}$

The Vesica Piscis is a form generator of the triangle, square, and pentagon—the basic planar elements of the five Platonic solids. The overlapping circles are an excellent representation of a cell or any unity in the midst of becoming dual. Medieval churches and cathedrals incorporated the fish-shaped geometry as a symbol of Christ.

To construct the Vesica Piscis: draw a circle of any radius about center A; at any chosen point on the circumference, draw another circle of equal radius (B). The area and shape defined by the two centers and the overlap of the two circumferences is known as the Vesica Piscis (fig. 3a).

Fig. 3b shows the generation of equilateral triangles.

In fig. 3c, we see that if AB = 1, then DG = 1, CG = 2, and, by the Pythagorean Theorem ($a^2 + b^2 = c^2$), the major axis

$$CD = \sqrt{(CG^2 - DG^2)} = \sqrt{3}$$

THE $\sqrt{5}$

The square root of 5 may be generated from a 1:2 rectangle (a double square); see fig. 4a. Fig. 4b demonstrates the relationship of the square root of 5, both with the number 5 (as the square of its root) and with the fivefold symmetry of the pentagon. The 3,4,5 "Pythagorean" triangle (fig. 4c) is derived from the crossing of three semidiagonals (square root of 5 divided by 2). The square root of 5 is the proportion that opens the way for the family of relationships called the Golden Proportion.

THE GOLDEN PROPORTION

Grand philosophical, natural, and aesthetic considerations have surrounded this proportion ever since humanity began to reflect on the geometric forms of its world. The Golden Proportion can be found in nature, where it governs plant growth patterns and human proportions. Its presence can be found in the sacred art and architecture of Egypt, India, China, Greece, Islamic countries, and other traditional cultures. It was hidden in Gothic cathedrals, celebrated in Renaissance art, and used by modernist architects such as Le Corbusier and Wright.

Discontinuous proportions contain four terms (a:b::c:d). Geometric relationships are of a three-term proportional type (a:b::b:c). There is only one proportional division that is possible with two terms; this is written a:b::b:(a + b). The unique two-term proportion (designated by the Greek letter ϕ) was called "golden" by the ancients because the original unity is always represented in its division, written

$$\frac{1}{\phi^3} : \frac{1}{\phi^2} : \frac{1}{\phi^2} : \frac{1}{\phi} : \frac{1}{\phi} :: 1 :: 1 : \phi :: \phi : \phi^2 :: \phi^2 : \phi^3 \quad \text{etc.}$$

Scot C. McBroom, AIA; Alexandria, Virginia

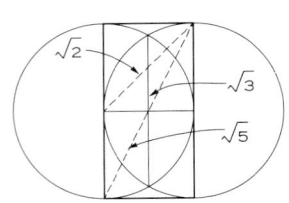

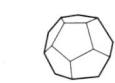

TETRAHEDRON OCTAHEDRON ICOSA-HEDRON

CUBE DODECAHEDRON

FIGURE 1A   **FIGURE 1B**   **FIGURE 1C**

GENERATIVE GEOMETRY

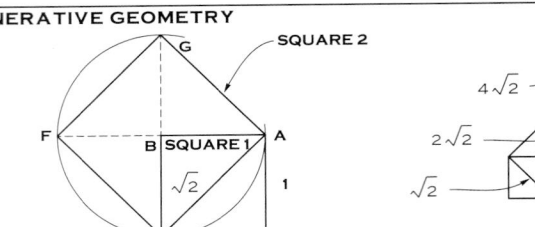
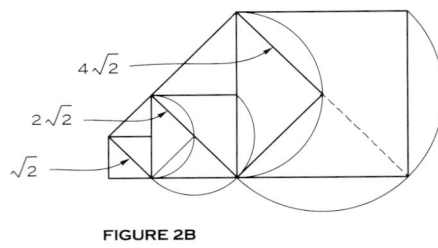

SQUARE 2

SQUARE 1

FIGURE 2A   **FIGURE 2B**

THE SQUARE ROOT OF 2

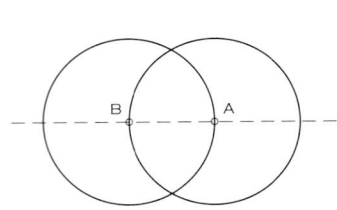
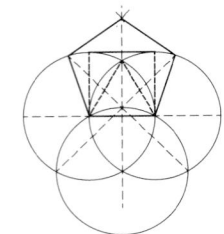
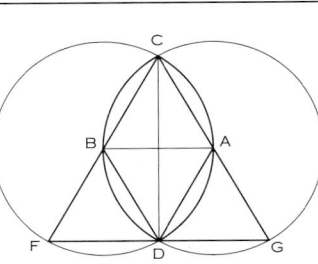

FIGURE 3A   **FIGURE 3B**   **FIGURE 3C**

THE SQUARE ROOT OF 3

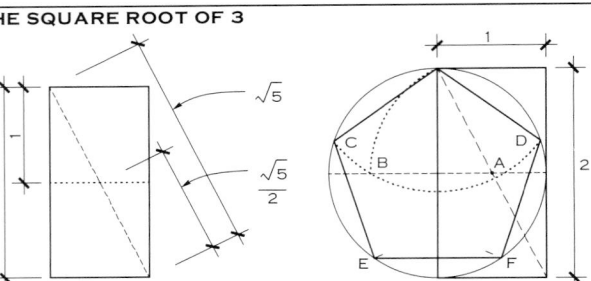
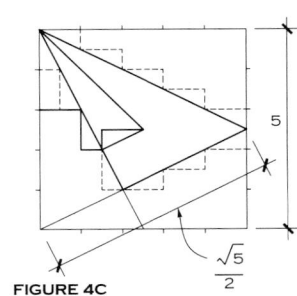

FIGURE 4A   **FIGURE 4B**   **FIGURE 4C**

THE SQUARE ROOT OF 5

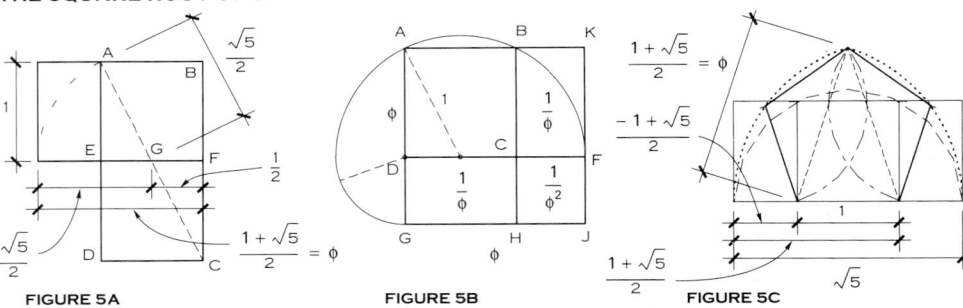

FIGURE 5A   **FIGURE 5B**   **FIGURE 5C**

GOLDEN PROPORTION

Fig. 5a shows the construction of the Golden Proportion from the 1:2 rectangle. Fig. 5b demonstrates the relationship of three squares related by ϕ. Fig. 5c reveals an important pentagonal relationship: the side of a pentagon is in relation to its diagonal as

$$1 : (1 + \sqrt{5})/2 \quad \text{or } 1 : \phi, \text{ the golden section}$$

ϕ represents a coinciding of the processes of addition and multiplication called the Fibonacci Series, which manifests itself in some biological growth patterns. The Fibonacci Series is an additive progression in which the two initial terms are added together to form the third term (1, 1, 2, 3, 5, 8, 13...). Any two successive terms tend to be approximately in relation to one another as 1: ϕ, and any three successive terms are as 1: ϕ : ϕ^2: ϕ^3....

REFERENCES

1. Brunes, T. *The Secret of Ancient Geometry and Its Use.* 2 vols. Copenhagen: Rhodos, 1967.

2. Critchlow, K. *Order in Space.* New York: Thames and Hudson, 1969.

3. Ghyka, M. *The Geometry of Art and Life.* New York: Dover, 1977.

4. Lawlor, R. *Sacred Geometry: Philosophy and Practice.* New York: Thames and Hudson, 1982. (The information presented on this page is based substantially on this work.)

5. Young, A. *The Geometry of Meaning.* New York: Delacorte Press, 1976.

 GEOMETRY

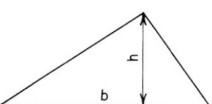

TRIANGLE
AREA = ½ ANY ALTITUDE × ITS BASE (ALTITUDE IS PERPENDICULAR DISTANCE TO OPPOSITE VERTEX OR CORNER.)
$A = \frac{1}{2} b \times h$

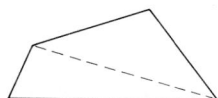

TRAPEZUM
(IRREGULAR QUADRILATERAL)
AREA = DIVIDE FIGURE INTO TWO TRIANGLES AND FIND AREAS AS ABOVE

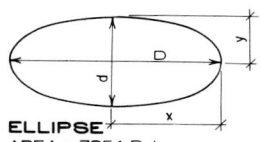

ELLIPSE
AREA = .7854 Dd
APPROX. PERIMETER
$= \pi\sqrt{2(x^2+y^2)}$

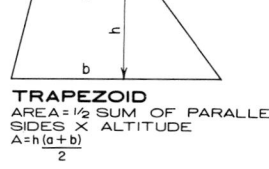

TRAPEZOID
AREA = ½ SUM OF PARALLEL SIDES × ALTITUDE
$A = h\frac{(a+b)}{2}$

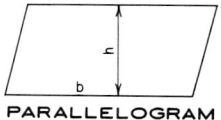

PARALLELOGRAM
AREA = EITHER SIDE × ALTITUDE

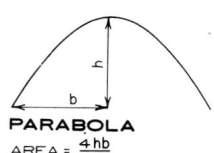

PARABOLA
AREA $= \frac{4hb}{3}$

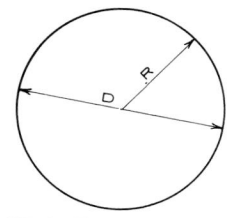

CIRCLE
AREA $= \frac{\pi D^2}{4} = \pi R^2$
CIRCUMFERENCE $= 2\pi R = \pi D$
($\pi = 3.14159265359$)

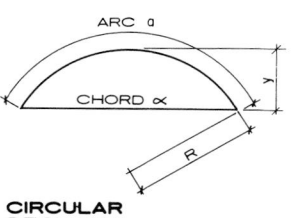

CIRCULAR SEGMENT
AREA = $\frac{(\text{LENGTH OF ARC } a) \times R - \propto(R-y)}{2}$
CHORD $\propto = 2\sqrt{2yR - y^2}$
$= 2R \sin\frac{A°}{2}$

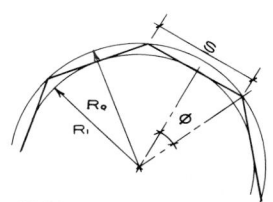

REGULAR POLYGON
AREA = $\frac{nSR_i}{2}$
(n = NUMBER OF SIDES)
ANY SIDE $S = 2\sqrt{R_o^2 - R_i^2}$
$R_i = \frac{S}{2\tan\emptyset}$ $R_o = \frac{S}{2\sin\emptyset}$

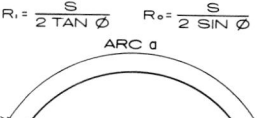
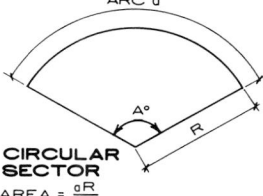

CIRCULAR SECTOR
AREA = $\frac{aR}{2}$
= AREA OF CIRCLE × $\frac{A°}{360}$
$= 0.0087R^2A°$
ARC $a = \frac{\pi R A°}{180°} = 0.0175 RA°$

GEOMETRIC PROPERTIES OF PLANE FIGURES

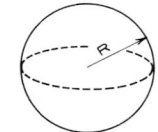

SPHERE
VOLUME = $\frac{4\pi R^3}{3}$
$= 0.5236D^3$
SURFACE = $4\pi R^2$
$= \pi D^2$

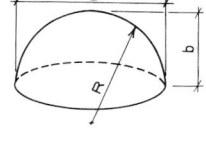

SEGMENT OF SPHERE
VOLUME = $\frac{\pi b^2(3R-b)}{3}$
(OR SECTOR – CONE)
SURFACE = $2\pi Rb$
(NOT INCLUDING SURFACE OF CIRCULAR BASE)

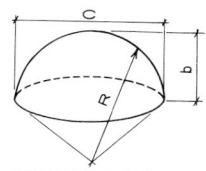

SECTOR OF SPHERE
VOLUME = $\frac{2\pi R^2 b}{3}$
SURFACE = $\frac{\pi R(4b+c)}{2}$
(OR: SEGMENT + CONE)

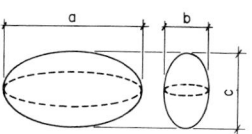

ELLIPSOID
VOLUME = $\frac{\pi abc}{6}$
SURFACE: NO SIMPLE RULE

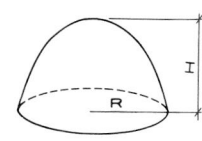

PARABOLOID OF REVOLUTION
VOLUME = AREA OF CIRCULAR BASE × ½ ALTITUDE.
SURFACE: NO SIMPLE RULE

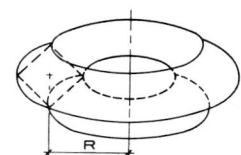

CIRCULAR RING OF ANY SECTION
R = DISTANCE FROM AXIS OF RING TO TRUE CENTER OF SECTION
VOLUME = AREA OF SECTION × $2\pi R$
SURFACE = PERIMETER OF SECTION × $2\pi R$ (CONSIDER THE SECTION ON ONE SIDE OF AXIS ONLY)

VOLUMES AND SURFACES OF DOUBLE - CURVED SOLIDS

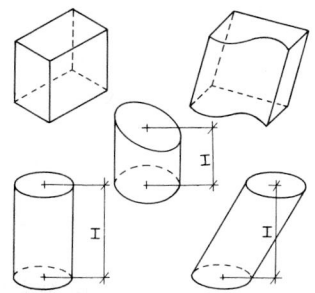

ANY PRISM OR CYLINDER, RIGHT OR OBLIQUE, REGULAR OR IRREGULAR.
Volume = area of base x altitude
Altitude = distance between parallel bases, measured perpendicular to the bases. When bases are not parallel, then Altitude = perpendicular distance from one base to the center of the other.

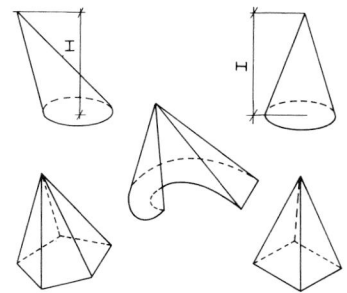

ANY PYRAMID OR CONE, RIGHT OR OBLIQUE, REGULAR OR IRREGULAR.
Volume = area of base x 1/3 altitude
Altitude = distance from base to apex, measured perpendicular to base.

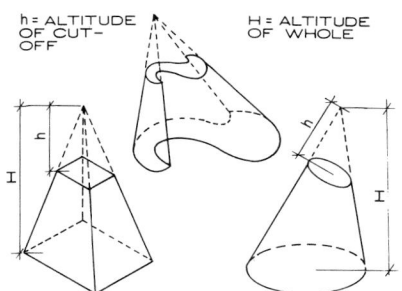

h = ALTITUDE OF CUT-OFF   H = ALTITUDE OF WHOLE

ANY FRUSTUM OR TRUNCATED PORTION OF THE SOLIDS SHOWN
Volume: From the volume of the whole solid, if complete, subtract the volume of the portion cut off.
The altitude of the cut-off part must be measured perpendicular to its own base.

SURFACES OF SOLIDS
The area of the surface is best found by adding together the areas of all the faces.

The area of a right cylindrical surface = perimeter of base x length of elements (average length if other base is oblique).

The area of a right conical surface = perimeter of base x 1/2 length of elements.

There is no simple rule for the area of an oblique conical surface, or for a cylindrical one where neither base is perpendicular to the elements. The best method is to construct a development, as if making a paper model, and measure its area by one of the methods given on the next page.

VOLUMES AND SURFACES OF TYPICAL SOLIDS

GEOMETRY A

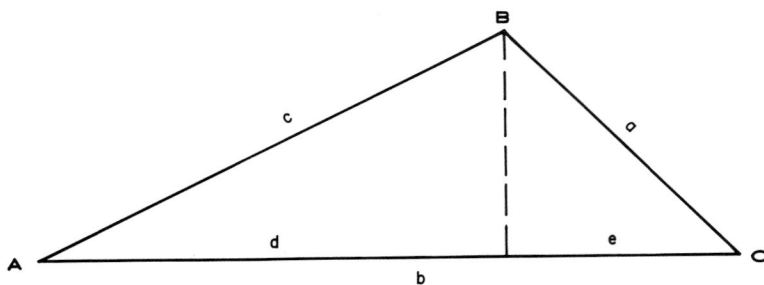

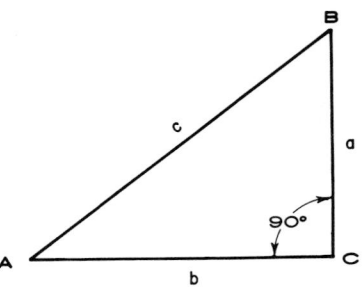

OBLIQUE TRIANGLES

FIND	GIVEN	SOLUTION
a	A B b	$b \sin A \div \sin B$
	A B c	$c \sin A \div \sin(A+B)$
	A C b	$b \sin A \div \sin(A+C)$
	A C c	$c \sin A \div \sin C$
	B C b	$b \sin(B+C) \div \sin B$
	B C c	$c \sin(B+C) \div \sin C$
	A b c	$\sqrt{b^2 + c^2 - 2bc \cdot \cos A}$
b	A B a	$a \sin B \div \sin A$
	A B c	$c \sin B \div \sin(A+B)$
	A C a	$a \sin(A+C) \div \sin A$
	A C c	$c \sin(A+C) \div \sin C$
	B C a	$a \sin B \div \sin(B+C)$
	B C c	$c \sin B \div \sin C$
	B a c	$\sqrt{a^2 + c^2 - 2ac \cdot \cos B}$
c	A B a	$a \sin(A+B) \div \sin A$
	A B b	$b \sin(A+B) \div \sin B$
	A C a	$a \sin C \div \sin A$
	A C b	$b \sin C \div \sin(A+C)$
	B C a	$a \sin C \div \sin(B+C)$
	B C b	$b \sin C \div \sin B$
	C a b	$\sqrt{a^2 + b^2 - 2ab \cdot \cos C}$
½(B+C)	A b c	$90° - \tfrac{1}{2}A$
½(B−C)		$\tan = [(b-c)\tan(90°-\tfrac{1}{2}A)] \div (b+c)$
½(A+C)	B a c	$90° - \tfrac{1}{2}B$
½(A−C)		$\tan = [(a-c)\tan(90°-\tfrac{1}{2}B)] \div (a+c)$
½(A+B)	C a b	$90° - \tfrac{1}{2}C$
½(A−B)		$\tan = [(a-b)\tan(90°-\tfrac{1}{2}C)] \div (a+b)$

FIND	GIVEN	SOLUTION
A	a b c s	$\sin \tfrac{1}{2}A = \sqrt{(s-b)(s-c) \div bc}$
		$\cos \tfrac{1}{2}A = \sqrt{s(s-a) \div bc}$
		$\tan \tfrac{1}{2}A = \sqrt{(s-b)(s-c) \div s(s-a)}$
	B a b	$\sin A = a \sin B \div b$
	B a c	$\tan A = \dfrac{a \sin B}{c - a \cos B}$
	C a b	$\tan A = \dfrac{a \sin C}{b - \cos C}$
	C a c	$\sin A = a \sin C \div c$
B	a b c s	$\sin \tfrac{1}{2}B = \sqrt{(s-a)(s-c) \div ac}$
		$\cos \tfrac{1}{2}B = \sqrt{s(s-b) \div ac}$
		$\tan \tfrac{1}{2}B = \sqrt{(s-a)(s-c) \div s(s-b)}$
	A a b	$\sin B = b \sin A \div a$
	A b c	$\tan B = \dfrac{b \sin A}{c - b \cos A}$
	C a b	$\tan B = \dfrac{b \sin C}{a - b \cos C}$
	C a c	$\sin B = b \sin C \div c$
C	a b c s	$\sin \tfrac{1}{2}C = \sqrt{(s-a)(s-b) \div ab}$
		$\cos \tfrac{1}{2}C = \sqrt{s(s-c) \div ab}$
		$\tan \tfrac{1}{2}C = \sqrt{(s-a)(s-b) \div s(s-c)}$
	A a c	$\sin C = c \sin A \div a$
	A b c	$\tan C = \dfrac{C \sin A}{b - c \cos A}$
	B a c	$C = \dfrac{C \sin B}{a - c \cos B}$
	B b c	$\sin C = c \sin B \div b$
AREA	a b c	$\sqrt{s(s-a)(s-b)(s-c)}$
	C a b	$\tfrac{1}{2} ab \sin C$
s	a b c	$(a + b + c) \div 2$
d	a b c s	$(b^2 + c^2 - a^2) \div 2b$
e	a b c s	$(a^2 + b^2 - c^2) \div 2b$

RIGHT TRIANGLES

FIND	GIVEN	SOLUTION
A	a b	$\tan A = a \div b$
	a c	$\sin A = a \div c$
	b c	$\cos A = b \div c$
B	a b	$\tan B = b \div a$
	a c	$\cos B = a \div c$
	b c	$\sin B = b \div c$
a	A b	$b \tan A$
	A c	$c \sin A$
b	A a	$a \div \tan A$
	A c	$c \cos A$
c	A a	$a \div \sin A$
	A b	$b \div \cos A$
AREA	a b	$ab \div 2$

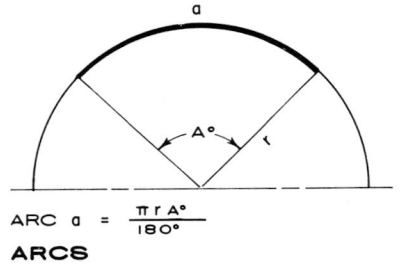

$$\text{ARC } a = \frac{\pi r A°}{180°}$$

ARCS

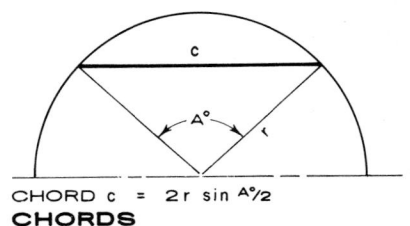

$$\text{CHORD } c = 2r \sin \tfrac{A°}{2}$$

CHORDS

  GEOMETRY

NATURAL SINES

ANGLE	0′	10′	20′	30′	40′	50′	60′	
0°	0.00000	0.00291	0.00582	0.00873	0.01164	0.01454	0.01745	89°
1	0.01745	0.02036	0.02327	0.02618	0.02908	0.03199	0.03490	88
2	0.03490	0.03781	0.04071	0.04362	0.04653	0.04943	0.05234	87
3	0.05234	0.05524	0.05814	0.06105	0.06395	0.06685	0.06976	86
4	0.06976	0.07266	0.07556	0.07846	0.08136	0.08426	0.08716	85
5	0.08716	0.09005	0.09295	0.09585	0.09874	0.10164	0.10453	84
6	0.10453	0.10742	0.11031	0.11320	0.11609	0.11898	0.12187	83
7	0.12187	0.12476	0.12764	0.13053	0.13341	0.13629	0.13917	82
8	0.13917	0.14205	0.14493	0.14781	0.15069	0.15356	0.15643	81
9	0.15643	0.15931	0.16218	0.16505	0.16792	0.17078	0.17365	80
10	0.17365	0.17651	0.17937	0.18224	0.18509	0.18795	0.19081	79
11	0.19081	0.19366	0.19652	0.19937	0.20222	0.20507	0.20791	78
12	0.20791	0.21076	0.21360	0.21644	0.21928	0.22212	0.22495	77
13	0.22495	0.22778	0.23062	0.23345	0.23627	0.23910	0.24192	76
14	0.24192	0.24474	0.24756	0.25038	0.25320	0.25601	0.25882	75
15	0.25882	0.26163	0.26443	0.26724	0.27004	0.27284	0.27564	74
16	0.27564	0.27843	0.28123	0.28402	0.28680	0.28959	0.29237	73
17	0.29237	0.29515	0.29793	0.30071	0.30348	0.30625	0.30902	72
18	0.30902	0.31178	0.31454	0.31730	0.32006	0.32282	0.32557	71
19	0.32557	0.32832	0.33106	0.33381	0.33655	0.33929	0.34202	70
20	0.34202	0.34475	0.34748	0.35021	0.35293	0.35565	0.35837	69
21	0.35837	0.36108	0.36379	0.36650	0.36921	0.37191	0.37461	68
22	0.37461	0.37730	0.37999	0.38268	0.38537	0.38805	0.39073	67
23	0.39073	0.39341	0.39608	0.39875	0.40141	0.40408	0.40674	66
24	0.40674	0.40939	0.41204	0.41469	0.41734	0.41998	0.42262	65
25	0.42262	0.42525	0.42788	0.43051	0.43313	0.43575	0.43837	64
26	0.43837	0.44098	0.44359	0.44620	0.44880	0.45140	0.45399	63
27	0.45399	0.45658	0.45917	0.46175	0.46433	0.46690	0.46947	62
28	0.46947	0.47204	0.47460	0.47716	0.47971	0.48226	0.48481	61
29	0.48481	0.48735	0.48989	0.49242	0.49495	0.49748	0.50000	60
30	0.50000	0.50252	0.50503	0.50754	0.51004	0.51254	0.51504	59
31	0.51504	0.51753	0.52002	0.52250	0.52498	0.52745	0.52992	58
32	0.52992	0.53238	0.53484	0.53730	0.53975	0.54220	0.54464	57
33	0.54464	0.54708	0.54951	0.55194	0.55436	0.55678	0.55919	56
34	0.55919	0.56160	0.56401	0.56641	0.56880	0.57119	0.57358	55
35	0.57358	0.57596	0.57833	0.58070	0.58307	0.58543	0.58779	54
36	0.58779	0.59014	0.59248	0.59482	0.59716	0.59949	0.60182	53
37	0.60182	0.60414	0.60645	0.60876	0.61107	0.61337	0.61566	52
38	0.61566	0.61795	0.62024	0.62251	0.62479	0.62706	0.62932	51
39	0.62932	0.63158	0.63383	0.63608	0.63832	0.64056	0.64279	50
40	0.64279	0.64501	0.64723	0.64945	0.65166	0.65386	0.65606	49
41	0.65606	0.65825	0.66044	0.66262	0.66480	0.66697	0.66913	48
42	0.66913	0.67129	0.67344	0.67559	0.67773	0.67987	0.68200	47
43	0.68200	0.68412	0.68624	0.68835	0.69046	0.69256	0.69466	46
44°	0.69466	0.69675	0.69883	0.70091	0.70298	0.70505	0.70711	45°
	60′	50′	40′	30′	20′	10′	0′	ANGLE

NATURAL COSINES

NATURAL TANGENTS

ANGLE	0′	10′	20′	30′	40′	50′	60′	
0°	0.00000	0.00291	0.00582	0.00873	0.01164	0.01455	0.01746	89°
1	0.01746	0.02036	0.02328	0.02619	0.02910	0.03201	0.03492	88
2	0.03492	0.03783	0.04075	0.04366	0.04658	0.04949	0.05241	87
3	0.05241	0.05533	0.05824	0.06116	0.06408	0.06700	0.06993	86
4	0.06993	0.07285	0.07578	0.07870	0.08163	0.08456	0.08749	85
5	0.08749	0.09042	0.09335	0.09629	0.09923	0.10216	0.10510	84
6	0.10510	0.10805	0.11099	0.11394	0.11688	0.11983	0.12278	83
7	0.12278	0.12574	0.12869	0.13165	0.13461	0.13758	0.14054	82
8	0.14054	0.14351	0.14648	0.14945	0.15243	0.15540	0.15838	81
9	0.15838	0.16137	0.16435	0.16734	0.17033	0.17333	0.17633	80
10	0.17633	0.17933	0.18233	0.18534	0.18835	0.19136	0.19438	79
11	0.19438	0.19740	0.20042	0.20345	0.20648	0.20952	0.21256	78
12	0.21256	0.21560	0.21864	0.22169	0.22475	0.22781	0.23087	77
13	0.23087	0.23393	0.23700	0.24008	0.24316	0.24624	0.24933	76
14	0.24933	0.25242	0.25552	0.25862	0.26172	0.26483	0.26795	75
15	0.26795	0.27107	0.27419	0.27732	0.28046	0.28360	0.28675	74
16	0.28675	0.28990	0.29305	0.29621	0.29938	0.30255	0.30573	73
17	0.30573	0.30891	0.31210	0.31530	0.31850	0.32171	0.32492	72
18	0.32492	0.32814	0.33136	0.33460	0.33783	0.34108	0.34433	71
19	0.34433	0.34758	0.35085	0.35412	0.35740	0.36068	0.36397	70
20	0.36397	0.36727	0.37057	0.37388	0.37720	0.38053	0.38386	69
21	0.38386	0.38721	0.39055	0.39391	0.39727	0.40065	0.40403	68
22	0.40403	0.40741	0.41081	0.41421	0.41763	0.42105	0.42447	67
23	0.42447	0.42791	0.43136	0.43481	0.43828	0.44175	0.44523	66
24	0.44523	0.44872	0.45222	0.45573	0.45924	0.46277	0.46631	65
25	0.46631	0.46985	0.47341	0.47698	0.48055	0.48414	0.48773	64
26	0.48773	0.49134	0.49495	0.49858	0.50222	0.50587	0.50953	63
27	0.50953	0.51320	0.51688	0.52057	0.52427	0.52798	0.53171	62
28	0.53171	0.53545	0.53920	0.54296	0.54673	0.55051	0.55431	61
29	0.55431	0.55812	0.56194	0.56577	0.56962	0.57348	0.57735	60
30	0.57735	0.58124	0.58513	0.58905	0.59297	0.59691	0.60086	59
31	0.60086	0.60483	0.60881	0.61280	0.61681	0.62083	0.62487	58
32	0.62487	0.62892	0.63299	0.63707	0.64117	0.64528	0.64941	57
33	0.64941	0.65355	0.65771	0.66189	0.66608	0.67028	0.67451	56
34	0.67451	0.67875	0.68301	0.68728	0.69157	0.69588	0.70021	55
35	0.70021	0.70455	0.70891	0.71329	0.71769	0.72211	0.72654	54
36	0.72654	0.73100	0.73547	0.73996	0.74447	0.74900	0.75355	53
37	0.75355	0.75812	0.76272	0.76733	0.77196	0.77661	0.78129	52
38	0.78129	0.78598	0.79070	0.79544	0.80020	0.80498	0.80978	51
39	0.80978	0.81461	0.81946	0.82434	0.82923	0.83415	0.83910	50
40	0.83910	0.84407	0.84906	0.85408	0.85912	0.86419	0.86929	49
41	0.96929	0.87441	0.87955	0.88473	0.88992	0.89515	0.90040	48
42	0.90040	0.90569	0.91099	0.91633	0.92170	0.92709	0.93252	47
43	0.93252	0.93797	0.94345	0.94896	0.95451	0.96008	0.96569	46
44°	0.96569	0.97133	0.97700	0.98270	0.98843	0.99420	1.00000	45°
	60′	50′	40′	30′	20′	10′	0′	ANGLE

NATURAL COTANGENTS

NATURAL SINES

ANGLE	0′	10′	20′	30′	40′	50′	60′	
45°	0.70711	0.70916	0.71121	0.71325	0.71529	0.71732	0.71934	44°
46	0.71934	0.72136	0.72337	0.72537	0.72737	0.72937	0.73135	43
47	0.73135	0.73333	0.73531	0.73728	0.73924	0.74120	0.74314	42
48	0.74314	0.74509	0.74703	0.74896	0.75088	0.75280	0.75471	41
49	0.75471	0.75661	0.75851	0.76041	0.76229	0.76417	0.76604	40
50	0.76604	0.76791	0.76977	0.77162	0.77347	0.77531	0.77715	39
51	0.77715	0.77897	0.78079	0.78261	0.78442	0.78622	0.78801	38
52	0.78801	0.78980	0.79158	0.79335	0.79512	0.79688	0.79864	37
53	0.79864	0.80038	0.80212	0.80386	0.80558	0.80730	0.80902	36
54	0.80902	0.81072	0.81242	0.81412	0.81580	0.81748	0.81915	35
55	0.81915	0.82082	0.82248	0.82413	0.82577	0.82741	0.82904	34
56	0.82904	0.83066	0.83228	0.83389	0.83549	0.83708	0.83867	33
57	0.83867	0.84025	0.84182	0.84339	0.84495	0.84650	0.84805	32
58	0.84805	0.84959	0.85112	0.85264	0.85416	0.85567	0.85717	31
59	0.85717	0.85866	0.86015	0.86163	0.86310	0.86457	0.86603	30
60	0.86603	0.86748	0.86892	0.87036	0.87178	0.87321	0.87462	29
61	0.87462	0.87603	0.87743	0.87882	0.88020	0.88158	0.88295	28
62	0.88295	0.88431	0.88566	0.88701	0.88835	0.88968	0.89101	27
63	0.89101	0.89232	0.89363	0.89493	0.89623	0.89752	0.89879	26
64	0.89879	0.90007	0.90133	0.90259	0.90383	0.90507	0.90631	25
65	0.90631	0.90753	0.90875	0.90996	0.91116	0.91236	0.91355	24
66	0.91355	0.91472	0.91590	0.91706	0.91822	0.91936	0.92050	23
67	0.92050	0.92164	0.92276	0.92388	0.92499	0.92609	0.92718	22
68	0.92718	0.92827	0.92935	0.93042	0.93148	0.93253	0.93358	21
69	0.93358	0.93462	0.93565	0.93667	0.93769	0.93869	0.93969	20
70	0.93969	0.94068	0.94167	0.94264	0.94361	0.94457	0.94552	19
71	0.94552	0.94646	0.94740	0.94832	0.94924	0.95015	0.95106	18
72	0.95106	0.95195	0.95284	0.95372	0.95459	0.95545	0.95630	17
73	0.95630	0.95715	0.95799	0.95882	0.95964	0.96046	0.96126	16
74	0.96126	0.96206	0.96285	0.96363	0.96440	0.96517	0.96593	15
75	0.96593	0.96667	0.96742	0.96815	0.96887	0.96959	0.97030	14
76	0.97030	0.97100	0.97169	0.97237	0.97304	0.97371	0.97437	13
77	0.97437	0.97502	0.97566	0.97630	0.97692	0.97754	0.97815	12
78	0.97815	0.97875	0.97934	0.97992	0.98050	0.98107	0.98163	11
79	0.98163	0.98218	0.98272	0.98325	0.98378	0.98430	0.98481	10
80	0.98481	0.98531	0.98580	0.98629	0.98676	0.98723	0.98769	9
81	0.98769	0.98814	0.98858	0.98902	0.98944	0.98986	0.99027	8
82	0.99027	0.99067	0.99106	0.99144	0.99182	0.99219	0.99255	7
83	0.99255	0.99290	0.99324	0.99357	0.99390	0.99421	0.99452	6
84	0.99452	0.99482	0.99511	0.99540	0.99567	0.99594	0.99619	5
85	0.99619	0.99644	0.99668	0.99692	0.99714	0.99736	0.99756	4
86	0.99756	0.99776	0.99795	0.99813	0.99831	0.99847	0.99863	3
87	0.99863	0.99878	0.99892	0.99905	0.99917	0.99929	0.99939	2
88	0.99939	0.99949	0.99958	0.99966	0.99973	0.99979	0.99985	1
89°	0.99985	0.99989	0.99993	0.99996	0.99998	1.00000	1.00000	0°
	60′	50′	40′	30′	20′	10′	0′	ANGLE

NATURAL COSINES

NATURAL TANGENTS

ANGLE	0′	10′	20′	30′	40′	50′	60′	
45°	1.00000	1.00583	1.01170	1.01761	1.02355	1.02952	1.03553	44°
46	1.03553	1.04158	1.04766	1.05378	1.05994	1.06613	1.07237	43
47	1.07237	1.07864	1.08496	1.09131	1.09770	1.10414	1.11061	42
48	1.11061	1.11713	1.12369	1.13029	1.13694	1.14363	1.15037	41
49	1.15037	1.15715	1.16398	1.17085	1.17777	1.18474	1.19175	40
50	1.19175	1.19882	1.20593	1.21310	1.22031	1.22758	1.23490	39
51	1.23490	1.24227	1.24969	1.25717	1.26471	1.27230	1.27994	38
52	1.27994	1.28764	1.29541	1.30323	1.31110	1.31904	1.32704	37
53	1.32704	1.33511	1.34323	1.35142	1.35968	1.36800	1.37638	36
54	1.37638	1.38484	1.39336	1.40195	1.41061	1.41934	1.42815	35
55	1.42815	1.43703	1.44598	1.45501	1.46411	1.47330	1.48256	34
56	1.48256	1.49190	1.50133	1.51084	1.52043	1.53010	1.53987	33
57	1.53987	1.54972	1.55966	1.56969	1.57981	1.59002	1.60033	32
58	1.60033	1.61074	1.62125	1.63185	1.64256	1.65337	1.66428	31
59	1.66428	1.67530	1.68643	1.69766	1.70901	1.72047	1.73205	30
60	1.73205	1.74375	1.75556	1.76749	1.77955	1.79174	1.80405	29
61	1.80405	1.81649	1.82906	1.84177	1.85462	1.86760	1.88073	28
62	1.88073	1.89400	1.90741	1.92098	1.93470	1.94858	1.96261	27
63	1.96261	1.97681	1.99116	2.00569	2.02039	2.03526	2.05030	26
64	2.05030	2.06553	2.08094	2.09654	2.11233	2.12832	2.14451	25
65	2.14451	2.16090	2.17749	2.19430	2.21132	2.22857	2.24604	24
66	2.24604	2.26374	2.28167	2.29984	2.31826	2.33693	2.35585	23
67	2.35585	2.37504	2.39449	2.41421	2.43422	2.45451	2.47509	22
68	2.47509	2.49597	2.51715	2.53865	2.56046	2.58261	2.60509	21
69	2.60509	2.62791	2.65109	2.67462	2.69853	2.72281	2.74748	20
70	2.74748	2.77254	2.79802	2.82391	2.85023	2.87700	2.90421	19
71	2.90421	2.93189	2.96004	2.98869	3.01783	3.04749	3.07768	18
72	3.07768	3.10842	3.13972	3.17159	3.20406	3.23714	3.27085	17
73	3.27085	3.30521	3.34023	3.37594	3.41236	3.44951	3.48741	16
74	3.48741	3.52609	3.56557	3.60588	3.64705	3.68909	3.73205	15
75	3.73205	3.77595	3.82083	3.86671	3.91364	3.96165	4.01078	14
76	4.01078	4.06107	4.11256	4.16530	4.21933	4.27471	4.33148	13
77	4.33148	4.38969	4.44942	4.51071	4.57363	4.63825	4.70463	12
78	4.70463	4.77286	4.84300	4.91516	4.98940	5.06584	5.14455	11
79	5.14455	5.22566	5.30928	5.39552	5.48451	5.57638	5.67128	10
80	5.67128	5.76937	5.87080	5.97576	6.08444	6.19703	6.31375	9
81	6.31375	6.43484	6.56055	6.69116	6.82694	6.96823	7.11537	8
82	7.11537	7.26873	7.42871	7.59575	7.77035	7.95302	8.14435	7
83	8.14435	8.34496	8.55555	8.77689	9.00983	9.25530	9.51436	6
84	9.51436	9.78817	10.07803	10.38540	10.71191	11.05943	11.43005	5
85	11.43005	11.82617	12.25051	12.70621	13.19688	13.72674	14.30067	4
86	14.30067	14.92442	15.60478	16.34986	17.16934	18.07498	19.08114	3
87	19.08114	20.20555	21.47040	22.90377	24.54176	26.43160	28.63625	2
88	28.63625	31.24158	34.36777	38.18846	42.96408	49.10388	57.28996	1
89°	57.28996	68.75009	85.93979	114.58865	171.88540	343.77371	Infinite	0°
	60′	50′	40′	30′	20′	10′	0′	ANGLE

NATURAL COTANGENTS

GEOMETRY A

NATURAL SECANTS

ANGLE	0′	10′	20′	30′	40′	50′	60′	
0°	1.00000	1.00001	1.00002	1.00004	1.00007	1.00011	1.00015	89°
1	1.00015	1.00021	1.00027	1.00034	1.00042	1.00051	1.00061	88
2	1.00061	1.00072	1.00083	1.00095	1.00108	1.00122	1.00137	87
3	1.00137	1.00153	1.00169	1.00187	1.00205	1.00224	1.00244	86
4	1.00244	1.00265	1.00287	1.00309	1.00333	1.00357	1.00382	85
5	1.00382	1.00408	1.00435	1.00463	1.00491	1.00521	1.00551	84
6	1.00551	1.00582	1.00614	1.00647	1.00681	1.00715	1.00751	83
7	1.00751	1.00787	1.00825	1.00863	1.00902	1.00942	1.00983	82
8	1.00983	1.01024	1.01067	1.01111	1.01155	1.01200	1.01247	81
9	1.01247	1.01294	1.01342	1.01391	1.01440	1.10491	1.01543	80
10	1.01543	1.01595	1.01649	1.01703	1.01758	1.01815	1.01872	79
11	1.01872	1.01930	1.01989	1.02049	1.02110	1.02171	1.02234	78
12	1.02234	1.02298	1.02362	1.02428	1.02494	1.02562	1.02630	77
13	1.02630	1.02700	1.02770	1.02842	1.02914	1.02987	1.03061	76
14	1.03061	1.03137	1.03213	1.03290	1.03368	1.03447	1.03528	75
15	1.03528	1.03609	1.03691	1.03774	1.03858	1.03944	1.04030	74
16	1.04030	1.04117	1.04206	1.04295	1.04385	1.04477	1.04569	73
17	1.04569	1.04663	1.04757	1.04853	1.04950	1.05047	1.05146	72
18	1.05146	1.05246	1.05347	1.05449	1.05552	1.05657	1.05762	71
19	1.05762	1.05869	1.05976	1.06085	1.06195	1.06306	1.06418	70
20	1.06418	1.06531	1.06645	1.06761	1.06878	1.06995	1.07115	69
21	1.07115	1.07235	1.07356	1.07479	1.07602	1.07727	1.07853	68
22	1.07853	1.07981	1.08109	1.08239	1.08370	1.08503	1.08636	67
23	1.08636	1.08771	1.08907	1.09044	1.09183	1.09323	1.09464	66
24	1.09464	1.09606	1.09750	1.09895	1.10041	1.10189	1.10338	65
25	1.10338	1.10488	1.10640	1.10793	1.10947	1.11103	1.11260	64
26	1.11260	1.11419	1.11579	1.11740	1.11903	1.12067	1.12233	63
27	1.12233	1.12400	1.12568	1.12738	1.12910	1.13083	1.13257	62
28	1.13257	1.13433	1.13610	1.13789	1.13970	1.14152	1.14335	61
29	1.14335	1.14521	1.14707	1.14896	1.15085	1.15277	1.15470	60
30	1.15470	1.15665	1.15861	1.16059	1.16259	1.16460	1.16663	59
31	1.16663	1.16868	1.17075	1.17283	1.17493	1.17704	1.17918	58
32	1.17918	1.18133	1.18350	1.18569	1.18790	1.19012	1.19236	57
33	1.19236	1.19463	1.19691	1.19920	1.20152	1.20386	1.20622	56
34	1.20622	1.20859	1.21099	1.21341	1.21584	1.21830	1.22077	55
35	1.22077	1.22327	1.22579	1.22833	1.23089	1.23347	1.23607	54
36	1.23607	1.23869	1.24134	1.24400	1.24669	1.24940	1.25214	53
37	1.25214	1.25489	1.25767	1.26047	1.26330	1.26615	1.26902	52
38	1.26902	1.27191	1.27483	1.27778	1.28075	1.28374	1.28676	51
39	1.28676	1.28980	1.29287	1.29597	1.29909	1.30223	1.30541	50
40	1.30541	1.30861	1.31183	1.31509	1.31837	1.32168	1.32501	49
41	1.32501	1.32838	1.33177	1.33519	1.33864	1.34212	1.34563	48
42	1.34563	1.34917	1.35274	1.35634	1.35997	1.36363	1.36733	47
43	1.36733	1.37105	1.37481	1.37860	1.38242	1.38628	1.39016	46
44°	1.39016	1.39409	1.39804	1.40203	1.40606	1.41012	1.41421	45°
	60′	50′	40′	30′	20′	10′	0′	ANGLE

NATURAL COSECANTS

NATURAL SECANTS

ANGLE	0′	10′	20′	30′	40′	50′	60′	
45°	1.41421	1.41835	1.42251	1.42672	1.43096	1.43524	1.43956	44°
46	1.43956	1.44391	1.44831	1.45274	1.45721	1.46173	1.46628	43
47	1.46628	1.47087	1.47551	1.48019	1.48491	1.48967	1.49448	42
48	1.49448	1.49933	1.50422	1.50916	1.51415	1.51918	1.52425	41
49	1.52425	1.52938	1.53455	1.53977	1.54504	1.55036	1.55572	40
50	1.55572	1.56114	1.56661	1.57213	1.57771	1.58333	1.58902	39
51	1.58902	1.59475	1.60054	1.60639	1.61229	1.61825	1.62427	38
52	1.62427	1.63035	1.63648	1.64268	1.64894	1.65526	1.66164	37
53	1.66164	1.66809	1.67460	1.68117	1.68782	1.69452	1.70130	36
54	1.70130	1.70815	1.71506	1.72205	1.72911	1.73624	1.74345	35
55	1.74345	1.75073	1.75808	1.76552	1.77303	1.78062	1.78829	34
56	1.78829	1.79604	1.80388	1.81180	1.81981	1.82790	1.83608	33
57	1.83608	1.84435	1.85271	1.86116	1.86970	1.87834	1.88708	32
58	1.88708	1.89591	1.90485	1.91388	1.92302	1.93226	1.94160	31
59	1.94160	1.95106	1.96062	1.97029	1.98008	1.98998	2.00000	30
60	2.00000	2.01014	2.02039	2.03077	2.04128	2.05191	2.06267	29
61	2.06267	2.07356	2.08458	2.09574	2.10704	2.11847	2.13005	28
62	2.13005	2.14178	2.15366	2.16568	2.17786	2.19019	2.20269	27
63	2.20269	2.21535	2.22817	2.24116	2.25432	2.26766	2.28117	26
64	2.28117	2.29487	2.30875	2.32282	2.33708	2.35154	2.36620	25
65	2.36620	2.38107	2.39614	2.41142	2.42692	2.44264	2.45859	24
66	2.45859	2.47477	2.49119	2.50784	2.52474	2.54190	2.55930	23
67	2.55930	2.57698	2.59491	2.61313	2.63162	2.65040	2.66947	22
68	2.66947	2.68884	2.70851	2.72850	2.74881	2.76945	2.79043	21
69	2.79043	2.81175	2.83342	2.85545	2.87785	2.90063	2.92380	20
70	2.92380	2.94737	2.97135	2.99574	3.02057	3.04584	3.07155	19
71	3.07155	3.09774	3.12440	3.15155	3.17920	3.20737	3.23607	18
72	3.23607	3.26531	3.29512	3.32551	3.35649	3.38808	3.42030	17
73	3.42030	3.45317	3.48671	3.52094	3.55587	3.59154	3.62796	16
74	3.62796	3.66515	3.70315	3.74198	3.78166	3.82223	3.86370	15
75	3.86370	3.90613	3.94952	3.99393	4.03938	4.08591	4.13357	14
76	4.13357	4.18238	4.23239	4.28366	4.33622	4.39012	4.44541	13
77	4.44541	4.50216	4.56041	4.62023	4.68167	4.74482	4.80973	12
78	4.80973	4.87649	4.94517	5.01585	5.08863	5.16359	5.24084	11
79	5.24084	5.32049	5.40263	5.48740	5.57493	5.66533	5.75877	10
80	5.75877	5.85539	5.95536	6.05886	6.16607	6.27719	6.39245	9
81	6.39245	6.51208	6.63633	6.76547	6.89979	7.03962	7.18530	8
82	7.18530	7.33719	7.49571	7.66130	7.83443	8.01565	8.20551	7
83	8.20551	8.40466	8.61379	8.83367	9.06515	9.30917	9.56677	6
84	9.56677	9.83912	10.12752	10.43343	10.75849	11.10455	11.47371	5
85	11.47371	11.86837	12.29125	12.74550	13.23472	13.76312	14.33559	4
86	14.33559	14.95788	15.63679	16.38041	17.19843	18.10262	19.10732	3
87	19.10732	20.23028	21.49368	22.92559	24.56212	26.45051	28.65371	2
88	28.65371	31.25758	34.38232	38.20155	42.97571	49.11406	57.29869	1
89°	57.29869	68.75736	85.94561	114.59301	171.88831	343.77516	Infinite	0°
	60′	50′	40′	30′	20′	10′	0′	ANGLE

NATURAL COSECANTS

FUNCTIONS OF NUMBERS

NO.	SQUARE	CUBE	SQUARE ROOT	CUBE ROOT	LOGARITHM	1000 x RECIPROCAL	NO. = DIAMETER CIRCUM.	AREA
1	1	1	1.0000	1.0000	0.00000	1000.000	3.142	0.7854
2	4	8	1.4142	1.2599	0.30103	500.000	6.283	3.1416
3	9	27	1.7321	1.4422	0.47712	333.333	9.425	7.0686
4	16	64	2.0000	1.5874	0.60206	250.000	12.566	12.5664
5	25	125	2.2361	1.7100	0.69897	200.000	15.708	19.6350
6	36	216	2.4495	1.8171	0.77815	166.667	18.850	28.2743
7	49	343	2.6458	1.9129	0.84510	142.857	21.991	38.4845
8	64	512	2.8284	2.0000	0.90309	125.000	25.133	50.2655
9	81	729	3.0000	2.0801	0.95424	111.111	28.274	63.6173
10	100	1000	3.1623	2.1544	1.00000	100.000	31.416	78.5398
11	121	1331	3.3166	2.2240	1.04139	90.9091	34.558	95.0332
12	144	1728	3.4641	2.2894	1.07918	83.3333	37.699	113.097
13	169	2197	3.6056	2.3513	1.11394	76.9231	40.841	132.732
14	196	2744	3.7417	2.4101	1.14613	71.4286	43.982	153.938
15	225	3375	3.8730	2.4662	1.17609	66.6667	47.124	176.715
16	256	4096	4.0000	2.5198	1.20412	62.5000	50.265	201.062
17	289	4913	4.1231	2.5713	1.23045	58.8235	53.407	226.980
18	324	5832	4.2426	2.6207	1.25527	55.5556	56.549	254.469
19	361	6859	4.3589	2.6684	1.27875	52.6316	59.690	283.529
20	400	8000	4.4721	2.7144	1.30103	50.0000	62.832	314.159
21	441	9261	4.5826	2.7589	1.32222	47.6190	65.973	346.361
22	484	10648	4.6904	2.8020	1.34242	45.4545	69.115	380.133
23	529	12167	4.7958	2.8439	1.36173	43.4783	72.257	415.476
24	576	13824	4.8990	2.8845	1.38021	41.6667	75.398	452.389
25	625	15625	5.0000	2.9240	1.39794	40.0000	78.540	490.874
26	676	17576	5.0990	2.9625	1.41497	38.4615	81.681	530.929
27	729	19683	5.1962	3.0000	1.43136	37.0370	84.823	572.555
28	784	21952	5.2915	3.0366	1.44716	35.7143	87.965	615.752
29	841	24389	5.3852	3.0723	1.46240	34.4828	91.106	660.520
30	900	27000	5.4772	3.1072	1.47712	33.3333	94.248	706.858
31	961	29791	5.5678	3.1414	1.49136	32.2581	97.389	754.768
32	1024	32768	5.6569	3.1748	1.50515	31.2500	100.531	804.248
33	1089	35937	5.7446	3.2075	1.51851	30.3030	103.673	855.299
34	1156	39304	5.8310	3.2396	1.53148	29.4118	106.814	907.920
35	1225	42875	5.9161	3.2711	1.54407	28.5714	109.956	962.113
36	1296	46656	6.0000	3.3019	1.55630	27.7778	113.097	1017.88
37	1369	50653	6.0828	3.3322	1.56820	27.0270	116.239	1075.21
38	1444	54872	6.1644	3.3620	1.57978	26.3158	119.381	1134.11
39	1521	59319	6.2450	3.3912	1.59106	25.6410	122.522	1194.59
40	1600	64000	6.3246	3.4200	1.60206	25.0000	125.66	1256.64
41	1681	68921	6.4031	3.4482	1.61278	24.3902	128.81	1320.25
42	1764	74088	6.4807	3.4760	1.62325	23.8095	131.95	1385.44
43	1849	79507	6.5574	3.5034	1.63347	23.2558	135.09	1452.20
44	1936	85184	6.6332	3.5303	1.64345	22.7273	138.23	1520.53
45	2025	91125	6.7082	3.5569	1.65321	22.2222	141.37	1590.43

FUNCTIONS OF NUMBERS

NO.	SQUARE	CUBE	SQUARE ROOT	CUBE ROOT	LOGARITHM	1000 x RECIPROCAL	NO. = DIAMETER CIRCUM.	AREA
46	2116	97336	6.7823	3.5830	1.66276	21.7391	144.51	1661.90
47	2209	103823	6.8557	3.6088	1.67210	21.2766	147.65	1734.94
48	2304	110592	6.9282	3.6342	1.68124	20.8333	150.80	1809.56
49	2401	117649	7.0000	3.6593	1.69020	20.4082	153.94	1885.74
50	2500	125000	7.0711	3.6840	1.69897	20.0000	157.08	1963.50
51	2601	132651	7.1414	3.7084	1.70757	19.6078	160.22	2042.82
52	2704	140608	7.2111	3.7325	1.71600	19.2308	163.36	2123.72
53	2809	148877	7.2801	3.7563	1.72428	18.8679	166.50	2206.18
54	2916	157464	7.3485	3.7798	1.73239	18.5185	169.65	2290.22
55	3025	166375	7.4162	3.8030	1.74036	18.1818	172.79	2375.83
56	3136	175616	7.4833	3.8259	1.74819	17.8571	175.93	2463.01
57	3249	185193	7.5498	3.8485	1.75587	17.5439	179.07	2551.76
58	3364	195112	7.6158	3.8709	1.76343	17.2414	182.21	2642.08
59	3481	205379	7.6811	3.8930	1.77085	16.9492	185.35	2733.97
60	3600	216000	7.7460	3.9149	1.77815	16.6667	188.50	2827.43
61	3721	226981	7.8102	3.9365	1.78533	16.3934	191.64	2922.47
62	3844	238328	7.8740	3.9579	1.79239	16.1290	194.78	3019.07
63	3969	250047	7.9373	3.9791	1.79934	15.8730	197.92	3117.25
64	4096	262144	8.0000	4.0000	1.80618	15.6250	201.06	3216.99
65	4225	274625	8.0623	4.0207	1.81291	15.3846	204.20	3318.31
66	4356	287496	8.1240	4.0412	1.81954	15.1515	207.35	3421.19
67	4489	300763	8.1854	4.0615	1.82607	14.9254	210.49	3525.65
68	4624	314432	8.2462	4.0817	1.83251	14.7059	213.63	3631.68
69	4761	328509	8.3066	4.1016	1.83885	14.4928	216.77	3739.28
70	4900	343000	8.3666	4.1213	1.84510	14.2857	219.91	3848.45
71	5041	357911	8.4261	4.1408	1.85126	14.0845	223.05	3959.19
72	5184	373248	8.4853	4.1602	1.85733	13.8889	226.19	4071.50
73	5329	389017	8.5440	4.1793	1.86332	13.6986	229.34	4185.39
74	5476	405224	8.6023	4.1983	1.86923	13.5135	232.48	4300.84
75	5625	421875	8.6603	4.2172	1.87506	13.3333	235.62	4417.86
76	5776	438976	8.7178	4.2358	1.88081	13.1579	238.76	4536.46
77	5929	456533	8.7750	4.2543	1.88649	12.9870	241.90	4656.63
78	6084	474552	8.8318	4.2727	1.89209	12.8205	245.04	4778.36
79	6241	493039	8.8882	4.2908	1.89763	12.6582	248.19	4901.67
80	6400	512000	8.9443	4.3089	1.90309	12.5000	251.33	5026.55
81	6561	531441	9.0000	4.3267	1.90849	12.3457	254.47	5153.00
82	6724	551368	9.0554	4.3445	1.91381	12.1951	257.61	5281.02
83	6889	571787	9.1104	4.3621	1.91908	12.0482	260.75	5410.61
84	7056	592704	9.1652	4.3795	1.92428	11.9048	263.89	5541.77
85	7225	614125	9.2195	4.3968	1.92942	11.7647	267.04	5674.50
86	7396	636056	9.2736	4.4140	1.93450	11.6279	270.18	5808.80
87	7569	658503	9.3274	4.4310	1.93952	11.4943	273.32	5944.68
88	7744	681472	9.3808	4.4480	1.94448	11.3636	276.46	6082.12
89	7921	704969	9.4340	4.4647	1.94939	11.2360	279.60	6221.14
90	8100	729000	9.4868	4.4814	1.95424	11.1111	282.74	6361.73

A GEOMETRY

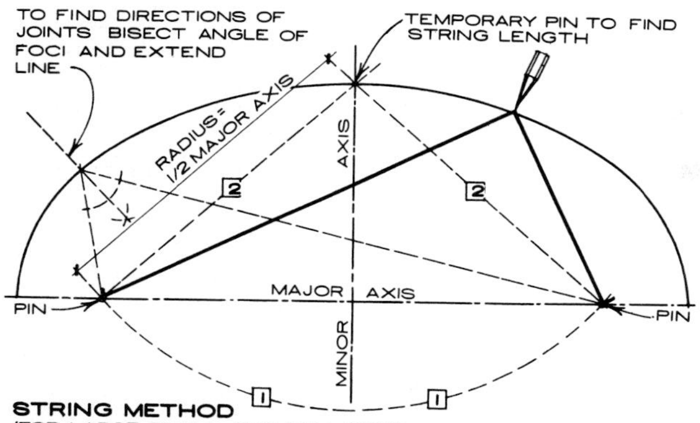

TO FIND DIRECTIONS OF JOINTS BISECT ANGLE OF FOCI AND EXTEND LINE
TEMPORARY PIN TO FIND STRING LENGTH
RADIUS = 1/2 MAJOR AXIS
AXIS
2
2
MAJOR AXIS
PIN
PIN
MINOR
1
1

STRING METHOD
(FOR LARGE SCALE AND FULL SIZE)

C
C
HALF MINOR AXIS
HALF MAJOR AXIS
B
B
A
A

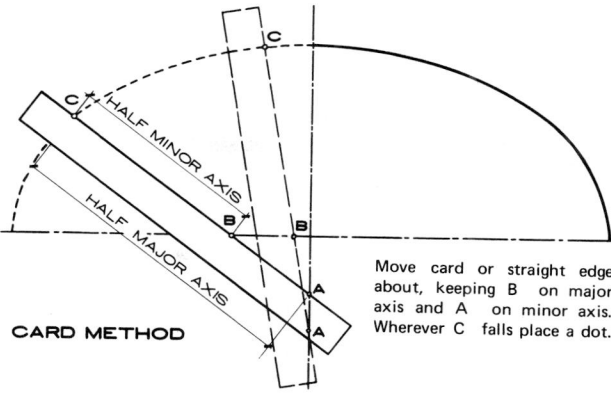

CARD METHOD

Move card or straight edge about, keeping B on major axis and A on minor axis. Wherever C falls place a dot.

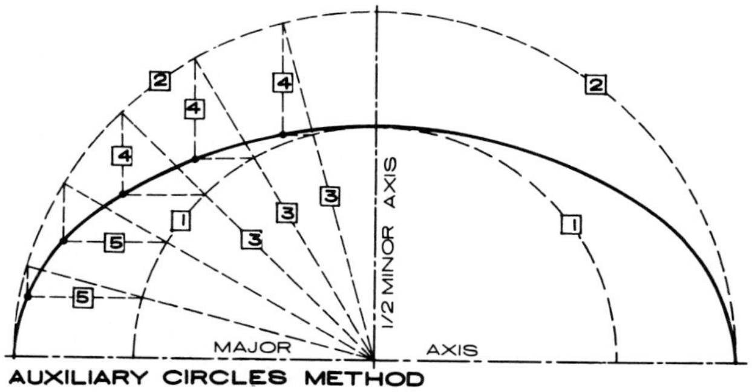

2
4
2
4
4
3
3
1
3
1
5
5
1/2 MINOR AXIS
MAJOR
AXIS

AUXILIARY CIRCLES METHOD

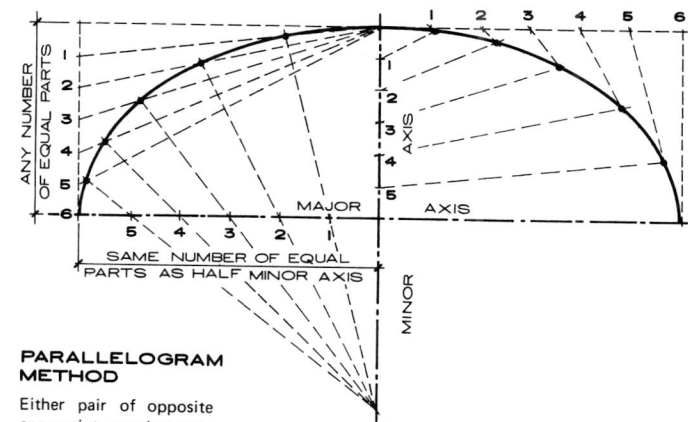

1 2 3 4 5 6
ANY NUMBER OF EQUAL PARTS
1
2
3
4
5
6
AXIS
MAJOR
AXIS
5 4 3 2 1
SAME NUMBER OF EQUAL PARTS AS HALF MINOR AXIS
MINOR

PARALLELOGRAM METHOD

Either pair of opposite apex points may be used.

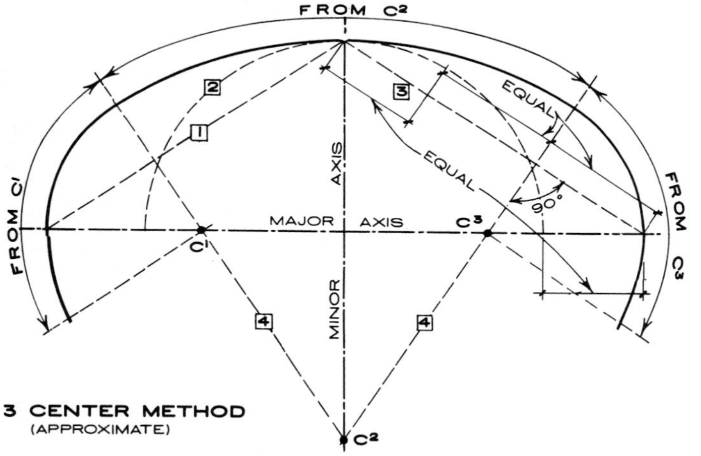

FROM C2
2
3
EQUAL
1
EQUAL
90°
FROM C1
AXIS
MAJOR AXIS
C3
FROM C3
C1
MINOR
4
4
C2

3 CENTER METHOD
(APPROXIMATE)

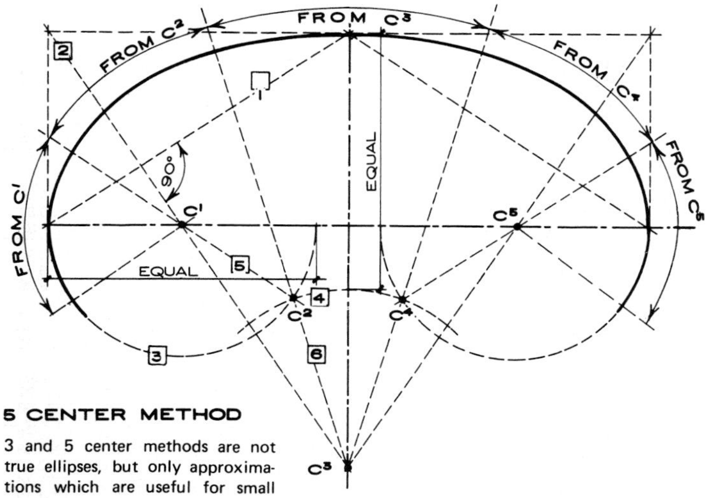

FROM C3
FROM C2
FROM C4
2
1
90°
FROM C1
FROM C5
EQUAL
C1
C5
EQUAL
5
4
C2
C4
3
6
C3

5 CENTER METHOD

3 and 5 center methods are not true ellipses, but only approximations which are useful for small scale drawings.

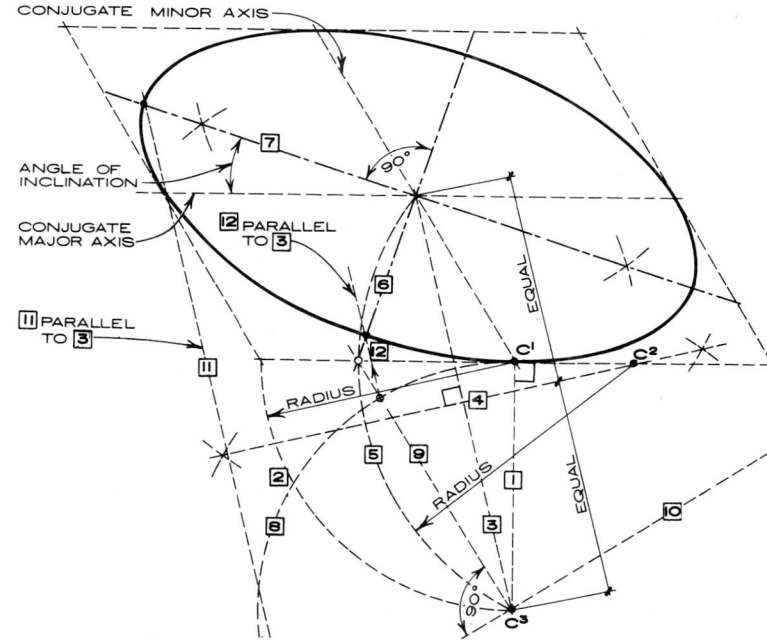

CONJUGATE MINOR AXIS
7
90°
ANGLE OF INCLINATION
CONJUGATE MAJOR AXIS
12 PARALLEL TO 3
6
EQUAL
11 PARALLEL TO 3
11
12
C1
C2
RADIUS
4
5
9
2
RADIUS
1
EQUAL
8
3
10
90°
C3

METHOD FOR FINDING THE ANGLE OF INCLINATION AND THEN THE TRUE LENGTHS OF THE MAJOR & MINOR AXES OF AN ELLIPSE TO BE INSCRIBED WITHIN A PARALLELOGRAM

NOTE

1. Using the conjugate axes, the ellipse can be drawn directly by using the parallelogram method.
2. Using the true lengths of the axes, the ellipse may be drawn with any one of the methods illustrated on this page.

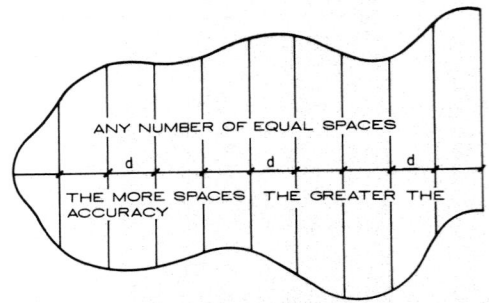

TO FIND THE AREA OF AN IRREGULAR PLANE FIGURE

1. Divide the figure into parallel strips by equally spaced parallel lines.

2. Measure the length of each of the parallel lines.

3. Obtain a summation of the unit areas by one of these 3 "rules".

TRAPEZOID RULE

Add together the length of the parallels, taking the first and last at $1/2$ value, and multiply by the width of the internal "d". This rule is sufficiently accurate for estimating and other ordinary purposes.

SIMPSON'S RULE

Add the parallels, taking the first and last at full value, second, the fourth, sixth, etc. from each end at 4 times full value, and the third, fifth, seventh, etc. from each end at 2 times the value, then multiply by $1/3$ d. This rule works only for an even number of spaces and is accurate for areas bounded by smooth curves.

DURAND'S RULE

Add the parallels taking the first and last at $5/12$ value, the second from each end at $13/12$ value, and all others at full value, then multiply by d. This rule is the most accurate for very irregular shapes.

NOTE

Irregular areas may be directly read off by means of a simple instrument called a Planimeter.

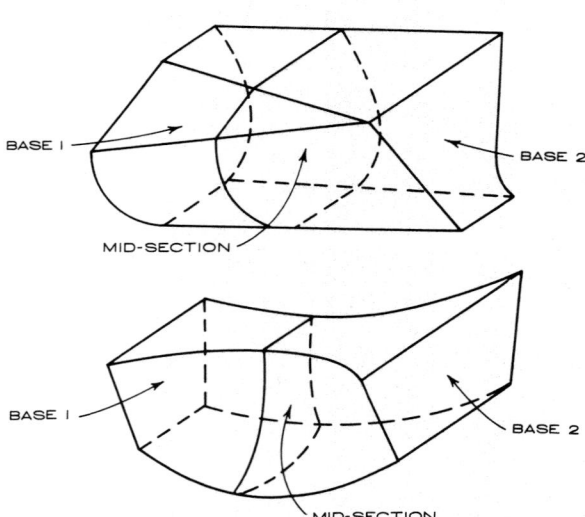

TO FIND THE VOLUME OF AN IRREGULAR FIGURE BY THE PRISMATOID FORMULA

Construct a section midway between the bases. Add 4 to the sum of the areas of the 2 bases and multiply the quantity by the area of the mid-section. Then multiply the total by $1/6$ the perpendicular distance between the bases.

V = [(area of base$_1$ + area of base$_2$ + 4) (area of midsection) x $1/6$ perpendicular distance between bases.

This formula is quite accurate for any solid with two parallel bases connected by a surface of straight line elements (upper figure), or smooth simple curves (lower figure).

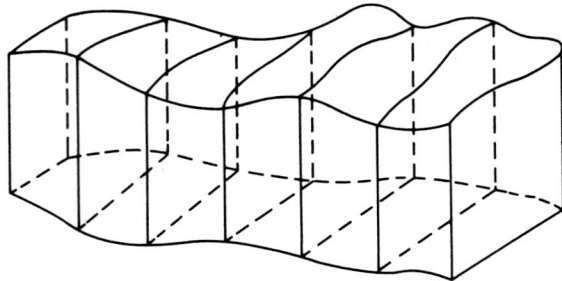

TO FIND THE VOLUME OF A VERY IRREGULAR FIGURE BY THE SECTIONING METHOD

1. Construct a series of equally spaced sections or profiles.

2. Determine the area of each section by any of the methods shown at left (preferably with a Planimeter).

3. Apply any one of the 3 summation "rules" given at left, to determine the total volume.

This method is in general use for estimating quantities of earthwork, etc.

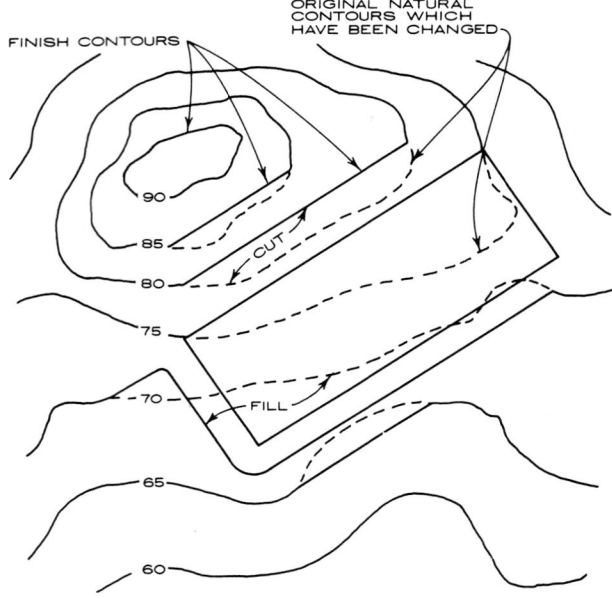

TO FIND THE VOLUME OF CUT AND FILL DIRECTLY FROM THE CONTOUR PLAN

1. Draw "finish" and "original" contours on same contour map.

2. Measure the differential areas between new and old contours of each contour and enter in columns according to whether cut or fill.

3. Add up each column and multiply by the contour interval to determine the volume in cubic feet.

EXAMPLE

CONTOUR	CUT		FILL	
85		300		
80		960		
75	2,460 ÷ 2 =	1,230	3,800 ÷ 2 =	1,900
70		20		2,200
		9,200		6,800
		x5		x5
TOTALS		46,000 cu. ft.		34,000 cu. ft.

NOTE

1. Where a cut or fill ends directly on a contour level use $1/2$ value.

2. The closer the contour interval, the greater the accuracy.

This method is more rapid than the sectioning method, and is sufficiently accurate for simple estimating purposes and for balancing of cut and fill.

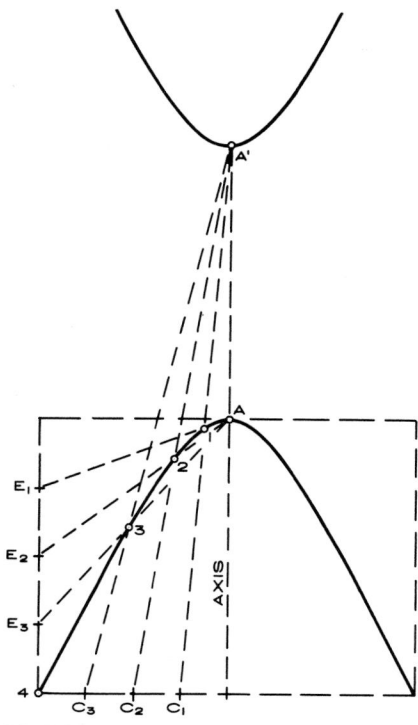

HYPERBOLA
PARALLELOGRAM METHOD
GIVEN:

Axis, two apexes (A and A') and a chord.

1. Draw surrounding parallelogram.
2. Divide chord in whole number of equal spaces (C_1, C_2, C_3, etc.).
3. Divide edge of parallelogram into same integral number of equal spaces (E_1, E_2, E_3, etc.).
4. Join A to points E on edge; join A' to points C on chord. Intersection of these rays are points on curve.

This method can be used equally well for any type of orthogonal or perspective projection, as shown by example of ellipse.

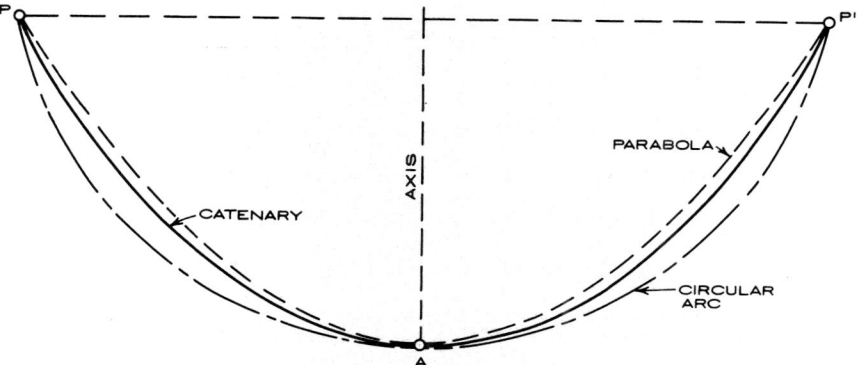

CATENARY

A catenary curve lies between a parabola and a circular arc drawn through the same three points, but is closer to the parabola. The catenary is not a conic section. The easiest method of drawing it is to tilt the drafting board and hang a very fine chain on it, and then prick guide points through the links of the chain.

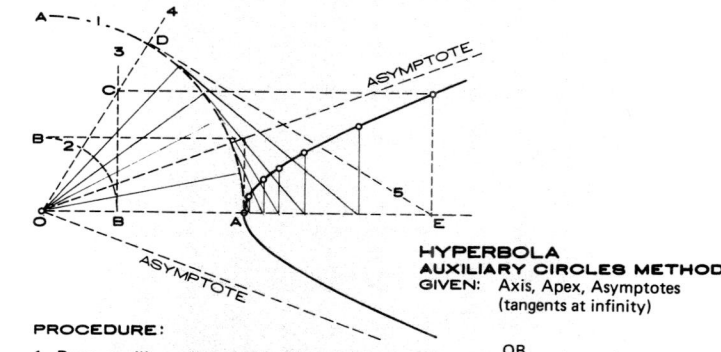

HYPERBOLA
AUXILIARY CIRCLES METHOD
GIVEN: Axis, Apex, Asymptotes
(tangents at infinity)

PROCEDURE:

1. Draw auxiliary circles with OB and OA as radii: note $\frac{OB}{OA}$ = slope of asymptote.
2. Erect perpendicular 3 where circle 2 intersects axis.
3. Draw any line 4 through 0, intersecting circle 1 at B and line 3 at C.
4. Draw line 5 through C parallel to axis.
5. Draw tangent 6 at D, intersecting axis at E.
6. Erect perpendicular 7 at E, intersecting 5 at P, a point on hyperbola.

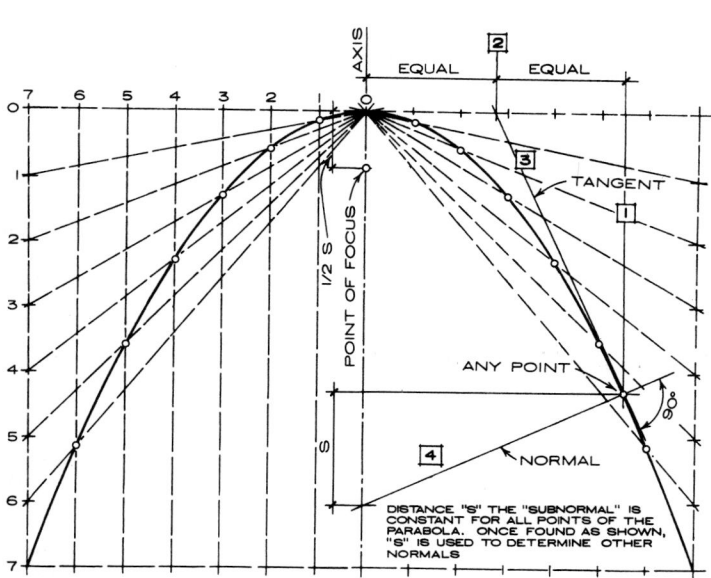

PARABOLA
PARALLELOGRAM METHOD

This method is comparable to the "Parallelogram Method" shown for the hyperbola above and the ellipse on previous page. The other apex 'A' is at infinity.

DISTANCE "S" THE "SUBNORMAL" IS CONSTANT FOR ALL POINTS OF THE PARABOLA. ONCE FOUND AS SHOWN, "S" IS USED TO DETERMINE OTHER NORMALS

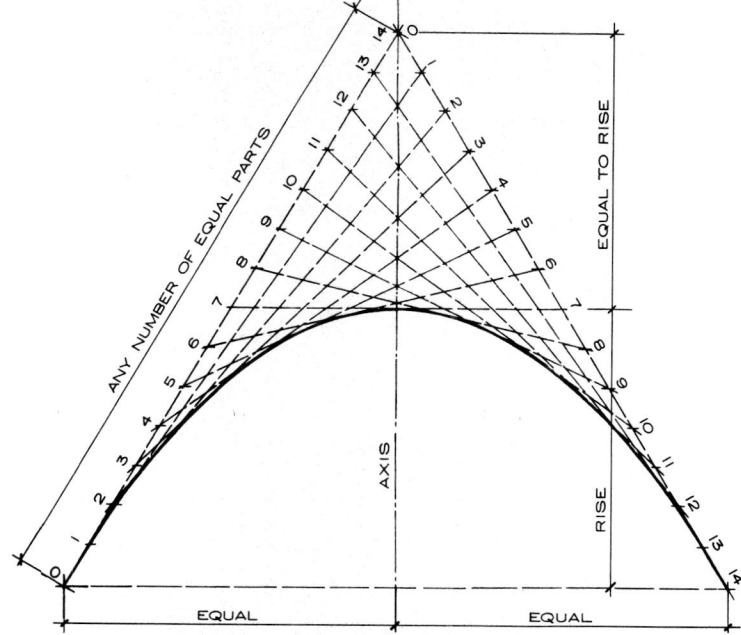

PARABOLA
ENVELOPE OF TANGENTS

This method does not give points on the curve, but a series of tangents within which the parabola can be drawn.

H. Seymour Howard, Jr.; Oyster Bay, New York

GEOMETRY

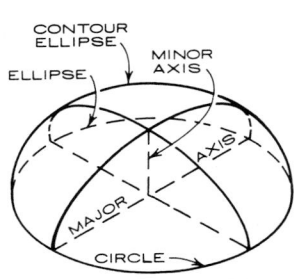

OBLATE SPHEROID

An ellipse rotated about its minor axis.

NOTES

1. The dome shapes shown above are SURFACES OF POSITIVE CUR-VATURE, that is, the centers of both principal radii of curvature are on the same side of the surface.

2. SURFACES OF NEGATIVE CURVATURE (saddle shapes) such as those shown below, are surfaces in which the centers of the two principal radii of curvature are on opposite sides of the surface.

PROLATE SPHEROID

An ellipse rotated about its major axis.

PARABOLOID OF REVOLUTION

A parabola rotated about its axis.

The elliptic paraboloid is similar, but its plan is an ellipse instead of circle, and vertical sections are varying parabolas.

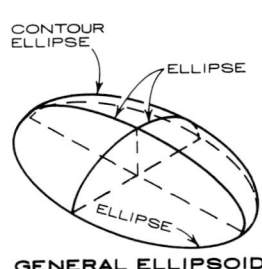

GENERAL ELLIPSOID

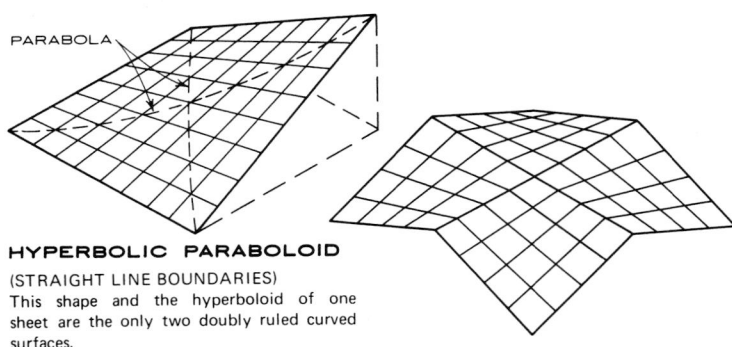

HYPERBOLIC PARABOLOID

(STRAIGHT LINE BOUNDARIES)
This shape and the hyperboloid of one sheet are the only two doubly ruled curved surfaces.

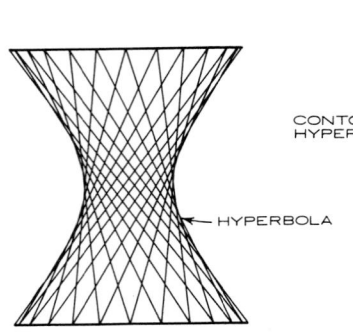

ELEVATION

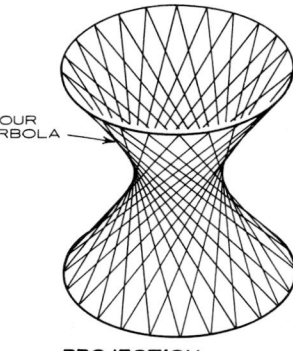

PROJECTION

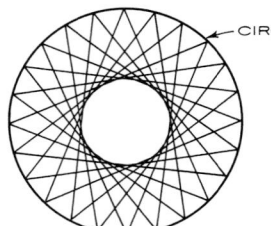

PLAN

NOTE

This shape is a doubly ruled surface, which can also be drawn with ellipses as plan sections instead of the circles shown.

HYPERBOLOID OF REVOLUTION
(OR HYPERBOLOID OF ONE SHEET)

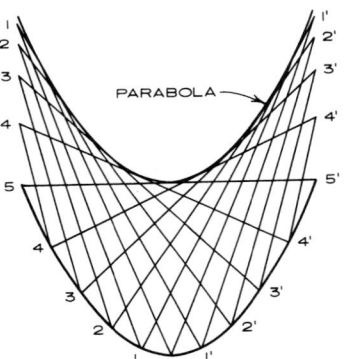

SECTION A-A

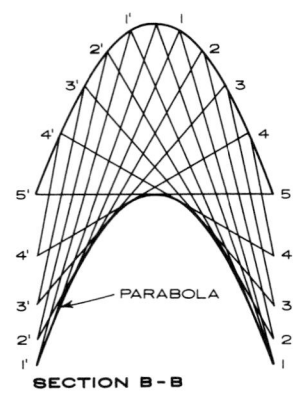

SECTION B-B

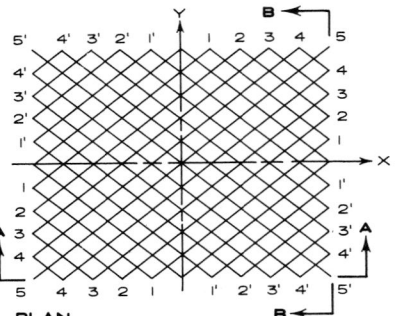

PLAN
HYPERBOLIC PARABOLOID
(PARABOLA BOUNDARIES)

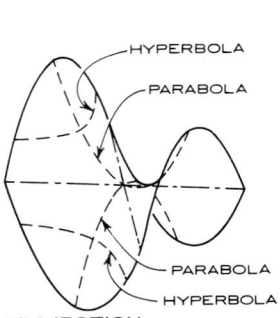

PROJECTION

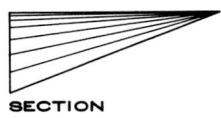

SECTION

PLAN
CONOID
(SINGLY RULED SURFACE)

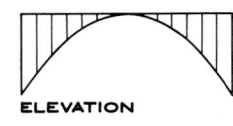

ELEVATION

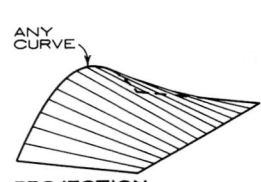

PROJECTION

A **GEOMETRY**

DECIMAL EQUIVALENTS

FRACTION	DECIMAL OF AN INCH	DECIMAL OF A FOOT
1/64	0.015625	
1/32	0.3125	
3/64	0.046875	
1/16	0.0625	0.0052
5/64	0.078125	
3/32	0.09375	
7/64	0.109375	
1/8	0.125	0.0104
9/64	0.140625	
5/32	0.15625	
11/64	0.171875	
3/16	0.1875	0.0156
13/64	0.203125	
7/32	0.21875	
15/64	0.234375	
1/4	0.250	0.0208
17/64	0.265625	
9/32	0.28125	
19/64	0.296875	
5/16	0.3125	0.0260
21/64	0.328125	
11/32	0.34375	
23/64	0.359375	
3/8	0.375	0.0313
25/64	0.390625	
13/32	0.40625	
27/64	0.421875	
7/16	0.4375	0.0365
29/64	0.453125	
15/32	0.46875	
31/64	0.484375	
1/2	0.500	0.0417
33/64	0.515625	
17/32	0.53125	
35/64	0.546875	
9/16	0.5625	0.0469
37/64	0.578125	
19/32	0.59375	
39/64	0.609375	
5/8	0.625	0.0521
41/64	0.640625	
21/32	0.65625	
43/64	0.671875	
11/16	0.6875	0.0573
45/64	0.703125	
23/32	0.71875	
47/64	0.734375	
3/4	0.750	0.0625
49/64	0.765625	
25/32	0.78125	
51/64	0.796875	
13/16	0.8125	0.0677
53/64	0.828125	
27/32	0.84375	
55/64	0.859375	
7/8	0.875	0.0729
57/64	0.890625	
29/32	0.90625	
59/64	0.921875	
15/16	0.9375	0.0781
61/64	0.953125	
31/32	0.96875	
63/64	0.984375	
1	1.00	0.0833
2	2.00	0.1667
3	3.00	0.2500
4	4.00	0.3333
5	5.00	0.4167
6	6.00	0.5000
7	7.00	0.5833
8	8.00	0.6667
9	9.00	0.7500
10	10.00	0.8333
11	11.00	0.9167
12	12.00	1.0000

SCIENTIFIC NOTATION

Scientific notation is used to abbreviate large numerical values in order to simplify calculations.

$4.2 \times 10^4 = 4.2 \times (10 \times 10 \times 10 \times 10) = 42{,}000$

$1.0 \times 10^1 = 1 \times 10 = 10$

$6.0 \times 10^{-4} = 6.0 \times (1 / 10 \times 10 \times 10 \times 10) = 0.0006$

MULTIPLYING AND DIVIDING POWERS

$$x^n x^m = x^{nm} \qquad (x^n)^m = x^{nm}$$

$$\frac{x^n}{x^m} = x^{n-m} \qquad x^{\frac{1}{n}} = \sqrt[n]{x}$$

PYTHAGOREAN THEOREM

$$c^2 = a^2 + b^2$$

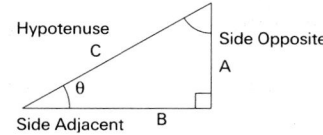

Hypotenuse C — Side Opposite A — θ — Side Adjacent B

BASIC TRIGONOMETRY FUNCTIONS

$$\sin \theta = \frac{\text{opposite}}{\text{hypotenuse}} = \frac{a}{c}$$

$$\cos \theta = \frac{\text{adjacent}}{\text{hypotenuse}} = \frac{b}{c}$$

$$\tan \theta = \frac{\text{opposite}}{\text{adjacent}} = \frac{\sin \theta}{\cos \theta} = \frac{a}{b}$$

$$\cot \theta = \frac{\text{adjacent}}{\text{opposite}} = \frac{1}{\tan \theta} = \frac{b}{a}$$

RADIANS AND DEGREES

A radian is a way of measuring angles in addition to degrees. Radians are the primary unit of angular measurement used in calculations.

$$1 \quad \text{rad} = \frac{180°}{\pi} = 57.3° \quad \text{(approx)}$$

$$1° = \frac{\pi}{180°} = 0.01745 \quad \text{rad} \quad \text{(approx)}$$

LINEAR DISTANCE

The distance **s** which a point **p** on the rim of a rotating wheel covers is called linear distance. The angle θ, the intercepting angle, is measured in radians.

$$s = r\theta$$

LINEAR SPEED

The linear speed **v**, of the point **p** around the rim of a rotating wheel, is the time taken **t** for point to travel the distance **s**.

$$v = \frac{s}{t}$$

ANGULAR SPEED

The angular speed ω, of the point **p** around the rim of a rotating wheel is the time taken, **t**, for the point to travel the angular distance, θ. The angular distance can be measured in degrees, revolutions, or radians. The resulting units of angular speed depend on the units used for angular distance and time.

$$\omega = \frac{\theta}{t}$$

LAW OF REFLECTION

A light ray reflects from a surface such that the angle of reflection equals the angle of incidence.

$$\theta'_1 = \theta_2$$

LAW OF REFRACTION

When a light ray traveling through a transparent medium strikes another transparent medium, part of the ray is reflected and part is refracted, entering the second medium. The angle of the refracted ray depends on the angle of incidence and the index of refraction of both mediums.

$$n_1 \sin \theta_1 = n_2 \sin \theta_2$$

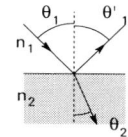

TOTAL INTERNAL REFLECTION

When light attempts to move from a medium with a high index of refraction to a medium with a low index of refraction, there is a particular angle of incidence large enough that the angle of refraction reaches 90°. The transmitted light ray moves parallel to the surface of the first medium and no more light is transmitted.

This angle of incidence is called the critical angle and depends on the indexes of refraction of the two mediums. Any angle of incidence larger than the critical angle is reflected back into the first medium.

$$\sin \theta_c = \frac{n_2}{n_1}$$

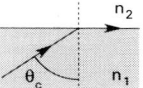

Speed of Light in Medium

$$C_{medium} = \frac{C_{vac}}{n_{medium}}$$

THERMAL EXPANSION OF LENGTH

An object of initial length L_o at some temperature. With a change in temperature of ΔT the length increases ΔL. The constant α is called the average coefficient of linear expansion for the given material.

$$\Delta L = \alpha L_o \Delta T$$

THERMAL EXPANSION OF AREA

An object of initial area A_o at some temperature. With a change in temperature of ΔT, the area increases ΔA. The constant γ is the average coefficient of area expansion for the given material.

$$\Delta A = \gamma A_o \Delta T \qquad \gamma = 2\alpha$$

THERMAL EXPANSION OF VOLUME

A mass of initial volume V_o at some temperature. With a change in temperature ΔT, the volume increases ΔV. The constant β is called the average coefficient of volume expansion for a given material.

$$\Delta V = \beta V_o \Delta T \qquad \beta = 3\alpha$$

USEFUL CONSTANTS
INDEXES OF REFRACTION (n)

Air at 20°c, 1 atm.	1.000

SOLIDS AND LIQUIDS AT 20°C

Water	1.333	Polystyrene	1.49
Ice (H₂O)	1.309	Glass, crown	1.52
Fused quartz	1.458	Glass, flint	1.66

LINEAR EXPANSION COEFFICENTS (α)

Aluminum	24×10^{-6}	Concrete	12×10^{-6}
Brass & bronze	19×10^{-6}	Lead	29×10^{-6}
Copper	17×10^{-6}	Steel	11×10^{-6}
Glass, ordinary	9×10^{-6}		

VOLUME EXPANSION COEFFICENTS (β) ($\beta = 3\alpha$)

Air	3.67×10^{-3}

NATURAL CONSTANTS

Speed of light in a vacuum	$C = 3.0 \times 10^8$ m/s
Standard gravity	$g = 9.80$ m/s²

MATHEMATICAL DATA

BRICK AND BLOCK MASONRY	PSF
4″ brickwork	40
4″ concrete block, stone or gravel	34
4″ concrete block, lightweight	22
4″ concrete brick, stone or gravel	46
4″ concrete brick, lightweight	33
6″ concrete block, stone or gravel	50
6″ concrete block, lightweight	31
8″ concrete block, stone or gravel	55
8″ concrete block, lightweight	35
12″ concrete block, stone or gravel	85
12″ concrete block, lightweight	55

CONCRETE		PCF
Plain	Cinder	108
	Expanded slag aggregate	100
	Expanded clay	90
	Slag	132
	Stone and cast stone	144
Reinforced	Cinder	111
	Slag	138
	Stone	150

FINISH MATERIALS	PSF
Acoustical tile unsupported per 1/2″	0.8
Building board, 1/2″	0.8
Cement finish, 1″	12
Fiberboard, 1/2″	0.75
Gypsum wallboard, 1/2″	2
Marble and setting bed	25–30
Plaster, 1/2″	4.5
Plaster on wood lath	8
Plaster suspended with lath	10
Plywood, 1/2″	1.5
Tile, glazed wall 3/8″	3
Tile, ceramic mosaic, 1/4″	2.5
Quarry tile, 1/2″	5.8
Quarry tile, 3/4″	8.6
Terrazzo 1″, 2″ in stone concrete	25
Vinyl tile, 1/8″	1.33
Hardwood flooring, 25/32″	4
Wood block flooring, 3″ on mastic	15

FLOOR AND ROOF (CONCRETE)		PSF
Flexicore, 6″ precast lightweight concrete		30
Flexicore, 6″ precast stone concrete		40
Plank, cinder concrete, 2″		15
Plank, gypsum, 2″		12
Concrete, reinforced, 1″	Stone	12.5
	Slag	11.5
	Lightweight	6–10
Concrete, plain, 1″	Stone	12
	Slag	11
	Lightweight	3–9

FUELS AND LIQUIDS	PCF
Coal, piled anthracite	47–58
Coal, piled bituminous	40–54
Ice	57.2
Gasoline	75
Snow	8
Water, fresh	62.4
Water, sea	64

GLASS	PSF
Polished plate, 1/4″	3.28
Polished plate, 1/2″	6.56
Double strength, 1/8″	26 oz
Sheet A, B, 1/32″	45 oz
Sheet A, B, 1/4″	52 oz

Insulating glass 5/8″ plate with airspace	3.25
1/4″ wire glass	3.5
Glass block	18

INSULATION AND WATERPROOFING	PSF
Batt, blankets per 1″ thickness	0.1–0.4
Corkboard per 1″ thickness	0.58
Foamed board insulation per 1″ thickness	2.6 oz
Five-ply membrane	5
Rigid insulation	0.75

LIGHTWEIGHT CONCRETE	PSF
Concrete, aerocrete	50–80
Concrete, cinder fill	60
Concrete, expanded clay	85–100
Concrete, expanded shale-sand	105–120
Concrete, perlite	35–50
Concrete, pumice	60–90

METALS	PCF
Aluminum, cast	165
Brass, cast, rolled	534
Bronze, commercial	552
Bronze, statuary	509
Copper, cast or rolled	556
Gold, cast, solid	1205
Gold coin in bags	509
Iron, cast gray, pig	450
Iron, wrought	480
Lead	710
Nickel	565
Silver, cast, solid	656
Silver coin in bags	590
Tin	459
Stainless steel, rolled	492–510
Steel, rolled, cold drawn	490
Zinc, rolled, cast or sheet	449

MORTAR AND PLASTER	PCF
Mortar, masonry	116
Plaster, gypsum, sand	104–120

PARTITIONS	PSF
2 x 4 wood stud, GWB, two sides	8
4″ metal stud, GWB, two sides	6
4″ concrete block, lightweight, GWB	26
6″ concrete block, lightweight, GWB	35
2″ solid plaster	20
4″ solid plaster	32

ROOFING MATERIALS	PSF
Built up	6.5
Concrete roof tile	9.5
Copper	1.5–2.5
Corrugated iron	2
Deck, steel without roofing or insulation	2.2–3.6
Fiberglass panels (2 1/2″ corrugated)	5–8 oz
Galvanized iron	1.2–1.7
Lead, 1/8″	6–8
Plastic sandwich panel, 2 1/2″ thick	2.6
Shingles, asphalt	1.7–2.8
Shingles, wood	2–3
Slate, 3/16″ to 1/4″	7–9.5
Slate, 3/8″ to 1/2″	14–18
Stainless steel	2.5
Tile, cement flat	13
Tile, cement ribbed	16
Tile, clay shingle type	8–16
Tile, clay flat with setting bed	15–20

Wood sheathing per inch	3

SOIL, SAND, AND GRAVEL	PCF
Ashes or cinder	40–50
Clay, damp and plastic	110
Clay, dry	63
Clay and gravel, dry	100
Earth, dry and loose	76
Earth, dry and packed	95
Earth, moist and loose	78
Earth, moist and packed	96
Earth, mud, packed	115
Sand or gravel, dry and loose	90–105
Sand or gravel, dry and packed	100–120
Sand or gravel, dry and wet	118–120
Silt, moist, loose	78
Silt, moist, packed	96

STONE (ASHLAR)	PCF
Granite, limestone, crystalline	165
Limestone, oolitic	135
Marble	173
Sandstone, bluestone	144
Slate	172

STONE VENEER	PSF
2″ granite, 1/2″ parging	30
4″ granite, 1/2″ parging	59
6″ limestone facing, 1/2″ parging	55
4″ sandstone or bluestone, 1/2″ parging	49
1″ marble	13
1″ slate	14

STRUCTURAL CLAY TILE	PSF
4″ hollow	23
6″ hollow	38
8″ hollow	45

STRUCTURAL FACING TILE	PSF
2″ facing tile	14
4″ facing tile	24
6″ facing tile	34
8″ facing tile	44

SUSPENDED CEILINGS	PSF
Mineral fiber tile 3/4″, 12″ x 12″	1.2–1.57
Mineral fiberboard 5/8″, 24″ x 24″	1.4
Acoustic plaster on gypsum lath base	10–11

WOOD	PCF
Ash, commercial white	40.5
Birch, red oak, sweet and yellow	44
Cedar, northern white	22.2
Cedar, western red	24.2
Cypress, southern	33.5
Douglas fir (coast region)	32.7
Fir, commercial white; Idaho white pine	27
Hemlock	28–29
Maple, hard (black and sugar)	44.5
Oak, white and red	47.3
Pine, northern white sugar	25
Pine, southern yellow	37.3
Pine, ponderosa, spruce: eastern and sitka	28.6
Poplar, yellow	29.4
Redwood	26
Walnut, black	38

NOTE

To establish uniform practice among designers, it is desirable to present a list of materials generally used in building construction, together with their proper weights. Many building codes prescribe the minimum weights of only a few building materials. It should be noted that there is a difference of more than 25% in some cases.

WEIGHTS OF MATERIALS

FORMULAS NOMENCLATURE

E — Modulus of Elasticity of steel at 29,000 ksi.

I — Moment of Inertia of beam (in.^{4}).

M_{MAX} — Maximum moment (kip in.).

M_1 — Maximum moment in left section of beam (kip in.).

M_2 — Maximum moment in right section of beam (kip in.).

M_3 — Maximum positive moment in beam with combined end moment conditions (kip in.).

M_x — Moment at distance x from end of beam (kip in.).

P — Concentrated load (kips).

P_1 — Concentrated load nearest left reaction (kips).

P_2 — Concentrated load nearest right reaction, and of different magnitude than P_1 (kips).

R — End beam reaction for any condition of symmetrical loading (kips).

R_1 — Left end beam reaction (kips).

R_2 — Right end or intermediate beam reaction (kips).

R_3 — Right end beam reaction (kips).

V — Maximum vertical shear for any condition of symmetrical loading (kips).

V_1 — Maximum vertical shear in left section of beam (kips).

V_2 — Vertical shear at right reaction point, or to left of intermediate reaction point of beam (kips).

V_3 — Vertical shear at right reaction point, or to right of intermediate reaction point of beam (kips).

V_x — Vertical shear at distance x from end of beam (kips).

W — Total load on beam (kips).

A — Measured distance along beam (in.).

B — Measured distance along beam which may be greater or less than "A" (in.).

L — Total length of beam between reaction points (in.).

w — Uniformly distributed load per unit of length (kips per in.).

w_1 — Uniformly distributed load per unit of length nearest left reaction (kips per in.).

w_2 — Uniformly distributed load per unit of length nearest right reaction, and of different magnitude than w_1 (kips per in.).

X — Any distance measured along beam from left reaction (in.).

X_1 — Any distance measured along overhang section of beam from nearest reaction point (in.).

Δ_{MAX} — Maximum deflection (in.).

Δ_A — Deflection at point of load (in.).

Δ_x — Deflection at any point x distance from left reaction (in.).

Δ_{x1} — Deflection of overhang section of beam at any distance from nearest reaction point (in.).

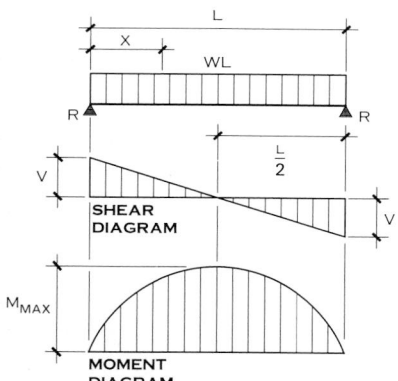

$$\frac{wL}{2} = V = R$$

$$w\left(\frac{L}{2} - x\right) = V_x$$

$$\frac{(wL)^2}{8} = M_{MAX}$$

$$\frac{5wL^4}{384EI} = \Delta_{MAX}$$

SIMPLE BEAM—UNIFORMLY DISTRIBUTED LOAD

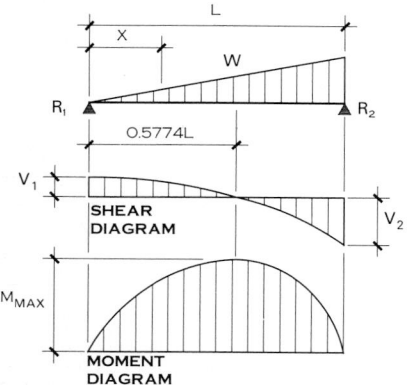

$$\frac{W}{3} = V_1 = R_1$$

$$\frac{2W}{3} = V_{2MAX} = R_2$$

$$\frac{W}{3} - \frac{Wx^2}{L^2} = V_x$$

$$\frac{2WL}{9\sqrt{3}} = M_{MAX}$$

$$0.01304\frac{WL^3}{EI} = \Delta_{MAX}$$

SIMPLE BEAM—LOAD INCREASING UNIFORMLY TO ONE END

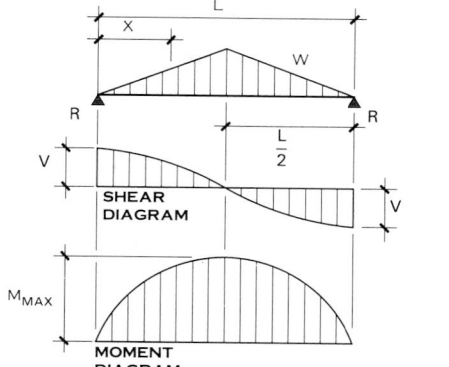
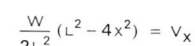

$$\frac{W}{2} = V = R$$

$$\frac{W}{2L^2}(L^2 - 4x^2) = V_x$$

$$\frac{WL}{6} = M_{MAX}$$

$$\frac{WL^3}{60EI} = \Delta_{MAX}$$

SIMPLE BEAM—LOAD INCREASING UNIFORMLY TO CENTER

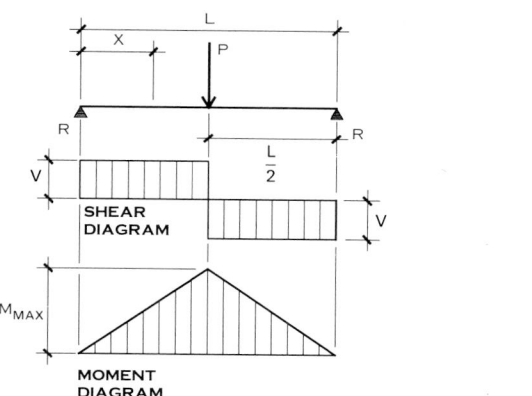

$$\frac{P}{2} = V = R$$

$$\frac{PL}{4} = M_{MAX}$$

$$\frac{PL^3}{48EI} = \Delta_{MAX}$$

SIMPLE BEAM—CONCENTRATED LOAD AT CENTER

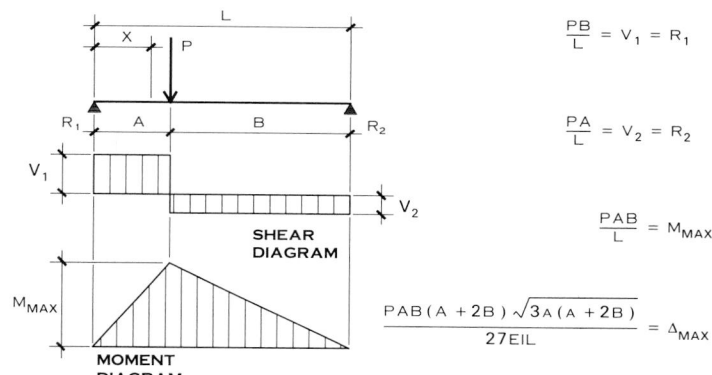

$$\frac{PB}{L} = V_1 = R_1$$

$$\frac{PA}{L} = V_2 = R_2$$

$$\frac{PAB}{L} = M_{MAX}$$

$$\frac{PAB(A+2B)\sqrt{3A(A+2B)}}{27EIL} = \Delta_{MAX}$$

SIMPLE BEAM—CONCENTRATED LOAD AT ANY POINT

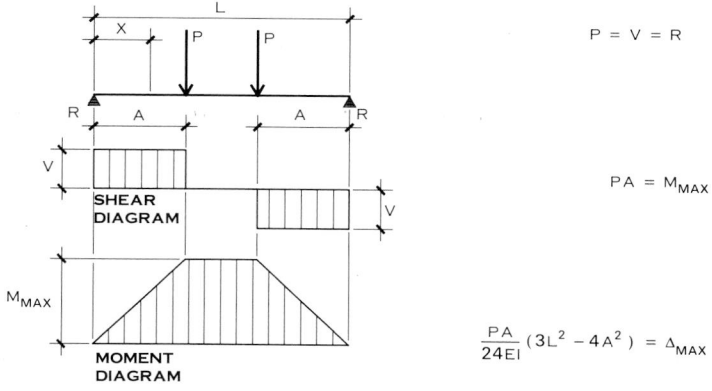

$$P = V = R$$

$$PA = M_{MAX}$$

$$\frac{PA}{24EI}(3L^2 - 4A^2) = \Delta_{MAX}$$

SIMPLE BEAM—TWO EQUAL CONCENTRATED LOADS SYMMETRICALLY PLACED

STRUCTURAL CALCULATIONS   △

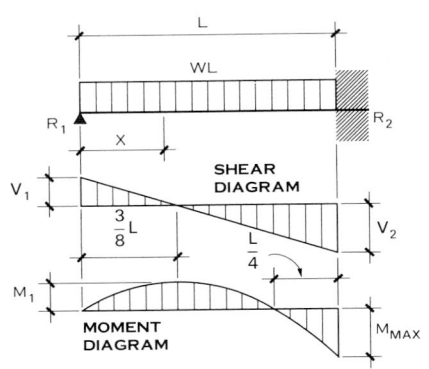

$$\frac{3WL}{8} = V_1 = R_1$$

$$\frac{5WL}{8} = V_{2max} = R_2$$

$$R1 - Wx = V_x$$

$$\frac{WL^2}{8} = M_{MAX}$$

$$\frac{WL^4}{185EI} = \Delta_{MAX}$$

FIXED BEAM AT ONE END AND SUPPORTED AT OTHER—UNIFORMLY DISTRIBUTED LOAD

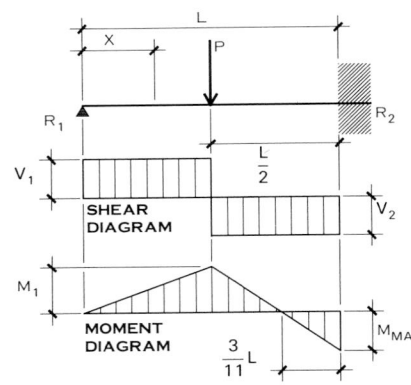

$$\frac{5P}{16} = V_1 = R_1$$

$$\frac{11P}{16} = V_{2MAX} = R_2$$

$$\frac{3PL}{16} = M_{MAX}$$

$$\frac{PL^3}{48EI\sqrt{5}} = \Delta_{MAX}$$

FIXED BEAM AT ONE END AND SUPPORTED AT OTHER—CONCENTRATED LOAD AT CENTER

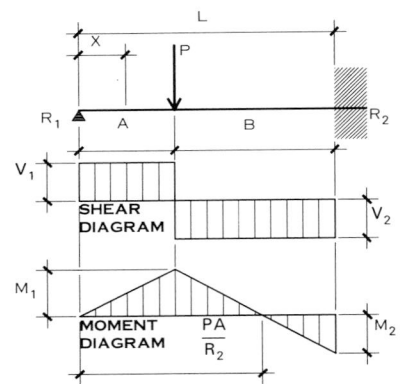

$$\frac{PB^2}{2L^3}(A + 2L) = V_1 = R_1$$

$$\frac{PA}{2L^3}(3L^2 - A^2) = V_2 = R_2$$

$$\frac{PA}{3EI}\frac{(L^2 - A^2)^3}{(3L^2 - A^2)^2} = \Delta_{MAX}$$

$$\frac{PAB^2}{6EI}\sqrt{\frac{A}{2L + A}} = \Delta_{MAX1}$$

FIXED BEAM AT ONE END AND SUPPORTED AT OTHER—CONCENTRATED LOAD AT ANY POINT

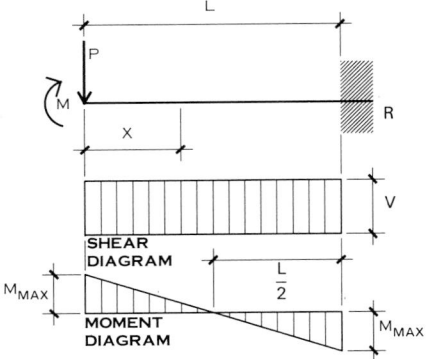

$$P = V = R$$

$$P\left(\frac{L}{2} - X\right) = M_x$$

$$\frac{PL}{2} = M_{MAX}$$

$$\frac{PL^3}{12EI} = \Delta_{MAX}$$

FIXED BEAM AT ONE END AND FREE TO DEFLECT VERTICALLY BUT NOT ROTATE AT OTHER—CONCENTRATED LOAD AT DEFLECTED END

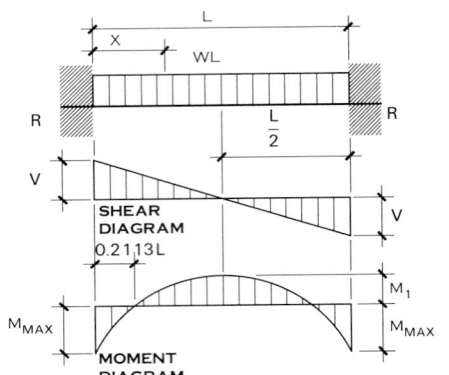

$$\frac{WL}{2} = V = R$$

$$\frac{WL^2}{12} = M_{MAX}$$

$$\frac{W}{12}(6LX - L^2 - 6X^2) = M_X$$

$$\frac{WL^4}{384EI} = \Delta_{MAX}$$

FIXED BEAM—UNIFORMLY DISTRIBUTED LOAD

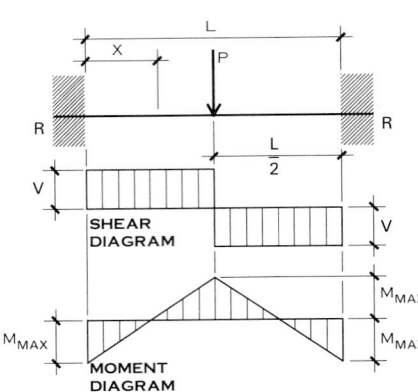

$$\frac{P}{2} = V = R$$

$$\frac{PL}{8} = M_{MAX}$$

$$\frac{P}{8}(4X - L) = M_X$$

$$\frac{PL^3}{192EI} = \Delta_{MAX}$$

FIXED BEAM—CONCENTRATED LOAD AT CENTER

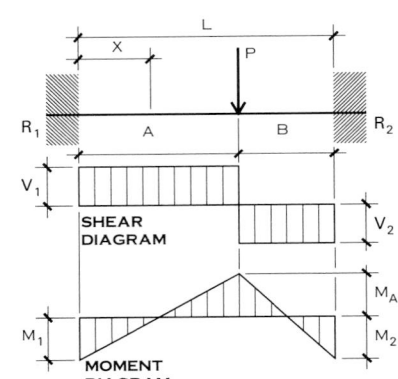

$$\frac{PB^2}{L^3}(3A + B) = V_1 = R_1$$

$$\frac{PA^2}{L^3}(A + 3B) = V_2 = R_2$$

$$XR_1 - \frac{PAB^2}{L^2} = M_X$$

$$\frac{2PA^3B^2}{3EI(3A + B)^2} = \Delta_{MAX}$$

FIXED BEAM—CONCENTRATED LOAD AT ANY POINT

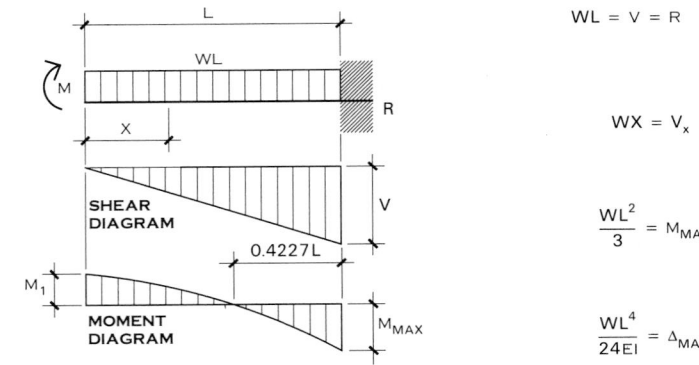

$$WL = V = R$$

$$WX = V_x$$

$$\frac{WL^2}{3} = M_{MAX}$$

$$\frac{WL^4}{24EI} = \Delta_{MAX}$$

FIXED BEAM AT ONE END AND FREE TO DEFLECT VERTICALLY BUT NOT ROTATE AT OTHER—UNIFORMLY DISTRIBUTED LOAD

 STRUCTURAL CALCULATIONS

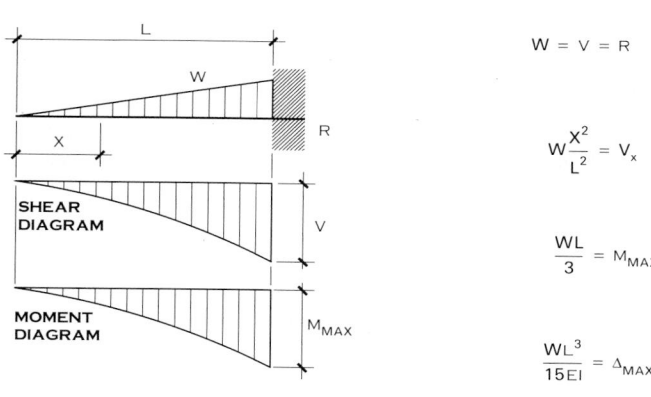

$$W = V = R$$

$$W\frac{X^2}{L^2} = V_x$$

$$\frac{WL}{3} = M_{MAX}$$

$$\frac{WL^3}{15EI} = \Delta_{MAX}$$

CANTILEVER BEAM—LOAD INCREASING UNIFORMLY TO FIXED END

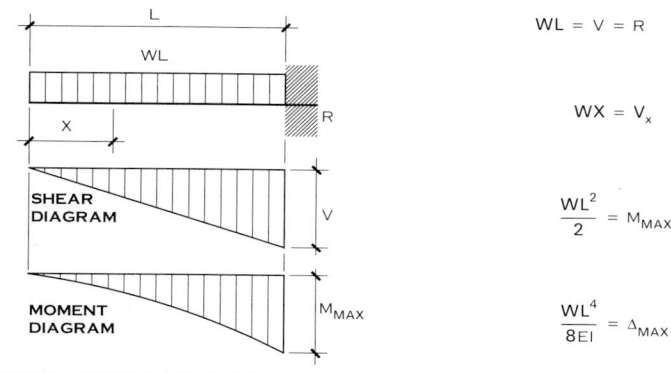

$$WL = V = R$$

$$WX = V_x$$

$$\frac{WL^2}{2} = M_{MAX}$$

$$\frac{WL^4}{8EI} = \Delta_{MAX}$$

CANTILEVER BEAM—UNIFORMLY DISTRIBUTED LOAD

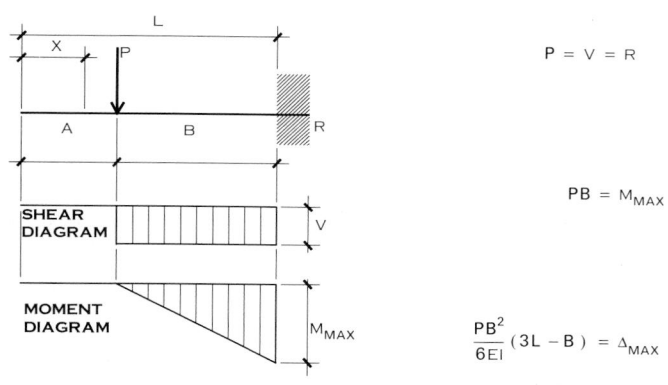

$$P = V = R$$

$$PB = M_{MAX}$$

$$\frac{PB^2}{6EI}(3L - B) = \Delta_{MAX}$$

CANTILEVER BEAM—CONCENTRATED LOAD AT ANY POINT

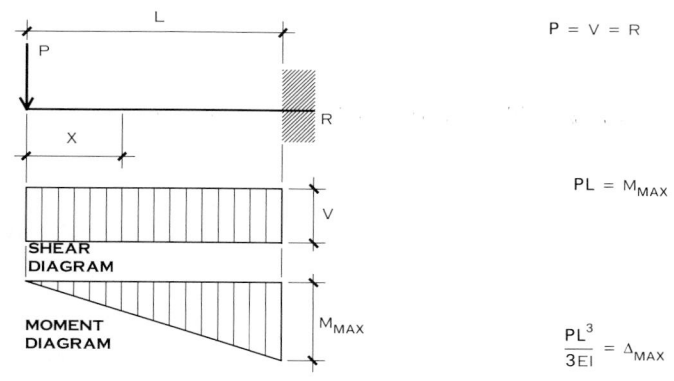

$$P = V = R$$

$$PL = M_{MAX}$$

$$\frac{PL^3}{3EI} = \Delta_{MAX}$$

CANTILEVER BEAM—CONCENTRATED LOAD AT FREE END

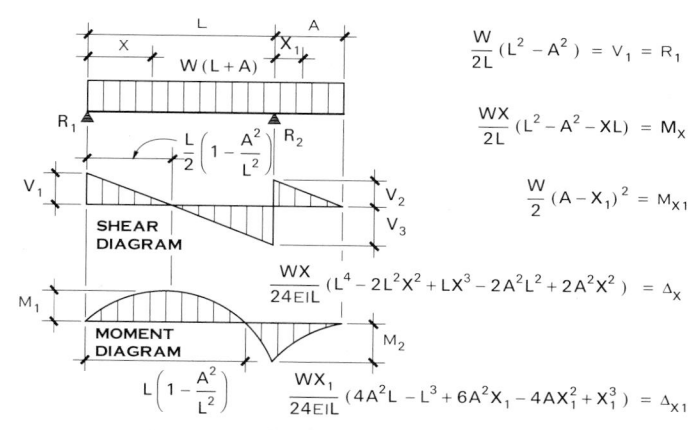

$$\frac{W}{2L}(L^2 - A^2) = V_1 = R_1$$

$$\frac{WX}{2L}(L^2 - A^2 - XL) = M_X$$

$$\frac{W}{2}(A - X_1)^2 = M_{X1}$$

$$\frac{WX}{24EIL}(L^4 - 2L^2X^2 + LX^3 - 2A^2L^2 + 2A^2X^2) = \Delta_X$$

$$\frac{WX_1}{24EIL}(4A^2L - L^3 + 6A^2X_1 - 4AX_1^2 + X_1^3) = \Delta_{X1}$$

BEAM OVERHANGING ONE SUPPORT—UNIFORMLY DISTRIBUTED LOAD

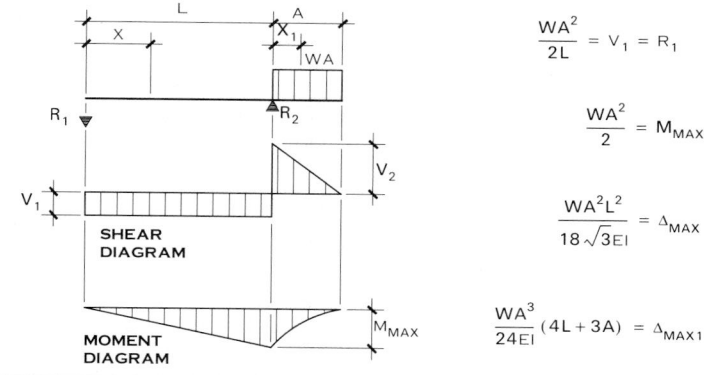

$$\frac{WA^2}{2L} = V_1 = R_1$$

$$\frac{WA^2}{2} = M_{MAX}$$

$$\frac{WA^2L^2}{18\sqrt{3}EI} = \Delta_{MAX}$$

$$\frac{WA^3}{24EI}(4L + 3A) = \Delta_{MAX1}$$

BEAM OVERHANGING ONE SUPPORT—UNIFORMLY DISTRIBUTED LOAD ON OVERHANG

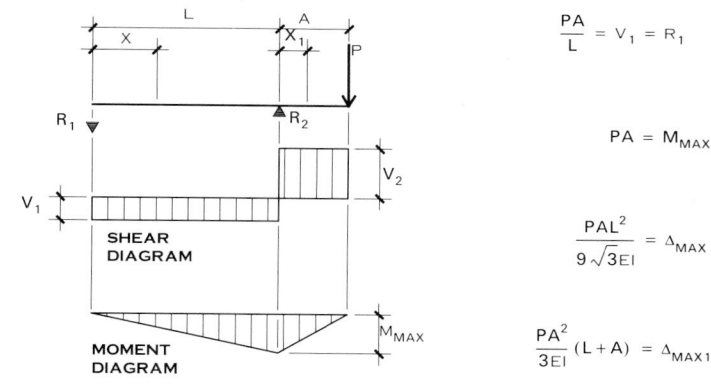

$$\frac{PA}{L} = V_1 = R_1$$

$$PA = M_{MAX}$$

$$\frac{PAL^2}{9\sqrt{3}EI} = \Delta_{MAX}$$

$$\frac{PA^2}{3EI}(L + A) = \Delta_{MAX1}$$

BEAM OVERHANGING ONE SUPPORT—CONCENTRATED LOAD AT END OF OVERHANG

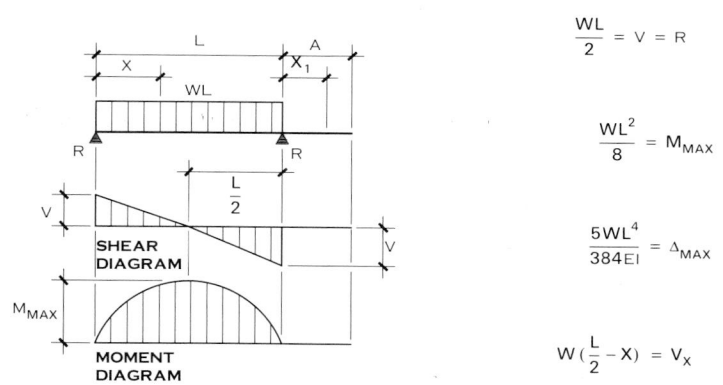

$$\frac{WL}{2} = V = R$$

$$\frac{WL^2}{8} = M_{MAX}$$

$$\frac{5WL^4}{384EI} = \Delta_{MAX}$$

$$W\left(\frac{L}{2} - X\right) = V_x$$

BEAM OVERHANGING ONE SUPPORT—UNIFORMLY DISTRIBUTED LOAD BETWEEN SUPPORTS

A SERIES/OWNER-CONTRACTOR DOCUMENTS

A101   Standard Form of Agreement Between Owner and Contractor—Stipulated Sum (1987) with instruction sheet wrapped

A101/CMa   Standard Form of Agreement Between Owner and Contractor—Stipulated Sum—Construction Manager-Adviser Edition (1992) with instruction sheet wrapped

A105   Standard Form of Agreement Between Owner and Contractor for a Small Project (1993)

A107   Abbreviated Owner-Contractor Agreement Form for Construction Projects of Limited Scope (1987) with instruction sheet wrapped

A111   Standard Form of Agreement Between Owner and Contractor—Cost Plus Fee (1987) with instruction sheet wrapped

A117   Abbreviated Owner-Contractor Agreement Form—Cost Plus Fee (1987) with instruction sheet wrapped

A121/CMc   Standard Form of Agreement Between Owner and Construction Manager where the Construction Manager is Also the Constructor (1991)

A171   Standard Form of Agreement Between Owner and Contractor for Furniture, Furnishings and Equipment (1990) with instruction sheet wrapped

A177   Abbreviated Owner-Contractor Agreement for Furniture, Furnishings and Equipment (1990) with instruction sheet wrapped

A191   Standard Form of Agreements Between Owner and Design/Build (1985)

A201   General Conditions of the Contract for Construction (1987)

A201/CMa   General Conditions of the Contract for Construction—Construction Manager-Adviser Edition (1992)

A201/SC   Federal Supplementary Conditions of the Contract for Construction (1990)

A205   General Conditions of the Contract for Construction of a Small Project (1993)

A271   General Conditions of the Contract for Furniture, Furnishings and Equipment (1990) with instruction sheet wrapped

A305   Contractor's Qualification Statement (1986)

A310   Bid Bond (1970)

A312   Performance Bond and Payment Bond (1984)

A401   Standard Form of Agreement Between Contractor and Subcontractor (1987)

A491   Standard Form of Agreements Between Design/Builder and Contractor (1985)

A501   Recommended Guide for Bidding Procedures and Contract Awards (1982)

A511   Guide for Supplementary Conditions (incorporates A512 1987)

A511/CMa   Guide for Supplementary Conditions—Construction Manager-Adviser Edition (1993)

A512   Additions to Guides for Supplementary Conditions (1989)

A521   Uniform Location Subject Matter (1981, reprinted 1983)

A571   Guide for Interiors Supplementary Conditions (1991)

A701   Instructions to Bidders (1987) with instruction sheet wrapped

A771   Instruction to Interiors Bidders (1990) with instruction sheet wrapped

B SERIES/OWNER-ARCHITECT DOCUMENTS

B141   Standard Form of Agreement Between Owner and Architect (1987) with instruction sheet wrapped

B141/CMa   Standard Form of Agreement Between Owner and Architect—Construction Manager-Adviser Edition (1992) with instruction sheet wrapped

B144/ARCH-CM   Standard Form of Amendment for the Agreement Between Owner and Architect Where the Architect Provides Construction Management Services as an Adviser to the Owner (1993)

B151   Abbreviated Owner-Architect Agreement Form (1987) with instruction sheet wrapped

B155   Standard Form of Agreement Between Owner and Architect for a Small Project (1993)

B163   Standard Form of Agreement Between Owner and Architect for Designated Services (1993)

B171   Standard Form of Agreement for Interior Design Services (1990) with instruction sheet wrapped

B177   Abbreviated Interior Design Services Agreement (1990) with instruction sheet wrapped

B181   Standard Form of Agreement Between Owner and Architect for Housing Services (1978) with instruction sheet wrapped

B352   Duties, Responsibilities, and Limitations of Authority of the Architect's Project Representative (1993)

B431   Architect's Qualification Statement (1993)

B511   Guide for Amendments to AIA Document B141 (1993)

B727   Standard Form of Agreement Between Owner and Architect for Special Services (1988) with instruction sheet wrapped

B801/CMa   Standard Form of Agreement Between Owner and Construction Manager Where the Construction Manager is Not a Constructor (1992) with instruction sheet wrapped

B901   Standard Form of Agreements Between Design/Builder and Architect (1985)

C SERIES/ARCHITECT-CONSULTANT DOCUMENTS

C141   Standard Form of Agreement Between Architect and Consultant (1987) with instructions wrapped

C142   Abbreviated Form of Agreement Between Architect and Consultant (1987)

C727   Standard Form of Agreement Between Architect and Consultant for Special Services (1982) with instructions wrapped

C801   Joint Venture Agreement (1993) with instructions wrapped

D SERIES/ARCHITECT-INDUSTRY DOCUMENTS

D101   Architectural Area and Volume of Buildings (1980)

D200   Project Checklist (1982)

F SERIES/COMPENSATION GUIDELINES FORMS AND WORKSHEETS

F800   F810 through F860—Complete set of 2 each of 24 forms needed (1978)

F SERIES/STANDARDIZED ACCOUNTING FOR ARCHITECTS FORMS

F1001 through F3002   These documents are included in the book *Standardized Accounting for Architects*, by Robert F. Mattox, FAIA (1982)

F5002   Invoice for Architectural Services (1978)

G SERIES/ARCHITECT'S OFFICE AND PROJECT FORMS

G601   Land Survey Agreement (1979) with instructions

G602   Request for Proposal—Geotechnical Services (1993)

G604   Professional Services Supplement (1993) with instructions

G612   Owner's Instructions Regarding the Construction Contract, Insurance and Bonds, and Bidding Procedures (1987)

G701   Change Order (1987)

G701/CMa   Change Order—Construction Manager-Adviser Edition (1992)

G702   Application and Certificate for Payment (1978, Rev. 1983)

G702/CMa   Application and Certificate for Payment—Construction Manager-Adviser Edition (1992)

G702/CR   Continuous Roll for Application and Certificate for Payment (1983)

G703   Continuation Sheet for G702 (1978, Rev. 1983)

G703/CR   Continuous Roll Continuation Sheet for G702 (1983)

G704   Certificate of Substantial Completion (1992)

G704/CMa   Certificate of Substantial Completion—Construction Manager-Adviser Edition (1992)

G706   Contractor's Affidavit of Payment of Debts and Claims (1970)

G706A   Contractor's Affidavit of Release of Liens (1970)

G707   Consent of Surety to Final Payment (1970)

G707A   Consent of Surety to Reduction in or Partial Release of Retainage (1971)

G709   Proposal Request (1993)

G710   Architect's Supplemental Instructions (1979) with instructions

G711   Architect's Field Report (1972)

G712   Shop Drawing and Sample Record (1972)

G714   Construction Change Directive (1987)

G714/CMa   Construction Change Directive—Construction Manager-Adviser Edition (1992)

G715   Instruction Sheet and Attachment for ACORD Certificate of Insurance (1991)

G722/CMa   Project Application and Project Certificate for Payment—Construction Manager-Adviser Edition (1992) with instructions

G723/CMa   Project Application Summary—Construction Manager-Adviser Edition (1992)

G804   Register of Bid Documents (1970)

G805   List of Subcontractors (1970)

G807   Project Directory (1970)

G809   Project Data (1970)

G810   Transmittal Letter (1970)

G811   Employment Record (1973)

G813   Temporary Placement of Employees (1974)

GENERAL

Editions shown (in parentheses) are the latest available documents at publication time. Before using any AIA document, consult the AIA, an AIA component chapter, or a current AIA Document List to determine the current edition of each document. AIA documents are revised on a cyclical basis, usually about ten years or fewer in duration.

Besides grouping the documents according to the various series shown, the AIA groups documents according to "families" of interrelated forms compatible in concept. Currently, there are five major families: A201, Small Project, Interiors, CM-Adviser/CM-Constructor, and Design/Build. Whenever possible, the AIA will publish all or nearly all the documents related to a single family at one time. For instance, the A201 family of documents was last revised in 1987, and they are scheduled for another revision in 1997. Some documents do not apply to any particular family but are for general use and information.

Since the 1970s the AIA has published more model forms in addition to standard documents. A model form, in contrast to a standard document, is a repository of provisions that may be borrowed and rewritten into a contract document to appear custom-made. The AIA publishes model documents with explanatory text under the rubric of "Guide." For instance, see AIA Document A511, Guide for Supplementary Conditions.

Most forms published by the American Institute of Architects are standard forms, such as A101 (Standard Form of Agreement Between Owner and Contractor—Stipulated Sum) and B141 (Standard Form of Agreement Between Owner and Architect). Standard forms are commercially printed documents intended for use as original, written agreements. The AIA aspires to establish and maintain, for nationwide application, standardized legal forms that can enhance the stability and order of design and construction legal transactions. For that reason, the AIA's standard contracts offer advantages many other standard forms fail to provide. To educate consumers of AIA Documents A201 (General Conditions of the Contract for Construction) and B141 (Standard Form of Agreement Between Owner and Architect), the AIA publishes commentaries, which contain annotated versions of those documents.

The AIA's standard forms are drafted using a process that seeks an industry consensus. This drafting process involves the efforts of architects, owners, contractors, engineers, and their legal counsel, who act as representatives of various professional and trade associations in the construction industry. In accordance with the AIA Documents Drafting Principles, the standard forms also seek "to establish a clear and equitable distribution of rights and duties, avoiding any unreasonable bias."

Regardless of the type, AIA forms lend predictability to the construction contract process. When used properly, they serve to lessen transaction costs, to encourage trust between parties, and, ultimately, to minimize risk.

AIA DOCUMENTS

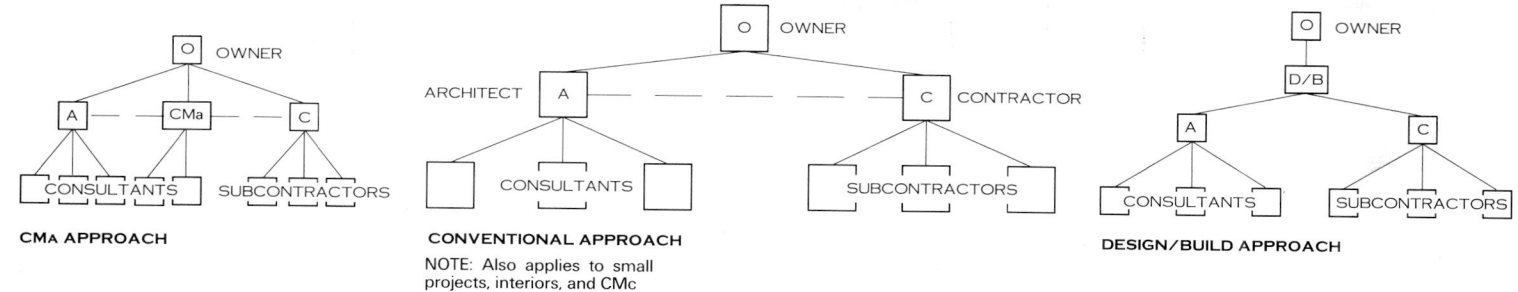

CMA APPROACH

CONVENTIONAL APPROACH
NOTE: Also applies to small projects, interiors, and CMc

DESIGN/BUILD APPROACH

A SERIES: OWNER—CONTRACTOR

	CMa	CONVENTIONAL			SMALL PROJECTS	INTERIORS		CMc	DESIGN/BUILD	
	STIPULATED SUM (CM-ADVISER)	STIPULATED SUM	COST PLUS	ABBREVIATED VERSION	STIPULATED SUM	STIPULATED SUM AND EXPENSES	ABBREVIATED VERSION	CM-CONSTRUCTOR VERSION	DESIGN	BUILD
AGREEMENT[2]	A101/CMa	A101	A111	A107/A117	A105	A171	A177	A121/CMc	A191 Part 1	A191 Part 2
General Conditions	A201/CMa	A201	A201	Incorp.	A205	A271	Incorp.	A201	—	—
Subcontractor	A401	A401	A401	A401	A401	A401	A401	A401	A491 Part 1	A491 Part 2
Contractor's Qualifications	A305	A305	A305	A305	A305	A305	A305	A305	—	—
Bidder's Instructions	A701	A701	—	A701	—	A771	A771	—	—	—
Bonds	A310 A312	A310 A312	A310 A312	A310 A312	A310 A312	A310 A312	A310 A312	A310 A312	—	—
Guides	A511/CMa	A511	A511	—	—	A571	—	A511	—	—

B SERIES: OWNER—ARCHITECT

	CMa	CONVENTIONAL			SMALL PROJECTS	INTERIORS		CMc	DESIGN/BUILD	
	CM-ADVISER VERSION	STANDARD VERSION	SPECIAL VERSION	ABBREVIATED VERSION	STIPULATED SUM	STANDARD VERSION	ABBREVIATED VERSION	CM-CONSTRUCTOR VERSION	DESIGN	BUILD
AGREEMENT[3]	B141/CMa	B141	B727	B151	B155	B171	B177	B141[4]	B901 Part 1	B901 Part 2
DESIGNATED SERVICE AGREEMENT[3]	—	B163	—	—	—	B163	—	—	—	—
HOUSING SERVICES AGREEMENT[3]	—	B181	B188	B151	B155	B171	B177	—	—	—
CM SERVICES AGREEMENT[3]	B801/CMa	—	B141 B144/Arch-CM	—	—	—	—	(see A121/CMc)	—	—
Project Rep. Services	B352	B352	B352	B352	—	B352	B352	—	—	—
Guides	B511	B511	B511	—	—	B511	—	—	—	—

C SERIES: ARCHITECT—CONSULTANT

	CONVENTIONAL			JOINT VENTURE
	STANDARD VERSION	SPECIAL VERSION	ABBREVIATED VERSION	STANDARD VERSION
AGREEMENT[3]	C141	C727	C142	C801
Guides	(Coordinate with B511)			

GENERAL NOTES

1. A dash (—) signifies that a particular type of document is currently unavailable or not applicable.

2. In the A series, the documents within each vertical column are related to or coordinated with the respective AGREEMENT form(s) at the top of the column.

3. In the B and C series, the various AGREEMENTS in each vertical column are compatible with the appropriate Project Representative form and Guide also listed in the same column.

4. B141 should be appropriately modified when used in conjunction with A121/CMc. Model provisions containing appropriate modifications or amendments may be found in B511.

5. The solid lines in the above diagrams indicate contractual relationships.

BASIC ORGANIZATION

The titles and numbers in MASTERFORMAT are grouped under the headings:

Bidding Requirements

Contract Forms

Conditions of the Contract

Specifications Divisions 1 Through 16

Documents under the first three headings are not specifications and should not be initiated or changed without specific coordination with the owner and the owner's legal and insurance counselors. However, MASTERFORMAT assigns standard locations and numbers for these documents for filing purposes and for coordination with the remainder of MASTERFORMAT.

The titles under the fourth heading are for specification sections. Specifications are the documents that define the quality of the products, materials, and workmanship upon which the construction contract is based.

DIVISIONS

The specification titles and numbers in MASTERFORMAT are organized into 16 basic groupings of related construction information called "divisions." Each division is identified by a fixed number and title. The divisions are the basic framework of MASTERFORMAT, and they indicate the location of the subordinate elements of the system. The numbers and titles of the divisions are:

DIVISION 1 GENERAL REQUIREMENTS

DIVISION 2 SITE WORK

DIVISION 3 CONCRETE

DIVISION 4 MASONRY

DIVISION 5 METALS

DIVISION 6 WOODS AND PLASTICS

DIVISION 7 THERMAL AND MOISTURE PROTECTION

DIVISION 8 DOORS AND WINDOWS

DIVISION 9 FINISHES

DIVISION 10 SPECIALTIES

DIVISION 11 EQUIPMENT

DIVISION 12 FURNISHINGS

DIVISION 13 SPECIAL CONSTRUCTION

DIVISION 14 CONVEYING SYSTEMS

DIVISION 15 MECHANICAL

DIVISION 16 ELECTRICAL

SECTIONS

Within each division specifications are written in numbered "sections," each of which covers one portion of the total work or requirements. MASTERFORMAT provides a standard system for numbering and titling these sections. The first two digits of the section number are the same as the division number.

BROADSCOPE, MEDIUMSCOPE, NARROWSCOPE

MASTERFORMAT identifies three levels of detail for a specification section—broadscope, mediumscope, and narrowscope.

Broadscope titles are for broad categories of work and provide the widest latitude in describing a unit of work.

Mediumscope titles cover units of work of more limited scope.

Narrowscope titles are for use in covering extremely limited and very specific elements of work.

In MASTERFORMAT the broadscope section titles are shown in boldface capital letters with five digit numbers.

The hyphenated three digit numbers with indented upper and lower case titles are recommended mediumscope sections. Unnumbered, indented titles, which in most cases follow a mediumscope title, are narrowscope section titles. These, when taken together with the mediumscope titles under a broadscope heading, describe the coverage of that broadscope section. For example:

02100 SITE PREPARATION

-110 Site Clearing
    Clearing and Grubbing
    Large Tract Tree Clearing

-115 Selective Clearing
    Sod Stripping
    Tree and Shrub Removal
    Tree Pruning

-120 Structure Moving

MASTERFORMAT provides five digit number only for the broadscope and mediumscope section titles. Unused numbers are available between mediumscope numbers to permit assignment of numbers to selected narrowscope titles needed to accommodate individual project requirements. A block of numbers has also been left unassigned at the beginning of each division to be used for filing general data and cost information applicable to the entire division.

BROADSCOPE SECTION EXPLANATIONS

A general description of the coverage of each broadscope section is provided opposite the listing of titles. The broadscope explanation together with the list of associated mediumscope and narrowscope titles provide an understanding of the scope of the broadscope section. Under the headings "Related Requirements and Sections," "Related Requirements," and "Related Sections" are lists of other documents and sections in MASTERFORMAT that contain elements of work related to the broadscope section. The listings include items about which there might be confusion as to proper location and items which might require coordination with the subject broadscope.

The "Notes" under the broadscope explanations provide additional information on the relationships to other documents and sections and options available for the location of information.

KEY WORD INDEX

An alphabetical index is included to help locate particular products, materials, systems, units of work, and requirements. Each entry references one or more broadscope number. Only broadscope numbers are referenced; however, the specific item may appear as a mediumscope or narrowscope listing under the referenced broadscope number and title.

BIDDING REQUIREMENTS, CONTRACT FORMS, AND CONDITIONS OF THE CONTRACT

00010 PRE-BID INFORMATION

00100 INSTRUCTIONS TO BIDDERS

00200 INFORMATION AVAILABLE TO BIDDERS

00300 BID FORMS

00400 SUPPLEMENTS TO BID FORMS

00500 AGREEMENT FORMS

00600 BONDS AND CERTIFICATES

00700 GENERAL CONDITIONS

00800 SUPPLEMENTARY CONDITIONS

00900 ADDENDA

NOTE

The items listed above are not specification sections and are referred to as "Documents" rather than "Sections" in the "Master List of Section Titles, Numbers, and Broadscope Section Explanations."

SPECIFICATIONS

The following is a list of the broadscope section numbers and titles from MASTERFORMAT.

DIVISION 1—GENERAL REQUIREMENTS

01010 SUMMARY OF WORK
01020 ALLOWANCES
01025 MEASUREMENT AND PAYMENT
01030 ALTERNATES/ALTERNATIVES
01035 MODIFICATION PROCEDURES
01040 COORDINATION
01050 FIELD ENGINEERING
01060 REGULATORY REQUIREMENTS
01070 IDENTIFICATION SYSTEMS
01090 REFERENCES
01100 SPECIAL PROJECT PROCEDURES
01200 PROJECT MEETINGS
01300 SUBMITTALS
01400 QUALITY CONTROL
01500 CONSTRUCTION FACILITIES AND TEMPORARY CONTROLS
01600 MATERIAL AND EQUIPMENT
01650 FACILITY STARTUP/COMMISSIONING
01700 CONTRACT CLOSEOUT
01800 MAINTENANCE

DIVISION 2—SITEWORK

02010 SUBSURFACE INVESTIGATION
02050 DEMOLITION
02100 SITE PREPARATION
02140 DEWATERING
02150 SHORING AND UNDERPINNING
02160 EXCAVATION SUPPORT SYSTEMS
02170 COFFERDAMS
02200 EARTHWORK
02300 TUNNELING
02350 PILES AND CAISSONS
02450 RAILROAD WORK
02480 MARINE WORK
02500 PAVING AND SURFACING
02600 UTILITY PIPING MATERIALS
02660 WATER DISTRIBUTION
02680 FUEL AND STEAM DISTRIBUTION
02700 SEWERAGE AND DRAINAGE
02760 RESTORATION OF UNDERGROUND PIPE
02770 PONDS AND RESERVOIRS
02780 POWER AND COMMUNICATIONS
02800 SITE IMPROVEMENTS
02900 LANDSCAPING

DIVISION 3—CONCRETE

03100 CONCRETE FORMWORK
03200 CONCRETE REINFORCEMENT
03250 CONCRETE ACCESSORIES
03300 CAST-IN-PLACE CONCRETE
03370 CONCRETE CURING
03400 PRECAST CONCRETE
03500 CEMENTITIOUS DECKS AND TOPPINGS
03600 GROUT
03700 CONCRETE RESTORATION AND CLEANING
03800 MASS CONCRETE

DIVISION 4—MASONRY

04100 MORTAR AND MASONRY GROUT
04150 MASONRY ACCESSORIES
04200 UNIT MASONRY
04400 STONE
04500 MASONRY RESTORATION AND CLEANING
04550 REFRACTORIES
04600 CORROSION RESISTANT MASONRY
04700 SIMULATED MASONRY

DIVISION 5—METALS

05010 METAL MATERIALS
05030 METAL COATINGS
05050 METAL FASTENING
05100 STRUCTURAL METAL FRAMING
05200 METAL JOISTS
05300 METAL DECKING
05400 COLD-FORMED METAL FRAMING
05500 METAL FABRICATIONS
05580 SHEET METAL FABRICATIONS
05700 ORNAMENTAL METAL
05800 EXPANSION CONTROL

The Construction Specifications Institute; Alexandria, Virginia
Construction Specifications Canada

 CSI DOCUMENTS

DIVISION 6—WOOD AND PLASTICS

06050 FASTENERS AND ADHESIVES
06100 ROUGH CARPENTRY
06130 HEAVY TIMBER CONSTRUCTION
06150 WOOD AND METAL SYSTEMS
06170 PREFABRICATED STRUCTURAL WOOD
06200 FINISH CARPENTRY
06300 WOOD TREATMENT
06400 ARCHITECTURAL WOODWORK
06500 STRUCTURAL PLASTICS
06600 PLASTIC FABRICATIONS
06650 SOLID POLYMER FABRICATIONS

DIVISION 7—THERMAL AND MOISTURE PROTECTION

07100 WATERPROOFING
07150 DAMPPROOFING
07180 WATER REPELLENTS
07190 VAPOR RETARDERS
07195 AIR BARRIERS
07200 INSULATION
07240 EXTERIOR INSULATION AND FINISH SYSTEMS
07250 FIREPROOFING
07270 FIRESTOPPING
07300 SHINGLES AND ROOFING TILES
07400 MANUFACTURED ROOFING AND SIDING
07480 EXTERIOR WALL ASSEMBLIES
07500 MEMBRANE ROOFING
07570 TRAFFIC COATINGS
07600 FLASHING AND SHEET METAL
07700 ROOF SPECIALTIES AND ACCESSORIES
07800 SKYLIGHTS
07900 JOINT SEALERS

DIVISION 8—DOORS AND WINDOWS

08100 METAL DOORS AND FRAMES
08200 WOOD AND PLASTIC DOORS
08250 DOOR OPENING ASSEMBLIES
08300 SPECIAL DOORS
08400 ENTRANCES AND STOREFRONTS
08500 METAL WINDOWS
08600 WOOD AND PLASTIC WINDOWS
08650 SPECIAL WINDOWS
08700 HARDWARE
08800 GLAZING
08900 GLAZED CURTAIN WALLS

DIVISION 9—FINISHES

09100 METAL SUPPORT SYSTEMS
09200 LATH AND PLASTER
09250 GYPSUM BOARD
09300 TILE
09400 TERRAZZO
09450 STONE FACING
09500 ACOUSTICAL TREATMENT
09540 SPECIAL WALL SURFACES
09545 SPECIAL CEILING SURFACES
09550 WOOD FLOORING
09600 STONE FLOORING
09630 UNIT MASONRY FLOORING
09650 RESILIENT FLOORING
09680 CARPET
09700 SPECIAL FLOORING
09780 FLOOR TREATMENT
09800 SPECIAL COATINGS
09900 PAINTING
09950 WALL COVERINGS

DIVISION 10—SPECIALTIES

10100 VISUAL DISPLAY BOARDS
10150 COMPARTMENTS AND CUBICLES
10200 LOUVERS AND VENTS
10240 GRILLES AND SCREENS
10250 SERVICE WALL SYSTEMS
10260 WALL AND CORNER GUARDS
10270 ACCESS FLOORING
10290 PEST CONTROL
10300 FIREPLACES AND STOVES
10340 MANUFACTURED EXTERIOR SPECIALTIES
10350 FLAGPOLES
10400 IDENTIFYING DEVICES
10450 PEDESTRIAN CONTROL DEVICES
10500 LOCKERS
10520 FIRE PROTECTION SPECIALTIES
10530 PROTECTIVE COVERS
10550 POSTAL SPECIALTIES
10600 PARTITIONS
10650 OPERABLE PARTITIONS
10670 STORAGE SHELVING
10700 EXTERIOR PROTECTION DEVICES FOR OPENINGS
10750 TELEPHONE SPECIALTIES
10800 TOILET AND BATH ACCESSORIES
10880 SCALES
10900 WARDROBE AND CLOSED SPECIALTIES

DIVISION 11—EQUIPMENT

11010 MAINTENANCE EQUIPMENT
11020 SECURITY AND VAULT EQUIPMENT
11030 TELLER AND SERVICE EQUIPMENT
11040 ECCLESIASTICAL EQUIPMENT
11050 LIBRARY EQUIPMENT
11060 THEATER AND STAGE EQUIPMENT
11070 INSTRUMENTAL EQUIPMENT
11080 REGISTRATION EQUIPMENT
11090 CHECKROOM EQUIPMENT
11100 MERCANTILE EQUIPMENT
11110 COMMERCIAL LAUNDRY AND DRY CLEANING EQUIPMENT
11120 VENDING EQUIPMENT
11130 AUDIO-VISUAL EQUIPMENT
11140 VEHICLE SERVICE EQUIPMENT
11150 PARKING CONTROL EQUIPMENT
11160 LOADING DOCK EQUIPMENT
11170 SOLID WASTE HANDLING EQUIPMENT
11190 DETENTION EQUIPMENT
11200 WATER SUPPLY AND TREATMENT EQUIPMENT
11280 HYDRAULIC GATES AND VALVES
11300 FLUID WASTE TREATMENT AND DISPOSAL EQUIPMENT
11400 FOOD SERVICE EQUIPMENT
11450 RESIDENTIAL EQUIPMENT
11460 UNIT KITCHENS
11470 DARKROOM EQUIPMENT
11480 ATHLETIC, RECREATIONAL, AND THERAPEUTIC EQUIPMENT
11500 INDUSTRIAL AND PROCESS EQUIPMENT
11600 LABORATORY EQUIPMENT
11650 PLANETARIUM EQUIPMENT
11660 OBSERVATORY EQUIPMENT
11680 OFFICE EQUIPMENT
11700 MEDICAL EQUIPMENT
11780 MORTUARY EQUIPMENT
11850 NAVIGATION EQUIPMENT
11870 AGRICULTURAL EQUIPMENT

DIVISION 12—FURNISHINGS

12050 FABRICS
12100 ARTWORK
12300 MANUFACTURED CASEWORK
12500 WINDOW TREATMENT
12600 FURNITURE AND ACCESSORIES
12670 RUGS AND MATS
12700 MULTIPLE SEATING
12800 INTERIOR PLANTS AND PLANTERS

DIVISION 13—SPECIAL CONSTRUCTION

13010 AIR-SUPPORTED STRUCTURES
13020 INTEGRATED ASSEMBLIES
13030 SPECIAL PURPOSE ROOMS
13080 SOUND, VIBRATION, AND SEISMIC CONTROL
13090 RADIATION PROTECTION
13100 NUCLEAR REACTORS
13120 PRE-ENGINEERED STRUCTURES
13150 AQUATIC FACILITIES
13175 ICE RINKS
13180 SITE CONSTRUCTED INCINERATORS
13185 KENNELS AND ANIMAL SHELTERS
13200 LIQUID AND GAS STORAGE TANKS
13220 FILTER UNDERDRAINS AND MEDIA
13230 DIGESTER COVERS AND APPURTENANCES
13240 OXYGENATION SYSTEMS
13260 SLUDGE CONDITIONING SYSTEMS
13300 UTILITY CONTROL SYSTEMS
13400 INDUSTRIAL AND PROCESS CONTROL SYSTEMS
13500 RECORDING INSTRUMENTATION
13550 TRANSPORTATION CONTROL INSTRUMENTATION
13600 SOLAR ENERGY SYSTEMS
13700 WIND ENERGY SYSTEMS
13750 COGENERATION SYSTEMS
13800 BUILDING AUTOMATION SYSTEMS
13900 FIRE SUPPRESSION AND SUPERVISORY SYSTEMS
13950 SPECIAL SECURITY CONSTRUCTION

DIVISION 14—CONVEYING SYSTEMS

14100 DUMBWAITERS
14200 ELEVATORS
14300 ESCALATORS AND MOVING WALKS
14400 LIFTS
14500 MATERIAL HANDLING SYSTEMS
14600 HOISTS AND CRANES
14700 TURNTABLES
14800 SCAFFOLDING
14900 TRANSPORTATION SYSTEMS

DIVISION 15—MECHANICAL SYSTEMS

15050 BASIC MECHANICAL MATERIALS AND METHODS
15250 MECHANICAL INSULATION
15300 FIRE PROTECTION
15400 PLUMBING
15500 HEATING, VENTILATING, AND AIR CONDITIONING
15550 HEAT GENERATION
15650 REFRIGERATION
15750 HEAT TRANSFER
15850 AIR HANDLING
15880 AIR DISTRIBUTION
15950 CONTROLS
15990 TESTING, ADJUSTING, AND BALANCING

DIVISION 16—ELECTRICAL

16050 BASIC ELECTRICAL MATERIALS AND METHODS
16200 POWER GENERATION-BUILT-UP SYSTEMS
16300 MEDIUM VOLTAGE DISTRIBUTION
16400 SERVICE AND DISTRIBUTION
16500 LIGHTING
16600 SPECIAL SYSTEMS
16700 COMMUNICATIONS
16850 ELECTRIC RESISTANCE HEATING
16900 CONTROLS
16950 TESTING

ORGANIZATION OF SPECIFICATIONS

The best known use of MASTERFORMAT is for organizing specifications. Titles are provided in a logical sequence for almost all conceivable specification sections that might be required for a construction project. The specifications writer striving for uniformity should use the titles and numbers as shown. Sections can be written and reproduced at any time without fear they will be incorrectly placed in the project manual. This is one of the major advantages in the use of MASTERFORMAT. Assembly of the final document in numerical sequence assures the correct grouping of sections.

MASTERFORMAT has been developed to provide the specifier with a standard yet flexible system for organizing specifications. However, the titles do not necessarily relate to the work accomplished by a single trade or subcontractor. It is not the intent of MASTERFORMAT to define the work of individual trades since each contractor will subdivide the work differently among subcontractors.

Broadscope and mediumscope section numbers and titles are shown in MASTERFORMAT in their recommended sequence. When selecting a narrowscope title, a five digit number will need to be assigned since these titles are unnumbered in MASTERFORMAT. Users may select needed narrowscope titles or combine titles into a single section and assign their own numerically sequenced numbers. Numbers have been left unassigned throughout MASTERFORMAT to allow for numbering narrowscope titles and any additional titles that may be required on a project. When assigning additional numbers for new titles, the specifications writer should review MASTERFORMAT and assign unused numbers from groupings of subject matter closely related to the product being specified.

DATA FILING

The MASTERFORMAT system of numbers and titles also serves as a system for filing and retrieving technical data and product literature. Because it is the same as the system used for organizing specifications it is easy to relate the filed material to the specification sections being written for a project. MASTERFORMAT is a system for organizing construction publications of all kind on the shelves of a technical library; for filing information on products, methods, manufacturers, suppliers, and subcontractors; for inventory of construction materials; for coding data stored electronically; and numerous other information storage and retrieval activities.

COST CLASSIFICATION

The MASTERFORMAT titles and numbers also serve as the basis for a system for the accumulation and organization of construction costs. Since the same format is used for project manuals as for filing construction information, the benefits of uniformity and standardization are further increased. Familiarity with MASTERFORMAT allows users to easily relate a specification section with both product information and cost data. This simplifies the storage and retrieval of information.

The Construction Specifications Institute; Alexandria, Virginia
Construction Specifications Canada

CSI DOCUMENTS

GENERAL

Developed at the time of the French Revolution, the metric system rapidly spread throughout Europe during the Napoleonic wars. It was promoted in the United States by Thomas Jefferson and later by John Quincy Adams, but the federal government did not legalize its use as a measurement system until 1866. In 1893, all standard United States measures were defined in metric units. Today, the United States remains the last industrialized country to commit to metric.

SYSTEM INTERNATIONAL (SI)

The modern metric system, know as "System International" (SI) was established by international agreement in 1960. It is the international standard of measurement and the system mandated by the *Metric Conversion Act* for use in the United States.

THE METRIC CONVERSION ACT

The *Metric Conversion Act of 1975*, as amended by the *Omnibus Trade and Competitiveness Act of 1988*, establishes the metric system as the preferred system of measurement in the United States. It requires that, to the extent feasible, the metric system be used in all federal procurement, grants, and business-related activities after September 30, 1992.

METRIC IN CONSTRUCTION

There has been much speculation about the difficulty of converting to metric in the United States construction industry. The experiences of the British, Australians, South Africans, and Canadians, all of whom converted from the inch-pound system to metric in the past 20 years, showed the following facts.

1. Metric conversion proved much less difficult than anticipated since most work is built in place.
2. There were no appreciable increases in design or construction costs, and conversion costs for most construction industry sectors were minimal or offset by later savings.
3. Architects and engineers liked metric dimensioning because it was less prone to error and easier to use than feet and inches and because engineering calculations were faster and more accurate since there were no unit conversions and no fractions.
4. Metric offered a one-time chance to reduce the many product sizes and shapes that are no longer useful, thus saving production, inventory, and procurement costs.

The following developments should make metric conversion in the United States construction industry easier:

1. The use of computer-aided design and drafting systems continues to increase; almost all engineering and cost calculations are now performed on computers.
2. The codes and construction standards of two of the country's three model building code organizations (BOCA and SBCCI), NFPA, and ASTM contain dual units that specify measurements. Many other standards-writing organizations have added metric measurements to their documents or are preparing to do so.
3. The preliminary results of several recent General Services Administration metric pilot projects in the Philadelphia area indicate no increase in design or construction costs.
4. American design and construction firms report no problems using metric in foreign work.
5. The costs of metric conversion in other industries have been far lower than expected, and the benefits greater. Total conversion costs were less than one percent of original estimates at General Motors, which now is fully metric. Rationalization of fastener sizes at IBM during metric conversion reduced fastener part numbers from 38,000 to 4,000. Some American manufacturers, such as Otis Elevator, are switching to metric to increase their international competitiveness and reduce their parts inventories. Others, such as the wood industry, have shipped exports in metric for many years.

CONVERSION AND ROUNDING

In a "soft" conversion, an exact inch-pound measurement is mathematically converted to its exact (or near exact) metric equivalent. In a "hard" conversion, a new rounded, rationalized metric number is created that is convenient to work with and remember.

When converting numbers from inch-pound to metric, round the metric value to the same number of digits as there were in the inch-pound number. In all cases, use professional rounding to determine the exact value.

With professional rounding, the basic module of metric design is 100 mm. Make every effort to keep design dimensions in this increment. Additional multimodules and submodules, in preferred order, are 6000, 3000, 1200, 600, 300, 50, 25, 20, and 10.

Example: 1990 BOCA Article 514.7 requires 36 inches (914 mm) of unobstructed pedestrian walkway width. However, 914 mm is not a clean and rational number. It should be rounded to facilitate the easiest construction possible. Since anything less than 914 mm would not meet the code requirements, the preferred number would be 1000 mm. Submodules will produce a rounding of 950, 925, or 920 mm.

SOFT AND HARD METRIC

Soft metric means "No Physical Change." This implies the product need not be physically modified to be used in a metric project. More than 95% of currently used building products will not change. In the future, as standard international metric product sizes are developed by the International Standards Organization (ISO) or another standards organization, these products may undergo modification to be compatible in the World market. Custom products, often made by computer controlled machinery, can be specified in any size.

Hard metric means "Product Requires Physical Change." The product must be physically modified to be efficiently used in a metric project, which is planned on a metric grid. A handful of current products must undergo hard metric conversion to new metric sizes.

HARD METRIC PRODUCTSNOTES

PRODUCT	SIZE (MM)
Brick	90 x 57 x 190[1]
Concrete masonry unit	190 x 190 x 390
Drywall	1200 x 2400[2]
Raised access flooring	600 x 600
Suspended ceiling tiles and grids	600 x 600 and 600 x 1200
Fluorescent lighting fixtures (lay-in type only)	600 x 600 and 600 x 1200
Air diffusers and grilles (lay-in type only)	600 and 1200 widths

1. Three vertical courses of metric modular brick with a joint of 10 mm equals 201 mm, which is rounded to 200. Three vertical rows of 200 equal 600 mm. 600 x 600 mm is a preferred nominal module for masonry.
2. Drywall thicknesses remain the same to minimize production impact. The standard thicknesses are 12.7 and 15.9 mm. Standard stud spacing is 400mm.

SPECIFICATIONS

Metric specifications should use "mm" for almost all measurements. The use of mm is consistent with the dimensions specified in major codes, such as BOCA and NEC. With the use of mm, the decimal point is used when extreme precision is indicated. Meters may be used only where large, round metric sizes are specified. Centimeters shall not be used in specifications. This is consistent with the recommendations of the AIA and ASTM.

RULES FOR WRITING METRIC SYMBOLS AND NAMES

1. Print the unit symbol in upright type and in lower case except for liter (L) or unless the unit name is derived from a proper name.
2. Print decimal prefixes in lower case for magnitudes 10^3 and lower; print the prefixes in upper case for magnitudes 10^6 and higher.
3. Leave a space between the numeral and symbol (example: 12 mm).
4. Do not use the degree mark with kelvin temperatures.
5. Do not leave a space between a unit symbol and its decimal prefix (example: km).
6. Do not use the plural of unit symbols, but do use the plural of written unit names (example: kg, kilograms).
7. For technical writing, use symbols in conjunction with numerals (example: 10 m^2) and write out unit names if numeral is not used (example: square meters).
8. Indicate the product of two or more units in symbolic form by using a dot positioned above the line (example: $kg \cdot m \cdot s^2$).
9. Do not mix names and symbols (example: N·meter).
10. Do not use a period after a symbol except when it occurs at the end of a sentence.

11. Always use decimals, not fractions.
12. Use a zero before the decimal marker for values less than one.
13. Use spaces instead of commas to separate blocks of three digits for any number over four digits (example: 45 138 kg or 0.004 46 kg). In the United States, the decimal marker is a period; in other countries a comma usually is used.

COMPARISON OF DRAWING SCALES

INCH-FOOT SCALES	INCH-FOOT RATIO	METRIC SCALE
Full size	1:1	1:1
Half size	1:2	1:2
4" = 1'-0"	1:3	
3" = 1'-0"	1:4	1:5
2" = 1'-0"	1:6	
1-1/2" = 1'-0"	1:8	1:10
1" = 1'-0"	1:12	
3/4" = 1'-0"	1:16	1:20
1/2" = 1'-0"	1:24	1:25
1/4" = 1'-0"	1:48	1:50
1" = 5'-0"	1:60	
1/8" = 1'-0"	1:96	1:100
1" = 10'-0"	1:120	
1/16" = 1'-0"	1:192	1:200
1" = 20'-0"	1:240	1:250
1" = 30'-0"	1:360	
1/32" = 1'-0"	1:384	
1" = 40'-0"	1:480	1:500
1" = 50'-0"	1:600	
1" = 60'-0"	1:720	
1" = 80'-0"	1:960	1:1000

NOTES

1. Metric drawing scales are expressed in nondimensional ratios.
2. Metric scales 1:2, 1:25, and 1:250 have limited use.

DRAWING SHEET DIMENSIONS

SIZE	SHEET SIZE
A0	1189 x 841 mm (46.8 x 33.1 inches)
A1	841 x 594 mm (33.1 x 23.4 inches)
A2	594 x 420 mm (23.4 x 16.5 inches)
A3	420 x 297 mm (16.5 x 11.7 inches)
A4	297 x 210 mm (11.7 x 8.3 inches)

NOTES

1. The ISO's "A" series drawing sizes are preferred metric sizes for design drawings.
2. A0 is the base size with an area of one square meter. Smaller sizes are half the long dimension of the previous size. All "A" sizes have a height-to-width ratio of one to the square root of two. Use a 35 mm microfilm frame to reduce these sizes.

METRIC PREFIXES

MULTIPLES	PREFIXES	SYMBOLS
$1\,000\,000\,000\,000 = 10^{12}$	tera	T
$1\,000\,000\,000 = 10^9$	giga	G
$1\,000\,000 = 10^6$	mega	M
$1\,000 = 10^3$	kilo	k*
$100 = 10^2$	hecto	h
$10 = 10$	deka	da
$0.1 = 10^{-1}$	deci	d
$0.01 = 10^{-2}$	centi	c
$0.001 = 10^{-3}$	milli	m*
$0.000\,001 = 10^{-6}$	micro	m
$0.000\,000\,001 = 10^{-9}$	nano	n
$0.000\,000\,000\,001 = 10^{-12}$	pico	p

*Commonly used with base units in design and construction

National Institute of Building Sciences; Washington, D.C.

METRIC

BASE UNITS

PHYSICAL QUALITY	UNIT	SYMBOL
Length	Meter	m
Mass[1]	Kilogram	kg
Time	Second	s
Electric current	Ampere	A
Thermodynamic temperature [2]	Kelvin	K
Luminous intensity	Candela	cd
Amount of substance [3]	Mole	mol

NOTES

1. "Weight" is often used to mean "mass."
2. Celsius temperature (°C) is more commonly used than kelvin (K), but both have the same temperature gradients. Celsius temperature is simply 273.15 degrees warmer than kelvin.
3. Mole is the amount of molecular substance and is used in physics.
4. Additional common units of measurement are the hectare (ha), liter (L), and metric ton (t). The hectare is used in surveying for land or sea areas and is equal to 10 000 square meters. The liter is a measurement for liquid volume that is equal to 1/1000 of a cubic meter. The metric ton is used to denote large loads such as those used in excavating and is equal to 1000 kilograms.

PLANE AND SOLID ANGLES

The radian (rad) and steradian (sr) denote plane and solid angles. They are used in lighting work and in various engineering calculations. In surveying, the units degree (°), minute ('), and second (") continue in use.

DERIVED UNITS

QUANTITY	NAME	SYMBOL	EXPRESSION
Frequency	hertz	Hz	$Hz = s^{-1}$
Force	newton	N	$N = kg\,m/s^2$
Pressure, stress	pascal	Pa	$Pa = N/m^2$
Energy, work, quantity of heat	joule	J	$J = Nm$
Power, radiant flux	watt	W	$W = J/s$
Electric charge, quantity	coulomb	C	$C = As$
Electric potential	volt	V	$V = W/A$ or J/C
Capacitance	farad	F	$F = C/V$
Electric resistance	ohm	W	$\Omega = V/A$
Electric conductance	siemens	S	$S = A/V$ or Ω^{-1}
Magnetic flux	weber	Wb	$Wb = Vs$
Magnetic flux density	tesla	T	$T = Wb/m^2$
Inductance	henry	H	$H = Wb/A$
Luminous flux	lumen	lm	$lm = cd\,sr$
Illuminance	lux	lx	$lx = lm/m^2$

CONVERSION FACTORS

QUANTITY	FROM INCH-POUND UNITS	TO METRIC UNITS	MULTIPLY BY
Length	mile	km	1.609 344*
	yard	m	0.914 4*
	foot	m	0.304 8*
		mm	304.8*
	inch	mm	25.4*
Area	square mile	km²	2.590 00
	acre	m²	4 046.87
		ha (10 000m2)	0.404 687
	square yard	m²	0.836 127 36*
	square foot	m²	0.092 903 04*
	square inch	mm²	645.16*
Volume	acre foot	m³	1 233.49
	cubic yard	m³	0.764 555
	cubic foot	m³	0.028 316 8
		cm³	28 316.85
		L (1000 cm³)	28.316 85
	100 board feet	m³	0.235 974
	gallon	L (1000 cm3)	3.785 41
	cubic inch	cm³	16.387 064*
		mm³	16 387.064*

*denotes an exact conversion

ADDITIONAL CONVERSION FACTORS

QUANTITY	FROM INCH-POUND UNITS	TO METRIC UNITS	MULTIPLY BY
Mass	lb	kg	0.453 592
	Kip (1,000 lb)	metric ton (1000 kg)	0.453 592
Mass/unit length	plf	kg/m	1.488 16
Mass/unit area	psf	kg/m²	4.882 43
Mass density	pcf	kg/m³	16.018 5
Force	lb	N	4.448 22
Force/unit length	plf	N/m	14.593 9
Pressure, stress, modulus of elasticity	psf	Pa	47.880 3
	psi	kPa	6.894 76
Bending moment, torque, moment of force	ft-lb	Nm	1.355 82
Moment of mass	lb ft	kg m	0.138 255
Moment of inertia	lb ft²	kg m²	0.042 140 1
Second moment of area	in⁴	mm⁴	416 231
Section modulus	in³	mm³	16 387.064*
Mass/area (density)	lb/ft²	kg/m²	4.882 428
Temperature	°F	°C	5/9(°F-32)
Energy, work, quantity of heat	kWh	MJ	3.6*
	Btu	J	1055.056
	ft lbf	J	1.355 82
Power	ton (refrig)	kW	3.517
	Btu/s	kW	1.055 056
	hp (electric)	W	745.700
	Btu/h	W	0.293 071
Heat flux	Btu/f²h	W/m	3.152 481
Rate of heat flow	Btu/s	kW	1.055 056
	Btu/h	W	0.293 071 1
Thermal conductivity (k value)	Btu/ft h °F	W/m K	1.730 73
Thermal conductance (U value)	Btu/ft² h °F	W/m² K	5.678 263
Thermal resistance (R value)	ft² h °F/Btu	m² K/W	0.176 110
Heat capacity, entrophy	Btu/°F	kJ/K	1.899 1
Specific heat capacity, specific entrophy	Btu/lb °F	kJ/kg K	4.186 8*
Specific energy, latent heat	Btu/lb	kJ/kg	2.326*
Vapor permeance	perm (23 ℃)	ng/(Pa s m²)	57.452 5
Vapor permeability	perm/in	ng/(Pa s m)	1.459 29
Volume rate of flow	ft³/s	m³/s	0.028 316 8
	cfm	m³/s	0.000 471 947 4
	cfm	L/s	0.471 947 4
Velocity, speed	ft/s	m/s	0.3048*
Acceleration	ft/s²	m/s²	0.3048*
Momentum	lb ft/s	kg m/s	0.138 255 0
Angular momentum	lb ft²/s	kg m²/s	0.042 140 11
Plane angle	degree	rad	0.017 453 3
Power, radiant flux	W	W	1 (same unit)
Radiant intensity	W/sr	W/sr	1 (same unit)
Radiance	W/(sr m²)	W/(sr m²)	1 (same unit)
Irradiance	W/m²	W/m²	1 (same unit)
Frequency	Hz	Hz	1 (same unit)
Electric Current	A	A	1 (same unit)
Electric Charge	A hr	C	3600*
Electric potential	V	V	1 (same unit)
Capacitance	F	F	1 (same unit)
Inductance	H	H	1 (same unit)
Resistance	W	W	1 (same unit)
Conductance	mho	S	100*
Magnetic flux	maxwell	Wb	10⁻⁸*
Magnetic flux density	gamma	T	10⁻⁹*
Luminous intensity	cd	cd	1 (same unit)
Luminance	lambert	kcd/m²	3.183 01
	cd/ft²	cd/m²	10.763 9
	footlambert	cd/m²	3.426 26
Luminous flux	lm	lm	1 (same unit)
Illuminance	footcandle	lx	10.763 9

*denotes an exact conversion

National Institute of Building Sciences; Washington, D.C.

METRIC

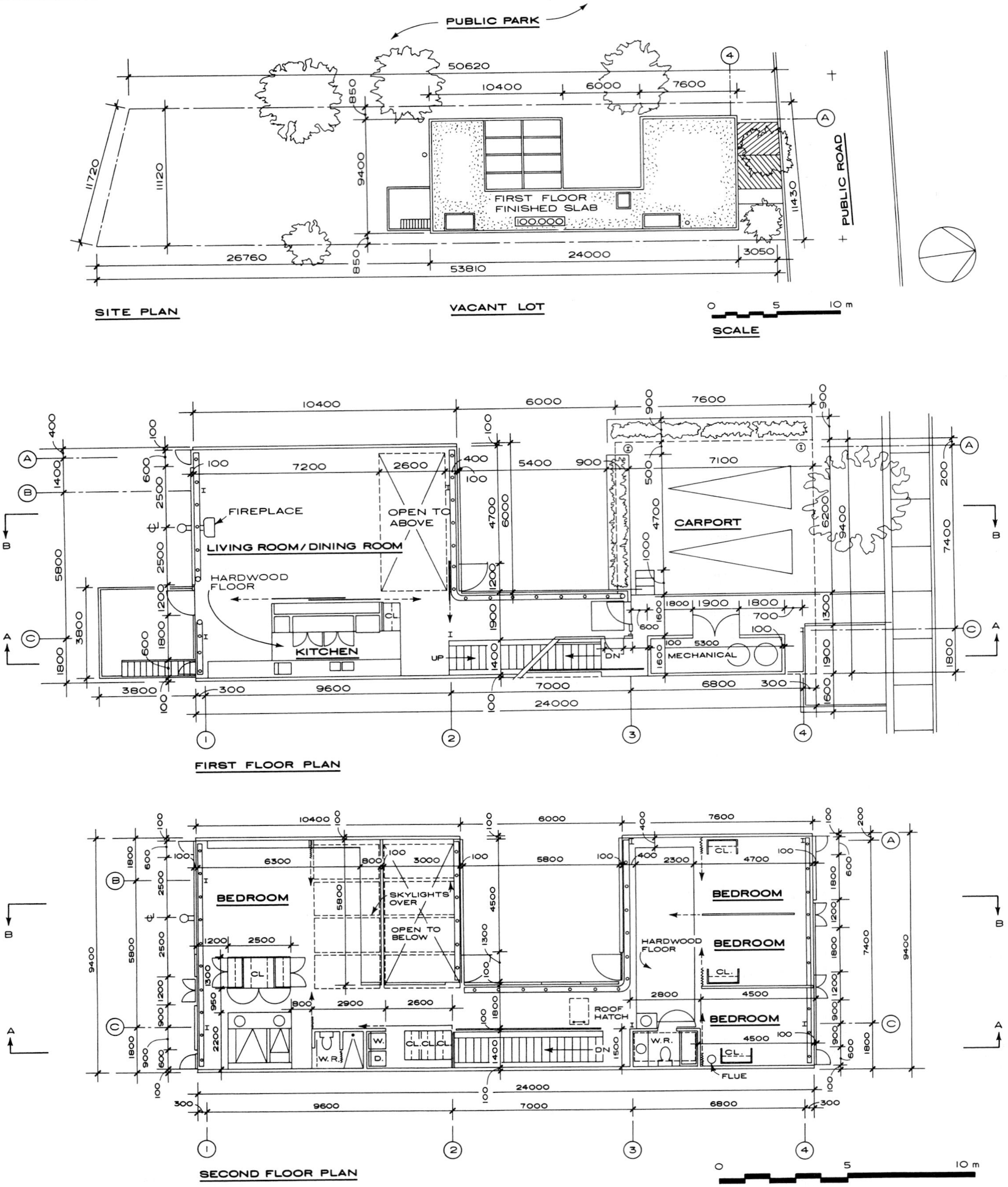

PUBLIC PARK

50620

10400   6000   7600

850

9400

FIRST FLOOR
FINISHED SLAB

100000

PUBLIC ROAD

11720   11120

26760   850   53810   24000   3050

11430

SITE PLAN   **VACANT LOT**

0   5   10 m

SCALE

10400   6000   900   7600   900

400   100   100

A   400   100   7200   2600   400   5400   900   7100

B   1400   600   100

FIREPLACE   OPEN TO
ABOVE   4700   6000   500   4700   CARPORT   6200   9400

2500   2500

LIVING ROOM/DINING ROOM

5800   HARDWOOD
FLOOR   1200   2500

B   1200   1900   1000   7400

CL   1800   1900   1800   700

C   3800   600   1800   **KITCHEN**   UP   1400   DN   600   1600   100   5300   100   1900   1800

1800   MECHANICAL   1900

3800   300   9600   7000   6800   300   1600

24000

1   2   3   4

FIRST FLOOR PLAN

10400   6000   400   7600

100   100   100   200

1800   600   100   **BEDROOM**   6300   800   3000   100   5800   100   400   2300   CL   4700   100

B   2500   100   SKYLIGHTS
OVER   400   **BEDROOM**   1800   600

5800   4500   **BEDROOM**

9400   5800   2500   1200   2500   1300   1300   HARDWOOD
FLOOR

1300   CL   100   1800   2800   4500

CL   OPEN TO
BELOW   100   ROOF
HATCH   **BEDROOM**

950   800   2900   2600   1800   W.R.   CL   4500   100

2200   W.   CL.CL.CL   DN   1500   FLUE

900   600   W.R.   D.   1400   900   600

100   100

300   9600   7000   6800   300

24000

1   2   3   4

SECOND FLOOR PLAN

0   5   10 m

THE WOLF RESIDENCE, TORONTO, CANADA, COMPLETED 1974. ARCHITECTS: A.J. DIAMOND AND BARTON MYERS. DESIGNED BY BARTON MYERS

Robert Hill, Barton Myers Associates; Toronto, Canada

 METRIC

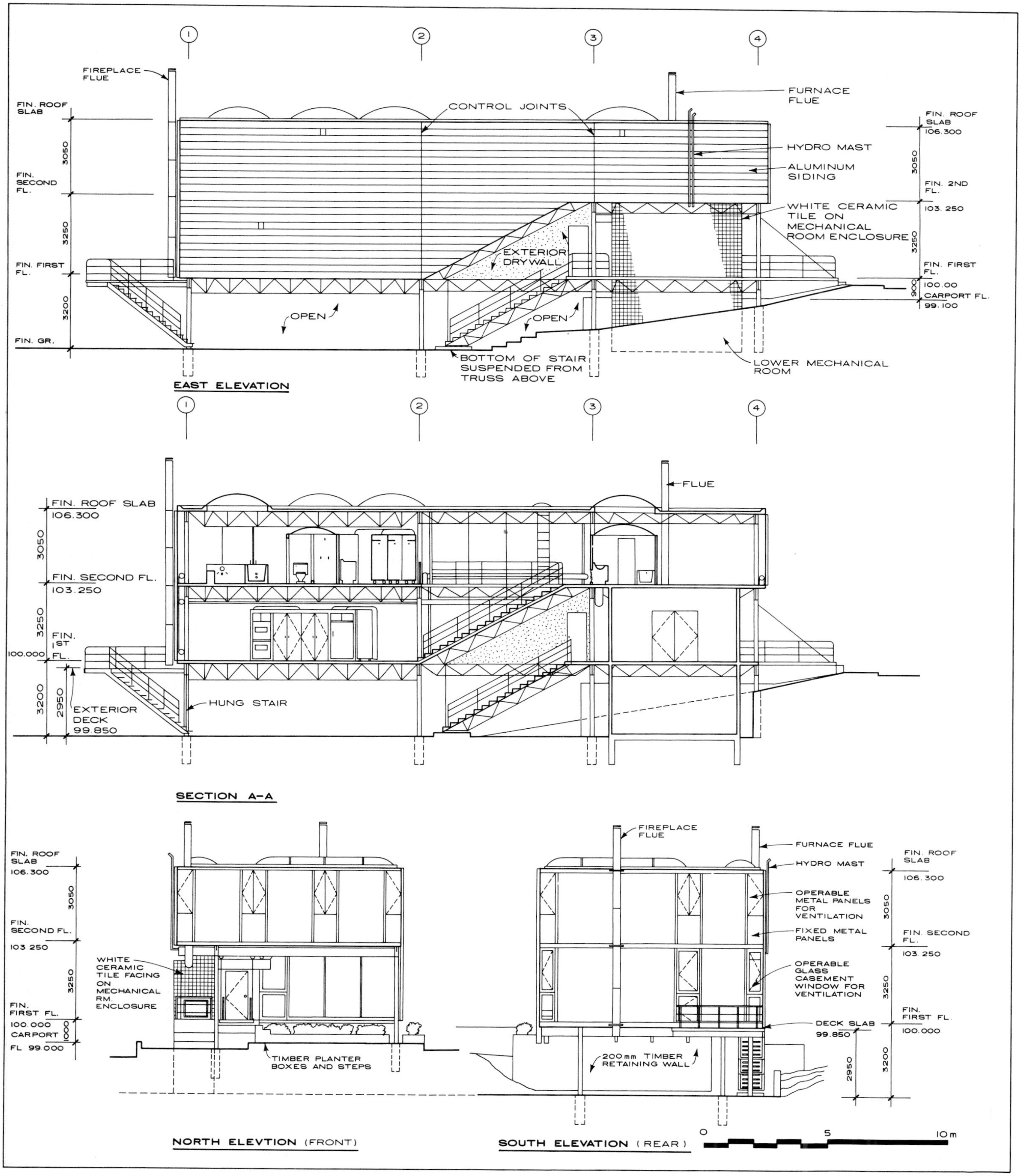

FIREPLACE
FLUE

CONTROL JOINTS

FURNACE
FLUE

FIN. ROOF
SLAB

FIN.
SECOND
FL.

HYDRO MAST

ALUMINUM
SIDING

FIN. ROOF
SLAB
106.300

FIN. 2ND
FL.

103.250

3050

3250

WHITE CERAMIC
TILE ON
MECHANICAL
ROOM ENCLOSURE

EXTERIOR
DRYWALL

FIN. FIRST
FL.

OPEN

OPEN

FIN. FIRST
FL.

100.00
CARPORT FL.
99.100

FIN. GR.

BOTTOM OF STAIR
SUSPENDED FROM
TRUSS ABOVE

LOWER MECHANICAL
ROOM

3200

900

3050

3250

EAST ELEVATION

FLUE

FIN. ROOF SLAB
106.300

FIN. SECOND FL.
103.250

FIN.
1ST
FL.

100.000

EXTERIOR
DECK
99.850

HUNG STAIR

3050

3250

3200

2950

SECTION A-A

FIN. ROOF
SLAB
106.300

FIN.
SECOND FL.

103.250

WHITE
CERAMIC
TILE FACING
ON
MECHANICAL
RM.
ENCLOSURE

FIN.
FIRST FL.
100.000
CARPORT
FL. 99.000

TIMBER PLANTER
BOXES AND STEPS

NORTH ELEVATION (FRONT)

3050

3250

FIREPLACE
FLUE

FURNACE FLUE

HYDRO MAST

OPERABLE
METAL PANELS
FOR
VENTILATION

FIXED METAL
PANELS

OPERABLE
GLASS
CASEMENT
WINDOW FOR
VENTILATION

DECK SLAB
99.850

200 mm TIMBER
RETAINING WALL

SOUTH ELEVATION (REAR)

FIN. ROOF
SLAB

106.300

FIN SECOND
FL.

103.250

FIN.
FIRST FL.
100.000

3050

3250

3200

2950

0   5   10 m

Robert Hill, Barton Myers Associates; Toronto, Canada

METRIC

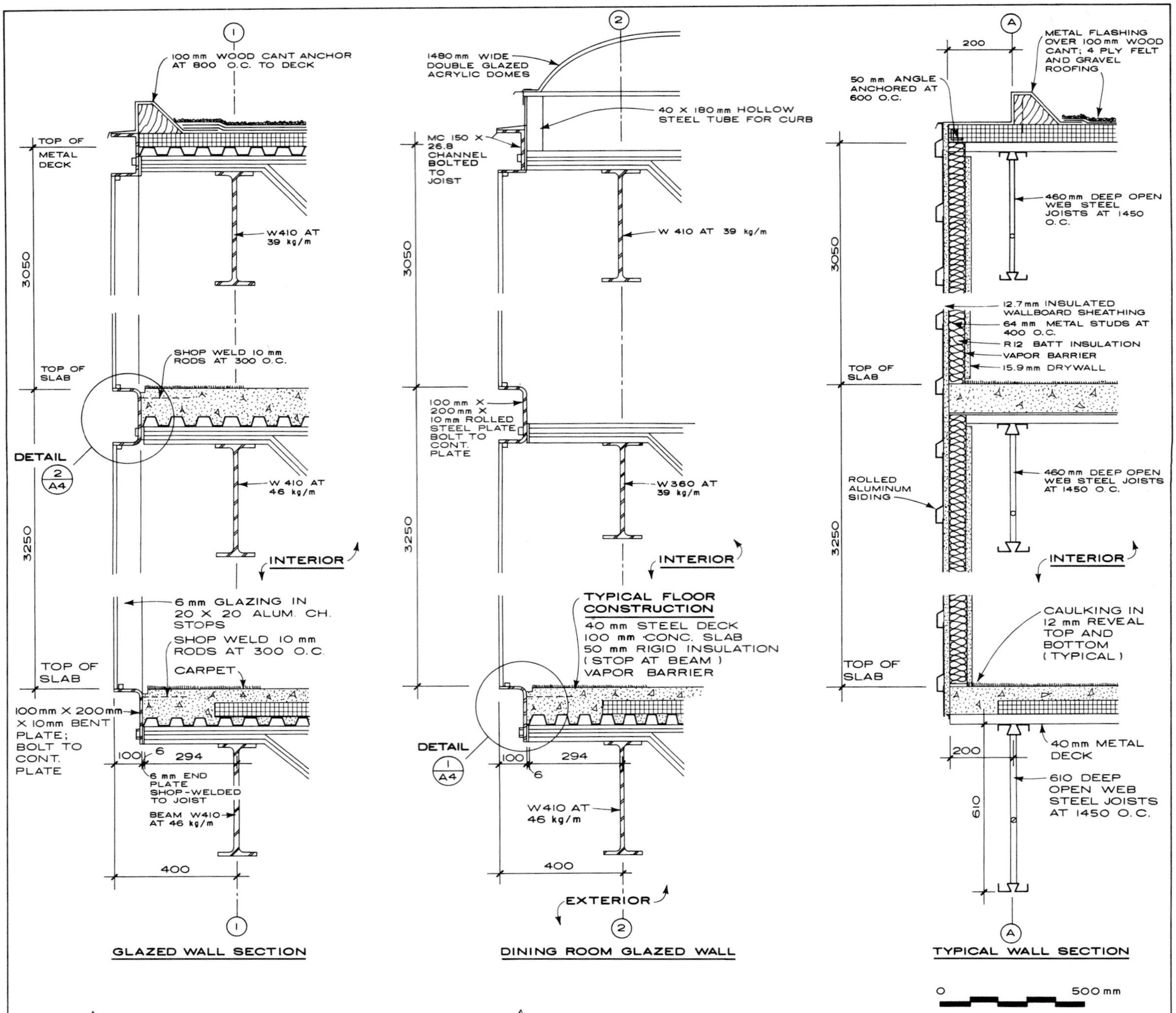

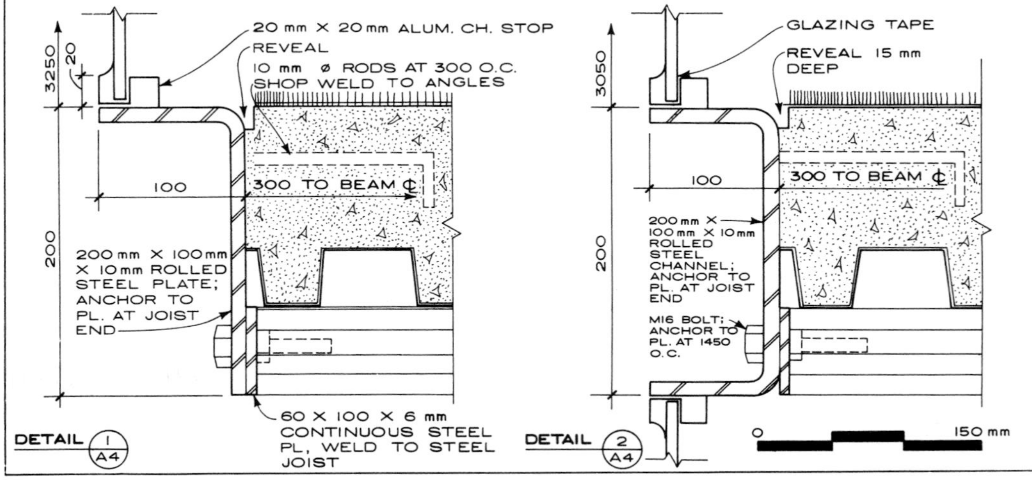

GLAZED WALL SECTION

100 mm WOOD CANT ANCHOR AT 800 O.C. TO DECK

TOP OF METAL DECK

W 410 AT 39 kg/m

3050

TOP OF SLAB

SHOP WELD 10 mm RODS AT 300 O.C.

DETAIL 2/A4

W 410 AT 46 kg/m

3250

INTERIOR

6 mm GLAZING IN 20 X 20 ALUM. CH. STOPS

SHOP WELD 10 mm RODS AT 300 O.C.

CARPET

TOP OF SLAB

100mm X 200mm X 10mm BENT PLATE; BOLT TO CONT. PLATE

100 6 294

6 mm END PLATE SHOP-WELDED TO JOIST

BEAM W410 AT 46 kg/m

400

DINING ROOM GLAZED WALL

1480mm WIDE DOUBLE GLAZED ACRYLIC DOMES

40 X 180 mm HOLLOW STEEL TUBE FOR CURB

MC 150 X 26.8 CHANNEL BOLTED TO JOIST

W 410 AT 39 kg/m

3050

100 mm X 200 mm X 10 mm ROLLED STEEL PLATE; BOLT TO CONT. PLATE

W 360 AT 39 kg/m

3250

INTERIOR

TYPICAL FLOOR CONSTRUCTION

40 mm STEEL DECK
100 mm CONC. SLAB
50 mm RIGID INSULATION (STOP AT BEAM)
VAPOR BARRIER

DETAIL 1/A4

100 6 294

W410 AT 46 kg/m

400

EXTERIOR

TYPICAL WALL SECTION

200

METAL FLASHING OVER 100 mm WOOD CANT; 4 PLY FELT AND GRAVEL ROOFING

50 mm ANGLE ANCHORED AT 600 O.C.

3050

460 mm DEEP OPEN WEB STEEL JOISTS AT 1450 O.C.

12.7 mm INSULATED WALLBOARD SHEATHING
64 mm METAL STUDS AT 400 O.C.
R 12 BATT INSULATION
VAPOR BARRIER
15.9 mm DRYWALL

TOP OF SLAB

ROLLED ALUMINUM SIDING

3250

460 mm DEEP OPEN WEB STEEL JOISTS AT 1450 O.C.

INTERIOR

CAULKING IN 12 mm REVEAL TOP AND BOTTOM (TYPICAL)

TOP OF SLAB

200

40 mm METAL DECK

610 DEEP OPEN WEB STEEL JOISTS AT 1450 O. C.

610

0   500 mm

DETAIL 1/A4

3250

20

20 mm X 20 mm ALUM. CH. STOP
REVEAL
10 mm ø RODS AT 300 O.C. SHOP WELD TO ANGLES

100

300 TO BEAM ℄

200

200 mm X 100mm X 10 mm ROLLED STEEL PLATE; ANCHOR TO PL. AT JOIST END

60 X 100 X 6 mm CONTINUOUS STEEL PL, WELD TO STEEL JOIST

DETAIL 2/A4

3050

GLAZING TAPE

REVEAL 15 mm DEEP

100

300 TO BEAM ℄

200

200 mm X 100 mm X 10 mm ROLLED STEEL CHANNEL; ANCHOR TO PL. AT JOIST END

M16 BOLT; ANCHOR TO PL. AT 1450 O.C.

0   150 mm

NOTES

1. All dimensions shown are in millimetres, using the axial technique of measurement and a grid plan based on a 100 mm plan module.
2. On site plan, sections, and elevations, note that all floor elevations are in metres.
3. All steel sections are dimensioned in millimetres, with weights of lengths in kilograms per metre.
4. Stock lumber dimensions have been "soft converted" to metric equivalents, since lumber will continue to be produced in imperial sizes to meet American Lumber Standards (ALS) requirements.
5. New metric stock door sizes for interior and exterior doors are employed throughout.

Robert Hill, Barton Myers Associates; Toronto, Canada

METRIC

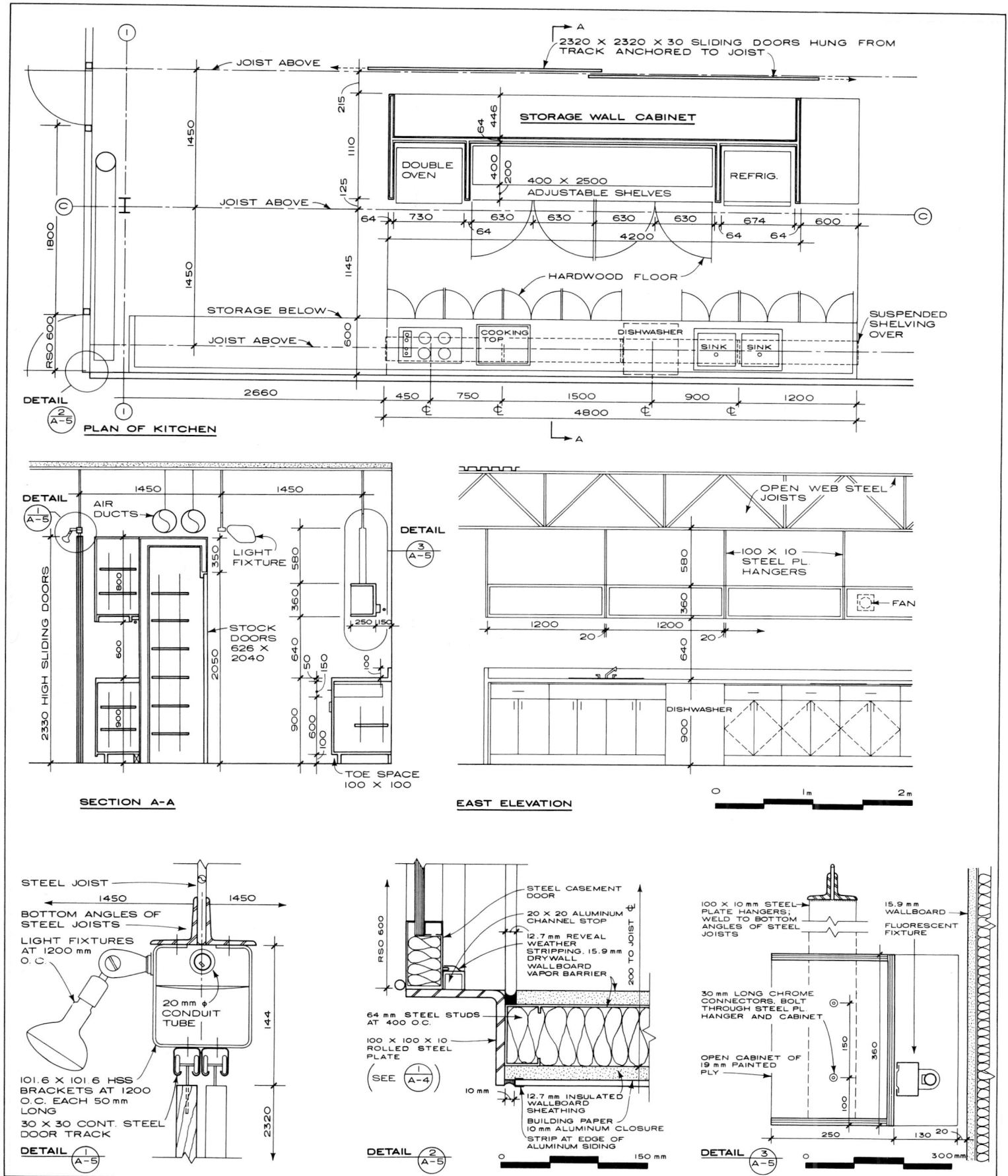

JOIST ABOVE

A

2320 X 2320 X 30 SLIDING DOORS HUNG FROM
TRACK ANCHORED TO JOIST

215

446
64

STORAGE WALL CABINET

1450

DOUBLE
OVEN

400
200

REFRIG.

1110

125

400 X 2500
ADJUSTABLE SHELVES

JOIST ABOVE

C

64   730

64

630   630   630   630

4200

674   600

64 64

C

1800

1450

1145

HARDWOOD FLOOR

STORAGE BELOW

JOIST ABOVE

600

COOKING
TOP

DISHWASHER

SINK   SINK

SUSPENDED
SHELVING
OVER

RSO 600

DETAIL
2
A-5

I

2660

450   750

1500

900

1200

4800

A

PLAN OF KITCHEN

DETAIL
1
A-5

1450

1450

AIR
DUCTS

350

LIGHT
FIXTURE

580

DETAIL
3
A-5

2330 HIGH SLIDING DOORS

900

600

STOCK
DOORS
626 X
2040

2050

360

250 150

640

50
150

900

600
100

TOE SPACE
100 X 100

SECTION A-A

OPEN WEB STEEL
JOISTS

100 X 10
STEEL PL.
HANGERS

580

FAN

1200   1200

360

20   20

640

DISHWASHER

900

EAST ELEVATION

0   1m   2m

STEEL JOIST

1450   1450

BOTTOM ANGLES OF
STEEL JOISTS

LIGHT FIXTURES
AT 1200 mm
O.C.

20 mm ⌀
CONDUIT
TUBE

144

101.6 X 101.6 HSS
BRACKETS AT 1200
O.C. EACH 50 mm
LONG

30 X 30 CONT. STEEL
DOOR TRACK

2320

DETAIL
1
A-5

STEEL CASEMENT
DOOR

20 X 20 ALUMINUM
CHANNEL STOP

12.7 mm REVEAL
WEATHER
STRIPPING, 15.9 mm
DRYWALL
WALLBOARD
VAPOR BARRIER

RSO 600

200 TO JOIST

64 mm STEEL STUDS
AT 400 O.C.

100 X 100 X 10
ROLLED STEEL
PLATE

SEE
1
A-4

10 mm

12.7 mm INSULATED
WALLBOARD
SHEATHING

BUILDING PAPER
10 mm ALUMINUM CLOSURE
STRIP AT EDGE OF
ALUMINUM SIDING

DETAIL
2
A-5

0   150 mm

100 X 10 mm STEEL
PLATE HANGERS;
WELD TO BOTTOM
ANGLES OF STEEL
JOISTS

15.9 mm
WALLBOARD

FLUORESCENT
FIXTURE

30 mm LONG CHROME
CONNECTORS, BOLT
THROUGH STEEL PL.
HANGER AND CABINET

360

150

OPEN CABINET OF
19 mm PAINTED
PLY

100

250   130 20

DETAIL
3
A-5

0   300mm

Robert Hill, Barton Myers Associates; Toronto, Canada

METRIC A

GENERAL REFERENCES

Allen, Edward. *Architectural Detailing: Function, Constructibility, Aesthetics.* New York: J. Wiley & Sons, 1993.

Allen, Edward. *Fundamentals of Building Construction,* 2nd ed. New York: J. Wiley & Sons, 1990.

Allen, Edward, and Joseph Iano. *The Architect´s Studio Companion.* New York: J. Wiley & Sons, 1989.

Ambrose, James. *Building Structures.* New York: J. Wiley & Sons, 1988.

Ambrose, James. *Construction Revisited: An Illustrated Guide to Construction Details of the Early 20th Century.* New York: J. Wiley & Sons, 1993.

Ambrose, James. *Simplified Design of Building Foundations.* New York: J. Wiley & Sons, 1981.

Ambrose, James. *Simplified Design of Building Structures,* 2nd ed. New York: J. Wiley & Sons, 1986.

Brown, Allen L., and William H. Haire. *Supplementary Education Handbook.* Washington, D.C.: AIA Press, 1992.

Burden, Ernest. *Perspective Grid Sourcebook.* Van Nostrand Reinhold, 1991.

Callendar, John. *Time-Saver Standards for Architectural Design Data.* McGraw-Hill, 1982.

Ching, Frank. *Architecture: Form, Space and Order.* Van Nostrand Reinhold, 1979.

Ching, Frank. *Architectural Graphics,* 2nd ed. Van Nostrand Reinhold, 1985.

Cowan, H. *Handbook of Architectural Technology.* New York: Van Nostrand Reinhold, 1991.

Cowan, H., and P. Smith. *The Science and Technology of Building Materials.* Van Nostrand Reinhold, 1988.

Cullinane, John J., AIA. *Understanding Architectural Drawings: A Guide for Non-Architects.* Washington, D.C.: Preservation Press, 1993.

Diekman, Norman, and John Pile. *Drawing Interior Architecture.* Lakewood, N.J.: Whitney Library of Design, 1990.

Dietz, Albert G. H. *Dwelling House Construction,* 5th ed. Cambridge, Mass.: MIT Press, 1990.

Elliot, Cecil D. *Technics and Architecture: The Development of Materials and Systems for Buildings.* Cambridge, Mass.: MIT Press, 1992.

Evan Terry Associates. *Americans with Disabilities Act Facilities Compliance: A Practical Guide.* New York: J. Wiley & Sons, 1993.

Evan Terry Associates. *Americans with Disabilities Act (ADA) Facilities Compliance Workbook.* 1992 with 1993 supplement.

Fletcher, Sir Bannister. *A History of Architecture,* 19th ed. Stoneham, Mass.: Butterworth, 1987.

Follis, John, and Dave Hammer. *Architectural Signing and Graphics.* Lakewood, N.J.: Whitney Library of Design, 1988.

Ford, Edward R. *The Details of Modern Architecture.* Cambridge, Mass.: MIT Press, 1990.

Harris, Cyril M., ed. *Dictionary of Architecture and Construction,* 2nd ed. McGraw-Hill, 1993.

Haviland, David S. *Architect´s Handbook of Professional Practice,* 12th ed. Washington, D.C.: AIA Press, 1994. [incl. AIA documents and forms]

Hornbostel, Caleb. *Construction Materials.* New York: J. Wiley & Sons, 1991.

Kliment, Stephen, ed. *Architectural Sketching and Rendering: Techniques for Designers and Artists.* Lakewood, N.J.: Whitney Library of Design, 1984.

Knoblock, Philip G. *Architectural Details from the Early Twentieth Century.* Washington, D.C.: AIA Press, 1991.

Lawlor, Robert. *Sacred Geometry, Philosophy and Practice.* Thames and Hudson, 1989.

Lorenz, Albert, and Stanley Salzman. *Drawing in Color: Rendering Techniques for Architects and Illustrators.* Lakewood, N.J.: Whitney Library of Design, 1991.

Masterformat, Construction Specifications Institute, 1988.

McGoodwin, Henry. *Architectural Shades and Shadows.* Washington, D.C.: AIA Press, 1989.

Nashed, Fred. *Time-Saving Techniques for Architectural Construction Drawings.* Van Nostrand Reinhold, 1993.

Neufert, Ernst. *Architect´s Data: The Handbook of Building Types,* 2nd English ed. Blackwell, 1981.

Panero, Julius and Martin Zelnik. *Human Dimension and Interior Space.* Lakewood, N.J.: Whitney Library of Design, 1979.

Parker, Harry. *Simplified Design of Reinforced Concrete,* 5th ed. New York: J. Wiley & Sons, 1984.

Parker, Harry. *Simplified Design of Structural Steel,* 5th ed. New York: J. Wiley & Sons, 1983.

Parker, Harry. *Simplified Design of Structural Wood,* 4th ed. New York: J. Wiley & Sons, 1988.

Parker, Harry. *Simplified Engineering for Architects and Builders,* 6th ed. New York: J. Wiley & Sons, 1984.

Parker, Harry. *Simplified Mechanics and Strength of Materials,* 4th ed. New York: J. Wiley & Sons, 1986.

Parker, Harry. *Simplified Site Engineering for Architects and Builders.* New York: J. Wiley & Sons, 1954.

Ramsey, Charles G., and Harold R. Sleeper. *Architectural Graphic Standards for Construction Details.* New York: J. Wiley & Sons, 1991.

Ramsey, Charles G., and Harold R. Sleeper. *Architectural Graphic Standards Facsimile of Original Edition.* New York: J. Wiley & Sons, 1932/90.

Reid, Grant W., ASLA. *Landscape Graphics.* Lakewood, N.J.: Whitney Library of Design, 1987.

Reznikorr, S.C. *Interior Graphic and Design Standards.* Lakewood, N.J.: Whitney Library of Design, 1986.

Ruegg, Rosalie T., and Harold E. Marshall. *Building Economics: Theory and Practice.* New York: Van Nostrand, Reinhold, 1990.

Staebler, Wendy W. *Architectural Detailing in Contract Interiors.* Lakewood, N.J.: Whitney Library of Design, 1993.

Stein, J. Stewart. *Construction Glossary: An Encyclopedic Reference and Manual.* New York: J. Wiley & Sons, 1986.

Stein, Benjamin and John S. Reynolds. *Mechanical and Electrical Equipment for Buildings.* 8th Ed. New York: J. Wiley & Sons, 1992.

Task Force on CAD. *CAD Layer Guidelines: Recommended Designations for Architecture, Engineering, and Facility Management Computer Aided Design.* Washington, DC: AIA Press, 1990.

Wakita, Osamu, and Richard Linde. *Professional Practice of Architectural Detailing,* 2nd ed. New York: J. Wiley & Sons, 1987.

Wakita, Osamu, and Richard Linde. *The Professional Practice of Architectural Working Drawings.* New York: J. Wiley & Sons, 1984.

Walker, Theodore D., and David A. Davis. *Plan Graphics,* 4th ed. Van Nostrand Reinhold, 1990.

White, Richard N. *Building Structural Design Handbook.* New York, J. Wiley & Sons, 1987.

Wiggins, Glenn E. *A Manual of Construction Documentation.* Lakewood, N.J.: Whitney Library, 1989.

Wiggins, Glenn E. *Construction Details for Commercial Buildings.* Lakewood, N.J.: Whitney Library, 1988.

Wilkes, Joseph, and Robert Packard, eds. *Encyclopedia of Architecture: Design, Engineering and Construction,* 5 vols. New York: J. Wiley & Sons, 1989.

INTERNATIONAL PERIODICALS

Abitare
Editrice Segesta s.p.a.
15 c.so Monfrote 20122
Milan, Italy

Architectural Design
42 Leicester Gardens
London W2 3AN England
Tel: (071) 402-2141

Architectural Record
1221 Avenue of the Americas
New York, NY 10020
Tel: (212) 512-2594

Architectural Review
Architectural Press, Ltd.
33-35 Bowling Green Lane
London EC1R ODA
England
Tel: (071) 837-1212

Architecture
1130 Connecticut Avenue, NW
Suite 625
Washington, DC 20036
Tel: (202) 828-0995

Architecture + Urbanism (A & U)
A & U Publishing Co., Ltd.
30-8 Yushima 2-chome
Bunkyo-ku
Tokyo 113, Japan
Tel: (03) 816-2935

Architecture d´Aujourd´hui
Group Expansion
67 Avenue de Wagram
75017 Paris, France
Tel: 763-12-11

Blueprint
26 Cramer Street
London W1M 3HE
England
Tel: (071) 486-7419

Daidalos
Bertelsmann Druck + Dienstlheistung
Berlin GmbH
Schlusterstrasse 42
D-1000 Berlin 15 Germany

Design Book Review
1418 Spring Way
Berkeley, CA 94708
Tel: (415) 486-1956

Domus
Editoriala Domus
Ufficio Abbonamenti
via A Grandi 5-720089 Rozzano
Milano, Italy

El Croquis
Barcelo 15
28004 Madrid, Spain
Tel: (91) 445-2194

House and Garden
Conde Naste Publications
350 Madison Avenue
New York, NY 10017
Tel: (212) 880-8800

Harvard Architecture Review
Harvard University
Graduate School of Design
Gund Hall
48 Quincy Street, #301
Cambridge, MA 02138
Tel: (617) 495-2591

Japan Architect
Japan Architect Co., Ltd.
31-2 Yushima 2-chome Bunkyo-ku
Tokyo 113, Japan
Tel: (03) 811-7101

L´Arca
L´Arca edizioni SpA
Ufficio Abbonamenti
viale Bianca Mariall
20122 Milan, Italy
Tel: (02) 790240

Lotus International
Electa Periodici Srl
via D. Trentacoste 7
20134 Milan, Italy
Tel: (02) 215631

Metropolis
177 East 87th Street
New York, NY 10028
Tel: (212) 722-5050

Ottagano
Co. P. IN.A.
via Melzi d´Eril 26
20154 Milan, Italy
Tel: (02) 315508

Process Architecture
Process Publishing, Co., Ltd.
3-1-3 Koishikawa Bunkyo-ku
Tokyo, Japan
Tel: (03) 816-1695-1696

Progressive Architecture
Reinhold Publishing, Inc.
600 Summer Street
P.O. Box 1361
Stamford, CT 06904
Tel: (203) 348-7531

INDEX